A Concordance to the Poems of

MATTHEW ARNOLD

THE CORNELL CONCORDANCES

Supervisory Committee

M. H. Abrams

William R. Keast

Stephen E. Whicher

S. M. Parrish, *General Editor*

POEMS OF MATTHEW ARNOLD

Edited by S. M. Parrish

A Concordance to the Poems of
MATTHEW ARNOLD

Edited by

STEPHEN MAXFIELD PARRISH

Cornell University Press

ITHACA, NEW YORK

To WILLIAM ANDRUS and JAMES PAINTER,

who made it possible,

this volume is gratefully dedicated.

PREFACE

WHEN Professor Lane Cooper of Cornell published his monumental *Concordance to the Poems of William Wordsworth* in 1911, he set down details of the method by which he had worked and named the persons who had helped him. His method, widely adopted thereafter, involved cutting out lines of printed text and pasting them on 3-by-5-inch slips of paper, each bearing an index word written in the upper left-hand corner. Line numbers were penciled, page numbers and poem titles stamped, on the slips. Sixty-seven people (three of whom died during the enterprise) took part in the truly heroic labor of cutting and pasting, alphabetizing the 211,000 slips, and proofreading. Testifying both to their industry and to his own executive powers, Professor Cooper was able to state that "the whole task of preparing the copy was accomplished, through careful planning, the division of the burden, the employment of labour-saving devices, and an exceptional spirit of co-operation, in the space of less than seven months." A year elapsed before a publisher could be found, and another year before the massive volume reached print.

These details may be of interest as background against which to read details of the Arnold concordance. This concordance was produced by an electronic computer, the IBM 704 Data Processing Machine. The lines of Arnold's verse, without punctuation, were punched on IBM cards, one line per card (this took one key-punch operator 69 hours). Line numbers were punched in automatically by running through an IBM Reproducer the deck of cards representing each poem along with a numbering deck on which the numbers from 1 to 999 had been punched in fixed locations. Page numbers were "gang-punched" on the same machine, by means of the same numbering deck, and one title card was punched for each poem (these operations, together with punching the variant lines of text, took the editor some 80 hours). The entire deck of 17,000 cards was then fed into an IBM Card Reader, which transferred the data to magnetic tape

(1 hour). Meanwhile a program had been written whereby the computer was instructed to search the tape and to index alphabetically every significant word on it (omitting 151 nonsignificant words previously stored in its "memory") by listing the entire line in which the word occurred, together with identifying information (the computer reads 15,000 characters per second and makes 42,000 logical decisions per second; the computer run took 38 hours, the printing 10 hours). The IBM print, spaced into pages, was reproduced for publication by offset.

It is only fair to confess that these totals exclude a good many sometimes lively, often weary, hours given to planning, devising, and testing the program. It is fair to confess, too, that while we have radically modernized Professor Cooper's indexing technique and shortened the drudgery involved, we have scarcely been able to improve upon the format he adopted, and we cannot claim to have produced a better volume. One of the largest concordances ever made, the Wordsworth remains a wholly admirable product. As we revive the Cornell tradition of concordance making, we look back with high respect to that tradition's distinguished inauguration.

Basic Text and Format

In the present series of concordances Matthew Arnold's name leads all the rest less for alphabetical than for textual reasons (it may reassure those who envision a remorseless, dreadful sequence—Arnold . . . Binyon . . . Clough . . . Davenant . . .—to learn that the second poet will be William Butler Yeats). The Arnold canon is established, there are few problems of variant spelling, and a modern variorum edition is available: C. B. Tinker and H. F. Lowry, eds., *The Poetical Works of Matthew Arnold* (1950). By permission of Oxford University Press this text was used for key-punching, and the poem titles, part divisions, and line numbering it shows were adopted without exception. The variant lines which it prints in footnotes were also included, except as indicated below (see "Omitted Variants," page xii). It seemed logical, further, to include variants found in *The Poetry of Matthew Arnold: A Commentary*, by Tinker and Lowry (Oxford University Press, 1940), and in Lowry's edition of *The Letters of Matthew Arnold to Arthur Hugh Clough* (Oxford University Press, 1932). From the *Commentary* we have also taken Arnold's specimens of translation from Homer, the "Unpublished Poems" (pp. 335–347), and the various other scraps of verse printed there. To these were added, for the sake of completeness, verse fragments found in Arnold's letters. The result is a concordance which may be said to be based upon Tinker and Lowry's edition of *The Poetical Works*, but which also contains all verse printed in their *Commentary*, in Lowry's *Letters to Clough*, and in the two-volume

edition of Arnold's *Letters* edited by G. W. E. Russell for Macmillan in 1895. (It was not possible to include the variants recorded in Kenneth Allott, "Matthew Arnold's Original Version of 'The River,'" *TLS*, March 28, 1958, p. 172.) The "List of Poems" (page xv) gives the precise source of each item.

In their collations of Arnold's texts the editors of *The Poetical Works* have, they state, recorded all changes of spelling "but not the alterations in punctuation to which Arnold was addicted." Unfortunately, variants of hyphenation are not recorded, even when they involved creating one word out of two or two out of one. (The result is that certain variants which would have turned up as separate concordance entries fail to appear.) Yet this is a matter we could hardly have mended. Hence the Tinker and Lowry readings have been followed virtually without exception. Furthermore, in punching MS readings from the *Commentary* we have adopted conventions set by the authors of that volume. Thus "bluebells" is not treated as a variant of "blue-bells" ("Stanzas from Carnac," line 20); "&" is converted to "and" and "th'" to "the"; "thro" is expanded to "through"; and obvious misspellings are corrected. Changes of this sort were normally made by Arnold himself in preparing MS for print.

On the concordance page each line of verse is followed by the page number of Tinker and Lowry's edition, the abbreviated title of the poem, and the line number, in that order. Variant lines are identified by a "v" preceding the line number; the absence of a line number indicates that the variant has no corresponding line in the final text. The absence of a page number indicates that the line has been supplied from another source than Tinker and Lowry's edition; its location may be found by consulting the "List of Poems" (page xv).

Distinctive Features of a Machine Concordance

This concordance has, of necessity, several peculiarities—not all of them, it must be admitted, wholly advantageous. Owing to the fact that the printing was done by an unmodified IBM Printer, all letters are Roman capitals and no punctuation is shown, save only hyphens. (The four other marks of punctuation available on the print wheels—left parenthesis, right parenthesis, comma, and period—seemed unhelpful without apostrophe, quotation marks, colon, semicolon, dash, question mark, and exclamation point.) The absence of capitalization, italics, and punctuation is occasionally misleading, not to say diverting. Consider

THEY SHINE UPON THE WORLD THEIR EARS

("Euphrosyne," line 21: "They shine upon the world! Their ears"), or

SUDDEN FOR FIFTEEN YEARS

("Rugby Chapel," line 30: "Sudden. For fifteen years,"). The omission of apostrophes can make individual words look peculiar (consider YEARLL, USD, THAMESS). What is more serious, it can make indistinguishable words which are wholly different. "She'll," for instance, appears as SHELL, "fee'd" as FEED, and "I'll" as ILL. (It could have been worse; Arnold never used "he'll.") But these disadvantages will, it is hoped, be minor ones. The context should make the desired word intelligible, even the oddest-looking lines can generally be parsed, and in any case the page number is nearly always provided.

In a concordance indexed by hand, variant forms of a word can be brought together under a single normalized index entry; where all indexing is mechanical, no such luxury can be offered. Hence separate entries will be found here for such words as NEATH and BENEATH, MID and AMID, FIXT and FIXD. Past participles frequently take two forms—one with, one without, an apostrophe (thus BATHD, BATHED; CALLD, CALLED; FIXT, FIXD, FIXED); happily the latter variants fall close together alphabetically, and the user should have little trouble with them.

A word needs to be said concerning the hyphen. In order to prevent the second halves of hyphenated words from getting lost in the index, the computer was instructed to sort the halves separately, treating the hyphen as a space, not as a letter. Thus "forest-skirts" ("Scholar-Gipsy," line 215) appears both under FOREST and under SKIRTS; there is no index entry for the compound. A glance at some other compounds in the same poem will suggest the advantages of this policy: "country-nook," "half-believers," "green-muffled," "summer-heats," "gipsy-crew," and so forth. One could wish that certain compounds might have been held together as index entries. Unfortunately we could not have it both ways. Saving "skirts," "nook," "believers," "muffled," "heats," and "crew" meant losing as index entries such common terms as "to-day" (which Arnold always hyphenated), "to-morrow," "to-night," "re-enter," "re-assembling," "a-tremble," and a few others less common, among them "Bab-lock-hithe," "clere-story," "Kara-kul," and "a-Kempis." (No one can feel any regret at losing "thus-wise.") But again, once the user is aware of this peculiarity, he can find the compounds readily enough by looking up their parts.

Lest the computer's limitations should lead readers to feel patronizing, notice ought to be taken of its distinctive talents. Most impressive, perhaps —apart from its dazzling speed—is its capacity to produce finished pages, ready for offset reproduction. Listing the lines of verse under each index word in the order in which the lines are fed to it—in page and line order, that is, except that the variant lines for a poem are grouped at the end of the poem—the machine spaces them neatly into pages, adds the abbreviated titles and other data, supplies dots to fill out short lines, doubles

back long lines where necessary, and prints "(CONTINUED)" wherever an index entry runs over a page break.

Hardly less impressive is the computer's ability to array the index words in order of frequency. The Appendix shows in this order 9,946 words of Arnold's poetic vocabulary (excluded are the 151 words not indexed). The total of 10,097 is somewhat inflated by the way in which hyphenated words and words containing apostrophes have been handled; individual frequencies, moreover, are often padded by the presence of variant lines. But the percentage of distortion is small, and the frequency list may be used with confidence to study Arnold's vocabulary or to compare it with that of other poets. The reader should perhaps be cautioned that the list cannot be compared directly with other lists of high-frequency words made up by combining variant forms. The Appendix gives raw frequencies transcribed from the indexing tapes. Thus MAN (230 occurrences), MANS (50), and MEN (194) are separate entries, as are CHANGE (38), CHANGED (15), CHANGD (2), CHANGES (5), CHANGING (5), and so forth. It was felt that to edit the list by making even the most elementary combinations might be to mask frequencies that certain users would wish to see; it would surely have been unwise, for example, to combine SPAKE (61) and SPOKE (37), or even OER (115) and OVER (81). As it stands, the list provides the greatest possible flexibility. Since every index word may be found twice— once in the concordance in alphabetical order, once in the Appendix in order of frequency—it should be relatively simple for the user to combine variant forms in any fashion he desires and, of course, to separate homographs (e.g., ROSE as a noun and ROSE as a verb, totaling 36 occurrences).

Among the computer's lesser, yet admirable, talents is its capacity to control errors. To ensure accurate selection of text lines (carried out by means of a line-number coding on the tapes), a program was devised whereby the machine automatically tested each line it picked up for the presence of the index word. To ensure errorless printing, a circuit was passed through the print wheels and the machine instructed, upon detection of a misprint (that is, an instance in which the print wheel may have failed to turn to the proper position), to stop, space the paper up, reprint the line correctly, then continue to the end of the page. Finally, the frequency list made possible a search for one other species of error— mispunches that may have survived proofreading; all entries with a frequency of one (there were 4,358 of them) were inspected to make sure that they represented authentic words. Errors detected by these and other means were corrected by a simple process of cutting and pasting (in the course of which a line of text was occasionally inserted out of its proper order). It would be highly incautious to claim that no errors of any sort remain: mispunches can come out as good English words; cards can be

lost or misfiled. We trust, however—and this trust has been sustained by extensive random checking—that the machine has performed its share of the labor with relentless accuracy and thoroughness.

One apparent mistake will quickly strike the eye: a line of text sometimes occurs doubled or even tripled. But here the machine is faithfully recording what it finds, and, except where a refrain is being repeated (as under MEMORY, for instance), a glance at the line should reveal two (or three) occurrences of the index word.

Omitted Variants

Of the variants recorded in the standard texts of Arnold (*The Poetical Works*, the *Commentary*, and the editions of letters), six kinds have been excluded from the concordance. These are:

1) Obvious misprints (as identified by the editors of the texts).

2) Variants involving punctuation, capitals, or italics only (these would not, of course, show up in the IBM print).

3) Variants of a refrain line after the *first* occurrence (thus "Ere the parting kiss be dry" for "Ere the parting hour go by," from "A Memory-Picture," lines 7, 15, 23, 31, 39, 47, and 63, is recorded once only, as an unnumbered variant line).

4) Variants which involve only the transposition or renumbering of identical lines (as in "Stagirius," lines 33 and 34).

5) Variant spellings of proper names occurring throughout a poem (the full list is as follows: "Rostom" for "Rustum," "Tristan" for "Tristram," "Hercules" for "Heracles," "Pisianax" for "Peisanax," "Panthea" for "Pantheia").

6) Variants that consist of fragmentary MS lines (as "But then I say . . ." in "Empedocles on Etna," Act I, Scene 2, line 411).

All other variant readings have been punched, even where, as in the case of certain deleted MS readings, it was necessary in effect to manufacture the lines in which they seemed to belong. The exclusion of variants that involved only nonsignificant words (i.e., words not indexed) was for a time considered. This would have got rid of numerous minor changes now scrupulously recorded: "has" for "hath," "that" for "which," "toward" for "towards," and the like. Yet variants of this sort frequently involved shifting the positions of words, so that a wholly new line resulted. Ultimately it was felt that they might often be of more interest to users than such variants of "significant" words as "received" for "receiv'dst"; hence all save two or three, overlooked until after the indexing had been finished, were included.

Omitted Index Words

The selection of common words to be omitted from the index proved to be exceptionally trying. In principle, it seemed well to keep the list short,

since the machine uncomplainingly performs any chores asked of it. Many words commonly omitted from concordance indexes are therefore retained here. Some examples are "about," "below," "down," "even," "more," "still," "under," "very," "while," and "yet," among many others omitted from the Dryden concordance and omitted or only partially listed in the Wordsworth and Tennyson, and "out" and "up," wholly omitted not only from the Dryden, Wordsworth, and Tennyson but also from the Gray, the Donne, and the Keats. "As," "like," and "than" are retained to provide a means of studying Arnold's similes; all first-person pronouns are likewise retained as a possible means of studying dramatic technique and personification; "O" is retained because it appears distinctively in apostrophes (where "oh" does not).

At the same time some omissions were clearly desirable; it seemed profitless to fill pages of the index with articles, prepositions, and conjunctions. Doubt arose mainly over homographs—both the genuine ones and those formed artificially by the absence of apostrophes. The computer being unable to index selectively, all words with one important meaning seemed worth retaining, even where unimportant meanings would overwhelmingly predominate. The choice was clear enough in some instances: words like "art," "will," "might," had to be retained. Even "wilt" and "till" could be argued for. But was the off-chance that Arnold may have used "can" to represent tin or "twill" to represent cloth important enough to warrant retaining those common terms? And was any user of the concordance likely to wish to plow through columns of verbs in search of "May" as a month?[1] In the end arbitrary decisions had to be made about these and other matters. While some readers may question the editor's

---

[1] When the computer run was started, my answer to these questions was a somewhat uneasy "no." Later I became troubled about MAY and decided to produce a special printing of that word alone. (The computer can locate all occurrences of even a high-frequency word in about 20 minutes.) Having scanned it, I can report that Arnold used May as a month 12 times, as follows:

ON A MAY EVENING IN THE DARKEND LANES	101	BALDER DEAD 1	233
AND OVERHEAD THE CLOUDLESS SKY OF MAY	133	TRISTRAM 1	96
LET THE BREATH OF THE MAY-WIND	135	TRISTRAM 1	156
THE GRASS HAD STILL THE GREEN OF MAY	222	EPILOG LAOCOON	38
TO DANCE AROUND THE FYFIELD ELM IN MAY	257	SCHOLAR-GIPSY	83
WITH BLOSSOMS RED AND WHITE OF FALLEN MAY	264	THYRSIS	55
WOODS WITH ANEMONIES IN FLOWER TILL MAY	268	THYRSIS	199
IN THE MILD EVENING OF THE MAY	274	STANZAS CARNAC	12
SLEEP OR ONLY WHEN MAY	285	HAWORTH CHURCH	113
SEE IN THE MAY-AFTERNOON	297	HEINES GRAVE	152
FRESHEND AND LIGHT WITH THE MAY	297	HEINES GRAVE	178
WHO OF LATE ON THE SOFT NIGHTS OF MAY	482	THEKLAS ANSWER	6

judgment, it is hoped that, as they look over the following list, none will think the decisions ill-considered. Whatever their merit, they cost much anxious reflection.

It may be worth noticing, finally, that titles are not indexed. This will explain why there are to be found under BEACH no entry from "Dover Beach," and for "Chartreuse," "Requiescat," and other such familiar title words, no entries at all.

OMITTED WORDS

A	EACH	MAYST	THEMSELVES	WAST
AGAIN	EITHER	MIGHTST	THEN	WERE
AH		MUST	THERE	WERT
ALSO	FOR		THEREFORE	WHAT
ALTHO	FROM	NEITHER	THERES	WHATEER
ALTHOUGH	HAD	NO	THESE	WHATEVER
AM	HADST	NOR	THEY	WHATS
AN	HAS	NOT	THINE	WHEN
AND	HAST	NOW	THIS	WHENEER
ARE	HATH		THO	WHENEVER
AT	HAVE	OF	THOSE	WHERE
ANOTHER	HE	OH	THOU	WHEREER
ANOTHERS	HER	ON	THOUGH	WHEREVER
	HERE	OR	THRO	WHETHER
BE	HERS	OTHER	THROUGH	WHICH
BECAUSE	HERSELF	OTHERS	THRU	WHICHEER
BEEN	HES		THUS	WHICHEVER
BOTH	HIM	SHALL	THY	WHO
BUT	HIMSELF	SHALLST	THYSELF	WHOM
BY	HIS	SHALT	TIS	WHOS
	HOW	SHE	TO	WHOSE
CAN	HOWEER	SHES	TOO	WHY
CANNOT	HOWEVER	SHOULD	TOWARD	WITH
CANST		SHOULDST	TOWARDS	WOULD
COULD	IF	SO	TOWRD	WOULDST
COULDST	IN		TOWRDS	
	INTO	THAT		YE
DID	IS	THATS	TWAS	YOU
DIDST	IT	THE	TWERE	YOUR
DO	ITS	THEE	TWILL	YOURS
DOES	ITSELF	THEIR	TWOULD	YOURSELF
DOST		THEIRS		YOURSELVES
DOTH	MAY	THEM	WAS	

Title Abbreviations

An effort has been made to devise abbreviations that will be intelligible even to the casual reader of Arnold's poems. Frequently the entire title, less articles, could be accommodated; whenever possible, at least the opening word has been used. Where a poem has gone under several titles, the one adopted in Arnold's final edition (and thus by Tinker and Lowry) has been taken as standard. Where the parts of a long poem begin a fresh sequence of line numbers, a fresh title has been assigned (thus "Balder Dead" has been treated as though it were made up of three separate poems, as has "Empedocles on Etna"). The "Switzerland" and "Faded Leaves" groups have been broken up and the poems that comprise them indexed separately.

List of Poems

In this list the abbreviated title, exactly as it appears in the concordance, is followed by the full title (or, where none has ever been assigned, by the opening words of text), and by the poem's location, given as the page number at which the poem begins in one of the following volumes:

Works: C. B. Tinker and H. F. Lowry, eds., *The Poetical Works of Matthew Arnold* (Oxford University Press, 1950).

Comm.: C. B. Tinker and H. F. Lowry, *The Poetry of Matthew Arnold: A Commentary* (Oxford University Press, 1940).

Clough: H. F. Lowry, ed., *The Letters of Matthew Arnold to Arthur Hugh Clough* (Oxford University Press, 1932).

Lett.: G. W. E. Russell, ed., *Letters of Matthew Arnold: 1848–1888*, 2 vols. (London and New York: Macmillan, 1895).

POEMS

ABSENCE	Switzerland 6. Absence	*Works,*	183
ALARIC AT ROME	Alaric at Rome	"	462
AUSTERITY POET	Austerity of Poetry	"	166
BACCHANALIA 1	Bacchanalia; or, The New Age (I)	"	217
BACCHANALIA 2	" " " " " (II)	"	219
BALDER DEAD 1	Balder Dead (I. Sending)	"	95
BALDER DEAD 2	" " (II. Journey to the Dead)	"	105
BALDER DEAD 3	" " (III. Funeral)	"	113
BELOW SURFACE	"Below the Surface-Stream"	"	483
BETTER PART	The Better Part	"	170
BURIED LIFE	The Buried Life	"	245
BUTLERS SERMONS	Written in Butler's Sermons	"	4
CALAIS SANDS	Calais Sands	"	204

CAUTION POETS	A Caution to Poets	*Works,*	228
CHURCH BROU 1	The Church of Brou (I. The Castle)	"	12
CHURCH BROU 2	" " " " (II. The Church)	"	16
CHURCH BROU 3	" " " " (III. The Tomb)	"	17
CONSOLATION	Consolation	"	50
COURAGE	Courage	"	481
CROMWELL	Cromwell	"	471
DESPONDENCY	Despondency	"	209
DESTINY	Destiny	"	481
DIVINITY	The Divinity	"	171
DOVER BEACH	Dover Beach	"	210
	(variant line 3)	*Comm.,*	173
DREAM	A Dream	*Works,*	24
DUKE WELLINGTON	To the Duke of Wellington on Hearing Him Mispraised	"	4
EARLY DEATH	Early Death and Fame	"	199
EAST AND WEST	East and West	"	170
EAST LONDON	East London	"	169
EDW QUILLINAN	Stanzas in Memory of Edward Quillinan	"	272
EMERSONS ESSAYS	Written in Emerson's Essays	"	3
	(variant lines 6–9, 11, 14)	*Comm.,*	27
EMPEDOCLES I 1	Empedocles on Etna: A Dramatic Poem (Act I, Scene 1)	*Works,*	406
EMPEDOCLES I 2	Empedocles on Etna (Act I, Scene 2)	"	412
	(11 variant lines, unnumbered)	*Comm.,*	292
EMPEDOCLES II	Empedocles on Etna (Act II)	*Works,*	428
EPILOG LAOCOON	Epilogue to Lessing's Laocoön	"	221
EUPHROSYNE	Euphrosyne	"	203
EVERLASTING SUB	"The Everlasting Substance of the Hills"	*Comm.,*	347
FAREWELL	Switzerland 3. A Farewell	*Works,*	177
FORSAKEN MERM	The Forsaken Merman	"	161
FRAG ANTIGONE	Fragment of an "Antigone"	"	195
FRAG DEJANEIRA	Fragment of Chorus of a "Dejaneira"	"	198
FRAGMENT 1	"Night comes:—with Night . . ."	*Clough,*	57
FRAGMENT 2	"Ye too, who stand beside . . ."	"	58
FRAGMENT 3	"this little which we are . . ."	"	85
FRAGMENT 4	"Where young Archestes . . ."	"	90
FRAGMENT 5	"Say this of her . . ."	"	93
		(also *Comm.,*	60)
FRAGMENT 6	"I believe . . ."	*Comm.,*	335
FRAGMENT 7	"The dropping patter . . ."	"	335
FRAGMENT 8	"The clouds of sickness . . ."	*Lett.,* I,	8

FRAGMENT 9	"It seems an idle thing . . ."	*Lett.*, II,	109
FUTURE	The Future	*Works*,	251
GEISTS GRAVE	Geist's Grave	"	449
GEO CRUIKSHANK	To George Cruikshank On Seeing, in the Country, His Picture of "The Bottle"	"	6
GIPSY CHILD	To a Gipsy Child by the Sea-Shore: Douglas, Isle of Man	*Works*,	41
GOOD SHEPHERD	The Good Shepherd with the Kid	"	172
GRANDE CHARTR	Stanzas from the Grande Chartreuse	"	299
GROWING OLD	Growing Old	"	212
HARMONY NATURE	In Harmony with Nature: To a Preacher	"	5
HAWORTH CHURCH	Haworth Churchyard: April, 1855	"	280
HAYSWATER BOAT	The Hayswater Boat	"	479
HEINES GRAVE	Heine's Grave	"	292
HOMER TRANS	Translations from Homer	*Comm.*,	329
HORATIAN ECHO	Horation Echo: (To an Ambitious Friend) (variant line 7; 4 unnumbered variant lines)	*Works*, *Comm.*,	47 59
HUMAN LIFE	Human Life	*Works*,	40
HUNGARIAN NAT	Sonnet to the Hungarian Nation	"	480
IMMORTALITY	Immortality	"	172
IN UTRUMQUE PAR	In Utrumque Paratus	"	45
ISOLATION MARG	Switzerland 4. Isolation. To Marguerite	"	180
KAISER DEAD	Kaiser Dead: April 6, 1887	"	458
KENSINGTON GARD	Lines Written in Kensington Gardens (variant lines 4–5, 7–11, 13–15, 17, 21, 24–26, 28–29, 32, 36, 39; 3 unnumbered variant lines)	" *Comm.*,	248 196
LAST WORD	The Last Word	*Works*,	215
LONGING	Faded Leaves 5. Longing	"	208
LORDS MESSENGER	The Lord's Messengers	"	216
LUCRETIUS 1	Fragments of "Lucretius" (1)	*Comm.*,	345
LUCRETIUS 2	" " " (2)	"	"
LUCRETIUS 3	" " " (3)	"	346
LUCRETIUS 5	" " " (5)	"	"
LUCRETIUS 6	" " " (6)	"	347
LUCRETIUS 7	" " " (7)	"	"
MEETING	Switzerland 1. Meeting	*Works*,	174
MEMORIAL VERSES	Memorial Verses: April, 1850	"	270
MEMORY-PICTURE	A Memory-Picture	"	22
MEROPE	Merope: A Tragedy	"	330
META CLOISTER	To Meta: The Cloister	*Comm.*,	339

MODERN SAPPHO	A Modern Sappho	Works,	19
MONICAS PRAYER	Monica's Last Prayer	"	173
MORALITY	Morality	"	241
MYCERINUS	Mycerinus	"	8
NAMELESS EPIT	A Nameless Epitaph	"	217
NECKAN	The Neckan	"	159
NEW ROME	New Rome: Lines Written for Miss Story's Album	"	214
NEW SIRENS	The New Sirens	"	26
OBERMANN	Stanzas in Memory of the Author of "Obermann": November, 1849	"	306
OBERMANN MORE	Obermann once more: (Composed Many Years After the Preceding)	"	312
ON THE RHINE	Faded Leaves 4. On the Rhine	"	207
PALLADIUM	Palladium	"	236
PARTING	Switzerland 2. Parting	"	174
	(variant lines 25, 27–28)	Clough,	110
PERSIST POETRY	Persistency of Poetry	Works,	227
PHILOMELA	Philomela	"	200
	(2 variant lines, unnumbered)	Comm.,	164
PICT NEWSTEAD	A Picture at Newstead	Works,	166
PILLARS UNIVERS	The Pillars of the Universe	Comm.,	338
PIS-ALLER	Pis-Aller	Works,	215
POOR MATTHIAS	Poor Matthias	"	452
PROGRESS	Progress	"	237
PROGRESS POESY	The Progress of Poesy: A Variation	"	213
QUESTION	A Question: To Fausta	"	44
QUIET WORK	Quiet Work	"	1
RACHEL 1	Rachel (I)	"	167
RACHEL 2	" (II)	"	"
RACHEL 3	" (III)	"	168
RELIGIOUS ISOL	Religious Isolation: To the Same Friend [see below]	"	8
REP FRIEND	To a Republican Friend, 1848	"	6
REP FRIEND CONT	Continued [see above]	"	7
REQUIESCAT	Requiescat	"	20
RESIGNATION	Resignation: To Fausta	"	52
REVOLUTIONS	Revolutions	"	239
RIVER	Faded Leaves 1. The River	"	206
ROME-SICKNESS	Rome-Sickness	"	483
RUDE ORATOR	Rude Orator	Comm.,	337
RUGBY CHAPEL	Rugby Chapel: November 1857	Works,	286

S S LUSITANIA	S.S. "Lusitania"	*Works,*	484
SAINT BRANDAN	Saint Brandan	"	156
SCHOLAR-GIPSY	The Scholar-Gipsy	"	255
SECOND BEST	The Second Best	"	49
	(variant lines 6–7, 10, 17–24)	*Comm.,*	60
SELF-DECEPTION	Self-Deception	*Works,*	209
SELF-DEPENDENCE	Self-Dependence	"	239
SEPARATION	Faded Leaves 3. Separation	"	207
SHAKESPEARE	Shakespeare	"	2
SICK KING BOKH	The Sick King in Bokhara	"	87
SOHRAB RUSTUM	Sohrab and Rustum: An Episode	"	61
SOUTHERN NIGHT	A Southern Night	"	275
STAGIRIUS	Stagirius	"	38
STANZAS CARNAC	Stanzas from Carnac	"	273
	(variant lines 7, 8, 16)	*Comm.,*	224
STRAYED REVEL	The Strayed Reveller	*Works,*	185
SUMMER NIGHT	A Summer Night	"	242
TERRACE BERNE	Switzerland 7. The Terrace at Berne: (Composed Ten Years after the Preceding [i.e., "Absence"])	"	183
THEKLAS ANSWER	Thekla's Answer: (From Schiller)	"	482
THYRSIS	Thyrsis: A Monody, to commemorate the author's friend, Arthur Hugh Clough, who died at Florence, 1861	"	262
TO A FRIEND	To a Friend	"	2
TO MARG CONT	Switzerland 5. To Marguerite—Continued	"	182
TOO LATE	Faded Leaves 2. Too Late	"	206
TRISTRAM 1	Tristram and Iseult (I. Tristram)	"	130
TRISTRAM 2	" " " (II. Iseult of Ireland)	"	142
TRISTRAM 3	" " " (III. Iseult of Brittany)	"	149
	(variant lines 1, 5, 7, 9–15, 18–19, 21–23, 32, 38, 43, 47, 49, 51, 53)	*Comm.,*	120
URANIA	Urania	*Works,*	201
VOICE	The Voice	"	35
WEST LONDON	West London	"	169
WESTMIN ABBEY	Westminster Abbey: July 25, 1881 (The Day of Burial, in the Abbey, of Arthur Penrhyn Stanley, Dean of Westminster.)	"	444
WISH	A Wish	"	249
WORLD QUIETIST	The World and the Quietist: To Critias	"	46
WORLDLY PLACE	Wordly Place	"	168
WORLDS TRIUMPHS	The World's Triumphs	"	37

YOUTH AND CALM Youth and Calm *Works,* 21

YOUTH OF NATURE The Youth of Nature " 228

YOUTH OF MAN The Youth of Man " 232

YOUTHS AGIT Youth's Agitations " 37

Acknowledgments

In the preface to the Spenser concordance Charles Grosvenor Osgood alludes darkly to "the help of many collaborators, a number of them volunteers." (One wonders about the others.) I should like to think that none of my own collaborators has been pressed into servitude, but whatever the case their co-operation and enthusiasm have done much to make this experiment successful.

My greatest debts are recorded in the dedication. William Andrus, now Manager, Applied Computations, Data Processing Division of the IBM Corporation, and formerly Manager of the IBM Scientific Computation Laboratory at Endicott, New York, put at my disposal his 704 computer, its peripheral equipment, and the services of his staff. Generosity of this sort beggars acknowledgment, and I can only hope that the wedding of literature and technology which we have staged will prove as satisfying to him as it has to me. James Painter, in charge of Systems Evaluation at the Scientific Computation Laboratory, wrote and checked out the computer program, at the cost of more hours of his time than I dare estimate. His skill at designing a program to meet our needs, his willingness to rewrite and recheck it almost endlessly, his good humor in the face of my whimsical and importunate demands, have put me very deeply in his debt.

Richard Lesser, Director of the Cornell Computing Center at Ithaca, has been equally generous with the IBM equipment under his control, allowing us to use key-punch and reproducing machines without cost. The expenses we did incur were met by a Cornell Faculty Research Grant and a portion of a Department of English Research Grant, for which I am deeply grateful.

To Yoline Chandler, Gail Sherrell, and especially to William Messenger, I owe thanks for proofreading and editorial assistance. They, Beverly Hillick (who punched the text cards), and I are the only participants in this venture who can claim to have enjoyed what Professor Osgood eloquently cited as the prime compensation of concordance making—the pleasure that arises "in handling from day to day bright ravelings from the rich fabric of Spenser's [Arnold's] poetry, or in hearing, until their cadence falls familiarly upon the ear, snatches of his incomparable music."

Uncompensated even by this reward, my colleagues at Cornell have rallied loyally to my aid. Professor Robert A. Donovan consented to cast his expert Arnoldian eye over this preface; Professor M. H. Abrams never

failed to make a wise and kindly response to my pleas for counsel; Professor William R. Keast by his encouragement and support at every step of the way helped enormously to convert a mere gleam in the eye into the series which this volume inaugurates.

S. M. PARRISH

Ithaca, New York
January 1959

A Concordance to the Poems of

MATTHEW ARNOLD

AAR
    AND THROUGH THOSE FIELDS COMES DOWN THE AAR · · 184 TERRACE BERNE 8

AARAU
    AT A MEAN INN IN GERMAN AARAU BORN · · · · · · 168 RACHEL 3 2

ABANDOND
    TO BATHE IN THE ABANDOND LASHER PASS · · · · · 258 SCHOLAR-GIPSY 95
    BEHIND ARE THE ABANDOND BATHS · · · · · · · 306 OBERMANN 5
    O HEAVEN-ABANDOND WRETCH THAT ENVIES THEE · · · · 397 MEROPE 1773

ABANDONS
    ABANDONS ALL WHICH MAKES · · · · · · · · · 420 EMPEDOCLES I 2 244
    ABANDONS ALL THAT MAKES · · · · · · · · · · 420 EMPEDOCLES I 2 V 244

ABBEY
    BEYOND THE ABBEY-TOWERS APPEARD · · · · · 223 EPILOG LAOCOON 70
    ABBEY RECALL IT WHAT A SPHERE · · · · · · 223 EPILOG LAOCOON 79
    BENEATH SOME OLD-WORLD ABBEY WALL · · · · 304 GRANDE CHARTR 170
    THEIR ABBEY AND ITS CLOSE OF GRAVES · · · · 305 GRANDE CHARTR 174
    COULDST THOU NO BETTER KEEP O ABBEY OLD · · 444 WESTMIN ABBEY 4
    THE WORLD-FAMED ABBEY BY THE WESTERING THAMES · 444 WESTMIN ABBEY 20
    SEEMD TO COME TRUE AT LAST O ABBEY OLD · · 446 WESTMIN ABBEY 73
    THEN FROM HIS ABBEY FADES · · · · · · 448 WESTMIN ABBEY 127
    AND THOU O ABBEY GREY · · · · · · · · 449 WESTMIN ABBEY 171
    AND FROM HIS ABBEY FADES · · · · · · · · 448 WESTMIN ABBEY V 127

ABBEYS
    THUS SLEEPING IN THINE ABBEYS FRIENDLY SHADE · · 449 WESTMIN ABBEY 164
    HERE SLEEPING IN THINE ABBEYS FRIENDLY SHADE · · 449 WESTMIN ABBEY V 164

ABHORRD
    FEELS THE ABHORRD APPROACHES OF OLD AGE · · · 63 SOHRAB RUSTUM 84
    HER STATELY PURPLE SHE ABHORRD · · · · · · 316 OBERMANN MORE 127
    NOT IN ABHORRD ESTRANGEMENT LET YOU STAND · · 339 MEROPE 300
    HATEFUL BY EACH MESSENIAN HEART ABHORRD · · · 366 MEROPE 1009

ABHORRED
    BETWIXT BLANK NOTHING AND ABHORRED DECAY · · · · FRAGMENT 5 5

ABHORRING
    NOT DAILY TO ENDURE ABHORRING GODS · · · · · · 125 BALDER DEAD 3 398

ABIDE
    OTHERS ABIDE OUR QUESTION THOU ART FREE · · · 2 SHAKESPEARE 1
    HE ESCAPES THENCE BUT WE ABIDE · · · · · · · 58 RESIGNATION 213
    THE LAW IS PLANTED TO ABIDE · · · · · · · 94 SICK KING BOKH 208
    HOWBEIT WE ABIDE OUR DAY TILL THEN · · · · · 111 BALDER DEAD 2 227
    THEY ABIDE AND THE FINEST OF SOULS · · · · 230 YOUTH OF NATURE 81
    HOW IT WERE GOOD TO ABIDE THERE AND BREATHE FREE · · 244 SUMMER NIGHT 90
    WHETHER IS BETTER TO ABIDE ALONE · · · · · 338 MEROPE 287
    WHERE HE WHO BEARS THEE MUST ABIDE · · · · · 435 EMPEDOCLES II 200
    AND WAIT WHILE HE DID THERE A SPACE ABIDE · · · 445 WESTMIN ABBEY 26

ABIDES
    IN MYSTERY OUR SOUL ABIDES · · · · · · · · 241 MORALITY 4
    THAT THERE ABIDES A PEACE OF THINE · · · · · 249 KENSINGTON GARD 39
    ABIDES ENTHROND AMID THE MIST AND STORM · · · 472 CROMWELL 18

ABJECT
    HOW MUCH MEN THINK ME ABJECT VOID OF HEART · · · 366 MEROPE 1016

ABLAZE
    DROVE ON ABLAZE ABOVE HER HULL WITH FIRE · · · 119 BALDER DEAD 3 192
    AND SET THE FIELDS OF GLOOM ABLAZE WITH LIGHT · · 120 BALDER DEAD 3 243

ABODE
    ERST ABODE AMBUSHD · · · · · · · · · · 51 CONSOLATION 32
    EVEN IN THE ABODE OF DEATH O BALDER HAIL · · · 112 BALDER DEAD 2 250
    THEIR ENDLESS ABODE · · · · · · · · · 442 EMPEDOCLES II 456
    MARKD WITH A STONE THY LAST ABODE · · · · · 452 GEISTS GRAVE 72

ABODES
    A LIGHT THAT SHINING FROM THE BLEST ABODES · · · 9 MYCERINUS 23
    TYRANNY PRIDE AND LUST FILL SICILYS ABODES · · · 416 EMPEDOCLES I 2 121
    IT STAYS IN YOUR ABODES · · · · · · · · · 423 EMPEDOCLES I 2 340

ABOUND
    WHERE WHERE DO THESE ABOUND · · · · · · · 309 OBERMANN 98
    BE JUDGE THYSELF IF IT ABOUND NOT HERE · · · · 336 MEROPE 211
    AND WHERE THE SOAKING SPRINGS ABOUND · · · · · 414 EMPEDOCLES I 2 64

ABOUT
    HIS ARMS ABOUT HIS NECK AND KISSD HIS LIPS · · · 81 SOHRAB RUSTUM 695
    THEN THEY WHO STOOD ABOUT THE KING · · · · · 91 SICK KING BOKH 105
    WHERE IDLY FLIT ABOUT THE FEEBLE SHADES · · · 110 BALDER DEAD 2 182
    TWINE ABOUT THEIR HEARTS AGAIN · · · · · · 135 TRISTRAM 1 152
    FLING THE FRESH HEAPS ABOUT · · · · · · · 218 BACCHANALIA 1 34
    FLING THE PILED SHEAVES ABOUT · · · · · · · 218 BACCHANALIA 1 V 34

2

ABOUT   (CONTINUED)
      SCATTERING THE PAST ABOUT   . . . .   220 BACCHANALIA 2   35
      EDDYING ABOUT IN BLIND UNCERTAINTY   . . . . .   246 BURIED LIFE   V   43
      BUT RUMOURS HUNG ABOUT THE COUNTRY-SIDE   . . .   256 SCHOLAR-GIPSY   52
      THE WHITE FOG CREEPS FROM BUSH TO BUSH ABOUT . .   267 THYRSIS   162
      MOST MEN EDDY ABOUT   . . . .   288 RUGBY CHAPEL   60
      CONDEMND TO CAST ABOUT   . . . .   307 OBERMANN   18
      AH TWO DESIRES TOSS ABOUT   . . . .   309 OBERMANN   93
      WITH QUESTIONINGS ABOUT AN IDLE TALE . . . . .   411 EMPEDOCLES I 1   155
      THE CUP ABOUT WHOSE DRAUGHTS BEGUILE . . . . .   431 EMPEDOCLES II   85
      CAME ABOUT THE YOUTHFUL GOD   . . . .   433 EMPEDOCLES II   158

ABOVE
      DOTH RUSTLINGLY ABOVE YOUR HEADS COMPLAIN   . . . . 18 CHURCH BROU 3   33
      AND ON THE LICHEN-CRUSTED LEADS ABOVE   . . . .   19 CHURCH BROU 3   45
      ON THIS MILD BANK ABOVE THE STREAM   . . . .   55 RESIGNATION   102
      CIRCLES ABOVE HIS EYRY WITH LOUD SCREAMS   . . .   78 SOHRAB RUSTUM   565
      AND HEAP A STATELY MOUND ABOVE MY BONES   . . .   84 SOHRAB RUSTUM   788
      AND HEAP A STATELY MOUND ABOVE THY BONES . . .   84 SOHRAB RUSTUM   803
      AND ZAL MIGHT WEEP ABOVE MY GRAVE NOT THINE   . .   85 SOHRAB RUSTUM   821
      DROVE ON ABLAZE ABOVE HER HULL WITH FIRE   . . .   119 BALDER DEAD 3   192
      THE EARTH AND OCEAN AND ABOVE THEM HEAVEN   . . . 121 BALDER DEAD 3   261
      HIGH ABOVE THE SOUNDING SEA   . . . . .   134 TRISTRAM 1   135
      ABOVE THE DIN HER VOICE IS IN MY EARS   . . . .   137 TRISTRAM 1   240
      EARTH SEA AND SKY AND GOD ABOVE   . . . . .   161 NECKAN   63
      WE SHALL SEE WHILE ABOVE US   . . . . .   165 FORSAKEN MERM   116
      ABOVE THE FRAGRANT WARM PROVENCAL SHORE   . . . . 167 RACHEL 2   2
      ABOVE THE HOWLING SENSES EBB AND FLOW   . . . .   169 EAST LONDON   11
      THOUGHT I ABOVE HER STATE THIS SPIRIT TOWERS . . 170 WEST LONDON   9
      THE LIQUID SKY ABOVE THE HILL   . . . .   218 BACCHANALIA 1   18
      A WORLD ABOVE MANS HEAD TO LET HIM SEE   . . .   244 SUMMER NIGHT   87
      AND ABOVE GODSTOW BRIDGE WHEN HAY-TIMES HERE . . 257 SCHOLAR-GIPSY   91
      ABOVE THE FOREST-GROUND CALLED THESSALY   . . . . 258 SCHOLAR-GIPSY   115
      ABOVE BY ENSHAM DOWN BY SANDFORD YIELDS . . . .   266 THYRSIS   109
      ABOVE THE LOCKS ABOVE THE BOATING THRONG . . .   266 THYRSIS   122
      ABOVE THE LOCKS ABOVE THE BOATING THRONG . . .   266 THYRSIS   122
      SEE LOW ABOVE THE TIDE AT FLOOD   . . . . .   274 STANZAS CARNAC   26
      EMBLEMS OF LIGHT ABOVE THE GRAVE   . . . . .   305 GRANDE CHARTR   V 201
      ABOVE HIS SUN-WARMD FIRS   . . . .   313 OBERMANN MORE   34
      O ARTS ABOVE THE VULGAR TYRANTS REACH   . . . .   339 MEROPE   310
      NOT ABOVE ALL IN THE DOUBTS   . . . . . .   370 MEROPE   1112
      BENT ABOVE ALL TO PACIFY TO RULE   . . . . .   388 MEROPE   1490
      ABOVE A RACE YOU KNOW NOT   . . . . . .   437 EMPEDOCLES II   296
      BRILLIANT ABOVE ME AND THOU FIERY WORLD   . . .   438 EMPEDOCLES II   305
      FOUR YEARS AND DIDST THOU STAY ABOVE   . . .   449 GEISTS GRAVE   1
      GREEN TURF ABOVE AND CRUMBLING DUST BELOW   . . . 464 ALARIC AT ROME   57
      AS TOWERED ON HIGH ABOVE THEIR MOONLIT ROAD   . . 466 ALARIC AT ROME   113
      AND TRANQUILLY ABOVE THAT TROUBLED BREAST   . . . 469 ALARIC AT ROME   195
      A FORM THAT TOWERD ABOVE HIS BROTHER MEN . . . . 476 CROMWELL   145
      BUT LET ME BE DEAD AND THE EARTH BE MOUNDED ABOVE ME   HOMER TRANS   37

ABREAST
      BUT WHEN THEY CAME ABREAST THE POINT THE RACE   . . 358 MEROPE   823

ABROAD
      DREW A WARM SCENT ABROAD BEHIND THE PINES   . . . . 25 DREAM   6
      AND WENT ABROAD INTO THE COLD WET FOG   . . . .   61 SOHRAB RUSTUM   10
      HIS HERALD TO HIS SIDE AND WENT ABROAD   . . . .   64 SOHRAB RUSTUM   103
      AND WENT ABROAD INTO THE COLD DIM AIR   . . . .   61 SOHRAB RUSTUM   V   10
      HE DROVE ABROAD IN FURIOUS GUISE   . . . . .   315 OBERMANN MORE   99
      ITS INMATES ON THEIR DAILY TASKS ABROAD   . . .   330 MEROPE   27
      EXILE ABROAD MORE SAFE THAN HEIRSHIP HERE   . . . 340 MEROPE   337

ABRUPTLY
      OF COURTLY SPEECH ABRUPTLY DIED   . . . . . .   146 TRISTRAM 2   119

ABSENCE
      MEANS PARTING THAT ONLY IN ABSENCE LIES PAIN . .   19 MODERN SAPPHO   V
      ABSENCE FROM FIELDS WHERE I COULD NOTHING AID   . . 127 BALDER DEAD 3   502
      AT THIS FIRST MEETING AFTER ABSENCE LONG . . . . 386 MEROPE   1452
      AND HAUNT HIM TILL THE ABSENCE FROM HIMSELF   . . 435 EMPEDOCLES II   225

ABSENT
      THOU HAST THINE ABSENT MASTERS TEAR   . . . . . . 451 GEISTS GRAVE   55

ABSOLVES
      THY CROWN CONDEMNS THEE WHILE THY TONGUE ABSOLVES   340 MEROPE   332

ABSTRACTED
      THY DARK VAGUE EYES AND SOFT ABSTRACTED AIR   . . 258 SCHOLAR-GIPSY   99

ABSURD
      DOOMD POMPOUS AND ABSURD   . . . .   48 HORATIAN ECHO   12

ABSURDITY
      BEHOLDING THE ABSURDITY OF MEN   . . . .   298 HEINES GRAVE   207

ABYSMAL
      AND CAST HIS TRUNK TO CHOKE THE ABYSMAL VOID . . 121 BALDER DEAD 3   259
      AND THREW HIS TRUNK TO CHOKE THE ABYSMAL VOID   . . 121 BALDER DEAD 3   V 259

ABYSS
    THE STORM THE ABYSS THE HOWLING AND THE PAIN   • • 109 BALDER DEAD 2   154
    THE GIANT YMIR WHOM THE ABYSS BROUGHT FORTH   • • 121 BALDER DEAD 3   257
    COME FLOATING UP FROM THE ABYSS OF YEARS   • • • • 469 ALARIC AT ROME   176

ACACIA
    AND THESE FRAIL ACACIA BOUGHS • • • • • • • • 200 PHILOMELA   V
    IN THE WHITE ACACIA FLOWERS • • • • • • • • 201 PHILOMELA   V

ACCENT
    WITH A MASTERS ACCENT HER FEIGND • • • • • • 280 HAWORTH CHURCH   11

ACCENTS
    ARE THE ACCENTS OF YOUR LURING • • • • • • • 27 NEW SIRENS   41
    O UNFORGOTTEN VOICE THY ACCENTS COME • • • • • • 36 VOICE   29
    ITS ACCENTS OF ANOTHER SPHERE • • • • • • • 306 GRANDE CHARTR   204
    HEARD ACCENTS OF THE ETERNAL TONGUE • • • • • 310 OBERMANN   125

ACCEPT
    ACCEPT THEM OR REJECT THEM BOTH HAVE GROUNDS • • 120 BALDER DEAD 3   226
    ACCEPT THEM AND THEY BIND US UNFULFILLD • • • • 120 BALDER DEAD 3   227
    ACCEPT THE CHANCE THOU CANST NO MORE OBTAIN • • 122 BALDER DEAD 3   290
    WHEREFORE ACCEPT THAT HAPPIER OMEN • • • • • 344 MEROPE   452
    ACCEPT THEM IN ONE WORD FOR GOOD OR BAD • • • • 355 MEROPE   713
    ACCEPT IT POLYPHONTES IS NO MORE • • • • • 401 MEROPE   1888

ACCEPTANCE
    AND STILL THE ACCEPTANCE FOLLOWS ME WHICH CROWND • • 126 BALDER DEAD 3   461
    AND SERVED MEN NOBLY AND ACCEPTANCE FOUND • • • • 448 WESTMIN ABBEY   143

ACCESS
    O EASY ACCESS TO THE HEARERS GRACE • • • • • • 265 THYRSIS   91

ACCLAIM
    WITH GLAD ACCLAIM ERE THEY FORESTALL MY NEWS • • 401 MEROPE   1887

ACCOMPANIES
    EVER ACCOMPANIES THE MARCH OF MAN • • • • • • 238 PROGRESS   V 38

ACCOMPANY
    FOR EVER DOTH ACCOMPANY MANKIND • • • • • • 238 PROGRESS   38

ACCOMPLICE
    INFER THEE THEIR ACCOMPLICE AND THEY SAY • • • • 334 MEROPE   143

ACCOMPLISH
    THAT HOW TO ACCOMPLISH WHAT THE GODS ENJOIN • • 379 MEROPE   1263

ACCOMPLISHD
    FAR NOISIER SCHEMES ACCOMPLISHD IN REPOSE • • • • 1 QUIET WORK   7
    MANS NOISY SCHEMES ACCOMPLISHD IN REPOSE • • • • 1 QUIET WORK   V 7
    MANS NOISY FEATS ACCOMPLISHD IN REPOSE • • • • 1 QUIET WORK   V 7
    MANS NOISY WORK ACCOMPLISHD IN REPOSE • • • • 1 QUIET WORK   V 7
    MUCH NOISIER WORK ACCOMPLISHD IN REPOSE • • • • 1 QUIET WORK   V 7

ACCOST
    BUT HE MUST STRAIGHT ACCOST THEIR SOLEMN QUEEN • • 100 BALDER DEAD 1   178

ACCOUNT
    FOR THAT HE PLOTS THY DEATH ACCOUNT IT FALSE • • 387 MEROPE   1485

ACCOUNTETH
    BUT ZEUS WHO ACCOUNTETH THY QUARREL HIS OWN • • 347 MEROPE   526

ACCURST
    POOR WORLD SHE CRIED SO DEEP ACCURST • • • • • 316 OBERMANN MORE   117
    NEVER TO EBB THE ACCURST • • • • • • • • 378 MEROPE   1245

ACCUSER
    OF MISTLETOE WHICH LOK THE ACCUSER GAVE • • • 95 BALDER DEAD 1   6
    THE FOE THE ACCUSER WHOM THOUGH GODS WE HATE • • 96 BALDER DEAD 1   38
    THE FOE THE ACCUSER WHOM THOUGH GODS WE HATE • • 98 BALDER DEAD 1   101
    IT IS THE ACCUSER LOK WHO FLOUTS US ALL • • • • 124 BALDER DEAD 3   370

ACCUSTOMD
    NOR FETCH TO TAKE THE ACCUSTOMD TOLL • • • • • • 250 WISH   21

ACHAIA
    WERE HUNTED OUT AND TO ACHAIA FLED • • • • • • 338 MEROPE   286

ACHAIAN
    BY ACHAIAN ARCADIAN SPEAR • • • • • • • • 345 MEROPE   480
    AS THY GRIEF WHEN IN TEARS SOME BRAZEN-COATED ACHAIAN   HOMER TRANS   27

ACHE
    TILL MINE EYES ACHE WITH THE LONG SPECTACLE • • 428 EMPEDOCLES I 2   475
    TILL MY EYES ACHE WITH THE LONG SPECTACLE • • • • 428 EMPEDOCLES I 2   V 475

4

ACHERON
STILL BY ACHERON STREAM . . . . 347 MEROPE 529

ACHIEVE
TO ACHIEVE HIS SONS DELIVERANCE O MY CHILD . . . . 198 FRAG ANTIGONE 103
WHAT ONE WEAK WOMAN CAN ACHIEVE ALONE . . . . . 368 MEROPE 1074
ACHIEVE YOUR GOOD WHO CAN . . . . 447 WESTMIN ABBEY 102

ACHIEVED
SAY HAVE THEIR SONS ACHIEVED MORE JOYS . . . . 303 GRANDE CHARTR 129

ACHIEVING
STRIVING BLINDLY ACHIEVING . . . . 288 RUGBY CHAPEL 65

ACHILLES
ACHILLES PONDERS IN HIS TENT . . . . 303 GRANDE CHARTR 115
THE YOUNG ACHILLES STANDING BY . . . . 414 EMPEDOCLES I 2 60
TRULY YET THIS TIME WILL WE SAVE THEE MIGHTY ACHILLES HOMER TRANS 47
THEN WITH A TROUBLED HEART THE SWIFT ACHILLES HOMER TRANS 58
ADDRESSD HIM

ACHING
WHAT THOU THINKST THIS ACHING BROW WAS COOLER . . 143 TRISTRAM 2 43
AN ACHING BODY AND A MIND . . . . 217 NAMELESS EPIT V
WITH ACHING HANDS AND BLEEDING FEET . . . . . . 241 MORALITY 7

ACONITE
THE ACONITE SPREADS . . . . 176 PARTING 52

ACQUAINTANCE
AND WITH THE COUNTRY-FOLK ACQUAINTANCE MADE . . 263 THYRSIS 33

ACQUIRE
MAY ACQUIRE IF NOT THE CALM . . . . 254 FUTURE 75

ACQUIRES
TIS ALL PERHAPS WHICH MAN ACQUIRES . . . . . 22 YOUTH AND CALM 24
TIS ALL PERHAPS THAT MAN ACQUIRES . . . . . 22 YOUTH AND CALM V 24

ACRID
THE ACRID MILK OF CAMELS AND THEIR WELLS . . . . 64 SOHRAB RUSTUM 125

ACROSS
FOR THIS THY TRACK ACROSS THE FRETFUL FOAM . . . 5 DUKE WELLINGTON 11
IN THE STILL NIGHT ACROSS THE STEAMING FLATS . . 12 MYCERINUS 126
AND RIDE ACROSS THE DRAWBRIDGE WITH THY HOUNDS . . 18 CHURCH BROU 3 10
TROOP ACROSS THE FLUSHING SANDS . . . . . 26 NEW SIRENS 14
FLITTING FAST ACROSS EACH MARBLE BROW . . . . 31 NEW SIRENS 162
WE STEM ACROSS THE SEA OF LIFE BY NIGHT . . . 41 HUMAN LIFE 27
WE STEM ACROSS THE SEA BY NIGHT . . . . . 41 HUMAN LIFE V 27
AND HE MUST FARE ACROSS THE DISMAL ICE . . . . 100 BALDER DEAD 1 165
BRUSHES ACROSS A TIRED TRAVELLERS FACE . . . . 101 BALDER DEAD 1 231
AND HE WILL FARE ACROSS THE DISMAL ICE . . . . 100 BALDER DEAD 1 V 165
THEIR KINE ACROSS A SNOWY MOUNTAIN-PASS . . . 107 BALDER DEAD 2 92
ACROSS THE BRIDGE THEN SHE TOOK POST AGAIN . . 108 BALDER DEAD 2 137
ACROSS THE SHAGGY BROWS OF TRISTRAMS HOUND . . 152 TRISTRAM 3 88
ACROSS THE HOLLOW WHITE ANEMONIES . . . . 155 TRISTRAM 3 207
HE HEARD ACROSS THE HOWLING SEAS . . . . 156 SAINT BRANDAN 5
ON HIS WHITE MULE ACROSS THE BRIDGE . . . . 160 NECKAN 47
ACROSS AND BEGGD AND CAME BACK SATISFIED . . . 170 WEST LONDON 7
AND GREET ACROSS INFINITY . . . . . . 180 FAREWELL 76
ACROSS THE SOUNDS AND CHANNELS POUR . . . . 182 TO MARG CONT 12
ACROSS MY HEART TO SAY THY THREAD . . . . 184 TERRACE BERNE 27
ACROSS THIS WIDE AERIAL PLAIN . . . . . 204 CALAIS SANDS 6
ACROSS THE GIRDLING CITYS HUM . . . . . 248 KENSINGTON GARD 6
THAT CHILD WHO DARTS ACROSS THE GLADE . . . KENSINGTON GARD V 9
I SEE HER VEIL DRAW SOFT ACROSS THE DAY . . . 266 THYRSIS 133
AND THERE ACROSS THE WATERY WAY . . . . 274 STANZAS CARNAC 25
BUT FARTHER YET ACROSS THE BRINE . . . . 277 SOUTHERN NIGHT 50
ACROSS THE VALLEY ON THAT SLOPE . . . . 312 OBERMANN MORE 13
ACROSS HER SPIRIT GREY . . . . 316 OBERMANN MORE 114
ACROSS THE GLIMMERING LAKE . . . . . 324 OBERMANN MORE 346
GULFS OF ESTRANGING BLOOD ACROSS THAT CHASM . 336 MEROPE 194
AND I ACROSS THE MOUNTAINS BROUGHT WITH HASTE . 358 MEROPE 845
HUGE IN THE GLOOM ACROSS IN THORNEY ISLE . . . 444 WESTMIN ABBEY 15

ACT
BUT ALL I LEFT OF MY OWN ACT AND FLED . . . 125 BALDER DEAD 3 405
DID THAT CHANCE ACT OF GOOD THAT ONE . . . 158 SAINT BRANDAN 58
WE SCHOOL OUR MANNERS ACT OUR PARTS . . . . 179 FAREWELL 45
AND LONG WE TRY IN VAIN TO SPEAK AND ACT . . . 247 BURIED LIFE 64
RANKS ANY MAN WITH MURDER SUCH AN ACT . . . 336 MEROPE 208
AND TO ONE ACT MANY MOST UNLIKE MOTIVES . . . 352 MEROPE 645
THOUGH TO HIS ACT EMPOWERD NAY IMPELLD . . . 385 MEROPE 1421
HIS DEATH A PUBLIC NOT A PERSONAL ACT . . . 387 MEROPE 1480
NOW NOT ANOTHER WORD BUT TO OUR ACT . . . 390 MEROPE 1586
YET OH COULDST THOU BUT ACT AS REASON BIDS . . . 396 MEROPE 1762
NATURAL VENGEANCE MAY MAINTAIN THINE ACT . . . 404 MEROPE 1998
ALIKE TO ANY ACT . . . . 422 EMPEDOCLES I 2 299
EVEN IN THE ACT TO BURST TWICE THREATENED TWICE 465 ALARIC AT ROME 84
DELAYED

ACTION
    ACTION AND SUFFERING THOUGH HE KNOW . . . . . .   56 RESIGNATION   152
    NOT WITHOUT ACTION TO DIE . . . .   288 RUGBY CHAPEL   80
    ACTION AND PLEASURE WILL YE ROAM . . . . . .   305 GRANDE CHARTR   194
    WHO WAS ON ACTION HURLD . . . .   311 OBERMANN   154
    NO PAUSE ITS ACTION KNEW . . . .   315 OBERMANN MORE   88
    ACTION I HAD NOT FOLLOWERS FAME . . . . . .   321 OBERMANN MORE   261
    THE ACTION OF MEN . . . .   443 EMPEDOCLES II   464
    TILL LIFE UNSTIRRD BY ACTION LIFE BECAME . . .   473 CROMWELL   59
    MOULDING ITSELF IN ACTION NOT IN WORD . . . .   478 CROMWELL   222

ACTIONS
    OF VEHEMENT ACTIONS WITHOUT SCOPE OR TERM . . . .   5 DUKE WELLINGTON   12
    IN ACTIONS DIZZYING EDDY WHIRLD . . . . . .   60 RESIGNATION   277
    COURAGEOUS FAITHFUL ACTIONS NOBLY DARED . . . . 333 MEROPE   88
    READ IN THESE ACTIONS INNOCENT IN THEE . . . .   333 MEROPE   90
    OF OUR OWN ACTIONS DIMLY TRACE THE CAUSES . . . 352 MEROPE   640
    BOLD ACTIONS PARENT AND A PIERCING KEN . . . .   478 CROMWELL   229

ACTIVE
    AND LAME THE ACTIVE MIND . . . .   237 PROGRESS   20
    WHAT ENDLESS ACTIVE LIFE IS HERE . . . . . .   248 KENSINGTON GARD   14
    WHAT ACTIVE ENDLESS LIFE IS HERE . . . . . .   KENSINGTON GARD V 14
    ACTIVE BENEFICENT PURE . . . .   281 HAWORTH CHURCH   V
    OR WITH THE ACTIVE RADIANT LIFE OF FIRE . . . . 439 EMPEDOCLES II   V 344

ACTIVITY
    BLAME OUR ACTIVITY . . . .   46 WORLD QUIETIST   6

ACTOR
    ASSIGND US BY THE ACTOR BE THE TRUE ONE . . . . 352 MEROPE   648

ACTS
    HIS ACTS THE WIFE HE CHOSE WAS FULL OF VIRTUES . . 337 MEROPE   240
    CONSTRUED HIS ACTS INDULGENTLY REVERED . . . .   337 MEROPE   255
    THEREFORE WHILE ACTS ARE FROM THEIR MOTIVES JUDGED 352 MEROPE   644
    DREAD THOUGH HIS ACTS TO WHOSE HAND . . . . . . 361 MEROPE   906
    BUT OUR OWN ACTS FOR GOOD OR ILL ARE MIGHTIER POWERS 420 EMPEDOCLES I 2 241

ADAMANTINE
    GRAVE IT ON BRASS WITH ADAMANTINE PEN . . . .   171 DIVINITY   2
    ALAS AN ADAMANTINE STRENGTH INDEED . . . . .   386 MEROPE   1434

ADD
    IT IS TO ADD IMMURED . . . .   212 GROWING OLD   23

ADDED
    ADDED THIS LAW . . . .   192 STRAYED REVEL   215

ADDERS
    BY THE THREE FOUNTAINS AND THE ADDERS HILL . . . 356 MEROPE   748
    THEN TURNING WESTWARD TO THE ADDERS HILL . . .   357 MEROPE   779

ADDRESS
    AND THUS ADDRESS THE GODS . . . .   423 EMPEDOCLES I 2   338
    AND THUS ADDRESS THE GODS . . . .   424 EMPEDOCLES I 2   373
    AND THEN ADDRESS THE GODS . . . .   424 EMPEDOCLES I 2   V 373

ADDRESSD
    TO HIM ADDRESSD WHO WOULD RECAST HER NEW . . . . 37 WORLDS TRIUMPHS   2
    TO HIM ADDRESSD WHO WOULD RECAST IT NEW . . . .   37 WORLDS TRIUMPHS V   2
    STRAIGHTWAY HE SPAKE AND THUS ADDRESSD THE GODS . 122 BALDER DEAD 3   298
    AND HE SHOOK HIS HEAD AND THUS ADDRESSD HIS OWN BOSOM HOMER TRANS   8
    THEN WITH A TROUBLED HEART THE SWIFT ACHILLES   HOMER TRANS   58
          ADDRESSD HIM

ADDRESSED
    THEN FROM BENEATH THE YOKE THE FLEET HORSE   HOMER TRANS   43
          XANTHUS ADDRESSED HIM

ADER
    THOU KNOWST IF SINCE FROM ADER-BAIJAN FIRST . .   62 SOHRAB RUSTUM   42
    MY MOTHER WHO IN ADER-BAIJAN DWELLS . . . . .   78 SOHRAB RUSTUM   590
    WHICH WAS IN ADER-BAIJAN BORN TO HIM . . . . .   79 SOHRAB RUSTUM   608
    IN ADER-BAIJAN AND HE SAW THAT YOUTH . . . . .   80 SOHRAB RUSTUM   631
    THOU KNOWEST IF SINCE FROM ADER-BAIJAN FIRST . . 62 SOHRAB RUSTUM   V 42

ADHERENCE
    AND WE PLEAD AS STAUNCH ADHERENCE . . . . . .   28 NEW SIRENS   59
    AND WE PLEAD AS FIRM ADHERENCE . . . .   28 NEW SIRENS   V 59

ADIEU
    ADIEU AND SAY THAT ONE AT LEAST . . . . . .   204 EUPHROSYNE   27
    THEN LOVE THY HAND AH NO ADIEU . . . .   207 TOO LATE   8
    AND THOU SAD GUIDE ADIEU . . . .   310 OBERMANN   130

ADMIRE
    BEARS TO ADMIRE UNCRAVINGLY . . . .   57 RESIGNATION   161
    ALLOW THEM WE ADMIRE WITH AWE . . . .   304 GRANDE CHARTR   163
    ADMIRE THEN MAIDENS HOW IN ONE SHORT HOUR . . . 360 MEROPE   875
    AND BYRON LET US DARE ADMIRE . . . .   482 COURAGE   17

ADMIRES
    WHEN IT ADMIRES AND LOVES ITS HEART AWAKES . . . . 382 MEROPE   1345

ADMIT
    NO NOR EXPECT THEE TO ADMIT THE GROUNDS   . . . . 340 MEROPE   339

ADMITS
    ADMITS NO MOMENTARY BRIGHTENING NOW . . . . . . 408 EMPEDOCLES I 1   69

ADOPTED
    BUT PRINCE ADOPTED BY THE WILL OF POWER   . . . . 335 MEROPE   171

ADORE
    NATURE IS STUBBORN MAN WOULD FAIN ADORE   . . . .   5 HARMONY NATURE   8
    MAKES IDOLS TO ADORE   . . . .   39 STAGIRIUS   23

ADORED
    PROUD IGNORANT SELF-ADORED YOU LIVE ALONE . . . . 198 FRAG DEJANEIRA   7

ADORND
    RADIANT ADORND OUTSIDE A HIDDEN GROUND   . . . . 166 AUSTERITY POET   13

ADOWN
    DROP WITH MINE ADOWN LIFES LATTER DAYS   . . . .   33 NEW SIRENS   210
    AND ROLL ADOWN A CHANNEL LARGE . . . .   224 EPILOG LAOCOON   101
    OF QUIET LOOK ADOWN THE DUSK HILL-SIDE   . . . . 267 THYRSIS   152

ADRIAN
    MOURNING AS WIDOWED VENICE OER HER ADRIAN TIDE   . . 468 ALARIC AT ROME   162

ADRIATIC
    THE ADRIATIC BREAKS IN A WARM BAY   . . . . . . 426 EMPEDOCLES I 2   428
    AND MURMURS OF THE ADRIATIC COME   . . . . . . 427 EMPEDOCLES I 2   455

ADVANCD
    WHICH SOHRAB HELD ADVANCD THE STEEL-SPIKED SPEAR . .   75 SOHRAB RUSTUM   V 492

ADVANCE
    OF LABOUR THAT IN STILL ADVANCE OUTGROWS   . . . .   1 QUIET WORK   V   6
    OF LABOUR THAT WITH MUTE ADVANCE OUTGOES   . . . .   1 QUIET WORK   V   6
    PATH OF ADVANCE BUT IT LEADS . . . .   288 RUGBY CHAPEL   86
    WHAT POINTED ROOFS ARE THESE ADVANCE . . . . . 300 GRANDE CHARTR   23
    BUT MEROPE THE YEARS ADVANCE I STAND . . . . . 334 MEROPE   151
    MARSHAL THEM TO AN ARMY THEN ADVANCE . . . . . 382 MEROPE   1324

ADVANCED
    AND RUSTUM TO THE PERSIAN FRONT ADVANCED   . . . .   70 SOHRAB RUSTUM   291
    ADVANCED TWO JAVELINS NOT NOW   . . . . 342 MEROPE   398
    TO HAVE ADVANCED TRUE FRIENDS AND BEAT DOWN   425 EMPEDOCLES I 2   401
        BAFFLING FOES

ADVANCEST
    ADVANCEST TO THE MIDDLE OF A DEED   . . . . . . 367 MEROPE   1061

ADVANCING
    AND SCANND WITH BLINKING EYES THE ADVANCING FORM . .   76 SOHRAB RUSTUM   518
    FROM STRENGTH TO STRENGTH ADVANCING ONLY HE   . . 172 IMMORTALITY   12

ADVANTAGE
    OF LIFE FOR MY ADVANTAGE AND MYSELF . . . . . . 382 MEROPE   1350

ADVENTUROUS
    THE UNKNOWN ADVENTUROUS YOUTH WHO FROM AFAR   . .   70 SOHRAB RUSTUM   309
    THE UNKNOWN ADVENTUROUS YOUTH WHO THROUGH THE WORLD   70 SOHRAB RUSTUM   V 309

ADVERSE
    DO ADVERSE VOICES FALL ON THE WORLDS EAR   . . . .   47 WORLD QUIETIST   19

ADVERSITY
    THITHER IN YOUR ADVERSITY   . . . . 198 FRAG DEJANEIRA   12

ADVISE
    HASTE AND ADVISE FOR DAY COMES ON APACE   . . . . 330 MEROPE   28
    THY PART IT WERE TO ADVISE AND MINE TO OBEY   . . 331 MEROPE   34

ADVISING
    ADVISING US A COURSE WHICH WOULD INDEED   . . . . 382 MEROPE   1337

AEGAEAN
    HEARD IT ON THE AEGEAN AND IT BROUGHT   . . . . 211 DOVER BEACH   16
    AMONG THE AEGAEAN ISLES   . . . . 262 SCHOLAR-GIPSY   236

AEGIMIUS
    AEGIMIUS GAVE OUR OUTCAST HOUSE A HOME   . . . . 337 MEROPE   224

AEOLIAN
    FROM THE AEOLIAN STOCK OF NELEUS SPRUNG   . . . . 337 MEROPE   236

AEPYTUS
    AEPYTUS THE MESSENIAN PRINCE IS DEAD . . . . . . 355 MEROPE   714
    NAMED AEPYTUS LIKE HIM HAVING GONE IN   . . . . 357 MEROPE   777
    TO AEPYTUS THE KING SEDUCED WITH GOLD   . . . . 364 MEROPE   970

```
AEPYTUS           ( CONTINUED )
       O AEPYTUS WEIGH WELL HER COUNSEL GIVEN    . . . .    382 MEROPE              1332
       OF AEPYTUS THY MURDERD MASTERS SON    . . . . . .    402 MEROPE              1926
       O AEPYTUS MY SON BEHOLD BEHOLD  . . . . . . . .      403 MEROPE              1963

AERIAL
       SPANND BY AERIAL ARCHES ALL OF GOLD    . . . . . .     4 BUTLERS SERMONS       12
       ACROSS THIS WIDE AERIAL PLAIN    . . . . . . . .      204 CALAIS SANDS          6
       THE WIDE AERIAL LANDSCAPE SPREAD    . . . . . .       250 WISH                 34

AERY
       WEIGHS LIKE OSSA ON THE AERY SOUL    . . . . . .       28 NEW SIRENS        V  72
       WEIGHD LIKE OSSA ON THE AERY SOUL    . . . . . .       28 NEW SIRENS        V  72

AETOLIAN
       THROUGH EUROPE TO THE AETOLIAN SHORE  . . . . . .     303 GRANDE CHARTR        135

AFAR
       SPIED PREY AFAR    . . . . . . . . .                   51 CONSOLATION          35
       THE UNKNOWN ADVENTUROUS YOUTH WHO FROM AFAR      . .   70 SOHRAB RUSTUM        309
       WHILE ON HIS ISLAND IN THE LAKE AFAR  . . . . . .     111 BALDER DEAD 2        214
       I LIKE THEE HAVE LEFT MY YOUTH AFAR    . . . . . .    143 TRISTRAM 2            22
       DRAGGING THEIR NETS THROUGH THE ROUGH WAVES AFAR  . . 151 TRISTRAM 3            80
       AFAR IN REST THE CATTLE LAY    . . . . . . . . .      224 EPILOG LAOCOON       109
       WE HEARD AFAR FAINT MUSIC PLAY  . . . . . . . .       224 EPILOG LAOCOON       110
       ITS FIRS AND AFAR ROSE THE PEAKS    . . . . . .       229 YOUTH OF NATURE       39
       ROSES THAT DOWN THE ALLEYS SHINE AFAR    . . . .      264 THYRSIS               67
       SOMEWHERE SURELY AFAR    . . . . . . . . .            287 RUGBY CHAPEL          40
       ALL-REGARDED AFAR  . . . . . . . . . . . . . .        345 MEROPE               484
       OF LYCAEUS AFAR    . . . . . . . . . . . .            347 MEROPE               519
       THOUGH FROM AFAR DISTINCTLY IT MAY SOOTHE HIM    . .  409 EMPEDOCLES I 1        89

AFFECTION
       I SHALL SUFFER BUT THEY WILL OUTLIVE THEIR AFFECTION   20 MODERN SAPPHO         17

AFFECTIONS
       AFFECTIONS INSTINCTS PRINCIPLES AND POWERS    . . . .   4 BUTLERS SERMONS        1
       OF THESE AFFECTIONS WIDER MADE  . . . . . . . .       58 RESIGNATION          219
       PRIVATE AFFECTIONS FOR THESE    . . . . . . . .      282 HAWORTH CHURCH     V

AFFECTS
       AFFECTS US WE COME NEAR  . . . . . . . . . . . .      418 EMPEDOCLES I 2       195

AFFINITIES
       OUR TRUE AFFINITIES OF SOUL    . . . . . . . .        179 FAREWELL              56

AFFIRM
       AFFORDS NO GROUND TO AFFIRM    . . . . . . . .        424 EMPEDOCLES I 2       349

AFFLICT
       SEEK TO AFFLICT OUR FOES WITH PETTY PANGS    . . . .  111 BALDER DEAD 2        229

AFFLICTS
       AFFLICTS GRAVE HEAVEN WITH ITS LONG SENSELESS ROAR    480 HUNGARIAN NAT          5

AFFORD
       AFFORD NO BALM    . . . . . . . . . . . .            200 PHILOMELA             15

AFFORDS
       AFFORDS NO GROUND TO AFFIRM    . . . . . . . .        424 EMPEDOCLES I 2       349

AFFRIGHT
       TO AFFRIGHT A FORTUNE WHICH THE GODS SECURE    . .    398 MEROPE              1782

AFGHANS
       MY FATHER WHOM THE ROBBER AFGHANS VEX    . . . .      68 SOHRAB RUSTUM        233

AFIELD
       AND AS AFIELD THE REAPERS CUT A SWATH    . . . .      70 SOHRAB RUSTUM        293
       AND AS AFIELD THE REAPERS CUT A SWATHE    . . . .     70 SOHRAB RUSTUM     V  293
       HANG IN THE AIR AFIELD AND DISAPPEAR  . . . . . .    104 BALDER DEAD 1        336
       AND SEEST MY STRIPLING HUNTER THERE AFIELD  . . . .  349 MEROPE               573

AFLAME
       AND WHEN MY ILL-SCHOOLD SPIRIT IS AFLAME    . . . .  169 WORLDLY PLACE         11
       WITH YELLOW SPIRES AFLAME    . . . . . . . .         313 OBERMANN MORE         22

AFLOAT
       BLACK CHAFING WATER AND AFLOAT  . . . . . . . .      479 HAYSWATER BOAT         2
       ALL ELSE BLACK WATER AND AFLOAT    . . . . . .       479 HAYSWATER BOAT        15
       SINCE THAT STRANGE CREW DID RIDE AFLOAT    . . . .   480 HAYSWATER BOAT        36

AFRAID
       HOVERING AND STOPPING OFT AS IF AFRAID    . . . .    124 BALDER DEAD 3        383
       WHOSE EYE THOU WAST AFRAID TO SEEK    . . . . . .    241 MORALITY              20
       WHOSE EYE THOU WERT AFRAID TO SEEK    . . . . . .    241 MORALITY          V   20
       SIGNS MAKE THY SOUL AFRAID    . . . . . . . .        416 EMPEDOCLES I 2       123

AFRASIAB
       FOR SO DID KING AFRASIAB BID ME SEEK  . . . . . .     62 SOHRAB RUSTUM         38
```

8

AFRASIAB   (CONTINUED)
        I HAVE STILL SERVED AFRASIAB WELL AND SHOWN   • • •   62 SOHRAB RUSTUM   44
        CHAMPIONS ENOUGH AFRASIAB HAS WHOM THOU   • • • •   74 SOHRAB RUSTUM   445

AFRASIABS
        AND WHEN TIS TRUCE THEN IN AFRASIABS TOWNS   • • • •   63 SOHRAB RUSTUM   73
        AND ON A FEAST-TIDE IN AFRASIABS HALL   • • • •   71 SOHRAB RUSTUM   355
        THOU ART NOT IN AFRASIABS GARDENS NOW   • • • •   75 SOHRAB RUSTUM   460
        AND BEAR THY TROPHIES TO AFRASIABS TENT   • • • •   77 SOHRAB RUSTUM   530
        AFRASIABS CITIES ONLY SAMARCAND   • • • • • •   83 SOHRAB RUSTUM   760
        AND ON A FEAST DAY IN AFRASIABS HALL • • • • • •   71 SOHRAB RUSTUM   V 355

AFRICA
        CITY OF AFRICA   • • • • • • • • • • •   51 CONSOLATION   28

AFTER
        MAN AFTER MAN THE WORLD SMILED AND PASSD BY   • •   3 EMERSONS ESSAYS   6
        MAN AFTER MAN THEY SMILED AND PASSED ON   • • • •   EMERSONS ESSAYS   V 6
        OF ALL ITS CHAFING TORRENTS AFTER THAW   • • • •   5 DUKE WELLINGTON   5
        AND AFTER CHURCH WHEN MASS IS DONE   • • • • •   17 CHURCH BROU 2   33
        AFTER SHORT COMMERCE WITH ME FEAR MY FROWN   • • • •   37 WORLDS TRIUMPHS   8
        AND AFTER THAT OF IGNORANT WITLESS MIND   • • • •   98 BALDER DEAD 1   98
        AND FOLLOWS THIS MAN AFTER THAT FOR HOURS   • • • •   114 BALDER DEAD 3   11
        MOST HONOURD AFTER FREA ODINS WIFE   • • • • •   116 BALDER DEAD 3   92
        AFTER THE FEAST IS DONE IN ODINS HALL   • • • •   117 BALDER DEAD 3   136
        AFTER AN HOUR A DRIPPING SOUND IS HEARD   • • • •   122 BALDER DEAD 3   310
        MUTE GAZING AFTER THEM IN TEARS AND FAIN   • • • •   129 BALDER DEAD 3   555
        ONE AFTER ONE TO-MORROW LIKE TO-DAY   • • • • •   151 TRISTRAM 3   67
        HOUR AFTER HOUR HER GOLD CURLS SWEEPING IT   • • • •   152 TRISTRAM 3   83
        STARS SHONE AFTER A DAY OF STORM   • • • • •   156 SAINT BRANDAN   14
        IT WAS THE FIRST AFTER I CAME   • • • • • •   157 SAINT BRANDAN   30
        KEPT ON AFTER THE GRAVE BUT NOT BEGUN   • • • •   172 IMMORTALITY   10
        STILL AFTER MANY YEARS IN DISTANT LANDS   • • • •   200 PHILOMELA   6
        AND IN THE AFTER-SILENCE SWEET   • • • • •   219 BACCHANALIA 2   13
        AND AFTER WE AWHILE HAD GONE   • • • • • •   221 EPILOG LAOCOON   4
        PAGE AFTER PAGE OF MUSIC TURN   • • • • • •   224 EPILOG LAOCOON   103
        RACE AFTER RACE MAN AFTER MAN   • • • • • •   232 YOUTH OF NATURE   129
        RACE AFTER RACE MAN AFTER MAN   • • • • • •   232 YOUTH OF NATURE   129
        WAY AFTER WAY CHANGES THAT NEVER CEASE   • • • •   239 REVOLUTIONS   7
        AND EMPIRE AFTER EMPIRE AT THEIR HEIGHT   • • • •   239 REVOLUTIONS   13
        AND AS YEAR AFTER YEAR   • • • • • • • •   243 SUMMER NIGHT   42
        AFTER THE KNOWLEDGE OF OUR BURIED LIFE   • • • •   246 BURIED LIFE   48
        BUT ONCE YEARS AFTER IN THE COUNTRY-LANES   • • • •   256 SCHOLAR-GIPSY   41
        THE AFTER-WORLD FORGETS MY NAME   • • • • •   321 OBERMANN MORE   263
        AFTER LONG DARKNESS RUDE   • • • • • •   322 OBERMANN MORE   294
        BY SILENCE EVER AFTER FOR BEHOLD   • • • • •   332 MEROPE   62
        MONTH AFTER MONTH I AWAIT   • • • • • •   347 MEROPE   517
        THE PRINCE IN CHASE AFTER A SWIMMING STAG   • • • •   363 MEROPE   959
        FLED FOR YEARS AFTER OER THE FACE OF EARTH   • • • •   385 MEROPE   1423
        AT THIS FIRST MEETING AFTER ABSENCE LONG   • • • •   386 MEROPE   1452
        EVEN AFTER NEWS OF THIS SAD DEATH OUR LEAGUE   • • •   394 MEROPE   1689
        FIRST WORK AFTER SUCH VICTORY LET US GO   • • •   405 MEROPE   2017
        MONTH AFTER MONTH THROUGH THE SLOW-DRAGGING YEAR   • •   347 MEROPE   V
        BY THE STREAM-SIDE AFTER THE DUSTY LANES   • • • •   406 EMPEDOCLES I 1   3
        AS DREW OF OLD THE PEOPLE AFTER HIM   • • • •   408 EMPEDOCLES I 1   63
        GIVES FLOWERS AFTER FLOWERS   • • • • • •   424 EMPEDOCLES I 2   358
        HAND AFTER HAND IN OURS   • • • • • • •   424 EMPEDOCLES I 2   360
        YEAR POSTING AFTER YEAR   • • • • • • •   424 EMPEDOCLES I 2   364
        SENSE AFTER SENSE DECAY   • • • • • • •   424 EMPEDOCLES I 2   365
        IN BREATHLESS QUIET AFTER ALL THEIR ILLS   • • • •   427 EMPEDOCLES I 2   438
        NIGHT AFTER NIGHT YOUR COURSES   • • • • •   437 EMPEDOCLES II   294
        AFTER LIGHTS TERM A TERM OF CECITY   • • • •   448 WESTMIN ABBEY   155
        AND AFTER THAT THOU DOST NOT CARE   • • • • •   451 GEISTS GRAVE   59
        HORDE AFTER HORDE STREAMED UP THY FROWNING CAPITOL   464 ALARIC AT ROME   72

AFTERNOON
        IN SEPTEMBERS BRIGHT AFTERNOON   • • • • • • •   292 HEINES GRAVE   7
        RUFFLES THE WARM AFTERNOON   • • • • • • •   293 HEINES GRAVE   40
        SEE IN THE MAY-AFTERNOON   • • • • • • • •   297 HEINES GRAVE   152

AGAINST
        THOU TOO WHEN THOU AGAINST MY CRIMES WOULDST CRY   • •   38 WORLDS TRIUMPHS   9
        THUS THOU WHEN THOU AGAINST MY CRIMES WOULDST CRY   38 WORLDS TRIUMPHS   V 9
        AGAINST THE ROBBERS AND HE SAW THAT HEAD   • • • •   71 SOHRAB RUSTUM   339
        AGAINST HIS BREAST HIS HEAVY MAILED HAND   • • • •   80 SOHRAB RUSTUM   663
        AGAINST THE HARBOUR BY THE CITY-WALL   • • • •   101 BALDER DEAD 1   225
        OVER AGAINST THE CURTAIN OF THE BED   • • • •   103 BALDER DEAD 1   286
        AND PERISH AGAINST FATE BEFORE THY DAY   • • • •   114 BALDER DEAD 3   29
        AGAINST THE BODIES AND STUCK TORCHES NEAR   • • • •   118 BALDER DEAD 3   167
        SET HIS STOUT SHOULDER HARD AGAINST THE STERN   • • •   118 BALDER DEAD 3   176
        AGAINST THE GODS UPON THE PLAINS OF HEAVEN   • • • •   127 BALDER DEAD 3   481
        AGAINST THE WOLVES AND ALL NIGHT LONG IT FLARES   • •   119 BALDER DEAD 3   V
        A GOLD HARP LEANS AGAINST THE BED   • • • •   131 TRISTRAM 1   17
        LEAND UP AGAINST THE COLUMN THERE   • • • • •   186 STRAYED REVEL   9
        AGAINST CREONS LAW POLYNICES   • • • • •   196 FRAG ANTIGONE   41
        AGAINST THE WEST I MISS IT IS IT GONE   • • • •   263 THYRSIS   27
        THAT LONELY TREE AGAINST THE WESTERN SKY   • • • •   268 THYRSIS   195
        AND AGAINST FEAR OUR BREAST TO STEEL   • • • •   272 MEMORIAL VERSES   65
        HAD STOOD AGAINST THE WAVE   • • • • • •   317 OBERMANN MORE   146
        AGAINST A POWER EXEMPT FROM COMMON CHECKS   • • •   336 MEROPE   206

AGAINST   (CONTINUED)
        RELUCTANTLY THE REST BUT AGAINST ALL . . . .   337 MEROPE   257
        IS CHARGED AGAINST THIS STRIPLING AGENTS FEED   . .   364 MEROPE   980
        AGAINST SURPRISE AND SUDDEN PANIC PROOF   . . . .   381 MEROPE   1305
        AGAINST THE ONE AND CERTAIN ARM OF POWER   . . . .   381 MEROPE   1313
        AGAINST THE KING HIMSELF ARRAY THE HOST   . . . .   382 MEROPE   1320
        ALAS AGAINST MY BROTHER SON AND FRIENDS   . . . .   390 MEROPE   1579
        SOME ILL DESIGN AGAINST HIM JEALOUSY . . . .   394 MEROPE   1700
        BUILT IN STRENGTH AGAINST THE VANQUISHD   . . . .   400 MEROPE   1854
        AGAINST THY MISTRESS LOVING HEART   . . . .   460 KAISER DEAD   53
        THIS BOAT THEY FOUND AGAINST THE SHORE   . . . .   480 HAYSWATER BOAT   25
        OF MEN WHO AGAINST HOPE REPELLD THE CHAIN   . . . .   480 HUNGARIAN NAT   10
        SORELY AGAINST THY WILL BY STRONG NECESSITYS ORDER   HOMER TRANS   31
        FOR ANY MAN TO FRET AGAINST HIS WEAKNESS   . . . .   LUCRETIUS 3   2
        AGAINST A SICKNESS OR DEFORMITY   . . . .   LUCRETIUS 3   4

AGAMEMNON
        WHO LED THE GREEKS TO ILIUM AGAMEMNON   . . . . .   367 MEROPE   1035

AGAMEMNONS
        SLEEPS AGAMEMNONS UNHAPPY   . . . .   344 MEROPE   439
        AGAMEMNONS SON IN MYCENAE   . . . .   368 MEROPE   1083

AGATE
        THE AGATE BROOCH-STONES   . . . .   186 STRAYED REVEL   17

AGE
        FROM FIRST YOUTH TESTED UP TO EXTREME OLD AGE   . .   2 TO A FRIEND   10
        IN GRAY AGE WITH PALSIED HANDS   . . . .   14 CHURCH BROU 1   66
        OF THAT PRIMAL AGE IS GONE   . . . .   27 NEW SIRENS   50
        AS OLD AGE YOUTHS FATAL MORROW . . . .   33 NEW SIRENS   217
        TO YOUTH AND AGE IN COMMON DISCONTENT   . . . .   .   37 YOUTHS AGIT   14
        SURELY THAN THOSE WHICH SHOULD THINE AGE EMPLOY   . .   41 GIPSY CHILD   V 11
        AGE-BOWD ASKS ALMS . . . .   51 CONSOLATION   30
        FEELS THE ABHORRD APPROACHES OF OLD AGE   . . . .   63 SOHRAB RUSTUM   84
        AND HE HAS NONE TO GUARD HIS WEAK OLD AGE   . . . .   68 SOHRAB RUSTUM   235
        AND REST MY AGE AND HEAR OF SOHRABS FAME   . . . .   68 SOHRAB RUSTUM   239
        TO GLAD THY FATHER IN HIS WEAK OLD AGE   . . . .   77 SOHRAB RUSTUM   536
        WITH AGE AND RULES OVER THE VALIANT KOORDS   . . . .   78 SOHRAB RUSTUM   592
        OF AGE AND LOOKS TO BE HIS OWN DEAR SON   . . . .   80 SOHRAB RUSTUM   632
        AND REAP A SECOND GLORY IN THINE AGE . . . . .   .   84 SOHRAB RUSTUM   776
        AND FULL OF BLOOD AND BATTLES IS MY AGE   . . . .   85 SOHRAB RUSTUM   825
        BETRAYD THEM AND OF WASTING AGE THEY DIED   . . . .   109 BALDER DEAD 2   167
        HERE MUST THOU LIE AND WAIT AN ENDLESS AGE   . . . .   126 BALDER DEAD 3   452
        WOULD TAKE A SCORE YEARS FROM A STRONG MANS AGE   . . 140 TRISTRAM 1   305
        BY AGE TAUGHT MANY THINGS   . . . .   189 STRAYED REVEL   119
        AGE AND THE MUSES . . . .   189 STRAYED REVEL   120
        IN AN EASY OLD AGE IN A HAPPY HOME   . . . .   199 FRAG DEJANEIRA   23
        THE QUIET MOSSY TRACK TO AGE   . . . .   199 EARLY DEATH   7
        THE MOSSY QUIET TRACK TO AGE   . . . .   199 EARLY DEATH   V 7
        WHICH GLOWS AS IF THE MIDDLE AGE   . . . .   204 CALAIS SANDS   7
        THE AGE HAS TALKD AND WORKD ITS FILL   . . . . .   .   219 BACCHANALIA 2   2
        AND OER THE PLAIN WHERE THE DEAD AGE   . . . . .   .   219 BACCHANALIA 2   19
        COMES THE NEW AGE . . . .   220 BACCHANALIA 2   36
        TEMPTS NOT THE BRIGHT NEW AGE . . . .   220 BACCHANALIA 2   51
        HE GREW OLD IN AN AGE HE CONDEMND   . . . .   229 YOUTH OF NATURE   28
        IN AN AGE WHICH CAN REAR THEM NO MORE   . . . . .   .   229 YOUTH OF NATURE   50
        SEES THE CONTRITION OF AGE   . . . .   232 YOUTH OF MAN   16
        CHILDREN OF MEN NOT THAT YOUR AGE EXCEL   . . . .   238 PROGRESS   45
        AND WE IMAGINE THEE EXEMPT FROM AGE   . . . .   . .   259 SCHOLAR-GIPSY   158
        PHYSICIAN OF THE IRON AGE   . . . .   270 MEMORIAL VERSES   17
        HE FOUND US WHEN THE AGE HAD BOUND   . . . .   . .   271 MEMORIAL VERSES   45
        O SPENT ONES OF A WORK-DAY AGE . . . .   279 SOUTHERN NIGHT   115
        AGE WHOM THE MOST OF US CHIDE . . . .   283 HAWORTH CHURCH   V
        OF A FORMER AGE ANY MORE . . . .   294 HEINES GRAVE   80
        FROM THE FIERCE TEMPEST OF THINE AGE   . . . . .   .   304 GRANDE CHARTR   148
        YEARS HENCE PERHAPS MAY DAWN AN AGE   . . . . .   .   304 GRANDE CHARTR   157
        THERE MAY PERHAPS YET DAWN AN AGE . . . .   304 GRANDE CHARTR   V 157
        THERE YET PERHAPS MAY DAWN AN AGE . . . .   304 GRANDE CHARTR   V 157
        BY ENGLANDS LAKES IN GREY OLD AGE . . . .   308 OBERMANN   49
        THE HOPELESS TANGLE OF OUR AGE . . . .   309 OBERMANN   83
        UPON THE THRESHOLD OF OLD AGE ALONE   . . . . .   .   334 MEROPE   152
        OLD AGE IS MORE SUSPICIOUS THAN THE FREE   . . . .   335 MEROPE   156
        FOR BEING OF LIKE AGE OF BIRTH NOT MEAN   . . . .   355 MEROPE   722
        NOT WITH THE FAILING BREATH AND FOOT OF AGE   . . . .   362 MEROPE   936
        AS CHILDREN OF WEAK AGE . . . .   421 EMPEDOCLES I 2   273
        THIS ENVIOUS MISERABLE AGE   . . . .   432 EMPEDOCLES II   107
        IN AN AGE LIKE THIS . . . .   432 EMPEDOCLES II   111
        FROM THAT ON WHICH HIS EXILED AGE IS THROWN   . . . .   436 EMPEDOCLES II   263
        AND EACH SUCCEEDING AGE IN WHICH WE ARE BORN . . . .   440 EMPEDOCLES II   377
        DOWN THE LONG AGE OF TRUTH THAT RIPENS SLOW   . .   448 WESTMIN ABBEY   148
        BUT AS AGE COMES ON I KNOW   . . . .   454 POOR MATTHIAS   77
        BROUGHT FROM THAT ANTERIOR AGE . . . .   456 POOR MATTHIAS   148
        A GLORIOUS MANHOOD YET A DIM OLD AGE   . . . . .   .   463 ALARIC AT ROME   39
        AGE OF ITS TEARS AND CHILDHOOD OF ITS SMILE   . . .   472 CROMWELL   6
        TO A MORTAL BUT YE ARE WITHOUT OLD AGE AND IMMORTAL   HOMER TRANS   10

AGED
        AND LETS THE AGED MOULDER TO THEIR GRAVES   . . . .   67 SOHRAB RUSTUM   225
        OF ZIRRAH AND THE AGED ZAL HIMSELF   . . . .   83 SOHRAB RUSTUM   752

AGED   (CONTINUED)
          HER WOMEN AND SIR TRISTRAMS AGED HOUND   • • • •   152 TRISTRAM 3   98
          A HEADLAND WITH ONE AGED PLANE-TREE CROWND • • • • 358 MEROPE   817
          CHIRON THE AGED CENTAUR LAY   • • • • • •   414 EMPEDOCLES I 2   59
          AND THERE THEY SAY TWO BRIGHT AND AGED SNAKES • •   427 EMPEDOCLES I 2   435

AGENT
          AND OF HIS UNSURE AGENT WHAT DEMANDS HE   • • • • • 380 MEROPE   1280

AGENTS
          IS CHARGED AGAINST THIS STRIPLING AGENTS FEED • •   364 MEROPE   980
          NEVER AGAIN IN LIFE NEXT AGENTS FEED • • • • • • 365 MEROPE   V

AGES
          AGES OR HOURS O WAKING ON LIFES STREAM   • • • •   45 IN UTRUMQUE PAR   11
          AND THUS THE FATHER OF THE AGES SPAKE   • • •   95 BALDER DEAD 1   17
          AND THUS THE FATHER OF THE AGES SPAKE   • • •   106 BALDER DEAD 2   40
          AND STRAIGHT THE FATHER OF THE AGES SAID • • •   115 BALDER DEAD 3   48
          BUT THEN THE FATHER OF THE AGES SAID • • • • •   118 BALDER DEAD 3   156
          AND THUS THE FATHER OF THE AGES SAID • • • • •   120 BALDER DEAD 3   224
          THE GENERATIONS PASS THE AGES GROW   • • • •   127 BALDER DEAD 3   473
          OF AGES AND MY LATE RETURN TO LIGHT   • • • •   128 BALDER DEAD 3   511
          TO SEVEN AGES   • • • • • • • • • •   192 STRAYED REVEL   222
          IN PRIDE OF LIFE THE AGES OF YOUR SIRES   • • •   238 PROGRESS   46
          BY FORMER AGES WHO ELSE   • • • • • • •   290 RUGBY CHAPEL   148
          AY AGES LONG ENDURED HIS SPAN   • • • • •   318 OBERMANN MORE   165
          THERE THE LAKE-WATERS WHICH IN AGES GONE   • • •   358 MEROPE   814
          FLOAT UP TO TELL OF AGES THAT ARE GONE   • • •   470 ALARIC AT ROME   208

AGING
          CHANGED AND AGING THEY AND WE   • • • • • • •   454 POOR MATTHIAS   51

AGITATED
          BUT AGITATED BRISK AND NEAR   • • • • •   224 EPILOG LAOCOON   111
          AND THE SAME AGITATED HEART WAS THERE   • • • •   242 SUMMER NIGHT   V 24

AGITATIONS
          THEN I SHALL WISH ITS AGITATIONS BACK   • • • •   37 YOUTHS AGIT   9

AGLOW
          AGLOW WITH ANGRY FIRE TO KEEP US TWAIN   • • • • 395 MEROPE   1736

AGNUS
          AND THE GREEN AGNUS-CASTUS   • • • • • • • •   391 MEROPE   1618

AGO
          BUT HE HAS MET THAT DOOM WHICH LONG AGO   • • • •   96 BALDER DEAD 1   23
          HER LONG AGO THE WANDERING ODER TOOK • • • • •   116 BALDER DEAD 3   93
          A THOUSAND YEARS AGO   • • • • • • • •   149 TRISTRAM 2   193
          WERE RESTLESS ONCE BUT LONG AGO   • • • •   208 ON THE RHINE   23
          SOPHOCLES LONG AGO • • • • • • • • •   211 DOVER BEACH   15
          YEARS AGO AT MY SIDE   • • • • • • • •   233 YOUTH OF MAN   24
          SO CHRIST SAID EIGHTEEN HUNDRED YEARS AGO • • •   237 PROGRESS   13
          AT WHOSE BEHEST I LONG AGO   • • • • • •   301 GRANDE CHARTR   74
          WHOSE BENT WAS TAKEN LONG AGO   • • • • •   305 GRANDE CHARTR   198
          YES TWENTY YEARS AGO THIS DAY BEHELD • • • • •   333 MEROPE   117
          THY SWORD REPELLD IT LONG AGO NOT I   • • • • •   341 MEROPE   355
          OF MY TWO ELDER SONS SLAIN LONG AGO   • • • •   367 MEROPE   1038
          THAT TO MY MIND THERE CAME HOW LONG AGO   • • •   446 WESTMIN ABBEY   83
          PEOPLE WHO LIVED HERE LONG AGO • • • • • •   452 GEISTS GRAVE   77
          SIX YEARS AGO I BROUGHT HIM DOWN   • • • • •   459 KAISER DEAD   13
          PEOPLED NIGHTS VOICELESS SHADES WITH FORMS OF LONG AGO 467 ALARIC AT ROME 126

AGOG
          TROPHY IN MOUTH AGOG TO START   • • • • • • • 460 KAISER DEAD   50

AGONE
          AND THIRTEEN HUNDRED YEARS AGONE THEY SAY • • • • 170 EAST AND WEST   3

AGONY
          STORMILY SWEET HIS TITAN-AGONY   • • • • • •   166 PICT NEWSTEAD   3
          WITH LOVE AND HATE TRIUMPH AND AGONY • • • • •   201 PHILOMELA   26
          VAIN IS THE AGONY OF GRIEF   • • • • • •   208 ON THE RHINE   6
          OF HUMAN AGONY   • • • • • • • • • •   307 OBERMANN   36
          AND WE SHALL FEEL THE AGONY OF THIRST   • • • •   439 EMPEDOCLES II   356
          OF THE PENT WINDS THAT SCREAM IN AGONY • • • •   472 CROMWELL   26
          NOT IN SUNK SPAINS PROLONGD DEATH AGONY   • • •   480 HUNGARIAN NAT   1

AGREED
          OLD MAN BE IT AGREED AS THOU HAST SAID   • • • • 66 SOHRAB RUSTUM   185

AGREES
          AGREES TO DEEM SOME DEEDS SO DARK IN GUILT • • • • 389 MEROPE   1524
          AGREES TO DEEM SOME DEEDS SO HORRIBLE   • • • •   389 MEROPE   V1524

AGRIGENTUM
          IN AGRIGENTUM AND OLYMPIA   • • • • • • •   408 EMPEDOCLES I 1   64
          THE WOMAN WHO AT AGRIGENTUM LAY   • • • • •   410 EMPEDOCLES I 1   109

AHEAD
FAR IN THE WOODS AHEAD THEIR MUSIC RANG • • • 357 MEROPE 792

AID
SLEEP ON I WATCH THEE AND AM HERE TO AID • • • 103 BALDER DEAD 1 292
WROUGHT BY THE GODS AND ASK THE GODS OUR AID • 111 BALDER DEAD 2 226
ABSENCE FROM FIELDS WHERE I COULD NOTHING AID • 127 BALDER DEAD 3 502
WHO ASKD THE PASSERS-BY FOR AID • • • • 157 SAINT BRANDAN 39
TO COME A LATE AVENGER TO THE AID • • • • 349 MEROPE 577
SOME STRAGGLING HUNTERS TO MY AID TO ROUSE • • • 358 MEROPE 836
THY KINSFOLK AND THY FATHERS FRIENDS FOR AID • • 384 MEROPE 1389
AND TO WHAT FRIENDS SHOULD I FOR AID APPLY • • • 384 MEROPE 1390
HIS ARGIVE OR HIS SPARTAN COUSINS AID • • 388 MEROPE 1499
WITH THE GODS AID AND IF THEY GIVE BUT AID • • • 391 MEROPE 1594
WITH THE GODS AID AND IF THEY GIVE BUT AID • • • 391 MEROPE 1594
THY GOODNESS NO MEN AID • • • • • • • • 416 EMPEDOCLES I 2 119

AIDS
THE AIDS TO NOBLE LIFE ARE ALL WITHIN • • • • 169 WORLDLY PLACE 14

AILEST
AND SAID THOU AILEST HERE AND HERE • • • • • 270 MEMORIAL VERSES 22

AILS
SHEPHERD WHAT AILS THEE THEN • • • • • • • 219 BACCHANALIA 1 40
POET WHAT AILS THEE THEN • • • • • • • • • 220 BACCHANALIA 2 45
AND ASKS WHAT AILS HIM SO AND GETS WHAT CURE HE CAN 416 EMPEDOCLES I 2 131
SINK IN THYSELF THERE ASK WHAT AILS THEE AT 417 EMPEDOCLES I 2 146
    THAT SHRINE

AIM
LET US NOT FRET AND FEAR TO MISS OUR AIM • • • 40 HUMAN LIFE 10
RATHER THYSELF FOR SOME AIM PRAY • • • • • 59 RESIGNATION 239
THOU HADST ONE AIM ONE BUSINESS ONE DESIRE • • • 259 SCHOLAR-GIPSY 152
NOT WITHOUT AIM TO GO ROUND • • • • • • 288 RUGBY CHAPEL 76
A LAST LONG-CHERISHD PROJECT IN MY AIM • • • • 360 MEROPE 880
NOT YET THOUGH SUCH NO DOUBT HIS FINAL AIM • • • 380 MEROPE 1283
INDEED THY LIFELONG PASSION AND SOLE AIM • • • 404 MEROPE 1983
HIS WELFARE HIS TRUE AIM • • • • • • • • 418 EMPEDOCLES I 2 174

AIMD
WERE AIMD AT THEIR PROMOTION OUR DECLINE • • • • 337 MEROPE 244

AIMLESS
AN AIMLESS UNALLAYD DESIRE • • • • • • • • 481 DESTINY 8

AIMS
WITH ITS SICK HURRY ITS DIVIDED AIMS • • • • • 261 SCHOLAR-GIPSY 204
AND THY CLEAR AIMS BE CROSS AND SHIFTING MADE • • 261 SCHOLAR-GIPSY 228

AIR
IN YOUR HIGH CHURCH MID THE STILL MOUNTAIN-AIR • • 17 CHURCH BROU 3 2
AND I FEEL THE COLD NIGHT-AIR • • • • • • 32 NEW SIRENS 190
POOR CHILD WHOM THE LIGHT AIR OF CHILDISH JOY • • 41 GIPSY CHILD V 9
SOME TWO HOURS MARCH WITH SERIOUS AIR • • • 54 RESIGNATION 68
BREATHES WHEN HE WILL IMMORTAL AIR • • • • • 58 RESIGNATION 207
CHOKED BY THE AIR AND SCARCE CAN THEY THEMSELVES • 66 SOHRAB RUSTUM 165
HIS SPIRITED AIR AND WONDERD WHO HE WAS • • • 70 SOHRAB RUSTUM 312
O THOU YOUNG MAN THE AIR OF HEAVEN IS SOFT • • • 70 SOHRAB RUSTUM 322
HEAVENS AIR IS BETTER THAN THE COLD DEAD GRAVE • • 71 SOHRAB RUSTUM 324
GREW BLACKER THUNDER RUMBLED IN THE AIR • • • 76 SOHRAB RUSTUM 500
AND WENT ABROAD INTO THE COLD DIM AIR • • • • 61 SOHRAB RUSTUM V 10
HIS FACE AND AIR AND WONDERD WHO HE WAS • • • 70 SOHRAB RUSTUM V 312
WHEN AIR IS CHILLIEST AND THE STARS SUNK LOW • 103 BALDER DEAD 1 281
HANG IN THE AIR AFIELD AND DISAPPEAR • • • • 104 BALDER DEAD 1 336
TO RIGHT AND LEFT AND WARM STEAM FILLS THE AIR • 107 BALDER DEAD 2 98
LIKE MEN WHO LIVE AND DRAW THE VITAL AIR • • • 108 BALDER DEAD 2 108
NOR LIT WITH SUN BUT THROUGH THE DARKSOME AIR • 108 BALDER DEAD 2 125
AND SLEIPNER SNORTED FOR HE SMELT THE AIR • • • 113 BALDER DEAD 2 302
NOT LIT WITH SUN BUT THROUGH THE DARKSOME AIR • • 108 BALDER DEAD 2 V 125
WITH THE OLD IMPERIOUS AIR • • • • • • 134 TRISTRAM 1 124
AND FOR THROUGH THE HAGGARD AIR • • • • • • 136 TRISTRAM 1 198
THE WIDE PLAIN RINGS THE DAZED AIR THROBS WITH BLOWS 137 TRISTRAM 1 235
THE MARCH THE LEAGUER HEAVENS BLITHE AIR • • • 138 TRISTRAM 1 258
THROUGH THE SOFT-OPEND LIPS THE AIR • • • • • 141 TRISTRAM 1 342
WHAT VOICES ARE THESE ON THE CLEAR NIGHT-AIR • • 142 TRISTRAM 1 372
THE AIR OF THE DECEMBER-NIGHT • • • • • • 147 TRISTRAM 2 147
WITH HEATED CHEEKS AND FLURRIED AIR • • • • 148 TRISTRAM 2 162
THE FIERCE HOUNDS SNUFF THE TAINTED AIR • • • 149 TRISTRAM 2 184
UNDER THE HOLLIES IN THE CLEAR STILL AIR • • • 150 TRISTRAM 3 39
LOOKD STERNLY THROUGH THE FROSTY EVENING-AIR • • 151 TRISTRAM 3 60
IN WHOSE HOT AIR OUR SPIRITS ARE UPCURLD • • • 153 TRISTRAM 3 120
BLOWING BETWEEN THE STEMS THE FOREST-AIR • • • 154 TRISTRAM 3 167
THE ICEBERG IN THE FROSTY AIR • • • • • • 158 SAINT BRANDAN V 76
ITS WHITE PEAKS IN AIR • • • • • • • • 175 PARTING 14
IN THE VOID AIR TOWARDS THEE • • • • • • • 176 PARTING 63
A TROUBLE IN THINE ALTERD AIR • • • • • • 178 FAREWELL 14
HOW SWEET TO FEEL ON THE BOON AIR • • • • • 180 FAREWELL 81
FAIL FROM EARTHS AIR AND I NOT KNOW • • • • • 184 TERRACE BERNE 32
AND THROUGH THE VOID AIR SANG • • • • • • 197 FRAG ANTIGONE 88
MY DARLING ON THIS LONELY AIR • • • • • • • 205 CALAIS SANDS 14
MY DARLING ON THIS QUIET AIR • • • • • • • 205 CALAIS SANDS V 14

AIR   (CONTINUED)
          AND WATCH THY AIR AND GUESS THY THOUGHTS   •   •   •   •   205 CALAIS SANDS   V 29
          COME TO THE WINDOW SWEET IS THE NIGHT-AIR   •   •   •   •   210 DOVER BEACH   6
          COME TO THE WINDOW HUSHD IS THE NIGHT-AIR   •   •   •   •   210 DOVER BEACH   V   6
          IN PUFFS OF BALM THE NIGHT-AIR BLOWS   •   •   •   •   •   218 BACCHANALIA 1   14
          TOSSING IN AIR   •   •   •   •   •   •   •   •   •   •   •   218 BACCHANALIA 1   25
          BRIGHT WAS THE MORN AND SOUTH THE AIR   •   •   •   •   •   222 EPILOG LAOCOON   42
          FULL OF SWEET BREATHINGS WAS THE AIR   •   •   •   •   •   223 EPILOG LAOCOON   63
          PERFUMES THE EVENING AIR   •   •   •   •   •   •   •   •   234 YOUTH OF MAN   69
          MOUNTAINS SURROUND IT AND SWEET VIRGIN AIR   •   •   •   •   236 PALLADIUM   10
          IN THE RUSTLING NIGHT-AIR CAME THE ANSWER   •   •   •   •   240 SELF-DEPENDENCE   15
          O AIR-BORN VOICE LONG SINCE SEVERELY CLEAR   •   •   •   •   240 SELF-DEPENDENCE   29
          NATURE WHOSE FREE LIGHT CHEERFUL AIR   •   •   •   •   •   241 MORALITY   17
          YET THAT SEVERE THAT EARNEST AIR   •   •   •   •   •   •   241 MORALITY   29
          BEHIND THROUGH THE SOFT AIR   •   •   •   •   •   •   •   242 SUMMER NIGHT   20
          AN AIR OF COOLNESS PLAYS UPON HIS FACE   •   •   •   •   •   247 BURIED LIFE   94
          AN AIR-STIRRD FOREST FRESH AND CLEAR   •   •   •   •   •   248 KENSINGTON GARD   16
          THE CEREMONIOUS AIR OF GLOOM   •   •   •   •   •   •   •   250 WISH   15
          AND AIR-SWEPT LINDENS YIELD   •   •   •   •   •   •   •   255 SCHOLAR-GIPSY   26
          THY DARK VAGUE EYES AND SOFT ABSTRACTED AIR   •   •   •   •   258 SCHOLAR-GIPSY   99
          HUMID THE AIR LEAFLESS YET SOFT AS SPRING   •   •   •   263 THYRSIS   17
          ARE FLOWERS FIRST OPEND ON SICILIAN AIR   •   •   •   •   •   265 THYRSIS   89
          AND HIGH THE MOUNTAIN-TOPS IN CLOUDY AIR   •   •   •   •   267 THYRSIS   143
          AND NOW IN HAPPIER AIR   •   •   •   •   •   •   •   •   268 THYRSIS   176
          NEATH THE MILD CANOPY OF ENGLISH AIR   •   •   •   •   •   268 THYRSIS   194
          NEATH THE SOFT CANOPY OF ENGLISH AIR   •   •   •   •   •   268 THYRSIS   V 194
          THE BLUE-BELLS PERFUME ALL THE AIR   •   •   •   •   •   •   274 STANZAS CARNAC   20
          OH COULD HE ONCE HAVE REACHD THIS AIR   •   •   •   •   •   275 STANZAS CARNAC   41
          THE FURZE-SCENT PERFUMES ALL THE AIR   •   •   •   •   •   274 STANZAS CARNAC   V 20
          WITH THE SINKING SUN AND THE AIR   •   •   •   •   •   •   297 HEINES GRAVE   163
          HOW CAN WE FLOWER IN FOREIGN AIR   •   •   •   •   •   •   306 GRANDE CHARTR   208
          HOW SHOULD WE FLOWER IN FOREIGN AIR   •   •   •   •   •   306 GRANDE CHARTR   V 208
          CLOSE OER IT IN THE AIR   •   •   •   •   •   •   •   •   306 OBERMANN   4
          THAT AIR OF LANGUOR COLD AND DEATH   •   •   •   •   •   •   306 OBERMANN   15
          YES THOUGH THE VIRGIN MOUNTAIN-AIR   •   •   •   •   •   •   307 OBERMANN   25
          BALMS FLOATING ON THY MOUNTAIN-AIR   •   •   •   •   •   •   309 OBERMANN   111
          AND ON THE AIR OF NIGHT   •   •   •   •   •   •   •   •   310 OBERMANN   124
          LIKE OURS IT LOOKD IN OUTWARD AIR   •   •   •   •   •   •   315 OBERMANN MORE   85
          AIR TO HIS UNWINGD FORM DENIES A WAY   •   •   •   •   •   351 MEROPE   624
          CLEARD WITH BLITHE TRAVEL AND THE MORNING AIR   •   •   •   355 MEROPE   734
          BROWND WITH THINE OPEN-AIR FREE HUNTERS LIFE   •   •   •   373 MEROPE   1164
          ONES BREATH CURLS IN THE AIR AND ON THESE PINES   •   •   •   406 EMPEDOCLES I 1   15
          THERE IS A SETTLED TROUBLE IN HIS AIR   •   •   •   •   •   408 EMPEDOCLES I 1   68
          IN THIS CLEAR MOUNTAIN-AIR A VOICE WILL RISE   •   •   •   409 EMPEDOCLES I 1   88
          DOWN ITS STEEP VERDANT SIDES THE AIR   •   •   •   •   •   414 EMPEDOCLES I 2   45
          WE PEOPLING THE VOID AIR   •   •   •   •   •   •   •   •   421 EMPEDOCLES I 2   278
          OF EARTH AND AIR AND SEA   •   •   •   •   •   •   •   •   422 EMPEDOCLES I 2   292
          THE GRASS IS COOL THE SEA-SIDE AIR   •   •   •   •   •   •   426 EMPEDOCLES I 2   432
          IN THE STILL MOUNTAIN AIR   •   •   •   •   •   •   •   •   430 EMPEDOCLES II   40
          THE AIR IS THIN THE VEINS SWELL   •   •   •   •   •   •   •   435 EMPEDOCLES II   215
          AIR AIR   •   •   •   •   •   •   •   •   •   •   •   •   •   435 EMPEDOCLES II   217
          AIR AIR   •   •   •   •   •   •   •   •   •   •   •   •   •   435 EMPEDOCLES II   217
          AND HE WILL FIND ITS AIR TOO KEEN FOR HIM   •   •   •   •   435 EMPEDOCLES II   228
          OH THAT IT BROODED OVER THE WORLD LIKE THE AIR   •   •   •   438 EMPEDOCLES II   326
          BREATH TO AIR   •   •   •   •   •   •   •   •   •   •   •   439 EMPEDOCLES II   336
          WE MIGHT HAVE JOY BLENT WITH THE ALL-BATHING AIR •   •   •   439 EMPEDOCLES II   343
          OVER THE UNRECOGNISING SEA WHILE AIR   •   •   •   •   •   439 EMPEDOCLES II   361
          WE SHOULD HAVE JOY BLENT WITH THE ALL-BATHING AIR   •   •   439 EMPEDOCLES II   V 343
          AND CAROLS FLOAT ALONG THE HAPPY AIR   •   •   •   •   •   445 WESTMIN ABBEY   39
          SONGS TO TRILL IN SURREY AIR   •   •   •   •   •   •   •   458 POOR MATTHIAS   197
          BREATHE THERE NOT SPIRITS ON THE PEOPLED AIR   •   •   •   468 ALARIC AT ROME   163
          AT LAST IN AIR FAR OFF DIM ROSE A HEIGHT   •   •   •   484 S S LUSITANIA   6

AIRIEST
          IN HIS GLADDEST AIRIEST SONG   •   •   •   •   •   •   •   231 YOUTH OF NATURE   96

AIRS
          BUT WE STOOD WITHOUT IN THE COLD BLOWING AIRS   •   •   163 FORSAKEN MERM   73
          WHEN SWEET AIRS COME SEAWARD   •   •   •   •   •   •   •   165 FORSAKEN MERM   128
          CRUSHD THEM WITH TOLLS OR FEVER-AIRS   •   •   •   •   •   193 STRAYED REVEL   251
          AIRS FROM THE EDEN OF YOUTH   •   •   •   •   •   •   •   235 YOUTH OF MAN   91
          COME AIRS AND FLOATING ECHOES AND CONVEY   •   •   •   •   247 BURIED LIFE   75
          CLEANSE TO SWEET AIRS THE BREATH OF POISONOUS STREAMS   410 EMPEDOCLES I 1   117
          AND DEADLY AIRS HIS STRENGTH DID UNDERMINE   •   •   •   •   448 WESTMIN ABBEY   126
          AND DEADLY AIRS HIS FORCE DID UNDERMINE   •   •   •   •   448 WESTMIN ABBEY   V 126

AIRY
          THAT LONG HAS TOWERD IN THE AIRY CLOUDS   •   •   •   •   73 SOHRAB RUSTUM   401
          PAINLESS AND SWIFT SET FREE HER AIRY SOUL   •   •   •   •   104 BALDER DEAD 1   340
          AIRY ANTE-MUNDANE THRONG   •   •   •   •   •   •   •   •   456 POOR MATTHIAS   135
          ALL AIRY HOPES THAT IDLE HEARTS CAN FRAME   •   •   •   •   474 CROMWELL   95

AISLE
          ON AISLE AND TRANSEPT AND YOUR MARBLE GRAVE   •   •   17 CHURCH BROU 3   6
          AND WE GAZED UP THE AISLE THROUGH THE SMALL   163 FORSAKEN MERM   75
              LEADED PANES

AISLES
          UP COLD AISLES OF BURIED GLADE   •   •   •   •   •   •   •   32 NEW SIRENS   180
          SHEEP MAKE THE DAISIED AISLES THEIR FOLD   •   •   •   •   274 STANZAS CARNAC   16
          SHEEP MAKE THE FURZE-GROWN AISLES THEIR FOLD   •   •   274 STANZAS CARNAC   V 16

AISLES   (CONTINUED)
        AND AS YEARS SPED THE MINSTER-AISLES DIVINE   • •   445 WESTMIN ABBEY   55

AJAX
        HECTOR AND AJAX WILL BE THERE AGAIN   • • • • • •   236 PALLADIUM   15

AKIN
        BUT AN ARCADIAN PRINCESS MORE AKIN   • • • • • •   337 MEROPE   241

ALACK
        ALACK FOR CORYDON NO RIVAL NOW • • • • • • • • •   265 THYRSIS   81

ALARM
        SPEAK IS THERE NEWS OR ANY NIGHT ALARM   • • • •   62 SOHRAB RUSTUM   32
        THE GOLDEN-CRESTED COCK SHALL SOUND ALARM • • • •   127 BALDER DEAD 3   496
        OF CHANGE ALARM SURPRISE • • • • • • • • • • •   308 OBERMANN   70
        KNOWST THOU THEN AUGHT THAT THUS THOU SOUNDST   396 MEROPE   1766
              THE ALARM

ALARMS
        SWEPT WITH CONFUSED ALARMS OF STRUGGLE AND FLIGHT   212 DOVER BEACH   36
        THE MOWERS CRY THE DOGS ALARMS • • • • • • •, • •   218 BACCHANALIA 1   6
        THE REAPERS CRY THE DOGS ALARMS   • • • • • •   218 BACCHANALIA 1   V   6

ALAS
        I AM DUMB ALAS TOO SOON ALL   • • • • • • • •   29 NEW SIRENS   89
        AND THOUGH WE WEAR OUT LIFE ALAS   • • • • • •   179 FAREWELL   49
        WHAT FAR TOO SOON ALAS I LEARND   • • • • • •   180 ISOLATION MARG   8
        SO ON THE SEA OF LIFE ALAS   • • • • • • •   185 TERRACE BERNE   47
        FOR ALAS HE LEFT US EACH RETAINING   • • • • • •   210 SELF-DECEPTION   17
        ALAS HOW FEW OF THEM ALL • • • • • • • • •   216 LORDS MESSENGER V 10
        WHAT THEY ARE ALAS WHAT THEY WERE   • • • • •   235 YOUTH OF MAN   94
        TOO HASTY HEADS FOR ORDERING WORLDS ALAS   • • • •   237 PROGRESS   9
        ALAS IS EVEN LOVE TOO WEAK   • • • • • • •   245 BURIED LIFE   12
        BUT DEEP ENOUGH ALAS NONE EVER MINES • • • • •   246 BURIED LIFE   56
        BECAUSE THOU HADST WHAT WE ALAS HAVE NOT   • • •   259 SCHOLAR-GIPSY   160
        ALAS YET TO THE SUFFERING MAN • • • • • •   273 EDW QUILLINAN   9
        STRANGE IRONY OF FATE ALAS   • • • • • •   277 SOUTHERN NIGHT   57
        OF THE EARLY-DYING ALAS   • • • • • • • •   283 HAWORTH CHURCH   67
        SAW THE FAMOUS ALAS   • • • • • • • •   281 HAWORTH CHURCH   V
        THE CHILDLESS FATHER ALAS • • • • • • • •   283 HAWORTH CHURCH   V
        THEIR HANGING RUIN ALAS   • • • • • • • •   289 RUGBY CHAPEL   100
        HEINE ALAS HE IS YOURS   • • • • • • • •   293 HEINES GRAVE   47
        ALAS TO HELP US FORGET   • • • • • • • •   296 HEINES GRAVE   118
        LEFT IT AND THOU ALAS   • • • • • • • •   298 HEINES GRAVE   197
        OF HEINE HIS STRANGE ALAS • • • • • • • •   299 HEINES GRAVE   224
        MORE FORTUNATE ALAS THAN WE   • • •• • • •   304 GRANDE CHARTR   158
        ALAS THAT HOW TO RULE IT WAS OUR BROIL   • • • •   334 MEROPE   127
        ALAS HOW FAIR A COLOUR CAN HIS TONGUE   • • • •   338 MEROPE   278
        THE YOUTH IS GONE WITHIN ALAS HE BEARS   • • • •   359 MEROPE   873
        TIS SO TIS SO ALAS FOR SEE THE PROOF • • • •   364 MEROPE   978
        PEACE WHAT IS IT ALAS   • • • • • • •   368 MEROPE   1086
        ALAS ALAS   • • • • • • • • • •   372 MEROPE   1148
        ALAS ALAS   • • • • • • • • • • •   372 MEROPE   1148
        ALAS OUR FOE ALONE STOOD FORWARD THEN   • • • •   383 MEROPE   1367
        ALAS AN ADAMANTINE STRENGTH INDEED   • • • •   386 MEROPE   1434
        ALAS AGAINST MY BROTHER SON AND FRIENDS   • • •   390 MEROPE   1579
        ALAS NO COMMON SEPULCHRE ART THOU   • • • •   464 ALARIC AT ROME   55
        ALAS IT NEEDS NOT IS IT HARD TO KNOW • • • •   466 ALARIC AT ROME   119
        ALAS NO WREATHS ARE HERE DESPAIR MAY TEACH • • •   467 ALARIC AT ROME   139
        ALAS THAT FIERY SPIRIT LITTLE KNEW   • •• • •   469 ALARIC AT ROME   187
        ALAS FAR OTHER THOUGHTS MIGHT WELL BE OURS • • •   470 ALARIC AT ROME   199
        A LITTLE WHILE ALAS A LITTLE WHILE   • • • •   470 ALARIC AT ROME   217
        THAT HAST SO MUCH REFLECTED BUT ALAS • • • • • •   LUCRETIUS 1   3

ALBAN
        ALONG THE GRACIOUS ALBAN HILL • • • • • • • •   484 ROME-SICKNESS   20

ALBEIT
        ALBEIT WITH LIPS UNAPT TO SELF-EXCUSE   • • • •   336 MEROPE   199

ALCMENAS
        ALCMENAS DREADFUL SON   • • • • • • • • • •   192 STRAYED REVEL   231

ALEHOUSE
        AT SOME LONE ALEHOUSE IN THE BERKSHIRE MOORS   • •   256 SCHOLAR-GIPSY   58

ALERT
        IS THIS THE EYE THE FORM ALERT • • • • • • •   276 SOUTHERN NIGHT V 37
        STILL ALERT THY STONE-CRUSHD FRAME   • • • • • •   430 EMPEDOCLES II   51
        TEEMING WITH PLANS ALERT AND GLAD   • • • • •   460 KAISER DEAD   45

ALEXANDER
        PRINCE ALEXANDER PHILIPS PEERLESS SON   • • • •   153 TRISTRAM 3   147

ALIEN
        SOME ANGELS IN AN ALIEN PLANET BORN   • • • • • •   42 GIPSY CHILD   26
        WHAT SERAPHS IN SOME ALIEN PLANET BORN   • • • •   42 GIPSY CHILD   V 26
        IN TIMES LESS ALIEN TO A SPIRIT MILD • • • • •   128 BALDER DEAD 3   512
        TRICKD IN DISGUISES ALIEN TO THE REST   • • • •   245 BURIED LIFE   21
        OF MEN AND ALIEN TO THEMSELVES AND YET   • • • •   245 BURIED LIFE   22

ALIENS
SHE WILL NOT ASK OF ALIENS BUT OF FRIENDS • • • •   170 WEST LONDON   10

ALIGHT
YE ALIGHT IN OUR VAN AT YOUR VOICE • • • • • •   292 RUGBY CHAPEL   196
ALIGHT AND SPARELY SUP AND WAIT • • • • • •   300 GRANDE CHARTR   26
HE WOULD NOT LET HIS SAVAGE CHIEFS ALIGHT • • • •   339 MEROPE   295

ALIKE
THIS DAY TO-MORROW YESTERDAY ALIKE • • • • • •   333 MEROPE   110
ALIKE TO ANY ACT • • • • • • • • • • • •   422 EMPEDOCLES I 2   299

ALIVE
MIGHT BE ONCE MORE ALIVE MY BITTEREST FOES • • • •   85 SOHRAB RUSTUM   810
ALIVE AND STILL THE RAYS WERE ROUND HIS HEAD • • •   103 BALDER DEAD 1   284
ALIVE I KEPT NOT FAR FROM THEE DEAR SOUL • • • •   103 BALDER DEAD 1   293
COWARDS WHO WERE IN SLOUGHS INTERRD ALIVE • • • •   109 BALDER DEAD 2   172
BEING ALIVE AND COME TO OCEANS SHORE • • • • •   110 BALDER DEAD 2   184
ALIVE THOU WAST OF GODS THE MOST BELOVED • • • •   112 BALDER DEAD 2   259
ALIVE THOU WERT OF GODS THE MOST BELOVED • • • •   112 BALDER DEAD 2   V 259
THE SWEETEST CHRISTIAN SOUL ALIVE • • • • •   132 TRISTRAM 1   54
ALIVE WITH BRIGHT GREEN LIZARDS • • • • • •   191 STRAYED REVEL   173
ALIVE WE WOULD HAVE CHANGED HIS LOT • • • • •   273 EDW QUILLINAN   19
TEMPER OF GENIUS ALIVE • • • • • • • •   293 HEINES GRAVE   V 26
SEEMD PUISSANT AND ALIVE • • • • • • • •   315 OBERMANN MORE   90
SAY IS IT MORE ALIVE • • • • • • • • •   320 OBERMANN MORE   228
THEIR DAILY-PRACTISED CHAFINGS KEEP ALIVE • • • •   331 MEROPE   44
A MOURNFUL FEUD ALIVE WHICH ELSE WOULD DIE • • • •   332 MEROPE   82
TO KEEP ALIVE THAT MEMORY IN MY HEART • • • • •   334 MEROPE   120
FOR THEE MY CHILD IF THOU WERT YET ALIVE • • • •   372 MEROPE   1157
NO BY THE GODS ALIVE AND LIKE TO LIVE • • • • •   377 MEROPE   1218
AND ONLY SLAVES AND TYRANTS LEFT ALIVE • • • •   383 MEROPE   1378
THEY ARE WITH ME NOT YOU YE ARE ALIVE • • • •   438 EMPEDOCLES II   303

ALL
ALL PAINS THE IMMORTAL SPIRIT MUST ENDURE • • •   3 SHAKESPEARE   12
ALL WEAKNESS WHICH IMPAIRS ALL GRIEFS WHICH BOW • •   3 SHAKESPEARE   13
ALL WEAKNESS WHICH IMPAIRS ALL GRIEFS WHICH BOW • •   3 SHAKESPEARE   13
ALL WEAKNESS THAT IMPAIRS ALL GRIEFS THAT BOW • • •   3 SHAKESPEARE   V 13
ALL WEAKNESS THAT IMPAIRS ALL GRIEFS THAT BOW • • •   3 SHAKESPEARE   V 13
EACH TO HIS LABOUR AND WHEN ALL WERE GONE • • • •   EMERSONS ESSAYS   V   7
SPANND BY AERIAL ARCHES ALL OF GOLD • • • •   4 BUTLERS SERMONS   12
OF ALL ITS CHAFING TORRENTS AFTER THAW • • • •   5 DUKE WELLINGTON   5
KNOW MAN HATH ALL WHICH NATURE HATH BUT MORE • •   5 HARMONY NATURE   5
AND IN THAT MORE LIE ALL HIS HOPES OF GOOD • • •   5 HARMONY NATURE   6
FRANCE FAMED IN ALL GREAT ARTS IN NONE SUPREME •   7 REP FRIEND CONT   4
IS ON ALL SIDES OERSHADOWD BY THE HIGH • • •   7 REP FRIEND CONT   6
ALL DIFFERENCE WITH HIS FELLOW-MORTAL CLOSED • •   7 REP FRIEND CONT   13
ALL DIFFERENCE WITH HIS FELLOW MAN COMPOSD • • •   7 REP FRIEND CONT   V 13
NATURES GREAT LAW AND LAW OF ALL MENS MINDS • •   8 RELIGIOUS ISOL   12
MANS JUSTICE FROM THE ALL-JUST GODS WAS GIVEN • •   9 MYCERINUS   20
AND PRAYERS AND GIFTS AND TEARS ARE FRUITLESS ALL •   10 MYCERINUS   71
MIGHT WANDER ALL DAY LONG AND NEVER TIRE • • •   11 MYCERINUS   91
FROM TREE TO TREE ALL THROUGH THE TWINKLING GROVE   11 MYCERINUS   95
REVEALING ALL THE TUMULT OF THE FEAST • • •   11 MYCERINUS   96
AND THE SIGHT FROZE ALL HER LIFE • • • • •   14 CHURCH BROU 1   52
IN MY CASTLE ALL IS SORROW • • • • • •   15 CHURCH BROU 1   73
LAST OF ALL THE BUILDERS REARD HER •• • • •   16 CHURCH BROU 1   103
BUT ALL THINGS NOW ARE ORDERED FAIR • • •   16 CHURCH BROU 2   15
THEY ARE GONE ALL IS STILL FOOLISH HEART DOST   19 MODERN SAPPHO   1
    THOU QUIVER
ARE ALL DEBTS PAID HAS ALL BEEN SAID • • • •   21 YOUTH AND CALM   8
ARE ALL DEBTS PAID HAS ALL BEEN SAID • • • •   21 YOUTH AND CALM   8
TIS ALL PERHAPS WHICH MAN ACQUIRES • • • •   22 YOUTH AND CALM   24
TIS ALL PERHAPS THAT MAN ACQUIRES • • • •   22 YOUTH AND CALM   V 24
ALL HER PALE SWEET-ROUNDED CHEEK • • • •   23 MEMORY-PICTURE   30
AH RETAIN WE ALL WE CAN • • • • • • •   24 MEMORY-PICTURE   60
THE MOUNTAIN-SKIRTS WITH ALL THEIR SYLVAN CHANGE •   25 DREAM   7
NOTES OF WILD PASTORAL MUSIC OVER ALL • • •   25 DREAM   12
TO ALL REEFS AND NARROWS WENDING • • • •   26 NEW SIRENS   15
STREAM ALL DAY THROUGH YOUR ENCHANTED LAWN • •   26 NEW SIRENS   24
I AM DUMB ALAS TOO SOON ALL • • • • • •   29 NEW SIRENS   89
AND MADE ALL YOUR CEDARS FROWN • • • • •   30 NEW SIRENS   124
ALL THE FRORE PEAKS AWFUL CROWN • • • • •   31 NEW SIRENS   144
IS THIS ALL THIS BALANCED MEASURE • • • •   33 NEW SIRENS   199
SPREADS ITS COLD LIGHT WIDER ALL THAT WHILE • •   33 NEW SIRENS   218
ALL TRUE SPEECH AND LARGE AVOWAL • • • • •   34 NEW SIRENS   227
ALL MANS HEART WHICH BROOKS BESTOWAL • • •   34 NEW SIRENS   229
ALL FRANK FAITH WHICH PASSION BREEDS • • •   34 NEW SIRENS   230
ALL THE MEANING OF YOUR EYES • • • •   34 NEW SIRENS   238
WIDENS SLOWLY WESTWARD ALL THAT WHILE • • •   33 NEW SIRENS   V 218
IN VAIN ALL ALL IN VAIN • • • • • • •   36 VOICE   32
IN VAIN ALL ALL IN VAIN • • • • • • •   36 VOICE   32
DRAIND ALL THE LIFE MY FULL HEART HAD TO SPILL •   36 VOICE   V 39
AND ALL ITS THWARTING CURRENTS OF DESIRE • •   37 YOUTHS AGIT   10
THOU TO WHOM ALL ARE KNOWN • • • • • •   38 STAGIRIUS   3
FROM DOUBT WHERE ALL IS DOUBLE • • • •   39 STAGIRIUS   39
LET ALL DOUBTS BE DUMB • • • • • • • •   39 STAGIRIUS   53
LET ALL WORDS BE MILD • • • • • • • •   40 STAGIRIUS   54
ALL STRIFES BE RECONCILED • • • • • • •   40 STAGIRIUS   55

ALL   (CONTINUED)

ALL PAINS BEGUILED	40 STAGIRIUS		56
FROM DOUBTS WHERE ALL IS DOUBLE	39 STAGIRIUS	V	39
UNRAVEL ALL HIS MANY-COLOURED LORE	43 GIPSY CHILD		34
WHOSE MIND HATH KNOWN ALL ARTS OF GOVERNING	43 GIPSY CHILD		35
HAVE KNOWN TOO MUCH OR ELSE FORGOTTEN ALL	43 GIPSY CHILD		48
TO HALVE A LODGING THAT WAS ALL HER OWN	44 GIPSY CHILD		64
BLITHE ALL ELSE STIRS THOU STIRREST NOT AVERSE	41 GIPSY CHILD	V	13
AND THOUGH THE JUST SUN GILD AS ALL MEN PRAY	43 GIPSY CHILD	V	59
TO HALVE A HOUSE THAT SHOULD BE ALL HER OWN	44 GIPSY CHILD	V	64
FOR THEIR DEAD HOPES AND ALL	44 QUESTION		12
IF IN THE SILENT MIND OF ONE ALL-PURE	45 IN UTRUMQUE PAR		1
TOOK THEN ITS ALL-SEEN WAY	45 IN UTRUMQUE PAR		7
BY LONELY PURENESS TO THE ALL-PURE FOUNT	45 IN UTRUMQUE PAR		12
CEASES NOT FROM ALL TIME TO HEAVE AND GROAN	45 IN UTRUMQUE PAR		26
OF ALL THE ENGINE-WORK OF STATE	48 HORATIAN ECHO		14
WHO THROUGH ALL HE MEETS CAN STEER HIM	49 SECOND BEST		17
IS PERSISTENCE ALL-ENDURING	SECOND BEST	V	22
BRINGS ROUND TO ALL MEN	52 CONSOLATION		74
TO THE DREAR EUXINE SO PRAY ALL	52 RESIGNATION		13
ON THIS SIDE THE ALL-COMMON CLOSE	53 RESIGNATION		16
HER OWN SWEET ERRANDS ALL FORGONE	53 RESIGNATION		36
ALL PAST AND THROUGH THE TREES WE GLIDE	54 RESIGNATION		58
FOR THEM FOR ALL TIMES BUSY TOUCH	56 RESIGNATION		126
ENVIES THE ALL-REGARDED PLACE	57 RESIGNATION		159
HEMS US ALL IN HE IS NOT BOUND	58 RESIGNATION		210
BUT ALL THE TARTAR CAMP ALONG THE STREAM	61 SOHRAB RUSTUM		3
SOHRAB ALONE HE SLEPT NOT ALL NIGHT LONG	61 SOHRAB RUSTUM		5
SLEEP BUT I SLEEP NOT ALL NIGHT LONG I LIE	62 SOHRAB RUSTUM		36
BUT IF THIS ONE DESIRE INDEED RULES ALL	63 SOHRAB RUSTUM		74
THESE ALL FILED OUT FROM CAMP INTO THE PLAIN	65 SOHRAB RUSTUM		135
A THRILL THROUGH ALL THE TARTAR SQUADRONS RAN	65 SOHRAB RUSTUM		158
OR ELSE TOO WEAK AND ALL EYES TURN TO THEE	67 SOHRAB RUSTUM		218
FOR WHAT CARE I THOUGH ALL SPEAK SOHRABS FAME	68 SOHRAB RUSTUM		228
THEE MOST OF ALL AND THOU WHOM MOST HE SEEKS	68 SOHRAB RUSTUM		245
RUKSH WHOSE RENOWN WAS NOISED THROUGH ALL THE EARTH	69 SOHRAB RUSTUM		272
ALL BEASTS OF CHASE ALL BEASTS WHICH HUNTERS KNOW	69 SOHRAB RUSTUM		279
ALL BEASTS OF CHASE ALL BEASTS WHICH HUNTERS KNOW	69 SOHRAB RUSTUM		279
AND ALL THE PERSIANS KNEW HIM AND WITH SHOUTS	69 SOHRAB RUSTUM		282
PLUNGING ALL DAY IN THE BLUE WAVES AT NIGHT	69 SOHRAB RUSTUM		287
ALL THE MOST VALIANT CHIEFS LONG HE PERUSED	70 SOHRAB RUSTUM		311
BESIDE THE OXUS ALL THE PERSIAN LORDS	72 SOHRAB RUSTUM		358
OXUS IN SUMMER WASH THEM ALL AWAY	72 SOHRAB RUSTUM		378
FOR WE ARE ALL LIKE SWIMMERS IN THE SEA	72 SOHRAB RUSTUM		390
REMEMBER ALL THY VALOUR TRY THY FEINTS	75 SOHRAB RUSTUM		466
AND CUNNING ALL THE PITY I HAD IS GONE	75 SOHRAB RUSTUM		467
NOR CLOVE ITS STEEL QUITE THROUGH BUT ALL THE CREST	76 SOHRAB RUSTUM		496
OF SOME PAIND DESERT-LION WHO ALL DAY	76 SOHRAB RUSTUM		504
HIS HEAD BUT THIS TIME ALL THE BLADE LIKE GLASS	76 SOHRAB RUSTUM		511
AND THE BRIGHT SUN BROKE FORTH AND MELTED ALL	76 SOHRAB RUSTUM		523
AND THEN THAT ALL THE TARTAR HOST WOULD PRAISE	77 SOHRAB RUSTUM		534
WHICH TROUBLES ALL MY HEART AND MADE MY SHIELD	77 SOHRAB RUSTUM		549
MY FATHER WHOM I SEEK THROUGH ALL THE WORLD	77 SOHRAB RUSTUM		554
HAD BEEN A PUNY GIRL NO BOY AT ALL	79 SOHRAB RUSTUM		609
AND ALL ITS BOUNDING RAPTURE AS AT DAWN	79 SOHRAB RUSTUM		620
WITH JOY AND ALL THE PLEASANT LIFE THEY LED	79 SOHRAB RUSTUM		627
HE SPOKE AND ALL THE BLOOD LEFT RUSTUMS CHEEKS	80 SOHRAB RUSTUM		661
AND ALL DAY LONG AND WHEN NIGHT COMES THE LAMP	81 SOHRAB RUSTUM		675
LET THEM ALL CROSS THE OXUS BACK IN PEACE	84 SOHRAB RUSTUM		782
THOU AND THE SNOW-HAIRD ZAL AND ALL THY FRIENDS	84 SOHRAB RUSTUM		786
AND PLANT A FAR-SEEN PILLAR OVER ALL	84 SOHRAB RUSTUM		789
WITH THE SNOW-HEADED ZAL AND ALL MY FRIENDS	84 SOHRAB RUSTUM		801
AND PLANT A FAR-SEEN PILLAR OVER ALL	84 SOHRAB RUSTUM		804
LET THEM ALL CROSS THE OXUS BACK IN PEACE	85 SOHRAB RUSTUM		807
FOR WOULD THAT ALL WHOM I HAVE EVER SLAIN	85 SOHRAB RUSTUM		809
FLOWD WITH THE STREAM ALL DOWN HIS COLD WHITE SIDE	86 SOHRAB RUSTUM		842
DEEP HEAVY GASPS QUIVERING THROUGH ALL HIS FRAME	86 SOHRAB RUSTUM		850
TILL NOW ALL STRENGTH WAS EBBD AND FROM HIS LIMBS	86 SOHRAB RUSTUM		853
AND DARKEND ALL AND A COLD FOG WITH NIGHT	86 SOHRAB RUSTUM		867
OR IF INDEED THIS ONE DESIRE RULES ALL	63 SOHRAB RUSTUM	V	74
FOR WOULD THAT ALL THAT I HAVE EVER SLAIN	85 SOHRAB RUSTUM	V	809
ALL RENT AND DUST UPON HIS HAIR	88 SICK KING BOKH		32
LIKE ALLAH HEARS AND JUDGES ALL	89 SICK KING BOKH		57
WITH ALL THE WATER THAT WAS THERE	90 SICK KING BOKH		69
AND CALLD MY MOTHER AND THEY ALL	90 SICK KING BOKH		80
AND ALL GRACE SHALL TO ME BE GRUDGED	91 SICK KING BOKH		102
BUT WHO THROUGH ALL THIS LENGTH OF TIME	92 SICK KING BOKH		145
THOUGH IT BE GREAT ALL THE EARTH ROUND	92 SICK KING BOKH		158
AND THESE ALL LABOURING FOR A LORD	93 SICK KING BOKH		169
WHICH IS THE HEAVIEST OF ALL PLAGUES	93 SICK KING BOKH		171
THERE ARE THE LEPERS AND ALL SICK	93 SICK KING BOKH		175
ALL THESE HAVE SORROW AND KEEP STILL	93 SICK KING BOKH		177
WILT THOU HAVE PITY ON ALL THESE	93 SICK KING BOKH		179
AND FOR THIS DROUGHT ALL KINDS OF FRUITS	94 SICK KING BOKH		195
AND THAT IT BE NOT FROM ALL TIME	94 SICK KING BOKH		207
WASH OFF ALL BLOOD SET SMOOTH EACH LIMB	95 SICK KING BOKH		230
WHICH ALL THE GODS IN SPORT HAD IDLY THROWN	95 BALDER DEAD 1		3
AND ALL THE GODS AND ALL THE HEROES CAME	95 BALDER DEAD 1		9
AND ALL THE GODS AND ALL THE HEROES CAME	95 BALDER DEAD 1		9
ALL YE WHO HEAR ME AND INHABIT HEAVEN	96 BALDER DEAD 1		29

ALL   (CONTINUED)
AND I TOO ODIN TOO THE LORD OF ALL   •   •   •   •   •   •   96 BALDER DEAD 1   30
BUT IN VALHALLA ALL THE GODS WENT BACK   •   •   •   •   97 BALDER DEAD 1   61
FROM AROUND BALDER ALL THE HEROES WENT   •   •   •   •   97 BALDER DEAD 1   62
WHO ALL WILL FLIT LIKE EDDYING LEAVES AROUND   •   •   100 BALDER DEAD 1   177
TELLING HER ALL THAT GRIEF THEY HAVE IN HEAVEN   •   •   100 BALDER DEAD 1   180
BUT THERE WAS ONE THE FIRST OF ALL THE GODS   •   •   101 BALDER DEAD 1   220
AND ALL THE GODS LAY DOWN IN THEIR OWN HOMES   •   •   102 BALDER DEAD 1   248
THEY THINK TO BURN AND ALL MY CHOICEST WEALTH   •   •   103 BALDER DEAD 1   299
AND ALL THE NOBLER SOULS OF MORTAL MEN   •   •   •   •   104 BALDER DEAD 1   320
FOR ALL THE NOBLER SOULS OF MORTAL MEN   •   •   •   •   104 BALDER DEAD 1   V 320
AND ALL THE GODS AND ALL THE HEROES WOKE   •   •   •   •   105 BALDER DEAD 2   10
AND ALL THE GODS AND ALL THE HEROES WOKE   •   •   •   •   105 BALDER DEAD 2   10
AND ALL DAY LONG THEY THERE ARE HACKD AND HEWN   •   •   105 BALDER DEAD 2   15
BUT ALL AT NIGHT RETURN TO ODINS HALL   •   •   •   •   105 BALDER DEAD 2   17
THERE ALL THE GODS IN SILENCE SATE THEM DOWN   •   •   106 BALDER DEAD 2   39
WITH ALL WHICH IT BESEEMS THE DEAD TO HAVE   •   •   •   106 BALDER DEAD 2   42
AND FROM THE GLENS ALL DAY AN ECHO CAME   •   •   •   •   106 BALDER DEAD 2   54
ALL DAY AND DAYLIGHT WANED AND NIGHT CAME ON   •   •   107 BALDER DEAD 2   81
AND ALL THAT NIGHT HE RODE AND JOURNEYD SO   •   •   •   107 BALDER DEAD 2   82
BUT ALL HE PASSD UNHAILD AND REACHD THE THRONE   •   •   109 BALDER DEAD 2   176
SHOW ME THROUGH ALL THE WORLD THE SIGNS OF GRIEF • •   111 BALDER DEAD 2   234
LET ALL THAT LIVES AND MOVES UPON THE EARTH   •   •   111 BALDER DEAD 2   236
WEEP HIM AND ALL THAT IS WITHOUT LIFE WEEP   •   •   •   111 BALDER DEAD 2   237
FEAR NOTHING BUT THAT ALL SHALL BE FULFILLD   •   •   112 BALDER DEAD 2   253
AND SURE OF ALL THE HAPPIEST FAR ART THOU   •   •   •   112 BALDER DEAD 2   257
HERE AND HAST HONOUR AMONG ALL THE DEAD   •   •   •   •   112 BALDER DEAD 2   261
CROWND HAVING HONOUR AMONG ALL THE DEAD   •   •   •   •   112 BALDER DEAD 2   278
FOR HIM FOR OTHERS ALL RETURN IS BARRD   •   •   •   113 BALDER DEAD 2   292
SHOW HER THROUGH ALL THE WORLD THE SIGNS OF GRIEF   114 BALDER DEAD 3   42
HE SPOKE AND ALL THE GODS TO ODIN LOOKD   •   •   •   •   115 BALDER DEAD 3   47
AND IN PROCESSION ALL COME NEAR AND WEEP   •   •   •   115 BALDER DEAD 3   51
FOR WE LOSE HIM WHO SMOOTHED ALL STRIFE IN HEAVEN   116 BALDER DEAD 3   88
HE SPAKE AND ALL THE GODS ASSENTING WAILD   •   •   •   •   116 BALDER DEAD 3   89
THE LOVELIEST GODDESS SHE IN HEAVEN BY ALL   •   •   •   •   116 BALDER DEAD 3   91
SHE SPAKE AND ALL THE GODDESSES BEWAILD   •   •   •   117 BALDER DEAD 3   123
AND ALL THESE GLADLY WHILE WE DRINK WE HEAR   •   •   117 BALDER DEAD 3   135
SO REGNER SPAKE AND ALL THE HEROES GROAND   •   •   •   117 BALDER DEAD 3   153
AND SOON HAD ALL THAT DAY BEEN SPENT IN WAIL   •   •   118 BALDER DEAD 3   155
AND BROUGHT HIS ARMS AND GOLD AND ALL HIS STUFF •   •   118 BALDER DEAD 3   169
REDDENING THE SEA AROUND AND ALL WAS DARK   •   •   •   •   119 BALDER DEAD 3   206
ALL NIGHT THEY ATE THE BOAR SERIMNERS FLESH   •   •   119 BALDER DEAD 3   210
AND MORNING OVER ALL THE WORLD WAS SPREAD   •   •   •   119 BALDER DEAD 3   213
ALL THE STRONG BROOD OF HEAVEN TO SWELL MY TRAIN • •   120 BALDER DEAD 3   241
FOR OF ALL POWERS THE MIGHTIEST FAR ART THOU   •   •   120 BALDER DEAD 3   250
FOR ALL WHICH HATH BEEN FIXT WAS FIXT BY THEE   •   •   121 BALDER DEAD 3   254
AND ALL THE RACE OF YMIR THOU DIDST DROWN   •   •   •   •   121 BALDER DEAD 3   271
BUT ALL THAT BROOD THOU HAST REMOVED FAR OFF   •   •   121 BALDER DEAD 3   274
A QUEEN AND EMPIRE OVER ALL THE DEAD   •   •   •   •   121 BALDER DEAD 3   278
AND ALL THAT IS TO COME I KNOW BUT LOCK   •   •   •   •   121 BALDER DEAD 3   286
ALL LIVING AND UNLIVING THINGS TO WEEP   •   •   •   •   122 BALDER DEAD 3   292
NOR DID THE ALL-RULING ODIN SLIGHT HER WORD   •   •   122 BALDER DEAD 3   297
GO QUICKLY FORTH THROUGH ALL THE WORLD AND PRAY •   •   122 BALDER DEAD 3   299
ALL LIVING AND UNLIVING THINGS TO WEEP   •   •   •   •   122 BALDER DEAD 3   300
THEIR HORSES AND RODE FORTH THROUGH ALL THE WORLD   122 BALDER DEAD 3   303
ENTREATING ALL THINGS TO WEEP BALDERS DEATH   •   •   122 BALDER DEAD 3   305
AND ALL THAT LIVED AND ALL WITHOUT LIFE WEPT   •   •   122 BALDER DEAD 3   306
AND ALL THAT LIVED AND ALL WITHOUT LIFE WEPT   •   •   122 BALDER DEAD 3   306
IN ALL THE FORESTS AND THE SOFT-STREWN SNOW   •   •   122 BALDER DEAD 3   311
OF ALL THINGS WEEPING TO BRING BALDER BACK   •   •   •   122 BALDER DEAD 3   318
THEY TWO SCOURD EVERY COAST AND ALL THINGS WEPT   •   123 BALDER DEAD 3   328
BUT WILL RESTORE IF ALL THINGS GIVE HIM TEARS   •   •   123 BALDER DEAD 3   348
BEGRUDGE NOT THINE TO ALL WAS BALDER DEAR   •   •   •   123 BALDER DEAD 3   349
WEEP HIM ALL OTHER THINGS IF WEEP THEY WILL   •   •   123 BALDER DEAD 3   353
IT IS THE ACCUSER LOK WHO FLOUTS US ALL   •   •   •   •   124 BALDER DEAD 3   370
BUT ALL I LEFT OF MY OWN ACT AND FLED   •   •   •   •   125 BALDER DEAD 3   405
BALDER UPBRAIDS ME NOT NOR HATES AT ALL   •   •   •   •   125 BALDER DEAD 3   407
THE LOVE ALL BEAR TOWARD THEE NOR TRAIN UP   •   •   •   126 BALDER DEAD 3   450
THOU HAST THEN ALL THE SOLACE DEATH ALLOWS   •   •   •   •   126 BALDER DEAD 3   469
AND ALL ARE MARSHALLD IN ONE FLAMING SQUARE   •   •   127 BALDER DEAD 3   480
AGAINST THE WOLVES AND ALL NIGHT LONG IT FLARES   •   119 BALDER DEAD 3   V
THE LOVE ALL BEAR TOWARDS THEE NOR TRAIN UP   •   •   126 BALDER DEAD 3   V 450
PASSING ALL HER YOUTHFUL HOUR   •   •   •   •   •   •   •   131 TRISTRAM 1   39
ALL THE SPRING-TIME OF HIS LOVE   •   •   •   •   •   •   136 TRISTRAM 1   173
ALL RED WITH BLOOD THE WHIRLING RIVER FLOWS   •   •   137 TRISTRAM 1   234
ALL ROUND THE FOREST SWEEPS OFF BLACK IN SHADE   •   139 TRISTRAM 1   276
ALL SHINING IN THE WHITE MOON-BEAMS   •   •   •   •   •   141 TRISTRAM 1   370
IN THE GREEN WOOD ALL OUR LIVES ALONE   •   •   •   •   143 TRISTRAM 2   36
THE CASTLE-COURT ALL WET WITH RAIN   •   •   •   •   •   148 TRISTRAM 2   170
NOT IN THE FREE GREEN WOOD AT ALL   •   •   •   •   •   149 TRISTRAM 2   179
IS LIGHT AND GREEN THE HEATHER WHICH ALL ROUND   •   150 TRISTRAM 3   14
NOR TO THE SNOW WHICH THOUGH TWAS ALL AWAY   •   •   •   151 TRISTRAM 3   50
CAN FORGET ALL TO HEAR THEM AS OF OLD   •   •   •   •   152 TRISTRAM 3   111
TO ALL THAT HAS DELIGHTED THEM BEFORE   •   •   •   •   152 TRISTRAM 3   114
POWER TO BE MOVED AND SOOTHED FOR ALL OUR PAIN   •   153 TRISTRAM 3   117
TO MAKE OUR FORMER PLEASURES ALL SEEM STALE   •   •   153 TRISTRAM 3   126
ALL WHICH WE DID BEFORE SHADOW AND DREAM   •   •   •   153 TRISTRAM 3   132
WHICH GLISTERING PLAYS ALL ROUND THEM LONE AND MILD   155 TRISTRAM 3   203
OVER THE WASTE BUT ALL THE HOLLOW OPEN GROUND   •   •   TRISTRAM 3   V 13
FIRST MEETS THE FRINGING HEATH AT ONCE ALL ROUND   •   •   TRISTRAM 3   V 14

ALL   (CONTINUED)

FIRST LEAVES THE FRINGING HEATH AT ONCE ALL ROUND   TRISTRAM 3   V   14
FIRST MEETS THE ENCIRCLING HEATH AT ONCE ALL ROUND   TRISTRAM 3   V   14
FIRST LEAVES THE ENCIRCLING HEATH AT ONCE ALL ROUND   TRISTRAM 3   V   14
IS GREEN AND CLEAR THE HEATHER WHICH ALL ROUND   • •   TRISTRAM 3   V   14
IS LIGHT AND GREEN THE HEATHER WHICH ALL ROUND   • •   TRISTRAM 3   V   14
TO ALL WHICH HAS DELIGHTED THEM BEFORE   • • • •   152 TRISTRAM 3   V 114
ALL THAT WE DID BEFORE SHADOW AND DREAM   • • • •   153 TRISTRAM 3   V 132
WHICH GLISTERING LAY ALL ROUND THEM LONE AND MILD   155 TRISTRAM 3   V 203
MY NAME IS UNDER ALL MENS BAN   • • • • • • •   157 SAINT BRANDAN   27
OF ALL HE SAW AND FELT ON EARTH   • • • • •   159 NECKAN   15
SHE WILL NOT COME THOUGH YOU CALL ALL DAY   • • • •   162 FORSAKEN MERM   28
WHERE THE WINDS ARE ALL ASLEEP   • • • • • • •   162 FORSAKEN MERM   36
WHERE THE SEA-BEASTS RANGED ALL ROUND   • • • •   162 FORSAKEN MERM   39
THROUGH THE NARROW PAVED STREETS WHERE ALL WAS STILL   163 FORSAKEN MERM   70
IN PARIS ALL LOOKD HOT AND LIKE TO FADE   • • •   167 RACHEL 1   1
ALL SPOTS MATCHD WITH THAT SPOT ARE LESS DIVINE   • •   167 RACHEL 1   13
THE AIDS TO NOBLE LIFE ARE ALL WITHIN   • • • •   169 WORLDLY PLACE   14
HOW ANGRILY THOU SPURNST ALL SIMPLER FARE   • • • •   170 BETTER PART   2
HIS SOUL WELL-KNIT AND ALL HIS BATTLES WON   • • • •   172 IMMORTALITY   13
YET FERVENT HAD HER LONGING BEEN THROUGH ALL   • • •   173 MONICAS PRAYER   6
ALL TIE WITH ALL BESIDE SEEMD VAIN AND CHEAP   • •   173 MONICAS PRAYER   10
ALL TIE WITH ALL BESIDE SEEMD VAIN AND CHEAP   • •   173 MONICAS PRAYER   10
TO ALL ALWAYS OPEN   • • • • • • • • • •   177 PARTING   81
TO ALL ALWAYS TRUE   • • • • • • • • • •   177 PARTING   82
ALL OUR UNQUIET PULSES CEASE   • • • • • • •   180 FAREWELL   82
WITH ALL THY BEING RE-ARRANGED   • • • • • • •   184 TERRACE BERNE   35
OF ALL THAT WAS MY MARGUERITES OWN   • • • • •   185 TERRACE BERNE   40
ALL DRENCHD IN DEW   • • • • • • • • • •   186 STRAYED REVEL   34
THE COURT ALL SILENT   • • • • • • • • •   187 STRAYED REVEL   47
THEY TURN ON ALL SIDES   • • • • • • • •   190 STRAYED REVEL   131
BAKED ON THE EMBERS ALL AROUND   • • • • • • •   191 STRAYED REVEL   167
ALL DAY LONG HAVE SEEN   • • • • • • • •   194 STRAYED REVEL   273
FOR LITTLE DO THE ALL-CONTAINING HOURS   • • •   195 FRAG ANTIGONE   2
THE ALL-HATED ORDER-BREAKING   • • • • • • •   195 FRAG ANTIGONE   25
DEATH WHO DISSEVERS ALL   • • • • • • • •   195 FRAG ANTIGONE   27
BUT STRANGELY MISINTERPRET ALL YOU HEAR   • • •   198 FRAG DEJANEIRA   14
IN ALL HIS LOVELY MIEN LET PIERCE   • • • • •   202 URANIA   23
FLED FLED AT ONCE BE ALL VESTIGE OF THEE   • • •   206 SEPARATION   10
AH QUIET ALL THINGS FEEL THY BALM   • • • •   208 ON THE RHINE   21
AS KIND TO ALL THE REST AS ME   • • • • • •   208 LONGING   V   8
IT IS LAST STAGE OF ALL   • • • • • • •   213 GROWING OLD   31
ALL THE CENTURIES PAST IT HAS HUNG SO   • • •   214 NEW ROME   V   19
VAIN THY ONSET ALL STANDS FAST   • • • • • •   215 LAST WORD   3
AH HOW FEW OF THEM ALL   • • • • • • • •   216 LORDS MESSENGER   10
ALAS HOW FEW OF THEM ALL   • • • • • • • •   216 LORDS MESSENGER   V   10
UNHEARD ALL DAY ASCENDS AGAIN   • • • • • •   217 BACCHANALIA 1   3
ALL HOUSED WITHIN THE SLEEPING FARMS   • • • •   218 BACCHANALIA 1   7
THE FAMOUS CRITICS JUDGED IT ALL   • • • • •   219 BACCHANALIA 2   9
ALL THINGS BEGIN AGAIN   • • • • • • • •   220 BACCHANALIA 2   41
POUR ALL THE SOUL OF THEIR COMPLAINT   • • • •   224 EPILOG LAOCOON   100
ALL CHANGES FAST AND HIES ALONG   • • • • •   225 EPILOG LAOCOON   124
THE THREAD WHICH BINDS IT ALL IN ONE   • • • •   225 EPILOG LAOCOON   141
YES ALL THIS EDDYING MOTLEY THRONG   • • • •   226 EPILOG LAOCOON   157
BUT AH HOW FEW OF ALL THAT TRY   • • • • • •   226 EPILOG LAOCOON   169
THEY SEE ALL ROUND A WILDERNESS   • • • • •   226 EPILOG LAOCOON   176
BUT HE WAS A PRIEST TO US ALL   • • • • •   229 YOUTH OF NATURE   53
SHARED AND REJOICED IN BY ALL   • • • • • •   230 YOUTH OF NATURE   67
HATH NOT BEEN THRILLD BY THEM ALL   • • • •   230 YOUTH OF NATURE   82
ALL THINGS HAVE SUFFERD A LOSS   • • • • • •   232 YOUTH OF NATURE   127
HAS NOT BEEN THRILLD BY THEM ALL   • • • •   230 YOUTH OF NATURE   V   82
THE SENSELESS WORLD WITH THEM ALL   • • • •   233 YOUTH OF MAN   34
AND FANCY THAT WE PUT FORTH ALL OUR LIFE   • • •   236 PALLADIUM   19
TILL ALL HAVE BEEN FULFILLD   • • • • • •   237 PROGRESS   12
TILL ALL SHALL BE FULFILLD   • • • • • • •   237 PROGRESS   V   12
TILL ALL HATH BEEN FULFILLD   • • • • • •   237 PROGRESS   V   12
ALL THE FEVER OF SOME DIFFERING SOUL   • • • •   240 SELF-DEPENDENCE   24
IN THEIR OWN TASKS ALL THEIR POWERS POURING   • •   240 SELF-DEPENDENCE   27
ALL WE HAVE BUILT DO WE DISCERN   • • • • •   241 MORALITY   12
LIKE ALL THE OTHER MEN I SEE   • • • • • •   243 SUMMER NIGHT   36
HARDLY HAD SKILL TO UTTER ONE OF ALL   • • • •   246 BURIED LIFE   61
OF ALL THE THOUSAND NOTHINGS OF THE HOUR   • • •   247 BURIED LIFE   69
A MELANCHOLY INTO ALL OUR DAY   • • • • • •   247 BURIED LIFE   76
STILL ALL THINGS IN THIS GLADE GO THROUGH   • • •   249 KENSINGTON GARD   31
CALM SOUL OF ALL THINGS MAKE IT MINE   • • • •   249 KENSINGTON GARD   37
ALL WHICH MAKES DEATH A HIDEOUS SHOW   • • • •   250 WISH   16
WHILE ALL AROUND IN SILENCE LIES   • • • •   250 WISH   30
BUT LIT FOR ALL ITS GENEROUS SUN   • • • •   251 WISH   39
ALL THAT MAKES DEATH A HIDEOUS SHOW   • • • •   250 WISH   V   16
AND THE TIRED MEN AND DOGS ALL GONE TO REST   • •   255 SCHOLAR-GIPSY   7
AND IN THE SUN ALL MORNING BINDS THE SHEAVES   • •   255 SCHOLAR-GIPSY   14
ALL THE LIVE MURMUR OF A SUMMERS DAY   • • • • •   255 SCHOLAR-GIPSY   20
HAVE KNOWN THEE EYING ALL AN APRIL-DAY   • • •   258 SCHOLAR-GIPSY   107
SEES THEE NOR STOPS HIS MEAL NOR FEARS AT ALL   •   258 SCHOLAR-GIPSY   117
AND ALL HIS STORE OF SAD EXPERIENCE HE   • • •   260 SCHOLAR-GIPSY   185
AND ALL HIS HOURLY VARIED ANODYNES   • • • •   260 SCHOLAR-GIPSY   190
AND WAIVE ALL CLAIM TO BLISS AND TRY TO BEAR   • •   260 SCHOLAR-GIPSY   193
HAVE KNOWN THEE WATCHING ALL AN APRIL-DAY   • • • •   258 SCHOLAR-GIPSY   V 107
HAVE KNOWN THEE HAUNTING ALL AN APRIL-DAY   • • • •   258 SCHOLAR-GIPSY   V 107
LOVELY ALL TIMES SHE LIES LOVELY TO-NIGHT   • • • •   263 THYRSIS   21

18

ALL   (CONTINUED)

WHEN GARDEN-WALKS AND ALL THE GRASSY FLOOR • • • • 264 THYRSIS   54
THEY ALL ARE GONE AND THOU ART GONE AS WELL • • • 266 THYRSIS   130
AND ALL THE MARVEL OF THE GOLDEN SKIES • • • • 268 THYRSIS   190
BUT ALL OUR HUSTLING MORROWS ONLY MAKE • 262 THYRSIS   V
FOR THESE ARE ALL THEIR OWN REWARD • • • • 273 EDW QUILLINAN   5
WITH ALL THE FORTUNATE HAVE NOT • • • • 273 EDW QUILLINAN   17
THE BLUE-BELLS PERFUME ALL THE AIR • • • • 274 STANZAS CARNAC   20
RISE UP ALL ROUND THE CHRISTIAN SPIRES • • • 274 STANZAS CARNAC   22
ALL ROUND NO SOUL NO BOAT NO HAIL • • • • 274 STANZAS CARNAC   30
THE FURZE-SCENT PERFUMES ALL THE AIR • • • • 274 STANZAS CARNAC V 20
THAT SPIRIT IF ALL HAVE NOT YET DIED • • • • 276 SOUTHERN NIGHT   35
AND SEE ALL SIGHTS FROM POLE TO POLE • • • • 277 SOUTHERN NIGHT   69
TWIXT MYRTLE-HEDGES ALL IN FLOWER • • • • 278 SOUTHERN NIGHT   103
ALL PLAINT IN HER OWN CAUSE CONTROLLD • • • 279 SOUTHERN NIGHT   122
WHAT ELSE IS ALL THESE WATERS ARE • • • • 279 SOUTHERN NIGHT   133
THEIR NAMES CHIEF GLORY OF ALL • • • • 281 HAWORTH CHURCH   22
INFERIOR ALL IN FAME • • • • 284 HAWORTH CHURCH   83
OF ALL THAT GIFTED RACE • • • • 285 HAWORTH CHURCH   103
THEIR NAMES CHIEF TREASURE OF ALL • • • • 281 HAWORTH CHURCH V 22
OF ALL HIS GIFTED RACE • • • • 285 HAWORTH CHURCH V 103
FROM DULL OBLIVION NOR ALL • • • 288 RUGBY CHAPEL   82
WHO ALL ROUND ME TO-DAY • • • • 290 RUGBY CHAPEL   156
RISING ALL ROUND OVERAWE • • • • 291 RUGBY CHAPEL   179
WE KNOW ALL THIS WE KNOW • • • • 295 HEINES GRAVE   115
ALL IN FERMENT BUT HE • • • • 298 HEINES GRAVE   195
WHAT ARE WE ALL BUT A MOOD • • • • 298 HEINES GRAVE   214
WHO ALONE IS ALL THINGS IN ONE • • • • 298 HEINES GRAVE   217
SPIRIT WHO FILLEST US ALL • 298 HEINES GRAVE   218
ALL ARE BEFORE ME I BEHOLD • • • • 301 GRANDE CHARTR   64
THEIR VOICES WERE IN ALL MENS EARS • • • • 303 GRANDE CHARTR   123
FOR WHAT AVAILD IT ALL THE NOISE • • • • 303 GRANDE CHARTR   127
AND SECRET FROM THE EYES OF ALL • • • • 305 GRANDE CHARTR   172
YES OBERMANN ALL SPEAKS OF THEE • • • • 306 OBERMANN   11
ALL SHIPWRECK IN THY OWN WEAK HEART • • • • 307 OBERMANN   19
WHOSE ONE BOND IS THAT ALL HAVE BEEN • • • • 311 OBERMANN   155
ALL MEANING FROM A NAME • • • • 312 OBERMANN MORE   2
AND YET I KNOW NOT ALL UNCHANGED • • • • 312 OBERMANN MORE   5
FOR ALL THAT MIGHT HAVE BEEN • • • • 314 OBERMANN MORE   52
SHE LEFT IT ALL BEHIND • • • • 317 OBERMANN MORE   134
AND UNSPENT ALL THAT TIME • • • • 318 OBERMANN MORE   162
HIS ALL TOO HUMAN CREEDS AND SCAN • • • • 319 OBERMANN MORE   187
ALL EUROPE FELT THAT FIERY BLAST • • • • 319 OBERMANN MORE   203
ALL IT BEFORE ENDEAVOURD • • • • 320 OBERMANN MORE   214
KNIT ALL YOUR PARTS AND KEPT YOU ONE • • • • 320 OBERMANN MORE   223
SEE I MAKE ALL THINGS NEW • • • • 320 OBERMANN MORE   232
AND JOY THAT SHOULD ALL HEARTS EMPLOY • • • 320 OBERMANN MORE   239
WHEREOF THY YOUTH FELT ALL THE SPELL • • • • 323 OBERMANN MORE   309
AND TRAVERSED ALL THE SHADE • • • • 323 OBERMANN MORE   310
AND PALSIED ALL OUR WORD WITH DOUBT • • • • 323 OBERMANN MORE   319
AND ALL OUR WORK WITH WOE • • • • 323 OBERMANN MORE   320
DOTH ALL THE HEAVENLY OPENING CLOSE • • • • 324 OBERMANN MORE   343
ALL THEY BEFORE ENDEAVOURD • • • • 320 OBERMANN MORE V 214
AND PALSIED ALL OUR DEED WITH DOUBT • • • • 323 OBERMANN MORE V 319
AND ALL OUR WORD WITH WOE • • • • 323 OBERMANN MORE V 320
SEVERER PALER STATELIER THAN THEY ALL • 331 MEROPE   57
ALL THIS I BEAR FOR WHAT I SEEK I KNOW • • • 333 MEROPE   100
DANGEROUS TO ALL TO BE BUT THUS ANNULLD • • • 336 MEROPE   207
ALL KNOW HOW WEAK THE EAGLE HERACLES • • 336 MEROPE   212
SOWING HIS VICTORS THINLY THROUGH THEM ALL • 337 MEROPE   250
RELUCTANTLY THE REST BUT AGAINST ALL • • 337 MEROPE   257
HOW OF ALL HUMAN RULES THE OVER-TENSE • • 339 MEROPE   307
HAST ALL IMPUNITY YET LEST THY FRIENDS • • • 341 MEROPE   372
HONOURD AND SUNG OF BY ALL • • • • 343 MEROPE   430
THE ALL-WEPT WAY • • • • • • • 344 MEROPE   448
THE ALL-WEPT WAY • • • • • • • 345 MEROPE   468
ALL-REGARDED AFAR • • • • • • 345 MEROPE   484
AND PRAY THE GODS AND PRAY THE ALL-SEEING SUN • • 349 MEROPE   570
FOR ALL WHO PASS PURSUERS AND PURSUED • • • 349 MEROPE   582
IF THIS BE ALL I KNOW NOT BUT I KNOW • • • 351 MEROPE   620
BUT MORE THAN ALL UNPLUMBD • • • • 352 MEROPE   629
MORE THAN ALL SECRETS HID THE WAY IT KEEPS • • • 352 MEROPE   631
FREE FROM ALL GUILT OF LAWLESSNESS • • • 353 MEROPE   660
COMMITS ALL DEEDS THE GUILTY OFTENEST DO • • 353 MEROPE   683
O KING ALL HAIL I COME WITH WEIGHTY NEWS • • • 354 MEROPE   710
MOST LIKELY GRATEFUL BUT IN ALL CASE SURE • • 354 MEROPE   711
THROUGH ALL THE LORDSHIPS OF THE ARCADIAN DALES • • 355 MEROPE   727
FROM ALL FOR HIS GREAT LINEAGE AND HIS WOES • • 356 MEROPE   762
ALL WHICH HE OWND AND PRAISED WITH GRATEFUL MIND • 356 MEROPE   763
ALL THE STYMPHALIAN PLAIN ARE NOW SUCKD DOWN • 358 MEROPE   816
ALL THIS O KING NOT PIECEMEAL AS TO THEE • • • • 358 MEROPE   827
WHILE ALL ELSE GRIEVES HIM THAT HIS GRANDCHILDS DEATH 359 MEROPE   851
ALL ENTERTAINMENT WHICH A TRAVELLER NEEDS • • • 359 MEROPE   870
O WERE BUT ARCAS COME ALL WOULD BE WELL • • • 362 MEROPE   933
WHILE LOYALTY WITH ALL HER SPEED IS SLOW • • • 363 MEROPE   963
WHEN ALL TURND TOWRDS ME ME HE WOULD HAVE SHOWN • • 366 MEROPE   1005
ALL CLAIM TO SUCCOUR FORFEIT TO MYSELF • • • 366 MEROPE   1008
WHILE ALL THIS TIME I BEAR TO LINGER ON • • • 366 MEROPE   1017
OR ELSE NOT LIVE AT ALL BUT HERE I HAUNT • • 366 MEROPE   1020
ALL VENGEANCE UNATTEMPTED AND DESCEND • • • • 367 MEROPE   1029

ALL   (CONTINUED)
TRIUMPHANT AND CONDEMNEST ALL OUR RACE . . . . 367 MEROPE 1051
SURE ALL-COMMON TO LOSE . . . . 369 MEROPE 1100
NOT ABOVE ALL IN THE DOUBTS . . . . 370 MEROPE 1112
ALL-COVERING DARKNESS O KING . . . . 372 MEROPE 1141
HE SLEEPS SLEEPS CALM O YE ALL-SEEING GODS . . . 372 MEROPE 1153
ALL-FLOODING OCEAN OF BLOOD . . . . 378 MEROPE 1246
FATHERS SONS GRANDSONS ARE ALL . . . . . . 379 MEROPE 1254
IN ALL ELSE WILLING TO BE TAUGHT IN THIS . . . 379 MEROPE 1258
FATAL TO ALL THE RACE OF HERACLES . . . . . 382 MEROPE 1330
THOUGH ALL FREE SPIRITS IN THIS LAND WERE DEAD . 383 MEROPE 1377
NOT TILL THE WAYS OF PRUDENCE ALL ARE TRIED . . 384 MEROPE 1386
BENT ABOVE ALL TO PACIFY TO RULE . . . . . 388 MEROPE 1490
NOT PRONE ALL SAY AVERSE TO BLOODSHED NOW . . . 388 MEROPE 1492
ALL THIS NO DOUBT THOU TO THYSELF HAST URGED . . 389 MEROPE 1529
JUSTICE AND WISDOM IS NO LIFE AT ALL . . . . 390 MEROPE 1576
TELLS ME ENOUGH THOU KNOWST THE NEWS WHICH ALL . 393 MEROPE 1685
THAT HE ENJOYD BUT PART BEING HEIR TO ALL . . . 394 MEROPE 1701
THAT ALL MAY BE ENDURED AND ALL FORGIVN . . . 394 MEROPE 1710
THAT ALL MAY BE ENDURED AND ALL FORGIVN . . . 394 MEROPE 1710
ALL THINGS BUT LIFE THOU LOSE NOT LIFE AS WELL . 396 MEROPE 1757
ALL I COULD DO TO SOOTHE THEE HAS BEEN TRIED . . 396 MEROPE 1764
STRIKES WITH ALL SAIL SET . . . . 400 MEROPE 1879
GROUPD AROUND ZEUSS ALTAR ALL IN ARMS . . . 401 MEROPE 1899
SILENCE AND EXPECTATION HELD US ALL . . . . 401 MEROPE 1902
TILL THEN WE ALL SEEMD STONE BUT THEN A CRY . . 402 MEROPE 1930
FOR FROM ALL SIDES A DELUGE AS IT SEEMD . . . 402 MEROPE 1937
MOTHER ALL THESE APPROVE ME BUT IF THOU . . . 403 MEROPE 1961
NONE SINCE A TWOFOLD COLOUR REIGNS IN ALL . . . 404 MEROPE 1994
THY MOTHERS PRAYERS AND THIS PRAYER LAST OF ALL . 405 MEROPE 2011
IN ALL BY THY EXPERIENCE TO BE RULED . . . . 405 MEROPE 2015
AND ALL THIS BY THE WILL OF THE GODS . . . . 405 MEROPE 2024
THOUGH ALL FREE SPIRITS IN THIS LAND BE DEAD . . 383 MEROPE V1377
NOT PRONE ALL SAY TO USELESS BLOODSHED NOW . . 388 MEROPE V1492
IN WHICH THEY HAVE TOILD ALL NIGHT FROM CATANA . 406 EMPEDOCLES I 1 4
I SADDLED MY WHITE MULE AND ALL NIGHT LONG . . 407 EMPEDOCLES I 1 44
AND ALL WHICH MIGHT RELAX HIS SETTLED GLOOM . . 409 EMPEDOCLES I 1 84
THOU HAST HEARD ALL MEN SPEAKING OF PANTHEIA . 410 EMPEDOCLES I 1 108
THIS HE COULD DO OF OLD BUT NOW SINCE ALL . . 410 EMPEDOCLES I 1 119
IN SUMMER TO ALL COUNTRY-FESTIVALS . . . . 412 EMPEDOCLES I 2 15
IT IS ENOUGH THAT ALL MEN SPEAK OF IT . . . 413 EMPEDOCLES I 2 22
OF ALL THE WOODY HIGH WELL-WATERD DELLS . . . 414 EMPEDOCLES I 2 42
AND ALL THE WISDOM OF HIS RACE . . . . . 414 EMPEDOCLES I 2 76
ALL KNOWLEDGE THAT I HAVE . . . . 415 EMPEDOCLES I 2 104
ALL SKILL I WIELD ARE FREE . . . . . . 415 EMPEDOCLES I 2 105
ALL STRIVE TO MAKE IT LESS . . . . . . 416 EMPEDOCLES I 2 120
BUT WE ARE ALL THE SAME THE FOOLS OF OUR OWN WOES 417 EMPEDOCLES I 2 166
CONDITION ALL WE DO . . . . 418 EMPEDOCLES I 2 185
EXPERIENCE LIKE A SEA SOAKS ALL-EFFACING IN . . 419 EMPEDOCLES I 2 201
THE WORLD IS WHAT IT IS FOR ALL OUR DUST AND DIN 419 EMPEDOCLES I 2 206
OUR WANTS HAVE ALL BEEN FELT OUR ERRORS MADE BEFORE 419 EMPEDOCLES I 2 211
WE WANT ALL PLEASANT ENDS BUT WILL USE NO HARSH MEANS 420 EMPEDOCLES I 2 236
ALL SIN IS JUST IS PURE . . . . 420 EMPEDOCLES I 2 243
ABANDONS ALL WHICH MAKES . . . . 420 EMPEDOCLES I 2 244
SEES ALL HER SONS AT PLAY . . . . . . 421 EMPEDOCLES I 2 258
ALL THINGS THE WORLD WHICH FILL . . . . . 422 EMPEDOCLES I 2 287
FAIN WOULD DO ALL THINGS WELL BUT SOMETIMES . 422 EMPEDOCLES I 2 296
    FAILS IN STRENGTH
AND WE WOULD KNOW IT ALL . . . . 423 EMPEDOCLES I 2 318
MANS MEASURES CANNOT METE THE IMMEASURABLE ALL . 423 EMPEDOCLES I 2 341
SURE ONLY THAT YOUR MIND SEES ALL THINGS WHICH BEFAL 423 EMPEDOCLES I 2 346
HE CANNOT ALL THINGS VIEW . . . . . . 424 EMPEDOCLES I 2 348
AND JUDGMENT ALL EMBROILD . . . . . . 425 EMPEDOCLES I 2 394
LOSE ALL OUR PRESENT STATE . . . . . . 425 EMPEDOCLES I 2 405
IN BREATHLESS QUIET AFTER ALL THEIR ILLS . . 427 EMPEDOCLES I 2 438
AND AT THE BANQUET ALL THE MUSES SANG . . . 427 EMPEDOCLES I 2 451
AND ALL THAT THEBAN WOE AND STRAY . . . . 427 EMPEDOCLES I 2 459
AND I SHALL DOUBTLESS SEE THEM ALL AGAIN . . 428 EMPEDOCLES I 2 476
ABANDONS ALL THAT MAKES . . . . 420 EMPEDOCLES I 2 V 244
ALL THINGS THE WORLD THAT FILL . . . . . 422 EMPEDOCLES I 2 V 287
MANS MEASURES CANNOT SPAN THE ILLIMITABLE ALL . 423 EMPEDOCLES I 2 V 341
AND JUDGMENTS ALL EMBROILD . . . . . . 425 EMPEDOCLES I 2 V 394
BEFORE THE SOUL LOSE ALL HER SOLEMN JOYS . . 429 EMPEDOCLES II 33
DROOPS ALL HIS SHEENY BROWN DEEP-FEATHERD NECK . 431 EMPEDOCLES II 76
BUT OVER ALL THE WORLD . . . . 432 EMPEDOCLES II 99
ALL THE FOOLS-ARMOURY OF MAGIC LIE THERE . . 432 EMPEDOCLES II 118
YOUNG APOLLO ALL THE PRIDE . . . . . . 433 EMPEDOCLES II 130
IN ALL THE ITALIAN CITIES LIKE OURSELVES . . 436 EMPEDOCLES II 237
IN ALL THINGS MY OWN DEADNESS . . . . . 438 EMPEDOCLES II 322
WE MIGHT HAVE JOY BLENT WITH THE ALL-BATHING AIR 439 EMPEDOCLES II 343
AND NEVER LET US CLASP AND FEEL THE ALL . . 439 EMPEDOCLES II 353
GO THROUGH THE SAD PROBATION ALL AGAIN . . 440 EMPEDOCLES II 368
NOT TO DIE WHOLLY NOT TO BE ALL ENSLAVED . . 441 EMPEDOCLES II 406
ALL ETNA HEAVES FIERCELY . . . . . . 441 EMPEDOCLES II 419
BUT ALL ARE DIVINE . . . . 442 EMPEDOCLES II 448
OF ALL THINGS AND THEN . . . . 443 EMPEDOCLES II 462
WE SHOULD HAVE JOY BLENT WITH THE ALL-BATHING AIR 439 EMPEDOCLES II V 343
LO ON A SUDDEN ALL THE PILE IS BRIGHT . . . 445 WESTMIN ABBEY 34
THEN ALL AGAIN IS DARK . . . . 445 WESTMIN ABBEY 41
AND TEMPER SWEET AND LOVE OF ALL THINGS PURE . 446 WESTMIN ABBEY 79
BUT ALL NIGHT LONG AMID THE FLAMES HE LAY . . 446 WESTMIN ABBEY 89

ALL   (CONTINUED)
         AND WENT WHERE ALL HIS FATHERS WENT BEFORE . . . . . 447 WESTMIN ABBEY   116
         AND BREAK HIS HEART WITH ALL THE BAFFLING CHANGE . . . 448 WESTMIN ABBEY   149
         AND ALL THE TEDIOUS TOSSING TO AND FRO   . . . . . 448 WESTMIN ABBEY   150
         AND ALL THAT LIFE AND ALL THAT LOVE . . . . . . 449 GEISTS GRAVE   3
         AND ALL THAT LIFE AND ALL THAT LOVE . . . . . . 449 GEISTS GRAVE   3
         OF ALL THE CENTURIES YET TO COME   . . . . . . 450 GEISTS GRAVE   22
         IN US WAS ALL THE WORLD TO THEE   . . . . . . 451 GEISTS GRAVE   60
         ALL CONVULSED HIS LITTLE FORM   . . . . 452 POOR MATTHIAS   4
         ALL THAT GAY COURAGEOUS CHEER   . . . . 454 POOR MATTHIAS   61
         ALL THAT HUMAN PATHOS DEAR   . . . . 454 POOR MATTHIAS   62
         FINDING NOT DO ALL THEY CAN   . . . . 455 POOR MATTHIAS   97
         BUT WITH ALL THIS TRAVAIL SAGE . . . . 456 POOR MATTHIAS   147
         WERE KNOWN TO ALL THE VILLAGE-STREET   . . . . . . 459 KAISER DEAD   8
         WHAT POOR KAI DEAD SAY ALL I MEET   . . . . . . 459 KAISER DEAD   9
         BUT ALL THOSE VIRTUES WHICH COMMEND . . . . . . 459 KAISER DEAD   31
         BY THEIR OWN CRIMES A LESSON TO ALL EYES . . . . 462 ALARIC AT ROME   11
         THAT FOR A MOMENT GLEAMS AND ALL AGAIN IS NIGHT . . 463 ALARIC AT ROME   30
         WHERE ALL WE SEE OR DO OR HEAR OR SAY   . . . . . 464 ALARIC AT ROME   47
         BUT ONE VAST FANE WHERE ALL UNCONSCIOUS SLEEP . . 464 ALARIC AT ROME   59
         YET HERE IT SPEAKS NOT YEA THOUGH ALL AROUND   . . 467 ALARIC AT ROME   143
         ALL NATURAL LOVE ALL HUMAN SYMPATHY . . . . . . 467 ALARIC AT ROME   147
         ALL NATURAL LOVE ALL HUMAN SYMPATHY . . . . . . 467 ALARIC AT ROME   147
         WHISPERING FROM ALL AROUND ALL EARTHLY THINGS MUST DIE 469 ALARIC AT ROME   180
         WHISPERING FROM ALL AROUND ALL EARTHLY THINGS MUST DIE 469 ALARIC AT ROME   180
         YET ALL HIGH SOUNDS THAT MOUNTAIN CHILDREN HEAR . . 472 CROMWELL   27
         ALL FREEDOMS MYSTIC LANGUAGE STORMS THAT ROAR . . 472 CROMWELL   29
         ALL THESE HAD STIRRD THY SPIRIT AND THINE EYE . . 472 CROMWELL   31
         TILL ALL BRIGHT THOUGHTS THAT HILLS OR WAVES CAN YIELD 472 CROMWELL   33
         BOUND ALL HIS BEING WITH A SILVER CHAIN . . . . 473 CROMWELL   63
         ALL IDLY FLUTTERD IN THE EASTERN GALE   . . . . . 473 CROMWELL   68
         ALL SHAPES THAT HAUNT REMEMBRANCE SOFT AND FAIR . . 474 CROMWELL   83
         LIKE A GREEN LAND AT SUNSET ALL WERE THERE . . . 474 CROMWELL   84
         ALL AIRY HOPES THAT IDLE HEARTS CAN FRAME . . . 474 CROMWELL   95
         ALL WONDROUS DEEDS THE COMING DAYS SHOULD SEE . . 475 CROMWELL   139
         AND ONE SWAYD ALL WHO WORE A KINGLY CROWN . . . 476 CROMWELL   143
         NO ALL WAS CHANGD THE MONARCH WEPT ALONE . . . . 477 CROMWELL   187
         THAT ALL NIGHT LONG ITS WEARY MOAN DOTH MAKE   . . 477 CROMWELL   191
         THEN ALL HIS DREAM WAS TROUBLED AND HIS SOUL   . . 477 CROMWELL   199
         THE YEARS OF TOIL ALL ALL WERE WRITTEN THERE   . . 478 CROMWELL   206
         THE YEARS OF TOIL ALL ALL WERE WRITTEN THERE   . . 478 CROMWELL   206
         THE IMPRISONING CHAINS FELL OFF AND ALL WAS CLEAR . 478 CROMWELL   214
         CHEERD ALL THE FAILING HEARTS THAT SORROWD THERE . 478 CROMWELL   218
         ALL THESE WERE THINE OH THOUGHT OF FEAR AND THOU . 479 CROMWELL   233
         THEN ALL HIS VISION FADED AND HIS SOUL . . . . . 479 CROMWELL   235
         ALL ELSE BLACK WATER AND AFLOAT . . . . 479 HAYSWATER BOAT   15
         ALL NIGHT THEY SATE THEN STOLE AWAY . . . . . . 480 HAYSWATER BOAT   31
         ALL THOU AUGUREST HERE OF LOVELY SEEMING . . . . 483 THEKLAS ANSWER   21
         WITH FRAGRANCE ALL FRASCATIS WOOD   . . . . . . 484 ROME-SICKNESS   19
         TO ALL WHO SINK TO ALL WHO STRAY   . . . . . . 484 ROME-SICKNESS   32
         TO ALL WHO SINK TO ALL WHO STRAY   . . . . . . 484 ROME-SICKNESS   32
         OF ALL LIVING THINGS THAT ON EARTH ARE BREATHING
            AND MOVING   HOMER TRANS   13
         SUDDEN HE BOWD HIS HEAD AND ALL HIS MANE AS HE BOWD IT HOMER TRANS   44
         FAR FROM MY FATHER AND MOTHER DEAR FOR ALL   HOMER TRANS   61
            THAT I WILL NOT
         OF ALL THIRST OF EARTHLY THINGS . . . . . .   META CLOISTER   2
         HERE WHERE LIFE AND ALL THINGS LIVING   . . . .   META CLOISTER   17
         ALL THE HEART ENJOINS BUT ONLY HERE . . . . .   META CLOISTER   24
         ALL YOUR SPIRITS HISTORY GLEANS . . . . . .   META CLOISTER   36
         THERE IS A SIGHT MORE SADDENING YET WHEN ALL . . LUCRETIUS 2   7
         WHAT ARE WE ALL . . . .   LUCRETIUS 6   1
         KEEP ALL O KEEP CONTINUAL HOLIDAY   . . . . .   FRAGMENT 2   5
         THE DOUBT THAT ASSAILS ALL THINGS NEVER WON   . . FRAGMENT 8   3

ALLAH
         FOR ALLAH SHUT MY EARS AND MIND   . . . . . . 88 SICK KING BOKH   24
         LIKE ALLAH HEARS AND JUDGES ALL   . . . . . . 89 SICK KING BOKH   57
         BUT HE PRAISED ALLAH WITH LOUD VOICE . . . . . . 91 SICK KING BOKH   123

ALLAYD
         DID EVER BURN IS LONG BY TIME ALLAYD . . . . . . 387 MEROPE   1471

ALLEDGE
         THOU DOST ALLEDGE FOR PROOF SUCH INSTANCES . . . . RUDE ORATOR   15

ALLEGIANCE
         IN THEIR ALLEGIANCE ME IN MY SONS DEATH-HOUR . . 366 MEROPE   1004
         BEQUEATHS THE ALLEGIANCE OF OUR SHEPHERD-TRIBES . . 389 MEROPE   1540

ALLEY
         HARK THROUGH THE ALLEY RESOUNDS   . . . . . . 293 HEINES GRAVE   37

ALLEYS
         DOWN THE STATUED ALLEYS CAME   . . . . 29 NEW SIRENS   102
         LEAVES WERE WHIRLING IN THE ALLEYS   . . . . . . 30 NEW SIRENS   125
         LEAVES ARE WHIRLING IN THE ALLEYS   . . . . . . 30 NEW SIRENS   V 125
         THROUGH SUN-PROOF ALLEYS . . . . 51 CONSOLATION   26
         ROSES THAT DOWN THE ALLEYS SHINE AFAR   . . . . 264 THYRSIS   67
         SWARDED ALLEYS THE LIMES . . . . 292 HEINES GRAVE   4

ALLIANCE
IMPIOUS I DEEM THE ALLIANCE WHICH HE ASKS . . . . . 348 MEROPE   550

ALLIED
THEY WERE ALLIED . . . . 279 SOUTHERN NIGHT   140

ALLIERE
WHENCE DROPS THE PATH TO ALLIERE DOWN . . . . 313 OBERMANN MORE   23

ALLOW
DEEPER TO THESE MUST NEEDS ALLOW . . . . . . 222 EPILOG LAOCOON   31
BUT WHILE WE WAIT ALLOW OUR TEARS . . . . . . 304 GRANDE CHARTR   162
ALLOW THEM WE ADMIRE WITH AWE . . . . 304 GRANDE CHARTR   163
BUT TILL THEY RISE ALLOW OUR TEARS . . . . . 304 GRANDE CHARTR   V 162
IF PARIS THAT BRIEF FLIGHT ALLOW . . . . . . 321 OBERMANN MORE   269
HE MAY FOR NEVER DID THE GODS ALLOW . . . . . 388 MEROPE   1508

ALLOWD
OR FOR THOU KNOWST THE FATES AND THINGS ALLOWD . . 98 BALDER DEAD 1   108
FAREWELL FOR LONGER SPEECH IS NOT ALLOWD . . . 129 BALDER DEAD 3   548
AND YET THE ONLY PEACE TO US ALLOWD . . . . . 378 MEROPE   1250
THE GODS PERHAPS ALLOWD YOU . . . . 398 MEROPE   1799
WHO HAS NO MINUTES BREATHING SPACE ALLOWD . . . 437 EMPEDOCLES II   272
ALLOWD NO FEAR . . . . 441 EMPEDOCLES II   403

ALLOWS
THOU HAST THEN ALL THE SOLACE DEATH ALLOWS . . . 126 BALDER DEAD 3   469
HAD SCORED HER WHITE RIGHT HAND WHICH SHE ALLOWS . . 154 TRISTRAM 3   174
WHOSE MIND ALLOWS A PLAN . . . . 415 EMPEDOCLES I 2   99
ALLOWS THE PROUDLY-RIDING AND THE FOUNDERING BARK . 421 EMPEDOCLES I 2   261
ALLOWS THE PROUDLY-RIDING AND THE FOUNDERD BARK . . 421 EMPEDOCLES I 2   V 261

ALLOY
AND GOODNESS WARM AND TRUTH WITHOUT ALLOY . . . . 446 WESTMIN ABBEY   78

ALLS
NAY ALLS WELL AGAIN THOU MUST NOT WEEP . . . . 144 TRISTRAM 2   72
LOOKS IN VAIN FOR ALLS OBSCURE . . . . 215 PIS-ALLER   4
WITHOUT THAT ALLS DARK FOR MEN . . . . 215 PIS-ALLER   10
IF SO ALLS WELL FOR LOOK THE OLD MAN SPEEDS . . 362 MEROPE   934
PEACE PEACE ALLS CLEAR THE WICKED WATCH AND WORK . 365 MEROPE   995
A FIT ALLS OVER . . . . 460 KAISER DEAD   64

ALLURING
THEIR FEET FROM ITS ALLURING WAVE . . . . . . 226 EPILOG LAOCOON   166

ALLY
HOW USELESS AN ALLY A PEOPLE IS . . . . . . 381 MEROPE   1312
A PEOPLE THEN IS AN ALLY INDEED . . . . . . 382 MEROPE   1347

ALMOST
THAT THY POOR HEAD ALMOST TURNS . . . . . . 49 SECOND BEST   8
FOLDS THE STILL VALLEY ALMOST ROUND . . . . . 57 RESIGNATION   175
POOR CHILD THOU ART ALMOST AS PALE AS I . . . 140 TRISTRAM 1   312
ALMOST BEFORE TIS PLANND COME GLOWING HATE . . . 367 MEROPE   1062
ALMOST AS MUCH AS THE NEW DANCING-GIRL . . . . 407 EMPEDOCLES I 1   35
BEGIN TO ROLL AND ALMOST DROWN . . . . 431 EMPEDOCLES II   63

ALMS
AGE-BOWD ASKS ALMS . . . . 51 CONSOLATION   30

ALOFT
ALOFT ARE HURLD IN THE DUST . . . . 288 RUGBY CHAPEL   64
BOILS OER ITS BORDERS ALOFT . . . . 289 RUGBY CHAPEL   98
AN OPEN GLADE NOW HE WAS HIGH ALOFT . . . . . 357 MEROPE   802
AN ARM ALOFT FOR HELP THEN SWEEP BENEATH . . . 358 MEROPE   833
ONE ARM ALOFT FOR HELP THEN SWEEP BENEATH . . . 358 MEROPE   V 833

ALONE
WHERE MANS ONE NATURE QUEEN-LIKE SITS ALONE . . 4 BUTLERS SERMONS   7
TOO FEARFUL OR TOO FOND TO PLAY ALONE . . . . 8 RELIGIOUS ISOL   5
THE PRINCELY PAIR ARE LEFT ALONE . . . . . . 17 CHURCH BROU 2   39
YET AH IS CALM ALONE IN TRUTH . . . . 21 YOUTH AND CALM   V 5
WITH THE DUMB WOODS AND THE NIGHT ALONE . . . 32 NEW SIRENS   194
THOU WHO DOST DWELL ALONE . . . . 38 STAGIRIUS   1
ALONE THE SUN ARISES AND ALONE . . . . . . 45 IN UTRUMQUE PAR   20
ALONE THE SUN ARISES AND ALONE . . . . . . 45 IN UTRUMQUE PAR   20
FORMS WHAT SHE FORMS ALONE . . . . 45 IN UTRUMQUE PAR   28
OH WHEN MOST SELF-EXALTED MOST ALONE . . . . 46 IN UTRUMQUE PAR   36
ALONE WE TREAD IT YOU AND I . . . . 55 RESIGNATION   88
AND DOES NOT SAY I AM ALONE . . . . 57 RESIGNATION   169
SOHRAB ALONE HE SLEPT NOT ALL NIGHT LONG . . . 61 SOHRAB RUSTUM   5
I SEEK ONE MAN ONE MAN AND ONE ALONE . . . . 62 SOHRAB RUSTUM   49
IN GLOOM THEY TWAIN WERE WRAPPD AND THEY ALONE . 75 SOHRAB RUSTUM   486
AND IN THE HAND THE HILT REMAIN ALONE . . . . 76 SOHRAB RUSTUM   513
AND RUSTUM AND HIS SON WERE LEFT ALONE . . . 86 SOHRAB RUSTUM   874
AND IN HIS HAND THE HILT REMAIN ALONE . . . . 76 SOHRAB RUSTUM   V 513
HOW IS IT WITH MY LORD ALONE . . . . 88 SICK KING BOKH   13
ALONE AND IN A DARKSOME PLACE . . . . 90 SICK KING BOKH   66
THIS PAIN ALONE WHICH MUST BE BORNE . . . . 92 SICK KING BOKH   151
GAINST THAT ALONE HAD BALDERS LIFE NO CHARM . . 95 BALDER DEAD 1   8

ALONE   (CONTINUED)
THAT I ALONE MUST TAKE THE BRANCH FROM LOK   • • • •   98 BALDER DEAD 1   100
GAINST THAT ALONE HAD BALDERS LIFE NO CHARM   • • •   98 BALDER DEAD 1   104
FOR MANY GODS IN HEAVEN NOT THOU ALONE   • • •   98 BALDER DEAD 1   119
TO RIDE BUT SLEIPNER ODINS HORSE ALONE   • • •   99 BALDER DEAD 1   138
AND IS ALONE NOT DIPT IN OCEANS STREAM   • • •   99 BALDER DEAD 1   158
SAVE ME ALONE AND HELA SOLEMN QUEEN   • •   • •   104 BALDER DEAD 1   319
NOR SHOOK THE BRIDGE SO MUCH AS THOU ALONE   • • •   107 BALDER DEAD 2   106
REMEMBRANCE IN OUR SOUL OF WARS ALONE   • • •   117 BALDER DEAD 3   138
WAS LOKS THE UNWITTING HAND ALONE WAS THINE   • •   125 BALDER DEAD 3   425
IN THE FOREST-DEPTHS ALONE   • • • • •   •   137 TRISTRAM 1   224
THIS STIR THEY HAVE AND THIS ALONE   • •   • • •   141 TRISTRAM 1   349
AH HARSH FLATTERER LET ALONE MY BEAUTY   • • •   143 TRISTRAM 2   21
IN THE GREEN WOOD ALL OUR LIVES ALONE   • • • •   143 TRISTRAM 2   36
HER CHILDRENS SHE MOVES SLOW HER VOICE ALONE   • •   151 TRISTRAM 3   72
TILL FOR ITS SAKE ALONE WE LIVE AND MOVE   • •   153 TRISTRAM 3   129
CHILDREN DEAR WERE WE LONG ALONE   • • • • •   163 FORSAKEN MERM   64
DEAR HEART I SAID WE ARE LONG ALONE   • • • • •   163 FORSAKEN MERM   78
AND ALONE DWELL FOR EVER   • • • • • • •   165 FORSAKEN MERM   122
AH NOT THE RADIANT SPIRIT OF GREECE ALONE   • •   168 RACHEL 3   9
THE HEART CAN BIND ITSELF ALONE   • • • • •   180 ISOLATION MARG   9
THOU HAST BEEN SHALT BE ART ALONE   • • • • •   181 ISOLATION MARG   30
OR IF NOT QUITE ALONE YET THEY   • • • • •   181 ISOLATION MARG   31
ALONE THAN THOU THEIR LONELINESS   • • • • •   181 ISOLATION MARG   42
WE MORTAL MILLIONS LIVE ALONE   • • • •   182 TO MARG CONT   4
TILL THE FATES COME AGAIN ALONE WITH DEATH   • • •   195 FRAG ANTIGONE   V 16
PROUD IGNORANT SELF-ADORED YOU LIVE ALONE   • •   198 FRAG DEJANEIRA   7
FOR NEITHER COULD SUBSIST ALONE   • • • • •   203 EUPHROSYNE   12
TO ONE DEMAND ALONE ARE COY   • • • • • •   203 EUPHROSYNE   22
YES BUT NOT THIS ALONE   • • • • •   212 GROWING OLD   5
AND NOT ITS SEPARATE PARTS ALONE   • • • • •   225 EPILOG LAOCOON   142
FOR ALONE THEY LIVE NOR PINE WITH NOTING   • •   240 SELF-DEPENDENCE V 23
IS THERE NO LIFE BUT THESE ALONE   • • • •   244 SUMMER NIGHT   74
HE WENDS UNFOLLOWD HE MUST HOUSE ALONE   • • •   269 THYRSIS   209
LEFT HUMAN HAUNT AND ON ALONE TILL NIGHT   • • •   269 THYRSIS   230
THOU SANKST ALONE   • • • • • • •   276 SOUTHERN NIGHT   28
BARE UNSHADED ALONE   • • • • • • • •   287 RUGBY CHAPEL   35
BUT THOU WOULDST NOT ALONE   • • • • • • •   290 RUGBY CHAPEL   124
BE SAVED MY FATHER ALONE   • • • • • • •   290 RUGBY CHAPEL   125
CHARM IS THE POETS ALONE   • • • • • • •   295 HEINES GRAVE   112
STANDEST AT NIGHTFALL ALONE   • • • • • •   297 HEINES GRAVE   175
WHO ALONE IS ALL THINGS IN ONE   • • • • •   298 HEINES GRAVE   217
AH LEAVE US NOT THE FRET ALONE   • • • • • •   302 GRANDE CHARTR   108
AH LEAVE US NOT THE PANG ALONE   • • • • • •   302 GRANDE CHARTR   V 108
SOUNDS NOW ONE WORD ALONE   • • • • • •   318 OBERMANN MORE   184
AND WHO CAN BE ALONE ELATE   • • • • • •   321 OBERMANN MORE   247
I PASSD OBSCURE ALONE   • • • • • • •   321 OBERMANN MORE   262
COMES NOW ONE WORD ALONE   • • • • • •   318 OBERMANN MORE   V 184
ALONE SELF-POISED HENCEFORWARD MAN   • • • •   319 OBERMANN MORE   V 185
UPON THE THRESHOLD OF OLD AGE ALONE   • • • •   334 MEROPE   152
WHETHER IS BETTER TO ABIDE ALONE   • • • • •   338 MEROPE   287
DANGEROUS ALONE TO THE DEER   • • • • •   342 MEROPE   399
THESE MANY YEARS I LIVE FOR THIS ALONE   • • •   351 MEROPE   621
AND TOOK THE LAKE TWO HOUNDS ALONE PURSUED   • • •   357 MEROPE   809
HE KEPT HIS TALE THEN FOR THE KING ALONE   • •   362 MEROPE   928
WHAT ONE WEAK WOMAN CAN ACHIEVE ALONE   • • •   368 MEROPE   1074
YES AND ALONE IS WITH ME HERE TO SHARE   • • •   379 MEROPE   1268
LAIAS ALONE NO ERRAND MINE FOR CROWDS   • • •   380 MEROPE   1285
O THOU LONG-LOST LONG SEEN IN DREAMS ALONE   • • •   381 MEROPE   1288
ALAS OUR FOE ALONE STOOD FORWARD THEN   • • •   383 MEROPE   1367
THE NOBLE THOUGHT WHICH IS ALONE THE MAN   • • •   385 MEROPE   1409
AND NOT ALONE DISSUADES HIM BUT COMPARES   • •   385 MEROPE   1416
ALONE I MASTERD POWER AND ALONE   • • • •   398 MEROPE   1792
ALONE I MASTERD POWER AND ALONE   • • • •   398 MEROPE   1792
THAT JUSTICE THAT SAGE ORDER NOT ALONE   • • •   404 MEROPE   1997
A THOUSAND TIMES HAVE I BEEN HERE ALONE   • • •   406 EMPEDOCLES I 1   7
PAUSANIAS AND ON FOOT ALONE AND THOU THEN   • • •   407 EMPEDOCLES I 1   30
TO BE LEFT MUSING THESE SOFT NIGHTS ALONE   • • •   409 EMPEDOCLES I 1   92
TO BRING THEE OUT WITH HIM ALONE ON ETNA   • • •   409 EMPEDOCLES I 1   107
ON ETNA HERE AND BE ALONE WITH HIM   • • • •   410 EMPEDOCLES I 1   129
FOR I MUST BE ALONE LEAVE ME ONE MULE   • • •   428 EMPEDOCLES I 2   465
ALONE   • • • • • • • • • •   428 EMPEDOCLES II   1
ROUND WHICH THE SULLEN VAPOUR ROLLS ALONE   • • •   429 EMPEDOCLES II   4
I HAVE BEEN ENOUGH ALONE   • • • • • • •   435 EMPEDOCLES II   219
NURSED AN IMMORTAL VIGOUR I ALONE   • • • •   438 EMPEDOCLES II   320
LIVE BESIDE US BUT ALONE   • • • • • • •   455 POOR MATTHIAS   96
AND WERE THERE NONE TO STAND AND WEEP ALONE   • •   467 ALARIC AT ROME   121
AND WHILE THEY RISE HERE MIGHT WE STAND ALONE • •   470 ALARIC AT ROME   203
NO ALL WAS CHANGD THE MONARCH WEPT ALONE   • •   477 CROMWELL   187
ONCE MORE ALONE BESIDE THE GLEAMING FLOOD   • • •   479 CROMWELL   240

ALONG
SWEEPS EARTH AND HEAVEN AND MEN AND GODS ALONG   • •   9 MYCERINUS   39
WHIRLS EARTH AND HEAVEN AND MEN AND GODS ALONG   • •   9 MYCERINUS   V 39
BEARS EARTH AND HEAVEN AND MEN AND GODS ALONG   • •   9 MYCERINUS   V 39
BUT ALL THE TARTAR CAMP ALONG THE STREAM   • • •   61 SOHRAB RUSTUM   3
THE SHORN AND PARCELLD OXUS STRAINS ALONG   • • •   87 SOHRAB RUSTUM   884
GREW DEEPER THUNDER CRASHD ALONG THE SKY   • • •   76 SOHRAB RUSTUM   V 500
HE CAME AND SADLY WENT ALONG THE SAND   • • •   97 BALDER DEAD 1   78
AND BACK ALONG THE BEACH TO ASGARD WENT   • • • •   101 BALDER DEAD 1   200

ALONG   (CONTINUED)
        ALONG THE FLINTY FLOOR OF ASGARD STREETS   . . . .   102 BALDER DEAD 1   261
        HER FLOCK ALONG THE WHITE NORWEGIAN BEACH . . . .   117 BALDER DEAD 3   150
        ALONG THIS IRON COAST KNOW LIKE A STAR   . . . .   151 TRISTRAM 3   81
        WHO LIES GUARDING HER FEET ALONG THE GROUND   . . .   152 TRISTRAM 3   89
        IN EVERY HUT ALONG THIS SEA-COAST WILD   . . . .   152 TRISTRAM 3   109
        YOU SAW THE BRIGHT-EYED SQUIRRELS DART ALONG . . .   155 TRISTRAM 3   195
        THE BALTIC SEA ALONG   . . . .   159 NECKAN   2
        THE BALTIC SEA ALONG   . . . .   161 NECKAN   66
        ALONG THE NEVER-SILENT STRAIT . . . .   204 CALAIS SANDS   3
        ALONG THE NEVER-SILENT BEACH   . . . .   204 CALAIS SANDS   V   3
        ALL CHANGES FAST AND HIES ALONG   . . . .   225 EPILOG LAOCOON   124
        THAT SPARKLES IN THE SUN ALONG . . . .   226 EPILOG LAOCOON   158
        ALONG THE APPIAN WAY   . . . .   315 OBERMANN MORE   100
        ALONG THE ROCKS OF NAYE   . . . .   324 OBERMANN MORE   336
        AND CAROLS FLOAT ALONG THE HAPPY AIR . . . . . .   445 WESTMIN ABBEY   39
        ALONG THE HOLY FLOOR   . . . .   445 WESTMIN ABBEY   52
        OF HEAVENS EMBATTLED MYRIADS SWEPT ALONG   . . . .   473 CROMWELL   44
        THE FUTURE ROLLD ITS GATHERING TIDES ALONG . . . .   475 CROMWELL   134
        ARE SWEPT LIKE HUDDLING SHEEP ALONG   . . . . . .   481 COURAGE   8
        ALONG THE GRACIOUS ALBAN HILL . . . .   484 ROME-SICKNESS   20

ALOOF
        WHAT CHURCH IS THIS FROM MEN ALOOF   . . . . . .   16 CHURCH BROU 2   7
        BUT RUSTUM CAME LAST NIGHT ALOOF HE SITS   . . . .   66 SOHRAB RUSTUM   178
        MEAN STILL TO KEEP ALOOF FROM DORIAN BROIL . . . .   384 MEROPE   1396
        MY MOTHER STANDS ALOOF AND BLAMES OUR DEED . . . .   386 MEROPE   1448
        BUT ALOOF ON THE LAKE-STRAND   . . . .   434 EMPEDOCLES II   165
        THOU KEEPEST ALOOF THE PROFANE . . . .   435 EMPEDOCLES II   207

ALOUD
        AND THEN HE TURND AND STERNLY SPAKE ALOUD . . . .   72 SOHRAB RUSTUM   364
        HE SPOKE AND AS HE CEASED HE WEPT ALOUD   . . . .   79 SOHRAB RUSTUM   602
        THAT THE HARD IRON CORSLET CLANKD ALOUD   . . . .   80 SOHRAB RUSTUM   664
        HIS ARMS ROUND HIS SONS NECK AND WEPT ALOUD   . . .   82 SOHRAB RUSTUM   728
        WHO CRY ALOUD TO LAY THE OLD WORLD LOW   . . . .   237 PROGRESS   15
        AND BEAUTY FILLD HER AND SHE SPAKE ALOUD   . . . .   447 WESTMIN ABBEY   100

ALPINE
        THE ALPINE PEASANTS TWO AND THREE . . . .   17 CHURCH BROU 2   18
        MARTIN AND I DOWN A GREEN ALPINE STREAM   . . . .   24 DREAM   2
        ROUND ALPINE SUMMITS EDDYING ROSE . . . .   52 RESIGNATION   8
        THROUGH ALPINE MEADOWS SOFT-SUFFUSED . . . . . .   299 GRANDE CHARTR   1
        STRONG CHILDREN OF THE ALPINE WILD . . . .   301 GRANDE CHARTR   57
        OR CHALETS NEAR THE ALPINE SNOW   . . . .   304 GRANDE CHARTR   150
        IN FRONT THE AWFUL ALPINE TRACK   . . . .   306 OBERMANN   1
        IN THIS STERN ALPINE DELL   . . . .   312 OBERMANN   182
        FULL-FOAMING MILK-PAILS ALPINE FARE   . . . . . .   313 OBERMANN MORE   17
        AND HEAR THE WILD BEES ALPINE HUM . . . .   313 OBERMANN MORE   47
        THERE AMONG ALPINE SNOWS   . . . .   321 OBERMANN MORE   250
        OUR LIFE TO ALPINE SNOW   . . . .   323 OBERMANN MORE   318

ALPS
        OF THE HIGH ALPS TO WHICH I GO . . . .   207 ON THE RHINE   4

ALREADY
        ALREADY FROM THE SILENT ROAD   . . . .   53 RESIGNATION   49
        FELT ALREADY SOME DEEPER SMART . . . .   131 TRISTRAM 1   46
        IS ALREADY GONE AND PAST . . . .   136 TRISTRAM 1   174

ALTAR
        BUT AT GODS ALTAR OH REMEMBER ME   . . . .   173 MONICAS PRAYER   4
        CREEDS PASS RITES CHANGE NO ALTAR STANDETH WHOLE . .   173 MONICAS PRAYER   12
        ON THE ALTAR THIS BOWL   . . . .   187 STRAYED REVEL   49
        QUENCH THEN THE ALTAR FIRES OF YOUR OLD GODS . . .   237 PROGRESS   V   27
        ZEUS HATH HIS ALTAR WHERE THY FATHER FELL . . . .   330 MEROPE   15
        I AT THAT ALTAR WHERE MID SHOUTING CROWDS . . . .   338 MEROPE   272
        FROM THE ALTAR OF ZEUS FROM THE CROWD CAME A WAIL   346 MEROPE   489
        FROM THE ALTAR THE UNAVENGED TOMB . . . .   371 MEROPE   1137
        AT THE DREAD ALTAR OF HER HUSBANDS TOMB   . . . .   385 MEROPE   1414
        GROUPD AROUND ZEUSS ALTAR ALL IN ARMS . . . . . .   401 MEROPE   1899
        THE ALTAR IN THE MIDDLE OF THE SQUARE . . . . . .   401 MEROPE   1908
        BURST OER THE ALTAR AND THE DORIAN LORDS   . . . .   402 MEROPE   1938

ALTARS
        ALTARS UNFED AND TEMPLES OVERTURND . . . .   8 MYCERINUS   3
        IN THE HIGH ALTARS DEPTH DIVINE   . . . .   306 GRANDE CHARTR   202

ALTER
        MAKE JUSTICE ALTER . . . .   398 MEROPE   1806

ALTERD
        SOMETHING ALTERD IN THY COURTLY TONE . . . . . .   143 TRISTRAM 2   34
        ALTERD TRISTRAM NOT IN COURTS BELIEVE ME   . . . .   143 TRISTRAM 2   37
        LOVE LIKE MINE IS ALTERD IN THE BREAST . . . . . .   143 TRISTRAM 2   38
        A TROUBLE IN THINE ALTERD AIR . . . .   178 FAREWELL   14

ALTERNATING
        SEASONS ALTERNATING AND NIGHT AND DAY . . . . . .   45 IN UTRUMQUE PAR   5
        ALTERNATING WITH WISDOMS TOO SHORT REIGN   . . . .   449 WESTMIN ABBEY   158

ALTOGETHER
    YES AND I FAIN WOULD ALTOGETHER WARD . . . . . . 104 BALDER DEAD 1   310

ALWAY
    THERE ARE THE POOR WHO FAINT ALWAY . . . . . . 93 SICK KING BOKH   176
    YET HADST THOU ALWAY VISIONS OF OUR LIGHT . . . . 269 THYRSIS   227
    ALWAY FROM THEIR PRESENCE BROKE . . . . . . 454 POOR MATTHIAS   53

ALWAYS
    STAND NEVER IDLE BUT GO ALWAYS ROUND . . . . . . 4 DUKE WELLINGTON   2
    FEAR ME NOT I WILL BE ALWAYS WITH THEE . . . . . 143 TRISTRAM 2   29
    AND HE WITH UNSUNND FACE DID ALWAYS GO . . . . 170 EAST AND WEST   8
    TO ALL ALWAYS OPEN . . . . 177 PARTING   81
    TO ALL ALWAYS TRUE . . . . 177 PARTING   82
    AH MIGHT I ALWAYS REST UNSEEN . . . . 205 CALAIS SANDS   31
    SO I MIGHT HAVE THEE ALWAYS NEAR . . . . . . 205 CALAIS SANDS   32
    OH MIGHT I ALWAYS REST UNSEEN . . . . 205 CALAIS SANDS   V 31
    WILLS THAT REMEMBRANCE SHOULD ALWAYS DECAY . . . . 206 SEPARATION   6
    SHALL ALWAYS SEE . . . . 279 SOUTHERN NIGHT   128
    ALWAYS IN ARMS ALWAYS IN FACE OF FOES . . . . . 334 MEROPE   153
    ALWAYS IN ARMS ALWAYS IN FACE OF FOES . . . . . 334 MEROPE   153
    HE IS NOW ALWAYS MOODY AND I FEAR HIM . . . . . 408 EMPEDOCLES I 1   74
    AND WHO CAN SAY I HAVE BEEN ALWAYS FREE . . . . 440 EMPEDOCLES II   392
    ALWAYS AND ALWAYS FIGHTING AMONG THE FIRST
        OF THE TROJANS   HOMER TRANS   18
    ALWAYS AND ALWAYS FIGHTING AMONG THE FIRST
        OF THE TROJANS   HOMER TRANS   18

AMAIN
    WHO SINCE IN YOUR DESPITE HATH WAXD AMAIN . . . . 110 BALDER DEAD 2   210
    LIFTING MANKIND AMAIN . . . . 323 OBERMANN MORE   V 324

AMASSD
    TO SORT WHATS HERE AMASSD . . . . 419 EMPEDOCLES I 2   215

AMAZE
    AND ONE LOUD CRY OF GRIEF AND OF AMAZE . . . . 11 MYCERINUS   80

AMAZED
    AND SHRANK AMAZED BACK HE RECOILD ONE STEP . . . . 76 SOHRAB RUSTUM   517
    AND SHRANK AMAZED BACK HE RECOILD ONE PACE . . . . 76 SOHRAB RUSTUM   V 517

AMBER
    A CEILING OF AMBER . . . . 165 FORSAKEN MERM   118
    FREIGHTED WITH AMBER GRAPES AND CHIAN WINE . . . . 262 SCHOLAR-GIPSY   238

AMBITION
    CALL IT AMBITION OR REMORSE OR LOVE . . . . . 153 TRISTRAM 3   130
    NO BUT TO THY AMBITION THEIR POOR LIVES . . . . 339 MEROPE   325
    CLOAK THINE AMBITION WITH THESE SPECIOUS WORDS . . 404 MEROPE   1985

AMBITIONS
    AMBITIONS BOLDEST DREAM MIGHT SOBER AND APPAL . . 463 ALARIC AT ROME   42

AMBITIOUS
    AH WARN SOME MORE AMBITIOUS HEART . . . . . . 174 MEETING   15

AMBROSIA
    HE SLUMBERD AND AMBROSIA BALMD THE CHILD . . . . 446 WESTMIN ABBEY   88

AMBUSHD
    MOCKERY EVER AMBUSHD IN . . . . 23 MEMORY-PICTURE   28
    ERST ABODE AMBUSHD . . . . 51 CONSOLATION   32

AMERICAN
    NOT IN AMERICAN VULGARITY . . . . 480 HUNGARIAN NAT   6

AMETHYST
    AND AMETHYST AND RUBY THEN UNCLOSE . . . . . . 18 CHURCH BROU 3   24
    OF TURQUOISE-EARTH AND AMETHYST . . . . . . 191 STRAYED REVEL   195

AMIABLE
    OF THIS AMIABLE HOME OF THE DEAD . . . . . . 293 HEINES GRAVE   45

AMID
    GAY OF OLD AMID THE GAYEST . . . . 14 CHURCH BROU 1   55
    OF GRASS PEEP OUT AMID SURROUNDING SNOW . . . . 122 BALDER DEAD 3   315
    IN HIS LIGHT YOUTH AMID A FESTAL THRONG . . . . 166 AUSTERITY POET   3
    OVER TOMBS AMID GRAVES . . . . 220 BACCHANALIA 2   32
    TO FEEL AMID THE CITYS JAR . . . . 249 KENSINGTON GARD   38
    THIS DAY AMID THESE RITES THIS BLACK-ROBED TRAIN . . 333 MEROPE   105
    IN SOME DARK FIR-TREES SHADOW AMID ROCKS . . . . 373 MEROPE   1167
    WAKE AMID GLOOM AND HOWLING AND THE NOISE . . . . 373 MEROPE   1185
    LAY ON THE HEARTH AMID A FIERY RING . . . . 446 WESTMIN ABBEY   84
    BUT ALL NIGHT LONG AMID THE FLAMES HE LAY . . . . 446 WESTMIN ABBEY   89
    DOWN SHE SANK AMID HER FUR . . . . 453 POOR MATTHIAS   36
    AND THUS AMID THE GLORIOUS HUES OF EVEN . . . . 466 ALARIC AT ROME   105
    ABIDES ENTHROND AMID THE MIST AND STORM . . . . 472 CROMWELL   18
    AMID THE WILD WAVES WELTERING . . . . 479 HAYSWATER BOAT   8

AMIDST
          AND SAW HER BABE AMIDST THE FIRE AND SCREAMD   . . 446 WESTMIN ABBEY   93

AMISS
          EVEN OF ANGELS SOUNDS AMISS   . . . . 295 HEINES GRAVE   102
          TASTED AMISS'TO THY SOUL . . . . 296 HEINES GRAVE   124
          MAIDENS AND READS EXPERIENCE MUCH AMISS   . . . . 382 MEROPE   1334
          AMISS FROM JUSTICE THE GODS   . . . . 348 MEROPE   V

AMITY
          THANKS TO HIM FOR OUR AMITY AS WELL   . . . . . . 395 MEROPE   1724

AMONG
          THE PRODIGY OF FULL-BLOWN CRIME AMONG   . . . .   6 GEO CRUIKSHANK   3
          AND THE WIND WAILS AMONG THE MOUNTAIN PINES   . .   18 CHURCH BROU 3   V 37
          I CAME AMONG THE TARTARS AND BORE ARMS   . . . .   62 SOHRAB RUSTUM   43
          CANST THOU NOT REST AMONG THE TARTAR CHIEFS   . .   63 SOHRAB RUSTUM   66
          A HELPLESS BABE AMONG THE MOUNTAIN-ROCKS   . . . .   81 SOHRAB RUSTUM   681
          BUT LODGED AMONG MY FATHERS FOES AND SEEN . . . .   83 SOHRAB RUSTUM   759
          WHILE WE YET LIVED AMONG THE OTHER GODS   . . . . 104 BALDER DEAD 1   330
          HERE AND HAST HONOUR AMONG ALL THE DEAD   . . . . 112 BALDER DEAD 2   261
          CROWND HAVING HONOUR AMONG ALL THE DEAD   . . . . 112 BALDER DEAD 2   278
          AMONG THE GODS AND HEROES HERE IN HEAVEN   . . . . 115 BALDER DEAD 3   80
          AS AMONG THOSE WHOSE JOY AND WORK IS WAR   . . . . 115 BALDER DEAD 3   81
          LAST FROM AMONG THE HEROES ONE CAME NEAR   . . . . 117 BALDER DEAD 3   124
          OF IDA AND AMONG THE GRASS SHALL FIND   . . . . 128 BALDER DEAD 3   538
          PASSD AMONG THESE HEATHS OF OURS   . . . . . . 137 TRISTRAM 1   230
          AMONG THE HOLLY-CLUMPS AND BROKEN GROUND   . . . . 150 TRISTRAM 3   28
          THE HUSH AMONG THE SHINING STARS   . . . . . . 180 FAREWELL   79
          AMONG THEIR SAVAGE GORGES AND COLD SPRINGS   . . . 198 FRAG DEJANEIRA   9
          AND FEEBLY RAKES AMONG THE STONES   . . . . . . 213 PROGRESS POESY   10
          HOW GREEN AMONG THE BOUGHS IT IS   . . . . . .   KENSINGTON GARD   V 7
          AMONG THE AEGAEAN ISLES   . . . . 262 SCHOLAR-GIPSY   236
          OF PROSERPINE AMONG WHOSE CROWNED HAIR   . . . . 265 THYRSIS   88
          RED LOOSESTRIFE AND BLOND MEADOW-SWEET AMONG   . . 266 THYRSIS   124
          OF THE LOWER HARTZ AMONG OAKS   . . . . 297 HEINES GRAVE   180
          WHERE THAT WET SMOKE AMONG THE WOODS . . . . . . 299 GRANDE CHARTR   11
          AMONG THE SWARMS OF MEN   . . . . 311 OBERMANN   176
          THERE AMONG ALPINE SNOWS   . . . . 321 OBERMANN MORE   250
          MERE PRISONERS MEANT OR NOT AMONG OUR FOES   . . . 337 MEROPE   251
          FROM SATURNS SEARCH AMONG THE NEW-YEAND LAMBS . . 355 MEROPE   738
          AMONG THE FORESTS ON CYLLENES SIDE   . . . . . . 364 MEROPE   974
          STRETCHD AMONG BRIARS AND STONES THE SLOW BLACK GORE 373 MEROPE   1172
          WERE NOT AMONG THE FEUDS OF WARRIOR-CHIEFS   . . . 388 MEROPE   1512
          WERT NOT AMONG THE FEUDS OF WARRIOR-CHIEFS   . . . 388 MEROPE   V1512
          AND WHEN HE COMES AMONG HIS FRIENDS AT FEASTS . . 408 EMPEDOCLES I 1   70
          TIS AS AN ORPHAN AMONG PROSPEROUS BOYS   . . . . 408 EMPEDOCLES I 1   71
          SOMETIMES AND WANDERS FAR AMONG THE GLENS . . . . 412 EMPEDOCLES I 2   17
          I KNOW THESE NOTES AMONG A THOUSAND HARK   . . . . 413 EMPEDOCLES I 2   35
          AMONG THE GREEN ILLYRIAN HILLS AND THERE   . . . . 426 EMPEDOCLES I 2   429
          WHERE THE SPHINX LIVED AMONG THE FROWNING HILLS . 427 EMPEDOCLES I 2   440
          I KNOW THOSE NOTES AMONG A THOUSAND HARK   . . . . 413 EMPEDOCLES I 2   V 35
          AMONG A PEOPLE OF CHILDREN   . . . . 432 EMPEDOCLES II   112
          AMONG AUGUST COMPANIONS   . . . . 437 EMPEDOCLES II   284
          THEY MOORD THEIR BOATS AMONG THE BULRUSH STEMS   . . 444 WESTMIN ABBEY   18
          ALWAYS AND ALWAYS FIGHTING AMONG THE FIRST   HOMER TRANS   18
               OF THE TROJANS
          BUT THAT PRINCE AMONG GODS THE SON OF THE LOVELY-HAIRD HOMER TRANS   52
               LETO

AMONGST
          AND THEN WE SUFFER AND AMONGST US ONE   . . . . 260 SCHOLAR-GIPSY   182
          WHAT AMONGST OURSELVES WE DO   . . . . 457 POOR MATTHIAS   158

AMPELUS
          THE YOUNG LANGUID-EYED AMPELUS   . . . . 188 STRAYED REVEL   78

AMPHIARAOS
          AMPHIARAOS OR MYCENAES KING   . . . . 367 MEROPE   1034

AMPLE
          HER CABIND AMPLE SPIRIT   . . . .   21 REQUIESCAT   13
          FORSAKE THIS AMPLE PROUD MESSENIAN REALM   . . . . 395 MEROPE   1744

AMPLER
          FOR MOVEMENT FOR AN AMPLER SPHERE   . . . . . .   60 RESIGNATION   273
          SOME NOBLER AMPLER STAGE OF LIFE TO WIN   . . . . 169 WORLDLY PLACE   12
          WITH TRIUMPHS A YET AMPLER BROOD   . . . . . . 222 EPILOG LAOCOON   24

AMUSE
          ASK NOT TO AMUSE BUT TO SET FREE   . . . . . .   59 RESIGNATION   242
          NOR YET TO AMUSE AS OURS ARE   . . . . 300 GRANDE CHARTR   52
          NOR YET TO AMUSE AS WORLDLINGS ARE   . . . . . . 300 GRANDE CHARTR   V 52

AMUSEMENT
          YIELD THEM LOVE AMUSEMENT SYMPATHY   . . . . . . 240 SELF-DEPENDENCE   20

ANARCHY
          THIS PEOPLES ANARCHY THY FOES PRETENCE   . . . . 404 MEROPE   2001

ANCESTOR
          THERE STANDS THE TEMPLE OF THINE ANCESTOR . . . . 330 MEROPE   13
          TO FOOT OF MORTAL WHERE HIS ANCESTOR . . . . . . 357 MEROPE   776

ANCESTOR   (CONTINUED)
    ANOTHER ANCESTOR NAMED TOO LIKE ME   • • • • • • 357 MEROPE   780

ANCHITUS
    ASK WHAT MOST HELPS WHEN KNOWN THOU SON OF ANCHITUS   416 EMPEDOCLES I 2   111

ANCHORITE
    SOLDIER AND ANCHORITE   • • • • • • • • • • 311 OBERMANN   150

ANCHORITES
    I SEEK THESE ANCHORITES NOT IN RUTH   • • • • • 301 GRANDE CHARTR   77
    AH ME WE ANCHORITES READ THINGS BEST   • • • • • 314 OBERMANN MORE   75
    AH ME WE ANCHORITES KNEW IT BEST   • • • • • • 314 OBERMANN MORE   V   75

ANCIENT
    COME ONCE MORE THAT ANCIENT LIGHTNESS   • • • •   32 NEW SIRENS   175
    UNTO THEIR ANCIENT HOME   • • • • • • • • •   36 VOICE   31
    AND ON WHOSE MARGE THE ANCIENT GIANTS DWELL   • •   99 BALDER DEAD 1   161
    AND WIFE AND CHILDREN AND OUR ANCIENT HOME   • • • 117 BALDER DEAD 3   144
    THAT AN ANCIENT RIVAL SHARES HER OFFICE   • • • 144 TRISTRAM 2   V   59
    OF FLANDERS TO THE ANCIENT RHINE   • • • • • 205 CALAIS SANDS   V   34
    YOUR STREETS ARE ANCIENT AND NARROW   • • • • • 214 NEW ROME   V   11
    YOUR STREETS HOW ANCIENT AND NARROW   • • • • • 214 NEW ROME   V   11
    AND KNEW THE INTRUDERS ON HIS ANCIENT HOME   • • • 262 SCHOLAR-GIPSY   240
    DEGRADING PYLOS FROM ITS ANCIENT RULE   • • • • 330 MEROPE   12
    FOR DEATH HIS ANCIENT TO HIS NEW-MADE FRIENDS   • 338 MEROPE   265
    THINE ANCIENT ROUT BY THE CILICIAN HILLS   • • • 430 EMPEDOCLES II   53
    THY ANCIENT ROUT BY THE CILICIAN HILLS   • • • 430 EMPEDOCLES II   V   53
    THE ANCIENT ROUT BY THE CILICIAN HILLS   • • • 430 EMPEDOCLES II   V   53
    AND TO MENS HEARTS THIS ANCIENT PLACE ENDEARD   • 444 WESTMIN ABBEY   9
    ANCIENT STREETS OF HASTINGS TOWN   • • • • • 457 POOR MATTHIAS   182

ANEMONES
    OF HYACINTHS AND ON LATE ANEMONES   • • • • • • 414 EMPEDOCLES I 2   V   50

ANEMONIES
    ACROSS THE HOLLOW WHITE ANEMONIES   • • • • • 155 TRISTRAM 3   207
    WOODS WITH ANEMONIES IN FLOWER TILL MAY   • • • 268 THYRSIS   199
    OF HYACINTHS AND ON LATE ANEMONIES   • • • • • 414 EMPEDOCLES I 2   50

ANEMONY
    OF FLOWERS THE FRAIL-LEAFD WHITE ANEMONY   • • • 257 SCHOLAR-GIPSY   87

ANEW
    MUSED ON WARM THE HEART ANEW   • • • • • • •   30 NEW SIRENS   134
    ON THE WIDE OCEAN OF LIFE ANEW   • • • • • • • 243 SUMMER NIGHT   53
    PEACE THAT RECALLD HIS CHILDISH HOURS ANEW   • • • 475 CROMWELL   115

ANGEL
    AND ON TWO ANGEL-HEADS DOTH PLAY   • • • • • 141 TRISTRAM 1   337
    AN ANGEL TOUCH MINE ARM AND SAY   • • • • • • 157 SAINT BRANDAN   35

ANGELIC
    AN ANGELIC GRAVITY   • • • • • • • • • • • •   24 MEMORY-PICTURE   46

ANGELS
    THE PASSAGE OF THE ANGELS WINGS WILL HEAR   • • •   19 CHURCH BROU 3   44
    SOME ANGELS IN AN ALIEN PLANET BORN   • • • • •   42 GIPSY CHILD   26
    NOR ANY ANGELS SORROW SO FORLORN   • • • • •   42 GIPSY CHILD   28
    OBLIVION IN LOST ANGELS CAN INFUSE   • • • • •   43 GIPSY CHILD   55
    AND NEVER ANGELS SORROW SO FORLORN   • • • • •   42 GIPSY CHILD   V   28
    OBLIVION IN LORN ANGELS CAN INFUSE   • • • • •   43 GIPSY CHILD   V   55
    AH SWEET ANGELS LET HIM DREAM   • • • • • • • 133 TRISTRAM 1   105
    CALL ON GOD AND ON THE HOLY ANGELS   • • • • • 145 TRISTRAM 2   79
    YE LIKE ANGELS APPEAR   • • • • • • • • • 291 RUGBY CHAPEL   190
    EVEN OF ANGELS SOUNDS AMISS   • • • • • • • 295 HEINES GRAVE   102

ANGER
    SO SPAKE HE HALF IN ANGER HALF IN SCORN   • • •   11 MYCERINUS   79
    ROUSE NO ANGER MAKE NO RIVALS MORE   • • • • • 144 TRISTRAM 2   64
    BEAR HERAS ANGER   • • • • • • • • • • 192 STRAYED REVEL   220
    THERE WITHOUT ANGER THOU WILT SEE   • • • • • 311 OBERMANN   157
    ANGER AND STRIFE AND SICKNESS ARE WITHIN   • • • 465 ALARIC AT ROME   81

ANGERBODE
    DID ANGERBODE THE GIANTESS BRING FORTH   • • • 110 BALDER DEAD 2   207

ANGERS
    IS IN MY SKIN WHICH ANGERS ME   • • • • • •   93 SICK KING BOKH   184
    AND YET I SWEAR IT ANGERS ME TO SEE   • • • • • 153 TRISTRAM 3   133

ANGLER
    WHERE THE TIRED ANGLER LIES STRETCHD OUT   • • • 248 KENSINGTON GARD   18
    WHERE THE LONE ANGLER LIES STRETCHD OUT   • • •   KENSINGTON GARD V   18

ANGLESEY
    IN THE BARE MIDST OF ANGLESEY THEY SHOW   • • • 170 EAST AND WEST   1

ANGRILY
    HOW ANGRILY THOU SPURNST ALL SIMPLER FARE   • • • 170 BETTER PART   2

ANGRILY   (CONTINUED)
        ANGRILY SMOTE ON THE CHORDS . . . .   285 HAWORTH CHURCH   128

ANGRY
        ON HIS BROW AN ANGRY FROWN . . . .   14 CHURCH BROU 1   48
        COME PLANT WE HERE IN EARTH OUR ANGRY SPEARS . .   74 SOHRAB RUSTUM   439
        AND RUSTUM PLUCKD IT BACK WITH ANGRY GROAN . . . .   76 SOHRAB RUSTUM   494
        AND DAILY STRIFES ARISE AND ANGRY WORDS . . . .   116 BALDER DEAD 3   82
        THIS MORNINGS ANGRY ANSWER FOR THY LAST   . . . .   394 MEROPE   1691
        AGLOW WITH ANGRY FIRE TO KEEP US TWAIN   . . . .   395 MEROPE   1736
        THESE ANGRY SMOKE-BURSTS . . . .   432 EMPEDOCLES II   96

ANGUISH
        WHOSE YOUTH IN THE FIRES OF ANGUISH HATH DIED . .   20 MODERN SAPPHO   28
        FROM THAT FIERCE ANGUISH . . . .   38 STAGIRIUS   8
        THE ANGUISH OF THE DEEP-FIXD SPEAR GREW FIERCE . .   80 SOHRAB RUSTUM   650
        HIS WOUNDS IMPERIOUS ANGUISH BUT THE BLOOD . . . . .   85 SOHRAB RUSTUM   840
        FROM VIOLENT ANGUISH SURELY FREE   . . . . . .   137 TRISTRAM 1   233
        THE PENITENT WITH ANGUISH BOWD   . . . .   225 EPILOG LAOCOON   155
        WITH PIERCING UNTOLD ANGUISH . . . .   235 YOUTH OF MAN   102
        YET EACH WILL HAVE ONE ANGUISH HIS OWN SOUL . .   238 PROGRESS   31
        FOR THERE WITH BODILY ANGUISH KEEN . . . . .   276 SOUTHERN NIGHT   25
        WHAT ANGUISH OF GREATNESS   . . . .   432 EMPEDOCLES II   104
        YET THAT IN ANGUISH DOUBT DESIRE . . . . . .   482 COURAGE   19

ANGUISHD
        WITH ANGUISHD FACE AND FLYING HAIR . . . . . .   244 SUMMER NIGHT   66

ANNIHILATE
        I WOULD ANNIHILATE . . . .   52 CONSOLATION   68

ANNIVERSARY
        THE TWENTIETH ANNIVERSARY OF STRIFE . . . . . .   333 MEROPE   115

ANNOUNCE
        TO ANNOUNCE THE RUIN OF MY HUSBANDS HOUSE . . . .   395 MEROPE   1738

ANNOUNCES
        ANNOUNCES ME THEIR RIGHTFUL PRINCE RETURND . . . .   383 MEROPE   1355

ANNOY
        NOR WEARINESS THE FULL-FED SOULS ANNOY   . . . .   42 GIPSY CHILD   11

ANNUAL
        BRINGING ME OF MY BOY THE ANNUAL NEWS . . . .   350 MEROPE   599
        SAVE FOR THIS ANNUAL CHARGE I HOPE TO HEAR . . . .   351 MEROPE   619

ANNUL
        THINK NOT THAT I TO ANNUL THE LAW HAVE WILLD . .   237 PROGRESS   10

ANNULLD
        DANGEROUS TO ALL TO BE BUT THUS ANNULLD   . . . .   336 MEROPE   207

ANODYNE
        AND THY GAY SMILES NO ANODYNE . . . .   245 BURIED LIFE   8

ANODYNES
        AND ALL HIS HOURLY VARIED ANODYNES . . . . .   260 SCHOLAR-GIPSY   190

ANON
        FAR OFF ANON HER MATE COMES WINGING BACK . . .   78 SOHRAB RUSTUM   561
        OF STAGSHORN FOR THEIR HATS ANON WITH SCREAMS . .   150 TRISTRAM 3   26
        AND ANON THERE BREAKS A SIGH . . . .   164 FORSAKEN MERM   101
        AND ANON THERE DROPS A TEAR . . . .   164 FORSAKEN MERM   102
        THEY DO BUT HALT THEY WILL BE HERE ANON . . .   408 EMPEDOCLES I 1   51
        IN JOY THY LAST MORN FLEW ANON . . . .   460 KAISER DEAD   63

ANSWER
        DUMB JUDGES ANSWER TRUTH OR MOCKERY . . . . .   4 EMERSONS ESSAYS   14
        SOME LARGE ANSWER YOU SHALL HEAR . . . . . .   29 NEW SIRENS   92
        LIGHT-PLASHING WAVES AN ANSWER MADE . . . . .   223 EPILOG LAOCOON   68
        AH FROM THE OLD WORLD LET SOME ONE ANSWER GIVE . .   237 PROGRESS   21
        IN THE RUSTLING NIGHT-AIR CAME THE ANSWER . . .   240 SELF-DEPENDENCE   15
        SADLY WE ANSWER WE BRING . . . .   289 RUGBY CHAPEL   117
        SHORT ANSWER IS SUFFICIENT LEAGUE WITH THEE . .   340 MEROPE   335
        WHAT SHALL I HAVE TO ANSWER TO SUCH WORDS . . .   367 MEROPE   1053
        THIS MORNINGS ANGRY ANSWER FOR THY LAST   . . .   394 MEROPE   1691
        TO THIS THOU WOULDST HAVE ANSWER TAKE IT FLY . .   395 MEROPE   1741
        AND HE MADE ANSWER I SHOULD COME AT NIGHT . . .   410 EMPEDOCLES I 1   128
        NO LACK OF ANSWER HAST THOU O MY HEART . . . .   RUDE ORATOR   13

ANSWERD
        FROM THE GATE THE WARDERS ANSWERD . . . . . .   15 CHURCH BROU 1   81
        IS ANSWERD FROM THE DEPTH OF DAWN . . . . . .   57 RESIGNATION   177
        HE SPOKE BUT RUSTUM ANSWERD WITH A SMILE . . .   67 SOHRAB RUSTUM   220
        HE SPOKE AND SOHRAB ANSWERD ON HIS FEET   . . .   72 SOHRAB RUSTUM   379
        HE SPOKE AND RUSTUM ANSWERD NOT BUT HURLD . . .   73 SOHRAB RUSTUM   398
        BUT SOHRAB ANSWERD HIM IN WRATH FOR NOW   . . .   80 SOHRAB RUSTUM   649
        AND THE BLIND HODER ANSWERD HER AND SAID . . .   99 BALDER DEAD 1   131
        SHE SPOKE BUT HODER ANSWERD HER AND SAID . . .   100 BALDER DEAD 1   184

ANSWERD   (CONTINUED)
    AND THE FLEET-FOOTED HERMOD ANSWERD HER   . . . .   108 BALDER DEAD 2   111
    SHE SPAKE AND HERMOD ANSWERD HER AND SAID   . . . .   111 BALDER DEAD 2   241
    SHE SPAKE BUT HERMOD ANSWERD HER AND SAID   . . . .   123 BALDER DEAD 3   345
    HE SPOKE BUT HODER ANSWERD HIM AND SAID   . . . .   124 BALDER DEAD 3   394
    AND THE BLIND HODER ANSWERD HIM AND SPAKE   . . . .   125 BALDER DEAD 3   431
    HE SPAKE AND BALDER ANSWERD HIM AND SAID   . . . .   126 BALDER DEAD 3   454
    HE SPAKE BUT BALDER ANSWERD HIM AND SAID   . . . .   127 BALDER DEAD 3   483
    AND THE RAY-CROWNED BALDER ANSWERD HIM   . . . .   128 BALDER DEAD 3   517
    WHEREAT HE ANSWERD THAT THE GIPSY-CREW   . . . .   256 SCHOLAR-GIPSY   44

ANSWERED
    HE SPAKE AND STRAIGHTWAY HELA ANSWERED HIM   . . . .   111 BALDER DEAD 2   246
    I AM NO KNIGHT HE ANSWERED   . . . .   159 NECKAN   25

ANSWEREST
    WELL THEN FOR CHRIST THOU ANSWEREST WHO CAN CARE . . .   171 BETTER PART   6
    SO ANSWEREST THOU BUT WHY NOT RATHER SAY   . . . .   171 BETTER PART   9

ANSWERS
    SIGNS THE CROSS AND ANSWERS SURELY   . . . . . .   META CLOISTER   39

ANTE
    AIRY ANTE-MUNDANE THRONG . . . .   456 POOR MATTHIAS   135

ANTERIOR
    BROUGHT FROM THAT ANTERIOR AGE . . . .   456 POOR MATTHIAS   148

ANTICIPANT
    O MEEK ANTICIPANT OF THAT SURE PAIN   . . . . . .   43 GIPSY CHILD   41

ANTIGONE
    BUT HUSH HAEMON WHOM ANTIGONE   . . . .   196 FRAG ANTIGONE   39
    O ANTIGONE   . . . .   196 FRAG ANTIGONE   52

ANTIQUE
    TO FORMS FROM ANTIQUE GREECE AND ROME UPTORN   . .   168 RACHEL 3   3
    IN HAT OF ANTIQUE SHAPE AND CLOAK OF GREY   . . . .   256 SCHOLAR-GIPSY   55
    LIKE STONE-SCULPTURED ANTIQUE KINGS   . . . . . .   META CLOISTER   4

ANTLERD
    WHOM ANTLERD REINDEER PULL OVER THE SNOW   . . .   96 BALDER DEAD 1   54
    BROKE BLACK WITH SWEAT THE ANTLERD MOUNTAIN-STAG . .   357 MEROPE   808

ANXIOUS
    BUT SUCH ANXIOUS SCHEMES THOU BREEDEST   . .   SECOND BEST   V   6
    BUT THROUGH THE ANXIOUS PERSIANS GUDURZ RAN   . .   66 SOHRAB RUSTUM   189
    BOTH HAVE BROUGHT THEIR ANXIOUS DAY TO EVENING . .   144 TRISTRAM 2   55
    THROUGH TWENTY YEARS HIS MOURNFUL ANXIOUS ZEAL . .   387 MEROPE   1477
    THE ANXIOUS MOTHER OF AN EXILED SON . . . . . .   403 MEROPE   1956

ANXIOUSLY
    SO ANXIOUSLY AND PAINFULLY   . . . .   36 VOICE   25

ANY
    NOR ANY ANGELS SORROW SO FORLORN   . . . . .   42 GIPSY CHILD   28
    SPEAK IS THERE NEWS OR ANY NIGHT ALARM   . . . .   62 SOHRAB RUSTUM   32
    IN SINGLE FIGHT WITH ANY MORTAL MAN . . . . .   69 SOHRAB RUSTUM   259
    WHAT SHOULD I DO WITH SLAYING ANY MORE   . . . .   85 SOHRAB RUSTUM   808
    IF ANY HERE MIGHT WEEP FOR BALDERS DEATH   . . . .   96 BALDER DEAD 1   20
    THOUGH HE HAS CAUSE HAVE ANY CAUSE BUT HE   . . . . 125 BALDER DEAD 3   408
    NOR LIGHTNESS WISDOM ANY MORE . . . .   179 FAREWELL   60
    LET THOSE WHO WILL IF ANY WEEP   . . . .   250 WISH   7
    WHO CAN SEE THE GREEN EARTH ANY MORE . . . . .   252 FUTURE   27
    ONCE PASSD I BLINDFOLD HERE AT ANY HOUR   . . . . 263 THYRSIS   24
    OF A FORMER AGE ANY MORE . . . .   294 HEINES GRAVE   80
    RANKS ANY MAN WITH MURDER SUCH AN ACT   . . . . 336 MEROPE   208
    NOR ANY OF OUR ORGANS SO OBTUSE   . . . . . .   352 MEROPE   632
    IF IN THE EVENT BE ANY PROOF   . . . . . .   354 MEROPE   701
    OF A PROTECTED EXILE ANY MORE . . . .   383 MEROPE   1381
    NOR ANY PLEADER ELSE SHALL BE INDULGED   . . . . 389 MEROPE   1527
    ALIKE TO ANY ACT   . . . .   422 EMPEDOCLES I 2   299
    PROCEEDS AT ANY NOD   . . . .   422 EMPEDOCLES I 2   300
    NOR THEBES NOR THE ISMENUS ANY MORE . . . . .   427 EMPEDOCLES I 2   442
    LIES ANY HOPE OF HEROISM MORE . . . .   480 HUNGARIAN NAT   8
    FOR ANY MAN TO FRET AGAINST HIS WEAKNESS   . . . .   LUCRETIUS 3   2

ANYTHING
    A GESTURE ANYTHING RETAIND   . . . .   185 TERRACE BERNE   39

APACE
    FADE INTO DIMNESS APACE   . . . .   286 RUGBY CHAPEL   5
    HASTE AND ADVISE FOR DAY COMES ON APACE   . . . . 330 MEROPE   28

APART
    BUT NOW HE KEEPS APART AND SITS AT HOME   . . . .   63 SOHRAB RUSTUM   81
    AND SULLEN AND HAS PITCHD HIS TENTS APART   . . . .   66 SOHRAB RUSTUM   179
    WE WERE APART YET DAY BY DAY . . . .   180 ISOLATION MARG   1
    SO FAR APART THEIR LIVES ARE THROWN . . . . .   206 TOO LATE   3
    WITH COMMON CARES UNMINGLING AND APART   . . . . 473 CROMWELL   57

APART   (CONTINUED)
        IF LIKE A COWARD I SKULKD BEHIND APART FROM THE BATTLE   HOMER TRANS   16

APATHETIC
        AND TOUCH THE APATHETIC GHOSTS WITH JOY   .   .   .   .   110 BALDER DEAD 2   196

APATHY
        NOT GODS BUT GHOSTS IN FROZEN APATHY   .   .   .   .   .   .   9 MYCERINUS   36

APENNINE
        WITHIN A FOLDING OF THE APENNINE   .   .   .   .   .   .   268 THYRSIS   180

APOLLO
        AND THE TIMES THAT BRIGHT APOLLO   .   .   .   .   .   .   214 NEW ROME   7
        SAYS APOLLO MODERNISE ROME   .   .   .   .   214 NEW ROME   10
        SAYS APOLLO MODERNISE ROME   .   .   .   .   214 NEW ROME   V 10
        APOLLO PEALD IT FROM HIS DELPHIAN CAVE   .   .   .   385 MEROPE   1401
        I HAVE MY HARP TOO THAT IS WELL APOLLO   .   .   .   407 EMPEDOCLES I 1   19
        HIS COUNSEL COULD ONCE SOOTHE HIM BUT APOLLO   .   428 EMPEDOCLES I 2   482
        YOUNG APOLLO ALL THE PRIDE   .   .   .   .   433 EMPEDOCLES II   130
        AND APOLLO BROUGHT HIS LYRE   .   .   .   .   433 EMPEDOCLES II   142
        THOU GUARDEST THEM APOLLO   .   .   .   .   435 EMPEDOCLES II   204
        NOT HERE O APOLLO   .   .   .   .   441 EMPEDOCLES II   421
        TIS APOLLO COMES LEADING .   .   .   .   442 EMPEDOCLES II   445

APOLLOS
        THEN APOLLOS MINISTER   .   .   .   .   433 EMPEDOCLES II   147
        NOT TO SEE APOLLOS SCORN .   .   .   .   434 EMPEDOCLES II   189
        SCORNFUL APOLLOS ENSIGN LIE THOU THERE   .   .   .   434 EMPEDOCLES II   193

APPAL
        AMBITIONS BOLDEST DREAM MIGHT SOBER AND APPAL   .   .   463 ALARIC AT ROME   42

APPALS
        APPALS ME SHAKES ME WITH AWE   .   .   .   .   372 MEROPE   1146

APPARENT
        TIS GOD HIMSELF BECOMES APPARENT WHEN   .   .   .   .   171 DIVINITY   3

APPEAR
        O JOY AGAIN THE FARMS APPEAR   .   .   .   .   54 RESIGNATION   74
        THE DRAWBRIDGE AND THE MOAT APPEAR   .   .   .   .   .   148 TRISTRAM 2   171
        ONCE MORE THE ROOFS OF BERNE APPEAR   .   .   .   .   .   183 TERRACE BERNE   2
        THE LIMITS OF HIS ART APPEAR   .   .   .   .   222 EPILOG LAOCOON   50
        ONE DAY THOU SAYST THERE WILL AT LAST APPEAR   .   .   239 REVOLUTIONS   17
        YE LIKE ANGELS APPEAR   .   .   .   .   291 RUGBY CHAPEL   190
        BEACONS OF HOPE YE APPEAR   .   .   .   .   292 RUGBY CHAPEL   192
        THE HUTS OF COURRERIE APPEAR   .   .   .   .   .   .   299 GRANDE CHARTR   18
        YET SHALL RESTORER APPEAR TO THE RACE   .   .   .   344 MEROPE   453
        O QUEEN FOR AN AVENGER TO APPEAR   .   .   .   .   .   348 MEROPE   545
        WHEN THE FLASHING TORCHES APPEAR   .   .   .   .   .   360 MEROPE   896
        YET SHALL RESTORERS APPEAR TO THE RACE   .   .   .   344 MEROPE   V 453
        LET BUT THE LIGHT APPEAR .   .   .   .   449 WESTMIN ABBEY   177

APPEARANCE
        AH YOU SAY THE LARGE APPEARANCE   .   .   .   .   .   .   28 NEW SIRENS   57
        COME YOU SAY THE LARGE APPEARANCE   .   .   .   .   .   28 NEW SIRENS   V 57

APPEARD
        TO AWAIT THEIR MARCH AND WHEN APPEARD   .   .   .   .   53 RESIGNATION   33
        THE CAMP AND TO THE PERSIAN HOST APPEARD   .   .   .   69 SOHRAB RUSTUM   281
        SO DELICATELY PRICKD THE SIGN APPEARD   .   .   .   .   81 SOHRAB RUSTUM   677
        AND INSTANTLY THE SACRED MORN APPEARD   .   .   .   .   104 BALDER DEAD 1   342
        BEYOND THE ABBEY-TOWERS APPEARD   .   .   .   .   .   223 EPILOG LAOCOON   70
        AGAIN APPEARD THE BLUE   .   .   .   .   319 OBERMANN MORE   208
        A CHILD OF LIGHT APPEARD .   .   .   .   444 WESTMIN ABBEY   7

APPEARING
        THROUGH THAT GLOOM HE WILL SEE BUT A SHADOW APPEARING   20 MODERN SAPPHO   25
        TROOPS WITH GOLD AND GIFTS APPEARING   .   .   .   .   .   26 NEW SIRENS   23
        TROOPS LIKE EASTERN KINGS APPEARING   .   .   .   .   .   26 NEW SIRENS   V 23

APPEARS
        WHERE MORN FIRST APPEARS   .   .   .   .   177 PARTING   86
        AND LONG THE WAY APPEARS WHICH SEEMD SO SHORT   .   267 THYRSIS   141
        A GREEN NEW EARTH APPEARS   .   .   .   .   322 OBERMANN MORE   286
        WAIT THEN UNTIL SUFFICIENT HELP APPEARS   .   .   .   384 MEROPE   1397
        BUT NOT A WORD APPEARS OF MURDER HERE   .   .   .   .   364 MEROPE   V
        CROSSING THE FROZEN LAKE APPEARS   .   .   .   .   .   451 GEISTS GRAVE   51

APPEASE
        RACHEL WITH EYES NO GAZING CAN APPEASE   .   .   .   .   167 RACHEL 1   7

APPEASED
        HOWBEIT STAY AND BE APPEASED AND TELL   .   .   .   .   125 BALDER DEAD 3   428
        MY FINAL VICTORY PROVES THE GODS APPEASED   .   .   .   397 MEROPE   1770
        THINKING APPEASED   .   .   .   .   400 MEROPE   1874

APPEASING
        OF THE APPEASING GRACIOUS HARMONY   .   .   .   .   .   431 EMPEDOCLES II   75

APPIAN
    ALONG THE APPIAN WAY   . . . . 315 OBERMANN MORE   100

APPLAUD
    SO WILL HE SPEAK PERHAPS WHILE MEN APPLAUD . . . .   72 SOHRAB RUSTUM   362
    TRY IT BUT I FOR ONE WILL NOT APPLAUD . . . . 121 BALDER DEAD 3   281
    TO HEAR THE WORLD APPLAUD THE HOLLOW GHOST . . . . 213 GROWING OLD   34

APPLAUDED
    HE SPAKE AND HIS FIERCE SONS APPLAUDED LOUD   . . 120 BALDER DEAD 3   245

APPLY
    OR HAVING LEARNT THEM WELL APPLY . . . . . . 354 MEROPE   699
    AND STRANGELY AS WE TALKD HE WOULD APPLY . . . . 356 MEROPE   766
    AND TO WHAT FRIENDS SHOULD I FOR AID APPLY . . . . 384 MEROPE   1390

APPOINTED
    BE STRICTLY CARED FOR IN THE APPOINTED DAY . . . .   96 BALDER DEAD 1   39
    FROM HIS APPOINTED END . . . . 197 FRAG ANTIGONE   83
    IT WAS NOT YET THE APPOINTED HOUR . . . . . . 321 OBERMANN MORE   253

APPOINTS
    APPOINTS THE WAY TO PEACE THROUGH SHEDDING BLOOD . . 378 MEROPE   1248

APPREHEND
    JOYS WE DIMLY APPREHEND . . . .   44 QUESTION   18

APPROACH
    FROM HER FALSE FRIENDS APPROACH IN HADES TURN . . 261 SCHOLAR-GIPSY   209
    APPROACH FOR WHAT WE SEEK IS HERE . . . . . . 300 GRANDE CHARTR   25
    WHAT BLACK PROCESSION SLOWLY MAKES APPROACH . . 331 MEROPE   52
    BOATS AND APPROACH NEAR AS WE DARED THE CHASM . . 358 MEROPE   838
    GREW USED TO THE APPROACH OF GLORYS WINGS . . . . 445 WESTMIN ABBEY   56

APPROACHD
    HE LAST APPROACHD THE CORPSE AND SPAKE AND SAID . . 117 BALDER DEAD 3   131

APPROACHES
    THE DAY APPROACHES WHEN WE MUST . . . .   48 HORATIAN ECHO   31
    FEELS THE ABHORRD APPROACHES OF OLD AGE . . . .   63 SOHRAB RUSTUM   84
    APPROACHES WITH UNDOUBTING HEART . . . . . . 400 MEROPE   1858

APPROACHING
    HUSH TIS VAIN I FEEL MY END APPROACHING . . . . 145 TRISTRAM 2   81
    FOLLOWS THE APPROACHING QUEEN WHO STOPS AS CALLD . . 332 MEROPE   64

APPROVE
    I ASK THEE NOT TO APPROVE THY HUSBANDS DEATH . . 340 MEROPE   338
    MOTHER ALL THESE APPROVE ME BUT IF THOU . . . . 403 MEROPE   1961
    APPROVE NOT TOO I HAVE BUT HALF MY JOY . . . . 403 MEROPE   1962

APPROVES
    APPROVES MY BROTHER LAIAS THIS INTENT . . . . 379 MEROPE   1267
    APPROVES MY BROTHER LAIAS THIS DESIGN . . . . 379 MEROPE   V1267

APPROVST
    APPROVST THOU THY WIFE NOW . . . . 372 MEROPE   1143

APRICOTS
    HARD BY A CLOSE OF APRICOTS . . . .   94 SICK KING BOKH   223

APRIL
    ONE APRIL WHEN THE WARM DAYS FIRST BEGAN . . . . 154 TRISTRAM 3   160
    IN THESE LONE SYLVAN GLADES THAT APRIL-DAY . . . 154 TRISTRAM 3   163
    HAVE KNOWN THEE EYING ALL AN APRIL-DAY . . . . 258 SCHOLAR-GIPSY   107
    HAVE KNOWN THEE WATCHING ALL AN APRIL-DAY . . . 258 SCHOLAR-GIPSY   V 107
    HAVE KNOWN THEE HAUNTING ALL AN APRIL-DAY . . . 258 SCHOLAR-GIPSY   V 107
    APRIL SHOWERS . . . . 286 HAWORTH CHURCH   129

APT
    ARE APT TO SNAP THE EASY-STRETCHD ENDURE . . . . 339 MEROPE   308

ARABIAN
    ON THE STARLIT ARABIAN WASTE . . . . 253 FUTURE   47

ARAL
    EMERGE AND SHINE UPON THE ARAL SEA . . . . . .   87 SOHRAB RUSTUM   892

ARALIAN
    OF ELBURZ FROM THE ARALIAN ESTUARIES . . . . . .   64 SOHRAB RUSTUM   114

ARCADE
    SINKS AND RISES THROUGH THIS COOL ARCADE . . . . META CLOISTER   16
    SINKS AND RISES THROUGH THIS CHARMD ARCADE . . . . META CLOISTER   V 16

ARCADES
    HOUSES ARCADES ENAMELLD MOSQUES . . . . . .   94 SICK KING BOKH   199

ARCADIA
OF PASTORAL ARCADIA WHERE A BABE . . . . . . 330 MEROPE 21
WHAT KEEPS HIM IN ARCADIA FROM RETURN . . . . 350 MEROPE 602
HE PERISHD IN ARCADIA WHERE HE DWELT . . . . . 355 MEROPE 717
A MESSENGER SENT FROM ARCADIA HERE . . . . . . 361 MEROPE 920
WHEREWITH FROM END TO END ARCADIA RINGS . . . . 362 MEROPE 943
LET HIM FETCH SUCCOURS FROM ARCADIA GAIN . . . 388 MEROPE 1498
BUT IN THE PASTORAL ARCADIA REARD . . . . . . 388 MEROPE 1514
TRUE BUT WHAT CAUSE TO OUR ARCADIA GIVES . . . 389 MEROPE 1534
A NEW-MADE WIFE I FROM ARCADIA CAME . . . . . 403 MEROPE 1972
HE PERISHD IN ARCADIA WHERE HE LIVD . . . . . 355 MEROPE V 717

ARCADIAN
MY GRANDFATHER THE GOOD ARCADIAN KING . . . . 331 MEROPE 33
BUT AN ARCADIAN PRINCESS MORE AKIN . . . . . 337 MEROPE 241
O ARCADIAN HILLS . . . . 342 MEROPE 392
BY ACHAIAN ARCADIAN SPEAR . . . . 345 MEROPE 480
FAR MID ARCADIAN HILLS . . . . 346 MEROPE 512
WHEN OER THE ARCADIAN FORESTS THOU ART COME . 349 MEROPE 572
THE SON OF AN ARCADIAN NOBLE I . . . . . . 355 MEROPE 723
THROUGH ALL THE LORDSHIPS OF THE ARCADIAN DALES . 355 MEROPE 727
CATES FROM OUR HUNTERS POUCH ARCADIAN FARE . . 356 MEROPE 753
OF BEASTS OF CHASE THAT HAUNT THE ARCADIAN HILLS . 356 MEROPE 757
LAST OF OUR QUARTERS WITH THE ARCADIAN CHIEFS . 356 MEROPE 759
AND WHAT ARCADIAN NEWS HAD HE TO TELL . . . . 361 MEROPE 926
OF AN ARCADIAN LORD OUR PRINCES FRIEND . . . 363 MEROPE 956
THIS YOUNG ARCADIAN NOBLE GUARD AND MATE . . . 364 MEROPE 969
IF THE ARCADIAN WITHIN . . . . 370 MEROPE 1121
ASLEEP IN THE ARCADIAN GLENS AT NOON . . . . 372 MEROPE 1160
AND WHAT OF THINE ARCADIAN MATE WHO BEARS . . 379 MEROPE 1269
AND WHAT ARCADIAN HELPERS BRINGST THOU HERE . 380 MEROPE 1284
MY FATHER THEN AND HIS ARCADIAN CHIEFS . . . 384 MEROPE 1395

ARCAS
TO RECEIVE ARCAS WHO TO-DAY SHOULD COME . . . 350 MEROPE 598
THUS MUCH FROM ARCAS MY OLD SERVANT TRUE . . . 351 MEROPE 616
THE BONES OF ARCAS WHENCE OUR RACE IS NAMED . 356 MEROPE 742
AND I CAME THINKING TO FIND ARCAS HERE . . . 361 MEROPE 916
HOW SO WAS ARCAS NOT THE MESSENGER . . . . . 361 MEROPE 924
O WERE BUT ARCAS COME ALL WOULD BE WELL . . . 362 MEROPE 933
ARCAS THOU HERE O MY DEAR MASTER O . . . . . 375 MEROPE 1206
AND ARCAS BUT I TREMBLE BOLDLY ASK . . . . . 375 MEROPE 1211
ARCAS SEEK OUT MY UNCLE LAIAS NOW . . . . . 379 MEROPE 1260
HID THE BABE HID ARCAS . . . . 391 MEROPE 1614
THE YOUTHFUL ARCAS BORN OF ZEUS . . . . . . 393 MEROPE 1657

ARCH
BUT THE ARCH-FIEND PRIDE . . . . 38 STAGIRIUS 18
THE LOVELY LIPS WITH THEIR ARCH SMILE THAT TELLS . 176 PARTING 39
LET THOSE ARCH EYES NOW SOFTLY SHINE . . . . 206 RIVER 5
THE LOW-BROWD CAVERN-ARCH AND DISAPPEAR . . . 358 MEROPE 834

ARCHES
SPANND BY AERIAL ARCHES ALL OF GOLD . . . . . 4 BUTLERS SERMONS 12
WHICH SPANS WITH GOLDEN ARCHES GIALLS STREAM . 99 BALDER DEAD 1 148
WHICH SPANS WITH GOLDEN ARCHES GIALLS STREAM . 107 BALDER DEAD 2 86

ARCHEST
TIED UNDER THE ARCHEST CHIN . . . . 23 MEMORY-PICTURE 27

ARCHESTES
WHERE YOUNG ARCHESTES DOTH WITH ISTER JOIN . . . FRAGMENT 4 1

ARCHETYPE
SOME BETTER ARCHETYPE WHOSE SEAT WAS HEAVEN . . 9 MYCERINUS 22

ARCHING
ARCHING HIS NECK AND GLAD TO BE BESTRODE . . . 107 BALDER DEAD 2 76

ARCHITECT
HER OLD ARCHITECT BESIDE . . . . 15 CHURCH BROU 1 98
WE BUT SURVEY HE IS THE ARCHITECT . . . . . . LUCRETIUS 5 3
WE BUT BEHOLD HE IS THE ARCHITECT . . . . . . LUCRETIUS 5 V 3

ARCTURUS
THE GUARD ARCTURUS . . . . 393 MEROPE 1677

ARDENT
THE ARDENT THE GIFTED HOW MOURN . . . . . . 282 HAWORTH CHURCH 49
ARDENT UNQUENCHABLE FIRES . . . . 288 RUGBY CHAPEL 74
EVEN OF THAT ARDENT SPIRIT HOPES AND FEARS . . 469 ALARIC AT ROME 178

ARDOUR
RELIGIOUS FERVOURS ARDOUR MISAPPLIED . . . . 237 PROGRESS 17
RADIANT WITH ARDOUR DIVINE . . . . 291 RUGBY CHAPEL 191
HOW SHALL I ROUSE THEIR LOVE THEIR ARDOUR SO . 382 MEROPE 1352

ARDRES
TO LOOK TOWRD ARDRES GOLDEN FIELD . . . . . 204 CALAIS SANDS 5
TO SEE TOWRD ARDRES GOLDEN FIELD . . . . . . 204 CALAIS SANDS V 5

ARENA
          TO MURDERS DREAD ARENA WHERE I SAW   . . . . . 387 MEROPE   1462

ARGIVE
          HIS BELOVED ARGIVE SEER WOULD ZEUS RETAIN   . . . 197 FRAG ANTIGONE   82
          HIS ARGIVE OR HIS SPARTAN COUSINS AID   . . . . 388 MEROPE   1499

ARGIVES
          SEE THAT YE BRING YOUR MASTER HOME TO THE HOST   HOMER TRANS   40
              OF THE ARGIVES

ARGO
          OF ARGO FIRST   . . . . 193 STRAYED REVEL   259

ARGOS
          I SPEAK NOT NOW OF ARGOS WHERE HIS BROTHER . . . 337 MEROPE   231
          FOR ASK AT ARGOS ASK IN LACEDAEMON   . . . . . 338 MEROPE   284
          THE ROYAL RACE OF TEMENUS IN ARGOS   . . . . . 384 MEROPE   1391
          ARGOS A JUGGLE TO CRESPHONTES GAVE   . . . . . 389 MEROPE   1551
          PERISHD IN ARGOS BY HIS JEALOUS SONS . . . . . 389 MEROPE   1557
          THEN PERHAPS THOU SHALT WORK AT THE LOOM OF   HOMER TRANS   29
              ANOTHER IN ARGOS

ARGUES
          WITH WOMEN THE HEART ARGUES NOT THE MIND   . . . . 340 MEROPE   341

ARGUMENT
          OUR DISCONTENT ITSELF IS ARGUMENT   . . . . . .   LUCRETIUS 3   10

ARID
          YOUTH RAMBLES ON LIFES ARID MOUNT   . . . . . 213 PROGRESS POESY   1
          HIDEOUS AND ARID AND VILE   . . . . 290 RUGBY CHAPEL   158
          OF SUN AND ARID STONE   . . . . 318 OBERMANN MORE   182

ARIGHT
          OFTENER PERFORM ARIGHT THEIR PARTS   . . . . . 221 EPILOG LAOCOON   10
          THINKING THAT SO I PRAYD ARIGHT I PRAYD   . . . . 348 MEROPE   546
          SO PASS WE ON BUT OH TO HARP ARIGHT   . . . . . 471 ALARIC AT ROME   223

ARIOSTO
          THE LAND OF ARIOSTO SHOWD   . . . . 222 EPILOG LAOCOON   22

ARISE
          WHERE THOU YOUNG PRINCE SHALT NEVER MORE ARISE   . .   18 CHURCH BROU 3   7
          IN SAMARCAND HE WILL ARISE AND CRY   . . . . .   72 SOHRAB RUSTUM   356
          NOR SEE THE SUN ARISE NOR SEE IT SET . . . . .   99 BALDER DEAD 1   154
          AND DAILY STRIFES ARISE AND ANGRY WORDS   . . . . 116 BALDER DEAD 3   82
          HATH REACHD IT THERE HEREAFTER SHALL ARISE   . . . 128 BALDER DEAD 3   520
          HASTE ARISE YE AND GO   . . . . 216 LORDS MESSENGER   5
          WHICH ARISE ON THE GLASS OF THE SAGE . . . . . 230 YOUTH OF NATURE   73
          THROUGH THE GATHERING DARKNESS ARISE . . . . . 286 RUGBY CHAPEL   11
          TO LIVE AND SEE ARISE   . . . . 449 WESTMIN ABBEY   157
          THEREFORE ARISE AND ARM THEE LO THE WORLD   . . . 465 ALARIC AT ROME   91
          ARISE AND ARM THEE SPREAD THY BANNERS FORTH   . . 465 ALARIC AT ROME   95

ARISES
          ALONE THE SUN ARISES AND ALONE   . . . .   45 IN UTRUMQUE PAR   20

ARISING
          ARISING FROM THE SINNERS LAKE   . . . . 158 SAINT BRANDAN   67

ARISTOPHANES
          STOLN FROM ARISTOPHANES . . . . 456 POOR MATTHIAS   154

ARM
          AND HE ROSE QUICKLY ON ONE ARM AND SAID   . . .   62 SOHRAB RUSTUM   30
          LET SOHRAB ARM AND WE WILL FIND A MAN   . . .   66 SOHRAB RUSTUM   186
          BUT THAT BELOVED NAME UNNERVED MY ARM   . . .   77 SOHRAB RUSTUM   547
          AND RISING STERNLY ON ONE ARM HE SAID   . . .   80 SOHRAB RUSTUM   654
          I TELL THEE PRICKD UPON THIS ARM I BEAR   . . .   80 SOHRAB RUSTUM   658
          HIS BELT AND NEAR THE SHOULDER BARED HIS ARM . .   81 SOHRAB RUSTUM   670
          ON SOHRABS ARM THE SIGN OF RUSTUMS SEAL   . . .   81 SOHRAB RUSTUM   678
          AND SOHRAB BARED THAT IMAGE ON HIS ARM   . . .   81 SOHRAB RUSTUM   684
          AND SOHRAB BARED THAT FIGURE ON HIS ARM   . . .   81 SOHRAB RUSTUM   V 684
          FOR IT GREW DARK BUT HODER TOUCHD HIS ARM   .   101 BALDER DEAD 1   229
          THEN WE SHALL MISS THY COUNSEL AND THY ARM . .   115 BALDER DEAD 3   70
          ONE LITTLE WANDERING ARM IS THROWN   . . . .   141 TRISTRAM 1   344
          AN ANGEL TOUCH MINE ARM AND SAY   . . . . .   157 SAINT BRANDAN   35
          DOWN ON ME THY RIGHT ARM . . . .   186 STRAYED REVEL   8
          WITH ONE ARM BARE   . . . .   189 STRAYED REVEL   107
          STOUT WAS ITS ARM EACH THEW AND BONE . . . .   315 OBERMANN MORE   89
          STOUT WAS ITS ARM EACH PULSE AND BONE . . . .   315 OBERMANN MORE   V 89
          AND PARALYSING CONSCIENCE STOP MY ARM   . .   333 MEROPE   98
          BUT WHEN FOR SOME GREAT PUBLIC CAUSE AN ARM   .   336 MEROPE   204
          ELECT HIMSELF HEAVENS DESTINED ARM   . . . .   353 MEROPE   691
          AN ARM ALOFT FOR HELP THEN SWEEP BENEATH . .   358 MEROPE   833
          INSPIRE THIS COWARD HEART THIS FLAGGING ARM   .   368 MEROPE   1066
          AGAINST THE ONE AND CERTAIN ARM OF POWER . .   381 MEROPE   1313
          ONE ARM ALOFT FOR HELP THEN SWEEP BENEATH . .   358 MEROPE   V 833
          IS THY FIRE-SCATHED ARM STILL RASH   . . . .   430 EMPEDOCLES II   50
          WITH ONE ARM OVER HIS HEAD   . . . .   434 EMPEDOCLES II   163
          THEREFORE ARISE AND ARM THEE LO THE WORLD . . .   465 ALARIC AT ROME   91

ARM   (CONTINUED)
      ARISE AND ARM THEE SPREAD THY BANNERS FORTH   •   •   465 ALARIC AT ROME   95
      HIS ARM HE RAISD IT DAUNTLESSLY   •   •   •   •   •   •   481 COURAGE   16

ARMADA
      AND THE ARMADA FLUNG TO THE FIERCE MAIN   •   •   •   •   481 HUNGARIAN NAT   14

ARMD
      SO ARMD HE ISSUED FORTH AND RUKSH HIS HORSE   •   •   69 SOHRAB RUSTUM   270
      AND SOHRAB ARMD IN HAMANS TENT AND CAME   •   •   •   70 SOHRAB RUSTUM   292
      AND ON THE BRIDGE A DAMSEL WATCHING ARMD   •   •   •   107 BALDER DEAD '2   87
      TO THE ARMD DAMSELS BRIDGE AND GIALLS STREAM   •   •   113 BALDER DEAD 2   290
      HE SPOKE AND THE GODS ARMD AND ODIN DONND   •   •   •   115 BALDER DEAD 3   57
      ARMD FOR RIGHT ONLY AND THE GENERAL GOOD   •   •   •   353 MEROPE   685
      AND HE WAS GIVEN A VOICE BY THE WHITE-ARMD   HOMER TRANS   46
            GODDESS HERA

ARMED
      TO ARMED WARRIORS I HEARD VENGEFUL CRIES   •   •   •   •   402 MEROPE   1940

ARMIES
      THE ARMIES OF THE HOMELESS AND UNFED   •   •   •   •   •   7 REP FRIEND   12
      LET THE TWO ARMIES REST TO-DAY BUT I   •   •   •   •   62 SOHRAB RUSTUM   55
      THE ARMIES ARE DRAWN OUT AND STAND AT GAZE   •   •   •   67 SOHRAB RUSTUM   210
      I CHALLENGED ONCE WHEN THE TWO ARMIES CAMPD   •   •   72 SOHRAB RUSTUM   357
      THE CLOUD AND THE TWO ARMIES SAW THE PAIR   •   •   •   77 SOHRAB RUSTUM   524
      BOTH ARMIES MOVED TO CAMP AND TOOK THEIR MEAL   •   •   86 SOHRAB RUSTUM   871
      THE WATCHERS OF TWO ARMIES STAND   •   •   •   •   •   93 SICK KING BOKH   162
      AND WILL NOT THEN THE IMMORTAL ARMIES SCORN   •   •   172 IMMORTALITY   5
      WHERE IGNORANT ARMIES CLASH BY NIGHT   •   •   •   •   •   212 DOVER BEACH   37
      COUNCILS AND ARMIES AND THE POMP OF WAR   •   •   •   476 CROMWELL   142

ARMLESS
      THE ARMLESS VATICAN CUPID   •   •   •   •   •   •   •   •   214 NEW ROME   1
      THE ARMLESS VATICAN CUPID   •   •   •   •   •   •   •   •   214 NEW ROME   17

ARMOUR
      ONE THE DUKE IN HELM AND ARMOUR   •   •   •   •   •   •   16 CHURCH BROU 1   107
      THERE WOULD I GO AND HANG MY ARMOUR UP   •   •   •   •   68 SOHRAB RUSTUM   236
      THERE WOULD I STAY AND HANG MY ARMOUR UP   •   •   •   68 SOHRAB RUSTUM   V 236
      NOT WOUNDS YET DYING THEY THEIR ARMOUR WORE   •   •   109 BALDER DEAD 2   168

ARMOURY
      ALL THE FOOLS-ARMOURY OF MAGIC LIE THERE   •   •   •   •   432 EMPEDOCLES II   118

ARMS
      LINKING THEIR CORAL ARMS UNDER THE SEA   •   •   •   •   4 BUTLERS SERMONS   10
      THEIR LIPS MOVED THEIR WHITE ARMS WAVED EAGERLY •   •   25 DREAM   28
      AND THOSE SLACKEND ARMS FORGO   •   •   •   •   •   •   27 NEW SIRENS   54
      DROOPD UNBRAIDED ON YOUR LISTLESS ARMS   •   •   •   30 NEW SIRENS   122
      AND YOUR SLACKEND ARMS FOREGO   •   •   •   •   •   •   27 NEW SIRENS   V 54
      OF RUGS AND FELTS AND NEAR HIM LAY HIS ARMS   •   •   61 SOHRAB RUSTUM   27
      I CAME AMONG THE TARTARS AND BORE ARMS   •   •   •   •   62 SOHRAB RUSTUM   43
      SEEK HIM IN PEACE AND CARRY TO HIS ARMS   •   •   •   63 SOHRAB RUSTUM   76
      BUT I WILL FIGHT UNKNOWN AND IN PLAIN ARMS   •   •   •   68 SOHRAB RUSTUM   257
      HIS FOLLOWERS IN AND BADE THEM BRING HIS ARMS   •   •   69 SOHRAB RUSTUM   264
      AND CLAD HIMSELF IN STEEL THE ARMS HE CHOSE   •   •   69 SOHRAB RUSTUM   265
      HIS STATELY CREST AND DIMMD HIS GLITTERING ARMS •   •   74 SOHRAB RUSTUM   454
      TO ARMS AND CRY FOR VENGEANCE UPON THEE   •   •   •   78 SOHRAB RUSTUM   585
      RUSTUM SHOULD SEEK THE BOY TO TRAIN IN ARMS   •   •   79 SOHRAB RUSTUM   611
      HIS ARMS ABOUT HIS NECK AND KISSD HIS LIPS   •   •   •   81 SOHRAB RUSTUM   695
      HIS HAIR AND FACE AND BEARD AND GLITTERING ARMS •   •   82 SOHRAB RUSTUM   702
      HIS ARMS ROUND HIS SONS NECK AND WEPT ALOUD   •   •   82 SOHRAB RUSTUM   728
      RUSTUM SHOULD TAKE THE BOY TO TRAIN IN ARMS   •   •   79 SOHRAB RUSTUM V 611
      HER ARMS TOWARDS HIM WITH A CRY BUT HE   •   •   •   •   104 BALDER DEAD 1   333
      THEIR ARMS AND LED THEIR HORSES FROM THE STALL   •   •   105 BALDER DEAD 2   12
      BUT NOW PUT ON YOUR ARMS AND MOUNT YOUR STEEDS   •   •   115 BALDER DEAD 3   50
      AND THRICE IN ARMS AROUND THE DEAD THEY RODE   •   •   115 BALDER DEAD 3   61
      WEEPING THE SANDS WERE WETTED AND THEIR ARMS   •   •   115 BALDER DEAD 3   62
      AND BROUGHT HIS ARMS AND GOLD AND ALL HIS STUFF •   •   118 BALDER DEAD 3   169
      IF I IF ODIN CLAD IN RADIANT ARMS   •   •   •   •   •   120 BALDER DEAD 3   238
      THE STAIND ARMS THE MATTED HAIR   •   •   •   •   •   •   136 TRISTRAM 1   199
      HAD FALLEN BACK HER ARMS OUTSPREAD   •   •   •   •   •   146 TRISTRAM 2   104
      FLASH ON HER WHITE ARMS STILL   •   •   •   •   •   •   •   146 TRISTRAM 2   111
      A BABE WAS IN HER ARMS AND AT HER SIDE   •   •   •   •   169 WEST LONDON   3
      THEIR YELLOWING ARMS   •   •   •   •   •   •   •   •   •   175 PARTING   8
      WOULD THESE ARMS REACH TO CLASP THEE   •   •   •   •   •   176 PARTING   61
      MY STRETCHD ARMS ARE CAST   •   •   •   •   •   •   •   176 PARTING   64
      THINE ARMS ROUND THY CHILD   •   •   •   •   •   •   •   177 PARTING   78
      MY STRAIND ARMS ARE CAST   •   •   •   •   •   •   •   176 PARTING   V 64
      LOCKD IN EACH OTHERS ARMS WE STOOD   •   •   •   •   •   178 FAREWELL   11
      AND HER BEAUTIFUL ARMS UNCLASPING   •   •   •   •   •   197 FRAG ANTIGONE   78
      AND THE CLANG OF ARMS IN HIS EAR   •   •   •   •   •   •   229 YOUTH OF NATURE   42
      HE SPREADS OUT HIS ARMS TO THE LIGHT   •   •   •   •   •   251 FUTURE   5
      HAVE TO HIS LITTLE ARMS BEGUILED   •   •· •   •   •   •   317 OBERMANN MORE   159
      I SMOTE HIM WHEN OUR WISHES CLASHD IN ARMS   •   •   •   334 MEROPE   130
      ALWAYS IN ARMS ALWAYS IN FACE OF FOES   •   •   •   •   334 MEROPE   153
      WHEN THEBES WHEN ATHENS DARED NOT WHO IN ARMS   •   •   337 MEROPE   225
      WITH ARMS THEN THEY SHOULD SEND HIM NOT BY STEALTH   •   351 MEROPE   606
      WITH ARMS THEY DARE NOT AND BY STEALTH THEY FEAR •   •   351 MEROPE   607
      THAT HE TO POWER MAKES WAY BY ARMS   •   •   •   •   •   353 MEROPE   681

ARMS   (CONTINUED)
         GROUPD AROUND ZEUSS ALTAR ALL IN ARMS   . . . .   401 MEROPE   1899
         LAIAS IN ARMS SPRANG TO HIS NEPHEWS SIDE   . . . .   402 MEROPE   1933
         ARTS CAME AND ARMS AND LAW   . . . .   445 WESTMIN ABBEY   57
         DID THE TROJANS OBTAIN TO STRIP THE ARMS FROM   HOMER TRANS   51
              PATROCLUS
         WITHIN THE MARBLE PRISON OF HER ARMS   . . . . . .   FRAGMENT 1   4

ARMY
         IN SAMARCAND BEFORE THE ARMY MARCHD   . . . . . .   62 SOHRAB RUSTUM   40
         THAT ARMY NOT ONE SHALL ARRIVE . . . .   291 RUGBY CHAPEL   184
         MARSHAL THEM TO AN ARMY THEN ADVANCE   . . . . .   382 MEROPE   1324
         A PEOPLE IS NO ARMY TRAIND TO FIGHT   . . . . .   382 MEROPE   1339

ARNE
         PAST ARNE SPRING WHERE RHEA GAVE THE BABE   . . . .   355 MEROPE   736
         TELLING US ARNE MINDED HIM HE TOO   . . . . . .   356 MEROPE   768

ARNO
         HEAR IT FROM THY BROAD LUCENT ARNO-VALE   . . . .   267 THYRSIS   167

AROANIAN
         THE AROANIAN STREAM   . . . .   391 MEROPE   1612

AROSE
         CREPT FROM THE OXUS SOON A HUM AROSE . . . . .   86 SOHRAB RUSTUM   868
         THEN FROM THEIR LOATHED FEAST THE GODS AROSE   . .   101 BALDER DEAD 1   203
         SO HAVING SPOKE THE KING OF GODS AROSE   . . . .   96 BALDER DEAD 1   V 46
         SO SAID HE AND THE GODS AROSE AND TOOK   . . .   106 BALDER DEAD 2   47
         BUT IN THE HILLS A STRONG EAST-WIND AROSE   . . .   118 BALDER DEAD 3   181
         THEN FROM THEIR LOATHED FEAST THE GODS AROSE   . .   119 BALDER DEAD 3   214
         BUT FREA MOTHER OF THE GODS AROSE   . . . . .   120 BALDER DEAD 3   246
         WHEN THE GODS HEARD THEY STRAIGHT AROSE AND TOOK . .   122 BALDER DEAD 3   302

AROSEST
         SINCE THOU AROSEST TO TREAD   . . . .   287 RUGBY CHAPEL   27

AROUND
         THE STRONG BAND WHICH PASSION AROUND HIM HATH FURLD   20 MODERN SAPPHO   22
         THE STRONG BAND WHICH BEAUTY AROUND HIM HATH FURLD   20 MODERN SAPPHO   V 22
         HER SOFT FACE HER HAIR AROUND   . . . .   23 MEMORY-PICTURE   26
         THE SOLEMN HILLS AROUND US SPREAD   . . . . . .   60 RESIGNATION   266
         WAS RUSTUMS AND HIS MEN LAY CAMPD AROUND   . . .   67 SOHRAB RUSTUM   194
         IN BOTH HIS HANDS THE DUST WHICH LAY AROUND   . .   81 SOHRAB RUSTUM   700
         FROM AROUND BALDER ALL THE HEROES WENT   . . . .   97 BALDER DEAD 1   62
         WHO ALL WILL FLIT LIKE EDDYING LEAVES AROUND   . .   100 BALDER DEAD 1   177
         SO AROUND HERMOD SWARMD THE TWITTERING GHOSTS   . .   109 BALDER DEAD 2   163
         AND THRICE IN ARMS AROUND THE DEAD THEY RODE   . .   115 BALDER DEAD 3   61
         REDDENING THE SEA AROUND AND ALL WAS DARK   . . .   119 BALDER DEAD 3   206
         AND ONCE MORE HERMOD SAW AROUND HIM SPREAD . . .   124 BALDER DEAD 3   379
         STEALS COLDLY AROUND THE CHAMBER BRIGHT   . . .   147 TRISTRAM 2   148
         BAKED ON THE EMBERS ALL AROUND   . . . .   191 STRAYED REVEL   167
         WHILE ALL AROUND IN SILENCE LIES   . . . . .   250 WISH   30
         AS THE PALE WASTE WIDENS AROUND HIM . . . . .   254 FUTURE   83
         TO DANCE AROUND THE FYFIELD ELM IN MAY   . . . .   257 SCHOLAR-GIPSY   83
         IS HEARD TO-NIGHT AROUND THY GRAVE   . . . . .   276 SOUTHERN NIGHT   22
         THAT OBERMANN THE WORLD AROUND   . . . . . .   307 OBERMANN   39
         GROUPD AROUND ZEUSS ALTAR ALL IN ARMS   . . . .   401 MEROPE   1899
         FOLD LIKE A SHROUD AROUND THY WITHERED BONES   . .   464 ALARIC AT ROME   64
         YET HERE IT SPEAKS NOT YEA THOUGH ALL AROUND   . .   467 ALARIC AT ROME   143
         WHISPERING FROM ALL AROUND ALL EARTHLY THINGS MUST DIE   469 ALARIC AT ROME   180
         AROUND WHOSE FEET THE EXULTING WAVES HAVE SUNG . .   472 CROMWELL   13
         SAD FACES WATCHD AROUND HIM AND HIS BREATH . . .   478 CROMWELL   207

ARRAIGN
         SO WE ARRAIGN HER HER SONS   . . . .   295 HEINES GRAVE   86
         YES WE ARRAIGN HER BUT SHE   . . . .   295 HEINES GRAVE   87
         STRAIGHTWAY THOU FALLEST TO ARRAIGN THE TIMES   . .   411 EMPEDOCLES I 1   144

ARRAIGNST
         SO THOU ARRAIGNST HER HER FOE   . . . .   295 HEINES GRAVE   85

ARRANGED
         WITH ALL THY BEING RE-ARRANGED   . . . .   184 TERRACE BERNE   35

ARRAS
         AND ON THE ARRAS WROUGHT YOU SEE   . . . . .   147 TRISTRAM 2   152

ARRAY
         AGAINST THE KING HIMSELF ARRAY THE HOST   . . .   382 MEROPE   1320
         FLASHT ON THE RUDE BARBARIANS WILD ARRAY   . . .   464 ALARIC AT ROME   70
         TWICE HAD THE PAGEANT OF THAT VAST ARRAY   . . .   465 ALARIC AT ROME   77
         THE SURGING BATTLE AND THE MAILD ARRAY   . . . .   475 CROMWELL   138
         TILL THE PALE MONARCH AND THE LONG ARRAY   . . .   477 CROMWELL   197

ARRAYD
         THE MAN OF THE BOLD WEST NOW COMES ARRAYD   . . .   170 EAST AND WEST   13
         IN CROWN AND SWORD ARRAYD   . . . .   316 OBERMANN MORE   122

ARRESTS
         ARRESTS THEM WITH A CHARMD SURPRISE . . . . .   305 GRANDE CHARTR   190

ARRIAN
    TAUGHT ARRIAN WHEN VESPASIANS BRUTAL SON   • • • •   2 TO A FRIEND   7

ARRIVE
    TILL DEATH ARRIVE TO SUPERSEDE • • • • • • •   56 RESIGNATION   142
    THAT ARMY NOT ONE SHALL ARRIVE • • • • • • • •   291 RUGBY CHAPEL   184
    BUT TRAVELLERS IN A HURRY TO ARRIVE • • • • •   LUCRETIUS 6   2

ARRIVED
    RIGHTLY THEY TOLD THEE AND THOU ART ARRIVED   • •   354 MEROPE   705
    ARRIVED FROM TEGEA WITH WEIGHTY NEWS • • • • •   361 MEROPE   915
    ARRIVED AND OF THE KING HAD SPEECH BUT NOW • • •   361 MEROPE   921
    A YOUTH ARRIVED BUT NOW THE SON HE SAID • • • •   363 MEROPE   955
    AND THE KIND CHANCE-ARRIVED WANDERER • • • • •   399 MEROPE   1836

ARRIVES
    TILL DEATH ARRIVES TO SUPERSEDE   • • • • •   56 RESIGNATION   V 142
    AND THERE ARRIVES A LULL IN THE HOT RACE • • • •   247 BURIED LIFE   91

ARRIVING
    LET MY TURN IF IT WILL COME BE SWIFT IN ARRIVING • •   20 MODERN SAPPHO   31

ARROW
    AND PIERCED HER WITH AN ARROW AS SHE ROSE • • •   78 SOHRAB RUSTUM   559
    LIES DYING WITH THE ARROW IN HER SIDE • • • •   78 SOHRAB RUSTUM   567
    BY A PITILESS ARROW OF DEATH • • • • • • • •   216 LORDS MESSENGER   18

ARROWS
    SPLINTERD THE SILVER ARROWS OF THE MOON   • • • •   11 MYCERINUS   99

ARROWY
    MINE EYES ARE DIZZY WITH THE ARROWY HAIL   • • • •   128 BALDER DEAD 3   507
    ARROWY LIGHTNINGS OF SOUL • • • • • • •   293 HEINES GRAVE   36
    ONCE IN THE BLACK AND ARROWY RACE AND CAST • • •   358 MEROPE   832

ART
    OTHERS ABIDE OUR QUESTION THOU ART FREE   • • • •   2 SHAKESPEARE   1
    WE ASK AND ASK THOU SMILEST AND ART STILL   • • • •   2 SHAKESPEARE   2
    WHISPERING A LITTLE SPACE AND THOU ART MINE   • •   11 MYCERINUS   106
    MURMURING ART THOU STILL UNKIND   • • • •   23 MEMORY-PICTURE   36
    OUT OF THIS STUFF THESE FORCES THOU ART GROWN   • •   46 IN UTRUMQUE PAR   V 38
    ONLY THAT WITH NO FINER ART • • • • • •   48 HORATIAN ECHO   19
    WHO ART THOU FOR IT IS NOT YET CLEAR DAWN   • • •   62 SOHRAB RUSTUM   31
    ART THOU NOT RUSTUM SPEAK ART THOU NOT HE   • • •   71 SOHRAB RUSTUM   344
    ART THOU NOT RUSTUM SPEAK ART THOU NOT HE   • • •   71 SOHRAB RUSTUM   344
    ART THOU SO FIERCE THOU WILT NOT FRIGHT ME SO   • •   72 SOHRAB RUSTUM   380
    BEGIN THOU ART MORE VAST MORE DREAD THAN I   • • •   72 SOHRAB RUSTUM   385
    AND THOU ART PROVED I KNOW AND I AM YOUNG   • • •   72 SOHRAB RUSTUM   386
    THOU SAYST THOU ART NOT RUSTUM BE IT SO   • • •   74 SOHRAB RUSTUM   431
    WHO ART THOU THEN THAT CANST SO TOUCH MY SOUL   • •   74 SOHRAB RUSTUM   432
    THOU ART NOT IN AFRASIABS GARDENS NOW   • • •   75 SOHRAB RUSTUM   460
    WITH TARTAR GIRLS WITH WHOM THOU ART WONT TO DANCE   75 SOHRAB RUSTUM   461
    FOOL THOU ART SLAIN AND BY AN UNKNOWN MAN   • • •   77 SOHRAB RUSTUM   537
    UNKNOWN THOU ART YET THY FIERCE VAUNT IS VAIN   • •   77 SOHRAB RUSTUM   541
    O SOHRAB THOU INDEED ART SUCH A SON   • • •   80 SOHRAB RUSTUM   641
    HAVE TOLD THEE FALSE THOU ART NOT RUSTUMS SON   • •   80 SOHRAB RUSTUM   644
    MAN WHO ART THOU WHO DOST DENY MY WORDS   • • •   80 SOHRAB RUSTUM   655
    IF THOU SHOW THIS THEN ART THOU RUSTUMS SON   • •   81 SOHRAB RUSTUM   668
    IN HEAVEN AND THOU ART HEAVENS UNCONSCIOUS HAND   • •   82 SOHRAB RUSTUM   710
    O RUKSH THOU ART MORE FORTUNATE THAN I   • • •   83 SOHRAB RUSTUM   747
    THOU ART MY FATHER AND THY GAIN IS MINE   • •   84 SOHRAB RUSTUM   777
    STILL THOU ART KING AND THE LAW STANDS   • •   92 SICK KING BOKH   138
    O VIZIER THOU ART OLD I YOUNG   • • • • •   93 SICK KING BOKH   181
    UNHAPPY BUT THAT ART HE DID NOT KNOW • • • •   101 BALDER DEAD 2   212
    WHO ART THOU ON THY BLACK AND FIERY HORSE   • • •   107 BALDER DEAD 2   101
    HERMOD FOR HE THOU ART THOU SON OF HEAVEN   • •   110 BALDER DEAD 2   202
    AND SURE OF ALL THE HAPPIEST FAR ART THOU   • • •   112 BALDER DEAD 2   257
    BALDER MY BROTHER THOU ART GONE A ROAD   • •   116 BALDER DEAD 3   99
    WHOM WE MAY BID TO SING THOUGH THOU ART GONE   • •   117 BALDER DEAD 3   134
    FOR OF ALL POWERS THE MIGHTIEST FAR ART THOU   • •   120 BALDER DEAD 3   250
    WHERE ART THOU WHO HADST HIS BLOOM   • • • •   132 TRISTRAM 1   77
    ART THOU COLD OR FALSE OR DEAD • • • • •   133 TRISTRAM 1   81
    MY PRINCESS ART THOU THERE SWEET DO NOT WAIT   • •   140 TRISTRAM 1   308
    POOR CHILD THOU ART ALMOST AS PALE AS I   • •   140 TRISTRAM 1   312
    MY PRINCESS ART THOU THERE SWEET TIS TOO LATE   • •   140 TRISTRAM 1   V 308
    THOU ART COME AT LAST THEN HAUGHTY QUEEN   • •   142 TRISTRAM 2   2
    THOU ART COME INDEED THOU HAST REJOIND ME   • •   142 TRISTRAM 2   9
    THOU ART PALER BUT THY SWEET CHARM ISEULT   • •   143 TRISTRAM 2   25
    TRISTRAM ART THOU CALLD FOR MY DEATHS SAKE   • • •   145 TRISTRAM 2   86
    AND WHO ART THOU THE PRIEST BEGAN • • • •   159 NECKAN   23
    THE BEAUTY AND THE GLORIOUS ART OF GREECE   • •   168 RACHEL 2   14
    THOU HAST BEEN SHALT BE ART ALONE   • • • •   181 ISOLATION MARG   30
    OR IS IT OVER ART THOU DEAD • • • • •   184 TERRACE BERNE   25
    WHENCE ART THOU SLEEPER • • • • • • •   186 STRAYED REVEL   23
    ART TIRED WITH HUNTING • • • • • •   188 STRAYED REVEL   72
    WONDERFUL GODDESS BY THY ART • • • •   188 STRAYED REVEL   77
    ART THOU NOT HE WHOM FAME • • • • •   189 STRAYED REVEL   108
    ART THOU HE STRANGER • • • • • • • •   189 STRAYED REVEL   111
    THOU ART TIRED BEST BE STILL • • • • •   215 LAST WORD   8

ART (CONTINUED)
```
ART SCIENCE WIT                                         220 BACCHANALIA 2         54
THE LIMITS OF HIS ART APPEAR                            222 EPILOG LAOCOON        50
CLEAR AS THE PAINTERS ART CAN DRESS                     225 EPILOG LAOCOON       134
AND I HE SAID THE SECRET OF THEIR ART                   256 SCHOLAR-GIPSY        48
AND THEN THEY LAND AND THOU ART SEEN NO MORE            257 SCHOLAR-GIPSY        81
AND THOU FROM EARTH ART GONE                            259 SCHOLAR-GIPSY       136
THEY ALL ARE GONE AND THOU ART GONE AS WELL            266 THYRSIS             130
YES THOU ART GONE AND ROUND ME TOO THE NIGHT          266 THYRSIS             131
THERE THOU ART GONE AND ME THOU LEAVEST HERE          268 THYRSIS             191
ART STILL HAS TRUTH TAKE REFUGE THERE                  271 MEMORIAL VERSES      28
STILL ART TO ME                                        276 SOUTHERN NIGHT       40
SOME IN ART SOME IN GIFT                                284 HAWORTH CHURCH       82
SOME IN GIFT SOME IN ART                                284 HAWORTH CHURCH    V  82
THOU MY FATHER ART LAID                                286 RUGBY CHAPEL         13
KNOCK PASS THE WICKET THOU ART COME                    300 GRANDE CHARTR        29
FLY HENCE POOR WRETCH WHOEER THOU ART                  307 OBERMANN             17
WHERE THOU O SEER ART SET                               309 OBERMANN            106
FOR THOU ART GONE AWAY FROM EARTH                      310 OBERMANN            141
AND WHO THOU ART WHO SPEAKEST TO ME I                  335 MEROPE              183
AND THOU ART POLYPHONTES FIRST HIS FRIEND             335 MEROPE              185
WHEN OER THE ARCADIAN FORESTS THOU ART COME          349 MEROPE              572
INTO THE QUIET GLOOM WHERE THOU ART NOW               350 MEROPE              593
RIGHTLY THEY TOLD THEE AND THOU ART ARRIVED          354 MEROPE              705
AND WHO ART THOU WHO BRINGEST ME SUCH NEWS           355 MEROPE              716
AND THOU THOU FAIR-SKINND SERPENT THOU ART LAID      373 MEROPE             1177
ART THOU THEN COME NEVER TO PART AGAIN               377 MEROPE             1221
THOU ART BEWILDERD THE SANE HEAD IS MINE             396 MEROPE             1759
FOR THAT IN THIS MY WARNING THOU ART PAID            396 MEROPE             1765
SISTER FROM THIS DAY FORTH THOU ART NO MORE          403 MEROPE             1954
THOU ART TOO YOUNG TO NOTE IT BUT HIS POWER          410 EMPEDOCLES I 1      112
BAH THOU A DOCTOR THOU ART SUPERSTITIOUS             410 EMPEDOCLES I 1      133
BUT THOU THOU ART NO COMPANY FOR HIM                 411 EMPEDOCLES I 1      140
THOU ART AS CROSS AS SOURD AS HIMSELF                411 EMPEDOCLES I 1      141
NOT MIRACLES THOU ART A LEARNED MAN                  411 EMPEDOCLES I 1      159
THOU ART MY FRIEND TO THEE                           415 EMPEDOCLES I 2      103
NO THOU ART COME TOO LATE EMPEDOCLES                 429 EMPEDOCLES II        16
AND BEING LONELY THOU ART MISERABLE                  429 EMPEDOCLES II        20
MARSYAS THOU ART VANQUISHED                          433 EMPEDOCLES II       146
BUT NO THIS HEART WILL GLOW NO MORE THOU ART         438 EMPEDOCLES II       327
NOR TO US ONLY ART THOU DEAR                         451 GEISTS GRAVE         53
TINY THOUGH THOU ART TO STRAY                        458 POOR MATTHIAS       208
AND THOU ART GONE WHERE GEIST HATH GONE              460 KAISER DEAD          65
OBLIVIONS DREARY FOUNTAIN WHERE ART THOU             462 ALARIC AT ROME        2
ALAS NO COMMON SEPULCHRE ART THOU                    464 ALARIC AT ROME       55
STRETCHD ON THAT BED OF DEATH ART NOTHING NOW        479 CROMWELL            234
WHICH MEN SAY IS THE FLEETEST OF WINDS TIS              HOMER TRANS          55
        THOU WHO ART FATED
WHEN THOU ART EITHER NOUGHT AND SO NOT LOVED            FRAGMENT 5            8

ARTEMIS
BY ARTEMIS SOFT SHAFTS                                  197 FRAG ANTIGONE       67

ARTHUR
OF CHILDHOOD ARTHUR DID SOME CHECK HAVE POWER          447 WESTMIN ABBEY      118
WHAT HAD OUR ARTHUR GAIND TO STOP AND SEE             448 WESTMIN ABBEY      154
OUR ARTHUR WILL AGAIN BE PRESENT HERE                 449 WESTMIN ABBEY      179

ARTHURS
FAMOUS IN ARTHURS COURT OF OLD                         131 TRISTRAM 1          20
AT ARTHURS SIDE HE FIGHTS ONCE MORE                   138 TRISTRAM 1         254

ARTIST
ARTIST WHOSE HAND WITH HORROR WINGD HATH TORN           6 GEO CRUIKSHANK       1
DO FOR THIS RADIANT GREEK-SOULD ARTIST CEASE          168 RACHEL 2            12
CAN THY PENCIL O ARTIST RESTORE                       231 YOUTH OF NATURE    110

ARTISTS
IN LAWS BY HUMAN ARTISTS BOUND                         223 EPILOG LAOCOON      76
AND ARTISTS ENVIOUS AND THE MOB PROFANE               295 HEINES GRAVE       114
HER ARTISTS COULD NOT PLEASE                          316 OBERMANN MORE      130

ARTS
FRANCE FAMED IN ALL GREAT ARTS IN NONE SUPREME          7 REP FRIEND CONT      4
WHOSE MIND HATH KNOWN ALL ARTS OF GOVERNING           43 GIPSY CHILD         35
FOR WISE HE WAS AND MANY CURIOUS ARTS                101 BALDER DEAD 1      210
OF WAR AND ARTS                                      189 STRAYED REVEL      125
WHY MUSIC AND THE OTHER ARTS                          221 EPILOG LAOCOON       9
HIS MATES HAD ARTS TO RULE AS THEY DESIRED           256 SCHOLAR-GIPSY       45
TO LEARN STRANGE ARTS AND JOIN A GIPSY-TRIBE         259 SCHOLAR-GIPSY      135
WHOSE TENDER WINNING ARTS                             317 OBERMANN MORE      158
O ARTS ABOVE THE VULGAR TYRANTS REACH                339 MEROPE             310
ARTS CAME AND ARMS AND LAW                            445 WESTMIN ABBEY       57
SUCH WAYS SUCH ARTS SUCH LOOKS HADST THOU            451 GEISTS GRAVE        44

ARUNDEL
IT WAS THE SIGHT OF THAT LORD ARUNDEL                 166 PICT NEWSTEAD        4

AS
AS THOUGH ONE SPAKE OF LIFE UNTO THE DEAD               3 EMERSONS ESSAYS      8
AS THOUGH ONE SPAKE OF NOISE UNTO THE DEAD             3 EMERSONS ESSAYS   V   8
```

AS   (CONTINUED)

AS THOUGH MEN SPAKE OF LIFE A JOY WAS FLED · · · ·   EMERSONS ESSAYS   V   8
CHILDREN AS SUCH FORGIVE THEM HAVE I KNOWN · · · ·   8 RELIGIOUS ISOL   1
NOW AS THE BARRIER CLOSES DIES AWAY · · · ·   10 MYCERINUS   58
WHO WRESTLES WITH HIS DREAM AS SOME PALE SHAPE   11 MYCERINUS   103
MY SAND RUNS SHORT AND AS YON STAR-SHOT RAY · ·   10 MYCERINUS   56
STANDS AS ERST THE BUILDERS LEFT IT · · · · ·   15 CHURCH BROU 1   69
BUT SHE DIED AS IT WAS BUILDING · · · · ·   14 CHURCH BROU 1   V   67
AS YESTERDAY WAS SO TO-MORROW WILL BE · · · ·   19 MODERN SAPPHO   12
AS HE DRIFTS TO FATIGUE DISCONTENT AND DEJECTION · ·   20 MODERN SAPPHO   19
PERCEIVE BUT A VOICE AS I COME TO HIS SIDE · · · ·   20 MODERN SAPPHO   26
RICH TO-MORROW AS TO-DAY · · · · · ·   22 MEMORY-PICTURE   3
SPEND AS MADLY AS YOU MAY · · · · ·   22 MEMORY-PICTURE   4
SPEND AS MADLY AS YOU MAY · · · · ·   22 MEMORY-PICTURE   4
MARGUERITE SAYS AS LAST YEAR WENT · · · · ·   23 MEMORY-PICTURE   17
AS SHE TOWRD ME LEAND HER FACE · · · · ·   23 MEMORY-PICTURE   34
TO PAINT ILL AS I HAVE DONE · · · · ·   24 MEMORY-PICTURE   51
HAST LIVD LIGHT AS THESE LIVE NOW · · · ·   22 MEMORY-PICTURE   V
AS THESE ARE THOU TOO WERT SUCH · · · · ·   22 MEMORY-PICTURE   V
AS SHE TOWARDS ME LEAND HER FACE · · · · ·   23 MEMORY-PICTURE   V   34
AND WE PLEAD AS STAUNCH ADHERENCE · · · · ·   28 NEW SIRENS   59
DUE TO PLEASURE AS TO PAIN · · · · ·   28 NEW SIRENS   60
BLEW SUCH MUSIC AS A GOD MAY FRAME · · · · ·   29 NEW SIRENS   104
DUMBLY SMILING AS YOU GO · · · · ·   31 NEW SIRENS   160
AS OLD AGE YOUTHS FATAL MORROW · · · · ·   33 NEW SIRENS   217
SOULS AS LITTLE GODLIKE AS THEIR OWN · · · ·   34 NEW SIRENS   250
SOULS AS LITTLE GODLIKE AS THEIR OWN · · · ·   34 NEW SIRENS   250
AND WE PLEAD AS FIRM ADHERENCE · · · · ·   28 NEW SIRENS   V   59
AS THE KINDLING GLANCES · · · · · ·   35 VOICE   1
AS THE TEARS OF SORROW · · · · · ·   36 VOICE   9
SO FAR AS I CONCEIVE THE WORLDS REBUKE · · · ·   37 WORLDS TRIUMPHS   1
HEAVY AS DEATH COLD AS THE GRAVE · · · · ·   38 STAGIRIUS   12
HEAVY AS DEATH COLD AS THE GRAVE · · · · ·   38 STAGIRIUS   12
HUNGRY AND BARREN AND SHARP AS THE SEA · · · ·   39 STAGIRIUS   47
NO AS THE FOAMING SWATH · · · · · ·   40 HUMAN LIFE   19
AS CHARTERD BY SOME UNKNOWN POWERS · · · · ·   41 HUMAN LIFE   26
NO AS THE FOAMING SWATHE · · · · · ·   40 HUMAN LIFE   V   19
GLOOMS THAT GO DEEP AS THINE I HAVE NOT KNOWN · ·   42 GIPSY CHILD   17
AND THOUGH THE JUST SUN GILD AS MORTALS PRAY · · ·   43 GIPSY CHILD   59
AND THOUGH THE JUST SUN GILD AS ALL MEN PRAY · · ·   43 GIPSY CHILD   V   59
HIGH AS THY LIFE BE RISEN TIS FROM THESE · · · ·   46 IN UTRUMQUE PAR   V   41
YET AS THE WHEEL FLIES ROUND · · · · · ·   47 WORLD QUIETIST   17
BREATHED DEEPLY AS IT DIED · · · · · ·   47 WORLD QUIETIST   31
AND JULIETS WAS AS FAIR A FACE · · · · · ·   48 HORATIAN ECHO   29
AND SCORN US AS OUR MISTRESS MAY · · · · ·   48 HORATIAN ECHO   33
OUR JOVIAL HOST AS FORTH WE FARE · · · · ·   53 RESIGNATION   42
THAT AS THE BALMY DARKNESS FELL · · · · ·   54 RESIGNATION   83
THE SELF-SAME SHADOWS NOW AS THEN · · · · ·   55 RESIGNATION   98
THEIR CHILDREN AS WHEN FIRST THEY CAME · · · ·   55 RESIGNATION   119
STILL SHARP AS EVER FREEZE AND PARCH · · · ·   56 RESIGNATION   131
IT SEEMS AS IF IN THEIR DECAY · · · · ·   56 RESIGNATION   134
CROWD AS WE WILL ITS NEUTRAL SPACE · · · · ·   59 RESIGNATION   258
EACH MOMENT AS IT FLIES TO WHOM · · · · ·   59 RESIGNATION   V 257
CROWD AS WE WILL ITS NEUTRAL ROOM · · · · ·   59 RESIGNATION   V 258
THY COUNSEL AND TO HEED THEE AS THY SON · · · ·   62 SOHRAB RUSTUM   39
FOR NOW IT IS NOT AS WHEN I WAS YOUNG · · · ·   63 SOHRAB RUSTUM   79
AS WHEN SOME GREY NOVEMBER MORN THE FILES · · ·   64 SOHRAB RUSTUM   111
AS IN THE COUNTRY ON A MORN IN JUNE · · · ·   65 SOHRAB RUSTUM   154
BUT AS A TROOP OF PEDLARS FROM CABOOL · · ·   65 SOHRAB RUSTUM   160
CROSSING SO HIGH THAT AS THEY MOUNT THEY PASS · ·   66 SOHRAB RUSTUM   163
OLD MAN BE IT AGREED AS THOU HAST SAID · · · ·   66 SOHRAB RUSTUM   185
AND DEAR AS THE WET DIVER TO THE EYES · · · ·   69 SOHRAB RUSTUM   284
AND AS AFIELD THE REAPERS CUT A SWATH · · · ·   70 SOHRAB RUSTUM   293
SOHRAB COME FORTH AND EYED HIM AS HE CAME · · ·   70 SOHRAB RUSTUM   301
AS SOME RICH WOMAN ON A WINTERS MORN · · · ·   70 SOHRAB RUSTUM   302
AS HE BEHELD HIM COMING AND HE STOOD · · · ·   70 SOHRAB RUSTUM   320
TO IRAN AND BE AS MY SON TO ME · · · ·   71 SOHRAB RUSTUM   331
THERE ARE NO YOUTHS IN IRAN BRAVE AS THOU · · ·   71 SOHRAB RUSTUM   333
AS ON SOME PARTRIDGE IN THE CORN A HAWK · · ·   73 SOHRAB RUSTUM   400
AND SPRANG ASIDE QUICK AS A FLASH THE SPEAR · ·   73 SOHRAB RUSTUM   403
LITHE AS THE GLANCING SNAKE AND THE CLUB CAME · ·   73 SOHRAB RUSTUM   418
BOY AS I AM I HAVE SEEN BATTLES TOO · · · ·   74 SOHRAB RUSTUM   433
TOGETHER AS TWO EAGLES ON ONE PREY · · · ·   75 SOHRAB RUSTUM   472
ROSE SUCH AS THAT THE SINEWY WOODCUTTERS · · ·   75 SOHRAB RUSTUM   476
AND OXUS CURDLED AS IT CROSSD HIS STREAM · · ·   76 SOHRAB RUSTUM   508
FOR WERE I MATCHD WITH TEN SUCH MEN AS THEE · ·   77 SOHRAB RUSTUM   544
AS WHEN SOME HUNTER IN THE SPRING HATH FOUND · ·   77 SOHRAB RUSTUM   556
AND PIERCED HER WITH AN ARROW AS SHE ROSE · · ·   78 SOHRAB RUSTUM   559
ECHO HER STORMY SCREAM AS SHE SAILS BY · · ·   78 SOHRAB RUSTUM   572
AS THAT POOR BIRD FLIES HOME NOR KNOWS HIS LOSS   78 SOHRAB RUSTUM   573
HE SPOKE AND AS HE CEASED HE WEPT ALOUD · · ·   79 SOHRAB RUSTUM   602
AND HIS SOUL SET TO GRIEF AS THE VAST TIDE · · ·   79 SOHRAB RUSTUM   616
AND ALL ITS BOUNDING RAPTURE AS AT DAWN · · ·   79 SOHRAB RUSTUM   620
PRICKD AS A CUNNING WORKMAN IN PEKIN · · · ·   81 SOHRAB RUSTUM   672
HIS HEAD AS IF INQUIRING WHAT THEIR GRIEF · · ·   82 SOHRAB RUSTUM   734
AS SOME ARE BORN TO BE OBSCURED AND DIE · · ·   84 SOHRAB RUSTUM   774
FEAR NOT AS THOU HAST SAID SOHRAB MY SON · · ·   84 SOHRAB RUSTUM   796
AS THOSE BLACK GRANITE PILLARS ONCE HIGH-REARD · ·   86 SOHRAB RUSTUM   860
AS OF A GREAT ASSEMBLY LOOSED AND FIRES · · ·   86 SOHRAB RUSTUM   869
WINDING SO HIGH THAT AS THEY MOUNT THEY PASS · ·   66 SOHRAB RUSTUM   V 163

AS   (CONTINUED)

AND DEAR AS THE WET FISHER TO THE EYES   .   .   .   .   69 SOHRAB RUSTUM   V 284
AND AS AFIELD THE REAPERS CUT A SWATHE   .   .   .   .   70 SOHRAB RUSTUM   V 293
AS SOME RICH LADY ON A WINTERS MORN   .   .   .   .   70 SOHRAB RUSTUM   V 302
AND OXUS CURDLED AS IT REACHD HIS STREAM   .   .   .   .   76 SOHRAB RUSTUM   V 508
FOR WERE I MATCHD WITH TEN SUCH MEN AS THOU   .   .   .   .   77 SOHRAB RUSTUM   V 544
AS THE LAW IS AND GO YOUR WAY   .   .   .   .   .   .   87 SICK KING BOKH   9
O VIZIER BE IT AS THOU SAYST   .   .   .   .   88 SICK KING BOKH   29
AS THE KING SAID SO IT WAS DONE   .   .   .   .   .   .   89 SICK KING BOKH   44
CARRIED BEFORE HIM AS IS RIGHT .   .   .   .   89 SICK KING BOKH   48
AS THEY WERE THIRSTY AND THE NIGHT   .   .   .   .   .   .   90 SICK KING BOKH   81
AS THE KING BADE SO WAS IT DONE   .   .   .   .   .   .   90 SICK KING BOKH   92
BUT SENTENCED HIM AS THE LAW IS   .   .   .   .   .   .   91 SICK KING BOKH   111
AND REMAIN KNEELING AS BEFORE   .   .   .   .   91 SICK KING BOKH   124
BUT BEING NOTHING AS HE IS   .   .   .   .   92 SICK KING BOKH   141
AS THE KING SAID SO WAS IT DONE   .   .   .   .   .   .   89 SICK KING BOKH   V 44
AS THE KING SAID SO WAS IT DONE   .   .   .   .   .   .   90 SICK KING BOKH   V 92
TO LIVE AS ERST YOUR DAILY LIFE IN HEAVEN   .   .   .   .   96 BALDER DEAD 1   36
AND EACH BESPAKE HIM AS HE LAID HIM DOWN   .   .   .   .   101 BALDER DEAD 1   215
HIM THE BLIND HODER MET AS HE CAME UP   .   .   .   .   101 BALDER DEAD 1   226
AND AS A SPRAY OF HONEYSUCKLE FLOWERS   .   .   .   .   101 BALDER DEAD 1   230
IN GARB IN FORM IN FEATURE AS HE WAS   .   .   .   .   .   .   103 BALDER DEAD 1   283
AND GAZED ON NANNA AS SHE SLEPT AND SPAKE   .   .   .   .   103 BALDER DEAD 1   287
AND AS THE WOODMAN SEES A LITTLE SMOKE   .   .   .   .   104 BALDER DEAD 1   335
BUT THE GODS WENT NOT NOW AS OTHERWHILE   .   .   .   .   105 BALDER DEAD 2   29
BUT AS WHEN COWHERDS IN OCTOBER DRIVE   .   .   .   .   107 BALDER DEAD 2   91
AND QUESTIOND HERMOD AS HE CAME AND SAID   .   .   .   .   107 BALDER DEAD 2   100
NOR SHOOK THE BRIDGE SO MUCH AS THOU ALONE   .   .   .   .   107 BALDER DEAD 2   106
AND AS THE SWALLOWS CROWD THE BULRUSH-BEDS   .   .   .   .   109 BALDER DEAD 2   157
WE DO NOT AS SOME FEEBLER HATERS DO   .   .   .   .   .   .   111 BALDER DEAD 2   228
HELA SUCH AS THOU SAYST THE TERMS SHALL BE   .   .   .   .   111 BALDER DEAD 2   242
THOU HEARST IF HEARING LIKE AS SPEECH IS THINE .   .   .   .   112 BALDER DEAD 2   251
BUT FEEBLY AS A VOICE FAR OFF HE SAID   .   .   .   .   112 BALDER DEAD 2   263
AND NOW I COUNT NOT OF THESE TERMS AS SAFE   .   .   .   .   112 BALDER DEAD 2   268
TO BE FULFILLD NOR MY RETURN AS SURE   .   .   .   .   112 BALDER DEAD 2   269
AND AS A TRAVELLER IN THE EARLY DAWN   .   .   .   .   .   .   113 BALDER DEAD 2   295
OF HEAVEN AND MIGHTILY AS WINGD HE FLEW   .   .   .   .   113 BALDER DEAD 2   303
LIKE AS A FARMER WHO HATH LOST HIS DOG   .   .   .   .   113 BALDER DEAD 3   8
AND LEAD AS ERST OUR DAILY LIFE IN HEAVEN   .   .   .   .   115 BALDER DEAD 3   56
AS AMONG THOSE WHOSE JOY AND WORK IS WAR   .   .   .   .   115 BALDER DEAD 3   81
BE YE THEN KIND AS BALDER TOO WAS KIND   .   .   .   .   116 BALDER DEAD 3   87
SUCH AS ON EARTH WE VALIANTLY HAVE WAGED   .   .   .   .   117 BALDER DEAD 3   139
BUT FAINTER AS THE STARS ROSE HIGH IT FLARED   .   .   .   .   119 BALDER DEAD 3   201
AND AS IN A DECAYING WINTER-FIRE   .   .   .   .   .   .   119 BALDER DEAD 3   203
AND AS IN WINTER WHEN THE FROST BREAKS UP   .   .   .   .   122 BALDER DEAD 3   307
LOOK AS IN SOME BOORS YARD A SWEET-BREATHD COW .   .   .   .   123 BALDER DEAD 3   340
AND AS SEAFARING MEN WHO LONG HAVE WROUGHT   .   .   .   .   123 BALDER DEAD 3   357
BUT AS HE ENTERD ON THE EXTREMEST BOUND   .   .   .   .   124 BALDER DEAD 3   381
HOVERING AND STOPPING OFT AS IF AFRAID   .   .   .   .   124 BALDER DEAD 3   383
HE SPAKE AND AS HE CEASED A PUFF OF WIND   .   .   .   .   126 BALDER DEAD 3   440
AS WHOLLY TO BE PITIED QUITE FORLORN   .   .   .   .   .   .   126 BALDER DEAD 3   458
BUT NOT TO ME SO GRIEVOUS AS I KNOW   .   .   .   .   .   .   127 BALDER DEAD 3   500
WHO THEN SHALL LIVE IN PEACE AS NOW IN WAR   .   .   .   .   128 BALDER DEAD 3   531
AND AS A STORK WHICH IDLE BOYS HAVE TRAPPD   .   .   .   .   129 BALDER DEAD 3   559
AND AS IN THE DARK NIGHT A TRAVELLING MAN   .   .   .   .   119 BALDER DEAD 3   V
BUT FAINTER AS THE STARS ROSE HIGH IT BURND   .   .   .   .   119 BALDER DEAD 3   V 201
AS THE DRIVEN SNOW ARE WHITE   .   .   .   .   131 TRISTRAM 1   31
SHE WHO AS THEY VOYAGED QUAFFD .   .   .   .   132 TRISTRAM 1   63
ONE SUCH KISS AS THOSE OF YORE .   .   .   .   132 TRISTRAM 1   78
AS HE WANDERS FAR FROM HERE   .   .   .   .   133 TRISTRAM 1   88
LET HER BE AS SHE WAS THEN   .   .   .   .   134 TRISTRAM 1   118
AS OF OLD SO LET HER BE .   .   .   .   134 TRISTRAM 1   125
AS HE STEERS HER OER THE SEA   .   .   .   .   134 TRISTRAM 1   128
LET HER AS SHE SITS ON BOARD   .   .   .   .   135 TRISTRAM 1   141
AS THEY FEEL THE FATAL BANDS   .   .   .   .   135 TRISTRAM 1   149
IDLE AS A MOSSY STONE   .   .   .   .   137 TRISTRAM 1   223
WE CANNOT KEEP HIM NOW AS THEN .   .   .   .   138 TRISTRAM 1   244
DANCES AS THE TRUMPETS BLOW   .   .   .   .   138 TRISTRAM 1   264
AS LITTLE AS DID SOLITUDE   .   .   .   .   139 TRISTRAM 1   293
AS LITTLE AS DID SOLITUDE   .   .   .   .   139 TRISTRAM 1   293
POOR CHILD THOU ART ALMOST AS PALE AS I   .   .   .   .   140 TRISTRAM 1   312
POOR CHILD THOU ART ALMOST AS PALE AS I   .   .   .   .   140 TRISTRAM 1   312
A LOOK AS IF THE HEART COMPLAINED   .   .   .   .   .   .   140 TRISTRAM 1   321
MAKES THEIR CHAMBER AS BRIGHT AS DAY   .   .   .   .   .   .   140 TRISTRAM 1   334
MAKES THEIR CHAMBER AS BRIGHT AS DAY   .   .   .   .   .   .   140 TRISTRAM 1   334
AS IF THEIR BABY-OWNER CHASED   .   .   .   .   141 TRISTRAM 1   347
THE BARE HEATHS SPREADING CLEAR AS DAY   .   .   .   .   141 TRISTRAM 1   364
AS HE MUTTERS BROKENLY .   .   .   .   133 TRISTRAM 1   V   93
AS PALE AND STILL AS WITHERD FLOWERS   .   .   .   .   .   .   147 TRISTRAM 2   127
AS PALE AND STILL AS WITHERD FLOWERS   .   .   .   .   .   .   147 TRISTRAM 2   127
A FRESHNESS BACK AS OF HER PRIME   .   .   .   .   .   .   147 TRISTRAM 2   142
COLD COLD AS THOSE WHO LIVED AND LOVED   .   .   .   .   149 TRISTRAM 2   192
AS ROOTED TO THE EARTH NOR SOUNDS   .   .   .   .   .   .   148 TRISTRAM 2   V
BUT STILL AS THEY PURSUED THEIR WARM DRY ROAD   .   .   .   .   150 TRISTRAM 3   44
SHE WOULD FIND ILL TO BEAR WEAK AS SHE IS   .   .   .   .   152 TRISTRAM 3   101
THESE ARE TO HER DEAR AS TO THEM THE TALES   .   .   .   .   152 TRISTRAM 3   106
CAN FORGET ALL TO HEAR THEM AS OF OLD   .   .   .   .   152 TRISTRAM 3   111
DEAR SAINTS IT IS NOT SORROW AS I HEAR   .   .   .   .   152 TRISTRAM 3   112
HIS MISTRESS USE HER EMPIRE AS SHE MAY   .   .   .   .   155 TRISTRAM 3   184
AND UP AS HIGH AS WHERE THEY STOOD TO LOOK   .   .   .   .   155 TRISTRAM 3   188

AS   (CONTINUED)

AND UP AS HIGH AS WHERE THEY STOOD TO LOOK   • • • •   155 TRISTRAM 3   188
AS IF TO ITSELF THE QUIET FOREST SMILED   • • • •   155 TRISTRAM 3   204
AND IN THAT DAISIED CIRCLE AS MEN SAY   • • • •   156 TRISTRAM 3   221
I FELT AS I IN TORMENT LAY   • • • •   157 SAINT BRANDAN   33
HE GAZED UPON ME AS I PASSD   • • • • • •   158 SAINT BRANDAN   49
FORGOT MY GOOD AS SOON AS DONE • • • • • • •   158 SAINT BRANDAN   60
FORGOT MY GOOD AS SOON AS DONE • • • • • • •,   158 SAINT BRANDAN   60
FORGOT MY DEED AS SOON AS DONE • • • • • • •   158 SAINT BRANDAN   V   60
FORGOT MY DEED AS SOON AS DONE • • • • • •   158 SAINT BRANDAN   V   60
O HUMAN SOUL AS LONG AS THOU CANST SO   • • • •   169 EAST LONDON   9
O HUMAN SOUL AS LONG AS THOU CANST SO   • • • •   169 EAST LONDON   9
CHRIST SOME ONE SAYS WAS HUMAN AS WE ARE   • • • •   170 BETTER PART   3
IF WE THEN TOO CAN BE SUCH MEN AS HE • • • •   171 BETTER PART   14
HAVE YET SO MUCH AS HEARD THIS SIMPLER LORE   • •   171 DIVINITY   12
YET WE HER MEMORY AS SHE PRAYD WILL KEEP   • • • •   173 MONICAS PRAYER   13
BUOYANT AS MORNING AND AS MORNING CLEAR   • • • •   175 PARTING   18
BUOYANT AS MORNING AND AS MORNING CLEAR   • • • •   175 PARTING   18
DISTRACTED AS A HOMELESS WIND   • • • •   179 FAREWELL   50
TO SEEM AS FREE FROM PRIDE AND GUILE • • • •   179 FAREWELL   63
AS GOOD AS GENEROUS AS THEY ARE   • • • •   179 FAREWELL   64
AS GOOD AS GENEROUS AS THEY ARE   • • • •   179 FAREWELL   64
AS GOOD AS GENEROUS AS THEY ARE   • • • •   179 FAREWELL   64
AS HAND IN HAND FACE EARTHLY LIFE   • • • •   179 FAREWELL   68
SHOULD BE AS SOON AS KINDLED COOLD   • • • •   182 TO MARG CONT   20
SHOULD BE AS SOON AS KINDLED COOLD   • • • •   182 TO MARG CONT   20
SCORN THEM AS BITTERLY AS SHE   • • • • • •   202 URANIA   16
SCORN THEM AS BITTERLY AS SHE   • • • • • •   202 URANIA   16
FOR THEY ARE HAPPY AS THEY ARE • • • • •   203 EUPHROSYNE   16
WHICH GLOWS AS IF THE MIDDLE AGE   • • • •   204 CALAIS SANDS   7
AS IS THE ETERNAL MOONLIT SNOW • • • • •   207 ON THE RHINE   3
AND AS THIS BRIMMD UNWRINKLED RHINE   • • • • •   208 ON THE RHINE   12
SO LET ME LIE AND CALM AS THEY • • • •   208 ON THE RHINE   16
COME AS THOU CAMST A THOUSAND TIMES   • • • •   208 LONGING   5
AS KIND TO OTHERS AS TO ME   • • • • •   208 LONGING   8
AS KIND TO OTHERS AS TO ME   • • • • •   208 LONGING   8
OR AS THOU NEVER CAMST IN SOOTH   • • • •   209 LONGING   9
AS KIND TO ALL THE REST AS ME   • • • • •   208 LONGING   V   8
AS KIND TO ALL THE REST AS ME   • • • • •   208 LONGING   V   8
THEN AS NOW THIS TREMULOUS EAGER BEING   • • •   210 SELF-DECEPTION   9
THEN AS NOW A POWER BEYOND OUR SEEING   • • •   210 SELF-DECEPTION   11
AND WE ARE HERE AS ON A DARKLING PLAIN   • • •   212 DOVER BEACH   35
MELLOWD AND SOFTEND AS WITH SUNSET-GLOW   • • •   212 GROWING OLD   14
AS FROM A HEIGHT WITH RAPT PROPHETIC EYES   • • •   212 GROWING OLD   17
HANGS DOWN HIS HEAD AS BEFORE   • • • •   214 NEW ROME   18
SOME AS PRISONERS DRAW BREATH   • • • •   216 LORDS MESSENGER   15
THE POET FEELS THE PAST AS WELL • • •   221 BACCHANALIA 2   66
ONE MORN AS THROUGH HYDE PARK WE WALKD   • • •   221 EPILOG LAOCOON   1
AS FROM THE KINGS OF SOUND ARE BLOWN   • • • •   222 EPILOG LAOCOON   34
THE SOFT-COUCHD CATTLE WERE AS FAIR   • • • •   222 EPILOG LAOCOON   43
AS THOSE WHICH PASTURED BY THE SEA   • • • •   222 EPILOG LAOCOON   44
THOSE CATTLE COUCHD OR AS THEY RISE   • • • •   222 EPILOG LAOCOON   53
SOUND AS OF WANDERING BREEZE BUT SOUND   • • •   223 EPILOG LAOCOON   75
CLEAR AS THE PAINTERS ART CAN DRESS   • • • •   225 EPILOG LAOCOON   134
SO DEEP AS THE MUSICIANS LORE   • • •   225 EPILOG LAOCOON   136
BUT CLEAR AS WORDS CAN MAKE REVEALING   • • • •   225 EPILOG LAOCOON   137
AND DEEP AS WORDS CAN FOLLOW FEELING   • • •   225 EPILOG LAOCOON   138
BUT NOT AS PAINTER CAN POURTRAY • • • •   226 EPILOG LAOCOON   182
BUT NOT AS THE MUSICIAN WELL   • • • •   226 EPILOG LAOCOON   184
NOR NO MUSICIAN MADE AS THEY   • • • •   227 EPILOG LAOCOON   202
AS THOSE THAT PASTURED BY THE SEA   • • • •   222 EPILOG LAOCOON   V   44
LOVELY AND SOFT AS A DREAM   • • • • •   228 YOUTH OF NATURE   3
NATURE IS FRESH AS OF OLD   • • • •   228 YOUTH OF NATURE   11
THEY ARE HERE I HEARD AS MEN HEARD   • • • •   230 YOUTH OF NATURE   75
AS SHE WAS IN HER MORNING OF SPRING   • • • •   231 YOUTH OF NATURE   112
OF HER EYES AS THEY RESTED ON THINE   • • • •   231 YOUTH OF NATURE   114
MUTE AS OF OLD DAYS FLEW   • • • •   233 YOUTH OF MAN   39
GROWS FROM SUCH SORROW AS THEIRS   • • • •   235 YOUTH OF MAN   100
AND WHEN IT FAILS FIGHT AS WE WILL WE DIE   • • •   236 PALLADIUM   23
LEAVE THEN THE CROSS AS YE HAVE LEFT CARVED GODS • •   237 PROGRESS   27
STILL STILL LET ME AS I GAZE UPON YOU   • • •   240 SELF-DEPENDENCE   11
WOULDST THOU BE AS THESE ARE LIVE AS THEY   • • •   240 SELF-DEPENDENCE   16
WOULDST THOU BE AS THESE ARE LIVE AS THEY   • • •   240 SELF-DEPENDENCE   16
REPELLENT AS THE WORLD BUT SEE • • • •   242 SUMMER NIGHT   5
AS CLEARLY AS AT NOON   • • • • • • • • •   242 SUMMER NIGHT   15
AS CLEARLY AS AT NOON   • • • • • • • • •   242 SUMMER NIGHT   15
AND AS YEAR AFTER YEAR   • • • • • •   243 SUMMER NIGHT   42
AS FROM AN INFINITELY DISTANT LAND   • • • •   247 BURIED LIFE   74
THINK OFTEN AS I HEAR THEM RAVE • • • •   249 KENSINGTON GARD   26
THINK SOMETIMES AS I HEAR THEM RAVE   • • • •   249 KENSINGTON GARD   26
THINK SADLY AS I HEAR THEM RAVE • • • •   KENSINGTON GARD V   26
AS WHAT HE SEES IS SO HAVE HIS THOUGHTS BEEN   • •   252 FUTURE   7
AS IS THE WORLD ON THE BANKS   • • • • • •   252 FUTURE   17
VAINLY DOES EACH AS HE GLIDES   • • • •   252 FUTURE   19
AS SHE WAS BY THE SOURCES OF TIME   • • • •   252 FUTURE   28
WHO IMAGINES HER FIELDS AS THEY LAY   • • •   252 FUTURE   29
WHO THINKS AS THEY THOUGHT   • • • •   252 FUTURE   31
NOW READS IN HER BOSOM AS CLEAR • • • •   252 FUTURE   35
AS REBEKAH READ WHEN SHE SATE   • • • •   252 FUTURE   36
AS DEEP AS PELLUCID A SPRING   • • • • •   252 FUTURE   39

AS   (CONTINUED)

AS DEEP AS PELLUCID A SPRING   252 FUTURE   39
OF FEELING AS TRANQUIL AS SURE   252 FUTURE   40
OF FEELING AS TRANQUIL AS SURE   252 FUTURE   40
WITH A PLAINNESS AS NEAR   253 FUTURE   44
AS FLASHING AS MOSES FELT   253 FUTURE   45
AS FLASHING AS MOSES FELT   253 FUTURE   45
ARE CONFUSED AS THE CRIES WHICH WE HEAR   253 FUTURE   56
CHANGING AND SHOT AS THE SIGHTS WHICH WE SEE   253 FUTURE   57
AS IT GROWS AS THE TOWNS ON ITS MARGE   253 FUTURE   72
AS IT GROWS AS THE TOWNS ON ITS MARGE   253 FUTURE   72
AS IT DRAWS TO THE OCEAN MAY STRIKE   254 FUTURE   81
AS THE PALE WASTE WIDENS AROUND HIM   254 FUTURE   83
AS THE BANKS FADE DIMMER AWAY   254 FUTURE   84
AS THE STARS COME OUT AND THE NIGHT-WIND   254 FUTURE   85
AND CAME AS MOST MEN DEEMD TO LITTLE GOOD   256 SCHOLAR-GIPSY   39
HIS MATES HAD ARTS TO RULE AS THEY DESIRED   256 SCHOLAR-GIPSY   45
AS THE PUNTS ROPE CHOPS ROUND   257 SCHOLAR-GIPSY   76
AND LIVING AS THOU LIVST ON GLANVILS PAGE   259 SCHOLAR-GIPSY   159
AND LIFE RAN GAILY AS THE SPARKLING THAMES   261 SCHOLAR-GIPSY   202
AVERSE AS DIDO DID WITH GESTURE STERN   261 SCHOLAR-GIPSY   208
FRESHEN THY FLOWERS AS IN FORMER YEARS   261 SCHOLAR-GIPSY   218
AS SOME GRAVE TYRIAN TRADER FROM THE SEA   262 SCHOLAR-GIPSY   232
AS THE SLOW PUNT SWINGS ROUND   257 SCHOLAR-GIPSY   V 76
HUMID THE AIR LEAFLESS YET SOFT AS SPRING   263 THYRSIS   17
WHERE ARE THE MOWERS WHO AS THE TINY SWELL   266 THYRSIS   127
THEY ALL ARE GONE AND THOU ART GONE AS WELL   266 THYRSIS   130
AND NIGHT AS WELCOME AS A FRIEND WOULD FALL   267 THYRSIS   150
AND NIGHT AS WELCOME AS A FRIEND WOULD FALL   267 THYRSIS   150
AS IN OLD DAYS JOVIAL AND TALKING RIDE   267 THYRSIS   154
MID CITY-NOISE NOT AS WITH THEE OF YORE   269 THYRSIS   232
AH MAY YE FEEL HIS VOICE AS WE   271 MEMORIAL VERSES   41
HE LAID US AS WE LAY AT BIRTH   271 MEMORIAL VERSES   48
ONCE MORE WE LAY AS ERST AT BIRTH   271 MEMORIAL VERSES V 48
AS THOUGH THE WIZARD MERLINS WILL   273 STANZAS CARNAC   7
AS IF THE WIZARD MERLINS WILL   273 STANZAS CARNAC   V   7
AS IF THE ENCHANTER MERLINS WILL   STANZAS CARNAC   V   7
AND TRANQUIL AS THE GLACIER-SNOWS   278 SOUTHERN NIGHT   90
THE DROWSY BEE AS OF OLD   285 HAWORTH CHURCH   120
RESTED AS UNDER THE BOUGHS   287 RUGBY CHAPEL   32
SUNSHINE AND RAIN AS WE MIGHT   287 RUGBY CHAPEL   34
PROMPT UNWEARIED AS HERE   287 RUGBY CHAPEL   48
STRIPPD WITHOUT FRIENDS AS WE ARE   289 RUGBY CHAPEL   121
NOT AS SERVANTS YE KNEW   291 RUGBY CHAPEL   164
HATH NOT AS YET IN ITS MARCH   291 RUGBY CHAPEL   169
FOLLOW YOUR STEPS AS YE GO   292 RUGBY CHAPEL   203
AH AS OF OLD FROM THE POMP   296 HEINES GRAVE   129
HAIL AS IT PASSES FROM EARTH   298 HEINES GRAVE   204
SUCH OF THY THOUGHTS AS THOU WILT   299 HEINES GRAVE   221
NOR YET TO AMUSE AS OURS ARE   300 GRANDE CHARTR   52
NOT AS THEIR FRIEND OR CHILD I SPEAK   301 GRANDE CHARTR   79
BUT AS ON SOME FAR NORTHERN STRAND   301 GRANDE CHARTR   80
AS IF THE WORLD HAD EVER HAD   302 GRANDE CHARTR   101
NOR YET TO AMUSE AS WORLDLINGS ARE   300 GRANDE CHARTR   V 52
THOUGH AS YOU READ YOU HEAR THE BELLS   307 OBERMANN   31
AS DEATH COMPOSED TO BEAR   309 OBERMANN   86
YES AS THE SON OF THETIS SAID   309 OBERMANN   89
THOU LEARNST TO THINK AS THEY   311 OBERMANN   148
THE CRACKLING HUSK-HEAPS BURN AS IF   312 OBERMANN MORE   11
THE WORLD AS IT WAS THEN   315 OBERMANN MORE   84
AND SHOOK AS IT RUSHD BY HER   319 OBERMANN MORE   204
AS WHEN THE PAST WAS NEW   320 OBERMANN MORE   240
DESPAIR NOT THOU AS I DESPAIRD   322 OBERMANN MORE   281
AS OUT OF SLEEP AND NO   323 OBERMANN MORE   326
THEIR CRACKLING HUSK-HEAPS BURN AS IF   312 OBERMANN MORE   V 11
FOLLOWS THE APPROACHING QUEEN WHO STOPS AS CALLD   332 MEROPE   64
AS I HAVE EVER FOUND THEE BENT TO KEEP   332 MEROPE   80
TOWRD THEE TOWARD THY SILENCE AS THY SPEECH   333 MEROPE   112
HENCEFORTH BE HONOURD AS THE DATE OF PEACE   333 MEROPE   116
HE HAD SMIT ME HAD HE BEEN SWIFT AS I   334 MEROPE   131
SHALL THEY NOT WEAR ONE HATRED OUT AS WELL   335 MEROPE   181
AS FROM A FASTNESS IN THE ROCKS OUR SCANT   337 MEROPE   247
DEEMING AS TYRANTS DEEM OUR SILENCE HATE   338 MEROPE   260
THOU HADST NO CAUSE AS FEIGND IN HIS MISRULE   338 MEROPE   283
INTO ONE PUISSANT FOLK AS HE DESIGND   338 MEROPE   290
SUCH CHANCE AS KILLD THE FATHER KILLD THE SONS   340 MEROPE   347
PRAY AS THOU POURST LIBATIONS ON THIS TOMB   342 MEROPE   382
GO AS IT WILL BUT IF THIS   348 MEROPE   536
AS THOSE WHEREWITH WE TRY TO TEST   352 MEROPE   634
AND AS WE ATE AND RESTED THERE WE TALKD   356 MEROPE   755
AS OF ONE SHADOWD BY IMPENDING DEATH   356 MEROPE   765
AND STRANGELY AS WE TALKD HE WOULD APPLY   356 MEROPE   766
EVEN AS THOSE DEAD UNEPITAPHD WHO LIE   356 MEROPE   772
WHERE AS LIFE EBBD HIS BEARERS LAID HIM DOWN   357 MEROPE   783
WASHD AS THE MARKS UPON THE HILLS STILL SHOW   358 MEROPE   815
CAUGHT THEM AS WIND TAKES FEATHERS WHIRLD THEM ROUND 358 MEROPE   824
ALL THIS O KING NOT PIECEMEAL AS TO THEE   358 MEROPE   827
BOATS AND APPROACH NEAR AS WE DARED THE CHASM   358 MEROPE   838
REFRESHMENT NEEDED BY THEE AS I JUDGE   359 MEROPE   867
AND SUCH AS FITS A ROYAL HOUSE TO SHOW   359 MEROPE   871

AS   (CONTINUED)

SWIFT AS I CAME HATH FALSEHOOD BEEN BEFORE   • • • • 363 MEROPE   954
AS MUCH TO THE KINGS WISH MORE TO HIS SHAME   • • 364 MEROPE   968
SUCH AS ERE NOW HATH SPURRD TO FEARFUL DEEDS   • • 366 MEROPE   1012
FAIN WOULD I FADE AWAY AS I HAVE LIVED   •   • • 366 MEROPE   1027
NO SOMETHING MUST BE DARED AND GREAT AS ERST   • • 367 MEROPE   1054
AS DEAD WE HELD THEE MOURND FOR THEE AS DEAD   • • 375 MEROPE   1208
AS DEAD WE HELD THEE MOURND FOR THEE AS DEAD   • • 375 MEROPE   1208
AS HITHERTO THEY KEPT HIM KEEP HIM NOW   •   • • 377 MEROPE   1226
FOR WHOM AS I SUPPOSE THOU PASSEST HERE   • • 379 MEROPE   1271
WHY WILT THOU FLY TO LOSE AS SOON AS FOUND   • • 381 MEROPE   1290
WHY WILT THOU FLY TO LOSE AS SOON AS FOUND   • • 381 MEROPE   1290
AND IF SO USED PROVES AS THOU SAYST UNSURE   • • 382 MEROPE   1341
HOW MIGHT NOT SUCH A SIGHT AS THIS REVIVE   •   • • 383 MEROPE   1358
WITH SUCH A DEED AS THIS THOU MATCHEST MINE   • • 385 MEROPE   1426
DEEP AS THOU CANST FOR HENCE NO SUCCOUR COMES   • • 386 MEROPE   1431
HERE AS I GUESS THE NOBLE LAIAS COMES   •   • • 386 MEROPE   1439
HEIRSHIP WITH FAIR INTENT AS I BELIEVE   • • 387 MEROPE   1484
MORE LOYAL AS OUR LINE CONTINUES MORE   • • 389 MEROPE   1541
AS OUR JUST CAUSE DESERVES I DO NOT FEAR   •   • • 391 MEROPE   1595
AS ERST THEY SHADOWD   • • • • • • •   •   • • 391 MEROPE   1600
THOUGH INJURED PAST FORGIVENESS AS MEN DEEM   • • 394 MEROPE   1707
THANKS TO HIM FOR OUR AMITY AS WELL   • •   •   • 395 MEROPE   1724
ALL THINGS BUT LIFE THOU LOSE NOT LIFE AS WELL   • • 396 MEROPE   1757
YET OH COULDST THOU BUT ACT AS REASON BIDS   •   • • 396 MEROPE   1762
UNARMD AND TRAVEL-SOILD JUST AS HE WAS   • • 401 MEROPE   1906
WHAT BLOOD SO MEET AS THINE TO WASH IT OUT   •   • • 402 MEROPE   1924
WHAT HAND TO STRIKE THEE MEET AS MINE THE HAND   • • 402 MEROPE   1925
THE SON TO PERISH AS YE LEFT THE SIRE   •   • • 402 MEROPE   1935
FOR FROM ALL SIDES A DELUGE AS IT SEEMD   • • 402 MEROPE   1937
OF DARING EASY AS IT SEEMS WHEN DONE   • • •   • • 403 MEROPE   1949
COULD FIND NO WAY TO FOUND THEM SURE AS THIS   • • 403 MEROPE   1960
INSCRUTABLE AS EVER SEE IT KEEPS   • •   •   • 403 MEROPE   1967
OF THE HERACLEIDAN CONQUERORS AS THOU SAIDST   • • 404 MEROPE   1982
OR DIDST THOU BUT AS CAUTIOUS SCHEMERS USE   • • 404 MEROPE   1984
AS THE CHIEFS RULE MY SON THE PEOPLE ARE   •   • • 404 MEROPE   2002
SO RULE THAT AS THY FATHER THOU BE LOVED   • • 404 MEROPE   2008
SO RULE THAT AS HIS FOE THOU BE OBEYD   •   • • 404 MEROPE   2009
FOLLOWS THE ISSUING QUEEN WHO STOPS AS CALLD   • • 332 MEROPE   V 64
TOWRDS THEE TOWARDS THY SILENCE AS THY SPEECH   • • 333 MEROPE   V 112
AS THOSE WITH WHICH WE TRY TO TEST   • • •   • • 352 MEROPE   V 634
AS THE CHIEFS RULE INDEED THE PEOPLE ARE   •   • • 404 MEROPE   V2002
SO RULE THAT AS THY FOE THOU BE OBEYD   • • 404 MEROPE   V2009
BUT IF AS MOST MEN SAY HE IS HALF MAD   • • • • 407 EMPEDOCLES I 1   23
TOUCHING THY HARP AS THE WHIM CAME ON THEE   • • 407 EMPEDOCLES I 1   33
ALMOST AS MUCH AS THE NEW DANCING-GIRL   •   • • 407 EMPEDOCLES I 1   35
ALMOST AS MUCH AS THE NEW DANCING-GIRL   •   • • 407 EMPEDOCLES I 1   35
AS I WAS LIFTING MY SOILD GARLAND OFF   • • 407 EMPEDOCLES I 1   40
PASSD YOU A LITTLE SINCE AS MORNING DAWND   • • 408 EMPEDOCLES I 1   46
AS DREW OF OLD THE PEOPLE AFTER HIM   •   • • 408 EMPEDOCLES I 1   63
TIS AS AN ORPHAN AMONG PROSPEROUS BOYS   • • 408 EMPEDOCLES I 1   71
AND HE WOULD TELL ME AS HIS OLD TRIED FRIEND   • • 410 EMPEDOCLES I 1   130
THOU ART AS CROSS AS SOURD AS HIMSELF   •   • • 411 EMPEDOCLES I 1   141
THOU ART AS CROSS AS SOURD AS HIMSELF   •   • • 411 EMPEDOCLES I 1   141
THOU ART AS CROSS AS SOURD AS HIMSELF   •   • • 411 EMPEDOCLES I 1   141
AS IF THE SKY WAS IMPIOUS NOT TO FALL   •   • • 411 EMPEDOCLES I 1   145
AS OF HIS GIFTED MASTER AND ONCE FRIEND   •   • • 411 EMPEDOCLES I 1   148
BUT CREDULOUS OF FABLES AS A GIRL   •   • • 411 EMPEDOCLES I 1   160
AS I HAVE PRAYD THEE THAT AND TO WHAT END   •   • • 412 EMPEDOCLES I 2   21
VISIT US AS THEY DO WITH SIGN AND PLAGUE   •   • • 413 EMPEDOCLES I 2   24
HOWBEIT I JUDGE AS LOST • • • • • • •   •   • • 415 EMPEDOCLES I 2   98
WHAT LIFE AND CHANCE GO HARD WITH THEE TOO AS WITH US 416 EMPEDOCLES I 2   116
TRUMPET IT AS THEY WILL IS BUT THE SAME AS THINE • • 417 EMPEDOCLES I 2   141
TRUMPET IT AS THEY WILL IS BUT THE SAME AS THINE • • 417 EMPEDOCLES I 2   141
AND SCEPTIC AS HE IS   • • • • • • •   •   • • 418 EMPEDOCLES I 2   170
AND BLENDS THEIR BLOODS AS THOSE • • • • •   • • 418 EMPEDOCLES I 2   189
BUT WE AS SOME RUDE GUEST • • • • • •   •   • • 419 EMPEDOCLES I 2   217
TO WORK AS BEST HE CAN • • • • • • •   •   • • 421 EMPEDOCLES I 2   269
AS CHILDREN OF WEAK AGE   • • • • • •   •   • • 421 EMPEDOCLES I 2   273
YET GRANT AS SENSE LONG MISSD • • • • •   •   • • 421 EMPEDOCLES I 2   282
BUT STILL AS WE PROCEED • • • • • • •   •   • • 423 EMPEDOCLES I 2   332
CLAIMS RAPTURE AS ITS RIGHT • • • • • • •   • • 424 EMPEDOCLES I 2   353
STILL HUNGRIER FOR DELIGHT AS DELIGHTS GROW MORE RARE 424 EMPEDOCLES I 2   371
HOW HIS BROW LIGHTEND AS THE MUSIC ROSE   • • 428 EMPEDOCLES I 2   483
WHAT LIFE AND TIME GO HARD WITH THEE TOO AS WITH US   416 EMPEDOCLES I 2 V 116
TO FIGHT AS BEST HE CAN   • • • • • •   •   • • 421 EMPEDOCLES I 2 V 269
AS VIRGINAL AND SWEET AS OURS   • • • • •   • • 426 EMPEDOCLES I 2 V 434
AS VIRGINAL AND SWEET AS OURS   • • • • •   • • 426 EMPEDOCLES I 2 V 434
AS HE LETS HIS LAX RIGHT HAND • • • • •   •   • • 431 EMPEDOCLES II   71
AS THE WELL-COUNSELLD ZEUS OPPRESSD • • • •   • • 432 EMPEDOCLES II   102
AS THE SKY-BRIGHTENING SOUTH-WIND CLEARS THE DAY • • 432 EMPEDOCLES II   121
AS THEY ARE DEAD TO ME   • • • • • • •   •   • • 437 EMPEDOCLES II   275
AS OF OLD IN THE FIELDS OF HEAVEN • • • •   • • 437 EMPEDOCLES II   278
OH THAT MY SOUL WERE FULL OF LIGHT AS THE STARS • • 438 EMPEDOCLES II   325
AND THEY WILL BE OUR LORDS AS THEY ARE NOW   •   • • 439 EMPEDOCLES II   351
AND WE SHALL BE UNSATISFIED AS NOW   • • •   • • 439 EMPEDOCLES II   355
AS IF THE REIGN OF JOY DID NOW BEGIN   • • •   • • 445 WESTMIN ABBEY   40
AND AS YEARS SPED THE MINSTER-AISLES DIVINE   • • 445 WESTMIN ABBEY   55
EVEN AS MY FATHER THOU   • • • • • • •   •   • • 449 WESTMIN ABBEY   167
EVEN AS THAT LOVED THAT WELL-RECORDED FRIEND   • • 449 WESTMIN ABBEY   168

AS   (CONTINUED)
              AND BE AS IF THOU NEER HADST BEEN   . . . . 451 GEISTS GRAVE   40
              AND THOU SHALT LIVE AS LONG AS WE   . . . . 451 GEISTS GRAVE   58
              AND THOU SHALT LIVE AS LONG AS WE   . . . . 451 GEISTS GRAVE   58
              BUT AS AGE COMES ON I KNOW   . . . . 454 POOR MATTHIAS   77
              WAS IT AS THE GRECIAN SINGS   . . . . 456 POOR MATTHIAS   131
              AS THEY SHOW AND DISAPPEAR   . . . . 456 POOR MATTHIAS   146
              OTHERS THERE ARE AS DEATHLESS FULL AS THEY . . . . . 462 ALARIC AT ROME   9
              OTHERS THERE ARE AS DEATHLESS FULL AS THEY . . . . . 462 ALARIC AT ROME   9
              THOU THAT HAST GAZED AS THE WORLD HURRIED BY   . . . 463 ALARIC AT ROME   23
              BUT FULL AND DEATHLESS AS THE DEEP DARK HUE   . . . 463 ALARIC AT ROME   35
              WHILE FULL AND CEASELESS AS THE OCEAN ROLL . . . . 464 ALARIC AT ROME   71
              AS TOWERED ON HIGH ABOVE THEIR MOONLIT ROAD   . . . 466 ALARIC AT ROME   113
              AND AS THE PAGEANT SWEPT BEFORE THEIR EYES . . . . 467 ALARIC AT ROME   122
              SO STERN A LESSON AS NECESSITY   . . . . 467 ALARIC AT ROME   142
              AND LO THE ETERNAL CITY AS THEY RISE   . . . . . 468 ALARIC AT ROME   155
              MOURNING AS WIDOWED VENICE OER HER ADRIAN TIDE   . . 468 ALARIC AT ROME   162
              AS THEY LOOKED STERNLY ON BEHELD NEW VICTORIES   . . 468 ALARIC AT ROME   174
              BUT AS ONE VOICELESS BLANK A PLACE OF GRAVES   . . 469 ALARIC AT ROME   182
              HOW BOTH WERE HASTENING AS THEY FLOWERED AND GREW   469 ALARIC AT ROME   189
              LIT WITH NO RAPTURE AS THE STORM SWEPT BY   . . . . 472 CROMWELL   22
              SOUNDS SUCH AS ERST THE LONE WAYFARING MAN . . . . 473 CROMWELL   39
              CAUGHT AS HE JOURNEYED FROM THE LIPS OF PAN   . . 473 CROMWELL   40
              THEN SLOWLY BRIGHTEND AS THE DAYS HAD FLOWN . . . 474 CROMWELL   76
              CRUSHD AS THEY ROSE BY MANHOODS STERNER WILL   . . 474 CROMWELL   80
              RANG AS HE TRODE THEM WITH THE VOICE OF WAR   . . 476 CROMWELL   152
              THERE AS HE GAZED A WONDROUS BAND THEY CAME   . . 476 CROMWELL   163
              STILL AS HE GAZD THE PHANTOMS MOURNFUL GLANCE   . . 477 CROMWELL   193
              THEN FROM THOSE WHITENING LIPS AS DEATH DREW NEAR   . 478 CROMWELL   213
              A LIFE THAT WAS NOT AS THE LIFE OF MAN   . . . . 478 CROMWELL   220
              AND LONELY AS A TRUANT CHILD   . . . . 479 HAYSWATER BOAT   3
              THE OARS HAVE MOULDERD AS THEY LAY   . . . . . 480 HAYSWATER BOAT   38
              OUR BANE DISGUISE IT AS WE MAY   . . . . 482 COURAGE   25
              AS LIGHT OF WHAT WE THINK WE FEEL THERE FLOWS   . . 483 BELOW SURFACE   3
              UNWEARIED AS FROM LAND TO LAND   . . . . 484 ROME-SICKNESS   29
              AS THY GRIEF WHEN IN TEARS SOME BRAZEN-COATED ACHAIAN   HOMER TRANS   27
              AND SOME MAN MAY SAY AS HE LOOKS AND SEES THY   HOMER TRANS   32
                  TEARS FALLING
              SUDDEN HE BOWD HIS HEAD AND ALL HIS MANE AS HE BOWD IT   HOMER TRANS   44
              TO ME IT SEEMS AS VAIN LUCRETIUS   . . . .   LUCRETIUS 3   1
              OF MENTAL NATURE AS FOR HIM TO FRET   . . . . .   LUCRETIUS 3   3
              BOTH HE MUST KEEP TORMENT HIM AS THEY MAY   . . . .   LUCRETIUS 3   V   7
              SOON SEEMS AS TEDIOUS AS EACH TEDIOUS STAGE   . .   LUCRETIUS 6   4
              SOON SEEMS AS TEDIOUS AS EACH TEDIOUS STAGE   . .   LUCRETIUS 6   4
              THIS MORN AS EVER   . . . .   EVERLASTING SUB   7

ASCENDED
              ASCENDED WITH UNDAUNTED HEART   . . . . 399 MEROPE   1833

ASCENDENCY
              WAS POLICY OF STATE THE ASCENDENCY   . . . . . . 404 MEROPE   1981

ASCENDING
              ASCENDING PURE THE BELL-LIKE FAME   . . . . . . 219 BACCHANALIA 2   15

ASCENDS
              UNHEARD ALL DAY ASCENDS AGAIN   . . . . 217 BACCHANALIA 1   3

ASCENT
              FORTH FROM THE EAST UP THE ASCENT OF HEAVEN   . . 105 BALDER DEAD 2   1

ASGARD
              IN ODINS HALL AND WENT THROUGH ASGARD STREETS   . . 97 BALDER DEAD 1   73
              TO ASGARD AND DECLARST THIS HIDDEN WAY   . . . 100 BALDER DEAD 1   190
              AND BACK ALONG THE BEACH TO ASGARD WENT   . . . 101 BALDER DEAD 1   200
              BUT NIGHT CAME DOWN AND DARKEND ASGARD STREETS . . 101 BALDER DEAD 1   202
              WHICH HE IN ASGARD BUILT HIM THERE TO DWELL   . . 101 BALDER DEAD 1   224
              TO ASGARD AND THE STARS CAME OUT IN HEAVEN . . . 102 BALDER DEAD 1   256
              HIGH OVER ASGARD TO LIGHT HOME THE KING   . . . 102 BALDER DEAD 1   257
              AND SWIFT TO ASGARD TO THE GATE HE CAME   . . . 102 BALDER DEAD 1   259
              ALONG THE FLINTY FLOOR OF ASGARD STREETS   . . . 102 BALDER DEAD 1   261
              ASGARD AND LED THEIR HORSES TO THE BEACH   . . . 106 BALDER DEAD 2   66
              FAR HENCE IN ASGARD IN THE CITY OF GODS   . . . 108 BALDER DEAD 2   114
              WHO SEE THE LIGHT AND BLEST IN ASGARD DWELL   . . 112 BALDER DEAD 2   255
              AND HERMOD SAW THE TOWERS OF ASGARD RISE   . . . 113 BALDER DEAD 2   304
              IN ASGARD AND THE GOLDEN HALLS WERE DUMB   . . . 113 BALDER DEAD 2   306
              IN ASGARD BUT THE GOLDEN HALLS WERE DUMB   . . . 113 BALDER DEAD 2   V 306
              TO ASGARD AND SATE DOWN IN ODINS HALL   . . . 119 BALDER DEAD 3   208
              AND ASGARD THOU DIDST BUILD AND MIDGARD FORT   . . 121 BALDER DEAD 3   266
              NO MORE TO ASGARD SHALT THOU COME NOR LODGE   . . 126 BALDER DEAD 3   448
              THE SECOND ASGARD WITH ANOTHER NAME   . . . . . 128 BALDER DEAD 3   521

ASGARDS
              THE DAY WILL COME WHEN FALL SHALL ASGARDS TOWERS   . . 127 BALDER DEAD 3   487
              THE DAY WILL COME WHEN ASGARDS TOWERS SHALL FALL   . . 127 BALDER DEAD 3   V 487

ASH
              AND THE FRAIL SCARLET-BERRIED ASH BEGAN   . . . . 25 DREAM   9
              BY THE ASH IGDRASIL IN IDAS PLAIN   . . . . . 105 BALDER DEAD 2   33
              THE BODIES WERE CONSUMED ASH CHOKED THE PILE   . . 119 BALDER DEAD 3   202
              TO THE ASH IGDRASIL AND IDAS PLAIN   . . . . . 120 BALDER DEAD 3   217

ASH   (CONTINUED)
        THE SWEET BLUE EYES THE SOFT ASH-COLOURD HAIR   • • 175 PARTING   37

ASHAMED
        NEITHER EXULTING NOR ASHAMED I STAND • • • • • • 398 MEROPE   1788

ASHES
        WHERE RED-BERRIED ASHES FRINGE • • • • • •   • • 190 STRAYED REVEL   146
        THY DEAR WIFES ASHES BURIED ARE   • • • • • •   • • 277 SOUTHERN NIGHT   51
        AND THE STRAIGHT ASHES GROW FOR SPEARS   • • • 414 EMPEDOCLES I 2   65
        TO MOAT THIS ISLE OF ASHES FROM THE WORLD   • • • • 438 EMPEDOCLES II   310
        THAT HOLDS THE ASHES OF YOUR HERO-DEAD   • • • 467 ALARIC AT ROME   136

ASHORE
        OF HIS PALE WIFE WHO WAITS AND WEEPS ASHORE   • •   69 SOHRAB RUSTUM   V 285
        AND SETS HIS FREIGHT ASHORE ON THORNEY STRAND   • • 445 WESTMIN ABBEY   30

ASHTREE
        OF WISDOM WHICH BENEATH THE ASHTREE SPRINGS   • • 120 BALDER DEAD 3   220

ASIA
        FAR HENCE IN ASIA • • • • • • • • • • • •   50 CONSOLATION   11

ASIAN
        SAW THE WIDE PROSPECT AND THE ASIAN FEN   • • • •   2 TO A FRIEND   3

ASIDE
        AND SPRANG ASIDE QUICK AS A FLASH THE SPEAR   • •   73 SOHRAB RUSTUM   403
        ONE STROKE BUT AGAIN SOHRAB SPRANG ASIDE   • • •   73 SOHRAB RUSTUM   417
        THE GOLDEN MACE-BEARERS ASIDE   • • • • • •   • •   88 SICK KING BOKH   34
        SHE SPAKE AND STEPPD ASIDE AND LEFT HIM ROOM   • • 108 BALDER DEAD 2   135
        ROLLD HEAVILY THE LEADEN MIST ASIDE   • • • • • 126 BALDER DEAD 3   441
        NOR LIGHTNINGS GO ASIDE   • • • • • • • • • 420 EMPEDOCLES I 2   254

ASK
        WE ASK AND ASK THOU SMILEST AND ART STILL   • • • •   2 SHAKESPEARE   2
        WE ASK AND ASK THOU SMILEST AND ART STILL   • • • •   2 SHAKESPEARE   2
        SHALL I ASK WHAT FADED MOURNER • • • • • •   • •   35 NEW SIRENS   273
        THESE FAUSTA ASK NOT THIS NOR THOU   • • • •   • •   53 RESIGNATION   38
        TIMES CHAFING PRISONER ASK IT NOW   • • • •   • •   53 RESIGNATION   39
        ASK NOT TO AMUSE BUT TO SET FREE   • • • •   • •   59 RESIGNATION   242
        COME THEN HEAR NOW AND GRANT ME WHAT I ASK   • • •   62 SOHRAB RUSTUM   54
        TO HELAS KINGDOM TO ASK BALDER BACK   • • • • 102 BALDER DEAD 1   237
        TO HELAS KINGDOM TO ASK BALDER BACK   • • • • 106 BALDER DEAD 2   46
        WROUGHT BY THE GODS AND ASK THE GODS OUR AID   • • 111 BALDER DEAD 2   226
        SHE WILL NOT ASK OF ALIENS BUT OF FRIENDS   • • • 170 WEST LONDON   10
        THEY ASK NOT KINDNESS GENTLE WAYS   • • • •   • • 178 FAREWELL   25
        THEY ASK A SOUL WHICH NEVER SWAYS   • • • •   • • 178 FAREWELL   27
        THEY ASK A SOUL THAT NEVER SWAYS   • • • •   • • 178 FAREWELL   V 27
        NAY ASK HIM • • • • • • • • • • • • 188 STRAYED REVEL   98
        WHY SHOULD THEY ASK IF TRUTH BE THERE   • • • • 203 EUPHROSYNE   4
        THESE ASK NO LOVE THESE PLIGHT NO FAITH   • • • 203 EUPHROSYNE   15
        THEY WILL NOT ASK IF TRUTH BE THERE   • • • • 203 EUPHROSYNE   V 4
        THEY SHOULD NOT ASK IF TRUTH BE THERE   • • • • 203 EUPHROSYNE   V 4
        ASK NOT MY NAME O FRIEND   • • • • • •   • • 217 NAMELESS EPIT   1
        ASK HOW SHE VIEWD THY SELF-CONTROL   • • • • 241 MORALITY   15
        I ASK NOT THAT MY BED OF DEATH • • • • • •   • • 249 WISH   1
        I ASK NOT EACH KIND SOUL TO KEEP   • • • •   • • 250 WISH   5
        I ASK BUT THAT MY DEATH MAY FIND   • • • •   • • 250 WISH   9
        ASK BUT THE FOLLY OF MANKIND   • • • • • •   • • 250 WISH   11
        I ASK IF THOU HAST PASSD THEIR QUIET PLACE   • • • 257 SCHOLAR-GIPSY   65
        DOST THOU ASK PROOF OUR TREE YET CROWNS THE HILL   • 269 THYRSIS   239
        QUIET TO ASK FOR CLOSED   • • • • • • • • 293 HEINES GRAVE   17
        THEY DO NOT ASK WHO PINED UNSEEN   • • • •   • • 311 OBERMANN   153
        SUCH ARE THEIR HOPES I ASK NOT IF BY THEE   • • • 334 MEROPE   147
        FOR ASK AT ARGOS ASK IN LACEDAEMON   • • • •   • • 338 MEROPE   284
        FOR ASK AT ARGOS ASK IN LACEDAEMON   • • • •   • • 338 MEROPE   284
        I ASK THEE NOT TO APPROVE THY HUSBANDS DEATH   • • 340 MEROPE   338
        AN AVENGER I ASK NOT SEND ME MY SON   • • • 348 MEROPE   544
        WHO SADLY ASK ME WHAT IF NOT REVENGE   • • • • 367 MEROPE   1039
        AND ARCAS BUT I TREMBLE BOLDLY ASK   • • • • 375 MEROPE   1211
        I ASK IF BLOODLESS MEANS MAY GAIN HIS END   • • • 387 MEROPE   1465
        FOR THE LAST TIME I ASK ASK EARNESTLY   • • • 394 MEROPE   1717
        FOR THE LAST TIME I ASK ASK EARNESTLY   • • • 394 MEROPE   1717
        AND ASK IF SOMETIMES   • • • • • • • • 398 MEROPE   1798
        MIGHT ASK WHY WE ENDURED THEIR YOKE SO LONG   • • 402 MEROPE   1947
        BLOOD I ASK NOT ENOUGH   • • • • • • • • 348 MEROPE   V
        ASK NOT THE LATEST NEWS OF THE LAST MIRACLE   • • 415 EMPEDOCLES I 2   106
        ASK NOT WHAT DAYS AND NIGHTS   • • • •   • • • 416 EMPEDOCLES I 2   107
        BUT ASK HOW THOU SUCH SIGHTS   • • • • • •   • • 416 EMPEDOCLES I 2   109
        ASK WHAT MOST HELPS WHEN KNOWN THOU SON OF ANCHITUS 416 EMPEDOCLES I 2   111
        SINK IN THYSELF THERE ASK WHAT AILS THEE AT   417 EMPEDOCLES I 2   146
                THAT SHRINE
        QUICK RAISED TO ASK WHICH WAY WE GO   • • • • 451 GEISTS GRAVE   50
        ASK OF THE POWERS THAT SPORT WITH MAN   • • • 481 DESTINY   4
        ASK WHERE NOW THOSE NIGHTINGALES ARE SINGING   • • 482 THEKLAS ANSWER   5

ASKANCE
        BUT RUSTUM EYED ASKANCE THE KNEELING YOUTH • • • •   71 SOHRAB RUSTUM   345

ASKD
WHO ASKD THE PASSERS-BY FOR AID   • • • • • •   157 SAINT BRANDAN   39
ASKD AN OUTFIT FOR ITS EARTHLY ROAD   • • • • • •   209 SELF-DECEPTION   8
THOU LEAPEST TO THY DEED AND HAST NOT ASKD   • • • •   384 MEROPE   1388
I ASKD HIM OF PANTHEIA YESTERDAY   • • • • • •   410 EMPEDOCLES I 1   126
AND ASKD NOT WISDOM   • • • • • • • •   432 EMPEDOCLES II   115
TRIBUTE ASKD BY THEE A VERSE   • • • • • • •   453 POOR MATTHIAS   V 18

ASKING
WEARY OF MYSELF AND SICK OF ASKING   • • • • • •   239 SELF-DEPENDENCE   1

ASKS
IT ASKS A REST IF NOT MORE DEEP   • • • • • •   22 YOUTH AND CALM   V 20
AGE-BOWD ASKS ALMS   • • • • • • • •   51 CONSOLATION   30
FOR IF I NOW CONFESS THIS THING HE ASKS   • • • •   71 SOHRAB RUSTUM   349
AND WHAT ASKS CUPID WILL SAVE US   • • • • • •   214 NEW ROME   V 9
AND WHAT ASKS CUPID IS COMING   • • • • • •   214 NEW ROME   V 9
PERISH AND NO ONE ASKS   • • • • • • • •   288 RUGBY CHAPEL   67
MORE THAN HE ASKS WHAT WAVES   • • • • • • •   288 RUGBY CHAPEL   69
OUR STORM-BEAT FIGURES AND ASKS   • • • • • •   289 RUGBY CHAPEL   114
IMPIOUS I DEEM THE ALLIANCE WHICH HE ASKS   • • • •   348 MEROPE   550
AND ASKS WHAT AILS HIM SO AND GETS WHAT CURE HE CAN   416 EMPEDOCLES I 2   131
WHO ASKS THIS FINAL SERVICE AT YOUR HANDS   • • •   429 EMPEDOCLES II   28

ASKST
WHO PROP THOU ASKST IN THESE BAD DAYS MY MIND   • •   2 TO A FRIEND   1
WHERE I AM THOU ASKST AND WHERE I WENDED   • • • •   482 THEKLAS ANSWER   1

ASLAUGA
AND SAW MY SHEPHERDESS ASLAUGA TEND   • • • • • •   117 BALDER DEAD 3   149

ASLEEP
WHEREIN WE LIE ASLEEP   • • • • • • • •   38 STAGIRIUS   11
AH NO SHE IS ASLEEP IN CORNWALL NOW   • • • • •   139 TRISTRAM 1   301
IN TYNTAGIL SHE IS ASLEEP IN CORNWALL NOW   • • •   139 TRISTRAM 1   V 301
THAT KNIGHTS ASLEEP AND AT HER PRAYER   • • • •   149 TRISTRAM 2   180
WHERE THE WINDS ARE ALL ASLEEP   • • • • • •   162 FORSAKEN MERM   36
ASLEEP IN THE ARCADIAN GLENS AT NOON   • • • •   372 MEROPE   1160
ASLEEP ON THE HILLS   • • • • • • • •   442 EMPEDOCLES II   436
ASLEEP YET LENDING HALF AN EAR   • • • • • • •   452 GEISTS GRAVE   69

ASOPUS
ASOPUS BANK   • • • • • • • • • • •   190 STRAYED REVEL   138
ASOPUS GLEAM ROCK-HEMMD   • • • • • • • •   197 FRAG ANTIGONE   63

ASPECT
MATCH THAT FUNEREAL ASPECT WITH HER PALL   • • • •   43 GIPSY CHILD   45
LIKE THESE AND IN ONE ASPECT BROUGHT   • • • • •   223 EPILOG LAOCOON   56
THE ASPECT OF THE MOMENT SHOW   • • • • •   225 EPILOG LAOCOON   131
THE ASPECT NOT I GRANT EXPRESS   • • • • •   225 EPILOG LAOCOON   133
THOU COME WITH ASPECT MARRD   • • • • • • •   322 OBERMANN MORE   302
ITS SOMBRE ASPECT OF MAJESTIC CARE   • • • • •   403 MEROPE   1968

ASPIRE
THERE BADE ME GAZE AND THERE ASPIRE   • • • • • •   301 GRANDE CHARTR   70

ASSAILD
UPBRAIDINGS OFTEN ASSAILD   • • • • • • •   294 HEINES GRAVE   71
THEN GORGED AND HELPLESS BE ASSAILD AND SLAIN   • •   339 MEROPE   298

ASSAILED
ROSE AND WITH FIRE AND SWORD ASSAILED MY HOUSE   • •   340 MEROPE   344

ASSAILS
THE DOUBT THAT ASSAILS ALL THINGS NEVER WON   • •   FRAGMENT 8   3

ASSAULT
TO FEAR ASSAULT OF ENVIOUS GODS   • • • • • •   197 FRAG ANTIGONE   81
VAINLY YOU HEDGE HIM FROM THE ASSAULT OF HARM   • •   359 MEROPE   855

ASSAY
DOST THOU ONCE MORE ASSAY   • • • • • • • •   201 PHILOMELA   22

ASSAYD
HERE TOO OUR SHEPHERD-PIPES WE FIRST ASSAYD   • •   263 THYRSIS   35

ASSEMBLAGE
A GENERAL ASSEMBLAGE OF THE REALM   • • • • • •   338 MEROPE   263

ASSEMBLING
THERE RE-ASSEMBLING WE SHALL SEE EMERGE   • • • •   128 BALDER DEAD 3   527

ASSEMBLY
AS OF A GREAT ASSEMBLY LOOSED AND FIRES   • • • •   86 SOHRAB RUSTUM   869

ASSENTING
HE SPAKE AND ALL THE GODS ASSENTING WAILD   • • • •   116 BALDER DEAD 3   89

ASSERTED
SURELY IF RIGHTS MAY BE BY FORCE ASSERTED   • • • •   352 MEROPE   656

```
ASSERTING
      IMPERIOUS SELF-ASSERTING VIOLENCE      •  •  •  •  •  •  353 MEROPE                 689

ASSIGND
      ASSIGND US BY THE ACTOR BE THE TRUE ONE      •  •  •  •  352 MEROPE                 648

ASSIST
      ASSIST ME TO RULE MILDLY LET US JOIN •  •  •  •  •  •  335 MEROPE                   164

ASSOILD
      BUT FOR THY CHILDRENS DEATH I STAND ASSOILD      •  •  340 MEROPE                   342

ASSUAGE
      REVOKE ASSUAGE HER SENTENCE      •  •  •  •  •  •  •  •  398 MEROPE                1807

ASSUME
      ASSUME THE ENSIGNS OF MY FATHERS POWER      •  •  •  •  405 MEROPE                2020

ASSURANCE
      FIND ASSURANCE IN TO-MORROW      •  •  •  •  •  •  •  •   31 NEW SIRENS             165
      WHERE YOU WHISPER IS ASSURANCE •  •  •  •  •  •  •  •     META CLOISTER            21

ASSURD
      FOR THAT DAY WILL COME MY SOUL IS ASSURD OF ITS COMING    HOMER TRANS              20

ASSURE
      MAIDENS ASSURE ME IF THEY TOLD ME TRUE      •  •  •  •  354 MEROPE                  703
      WHO ASSURE US SUNDERING POWERS •  •  •  •  •  •  •  •  •  457 POOR MATTHIAS         171

ASSURING
      THAT THE ONE LORE THATS ASSURING      •  •  •  •  •  •     SECOND BEST           V  21

ASTERN
      STANDS AT THE PROW AND GUIDES THEM BUT ASTERN      •  •  191 STRAYED REVEL         190

ASTONISHD
      BACK THROUGH THE ASTONISHD TRIBES OF DEAD TO HEAVEN      112 BALDER DEAD 2         285

ASTRAY
      AND BE ASTRAY FOR EVER SLAVE OF SENSE      •  •  •  •  440 EMPEDOCLES II          390
      OF MEN WITH MIND THUS DARKEND AND ASTRAY      •  •  •  •  446 WESTMIN ABBEY         68
      OF MEN WHOSE MINDS WERE DARKEND AND ASTRAY      •  •  •  446 WESTMIN ABBEY       V  68

ATE
      WAILING NO MORE IN SILENCE ATE AND DRANK      •  •  •   97 BALDER DEAD 1           70
      AND ATE THE SHRIVELLING SAILS BUT STILL THE SHIP •  •  119 BALDER DEAD 3          191
      ALL NIGHT THEY ATE THE BOAR SERIMNERS FLESH      •  •  119 BALDER DEAD 3          210
      AND AS WE ATE AND RESTED THERE WE TALKD      •  •  •  •  356 MEROPE               755

ATHENS
      GERMANY FRANCE CHRIST MOSES ATHENS ROME      •  •  •  168 RACHEL 3                 12
      WHEN THEBES WHEN ATHENS DARED NOT WHO IN ARMS      •  •  337 MEROPE               225

ATHIRST
      THOU WAST ATHIRST AND DIDST NOT SEE      •  •  •  •  •   94 SICK KING BOKH         210
      THOU WERT ATHIRST AND DIDST NOT SEE      •  •  •  •  •   94 SICK KING BOKH       V 210

ATLANTEAN
      ATLANTEAN THE LOAD •  •  •  •  •  •  •  •  •  •  •  •  295 HEINES GRAVE             94

ATLANTIC
      BEATING FROM THE ATLANTIC SEA      •  •  •  •  •  •  •  131 TRISTRAM 1              34
      NOT THIS FIERCE ATLANTIC DEEP •  •  •  •  •  •  •  •  •  133 TRISTRAM 1             92
      OUR SNOWDROP BY THE ATLANTIC SEA      •  •  •  •  •  •  136 TRISTRAM 1             196
      BY THE GREY ATLANTIC SEA •  •  •  •  •  •  •  •  •  •  137 TRISTRAM 1              231
      THE UNQUIET BRIGHT ATLANTIC PLAIN      •  •  •  •  •  148 TRISTRAM 2              174
      BORE UP FROM WHERE THE BRIGHT ATLANTIC GLEAMS      •  •  151 TRISTRAM 3            53
      CAME IN FROM WHERE THE BRIGHT ATLANTIC GLEAMS      •  •     TRISTRAM 3          V  53
      TO WHERE THE ATLANTIC RAVES      •  •  •  •  •  •  •  262 SCHOLAR-GIPSY           246
      IT LAY BESIDE THE ATLANTIC WAVE      •  •  •  •  •  •  273 STANZAS CARNAC           6
      AND BEYOND THAT THE ATLANTIC WIDE      •  •  •  •  •  274 STANZAS CARNAC          29
      HE ENTERS NOT THE ATLANTIC MAIN      •  •  •  •  •  •  275 STANZAS CARNAC          40

ATLAS
      NEAR WHERE ATLAS HATH HIS STAND      •  •  •  •  •  •     PILLARS UNIVERS           2

ATONE
      AND HE IS LOST AND THOU HAST THAT TO ATONE •  •  •  •  368 MEROPE                1070

ATONED
      MY DEED IS OF OLD DATE AND LONG ATONED      •  •  •  •  396 MEROPE               1768
      ATONED THIS VERY DAY PERHAPS IT IS      •  •  •  •  •  397 MEROPE               1769
      THINKING ATONED-FOR      •  •  •  •  •  •  •  •  •  •  400 MEROPE               1872

ATOP
      AND FROM THE FLUTED SPINE ATOP A PLUME      •  •  •  •   69 SOHRAB RUSTUM          268

ATOSSA
      GREAT ATOSSA THEY ARE DEAD      •  •  •  •  •  •  •  •  453 POOR MATTHIAS          26
      THOU HAST SEEN ATOSSA SAGE      •  •  •  •  •  •  •  •  453 POOR MATTHIAS          31
```

ATOSSA   (CONTINUED)
        ROVER DIED ATOSSA TOO   . . . . 453 POOR MATTHIAS   43

ATTACH
        TO ATTACH BLAME ELSEWHERE   . . . . 422 EMPEDOCLES I 2   308

ATTAIN
        TO DIE BE GIVEN US OR ATTAIN   . . . . 52 RESIGNATION   1
        WHICH NOW IS MINE MUST RE-ATTAIN   . . . . . . 206 RIVER   14
        ENDS WE SEEK WE NEVER SHALL ATTAIN   . . . . . 210 SELF-DECEPTION   26
        THESE ATTAIN THE MIGHTY LIFE YOU SEE   . . . . 240 SELF-DEPENDENCE   28
        TOO HARASSD TO ATTAIN   . . . . 308 OBERMANN   78
        THAT END TO HELP ATTAIN   . . . . 323 OBERMANN MORE   322
        THIS END TO HELP ATTAIN   . . . . 323 OBERMANN MORE   V 322
        THERE LIES THY GOAL TO MISS OR TO ATTAIN   . . . 465 ALARIC AT ROME   87

ATTAIND
        I KNOW BUT TWO WHO HAVE ATTAIND   . . . . . . 307 OBERMANN   47

ATTAINTS
        SHEDS BLOOD IMPRISONS BANISHES ATTAINTS   . . . . 353 MEROPE   682

ATTEMPT
        NOW THEREFORE WHAT TO ATTEMPT OR WHITHER FLY   . . 98 BALDER DEAD 1   105
        STILL THE ATTEMPT TO USE THEM PROVES THEM NULL   . . 210 SELF-DECEPTION   20
        HERE STAND I NOW AND THE ATTEMPT SHALL BE   . . . 383 MEROPE   1383
        IF HAPLY AT THIS MOMENT SUCH ATTEMPT . . . . . 388 MEROPE   1505
        I TREMBLED FOR OUR PRINCE AND HIS ATTEMPT   . . . 401 MEROPE   1901

ATTEMPTING
        ATTEMPTING DEEDS BEYOND THY POWER TO DO   . . . . 368 MEROPE   1079

ATTEND
        UNARMD INGLORIOUS I ATTEND THE COURSE   . . . . 128 BALDER DEAD 3   510
        ATTEND IT FROM ITS PRIMAL SOURCE   . . . . 225 EPILOG LAOCOON   148
        ATTEND IT OF ITS MID CAREER   . . . . 225 EPILOG LAOCOON   150
        ATTEND IT TO THE LAST REPOSE   . . . . 225 EPILOG LAOCOON   151
        UNTIRED ITS MOVEMENT BRIGHT ATTEND   . . . . . . 227 EPILOG LAOCOON   191

ATTENDS
        SHE TURNS FROM THAT COLD SUCCOUR WHICH ATTENDS   . . 170 WEST LONDON   12

ATTENTIVE
        SWELL HIS ATTENTIVE SOUL . . . . 47 WORLD QUIETIST   30
        AND THE ATTENTIVE MUSES SAID   . . . . 433 EMPEDOCLES II   145

ATTIC
        THE MELLOW GLORY OF THE ATTIC STAGE . . . . . . 2 TO A FRIEND   13

ATTIRD
        WHATEVER SHOWN HOWEER ATTIRD   . . . . 279 SOUTHERN NIGHT V 131

ATTIRE
        WHAT LADY IS THIS WHOSE SILK ATTIRE . . . . . . 131 TRISTRAM 1   24
        OF CITIZENS IN HOLIDAY ATTIRE . . . . 401 MEROPE   1897

ATTITUDE
        THINE ATTITUDE OF COLD ESTRANGED REPROACH   . . . 332 MEROPE   85
        THE LONG REPRESSIVE ATTITUDE OF RULE . . . . . . 334 MEROPE   154

ATTRIBUTES
        FOR GOD OF THESE HIS ATTRIBUTES IS MADE   . . . . 171 DIVINITY   5

ATTRUCK
        AND THOSE FROM ATTRUCK AND THE CASPIAN SANDS   . . 64 SOHRAB RUSTUM   123

AUDIENCE
        DIDST FORCE AN AUDIENCE ERE I STRUCK THE SCALE   . .   RUDE ORATOR   6

AUGHT
        THIS MIGHTY MARCH DO AUGHT BUT DIE   . . . . . . 226 EPILOG LAOCOON   170
        REMOVE YET FURTHER OFF IF AUGHT COMES NEAR . . . 332 MEROPE   69
        LET HIM DO THIS DO AUGHT BUT RECOMMENCE   . . . . 388 MEROPE   1500
        KNOWST THOU THEN AUGHT THAT THUS THOU SOUNDST   396 MEROPE   1766
            THE ALARM

AUGUR
        I AUGUR THOU WILT HEAR SOME BOLD RESOLVE   . . . . 351 MEROPE   610
        VAIN TO AUGUR THEY OR I . . . . 454 POOR MATTHIAS   76

AUGUREST
        ALL THOU AUGUREST HERE OF LOVELY SEEMING   . . . . 483 THEKLAS ANSWER   21

AUGUST
        THE PORT LIES BRIGHT UNDER THE AUGUST SUN   . . . 41 GIPSY CHILD   V 5
        TWAS AUGUST AND THE FIERCE SUN OVERHEAD   . . . . 169 EAST LONDON   1
        A SYMPATHY AUGUST AND PURE   . . . . 179 FAREWELL   70
        AUGUST LAWS DOTH MIGHTILY VINDICATE . . . . . . 196 FRAG ANTIGONE   49
        AND BOWER ME FROM THE AUGUST SUN WITH SHADE   . . 256 SCHOLAR-GIPSY   29
        AUGUST INDEED WAS THE FOUNDATION HERE   . . . . 389 MEROPE   1554
        AMONG AUGUST COMPANIONS . . . . 437 EMPEDOCLES II   284

AURELIUS
    MARCUS AURELIUS BUT THE STIFLING DEN • • • • • •   168 WORLDLY PLACE   3

AUSTERE
    SEEMS IT SO LIGHT A THING THEN AUSTERE POWERS • •   9 MYCERINUS   31
    WHOM HELA WITH AUSTERE CONTROL PRESIDES • • •   104 BALDER DEAD 1   317
    BIRTH-GODDESS AND THE AUSTERE FATES FIRST GAVE • •   195 FRAG ANTIGONE   10
    SOME GREY CRUSADING KNIGHT AUSTERE • • • •   278 SOUTHERN NIGHT   93
    SOLEMN UNLIGHTED AUSTERE • • • • • • • •   286 RUGBY CHAPEL   10
    AUSTERE DANTE NO GRAVE • • • • • • •   294 HEINES GRAVE   62
    THE HOUSE THE BROTHERHOOD AUSTERE • • • •   301 GRANDE CHARTR   65
    EVEN IN DEATH THAT COUNTENANCE AUSTERE • • •   403 MEROPE   1970
    IN HIS SNOWY LIGHT AUSTERE • • • • • • •   PILLARS UNIVERS   9
    IN HIS ROSEATE LIGHT AUSTERE • • • • • •   PILLARS UNIVERS V   9
    IN HIS WINTRY LIGHT AUSTERE • • • • • •   PILLARS UNIVERS V   9
    TEARS HAVE WASHED THEIR AUSTERE FACES • • •   META CLOISTER   7

AUSTERELY
    IS WITHOUT LOVE OR HATE AUSTERELY RAISED • • • •   336 MEROPE   205

AUSTERER
    LEAVES ME AUSTERER STERNER THAN I WOULD • • • •   335 MEROPE   155

AUSTERITY
    OF THOUGHT AND OF AUSTERITY WITHIN • • • • •   166 AUSTERITY POET   14

AUSTRALIAN
    DROPT BY THE FAR AUSTRALIAN FOAM • • • • •   451 GEISTS GRAVE   56

AUSTRIAN
    AUSTRIAN KNIGHTS FROM SYRIA CAME • • • •   15 CHURCH BROU 1   78
    AUSTRIAN WANDERERS BRING O WARDERS • • • •   15 CHURCH BROU 1   79
    HOMAGE TO YOUR AUSTRIAN DAME • • • • •   15 CHURCH BROU 1   80
    AUSTRIAN KNIGHTS AND MARCH-WORN PALMERS • • •   15 CHURCH BROU 1   85

AUTHENTIC
    AUTHENTIC PROOF OF WHAT THOU TELLST OUR EARS • •   403 MEROPE   1952

AUTHOR
    FIX HIM THE AUTHOR OF MY DEATH I KNOW NOT • • •   379 MEROPE   1273
    OF DARKNESS SO TREMENDOUS THAT ITS AUTHOR • • •   385 MEROPE   1420
    FIXD HIM THE AUTHOR OF MY DEATH I KNEW NOT • • •   379 MEROPE   V1273

AUTUMN
    NO NOR GREW DARK WHEN AUTUMN BROUGHT THE CLOUDS • •   12 MYCERINUS   121
    NOW THE AUTUMN CRISPS THE FOREST • • • •   13 CHURCH BROU 1   15
    ON AUTUMN-MORNINGS WHEN THE BUGLE SOUNDS • • •   18 CHURCH BROU 3   9
    OR LET IT BE ON AUTUMN NIGHTS WHEN RAIN • • •   18 CHURCH BROU 3   32
    BLAZED BRIGHT AND BALEFUL LIKE THAT AUTUMN-STAR • •   74 SOHRAB RUSTUM   452
    ON AUTUMN-DAYS BEFORE THEY CROSS THE SEA • • •   109 BALDER DEAD 2   159
    AND TIED HIM IN A YARD AT AUTUMN SEES • • •   129 BALDER DEAD 3   560
    YE STORM-WINDS OF AUTUMN • • • • • • •   174 PARTING   1
    IN AUTUMN ON THE SKIRTS OF BAGLEY WOOD • • •   258 SCHOLAR-GIPSY   111
    THE AUTUMN-EVENING THE FIELD • • • • • •   286 RUGBY CHAPEL   2
    OF THE AUTUMN EVENING BUT AH • • • • • •   286 RUGBY CHAPEL   15
    IN THE AUTUMN EVENING AND THINK • • • •   287 RUGBY CHAPEL   24
    THE AUTUMN STORM-WINDS DRIVE THE RACK • • •   306 OBERMANN   3
    HAST THOU NOT MARKED ON A WILD AUTUMN DAY • • •   466 ALARIC AT ROME   97

AUTUMNAL
    THE AUTUMNAL EVENING DARKENS ROUND • • • • •   299 GRANDE CHARTR   7

AUTUMNS
    LORN AUTUMNS AND TRIUMPHANT SPRINGS • • • • •   181 ISOLATION MARG   34
    OF BYGONE AUTUMNS WITH THEE • • • • • • •   287 RUGBY CHAPEL   25

AVAIL
    WEEP HIM AN HOUR BUT WHAT CAN GRIEF AVAIL • • •   96 BALDER DEAD 1   27
    THY WAY AND THIS AT LEAST MY PRAYERS AVAIL • • •   104 BALDER DEAD 1   309
    I WHAT WERE I WHEN THESE CAN NOUGHT AVAIL • • •   127 BALDER DEAD 3   493
    BUT TAKES AWAY THE POWER THIS CAN AVAIL • • •   153 TRISTRAM 3   124

AVAILD
    FOR WHAT AVAILD IT ALL THE NOISE • • • • •   303 GRANDE CHARTR   127

AVALANCHE
    THERE THE AVALANCHE THUNDERS • • • • • •   175 PARTING   31
    THE AVALANCHE SWEPT FROM OUR SIDE • • • • •   289 RUGBY CHAPEL   123

AVANT
    THE HUTS OF AVANT SHINE • • • • • • • •   312 OBERMANN MORE   14

AVARICE
    LUST AVARICE ENVY LIBERATED MAN • • • • •   7 REP FRIEND CONT   12

AVENGE
    THE MIGHTY RUSTUM SHALL AVENGE MY DEATH • • •   77 SOHRAB RUSTUM   553
    HE SHALL AVENGE MY DEATH AND PUNISH THEE • • •   77 SOHRAB RUSTUM   555
    TO AVENGE THAT FALL AND BRING THEM BACK TO POWER • •   334 MEROPE   146

AVENGE   (CONTINUED)
          THAN THINE ILLUSTRIOUS HUSBANDS TO AVENGE   . . . .   390 MEROPE   1569

AVENGED
          BETRAYD LIKE HIM BUT NOT LIKE HIM AVENGED   . . . .   367 MEROPE   1036
          WELL-MOURND BUT ILL-AVENGED   . . . .   372 MEROPE   1142
          THEIR MURDERD RULERS TERRIBLY AVENGED   . . . .   390 MEROPE   1566

AVENGER
          THY HUSBAND WEAK AVENGER THROUGH THYSELF   . . .   201 PHILOMELA   V
          SEND AN AVENGER GODS OF THE DEAD   . . . . . .   348 MEROPE   543
          AN AVENGER I ASK NOT SEND ME MY SON   . . . . .   348 MEROPE   544
          O QUEEN FOR AN AVENGER TO APPEAR   . . . . . .   348 MEROPE   545
          TO COME A LATE AVENGER TO THE AID   . . . . . .   349 MEROPE   577
          THINK YE THE AVENGER LOITERS ON HIS WAY   . . . .   466 ALARIC AT ROME   116

AVENGERS
          THE TRUE AVENGERS THESE I LEAVE HIS DEED   . . . .   349 MEROPE   555
          WHO KNOWS BUT THAT AVENGERS THOU HADST FOUND   . .   383 MEROPE   1372
          YEA ON YOUR FATHERS BONES THE AVENGERS TREAD   . .   467 ALARIC AT ROME   134

AVENGING
          TO HIS AVENGING SHADE AND TO THE GODS   . . . .   332 MEROPE   73
          NO THE AVENGING GODS WHO PUNISH CRIME   . . . .   341 MEROPE   359

AVENUE
          THE POPLAR AVENUE WAS PASSD   . . . .   177 FAREWELL   5

AVER
          WHO WITHOUT CHECK OF CONSCIENCE CAN AVER   . . . .   353 MEROPE   680

AVERSE
          THOU DRUGGING PAIN BY PATIENCE HALF AVERSE   . . .   42 GIPSY CHILD   13
          BLITHE ALL ELSE STIRS THOU STIRREST NOT AVERSE   . .   41 GIPSY CHILD   V 13
          AVERSE AS DIDO DID WITH GESTURE STERN   . . . .   261 SCHOLAR-GIPSY   208
          NOT PRONE ALL SAY AVERSE TO BLOODSHED NOW   . . . .   388 MEROPE   1492

AVERSION
          OUTLASTS AVERSION OUTLASTS LOVE   . . . . . .   58 RESIGNATION   216

AVERT
          BUT WORDSWORTHS EYES AVERT THEIR KEN   . . . . .   308 OBERMANN   53
          A WOMAN AND A MOTHER TO AVERT   . . . .   387 MEROPE   1455

AVERTED
          TURN WITH AVERTED EYES FROM DEEDS OF BLOOD   . . .   354 MEROPE   695

AVOID
          IGNORANT WHERE TO STAND OR WHOM TO AVOID   . . . .   195 FRAG ANTIGONE   19

AVOIDS
          OUT OF THE LIGHT AND MUTELY WHICH AVOIDS   . . . .   199 EARLY DEATH   3

AVON
          BY THE AVON SIDE IN THE BRIGHT   . . . .   294 HEINES GRAVE   63

AVOWAL
          ALL TRUE SPEECH AND LARGE AVOWAL   . . . . . .   34 NEW SIRENS   227

AWAIT
          TO AWAIT THEIR MARCH AND WHEN APPEARD   . . . .   53 RESIGNATION   33
          YET THEY BELIEVE ME WHO AWAIT   . . . .   59 RESIGNATION   247
          BUT HIM TOO FOES AWAIT AND NETTED SNARES   . . . .   111 BALDER DEAD 2   219
          AH DO NOT WE WANDERER AWAIT IT TOO   . . . . .   260 SCHOLAR-GIPSY   180
          YES WE AWAIT IT BUT IT STILL DELAYS   . . . . .   260 SCHOLAR-GIPSY   181
          MONTH AFTER MONTH I AWAIT   . . . .   347 MEROPE   517

AWAITS
          DANGER OR DEATH AWAITS THEE ON THIS FIELD   . . . .   63 SOHRAB RUSTUM   87

AWAKE
          O SEEMING SOLE TO AWAKE THY SUN-BATHED HEAD   . .   45 IN UTRUMQUE PAR   29
          AWAKE AND STIR IN THEIR SOUL   . . . .   235 YOUTH OF MAN   92
          YEARLY AWAKE TO BEHOLD   . . . .   285 HAWORTH CHURCH   117
          WHILE TROUBLED INNOCENTS TOSS AND LIE AWAKE   . .   372 MEROPE   1155

AWAKES
          WHEN IT ADMIRES AND LOVES ITS HEART AWAKES   . . .   382 MEROPE   1345

AWAKING
          DISENCHANTED BY HABIT AND NEWLY AWAKING   . . . .   20 MODERN SAPPHO   23

AWARD
          LOVE ME AND GLADLY BRING FOR MY AWARD   . . . .   126 BALDER DEAD 3   465
          TRUST ME AND GLADLY BRING FOR MY AWARD   . . . .   126 BALDER DEAD 3   V 465

AWARE
          A MAN BECOMES AWARE OF HIS LIFES FLOW   . . . .   247 BURIED LIFE   88

AWAY

NOW AS THE BARRIER CLOSES DIES AWAY	10	MYCERINUS	58
THEN THEY DROP AWAY	17	CHURCH BROU 2	38
AH I HOPE YET ONCE AWAY	23	MEMORY-PICTURE	21
FREELY GAVE IT BUT IT DIES AWAY	35	NEW SIRENS	258
FALLS HEAVILY AWAY WITH LONG-DRAWN ROAR	40	HUMAN LIFE	21
BUT IN DISDAINFUL SILENCE TURN AWAY	42	GIPSY CHILD	31
AND TURND AWAY AND SPAKE TO HIS OWN SOUL	71	SOHRAB RUSTUM	346
CHANGED GIFTS AND WENT ON EQUAL TERMS AWAY	72	SOHRAB RUSTUM	361
OXUS IN SUMMER WASH THEM ALL AWAY	72	SOHRAB RUSTUM	378
HE SHORE AWAY AND THAT PROUD HORSEHAIR PLUME	76	SOHRAB RUSTUM	497
I CAME AND LIKE THE WIND I GO AWAY	82	SOHRAB RUSTUM	723
AND CARRY THEE AWAY TO SEISTAN	84	SOHRAB RUSTUM	799
UNWILLINGLY THE SPIRIT FLED AWAY	86	SOHRAB RUSTUM	854
AND TURND AWAY AND SPOKE TO HIS OWN SOUL	71	SOHRAB RUSTUM V	346
O MOST JUST VIZIER SEND AWAY	87	SICK KING BOKH	1
SEND HIM AWAY SIRS AND MAKE ON	90	SICK KING BOKH	90
AND FROM THE HALL OF HEAVEN HE RODE AWAY	96	BALDER DEAD 1	48
SO BALDER FADED IN THE NIGHT AWAY	104	BALDER DEAD 1	337
ONE LAST KISS FIRST TIS VAIN TO HORSE AWAY	135	TRISTRAM 1	169
MOOR BEHIND MOOR FAR FAR AWAY	141	TRISTRAM 1	365
WOULD NOT FADE WITH THE DULL YEARS AWAY	143	TRISTRAM 2	26
SWELLS MY HEART AND TAKES MY BREATH AWAY	145	TRISTRAM 2	74
THE SUNKEN REEFS AND FAR AWAY	148	TRISTRAM 2	173
A YEAR HAD FLOWN AND OER THE SEA AWAY	149	TRISTRAM 3	1
NOR TO THE SNOW WHICH THOUGH TWAS ALL AWAY	151	TRISTRAM 3	50
SLIP WITHOUT BRINGING BLISS SLOWLY AWAY	151	TRISTRAM 3	66
HER WORK AWAY AND LET HER FINGERS ROVE	152	TRISTRAM 3	87
BUT TAKES AWAY THE POWER THIS CAN AVAIL	153	TRISTRAM 3	124
AWAY THE OTHER SIDE OF BRITTANY	154	TRISTRAM 3	154
PEERD TWIXT THE STEMS AND THE GROUND BROKE AWAY	155	TRISTRAM 3	186
COME DEAR CHILDREN LET US AWAY	161	FORSAKEN MERM	1
DOWN AND AWAY BELOW	161	FORSAKEN MERM	2
CHILDREN DEAR LET US AWAY	161	FORSAKEN MERM	8
CALL HER ONCE AND COME AWAY	162	FORSAKEN MERM	18
COME DEAR CHILDREN COME AWAY DOWN	162	FORSAKEN MERM	23
COME AWAY COME AWAY	162	FORSAKEN MERM	29
COME AWAY COME AWAY	162	FORSAKEN MERM	29
CALL YET ONCE THAT SHE WENT AWAY	162	FORSAKEN MERM	49
COME AWAY CHILDREN CALL NO MORE	164	FORSAKEN MERM	83
COME AWAY COME DOWN CALL NO MORE	164	FORSAKEN MERM	84
COME AWAY AWAY CHILDREN	164	FORSAKEN MERM	108
COME AWAY AWAY CHILDREN	164	FORSAKEN MERM	108
THIS STARTING FEVERISH HEART AWAY	178	FAREWELL	32
I BADE IT KEEP THE WORLD AWAY	180	ISOLATION MARG	3
I PRAISE THE LIFE WHICH SLIPS AWAY	199	EARLY DEATH	2
THAT LIFE IS BEST WHICH SLIPS AWAY	199	EARLY DEATH V	2
SPREAD WIDE AWAY THE LUMINOUS PLAIN	204	CALAIS SANDS V	6
MUST WHEN UNSEEN FROM THE SOUL FADE AWAY	206	SEPARATION	8
DELICATE SPIRITS PUSHD AWAY	219	BACCHANALIA 2	17
THOUGH THE MUSE BE GONE AWAY	227	PERSIST POETRY	1
FALL AWAY FROM THEIR EYES	235	YOUTH OF MAN	107
THE BLUE HAZE-CRADLED MOUNTAINS SPREAD AWAY	242	SUMMER NIGHT	21
THAT WHIRLS THE SPIRIT FROM ITSELF AWAY	243	SUMMER NIGHT	30
WHEN I WHO WATCH THEM AM AWAY	249	KENSINGTON GARD	30
AS THE BANKS FADE DIMMER AWAY	254	FUTURE	84
WHILE TO MY EAR FROM UPLANDS FAR AWAY	255	SCHOLAR-GIPSY	17
THROUGH THE LONG DEWY GRASS MOVE SLOW AWAY	258	SCHOLAR-GIPSY	110
WHO HESITATE AND FALTER LIFE AWAY	260	SCHOLAR-GIPSY	178
AND EVERY DOUBT LONG BLOWN BY TIME AWAY	261	SCHOLAR-GIPSY	200
WAVE US AWAY AND KEEP THY SOLITUDE	261	SCHOLAR-GIPSY	210
BUT THYRSIS OF HIS OWN WILL WENT AWAY	264	THYRSIS	40
WHEN GOETHE PASSD AWAY WE SAID	270	MEMORIAL VERSES V	15
CURVES WITH THE CURVING BEACH AWAY	275	SOUTHERN NIGHT	10
SLOW ROUND HER PADDLES DIES AWAY	276	SOUTHERN NIGHT	31
THEN LEARNT HIS DEATH AND PINED AWAY	279	SOUTHERN NIGHT	110
PANIC DESPAIR FLEE AWAY	292	RUGBY CHAPEL	197
THE STRANGE GUEST SPARKLED NOW TIS PASSD AWAY	298	HEINES GRAVE	211
AH IF IT BE PASSD TAKE AWAY	302	GRANDE CHARTR	103
CARRIED THY LOVELY WAIL AWAY	303	GRANDE CHARTR	140
LONG SINCE HATH FLUNG HER WEEDS AWAY	304	GRANDE CHARTR	154
LONG SINCE HATH THROWN HER WEEDS AWAY	304	GRANDE CHARTR V	154
LISTEND AND WEPT AWAY	310	OBERMANN	128
AWAY THE DREAMS THAT BUT DECEIVE	310	OBERMANN	129
FOR THOU ART GONE AWAY FROM EARTH	310	OBERMANN	141
FILLD EARTH AND HEAVEN AND CAUGHT AWAY	317	OBERMANN MORE	143
OF OBERMANN AWAY	324	OBERMANN MORE	334
THEIR LOAD AND GONE AWAY	315	OBERMANN MORE V	82
HATE TO THEIR RULE WHICH ELSE WOULD DIE AWAY	331	MEROPE	43
BUT WHITHER GOST THOU HENCE O QUEEN AWAY	350	MEROPE	597
FAIN WOULD I FADE AWAY AS I HAVE LIVED	366	MEROPE	1027
WHAT WAVST THOU OFF THAT MURDEROUS AXE AWAY	376	MEROPE	1215
AND ON WHOSE LIGHTNESS BLAME IS THROWN AWAY	411	EMPEDOCLES I 1	162
HE SHOWD HIM PHTHIA FAR AWAY	414	EMPEDOCLES I 2	68
THE WIND SWEEP MAN AWAY	421	EMPEDOCLES I 2	260
IN SIGHT OF BLOOD BUT WERE RAPT FAR AWAY	427	EMPEDOCLES I 2	453
THE MUSIC OF THE LYRE BLOWS AWAY	432	EMPEDOCLES II	123
OR WHETHER WE WILL ONCE MORE FALL AWAY	440	EMPEDOCLES II	373
SHE SPAKE AND FROM THE PORTAL PASSD AWAY	447	WESTMIN ABBEY	110
NO AWAY WITH TALES LIKE THESE	456	POOR MATTHIAS	153
OR TIMES STERN HAND WHY BLOTS IT NOT AWAY	462	ALARIC AT ROME	5

AWAY   (CONTINUED)
          THERE ARE WHOSE GLORY PASSETH NOT AWAY   .   .   .   .   462 ALARIC AT ROME   7
          HOW SHOULD THAT MIGHTIEST CITY PASS AWAY   .   .   .   .   467 ALARIC AT ROME   129
          PERCHANCE HIS WANDERING HEART WAS FAR AWAY   .   .   .   .   468 ALARIC AT ROME   169
          SHOULD FLEET BEFORE US BUT TO MELT AWAY   .   .   .   .   470 ALARIC AT ROME   212
          ONE MOMENTS SPACE MIGHT WAFT HIM FAR AWAY   .   .   .   .   475 CROMWELL   111
          PASSD LIKE A MORNING MIST IN TEARS AWAY   .   .   .   .   477 CROMWELL   198
          BATHD IN A BLAZE OF SUNSET MELT AWAY   .   .   .   .   .   .   478 CROMWELL   216
          ALL NIGHT THEY SATE THEN STOLE AWAY   .   .   .   .   .   .   480 HAYSWATER BOAT   31
          SHALL TRANSPORT THEE AWAY AND THE DAY OF THY   HOMER TRANS   28
             FREEDOM BE ENDED
          WHEN HIS FINE GENIUS FOAMS ITSELF AWAY   .   .   .   .   LUCRETIUS 2   4

AWE
          MY CRIME THAT RAPT IN REVERENTIAL AWE   .   .   .   .   9 MYCERINUS   8
          AND KISSD HIM AND AWE FELL ON BOTH THE HOSTS   .   .   82 SOHRAB RUSTUM   729
          WHEN HIS AWE-STRUCK CAPTORS LED   .   .   .   .   .   229 YOUTH OF NATURE   43
          GIVES US A SENSE OF THE AWE   .   .   .   .   231 YOUTH OF NATURE   100
          AND YET WITH REVERENTIAL AWE   .   .   .   .   270 MEMORIAL VERSES   12
          IN PITY AND SILENT AWE   .   .   .   .   283 HAWORTH CHURCH   V
          WITH HALF CENSURE WITH AWE   .   .   .   .   298 HEINES GRAVE   203
          IN PITY AND MOURNFUL AWE MIGHT STAND   .   .   .   .   .   301 GRANDE CHARTR   82
          ALLOW THEM WE ADMIRE WITH AWE   .   .   .   .   304 GRANDE CHARTR   163
          THEY AWE US BUT THEY ARE NOT OURS   .   .   .   .   .   .   304 GRANDE CHARTR   V 168
          THE BROODING EAST WITH AWE BEHELD   .   .   .   .   .   .   316 OBERMANN MORE   105
          APPALS ME SHAKES ME WITH AWE   .   .   .   .   372 MEROPE   1146
          THIS AWE WHICH GUARDS OUR EARTH-SPRUNG LINEAL KINGS   389 MEROPE   1543
          WHAT HATE AND AWE AND SHAME   .   .   .   .   416 EMPEDOCLES I 2   112
          AND AWE BE DEAD AND HOPE IMPOSSIBLE   .   .   .   .   .   429 EMPEDOCLES II   34
          AWE-STRUCK FAIN WOULD CEASE TO BE   .   .   .   .   .   .   META CLOISTER   18

AWED
          STRUCK ONCE AND AWED HIS MOB AND SAVED THIS REALM   338 MEROPE   275
          THE FISHER AWED OBEYS   .   .   .   .   445 WESTMIN ABBEY   27

AWFUL
          LEFT OUR AWFUL LAURELS HANGING   .   .   .   .   27 NEW SIRENS   31
          ALL THE FRORE PEAKS AWFUL CROWN   .   .   .   .   .   .   31 NEW SIRENS   144
          IN FRONT THE AWFUL ALPINE TRACK   .   .   .   .   .   .   306 OBERMANN   1
          FOR THE AWFUL MONARCHS BELOW   .   .   .   .   345 MEROPE   476
          WHICH STYXS AWFUL WATERS TRICKLE DOWN   .   .   .   .   .   368 MEROPE   1065
          A DEED SO AWFUL THAT THE GENERAL TONGUE   .   .   .   .   385 MEROPE   1418
          CROWND BY THE AWFUL PEAK ETNAS GREAT MOUTH   .   .   .   .   429 EMPEDOCLES II   3
          BUT AN AWFUL PLEASURE BLAND   .   .   .   .   431 EMPEDOCLES II   67

AWHILE
          AWHILE WITH THEM BEFORE THEY SLEEP AND THEN   .   .   151 TRISTRAM 3   78
          AWHILE LET ME WITH THOUGHT HAVE DONE   .   .   .   .   .   208 ON THE RHINE   11
          AND AFTER WE AWHILE HAD GONE   .   .   .   .   221 EPILOG LAOCOON   4
          AWHILE HE HOLDS SOME FALSE WAY UNDEBARRD   .   .   .   244 SUMMER NIGHT   59
          GIVE ME THY HAND AND HUSH AWHILE   .   .   .   .   .   .   245 BURIED LIFE   9
          SUCH BARREN KNOWLEDGE AWHILE   .   .   .   .   296 HEINES GRAVE   119
          SUSPEND YOUR MELANCHOLY RITES AWHILE   .   .   .   .   .   332 MEROPE   77
          AND SEEMD TO MUSE AWHILE THEN RAISED HIS EYES   .   .   402 MEROPE   1913
          AND WE SHALL STRUGGLE AWHILE GASP AND REBEL   .   .   440 EMPEDOCLES II   382

AWOKE
          A CONQUERING NEW-BORN JOY AWOKE   .   .   .   .   .   .   316 OBERMANN MORE   115
          THE VISION ENDED I AWOKE   .   .   .   .   323 OBERMANN MORE   325
          THAT BOUND HIS SPIRIT AND HIS HEART AWOKE   .   .   .   .   475 CROMWELL   132

AWRY
          CONSTRUED AWRY MISPLANND INVASIONS WORE   .   .   .   .   336 MEROPE   216
          CONSTRUED AWRY MISPLANND INVASIONS USD   .   .   .   .   336 MEROPE   V 216

AXE
          AH BLOODY AXE DIZZY BLOWS   .   .   .   .   346 MEROPE   499
          FETCH ME THE SACRIFICE-AXE   .   .   .   .   371 MEROPE   1138
          THE AXE WHO BRINGS IT TIS HERE   .   .   .   .   372 MEROPE   1144
          WHAT WAVST THOU OFF THAT MURDEROUS AXE AWAY   .   .   376 MEROPE   1215
          THE SACRIFICERS AXE WILL SERVE THY TURN   .   .   .   .   391 MEROPE   1592
          AND STANDS SHOUTING FOR A SLAUGHTEROUS AXE   .   .   .   400 MEROPE   1860
          DRIVES THE AXE TO ITS GOAL   .   .   .   .   400 MEROPE   1864
          THE AXE AND ON THE FOREHEAD OF THE KING   .   .   .   .   402 MEROPE   1920

AXES
          OF HEWING AXES CRASHING TREES SUCH BLOWS   .   .   .   .   75 SOHRAB RUSTUM   478
          LAY THICKLY STREWN SWORDS AXES DARTS AND SPEARS .   .   95 BALDER DEAD 1   2
          AXES AND ROPES AND AT THEIR HEAD CAME THOR   .   .   .   .   106 BALDER DEAD 2   48

AY
          AY WE WOULD EACH FAIN DRIVE   .   .   .   .   40 HUMAN LIFE   13
          GODS WISDOM AND GODS GOODNESS AY BUT FOOLS   .   .   .   171 DIVINITY   9
          AY AGES LONG ENDURED HIS SPAN   .   .   .   .   318 OBERMANN MORE   165
          LISTEN PAUSANIUS AY TIS CALLICLES   .   .   .   .   .   .   413 EMPEDOCLES I 2   34
          AY ME TIS DEAF THAT EAR   .   .   .   .   449 WESTMIN ABBEY   161

AYE
          ROUND THE WORLD FOR EVER AND AYE   .   .   .   .   .   .   162 FORSAKEN MERM   45
          SO IT IS SO IT WILL BE FOR AYE   .   .   .   .   228 YOUTH OF NATURE   10

BAB

CROSSING THE STRIPLING THAMES AT BAB-LOCK-HITHE • •   257 SCHOLAR-GIPSY   74

BABE

FOR HE HAD HAD SURE TIDINGS THAT THE BABE • • •   79 SOHRAB RUSTUM   607
THAT SHE MIGHT PRICK IT ON THE BABE SHE BORE • •   80 SOHRAB RUSTUM   660
A HELPLESS BABE AMONG THE MOUNTAIN-ROCKS • • •   81 SOHRAB RUSTUM   681
A BABE WAS IN HER ARMS AND AT HER SIDE • • •   169 WEST LONDON   3
OF PASTORAL ARCADIA WHERE A BABE • • •   330 MEROPE   21
WHO SAVED HIM FROM THESE MURDEROUS HALLS A BABE • •   351 MEROPE   617
PAST ARNE SPRING WHERE RHEA GAVE THE BABE • •   355 MEROPE   736
WAS SAVED A BABE BUT TO A LIFE OBSCURE • • •   356 MEROPE   769
A BABE THOU SMILEST AGAIN • • • • •   378 MEROPE   1237
HID THE BABE HID ARCAS • • • • • •   391 MEROPE   1614
THE CHARMD BABE OF THE ELEUSINIAN KING • •   446 WESTMIN ABBEY   85
AND SAW HER BABE AMIDST THE FIRE AND SCREAMD • •   446 WESTMIN ABBEY   93

BABES

TWO UNOFFENDING BABES HIS INNOCENT SONS • • • •   339 MEROPE   319

BABY

AS IF THEIR BABY-OWNER CHASED • • • • •   141 TRISTRAM 1   347
HOW FRIVOLOUS A BABY MAN WOULD BE • • • •   246 BURIED LIFE   31
A BABY DOG FROM LONDON TOWN • • • • •   459 KAISER DEAD   14
DEEP ON HIS LIFE AND CHILDHOODS BABY WAVES • • •   473 CROMWELL   48

BABYLON

TO DIE AT THIRTY-FIVE IN BABYLON • • • • •   154 TRISTRAM 3   150

BACK

TIS MY LORD COME BACK FROM HUNTING • • • •   14 CHURCH BROU 1   39
SADLY BACK THE SEATS OF MEN • • • • •   31 NEW SIRENS   150
THEN I SHALL WISH ITS AGITATIONS BACK • •   37 YOUTHS AGIT   9
PAIN TO THREAD BACK AND TO RENEW • • •   53 RESIGNATION   20
AND TO A HILLOCK CAME A LITTLE BACK • • •   61 SOHRAB RUSTUM   17
AND BEAT THE PERSIANS BACK ON EVERY FIELD • •   62 SOHRAB RUSTUM   48
AND WITH HIS STAFF KEPT BACK THE FOREMOST RANKS • •   65 SOHRAB RUSTUM   143
THAT PERAN-WISA KEPT THE TARTARS BACK • •   65 SOHRAB RUSTUM   145
BACK THROUGH THE OPENING SQUADRONS TO HIS TENT • •   66 SOHRAB RUSTUM   188
BACK QUICKLY THROUGH THE CAMP IN FEAR AND JOY • •   69 SOHRAB RUSTUM   261
BACK OUT TO SEA TO THE DEEP WAVES OF DEATH • •   73 SOHRAB RUSTUM   395
BUT COURTEOUSLY DREW BACK AND SPOKE AND SAID • •   74 SOHRAB RUSTUM   426
AND RUSTUM PLUCKD IT BACK WITH ANGRY GROAN • •   76 SOHRAB RUSTUM   494
AND SHRANK AMAZED BACK HE RECOILD ONE STEP • •   76 SOHRAB RUSTUM   517
HE REELD AND STAGGERING BACK SANK TO THE GROUND • •   76 SOHRAB RUSTUM   521
FAR OFF ANON HER MATE COMES WINGING BACK • •   78 SOHRAB RUSTUM   561
CHIDING HIS MATE BACK TO HER NEST BUT SHE • •   78 SOHRAB RUSTUM   566
WHO SPOKE ALTHOUGH HE CALLD BACK NAMES HE KNEW • •   79 SOHRAB RUSTUM   606
TRYING TO CALL HIM BACK TO LIFE AND LIFE • •   81 SOHRAB RUSTUM   697
CAME BACK TO RUSTUM AND HE OPED HIS EYES • •   81 SOHRAB RUSTUM   698
LET THEM ALL CROSS THE OXUS BACK IN PEACE • •   84 SOHRAB RUSTUM   782
LET THEM ALL CROSS THE OXUS BACK IN PEACE • •   85 SOHRAB RUSTUM   807
CONVULSED HIM BACK TO LIFE HE OPEND THEM • •   86 SOHRAB RUSTUM   851
AND SHRANK AMAZED BACK HE RECOILD ONE PACE • •   76 SOHRAB RUSTUM   V 517
HE REELD AND STAGGERING BACK SUNK TO THE GROUND • •   76 SOHRAB RUSTUM   V 521
BUT IN VALHALLA ALL THE GODS WENT BACK • •   97 BALDER DEAD 1   61
CAN I O MOTHER BRING THEM BALDER BACK • •   98 BALDER DEAD 1   107
WOULD FREELY DIE TO PURCHASE BALDER BACK • •   98 BALDER DEAD 1   120
AND MAKE HER YIELD AND GIVE HIM BALDER BACK • •   100 BALDER DEAD 1   183
AND BACK ALONG THE BEACH TO ASGARD WENT • •   101 BALDER DEAD 1   200
TO HELAS KINGDOM TO ASK BALDER BACK • •   102 BALDER DEAD 1   237
AND NANNA ON HER BED SANK BACK BUT THEN • •   104 BALDER DEAD 1   338
AND NANNA ON HER BED SUNK BACK BUT THEN • •   104 BALDER DEAD 1   V 338
WHOM THEY BRING BACK WITH THEM AT NIGHT TO HEAVEN • •   105 BALDER DEAD 2   27
TO HELAS KINGDOM TO ASK BALDER BACK • • •   106 BALDER DEAD 2   46
ON HIS BROAD BACK NO LESSER RIDER BORE • •   107 BALDER DEAD 2   74
AND BEND MY HEART AND GIVE HIM BACK TO HEAVEN • •   111 BALDER DEAD 2   240
BACK THROUGH THE ASTONISHD TRIBES OF DEAD TO HEAVEN   112 BALDER DEAD 2   285
SEE HERE IS HERMOD WHO COMES SINGLE BACK • •   113 BALDER DEAD 3   6
AND BEND HER HEART AND GIVE YOU BALDER BACK • •   115 BALDER DEAD 3   46
TO GOD OR HERO BUT THOU KEPTEST BACK • • •   116 BALDER DEAD 3   85
AND BRING IN TRIUMPH BALDER BACK TO HEAVEN • •   120 BALDER DEAD 3   244
HELA AND WIN THE LOVED ONE BACK TO HEAVEN • •   122 BALDER DEAD 3   294
OF ALL THINGS WEEPING TO BRING BALDER BACK • •   122 BALDER DEAD 3   318
RIDE BACK AND TELL IN HEAVEN THIS HEAVY NEWS • •   124 BALDER DEAD 3   371
HE SPOKE AND NIORD SET FORTH BACK TO HEAVEN • •   124 BALDER DEAD 3   373
AT LAST HE SIGHD AND SET FORTH BACK TO HEAVEN • •   129 BALDER DEAD 3   566
AND THE KNIGHT SINKS BACK ON HIS PILLOWS AGAIN • •   133 TRISTRAM 1   84
AND SHAKE BACK HER RAVEN HAIR • • • •   134 TRISTRAM 1   123
HEAVEN HIS HEAD SINKS BACK UPON THE PILLOW • •   145 TRISTRAM 2   77
HAD FALLEN BACK HER ARMS OUTSPREAD • • •   146 TRISTRAM 2   104
A FRESHNESS BACK AS OF HER PRIME • • •   147 TRISTRAM 2   142
WHERE THE SUNS RAYS STRUCK FULL AND FLASHD BACK KEEN   TRISTRAM 3   V 21
SAY THY PRAYER AND COME BACK TO THE KIND SEA-CAVES   163 FORSAKEN MERM   61
AND THEN COME BACK DOWN • • • • • •   165 FORSAKEN MERM   139
ACROSS AND BEGGD AND CAME BACK SATISFIED • •   170 WEST LONDON   7
BACK TO THY SOLITUDE AGAIN • • • •   181 ISOLATION MARG   18
BACK WITH THE CONSCIOUS THRILL OF SHAME • •   181 ISOLATION MARG   19
OR HAST THOU LONG SINCE WANDERD BACK • •   184 TERRACE BERNE   17
SHAKE BACK THY BANDS OF SOFT BROWN HAIR • •   205 CALAIS SANDS   V 16

BACK   (CONTINUED)
        STAVED US BACK AND GAVE OUR CHOICE THE LAW . . . . . 210 SELF-DECEPTION   12
        OF PEBBLES WHICH THE WAVES DRAW BACK AND FLING   . . 211 DOVER BEACH   10
        OF PEBBLES WHICH THE WAVES SUCK BACK AND FLING   . . 211 DOVER BEACH   V 10
        BACK TO HIS MASTER AGAIN . . . . 217 LORDS MESSENGER   24
        A BOLT IS SHOT BACK SOMEWHERE IN OUR BREAST   . . 247 BURIED LIFE   84
        THEN HERE AT NOON COMES BACK HIS STORES TO USE   . . 255 SCHOLAR-GIPSY   15
        SEE HIM COME BACK AND CUT A SMOOTHER REED   . . . . 265 THYRSIS   78
        OUR YOUTH CAME BACK FOR THERE WAS SHED   . . . . 271 MEMORIAL VERSES   V 54
        ECHOED HER BACK BY THE CROWD   . . . . 281 HAWORTH CHURCH   43
        BACK TO YOUR NATIVE HEATHS   . . . . 285 HAWORTH CHURCH   115
        CHIDE AND PUT BACK AND DELAY   . . . . 283 HAWORTH CHURCH   V
        BRINGS THEE BACK IN THE LIGHT . . . . 286 RUGBY CHAPEL   17
        LONGD HIMSELF BACK TO THE FIELDS   . . . . 296 HEINES GRAVE   137
        BACK TO THE TRANQUIL THE COOL . . . . 296 HEINES GRAVE   150
        BUT STOP TO FETCH BACK THOUGHTS THAT STRAY   . . . . 313 OBERMANN MORE   29
        BACK TO THY YOUTH AND ME   . . . . 314 OBERMANN MORE   72
        AH CARRY BACK THY KEN   . . . . 315 OBERMANN MORE   82
        THE HERACLEIDAE BACK TO PELOPS ISLE   . . . . . . 330 MEROPE   7
        SOFTLY STAND BACK SEE TO THESE PALACE GATES . . . . 331 MEROPE   51
        SET DOWN YOUR PITCHERS MAIDENS AND FALL BACK . . . . 332 MEROPE   76
        TO AVENGE THAT FALL AND BRING THEM BACK TO POWER . . 334 MEROPE   146
        WHO CAN EXTEND THEIR HANDS MAIDENS TAKE BACK . . . . 336 MEROPE   195
        HOTLIER THAN THOU AND WERE BY THEE KEPT BACK . . . . 339 MEROPE   330
        PROSPEROUS MIGHTY CAME BACK   . . . . 343 MEROPE   411
        CAN VENGEANCE GIVE ME BACK THE MURDERED NO   . . . . 349 MEROPE   567
        AND CHECK THY FIERY STEEDS AND LEANING BACK . . . . 349 MEROPE   575
        IF THIS WILL BRING HIM BACK BE THIS MY PRAYER   . . 349 MEROPE   579
        BRING BACK OUR SON IF MAY BE WITHOUT BLOOD   . . . . 350 MEROPE   587
        WELL PURPOSE TO PEN BACK . . . . 353 MEROPE   671
        HIS BOAR-SPEARS BROKEN SHAFT BACK ON THE LAKE   . . 358 MEROPE   840
        COME COME BACK TO OUR PRAYER   . . . . 360 MEROPE   892
        THRUST BACK NOW THE BOLT OF THAT DOOR   . . . . . 372 MEROPE   1147
        FLY BACK MY CHILD AND THOU SEEMST   . . . . 377 MEROPE   1229
        ONCE MORE ROLL BACK ON MY HOUSE   . . . . 378 MEROPE   1244
        HERE BRING HIM ERE THE KING COME BACK FROM COUNCIL   379 MEROPE   1262
        THOU COUNTEST ON TO BACK THEE GAINST HIS LORDS   . . 382 MEROPE   1321
        SOMETIMES WHEN HE WAS GONE I WISHD HIM BACK . . . . 387 MEROPE   1457
        SOFTLY STAND BACK SEE TOWRD THE PALACE GATES . . . . 331 MEROPE   V 51
        HE WHO WAS SENT HATH SPED AND NOW COMES BACK . . . . 366 MEROPE   V
        AND NOW AND NOW BACK TO THE TOWN WITH SPEED . . . . 408 EMPEDOCLES I 1   49
        AND WHOM EMPEDOCLES CALLD BACK TO LIFE   . . . . . 410 EMPEDOCLES I 1   111
        BUT HE IS STRANGELY WROUGHT I WILL SPEED BACK   . . 428 EMPEDOCLES I 2   480
        WHERE SHALL THY VOTARY FLY THEN BACK TO MEN . . . . 435 EMPEDOCLES II   220
        AND SO CHANGE BACK AND MANY THOUSAND TIMES   . . . . 435 EMPEDOCLES II   229
        WILL BLOW US FIERCELY BACK TO SEA AND EARTH . . . . 439 EMPEDOCLES II   362
        BACK TO THIS MEADOW OF CALAMITY   . . . . 440 EMPEDOCLES II   365
        AND THE REALITY WILL PLUCK US BACK   . . . . 440 EMPEDOCLES II   385
        SEEMS STRANGELY ECHOED BACK BY TONES OF YESTERDAY   464 ALARIC AT ROME   48
        SHOOK BACK HIS TANGLED LOCKS AND MURMURD PEACE   . . 477 CROMWELL   174

BACKD
        BACKD BY THE PINES A PLANK-BUILT COTTAGE STOOD   . . 25 DREAM   15
        BACKD BY THE SUNSET WHICH DOTH GLORIFY   . . . . . 267 THYRSIS   158

BACKWARD
        AND YOUR PROUD HEADS BACKWARD THROWN . . . . 32 NEW SIRENS   192
        BACKWARD AND FORWARD ROLLD THE WAVES OF FIGHT   . . 236 PALLADIUM   7
        AND LEANING BACKWARD IN A PENSIVE DREAM . . . . . 257 SCHOLAR-GIPSY   77

BACKWARDS
        AND LEANING BACKWARDS IN A PENSIVE DREAM   . . . . 257 SCHOLAR-GIPSY   V 77

BAD
        WHO PROP THOU ASKST IN THESE BAD DAYS MY MIND   . . 2 TO A FRIEND   1
        STERNLY REPRESSEST THE BAD   . . . . 287 RUGBY CHAPEL   51
        AND STAMP HIMSELF THEREAFTER BAD OR GOOD   . . . . 352 MEROPE   651
        THE MOST ARE BAD WISE MEN HAVE SAID . . . . 352 MEROPE   652
        I THE ONE RIGHTEOUS THEY THE MANY BAD   . . . . . 353 MEROPE   679
        ACCEPT THEM IN ONE WORD FOR GOOD OR BAD . . . . . 355 MEROPE   713
        AND ONLY BAD MEN JOY TO SEE UNDONE   . . . . 386 MEROPE   1429

BADE
        INTO THE OPEN PLAIN SO HAMAN BADE   . . . . 64 SOHRAB RUSTUM   107
        HIS FOLLOWERS IN AND BADE THEM BRING HIS ARMS   . . 69 SOHRAB RUSTUM   264
        AS THE KING BADE SO WAS IT DONE   . . . . 90 SICK KING BOKH   92
        I BADE MY HEART MORE CONSTANT BE   . . . . 180 ISOLATION MARG   2
        I BADE IT KEEP THE WORLD AWAY . . . . 180 ISOLATION MARG   3
        AND BADE BETWIXT THEIR SHORES TO BE . . . . 182 TO MARG CONT   23
        AND BADE HIM MAKE WITH THEM WHAT WORD HE COULD   . . 239 REVOLUTIONS   4
        BADE THROUGH THE DEEP RECESSES OF OUR BREAST . . . . 246 BURIED LIFE   38
        THERE BADE ME GAZE AND THERE ASPIRE . . . . 301 GRANDE CHARTR   70
        AND THEN HE BADE REMEMBER HOW WE PASSD   . . . . . 356 MEROPE   774
        AND BADE THE WINDS THROUGH SPACE IMPEL THE GUSTY TOY 415 EMPEDOCLES I 2   81
        WHO BADE HIM LOOSE HIS BOAT AND FIX HIS OAR . . . 444 WESTMIN ABBEY   24
        LIKE SUNSHINE WENT AND CAME AND BADE . . . . 460 KAISER DEAD   47

BADEN
        TO SWITZERLAND TO BADEN TO THE RHINE . . . . 167 RACHEL 1   10

BADNESS
          FOR I FIND WORTH IN THEE AND BADNESS TOO   . . . .   404 MEROPE   1990

BAFFLED
          MOCKD AND BAFFLED BY YOUR GLADNESS   . . . . . .   32 NEW SIRENS   169
          SHAMD AND BAFFLED BY YOUR GLADNESS   . . . . . .   32 NEW SIRENS   V 169
          TURNING SICK AND BAFFLED LEARNS   . . . . . .   SECOND BEST   V   20
          BAFFLED BEWILDERD THEY STRAY   . . . .   216 LORDS MESSENGER   14
          WHICH MUCH TO HAVE TRIED IN MUCH BEEN BAFFLED BRINGS   260 SCHOLAR-GIPSY   165
          BAFFLED UNKNOWN SELF-CONSUMED   . . . .   285 HAWORTH CHURCH   98
          OF CONCORD AND BEEN BAFFLED WITH DISDAIN   . . . .   360 MEROPE   V 881
          BAFFLED FOR EVER AND STILL THOUGHT AND MIND   . .   439 EMPEDOCLES II   358
          THE TRUE HEART-BREAKING BAFFLED HOPE AND SHAME   . .   LUCRETIUS 2   13

BAFFLERS
          BAFFLERS OF OUR OWN PRAYERS FROM YOUTH TO LIFES   420 EMPEDOCLES I 2   231
               LAST SCENES

BAFFLING
          BUT THE WIT-BAFFLING WILL AND HAND OF HEAVEN   . .   363 MEROPE   952
          TO HAVE ADVANCED TRUE FRIENDS AND BEAT DOWN   425 EMPEDOCLES I 2   401
               BAFFLING FOES
          AND BREAK HIS HEART WITH ALL THE BAFFLING CHANGE . .   448 WESTMIN ABBEY   149

BAGLEY
          IN AUTUMN ON THE SKIRTS OF BAGLEY WOOD   . . . .   258 SCHOLAR-GIPSY   111

BAH
          BAH THOU A DOCTOR THOU ART SUPERSTITIOUS   . . . .   410 EMPEDOCLES I 1   133

BAHREIN
          BY SANDY BAHREIN IN THE PERSIAN GULF . . . . . .   69 SOHRAB RUSTUM   286

BAIJAN
          THOU KNOWST IF SINCE FROM ADER-BAIJAN FIRST   . .   62 SOHRAB RUSTUM   42
          MY MOTHER WHO IN ADER-BAIJAN DWELLS   . . . . . .   78 SOHRAB RUSTUM   590
          WHICH WAS IN ADER-BAIJAN BORN TO HIM . . . . . .   79 SOHRAB RUSTUM   608
          IN ADER-BAIJAN AND HE SAW THAT YOUTH . . . . . .   80 SOHRAB RUSTUM   631
          THOU KNOWEST IF SINCE FROM ADER-BAIJAN FIRST   . .   62 SOHRAB RUSTUM   V   42

BAKED
          BAKED ON THE EMBERS ALL AROUND   . . . .   191 STRAYED REVEL   167

BALANCE
          IT WERE NOT MEET THE BALANCE SWERVED   . . . . . .   92 SICK KING BOKH   139
          WE HAD NOT LOST OUR BALANCE THEN NOR GROWN   . . . .   436 EMPEDOCLES II   248
          WITHIN THE BALANCE OF A SLOW SUSPENSE   . . . . .   RUDE ORATOR   5

BALANCED
          MY SPECIAL THANKS WHOSE EVEN-BALANCED SOUL   . . . .   2 TO A FRIEND   9
          IS THIS ALL THIS BALANCED MEASURE   . . . . . .   33 NEW SIRENS   199
          AH ON WHICH IF BOTH OUR LOTS WERE BALANCED   . . . .   144 TRISTRAM 2   49

BALCONY
          ON THE BROWN RUDE-CARVED BALCONY TWO FORMS   . . . .   25 DREAM   21

BALD
          LIKE THAT BALD CAESAR THE FAMED ROMAN WIGHT   . .   153 TRISTRAM 3   143

BALDER
          SO ON THE FLOOR LAY BALDER DEAD AND ROUND   . . . .   95 BALDER DEAD 1   1
          AT BALDER WHOM NO WEAPON PIERCED OR CLOVE   . . . .   95 BALDER DEAD 1   4
          AND STOOD ROUND BALDER ON THE BLOODY FLOOR   . . . .   95 BALDER DEAD 1   10
          BALDER HAS MET HIS DEATH AND YE SURVIVE   . . . .   96 BALDER DEAD 1   26
          FROM AROUND BALDER ALL THE HEROES WENT   . . . .   97 BALDER DEAD 1   62
          CAN I O MOTHER BRING THEM BALDER BACK   . . . . .   98 BALDER DEAD 1   107
          ON BALDER DEATH HATH LAID HER HAND NOT THEE . . . .   98 BALDER DEAD 1   117
          WOULD FREELY DIE TO PURCHASE BALDER BACK   . . . .   98 BALDER DEAD 1   120
          BALDER THEIR JOY SO BRIGHT SO LOVED A GOD   . . . .   98 BALDER DEAD 1   126
          AND BALDER SITTING CROWND AND HELAS THRONE   . . . .   100 BALDER DEAD 1   175
          FOR BALDER WHOM SHE HOLDS BY RIGHT BELOW   . . . .   100 BALDER DEAD 1   181
          AND MAKE HER YIELD AND GIVE HIM BALDER BACK   . .   100 BALDER DEAD 1   183
          OF BALDER FROM THE FLOOR OF ODINS HALL   . . . .   101 BALDER DEAD 1   205
          BREIDABLIK ON WHOSE COLUMNS BALDER GRAVED   . . . .   101 BALDER DEAD 1   208
          THERE TO HIS HALL THE GODS BROUGHT BALDER HOME   . .   101 BALDER DEAD 1   214
          WOULD THAT OURSELVES O BALDER WE WERE BORNE . . . .   101 BALDER DEAD 1   216
          HEAVY IN HEART FOR BALDER TO HIS HOUSE . . . . .   101 BALDER DEAD 1   223
          TO HELAS KINGDOM TO ASK BALDER BACK . . . . . .   102 BALDER DEAD 1   237
          AND STOOD BY BALDER LYING ON HIS BIER   . . . . .   102 BALDER DEAD 1   270
          SO BALDER FADED IN THE NIGHT AWAY   . . . . . .   104 BALDER DEAD 1   337
          AND STOOD ROUND BALDER LYING ON HIS BIER   . . . .   102 BALDER DEAD 1   V 270
          TO HELAS KINGDOM TO ASK BALDER BACK . . . . . .   106 BALDER DEAD 2   46
          BALDER HATH GONE THIS WAY AND TAEN THE ROAD . . . .   108 BALDER DEAD 2   122
          HELAS PALE SWARMS AND THERE WAS BALDER BOUND   . .   108 BALDER DEAD 2   133
          OF HELA AND SAW NEAR IT BALDER CROWND   . . . . .   109 BALDER DEAD 2   177
          FOR BALDER WHOM THOU HOLDST BY RIGHT BELOW   . . . .   110 BALDER DEAD 2   193
          FOR HEAVEN WAS BALDER BORN THE CITY OF GODS   . .   110 BALDER DEAD 2   198
          COME THEN IF BALDER WAS SO DEAR BELOVED   . . . .   111 BALDER DEAD 2   231
          HEAR HOW TO HEAVEN MAY BALDER BE RESTORED   . . . .   111 BALDER DEAD 2   233
          FAILS BUT ONE THING TO GRIEVE HERE BALDER STOPS   . .   111 BALDER DEAD 2   235
          MAY I ERE I DEPART BID BALDER HAIL   . . . . . .   111 BALDER DEAD 2   244
          HERMOD GREET BALDER IF THOU WILT AND HOLD   . . . .   111 BALDER DEAD 2   247

54

BALDER   (CONTINUED)
            AND STRAIGHT TO BALDER HERMOD TURND AND SPAKE   • • 111 BALDER DEAD 2   249
            EVEN IN THE ABODE OF DEATH O BALDER HAIL   • • • 112 BALDER DEAD 2   250
            HE SPAKE AND BALDER UTTERD HIM REPLY • • • • •   112 BALDER DEAD 2   262
            FAILS BUT ONE THING TO GRIEVE THERE BALDER STOPS • • 114 BALDER DEAD 3   43
            AND BEND HER HEART AND GIVE YOU BALDER BACK   • • • 115 BALDER DEAD 3   46
            BALDER FOR THAT IS WHAT THE DEAD DESIRE   • • • •   115 BALDER DEAD 3   52
            FAREWELL O BALDER BRIGHT AND LOVED MY SON   • • •   115 BALDER DEAD 3   67
            BUT FROM THY LIPS O BALDER NIGHT OR DAY   • • • •   116 BALDER DEAD 3   83
            BE YE THEN KIND AS BALDER TOO WAS KIND   • • • •   116 BALDER DEAD 3   87
            BALDER MY BROTHER THOU ART GONE A ROAD   • • • •   116 BALDER DEAD 3   99
            THOU ONLY BALDER WAST FOR EVER KIND   • • • •   116 BALDER DEAD 3   112
            SO BALDER SAID BUT ODER WELL I KNOW   • • • • •   117 BALDER DEAD 3   119
            TO THE WORLDS END AND BALDER NOW IS GONE   • • •   117 BALDER DEAD 3   121
            BALDER THERE YET ARE MANY SCALDS IN HEAVEN   • • •   117 BALDER DEAD 3   132
            BUT WHEN THOU SANGEST BALDER THOU DIDST STRIKE   • • 117 BALDER DEAD 3   141
            OF BALDER ON THE HIGHEST TOP THEY LAID   • • • •   118 BALDER DEAD 3   163
            TO LEAVE FOR EVER BALDER IN THE GRAVE   • • • •   120 BALDER DEAD 3   228
            FOR DEAR-BELOVED WAS BALDER WHILE HE LIVED   • • •   120 BALDER DEAD 3   232
            AND BRING IN TRIUMPH BALDER BACK TO HEAVEN   • • •   120 BALDER DEAD 3   244
            FOR BALDER IF THOU HAPLY THUS MAYST MELT   • • •   122 BALDER DEAD 3   293
            BALDER IF HAPLY HE MAY THUS BE WON   • • •   122 BALDER DEAD 3   301
            OF ALL THINGS WEEPING TO BRING BALDER BACK   • • •   122 BALDER DEAD 3   318
            BALDER IS DEAD AND HELA HOLDS HER PREY   • • • •   123 BALDER DEAD 3   347
            BEGRUDGE NOT THINE TO ALL WAS BALDER DEAR   • • •   123 BALDER DEAD 3   349
            IS BALDER DEAD AND DO YE COME FOR TEARS   • • • • 123 BALDER DEAD 3   351
            NO LESS THAN BALDER HAVE I LOST THE LIGHT   • • •   125 BALDER DEAD 3   401
            BALDER UPBRAIDS ME NOT NOR HATES AT ALL   • • • • 125 BALDER DEAD 3   407
            SITS BALDER STILL IN POMP BY HELAS SIDE   • • • • 125 BALDER DEAD 3   429
            BALDER AND NANNA AND TO BALDER SAID   • • • •   126 BALDER DEAD 3   445
            BALDER AND NANNA AND TO BALDER SAID   • • • •   126 BALDER DEAD 3   445
            BALDER TOO TRULY THOU FORESAWST A SNARE   • • • • 126 BALDER DEAD 3   446
            THEREFORE FOR THE LAST TIME O BALDER HAIL   • • •   126 BALDER DEAD 3   453
            HE SPAKE AND BALDER ANSWERD HIM AND SAID   • • •   126 BALDER DEAD 3   454
            YET HERE THOU LIEST BALDER UNDERGROUND   • • • •   127 BALDER DEAD 3   471
            HE SPAKE BUT BALDER ANSWERD HIM AND SAID   • • •   127 BALDER DEAD 3   483
            AND THE RAY-CROWNED BALDER ANSWERD HIM   •   • • •   128 BALDER DEAD 3   517
            THOU ONLY BALDER WERT FOR EVER KIND   • • • • •   116 BALDER DEAD 3   V 112

BALDERS
            GAINST THAT ALONE HAD BALDERS LIFE NO CHARM   • •   95 BALDER DEAD 1   8
            IF ANY HERE MIGHT WEEP FOR BALDERS DEATH   • • • •   96 BALDER DEAD 1   20
            BRING WOOD TO THE SEASHORE TO BALDERS SHIP   • • •   96 BALDER DEAD 1   41
            AND ON THE TOP LAY BALDERS CORPSE AND PUT   • • •   96 BALDER DEAD 1   43
            AND CEASE TO MOURN AND THINK OF BALDERS PYRE   • •   97 BALDER DEAD 1   60
            AND CAST IT AT THE DEAR-LOVED BALDERS BREAST   • •   98 BALDER DEAD 1   102
            GAINST THAT ALONE HAD BALDERS LIFE NO CHARM   • •   98 BALDER DEAD 1   104
            THAT ONE SHOULD GRUDGE ITS LOSS FOR BALDERS SAKE • •   98 BALDER DEAD 1   125
            BUT IN BREIDABLIK NANNA BALDERS WIFE • • • •   102 BALDER DEAD 1   268
            THEN BALDERS SPIRIT THROUGH THE GLOOM DREW NEAR   • • 103 BALDER DEAD 1   282
            WHICH TOOK ON BALDERS TRACK THE WAY BELOW   • • •   104 BALDER DEAD 1   341
            AND MAKE A FUNERAL-PILE ON BALDERS SHIP   • • •   106 BALDER DEAD 2   43
            AND RANGED THE WOOD IN STACKS BY BALDERS SHIP   • •   106 BALDER DEAD 2   68
            AND I COME SENT THIS ROAD ON BALDERS TRACK   • • •   108 BALDER DEAD 2   116
            THE GODS ON THE SEA-SHORE BY BALDERS SHIP   • • •   113 BALDER DEAD 2   310
            ROUND BALDERS CORPSE WHICH THEY HAD THITHER BORNE   113 BALDER DEAD 3   2
            IF CLEAR FROM PLOTTING BALDERS DEATH TO SWIM   • •   114 BALDER DEAD 3   27
            ON BALDERS BREAST AND THUS BEGAN THE WAIL   • • •   115 BALDER DEAD 3   66
            AND OVER BALDERS CORPSE THESE WORDS DIDST SAY   • •   115 BALDER DEAD 3   74
            SHE IN HER HANDS TOOK BALDERS HEAD AND SPAKE   • •   116 BALDER DEAD 3   98
            BRING NOW THE GATHERD WOOD TO BALDERS SHIP   • • •   118 BALDER DEAD 3   158
            THE WOOD TO BALDERS SHIP AND BUILT A PILE   • • •   118 BALDER DEAD 3   161
            AND HIS HORSE BALDERS HORSE WHOM MOST HE LOVED   • • 118 BALDER DEAD 3   171
            AND LONG IN THE FAR DARK BLAZED BALDERS PILE   • •   119 BALDER DEAD 3   200
            ENTREATING ALL THINGS TO WEEP BALDERS DEATH   • •   122 BALDER DEAD 3   305
            THOK WITH DRY EYES WILL WEEP OER BALDERS PYRE   • •   123 BALDER DEAD 3   352
            DOUBTLESS THOU FEAREST TO MEET BALDERS VOICE   • •   124 BALDER DEAD 3   392
            SO FLARD IN THE FAR DARKNESS BALDERS PYRE   • • •   119 BALDER DEAD 3   V 200
            SO SHOWED IN THE FAR DARKNESS BALDERS PYRE   • • •   119 BALDER DEAD 3   V 200

BALE
            MOTHER A CHILD OF BALE THOU BARST IN ME   • • • •   98 BALDER DEAD 1   95
            HODER ILL-FATED CHILD OF BALE MY SON • • • • •   98 BALDER DEAD 1   112
            AND BIND THY CARCASE LIKE A BALE WITH CORDS   • •   114 BALDER DEAD 3   25
            TYRANNOUS TEMPESTS OF BALE   • • • • • • •   293 HEINES GRAVE   35

BALEFUL
            BLAZED BRIGHT AND BALEFUL LIKE THAT AUTUMN-STAR   • •   74 SOHRAB RUSTUM   452
            THE BALEFUL SIGN OF FEVERS DUST HAD SOILD   • • •   74 SOHRAB RUSTUM   453

BALES
            OF SILK-BALES AND OF BALSAM-DROPS   • • • • • •   191 STRAYED REVEL   193
            AND ON THE BEACH UNDID HIS CORDED BALES   • • • •   262 SCHOLAR-GIPSY   250

BALIUS
            XANTHUS AND BALIUS BOTH YE FAR-FAMD SEED OF PODARGA   HOMER TRANS   39

BALL
            WE MINE THIS EARTHEN BALL   • • • • • • • • •   423 EMPEDOCLES I 2   320

BALM

BUT THEY TOO DOUBTLESS WILL HAVE BREATHED THE BALM	126 BALDER DEAD 3	437
ONLY DEATH CAN BALM THY WOE	139 TRISTRAM 1	289
WITH SILENCE BALM MY WHIRLING BRAIN	158 SAINT BRANDAN	70
AFFORD NO BALM	200 PHILOMELA	15
AH QUIET ALL THINGS FEEL THY BALM	208 ON THE RHINE	21
IN PUFFS OF BALM THE NIGHT-AIR BLOWS	218 BACCHANALIA 1	14

BALMD

HE SLUMBERD AND AMBROSIA BALMD THE CHILD	446 WESTMIN ABBEY	88

BALMS

AND THEY ARE SWEPT BY BALMS OF SPRING	182 TO MARG CONT	8
BALMS FLOATING ON THY MOUNTAIN-AIR	309 OBERMANN	111

BALMY

THAT AS THE BALMY DARKNESS FELL	54 RESIGNATION	83
THE NIGHTS BALMY PRIME	442 EMPEDOCLES II	444

BALSAM

OF SILK-BALES AND OF BALSAM-DROPS	191 STRAYED REVEL	193

BALTIC

THE BALTIC SEA ALONG	159 NECKAN	2
GREEN ROLLS THE BALTIC SEA	159 NECKAN	6
THE BALTIC SEA ALONG	161 NECKAN	66

BALUSTRADE

HERE LEAN MY HEAD ON THIS COLD BALUSTRADE	19 MODERN SAPPHO		4
HERE LEAN MY HEAD ON THIS COOL BALUSTRADE	19 MODERN SAPPHO	V	4
HERE WHERE THIS GREY BALUSTRADE	234 YOUTH OF MAN		62

BAN

MY NAME IS UNDER ALL MENS BAN	157 SAINT BRANDAN	27
THEREFORE WITH UNEXCEPTING BAN	353 MEROPE	687

BAND

THE STRONG BAND WHICH PASSION AROUND HIM HATH FURLD	20 MODERN SAPPHO		22
THE STRONG BAND WHICH BEAUTY AROUND HIM HATH FURLD	20 MODERN SAPPHO	V	22
WHEN FROM THE SOUTH SHALL MARCH THE FIERY BAND	127 BALDER DEAD 3		475
BOUND I WAS I COULD NOT BREAK THE BAND	142 TRISTRAM 2		6
CIRCLED TRISTRAM BY A BAND OF GOLD	143 TRISTRAM 2		44
I WAS BOUND I COULD NOT BREAK THE BAND	142 TRISTRAM 2	V	6
SHAKE LOOSE SOME BAND OF SOFT BROWN HAIR	205 CALAIS SANDS		16
THE BAND WILL QUIT MANS HEART HE WILL BREATHE FREE	239 REVOLUTIONS		20
LOVING A SISTERLY BAND	284 HAWORTH CHURCH		81
AND WITH THAT SMALL TRANSFIGURED BAND	311 OBERMANN		145
A WOLFISH BAND IN A DISPEOPLED REALM	338 MEROPE		288
THERE THE YOUNGEST OF THE BAND OF CONQUERORS	345 MEROPE		465
I PRAY THE FURIES EVER-RESTLESS BAND	349 MEROPE		569
THESE ARE NOT NOW THE SAVAGE BAND WHO ERST	381 MEROPE		1299
THEIR MASTER FALLN THESE WILL NOT FLINCH BUT BAND	381 MEROPE		1306
WITH A GAY REVELLING BAND HE BREAKS FROM THEM	412 EMPEDOCLES I 2		16
THERE AS HE GAZED A WONDROUS BAND THEY CAME	476 CROMWELL		163
OF THAT DUSK SLOW-MOVING BAND	META CLOISTER		10

BANDIED

BE MISERABLY BANDIED TO AND FRO	435 EMPEDOCLES II	230

BANDS

REVIEWS AND RANKS HIS MOTLEY BANDS	53 RESIGNATION		45
AS THEY FEEL THE FATAL BANDS	135 TRISTRAM 1		149
SHAKE BACK THY BANDS OF SOFT BROWN HAIR	205 CALAIS SANDS	V	16
FROM BANDS OF GREEDY HEIRS BE FREE	249 WISH		2

BANE

BLIND LEADERS TO THEIR BANE	353 MEROPE	675
OUR BANE DISGUISE IT AS WE MAY	482 COURAGE	25

BANEFUL

COME BANEFUL MISCHIEF FROM THY MURKY DEN	367 MEROPE	1063

BANISHD

THE LOVE-DESPERATE BANISHD KNIGHT	136 TRISTRAM 1	186
WHERE HE WAS PARAMOUNT SINCE HE IS BANISHD	410 EMPEDOCLES I 1	123
AND THEN THY FRIEND IS BANISHD AND ON THAT	411 EMPEDOCLES I 1	143
THE WEARY MAN THE BANISHD CITIZEN	429 EMPEDOCLES II	11

BANISHES

SHEDS BLOOD IMPRISONS BANISHES ATTAINTS	353 MEROPE	682

BANISHMENT

WHEN HIS STAR REIGND BEFORE HIS BANISHMENT	408 EMPEDOCLES I 1	65
WHOSE' BANISHMENT IS NOT HIS GREATEST ILL	429 EMPEDOCLES II	12

BANK

BORDERD EACH BANK WITH PINES THE MORNING SUN	24 DREAM	3
HIGH ON A BANK OUR LEADER STANDS	53 RESIGNATION	44
ON THIS MILD BANK ABOVE THE STREAM	55 RESIGNATION	102
WASHD EDDYING FROM THIS BANK THEIR HOME	58 RESIGNATION	202

BANK   (CONTINUED)
        LEFT FRESHLY GATHERD ON THEIR NATIVE BANK   . .   .   86 SOHRAB RUSTUM   845
        ASOPUS BANK   . . . .   190 STRAYED REVEL   138
        MOORD TO THE COOL BANK IN THE SUMMER-HEATS   . . .   257 SCHOLAR-GIPSY   67
        SITTING UPON THE RIVER BANK OERGROWN   . . . . .   258 SCHOLAR-GIPSY   97
        DOWN EACH GREEN BANK HATH GONE THE PLOUGHBOYS TEAM   266 THYRSIS   118
        IN A BANK OF VAPOURS AGAIN   . . . .   297 HEINES GRAVE   174
        ON THE HIGH SEA-BANK IN THE SIGHT   . . . . .   345 MEROPE   482
        ON EVERY BANK THE VIRGIN SAXIFRAGE   . . . . .   EVERLASTING SUB   5

BANKS
        HEMMD BY TWO BANKS OF CLOUD PEERS PALE AND WEAK   . .   10 MYCERINUS   57
        THERE BY THE RIVER-BANKS HE WANDERD ON   . . . .   11 MYCERINUS   85
        THE TARTARS OF FERGHANA FROM THE BANKS   . . . .   64 SOHRAB RUSTUM   128
        PLUNGING THROUGH DEEP UNTRODDEN BANKS OF SNOW   . .   107 BALDER DEAD 2   97
        AND THEIR QUICK TWITTERING FILLS THE BANKS AND SHORES 109 BALDER DEAD 2   162
        THE HOLLOWS GRASSY BANKS ARE SOFT-INCLINED   . . . . 149 TRISTRAM 3   10
        THE OPENINGS GRASSY BANKS ARE SOFT INCLINED   . .   TRISTRAM 3   V   10
        THE OPENINGS GRASSY BANKS WERE SOFT INCLINED   .   TRISTRAM 3   V   10
        OVER BANKS OF BRIGHT SEAWEED   . . . .   165 FORSAKEN MERM   134
        THE ROCKY BANKS THE TERRACE HIGH   . . . . .   183 TERRACE BERNE   3
        RIVETS HIS GAZE ON THE BANKS OF THE STREAM   . . .   251 FUTURE   6
        AS IS THE WORLD ON THE BANKS   . . . .   252 FUTURE   17
        THAT THE DIN WILL BE MORE ON ITS BANKS   . . . .   253 FUTURE   62
        AS THE BANKS FADE DIMMER AWAY   . . . .   254 FUTURE   84
        THAT MUFFLE ITS WET BANKS BUT GLADE   . . . . .   414 EMPEDOCLES I 2   51

BANNER
        TO-DAY A HEROS BANNER IS UNFURLD   . . . . . .   3 EMERSONS ESSAYS   4
        AND FIGHT BENEATH MY BANNER TILL I DIE   . . . .   71 SOHRAB RUSTUM   332
        BANNER BY TURNS AND BUGLE WOO   . . . .   305 GRANDE CHARTR   191

BANNERS
        US WHO WITH BANNERS UNFURLD   . . . .   216 LORDS MESSENGER   V
        THE BANNERS FLASHING THROUGH THE TREES   . . . .   305 GRANDE CHARTR   187
        PASS BANNERS PASS AND BUGLES CEASE   . . . . .   306 GRANDE CHARTR   209
        ARISE AND ARM THEE SPREAD THY BANNERS FORTH   . .   465 ALARIC AT ROME   95

BANQUET
        WITH THEIR MILD DARK HIS GRASSY BANQUET-HALL   . .   12 MYCERINUS   119
        IN THE BANQUET-HALL OF TYNTAGIL   . . . . . .   146 TRISTRAM 2   V 115
        IN THE BANQUET AND LEARND HIS SONGS   . . . . .   189 STRAYED REVEL   123
        FROM THE HALF-TRIED BANQUET OF LIFE   . . . . .   199 EARLY DEATH   10
        AND AT THE BANQUET ALL THE MUSES SANG   . . . .   427 EMPEDOCLES I 2   451

BANQUETINGS
        LOVE FREE TO RANGE AND REGAL BANQUETINGS   . . . .   9 MYCERINUS   34

BAPTISMAL
        WHO SINS ONCE WASHD BY THE BAPTISMAL WAVE   . . . .   172 GOOD SHEPHERD   5

BAR
        WERE BAR AND THIS TOO WAS THEIR FATHERS CRIME   . .   339 MEROPE   326
        OR OUR OWN WANT OF EFFORT BE THE BAR   . . . . .   352 MEROPE   643
        TO BREATHE A SYLLABLE TO BAR REVENGE   . . . . .   389 MEROPE   1528

BARBARIANS
        FLASHT ON THE RUDE BARBARIANS WILD ARRAY   . . . .   464 ALARIC AT ROME   70

BARD
        THROUGH THE ISLANDS SOME DIVINE BARD   . . . . . .   189 STRAYED REVEL   118
        WHAT BARD   . . . .   253 FUTURE   41
        KEPT THE MEMORIAL BARD   . . . .   281 HAWORTH CHURCH   20
        HELD MEMORIAL BARD   . . . .   281 HAWORTH CHURCH   V 20
        SURELY IT WAS THAT BARD   . . . .   295 HEINES GRAVE   98
        WHICH BEST BEFITS ITS BARD   . . . .   322 OBERMANN MORE   304
        WHICH BEST BESEEM ITS BARD   . . . .   322 OBERMANN MORE   V 304
        OR WITH PEN-BRYNS BOLD BARD PURSUES   . . . . .   458 KAISER DEAD   5

BARDS
        GODS ARE WE BARDS SAINTS HEROES IF WE WILL   . . . .   4 EMERSONS ESSAYS   13
        THE WISE BARDS ALSO   . . . .   192 STRAYED REVEL   208
        BARDS MAKE NEW POEMS   . . . .   220 BACCHANALIA 2   37
        OF BARDS FULL MANY A STROKE DIVINE   . . . . . .   222 EPILOG LAOCOON   20
        YE KNOW NOT YOURSELVES AND YOUR BARDS   . . . .   231 YOUTH OF NATURE   103

BARE
        O MAN WHOM EARTH THY LONG-VEXT MOTHER BARE   . . . .   46 IN UTRUMQUE PAR   32
        AND IN THE MIDST A STUBBLE SHORT AND BARE   . . .   70 SOHRAB RUSTUM   296
        THE NORNIES WHEN HIS MOTHER BARE HIM SPUN   . . .   96 BALDER DEAD 1   24
        AND LAID IT ON A BIER AND BARE HIM HOME   . . . .   101 BALDER DEAD 1   206
        THE BARE HEATHS SPREADING CLEAR AS DAY   . . . .   141 TRISTRAM 1   364
        A GIRL THEIR CLOTHES THEIR RAGS THEIR FEET WERE BARE   169 WEST LONDON   4
        IN THE BARE MIDST OF ANGLESEY THEY SHOW   . . . .   170 EAST AND WEST   1
        WITH ONE ARM BARE   . . . .   189 STRAYED REVEL   107
        PARCH THEM IN WINTER-TIME ON THE BARE STEPP   . .   193 STRAYED REVEL   241
        LAYS BARE OF WRETCHED DAYS   . . . .   260 SCHOLAR-GIPSY   186
        TOPS IN LIFES MORNING-SUN SO BRIGHT AND BARE   . .   267 THYRSIS   145
        BARE ON ITS LONELY RIDGE THE TREE THE TREE   . . .   267 THYRSIS   160
        BARE UNSHADED ALONE   . . . .   287 RUGBY CHAPEL   35

BARE   (CONTINUED)
        AND WRESTLE RISING THEN WITH BARE   . . . . . 300 GRANDE CHARTR   40
        AND THE BLANCHD SUMMIT BARE   . . . . 324 OBERMANN MORE   338
        OF THIS POOR SOUL WHO BARE HIM AND HIS SIRE   349 MEROPE   578
        SLOPE BEHIND SLOPE UP TO THE PEAK LIES BARE   . . 414 EMPEDOCLES I 2   55
        ON SOME BARE HEADLAND STRAINING MOURNFULLY . . . . 477 CROMWELL   190

BARED
        BUT HE LOOKD ON AND SMILED NOR BARED HIS SWORD   . . 74 SOHRAB RUSTUM 425
        HIS BELT AND NEAR THE SHOULDER BARED HIS ARM   . . 81 SOHRAB RUSTUM 670
        AND SOHRAB BARED THAT IMAGE ON HIS ARM   . . . . 81 SOHRAB RUSTUM   684
        AND SOHRAB BARED THAT FIGURE ON HIS ARM   . . . . 81 SOHRAB RUSTUM V 684

BAREST
        FOR FIRST THOU BAREST ME WITH BLINDED EYES . . . . 98 BALDER DEAD 1   96
        THOU BAREST ME AND UNFORESEEING SOUL . . . . . . 98 BALDER DEAD 1   99

BARGE
        SITTING IN THE GILDED BARGE   . . . . 134 TRISTRAM 1   111
        NOR IS THAT WIND LESS ROUGH WHICH BLOWS A GOOD   420 EMPEDOCLES I 2   256
            MANS BARGE
        NOR IS THE WIND LESS ROUGH THAT BLOWS A GOOD   420 EMPEDOCLES I 2 V 256
            MANS BARGE

BARING
        BARING HIS DUMB REMORSE TO FUTURE DAYS   . . . . 167 PICT NEWSTEAD   13

BARK
        FAINTLY THE BARK OF A DOG   . . . . 234 YOUTH OF MAN   73
        ALLOWS THE PROUDLY-RIDING AND THE FOUNDERING BARK   421 EMPEDOCLES I 2 261
        ALLOWS THE PROUDLY-RIDING AND THE FOUNDERD BARK . . 421 EMPEDOCLES I 2 V 261
        AND BY THE FISHERS BARK   . . . . 445 WESTMIN ABBEY   42

BARLEY
        SWEET CHESTNUTS BARLEY-CAKES AND BOARS-FLESH DRIED   356 MEROPE   754
        BY THEIR CHARIOTS STOOD THE STEEDS AND CHAMPD   HOMER TRANS   5
            THE WHITE BARLEY

BARN
        BY BARN IN THRESHING-TIME BY NEW-BUILT RICK   . . 263 THYRSIS   34

BARNS
        TO WATCH THE THRESHERS IN THE MOSSY BARNS   . . . . 258 SCHOLAR-GIPSY 104

BARRD
        FOR HIM FOR OTHERS ALL RETURN IS BARRD   . . . . 113 BALDER DEAD 2 292
        AND MILK-BARRD ONYX-STONES   . . . . 192 STRAYED REVEL   197
        AT THEIR RETURN UP THE BARRD STRAND   . . . . . . 211 DOVER BEACH   V 11

BARREN
        O BARREN BOAST O JOYLESS MOCKERY   . . . . . .   EMERSONS ESSAYS V 14
        THE BARREN OPTIMISTIC SOPHISTRIES   . . . .   7 REP FRIEND   5
        HUNGRY AND BARREN AND SHARP AS THE SEA   . . . . 39 STAGIRIUS   47
        UPON TIMES BARREN STORMY FLOW   . . . . 183 ABSENCE   19
        FRESH PRODUCTS OF THEIR BARREN LABOUR FALL . . . . 243 SUMMER NIGHT   43
        SUCH BARREN KNOWLEDGE AWHILE   . . . . 296 HEINES GRAVE   119
        WHO WOULD NOT TURN HIM FROM THE BARREN SEA . . . . 470 ALARIC AT ROME 221
        BETWEEN THE BARREN MOUNTAINS AND THE STORMY SEA . . 475 CROMWELL   118

BARRIER
        NOW AS THE BARRIER CLOSES DIES AWAY   . . . . . . 10 MYCERINUS   58
        WHERE YOUR COLD DISTANT BARRIER   . . . . 175 PARTING   11

BARRING
        BARRING HIS WAY AND IN THE WALL A GRATE   . . . . 100 BALDER DEAD 1 167
        BARRING HIS WAY AND IN THE WALL A GRATE   . . . . 109 BALDER DEAD 2 145

BARS
        BUT RIGHT BARS THIS NOT ONLY THY DESIRE   . . . . 104 BALDER DEAD 1 313
        OR HOW OERLEAP THE GRATE THAT BARS THE WALL   . . 110 BALDER DEAD 2   185
        LISTLESSLY THROUGH THE WINDOW-BARS   . . . . . . 131 TRISTRAM 1   41

BARST
        MOTHER A CHILD OF BALE THOU BARST IN ME   . . . . 98 BALDER DEAD 1   95

BASE
        SPARES BUT THE CLOUDY BORDER OF HIS BASE   . . . .   3 SHAKESPEARE   7
        SPARES OFTEN BUT THE BORDER OF HIS BASE   . . . .   3 SHAKESPEARE   V 7
        SPARES BUT THE BORDER OFTEN OF HIS BASE   . . . .   3 SHAKESPEARE   V 7
        INVOLVED IN ONE SUSPICION WITH THE BASE   . . . . 341 MEROPE   367
        THERE IS A CHASM RIFTED IN THE BASE   . . . . . . 358 MEROPE   811
        FROM THEIR DEEP BASE THY BEETLING CLIFFS DUNBAR . . 476 CROMWELL   151

BASED
        BASED ON PURE PUBLIC WELFARE LET US BE   . . . . 394 MEROPE   1718

BASELY
        HAD IN A FATHERS PLACE HE BASELY MURDERD   . . . . 364 MEROPE   977

BASENESS
        BUT FROM THEIR BASENESS WHO WOULD WORK HER RUE . . 37 WORLDS TRIUMPHS V 4

BASILIS
    TO CYPSELUS AT BASILIS THIS NEWS . . . . . . 359 MEROPE   846
    BASILIS HIS NEW CITY WHICH HE NOW . . . . . . 359 MEROPE   847
    TO CYPSELUS AT BASILIS HE BROUGHT . . . . . . 364 MEROPE   V

BASINS
    INTO THEIR STONE-CARVED BASINS COLD . . . . . . 300 GRANDE CHARTR   32

BASIS
    WHO DWELL ON A FIRM BASIS OF CONTENT . . . . . . 436 EMPEDOCLES II   260

BASK
    DRY THEIR MAIL AND BASK IN THE BRINE . . . . . . 162 FORSAKEN MERM   42
    WHEN THOU DOST BASK IN NATURES EYE . . . . . . 241 MORALITY   14
    BASK IN THE GLENS OR ON THE WARM SEA-SHORE . . . . 427 EMPEDOCLES I 2 437

BASKET
    AND EASED OF BASKET AND OF ROD . . . . 248 KENSINGTON GARD 19
    HIS COAT HIS BASKET AND HIS EARTHEN CRUSE . . . . 255 SCHOLAR-GIPSY   13

BASKING
    THE BASKING TORTOISES . . . . 392 MEROPE   1627

BASKS
    BASKS IN HIS MORNING OF YOUTH . . . . 347 MEROPE   521
    THE HAPPY HUNTER HE BASKS . . . . 347 MEROPE   V

BASTIOND
    THAN THE ICE-BASTIOND CAUCASIAN MOUNT . . . . 395 MEROPE   1749

BATH
    LIFE ONE PERPETUAL FIGHT A BATH OF BLOOD . . . . 128 BALDER DEAD 3   506

BATHD
    BATHD IN A BLAZE OF SUNSET MELT AWAY . . . . . . 478 CROMWELL   216

BATHE
    RIDE DOWN AND BATHE MY HOT BROW IN THE FLOOD . . 139 TRISTRAM 1   282
    TO BATHE IN THE ABANDOND LASHER PASS . . . . . 258 SCHOLAR-GIPSY   95
    THEY BATHE ON THIS MOUNTAIN . . . . 442 EMPEDOCLES II   453

BATHED
    SHE BATHED IT IN SMILES OF GLEE . . . . 21 REQUIESCAT   6
    O SEEMING SOLE TO AWAKE THY SUN-BATHED HEAD . . 45 IN UTRUMQUE PAR   29
    WE BATHED OUR HANDS WITH SPEECHLESS GLEE . . . 54 RESIGNATION   84
    AND TRANQUIL FROM WHOSE FLOOR THE NEW-BATHED STARS 87 SOHRAB RUSTUM   891
    THEIR SPEARS ARE DOWN THEIR STEEDS ARE BATHED IN FOAM 137 TRISTRAM 1   237
    HER PALFREYS FLANKS WERE MIRED AND BATHED IN SWEAT 154 TRISTRAM 3   171
    IN THE TWILIGHT AND BATHED IN DEW . . . . . . 234 YOUTH OF MAN   78
    BATHED IN THE SACRED DEWS OF MORN . . . . . . 250 WISH   33
    WHICH BATHED OUR LIFE RETIRED . . . . 319 OBERMANN MORE   190
    ON THE SWEET AND MOON-BATHED LAND . . . . . . META CLOISTER   12

BATHES
    THERE ON A HIGH GREEN SPUR WHICH BATHES ITS POINT 356 MEROPE   751
    THERE ON A GRASSY SPUR WHICH BATHES ITS ROOT . . 356 MEROPE   V 751

BATHING
    BUT WHEN THEY CAME FROM BATHING THOU WAST GONE . . 258 SCHOLAR-GIPSY   100
    BUT WHEN THEY CAME FROM BATHING THOU WERT GONE . . 258 SCHOLAR-GIPSY V 100
    LIKE CHILDREN BATHING ON THE SHORE . . . . . . 308 OBERMANN   73
    WE MIGHT HAVE JOY BLENT WITH THE ALL-BATHING AIR . . 439 EMPEDOCLES II   343
    WE SHOULD HAVE JOY BLENT WITH THE ALL-BATHING AIR 439 EMPEDOCLES II V 343

BATHS
    BEHIND ARE THE ABANDOND BATHS . . . . 306 OBERMANN   5

BATTALIONS
    MARSHALLD BATTALIONS BRIGHT IN BURNISHD STEEL . . 65 SOHRAB RUSTUM   140

BATTER
    BATTER FOR EVER IN VAIN . . . . 291 RUGBY CHAPEL V 186

BATTERD
    OF THE LONG-BATTERD WORLD UPLIFTS ITS WALL . . . . 267 THYRSIS   147
    THE BOAT WAS OLD A BATTERD BOAT . . . . . . 480 HAYSWATER BOAT   34

BATTLE
    SITS RAPT AND HEARS THE BATTLE BREAK BELOW . . . 42 GIPSY CHILD   23
    OF BATTLE AND WITH ME WHO MAKE NO PLAY . . . . 75 SOHRAB RUSTUM   463
    BUT THAT IN BATTLE WITH A NAMELESS FOE . . . . 79 SOHRAB RUSTUM   600
    ON BATTLE-FIELD HAVE MET THEIR DEATH AND NOW . . 104 BALDER DEAD 1   321
    THERE THROUGH SOME BATTLE-FIELD WHERE MEN FALL FAST 105 BALDER DEAD 2   24
    YET DOUBTLESS WHEN THE DAY OF BATTLE COMES . . . 127 BALDER DEAD 3   494
    THE RUSHING BATTLE CLEARD THY BLOOD . . . . . 139 TRISTRAM 1   292
    SEE YE THE BATTLE BELOW . . . . 216 LORDS MESSENGER V   2
    WE SHALL RENEW THE BATTLE IN THE PLAIN . . . . 236 PALLADIUM   13
    MEN WILL RENEW THE BATTLE IN THE PLAIN . . . . 236 PALLADIUM   V 13
    IN SOME CHANCE BATTLE ON CITHAERON-SIDE . . . 447 WESTMIN ABBEY   114
    THE DOOM PRONOUNCED THE BATTLE-FLAG UNFURLED . . 465 ALARIC AT ROME   93

BATTLE   (CONTINUED)
        THE SURGING BATTLE AND THE MAILD ARRAY   .   .   .   . 475 CROMWELL   138
        STILL TURND TO WATCH THE BATTLE STILL FORGOT   .   .   . 476 CROMWELL   171
        IF LIKE A COWARD I SKULKD BEHIND APART FROM THE BATTLE   HOMER TRANS   16
        IN SOME OTHER SORT THAN YOUR LAST WHEN THE   HOMER TRANS   41
            BATTLE IS ENDED
        SO HE SPAKE AND DROVE WITH A CRY HIS STEEDS   HOMER TRANS   63
            INTO BATTLE

BATTLES
        AND SHARE THE BATTLES COMMON CHANCE WITH US   .   .   63 SOHRAB RUSTUM   67
        BOY AS I AM I HAVE SEEN BATTLES TOO .   .   .   .   .   74 SOHRAB RUSTUM   433
        BUT NOW IN BLOOD AND BATTLES WAS MY YOUTH   .   .   85 SOHRAB RUSTUM   824
        AND FULL OF BLOOD AND BATTLES IS MY AGE   .   .   .   85 SOHRAB RUSTUM   825
        HIS SOUL WELL-KNIT AND ALL HIS BATTLES WON .   .   .   172 IMMORTALITY   13

BATTLING
        WRAPT IN THY CLOAK AND BATTLING WITH THE SNOW   .   .   258 SCHOLAR-GIPSY   124

BAWLING
        NOR LET THY BAWLING FELLOWS RACK THEIR THROATS   .   . 255 SCHOLAR-GIPSY   4

BAY
        AND TMOLUS HILL AND SMYRNA BAY THOUGH BLIND   .   .   2 TO A FRIEND   4
        AND TMOLUS HILL AND SMYRNAS BAY THOUGH BLIND   .   .   2 TO A FRIEND   V   4
        AND REARD HIM A BRIGHT BAY WITH LOFTY CREST   .   .   69 SOHRAB RUSTUM   276
        AND TRAIND HIM A BRIGHT BAY WITH LOFTY CREST   .   .   69 SOHRAB RUSTUM   V 276
        NOW MY BROTHERS CALL FROM THE BAY   .   .   .   .   .   161 FORSAKEN MERM   3
        WE HEARD THE SWEET BELLS OVER THE BAY   .   .   .   162 FORSAKEN MERM   31
        SHE SMILED SHE WENT UP THROUGH THE SURF IN THE BAY   163 FORSAKEN MERM   62
        COME I SAID AND WE ROSE THROUGH THE SURF IN THE BAY   163 FORSAKEN MERM   67
        EACH GLISTENING STRAND EACH HEATH-FRINGED BAY   .   177 FAREWELL   4
        GLIMMERING AND VAST OUT IN THE TRANQUIL BAY   .   .   210 DOVER BEACH   5
        AND GALATEA FROM THE BAY .   .   .   .   222 EPILOG LAOCOON   47
        GIRDLED THE GLISTENING BAY   .   .   .   .   .   .   242 SUMMER NIGHT   19
        THE SICKLE-SWEEP OF QUIBERON BAY   .   .   .   .   .   274 STANZAS CARNAC   27
        FAR IN THE BAY   .   .   .   .   275 SOUTHERN NIGHT   12
        NAPLES BAY FOR A SWEET   .   .   .   .   294 HEINES GRAVE   58
        WHICH FRINGE THY SOFT BLUE SPEZZIAN BAY   .   .   .   303 GRANDE CHARTR   142
        WHERE HUNTERS GATHER STAGHOUNDS BAY   .   .   .   .   305 GRANDE CHARTR   183
        THAT FRINGE THY SOFT BLUE SPEZZIAN BAY   .   .   .   303 GRANDE CHARTR   V 142
        THAT FRINGE THY DARK BLUE SPEZZIAN BAY   .   .   .   303 GRANDE CHARTR   V 142
        PARTS FROM THIS CAVE-PIERCED CLIFF THE SHELVING BAY   358 MEROPE   818
        WHERE FIRST THE CHASE PLUNGED IN THE BAY IS SMOOTH   358 MEROPE   819
        HIS BROAD-BRIMMD HUNTERS HAT WHICH IN THE BAY   .   .   358 MEROPE   843
        PARTS FROM THE CAVE-PIERCD CLIFF THE SHELVING BAY   358 MEROPE   V 818
        THE ADRIATIC BREAKS IN A WARM BAY   .   .   .   .   .   426 EMPEDOCLES I 2   428
        SMILINGLY FORTH UPON HER SUNNY BAY   .   .   .   .   468 ALARIC AT ROME   160
        AND LEFT IT ROCKING IN THE BAY .   .   .   .   .   .   480 HAYSWATER BOAT   32
        THE BOAT HATH DRIFTED IN THE BAY   .   .   .   .   .   480 HAYSWATER BOAT   37

BEACH
        AND BACK ALONG THE BEACH TO ASGARD WENT   .   .   .   101 BALDER DEAD 1   200
        ASGARD AND LED THEIR HORSES TO THE BEACH   .   .   .   106 BALDER DEAD 2   66
        HER FLOCK ALONG THE WHITE NORWEGIAN BEACH   .   .   .   117 BALDER DEAD 3   150
        AND THE GODS STOOD UPON THE BEACH AND GAZED   .   .   119 BALDER DEAD 3   193
        AND THEN THE BEACH AND MARKD WITH SPRAY   .   .   .   148 TRISTRAM 2   172
        WE WENT UP THE BEACH BY THE SANDY DOWN   .   .   .   163 FORSAKEN MERM   68
        ALONG THE NEVER-SILENT BEACH   .   .   .   .   .   .   204 CALAIS SANDS   V   3
        WHEN ON THE BEACH THE CYCLOPS LAY   .   .   .   .   .   222 EPILOG LAOCOON   46
        AND ON THE BEACH UNDID HIS CORDED BALES   .   .   .   262 SCHOLAR-GIPSY   250
        WHOSE BEACH ONCE RAN WITH LOYAL BLOOD   .   .   .   .   274 STANZAS CARNAC   28
        CURVES WITH THE CURVING BEACH AWAY .   .   .   .   .   275 SOUTHERN NIGHT   10

BEACHED
        FROM THOSE TWIN BROOKS THAT BEACHED STRAND .   .   .   480 HAYSWATER BOAT   21

BEACHES
        BEACHES THE PINNACE IN A DARKENING COVE   .   .   .   . 69 SOHRAB RUSTUM   V 288
        TO SHOW HIM SPITS AND BEACHES OF THE SEA   .   .   .   . 122 BALDER DEAD 3   321
        UP THE STILL GLISTENING BEACHES   .   .   .   .   .   . 165 FORSAKEN MERM   132

BEACONS
        TO WHERE THE LIGHTHOUSE BEACONS BRIGHT   .   .   .   . 275 SOUTHERN NIGHT   11
        BEACONS OF HOPE YE APPEAR   .   .   .   . 292 RUGBY CHAPEL   192
        BEACONS OF VENGEANCE NOT TO BE LET DIE   .   .   .   . 333 MEROPE   93

BEADED
        OF SHORT GRASS BEADED WITH DEW .   .   .   . 399 MEROPE   1823

BEADS
        HER ROSARY-BEADS OF EBONY TIPPD WITH GOLD   .   .   .   . 152 TRISTRAM 3   93
        CLUSTERD IN THICK BEADS DIM   .   .   .   . 186 STRAYED REVEL   16

BEAK
        TOUCH HIS TREMBLING BEAK WITH WINE .   .   .   .   .   . 452 POOR MATTHIAS   12

BEAM
        A LIGHT THAT FROM SOME UPPER FOUNT DID BEAM   .   .   9 MYCERINUS   21
        LED BY THY TAPERS STARLIKE BEAM   .   .   .   .   .   . 177 FAREWELL   8
        LIT BY THY TAPERS STARLIKE BEAM   .   .   .   .   .   . 177 FAREWELL   V   8
        LET BEAM UPON MY INWARD VIEW   .   .   .   . 208 ON THE RHINE   17

BEAM   (CONTINUED)
        OF PASSING TROOPS IN THE SUNS BEAM   . . . . . .   305 GRANDE CHARTR   177
        ON ETNA AND THE BEAM   . . . .   414 EMPEDOCLES I 2   43

BEAMD
        A HUNDRED LAMPS BEAMD IN THE TRANQUIL GLOOM   . .   11 MYCERINUS   94
        THEN RAISED HER FACE AND GLORY ROUND HER BEAMD   . . 447 WESTMIN ABBEY   V 96

BEAMS
        BUT TO THE STARS AND THE COLD LUNAR BEAMS   . . . .   45 IN UTRUMQUE PAR   19
        ALL SHINING IN THE WHITE MOON-BEAMS   . . . . . .   141 TRISTRAM 1   370

BEAR
        AND LET US BEAR THAT THEY DEBATE   . . . . . .   48 HORATIAN ECHO   13
        SEEM TO BEAR RATHER THAN REJOICE   . . . . . .   60 RESIGNATION   270
        THIS TOO THOU KNOWST THAT WHILE I STILL BEAR ON   . . 62 SOHRAB RUSTUM   46
        AND BEAR THY TROPHIES TO AFRASIABS TENT   . . . .   77 SOHRAB RUSTUM   530
        I TELL THEE PRICKD UPON THIS ARM I BEAR   . . . .   80 SOHRAB RUSTUM   658
        AND SAID O RUKSH BEAR RUSTUM WELL BUT I   . . . .   83 SOHRAB RUSTUM   755
        BUT ME THOU MUST BEAR HENCE NOT SEND WITH THEM   . .   84 SOHRAB RUSTUM   783
        AND QUIT THE HOST AND BEAR THEE HENCE WITH ME   . .   84 SOHRAB RUSTUM   798
        BY JEMSHID IN PERSEPOLIS TO BEAR   . . . . . .   86 SOHRAB RUSTUM   861
        COULD BEAR THE BURDEN OF HIS YEARS   . . . . . .   92 SICK KING BOKH   146
        ONE MAN IS NOT WELL MADE TO BEAR   . . . . . .   92 SICK KING BOKH   154
        IF A MAN BEAR TO HAVE IT SO   . . . .   92 SICK KING BOKH   159
        THEY THAT BEAR RULE AND ARE OBEYD   . . . . . .   93 SICK KING BOKH   186
        THITHER O VIZIER WILL I BEAR   . . . .   95 SICK KING BOKH   225
        FOR WHO WILL BEAR MY HATEFUL SIGHT IN HEAVEN   . .   98 BALDER DEAD 1   106
        BUT HE MUST EVER WATCH THE NORTHERN BEAR   . . . .   99 BALDER DEAD 1   155
        THE LOVE ALL BEAR TOWARD THEE NOR TRAIN UP . . . .   126 BALDER DEAD 3   450
        THE LOVE ALL BEAR TOWARDS THEE NOR TRAIN UP   . . .   126 BALDER DEAD 3   V 450
        SHE WOULD FIND ILL TO BEAR WEAK AS SHE IS   . . . .   152 TRISTRAM 3   101
        SOONER SHALL THIS MY STAFF BEAR LEAVES   . . . .   160 NECKAN   51
        I BEAR THAT YE REMOVE   . . . .   183 ABSENCE   16
        THAT THEY SHOULD BEAR TOO   . . . .   192 STRAYED REVEL   216
        BEAR HERAS ANGER   . . . .   192 STRAYED REVEL   220
        NOR IF FATE BINDS NOT BEAR   . . . .   196 FRAG ANTIGONE   38
        BUT THAT YE THINK CLEAR FEEL DEEP BEAR FRUIT WELL   238 PROGRESS   47
        BUT THAT YOU TOO FEEL DEEPLY BEAR FRUIT WELL   . .   238 PROGRESS   V 47
        BUT THAT YOU THINK CLEAR FEEL DEEP BEAR FRUIT WELL   238 PROGRESS   V 47
        WE BEAR THE BURDEN AND THE HEAT   . . . . . .   241 MORALITY   9
        AND WAIVE ALL CLAIM TO BLISS AND TRY TO BEAR   . .   260 SCHOLAR-GIPSY   193
        OTHERS WILL STRENGTHEN US TO BEAR   . . . . . .   272 MEMORIAL VERSES   66
        AS DEATH COMPOSED TO BEAR   . . . .   309 OBERMANN   86
        COMPOSED TO BEAR I LIVED AND DIED   . . . . . .   321 OBERMANN MORE   265
        DOUBTLESS THEY BEAR THEM TO MY FATHERS TOMB   . .   331 MEROPE   55
        ALL THIS I BEAR FOR WHAT I SEEK I KNOW   . . . .   333 MEROPE   100
        WHAT SHALL I BEAR O LOST   . . . .   342 MEROPE   400
        WILD HOG AND BEAR AND MOUNTAIN-DEER AND ROE   . .   356 MEROPE   758
        WHILE ALL THIS TIME I BEAR TO LINGER ON   . . . .   366 MEROPE   1017
        BEAR WITNESS SEE MARK WELL ON WHAT A HEAD   . . . .   377 MEROPE   1223
        THE SHY MOUNTAIN-BEAR   . . . .   392 MEROPE   1640
        THE GUARD-WATCHD BEAR   . . . .   393 MEROPE   1678
        THE ILLS WE OUGHT TO BEAR   . . . .   421 EMPEDOCLES I 2   280
        FAILD TO FILL UP THE VOID WHICH IN OUR BREASTS WE BEAR 424 EMPEDOCLES I 2   376
        WHICH MAN PROUD MAN FINDS HARD TO BEAR   . . . .   450 GEISTS GRAVE   30
        MUST BEAR IN SILENCE MANY AN ILL   . . . . . .   481 COURAGE   3
        OR BEAR PAILS TO THE WELL OF MESSEIS OR HYPEREIA . .   HOMER TRANS   30

BEARABLE
        THOUGH BEARABLE SEEM HARDLY WORTH   . . . . . .   60 RESIGNATION   263

BEARD
        HIS HAIR AND FACE AND BEARD AND GLITTERING ARMS   . . 82 SOHRAB RUSTUM   702

BEARDED
        SMOTE MID THE ROCKS THE LICHEN-BEARDED PINES   . .   106 BALDER DEAD 2   56
        BEARDED WITH LICHEN SCRAWLD AND GREY   . . . . . .   274 STANZAS CARNAC   10
        BEARDED WITH LICHEN OLD AND GREY   . . . . . .   274 STANZAS CARNAC   V 10

BEARDS
        OF THE JAXARTES MEN WITH SCANTY BEARDS   . . . .   64 SOHRAB RUSTUM   129

BEARER
        BUT THOU THE ZEALOUS BEARER HAST NO PART   . . . .   359 MEROPE   863

BEARERS
        THE GOLDEN MACE-BEARERS ASIDE   . . . .   88 SICK KING BOKH   34
        I HEAR THE BEARERS ON THE STAIR   . . . . . .   92 SICK KING BOKH   130
        WHERE AS LIFE EBBD HIS BEARERS LAID HIM DOWN   . .   357 MEROPE   783

BEARING
        BUT DEEPER THEIR VOICE GROWS AND NOBLER THEIR BEARING 20 MODERN SAPPHO   27
        LOFTIER BEARING AND A PROUDER EYE   . . . . . .   28 NEW SIRENS   64
        HIS GENTLE BEARING AT THE SIDE   . . . .   137 TRISTRAM 1   213
        THE DEEP DRAUGHTS OF DEATH IN BEARING ME   . . . .   145 TRISTRAM 2   84
        HE IS DEAD AND THE FRUIT-BEARING DAY   . . . . . .   229 YOUTH OF NATURE   56
        THAT CORDIAL HAND THAT BEARING FREE   . . . . . .   279 SOUTHERN NIGHT   126
        BEARING ON SHOULDERS IMMENSE   . . . .   295 HEINES GRAVE   93
        BEARING WITH IT TO OLYMPUS   . . . .   399 MEROPE   1841

BEARING   (CONTINUED)
    BEARING WITH IT TO ERINNYS   . . . .   400 MEROPE   1866
    BEARING ON HIS SHOULDERS BROAD . . . .   PILLARS UNIVERS   3

BEARS
    BEARS EARTH AND HEAVEN AND MEN AND GODS ALONG   . .   9 MYCERINUS   V 39
    BEARS TO ADMIRE UNCRAVINGLY   . . . .   57 RESIGNATION   161
    AT THIS VESSELS PROW I STAND WHICH BEARS ME   . .   239 SELF-DEPENDENCE   3
    AT THE VESSELS PROW I STAND WHICH BEARS ME   . . .   239 SELF-DEPENDENCE V   3
    IT BEARS ETERNITY BE THOU   . . . .   321 OBERMANN MORE   271
    HE BEARS THE SEED OF RUIN IN HIMSELF . . . . . .   359 MEROPE   856
    THE YOUTH IS GONE WITHIN ALAS HE BEARS   . . . .   359 MEROPE   873
    BEARS SAD WITNESS IS LOST   . . . .   369 MEROPE   1092
    AND WHAT OF THINE ARCADIAN MATE WHO BEARS   . . . . 379 MEROPE   1269
    ONLY THE LOVED HEBE BEARS   . . . .   431 EMPEDOCLES II   84
    WHERE HE WHO BEARS THEE MUST ABIDE   . . . . . .   435 EMPEDOCLES II   200

BEAST
    THROUGH MANY STREETS THE POOR BEAST RUNS IN VAIN . . 114 BALDER DEAD 3   10
    HE TETHERS HIS BEAST DOWN AND MAKES HIS MEAL   . . 191 STRAYED REVEL   165

BEASTS
    THEY SEE THEIR SHACKLED BEASTS AGAIN . . . . . .   55 RESIGNATION   120
    ALL BEASTS OF CHASE ALL BEASTS WHICH HUNTERS KNOW   69 SOHRAB RUSTUM   279
    ALL BEASTS OF CHASE ALL BEASTS WHICH HUNTERS KNOW   69 SOHRAB RUSTUM   279
    WHERE THE SEA-BEASTS RANGED ALL ROUND   . . . .   162 FORSAKEN MERM   39
    OF BEASTS OF CHASE THAT HAUNT THE ARCADIAN HILLS . . 356 MEROPE   757
    WILD BEASTS AND VULTURES SAILING OVERHEAD   . . .   373 MEROPE   1170

BEAT
    THEY BEAT UPON MINE EAR AGAIN . . . .   36 VOICE   33
    AND BEAT THE PERSIANS BACK ON EVERY FIELD   . . . .   62 SOHRAB RUSTUM   48
    FOR THE SURGE-BEAT CORNISH STRAND   . . . . .   134 TRISTRAM 1   132
    TYNTAGEL ON ITS SURGE-BEAT HILL   . . . .   136 TRISTRAM 1   177
    VOW TO BEAT HENCEFORTH SIDE BY SIDE . . . . . .   203 EUPHROSYNE   8
    OUR STORM-BEAT FIGURES AND ASKS   . . . . . .   289 RUGBY CHAPEL   114
    MADE IT A BEAT OF THY JOY   . . . .   299 HEINES GRAVE   232
    TO HAVE ADVANCED TRUE FRIENDS AND BEAT DOWN   425 EMPEDOCLES I 2   401
        BAFFLING FOES
    KNOWING CLASP IT AND SERENELY BEAT   . . . . . .   META CLOISTER   32

BEATERS
    WITH BEATERS HOUNDS AND HUNTSMEN HE AND I   . . . . 355 MEROPE   731

BEATING
    BEATING FROM THE ATLANTIC SEA . . . .   131 TRISTRAM 1   34
    IN BEATING WHERE WE MUST NOT PASS   . . . . .   179 FAREWELL   51
    AND THE BEATING OF HIS OWN HEART   . . . . . .   435 EMPEDOCLES II   214

BEATS
    IF ONES OWN HEART BEATS NOT LIGHT   . . . . . .   138 TRISTRAM 1   265
    THE SAME HEART BEATS IN EVERY HUMAN BREAST . . . . 245 BURIED LIFE   23
    INTO THE MYSTERY OF THIS HEART WHICH BEATS . . .   246 BURIED LIFE   52
    THERE BEATS ONE HEART IN EVERY HUMAN BREAST   . . . 245 BURIED LIFE   V   23
    INTO THE MYSTERY OF THIS HEART THAT BEATS   . . .   246 BURIED LIFE   V   52

BEAUTEOUS
    AND MAKE LEAP UP WITH JOY THE BEAUTEOUS HEAD   . . 265 THYRSIS   87
    BUT HE TURND HIS BEAUTEOUS FACE   . . . . . .   433 EMPEDOCLES II   159

BEAUTIFUL
    STRONG IS THE SOUL AND WISE AND BEAUTIFUL   . . .   4 EMERSONS ESSAYS   11
    STRONG IS THE SOUL AND FRESH AND BEAUTIFUL . . . .   EMERSONS ESSAYS V   11
    BEAUTIFUL EYES MEET HIS AND HE . . . .   57 RESIGNATION   160
    AND HER BEAUTIFUL ARMS UNCLASPING   . . . . .   197 FRAG ANTIGONE   78
    SO VARIOUS SO BEAUTIFUL SO NEW . . . .   211 DOVER BEACH   32
    HANGS DOWN HIS BEAUTIFUL HEAD . . . .   214 NEW ROME   2
    BEAUTIFUL SOULS . . . .   221 BACCHANALIA 2   60
    UNHAPPY BEAUTIFUL THE CAUSE   . . . .   285 HAWORTH CHURCH   V 105
    MOST BEAUTIFUL OF WATERS   . . . .   391 MEROPE   1609
    AND MAKES THY VERY RUIN FRESH AND BEAUTIFUL   . .   464 ALARIC AT ROME   54
    HOW CALMLY SAD HOW SADLY BEAUTIFUL   . . . . .   466 ALARIC AT ROME   100
    BEAUTIFUL CITY IF DEPARTED THINGS   . . . . . .   470 ALARIC AT ROME   205

BEAUTY
    FOR COLD IS HIS EYE TO MERE BEAUTY WHO BREAKING   . . 20 MODERN SAPPHO   21
    THE STRONG BAND WHICH BEAUTY AROUND HIM HATH FURLD   20 MODERN SAPPHO   V   22
    HER BEAUTY WILL NO BETTER BE   . . . .   48 HORATIAN ECHO   34
    AND THY BEAUTY NEVER WAS MORE FAIR   . . . . .   142 TRISTRAM 2   20
    AH HARSH FLATTERER LET ALONE MY BEAUTY   . . . .   143 TRISTRAM 2   21
    CONSUMED HER BEAUTY LIKE A FLAME   . . . . . .   147 TRISTRAM 2   134
    THE BEAUTY AND THE GLORIOUS ART OF GREECE   . . .   168 RACHEL 2   14
    WITH SPIRIT VANISHD BEAUTY WANED   . . . . . .   185 TERRACE BERNE   37
    IS IT FOR BEAUTY TO FOREGO HER WREATH   . . . .   212 GROWING OLD   4
    AND ITS LOCKD FOUNT OF BEAUTY USE   . . . . .   223 EPILOG LAOCOON   84
    IS IT YOU O BEAUTY O GRACE   . . . .   230 YOUTH OF NATURE   63
    HATH NEITHER BEAUTY NOR WARMTH   . . . .   233 YOUTH OF MAN   30
    HAS NEITHER BEAUTY NOR WARMTH . . . .   233 YOUTH OF MAN   V   30
    AND BEAUTY FILLD HER AND SHE SPAKE ALOUD   . . .   447 WESTMIN ABBEY   100
    BURSTS IN MAJESTIC BEAUTY ON HER CONQUERORS EYES . . 468 ALARIC AT ROME   156
    FAIR BEYOND HUMAN BEAUTY AND HIS EYE   . . . . .   477 CROMWELL   177

BEAUTYS
    SHE NEEDS NOT JUNE FOR BEAUTYS HEIGHTENING • • • • 263 THYRSIS 20

BECALMD
    YEARS THAT WERE SWEET OR SAD BECALMD OR TOSSD • • 474 CROMWELL 77

BECAME
    TILL LIFE UNSTIRRD BY ACTION LIFE BECAME • • • • 473 CROMWELL 59

BECK
    THE BECK OF THE SPIRIT LIKE HIM • • • • • • 253 FUTURE 49
    AND THE EAGLE AT THE BECK • • • • • • • • 431 EMPEDOCLES II 74

BECKOND
    AND BECKOND TO HIM WITH HIS HAND AND SAID • • • • 70 SOHRAB RUSTUM 321
    BECKOND HIM ON WITH QUIVERING LIP • • • • • • 278 SOUTHERN NIGHT 107

BECKONEDST
    BECKONEDST THE TREMBLER AND STILL • • • • • • 290 RUGBY CHAPEL 132

BECKONING
    WITH BLOWN TRESSES AND WITH BECKONING HANDS • • 26 NEW SIRENS 16

BECKONS
    BECKONS TOO EARLY THE GUEST • • • • • • • • 199 EARLY DEATH 9

BECOME
    HAST LABOURD BUT WITH PURPOSE HAST BECOME • • • • 5 DUKE WELLINGTON 9
    HAST LABOURD WITH THE FOREMOST HAST BECOME • • • • 5 DUKE WELLINGTON V 9
    TO BECOME WHAT WE SING • • • • • • • • 193 STRAYED REVEL 234
    BECOME LIKE GLORIOUS LONDON • • • • • • • • 214 NEW ROME V 13
    THERE LET ME GAZE TILL I BECOME • • • • • • 251 WISH 41
    IS BECOME INVINCIBLE • • • • • • • • • 431 EMPEDOCLES II 94
    ARE YOU TOO WHAT I FEAR TO BECOME • • • • 437 EMPEDOCLES II 281
    MADE ROUGH WITH CARE BECOME THE CHANGEFUL SEA • • 473 CROMWELL 49

BECOMES
    TIS GOD HIMSELF BECOMES APPARENT WHEN • • • • 171 DIVINITY 3
    A MAN BECOMES AWARE OF HIS LIFES FLOW • • • • 247 BURIED LIFE 88

BECOMING
    FEEL MY SOUL BECOMING VAST LIKE YOU • • • • • 240 SELF-DEPENDENCE 12

BED
    IN ITS CLEAR SHALLOW TURF-FRINGED BED • • • • 55 RESIGNATION 91
    HE HAD LAIN WAKEFUL TOSSING ON HIS BED • • • • 61 SOHRAB RUSTUM 6
    AND FOUND THE OLD MAN SLEEPING ON HIS BED • • • • 61 SOHRAB RUSTUM 26
    HIS BED AND THE WARM RUGS WHEREON HE LAY • • • • 63 SOHRAB RUSTUM 95
    OR SOME FRORE CASPIAN REED-BED SOUTHWARD BOUND • • 64 SOHRAB RUSTUM 115
    MOWING THE GARDEN GRASS-PLOTS NEAR ITS BED • • 80 SOHRAB RUSTUM 636
    AND PLACE ME ON A BED AND MOURN FOR ME • • • • 84 SOHRAB RUSTUM 785
    AND PLACE THEE ON A BED AND MOURN FOR THEE • • • • 84 SOHRAB RUSTUM 800
    OVER AGAINST THE CURTAIN OF THE BED • • • • • 103 BALDER DEAD 1 286
    AND NANNA ON HER BED SANK BACK BUT THEN • • • • 104 BALDER DEAD 1 338
    AND NANNA ON HER BED SUNK BACK BUT THEN • • • • 104 BALDER DEAD 1 V 338
    AND IN A CAVE A BED OF NEEDLE-ROCKS • • • • • 111 BALDER DEAD 2 220
    PROPT ON PILLOWS IN HIS BED • • • • • • • 130 TRISTRAM 1 11
    A GOLD HARP LEANS AGAINST THE BED • • • • • 131 TRISTRAM 1 17
    WATCHES PALE BY TRISTRAMS BED • • • • • • • 132 TRISTRAM 1 75
    TO BED AND SLEEP MY FEVER IS GONE BY • • • • • 140 TRISTRAM 1 309
    TO BED GOOD NIGHT • • • • • • • • • • 140 TRISTRAM 1 314
    SHE CAME TO THE BED-SIDE • • • • • • • • 140 TRISTRAM 1 316
    IS BOWD HALF-BURIED ON THE BED • • • • • • 146 TRISTRAM 2 106
    AND THOUGH THE BED-CLOTHES HIDE HER FACE • • • • 147 TRISTRAM 2 136
    THAT LADY BY THE BED DOTH KNEEL • • • • • • 149 TRISTRAM 2 181
    FALSE NECKAN SHARES MY BED SHE WEEPS • • • • 160 NECKAN 35
    POLYMNIA FULL ON HER DEATH-BED TWAS WELL • • • • 168 RACHEL 2 8
    WHERE THE NICHED SNOW-BED SPRAYS DOWN • • • • 176 PARTING 49
    CREEP INTO THY NARROW BED • • • • • • • 215 LAST WORD 1
    THE CHILD SLEEPS WARMLY IN HIS BED • • • • • 249 KENSINGTON GARD 36
    THE CHILD SLEEPS SWEETLY IN HIS BED • • • • • KENSINGTON GARD V 36
    I ASK NOT THAT MY BED OF DEATH • • • • • • 249 WISH 1
    HEMS IN ITS GORGES THE BED • • • • • • • • 252 FUTURE 11
    WHO MADE THE ROOTS OF TREES HIS BED • • • • • 277 SOUTHERN NIGHT 79
    THE TRACK THE STREAM-BED DESCENDS • • • • • • 289 RUGBY CHAPEL 95
    AND WHERE THEY SLEEP THAT WOODEN BED • • • • • 300 GRANDE CHARTR 47
    HERE ON ITS BED OF PAIN • • • • • • • • 307 OBERMANN 24
    IN A RICH CHAMBER ON A HAPPY BED • • • • • • 373 MEROPE 1178
    STRETCHD ON THAT BED OF DEATH ART NOTHING NOW • • 479 CROMWELL 234
    SO SHONE FORTH IN FRONT OF TROY BY THE BED OF XANTHUS   HOMER TRANS 1

BEDECKD
    STRAW HATS BEDECKD THEIR HEADS WITH RIBBONS BLUE • • 25 DREAM 24

BEDIMMD
    AND DEATHS COLD DEWS BEDIMMD HIS EARNEST BROW • • 476 CROMWELL 170

BEDS
    AND RISE UPON YOUR COLD WHITE MARBLE BEDS • • • • 18 CHURCH BROU 3 27

BEDS   (CONTINUED)
        AND RAISE YOU ON YOUR COLD WHITE MARBLE BEDS   . .   18 CHURCH BROU 3   V 27
        THROUGH BEDS OF SAND AND MATTED RUSHY ISLES   . .   87 SOHRAB RUSTUM   885
        AND THE GODS TREMBLED ON THEIR GOLDEN BEDS   . . . .   102 BALDER DEAD 1   262
        AND FROM THEIR BEDS THE HEROES ROSE AND DONND   . .   105 BALDER DEAD 2   11
        AND AS THE SWALLOWS CROWD THE BULRUSH-BEDS . . . .   109 BALDER DEAD 2   157
        HER LAUGHING CHILDREN IN THEIR BEDS AND PLAY   . .   151 TRISTRAM 3   77
        LEAVING THE SALT SEA-BEDS   . . . .   196 FRAG ANTIGONE   57
        THE UNSEEN SNOW-BEDS DISLODGE . . . .   289 RUGBY CHAPEL   99
        WHERE THE LONG GREEN REED-BEDS SWAY . . . . .   433 EMPEDOCLES II   133

BEDSIDE
        BUT SOHRAB CAME TO THE BEDSIDE AND SAID   . . .   62 SOHRAB RUSTUM   33
        WHILE BY HER BEDSIDE HEBREW RITES HAVE PLACE   . .   168 RACHEL 3   8

BEE
        CLUSTERING LIKE BEE-HIVES ON THE LOW FLAT STRAND . .   61 SOHRAB RUSTUM   13
        THE DROWSY BEE AS OF OLD . . . .   285 HAWORTH CHURCH   120
        AND BROODING MOUNTAIN-BEE   . . . .   307 OBERMANN   34

BEECH
        BETWEEN THE HOLLY AND THE BEECH   . . . . . .   451 GEISTS GRAVE   67

BEECHEN
        AND BEECHEN COVERTS AND COPSE   . . . .   297 HEINES GRAVE   181

BEECHES
        ON MY LEFT THROUGH THE BEECHES . . . .   187 STRAYED REVEL   43

BEES
        THE MOUNTAIN-BEES HUM   . . . .   176 PARTING   56
        AND HEAR THE WILD BEES ALPINE HUM   . . . . .   313 OBERMANN MORE   47

BEETHOVEN
        MOZART BEETHOVEN MENDELSSOHN   . . . .   222 EPILOG LAOCOON   35
        BEETHOVEN TAKES THEM THEN THOSE TWO   . . . . .   224 EPILOG LAOCOON   95
        BEETHOVEN RAPHAEL CANNOT REACH . . . .   227 EPILOG LAOCOON   205

BEETLING
        FROM THEIR DEEP BASE THY BEETLING CLIFFS DUNBAR   . .   476 CROMWELL   151

BEFAL
        SURE ONLY THAT YOUR MIND SEES ALL THINGS WHICH BEFAL   423 EMPEDOCLES I 2   346

BEFALLN
        TO WHAT HATH IN THIS HOUSE BEFALLN   . . . . . .   354 MEROPE   700

BEFALLS
        BEFALLS ME WANDERING THROUGH THIS UPLAND DIM   . .   263 THYRSIS   23

BEFITS
        BEFITS YOU ILL   . . . .   279 SOUTHERN NIGHT   116
        WHICH BEST BEFITS ITS BARD   . . . .   322 OBERMANN MORE   304

BEFORE
        IF THOUGHTS NOT IDLE WHILE BEFORE ME FLOW   . . .   7 REP FRIEND   11
        WOULD THRUST A HAND BEFORE THE LIFTED BOWL . . .   11 MYCERINUS   105
        LAY BEFORE HIS YOUTHFUL WIFE   . . . .   14 CHURCH BROU 1   50
        BEFORE HIM HE SEES LIFE UNROLL . . . .   57 RESIGNATION   189
        IN SAMARCAND BEFORE THE ARMY MARCHD   . . . .   62 SOHRAB RUSTUM   40
        THE TABLE STOOD BEFORE HIM CHARGED WITH FOOD   67 SOHRAB RUSTUM   197
        BEFORE HIM AND HE LOOKD AND SAW HIM STAND   . .   67 SOHRAB RUSTUM   202
        BEFORE THY FACE THIS DAY AND WERE REVEALD   . .   72 SOHRAB RUSTUM   371
        BUT NEVER WAS MY HEART THUS TOUCHD BEFORE   . .   74 SOHRAB RUSTUM   436
        BECAUSE THOU HAST SHAMED ME BEFORE BOTH THE HOSTS   75 SOHRAB RUSTUM   468
        AND THEN A DARK CLOUD PASSD BEFORE HIS EYES   . .   81 SOHRAB RUSTUM   692
        CARRIED BEFORE HIM AS IS RIGHT . . . .   89 SICK KING BOKH   48
        BEFORE THE PRIESTS THOU SHALT BE HEARD   . .   91 SICK KING BOKH   108
        AND REMAIND KNEELING AS BEFORE . . . .   91 SICK KING BOKH   124
        AND BEFORE EACH THE COOKS WHO SERVED THEM PLACED . .   97 BALDER DEAD 1   66
        FORTH WENDED THEY AND DRAVE THEIR STEEDS BEFORE   . .   106 BALDER DEAD 2   50
        AND SADDLED HIM BEFORE THAT SLEIPNER BROOKD   . .   107 BALDER DEAD 2   72
        ON AUTUMN-DAYS BEFORE THEY CROSS THE SEA   . . .   109 BALDER DEAD 2   159
        AND FELL BEFORE HER FEET AND CLASPD HER KNEES   . .   110 BALDER DEAD 2   187
        FORTH WENDED THEY AND DROVE THEIR STEEDS BEFORE   . .   106 BALDER DEAD 2   V 50
        BEFORE A STRANGERS THRESHOLD NOT HIS HOME   . .   114 BALDER DEAD 3   13
        AND PERISH AGAINST FATE BEFORE THY DAY   . .   114 BALDER DEAD 3   29
        BEFORE THE HEAVENS WERE BUILDED THOU DIDST SLAY   . .   121 BALDER DEAD 3   256
        AT WINTERS END BEFORE THE SPRING BEGINS   . .   122 BALDER DEAD 3   308
        THERE IN THE WOOD BEFORE A CAVE THEY CAME   . .   123 BALDER DEAD 3   332
        WHICH FLOATS BEFORE A VISITANT FROM HEAVEN . .   126 BALDER DEAD 3   438
        BEFORE US ARE THE SWEET GREEN FIELDS OF WALES   133 TRISTRAM 1   95
        THINND AND PALED BEFORE HIS TIME   . . . .   134 TRISTRAM 1   108
        POURD IN PRAYER BEFORE THE VIRGIN-MOTHER   . .   144 TRISTRAM 2   63
        POURD IN GRIEF BEFORE THE VIRGIN-MOTHER   . .   144 TRISTRAM 2   V 63
        NOW STAND CLEAR BEFORE ME IN THE MOONLIGHT . .   145 TRISTRAM 2   V 97
        AWHILE WITH THEM BEFORE THEY SLEEP AND THEN   . .   151 TRISTRAM 3   78
        TO ALL THAT HAS DELIGHTED THEM BEFORE . . . .   152 TRISTRAM 3   114
        ALL WHICH WE DID BEFORE SHADOW AND DREAM   . . .   153 TRISTRAM 3   132
        BEFORE THE CHILDRENS FANCY HIM AND HER   . . .   154 TRISTRAM 3   166

BEFORE   (CONTINUED)
        TO ALL WHICH HAS DELIGHTED THEM BEFORE   • • • • 152 TRISTRAM 3   V 114
        ALL THAT WE DID BEFORE SHADOW AND DREAM   • • • • 153 TRISTRAM 3   V 132
        CALL HER ONCE BEFORE YOU GO   • • • • • • 161 FORSAKEN MERM   10
        AND UNION BEFORE GOD THE ONLY CARE   • • • • • 173 MONICAS PRAYER   11
        HE MAKES HIS MEAL BEFORE HIM FOR LONG MILES   • • 191 STRAYED REVEL   172
        YE FADE YE SWIM YE WAVER BEFORE ME   • • • • • 194 STRAYED REVEL   290
        BEFORE I DIE BEFORE THE SOUL   • • • • • • 206 RIVER   13
        BEFORE I DIE BEFORE THE SOUL   • • • • • • 206 RIVER   13
        BEFORE THIS TEASED OERLABOURD HEART   • • • • • 206 RIVER   17
        BUT BEFORE WE WOKE ON EARTH WE WERE   • • • • • 209 SELF-DECEPTION   4
        TO LIE BEFORE US LIKE A LAND OF DREAMS   • • • • 211 DOVER BEACH   31
        HANGS DOWN HIS HEAD AS BEFORE   • • • • • • 214 NEW ROME   18
        BETTER MEN FARED THUS BEFORE THEE   • • • • • 215 LAST WORD   10
        BEFORE MAN PARTED FOR THIS EARTHLY STRAND   • • • • 239 REVOLUTIONS   1
        BEFORE I HAVE BEGUN TO LIVE   • • • • • • • 249 KENSINGTON GARD   44
        ONCE MORE BEFORE MY DYING EYES   • • • • • • 250 WISH   32
        TO HAVE BEFORE MY MIND INSTEAD   • • • • • • 251 WISH   44
        BUT WHAT WAS BEFORE US WE KNOW NOT   • • • • • 253 FUTURE   69
        BEFORE THIS STRANGE DISEASE OF MODERN LIFE   • • • • 261 SCHOLAR-GIPSY   203
        BEFORE THE ROSES AND THE LONGEST DAY   • • • • • 264 THYRSIS   53
        BEFORE WE DIE   • • • • • • • • • 277 SOUTHERN NIGHT   72
        LAY BEFORE BOTH AND A FAME   • • • • • • • 281 HAWORTH CHURCH   28
        TRUST ITS OWN THOUGHTS BEFORE YET   • • • • • 281 HAWORTH CHURCH   42
        ALL ARE BEFORE ME I BEHOLD   • • • • • • • 301 GRANDE CHARTR   64
        BEFORE SOME FALLEN RUNIC STONE   • • • • • • 301 GRANDE CHARTR   83
        TILL FREE MY THOUGHTS BEFORE ME ROLL   • • • • • 302 GRANDE CHARTR   95
        THE SECOND WAVE SUCCEEDS BEFORE   • • • • • • 308 OBERMANN   75
        BEFORE HE CLIMB THE PASS   • • • • • • • 313 OBERMANN MORE   20
        EARTH HAPPIER THAN BEFORE   • • • • • • • 314 OBERMANN MORE   56
        ON MY MIND YEARS BEFORE   • • • • • • • 314 OBERMANN MORE   62
        THE EAST BOWD LOW BEFORE THE BLAST   • • • • • 316 OBERMANN MORE   109
        ALL IT BEFORE ENDEAVOURD   • • • • • • • 320 OBERMANN MORE   214
        ALL THEY BEFORE ENDEAVOURD   • • • • • • • 320 OBERMANN MORE   V 214
        BEFORE THY FEET THIS RECENT CITY SPREADS   • • • • 330 MEROPE   9
        LET US CONSULT BEFORE THIS PALACE SENDS   • • • • 330 MEROPE   26
        AND FUTURE KING BEFORE THIS PEOPLES EYES   • • • • 335 MEROPE   172
        TO ZEUS BEFORE HE STRUCK HIS BLOW STRUCK MINE   • • 338 MEROPE   274
        SWIFT AS I CAME HATH FALSEHOOD BEEN BEFORE   • • • • 363 MEROPE   954
        ALMOST BEFORE TIS PLANND COME GLOWING HATE   • • • • 367 MEROPE   1062
        PERISHD BEFORE THEIR EYES YET NO MAN STIRRD   • • • 381 MEROPE   1315
        DEALT AT MY OWN SOLE RISK BEFORE THEIR EYES   • • • 383 MEROPE   1354
        BEFORE HIM AT HIS SIDE THE PRINCE THY SON   • • • • 401 MEROPE   1905
        WHEN HIS STAR REIGND BEFORE HIS BANISHMENT   • • • • 408 EMPEDOCLES I 1   65
        BEFORE THEY REACH THE ELYSIAN PLACE   • • • • • 414 EMPEDOCLES I 2   74
        OUR WANTS HAVE ALL BEEN FELT OUR ERRORS MADE BEFORE   • 419 EMPEDOCLES I 2   211
        BEFORE THE SOPHIST-BROOD HATH OVERLAID   • • • • 429 EMPEDOCLES II   29
        BEFORE THE SOUL LOSE ALL HER SOLEMN JOYS   • • • • 429 EMPEDOCLES II   33
        AND WENT WHERE ALL HIS FATHERS WENT BEFORE   • • • • 447 WESTMIN ABBEY   116
        AND STOP BEFORE THE STONE AND SAY   • • • • • 452 GEISTS GRAVE   76
        BEFORE THE SUN BEFORE THE WIND   • • • • • • 456 POOR MATTHIAS   133
        BEFORE THE SUN BEFORE THE WIND   • • • • • • 456 POOR MATTHIAS   133
        BEFORE THE GODS BEFORE MANKIND   • • • • • • 456 POOR MATTHIAS   134
        BEFORE THE GODS BEFORE MANKIND   • • • • • • 456 POOR MATTHIAS   134
        AND AS THE PAGEANT SWEPT BEFORE THEIR EYES   • • • • 467 ALARIC AT ROME   122
        SHOULD FLEET BEFORE US BUT TO MELT AWAY   • • • • 470 ALARIC AT ROME   212
        THE STATESMAN QUAILD BEFORE HIS GLANCE OF IRE   • • • 476 CROMWELL   154
        ON THAT DARK FORM HIS EYES HAD GAZD BEFORE   • • • • 477 CROMWELL   201
        BEFORE A STONE WAS LIFTED AND WE MEMMIUS   • • • • LUCRETIUS 5   5

BEFOREHAND
        JUDGE VAIN BEFOREHAND HUMAN CARES   • • • • • • 59 RESIGNATION   232

BEGAN
        WHICH THE DUCHESS MAUD BEGAN   • • • • • • • 14 CHURCH BROU 1   64
        OLD THAT DUCHESS STERN BEGAN IT   • • • • • • 14 CHURCH BROU 1   65
        AND THE FRAIL SCARLET-BERRIED ASH BEGAN   • • • • 25 DREAM   9
        THEN WITH A BITTER SMILE RUSTUM BEGAN   • • • • • 77 SOHRAB RUSTUM   527
        BEGAN TO TWINKLE THROUGH THE FOG FOR NOW   • • • • 86 SOHRAB RUSTUM   870
        RIGHT OPPOSITE AND THUS BEGAN   • • • • • • • 90 SICK KING BOKH   96
        BEGAN AGAIN TO HEAP THE SACRED FIRE   • • • • • 100 BALDER DEAD 1   196
        HE SPAKE AND STRAIGHT HIS LINEAMENTS BEGAN   • • • • 104 BALDER DEAD 1   331
        THE GOLDEN-CRESTED COCK BEGAN TO CROW   • • • • • 105 BALDER DEAD 2   4
        WERE RANGED AND THEN THE DAILY FRAY BEGAN   • • • • 105 BALDER DEAD 2   14
        ON BALDERS BREAST AND THUS BEGAN THE WAIL   • • • • 115 BALDER DEAD 3   66
        AT TABLE AND THE FUNERAL-FEAST BEGAN   • • • • • 119 BALDER DEAD 3   209
        ONE APRIL WHEN THE WARM DAYS FIRST BEGAN   • • • • 154 TRISTRAM 3   160
        THE UNDERWOOD AND TREES BEGAN AGAIN   • • • • • 155 TRISTRAM 3   190
        AND WHO ART THOU THE PRIEST BEGAN   • • • • • • 159 NECKAN   23
        SINCE FIRST THE WORLD BEGAN   • • • • • • • 238 PROGRESS   V 40
        AND BEGAN TO WHET HIS KNIFE   • • • • • • • 433 EMPEDOCLES II   150
        FOR MAX THY BROTHER-DOG BEGAN   • • • • • • 459 KAISER DEAD   37
        STILL TOILS TO PERFECT WHAT THE CHILD BEGAN   • • • 473 CROMWELL   46

BEGET
        BEGET A CRUEL TEMPER HELP ME QUELL   • • • • • • 335 MEROPE   162

BEGGAR
        A BLIND LED BEGGAR   • • • • • • • • • • 51 CONSOLATION   29

BEGGD
        ACROSS AND BEGGD AND CAME BACK SATISFIED   . . . .   170 WEST LONDON   7

BEGIN
        MAN MUST BEGIN KNOW THIS WHERE NATURE ENDS   . . . .   5 HARMONY NATURE   12
        AH NO FOR THEN I SHALL BEGIN TO FIND   . . . . . .   37 YOUTHS AGIT   7
        BEGIN THOU ART MORE VAST MORE DREAD THAN I . . . .   72 SOHRAB RUSTUM   385
        BRIMMING AND BRIGHT AND LARGE THEN SANDS BEGIN   . .   87 SOHRAB RUSTUM   881
        AND BUCKLERS CLASH AND SPEARS BEGIN TO POUR   . . .   127 BALDER DEAD 3   498
        BEGIN AND CEASE AND THEN AGAIN BEGIN   . . . . . .   211 DOVER BEACH   12
        BEGIN AND CEASE AND THEN AGAIN BEGIN   . . . . . .   211 DOVER BEACH   12
        CEASE AND BEGIN AND THEN AGAIN BEGIN   . . . . . .   211 DOVER BEACH   V 12
        CEASE AND BEGIN AND THEN AGAIN BEGIN   . . . . . .   211 DOVER BEACH   V 12
        BEGIN TO QUAKE AND DISBAND   . . . .   214 NEW ROME   6
        ALL THINGS BEGIN AGAIN   . . . .   220 BACCHANALIA 2   41
        BEGIN TO STEAL TO THEIR EYES   . . . .   235 YOUTH OF MAN   98
        COME SHEPHERD AND AGAIN BEGIN THE QUEST   . . . .   255 SCHOLAR-GIPSY   10
        BEGIN TO ROLL AND ALMOST DROWN   . . . .   431 EMPEDOCLES II   63
        WHO SLOWLY BEGIN TO MARSHAL   . . . .   437 EMPEDOCLES II   277
        AS IF THE REIGN OF JOY DID NOW BEGIN   . . . . . .   445 WESTMIN ABBEY   40

BEGINNING
        IN THE BEGINNING ERE THE GODS WERE BORN   . . . .   121 BALDER DEAD 3   255
        FROM THE BEGINNING CAN   . . . .   217 NAMELESS EPIT   3

BEGINNINGS
        BREEDS NEW BEGINNINGS DISAPPOINTMENTS NEW   . . . .   260 SCHOLAR-GIPSY   177

BEGINS
        AT WINTERS END BEFORE THE SPRING BEGINS   . . . .   122 BALDER DEAD 3   308

BEGRUDGE
        BEGRUDGE NOT THINE TO ALL WAS BALDER DEAR   . . . .   123 BALDER DEAD 3   349

BEGUILE
        EVEN FOR YOURSELVES TO CONQUER OR BEGUILE   . . . .   9 MYCERINUS   38
        THE CUP ABOUT WHOSE DRAUGHTS BEGUILE   . . . . . .   431 EMPEDOCLES II   85
        SOUNDS OF DEEP IMPORT VOICES THAT BEGUILE   . . . .   472 CROMWELL   5

BEGUILED
        FEAST AND DANCE HER YOUTH BEGUILED   . . . . . .   14 CHURCH BROU 1   58
        ALL PAINS BEGUILED   . . . .   40 STAGIRIUS   56
        WITH WHICH THIS DAY THE CHILDREN SHE BEGUILED   . .   152 TRISTRAM 3   107
        HAVE TO HIS LITTLE ARMS BEGUILED   . . . .   317 OBERMANN MORE   159
        BEGUILED HIS WALK   . . . .   460 KAISER DEAD   72

BEGUN
        PROVES FORGETFULNESS BEGUN   . . . .   24 MEMORY-PICTURE   52
        KEPT ON AFTER THE GRAVE BUT NOT BEGUN   . . . . .   172 IMMORTALITY   10
        BEFORE I HAVE BEGUN TO LIVE   . . . .   249 KENSINGTON GARD   44
        IF YOUR OWN HANDS THE GOOD BEGUN UNDO   . . . . .   447 WESTMIN ABBEY   103

BEHELD
        AS HE BEHELD HIM COMING AND HE STOOD   . . . . .   70 SOHRAB RUSTUM   320
        AND ON THE TENTH MORN HE BEHELD THE BRIDGE   . . .   107 BALDER DEAD 2   85
        AND HE BEHELD SPREAD ROUND HIM HELAS REALM   . . .   109 BALDER DEAD 2   149
        OF HELL BEHELD THEM AND THE GHOSTS STOOD DUMB   . .   112 BALDER DEAD 2   281
        BEHELD HIM COME AND TO HIS NEIGHBOUR SPAKE   . . .   113 BALDER DEAD 3   5
        ROUND WHERE THEY STOOD AND THEY BEHELD TWO FORMS   .   126 BALDER DEAD 3   442
        TREMBLING I ENTERD BEHELD   . . . .   187 STRAYED REVEL   46
        MOST IN THEMSELVES HAVE BEHELD   . . . .   231 YOUTH OF NATURE   105
        I BEHELD THE OBSCURE   . . . .   281 HAWORTH CHURCH   V
        THE BROODING EAST WITH AWE BEHELD   . . . . . .   316 OBERMANN MORE   105
        YES TWENTY YEARS AGO THIS DAY BEHELD   . . . . .   333 MEROPE   117
        SOON HAVING ONCE BEHELD HIM TO DESCEND   . . . .   350 MEROPE   592
        BEHELD HIS EXPIATION FOR HE DIED   . . . . . .   399 MEROPE   1819
        BEHELD HIM MASTER OF IMPERIAL ROME   . . . . . .   468 ALARIC AT ROME   172
        AS THEY LOOKED STERNLY ON BEHELD NEW VICTORIES   . .   468 ALARIC AT ROME   174

BEHEST
        AT WHOSE BEHEST I LONG AGO   . . . .   301 GRANDE CHARTR   74

BEHESTS
        PERMIT NO PEACE TILL YOUR BEHESTS ARE DONE   . . . .   367 MEROPE   1057

BEHIND
        DREW A WARM SCENT ABROAD BEHIND THE PINES   . . . .   25 DREAM   6
        SHALL I NOT JOY YOUTHS HEATS ARE LEFT BEHIND   . .   37 YOUTHS AGIT   5
        EVEN SO WE LEAVE BEHIND   . . . .   41 HUMAN LIFE   25
        SLOWLY BEHIND HIS HEAVY TREAD   . . . .   57 RESIGNATION   184
        SLOWLY BEHIND THE HEAVY TREAD   . . . .   57 RESIGNATION   V 184
        THE ILYATS OF KHORASSAN AND BEHIND   . . . . . .   65 SOHRAB RUSTUM   138
        AND CROSSD THE CAMP WHICH LAY BEHIND AND REACHD   . .   66 SOHRAB RUSTUM   190
        I HID THE CAN BEHIND THE DOOR   . . . .   90 SICK KING BOKH   72
        BEHIND THE DOOR UPON THE GROUND   . . . .   90 SICK KING BOKH   79
        FROM THE HIGH MOORS BEHIND AND MEETS THE SEA   . .   97 BALDER DEAD 2   83
        BUT THEY WENT ODIN FIRST THE REST BEHIND   . . .   105 BALDER DEAD 2   35
        AND BOUND THE LOGS BEHIND THEIR STEEDS TO DRAW   . .   106 BALDER DEAD 2   60
        BEHIND FLOCKD WRANGLING UP A PITEOUS CREW   . . . .   109 BALDER DEAD 2   170
        MOOR BEHIND MOOR FAR FAR AWAY   . . . .   141 TRISTRAM 1   365

BEHIND   (CONTINUED)
    CREEPS OVER IT FROM THE TILLD FIELDS BEHIND   • •   149 TRISTRAM 3   9
    RAN OUT FROM THE DARK UNDERWOOD BEHIND   • • •   155 TRISTRAM 3   209
    CREEPS OVER IT FROM THE TILLD LAND BEHIND   • • •   TRISTRAM 3   V   9
    STEALS OVER IT FROM THE TILLD LAND BEHIND   • • •   TRISTRAM 3   V   9
    STEALS OVER IT FROM THE TILLD FIELDS BEHIND   •   TRISTRAM 3   V   9
    THIS SENTENCE HAVE I LEFT BEHIND   • • • •   217 NAMELESS EPIT   V
    ON FOOT BEHIND THEM GO AND COME   • • • •   224 EPILOG LAOCOON   114
    THEBES WAS BEHIND HIM IN FLAMES   • • • •   229 YOUTH OF NATURE   41
    CROWNS THE STILL VALLEY BEHIND   • • • • • •   234 YOUTH OF MAN   63
    THE MOON AND LOST BEHIND HER FADING DIM   • •   242 SUMMER NIGHT   7
    BEHIND THROUGH THE SOFT AIR   • • • • • •   242 SUMMER NIGHT   20
    THE HILL BEHIND WHOSE RIDGE THE SUNSET FLAMES   263 THYRSIS   13
    AND LEAVE NO GOOD BEHIND • • • • • • • •   273 EDW QUILLINAN   6
    AND LEAVE NO TRACE BEHIND   • • • • • • •   273 EDW QUILLINAN   V   6
    BEHIND ME ON THEIR GRASSY SWEEP   • • • •   274 STANZAS CARNAC   9
    BEHIND THAT LOVELY MOUNTAIN-LINE   • • • •   275 SOUTHERN NIGHT   7
    WHERE BEHIND KEIGHLEY THE ROAD   • • • • •   282 HAWORTH CHURCH   55
    BEHIND ARE THE ABANDOND BATHS   • • • • •   306 OBERMANN   5
    SHE LEFT IT ALL BEHIND   • • • • • • • •   317 OBERMANN MORE   134
    BEHIND THE UPCROWDING HILLS • • • • • •   324 OBERMANN MORE   342
    BEHIND THE SHELTER OF THY FATHERS TOMB   • •   332 MEROPE   68
    YET GRANT THAT IT SUCCEEDS THOU HAST BEHIND   •   381 MEROPE   1296
    BEHIND HIS CORPSE THEIR HEDGE OF SERRIED SPEARS • • 381 MEROPE   1308
    SLOPE BEHIND SLOPE UP TO THE PEAK LIES BARE   414 EMPEDOCLES I 2   55
    BEHIND A BURIED VALE DOTH SLEEP   • • • • •   479 HAYSWATER BOAT   9
    IF LIKE A COWARD I SKULKD BEHIND APART FROM THE BATTLE   HOMER TRANS   16
    AND NOT LEAVE HIM BEHIND A CORPSE ON THE PLAIN   HOMER TRANS   42
        LIKE PATROCLUS

BEHOLD
    AND THE DULL GODS BEHOLD ERE THESE ARE FLOWN   • •   10 MYCERINUS   65
    BEHOLD THE PAVEMENT OF THE COURTS OF HEAVEN   • •   18 CHURCH BROU 3   31
    BEHOLD SHE CRIES SO MANY RAGES LULLD • • • •   37 WORLDS TRIUMPHS   5
    AND NOW IN FRONT BEHOLD OUTSPREAD   • • • •   54 RESIGNATION   64
    BEHOLD ME I AM VAST AND CLAD IN IRON • • • •   71 SOHRAB RUSTUM   325
    IN THE KINGS PATH BEHOLD THE MAN   • • • •   90 SICK KING BOKH   94
    BEHOLD HER HERE THE PATIENT FLOWER   • • • •   132 TRISTRAM 1   72
    THAN THOU SHALT HEAVEN BEHOLD   • • • •   160 NECKAN   52
    BEHOLD THE STERN MAILD FATHER STAFF IN HAND   • •   167 PICT NEWSTEAD   9
    MY SISTER TO BEHOLD WITH THEE   • • • • •   180 FAREWELL   V 78
    THE GODS BEHOLD THEM   • • • • • • •   192 STRAYED REVEL   200
    BEHOLD AND SING   • • • • • • • •   192 STRAYED REVEL   209
    HIM YOU EXPECT TO BEHOLD   • • • • • •   199 FRAG DEJANEIRA   22
    DOST THOU TO-NIGHT BEHOLD   • • • • • •   201 PHILOMELA   16
    DOST THOU STILL BEHOLD   • • • • • • •   201 PHILOMELA   V 16
    BEHOLD I SAID THE PAINTERS SPHERE   • • • •   222 EPILOG LAOCOON   49
    BEHOLD AT LAST THE POETS SPHERE   • • • •   225 EPILOG LAOCOON   127
    BEHOLD O NATURE THIS PAIR   • • • • •   232 YOUTH OF MAN   17
    BEHOLD THE NEW WORLD RISE   • • • • •   237 PROGRESS   4
    AND NO MAN MAY THE OTHERS HURT BEHOLD   •   238 PROGRESS   30
    BEHOLD WITH TEARS MINE EYES ARE WET   • • • •   245 BURIED LIFE   2
    BEHOLD WITH TEARS MY EYES ARE WET   • • • •   245 BURIED LIFE   V   2
    BEHOLD THE ELDER TO-DAY   • • • • •   281 HAWORTH CHURCH   30
    YEARLY AWAKE TO BEHOLD   • • • • • •   285 HAWORTH CHURCH   117
    SHE WILL BEHOLD NO MORE • • • • • •   282 HAWORTH CHURCH   V
    THE HUMID CORRIDORS BEHOLD   • • • • •   300 GRANDE CHARTR   34
    ALL ARE BEFORE ME I BEHOLD   • • • • •   301 GRANDE CHARTR   64
    BEHOLD THY HERITAGE THY FATHERS REALM   • •   330 MEROPE   3
    SOUTHWARD AND WEST BEHOLD THOSE SNOWY PEAKS   •   330 MEROPE   16
    BY SILENCE EVER AFTER FOR BEHOLD   • • • •   332 MEROPE   62
    AND EVEN NOW IF TO BEHOLD ME HERE   • • • •   333 MEROPE   104
    BEHOLD O KING FROM THE DARK   • • • • •   342 MEROPE   390
    BEHOLD THE FASTENINGS WITHDRAWN   • • • •   372 MEROPE   1149
    BEHOLD IN SUMMER   • • • • • •   392 MEROPE   1651
    O AEPYTUS MY SON BEHOLD BEHOLD   • • • • •   403 MEROPE   1963
    O AEPYTUS MY SON BEHOLD BEHOLD   • • • • •   403 MEROPE   1963
    THENCE TO THE SOUTH BEHOLD THOSE SNOWY PEAKS •   330 MEROPE   V 16
    SLOWLY THREAD THEM WHEN BEHOLD   • • • • •   457 POOR MATTHIAS   183
    WE BUT BEHOLD HE IS THE ARCHITECT   • • • •   LUCRETIUS 5   V   3

BEHOLDING
    BEHOLDING HIM WHERE THE TWO PILLARS STAND   • • •   198 FRAG ANTIGONE   91
    BEHOLDING THE ABSURDITY OF MEN   • • • • • •   298 HEINES GRAVE   207

BEHOOF
    THIS COMMERCE FOR MY BEST BEHOOF HE PLIES   • • •   380 MEROPE   1277

BEING
    BUT BEING WHAT I AM I TELL THEE THIS • • • •   72 SOHRAB RUSTUM   373
    NOW MARK I BEING FEVERD SICK   • • • • •   90 SICK KING BOKH   85
    BUT BEING NOTHING AS HE IS   • • • • • •   92 SICK KING BOKH   141
    BEING ALIVE AND COME TO OCEANS SHORE • • • •   110 BALDER DEAD 2   184
    AND HAVE NOW SHORT SPACE FOR BEING GLAD   • •   144 TRISTRAM 2   56
    BEING IN TRUTH BUT A DISEASED UNREST • • • •   153 TRISTRAM 3   135
    WITH ALL THY BEING RE-ARRANGED   • • • • •   184 TERRACE BERNE   35
    THEN AS NOW THIS TREMULOUS EAGER BEING   • •   210 SELF-DECEPTION   9
    THAT BEING ONLY WHICH HATH KNOWN EACH MAN   •   217 NAMELESS EPIT   2
    TIS THAT FROM CHANGE TO CHANGE THEIR BEING ROLLS •   259 SCHOLAR-GIPSY   143
    AND THE PURE GOAL OF BEING REACH   • • • •   278 SOUTHERN NIGHT   85
    OF BEING IS PRACTISED THAT STRENGTH   • • • •   287 RUGBY CHAPEL   42

BEING   (CONTINUED)
        OF THE BEING IN WHOM WE EXIST . . . .   298 HEINES GRAVE   V 216
        FOR BEING OF LIKE AGE OF BIRTH NOT MEAN . . . . 355 MEROPE   722
        THAT HE ENJOYD BUT PART BEING HEIR TO ALL . . . . 394 MEROPE   1701
        TO TUNES WE DID NOT CALL OUR BEING MUST KEEP CHIME 418 EMPEDOCLES I 2 196
        NOR DOES BEING WEARY PROVE THAT HE HAS WHERE TO REST 424 EMPEDOCLES I 2 351
        AND BEING LONELY THOU ART MISERABLE . . . . . .   429 EMPEDOCLES II   20
        ERE QUITE THE BEING OF MAN ERE QUITE THE WORLD . . 429 EMPEDOCLES II   31
        BEING ONE WITH WHICH WE ARE ONE WITH THE WHOLE WORLD 440 EMPEDOCLES II 372
        BOUND ALL HIS BEING WITH A SILVER CHAIN . . . . 473 CROMWELL   63

BEINGS
        AND COUNTLESS BEINGS . . . .   50 CONSOLATION   9
        CLEAR PROSPECT OER OUR BEINGS WHOLE . . . . . . 179 FAREWELL   54
        EVEN IN HIS OWN DESPITE HIS BEINGS LAW . . . . 246 BURIED LIFE   37

BELATED
        THE LAST BELATED GLEANER GONE . . . .   218 BACCHANALIA 1   V 9

BELEAGUER
        WHEN MUSPELS CHILDREN SHALL BELEAGUER HEAVEN . . 115 BALDER DEAD 3   69

BELGRAVE
        CROUCHD ON THE PAVEMENT CLOSE BY BELGRAVE SQUARE . . 169 WEST LONDON   1

BELIEVE
        YET THEY BELIEVE ME WHO AWAIT . . . .   59 RESIGNATION   247
        NOR DID HE YET BELIEVE IT WAS HIS SON . . . .   79 SOHRAB RUSTUM   605
        ALTERD TRISTRAM NOT IN COURTS BELIEVE ME . . . . 143 TRISTRAM 2   37
        THAT OR NOTHING I BELIEVE . . . .   215 PIS-ALLER   11
        FOR GODS SAKE BELIEVE IT THEN . . . .   215 PIS-ALLER   12
        AND THROUGH THEE I BELIEVE . . . .   290 RUGBY CHAPEL   145
        YES I BELIEVE THAT THERE LIVED . . . .   290 RUGBY CHAPEL   153
        LAST OF THE PEOPLE WHO BELIEVE . . . .   302 GRANDE CHARTR   112
        WITH OLD-WORLD CURES MEN HALF BELIEVE . . . .   320 OBERMANN MORE   235
        REPEATED ARE IN THEE I WELL BELIEVE . . . . .   333 MEROPE   87
        AND ME BELIEVE IT WISE MEN GRAVELY BLAME . . . 333 MEROPE   94
        BUT IT IS SOMETIMES TRODDEN OH BELIEVE IT . . . 341 MEROPE   370
        YET HOW CANST THOU BELIEVE IT THEREFORE THOU . . 341 MEROPE   371
        BY HIM SHOWN FAIR BUT I BELIEVE MOST FOUL . . . 349 MEROPE   556
        HEIRSHIP WITH FAIR INTENT AS I BELIEVE . . . . 387 MEROPE   1484
        WHO KNOWS NOT WHAT TO BELIEVE . . . .   415 EMPEDOCLES I 2   89
        BELIEVE AND THOU SHALT FIND THE HOLY NIGH . . . 483 THEKLAS ANSWER   20
        I BELIEVE . . . .   FRAGMENT 6   1

BELIEVED
        BECAUSE THOU HAST BELIEVED THE WHEELS OF LIFE . .   4 DUKE WELLINGTON   1
        HE LIVED WHILE WE BELIEVED . . . .   318 OBERMANN MORE   168
        WHILE WE BELIEVED ON EARTH HE WENT . . . . . .   318 OBERMANN MORE   169
        MOTHER I WELL BELIEVED THOU LIVEDST ON . . . .   367 MEROPE   1043
        WHICH IS NOT YET BELIEVED . . . .   421 EMPEDOCLES I 2   285

BELIEVERS
        LIGHT HALF-BELIEVERS OF OUR CASUAL CREEDS . . . 260 SCHOLAR-GIPSY   172
        VAGUE HALF-BELIEVERS OF OUR CASUAL CREEDS . . . 260 SCHOLAR-GIPSY   V 172

BELIEVES
        AND BELIEVES NATURE OUTRAGED IF HIS WILLS GAINSAID 417 EMPEDOCLES I 2   156

BELIEVING
        GOD DOTH MATCH HIS GIFTS TO MANS BELIEVING . . . . 483 THEKLAS ANSWER   19

BELL
        HARK WHAT BELL FOR CHURCH IS TOLLD . . . . . .   12 CHURCH BROU 1   4
        THE FAR-OFF SOUND OF A SILVER BELL . . . . . .   162 FORSAKEN MERM   34
        WHEN DOWN SWUNG THE SOUND OF A FAR-OFF BELL . . 163 FORSAKEN MERM   54
        FOR THE PRIEST AND THE BELL AND THE HOLY WELL . . 164 FORSAKEN MERM   91
        WHEN DOWN SWUNG THE SOUND OF THE FAR-OFF BELL . . 163 FORSAKEN MERM   V 54
        ASCENDING PURE THE BELL-LIKE FAME . . . . . .   219 BACCHANALIA 2   15

BELLS
        YOUR EYES PURSUE THE BELLS OF FOAM . . . . . .   58 RESIGNATION   201
        CHIME CONVENT-BELLS ON WINTRY NIGHTS . . . . .   156 SAINT BRANDAN   6
        AND NOW NO BELLS NO CONVENTS MORE . . . . . .   156 SAINT BRANDAN   10
        WE HEARD THE SWEET BELLS OVER THE BAY . . . .   162 FORSAKEN MERM   31
        AND BLUE-BELLS TREMBLING BY THE FOREST-WAYS . . 265 THYRSIS   75
        THYRSIS IN REACH OF SHEEP-BELLS IS MY HOME . . 269 THYRSIS   233
        THE BLUE-BELLS PERFUME ALL THE AIR . . . . . .   274 STANZAS CARNAC   20
        THOUGH AS YOU READ YOU HEAR THE BELLS . . . .   307 OBERMANN   31
        THEIR TINKLING BELLS MIXD WITH THE SONG OF BIRDS . . 407 EMPEDOCLES I 1 28
        OF IVY-PLANTS AND FRAGRANT HANGING BELLS . . . 414 EMPEDOCLES I 2   49

BELONG
        YOUTH LIKE A STAR AND WHAT TO YOUTH BELONG . . . 166 AUSTERITY POET   6
        NO THOUGHTS THAT TO THE WORLD BELONG . . . . .   317 OBERMANN MORE   145

BELOVED
        BUT THAT BELOVED NAME UNNERVED MY ARM . . . . .   77 SOHRAB RUSTUM   547
        COME THEN IF BALDER WAS SO DEAR BELOVED . . . . 111 BALDER DEAD 2   231
        ALIVE THOU WAST OF GODS THE MOST BELOVED . . . 112 BALDER DEAD 2   259

BELOVED   (CONTINUED)
    ALIVE THOU WERT OF GODS THE MOST BELOVED   •   •   •   •   112 BALDER DEAD 2   V 259
    FOR DEAR-BELOVED WAS BALDER WHILE HE LIVED   •   •   •   •   120 BALDER DEAD 3   232
    FORSET THY SON TO BE BELOVED LIKE THEE   •   •   •   •   126 BALDER DEAD 3   451
    OR SOME YOUTH BELOVED OF PAN   •   •   •   •   •   •   188 STRAYED REVEL   80
    FLOWING-ROBED THE BELOVED   •   •   •   •   •   •   194 STRAYED REVEL   279
    BELOVED IACCHUS   •   •   •   •   •   •   194 STRAYED REVEL   281
    HIS BELOVED ARGIVE SEER WOULD ZEUS RETAIN   •   •   •   197 FRAG ANTIGONE   82
    WHEN A BELOVED HAND IS LAID IN OURS   •   •   •   247 BURIED LIFE   78
    AND STILL THE HAUNT BELOVED A VIRTUE YIELDS   •   269 THYRSIS   220
    RATHER ON THEE I CALL HUSBAND BELOVED   •   •   •   349 MEROPE   584
    MY CHILD MY CHARGE BELOVED WELCOME TO LIFE   •   •   375 MEROPE   1207
    MY NEW-WON TREASURE THY BELOVED LIFE   •   •   •   381 MEROPE   1291
    THAT DEAR-BELOVED THAT YOUNG THAT GRACIOUS HEAD   •   382 MEROPE   1327
    THE SOUND BELOVED OF HIS VICTORIOUS BREATH   •   •   448 WESTMIN ABBEY   128

BELOW
    HARK BELOW THE GATES UNBARRING   •   •   •   •   •   14 CHURCH BROU 1   37
    BY THE STREAM BELOW THE PINES   •   •   •   •   •   15 CHURCH BROU 1   92
    MID BRIGHT GREEN FIELDS BELOW THE PINES   •   •   •   16 CHURCH BROU 2   5
    SITS RAPT AND HEARS THE BATTLE BREAK BELOW   •   •   42 GIPSY CHILD   23
    THE GIPSIES WHOM WE MET BELOW   •   •   •   •   55 RESIGNATION   108
    BELOW THERE IN THE REGISTAN   •   •   •   •   •   93 SICK KING BOKH   192
    FOR BALDER WHOM SHE HOLDS BY RIGHT BELOW   •   •   100 BALDER DEAD 1   181
    ONLY THE INGLORIOUS SORT ARE THERE BELOW   •   •   104 BALDER DEAD 1   323
    WHICH TOOK ON BALDERS TRACK THE WAY BELOW   •   •   104 BALDER DEAD 1   341
    BOUND ON THEIR WAY BELOW TO HELAS REALM   •   •   107 BALDER DEAD 2   105
    SOULS BOUND BELOW MY DAILY PASSERS HERE   •   •   108 BALDER DEAD 2   110
    BELOW THERE TO THE NORTH TOWRD HELAS REALM   •   •   108 BALDER DEAD 2   123
    BUT NORTHWARD HERMOD RODE THE WAY BELOW   •   •   108 BALDER DEAD 2   138
    FOR BALDER WHOM THOU HOLDST BY RIGHT BELOW   •   •   110 BALDER DEAD 2   193
    ME SITTING HERE BELOW BY HELAS SIDE   •   •   112 BALDER DEAD 2   277
    BELOW AND LOOKD UPON THE SHADOWY TRIBES   •   •   114 BALDER DEAD 3   39
    I MUST AGAIN BELOW TO HELAS REALM   •   •   •   124 BALDER DEAD 3   372
    BUT NORTHWARD HERMOD RODE THE WAY BELOW   •   •   124 BALDER DEAD 3   374
    BELOW AND DOST THOU HATE ME EVEN HERE   •   •   125 BALDER DEAD 3   406
    LATELY BELOW AND JOIND HIM AND THE PAIR   •   •   125 BALDER DEAD 3   434
    OUT OF THE BLACK WASTE FOREST FAR BELOW   •   •   119 BALDER DEAD 3   V
    INTO THE TANGLED GLEN BELOW   •   •   •   •   148 TRISTRAM 2   V
    AND THERE BELOW THE NECKANS FEET   •   •   •   159 NECKAN   7
    DOWN AND AWAY BELOW   •   •   •   •   •   161 FORSAKEN MERM   2
    AND SEE BELOW THEM   •   •   •   •   •   190 STRAYED REVEL   133
    SEE YE THE TROUBLE BELOW   •   •   •   •   216 LORDS MESSENGER   2
    MADLY BELOW IN THE PLAIN   •   •   •   •   216 LORDS MESSENGER   V
    SEE YE THE BATTLE BELOW   •   •   •   •   216 LORDS MESSENGER   V   2
    WHILE THROUGH THEIR EARTH-MOORD NAVE BELOW   •   •   223 EPILOG LAOCOON   73
    WHILE THROUGH THE EARTH-MOORD NAVE BELOW   •   •   223 EPILOG LAOCOON   V   73
    AND HECTOR WAS IN ILIUM FAR BELOW   •   •   236 PALLADIUM   3
    CAUSES OF THINGS AND FAR BELOW   •   •   •   •   271 MEMORIAL VERSES   30
    LAKE LEMANS WATERS FAR BELOW   •   •   •   •   310 OBERMANN   121
    HIS BIRTH-NAME JUST BELOW   •   •   •   •   313 OBERMANN MORE   26
    THE SILENCE FAR BELOW   •   •   •   •   323 OBERMANN MORE   328
    IF THAT MIGHT SOOTHE HIM BELOW   •   •   •   •   343 MEROPE   410
    FOR THE AWFUL MONARCHS BELOW   •   •   •   •   345 MEROPE   476
    MY WORDS BELOW TO THEE AND MAKE THEE HEAR   •   •   350 MEROPE   586
    AND RESTING THERE TO BREATHE I SAW BELOW   •   •   357 MEROPE   V 797
    THE MULES MUST BE BELOW FAR DOWN I HEAR   •   •   407 EMPEDOCLES I 1   27
    ROSE FROM BELOW IF IT WERE POSSIBLE   •   •   •   412 EMPEDOCLES I 2   9
    I SAW HIM THROUGH THE CHESTNUTS FAR BELOW   •   •   428 EMPEDOCLES I 2   485
    GREEN TURF ABOVE AND CRUMBLING DUST BELOW   •   •   464 ALARIC AT ROME   57
    ONE FORM STANDS GAZING SILENTLY BELOW   •   •   468 ALARIC AT ROME   153
    NOR WAKE THE WEARY SOUL THAT SLUMBERS ON BELOW   •   469 ALARIC AT ROME   198
    BELOW THE SURFACE-STREAM SHALLOW AND LIGHT   •   •   483 BELOW SURFACE   1
    OF WHAT WE SAY WE FEEL BELOW THE STREAM   •   •   483 BELOW SURFACE   2

BELT
    A BELT OR SWORD PERHAPS AND GO HIS WAY   •   •   •   71 SOHRAB RUSTUM   354
    HIS BELT AND NEAR THE SHOULDER BARED HIS ARM   •   •   81 SOHRAB RUSTUM   670
    THE FORESTS ROUND THAT BELT CYLLENES SIDE   •   •   357 MEROPE   794
    THE FORESTS ROUND WHICH BELT CYLLENES SIDE   •   •   357 MEROPE   V 794

BENCH
    ON THE WARM INGLE-BENCH THE SMOCK-FROCKD BOORS   •   256 SCHOLAR-GIPSY   59
    AH GENTLY PLACE HIM ON THE BENCH   •   •   •   •   276 SOUTHERN NIGHT   34
    AND THE OLD MEN RISE FROM THEIR BENCH   •   •   360 MEROPE   900

BEND
    BEND YE ON THESE INDEED AN UNMOVED EYE   •   •   •   9 MYCERINUS   35
    AND BEND MY HEART AND GIVE HIM BACK TO HEAVEN   •   111 BALDER DEAD 2   240
    AND BEND HER HEART AND GIVE YOU BALDER BACK   •   115 BALDER DEAD 3   46
    BEND BEND DOWN I YET HAVE MUCH TO SAY   •   •   145 TRISTRAM 2   76
    BEND BEND DOWN I YET HAVE MUCH TO SAY   •   •   145 TRISTRAM 2   76
    AH THEY BEND NEARER   •   •   •   •   •   •   176 PARTING   41
    WITH STAFF AND GOURD HIS WAY DID BEND   •   •   278 SOUTHERN NIGHT   81
    NOR BEND MYSELF TOO LOW TO MAKE IT YIELD   •   •   398 MEROPE   1786
    AND BEND THEIR LITTLE FISTS AND RATE THE SENSELESS   421 EMPEDOCLES I 2   276
        GROUND
    TO BEND IN RAPTURE AT SOME IDOL THRONE   •   •   •   474 CROMWELL   99

BENDING
    BENDING GAILY OER THY HAND   •   •   •   •   •   •   •   134 TRISTRAM 1   113

BENDING   (CONTINUED)
        THAT HE SITS BENDING DOWNWARD   . . . .   188 STRAYED REVEL   82

BENEATH
        THEIR SMOOTH TOPS SHINING SUNWARD AND BENEATH   . .   11 MYCERINUS   87
        THEIR SMOOTH TOPS SHINING SUNWARDS AND BENEATH   . .   11 MYCERINUS   V 87
        CLOTHED IN SMILES BENEATH THE DAIS   . . . . . .   13 CHURCH BROU 1   35
        FAR UP SHINES THE HOUSE AND BENEATH FLOWS THE RIVER   19 MODERN SAPPHO   3
        FAR UP GLEAMS THE HOUSE AND BENEATH FLOWS THE RIVER   19 MODERN SAPPHO   V 3
        WE SHOT BENEATH THE COTTAGE WITH THE STREAM   . .   25 DREAM   20
        A COLT BENEATH ITS DAM AND DROVE HIM HOME   . . . .   69 SOHRAB RUSTUM   275
        AND FIGHT BENEATH MY BANNER TILL I DIE   . . . .   71 SOHRAB RUSTUM   332
        THROUGH WHICH A RIVER FLOWS AND SEES BENEATH   . .   113 BALDER DEAD 2   297
        OF WISDOM WHICH BENEATH THE ASHTREE SPRINGS   . .   120 BALDER DEAD 3   220
        AND CAME BENEATH THE WALL AND FOUND THE GRATE   . .   124 BALDER DEAD 3   377
        FOR THIS I DIED AND FLED BENEATH THE GLOOM   . . . .   124 BALDER DEAD 3   397
        GREEN ROLLS BENEATH THE HEADLANDS   . . . .   159 NECKAN   5
        BENEATH THE SALT SEA-TIDE   . . . .   160 NECKAN   32
        BENEATH THE BIRCH-TREES COOL   . . . .   160 NECKAN   42
        BENEATH THE COLD SEA TIDE   . . . .   160 NECKAN   V 32
        BENEATH ONE ROOF MY QUEEN WITH MINE   . . . . . .   205 CALAIS SANDS   36
        I CLIMBD BENEATH ME BRIGHT AND WIDE   . . . . . .   273 STANZAS CARNAC   3
        AND CHEERFUL WORKS BENEATH THE SUN   . . . . . .   301 GRANDE CHARTR   60
        BENEATH SOME OLD-WORLD ABBEY WALL   . . . . . .   304 GRANDE CHARTR   170
        BENEATH THE CALM THEY FEIGN   . . . .   307 OBERMANN   22
        BURIED A WAVE BENEATH   . . . .   308 OBERMANN   74
        BENEATH THE PINY SWARD   . . . .   310 OBERMANN   120
        AN ARM ALOFT FOR HELP THEN SWEEP BENEATH   . . .   358 MEROPE   833
        ONE ARM ALOFT FOR HELP THEN SWEEP BENEATH   . . .   358 MEROPE   V 833
        FALLN BENEATH HIS PERCH AND DYING   . . . . . .   452 POOR MATTHIAS   2
        STILL BENEATH THEIR FEATHERD BREAST   . . . . . .   455 POOR MATTHIAS   101
        AND THUS BENEATH THE CLEAR CALM VAULT OF HEAVEN   . .   466 ALARIC AT ROME   103
        WAS COLD AND SAD BENEATH THAT BREATHLESS VOICELESS   466 ALARIC AT ROME   108
            NIGHT
        AND THERE BENEATH HIS FEET HIS CONQUEST LAY   . .   468 ALARIC AT ROME   158
        HIDE HIS TORN HEAD BENEATH HIS SUNLESS CAVE   . .   472 CROMWELL   24
        ONCE MORE BENEATH HIM AND THE FLUTTERING SAIL   . .   479 CROMWELL   237
        IN THE BLOODY DUST BENEATH THE FEET OF THEIR FOEMEN   HOMER TRANS   26
        THEN FROM BENEATH THE YOKE THE FLEET HORSE   HOMER TRANS   43
            XANTHUS ADDRESSED HIM

BENEFICENT
        ACTIVE BENEFICENT PURE   . . . .   281 HAWORTH CHURCH   V
        ZEALOUS BENEFICENT FIRM . . . .   287 RUGBY CHAPEL   43

BENIGHTED
        COMING BENIGHTED TO THE CASTLE-GATE   . . . . . .   18 CHURCH BROU 3   15

BENIGNANT
        STRETCHD FORTH HIS HAND AND WITH BENIGNANT VOICE   . .   125 BALDER DEAD 3   410
        BUT SOULS WHOM SOME BENIGNANT BREATH   . . . . . .   203 EUPHROSYNE   13
        MARS THE BENIGNANT REPOSE   . . . .   293 HEINES GRAVE   44

BENT
        TO PAIN TO DEATH THE BENT OF HIS OWN DAYS   . . .   6 GEO CRUIKSHANK   13
        EVER IN THEIR OWN EAGER PASTIME BENT   . . . . . .   8 RELIGIOUS ISOL   2
        GIRT WITH A THRONG OF REVELLERS BENT HIS WAY   . .   11 MYCERINUS   83
        BENT TO THE COLD WINDS OF THE SHOWERLESS SPRING   . .   12 MYCERINUS   120
        AND ON THE CONJURING LAPPS HE BENT HIS GAZE   . .   96 BALDER DEAD 1   53
        LIFTING HER SOFT-BENT HEAD ONLY TO MIND   . . .   152 TRISTRAM 3   84
        KNOWS THAT THE BENT OF BOTH OUR HEARTS   . . .   179 FAREWELL   47
        WITH HEADS BENT OER THEIR TOIL THEY LANGUIDLY   . .   243 SUMMER NIGHT   39
        STILL BENT TO MAKE SOME PORT HE KNOWS NOT WHERE   . .   244 SUMMER NIGHT   68
        OF BLOOM ON THE BENT GRASS WHERE I AM LAID   . . .   256 SCHOLAR-GIPSY   28
        WHOSE BENT WAS TAKEN LONG AGO   . . . . . .   305 GRANDE CHARTR   198
        BENT ON MY FACE WITH GAZE WHICH SCANND   . . .   314 OBERMANN MORE   67
        BENT ON MY FACE WITH GAZE THAT SCANND   . . .   314 OBERMANN MORE   V 67
        AS I HAVE EVER FOUND THEE BENT TO KEEP   . . .   332 MEROPE   80
        BENT ONLY TO SERVE VIRTUE   . . . .   353 MEROPE   662
        BENT TO DIMINISH WRONG   . . . .   353 MEROPE   663
        BENT ABOVE ALL TO PACIFY TO RULE   . . . . . .   388 MEROPE   1490
        HAVE LEARND THAT WE MUST SACRIFICE THE BENT   . .   394 MEROPE   1711
        THERE HAMPDEN BENT HIM OER HIS SADDLE BOW   . . .   476 CROMWELL   169
        NOT IN RICH ENGLAND BENT BUT TO MAKE POUR   . . .   480 HUNGARIAN NAT   2
        MAN ONLY WITH ETERNAL BENT   . . . .   484 ROME-SICKNESS   21

BENUMB
        BUT WE MY LOVE DOTH A LIKE SPELL BENUMB   . . .   245 BURIED LIFE   24
        AH YES AND THEY BENUMB US AT OUR CALL   . . .   247 BURIED LIFE   71
        BUT WE MY LOVE DOES A LIKE SPELL BENUMB   . . .   245 BURIED LIFE   V 24

BENUMBD
        AND NEVER QUITE BENUMBD BY THE WORLDS SWAY   . . . .   243 SUMMER NIGHT   33

BENUMBING
        OUR SOULS IN ITS BENUMBING ROUND   . . . . . .   271 MEMORIAL VERSES   46
        LAY THY BENUMBING HAND   . . . .   283 HAWORTH CHURCH   V

BEQUEATHS
        BEQUEATHS THE ALLEGIANCE OF OUR SHEPHERD-TRIBES   . .   389 MEROPE   1540

BERGELMER
    SAVE ONE BERGELMER HE ON SHIPBOARD FLED • • • • • 121 BALDER DEAD 3   272

BERKSHIRE
    AT SOME LONE ALEHOUSE IN THE BERKSHIRE MOORS • • 256 SCHOLAR-GIPSY   58
    FROM HUNTING WITH THE BERKSHIRE HOUNDS THEY COME • • 267 THYRSIS   155

BERNARD
    YES WRITE IT IN THE ROCK SAINT BERNARD SAID • • 171 DIVINITY   1

BERNE
    ONCE MORE THE ROOFS OF BERNE APPEAR • • • • • • 183 TERRACE BERNE   2

BERRIED
    AND THE FRAIL SCARLET-BERRIED ASH BEGAN • • • • 25 DREAM   9
    WHERE RED-BERRIED ASHES FRINGE • • • • • • • 190 STRAYED REVEL   146

BERRIES
    WITH SCARLET BERRIES GEMMD THE FELL-FARES FOOD • • 150 TRISTRAM 3   22
    WITH SCARLET BERRIES BRIGHT THE FELLFARES FOOD • • TRISTRAM 3 V 22

BESEECH
    AH I BESEECH THEE WITH TEARS • • • • • • • 372 MEROPE   1151

BESEEM
    WHICH BEST BESEEM ITS BARD • • • • • • 322 OBERMANN MORE V 304

BESEEMS
    WITH ALL WHICH IT BESEEMS THE DEAD TO HAVE • • • 106 BALDER DEAD 2   42

BESIDE
    GOD THE DUKE LIES STRETCHD BESIDE HIM • • • 13 CHURCH BROU 1   27
    HER OLD ARCHITECT BESIDE • • • • • • • 15 CHURCH BROU 1   98
    BESIDE THE OXUS ALL THE PERSIAN LORDS • • • 72 SOHRAB RUSTUM   358
    COME SIT BESIDE ME ON THIS SAND AND TAKE • • 82 SOHRAB RUSTUM   718
    THE TABLE STOOD BESIDE HIM CHARGED WITH FOOD • • 67 SOHRAB RUSTUM V 197
    THE TABLE STOOD BESIDE HIM CHARGED WITH CATES • • 67 SOHRAB RUSTUM V 197
    A COLT BESIDE ITS DAM AND DROVE HIM HOME • • 69 SOHRAB RUSTUM V 275
    BESIDE THE TABLES IN THE HALL OF HEAVEN • • 97 BALDER DEAD 1   65
    DRAWN IN HIS CAR BESIDE ME AND MY SONS • • 120 BALDER DEAD 3   240
    BUT HERMOD STOOD BESIDE HIS DROOPING HORSE • • 129 BALDER DEAD 3   554
    COUCHD BESIDE HIM ON THE GROUND • • • • 137 TRISTRAM 1   226
    FAST BESIDE THE SOUNDING SEA • • • • 134 TRISTRAM 1 V 135
    SAY I WILLD SO THAT THOU STAY BESIDE ME • • 145 TRISTRAM 2   95
    SAY I CHARGD HER THAT THOU STAY BESIDE ME • • 145 TRISTRAM 2 V 95
    SAY I CHARGD THEE THAT THOU STAY BESIDE HER • • 145 TRISTRAM 2 V 95
    BESIDE THE RIVER-POOL • • • • • • • 160 NECKAN   44
    BESIDE THE POOL SATE NECKAN • • • • • 160 NECKAN   45
    ALL TIE WITH ALL BESIDE SEEMD VAIN AND CHEAP • • 173 MONICAS PRAYER   10
    MY HORSES FEET BESIDE THE LAKE • • • • • 177 FAREWELL   1
    SIT PALE BESIDE THEIR WEALTH • • • • 191 STRAYED REVEL   192
    SILENT THE SWANS BESIDE US FLOAT • • • 206 RIVER   3
    IT LAY BESIDE THE ATLANTIC WAVE • • • 273 STANZAS CARNAC   6
    AND LIE BESIDE ITS DOOR • • • • • • 313 OBERMANN MORE   46
    SIT FOR HOURS BESIDE THY CAGE • • • • • 453 POOR MATTHIAS   32
    LIVE BESIDE US BUT ALONE • • • • • • 455 POOR MATTHIAS   96
    ONCE MORE ALONE BESIDE THE GLEAMING FLOOD • • 479 CROMWELL   240
    YE TOO WHO STAND BESIDE THE HOARY THRONE • • • FRAGMENT 2   1

BESIDES
    BESIDES TO EACH ARE HIS OWN FRIENDS • • • • 92 SICK KING BOKH   155
    BESIDES WHAT WASTE HE MAKES • • • • • 195 FRAG ANTIGONE   24
    NOTHING BESIDES IN FRONT • • • • • • 234 YOUTH OF MAN   75
    BESIDES FOR FROM MY BROTHER AND MY SON • • • 387 MEROPE   1473
    AND COLD BESIDES HIS BLUE BLOOD RAN • • • • 460 KAISER DEAD   39

BESIEGE
    FOR THESE BESIEGE THE LATEST BREATH • • • • • 249 WISH   3

BESPAKE
    AND EACH BESPAKE HIM AS HE LAID HIM DOWN • • • 101 BALDER DEAD 1   215
    AND THUS BESPAKE HIM FIRST THE SOLEMN QUEEN • • 110 BALDER DEAD 2   179

BESPATTERD
    WITH BLOOD-BESPATTERD ROBES AND CHAPLET SHORN • • 403 MEROPE   1966

BEST
    AND OUR BEST IMPRESSIONS ARE • • • • • 23 MEMORY-PICTURE   11
    FOR THAT BEST WHICH SHE DISCERNS • • • • 49 SECOND BEST   12
    OF HIS DEEPEST BEST EXISTENCE • • • • • 49 SECOND BEST   22
    THAT WERE FAR BEST MY SON TO STAY WITH US • • 63 SOHRAB RUSTUM   71
    AND AN UNNATURAL OVERHEAT AT BEST • • • 153 TRISTRAM 3   136
    FORGOT HIS CRAFT AND HIS BEST WITS TOOK FLIGHT • • 155 TRISTRAM 3   182
    THAT LIFE IS BEST WHICH SLIPS AWAY • • • 199 EARLY DEATH V 2
    THOU ART TIRED BEST BE STILL • • • • • 215 LAST WORD   8
    WHERE BEST THE POET FRAMED HIS PIECE • • • 221 EPILOG LAOCOON   14
    HARDLY HIS VOICE AT ITS BEST • • • • • 231 YOUTH OF NATURE   99
    THE CLEAREST THE BEST WHO HAVE READ • • • 231 YOUTH OF NATURE   104
    SING HIM THY BEST FOR FEW OR NONE • • • 272 MEMORIAL VERSES   73
    SILENT THE BEST ARE SILENT NOW • • • • • 302 GRANDE CHARTR   114
    AH ME WE ANCHORITES READ THINGS BEST • • • 314 OBERMANN MORE   75

BEST   (CONTINUED)
    WHICH BEST BEFITS ITS BARD   . . . .   322 OBERMANN MORE   304
    AH ME WE ANCHORITES KNEW IT BEST   . . . .   314 OBERMANN MORE   V 75
    BEST CAN ITS COURSE DISCERN   . . . .   314 OBERMANN MORE   V 76
    WHICH BEST BESEEM ITS BARD   . . . .   322 OBERMANN MORE   V 304
    WE JUDGED THE BEST CHANCE FINDS NO BETTER WAY   . . .   331 MEROPE   36
    LET THE BEST RULE THEY SAY AGAIN   . . . . . .   352 MEROPE   653
    THE BEST THEN TO DOMINION HATH THE RIGHT   . . . . .   352 MEROPE   654
    THE BEST THEN TO THE THRONE MAY CARVE HIS WAY   . . .   352 MEROPE   658
    THAT BEST WHO OUGHT TO RULE AM I   . . . . . .   353 MEROPE   677
    OF IMPORT AND IN SILENCE BEST RECEIVED   . . . . .   359 MEROPE   861
    THOU FOR THY LABOUR HAST DESERVED OUR BEST   . . . .   359 MEROPE   866
    THIS COMMERCE FOR MY BEST BEHOOF HE PLIES   . . . .   380 MEROPE   1277
    O MOTHER MY BEST DILIGENCE SHALL BE   . . . . . .   405 MEROPE   2014
    THE BEST THEN TO DOMINION HAVE THE RIGHT   . . . . .   352 MEROPE   V 654
    AND HE TREATS DOUBT THE BEST WHO TRIES TO SEE   415 EMPEDOCLES I 2   101
        LEAST ILL
    HOW MAN MAY HERE BEST LIVE NO CARE TOO GREAT   419 EMPEDOCLES I 2   216
        TO EXPLORE
    TO WORK AS BEST HE CAN   . . . .   421 EMPEDOCLES I 2   269
    TO FIGHT AS BEST HE CAN   . . . .   421 EMPEDOCLES I 2   V 269

BESTOW
    WOULD I BESTOW TO HELP EMPEDOCLES   . . . .   409 EMPEDOCLES I 1   102
    THE WORLD DOES BUT EXIST THAT WELFARE TO BESTOW   . .   418 EMPEDOCLES I 2   176
    KINDNESS WE BESTOW AND PRAISE   . . . .   455 POOR MATTHIAS   99

BESTOWAL
    ALL MANS HEART WHICH BROOKS BESTOWAL   . . . . . .   34 NEW SIRENS   229

BESTOWD
    WEAKNESS AND WORSE WEAKNESS BESTOWD IN VAIN   . .   40 HUMAN LIFE   15
    SCOTT HAD BESTOWD THERE HIS LAST   . . . . . .   281 HAWORTH CHURCH   23
    AND HALF-BESTOWD HALF YIELDED UP THEIR SOIL   . .   339 MEROPE   294
    OF THAT STOCK BORN WHO BESTOWD   . . . .   343 MEROPE   426

BESTOWS
    WHEN ON THE STRENUOUS JUST MAN HEAVEN BESTOWS   . .   9 MYCERINUS   29

BESTRODE
    ARCHING HIS NECK AND GLAD TO BE BESTRODE   . . . .   107 BALDER DEAD 2   76

BETAKE
    DO YOU BETAKE YOURSELVES FOR LIGHT   . . . . . .   198 FRAG DEJANEIRA   13

BETHINK
    FIERCE MAN BETHINK THEE FOR AN ONLY SON   . . . .   78 SOHRAB RUSTUM   586
    BETHINK YE GODS IS THERE NO OTHER WAY   . . . . .   120 BALDER DEAD 3   236
    AND NOT BETHINK HER OF HER GLORIOUS PRIME   . . . .   467 ALARIC AT ROME   130
    WOMAN I TOO TAKE THOUGHT FOR THIS BUT THEN   HOMER TRANS   14
        I BETHINK*ME

BETHNAL
    SMOTE ON THE SQUALID STREETS OF BETHNAL GREEN   . .   169 EAST LONDON   2

BETRAY
    YE TOO YE TOO JOIN TO BETRAY THEN   . . . .   371 MEROPE   1125

BETRAYD
    BETRAYD THEM AND OF WASTING AGE THEY DIED   .   . . .   109 BALDER DEAD 2   167
    TRISTRAM SWEET LOVE WE ARE BETRAYD OUT-PLANND   . .   135 TRISTRAM 1   167
    BETRAYD LIKE HIM BUT NOT LIKE HIM AVENGED   . . . .   367 MEROPE   1036
    HOW RIGHTEND HOW BETRAYD . . . .   423 EMPEDOCLES I 2   330

BETRAYS
    FAUSTA BETRAYS YOU COLD THE WHILE   . . . .   58 RESIGNATION   200

BETTER
    DIDST TREAD ON EARTH UNGUESSD AT BETTER SO . . . .   3 SHAKESPEARE   11
    DIDST WALK ON EARTH UNGUESSD AT BETTER SO   . . . .   3 SHAKESPEARE   V 11
    DIDST PASS ON EARTH UNGUESSD AT BETTER SO   . . . .   3 SHAKESPEARE   V 11
    DIDST STAND ON EARTH UNGUESSD AT BETTER SO . . . .   3 SHAKESPEARE   V 11
    DIDST LIVE ON EARTH UNGUESSD AT BETTER SO   . . . .   3 SHAKESPEARE   V 11
    SOME BETTER ARCHETYPE WHOSE SEAT WAS HEAVEN   . .   9 MYCERINUS   22
    HER BEAUTY WILL NO BETTER BE   . . . .   48 HORATIAN ECHO   34
    WELCOME THESE EYES COULD SEE NO BETTER SIGHT   . .   67 SOHRAB RUSTUM   205
    THOU KNOWEST BETTER WORDS THAN THIS TO SAY . . .   68 SOHRAB RUSTUM   251
    HEAVENS AIR IS BETTER THAN THE COLD DEAD GRAVE   . .   71 SOHRAB RUSTUM   324
    HELPLESS TO BETTER US OR RUIN THEM   . . . .   111 BALDER DEAD 2   230
    BETTER TO LIVE A SERF A CAPTURED MAN   . . . . . .   112 BALDER DEAD 2   265
    BETTER TO LIVE A SLAVE A CAPTURED MAN   . . . . .   112 BALDER DEAD 2   V 265
    THE TRISTRAM WHO IN BETTER DAYS   . . . .   136 TRISTRAM 1   202
    AND POINTS US TO A BETTER TIME THAN OURS   . . . .   170 WEST LONDON   14
    ONE OF SOME BETTER RACE THAN WE   . . . . . .   202 URANIA   V 18
    BETTER MEN FARED THUS BEFORE THEE   . . . . . .   215 LAST WORD   10
    WE JUDGED THE BEST CHANCE FINDS NO BETTER WAY   . .   331 MEROPE   36
    WHETHER IS BETTER TO ABIDE ALONE   . . . . . .   338 MEROPE   287
    BETTER FROM THINE THAN FROM AN ENEMYS TONGUE   . ^   363 MEROPE   950
    THAT NEEDS NO THANKS ONE IS FAR BETTER HERE   . . .   409 EMPEDOCLES I 1   103
    COULDST THOU NO BETTER KEEP O ABBEY OLD   . . . .   444 WESTMIN ABBEY   4
    WHAT COULD HE BETTER WISH THAN THEN TO DIE . . . .   448 WESTMIN ABBEY   145
    WHAT CAN HE BETTER CRAVE THAN THEN TO DIE   . . . .   448 WESTMIN ABBEY   V 145
    BETTER THAN WE SPENT WITH THEE   . . . .   458 POOR MATTHIAS   213

BETWEEN
    OR CLUSTERD PEAKS WITH PLUNGING GULFS BETWEEN   • •   4 BUTLERS SERMONS   11
    LET THERE BE TRUCE BETWEEN THE HOSTS TO-DAY   • •   65 SOHRAB RUSTUM 151
    BETWEEN THE WAVES AND BLACK OERHANGING CLIFFS   • •   97 BALDER DEAD 1   79
    WHERE THE ROAD ISSUES BETWEEN WALLING ROCKS   • • 107 BALDER DEAD 2   89
    SO HERMOD OER THE FOG BETWEEN SAW HEAVEN   •   • • 113 BALDER DEAD 2 301
    HANGS QUIVERING OUT BETWEEN HIS DUST-SMEARD JAWS • • 114 BALDER DEAD 3   15
    AND THE PILE CRACKLED AND BETWEEN THE LOGS • • • 118 BALDER DEAD 3 187
    BLOWING BETWEEN THE STEMS THE FOREST-AIR   • • • 154 TRISTRAM 3 167
    BUT A SEA ROLLS BETWEEN US   • • • • • • 176 PARTING   65
    WITH ECHOING STRAITS BETWEEN US THROWN   • • • 182 TO MARG CONT   2
    A BREAK BETWEEN THE HOUSETOPS SHOWS   • • • • 242 SUMMER NIGHT   6
    HEAVED DAZZLINGLY BETWEEN   • • • • • • 242 SUMMER NIGHT   17
    AND THEN THE TEMPEST STRIKES HIM AND BETWEEN   • • 244 SUMMER NIGHT   62
    HOW GREEN BETWEEN THE STEMS IT IS   • • • KENSINGTON GARD V   7
    BETWEEN HEATH-CLAD SHOWERY HILLS   • • • • 282 HAWORTH CHURCH   57
    WANDERING BETWEEN TWO WORLDS ONE DEAD   • • • 302 GRANDE CHARTR   85
    LAUGHTER AND CRIES THOSE NOTES BETWEEN   • • • 305 GRANDE CHARTR 186
    BETWEEN THE DUSTY VINEYARD-WALLS   • • • • 311 OBERMANN 169
    WHERE BETWEEN GRANITE TERRACES   • • • • • 312 OBERMANN 177
    THE BREACH BETWEEN OUR PARTIES HELP ME CLOSE   • • 335 MEROPE 163
    BETWEEN THE PINE-WOODS AND THE CLIFFS   • • • 399 MEROPE 1824
    BETWEEN THE HOLLY AND THE BEECH   • • • • • 451 GEISTS GRAVE   67
    LIKE DREAMS BETWEEN TWO SORROWS WENT AND CAME • • 474 CROMWELL   96
    BETWEEN THE BARREN MOUNTAINS AND THE STORMY SEA • • 475 CROMWELL 118
    BETWEEN A RUIND CHURCH AND SHATTERD THRONE • • • 477 CROMWELL 188
    BETWEEN THAT AND THE SHIPS THE TROJANS NUMEROUS FIRES   HOMER TRANS   2

BETWIXT
    BETWIXT OUR SENSES AND OUR SORROW KEEPS   • • • • 43 GIPSY CHILD   50
    BETWIXT THY WAKING AND THE BIRTH OF THINGS • • • 45 IN UTRUMQUE PAR   10
    BETWIXT THE SILENT HOSTS AND SPAKE AND SAID   • • 65 SOHRAB RUSTUM 149
    MY HEAD BETWIXT THY HANDS AND KISS MY CHEEKS   • 82 SOHRAB RUSTUM 719
    BETWIXT THE SILENT HOSTS AND SPOKE AND SAID   • • 65 SOHRAB RUSTUM V 149
    AND BADE BETWIXT THEIR SHORES TO BE   • • • • 182 TO MARG CONT   23
    BETWIXT THE SYRTES AND SOFT SICILY   • • • • 262 SCHOLAR-GIPSY 245
    LIKE A SEA-WAVE BETWIXT THE WORLD AND THEE • • 436 EMPEDOCLES II 231
    SET BETWIXT OURSELVES AND THEE   • • • • 456 POOR MATTHIAS 128
    BETWIXT SUCH UNLIKE POWERS   • • • • • LUCRETIUS 5   10
    BETWIXT BLANK NOTHING AND ABHORRED DECAY   • • • FRAGMENT 5   5

BEWAIL
    HOW I BEWAIL YOU   • • • • • • • • • 198 FRAG DEJANEIRA   4

BEWAILD
    THEN WITH A HEAVY GROAN RUSTUM BEWAILD   • • • 83 SOHRAB RUSTUM 767
    SHE SPAKE AND ALL THE GODDESSES BEWAILD   • • • 117 BALDER DEAD 3 123

BEWAILING
    PROUDLY LIKE A KING BEWAILING   • • • • • • 34 NEW SIRENS 225
    AND WITH PITY THE SON OF SATURN SAW THEM BEWAILING   HOMER TRANS   7

BEWAILS
    THOUGH MAN BEWAILS YOU NOT   • • • • • • • 198 FRAG DEJANEIRA   3

BEWARE
    BEWARE FROM THEE UPBRAIDINGS I RECEIVE   • • • 341 MEROPE 360
    WITH PITY NAY WITH REVERENCE YET BEWARE   • • • 341 MEROPE 361
    AND HAVE TO THANK THEE FOR A FALL BEWARE   • • • 342 MEROPE 375

BEWEEP
    LET GODS MEN BRUTES BEWEEP HIM PLANTS AND STONES • • 111 BALDER DEAD 2 238
    LET GODS MEN BRUTES BEWEEP HIM PLANTS AND STONES • • 114 BALDER DEAD 3   44

BEWILDERD
    AND THEN HE STOOD BEWILDERD AND HE DROPPD • • • 76 SOHRAB RUSTUM 519
    STILL NOURISHING IN THY BEWILDERD BRAIN   • • • 200 PHILOMELA   7
    BAFFLED BEWILDERD THEY STRAY   • • • • • 216 LORDS MESSENGER   14
    THOU ART BEWILDERD THE SANE HEAD IS MINE   • • • 396 MEROPE 1759

BEWILDERMENT
    WHAT MAD BEWILDERMENT OF GRIEF IS THIS   • • • 396 MEROPE 1758

BEYOND
    FROM THE WALLD TOWN BEYOND THE PASS   • • • • • 17 CHURCH BROU 2   26
    AND NOW BEYOND THE RUDE STONE BRIDGE   • • • • 54 RESIGNATION   52
    BEYOND HIS PASSIONS WIDEST RANGE   • • • • • 58 RESIGNATION 221
    OUT ON THE SANDS BEYOND IT RUSTUMS TENTS   • • • 66 SOHRAB RUSTUM 191
    THEIR SHIPS AND THROUGH THE GATE BEYOND THE WALL • • 97 BALDER DEAD 1   75
    FAR FAR BEYOND THE OUTMOST GIANTS HOME   • • • 100 BALDER DEAD 1 163
    AT THE DREAR ICE BEYOND THE GIANTS HOME   • • • 108 BALDER DEAD 2 142
    FAR TO THE SOUTH BEYOND THE BLUE THERE SPREADS • • 128 BALDER DEAD 3 518
    BEYOND THE MOUNTAINS WILL HE SEE   • • • • • 138 TRISTRAM 1 250
    AND FAR BEYOND THE SPARKLING TREES   • • • • 141 TRISTRAM 1 362
    BEYOND THE HEATHS EDGED BY THE LONELY SEA   • • 154 TRISTRAM 3 155
    THEN AS NOW A POWER BEYOND OUR SEEING   • • • 210 SELF-DECEPTION   11
    BEYOND THE ABBEY-TOWERS APPEARD   • • • • 223 EPILOG LAOCOON   70
    DREAMING OF NOUGHT BEYOND THEIR PRISON-WALL   • 243 SUMMER NIGHT   41
    AND BEYOND THAT THE ATLANTIC WIDE   • • • • 274 STANZAS CARNAC   29

BEYOND   (CONTINUED)
        BEYOND THIS GRACIOUS BOUND   . . . . 313 OBERMANN MORE   30
        FOR TYRANTS MAKE MAN GOOD BEYOND HIMSELF   . .   . . 331 MEROPE   42
        ATTEMPTING DEEDS BEYOND THY POWER TO DO   . .   . . 368 MEROPE   1079
        END HERE ETNA BEYOND IN THE BROAD GLARE   . .   . . 414 EMPEDOCLES I 2   53
        EVEN TO A DATE BEYOND OUR OWN   . . . . 451 GEISTS GRAVE   62
        OH YES IF FANCY FEELS BEYOND TO DAY   . . . . .   . 467 ALARIC AT ROME   127
        NO LIFE OF DREAMS NO HOME BEYOND THE DEEP   . .   . . 475 CROMWELL   124
        FAIR BEYOND HUMAN BEAUTY AND HIS EYE . . . . .   . 477 CROMWELL   177
        THAT IN THE SOLITUDE BEYOND THE STARS   . .   .   FRAGMENT 6   2

BIAS
        A BIAS WITH US HERE   . . . . 418 EMPEDOCLES I 2   193

BID
        FOR SO DID KING AFRASIAB BID ME SEEK . . . . .   .   62 SOHRAB RUSTUM   38
        AND SHE WILL BID HIM NORTHWARD STEER HIS COURSE   . .   99 BALDER DEAD 1   152
        MAY I ERE I DEPART BID BALDER HAIL   . . . . .   . 111 BALDER DEAD 2   244
        WHOM WE MAY BID TO SING THOUGH THOU ART GONE   . . . 117 BALDER DEAD 3   134
        I AM NOW THY NURSE I BID THEE SLEEP   . . . . .   . 144 TRISTRAM 2   70
        BID IT RISE BOLDLY AT THE SIGNAL GIVEN   . . . . 331 MEROPE   46
        AND BID THE CHIEF TORMENTORS THERE PROVIDE   . . . . 373 MEROPE   1188
        HER SWORD WILL BE THE FIRST TO BID IT FALL   . . . . 388 MEROPE   1504
        WHO SPARED NOT OTHERS BID NOT US TO SPARE   . . . . 390 MEROPE   1578
        TO BID HER SHARE THINE UNENDANGERD THRONE   . . . . 395 MEROPE   1740
        AND BID THE SUN THINE ONLY VISITANT . . . . .   . 395 MEROPE   1752
        WE BID THEE TO THY VACANT CHAIR   . . . . .   . 451 GEISTS GRAVE   46
        NOR WOULD MY OWN HEART LET ME MY HEART WHICH   HOMER TRANS   17
             HAS BID ME BE VALIANT

BIDS
        FEROOD SHAME BIDS US TAKE THEIR CHALLENGE UP   . .   66 SOHRAB RUSTUM   175
        SINCE POLICY BIDS THUS WHAT FOULER DEATH   . . . . 390 MEROPE   1568
        YET OH COULDST THOU BUT ACT AS REASON BIDS   . . . . 396 MEROPE   1762

BIER
        AND LAID IT ON A BIER AND BARE HIM HOME   . . . . 101 BALDER DEAD 1   206
        AND STOOD BY BALDER LYING ON HIS BIER   . . . . 102 BALDER DEAD 1   270
        AND STOOD ROUND BALDER LYING ON HIS BIER   . . . . 102 BALDER DEAD 1   V 270
        NOT THIS THE TIME TO WEEP UPON THE BIER   . . . . 467 ALARIC AT ROME   135

BIFROST
        OER THE BRIDGE BIFROST WHERE IS HEIMDALLS WATCH . .   99 BALDER DEAD 1   141
        NOT BIFROST BUT THAT BRIDGE A DAMSEL KEEPS   . . .   99 BALDER DEAD 1   149
        AND OVER BIFROST WHERE IS HEIMDALLS WATCH   . . . . 105 BALDER DEAD 2   22
        OER THE BRIDGE BIFROST WHERE IS HEIMDALLS WATCH . . 119 BALDER DEAD 3   216

BIG
        THE BIG WARM TEARS ROLLD DOWN AND CAKED THE SAND . .   82 SOHRAB RUSTUM   736

BILLOW
        IN THEBES THE BILLOW OF CALAMITY   . . . . .   . 427 EMPEDOCLES I 2   445

BILLOWS
        HE SINGS HOW THROUGH THE BILLOWS   . . . . .   . 160 NECKAN   37

BILLOWY
        THAT HEAVES ITS WHITE AND BILLOWY VAPOURS UP   . . 438 EMPEDOCLES II   309

BIND
        COME BIND UP THOSE RINGLET SHOWERS   . . . . .   .   32 NEW SIRENS   173
        AND BIND THY CARCASE LIKE A BALE WITH CORDS   . . 114 BALDER DEAD 3   25
        ACCEPT THEM AND THEY BIND US UNFULFILLD   . . . . 120 BALDER DEAD 3   227
        THE HEART CAN BIND ITSELF ALONE   . . . . .   . 180 ISOLATION MARG   9
        OF BLOOD CAN HE NOT BIND . . . . 196 FRAG ANTIGONE   37
        AND THEY CAN BIND THEM TO WHAT THOUGHTS THEY WILL   256 SCHOLAR-GIPSY   47

BINDS
        THROUGH THEIR BLOOD AND BINDS THEIR SOULS   . . . . 132 TRISTRAM 1   66
        NOR IF FATE BINDS NOT BEAR   . . . . 196 FRAG ANTIGONE   38
        THE THREAD WHICH BINDS IT ALL IN ONE . . . . .   . 225 EPILOG LAOCOON   141
        AND IN THE SUN ALL MORNING BINDS THE SHEAVES   . . . 255 SCHOLAR-GIPSY   14
        THAT BINDS THE HEART OF MAN WITH MIGHTIEST POWER   . . 467 ALARIC AT ROME   146

BIONS
        PIPING A DITTY SAD FOR BIONS FATE   . . . . .   . 265 THYRSIS   84

BIRCH
        BENEATH THE BIRCH-TREES COOL   . . . . 160 NECKAN   42

BIRD
        AND WITH A CRY SPRANG UP AND DROPPD THE BIRD   . .   67 SOHRAB RUSTUM   203
        AS THAT POOR BIRD FLIES HOME NOR KNOWS HIS LOSS   . .   78 SOHRAB RUSTUM   573
        WITH SHRILL AND DISMAL CRIES THAT BIRD SHALL CROW   105 BALDER DEAD 2   6
        ANOTHER NOTE AND LIKE A BIRD IN SPRING   . . . .   117 BALDER DEAD 3   142
        AND HIS BLACK BROTHER-BIRD FROM HENCE REPLY   . . 127 BALDER DEAD 3   497
        SAY HAS SOME WET BIRD-HAUNTED ENGLISH LAWN   . . . . 175 PARTING   19
        HAST THOU NOT YET POOR BIRD   . . . . 200 PHILOMELA   V
        BIRDS HERE MAKE SONG EACH BIRD HAS HIS   . . . . 248 KENSINGTON GARD   5
        FRIENDS MORE NEAR US THAN A BIRD   . . . . .   . 453 POOR MATTHIAS   23
        THOU WOULDST CHIRP THOU FOOLISH BIRD . . . . .   . 453 POOR MATTHIAS   33

BIRD   (CONTINUED)
        YET POOR BIRD THY TINY CORSE . . . .   454 POOR MATTHIAS   83
        DEAD CANARY BIRD A STAVE . . . .   457 POOR MATTHIAS   176
        THERE A BIRD HIGH-COLOURED FAT . . . . 457 POOR MATTHIAS   188
        ON HIS PERCH A SPRIGHTLIER BIRD . . . .   458 POOR MATTHIAS   193

BIRDS
        NOR IDLY DO THESE SEA-BIRDS HOVER NEAR . . . .   42 GIPSY CHILD   8
        AND BLITHELY DO THESE SEA-BIRDS HOVER NEAR . . . 41 GIPSY CHILD   V   8
        LONG FLOCKS OF TRAVELLING BIRDS DEAD ON THE SNOW 66 SOHRAB RUSTUM   164
        LIKE HELPLESS BIRDS IN THE WARM NEST . . . . . 140 TRISTRAM 1   328
        THE SAND THE SEA-BIRDS AND THE DISTANT SAILS . 152 TRISTRAM 3   105
        OH THAT YON SEA-BIRDS WINGS WERE MINE . . . .   205 CALAIS SANDS   23
        OH THAT THAT SEA-BIRDS WINGS WERE MINE . . . . 205 CALAIS SANDS   V 23
        BIRDS HERE MAKE SONG EACH BIRD HAS HIS . . . . 248 KENSINGTON GARD   5
        THE FLOWERS UPCLOSE THE BIRDS ARE FED . . . .   249 KENSINGTON GARD   34
        THE BIRDS SING SWEETLY IN THESE TREES . . . .   248 KENSINGTON GARD   V   5
        THE BIRDS SING SWEETLY IN THEIR TREES . . . .   KENSINGTON GARD   V   5
        THE FLOWERS CLOSE THE BIRDS ARE FED . . . . .   249 KENSINGTON GARD   V 34
        THE WHITE MOUNTAIN-BIRDS . . . .   392 MEROPE   1625
        THEIR TINKLING BELLS MIXD WITH THE SONG OF BIRDS 407 EMPEDOCLES I 1   28
        BIRDS COMPANIONS MORE UNKNOWN . . . .   455 POOR MATTHIAS   95
        BIRDS WERE BORN THE FIRST OF THINGS . . . . .   456 POOR MATTHIAS   132
        BIRDS WE BUT REPEAT ON YOU . . . .   457 POOR MATTHIAS   157

BIRTH
        BETWIXT THY WAKING AND THE BIRTH OF THINGS . . . 45 IN UTRUMQUE PAR   10
        BUT IF THE WILD UNFATHERD MASS NO BIRTH . . .   45 IN UTRUMQUE PAR   22
        HATH MADE OR BIRTH HATH FOUND RESIGND . . . .   53 RESIGNATION   27
        HE SEES THE GENTLE STIR OF BIRTH . . . . . .   57 RESIGNATION   170
        IF BIRTH PROCEEDS IF THINGS SUBSIST . . . . .   58 RESIGNATION   194
        THIS POMP OF WORLDS THIS PAIN OF BIRTH . . . .   60 RESIGNATION   264
        SOHRAB MEN CALL HIM BUT HIS BIRTH IS HID . . .   67 SOHRAB RUSTUM   214
        THE DOOM WHICH AT MY BIRTH WAS WRITTEN DOWN . . 82 SOHRAB RUSTUM   709
        THE DOOM THAT AT MY BIRTH WAS WRITTEN DOWN . .   82 SOHRAB RUSTUM   V 709
        BIRTH-GODDESS AND THE AUSTERE FATES FIRST GAVE 195 FRAG ANTIGONE   10
        HATH CHARMD AT BIRTH FROM GLOOM AND CARE . . . 203 EUPHROSYNE   14
        HAS CHARMD AT BIRTH FROM GLOOM AND CARE . . .   203 EUPHROSYNE   V 14
        ROAMD ERE BIRTH THE TREASURIES OF GOD . . . .   209 SELF-DECEPTION   6
        WARFARE OF MAN FROM HIS BIRTH . . . .   216 LORDS MESSENGER   3
        TURMOIL OF DEATH AND OF BIRTH . . . .   216 LORDS MESSENGER   V   3
        A WANDERER IS MAN FROM HIS BIRTH . . . . . .   251 FUTURE   1
        TELLS US HIS MISERYS BIRTH AND GROWTH AND SIGNS 260 SCHOLAR-GIPSY   187
        HE LAID US AS WE LAY AT BIRTH . . . .   271 MEMORIAL VERSES   48
        ONCE MORE WE LAY AS ERST AT BIRTH . . . . .   271 MEMORIAL VERSES   V 48
        THE CHILDREN OF THE SECOND BIRTH . . . . . .   310 OBERMANN   143
        HIS BIRTH-NAME JUST BELOW . . . .   313 OBERMANN MORE   26
        RETURNST THOU IN HER HOUR OF BIRTH . . . . .   315 OBERMANN MORE   79
        FOR BEING OF LIKE AGE OF BIRTH NOT MEAN . . .   355 MEROPE   722
        ON THE BLOOD-STAIND HOME OF HIS BIRTH . . . .   347 MEROPE   V
        HOW EVERY BIRTH OF TIMES MIRACULOUS WOMB . . . 469 ALARIC AT ROME   191

BITE
        DIED OF A SNAKE-BITE SAID HE ON THAT BROW . . . 357 MEROPE   781

BITING
        THEY FEEL THE BITING SPEARS . . . .   192 STRAYED REVEL   227

BITTER
        OF BITTER KNOWLEDGE YET THE WILL IS FREE . . .   4 EMERSONS ESSAYS   10
        WHAT EXILES CHANGING BITTER THOUGHTS WITH GLAD   42 GIPSY CHILD   V 25
        MEN DIG GRAVES WITH BITTER TEARS . . . . . .   44 QUESTION   11
        THEN WITH A BITTER SMILE RUSTUM BEGAN . . . .   77 SOHRAB RUSTUM   527
        WHAT I HEAR THESE BITTER WORDS FROM THEE . . . 142 TRISTRAM 2   14
        STOP NOT TO ME AT THIS BITTER DEPARTING . . .   206 SEPARATION   1
        BITTER SPIRITS YE CLAIM . . . .   293 HEINES GRAVE   46
        BITTER AND STRANGE WAS THE LIFE . . . . . .   299 HEINES GRAVE   223
        HIS BITTER LIFE MAY A LIFE . . . .   299 HEINES GRAVE   225
        UPON THE BITTER TREE . . . .   317 OBERMANN MORE   V 156
        HE IS TOO SCORNFUL TOO HIGH-WROUGHT TOO BITTER 411 EMPEDOCLES I 1   149
        BE CRUSHT AND OUTRAGED IN THIS BITTER HOUR . . 468 ALARIC AT ROME   148
        OH IT IS BITTER THAT EACH FAIREST DREAM . . .   470 ALARIC AT ROME   211
        CALMD BY BITTER DISABUSINGS . . . .   META CLOISTER   1

BITTERER
        OF PORT THEY HAD MAKES BITTERER FAR THEIR TOIL . 124 BALDER DEAD 3   367
        SO THE GODS CROSS WAS BITTERER FOR THEIR JOY . 124 BALDER DEAD 3   368

BITTEREST
        MIGHT BE ONCE MORE ALIVE MY BITTEREST FOES . .   85 SOHRAB RUSTUM   810
        AND THANK THY BITTEREST FOE THAT HAVING LOST . 396 MEROPE   1756

BITTERLY
        SCORN THEM AS BITTERLY AS SHE . . . .   202 URANIA   16
        DESIRE IT BITTERLY . . . .   LUCRETIUS 7   3

BIVOUACS
        WHO BIVOUACS IN A FOREST MID THE HILLS . . . . 119 BALDER DEAD 3   V

BLACK
CLAD IN BLACK ON HER WHITE PALFREY . . . . . . 15 CHURCH BROU 1 97
BLACK UNDER CLIFFS IT RACED ROUND HEADLANDS SHONE 25 DREAM 34
THROUGH BLACK DEPTHS OF SERRIED SHADOWS . . . . 32 NEW SIRENS 179
ON EITHER SIDE THE BLACK DEEP-FURROWD PATH . . . 41 HUMAN LIFE 22
THROUGH THE BLACK TARTAR TENTS HE PASSD WHICH STOOD 61 SOHRAB RUSTUM 12
THROUGH THE BLACK TENTS HE PASSD OER THAT LOW STRAND 61 SOHRAB RUSTUM 16
BLACK GLOSSY CURLD THE FLEECE OF KARA-KUL . . . . 64 SOHRAB RUSTUM 101
FROM THEIR BLACK TENTS LONG FILES OF HORSE 64 SOHRAB RUSTUM 110
    THEY STREAMD
FIRST WITH BLACK SHEEP-SKIN CAPS AND WITH LONG SPEARS 64 SOHRAB RUSTUM 118
NEVER THE BLACK AND DRIPPING PRECIPICES . . . . 78 SOHRAB RUSTUM 571
AND THE BLACK TOORKMUN TENTS AND ONLY DRUNK . . 83 SOHRAB RUSTUM 762
AS THOSE BLACK GRANITE PILLARS ONCE HIGH-REARD . 86 SOHRAB RUSTUM 860
BETWEEN THE WAVES AND BLACK OERHANGING CLIFFS . 97 BALDER DEAD 1 79
WHO ART THOU ON THY BLACK AND FIERY HORSE . . . 107 BALDER DEAD 2 101
RAN BLACK OER THE SEAS FACE THEN STEADY RUSHD . 118 BALDER DEAD 3 183
AND HIS BLACK BROTHER-BIRD FROM HENCE REPLY . 127 BALDER DEAD 3 497
OUT OF THE BLACK WASTE FOREST FAR BELOW . . 119 BALDER DEAD 3 V
ALL ROUND THE FOREST SWEEPS OFF BLACK IN SHADE . 139 TRISTRAM 1 276
IS IT THAT THE BLACK SEA-GALE . . . . 131 TRISTRAM 1 V 33
OF HAIR THAT BLACK AND TUFTED FELL . . . . . 157 SAINT BRANDAN V 18
THE TRACK A STRAIGHT BLACK LINE . . . . . 191 STRAYED REVEL 175
BUT SEE HIS BLACK-COATED GAOLERS . . . . . 214 NEW ROME V 5
THOSE BLACK-CROWND RED-BOLED PINE-TREES STAND . 248 KENSINGTON GARD 4
THOSE BLACK-TOPPD RED-BOLED PINE-TREES STAND . 248 KENSINGTON GARD V 4
WHERE BLACK-WINGD SWALLOWS HAUNT THE GLITTERING THAMES 257 SCHOLAR-GIPSY 94
THAT BLACK TOMBSTONE THE NAME . . . . 292 HEINES GRAVE 2
YELLOW AND BLACK ON THE GRAVES . . . . 292 HEINES GRAVE 12
THE BLACK TOMBSTONE THE NAME . . . . 292 HEINES GRAVE V 2
WHAT BLACK PROCESSION SLOWLY MAKES APPROACH 331 MEROPE 52
THIS DAY AMID THESE RITES THIS BLACK-ROBED TRAIN . 333 MEROPE 105
BROKE BLACK WITH SWEAT THE ANTLERD MOUNTAIN-STAG . 357 MEROPE 808
STRONG BLACK TEMPESTUOUS TO THE CAVERN-MOUTH 358 MEROPE 821
ONCE IN THE BLACK AND ARROWY RACE AND CAST . . 358 MEROPE 832
NOT THE BLACK CREDIT OF HIS MURDERER . . . 365 MEROPE 991
UNDER THE DRIPPING BLACK TARTAREAN CLIFF . . 368 MEROPE 1064
ON THE BLACK WAVE BORNE TO AND FRO . . . . 370 MEROPE 1119
STRETCHD AMONG BRIARS AND STONES THE SLOW BLACK GORE 373 MEROPE 1172
THAT BLACK-ROBED SWOONING FIGURE MEROPE . . 376 MEROPE 1212
BUT THAT SINCE FIRST THE BLACK AND FRUITFUL EARTH 389 MEROPE 1536
WHICH MAKES THE TIME LOOK BLACK AND SAD TO HIM . 411 EMPEDOCLES I 1 153
WHICH MAKES THE TIMES LOOK BLACK AND SAD TO HIM . 411 EMPEDOCLES I 1 V 153
THROUGH THE BLACK RUSHING SMOKE-BURSTS . . . 441 EMPEDOCLES II 417
THY SMALL BLACK FIGURE ON THE SNOW . . . . 451 GEISTS GRAVE 52
ROUND HIS SMALL THROAT OF BLACK AND BROWN . . 459 KAISER DEAD 15
BLACK CHAFING WATER AND AFLOAT . . . . . . 479 HAYSWATER BOAT 2
ALL ELSE BLACK WATER AND AFLOAT . . . . . . 479 HAYSWATER BOAT 15
IN HIS LONG BLACK SHIP SPEEDING NIGHT AND DAY . . 485 S S LUSITANIA 10

BLACKBIRD
THE BLACKBIRD WHISTLED FROM THE DINGLES NEAR . . 155 TRISTRAM 3 197
THE BLACKBIRD PICKING FOOD . . . . 258 SCHOLAR-GIPSY 116

BLACKEND
WHO WITH NUMB BLACKEND FINGERS MAKES HER FIRE . 70 SOHRAB RUSTUM 304
THE FEARD AND BLACKEND RULER OF THEIR RACE . . . 336 MEROPE 198
ON THIS CHARRD BLACKEND MELANCHOLY WASTE . . . 428 EMPEDOCLES II 2

BLACKENING
THE FRESHENING WIND AND BLACKENING WAVES . . . 244 SUMMER NIGHT 61

BLACKER
GREW BLACKER THUNDER RUMBLED IN THE AIR . . . . 76 SOHRAB RUSTUM 500
IN A BLACKER INCESSANTER LINE . . . . 253 FUTURE 61

BLACKEST
HEREAFTER IN THE BLACKEST DEAD OF NIGHT . . . . 105 BALDER DEAD 2 5

BLADE
HIS HEAD BUT THIS TIME ALL THE BLADE LIKE GLASS . . 76 SOHRAB RUSTUM 511

BLAME
LAUGH MY FRIENDS AND WITHOUT BLAME . . . . . 22 MEMORY-PICTURE 1
BLAME THE MUSIC OF YOUR FEASTS IN VAIN . . . . 32 NEW SIRENS V 170
BLAME OUR ACTIVITY . . . . 46 WORLD QUIETIST 6
BLAME THOU NOT THEREFORE HIM WHO DARES . . . 59 RESIGNATION 231
HIM BLAME NOT FAUSTA RATHER PRAISE . . . . 59 RESIGNATION 238
WHEN THEY HAVE WOE THEY BLAME THE NEAREST CAUSE . 125 BALDER DEAD 3 427
BLAME ME NOT POOR SUFFERER THAT I TARRIED . . . 142 TRISTRAM 2 5
I BLAME THEE NOT THIS HEART I KNOW . . . . 178 FAREWELL 17
WITH BLANK INDIFFERENCE OR WITH BLAME REPROVED . 245 BURIED LIFE 19
ECHO THE BLAME OF HER FOES . . . . 294 HEINES GRAVE 75
I BLAME THEE NOT I DO THY HEART NO WRONG . . . 332 MEROPE 83
AND ME BELIEVE IT WISE MEN GRAVELY BLAME . . . 333 MEROPE 94
AND ON WHOSE LIGHTNESS BLAME IS THROWN AWAY . 411 EMPEDOCLES I 1 162
NOR IS THE THIRST TO BLAME . . . . . . 418 EMPEDOCLES I 2 172
TO ATTACH BLAME ELSEWHERE . . . . 422 EMPEDOCLES I 2 308
NOR IS THAT THIRST TO BLAME . . . . 418 EMPEDOCLES I 2 V 172

BLAMED
WHICH BLAMED THE LIVING MAN . . . . 213 GROWING OLD 35

BLAMES
    MY MOTHER STANDS ALOOF AND BLAMES OUR DEED • • • • 386 MEROPE   1448

BLAMING
    STILL WORKING BLAMING STILL OUR VAIN TURMOIL • •   2 QUIET WORK   13

BLANCHD
    HA DOST THOU START ARE THY LIPS BLANCHD LIKE MINE   133 TRISTRAM 1   102
    OER THE BLANCHD SHEET HER RAVEN HAIR • • • • • 146 TRISTRAM 2   107
    ON THE BLANCHD SANDS A GLOOM • • • • • • 165 FORSAKEN MERM   131
    AND THESE BLANCHD SONG-STIRRD BOUGHS • • • • 200 PHILOMELA   V
    WHERE THE SEA MEETS THE MOON-BLANCHD LAND • • • • 211 DOVER BEACH   8
    WHERE THE EBB MEETS THE MOON-BLANCHD SAND • • • • 211 DOVER BEACH   V   8
    WHERE THE SEA MEETS THE MOON-BLANCHD SAND • • • • 211 DOVER EEACH   V   8
    IN THE DESERTED MOON-BLANCHD STREET • • • • • 242 SUMMER NIGHT   1
    CROSS AND RECROSS THE STRIPS OF MOON-BLANCHD GREEN 255 SCHOLAR-GIPSY   9
    AND THE BLANCHD SUMMIT BARE • • • • • • • 324 OBERMANN MORE   338

BLAND
    THAT MOCKING MOUTH GROW SWEETLY BLAND • • • • 206 RIVER   6
    AND IN THAT GRACIOUS REGION BLAND • • • • • 311 OBERMANN   165
    BUT AN AWFUL PLEASURE BLAND • • • • • • 431 EMPEDOCLES II   67
    CRUEL BUT COMPOSED AND BLAND • • • • • • 453 POOR MATTHIAS   39

BLANK
    THOUGH THAT BLANK SUNSHINE BLIND THEE THOUGH THE CLOUD 44 GIPSY CHILD   61
    IN THE BLANK ECHOING SOLITUDE IF EARTH • • • 45 IN UTRUMQUE PAR   24
    IT SHINES UPON THE BLANK WHITE WALLS • • • • • 141 TRISTRAM 1   335
    SATE IN THE BROUGHAM AND THOSE BLANK WALLS SURVEYD 167 RACHEL 1   8
    MANS BLANK SPIRIT SINCE IT WAS NOT WE • • • 210 SELF-DECEPTION V 14
    WITH BLANK INDIFFERENCE OR WITH BLAME REPROVED • • 245 BURIED LIFE   19
    WE SEE IN BLANK DISMAY • • • • • • • 424 EMPEDOCLES I 2   363
    BUT AS ONE VOICELESS BLANK A PLACE OF GRAVES • • 469 ALARIC AT ROME   182
    BETWIXT BLANK NOTHING AND ABHORRED DECAY • • • FRAGMENT 5   5

BLANKETS
    LIE WRAPT IN THEIR BLANKETS • • • • • • • 442 EMPEDOCLES II   435

BLAST
    THE FLYING LEAVES THE STRAINING BLAST • • • • 136 TRISTRAM 1   179
    AND DIMMD IT LIKE THE DESERT-BLAST • • • • • 147 TRISTRAM 2   135
    AND DIMMD HER LIKE THE DESERT-BLAST • • • • 147 TRISTRAM 2   V 135
    STIRRD LIKE A CLARION-BLAST MY SOUL • • • • 285 HAWORTH CHURCH   100
    SHOOK LIKE A CLARION-BLAST MY SOUL • • • • 284 HAWORTH CHURCH   V 100
    FOR THOUGH HIS MANHOOD BORE THE BLAST • • • 308 OBERMANN   65
    THE EAST BOWD LOW BEFORE THE BLAST • • • • 316 OBERMANN MORE   109
    ALL EUROPE FELT THAT FIERY BLAST • • • • 319 OBERMANN MORE   203
    THE STRONG BLAST BROUGHT A PIGMY THRONG • • • 479 HAYSWATER BOAT   19
    WE CHEERD BUT FROM IT RUSHD A BLAST OF MIGHT • • 484 S S LUSITANIA   7

BLAZE
    BATHD IN A BLAZE OF SUNSET MELT AWAY • • • • • 478 CROMWELL   216

BLAZED
    BLAZED BRIGHT AND BALEFUL LIKE THAT AUTUMN-STAR • • 74 SOHRAB RUSTUM   452
    AND LONG IN THE FAR DARK BLAZED BALDERS PILE • • 119 BALDER DEAD 3   200

BLAZING
    IN THE HALL WITH SCONCES BLAZING • • • • • 13 CHURCH BROU 1   33
    BLAZING AND BRILLIANT CROWDS • • • • • • 296 HEINES GRAVE   142

BLEACH
    BLEACH THEM OR OXUS WITH HIS SUMMER-FLOODS • • • 72 SOHRAB RUSTUM   377

BLEAK
    THE BLEAK STERN HOUR • • • • • • • • 52 CONSOLATION   66
    IS IT THAT THE BLEAK SEA-GALE • • • • • • • 131 TRISTRAM 1   33
    LONELY AND BLEAK AT ITS SIDE • • • • • • • 283 HAWORTH CHURCH   64

BLEARD
    GREY RAIN-BLEARD STATUES OVERPEER • • • • • • 191 STRAYED REVEL   179

BLEATING
    THE BLEATING OF THE FOLDED FLOCKS IS BORNE • • • 255 SCHOLAR-GIPSY   18

BLEED
    NO VICTIMS BLEED NO DRUIDS BOW • • • • • • 274 STANZAS CARNAC   15
    TO SEE ANOTHER MIGHTY VICTIM BLEED • • • • • 349 MEROPE   563

BLEEDING
    TRUTH WHAT IS TRUTH TWO BLEEDING HEARTS • • • 203 EUPHROSYNE   5
    WITH ACHING HANDS AND BLEEDING FEET • • • • 241 MORALITY   7
    THE PAGEANT OF HIS BLEEDING HEART • • • • • 303 GRANDE CHARTR   136

BLEND
    HAVE DREAMD TWO HUMAN HEARTS MIGHT BLEND • • • 181 ISOLATION MARG   38
    AND BLEND HIS HAPPY LIFE • • • • • • • • 197 FRAG ANTIGONE   73

BLENDING
    TWO BLENDING DUTIES HARMONISD IN ONE • • • • • •   1 QUIET WORK   V   3

BLENDS
    AND BLENDS THEIR BLOODS AS THOSE   • • • • • 418 EMPEDOCLES I 2   189

BLENT
    OF THEIRS ARE BLENT IN THEM • • • • • • 418 EMPEDOCLES I 2   190
    WE MIGHT HAVE JOY BLENT WITH THE ALL-BATHING AIR • • 439 EMPEDOCLES II   343
    WE SHOULD HAVE JOY BLENT WITH THE ALL-BATHING AIR   439 EMPEDOCLES II   V 343

BLESSED
    ONLY THE BLESSED SAINTS ARE SMILING DUMB • • • • 17 CHURCH BROU 3   4
    ARE THE BLESSED GODS DISMAYD • • • • • 34 NEW SIRENS   246
    AND LABEL WITH THE BLESSED SIGN • • • • • 138 TRISTRAM 1   252
    TELL THEM ONE BLESSED CHRISTMAS-NIGHT • • • 157 SAINT BRANDAN   29
    AND THE BLESSED LIGHT OF THE SUN • • • • 164 FORSAKEN MERM   93
    MACARIA BLESSED CHILD • • • • • • • • 343 MEROPE   433

BLESSING
    WHAT BLESSING MUST FULL GOODNESS SHOWER • • • 158 SAINT BRANDAN   54
    WHAT BLESSING MUST TRUE GOODNESS SHOWER • • • 158 SAINT BRANDAN   V 54
    SO SAITH HE BLESSING HIM WITH OUTSPREAD HANDS • • 445 WESTMIN ABBEY   46

BLEST
    MAN WOULD BE MILD AND WITH SAFE CONSCIENCE BLEST • • 5 HARMONY NATURE   11
    A LIGHT THAT SHINING FROM THE BLEST ABODES • • • • 9 MYCERINUS   23
    DO THE GODS SEND TO ME TO MAKE THEM BLEST • • • 110 BALDER DEAD 2   204
    WHO SEE THE LIGHT AND BLEST IN ASGARD DWELL • 112 BALDER DEAD 2   255
    ON ONE SHE SMILED AND HE WAS BLEST • • • • 204 EUPHROSYNE   V
    PURE SOULS HONOURD AND BLEST • • • • • • 290 RUGBY CHAPEL   147
    FAIL TO MAKE BLEST THY STATE • • • • • • 426 EMPEDOCLES I 2   420

BLEW
    BLEW SUCH MUSIC AS A GOD MAY FRAME • • • • 29 NEW SIRENS   104
    BLEW SUCH A THRILLING SUMMONS TO MY WILL • • • 36 VOICE   37
    THE BREEZE AND FILLD THE SAILS AND BLEW THE FIRE • • 118 BALDER DEAD 3   184

BLIGHTING
    IS IT THE BLIGHTING TAINT DISHONOUR BREATHES • • 463 ALARIC AT ROME   27

BLIND
    AND TMOLUS HILL AND SMYRNA BAY THOUGH BLIND • • 2 TO A FRIEND   4
    AND TMOLUS HILL AND SMYRNAS BAY THOUGH BLIND • • 2 TO A FRIEND   V 4
    BLIND DIVINATIONS OF A WILL SUPREME • • • • • 10 MYCERINUS   52
    THOUGH THAT BLANK SUNSHINE BLIND THEE THOUGH THE CLOUD   44 GIPSY CHILD   61
    A BLIND LED BEGGAR • • • • • • • • 51 CONSOLATION   29
    BUT THE BLIND HODER LEFT THE FEASTING GODS • • • 97 BALDER DEAD 1   72
    AND THE BLIND HODER ANSWERD HER AND SAID • • • 99 BALDER DEAD 1   131
    HIM THE BLIND HODER MET AS HE CAME UP • • • 101 BALDER DEAD 1   226
    HODER ILL-FATED BLIND IN HEART AND EYES • • • 124 BALDER DEAD 3   387
    THOU DOEST WELL TO CHIDE ME HODER BLIND • • • 125 BALDER DEAD 3   423
    AND THE BLIND HODER ANSWERD HIM AND SPAKE • • • 125 BALDER DEAD 3   431
    TO NANNA AND SHE GAVE THEIR BROTHER BLIND • • • 129 BALDER DEAD 3   550
    WITH THE BLIND GUSTS THAT SHAKE THEIR OWN • • • 178 FAREWELL   28
    WITH THE BLIND GUSTS WHICH SHAKE THEIR OWN • • • 178 FAREWELL   V 28
    MAN IS BLIND BECAUSE OF SIN • • • • • • 215 PIS-ALLER   1
    NOT WHOLLY CLEAR NOR WHOLLY BLIND • • • • 217 NAMELESS EPIT   V
    THEY DROOPD THEY GREW BLIND THEY GREW OLD • • • 233 YOUTH OF MAN   48
    AND FLUCTUATE TWIXT BLIND HOPES AND BLIND DESPAIRS • 236 PALLADIUM   18
    AND FLUCTUATE TWIXT BLIND HOPES AND BLIND DESPAIRS • 236 PALLADIUM   18
    HENCE HENCE THEY CRY YE DO BUT KEEP MAN BLIND • 237 PROGRESS   18
    EDDYING AT LARGE IN BLIND UNCERTAINTY • • • • 246 BURIED LIFE   43
    EDDYING ABOUT IN BLIND UNCERTAINTY • • • • 246 BURIED LIFE   V 43
    HALF BLIND PALSIED IN PAIN • • • • • • 292 HEINES GRAVE   13
    BY NIGHT IN THAT BLIND TUMULT THEY WERE SLAIN • 340 MEROPE   345
    WHAT HATH INVOLVED THEM BUT BLIND • • • • 343 MEROPE   423
    BLIND LEADERS TO THEIR BANE • • • • • • 353 MEROPE   675
    HATRED AND PASSIONATE ENVY BLIND THINE EYES • 397 MEROPE   1772
    BE NOT THEN FEARS BLIND SLAVE • • • • • 415 EMPEDOCLES I 2   102
    TO THE BLIND SLAVES OF POWER TO MAKE IT KNOWN • •   FRAGMENT 2   3

BLINDED
    FOR FIRST THOU BAREST ME WITH BLINDED EYES • • • 98 BALDER DEAD 1   96
    HIS SHEEP HIS HAPLESS LOVE HIS BLINDED EYES • • 268 THYRSIS   187
    WAS BLINDED BY THE OUTGUSHING SPRINGS OF BRINE • • 357 MEROPE   778

BLINDFOLD
    ONCE PASSD I BLINDFOLD HERE AT ANY HOUR • • • • 263 THYRSIS   24

BLINDING
    IN BLINDING MASSES SHOWERD THE GOLDEN HAIR • • • • 150 TRISTRAM 3   34

BLINDLY
    STRIVING BLINDLY ACHIEVING • • • • • • • • 288 RUGBY CHAPEL   65
    WHO BLINDLY FOLLOW EVER • • • • • • • • 353 MEROPE   674

BLINDNESS
    LIGHT BRING NO BLINDNESS • • • • • • • • 40 STAGIRIUS   57
    HIS GROPING BLINDNESS • • • • • • • • • 192 STRAYED REVEL   217

BLINDS
 CLOSE THINE EYES THIS FLOODING MOONLIGHT BLINDS THEM 144 TRISTRAM 2 71
 SAY WHAT BLINDS US THAT WE CLAIM THE GLORY • • • • 209 SELF-DECEPTION 1

BLINKING
 AND SCANND WITH BLINKING EYES THE ADVANCING FORM • • 76 SOHRAB RUSTUM 518

BLISS
 SAY WHAT IS THIS WE ARE IN BLISS FORGIVEN • • • • 18 CHURCH BROU 3 30
 AH NO THE BLISS YOUTH DREAMS IS ONE • • • • • • 22 YOUTH AND CALM 16
 YOUTH DREAMS A BLISS ON THIS SIDE DEATH • • • • • 22 YOUTH AND CALM 19
 SMALL BLISS MY RACE HATH OF THE GODS OBTAINED • • 110 BALDER DEAD 2 205
 THAT WAS BLISS TO MAKE MY SORROWS FLEE • • • 144 TRISTRAM 2 46
 SLIP WITHOUT BRINGING BLISS SLOWLY AWAY • • • • 151 TRISTRAM 3 66
 AGAIN I SEE MY BLISS AT HAND • • • • • • • 174 MEETING 1
 FAIR CHILD IT WAS THE BLISS WITHIN • • • • • • 204 EUPHROSYNE 26
 TILL HAVING USED OUR NERVES WITH BLISS AND TEEN • 259 SCHOLAR-GIPSY 147
 AND WAIVE ALL CLAIM TO BLISS AND TRY TO BEAR • 260 SCHOLAR-GIPSY 193
 WHICH THOUGH IT GIVES NO BLISS YET SPOILS FOR REST • 261 SCHOLAR-GIPSY 223
 THOU HAST NO RIGHT TO BLISS • • • • • • • • 417 EMPEDOCLES I 2 160
 WHENEER OF BLISS DEBARRD • • • • • • • • • 417 EMPEDOCLES I 2 163
 OF LIFE THE THIRST FOR BLISS • • • • • • • 418 EMPEDOCLES I 2 168
 OUR CRY FOR BLISS OUR PLEA • • • • • • • • 419 EMPEDOCLES I 2 209
 WHY SHOULD I SAY THAT LIFE NEED YIELD BUT MODERATE 425 EMPEDOCLES I 2 391
  BLISS
 SHALL WE JUDGE WHAT FOR MAN IS NOT TRUE BLISS OR IS 425 EMPEDOCLES I 2 396
 THAT WE MUST FEIGN A BLISS • • • • • • • 425 EMPEDOCLES I 2 402
 WHENEER FROM BLISS DEBARRD 417 EMPEDOCLES I 2 V 163
 SHALL WE JUDGE WHAT FOR MAN IS NOT HIGH BLISS OR IS 425 EMPEDOCLES I 2 V 396
 THAT WE DEMAND A BLISS • • • • • • • 425 EMPEDOCLES I 2 V 402
 THAT WE MUST CLAIM SOME BLISS • • • • • • • 425 EMPEDOCLES I 2 V 402

BLISTERD
 WHEN THE SHIRT-WRAPT POISON-BLISTERD HERO • • • • 399 MEROPE 1832

BLITHE
 BLITHE ALL ELSE STIRS THOU STIRREST NOT AVERSE • • 41 GIPSY CHILD V 13
 THE MARCH THE LEAGUER HEAVENS BLITHE AIR • • • 138 TRISTRAM 1 258
 TEMPTS NOT THE REVEL BLITHE • • • • • • • 219 BACCHANALIA 1 44
 THEE AT THE FERRY OXFORD RIDERS BLITHE • • 257 SCHOLAR-GIPSY 72
 CLEARD WITH BLITHE TRAVEL AND THE MORNING AIR • 355 MEROPE 734

BLITHELY
 BLITHELY THIS MORN OLD OCEANS WORK IS DONE • • • • 41 GIPSY CHILD V 7
 AND BLITHELY DO THESE SEA-BIRDS HOVER NEAR • • • 41 GIPSY CHILD V 8

BLOCK
 LIVING HIS OWN SACRIFICE-BLOCK • • • • • • • 400 MEROPE 1859

BLOCKD
 SO ON THE BRIDGE THAT DAMSEL BLOCKD THE WAY • • 107 BALDER DEAD 2 99

BLOCKS
 BLOCKS OF THE PAST LIKE ICEBERGS HIGH • • • • 319 OBERMANN MORE 211

BLOND
 RED LOOSESTRIFE AND BLOND MEADOW-SWEET AMONG • • 266 THYRSIS 124
 HEAVY WITH FRAGRANCE THE BLOND • • • • • • • 296 HEINES GRAVE 135

BLOOD
 NATURE IS CRUEL MAN IS SICK OF BLOOD • • • 5 HARMONY NATURE 7
 ON HIS COAT WERE LEAVES AND BLOOD-STAINS • • • 14 CHURCH BROU 1 47
 MADE MY TOST HEART ITS VERY LIFE-BLOOD SPILL • • 36 VOICE 39
 OF BLOOD AND I HAVE FOUGHT WITH MANY A FOE • • 71 SOHRAB RUSTUM 327
 AND LET THE BLOOD FLOW FREE AND SO TO DIE • • 80 SOHRAB RUSTUM 652
 HE SPOKE AND ALL THE BLOOD LEFT RUSTUMS CHEEKS • • 80 SOHRAB RUSTUM 661
 BUT NOW IN BLOOD AND BATTLES WAS MY YOUTH • • • 85 SOHRAB RUSTUM 824
 AND FULL OF BLOOD AND BATTLES IS MY AGE • • • 85 SOHRAB RUSTUM 825
 AND I SHALL NEVER END THIS LIFE OF BLOOD • • • 85 SOHRAB RUSTUM 826
 A LIFE OF BLOOD INDEED THOU DREADFUL MAN • • • 85 SOHRAB RUSTUM 828
 HIS WOUNDS IMPERIOUS ANGUISH BUT THE BLOOD • • • • 85 SOHRAB RUSTUM 840
 MY MAN COMES RUNNING FLECKD WITH BLOOD • • • 89 SICK KING BOKH 50
 IS HE THY FRIEND OR OF THY BLOOD • • • • • 92 SICK KING BOKH 135
 WASH OFF ALL BLOOD SET SMOOTH EACH LIMB • • • 95 SICK KING BOKH 230
 MID DUST AND GROANS AND LIMBS LOPPD OFF AND BLOOD • 105 BALDER DEAD 2 16
 THEIR HORSES FETLOCK-DEEP IN BLOOD THEY RIDE • • 105 BALDER DEAD 2 25
 AND BLOOD AND RINGING BLOWS AND VIOLENT DEATH • 117 BALDER DEAD 3 140
 LIFE ONE PERPETUAL FIGHT A BATH OF BLOOD • • • 128 BALDER DEAD 3 506
 THROUGH THEIR BLOOD AND BINDS THEIR SOULS • • • 132 TRISTRAM 1 66
 FROM THE FEVER IN HIS BLOOD • • • • • • 136 TRISTRAM 1 172
 ALL RED WITH BLOOD THE WHIRLING RIVER FLOWS • • 137 TRISTRAM 1 234
 THEY CLOUD THE BRAIN THEY DULL THE BLOOD • • • 138 TRISTRAM 1 248
 I THINK I HAVE A FEVER IN MY BLOOD • • • • 139 TRISTRAM 1 280
 THE RUSHING BATTLE CLEARD THY BLOOD • • • • 139 TRISTRAM 1 292
 AND WITH A BLOOD LIKE MINE WILL LEAVE I FEAR • 140 TRISTRAM 1 306
 SPEAK HER FAIR SHE IS OF ROYAL BLOOD • • • 145 TRISTRAM 2 94
 SPRUNG FROM THE BLOOD OF ISRAELS SCATTERD RACE • 168 RACHEL 3 1
 I CAME I SAW THEE RISE THE BLOOD • • • • • 178 FAREWELL 9
 WHICH CONSECRATES THE TIES OF BLOOD FOR THESE INDEED 196 FRAG ANTIGONE 31
 OF BLOOD CAN HE NOT BIND • • • • • • • • 196 FRAG ANTIGONE 37
 MADDENING THEIR BLOOD • • • • • • • • • 218 BACCHANALIA 1 31

BLOOD   (CONTINUED)
          THE MANTLING BLOOD TO THY CHEEK . . . . .   235 YOUTH OF MAN   115
          TO—MORROW RED WITH BLOOD WILL XANTHUS BE . . . 236 PALLADIUM   14
          WHOSE BEACH ONCE RAN WITH LOYAL BLOOD . . . . 274 STANZAS CARNAC   28
          THOSE OF THY BLOOD WHOM THOU LOVDST . . . . . 284 HAWORTH CHURCH   79
          THEREFORE WITH BLOOD OF THY FOES . . . . .   296 HEINES GRAVE   125
          THEIR DROPS OF BLOOD THEIR DEATH IN LIFE . . . 301 GRANDE CHARTR   54
          MAKE THEIR BLOOD DANCE AND CHAIN THEIR EYES . . 305 GRANDE CHARTR   188
          THE POETS FEVERISH BLOOD . . . .   309 OBERMANN   94
          WHEN BLOOD AND WARMTH WERE FLED . . . . . . 319 OBERMANN MORE   194
          CLOSING IN BLOOD AND GLOOM HIS SULLEN REIGN . . 335 MEROPE   160
          GULFS OF ESTRANGING BLOOD ACROSS THAT CHASM . . 336 MEROPE   194
          AND SHED THEIR BLOOD LIKE WATER IN OUR CAUSE . . 337 MEROPE   227
          THOUGH FOUND PERVERSE THE BLOOD OF HERACLES . . 337 MEROPE   256
          RAVIN A LITTLE WHILE IN SPOIL AND BLOOD . . . 339 MEROPE   297
          FORSWORN THEIR BLOOD UNGRATEFULLY HAD THEY . .   339 MEROPE   323
          ERROR ON ERROR AND BLOOD . . . .   343 MEROPE   424
          HER BLOOD THAT SO SHE MIGHT MAKE . . . . .   343 MEROPE   427
          JEALOUS BLOOD-EXACTING FRIENDS . . . . . .   344 MEROPE   461
          SULLYING HIS GARMENT WITH DARK—STREAMING BLOOD . 346 MEROPE   491
          BRING BACK OUR SON IF MAY BE WITHOUT BLOOD . . 350 MEROPE   587
          INSTALL HIM IN THY THRONE STILL WITHOUT BLOOD . 350 MEROPE   588
          SHEDS BLOOD IMPRISONS BANISHES ATTAINTS . . . 353 MEROPE   682
          TURN WITH AVERTED EYES FROM DEEDS OF BLOOD . .   354 MEROPE   695
          IN THIS BLOOD-DELUGED PALACE IN WHOSE HALLS . . 366 MEROPE   1018
          ALL—FLOODING OCEAN OF BLOOD . . . .   378 MEROPE   1246
          APPOINTS THE WAY TO PEACE THROUGH SHEDDING BLOOD . 378 MEROPE   1248
          FRESH BLOOD FLOWS CALLING FOR BLOOD . . . .   379 MEROPE   1253
          FRESH BLOOD FLOWS CALLING FOR BLOOD . . . .   379 MEROPE   1253
          THE UNDEGENERATE BLOOD OF HERACLES . . . .   383 MEROPE   1356
          WHICH NATURE SANCTIONS WHICH THE INNOCENT BLOOD . 386 MEROPE   1427
          I LOATHE FOR HIM THE SLIPPERY WAY OF BLOOD . .   387 MEROPE   1464
          OUR OWN RIGHT HAND IN THE DETESTED BLOOD . .   387 MEROPE   1468
          BLOOD—FOUNDED THRONES THOU SAYST ARE INSECURE . 389 MEROPE   1532
          ITS PRIVILEGED IMMUNITY FROM BLOOD . . . .   389 MEROPE   1535
          WHETHER BLOOD FLOWS OR NO CAN YET INVEST . .   389 MEROPE   1545
          BLOOD—SEVERD BUT MESSENIAS KING AND QUEEN . .   394 MEROPE   1720
          POSSESSD IN HATRED LOST IN BLOOD . . . . .   399 MEROPE   1849
          THAT THE BLOOD RUSHES IN STREAMS TO THE DUST .   400 MEROPE   1865
          AND CRIED O ZEUS LET WHAT BLOOD—GUILTINESS . .   402 MEROPE   1915
          YET STAINS OUR LAND BE BY THIS BLOOD WASHD OUT . 402 MEROPE   1916
          WHAT BLOOD SO MEET AS THINE TO WASH IT OUT . .   402 MEROPE   1924
          WITH BLOOD—BESPATTERD ROBES AND CHAPLET SHORN . 403 MEROPE   1966
          HIS BLOOD TO ME FOR I CONFESS IT KIND . . .   404 MEROPE   1976
          WHICH LAID THEE LOW FOR BLOOD REQUIRES BLOOD .   404 MEROPE   1987
          WHICH LAID THEE LOW FOR BLOOD REQUIRES BLOOD .   404 MEROPE   1987
          ON THE BLOOD-STAIND HOME OF HIS BIRTH . . .   347 MEROPE   V
          BLOOD I ASK NOT ENOUGH . . . .   348 MEROPE   V
          ARE MINE EYES WITH BLOOD BUT IF THIS . . . .   348 MEROPE   V
          AGAIN OUR YOUTHFUL BLOOD . . . .   424 EMPEDOCLES I 2   352
          IN SIGHT OF BLOOD BUT WERE RAPT FAR AWAY . .   427 EMPEDOCLES I 2   453
          OUR BLOOD TO WATER . . . .   439 EMPEDOCLES II   334
          OF BLOOD—UNMIXD FROM POTSDAM CAME . . . . .   459 KAISER DEAD   20
          AND COLD BESIDES HIS BLUE BLOOD RAN . . . .   460 KAISER DEAD   39
          THAT STREWD THE BLOOD-STAIND PATH WHERE EMPIRE LED 478 CROMWELL   226
          YET HAPPY SINCE HIS FEVERISH BLOOD . . . .   484 ROME—SICKNESS   25

BLOODLESS
          I ASK IF BLOODLESS MEANS MAY GAIN HIS END . .   387 MEROPE   1465
          PRACTISE THE INDULGENT BLOODLESS POLICY . . . 390 MEROPE   1561

BLOODS
          AND BLENDS THEIR BLOODS AS THOSE . . . . .   418 EMPEDOCLES I 2   189

BLOODSHED
          NOT PRONE ALL SAY AVERSE TO BLOODSHED NOW . .   388 MEROPE   1492
          NOT PRONE ALL SAY TO USELESS BLOODSHED NOW . .   388 MEROPE   V1492

BLOODSHOT
          BUT IN THE GLOOM THEY FOUGHT WITH BLOODSHOT EYES . 75 SOHRAB RUSTUM   490
          DO THY BLOODSHOT EYES STILL WEEP . . . . .   430 EMPEDOCLES II   55
          DO THY BLOODSHOT EYES STILL SEE . . . . .   430 EMPEDOCLES II V 55
          DO THY BLOODSHOT EYES STILL FLEE . . . . .   430 EMPEDOCLES II V 55

BLOODY
          BLOODY NEATH THE FLARING SCONCES . . . . .   14 CHURCH BROU 1   51
          THE JADED HUNTERS WITH THEIR BLOODY FREIGHT . .   18 CHURCH BROU 3   14
          HAVE WADED FOREMOST IN THEIR BLOODY WAVES . .   74 SOHRAB RUSTUM   434
          AND SOHRAB WOUNDED ON THE BLOODY SAND . . .   77 SOHRAB RUSTUM   526
          MIGHT NOW BE LYING ON THIS BLOODY SAND . . .   85 SOHRAB RUSTUM   817
          SO ON THE BLOODY SAND SOHRAB LAY DEAD . . .   86 SOHRAB RUSTUM   857
          AND STOOD ROUND BALDER ON THE BLOODY FLOOR . .   95 BALDER DEAD 1   10
          AH BLOODY AXE DIZZY BLOWS . . . .   346 MEROPE   499
          PERFORMD GOOD SERVICE FOR HIS BLOODY WAGE . .   364 MEROPE   975
          WHICH WAY TO LEAN I KNOW NOT BLOODY STROKES . . 388 MEROPE   1521
          TRACKD BY MURDERS BLOODY SWORD NO MORE . . .   482 THEKLAS ANSWER   16
          IN THE BLOODY DUST BENEATH THE FEET OF THEIR FOEMEN   HOMER TRANS   26

BLOOM
          HIS YOUTH SAW SOHRABS MOTHER IN HER BLOOM . .   79 SOHRAB RUSTUM   624

BLOOM   (CONTINUED)
    AND LIES A FRAGRANT TOWER OF PURPLE BLOOM • • • •   80 SOHRAB RUSTUM   637
    AND YOUTH AND BLOOM AND THIS DELIGHTFUL WORLD • •   86 SOHRAB RUSTUM   856
    WHERE ART THOU WHO HADST HIS BLOOM • • • • • 132 TRISTRAM 1   77
    IF HER BLOOM BE NOW LESS RARE • • • • • • 134 TRISTRAM 1   116
    WHICH KILLS IN US THE BLOOM THE YOUTH THE SPRING • 153 TRISTRAM 3   122
    WHERE THE SEA-STOCKS BLOOM TO THE WHITE-WALLD TOWN 163 FORSAKEN MERM   69
    YOUNG IN THE BLOOM OF HIS DAYS • • • • 199 EARLY DEATH   11
    NOT OUR BLOOM ONLY BUT OUR STRENGTH DECAY • • • 212 GROWING OLD   7
    OF THE WONDER AND BLOOM OF THE WORLD • • • • 229 YOUTH OF NATURE   54
    THE FIGURE THE BLOOM OF THY LOVE • • • • 231 YOUTH OF NATURE 111
    BRUSHD OFF THE BLOOM FROM THEIR SOUL • • • • 233 YOUTH OF MAN   42
    OF BLOOM ON THE BENT GRASS WHERE I AM LAID • • 256 SCHOLAR-GIPSY   28
    WHEN THE YEARS PRIMAL BURST OF BLOOM IS OER • 264 THYRSIS   52
    THE BLOOM IS GONE AND WITH THE BLOOM GO I • • 264 THYRSIS   60
    THE BLOOM IS GONE AND WITH THE BLOOM GO I • • 264 THYRSIS   60
    CALL FROM THE HEATHER IN BLOOM • • • • 285 HAWORTH CHURCH 122
    OF HOPES AND HEARTS IN BLOOM • • • • • 315 OBERMANN MORE   80
    SHORN OF THE JOY THE BLOOM THE POWER • • • 322 OBERMANN MORE 303
    THAT MY SON STILL SURVIVES IN HEALTH IN BLOOM • 351 MEROPE   612
    SEE HOW THE GIANT SPIRES OF YELLOW BLOOM • • • 412 EMPEDOCLES I 2   4

BLOOMS
    BLOOMS THICKLY GROWS NOT HERE • • • • • • TRISTRAM 3   V 15
    WAVING HER MYRIADS OF WHITE FAIRY BLOOMS • • • EVERLASTING SUB   6

BLOSSOM
    THEN WHITE WITH BLOSSOM AND YOU SAW THE HORNS • 155 TRISTRAM 3   192
    AND FROM THE ELDER-BLOSSOM WHITE • • • • 218 BACCHANALIA 1   11
    GOLD FURZE WITH BROOM IN BLOSSOM VIES • • • 274 STANZAS CARNAC   19
    GOLD BROOM WITH FURZE IN BLOSSOM VIES • • • 274 STANZAS CARNAC V 19

BLOSSOMD
    THE BLOSSOMD THORN-TREE AND HER SLEEPING LOVER • 156 TRISTRAM 3   218
    OF BLOSSOMD CLUSTERS PALE • • • • • • 200 PHILOMELA   V
    THE GRASS THE ELMS THAT BLOSSOMD THORN • • 222 EPILOG LAOCOON   52
    WITH THORNS ONCE STUDDED OLD WHITE-BLOSSOMD TREES 266 THYRSIS 113
    OER FLOWERING PLAIN AND BLOSSOMD MEADOW FLING • 474 CROMWELL   91

BLOSSOMS
    WITH BLOSSOMS RED AND WHITE OF FALLEN MAY • • 264 THYRSIS   55
    THE CYCLAMENS WHOSE BLOSSOMS FILL • • • • 484 ROME-SICKNESS   18

BLOT
    OF WISER THOUGHTS AND FEELINGS BLOT • • • • 183 ABSENCE   7
    MAX A DACHSHOUND WITHOUT BLOT • • • • • 454 POOR MATTHIAS   69
    YES THERE ARE STAINS TIMES FINGERS CANNOT BLOT • 462 ALARIC AT ROME   14
    YET STAINS THERE ARE TO BLOT THY BRIGHTEST PAGE • 463 ALARIC AT ROME   37

BLOTS
    OR TIMES STERN HAND WHY BLOTS IT NOT AWAY • • • 462 ALARIC AT ROME   5

BLOTTED
    BY THE DIM VAPOUR-BLOTTED LIGHT OF STARS • • • 108 BALDER DEAD 2 126
    BUT BY THE BLOTTED LIGHT OF STARS HE FARED • • 108 BALDER DEAD 2 140

BLOTTING
    BLOTTING THIS SIX YEARS SPACE WHICH YET IS MINE • 10 MYCERINUS   60
    SHOWING THEN BLOTTING FROM OUR SIGHT • • • • 299 GRANDE CHARTR   15

BLOW
    GUST ON GUST THE HARSH WINDS BLOW • • • • 32 NEW SIRENS   172
    GUST ON GUST THE HOARSE WINDS BLOW • • • • 32 NEW SIRENS V 172
    AND RUSTUM FOLLOWD HIS OWN BLOW AND FELL • • 73 SOHRAB RUSTUM 420
    DANCES AS THE TRUMPETS BLOW • • • • • 138 TRISTRAM 1 264
    THY GOLDEN-TASSELLD BUGLE BLOW • • • • • 149 TRISTRAM 2 188
    NOW THE GREAT WINDS SHOREWARD BLOW • • • 161 FORSAKEN MERM   4
    WHEN SOFT THE WINDS BLOW • • • • • 165 FORSAKEN MERM 125
    NOW THE GREAT WINDS SHOREWARDS BLOW • • • 161 FORSAKEN MERM V 4
    THAT SON OF ITALY WHO TRIED TO BLOW • • • 166 AUSTERITY POET   1
    BLOW YE WINDS LIFT ME WITH YOU • • • • 177 PARTING   75
    ANOTHER BREATH OF WIND DOTH BLOW • • • • 223 EPILOG LAOCOON   74
    AND STOCKS IN FRAGRANT BLOW • • • • • 264 THYRSIS   66
    AND BLOW A STRAIN THE WORLD AT LAST SHALL HEED • 265 THYRSIS   79
    BLOW FROM THEIR GRAVES TOWARD THINE • • • 284 HAWORTH CHURCH V 89
    TOO LATE FOR US YOUR CALL YE BLOW • • • 305 GRANDE CHARTR 197
    BLOW OFF THE SPOT OF MURDER FROM HIS NAME • • 336 MEROPE 200
    TO ZEUS BEFORE HE STRUCK HIS BLOW STRUCK MINE • 338 MEROPE 274
    A BLOW A BLOW WAS STRUCK AND HE FELL • • • 346 MEROPE 490
    A BLOW A BLOW WAS STRUCK AND HE FELL • • • 346 MEROPE 490
    DIRE IS THIS BLOW FOR MEROPE AND I • • • 360 MEROPE 885
    WITHOUT A CRY A STRUGGLE OR A BLOW • • • 367 MEROPE 1028
    O GODS FOOLISH OLD MAN THOU SPOILST MY BLOW • 374 MEROPE 1194
    UNHAPPY ONE THOU STRIKST A MOST JUST BLOW • • 374 MEROPE 1200
    JUSTICE MY SISTER LONG DEMANDS THIS BLOW • • 390 MEROPE 1572
    BE WITH HIM CHOOSE THE MOMENT STRIKE THY BLOW • 391 MEROPE 1590
    WHERE TWINES THE CHAPLET DEALT A MIGHTY BLOW • 402 MEROPE 1921
    AT ONE BOLD WORD ONE ENTERPRISING BLOW • • 402 MEROPE 1946
    GO WITH HIM CHOOSE THE MOMENT STRIKE THY BLOW • 391 MEROPE V1590
    WILL BLOW US FIERCELY BACK TO SEA AND EARTH • 439 EMPEDOCLES II 362

BLOW   (CONTINUED)
      LIKE FROZEN WINDS ON SOUTHERN VALES THAT BLOW   • •   474 CROMWELL   89

BLOWETH
      THE SPIRIT BLOWETH AND IS STILL   • • • • • •   241 MORALITY   3

BLOWING
      BUT I HEAR THE NORTH WIND BLOWING   • • • • •   32 NEW SIRENS   189
      BLOWING BETWEEN THE STEMS THE FOREST-AIR   • • •   154 TRISTRAM 3   167
      BUT WE STOOD WITHOUT IN THE COLD BLOWING AIRS   • •   163 FORSAKEN MERM   73
      WHAT BLOWING DAISIES FRAGRANT GRASS • • • • • •   248 KENSINGTON GARD   15
      OER THEIR POLISHD BOSOMS BLOWING   • • • • • •   433 EMPEDOCLES II   154

BLOWN
      ONE LESSON WHICH IN EVERY WIND IS BLOWN   • • • •   1 QUIET WORK   2
      TWO LESSONS THAT IN EVERY WIND ARE BLOWN   • • • •   1 QUIET WORK   V   2
      THE PRODIGY OF FULL-BLOWN CRIME AMONG   • • • • • •   6 GEO CRUIKSHANK   3
      WITH BLOWN TRESSES AND WITH BECKONING HANDS   • •   26 NEW SIRENS   16
      AND THOSE BLOWN RUSHES ON THE FLOOR   • • • • •   148 TRISTRAM 2   160
      AND THE BLOWN RUSHES ON THE FLOOR   • • • • •   148 TRISTRAM 2   V 160
      AS FROM THE KINGS OF SOUND ARE BLOWN   • • • • •   222 EPILOG LAOCOON   34
      AND EVERY DOUBT LONG BLOWN BY TIME AWAY   • • • •   261 SCHOLAR-GIPSY   200
      A WIND-BLOWN THREAD   • • • • • • • • •   392 MEROPE   1654

BLOWS
      BECAUSE ON ITS HOT BROW THERE BLOWS   • • • • • •   21 YOUTH AND CALM   11
      BECAUSE ON ITS HOT HOUR THERE BLOWS   • • • • • •   21 YOUTH AND CALM   V 11
      OF HEWING AXES CRASHING TREES SUCH BLOWS   • • • •   75 SOHRAB RUSTUM   478
      AND BLOOD AND RINGING BLOWS AND VIOLENT DEATH • •   117 BALDER DEAD 3   140
      AND A WARM WEST-WIND BLOWS AND THAW SETS IN   • •   122 BALDER DEAD 3   309
      MINE EARS ARE STUNND WITH BLOWS AND SICK FOR CALM   128 BALDER DEAD 3   508
      CHILL BLOWS THE WIND THE PLEASAUNCE-WALKS ARE DREAR 135 TRISTRAM 1   161
      THE WIDE PLAIN RINGS THE DAZED AIR THROBS WITH BLOWS 137 TRISTRAM 1   235
      THE NEIGHING STEEDS THE RINGING BLOWS   • • • •   138 TRISTRAM 1   259
      THE HOARSE WIND BLOWS COLDLY   • • • • • •   164 FORSAKEN MERM   110
      THE HOARSE WIND BLOWS COLDER   • • • • • •   164 FORSAKEN MERM   V 110
      BLOWS THROUGH THE PORTICO   • • • • • •   186 STRAYED REVEL   20
      IN PUFFS OF BALM THE NIGHT-AIR BLOWS   • • • • •   218 BACCHANALIA 1   14
      STILL BLOWS IN THE QUANTOCK COOMBS   • • • • •   229 YOUTH OF NATURE   23
      BLOWS FROM THEIR GRAVES TO THY OWN   • • • • •   284 HAWORTH CHURCH   89
      WITH RAIN WHERE THICK THE CROCUS BLOWS   • • • •   299 GRANDE CHARTR   2
      FRESH THROUGH THESE PAGES BLOWS   • • • • • •   307 OBERMANN   26
      AH BLOODY AXE DIZZY BLOWS   • • • • • •   346 MEROPE   499
      HOW TWENTYFOLD WORSE ARE YE WHEN YOUR BLOWS   • •   385 MEROPE   1407
      NOR IS THAT WIND LESS ROUGH WHICH BLOWS A GOOD   420 EMPEDOCLES I 2   256
            MANS BARGE
      NOR IS THE WIND LESS ROUGH THAT BLOWS A GOOD   420 EMPEDOCLES I 2   V 256
            MANS BARGE
      THE MUSIC OF THE LYRE BLOWS AWAY   • • • • •   432 EMPEDOCLES II   123

BLUE
      PAINT THOSE EYES SO BLUE SO KIND   • • • • •   24 MEMORY-PICTURE   41
      STRAW HATS BEDECKD THEIR HEADS WITH RIBBONS BLUE • •   25 DREAM   24
      YOU CRUSH THEM THE BLUE GENTIANS GLEAM   • • •   55 RESIGNATION   103
      PLUNGING ALL DAY IN THE BLUE WAVES AT NIGHT   • •   69 SOHRAB RUSTUM   287
      RETURNING HOME OVER THE SALT BLUE SEA   • • •   85 SOHRAB RUSTUM   833
      FAR TO THE SOUTH BEYOND THE BLUE THERE SPREADS   •   128 BALDER DEAD 3   518
      BLUE AND OER ITS MIRROR KIND   • • • • • •   135 TRISTRAM 1   155
      AND STILL THE CHILDREN LISTEND THEIR BLUE EYES   •   150 TRISTRAM 3   46
      OR ELSE SHE WILL FALL MUSING HER BLUE EYES • • •   152 TRISTRAM 3   90
      WHICH PLAYD ON HER FLUSHD CHEEK AND HER BLUE EYES •   154 TRISTRAM 3   169
      BUT STILL SHE CHATTED ON WITH HER BLUE EYES   • •   154 TRISTRAM 3   177
      TEARS FILLD HIS MILD BLUE EYE   • • • • • •   160 NECKAN   46
      TEARS FILLD HIS COLD BLUE EYE   • • • • • •   160 NECKAN   V 46
      TEARS FILLD HIS KIND BLUE EYE   • • • • • •   160 NECKAN   V 46
      AND THOSE SWEET EYES OF BLUE   • • • • • •   174 MEETING   8
      THE SWEET BLUE EYES THE SOFT ASH-COLOURD HAIR   •   175 PARTING   37
      THERE ITS DUSKY BLUE CLUSTERS   • • • • • •   176 PARTING   51
      AND FROM THE BLUE TWIN-LAKES IT COMES   • • •   184 TERRACE BERNE   9
      ON THE BLUE STRAIT MINE EYES I STRAIN   • • •   205 CALAIS SANDS   20
      ON THE BLUE SEA MY GAZE I STRAIN   • • • • •   205 CALAIS SANDS   V 20
      OER THE BLUE STRAIT MINE EYES I STRAIN   • • •   205 CALAIS SANDS   V 20
      EYES TOO EXPRESSIVE TO BE BLUE   • • • • • •   208 ON THE RHINE   19
      THOSE BLUE HILLS TOO THIS RIVERS FLOW   • • •   208 ON THE RHINE   22
      THE BLUE HAZE-CRADLED MOUNTAINS SPREAD AWAY   •   242 SUMMER NIGHT   21
      OER THE BLUE MIDLAND WATERS WITH THE GALE • • •   262 SCHOLAR-GIPSY   244
      PALE BLUE CONVOLVULUS IN TENDRILS CREEP   • • •   255 SCHOLAR-GIPSY   V 25
      AND BLUE-BELLS TREMBLING BY THE FOREST-WAYS   •   265 THYRSIS   75
      THE BLUE-BELLS PERFUME ALL THE AIR   • • • •   274 STANZAS CARNAC   20
      IN THE LAURELLD ROCK OER THE BLUE   • • • •   294 HEINES GRAVE   57
      WHICH FRINGE THY SOFT BLUE SPEZZIAN BAY   • • •   303 GRANDE CHARTR   142
      THAT FRINGE THY SOFT BLUE SPEZZIAN BAY   • • •   303 GRANDE CHARTR   V 142
      THAT FRINGE THY DARK BLUE SPEZZIAN BAY   • • •   303 GRANDE CHARTR   V 142
      THE RIPPLES OF WHOSE BLUE WAVES CHEER   • • •   311 OBERMANN   163
      THE BLUE SEINE ROLLS HER WAVE   • • • • • •   312 OBERMANN   178
      SEE IN THE BLUE PROFOUND   • • • • • • • •   313 OBERMANN MORE   32
      AGAIN APPEARD THE BLUE   • • • • • • • •   319 OBERMANN MORE   208
      THE CURTAINS OF THE BLUE FILMS SLOWLY MEET • • •   431 EMPEDOCLES II   79
      A RIBBON BLUE   • • • • • • • • •   459 KAISER DEAD   16
      AND COLD BESIDES HIS BLUE BLOOD RAN   • • • •   460 KAISER DEAD   39
      OF OCEANS SLEEPING FACE OR HEAVENS UNBROKEN BLUE •   463 ALARIC AT ROME   36
      A FRETTED WALL OF BLUE AND GREY   • • • • •   479 HAYSWATER BOAT   12

BLUE   (CONTINUED)
           SOFTLY GLEAM THE FAR BLUE MOUNTAINS   . . . .   META CLOISTER   13
           HER VALLIES AND BLUE HILLS   . . . .   FRAGMENT 8   2

BLUEBELLS
           DARK BLUEBELLS DRENCHD WITH DEWS OF SUMMER EVES   . .   257 SCHOLAR-GIPSY   88

BLURRD
           LOOM THE BLURRD HILLS THE RAIN   . . . .   286 HAWORTH CHURCH   132

BLUSHING
           EACH ROSE WITH BLUSHING FACE   . . . .   265 THYRSIS   96

BLUSTER
           BLUSTER OR CRINGE AND MAKE LIFE   . . . .   290 RUGBY CHAPEL   157

BOAR
           HORSES FRET AND BOAR-SPEARS GLANCE   . . . .   13 CHURCH BROU 1   18
           ON THE TURF DEAD LIES THE BOAR . . . .   13 CHURCH BROU 1   26
           TO HUNT THE BOAR IN THE CRISP WOODS TILL EVE   . . .   18 CHURCH BROU 3   11
           NEW MESSES OF THE BOAR SERIMNERS FLESH   . . . .   97 BALDER DEAD 1   67
           ALL NIGHT THEY ATE THE BOAR SERIMNERS FLESH   . .   119 BALDER DEAD 3   210
           THE WILD BOAR RUSTLES IN HIS LAIR   . . . . . .   149 TRISTRAM 2   183
           THE WILD BOAR HARBOURS CLOSE AND FEEDS   . . . .   148 TRISTRAM 2   V
           HIS BOAR-SPEARS BROKEN SHAFT BACK ON THE LAKE . .   358 MEROPE   840

BOARD
           FOR THE WARM PERSIAN SEA-BOARD SO THEY STREAMD   . .   64 SOHRAB RUSTUM   116
           NOT PENT ON SHIP-BOARD THIS DELICIOUS DAY   . . . .   133 TRISTRAM 1   98
           LET HER AS SHE SITS ON BOARD   . . . .   135 TRISTRAM 1   141

BOARS
           SWEET CHESTNUTS BARLEY-CAKES AND BOARS-FLESH DRIED   356 MEROPE   754

BOAST
           O BARREN BOAST O JOYLESS MOCKERY   . . . . . .   EMERSONS ESSAYS   V 14
           NOT LESS THY BOAST ILLUMINATES CONTROL   . . . .   8 RELIGIOUS ISOL   7
           BY A FALSE BOAST THE STYLE OF RUSTUMS SON . . . .   79 SOHRAB RUSTUM   613
           WHOM THIS REALM OF FRANCE CAN BOAST   . . . . . .   136 TRISTRAM 1   195
           THAT THIS REALM OF FRANCE CAN BOAST   . . . . . .   136 TRISTRAM 1   V 195
           NO SMALL BOAST FOR A WEAK   . . . .   293 HEINES GRAVE   29
           I SPEAK NO WORD OF BOAST BUT THIS I SAY   . . . .   360 MEROPE   888

BOASTEST
           AND NOW THOU BOASTEST AND INSULTST MY FATE   . . . .   77 SOHRAB RUSTUM   551

BOASTFUL
           FALSE WILY BOASTFUL ARE THESE TARTAR BOYS   . . . .   71 SOHRAB RUSTUM   348
           THOU DOST NOT SLAY ME PROUD AND BOASTFUL MAN   . .   77 SOHRAB RUSTUM   542

BOASTING
           THE PROUD BOASTING OF THEIR YOUTH   . . . .   235 YOUTH OF MAN   103

BOAT
           ERE HE COME ERE THE BOAT BY THE SHINING-BRANCHD BORDER   19 MODERN SAPPHO   5
           ERE THEIR BOAT-MUSIC SOUND ERE THEIR BROIDERD   19 MODERN SAPPHO   8
                 FLAGS GLEAM
           TIS HE TIS THE BOAT SHOOTING ROUND BY THE TREES   . .   20 MODERN SAPPHO   V 30
           ONE MOMENT ON THE RAPIDS TOP OUR BOAT   . . . .   25 DREAM   30
           FROM THE STREAMS BRINK THE SPOT WHERE FIRST A BOAT   61 SOHRAB RUSTUM   18
           HIS FRAIL BOAT MOORD TO . . . .   190 STRAYED REVEL   153
           THE FERRY-BOAT WITH WOVEN ROPES   . . . .   191 STRAYED REVEL   186
           THE LOADED BOAT SWINGS GROANING   . . . .   192 STRAYED REVEL   198
           STILL GLIDES THE STREAM SLOW DROPS THE BOAT   . .   206 RIVER   1
           SILENT THE BOAT THE LAKE   . . . .   228 YOUTH OF NATURE   2
           OR IN MY BOAT I LIE   . . . .   257 SCHOLAR-GIPSY   66
           OF OUR BOAT PASSING HEAVED THE RIVER-GRASS . . . .   266 THYRSIS   128
           ALL ROUND NO SOUL NO BOAT NO HAIL   . . . . . .   274 STANZAS CARNAC   30
           A BOAT IS LOWERD FROM HER SIDE . . . .   276 SOUTHERN NIGHT   33
           ENOUGH THE BOAT WITH QUIET SHOCK   . . . . . .   276 SOUTHERN NIGHT   45
           WHO BADE HIM LOOSE HIS BOAT AND FIX HIS OAR   . .   444 WESTMIN ABBEY   24
           IN A WASTE WOOD A SINGLE BOAT   . . . .   479 HAYSWATER BOAT   4
           ONE ROOD FROM SHORE THAT SINGLE BOAT . . . . . .   479 HAYSWATER BOAT   16
           THIS BOAT THEY FOUND AGAINST THE SHORE   . . . .   480 HAYSWATER BOAT   25
           THE BOAT WAS OLD A BATTERD BOAT   . . . . . .   480 HAYSWATER BOAT   34
           THE BOAT WAS OLD A BATTERD BOAT   . . . . . .   480 HAYSWATER BOAT   34
           THE BOAT HATH DRIFTED IN THE BAY   . . . . . .   480 HAYSWATER BOAT   37

BOATING
           ABOVE THE LOCKS ABOVE THE BOATING THRONG   . . . .   266 THYRSIS   122

BOATMANS
           WHERE IS THE GIRL WHO BY THE BOATMANS DOOR . . . .   266 THYRSIS   121

BOATS
           TO BUILD THEM BOATS FISH FROM THE FLOODED RIVERS   . .   73 SOHRAB RUSTUM   411
           THE LANTERNS OF THE FISHING-BOATS AT SEA   . . . .   130 TRISTRAM 1   6
           AND MIMIC BOATS THEIR HAVEN NEARD   . . . . . .   223 EPILOG LAOCOON   69
           BOATS AND APPROACH NEAR AS WE DARED THE CHASM   . . 358 MEROPE   838
           THEY MOORD THEIR BOATS AMONG THE BULRUSH STEMS   . . 444 WESTMIN ABBEY   18

BODIES
AGAINST THE BODIES AND STUCK TORCHES NEAR • • • • 118 BALDER DEAD 3 167
THE BODIES WERE CONSUMED ASH CHOKED THE PILE • • 119 BALDER DEAD 3 202
STILL USE OUR BODIES ILL • • • • • • • • • • • 420 EMPEDOCLES I 2 230
OUR BODIES TO EARTH • • • • • • • • • • • 439 EMPEDOCLES II 333

BODILY
FOR THERE WITH BODILY ANGUISH KEEN • • • • • • 276 SOUTHERN NIGHT 25

BODING
OF SWAY HAVE FELT THIS BODING SENSE COME ON • • 239 REVOLUTIONS 14
THE ILL-BODING NOTE WHICH FRANTIC HATRED SOUNDS • • 397 MEROPE 1781
THE ILL-BODING NOTE WHICH FRANTIC ENVY SOUNDS • • 397 MEROPE V1781

BODY
ROCKING HER OBSCURE BODY TO AND FRO • • • • • • 45 IN UTRUMQUE PAR 25
THERE LAY HIS BODY IN MY GRAVE • • • • • • • • 95 SICK KING BOKH 228
AND LEFT HIS BODY STRETCHD UPON THE FLOOR • • • • 97 BALDER DEAD 1 63
FIND THY BODY BY THE WALL • • • • • • • • • 215 LAST WORD 16
AN ACHING BODY AND A MIND • • • • • • • • • 217 NAMELESS EPIT V
THE CONQUERORS WITH THE KINGS DEAD BODY COME • • 403 MEROPE 1953
NEITHER HIS MIND NOR BODY DID HE MAKE • • • • LUCRETIUS 3 5
NEITHER HIS MIND NOR BODY CAN HE CHANGE • • • • LUCRETIUS 3 6

BOIL
AH BOIL UP YE VAPOURS • • • • • • • • • • 441 EMPEDOCLES II 410

BOILING
OVER HIS BOILING CAULDRON BROODS • • • • • • 299 GRANDE CHARTR 12
OVER HIS BOILING CAULDRONS BROODS • • • • • • 299 GRANDE CHARTR V 12

BOILS
BOILS OER ITS BORDERS ALOFT • • • • • • • • 289 RUGBY CHAPEL 98

BOISTEROUS
GHOSTS OF THAT BOISTEROUS COMPANY • • • • • • 55 RESIGNATION 89
BY NIGHT WITH BOISTEROUS BUGLE-PEAL • • • • • 148 TRISTRAM 2 177
THEN HUSH THOU BOISTEROUS BUGLE-PEAL • • • • • 149 TRISTRAM 2 182

BOKHARA
LARGE MEN LARGE STEEDS WHO FROM BOKHARA COME • • 64 SOHRAB RUSTUM 119
DID IN BOKHARA BY THE RIVER FIND • • • • • • 69 SOHRAB RUSTUM 274
BOKHARA AND LONE KHIVA IN THE WASTE • • • • • 83 SOHRAB RUSTUM 761
THE TARTARS OF BOKHARA THE KINGS GUARD • • • • 64 SOHRAB RUSTUM V 117
HERE IN BOKHARA BUT AT NOON • • • • • • • 87 SICK KING BOKH 6

BOLD
LIKE THAT BOLD CAESAR THE FAMED ROMAN WIGHT • • 153 TRISTRAM 3 V 143
THE MAN OF THE BOLD WEST NOW COMES ARRAYD • • • 170 EAST AND WEST 13
BUT THOU TOO-BOLD HEADSTRONG PITILESS • • • • 196 FRAG ANTIGONE 50
ON THE HEIGHT OF THEIR BOLD-FOLLOWD WAY • • • • 216 LORDS MESSENGER V 17
GIRL STATESMAN MERCHANT SOLDIER BOLD • • • • • 226 EPILOG LAOCOON 159
THOSE DARK-TOPPD RED-BOLD PINETREES STAND • • KENSINGTON GARD V 4
WHOSE TOO BOLD DYING SONG • • • • • • • • 285 HAWORTH CHURCH 99
TORTURED THEE BRILLIANT AND BOLD • • • • • • 296 HEINES GRAVE 122
I AUGUR THOU WILT HEAR SOME BOLD RESOLVE • • • • 351 MEROPE 610
STERNLY CONDEMN THE TOO BOLD MAN WHO DARES • • • 353 MEROPE 690
AT ONE BOLD WORD ONE ENTERPRISING BLOW • • • • 402 MEROPE 1946
OR WITH PEN-BRYNS BOLD BARD PURSUES • • • • • 458 KAISER DEAD 5
THEN FANCYS ROVING VISIONS BOLD AND FREE • • • • 474 CROMWELL 93
BOLD ACTIONS PARENT AND A PIERCING KEN • • • • 478 CROMWELL 229

BOLDER
NO BOLDER ROBBER • • • • • • • • • • • 51 CONSOLATION 31
AND TWINE WITH BOLDER HAND THY LAST MEMORIAL WREATH 471 ALARIC AT ROME 228

BOLDEST
AMBITIONS BOLDEST DREAM MIGHT SOBER AND APPAL • • 463 ALARIC AT ROME 42
YET NOW WHEN BOLDEST WILLS GIVE PLACE • • • • 481 COURAGE 5

BOLDLY
BID IT RISE BOLDLY AT THE SIGNAL GIVEN • • • • 331 MEROPE 46
AND ARCAS BUT I TREMBLE BOLDLY ASK • • • • • 375 MEROPE 1211

BOLDNESS
WOULD YOU FREEZE MY TOO LOUD BOLDNESS • • • • 31 NEW SIRENS 159
WOULD YOU FREEZE MY LOUDER BOLDNESS • • • • • 31 NEW SIRENS V 159

BOLED
THOSE BLACK-CROWND RED-BOLED PINE-TREES STAND • • 248 KENSINGTON GARD 4
THOSE BLACK-TOPPD RED-BOLED PINE-TREES STAND • • 248 KENSINGTON GARD V 4

BOLT
A BOLT IS SHOT BACK SOMEWHERE IN OUR BREAST • • 247 BURIED LIFE 84
HIS BOLT-SCATHED FRONT TO THE STARS • • • • • 293 HEINES GRAVE 32
THRUST BACK NOW THE BOLT OF THAT DOOR • • • • 372 MEROPE 1147

BOND
WITH STRANGERS BUT THE BOND • • • • • • • • 196 FRAG ANTIGONE 35
WHOSE ONE BOND IS THAT ALL HAVE BEEN • • • • • 311 OBERMANN 155

BONDAGE

INTO SOME BONDAGE OF THE FLESH OR MIND	440	EMPEDOCLES II	374
AT THY WANT OF A MAN LIKE ME TO SAVE THEE FROM BONDAGE		HOMER TRANS	36

BONDS

YET HE SHALL ONE DAY RISE AND BURST HIS BONDS	111	BALDER DEAD 2	222
BUT I HAVE NOT GROWN EASY IN THESE BONDS	440	EMPEDOCLES II	397
BUT I HAVE NOT DENIED WHAT BONDS THESE WERE	440	EMPEDOCLES II	398
WHO WOULD NOT BURST HIS BONDS AND IN HIS TURN BE FREE	465	ALARIC AT ROME	90

BONE

AND YON WHITENING BONE-MOUNDS DO NOT GROW	27	NEW SIRENS		56
AND THOSE WHITENING BONE-MOUNDS DO NOT GROW	27	NEW SIRENS	V	56
STOUT WAS ITS ARM EACH THEW AND BONE	315	OBERMANN MORE		89
STOUT WAS ITS ARM EACH PULSE AND BONE	315	OBERMANN MORE	V	89

BONES

BE CRUMBLING BONES AND WINDY DUST	48	HORATIAN ECHO	32
OR ELSE THY BONES SHALL STREW THIS SAND TILL WINDS	72	SOHRAB RUSTUM	376
UPON THE SUMMER-FLOODS AND NOT MY BONES	74	SOHRAB RUSTUM	428
AND HEAP A STATELY MOUND ABOVE MY BONES	84	SOHRAB RUSTUM	788
AND HEAP A STATELY MOUND ABOVE THY BONES	84	SOHRAB RUSTUM	803
DRIVE CRASHING THROUGH THEIR BONES THEY FEEL	192	STRAYED REVEL	229
AND DOWN HE LAYS HIS WEARY BONES	213	PROGRESS POESY	12
RIVE ITS DRY BONES AND WITH NEW FORCE	319	OBERMANN MORE	199
THE BONES OF ARCAS WHENCE OUR RACE IS NAMED	356	MEROPE	742
FOLD LIKE A SHROUD AROUND THY WITHERED BONES	464	ALARIC AT ROME	64
YEA ON YOUR FATHERS BONES THE AVENGERS TREAD	467	ALARIC AT ROME	134
THE TOO-DARING TITANS BONES		PILLARS UNIVERS	12

BONNET

HIS SAILORS BONNET	189	STRAYED REVEL	105

BOOK

WENT FORTH AGAIN THE HOLY BOOK	89	SICK KING BOKH		47
FOR HER EYES WERE SEALD TO THE HOLY BOOK	163	FORSAKEN MERM		81
AND NEAR ME ON THE GRASS LIES GLANVILS BOOK	256	SCHOLAR-GIPSY		31
IN A BOOK WHICH OF WORLD-FAMOUS SOULS	280	HAWORTH CHURCH		19
IN A BOOK WHICH OF GLORIOUS SOULS	280	HAWORTH CHURCH	V	19
A BOOK WAS IN HIS BREAST	314	OBERMANN MORE		66
I DROPPD THE BOOK AND OF MY CHILD I THOUGHT	485	S S LUSITANIA		9

BOOKS

BUT SO MANY BOOKS THOU READEST	49	SECOND BEST	5
SHE TORE HER BOOKS SHE SHUT HER COURTS	316	OBERMANN MORE	131

BOON

THE PRAISE OF GODS RICH BOON AND LENGTH OF DAYS	11	MYCERINUS		78
AND WHEN THIS BOON REWARDS THE DEAD	21	YOUTH AND CALM		7
HOW SWEET TO FEEL ON THE BOON AIR	180	FAREWELL		81
TO A BOON SOUTHERN COUNTRY HE IS FLED	268	THYRSIS		175
SUCH A BOON TO BRING HATH BEEN GIVEN	361	MEROPE		907
OF THIS FAR-SCHEMING TYRANT AND HIS BOON	366	MEROPE		998
THE BOON THY DEDICATION-SIGN FORETOLD	444	WESTMIN ABBEY		5
HIS BOON OF LIFE AND IMMORTALITY	446	WESTMIN ABBEY		63
AND SCARCE THE BOON OF LIFE COULD STRUGGLE THROUGH	446	WESTMIN ABBEY		69
FOR WANT OF LIGHT WHICH SHOULD THE BOON CONVEY	446	WESTMIN ABBEY		70
DEATH DEATH WAS JUDGED THE BOON SUPREME INDEED	448	WESTMIN ABBEY		140
THE BOON TO THY FOUNDATION-HOUR FORETOLD	444	WESTMIN ABBEY	V	5
FOR LACK OF LIGHT WHICH SHOULD THE BOON CONVEY	446	WESTMIN ABBEY	V	70

BOORS

LOOK AS IN SOME BOORS YARD A SWEET-BREATHD COW	123	BALDER DEAD 3	340
ON THE WARM INGLE-BENCH THE SMOCK-FROCKD BOORS	256	SCHOLAR-GIPSY	59
THE BOORS WITH WHOM HE TALKD THE COUNTRY-SPOTS HE KNEW	426	EMPEDOCLES I 2	416

BOOTHS

WHERE THROUGH THE SELLERS BOOTHS THE SLAVES	88	SICK KING BOKH	18
WHO LOITERS BY THE HIGH-HEAPD BOOTHS	93	SICK KING BOKH	191

BOOTS

AH WHAT BOOTS IT THAT THE JEST	138	TRISTRAM 1	261
WHAT BOOTS IT SHELLEY THAT THE BREEZE	303	GRANDE CHARTR	139

BOR

THOU AND THY BRETHREN FIERCE THE SONS OF BOR	121	BALDER DEAD 3	258

BORDER

SPARES BUT THE CLOUDY BORDER OF HIS BASE	3	SHAKESPEARE		7
SPARES OFTEN BUT THE BORDER OF HIS BASE	3	SHAKESPEARE	V	7
SPARES BUT THE BORDER OFTEN OF HIS BASE	3	SHAKESPEARE	V	7
ERE HE COME ERE THE BOAT BY THE SHINING-BRANCHD BORDER	19	MODERN SAPPHO		5
ITS WOODY BORDER AND THE LAST	54	RESIGNATION		54
WHICH BORDER ENNERDALE LAKE	228	YOUTH OF NATURE		16
THAT BORDER ENNERDALE LAKE	228	YOUTH OF NATURE	V	16
TREAD THE BORDER-LAND DIM	288	RUGBY CHAPEL		54
TAYGETUS LACONIAS BORDER-WALL	330	MEROPE		17

BORDERD
```
      BORDERD EACH BANK WITH PINES THE MORNING SUN      • •    24 DREAM                3
      BY MOSS-BORDERD STATUES SITTING      • • • • • •    34 NEW SIRENS          239
      BORDERD BY CITIES AND HOARSE      • • • • • • • •   253 FUTURE              53
      BORDERD BY STATUES AND WALKS      • • • • • • • •   296 HEINES GRAVE        133
```

BORDERING
```
      AND TWAS WHEN NIGHT IS BORDERING HARD ON DAWN      • •   103 BALDER DEAD 1        280
      BORDERING THE GIANTS WHERE THE TREES ARE IRON      • •   123 BALDER DEAD 3        331
```

BORDERS
```
      AND CLIP HIS BORDERS SHORT AND DRIVE HIS HERDS      • •    68 SOHRAB RUSTUM        234
      AND CLIP HIS BORDERS ROUND AND DRIVE HIS HERDS      • •    68 SOHRAB RUSTUM      V 234
      WHICH BORDERS THE SEA-SHORE A COUNTRY PATH      • • • •   149 TRISTRAM 3            8
      BOILS OER ITS BORDERS ALOFT      • • • • • • • •   289 RUGBY CHAPEL         98
```

BORE
```
      LOUD THUNDERING BORE US BY SWIFT SWIFT IT FOAMD      • •    25 DREAM               33
      THAN THE CHARMS ULYSSES BORE      • • • • • • •    27 NEW SIRENS           44
      I CAME AMONG THE TARTARS AND BORE ARMS      • • • •    62 SOHRAB RUSTUM        43
      THAT SHE MIGHT PRICK IT ON THE BABE SHE BORE      • •    80 SOHRAB RUSTUM       660
      WHEN FIRST THEY BORE THY MASTER TO THIS FIELD      • •    83 SOHRAB RUSTUM      V 740
      ON HIS BROAD BACK NO LESSER RIDER BORE      • • • •   107 BALDER DEAD 2        74
      FROM IRELAND TO CORNWALL BORE      • • • • • •   132 TRISTRAM 1           60
      TO TYNTAGIL FROM IRELAND BORE      • • • • • •   132 TRISTRAM 1         V 60
      THERE IN A SHIP THEY BORE THOSE LOVERS COLD      • •   149 TRISTRAM 3            4
      BORE UP FROM WHERE THE BRIGHT ATLANTIC GLEAMS      •   151 TRISTRAM 3           53
      AND BORE HER DOWN TO THE SEA-HALLS      • • • • •   160 NECKAN               31
      THE DYING RACHEL IN A CHAIR THEY BORE      • • • •   167 RACHEL 2             3
      WELL SPAKE THE IMPETUOUS SAINT AND BORE OF MEN      •   171 DIVINITY             6
      I TOO HAVE FELT THE LOAD I BORE      • • • • • •   178 FAREWELL             29
      WHICH THE DAWN-GODDESS BORE      • • • • • • •   196 FRAG ANTIGONE        55
      WHO BORE SAINT LOUIS COMPANY      • • • • • • •   278 SOUTHERN NIGHT       94
      WHAT HELPS IT NOW THAT BYRON BORE      • • • • •   303 GRANDE CHARTR       133
      FOR THOUGH HIS MANHOOD BORE THE BLAST      • • • •   308 OBERMANN            65
      IN THE PRIMEVAL MOUNTAIN-FORESTS BORE      • • • •   389 MEROPE            1537
      OF THIS POOR SOUL WHO BORE HIM AND HIS SIRE      • •   349 MEROPE            V 578
      AND BORE A MORTAL LOT      • • • • • • • •   447 WESTMIN ABBEY       112
      AND TO THE GRAVE HE BORE A CHERISHD WIFE      • • •   447 WESTMIN ABBEY     V 124
      AND SO HE BORE THE IMPERIAL NAME      • • • • •   459 KAISER DEAD          23
      WHEN THOU TOO HAST BORNE THE LOVE WE BORE      • • •   482 THEKLAS ANSWER       14
```

BORED
```
      MADE FAST TO THE BORED CRAG BY WILE NOT STRENGTH      • •   111 BALDER DEAD 2        215
```

BORN
```
      VALLEYS AND MEN TO MIDDLE FORTUNE BORN      • • • •     6 GEO CRUIKSHANK        4
      SOME ANGELS IN AN ALIEN PLANET BORN      • • • • •    42 GIPSY CHILD          26
      WHAT SERAPHS IN SOME ALIEN PLANET BORN      • • • •    42 GIPSY CHILD        V 26
      HOPES BORN HERE AND BORN TO END      • • • • • •    44 QUESTION             20
      HOPES BORN HERE AND BORN TO END      • • • • • •    44 QUESTION             20
      WHICH WAS IN ADER-BAIJAN BORN TO HIM      • • • • •    79 SOHRAB RUSTUM       608
      FOR SOME ARE BORN TO DO GREAT DEEDS AND LIVE      • •    84 SOHRAB RUSTUM       773
      AS SOME ARE BORN TO BE OBSCURED AND DIE      • • •    84 SOHRAB RUSTUM       774
      FOR HEAVEN WAS BALDER BORN THE CITY OF GODS      • •   110 BALDER DEAD 2       198
      AND TELL THE HEAVEN-BORN GODS HOW THOU HAST SEEN      •   112 BALDER DEAD 2       276
      IN THE BEGINNING ERE THE GODS WERE BORN      • • •   121 BALDER DEAD 3       255
      THEN ME THOU MADST OF US THE GODS WERE BORN      • •   121 BALDER DEAD 3       267
      FOR I TOO AM A GODDESS BORN OF THEE      • • • •   121 BALDER DEAD 3       284
      NOT BORN IN HEAVEN HE WAS IN VANHEIM REARD      • •   122 BALDER DEAD 3       324
      AT A MEAN INN IN GERMAN AARAU BORN      • • • • •   168 RACHEL 3             2
      SHE THOUGH A GODDESS BORN      • • • • • • •   197 FRÄG ANTIGONE        68
      SEE PULSING WITH THE FIRST-BORN STAR      • • • •   218 BACCHANALIA 1        17
      THOU MUST BE BORN AGAIN      • • • • • • • •   238 PROGRESS             44
      O AIR-BORN VOICE LONG SINCE SEVERELY CLEAR      • •   240 SELF-DEPENDENCE      29
      THE WORLD WHICH WAS ERE I WAS BORN      • • • • •   250 WISH                 35
      HE WAS BORN IN A SHIP      • • • • • • • •   251 FUTURE                2
      OF THE NEW-BORN CLEAR-FLOWING STREAM      • • • •   252 FUTURE               12
      O BORN IN DAYS WHEN WITS WERE FRESH AND CLEAR      •   261 SCHOLAR-GIPSY       201
      THE OTHER POWERLESS TO BE BORN      • • • • • •   302 GRANDE CHARTR        86
      A CONQUERING NEW-BORN JOY AWOKE      • • • • • •   316 OBERMANN MORE       115
      THE NEW IS NOT YET BORN      • • • • • • • •   321 OBERMANN MORE       246
      THE FUTURE NOT YET BORN      • • • • • • • •   321 OBERMANN MORE     V 246
      OF THAT STOCK BORN WHO BESTOWD      • • • • • •   343 MEROPE              426
      OR HOW REPLY TO THEE MY CHILD LAST-BORN      • • •   367 MEROPE             1041
      FROM THE FIRST-WROUGHT VENGEANCE IS BORN      • • •   379 MEROPE             1251
      EACH SOVEREIGN FOR HIS DEAR-BOUGHT HOUR BORN      • •   388 MEROPE             1513
      THE YOUTHFUL ARCAS BORN OF ZEUS      • • • • • •   393 MEROPE             1657
      DEEP IN MANS HEART IS BORN      • • • • • • •   418 EMPEDOCLES I 2       169
      BORN INTO LIFE WE ARE AND LIFE MUST BE OUR MOULD      •   418 EMPEDOCLES I 2       186
      BORN INTO LIFE MAN GROWS      • • • • • • • •   418 EMPEDOCLES I 2       187
      BORN INTO LIFE WE BRING      • • • • • • • •   418 EMPEDOCLES I 2       192
      BORN INTO LIFE IN VAIN      • • • • • • • •   419 EMPEDOCLES I 2       197
      BORN INTO LIFE WHO LISTS      • • • • • • • •   419 EMPEDOCLES I 2       202
      BORN INTO LIFE TIS WE      • • • • • • • •   419 EMPEDOCLES I 2       207
      WHERE MAEANDERS SPRINGS ARE BORN      • • • • •   433 EMPEDOCLES II       136
      YE SUN-BORN VIRGINS ON THE ROAD OF TRUTH      • • •   436 EMPEDOCLES II       239
      THEY WERE WELL BORN THEY WILL BE WELL ENTOMBD      •   439 EMPEDOCLES II       337
      AND EACH SUCCEEDING AGE IN WHICH WE ARE BORN      • •   440 EMPEDOCLES II       377
      HITHER HE CAME LATE-BORN AND LONG-DESIRED      • • •   444 WESTMIN ABBEY         8
      BIRDS WERE BORN THE FIRST OF THINGS      • • • • •   456 POOR MATTHIAS       132
```

BORN   (CONTINUED)
        NO PASSING PAGEANT BORN BUT TO EXPIRE   .   .   .   .   463 ALARIC AT ROME   34
        BORN REASONS HEIRS AND OF THAT HERITAGE   .   .   .   .   RUDE ORATOR   3
        FEEBLE HE RESTS IF FEEBLE HE WAS BORN   .   .   .   .   LUCRETIUS 3   7
        ISTER TETHYS AND OCEANS SIXTH-BORN SON   .   .   .   .   FRAGMENT 4   2

BORNE
        THOUGH HE HATH BORNE IMMORTAL PAINS   . . . . .   56 RESIGNATION   151
        AND I NOT THOU BE BORNE TO SEISTAN   . . . . .   85 SOHRAB RUSTUM   820
        THIS PAIN ALONE WHICH MUST BE BORNE   . . . . .   92 SICK KING BOKH   151
        WOULD THAT OURSELVES O BALDER WE WERE BORNE   . . 101 BALDER DEAD 1   216
        ROUND BALDERS CORPSE WHICH THEY HAD THITHER BORNE   113 BALDER DEAD 3   2
        THE WORLD SHALL BE THRUST DOWN AND WE UP-BORNE   . . 172 IMMORTALITY   4
        HAD BORNE ME FAR FROM THEE   . . . .   183 ABSENCE   4
        THE BLEATING OF THE FOLDED FLOCKS IS BORNE . . . 255 SCHOLAR-GIPSY   18
        WHOSE INSIGHT NEVER HAS BORNE FRUIT IN DEEDS . . 260 SCHOLAR-GIPSY   174
        WELLNIGH NOT TO BE BORNE . . . .   295 HEINES GRAVE   95
        FAINT BUGLE-NOTES FROM FAR ARE BORNE . . . . .   305 GRANDE CHARTR   182
        ON THE BLACK WAVE BORNE TO AND FRO   . . . . .   370 MEROPE   1119
        THE WIND-BORNE MIRRORING SOUL   . . . . . .   415 EMPEDOCLES I 2   83
        AND BORNE TO LIGHT AND RIGHT HIS WITNESS HIGH   . 448 WESTMIN ABBEY   144
        PAIN HEROICALLY BORNE   . . . .   454 POOR MATTHIAS   64
        OR WONDROUS SOUNDS FROM TRANQUIL SKIES WERE BORNE   472 CROMWELL   35
        WHEN THOU TOO HAST BORNE THE LOVE WE BORE . . . 482 THEKLAS ANSWER   14

BOSOM
        SHOOK HER WEAK BOSOM DAY AND NIGHT   . . . . .   147 TRISTRAM 2   133
        NOW READS IN HER BOSOM AS CLEAR   . . . . . .   252 FUTURE   35
        WHO IN MANS INMOST BOSOM SIT AND JUDGE   . . . .   349 MEROPE   554
        IF IN THIS FEEBLE BOSOM SUCH A FIRE   . . . . .   387 MEROPE   1470
        IN HIS OWN BOSOM DELVES   . . . .   416 EMPEDOCLES I 2   130
        AND HE SHOOK HIS HEAD AND THUS ADDRESSD HIS OWN BOSOM   HOMER TRANS   8

BOSOMS
        THEY SAW US THEY CONFERRD THEIR BOSOMS HEAVED   . .   25 DREAM   26
        OER THEIR POLISHD BOSOMS BLOWING   . . . . . .   433 EMPEDOCLES II   154

BOTTOM
        AND IN THE BOTTOM OF THE GLADE SHINE CLEAR . . .   139 TRISTRAM 1   278
        YET IN THE SEDGY BOTTOM THERE   . . . . . .   148 TRISTRAM 2   V
        YET LOW AND FROM THE BOTTOM YET TO ONE STANDING IN IT   TRISTRAM 3   V 11

BOUGH
        BUT IN HIS BREAST STOOD FIXT THE FATAL BOUGH   . .   95 BALDER DEAD 1   5
        AND UPON EVERY GIANT-BOUGH   . . . .   141 TRISTRAM 1   358
        TO GAZE ON THE LIGHT SEA OF LEAF AND BOUGH . . .   155 TRISTRAM 3   202
        TO GAZE ON THE GREEN SEA OF LEAF AND BOUGH . . .   155 TRISTRAM 3   V 202
        MY LAUREL BOUGH   . . . .   434 EMPEDOCLES II   192
        MY LAUREL BOUGH   . . . .   435 EMPEDOCLES II   197
        TAKE THY BOUGH SET ME FREE FROM MY SOLITUDE   . .   435 EMPEDOCLES II   218

BOUGHD
        OF MANY A DARK-BOUGHD PINE   . . . . 307 OBERMANN   30

BOUGHS
        HEARD THE HOARSE BOUGHS LABOUR IN THE WIND . . .   26 NEW SIRENS   8
        WHEN THE PINE-BOUGHS YIELDED ROUND YOU   . . . .   29 NEW SIRENS   99
        SAW THE HOARSE BOUGHS LABOUR IN THE WIND . . . .   26 NEW SIRENS   V 8
        AND STREWN THE CHANNELS WITH TORN BOUGHS SO HUGE . 73 SOHRAB RUSTUM   415
        AND STREWN THE CHANNELS WITH TORN BOUGHS SO ROUGH   73 SOHRAB RUSTUM   V 415
        AND LOPPD THEIR BOUGHS AND CLOVE THEM ON THE SWARD 106 BALDER DEAD 2   59
        FOLLOWD AND ON THEIR SHOULDERS CARRIED BOUGHS   . . 106 BALDER DEAD 2   64
        AND FROM THE BOUGHS THE SNOWLOADS SHUFFLE DOWN . . 122 BALDER DEAD 3   313
        THROUGH WHOSE GREEN BOUGHS THE GOLDEN SUNSHINE CREEPS 154 TRISTRAM 3   157
        THE OTHER WARDED OFF THE DROOPING BOUGHS . . . . 154 TRISTRAM 3   176
        AND THESE FRAIL ACACIA BOUGHS   . . . . 200 PHILOMELA   V
        AND THESE BLANCHD SONG-STIRRD BOUGHS . . . . .   200 PHILOMELA   V
        SCREEND BY DEEP BOUGHS ON EITHER HAND   . . . .   248 KENSINGTON GARD   2
        HOW GREEN UNDER THE BOUGHS IT IS   . . . . .   248 KENSINGTON GARD   7
        HOW GREEN AMONG THE BOUGHS IT IS   . . . . . .   KENSINGTON GARD   V 7
        RESTED AS UNDER THE BOUGHS   . . . .   287 RUGBY CHAPEL   32
        OF NOON IS BROKEN THERE BY CHESTNUT-BOUGHS . . .   414 EMPEDOCLES I 2   44

BOUGHT
        WITH CURIOUS FRUIT TREES BOUGHT FROM FAR . . . .   94 SICK KING BOKH   V 201
        TIS NOT IN THE WORLDS MARKET BOUGHT AND SOLD   . . 268 THYRSIS   205
        EACH SOVEREIGN FOR HIS DEAR-BOUGHT HOUR BORN   . . 388 MEROPE   1513

BOULDERS
        MOSS-HUNG BOULDERS AND THIN   . . . . 297 HEINES GRAVE   160

BOUND
        PAINT THAT LILAC KERCHIEF BOUND   . . . . . .   23 MEMORY-PICTURE   25
        FOR A BOUND WAS SET TO MEETINGS   . . . . . .   30 NEW SIRENS   115
        FROM THEIR EARTHWARD-BOUND DEVOTION   . . . . .   31 NEW SIRENS   157
        MIRTH TO-DAY AND VINE-BOUND TRESSES   . . . . .   33 NEW SIRENS   197
        BUT A BOUND WAS SET TO MEETINGS   . . . . . .   30 NEW SIRENS   V 115
        SO PILGRIMS BOUND FOR MECCA PRAYD   . . . . . .   52 RESIGNATION   3
        THE GOTH BOUND ROME-WARDS SO THE HUN . . . . .   52 RESIGNATION   9
        LOW WOODY HILL WITH GRACIOUS BOUND . . . . . .   57 RESIGNATION   174

BOUND   (CONTINUED)
     HEMS US ALL IN HE IS NOT BOUND . . . .   58 RESIGNATION   210
     OR SOME FRORE CASPIAN REED-BED SOUTHWARD BOUND   . . 64 SOHRAB RUSTUM   115
     AND BOUND THE LOGS BEHIND THEIR STEEDS TO DRAW   . . 106 BALDER DEAD 2   60
     BOUND ON THEIR WAY BELOW TO HELAS REALM   . . .   107 BALDER DEAD 2   105
     SOULS BOUND BELOW MY DAILY PASSERS HERE   . . .   108 BALDER DEAD 2   110
     HELAS PALE SWARMS AND THERE WAS BALDER BOUND   108 BALDER DEAD 2   133
     SUBDUED WITH LIMBER CHAINS LIVES FENRIS BOUND   111 BALDER DEAD 2   216
     BUT AS HE ENTERD ON THE EXTREMEST BOUND   . . .   124 BALDER DEAD 3   381
     THOUGH THEY TO DEATH WERE BOUND AND HE TO HEAVEN . . 129 BALDER DEAD 3   557
     BOUND I WAS I COULD NOT BREAK THE BAND   . . . .   142 TRISTRAM 2   6
     I WAS BOUND I COULD NOT BREAK THE BAND   . . . .   142 TRISTRAM 2   V   6
     OF MAD DELIGHT THEY DROP THEIR SPOILS AND BOUND   . . 150 TRISTRAM 3   27
     YE ARE BOUND FOR THE MOUNTAINS . . . .   175 PARTING   9
     THE FRAUDULENT OATH WHICH BOUND   . . . . . .   198 FRAG ANTIGONE   95
     IN LAWS BY HUMAN ARTISTS BOUND . . . .   223 EPILOG LAOCOON   76
     AND TO WHAT GOAL WHAT ENDING BOUND   . . . . .   225 EPILOG LAOCOON   126
     OF THE POOR SINNER BOUND FOR DEATH   . . . . .   250 WISH   22
     THOU TOO O THYRSIS ON LIKE QUEST WAST BOUND   269 THYRSIS   211
     THOU TOO O THYRSIS ON LIKE QUEST WERT BOUND   269 THYRSIS   V   211
     HE FOUND US WHEN THE AGE HAD BOUND   . . . . .   271 MEMORIAL VERSES   45
     YET BOUND IT FROM HIS FOREST GRAVE   . . . . .   STANZAS CARNAC V   8
     THE CHAPEL-WALLS IN WHOSE BOUND   . . . . . .   286 RUGBY CHAPEL   12
     ON TO THE BOUND OF THE WASTE . . . .   292 RUGBY CHAPEL   207
     BEYOND THIS GRACIOUS BOUND . . . .   313 OBERMANN MORE   30
     WHEREWITH FATIGUE AND YOUTH HAD BOUND MINE EYES . . 375 MEROPE   1204
     WHOSE SPELL-BOUND SENSE FROM CHILDHOODS HOUR   471 CROMWELL   3
        HATH KNOWN
     BOUND ALL HIS BEING WITH A SILVER CHAIN   . . . .   473 CROMWELL   63
     THAT BOUND HIS SPIRIT AND HIS HEART AWOKE   . . .   475 CROMWELL   132

BOUNDARY
     THE VALLEYS WESTERN BOUNDARY . . . .   53 RESIGNATION   47

BOUNDED
     POOR BOUNDED WORDS AND MAKES THEM NEW   . . . .   224 EPILOG LAOCOON   96
     BOUNDED BY THEMSELVES AND UNREGARDFUL   . . . .   240 SELF-DEPENDENCE   25
     BOUNDED BY THEMSELVES AND UNOBSERVANT   . . . .   240 SELF-DEPENDENCE V 25
     BOUNDED IN OUR OWN BREAST WE HARDLY KNOW   . . .   352 MEROPE   639
     WE BOUNDED DOWN THE SWARDED SLOPE WE PLUNGED   . . 357 MEROPE   790
     OH THAT MY HEART BOUNDED WITH THE SWELL OF THE SEA 438 EMPEDOCLES II   324

BOUNDING
     AND ALL ITS BOUNDING RAPTURE AS AT DAWN   . . .   79 SOHRAB RUSTUM   620
     LIKE STARS OVER THE BOUNDING HILL   . . . . .   220 BACCHANALIA 2   27
     THE HEART LESS BOUNDING AT EMOTION NEW   . . .   266 THYRSIS   139

BOUNDLESS
     ANOTHER HEAVEN THE BOUNDLESS NO ONE YET   . . .   128 BALDER DEAD 3   519
     LONG FED ON BOUNDLESS HOPES O RACE OF MAN   . . .   170 BETTER PART   1
     UPON THE BOUNDLESS OCEAN-PLAIN . . . .   185 TERRACE BERNE   46
     THE BOUNDLESS WAVING GRASS-PLAINS STRETCH THICK-STARRD 191 STRAYED REVEL 168
     HOW BOUNDLESS MIGHT HIS SOULS HORIZONS BE   . . .   244 SUMMER NIGHT   88
     THAT DAY OF BOUNDLESS HOPE AND PROMISE HIGH   . .   478 CROMWELL   211

BOUNDS
     AND THEN THEIR ENDLESS BOUNDS THEY KNOW   . . .   182 TO MARG CONT   6
     WITH SAUNTER WITH BOUNDS . . . .   218 BACCHANALIA 1   21
     IS MY SON SAFE THAT QUESTION BOUNDS MY CARE   . .   401 MEROPE   1889
     THE BOUNDS OF EFFACED STATES . . . .   423 EMPEDOCLES I 2   324

BOURNE
     WHEN HE GUIDES MUSPELS CHILDREN TO THEIR BOURNE . . 111 BALDER DEAD 2   224

BOW
     ALL WEAKNESS WHICH IMPAIRS ALL GRIEFS WHICH BOW . .   3 SHAKESPEARE   13
     ALL WEAKNESS THAT IMPAIRS ALL GRIEFS THAT BOW   . .   3 SHAKESPEARE V   13
     TO EITHER BOW . . . .   191 STRAYED REVEL   187
     PLY HIS BOW SUCH A PRICE . . . .   193 STRAYED REVEL   232
     UPHUNG THE SPEAR UNBENT THE BOW   . . . . . .   219 BACCHANALIA 2   11
     YET EVEN I AND NONE WILL BOW . . . .   222 EPILOG LAOCOON   30
     NO VICTIMS BLEED NO DRUIDS BOW . . . .   274 STANZAS CARNAC   15
     THE INHERITOR OF THE BOW . . . .   399 MEROPE   1837
     THEIR WAY THROUGH LIFE AND BOW . . . .   425 EMPEDOCLES I 2   389
     THERE HAMPDEN BENT HIM OER HIS SADDLE BOW   . . .   476 CROMWELL   169
     TRUE WE MUST BOW TO NATURES LAW   . . . . . .   481 COURAGE   2

BOWD
     WORLD HAVE THY CHILDREN YET BOWD AT HIS KNEE   . .   20 MODERN SAPPHO   34
     AGE-BOWD ASKS ALMS . . . .   51 CONSOLATION   30
     AND RUSTUM BOWD HIS HEAD BUT THEN THE GLOOM   . .   76 SOHRAB RUSTUM   499
     AND STRUCK AGAIN AND AGAIN RUSTUM BOWD   . . .   76 SOHRAB RUSTUM   510
     AND BOWD HER HEAD AND SATE WITH FOLDED HANDS   . . 100 BALDER DEAD 1   193
     AND BOWD HER HEAD AND SATE WITH FOLDED HANDS   . . 122 BALDER DEAD 3   296
     IS BOWD HALF-BURIED ON THE BED . . . .   146 TRISTRAM 2   106
     HE BOWD HIS HEAD HE BREATHED A PRAYER   . . . .   158 SAINT BRANDAN   74
     THE PENITENT WITH ANGUISH BOWD . . . .   225 EPILOG LAOCOON   155
     WE BOWD OUR HEAD AND HELD OUR BREATH   . . . .   270 MEMORIAL VERSES   7
     WE BOWD OUR HEADS AND HELD OUR BREATH   . . . .   270 MEMORIAL VERSES V 7
     WITH VEILD FACE AND BOWD HEAD . . . .   283 HAWORTH CHURCH V
     THE EAST BOWD LOW BEFORE THE BLAST   . . . . .   316 OBERMANN MORE   109

BOWD   (CONTINUED)
        HE BOWD HIS HEAD AND DEEPLY GROAND AND DIED   • •   402 MEROPE   1929
        MANTLED HER FORM NO MORE HER HEAD WAS BOWD • • • •   447 WESTMIN ABBEY   98
        SUDDEN HE BOWD HIS HEAD AND ALL HIS MANE AS HE BOWD IT   HOMER TRANS   44
        SUDDEN HE BOWD HIS HEAD AND ALL HIS MANE AS HE BOWD IT   HOMER TRANS   44

BOWED
        TWICE HAD THE ETERNAL CITY BOWED HER LOW   • • • •   465 ALARIC AT ROME   75
        THE WORLD HATH BOWED TO ROME OH COLD WERE HE   • •   465 ALARIC AT ROME   89
        HIS DROOPING HEAD BOWED MEEKLY ON HIS BREAST   • •   476 CROMWELL   167

BOWER
        AND HER BOWER IN IRELAND • • • • • • • • •   134 TRISTRAM 1   131
        AND BOWER ME FROM THE AUGUST SUN WITH SHADE   • •   256 SCHOLAR-GIPSY   29
        SOME GIRL WHO HERE FROM CASTLE-BOWER • • • • •   278 SOUTHERN NIGHT   101
        SOME GIRL WHO HERE FROM PALACE-BOWER • • • • •   278 SOUTHERN NIGHT   V 101

BOWERING
        STILL FLY PLUNGE DEEPER IN THE BOWERING WOOD   • •   261 SCHOLAR-GIPSY   207

BOWERS
        SITTING CHEERLESS IN YOUR BOWERS • • • • • • •   30 NEW SIRENS   127
        PLUCKD IN SHY FIELDS AND DISTANT WYCHWOOD BOWERS • •   257 SCHOLAR-GIPSY   79
        PLUCKD IN SHY FIELDS AND DISTANT WOODLAND BOWERS • •   257 SCHOLAR-GIPSY   V 79
        TERRACED AND ORANGE-BOWERS   • • • • • • •   296 HEINES GRAVE   134

BOWING
        WITH HIS HEAD BOWING TO THE GROUND AND MANE   • •   82 SOHRAB RUSTUM   731

BOWL
        WOULD THRUST A HAND BEFORE THE LIFTED BOWL • • • •   11 MYCERINUS   105
        AND DRAIND HIS MIGHTY BOWL   • • • • • • • •   47 WORLD QUIETIST   32
        ON THE ALTAR THIS BOWL • • • • • • • • •   187 STRAYED REVEL   49
        DENY THEE NOT MY BOWL   • • • • • • • • •   187 STRAYED REVEL   60

BOWS
        MAKES THE HEAD WHITE AND BOWS THE KNEES   • • • •   92 SICK KING BOKH   152

BOY
        RASH BOY MEN LOOK ON RUSTUMS FACE AND FLEE • • •   72 SOHRAB RUSTUM   369
        BOY AS I AM I HAVE SEEN BATTLES TOO • • • • •   74 SOHRAB RUSTUM   433
        HAD BEEN A PUNY GIRL NO BOY AT ALL • • • • •   79 SOHRAB RUSTUM   609
        RUSTUM SHOULD SEEK THE BOY TO TRAIN IN ARMS   • •   79 SOHRAB RUSTUM   611
        O BOY THY FATHER AND HIS VOICE CHOKED THERE   • •   81 SOHRAB RUSTUM   691
        RUSTUM SHOULD TAKE THE BOY TO TRAIN IN ARMS   • •   79 SOHRAB RUSTUM   V 611
        FOOLISH BOY WHY TREMBLEST THOU • • • • • • •   187 STRAYED REVEL   53
        ROAMING THE COUNTRY-SIDE A TRUANT BOY   • • •   261 SCHOLAR-GIPSY   198
        POOR GALLANT BOY FOR SUCH THOU WAST • • • • •   276 SOUTHERN NIGHT   39
        POOR GALLANT BOY FOR SUCH THOU WERT • • • • •   276 SOUTHERN NIGHT   V 39
        O BOY IF HERE THOU SLEEPST SLEEP WELL   • • •   285 HAWORTH CHURCH   107
        STILL THE DORIAN BOY   • • • • • • • • •   347 MEROPE   532
        A RETURN O FATHER GIVE TO THY BOY   • • • • •   348 MEROPE   542
        BRINGING ME OF MY BOY THE ANNUAL NEWS   • • •   350 MEROPE   599
        WAS CHOSEN HIS COMPANION FROM A BOY • • • • •   355 MEROPE   724
        OLD MAN OLD MAN THOU HADST MY BOY IN CHARGE   • •   368 MEROPE   1069
        AND WHERE DOST THOU SLEEP NOW MY INNOCENT BOY   •   373 MEROPE   1166
        CALLISTO AND HER BOY   • • • • • • • • •   391 MEROPE   1605
        THEN A BOY HE STARTLED • • • • • • • • •   392 MEROPE   1622
        AND THOU A BOY WHOSE TONGUE OUTRUNS HIS KNOWLEDGE   411 EMPEDOCLES I 1   161
        HARK THERE AGAIN TIS THE BOY CALLICLES   • • •   412 EMPEDOCLES I 2   12
        AND SAID O BOY I TAUGHT THIS LORE   • • • • •   414 EMPEDOCLES I 2   69
        IMMORTAL HAD I MADE THIS BOY OF MINE • • • • •   447 WESTMIN ABBEY   105
        THE BOY HIS NURSE FORGOT • • • • • • • • •   447 WESTMIN ABBEY   111
        HE TOO WAS THERE IT WAS THE PRINCELY BOY   • • •   477 CROMWELL   179

BOYS
        AT MY BOYS YEARS THE COURAGE OF A MAN   • • •   62 SOHRAB RUSTUM   45
        FALSE WILY BOASTFUL ARE THESE TARTAR BOYS • • •   71 SOHRAB RUSTUM   348
        A FIRE OF WITHERD FURZE WHICH BOYS HAVE LIT   • •   124 BALDER DEAD 3   361
        AND AS A STORK WHICH IDLE BOYS HAVE TRAPPD • • •   129 BALDER DEAD 3   559
        AND BOYS WHO IN LONE WHEATFIELDS SCARE THE ROOKS • •   257 SCHOLAR-GIPSY   64
        FROM A FEW BOYS LATE AT THEIR PLAY • • • • •   286 RUGBY CHAPEL   7
        POSEIDON TO THE SHEPHERD-BOYS TO HIDE   • • •   355 MEROPE   737
        WITH DANCING MAIDENS AND BOYS   • • • • • •   360 MEROPE   898
        MESSENIA TO THOSE HELPLESS BOYS THE LOT   • • •   389 MEROPE   1552
        TIS AS AN ORPHAN AMONG PROSPEROUS BOYS   • • •   408 EMPEDOCLES I 1   71

BRACELET
        KAIS BRACELET TAIL KAIS BUSY FEET   • • • • •   459 KAISER DEAD   7
        I SEE THE TAIL LIKE BRACELET TWIRLD • • • • •   460 KAISER DEAD   55

BRACELETS
        AND THE GOLDEN BRACELETS HEAVY AND RARE   • • • •   146 TRISTRAM 2   110

BRAGE
        STILL LEFT AND THAT CHIEF SCALD THY BROTHER BRAGE   117 BALDER DEAD 3   133

BRAIN
        COME YOU SAY THE BRAIN IS SEEKING   • • • • • •   28 NEW SIRENS   77
        WITH A FIRE IN HIS BRAIN • • • • • • • • •   136 TRISTRAM 1   187

BRAIN   (CONTINUED)
        THEY CLOUD THE BRAIN THEY DULL THE BLOOD   •   •   •   •   138 TRISTRAM 1   248
        WITH SILENCE BALM MY WHIRLING BRAIN   •   •   •   •   •   158 SAINT BRANDAN   70
        OUR PASSIONS FROM OUR BRAIN   •   •   •   •   •   •   •   183 ABSENCE   8
        STILL NOURISHING IN THY BEWILDERD BRAIN   •   •   •   •   200 PHILOMELA   7
        TO THY RACKD HEART AND BRAIN   •   •   •   •   •   •   •   200 PHILOMELA   14
        TO THY TORN HEART AND BRAIN   •   •   •   •   •   •   •   200 PHILOMELA   V   14
        MY PENT-UP TEARS OPPRESS MY BRAIN   •   •   •   •   •   •   206 RIVER   9
        OF PREGNANT PARTS AND QUICK INVENTIVE BRAIN   •   •   256 SCHOLAR-GIPSY   34
        OF SHINING PARTS AND QUICK INVENTIVE BRAIN •   •   •   256 SCHOLAR-GIPSY   V   34
        OF PRAISE HOT HEADY FUMES TO THE POOR BRAIN   •   •   296 HEINES GRAVE   146
        THE WANT WHICH RACKD OUR BRAIN •   •   •   •   •   •   •   323 OBERMANN MORE   314
        THE DREAM WHICH FILLD OUR BRAIN   •   •   •   •   •   •   323 OBERMANN MORE   V   314
        THE WANT WHICH CRAZED OUR BRAIN   •   •   •   •   •   •   323 OBERMANN MORE   V   314
        THE WANT WHICH WORE OUR BRAIN   •   •   •   •   •   •   •   323 OBERMANN MORE   V   314
        AND IF THE SACRED LOAD OPPRESSD OUR BRAIN   •   •   •   •   436 EMPEDOCLES II   244

BRAINS
        THE WORKINGS OF MENS BRAINS   •   •   •   •   •   •   •   256 SCHOLAR-GIPSY   46

BRAKE
        BRAKE FORTH AND CURSED THEM DOST THOU HEAR •   •   •   •   90 SICK KING BOKH   87
        CHEER CHEER THY DOGS INTO THE BRAKE   •   •   •   •   •   149 TRISTRAM 2   186
        RARE STRAGGLING HUNTERS FOILD BY BRAKE AND CRAG   •   •   357 MEROPE   798

BRAKES
        IN THE LONE BRAKES OF FONTAINEBLEAU   •   •   •   •   •   304 GRANDE CHARTR   149
        AND BY THE SEA AND IN THE BRAKES   •   •   •   •   •   •   426 EMPEDOCLES I 2   431
        THERE THOSE TWO LIVE FAR IN THE ILLYRIAN BRAKES   •   •   427 EMPEDOCLES I 2   443

BRAMBLES
        THESE BRAMBLES PALE WITH MIST ENGARLANDED   •   •   •   •   267 THYRSIS   173

BRANCH
        THAT I ALONE MUST TAKE THE BRANCH FROM LOK •   •   •   •   98 BALDER DEAD 1   100

BRANCHD
        ERE HE COME ERE THE BOAT BY THE SHINING-BRANCHD BORDER   19 MODERN SAPPHO   5
        IT GREEND IT BRANCHD IT WAVED   •   •   •   •   •   •   •   160 NECKAN   54

BRANCHES
        THESE VEXT BRANCHES AND THIS HOWLING SKY   •   •   •   27 NEW SIRENS   48
        WHICH BRANCHES FROM THE NORTH OF HEAVEN AND RIDE   •   •   99 BALDER DEAD 1   144
        WHICH BRANCHES FROM THE NORTH OF HEAVEN AND WENT   •   •   107 BALDER DEAD 2   80
        BY NIGHT THE SILVERD BRANCHES OF THE GLADE •   •   •   •   261 SCHOLAR-GIPSY   214
        THROUGH THE PINE BRANCHES PLAY •   •   •   •   •   •   •   310 OBERMANN   126
        ITS PINES UNDER THEIR BRANCHES OPE •   •   •   •   •   •   312 OBERMANN MORE   15

BRANCHING
        HANGD UPON A BRANCHING FIR   •   •   •   •   •   •   •   433 EMPEDOCLES II   148

BRAND
        WE CALL IT MURDER CRUSH HIM BRAND HIS NAME •   •   •   •   336 MEROPE   203
        ZEUS AND PURE-THOUGHTED JUSTICE BRAND   •   •   •   •   •   353 MEROPE   688

BRANDAN
        SAINT BRANDAN SAILS THE NORTHERN MAIN   •   •   •   •   •   156 SAINT BRANDAN   1
        BUT NORTH STILL NORTH SAINT BRANDAN STEERD •   •   •   •   156 SAINT BRANDAN   9
        IT IS OH WHERE SHALL BRANDAN FLY   •   •   •   •   •   •   157 SAINT BRANDAN   19
        PALSIED WITH TERROR BRANDAN SATE   •   •   •   •   •   •   157 SAINT BRANDAN   21
        OH BRANDAN THINK WHAT GRACE DIVINE •   •   •   •   •   •   158 SAINT BRANDAN   53
        O BRANDAN TO THIS HOUR OF REST •   •   •   •   •   •   •   158 SAINT BRANDAN   71

BRANDANS
        TEARS STARTED TO SAINT BRANDANS EYES   •   •   •   •   •   158 SAINT BRANDAN   73

BRASS
        GRAVE IT ON BRASS WITH ADAMANTINE PEN   •   •   •   •   171 DIVINITY   2

BRAVE
        PROPHETS TRANSFIGURED SAINTS AND MARTYRS BRAVE   •   •   18 CHURCH BROU 3   20
        A SON SO FAMED SO BRAVE TO SEND TO WAR •   •   •   •   68 SOHRAB RUSTUM   231
        THERE ARE NO YOUTHS IN IRAN BRAVE AS THOU   •   •   •   •   71 SOHRAB RUSTUM   333
        MY MOTHER TOLD ME OF THEE THOU BRAVE STEED •   •   •   •   83 SOHRAB RUSTUM   743
        A SON SO PRAISD SO BRAVE TO SEND TO WAR   •   •   •   •   68 SOHRAB RUSTUM   V   231
        AT THE STRAITS FAILD THAT SPIRIT BRAVE •   •   •   •   275 STANZAS CARNAC   46
        PRAISE RE-INSPIRE THE BRAVE   •   •   •   •   •   •   •   292 RUGBY CHAPEL   200
        THE BRAVE IMPETUOUS HEART YIELDS EVERYWHERE   •   •   431 EMPEDOCLES II   90
        THE BRAVE IMPETUOUS HAND YIELDS EVERYWHERE •   •   •   431 EMPEDOCLES II   V   90
        NOR MY BRETHRENS MANY AND BRAVE WHO THEN WILL BE LYING   HOMER TRANS   25
        SO MANIFOLD SO FRESH SO BRAVE A WORLD   •   •   •   •   LUCRETIUS 1   2

BRAVELIER
        MAY BRAVELIER FRONT HIS LIFE AND IN HIMSELF   •   •   429 EMPEDOCLES II   9

BRAVELY
        BRAVELY SAID HE FOR I OF LATE HAVE BEEN   •   •   •   •   169 EAST LONDON   7

BRAVES
        BY THWARTING SIGNS AND BRAVES   •   •   •   •   •   •   •   244 SUMMER NIGHT   60

BRAVEST
WILL CHALLENGE FORTH THE BRAVEST PERSIAN LORDS • •   62 SOHRAB RUSTUM   56
WHEN SOHRAB DARES OUR BRAVEST FORTH AND SEEKS • •   68 SOHRAB RUSTUM 244
AND PICK THE BRAVEST WARRIORS OUT FOR DEATH • • 105 BALDER DEAD 2   26
OTHERS THE BRAVEST ARE CROSSD • • • • • • • 216 LORDS MESSENGER V 16

BRAWLING
IN A SLOPED SWARD DOWN TO A BRAWLING BROOK • • • • 155 TRISTRAM 3 187

BRAWLS
THE OTHERS LABOURING TO COMPOSE THEIR BRAWLS • • 116 BALDER DEAD 3   86

BRAZEN
FOR MOST MEN IN A BRAZEN PRISON LIVE • • • • • 243 SUMMER NIGHT   37
OUR SPIRITS IN A BRAZEN ROUND • • • • • • • 271 MEMORIAL VERSES V 46
THE BRAZEN-FOOTED FURY EVER STALKS • • • • • • 395 MEROPE 1734
AS THY GRIEF WHEN IN TEARS SOME BRAZEN-COATED ACHAIAN   HOMER TRANS   27

BREACH
ITS FRAME YET STOOD WITHOUT A BREACH • • • • • 319 OBERMANN MORE 193
THE BREACH BETWEEN OUR PARTIES HELP ME CLOSE • • 335 MEROPE 163
THAT MURDER MOVES THIS BREACH THAT THOU WOULDST CLOSE 335 MEROPE 187
THAT MURDER DRAWS THIS BREACH THAT THOU WOULDST CLOSE 335 MEROPE V 187

BREACHD
ROARING TORRENTS HAVE BREACHD • • • • • • • 289 RUGBY CHAPEL   94

BREAD
A SIDE OF ROASTED SHEEP AND CAKES OF BREAD • • •   67 SOHRAB RUSTUM 198
A SIDE OF ROASTED SHEEP AND LOAVES OF BREAD • •   67 SOHRAB RUSTUM V 198
OUR FREEDOM FOR A LITTLE BREAD WE SELL • • • • 169 WORLDLY PLACE   5
MUCH CHEERD WITH THOUGHTS OF CHRIST THE LIVING BREAD 169 EAST LONDON   8
MARES MILK AND BREAD • • • • • • • • • 191 STRAYED REVEL 166

BREADTH
FULL THE DECKS BREADTH AND LOFTY THEN THE CORPSE • • 118 BALDER DEAD 3 162
ONE WITH THE OERLABOURD POWER THAT THROUGH   422 EMPEDOCLES I 2 291
    THE BREADTH AND LENGTH

BREAK
WAS NEW MADE TO BREAK AGAIN • • • • • • • •   23 MEMORY-PICTURE   38
YET COULD NOT BREAK IT • • • • • • • •   36 VOICE   40
SITS RAPT AND HEARS THE BATTLE BREAK BELOW • • •   42 GIPSY CHILD   23
ON THIS GREAT SINNER WHO DID BREAK • • • • •   89 SICK KING BOKH   37
THEN BUT A POWER HE COULD NOT BREAK WITHHELD • • 129 BALDER DEAD 3 558
AH HIS EYELIDS SLOWLY BREAK • • • • • • • • 139 TRISTRAM 1 294
BOUND I WAS I COULD NOT BREAK THE BAND • • • 142 TRISTRAM 2   6
I WAS BOUND I COULD NOT BREAK THE BAND • • • 142 TRISTRAM 2 V   6
THOU THYSELF MUST BREAK AT LAST • • • • • • 215 LAST WORD   4
BREAK FROM THE WOOD • • • • • • • • • 218 BACCHANALIA 1   29
A BREAK BETWEEN THE HOUSETOPS SHOWS • • • • 242 SUMMER NIGHT   6
SOON WILL THE MUSK CARNATIONS BREAK AND SWELL • • 264 THYRSIS   63
BREAK YOUR UNITED REPOSE • • • • • • • • 285 HAWORTH CHURCH 124
THREATENS TO BREAK TO DISSOLVE • • • • • • 291 RUGBY CHAPEL 181
I SAW THE MORNING BREAK • • • • • • • • 324 OBERMANN MORE 348
BREAK OFF BREAK OFF YOUR TALKING AND DEPART • • 386 MEROPE 1440
BREAK OFF BREAK OFF YOUR TALKING AND DEPART • • 386 MEROPE 1440
AT DAY-BREAK THROUGH THE DEW • • • • • • 392 MEROPE 1645
TO WHAT THEY CANNOT BREAK • • • • • • • 425 EMPEDOCLES I 2 390
AND THE WORLD HATH THE DAY AND MUST BREAK THEE • • 429 EMPEDOCLES II   17
OF MESSOGIS WESTWARD BREAK • • • • • • 433 EMPEDOCLES II 138
AND BREAK HIS HEART WITH ALL THE BAFFLING CHANGE • • 448 WESTMIN ABBEY 149
I WOULD NOT BREAK THY REST NOR CHANGE THY DOOM • • 449 WESTMIN ABBEY 166

BREAKING
FOR COLD IS HIS EYE TO MERE BEAUTY WHO BREAKING • •   20 MODERN SAPPHO   21
SCORES OF TRUE LOVE KNOTS ARE BREAKING • • •   35 NEW SIRENS 261
CAME BREAKING GODDESS • • • • • • • • • 186 STRAYED REVEL   28
THE ALL-HATED ORDER-BREAKING • • • • • • 195 FRAG ANTIGONE   25
THE TRUE HEART-BREAKING BAFFLED HOPE AND SHAME • •   LUCRETIUS 2   13

BREAKS
UNTIL HE CAME TO WHERE A GULLY BREAKS • • •   97 BALDER DEAD 1   81
AND AS IN WINTER WHEN THE FROST BREAKS UP • • • 122 BALDER DEAD 3 307
AND ANON THERE BREAKS A SIGH • • • • • • 164 FORSAKEN MERM 101
THE SOFT MEDITERRANEAN BREAKS • • • • • • 275 SOUTHERN NIGHT   3
IN A THOUSAND WATER-BREAKS LIGHT • • • • • 297 HEINES GRAVE 184
THE ETERNAL TRIFLER BREAKS YOUR SPELL • • • • 304 GRANDE CHARTR 155
THE ETERNAL TRIFLER BREAKS THEIR SPELL • • • • 304 GRANDE CHARTR V 155
HE BREAKS THE WINTER OF THE PAST • • • • • 322 OBERMANN MORE 285
MISERY WHICH ROUSES OTHERS BREAKS THE SPRING • • 366 MEROPE 1025
WITH A GAY REVELLING BAND HE BREAKS FROM THEM • • 412 EMPEDOCLES I 2   16
THE ADRIATIC BREAKS IN A WARM BAY • • • • • 426 EMPEDOCLES I 2 428
WHERE THE SHOREWARD RIPPLE BREAKS • • • • • 434 EMPEDOCLES II 178
THICK BREAKS THE RED FLAME • • • • • • • 441 EMPEDOCLES II 418
BUT WHERE HELICON BREAKS DOWN • • • • • • 441 EMPEDOCLES II 423
QUICK BREAKS THE RED FLAME • • • • • • • 441 EMPEDOCLES II V 418
BREAKS OUT AND LONGS FOR SWITZERLAND • • • • 483 ROME-SICKNESS   3

BREAST

CLAD WERE THEY BOTH IN WHITE FLOWERS IN THEIR BREAST	25 DREAM	23
FALL ON THE THROBBING BROW FALL ON THE BURNING BREAST	36 VOICE	15
FROM THINE OWN MOTHERS BREAST THAT KNOWS NOT THEE	42 GIPSY CHILD	14
HIS BREAST HEAVED HIS LIPS FOAMD AND TWICE HIS VOICE	74 SOHRAB RUSTUM	455
AGAINST HIS BREAST HIS HEAVY MAILED HAND	80 SOHRAB RUSTUM	663
AND STRONG CONVULSIVE GROANINGS SHOOK HIS BREAST	82 SOHRAB RUSTUM	703
BUT IN HIS BREAST STOOD FIXT THE FATAL BOUGH	95 BALDER DEAD 1	5
AND CAST IT AT THE DEAR-LOVED BALDERS BREAST	98 BALDER DEAD 1	102
ON BALDERS BREAST AND THUS BEGAN THE WAIL	115 BALDER DEAD 3	66
IN MINE OWN BREAST AND HAVE TO NONE REVEALD	121 BALDER DEAD 3	287
LONGING WILL STIR WITHIN MY BREAST THOUGH VAIN	127 BALDER DEAD 3	499
IN MY OWN BREAST AND HAVE TO NONE REVEALD	121 BALDER DEAD 3 V	287
THERES A SECRET IN HIS BREAST	138 TRISTRAM 1	245
WHAT THAT EVERY OTHER BREAST	138 TRISTRAM 1	263
LOVE LIKE MINE IS ALTERD IN THE BREAST	143 TRISTRAM 2	38
I STANCH WITH ICE MY BURNING BREAST	158 SAINT BRANDAN	69
SHE HAD ONE POWER WHICH MADE HER BREAST ITS HOME	168 RACHEL 3	10
WERE STRAIND TO THAT BREAST	176 PARTING	70
WERE CLASPD TO THAT BREAST	176 PARTING V	70
IT WAS NOT LOVE WHICH HEAVED THY BREAST	204 EUPHROSYNE	25
IT WAS NOT LOVE THAT HEAVED THY BREAST	204 EUPHROSYNE V	25
BUT TWAS NOT LOVE WHICH HEAVED HER BREAST	204 EUPHROSYNE V	25
OF THE THOUGHTS THAT FERMENT IN MY BREAST	231 YOUTH OF NATURE	120
AND LAY UPON THE BREAST OF GOD	242 MORALITY	36
HAST THOU THEN STILL THE OLD UNQUIET BREAST	243 SUMMER NIGHT	27
GLOOM SETTLES SLOWLY DOWN OVER THEIR BREAST	243 SUMMER NIGHT	46
BUT THERES A SOMETHING IN THIS BREAST	245 BURIED LIFE	6
THE SAME HEART BEATS IN EVERY HUMAN BREAST	245 BURIED LIFE	23
BADE THROUGH THE DEEP RECESSES OF OUR BREAST	246 BURIED LIFE	38
AND MANY A MAN IN HIS OWN BREAST THEN DELVES	246 BURIED LIFE	55
THE NAMELESS FEELINGS THAT COURSE THROUGH OUR BREAST	246 BURIED LIFE	62
A BOLT IS SHOT BACK SOMEWHERE IN OUR BREAST	247 BURIED LIFE	84
AND AN UNWONTED CALM PERVADES HIS BREAST	247 BURIED LIFE	95
THERE BEATS ONE HEART IN EVERY HUMAN BREAST	245 BURIED LIFE V	23
ON THE BREAST OF THE RIVER OF TIME	251 FUTURE	3
HAD LEFT ERE HE WOKE ON ITS BREAST	252 FUTURE	22
THE TRIBES WHO THEN ROAMD ON HER BREAST	252 FUTURE	32
WHO GUARDS IN HER BREAST	252 FUTURE	38
AND WE ON ITS BREAST OUR MINDS	253 FUTURE	55
THAT NEVER WILL THOSE ON ITS BREAST	253 FUTURE	66
PEACE TO THE SOUL OF THE MAN ON ITS BREAST	254 FUTURE	82
THE TRIBES WHO THEN LIVD ON HER BREAST	252 FUTURE V	32
AND HOW THE BREAST WAS SOOTHED AND HOW THE HEAD	260 SCHOLAR-GIPSY	189
AND AGAINST FEAR OUR BREAST TO STEEL	272 MEMORIAL VERSES	65
TRAVERSE IN TROOPS WITH CARE-FILLD BREAST	277 SOUTHERN NIGHT	66
A BOOK WAS IN HIS BREAST	314 OBERMANN MORE	66
SHE FELT THE VOID WHICH MINED HER BREAST	316 OBERMANN MORE	123
BOUNDED IN OUR OWN BREAST WE HARDLY KNOW	352 MEROPE	639
AND LOCKD MY SPEECH FOR EVER IN MY BREAST	362 MEROPE	941
NEVER BEEN TORN FROM THIS BREAST	377 MEROPE	1231
AT THE UNDRIED FOUNT OF THIS BREAST	378 MEROPE	1236
ONCE READ THY OWN BREAST RIGHT	417 EMPEDOCLES I 2	142
DRAWS IN THE ENAMOURD GAZER TO ITS SHINING BREAST	424 EMPEDOCLES I 2	356
OF HIS OWN BREAST FETTERED TO WHAT HE GUARDS	437 EMPEDOCLES II	269
WARM IN HER BREAST BY DAY	446 WESTMIN ABBEY	87
VAINLY WARM HIM IN YOUR BREAST	452 POOR MATTHIAS	9
STILL BENEATH THEIR FEATHERD BREAST	455 POOR MATTHIAS	101
THE THOUGHTS THAT TOUCHT THY BREAST THOU LONELY CONQUEROR THEN	468 ALARIC AT ROME	168
AND TRANQUILLY ABOVE THAT TROUBLED BREAST	469 ALARIC AT ROME	195
IN THE DEEP STILLNESS OF ITS SHELTRING BREAST	472 CROMWELL	12
HIS DROOPING HEAD BOWED MEEKLY ON HIS BREAST	476 CROMWELL	167
AND PILLOWS ON HER FROZEN BREAST AND LOCKS	FRAGMENT 1	3

BREASTS

BREASTS HER OWN GRIEFS AND URGED TOO FIERCELY SAYS	6 GEO CRUIKSHANK	10
CLAD WERE THEY BOTH IN WHITE FLOWERS IN THEIR BREASTS	25 DREAM V	23
FAILD TO FILL UP THE VOID WHICH IN OUR BREASTS WE BEAR	424 EMPEDOCLES I 2	376

BREATH

IT FLUTTERD AND FAILD FOR BREATH	21 REQUIESCAT	14
FOR FEELING NERVES AND LIVING BREATH	22 YOUTH AND CALM	18
THIS WORLD IN WHICH WE DRAW OUR BREATH	59 RESIGNATION	229
IN SINGLE FILE THEY MOVE AND STOP THEIR BREATH	66 SOHRAB RUSTUM	167
SO THE PALE PERSIANS HELD THEIR BREATH WITH FEAR	66 SOHRAB RUSTUM	169
BUT YET SUCCESS SWAYS WITH THE BREATH OF HEAVEN	72 SOHRAB RUSTUM	387
AND LABOURING BREATH FIRST RUSTUM STRUCK THE SHIELD	75 SOHRAB RUSTUM	491
IN SINGLE FILE THEY PASS AND STOP THEIR BREATH	66 SOHRAB RUSTUM V	167
IN SINGLE FILE THEY WIND AND STOP THEIR BREATH	66 SOHRAB RUSTUM V	167
LET THE BREATH OF THE MAY-WIND	135 TRISTRAM 1	156
SWELLS MY HEART AND TAKES MY BREATH AWAY	145 TRISTRAM 2	74
AND A FRESH BREATH OF SPRING STIRRD EVERYWHERE	155 TRISTRAM 3	200
BUT SOULS WHOM SOME BENIGNANT BREATH	203 EUPHROSYNE	13
RETREATING TO THE BREATH	211 DOVER BEACH	26
SOME AS PRISONERS DRAW BREATH	216 LORDS MESSENGER	15
ANOTHER BREATH OF WIND DOTH BLOW	223 EPILOG LAOCOON	74
COME LIKE THE BREATH OF THE SPRING	234 YOUTH OF MAN	56
FROM THE GREY-WALLD GARDENS A BREATH	234 YOUTH OF MAN	67
FOR THESE BESIEGE THE LATEST BREATH	249 WISH	3
TO CANVASS WITH OFFICIAL BREATH	250 WISH	24
THE TURMOIL FOR A LITTLE BREATH	251 WISH	46

BREATH   (CONTINUED)
        A TURMOIL FOR A LITTLE BREATH . . . . 251 WISH   V 46
        I FEEL HER SLOWLY CHILLING BREATH INVADE . . . . 266 THYRSIS   134
        WE BOWD OUR HEADS AND HELD OUR BREATH . . . . . . 270 MEMORIAL VERSES   7
        WE BOWD OUR HEADS AND HELD OUR BREATH . . . . . 270 MEMORIAL VERSES   V 7
        HAVE FELT THIS BREATH HE LOVED OF FAIR   . . . . 275 STANZAS CARNAC   43
        A BREATH MIGHT QUENCH . . . . 276 SOUTHERN NIGHT   36
        I TURN THY LEAVES I FEEL THEIR BREATH   . . . . 306 OBERMANN   13
        NOT WITH THE FAILING BREATH AND FOOT OF AGE . . 362 MEROPE   936
        HAD ON THE JOURNEY CHOKED MY LABOURING BREATH . . 362 MEROPE   940
        ONES BREATH CURLS IN THE AIR AND ON THESE PINES . . 406 EMPEDOCLES I 1   15
        CLEANSE TO SWEET AIRS THE BREATH OF POISONOUS STREAMS . 410 EMPEDOCLES I 1 117
        ARE NOT THE PASSIONATE BREATH . . . . 432 EMPEDOCLES II   97
        BREATH TO AIR . . . . 439 EMPEDOCLES II   336
        THEIR SOUL OF UNWORN YOUTH THEIR BREATH OF GREATNESS . 440 EMPEDOCLES II   384
        THE SOUND BELOVED OF HIS VICTORIOUS BREATH . . . 448 WESTMIN ABBEY   128
        TO CHANT THY REQUIEM WITH MORE PASSIONATE BREATH . . 471 ALARIC AT ROME   227
        SAD FACES WATCHD AROUND HIM AND HIS BREATH . . . . 478 CROMWELL   207
        QUICKENED AND MOVED A HAPPY BREATH . . . . . . 483 ROME-SICKNESS   7
        BUT FOR US WE VIE IN SPEED WITH THE BREATH   HOMER TRANS   54
                OF THE WEST-WIND

BREATHD
        LOOK AS IN SOME BOORS YARD A SWEET-BREATHD COW   . . 123 BALDER DEAD 3   340

BREATHE
        AND BREATHE MORE HAPPY IN AN EVEN CLIME   . . . . 37 YOUTHS AGIT   6
        THE BAND WILL QUIT MANS HEART HE WILL BREATHE FREE   239 REVOLUTIONS   20
        HOW IT WERE GOOD TO ABIDE THERE AND BREATHE FREE . . 244 SUMMER NIGHT   90
        HOW IT WERE GOOD TO SINK THERE AND BREATHE FREE . . 244 SUMMER NIGHT   V 90
        HOW IT WERE GOOD TO LIVE THERE AND BREATHE FREE . . 244 SUMMER NIGHT   V 90
        WE HAVE HAD TIME TO BREATHE . . . . 308 OBERMANN   76
        AND RESTING THERE TO BREATHE I WATCHD THE CHASE . . 357 MEROPE   797
        TO BREATHE A SYLLABLE TO BAR REVENGE . . . . . 389 MEROPE   1528
        AND RESTING THERE TO BREATHE I SAW BELOW . . . . 357 MEROPE   V 797
        SOME OF US TO THE PORTICO TO BREATHE . . . . . 407 EMPEDOCLES I 1   38
        MOUNTS OFF MY SOUL I FEEL IT I BREATHE FREE   . . 441 EMPEDOCLES II   408
        BREATHE THERE NOT SPIRITS ON THE PEOPLED AIR   . . 468 ALARIC AT ROME   163

BREATHED
        BREATHED DEEPLY AS IT DIED . . . . 47 WORLD QUIETIST   31
        BUT THEY TOO DOUBTLESS WILL HAVE BREATHED THE BALM   126 BALDER DEAD 3   437
        HE BOWD HIS HEAD HE BREATHED A PRAYER   . . . . 158 SAINT BRANDAN   74
        WAS BREATHED ON BY THE RURAL PAN . . . . . . 249 KENSINGTON GARD   24

BREATHES
        BREATHES WHEN HE WILL IMMORTAL AIR . . . . . . 58 RESIGNATION   207
        IS IT THE BLIGHTING TAINT DISHONOUR BREATHES   . . 463 ALARIC AT ROME   27
        FOR THAN MAN INDEED THERE BREATHES NO WRETCHEDER   HOMER TRANS   12
                CREATURE

BREATHING
        BREATHING SELF-MURDER FRENZY SPITE . . . . . . 157 SAINT BRANDAN   31
        WHO HAS NO MINUTES BREATHING SPACE ALLOWD . . . . 437 EMPEDOCLES II   272
        WHAT SWEET-BREATHING PRESENCE . . . . 442 EMPEDOCLES II   441
        OF ALL LIVING THINGS THAT ON EARTH ARE BREATHING   HOMER TRANS   13
                AND MOVING

BREATHINGS
        FULL OF SWEET BREATHINGS WAS THE AIR . . . . . . 223 EPILOG LAOCOON   63
        BREATHINGS OF SONG WITH A PEN . . . . 281 HAWORTH CHURCH   24

BREATHLESS
        SHALL BREATHLESS GLADES CHEERD BY SHY DIANS HORN . . 6 GEO CRUIKSHANK   8
        PALE AND BREATHLESS CAME THE HUNTERS . . . . . . 13 CHURCH BROU 1   25
        UPON THESE BREATHLESS SOLITUDES . . . . 54 RESIGNATION   73
        IN BREATHLESS QUIET AFTER ALL THEIR ILLS   . . . 427 EMPEDOCLES I 2   438
        WAS COLD AND SAD BENEATH THAT BREATHLESS VOICELESS   466 ALARIC AT ROME   108
                NIGHT

BRED
        THE GREEN ISLE WHERE SHE WAS BRED   . . . . . . 134 TRISTRAM 1   130

BREED
        WHAT WONDER SHALL TIME BREED TO SWELL THY STRAIN . . 43 GIPSY CHILD   43

BREEDEST
        BUT SO MANY SCHEMES THOU BREEDEST   . . . . . . 49 SECOND BEST   6
        BUT SUCH ANXIOUS SCHEMES THOU BREEDEST   . . . . SECOND BEST   V 6

BREEDING
        A BREEDING EAGLE SITTING ON HER NEST . . . . . . 77 SOHRAB RUSTUM   557

BREEDS
        ALL FRANK FAITH WHICH PASSION BREEDS . . . . . . 34 NEW SIRENS   230
        BREEDS NEW BEGINNINGS DISAPPOINTMENTS NEW . . . . 260 SCHOLAR-GIPSY   177

BREEZE
        THE BREEZE AND FILLD THE SAILS AND BLEW THE FIRE . . 118 BALDER DEAD 3   184
        HOW SWEETLY WOULD THE FRESH SEA-BREEZE   . . . . 205 CALAIS SANDS   15
        DOWN OER THE STATELY BRIDGE THE BREEZE   . . . . 223 EPILOG LAOCOON   65
        SOUND AS OF WANDERING BREEZE BUT SOUND   . . . . 223 EPILOG LAOCOON   75
        THIS BREEZE THAT RUSTLES BY THAT FAMED   . . . . 223 EPILOG LAOCOON   78
        THE MEADOWS WHERE IT GLIDES THE SUN THE BREEZE   . . 247 BURIED LIFE   90

BREEZE   (CONTINUED)
        COME WITH THE VOLLEYING RAIN AND TOSSING BREEZE   . .   264 THYRSIS   59
        THE HILLS WERE ROUND US AND THE BREEZE   .   .   .   .   271 MEMORIAL VERSES   51
        SO SANG I BUT THE MIDNIGHT BREEZE   .   .   .   .   .   279 SOUTHERN NIGHT   117
        CREEPS OER THE SUNSHINE A BREEZE   .   .   .   .   .   .   293 HEINES GRAVE   39
        WHAT BOOTS IT SHELLEY THAT THE BREEZE   .   .   .   .   303 GRANDE CHARTR   139
        THAT BUGLE-MUSIC ON THE BREEZE   .   .   .   .   305 GRANDE CHARTR   189

BREEZES
        AND SNUFFD THE BREEZES OF MY FATHERS HOME   .   .   .   .   83 SOHRAB RUSTUM   749

BREEZY
        MEN WHO THROUGH THOSE WIDE FIELDS OF BREEZY GRASS   257 SCHOLAR-GIPSY   93

BREIÐABLIK
        BREIÐABLIK ON WHOSE COLUMNS BALDER GRAVED   .   .   .   .   101 BALDER DEAD 1   208
        BUT IN BREIÐABLIK NANNA BALDERS WIFE .   .   .   .   .   .   102 BALDER DEAD 1   268
        IN THY OWN HOUSE BREIÐABLIK NOR ENJOY   .   .   .   .   126 BALDER DEAD 3   449

BRETHREN
        NOW MEANWHILE HAD MY BRETHREN FOUND   .   .   .   .   .   .   90 SICK KING BOKH   77
        THOU AND THY BRETHREN FIERCE THE SONS OF BOR   .   .   121 BALDER DEAD 3   258
        OUTLIVED HIS BRETHREN HIS PEERS   .   .   .   .   .   .   229 YOUTH OF NATURE   33
        HIS FATHER AND HIS ILL-STARRD BRETHREN FALL   .   .   387 MEROPE   1463

BRETHRENS
        WHOSE CULTURE IS THE BRETHRENS CARE   .   .   .   .   .   .   301 GRANDE CHARTR   58
        NOR MY BRETHRENS MANY AND BRAVE WHO THEN WILL BE LYING   HOMER TRANS   25

BRETON
        TOLD THEM AN OLD-WORLD BRETON HISTORY   .   .   .   .   150 TRISTRAM 3   37
        SHE GLEANED FROM BRETON GRANDAMES WHEN A CHILD   .   .   152 TRISTRAM 3   108

BREWS
        FROM WHERE IN FARRINGFORD SHE BREWS   .   .   .   .   .   .   458 KAISER DEAD   3

BRIAR
        A BRIAR IN THAT TANGLED WILDERNESS   .   .   .   .   .   .   154 TRISTRAM 3   V 173

BRIARS
        STRETCHD AMONG BRIARS AND STONES THE SLOW BLACK GORE   373 MEROPE   1172

BRICK
        I HAVE A FRETTED BRICK-WORK TOMB   .   .   .   .   .   .   94 SICK KING BOKH   221

BRIDAL
        SINGS OF HIS EARTHLY BRIDAL   .   .   .   .   159 NECKAN   21

BRIDE
        SAVOYS DUKE HAD LEFT HIS BRIDE   .   .   .   .   13 CHURCH BROU 1   6
        HERE SHE CAME A BRIDE IN SPRING   .   .   .   .   .   .   13 CHURCH BROU 1   14
        OF KING MARC TO BE HIS BRIDE   .   .   .   .   132 TRISTRAM 1   62
        OF HIS TIMID YOUTHFUL BRIDE   .   .   .   .   137 TRISTRAM 1   214
        THIS HIS IDOL THIS THAT ROYAL BRIDE   .   .   .   .   .   144 TRISTRAM 2   66
        HE VANISHD WITH HIS BRIDE   .   .   .   .   160 NECKAN   30
        SATE WITH HIS BRIDE TO SEE A PUBLIC SHOW   .   .   .   166 AUSTERITY POET   4
        FAIR WAS THE BRIDE AND ON HER FRONT DID GLOW   .   .   166 AUSTERITY POET   5
        SUCH POETS IS YOUR BRIDE THE MUSE YOUNG GAY   .   .   166 AUSTERITY POET   12
        ROBS OF A LOVED BRIDE PALE IMPLORING   .   .   .   .   .   196 FRAG ANTIGONE   42
        WHEN THE YOUTHS BRING HOME THE BRIDE .   .   .   .   .   .   360 MEROPE   901

BRIDGE
        AND NOW BEYOND THE RUDE STONE BRIDGE .   .   .   .   .   .   54 RESIGNATION   52
        OER THE BRIDGE BIFROST WHERE IS HEIMDALLS WATCH   .   .   99 BALDER DEAD 1   141
        AND HE WILL REACH ON THE TENTH MORN A BRIDGE   .   .   99 BALDER DEAD 1   147
        NOT BIFROST BUT THAT BRIDGE A DAMSEL KEEPS   .   .   .   99 BALDER DEAD 1   149
        AND ON THE TENTH MORN HE BEHELD THE BRIDGE   .   .   .   107 BALDER DEAD 2   85
        AND ON THE BRIDGE A DAMSEL WATCHING ARMD   .   .   .   107 BALDER DEAD 2   87
        SO ON THE BRIDGE THAT DAMSEL BLOCKD THE WAY   .   .   107 BALDER DEAD 2   99
        UNDER WHOSE HOOFS THE BRIDGE OER GIALLS STREAM   .   .   107 BALDER DEAD 2   102
        NOR SHOOK THE BRIDGE SO MUCH AS THOU ALONE   .   .   .   107 BALDER DEAD 2   106
        SAY THEN IF HE HATH CROSSD THY BRIDGE OR NO   .   .   108 BALDER DEAD 2   117
        HE SPAKE THE WARDER OF THE BRIDGE REPLIED   .   .   .   108 BALDER DEAD 2   118
        UPON MY BRIDGE AND WHEN THEY CROSS I KNOW   .   .   .   108 BALDER DEAD 2   121
        ACROSS THE BRIDGE THEN SHE TOOK POST AGAIN   .   .   .   108 BALDER DEAD 2   137
        HOW DIDST THOU CROSS THE BRIDGE OER GIALLS STREAM   110 BALDER DEAD 2   183
        TO THE ARMD DAMSELS BRIDGE AND GIALLS STREAM   .   .   113 BALDER DEAD 2   290
        OER THE BRIDGE BIFROST WHERE IS HEIMDALLS WATCH   .   .   119 BALDER DEAD 3   216
        AND CROSS THE BRIDGE OF HEAVEN WITH LOK FOR GUIDE   127 BALDER DEAD 3   476
        ON HIS WHITE MULE ACROSS THE BRIDGE   .   .   .   .   .   160 NECKAN   47
        AND THE ROOFD BRIDGE THAT SPANS THE STREAM   .   .   .   177 FAREWELL   6
        AND NOW UPON THE BRIDGE WE STOOD   .   .   .   .   .   223 EPILOG LAOCOON   62
        DOWN OER THE STATELY BRIDGE THE BREEZE   .   .   .   .   223 EPILOG LAOCOON   65
        AND ABOVE GODSTOW BRIDGE WHEN HAY-TIMES HERE   .   .   257 SCHOLAR-GIPSY   91
        HAVE I NOT PASSD THEE ON THE WOODEN BRIDGE   .   .   .   258 SCHOLAR-GIPSY   123
        THE BRIDGE IS CROSSD AND SLOW WE RIDE   .   .   .   .   299 GRANDE CHARTR   5

BRIEF
        AND TURNING LEFT THEM THERE AND WITH BRIEF PAUSE .   .   11 MYCERINUS   82
        A LITTLE POOL AND IN BRIEF SPACE   .   .   .   .   .   .   90 SICK KING BOKH   V 68

BRIEF   (CONTINUED)
          IF PARIS THAT BRIEF FLIGHT ALLOW   . . . . . .   321 OBERMANN MORE   269
          FOOLS THAT IN MANS BRIEF TERM   . . . .   424 EMPEDOCLES I 2   347
          OR THE BRIEF SPLENDOUR OF THAT METEOR LIGHT   . .   463 ALARIC AT ROME   29

BRIER
          A BRIER IN THAT TANGLED WILDERNESS   . . . . . .   154 TRISTRAM 3   173

BRIERS
          THE TENDER PURPLE SPRAY ON COPSE AND BRIERS   . .   263 THYRSIS   18

BRIGHT
          IN THE BRIGHT OCTOBER MORNING   . . . .   13 CHURCH BROU 1   5
          ON THE WORK THE BRIGHT SUN SHINES   . . . .   15 CHURCH BROU 1   90
          MID BRIGHT GREEN FIELDS BELOW THE PINES   . . . .   16 CHURCH BROU 2   5
          STREAMS FROM THE SETTING SUN AND COLOURS BRIGHT . . 18 CHURCH BROU 3   19
          ITS STEP SO FIRM ITS EYE SO BRIGHT   . . . . .   21 YOUTH AND CALM   10
          ITS STEP SO FIRM ITS EYES SO BRIGHT   . . . . .   21 YOUTH AND CALM   V   10
          ITS STEP SO GAY ITS EYE SO BRIGHT   . . . . .   21 YOUTH AND CALM   V   10
          OF BRIGHT-LEAFD CHESTNUTS AND MOSSD WALNUT-TREES . . 25 DREAM   8
          RANGED DIAMOND-BRIGHT THE ETERNAL WALL OF SNOW . . 25 DREAM   13
          BRIGHT IN THE SUN THE CLIMBING GOURD-PLANTS LEAVES . 25 DREAM   16
          AND THE BRIGHT AND MORNING STAR   . . . . . .   27 NEW SIRENS   36
          WHICH THE BRIGHT MOON LANCES   . . . .   35 VOICE   3
          LIKE BRIGHT WAVES THAT FALL   . . . .   36 VOICE   17
          THE PORT LIES BRIGHT UNDER THE AUGUST SUN   . . .   41 GIPSY CHILD   V   5
          BRIGHT SHINES THE SUN   . . . . . .   50 CONSOLATION   15
          BRIGHT COMRADE TO THE NOISY TOWN   . . . . .   54 RESIGNATION   77
          MARSHALLD BATTALIONS BRIGHT IN BURNISHD STEEL   . . 65 SOHRAB RUSTUM   140
          AND REARD HIM A BRIGHT BAY WITH LOFTY CREST   . .   69 SOHRAB RUSTUM   276
          BLAZED BRIGHT AND BALEFUL LIKE THAT AUTUMN-STAR . . 74 SOHRAB RUSTUM   452
          AND THE BRIGHT SUN BROKE FORTH AND MELTED ALL   . . 76 SOHRAB RUSTUM   523
          OF THE BRIGHT ROCKING OCEAN SETS TO SHORE   . . .   79 SOHRAB RUSTUM   617
          A FAR BRIGHT CITY SMITTEN BY THE SUN . . . . .   79 SOHRAB RUSTUM   622
          BRIMMING AND BRIGHT AND LARGE THEN SANDS BEGIN . . 87 SOHRAB RUSTUM   881
          OXUS FORGETTING THE BRIGHT SPEED HE HAD   . . .   87 SOHRAB RUSTUM   886
          HIS LUMINOUS HOME OF WATERS OPENS BRIGHT   . . . .   87 SOHRAB RUSTUM   890
          AND TRAIND HIM A BRIGHT BAY WITH LOFTY CREST   . . 69 SOHRAB RUSTUM   V   276
          STOOD IN BRIGHT DAYLIGHT AND THE SKY WAS PURE   . . 75 SOHRAB RUSTUM   V   488
          I LOSE TO-DAY SO BRIGHT SO LOVED A GOD   . .   96 BALDER DEAD 1   22
          BALDER THEIR JOY SO BRIGHT SO LOVED A GOD   . . .   98 BALDER DEAD 1   126
          VINEYARDS AND CROFTS AND PASTURES BRIGHT WITH SUN . 113 BALDER DEAD 2   300
          THEY MOURND THAT DAY SO BRIGHT SO LOVED A GOD   . . 115 BALDER DEAD 3   64
          FAREWELL O BALDER BRIGHT AND LOVED MY SON   . . .   115 BALDER DEAD 3   67
          FROM THE BRIGHT OCEAN AT OUR FEET AN EARTH   . . .   128 BALDER DEAD 3   528
          THAT FIRST ISEULT PRINCESS BRIGHT   . . . . .   134 TRISTRAM 1   126
          GOD TIS HER FACE PLAYS IN THE WATERS BRIGHT   . .   139 TRISTRAM 1   284
          UPON THE WINDOW-PANES THE MOON SHINES BRIGHT   . .   139 TRISTRAM 1   299
          MAKES THEIR CHAMBER AS BRIGHT AS DAY   . . . .   140 TRISTRAM 1   334
          ARE JEWELLD WITH BRIGHT DROPS OF RAIN   . . . .   141 TRISTRAM 1   360
          YOU SEE THEM CLEAR THE MOON SHINES BRIGHT   . .   146 TRISTRAM 2   101
          STEALS COLDLY AROUND THE CHAMBER BRIGHT   . . .   147 TRISTRAM 2   148
          AT THAT BRIGHT IRON-FIGURED DOOR   . . . . .   148 TRISTRAM 2   159
          HOW COMES IT HERE THIS CHAMBER BRIGHT   . . . .   148 TRISTRAM 2   168
          THE UNQUIET BRIGHT ATLANTIC PLAIN   . . . . .   148 TRISTRAM 2   174
          AT THE BRIGHT IRON-FIGURED DOOR   . . . . .   148 TRISTRAM 2   V   159
          THE YOUNG SURVIVING ISEULT ONE BRIGHT DAY   . .   149 TRISTRAM 3   5
          THE LONE UNBROKEN VIEW SPREADS BRIGHT AND CLEAR .   150 TRISTRAM 3   12
          NOR TO THE BROWN HEATHS ROUND THEM BRIGHT AND WIDE   151 TRISTRAM 3   49
          BORE UP FROM WHERE THE BRIGHT ATLANTIC GLEAMS   . . 151 TRISTRAM 3   53
          CAME KEEN AND CHILL DOWN ON THE HEATHER BRIGHT . . 151 TRISTRAM 3   57
          UNDER THE HOLLIES THAT BRIGHT WINTERS DAY   . .   154 TRISTRAM 3   152
          YOU SAW THE BRIGHT-EYED SQUIRRELS DART ALONG   . .   155 TRISTRAM 3   195
          THE YEAR HAD TRAVELLD ROUND AND ONE BRIGHT DAY . .   TRISTRAM 3   V   1
          THE LONE UNBROKEN VIEW STRETCHD BRIGHT AND CLEAR .   TRISTRAM 3   V   12
          WITH SCARLET BERRIES BRIGHT THE FELLFARES FOOD . .   TRISTRAM 3   V   22
          CAME IN FROM WHERE THE BRIGHT ATLANTIC GLEAMS   . .   TRISTRAM 3   V   53
          THE MOON WAS BRIGHT THE ICEBERG NEAR   . . . .   157 SAINT BRANDAN   22
          SHE COMBD ITS BRIGHT HAIR AND SHE TENDED IT WELL   163 FORSAKEN MERM   53
          OVER BANKS OF BRIGHT SEAWEED   . . . . . .   165 FORSAKEN MERM   134
          SEIRIOL THE BRIGHT KYBI THE DARK MEN SAID   . .   170 EAST AND WEST   9
          AH NOW TIS CHANGED IN CONQUERING SUNSHINE BRIGHT . 170 EAST AND WEST   12
          BUT BRIGHT ARE THOSE GREEN FIELDS AT HAND   . .   184 TERRACE BERNE   7
          THE BRIGHT PROCESSION   . . . .   185 STRAYED REVEL   4
          OF THY CUP THE BRIGHT GLANCING VINE-LEAVES   . .   188 STRAYED REVEL   85
          ALIVE WITH BRIGHT GREEN LIZARDS   . . . . .   191 STRAYED REVEL   173
          THE BRIGHT PROCESSION   . . . .   194 STRAYED REVEL   295
          LAY LIKE THE FOLDS OF A BRIGHT GIRDLE FURLD   . .   211 DOVER BEACH   23
          LAY LIKE THE FOLDS OF A BRIGHT GARMENT FURLD   . .   211 DOVER BEACH   V   23
          FOR THE BRIGHT STREAM A CHANNEL GRAND   . . .   213 PROGRESS POESY   6
          AND THE TIMES THAT BRIGHT APOLLO   . . . .   214 NEW ROME   7
          COME WITH COUNTENANCE BRIGHT   . . . . . .   217 LORDS MESSENGER   20
          TEMPTS NOT THE BRIGHT NEW AGE   . . . . . .   220 BACCHANALIA 2   51
          BRIGHT WAS THE MORN AND SOUTH THE AIR   . . .   222 EPILOG LAOCOON   42
          UNTIRED ITS MOVEMENT BRIGHT ATTEND   . . . .   227 EPILOG LAOCOON   191
          COPAIS LAY BRIGHT IN THE MOON   . . . . .   229 YOUTH OF NATURE   37
          BRIGHT ELSE AND FAST THE STREAM OF LIFE MAY ROLL . 238 PROGRESS   29
          AND THE SAME BRIGHT CALM MOON   . . . . . .   242 SUMMER NIGHT   25
          THAT SINGLE ELM-TREE BRIGHT   . . . . . .   263 THYRSIS   26

BRIGHT   (CONTINUED)
    TOPS IN LIFES MORNING-SUN SO BRIGHT AND BARE   • •   267 THYRSIS   145
    THE WEST UNFLUSHES THE HIGH STARS GROW BRIGHT   • •   267 THYRSIS   163
    I CLIMBD BENEATH ME BRIGHT AND WIDE   • • • • •   273 STANZAS CARNAC   3
    BRIGHT IN THE SUNSET WEIRD AND STILL   • • • • •   273 STANZAS CARNAC   5
    TO WHERE THE LIGHTHOUSE BEACONS BRIGHT   • •   275 SOUTHERN NIGHT   11
    WHAT ELSE IS BRIGHT WHAT ELSE IS FAIR   • • •   279 SOUTHERN NIGHT   135
    BRIGHT IN THY CRADLE SMILE   • • • • • • •   285 HAWORTH CHURCH   109
    IN SEPTEMBERS BRIGHT AFTERNOON   • • • • • • • •   292 HEINES GRAVE   7
    BY THE AVON SIDE IN THE BRIGHT   • • • • • • •   294 HEINES GRAVE   63
    AND THERE THEY SAY TWO BRIGHT AND AGED SNAKES   • •   427 EMPEDOCLES I 2   435
    LO ON A SUDDEN ALL THE PILE IS BRIGHT   • • •   445 WESTMIN ABBEY   34
    BRIGHT WITS AND INSTINCTS SURE   • • • • • •   446 WESTMIN ABBEY   77
    AND ON THAT COUNTENANCE BRIGHT   • • • • • •   446 WESTMIN ABBEY   81
    HATH RUN HIS BRIGHT CAREER   • • • • • • • •   448 WESTMIN ABBEY   142
    THOUGH SUNK BE NOW THIS BRIGHT THIS GRACIOUS HEAD   449 WESTMIN ABBEY   176
    BRIGHT WITS AND INSTINCT SURE   • • • • • •   446 WESTMIN ABBEY   V 77
    THOUGH SUNK IS NOW THIS BRIGHT THIS GRACIOUS HEAD   449 WESTMIN ABBEY   V 176
    THINE EYE WAS BRIGHT THY COAT IT SHONE   • • •   460 KAISER DEAD   61
    HOW EACH BRIGHT TINT OF TREE AND FLOWER AND HEATH   466 ALARIC AT ROME   101
    TILL WHAT AT MORNINGS HOUR LOOKT WARM AND BRIGHT •   466 ALARIC AT ROME   107
    TILL ALL BRIGHT THOUGHTS THAT HILLS OR WAVES CAN YIELD 472 CROMWELL   33
    CHILDHOODS BRIGHT GLANCE AND SUNNY SMILE NO MORE   • • 477 CROMWELL   182

BRIGHTEN
    DO I BRIGHTEN AT YOUR SORROW   • • • • •   • • •   31 NEW SIRENS   163
    ROSILY BRIGHTEN AND THE SOOTHED GODS SMILE   • • • •   431 EMPEDOCLES II   81

BRIGHTEND
    THEN SLOWLY BRIGHTEND AS THE DAYS HAD FLOWN   • •   474 CROMWELL   76

BRIGHTENING
    ADMITS NO MOMENTARY BRIGHTENING NOW   • • • • •   408 EMPEDOCLES I 1   69
    AS THE SKY-BRIGHTENING SOUTH-WIND CLEARS THE DAY • •   432 EMPEDOCLES II   121

BRIGHTEST
    AND BRIGHTEST IS THEIR GLORYS SHEEN   • • • • •   227 EPILOG LAOCOON   209
    YET STAINS THERE ARE TO BLOT THY BRIGHTEST PAGE   • •   463 ALARIC AT ROME   37

BRIGHTNESS
    LET YOUR BROAD LAMPS FLASH THE BRIGHTNESS   • • • •   32 NEW SIRENS   177
    NO METEOR BRIGHTNESS TO BE SEEN AND DIE   • • • •   463 ALARIC AT ROME   33

BRILLIANT
    BUT THE BRILLIANT YOUTHFUL KNIGHT   • • • • •   134 TRISTRAM 1   109
    WITH HOT-FLUSHD CHEEKS AND BRILLIANT EYES   • • •   146 TRISTRAM 2   117
    BRILLIANT WITH RECENT RENOWN   • • • • •   •   280 HAWORTH CHURCH   9
    TORTURED THEE BRILLIANT AND BOLD   • • • • •   296 HEINES GRAVE   122
    BLAZING AND BRILLIANT CROWDS   • • • • •   •   296 HEINES GRAVE   142
    IS SHINING ON THE BRILLIANT MOUNTAIN-CRESTS   • •   406 EMPEDOCLES I 1   10
    BRILLIANT ABOVE ME AND THOU FIERY WORLD   • • • •   438 EMPEDOCLES II   305

BRIMMD
    AND AS THIS BRIMMD UNWRINKLED RHINE   • • • • •   208 ON THE RHINE   12
    DOWN TO THE BRIMMD MOON-CHARMED MAIN   • • • •   • • 279 SOUTHERN NIGHT   118
    HIS BROAD-BRIMMD HUNTERS HAT WHICH IN THE BAY   • • 358 MEROPE   843

BRIMMEST
    THOU TOO BRIMMEST WITH LIFE THE SEA OF CLOUD   • •   438 EMPEDOCLES II   308

BRIMMING
    AND WITH EYES BRIMMING   • • • • • • • •   • • •   51 CONSOLATION   47
    BRIMMING AND BRIGHT AND LARGE THEN SANDS BEGIN   • •   87 SOHRAB RUSTUM   881
    THEN FROM ITS BRIMMING WAVES THEIR EYE   • • •   227 EPILOG LAOCOON   193
    THE SPRING-TIDES BRIMMING FLOW   • • • • • • •   242 SUMMER NIGHT   16
    BRIMMING WITH WONDER AND JOY   • • • • • • •   251 FUTURE   4

BRINE
    DRY THEIR MAIL AND BASK IN THE BRINE   • • • •   162 FORSAKEN MERM   42
    GREEN BURSTING FIGS AND TUNNIES STEEPD IN BRINE   • •   262 SCHOLAR-GIPSY   239
    BUT FARTHER YET ACROSS THE BRINE   • • • • •   277 SOUTHERN NIGHT   50
    WAS BLINDED BY THE OUTGUSHING SPRINGS OF BRINE   • •   357 MEROPE   778

BRING
    OF THE GREAT GODS IS PLAIN AND YE MUST BRING   • •   11 MYCERINUS   75
    AUSTRIAN WANDERERS BRING O WARDERS   • • • •   •   15 CHURCH BROU 1   79
    MAY BRING ONE OF THE OLD HAPPY MOMENTS AGAIN   • •   19 MODERN SAPPHO   V
    FROM TEARS THAT BRING NO HEALING   • • • • •   39 STAGIRIUS   35
    LIGHT BRING NO BLINDNESS   • • • • • • • •   • •   40 STAGIRIUS   57
    HIS FOLLOWERS IN AND BADE THEM BRING HIS ARMS   • •   69 SOHRAB RUSTUM   264
    BRING THOU TO ME HIS CORPSE HE SAID   • • • •   •   91 SICK KING BOKH   128
    WILT THOU THEY STRAIGHTWAY BRING HIM IN   • • •   92 SICK KING BOKH   131
    BRING WATER NARD AND LINEN ROLLS   • • • • •   •   95 SICK KING BOKH   229
    BRING WOOD TO THE SEASHORE TO BALDERS SHIP   • •   96 BALDER DEAD 1   41
    CAN I O MOTHER BRING THEM BALDER BACK   • • •   98 BALDER DEAD 1   107
    WHOM THEY BRING BACK WITH THEM AT NIGHT TO HEAVEN   105 BALDER DEAD 2   27
    GO QUICKLY GODS BRING WOOD TO THE SEASHORE   • • •   106 BALDER DEAD 2   41
    DID ANGERBODE THE GIANTESS BRING FORTH   • • •   110 BALDER DEAD 2   207
    BRING NOW THE GATHERD WOOD TO BALDERS SHIP   • •   118 BALDER DEAD 3   158
    AND BRING IN TRIUMPH BALDER BACK TO HEAVEN   • • •   120 BALDER DEAD 3   244

```
BRING                ( CONTINUED )
          OF ALL THINGS WEEPING TO BRING BALDER BACK   • • • •   122 BALDER DEAD 3      318
          LOVE ME AND GLADLY BRING FOR MY AWARD          • • • •   126 BALDER DEAD 3      465
          AND BRING US NEARER TO THE FINAL DAY  • • • • •        127 BALDER DEAD 3      474
          AND THAT WILL BRING TO MIND THE FORMER LIFE     • •     128 BALDER DEAD 3      540
          TRUST ME AND GLADLY BRING FOR MY AWARD        • • • •   126 BALDER DEAD 3    V 465
          WHICH VENICE SHIPS DO FROM SWART EGYPT BRING    • •     150 TRISTRAM 3          41
          BRING HIM A WEEPING CHILD         • • • • • • •         195 FRAG ANTIGONE       12
          BUT THEY BRING MORE THAN THEY RECEIVE           • • • • 203 EUPHROSYNE          20
          THEY BRING US LIGHT AND WARMTH AND JOY          • • • • 203 EUPHROSYNE          24
          WITH TREMULOUS CADENCE SLOW AND BRING           • • • • 211 DOVER BEACH         13
          WITH REGULAR CADENCE SLOW AND BRING   • • • • •        211 DOVER BEACH       V 13
          WITH MOURNFUL CADENCE SLOW AND BRING • • • • • •       211 DOVER BEACH       V 13
          TO WHICH THY LIGHT WORDS BRING NO REST          • • • • 245 BURIED LIFE          7
          NOR BRING TO SEE ME CEASE TO LIVE    • • • • •        250 WISH                17
          BRING NONE OF THESE BUT LET ME BE     • • • • •        250 WISH                29
          AH SINCE DARK DAYS STILL BRING TO LIGHT         • • • • 272 MEMORIAL VERSES     58
          WHOM IN OUR PARTY WE BRING       • • • • •            289 RUGBY CHAPEL       115
          SADLY WE ANSWER WE BRING  • • • • • • • • •            289 RUGBY CHAPEL       117
          TO AVENGE THAT FALL AND BRING THEM BACK TO POWER  • •  334 MEROPE             146
          SOON SOON SHALL ZEUS BRING HIM HOME  • • • • •        347 MEROPE             514
          BRING TO ME SAFE LET THE REST    • • • • • •          348 MEROPE             535
          SO BE IT YET WILL THAT MORE SOLACE BRING        • • • • 349 MEROPE             559
          CAN IT BRING HOME MY CHILD AH IF IT CAN         • • • • 349 MEROPE             568
          IF THIS WILL BRING HIM BACK BE THIS MY PRAYER   • •     349 MEROPE             579
          BRING BACK OUR SON IF MAY BE WITHOUT BLOOD    • • • •   350 MEROPE             587
          WHEN THE YOUTHS BRING HOME THE BRIDE • • • • •        360 MEROPE             901
          SUCH A BOON TO BRING HATH BEEN GIVEN    • • • •        361 MEROPE             907
          YET THEN ANOTHER MAN WOULD BRING THIS NEWS    • • • •   362 MEROPE             942
          HERE BRING HIM ERE THE KING COME BACK FROM COUNCIL     379 MEROPE            1262
          OF YOUR DEAD MASTERS LINE I BRING YOU NEWS      • • • • 400 MEROPE            1883
          YET YET SHALL ZEUS BRING HIM HOME    • • • • •        347 MEROPE           V 514
          BRING TO HIS MOTHER THE REST I COMMIT           • • • • 348 MEROPE           V
          TO BRING THEE OUT WITH HIM ALONE ON ETNA        • • • • 409 EMPEDOCLES I 1     107
          BORN INTO LIFE WE BRING     • • • • • • • •            418 EMPEDOCLES I 2     192
          THAT CHANCE WILL BRING US THROUGH     • • • • •        420 EMPEDOCLES I 2     240
          AND BRING PEISIANAX TO HIM FROM THE CITY    • • • •    428 EMPEDOCLES I 2     481
          BRING HIM TO POISE THERE IS NO OTHER WAY     • • • •   436 EMPEDOCLES II      234
          IT SEEMD A CHILD OF LIGHT DID BRING THE DOWER   • •     446 WESTMIN ABBEY       74
          SOON SOON THE DAYS CONVICTION BRING  • • • • • •      459 KAISER DEAD         25
          SEE THAT YE BRING YOUR MASTER HOME TO THE HOST         HOMER TRANS         40
               OF THE ARGIVES

BRINGER
          FORGIVE FORGIVE THE BRINGER OF SUCH NEWS      • • • •   363 MEROPE             949
          BRINGER OF HEAVENLY LIGHT A HUMAN HOUR        • • • •   447 WESTMIN ABBEY      120

BRINGEST
          AND WHO ART THOU WHO BRINGEST ME SUCH NEWS    • • • •   355 MEROPE             716
          STRANGER THIS NEWS THOU BRINGEST IS TOO GREAT   • •     359 MEROPE             859
          STRANGER THE NEWS THOU BRINGEST IS TOO GREAT    • •     359 MEROPE           V 859

BRINGING
          BRINGING NO REST     • • • • • • • •                   36 VOICE              16
          ARE THIS WAY BRINGING THE DEAD MAN     • • • • • •      88 SICK KING BOKH     19
          SLIP WITHOUT BRINGING BLISS SLOWLY AWAY         • • • • 151 TRISTRAM 3          66
          BRINGING THY SHEEP IN THY HAND   • • • • • •          290 RUGBY CHAPEL       144
          AN UNKNOWN GUEST WILL ENTER BRINGING WORD     • • • •   331 MEROPE             48
          BRINGING ME OF MY BOY THE ANNUAL NEWS           • • • • 350 MEROPE             599

BRINGS
          BRINGS ROUND TO ALL MEN      • • • • • • • • •        52 CONSOLATION         74
          BUT EACH DAY BRINGS ITS PETTY DUST      • • • • • •    183 ABSENCE             9
          SEE WHAT THE DAY BRINGS   • • • • • •                  188 STRAYED REVEL       74
          AND BRINGS THE WATER FROM THE FOUNT   • • • • •        213 PROGRESS POESY      3
          THAT TRAVAILS SORE AND BRINGS FORTH WIND      • • • •   217 NAMELESS EPIT    V
          BRINGS UP THE STREAM     • • • • • • • • • •          254 FUTURE             86
          WHICH MUCH TO HAVE TRIED IN MUCH BEEN BAFFLED BRINGS   260 SCHOLAR-GIPSY      165
          BRINGS THEE BACK IN THE LIGHT    • • • • • •          286 RUGBY CHAPEL       17
          THE AXE WHO BRINGS IT TIS HERE   • • • • • •          372 MEROPE            1144
          TO THOSE HE BRINGS FROM HOME     • • • • • •          419 EMPEDOCLES I 2     220
          NOW THY MISTRESS BRINGS THEE HERE     • • • • •        452 POOR MATTHIAS      16
          SOMETHING HAUNTS MY CONSCIENCE BRINGS           • • • • 455 POOR MATTHIAS      85
          BUT SHE WITH PRODIGALITY BRINGS FORTH           • • • • EVERLASTING SUB     4

BRINGST
          AND WHAT ARCADIAN HELPERS BRINGST THOU HERE     • •     380 MEROPE            1284

BRINK
          FROM THE STREAMS BRINK THE SPOT WHERE FIRST A BOAT     61 SOHRAB RUSTUM      18
          THE YELLOW OXUS BY WHOSE BRINK I DIE • • • • • •      83 SOHRAB RUSTUM     766
          AND HEAVENWARD FROM THE FOUNTAIN-BRINK HE SPRANG  • •  268 THYRSIS           189
          OER GLION FRINGE THE MOUNTAINS BRINK • • • • • •      483 ROME-SICKNESS      11

BRISK
          BUT AGITATED BRISK AND NEAR     • • • • • • • •        224 EPILOG LAOCOON    111

BRISTLED
          BRISTLED WITH CITIES US THE SEA RECEIVED      • • • •   25 DREAM              37
```

BRISTLING
    BRISTLING AND IN THE MIDST THE OPEN SAND   • • • •   70 SOHRAB RUSTUM   298

BRITTANY
    ON THIS COAST OF BRITTANY • • • • • • • • 131 TRISTRAM 1   35
    ISEULT OF BRITTANY • • • • • • • • • 132 TRISTRAM 1   55
    ISEULT OF BRITTANY BUT WHERE • • • • • • 132 TRISTRAM 1   56
    ISEULT OF BRITTANY • • • • • • • • • 136 TRISTRAM 1   197
    INTO THE HEART OF BRITTANY • • • • • • 141 TRISTRAM 1   366
    AWAY THE OTHER SIDE OF BRITTANY • • • • • 154 TRISTRAM 3   154
    LAY THE LONE COAST OF BRITTANY • • • • • • 273 STANZAS CARNAC   4

BROAD
    VAIN LABOUR DEEP AND BROAD WHERE NONE MAY SEE • •   4 BUTLERS SERMONS   5
    LIKE THE BROAD VOLUME OF THE INSURGENT NILE • • 10 MYCERINUS   40
    LIKE THE BROAD RUSHING OF THE INSURGENT NILE • • 10 MYCERINUS V 40
    LIKE THE BROAD RUSHING OF THE COLUMND NILE • • • 10 MYCERINUS V 40
    LIKE THE BROAD RUSHING OF THE INSURGED NILE • • 10 MYCERINUS V 40
    LET YOUR BROAD LAMPS FLASH THE BRIGHTNESS • • • 32 NEW SIRENS   177
    FROM THE BROAD OXUS AND THE GLITTERING SANDS • • 64 SOHRAB RUSTUM   105
    STOOD IN BROAD DAYLIGHT AND THE SKY WAS PURE • • 75 SOHRAB RUSTUM   488
    ON HIS BROAD BACK NO LESSER RIDER BORE • • • • 107 BALDER DEAD 2   74
    ON THE BROAD CLAY-LADEN • • • • • • • • 191 STRAYED REVEL   182
    THE BROAD EARTH OPEND AND WHELMD THEM AND HIM • 197 FRAG ANTIGONE   87
    HEAR IT FROM THY BROAD LUCENT ARNO-VALE • • • 267 THYRSIS   167
    THE BROAD RED SUN OVER FIELD • • • • • • 297 HEINES GRAVE   170
    WITH THE LOW BROAD HAT OF THE TANND • • • • 342 MEROPE   395
    HIS BROAD-BRIMMD HUNTERS HAT WHICH IN THE BAY • 358 MEROPE   843
    END HERE ETNA BEYOND IN THE BROAD GLARE • • • 414 EMPEDOCLES I 2   53
    WE STROKE THY BROAD BROWN PAWS AGAIN • • • • 451 GEISTS GRAVE   45
    AND SOONEST FADE IN THE BROAD GLARE OF DAY • • • 470 ALARIC AT ROME   214
    IN BROAD CLEAR LIGHT THE GHASTLY VISION SHONE • • 477 CROMWELL   203
    BEARING ON HIS SHOULDERS BROAD • • • • • •   PILLARS UNIVERS   3

BROCE
    OF THE DEEP FOREST-GLADES OF BROCE-LIANDE • • • • 154 TRISTRAM 3   156

BROCKEN
    ON THE ROOF OF THE BROCKEN-TOWER • • • • • • 297 HEINES GRAVE   168

BROIDERD
    AND FROM YOUR BROIDERD PILLOWS LIFT YOUR HEADS • • 18 CHURCH BROU 3   26
    ERE THEIR BOAT-MUSIC SOUND ERE THEIR BROIDERD   19 MODERN SAPPHO   8
        FLAGS GLEAM
    DIGHT WITH A SADDLE-CLOTH OF BROIDERD GREEN • • 69 SOHRAB RUSTUM   277

BROIDERIES
    AND PRAISE THE CHISELLD BROIDERIES RARE • • • 17 CHURCH BROU 2   37

BROIDERY
    AND TAKE HER BROIDERY-FRAME AND THERE SHELL SIT • • 152 TRISTRAM 3   82

BROIL
    ALAS THAT HOW TO RULE IT WAS OUR BROIL • • • • 334 MEROPE   127
    WISHD TRULY WISHD SOLUTION TO OUR BROIL • • • • 360 MEROPE   886
    MEAN STILL TO KEEP ALOOF FROM DORIAN BROIL • • • 384 MEROPE   1396

BROILING
    THAN IN THE BROILING CITY IN THESE HEATS • • • • 409 EMPEDOCLES I 1   104

BROILS
    SOMETHING TOO MUCH OF WAR AND BROILS WHICH MAKE • 128 BALDER DEAD 3   505
    SINCE BROILS TEAR US IN TWAIN SINCE THIS NEW SWARM 410 EMPEDOCLES I 1   121

BROKE
    BROKE FROM HIS SORROWING PEOPLE SO HE SPAKE • • 11 MYCERINUS   81
    WAS CHOKED WITH RAGE AT LAST THESE WORDS BROKE WAY 74 SOHRAB RUSTUM   456
    AND THE BRIGHT SUN BROKE FORTH AND MELTED ALL • • 76 SOHRAB RUSTUM   523
    OF RUSTUM AND HIS TEARS BROKE FORTH HE CAST • • 82 SOHRAB RUSTUM   727
    ON THIS GREAT SINNER WHO HATH BROKE • • • • 89 SICK KING BOKH V 37
    PEERD TWIXT THE STEMS AND THE GROUND BROKE AWAY • 155 TRISTRAM 3   186
    HOTLY CHARGED AND BROKE AT LAST • • • • 215 LAST WORD V 12
    SMILES BROKE FROM US AND WE HAD EASE • • • • 271 MEMORIAL VERSES   50
    BROKE ON THE FIELD OF HIS FAME • • • • • 296 HEINES GRAVE   128
    SO WELL SHE MUSED A MORNING BROKE • • • • 316 OBERMANN MORE   113
    SHE BROKE HER FLUTES SHE STOPPD HER SPORTS • • 316 OBERMANN MORE   129
    VOICE MOVED ONLY THE TORRENT BROKE • • • • 323 OBERMANN MORE   327
    BY THE LAKE-EDGE BROKE THE SHARP CRY OF HOUNDS • • 357 MEROPE   787
    BROKE BLACK WITH SWEAT THE ANTLERD MOUNTAIN-STAG • 357 MEROPE   808
    BROKE FROM THE DORIAN LORDS FORWARD THEY RUSHD • • 402 MEROPE   1931
    ALWAY FROM THEIR PRESENCE BROKE • • • • • 454 POOR MATTHIAS   53
    THEN HIS EYE SLUMBERD AND THE CHAIN WAS BROKE • • 475 CROMWELL   131

BROKEN
    MANY A BROKEN PROMISE THEN • • • • • • • 23 MEMORY-PICTURE   37
    DEEP AND FAR A BROKEN GLEAMING • • • • • • 32 NEW SIRENS   185
    HIS HOUSE NOW MID THEIR BROKEN FLIGHTS OF STEPS • • 86 SOHRAB RUSTUM   862
    THE SWORD WERE BROKEN IN THY HANDS • • • • 92 SICK KING BOKH   140
    AND FENRIS AT HIS HEEL WITH BROKEN CHAIN • • • 127 BALDER DEAD 3   477
    AMONG THE HOLLY-CLUMPS AND BROKEN GROUND • • • 150 TRISTRAM 3   28
    TO TAKE HIS NURSE HIS BROKEN TOY • • • • • 248 KENSINGTON GARD   10
    DRAGS TO HIS NURSE HIS BROKEN TOY • • • • •   KENSINGTON GARD V 10

BROKEN   (CONTINUED)
    O UNSTRUNG WILL O BROKEN HEART . . . .   312 OBERMANN   183
    POOR FRAGMENTS OF A BROKEN WORLD . . . .   320 OBERMANN MORE   217
    HIS BOAR-SPEARS BROKEN SHAFT BACK ON THE LAKE . . 358 MEROPE   840
    THE BROKEN ORDER OF YOUR DORIAN THRONES . . . .   389 MEROPE   1546
    SWEPT DOWN A CHASM BROKEN IN THE CLIFF . . . .   363 MEROPE   V 960
    OF NOON IS BROKEN THERE BY CHESTNUT-BOUGHS . . . 414 EMPEDOCLES I 2   44
    SOON WAS THAT STILLNESS BROKEN LIKE THE CRY . .   466 ALARIC AT ROME   109

BROKENLY
    WHILE HE MUTTERS BROKENLY   . . . . 133 TRISTRAM 1   93
    AS HE MUTTERS BROKENLY . . . .   133 TRISTRAM 1   V 93

BROOCH
    THE AGATE BROOCH-STONES . . . .   186 STRAYED REVEL   17

BROOD
    ALL THE STRONG BROOD OF HEAVEN TO SWELL MY TRAIN . . 120 BALDER DEAD 3 241
    BUT ALL THAT BROOD THOU HAST REMOVED FAR OFF . . 121 BALDER DEAD 3   274
    WITH TRIUMPHS A YET AMPLER BROOD . . . .   222 EPILOG LAOCOON   24
    WHO BUT THE KINSMEN OF THE ROYAL BROOD   . . . . 336 MEROPE   221
    BEFORE THE SOPHIST-BROOD HATH OVERLAID   . . . . 429 EMPEDOCLES II   29
    THEY ENVY NOT THIS TRANQUIL BROOD . . . . . .   484 ROME-SICKNESS   17

BROODED
    WHICH BROODED OER THY SOUL . . . .   306 OBERMANN   16
    OH THAT IT BROODED OVER THE WORLD LIKE THE AIR . . 438 EMPEDOCLES II   326

BROODING
    AND BROODING MOUNTAIN-BEE . . . .   307 OBERMANN   34
    THE BROODING EAST WITH AWE BEHELD . . . . . .   316 OBERMANN MORE   105
    WITH EXILE AND WITH BROODING ON HIS WRONGS . . . 407 EMPEDOCLES I 1   24

BROODS
    THE PILLAR STILL BROODS OER THE FIELDS   . . .   228 YOUTH OF NATURE   15
    OVER HIS BOILING CAULDRON BROODS   . . . . . .   299 GRANDE CHARTR   12
    OVER HIS BOILING CAULDRONS BROODS . . . . . .   299 GRANDE CHARTR   V 12
    WITH GLOOMING CLOUDS BROODS DARK AND HEAVILY . . 475 CROMWELL   130
    WHERE BROODS THE UNCOMPANIONED LIFE OF GOD . . .   FRAGMENT 6   3

BROOK
    THERE SPRINGS THE BROOK WILL GUIDE US DOWN . . .   54 RESIGNATION   76
    HERE WHERE THE BROOK SHINES NEAR ITS HEAD . . .   55 RESIGNATION   90
    STILL THIS WILD BROOK THE RUSHES COOL . . . .   55 RESIGNATION   104
    IN A SLOPED SWARD DOWN TO A BRAWLING BROOK . . . 155 TRISTRAM 3   187
    OR WAS IT FROM SOME SUN-FLECKD MOUNTAIN-BROOK . . 175 PARTING   21

BROOKD
    AND SADDLED HIM BEFORE THAT SLEIPNER BROOKD   . . 107 BALDER DEAD 2   72

BROOKS
    ALL MANS HEART WHICH BROOKS BESTOWAL . . . . . .   34 NEW SIRENS   229
    ERE THE LONG NIGHT WHOSE STILLNESS BROOKS NO STAR   43 GIPSY CHILD   45
    ON THE BROOKS FARTHER SIDE WAS CLEAR BUT THEN . . 155 TRISTRAM 3   189
    ON THE BROOKS FURTHER SIDE WAS CLEAR BUT THEN . . 155 TRISTRAM 3   V 189
    AND WHAT SEDGED BROOKS ARE THAMESS TRIBUTARIES . . 266 THYRSIS   110
    FROM THOSE TWIN BROOKS THAT BEACHED STRAND . . .   480 HAYSWATER BOAT   21

BROOKSIDE
    AND ONLY IN THE HIDDEN BROOKSIDE GLEAM   . . . .   266 THYRSIS   119

BROOM
    FROM HEATHS STARRD WITH BROOM . . . .   165 FORSAKEN MERM   129
    GOLD FURZE WITH BROOM IN BLOSSOM VIES   . . . .   274 STANZAS CARNAC   19
    GOLD BROOM WITH FURZE IN BLOSSOM VIES   . . . .   274 STANZAS CARNAC   V 19
    THE GOLD-FLOWERD BROOM . . . .   442 EMPEDOCLES II   440

BROTHER
    ROUND THY STILL DREAMING BROTHER-WORLD OUTSPREAD . . 45 IN UTRUMQUE PAR   31
    THY BROTHER-WORLD STIRS AT THY FEET UNKNOWN . .   46 IN UTRUMQUE PAR   38
    AND TO FEROOD HIS BROTHER CHIEFS CAME UP   . . .   66 SOHRAB RUSTUM   170
    BROTHER THOU DWELLEST IN THE DARKSOME LAND . . . 115 BALDER DEAD 3   75
    BALDER MY BROTHER THOU ART GONE A ROAD   . . .   116 BALDER DEAD 3   99
    STILL LEFT AND THAT CHIEF SCALD THY BROTHER BRAGE 117 BALDER DEAD 3   133
    HODER HIS BROTHER WHOM HIS OWN HAND SLEW . . . . 118 BALDER DEAD 3   165
    THY BROTHER WHOM THROUGH FOLLY THOU DIDST SLAY . . 124 BALDER DEAD 3   393
    BROTHER AND FELLOW-SPORT OF LOK WITH ME . . .   125 BALDER DEAD 3   412
    TO FEEL THE PRESENCE OF A BROTHER GOD . . . .   125 BALDER DEAD 3   418
    AND HIS BLACK BROTHER-BIRD FROM HENCE REPLY . . 127 BALDER DEAD 3   497
    BROTHER WHAT SEATS ARE THESE WHAT HAPPIER DAY . . 128 BALDER DEAD 3   515
    TO NANNA AND SHE GAVE THEIR BROTHER BLIND . . . 129 BALDER DEAD 3   550
    HIS BROTHER-DOCTOR OF THE SOUL . . . .   250 WISH   23
    MY BROTHER AND THINE EARLY LOT . . . .   276 SOUTHERN NIGHT   19
    OF THEE I THINK MY BROTHER YOUNG   . . . . . .   279 SOUTHERN NIGHT   123
    A BROTHER SLEEPS HE HERE . . . .   285 HAWORTH CHURCH   102
    O BROTHER OF MY MOTHER GUARDIAN TRUE . . . . .   330 MEROPE   29
    I SPEAK NOT NOW OF ARGOS WHERE HIS BROTHER . . . 337 MEROPE   231
    BROTHER FOLLOWD SISTER . . . .   344 MEROPE   447
    APPROVES MY BROTHER LAIAS THIS INTENT   . . . . 379 MEROPE   1267
    THY SPARTAN COUSINS PROCLES AND HIS BROTHER . . 384 MEROPE   1393

BROTHER   (CONTINUED)
    BROTHER IT SEEMS THY SISTER MUST PRESENT • • • 386 MEROPE   1451
    BESIDES FOR FROM MY BROTHER AND MY SON • • • 387 MEROPE   1473
    DESPISE THEM NOT FOR BROTHER THOU AND I • • • 388 MEROPE   1511
    THE ELDEST MIGHTIEST BROTHER TEMENUS TOOK • • • 389 MEROPE   1550
    ALAS AGAINST MY BROTHER SON AND FRIENDS • • • 390 MEROPE   1579
    O BROTHER THOU HAST CONQUERD YET I FEAR • • • 390 MEROPE   1581
    APPROVES MY BROTHER LAIAS THIS DESIGN • • • 379 MEROPE   V1267
    DESPISE THEM NOT FOR BROTHER THOU LIKE ME • • • 388 MEROPE   V1511
    BROTHER MANS DESPAIRING SIGN • • • • • 457 POOR MATTHIAS   169
    FOR MAX THY BROTHER-DOG BEGAN • • • • • 459 KAISER DEAD   37
    A FORM THAT TOWERD ABOVE HIS BROTHER MEN • • • 476 CROMWELL   145

BROTHERHOOD
    OF RAPHAEL AND HIS BROTHERHOOD • • • • • • • • 222 EPILOG LAOCOON   25
    AND ROAMD THE WORLD WITH THAT WILD BROTHERHOOD • 256 SCHOLAR-GIPSY   38
    THE HOUSE THE BROTHERHOOD AUSTERE • • • • • 301 GRANDE CHARTR   65

BROTHERHOODS
    THE BROTHERHOODS OF SAINTS ARE GLAD • • • • • 156 SAINT BRANDAN   2

BROTHERS
    WHO HATH A MONARCHS HATH NO BROTHERS PART • • • 46 IN UTRUMQUE PAR   39
    NOR YET COULD HERMOD SEE HIS BROTHERS FACE • • • 101 BALDER DEAD 1   228
    AND HERMOD LOOKD AND KNEW HIS BROTHERS GHOST • 124 BALDER DEAD 3   385
    NOW MY BROTHERS CALL FROM THE BAY • • • • • 161 FORSAKEN MERM   3
    NO MAN CAN SAVE HIS BROTHERS SOUL • • • • 318 OBERMANN MORE   V
    NOR PAY HIS BROTHERS DEBT • • • • • • 318 OBERMANN MORE   V
    BECAUSE THOU SLEWST HIS BROTHERS WITH THEIR FATHER • 336 MEROPE   191
    THREE BROTHERS WON THE FIELD • • • • • • 344 MEROPE   454
    THY BROTHERS PLAY AT MY FEET • • • • • • 378 MEROPE   1238
    TWO BROTHERS AND THEIR ORPHAN NEPHEWS STROVE • 389 MEROPE   1548
    THE SPARTAN BROTHERS WITH THEIR GUARDIAN STRIVE • 390 MEROPE   1558
    REGARDS HIS BROTHERS FORM OUTSPREAD • • • • • 460 KAISER DEAD   68

BROU
    SEEK HER AT THE CHURCH OF BROU • • • • • • • 15 CHURCH BROU 1   84
    TIS THE CHURCH OF BROU • • • • • • • • 16 CHURCH BROU 2   8
    ROUND THE CHURCH OF BROU • • • • • • • 16 CHURCH BROU 2   16
    ROUND THE CHURCH OF BROU • • • • • • • 17 CHURCH BROU 2   24
    ROUND THE CHURCH OF BROU • • • • • • • 17 CHURCH BROU 2   32
    IN THE CHURCH OF BROU • • • • • • • • 17 CHURCH BROU 2   40

BROUGHAM
    TWAS DAWN A BROUGHAM ROLLD THROUGH THE STREETS   167 RACHEL 1   4
        AND MADE
    SATE IN THE BROUGHAM AND THOSE BLANK WALLS SURVEYD   167 RACHEL 1   8

BROUGHT
    NO NOR GREW DARK WHEN AUTUMN BROUGHT THE CLOUDS • • 12 MYCERINUS   121
    WILL BE BROUGHT THOU POOR HEART HOW MUCH NEARER   20 MODERN SAPPHO   20
        TO THEE
    FOR FROM THE TARTARS IS A CHALLENGE BROUGHT • • 67 SOHRAB RUSTUM   211
    OR ERE THEY BROUGHT THY MASTER TO THIS FIELD • • 83 SOHRAB RUSTUM   740
    OF SAMARCAND IS BROUGHT THIS WAY • • • • 89 SICK KING BOKH   63
    WITH CURIOUS FRUIT-TREES BROUGHT FROM FAR • • • 94 SICK KING BOKH   201
    THERE TO HIS HALL THE GODS BROUGHT BALDER HOME • 101 BALDER DEAD 1   214
    BUT WHEN THE GODS AND HEROES HEARD THEY BROUGHT • 118 BALDER DEAD 3   160
    AND BROUGHT HIS ARMS AND GOLD AND ALL HIS STUFF • 118 BALDER DEAD 3   169
    YE GODS THE TERMS YE KNOW WHICH HERMOD BROUGHT • 120 BALDER DEAD 3   225
    THE GIANT YMIR WHOM THE ABYSS BROUGHT FORTH • 121 BALDER DEAD 3   257
    BOTH HAVE BROUGHT THEIR ANXIOUS DAY TO EVENING • 144 TRISTRAM 2   55
    FILLD UP THE HOLLOW CHEEK AND BROUGHT • • • 147 TRISTRAM 2   141
    AND BROUGHT HER TALE TO AN END AND FOUND THE PATH • 151 TRISTRAM 3   62
    WAS THE ONE ISEULT CHOSE AND SHE BROUGHT CLEAR • 154 TRISTRAM 3   165
    MAY TO EACH OTHER BE BROUGHT NEAR • • • • 180 FAREWELL   75
    THE FAVOURD GUEST OF CIRCE BROUGHT BY THE WAVES • 189 STRAYED REVEL   110
    HEARD IT ON THE AEGAEAN AND IT BROUGHT • • 211 DOVER BEACH   16
    LIKE THESE AND IN ONE ASPECT BROUGHT • • • • 223 EPILOG LAOCOON   56
    IS ON A SUDDEN BROUGHT • • • • • • • 242 SUMMER NIGHT   12
    BROUGHT BY THE WEST-WIND RETURNS • • • • • 285 HAWORTH CHURCH   114
    BUT WE BROUGHT FORTH AND REARD IN HOURS • • • 308 OBERMANN   69
    WELLNIGH TWO THOUSAND YEARS HAVE BROUGHT • • 315 OBERMANN MORE V 81
    THE LATE-RELENTING GODS WITH VICTORY BROUGHT • 330 MEROPE   6
    WHITHER FROM WINTRY MAENALUS WERE BROUGHT • • 356 MEROPE   741
    AND I ACROSS THE MOUNTAINS BROUGHT WITH HASTE • 358 MEROPE   845
    THE MESSAGE BROUGHT WAS FOR THE KING DESIGND • 361 MEROPE   923
    HE BROUGHT REPORT THAT HIS OWN EYES HAD SEEN • 363 MEROPE   958
    AND THE STERN DESTINY-BROUGHT STRANGER • • • 400 MEROPE   1861
    TO CYPSELUS AT BASILIS HE BROUGHT • • • • 364 MEROPE   V
    THERE THE PHRYGIAN BROUGHT HIS FLUTES • • • 433 EMPEDOCLES II   141
    AND APOLLO BROUGHT HIS LYRE • • • • • • 433 EMPEDOCLES II   142
    BROUGHT FROM THAT ANTERIOR AGE • • • • • 456 POOR MATTHIAS   148
    HOME WE BROUGHT HIM YOUNG AND FAIR • • • • 458 POOR MATTHIAS   196
    SIX YEARS AGO I BROUGHT HIM DOWN • • • • 459 KAISER DEAD   13
    THE STRONG BLAST BROUGHT A PIGMY THRONG • • 479 HAYSWATER BOAT   19
    WHAT LIVING HAND HATH BROUGHT IT HERE • • • 480 HAYSWATER BOAT   40
    THEN THE DOOR OPENS AND THIS CARD IS BROUGHT • 485 S S LUSITANIA   13

BROW
    FIND THEIR SOLE SPEECH IN THAT VICTORIOUS BROW • • 3 SHAKESPEARE   14
    FIND THEIR SOLE VOICE IN THAT VICTORIOUS BROW • • 3 SHAKESPEARE V 14

BROW
    (CONTINUED)
IT MAY BE BUT NOT LESS HIS BROW WAS SMOOTH • • • •   12 MYCERINUS   112
ON HIS BROW AN ANGRY FROWN • • • • • • •   14 CHURCH BROU 1   48
THE SMOOTHNESS OF THAT LIMPID BROW • • • • • •   21 YOUTH AND CALM   4
BECAUSE ON ITS HOT BROW THERE BLOWS • • • • •   21 YOUTH AND CALM   11
FLITTING FAST ACROSS EACH MARBLE BROW • • • •   31 NEW SIRENS   162
ROSES FOR THAT DREAMING BROW • • • • • • •   32 NEW SIRENS   174
FALL ON THE THROBBING BROW FALL ON THE BURNING BREAST   36 VOICE   15
WHO MASSD ROUND THAT SLIGHT BROW THESE CLOUDS OF DOOM   41 GIPSY CHILD   4
AH WHAT TROUBLES ON HIS BROW • • • • • • • •   137 TRISTRAM 1   227
LIGHTENS EVERY OTHER BROW • • • • • • • •   138 TRISTRAM 1   262
RIDE DOWN AND BATHE MY HOT BROW IN THE FLOOD • •   139 TRISTRAM 1   282
FAR HENCE HER DREAMS ARE FAIR SMOOTH IS HER BROW • •   139 TRISTRAM 1   302
ROUND EACH SWEET BROW THE CAP CLOSE-SET • • •   141 TRISTRAM 1   340
WHAT THOU THINKST THIS ACHING BROW WAS COOLER • •   143 TRISTRAM 2   43
THE SWEET EXPRESSION OF HER BROW • • • • • •   147 TRISTRAM 2   138
THEIR CHEEKS WERE FLUSHD AND OVER EACH HOT BROW • •   150 TRISTRAM 3   32
MERLIN AND VIVIAN STOPPD ON THE SLOPES BROW • •   155 TRISTRAM 3   201
UPON THE BROW-TOP GREW A THORN AND HERE • • •   155 TRISTRAM 3   205
THEIR CHEEKS GREW FLUSHD AND OVER EACH HOT BROW • •   TRISTRAM 3   V 32
OF STARTLED PLEASURE FLOODS THY BROW • • • • •   184 TERRACE BERNE   14
AND PART MY HAIR AND KISS MY BROW • • • • •   209 LONGING   11
THERE IS NO EFFORT ON MY BROW • • • • • • •   241 MORALITY   25
AND GAIND THE WHITE BROW OF THE CUMNER RANGE • •   259 SCHOLAR-GIPSY   127
THE FRINGES OF A SOUTHWARD-FACING BROW • • •   262 SCHOLAR-GIPSY   235
AND RELAX PLUTOS BROW • • • • • • • • •   265 THYRSIS   86
AND UNBEND PLUTOS BROW • • • • • • • •   265 THYRSIS   V 86
WITH GENTLE VOICE AND BROW • • • • • • •   273 EDW QUILLINAN   18
OF FINISTERES UNQUIET BROW • • • • • • •   274 STANZAS CARNAC   36
THAT COMELY FACE THAT CLUSTERD BROW • • • •   279 SOUTHERN NIGHT   125
GRATEFULLY COLD ON THIS BROW • • • • • • •   283 HAWORTH CHURCH   V
WEARINESS NOT ON YOUR BROW • • • • • • •   292 RUGBY CHAPEL   195
SILENT WHILE YEARS ENGRAVE THE BROW • • • •   302 GRANDE CHARTR   113
WITH HOPE EXTINCT AND BROW COMPOSED • • • •   322 OBERMANN MORE   297
A GOLDEN CIRCLET ON HER QUEENLY BROW • • • •   331 MEROPE   58
HUNTER OERSHADOWING HIS BROW • • • • • • •   342 MEROPE   396
DIED OF A SNAKE-BITE SAID HE ON THAT BROW • • •   357 MEROPE   781
HIS FLOWING LOCKS AND GOLD-ENCIRCLED BROW • • •   408 EMPEDOCLES I 1   60
HOW HIS BROW LIGHTEND AS THE MUSIC ROSE • • •   428 EMPEDOCLES I 2   483
THE BROW UNBOUND THE THOUGHTS FLOW FREE AGAIN • •   436 EMPEDOCLES II   246
THAT TROUBLOUS NIGHT IS OVER ON THE BROW • • •   468 ALARIC AT ROME   151
LIKE ISLES OF SUNLIGHT ON A MOUNTAINS BROW • • •   475 CROMWELL   127
WORN WAS HIS BROW WITH CARES NO THOUGHT COULD SCAN   476 CROMWELL   155
AND DEATHS COLD DEWS BEDIMMD HIS EARNEST BROW • •   476 CROMWELL   170
THAT BROW SO SAD SO PALE SO FULL OF CARE • • • •   477 CROMWELL   183

BROWD
THE LOW-BROWD CAVERN-ARCH AND DISAPPEAR • • • •   358 MEROPE   834

BROWN
ON THE BROWN RUDE-CARVED BALCONY TWO FORMS • • •   25 DREAM   21
THOUGH THE LOCKS ARE YET BROWN ON HIS NOBLE HEAD • •   130 TRISTRAM 1   10
NOR TO THE BROWN HEATHS ROUND THEM BRIGHT AND WIDE   151 TRISTRAM 3   49
HAD LOOSEND THE BROWN LOCKS OF VIVIANS HAIR • •   154 TRISTRAM 3   168
AND FROM HER BROWN-LOCKD HEAD THE WIMPLE THROWS • •   156 TRISTRAM 3   216
NOR TO THE BROWN HEATHS ROUND THEM WARM AND WIDE • •   TRISTRAM 3   V 49
HAD LOOSEND THE BROWN CURLS OF VIVIANS HAIR • •   154 TRISTRAM 3   V 168
BROWN IN THE GARDEN OF THE TUILERIES • • • • •   167 RACHEL 1   V 2
BROWN WITH SEPTEMBER DROOPD THE CHESTNUT-TREES • •   167 RACHEL 1   V 3
THE CLEAR-BROWN SHALLOW POOLS • • • • • •   190 STRAYED REVEL   147
SHAKE LOOSE SOME BAND OF SOFT BROWN HAIR • • •   205 CALAIS SANDS   16
SHAKE BACK THY BANDS OF SOFT BROWN HAIR • • •   205 CALAIS SANDS   V 16
SHAKE LOOSE SOME LOCK OF SOFT BROWN HAIR • • •   205 CALAIS SANDS   V 16
WITH THE GREY EYES AND THE LOVELY BROWN HAIR • •   206 SEPARATION   16
WHILE THE LOCKS ARE YET BROWN ON THY HEAD • • •   235 YOUTH OF MAN   112
THE BROWN THRUSH CROSSES OVERHEAD   KENSINGTON GARD   V 11
THE CHEEK GROWN THIN THE BROWN HAIR SPRENT WITH GREY   266 THYRSIS   135
DROOPS ALL HIS SHEENY BROWN DEEP-FEATHERD NECK • •   431 EMPEDOCLES II   76
WITH LONG PLUMES AND SOFT BROWN SEEDS • • • •   434 EMPEDOCLES II   175
WE STROKE THY BROAD BROWN PAWS AGAIN • • • • •   451 GEISTS GRAVE   45
ROVER WITH THE GOOD BROWN HEAD • • • • • •   453 POOR MATTHIAS   25
ROUND HIS SMALL THROAT OF BLACK AND BROWN • • •   459 KAISER DEAD   15

BROWND
BROWND WITH THINE OPEN-AIR FREE HUNTERS LIFE • •   373 MEROPE   1164

BROWS
AND YOUR BROWS WERE STARRD WITH DEW • • • • •   29 NEW SIRENS   100
ACROSS THE SHAGGY BROWS OF TRISTRAMS HOUND • • •   152 TRISTRAM 3   88
CROWNING THEIR BROWS WITH ITS LIGHT • • • • • •   232 YOUTH OF MAN   20

BROWSING
MOVE BROWSING UP THE GRAY-WALLD LANE • • • • •   55 RESIGNATION   121

BRUISED
THAT THEY FLEW THICK AND BRUISED HIM SORE • • • •   91 SICK KING BOKH   122

BRUITED
BUT A DARK RUMOUR WILL BE BRUITED UP • • • • •   79 SOHRAB RUSTUM   596

BRUSH
    QUICK THROUGH THE OLEANDERS BRUSH   • • • • •   184 TERRACE BERNE   15
    COWLD FORMS BRUSH BY IN GLEAMING WHITE   • • • •   300 GRANDE CHARTR   36

BRUSHD
    SO HODER BRUSHD BY HERMODS SIDE AND SAID   101 BALDER DEAD 1   235
    HE SPAKE AND BRUSHD SOFT BY AND DISAPPEARD • • • •   102 BALDER DEAD 1   239
    BRUSHD OFF THE BLOOM FROM THEIR SOUL • • • • • •   233 YOUTH OF MAN   42

BRUSHES
    BRUSHES ACROSS A TIRED TRAVELLERS FACE   • • • •   101 BALDER DEAD 1   231

BRUSHING
    WITH A FREE ONWARD IMPULSE BRUSHING THROUGH   • •   261 SCHOLAR-GIPSY   213

BRUSHWOOD
    WENT STRAINING THROUGH THE CRACKLING BRUSHWOOD DOWN   106 BALDER DEAD 2   62
    THEY CAME TO WHERE THE BRUSHWOOD CEASED AND DAY • •   155 TRISTRAM 3   185
    AND THROUGH THE BRUSHWOOD TO THE PEBBLY STRAND • •   357 MEROPE   807
    CROUCH IN THE BRUSHWOOD TILL THE MULES HAVE PASSD   411 EMPEDOCLES I 1   166

BRUTAL
    TAUGHT ARRIAN WHEN VESPASIANS BRUTAL SON • • • •   2 TO A FRIEND   7
    WE LEAVE THE BRUTAL WORLD TO TAKE ITS WAY • • • •   172 IMMORTALITY   2

BRUTES
    LET GODS MEN BRUTES BEWEEP HIM PLANTS AND STONES • •   111 BALDER DEAD 2   238
    LET GODS MEN BRUTES BEWEEP HIM PLANTS AND STONES • •   114 BALDER DEAD 3   44
    LIVE WE LIKE BRUTES OUR LIFE WITHOUT A PLAN • •   171 BETTER PART   8

BRYNS
    OR WITH PEN-BRYNS BOLD BARD PURSUES • • • • • •   458 KAISER DEAD   5

BUBBLED
    COLD BUBBLED THE SPRING OF TILPHUSA • • • • • •   229 YOUTH OF NATURE   36

BUBBLES
    THE SPRING THAT BUBBLES UP BY HELAS THRONE • • • •   108 BALDER DEAD 2   131

BUBBLING
    COLD-BUBBLING SPRINGS OR CAVES NOT SO THE SOUL • •   6 GEO CRUIKSHANK   9
    BY MIDNIGHT TO A BUBBLING FOUNTAINS SOUND • • •   70 SOHRAB RUSTUM   317

BUCKLERS
    AND BUCKLERS CLASH AND SPEARS BEGIN TO POUR • •   127 BALDER DEAD 3   498

BUDDED
    BUT LO THE STAFF IT BUDDED • • • • • • • •   160 NECKAN   53

BUDGE
    AND SCARCELY WILL THEY BUDGE A YARD O PAN • • • •   406 EMPEDOCLES I 1   5

BUFFETING
    OF BUFFETING WIND AND SURGING TIDE • • • • • •   140 TRISTRAM 1   331

BUGLE
    ON AUTUMN-MORNINGS WHEN THE BUGLE SOUNDS • • • •   18 CHURCH BROU 3   9
    BY NIGHT WITH BOISTEROUS BUGLE-PEAL • • • • •   148 TRISTRAM 2   177
    THEN HUSH THOU BOISTEROUS BUGLE-PEAL • • • • •   149 TRISTRAM 2   182
    THY GOLDEN-TASSELLD BUGLE BLOW • • • • • •   149 TRISTRAM 2   188
    FAINT BUGLE-NOTES FROM FAR ARE BORNE • • • • •   305 GRANDE CHARTR   182
    THAT BUGLE-MUSIC ON THE BREEZE • • • • • • •   305 GRANDE CHARTR   189
    BANNER BY TURNS AND BUGLE WOO • • • • • • •   305 GRANDE CHARTR   191

BUGLES
    HUNTERS GATHER BUGLES RING • • • • • • • •   13 CHURCH BROU 1   16
    PASS BANNERS PASS AND BUGLES CEASE • • • • • •   306 GRANDE CHARTR   209

BUILD
    WE WILL BUILD THE CHURCH AGAIN • • • • • • •   15 CHURCH BROU 1   76
    TO BUILD THEM BOATS FISH FROM THE FLOODED RIVERS • •   73 SOHRAB RUSTUM   411
    IN VAIN HATH A KING POWER TO BUILD • • • •   94 SICK KING BOKH   198
    AND ON THE DECK BUILD HIGH A FUNERAL-PILE • • •   96 BALDER DEAD 1   42
    TO GATHER WOOD AND BUILD A FUNERAL-PILE • • •   103 BALDER DEAD 1   296
    WHEN YE ENOUGH HAVE WEPT THEN BUILD A PILE • •   115 BALDER DEAD 3   53
    HEAP ON THE DECK THE LOGS AND BUILD THE PYRE • •   118 BALDER DEAD 3   159
    BUT OF HIS FLESH AND MEMBERS THOU DIDST BUILD • •   121 BALDER DEAD 3   260
    AND ASGARD THOU DIDST BUILD AND MIDGARD FORT • •   121 BALDER DEAD 3   266
    I AM DYING BUILD THOU MAYST MY GRAVE • • • • •   142 TRISTRAM 2   12
    AND THE SEA-EAGLES BUILD THEIR NEST • • • • •   414 EMPEDOCLES I 2   67
    THERE BUILD WE THEE O GUARDIAN DEAR • • • • •   452 GEISTS GRAVE   71

BUILDED
    HATH BUILDED ON THE WASTE IN FORMER YEARS • • •   71 SOHRAB RUSTUM   338
    HAS BUILDED ON THE WASTE IN FORMER YEARS • • •   71 SOHRAB RUSTUM   V 338
    HATH BUILDED ON THE WASTE IN FORMER DAYS • • •   71 SOHRAB RUSTUM   V 338
    HAS BUILDED ON THE WASTE IN FORMER DAYS • • •   71 SOHRAB RUSTUM   V 338
    BEFORE THE HEAVENS WERE BUILDED THOU DIDST SLAY • •   121 BALDER DEAD 3   256

```
BUILDERS
      STANDS AS ERST THE BUILDERS LEFT IT      • • • • •      15 CHURCH BROU 1       69
      THERE SHE SATE AND WATCHD THE BUILDERS      • • • •      16 CHURCH BROU 1      101
      LAST OF ALL THE BUILDERS REARD HER      • • • • • •      16 CHURCH BROU 1      103

BUILDEST
      WHEREON THOU BUILDEST SUCH A GOODLY PRIDE      • • • •      RUDE ORATOR         8

BUILDING
      BUT SHE DIED WHILE IT WAS BUILDING      • • • • • •      14 CHURCH BROU 1       67
      BUT SHE DIED AS IT WAS BUILDING      • • • • • • •      14 CHURCH BROU 1   V   67

BUILDS
      NEAR LYCOSURA BUILDS LYCAONS TOWN      • • • • • •      359 MEROPE            848
      AND BUILDS HIMSELF I KNOW NOT WHAT      • • • • • •      450 GEISTS GRAVE      31

BUILT
      BACKD BY THE PINES A PLANK-BUILT COTTAGE STOOD      • •      25 DREAM           15
      WHERE FAITHS ARE BUILT ON DUST      • • • • • • •      39 STAGIRIUS           45
      THE TARTARS BUILT THERE PERAN-WISAS TENT      • • •      61 SOHRAB RUSTUM      22
      WHICH HE IN ASGARD BUILT HIM THERE TO DWELL      • •      101 BALDER DEAD 1    224
      TO THE HALL GLADHEIM WHICH IS BUILT OF GOLD      • •      106 BALDER DEAD 2     36
      OF ODIN AND MY HIGH-ROOFD HOUSE IS BUILT      • • •      108 BALDER DEAD 2    113
      THE WOOD TO BALDERS SHIP AND BUILT A PILE      • • •      118 BALDER DEAD 3    161
      FROM HER LONELY SHORE-BUILT TOWER      • • • • •      131 TRISTRAM 1           43
      INLAND OR BUILT      • • • • • • • • •      189 STRAYED REVEL               127
      ON THE PURE COLUMNS OF ITS GLEN-BUILT HALL      • • •      236 PALLADIUM         6
      ALL WE HAVE BUILT DO WE DISCERN      • • • • •      241 MORALITY              12
      BY BARN IN THRESHING-TIME BY NEW-BUILT RICK      • •      263 THYRSIS           34
      THERE ON ITS SLOPE IS BUILT      • • • • • • •      283 HAWORTH CHURCH        61
      HERE NO SEPULCHRE BUILT      • • • • • • • •      294 HEINES GRAVE           56
      O STENYCLAROS WHICH HE BUILT AND MADE      • • •      330 MEROPE              10
      SO WOULD HAVE BUILT YOU IN A FEW SHORT YEARS      • •      339 MEROPE          304
      IN THE TEMPLE-BUILT GORGE      • • • • • • •      345 MEROPE                464
      STILL AT HIS MOUNTAIN-TOMB MEN MARVEL BUILT      • •      357 MEROPE          782
      PAST EXPECTATION HATH THY MURDERER BUILT      • • •      386 MEROPE          1435
      FROM THE OAK-BUILT FIERCELY-BURNING PYRE      • • •      399 MEROPE          1827
      BUILT IN STRENGTH AGAINST THE VANQUISHD      • • •      400 MEROPE          1854
      YE WITNESS YE NEW-BUILT TOWERS      • • • • • •      400 MEROPE            1856

BULL
      THE FLOWER-DRESSD VICTIM STOOD A MILK-WHITE BULL      • •      401 MEROPE      1910

BULRUSH
      AND AS THE SWALLOWS CROWD THE BULRUSH-BEDS      • • •      109 BALDER DEAD 2    157
      AND TO EACH BULRUSH-CREST A SWALLOW HANGS      • • •      109 BALDER DEAD 2    160
      THEY MOORD THEIR BOATS AMONG THE BULRUSH STEMS      • •      444 WESTMIN ABBEY   18

BULWARKS
      TWICE FROM WITHOUT THY BULWARKS HATH THE DIN      • •      465 ALARIC AT ROME    79

BUOYANT
      BUOYANT AS MORNING AND AS MORNING CLEAR      • • •      175 PARTING             18
      OF THY BUOYANT CHEERFULNESS CLEAR      • • • • •      287 RUGBY CHAPEL         22
      BUOYANT AND FRESH THE MOUNTAIN FLOWERS      • • •      426 EMPEDOCLES I 2      433
      AND GLADSOME GREETINGS OF THE BUOYANT SEA      • • •      472 CROMWELL           8
      CHILLD EVERY BUOYANT HOPE THAT FLOATED BY      • • •      474 CROMWELL          88

BURDEN
      COULD BEAR THE BURDEN OF HIS YEARS      • • • • •      92 SICK KING BOKH      146
      WAS INDEED THE HEAVIEST BURDEN THROWN      • • •      144 TRISTRAM 2           50
      WE BEAR THE BURDEN AND THE HEAT      • • • • •      241 MORALITY              9
      THE BURDEN OF OURSELVES      • • • • • • • •      416 EMPEDOCLES I 2         128

BURGHERS
      BURGHERS AND DAMES AT SUMMERS PRIME      • • • • •      17 CHURCH BROU 2        20

BURIAL
      HER COURSE FOR HOME AT LAST AND BURIAL      • • • •      173 MONICAS PRAYER     7

BURIED
      LOOKS LANGUIDLY ROUND ON A GLOOM-BURIED WORLD      • •      20 MODERN SAPPHO     24
      UP COLD AISLES OF BURIED GLADE      • • • • • • •      32 NEW SIRENS          180
      IS BOWD HALF-BURIED ON THE BED      • • • • • • •      146 TRISTRAM 2         106
      THE BURIED STREAM AND SEEM TO BE      • • • • •      246 BURIED LIFE          42
      AFTER THE KNOWLEDGE OF OUR BURIED LIFE      • • •      246 BURIED LIFE          48
      THY DEAR WIFES ASHES BURIED ARE      • • • • •      277 SOUTHERN NIGHT       51
      BURIED I KNEW HE WAS YOURS      • • • • • • •      294 HEINES GRAVE          54
      IS BURIED IN HIS COWL ONCE MORE      • • • • •      300 GRANDE CHARTR        44
      BURIED A WAVE BENEATH      • • • • • • • •      308 OBERMANN               74
      LAY IN THY SON IS BURIED IN HIS GRAVE      • • •      394 MEROPE            1694
      TO OUR OWN ONLY TRUE DEEP-BURIED SELVES      • • •      440 EMPEDOCLES II      371
      BEHIND A BURIED VALE DOTH SLEEP      • • • • •      479 HAYSWATER BOAT        9

BURN
      THEIR PASSION BURN MORE ERE IT CEASES TO BURN      • •      19 MODERN SAPPHO     14
      THEIR PASSION BURN MORE ERE IT CEASES TO BURN      • •      19 MODERN SAPPHO     14
      SO SHALL IT BE FOR I WILL BURN MY TENTS      • • •      84 SOHRAB RUSTUM       797
      TO BURN FOR THAT IS WHAT THE DEAD DESIRE      • •      96 SOHRAB RUSTUM        45
      UPON MY SHIP AND BURN MY CORPSE WITH FIRE      • •      103 BALDER DEAD 1      297
      THEY THINK TO BURN AND ALL MY CHOICEST WEALTH      • •      103 BALDER DEAD 1    299
```

BURN   (CONTINUED)
        AND THEY SHALL BURN THY CORPSE WITH MINE NOT THEE   103 BALDER DEAD 1   304
        ON THE TWELFTH DAY THE GODS SHALL BURN HIS CORPSE   106 BALDER DEAD 2   44
        OF THE HEAPD WOOD AND BURN HIS CORPSE WITH FIRE   • • 115 BALDER DEAD 3   54
        AND STILL THEY LIVE AND STILL THEY BURN   • • • •   224 EPILOG LAOCOON   104
        THE CRACKLING HUSK-HEAPS BURN AS IF   • • • • • • 312 OBERMANN MORE   11
        THEIR CRACKLING HUSK-HEAPS BURN AS IF   • • • • •   312 OBERMANN MORE   V 11
        DID EVER BURN IS LONG BY TIME ALLAYD • • • • • •   387 MEROPE   1471
        FEAR NOT BUT THAT THY LIGHT ONCE MORE SHALL BURN • •   449 WESTMIN ABBEY   174

BURND
        IN THESE LAST DAYS THE SUN HATH BURND   • • • •   89 SICK KING BOKH   59
        BUT FAINTER AS THE STARS ROSE HIGH IT BURND   • •   119 BALDER DEAD 3   V 201

BURNING
        FADED THE MOSS THE ROCKS US BURNING PLAINS • • • •   25 DREAM   36
        WILL IT WEEP OUR BURNING TEARS • • • • • • • •   29 NEW SIRENS   86
        STARS SET DEEP YET INLY BURNING • • • • • • •   30 NEW SIRENS   137
        FALL ON THE THROBBING BROW FALL ON THE BURNING BREAST   36 VOICE   15
        AT BURNING NOON SO WARRIORS SAID   • • • • • •   52 RESIGNATION   4
        AND BURNING DUST AGAIN I CREEP • • • • • • • •   90 SICK KING BOKH   75
        MY HEAD IS BURNING AND A HEAT • • • • • • • •   93 SICK KING BOKH   183
        BUT THROUGH THE DARK THEY WATCHD THE BURNING SHIP   119 BALDER DEAD 3   197
        UPON THE CLIFFS OR SMOKE OF BURNING WEEDS   • • • • 124 BALDER DEAD 3   362
        AND HIS BURNING FEVER-PAIN   • • • • • • • •   136 TRISTRAM 1   182
        ITS STORMS OF DUST WITH BURNING HEAT   • • • • •   157 SAINT BRANDAN   44
        I STANCH WITH ICE MY BURNING BREAST   • • • • •   158 SAINT BRANDAN   69
        NOR DID THERE NEED LESS THAN THE BURNING PILE   • •   198 FRAG ANTIGONE   98
        FROM THE OAK-BUILT FIERCELY-BURNING PYRE   • • • • 399 MEROPE   1827

BURNISHD
        WHILE THE DEEP-BURNISHD FOLIAGE OVERHEAD   • • • •   11 MYCERINUS   98
        UNDER THEIR BURNISHD SYCAMORES • • • • • • • •   54 RESIGNATION   57
        MARSHALLD BATTALIONS BRIGHT IN BURNISHD STEEL   • •   65 SOHRAB RUSTUM   140
        WITH THE CLASP OF BURNISHD GOLD • • • • • • •   131 TRISTRAM 1   28
        WARM WITH THE WINTER-SUN OF BURNISHD GREEN   • • •   150 TRISTRAM 3   21
        UNDER THE BURNISHD HOLLIES ISEULT STANDS   • • •   TRISTRAM 3   V 23

BURNOUS
        AND WHITER THAN THY WHITE BURNOUS   • • • • • •   276 SOUTHERN NIGHT   43

BURNS
        STRONGLY SETS AND TRULY BURNS   • • • • • • •   49 SECOND BEST   24
        STRONGLY STIRS AND TRULY BURNS   • • • • • • •   49 SECOND BEST   V 24
        DEEPLY STIRS AND TRULY BURNS • • • • • • • •   SECOND BEST   V 24
        RATHER THAT HEART WHICH BURNS IN THEE   • • • •   59 RESIGNATION   241
        A FEVER IN THESE PAGES BURNS • • • • • • • •   307 OBERMANN   21
        BURNS EVER UNCONSUMED   • • • • • • • • • •   424 EMPEDOCLES I 2   370

BURNT
        THEY STRAIGHTWAY ARE BURNT UP WITH FUME AND CARE • • 153 TRISTRAM 3   139

BURST
        AND THE BURST OF JOYFUL GREETINGS   • • • • • • • 30 NEW SIRENS   117
        AND BURST THEIR ROOTS WHILE TO THEIR TOPS THE GODS   106 BALDER DEAD 2   57
        YET HE SHALL ONE DAY RISE AND BURST HIS BONDS   • •   111 BALDER DEAD 2   222
        A CLOUD OF DESERT ROBBER-HORSE HAVE BURST   • • •   193 STRAYED REVEL   248
        A CLOUD OF DESERT ROBBER-HORSE HAS BURST   • • •   193 STRAYED REVEL   V 248
        HARK FROM THAT MOONLIT CEDAR WHAT A BURST   • • •   200 PHILOMELA   3
        WHEN THE YEARS PRIMAL BURST OF BLOOM IS OER   • •   264 THYRSIS   52
        BURST OER THE ALTAR AND THE DORIAN LORDS   • • • • 402 MEROPE   1938
        EVEN IN THE ACT TO BURST TWICE THREATENED TWICE   465 ALARIC AT ROME   84
            DELAYED
        WHO WOULD NOT BURST HIS BONDS AND IN HIS TURN BE FREE   465 ALARIC AT ROME   90

BURSTING
        WHEN BURSTING THROUGH THE NETWORK SUPERPOSED   • •   7 REP FRIEND CONT   10
        SWELL THEIR LARGE VEINS TO BURSTING IN WILD PAIN • • 192 STRAYED REVEL   226
        THUNDERING AND BURSTING • • • • • • • • • •   220 BACCHANALIA 2   29
        GREEN BURSTING FIGS AND TUNNIES STEEPD IN BRINE   • • 262 SCHOLAR-GIPSY   239
        O THAT MY OVER-SPEED AND BURSTING GRIEF   • • • •   362 MEROPE   939
        JARRD WITH THE BURSTING SHOUT THEY COME THE   467 ALARIC AT ROME   132
            GOTH THEY COME

BURSTS
        HOW THICK THE BURSTS COME CROWDING THROUGH THE LEAVES 201 PHILOMELA   29
        THE LIGHTNING-BURSTS IS SEEN   • • • • • • • •   244 SUMMER NIGHT   63
        THESE ANGRY SMOKE-BURSTS • • • • • • • • • •   432 EMPEDOCLES II   96
        THROUGH THE BLACK RUSHING SMOKE-BURSTS   • • • •   441 EMPEDOCLES II   417
        BURSTS IN MAJESTIC BEAUTY ON HER CONQUERORS EYES • • 468 ALARIC AT ROME   156

BURWOOD
        AND GLORY STRETCHD AT BURWOOD GATE   • • • • • • 461 KAISER DEAD   73

BURY
        O VIZIER I MAY BURY HIM • • • • • • • • • •   88 SICK KING BOKH   21
        BECAUSE A KING SHALL BURY HIM • • • • • • • •   95 SICK KING BOKH   232

BURYING
        BURYING THEIR UNSUNND STEMS IN GRASS AND FLOWERS • •   11 MYCERINUS   88
        ROBBING HERSELF OF LIFE IN BURYING   • • • • • • 196 FRAG ANTIGONE   40

BUSH
PITCH THEIR SMOKED TENTS AND EVERY BUSH YOU SEE • • 258 SCHOLAR-GIPSY 113
THE WHITE FOG CREEPS FROM BUSH TO BUSH ABOUT • • 267 THYRSIS 162
THE WHITE FOG CREEPS FROM BUSH TO BUSH ABOUT • • 267 THYRSIS 162
FROM BUSH TO BUSH THE CUCKOO FLIES • • • • • 274 STANZAS CARNAC 17
FROM BUSH TO BUSH THE CUCKOO FLIES • • • • • 274 STANZAS CARNAC 17

BUSINESS
BUSINESS COULD NOT MAKE DULL NOR PASSION WILD • • 2 TO A FRIEND 11
AND TO MENS BUSINESS NOT TOO NEAR • • • • • 59 RESIGNATION 250
THE BUSINESS OF THE DAY IS DONE • • • • • 218 BACCHANALIA 1 8
THOU HADST ONE AIM ONE BUSINESS ONE DESIRE • • • • 259 SCHOLAR-GIPSY 152
OUR BUSINESS WITH UNSLACKENING STRIDE • • • • 277 SOUTHERN NIGHT 65
OF MECHANIC BUSINESS AND LETS • • • • • • • 295 HEINES GRAVE 82
NEWS OF MY BUSINESS PASTIME TEMPER FRIENDS • • • • 380 MEROPE 1281

BUSTARD
AND THE SPRINGING BUSTARD-FOWL • • • • • • • 191 STRAYED REVEL 174

BUSTLE
AND GLANCE AND NOD AND BUSTLE BY • • • • • • 277 SOUTHERN NIGHT 70

BUSY
FOR THEM FOR ALL TIMES BUSY TOUCH • • • • • • 56 RESIGNATION 126
ARE BUSY GATHERING SPARS OF QUARTZ AND STREAMS • • 150 TRISTRAM 3 25
KAIS BRACELET TAIL KAIS BUSY FEET • • • • • • 459 KAISER DEAD 7
BUSY FOR PRIAMS FAME AND MY OWN IN SPITE OF THE FUTURE HOMER TRANS 19

BUTTERCUPS
BUTTERCUPS CLOVER DAISIES GRASS • • • • • • • KENSINGTON GARD V 15

BUTTERFLIES
THE BUTTERFLIES AGAIN • • • • • • • • • • 141 TRISTRAM 1 348

BYGONE
THOSE LUTE-LIKE TONES WHICH IN THE BYGONE YEAR • • 36 VOICE 35
OF BYGONE AUTUMNS WITH THEE • • • • • • • • 287 RUGBY CHAPEL 25

BYRON
TWAS NOT THE THOUGHT OF BYRON OF HIS CRY • • • 166 PICT NEWSTEAD 2
DARING SINCE BYRON DIED • • • • • • • • • 284 HAWORTH CHURCH 96
WHAT HELPS IT NOW THAT BYRON BORE • • • • • 303 GRANDE CHARTR 133
AND WALLS WHERE BYRON CAME • • • • • • • • 313 OBERMANN MORE 24
AND BYRON LET US DARE ADMIRE • • • • • • • 482 COURAGE 17

BYRONS
WAS WOE THAN BYRONS WOE MORE TRAGIC FAR • • • 167 PICT NEWSTEAD 14
LONG SINCE SAW BYRONS STRUGGLE CEASE • • • • • 270 MEMORIAL VERSES 2
WHEN BYRONS EYES WERE SHUT IN DEATH • • • • • 270 MEMORIAL VERSES 6
GOETHES SAGE MIND AND BYRONS FORCE • • • • • 272 MEMORIAL VERSES 61

BYSTANDER
TO MAKE THE INCURIOUS BYSTANDER INTENT • • • • 8 RELIGIOUS ISOL 3

CABAL
STUPID DETRACTION JEALOUSY CABAL • • • • • • 199 EARLY DEATH 5

CABIND
HER CABIND AMPLE SPIRIT • • • • • • • • • 21 REQUIESCAT 13

CABOOL
BUT AS A TROOP OF PEDLARS FROM CABOOL • • • • 65 SOHRAB RUSTUM 160

CADENCE
WITH TREMULOUS CADENCE SLOW AND BRING • • • • 211 DOVER BEACH 13
WITH REGULAR CADENCE SLOW AND BRING • • • • • • 211 DOVER BEACH V 13
WITH MOURNFUL CADENCE SLOW AND BRING • • • • • • 211 DOVER BEACH V 13
WITH SOLEMN CADENCE ROUND HER CITADEL • • • • 472 CROMWELL 20

CADMUS
WHO ONCE WERE CADMUS AND HARMONIA • • • • • • 427 EMPEDOCLES I 2 436

CAESAR
LIKE THAT BALD CAESAR THE FAMED ROMAN WIGHT • • 153 TRISTRAM 3 143
LIKE THAT BOLD CAESAR THE FAMED ROMAN WIGHT • • 153 TRISTRAM 3 V 143
SOLDIERS LIKE CAESAR • • • • • • • • • 220 BACCHANALIA 2 55
SCENES WHERE A CAESAR TRIUMPHT OR A SCIPIO TROD • • 466 ALARIC AT ROME 114

CAGE •
SIT FOR HOURS BESIDE THY CAGE • • • • • • • 453 POOR MATTHIAS 32

CAGES
FIELDS WHERE SOFT SHEEP FROM CAGES PULL THE HAY • • 268 THYRSIS 198
FIELDS WHERE THE SHEEP FROM CAGES PULL THE HAY • • 268 THYRSIS V 198

CAKE
CAKE WE OFFERD SUGAR SEED • • • • • • • • 455 POOR MATTHIAS 115

CAKED
THE BIG WARM TEARS ROLLD DOWN AND CAKED THE SAND • • 82 SOHRAB RUSTUM 736

CAKES
    A SIDE OF ROASTED SHEEP AND CAKES OF BREAD • • • •   67 SOHRAB RUSTUM   198
    LAY HONEY-CAKES ON ITS MARGE • • • • • • • • •   342 MEROPE   386
    SWEET CHESTNUTS BARLEY-CAKES AND BOARS-FLESH DRIED   356 MEROPE   754

CALAIS
    TO CALAIS GLITTERING IN THE SUN • • • • • •   204 CALAIS SANDS   4
    OER CALAIS AND ITS FAMOUS PLAIN • • • • • •   205 CALAIS SANDS   18
    TO CALAIS SPARKLING IN THE SUN • • • • • • •   204 CALAIS SANDS   V   4
    ON CALAIS AND ITS SHINING PLAIN • • • • • •   205 CALAIS SANDS   V 18

CALAMITY
    RACE OF CALAMITY MINE • • • • • • • • • •   370 MEROPE   1108
    O SUFFERING O CALAMITY HOW TEN • • • • • • •   385 MEROPE   1406
    IN THEBES THE BILLOW OF CALAMITY • • • • •   427 EMPEDOCLES I 2   445
    BACK TO THIS MEADOW OF CALAMITY • • • • •   440 EMPEDOCLES II   365

CALL
    WE HAVE LOST THEM AT YOUR CALL • • • • • • • •   27 NEW SIRENS   38
    AND CALL THIS HURRYING FEVER GENEROUS FIRE • • • •   37 YOUTHS AGIT   12
    SOHRAB MEN CALL HIM BUT HIS BIRTH IS HID • • •   67 SOHRAB RUSTUM   214
    TRYING TO CALL HIM BACK TO LIFE AND LIFE • • • •   81 SOHRAB RUSTUM   697
    BY CHILDREN WHOM THEIR NURSES CALL WITH HASTE • •   86 SOHRAB RUSTUM   846
    BY ROMPING CHILDREN WHOM THEIR NURSES CALL • • •   86 SOHRAB RUSTUM   V 846
    NOW MUST I CALL THY GRIEF NOT WISE • • • • •   92 SICK KING BOKH   134
    THEY CALL HER FREYA IS HER NAME IN HEAVEN • • • •   116 BALDER DEAD 3   97
    CALL ON GOD AND ON THE HOLY ANGELS • • • • • •   145 TRISTRAM 2   79
    CALL IT AMBITION OR REMORSE OR LOVE • • • • • •   153 TRISTRAM 3   130
    NOW MY BROTHERS CALL FROM THE BAY • • • • • •   161 FORSAKEN MERM   3
    CALL HER ONCE BEFORE YOU GO • • • • • • • •   161 FORSAKEN MERM   10
    CALL ONCE YET • • • • • • • • • •   161 FORSAKEN MERM   11
    CALL ONCE MORE TO A MOTHERS EAR • • • • • •   161 FORSAKEN MERM   15
    CALL HER ONCE AND COME AWAY • • • • • • • •   162 FORSAKEN MERM   18
    CALL NO MORE • • • • • • • • • • • •   162 FORSAKEN MERM   24
    SHE WILL NOT COME THOUGH YOU CALL ALL DAY • • • •   162 FORSAKEN MERM   28
    CALL YET ONCE THAT SHE WENT AWAY • • • • • •   162 FORSAKEN MERM   49
    COME AWAY CHILDREN CALL NO MORE • • • • • •   164 FORSAKEN MERM   83
    COME AWAY COME DOWN CALL NO MORE • • • • • •   164 FORSAKEN MERM   84
    EVERYWHERE HEARD WILL BE THE JUDGMENT-CALL • • •   173 MONICAS PRAYER   3
    WE SHALL NOT THEN CALL HARDNESS FORCE • • • •   179 FAREWELL   59
    GLADLY THEY RISE AT HIS CALL • • • • • •   216 LORDS MESSENGER   7
    AH YES AND THEY BENUMB US AT OUR CALL • • •   247 BURIED LIFE   71
    GO FOR THEY CALL YOU SHEPHERD FROM THE HILL • •   255 SCHOLAR-GIPSY   1
    AND HOW A CALL CELESTIAL ROUND HIM RANG • • • •   268 THYRSIS   188
    CALL FROM THE HEATHER IN BLOOM • • • • • •   285 HAWORTH CHURCH   122
    OF DEATH AT A CALL UNFORESEEN • • • • • •   287 RUGBY CHAPEL   29
    SHALL I NOT CALL YOU BECAUSE • • • • • • •   291 RUGBY CHAPEL   163
    AND CALL US BUT TOO LATE YE COME • • • • • •   305 GRANDE CHARTR   196
    TOO LATE FOR US YOUR CALL YE BLOW • • • • • •   305 GRANDE CHARTR   197
    WE CALL IT MURDER CRUSH HIM BRAND HIS NAME • • •   336 MEROPE   203
    MURDER LET OTHERS CALL THIS IF THEY WILL • • • •   338 MEROPE   276
    RATHER ON THEE I CALL HUSBAND BELOVED • • • •   349 MEROPE   584
    AND WHAT I COULD I DID TO CALL BY CRIES • • • •   358 MEROPE   835
    HATE DUTY INTEREST PASSION CALL ONE WAY • • • •   383 MEROPE   1382
    MOST HONOURABLY I MEANT I CALL THE GODS • • • •   394 MEROPE   1695
    WHAT MOOD OF SPIRIT THEREFORE SHALL WE CALL • • •   404 MEROPE   1991
    TO TUNES WE DID NOT CALL OUR BEING MUST KEEP CHIME   418 EMPEDOCLES I 2   196
    WHAT WILL RECEIVE THEM WHO WILL CALL THEM HOME • •   439 EMPEDOCLES II   348
    NOW IN VAIN YOU CALL HIS NAME • • • • • • •   452 POOR MATTHIAS   7

CALLD
    CALLD HISTORY KEEPS A SPLENDOUR DUE TO WIT • • •   5 DUKE WELLINGTON   13
    AND RAISED THE CURTAIN OF HIS TENT AND CALLD • •   64 SOHRAB RUSTUM   102
    BUT RUSTUM STRODE TO HIS TENT-DOOR AND CALLD • •   69 SOHRAB RUSTUM   263
    OF RUSTUM I AM HERE WHOM THOU HAST CALLD • • • •   72 SOHRAB RUSTUM   366
    WHO SPOKE ALTHOUGH HE CALLD BACK NAMES HE KNEW • •   79 SOHRAB RUSTUM   606
    AND THEY WHO WERE CALLD CHAMPIONS IN THEIR TIME • •   85 SOHRAB RUSTUM   811
    AND CALLD MY MOTHER AND THEY ALL • • • • • •   90 SICK KING BOKH   80
    O DAMSEL HERMOD AM I CALLD THE SON • • • • • •   108 BALDER DEAD 2   112
    THOK IS SHE CALLD BUT NOW LOK WORE HER SHAPE • •   123 BALDER DEAD 3   335
    AND CALLD HIM BY HIS NAME AND STERNLY SAID • • •   124 BALDER DEAD 3   386
    TRISTRAM ART THOU CALLD FOR THY DEATHS SAKE • • •   145 TRISTRAM 2   86
    THEN ISEULT CALLD THEM TO HER AND THE THREE • • •   150 TRISTRAM 3   35
    MEN CALLD FROM CHAMBER CHURCH AND TENT • • • •   318 OBERMANN MORE   171
    FOLLOWS THE APPROACHING QUEEN WHO STOPS AS CALLD • •   332 MEROPE   64
    HAD TO THIS CITY STENYCLAROS CALLD • • • • •   338 MEROPE   262
    FOLLOWS THE ISSUING QUEEN WHO STOPS AS CALLD • •   332 MEROPE   V 64
    AND WHOM EMPEDOCLES CALLD BACK TO LIFE • • • •   410 EMPEDOCLES I 1   111
    CALLD US TO PET THEE OR TO PRAISE • • • • • •   450 GEISTS GRAVE   7

CALLED
    ABOVE THE FOREST-GROUND CALLED THESSALY • • • •   258 SCHOLAR-GIPSY   115

CALLICLES
    AND TRY THY NOBLEST STRAINS MY CALLICLES • • • •   409 EMPEDOCLES I 1   97
    HARK THERE AGAIN TIS THE BOY CALLICLES • • • •   412 EMPEDOCLES I 2   12
    LISTEN PAUSANIUS AY TIS CALLICLES • • • • •   413 EMPEDOCLES I 2   34
    AND FOR YOUNG CALLICLES THANK HIM FROM ME • • •   428 EMPEDOCLES I 2   467
    CALLICLES MUST WAIT HERE AND PLAY TO HIM • • • •   428 EMPEDOCLES I 2   484

CALLICLES   (CONTINUED)
        JUST SINCE DOWN AT THE STREAM HO CALLICLES   .   .   .   .   428 EMPEDOCLES I 2   486

CALLING
        O YE FALSE ONES AT YOUR CALLING   .   .   .   .   .   .   27 NEW SIRENS   39
        IN CALLING VENGEANCE ON A MURDERERS HEAD   .   .   .   .   348 MEROPE   549
        FRESH BLOOD FLOWS CALLING FOR BLOOD   .   .   .   .   .   .   379 MEROPE   1253
        CUCKOO CALLING FROM THE HILL   .   .   .   .   456 POOR MATTHIAS   141

CALLISTO
        CALLISTO AND HER BOY   .   .   .   .   391 MEROPE   1605
        BUT HIS MOTHER CALLISTO   .   .   .   .   392 MEROPE   1631
        TRANSFORMD CALLISTO   .   .   .   .   393 MEROPE   1659

CALLOW
        HIS PUNY CALLOW EAGLETS AND WHAT TRIALS   .   .   .   .   336 MEROPE   214

CALLS
        IS ILL AT EASE AND CALLS FOR THEE   .   .   .   .   .   .   87 SICK KING BOKH   4
        EACH TO HIS POST WHERE THE OCCASION CALLS   .   .   .   .   386 MEROPE   1441
        O PRINCELY LAIAS TO WHAT PURPOSE CALLS   .   .   .   .   386 MEROPE   1446
        POST-HASTE TO COBHAM CALLS THE MUSE   .   .   .   .   .   .   458 KAISER DEAD   2

CALM
        SAY WHAT SHALL CALM US WHEN SUCH GUESTS INTRUDE   .   .   6 GEO CRUIKSHANK   6
        BUT IS A CALM LIKE THIS IN TRUTH   .   .   .   .   .   .   21 YOUTH AND CALM   5
        CALMS NOT LIFES CROWN THOUGH CALM IS WELL   .   .   .   .   22 YOUTH AND CALM   23
        YET IS A CALM LIKE THIS IN TRUTH   .   .   .   .   .   .   21 YOUTH AND CALM   V   5
        YET AH IS CALM ALONE IN TRUTH   .   .   .   .   21 YOUTH AND CALM   V   5
        IS THE CALM THINE OF STOIC SOULS WHO WEIGH .   .   .   .   42 GIPSY CHILD   29
        THEIR NOBLE CALM   .   .   .   .   50 CONSOLATION   25
        THEN THE WIND FELL WITH NIGHT AND THERE WAS CALM .   .   119 BALDER DEAD 3   196
        MINE EARS ARE STUNND WITH BLOWS AND SICK FOR CALM   .   128 BALDER DEAD 3   508
        THE CALM SEA SHINES LOOSE HANG THE VESSELS SAILS .   .   133 TRISTRAM 1   94
        AH CALM ME RESTORE ME   .   .   .   .   177 PARTING   83
        THE CALM UPON THE MOONLIT SEA   .   .   .   .   180 FAREWELL   80
        SO LET ME LIE AND CALM AS THEY   .   .   .   .   208 ON THE RHINE   16
        THEIR JOY IS IN THEIR CALM   .   .   .   .   208 ON THE RHINE   25
        THE SEA IS CALM TO-NIGHT .   .   .   .   210 DOVER BEACH   1
        MILD AND INSCRUTABLY CALM   .   .   .   .   232 YOUTH OF MAN   10
        CALM ME AH COMPOSE ME TO THE END   .   .   .   .   .   .   240 SELF-DEPENDENCE   8
        AND THE SAME BRIGHT CALM MOON   .   .   .   .   242 SUMMER NIGHT   25
        AND THE CALM MOONLIGHT SEEMS TO SAY   .   .   .   .   .   .   243 SUMMER NIGHT   26
        OF LANGUOR THOUGH SO CALM AND THOUGH SO GREAT   .   .   244 SUMMER NIGHT   79
        AND AN UNWONTED CALM PERVADES HIS BREAST   .   .   .   .   247 BURIED LIFE   95
        CALM SOUL OF ALL THINGS MAKE IT MINE .   .   .   .   .   .   249 KENSINGTON GARD   37
        CALM CALM ME MORE NOR LET ME DIE   .   .   .   .   .   .   249 KENSINGTON GARD   43
        CALM CALM ME MORE NOR LET ME DIE   .   .   .   .   .   .   249 KENSINGTON GARD   43
        BUT HERE THIS CALM IS NOTHING NEW   .   .   .   .   .   .   KENSINGTON GARD V 29
        GONE IS THE CALM OF ITS EARLIER SHORE   .   .   .   .   .   253 FUTURE   52
        MAY ACQUIRE IF NOT THE CALM   .   .   .   .   254 FUTURE   75
        POET AND STEEP HIM IN CALM   .   .   .   .   294 HEINES GRAVE   51
        BENEATH THE CALM THEY FEIGN   .   .   .   .   307 OBERMANN   22
        WORDSWORTHS SWEET CALM OR GOETHES WIDE   .   .   .   .   308 OBERMANN   79
        THEIR MOURNFUL CALM SERENE   .   .   .   .   314 OBERMANN MORE   50
        PEACE PEACE IS WHAT I SEEK AND PUBLIC CALM .   .   .   .   333 MEROPE   101
        BUT CALM BUT UNRESENTFUL I ENDURED   .   .   .   .   .   .   366 MEROPE   1014
        HE SLEEPS SLEEPS CALM O YE ALL-SEEING GODS .   .   .   .   372 MEROPE   1153
        RIGIDLY YET IN SETTLED CALM THIS REALM   .   .   .   .   388 MEROPE   1491
        WELFARE TO THE MESSENIAN STATE AND CALM   .   .   .   .   403 MEROPE   1959
        SCARCE CAN ONE THINK IN CALM SO THREATENING   416 EMPEDOCLES I 2   126
                ARE THE GODS
        THE STARS IN THEIR CALM   .   .   .   .   443 EMPEDOCLES II   468
        AND THUS BENEATH THE CLEAR CALM VAULT OF HEAVEN   .   .   466 ALARIC AT ROME   103
        THESE HAD NO SOUND FOR THEE THAT COLD CALM EYE   .   .   472 CROMWELL   21
        AND MEMORYS CALM CLEAR VOICE AND MOURNFUL EYE   .   .   474 CROMWELL   87
        MIGHT PAINT THE CALM SWEET PEACE THE REST OF HOME   475 CROMWELL   113
        MORE CALM MORE DEEP THAN CHILDHOOD EVER KNEW   .   .   475 CROMWELL   116
        SO SADLY CALM SO KINGLY SO SERENE   .   .   .   .   .   .   477 CROMWELL   186
        THAT CALM EYE FOLLOWD TURN HIM WHERE HE WILL   .   .   477 CROMWELL   196
        AND WITH ITS CLEAR CALM TONES THAT DYING PRAYER   .   .   478 CROMWELL   217
        CALM THE MURMUR OF THE FOUNTAINS   .   .   .   .   .   .   META CLOISTER   15
        OF CALM WISHES MILD ENDURANCE   .   .   .   .   META CLOISTER   23

CALMD
        WAS CALMD ENNOBLED COMFORTED SUSTAIND   .   .   .   .   .   12 MYCERINUS   111
        YE WHO FROM MY CHILDHOOD UP HAVE CALMD ME   .   .   .   .   240 SELF-DEPENDENCE   7
        CALMD BY BITTER DISABUSINGS   .   .   .   .   META CLOISTER   1

CALMER
        A NOBLER CALMER TRAIN   .   .   .   .   183 ABSENCE   6
        I PITY THEE AND WISH THEE CALMER MIND   .   .   .   .   .   396 MEROPE   1760

CALMEST
        HER YOUNGER RIVALS CALMEST GRACE   .   .   .   .   .   .   147 TRISTRAM 2   V 146

CALMLY
        HOW CALMLY SAD HOW SADLY BEAUTIFUL   .   .   .   .   .   .   466 ALARIC AT ROME   100

CALMNESS
        THY SORROW AND THY CALMNESS ARE THINE OWN   .   .   .   .   42 GIPSY CHILD   19

CALMS

CALMS NOT LIFES CROWN THOUGH CALM IS WELL • • • • 22 YOUTH AND CALM 23
AND ON RAPTURES FOLLOW CALMS • • • • • • • • 30 NEW SIRENS 120
MAD DELIGHT AND FROZEN CALMS • • • • • • • • • 33 NEW SIRENS 196

CAME

HERE CAME THE KING HOLDING HIGH FEAST AT MORN • • 11 MYCERINUS 92
SOMETIMES FROM THE GROVES CENTRE ECHOES CAME • • 12 MYCERINUS 124
HERE SHE CAME A BRIDE IN SPRING • • • • • • 13 CHURCH BROU 1 14
PALE AND BREATHLESS CAME THE HUNTERS • • • • • • 13 CHURCH BROU 1 25
CAME THE HUNTERS WITH THEIR LOAD • • • • • • 13 CHURCH BROU 1 32
SLOW AND TIRED CAME THE HUNTERS • • • • • • 14 CHURCH BROU 1 41
AUSTRIAN KNIGHTS FROM SYRIA CAME • • • • • • 15 CHURCH BROU 1 78
LIGHTLY QUIT WHAT LIGHTLY CAME • • • • • • • 22 MEMORY-PICTURE 2
AND FROM SOME SWARDED SHELF HIGH UP THERE CAME • • 25 DREAM 11
CAME FORTH OLIVIAS MARGUERITE AND THINE • • • • 25 DREAM 22
AND CAME HEAPD WITH MYRTLES TO YOUR THRONE • • • • 27 NEW SIRENS 32
DOWN THE STATUED ALLEYS CAME • • • • • • 29 NEW SIRENS 102
THEIR CHILDREN AS WHEN FIRST THEY CAME • • • • 55 RESIGNATION 119
AND TO A HILLOCK CAME A LITTLE BACK • • • • • 61 SOHRAB RUSTUM 17
AND SOHRAB CAME THERE AND WENT IN AND STOOD • • 61 SOHRAB RUSTUM 24
BUT SOHRAB CAME TO THE BEDSIDE AND SAID • • • • 62 SOHRAB RUSTUM 33
I CAME AMONG THE TARTARS AND BORE ARMS • • 62 SOHRAB RUSTUM 43
AND THEN A SWARM OF WANDERING HORSE WHO CAME • • 64 SOHRAB RUSTUM 126
BUT PERAN-WISA WITH HIS HERALD CAME • • • • • • 65 SOHRAB RUSTUM 141
HE TOOK HIS SPEAR AND TO THE FRONT HE CAME • • 65 SOHRAB RUSTUM 146
AND THE OLD TARTAR CAME UPON THE SAND • • • • 65 SOHRAB RUSTUM 148
AND TO FEROOD HIS BROTHER CHIEFS CAME UP • • • • 66 SOHRAB RUSTUM 170
TO COUNSEL GUDURZ AND ZOARRAH CAME • • • • 66 SOHRAB RUSTUM 171
THESE CAME AND COUNSELLD AND THEN GUDURZ SAID • • 66 SOHRAB RUSTUM 174
BUT RUSTUM CAME LAST NIGHT ALOOF HE SITS • • • • 66 SOHRAB RUSTUM 178
AND PLAYD WITH IT BUT GUDURZ CAME AND STOOD • • 67 SOHRAB RUSTUM 201
FEAR AT HIS WRATH BUT JOY THAT RUSTUM CAME • • • • 69 SOHRAB RUSTUM 262
SO DEAR TO THE PALE PERSIANS RUSTUM CAME • • • • 70 SOHRAB RUSTUM 290
AND SOHRAB ARMD IN HAMANS TENT AND CAME • • • • 70 SOHRAB RUSTUM 292
AND RUSTUM CAME UPON THE SAND AND CAST • • • • 70 SOHRAB RUSTUM 299
SOHRAB COME FORTH AND EYED HIM AS HE CAME • • • • 70 SOHRAB RUSTUM 301
CAME SEEKING RUSTUM AND DEFYING FORTH • • • • 70 SOHRAB RUSTUM 310
HIS SPEAR DOWN FROM THE SHOULDER DOWN IT CAME • • 73 SOHRAB RUSTUM 399
LITHE AS THE GLANCING SNAKE AND THE CLUB CAME • • 73 SOHRAB RUSTUM 418
CAME BACK TO RUSTUM AND HE OPED HIS EYES • • • • 81 SOHRAB RUSTUM 698
I CAME AND LIKE THE WIND I GO AWAY • • • • 82 SOHRAB RUSTUM 723
SWEEPING THE DUST CAME NEAR AND IN MUTE WOE • • 82 SOHRAB RUSTUM 732
CAME WELLING FROM THE OPEN GASH AND LIFE • • • • 85 SOHRAB RUSTUM 841
AND NIGHT CAME DOWN OVER THE SOLEMN WASTE • • 86 SOHRAB RUSTUM 865
AND PERAN WISA CAME UPON THE SAND • • • • 65 SOHRAB RUSTUM V 148
FEAR AT HIS WRATH AND JOY THAT RUSTUM CAME • • • • 69 SOHRAB RUSTUM V 262
THEIR LIPS STILL WET WHEN I CAME DOWN • • • • 90 SICK KING BOKH 84
AND ALL THE GODS AND ALL THE HEROES CAME • • 95 BALDER DEAD 1 9
WHILE TWILIGHT FELL AND SACRED NIGHT CAME ON • • 97 BALDER DEAD 1 71
HE CAME AND SADLY WENT ALONG THE SAND • • • • 97 BALDER DEAD 1 78
UNTIL HE CAME TO WHERE A GULLY BREAKS • • • • 97 BALDER DEAD 1 81
AND CAME AGAIN DOWN TO THE ROARING WAVES • • 101 BALDER DEAD 1 199
BUT NIGHT CAME DOWN AND DARKEND ASGARD STREETS • • 101 BALDER DEAD 1 202
HIM THE BLIND HODER MET AS HE CAME UP • • • • 101 BALDER DEAD 1 226
SO SPEAKING THE FLEET-FOOTED HERMOD CAME • • • • 102 BALDER DEAD 1 246
AND HODER TOO CAME HOME DISTRAUGHT WITH GRIEF • • 102 BALDER DEAD 1 249
TO ASGARD AND THE STARS CAME OUT IN HEAVEN • • 102 BALDER DEAD 1 256
AND SWIFT TO ASGARD TO THE GATE HE CAME • • • • 102 BALDER DEAD 1 259
FOR DREAD FOR LIKE A WHIRLWIND ODIN CAME • • • • 102 BALDER DEAD 1 264
CAME WITH THE GODDESSES WHO WROUGHT HER WILL • • 102 BALDER DEAD 1 269
PAST MIDGARD FORTRESS DOWN TO EARTH THEY CAME • • 105 BALDER DEAD 2 23
AXES AND ROPES AND AT THEIR HEAD CAME THOR • • 106 BALDER DEAD 2 48
AND FROM THE GLENS ALL DAY AN ECHO CAME • • 106 BALDER DEAD 2 54
AND THEY CAME OUT UPON THE PLAIN AND PASSD • • 106 BALDER DEAD 2 65
ALL DAY AND DAYLIGHT WANED AND NIGHT CAME ON • • 107 BALDER DEAD 2 81
AND QUESTIOND HERMOD AS HE CAME AND SAID • • • • 107 BALDER DEAD 2 100
AND HE CAME DOWN TO OCEANS NORTHERN STRAND • • 108 BALDER DEAD 2 141
AND MADE HIM LEAP THE GRATE AND CAME WITHIN • • 109 BALDER DEAD 2 148
AND TO THE WALL HE CAME AND FOUND THE GRATE • • 113 BALDER DEAD 2 286
AND HERMOD CAME DOWN TOWRDS THEM FROM THE GATE • • 113 BALDER DEAD 3 3
AND HERMOD CAME AND LEAPT FROM SLEIPNER DOWN • • 114 BALDER DEAD 3 33
AND ODIN CAME AND LAID HIS KINGLY HANDS • • 115 BALDER DEAD 3 65
AND FREYA NEXT CAME NIGH WITH GOLDEN TEARS • • • • 116 BALDER DEAD 3 90
LAST FROM AMONG THE HEROES ONE CAME NEAR • • • • 117 BALDER DEAD 3 124
AND CAME DOWN MOANING TO THE SEA FIRST SQUALLS • • 118 BALDER DEAD 3 182
INTO THE SMOKE-WRAPT SEA AND NIGHT CAME ON • • 119 BALDER DEAD 3 195
THOR CAME ON FOOT THE REST ON HORSEBACK RODE • • 120 BALDER DEAD 3 218
THERE CAME THE GODS AND SATE THEM DOWN ON STONES • • 120 BALDER DEAD 3 223
THERE IN THE WOOD BEFORE A CAVE THEY CAME • • • • 123 BALDER DEAD 3 332
AND CAME BENEATH THE WALL AND FOUND THE GRATE • • 124 BALDER DEAD 3 377
WHEN THAT WITH DOWNCAST LOOKS I HITHER CAME • • 125 BALDER DEAD 3 409
MY HATED CONVERSE ON THEE CAME I UP • • • • 125 BALDER DEAD 3 414
BUT EMPTY FOR HIS WIFE FOR NANNA CAME • • • • 125 BALDER DEAD 3 433
OF THE NEAR WAVES CAME SADLY GRAND • • • • • 137 TRISTRAM 1 217
SHE CAME TO THE BED-SIDE • • • • • • • • 140 TRISTRAM 1 316
CAME KEEN AND CHILL DOWN ON THE HEATHER BRIGHT • • 151 TRISTRAM 3 57
FOR HERE HE CAME WITH THE FAY VIVIAN • • • • • 154 TRISTRAM 3 159
THEY CAME TO WHERE THE BRUSHWOOD CEASED AND DAY • • 155 TRISTRAM 3 185

CAME   (CONTINUED)
        CAME IN FROM WHERE THE BRIGHT ATLANTIC GLEAMS   • •   TRISTRAM 3   V 53
        IT WAS THE FIRST AFTER I CAME • • • • • • • •   157 SAINT BRANDAN   30
        FROM THE CHURCH CAME A MURMUR OF FOLK AT THEIR PRAYERS   163 FORSAKEN MERM   72
        SINGING HERE CAME A MORTAL • • • • • • • •   165 FORSAKEN MERM   120
        ERE DANTE CAME THE TRUMP OF SACRED SONG   • • • • 166 AUSTERITY POET   2
        WHO SPOKE THESE WORDS NO SHADOW EVER CAME   • • • 169 WORLDLY PLACE   10
        ACROSS AND BEGGD AND CAME BACK SATISFIED   • • • 170 WEST LONDON   7
        ONE CAME FROM PENMON WESTWARD AND A GLOW   • • • 170 EAST AND WEST   5
        I CAME I SAW THEE RISE THE BLOOD   • • • • •   178 FAREWELL   9
        CAME FLOODING TO THY LANGUID CHEEK   • • • • •   178 FAREWELL   V 10
        CAME FLUSHING TO THY LANGUID CHEEK   • • • • •   178 FAREWELL   V 10
        CAME BREAKING GODDESS   • • • • • • • •   186 STRAYED REVEL   28
        CAME SWIFT DOWN TO JOIN • • • • • • • •   186 STRAYED REVEL   35
        CAME LOLLING IN THE SUNSHINE   • • • • • •   193 STRAYED REVEL   262
        HIS FLYING STEEDS CAME NEAR   • • • • • •   197 FRAG ANTIGONE   85
        CAME RUSTLING FROM THE GARDEN-TREES • • • • •   223 EPILOG LAOCOON   66
        IN THE RUSTLING NIGHT-AIR CAME THE ANSWER   • • • 240 SELF-DEPENDENCE   15
        AND CAME AS MOST MEN DEEMD TO LITTLE GOOD   • • • 256 SCHOLAR-GIPSY   39
        BUT CAME TO OXFORD AND HIS FRIENDS NO MORE   • • • 256 SCHOLAR-GIPSY   40
        BUT WHEN THEY CAME FROM BATHING THOU WAST GONE   258 SCHOLAR-GIPSY   100
        BUT WHEN THEY CAME FROM BATHING THOU WERT GONE   258 SCHOLAR-GIPSY   V 100
        HERE CAME I OFTEN OFTEN IN OLD DAYS • • • • •   263 THYRSIS   9
        NOW SELDOM COME I SINCE I CAME WITH HIM   • •   263 THYRSIS   25
        OUR YOUTH CAME BACK FOR THERE WAS SHED   • • •   271 MEMORIAL VERSES   V 54
        AND CAME HOME HURT TO DEATH AND HERE   • • • •   278 SOUTHERN NIGHT   95
        BY MOONLIGHT CAME • • • • • • • • • •   278 SOUTHERN NIGHT   104
        BUT SOME DARK SHADOW CAME   • • • • • •   285 HAWORTH CHURCH   110
        IN THE LONG-PAST WINTER HE CAME   • • • • •   298 HEINES GRAVE   192
        AND WALLS WHERE BYRON CAME   • • • • •   313 OBERMANN MORE   24
        AND CENTURIES CAME AND RAN THEIR COURSE   • •   318 OBERMANN MORE   161
        DOWN CAME THE STORM OER FRANCE IT PASSD   • •   319 OBERMANN MORE   201
        DOWN CAME THE STORM IN RUINS FELL   • • •   319 OBERMANN MORE   205
        DOWN CAME THE STORM IN RUIN FELL   • • • • •   319 OBERMANN MORE   V 205
        THE PRAYER I CAME TO URGE I WILL DEFER   • • •   333 MEROPE   109
        TOGETHER TO THIS ISLE OF PELOPS CAME • • • • •   334 MEROPE   124
        WHO TO MESSENIA WITH THY HUSBAND CAME   • • •   337 MEROPE   230
        WHOSE PEOPLE WHEN THE HERACLEIDAE CAME   • • •   338 MEROPE   285
        PROSPEROUS MIGHTY CAME BACK • • • • • • •   343 MEROPE   411
        FROM THE ALTAR OF ZEUS FROM THE CROWD CAME A WAIL 346 MEROPE   489
        BUT HER NURSLING HER HOPE CAME AT LAST   • • •   346 MEROPE   510
        THAT WILL I DO AND TO THIS END I CAME   • • •   355 MEROPE   721
        TILL I THROWN OUT AND TIRED CAME TO HALT   • • •   357 MEROPE   795
        THEN CAME THE PRINCE HE SHOUTED AND PLUNGED IN   358 MEROPE   810
        BUT WHEN THEY CAME ABREAST THE POINT THE RACE • • 358 MEROPE   823
        AND I CAME THINKING TO FIND ARCAS HERE   • • •   361 MEROPE   916
        SWIFT AS I CAME HATH FALSEHOOD BEEN BEFORE   • •   363 MEROPE   954
        TO WHOM THIS DAY HE CAME TO PROFFER PEACE   • •   387 MEROPE   1482
        CAME UPON HER STEALING   • • • • • • • •   392 MEROPE   1644
        TILL PRESENTLY THE KING CAME FORTH IN ROBE   • •   401 MEROPE   1903
        AND SHOUTED SINCE BY THEE DEFILEMENT CAME   • •   402 MEROPE   1923
        A NEW-MADE WIFE I FROM ARCADIA CAME   • • • •   403 MEROPE   1972
        THEN EVIDENCE CAME HIS COMRADES OF THE HUNT   •   365 MEROPE   V
        TO OFFER THAT I CAME NOT BUT TO URGE • • • • •   394 MEROPE   V1688
        TOUCHING THY HARP AS THE WHIM CAME ON THEE   • •   407 EMPEDOCLES I 1   33
        TO THE PHRYGIAN HIGHLANDS CAME • • • • • •   433 EMPEDOCLES II   132
        CAME ABOUT THE YOUTHFUL GOD   • • • • • •   433 EMPEDOCLES II   158
        TO THE ELEMENTS IT CAME FROM   • • • • • •   439 EMPEDOCLES II   331
        HITHER HE CAME LATE-BORN AND LONG-DESIRED   • •   444 WESTMIN ABBEY   8
        ARTS CAME AND ARMS AND LAW   • • • • • •   445 WESTMIN ABBEY   57
        THAT TO MY MIND THERE CAME HOW LONG AGO   • •   446 WESTMIN ABBEY   83
        GEIST CAME NEXT OUR LITTLE FRIEND   • • • •   454 POOR MATTHIAS   57
        OF BLOOD-UNMIXD FROM POTSDAM CAME   • • • •   459 KAISER DEAD   20
        LIKE SUNSHINE WENT AND CAME AND BADE   • • •   460 KAISER DEAD   47
        LIKE DREAMS BETWEEN TWO SORROWS WENT AND CAME •   474 CROMWELL   96
        BY LEAGUERD TOWER AND TENTED FIELD IT CAME • • •   476 CROMWELL   148
        THERE AS HE GAZED A WONDROUS BAND THEY CAME   • • 476 CROMWELL   163
        CAME FAINT AND FEEBLE IN THE EMBRACE OF DEATH   478 CROMWELL   208

CAMELS
        THE ACRID MILK OF CAMELS AND THEIR WELLS   • • • • 64 SOHRAB RUSTUM   125

CAMEST
        THOU CAMEST NEAR THE NEXT O WARRIOR THOR   • • • • 115 BALDER DEAD 3   71
        NOT TOO FAR OFF WHEN THAT THOU CAMEST BY   • • • • 125 BALDER DEAD 3   417

CAMP
        BUT ALL THE TARTAR CAMP ALONG THE STREAM   • • •   61 SOHRAB RUSTUM   3
        THROUGH THE DIM CAMP TO PERAN-WISAS TENT   • • •   61 SOHRAB RUSTUM   11
        THESE ALL FILED OUT FROM CAMP INTO THE PLAIN   •   65 SOHRAB RUSTUM   135
        AND CROSSD THE CAMP WHICH LAY BEHIND AND REACHD   66 SOHRAB RUSTUM   190
        BACK QUICKLY THROUGH THE CAMP IN FEAR AND JOY   •   69 SOHRAB RUSTUM   261
        THE CAMP AND TO THE PERSIAN HOST APPEARD   • • •   69 SOHRAB RUSTUM   281
        SOHRAB RETURNING FROM THE TARTAR CAMP   • • •   79 SOHRAB RUSTUM   594
        BOTH ARMIES MOVED TO CAMP AND TOOK THEIR MEAL   •   86 SOHRAB RUSTUM   871
        THROUGH THE HUSHD CAMP TO PERAN-WISAS TENT • • •   61 SOHRAB RUSTUM   V 11

CAMPD
        WAS RUSTUMS AND HIS MEN LAY CAMPD AROUND   • • •   67 SOHRAB RUSTUM   194
        I CHALLENGED ONCE WHEN THE TWO ARMIES CAMPD   • • 72 SOHRAB RUSTUM   357

CAMST
    COME AS THOU CAMST A THOUSAND TIMES • • • • • •   208 LONGING   5
    OR AS THOU NEVER CAMST IN SOOTH   • • • • • •   209 LONGING   9
    HERE CAMST THOU IN THY JOCUND YOUTHFUL TIME   • •   269 THYRSIS   218
    CAMST THOU FROM HEAVEN O CHILD • • • • • • • •   295 HEINES GRAVE   116

CANAL
    AND THE CANAL WHICH FROM THE STREAM • • • • • •   89 SICK KING BOKH   62
    AND THE CANAL THAT FROM THE STREAM • • • • • •   89 SICK KING BOKH V 62

CANARY
    POOR CANARY MANY A YEAR • • • • • • • • •   452 POOR MATTHIAS   5
    DEAD CANARY BIRD A STAVE • • • • • • • • •   457 POOR MATTHIAS   176
    FRENCH CANARY-MERCHANT OLD   • • • • • • •   457 POOR MATTHIAS   184

CANNOND
    THERE WHERE GIBRALTARS CANNOND STEEP • • • • • •   276 SOUTHERN NIGHT   23

CANOPY
    NEATH THE MILD CANOPY OF ENGLISH AIR • • • • • •   268 THYRSIS   194
    NEATH THE SOFT CANOPY OF ENGLISH AIR • • • • • •   268 THYRSIS   V 194

CANVAS
    AND YET EEN THERE THE CANVAS GLOWD • • • • • •   222 EPILOG LAOCOON   23

CANVASS
    TO CANVASS WITH OFFICIAL BREATH   • • • • • •   250 WISH   24

CAP
    AND ON HIS HEAD HE SET HIS SHEEP-SKIN CAP • • • •   64 SOHRAB RUSTUM   100
    AND ON HIS HEAD HE PLACD HIS SHEEP-SKIN CAP   • •   64 SOHRAB RUSTUM V 100
    ROUND EACH SWEET BROW THE CAP CLOSE-SET • • • •   141 TRISTRAM 1   340

CAPACIOUS
    IN WHOSE CAPACIOUS SPIRIT LAY HIS PLAN • • • •   LUCRETIUS 5   4

CAPE
    REACHD CAPE VERDE ISLANDS LUSITANIA • • • • • •   485 S S LUSITANIA   14

CAPHYAE
    AND THE STONE COFFINS THEN BY CAPHYAE CLIFFS • •   356 MEROPE   744

CAPITAL
    THE CAPITAL OF PLEASURE SEES • • • • • • • •   312 OBERMANN   179

CAPITOL
    HORDE AFTER HORDE STREAMED UP THY FROWNING CAPITOL   464 ALARIC AT ROME   72
    OF THY STERN HILL THOU MIGHTY CAPITOL   • • • •   468 ALARIC AT ROME   152

CAPPD
    CAPPD WITH FAINT SMOKE THE NOISY TOWN   • • • •   55 RESIGNATION   93

CAPRICIOUS
    THAT IT MIGHT KEEP FROM HIS CAPRICIOUS PLAY   • •   246 BURIED LIFE   35

CAPS
    FIRST WITH BLACK SHEEP-SKIN CAPS AND WITH LONG SPEARS   64 SOHRAB RUSTUM   118
    AND CLOSE-SET SKULL-CAPS AND THOSE WILDER HORDES • •   64 SOHRAB RUSTUM   130

CAPT
    WHO SCALE THE CLOUD-CAPT HEIGHT OR SINK TO REST • •   472 CROMWELL   11

CAPTAIN
    THE CAPTAIN OF HIS SQUIRES AND HIS GUARD • • • •   355 MEROPE   729
    SEE THE WIFE OF HECTOR THAT GREAT PRE-EMINENT CAPTAIN   HOMER TRANS   33

CAPTIVE
    THE SUFFRAGE CAPTIVE NOW NOT ONE IN TEN • • • •   171 DIVINITY   7
    THEREFORE NO WORDS A MURDERER AND A CAPTIVE   • •   374 MEROPE   1196
    HADST THOU FROM THY FORLORN AND CAPTIVE STATE   • •   383 MEROPE   1369

CAPTIVITY
    ERE I HEAR THY CRIES AND THY CAPTIVITY TOLD OF   • •   HOMER TRANS   38

CAPTORS
    WHEN HIS AWE-STRUCK CAPTORS LED • • • • • •   229 YOUTH OF NATURE   43

CAPTURED
    BETTER TO LIVE A SERF A CAPTURED MAN • • • • • •   112 BALDER DEAD 2   265
    BETTER TO LIVE A SLAVE A CAPTURED MAN   • • • •   112 BALDER DEAD 2 V 265
    LIVING BUT ELLA CAPTURED HIM AND SLEW   • • • •   117 BALDER DEAD 3   128

CAR
    DRAWN IN HIS CAR BESIDE ME AND MY SONS • • • •   120 BALDER DEAD 3   240

CARAVAN
    UPON THEIR CARAVAN OR GREEDY KINGS • • • • • •   193 STRAYED REVEL   249

CARCASE
    AND BIND THY CARCASE LIKE A BALE WITH CORDS   • • 114 BALDER DEAD 3   25

CARD
    THEN THE DOOR OPENS AND THIS CARD IS BROUGHT   • • 485 S S LUSITANIA   13

CARE
    WHICH YEARS TO MOST AND CARE AND SUFFERING GIVE • • 43 GIPSY CHILD V 38
    SUCH HAPPY ISSUE CROWND HER PAINFUL CARE • • • • 46 IN UTRUMQUE PAR   34
    WITH PLEASANT SMILE LET US TAKE CARE • • • • • 48 HORATIAN ECHO   21
    FOR WHAT CARE I THOUGH ALL SPEAK SOHRABS FAME • • 68 SOHRAB RUSTUM   228
    FOR WHAT CARE I THAT SOHRABS FAME QUENCH THEIRS • • 68 SOHRAB RUSTUM V 228
    TO MOURN WITH HIM AND SHOW HIM CARE • • • • • • 92 SICK KING BOKH   156
    WILL HELP HIM TO FORGET HIS CARE • • • • • • 138 TRISTRAM 1   257
    THEY STRAIGHTWAY ARE BURNT UP WITH FUME AND CARE • • 153 TRISTRAM 3   139
    WELL THEN FOR CHRIST THOU ANSWEREST WHO CAN CARE • • 171 BETTER PART   6
    CARE NOT FOR THAT AND LAY ME WHERE I FALL • • • • 173 MONICAS PRAYER   2
    AND UNION BEFORE GOD THE ONLY CARE • • • • • 173 MONICAS PRAYER   11
    ON THE OXUS STREAM BUT CARE • • • • • • • • 193 STRAYED REVEL   245
    ARE TO THE GODS A CARE • • • • • • • • • 196 FRAG ANTIGONE   32
    HATH CHARMD AT BIRTH FROM GLOOM AND CARE • • • 203 EUPHROSYNE   14
    HAS CHARMD AT BIRTH FROM GLOOM AND CARE • • • 203 EUPHROSYNE V 14
    AND LONG WITH MEN OF CARE THOU COULDST NOT STAY • • 269 THYRSIS   228
    TRAVERSE IN TROOPS WITH CARE-FILLD BREAST • • • • 277 SOUTHERN NIGHT   66
    WHOSE CULTURE IS THE BRETHRENS CARE • • • • 301 GRANDE CHARTR   58
    SOUL THAT THAN THEY WE TAKE MORE CARE • • • • 315 OBERMANN MORE V
    SOUL THAT WE TAKE MORE COUNT AND CARE • • • • 315 OBERMANN MORE V
    IS MY SON SAFE THAT QUESTION BOUNDS MY CARE • • 401 MEROPE   1889
    ITS SOMBRE ASPECT OF MAJESTIC CARE • • • • 403 MEROPE   1968
    WILLING PATIENT TO ZEUS TO HIS CARE • • • • 348 MEROPE V
    HOW MAN MAY HERE BEST LIVE NO CARE TOO GREAT   419 EMPEDOCLES I 2   216
        TO EXPLORE
    STERN POWERS WHO MAKE THEIR CARE • • • • • 422 EMPEDOCLES I 2   310
    PAIN AND CARE WITH A DARK STORE • • • • • • 431 EMPEDOCLES II   86
    KNEW CARE AND KNEW UNREST • • • • • • • • 447 WESTMIN ABBEY   122
    AND AFTER THAT THOU DOST NOT CARE • • • • • 451 GEISTS GRAVE   59
    MADE ROUGH WITH CARE BECOME THE CHANGEFUL SEA • • 473 CROMWELL   49
    THAT BROW SO SAD SO PALE SO FULL OF CARE • • • 477 CROMWELL   183
    THE NIGHT OF TERRORS AND THE DAY OF CARE • • • 478 CROMWELL   205
    THAT THEY SHOULD EASE GRAVE COUNSEL OF ITS CARE • • RUDE ORATOR   10

CARED
    BE STRICTLY CARED FOR IN THE APPOINTED DAY • • • • 96 BALDER DEAD 1   39

CAREER
    ATTEND IT OF ITS MID CAREER • • • • • • • • 225 EPILOG LAOCOON   150
    HATH RUN HIS BRIGHT CAREER • • • • • • • • 448 WESTMIN ABBEY   142

CAREEREST
    SUN WHO CAREEREST THROUGH THE HEIGHT OF HEAVEN • • 349 MEROPE   571

CARELESS
    BUT HIDES IF GODS GODS CARELESS OF OUR DOOM • • 10 MYCERINUS   54
    THE CARELESS GLANCE THE COLD UNMEANING SMILE • • 470 ALARIC AT ROME   219
    WHAT TRACE OF CARELESS CHILDHOOD LINGERD THERE • • 477 CROMWELL   184
    RETAIND SO LITTLE IN THY CARELESS DEPTHS • • • • LUCRETIUS 1   4

CARES
    JUDGE VAIN BEFOREHAND HUMAN CARES • • • • • • 59 RESIGNATION   232
    SCORN YE THIS WORLD THEIR TEARS THEIR INWARD CARES 237 PROGRESS   22
    COUNTRY AND PUBLIC CARES • • • • • • • • • 282 HAWORTH CHURCH V
    PUBLIC CARES WHICH MOVE • • • • • • • • • 282 HAWORTH CHURCH V
    THE CARES WHICH MIGHT IN ME WITH TIME I FEEL • • 335 MEROPE   161
    WITH COMMON CARES UNMINGLING AND APART • • • 473 CROMWELL   57
    WITH CARES TO CONQUER AND A GOAL TO WIN • • • 475 CROMWELL   122
    WORN WAS HIS BROW WITH CARES NO THOUGHT COULD SCAN 476 CROMWELL   155

CARESSD
    IS BY THE TONES OF A LOVED VOICE CARESSD • • • • 247 BURIED LIFE   83

CARESSES
    ROUND OUR HEARTS WITH LONG CARESSES • • • • • • 28 NEW SIRENS   69

CAREWORN
    POINTING TO EARTHS CAREWORN CREATURES • • • • 28 NEW SIRENS   61

CARNAC
    THE GIANT STONES OF CARNAC SLEEP • • • • • 274 STANZAS CARNAC   11
    THE CHURCH OF CARNAC BY THE STRAND • • • • • 274 STANZAS CARNAC   23

CARNAGE
    OF CARNAGE AND FIND HERMOD IN YOUR LIFE • • • • 127 BALDER DEAD 3   504

CARNATIONS
    SOON WILL THE MUSK CARNATIONS BREAK AND SWELL • • 264 THYRSIS   63

CAROLLING
    CAROLLING AND SHOUTING • • • • • • • • • • 220 BACCHANALIA 2   31

CAROLS
    ONCE EVERY YEAR WHEN CAROLS WAKE • • • • • 158 SAINT BRANDAN   65
    AND CAROLS FLOAT ALONG THE HAPPY AIR • • • • • • 445 WESTMIN ABBEY   39

CARPETS
       UPON THE THICK PILED CARPETS IN THE TENT   • • • •   61 SOHRAB RUSTUM   25

CARRIED
       CARRIED BEFORE HIM AS IS RIGHT   • • • • • • • •   89 SICK KING BOKH   48
       FOLLOWD AND ON THEIR SHOULDERS CARRIED BOUGHS   • •   106 BALDER DEAD 2   64
       STILL CARRIED OER THE DISTANT WATERS ON   • • • •   119 BALDER DEAD 3   198
       WHO CARRIED THE GREAT WAR FROM MACEDON   • • • •   154 TRISTRAM 3   148
       CARRIED THY LOVELY WAIL AWAY   • • • • • • • •   303 GRANDE CHARTR   140

CARRIES
       THE ORGAN CARRIES TO OUR EAR   • • • • • • • •   306 GRANDE CHARTR   203

CARRY
       SEEK HIM IN PEACE AND CARRY TO HIS ARMS   • • • •   63 SOHRAB RUSTUM   76
       O SOHRAB CARRY AN UNWOUNDED SON   • • • • • • •   63 SOHRAB RUSTUM   77
       HIM WILL I SEEK AND CARRY TO HIS EAR   • • • • • •   66 SOHRAB RUSTUM   180
       BUT CARRY ME WITH THEE TO SEISTAN   • • • • • •   84 SOHRAB RUSTUM   784
       AND CARRY THEE AWAY TO SEISTAN   • • • • • • • •   84 SOHRAB RUSTUM   799
       CARRY MY PEACE UPON EARTH   • • • • • • • •   216 LORDS MESSENGER   6
       AH CARRY BACK THY KEN   • • • • • • • •   315 OBERMANN MORE   82
       CARRY HIS MESSENGER BUT LEFT HIM HERE   • • • •   374 MEROPE   1193
       WE STRIVE TO CARRY DOWN THY NAME   • • • • •   451 GEISTS GRAVE   63

CARS
       OR IN MID-HEAVEN PERHAPS YOUR GOLDEN CARS   • • •   10 MYCERINUS   43

CART
       THE WOOD-CUTTERS CART-TRACK   • • • • • • • •   187 STRAYED REVEL   41
       SITTING IN HIS CART   • • • • • • • • • •   191 STRAYED REVEL   171

CARTHAGE
       AH COULD THY GRAVE AT HOME AT CARTHAGE BE   • • •   173 MONICAS PRAYER   1
       OH COULD THY GRAVE AT HOME AT CARTHAGE BE   • • •   173 MONICAS PRAYER   V   1

CARTHUSIANS
       TO THE CARTHUSIANS WORLD-FAMED HOME   • • • • •   300 GRANDE CHARTR   30

CARTS
       RUNS AND COLLIERS CARTS   • • • • • • • • •   282 HAWORTH CHURCH   58

CARVE
       THE BEST THEN TO THE THRONE MAY CARVE HIS WAY   • •   352 MEROPE   658

CARVED
       ROUND THE TOMB THE CARVED STONE FRETWORK   • • • •   16 CHURCH BROU 1   109
       ON THE CARVED WESTERN FRONT A FLOOD OF LIGHT   • •   18 CHURCH BROU 3   18
       ON THE BROWN RUDE-CARVED BALCONY TWO FORMS   • •   25 DREAM   21
       LEAVE THEN THE CROSS AS YE HAVE LEFT CARVED GODS   • • 237 PROGRESS   27
       CARVED THERE NO MORE AND THE SMOOTH   • • • • •   292 HEINES GRAVE   3
       INTO THEIR STONE-CARVED BASINS COLD   • • • • •   300 GRANDE CHARTR   32
       AND HAD CARVED THEM INTO FLUTES   • • • • • •   434 EMPEDOCLES II   176

CARVERS
       FLEMISH CARVERS LOMBARD GILDERS   • • • • • •   15 CHURCH BROU 1   95

CARVES
       DECLINES HER MINISTRY AND CARVES HIS OWN   • • • •   195 FRAG ANTIGONE   6

CARVING
       WHILE TONGUES OF FIRE ON COIGN AND CARVING PLAY   • • 445 WESTMIN ABBEY   36

CASBIN
       STREAM OVER CASBIN AND THE SOUTHERN SLOPES   • • • •   64 SOHRAB RUSTUM   113

CASD
       CASD IN ONE MANS DIMENSIONS CAN DISTIL   • • • •   50 CONSOLATION   V

CASE
       MOST LIKELY GRATEFUL BUT IN ALL CASE SURE   • • • •   354 MEROPE   711
       I KNOW NOT JUST IN EITHER CASE THE STROKE   • • • •   404 MEROPE   1986
       THE CASE WAS CLEAR A MONGREL THING   • • • • •   459 KAISER DEAD   29

CASEMENT
       FROM HER MULLIOND CHAMBER-CASEMENT   • • • • • •   13 CHURCH BROU 1   11

CASPIAN
       OR SOME FRORE CASPIAN REED-BED SOUTHWARD BOUND   • •   64 SOHRAB RUSTUM   115
       AND THOSE FROM ATTRUCK AND THE CASPIAN SANDS   • •   64 SOHRAB RUSTUM   123
       TO MAINTAIN THE CASPIAN FREE   • • • • • • • •   PILLARS UNIVERS   7

CASSOCKD
       A CASSOCKD PRIEST RODE BY   • • • • • • • •   160 NECKAN   48
       THE CASSOCKD PRIEST RODE ONWARDS   • • • • • •   161 NECKAN   57

CAST
       AND RUSTUM CAME UPON THE SAND AND CAST   • • • •   70 SOHRAB RUSTUM   299
       BUT SOHRAB CRAWLD TO WHERE HE LAY AND CAST   • • • •   81 SOHRAB RUSTUM   694
       OF RUSTUM AND HIS TEARS BROKE FORTH HE CAST   • •   82 SOHRAB RUSTUM   727

CAST   (CONTINUED)
          AND CAST IT SOFTLY BUT THE MAN . . . .   91 SICK KING BOKH   118
          SO THEY WHOSE LOT IT WAS CAST STONES . . . . . .   91 SICK KING BOKH   121
          AND CAST IT AT THE DEAR-LOVED BALDERS BREAST . .   98 BALDER DEAD 1   102
          OF THESE THE SERPENT IN THE SEA YE CAST   . . . .   110 BALDER DEAD 2   209
          AND CAST HIS TRUNK TO CHOKE THE ABYSMAL VOID . .   121 BALDER DEAD 3   259
          TO THE POOR WRETCH MY CLOAK I CAST . . . . . .   158 SAINT BRANDAN   51
          MY STRETCHD ARMS ARE CAST   . . . .   176 PARTING   64
          MY STRAIND ARMS ARE CAST . . . .   176 PARTING   V   64
          CONDEMND TO CAST ABOUT . . . .   307 OBERMANN   18
          THOUGH ROUND THY FIRMER MANHOOD CAST . . . . .   323 OBERMANN MORE   307
          ONCE IN THE BLACK AND ARROWY RACE AND CAST . . .   358 MEROPE   832
          CAST BY THE RUMBLING SUBTERRANEAN STREAM . . .   358 MEROPE   841
          ON THIS SUSPICION CAST HIM INTO CHAINS . . . .   365 MEROPE   V
          THE CLOUDS OF SICKNESS CAST NO STAIN UPON . . .   FRAGMENT 8   1

CASTLE
          ECHOING ROUND THIS CASTLE OLD . . . .   12 CHURCH BROU 1   2
          FROM THE CASTLE PAST THE DRAWBRIDGE . . . . .   13 CHURCH BROU 1   7
          TO THE CASTLE PAST THE DRAWBRIDGE . . . . . .   13 CHURCH BROU 1   31
          IN MY CASTLE ALL IS SORROW . . . .   15 CHURCH BROU 1   73
          COMING BENIGHTED TO THE CASTLE-GATE . . . . .   18 CHURCH BROU 3   15
          THE CASTLE AND THE DEWY WOODS AND HUNT . . . .   79 SOHRAB RUSTUM   629
          IN HER CASTLE BY THE COAST . . . .   136 TRISTRAM 1   193
          OF THE CASTLE-PARK ONE SEES . . . .   141 TRISTRAM 1   363
          THE CASTLE-COURT ALL WET WITH RAIN . . . . .   148 TRISTRAM 2   170
          AND THE GREY TURRETS OF THE CASTLE OLD . . . .   151 TRISTRAM 3   59
          BY CASTLE FIELD AND TOWN . . . .   159 NECKAN   18
          SOME GIRL WHO HERE FROM CASTLE-BOWER . . . . .   278 SOUTHERN NIGHT   101

CASTLED
          IS THE CASTLED HOUSE WITH ITS WOODS . . . . . .   234 YOUTH OF MAN   64
          IN THE CASTLED HOUSE WITH ITS WOODS . . . . . .   234 YOUTH OF MAN   V   64

CASTLES
          ON THE CASTLES SOUTHERN SIDE   . . . .   140 TRISTRAM 1   329

CASTS
          WHOSE FIGURE CASTS A SHADOW ON THE FLOOR   . . . . 175 PARTING   36

CASTUS
          AND THE GREEN AGNUS-CASTUS   . . . .   391 MEROPE   1618

CASUAL
          LIGHT HALF-BELIEVERS OF OUR CASUAL CREEDS . . . . 260 SCHOLAR-GIPSY   172
          VAGUE HALF-BELIEVERS OF OUR CASUAL CREEDS . . . . 260 SCHOLAR-GIPSY   V 172
          ARE BUT THE CASUAL PASSERS BY WHO COME   . . . .   LUCRETIUS 5   6

CAT
          HAD TIBERIUS BEEN A CAT . . . .   453 POOR MATTHIAS   42

CATACOMBS
          AND THEN SHE SMILED AND IN THE CATACOMBS   . . . . 172 GOOD SHEPHERD   9

CATALOGUE
          FOR SUCH A DAMNING CATALOGUE OF ILLS . . . . . .   RUDE ORATOR   14

CATANA
          IN WHICH THEY HAVE TOILD ALL NIGHT FROM CATANA . . 406 EMPEDOCLES I 1   4
          THE SWEETEST HARP-PLAYER IN CATANA   . . . . . .   412 EMPEDOCLES I 2   13
          TAKE DOWN WITH THEE THE REST TO CATANA . . . .   428 EMPEDOCLES I 2   466
          GOOD FRIEND I SHALL REVISIT CATANA . . . . . .   428 EMPEDOCLES I 2   473

CATARACTS
          TO ROCK THE CATARACTS REPLY   . . . .   289 RUGBY CHAPEL   92

CATCH
          TO CATCH THY SMILE TO SEEK THINE EYE . . . . . .   205 CALAIS SANDS   V 26
          THEY CATCH OF THE MYSTERIOUS STREAM . . . . . .   226 EPILOG LAOCOON   178
          OFT THROUGH THE TREES THEY CATCH A GLANCE . . .   305 GRANDE CHARTR   176

CATCHES
          CATCHES THEM AND DRIVES OUT AGAIN TO SEA   . . .   124 BALDER DEAD 3   364
          CATCHES THE WESTERING SUNS LAST FIRES   . . . .   274 STANZAS CARNAC   24

CATES
          THE TABLE STOOD BESIDE HIM CHARGED WITH CATES   . . 67 SOHRAB RUSTUM   V 197
          CATES FROM OUR HUNTERS POUCH ARCADIAN FARE . . .   356 MEROPE   753

CATO
          YES BE THE SECOND CATO PRAISD . . . .   481 COURAGE   13

CATS
          AND THOU DEEMEDST CATS WERE KIND   . . . . . .   453 POOR MATTHIAS   38

CATTLE
          WITH GOAD AND SHOUTING URGE THEIR CATTLE PAST   . . 107 BALDER DEAD 2   96
          THE SOFT-COUCHD CATTLE WERE AS FAIR . . . . . .   222 EPILOG LAOCOON   43
          THOSE CATTLE COUCHD OR AS THEY RISE . . . . .   222 EPILOG LAOCOON   53
          AFAR IN REST THE CATTLE LAY   . . . .   224 EPILOG LAOCOON   109

CATTLE   (CONTINUED)
        THE CATTLE RISING FROM THE GRASS   . . . . . .   225 EPILOG LAOCOON   153
        THE CATTLE LOVE TO GATHER ON THEIR WAY   . . . . .   413 EMPEDOCLES I 2   38

CAUCASIAN
        THAN THE ICE-BASTIOND CAUCASIAN MOUNT   . . . .   395 MEROPE   1749

CAUCASUS
        CROSS UNDERNEATH THE INDIAN CAUCASUS   . . . . . .   65 SOHRAB RUSTUM   161
        WIND UNDERNEATH THE INDIAN CAUCASUS   . . . . . .   66 SOHRAB RUSTUM   V 161
        CLIMB UNDERNEATH THE INDIAN CAUCASUS   . . . . . .   66 SOHRAB RUSTUM   V 161

CAUGHT
        CAUGHT NOT TILL THEN A SENSE   . . . .   47 WORLD QUIETIST   22
        OF MERCY CAUGHT DID NOT EXPIRE   . . . .   158 SAINT BRANDAN   62
        THESE OR MUCH GREATER THINGS BUT CAUGHT   . . . . 223 EPILOG LAOCOON   55
        SOULS EREWHILE WHO CAUGHT HER WORD   . . . . . .   227 PERSIST POETRY   3
        FILLD EARTH AND HEAVEN AND CAUGHT AWAY   . . . .   317 OBERMANN MORE   143
        CAUGHT THEM AS WIND TAKES FEATHERS WHIRLD THEM ROUND 358 MEROPE   824
        CAUGHT AS HE JOURNEYED FROM THE LIPS OF PAN   . .   473 CROMWELL   40

CAULDRON
        OVER HIS BOILING CAULDRON BROODS   . . . .   299 GRANDE CHARTR   12

CAULDRONS
        OVER HIS BOILING CAULDRONS BROODS   . . . . . .   299 GRANDE CHARTR   V 12

CAUSE
        WHY FOR NO CAUSE MAKE SAD THY FACE   . . . . . .   92 SICK KING BOKH   142
        THOUGH HE HAS CAUSE HAVE ANY CAUSE BUT HE   . . . . 125 BALDER DEAD 3   408
        THOUGH HE HAS CAUSE HAVE ANY CAUSE BUT HE   . . . . 125 BALDER DEAD 3   408
        WHEN THEY HAVE WOE THEY BLAME THE NEAREST CAUSE . . 125 BALDER DEAD 3   427
        ALL PLAINT IN HER OWN CAUSE CONTROLLD   . . . .   279 SOUTHERN NIGHT   122
        UNHAPPY BEAUTIFUL THE CAUSE   . . . .   285 HAWORTH CHURCH   V 105
        BUT WHEN FOR SOME GREAT PUBLIC CAUSE AN ARM   . .   336 MEROPE   204
        FIND THEN SUCH CAUSE THE CHARGE OF MURDER FALLS . . 336 MEROPE   210
        AND SHED THEIR BLOOD LIKE WATER IN OUR CAUSE   . .   337 MEROPE   227
        THOU HADST NO CAUSE AS FEIGND IN HIS MISRULE   . .   338 MEROPE   283
        POWER FAILS US TO TRY CLEARLY IF THAT CAUSE   . .   352 MEROPE   647
        THE CAUSE WHICH DREW HIM TO HIS DEED . . . . . .   352 MEROPE   650
        TO FRIENDS STILL MORE AND LABOURERS IN OUR CAUSE . 359 MEROPE   872
        THY FATHER PERISHD IN THIS PEOPLES CAUSE   . . . . 381 MEROPE   1314
        FIRST RALLY THE MESSENIANS TO THY CAUSE   . . . . 382 MEROPE   1322
        DISCREDITING THE SUCCOUR WHICH OUR CAUSE   . . . . 382 MEROPE   1335
        LOVE A WON CAUSE BUT NOT A CAUSE TO WIN   . . . . 384 MEROPE   1394
        LOVE A WON CAUSE BUT NOT A CAUSE TO WIN   . . . . 384 MEROPE   1394
        MY ROYAL SISTER BUT WITHOUT SOME CAUSE   . . . . 386 MEROPE   1449
        TRUE BUT WHAT CAUSE TO OUR ARCADIA GIVES   . . . . 389 MEROPE   1534
        AS OUR JUST CAUSE DESERVES I DO NOT FEAR   . . . . 391 MEROPE   1595
        ARE THE SOLE CLAIMANTS LEFT WHAT CAUSE OF STRIFE . 394 MEROPE   1693

CAUSES
        CAUSES OF THINGS AND FAR BELOW . . . .   271 MEMORIAL VERSES   30
        OF OUR OWN ACTIONS DIMLY TRACE THE CAUSES   . . . . 352 MEROPE   640
        THAT NATURAL CAUSES MAR THY EFFORTS AND NOT FATE . .   EMPEDOCLES I 2   V
        THAT NATURAL CAUSES THWART THY WELFARE AND NOT FATE   EMPEDOCLES I 2   V

CAUSEWAY
        AND ONCE IN WINTER ON THE CAUSEWAY CHILL   . . . . 258 SCHOLAR-GIPSY   121

CAUTION
        I DOUBT THEIR CAUTION LITTLE SUITS THEIR WARD   . . 351 MEROPE   608

CAUTIOUS
        OR DIDST THOU BUT AS CAUTIOUS SCHEMERS USE . . . . 404 MEROPE   1984

CAVE
        LODGERS IN THE FOREST AND THE CAVE   . . . . . .   34 NEW SIRENS   234
        AND IN A CAVE A BED OF NEEDLE-ROCKS   . . . . . .   111 BALDER DEAD 2   220
        THERE IN THE WOOD BEFORE A CAVE THEY CAME   . . . . 123 BALDER DEAD 3   332
        PARTS FROM THIS CAVE-PIERCED CLIFF THE SHELVING BAY 358 MEROPE   818
        APOLLO PEALD IT FROM HIS DELPHIAN CAVE   . . . .   385 MEROPE   1401
        PARTS FROM THE CAVE-PIERCD CLIFF THE SHELVING BAY   358 MEROPE   V 818
        HIDE HIS TORN HEAD BENEATH HIS SUNLESS CAVE   . .   472 CROMWELL   24

CAVERN
        STRONG BLACK TEMPESTUOUS TO THE CAVERN-MOUTH   . .   358 MEROPE   821
        THE LOW-BROWD CAVERN-ARCH AND DISAPPEAR   . . . . 358 MEROPE   834

CAVERNS
        SHE SPAKE AND TO THE CAVERNS DEPTH SHE FLED   . .   123 BALDER DEAD 3   355
        IN THE CAVERNS WHERE WE LAY   . . . .   162 FORSAKEN MERM   32
        SAND-STREWN CAVERNS COOL AND DEEP   . . . . . .   162 FORSAKEN MERM   35
        IS TO THEIR FARTHEST CAVERNS SENT   . . . . . .   182 TO MARG CONT   14

CAVES
        COLD-BUBBLING SPRINGS OR CAVES NOT SO THE SOUL . .   6 GEO CRUIKSHANK   9
        WHERE SATE IN THE CAVES MOUTH A SKINNY HAG . . . . 123 BALDER DEAD 3   333
        SAY THY PRAYER AND COME BACK TO THE KIND SEA-CAVES   163 FORSAKEN MERM   61
        WHEN THROUGH THY CAVES THOU HEAREST MUSIC SWELL . . 431 EMPEDOCLES II   66

CAVES   (CONTINUED)
     OF THE MOONLIT PEAKS AND THE CAVES   . . . . .   435 EMPEDOCLES II   203

CEASE
     THAT GENERAL LIFE WHICH DOES NOT CEASE   . . .   58 RESIGNATION   191
     AND CEASE TO MOURN AND THINK OF BALDERS PYRE . . 97 BALDER DEAD 1   60
     DO FOR THIS RADIANT GREEK-SOULD ARTIST CEASE . . 168 RACHEL 2   12
     ALL OUR UNQUIET PULSES CEASE   . . . .   180 FAREWELL   82
     BEGIN AND CEASE AND THEN AGAIN BEGIN . . . . .   211 DOVER BEACH   12
     CEASE AND BEGIN AND THEN AGAIN BEGIN . . . . .   211 DOVER BEACH   V 12
     LET THE LONG CONTENTION CEASE   . . . .   215 LAST WORD   5
     AND WHEN AT LAST THEIR SNATCHES CEASE   . . . . 226 EPILOG LAOCOON   185
     AND WHEN AT LAST THESE SNATCHES CEASE   . . . . 226 EPILOG LAOCOON   V 185
     WAY AFTER WAY CHANGES THAT NEVER CEASE . . . . 239 REVOLUTIONS   7
     NOR BRING TO SEE ME CEASE TO LIVE   . . . . .   250 WISH   17
     LONG SINCE SAW BYRONS STRUGGLE CEASE . . . . . 270 MEMORIAL VERSES   2
     PASS BANNERS PASS AND BUGLES CEASE . . . . . . 306 GRANDE CHARTR   209
     WE WOULD HAVE MISERY CEASE   . . . .   420 EMPEDOCLES I 2   234
     YET WILL NOT CEASE FROM SIN   . . . .   420 EMPEDOCLES I 2   235
     NEVER TO CEASE TO WRITHE AND TRY TO REST . . . 430 EMPEDOCLES II   60
     NEVER TO CEASE TO WRITHE AND TRY TO SLEEP . . . 430 EMPEDOCLES II   V 60
     THINGS THAT MAY CEASE BUT NEVER BE FORGOT . . . 462 ALARIC AT ROME   16
     THERE FALKLAND EYD THE STRIFE THAT WOULD NOT CEASE 477 CROMWELL   173
     AWE-STRUCK FAIN WOULD CEASE TO BE   . . . . . .   META CLOISTER   18

CEASED
     HE CEASED BUT WHILE HE SPAKE RUSTUM HAD RISEN . . 74 SOHRAB RUSTUM   448
     HE SPOKE AND AS HE CEASED HE WEPT ALOUD   . . . .   79 SOHRAB RUSTUM   602
     WHO WHILE THE MOTHER SPAKE HAD CEASED THEIR TOIL . 100 BALDER DEAD 1   195
     HE SPAKE AND AS HE CEASED A PUFF OF WIND   . . . . 126 BALDER DEAD 3   440
     THEY CAME TO WHERE THE BRUSHWOOD CEASED AND DAY . 155 TRISTRAM 3   185
     HAD CEASED TO LIVE AND THRIVE   . . . .   320 OBERMANN MORE   226

CEASELESS
     WITH THE CEASELESS STROKE OF HIS WINGS   . . . . 233 YOUTH OF MAN   41
     IN CEASELESS OPPOSITION BE THE GUARD . . . . .   437 EMPEDOCLES II   268
     WHILE FULL AND CEASELESS AS THE OCEAN ROLL . . . 464 ALARIC AT ROME   71

CEASES
     THEIR PASSION BURN MORE ERE IT CEASES TO BURN . . 19 MODERN SAPPHO   14
     CEASES NOT FROM ALL TIME TO HEAVE AND GROAN   . .   45 IN UTRUMQUE PAR   26

CECITY
     AFTER LIGHTS TERM A TERM OF CECITY   . . . . . . 448 WESTMIN ABBEY   155

CEDAR
     IN THE CEDAR SHADOW SLEEPING   . . . .   26 NEW SIRENS   V 1
     HARK FROM THAT MOONLIT CEDAR WHAT A BURST   . . . 200 PHILOMELA   3

CEDARN
     IN THE CEDARN SHADOW SLEEPING   . . . .   26 NEW SIRENS   1
     IN THE SLUMBROUS CEDARN SHADE   . . . .   28 NEW SIRENS   68
     IN THIS SLUMBROUS CEDARN SHADE   . . . .   28 NEW SIRENS   V 68

CEDARS
     AND MADE ALL YOUR CEDARS FROWN   . . . .   30 NEW SIRENS   124
     SAW THE CEDARS OF PAINS HILL   . . . .   458 POOR MATTHIAS   199

CEILED
     SEEKING CEILED CHAMBERS AND A PALACE-HALL   . . . 27 NEW SIRENS   40

CEILING
     A CEILING OF AMBER   . . . .   165 FORSAKEN MERM   118

CEILING
     AND HOW A CALL CELESTIAL ROUND HIM RANG   . . . . 268 THYRSIS   188
     BUT RAIMENT OF CELESTIAL SHEEN SHE WORE   . . . . 447 WESTMIN ABBEY   99

CELL
     HE TORE US FROM THE PRISON-CELL   . . . . 271 MEMORIAL VERSES V

CELLS
     THE CELLS THE SUFFERING SON OF MAN   . . . . . . 300 GRANDE CHARTR   45

CEMENTED
     UNION CEMENTED FOR THIS NATIONS WEAL . . . . . 333 MEROPE   103

CENAEUM
     AND THE PROMONTORY OF CENAEUM   . . . . 399 MEROPE   1816

CENSURE
     AND SHE WHOSE CENSURE THOU DOST DREAD   . . . . 241 MORALITY   19
     WITH HALF CENSURE WITH AWE   . . . .   298 HEINES GRAVE   203
     THEREFORE WITH CENSURE UNALLAYD   . . . . . .   353 MEROPE   686

CENTAUR
     CHIRON THE AGED CENTAUR LAY   . . . .   414 EMPEDOCLES I 2   59
     THE CENTAUR TAUGHT HIM TO EXPLORE   . . . . . . 414 EMPEDOCLES I 2   61

CENTAURS
          THEY SEE THE CENTAURS   . . . .   190 STRAYED REVEL   143
          THEY SEE THE CENTAURS   . . . .   192 STRAYED REVEL   223
          AND THE TIRED CENTAURS COME TO REST . . . . . .   414 EMPEDOCLES I 2   63

CENTRAL
          BUT AT THE CENTRAL HEARTH THOSE WOMEN OLD . . . .   100 BALDER DEAD 1   194
          THAT GLOW OF CENTRAL FIRE IS DONE   . . . . . .   320 OBERMANN MORE   221
          THE GLOW OF CENTRAL FIRE IS DONE   . . . . . .   320 OBERMANN MORE   V 221
          WHICH FROM ONE CENTRAL CITYS GUARDED SEAT . . . .   337 MEROPE   246
          THE CENTRAL STREAM OF WHAT WE FEEL INDEED . . . .   483 BELOW SURFACE   5

CENTRE
          SOMETIMES FROM THE GROVES CENTRE ECHOES CAME   . .   12 MYCERINUS   124
          OUTMOST THE OTHERS NEAR THE CENTRE RUN   . . . .   109 BALDER DEAD 2   153
          IN THE SMOOTH CENTRE OF THE OPENING STOOD . . .   150 TRISTRAM 3   19
          IN THE SMOOTH CENTRE OF THE HOLLOW STOOD   . . .   TRISTRAM 3   V 19

CENTRED
          CENTRED IN A MAJESTIC UNITY   . . . .   4 BUTLERS SERMONS   8
          STAND MUTE SELF-CENTRED STERN AND DREAM NO MORE . .   42 GIPSY CHILD   32

CENTURIES
          THROUGH CENTURIES PAST IT HAS HUNG SO   . . . .   214 NEW ROME   19
          AND WILL THROUGH CENTURIES MORE   . . . . . .   214 NEW ROME   20
          ALL THE CENTURIES PAST IT HAS HUNG SO   . . . .   214 NEW ROME   V 19
          AND WILL FOR CENTURIES MORE   . . . .   214 NEW ROME   V 20
          AND CENTURIES CAME AND RAN THEIR COURSE   . . .   318 OBERMANN MORE   161
          OF ALL THE CENTURIES YET TO COME   . . . . .   450 GEISTS GRAVE   22

CEPHISSIAN
          LONE DAULIS AND THE HIGH CEPHISSIAN VALE   . . . .   201 PHILOMELA   27

CEREMONIOUS
          THE CEREMONIOUS AIR OF GLOOM   . . . .   250 WISH   15

CERTAIN
          A CERTAIN MOOLLAH WITH HIS ROBE   . . . . . .   88 SICK KING BOKH   31
          NO CERTAIN NEWS IF LIKE THE REST IT RUN   . . .   350 MEROPE   600
          CERTAIN IN THIS THAT TIS UNCERTAIN STILL   . . .   350 MEROPE   601
          AGAINST THE ONE AND CERTAIN ARM OF POWER   . . .   381 MEROPE   1313
          SINGLE AND FRIENDLESS GIVE TO CERTAIN DEATH . .   382 MEROPE   1326
          SINGLE AND FRIENDLESS THROW TO CERTAIN DEATH   . .   382 MEROPE   V1326

CERTAINTY
          WITH CERTAINTY OF FAVOUR . . . .   391 MEROPE   1599

CERTITUDE
          NOR CERTITUDE NOR PEACE NOR HELP FOR PAIN . . . .   212 DOVER BEACH   34

CESSION
          MAKE CESSION OF HER SCEPTRE DOOM HERSELF . . . .   RUDE ORATOR   19

CETTE
          CETTE WITH ITS GLISTENING HOUSES WHITE   . . . .   275 SOUTHERN NIGHT   9

CEUTA
          AND CEUTA ON THE LEFT THEN SOUTHWARD SPED . . . .   484 S S LUSITANIA   5

CHAFE
          CHAMP AND CHAFE AND TOSS IN THE SPRAY   . . . .   161 FORSAKEN MERM   7
          I CHAFE NOT WITH THEE THAT THY HATE ENDURES . .   398 MEROPE   1785

CHAFED
          NOT CHAFED BY HOURLY FALSE CONTROL   . . . . .   302 GRANDE CHARTR   96
          NOT CHAFED BY HOURLY FALSE CONTROUL . . . . .   302 GRANDE CHARTR   V 96
          TO THE CHAFED HEART OF JUSTICE THAN TO MINE . .   349 MEROPE   560

CHAFES
          CHAFES IN HIS PLACE AND PINES FOR CHANGE   . . .   484 ROME-SICKNESS   24

CHAFING
          OF ALL ITS CHAFING TORRENTS AFTER THAW   . . . .   5 DUKE WELLINGTON   5
          TIMES CHAFING PRISONER ASK IT NOW   . . . . .   53 RESIGNATION   39
          BLACK CHAFING WATER AND AFLOAT   . . . .   479 HAYSWATER BOAT   2

CHAFINGS
          THEIR DAILY-PRACTISED CHAFINGS KEEP ALIVE . . .   331 MEROPE   44

CHAIN
          WHAT MAY CHAIN US WHO CAN SAY   . . . .   23 MEMORY-PICTURE   22
          THIS FAR-REACHING MAGIC CHAIN . . . .   33 NEW SIRENS   204
          OH ONCE ERE NIGHT IN THY SUCCESS THY CHAIN   . .   44 GIPSY CHILD   66
          AND FENRIS AT HIS HEEL WITH BROKEN CHAIN   . . .   127 BALDER DEAD 3   477
          MAKE THEIR BLOOD DANCE AND CHAIN THEIR EYES . .   305 GRANDE CHARTR   188
          ONCE MORE I SLIP MY CHAIN . . . .   313 OBERMANN MORE   44
          TILL NOW AND I HAVE STRENGTH TO CHAIN IT STILL . .   334 MEROPE   150
          NO VIGOUR AND SEVERITY MUST CHAIN   . . . . .   390 MEROPE   1563
          CHAIN MADMEN BY THE MUSIC OF HIS LYRE   . . . .   410 EMPEDOCLES I 1   116
          SKIES THAT UNBOUND BY CLASP OF MOUNTAIN CHAIN . .   473 CROMWELL   37
          BOUND ALL HIS BEING WITH A SILVER CHAIN   . . .   473 CROMWELL   63

CHAIN   (CONTINUED)
        THEN HIS EYE SLUMBERD AND THE CHAIN WAS BROKE   • •   475 CROMWELL   131
        OF MEN WHO AGAINST HOPE REPELLD THE CHAIN   • • • •   480 HUNGARIAN NAT   10

CHAIND
        FOR I HAVE KEPT CONSPIRACY FAST-CHAIND   • • • •   334 MEROPE   149

CHAINS
        THOUGH HE HATH LOOSED A THOUSAND CHAINS   • • • •   56 RESIGNATION   150
        SUBDUED WITH LIMBER CHAINS LIVES FENRIS BOUND   • •   111 BALDER DEAD 2   216
        ON THIS SUSPICION CAST HIM INTO CHAINS   • • • •   365 MEROPE   V
        THE IMPRISONING CHAINS FELL OFF AND ALL WAS CLEAR • • 478 CROMWELL   214

CHAIR
        SHOUTS GREETING FROM HIS EASY CHAIR   • • • • • •   53 RESIGNATION   43
        UPON HER GOLDEN CHAIR THE MOTHER SATE   • • • •   98 BALDER DEAD 1   92
        THE DYING RACHEL IN A CHAIR THEY BORE   • • • •   167 RACHEL 2   3
        WE BID THEE TO THY VACANT CHAIR   • • • • • •   451 GEISTS GRAVE   46

CHAIRS
        AND ON THEIR GOLDEN CHAIRS THEY SATE AGAIN • • • •   97 BALDER DEAD 1   64
        WHERE ARE IN CIRCLE RANGED TWELVE GOLDEN CHAIRS   • • 106 BALDER DEAD 2   37
        AT ONE ANOTHER FROM THEIR GOLDEN CHAIRS   • • • •   431 EMPEDOCLES II   82

CHALCEDONY
        JASPER AND CHALCEDONY   • • • • • • • • • •   191 STRAYED REVEL   196

CHALET
        BY SOME HIGH CHALET-DOOR AND SEEN   • • • • •   310 OBERMANN   115
        AND TO THY MOUNTAIN-CHALET COME   • • • • •   313 OBERMANN MORE   45

CHALETS
        MID THE DISTANT MOUNTAIN-CHALETS   • • • • • •   12 CHURCH BROU 1   3
        SWISS CHALETS GLITTERD ON THE DEWY SLOPES   • • • •   25 DREAM   10
        OR CHALETS NEAR THE ALPINE SNOW   • • • • • •   304 GRANDE CHARTR   150

CHALLENGE
        WILL CHALLENGE FORTH THE BRAVEST PERSIAN LORDS   • •   62 SOHRAB RUSTUM   56
        FEROOD SHAME BIDS US TAKE THEIR CHALLENGE UP   • •   66 SOHRAB RUSTUM   175
        THE TARTAR CHALLENGE AND THIS YOUNG MANS NAME   • •   66 SOHRAB RUSTUM   181
        STAND FORTH THE WHILE AND TAKE THEIR CHALLENGE UP   66 SOHRAB RUSTUM   183
        FOR FROM THE TARTARS IS A CHALLENGE BROUGHT   • •   67 SOHRAB RUSTUM   211
        BY CHALLENGE FORTH MAKE GOOD THY VAUNT OR YIELD   • •   72 SOHRAB RUSTUM   367

CHALLENGED
        I CHALLENGED ONCE WHEN THE TWO ARMIES CAMPD   • •   72 SOHRAB RUSTUM   357

CHALLENGING
        AND TO UPHOLD THY DESPERATE CHALLENGING   • • • •   RUDE ORATOR   17

CHAMBER
        FROM HER MULLIOND CHAMBER-CASEMENT   • • • • •   13 CHURCH BROU 1   11
        INTO AN UPPER CHAMBER AND LAY DOWN   • • • • •   103 BALDER DEAD 1   278
        MAKES THEIR CHAMBER AS BRIGHT AS DAY   • • • • •   140 TRISTRAM 1   334
        STEALS COLDLY AROUND THE CHAMBER BRIGHT   • • • •   147 TRISTRAM 2   148
        HOW COMES IT HERE THIS CHAMBER BRIGHT   • • • •   148 TRISTRAM 2   168
        MEN CALLD FROM CHAMBER CHURCH AND TENT   • • • •   318 OBERMANN MORE   171
        TO THE GUEST-CHAMBER LEAD HIM SOME ONE GIVE   • •   359 MEROPE   869
        HE IN THE GUEST-CHAMBER NOW   • • • • • • •   371 MEROPE   1123
        OF THE GUEST-CHAMBER DOOR   • • • • • • •   372 MEROPE   1150
        IN A RICH CHAMBER ON A HAPPY BED   • • • • •   373 MEROPE   1178
        LEST FROM THE COUNCIL-CHAMBER PRESENTLY   • • • •   386 MEROPE   1442

CHAMBERS
        SEEKING CEILED CHAMBERS AND A PALACE-HALL   • • •   27 NEW SIRENS   40
        WHAT THOU THINKST MEN SPEAK IN COURTLY CHAMBERS   • • 143 TRISTRAM 2   41
        HAUNTING THE SHROUDED CHAMBERS OF HIS HEART   • •   473 CROMWELL   58
        THRO THE DARK CHAMBERS OF THE HEARTS OF MEN   • •   478 CROMWELL   230

CHAMBERY
        RIDE OUT TO CHURCH FROM CHAMBERY   • • • • • •   17 CHURCH BROU 2   21

CHAMP
        CHAMP AND CHAFE AND TOSS IN THE SPRAY   • • • •   161 FORSAKEN MERM   7

CHAMPD
        BY THEIR CHARIOTS STOOD THE STEEDS AND CHAMPD   HOMER TRANS   5
            THE WHITE BARLEY

CHAMPION
        BUT CHOOSE A CHAMPION FROM THE PERSIAN LORDS   • •   65 SOHRAB RUSTUM   152
        TO FIGHT OUR CHAMPION SOHRAB MAN TO MAN   • • • •   65 SOHRAB RUSTUM   153
        YET CHAMPION HAVE WE NONE TO MATCH THIS YOUTH   • •   66 SOHRAB RUSTUM   176
        TO PICK A CHAMPION FROM THE PERSIAN LORDS   • • •   67 SOHRAB RUSTUM   212
        TO FIGHT THEIR CHAMPION AND THOU KNOWST HIS NAME   •   67 SOHRAB RUSTUM   213
        AND CHAMPION TO THE THRONE I HONOURING MOST   • •   338 MEROPE   268
        SOMEWHERE FOR VENGEANCE A CHAMPION A LIGHT   • •   346 MEROPE   513

CHAMPIONS
        CHAMPIONS ENOUGH AFRASIAB HAS WHOM THOU   • • •   74 SOHRAB RUSTUM   445
        AND THEY WHO WERE CALLD CHAMPIONS IN THEIR TIME   • •   85 SOHRAB RUSTUM   811

CHANCD
      FIGHT LIFES MANY—CHANCD FIGHT • • • • • • • • 216 LORDS MESSENGER V

CHANCE
      CHANCE GUIDES THE MIGRATORY RACE • • • • • • 55 RESIGNATION 113
      FATE GAVE WHAT CHANCE SHALL NOT CONTROL • • • • 58 RESIGNATION 197
      NO GIFTS FROM CHANCE HAVE CONQUERD FATE • • • • 59 RESIGNATION 248
      AND SHARE THE BATTLES COMMON CHANCE WITH US • • 63 SOHRAB RUSTUM 67
      ACCEPT THE CHANCE THOU CANST NO MORE OBTAIN • • 122 BALDER DEAD 3 290
      DID THAT CHANCE ACT OF GOOD THAT ONE • • • • 158 SAINT BRANDAN 58
      MY FRIEND AND I BY CHANCE WE TALKD • • • • • 221 EPILOG LAOCOON 2
      WE JUDGED THE BEST CHANCE FINDS NO BETTER WAY • 331 MEROPE 36
      WILL LIE MY GRANDSIRE SAID OUR FAIREST CHANCE • 331 MEROPE 41
      TO CHANCE IMPUTE THEIR DEATHS THEN NOT TO ME • 340 MEROPE 346
      SUCH CHANCE AS KILLD THE FATHER KILLD THE SONS • • 340 MEROPE 347
      AND THE KIND CHANCE—ARRIVED WANDERER • • • • • 399 MEROPE 1836
      WHAT LIFE AND CHANCE GO HARD WITH THEE TOO AS WITH US 416 EMPEDOCLES I 2 116
      THAT CHANCE WILL BRING US THROUGH • • • • • • 420 EMPEDOCLES I 2 240
      IN SOME CHANCE BATTLE ON CITHAERON—SIDE • • • • 447 WESTMIN ABBEY 114

CHANCED
      IT CHANCED I KNOW NOT HOW MY DREAM WAS FLED • • EMERSONS ESSAYS V 8
      IT CHANCED I KNOW NOT HOW MY JOY WAS FLED • • • • EMERSONS ESSAYS V 8
      TO SPEAK IN ORDER WHAT HATH CHANCED • • • • • • 88 SICK KING BOKH 28

CHANCEL
      MOUNTAIN GREENSWARD PAVES THE CHANCEL • • • • 15 CHURCH BROU 1 71

CHANCES
      MAN CANNOT THOUGH HE WOULD LIVE CHANCES FOOL • • 40 HUMAN LIFE 18

CHANGD
      BUT OH HOW CHANGD THOSE DEATHLIKE FEATURES WORE • • 477 CROMWELL 181
      NO ALL WAS CHANGD THE MONARCH WEPT ALONE • • • • 477 CROMWELL 187

CHANGE
      THE MOUNTAIN—SKIRTS WITH ALL THEIR SYLVAN CHANGE • • 25 DREAM 7
      THEN WHEN CHANGE ITSELF IS OVER • • • • • • 33 NEW SIRENS 219
      AND OH WITH SUCH INTOLERABLE CHANGE • • • • • 36 VOICE 27
      CHANGE DOTH UNKNIT THE TRANQUIL STRENGTH OF MEN • • 44 QUESTION 3
      FAR REGIONS OF ETERNAL CHANGE • • • • • • 58 RESIGNATION 222
      SHOULD CHANGE HIS LOT AND FILL ANOTHERS LIFE • • 98 BALDER DEAD 1 115
      LOVERS OF CHANGE YE ARE FASTIDIOUS SPRITES • • • • 123 BALDER DEAD 3 339
      WHAT NEW CHANGE SHALL WE NOW SEE • • • • • 139 TRISTRAM 1 296
      THIS TOO CAN CHANGE US WHOLLY AND MAKE SEEM • • 153 TRISTRAM 3 131
      CREEDS PASS RITES CHANGE NO ALTAR STANDETH WHOLE • • 173 MONICAS PRAYER 12
      POOR FUGITIVE THE FEATHERY CHANGE • • • • • • 201 PHILOMELA 24
      CAN CHANGE OF SCENE AND NIGHT • • • • • • • 200 PHILOMELA V
      FESTERS THE DULL REMEMBRANCE OF A CHANGE • • • 213 GROWING OLD 29
      WHAT POWER OF PASSION WEALTH OF CHANGE • • • • 223 EPILOG LAOCOON 82
      FROM CHANGE TO CHANGE AND YEAR TO YEAR • • • • 225 EPILOG LAOCOON 149
      FROM CHANGE TO CHANGE AND YEAR TO YEAR • • • • 225 EPILOG LAOCOON 149
      SEEST US CHANGE WHILE WE LIVE • • • • • • • 232 YOUTH OF MAN 6
      WELL FOR US THAT WE CHANGE • • • • • • • • 232 YOUTH OF MAN 11
      AND WELL—NIGH CHANGE HIS OWN IDENTITY • • • • 246 BURIED LIFE 34
      TIS THAT FROM CHANGE TO CHANGE THEIR BEING ROLLS • • 259 SCHOLAR—GIPSY 143
      TIS THAT FROM CHANGE TO CHANGE THEIR BEING ROLLS • • 259 SCHOLAR—GIPSY 143
      WE WOULD NOT CHANGE IT NOW • • • • • • • 273 EDW QUILLINAN 20
      OF CHANGE ALARM SURPRISE • • • • • • • • • 308 OBERMANN 70
      BY THEIR GREEN RIVER WHO DOTH CHANGE • • • • 313 OBERMANN MORE 25
      PERCEIVST THOU NOT THE CHANGE OF DAY • • • • • 315 OBERMANN MORE 81
      EXPECT NO WAVERING NO RETREAT NO CHANGE • • • 342 MEROPE 378
      WOULD CHANGE WHEREER HE ROAM • • • • • • • 419 EMPEDOCLES I 2 218
      AND SO CHANGE BACK AND MANY THOUSAND TIMES • • • 435 EMPEDOCLES II 229
      WHOSE HABIT OF THOUGHT IS FIXD WHO WILL NOT CHANGE 437 EMPEDOCLES II 266
      KNEAD US IN ITS HOT HAND AND CHANGE OUR NATURE • • 440 EMPEDOCLES II 386
      AND BREAK HIS HEART WITH ALL THE BAFFLING CHANGE • • 448 WESTMIN ABBEY 149
      I WOULD NOT BREAK THY REST NOR CHANGE THY DOOM • • 449 WESTMIN ABBEY 166
      NOTE NO CHANGE AND LET THEM DIE • • • • • • 455 POOR MATTHIAS 108
      THE CHANGE OF LIFE THE NOTHINGNESS OF POWER • • 469 ALARIC AT ROME 188
      CHAFES IN HIS PLACE AND PINES FOR CHANGE • • • • 484 ROME—SICKNESS 24
      LEAVES HIM NO REST AND CHANGE HE WILL • • • • 484 ROME—SICKNESS 26
      NEITHER HIS MIND NOR BODY CAN HE CHANGE • • • LUCRETIUS 3 6
      AND WHEREFORE THEN IF HE CAN NEVER CHANGE • • • LUCRETIUS 3 V 8

CHANGED
      THESE ARE NOT CHANGED AND WE YOU SAY • • • • • 55 RESIGNATION 106
      ARE SCARCE MORE CHANGED IN TRUTH THAN THEY • • • 55 RESIGNATION 107
      CHANGED GIFTS AND WENT ON EQUAL TERMS AWAY • • • 72 SOHRAB RUSTUM 361
      AH NOW TIS CHANGED IN CONQUERING SUNSHINE BRIGHT • • 170 EAST AND WEST 12
      OR SHALL I FIND THEE STILL BUT CHANGED • • • • 184 TERRACE BERNE 33
      THEY ARE DUST THEY ARE CHANGED THEY ARE GONE • • 232 YOUTH OF NATURE 133
      THEY NOT NATURE ARE CHANGED • • • • • • • 235 YOUTH OF MAN 95
      HOW CHANGED IS HERE EACH SPOT MAN MAKES OR FILLS • • 262 THYRSIS 1
      ARE YE TOO CHANGED YE HILLS • • • • • • • • 263 THYRSIS 6
      ALIVE WE WOULD HAVE CHANGED HIS LOT • • • • • 273 EDW QUILLINAN 19
      SHE CHANGED INTO A CHILD • • • • • • • • • 317 OBERMANN MORE 138
      FIXD YESTERDAY AND TEN TIMES CHANGED SINCE THEN • • 389 MEROPE 1547
      BUT OH PAUSANIAS HE IS CHANGED OF LATE • • • • 408 EMPEDOCLES I 1 67

CHANGED   (CONTINUED)
         PLACED SAFELY IN CHANGED FORMS THE PAIR   • • • •   427 EMPEDOCLES I 2   457
         CHANGED AND AGING THEY AND WE • • • • • • • •   454 POOR MATTHIAS   51

CHANGEFUL
         CHANGEFUL TILL NOW WE STILL   • • • • • • •   425 EMPEDOCLES I 2   377
         MADE ROUGH WITH CARE BECOME THE CHANGEFUL SEA   • •   473 CROMWELL   49

CHANGELESS
         LET US WITH CHANGELESS WILL   • • • • • • •   425 EMPEDOCLES I 2   379
         ON THE DARK CURRENT OF HIS CHANGELESS DAY   • • • •   473 CROMWELL   62

CHANGELING
         POOR CHANGELING TREMBLED • • • • • • • • • • •   392 MEROPE   1636

CHANGES
         CHANGES PLACE AND TIME OF YEAR • • • • • •   133 TRISTRAM 1   89
         SCANNING MY FACE AND THE CHANGES WROUGHT THERE • •   206 SEPARATION   14
         ALL CHANGES FAST AND HIES ALONG   • • • • •   225 EPILOG LAOCOON   124
         WAY AFTER WAY CHANGES THAT NEVER CEASE • • • •   239 REVOLUTIONS   7
         THE CHANGES OF THEIR QUIET DAY • • • • • • •   249 KENSINGTON GARD   32

CHANGING
         CHANGING THE PURE EMOTION   • • • • • • • •   39 STAGIRIUS   24
         WHAT EXILES CHANGING BITTER THOUGHTS WITH GLAD • •   42 GIPSY CHILD   V 25
         CHANGING AND SHOT AS THE SIGHTS WHICH WE SEE   • •   253 FUTURE   57
         A NEVER-CHANGING INDEX TO REVENGE   • • • • • •   381 MEROPE   1317
         FORMS THAT WITH HIM SHALL TREAD LIFES CHANGING STAGE 476 CROMWELL   161

CHANNEL
         FOR THE BRIGHT STREAM A CHANNEL GRAND   • • • •   213 PROGRESS POESY   6
         THE MOUNT IS MUTE THE CHANNEL DRY   • • • • •   213 PROGRESS POESY   11
         AND ROLL ADOWN A CHANNEL LARGE • • • • • • •   224 EPILOG LAOCOON   101

CHANNELS
         AND STREWN THE CHANNELS WITH TORN BOUGHS SO HUGE • • 73 SOHRAB RUSTUM   415
         AND STREWN THE CHANNELS WITH TORN BOUGHS SO ROUGH   73 SOHRAB RUSTUM   V 415
         ACROSS THE SOUNDS AND CHANNELS POUR   • • • • •   182 TO MARG CONT   12

CHANT
         TO CHANT THY REQUIEM WITH MORE PASSIONATE BREATH • • 471 ALARIC AT ROME   227

CHANTING
         SAD-CHANTING MAIDENS CLAD IN MOURNING ROBES   • •   331 MEROPE   53

CHANTS
         THOU HEAREST THE IMMORTAL CHANTS OF OLD   • • • •   268 THYRSIS   181

CHAOS
         THOU WONDROUS CHAOS WHERE TOGETHER DWELL • • • •   463 ALARIC AT ROME   43

CHAPEL
         THE FOREST-CHAPEL AND THE FOUNTAIN NEAR   • • • •   139 TRISTRAM 1   279
         I A STATUE ON THY CHAPEL-FLOOR • • • • •   • •   144 TRISTRAM 2   62
         IN KING MARCS CHAPEL IN TYNTAGEL OLD • • • • •   149 TRISTRAM 3   3
         A YEAR HAD FLOWN AND IN THE CHAPEL OLD • • • •   149 TRISTRAM 3   V 1
         AT TYNTAGIL IN KING MARCS CHAPEL OLD   • • • • •   149 TRISTRAM 3   V 3
         HE SINGS HOW FROM THE CHAPEL   • • • • • •   160 NECKAN   29
         SAINT MICHAELS CHAPEL CUTS THE SKY   • • • • •   273 STANZAS CARNAC   2
         THE CHAPEL-WALLS IN WHOSE BOUND   • • • • •   286 RUGBY CHAPEL   12
         THE CHAPEL WHERE NO ORGANS PEAL   • • • • •   300 GRANDE CHARTR   37

CHAPLET
         WHERE TWINES THE CHAPLET DEALT A MIGHTY BLOW   • •   402 MEROPE   1921
         WITH BLOOD-BESPATTERD ROBES AND CHAPLET SHORN • •   403 MEROPE   1966

CHARGD
         SAY I CHARGD HER THAT YE LIVE TOGETHER • • • •   145 TRISTRAM 2   V 95
         SAY I CHARGD HER THAT THOU STAY BESIDE ME • • •   145 TRISTRAM 2   V 95
         SAY I CHARGD THEE THAT THOU STAY BESIDE HER   • •   145 TRISTRAM 2   V 95
         SO CHARGD HE STOOD DUMB-FOUNDERD CYPSELUS   • • •   365 MEROPE   V

CHARGE
         AT THY SIDE THOU LOVELY CHARGE • • • • • • •   134 TRISTRAM 1   112
         CHARGE ONCE MORE THEN AND BE DUMB   • • • • • •   215 LAST WORD   13
         THE WEALTH DIVINE THEY HAVE IN CHARGE   • • • •   224 EPILOG LAOCOON   102
         FIND THEN SUCH CAUSE THE CHARGE OF MURDER FALLS • • 336 MEROPE   210
         SAVE FOR THIS ANNUAL CHARGE I HOPE TO HEAR • • • •   351 MEROPE   619
         O HONOURD QUEEN THY SON MY CHARGE IS GONE   • • • •   362 MEROPE   944
         OLD MAN OLD MAN THOU HADST MY BOY IN CHARGE   • •   368 MEROPE   1069
         MY CHILD MY CHARGE BELOVED WELCOME TO LIFE • • • •   375 MEROPE   1207

CHARGED
         THE TABLE STOOD BEFORE HIM CHARGED WITH FOOD   • •   67 SOHRAB RUSTUM   197
         THE TABLE STOOD BESIDE HIM CHARGED WITH FOOD   • •   67 SOHRAB RUSTUM   V 197
         THE TABLE STOOD BESIDE HIM CHARGED WITH CATES • •   67 SOHRAB RUSTUM   V 197
         NOW THE KING CHARGED US SECRETLY   • • • • • •   91 SICK KING BOKH   113
         HOTLY CHARGED AND SANK AT LAST • • • • • • •   215 LAST WORD   12
         HOTLY CHARGED AND BROKE AT LAST   • • • • •   215 LAST WORD   V 12
         IS CHARGED AGAINST THIS STRIPLING AGENTS FEED • •   364 MEROPE   980

CHARIOT
    WHEREOER THE CHARIOT WHEELS OF LIFE ARE ROLLD   •   •   4 BUTLERS SERMONS   13
    SHOULDERING THY HAMMER IN THY CHARIOT DRAWN   •   •   115 BALDER DEAD 3   72

CHARIOTS
    BY THEIR CHARIOTS STOOD THE STEEDS AND CHAMPD   HOMER TRANS   5
        THE WHITE BARLEY

CHARITY
    IN JOPPA AND THY CHARITY • • • • • • • • • • •   157 SAINT BRANDAN   40

CHARM
    GAINST THAT ALONE HAD BALDERS LIFE NO CHARM   •   •   95 BALDER DEAD 1   8
    GAINST THAT ALONE HAD BALDERS LIFE NO CHARM   •   •   98 BALDER DEAD 1   104
    THOU ART PALER BUT THY SWEET CHARM ISEULT   •   •   •   143 TRISTRAM 2   25
    WOULD CHARM THE GAZER TILL HIS THOUGHT   •   •   •   147 TRISTRAM 2   139
    THE CHARM WHICH HOMER SHAKESPEARE TEACH   •   •   •   227 EPILOG LAOCOON   206
    O CHARM O ROMANCE THAT WE FEEL • • • • • •   230 YOUTH OF NATURE   64
    NATURE IS NOTHING HER CHARM   •   •   •   233 YOUTH OF MAN   35
    ON MY HEART YOUR MIGHTY CHARM RENEW • • • • •   240 SELF-DEPENDENCE   10
    AND NEAR AND REAL THE CHARM OF THY REPOSE   •   •   267 THYRSIS   149
    IS GRACE IS CHARM • • • • • • • • • •   279 SOUTHERN NIGHT   132
    CHARM IS THE GLORY WHICH MAKES • • • • • • •   295 HEINES GRAVE   103
    LOVE IS THE FOUNTAIN OF CHARM • • • • • • •   295 HEINES GRAVE   105
    HOW WITHOUT CHARM WILT THOU DRAW   •   •   •   295 HEINES GRAVE   106
    CHARM IS THE POETS ALONE   •   •   •   295 HEINES GRAVE   112
    BUT DRUGS TO CHARM WITH • • • • • • • • •   432 EMPEDOCLES II   116
    ONE MOMENTS SPACE PERCHANCE MIGHT CHARM HIS EYE   •   •   475 CROMWELL   109

CHARMD
    WHICH THE CHARMD WINDS NEVER DROWN   •   •   •   •   27 NEW SIRENS   28
    HATH CHARMD AT BIRTH FROM GLOOM AND CARE   •   •   •   203 EUPHROSYNE   14
    HAS CHARMD AT BIRTH FROM GLOOM AND CARE   •   •   •   203 EUPHROSYNE   V   14
    WHAT CHARMD YOU IN OTHERS RE-LIVE   •   •   •   231 YOUTH OF NATURE   109
    YET CHARMD IT FROM HIS FOREST-GRAVE   •   •   •   273 STANZAS CARNAC   8
    ARRESTS THEM WITH A CHARMD SURPRISE   •   •   •   305 GRANDE CHARTR   190
    THE CHARMD BABE OF THE ELEUSINIAN KING   •   •   •   446 WESTMIN ABBEY   85
    SINKS AND RISES THROUGH THIS CHARMD ARCADE   •   •   •   META CLOISTER   V   16

CHARMED
    DOWN TO THE BRIMMD MOON-CHARMED MAIN • • • • •   279 SOUTHERN NIGHT   118
    AND NO ONE ROUND THE CHARMED CIRCLE SPEAKS • • • •   431 EMPEDOCLES II   83

CHARMS
    THAN THE CHARMS ULYSSES BORE   • • • • • • •   27 NEW SIRENS   44

CHARRD
    A CHARRD LOG FALLING MAKES A SHOWER OF SPARKS   •   •   119 BALDER DEAD 3   204
    ON THIS CHARRD BLACKEND MELANCHOLY WASTE   •   •   •   428 EMPEDOCLES II   2
    UPON WHOSE CHARRD AND QUAKING CRUST I STAND   •   •   438 EMPEDOCLES II   307

CHART
    THE INLY-WRITTEN CHART THOU GAVEST ME   •   •   •   •   40 HUMAN LIFE   5

CHARTERD
    AS CHARTERD BY SOME UNKNOWN POWERS   •   •   •   •   41 HUMAN LIFE   26

CHASE
    ALL BEASTS OF CHASE ALL BEASTS WHICH HUNTERS KNOW   69 SOHRAB RUSTUM   279
    THE CHASE NEGLECTED AND HIS HOUND   • • • • • • •   137 TRISTRAM 1   225
    WHEREIN HE DOTH FOR EVER CHASE • • • • • • • •   247 BURIED LIFE   92
    TO CHASE FATIGUE AND FEAR   • • • • • • • •   269 THYRSIS   236
    GIRT WITH HIS COAT FOR THE CHASE   • • • • •   342 MEROPE   394
    OF BEASTS OF CHASE THAT HAUNT THE ARCADIAN HILLS • •   356 MEROPE   757
    AND RESTING THERE TO BREATHE I WATCHD THE CHASE   •   357 MEROPE   797
    WHERE FIRST THE CHASE PLUNGED IN THE BAY IS SMOOTH   358 MEROPE   819
    THE PRINCE IN CHASE AFTER A SWIMMING STAG   •   •   •   363 MEROPE   959

CHASED
    AS IF THEIR BABY-OWNER CHASED   • • • • • • • •   141 TRISTRAM 1   347

CHASM
    GULFS OF ESTRANGING BLOOD ACROSS THAT CHASM   •   •   336 MEROPE   194
    THERE IS A CHASM RIFTED IN THE BASE • • • • •   •   358 MEROPE   811
    BOATS AND APPROACH NEAR AS WE DARED THE CHASM   •   358 MEROPE   838
    SWEPT DOWN A CHASM RIFTED IN THE CLIFF   •   •   •   363 MEROPE   960
    SWEPT DOWN A CHASM BROKEN IN THE CLIFF   •   •   •   363 MEROPE   V 960

CHASTE
    YET SHE CHASTE QUEEN HAD NEVER PROVED   •   •   •   181 ISOLATION MARG   25

CHATELAINE
    THE YOUNGEST FAIREST CHATELAINE   • · • • • • •   136 TRISTRAM 1   194

CHATTED
    BUT STILL SHE CHATTED ON WITH HER BLUE EYES   •   •   154 TRISTRAM 3   177

CHATTER
    CHATTER AND LOVE AND HATE   • • • • • • • •   288 RUGBY CHAPEL   62
    AND KEEP THEIR FRIENDLY CHATTER AT HIS EAR • • • •   435 EMPEDOCLES II   224
    TROUBLING WITH OUR CHATTER VAIN   • • • • • •   456 POOR MATTHIAS   123

CHATTING
    CHATTING WITH HER YOUTHFUL KNIGHT • • • • • • 134 TRISTRAM 1   127

CHAUNT
    DID THE WAVES CHAUNT THEIR SONG OF LIBERTY • • • • 472 CROMWELL   16

CHEAP
    ALL TIE WITH ALL BESIDE SEEMD VAIN AND CHEAP • • 173 MONICAS PRAYER   10
    THOU HOLDST SO CHEAP THEN THE MESSENIAN CROWN • • 397 MEROPE   1774

CHEAT
    OH WHEREFORE CHEAT OUR YOUTH IF THUS IT BE • • • • 10 MYCERINUS   49
    BUT WE AN EASIER WAY TO CHEAT OUR PAINS HAVE FOUND 421 EMPEDOCLES I 2   271

CHECK
    LET THY FOREBODED HOMAGE CHECK THY TONGUE • • • • 38 WORLDS TRIUMPHS   10
    LET THY FOREBODED TREASON CHECK THY TONGUE • • • • 38 WORLDS TRIUMPHS V 10
    AND CHECK THY FIERY STEEDS AND LEANING BACK • • 349 MEROPE   575
    WHO WITHOUT CHECK OF CONSCIENCE CAN AVER • • • • 353 MEROPE   680
    OF CHILDHOOD ARTHUR DID SOME CHECK HAVE POWER • • 447 WESTMIN ABBEY   118

CHECKD
    AND CHECKD HIS RANKS AND FIXD THEM WHERE THEY STOOD 65 SOHRAB RUSTUM   147

CHECKS
    HIS HUDDLING YOUNG LEFT SOLE AT THAT HE CHECKS • • 78 SOHRAB RUSTUM   563
    AND CHECKS MY STRAIN • • • • • • • • 279 SOUTHERN NIGHT   120
    AGAINST A POWER EXEMPT FROM COMMON CHECKS • • • • 336 MEROPE   206
    SHAME RARELY CHECKS THE GENUINE TYRANTS WILL • •. • 340 MEROPE   352

CHEEK
    ALL HER PALE SWEET-ROUNDED CHEEK • • • • • • 23 MEMORY-PICTURE   30
    ON THE PEERLESS CHEEK OF QUEENS • • • • 33 NEW SIRENS   214
    DOWN THE PALE CHEEK LONG LINES OF SHADOW SLOPE • • 43 GIPSY CHILD   37
    DOWN THY PALE CHEEK THOSE LINES OF SHADOW SLOPE • • 43 GIPSY CHILD V 37
    TEARS WET THE PILLOW BY THY CHEEK BUT THOU • • • 103 BALDER DEAD 1   290
    SEE MY CHEEK AND LIPS HOW WHITE THEY ARE • • • • • 143 TRISTRAM 2   24
    FILLD UP THE HOLLOW CHEEK AND BROUGHT • • • 147 TRISTRAM 2   141
    WHICH PLAYD ON HER FLUSHD CHEEK AND HER BLUE EYES • 154 TRISTRAM 3   169
    THAT CHEEK OF LANGUID HUE • • • • • • • 174 MEETING   6
    POURD FLUSHING TO THY LANGUID CHEEK • • • • 178 FAREWELL   10
    THY CHEEK WAS GRAVE THY SPEECH GREW RARE • • • • 178 FAREWELL   16
    CAME FLOODING TO THY LANGUID CHEEK • • • • • 178 FAREWELL V 10
    CAME FLUSHING TO THY LANGUID CHEEK • • • • • 178 FAREWELL V 10
    PROPS THY SOFT CHEEK • • • • • • • 186 STRAYED REVEL   10
    THE MANTLING BLOOD TO THY CHEEK • • • • • 235 YOUTH OF MAN   115
    A STRONG EMOTION ON HER CHEEK • • • • • • • 241 MORALITY   22
    THE CHEEK GROWN THIN THE BROWN HAIR SPRENT WITH GREY 266 THYRSIS   135
    THAT WASTED CHEEK • • • • • • • • 276 SOUTHERN NIGHT   44
    WITH FURTIVE STEP AND CHEEK OF FLAME • • • • • • 278 SOUTHERN NIGHT   102

CHEEKS
    HE SPOKE AND ALL THE BLOOD LEFT RUSTUMS CHEEKS • • 80 SOHRAB RUSTUM   661
    AND WITH FOND FALTERING FINGERS STROKED HIS CHEEKS 81 SOHRAB RUSTUM   696
    MY HEAD BETWIXT THY HANDS AND KISS MY CHEEKS • • 82 SOHRAB RUSTUM   719
    AND THOU HAST FLESH AND COLOUR ON THY CHEEKS • • 108 BALDER DEAD 2   107
    BUT HER CHEEKS ARE SUNK AND PALE • • • • • • 131 TRISTRAM 1   32
    TREMBLE AND THEIR CHEEKS BE FLAME • • • • • 135 TRISTRAM 1   148
    THE LASHES ON THE CHEEKS REPOSED • • • • • 141 TRISTRAM 1   339
    AND HER CHEEKS ARE SUNK AND PALE • • • • • 131 TRISTRAM 1 V 32
    WITH HOT-FLUSHD CHEEKS AND BRILLIANT EYES • • • 146 TRISTRAM 2   117
    AND HAS A COLOUR IN HER CHEEKS • • • • • • • 147 TRISTRAM 2   129
    WITH HEATED CHEEKS AND FLURRIED AIR • • • • • 148 TRISTRAM 2   162
    THEIR CHEEKS WERE FLUSHD AND OVER EACH HOT BROW • • 150 TRISTRAM 3   32
    THEIR CHEEKS GREW FLUSHD AND OVER EACH HOT BROW • • TRISTRAM 3 V 32
    THE CHEEKS THAT STILL THEIR GENTLE PALENESS WEAR • • 175 PARTING   38
    THY CHEEKS SOFT HUE AND FLUTTERING LACE • • • 184 TERRACE BERNE   23
    WITH HOT CHEEKS AND SEARD EYES • • • • • 201 PHILOMELA   20
    IS NOT ON CHEEKS LIKE THOSE • • • • • • 219 BACCHANALIA 1   48
    SEE ON THEIR GLOWING CHEEKS • • • • • • • 221 BACCHANALIA 2   61
    THE SHORT PROUD LIP SHOWING THY RACE THY CHEEKS • • 373 MEROPE   1163
    ONCE HUMAN CHEEKS • • • • • • • • • • 393 MEROPE   1671

CHEER
    CLING TO WHAT CAN TRULY CHEER HIM • • • • • 49 SECOND BEST   19
    COOL SHADE IS THERE AND RUSTIC CHEER • • • • • 54 RESIGNATION   75
    RUNS HIS OLD ROUND OF DUBIOUS CHEER • • • • • 56 RESIGNATION   129
    WHILST OTHER MEN MAKE CHEER AND SING • • • • 93 SICK KING BOKH   178
    SHALL HE SHED CHEER OVER THE CHEERLESS SEATS • • 110 BALDER DEAD 2   195
    CHEER CHEER THY DOGS INTO THE BRAKE • • • • 149 TRISTRAM 2   186
    CHEER CHEER THY DOGS INTO THE BRAKE • • • • • 149 TRISTRAM 2   186
    TO CHEER THEE AND TO RIGHT THEE IF THOU ROAM • • 169 EAST LONDON   12
    SOON SOON THY CHEER WOULD DIE • • • • • • 261 SCHOLAR-GIPSY   226
    THE RIPPLES OF WHOSE BLUE WAVES CHEER • • • • 311 OBERMANN   163
    ALL THAT GAY COURAGEOUS CHEER • • • • • • 454 POOR MATTHIAS   61
    WHAT SENSE WHAT CHEER • • • • • • • • • 459 KAISER DEAD   34

CHEERD
    SHALL BREATHLESS GLADES CHEERD BY SHY DIANS HORN • • 6 GEO CRUIKSHANK   8

CHEERD   (CONTINUED)
          MUCH CHEERD WITH THOUGHTS OF CHRIST THE LIVING BREAD   169 EAST LONDON   8
          CHEERD US AND NOW IS PASSD INTO THE NIGHT   .   .   .   444 WESTMIN ABBEY   3
          CHEERD ALL THE FAILING HEARTS THAT SORROWD THERE   .   . 478 CROMWELL   218
          WE CHEERD BUT FROM IT RUSHD A BLAST OF MIGHT   .   .   484 S S LUSITANIA   7

CHEERED
          WE CHEERED HIM BUT THAT MOMENT FROM THE COPSE   .   .   357 MEROPE   786

CHEERFUL
          FOR DAYLIGHT FOR THE CHEERFUL SUN   .   .   .   .   .   22 YOUTH AND CALM   17
          THE CHEERFUL SILENCE OF THE FELLS   .   .   .   .   .   54 RESIGNATION   67
          BUT NOW HE CREW AT DAWN A CHEERFUL NOTE   .   .   .   105 BALDER DEAD 2   8
          NATURE WHOSE FREE LIGHT CHEERFUL AIR   .   .   .   .   241 MORALITY   17
          CHEERFUL WITH FRIENDS WE SET FORTH   .   .   .   .   .   289 RUGBY CHAPEL   89
          CHEERFUL AND HELPFUL AND FIRM .   .   .   .   290 RUGBY CHAPEL   139
          AND CHEERFUL WORKS BENEATH THE SUN   .   .   .   .   .   301 GRANDE CHARTR   60
          WAS PAST OF CHEERFUL YOUTH   .   .   .   .   322 OBERMANN MORE   278

CHEERFULNESS
          OF THY BUOYANT CHEERFULNESS CLEAR   .   .   .   .   .   287 RUGBY CHAPEL   22
          OF THINE EVEN CHEERFULNESS CLEAR   .   .   .   .   .   287 RUGBY CHAPEL   V 22

CHEERING
          SUCH LOVELY FLOWERS FOR CHEERING SOULS   .   .   .   .   227 EPILOG LAOCOON   204
          CHEERING WITH HAND AND VOICE AND HORN HIS DOGS   .   .   357 MEROPE   805

CHEERLESS
          SITTING CHEERLESS IN YOUR BOWERS   .   .   .   .   .   30 NEW SIRENS   127
          THE LIGHT AND JOURNEY TO THE CHEERLESS LAND   .   .   110 BALDER DEAD 2   181
          SHALL HE SHED CHEER OVER THE CHEERLESS SEATS   .   .   110 BALDER DEAD 2   195
          ME ON THIS CHEERLESS NETHER WORLD YE THREW   .   .   .   110 BALDER DEAD 2   212
          AND LOVE HIS CHEERLESS TRUTH   .   .   .   . 322 OBERMANN MORE   280

CHEERS
          MY FORMER LIFE AND CHEERS ME EVEN HERE   .   .   .   .   126 BALDER DEAD 3   462
          HIS LIFTED HORN NOR CHEERS HIS HOUNDS   .   .   .   .   148 TRISTRAM 2   V

CHEQUER
          A CHEQUER-WORK OF GLOWING SAPPHIRE-TINTS   .   .   .   18 CHURCH BROU 3   23
          WHICH CHEQUER AT YOUR FEET THE ILLUMINED FLINTS   .   .   18 CHURCH BROU 3   29
          THAT CHEQUER AT YOUR FEET THE ILLUMINED FLINTS   .   .   18 CHURCH BROU 3   V 29

CHEQUERING
          CHEQUERING THE GRASS WITH THEIR SHADE   .   .   .   .   297 HEINES GRAVE   158

CHERISHD
          IF THE LOVED FORM AND THE DEEP-CHERISHD FEATURE   .   .   206 SEPARATION   7
          A LAST LONG-CHERISHD PROJECT IN MY AIM   .   .   .   .   360 MEROPE   880
          AND IN THE GRAVE HE LAID A CHERISHD WIFE   .   .   .   447 WESTMIN ABBEY   124
          AND TO THE GRAVE HE BORE A CHERISHD WIFE   .   .   .   447 WESTMIN ABBEY   V 124
          FELL ON THE CHERISHD PAST WITH TEARFUL SMILE   .   .   474 CROMWELL   70

CHERRIES
          WITH CHERRIES SERVD IN DRIFTS OF SNOW   .   .   .   .   94 SICK KING BOKH   197

CHESTNUT
          SERE WITH SEPTEMBER DROOPD THE CHESTNUT-TREES   .   .   167 RACHEL 1   3
          BROWN WITH SEPTEMBER DROOPD THE CHESTNUT-TREES   .   .   167 RACHEL 1   V   3
          AND CHESTNUT-FLOWERS ARE STREWN   .   .   .   .   .   .   264 THYRSIS   56
          AND NEATH THOSE CHESTNUT-TREES WHERE STIFF   .   .   .   312 OBERMANN MORE   9
          OF NOON IS BROKEN THERE BY CHESTNUT-BOUGHS   .   .   .   414 EMPEDOCLES I 2   44
          AND STREAM AND SWARD AND CHESTNUT-TREES   .   .   .   .   414 EMPEDOCLES I 2   52

CHESTNUTS
          OF BRIGHT-LEAFD CHESTNUTS AND MOSSD WALNUT-TREES   .   .   25 DREAM   8
          OF MY HUT BY THE CHESTNUTS   .   .   .   .   186 STRAYED REVEL   26
          LIGHT THE GREEN-FOLIAGD CHESTNUTS PLAY   .   .   .   .   248 KENSINGTON GARD V
          LIGHT THE CLEAR FOLIAGED CHESTNUTS PLAY   .   .   .   KENSINGTON GARD V
          SWEET CHESTNUTS BARLEY-CAKES AND BOARS-FLESH DRIED   356 MEROPE   754
          I SAW HIM THROUGH THE CHESTNUTS FAR BELOW   .   .   .   428 EMPEDOCLES I 2   485

CHEW
          TO CHEW THE STRAW HER LITTER AT HER FEET   .   .   .   123 BALDER DEAD 3   343

CHIAN
          FREIGHTED WITH AMBER GRAPES AND CHIAN WINE   .   .   .   262 SCHOLAR-GIPSY   238

CHID
          BUT RUSTUM CHID HIM WITH STERN VOICE AND SAID   .   .   82 SOHRAB RUSTUM   737

CHIDE
          THOU DOEST WELL TO CHIDE ME HODER BLIND   .   .   .   125 BALDER DEAD 3   423
          CHIDE NOT WITH THE PAST BUT FEEL THE PRESENT   .   .   142 TRISTRAM 2   7
          DRINK THEN I CHIDE THEE NOT   .   .   .   .   187 STRAYED REVEL   59
          AGE WHOM THE MOST OF US CHIDE   .   .   .   .   .   .   283 HAWORTH CHURCH   V
          CHIDE AND PUT BACK AND DELAY   .   .   .   .   .   .   283 HAWORTH CHURCH   V
          I CHIDE WITH THEE NOT THAT THY SHARP   .   .   .   .   294 HEINES GRAVE   70
          WITH FATE I MURMUR NOT NOR CHIDE   .   .   .   .   .   321 OBERMANN MORE   267

CHIDES
    PRESSES ME CHIDES ME WILL NOT LET ME WEEP • • • • 378 MEROPE 1233

CHIDING
    STILL WORKING CHIDING STILL OUR VAIN TURMOIL • • 2 QUIET WORK V 13
    CHIDING HIS MATE BACK TO HER NEST BUT SHE • • • • 78 SOHRAB RUSTUM 566

CHIEF
    CHIEF DREAMER OWN THY DREAM • • • • • • 46 IN UT.RUMQUE PAR 37
    SOLE LIKE SOME SINGLE TOWER WHICH A CHIEF • • • 71 SOHRAB RUSTUM 337
    AND NOW HAVE CHIEF REGARD IN HELAS REALM • • • 109 BALDER DEAD 2 169
    NO GOD BUT OF THE HERO—TROOP THE CHIEF • • • 117 BALDER DEAD 3 125
    STILL LEFT AND THAT CHIEF SCALD THY BROTHER BRAGE • 117 BALDER DEAD 3 133
    FIRM HARNESSD BY THE MANE A CHIEF • • • • • 191 STRAYED REVEL 188
    THEIR NAMES CHIEF GLORY OF ALL • • • • • • 281 HAWORTH CHURCH 22
    THEIR NAMES CHIEF TREASURE OF ALL • • • • 281 HAWORTH CHURCH V 22
    I HIS CHIEF KINSMAN I HIS PIONEER • • • • • 338 MEROPE 267
    EVEN FANCIED AND HIS DEATH THOU WROUGHTEST CHIEF • 339 MEROPE 328
    HYLLUS THE CHIEF OF HIS HOUSE • • • • • • 344 MEROPE 446
    OF A VALIANT CHIEF TO HIS OWN • • • • • • 345 MEROPE 486
    FROM CHIEF TO CHIEF I WANDERD AT HIS SIDE • • 355 MEROPE 728
    FROM CHIEF TO CHIEF I WANDERD AT HIS SIDE • • • 355 MEROPE 728
    THERE WITH THE CHIEF OF THAT HILL—TOWN WE LODGED • 356 MEROPE 746
    AND BID THE CHIEF TORMENTORS THERE PROVIDE • • • 373 MEROPE 1188
    THEIR CHIEF HATH TRAIND THEM MADE THEM LIKE HIMSELF • 381 MEROPE 1303
    THE OCCASION IF OUR CHIEF CONFEDERATE FAILS • • 386 MEROPE 1447
    I HEAR GORGIAS THEIR CHIEF SPEAKS NOBLY OF HIM • • 411 EMPEDOCLES I 1 147
    YET ONCE AGAIN STERN CHIEF YET ONCE AGAIN • • • • 465 ALARIC AT ROME 85

CHIEFLY
    WHO CHIEFLY PROFIT RUN NO MORE THAN THEY • • • • 382 MEROPE 1351

CHIEFS
    CANST THOU NOT REST AMONG THE TARTAR CHIEFS • • 63 SOHRAB RUSTUM 66
    AND TO FEROOD HIS BROTHER CHIEFS CAME UP • • • 66 SOHRAB RUSTUM 170
    AND HE IS YOUNG AND IRANS CHIEFS ARE OLD • • • 67 SOHRAB RUSTUM 217
    GO TO IF IRANS CHIEFS ARE OLD THEN I • • • • 67 SOHRAB RUSTUM 221
    ALL THE MOST VALIANT CHIEFS LONG HE PERUSED • • 70 SOHRAB RUSTUM 311
    THEN WERE THE CHIEFS OF IRAN SHAMED THROUGH ME • 72 SOHRAB RUSTUM 363
    THE CHIEFS AND PEOPLE • • • • • • • • 189 STRAYED REVEL 122
    THE CHIEFS AND THE PEOPLE • • • • • • • 189 STRAYED REVEL V 122
    OUR FACTIONS WITH THE FRIENDSHIP OF THEIR CHIEFS • 335 MEROPE 166
    WERE THE MESSENIAN CHIEFS THE LAWS HE FRAMED • • 337 MEROPE 243
    HE WOULD NOT LET HIS SAVAGE CHIEFS ALIGHT • • • 339 MEROPE 295
    FOR WELL HE KNEW WHAT YOU HIS CHIEFS DID NOT • • 339 MEROPE 306
    LAST OF OUR QUARTERS WITH THE ARCADIAN CHIEFS • • 356 MEROPE 759
    MY FATHER THEN AND HIS ARCADIAN CHIEFS • • • • 384 MEROPE 1395
    WERE NOT AMONG THE FEUDS OF WARRIOR—CHIEFS • • • 388 MEROPE 1512
    HOW CAN YOUR HERACLEIDAN CHIEFS INSPIRE • • • • 389 MEROPE 1542
    AS THE CHIEFS RULE MY SON THE PEOPLE ARE • • • 404 MEROPE 2002
    UNHAPPY PEOPLE WHERE THE CHIEFS THEMSELVES • • • 404 MEROPE 2003
    WERT NOT AMONG THE FEUDS OF WARRIOR—CHIEFS • • • 388 MEROPE V1512
    AS THE CHIEFS RULE INDEED THE PEOPLE ARE • • • 404 MEROPE V2002

CHIEL
    THE CHIEL FROM SKYE • • • • • • • • • • 461 KAISER DEAD 76

CHILD
    SINGER OF SWEET COLONUS AND ITS CHILD • • • • 2 TO A FRIEND 14
    WHO LENT THEE CHILD THIS MEDITATIVE GUISE • • • 41 GIPSY CHILD 3
    POOR CHILD WHOM THE LIGHT AIR OF CHILDISH JOY • • 41 GIPSY CHILD V 9
    HIS WANDERING GUEST AND GAVE HIM HIS FAIR CHILD • • 79 SOHRAB RUSTUM 626
    FOR RUSTUM HAD NO SON ONE CHILD HE HAD • • • • 80 SOHRAB RUSTUM 645
    FATHERS WE MUST HAVE WIFE AND CHILD • • • • 92 SICK KING BOKH 149
    MOTHER A CHILD OF BALE THOU BARST IN ME • • • 98 BALDER DEAD 1 95
    HODER ILL—FATED CHILD OF BALE MY SON • • • • • 98 BALDER DEAD 1 112
    LIKE A YOUNG CHILD HAST CRIED THYSELF TO SLEEP • • 103 BALDER DEAD 1 291
    I TOO HAD ONCE A WIFE AND ONCE A CHILD • • • • 125 BALDER DEAD 3 403
    CHILD TIS NO TRUE DRAUGHT THIS TIS POISOND WINE • • 133 TRISTRAM 1 103
    THE LOVELY ORPHAN CHILD AGAIN • • • • • • 136 TRISTRAM 1 192
    POOR CHILD THOU ART ALMOST AS PALE AS I • • • 140 TRISTRAM 1 312
    CHILD TIS NO WATER THIS TIS POISOND WINE • • • 133 TRISTRAM 1 V 103
    SHE GLEANED FROM BRETON GRANDAMES WHEN A CHILD • • 152 TRISTRAM 3 108
    FOR THE HUMMING STREET AND THE CHILD WITH ITS TOY • 164 FORSAKEN MERM 90
    WHO STRUCK IN HEAT HIS CHILD HE LOVED SO WELL • • 166 PICT NEWSTEAD 5
    WHO STRUCK IN HEAT THE CHILD HE LOVED SO WELL • • 166 PICT NEWSTEAD V 5
    THINE ARMS ROUND THY CHILD • • • • • • • 177 PARTING 78
    BRING HIM A WEEPING CHILD • • • • • • • 195 FRAG ANTIGONE 12
    TO ACHIEVE HIS SONS DELIVERANCE O MY CHILD • • • 198 FRAG ANTIGONE 103
    FAIR CHILD IT WAS THE BLISS WITHIN • • • • • 204 EUPHROSYNE 26
    GRAVE GAY CHILD PARENT HUSBAND WIFE • • • • • 226 EPILOG LAOCOON 161
    AH CHILD SHE CRIES THAT STRIFE DIVINE • • • • 241 MORALITY 23
    SOMETIMES A CHILD WILL CROSS THE GLADE • • • • 248 KENSINGTON GARD 9
    THE CHILD SLEEPS WARMLY IN HIS BED • • • • • 249 KENSINGTON GARD 36
    THAT CHILD WHO DARTS ACROSS THE GLADE • • • • KENSINGTON GARD V 9
    THE CHILD SLEEPS SWEETLY IN HIS BED • • • • • KENSINGTON GARD V 36
    UNHAPPY ELOQUENT THE CHILD • • • • • • • 285 HAWORTH CHURCH 105
    CAMST THOU FROM HEAVEN O CHILD • • • • • • 295 HEINES GRAVE 116
    NOT AS THEIR FRIEND OR CHILD I SPEAK • • • • • 301 GRANDE CHARTR 79
    SHE CHANGED INTO A CHILD • • • • • • • • 317 OBERMANN MORE 138

CHILD   (CONTINUED)
          COULD SEE THE MOTHER WITH HER CHILD . . . . .   317 OBERMANN MORE   157
          THAT GRACIOUS CHILD THAT THORN-CROWND MAN . . . .   318 OBERMANN MORE   167
          COULD SEE THE MOTHER WITH THE CHILD . . . . .   317 OBERMANN MORE   V 157
          WAS BY THAT MURDER OPEND THAT ONE CHILD . . .   335 MEROPE   188
          MACARIA BLESSED CHILD . . . .   343 MEROPE   433
          ONLY TO ME GIVE MY CHILD . . . .   348 MEROPE   540
          CAN IT BRING HOME MY CHILD AH IF IT CAN . . .   349 MEROPE   568
          OR HOW REPLY TO THEE MY CHILD LAST-BORN . . .   367 MEROPE   1041
          ONE LAST MURDER-SAVED CHILD . . . . . .   369 MEROPE   1102
          MY CHILD LIES IN HIS JAGGD . . . . . .   370 MEROPE   1117
          FOR THEE MY CHILD IF THOU WERT YET ALIVE . . .   372 MEROPE   1157
          THERE THERE THOU LIEST NOW MY HAPLESS CHILD . .   373 MEROPE   1171
          MY CHILD MY CHARGE BELOVED WELCOME TO LIFE . . .   375 MEROPE   1207
          MY CHILD UNHURT ONLY BY OVER JOY . . . . .   377 MEROPE   1220
          FLY BACK MY CHILD AND THOU SEEMST . . . .   377 MEROPE   1229
          AND ENTERTAINST THOU CHILD SUCH DANGEROUS FRIENDS   380 MEROPE   1276
          BUT NOW SEEN FACE TO FACE MY ONLY CHILD . . .   381 MEROPE   1289
          ON WHAT A REED MY CHILD THOU LEANEST THERE . .   381 MEROPE   1310
          I SHUDDER LAIAS TO COMMIT MY CHILD . . . .   387 MEROPE   1461
          SO OER THEE AND THY CHILD . . . . . .   393 MEROPE   1679
          MY CHILD LIES IN A JAGGD . . . .   370 MEROPE   V1117
          DARED ONE BUT TRY THOU WAST A KIND CHILD EVER .   408 EMPEDOCLES I 1   76
          DARED ONE BUT TRY THOU WERT A KIND CHILD EVER .   409 EMPEDOCLES I 1   V 76
          A CHILD OF LIGHT APPEARD . . . .   444 WESTMIN ABBEY   7
          IT SEEMD A CHILD OF LIGHT DID BRING THE DOWER .   446 WESTMIN ABBEY   74
          HE SLUMBERD AND AMBROSIA BALMD THE CHILD . . .   446 WESTMIN ABBEY   88
          PLUCKD FROM THE FIRE THE CHILD AND LAID HIM DOWN   447 WESTMIN ABBEY   95
          STILL TOILS TO PERFECT WHAT THE CHILD BEGAN . .   473 CROMWELL   46
          SWEPT OER THE FANCY OF THE HEEDLESS CHILD . . .   473 CROMWELL   52
          THE CHILD-COMPANION OF HIS CHILDISH JOY . . .   477 CROMWELL   180
          AND LONELY AS A TRUANT CHILD . . . . .   479 HAYSWATER BOAT   3
          I DROPPD THE BOOK AND OF MY CHILD I THOUGHT . .   485 S S LUSITANIA   9

CHILDHOOD
          WHICH SHELTERD THEIR CHILDHOOD THE SUN . . . .   234 YOUTH OF MAN   65
          YE WHO FROM MY CHILDHOOD UP HAVE CALMD ME . . .   240 SELF-DEPENDENCE   7
          OF CHILDHOOD ARTHUR DID SOME CHECK HAVE POWER .   447 WESTMIN ABBEY   118
          AGE OF ITS TEARS AND CHILDHOOD OF ITS SMILE . .   472 CROMWELL   6
          NO WONDERS NURSD THY CHILDHOOD NOT FOR THEE . .   472 CROMWELL   15
          THE PEACE OF CHILDHOOD AND THE THOUGHTS THAT ROAM   474 CROMWELL   73
          MORE CALM MORE DEEP THAN CHILDHOOD EVER KNEW .   475 CROMWELL   116
          WHAT TRACE OF CARELESS CHILDHOOD LINGERD THERE .   477 CROMWELL   184

CHILDHOODS
          WHOSE SPELL-BOUND SENSE FROM CHILDHOODS HOUR   471 CROMWELL   3
               HATH KNOWN
          DEEP ON HIS LIFE AND CHILDHOODS BABY WAVES . . .   473 CROMWELL   48
          LIKE LOVING SHADOWS ROUND THAT CHILDHOODS HOME .   474 CROMWELL   74
          AND THE FIRST SORROW WHICH IS CHILDHOODS GRAVE .   474 CROMWELL   82
          CHILDHOODS BRIGHT GLANCE AND SUNNY SMILE NO MORE .   477 CROMWELL   182

CHILDISH
          POOR CHILD WHOM THE LIGHT AIR OF CHILDISH JOY .   41 GIPSY CHILD   V 9
          OR DROWND IN MISTS OF CHILDISH WONDERMENT . . .   446 WESTMIN ABBEY   65
          PEACE THAT RECALLD HIS CHILDISH HOURS ANEW . .   475 CROMWELL   115
          THE CHILD-COMPANION OF HIS CHILDISH JOY . . .   477 CROMWELL   180
          LOFTY THOUGHT LIES OFT IN CHILDISH PLAY . . .   483 THEKLAS ANSWER   24

CHILDLESS
          THE CHILDLESS FATHER ALAS . . . .   283 HAWORTH CHURCH   V

CHILDREN
          CHILDREN AS SUCH FORGIVE THEM HAVE I KNOWN . . .   8 RELIGIOUS ISOL   1
          WORLD HAVE THY CHILDREN YET BOWD AT HIS KNEE .   20 MODERN SAPPHO   34
          THEIR CHILDREN AS WHEN FIRST THEY CAME . . .   55 RESIGNATION   119
          BY CHILDREN WHOM THEIR NURSES CALL WITH HASTE .   86 SOHRAB RUSTUM   846
          BY ROMPING CHILDREN WHOM THEIR NURSES CALL . . .   86 SOHRAB RUSTUM   V 846
          THREE MIGHTY CHILDREN TO MY FATHER LOK . . .   110 BALDER DEAD 2   206
          WHEN HE GUIDES MUSPELS CHILDREN TO THEIR BOURNE .   111 BALDER DEAD 2   224
          WHEN MUSPELS CHILDREN SHALL BELEAGUER HEAVEN .   115 BALDER DEAD 3   69
          AND WIFE AND CHILDREN AND OUR ANCIENT HOME . . .   117 BALDER DEAD 3   144
          WITH HER CHILDREN AT HER SIDE . . . . .   138 TRISTRAM 1   271
          WHERE DO THE CHILDREN SLEEP KISS THEM FOR ME .   140 TRISTRAM 1   311
          HAD WANDERD FORTH HER CHILDREN WERE AT PLAY . .   149 TRISTRAM 3   6
          WATCHING HER CHILDREN PLAY THEIR LITTLE HANDS .   150 TRISTRAM 3   24
          AND STILL THE CHILDREN LISTEND THEIR BLUE EYES .   150 TRISTRAM 3   46
          THEN ISEULT TOOK BY THE HAND THOSE CHILDREN FAIR .   151 TRISTRAM 3   61
          HER LAUGHING CHILDREN IN THEIR BEDS AND PLAY .   151 TRISTRAM 3   77
          HER CHILDREN OR TO LISTEN TO THE WIND . . .   152 TRISTRAM 3   85
          THE CHILDREN AND THE GREY-HAIRD SENESCHAL . . .   152 TRISTRAM 3   97
          SHE HAS HER CHILDREN TOO AND NIGHT AND DAY . .   152 TRISTRAM 3   102
          WITH WHICH THIS DAY THE CHILDREN SHE BEGUILED .   152 TRISTRAM 3   107
          WHAT TALE DID ISEULT TO THE CHILDREN SAY . . .   154 TRISTRAM 3   151
          DREW ISEULT FORTH HER CHILDREN WERE AT PLAY .   TRISTRAM 3   V 5
          HIS WIFE AND CHILDREN BE . . . .   159 NECKAN   8
          THAN THE SEA-CHILDREN OWN . . . .   159 NECKAN   20
          COME DEAR CHILDREN LET US AWAY . . . . .   161 FORSAKEN MERM   1
          CHILDREN DEAR LET US AWAY . . . .   161 FORSAKEN MERM   8
          COME DEAR CHILDREN COME AWAY DOWN . . . .   162 FORSAKEN MERM   23
          CHILDREN DEAR WAS IT YESTERDAY . . . . .   162 FORSAKEN MERM   30

CHILDREN   (CONTINUED)
         CHILDREN DEAR WAS IT YESTERDAY . . . .   162 FORSAKEN MERM   47
         CHILDREN DEAR WAS IT YESTERDAY . . . .   162 FORSAKEN MERM   48
         CHILDREN DEAR WAS IT YESTERDAY . . . .   163 FORSAKEN MERM   63
         CHILDREN DEAR WERE WE LONG ALONE   . . . . . .   163 FORSAKEN MERM   64
         COME AWAY CHILDREN CALL NO MORE   . . . . . .   164 FORSAKEN MERM   83
         COME AWAY AWAY CHILDREN . . . .   164 FORSAKEN MERM   108
         COME CHILDREN COME DOWN . . . .   164 FORSAKEN MERM   109
         BUT CHILDREN AT MIDNIGHT . . . .   165 FORSAKEN MERM   124
         THEIR CHILDREN PLAY ON THE LAWNS   . . . . .   234 YOUTH OF MAN   70
         CHILDREN OF MEN THE UNSEEN POWER WHOSE EYE . . . . 238 PROGRESS   37
         CHILDREN OF MEN NOT THAT YOUR AGE EXCEL . . . .   238 PROGRESS   45
         CHILDREN WHO EARLY RANGE THESE SLOPES AND LATE . . 258 SCHOLAR-GIPSY   105
         STRONG CHILDREN OF THE ALPINE WILD . . . . .   301 GRANDE CHARTR   57
         WE ARE LIKE CHILDREN REARD IN SHADE . . . . .   304 GRANDE CHARTR   169
         O CHILDREN WHAT DO YE REPLY   . . . .   305 GRANDE CHARTR   193
         LIKE CHILDREN BATHING ON THE SHORE   . . . . .   308 OBERMANN   73
         THE CHILDREN OF THE SECOND BIRTH   . . . . .   310 OBERMANN   143
         FROM THE CHILDREN FROM THE FURY TO THEM   . . . . 346 MEROPE   497
         OR THE CHILDREN PLUCKING . . . .   392 MEROPE   1637
         WOMEN AND CHILDREN INTERMIXD AND THEN   . . . .   401 MEROPE   1898
         AS CHILDREN OF WEAK AGE . . . .   421 EMPEDOCLES I 2   273
         OVER THEIR OWN DEAR CHILDREN ROLLD   . . . . .   427 EMPEDOCLES I 2   446
         AMONG A PEOPLE OF CHILDREN   . . . .   432 EMPEDOCLES II   112
         YET ALL HIGH SOUNDS THAT MOUNTAIN CHILDREN HEAR . .472 CROMWELL   27
         FROM A FAR LAND THE CHILDREN OF THE SNOW . . . . 474 CROMWELL   90

CHILDRENS
         SWEET FLOWER THY CHILDRENS EYES   . . . . .   140 TRISTRAM 1   325
         HER CHILDRENS SHE MOVES SLOW HER VOICE ALONE . . 151 TRISTRAM 3   72
         BEFORE THE CHILDRENS FANCY HIM AND HER   . . . .   154 TRISTRAM 3   166
         CHILDRENS VOICES SHOULD BE DEAR   . . . . .   161 FORSAKEN MERM   14
         CHILDRENS VOICES WILD WITH PAIN   . . . . .   162 FORSAKEN MERM   16
         THE CHILDRENS SHOUTS AND AT TIMES . . . . . .   234 YOUTH OF MAN   72
         BUT FOR THY CHILDRENS DEATH I STAND ASSOILD . .   340 MEROPE   342

CHILDS
         AND HIS CHILDS REASON FLICKERD AND DID DIE . . . 166 PICT NEWSTEAD   6
         AND THE CHILDS REASON FLICKERD AND DID DIE . .   166 PICT NEWSTEAD   V   6
         STILL STILL WENT FORTH THAT CHILDS DEAR FORCE . . 318 OBERMANN MORE   163
         THE DROPPING PATTER OF A CHILDS SMALL FEET . . .   FRAGMENT 7   1

CHILDSWORTH
         RUNS IT NOT HERE THE TRACK BY CHILDSWORTH FARM . . 263 THYRSIS   11

CHILL
         CHILL BLOWS THE WIND THE PLEASAUNCE-WALKS ARE DREAR 135 TRISTRAM 1   161
         CAME KEEN AND CHILL DOWN ON THE HEATHER BRIGHT . . 151 TRISTRAM 3   57
         WHILE YET THE NIGHT IS CHILL   . . . . . .   183 ABSENCE   18
         AND ONCE IN WINTER ON THE CAUSEWAY CHILL   . . . . 258 SCHOLAR-GIPSY   121
         SADDENS MY SOUL WITH ITS CHILL   . . . .   293 HEINES GRAVE   41
         CHILL AND THE SHADOWS NOW   . . . .   297 HEINES GRAVE   164
         THY HEAD IS CLEAR THY FEELING CHILL . . . . . .   309 OBERMANN   87

CHILLD
         CHILLD EVERY BUOYANT HOPE THAT FLOATED BY   . . . . 474 CROMWELL   88

CHILLIEST
         WHEN AIR IS CHILLIEST AND THE STARS SUNK LOW . . 103 BALDER DEAD 1   281

CHILLING
         I FEEL HER SLOWLY CHILLING BREATH INVADE   . . . . 266 THYRSIS   134

CHILLON
         THE LAKE WITH CHILLON BY . . . .   312 OBERMANN MORE   8

CHILLY
         CHILLY THEY GROW YET WINDS IN MARCH . . . . .   56 RESIGNATION   130
         AND OER HIS CHILLY LIMBS HIS WOOLLEN COAT . . . . 63 SOHRAB RUSTUM   96
         HATH COME ON HER A CHILLY FEAR . . . .   131 TRISTRAM 1   38

CHIME
         ON SUNDAYS AT THE MATIN-CHIME   . . . .   17 CHURCH BROU 2   17
         CHIME CONVENT-BELLS ON WINTRY NIGHTS . . . . . . 156 SAINT BRANDAN   6
         SHAKEN AND OUT OF CHIME . . . .   416 EMPEDOCLES I 2   115
         TO TUNES WE DID NOT CALL OUR BEING MUST KEEP CHIME 418 EMPEDOCLES I 2   196

CHIMNEY
         AND FROM THE ROOFS THE TWISTED CHIMNEY-STACKS . . 263 THYRSIS   5

CHIMNEYS
         BY MIST AND CHIMNEYS UNCONFINED   . . . .   223 EPILOG LAOCOON   71

CHIN
         TIED UNDER THE ARCHEST CHIN   . . . .   23 MEMORY-PICTURE   27

CHINKD
         AT THE CHINKD FIELDS OF ICE THE WASTE OF SNOW . . 100 BALDER DEAD 1   164

CHINKS
          AND IN THE MOUNTAIN-CHINKS INTER THE WINDS . . . .   410 EMPEDOCLES I 1   118

CHIPPING
          AND THE WEIRD CHIPPING OF THE WOODPECKER   . . . .   155 TRISTRAM 3   198
          AND THE LIGHT CHIPPING OF THE WOODPECKER   . . . .   155 TRISTRAM 3   V 198

CHIRON
          CHIRON THE AGED CENTAUR LAY   . . . .   414 EMPEDOCLES I 2   59

CHIRP
          THOU WOULDST CHIRP THOU FOOLISH BIRD . . . . . .   453 POOR MATTHIAS   33
          FLUTTER CHIRP SHE NEVER STIRRD . . . .   453 POOR MATTHIAS   34

CHISELLD
          AND PRAISE THE CHISELLD BROIDERIES RARE   . . . .   17 CHURCH BROU 2   37

CHIVALRY
          UPON US ARE THE CHIVALRY OF ROME   . . . . . .   137 TRISTRAM 1   236
          OR THAT RENOWND MIRROR OF CHIVALRY   . . . . . .   153 TRISTRAM 3   146

CHOICE
          A LAST CHOICE GIFT THEREON HIS GOLDEN RING . . . .   118 BALDER DEAD 3   173
          AGAIN I SPRING TO MAKE MY CHOICE   . . . . . .   174 MEETING   9
          STAVED US BACK AND GAVE OUR CHOICE THE LAW . . . .   210 SELF-DECEPTION   12
          AH WHO SWAYD OUR CHOICE AND WHO DECIDED . . . .   210 SELF-DECEPTION   15

CHOICEST
          THEY THINK TO BURN AND ALL MY CHOICEST WEALTH   . .   103 BALDER DEAD 1   299

CHOIR
          HIS CHOIR THE NINE . . . .   442 EMPEDOCLES II   446
          NAVE CHOIR AND TRANSEPT GLORIFIED WITH LIGHT   . .   445 WESTMIN ABBEY   35

CHOKD
          DEEP THRO HIS SOUL AND CHOKD HIS FALTERING TONGUE   478 CROMWELL   224

CHOKE
          AND CAST HIS TRUNK TO CHOKE THE ABYSMAL VOID   . .   121 BALDER DEAD 3   259
          AND THREW HIS TRUNK TO CHOKE THE ABYSMAL VOID   . .   121 BALDER DEAD 3   V 259

CHOKED
          CHOKED BY THE AIR AND SCARCE CAN THEY THEMSELVES . .   66 SOHRAB RUSTUM   165
          DIZZY AND ON HIS KNEES AND CHOKED WITH SAND   . .   74 SOHRAB RUSTUM   424
          WAS CHOKED WITH RAGE AT LAST THESE WORDS BROKE WAY   74 SOHRAB RUSTUM   456
          O BOY THY FATHER AND HIS VOICE CHOKED THERE   . .   81 SOHRAB RUSTUM   691
          AND HIS SOBS CHOKED HIM AND HE CLUTCHD HIS SWORD . .   82 SOHRAB RUSTUM   704
          THE BODIES WERE CONSUMED ASH CHOKED THE PILE   . .   119 BALDER DEAD 3   202
          OUR SOON-CHOKED SOULS TO FILL . . . .   183 ABSENCE   10
          HAD ON THE JOURNEY CHOKED MY LABOURING BREATH   . .   362 MEROPE   940
          IN THE THORN-CHOKED GULLIES   . . . .   392 MEROPE   1638

CHOKES
          AND ON THE RIDGE A WAGGON CHOKES THE WAY   . . . .   107 BALDER DEAD 2   94

CHOOSE
          BUT CHOOSE A CHAMPION FROM THE PERSIAN LORDS   . .   65 SOHRAB RUSTUM   152
          NOR MUST HE CHOOSE THAT COMMON PATH OF GODS   . .   99 BALDER DEAD 1   139
          THEN LET HIM CHOOSE HIS MOMENT WELL . . . . .   223 EPILOG LAOCOON   59
          SOME SOURCE OF FEELING HE MUST CHOOSE   . . . .   223 EPILOG LAOCOON   83
          TO CHOOSE IT RIGHTLY IS HIS PART   . . . . .   223 EPILOG LAOCOON   87
          SOME PULSE OF FEELING HE MUST CHOOSE . . . . .   223 EPILOG LAOCOON   V 83
          BE WITH HIM CHOOSE THE MOMENT STRIKE THY BLOW   . .   391 MEROPE   1590
          GO WITH HIM CHOOSE THE MOMENT STRIKE THY BLOW   . .   391 MEROPE   V1590
          THERE CHOOSE WE THEE O GUARDIAN DEAR . . . . .   452 GEISTS GRAVE   V 71

CHOOSEST
          CHOOSEST THOU NOW TO TURN   . . . .   314 OBERMANN MORE   74

CHOPS
          THE MAN MATURE WITH LABOUR CHOPS   . . . . . .   213 PROGRESS POESY   5
          AS THE PUNTS ROPE CHOPS ROUND   . . . .   257 SCHOLAR-GIPSY   76

CHORASMIAN
          REJOICING THROUGH THE HUSHD CHORASMIAN WASTE   . .   87 SOHRAB RUSTUM   878
          LONE CHORASMIAN STREAM THEREON . . . .   191 STRAYED REVEL   183

CHORD
          THAT THRILLS IN HIS MOURNFULLEST CHORD   . . . .   231 YOUTH OF NATURE   93
          WHILST EVERY CHORD THAT THRILLS AT THOUGHTS OF HOME   467 ALARIC AT ROME   131

CHORDS
          ANGRILY SMOTE ON THE CHORDS   . . . .   285 HAWORTH CHURCH   128

CHOSE
          AND CLAD HIMSELF IN STEEL THE ARMS HE CHOSE   . .   69 SOHRAB RUSTUM   265
          WAS THE ONE ISEULT CHOSE AND SHE BROUGHT CLEAR . .   154 TRISTRAM 3   165
          HIS ACTS THE WIFE HE CHOSE WAS FULL OF VIRTUES . .   337 MEROPE   240

CHOSEN
          WE WE HAVE CHOSEN OUR PATH   . . . .   288 RUGBY CHAPEL   84

CHOSEN   (CONTINUED)
```
WAS CHOSEN HIS COMPANION FROM A BOY      • • • • • •   355 MEROPE              724
CHOSEN A PRISON FOR PROMETHEUS CLIMB     • • • • • •   395 MEROPE             1750
OF RICH SOIL CHOSEN BY CRAFT       • • • • • • • •     399 MEROPE             1848
```

CHRIST
```
CHRIST WHAT A NIGHT HOW THE SLEET WHIPS THE PANE • •   130 TRISTRAM 1            4
WHAT LOVE COURAGE CHRIST HE IS SO PALE       • • •     145 TRISTRAM 2           80
CHRIST KEEP US FROM SUCH FANTASY     • • • • • •       147 TRISTRAM 2          130
AND ON IT CHRIST A LIVING FORM   • • • • • • •         156 SAINT BRANDAN        16
GERMANY FRANCE CHRIST MOSES ATHENS ROME    • • • •     168 RACHEL 3             12
MUCH CHEERD WITH THOUGHTS OF CHRIST THE LIVING BREAD   169 EAST LONDON           8
CHRIST SOME ONE SAYS WAS HUMAN AS WE ARE   • • • •     170 BETTER PART           3
WELL THEN FOR CHRIST THOU ANSWEREST WHO CAN CARE • •   171 BETTER PART           6
WAS CHRIST A MAN LIKE US AH LET US TRY     • • • •     171 BETTER PART          13
SO CHRIST SAID EIGHTEEN HUNDRED YEARS AGO   • • • •    237 PROGRESS             13
THE LINE OF FESTAL LIGHT IN CHRIST-CHURCH HALL   • •   259 SCHOLAR-GIPSY       129
AND CHRIST WAS BY TO SAVE    • • • • • • • •           318 OBERMANN MORE       172
```

CHRISTIAN
```
THE SWEETEST CHRISTIAN SOUL ALIVE    • • • • •         132 TRISTRAM 1           54
NO CHRISTIAN MATE HAVE I  • • • • • • • • • •          160 NECKAN               36
THEN SOOTHING WITH THY CHRISTIAN STRAIN FORLORN  • •   168 RACHEL 3              6
RISE UP ALL ROUND THE CHRISTIAN SPIRES     • • • •     274 STANZAS CARNAC       22
CHRISTIAN AND PAGAN KING AND SLAVE   • • • • •         311 OBERMANN            149
```

CHRISTMAS
```
AT LAST IT WAS THE CHRISTMAS NIGHT   • • • • •         156 SAINT BRANDAN        13
TELL THEM ONE BLESSED CHRISTMAS-NIGHT    • • • •       157 SAINT BRANDAN        29
ON EARTH THE CHRISTMAS-NIGHTS REPOSE • • • • •         158 SAINT BRANDAN        66
```

CHRISTS
```
FROM CHRISTS THEN OPEN GRAVE     • • • • • • •         317 OBERMANN MORE       148
```

CHUCKLE
```
TO CHUCKLE WITH HIS SENDER OER THE GAME    • • • •     366 MEROPE                V
```

CHURCH
```
HARK WHAT BELL FOR CHURCH IS TOLLD   • • • • •          12 CHURCH BROU 1         4
STANDS A LONELY CHURCH UNFINISHD     • • • • •          14 CHURCH BROU 1        63
AND THE CHURCH UNFINISHD STANDS      • • • • •          14 CHURCH BROU 1        68
WE WILL BUILD THE CHURCH AGAIN   • • • • • • •          15 CHURCH BROU 1        76
SEEK HER AT THE CHURCH OF BROU   • • • • • • •          15 CHURCH BROU 1        84
TILL THE CHURCH WAS ROOFD AND DONE   • • • • •          16 CHURCH BROU 1       102
STANDS THE CHURCH ON HIGH    • • • • • • • •            16 CHURCH BROU 2         6
WHAT CHURCH IS THIS FROM MEN ALOOF   • • • • •          16 CHURCH BROU 2         7
TIS THE CHURCH OF BROU   • • • • • • • • •              16 CHURCH BROU 2         8
ROUND THE CHURCH OF BROU   • • • • • • • •              16 CHURCH BROU 2        16
RIDE OUT TO CHURCH FROM CHAMBERY     • • • • •          17 CHURCH BROU 2        21
ROUND THE CHURCH OF BROU   • • • • • • • •              17 CHURCH BROU 2        24
ROUND THE CHURCH OF BROU   • • • • • • • •              17 CHURCH BROU 2        32
AND AFTER CHURCH WHEN MASS IS DONE   • • • • •          17 CHURCH BROU 2        33
IN THE CHURCH OF BROU    • • • • • • • •                17 CHURCH BROU 2        40
IN YOUR HIGH CHURCH MID THE STILL MOUNTAIN-AIR   • •    17 CHURCH BROU 3         2
AND THE LITTLE GREY CHURCH ON THE WINDY SHORE  • •     162 FORSAKEN MERM        26
IN THE LITTLE GREY CHURCH ON THE SHORE TO-DAY  • •     163 FORSAKEN MERM        57
TO THE LITTLE GREY CHURCH ON THE WINDY HILL  • •       163 FORSAKEN MERM        71
FROM THE CHURCH CAME A MURMUR OF FOLK AT THEIR PRAYERS 163 FORSAKEN MERM        72
AT THE CHURCH ON THE HILL-SIDE   • • • • • • •         165 FORSAKEN MERM       138
THIS NO SAINT PREACHES AND THIS NO CHURCH RULES  • •   171 DIVINITY             13
THE INFANT CHURCH OF LOVE SHE FELT THE TIDE  • •       172 GOOD SHEPHERD         7
THE LINE OF FESTAL LIGHT IN CHRIST-CHURCH HALL   • •   259 SCHOLAR-GIPSY       129
THE CHURCH OF CARNAC BY THE STRAND   • • • • •         274 STANZAS CARNAC       23
THE MOORLAND TOWN BUT THE CHURCH     • • • • •         283 HAWORTH CHURCH       62
THE MOORLAND PLACE BUT THE CHURCH    • • • • •         283 HAWORTH CHURCH    V  62
MEN CALLD FROM CHAMBER CHURCH AND TENT     • • •       318 OBERMANN MORE       171
HOW HIS ST PETERS CHURCH IN THORNEY ISLE   • • • •     445 WESTMIN ABBEY        49
A CHURCH ONCE LARGE AND THEN GROWN STRAIT IN SOUL      449 WESTMIN ABBEY       156
BETWEEN A RUIND CHURCH AND SHATTERD THRONE • • • •     477 CROMWELL            188
```

CHURCHYARD
```
THE CHURCHYARD WALL THAT CLIPS THE SQUARE  • • • •      16 CHURCH BROU 2        12
FLOWS BY THE TOWN THE CHURCHYARD FAIR    • • •         184 TERRACE BERNE        10
LONG SINCE AND IN SOME QUIET CHURCHYARD LAID   • •     259 SCHOLAR-GIPSY       137
IN A CHURCHYARD HIGH MID THE MOORS   • • • • •         282 HAWORTH CHURCH       52
NOW FOR YEARS IN CHURCHYARD MOULD    • • • • •         453 POOR MATTHIAS        48
```

CHURL
```
AND YET THE VILLAGE-CHURL FEELS THE TRUTH MORE         426 EMPEDOCLES I 2      411
        THAN YOU
```

CHUSE
```
THOU WILT BE MOST UNLOVELY SHALL I CHUSE   • • • •         FRAGMENT 5            3
```

CILICIAN
```
THINE ANCIENT ROUT BY THE CILICIAN HILLS   • • • •     430 EMPEDOCLES II        53
THY ANCIENT ROUT BY THE CILICIAN HILLS     • • • •     430 EMPEDOCLES II     V  53
THE ANCIENT ROUT BY THE CILICIAN HILLS     • • • •     430 EMPEDOCLES II     V  53
```

CINCTURED
    THE DEEP CUP IVY-CINCTURED . . . . 186 STRAYED REVEL 12

CIRCE
    O CIRCE GODDESS . . . . 185 STRAYED REVEL 2
    THE FAVOURD GUEST OF CIRCE BROUGHT BY THE WAVES . . 189 STRAYED REVEL 110
    O CIRCE GODDESS . . . . 194 STRAYED REVEL 293

CIRCLE
    WHERE ARE IN CIRCLE RANGED TWELVE GOLDEN CHAIRS . . 106 BALDER DEAD 2 37
    AND IN THAT DAISIED CIRCLE AS MEN SAY . . . . 156 TRISTRAM 3 221
    IN EVER-NEARING CIRCLE WEAVES HER SHADE . . . . 266 THYRSIS 132
    HAVE RUN THEIR CIRCLE AND LEFT . . . . 282 HAWORTH CHURCH V
    TO CIRCLE THE PRINCE ROUND WHEN SUDDENLY . . . . 402 MEROPE 1932
    AND NO ONE ROUND THE CHARMED CIRCLE SPEAKS . . . . 431 EMPEDOCLES II 83

CIRCLED
    CIRCLED TRISTRAM BY A BAND OF GOLD . . . . . . 143 TRISTRAM 2 44

CIRCLES
    IN CLOUDY CIRCLES TO ETERNITY . . . . 4 BUTLERS SERMONS 14
    CIRCLES ABOVE HIS EYRY WITH LOUD SCREAMS . . . . 78 SOHRAB RUSTUM 565

CIRCLET
    A GOLDEN CIRCLET ON HER QUEENLY BROW . . . . . . 331 MEROPE 58
    MY GOLDEN CIRCLET . . . . 432 EMPEDOCLES II 119

CIRCLING
    FLICKERING AND CIRCLING . . . . 218 BACCHANALIA 1 22
    OR HEAR MID CIRCLING CRAGS THE IMPATIENT CRY . . 472 CROMWELL 25

CIRCUITOUS
    A FOILD CIRCUITOUS WANDERER TILL AT LAST . . . . 87 SOHRAB RUSTUM 888

CIRCULAR
    IN A GREEN CIRCULAR HOLLOW IN THE HEATH . . . 149 TRISTRAM 3 7
    IN THAT GREEN CIRCULAR OPENING IN THE HEATH . . TRISTRAM 3 V 7
    IN A GREEN CIRCULAR OPENING IN THE HEATH . . . TRISTRAM 3 V 7

CIRCUMAMBIENT
    LOST LABOUR WHEN THE CIRCUMAMBIENT GLOOM . . . . 10 MYCERINUS 53

CIRCUMSTANCE
    WHEN FATE AND CIRCUMSTANCE ARE STRONG . . . . 481 COURAGE 6

CIRQUE
    OVER THE WASTE THIS CIRQUE OF OPEN GROUND . . . . 150 TRISTRAM 3 13

CISTERNS
    WITH CISTERNS FOR THE WINTER-RAIN . . . . . . 94 SICK KING BOKH 202

CITADEL
    TO PHENEOS WITH ITS CRAGGY CITADEL . . . . . . 356 MEROPE 745
    WITH SOLEMN CADENCE ROUND HER CITADEL . . . . 472 CROMWELL 20

CITHAERON
    IN SOME CHANCE BATTLE ON CITHAERON-SIDE . . . . 447 WESTMIN ABBEY 114

CITIES
    BRISTLED WITH CITIES US THE SEA RECEIVED . . . . 25 DREAM 37
    AFRASIABS CITIES ONLY SAMARCAND . . . . . . 83 SOHRAB RUSTUM 760
    AND PEOPLED CITIES . . . . 189 STRAYED REVEL 126
    IN THE WALLD CITIES THE WAY PASSES THROUGH . . . 193 STRAYED REVEL 250
    BORDERD BY CITIES AND HOARSE . . . . 253 FUTURE 53
    THAT CITIES WILL CROWD TO ITS EDGE . . . . . 253 FUTURE 60
    IN CITIES SHOULD WE ENGLISH LIE . . . . . . 277 SOUTHERN NIGHT 61
    TO LIFE TO CITIES AND TO WAR . . . . . . 305 GRANDE CHARTR 180
    I HAVE SEEN MANY CITIES IN MY TIME . . . . . 428 EMPEDOCLES I 2 474
    WHO THRONGD ME IN THEIR CITIES . . . . 432 EMPEDOCLES II 113
    IN ALL THE ITALIAN CITIES LIKE OURSELVES . . . 436 EMPEDOCLES II 237

CITIZEN
    THE WEARY MAN THE BANISHD CITIZEN . . . . . . 429 EMPEDOCLES II 11

CITIZENS
    OF CITIZENS IN HOLIDAY ATTIRE . . . . 401 MEROPE 1897
    OF HOLIDAY-CLAD CITIZENS TRANSFORMD . . . . . 402 MEROPE 1939
    THOU HAST SOME WRONG FROM THINE OWN CITIZENS . . 411 EMPEDOCLES I 1 142
    THY CITIZENS TIS SAID . . . . 416 EMPEDOCLES I 2 117

CITY
    AND FAINT THE CITY GLEAMS . . . . 45 IN UTRUMQUE PAR 16
    CITY OF AFRICA . . . . 51 CONSOLATION 28
    A FAR BRIGHT CITY SMITTEN BY THE SUN . . . . . 79 SOHRAB RUSTUM 622
    AGAINST THE HARBOUR BY THE CITY-WALL . . . . . 101 BALDER DEAD 1 225
    FAR HENCE IN ASGARD IN THE CITY OF GODS . . . . 108 BALDER DEAD 2 114
    FOR HEAVEN WAS BALDER BORN THE CITY OF GODS . . 110 BALDER DEAD 2 198
    BY CITY AND HOUSEHOLD GROUPD WE LIVE AND MANY SHOCKS 195 FRAG ANTIGONE 20
    WITHOUT FRIEND CITY OR HOME . . . . 195 FRAG ANTIGONE 26
    OF THE CITY OF DEATH HAVE FOR EVER CLOSED . . . 199 FRAG DEJANEIRA 30
    STILL PLAYS ON THE CITY SPIRES . . . . 234 YOUTH OF MAN 82

CITY   (CONTINUED)
        AND THAT SWEET CITY WITH HER DREAMING SPIRES   •   •   •   263 THYRSIS   19
        MID CITY-NOISE NOT AS WITH THEE OF YORE   •   •   •   •   269 THYRSIS   232
        ON TO THE CITY OF GOD   •   •   •   •   •   •   •   •   •   292 RUGBY CHAPEL   208
        FOREST AND CITY AND SPIRE   •   •   •   •   •   •   •   •   297 HEINES GRAVE   171
        BEFORE THY FEET THIS RECENT CITY SPREADS   •   •   •   •   330 MEROPE   9
        GO THOU INTO THE CITY AND SEEK OUT   •   •   •   •   •   331 MEROPE   37
        NO LINGERING NOW STRAIGHT TO THE CITY I   •   •   •   •   332 MEROPE   65
        HAD TO THIS CITY STENYCLAROS CALLD   •   •   •   •   •   •   338 MEROPE   262
        BASILIS HIS NEW CITY WHICH HE NOW   •   •   •   •   •   •   359 MEROPE   847
        FIRST CITY FOUNDED ON THE EARTH BY MEN   •   •   •   •   •   359 MEROPE   849
        UP FROM THE CITY TOWRD THIS GATED HILL   •   •   •   •   •   362 MEROPE   935
        CONFERRING IN THE CITY WITH OUR FRIENDS •   •   •   •   •   379 MEROPE   1261
        WHATEER IN THE MESSENIAN CITY STIRS   •   •   •   •   •   •   331 MEROPE   V 38
        UP FROM THE CITY TOWRDS THIS GATED HILL •   •   •   •   •   362 MEROPE   V 935
        CONCERTING IN THE CITY WITH OUR FRIENDS •   •   •   •   •   379 MEROPE   V1261
        THAN IN THE BROILING CITY IN THESE HEATS   •   •   •   •   409 EMPEDOCLES I 1   104
        THOU WILT RETURN TO-MORROW TO THE CITY   •   •   •   •   •   428 EMPEDOCLES I 2   470
        AND BRING PEISIANAX TO HIM FROM THE CITY   •   •   •   •   428 EMPEDOCLES I 2   481
        IN THE COURT OF GODS IN THE CITY OF MEN •   •   •   •   •   430 EMPEDOCLES II   38
        BUT THOU IMPERIAL CITY THAT HAST STOOD   •   •   •   •   •   463 ALARIC AT ROME   19
        TWICE HAD THE ETERNAL CITY BOWED HER LOW   •   •   •   •   465 ALARIC AT ROME   75
        IN MOURNFUL LOVELINESS THAT CITY LAY •   •   •   •   •   •   466 ALARIC AT ROME   104
        THAT CITY TOLD OF LANGUOR AND DECAY   •   •   •   •   •   •   466 ALARIC AT ROME   106
        HOW SHOULD THAT MIGHTIEST CITY PASS AWAY   •   •   •   •   467 ALARIC AT ROME   129
        AND LO THE ETERNAL CITY AS THEY RISE •   •   •   •   •   •   468 ALARIC AT ROME   155
        UNLIKE THAT OCEAN-CITY GAZING STILL   •   •   •   •   •   •   468 ALARIC AT ROME   159
        PERCHANCE THAT WONDROUS CITY WAS TO HIM •   •   •   •   •   469 ALARIC AT ROME   181
        BEAUTIFUL CITY IF DEPARTED THINGS   •   •   •   •   •   •   470 ALARIC AT ROME   205
        OF THE HORSEMEN OF TROY IN THE DAY THEY FOUGHT   HOMER TRANS   34
                FOR THEIR CITY

CITYS
        ACROSS THE GIRDLING CITYS HUM   •   •   •   •   •   •   •   248 KENSINGTON GARD   6
        TO FEEL AMID THE CITYS JAR   •   •   •   •   •   •   •   •   249 KENSINGTON GARD   38
        WHICH FROM ONE CENTRAL CITYS GUARDED SEAT   •   •   •   •   337 MEROPE   246

CITYWARD
        FROM THE SEA CITYWARD AND KNEW HIS STEP   •   •   •   •   101 BALDER DEAD 1   227

CIVIL
        WHAT GODS THE GODS OF CONCORD CIVIL WEAL   •   •   •   •   341 MEROPE   358

CLAD
        CLAD IN BLACK ON HER WHITE PALFREY   •   •   •   •   •   •   15 CHURCH BROU 1   97
        CLAD WERE THEY BOTH IN WHITE FLOWERS IN THEIR BREAST   25 DREAM   23
        CLAD WERE THEY BOTH IN WHITE FLOWERS IN THEIR BREASTS   25 DREAM   V 23
        HE ROSE AND CLAD HIMSELF AND GIRT HIS SWORD   •   •   •   61 SOHRAB RUSTUM   8
        AND CLAD HIMSELF IN STEEL THE ARMS HE CHOSE   •   •   •   69 SOHRAB RUSTUM   265
        BEHOLD ME I AM VAST AND CLAD IN IRON •   •   •   •   •   •   71 SOHRAB RUSTUM   325
        IF I IF ODIN CLAD IN RADIANT ARMS   •   •   •   •   •   •   120 BALDER DEAD 3   238
        A STATELY HUNTSMAN CLAD IN GREEN   •   •   •   •   •   •   •   147 TRISTRAM 2   153
        HOAR-HEADED WRINKLED CLAD IN WHITE   •   •   •   •   •   •   278 SOUTHERN NIGHT   86
        GREY-HEADED WRINKLED CLAD IN WHITE   •   •   •   •   •   •   278 SOUTHERN NIGHT   V 86
        BETWEEN HEATH-CLAD SHOWERY HILLS   •   •   •   •   •   •   •   282 HAWORTH CHURCH   57
        SAD-CHANTING MAIDENS CLAD IN MOURNING ROBES •   •   •   •   331 MEROPE   53
        JADED WITH TRAVEL CLAD IN HUNTERS GARB   •   •   •   •   •   363 MEROPE   957
        OF HOLIDAY-CLAD CITIZENS TRANSFORMD   •   •   •   •   •   •   402 MEROPE   1939

CLAIM
        AH LET US MAKE NO CLAIM   •   •   •   •   •   •   •   •   •   40 HUMAN LIFE   7
        THESE CLAIM NOT EVERY LAUGHING HOUR   •   •   •   •   •   •   53 RESIGNATION   30
        OLD MAN THE DEAD NEED NO ONE CLAIM NO KIN   •   •   •   •   62 SOHRAB RUSTUM   59
        SAY WHAT BLINDS US THAT WE CLAIM THE GLORY   •   •   •   •   209 SELF-DECEPTION   1
        WILL YE CLAIM FOR YOUR GREAT ONES THE GIFT   •   •   •   •   231 YOUTH OF NATURE   122
        AND WAIVE ALL CLAIM TO BLISS AND TRY TO BEAR   •   •   •   260 SCHOLAR-GIPSY   193
        BITTER SPIRITS YE CLAIM   •   •   •   •   •   •   •   •   •   293 HEINES GRAVE   46
        AND PLACE WITH THOSE DOST CLAIM   •   •   •   •   •   •   •   310 OBERMANN   142
        ALL CLAIM TO SUCCOUR FORFEIT TO MYSELF   •   •   •   •   •   366 MEROPE   1008
        NONE CAN TRULY CLAIM THAT   •   •   •   •   •   •   •   •   370 MEROPE   1109
        REFRESHD AND CLAIM THY MASTERS THANKS AND GOLD   •   •   •   373 MEROPE   1182
        THOU SMILING FIEND AND CLAIM THY GUERDON THERE   •   •   •   373 MEROPE   1184
        THAT WE MUST CLAIM SOME BLISS   •   •   •   •   •   •   •   •   425 EMPEDOCLES I 2   V 402
        AND WHEREFORE THEN HAVING NO CLAIM TO MORE   •   •   •   •   LUCRETIUS 3   8

CLAIMANT
        THE DARING CLAIMANT OF A PERILOUS THRONE   •   •   •   •   383 MEROPE   1357

CLAIMANTS
        ARE THE SOLE CLAIMANTS LEFT WHAT CAUSE OF STRIFE •   •   394 MEROPE   1693

CLAIMS
        WHEN THE DUPED SOUL SELF-MASTERD CLAIMS ITS MEED •   •   9 MYCERINUS   28
        CLAIMS EVER HOSTILE ELSE AND SET THY SON   •   •   •   •   335 MEROPE   168
        CLAIMS RAPTURE AS ITS RIGHT   •   •   •   •   •   •   •   •   424 EMPEDOCLES I 2   353

CLAIMST
        MORE THAN PITY CLAIMST A STAVE •   •   •   •   •   •   •   •   453 POOR MATTHIAS   22

CLAMOURS
        CLAMOURS TO FIND FULFILLD WHICH GOOD MEN PRAISE •   •   386 MEROPE   1428

CLANG
         DASHD WITH A CLANG TOGETHER AND A DIN   • • • • •   75 SOHRAB RUSTUM   475
         AND THE CLANG OF ARMS IN HIS EAR   • • • • • •   229 YOUTH OF NATURE   42

CLANKD
         THAT THE HARD IRON CORSLET CLANKD ALOUD   • • • • •   80 SOHRAB RUSTUM   664

CLAP
         AND CLAP THY HANDS AND CRY TIS THOU   • • • • • •   184 TERRACE BERNE   16

CLAPS
         AND THE DUCHESS CLAPS HER HANDS   • • • • • • •   14 CHURCH BROU 1   40

CLARION
         STIRRD LIKE A CLARION-BLAST MY SOUL   • • • • •   285 HAWORTH CHURCH   100
         SHOOK LIKE A CLARION-BLAST MY SOUL   • • • • •   284 HAWORTH CHURCH   V 100
         OF GOTHIC CLARION SMOTE THY STARTLED EAR   • • •   465 ALARIC AT ROME   80

CLASH
         AND BUCKLERS CLASH AND SPEARS BEGIN TO POUR   • •   127 BALDER DEAD 3   498
         WHERE IGNORANT ARMIES CLASH BY NIGHT   • • • • •   212 DOVER BEACH   37
         CLASH WITH JUSTICE THE GODS   • • • • • • •   348 MEROPE   537
         I HEARD THE CLASH OF WEAPONS THEN I SAW   • • • •   402 MEROPE   1941
         OTHER EXISTENCES THERE ARE THAT CLASH WITH OURS   • • 420 EMPEDOCLES I 2   246
         OTHER EXISTENCES THERE ARE WHICH CLASH WITH OURS   • • 420 EMPEDOCLES I 2   V 246

CLASHD
         IN HER LIKE US THERE CLASHD CONTENDING POWERS   • •   168 RACHEL 3   11
         I SMOTE HIM WHEN OUR WISHES CLASHD IN ARMS   • • • • 334 MEROPE   130

CLASHING
         DOUBLE AND CLASHING THAT HANG   • • • • • • • •   370 MEROPE   1113

CLASP
         WITH THE CLASP OF BURNISHD GOLD   • • • • • •   131 TRISTRAM 1   28
         WOULD THESE ARMS REACH TO CLASP THEE   • • • • • • 176 PARTING   61
         HEAR THAT FRESH VOICE AND CLASP THAT GOLD-LOCKD HEAD 387 MEROPE   1460
         WITH PASSIONATE WARMTH WE CLASP   • • • • •   424 EMPEDOCLES I 2   359
         AND CLASP CONJECTURED JOYS OR DREAD CONJECTURED WOES 425 EMPEDOCLES I 2   V 406
         AND NEVER LET US CLASP AND FEEL THE ALL   • • • •   439 EMPEDOCLES II   353
         SKIES THAT UNBOUND BY CLASP OF MOUNTAIN CHAIN   • • 473 CROMWELL   37
         KNOWING CLASP IT AND SERENELY BEAT   • • • • • •   META CLOISTER   32

CLASPD
         AND CLASPD HIS HAND WITHIN HIS OWN AND SAID   • •   71 SOHRAB RUSTUM   342
         AND FELL BEFORE HER FEET AND CLASPD HER KNEES   • • 110 BALDER DEAD 2   187
         FIXT HER SLIGHT HANDS CLASPD ON HER LAP THEN RISE   152 TRISTRAM 3   91
         WERE CLASPD TO THAT BREAST   • • • • • • • •   176 PARTING   V 70

CLASSES
         SINCE GAINST THE CLASSES   • • • • • • • • • •   460 KAISER DEAD   40

CLASSIC
         IMPARTING LIFE RENEWD OLD CLASSIC GRACE   • • • •   168 RACHEL 3   5

CLATTER
         BUT MID THEIR DRINK AND CLATTER HE WOULD FLY   • • 257 SCHOLAR-GIPSY   61

CLAY
         WITH A CLAY FORT BUT THAT WAS FALLN AND NOW   • •   61 SOHRAB RUSTUM   21
         ON THE BROAD CLAY-LADEN   • • • • • • • • • •   191 STRAYED REVEL   182
         WHEN WE TOO LIKE THYSELF ARE CLAY   • • • • •   452 GEISTS GRAVE   74
         THAT FRAME OF VIGOUR SHALL BE CRUMBLING CLAY   • • 469 ALARIC AT ROME   194

CLEANSE
         CLEANSE TO SWEET AIRS THE BREATH OF POISONOUS STREAMS 410 EMPEDOCLES I 1   117

CLEAR
         AND HIS CLEAR LAUGH FLED RINGING THROUGH THE GLOOM   12 MYCERINUS   113
         IF THE CLEAR IMPRESSION DIES   • • • • • • •   24 MEMORY-PICTURE   61
         QUEEN-LIKE AND CLEAR   • • • • • • • • • •   35 VOICE   2
         CAN REJECT WHAT CANNOT CLEAR HIM   • • • • • •   49 SECOND BEST   18
         MAKES CLEAR OUR GOAL TO EVERY EYE   • • • • • •   53 RESIGNATION   46
         MILD HOLLOWS AND CLEAR HEATHY SWELLS   • • • •   54 RESIGNATION   66
         IN ITS CLEAR SHALLOW TURF-FRINGED BED   • • • •   55 RESIGNATION   91
         WHO ART THOU FOR IT IS NOT YET CLEAR DAWN   • • •   62 SOHRAB RUSTUM   31
         BUT OF A SINGLE COMBAT FAME SPEAKS CLEAR   • • •   62 SOHRAB RUSTUM   62
         PRICKS WITH VERMILION SOME CLEAR PORCELAIN VASE   • 81 SOHRAB RUSTUM   673
         NOR SLAKED MY THIRST AT THE CLEAR HELMUND STREAM   • 83 SOHRAB RUSTUM   758
         CLEAR IN THESE THINGS I CANNOT SEE   • • • •   93 SICK KING BOKH   182
         OF SOME CLEAR RIVER ISSUING FROM A LAKE   • • •   109 BALDER DEAD 2   158
         IF CLEAR FROM PLOTTING BALDERS DEATH TO SWIM   • • 114 BALDER DEAD 3   27
         DIVIDING CLEAR THE PATHS OF NIGHT AND DAY   • • •   121 BALDER DEAD 3   265
         OF THEIR OWN COUNTRY AND CAN CLEAR DESCRY   • • •   123 BALDER DEAD 3   V 360
         AND HIS SPIRIT IS NOT CLEAR   • • • • • • •   133 TRISTRAM 1   86
         AND IN THE BOTTOM OF THE GLADE SHINE CLEAR   • • • 139 TRISTRAM 1   278
         MILD SHINES THE COLD SPRING IN THE MOONS CLEAR LIGHT 139 TRISTRAM 1   283
         THE BARE HEATHS SPREADING CLEAR AS DAY   • • • •   141 TRISTRAM 1   364
         WHAT VOICES ARE THESE ON THE CLEAR NIGHT-AIR   • • 142 TRISTRAM 1   372

CLEAR   (CONTINUED)

YOU SEE THEM CLEAR THE MOON SHINES BRIGHT	146	TRISTRAM 2	101
ON THAT CLEAR FOREST-KNOLL HE STAYS	148	TRISTRAM 2	155
THROUGH WHOSE MULLIOND WINDOWS CLEAR	148	TRISTRAM 2	169
NOW STAND CLEAR BEFORE ME IN THE MOONLIGHT	145	TRISTRAM 2	V 97
THE LONE UNBROKEN VIEW SPREADS BRIGHT AND CLEAR	150	TRISTRAM 3	12
UNDER THE HOLLIES IN THE CLEAR STILL AIR	150	TRISTRAM 3	39
SWOOPING TO LANDWARD NOR TO WHERE QUITE CLEAR	151	TRISTRAM 3	54
WAS THE ONE ISEULT CHOSE AND SHE BROUGHT CLEAR	154	TRISTRAM 3	165
HER HAVIOUR HAD THE MORNINGS FRESH CLEAR GRACE	154	TRISTRAM 3	179
ON THE BROOKS FARTHER SIDE WAS CLEAR BUT THEN	155	TRISTRAM 3	189
THE GRASS WAS DRY AND MOSSD AND YOU SAW CLEAR	155	TRISTRAM 3	206
THE LONE UNBROKEN VIEW STRETCHD BRIGHT AND CLEAR		TRISTRAM 3	V 12
THE LONE UNBROKEN VIEW GOES SPREADING CLEAR		TRISTRAM 3	V 12
IS GREEN AND CLEAR THE HEATHER WHICH ALL ROUND		TRISTRAM 3	V 14
ON THE BROOKS FURTHER SIDE WAS CLEAR BUT THEN	155	TRISTRAM 3	V 189
SHE SIGHD SHE LOOKD UP THROUGH THE CLEAR GREEN SEA	163	FORSAKEN MERM	55
SHE SATE BY THE PILLAR WE SAW HER CLEAR	163	FORSAKEN MERM	76
WHEN CLEAR FALLS THE MOONLIGHT	165	FORSAKEN MERM	126
BUOYANT AS MORNING AND AS MORNING CLEAR	175	PARTING	18
TO THE CLEAR WANING HILL-SIDE	176	PARTING	45
CLEAR PROSPECT OER OUR BEINGS WHOLE	179	FAREWELL	54
THE CLEAR-BROWN SHALLOW POOLS	190	STRAYED REVEL	147
THE TOO CLEAR WEB AND THY DUMB SISTERS SHAME	201	PHILOMELA	21
FAILD TO PLACE THAT MASTER-FEELING CLEAR	210	SELF-DECEPTION	24
FAILD TO PLACE OUR MASTER-FEELING CLEAR	210	SELF-DECEPTION	V 24
CLEAR PRESCRIBED WITHOUT YOUR CREED	215	PIS-ALLER	8
NOT WHOLLY CLEAR NOR WHOLLY BLIND	217	NAMELESS EPIT	V
CLEAR AS THE PAINTERS ART CAN DRESS	225	EPILOG LAOCOON	134
BUT CLEAR AS WORDS CAN MAKE REVEALING	225	EPILOG LAOCOON	137
CLEAR IN THE PURE JUNE-NIGHT	228	YOUTH OF NATURE	6
OF PARNASSUS SNOWILY CLEAR	229	YOUTH OF NATURE	40
TO CLEAR THE NEW WORLDS WAY	237	PROGRESS	16
BUT THAT YE THINK CLEAR FEEL DEEP BEAR FRUIT WELL	238	PROGRESS	47
BUT THAT YOU THINK CLEAR FEEL DEEP BEAR FRUIT WELL	238	PROGRESS	V 47
FROM THE INTENSE CLEAR STAR-SOWN VAULT OF HEAVEN	240	SELF-DEPENDENCE	13
O AIR-BORN VOICE LONG SINCE SEVERELY CLEAR	240	SELF-DEPENDENCE	29
HOW VAST YET OF WHAT CLEAR TRANSPARENCY	244	SUMMER NIGHT	89
OUR EYES CAN IN ANOTHERS EYES READ CLEAR	247	BURIED LIFE	81
AN AIR-STIRRD FOREST FRESH AND CLEAR	248	KENSINGTON GARD	16
LIGHT THE CLEAR FOLIAGED CHESTNUTS PLAY		KENSINGTON GARD	V
COMPOSED REFRESHD ENNOBLED CLEAR	251	WISH	50
OF THE NEW-BORN CLEAR-FLOWING STREAM	252	FUTURE	12
NOW READS IN HER BOSOM AS CLEAR	252	FUTURE	35
O BORN IN DAYS WHEN WITS WERE FRESH AND CLEAR	261	SCHOLAR-GIPSY	201
AND THY CLEAR AIMS BE CROSS AND SHIFTING MADE	261	SCHOLAR-GIPSY	228
STILL STILL THESE SLOPES TIS CLEAR	268	THYRSIS	196
HE READ EACH WOUND EACH WEAKNESS CLEAR	270	MEMORIAL VERSES	20
HEARD THE CLEAR SONG OF ORPHEUS COME	271	MEMORIAL VERSES	38
OF THY BUOYANT CHEERFULNESS CLEAR	287	RUGBY CHAPEL	22
PATH TO A CLEAR-PURPOSED GOAL	288	RUGBY CHAPEL	85
OF THINE EVEN CHEERFULNESS CLEAR	287	RUGBY CHAPEL	V 22
FROM MISTS AND SANE AND CLEAR	308	OBERMANN	62
THY HEAD IS CLEAR THY FEELING CHILL	309	OBERMANN	87
WHERE WITH CLEAR-RUSTLING WAVE	311	OBERMANN	166
AND STOOPS TO CLEAR THY MOSS-GROWN DATE	311	OBERMANN	173
ITS HEAD WAS CLEAR AND TRUE	315	OBERMANN MORE	86
SELF-POISED CLEAR-MINDED HENCEFORTH MAN	319	OBERMANN MORE	V 185
PEACE PEACE ALLS CLEAR THE WICKED WATCH AND WORK	365	MEROPE	995
INSTRUCT ME NOT I HAVE MY LESSON CLEAR	379	MEROPE	1259
THE GODS COMMAND NOT WHERE THE HEART SPEAKS CLEAR	385	MEROPE	1404
WHERE CLEAR-FLOWING LADON	391	MEROPE	1608
AND FROM THAT MOMENT I SAW NOTHING CLEAR	402	MEROPE	1936
SUSPICION GRAVE I SEE BUT NO CLEAR PROOF	365	MEROPE	V 994
IN THIS CLEAR MOUNTAIN-AIR A VOICE WILL RISE	409	EMPEDOCLES I 1	88
THE WIT AND COUNSEL OF MAN WAS NEVER CLEAR	413	EMPEDOCLES I 2	30
THE TRACK WINDS DOWN TO THE CLEAR STREAM	413	EMPEDOCLES I 2	36
SINCE HE SEES NOTHING CLEAR	415	EMPEDOCLES I 2	90
HE FAILS NOT TO JUDGE CLEAR IF THIS BE QUENCHD OR NO	418	EMPEDOCLES I 2	171
THROUGH WHICH TO SEE LESS CLEAR	419	EMPEDOCLES I 2	205
AT ONCE OUR EYES GROW CLEAR	424	EMPEDOCLES I 2	362
WHERE HE SEES NOTHING CLEAR	415	EMPEDOCLES I 2	V 90
HE FAILS NOT TO JUDGE CLEAR IF THIS IS QUENCHD OR NO	418	EMPEDOCLES I 2	V 171
THAT VOICE HAD NOTE SO CLEAR OF SWEET COMMAND	445	WESTMIN ABBEY	28
THE CASE WAS CLEAR A MONGREL THING	459	KAISER DEAD	29
AND THUS BENEATH THE CLEAR CALM VAULT OF HEAVEN	466	ALARIC AT ROME	103
AND MEMORYS CALM CLEAR VOICE AND MOURNFUL EYE	474	CROMWELL	87
IN BROAD CLEAR LIGHT THE GHASTLY VISION SHONE	477	CROMWELL	203
THE IMPRISONING CHAINS FELL OFF AND ALL WAS CLEAR	478	CROMWELL	214
AND WITH ITS CLEAR CALM TONES THAT DYING PRAYER	478	CROMWELL	217
LAST NIGHT I LOOKD THE SKY WAS CLEAR	480	HAYSWATER BOAT	33
GREAT ELBRUIS WHITENS CLEAR		PILLARS UNIVERS	10
OF A SPIRIT SOFTLY CLEAR		META CLOISTER	22
PLEADING GAZE THAT FOREHEAD CLEAR		META CLOISTER	38

CLEARD

CLEARD ROME OF WHAT MOST SHAMED HIM BUT BE HIS	2	TO A FRIEND	8
THE SUN BY THIS HAD RISEN AND CLEARD THE FOG	64	SOHRAB RUSTUM	104
BY THIS THE SUN HAD RISEN AND CLEARD THE FOG	64	SOHRAB RUSTUM	V 104
THE RUSHING BATTLE CLEARD THY BLOOD	139	TRISTRAM 1	292

CLEARD   (CONTINUED)
      CLEARD WITH BLITHE TRAVEL AND THE MORNING AIR   •   •   355 MEROPE   734

CLEARER
      WHEN THE SOUL GROWING CLEARER   •   •   •   •   •   •   •   38 STAGIRIUS   14
      WHEN THE MIND WAXING CLEARER SEES GOD NO NEARER   •   •   38 STAGIRIUS   V 16
      NO CLEARER EYESIGHT   •   •   •   •   •   •   •   •   51 CONSOLATION   34
      MUST NEEDS READ CLEARER SURE THAN HE   •   •   •   •   •   •   250 WISH   28
      CLEARER HOW MUCH THAN OURS YET WE   •   •   •   •   •   •   308 OBERMANN   63
      DIVINELIER IMAGED CLEARER SEEN   •   •   •   •   •   •   •   322 OBERMANN MORE   295

CLEAREST
      HE MUCH THE OLD MAN WHO CLEAREST-SOULD OF MEN   •   •   2 TO A FRIEND   2
      THE CLEAREST THE BEST WHO HAVE READ   •   •   •   •   •   231 YOUTH OF NATURE   104
      CLEAREST THEIR COURSE DISCERN   •   •   •   •   •   •   •   314 OBERMANN MORE   76

CLEARING
      CLEARING A STAGE   •   •   •   •   •   •   •   •   •   220 BACCHANALIA 2   34
      OF SACRIFICE HIS GUARDS CLEARING THE WAY   •   •   •   401 MEROPE   1904

CLEARLY
      AS CLEARLY AS AT NOON   •   •   •   •   •   •   •   •   •   242 SUMMER NIGHT   15
      WHO NEVER DEEPLY FELT NOR CLEARLY WILLD   •   •   •   260 SCHOLAR-GIPSY   173
      POWER FAILS US TO TRY CLEARLY IF THAT CAUSE   •   •   352 MEROPE   647

CLEARNESS
      THAT THE SWEET VOICE ITS UPLAND CLEARNESS TOOK   •   •   175 PARTING   22
      PLAINNESS AND CLEARNESS WITHOUT SHADOW OF STAIN   •   •   244 SUMMER NIGHT   76
      CLEARNESS DIVINE   •   •   •   •   •   •   •   •   •   244 SUMMER NIGHT   77
      JOIND TO ITS CLEARNESS OF THEIR FORCE   •   •   •   •   482 COURAGE   28

CLEARS
      AS THE SKY-BRIGHTENING SOUTH-WIND CLEARS THE DAY   •   •   432 EMPEDOCLES II   121

CLEAVES
      FAR DOWN THE TORRENT CLEAVES ITS WAY   •   •   •   •   •   •   479 HAYSWATER BOAT   10

CLEMENT
      CLEMENT IF MAY BE BUT TO RULE IT THERE   •   •   •   •   342 MEROPE   377

CLENCHD
      YET STARK FROM THE DEATH-STRUGGLE TIGHT-CLENCHD HANDS   373 MEROPE   1174

CLERE
      THE MOON THROUGH THE CLERE-STORY WINDOWS SHINES   •   •   18 CHURCH BROU 3   36

CLIFF
      THROUGH THE CLIFF-WALL AND A FRESH STREAM RUNS DOWN   97 BALDER DEAD 1   82
      THE HOLLIES AND THE CLIFF AND THE SEA-SHORE   •   •   152 TRISTRAM 3   104
      PEERING TO SPY A GOAT-TRACK DOWN THE CLIFF   •   •   •   357 MEROPE   804
      PARTS FROM THIS CAVE-PIERCED CLIFF THE SHELVING BAY   358 MEROPE   818
      SWEPT DOWN A CHASM RIFTED IN THE CLIFF   •   •   •   •   363 MEROPE   960
      UNDER THE DRIPPING BLACK TARTAREAN CLIFF   •   •   •   368 MEROPE   1064
      PARTS FROM THE CAVE-PIERCD CLIFF THE SHELVING BAY   358 MEROPE   V 818
      SWEPT DOWN A CHASM BROKEN IN THE CLIFF   •   •   •   •   363 MEROPE   V 960
      IN CLIFF TO THE SEA   •   •   •   •   •   •   •   •   •   441 EMPEDOCLES II   424
      ON THE SWARD AT THE CLIFF-TOP   •   •   •   •   •   •   •   442 EMPEDOCLES II   429
      ON THE CLIFF-SIDE THE PIGEONS   •   •   •   •   •   •   •   442 EMPEDOCLES II   431
      OF SHOOTING CLIFF AND CRUMBLED STONE   •   •   •   •   •   479 HAYSWATER BOAT   13

CLIFFS
      BLACK UNDER CLIFFS IT RACED ROUND HEADLANDS SHONE   25 DREAM   34
      BETWEEN THE WAVES AND BLACK OERHANGING CLIFFS   •   •   97 BALDER DEAD 1   79
      UPON THE CLIFFS OR SMOKE OF BURNING WEEDS   •   •   •   124 BALDER DEAD 3   362
      TO ENGLANDS CLIFFS MY GAZE IS TURND   •   •   •   •   •   205 CALAIS SANDS   19
      TO ENGLANDS CLIFFS MY LOOK IS TURND   •   •   •   •   •   205 CALAIS SANDS   V 19
      GLEAMS AND IS GONE THE CLIFFS OF ENGLAND STAND   •   •   210 DOVER BEACH   4
      SHINES AND IS GONE THE CLIFFS OF ENGLAND   •   •   •   210 DOVER BEACH   V   4
      THERE WHERE DOWN CLOUDY CLIFFS THROUGH SHEETS OF FOAM   262 SCHOLAR-GIPSY   248
      AND THE STONE COFFINS THEN BY CAPHYAE CLIFFS   •   •   356 MEROPE   744
      OER WHOSE CLIFFS THE TOWNSMEN   •   •   •   •   •   •   392 MEROPE   1649
      BETWEEN THE PINE-WOODS AND THE CLIFFS   •   •   •   •   399 MEROPE   1824
      O CLIFFS LEFT BY THE EAGLES   •   •   •   •   •   •   •   399 MEROPE   1825
      FROM THEIR DEEP BASE THY BEETLING CLIFFS DUNBAR   •   •   476 CROMWELL   151

CLIMATES
      OUR JANGLE OF FALSE WITS OUR CLIMATES FROWNS   •   •   168 RACHEL 2   11

CLIMB
      CLIMB THE WINDING MOUNTAIN-WAY   •   •   •   •   •   •   •   15 CHURCH BROU 1   86
      CLIMB UP HERE TO PRAY   •   •   •   •   •   •   •   •   17 CHURCH BROU 2   19
      CLIMB UNDERNEATH THE INDIAN CAUCASUS   •   •   •   •   •   66 SOHRAB RUSTUM   V 161
      BEFORE HE CLIMB THE PASS   •   •   •   •   •   •   •   •   313 OBERMANN MORE   20
      CHOSEN A PRISON FOR PROMETHEUS CLIMB   •   •   •   •   •   395 MEROPE   1750
      THAT CLIMB FROM THE STREAMS EDGE THE LONG GREY TUFTS   406 EMPEDOCLES I 1   16
      TILL THE SLOW MULES SHOULD CLIMB IN SIGHT AGAIN   •   •   408 EMPEDOCLES I 1   48
      SAW BUT ANOTHER STEP TO CLIMB TO VICTORY   •   •   •   469 ALARIC AT ROME   186

CLIMBD
      WE CLIMBD ON THE GRAVES ON THE STONES WORN WITH RAINS   163 FORSAKEN MERM   74

CLIMBD   (CONTINUED)
        AND THOU HAST CLIMBD THE HILL . . . .   258 SCHOLAR-GIPSY   126
        I CLIMBD BENEATH ME BRIGHT AND WIDE . . . . . .   273 STANZAS CARNAC   3

CLIMBEST
        HEINE THOU CLIMBEST AGAIN   . . . .   297 HEINES GRAVE   155

CLIMBING
        BRIGHT IN THE SUN THE CLIMBING GOURD-PLANTS LEAVES   25 DREAM   16
        FELL LIKE OSSA ON THE CLIMBING SOUL . . . . . .   28 NEW SIRENS   72
        A WILD ROSE CLIMBING UP A MOULDERING WALL . . . .   36 VOICE   20
        THERE CLIMBING HANGS A FAR-SEEN SIGN . . . . . .   54 RESIGNATION   60
        CLIMBING THE ROCK WHICH JUTS . . . .   297 HEINES GRAVE   186

CLIMBS
        WHERE EARTHLY VOICE CLIMBS NEVER WING THEIR FLIGHT   10 MYCERINUS   44
        WHEN THE SOUND CLIMBS NEAR HIS SEAT . . . . . .   431 EMPEDOCLES II   69

CLIME
        AND BREATHE MORE HAPPY IN AN EVEN CLIME   . . . .   37 YOUTHS AGIT   6
        I FELT IT IN SOME OTHER CLIME . . . .   242 MORALITY   33
        HE TOO UPON A WINTRY CLIME   . . . .   271 MEMORIAL VERSES   42

CLIMES
        LEARND IN MORE LANGUID CLIMES . . . .   46 WORLD QUIETIST   5
        A MESSENGER FROM RADIANT CLIMES   . . . . . .   208 LONGING   6

CLING
        CLING TO WHAT CAN TRULY CHEER HIM   . . . . . .   49 SECOND BEST   19

CLINGEST
        CLINGEST WITH SMILES WITH A SIGH   . . . . . .   298 HEINES GRAVE   190

CLINGST
        ONCE MORE THOU CLINGST TO THE CROSS . . . . . .   298 HEINES GRAVE   189

CLIP
        AND CLIP HIS BORDERS SHORT AND DRIVE HIS HERDS   . .   68 SOHRAB RUSTUM   234
        AND CLIP HIS BORDERS ROUND AND DRIVE HIS HERDS   . .   68 SOHRAB RUSTUM   V 234

CLIPS
        THE CHURCHYARD WALL THAT CLIPS THE SQUARE   . . . .   16 CHURCH BROU 2   12

CLOAK
        THEY CLOAK THE TROUBLES OF THE HEART . . . . . .   48 HORATIAN ECHO   20
        AND TOOK HIS HORSEMANS CLOAK AND LEFT HIS TENT   . .   61 SOHRAB RUSTUM   9
        AND THREW A WHITE CLOAK ROUND HIM AND HE TOOK   . .   64 SOHRAB RUSTUM   98
        AND THE GREAT RUSTUM DREW HIS HORSEMANS CLOAK   . .   86 SOHRAB RUSTUM   858
        YES THE SPRAY IS ON THY CLOAK AND HAIR   . . . .   142 TRISTRAM 2   18
        TO THE POOR WRETCH MY CLOAK I CAST   . . . . . .   158 SAINT BRANDAN   51
        IN HAT OF ANTIQUE SHAPE AND CLOAK OF GREY   . . . .   256 SCHOLAR-GIPSY   55
        WRAPT IN THY CLOAK AND BATTLING WITH THE SNOW   . .   258 SCHOLAR-GIPSY   124
        CLOAK THINE AMBITION WITH THESE SPECIOUS WORDS   . .   404 MEROPE   1985

CLOAKD
        NOW FOR THYSELF THOU COMST WITH WELL-CLOAKD JOY   . .   395 MEROPE   1737

CLOCK
        AND WHEN THE CLOCK PEALS MIDNIGHT SHE WILL MOVE   . .   152 TRISTRAM 3   86

CLOG
        FROM THE CLOG OF MISERY   . . . .   138 TRISTRAM 1   268

CLOGS
        MIST CLOGS THE SUNSHINE   . . . .   50 CONSOLATION   1

CLOISTER
        NO CLOISTER-FLOOR OF HUMID STONE   . . . . . .   317 OBERMANN MORE   149
        OF THEIR CLOISTER SEE THEY GLIDE   . . . . . .   META CLOISTER   6

CLOISTRAL
        FENCED EARLY IN THIS CLOISTRAL ROUND . . . . . .   306 GRANDE CHARTR   205

CLOSE
        CROWN OF HIS STRUGGLING LIFE AN UNJUST CLOSE   . .   9 MYCERINUS   30
        ERE THE LONG EVENING CLOSE THOU SHALT RETURN   . .   44 GIPSY CHILD   67
        ON THIS SIDE THE ALL-COMMON CLOSE . . . . . .   53 RESIGNATION   16
        AND CLOSE-SET SKULL-CAPS AND THOSE WILDER HORDES . .   64 SOHRAB RUSTUM   130
        DREW CLOSE TOGETHER AND CONFERRD   . . . . . .   91 SICK KING BOKH   106
        HARD BY A CLOSE OF APRICOTS   . . . .   94 SICK KING BOKH   223
        ROUND EACH SWEET BROW THE CAP CLOSE-SET   . . . .   141 TRISTRAM 1   340
        AND OFTEN THE FINGERS CLOSE IN HASTE . . . . . .   141 TRISTRAM 1   346
        CLOSE THINE EYES THIS FLOODING MOONLIGHT BLINDS THEM   144 TRISTRAM 2   71
        CLOSE MINE EYES THEN SEEK THE PRINCESS ISEULT   . .   145 TRISTRAM 2   93
        THE WILD BOAR HARBOURS CLOSE AND FEEDS   . . . .   148 TRISTRAM 2   V
        CROUCHD ON THE PAVEMENT CLOSE BY BELGRAVE SQUARE . .   169 WEST LONDON   1
        TWO SPRINGS WHICH CLOSE BY ONE ANOTHER PLAY   . .   170 EAST AND WEST   2
        TO-NIGHT THOSE SOFT-FRINGED EYES SHALL CLOSE   . .   205 CALAIS SANDS   35
        TO-NIGHT THOSE SOFT-VEILED EYES SHALL CLOSE   . .   205 CALAIS SANDS   V 35
        AT THE CLOSE OF DAY FROM THE PLAIN   . . . . . .   217 LORDS MESSENGER   21

CLOSE   (CONTINUED)
          AND SOLEMN SILENCE OF ITS CLOSE   . . . . . .   225 EPILOG LAOCOON   152
          THE FLOWERS CLOSE THE BIRDS ARE FED   . . . .   249 KENSINGTON GARD   V 34
          WITH CLOSE-LIPPD PATIENCE FOR OUR ONLY FRIEND   . .   260 SCHOLAR-GIPSY   194
          THEIR ABBEY AND ITS CLOSE OF GRAVES   . . . . . .   305 GRANDE CHARTR   174
          CLOSE OER IT IN THE AIR   . . . .   306 OBERMANN   4
          DOTH ALL THE HEAVENLY OPENING CLOSE   . . . . . .   324 OBERMANN MORE   343
          TO GUIDE OUR VENGEANCE TO A PROSPEROUS CLOSE   . .   332 MEROPE   75
          THE BREACH BETWEEN OUR PARTIES HELP ME CLOSE   . .   335 MEROPE   163
          THAT MURDER MOVES THIS BREACH THAT THOU WOULDST CLOSE 335 MEROPE   187
          TO CLOSE AN OLD WOUND NOT TO OPEN NEW   . . . . .   379 MEROPE   1257
          PROOF NOT SURMISE SHOWS HIM IN COMMERCE CLOSE   . .   380 MEROPE   1274
          TO GUIDE OUR EFFORT TO A PROSPEROUS CLOSE   . . . .   332 MEROPE   V 75
          THAT MURDER DRAWS THIS BREACH THAT THOU WOULDST CLOSE 335 MEROPE   V 187
          EXAMIND CLOSE HE OWND THIS STORY FALSE   . . . .   365 MEROPE   V
          WE LAY THEE CLOSE WITHIN OUR REACH   . . . .   451 GEISTS GRAVE   65
          LIKE LOWERING CLOUDS THAT AT THE CLOSE OF DAY   . .   478 CROMWELL   215

CLOSED
          ALL DIFFERENCE WITH HIS FELLOW-MORTAL CLOSED   . .   7 REP FRIEND CONT   13
          THEN THE DUCHESS CLOSED HER LABOURS   . . . . . .   16 CHURCH BROU 1   111
          WHITE WITH EYES CLOSED ONLY WHEN HEAVY GASPS   . .   86 SOHRAB RUSTUM   849
          AND HIS CLOSED EYE DOTH SWEEP   . . . .   133 TRISTRAM 1   90
          TURND TO EACH OTHER THE EYES CLOSED   . . . . . .   141 TRISTRAM 1   338
          OF LIFE WAS CUT AND CLOSED THY SPAN   . . . . . .   184 TERRACE BERNE   28
          OF THE CITY OF DEATH HAVE FOR EVER CLOSED   . . .   199 FRAG DEJANEIRA   30
          OR SHALL REACH WHEN HIS EYES HAVE BEEN CLOSED   . .   252 FUTURE   23
          QUIET TO ASK FOR CLOSED   . . . .   293 HEINES GRAVE   17
          ITS TERM OF LIFE WAS NEARLY CLOSED   . . . . . .   322 OBERMANN MORE   299
          NOR OUTWARD THINGS WERE CLOSED AND DEAD TO US   . .   436 EMPEDOCLES II   241

CLOSELY
          FOLD CLOSELY O NATURE   . . . .   177 PARTING   77
          SPIRITS DRIED UP AND CLOSELY FURLD   . . . . . .   272 MEMORIAL VERSES   56
          SPIRITS DEEP-CRUSHED AND CLOSELY FURLD   . . . . .   272 MEMORIAL VERSES   V 56

CLOSER
          NAY LOOK CLOSER INTO MAN . . . .   215 PIS-ALLER   5
          CLOSER KNIT THEIR LIFE WITH OURS   . . . .   453 POOR MATTHIAS   46

CLOSES
          NOW AS THE BARRIER CLOSES DIES AWAY   . . . . . .   10 MYCERINUS   58
          AND TO MAKE ORCHARD-CLOSES FILLD   . . . .   94 SICK KING BOKH   200

CLOSING
          HAVE YOU SEEN IT AT THE CLOSING   . . . .   33 NEW SIRENS   207
          MOURN WILL WE NOT YOUR CLOSING HOUR   . . . . . .   48 HORATIAN ECHO   10
          CLOSING IN BLOOD AND GLOOM HIS SULLEN REIGN   . .   335 MEROPE   160
          NEARER AND NEARER TO THEIR CLOSING HOUR   . . . .   469 ALARIC AT ROME   190

CLOTH
          OF SCARLET CLOTH THEY WERE AND GLITTERING GAY   . .   66 SOHRAB RUSTUM   192
          DIGHT WITH A SADDLE-CLOTH OF BROIDERD GREEN   . .   69 SOHRAB RUSTUM   277
          THE CLOTH-MERCHANTS AND LET THEM BE   . . . . . .   87 SICK KING BOKH   2
          EACH FORTIETH WEB OF CLOTH TO ME   . . . .   87 SICK KING BOKH   8

CLOTHE
          FOND HEARTS THAT FAIN WOULD CLOTHE THE UNWELCOME TRUTH   474 CROMWELL   97

CLOTHED
          CLOTHED IN SMILES BENEATH THE DAIS   . . . . . .   13 CHURCH BROU 1   35
          THE HILLS ARE CLOTHED WITH PINES SUN-PROOF   . . .   16 CHURCH BROU 2   4
          WELL-FED WELL-CLOTHED WELL-FRIENDED I   . . . .   158 SAINT BRANDAN   57
          O HUSBAND O CLOTHED   . . . .   371 MEROPE   1139
          HER FOREST-CLOTHED FRAME . . . .   441 EMPEDOCLES II   420

CLOTHES
          AND THOUGH THE BED-CLOTHES HIDE HER FACE   . . . .   147 TRISTRAM 2   136
          A GIRL THEIR CLOTHES WERE RAGS THEIR FEET WERE BARE   169 WEST LONDON   4

CLOTHING
          SUMPTUOUS ITS CLOTHING RICH ITS FARE   . . . . . .   315 OBERMANN MORE   87

CLOUD
          HEMMD BY TWO BANKS OF CLOUD PEERS PALE AND WEAK   . .   10 MYCERINUS   57
          THOUGH THAT BLANK SUNSHINE BLIND THEE THOUGH THE CLOUD   44 GIPSY CHILD   61
          PIERCING THE SOLEMN CLOUD   . . . .   45 IN UTRUMQUE PAR   30
          FIRST A LIGHT CLOUD OF HORSE TARTARS THEY SEEMD   . .   65 SOHRAB RUSTUM   137
          IN THAT UNNATURAL CONFLICT FOR A CLOUD   . . . .   75 SOHRAB RUSTUM   481
          AND LIGHTNINGS RENT THE CLOUD AND RUKSH THE HORSE   76 SOHRAB RUSTUM   501
          THE CLOUD AND THE TWO ARMIES SAW THE PAIR   . . .   77 SOHRAB RUSTUM   524
          AND THEN A DARK CLOUD PASSD BEFORE HIS EYES   . .   81 SOHRAB RUSTUM   692
          THEY CLOUD THE BRAIN THEY DULL THE BLOOD   . . .   138 TRISTRAM 1   248
          THERE THE PINES SLOPE THE CLOUD-STRIPS   . . . .   176 PARTING   53
          A CLOUD OF DESERT ROBBER-HORSE HAVE BURST   . . .   193 STRAYED REVEL   248
          A CLOUD OF DESERT ROBBER-HORSE HAS BURST   . . .   193 STRAYED REVEL   V 248
          THOU COMEST YES THE VESSELS CLOUD   . . . . . .   205 CALAIS SANDS   21
          OER THE CLOUD-WRAPT PERILOUS PLAIN   . . . . . .   217 LORDS MESSENGER   V 21
          THE CLOUD OF MORTAL DESTINY   . . . .   272 MEMORIAL VERSES   68
          HALT THROUGH THE CLOUD-DRIFT SOMETHING SHINES   . .   299 GRANDE CHARTR   16

CLOUD   (CONTINUED)
        A CLOUD OF VULTURES ON THIS VIGOROUS RACE   • • • •   339 MEROPE   296
        THAT REGION IN PERPETUAL CLOUD • • • • • • •   352 MEROPE   642
        CLOUD-ENVELOPED OBSCURE   370 MEROPE   1106
        ON THAT MORN WHEN THE SMOKE-CLOUD   • • • • • •   399 MEROPE   1826
        THOU TOO BRIMMEST WITH LIFE THE SEA OF CLOUD   • •   438 EMPEDOCLES II   308
        I FEEL IT IN THIS HOUR THE NUMBING CLOUD   • • • •   441 EMPEDOCLES II   407
        TWICE HATH THE CLOUD HUNG OER THEE TWICE BEEN STAYED   465 ALARIC AT ROME   83
        WHO SCALE THE CLOUD-CAPT HEIGHT OR SINK TO REST • •   472 CROMWELL   11

CLOUDED
        HAVE YOU TRACKD ITS CLOUDED WAYS   • • • • • • •   33 NEW SIRENS   208
        FROM A SORROW-CLOUDED EYE   • • • • • • • •   164 FORSAKEN MERM   103
        CLOUDED AND DIM GREW THEIR EYE • • • • • • •   233 YOUTH OF MAN   43
        THE CLOUDED SKY IS STILL AND GREY   • • • • •   248 KENSINGTON GARD   V

CLOUDLESS
        HATH SOWN WITH CLOUDLESS PASSAGES THE TALE   • • • •   43 GIPSY CHILD   51
        KEPT THEY MORE CLOUDLESS • • • • • • • • •   50 CONSOLATION   24
        AND OVERHEAD THE CLOUDLESS SKY OF MAY   • • • •   133 TRISTRAM 1   96

CLOUDS
        NO NOR GREW DARK WHEN AUTUMN BROUGHT THE CLOUDS • •   12 MYCERINUS   121
        WHO MASSD ROUND THAT SLIGHT BROW THESE CLOUDS OF DOOM   41 GIPSY CHILD   4
        WHAT CLOUDS THY FOREHEAD AND FORE-DATES THY DOOM • •   41 GIPSY CHILD   V   4
        THROUGH CLOUDS OF INDIVIDUAL STRIFE • • • • • •   59 RESIGNATION   251
        THAT LONG HAS TOWERD IN THE AIRY CLOUDS   • • • •   73 SOHRAB RUSTUM   401
        COME RUSHING DOWN TOGETHER FROM THE CLOUDS   • • • •   75 SOHRAB RUSTUM   473
        THROUGH MANY ROLLING CLOUDS SO RUSTUM SAW   • • • •   79 SOHRAB RUSTUM   623
        CLOUDS OF WHITE ROLLING VAPOURS FILL THE VALE   • • •   113 BALDER DEAD 2   298
        THROUGH THE LOOSE CLOUDS LIFTS DIMLY   • • • • •   175 PARTING   13
        OCEAN AND CLOUDS AND NIGHT AND DAY   • • • • • •   181 ISOLATION MARG   33
        THE CLOUDS ARE ON THE OBERLAND • • • • • •   184 TERRACE BERNE   5
        THEN WHEN THE CLOUDS ARE OFF THE SOUL   • • • •   241 MORALITY   13
        TO THEE WE COME THEN CLOUDS ARE ROLLD   • • • •   309 OBERMANN   105
        CLOUDS AND GROWS DAILY WORSE IN SICILY   • • • •   410 EMPEDOCLES I 1   120
        THE PEAK ROUND WHICH THE WHITE CLOUDS PLAY   • • • •   414 EMPEDOCLES I 2   56
        AND MAKES THE MASSD CLOUDS ROLL   • • • • • •   432 EMPEDOCLES II   122
        THE CLOUDS WHICH WRAP THE SOUL • • • • • • •   432 EMPEDOCLES II   124
        THE CLOUDS THAT WRAP THE SOUL   • • • • • • •   432 EMPEDOCLES II   V 124
        WITH GLOOMING CLOUDS BROODS DARK AND HEAVILY   • •   475 CROMWELL   130
        LIKE LOWERING CLOUDS THAT AT THE CLOSE OF DAY   • •   478 CROMWELL   215
        THE CLOUDS OF SICKNESS CAST NO STAIN UPON   • • • •   FRAGMENT 8   1

CLOUDY
        SPARES BUT THE CLOUDY BORDER OF HIS BASE   • • • •   3 SHAKESPEARE   7
        IN CLOUDY CIRCLES TO ETERNITY   • • • • • • •   4 BUTLERS SERMONS   14
        MAKE TOWARD THEM OER THE STRETCHING CLOUDY PLAIN • •   126 BALDER DEAD 3   443
        DEPARTED OER THE CLOUDY PLAIN AND SOON   • • • •   129 BALDER DEAD 3   552
        MAKE TOWARDS THEM OER THE STRETCHING CLOUDY PLAIN   • •   126 BALDER DEAD 3   V 443
        THERE WHERE DOWN CLOUDY CLIFFS THROUGH SHEETS OF FOAM   262 SCHOLAR-GIPSY   248
        AND HIGH THE MOUNTAIN-TOPS IN CLOUDY AIR   • • • •   267 THYRSIS   143

CLOVE
        NOR CLOVE ITS STEEL QUITE THROUGH BUT ALL THE CREST   76 SOHRAB RUSTUM   496
        AT BALDER WHOM NO WEAPON PIERCED OR CLOVE   • • • •   95 BALDER DEAD 1   4
        AND LOPPD THEIR BOUGHS AND CLOVE THEM ON THE SWARD   106 BALDER DEAD 2   59

CLOVER
        BUTTERCUPS CLOVER DAISIES GRASS   • • • • • • •   KENSINGTON GARD   V 15

CLOWN
        HE SEES THE DROWSY NEW-WAKED CLOWN   • • • • • • •   57 RESIGNATION   181

CLOY
        WHERE SWEET THINGS SOONEST CLOY   • • • • • • •   39 STAGIRIUS   44

CLUB
        AND RUSTUM SEIZED HIS CLUB WHICH NONE BUT HE   • •   73 SOHRAB RUSTUM   408
        THE CLUB WHICH RUSTUM LIFTED NOW AND STRUCK • •   73 SOHRAB RUSTUM   416
        LITHE AS THE GLANCING SNAKE AND THE CLUB CAME   • •   73 SOHRAB RUSTUM   418
        THOU STRIKST TOO HARD THAT CLUB OF THINE WILL FLOAT   74 SOHRAB RUSTUM   427
        AND STOOD ERECT TREMBLING WITH RAGE HIS CLUB   • •   74 SOHRAB RUSTUM   449
        THEN RUSTUM SEIZED HIS CLUB WHICH NONE BUT HE   • •   73 SOHRAB RUSTUM   V 408

CLUE
        WHICH SAW ONE CLUE TO LIFE AND FOLLOWD IT   • • • •   5 DUKE WELLINGTON   14
        HE DOES WELL TOO WHO KEEPS THAT CLUE THE MILD   • •   195 FRAG ANTIGONE   9
        THE CLUE TO HAPPINESS   • • • • • • • • • •   EMPEDOCLES I 2   V

CLUMPS
        AMONG THE HOLLY-CLUMPS AND BROKEN GROUND   • • • •   150 TRISTRAM 3   28
        STARRD THE COOL TURF AND CLUMPS OF PRIMROSES   • •   155 TRISTRAM 3   208

CLUSTER
        SLEEP O CLUSTER OF FRIENDS • • • • • • • •   285 HAWORTH CHURCH   112

CLUSTERD
        OR CLUSTERD PEAKS WITH PLUNGING GULFS BETWEEN   • •   4 BUTLERS SERMONS   11
        THE SWINGING WATERS AND THE CLUSTERD PIER   • • • •   42 GIPSY CHILD   6

CLUSTERD   (CONTINUED)
        GAY SHINE THE WATERS AND THE CLUSTERD PIER   • • • •   41 GIPSY CHILD   V   6
        CLUSTERD UNDER THE HOLLY-SCREEN AND SHE   • • • •   150 TRISTRAM 3   36
        CLUSTERD IN THICK BEADS DIM   • • • • • • • • •   186 STRAYED REVEL   16
        THAT COMELY FACE THAT CLUSTERD BROW   • • • • • •   279 SOUTHERN NIGHT   125

CLUSTERING
        CLUSTERING LIKE BEE-HIVES ON THE LOW FLAT STRAND   • •   61 SOHRAB RUSTUM   13
        CLUSTERING OER THY WHITE FOREHEAD LIKE A GIRLS   • •   373 MEROPE   1162

CLUSTERS
        THERE ITS DUSKY BLUE CLUSTERS   • • • • • • • •   176 PARTING   51
        CLUSTERS OF LONELY MOUNDS   • • • • • • • • •   191 STRAYED REVEL   177
        OF BLOSSOMD CLUSTERS PALE   • • • • • • • • •   200 PHILOMELA   V

CLUTCHD
        TO HIS KNEES AND WITH HIS FINGERS CLUTCHD THE SAND   73 SOHRAB RUSTUM   421
        AND HIS SOBS CHOKED HIM AND HE CLUTCHD HIS SWORD   • •   82 SOHRAB RUSTUM   704

CLUTCHING
        STILL CLUTCHING THE INVIOLABLE SHADE   • • • • • •   261 SCHOLAR-GIPSY   212

COAST
        IF SOME FAIR COAST HAVE LURED US TO MAKE STAY   • •   40 HUMAN LIFE   11
        IF SOME FAIR COAST HAS LURED US TO MAKE STAY   • •   40 HUMAN LIFE   V   11
        NOR ELLAS VICTORY ON THE ENGLISH COAST   • • •   117 BALDER DEAD 3   147
        THEY TWO SCOURD EVERY COAST AND ALL THINGS WEPT   • •   123 BALDER DEAD 3   328
        ON THIS COAST OF BRITTANY   • • • • • • • •   131 TRISTRAM 1   35
        IN HER CASTLE BY THE COAST   • • • • • • • • •   136 TRISTRAM 1   193
        ALONG THIS IRON COAST KNOW LIKE A STAR   • • •   151 TRISTRAM 3   81
        IN EVERY HUT ALONG THIS SEA-COAST WILD   • • •   152 TRISTRAM 3   109
        UPON THE STRAITS ON THE FRENCH COAST THE LIGHT   • •   210 DOVER BEACH   3
        UPON THE STRAIT ON THE FRENCH COAST THE LIGHT   • • •   DOVER BEACH   V   3
        LAY THE LONE COAST OF BRITTANY   • • • • • • • •   273 STANZAS CARNAC   4

COASTER
        AND SAW THE MERRY GRECIAN COASTER COME   • • • •   262 SCHOLAR-GIPSY   237

COASTS
        WE RUSH BY COASTS WHERE WE HAD LIEF REMAIN   • • • •   40 HUMAN LIFE   17
        TO WARMER LANDS AND COASTS THAT KEEP THE SUN   • •   129 BALDER DEAD 3   562

COAT
        ON HIS COAT WERE LEAVES AND BLOOD-STAINS   • • • •   14 CHURCH BROU 1   47
        AND OER HIS CHILLY LIMBS HIS WOOLLEN COAT   • • • •   63 SOHRAB RUSTUM   96
        HIS SHORT COAT TRAVEL-TARNISHD   • • • • • • • •   189 STRAYED REVEL   106
        HIS COAT HIS BASKET AND HIS EARTHEN CRUSE   • • • •   255 SCHOLAR-GIPSY   13
        GIRT WITH HIS COAT FOR THE CHASE   • • • • • • •   342 MEROPE   394
        WITH THY SOILD HUNTING-COAT AND SANDALS TORN   • •   372 MEROPE   1159
        MAX WITH SHINING YELLOW COAT   • • • • • • • •   454 POOR MATTHIAS   71
        THINE EYE WAS BRIGHT THY COAT IT SHONE   • • • •   460 KAISER DEAD   61

COATED
        BUT SEE HIS BLACK-COATED GAOLERS   • • • • • • •   214 NEW ROME   V   5
        AS THY GRIEF WHEN IN TEARS SOME BRAZEN-COATED ACHAIAN   HOMER TRANS   27

COBHAM
        POST-HASTE TO COBHAM CALLS THE MUSE   • • • • • •   458 KAISER DEAD   2

COCK
        AT COCK-CROW ON A STARLIT WINTERS MORN   • • • •   70 SOHRAB RUSTUM   305
        THE GOLDEN-CRESTED COCK BEGAN TO CROW   • • • •   105 BALDER DEAD 2   4
        THE GOLDEN-CRESTED COCK SHALL SOUND ALARM   • • • •   127 BALDER DEAD 3   496

COFFIN
        WHICH SHALL THEIR COFFIN BE WHEN DEAD   • • • •   300 GRANDE CHARTR   48

COFFINS
        AND THE STONE COFFINS THEN BY CAPHYAE CLIFFS   • •   356 MEROPE   744
        IN THE STONE COFFINS AT ORCHOMENUS   • • • • • •   356 MEROPE   773

COHESION
        GIVE THEM COHESION PURPOSE AND RESOLVE   • • • •   382 MEROPE   1323

COIGN
        WHILE TONGUES OF FIRE ON COIGN AND CARVING PLAY   • •   445 WESTMIN ABBEY   36

COIL
        WHERE THE SEA-SNAKES COIL AND TWINE   • • • • • •   162 FORSAKEN MERM   41

COINER
        CURLD MINION DANCER COINER OF SWEET WORDS   • • • •   74 SOHRAB RUSTUM   458

COLD
        COLD-BUBBLING SPRINGS OR CAVES NOT SO THE SOUL   • •   6 GEO CRUIKSHANK   9
        COLD HEARTS AND THANKLESS TONGUES WHERE THANKS ARE DUE   8 MYCERINUS   4
        BENT TO THE COLD WINDS OF THE SHOWERLESS SPRING   • •   12 MYCERINUS   120
        COLD HEARTS AND THANKLESS TONGUES WHERE THANKS   8 MYCERINUS   V   4
            WERE DUE
        AND RISE UPON YOUR COLD WHITE MARBLE BEDS   • • • •   18 CHURCH BROU 3   27
        AND RAISE YOU ON YOUR COLD WHITE MARBLE BEDS   • •   18 CHURCH BROU 3   V   27

COLD (CONTINUED)
HERE LEAN MY HEAD ON THIS COLD BALUSTRADE . . . . 19 MODERN SAPPHO 4
FOR COLD IS HIS EYE TO MERE BEAUTY WHO BREAKING . . 20 MODERN SAPPHO 21
UP COLD AISLES OF BURIED GLADE . . . . 32 NEW SIRENS 180
AND I FEEL THE COLD NIGHT-AIR . . . . 32 NEW SIRENS 190
SPREADS ITS COLD LIGHT WIDER ALL THAT WHILE . . . 33 NEW SIRENS 218
COLD IN THAT UNLOVELY DAWNING . . . . 35 NEW SIRENS 265
HEAVY AS DEATH COLD AS THE GRAVE . . . . . . 38 STAGIRIUS 12
BOTH ARE LAID IN ONE COLD PLACE . . . . 44 QUESTION 6
BUT TO THE STARS AND THE COLD LUNAR BEAMS . . . . 45 IN UTRUMQUE PAR 19
BUT IS THY FAIR EUGENIA COLD . . . . 48 HORATIAN ECHO 27
THROUGH THE COLD GLOOM WITH MEASURED RACE . . . . 53 RESIGNATION 34
FAUSTA BETRAYS YOU COLD THE WHILE . . . . . . 58 RESIGNATION 200
AND WENT ABROAD INTO THE COLD WET FOG . . . . . 61 SOHRAB RUSTUM 10
AND WARM AND PLEASANT BUT THE GRAVE IS COLD . . . 71 SOHRAB RUSTUM 323
HEAVENS AIR IS BETTER THAN THE COLD DEAD GRAVE . . 71 SOHRAB RUSTUM 324
BUT WITH A COLD INCREDULOUS VOICE HE SAID . . . . 78 SOHRAB RUSTUM 576
FLOWD WITH THE STREAM ALL DOWN HIS COLD WHITE SIDE . 86 SOHRAB RUSTUM 842
AND DARKEND ALL AND A COLD FOG WITH NIGHT . . . . 86 SOHRAB RUSTUM 867
AND WENT ABROAD INTO THE COLD DIM AIR . . . . . 61 SOHRAB RUSTUM V 10
AND WITH A COLD INCREDULOUS VOICE HE SAID . . . . 78 SOHRAB RUSTUM V 576
WITH COLD DRY EYES AND HEARTS COMPOSED AND STERN . 96 BALDER DEAD 1 35
FROM HERE THE COLD WHITE MIST CAN BE DISCERND . . 108 BALDER DEAD 2 124
ART THOU COLD OR FALSE OR DEAD . . . . 133 TRISTRAM 1 81
MILD SHINES THE COLD SPRING IN THE MOONS CLEAR LIGHT 139 TRISTRAM 1 283
COLD COLD AS THOSE WHO LIVED AND LOVED . . . . . 149 TRISTRAM 2 192
COLD COLD AS THOSE WHO LIVED AND LOVED . . . . . 149 TRISTRAM 2 192
THERE IN A SHIP THEY BORE THOSE LOVERS COLD . . . 149 TRISTRAM 3 4
BUT WHEN THE RED GLOW ON THE SEA GREW COLD . . . 151 TRISTRAM 3 58
LAY TRISTRAM AND QUEEN ISEULT DEAD AND COLD . . . 149 TRISTRAM 3 V 2
BENEATH THE COLD SEA TIDE . . . . 160 NECKAN V 32
TEARS FILLD HIS COLD BLUE EYE . . . . 160 NECKAN V 46
BUT WE STOOD WITHOUT IN THE COLD BLOWING AIRS . . 163 FORSAKEN MERM 73
FOR THE COLD STRANGE EYES OF A LITTLE MERMAIDEN . . 164 FORSAKEN MERM 106
SHE TURNS FROM THAT COLD SUCCOUR WHICH ATTENDS . . 170 WEST LONDON 12
WHERE YOUR COLD DISTANT BARRIER . . . . . . 175 PARTING 11
AMONG THEIR SAVAGE GORGES AND COLD SPRINGS . . . . 198 FRAG DEJANEIRA 9
SHE IS NOT COLD THOUGH SHE SEEMS SO . . . . . 201 URANIA 2
SHE IS NOT COLD SHE IS NOT LIGHT . . . . . . 201 URANIA 3
SOME DAY I SHALL BE COLD I KNOW . . . . . . 207 ON THE RHINE 2
LIKE STARS ON LIFES COLD SEA . . . . 209 DESPONDENCY 2
COLD BUBBLED THE SPRING OF TILPHUSA . . . . . 229 YOUTH OF NATURE 36
COLD THE ELATION OF JOY . . . . 231 YOUTH OF NATURE 95
COLD PLASHING PAST IT CRYSTAL WATERS ROLL . . . 236 PALLADIUM 11
WHICH PERISHES OF COLD . . . . 238 PROGRESS 32
FACES UNGREETING AND COLD . . . . 284 HAWORTH CHURCH 76
GRATEFULLY COLD ON THIS BROW . . . . 283 HAWORTH CHURCH V
IN THE SCHOOL-ROOM WINDOWS BUT COLD . . . . . 286 RUGBY CHAPEL 9
INTO THEIR STONE-CARVED BASINS COLD . . . . . 300 GRANDE CHARTR 32
SHOWD ME THE PALE COLD STAR OF TRUTH . . . . . 301 GRANDE CHARTR V 69
THAT AIR OF LANGUOR COLD AND DEATH . . . . . 306 OBERMANN 15
THY REALM OF THOUGHT IS DREAR AND COLD . . . . 309 OBERMANN 107
HAD BEEN TOO COLD FOR ME . . . . 317 OBERMANN MORE 150
NOR BE COLD GLOOM THY PRISON . . . . 322 OBERMANN MORE 282
THINE ATTITUDE OF COLD ESTRANGED REPROACH . . . 332 MEROPE 85
HIS OFFERS COLDLY HEARD THEM COLD REPELLD . . . 366 MEROPE 1015
THIRTY LONG DAYS IN A COLD TRANCE OF DEATH . . . 410 EMPEDOCLES I 1 110
YOUR LONELY COLD-SHINING LIGHTS . . . . . 437 EMPEDOCLES II 289
HANDS HAD STROKED THEM WHICH ARE COLD . . . . 453 POOR MATTHIAS 47
AND COLD BESIDES HIS BLUE BLOOD RAN . . . . . 460 KAISER DEAD 39
THE WORLD HATH BOWED TO ROME OH COLD WERE HE . . 465 ALARIC AT ROME 89
WAS COLD AND SAD BENEATH THAT BREATHLESS VOICELESS 466 ALARIC AT ROME 108
    NIGHT
THE CARELESS GLANCE THE COLD UNMEANING SMILE . . 470 ALARIC AT ROME 219
THESE HAD NO SOUND FOR THEE THAT COLD CALM EYE . . 472 CROMWELL 21
THE COLD DULL SOIL OF HIS UNFRUITFUL YOUTH . . . 473 CROMWELL 54
THE COLD DULL SHADOW OF THEIR ICY WING . . . 474 CROMWELL 92
AND DEATHS COLD DEWS BEDIMMD HIS EARNEST BROW . . 476 CROMWELL 170
STILL WOULD BE TRUE YET STILL GROWS COLD . . . 481 DESTINY 3
DID WITH SUCH COLD DERISION SHINE . . . . . 482 COURAGE 22

COLDER
THE HOARSE WIND BLOWS COLDER . . . . 164 FORSAKEN MERM V 110
THE WORLD IS COLDER YET . . . . 309 OBERMANN 108

COLDLY
STEALS COLDLY AROUND THE CHAMBER BRIGHT . . . 147 TRISTRAM 2 148
THE HOARSE WIND BLOWS COLDLY . . . . . 164 FORSAKEN MERM 110
COLDLY SHE MOCKS THE SONS OF MEN . . . . 202 URANIA 30
COLDLY SADLY DESCENDS . . . . 286 RUGBY CHAPEL 1
HIS OFFERS COLDLY HEARD THEM COLD REPELLD . . . 366 MEROPE 1015

COLDNESS
ONE FAINT FROWN OF DISTANT COLDNESS . . . . . . 31 NEW SIRENS 161

COLLAR
WELL FETCH HIS GRAVEN COLLAR FINE . . . . . 461 KAISER DEAD 79
STREAMD TO THE GROUND BY THE YOKE ESCAPING   HOMER TRANS 45
    FROM UNDER THE COLLAR

COLLEGE
TWO SCHOLARS WHOM AT COLLEGE ERST HE KNEW . . . . 256 SCHOLAR-GIPSY 42

COLLIE
    KAISER WITH HIS COLLIE FACE • • • • • • • • 454 POOR MATTHIAS 73
    THE COLLIE HAIR THE COLLIE SWING • • • • • • 459 KAISER DEAD 26
    THE COLLIE HAIR THE COLLIE SWING • • • • • • 459 KAISER DEAD 26

COLLIERS
    RUNS AND COLLIERS CARTS • • • • • • • • • • 282 HAWORTH CHURCH 58

COLONNADE
    HALT AT THE WHITE AND SILENT COLONNADE • • • • 167 RACHEL 1 5

COLONUS
    SINGER OF SWEET COLONUS AND ITS CHILD • • • • 2 TO A FRIEND 14

COLOUR
    FROM THOSE STILL DEEPS IN FORM AND COLOUR DREST • • 45 IN UTRUMQUE PAR 4
    AND THOU HAST FLESH AND COLOUR ON THY CHEEKS • • 108 BALDER DEAD 2 107
    AND HAS A COLOUR IN HER CHEEKS • • • • • • • 147 TRISTRAM 2 129
    WITH MARBLE WITH COLOUR WITH WORD • • • • • 231 YOUTH OF NATURE 108
    ALAS HOW FAIR A COLOUR CAN HIS TONGUE • • • • 338 MEROPE 278
    NONE SINCE A TWOFOLD COLOUR REIGNS IN ALL • • • • 404 MEROPE 1994
    ONE COLOUR IN THY LIFE THE HUE OF TRUTH • • • • 404 MEROPE 1996

COLOURD
    UNRAVEL ALL HIS MANY-COLOURD LORE • • • • • 43 GIPSY CHILD 34
    ONLY BY THIS THOU CANST THE COLOURD DREAM • • • • 45 IN UTRUMQUE PAR 13
    OUR WAVERING MANY-COLOURD LINE • • • • • • • 54 RESIGNATION 61
    GRAPE-SYRUP SQUARES OF COLOURD ICE • • • • • 94 SICK KING BOKH 196
    THE SWEET BLUE EYES THE SOFT ASH-COLOURD HAIR • • 175 PARTING 37

COLOURED
    THERE A BIRD HIGH-COLOURED FAT • • • • • • • 457 POOR MATTHIAS 188

COLOURS
    STREAMS FROM THE SETTING SUN AND COLOURS BRIGHT • • 18 CHURCH BROU 3 19

COLT
    A COLT BENEATH ITS DAM AND DROVE HIM HOME • • • • 69 SOHRAB RUSTUM 275
    A COLT BESIDE ITS DAM AND DROVE HIM HOME • • • • 69 SOHRAB RUSTUM V 275

COLUMN
    LEAND UP AGAINST THE COLUMN THERE • • • • • • 186 STRAYED REVEL 9

COLUMND
    LIKE THE BROAD RUSHING OF THE COLUMND NILE • • • • 10 MYCERINUS V 40

COLUMNS
    THE COLUMNS OF THE HEAVENLY PALACES • • • • • • 19 CHURCH BROU 3 42
    BREIDABLIK ON WHOSE COLUMNS BALDER GRAVED • • • • 101 BALDER DEAD 1 208
    ON THE PURE COLUMNS OF ITS GLEN-BUILT HALL • • • • 236 PALLADIUM 6

COMBAT
    BUT OF A SINGLE COMBAT FAME SPEAKS CLEAR • • • • 62 SOHRAB RUSTUM 62

COMBATANTS
    THE COMBATANTS ARE PARTED NOW • • • • • • • • 219 BACCHANALIA 2 10

COMBATINGS
    NOT HUMAN COMBATINGS WITH DEATH • • • • • • • 251 WISH 48

COMBD
    SHE COMBD ITS BRIGHT HAIR AND SHE TENDED IT WELL • • 163 FORSAKEN MERM 53

COMBINED
    THE LETTERS HAVE COMBINED SOMETHING WAS MADE • • 239 REVOLUTIONS 8
    AH KEEP KEEP THEM COMBINED • • • • • • • • • 291 RUGBY CHAPEL 182

COME
    TIS MY LORD COME BACK FROM HUNTING • • • • • • 14 CHURCH BROU 1 39
    ON SUNDAYS TOO A PRIEST DOTH COME • • • • • • • 17 CHURCH BROU 2 25
    WHERE HORN AND HOUND AND VASSALS NEVER COME • • 17 CHURCH BROU 3 3
    ERE HE COME ERE THE BOAT BY THE SHINING-BRANCHD BORDER 19 MODERN SAPPHO 5
    PERCEIVE BUT A VOICE AS I COME TO HIS SIDE • • • • 20 MODERN SAPPHO 26
    LET MY TURN IF IT WILL COME BE SWIFT IN ARRIVING • • 20 MODERN SAPPHO 31
    OF DARK ELMS COME ROUND DROPPING DOWN THE PROUD STREAM 19 MODERN SAPPHO V 6
    BECAUSE IT HATH THE HOPE TO COME • • • • • • • 21 YOUTH AND CALM 14
    BECAUSE IT HAS THE HOPE TO COME • • • • • • • 21 YOUTH AND CALM V 14
    COME YOU MURMUR WITH A SIGH • • • • • • • • 28 NEW SIRENS 62
    COME YOU SAY THE HOURS WERE DREARY • • • • • • 28 NEW SIRENS 65
    COME YOU SAY THE SOUL IS FAINTING • • • • • • • 28 NEW SIRENS 73
    COME YOU SAY THE BRAIN IS SEEKING • • • • • • • 28 NEW SIRENS 77
    COME YOU SAY OPINION TREMBLES • • • • • • • • 29 NEW SIRENS 81
    COME BIND UP THOSE RINGLET SHOWERS • • • • • • 32 NEW SIRENS 173
    COME ONCE MORE THAT ANCIENT LIGHTNESS • • • • • 32 NEW SIRENS 175
    COME LOOSE HANDS THE WINGED FLEETNESS • • • • • 34 NEW SIRENS 251
    COME YOU SAY THE LARGE APPEARANCE • • • • • • 28 NEW SIRENS V 57
    COME YOU SAY THE HOURS ARE DREARY • • • • • • 28 NEW SIRENS V 65
    O UNFORGOTTEN VOICE THY ACCENTS COME • • • • • • 36 VOICE 29
    O UNFORGOTTEN VOICE THY WHISPERS COME • • • • • 36 VOICE V 29

138

COME   (CONTINUED)

O WHERE THY VOICE DOTH COME . . . . 39 STAGIRIUS 52
TOSSING AND WAKEFUL AND I COME TO THEE . . . . 62 SOHRAB RUSTUM 37
COME THEN HEAR NOW AND GRANT ME WHAT I ASK . . . 62 SOHRAB RUSTUM 54
LARGE MEN LARGE STEEDS WHO FROM BOKHARA COME . . . 64 SOHRAB RUSTUM 119
WHO COME ON SHAGGY PONIES FROM PAMERE . . . . . 65 SOHRAB RUSTUM 134
NOT NOW A TIME WILL COME TO EAT AND DRINK . . . . 67 SOHRAB RUSTUM 208
COME DOWN AND HELP US RUSTUM OR WE LOSE . . . . 67 SOHRAB RUSTUM 219
COME THOU SHALT SEE HOW RUSTUM HOARDS HIS FAME . . 68 SOHRAB RUSTUM 256
SOHRAB COME FORTH AND EYED HIM AS HE CAME . . . 70 SOHRAB RUSTUM 301
BE GOVERND QUIT THE TARTAR HOST AND COME . . . . 71 SOHRAB RUSTUM 330
DROPS LIKE A PLUMMET SOHRAB SAW IT COME . . . . 73 SOHRAB RUSTUM 402
COME PLANT WE HERE IN EARTH OUR ANGRY SPEARS . . . 74 SOHRAB RUSTUM 439
COME RUSHING DOWN TOGETHER FROM THE CLOUDS . . . 75 SOHRAB RUSTUM 473
OR ELSE THAT THE GREAT RUSTUM WOULD COME DOWN . . 77 SOHRAB RUSTUM 531
COME SIT BESIDE ME ON THIS SAND AND TAKE . . . . 82 SOHRAB RUSTUM 718
COME LET ME LAY MY HAND UPON THY MANE . . . . . 83 SOHRAB RUSTUM 746
BUT COME THOU SEEST THIS GREAT HOST OF MEN . . . 84 SOHRAB RUSTUM 778
WHO COME FROM KIPCHAK AND THE NORTHERN WASTE . . 65 SOHRAB RUSTUM V 131
TO-MORROW COME AND YE SHALL PAY . . . . . . 87 SICK KING BOKH 7
WITH FOLDED HANDS REVOLVING THINGS TO COME . . . . 98 BALDER DEAD 1 93
WHICH EVERY DAY THEY COME AND GO IN HEAVEN . . . 99 BALDER DEAD 1 140
AND STRAIGHT HE WILL COME DOWN TO OCEANS STRAND . . 99 BALDER DEAD 1 159
AND MAKE HIM LEAP THE GRATE AND COME WITHIN . . . 100 BALDER DEAD 1 170
BUT PAINLESS SHALL A STROKE FROM FREA COME . . . 103 BALDER DEAD 1 302
AND I COME SENT THIS ROAD ON BALDERS TRACK . . . 108 BALDER DEAD 2 116
BEING ALIVE AND COME TO OCEANS SHORE . . . . . 110 BALDER DEAD 2 184
COME THEN IF BALDER WAS SO DEAR BELOVED . . . . 111 BALDER DEAD 2 231
BUT COME DECLARE ME THIS AND TRULY TELL . . . . 111 BALDER DEAD 2 243
BEHELD HIM COME AND TO HIS NEIGHBOUR SPAKE . . . 113 BALDER DEAD 3 5
LO HOME HAVING PERFORMD YOUR WILL I COME . . . . 114 BALDER DEAD 3 37
AND IN PROCESSION ALL COME NEAR AND WEEP . . . . 115 BALDER DEAD 3 51
BUT FROM THE TRAITOROUS SEED OF LOK THEY COME . . 120 BALDER DEAD 3 234
AND ALL THAT IS TO COME I KNOW BUT LOCK . . . 121 BALDER DEAD 3 286
COME THEN SINCE HELA HOLDS BY RIGHT HER PREY . . 121 BALDER DEAD 3 288
THAT YE COME PLEASURING TO THOKS IRON WOOD . . . 123 BALDER DEAD 3 338
THOK NOT FOR GIBES WE COME WE COME FOR TEARS . . 123 BALDER DEAD 3 346
THOK NOT FOR GIBES WE COME WE COME FOR TEARS . . 123 BALDER DEAD 3 346
IS BALDER DEAD AND DO YE COME FOR TEARS . . . 123 BALDER DEAD 3 351
IN THE GREAT DEEP FOR GAIN AT LAST COME HOME . . 123 BALDER DEAD 3 358
OF NIFLHEIM HE SAW ONE GHOST COME NEAR . . . . 124 BALDER DEAD 3 382
NO MORE TO ASGARD SHALT THOU COME NOR LODGE . . 126 BALDER DEAD 3 448
THE DAY WILL COME WHEN FALL SHALL ASGARDS TOWERS . 127 BALDER DEAD 3 487
THE DAY WILL COME WHEN ASGARDS TOWERS SHALL FALL . 127 BALDER DEAD 3 V 487
IS SHE NOT COME THE MESSENGER WAS SURE . . . 130 TRISTRAM 1 1
HATH COME ON HER A CHILLY FEAR . . . . . . 131 TRISTRAM 1 38
COME LET ME LEAVE THE SHADOW OF THIS WOOD . . . 139 TRISTRAM 1 281
IS MY PAGE HERE COME TURN ME TO THE FIRE . . . 139 TRISTRAM 1 298
THE WIND IS DOWN BUT SHELL NOT COME TO-NIGHT . . 139 TRISTRAM 1 300
THOU ART COME AT LAST THEN HAUGHTY QUEEN . . . 142 TRISTRAM 2 2
THOU ART COME INDEED THOU HAST REJOIND ME . . . 142 TRISTRAM 2 9
THROUGH A MIST I SEE THEE NEAR COME NEARER . . . 145 TRISTRAM 2 75
TRISTRAM TRISTRAM STAY I COME AH SORROW . . . . 146 TRISTRAM 2 V 99
WHO COME AT NOON DOWN TO THE WATER HERE . . . 155 TRISTRAM 3 194
WHICH COME AT NOON DOWN TO THE WATER HERE . . . 155 TRISTRAM 3 V 194
FROM THE SEA-WAVES I COME . . . . 159 NECKAN 26
COME DEAR CHILDREN LET US AWAY . . . . . . 161 FORSAKEN MERM 1
SURELY SHE WILL COME AGAIN . . . . 162 FORSAKEN MERM 17
CALL HER ONCE AND COME AWAY . . . . 162 FORSAKEN MERM 18
COME DEAR CHILDREN COME AWAY DOWN . . . . . 162 FORSAKEN MERM 23
COME DEAR CHILDREN COME AWAY DOWN . . . . . 162 FORSAKEN MERM 23
THEN COME DOWN . . . . 162 FORSAKEN MERM 27
SHE WILL NOT COME THOUGH YOU CALL ALL DAY . . . 162 FORSAKEN MERM 28
COME AWAY COME AWAY . . . . 162 FORSAKEN MERM 29
COME AWAY COME AWAY . . . . 162 FORSAKEN MERM 29
WHERE GREAT WHALES COME SAILING BY . . . . . 162 FORSAKEN MERM 43
WHEN DID MUSIC COME THIS WAY . . . . . . 162 FORSAKEN MERM 46
SAY THY PRAYER AND COME BACK TO THE KIND SEA-CAVES 163 FORSAKEN MERM 61
COME I SAID AND WE ROSE THROUGH THE SURF IN THE BAY 163 FORSAKEN MERM 67
MARGARET HIST COME QUICK WE ARE HERE . . . . 163 FORSAKEN MERM 77
COME AWAY CHILDREN CALL NO MORE . . . . . . 164 FORSAKEN MERM 83
COME AWAY COME DOWN CALL NO MORE . . . . . 164 FORSAKEN MERM 84
COME AWAY COME DOWN CALL NO MORE . . . . . 164 FORSAKEN MERM 84
COME AWAY AWAY CHILDREN . . . . 164 FORSAKEN MERM 108
COME CHILDREN COME DOWN . . . . 164 FORSAKEN MERM 109
COME CHILDREN COME DOWN . . . . 164 FORSAKEN MERM 109
WHEN SWEET AIRS COME SEAWARD . . . . . . 165 FORSAKEN MERM 128
AND THEN COME BACK DOWN . . . . 165 FORSAKEN MERM 139
I COME O YE MOUNTAINS . . . . 175 PARTING 33
YE TORRENTS I COME . . . . 175 PARTING 34
I COME O YE MOUNTAINS . . . . 176 PARTING 57
YE PINE-WOODS I COME . . . . 176 PARTING 58
I COME TO THE WILD . . . . 177 PARTING 76
WHERE FEET LIKE THINE TOO LIGHTLY COME . . . . 184 TERRACE BERNE 20
COME STRETCH FORTH THY HAND THEN SO . . . . . 187 STRAYED REVEL 61
COME FORTH ULYSSES . . . . 188 STRAYED REVEL 71
TILL THE FATES COME AGAIN THIS TIME WITH DEATH . . 195 FRAG ANTIGONE 16
TILL THE FATES COME AGAIN ALONE WITH DEATH . . . 195 FRAG ANTIGONE V 16
THY FLIGHT AND FEEL COME OVER THEE . . . . . 201 PHILOMELA 23
HOW THICK THE BURSTS COME CROWDING THROUGH THE LEAVES 201 PHILOMELA 29

COME   (CONTINUED)

HOW EXQUISITE THY VOICE WOULD COME	205	CALAIS SANDS	13
COME TO ME IN MY DREAMS AND THEN	208	LONGING	1
COME AS THOU CAMST A THOUSAND TIMES	208	LONGING	5
COME NOW AND LET ME DREAM IT TRUTH	209	LONGING	10
COME TO ME IN MY DREAMS AND THEN	209	LONGING	13
COME NOW AND LET ME DEEM IT TRUTH	209	LONGING	V 10
AND NEVER COME AGAIN	209	DESPONDENCY	8
COME TO THE WINDOW SWEET IS THE NIGHT-AIR	210	DOVER BEACH	6
COME TO THE WINDOW HUSHD IS THE NIGHT-AIR	210	DOVER BEACH	V 6
LET THE VICTORS WHEN THEY COME	215	LAST WORD	14
COME WITH COUNTENANCE BRIGHT	217	LORDS MESSENGER	20
ON FOOT BEHIND THEM GO AND COME	224	EPILOG LAOCOON	114
COME LIKE THE BREATH OF THE SPRING	234	YOUTH OF MAN	56
HELEN WILL COME UPON THE WALL TO SEE	236	PALLADIUM	16
THE OLD LAW THEY CRIED IS WHOLLY COME TO NOUGHT	237	PROGRESS	3
THE OLD LAW THEY SAID IS WHOLLY COME TO NOUGHT	237	PROGRESS	V 3
OF SWAY HAVE FELT THIS BODING SENSE COME ON	239	REVOLUTIONS	14
WHENCE OUR LIVES COME AND WHERE THEY GO	246	BURIED LIFE	54
COME AIRS AND FLOATING ECHOES AND CONVEY	247	BURIED LIFE	75
WHENCE OUR THOUGHTS COME AND WHERE THEY GO	246	BURIED LIFE	V 54
HOW THICK THE TREMULOUS SHEEP-CRIES COME	248	KENSINGTON GARD	8
HOW STRANGE THE TREMULOUS SHEEP-CRIES COME		KENSINGTON GARD	V 8
THE FRIENDS WHO COME AND GAPE AND GO	250	WISH	14
AS THE STARS COME OUT AND THE NIGHT-WIND	254	FUTURE	85
COME SHEPHERD AND AGAIN BEGIN THE QUEST	255	SCHOLAR-GIPSY	10
COME LET ME READ THE OFT-READ TALE AGAIN	256	SCHOLAR-GIPSY	32
MAIDENS WHO FROM THE DISTANT HAMLETS COME	257	SCHOLAR-GIPSY	82
AND MARKD THEE WHEN THE STARS COME OUT AND SHINE	258	SCHOLAR-GIPSY	109
AND SAW THE MERRY GRECIAN COASTER COME	262	SCHOLAR-GIPSY	237
SHY TRAFFICKERS THE DARK IBERIANS COME	262	SCHOLAR-GIPSY	249
COME SHEPHERD AND AGAIN RENEW THE QUEST	255	SCHOLAR-GIPSY	V 10
NOW SELDOM COME I SINCE I CAME WITH HIM	263	THYRSIS	25
COME WITH THE VOLLEYING RAIN AND TOSSING BREEZE	264	THYRSIS	59
SOON WILL THE HIGH MIDSUMMER POMPS COME ON	264	THYRSIS	62
SEE HIM COME BACK AND CUT A SMOOTHER REED	265	THYRSIS	78
FROM HUNTING WITH THE BERKSHIRE HOUNDS THEY COME	267	THYRSIS	155
AND IN THE SCATTERD FARMS THE LIGHTS COME OUT	267	THYRSIS	164
THIS DOES NOT COME WITH HOUSES OR WITH GOLD	268	THYRSIS	203
LET IN THY VOICE A WHISPER OFTEN COME	269	THYRSIS	235
THUS YESTERDAY TO-DAY TO-MORROW COME	262	THYRSIS	V
BUT ONE SUCH DEATH REMAINT TO COME	270	MEMORIAL VERSES	3
HEARD THE CLEAR SONG OF ORPHEUS COME	271	MEMORIAL VERSES	38
AH WHERE IS HE WHO SHOULD HAVE COME	274	STANZAS CARNAC	33
I SEE THE SMOKE-CROWND VESSEL COME	276	SOUTHERN NIGHT	30
COME UNUPBRAIDED FOR ONCE	283	HAWORTH CHURCH	V
THE LIGHTS COME OUT IN THE STREET	286	RUGBY CHAPEL	8
COME TO THE END OF OUR WAY	289	RUGBY CHAPEL	108
CONQUER AND COME TO THY GOAL	290	RUGBY CHAPEL	126
O FAITHFUL SHEPHERD TO COME	290	RUGBY CHAPEL	143
HITHER TO COME FROM THE STREETS	292	HEINES GRAVE	14
HITHER TO COME AND TO SLEEP	293	HEINES GRAVE	21
KNOCK PASS THE WICKET THOU ART COME	300	GRANDE CHARTR	29
I COME NOT HERE TO BE YOUR FOE	301	GRANDE CHARTR	76
I COME TO SHED THEM AT THEIR SIDE	302	GRANDE CHARTR	90
AND WAIT TO SEE THE FUTURE COME	303	GRANDE CHARTR	118
AND CALL US BUT TOO LATE YE COME	305	GRANDE CHARTR	196
TO THEE WE COME THEN CLOUDS ARE ROLLD	309	OBERMANN	105
WITH THOSE WHO COME TO THEE	309	OBERMANN	110
AND TO THY MOUNTAIN-CHALET COME	313	OBERMANN MORE	45
AND WAIT FOR WORDS TO COME	318	OBERMANN MORE	180
COME TO MY MOUNTAIN-SOLITUDE	322	OBERMANN MORE	275
THOU COME WITH ASPECT MARRD	322	OBERMANN MORE	302
THEY COME AND GO THEY WORK AND PLAN	320	OBERMANN MORE	V 215
NOT TO THEE ONLY HATH COME	346	MEROPE	505
WHEN OER THE ARCADIAN FORESTS THOU ART COME	349	MEROPE	572
TO COME A LATE AVENGER TO THE AID	349	MEROPE	577
TO RECEIVE ARCAS WHO TO-DAY SHOULD COME	350	MEROPE	598
O KING ALL HAIL I COME WITH WEIGHTY NEWS	354	MEROPE	710
OTHER THAN BY THIS DEATH BUT IT HATH COME	360	MEROPE	887
COME COME BACK TO OUR PRAYER	360	MEROPE	892
COME COME BACK TO OUR PRAYER	360	MEROPE	892
WHILE THE MATRONS COME TO THE DOORS	360	MEROPE	899
LET HER COME FAIR PEACE LET HER COME	361	MEROPE	908
LET HER COME FAIR PEACE LET HER COME	361	MEROPE	908
TELL ME HATH ONE NOT COME OR WORSE MISCHANCE	361	MEROPE	918
COME BUT BEEN INTERCEPTED BY THE KING	361	MEROPE	919
O WERE BUT ARCAS COME ALL WOULD BE WELL	362	MEROPE	933
COME FORTH DENOUNCE THE TRAFFIC AND THE TRAITOR	364	MEROPE	982
COME YE SWIFT FURIES WHO TO HIM YE HAUNT	367	MEROPE	1056
COME HERMES WHO DOST FRIEND THE UNJUSTLY KILLD	367	MEROPE	1058
COME LIGHTNING PASSION THAT WITH FOOT OF FIRE	367	MEROPE	1060
ALMOST BEFORE TIS PLANND COME GLOWING HATE	367	MEROPE	1062
COME BANEFUL MISCHIEF FROM THY MURKY DEN	367	MEROPE	1063
WHERE TRAVELLERS NEVER PASS WHERE ONLY COME	373	MEROPE	1169
ART THOU THEN COME NEVER TO PART AGAIN	377	MEROPE	1221
REMEMBER TO REVENGE HIS DEATH I COME	378	MEROPE	1241
MOTHER THY FEARS ARE IDLE FOR I COME	379	MEROPE	1256
HERE BRING HIM ERE THE KING COME BACK FROM COUNCIL	379	MEROPE	1262
A TIME WILL COME FOR GREETINGS BUT TO-DAY	386	MEROPE	1444

COME   (CONTINUED)
        THE HOUR FOR WORDS IS GONE IS COME FOR DEEDS   • •   386 MEROPE   1445
        OF STYX COME DANCING   • • • • • • • •   392 MEROPE   1653
        TO OFFER THAT I COME NOT BUT TO URGE   • • • •   394 MEROPE   1688
        YES ONCE AGAIN I COME I WILL NOT TAKE   • • •   394 MEROPE   1690
        THE CONQUERORS WITH THE KINGS DEAD BODY COME   • •   403 MEROPE   1953
        COME HERMES WHO DOST WATCH THE UNJUSTLY KILLD   367 MEROPE   V1058
        AND HE MADE ANSWER I SHOULD COME AT NIGHT   • • • •   410 EMPEDOCLES I 1   128
        WE SHALL HAVE LEFT THE WOODY TRACT AND COME   • •   412 EMPEDOCLES I 2   2
        AND THE TIRED CENTAURS COME TO REST   • • • • •   414 EMPEDOCLES I 2   63
        AND WHERE THE HILL-GOATS COME TO FEED   • • • •   414 EMPEDOCLES I 2   66
        AFFECTS US WE COME NEAR   • • • • • • • •   418 EMPEDOCLES I 2   195
        THE GODS HAD TO THEIR MARRIAGE COME   • • • • •   427 EMPEDOCLES I 2   450
        AND MURMURS OF THE ADRIATIC COME   • • • • •   427 EMPEDOCLES I 2   455
        NO THOU ART COME TOO LATE EMPEDOCLES   • • • • •   429 EMPEDOCLES II   16
        AND THE SOULS DEEP ETERNAL NIGHT COME ON   • • •   429 EMPEDOCLES II   35
        COME STREAMING WITH THE FLOODS OF GLORY IN   • • •   445 WESTMIN ABBEY   38
        SEEMD TO COME TRUE AT LAST O ABBEY OLD   • • •   446 WESTMIN ABBEY   73
        OF ALL THE CENTURIES YET TO COME   • • • • •   450 GEISTS GRAVE   22
        TEACH US WHILE THEY COME AND GO   • • • • •   456 POOR MATTHIAS   139
        CRYING COME ON AND RANGE THE WORLD   • • • •   460 KAISER DEAD   59
        JARRD WITH THE BURSTING SHOUT THEY COME THE   467 ALARIC AT ROME   132
               GOTH THEY COME
        JARRD WITH THE BURSTING SHOUT THEY COME THE   467 ALARIC AT ROME   132
               GOTH THEY COME
        COME FLOATING UP FROM THE ABYSS OF YEARS   • • •   469 ALARIC AT ROME   176
        JOYS THAT HAD COME AND VANISHD HALF UNKNOWN   • •   474 CROMWELL   75
        TO COME AND GO TO SHIFT AND RANGE   • • • • •   484 ROME-SICKNESS   22
        FOR THAT DAY WILL COME MY SOUL IS ASSURD OF ITS COMING   HOMER TRANS   20
        IT WILL COME WHEN SACRED TROY SHALL GO TO DESTRUCTION   HOMER TRANS   21
        ARE BUT THE CASUAL PASSERS BY WHO COME   • • • •   LUCRETIUS 5   6

COMELY
        THAT COMELY FACE THAT CLUSTERD BROW   • • • • • •   279 SOUTHERN NIGHT   125

COMER
        HE HEARKENS NOT LIGHT COMER HE IS FLOWN   • • • •   265 THYRSIS   71
        HE HEARKENS NOT LIGHT COMER HE IS GONE   • • • •   265 THYRSIS   V 71
        THIS COMER GREET HER WITH JOY   • • • • • • •   284 HAWORTH CHURCH   85

COMES
        TO GOD COMES NO NIGHER   • • • • • • • •   38 STAGIRIUS   17
        WHEN THE SOUL RISING HIGHER TO GOD COMES NO NIGHER   38 STAGIRIUS   V 14
        IN THE THRONGD FIELDS WHERE WINNING COMES BY STRIFE   43 GIPSY CHILD   58
        IN EARTHS THRONGD FIELDS WHERE WINNING COMES BY STRIFE   43 GIPSY CHILD   V 58
        JOY COMES AND GOES HOPE EBBS AND FLOWS   • • • •   44 QUESTION   1
        AND COMES AT NIGHT TO DIE UPON THE SAND   • • • •   76 SOHRAB RUSTUM   506
        FAR OFF ANON HER MATE COMES WINGING BACK   • • •   78 SOHRAB RUSTUM   561
        AND ALL DAY LONG AND WHEN NIGHT COMES THE LAMP   • •   81 SOHRAB RUSTUM   675
        MY MAN COMES RUNNING FLECKD WITH BLOOD   • • • •   89 SICK KING BOKH   50
        BUT OURS WE SHALL NOT MEET WHEN THAT DAY COMES   • •   96 BALDER DEAD 1   31
        TO THE STEEP EDGE OF SOME GREAT VALLEY COMES   • •   113 BALDER DEAD 2   296
        SEE HERE IS HERMOD WHO COMES SINGLE BACK   • • •   113 BALDER DEAD 3   6
        BUT HOME HIS MASTER COMES TO HIS OWN FARM   • • •   114 BALDER DEAD 3   17
        SO HERMOD COMES TO-DAY UNFOLLOWD HOME   • • • •   114 BALDER DEAD 3   19
        YET DOUBTLESS WHEN THE DAY OF BATTLE COMES   • • •   127 BALDER DEAD 3   494
        SICK PINING COMES NOT WHERE THESE ARE   • • • •   138 TRISTRAM 1   260
        THIS COMES OF NURSING LONG AND WATCHING LATE   • •   140 TRISTRAM 1   313
        WHERE FEEBLY COMES THE MOURNFUL ROAR   • • • • •   140 TRISTRAM 1   330
        HOW COMES IT HERE THIS CHAMBER BRIGHT   • • • •   148 TRISTRAM 2   168
        BUT EVEN THAT COMES LANGUIDLY IN TRUTH   • • • •   151 TRISTRAM 3   74
        THE MAN OF THE BOLD WEST NOW COMES ARRAYD   • • • •   170 EAST AND WEST   13
        AH IT COMES NEARER   • • • • • • • • •   175 PARTING   23
        AND THROUGH THOSE FIELDS COMES DOWN THE AAR   • •   184 TERRACE BERNE   8
        AND FROM THE BLUE TWIN-LAKES IT COMES   • • • •   184 TERRACE BERNE   9
        WHO SPEAKS AH WHO COMES FORTH   • • • • • • •   189 STRAYED REVEL   99
        FORTH FROM THE PALACE HITHERWARD COMES   • • • •   196 FRAG ANTIGONE   44
        THY VOICE IN GUSHES COMES   • • • • • • • •   200 PHILOMELA   V
        THY VOICE BY GUSHES COMES   • • • • • • • •   200 PHILOMELA   V
        THE EVENING COMES THE FIELDS ARE STILL   • • • •   217 BACCHANALIA 1   1
        THE EVENING COMES THE FIELDS ARE STILL   • • • •   218 BACCHANALIA 1   19
        THE EVENING COMES THE FIELD IS STILL   • • • • • •   217 BACCHANALIA 1   V   1
        THE EVENING COMES THE FIELD IS STILL   • • • • • •   218 BACCHANALIA 1   V 19
        COMES THE NEW AGE   • • • • • • • • • •   220 BACCHANALIA 2   36
        BUT AH THEN COMES HIS SOREST SPELL   • • • • •   225 EPILOG LAOCOON   139
        AH WE SHALL KNOW THAT WELL WHEN IT COMES NEAR   • •   239 REVOLUTIONS   19
        NEVER YET COMES MORE NEAR   • • • • • • • •   243 SUMMER NIGHT   45
        AND STERNER COMES THE ROAR   • • • • • • •   244 SUMMER NIGHT   70
        AND HE TOO DISAPPEARS AND COMES NO MORE   • • •   244 SUMMER NIGHT   73
        THE NIGHT COMES DOWN UPON THE GRASS   • • • • •   249 KENSINGTON GARD   35
        THEN HERE AT NOON COMES BACK HIS STORES TO USE   • •   255 SCHOLAR-GIPSY   15
        COMES SOFTLY THROUGH THE OLIVE-TREES   • • • • • •   279 SOUTHERN NIGHT   119
        THEN ON THE HEIGHT COMES THE STORM   • • • • • •   289 RUGBY CHAPEL   90
        COMES NOW ONE WORD ALONE   • • • • • • • • •   318 OBERMANN MORE   V 184
        HASTE AND ADVISE FOR DAY COMES ON APACE   • • • •   330 MEROPE   28
        THE HAPPY MOMENT COMES LURK HERE UNSEEN   • • • •   332 MEROPE   67
        REMOVE YET FURTHER OFF IF AUGHT COMES NEAR   • • • •   332 MEROPE   69
        INFORM HIM THAT THYSELF FOR HERE HE COMES   • • • •   354 MEROPE   709
        MY FAITHFUL FOLLOWER COMES WELCOME OLD FRIEND   • •   362 MEROPE   937
        HE COMES TO TELL HIS PROMPTER HE HATH SPED   • • •   365 MEROPE   986
        AND TRIED IN VAIN THE TURN OF RASHNESS COMES   • •   384 MEROPE   1387
        DEEP AS THOU CANST FOR HENCE NO SUCCOUR COMES   • •   386 MEROPE   1431

COMES   (CONTINUED)
        HERE AS I GUESS THE NOBLE LAIAS COMES   • • • 386 MEROPE   1439
        BUT HE COMES NOT WHAT DELL   • • • • • •   347 MEROPE   V
        HE WHO WAS SENT HATH SPED AND NOW COMES BACK • • 366 MEROPE   V
        HERE WILL I STAY TILL THE SLOW LITTER COMES   • • 407 EMPEDOCLES I 1   18
        AND WHEN HE COMES AMONG HIS FRIENDS AT FEASTS • • 408 EMPEDOCLES I 1   70
        PLAY WHEN WE HALT AND WHEN THE EVENING COMES • • 409 EMPEDOCLES I 1   90
        TIS APOLLO COMES LEADING • • • • • • • • • • • 442 EMPEDOCLES II   445
        BUT AS AGE COMES ON I KNOW   • • • • • • • • 454 POOR MATTHIAS   77
        FATES THREATNINGS ARE NOT VAIN THE SPOILER   466 ALARIC AT ROME   120
             COMES NOT SLOW
        NIGHT COMES WITH NIGHT COMES SILENCE HAND IN HAND   FRAGMENT 1   1
        NIGHT COMES WITH NIGHT COMES SILENCE HAND IN HAND   FRAGMENT 1   1
        WITH NIGHT COMES SILENCE AND WITH THAT REPOSE • • FRAGMENT 1   2

COMEST
        LATE THOU COMEST CRUEL THOU HAST BEEN   • • • • 142 TRISTRAM 2   4
        I FORGOT THOU COMEST FROM THY VOYAGE • • • • • • 142 TRISTRAM 2   17
        THOU COMEST YES THE VESSELS CLOUD • • • • • • • 205 CALAIS SANDS   21

COMETS
        LIKE COMETS ON THE HEAVENLY SOLITUDE • • • • • •   6 GEO CRUIKSHANK   7

COMFORT
        WHERE COMFORT TURNS TO TROUBLE • • • • • • • • 39 STAGIRIUS   41
        FOR COMFORT FROM WITHOUT • • • • • • • •   307 OBERMANN   20
        SMALL COMFORT OFFERS FOR A WOMAN THERE   • • • • 349 MEROPE   564
        LOOK UP AND SEE THY FRIENDS WHO COMFORT THEE • • 363 MEROPE   947
        THERE IS SMALL COMFORT FOR A WOMAN HERE   • • • • 349 MEROPE   V 564

COMFORTABLE
        OF COMFORTABLE MOLES WHOM WHAT THEY DO   • • • •   7 REP FRIEND   6

COMFORTED
        WAS CALMD ENNOBLED COMFORTED SUSTAIND   • • • • 12 MYCERINUS   111

COMFORTERS
        O MY COMFORTERS STRAYS   • • • • • • • • • • • 348 MEROPE   V

COMING
        COMING BENIGHTED TO THE CASTLE-GATE • • • • • • 18 CHURCH BROU 3   15
        SO THE COMING YEARLL BE SPENT   • • • • • • • • 23 MEMORY-PICTURE   18
        AS HE BEHELD HIM COMING AND HE STOOD • • • • • • 70 SOHRAB RUSTUM   320
        WATCHD MY LORDS COMING FORTH AND PUSHD   • • • • 88 SICK KING BOKH   33
        HEARING THE WRATHFUL FATHER COMING HOME   • • • • 102 BALDER DEAD 1   263
        AND COMING FLUSHD OVER THE STORMY FRITH • • • • 196 FRAG ANTIGONE   58
        AND WHAT ASKS CUPID IS COMING • • • • • • • •   214 NEW ROME   V 9
        UNTO ITS HAVEN COMING NIGH   • • • • • • • •   276 SOUTHERN NIGHT   46
        POACH THE DEEP WAYS COMING DOWN • • • • • • • 282 HAWORTH CHURCH   59
        OER THE GRACIOUS SPURS COMING DOWN   • • • • • • 297 HEINES GRAVE   179
        NEW-COMING SON OF MANKIND   • • • • • • • •   298 HEINES GRAVE   220
        IN THE MARRIAGE-TRAIN COMING ON • • • • • • • 360 MEROPE   897
        FOR A GRAND CULPRIT SHORTLY COMING DOWN • • • • 373 MEROPE   1189
        COMING SWIFTLY THROUGH THE SAD TRACHINIANS • • • 399 MEROPE   1838
        COMING SWIFTLY THROUGH THE JOCUND DORIANS   • • • 400 MEROPE   1863
        WHOSE MULES I FOLLOWD MAY BE COMING UP   • • • • 407 EMPEDOCLES I 1   22
        HE IS FOR EVER COMING ON THESE HILLS • • • • • • 412 EMPEDOCLES I 2   14
        WHAT FORMS ARE THESE COMING • • • • • • • •   442 EMPEDOCLES II   437
        A STRANGE WAYFARER COMING TO HIS SIDE   • • • • 444 WESTMIN ABBEY   23
        ALL WONDROUS DEEDS THE COMING DAYS SHOULD SEE • • 475 CROMWELL   139
        THE COMING SPRING-TIMES EARLIEST STIR   • • • • 483 ROME-SICKNESS   6
        FOR THAT DAY WILL COME MY SOUL IS ASSURD OF ITS COMING HOMER TRANS   20

COMMAND
        FOR THERE RANG NOTE DIVINE IN THAT COMMAND • • • 102 BALDER DEAD 1   245
        WITH ITS GESTURE OF COMMAND   • • • • • • • • • 134 TRISTRAM 1   122
        GLADLY OBEY HIS COMMAND • • • • • • • • • • • 216 LORDS MESSENGER   8
        GLADLY THEY TAKE HIS COMMAND • • • • • • • • • 216 LORDS MESSENGER V 8
        THE GODS COMMAND NOT WHERE THE HEART SPEAKS CLEAR 385 MEROPE   1404
        THAT VOICE HAD NOTE SO CLEAR OF SWEET COMMAND • • 445 WESTMIN ABBEY   28

COMMANDMENT
        BUT IF THE STEDFAST COMMANDMENT OF NATURE   • • • 206 SEPARATION   5

COMMANDS
        TRAMP OF MEN AND QUICK COMMANDS   • • • • • • • 14 CHURCH BROU 1   38

COMMEND
        BUT ALL THOSE VIRTUES WHICH COMMEND • • • • • • 459 KAISER DEAD   31

COMMENT
        FOR INSTANT COMMENT HAVING MANY SIDES   • • • • 359 MEROPE   860

COMMERCE
        AFTER SHORT COMMERCE WITH ME FEAR MY FROWN • • • 37 WORLDS TRIUMPHS 8
        OF COMMERCE LAWS AND POLICY   • • • • • • • • 48 HORATIAN ECHO   15
        PROOF NOT SURMISE SHOWS HIM IN COMMERCE CLOSE • • 380 MEROPE   1274
        THIS COMMERCE FOR MY BEST BEHOOF HE PLIES   • • • 380 MEROPE   1277
        IN THE DELIGHTFUL COMMERCE OF THE WORLD   • • • • 436 EMPEDOCLES II   247
        THE FLOOD OF THE WORLDS COMMERCE ON HER SHORE • • 480 HUNGARIAN NAT   3

COMMISSION
          HAST THY COMMISSION DONE YE BOTH MAY NOW   • • • •   449 WESTMIN ABBEY   169

COMMIT
          I SHUDDER LAIAS TO COMMIT MY CHILD   • • • • •   387 MEROPE   1461
          BRING TO HIS MOTHER THE REST I COMMIT   • • • •   348 MEROPE   V

COMMITS
          COMMITS ALL DEEDS THE GUILTY OFTENEST DO   • • • •   353 MEROPE   683

COMMITTER
          HOWEVER NOBLE THE COMMITTER BE   • • • • • • • • •   353 MEROPE   693

COMMON
          TO SPURN MANS COMMON LURE LIFES PLEASANT THINGS   • •   9 MYCERINUS   32
          TO YOUTH AND AGE IN COMMON DISCONTENT   • • • •   37 YOUTHS AGIT   14
          ON THIS SIDE THE ALL-COMMON CLOSE   • • • • •   53 RESIGNATION   16
          AND FLEES THE COMMON LIFE OF MEN   • • • • • •   58 RESIGNATION   212
          DIM IS THE RUMOUR OF A COMMON FIGHT   • • • • •   62 SOHRAB RUSTUM   60
          AND SHARE THE BATTLES COMMON CHANCE WITH US   • •   63 SOHRAB RUSTUM   67
          LOVELY IN DEATH UPON THE COMMON SAND   • • • • • •   80 SOHRAB RUSTUM   639
          AND I WERE NOTHING BUT A COMMON MAN   • • • • •   85 SOHRAB RUSTUM   813
          NOR MUST HE CHOOSE THAT COMMON PATH OF GODS   • •   99 BALDER DEAD 1   139
          WITH ME FOR THUS ORDAINS THE COMMON RITE   • • •   103 BALDER DEAD 1   300
          OF COMMON LIFE WHERE CROWDED UP PELL-MELL   • • •   168 WORLDLY PLACE   4
          OF SHARERS IN A COMMON HUMAN FATE   • • • • •   170 WEST LONDON   11
          CONDUCTED TO THEIR COMMON LAND   • • • • • •   311 OBERMANN   147
          BUT SLOW THAT TIDE OF COMMON THOUGHT   • • • • •   319 OBERMANN MORE   189
          ITS COMMON HOPE WERE VAIN   • • • • • •   321 OBERMANN MORE   242
          ONE COMMON WAVE OF THOUGHT AND JOY   • • • • •   323 OBERMANN MORE   323
          AGAINST A POWER EXEMPT FROM COMMON CHECKS   • • •   336 MEROPE   206
          SURE ALL-COMMON TO LOSE   • • • • • • • •   369 MEROPE   1100
          A PEOPLE LIKE A COMMON MAN IS DULL   • • • • •   382 MEROPE   1342
          O MEROPE THE COMMON HEART OF MAN   • • • • •   389 MEROPE   1523
          AND TALK TO HIM OF THINGS AT HAND AND COMMON   • •   411 EMPEDOCLES I 1   158
          ALAS NO COMMON SEPULCHRE ART THOU   • • • • •   464 ALARIC AT ROME   55
          IN COMMON SIGHTS READ SECRET SYMPATHY   • • • •   472 CROMWELL   32
          WITH COMMON CARES UNMINGLING AND APART   • • • •   473 CROMWELL   57

COMMUNED
          OF GHOSTS AND COMMUNED WITH THEIR SOLEMN QUEEN   • •   114 BALDER DEAD 3   40

COMMUNION
          OF HEAVEN AND COMMUNION WITH MY KIN   • • • • • •   125 BALDER DEAD 3   402
          STILL SHOULD THE SPIRIT HOLD COMMUNION ROME WITH THEE   470 ALARIC AT ROME   210

COMPACT
          CAN I WITH HELAS POWER A COMPACT STRIKE   • • • •   98 BALDER DEAD 1   109
          WITH COMPACT IN THAT CONCOURSE TO DELIVER   • • • •   338 MEROPE   264

COMPANIES
          IN LITTLE COMPANIES   • • • • • • • • • •   195 FRAG ANTIGONE   17

COMPANION
          WITHOUT COMPANION WITHOUT SPEECH   • • • • •   278 SOUTHERN NIGHT   87
          WAS CHOSEN HIS COMPANION FROM A BOY   • • • • • •   355 MEROPE   724
          FARE THEE WELL COMPANION DEAR   • • • • • •   458 POOR MATTHIAS   206
          THE CHILD-COMPANION OF HIS CHILDISH JOY   • • • •   477 CROMWELL   180

COMPANIONS
          ARE THERE THE SOLE COMPANIONS TO BE FOUND   • • •   152 TRISTRAM 3   99
          FRIENDS COMPANIONS AND TRAIN   • • • • • •   289 RUGBY CHAPEL   122
          AMONG AUGUST COMPANIONS   • • • • • • • •   437 EMPEDOCLES II   284
          BIRDS COMPANIONS MORE UNKNOWN   • • • • • •   455 POOR MATTHIAS   95
          OUR COMPANIONS DYING SIGN   • • • • • • •   456 POOR MATTHIAS   126

COMPANY
          OR SOME FRIEND HAILD US TO KEEP COMPANY   • • •   40 HUMAN LIFE   12
          GHOSTS OF THAT BOISTEROUS COMPANY   • • • • •   55 RESIGNATION   89
          TO-NIGHT MY PAGE SHALL KEEP ME COMPANY   • • •   140 TRISTRAM 1   310
          WHO BORE SAINT LOUIS COMPANY   • • • • • •   278 SOUTHERN NIGHT   94
          BUT THOU THOU ART NO COMPANY FOR HIM   • • • • •   411 EMPEDOCLES I 1   140

COMPARE
          SO MIGHT THEY REASON SO COMPARE   • • • • • •   56 RESIGNATION   136

COMPARES
          AND NOT ALONE DISSUADES HIM BUT COMPARES   • • • •   385 MEROPE   1416

COMPARISON
          OF LIKENESS OR COMPARISON CAN BE   • • • • • •   LUCRETIUS 5   9

COMPASSION
          PITY THYSELF NONE NEEDS COMPASSION MORE   • • • •   396 MEROPE   1761

COMPASSIONATE
          MIGHT MEAN AND FROM HIS DARK COMPASSIONATE EYES   • •   82 SOHRAB RUSTUM   735

COMPEERS
          MY HUSBAND WANDERING WITH HIS STERN COMPEERS   • •   367 MEROPE   1033

COMPELLD
    WHICH COMPELLD FOR GEIST A SONG . . . . . . 454 POOR MATTHIAS 60

COMPLAIN
    DOTH RUSTLINGLY ABOVE YOUR HEADS COMPLAIN . . . . 18 CHURCH BROU 3 33
    TO OUR LONELY SEA COMPLAIN . . . . 139 TRISTRAM 1 274
    DOTH THE DEAD GUIERS STREAM COMPLAIN . . . . . . 299 GRANDE CHARTR 10
    WHICH WOULD OF DEATH COMPLAIN . . . . 448 WESTMIN ABBEY 132

COMPLAIND
    TIME SO COMPLAIND OF . . . . 52 CONSOLATION 71

COMPLAINED
    A LOOK AS IF THE HEART COMPLAINED . . . . . . 140 TRISTRAM 1 321

COMPLAINING
    HAVE WHISPERD IT TO THE COMPLAINING SEA . . . . 8 RELIGIOUS ISOL 11
    FROM WILD AND WEAK COMPLAINING . . . . 39 STAGIRIUS 36
    WITH WOMENS TEARS AND WEAK COMPLAINING CRIES . . 96 BALDER DEAD 1 32
    WITH WOMANS TEARS AND WEAK COMPLAINING CRIES . . 96 BALDER DEAD 1 V 32
    FOLLOWS THEM WITH A LONG COMPLAINING CRY . . . . 129 BALDER DEAD 3 564
    BUT LIKE ME SHE WROTH COMPLAINING . . . . . . 197 FRAG ANTIGONE 76
    THE COMPLAINING MILLIONS OF MEN . . . . . . 229 YOUTH OF NATURE 51
    WHAT FORMS ARE THESE THAT WITH COMPLAINING SOUND . . 476 CROMWELL 159

COMPLAININGS
    MANS WEAK COMPLAININGS MINGLING WITH HIS TOIL . . 1 QUIET WORK V 10

COMPLAINT
    POUR ALL THE SOUL OF THEIR COMPLAINT . . . . . . 224 EPILOG LAOCOON 100

COMPLETE
    ARE BY A STROKE THOUGH UNDESIRED COMPLETE . . . . 360 MEROPE 877

COMPLEXION
    WHAT MOOD WEARS LIKE COMPLEXION TO THY WOE . . . . 42 GIPSY CHILD 21
    THE CREDULOUS COMPLEXION OF THY DREAMS . . . . RUDE ORATOR 12
    THE CREDULOUS COMPLEXION OF THY WOE . . . . . . RUDE ORATOR V 12

COMPOSD
    ALL DIFFERENCE WITH HIS FELLOW MAN COMPOSD . . . . 7 REP FRIEND CONT V 13

COMPOSE
    THE OTHERS LABOURING TO COMPOSE THEIR BRAWLS . . 116 BALDER DEAD 3 86
    CALM ME AH COMPOSE ME TO THE END . . . . . . 240 SELF-DEPENDENCE 8

COMPOSED
    WITH COLD DRY EYES AND HEARTS COMPOSED AND STERN . . 96 BALDER DEAD 1 35
    COMPOSED REFRESHD ENNOBLED CLEAR . . . . . . 251 WISH 50
    AS DEATH COMPOSED TO BEAR . . . . 309 OBERMANN 86
    COMPOSED TO BEAR I LIVED AND DIED . . . . . . 321 OBERMANN MORE 265
    WITH HOPE EXTINCT AND BROW COMPOSED . . . . . . 322 OBERMANN MORE 297
    CRUEL BUT COMPOSED AND BLAND . . . . 453 POOR MATTHIAS 39

COMPREHEND
    AH NOW I COMPREHEND THE LIBERAL GRACE . . . . 366 MEROPE V 997

COMPREHENDING
    SCARCE COMPREHENDING THE VOICE . . . . 294 HEINES GRAVE 78

COMPRESSD
    STERNLY COMPRESSD WE STRAIN ON . . . . 289 RUGBY CHAPEL 106

COMPUNCTIOUS
    SAD COMPUNCTIOUS VISITINGS . . . . 455 POOR MATTHIAS 86

COMRADE
    BRIGHT COMRADE TO THE NOISY TOWN . . . . . . 54 RESIGNATION 77

COMRADES
    THEN EVIDENCE CAME HIS COMRADES OF THE HUNT . . 365 MEROPE V
    COMRADES OF OUR PAST WERE THEY . . . . 453 POOR MATTHIAS 49

COMST
    BUT HE WHOM FIRST THOU MEETEST WHEN THOU COMST . . 100 BALDER DEAD 1 189
    FOR THE LAST TIME FOR HERE THOU COMST NO MORE . . 125 BALDER DEAD 3 420
    HAIL AND FAREWELL FOR HERE THOU COMST NO MORE . . 126 BALDER DEAD 3 455
    OR HOW EXPECTEST NOT TO LOSE WHO COMST . . . . 381 MEROPE 1292
    NOW FOR THYSELF THOU COMST WITH WELL-CLOAKD JOY . . 395 MEROPE 1737
    COMST THOU GUIDED SAFE TO THY HOME . . . . . . 405 MEROPE 2022

CONCEAL
    YET STILL FOR I CONCEAL IT NOT FERMENTS . . . . 334 MEROPE 137

CONCEALD
    I KNEW THE MASS OF MEN CONCEALD . . . . . . 245 BURIED LIFE 16
    WHAT I KNEW I CONCEALD . . . . 371 MEROPE 1132

CONCEALS
     CONCEALS FROM MAN WHO CANNOT PLUMB ITS DEPTHS   •   •   351 MEROPE   623
     O LYCAEUS CONCEALS • • • • • • • • • • • •   347 MEROPE   V

CONCEDES
     WHICH THE JEALOUS SOUL CONCEDES   • • • • • •   34 NEW SIRENS   228

CONCEIVE
     SO FAR AS I CONCEIVE THE WORLDS REBUKE   • • • •   37 WORLDS TRIUMPHS   1
     YES YES NOW I CONCEIVE THE LIBERAL GRACE   • • • •   366 MEROPE   997

CONCERN
     IS NO CONCERN OF OURS   • • • • • • • • • •   47 HORATIAN ECHO   6

CONCERTING
     CONCERTING IN THE CITY WITH OUR FRIENDS   • • • •   379 MEROPE   V1261

CONCLUDED
     AM I NOT CONCLUDED NOW AND ENDED   • • • • • •   482 THEKLAS ANSWER   3

CONCORD
     WHAT GODS THE GODS OF CONCORD CIVIL WEAL   • • • •   341 MEROPE   358
     OF CONCORD AND BEEN BAFFLED WITH DISDAIN   • • • •   360 MEROPE   V 881

CONCOURSE
     WITH COMPACT IN THAT CONCOURSE TO DELIVER   • • • •   338 MEROPE   264

CONDEMN
     CONDEMN ME NOR UPBRAID   • • • • • • • • • •   310 OBERMANN   140
     IF THESE CONDEMN HIM LET THEM PASS HIS DOOM   • •   349 MEROPE   557
     STERNLY CONDEMN THE TOO BOLD MAN WHO DARES • • • •   353 MEROPE   690

CONDEMND
     HE GREW OLD IN AN AGE HE CONDEMND   • • • • • •   229 YOUTH OF NATURE   28
     CONDEMND TO CAST ABOUT   • • • • • • • • • •   307 OBERMANN   18
     NOT CONDEMND BY MY VOICE • • • • • • • • • •   360 MEROPE   902
     CONDEMND BY PRUDENCE HAVE SOMETIMES GONE WELL   • •   383 MEROPE   1385

CONDEMNEST
     TRIUMPHANT AND CONDEMNEST ALL OUR RACE   • • • •   367 MEROPE   1051

CONDEMNS
     THY CROWN CONDEMNS THEE WHILE THY TONGUE ABSOLVES   340 MEROPE   332

CONDITION
     HIS FIXD CONDITION AND PERPETUAL WALK   • • • •   404 MEROPE   1993
     CONDITION ALL WE DO   • • • • • • • • • •   418 EMPEDOCLES I 2   185

CONDUCTED
     CONDUCTED TO THEIR COMMON LAND • • • • • • • •   311 OBERMANN   147

CONDUCTS
     THE SEINE CONDUCTS HER WAVE   • • • • • • • •   312 OBERMANN   V 178

CONE
     THE CONE OF JAMAN PALE AND GREY   • • • • • •   313 OBERMANN MORE   31
     SOMETIMES TO ETNAS TOP AND TO THE CONE   • • • •   409 EMPEDOCLES I 1   95

CONFEDERATE
     HE PARCELLD OUT IN FIVE CONFEDERATE STATES • • • •   337 MEROPE   249
     THE OCCASION IF OUR CHIEF CONFEDERATE FAILS   • •   386 MEROPE   1447

CONFER
     FLY FIND ME ON THE INSTANT WHERE CONFER   • • • •   368 MEROPE   1071

CONFERRD
     THEY SAW US THEY CONFERRD THEIR BOSOMS HEAVED   • •   25 DREAM   26
     DREW CLOSE TOGETHER AND CONFERRD   • • • • • •   91 SICK KING BOKH   106

CONFERRING
     CONFERRING IN THE CITY WITH OUR FRIENDS   • • • •   379 MEROPE   1261
     WITH HIM CONFERRING THE KING SLOWLY REACHD • • • •   401 MEROPE   1907

CONFERS
     ITS GOLDEN RAIN ON EARTH CONFERS   • • • • • •   277 SOUTHERN NIGHT   54

CONFESS
     FOR IF I NOW CONFESS THIS THING HE ASKS   • • • •   71 SOHRAB RUSTUM   349
     THAT NAME AND SOMETHING I CONFESS IN THEE   • • • •   77 SOHRAB RUSTUM   548
     HIS BLOOD TO ME FOR I CONFESS IT KIND   • • • •   404 MEROPE   1976

CONFESSEST
     THOU CONFESSEST THE PRIZE   • • • • • • • •   370 MEROPE   1104

CONFEST
     KAI STOOD CONFEST • • • • • • • • • • • • •   459 KAISER DEAD   30

CONFIDENCE
     HAD MOST THY HUSBANDS CONFIDENCE CONSULT   • • • •   337 MEROPE   239

CONFIRMS
    REASON THE PROOF CONFIRMS   . . . . 419 EMPEDOCLES I 2   224
    REASON ITS VOICE CONFIRMS   . . . . 419 EMPEDOCLES I 2 V 224

CONFLICT
    IN THAT UNNATURAL CONFLICT FOR A CLOUD   . . . . 75 SOHRAB RUSTUM   481
    RENT WITH TUMULTUOUS THOUGHTS WHOSE CONFLICT RUNG   478 CROMWELL   223

CONFLUENT
    AND ON THIS SIDE THOSE CONFLUENT STREAMS WHICH MAKE   330 MEROPE   18

CONFOUND
    TROUBLES CONFOUND THE LITTLE WIT HE HAS   . . . . 413 EMPEDOCLES I 2   31

CONFOUNDST
    THOU FRIGHTENEST AND CONFOUNDST ME BY THY WORDS . . 362 MEROPE   932

CONFRONT
    MAYST FIGHT FIGHT THEM WHEN THEY CONFRONT THY SPEAR   74 SOHRAB RUSTUM   446

CONFRONTS
    CONFRONTS THE DOG AND HUNTER IN THE SOUTH   . . . . 99 BALDER DEAD 1   157

CONFUSE
    TROUBLES CONFUSE THE LITTLE WIT HE HAS   . . . . 413 EMPEDOCLES I 2 V 31

CONFUSED
    SWEPT WITH CONFUSED ALARMS OF STRUGGLE AND FLIGHT   212 DOVER BEACH   36
    ARE CONFUSED AS THE CRIES WHICH WE HEAR   . . . . 253 FUTURE   56

CONJECTURED
    AND CLASP CONJECTURED JOYS OR DREAD CONJECTURED WOES   425 EMPEDOCLES I 2 V 406
    AND CLASP CONJECTURED JOYS OR DREAD CONJECTURED WOES   425 EMPEDOCLES I 2 V 406
    AND KISS CONJECTURED JOYS OR FEAR CONJECTURED WOES   425 EMPEDOCLES I 2 V 406
    AND KISS CONJECTURED JOYS OR FEAR CONJECTURED WOES   425 EMPEDOCLES I 2 V 406

CONJURING
    AND ON THE CONJURING LAPPS HE BENT HIS GAZE   . . 96 BALDER DEAD 1   53

CONQUER
    EVEN FOR YOURSELVES TO CONQUER OR BEGUILE   . . . .   9 MYCERINUS   38
    BUT I SHALL CONQUER THAT MY HEART FOREBODES   . . 62 SOHRAB RUSTUM V
    CONQUER AND COME TO THY GOAL   . . . . 290 RUGBY CHAPEL   126
    COWARDS TO CONQUER AND THE WEAK TO DIE   . . . . 467 ALARIC AT ROME   140
    WITH CARES TO CONQUER AND A GOAL TO WIN   . . . . 475 CROMWELL   122

CONQUERD
    NO GIFTS FROM CHANCE HAVE CONQUERD FATE   . . . . 59 RESIGNATION   248
    FOR TIME NOT CORYDON HATH CONQUERD THEE   . . . . 265 THYRSIS   80
    OF HIS FRESH-CONQUERD REALM THE ROYAL SEAT   . . . 330 MEROPE   11
    SUCH WERE THE CONQUERD SUCH THE CONQUERORS WHO   . . 337 MEROPE   238
    OR CONQUERORS WITH CONQUERD TO UNITE   . . . . 338 MEROPE   289
    GIVE THE THRONES THAT THEY CONQUERD   . . . . . 344 MEROPE   456
    FOR THE THREE CONQUERD KINGDOMS OF THIS ISLE   . . 389 MEROPE   1549
    O BROTHER THOU HAST CONQUERD YET I FEAR   . . . . 390 MEROPE   1581
    NO SHAME THAT SUNS SHOULD RISE TO LIGHT A CONQUERD   468 ALARIC AT ROME   150
        ROME

CONQUERING
    THE CONQUERING TARTAR ENSIGNS THROUGH THE WORLD . . 62 SOHRAB RUSTUM   47
    AH NOW TIS CHANGED IN CONQUERING SUNSHINE BRIGHT . . 170 EAST AND WEST   12
    TO HYMN THE CONQUERING MARCH OF ROME   . . . . . . 300 GRANDE CHARTR   51
    A CONQUERING NEW-BORN JOY AWOKE   . . . . 316 OBERMANN MORE   115
    A CONQUERING SIGN   . . . . 460 KAISER DEAD   58

CONQUEROR
    THE THOUGHTS THAT TOUCHT THY BREAST THOU LONELY   468 ALARIC AT ROME   168
        CONQUEROR THEN

CONQUERORS
    SUCH WERE THE CONQUERD SUCH THE CONQUERORS WHO . . 337 MEROPE   238
    HANDFUL OF DORIAN CONQUERORS MIGHT HAVE CURBD . . 337 MEROPE   248
    OR CONQUERORS WITH CONQUERD TO UNITE . . . . . 338 MEROPE   289
    THERE THE YOUNGEST OF THE BAND OF CONQUERORS . . 345 MEROPE   465
    THE CONQUERORS WITH THE KINGS DEAD BODY COME . . 403 MEROPE   1953
    OF THE HERACLEIDAN CONQUERORS AS THOU SAIDST . . 404 MEROPE   1982
    BURSTS IN MAJESTIC BEAUTY ON HER CONQUERORS EYES . . 468 ALARIC AT ROME   156
    WHOSE SONS WERE CONQUERORS ONCE AND NOW WERE SLAVES   469 ALARIC AT ROME   184

CONQUEST
    SAILD BY THE FATE-MEANT GULF TO THEIR CONQUEST . . 344 MEROPE   450
    AND THERE BENEATH HIS FEET HIS CONQUEST LAY . . 468 ALARIC AT ROME   158
    AND HIS YOUNG DREAMS OF CONQUEST HOW TO-DAY . . 468 ALARIC AT ROME   171

CONSCIENCE
    MAN WOULD BE MILD AND WITH SAFE CONSCIENCE BLEST . .   5 HARMONY NATURE   11
    AND PARALYSING CONSCIENCE STOP MY ARM   . . . 333 MEROPE   98
    THAT RIGHT THAT CONSCIENCE POINTED TO A DEED . . 341 MEROPE   363
    WHO WITHOUT CHECK OF CONSCIENCE CAN AVER   . . . 353 MEROPE   680
    DID CONSCIENCE GOAD HIM TO DENOUNCE HIMSELF   . . 364 MEROPE V
    SOMETHING HAUNTS MY CONSCIENCE BRINGS   . . . . 455 POOR MATTHIAS   85

CONSCIOUS
       BACK WITH THE CONSCIOUS THRILL OF SHAME   . . . .   181 ISOLATION MARG   19
       CONSCIOUS OR NOT OF THE PAST   . . . .   287 RUGBY CHAPEL   45

CONSCIOUSNESS
       THE LAST SPARK OF MANS CONSCIOUSNESS WITH WORDS   . . 429 EMPEDOCLES II   30
       AND KEEP US PRISONERS OF OUR CONSCIOUSNESS . . . . 439 EMPEDOCLES II   352

CONSECRATE
       PETER HIS FRIEND WITH LIGHT DID CONSECRATE . . . . 445 WESTMIN ABBEY   50

CONSECRATES
       WHICH CONSECRATES THE TIES OF BLOOD FOR THESE INDEED   196 FRAG ANTIGONE   31

CONSECRATION
       WON CONSECRATION FROM TIME   . . . .   281 HAWORTH CHURCH   46
       FORESHOWN THEE IN THY CONSECRATION-HOUR   . . . . 446 WESTMIN ABBEY   75

CONSIDER
       CONSIDER HIM CONSIDER NOT OLD HATES   . . . . . . 335 MEROPE   173
       CONSIDER HIM CONSIDER NOT OLD HATES   . . . . . . 335 MEROPE   173
       CONSIDER TOO THIS PEOPLE WHO WERE DEAR   . . . .   335 MEROPE   174

CONSIDERATE
       AND PURGED CONSIDERATE MINDS   . . . .   198 FRAG DEJANEIRA   17

CONSIGND
       SCOTT HAD CONSIGND THERE HIS LAST   . . . . . . 281 HAWORTH CHURCH   V 23

CONSOLATION
       NOT FROM MY LIPS SHOULD CONSOLATION FALL   . . . . 393 MEROPE   1687

CONSOLATIONS
       SPEAK OF THE SURE CONSOLATIONS OF TIME   . . . .   206 SEPARATION   2

CONSOLE
       CONSOLE WE CANNOT HER EAR   . . . .   282 HAWORTH CHURCH   50
       WHAT MIGHT WE SAY TO CONSOLE   . . . .   282 HAWORTH CHURCH   V

CONSOLED
       WORDS BY WHICH THE WRETCHED ARE CONSOLED   . . . . 143 TRISTRAM 2   42
       THAT STEADFAST MOURNFUL STRAIN CONSOLED   . . . . 450 GEISTS GRAVE   17

CONSORT
       WINDS FROM OUR SIDE THE UNSUITING CONSORT RIVE   . .   40 HUMAN LIFE   16

CONSPIRACY
       FOR I HAVE KEPT CONSPIRACY FAST-CHAIND   . . . . 334 MEROPE   149
       UNADULATING GRIEF CONSPIRACY   . . . .   338 MEROPE   261

CONSPIRE
       WHEN JEALOUS PAN WITH MARSYAS DID CONSPIRE . . . . 432 EMPEDOCLES II   128

CONSTANCY
       MUCH TURBULENCE AND LITTLE CONSTANCY . . . . . . 337 MEROPE   234

CONSTANT
       I BADE MY HEART MORE CONSTANT BE   . . . . . . 180 ISOLATION MARG   2

CONSTRAIND
       BOTH HAVE PASSD A YOUTH CONSTRAIND AND SAD . . . . 144 TRISTRAM 2   V 54

CONSTRAINT
       WHERE THEY CAN NOW WITHOUT CONSTRAINT   . . . .   224 EPILOG LAOCOON   99

CONSTRUCTED
       HAVE FELT THEIR HUGE FRAMES NOT CONSTRUCTED RIGHT   239 REVOLUTIONS   15

CONSTRUCTION
       BY THE CONSTRUCTION AND REPORT OF MEN   . . . .   398 MEROPE   1790

CONSTRUED
       CONSTRUED AWRY MISPLANND INVASIONS WORE   . . . . 336 MEROPE   216
       CONSTRUED HIS ACTS INDULGENTLY REVERED   . . . . 337 MEROPE   255
       CONSTRUED AWRY MISPLANND INVASIONS USD   . . . . 336 MEROPE   V 216

CONSULT
       LET US CONSULT BEFORE THIS PALACE SENDS   . . . . 330 MEROPE   26
       HAD MOST THY HUSBANDS CONFIDENCE CONSULT   . . . . 337 MEROPE   239
       WE TWO WITH THEE MY MOTHER MAY CONSULT   . . . . 379 MEROPE   1265

CONSUMD
       CONSUMD OUR SOUL WITH THIRST LIKE FIRE   . . . . 323 OBERMANN MORE   V 315

CONSUMED
       THE BODIES WERE CONSUMED ASH CHOKED THE PILE   . .   119 BALDER DEAD 3   202
       BOTH HAVE PASSD A YOUTH CONSUMED AND SAD   . . . . 144 TRISTRAM 2   54
       CONSUMED HER BEAUTY LIKE A FLAME   . . . . . . 147 TRISTRAM 2   134
       BAFFLED UNKNOWN SELF-CONSUMED . . . . 285 HAWORTH CHURCH   98
       CONSUMED OUR HEART WITH THIRST LIKE FIRE   . . . . 323 OBERMANN MORE   315

CONSUMING
    THE DEPTH OF THAT CONSUMING RESTLESSNESS . . . . 238 PROGRESS   V

CONTACT
    FLY HENCE OUR CONTACT FEAR   . . . . 261 SCHOLAR-GIPSY   206
    BUT FLY OUR PATHS OUR FEVERISH CONTACT FLY . . . 261 SCHOLAR-GIPSY   221

CONTAIN
    THOSE HALLS TOO DESTINED TO CONTAIN . . . . . . 301 GRANDE CHARTR   61

CONTAINING
    FOR LITTLE DO THE ALL-CONTAINING HOURS . . . . 195 FRAG ANTIGONE   2

CONTEMPLATING
    PLEASURE IN CONTEMPLATING   . . . . 228 CAUTION POETS   4

CONTEMPLATION
    BY CONTEMPLATION OF DIVINER THINGS . . . . . .   9 MYCERINUS   12

CONTEND
    BUT THEY CONTEND AND CRY NO MORE   . . . . . . 303 GRANDE CHARTR   120

CONTENDING
    IN HER LIKE US THERE CLASHD CONTENDING POWERS . . 168 RACHEL 3   11

CONTENT
    SILENT THEY ARE THOUGH NOT CONTENT . . . . . . 303 GRANDE CHARTR   117
    ON WHICH MAN WINS CONTENT   . . . . 419 EMPEDOCLES I 2   223
    WHO DWELL ON A FIRM BASIS OF CONTENT . . . . . 436 EMPEDOCLES II   260
    AT LIFE AND LIVING NOT CONTENT . . . . 484 ROME-SICKNESS   23

CONTENTION
    LET THE LONG CONTENTION CEASE . . . . 215 LAST WORD   5
    OF MEN CONTENTION-TOST OF MEN WHO GROAN . . . 269 THYRSIS   224

CONTINENT
    PARTS OF A SINGLE CONTINENT   . . . . 182 TO MARG CONT   16

CONTINUAL
    KEEP ALL O KEEP CONTINUAL HOLIDAY   . . . . . .   FRAGMENT 2   5

CONTINUALLY
    TOSSING CONTINUALLY   . . . .   39 STAGIRIUS   51

CONTINUE
    STABLISH CONTINUE OUR MARCH   . . . . 292 RUGBY CHAPEL   206

CONTINUES
    MORE LOYAL AS OUR LINE CONTINUES MORE   . . . . 389 MEROPE   1541

CONTINUOUS
    A PLACID AND CONTINUOUS WHOLE . . . . 57 RESIGNATION   190

CONTRAST
    OF THOUGHT SUCH CONTRAST STRANGE . . . . . .   36 VOICE   28

CONTRITION
    AND BY CONTRITION SEALD THRICE SURE . . . . . 179 FAREWELL   72
    SEES THE CONTRITION OF AGE   . . . . 232 YOUTH OF MAN   16

CONTRIVING
    TO THE SUBTLE CONTRIVING HEAD . . . . 431 EMPEDOCLES II   91

CONTROL
    IMPULSE AND REASON FREEDOM AND CONTROL . . . .   4 BUTLERS SERMONS   2
    MAY BE BY MAN EFFACED MAN CAN CONTROL   . . . .   6 GEO CRUIKSHANK   12
    NOT LESS THY BOAST ILLUMINATES CONTROL . . . .   8 RELIGIOUS ISOL   7
    FATE GAVE WHAT CHANCE SHALL NOT CONTROL . . . 58 RESIGNATION   197
    WHOM HELA WITH AUSTERE CONTROL PRESIDES . . . 104 BALDER DEAD 1   317
    STERN STRENGTH AND PROMISE OF CONTROL   . . . 178 FAREWELL   24
    IMMUNITY FROM MY CONTROL . . . . 206 RIVER   15
    ASK HOW SHE VIEWD THY SELF-CONTROL . . . . . 241 MORALITY   15
    NOT CHAFED BY HOURLY FALSE CONTROL . . . . . 302 GRANDE CHARTR   96
    SEES MAN CONTROL THE WIND   . . . . 421 EMPEDOCLES I 2   259
    THRILLD WITH A DREAD NO SLUMBER COULD CONTROL . . 477 CROMWELL   200

CONTROLLD
    ALL PLAINT IN HER OWN CAUSE CONTROLLD   . . . . 279 SOUTHERN NIGHT   122

CONTROLS
    LIFES MOVEMENT FASCINATES CONTROLS . . . . . . 226 EPILOG LAOCOON   164

CONTROUL
    NOT CHAFED BY HOURLY FALSE CONTROUL . . . . . . 302 GRANDE CHARTR   V 96

CONVENT
    ON THE SMOOTH CONVENT-ROOFS   . . . . 50 CONSOLATION   12
    CHIME CONVENT-BELLS ON WINTRY NIGHTS . . . . . 156 SAINT BRANDAN   6

CONVENTS
    AND NOW NO BELLS NO CONVENTS MORE   • • • • • •   156 SAINT BRANDAN   10

CONVERSE
    WITH EYES WHICH SOUGHT THINE EYES THOU DIDST CONVERSE   42 GIPSY CHILD   15
    WITH EYES WHICH SEEK THINE EYES THOU DOST CONVERSE   41 GIPSY CHILD   V   15
    WITH EYES THAT SOUGHT THINE EYES THOU DIDST CONVERSE   42 GIPSY CHILD   V   15
    CONVERSE HIS SPEECH REMAINS THOUGH HE BE DEAD   • •   111 BALDER DEAD 2   248
    MY HATED CONVERSE ON THEE CAME I UP   • • • • •   125 BALDER DEAD 3   414
    OF HELA AND HOLD CONVERSE UNDISTURBD   • • • • •   126 BALDER DEAD 3   436
    THE TWO HELD CONVERSE THEY WROTE   • • • • • •   280 HAWORTH CHURCH   18
    THEY MET HELD CONVERSE THEY WROTE   • • • • • •   280 HAWORTH CHURCH   V   18
    OF DAZZLING CONVERSE FROM FUMES   • • • • • •   296 HEINES GRAVE   145
    OF DAZZLING CONVERSE AND FUMES   • • • • • •   296 HEINES GRAVE   V 145

CONVEY
    COME AIRS AND FLOATING ECHOES AND CONVEY   • • • •   247 BURIED LIFE   75
    MAY HERMES HERALD OF THE DEAD CONVEY   • • • • • •   349 MEROPE   585
    FOR WANT OF LIGHT WHICH SHOULD THE BOON CONVEY   • •   446 WESTMIN ABBEY   70
    FOR LACK OF LIGHT WHICH SHOULD THE BOON CONVEY   • •   446 WESTMIN ABBEY   V   70

CONVEYD
    BEEN TO YOUR SHADOWY WORLD CONVEYD   • • • • • •   271 MEMORIAL VERSES   36

CONVICTION
    SOON SOON THE DAYS CONVICTION BRING   • • • • • •   459 KAISER DEAD   25

CONVICTIONS
    JUDGMENT SHIFTS CONVICTIONS GO   • • • • • • • •   29 NEW SIRENS   82

CONVINCE
    BUT FIRST HE WOULD CONVINCE HIS STUBBORN FOE   • •   80 SOHRAB RUSTUM   653

CONVOLVULUS
    PALE PINK CONVOLVULUS IN TENDRILS CREEP   • • • •   255 SCHOLAR-GIPSY   25
    PALE BLUE CONVOLVULUS IN TENDRILS CREEP   • • • •   255 SCHOLAR-GIPSY   V   25

CONVULSED
    CONVULSED HIM BACK TO LIFE HE OPEND THEM   • • •   86 SOHRAB RUSTUM   851
    ALL CONVULSED HIS LITTLE FORM   • • • • • • •   452 POOR MATTHIAS   4

CONVULSIVE
    AND STRONG CONVULSIVE GROANINGS SHOOK HIS BREAST   • •   82 SOHRAB RUSTUM   703

COOKS
    AND BEFORE EACH THE COOKS WHO SERVED THEM PLACED   • •   97 BALDER DEAD 1   66

COOL
    TO BE LIKE NATURE STRONG LIKE NATURE COOL   • • • •   5 HARMONY NATURE   4
    TO THE COOL REGION OF THE GROVES HE LOVED   • • • •   11 MYCERINUS   84
    HERE LEAN MY HEAD ON THIS COOL BALUSTRADE   • • • •   19 MODERN SAPPHO   V   4
    WHERE COOL GRASS AND FRAGRANT GLOOMS   • • • • • •   26 NEW SIRENS   2
    IN THEIR COOL GALLERY   • • • • • • • • •   50 CONSOLATION   18
    COOL FARMS WITH OPEN-LYING STORES   • • • • • •   54 RESIGNATION   56
    COOL SHADE IS THERE AND RUSTIC CHEER   • • • • •   54 RESIGNATION   75
    STILL THIS WILD BROOK THE RUSHES COOL   • • • •   55 RESIGNATION   104
    STARRD THE COOL TURF AND CLUMPS OF PRIMROSES   • •   155 TRISTRAM 3   208
    GO HENCE AND COOL THYSELF AN HOUR   • • • • • •   157 SAINT BRANDAN   36
    BENEATH THE BIRCH-TREES COOL   • • • • • • • •   160 NECKAN   42
    SAND-STREWN CAVERNS COOL AND DEEP   • • • • • •   162 FORSAKEN MERM   35
    THE COOL NIGHT-WIND TOO   • • • • • • • •   186 STRAYED REVEL   19
    FLOW THE COOL LAKE-WAVES   • • • • • • • • •   190 STRAYED REVEL   160
    AH COOL NIGHT-WIND TREMULOUS STARS   • • • • • •   194 STRAYED REVEL   282
    WITH ITS COOL TREES AND NIGHT   • • • • • • •   200 PHILOMELA   11
    MOORD TO THE COOL BANK IN THE SUMMER-HEATS   • • •   257 SCHOLAR-GIPSY   67
    TRAILING IN THE COOL STREAM THY FINGERS WET   • •   257 SCHOLAR-GIPSY   75
    LIFTING THE COOL-HAIRD CREEPERS STEALTHILY   • • •   262 SCHOLAR-GIPSY   234
    ON THE COOL FLOWERY LAP OF EARTH   • • • • •   271 MEMORIAL VERSES   49
    COOL NORTHERN FIELDS AND GRASS AND FLOWERS   • • •   275 STANZAS CARNAC   44
    SHADOW AND VERDURE AND COOL   • • • • • • •   292 HEINES GRAVE   8
    AND COOL DRINKS AND AN EASED   • • • • • • •   293 HEINES GRAVE   19
    BACK TO THE TRANQUIL THE COOL   • • • • • • •   296 HEINES GRAVE   150
    IN HIS COOL HALL WITH HAGGARD EYES   • • • • •   315 OBERMANN MORE   97
    THEY FEEL THE COOL WET TURF UNDER THEIR FEET   •   406 EMPEDOCLES I 1   2
    THROUGH THE COOL LOVELY COUNTRY FOLLOWD YOU   •   407 EMPEDOCLES I 1   45
    KNEE-DEEP IN THE COOL FORD FOR TIS THE LAST   •   413 EMPEDOCLES I 2   41
    THE GRASS IS COOL THE SEA-SIDE AIR   • • • • •   426 EMPEDOCLES I 2   432
    SINKS AND RISES THROUGH THIS COOL ARCADE   • • • •   META CLOISTER   16
    COOL THE MURMUR OF THE FOUNTAINS   • • • • •   META CLOISTER   V   15

COOLD
    SO MANY FIERY SPIRITS QUITE COOLD DOWN   • • • •   37 WORLDS TRIUMPHS   6
    SHOULD BE AS SOON AS KINDLED COOLD   • • • • •   182 TO MARG CONT   20

COOLER
    WHAT THOU THINKST THIS ACHING BROW WAS COOLER   • •   143 TRISTRAM 2   43

COOLING
    I SHALL WEEP BUT THEIR LOVE WILL BE COOLING AND HE   20 MODERN SAPPHO   18

COOLNESS
AN AIR OF COOLNESS PLAYS UPON HIS FACE   • • • •   247 BURIED LIFE   94

COOMBS
STILL BLOWS IN THE QUANTOCK COOMBS   • • • • • •   229 YOUTH OF NATURE   23

COPAIS
COPAIS LAY BRIGHT IN THE MOON   • • • • • • •   229 YOUTH OF NATURE   37

COPE
TO COPE WITH ME IN SINGLE FIGHT BUT THEY   • • • •   72 SOHRAB RUSTUM   359
WITH SUCH SLIGHT MEANS TO COPE WITH SUCH A FOE   • •   381 MEROPE   1293

COPSE
CORN-FIELD AND HAMLET AND COPSE   • • • • •   234 YOUTH OF MAN   79
THE TENDER PURPLE SPRAY ON COPSE AND BRIERS   • •   263 THYRSIS   18
AND BEECHEN COVERTS AND COPSE   • • • • • • •   297 HEINES GRAVE   181
WE CHEERED HIM BUT THAT MOMENT FROM THE COPSE   • •   357 MEROPE   786
THERE IN THE LEAF-STREWN COPSE I FOUND   • • • •   484 ROME-SICKNESS   14

CORAL
LINKING THEIR CORAL ARMS UNDER THE SEA   • • • •   4 BUTLERS SERMONS   10

CORD
A CORD THE GODS FIRST SLUNG   • • • • • • • •   415 EMPEDOCLES I 2   78

CORDED
AND ON THE BEACH UNDID HIS CORDED BALES   • • • •   262 SCHOLAR-GIPSY   250

CORDIAL
THAT CORDIAL HAND THAT BEARING FREE   • • • • • •   279 SOUTHERN NIGHT   126
WHOSE CORDIAL TALK   • • • • • • • • • • •   460 KAISER DEAD   70

CORDS
AND BIND THY CARCASE LIKE A BALE WITH CORDS   • •   114 BALDER DEAD 3   25

CORE
OR SUNK AT THE CORE OF THE WORLD   • • • • •   230 YOUTH OF NATURE   70
DEEP HAVE EMBREATHED AT ITS CORE   • • • • • •   299 HEINES GRAVE   230

CORN
UNDER THE EAVES PEERD ROWS OF INDIAN CORN   • • •   25 DREAM   19
A SHIVER RUNS THROUGH THE DEEP CORN FOR JOY   • •   65 SOHRAB RUSTUM   156
DOWN THROUGH THE MIDDLE OF A RICH MANS CORN   • •   70 SOHRAB RUSTUM   294
AND ON EACH SIDE ARE SQUARES OF STANDING CORN   •   70 SOHRAB RUSTUM   295
AS ON SOME PARTRIDGE IN THE CORN A HAWK   • • •   73 SOHRAB RUSTUM   400
CORN IN A GOLDEN PLATTER SOAKD WITH WINE   • • •   83 SOHRAB RUSTUM   754
SEE THROUGH THE QUIET CORN   • • • • • • •   218 BACCHANALIA 1   V   32
CORN-FIELD AND HAMLET AND COPSE   • • • • •   234 YOUTH OF MAN   79
WITH DISTANT CRIES OF REAPERS IN THE CORN   • • •   255 SCHOLAR-GIPSY   19
THROUGH THE THICK CORN THE SCARLET POPPIES PEEP   •   255 SCHOLAR-GIPSY   23
DOTTING THE FIELDS OF CORN AND VINE   • • • • •   275 SOUTHERN NIGHT   5
WEALTHY IN CORN AND FLOCKS WHICH WHEN AT LAST   •   330 MEROPE   5
THE REAPERS IN THE CORN   • • • • • • • •   436 EMPEDOCLES II   255
FAR OER THE GLISTENING SHEETS OF WINDY CORN   • •   473 CROMWELL   36

CORNER
IN THIS HIGH FIELDS DARK CORNER WHERE HE LEAVES   • •   255 SCHOLAR-GIPSY   12

CORNFIELD
IN THE HOT CORNFIELD OF THE PHRYGIAN KING   • • • •   268 THYRSIS   183

CORNISH
FOR THE SURGE-BEAT CORNISH STRAND   • • • • • •   134 TRISTRAM 1   132

CORNWALL
FROM IRELAND TO CORNWALL BORE   • • • • • • •   132 TRISTRAM 1   60
AH NO SHE IS ASLEEP IN CORNWALL NOW   • • • • •   139 TRISTRAM 1   301
IN TYNTAGIL SHE IS ASLEEP IN CORNWALL NOW   • • •   139 TRISTRAM 1   V 301
IN CORNWALL TRISTRAM AND QUEEN ISEULT LAY   • • •   149 TRISTRAM 3   2

CORNWALLS
THAT PROUD FIRST ISEULT CORNWALLS QUEEN   • • • •   132 TRISTRAM 1   58
TO CORNWALLS PALACE TO THE SIDE   • • • • •   132 TRISTRAM 1   V 61

CORONALS
THE CORONALS OF THAT FORGOTTEN TIME   • • • • •   266 THYRSIS   117

CORPSE
A PERSIAN LORD THIS DAY AND STRIP HIS CORPSE   • •   77 SOHRAB RUSTUM   529
BRING THOU TO ME HIS CORPSE HE SAID   • • • • •   91 SICK KING BOKH   128
AND ON THE TOP LAY BALDERS CORPSE AND PUT   • • •   96 BALDER DEAD 1   43
AND LIGHTED TORCHES AND TOOK UP THE CORPSE   • • •   101 BALDER DEAD 1   204
THESE OER THE CORPSE INTONED A PLAINTIVE STRAIN   •   103 BALDER DEAD 1   273
UPON MY SHIP AND BURN MY CORPSE WITH FIRE   • • •   103 BALDER DEAD 1   297
AND THEY SHALL BURN THY CORPSE WITH MINE NOT THEE   103 BALDER DEAD 1   304
ON THE TWELFTH DAY THE GODS SHALL BURN HIS CORPSE   106 BALDER DEAD 2   44
ROUND BALDERS CORPSE WHICH THEY HAD THITHER BORNE   113 BALDER DEAD 3   2
OF THE HEAPD WOOD AND BURN HIS CORPSE WITH FIRE   •   115 BALDER DEAD 3   54
AND OVER BALDERS CORPSE THESE WORDS DIDST SAY   • •   115 BALDER DEAD 3   74
HE LAST APPROACHD THE CORPSE AND SPAKE AND SAID   • •   117 BALDER DEAD 3   131

CORPSE   (CONTINUED)
        FULL THE DECKS BREADTH AND LOFTY THEN THE CORPSE . . 118 BALDER DEAD 3   162
        A DEAD IGNORANT THANKLESS CORPSE . . . . . . 196 FRAG ANTIGONE   53
        BEHIND HIS CORPSE THEIR HEDGE OF SERRIED SPEARS . . 381 MEROPE   1308
        OVER THY CORPSE TRIUMPH NOT NEITHER MOURN . . . . 404 MEROPE   1989
        TAKE THESE MY SON OVER THINE ENEMYS CORPSE . . . . 404 MEROPE   2010
        AND NOT LEAVE HIM BEHIND A CORPSE ON THE PLAIN   HOMER TRANS   42
            LIKE PATROCLUS

CORRIDOR
        THROUGH MANY A ROOM AND CORRIDOR   . . . . 140 TRISTRAM 1   332

CORRIDORS
        THE HUMID CORRIDORS BEHOLD   . . . . 300 GRANDE CHARTR   34

CORRUPT
        WHEN THEY CORRUPT THE SOULS OF THOSE THEY RULE . . 386 MEROPE   1437

CORSE
        AND OH WE CRIED THAT ON THIS CORSE . . . . 319 OBERMANN MORE   197
        YET POOR BIRD THY TINY CORSE . . . . 454 POOR MATTHIAS   83

CORSLET
        THAT THE HARD IRON CORSLET CLANKD ALOUD . . . .   80 SOHRAB RUSTUM   664
        HIS DAZZLING CORSLET AND HIS HELM OF GOLD . . . . 115 BALDER DEAD 3   58

CORYDON
        FOR TIME NOT CORYDON HATH CONQUERD THEE . . . . 265 THYRSIS   80
        ALACK FOR CORYDON NO RIVAL NOW . . . . 265 THYRSIS   81

COST
        TOO DEAR HIS SECRET WILES HAVE COST OUR HOUSE   . . 380 MEROPE   1279

COTES
        GO SHEPHERD AND UNTIE THE WATTLED COTES   . . . . 255 SCHOLAR-GIPSY   2

COTTAGE
        BACKD BY THE PINES A PLANK-BUILT COTTAGE STOOD   . .   25 DREAM   15
        WE SHOT BENEATH THE COTTAGE WITH THE STREAM   . .   25 DREAM   20
        SOON THE PLANKD COTTAGE BY THE SUN-WARMD PINES   . .   25 DREAM   35
        SOON THE PLANKD COTTAGE MID THE SUN-WARMD PINES . .   25 DREAM   V 35
        SWEET-WILLIAM WITH HIS HOMELY COTTAGE-SMELL   . . 264 THYRSIS   65

COUCHANT
        WHERE OFT WE WATCHD THY COUCHANT FORM   . . . . 451 GEISTS GRAVE   68

COUCHD
        COUCHD BESIDE HIM ON THE GROUND   . . . . 137 TRISTRAM 1   226
        THE SOFT-COUCHD CATTLE WERE AS FAIR   . . . . . . 222 EPILOG LAOCOON   43
        THOSE CATTLE COUCHD OR AS THEY RISE   . . . . . . 222 EPILOG LAOCOON   53

COUNCIL
        WHERE THEY HOLD COUNCIL AND GIVE LAWS FOR MEN   . . 105 BALDER DEAD 2   34
        I GO I GO THE KING HOLDS COUNCIL THERE   . . . . 368 MEROPE   1077
        TAKE NOT WITH THEE TO COUNCIL DID THE KING   . . . 373 MEROPE   1192
        HERE BRING HIM ERE THE KING COME BACK FROM COUNCIL   379 MEROPE   1262
        LEST FROM THE COUNCIL-CHAMBER PRESENTLY   . . . . 386 MEROPE   1442
        THE OLYMPIAN COUNCIL SEES   . . . . 431 EMPEDOCLES II   70

COUNCILS
        COUNCILS AND ARMIES AND THE POMP OF WAR   . . . . 476 CROMWELL   142

COUNSEL
        THY COUNSEL AND TO HEED THEE AS THY SON   . . . .   62 SOHRAB RUSTUM   39
        TO COUNSEL GUDURZ AND ZOARRAH CAME   . . . . . .   66 SOHRAB RUSTUM   171
        WHEREFORE THAT I MAY COUNSEL THEE   . . . .   88 SICK KING BOKH   26
        THEN WE SHALL MISS THY COUNSEL AND THY ARM . . . . 115 BALDER DEAD 3   70
        DO YOU SEEK COUNSEL OF THE GODS   . . . . 198 FRAG DEJANEIRA   6
        HE HAD HIS COUNSEL PARTY FRIENDS I MINE   . . . . 334 MEROPE   128
        THAT THOU MAYST READ THINE ENEMYS COUNSEL PLAIN . . 380 MEROPE   1278
        BE GUIDED O MY SON SPURN COUNSEL NOT . . . . . . 382 MEROPE   1328
        O AEPYTUS WEIGH WELL HER COUNSEL GIVEN   . . . . 382 MEROPE   1332
        ILL COUNSEL IN MY JUDGMENT GIVES SHE HERE . . . . 382 MEROPE   1333
        THE WIT AND COUNSEL OF MAN WAS NEVER CLEAR . . . . 413 EMPEDOCLES I 2   30
        HIS COUNSEL COULD ONCE SOOTHE HIM BUT APOLLO   . . 428 EMPEDOCLES I 2   482
        THAT THEY SHOULD EASE GRAVE COUNSEL OF ITS CARE . .   RUDE ORATOR   10

COUNSELLD
        THESE CAME AND COUNSELLD AND THEN GUDURZ SAID   . .   66 SOHRAB RUSTUM   174
        BE COUNSELLD AND RETIRE . . . . 174 MEETING   12
        YES BUT HIS SEED STILL WISER-COUNSELLD   . . . . 344 MEROPE   449
        YES BUT HIS SONS SEED WISER-COUNSELLD   . . . . 344 MEROPE   V 449
        AS THE WELL-COUNSELLD ZEUS OPPRESSD . . . . . . 432 EMPEDOCLES II   102

COUNSELS
        IF PRUDENCE COUNSELS THEE TO GO UNARMD   . . . . 391 MEROPE   1591

COUNT
        COUNT THE HOURS   . . . .   44 QUESTION   14
        WE COUNT THE HOURS THESE DREAMS OF OURS   . . . .   44 QUESTION   15
        WHETHER IT NEEDS THEE COUNT   . . . .   45 IN UTRUMQUE PAR   9

COUNT   (CONTINUED)
```
        NOR DOTH SHE COUNT THIS LIFE A PRICE FOR THAT    • •     98 BALDER DEAD 1      118
        AND NOW I COUNT NOT OF THESE TERMS AS SAFE  • • • •    112 BALDER DEAD 2      268
        HIM I COUNT HIM WELL-STARRD    • • • • •    199 FRAG DEJANEIRA     31
        SOUL THAT WE TAKE MORE COUNT AND CARE    • • • •    315 OBERMANN MORE       V
        AND COUNT ON LIKE IMPUNITY AND RISE  • • • • •    342 MEROPE            374
        AND RIGHTEOUS IF HE FALLS I COUNT HIS FALL  • • •    349 MEROPE            552
        FOR WHOSE HELP DARE I COUNT ON IF NOT THINE    • •    379 MEROPE           1266
        OF ENEMIES AND COUNT THEIR DYING GROANS    • • • •    387 MEROPE           1469
```

COUNTED
```
        THAT THOUSANDS COUNTED EVERY GROAN    • • • • • •    303 GRANDE CHARTR     137
```

COUNTENANCE
```
        AND HELA SET THEREON WITH COUNTENANCE STERN    • •    110 BALDER DEAD 2      178
        AND HELA SAT THEREON WITH COUNTENANCE STERN    • •    110 BALDER DEAD 2    V 178
        COME WITH COUNTENANCE BRIGHT    • • • • • •    217 LORDS MESSENGER    20
        EVEN IN DEATH THAT COUNTENANCE AUSTERE    • • •    403 MEROPE           1970
        AND ON THAT COUNTENANCE BRIGHT  • • • • • • •    446 WESTMIN ABBEY      81
```

COUNTERPANE
```
        AT RANDOM ON THE COUNTERPANE    • • • • • • •    141 TRISTRAM 1        345
```

COUNTEST
```
        THOU COUNTEST ON TO BACK THEE GAINST HIS LORDS    • •    382 MEROPE           1321
```

COUNTING
```
        COUNTING TILL I GREW UP THE LAGGARD YEARS    • • • •    367 MEROPE           1046
```

COUNTLESS
```
        EVERYWHERE COUNTLESS    • • • • • • • •     50 CONSOLATION         7
        AND COUNTLESS BEINGS    • • • • • • • • •     50 CONSOLATION         9
        PASS COUNTLESS MOODS    • • • • • • • •     50 CONSOLATION        10
        HOLDS COUNTLESS TRACTS UNTROD  • • • • • • •    352 MEROPE            628
        OF NATURE WITH HER COUNTLESS SUM    • • • •    450 GEISTS GRAVE       24
        A HEART THAT RECKD NOT OF THE COUNTLESS DEAD    • •    478 CROMWELL          225
```

COUNTRIES
```
        IN A THOUSAND COUNTRIES A THOUSAND    • • • • •    369 MEROPE           1094
```

COUNTRY
```
        CROWDED AND KEEN THE COUNTRY GROWS    • • • • •     56 RESIGNATION       133
        AS IN THE COUNTRY ON A MORN IN JUNE  • • • • •     65 SOHRAB RUSTUM     154
        FAR IN THE COUNTRY WONDERING WHERE HE IS    • • •    114 BALDER DEAD 3      18
        OF THEIR DEAR COUNTRY AND CAN PLAIN DESCRY  • • •    123 BALDER DEAD 3     360
        OF THEIR OWN COUNTRY AND CAN CLEAR DESCRY  • • •    123 BALDER DEAD 3   V 360
        WHICH BORDERS THE SEA-SHORE A COUNTRY PATH  • • •    149 TRISTRAM 3         8
        A COUNTRY FOR HIM KINSFOLK AND A HOME    • • •    195 FRAG ANTIGONE      14
        BUT ONCE YEARS AFTER IN THE COUNTRY-LANES    • •    256 SCHOLAR-GIPSY      41
        BUT RUMOURS HUNG ABOUT THE COUNTRY-SIDE    • • •    256 SCHOLAR-GIPSY      52
        SOME COUNTRY-NOOK WHERE OER THY UNKNOWN GRAVE  • •    259 SCHOLAR-GIPSY     138
        ROAMING THE COUNTRY-SIDE A TRUANT BOY    • • •    261 SCHOLAR-GIPSY     198
        AND WITH THE COUNTRY-FOLK ACQUAINTANCE MADE  • •    263 THYRSIS            33
        HE LOVED EACH SIMPLE JOY THE COUNTRY YIELDS    • •    264 THYRSIS            42
        TO A BOON SOUTHERN COUNTRY HE IS FLED  • • • •    268 THYRSIS           175
        KEPT NOT FOR LONG ITS HAPPY COUNTRY TONE  • • •    269 THYRSIS           222
        TO THE SILENT COUNTRY AND LEAVES    • • • •    283 HAWORTH CHURCH     69
        SHE WILL NOT SEE HER COUNTRY LOSE    • • • •    282 HAWORTH CHURCH      V
        COUNTRY AND PUBLIC CARES  • • • • • • • •    282 HAWORTH CHURCH      V
        ENGLAND MY COUNTRY FOR WE  • • • • • • •    294 HEINES GRAVE       72
        THROUGH THE COOL LOVELY COUNTRY FOLLOWD YOU    • •    407 EMPEDOCLES I 1     45
        IN SUMMER TO ALL COUNTRY-FESTIVALS    • • • •    412 EMPEDOCLES I 2     15
        THE BOORS WITH WHOM HE TALKD THE COUNTRY-SPOTS HE KNEW  426 EMPEDOCLES I 2    416
        NOR DO THEY SEE THEIR COUNTRY NOR THE PLACE    • •    427 EMPEDOCLES I 2    439
        THE SPORTS OF THE COUNTRY-PEOPLE    • • • • •    436 EMPEDOCLES II     251
```

COUNTRYS
```
        HIMSELF HIS SUFFERINGS IN HIS COUNTRYS LOT  • • • •    477 CROMWELL          172
```

COUNTS
```
        COUNTS HIS DAYS SPOIL THE SPOTTED TROUT    • • • •    248 KENSINGTON GARD    20
```

COURAGE
```
        AT MY BOYS YEARS THE COURAGE OF A MAN    • • • •     62 SOHRAB RUSTUM      45
        THY COURAGE OR THY CRAFT AND SPREAD THY FAME    • •     77 SOHRAB RUSTUM     535
        WHAT LOVE COURAGE CHRIST HE IS SO PALE    • • •    145 TRISTRAM 2         80
        HAIL TO THE COURAGE WHICH GAVE  • • • • • •    281 HAWORTH CHURCH     44
        ORDER COURAGE RETURN  • • • • • • • • •    292 RUGBY CHAPEL      201
        AND FOR WHOSE HURT COURAGE IS NOT THE CURE  • • •    429 EMPEDOCLES II      14
        MAINTAIND COURAGE AND FORCE AND IN MYSELF  • • •    438 EMPEDOCLES II     319
        THY FIERY COURAGE STILL WAS STRONG    • • • •    482 COURAGE            20
```

COURAGEOUS
```
        COURAGEOUS FAITHFUL ACTIONS NOBLY DARED    • • • •    333 MEROPE             88
        ALL THAT GAY COURAGEOUS CHEER  • • • • • • •    454 POOR MATTHIAS      61
```

COURRERIE
```
        THE HUTS OF COURRERIE APPEAR  • • • • • • •    299 GRANDE CHARTR      18
```

COURSE
    THEIR GLORIOUS COURSE IN SILENCE PERFECTING   • •   2 QUIET WORK   V   12
    NOT HIS OWN COURSE BUT THAT OF MAN • • • • • •   56 RESIGNATION   147
    AND SHE WILL BID HIM NORTHWARD STEER HIS COURSE • •   99 BALDER DEAD 1   152
    UNARMD INGLORIOUS I ATTEND THE COURSE   • • •   128 BALDER DEAD 3   510
    HER COURSE FOR HOME AT LAST AND BURIAL   • • • •   173 MONICAS PRAYER   7
    HAVE PRAISED THE KEEN UNSCRUPULOUS COURSE • • • •   178 FAREWELL   35
    WE SHALL NOT THEN DENY A COURSE • • • • •   179 FAREWELL   57
    FROM THY REMOTE AND SPHERED COURSE • • • • • •   181 ISOLATION MARG   16
    TO THINGS BY MORTAL COURSE THAT LIVE • • • •   185 TERRACE BERNE   42
    WITH THE GREY MIST MARKING ITS COURSE   • • • •   234 YOUTH OF MAN   84
    IN TRACKING OUT OUR TRUE ORIGINAL COURSE   • • • •   246 BURIED LIFE   50
    THE NAMELESS FEELINGS THAT COURSE THROUGH OUR BREAST   246 BURIED LIFE   62
    BUT THEY COURSE ON FOR EVER UNEXPRESSD • • • •   246 BURIED LIFE   63
    THE PURE ETERNAL COURSE OF LIFE • • • • •   251 WISH   47
    FOR EVER THE COURSE OF THE RIVER OF TIME • • • •   253 FUTURE   59
    TIME MAY RESTORE US IN HIS COURSE • • • • •   272 MEMORIAL VERSES   60
    TIME MAY RESTORE US IN ITS COURSE • • • • •   272 MEMORIAL VERSES V   60
    LAURELS SHE HAD AND A COURSE • • • • • •   283 HAWORTH CHURCH   72
    WHAT IS THE COURSE OF THE LIFE • • • • • •   288 RUGBY CHAPEL   58
    AND GOETHES COURSE FEW SONS OF MEN • • • • •   308 OBERMANN   55
    HAVE A WORSE COURSE TO STEER • • • • • •   308 OBERMANN   64
    CLEAREST THEIR COURSE DISCERN • • • • • •   314 OBERMANN MORE   76
    AND CENTURIES CAME AND RAN THEIR COURSE • • • •   318 OBERMANN MORE   161
    BEST CAN ITS COURSE DISCERN • • • • • •   314 OBERMANN MORE V   76
    PASSIVE PERMITTING THEE WHAT COURSE THOU WILT • •   333 MEROPE   96
    ADVISING US A COURSE WHICH WOULD INDEED • • • •   382 MEROPE   1337
    WE MARK NOT THE WORLDS COURSE BUT WOULD HAVE   419 EMPEDOCLES I 2   221
        IT TAKE OURS
    THE WORLDS COURSE PROVES THE TERMS   • • • • •   419 EMPEDOCLES I 2   222
    A FALSE COURSE FOR THE WORLD AND FOR OURSELVES   419 EMPEDOCLES I 2   226
        FALSE POWERS
    TO RUN THEIR COURSE AND REACH THEIR GOAL   • • • •   450 GEISTS GRAVE   11
    YES ONLY FOUR AND NOT THE COURSE • • • • •   450 GEISTS GRAVE   21
    UPON ITS HEADLONG COURSE WITH SAD PROPHETIC EYE   • •   463 ALARIC AT ROME   24
    NOT THAT HE TOOK THE COURSE TO DIE • • • • •   481 COURAGE   14
    IS WEAKNESS IS A FALTERING COURSE • • • • •   482 COURAGE   26
    WHEN HE IS TIED AND THWARTED FROM HIS COURSE • •   LUCRETIUS 2   3

COURSED
    AND MANY TIMES THAT MORN WE COURSED IN RING   • •   357 MEROPE   793
    TEARS COURSED TEARS HUMAN • • • • • • •   393 MEROPE   1669

COURSER
    DAY DROVE HIS COURSER WITH THE SHINING MANE   • •   105 BALDER DEAD 2   2

COURSES
    MAY THEN MORE NEIGHBOURING COURSES PLY   • • • •   180 FAREWELL   74
    NIGHT AFTER NIGHT YOUR COURSES • • • • • • •   437 EMPEDOCLES II   294

COURT
    STOPPD IN DARKNESS IN THE COURT • • • • •   14 CHURCH BROU 1   42
    AND MOUNTED THEM AND IN VALHALLAS COURT   • • •   105 BALDER DEAD 2   13
    FAMOUS IN ARTHURS COURT OF OLD • • • • •   131 TRISTRAM 1   20
    WHAT LIGHTS IN THE COURT WHAT STEPS ON THE STAIR   •   142 TRISTRAM 1   373
    KEEPS HIS COURT IN TYNTAGIL • • • • • • •   134 TRISTRAM 1 V 134
    THE CASTLE-COURT ALL WET WITH RAIN • • • • •   148 TRISTRAM 2   170
    THE COURT ALL SILENT • • • • • • • •   187 STRAYED REVEL   47
    I SAW THE MULES AND LITTER IN THE COURT   • • • •   407 EMPEDOCLES I 1   41
    IN THE COURT OF GODS IN THE CITY OF MEN   • • • •   430 EMPEDOCLES II   38

COURTEOUS
    AND PRAISE MY FAME AND PROFFER COURTEOUS GIFTS   • •   71 SOHRAB RUSTUM   353
    FOR COURTEOUS ENTERTAINMENT WELCOME WARM   • • • •   356 MEROPE   760
    PRAISED PERHAPS THY COURTEOUS EYE • • • • •   455 POOR MATTHIAS   117
    COURTEOUS-EYED ERECT AND SLIM • • • • • • •   458 POOR MATTHIAS   194

COURTEOUSLY
    BUT COURTEOUSLY DREW BACK AND SPOKE AND SAID   • •   74 SOHRAB RUSTUM   426

COURTESY
    TRISTRAM I PRAY THEE OF THY COURTESY • • • •   133 TRISTRAM 1   99
    BUT PLEDGE ME IN IT FIRST FOR COURTESY   • • • •   133 TRISTRAM 1   101
    SIR TRISTRAM OF THY COURTESY • • • • • •   135 TRISTRAM 1   145
    AND PLEDGE ME IN IT FIRST FOR COURTESY   • • • •   133 TRISTRAM 1 V 101

COURTIERS
    SILKEN COURTIERS WHISPERING HONIED NOTHINGS   • •   144 TRISTRAM 2   47

COURTLY
    SOMETHING ALTERD IN THY COURTLY TONE • • • •   143 TRISTRAM 2   34
    COURTLY LIFE IS LIGHT AND CANNOT REACH IT • • • •   143 TRISTRAM 2   39
    WHAT THOU THINKST MEN SPEAK IN COURTLY CHAMBERS   • •   143 TRISTRAM 2   41
    OF COURTLY SPEECH ABRUPTLY DIED • • • • •   146 TRISTRAM 2   119

COURTS
    BEHOLD THE PAVEMENT OF THE COURTS OF HEAVEN   • •   18 CHURCH BROU 3   31
    ALTERD TRISTRAM NOT IN COURTS BELIEVE ME   • • • •   143 TRISTRAM 2   37
    THE SILENT COURTS WHERE NIGHT AND DAY • • • •   300 GRANDE CHARTR   31
    SHE TORE HER BOOKS SHE SHUT HER COURTS   • • • •   316 OBERMANN MORE   131
    AND IN THY COURTS HIS SHINING FREIGHT UNROLLD   • •   446 WESTMIN ABBEY   76

COUSINS
  THY SPARTAN COUSINS PROCLES AND HIS BROTHER   • •   384 MEROPE   1393
  HIS ARGIVE OR HIS SPARTAN COUSINS AID   • • • •   388 MEROPE   1499

COVE
  BEACHES THE PINNACE IN A DARKENING COVE   • • • •   69 SOHRAB RUSTUM   V 288

COVERD
  MY LORD HAD COVERD UP HIS FACE • • • • • • • • •   91 SICK KING BOKH   125

COVERING
  HIS COVERING SHIELD AND THE SPEAR PIERCED HIS SIDE   76 SOHRAB RUSTUM   520
  ALL—COVERING DARKNESS O KING   • • • • • • • •   372 MEROPE   1141

COVERLET
  SCARCELY MOVES THE COVERLET   • • • • • • • • •   141 TRISTRAM 1   343

COVERTS
  OUT OF THEIR GLOSSY COVERTS BUT WHEN NOW   • • • •   150 TRISTRAM 3   31
  FROM THE DEWY FOREST—COVERTS   • • • • • • • •   193 STRAYED REVEL   263
  AND BEECHEN COVERTS AND COPSE • • • • • • • •   297 HEINES GRAVE   181
  TO DRAW THE COVERTS ON CYLLENES SIDE • • • • • •   356 MEROPE   750

COW
  LOOK AS IN SOME BOORS YARD A SWEET—BREATHD COW   • • 123 BALDER DEAD 3   340
  TILL THE ROUGH COW—HERDS DRIVE THEM PAST   • • • •   413 EMPEDOCLES I 2   40

COWARD
  INSPIRE THIS COWARD HEART THIS FLAGGING ARM   • •   368 MEROPE   1066
  THOSE LINGERING HOPES OF COWARD HEARTS THAT STILL   475 CROMWELL   107
  IF LIKE A COWARD I SKULKD BEHIND APART FROM THE BATTLE   HOMER TRANS   16

COWARDS
  THE OLD THE COWARDS AND THE WEAK ARE THERE • • • •   104 BALDER DEAD 1   324
  COWARDS WHO WERE IN SLOUGHS INTERRD ALIVE   • • • •   109 BALDER DEAD 2   172
  COWARDS TO CONQUER AND THE WEAK TO DIE   • • • •   467 ALARIC AT ROME   140

COWERING
  THE COWERING MERCHANTS IN LONG ROBES   • • • • • •   191 STRAYED REVEL   191

COWHERDS
  BUT AS WHEN COWHERDS IN OCTOBER DRIVE   • • • •   107 BALDER DEAD 2   91

COWL
  IS BURIED IN HIS COWL ONCE MORE   • • • • • • •   300 GRANDE CHARTR   44

COWLD
  COWLD FORMS BRUSH BY IN GLEAMING WHITE   • • • •   300 GRANDE CHARTR   36
  TAKE ME COWLD FORMS AND FENCE ME ROUND   • • • •   302 GRANDE CHARTR   93

COWSLIPS
  HER FOOT THE CUMNER COWSLIPS NEVER STIRRD   • • • •   265 THYRSIS   99
  WHERE THICK THE COWSLIPS GREW AND FAR DESCRIED   • • 266 THYRSIS   114
  HER FOOT THE CUMNOR COWSLIPS NEVER STIRRD   • • • •   265 THYRSIS   V 99

COY
  TO ONE DEMAND ALONE ARE COY   • • • • • • • •   203 EUPHROSYNE   22

CRACKLED
  AND THE PILE CRACKLED AND BETWEEN THE LOGS • • • •   118 BALDER DEAD 3   187

CRACKLING
  WENT STRAINING THROUGH THE CRACKLING BRUSHWOOD DOWN   106 BALDER DEAD 2   62
  THE CRACKLING HUSK—HEAPS BURN AS IF • • • • • •   312 OBERMANN MORE   11
  THEIR CRACKLING HUSK—HEAPS BURN AS IF   • • • •   312 OBERMANN MORE   V 11

CRADLE
  FROM THE CRADLE TO THE GRAVE   • • • • • • • •   38 STAGIRIUS   4
  FROM THE CRADLE TO THE GRAVE   • • • • • • • •   40 STAGIRIUS   61
  IN HIS HIGH MOUNTAIN—CRADLE IN PAMERE   • • • • •   87 SOHRAB RUSTUM   887
  BUT IN MY HELPLESS CRADLE I   • • • • • • • •   249 KENSINGTON GARD   23
  BRIGHT IN THY CRADLE SMILE   • • • • • • • •   285 HAWORTH CHURCH   109
  RUSTLED ROUND HIS CRADLE • • • • • • • • •   392 MEROPE   1620

CRADLED
  THE BLUE HAZE—CRADLED MOUNTAINS SPREAD AWAY   • •   242 SUMMER NIGHT   21

CRAFT
  THY COURAGE OR THY CRAFT AND SPREAD THY FAME   • •   77 SOHRAB RUSTUM   535
  FORGOT HIS CRAFT AND HIS BEST WITS TOOK FLIGHT • •   155 TRISTRAM 3   182
  IMMERSED IN SERIOUS STATE—CRAFT IS THE KING   • •   387 MEROPE   1489
  OF RICH SOIL CHOSEN BY CRAFT   • • • • • • • •   399 MEROPE   1848
  THEIR CRAFT THE FISHERS LEAVE • • • • • • • •   444 WESTMIN ABBEY   12

CRAG
  MADE FAST TO THE BORED CRAG BY WILE NOT STRENGTH • • 111 BALDER DEAD 2   215
  RARE STRAGGLING HUNTERS FOILD BY BRAKE AND CRAG • • 357 MEROPE   798
  OF CRAG—PERCHD NONACRIS • • • • • • • • • •   392 MEROPE   1650

CRAGGY
  UPON THE CRAGGY ISLE OF A HILL—LAKE • • • • • •   78 SOHRAB RUSTUM   558

CRAGGY   (CONTINUED)
        TO PHENEOS WITH ITS CRAGGY CITADEL   • • • • • •   356 MEROPE   745

CRAGS
        UNDER THE TOWERING TRACHIS CRAGS   • • • • • •   198 FRAG ANTIGONE   99
        OR HEAR MID CIRCLING CRAGS THE IMPATIENT CRY   • •   472 CROMWELL   25

CRANES
        IN MARCHING ORDER SPREAD OF LONG-NECKD CRANES   • •   64 SOHRAB RUSTUM   112

CRASH
        HARK A SHOUT A CRASH A GROAN   • • • • • • • •   13 CHURCH BROU 1   24
        A PROP GAVE WAY CRASH FELL A PLATFORM LO   • • • •   166 AUSTERITY POET   8
        AND THEN THAT MIGHTIEST CRASH THAT GIANT FALL   • •   463 ALARIC AT ROME   41

CRASHD
        GREW DEEPER THUNDER CRASHD ALONG THE SKY   • • • •   76 SOHRAB RUSTUM   V 500

CRASHES
        THUNDER CRASHES FROM ROCK   • • • • • • • •   289 RUGBY CHAPEL   91

CRASHING
        OF HEWING AXES CRASHING TREES SUCH BLOWS   • • • •   75 SOHRAB RUSTUM   478
        OF CRASHING FALLS FOR WITH HIS HAMMER THOR   • • • •   106 BALDER DEAD 2   55
        DRIVE CRASHING THROUGH THEIR BONES THEY FEEL   • •   192 STRAYED REVEL   229
        GAINST THICK-CRASHING INSANE   • • • • • • • •   293 HEINES GRAVE   34

CRAVE
        WHAT CAN HE BETTER CRAVE THAN THEN TO DIE   • • • •   448 WESTMIN ABBEY   V 145

CRAVEN
        VALIANT OR CRAVEN YOUNG OR OLD TO ME   • • • • • •   68 SOHRAB RUSTUM   253
        A CRAVEN MOB BUT A DEVOURING FIRE   • • • • • •   383 MEROPE   1361

CRAVES
        THE LIFE HE CRAVES IF NOT IN VAIN   • • • • • •   58 RESIGNATION   196

CRAWL
        TILL THEY TOO FADE LIKE GRASS THEY CRAWL   • • • •   193 STRAYED REVEL   242

CRAWLD
        BUT SOHRAB CRAWLD TO WHERE HE LAY AND CAST   • • • •   81 SOHRAB RUSTUM   694

CRAWLS
        CRAWLS UP ITS ROCKY STAIR   • • • • • • • •   306 OBERMANN   2

CRAZED
        THE WANT WHICH CRAZED OUR BRAIN   • • • • • •   323 OBERMANN MORE   V 314
        NOR THINK THE GODS WERE CRAZED   • • • • • • • •   417 EMPEDOCLES I 2   164

CREAMING
        THE RED CREAMING LIQUOR   • • • • • • • • • • •   187 STRAYED REVEL   57

CREATING
        A PLEASURE IN CREATING   • • • • • • • • • • •   228 CAUTION POETS   2

CREATION
        OF NEW CREATION EVERMORE   • • • • • • • • • •   450 GEISTS GRAVE   26

CREATURE
        TO ITS OWN IMPULSE EVERY CREATURE STIRS   • • • •   8 RELIGIOUS ISOL   13
        THAT MARS THY CONSCIENCE   • • • • • • • • •   39 STAGIRIUS   32
        HIM THAT KIND CREATURE FOUND AND REARD AND LOVED • •   81 SOHRAB RUSTUM   682
        THIS LOST SEA-CREATURE SAVED   • • • • • • • •   160 NECKAN   56
        FOR THAN MAN INDEED THERE BREATHES NO WRETCHEDER   HOMER TRANS   12
                CREATURE

CREATURES
        POINTING TO EARTHS CAREWORN CREATURES   • • • • •   28 NEW SIRENS   61
        OF UNSPHERED DISCROWNED CREATURES   • • • • • •   34 NEW SIRENS   249
        POINTING TO SOME WORLD-WORN CREATURES   • • • • •   28 NEW SIRENS   V 61

CREDIT
     NOT THE BLACK CREDIT OF HIS MURDERER   • • • • • •   365 MEROPE   991

CREDULOUS
        LONG SINCE WITH CREDULOUS ZEAL   • • • • • • • •   46 WORLD QUIETIST   12
        BUT CREDULOUS OF FABLES AS A GIRL   • • • • • •   411 EMPEDOCLES I 1   160
        THE CREDULOUS COMPLEXION OF THY DREAMS   • • • • •   RUDE ORATOR   12
        THE CREDULOUS COMPLEXION OF THY WOE   • • • • • •   RUDE ORATOR   V 12

CREED
        CLEAR PRESCRIBED WITHOUT YOUR CREED   • • • • • •   215 PIS-ALLER   8
        VOICE TO ITS CREED ERE THE CREED   • • • • • •   281 HAWORTH CHURCH   45
        VOICE TO ITS CREED ERE THE CREED   • • • • • •   281 HAWORTH CHURCH   45

CREEDS
        CREEDS PASS RITES CHANGE NO ALTAR STANDETH WHOLE • •   173 MONICAS PRAYER   12
        LIGHT HALF-BELIEVERS OF OUR CASUAL CREEDS   • • •   260 SCHOLAR-GIPSY   172
        VAGUE HALF-BELIEVERS OF OUR CASUAL CREEDS   • • •   260 SCHOLAR-GIPSY V 172
        HIS ALL TOO HUMAN CREEDS AND SCAN   • • • • • •   319 OBERMANN MORE   187

CREEDS   (CONTINUED)
    YOUR CREEDS ARE DEAD YOUR RITES ARE DEAD . . . . 320 OBERMANN MORE   229

CREEK
    HE KNOWS EACH FRITH AND EVERY ROCKY CREEK . . . . 123 BALDER DEAD 3   326

CREEKS
    UP THE CREEKS WE WILL HIE   . . . . 165 FORSAKEN MERM   133

CREEP
    AND BURNING DUST AGAIN I CREEP . . . . 90 SICK KING BOKH   75
    CREEP INTO THY NARROW BED   . . . . 215 LAST WORD   1
    CREEP AND LET NO MORE BE SAID   . . . . 215 LAST WORD   2
    PALE PINK CONVOLVULUS IN TENDRILS CREEP   . . . 255 SCHOLAR-GIPSY   25
    PALE BLUE CONVOLVULUS IN TENDRILS CREEP   . . . 255 SCHOLAR-GIPSY   V 25

CREEPERS
    LIFTING THE COOL-HAIRD CREEPERS STEALTHILY . . . 262 SCHOLAR-GIPSY   234

CREEPING
    FORTH AT NOON HAD LURED ME CREEPING   . . . . . . 26 NEW SIRENS   3
    OFT AT NOON HAVE LURED ME CREEPING   . . . . . . 26 NEW SIRENS   V   3
    LATE AT EVE HAD LURED ME CREEPING   . . . . . . 26 NEW SIRENS   V   3
    WITH LARGE-LEAVED LOW-CREEPING MELON-PLANTS . . 190 STRAYED REVEL   155

CREEPS
    WHERE THE DEEP FOREST STREAM CREEPS SLOW   . . . 148 TRISTRAM 2   V
    CREEPS OVER IT FROM THE TILLD FIELDS BEHIND   . . 149 TRISTRAM 3   9
    CREEPS THICKLY GROWS NOT HERE BUT THE PALE GRASS . . 150 TRISTRAM 3   15
    THROUGH WHOSE GREEN BOUGHS THE GOLDEN SUNSHINE CREEPS 154 TRISTRAM 3   157
    CREEPS OVER IT FROM THE TILLD LAND BEHIND . . .   TRISTRAM 3   V   9
    CREEPS THICKLY GROWS NOT HERE   . . . .   TRISTRAM 3   V 15
    THE WHITE FOG CREEPS FROM BUSH TO BUSH ABOUT . . 267 THYRSIS   162
    CREEPS OER THE SUNSHINE A BREEZE   . . . . . . 293 HEINES GRAVE   39

CREON
    NO NO OLD MEN CREON I CURSE NOT   . . . . . . 196 FRAG ANTIGONE   45
    ONE THAN CREON CRUELLER FAR   . . . . 196 FRAG ANTIGONE   47

CREONS
    AGAINST CREONS LAW POLYNICES   . . . . 196 FRAG ANTIGONE   41

CREPT
    CREPT FROM THE OXUS SOON A HUM AROSE . . . . . . 86 SOHRAB RUSTUM   868

CRESPHONTES
    SON OF CRESPHONTES WE HAVE REACHD THE GOAL . . . 330 MEROPE   1
    THE KING CRESPHONTES THY GREAT HUSBAND FALL . . 333 MEROPE   118
    NOT OF HIM OF CRESPHONTES THOU SHAREDST THE LOT . 345 MEROPE   471
    ARGOS A JUGGLE TO CRESPHONTES GAVE   . . . . . . 389 MEROPE   1551
    CRESPHONTES IN MESSENIA TEMENUS   . . . . . . 389 MEROPE   1556
    SON OF CRESPHONTES PAST WHAT PERILS   . . . . . . 405 MEROPE   2021

CRESSES
    FOR CRESSES FROM THE RILLS   . . . . 258 SCHOLAR-GIPSY   106

CREST
    AND REARD HIM A BRIGHT BAY WITH LOFTY CREST . . 69 SOHRAB RUSTUM   276
    HIS STATELY CREST AND DIMMD HIS GLITTERING ARMS . . 74 SOHRAB RUSTUM   454
    NOR CLOVE ITS STEEL QUITE THROUGH BUT ALL THE CREST 76 SOHRAB RUSTUM   496
    AND TRAIND HIM A BRIGHT BAY WITH LOFTY CREST . . 69 SOHRAB RUSTUM   V 276
    AND TO EACH BULRUSH-CREST A SWALLOW HANGS . . . 109 BALDER DEAD 2   160
    STANDS ON THE CREST OF THE HILL   . . . . . . 283 HAWORTH CHURCH   63
    VAINLY KISS HIS GOLDEN CREST   . . . . 452 POOR MATTHIAS   10
    TO MARK WITH SHIVERD CREST THE REELING WAVE . . 472 CROMWELL   23

CRESTED
    THE GOLDEN-CRESTED COCK BEGAN TO CROW . . . . . 105 BALDER DEAD 2   4
    THE GOLDEN-CRESTED COCK SHALL SOUND ALARM . . . 127 BALDER DEAD 3   496
    THE TALL CRESTED WATER-REEDS   . . . . 434 EMPEDOCLES II   174

CRESTS
    IS SHINING ON THE BRILLIANT MOUNTAIN-CRESTS . . 406 EMPEDOCLES I 1   10

CRETE
    OF THE MIGHTY MOTHER OR CRETE   . . . . 230 YOUTH OF NATURE   77

CREVICD
    PRISONING IN HIS CREVICD STONES   . . . . . .   PILLARS UNIVERS   11

CREW
    BUT NOW HE CREW AT DAWN A CHEERFUL NOTE   . . . 105 BALDER DEAD 2   8
    BEHIND FLOCKD WRANGLING UP A PITEOUS CREW . . . 109 BALDER DEAD 2   170
    WHEREAT HE ANSWERD THAT THE GIPSY-CREW   . . . 256 SCHOLAR-GIPSY   44
    WITH PLACE WITH HONOUR AND A FLATTERING CREW . . 268 THYRSIS   204
    SINCE THAT STRANGE CREW DID RIDE AFLOAT   . . . 480 HAYSWATER BOAT   36

CRIED
    SO SPAKE HE AND FEROOD STOOD FORTH AND CRIED . . 66 SOHRAB RUSTUM   184
    SURELY MY HEART CRIED OUT THAT IT WAS THOU . . . 82 SOHRAB RUSTUM   711

CRIED   (CONTINUED)
        AND FELL AT THE KINGS FEET AND CRIED . . . . .   88 SICK KING BOKH   35
        KNEELD DOWN AND CRIED NOT NEITHER RAN   . . . .   91 SICK KING BOKH   120
        LIKE A YOUNG CHILD HAST CRIED THYSELF TO SLEEP . . 103 BALDER DEAD 1   291
        HIS MESSENGER AND HE STOOD FORTH AND CRIED . . . . 114 BALDER DEAD 3   32
        O RUTH OF GOD THE PRIEST CRIED OUT   . . . . .   160 NECKAN   55
        OF THAT UNPITYING PHRYGIAN SECT WHICH CRIED   . .   172 GOOD SHEPHERD   3
        THE OLD LAW THEY CRIED IS WHOLLY COME TO NOUGHT . . 237 PROGRESS   3
        WHICH HAS NOT CRIED TO SUNK SELF-WEARY MAN . . .   238 PROGRESS   43
        AH ONCE MORE I CRIED YE STARS YE WATERS   . . . .   240 SELF-DEPENDENCE   9
        AND IS IT THOU HE CRIED SO LONG   . . . . .   314 OBERMANN MORE   69
        POOR WORLD SHE CRIED SO DEEP ACCURST   . . . . .   316 OBERMANN MORE   117
        AND OH WE CRIED THAT ON THIS CORSE   . . . . .   319 OBERMANN MORE   197
        YE LIVE I CRIED YE WORK AND PLAN   . . . . .   320 OBERMANN MORE   215
        AND CRIED O ZEUS LET WHAT BLOOD-GUILTINESS . . . . 402 MEROPE   1915

CRIES
        BEHOLD SHE CRIES SO MANY RAGES LULLD . . . . . .   37 WORLDS TRIUMPHS   5
        CRIES OUT MOST EARNESTLY O KING   . . . . . .   89 SICK KING BOKH   52
        UP TO ITS GOLDEN ROOF WITH SOBS AND CRIES . . . .   95 BALDER DEAD 1   12
        WITH WOMENS TEARS AND WEAK COMPLAINING CRIES   . .   96 BALDER DEAD 1   32
        WITH WOMANS TEARS AND WEAK COMPLAINING CRIES   . .   96 BALDER DEAD 1   V   32
        WITH SHRILL AND DISMAL CRIES THAT BIRD SHALL CROW   105 BALDER DEAD 2   6
        AND WHAT CRIES CUPID WILL SAVE US   . . . . . .   214 NEW ROME   9
        FILL WITH THEIR CRIES   . . . .   218 BACCHANALIA 1   39
        LURE NOT THEIR CRIES   . . . .   219 BACCHANALIA 1   45
        FILL WITH THEIR CRIES   . . . .   220 BACCHANALIA 2   44
        AH CRIES MY FRIEND BUT WHO HATH TAUGHT   . . .   221 EPILOG LAOCOON   8
        AH CHILD SHE CRIES THAT STRIFE DIVINE   . . .   241 MORALITY   23
        HOW THICK THE TREMULOUS SHEEP-CRIES COME   . . .   248 KENSINGTON GARD   8
        HOW STRANGE THE TREMULOUS SHEEP-CRIES COME . . .   KENSINGTON GARD   V 8
        WITH A THOUSAND CRIES IS ITS STREAM   . . . . .   253 FUTURE   54
        ARE CONFUSED AS THE CRIES WHICH WE HEAR   . . .   253 FUTURE   56
        WITH DISTANT CRIES OF REAPERS IN THE CORN . . .   255 SCHOLAR-GIPSY   19
        WHERE CRIES ARE RISING EVER NEW   . . . . .   277 SOUTHERN NIGHT   62
        STRIKE LEFTWARD CRIES OUR GUIDE AND HIGHER . . .   300 GRANDE CHARTR   19
        WITH PENITENTIAL CRIES THEY KNEEL   . . . . .   300 GRANDE CHARTR   39
        FOR THE WORLD CRIES YOUR FAITH IS NOW   . . . .   302 GRANDE CHARTR   97
        LAUGHTER AND CRIES THOSE NOTES BETWEEN   . . .   305 GRANDE CHARTR   186
        THE GLOW HE CRIES THE THRILL OF LIFE . . . . .   309 OBERMANN   97
        WAR-CRIES TO FACTION YEAR BY YEAR RENEWD   . . .   333 MEROPE   92
        AND WHAT I COULD I DID TO CALL BY CRIES   . . .   358 MEROPE   835
        TO ARMED WARRIORS I HEARD VENGEFUL CRIES   . . .   402 MEROPE   1940
        AT HIS MASTERS PITEOUS CRIES   . . . .   434 EMPEDOCLES II   186
        ERE I HEAR THY CRIES AND THY CAPTIVITY TOLD OF . .   HOMER TRANS   38

CRIME
        THE PRODIGY OF FULL-BLOWN CRIME AMONG   . . . .   6 GEO CRUIKSHANK   3
        I WILL UNFOLD MY SENTENCE AND MY CRIME   . . . .   9 MYCERINUS   7
        MY CRIME THAT RAPT IN REVERENTIAL AWE   . . . .   9 MYCERINUS   8
        ON EARTH MY CRIME MY DEATH THEY KNEW . . . . .   157 SAINT BRANDAN   26
        YET NOT FOR THIS ELSE MIGHT THY CRIME IN PART   . . 339 MEROPE   314
        WERE BAR AND THIS TOO WAS THEIR FATHERS CRIME   . . 339 MEROPE   326
        NO THE AVENGING GODS WHO PUNISH CRIME   . . . .   341 MEROPE   359
        THOU KNOWST NOT WHOM THOU STRIKST I KNOW HIS CRIME 374 MEROPE   1199
        TO EFFACE IN ME THE MEMORY OF HIS CRIME   . . . .   387 MEROPE   1478
        THY CRIME THAT WERE ENOUGH TO MAKE ONE FEAR . .   396 MEROPE   1767
        SUCCESS OF CRIME   . . . .   398 MEROPE   1797
        AND YEARS OF CRIME AND NOTHINGNESS AND GLOOM . .   463 ALARIC AT ROME   40

CRIMES
        THOU TOO WHEN THOU AGAINST MY CRIMES WOULDST CRY . . 38 WORLDS TRIUMPHS   9
        THUS THOU WHEN THOU AGAINST MY CRIMES WOULDST CRY   38 WORLDS TRIUMPHS   V 9
        A LONG SUCCESSION OF CRIMES   . . . .   379 MEROPE   1252
        BY THEIR OWN CRIMES A LESSON TO ALL EYES   . . .   462 ALARIC AT ROME   11

CRIMSON
        THE CRIMSON TORRENT RAN DIM NOW AND SOILD . . . .   86 SOHRAB RUSTUM   843
        THE CRIMSON TORRENT POURD DIM NOW AND SOILD   . .   86 SOHRAB RUSTUM   V 843

CRINGE
        BLUSTER OR CRINGE AND MAKE LIFE   . . . . . . 290 RUGBY CHAPEL   157

CRISP
        TO HUNT THE BOAR IN THE CRISP WOODS TILL EVE   . .   18 CHURCH BROU 3   11
        CRISP EVERLASTING-FLOWERS   . . . .   292 HEINES GRAVE   11
        AND CRISP THYME TUFTED   . . . .   392 MEROPE   1643

CRISPS
        NOW THE AUTUMN CRISPS THE FOREST   . . . . . .   13 CHURCH BROU 1   15

CRITIAS
        WHY YOU SAY CRITIAS BE DEBATING STILL   . . . .   46 WORLD QUIETIST   3
        CRITIAS LONG SINCE I KNOW   . . . .   46 WORLD QUIETIST   9

CRITICS
        THE FAMOUS CRITICS JUDGED IT ALL   . . . . . .   219 BACCHANALIA 2   9
        CRITICS NEW RULES . . . .   220 BACCHANALIA 2   40

CROCUS
```
        WITH RAIN WHERE THICK THE CROCUS BLOWS      •  •  •  •   299 GRANDE CHARTR        2
        WITH THE PALE CROCUS STARRD    •  •  •  •  •  •  •      310 OBERMANN            118
        I WATCHD THE CROCUS FADE AND FLOWER  •  •  •  •  •  •   321 OBERMANN MORE       255
```

CROFT
```
        ORCHARD AND CROFT AND FULL-STORED GRANGE    •  •  •  •   313 OBERMANN MORE        27
```

CROFTS
```
        VINEYARDS AND CROFTS AND PASTURES BRIGHT WITH SUN      113 BALDER DEAD 2        300
```

CROON
```
        O FOR THE CROON PATHETIC SWEET  •  •  •  •  •  •  •  •   459 KAISER DEAD          11
```

CROPPD
```
        NOR THE CROPPD HERBAGE SHOOT ANOTHER HEAD   •  •  •  •   255 SCHOLAR-GIPSY         5
        NOR THE CROPPD GRASSES SHOOT ANOTHER HEAD   •  •  •  •   255 SCHOLAR-GIPSY    V    5
```

CROSS
```
        SCARFD WITH THE CROSS WHO WATCHD THE MILES  •  •  •  •    52 RESIGNATION          5
        CROSS UNDERNEATH THE INDIAN CAUCASUS   •  •  •  •        65 SOHRAB RUSTUM       161
        LET THEM ALL CROSS THE OXUS BACK IN PEACE   •  •  •  •    84 SOHRAB RUSTUM       782
        LET THEM ALL CROSS THE OXUS BACK IN PEACE   •  •  •  •    85 SOHRAB RUSTUM       807
        UPON MY BRIDGE AND WHEN THEY CROSS I KNOW   •  •  •  •   108 BALDER DEAD 2       121
        ON AUTUMN-DAYS BEFORE THEY CROSS THE SEA    •  •  •  •   109 BALDER DEAD 2       159
        HOW DIDST THOU CROSS THE BRIDGE OER GIALLS STREAM       110 BALDER DEAD 2       183
        SO THE GODS CROSS WAS BITTERER FOR THEIR JOY   •  •     124 BALDER DEAD 3       368
        AND CROSS THE BRIDGE OF HEAVEN WITH LOK FOR GUIDE       127 BALDER DEAD 3       476
        AND SOUGHT A PRIEST TO SIGN THE CROSS    •  •  •  •     160 NECKAN               39
        WHO CROSS TO THE HILL-SIDE   •  •  •  •  •  •  •        175 PARTING               5
        TO CROSS THE STEEP ISMENIAN GLEN    •  •  •  •  •       197 FRAG ANTIGONE        86
        LEAVE THEN THE CROSS AS YE HAVE LEFT CARVED GODS  •  •  237 PROGRESS             27
        TRADE-WINDS WHICH CROSS IT FROM ETERNITY   •  •  •  •   243 SUMMER NIGHT         58
        TRADE-WINDS THAT CROSS IT FROM ETERNITY    •  •  •  •   243 SUMMER NIGHT     V   58
        SOMETIMES A CHILD WILL CROSS THE GLADE     •  •  •  •   248 KENSINGTON GARD       9
        CROSS AND RECROSS THE STRIPS OF MOON-BLANCHD GREEN     255 SCHOLAR-GIPSY         9
        OR CROSS A STILE INTO THE PUBLIC WAY  •  •  •  •  •     257 SCHOLAR-GIPSY        85
        AND THY CLEAR AIMS BE CROSS AND SHIFTING MADE   •  •   261 SCHOLAR-GIPSY       228
        AND CROSS THE UNPERMITTED FERRYS FLOW      •  •  •  •   265 THYRSIS              85
        QUICK LET ME FLY AND CROSS    •  •  •  •  •  •  •       267 THYRSIS             156
        ROCK TO ITS IRON CROSS   •  •  •  •  •  •  •  •  •      298 HEINES GRAVE        188
        ONCE MORE THOU CLINGST TO THE CROSS   •  •  •  •  •     298 HEINES GRAVE        189
        THEN CROSS THE SWARD AND REACH THAT GATE   •  •  •  •   300 GRANDE CHARTR        28
        UPON HIS CROSS WITH HEAD SUNK LOW    •  •  •  •  •      317 OBERMANN MORE       155
        NOW IN THE WOODS FAR DOWN I SAW THEM CROSS  •  •  •     357 MEROPE              801
        STRUGGLING IN VAIN TO CROSS IT SWEPT THEM ON    •  •   358 MEROPE              825
        THOU ART AS CROSS AS SOURD AS HIMSELF      •  •  •  •   411 EMPEDOCLES I 1      141
        TO CROSS THE SPARKLING SHALLOWS THERE      •  •  •     413 EMPEDOCLES I 2       37
        CROSS HIS LONE PATH OR SHARE HIS PILGRIMAGE     •  •   476 CROMWELL            162
        SIGNS THE CROSS AND ANSWERS SURELY    •  •  •  •  •         META CLOISTER       39
```

CROSSD
```
        AND CROSSD THE CAMP WHICH LAY BEHIND AND REACHD  •  •   66 SOHRAB RUSTUM        190
        SO FOLLOWD RUSTUM LEFT HIS TENTS AND CROSSD     •  •   69 SOHRAB RUSTUM        280
        AND OXUS CURDLED AS IT CROSSD HIS STREAM   •  •  •  •   76 SOHRAB RUSTUM        508
        SO FOLLOWD RUSTUM ISSUED FORTH AND CROSSD  •  •  •  •   69 SOHRAB RUSTUM    V  280
        SAY THEN IF HE HATH CROSSD THY BRIDGE OR NO     •  •  108 BALDER DEAD 2       117
        AND DOWN TO OCEAN GROPED AND CROSSD THE ICE     •  •  124 BALDER DEAD 3       376
        SOME UNCONQUERD ARE CROSSD   •  •  •  •  •  •  •  •    216 LORDS MESSENGER      16
        OTHERS THE BRAVEST ARE CROSSD   •  •  •  •  •  •  •    216 LORDS MESSENGER  V   16
        THE BRIDGE IS CROSSD AND SLOW WE RIDE      •  •  •  •  299 GRANDE CHARTR         5
        THE NOON IS HOT WHEN WE HAVE CROSSD THE STREAM  •  •  412 EMPEDOCLES I 2        1
        I CROSSD ST GEORGES HILL TO-DAY     •  •  •  •  •  •  484 ROME-SICKNESS        13
```

CROSSES
```
        THE BROWN THRUSH CROSSES OVERHEAD     •  •  •  •  •  •      KENSINGTON GARD  V  11
```

CROSSING
```
        CROSSING THE STREAM THE KINE ARE SEEN      •  •  •  •    16 CHURCH BROU 2        10
        CROSSING THE STREAM IN SUMMER SCRAPES THE LAND  •  •    61 SOHRAB RUSTUM        19
        CROSSING SO HIGH THAT AS THEY MOUNT THEY PASS   •  •    66 SOHRAB RUSTUM       163
        CROSSING THE STREAM IN SUMMER MEETS THE LAND    •  •    61 SOHRAB RUSTUM    V   19
        I SEE HER FORM GLIDE THROUGH THE CROSSING SPEARS   •  138 TRISTRAM 1          241
        CROSSING THE STRIPLING THAMES AT BAB-LOCK-HITHE    •  257 SCHOLAR-GIPSY        74
        CROSSING THE FROZEN LAKE APPEARS    •  •  •  •  •  •   451 GEISTS GRAVE         51
```

CROUCH
```
        IN DARK KNOTS CROUCH ROUND THE WILD FLAME  •  •  •  •    55 RESIGNATION        118
        CROUCH IN THE WOOD FIRST TILL THE MULES HAVE PASSD    408 EMPEDOCLES I 1       50
        CROUCH IN THE BRUSHWOOD TILL THE MULES HAVE PASSD     411 EMPEDOCLES I 1      166
```

CROUCHD
```
        CROUCHD ON HIS SADDLE WHILE THE SUN   •  •  •  •  •  •   52 RESIGNATION         10
        CROUCHD ON HIS SADDLE WHEN THE SUN    •  •  •  •  •  •   52 RESIGNATION     V   10
        CROUCHD ON THE PAVEMENT CLOSE BY BELGRAVE SQUARE   •  169 WEST LONDON          1
```

CROW
```
        AT COCK-CROW ON A STARLIT WINTERS MORN     •  •  •  •   70 SOHRAB RUSTUM       305
        THE GOLDEN-CRESTED COCK BEGAN TO CROW      •  •  •  •  105 BALDER DEAD 2        4
        WITH SHRILL AND DISMAL CRIES THAT BIRD SHALL CROW     105 BALDER DEAD 2        6
```

CROWD
    THEY PASS HE MINGLED WITH THE CROWD . . . . . .   57 RESIGNATION   162
    CROWD AS WE WILL ITS NEUTRAL SPACE . . . . . .   59 RESIGNATION   258
    CROWD AS WE WILL ITS NEUTRAL ROOM . . . . . .   59 RESIGNATION   V 258
    AND AS THE SWALLOWS CROWD THE BULRUSH-BEDS . . . . 109 BALDER DEAD 2   157
    HIS THOUGHT MUST FOLLOW THROUGH THE CROWD . . . . 225 EPILOG LAOCOON   156
    THAT CITIES WILL CROWD TO ITS EDGE . . . . . .   253 FUTURE   60
    ECHOED HER BACK BY THE CROWD . . . . . .   281 HAWORTH CHURCH   43
    NOT WITH THE CROWD TO BE SPENT . . . . . .   288 RUGBY CHAPEL   75
    NOT LIKE THE MEN OF THE CROWD . . . .   290 RUGBY CHAPEL   155
    YES THE CROWD MUTTERS THAT REMORSEFUL FEAR . . . 333 MEROPE   97
    FROM THE ALTAR OF ZEUS FROM THE CROWD CAME A WAIL 346 MEROPE   489

CROWDED
    CROWDED AND KEEN THE COUNTRY GROWS . . . . . .   56 RESIGNATION   133
    SOME MORN AT MARKET IN A CROWDED TOWN . . . .   114 BALDER DEAD 3   9
    ONE MORN AT MARKET IN A CROWDED TOWN . . . . .   114 BALDER DEAD 3   V 9
    AND A GLANCE WHICH OVER THE CROWDED FLOOR . . .   146 TRISTRAM 2   120
    AND A GLANCE WHICH OVER THE CROWDED FLOOR . . .   146 TRISTRAM 2   V 120
    OF COMMON-LIFE WHERE CROWDED UP PELL-MELL . . .   168 WORLDLY PLACE   4
    BUT OFTEN IN THE WORLDS MOST CROWDED STREETS . . 246 BURIED LIFE   45
    SPARE ME THE WHISPERING CROWDED ROOM . . . . .   250 WISH   13
    WERE CROWDED GEIST INTO NO MORE . . . . . .   449 GEISTS GRAVE   4

CROWDING
    HOW THICK THE BURSTS COME CROWDING THROUGH THE LEAVES 201 PHILOMELA   29

CROWDS
    BLAZING AND BRILLIANT CROWDS . . . .   296 HEINES GRAVE   142
    I AT THAT ALTAR WHERE MID SHOUTING CROWDS . . .   338 MEROPE   272
    LAIAS ALONE NO ERRAND MINE FOR CROWDS . . . .   380 MEROPE   1285
    HARK HOW THE SHOUTING CROWDS TRAMP HITHERWARD . . 401 MEROPE   1886
    I TOOK MY STAND AND SAW THE UNARMD CROWDS . . .   401 MEROPE   1896

CROWN
    CROWN OF HIS STRUGGLING LIFE AN UNJUST CLOSE . .   9 MYCERINUS   30
    CROWN CROWN HIM QUICKLY AND LEAVE HIM FOR ME . .   20 MODERN SAPPHO   36
    CROWN CROWN HIM QUICKLY AND LEAVE HIM FOR ME . .   20 MODERN SAPPHO   36
    CALMS NOT LIFES CROWN THOUGH CALM IS WELL . . .   22 YOUTH AND CALM   23
    ALL THE FRORE PEAKS AWFUL CROWN . . . . . .   31 NEW SIRENS   144
    TO CROWN EUGENIAS HAIR . . . .   48 HORATIAN ECHO   24
    I SNATCHD UP MY VINE-CROWN MY FIR-STAFF . . .   186 STRAYED REVEL   33
    THAT CROWN HIS HAIR . . . .   188 STRAYED REVEL   86
    THE GENTIAN-FLOWERD PASS ITS CROWN . . . . . .   313 OBERMANN MORE   21
    IN CROWN AND SWORD ARRAYD . . . .   316 OBERMANN MORE   122
    AND HER IMPERIAL CROWN . . . .   316 OBERMANN MORE   128
    WHY NOT ON THEM HAVE PLACED THE FORFEIT CROWN .   339 MEROPE   320
    THY CROWN CONDEMNS THEE WHILE THY TONGUE ABSOLVES 340 MEROPE   332
    FROM HIS UNATTAIND CROWN . . . .   344 MEROPE   458
    WHERE SIRE TO SON TRANSMITS THE UNQUESTIOND CROWN 388 MEROPE   1517
    FLING OFF THY CROWN SUPPOSED AT LAST SECURE . .   395 MEROPE   1743
    THOU HOLDST SO CHEAP THEN THE MESSENIAN CROWN .   397 MEROPE   1774
    DIRGE FROM ME TO CROWN THEIR GRAVE . . . . .   454 POOR MATTHIAS   82
    DIRGE OF MINE TO CROWN THEIR GRAVE . . . . .   454 POOR MATTHIAS V 82
    IS THINE THE LAUREL-CROWN THAT GREATNESS WREATHES 463 ALARIC AT ROME   25
    AND ONE SWAYD ALL WHO WORE A KINGLY CROWN . . .   476 CROMWELL   143
    THE LOUD RAINS LASHD THE MOUNTAINS CROWN . . .   480 HAYSWATER BOAT   29

CROWND
    CROWND WITH GRAY HAIRS HE DIED AND FULL OF SWAY .   9 MYCERINUS   14
    SEEMS THERE NO JOY IN DANCES CROWND WITH FLOWERS . 9 MYCERINUS   33
    ROSE-CROWND AND EVER WHEN THE SUN WENT DOWN . .   11 MYCERINUS   93
    HAST THOU WITH MYRTLE-LEAF CROWND HIM O PLEASURE . 20 MODERN SAPPHO   35
    SUCH HAPPY ISSUE CROWND HER PAINFUL CARE . . .   46 IN UTRUMQUE PAR 34
    THE MEN OF FORMER TIMES HAD CROWND THE TOP . .   61 SOHRAB RUSTUM   20
    AND THE VALKYRIES CROWND THEIR HORNS WITH MEAD .   97 BALDER DEAD 1   68
    AND BALDER SITTING CROWND AND HELAS THRONE . . . 100 BALDER DEAD 1   175
    OF HELA AND SAW NEAR IT BALDER CROWND . . .   109 BALDER DEAD 2   177
    AND NOW THOU SITTEST CROWND BY HELAS SIDE . . .   112 BALDER DEAD 2   260
    THAN BE A CROWND KING HERE AND RULE THE DEAD .   112 BALDER DEAD 2   267
    CROWND HAVING HONOUR AMONG ALL THE DEAD . . .   112 BALDER DEAD 2   278
    AND STILL THE ACCEPTANCE FOLLOWS ME WHICH CROWND 126 BALDER DEAD 3   461
    THE ROSE-CROWND QUEEN OF LEGENDARY LORE . . .   168 RACHEL 2   7
    THE PUISSANT CROWND THE WEAK LAID LOW . . .   219 BACCHANALIA 2   12
    THOSE BLACK-CROWND RED-BOLED PINE-TREES STAND .   248 KENSINGTON GARD   4
    I SEE THE SMOKE-CROWND VESSEL COME . . . . .   276 SOUTHERN NIGHT   30
    AND CROWND HIS HAIR WITH FLOWERS . . . . .   316 OBERMANN MORE   102
    THAT GRACIOUS CHILD THAT THORN-CROWND MAN . . .   318 OBERMANN MORE   167
    A HEADLAND WITH ONE AGED PLANE-TREE CROWND . .   358 MEROPE   817
    CROWND WITH SUCCESS NOT IN MY WAY BUT HEAVENS .   360 MEROPE   878
    WITH THY HEAD FULL OF WINE AND THY HAIR CROWND . 407 EMPEDOCLES I 1   32
    CROWND BY THE AWFUL PEAK ETNAS GREAT MOUTH . .   429 EMPEDOCLES II   3
    THE FIGHT WHICH CROWND THINE ILLS . . . . .   430 EMPEDOCLES II   56
    THE FIGHT THAT CROWND THY ILLS . . . . . .   430 EMPEDOCLES II V 56

CROWNED
    AND THE RAY-CROWNED BALDER ANSWERD HIM . . . .   128 BALDER DEAD 3   517
    OF PROSERPINE AMONG WHOSE CROWNED HAIR . . . .   265 THYRSIS   88
    THAT NAILD THORN-CROWNED MAN . . . .   317 OBERMANN MORE   156
    WHEN THE WHITE-ROBED GARLAND-CROWNED MONARCH . . 400 MEROPE   1857

CROWNING
 THE CROWNING END OF LIFE AND YOUTH   • • • • •   21 YOUTH AND CALM   6
 CROWNING MOMENTS WITH THE WEALTH OF YEARS   • • • •   29 NEW SIRENS   88
 CROWNING MOMENTS WITH THE WEIGHT OF YEARS   • • • •   29 NEW SIRENS   V 88
 CROWNING THEIR BROWS WITH ITS LIGHT   • • • • •   232 YOUTH OF MAN   20
 AND NEXT THE CROWNING IMPOTENCE OF DEATH   • • • •   448 WESTMIN ABBEY   130
 AND THEN THE CROWNING IMPOTENCE OF DEATH   • • • •   448 WESTMIN ABBEY   V 130
 CROWNING HIS WILDEST HOPES PERCHANCE HIS EYES   • •   468 ALARIC AT ROME   173

CROWNS
 CROWNS THE STILL VALLEY BEHIND   • • • • • • • •   234 YOUTH OF MAN   63
 PAST THE HIGH WOOD TO WHERE THE ELM-TREE CROWNS   • •   263 THYRSIS   12
 DOST THOU ASK PROOF OUR TREE YET CROWNS THE HILL   • •   269 THYRSIS   239
 UP PAST THE WOOD TO WHERE THE ELM-TREE CROWNS   • •   263 THYRSIS   V 12

CRUCIBLE
 PASSD THROUGH THE CRUCIBLE OF TIME   • • • • • •   184 TERRACE BERNE   36

CRUEL
 NATURE IS CRUEL MAN IS SICK OF BLOOD   • • • • •   5 HARMONY NATURE   7
 LOVE HAS FLUSHD THOSE CRUEL FACES   • • • • • •   27 NEW SIRENS   53
 LATE THOU COMEST CRUEL THOU HAST BEEN   • • • • •   142 TRISTRAM 2   4
 BUT CRUEL IS SHE   • • • • • • • • •   165 FORSAKEN MERM   141
 BEGET A CRUEL TEMPER HELP ME QUELL   • • • • • •   335 MEROPE   162
 CRUEL BUT COMPOSED AND BLAND   • • • • • • • •   453 POOR MATTHIAS   39

CRUELLER
 ONE THAN CREON CRUELLER FAR   • • • • • • • •   196 FRAG ANTIGONE   47

CRUMBLE
 UNTIL THEY CRUMBLE OR ELSE GROW LIKE STEEL   • • • •   153 TRISTRAM 3   121

CRUMBLED
 OF SHOOTING CLIFF AND CRUMBLED STONE   • • • • • •   479 HAYSWATER BOAT   13

CRUMBLING
 BE CRUMBLING BONES AND WINDY DUST   • • • • • •   48 HORATIAN ECHO   32
 AND CRUMBLING WALL AND SULTRY SAND   • • • • • •   318 OBERMANN MORE   183
 GREEN TURF ABOVE AND CRUMBLING DUST BELOW   • • •   464 ALARIC AT ROME   57
 THAT FRAME OF VIGOUR SHALL BE CRUMBLING CLAY   • •   469 ALARIC AT ROME   194

CRUSADING
 SOME GREY CRUSADING KNIGHT AUSTERE   • • • • • •   278 SOUTHERN NIGHT   93

CRUSE
 HIS COAT HIS BASKET AND HIS EARTHEN CRUSE   • • • •   255 SCHOLAR-GIPSY   13

CRUSH
 YOU CRUSH THEM THE BLUE GENTIANS GLEAM   • • • •   55 RESIGNATION   103
 WE CALL IT MURDER CRUSH HIM BRAND HIS NAME   • • •   336 MEROPE   203
 ON WHAT RELYING TO CRUSH SUCH A FOE   • • • • • •   380 MEROPE   1286

CRUSHD
 CRUSHD THEM WITH TOLLS OR FEVER-AIRS   • • • • •   193 STRAYED REVEL   251
 AND HOPE ONCE CRUSHD LESS QUICK TO SPRING AGAIN   • •   266 THYRSIS   140
 NOW CRUSHD BUT NOT QUITE LIFELESS BY HIS FALL   • •   334 MEROPE   140
 RUTHLESSLY THEIR REBELLIOUS SUBJECTS CRUSHD   • •   390 MEROPE   1567
 ONE SEES ONES FOOTPRINTS CRUSHD IN THE WET GRASS   • •   406 EMPEDOCLES I 1   14
 STILL ALERT THY STONE-CRUSHD FRAME   • • • • •   430 EMPEDOCLES II   51
 OF THE MOUNTAIN-CRUSHD TORTURED INTRACTABLE TITAN KING   432 EMPEDOCLES II   98
 CRUSHD AS THEY ROSE BY MANHOODS STERNER WILL   • •   474 CROMWELL   80
 HE CRUSHD THEE NOT WITH HIS DISDAIN   • • • • • •   482 COURAGE   23

CRUSHED
 SPIRITS DEEP-CRUSHED AND CLOSELY FURLD   • • • •   272 MEMORIAL VERSES   V 56

CRUSHT
 BE CRUSHT AND OUTRAGED IN THIS BITTER HOUR   • • • •   468 ALARIC AT ROME   148

CRUST
 UPON WHOSE CHARRD AND QUAKING CRUST I STAND   • •   438 EMPEDOCLES II   307

CRUSTED
 AND ON THE LICHEN-CRUSTED LEADS ABOVE   • • • •   19 CHURCH BROU 3   45
 CRUSTED WITH GOLD AND ON THE GROUND WERE WORKD   • •   69 SOHRAB RUSTUM   278

CRY
 AND ONE LOUD CRY OF GRIEF AND OF AMAZE   • • •   11 MYCERINUS   80
 PLEASED YOU MOCK THE FRUITLESS CRY   • • • • •   24 MEMORY-PICTURE   55
 THOU TOO WHEN THOU AGAINST MY CRIMES WOULDST CRY   • •   38 WORLDS TRIUMPHS   9
 THUS THOU WHEN THOU AGAINST MY CRIMES WOULDST CRY   38 WORLDS TRIUMPHS   V 9
 AH THEY CRY DESTINY   • • • • • • • • • •   51 CONSOLATION   48
 AND WITH A CRY SPRANG UP AND DROPPD THE BIRD   • •   67 SOHRAB RUSTUM   203
 IN SAMARCAND HE WILL ARISE AND CRY   • • • • •   72 SOHRAB RUSTUM   356
 WHO STOOD AT HAND UTTERD A DREADFUL CRY   • • •   76 SOHRAB RUSTUM   502
 NO HORSES CRY WAS THAT MOST LIKE THE ROAR   • • •   76 SOHRAB RUSTUM   503
 THE TWO HOSTS HEARD THAT CRY AND QUAKED FOR FEAR   •   76 SOHRAB RUSTUM   507
 TO ARMS AND CRY FOR VENGEANCE UPON THEE   • • •   78 SOHRAB RUSTUM   585
 SPEECHLESS AND THEN HE UTTERD ONE SHARP CRY   • •   81 SOHRAB RUSTUM   690

CRY   (CONTINUED)
        MAY SEE MY TOMB A GREAT WAY OFF AND CRY   • • • •   84 SOHRAB RUSTUM   791
        HER ARMS TOWARDS HIM WITH A CRY BUT HE   • • • •   104 BALDER DEAD 1   333
        FOLLOWS THEM WITH A LONG COMPLAINING CRY   • • • •   129 BALDER DEAD 3   564
        UP TRISTRAM UP MEN CRY THOU MOONSTRUCK KNIGHT   • • 137 TRISTRAM 1   238
        SHE WILL CRY IS THIS THE FOE I DREADED   • • • •   144 TRISTRAM 2   65
        TWAS NOT THE THOUGHT OF BYRON OF HIS CRY   • • • •   166 PICT NEWSTEAD   2
        AND CLAP THY HANDS AND CRY TIS THOU   • • • • •   184 TERRACE BERNE   16
        AND CRY LONG LONG IVE LOOKD FOR THEE   • • • • •   202 URANIA   28
        THE MOWERS CRY THE DOGS ALARMS   • • • • • • •   218 BACCHANALIA 1   6
        THE REAPERS CRY THE DOGS ALARMS • • • • • • •   218 BACCHANALIA 1   V   6
        WHO CRY ALOUD TO LAY THE OLD WORLD LOW   • • • •   237 PROGRESS   15
        HENCE HENCE THEY CRY YE DO BUT KEEP MAN BLIND   • •   237 PROGRESS   18
        A CRY LIKE THINE IN MINE OWN HEART I HEAR   • • • •   240 SELF-DEPENDENCE   30
        A CRY LIKE THINE IN MY OWN HEART I HEAR   • • • •   240 SELF-DEPENDENCE   V 30
        THE WILL TO NEITHER STRIVE NOR CRY   • • • • •   249 KENSINGTON GARD   41
        SO HAVE I HEARD THE CUCKOOS PARTING CRY   • • • •   264 THYRSIS   57
        SEEMD BUT A CRY OF DESIRE   • • • • • • • •   290 RUGBY CHAPEL   152
        BUT THEY CONTEND AND CRY NO MORE   • • • • • •   303 GRANDE CHARTR   120
        THROUGH THESE SECLUDED DELLS TO CRY   • • • • •   305 GRANDE CHARTR   195
        THERE ROSE UP A CRY IN THE STREETS   • • • • •   345 MEROPE   487
        MORE PIERCING THE SECOND CRY RANG   • • • • • •   346 MEROPE   495
        BY THE LAKE-EDGE BROKE THE SHARP CRY OF HOUNDS   • •   357 MEROPE   787
        AT LAST THE CRY DREW TO THE WATERS EDGE   • • • •   357 MEROPE   806
        WITHOUT A CRY A STRUGGLE OR A BLOW   • • • • •   367 MEROPE   1028
        THY PRISON-HOUSE RAISED ONE IMPLORING CRY   • • • •   383 MEROPE   1371
        TILL THEN WE ALL SEEMD STONE BUT THEN A CRY   • • • 402 MEROPE   1930
        GAPE AND CRY WIZARD AT HIM IF THEY LIST   • • • •   410 EMPEDOCLES I 1   139
        WE HAVE THE TRUTH THEY CRY   • • • • • • •   417 EMPEDOCLES I 2   139
        OUR CRY FOR BLISS OUR PLEA   • • • • • • •   419 EMPEDOCLES I 2   209
        HE HEARS NOTHING BUT THE CRY OF THE TORRENTS   • •   435 EMPEDOCLES II   213
        HAD HUMAN CRY NOT MARRD THE WORK DIVINE   • • • •   447 WESTMIN ABBEY   104
        SEEMD SURGING THE VIRGILIAN CRY   • • • • •   450 GEISTS GRAVE   15
        SOON WAS THAT STILLNESS BROKEN LIKE THE CRY   • •   466 ALARIC AT ROME   109
        OR HEAR MID CIRCLING CRAGS THE IMPATIENT CRY   • •   472 CROMWELL   25
        OR THAT MYSTERIOUS CRY THAT SMOTE WITH FEAR   • •   473 CROMWELL   41
        NOT IN THAT MADHOUSE FRANCE FROM WHENCE THE CRY   • •   480 HUNGARIAN NAT   4
        SO HE SPAKE AND DROVE WITH A CRY HIS STEEDS   HOMER TRANS   63
                INTO BATTLE

CRYING
        CRYING O YE MESSENIANS WILL YE LEAVE   • • • • • • 402 MEROPE   1934
        CRYING COME ON AND RANGE THE WORLD   • • • • • • 460 KAISER DEAD   59

CRYSTAL
        COLD PLASHING PAST IT CRYSTAL WATERS ROLL   • • • •   236 PALLADIUM   11

CUB
        IN VAIN BUT WHO CAN KEEP THE LIONS CUB   • • • •   63 SOHRAB RUSTUM   91

CUBIT
        SEVEN-CUBIT-STATURED SON • • • • • • • • • • • 344 MEROPE   441

CUCKOO
        THE CUCKOO LOUD ON SOME HIGH LAWN   • • • • • •   57 RESIGNATION   176
        FROM BUSH TO BUSH THE CUCKOO FLIES   • • • • • •   274 STANZAS CARNAC   17
        CUCKOO CALLING FROM THE HILL   • • • • • • • •   456 POOR MATTHIAS   141

CUCKOOS
        SO HAVE I HEARD THE CUCKOOS PARTING CRY   • • • •   264 THYRSIS   57

CUCUMBER
        AND THE DARK CUCUMBER   • • • • • • • • • • •   190 STRAYED REVEL   156

CULPRIT
        FOR A GRAND CULPRIT SHORTLY COMING DOWN   • • • •   373 MEROPE   1189

CULTURE
        WHOSE CULTURE IS THE BRETHRENS CARE   • • • • • • 301 GRANDE CHARTR   58

CUMBER
        NOR WITH A HATEFUL PRESENCE CUMBER HEAVEN   • • • •   125 BALDER DEAD 3   399
        ME LET NO HALF-EFFACED MEMORIES CUMBER   • • • •   206 SEPARATION   9

CUMBERD
        THEIR FRAGMENTS ON THE CUMBERD GRASS   • • • • •   55 RESIGNATION   111
        TO THE ICE-CUMBERD GORGES   • • • • • • • •   175 PARTING   27
        TOWARDS THE ICE-CUMBERD GORGES   • • • • • • • •   PARTING   V   27
        SEE ON THE CUMBERD PLAIN • • • • • • • • •   220 BACCHANALIA 2   33

CUMNER
        AND WATCH THE WARM GREEN-MUFFLED CUMNER HILLS   • •   257 SCHOLAR-GIPSY   69
        AT SOME LONE HOMESTEAD IN THE CUMNER HILLS   • • •   258 SCHOLAR-GIPSY   101
        AND GAIND THE WHITE BROW OF THE CUMNER RANGE   • •   259 SCHOLAR-GIPSY   127
        HER FOOT THE CUMNER COWSLIPS NEVER STIRRD   • • • •   265 THYRSIS   99
        AND THIS RUDE CUMNER GROUND   • • • • • • • •   269 THYRSIS   216

CUMNOR
        HER FOOT THE CUMNOR COWSLIPS NEVER STIRRD   • • • •   265 THYRSIS   V   99
        AND THIS RUDE CUMNOR GROUND   • • • • • • • •   269 THYRSIS   V 216

CUNNING
    AND CUNNING ALL THE PITY I HAD IS GONE   • • • •   75 SOHRAB RUSTUM   467
    PRICKD AS A CUNNING WORKMAN IN PEKIN • • • • • •   81 SOHRAB RUSTUM   672
    OF PLAINNESS OPPRESSD BY CUNNING • • • • • •   432 EMPEDOCLES II   101

CUP
    PLEDGE ME IN MY GOLDEN CUP • • • • •   135 TRISTRAM 1   146
    REACH ME MY GOLDEN CUP THAT STANDS BY THEE • • •   133 TRISTRAM 1   V 100
    AND THAT GOLDEN CUP HER MOTHER • • • • • •   134 TRISTRAM 1   V 136
    THE DEEP CUP IVY-CINCTURED • • • • • •   186 STRAYED REVEL   12
    OF THY CUP THE BRIGHT GLANCING VINE-LEAVES • • • •   188 STRAYED REVEL   85
    THE CUP AGAIN • • • • • • • • •   194 STRAYED REVEL   291
    THE CUP ABOUT WHOSE DRAUGHTS BEGUILE • • • • •   431 EMPEDOCLES II   85

CUPID
    THE ARMLESS VATICAN CUPID • • • • • • •   214 NEW ROME   1
    AND WHAT CRIES CUPID WILL SAVE US • • • • •   214 NEW ROME   9
    THE ARMLESS VATICAN CUPID • • • • • • •   214 NEW ROME   17
    AND WHAT ASKS CUPID WILL SAVE US • • • • •   214 NEW ROME   V 9
    AND WHAT ASKS CUPID IS COMING • • • • • •   214 NEW ROME   V 9

CURB
    STREAMS WILL NOT CURB THEIR PRIDE • • • • •   420 EMPEDOCLES I 2   252

CURBD
    HANDFUL OF DORIAN CONQUERORS MIGHT HAVE CURBD • •   337 MEROPE   248

CURDLED
    AND OXUS CURDLED AS IT CROSSD HIS STREAM • • • •   76 SOHRAB RUSTUM   508
    AND OXUS CURDLED AS IT REACHD HIS STREAM • • • •   76 SOHRAB RUSTUM   V 508

CURE
    THE ILL HE CANNOT CURE A NAME • • • • • •   250 WISH   20
    COULD SCARCE HAVE LIGHTED ON A LOVELIER CURE • •   407 EMPEDOCLES I 1   26
    AND ASKS WHAT AILS HIM SO AND GETS WHAT CURE HE CAN   416 EMPEDOCLES I 2   131
    AND FOR WHOSE HURT COURAGE IS NOT THE CURE • • • •   429 EMPEDOCLES II   14

CURES
    WITH OLD-WORLD CURES MEN HALF BELIEVE • • • •   320 OBERMANN MORE   235

CURIOUS
    WHICH YEARS AND CURIOUS THOUGHT AND SUFFERING GIVE   43 GIPSY CHILD   38
    WITH CURIOUS FRUIT-TREES BROUGHT FROM FAR • • • •   94 SICK KING BOKH   201
    WITH CURIOUS FRUIT TREES BOUGHT FROM FAR • • • •   94 SICK KING BOKH   V 201
    FOR WISE HE WAS AND MANY CURIOUS ARTS • • •   101 BALDER DEAD 1   210

CURLD
    BLACK GLOSSY CURLD THE FLEECE OF KARA-KUL • • • •   64 SOHRAB RUSTUM   101
    CURLD MINION DANCER COINER OF SWEET WORDS • • • •   74 SOHRAB RUSTUM   458
    ON THE FAIR CURLD HEADS OF MY SONS • • • • •   346 MEROPE   504

CURLING
    CURLING AND DARTING HIGHER UNTIL THEY LICKD • •   119 BALDER DEAD 3   189

CURLS
    HOUR AFTER HOUR HER GOLD CURLS SWEEPING IT • • •   152 TRISTRAM 3   83
    HAD LOOSEND THE BROWN CURLS OF VIVIANS HAIR • •   154 TRISTRAM 3   V 168
    THY HEAD DROOPD SOFTLY AND THE GOLDEN CURLS • •   373 MEROPE   1161
    ONES BREATH CURLS IN THE AIR AND ON THESE PINES •   406 EMPEDOCLES I 1   15

CURRENT
    AH TOO TRUE TIMES CURRENT STRONG • • • •   24 MEMORY-PICTURE   57
    ROLL TUMBLING IN THE CURRENT OER MY HEAD • • •   83 SOHRAB RUSTUM   770
    FRESHENING ITS CURRENT AND SPOTTED WITH FOAM •   254 FUTURE   80
    BUT ROUND THE HEADLANDS POINT A CURRENT SETS •   358 MEROPE   820
    ON THE DARK CURRENT OF HIS CHANGELESS DAY • • •   473 CROMWELL   62
    WITH NOISELESS CURRENT STRONG OBSCURE AND DEEP •   483 BELOW SURFACE   4

CURRENTS
    AND ALL ITS THWARTING CURRENTS OF DESIRE • • •   37 YOUTHS AGIT   10
    PAST STRAITS AND CURRENTS LONG STEERD THROUGH • •   53 RESIGNATION   21
    AND SPLIT HIS CURRENTS THAT FOR MANY A LEAGUE • •   87 SOHRAB RUSTUM   883
    WHERE ERST THE STRONG SEA-CURRENTS SUCKD THEE DOWN   430 EMPEDOCLES II   59

CURSE
    THE KAFFIRS ALSO WHOM GOD CURSE • • • • • •   93 SICK KING BOKH   173
    THIS IS THE CURSE OF LIFE THAT NOT • • • • •   183 ABSENCE   5
    NO NO OLD MEN CREON I CURSE NOT • • • • • •   196 FRAG ANTIGONE   45
    TO CURSE AND TO DENY YOUR TRUTH • • • • • •   301 GRANDE CHARTR   78
    YET HE CAN CURSE BUT THIS • • • • • • •   422 EMPEDOCLES I 2   303
    AND WHAT WE MADE TO CURSE • • • • • • •   422 EMPEDOCLES I 2   314
    CURSE UPON CURSE PANG UPON PANG • • • • • •   427 EMPEDOCLES I 2   447
    CURSE UPON CURSE PANG UPON PANG • • • • • •   427 EMPEDOCLES I 2   447

CURSED
    BRAKE FORTH AND CURSED THEM DOST THOU HEAR • • • •   90 SICK KING BOKH   87

CURSINGS
    AND QUIETLY DECLAIMS THE CURSINGS OF HIMSELF • •   422 EMPEDOCLES I 2   301
    AND PATIENTLY DECLAIMS THE CURSINGS OF HIMSELF • •   422 EMPEDOCLES I 2   V 301

CURST
AND THAT CURST TREACHERY ON THE MOUNT OF GORE • • 430 EMPEDOCLES II 54
HOW FIRS LESS CURST BY FORTUNES FROWN • • • • 483 ROME-SICKNESS 10

CURTAIN
AND RAISED THE CURTAIN OF HIS TENT AND CALLD • • 64 SOHRAB RUSTUM 102
OVER AGAINST THE CURTAIN OF THE BED • • • • • • 103 BALDER DEAD 1 286

CURTAINS
EYES THROUGH HER SILKEN CURTAINS THE POOR DRUDGE • • 70 SOHRAB RUSTUM 303
AND THOUGH THE CURTAINS HIDE HER FACE • • • • 147 TRISTRAM 2 V 136
THE CURTAINS OF THE BLUE FILMS SLOWLY MEET • • • • 431 EMPEDOCLES II 79

CURVED
WHERE SOME MUSE WITH HALF-CURVED FROWN • • • • 27 NEW SIRENS 26

CURVES
CURVES WITH THE CURVING BEACH AWAY • • • • • • 275 SOUTHERN NIGHT 10

CURVING
CURVES WITH THE CURVING BEACH AWAY • • • • • • 275 SOUTHERN NIGHT 10

CUT
CUT BY AN ONWARD-LABOURING VESSELS PRORE • • • • 41 HUMAN LIFE 23
AND AS AFIELD THE REAPERS CUT A SWATH • • • • 70 SOHRAB RUSTUM 293
OF AN UNSKILFUL GARDENER HAS BEEN CUT • • • • 80 SOHRAB RUSTUM 635
AND AS AFIELD THE REAPERS CUT A SWATHE • • • • 70 SOHRAB RUSTUM V 293
TO CUT THY THREAD OF LIFE AND FREE THY SOUL • • 103 BALDER DEAD 1 303
OF LIFE WAS CUT AND CLOSED THY SPAN • • • • 184 TERRACE BERNE 28
SEE HIM COME BACK AND CUT A SMOOTHER REED • • • • 265 THYRSIS 78
SWEET HEAPS OF FRESH-CUT GRASS • • • • • • 313 OBERMANN MORE 18
CUT SHORT THY TRIUMPH SEEMING AT ITS HEIGHT • • 395 MEROPE 1742
TO HAVE RAISD FAITHFUL FRIENDS AND CUT DOWN 425 EMPEDOCLES I 2 V 401
    SPITEFUL FOES
CAN CUT HIS OSCILLATIONS SHORT AND SO • • • • 436 EMPEDOCLES II 233
SHALL CUT HIS OSCILLATIONS SHORT AND SO • • • • 436 EMPEDOCLES II V 233

CUTS
SAINT MICHAELS CHAPEL CUTS THE SKY • • • • • 273 STANZAS CARNAC 2
GLION AH TWENTY YEARS IT CUTS • • • • • • • • 312 OBERMANN MORE 1
CUTS SHORT THE FEIGNINGS OF FANTASTIC GRIEF • • FRAGMENT 1 6

CUTTERS
THE WOOD-CUTTERS CART-TRACK • • • • • • • • 187 STRAYED REVEL 41

CYCLAMENS
THE CYCLAMENS WHOSE BLOSSOMS FILL • • • • • • 484 ROME-SICKNESS 18

CYCLOPS
WHEN ON THE BEACH THE CYCLOPS LAY • • • • • • 222 EPILOG LAOCOON 46

CYLLENE
OF HIGH CYLLENE • • • • • • • • • • • • 392 MEROPE 1624

CYLLENES
TO DRAW THE COVERTS ON CYLLENES SIDE • • • • 356 MEROPE 750
THE FORESTS ROUND THAT BELT CYLLENES SIDE • • • • 357 MEROPE 794
AMONG THE FORESTS ON CYLLENES SIDE • • • • • 364 MEROPE 974
UNTRODDEN ON CYLLENES DESOLATE SIDE • • • • • 373 MEROPE 1168
THE FORESTS ROUND WHICH BELT CYLLENES SIDE • • • • 357 MEROPE V 794

CYPRESS
PLUCK PLUCK CYPRESS O PALE MAIDENS • • • • • • 30 NEW SIRENS 113
PLUCK PLUCK CYPRESS O PALE MAIDENS • • • • • • 35 NEW SIRENS 269
PLUCK PLUCK CYPRESS O PALE MAIDENS • • • • • • 35 NEW SIRENS 275
LIKE SOME YOUNG CYPRESS TALL AND DARK AND STRAIGHT 70 SOHRAB RUSTUM 314

CYPSELUS
AN INFANT AT THE HEARTH OF CYPSELUS • • • • • 331 MEROPE 32
WITH CYPSELUS AND TWO DAYS SINCE HE DIED • • • • 355 MEROPE 718
ONE OF THE TRAIN OF CYPSELUS AM I • • • • • • 355 MEROPE 719
TO CYPSELUS AT BASILIS THIS NEWS • • • • • • 359 MEROPE 846
WITH CYPSELUS OUR FATHER WHERE WE SAW • • • • 388 MEROPE 1515
TO CYPSELUS AT BASILIS HE BROUGHT • • • • • 364 MEROPE V
SO CHARGD HE STOOD DUMB-FOUNDERD CYPSELUS • • • • 365 MEROPE V

CZAR
AND WHAT THE RUSSIAN CZAR INTENDS • • • • • • 47 HORATIAN ECHO 5

DACHS
THE DACHS-HOUND GEIST THEIR LITTLE FRIEND • • • • 452 GEISTS GRAVE 80

DACHSHOUND
MAX A DACHSHOUND WITHOUT BLOT • • • • • • • 454 POOR MATTHIAS 69
A DACHSHOUND TRUE • • • • • • • • • • • 459 KAISER DEAD 18

DAFFODIL
I KNOW THE WOOD WHICH HIDES THE DAFFODIL • • • • 266 THYRSIS 105

DAILY
```
      NOT DAILY LABOURS DULL LETHAEAN SPRING    .  .  .  .    43 GIPSY CHILD         54
      US NOT THE DAILY QUICKENING RACE      .  .  .  .  .    48 HORATIAN ECHO        7
      TO LIVE AS ERST YOUR DAILY LIFE IN HEAVEN  .  .  .  .   96 BALDER DEAD 1       36
      WERE RANGED AND THEN THE DAILY FRAY BEGAN  .  .  .  .  105 BALDER DEAD 2       14
      SOULS BOUND BELOW MY DAILY PASSERS HERE    .  .  .  .  108 BALDER DEAD 2      110
      AND LEAD AS ERST OUR DAILY LIFE IN HEAVEN  .  .  .  .  115 BALDER DEAD 3       56
      AND DAILY STRIFES ARISE AND ANGRY WORDS    .  .  .  .  116 BALDER DEAD 3       82
      NOT DAILY TO ENDURE ABHORRING GODS    .  .  .  .  .  .  125 BALDER DEAD 3      398
      ITS INMATES ON THEIR DAILY TASKS ABROAD             .  330 MEROPE             27
      THEIR DAILY-PRACTISED CHAFINGS KEEP ALIVE  .  .  .  .  331 MEROPE             44
      CLOUDS AND GROWS DAILY WORSE IN SICILY     .  .  .  .  410 EMPEDOCLES I 1    120
      MEED FOR DAILY SONG OF YORE  .  .  .  .  .  .  .  .  .  453 POOR MATTHIAS      19
      TILL WITH HIS DAILY LIFE A LIFE THAT THREW  .  .  .  .  473 CROMWELL           55
      TO DAILY TASKS WE SET OUR HAND  .  .  .  .  .  .  .  .  483 ROME-SICKNESS       1
```

DAINTILY
```
      SNUFFS AT IT DAINTILY AND STOOPS HER HEAD  .  .  .  .  123 BALDER DEAD 3      342
```

DAIS
```
      CLOTHED IN SMILES BENEATH THE DAIS    .  .  .  .  .  .   13 CHURCH BROU 1      35
```

DAISIED
```
      AND IN THAT DAISIED CIRCLE AS MEN SAY  .  .  .  .  .  156 TRISTRAM 3         221
      SHEEP MAKE THE DAISIED AISLES THEIR FOLD   .  .  .  .  274 STANZAS CARNAC     16
```

DAISIES
```
      WHAT BLOWING DAISIES FRAGRANT GRASS   .  .  .  .  .  .  248 KENSINGTON GARD    15
      BUTTERCUPS CLOVER DAISIES GRASS       .  .  .  .  .  .      KENSINGTON GARD  V 15
```

DALES
```
      THROUGH ALL THE LORDSHIPS OF THE ARCADIAN DALES  .  .  355 MEROPE            727
```

DAM
```
      A COLT BENEATH ITS DAM AND DROVE HIM HOME  .  .  .  .   69 SOHRAB RUSTUM     275
      TO HEM HIS WATERY MARCH AND DAM HIS STREAMS  .  .  .    87 SOHRAB RUSTUM     882
      A COLT BESIDE ITS DAM AND DROVE HIM HOME   .  .  .  .   69 SOHRAB RUSTUM   V 275
```

DAME
```
      HOMAGE TO YOUR AUSTRIAN DAME   .  .  .  .  .  .  .  .   15 CHURCH BROU 1      80
      HIS MOTHER MOST MAJESTIC DAME  .  .  .  .  .  .  .  .  459 KAISER DEAD        19
```

DAMES
```
      BURGHERS AND DAMES AT SUMMERS PRIME   .  .  .  .  .  .   17 CHURCH BROU 2      20
      AND THE DAMES WHISPERED SCOFFINGLY    .  .  .  .  .  .  146 TRISTRAM 2        124
      GAY DAMES ARE THERE IN SYLVAN GREEN   .  .  .  .  .  .  305 GRANDE CHARTR     185
```

DAMNING
```
      FOR SUCH A DAMNING CATALOGUE OF ILLS  .  .  .  .  .  .      RUDE ORATOR        14
```

DAMSEL
```
      NOT BIFROST BUT THAT BRIDGE A DAMSEL KEEPS  .  .  .  .   99 BALDER DEAD 1     149
      AND ON THE BRIDGE A DAMSEL WATCHING ARMD   .  .  .  .  107 BALDER DEAD 2      87
      SO ON THE BRIDGE THAT DAMSEL BLOCKD THE WAY     .  .  107 BALDER DEAD 2      99
      O DAMSEL HERMOD AM I CALLD THE SON    .  .  .  .  .  .  108 BALDER DEAD 2     112
```

DAMSELS
```
      TO THE ARMD DAMSELS BRIDGE AND GIALLS STREAM   .  .  113 BALDER DEAD 2      290
```

DANCD
```
      THOU MIRROR THAT HAST DANCD THROUGH SUCH A WORLD  .  .      LUCRETIUS 1         1
```

DANCE
```
      FEAST AND DANCE HER YOUTH BEGUILED    .  .  .  .  .  .   14 CHURCH BROU 1      58
      WITH TARTAR GIRLS WITH WHOM THOU ART WONT TO DANCE     75 SOHRAB RUSTUM     461
      BUT ON THE OXUS-SANDS AND IN THE DANCE     .  .  .  .   75 SOHRAB RUSTUM     462
      TO DANCE AROUND THE FYFIELD ELM IN MAY     .  .  .  .  257 SCHOLAR-GIPSY      83
      MAKE THEIR BLOOD DANCE AND CHAIN THEIR EYES    .  .  305 GRANDE CHARTR     188
```

DANCED
```
      WHICH DANCED AND ON THEIR SHOULDERS FLUTTERING PLAYD    25 DREAM             25
```

DANCER
```
      CURLD MINION DANCER COINER OF SWEET WORDS  .  .  .  .   74 SOHRAB RUSTUM     458
```

DANCERS
```
      THE DANCERS AND THE FESTIVE HOST      .  .  .  .  .  .  146 TRISTRAM 2        121
```

DANCES
```
      SEEMS THERE NO JOY IN DANCES CROWND WITH FLOWERS  .  .    9 MYCERINUS         33
      DANCES AS THE TRUMPETS BLOW  .  .  .  .  .  .  .  .  .  138 TRISTRAM 1        264
      FLASHING IN THE DANCES WHIRLS  .  .  .  .  .  .  .  .  434 EMPEDOCLES II     182
```

DANCING
```
      WITH DANCING MAIDENS AND BOYS  .  .  .  .  .  .  .  .  360 MEROPE            898
      OF STYX COME DANCING     .  .  .  .  .  .  .  .  .  .  392 MEROPE           1653
      ALMOST AS MUCH AS THE NEW DANCING-GIRL     .  .  .  .  407 EMPEDOCLES I 1     35
```

DANGER
```
      DANGER OR DEATH AWAITS THEE ON THIS FIELD  .  .  .  .   63 SOHRAB RUSTUM      87
```

DANGEROUS
DANGEROUS TO ALL TO BE BUT THUS ANNULLD	336 MEROPE	207
DANGEROUS ALONE TO THE DEER	342 MEROPE	399
BUT VENGEANCE TRAVELS IN A DANGEROUS WAY	349 MEROPE	580
AND ENTERTAINST THOU CHILD SUCH DANGEROUS FRIENDS	380 MEROPE	1276
SCARCE DANGEROUS LESS THAN HIM THE DORIAN LORDS	381 MEROPE	1298
IN DANGEROUS TRIAL	391 MEROPE	1598
IN DANGEROUS HOUR STRETCHES HIS HAND	393 MEROPE	1681

DANK
STREWN WITH ITS DANK YELLOW DRIFTS	286 RUGBY CHAPEL	3

DANTE
ERE DANTE CAME THE TRUMP OF SACRED SONG	166 AUSTERITY POET	2
AUSTERE DANTE NO GRAVE	294 HEINES GRAVE	62
I READ IN DANTE HOW THAT HORNED LIGHT	484 S S LUSITANIA	1

DANTES
IN DANTES PETRARCHS TASSOS LINE	222 EPILOG LAOCOON	21

DANUBE
FROM VIENNA BY THE DANUBE	13 CHURCH BROU 1	13
IN VIENNA BY THE DANUBE	14 CHURCH BROU 1	53
IN VIENNA BY THE DANUBE	14 CHURCH BROU 1	57
THROUGH WHICH THE GROANING DANUBE STRAINS	52 RESIGNATION	12

DAPHNIS
YOUNG DAPHNIS WITH HIS SILVER VOICE DOTH SING	268 THYRSIS	185

DAPPLED
MY DAPPLED FAWN-SKIN	186 STRAYED REVEL	30

DARE
COULD EVER YET DARE TELL HIM FEARLESSLY	40 HUMAN LIFE	3
OF A LOVE THEY DARE NOT NAME	135 TRISTRAM 1	150
FLY SAVE THYSELF SAVE ME I DARE NOT STAY	135 TRISTRAM 1	168
OUR SOOTHED ENCOURAGED SOULS WILL DARE	179 FAREWELL	62
OTHERS WILL TEACH US HOW TO DARE	272 MEMORIAL VERSES	64
WITH ARMS THEY DARE NOT AND BY STEALTH THEY FEAR	351 MEROPE	607
I DARE NOT WISH IT BUT AT LEAST TO HEAR	351 MEROPE	611
FOR WHOSE HELP DARE I COUNT ON IF NOT THINE	379 MEROPE	1266
SINCE SO THOU WILT I DARE MAINTAIN IT STILL	398 MEROPE	1793
TREMBLEST AND WILT NOT DARE TO TRUST THE JOYS THERE ARE	426 EMPEDOCLES I 2	421
I DARE NOT URGE HIM FURTHER HE MUST GO	428 EMPEDOCLES I 2	479
AND BYRON LET US DARE ADMIRE	482 COURAGE	17
DARE O FRIEND BE WANDERING DARE BE DREAMING	483 THEKLAS ANSWER	23
DARE O FRIEND BE WANDERING DARE BE DREAMING	483 THEKLAS ANSWER	23

DARED
SHRANK ONLY RUSTUM DARED THEN HE AND I		72 SOHRAB RUSTUM	360
THOU HAST DARED IT BUT TOO LATE TO SAVE		142 TRISTRAM 2	10
HAIL TO THE SPIRIT WHICH DARED		281 HAWORTH CHURCH	41
COURAGEOUS FAITHFUL ACTIONS NOBLY DARED		333 MEROPE	88
WHEN THEBES WHEN ATHENS DARED NOT WHO IN ARMS		337 MEROPE	225
WHAT HIS FOES DARED NOT I HIS LOVER DARED		338 MEROPE	271
WHAT HIS FOES DARED NOT I HIS LOVER DARED		338 MEROPE	271
BOATS AND APPROACH NEAR AS WE DARED THE CHASM		358 MEROPE	838
NO SOMETHING MUST BE DARED AND GREAT AS ERST		367 MEROPE	1054
DARED ONE BUT TRY THOU WAST A KIND CHILD EVER		408 EMPEDOCLES I 1	76
DARED ONE BUT TRY THOU WERT A KIND CHILD EVER		409 EMPEDOCLES I 1	V 76
AND DARED PRONOUNCE IT HAPPY WHAT ARE THESE		RUDE ORATOR	7
AND DARED PRONOUNCE THEM HAPPY WHAT ARE THESE		RUDE ORATOR	V 7

DARES
WHICH ON THE SWEETS THAT WOO IT DARES NOT FEED	9 MYCERINUS	26
BLAME THOU NOT THEREFORE HIM WHO DARES	59 RESIGNATION	231
WHEN SOHRAB DARES OUR BRAVEST FORTH AND SEEKS	68 SOHRAB RUSTUM	244
HIM THEN I PRAISE WHO DARES	196 FRAG ANTIGONE	28
STERNLY CONDEMN THE TOO BOLD MAN WHO DARES	353 MEROPE	690
AND DARES STAMP NOTHING FALSE WHERE HE FINDS NOTHING SURE	415 EMPEDOCLES I 2	91

DARING
DARING SINCE BYRON DIED	284 HAWORTH CHURCH	96
OUR DASTARD PATIENCE BE OUR DARING NOW	367 MEROPE	1055
THE DARING CLAIMANT OF A PERILOUS THRONE	383 MEROPE	1357
HAPLY HAD BUT ONE DARING SOUL STOOD FORTH	383 MEROPE	1364
MORE DARING AND MORE GRAND OFFENDER FIND	390 MEROPE	1571
O LAWLESS DARING OF THE STRONG	398 MEROPE	1800
OF DARING EASY AS IT SEEMS WHEN DONE	403 MEROPE	1949
WHAT THINGS DARING WHAT ENDURING	405 MEROPE	2023
A DARING HAND THAT SHRUNK NOT TO FULFIL	478 CROMWELL	227
THE TOO-DARING TITANS BONES	PILLARS UNIVERS	12

DARK
WITH THEIR MILD DARK HIS GRASSY BANQUET-HALL	12 MYCERINUS	119
NO NOR GREW DARK WHEN AUTUMN BROUGHT THE CLOUDS	12 MYCERINUS	121
OF DARK ELMS SHOOT ROUND DROPPING DOWN THE PROUD STREAM	19 MODERN SAPPHO	6
FASTEND ON HER DARK HAIR AND HER WREATH OF WHITE HEATHER	19 MODERN SAPPHO	11
OF DARK ELMS COME ROUND DROPPING DOWN THE PROUD STREAM	19 MODERN SAPPHO	V 6
THE GUIDE OF OUR DARK STEPS A TRIPLE VEIL	43 GIPSY CHILD	49

DARK   (CONTINUED)
        AND THY DARK MOURNFUL VISION RESTS ON ME   41 GIPSY CHILD   V   16
        OF ITS DARK UPLAND FARMS IS PAST   54 RESIGNATION   55
        THE LOOSE DARK STONES ON THE GREEN WAY   55 RESIGNATION   100
        IN DARK KNOTS CROUCH ROUND THE WILD FLAME   55 RESIGNATION   118
        AND DARK GREEN MELONS AND THERE RUSTUM SATE   67 SOHRAB RUSTUM   199
        LIKE SOME YOUNG CYPRESS TALL AND DARK AND STRAIGHT 70 SOHRAB RUSTUM   314
        ITS SLIGHT DARK SHADOW ON THE MOONLIT TURF   70 SOHRAB RUSTUM   316
        BY THEIR DARK SPRINGS THE WIND IN WINTER-TIME   73 SOHRAB RUSTUM   413
        BUT A DARK RUMOUR WILL BE BRUITED UP   79 SOHRAB RUSTUM   596
        AND THEN A DARK CLOUD PASSD BEFORE HIS EYES   81 SOHRAB RUSTUM   692
        MIGHT MEAN AND FROM HIS DARK COMPASSIONATE EYES   82 SOHRAB RUSTUM   735
        BUT HE MUST TREAD A DARK UNTRAVELLD ROAD   99 BALDER DEAD 1   143
        FOR IT GREW DARK BUT HODER TOUCHD HIS ARM   101 BALDER DEAD 1   229
        WHO IS IT UTTERS THROUGH THE DARK HIS HEST   102 BALDER DEAD 1   241
        TO THE DARK FORESTS IN THE EARLY DAWN   106 BALDER DEAD 2   52
        IN SILENCE UP THE DARK UNTRAVELLD ROAD   107 BALDER DEAD 2   79
        AND FROM THE DARK FLOCKD UP THE SHADOWY TRIBES   109 BALDER DEAD 2   156
        BUT THROUGH THE DARK THEY WATCHD THE BURNING SHIP 119 BALDER DEAD 3   197
        AND LONG IN THE FAR DARK BLAZED BALDERS PILE   119 BALDER DEAD 3   200
        REDDENING THE SEA AROUND AND ALL WAS DARK   119 BALDER DEAD 3   206
        AND IN FIELDS SLOPING TO THE SOUTH DARK PLOTS   122 BALDER DEAD 3   314
        FRINGED WITH DARK PINES AND SANDS WHERE SEAFOWL SCREAM 123 BALDER DEAD 3   327
        AND AS IN THE DARK NIGHT A TRAVELLING MAN   119 BALDER DEAD 3   V
        A DARK GREEN FOREST-DRESS   131 TRISTRAM 1   16
        LET HER HAVE HER PROUD DARK EYES   134 TRISTRAM 1   119
        THROUGH THE DARK UP THE DROWND SAND   137 TRISTRAM 1   218
        BUT THY DARK EYES ARE NOT DIMMD PROUD ISEULT   142 TRISTRAM 2   19
        AND THEY WOULD STILL HAVE LISTEND TILL DARK NIGHT 151 TRISTRAM 3   56
        RAN OUT FROM THE DARK UNDERWOOD BEHIND   155 TRISTRAM 3   209
        SEIRIOL THE BRIGHT KYBI THE DARK MEN SAID   170 EAST AND WEST   9
        DOWN THE DARK VALLEY I SAW   187 STRAYED REVEL   42
        STROWN WITH DARK SEEDS   187 STRAYED REVEL   58
        WITH THE DARK IVY-PLANTS   188 STRAYED REVEL   88
        THIS SPARE DARK-FEATURED   189 STRAYED REVEL   102
        AND THE DARK CUCUMBER   190 STRAYED REVEL   156
        SITTING IN THE DARK SHIP   192 STRAYED REVEL   202
        HIS DARK FOREBODING   192 STRAYED REVEL   218
        PASSING THROUGH THE DARK STEMS   194 STRAYED REVEL   278
        HANGS DARK UPON THE ROLLING SEA   205 CALAIS SANDS   22
        WITHOUT THAT ALLS DARK FOR MEN   215 PIS-ALLER   10
        INTO THE DEWY DARK OBSCURITY   242 SUMMER NIGHT   8
        YE HEAVENS WHOSE PURE DARK REGIONS HAVE NO SIGN 244 SUMMER NIGHT   78
        SCREEND BY DARK TREES ON EITHER HAND   248 KENSINGTON GARD   V   2
        THOSE DARK-TOPPD RED-BOLD PINETREES STAND   KENSINGTON GARD   V   4
        IN THIS HIGH FIELDS DARK CORNER WHERE HE LEAVES 255 SCHOLAR-GIPSY   12
        DARK BLUEBELLS DRENCHD WITH DEWS OF SUMMER EVES 257 SCHOLAR-GIPSY   88
        THY DARK VAGUE EYES AND SOFT ABSTRACTED AIR   258 SCHOLAR-GIPSY   99
        UNDER A DARK RED-FRUITED YEW-TREES SHADE   259 SCHOLAR-GIPSY   140
        FROM THE DARK DINGLES TO THE NIGHTINGALES   261 SCHOLAR-GIPSY   220
        SHY TRAFFICKERS THE DARK IBERIANS COME   262 SCHOLAR-GIPSY   249
        AH SINCE DARK DAYS STILL BRING TO LIGHT   272 MEMORIAL VERSES   58
        BUT SOME DARK SHADOW CAME   285 HAWORTH CHURCH   110
        IN THE DARK FERMENTATION OF EARTH   286 HAWORTH CHURCH   135
        DAYS NOT DARK AT THY SIDE   287 RUGBY CHAPEL   20
        UP THROUGH THE TALL DARK FIRS   297 HEINES GRAVE   156
        PAST THE DARK FORGES LONG DISUSED   299 GRANDE CHARTR   3
        THAT FRINGE THY DARK BLUE SPEZZIAN BAY   303 GRANDE CHARTR   V 142
        OF MANY A DARK-BOUGHD PINE   307 OBERMANN   30
        STAND DARK ROUND THY GREEN GRAVE   311 OBERMANN   168
        BEHOLD O KING FROM THE DARK   342 MEROPE   390
        SULLYING HIS GARMENT WITH DARK-STREAMING BLOOD   346 MEROPE   491
        ON SOME TALL SCAR FRINGED WITH DARK FEATHERY PINES 357 MEROPE   803
        IN SOME DARK FIR-TREES SHADOW AMID ROCKS   373 MEROPE   1167
        AGREES TO DEEM SOME DEEDS SO DARK IN GUILT   389 MEROPE   1524
        IS DARK AND ON THE STREAM THE MIST STILL HANGS   406 EMPEDOCLES I 1   13
        OF TREES AND VEINS OF TURF AND LONG DARK SHOOTS 414 EMPEDOCLES I 2   48
        THE ILL DEEDS OF OTHER MEN MAKE OFTEN OUR LIFE DARK 421 EMPEDOCLES I 2   266
        THROUGH THE DARK NIGHT SUDDENLY   430 EMPEDOCLES II   47
        PAIN AND CARE WITH A DARK STORE   431 EMPEDOCLES II   86
        IN THE WIND AND LOOSE DARK HAIR   433 EMPEDOCLES II   153
        YE AND THE PURE DARK ETHER WHERE YE RIDE   438 EMPEDOCLES II   304
        THEN ALL AGAIN IS DARK   445 WESTMIN ABBEY   41
        BUT FULL AND DEATHLESS AS THE DEEP DARK HUE   463 ALARIC AT ROME   35
        ON THE DARK CURRENT OF HIS CHANGELESS DAY   473 CROMWELL   62
        WHERE RODE THE TALL DARK SHIPS WHOSE LOOSEND SAIL 473 CROMWELL   67
        WITH GLOOMING CLOUDS BROODS DARK AND HEAVILY   475 CROMWELL   130
        ON THAT DARK FORM HIS EYES HAD GAZD BEFORE   477 CROMWELL   201
        THRO THE DARK CHAMBERS OF THE HEARTS OF MEN   478 CROMWELL   230
        WHERE THE DARK SHIPS RODE PROUDLY WOOD THE GALE 479 CROMWELL   238
        OER THOSE SAME SEAS DARK TENERIFFE ROSE FRAUGHT 485 S S LUSITANIA   11
        DARK THE VALLEY SLEEPS IN SHADE   META CLOISTER   14

DARKD
        GREW SUDDENLY IN HEAVEN AND DARKD THE SUN   75 SOHRAB RUSTUM   482

DARKEN
        DARKEN IN LABOUR AND PAIN   229 YOUTH OF NATURE   52

DARKEND
FROM YOUR DARKEND PALACE ROOMS	26	NEW SIRENS	4
AND DARKEND ALL AND A COLD FOG WITH NIGHT	86	SOHRAB RUSTUM	867
BUT NIGHT CAME DOWN AND DARKEND ASGARD STREETS	101	BALDER DEAD 1	202
ON A MAY EVENING IN THE DARKEND LANES	101	BALDER DEAD 1	233
SHUTTERS AND DARKEND ROOM	293	HEINES GRAVE	18
WHERE THE RIDGD PINE-DARKEND ROOTS	433	EMPEDOCLES II	V 137
OF MEN WITH MIND THUS DARKEND AND ASTRAY	446	WESTMIN ABBEY	68
OF MEN WHOSE MINDS WERE DARKEND AND ASTRAY	446	WESTMIN ABBEY	V 68
LIKE SUMMER LIGHTNINGS OER A DARKEND SKY	474	CROMWELL	72

DARKENING
BEACHES THE PINNACE IN A DARKENING COVE	69	SOHRAB RUSTUM	V 288
THROUGH THE FAST-DARKENING STREETS TO HIS OWN HOUSE	101	BALDER DEAD 1	207
AND LED THEM HOME OVER THE DARKENING HEATH	151	TRISTRAM 3	63
DARKENING FAST BUT A LIGHT	234	YOUTH OF MAN	80
OFT THROUGH THE DARKENING FIELDS HAVE SEEN THEE ROAM	257	SCHOLAR-GIPSY	84

DARKENS
THE AUTUMNAL EVENING DARKENS ROUND	299	GRANDE CHARTR	7

DARKER
WHO POSSESSD HIS DARKER HOUR	132	TRISTRAM 1	73
THE DARKER ELMS STAND GRAVE AND DUN	248	KENSINGTON GARD	V

DARKLING
AND BY THE DARKLING FOREST-PATHS THE GODS	106	BALDER DEAD 2	63
AND WE ARE HERE AS ON A DARKLING PLAIN	212	DOVER BEACH	35

DARKNESS
STOPPD IN DARKNESS IN THE COURT	14	CHURCH BROU 1	42
THAT AS THE BALMY DARKNESS FELL	54	RESIGNATION	83
WAITING THE DARKNESS OF THE FINAL TIMES	98	BALDER DEAD 1	124
AND MOUNTED SLEIPNER AND IN DARKNESS RODE	102	BALDER DEAD 1	255
HER DARKNESS FROM HER GRASP A SUBJECT TEAR	121	BALDER DEAD 3	280
SO FLARD IN THE FAR DARKNESS BALDERS PYRE	119	BALDER DEAD 3	V 200
SO SHOWED IN THE FAR DARKNESS BALDERS PYRE	119	BALDER DEAD 3	V 200
DEEP BE THE DARKNESS AND STILL BE THE SLUMBER	206	SEPARATION	11
AND DARKNESS RETURNS TO OUR EYES	229	YOUTH OF NATURE	58
TO GROW OLD IN DARKNESS AND PAIN	234	YOUTH OF MAN	58
THROUGH THE GATHERING DARKNESS ARISE	286	RUGBY CHAPEL	11
AND DARKNESS STEAL OER THE WET GRASS	310	OBERMANN	117
AFTER LONG DARKNESS RUDE	322	OBERMANN MORE	294
SOFT DARKNESS ON THE TURF DID LIE	323	OBERMANN MORE	329
ALL-COVERING DARKNESS O KING	372	MEROPE	1141
OF DARKNESS SO TREMENDOUS THAT ITS AUTHOR	385	MEROPE	1420
THAT I HAVE LOVED NO DARKNESS	441	EMPEDOCLES II	400
AND DOWN OVER THE THAMES THE DARKNESS DREW	444	WESTMIN ABBEY	13

DARKSOME
ALONE AND IN A DARKSOME PLACE	90	SICK KING BOKH	66
NOR LIT WITH SUN BUT THROUGH THE DARKSOME AIR	108	BALDER DEAD 2	125
AND OER A DARKSOME TRACT WHICH KNOWS NO SUN	108	BALDER DEAD 2	139
NOT LIT WITH SUN BUT THROUGH THE DARKSOME AIR	108	BALDER DEAD 2	V 125
BROTHER THOU DWELLEST IN THE DARKSOME LAND	115	BALDER DEAD 3	75

DARLING
IACCHUS DARLING	188	STRAYED REVEL	79
MY DARLING ON THIS LONELY AIR	205	CALAIS SANDS	14
MY DARLING ON THIS QUIET AIR	205	CALAIS SANDS	V 14

DARNS
WHERE AT HER OPEN DOOR THE HOUSEWIFE DARNS	258	SCHOLAR-GIPSY	102

DART
YOU SAW THE BRIGHT-EYED SQUIRRELS DART ALONG	155	TRISTRAM 3	195

DARTING
HUNG POISED AND THEN THE DARTING RIVER OF LIFE	25	DREAM	31
CURLING AND DARTING HIGHER UNTIL THEY LICKD	119	BALDER DEAD 3	189
AND DARTING SWALLOWS AND LIGHT WATER-GNATS	266	THYRSIS	125

DARTS
LAY THICKLY STREWN SWORDS AXES DARTS AND SPEARS	95	BALDER DEAD 1	2
THAT CHILD WHO DARTS ACROSS THE GLADE		KENSINGTON GARD	V 9

DASH
THE LONGD-FOR DASH OF WAVES IS HEARD AND WIDE	87	SOHRAB RUSTUM	889
AND DASH OUR HOLIEST RAPTURES WHILE WE GAZE	470	ALARIC AT ROME	200

DASHD
DASHD WITH A CLANG TOGETHER AND A DIN	75	SOHRAB RUSTUM	475

DASTARD
OUR DASTARD PATIENCE BE OUR DARING NOW	367	MEROPE	1055

DATE
AND STOOPS TO CLEAR THY MOSS-GROWN DATE	311	OBERMANN	173
BUT NOW THE OLD IS OUT OF DATE	321	OBERMANN MORE	245
BUT NOW THE PAST IS OUT OF DATE	321	OBERMANN MORE	V 245
HENCEFORTH BE HONOURD AS THE DATE OF PEACE	333	MEROPE	116

DATE   (CONTINUED)
       MY DEED IS OF OLD DATE AND LONG ATONED   • • • •   396 MEROPE   1768
       OF DOUBTFUL FUTURE DATE • • • • • • • • •   425 EMPEDOCLES I 2   403
       EVEN TO A DATE BEYOND OUR OWN • • • • • • • •   451 GEISTS GRAVE   62

DATED
       TO THESE OUT-DATED 'STINGS AGAIN   • • • • • •   302 GRANDE CHARTR   106

DATES
       WHAT CLOUDS THY FOREHEAD AND FORE-DATES THY DOOM • •   41 GIPSY CHILD   V 4
       WE SCRUTINISE THE DATES • • • • • • • • • •   423 EMPEDOCLES I 2   322

DAUGHTER
       DAUGHTER AND WIFE OF ODIN THUS SHE SAID   • • • •   120 BALDER DEAD 3   247
       DAUGHTER OF FRANCE TO FRANCE THY HOME   • • • •   184 TERRACE BERNE   18
       DROVE MY DAUGHTER SMALL AND ME   • • • •   457 POOR MATTHIAS   179
       YOU SAY TRUE MY DAUGHTER PEACE IS HERE   • • • •   META CLOISTER   40

DAULIS
       LONE DAULIS AND THE HIGH CEPHISSIAN VALE   • • • •   201 PHILOMELA   27

DAUNTLESS
       THE THOUGHT THAT SPURRD IT AND A DAUNTLESS WILL   • •   478 CROMWELL   228

DAUNTLESSLY
       HIS ARM HE RAISD IT DAUNTLESSLY   • • • • • •   481 COURAGE   16

DAVIDS
       FROM DAVIDS LIPS THIS WORD DID ROLL   • • • • •   318 OBERMANN MORE   V
       FROM DAVIDS LIPS THAT WORD DID ROLL   • • • • •   318 OBERMANN MORE   V

DAWN
       NOR WILL THAT DAY DAWN AT A HUMAN NOD   • • • •   7 REP FRIEND CONT   9
       FROM THE JEWELLD LANDS OF DAWN   • • • • • •   26 NEW SIRENS   22
       AND THE JOYFUL DAWN WERE GONE   • • • • • •   30 NEW SIRENS   118
       WHEN A DREARY DAWN IS WADING   • • • • • •   33 NEW SIRENS   211
       FROM THE GOLDEN SPRINGS OF DAWN   • • • •   26 NEW SIRENS   V 22
       DREAMS DAWN AND FLY FRIENDS SMILE AND DIE   • •   44 QUESTION   8
       IS ANSWERD FROM THE DEPTH OF DAWN   • • •   57 RESIGNATION   177
       BUT WHEN THE GREY DAWN STOLE INTO HIS TENT   • • •   61 SOHRAB RUSTUM   7
       WHO ART THOU FOR IT IS NOT YET CLEAR DAWN   • •   62 SOHRAB RUSTUM   31
       AND ALL ITS BOUNDING RAPTURE AS AT DAWN   • • • •   79 SOHRAB RUSTUM   620
       TAKE SLEIPNER HERMOD AND SET FORTH WITH DAWN   • • •   102 BALDER DEAD 1   236
       LOATHING TO MEET AT DAWN THE OTHER GODS   • • •   102 BALDER DEAD 1   250
       AND TWAS WHEN NIGHT IS BORDERING HARD ON DAWN   •   103 BALDER DEAD 1   280
       FOR WITH TO-MORROWS DAWN THE GODS PREPARE   • •   103 BALDER DEAD 1   295
       BUT NOW HE CREW AT DAWN A CHEERFUL NOTE   • • •   105 BALDER DEAD 2   8
       TO THE DARK FORESTS IN THE EARLY DAWN   • • •   106 BALDER DEAD 2   52
       AND AS A TRAVELLER IN THE EARLY DAWN • • • •   113 BALDER DEAD 2   295
       TWAS DAWN A BROUGHAM ROLLD THROUGH THE STREETS   167 RACHEL 1   4
                AND MADE
       LENT IT THE MUSIC OF ITS TREES AT DAWN   • • •   175 PARTING   20
       WHEN THE WHITE DAWN FIRST   • • • • •   186 STRAYED REVEL   24
       WHICH THE DAWN-GODDESS BORE   • • • • •   196 FRAG ANTIGONE   55
       YEARS HENCE PERHAPS MAY DAWN AN AGE   • • • •   304 GRANDE CHARTR   157
       THERE MAY PERHAPS YET DAWN AN AGE   • • • •   304 GRANDE CHARTR V 157
       THERE YET PERHAPS MAY DAWN AN AGE   • • • •   304 GRANDE CHARTR V 157
       SOME NEW SUCH HOPE MUST DAWN AT LAST   • • •   321 OBERMANN MORE   243
       A NEW SUCH HOPE MUST DAWN AT LAST   • • • •   321 OBERMANN MORE V 243
       SOON SHALL HE DAWN ON THIS LAND   • • • • •   347 MEROPE   515
       ONE NIGHT AND THE NEXT DAY AT DAWN FARED ON   • •   356 MEROPE   747
       YET SHALL HE DAWN ON THIS LAND   • • • • •   347 MEROPE   V 515
       AT DAWN THOU TO KING SEBERT SHALT RELATE   • • •   445 WESTMIN ABBEY   48

DAWND
       PASSD YOU A LITTLE SINCE AS MORNING DAWND   • • • •   408 EMPEDOCLES I 1   46

DAWNING
       YES I MUSE AND IF THE DAWNING   • • • • • •   29 NEW SIRENS   105
       COLD IN THAT UNLOVELY DAWNING   • • • • • •   35 NEW SIRENS   265
       WHILE THE DAWNING OF THE MORROW   • • • • •   33 NEW SIRENS   V 217

DAWNS
       WHEN DAWNS THAT DAY THAT DAY   • • • • • •   48 HORATIAN ECHO   36
       MEANWHILE TO-MORROW WHEN THE MORNING DAWNS • • • •   96 BALDER DEAD 1   40
       THE WORLDS GREAT ORDER DAWNS IN SHEEN   • • • •   322 OBERMANN MORE   293
       SO LIKE A STAR DAWNS THY SON   • • • • • •   393 MEROPE   1682

DAY
       A VOICE ORACULAR HATH PEALD TO-DAY   • • • •   3 EMERSONS ESSAYS   3
       TO-DAY A HEROS BANNER IS UNFURLD   • • • •   3 EMERSONS ESSAYS   4
       NOR WILL THAT DAY DAWN AT A HUMAN NOD   • • • •   7 REP FRIEND CONT   9
       THE GODS DECLARE MY RECOMPENCE TO-DAY   • • •   9 MYCERINUS   16
       MIGHT WANDER ALL DAY LONG AND NEVER TIRE   • • •   11 MYCERINUS   91
       AND BY THAT SILENT KNOWLEDGE DAY BY DAY   • • •   12 MYCERINUS   110
       AND BY THAT SILENT KNOWLEDGE DAY BY DAY   • • •   12 MYCERINUS   110
       SO SIX LONG YEARS HE REVELLD NIGHT AND DAY   • •   12 MYCERINUS   122
       RISES HIGHER DAY BY DAY • • • • • • • •   15 CHURCH BROU 1   88
       RISES HIGHER DAY BY DAY • • • • • • • •   15 CHURCH BROU 1   88
       ONE DAY TO HARBOUR IN THE TOMB   • • • • •   22 YOUTH AND CALM   15
       RICH TO-MORROW AS TO-DAY • • • • • • • •   22 MEMORY-PICTURE   3

DAY   (CONTINUED)

SOME DAY NEXT YEAR I SHALL BE . . . .   23 MEMORY-PICTURE   19
STREAM ALL DAY THROUGH YOUR ENCHANTED LAWN . . . .   26 NEW SIRENS   24
OR THE DAY WERE SOONER DONE . . . .   29 NEW SIRENS   110
AND THE SOMBRE DAY DRAGGD ON . . . .   30 NEW SIRENS   116
WHICH THE SORROW-STRICKEN DAY DENIES . . . . . .   32 NEW SIRENS   178
MIRTH TO-DAY AND VINE-BOUND TRESSES . . . . . .   33 NEW SIRENS   197
EVEN BY MOMENTS OF TO-DAY . . . .   33 NEW SIRENS   222
HALF THEIR GLORIES TO THE DAY . . . .   35 NEW SIRENS   256
HIS WHO IN MOUNTAIN GLENS AT NOON OF DAY . . .   42 GIPSY CHILD   22
ONCE ERE THE DAY DECLINE THOU SHALT DISCERN . .   44 GIPSY CHILD   65
SOME DREAMERS WHO FAR OFF A SUMMERS DAY . . . .   42 GIPSY CHILD   V 22
ONCE ERE THY DAY GO DOWN THOU SHALT DISCERN . .   44 GIPSY CHILD   V 65
SEASONS ALTERNATING AND NIGHT AND DAY . . . . .   45 IN UTRUMQUE PAR   5
THE DAY APPROACHES WHEN WE MUST . . . . . .   48 HORATIAN ECHO   31
WHEN DAWNS THAT DAY THAT DAY . . . .   48 HORATIAN ECHO   36
WHEN DAWNS THAT DAY THAT DAY . . . .   48 HORATIAN ECHO   36
WHO EACH DAY MORE SURELY LEARNS . . . . . .   49 SECOND BEST   20
OBEDIENCE TO THE PASSING DAY . . . .   53 RESIGNATION   29
THAT WAYSIDE INN WE LEFT TO-DAY . . . .   53 RESIGNATION   41
PARCHD AND ROAD-WORN WE MADE THAT DAY . . . . .   54 RESIGNATION   81
THE LAW GREW STRONGER EVERY DAY . . . . . .   56 RESIGNATION   135
THOUGH HE MOVE MOUNTAINS THOUGH HIS DAY . . .   56 RESIGNATION   148
NOBLER THAN THIS TO FILL THE DAY . . . . . .   59 RESIGNATION   240
SHOULD ONE DAY GREET UPON SOME WELL-FOUGHT FIELD . . 62 SOHRAB RUSTUM   51
LET THE TWO ARMIES REST TO-DAY BUT I . . . . .   62 SOHRAB RUSTUM   55
LET THERE BE TRUCE BETWEEN THE HOSTS TO-DAY . .   65 SOHRAB RUSTUM   151
BUT NOT TO-DAY TO-DAY HAS OTHER NEEDS . . . .   67 SOHRAB RUSTUM   209
BUT NOT TO-DAY TO-DAY HAS OTHER NEEDS . . . .   67 SOHRAB RUSTUM   209
PLUNGING ALL DAY IN THE BLUE WAVES AT NIGHT . .   69 SOHRAB RUSTUM   287
BEFORE THY FACE THIS DAY AND WERE REVEALD . .   72 SOHRAB RUSTUM   371
OF SOME PAIND DESERT-LION WHO ALL DAY . . . .   76 SOHRAB RUSTUM   504
A PERSIAN LORD THIS DAY AND STRIP HIS CORPSE . .   77 SOHRAB RUSTUM   529
AND I WERE THAT WHICH TILL TO-DAY I WAS . . .   77 SOHRAB RUSTUM   545
SURELY THE NEWS WILL ONE DAY REACH HIS EAR . . .   78 SOHRAB RUSTUM   581
AND ALL DAY LONG AND WHEN NIGHT COMES THE LAMP . .   81 SOHRAB RUSTUM   675
FATHER FORBEAR FOR I BUT MEET TO-DAY . . . .   82 SOHRAB RUSTUM   708
THAT I SHOULD ONE DAY FIND THY LORD AND THEE . .   83 SOHRAB RUSTUM   745
NOT YET BUT THOU SHALT HAVE IT ON THAT DAY . . .   85 SOHRAB RUSTUM   830
SOON BE THAT DAY MY SON AND DEEP THAT SEA . .   85 SOHRAB RUSTUM   836
AND ON A FEAST DAY IN AFRASIABS HALL . . . .   71 SOHRAB RUSTUM   V 355
AND I WERE HE WHO TILL TO-DAY I WAS . . . . .   77 SOHRAB RUSTUM   V 545
THEM AND THEIR DUES THIS DAY THE KING . . . .   87 SICK KING BOKH   3
O MERCHANTS TARRY YET A DAY . . . .   87 SICK KING BOKH   5
WASTES AND RUNS THINNER EVERY DAY . . . . .   89 SICK KING BOKH   64
VEX ONE ANOTHER NIGHT AND DAY . . . .   93 SICK KING BOKH   174
I LOSE TO-DAY SO BRIGHT SO LOVED A GOD . . .   96 BALDER DEAD 1   22
BUT OURS WE SHALL NOT MEET WHEN THAT DAY COMES . .   96 BALDER DEAD 1   31
BE STRICTLY CARED FOR IN THE APPOINTED DAY . .   96 BALDER DEAD 1   39
BOTH NIGHT AND DAY AND BY THE INNER WALL . . .   98 BALDER DEAD 1   91
WHICH EVERY DAY THEY COME AND GO IN HEAVEN . .   99 BALDER DEAD 1   140
DAY DROVE HIS COURSER WITH THE SHINING MANE . .   105 BALDER DEAD 2   2
AND ALL DAY LONG THEY THERE ARE HACKD AND HEWN . . 105 BALDER DEAD 2   15
ON THE TWELFTH DAY THE GODS SHALL BURN HIS CORPSE 106 BALDER DEAD 2   44
AND FROM THE GLENS ALL DAY AN ECHO CAME . . .   106 BALDER DEAD 2   54
ALL DAY AND DAYLIGHT WANED AND NIGHT CAME ON . .   107 BALDER DEAD 2   81
YET HE SHALL ONE DAY RISE AND BURST HIS BONDS . . 111 BALDER DEAD 2   222
HOWBEIT WE ABIDE OUR DAY TILL THEN . . . .   111 BALDER DEAD 2   227
SO HERMOD COMES TO-DAY UNFOLLOWD HOME . . . .   114 BALDER DEAD 3   19
AND PERISH AGAINST FATE BEFORE THY DAY . . . .   114 BALDER DEAD 3   29
YE GODS THESE TERMS MAY KEEP ANOTHER DAY . . .   115 BALDER DEAD 3   49
THEY MOURND THAT DAY SO BRIGHT SO LOVED A GOD . . 115 BALDER DEAD 3   64
IN THAT GREAT DAY THE TWILIGHT OF THE GODS . .   115 BALDER DEAD 3   68
BUT FROM THY LIPS O BALDER NIGHT OR DAY . . .   116 BALDER DEAD 3   83
ONE DAY THE WANDERING ODER WILL RETURN . . .   116 BALDER DEAD 3   115
AND SOON HAD ALL THAT DAY BEEN SPENT IN WAIL . .   118 BALDER DEAD 3   155
DIVIDING CLEAR THE PATHS OF NIGHT AND DAY . . .   121 BALDER DEAD 3   265
AND BRING US NEARER TO THE FINAL DAY . . . .   127 BALDER DEAD 3   474
WHO LIVE AND WITH THEIR EYES SHALL SEE THAT DAY .   127 BALDER DEAD 3   486
THE DAY WILL COME WHEN FALL SHALL ASGARDS TOWERS . 127 BALDER DEAD 3   487
YET DOUBTLESS WHEN THE DAY OF BATTLE COMES . .   127 BALDER DEAD 3   494
IN NEW-RECOVERD SEATS THE HAPPIER DAY . . . .   128 BALDER DEAD 3   513
BROTHER WHAT SEATS ARE THESE WHAT HAPPIER DAY . . 128 BALDER DEAD 3   515
THE DAY WILL COME WHEN ASGARDS TOWERS SHALL FALL   127 BALDER DEAD 3   V 487
EACH HER HOUR OF TRISTRAMS DAY . . . . . .   132 TRISTRAM 1   69
NOT PENT ON SHIP-BOARD THIS DELICIOUS DAY . . .   133 TRISTRAM 1   98
MIGHT DRINK IT ON THEIR MARRIAGE-DAY . . . . .   135 TRISTRAM 1   139
HAD BEEN THE LIKELIEST TRYSTING-PLACE TO-DAY . .   135 TRISTRAM 1   165
PASSING THE LONG SUMMERS DAY . . . .   137 TRISTRAM 1   222
MAKES THEIR CHAMBER AS BRIGHT AS DAY . . . .   140 TRISTRAM 1   334
FAR LOVELIER THAN THEY ARE BY DAY . . . . .   141 TRISTRAM 1   356
THE BARE HEATHS SPREADING CLEAR AS DAY . . . .   141 TRISTRAM 1   364
BOTH HAVE BROUGHT THEIR ANXIOUS DAY TO EVENING . . 144 TRISTRAM 2   55
SHOOK HER WEAK BOSOM DAY AND NIGHT . . . .   147 TRISTRAM 2   133
THE YOUNG SURVIVING ISEULT ONE BRIGHT DAY . .   149 TRISTRAM 3   5
ONE AFTER ONE TO-MORROW LIKE TO-DAY . . . .   151 TRISTRAM 3   67
SHE HAS HER CHILDREN TOO AND NIGHT AND DAY . .   152 TRISTRAM 3   102
WITH WHICH THIS DAY THE CHILDREN SHE BEGUILED . . 152 TRISTRAM 3   107
UNDER THE HOLLIES THAT BRIGHT WINTERS DAY . .   154 TRISTRAM 3   152
IN THESE LONE SYLVAN GLADES THAT APRIL-DAY . .   154 TRISTRAM 3   163

DAY (CONTINUED)

THEY CAME TO WHERE THE BRUSHWOOD CEASED AND DAY	155	TRISTRAM 3	185
IS MERLIN PRISONER TILL THE JUDGMENT-DAY	156	TRISTRAM 3	222
THE YEAR HAD TRAVELLD ROUND AND ONE BRIGHT DAY		TRISTRAM 3	V 1
STARS SHONE AFTER A DAY OF STORM	156	SAINT BRANDAN	14
SIR KNIGHT WHO WEDDST TO-DAY	159	NECKAN	24
SHE WILL NOT COME THOUGH YOU CALL ALL DAY	162	FORSAKEN MERM	28
IN THE LITTLE GREY CHURCH ON THE SHORE TO-DAY	163	FORSAKEN MERM	57
IN THIS HER LIFES LAST DAY OUR POOR OUR PAIN	168	RACHEL 2	10
EASTWARD THE OTHER FROM THE DYING DAY	170	EAST AND WEST	7
WHO FAILD UNDER THE HEAT OF THIS LIFES DAY	172	IMMORTALITY	7
THOU TOO WILT SURELY ONE DAY PROVE	178	FAREWELL	38
YET WE SHALL ONE DAY GAIN LIFE PAST	179	FAREWELL	53
WE WERE APART YET DAY BY DAY	180	ISOLATION MARG	1
WE WERE APART YET DAY BY DAY	180	ISOLATION MARG	1
LIKE MINE EACH DAY MORE TRIED MORE TRUE	180	ISOLATION MARG	6
OCEAN AND CLOUDS AND NIGHT AND DAY	181	ISOLATION MARG	33
I SHIVER FOR THE PASSING DAY	183	ABSENCE	3
BUT EACH DAY BRINGS ITS PETTY DUST	183	ABSENCE	9
I SHUDDER FOR THE PASSING DAY	183	ABSENCE	V 3
SEE WHAT THE DAY BRINGS	188	STRAYED REVEL	74
ALL DAY LONG HAVE SEEN	194	STRAYED REVEL	273
FOR FROM THE DAY WHEN THESE	195	FRAG ANTIGONE	11
MUST EVERY DAY ENDURE	195	FRAG ANTIGONE	22
FOR EVERY DAY MAN MAY BE LINKD AND LOOSED	196	FRAG ANTIGONE	34
NOT ONCE TO DAY THESE EYES HAVE STAYD	205	CALAIS SANDS	V 17
SOME DAY I SHALL BE COLD I KNOW	207	ON THE RHINE	2
BY DAY I SHALL BE WELL AGAIN	208	LONGING	2
THE HOPELESS LONGING OF THE DAY	208	LONGING	4
BY DAY I SHALL BE WELL AGAIN	209	LONGING	14
THE HOPELESS LONGING OF THE DAY	209	LONGING	16
AH WHOSE HAND THAT DAY THROUGH HEAVEN GUIDED	210	SELF-DECEPTION	13
NOT YET HALF THROUGH THE DAY	216	LORDS MESSENGER	17
AT THE CLOSE OF DAY FROM THE PLAIN	217	LORDS MESSENGER	21
UNHEARD ALL DAY ASCENDS AGAIN	217	BACCHANALIA 1	3
THE BUSINESS OF THE DAY IS DONE	218	BACCHANALIA 1	8
THE PERFUME WHICH THE DAY FORGOES	218	BACCHANALIA 1	15
IN THE HOT PRESS OF THE NOON-DAY	219	BACCHANALIA 2	18
AND NOBLY PERFECT IN OUR DAY	222	EPILOG LAOCOON	26
THOUGH SHE MOVE NOT EARTH TO-DAY	227	PERSIST POETRY	2
THOUGH SHE RULE NOT EARTH TO-DAY	227	PERSIST POETRY	V 2
DIED IN HIS ENEMIES DAY	229	YOUTH OF NATURE	35
HE IS DEAD AND THE FRUIT-BEARING DAY	229	YOUTH OF NATURE	56
FAR OFF A GLORY OF DAY	234	YOUTH OF MAN	81
AND WHAT THEN SHALL BE SAID TO THOSE TO-DAY	237	PROGRESS	14
ONE DAY THOU SAYST THERE WILL AT LAST APPEAR	239	REVOLUTIONS	17
OF THE LONG DAY AND WISH TWERE DONE	241	MORALITY	10
A MELANCHOLY INTO ALL OUR DAY	247	BURIED LIFE	76
THE CHANGES OF THEIR QUIET DAY	249	KENSINGTON GARD	32
THE STAGES OF THEIR QUIET DAY		KENSINGTON GARD	V 32
ALL THE LIVE MURMUR OF A SUMMERS DAY	255	SCHOLAR-GIPSY	20
HAVE KNOWN THEE EYING ALL AN APRIL-DAY	258	SCHOLAR-GIPSY	107
AND LOSE TO-MORROW THE GROUND WON TO-DAY	260	SCHOLAR-GIPSY	179
AND DAY AND NIGHT HELD ON INDIGNANTLY	262	SCHOLAR-GIPSY	243
HAVE KNOWN THEE WATCHING ALL AN APRIL-DAY	258	SCHOLAR-GIPSY	V 107
HAVE KNOWN THEE HAUNTING ALL AN APRIL-DAY	258	SCHOLAR-GIPSY	V 107
BEFORE THE ROSES AND THE LONGEST DAY	264	THYRSIS	53
HATH SINCE OUR DAY PUT BY	266	THYRSIS	116
I SEE HER VEIL DRAW SOFT ACROSS THE DAY	266	THYRSIS	133
THUS YESTERDAY TO-DAY TO-MORROW COME	262	THYRSIS	V
THE SMOOTH TO-DAY OF GOD	262	THYRSIS	V
WE STAND TO-DAY BY WORDSWORTHS TOMB	270	MEMORIAL VERSES	5
WE STAND TO-DAY AT WORDSWORTHS TOMB	270	MEMORIAL VERSES	V 5
AND ONCE A DAY	277	SOUTHERN NIGHT	80
BY DAY AND NIGHT	278	SOUTHERN NIGHT	88
O SPENT ONES OF A WORK-DAY AGE	279	SOUTHERN NIGHT	115
BEHOLD THE ELDER TO-DAY	281	HAWORTH CHURCH	30
THOU O MOURND ONE TO-DAY	284	HAWORTH CHURCH	77
AND AT THE END OF THY DAY	290	RUGBY CHAPEL	142
WHO ALL ROUND ME TO-DAY	290	RUGBY CHAPEL	156
THE SILENT COURTS WHERE NIGHT AND DAY	300	GRANDE CHARTR	31
THE WORLD WHICH FOR AN IDLE DAY	304	GRANDE CHARTR	152
IN THIS OUR TROUBLED DAY	307	OBERMANN	46
KNOWS HOW THE DAY HATH GONE	309	OBERMANN	102
THE SUMMER-DAY GROW LATE	310	OBERMANN	116
PERCEIVST THOU NOT THE CHANGE OF DAY	315	OBERMANN MORE	81
AND FILLD HER LIFE WITH DAY	316	OBERMANN MORE	116
OH HAD I LIVED IN THAT GREAT DAY	317	OBERMANN MORE	141
WHEN YOUR WORLDS DAY WAS SPENT	320	OBERMANN MORE	220
THE DAY I LIVED IN WAS NOT MINE	321	OBERMANN MORE	257
MAN GETS NO SECOND DAY	321	OBERMANN MORE	258
A WORLD LIKE OURS TO-DAY	315	OBERMANN MORE	V 84
HASTE AND ADVISE FOR DAY COMES ON APACE	330	MEROPE	28
THIS DAY AMID THESE RITES THIS BLACK-ROBED TRAIN	333	MEROPE	105
THIS DAY TO-MORROW YESTERDAY ALIKE	333	MEROPE	110
HEAR ME THEN SPEAK AND LET THIS MOURNFUL DAY	333	MEROPE	114
YES TWENTY YEARS AGO THIS DAY BEHELD	333	MEROPE	117
THESE OFFERINGS HOME OUR RITES ARE SPOILD TO-DAY	336	MEROPE	196
FOR FROM THE DAY WHEN THE FIRST	343	MEROPE	420
NIGHT AND DAY SEE THEM FALL	346	MEROPE	502

DAY   (CONTINUED)
        TO RECEIVE ARCAS WHO TO-DAY SHOULD COME   •   •   •   350 MEROPE   598
        AND SINCE HAS FONDLY WATCHD HIM NIGHT AND DAY   •   •   351 MEROPE   618
        ONE NIGHT AND THE NEXT DAY AT DAWN FARED ON   •   •   356 MEROPE   747
        WHILE THE GOOD SLEEP THE WORKERS HAVE THE DAY   •   •   366 MEROPE   996
        THAT I TO-DAY RETURNING FIND MYSELF   •   •   •   •   385 MEROPE   1410
        A TIME WILL COME FOR GREETINGS BUT TO-DAY   •   •   •   386 MEROPE   1444
        TO WHOM THIS DAY HE CAME TO PROFFER PEACE   •   •   •   387 MEROPE   1482
        AT DAY-BREAK THROUGH THE DEW   •   •   •   •   •   •   392 MEROPE   1645
        ATONED THIS VERY DAY PERHAPS IT IS   •   •   •   •   397 MEROPE   1769
        TO-DAY I REIGN THE REST I LEAVE TO FATE   •   •   •   397 MEROPE   1776
        A WILLING A WILLING SACRIFICE ON THAT DAY   •   •   •   399 MEROPE   1830
        ANOTHER ANOTHER SACRIFICE ON THIS DAY   •   •   •   •   400 MEROPE   1855
        SISTER FROM THIS DAY FORTH THOU ART NO MORE   •   •   403 MEROPE   1954
        SO LOOKD HE IN THAT DREADFUL DAY OF DEATH   •   •   •   404 MEROPE   1977
        MORE THAN A DAY AND NIGHT PAUSANIAS   •   •   •   •   409 EMPEDOCLES I 1   100
        IN SUCH A GLEN ON SUCH A DAY   •   •   •   •   •   •   414 EMPEDOCLES I 2   57
        AND WE FEEL DAY AND NIGHT   •   •   •   •   •   •   •   416 EMPEDOCLES I 2   127
        BUT THE DAY WEARS GO NOW PAUSANIAS   •   •   •   •   427 EMPEDOCLES I 2   464
        EITHER TO-MORROW OR SOME OTHER DAY   •   •   •   •   428 EMPEDOCLES I 2   471
        FILL THEE TO SEE OUR DAY   •   •   •   •   •   •   •   416 EMPEDOCLES I 2   V 113
        AND THE WORLD HATH THE DAY AND MUST BREAK THEE   •   •   429 EMPEDOCLES II   17
        AS THE SKY-BRIGHTENING SOUTH-WIND CLEARS THE DAY   •   •   432 EMPEDOCLES II   121
        BY OTHER RULES THAN ARE IN VOGUE TO-DAY   •   •   •   436 EMPEDOCLES II   265
        THE DAY IN HIS HOTNESS   •   •   •   •   •   •   •   •   443 EMPEDOCLES II   465
        THE DAY IN ITS HOTNESS   •   •   •   •   •   •   •   •   443 EMPEDOCLES II   V 465
        WARM IN HER BREAST BY DAY   •   •   •   •   •   •   •   446 WESTMIN ABBEY   87
        ON THEE TOO IN THY DAY   •   •   •   •   •   •   •   •   447 WESTMIN ABBEY   117
        ONE DAY THINE IMMEMORIAL GLEAM RETURN   •   •   •   •   449 WESTMIN ABBEY   V 175
        WHAT WAS FOUR YEARS THEIR WHOLE SHORT DAY   •   •   •   450 GEISTS GRAVE   20
        OF THAT UNRETURNING DAY   •   •   •   •   •   •   •   453 POOR MATTHIAS   50
        MAX AND KAISER WE TO-DAY   •   •   •   •   •   •   •   454 POOR MATTHIAS   67
        TELLING HOW ONE STORMY DAY   •   •   •   •   •   •   457 POOR MATTHIAS   177
        LIVE OUT THE DAY   •   •   •   •   •   •   •   •   •   460 KAISER DEAD   48
        TWICE ERE THAT DAY OF SHAME THE EMBATTLED FOE   •   •   465 ALARIC AT ROME   73
        HAST THOU NOT MARKED ON A WILD AUTUMN DAY   •   •   •   466 ALARIC AT ROME   97
        OH YES IF FANCY FEELS BEYOND TO DAY   •   •   •   •   467 ALARIC AT ROME   127
        AND HIS YOUNG DREAMS OF CONQUEST HOW TO-DAY   •   •   468 ALARIC AT ROME   171
        AND SOONEST FADE IN THE BROAD GLARE OF DAY   •   •   •   470 ALARIC AT ROME   214
        THE VANISHT GLORIES OF THINE EARLY DAY   •   •   •   471 ALARIC AT ROME   224
        ON THE DARK CURRENT OF HIS CHANGELESS DAY   •   •   •   473 CROMWELL   62
        TO WESTERN SHORES THE DEATH-PLACE OF THE DAY   •   •   475 CROMWELL   112
        O HAPPY SLUMBER IF THE DAY WERE DONE   •   •   •   •   475 CROMWELL   120
        THE NIGHT OF TERRORS AND THE DAY OF CARE   •   •   •   478 CROMWELL   205
        THAT DAY OF BOUNDLESS HOPE AND PROMISE HIGH   •   •   478 CROMWELL   211
        THAT DAY THAT HAILD HIS TRIUMPHS SAW HIM DIE   •   •   478 CROMWELL   212
        LIKE LOWERING CLOUDS THAT AT THE CLOSE OF DAY   •   •   478 CROMWELL   215
        OH THAT PAST TIMES COULD GIVE OUR DAY   •   •   •   •   482 COURAGE   27
        THERE SHALL FIND FULFILMENT IN ITS DAY   •   •   •   483 THEKLAS ANSWER   22
        I PASSD TO-DAY OER WALTON HEATH   •   •   •   •   •   483 ROME-SICKNESS   5
        I CROSSD ST GEORGES HILL TO-DAY   •   •   •   •   •   484 ROME-SICKNESS   13
        IN HIS LONG BLACK SHIP SPEEDING NIGHT AND DAY   •   •   485 S S LUSITANIA   10
        FOR THAT DAY WILL COME MY SOUL IS ASSURD OF ITS COMING   HOMER TRANS   20
        SHALL TRANSPORT THEE AWAY AND THE DAY OF THY   HOMER TRANS   28
                FREEDOM BE ENDED
        OF THE HORSEMEN OF TROY IN THE DAY THEY FOUGHT   HOMER TRANS   34
                FOR THEIR CITY
        BUT THY DAY OF DEATH IS AT HAND NOR SHALL WE   HOMER TRANS   48
                BE THE REASON
        THE DAY WAS THOU WERT NOT THE DAY WILL BE   •   •   •   FRAGMENT 5   2
        THE DAY WAS THOU WERT NOT THE DAY WILL BE   •   •   •   FRAGMENT 5   2

DAYBREAK
        STANDS AT DAYBREAK WEEPING BY MY SIDE   •   •   •   •   35 NEW SIRENS   274

DAYLIGHT
        FOR DAYLIGHT FOR THE CHEERFUL SUN   •   •   •   •   22 YOUTH AND CALM   17
        INTO DAYLIGHT NEVER GREW   •   •   •   •   •   •   •   •   29 NEW SIRENS   106
        STOOD IN BROAD DAYLIGHT AND THE SKY WAS PURE   •   •   75 SOHRAB RUSTUM   488
        STOOD IN BRIGHT DAYLIGHT AND THE SKY WAS PURE   •   •   75 SOHRAB RUSTUM   V 488
        ALL DAY AND DAYLIGHT WANED AND NIGHT CAME ON   •   •   107 BALDER DEAD 2   81
        ARE YE LIKE DAYLIGHT AND SUN   •   •   •   •   •   •   •   230 YOUTH OF NATURE   66

DAYS
        WHO PROP THOU ASKST IN THESE BAD DAYS MY MIND   •   •   2 TO A FRIEND   1
        TO PAIN TO DEATH THE BENT OF HIS OWN DAYS   •   •   •   6 GEO CRUIKSHANK   13
        THE PRAISE OF GODS RICH BOON AND LENGTH OF DAYS   •   •   11 MYCERINUS   78
        IN THE RICH LANGUOR OF LONG SUMMER-DAYS   •   •   •   12 MYCERINUS   117
        DROP WITH MINE ADOWN LIFES LATTER DAYS   •   •   •   33 NEW SIRENS   210
        BY WELL-HEADS IN SUMMER DAYS   •   •   •   •   •   •   34 NEW SIRENS   240
        THE GHOST IN THEM OF FORMER DAYS   •   •   •   •   •   56 RESIGNATION   123
        IN THE DAYS LIFE WHOSE IRON ROUND   •   •   •   •   •   58 RESIGNATION   209
        THE GHOSTS IN THEM OF FORMER DAYS   •   •   •   •   •   56 RESIGNATION   V 123
        IS THIS THEN RUKSH HOW OFTEN IN PAST DAYS   •   •   •   83 SOHRAB RUSTUM   742
        HATH BUILDED ON THE WASTE IN FORMER DAYS   •   •   •   71 SOHRAB RUSTUM   V 338
        HAS BUILDED ON THE WASTE IN FORMER DAYS   •   •   •   71 SOHRAB RUSTUM   V 338
        THESE MANY DAYS AND HEARD NO THING   •   •   •   •   88 SICK KING BOKH   23
        THREE DAYS SINCE AT THE TIME OF PRAYER   •   •   •   88 SICK KING BOKH   30
        IN THESE LAST DAYS THE SUN HATH BURND   •   •   •   89 SICK KING BOKH   59
        NINE DAYS NINE NIGHTS TOWARD THE NORTHERN ICE   •   •   99 BALDER DEAD 1   145
        NINE DAYS NINE NIGHTS TOWARDS THE NORTHERN ICE   •   •   99 BALDER DEAD 1   V 145
        NINE DAYS NINE NIGHTS TOWARD THE NORTHERN ICE   •   •   107 BALDER DEAD 2   83
        ON AUTUMN-DAYS BEFORE THEY CROSS THE SEA   •   •   •   109 BALDER DEAD 2   159

DAYS   (CONTINUED)
        NINE DAYS HE TOOK TO GO TWO TO RETURN   • •   • •   113 BALDER DEAD 2   293
        NINE DAYS NINE NIGHTS TOWARDS THE NORTHERN ICE • •   107 BALDER DEAD 2   V 83
        AND THEY GO LONG DAYS TOSSING UP AND DOWN   • •   •   124 BALDER DEAD 3   365
        THE TEMPEST OF THE LATTER DAYS HATH SWEPT   • •   •   128 BALDER DEAD 3   523
        OF ODIN THE DELIGHTS OF OTHER DAYS   • •   •   •   129 BALDER DEAD 3   542
        THE TRISTRAM WHO IN BETTER DAYS   • •   •   •   136 TRISTRAM 1   202
        JOIND AT EVENING OF THEIR DAYS AGAIN • •   •   •   •   143 TRISTRAM 2   32
        THE DAYS IN WHICH SHE MIGHT HAVE LIVED AND LOVED • •   151 TRISTRAM 3   65
        TO-DAYS EXACT REPEATED EFFIGY   • •   •   •   •   •   • 152 TRISTRAM 3   95
        ONE APRIL WHEN THE WARM DAYS FIRST BEGAN   • •   •   154 TRISTRAM 3   160
        BARING HIS DUMB REMORSE TO FUTURE DAYS   • •   •   167 PICT NEWSTEAD   13
        DAYS FLEW AH SOON I COULD DISCERN   • •   •   •   178 FAREWELL   13
        YOUNG IN THE BLOOM OF HIS DAYS • •   •   •   •   •   • 199 EARLY DEATH   11
        A GOLDEN DAYS DECLINE   • •   •   •   •   •   •   • 212 GROWING OLD   15
        IT IS TO SPEND LONG DAYS   • •   •   •   •   •   •   • 212 GROWING OLD   21
        MUTE AS OF OLD DAYS FLEW • •   •   •   •   •   •   •   • 233 YOUTH OF MAN   39
        DAYS AND YEARS AND TIME   • •   •   •   •   •   •   •   • 233 YOUTH OF MAN   40
        DEEP IN HER UNKNOWN DAYS EMPLOY   • •   •   •   •   248 KENSINGTON GARD   12
        COUNTS HIS DAYS SPOIL THE SPOTTED TROUT   • •   •   248 KENSINGTON GARD   20
        LAYS BARE OF WRETCHED DAYS   • •   •   •   •   •   • 260 SCHOLAR-GIPSY   186
        O BORN IN DAYS WHEN WITS WERE FRESH AND CLEAR • •   • 261 SCHOLAR-GIPSY   201
        HERE CAME I OFTEN OFTEN IN OLD DAYS   • •   •   •   •   263 THYRSIS   9
        AND WE SHALL HAVE HIM IN THE SWEET SPRING-DAYS • •   265 THYRSIS   73
        AS IN OLD DAYS JOVIAL AND TALKING RIDE   • •   •   •   267 THYRSIS   154
        AH SINCE DARK DAYS STILL BRING TO LIGHT   • •   •   272 MEMORIAL VERSES   58
        DAYS NOT DARK AT THY SIDE   • •   •   •   •   •   •   • 287 RUGBY CHAPEL   20
        DAYS NOT OF GLOOM AT THY SIDE • •   •   •   •   •   • 287 RUGBY CHAPEL   V 20
        WITH CYPSELUS AND TWO DAYS SINCE HE DIED   • •   •   355 MEROPE   718
        HE ON A HUNTING PARTY TWO DAYS SINCE • •   •   •   •   364 MEROPE   973
        HE ON A HUNTING PARTY THREE DAYS SINCE   • •   •   •   364 MEROPE   V 973
        THIRTY LONG DAYS IN A COLD TRANCE OF DEATH   • •   •   410 EMPEDOCLES I 1   110
        HE COULD STAY SWIFT DISEASES IN OLD DAYS   • •   •   410 EMPEDOCLES I 1   115
        ASK NOT WHAT DAYS AND NIGHTS   • •   •   •   •   •   • 416 EMPEDOCLES I 2   107
        THEREFORE THEY DID NOT END THEIR DAYS   • •   •   •   427 EMPEDOCLES I 2   452
        AND YET WHAT DAYS WERE THOSE PARMENIDES   • •   •   436 EMPEDOCLES II   235
        BUT HE WHO HAS OUTLIVED HIS PROSPEROUS DAYS • •   •   436 EMPEDOCLES II   261
        SEVEN DAYS THE GOD REPLIED • •   •   •   •   •   •   • 448 WESTMIN ABBEY   137
        SOON SOON THE DAYS CONVICTION BRING   • •   •   •   •   459 KAISER DEAD   25
        AND THE DIM GLORIES OF DEPARTED DAYS • •   •   •   •   464 ALARIC AT ROME   63
        THE SADDENING VISIONS OF DEPARTED DAYS   • •   •   •   470 ALARIC AT ROME   202
        THEN SLOWLY BRIGHTEND AS THE DAYS HAD FLOWN • •   •   474 CROMWELL   76
        ALL WONDROUS DEEDS THE COMING DAYS SHOULD SEE • •   475 CROMWELL   139

DAZED
        THE WIDE PLAIN RINGS THE DAZED AIR THROBS WITH BLOWS   137 TRISTRAM 1   235

DAZZLE
        LIGHTNINGS DAZZLE OUR EYES   • •   •   •   •   •   • 289 RUGBY CHAPEL   93

DAZZLED
        FROM YOUR DAZZLED WINDOWS STREAMING   • •   •   •   •   32 NEW SIRENS   183
        FOES DAZZLED WITH YOUR PROWESS WELL INCLINED   • •   • 339 MEROPE   302
        DAZZLED NELLYS YOUTHFUL EYNE   • •   •   •   •   •   • 458 POOR MATTHIAS   191

DAZZLING
        OR IN DEAF EASE ON THRONES OF DAZZLING SHEEN   • •   10 MYCERINUS   47
        AND THE SKIN OF DAZZLING SMOOTHNESS   • •   •   •   •   27 NEW SIRENS   51
        HIS DAZZLING CORSLET AND HIS HELM OF GOLD   • •   •   115 BALDER DEAD 3   58
        LET HER SWEEP HER DAZZLING HAND   • •   •   •   •   134 TRISTRAM 1   121
        OF DAZZLING CONVERSE FROM FUMES   • •   •   •   •   296 HEINES GRAVE   145
        OF DAZZLING CONVERSE AND FUMES • •   •   •   •   •   • 296 HEINES GRAVE   V 145
        THY DAZZLING LIGHT AN EAGLES GAZE SHOULD TIRE • •   463 ALARIC AT ROME   32

DAZZLINGLY
        HEAVED DAZZLINGLY BETWEEN   • •   •   •   •   •   • 242 SUMMER NIGHT   17

DEAD
        O MONSTROUS DEAD UNPROFITABLE WORLD   • •   •   •   3 EMERSONS ESSAYS   1
        AS THOUGH ONE SPAKE OF LIFE UNTO THE DEAD   • •   •   3 EMERSONS ESSAYS   8
        AS THOUGH ONE SPAKE OF NOISE UNTO THE DEAD   • •   •   3 EMERSONS ESSAYS   V 8
        ON THE TURF DEAD LIES THE BOAR • •   •   •   •   •   13 CHURCH BROU 1   26
        DEAD HER PRINCELY YOUTHFUL HUSBAND   • •   •   •   •   14 CHURCH BROU 1   49
        DEAD OUR DUKE AND GONE HIS DUCHESS   • •   •   •   •   15 CHURCH BROU 1   83
        AND WHEN THIS BOON REWARDS THE DEAD   • •   •   •   •   21 YOUTH AND CALM   7
        WHILE THE SOVRAN HEART IS DEAD • •   •   •   •   •   •   28 NEW SIRENS   78
        WHEN THE PRINCELY HEART IS DEAD   • •   •   •   •   28 NEW SIRENS   V 78
        WHILE THE PRINCELY HEART IS DEAD   • •   •   •   •   28 NEW SIRENS   V 78
        LIES FROZEN AND DEAD   • •   •   •   •   •   •   •   36 VOICE   14
        FOR THEIR DEAD HOPES AND ALL   • •   •   •   •   •   •   44 QUESTION   12
        DO WE GO HENCE AND FIND THEY ARE NOT DEAD   • •   •   44 QUESTION   17
        SHALL WE GO HENCE AND FIND THEY ARE NOT DEAD   • •   44 QUESTION   V 17
        WONDER NOT DEAD AND THIRST NOT DRIED • •   •   •   •   59 RESIGNATION   226
        OLD MAN THE DEAD NEED NO ONE CLAIM NO KIN   • •   •   62 SOHRAB RUSTUM   59
        LONG FLOCKS OF TRAVELLING BIRDS DEAD ON THE SNOW • •   66 SOHRAB RUSTUM   164
        HEAVENS AIR IS BETTER THAN THE COLD DEAD GRAVE • •   71 SOHRAB RUSTUM   324
        SO ON THE BLOODY SAND SOHRAB LAY DEAD   • •   •   •   86 SOHRAB RUSTUM   857
        DOWN OER HIS FACE AND SATE BY HIS DEAD SON   • •   •   86 SOHRAB RUSTUM   859
        ARE THIS WAY BRINGING THE DEAD MAN   • •   •   •   •   88 SICK KING BOKH   19
        BUT WHEN ONE TOLD HIM HE IS DEAD   • •   •   •   •   91 SICK KING BOKH   126

DEAD   (CONTINUED)

NO NOR ON THIS DEAD DOG O KING . . . .   93 SICK KING BOKH   180
WHEN I AM DEAD WILL SOON GROW STILL . . . . . .   94 SICK KING BOKH   218
SO ON THE FLOOR LAY BALDER DEAD AND ROUND . . . .   95 BALDER DEAD 1   1
TO BURN FOR THAT IS WHAT THE DEAD DESIRE . . . .   96 BALDER DEAD 1   45
WHO TELLS THE PASSING TROOPS OF DEAD THEIR WAY . .   99 BALDER DEAD 1   150
THE PLAINS OF NIFLHEIM WHERE DWELL THE DEAD . . .   100 BALDER DEAD 1   172
THE ENCHANTMENTS THAT RECALL THE DEAD TO LIFE . .   101 BALDER DEAD 1   209
NEITHER DO I NEGLECT THEE NOW THOUGH DEAD . . . .   103 BALDER DEAD 1   294
THAT SAD SOLE HONOUR OF THE DEAD AND THEE . . . .   103 BALDER DEAD 1   298
AND DOLEFUL ARE THE GHOSTS THE TROOPS OF DEAD . .   104 BALDER DEAD 1   316
HEREAFTER IN THE BLACKEST DEAD OF NIGHT . . . .   105 BALDER DEAD 2   5
WITH ALL WHICH IT BESEEMS THE DEAD TO HAVE . . .   106 BALDER DEAD 2   42
BUT YESTERMORN FIVE TROOPS OF DEAD PASSD BY . . .   107 BALDER DEAD 2   104
THE PLAINS OF NIFLHEIM WHERE DWELL THE DEAD . . .   109 BALDER DEAD 2   150
OR IS IT HERE WITHHELD TO GREET THE DEAD . . . .   111 BALDER DEAD 2   245
CONVERSE HIS SPEECH REMAINS THOUGH HE BE DEAD . .   111 BALDER DEAD 2   248
HERE AND HAST HONOUR AMONG ALL THE DEAD . . . .   112 BALDER DEAD 2   261
THAN BE A CROWND KING HERE AND RULE THE DEAD . .   112 BALDER DEAD 2   267
CROWND HAVING HONOUR AMONG ALL THE DEAD . . . .   112 BALDER DEAD 2   278
BACK THROUGH THE ASTONISHD TRIBES OF DEAD TO HEAVEN   112 BALDER DEAD 2   285
BALDER FOR THAT IS WHAT THE DEAD DESIRE . . . .   115 BALDER DEAD 3   52
AND THRICE IN ARMS AROUND THE DEAD THEY RODE . .   115 BALDER DEAD 3   61
MY DUNGEON WHERE THE SERPENTS STUNG ME DEAD . . .   117 BALDER DEAD 3   146
THEREFORE WITH GRATEFUL HEART I MOURN THEE DEAD .   117 BALDER DEAD 3   152
THE SUMMIT OF THE PILE THE DEAD THE MAST . . . .   119 BALDER DEAD 3   190
A QUEEN AND EMPIRE OVER ALL THE DEAD . . . . .   121 BALDER DEAD 3   278
BALDER IS DEAD AND HELA HOLDS HER PREY . . . .   123 BALDER DEAD 3   347
IS BALDER DEAD AND DO YE COME FOR TEARS . . . .   123 BALDER DEAD 3   351
OR IS HE MINGLED WITH THE UNNUMBERD DEAD . . . .   125 BALDER DEAD 3   430
WHEN I DRAW NIGH AND THE WAN TRIBES OF DEAD . . .   126 BALDER DEAD 3   464
ART THOU COLD OR FALSE OR DEAD . . . .   133 TRISTRAM 1   81
FRINGD WITH DEAD LEAVES AND MOSSES RARE . . . .   148 TRISTRAM 2   V
LAY TRISTRAM AND QUEEN ISEULT DEAD AND COLD . .   149 TRISTRAM 3   V   2
OR IS IT OVER ART THOU DEAD . . . .   184 TERRACE BERNE   25
DEAD AND NO WARNING SHIVER RAN . . . .   184 TERRACE BERNE   26
A DEAD IGNORANT THANKLESS CORPSE . . . . . .   196 FRAG ANTIGONE   53
DEAD TO ITS DEEP HABITUAL SMART . . . .   206 RIVER   19
AND DEAD TO HOPES OF FUTURE JOY . . . .   206 RIVER   20
DEAD BE THE PAST AND ITS PHANTOMS TO ME . . . .   206 SEPARATION   12
AND PSYCHE LONG HAS BEEN DEAD . . . .   214 NEW ROME   4
AND OER THE PLAIN WHERE THE DEAD AGE . . . . .   219 BACCHANALIA 2   19
IN THE SHADOW WORDSWORTH LIES DEAD . . . . . .   228 YOUTH OF NATURE   9
IS LOVELY A MORTAL IS DEAD . . . .   228 YOUTH OF NATURE   12
HE IS DEAD AND THE FRUIT-BEARING DAY . . . . .   229 YOUTH OF NATURE   56
NOR THE DULLEST BEEN DEAD TO THEM QUITE . . . .   230 YOUTH OF NATURE   83
WHEN YE MOURN THAT A POET IS DEAD . . . . . .   230 YOUTH OF NATURE   88
THE WORLD WHICH LASTS WHEN I AM DEAD . . . . .   250 WISH   36
ELSE WERT THOU LONG SINCE NUMBERD WITH THE DEAD .   259 SCHOLAR-GIPSY   153
OUR FRIEND THE GIPSY-SCHOLAR WAS NOT DEAD . . .   263 THYRSIS   29
HE COULD NOT WAIT THEIR PASSING HE IS DEAD . . .   264 THYRSIS   50
AND FLUTE HIS FRIEND LIKE ORPHEUS FROM THE DEAD .   265 THYRSIS   90
OUR FRIEND THE SCHOLAR-GIPSY WAS NOT DEAD . . .   263 THYRSIS   V 29
ON SPIRITS THAT HAD LONG BEEN DEAD . . . . . .   272 MEMORIAL VERSES   55
SOME SAGE TO WHOM THE WORLD WAS DEAD . . . . .   277 SOUTHERN NIGHT   77
OF A GENTLE SPIRIT NOW DEAD . . . .   280 HAWORTH CHURCH   5
SUMMONS THE YOUNGER IS DEAD . . . .   281 HAWORTH CHURCH   33
TURN WE NEXT TO THE DEAD . . . .   282 HAWORTH CHURCH   47
FRIENDLY AND GENTLE NOW DEAD . . . .   280 HAWORTH CHURCH   V   5
OF THIS AMIABLE HOME OF THE DEAD . . . . . .   293 HEINES GRAVE   45
DOTH THE DEAD GUIERS STREAM COMPLAIN . . . . .   299 GRANDE CHARTR   10
WHICH SHALL THEIR COFFIN BE WHEN DEAD . . . .   300 GRANDE CHARTR   48
WANDERING BETWEEN TWO WORLDS ONE DEAD . . . .   302 GRANDE CHARTR   85
BUT A DEAD TIMES EXPLODED DREAM . . . . . .   302 GRANDE CHARTR   98
GREATER BY FAR THAN THOU ARE DEAD . . . . . .   309 OBERMANN   91
NOW HE IS DEAD FAR HENCE HE LIES . . . . . .   318 OBERMANN MORE   173
BUT EVERY WORD WAS DEAD . . . .   319 OBERMANN MORE   196
YOUR CREEDS ARE DEAD YOUR RITES ARE DEAD . . .   320 OBERMANN MORE   229
YOUR CREEDS ARE DEAD YOUR RITES ARE DEAD . . .   320 OBERMANN MORE   229
OF THY DEAD HUSBANDS FACTION VIGOROUS ONCE . . .   334 MEROPE   139
TO THEIR DEAD KING THY HUSBAND YEA TOO DEAR . .   335 MEROPE   175
SEND AN AVENGER GODS OF THE DEAD . . . . . .   348 MEROPE   543
MAY HERMES HERALD OF THE DEAD CONVEY . . . .   349 MEROPE   585
THE DEAD HATH NOW HIS OFFERINGS DULY PAID . . .   350 MEROPE   596
AEPYTUS THE MESSENIAN PRINCE IS DEAD . . . .   355 MEROPE   714
DEAD AND WHEN DIED HE WHERE AND BY WHAT HAND . .   355 MEROPE   715
EVEN AS THOSE DEAD UNEPITAPHD WHO LIE . . . .   356 MEROPE   772
IN ONE THING ONLY THAT THE PRINCE IS DEAD . . .   364 MEROPE   966
AS DEAD WE HELD THEE MOURND FOR THEE AS DEAD . .   375 MEROPE   1208
AS DEAD WE HELD THEE MOURND FOR THEE AS DEAD . .   375 MEROPE   1208
THOUGH ALL FREE SPIRITS IN THIS LAND WERE DEAD .   383 MEROPE   1377
I KNOW SHE HONOURS NOT THE DEAD SO ILL . . . .   386 MEROPE   1450
MESSENIA SPEAKS THE PRINCE THY SON IS DEAD . . .   393 MEROPE   1686
TO THE DEAD UNAVENGED . . . .   400 MEROPE   1868
OF YOUR DEAD MASTERS LINE I BRING YOU NEWS . . .   400 MEROPE   1883
AT THY DEAD HUSBANDS NAME THE PEOPLE SHOW . . .   401 MEROPE   1894
THE DORIANS LYING DEAD THY SON HAILD KING . . .   402 MEROPE   1942
THE CONQUERORS WITH THE KINGS DEAD BODY COME . .   403 MEROPE   1953
THOUGH ALL FREE SPIRITS IN THIS LAND BE DEAD . .   383 MEROPE   V1377
THE DEAD RETURN TO LIFE . . . .   416 EMPEDOCLES I 2   124

DEAD   (CONTINUED)
        WE SEARCH OUT DEAD MENS WORDS AND WORKS OF   423 EMPEDOCLES I 2   326
                DEAD MENS HANDS
        WE SEARCH OUT DEAD MENS WORDS AND WORKS OF   423 EMPEDOCLES I 2   326
                DEAD MENS HANDS
        AND AWE BE DEAD AND HOPE IMPOSSIBLE . . . .   429 EMPEDOCLES II   34
        NOR OUTWARD THINGS WERE CLOSED AND DEAD TO US   . .   436 EMPEDOCLES II   241
        THOUGHTS SLAVES AND DEAD TO EVERY NATURAL JOY   . .   436 EMPEDOCLES II   249
        AS THEY ARE DEAD TO ME   . . . .   437 EMPEDOCLES II   275
        AM DEAD TO LIFE AND JOY THEREFORE I READ   . . . .   438 EMPEDOCLES II   321
        DEAD AND MUTE OUR TINY FRIEND   . . . .   452 POOR MATTHIAS   14
        GREAT ATOSSA THEY ARE DEAD   . . . .   453 POOR MATTHIAS   26
        DEAD AND NEITHER PROSE NOR RHYME   . . . .   453 POOR MATTHIAS   27
        DEAD CANARY BIRD A STAVE . . . .   457 POOR MATTHIAS   176
        WHAT KAISER DEAD THE HEAVY NEWS   . . . .   458 KAISER DEAD   1
        WHAT POOR KAI DEAD SAY ALL I MEET   . . . .   459 KAISER DEAD   9
        FULL WELL MAX KNOWS THE FRIEND IS DEAD   . . . . .   460 KAISER DEAD   69
        UNWELCOME SHROUD OF THE FORGOTTEN DEAD   . . . . .   462 ALARIC AT ROME   1
        ROUND THE WAN TEMPLES OF THE HALLOWED DEAD . . . .   463 ALARIC AT ROME   26
        PRESENT AND PAST THE LIVING AND THE DEAD   . . . .   463 ALARIC AT ROME   44
        NO HABITATION FOR THE NAMELESS DEAD   . . . . . .   464 ALARIC AT ROME   56
        THY DEAD ARE KINGS THY DUST ARE PALACES   . . . .   464 ALARIC AT ROME   61
        THAT HOLDS THE ASHES OF YOUR HERO–DEAD   . . . . .   467 ALARIC AT ROME   136
        A HEART THAT RECKD NOT OF THE COUNTLESS DEAD   . .   478 CROMWELL   225
        AND MAKE THE WORLDS DEAD SPIRIT LEAP AGAIN . . . .   481 HUNGARIAN NAT   11
        BUT LET ME BE DEAD AND THE EARTH BE MOUNDED ABOVE ME   HOMER TRANS   37

DEADEN
        DEADEN THE INFINITE PAIN . . . .   283 HAWORTH CHURCH   V

DEADENS
        WHICH NEITHER DEADENS INTO REST   . . . .   243 SUMMER NIGHT   28
        THAT NEITHER DEADENS INTO REST . . . .   243 SUMMER NIGHT   V 28
        WHICH NEVER DEADENS INTO REST   . . . .   243 SUMMER NIGHT   V 28

DEADLY
        EVEN IN THE DEADLY PALACE OF MY FOE   . . . . . .   375 MEROPE   1205
        AND DEADLY AIRS HIS STRENGTH DID UNDERMINE . . . .   448 WESTMIN ABBEY   126
        AND DEADLY AIRS HIS FORCE DID UNDERMINE   . . . .   448 WESTMIN ABBEY   V 126

DEADNESS
        IN ALL THINGS MY OWN DEADNESS   . . . .   438 EMPEDOCLES II   322

DEAF
        OR IN DEAF EASE ON THRONES OF DAZZLING SHEEN   . .   10 MYCERINUS   47
        MOST DEAF WHERE THOU SHOULDST MOST GIVE EAR   . .   91 SICK KING BOKH   98
        IS DEAF FAR NORTHWARD FROM HERE   . . . .   282 HAWORTH CHURCH   51
        THE WEARY TITAN WITH DEAF   . . . .   295 HEINES GRAVE   88
        AY ME TIS DEAF THAT EAR   . . . .   449 WESTMIN ABBEY   161

DEAFEND
        DEAFEND BY HIS OWN STIR   . . . .   47 WORLD QUIETIST   20
        WHEN OUR WORLD–DEAFEND EAR   . . . .   247 BURIED LIFE   82
        GAINS NOT AN EARTH–DEAFEND EAR . . . .   281 HAWORTH CHURCH   36

DEALING
        ONE DEATH–DEALING VENGEFUL TRAIN   . . . .   379 MEROPE   1255

DEALT
        HAST THOU YET DEALT HIM O LIFE THY FULL MEASURE   . .   20 MODERN SAPPHO   33
        DEALT AT MY OWN SOLE RISK BEFORE THEIR EYES   . .   383 MEROPE   1354
        WHERE TWINES THE CHAPLET DEALT A MIGHTY BLOW   . .   402 MEROPE   1921

DEAR
        AND DEAR AS THE WET DIVER TO THE EYES   . . . .   69 SOHRAB RUSTUM   284
        SO DEAR TO THE PALE PERSIANS RUSTUM CAME   . . . .   70 SOHRAB RUSTUM   290
        OF AGE AND LOOKS TO BE HIS OWN DEAR SON   . . . .   80 SOHRAB RUSTUM   632
        FROM LAYING THY DEAR MASTER IN HIS GRAVE   . . . .   85 SOHRAB RUSTUM   834
        AND DEAR AS THE WET FISHER TO THE EYES   . . . .   69 SOHRAB RUSTUM   V 284
        AND CAST IT AT THE DEAR–LOVED BALDERS BREAST   . .   98 BALDER DEAD 1   102
        ALIVE I KEPT NOT FAR FROM THEE DEAR SOUL   . . . .   103 BALDER DEAD 1   293
        KNOWING THE GOD THEY WENT TO SEEK HOW DEAR . . . .   107 BALDER DEAD 2   77
        COME THEN IF BALDER WAS SO DEAR BELOVED   . . . .   111 BALDER DEAD 2   231
        SO SHALL I KNOW THE LOST WAS DEAR INDEED   . . . .   111 BALDER DEAD 2   239
        SO SHALL SHE KNOW YOUR LOSS WAS DEAR INDEED   . .   115 BALDER DEAD 3   45
        FOR DEAR–BELOVED WAS BALDER WHILE HE LIVED . . . .   120 BALDER DEAD 3   232
        BEGRUDGE NOT THINE TO ALL WAS BALDER DEAR   . . . .   123 BALDER DEAD 3   349
        OF THEIR DEAR COUNTRY AND CAN PLAIN DESCRY . . . .   123 BALDER DEAD 3   360
        TAKE MY HAND DEAR TRISTRAM LOOK ON ME   . . . .   142 TRISTRAM 2   16
        THESE ARE TO HER DEAR AS TO THEM THE TALES . . . .   152 TRISTRAM 3   106
        DEAR SAINTS IT IS NOT SORROW AS I HEAR   . . . .   152 TRISTRAM 3   112
        COME DEAR CHILDREN LET US AWAY . . . .   161 FORSAKEN MERM   1
        CHILDREN DEAR LET US AWAY   . . . .   161 FORSAKEN MERM   8
        CHILDRENS VOICES SHOULD BE DEAR   . . . .   161 FORSAKEN MERM   14
        MOTHER DEAR WE CANNOT STAY   . . . .   162 FORSAKEN MERM   20
        COME DEAR CHILDREN COME AWAY DOWN   . . . . . .   162 FORSAKEN MERM   23
        CHILDREN DEAR WAS IT YESTERDAY . . . .   162 FORSAKEN MERM   30
        CHILDREN DEAR WAS IT YESTERDAY . . . .   162 FORSAKEN MERM   47
        CHILDREN DEAR WAS IT YESTERDAY . . . .   162 FORSAKEN MERM   48
        I SAID GO UP DEAR HEART THROUGH THE WAVES   . . . .   163 FORSAKEN MERM   60
        CHILDREN DEAR WAS IT YESTERDAY . . . .   163 FORSAKEN MERM   63
        CHILDREN DEAR WERE WE LONG ALONE   . . . . . .   163 FORSAKEN MERM   64

DEAR   (CONTINUED)
    DEAR HEART I SAID WE ARE LONG ALONE . . . . . . 163 FORSAKEN MERM   78
    THY DEAR WIFES ASHES BURIED ARE . . . . . . 277 SOUTHERN NIGHT   51
    STILL WENT FORTH THAT CHILDS DEAR FORCE . . . 318 OBERMANN MORE   163
    CONSIDER TOO THIS PEOPLE WHO WERE DEAR . . . . 335 MEROPE   174
    TO THEIR DEAD KING THY HUSBAND YEA TOO DEAR . . 335 MEROPE   175
    LOOK UP O QUEEN LOOK UP O MISTRESS DEAR . . . . 363 MEROPE   946
    TO THE DEAR NEXT-OF-KIN OF HIM HE MURDERD . . . 374 MEROPE   1197
    ARCAS THOU HERE O MY DEAR MASTER O . . . . . . 375 MEROPE   1206
    WE SEE DEAR MISTRESS AND WE SAY THE GODS . . . 377 MEROPE   1225
    TOO DEAR HIS SECRET WILES HAVE COST OUR HOUSE . 380 MEROPE   1279
    THAT DEAR-BELOVED THAT YOUNG THAT GRACIOUS HEAD . 382 MEROPE   1327
    EACH SOVEREIGN FOR HIS DEAR-BOUGHT HOUR BORN . . 388 MEROPE   1513
    THE GODS O MISTRESS DEAR THE HARD-SOULD MAN . . 390 MEROPE   1577
    MAY WHAT IS FALSE HOLD DEAR . . . . 419 EMPEDOCLES I 2   203
    OVER THEIR OWN DEAR CHILDREN ROLLD . . . . . 427 EMPEDOCLES I 2   446
    BY THIS DEAR GUEST OVER THY PRECINCT SHED . . . 449 WESTMIN ABBEY   173
    BY THIS DEAR SOUL OVER THY PRECINCT SHED . . . 449 WESTMIN ABBEY V 173
    DEAR LITTLE FRIEND AT EVERY TURN . . . . . . 450 GEISTS GRAVE   8
    NOR TO US ONLY ART THOU DEAR . . . . 451 GEISTS GRAVE   53
    THERE BUILD WE THEE O GUARDIAN DEAR . . . . . 452 GEISTS GRAVE   71
    THERE CHOOSE WE THEE O GUARDIAN DEAR . . . . . 452 GEISTS GRAVE   V 71
    WELL HE KNEW HIS MISTRESS DEAR . . . . 452 POOR MATTHIAS   6
    ALL THAT HUMAN PATHOS DEAR . . . . 454 POOR MATTHIAS   62
    GRAVELY THOU THE WHILE POOR DEAR . . . . . . 455 POOR MATTHIAS   119
    FARE THEE WELL COMPANION DEAR . . . . 458 POOR MATTHIAS   206
    A MATE HOW DEAR . . . . 459 KAISER DEAD   36
    FAR FROM MY FATHER AND MOTHER DEAR FOR ALL   HOMER TRANS   61
        THAT I WILL NOT

DEARER
    DEARER TO THE RED JACKALS SHALT THOU BE . . . . 77 SOHRAB RUSTUM   538

DEARLY
    WE PRIZED IT DEARLY WHILE IT STOOD WE SAID . . . 263 THYRSIS   28

DEATH
    TO PAIN TO DEATH THE BENT OF HIS OWN DAYS . . .   6 GEO CRUIKSHANK   13
    THE VASTY HALL OF DEATH . . . . 21 REQUIESCAT   16
    TIS DEATH AND PEACE INDEED IS HERE . . . . . 21 YOUTH AND CALM   1
    YOUTH DREAMS A BLISS ON THIS SIDE DEATH . . . 22 YOUTH AND CALM   19
    YOUTH DREAMS A JOY ON THIS SIDE DEATH . . . . 22 YOUTH AND CALM   V   19
    THE DELIGHT OF DEATH-EMBRACES . . . . 27 NEW SIRENS   55
    HEAVY AS DEATH COLD AS THE GRAVE . . . . . . 38 STAGIRIUS   12
    TILL DEATH ARRIVE TO SUPERSEDE . . . . 56 RESIGNATION   142
    NAY AND SINCE DEATH WHICH WIPES OUT MAN . . . 58 RESIGNATION   223
    IN SOME SENSE FAUSTA OUTLASTS DEATH . . . . . 59 RESIGNATION   230
    WHENCE EQUALLY THE SEAS OF LIFE AND DEATH ARE FED 60 RESIGNATION   260
    TILL DEATH ARRIVES TO SUPERSEDE . . . . 56 RESIGNATION   V 142
    DANGER OR DEATH AWAITS THEE ON THIS FIELD . . . 63 SOHRAB RUSTUM   87
    AND LEAVE TO DEATH THE HOSTS OF THANKLESS KINGS 68 SOHRAB RUSTUM   240
    O SOHRAB WHEREFORE WILT THOU RUSH ON DEATH . . 71 SOHRAB RUSTUM   329
    BACK OUT TO SEA TO THE DEEP WAVES OF DEATH . . 73 SOHRAB RUSTUM   395
    THE MIGHTY RUSTUM SHALL AVENGE MY DEATH . . . 77 SOHRAB RUSTUM   553
    HE SHALL AVENGE MY DEATH AND PUNISH THEE . . . 77 SOHRAB RUSTUM   555
    THINKING OF HER HE LEFT AND HIS OWN DEATH . . . 79 SOHRAB RUSTUM   603
    LOVELY IN DEATH UPON THE COMMON SAND . . . . . 80 SOHRAB RUSTUM   639
    AND THROUGH WHOSE DEATH I WON THAT FAME I HAVE . 85 SOHRAB RUSTUM   812
    NEAR DEATH AND BY AN IGNORANT STROKE OF THINE . 85 SOHRAB RUSTUM   818
    THEN AT THE POINT OF DEATH SOHRAB REPLIED . . . 85 SOHRAB RUSTUM   827
    IF ANY HERE MIGHT WEEP FOR BALDERS DEATH . . . 96 BALDER DEAD 1   20
    BALDER HAS MET HIS DEATH AND YE SURVIVE . . . 96 BALDER DEAD 1   26
    THAT ONE LONG PORTIOND WITH HIS DOOM OF DEATH . 98 BALDER DEAD 1   114
    ON BALDER DEATH HATH LAID HER HAND NOT THEE . . 98 BALDER DEAD 1   117
    AND WELL I KNOW THAT BY NO STROKE OF DEATH . . . 103 BALDER DEAD 1   305
    DEATH FROM THY HEAD AND WITH THE GODS IN HEAVEN . 104 BALDER DEAD 1   311
    ON BATTLE-FIELD HAVE MET THEIR DEATH AND NOW . . 104 BALDER DEAD 1   321
    AND PICK THE BRAVEST WARRIORS OUT FOR DEATH . . 105 BALDER DEAD 2   26
    EVEN IN THE ABODE OF DEATH O BALDER HAIL . . . 112 BALDER DEAD 2   250
    HERMOD THE NIMBLE GILD ME NOT MY DEATH . . . . 112 BALDER DEAD 2   264
    THOUGH I BE LOVED AND MANY MOURN MY DEATH . . . 112 BALDER DEAD 2   270
    IF CLEAR FROM PLOTTING BALDERS DEATH TO SWIM . . 114 BALDER DEAD 3   27
    AND BLOOD AND RINGING BLOWS AND VIOLENT DEATH . 117 BALDER DEAD 3   140
    ENTREATING ALL THINGS TO WEEP BALDERS DEATH . . 122 BALDER DEAD 3   305
    THOU HAST THEN ALL THE SOLACE DEATH ALLOWS . . 126 BALDER DEAD 3   469
    DEATH AND THE GLOOM WHICH ROUND ME EVEN NOW . . 129 BALDER DEAD 3   546
    THOUGH THEY TO DEATH WERE BOUND AND HE TO HEAVEN 129 BALDER DEAD 3   557
    ONLY DEATH CAN BALM THY WOE . . . . 139 TRISTRAM 1   289
    THE DEEP DRAUGHTS OF DEATH IN BEARING ME . . . 145 TRISTRAM 2   84
    NOW TO SAIL THE SEAS OF DEATH I LEAVE THEE . . 145 TRISTRAM 2   97
    FELL UPON MERLIN MORE LIKE DEATH SO DEEP . . . 155 TRISTRAM 3   214
    ON EARTH MY CRIME MY DEATH THEY KNEW . . . . . 157 SAINT BRANDAN   26
    MID STRUGGLING SUFFERERS HURT TO DEATH SHE LAY . 166 AUSTERITY POET   9
    POLYMNIA FULL ON HER DEATH-BED TWAS WELL . . . 168 RACHEL 2   8
    HER HEAD MID IGNOMINY DEATH AND TOMBS . . . . 172 GOOD SHEPHERD   12
    HER HEAD IN IGNOMINY DEATH AND TOMBS . . . . . 172 GOOD SHEPHERD   V 12
    TILL THE FATES COME AGAIN THIS TIME WITH DEATH . 195 FRAG ANTIGONE   16
    DEATH WHO DISSEVERS ALL . . . . 195 FRAG ANTIGONE   27
    TILL THE FATES COME AGAIN ALONE WITH DEATH . . 195 FRAG ANTIGONE   V 16
    OF THE CITY OF DEATH HAVE FOR EVER CLOSED . . . 199 FRAG DEJANEIRA   30
    BUT WHEN IMMATURE DEATH . . . . 199 EARLY DEATH   8

DEATH   (CONTINUED)
     AND SOME FIND DEATH ERE THEY FIND LOVE   . . . .   206 TOO LATE   2
     BY A PITILESS ARROW OF DEATH   . . . .   216 LORDS MESSENGER   18
     TURMOIL OF DEATH AND OF BIRTH   . . . .   216 LORDS MESSENGER   V   3
     BY THE SWIFT-RUSHING MISSILE OF DEATH   . . . .   216 LORDS MESSENGER   V 18
     DEATH IN THEIR PRISON REACHES THEM   . . . .   243 SUMMER NIGHT   49
     I ASK NOT THAT MY BED OF DEATH   . . . .   249 WISH   1
     TEARLESS WHEN OF MY DEATH HE HEARS   . . . .   250 WISH   6
     I ASK BUT THAT MY DEATH MAY FIND   . . . .   250 WISH   9
     ALL WHICH MAKES DEATH A HIDEOUS SHOW . . . .   250 WISH   16
     OF THE POOR SINNER BOUND FOR DEATH   . . . .   250 WISH   22
     NOT HUMAN COMBATINGS WITH DEATH . . . .   251 WISH   48
     ALL THAT MAKES DEATH A HIDEOUS SHOW . . . .   250 WISH   V 16
     BUT ONE SUCH DEATH REMAIN TO COME   . . . .   270 MEMORIAL VERSES   3
     WHEN BYRONS EYES WERE SHUT IN DEATH . . . .   270 MEMORIAL VERSES   6
     WHEN GOETHES DEATH WAS TOLD WE SAID . . . .   270 MEMORIAL VERSES   15
     AND CAME HOME HURT TO DEATH AND HERE . . . .   278 SOUTHERN NIGHT   95
     THEN LEARNT HIS DEATH AND PINED AWAY . . . .   279 SOUTHERN NIGHT   110
     TOTTERING A DEATH-STRICKEN HAND . . . .   281 HAWORTH CHURCH   25
     LIES EXPECTING FROM DEATH   . . . .   281 HAWORTH CHURCH   31
     TURN O DEATH ON THE VILE   . . . .   281 HAWORTH CHURCH   V
     OF DEATH AT A CALL UNFORESEEN   . . . .   287 RUGBY CHAPEL   29
     THEIR DROPS OF BLOOD THEIR DEATH IN LIFE   . . . .   301 GRANDE CHARTR   54
     THAT AIR OF LANGUOR COLD AND DEATH   . . . .   306 OBERMANN   15
     AS DEATH COMPOSED TO BEAR   . . . .   309 OBERMANN   86
     REGARD HIS DEATH-PLACE DUMB . . . .   318 OBERMANN MORE   178
     WHY WERE YE TOO TO DEATH NOT HURLD   . . . .   320 OBERMANN MORE   219
     OF MY OWN DEATH BUT LAIAS WELL I HOPE   . . . .   331 MEROPE   49
     THROUGH THAT PRETENDED DEATH TO LIVE AND REIGN . . . .   331 MEROPE   50
     SOARING FROM HIS DEATH-PILE ON OETA LEFT   . . . .   336 MEROPE   213
     FOR DEATH HIS ANCIENT TO HIS NEW-MADE FRIENDS   . . . .   338 MEROPE   265
     EVEN FANCIED AND HIS DEATH THOU WROUGHTEST CHIEF . .   339 MEROPE   328
     WHY DOST THOU ONLY PROFIT BY HIS DEATH   . . . .   340 MEROPE   331
     I ASK THEE NOT TO APPROVE THY HUSBANDS DEATH   . . . .   340 MEROPE   338
     BUT FOR THY CHILDRENS DEATH I STAND ASSOILD   . . . .   340 MEROPE   342
     SUFFERING SENT THEM DEATH   . . . .   343 MEROPE   417
     SHE LED THE WAY OF DEATH   . . . .   344 MEROPE   434
     FIERY PHANTOMS OF DEATH   . . . .   346 MEROPE   503
     A PALACE DEFILED BY A DEATH UNAVENGED   . .   . . . .   346 MEROPE   508
     PRISONERS OF DEATH FROM THE GRAVE   . . . .   347 MEROPE   525
     INSTRUCT ME OF THE MANNER OF HIS DEATH   . . . .   355 MEROPE   720
     AS OF ONE SHADOWD BY IMPENDING DEATH . . . .   356 MEROPE   765
     WHILE ALL ELSE GRIEVES HIM THAT HIS GRANDCHILDS DEATH   359 MEROPE   851
     THE MAN WHO TO UNTIMELY DEATH IS DOOMD   . . . .   359 MEROPE   854
     OTHER THAN BY THIS DEATH BUT IT HATH COME   . . . .   360 MEROPE   887
     UNCLE AND NEPHEW DISAPPEAR THEIR DEATH   . . . .   364 MEROPE   979
     YOUR KING DESIRED THE PROFIT OF HIS DEATH   . . . .   365 MEROPE   990
     IN THEIR ALLEGIANCE ME IN MY SONS DEATH-HOUR   366 MEROPE   1004
     WITH PATIENCE ON THY FACE DEATH IN THY HEART   . . . .   367 MEROPE   1045
     MY DEATH MAKES MY DEBT VOID AND DOUBLES THINE   . . . .   367 MEROPE   1049
     LIVED FOR THE DEATH OF HIS FOES . . . .   368 MEROPE   1085
     YET STARK FROM THE DEATH-STRUGGLE TIGHT-CLENCHD HANDS   373 MEROPE   1174
     REMEMBER TO REVENGE HIS DEATH I COME . . . .   378 MEROPE   1241
     ONE DEATH-DEALING VENGEFUL TRAIN   . . . .   379 MEROPE   1255
     SUSPICION FROM THY GRANDSIRE OF THY DEATH   . . . .   379 MEROPE   1270
     FIX HIM THE AUTHOR OF MY DEATH I KNOW NOT   . . . .   379 MEROPE   1273
     SINGLE AND FRIENDLESS GIVE TO CERTAIN DEATH   . . . .   382 MEROPE   1326
     HIS DEATH A PUBLIC NOT A PERSONAL ACT . .   . . . .   387 MEROPE   1480
     FOR THAT HE PLOTS THY DEATH ACCOUNT IT FALSE   . . . .   387 MEROPE   1485
     SINCE POLICY BIDS THUS WHAT FOULER DEATH   . . . .   390 MEROPE   1568
     EVEN AFTER NEWS OF THIS SAD DEATH OUR LEAGUE   . . . .   394 MEROPE   1689
     EVEN IN DEATH THAT COUNTENANCE AUSTERE   . . . .   403 MEROPE   1970
     SO LOOKD HE IN THAT DREADFUL DAY OF DEATH   . . . .   404 MEROPE   1977
     FIXD HIM THE AUTHOR OF MY DEATH I KNEW NOT   . . . .   379 MEROPE   V1273
     SINGLE AND FRIENDLESS THROW TO CERTAIN DEATH   . . . .   382 MEROPE   V1326
     THIRTY LONG DAYS IN A COLD TRANCE OF DEATH   . . . .   410 EMPEDOCLES I 1   110
     HE GRASPS THE VERY REINS OF LIFE AND DEATH   . . . .   410 EMPEDOCLES I 1   125
     THOU YOUNG IMPLACABLE GOD AND ONLY DEATH   . . . .   436 EMPEDOCLES II   232
     NO NO YE STARS THERE IS NO DEATH WITH YOU   . . . .   438 EMPEDOCLES II   301
     NO LANGUOR NO DECAY LANGUOR AND DEATH   . . . .   438 EMPEDOCLES II   302
     BUT NOW HIS HEAD TO DEATH AGAIN IS DUE   . . . .   447 WESTMIN ABBEY   106
     AND NEXT THE CROWNING IMPOTENCE OF DEATH   . . . .   448 WESTMIN ABBEY   130
     WHICH WOULD OF DEATH COMPLAIN   . . . .   448 WESTMIN ABBEY   132
     DEATH DEATH WAS JUDGED THE BOON SUPREME INDEED . . . .   448 WESTMIN ABBEY   140
     DEATH DEATH WAS JUDGED THE BOON SUPREME INDEED . . . .   448 WESTMIN ABBEY   140
     AND THEN THE CROWNING IMPOTENCE OF DEATH   . . . .   448 WESTMIN ABBEY   V 130
     DULL LOOK ON WHEN DEATH IS NIGH . . . .   455 POOR MATTHIAS   107
     WERE MINGLING WITH THE SERE AND WITHERED HUES OF DEATH   466 ALARIC AT ROME   102
     TO WESTERN SHORES THE DEATH-PLACE OF THE DAY   . . . .   475 CROMWELL   112
     CAME FAINT AND FEEBLE IN THE EMBRACE OF DEATH   . . . .   478 CROMWELL   208
     THEN FROM THOSE WHITENING LIPS AS DEATH DREW NEAR   478 CROMWELL   213
     STRETCHD ON THAT BED OF DEATH ART NOTHING NOW   . . . .   479 CROMWELL   234
     NOT IN SUNK SPAINS PROLONGD DEATH AGONY   . . . .   480 HUNGARIAN NAT   1
     BUT THY DAY OF DEATH IS AT HAND NOR SHALL WE   HOMER TRANS   48
          BE THE REASON
     TO LIE LOW IN DEATH BY THE HAND OF A GOD AND A MORTAL   HOMER TRANS   56
     WHY DOST THOU PROPHESY SO MY DEATH TO ME XANTHUS   HOMER TRANS   59
          IT NEEDS NOT

DEATHLESS
     OTHERS THERE ARE AS DEATHLESS FULL AS THEY . . . .   462 ALARIC AT ROME   9
     BUT FULL AND DEATHLESS AS THE DEEP DARK HUE   . .   463 ALARIC AT ROME   35

DEATHLIKE
WHY SPEEDST THOU NOT THY DEATHLIKE WAVE TO SHED . . 462 ALARIC AT ROME 3
WHAT DEATHLIKE STILLNESS OER THE LANDSCAPE LAY . . 466 ALARIC AT ROME 99
BUT OH HOW CHANGD THOSE DEATHLIKE FEATURES WORE . . 477 CROMWELL 181
SHOOK THE DEEP SLUMBER OF HIS DEATHLIKE TRANCE . . 477 CROMWELL 194

DEATHS
TRISTRAM ART THOU CALLD FOR MY DEATHS SAKE . . . . 145 TRISTRAM 2 86
WHICH ONE WHO FEELS DEATHS WINNOWING WINGS . . . . 250 WISH 27
DEATHS FROZEN HOUR IS DONE . . . . . . 322 OBERMANN MORE 292
TO CHANCE IMPUTE THEIR DEATHS THEN NOT TO ME . . 340 MEROPE 346
WHAT DO I SEE A MURDERER AT DEATHS DOOR . . . . 374 MEROPE 1195
AND VIOLENT DEATHS TO VIOLENT MEN . . . . . 398 MEROPE 1809
AND DEATHS COLD DEWS BEDIMMD HIS EARNEST BROW . . 476 CROMWELL 170

DEBAR
AND FROM HIS NATURAL RIGHTS MY SON DEBAR . . . . 388 MEROPE 1495

DEBARRD
WHENEER OF BLISS DEBARRD . . . . 417 EMPEDOCLES I 2 163
WHENEER FROM BLISS DEBARRD . . . . 417 EMPEDOCLES I 2 V 163

DEBATE
AND LET US BEAR THAT THEY DEBATE . . . . . 48 HORATIAN ECHO 13
VAIN AND STRANGE DEBATE WHERE BOTH HAVE SUFFERD . . 144 TRISTRAM 2 53

DEBATING
WHY YOU SAY CRITIAS BE DEBATING STILL . . . . 46 WORLD QUIETIST 3

DEBT
NATURE FORGIVES NO DEBT AND FEARS NO GRAVE . . . . 5 HARMONY NATURE 10
NOR PAY HIS BROTHERS DEBT . . . . 318 OBERMANN MORE V
TO OUR UNHAPPY HOUSE THE DEBT WE OWE . . . . . 367 MEROPE 1048
MY DEATH MAKES MY DEBT VOID AND DOUBLES THINE . . 367 MEROPE 1049
TO ONE UNHAPPY HOUSE THE DEBT WE OWE . . . . . 367 MEROPE V1048

DEBTS
ARE ALL DEBTS PAID HAS ALL BEEN SAID . . . . . 21 YOUTH AND CALM 8
HE HATH HIS LESSON TOO AND THAT DEBTS PAID . . . 429 EMPEDOCLES II 7
HE HAS HIS LESSON TOO AND THAT DEBTS PAID . . . 429 EMPEDOCLES II V 7

DECAY
IT SEEMS AS IF IN THEIR DECAY . . . . . . 56 RESIGNATION 134
MEN SPENT BY SICKNESS OR OBSCURE DECAY . . . 104 BALDER DEAD 1 325
WILLS THAT REMEMBRANCE SHOULD ALWAYS DECAY . . . 206 SEPARATION 6
NOT OUR BLOOM ONLY BUT OUR STRENGTH DECAY . . . 212 GROWING OLD 7
HE LOOKD ON THE RUSHING DECAY . . . . . . 229 YOUTH OF NATURE 29
SENSE AFTER SENSE DECAY . . . . 424 EMPEDOCLES I 2 365
NO LANGUOR NO DECAY LANGUOR AND DEATH . . . 438 EMPEDOCLES II 302
KNOW THEM IN THEIR SAD DECAY . . . . . . 453 POOR MATTHIAS 30
SOOTHED THEM IN THEIR LAST DECAY . . . . . 455 POOR MATTHIAS 92
THE SADDENING TALE THAT TELLS OF SORROW AND DECAY 462 ALARIC AT ROME 6
THAT CITY TOLD OF LANGUOR AND DECAY . . . . 466 ALARIC AT ROME 106
MATERIAL GRANDEURS DO IN HEAVEN DECAY . . . . FRAGMENT 2 4
BETWIXT BLANK NOTHING AND ABHORRED DECAY . . . FRAGMENT 5 5

DECAYING
AND AS IN A DECAYING WINTER-FIRE . . . . . 119 BALDER DEAD 3 203

DECEASED
NOR LOOKST THOU PALE AND WAN LIKE MEN DECEASED . . 108 BALDER DEAD 2 109
THE LINES OF DECEASED KINGS . . . . . . 423 EMPEDOCLES I 2 325

DECEIVE
STRONG TO DECEIVE STRONG TO ENSLAVE . . . . 39 STAGIRIUS 28
AWAY THE DREAMS THAT BUT DECEIVE . . . . . 310 OBERMANN 129

DECEIVER
DECEIVER FAIR IN FORM BUT FALSE IN HEART . . . 114 BALDER DEAD 3 21

DECEIVING
THERE HE FEELS IT WAS NO DREAM DECEIVING . . . 483 THEKLAS ANSWER 17

DECEMBER
ON THIS WILD DECEMBER NIGHT . . . . . . 130 TRISTRAM 1 14
AND THIS ROUGH DECEMBER-NIGHT . . . . . . 136 TRISTRAM 1 181
THE AIR OF THE DECEMBER-NIGHT . . . . . . 147 TRISTRAM 2 147

DECIDED
AH WHO SWAYD OUR CHOICE AND WHO DECIDED . . . 210 SELF-DECEPTION 15

DECK
AND ON THE DECK BUILD HIGH A FUNERAL-PILE . . . 96 BALDER DEAD 1 42
HEAP ON THE DECK THE LOGS AND BUILD THE PYRE . . 118 BALDER DEAD 3 159
AND THE PALE MASTER ON HIS SPAR-STREWN DECK . . 244 SUMMER NIGHT 65
DECK IT WITH GARLANDS OF FLOWERS . . . . . 342 MEROPE 388
THEY SHALL NOT DECK YOUR LIFE BUT SANCTIFY YOUR GRAVE 467 ALARIC AT ROME 138

DECKD
    BUT THEN THEY DECKD A RESTLESS GHOST . . . . 146 TRISTRAM 2   116
    DECKD THE DULL WASTE AND THE FAMILIAR FIELD . . 472 CROMWELL   34

DECKS
    FULL THE DECKS BREADTH AND LOFTY THEN THE CORPSE . . 118 BALDER DEAD 3   162

DECLAIMS
    AND QUIETLY DECLAIMS THE CURSINGS OF HIMSELF . . 422 EMPEDOCLES I 2   301
    AND PATIENTLY DECLAIMS THE CURSINGS OF HIMSELF . . 422 EMPEDOCLES I 2   V 301

DECLARE
    THE GODS DECLARE MY RECOMPENCE TO-DAY . . . . 9 MYCERINUS   16
    O HELA WHEREFORE SHOULD THE GODS DECLARE . . . 110 BALDER DEAD 2   189
    BUT COME DECLARE ME THIS AND TRULY TELL . . . . 111 BALDER DEAD 2   243
    YET SHE COULD LOVE THOSE EYES DECLARE . . . . 202 URANIA   7
    OF LIGHT BUT THIS TO DECLARE . . . . 296 HEINES GRAVE   117

DECLARED
    THEY HAVE DECLARED THE SPIRITS SORE . . . . . . 224 EPILOG LAOCOON   93

DECLARST
    TO ASGARD AND DECLARST THIS HIDDEN WAY . . . . 100 BALDER DEAD 1   190

DECLINE
    ONCE ERE THE DAY DECLINE THOU SHALT DISCERN . . 44 GIPSY CHILD   65
    A GOLDEN DAYS DECLINE . . . . 212 GROWING OLD   15
    HELPLESSLY GAZING ON THEIR OWN DECLINE . . . 282 HAWORTH CHURCH   V
    UNCLOUDED REASON I WOULD NOT DECLINE . . . . 335 MEROPE   158
    WERE AIMD AT THEIR PROMOTION OUR DECLINE . . . 337 MEROPE   244
    IS POTENT STILL ON ME IN HIS DECLINE . . . . 408 EMPEDOCLES I 1   66
    AND WEAKNESS WARND HIM AND HE FEARD DECLINE . . 447 WESTMIN ABBEY   123

DECLINES
    SHOW YOU SAY MY LOVE DECLINES . . . . 24 MEMORY-PICTURE   50
    DECLINES HER MINISTRY AND CARVES HIS OWN . . . 195 FRAG ANTIGONE   6

DECLINING
    TO US DECLINING TOWRDS OUR END . . . . 459 KAISER DEAD   35

DECREE
    GOES AN UNREVERSED DECREE . . . . 456 POOR MATTHIAS   149

DECREED
    FOR FATE DECREED IT SO . . . . 46 WORLD QUIETIST   10

DECREES
    DECREES OF HEAVEN . . . . 398 MEROPE   1805
    THE OBSTINATE MIND DECREES . . . . 419 EMPEDOCLES I 2   200

DECRIED
    NOT DECRIED BY MY VOICE . . . . 360 MEROPE   V 902

DEDICATION
    THE BOON THY DEDICATION-SIGN FORETOLD . . . . 444 WESTMIN ABBEY   5

DEED
    FORGOT MY DEED AS SOON AS DONE . . . . 158 SAINT BRANDAN   V 60
    AND PALSIED ALL OUR DEED WITH DOUBT . . . . . 323 OBERMANN MORE   V 319
    IN REASON GOOD WHICH JUSTIFIED MY DEED . . . . 340 MEROPE   340
    THAT RIGHT THAT CONSCIENCE POINTED TO A DEED . . 341 MEROPE   363
    WHICH IN A DEED LIKE MINE A JUST MAN TREADS . . 341 MEROPE   369
    THE TRUE AVENGERS THESE I LEAVE HIS DEED . . . 349 MEROPE   555
    THE CAUSE WHICH DREW HIM TO HIS DEED . . . . 352 MEROPE   650
    ADVANCEST TO THE MIDDLE OF A DEED . . . . 367 MEROPE   1061
    UNHAPPY ONE WHAT DEED . . . . 371 MEROPE   1134
    IN WORD I DIED THAT I IN DEED MIGHT LIVE . . . 375 MEROPE   1209
    THOU LEAPEST TO THY DEED AND HAST NOT ASKD . . 384 MEROPE   1388
    HIS JUST REVENGE TO AN UNNATURAL DEED . . . 385 MEROPE   1417
    A DEED SO AWFUL THAT THE GENERAL TONGUE . . . 385 MEROPE   1418
    WITH SUCH A DEED AS THIS THOU MATCHEST MINE . . 385 MEROPE   1426
    MY MOTHER STANDS ALOOF AND BLAMES OUR DEED . . 386 MEROPE   1448
    SHALL BE IMPOSED TO US SHALL BE THE DEED . . . 390 MEROPE   1585
    MY DEED IS OF OLD DATE AND LONG ATONED . . . 396 MEROPE   1768
    WHAT I HAVE DONE IS DONE BY MY OWN DEED . . . 398 MEROPE   1787

DEEDS
    ILL DEEDS ILL PASSIONS ZEALOUS TO FULFIL . . . 11 MYCERINUS   76
    BUT WHO FOR MEN OF NOUGHT WOULD DO GREAT DEEDS . 68 SOHRAB RUSTUM   255
    AND THOU SHALT TALK TO ME OF RUSTUMS DEEDS . . 74 SOHRAB RUSTUM   442
    FOR SOME ARE BORN TO DO GREAT DEEDS AND LIVE . 84 SOHRAB RUSTUM   773
    DO THOU THE DEEDS I DIE TOO YOUNG TO DO . . . 84 SOHRAB RUSTUM   775
    NOW TIME OBSCURES IT AND MENS LATER DEEDS . . 117 BALDER DEAD 3   130
    EARTH WITH THEIR DEEDS THEY FILL . . . . 220 BACCHANALIA 2   43
    WHOSE INSIGHT NEVER HAS BORNE FRUIT IN DEEDS . 260 SCHOLAR-GIPSY   174
    WHO UNDER EARTH WATCH GUILTY DEEDS OF MEN . . 332 MEROPE   74
    WITH GRIEVOUS DEEDS PERHAPS WITH MURDER NO . . 336 MEROPE   209
    WHO SELF-EXCULPATES LEND TO FOULEST DEEDS . . 338 MEROPE   279
    COMMITS ALL DEEDS THE GUILTY OFTENEST DO . . 353 MEROPE   683
    TURN WITH AVERTED EYES FROM DEEDS OF BLOOD . . 354 MEROPE   695
    SUCH AS ERE NOW HATH SPURRD TO FEARFUL DEEDS . 366 MEROPE   1012

DEEDS   (CONTINUED)
          ATTEMPTING DEEDS BEYOND THY POWER TO DO   • • • •   368 MEROPE   1079
          PRUDENCE IS ON THE OTHER SIDE BUT DEEDS   • • • •   383 MEROPE   1384
          THE HOUR FOR WORDS IS GONE IS COME FOR DEEDS   • • • •   386 MEROPE   1445
          AGREES TO DEEM SOME DEEDS SO DARK IN GUILT   • • • •   389 MEROPE   1524
          HAVE LEARND THAT THERE ARE GUILTY DEEDS WHICH LEAVE   394 MEROPE   1713
          WHICH DOOMS DREAD ENDS TO DREADFUL DEEDS   • • • •   398 MEROPE   1808
          DEEDS UNATONABLE   • • • • • • • • • • • •   400 MEROPE   1873
          AGREES TO DEEM SOME DEEDS SO HORRIBLE   • • • •   389 MEROPE   V1524
          THE ILL DEEDS OF OTHER MEN MAKE OFTEN OUR LIFE DARK   421 EMPEDOCLES I 2   266
          DEEDS THAT SHALL LIVE WHEN THEY WHO DID THEM DIE   • •   462 ALARIC AT ROME   15
          ALL WONDROUS DEEDS THE COMING DAYS SHOULD SEE • •   475 CROMWELL   139

DEEM
          SPARING US NARROWER MARGIN THAN WE DEEM   • • • •   7 REP FRIEND CONT   8
          YET SURELY O MY PEOPLE DID I DEEM   • • • • •   9 MYCERINUS   19
          COME NOW AND LET ME DEEM IT TRUTH   • • • • •   209 LONGING   V 10
          AT THE HEIGHT OF HIS VISION CAN DEEM   • • • • •   253 FUTURE   42
          DEEMING AS TYRANTS DEEM OUR SILENCE HATE   • • • •   338 MEROPE   260
          FOR ME I DEEM SUCH IMPIOUS AND FOR HIM   • • • •   340 MEROPE   336
          IMPIOUS I DEEM THE ALLIANCE WHICH HE ASKS   • • • •   348 MEROPE   550
          AGREES TO DEEM SOME DEEDS SO DARK IN GUILT   • • • •   389 MEROPE   1524
          THOUGH INJURED PAST FORGIVENESS AS MEN DEEM   • • •   394 MEROPE   1707
          AGREES TO DEEM SOME DEEDS SO HORRIBLE   • • • •   389 MEROPE   V1524
          FAIN WOULD WE DEEM THAT THOU HAST RISEN SO HIGH   • •   463 ALARIC AT ROME   31

DEEMD
          AND SO HE DEEMD THAT EITHER SOHRAB TOOK   • • • •   79 SOHRAB RUSTUM   612
          SO DEEMD HE YET HE LISTEND PLUNGED IN THOUGHT • •   79 SOHRAB RUSTUM   615
          AND CAME AS MOST MEN DEEMD TO LITTLE GOOD   • • • •   256 SCHOLAR-GIPSY   39
          BE ERROR DEEMD BUT THAT PRETENCE IS VAIN   • • • •   339 MEROPE   315
          AND KAISERS RACE WE DEEMD THE SAME   • • • •   459 KAISER DEAD   21

DEEMEDST
          AND THOU DEEMEDST CATS WERE KIND   • • • • •   453 POOR MATTHIAS   38

DEEMING
          DEEMING AS TYRANTS DEEM OUR SILENCE HATE   • • • •   338 MEROPE   260

DEEMS
          MAN ERRS NOT THAT HE DEEMS   • • • • • • • •   418 EMPEDOCLES I 2   173

DEEP
          VAIN LABOUR DEEP AND BROAD WHERE NONE MAY SEE   • •   4 BUTLERS SERMONS   5
          DRINKING DEEP DRAUGHTS OF JOY YE DWELL SERENE   • •   10 MYCERINUS   48
          REVELS MORE DEEP JOY KEENER THAN THEIR OWN   • • •   10 MYCERINUS   66
          WHILE THE DEEP-BURNISHD FOLIAGE OVERHEAD   • • •   11 MYCERINUS   98
          IT DREAMS A REST IF NOT MORE DEEP   • • • • •   22 YOUTH AND CALM   20
          IT ASKS A REST IF NOT MORE DEEP   • • • • •   22 YOUTH AND CALM   V 20
          THOSE FRANK EYES WHERE DEEP I SEE   • • • • •   24 MEMORY-PICTURE   45
          THOSE FRANK EYES WHERE DEEP DOTH LIE   • • • • •   24 MEMORY-PICTURE   V 45
          THOSE FRANK EYES WHERE DEEP DOTH BE   • • • • •   24 MEMORY-PICTURE   V 45
          THOSE FRANK EYES WHERE DEEP WILL BE   • • • • •   24 MEMORY-PICTURE   V 45
          OF THE DEEP ARE NOT YOUR LAIR   • • •   • •   26 NEW SIRENS   18
          STARS SET DEEP YET INLY BURNING   • • • • •   30 NEW SIRENS   137
          DEEP AND FAR A BROKEN GLEAMING   • • • • •   32 NEW SIRENS   185
          TO THIS DEEP-SOBERD HEART   • • • • •   •   36 VOICE   24
          FROM THAT TORPOR DEEP   • • • • • •   • •   38 STAGIRIUS   10
          TO A SKIN-DEEP SENSE   • • • • • •   • •   39 STAGIRIUS   26
          ON EITHER SIDE THE BLACK DEEP-FURROWD PATH   • • • •   41 HUMAN LIFE   22
          GLOOMS THAT GO DEEP AS THINE I HAVE NOT KNOWN • •   42 GIPSY CHILD   17
          HUMAN THINGS SO DEEP ENTANGLED   • • • • • • • •   SECOND BEST   V 10
          DEEP IN THE SANDY WASTE   • • • • • •   • •   51 CONSOLATION   33
          THROUGH THE DEEP NOONTIDE HEATS WE FARE   • • •   54 RESIGNATION   69
          NOT DEEP THE POET SEES BUT WIDE   • • •   • • •   58 RESIGNATION   214
          A SHIVER RUNS THROUGH THE DEEP CORN FOR JOY   • •   65 SOHRAB RUSTUM   156
          AND A DEEP PITY ENTERD RUSTUMS SOUL   • • •   70 SOHRAB RUSTUM   319
          BACK OUT TO SEA TO THE DEEP WAVES OF DEATH   • • •   73 SOHRAB RUSTUM   395
          THE ANGUISH OF THE DEEP-FIXD SPEAR GREW FIERCE •   80 SOHRAB RUSTUM   650
          SOON BE THAT DAY MY SON AND DEEP THAT SEA   • • •   85 SOHRAB RUSTUM   836
          DEEP HEAVY GASPS QUIVERING THROUGH ALL HIS FRAME •   86 SOHRAB RUSTUM   850
          THROUGH VALLEYS DEEP-ENGULPHD WITH ROARING STREAMS   99 BALDER DEAD 1   146
          WHO SHUFFLES THROUGH THE DEEP DEW-MOISTEND DUST   •   101 BALDER DEAD 1   232
          THEIR HORSES FETLOCK-DEEP IN BLOOD THEY RIDE   • •   105 BALDER DEAD 2   25
          THROUGH VALLEYS DEEP-ENGULPHD BY ROARING STREAMS •   107 BALDER DEAD 2   84
          PLUNGING THROUGH DEEP UNTRODDEN BANKS OF SNOW •   107 BALDER DEAD 2   97
          WHEREWITH THEY STAMPD THEM DOWN AND TROD THEM DEEP   109 BALDER DEAD 2   174
          BUT DEEP IF THOU DEVISEDST IT TO DROWN   • • •   114 BALDER DEAD 3   28
          FROM THE DEEP TRENCH SHE PLOUGHD SO STRONG A GOD •   118 BALDER DEAD 3   178
          IN THE GREAT DEEP FOR GAIN AT LAST COME HOME   • •   123 BALDER DEAD 3   358
          OF THE DEEP INNER GLOOM BUT FLITTEST HERE   • • •   124 BALDER DEAD 3   389
          FROM THE DEEP GLOOM WHERE I WILL NOW RETURN   • •   125 BALDER DEAD 3   415
          IS IT THAT A DEEP FATIGUE   • • • • • • •   •   131 TRISTRAM 1   37
          NOT THIS FIERCE ATLANTIC DEEP   • • • • •   • •   133 TRISTRAM 1   92
          IN HIS STATELY DEEP DISTRESS   • • • • •   • •   137 TRISTRAM 1   209
          AH IT LIVES BECAUSE SO DEEP-SUPPRESSD   • • •   143 TRISTRAM 2   40
          ROYAL STATE WITH MARC MY DEEP-WRONGD HUSBAND   •   144 TRISTRAM 2   45
          THE DEEP DRAUGHTS OF DEATH IN BEARING ME   • • •   145 TRISTRAM 2   84
          WHERE THE DEEP FOREST STREAM CREEPS SLOW   • • •   148 TRISTRAM 2   V
          MANTLES WITH THOSE RICH FURS DEEP GLISTERING   • •   150 TRISTRAM 3   40

DEEP   (CONTINUED)
      OF THE DEEP FOREST-GLADES OF BROCE-LIANDE   • • • •   154 TRISTRAM 3   156
      FELL UPON MERLIN MORE LIKE DEATH SO DEEP   • • • •   155 TRISTRAM 3   214
      BUT THEIR SLOPE WAS NOT DEEP AND FAR AND NEAR   • •   TRISTRAM 3   V 11
      SAND-STREWN CAVERNS COOL AND DEEP   • • • • •   162 FORSAKEN MERM   35
      HOW DEEP IS THEIR STILLNESS   • • • • • • •   175 PARTING   15
      WHO RENDERS VAIN THEIR DEEP DESIRE   • • • • •   182 TO MARG CONT   21
      THE DEEP CUP IVY-CINCTURED   • • • • • • • •   186 STRAYED REVEL   12
      ORIGINAL DEEP-INWOUND   • • • • • • • • •   196 FRAG ANTIGONE   36
      THAT WILD UNQUENCHD DEEP-SUNKEN OLD-WORLD PAIN   • •   200 PHILOMELA   8
      THEIR PURE UNWAVERING DEEP DISDAIN   • • • • • •   202 URANIA   32
      THEIR GAY UNWAVERING DEEP DISDAIN   • • • • • •   202 URANIA   V 32
      DEAD TO ITS DEEP HABITUAL SMART   • • • • • •   206 RIVER   19
      IF THE LOVED FORM AND THE DEEP-CHERISHD FEATURE   • •   206 SEPARATION   7
      DEEP BE THE DARKNESS AND STILL BE THE SLUMBER   • •   206 SEPARATION   11
      THOSE EYES OF DEEP SOFT LUCENT HUE   • • • • • •   208 ON THE RHINE   18
      DEEP IN OUR HIDDEN HEART   • • • • • • • •   213 GROWING OLD   28
      DEEP IS THEIR PENITENTIAL MOAN   • • • • • • • •   224 EPILOG LAOCOON   91
      SO DEEP AS THE MUSICIANS LORE   • • • • • • •   225 EPILOG LAOCOON   136
      AND DEEP AS WORDS CAN FOLLOW FEELING   • • • • •   225 EPILOG LAOCOON   138
      AND ITS DEEP-TONED MELODIOUS VOICE   • • • • •   227 EPILOG LAOCOON   195
      TOO DEEP FOR THE MOST TO DISCERN   • • • • • •   230 YOUTH OF NATURE   71
      LIKE STARS IN THE DEEP OF THE SKY   • • • • •   230 YOUTH OF NATURE   72
      BUT THAT YE THINK CLEAR FEEL DEEP BEAR FRUIT WELL   •   238 PROGRESS   47
      BUT THAT YOU THINK CLEAR FEEL DEEP BEAR FRUIT WELL •   238 PROGRESS   V 47
      HEADLANDS STOOD OUT INTO THE MOONLIT DEEP   • • • •   242 SUMMER NIGHT   14
      FOR THAT WHICH SEALS THEM HATH BEEN DEEP-ORDAIND   • •   245 BURIED LIFE   29
      BADE THROUGH THE DEEP RECESSES OF OUR BREAST   • •   246 BURIED LIFE   38
      SO WILD SO DEEP IN US TO KNOW   • • • • • •   246 BURIED LIFE   53
      BUT DEEP ENOUGH ALAS NONE EVER MINES   • • • • •   246 BURIED LIFE   56
      SCREEND BY DEEP BOUGHS ON EITHER HAND   • • •   248 KENSINGTON GARD   2
      DEEP IN HER UNKNOWN DAYS EMPLOY   • • • • • •   248 KENSINGTON GARD   12
      AS DEEP AS PELLUCID A SPRING   • • • • • •   252 FUTURE   39
      SPIRITS DEEP-CRUSHED AND CLOSELY FURLD   • • •   272 MEMORIAL VERSES V 56
      THE MURMUR OF THIS MIDLAND DEEP   • • • • •   276 SOUTHERN NIGHT   21
      POACH THE DEEP WAYS COMING DOWN   • • • •   282 HAWORTH CHURCH   59
      LONG SINCE DEEP IN OUR HEARTS   • • • • • •   294 HEINES GRAVE   74
      DEEP HAVE EMBREATHED AT ITS CORE   • • • • •   299 HEINES GRAVE   230
      DEEP DEEP THE GREENWOOD ROUND THEM WAVES   • • •   305 GRANDE CHARTR   173
      DEEP DEEP THE GREENWOOD ROUND THEM WAVES   • • •   305 GRANDE CHARTR   173
      IS FRAUGHT TOO DEEP WITH PAIN   • • • • • •   307 OBERMANN   38
      TO TELL TOO DEEP ONES IS NOT WELL   • • • •   307 OBERMANN   43
      DEEP WEARINESS AND SATED LUST   • • • • • •   315 OBERMANN MORE   95
      IN PATIENT DEEP DISDAIN   • • • • • •   316 OBERMANN MORE   110
      POOR WORLD SHE CRIED SO DEEP ACCURST   • • • •   316 OBERMANN MORE   117
      OF LOVE WHICH SET SO DEEP AND STRONG   • • • •   317 OBERMANN MORE   147
      HELP IT TO FILL THAT DEEP DESIRE   • • • • •   323 OBERMANN MORE   313
      HELP IT TO REACH OUR DEEP DESIRE   • • • • •   323 OBERMANN MORE   V 313
      THY DEEP SECLUSION THINE UNYIELDING GLOOM   • • •   332 MEROPE   84
      WALLS ON ONE SIDE THE DEEP STYMPHALIAN LAKE   • •   358 MEROPE   813
      DEEP AS THOU CANST FOR HENCE NO SUCCOUR COMES   • •   386 MEROPE   1431
      I HIDE NOT EVEN THIS THE REVERENCE DEEP   • • •   387 MEROPE   1474
      WHAT DEEP-GRASSD MEADOW   • • • • • •   391 MEROPE   1606
      KNEE-DEEP IN THE COOL FORD FOR TIS THE LAST   •   413 EMPEDOCLES I 2   41
      HOW DEEP A FAULT IS THIS   • • • • • • •   417 EMPEDOCLES I 2   158
      DEEP IN MANS HEART IS BORN   • • • • • • •   418 EMPEDOCLES I 2   169
      AND THE SOULS DEEP ETERNAL NIGHT COME ON   • • •   429 EMPEDOCLES II   35
      THY LAST MISCHANCE ON THIS SICILIAN DEEP   • • •   430 EMPEDOCLES II   57
      DROOPS ALL HIS SHEENY BROWN DEEP-FEATHERD NECK   •   431 EMPEDOCLES II   76
      TO OUR OWN ONLY TRUE DEEP-BURIED SELVES   • •   440 EMPEDOCLES II   371
      ROOST DEEP IN THE ROCKS   • • • • • •   442 EMPEDOCLES II   432
      THAT THY GROANS LIKE THUNDER DEEP   • • • •   430 EMPEDOCLES II   V 62
      WITH WHAT ROLLD OF US IN THE STORMY DEEP   • • •   439 EMPEDOCLES II   V 342
      BUT ONCE AT MIDNIGHT DEEP   • • • • • •   446 WESTMIN ABBEY   91
      FAIL TO TRACK THEIR DEEP DISTRESS   • • • •   455 POOR MATTHIAS   106
      BUT FULL AND DEATHLESS AS THE DEEP DARK HUE   •   463 ALARIC AT ROME   35
      AND MEMORYS GUSHING TIDE SWELLS DEEP AND FULL   •   464 ALARIC AT ROME   53
      EARTHS OLD HEROIC FORMS IN PEACEFUL SLUMBERS DEEP •   464 ALARIC AT ROME   60
      AND THE DEEP HUES OF AN ITALIAN SKY   • • • •   464 ALARIC AT ROME   69
      SOUNDS OF DEEP IMPORT VOICES THAT BEGUILE   • • •   472 CROMWELL   5
      IN THE DEEP STILLNESS OF ITS SHELTRING BREAST   •   472 CROMWELL   12
      DEEP ON HIS LIFE AND CHILDHOODS BABY WAVES   • • •   473 CROMWELL   48
      MORE CALM MORE DEEP THAN CHILDHOOD EVER KNEW   • •   475 CROMWELL   116
      NO LIFE OF DREAMS NO HOME BEYOND THE DEEP   • •   475 CROMWELL   124
      FROM THEIR DEEP BASE THY BEETLING CLIFFS DUNBAR   •   476 CROMWELL   151
      SHOOK THE DEEP SLUMBER OF HIS DEATHLIKE TRANCE   •   477 CROMWELL   194
      DEEP THRO HIS SOUL AND CHOKD HIS FALTERING TONGUE •   478 CROMWELL   224
      WITH NOISELESS CURRENT STRONG OBSCURE AND DEEP   • •   483 BELOW SURFACE   4
      SHARP SENSE OF DEEP SELF-IGNORANCE FEAR OF LOOKS   • •   LUCRETIUS 2   14

DEEPENING
      OF SEA AND WIND AND THROUGH THE DEEPENING GLOOM   • •   244 SUMMER NIGHT   71
      WHERE GHOSTLIKE IN THE DEEPENING NIGHT   • • • •   300 GRANDE CHARTR   35

DEEPER
      BUT DEEPER THEIR VOICE GROWS AND NOBLER THEIR BEARING   20 MODERN SAPPHO   27
      DEEPER THE POET FEELS BUT HE   • • • • • • • •   58 RESIGNATION   206
      GREW DEEPER THUNDER CRASHD ALONG THE SKY   • • •   76 SOHRAB RUSTUM   V 500
      FELT ALREADY SOME DEEPER SMART   • • • • • • •   131 TRISTRAM 1   46
      DEEPER TO THESE MUST NEEDS ALLOW   • • • • • •   222 EPILOG LAOCOON   31

DEEPER   (CONTINUED)
        A DEEPER LIFE THAN THEIRS   · · · · ·   · · ·   237 PROGRESS   24
        STILL FLY PLUNGE DEEPER IN THE BOWERING WOOD   · ·   261 SCHOLAR-GIPSY   207

DEEPEST
        OF HIS DEEPEST BEST EXISTENCE   · · · · · · · ·   · ·   49 SECOND BEST   22

DEEPLY
        BREATHED DEEPLY AS IT DIED   · · · · · · ·   · ·   47 WORLD QUIETIST   31
        DEEPLY STIRS AND TRULY BURNS   · · · · · ·   · · ·   SECOND BEST   V 24
        DEEPLY THE POET FEELS BUT HE   · · · · · · ·   · ·   58 RESIGNATION   V 206
        FARE FAREWELL THOU LONG THOU DEEPLY LOVD   · · · ·   ·   145 TRISTRAM 2   V 98
        NO WE MAY SUFFER DEEPLY YET RETAIN · · · · · ·   · · ·   153 TRISTRAM 3   116
        HOW DEEPLY SHE WHO SCORNS CAN LOVE · · · ·   · · · ·   202 URANIA   20
        BUT THAT YOU TOO FEEL DEEPLY BEAR FRUIT WELL   ·   · ·   238 PROGRESS   V 47
        WHO HAVE LONGD DEEPLY ONCE AND LONGD IN VAIN   ·   · ·   244 SUMMER NIGHT   85
        WHO NEVER DEEPLY FELT NOR CLEARLY WILLD   · · · ·   ·   260 SCHOLAR-GIPSY   173
        BUT THOU O MEROPE THOUGH DEEPLY WRONGD   · · · · ·   ·   394 MEROPE   1706
        HE BOWD HIS HEAD AND DEEPLY GROAND AND DIED   ·   · ·   402 MEROPE   1929
        TO LOVE MORE DEEPLY THAN HE CAN   · · · · ·   · ·   481 DESTINY   2

DEEPS
        FROM THOSE STILL DEEPS IN FORM AND COLOUR DREST   ·   ·   45 IN UTRUMQUE PAR   4
        I WILL NOT SAY THAT YOUR MILD DEEPS RETAIN   · · · ·   ·   244 SUMMER NIGHT   83

DEER
        WHERE THE LOOMING DEER ARE LAID   · · · · ·   · ·   32 NEW SIRENS   V 182
        THROUGH LAST YEARS FERN OF THE SHY FALLOW-DEER   ·   ·   155 TRISTRAM 3   193
        THROUGH THE GREEN FERN OF THE SHY FALLOW-DEER   ·   ·   155 TRISTRAM 3   V 193
        DANGEROUS ALONE TO THE DEER   · · · · · ·   · ·   342 MEROPE   399
        A GLADSOME HUNTER OF DEER   · · · · · · · ·   ·   347 MEROPE   520
        WILD HOG AND BEAR AND MOUNTAIN-DEER AND ROE   · ·   356 MEROPE   758

DEFACD
        NEVER DEFACD TILL NOW SHAMD TO THE DUST   · · · ·   ·   76 SOHRAB RUSTUM   V 498

DEFEAT
        THY LAST DEFEAT IN THIS SICILIAN SEA   · · · · · ·   ·   430 EMPEDOCLES II   V 57

DEFENCE
        I SELF-DEFENCE AND RIGHTEOUS EXECUTION   · · · ·   ·   338 MEROPE   277

DEFENCELESS
        AND THEN WILL THAT DEFENCELESS WOMAN LEARN   · · ·   79 SOHRAB RUSTUM   598

DEFER
        THE PRAYER I CAME TO URGE I WILL DEFER   · · · ·   ·   333 MEROPE   109

DEFERRD
        WHO MADE THAT TRIUMPH THOUGH DEFERRD SECURE   · ·   336 MEROPE   220

DEFILED
        NEVER TILL NOW DEFILED SANK TO THE DUST   · · · ·   ·   76 SOHRAB RUSTUM   498
        NEVER TILL NOW DEFILED SUNK TO THE DUST   · · · ·   ·   76 SOHRAB RUSTUM   V 498
        A PALACE DEFILED BY A DEATH UNAVENGED   · · · ·   ·   346 MEROPE   508

DEFILEMENT
        AND SHOUTED SINCE BY THEE DEFILEMENT CAME   · · ·   402 MEROPE   1923

DEFINE
        MIS-DEFINE THESE TILL GOD KNOWS THEM NO MORE   ·   ·   171 DIVINITY   10

DEFORMITY
        AGAINST A SICKNESS OR DEFORMITY   · · · · · ·   ·   LUCRETIUS 3   4

DEFYING
        CAME SEEKING RUSTUM AND DEFYING FORTH   · · · ·   ·   70 SOHRAB RUSTUM   310
        WENT SEEKING RUSTUM AND DEFYING FORTH   · · · ·   ·   70 SOHRAB RUSTUM   V 310

DEGRADE
        WHICH WOULD DEGRADE IT MOST   · · · · · · ·   ·   415 EMPEDOCLES I 2   100

DEGRADING
        DEGRADING PYLOS FROM ITS ANCIENT RULE   · · · ·   ·   330 MEROPE   12

DEIGN
        EMPEDOCLES WOULD SAY SO DID HE DEIGN   · · · · ·   ·   410 EMPEDOCLES I 1   137

DEITIES
        TERRIBLE DEITIES THRONED   · · · · · · ·   · ·   347 MEROPE   530
        TO EMBITTER HUMAN LIFE MALIGNANT DEITIES   · · · ·   ·   422 EMPEDOCLES I 2   311

DEJECTEDLY
        WHO MOST HAS SUFFERD TAKES DEJECTEDLY   · · ·   · ·   260 SCHOLAR-GIPSY   183

DEJECTION
        AS HE DRIFTS TO FATIGUE DISCONTENT AND DEJECTION   · ·   20 MODERN SAPPHO   19
        A VAGUE DEJECTION   · · · · · · · ·   · ·   50 CONSOLATION   4
        PAIN AND DEJECTION TO-NIGHT   · · · · · · · ·   · ·   229 YOUTH OF NATURE   26
        TOIL OR DEJECTION HAVE TRIED   · · · · · · · ·   · ·   290 RUGBY CHAPEL   136

```
DELAY
        THE DOOM THEY PASS REVOKE NOT NOR DELAY    . . . .    10 MYCERINUS          70
        CHIDE AND PUT BACK AND DELAY    . . . . . . . .   283 HAWORTH CHURCH    V

DELAYED
        EVEN IN THE ACT TO BURST TWICE THREATENED TWICE       465 ALARIC AT ROME      84
            DELAYED

DELAYS
        WITH HIS PACK ROUND HIM AND DELAYS    . . . . .   148 TRISTRAM 2          156
        YES WE AWAIT IT BUT IT STILL DELAYS    . . . . .   260 SCHOLAR-GIPSY       181
        BUT THE THIRD WHAT DELAYS HIM    . . . . . . . .   344 MEROPE              457

DELIBERATE
        AND WIN DELIBERATE REASON TO PUT ON FEAR    . . . .      RUDE ORATOR         11

DELICATE
        THROUGH THE DELICATE FLUSHD MARBLE    . . . . . .   187 STRAYED REVEL       56
        HIS WHITE DELICATE NECK    . . . . . . . . . .   188 STRAYED REVEL       83
        DELICATE SPIRITS PUSHD AWAY    . . . . . . . .   219 BACCHANALIA 2       17

DELICATELY
        SO DELICATELY PRICKD THE SIGN APPEARD    . . . .    81 SOHRAB RUSTUM      677
        AH JAMAN DELICATELY TALL    . . . . . . . . . .   313 OBERMANN MORE      33

DELICIOUS
        NOT PENT ON SHIP-BOARD THIS DELICIOUS DAY    . . . .   133 TRISTRAM 1          98
        WITH A WILD DELICIOUS PAIN    . . . . . . . .   135 TRISTRAM 1         151

DELIGHT
        THE DELIGHT OF DEATH-EMBRACES    . . . . . . . .    27 NEW SIRENS          55
        MAD DELIGHT AND FROZEN CALMS    . . . . . . . .    33 NEW SIRENS         196
        THE DELIGHT OF FIERCE EMBRACES    . . . . . . .    27 NEW SIRENS        V  55
        NO MEDITATION NO DELIGHT NO SORROW    . . . . .    50 CONSOLATION        V
        SO THOU MIGHTST LIVE AND STILL DELIGHT THE GODS    . .   101 BALDER DEAD 1      218
        OF MAD DELIGHT THEY DROP THEIR SPOILS AND BOUND    . .   150 TRISTRAM 3          27
        OF THAT FRESH VOICE THE GAY DELIGHT    . . . . .   184 TERRACE BERNE       31
        HEAR WITH DELIGHT OF THY FAME    . . . . . . .   284 HAWORTH CHURCH      87
        PEACE WITH DELIGHT IN THY TRAIN    . . . . . .   360 MEROPE             891
        TO IMMORTAL DELIGHT    . . . . . . . . . . .   399 MEROPE            1843
        OF NEWNESS AND DELIGHT    . . . . . . . . . .   424 EMPEDOCLES I 2     355
        STILL HUNGRIER FOR DELIGHT AS DELIGHTS GROW MORE RARE   424 EMPEDOCLES I 2     371

DELIGHTED
        TO ALL THAT HAS DELIGHTED THEM BEFORE    . . . .   152 TRISTRAM 3         114
        TO ALL WHICH HAS DELIGHTED THEM BEFORE    . . . .   152 TRISTRAM 3       V 114
        DRINKS UP DELIGHTED ECSTASY    . . . . . . . .   227 EPILOG LAOCOON     194

DELIGHTFUL
        AND HOUND AND MORN ON THOSE DELIGHTFUL HILLS    . .    80 SOHRAB RUSTUM      630
        AND YOUTH AND BLOOM AND THIS DELIGHTFUL WORLD    . .    86 SOHRAB RUSTUM      856
        IN THE DELIGHTFUL COMMERCE OF THE WORLD    . . .   436 EMPEDOCLES II      247

DELIGHTING
        AND HEARD HIM DELIGHTING    . . . . . . . . . .   189 STRAYED REVEL      121

DELIGHTS
        OF ODIN THE DELIGHTS OF OTHER DAYS    . . . . .   129 BALDER DEAD 3      542
        LIKE US THE LIBYAN WIND DELIGHTS TO ROAM AT LARGE    420 EMPEDOCLES I 2     251
        STILL HUNGRIER FOR DELIGHT AS DELIGHTS GROW MORE RARE   424 EMPEDOCLES I 2     371

DELIVER
        WITH COMPACT IN THAT CONCOURSE TO DELIVER    . . .   338 MEROPE             264

DELIVERANCE
        TO ACHIEVE HIS SONS DELIVERANCE O MY CHILD    . . .   198 FRAG ANTIGONE      103

DELIVERD
        TO BE DELIVERD FROM THY FOSTERD HATE    . . . . .   342 MEROPE             383
        THERE FROM SIN DELIVERD DWELLS MY FATHER    . . .   482 THEKLAS ANSWER      15

DELL
        UNTO A LONELY VILLA IN A DELL    . . . . . . .   167 RACHEL 2             1
        IN THIS STERN ALPINE DELL    . . . . . . . . .   312 OBERMANN           182
        BUT HE COMES NOT WHAT DELL    . . . . . . . .   347 MEROPE             V

DELLS
        THROUGH THESE SECLUDED DELLS TO CRY    . . . . .   305 GRANDE CHARTR      195
        THE NURSLING OF THE DELLS    . . . . . . . . .   391 MEROPE            1615
        OF ALL THE WOODY HIGH WELL-WATERD DELLS    . . .   414 EMPEDOCLES I 2      42

DELOS
        SAW IN THE ROCKY ISLE OF DELOS DIE    . . . . .   197 FRAG ANTIGONE       69

DELPHI
        IN THE PASSES OF DELPHI    . . . . . . . . . .   344 MEROPE             463
        OF THE GORGE OF DELPHI    . . . . . . . . . .   435 EMPEDOCLES II      202

DELPHIAN
        APOLLO PEALD IT FROM HIS DELPHIAN CAVE    . . . .   385 MEROPE            1401
```

DELPHIC
    THAT DELPHIC HEST TO RETURN • • • • • • • • 343 MEROPE 422

DELUGE
    THY DELUGE AND FROM HIM THE GIANTS SPRANG • • • • 121 BALDER DEAD 3 273
    FOR FROM ALL SIDES A DELUGE AS IT SEEMD • • • • 402 MEROPE 1937

DELUGED
    IN THIS BLOOD-DELUGED PALACE IN WHOSE HALLS • • 366 MEROPE 1018

DELUSION
    AND THE MISTS OF DELUSION • • • • • • • • 235 YOUTH OF MAN 105
    NURSED NO DELUSION • • • • • • • • • • • 441 EMPEDOCLES II 402

DELVES
    AND MANY A MAN IN HIS OWN BREAST THEN DELVES • • 246 BURIED LIFE 55
    IN HIS OWN BOSOM DELVES • • • • • • • • • • 416 EMPEDOCLES I 2 130

DEMAND
    TO ONE DEMAND ALONE ARE COY • • • • • • • 203 EUPHROSYNE 22
    THESE DEMAND NOT THAT THE THINGS WITHOUT THEM • • 240 SELF-DEPENDENCE 19
    WITH INWARD STRIVING AND DEMAND • • • • • 247 BURIED LIFE 68
    PLUNGD IN THEMSELVES WHO DEMAND • • • • • • 282 HAWORTH CHURCH V
    THAT WE DEMAND A BLISS • • • • • • • • • 425 EMPEDOCLES I 2 V 402

DEMANDEST
    DEMANDEST VENGEANCE NOT GRIEF • • • • • • • 343 MEROPE 405

DEMANDS
    AND OF HIS UNSURE AGENT WHAT DEMANDS HE • • • • 380 MEROPE 1280
    JUSTICE MY SISTER LONG DEMANDS THIS BLOW • • • • 390 MEROPE 1572
    AND WISDOM NOW THOU SEEST DEMANDS IT TOO • • • • 390 MEROPE 1573

DEMONS
    BUT THE DEMONS LONG NOURISHD HERE • • • • • 361 MEROPE 909

DEN
    MARCUS AURELIUS BUT THE STIFLING DEN • • • • • 168 WORLDLY PLACE 3
    COME BANEFUL MISCHIEF FROM THY MURKY DEN • • • • 367 MEROPE 1063

DENIED
    MOUNTING TO POWER LONG DENIED • • • • • • • HORATIAN ECHO V
    THE FREEDOM TO MY LIFE DENIED • • • • • • • 250 WISH 10
    AT THE FATE-DENIED STRAITS • • • • • • • • 344 MEROPE 444
    RIGHTS UNCONCEDED AND DENIED • • • • • • • 352 MEROPE 655
    BUT I HAVE NOT DENIED WHAT BONDS THESE WERE • • 440 EMPEDOCLES II 398

DENIES
    WHICH THE SORROW-STRICKEN DAY DENIES • • • • • 32 NEW SIRENS 178
    AIR TO HIS UNWINGD FORM DENIES A WAY • • • • • 351 MEROPE 624
    IT IS A SAD SIGHT WHEN THE WORLD DENIES • • • • LUCRETIUS 2 1

DENIZEN
    FIT DENIZEN THE LAMPLESS UNDER-WORLD • • • • • 367 MEROPE 1031

DENMARK
    AND RULED OER DENMARK AND THE HEATHY ISLES • • • • 117 BALDER DEAD 3 127

DENOUNCE
    COME FORTH DENOUNCE THE TRAFFIC AND THE TRAITOR • • 364 MEROPE 982
    DID CONSCIENCE GOAD HIM TO DENOUNCE HIMSELF • • 364 MEROPE V

DENSE
    THROUGH THE DENSE ILEX-THICKETS TO THE DOGS • • 357 MEROPE 791

DENSER
    DENSER THE TRADE ON ITS STREAM • • • • • • • • 253 FUTURE 63

DENY
    MAN WHO ART THOU WHO DOST DENY MY WORDS • • • • 80 SOHRAB RUSTUM 655
    WE SHALL NOT THEN DENY A COURSE • • • • • • 179 FAREWELL 57
    DENY THEE NOT MY BOWL • • • • • • • • • 187 STRAYED REVEL 60
    TO CURSE AND TO DENY YOUR TRUTH • • • • • • 301 GRANDE CHARTR 78

DEPART
    VAIN DREAMS WHICH QUENCH OUR PLEASURES THEN DEPART 9 MYCERINUS 27
    VAIN DREAMS THAT QUENCH OUR PLEASURES THEN DEPART 9 MYCERINUS V 27
    MAY I ERE I DEPART BID BALDER HAIL • • • • • • 111 BALDER DEAD 2 244
    EVEN FOR A MOMENT DIDST DEPART • • • • • • • 181 ISOLATION MARG 15
    WHEN YOUR GREAT ONES DEPART WILL YE SAY • • • • 231 YOUTH OF NATURE 126
    WE O NATURE DEPART • • • • • • • • • • • 232 YOUTH OF MAN 1
    SEEST OUR ERRORS DEPART • • • • • • • • • 232 YOUTH OF MAN 8
    ESCAPE THEIR PRISON AND DEPART • • • • • • 243 SUMMER NIGHT 52
    INTO THE WORLD AND WAVE OF MEN DEPART • • • 264 THYRSIS 39
    BREAK OFF BREAK OFF YOUR TALKING AND DEPART • • 386 MEROPE 1440
    NOR LET THEE UTTERLY DEPART • • • • • • • • 451 GEISTS GRAVE 39
    THEN HOME RETURND ONCE MORE DEPART • • • • • • 460 KAISER DEAD 51

DEPARTED
    DEPARTED OER THE CLOUDY PLAIN AND SOON   • • • •   129 BALDER DEAD 3   552
    AND THE DIM GLORIES OF DEPARTED DAYS • • • • • •   464 ALARIC AT ROME   63
    THE SADDENING VISIONS OF DEPARTED DAYS   • • • •   470 ALARIC AT ROME   202
    BEAUTIFUL CITY IF DEPARTED THINGS   • • • • •   470 ALARIC AT ROME   205

DEPARTING
    A-KEMPIS HER DEPARTING SOUL OUTWORN   • • • • •   168 RACHEL 3   7
    STOP NOT TO ME AT THIS BITTER DEPARTING   • • • •   206 SEPARATION   1

DEPLORE
    LIFE WELL AND FIND IT WANTING NOR DEPLORE   • • • •   42 GIPSY CHILD   30
    VEXT HEART DEPLORE • • • • • • • • • • • •   275 SOUTHERN NIGHT   16
    DOTH THY FIERCE SOUL STILL DEPLORE   • • • • •   430 EMPEDOCLES II   52

DEPLORED
    BUT I FROM OUR DEPLORED MISCHANCE LEARN THIS   • •   359 MEROPE   853

DEPRESSD
    FOILD BY OUR FELLOW-MEN DEPRESSD OUTWORN   • • • •   172 IMMORTALITY   1

DEPTH
    IS ANSWERD FROM THE DEPTH OF DAWN   • • • • •   57 RESIGNATION   177
    MAKE OFTEN IN THE FORESTS DEPTH AT MORN   • • • •   75 SOHRAB RUSTUM   V 477
    SHE SPAKE AND TO THE CAVERNS DEPTH SHE FLED   • • •   123 BALDER DEAD 3   355
    THE DEPTH OF THAT CONSUMING RESTLESSNESS   • • • •   238 PROGRESS   V
    FROM THE SOULS SUBTERRANEAN DEPTH UPBORNE   • • • •   247 BURIED LIFE   73
    WROUGHT TO ERASE FROM ITS DEPTH   • • • • •   281 HAWORTH CHURCH   39
    SELDOM AND FAINTLY THE DEPTH   • • • • • •   282 HAWORTH CHURCH   V
    OF HAZELS GREEN IN WHOSE DEPTH • • • • • • •   297 HEINES GRAVE   182
    IN THE HIGH ALTARS DEPTH DIVINE   • • • • •   306 GRANDE CHARTR   202
    HIGH IN THE VALAIS-DEPTH PROFOUND   • • • • • •   324 OBERMANN MORE   347
    FAITHFUL LOVE IN DEPTH DIVINE   • • • • • •   454 POOR MATTHIAS   65

DEPTHS
    THROUGH BLACK DEPTHS OF SERRIED SHADOWS   • • • •   32 NEW SIRENS   179
    IN THE FOREST-DEPTHS ALONE   • • • • • • • •   137 TRISTRAM 1   224
    DOWN TO THE DEPTHS OF THE SEA • • • • • • •   164 FORSAKEN MERM   86
    FOR SOMETHING IN ITS DEPTHS DOTH GLOW   • • •   178 FAREWELL   19
    RALLY THE GOOD IN THE DEPTHS OF THYSELF   • • •   235 YOUTH OF MAN   118
    CONCEALS FROM MAN WHO CANNOT PLUMB ITS DEPTHS   •   351 MEROPE   623
    RETAIND SO LITTLE IN THY CARELESS DEPTHS   • • •   LUCRETIUS 1   4

DERIDE
    THEIR FAITH MY TEARS THE WORLD DERIDE   • • • •   302 GRANDE CHARTR   89

DERISION
    DID WITH SUCH COLD DERISION SHINE   • • • • • •   482 COURAGE   22

DERISIVE
    OF PITYING FRIENDS DERISIVE ENEMIES   • • • • • •   LUCRETIUS 2   15

DESCEND
    AT LAST SHALL DESCEND UNDISTURBD   • • • • •   199 FRAG DEJANEIRA   21
    GLADLY DESCEND TO THE PLAIN   • • • • • • •   216 LORDS MESSENGER   9
    SOON HAVING ONCE BEHELD HIM TO DESCEND   • • •   350 MEROPE   592
    ALL VENGEANCE UNATTEMPTED AND DESCEND   • • • •   367 MEROPE   1029

DESCENDS
    INSINCERE PRAISES WHICH DESCENDS   • • • • •   199 EARLY DEATH   6
    COLDLY SADLY DESCENDS   • • • • • • • • •   286 RUGBY CHAPEL   1
    THE TRACK THE STREAM-BED DESCENDS   • • • • •   289 RUGBY CHAPEL   95

DESCRIED
    DESCRIED AT SUNRISE AN EMERGING PROW   • • • •   262 SCHOLAR-GIPSY   233
    WHERE THICK THE COWSLIPS GREW AND FAR DESCRIED   •   266 THYRSIS   114
    FAR ON ITS ROCKY KNOLL DESCRIED   • • • • •   273 STANZAS CARNAC   1
    BUT ON THE HORIZONS VERGE DESCRIED   • • • • •   274 STANZAS CARNAC   31

DESCRIES
    FROM HUNTING AND A GREAT WAY OFF DESCRIES   • • •   78 SOHRAB RUSTUM   562
    THE SHEPHERD FROM HIS MOUNTAIN-LODGE DESCRIES   •   79 SOHRAB RUSTUM   621
    BUT OER THEM ON THE FARTHER SLOPE DESCRIES   • • •   113 BALDER DEAD 2   299

DESCRY
    TILL AT EVENING WE DESCRY   • • • • •   27 NEW SIRENS   46
    OF THEIR DEAR COUNTRY AND CAN PLAIN DESCRY   • • •   123 BALDER DEAD 3   360
    OF THEIR OWN COUNTRY AND CAN CLEAR DESCRY   • • •   123 BALDER DEAD 3   V 360
    DESPAIR I WILL NOT WHILE I YET DESCRY   • • •   268 THYRSIS   193

DESERT
    OF SOME PAIND DESERT-LION WHO ALL DAY   • • •   76 SOHRAB RUSTUM   504
    THE DESERT RIVERS MOORGHAB AND TEJEND   • • •   83 SOHRAB RUSTUM   763
    AND IN THE DESERT SPACIOUS INNS   • • • • •   94 SICK KING BOKH   203
    AND DIMMD IT LIKE THE DESERT-BLAST   • • • • •   147 TRISTRAM 2   135
    AND DIMMD HER LIKE THE DESERT-BLAST   • • • • •   147 TRISTRAM 2   V 135
    TIS IN THE DESERT NOW AND HERETOFORE • • • •   171 DIVINITY   14
    A CLOUD OF DESERT ROBBER-HORSE HAVE BURST   • • •   193 STRAYED REVEL   248
    A CLOUD OF DESERT ROBBER-HORSE HAS BURST   • • •   193 STRAYED REVEL   V 248
    STRETCHING OUT LIKE THE DESERT   • • • • • •   235 YOUTH OF MAN   109
    AND LEAVE OUR DESERT TO ITS PEACE   • • • • • •   306 GRANDE CHARTR   210

DESERT   (CONTINUED)
     FOR ME NO EASTERN DESERT LONE . . . . . . 317 OBERMANN MORE   151
     UNFAITHFUL SERVANT DOST THOU TOO DESERT ME . . . . 368 MEROPE   1076
     IN DESERT ICE OF SUBTLETIES WAS SPENT . . . . 446 WESTMIN ABBEY   64

DESERTED
     DESERTED IS THE HALF-MOWN PLAIN . . . . . . 217 BACCHANALIA 1   4
     DESERTED IS THE NEW-REAPD GRAIN . . . . . . 217 BACCHANALIA 1   V 4
     IN THE DESERTED MOON-BLANCHD STREET . . . . . . 242 SUMMER NIGHT   1

DESERVED
     THOU FOR THY LABOUR HAST DESERVED OUR BEST . . . . 359 MEROPE   866

DESERVES
     AS OUR JUST CAUSE DESERVES I DO NOT FEAR . . . . 391 MEROPE   1595

DESIGN
     I FEAR NOT BUT I THINK ON MY DESIGN . . . . . . 378 MEROPE   1235
     SOME ILL DESIGN AGAINST HIM JEALOUSY . . . . . . 394 MEROPE   1700
     APPROVES MY BROTHER LAIAS THIS DESIGN . . . . 379 MEROPE   V1267
     THE WORLDS IMMENSE DESIGN . . . . 423 EMPEDOCLES I 2   343

DESIGND
     THE JOYS WHICH WERE NOT FOR OUR USE DESIGND . . 41 HUMAN LIFE   28
     INTO ONE PUISSANT FOLK AS HE DESIGND . . . . . . 338 MEROPE   290
     THE MESSAGE BROUGHT WAS FOR THE KING DESIGND . . 361 MEROPE   923

DESIGNED
     BUT HIS THE PRIOR PATTERN HE DESIGNED . . . . LUCRETIUS 5   2
     HIS IS THE PRIOR PATTERN HE DESIGNED . . . . . . LUCRETIUS 5   V 2

DESIRE
     AND YOU WEARIED IN DESIRE . . . . . 31 NEW SIRENS   142
     AND ALL ITS THWARTING CURRENTS OF DESIRE . . . . 37 YOUTHS AGIT   10
     BUT IF THIS ONE DESIRE INDEED RULES ALL . . . . 63 SOHRAB RUSTUM   74
     DESIRE NOT THAT MY FATHER THOU MUST LIVE . . . . 84 SOHRAB RUSTUM 772
     OR IF INDEED THIS ONE DESIRE RULES ALL . . . . 63 SOHRAB RUSTUM V 74
     THAT THOUGH WE TAKE WHAT WE DESIRE . . . . 94 SICK KING BOKH   211
     THAT THOUGH WE SNATCH WHAT WE DESIRE . . . . 94 SICK KING BOKH V 211
     TO BURN FOR THAT IS WHAT THE DEAD DESIRE . . . . 96 BALDER DEAD 1   45
     BUT RIGHT BARS THIS NOT ONLY THY DESIRE . . . . 104 BALDER DEAD 1 313
     BALDER FOR THAT IS WHAT THE DEAD DESIRE . . . . 115 BALDER DEAD 3   52
     ISEULT AH NOT THE ISEULT I DESIRE . . . . . . 130 TRISTRAM 1   8
     OF ME SHE RECKS NOT NOR MY VAIN DESIRE . . . . 140 TRISTRAM 1   303
     OF ME SHE RECKS NOT NOR OF MY DESIRE . . . . 140 TRISTRAM 1   V 303
     WHO RENDERS VAIN THEIR DEEP DESIRE . . . . . 182 TO MARG CONT   21
     BUT HE PREFERRD FATE TO HIS STRONG DESIRE . . . . 198 FRAG ANTIGONE 97
     AND A LOOK OF PASSIONATE DESIRE . . . . 240 SELF-DEPENDENCE   5
     THERE RISES AN UNSPEAKABLE DESIRE . . . . 246 BURIED LIFE   47
     THOU HADST ONE AIM ONE BUSINESS ONE DESIRE . . . . 259 SCHOLAR-GIPSY 152
     SEEMD BUT A CRY OF DESIRE . . . . 290 RUGBY CHAPEL   152
     YET TINGED WITH INFINITE DESIRE . . . . . 314 OBERMANN MORE   51
     HELP IT TO FILL THAT DEEP DESIRE . . . . . . 323 OBERMANN MORE   313
     HELP IT TO REACH OUR DEEP DESIRE . . . . . 323 OBERMANN MORE   V 313
     A WOMAN O MY FRIENDS HAS ONE DESIRE . . . . 349 MEROPE   565
     WELL SOMETIMES MAY THE GOOD DESIRE . . . . 353 MEROPE   665
     WHAT SWEETER SLEEP THAN THIS COULD I DESIRE . . 372 MEROPE   1156
     MAKE US NOT FLY TO DREAMS BUT MODERATE DESIRE . . 425 EMPEDOCLES I 2 386
     AN AIMLESS UNALLAYD DESIRE . . . . 481 DESTINY   8
     YET THAT IN ANGUISH DOUBT DESIRE . . . . . . 482 COURAGE   19
     DESIRE IT BITTERLY . . . . LUCRETIUS 7   3

DESIRED
     AND HE DESIRED TO DRAW FORTH THE STEEL . . . 80 SOHRAB RUSTUM   651
     PROLONG THY LIFE THOUGH NOT BY THEE DESIRED . . 104 BALDER DEAD 1 312
     THE DESIRED THE DIVINE . . . . 194 STRAYED REVEL   280
     FOR SHE DESIRED TO MAKE . . . . 197 FRAG ANTIGONE   71
     HIS MATES HAD ARTS TO RULE AS THEY DESIRED . . 256 SCHOLAR-GIPSY   45
     FOR IF THE OTHER LORDS DESIRED HIS FALL . . . . 339 MEROPE   329
     YOUR KING DESIRED THE PROFIT OF HIS DEATH . . 365 MEROPE   990
     HITHER HE CAME LATE-BORN AND LONG-DESIRED . . 444 WESTMIN ABBEY   8
     LEARN TO KNOW WHAT IT DESIRED . . . . META CLOISTER   31

DESIREDST
     DESIREDST THOU WHAT TRULY SPURRD THEE ON . . . . 404 MEROPE   1980

DESIRES
     BUT TIS NOT WHAT OUR YOUTH DESIRES . . . . . 22 YOUTH AND CALM   25
     AND I WILL TELL THEE WHAT MY HEART DESIRES . . 62 SOHRAB RUSTUM   41
     GO I WILL GRANT THEE WHAT THY HEART DESIRES . . 63 SOHRAB RUSTUM   93
     THE FRIEND OF MAN DESIRES . . . . 238 PROGRESS   48
     AH TWO DESIRES TOSS ABOUT . . . . 309 OBERMANN   93
     THE STREAM LIKE US DESIRES . . . . 420 EMPEDOCLES I 2   249

DESOLATE
     SEE IN THE DESOLATE HOUSE . . . . 283 HAWORTH CHURCH   V
     IN THE STORMY DESOLATE WAVES . . . . 361 MEROPE   911
     UNTRODDEN ON CYLLENES DESOLATE SIDE . . . . 373 MEROPE   1168
     IT MAY BE IN THAT DESOLATE SIGHT HIS EYE . . . . 469 ALARIC AT ROME 185
     A REGION DESOLATE AND WILD . . . . 479 HAYSWATER BOAT   1

DESPAIR
    PASSIVE AT THE MIDNIGHT OF DESPAIR   • • • • • • • •   33 NEW SIRENS   V 202
    OH THEN A LONGING LIKE DESPAIR • • • • • • • • 182 TO MARG CONT   13
    BUT IS DESPAIR RELIEF   • • • • • • • • 208 ON THE RHINE   10
    OFT MADE THEE IN THY GLOOM DESPAIR • • • • • 241 MORALITY   18
    SAD PATIENCE TOO NEAR NEIGHBOUR TO DESPAIR • • • 261 SCHOLAR-GIPSY   195
    SOLE IN THESE FIELDS YET WILL I NOT DESPAIR • • 268 THYRSIS   192
    DESPAIR I WILL NOT WHILE I YET DESCRY • • • • 268 THYRSIS   193
    SHUT OUT THE GRIEF THE DESPAIR • • • • • • 283 HAWORTH CHURCH   V
    PANIC DESPAIR FLEE AWAY • • • • • • • • 292 RUGBY CHAPEL   197
    AND ICY THY DESPAIR • • • • • • • • 309 OBERMANN   88
    DESPAIR NOT THOU AS I DESPAIRD • • • • • • 322 OBERMANN MORE   281
    GIVE NOT THY HEART TO DESPAIR • • • • • • 347 MEROPE   523
    PURPOSES THY DESPAIR • • • • • • • 371 MEROPE   1135
    BECAUSE THOU MUST NOT DREAM THOU NEEDST NOT   426 EMPEDOCLES I 2   426
        THEN DESPAIR
    ALAS NO WREATHS ARE HERE DESPAIR MAY TEACH • • • 467 ALARIC AT ROME   139

DESPAIRD
    DESPAIR NOT THOU AS I DESPAIRD • • • • • • • 322 OBERMANN MORE   281

DESPAIRER
    TOO QUICK DESPAIRER WHEREFORE WILT THOU GO • • • • 264 THYRSIS   61

DESPAIRING
    BROTHER MANS DESPAIRING SIGN • • • • • • • 457 POOR MATTHIAS   169

DESPAIRS
    AND FLUCTUATE TWIXT BLIND HOPES AND BLIND DESPAIRS   236 PALLADIUM   18

DESPERATE
    THE LOVE-DESPERATE BANISHD KNIGHT • • • • • • 136 TRISTRAM 1   186
    THE STROKE THOU PURPOSEST IS DESPERATE RASH • • 381 MEROPE   1295
    THE FLEET DESPERATE HUNTER • • • • • • 393 MEROPE   1656
    OUR DESPERATE SEARCH WAS SIN • • • • • • 423 EMPEDOCLES I 2   344
    AND TO UPHOLD THY DESPERATE CHALLENGING • • • RUDE ORATOR   17

DESPISE
    MANS FUNDAMENTAL LIFE IF TO DESPISE • • • • 6 REP FRIEND   4
    AND IGNORANT MEN DESPISE ME THAT I STAND • • • 333 MEROPE   95
    DESPISE THEM NOT FOR BROTHER THOU AND I • • • 388 MEROPE   1511
    DESPISE THEM NOT FOR BROTHER THOU LIKE ME • • • 388 MEROPE   V1511

DESPISED
    TO MY MESSENIANS DUPED DISARMD DESPISED • • • • 366 MEROPE   1006

DESPITE
    WHO SINCE IN YOUR DESPITE HATH WAXD AMAIN • • • • 110 BALDER DEAD 2   210
    EVEN IN HIS OWN DESPITE HIS BEINGS LAW • • • • 246 BURIED LIFE   37

DESPONDED
    IN THY DESPONDENCY DESPONDED TOO • • • • • 383 MEROPE   1374

DESPONDENCY
    IN THY DESPONDENCY DESPONDED TOO • • • • • 383 MEROPE   1374
    OF DESPONDENCY AND GLOOM • • • • • • • • 441 EMPEDOCLES II   414

DESPONDENT
    ON US WHO STOOD DESPONDENT BY • • • • • • • 450 GEISTS GRAVE   34

DESPOTIC
    AT SUCH DESPOTIC LENGTH TO PROVE • • • • • HORATIAN ECHO   V
    DESPOTIC ON THAT SEA • • • • • • • • 243 SUMMER NIGHT   57
    DESPOTIC ON LIFES SEA • • • • • • • • 243 SUMMER NIGHT   V 57

DESTINATION
    TO WHOM THEIR DESTINATION WHEN TIS REACHD • • • LUCRETIUS 6   3

DESTIND
    THAN I WERT DESTIND TO THIS LORE • • • • • 179 FAREWELL   V 44
    I OF MYSELF KNOW WELL THAT HERE I AM DESTIND TO PERISH   HOMER TRANS   60
    THAT WE WERE DESTIND TO A HAPPIER STATE • • • • LUCRETIUS 3   11

DESTINED
    THE HOMES THAT WERE NOT DESTINED TO BE OURS • • 41 HUMAN LIFE   30
    TO USHER FOR A DESTINED SPACE • • • • • • 53 RESIGNATION   35
    THAN I WAST DESTINED TO THIS LORE • • • • • 179 FAREWELL   44
    DESTINED TO WORK AND TO LIVE • • • • • • 298 HEINES GRAVE   196
    THOSE HALLS TOO DESTINED TO CONTAIN • • • • 301 GRANDE CHARTR   61
    ELECT HIMSELF HEAVENS DESTINED ARM • • • • 353 MEROPE   691

DESTINY
    STERN SENTENCE OF THE POWERS OF DESTINY • • • • 8 MYCERINUS   6
    AH THEY CRY DESTINY • • • • • • • • 51 CONSOLATION   48
    THE CLOUD OF MORTAL DESTINY • • • • • • 272 MEMORIAL VERSES   68
    AND TO TWO DID DESTINY • • • • • • • 344 MEROPE   455
    AND THE STERN DESTINY-BROUGHT STRANGER • • • • 400 MEROPE   1861

DESTROY
    THOU WILT DESTROY I SEE THYSELF AND US • • • • 385 MEROPE   1405

DESTROYD
    FOR THAT DESTROYD HIM GIVE THEM PEACE THOU CANST   •   •   335 MEROPE   176

DESTROYEST
    THOU DESTROYEST ME HOW   •   •   •   •   •   •   •   •   •   369 MEROPE   1087

DESTRUCTION
    PATIENCE WAS THENCEFORTH SELF DESTRUCTION I   •   •   338 MEROPE   266
    IT WILL COME WHEN SACRED TROY SHALL GO TO DESTRUCTION   HOMER TRANS   21

DETESTED
    IN THE DETESTED PALACE OF THY FOE   •   •   •   •   367 MEROPE   1044
    OUR OWN RIGHT HAND IN THE DETESTED BLOOD   •   •   •   387 MEROPE   1468

DETRACTION
    STUPID DETRACTION JEALOUSY CABAL   •   •   •   •   •   199 EARLY DEATH   5

DEVICE
    WERE PLAIN AND ON HIS SHIELD WAS NO DEVICE   •   •   •   69 SOHRAB RUSTUM   266

DEVISEDST
    BUT DEEP IF THOU DEVISEDST IT TO DROWN   •   •   •   114 BALDER DEAD 3   28

DEVOTION
    FROM THEIR EARTHWARD-BOUND DEVOTION   •   •   •   •   31 NEW SIRENS   157
    OF HER HIGH DEVOTION   •   •   •   •   •   •   •   39 STAGIRIUS   25

DEVOURING
    GLUT THE DEVOURING GRAVE   •   •   •   •   •   •   288 RUGBY CHAPEL   83
    FOR YEARS IN SILENCE DEVOURING HER HEART   •   •   346 MEROPE   509
    A CRAVEN MOB BUT A DEVOURING FIRE   •   •   •   383 MEROPE   1361
    NOTHING BUT A DEVOURING FLAME OF THOUGHT   •   •   438 EMPEDOCLES II   329

DEW
    AND YOUR BROWS WERE STARRD WITH DEW   •   •   •   29 NEW SIRENS   100
    ON THE DRY NOON SHOOK THEIR DEW   •   •   •   •   29 NEW SIRENS   108
    LEAVE THE LILIES IN THEIR DEW   •   •   •   •   •   35 NEW SIRENS   268
    PALE DEW-DRENCHD HALF-SHUT ROSES GLEAM   •   •   57 RESIGNATION   179
    WHEN THE DEW GLISTENS ON THE PEARLED EARS   •   •   65 SOHRAB RUSTUM   155
    WHO SHUFFLES THROUGH THE DEEP DEW-MOISTEND DUST   •   101 BALDER DEAD 1   232
    OF THAT WORLD-SHADOWING TREE WITH HONEY-DEW   •   120 BALDER DEAD 3   222
    ALL DRENCHD IN DEW   •   •   •   •   •   •   •   186 STRAYED REVEL   34
    AND MOONSHINE AND THE DEW   •   •   •   •   •   200 PHILOMELA   13
    AND MOONLIGHT AND THE DEW   •   •   •   •   •   200 PHILOMELA   V
    IN THE TWILIGHT AND BATHED IN DEW   •   •   •   234 YOUTH OF MAN   78
    WITH DEW OR LISTEN WITH ENCHANTED EARS   •   •   261 SCHOLAR-GIPSY   219
    THE FOOT LESS PROMPT TO MEET THE MORNING DEW   •   266 THYRSIS   138
    AT DAY-BREAK THROUGH THE DEW   •   •   •   •   392 MEROPE   1645
    OF SHORT GRASS BEADED WITH DEW   •   •   •   •   399 MEROPE   1823
    WHICH THE GOATS LOVE ARE JEWELLD THICK WITH DEW   •   407 EMPEDOCLES I 1   17

DEWLAP
    PRINKING EARS AND DEWLAP THROAT   •   •   •   •   454 POOR MATTHIAS   72

DEWS
    SO SOON I SEE THE NIGHT-DEWS   •   •   •   •   •   186 STRAYED REVEL   15
    BATHED IN THE SACRED DEWS OF MORN   •   •   •   250 WISH   33
    DARK BLUEBELLS DRENCHD WITH DEWS OF SUMMER EVES   •   257 SCHOLAR-GIPSY   88
    AND DEATHS COLD DEWS BEDIMMD HIS EARNEST BROW   •   476 CROMWELL   170

DEWY
    AT SUNRISE FROM THEIR DEWY LAIR   •   •   •   •   16 CHURCH BROU 2   9
    SWISS CHALETS GLITTERD ON THE DEWY SLOPES   •   •   25 DREAM   10
    FRESH GARLANDS OF THIS DEWY ROSE   •   •   •   48 HORATIAN ECHO   23
    THE CASTLE AND THE DEWY WOODS AND HUNT   •   •   79 SOHRAB RUSTUM   629
    AND UP THE DEWY MOUNTAIN-TRACKS THEY FARED   •   •   106 BALDER DEAD 2   51
    FROM THE DEWY FOREST-COVERTS   •   •   •   •   193 STRAYED REVEL   263
    INTO THE DEWY DARK OBSCURITY   •   •   •   •   •   242 SUMMER NIGHT   8
    THROUGH THE LONG DEWY GRASS MOVE SLOW AWAY   •   •   258 SCHOLAR-GIPSY   110

DIAMOND
    RANGED DIAMOND-BRIGHT THE ETERNAL WALL OF SNOW   •   25 DREAM   13

DIANS
    SHALL BREATHLESS GLADES CHEERD BY SHY DIANS HORN   •   6 GEO CRUIKSHANK   8

DIBBLED
    UNDER THE TREES IS DIBBLED THICK WITH HOLES   •   •   122 BALDER DEAD 3   312

DICE
    THE GOLDEN DICE WHEREWITH WE PLAYD OF YORE   •   •   •   128 BALDER DEAD 3   539
    THE GOLDEN DICE WITH WHICH WE PLAYD OF YORE   •   •   128 BALDER DEAD 3   V 539

DIDO
    AVERSE AS DIDO DID WITH GESTURE STERN   •   •   •   261 SCHOLAR-GIPSY   208

DIE
    AND WHEN SIX YEARS ARE MEASURED LO I DIE   •   •   •   9 MYCERINUS   18
    AND OLD MEN DIE AND YOUNG MEN PASS THEIR PRIME   •   •   10 MYCERINUS   63

DIE   (CONTINUED)

SHIVER AND DIE · · · · · · · · · · ·   35 VOICE   8
DREAMS DAWN AND FLY FRIENDS SMILE AND DIE · · · ·   44 QUESTION   8
TO DIE BE GIVEN US OR ATTAIN · · · · · · · ·   52 RESIGNATION   1
AND FIGHT BENEATH MY BANNER TILL I DIE · · · · ·   71 SOHRAB RUSTUM   332
AND COMES AT NIGHT TO DIE UPON THE SAND · · · · ·   76 SOHRAB RUSTUM   506
AND LET THE BLOOD FLOW FREE AND SO TO DIE · · · ·   80 SOHRAB RUSTUM   652
RUSTUMS GREAT FATHER WHOM THEY LEFT TO DIE · · · ·   81 SOHRAB RUSTUM   680
THE YELLOW OXUS BY WHOSE BRINK I DIE · · · · · ·   83 SOHRAB RUSTUM   766
AS SOME ARE BORN TO BE OBSCURED AND DIE · · · · ·   84 SOHRAB RUSTUM   774
DO THOU THE DEEDS I DIE TOO YOUNG TO DO · · · · ·   84 SOHRAB RUSTUM   775
NOT THOU OF MINE AND I MIGHT DIE NOT THOU · · · ·   85 SOHRAB RUSTUM   819
THE LAW AND BY THE LAW MUST DIE · · · · · ·   89 SICK KING BOKH   38
TO DIE BY STONING ON THE SPOT · · · · · · ·   91 SICK KING BOKH   112
WOULD FREELY DIE TO PURCHASE BALDER BACK · · · · ·   98 BALDER DEAD 1   120
TARDY OR SWIFT WOULDST THOU BE LOATH TO DIE · · · ·   103 BALDER DEAD 1   306
DIE ON THE GREEN FIELDS OF WALES · · · · · ·   135 TRISTRAM 1   158
TO DIE AT THIRTY-FIVE IN BABYLON · · · · · ·   154 TRISTRAM 3   150
AND MURMURD HELP ME OR I DIE · · · · · · ·   158 SAINT BRANDAN   50
AND HIS CHILDS REASON FLICKERD AND DID DIE · · · ·   166 PICT NEWSTEAD   6
AND THE CHILDS REASON FLICKERD AND DID DIE · · · ·   166 PICT NEWSTEAD   V   6
SAW IN THE ROCKY ISLE OF DELOS DIE · · · · · ·   197 FRAG ANTIGONE   69
WHILE WE FOR HOPELESS PASSION DIE · · · · · ·   202 URANIA   6
BEFORE I DIE BEFORE THE SOUL · · · · · · ·   206 RIVER   13
THIS MIGHTY MARCH DO AUGHT BUT DIE · · · · · ·   226 EPILOG LAOCOON   170
THE POET WHO SINGS THEM MAY DIE · · · · · · ·   230 YOUTH OF NATURE   84
THOU WHO SEEST US DIE · · · · · · · · ·   232 YOUTH OF MAN   5
AND WHEN IT FAILS FIGHT AS WE WILL WE DIE · · · ·   236 PALLADIUM   23
HATH WITHOUT PAIN SEEN NO RELIGION DIE · · · · ·   238 PROGRESS   V 39
CALM CALM ME MORE NOR LET ME DIE · · · · · ·   249 KENSINGTON GARD   43
SOON SOON THY CHEER WOULD DIE · · · · · · ·   261 SCHOLAR-GIPSY   226
FADE AND GROW OLD AT LAST AND DIE LIKE OURS · · · ·   261 SCHOLAR-GIPSY   230
LANDS THEE TO DIE · · · · · · · · · · ·   276 SOUTHERN NIGHT   48
BEFORE WE DIE · · · · · · · · · · · ·   277 SOUTHERN NIGHT   72
LANDED TO DIE · · · · · · · · · · · ·   278 SOUTHERN NIGHT   96
TOUCHD SHORE TO DIE · · · · · · · · · ·   278 SOUTHERN NIGHT   V 96
NOTHING AND THEN THEY DIE · · · · · · · ·   288 RUGBY CHAPEL   66
NOT WITHOUT ACTION TO DIE · · · · · · · ·   288 RUGBY CHAPEL   80
FAIN TO DROP DOWN AND TO DIE · · · · · · ·   290 RUGBY CHAPEL   130
DIE ONE BY ONE IN THE WASTE · · · · · · · ·   291 RUGBY CHAPEL   187
SLOW DIE OUT OF HER LIFE · · · · · · · · ·   295 HEINES GRAVE   83
ONLY TO LAUGH AND TO DIE · · · · · · · · ·   298 HEINES GRAVE   198
HERE LEAVE US TO DIE OUT WITH THESE · · · · · ·   302 GRANDE CHARTR   111
STRIVE NOT DIE ALSO THOU · · · · · · · · ·   309 OBERMANN   92
I MARKD THE PRESENT DIE · · · · · · · · ·   322 OBERMANN MORE   298
HATE TO THEIR RULE WHICH ELSE WOULD DIE AWAY · · ·   331 MEROPE   43
A MOURNFUL FEUD ALIVE WHICH ELSE WOULD DIE · · · ·   332 MEROPE   82
BEACONS OF VENGEANCE NOT TO BE LET DIE · · · · ·   333 MEROPE   93
YET FOR ME MOTHER I HAD LIEFER DIE · · · · · ·   383 MEROPE   1379
JOY AND THE OUTWARD WORLD MUST DIE TO HIM · · · ·   437 EMPEDOCLES II   274
NOT TO DIE WHOLLY NOT TO BE ALL ENSLAVED · · · ·   441 EMPEDOCLES II   406
WHAT COULD HE BETTER WISH THAN THEN TO DIE · · · ·   448 WESTMIN ABBEY   145
WHAT CAN HE BETTER CRAVE THAN THEN TO DIE · · · ·   448 WESTMIN ABBEY   V 145
AND HUMBLY LAY THEE DOWN TO DIE · · · · · ·   450 GEISTS GRAVE   36
WHICH MAY BE THE FIRST TO DIE · · · · · · ·   454 POOR MATTHIAS   75
NOTE NO CHANGE AND LET THEM DIE · · · · · ·   455 POOR MATTHIAS   108
THY MEMORY DIE · · · · · · · · · · · ·   461 KAISER DEAD   78
DEEDS THAT SHALL LIVE WHEN THEY WHO DID THEM DIE · ·   462 ALARIC AT ROME   15
NO METEOR BRIGHTNESS TO BE SEEN AND DIE · · · ·   463 ALARIC AT ROME   33
COWARDS TO CONQUER AND THE WEAK TO DIE · · · · ·   467 ALARIC AT ROME   140
WHISPERING FROM ALL AROUND ALL EARTHLY THINGS MUST DIE   469 ALARIC AT ROME   180
STOOPS TO THE SOARING MOUNTAINS LIVE AND DIE · ·   472 CROMWELL   10
THAT DAY THAT HAILD HIS TRIUMPHS SAW HIM DIE · ·   478 CROMWELL   212
NOT THAT HE TOOK THE COURSE TO DIE · · · · · ·   481 COURAGE   14

DIED

CROWND WITH GRAY HAIRS HE DIED AND FULL OF SWAY · ·   9 MYCERINUS   14
NOR PALLD WITH ITS OWN FULNESS EBBD AND DIED · ·   12 MYCERINUS   116
BUT SHE DIED WHILE IT WAS BUILDING · · · · · ·   14 CHURCH BROU 1   67
AND SHE DIED AT THE ST JOHN · · · · · · · ·   16 CHURCH BROU 1   112
BUT SHE DIED AS IT WAS BUILDING · · · · · · ·   14 CHURCH BROU 1   V 67
WHOSE YOUTH IN THE FIRES OF ANGUISH HATH DIED · ·   20 MODERN SAPPHO   28
BREATHED DEEPLY AS IT DIED · · · · · · · ·   47 WORLD QUIETIST   31
HIS SWORD UPRIGHT AND FELL ON IT AND DIED · · ·   102 BALDER DEAD 1   252
WOMEN AND INFANTS AND YOUNG MEN WHO DIED · · · ·   109 BALDER DEAD 2   164
BETRAYD THEM AND OF WASTING AGE THEY DIED · · · ·   109 BALDER DEAD 2   167
FOR THIS I DIED AND FLED BENEATH THE GLOOM · · ·   124 BALDER DEAD 3   397
SO SHE SAID AND DIED IN THE DREAR FOREST · · · ·   145 TRISTRAM 2   87
OF COURTLY SPEECH ABRUPTLY DIED · · · · · · ·   146 TRISTRAM 2   119
THUS MONICA AND DIED IN ITALY · · · · · · · ·   173 MONICAS PRAYER   5
DIED IN HIS ENEMIES DAY · · · · · · · · · ·   229 YOUTH OF NATURE   35
TIRESIAS DRANK AND DIED · · · · · · · · · ·   229 YOUTH OF NATURE   45
AND DROOPD AND SLOWLY DIED UPON THEIR THRONE · · ·   239 REVOLUTIONS   16
WHY FAINTEST THOU I WANDERD TILL I DIED · · · ·   269 THYRSIS   237
THAT SPIRIT IF ALL HAVE NOT YET DIED · · · · ·   276 SOUTHERN NIGHT   35
DARING SINCE BYRON DIED · · · · · · · · · ·   284 HAWORTH CHURCH   96
FAINTED AND FALLEN AND DIED · · · · · · · ·   291 RUGBY CHAPEL   170
THE SUFFERERS DIED THEY LEFT THEIR PAIN · · · ·   303 GRANDE CHARTR   131
COMPOSED TO BEAR I LIVED AND DIED · · · · · ·   321 OBERMANN MORE   265
GLOOM-WRAPPED WITHIN I LIVED AND DIED · · · ·   321 OBERMANN MORE   V 265

DIED   (CONTINUED)
          THIS GOOD HE MEANT YOU AND FOR THIS HE DIED   • •   339 MEROPE   313
          THAT THOU MIGHTST REIGN HE DIED NOT FOR HIS FAULT • •   339 MEROPE   327
          DEAD AND WHEN DIED HE WHERE AND BY WHAT HAND   • •   355 MEROPE   715
          WITH CYPSELUS AND TWO DAYS SINCE HE DIED   • • • • 355 MEROPE   718
          DIED OF A SNAKE-BITE SAID HE ON THAT BROW   • • • • 357 MEROPE   781
          ORESTES DIED BUT IN NAME • • • • • • • • • •   368 MEROPE   1084
          IN WORD I DIED THAT I IN DEED MIGHT LIVE   • • • • 375 MEROPE   1209
          BEHELD HIS EXPIATION FOR HE DIED   • • • • • •   399 MEROPE   1819
          HE BOWD HIS HEAD AND DEEPLY GROAND AND DIED   • • • • 402 MEROPE   1929
          THE NURSLING OF THE MIGHTY MOTHER DIED   • • • • 447 WESTMIN ABBEY   115
          QUIET IN SLEEP THE SEVENTH NIGHT THEY DIED   • • • • 448 WESTMIN ABBEY   139
          ROVER DIED ATOSSA TOO • • • • • • • • • • •   453 POOR MATTHIAS   43
          YET THEY DIED AND DIED UNSUNG   • • • • • • • •   454 POOR MATTHIAS   56
          YET THEY DIED AND DIED UNSUNG   • • • • • • • •   454 POOR MATTHIAS   56

DIES
          NOW AS THE BARRIER CLOSES DIES AWAY   • • • • • •   10 MYCERINUS   58
          IF THE CLEAR IMPRESSION DIES   • • • • • • • •   24 MEMORY-PICTURE   61
          FREELY GAVE IT BUT IT DIES AWAY   • • • • • •   35 NEW SIRENS   258
          SLOW ROUND HER PADDLES DIES AWAY   • • • • • •   276 SOUTHERN NIGHT   31
          SO DIES THE LAST SHOOT OF OUR ROYAL TREE   • • • • 359 MEROPE   857
          AND HE DIES FRUITLESS HAVING FOUND NO FIELD   • •   LUCRETIUS 2   6

DIEU
          AND AT HER PRIE-DIEU KNEEL UNTIL SHE HAVE TOLD   • •   152 TRISTRAM 3   92

DIFFERENCE
          ALL DIFFERENCE WITH HIS FELLOW-MORTAL CLOSED   • •   7 REP FRIEND CONT   13
          ALL DIFFERENCE WITH HIS FELLOW MAN COMPOSD • • • •   7 REP FRIEND CONT V 13

DIFFERENT
          OUR DIFFERENT PAST • • • • • • • • • • • •   176 PARTING   66
          OF A PAST NIGHT AND A FAR DIFFERENT SCENE   • • • • 242 SUMMER NIGHT   13
          AND EACH HALF LIVES A HUNDRED DIFFERENT LIVES   • •   260 SCHOLAR-GIPSY   169
          WHOM MANY A DIFFERENT WAY • • • • • • • • • •   311 OBERMANN   146
          A YOUNGER MAN AND OF A DIFFERENT NAME   • • • • • 361 MEROPE   925
          BUT HE WHOSE YOUTH FELL ON A DIFFERENT WORLD   • •   436 EMPEDOCLES II   262

DIFFERING
          ALL THE FEVER OF SOME DIFFERING SOUL   • • • • • • 240 SELF-DEPENDENCE   24

DIG
          MEN DIG GRAVES WITH BITTER TEARS   • • • • • •   44 QUESTION   11
          WE DIG AND HEAP LAY STONE ON STONE   • • • • • • 241 MORALITY   8

DIGHT
          DIGHT WITH MANTLES GAY • • • • • • • • • • •   17 CHURCH BROU 2   22
          DIGHT WITH A SADDLE-CLOTH OF BROIDERD GREEN   • • • •   69 SOHRAB RUSTUM   277
          WHEREIN AT FIRST WAS DIGHT • • • • • • • • • •   446 WESTMIN ABBEY   62
          WHEREWITH AT FIRST WAS DIGHT   • • • • • • • •   446 WESTMIN ABBEY   V 62

DILIGENCE
          O MOTHER MY BEST DILIGENCE SHALL BE   • • • • • • 405 MEROPE   2014

DIM
          THE GAZING UP MID THE DIM PILLARS HIGH   • • • •   18 CHURCH BROU 3   38
          THEN GAZING UP THROUGH THE DIM PILLARS HIGH   • • •   18 CHURCH BROU 3   V 38
          IS IT HOPE MAKES ME LINGER THE DIM THOUGHT THAT SORROW   19 MODERN SAPPHO   V
          AH THE DIM REMEMBRANCE PRIZE   • • • • • • • •   24 MEMORY-PICTURE   62
          THROUGH THE DIM CAMP TO PERAN-WISAS TENT   • • •   61 SOHRAB RUSTUM   11
          DIM IS THE RUMOUR OF A COMMON FIGHT   • • • • •   62 SOHRAB RUSTUM   60
          THE CRIMSON TORRENT RAN DIM NOW AND SOILD   • • •   86 SOHRAB RUSTUM   843
          AND WENT ABROAD INTO THE COLD DIM AIR • • • • •   61 SOHRAB RUSTUM   V 10
          THE CRIMSON TORRENT POURD DIM NOW AND SOILD   • • •   86 SOHRAB RUSTUM   V 843
          IN THAT DIM WORLD IN HELAS MOULDERING REALM   • • •   104 BALDER DEAD 1   315
          BY THE DIM VAPOUR-BLOTTED LIGHT OF STARS   • • •   108 BALDER DEAD 2   126
          CLUSTERD IN THICK BEADS DIM   • • • • • • • •   186 STRAYED REVEL   16
          OR AT HIS WORK IN THAT DIM LOWER WORLD   • • • •   198 FRAG ANTIGONE   93
          CLOUDED AND DIM GREW THEIR EYE   • • • • • • • •   233 YOUTH OF MAN   43
          TO THE DIM HORIZON REPOSED • • • • • • • • • •   234 YOUTH OF MAN   77
          THE MOON AND LOST BEHIND HER FADING DIM   • • • •   242 SUMMER NIGHT   7
          BEFALLS ME WANDERING THROUGH THIS UPLAND DIM • • •   263 THYRSIS   23
          AH VAIN THESE ENGLISH FIELDS THIS UPLAND DIM • • •   267 THYRSIS   172
          TREAD THE BORDER-LAND DIM • • • • • • • • • •   288 RUGBY CHAPEL   54
          ROSE DIM FROM THE MORASS   • • • • • • • • • •   445 WESTMIN ABBEY   32
          IN A LOW DIM-LIGHTED PEN   • • • • • • • • • •   457 POOR MATTHIAS   186
          A GLORIOUS MANHOOD YET A DIM OLD AGE   • • • • • •   463 ALARIC AT ROME   39
          AND THE DIM GLORIES OF DEPARTED DAYS   • • • • • •   464 ALARIC AT ROME   63
          TO HEAR A DIM AND LONG FORGOTTEN TONE • • • • • •   467 ALARIC AT ROME   123
          LOST IN DIM MEMORIES OF HIS EARLY HOME • • • • • •   468 ALARIC AT ROME   170
          AND RECOLLECTIONS INDISTINCT AND DIM   • • • • • •   469 ALARIC AT ROME   183
          FAR ON THE DIM HORIZON WHEN THE SKY   • • • • • •   475 CROMWELL   129
          AT LAST IN AIR FAR OFF DIM ROSE A HEIGHT   • • •   484 S S LUSITANIA   6

DIMENSIONS
          CASD IN ONE MANS DIMENSIONS CAN DISTIL   • • • •   50 CONSOLATION   V

DIMINISH
          BENT TO DIMINISH WRONG • • • • • • • • • • •   353 MEROPE   663

DIMLY
    JOYS WE DIMLY APPREHEND . . . . 44 QUESTION 18
    THROUGH THE LOOSE CLOUDS LIFTS DIMLY . . . . . . 175 PARTING 13
    OF OUR OWN ACTIONS DIMLY TRACE THE CAUSES . . . . 352 MEROPE 640

DIMMD
    HIS STATELY CREST AND DIMMD HIS GLITTERING ARMS . . 74 SOHRAB RUSTUM 454
    BUT THY DARK EYES ARE NOT DIMMD PROUD ISEULT . . 142 TRISTRAM 2 19
    AND DIMMD IT LIKE THE DESERT-BLAST . . . . . . 147 TRISTRAM 2 135
    AND DIMMD HER LIKE THE DESERT-BLAST . . . . . . 147 TRISTRAM 2 V 135
    EARS AND LABOUR-DIMMD EYES . . . . 295 HEINES GRAVE 89
    THOUGH LATE THOUGH DIMMD THOUGH WEAK YET TELL . . 323 OBERMANN MORE 311
    OUR HAIR GROWS GREY OUR EYES ARE DIMMD OUR . . 423 EMPEDOCLES I 2 336
        HEAT IS TAMED

DIMMER
    AS THE BANKS FADE DIMMER AWAY . . . . 254 FUTURE 84

DIMNESS
    FADE INTO DIMNESS APACE . . . . 286 RUGBY CHAPEL 5

DIN
    DASHD WITH A CLANG TOGETHER AND A DIN . . . . 75 SOHRAB RUSTUM 475
    ABOVE THE DIN HER VOICE IS IN MY EARS . . . . 137 TRISTRAM 1 240
    SHE SMILES ELSEWHERE WE MAKE A DIN . . . . . 204 EUPHROSYNE V
    BUT OFTEN IN THE DIN OF STRIFE . . . . 246 BURIED LIFE 46
    THAT THE DIN WILL BE MORE ON ITS BANKS . . . . 253 FUTURE 62
    LONGD ITSELF OUT OF THE DIN . . . . 296 HEINES GRAVE 149
    THE WORLD IS WHAT IT IS FOR ALL OUR DUST AND DIN . . 419 EMPEDOCLES I 2 206
    TWICE FROM WITHOUT THY BULWARKS HATH THE DIN . . 465 ALARIC AT ROME 79

DINGLE
    BUT MANY A DINGLE ON THE LOVED HILL-SIDE . . . . 266 THYRSIS 112

DINGLES
    THE BLACKBIRD WHISTLED FROM THE DINGLES NEAR . . 155 TRISTRAM 3 197
    FROM THE DARK DINGLES TO THE NIGHTINGALES . . . . 261 SCHOLAR-GIPSY 220

DINGY
    THE DINGY TENTS ARE PITCHD THE FIRES . . . . . . 55 RESIGNATION 116

DIPT
    AND IS ALONE NOT DIPT IN OCEANS STREAM . . . . 99 BALDER DEAD 1 158

DIRE
    DIRE IS THIS BLOW FOR MEROPE AND I . . . . . . 360 MEROPE 885

DIRECT
    DIRECT TO THY DISSUASIONS I REPLY . . . . . . 389 MEROPE 1531

DIRGE
    A DIRGE AND NANNA AND HER TRAIN REPLIED . . . . 103 BALDER DEAD 1 274
    AND FAR INTO THE NIGHT THEY WAILD THEIR DIRGE . . 103 BALDER DEAD 1 275
    DIRGE FROM ME TO CROWN THEIR GRAVE . . . . . . 454 POOR MATTHIAS 82
    DIRGE OF MINE TO CROWN THEIR GRAVE . . . . . . 454 POOR MATTHIAS V 82

DISABUSINGS
    CALMD BY BITTER DISABUSINGS . . . . META CLOISTER 1

DISAPPEAR
    MANS GRAVE REASONS DISAPPEAR . . . . 29 NEW SIRENS 90
    HANG IN THE AIR AFIELD AND DISAPPEAR . . . . 104 BALDER DEAD 1 336
    POWERS STIR IN US STIR AND DISAPPEAR . . . . . 210 SELF-DECEPTION 22
    THE LOW-BROWD CAVERN-ARCH AND DISAPPEAR . . . . 358 MEROPE 834
    UNCLE AND NEPHEW DISAPPEAR THEIR DEATH . . . . 364 MEROPE 979
    AS THEY SHOW AND DISAPPEAR . . . . 456 POOR MATTHIAS 146

DISAPPEARD
    HE SPAKE AND BRUSHD SOFT BY AND DISAPPEARD . . . 102 BALDER DEAD 1 239
    MOURNFULLY SHOOK HIS HEAD AND DISAPPEARD . . . 104 BALDER DEAD 1 334
    AND THEY FROM SIGHT HAVE DISAPPEARD AND SUNK . . 128 BALDER DEAD 3 524

DISAPPEARS
    THE HEATHER DISAPPEARS AND THE PALE GRASS . . . TRISTRAM 3 V 15
    AND HE TOO DISAPPEARS AND COMES NO MORE . . . 244 SUMMER NIGHT 73

DISAPPOINTMENTS
    BREEDS NEW BEGINNINGS DISAPPOINTMENTS NEW . . . 260 SCHOLAR-GIPSY 177

DISARMD
    TO MY MESSENIANS DUPED DISARMD DESPISED . . . 366 MEROPE 1006

DISARRAY
    OF HASTE HALF-WORK AND DISARRAY . . . . . . 222 EPILOG LAOCOON 27

DISARRAYD
    BE DISARRAYD OF THEIR DIVINITY . . . . 429 EMPEDOCLES II 32

DISBAND
    BEGIN TO QUAKE AND DISBAND . . . . 214 NEW ROME 6

DISCERN
    WHAT HEAVENS WHAT EARTH WHAT SUN SHALT THOU DISCERN   43 GIPSY CHILD   44
    ONCE ERE THE DAY DECLINE THOU SHALT DISCERN   • •   44 GIPSY CHILD   65
    WHAT HEAVENS WHAT EARTH WHAT SUNS SHALT THOU DISCERN   43 GIPSY CHILD   V 44
    ONCE ERE THY DAY GO DOWN THOU SHALT DISCERN   • •   44 GIPSY CHILD   V 65
    WHOSE NATURAL INSIGHT CAN DISCERN   • • • • •   59 RESIGNATION   233
    HOW CANST THOU ERE THOU HEAR DISCERN   • • • • •   89 SICK KING BOKH   54
    DAYS FLEW AH SOON I COULD DISCERN   • • • • •   178 FAREWELL   13
    TOO DEEP FOR THE MOST TO DISCERN   • • • • • •   230 YOUTH OF NATURE   71
    ALL WE HAVE BUILT DO WE DISCERN   • • • • • •   241 MORALITY   12
    CLEAREST THEIR COURSE DISCERN   • • • • • • •   314 OBERMANN MORE   76
    BEST CAN ITS COURSE DISCERN   • • • • • • •   314 OBERMANN MORE   V 76
    COULDST THOU BUT ONCE DISCERN   • • • • • • •   417 EMPEDOCLES I 2   159

DISCERND
    FROM HERE THE COLD WHITE MIST CAN BE DISCERND   • •   108 BALDER DEAD 2   124
    WILL MAKE OURSELVES HARDER TO BE DISCERND   • • •   440 EMPEDOCLES II   381

DISCERNS
    FOR THAT BEST WHICH SHE DISCERNS   • • • • • •   49 SECOND BEST   12

DISCIPLES
    HE SAW A FIRE IN HIS DISCIPLES EYES   • • • • •   237 PROGRESS   2

DISCLOSE
    DOTH A WHOLE TRACT OF HEAVEN DISCLOSE   • • • •   242 SUMMER NIGHT   10

DISCONTENT
    AS HE DRIFTS TO FATIGUE DISCONTENT AND DEJECTION   • • 20 MODERN SAPPHO   19
    TO YOUTH AND AGE IN COMMON DISCONTENT   • • •   37 YOUTHS AGIT   14
    OUR SHIVERING HEART IS MINED BY SECRET DISCONTENT   424 EMPEDOCLES I 2   366
    OUR DISCONTENT ITSELF IS ARGUMENT   • • • • •   LUCRETIUS 3   10

DISCONTENTED
    DISCONTENTED PERHAPS   • • • • • • • • • •   343 MEROPE   404

DISCORD
    MURDER DISCORD AND HATE   • • • • • • • • •   361 MEROPE   910

DISCORDS
    YES WHILE ON EARTH A THOUSAND DISCORDS RING   • •   1 QUIET WORK   9

DISCOURSE
    AND PASTIME OF THE GODS THE WISE DISCOURSE   • • •   129 BALDER DEAD 3   541

DISCOURSED
    WHILE THUS MY FRIEND DISCOURSED WE PASS   • • • •   222 EPILOG LAOCOON   36

DISCOVERY
    DISCOVERY OF A VISIT MADE BY STEALTH   • • • • •   351 MEROPE   605

DISCREDITING
    DISCREDITING THE SUCCOUR WHICH OUR CAUSE   • • • •   382 MEROPE   1325

DISCROWNED
    OF UNSPHERED DISCROWNED CREATURES   • • • •   34 NEW SIRENS   249
    THE VANISHT MIGHT OF THAT DISCROWNED HEAD   • • •   464 ALARIC AT ROME   46

DISDAIN
    THEIR PURE UNWAVERING DEEP DISDAIN   • • • • •   202 URANIA   32
    THEIR GAY UNWAVERING DEEP DISDAIN   • • • • •   202 URANIA   V 32
    IN PATIENT DEEP DISDAIN   • • • • • • • •   316 OBERMANN MORE   110
    OF CONCORD AND BEEN BAFFLED WITH DISDAIN   • • •   360 MEROPE   V 881
    HE CRUSHD THEE NOT WITH HIS DISDAIN   • • • • •   482 COURAGE   23

DISDAINFUL
    BUT IN DISDAINFUL SILENCE TURN AWAY   • • • • •   42 GIPSY CHILD   31

DISEASE
    AND PROUD SELF-SEVERANCE FROM THEM WERE DISEASE   • •   46 IN UTRUMQUE PAR V 39
    OF THE FRENCH THEATRE WORN WITH DISEASE   • • •   167 RACHEL 1   6
    BEFORE THIS STRANGE DISEASE OF MODERN LIFE   • • •   261 SCHOLAR-GIPSY   203

DISEASED
    BEING IN TRUTH BUT A DISEASED UNREST   • • • • •   153 TRISTRAM 3   135

DISEASES
    HE COULD STAY SWIFT DISEASES IN OLD DAYS   • • • •   410 EMPEDOCLES I 1   115

DISENCHANTED
    DISENCHANTED BY HABIT AND NEWLY AWAKING   • • •   20 MODERN SAPPHO   23

DISFEATURED
    GREETED OF NONE DISFEATURED AND FORLORN   • • • •   109 BALDER DEAD 2   171

DISFIGURED
    DOWN THOSE DISFIGURED   • • • • • • • • • •   393 MEROPE   1670

DISGRACE
    IN MOMENTS OF DISGRACE UNCURLD • • • • • • • • 460 KAISER DEAD   56

DISGUISE
    OUR BANE DISGUISE IT AS WE MAY • • • • • • • • 482 COURAGE   25

DISGUISES
    TRICKD IN DISGUISES ALIEN TO THE REST   • • • • 245 BURIED LIFE   21

DISGUST
    ON THAT HARD PAGAN WORLD DISGUST   • • • • • 315 OBERMANN MORE   93

DISHONOUR
    IS IT THE BLIGHTING TAINT DISHONOUR BREATHES   • • 463 ALARIC AT ROME   27

DISLODGE
    FOR FEAR THEY SHOULD DISLODGE THE OERHANGING SNOWS   66 SOHRAB RUSTUM   168
    THE UNSEEN SNOW-BEDS DISLODGE • • • • • • • 289 RUGBY CHAPEL   99

DISMAL
    AND HE MUST FARE ACROSS THE DISMAL ICE   • • • 100 BALDER DEAD 1   165
    AND HE WILL FARE ACROSS THE DISMAL ICE   • • • 100 BALDER DEAD 1   V 165
    WITH SHRILL AND DISMAL CRIES THAT BIRD SHALL CROW   105 BALDER DEAD 2   6

DISMARBLE
    THERES NOTHING CAN DISMARBLE NOW   • • • • • 21 YOUTH AND CALM   3
    THOUGH NOTHING CAN DISMARBLE NOW   • • • • • 21 YOUTH AND CALM   V 3

DISMAY
    PASSIVE AT THE NADIR OF DISMAY • • • • • • • 33 NEW SIRENS   202
    MAYST SEE WITHOUT DISMAY • • • • • • • • 416 EMPEDOCLES I 2   110
    WE SEE IN BLANK DISMAY • • • • • • • • 424 EMPEDOCLES I 2   363
    SHAKEN AND IN DISMAY • • • • • • • • 416 EMPEDOCLES I 2   V 115

DISMAYD
    ARE THE BLESSED GODS DISMAYD • • • • • • 34 NEW SIRENS   246
    ARE THE HAPPY GODS DISMAYD • • • • • • 34 NEW SIRENS   V 246
    MAN STILL WOULD SEE AND SEE DISMAYD • • • • • 58 RESIGNATION   220

DISMISSD
    WE DISMISSD WITHOUT A WORD   • • • • • • • 453 POOR MATTHIAS   24

DISMOUNT
    BUT THEN HE MUST DISMOUNT AND ON THE ICE   • • • 100 BALDER DEAD 1   168

DISMOUNTED
    THEN HE DISMOUNTED AND DREW TIGHT THE GIRTHS   • • 109 BALDER DEAD 2   146

DISOBEDIENT
    FOR TO LIVE DISOBEDIENT TO THESE TWO • • • • • 390 MEROPE   1575

DISORDERD
    LIES IN DISORDERD STREAMS AND THERE • • • • • 146 TRISTRAM 2   108

DISPEOPLED
    A WOLFISH BAND IN A DISPEOPLED REALM • • • • • 338 MEROPE   288

DISPERSED
    AND THEN THE GLOOM DISPERSED AND THE WIND FELL   • • 76 SOHRAB RUSTUM   522
    WELL WIND-DISPERSED AND VAIN THE WORDS WILL BE   • • 265 THYRSIS   101

DISPIRITED
    IN SPITALFIELDS LOOKD THRICE DISPIRITED   • • • • 169 EAST LONDON   4
    OF YOUR FAINTING DISPIRITED RACE   • • • • • 291 RUGBY CHAPEL   189

DISPLAY
    FEWER FINE SUCCESSES CAN DISPLAY   • • • • • 221 EPILOG LAOCOON   12
    FEWER REAL SUCCESSES CAN DISPLAY   • • • • • 221 EPILOG LAOCOON   V 12
    THE TENDER FOXGLOVE-PLANTS DISPLAY   • • • • • 484 ROME-SICKNESS   15

DISPLAYD
    GODS WISDOM AND GODS GOODNESS ARE DISPLAYD • • • 171 DIVINITY   4

DISPLAYS
    NOT MUCH A TYRANT THY FREE SPEECH DISPLAYS ME   • • 340 MEROPE   350

DISPLEASE
    HENCEFORTH IF WHAT I URGE DISPLEASE I MAY • • • 395 MEROPE   1727

DISPOSE
    NOR WITH A LIGHTER HAND DISPOSE   • • • • • 48 HORATIAN ECHO   22

DISPOSSESSD
    A MOMENT DISPOSSESSD REALITY • • • • • • • 474 CROMWELL   94

DISPOSSESSED
    WERE THEY WE DISPOSSESSED OF US I SPEAK   • • • 337 MEROPE   229

DISPOSSESSORS
    SUCH WERE THE DISPOSSESSORS OF WHAT STAMP   • • • 337 MEROPE   228

DISPUTATIOUS
    FIERCE DISPUTATIOUS EVER AT WAR WITH MAN　　• • • •　440 EMPEDOCLES II　395

DISPUTES
    OF DOUBTS DISPUTES DISTRACTIONS FEARS　　• • • •　271 MEMORIAL VERSES　44

DISQUIETED
    WHEREIN EARTHS GREAT ONES ARE DISQUIETED　　• • • •　7 REP FRIEND　10

DISQUIETUDE
    SUGGESTIONS TO DISQUIETUDE　　• • • • • • • •　56 RESIGNATION　125

DISSATISFIED
    ARE WE DISSATISFIED WITH WHAT WE ARE　• • • • •　LUCRETIUS 3　9
    ARE WE DISSATISFIED WITH WHAT WE HAVE　• • • •　LUCRETIUS 3　V 9

DISSEMBLES
    LIFE DRIES UP THE HEART DISSEMBLES　　• • • • • •　29 NEW SIRENS　83

DISSENSIONS
    VOYAGES EXILES HATES DISSENSIONS WARS　　• • • •　195 FRAG ANTIGONE　23

DISSEVERS
    DEATH WHO DISSEVERS ALL　• • • • • • • • • •　195 FRAG ANTIGONE　27

DISSOLVE
    THREATENS TO BREAK TO DISSOLVE　• • • • • • •　291 RUGBY CHAPEL　181

DISSOLVING
    FELT THE DISSOLVING THROES　　• • • • • • • •　229 YOUTH OF NATURE　31

DISSUADE
    TO STRIKE IT THEN DISSUADE THY SON NO MORE　• • • •　390 MEROPE　1574

DISSUADES
    FOR THIS IS NOT MY MOTHER WHO DISSUADES　• • • •　385 MEROPE　1413
    AND NOT ALONE DISSUADES HIM BUT COMPARES　• • • •　385 MEROPE　1416

DISSUASIONS
    DIRECT TO THY DISSUASIONS I REPLY　• • • • • •　389 MEROPE　1531

DISTANCE
    THAT AN IMPULSE FROM THE DISTANCE　• • • • •　49 SECOND BEST　21
    FROM A FAR LONELIER DISTANCE LIKE THE WIND　• • • •　238 PROGRESS　34
    BUT AT A DISTANCE IN THESE SOLITUDES　• • • • •　409 EMPEDOCLES I 1　87
    NO GLITTERING HOPES ON LIFES GREY DISTANCE SMILED　475 CROMWELL　126

DISTANT
    MID THE DISTANT MOUNTAIN-CHALETS　• • • • •　12 CHURCH BROU 1　3
    ONE FAINT FROWN OF DISTANT COLDNESS　• • • • •　31 NEW SIRENS　161
    THOSE LUTE-LIKE TONES WHICH IN LONG DISTANT YEARS　36 VOICE　V 35
    BY THE FAR-DISTANT OXUS HE IS SLAIN　• • • • •　79 SOHRAB RUSTUM　601
    THEY THREE IN THAT LONG-DISTANT SUMMER-TIME　• •　79 SOHRAB RUSTUM　628
    TO MATE BUT LEFT HER TO ROAM DISTANT LANDS　• •　116 BALDER DEAD 3　94
    FIRST DROVE HIM FROM ME INTO DISTANT LANDS　• •　116 BALDER DEAD 3　108
    STILL CARRIED OER THE DISTANT WATERS ON　• •　119 BALDER DEAD 3　198
    THE SAND THE SEA-BIRDS AND THE DISTANT SAILS　• •　152 TRISTRAM 3　105
    WHERE YOUR COLD DISTANT BARRIER　• • • • •　175 PARTING　11
    STILL AFTER MANY YEARS IN DISTANT LANDS　• •　200 PHILOMELA　6
    HEARING IT BY THIS DISTANT NORTHERN SEA　• •　211 DOVER BEACH　20
    FROM A DISTANT FARM IN THE HILLS　• • • •　234 YOUTH OF MAN　74
    AS FROM AN INFINITELY DISTANT LAND　• • • •　247 BURIED LIFE　74
    WITH DISTANT CRIES OF REAPERS IN THE CORN　• •　255 SCHOLAR-GIPSY　19
    PLUCKD IN SHY FIELDS AND DISTANT WYCHWOOD BOWERS　•　257 SCHOLAR-GIPSY　79
    MAIDENS WHO FROM THE DISTANT HAMLETS COME　• • •　257 SCHOLAR-GIPSY　82
    PLUCKD IN SHY FIELDS AND DISTANT WOODLAND BOWERS　257 SCHOLAR-GIPSY　V 79
    HANGS TOUCHD WITH LIGHT ONE DISTANT SAIL　• • •　274 STANZAS CARNAC　V 32
    FADE FROM THE DISTANT PEAKS OF SNOW　• • • •　310 OBERMANN　123
    TO PELEUS IN LONG DISTANT YEARS　• • • •　414 EMPEDOCLES I 2　70
    AND RELEGATE TO WORLDS YET DISTANT OUR REPOSE　• •　425 EMPEDOCLES I 2　406
    YOUR DISTANT MELANCHOLY LINES　• • • • • •　437 EMPEDOCLES II　279

DISTIL
    CASD IN ONE MANS DIMENSIONS CAN DISTIL　• • • •　50 CONSOLATION　V

DISTILS
    HEINE DISTILS FROM THY LIFE　• • • • • • • •　294 HEINES GRAVE　68

DISTINCTIONS
    DISTINCTIONS WE ESTEEM SO GRAVE　• • • • • •　311 OBERMANN　151

DISTINCTLY
    POWER FAILS THE MAN HIMSELF TO FIX DISTINCTLY　• •　352 MEROPE　649
    THOUGH FROM AFAR DISTINCTLY IT MAY SOOTHE HIM　• •　409 EMPEDOCLES I 1　89

DISTRACTED
    DISTRACTED AS A HOMELESS WIND　• • • • •　179 FAREWELL　50
    LIKE US DISTRACTED AND LIKE US UNBLEST　• • • •　261 SCHOLAR-GIPSY　225

DISTRACTIONS
        BY WHAT DISTRACTIONS HE WOULD BE POSSESSD   .   .   .   .   246 BURIED LIFE   32
        OF DOUBTS DISPUTES DISTRACTIONS FEARS   .   .   .   .   271 MEMORIAL VERSES   44

DISTRAUGHT
        AND HODER TOO CAME HOME DISTRAUGHT WITH GRIEF   .   .   102 BALDER DEAD 1   249

DISTRESS
        DISTRESS ELSEWHERE   .   .   .   .   51 CONSOLATION   60
        SHADOWS OF HATES BUT THEY DISTRESS THEM STILL   .   .   126 BALDER DEAD 3   467
        IN HIS STATELY DEEP DISTRESS   .   .   .   .   137 TRISTRAM 1   209
        HOW THEY ARE FULL OF LANGUOR AND DISTRESS   .   .   .   153 TRISTRAM 3   137
        IN PAIN IN TERROR IN DISTRESS   .   .   .   .   .   .   226 EPILOG LAOCOON   175
        OF TERROR AND INSANE DISTRESS   .   .   .   .   .   .   271 MEMORIAL VERSES   32
        INHERITORS OF THY DISTRESS   .   .   .   .   303 GRANDE CHARTR   143
        SINGLE NOT FOR DISTRESS   .   .   .   .   EMPEDOCLES I 2   V
        FAIL TO TRACK THEIR DEEP DISTRESS   .   .   .   .   .   455 POOR MATTHIAS   106

DISTRESSFUL
        QUICK FROM DISTRESSFUL THOUGHT AND FLOATS IN JOY   .   .   351 MEROPE   615
        DISTRESSFUL LONGING   .   .   .   .   393 MEROPE   1663

DISTRUST
        EXTINGUISHES DISTRUST TWIXT HIM AND THEE   .   .   .   .   359 MEROPE   852

DISTURB
        YET WOULD I NOT DISTURB THEE FROM THY TOMB   .   .   .   .   449 WESTMIN ABBEY   163

DISUSED
        PAST THE DARK FORGES LONG DISUSED   .   .   .   .   .   .   299 GRANDE CHARTR   3

DITTY
        PIPING A DITTY SAD FOR BIONS FATE   .   .   .   .   .   .   265 THYRSIS   84

DIVER
        AND DEAR AS THE WET DIVER TO THE EYES   .   .   .   .   69 SOHRAB RUSTUM   284

DIVERGING
        DIVERGING TO ANOTHER THOUGHT   .   .   .   .   221 EPILOG LAOCOON   7

DIVERS
        IN DIVERS PLACES IF THAT PAIN   .   .   .   .   94 SICK KING BOKH   204

DIVIDE
        FACTIONS DIVIDE THEM THEIR HOST   .   .   .   .   .   .   291 RUGBY CHAPEL   180

DIVIDED
        WITH ITS SICK HURRY ITS DIVIDED AIMS   .   .   .   .   .   261 SCHOLAR-GIPSY   204

DIVIDING
        DIVIDING CLEAR THE PATHS OF NIGHT AND DAY   .   .   .   121 BALDER DEAD 3   265
        AND WILL LIKE A DIVIDING SPEAR   .   .   .   .   .   .   178 FAREWELL   34

DIVINATIONS
        BLIND DIVINATIONS OF A WILL SUPREME   .   .   .   .   .   10 MYCERINUS   52

DIVINE
        IS THERE DOUBT ON DIVINE FACES   .   .   .   .   .   .   34 NEW SIRENS   245
        IN DIVINE SEATS HATH KNOWN   .   .   .   .   45 IN UTRUMQUE PAR   23
        FOR THERE RANG NOTE DIVINE IN THAT COMMAND   .   .   .   102 BALDER DEAD 1   245
        THE GAZE OF ONE WHO CAN DIVINE   .   .   .   .   .   .   140 TRISTRAM 1   323
        OH BRANDAN THINK WHAT GRACE DIVINE   .   .   .   .   .   158 SAINT BRANDAN   53
        ALL SPOTS MATCHD WITH THAT SPOT ARE LESS DIVINE   .   .   167 RACHEL 1   13
        THROUGH THE ISLANDS SOME DIVINE BARD   .   .   .   .   189 STRAYED REVEL   118
        THE DESIRED THE DIVINE   .   .   .   .   194 STRAYED REVEL   280
        LIE SWEETLY IN THE LOOK DIVINE   .   .   .   .   .   .   208 ON THE RHINE   14
        OF BARDS FULL MANY A STROKE DIVINE   .   .   .   .   .   222 EPILOG LAOCOON   20
        WITH POWER DIVINE ITS STORY TELL   .   .   .   .   .   223 EPILOG LAOCOON   60
        THE WEALTH DIVINE THEY HAVE IN CHARGE   .   .   .   .   224 EPILOG LAOCOON   102
        THEY SPEAK THE HAPPINESS DIVINE   .   .   .   .   .   .   227 EPILOG LAOCOON   197
        FILLD HIM AND MADE HIM DIVINE   .   .   .   .   .   .   231 YOUTH OF NATURE   98
        AH CHILD SHE CRIES THAT STRIFE DIVINE   .   .   .   .   241 MORALITY   23
        CLEARNESS DIVINE   .   .   .   .   244 SUMMER NIGHT   77
        SHE KNEW THE DORIAN WATERS GUSH DIVINE   .   .   .   .   265 THYRSIS   94
        WANDERING WITH THE GREAT MOTHERS TRAIN DIVINE   .   .   268 THYRSIS   177
        TO THAT IN YOU WHICH IS DIVINE   .   .   .   .   .   .   279 SOUTHERN NIGHT   139
        RADIANT WITH ARDOUR DIVINE   .   .   .   .   291 RUGBY CHAPEL   191
        SONG OF THE POET DIVINE   .   .   .   .   295 HEINES GRAVE   104
        IN THE HIGH ALTARS DEPTH DIVINE   .   .   .   .   .   .   306 GRANDE CHARTR   202
        SIMPLY THE WAY DIVINE   .   .   .   .   319 OBERMANN MORE   188
        A MOTHERS MURDER NEEDED HEST DIVINE   .   .   .   .   .   385 MEROPE   1402
        BUT ALL ARE DIVINE   .   .   .   .   442 EMPEDOCLES II   448
        AND AS YEARS SPED THE MINSTER-AISLES DIVINE   .   .   445 WESTMIN ABBEY   55
        HAD HUMAN CRY NOT MARRD THE WORK DIVINE   .   .   .   447 WESTMIN ABBEY   104
        FAITHFUL LOVE IN DEPTH DIVINE   .   .   .   .   .   .   454 POOR MATTHIAS   65
        US UNABLE TO DIVINE   .   .   .   .   456 POOR MATTHIAS   125
        WHO MAY TRUST US TO DIVINE   .   .   .   .   457 POOR MATTHIAS   170

DIVINELIER
        DIVINELIER IMAGED CLEARER SEEN   .   .   .   .   322 OBERMANN MORE   295

DIVINELY
    THE NIGHTINGALES DIVINELY SING . . . . 182 TO MARG CONT   10

DIVINER
    BY CONTEMPLATION OF DIVINER THINGS . . . .   9 MYCERINUS   12
    AH WE OWN DIVINER FEATURES . . . . 28 NEW SIRENS   63
    THERE NEEDS A MINSTREL OF DIVINER MIGHT . . . . 471 ALARIC AT ROME   225

DIVINITY
    BE DISARRAYD OF THEIR DIVINITY . . . . 429 EMPEDOCLES II   32

DIVORCE
    AT DIVORCE WHICH IT PROCLAIMS . . . . 35 NEW SIRENS   262

DIVORCED
    WHEN I SHALL BE DIVORCED SOME TEN YEARS HENCE . . 37 YOUTHS AGIT   1

DIVULGE
    DIVULGE NOT TO THE FAR-OFF WORLD OF MEN . . . . 396 MEROPE   1753

DIZZILY
    OER THE VALLEY THE DIZZILY PERCHD . . . . . . 297 HEINES GRAVE   187

DIZZY
    DIZZY AND ON HIS KNEES AND CHOKED WITH SAND . . 74 SOHRAB RUSTUM   424
    MINE EYES ARE DIZZY WITH THE ARROWY HAIL . . . . 128 BALDER DEAD 3   507
    DIZZY THE PATH AND PERILOUS THE WAY . . . . . 341 MEROPE   368
    AH BLOODY AXE DIZZY BLOWS . . . . 346 MEROPE   499

DIZZYING
    IN ACTIONS DIZZYING EDDY WHIRLD . . . . . . 60 RESIGNATION   277

DOCILE
    YET DOCILE NOW HE STOOD AT HERMODS SIDE . . . . 107 BALDER DEAD 2   75

DOCTOR
    SOME DOCTOR FULL OF PHRASE AND FAME . . . . . 250 WISH   18
    HIS BROTHER-DOCTOR OF THE SOUL . . . . 250 WISH   23
    BAH THOU A DOCTOR THOU ART SUPERSTITIOUS . . . . 410 EMPEDOCLES I 1   133

DOCTORS
    THESE HUNDRED DOCTORS TRY . . . . 417 EMPEDOCLES I 2   137

DOEST
    THOU DOEST WELL TO CHIDE ME HODER BLIND . . . . 125 BALDER DEAD 3   423

DOG
    NO NOR ON THIS DEAD DOG O KING . . . . 93 SICK KING BOKH   180
    CONFRONTS THE DOG AND HUNTER IN THE SOUTH . . . 99 BALDER DEAD 1   157
    LIKE AS A FARMER WHO HATH LOST HIS DOG . . . . 113 BALDER DEAD 3   8
    AND PALE DOG-ROSES IN THE HEDGE . . . . . 218 BACCHANALIA 1   12
    FAINTLY THE BARK OF A DOG . . . . 234 YOUTH OF MAN   73
    A BABY DOG FROM LONDON TOWN . . . . 459 KAISER DEAD   14
    FOR MAX THY BROTHER-DOG BEGAN . . . . 459 KAISER DEAD   37

DOGGD
    WHICH DOGGD BY FEAR AND FOUGHT BY SHAME . . . . 147 TRISTRAM 2   132

DOGGISH
    AND JOKES IN DOGGISH LANGUAGE SAID . . . . . . 460 KAISER DEAD   71

DOGS
    THE SHIAH DOGS WHO PASTURE SHEEP . . . . . 93 SICK KING BOKH   167
    AND SLEW THE DOGS WHO AT HIS TABLE FED . . . 118 BALDER DEAD 3   170
    AND SLEW THE DOGS WHICH AT HIS TABLE FED . . . 118 BALDER DEAD 3 V 170
    AND SENT ME WITH MY DOGS TO SWEEP . . . . . . 148 TRISTRAM 2   176
    CHEER CHEER THY DOGS INTO THE BRAKE . . . . . 149 TRISTRAM 2   186
    AND SENT HIM WITH HIS DOGS TO SWEEP . . . . . 148 TRISTRAM 2 V 176
    THE MOWERS CRY THE DOGS ALARMS . . . . . . 218 BACCHANALIA 1   6
    THE REAPERS CRY THE DOGS ALARMS . . . . . . 218 BACCHANALIA 1 V 6
    AND THE TIRED MEN AND DOGS ALL GONE TO REST . . 255 SCHOLAR-GIPSY   7
    THROUGH THE DENSE ILEX-THICKETS TO THE DOGS . . 357 MEROPE   791
    CHEERING WITH HAND AND VOICE AND HORN HIS DOGS . 357 MEROPE   805
    STAG DOGS AND HUNTER TO THE YAWNING GULPH . . . 358 MEROPE   826
    AND TOOK THREE STRIDES QUARRY AND DOGS WERE GONE . . 358 MEROPE   830

DOING
    AND FOR SUCH DOING THEY REQUIRE NOT EYES . . . . 7 REP FRIEND   8
    AND FOR SUCH DOING HAVE NO NEED OF EYES . . . . 7 REP FRIEND V 8
    AND FOR SUCH DOING THEY REQUIRE NO EYES . . . . 7 REP FRIEND V 8

DOLEFUL
    AND DOLEFUL ARE THE GHOSTS THE TROOPS OF DEAD . . 104 BALDER DEAD 1   316

DOLOUR
    OF TOIL AND DOLOUR UNTOLD . . . . 199 FRAG DEJANEIRA   19

DOME
    A DOME OF LATHS AND OER IT FELTS WERE SPREAD . . 61 SOHRAB RUSTUM   23
    TOO MUCH OF PALACE AND DOME . . . . 214 NEW ROME   12

DOMED

AND THE DOMED VELAN WITH HIS SNOWS · · · · · · · 324 OBERMANN MORE 341

DOMES

FROM THOSE WEIRD DOMES OF MOUNDED GREEN · · · · 480 HAYSWATER BOAT 23

DOMINE

MISERERE DOMINE · · · · · · · · · 224 EPILOG LAOCOON 89
MISERERE DOMINE · · · · · · · · · 224 EPILOG LAOCOON 106

DOMINION

THE BEST THEN TO DOMINION HATH THE RIGHT · · · · 352 MEROPE 654
TO GIVE TO VIRTUE HER DOMINION DUE · · · · · 353 MEROPE 666
THE BEST THEN TO DOMINION HAVE THE RIGHT · · · · 352 MEROPE V 654
NEW DREAMS OF WIDE DOMINION MIGHTIER HIGHER · · 469 ALARIC AT ROME 175

DONE

TILL THE CHURCH WAS ROOFD AND DONE · · · · · 16 CHURCH BROU 1 102
AND AFTER CHURCH WHEN MASS IS DONE · · · · · 17 CHURCH BROU 2 33
TO PAINT ILL AS I HAVE DONE · · · · · · 24 MEMORY-PICTURE 51
OR THE DAY WERE SOONER DONE · · · · · · 29 NEW SIRENS 110
WHEN YOUTH HAS DONE ITS TEDIOUS VAIN EXPENSE · · 37 YOUTHS AGIT 3
LIFES VOYAGE DONE HIS HEAVENLY FRIEND · · · · 40 HUMAN LIFE 2
BLITHELY THIS MORN OLD OCEANS WORK IS DONE · · · 41 GIPSY CHILD V 7
RUSTUM HIS MORNING MEAL WAS DONE BUT STILL · · · 67 SOHRAB RUSTUM 196
WITH SPOILS AND HONOUR WHEN THE WAR IS DONE · · 79 SOHRAB RUSTUM 595
LET ME ENTREAT FOR THEM WHAT HAVE THEY DONE · · 84 SOHRAB RUSTUM 780
AS THE KING SAID SO IT WAS DONE · · · · · 89 SICK KING BOKH 44
AS THE KING BADE SO WAS IT DONE · · · · · 90 SICK KING BOKH 92
AS THE KING SAID SO WAS IT DONE · · · · · 89 SICK KING BOKH V 44
AS THE KING SAID SO WAS IT DONE · · · · · 90 SICK KING BOKH V 92
AFTER THE FEAST IS DONE IN ODINS HALL · · · · 117 BALDER DEAD 3 136
FORGOT MY GOOD AS SOON AS DONE · · · · · 158 SAINT BRANDAN 60
FORGOT MY DEED AS SOON AS DONE · · · · · 158 SAINT BRANDAN V 60
WE LIVE NO MORE WHEN WE HAVE DONE OUR SPAN · · 171 BETTER PART 5
WELL HATH HE DONE WHO HATH SEIZED HAPPINESS · · 195 FRAG ANTIGONE 1
AWHILE LET ME WITH THOUGHT HAVE DONE · · · · 208 ON THE RHINE 11
HIS MASTERS ERRAND WELL DONE · · · · · · 217 LORDS MESSENGER 22
THE BUSINESS OF THE DAY IS DONE · · · · · 218 BACCHANALIA 1 8
WHATEVER MEN HAVE DONE MIGHT DO · · · · · 221 BACCHANALIA 2 67
THE FAMOUS ORATORS HAVE DONE · · · · · · 219 BACCHANALIA 2 V 3
OF THE LONG DAY AND WISH TWERE DONE · · · · 241 MORALITY 10
INTO YON FARTHER FIELD TIS DONE AND SEE · · · 267 THYRSIS 157
INTO YON FURTHER FIELD TIS DONE AND SEE · · · 267 THYRSIS V 157
GOETHE HAS DONE HIS PILGRIMAGE · · · · · 270 MEMORIAL VERSES 18
THAT GLOW OF CENTRAL FIRE IS DONE · · · · · 320 OBERMANN MORE 221
DEATHS FROZEN HOUR IS DONE · · · · · · 322 OBERMANN MORE 292
THE GLOW OF CENTRAL FIRE IS DONE · · · · · 320 OBERMANN MORE V 221
PERMIT NO PEACE TILL YOUR BEHESTS ARE DONE · · 367 MEROPE 1057
THROW THE DOOR OPEN TIS DONE · · · · · · 372 MEROPE 1152
WHAT I HAVE DONE IS DONE BY MY OWN DEED · · · 398 MEROPE 1787
WHAT I HAVE DONE IS DONE BY MY OWN DEED · · · 398 MEROPE 1787
OF DARING EASY AS IT SEEMS WHEN DONE · · · · 403 MEROPE 1949
AND THOU HAST DONE WITH FEARS · · · · · · 417 EMPEDOCLES I 2 143
TO HAVE LOVED TO HAVE THOUGHT TO HAVE DONE · · 425 EMPEDOCLES I 2 400
TOUCHD THE HILLS THE STRIFE WAS DONE · · · · 433 EMPEDOCLES II 144
HAST THY COMMISSION DONE YE BOTH MAY NOW · · · 449 WESTMIN ABBEY 169
O HAPPY SLUMBER IF THE DAY WERE DONE · · · · 475 CROMWELL 120

DONND

AND FROM THEIR BEDS THE HEROES ROSE AND DONND · · 105 BALDER DEAD 2 11
HE SPOKE AND THE GODS ARMD AND ODIN DONND · · · 115 BALDER DEAD 3 57

DOOM

THE DOOM THEY PASS REVOKE NOT NOR DELAY · · · · 10 MYCERINUS 70
BUT HIDES IF GODS GODS CARELESS OF OUR DOOM · · 10 MYCERINUS 54
WHO MASSD ROUND THAT SLIGHT BROW THESE CLOUDS OF DOOM 41 GIPSY CHILD 4
WHAT CLOUDS THY FOREHEAD AND FORE-DATES THY DOOM · · 41 GIPSY CHILD V 4
THE DOOM WHICH AT MY BIRTH WAS WRITTEN DOWN · · 82 SOHRAB RUSTUM 709
THE DOOM THAT AT MY BIRTH WAS WRITTEN DOWN · · · 82 SOHRAB RUSTUM V 709
BUT HE HAS MET THAT DOOM WHICH LONG AGO · · · 96 BALDER DEAD 1 23
FOR YE YOURSELVES YE GODS SHALL MEET YOUR DOOM · · 96 BALDER DEAD 1 28
THAT ONE LONG PORTION WITH HIS DOOM OF DEATH · · 98 BALDER DEAD 1 114
FOR YOU YOURSELVES YE GODS SHALL MEET YOUR DOOM · · 96 BALDER DEAD 1 V 28
OUTLIVES MY GUILT OUTLIVES MY DOOM · · · · · 158 SAINT BRANDAN 63
THE DOOM OF THEBES · · · · · · · · 190 STRAYED REVEL 142
IF THESE CONDEMN HIM LET THEM PASS HIS DOOM · · 349 MEROPE 557
THAT DOOM OBTAIN EFFECT FROM GODS OR MEN · · · 349 MEROPE 558
I WOULD NOT BREAK THY REST NOR CHANGE THY DOOM · · 449 WESTMIN ABBEY 166
THE DOOM PRONOUNCED THE BATTLE-FLAG UNFURLED · · 465 ALARIC AT ROME 93
MAKE CESSION OF HER SCEPTRE DOOM HERSELF · · · · RUDE ORATOR. 19

DOOMD

DOOMD POMPOUS AND ABSURD · · · · · · · 48 HORATIAN ECHO 12
WHERE WE HAD LONG BEEN DOOMD TO DWELL · · · · 271 MEMORIAL VERSES V
THE MAN WHO TO UNTIMELY DEATH IS DOOMD · · · · 359 MEROPE 854

DOOMS

WHICH DOOMS DREAD ENDS TO DREADFUL DEEDS · · · · 398 MEROPE 1808

DOOR
BUT GUDURZ STOOD IN THE TENT-DOOR AND SAID	• • •	67 SOHRAB RUSTUM	207
BUT RUSTUM STRODE TO HIS TENT-DOOR AND CALLD	• •	69 SOHRAB RUSTUM	263
O VIZIER HERE IS THE KINGS DOOR	• • • •	88 SICK KING BOKH	20
I HID THE CAN BEHIND THE DOOR	• • • • •	90 SICK KING BOKH	72
BEHIND THE DOOR UPON THE GROUND	• • • •	90 SICK KING BOKH	79
AND HE WENT IN AND SHUT THE DOOR AND FIXT	• •	102 BALDER DEAD 1	251
FLEW EVER TO THE DOOR	• • • • • •	146 TRISTRAM 2	122
AT THAT BRIGHT IRON-FIGURED DOOR	• • • •	148 TRISTRAM 2	159
AT THE BRIGHT IRON-FIGURED DOOR	• • • •	148 TRISTRAM 2	V 159
LOUD PRAYS THE PRIEST SHUT STANDS THE DOOR	• •	163 FORSAKEN MERM	82
WHEN GUSTS SHAKE THE DOOR	• • • • • •	164 FORSAKEN MERM	113
BUT WHO IS THIS BY THE HALF-OPEND DOOR	• •	175 PARTING	35
WHERE THEY LAY BY THE HUT DOOR	• • • •	186 STRAYED REVEL	32
WHO TIRED OF KNOCKING AT PREFERMENTS DOOR	• •	256 SCHOLAR-GIPSY	35
WHERE AT HER OPEN DOOR THE HOUSEWIFE DARNS	• •	258 SCHOLAR-GIPSY	102
WHERE IS THE GIRL WHO BY THE BOATMANS DOOR	• •	266 THYRSIS	121
BY SOME HIGH CHALET-DOOR AND SEEN	• • • •	310 OBERMANN	115
AND LIE BESIDE ITS DOOR	• • • • • •	313 OBERMANN MORE	46
THRUST BACK NOW THE BOLT OF THAT DOOR	• •	372 MEROPE	1147
OF THE GUEST-CHAMBER DOOR	• • • • •	372 MEROPE	1150
THROW THE DOOR OPEN TIS DONE	• • • •	372 MEROPE	1152
WHAT DO I SEE A MURDERER AT DEATHS DOOR	• •	374 MEROPE	1195
THEN THE DOOR OPENS AND THIS CARD IS BROUGHT	• •	485 S S LUSITANIA	13

DOORS
THERE HE WENT UP AND PASSD THE OPEN DOORS	• • • •	97 BALDER DEAD 1	87
A PRESENCE SAD FOR SOME ONE THROUGH THOSE DOORS	• •	359 MEROPE	874
WHILE THE MATRONS COME TO THE DOORS	• • • •	360 MEROPE	899

DORIAN
WHEN DORIAN SHEPHERDS SANG TO PROSERPINE	• • •	265 THYRSIS	92
SHE KNEW THE DORIAN WATERS GUSH DIVINE	• • •	265 THYRSIS	94
SHE LOVED THE DORIAN PIPE THE DORIAN STRAIN	• •	265 THYRSIS	97
SHE LOVED THE DORIAN PIPE THE DORIAN STRAIN	• •	265 THYRSIS	97
THAN THEY THESE AND THE DORIAN LORDS WHOSE KING	• •	337 MEROPE	223
HANDFUL OF DORIAN CONQUERORS MIGHT HAVE CURBD	• •	337 MEROPE	248
INJUSTICE TO HIS KIN AND DORIAN FRIENDS	• • •	339 MEROPE	317
PREFERRD MESSENIAN SERFS TO DORIAN LORDS	• • •	339 MEROPE	324
STILL STILL THE DORIAN BOY	• • • • • •	347 MEROPE	532
SCARCE DANGEROUS LESS THAN HIM THE DORIAN LORDS	• •	381 MEROPE	1298
MEAN STILL TO KEEP ALOOF FROM DORIAN BROIL	• •	384 MEROPE	1396
THE BROKEN ORDER OF YOUR DORIAN THRONES	• • •	389 MEROPE	1546
SERRIED AND GRIM THE RING OF DORIAN LORDS	• • •	401 MEROPE	1900
BROKE FROM THE DORIAN LORDS FORWARD THEY RUSHD	• •	402 MEROPE	1931
BURST OER THE ALTAR AND THE DORIAN LORDS	• • •	402 MEROPE	1938

DORIANS
WHO TO THE INVADING DORIANS STRETCHD A HAND	• •	338 MEROPE	293
COMING SWIFTLY THROUGH THE JOCUND DORIANS	• • •	400 MEROPE	1863
THE DORIANS LYING DEAD THY SON HAILD KING	• • •	402 MEROPE	1942

DORIS
FROM THE FOUR-TOWND MOUNTAIN-SHADOWD DORIS	• • • •	400 MEROPE	1852

DOT
OR DOT THE SLOPES TO VEVEY DOWN	• • • • • •	483 ROME-SICKNESS	12

DOTTED
DOTTED WITH HOLLY-TREES AND JUNIPER	• • • •	150 TRISTRAM 3	18
FROM THE PINE-DOTTED SPURS	• • • • • • •	197 FRAG ANTIGONE	61

DOTTING
DOTTING THE SHORELESS WATERY WILD	• • • • •	182 TO MARG CONT	3
DOTTING THE FIELDS OF CORN AND VINE	• • • • •	275 SOUTHERN NIGHT	5

DOUBLE
FROM DOUBT WHERE ALL IS DOUBLE	• • • • • •	39 STAGIRIUS	39
FROM DOUBTS WHERE ALL IS DOUBLE	• • • • •	39 STAGIRIUS	V 39
FOR DOUBLE-MINDED EVER WAS THE SEED	• • • •	112 BALDER DEAD 2	271
OF LOK AND DOUBLE ARE THE GIFTS THEY GIVE	• •	112 BALDER DEAD 2	272
WIDE STREETS WITH FINE DOUBLE TROTTOIRS	• • • •	214 NEW ROME	15
NEW STREETS WITH FINE DOUBLE TROTTOIRS	• • • •	214 NEW ROME	V 15
DOUBLE OF ISSUE FULL OF PITS AND SNARES	• • •	349 MEROPE	581
DOUBLE AND CLASHING THAT HANG	• • • • •	370 MEROPE	1113

DOUBLES
MY DEATH MAKES MY DEBT VOID AND DOUBLES THINE	• •	367 MEROPE	1049

DOUBT
HALF IN DOUBT THEY SAY AND GAZING	• • • • •	31 NEW SIRENS	149
DOUBT NOT WHAT WE HAD WE GAVE	• • • • • •	34 NEW SIRENS	232
IS THERE DOUBT ON DIVINE FACES	• • • • •	34 NEW SIRENS	245
FROM DOUBT WHERE ALL IS DOUBLE	• • • • •	39 STAGIRIUS	39
WHICH KNOWS NO DOUBT WHICH FEELS NO FEAR	• • •	178 FAREWELL	36
FREE FROM THE SICK FATIGUE THE LANGUID DOUBT	• •	260 SCHOLAR-GIPSY	164
AND EVERY DOUBT LONG BLOWN BY TIME AWAY	• • •	261 SCHOLAR-GIPSY	200
AND PALSIED ALL OUR WORD WITH DOUBT	• • • •	323 OBERMANN MORE	319
AND PALSIED ALL OUR DEED WITH DOUBT	• • • •	323 OBERMANN MORE	V 319

DOUBT   (CONTINUED)
    WHEN THE FIGHT HUNG IN DOUBT BUT SHE NOW   •   • • 343 MEROPE   429
    I DOUBT THEIR CAUTION LITTLE SUITS THEIR WARD   • • 351 MEROPE   608
    NOT YET THOUGH SUCH NO DOUBT HIS FINAL AIM •   • • 380 MEROPE   1283
    ARE NEVER FREE FROM DOUBT THOUGH SOMETIMES DUE   • • 388 MEROPE   1522
    ALL THIS NO DOUBT THOU TO THYSELF HAST URGED   • • 389 MEROPE   1529
    TO WATCH MAN DOUBT AND FEAR   •   •   •   •   • • 415 EMPEDOCLES I 2   88
    AND HE TREATS DOUBT THE BEST WHO TRIES TO SEE   • • 415 EMPEDOCLES I 2   101
        LEAST ILL
    MUCH I DOUBT IF THEY SHALL HAVE   •   •   •   • • 454 POOR MATTHIAS   81
    YET THAT IN ANGUISH DOUBT DESIRE   •   •   •   • 482 COURAGE   19
    DOUBT IT NOT WE MET AND WE ARE ONE   •   •   •   • 482 THEKLAS ANSWER   10
    THE DOUBT THAT ASSAILS ALL THINGS NEVER WON   • • FRAGMENT 8   3

DOUBTED
    AND THE THING HEARD THEY DOUBTED NOT • • • • • • 91 SICK KING BOKH   110

DOUBTFUL
    FROM FAR AND A MORE DOUBTFUL SERVICE OWND   •   •   • 64 SOHRAB RUSTUM   127
    OF DOUBTFUL FUTURE DATE •   •   •   •   •   •   • 425 EMPEDOCLES I 2   403
    NEVER DOUBTFUL OF THY NEED   •   •   •   •   •   • 455 POOR MATTHIAS   116

DOUBTFULLY
    SO DREARILY AND DOUBTFULLY   •   •   •   •   •   • 36 VOICE   26

DOUBTING
    SON WITH A DOUBTING HEART THY MOTHER YIELDS   • • 390 MEROPE   1582

DOUBTLESS
    DOUBTLESS YOU ARE PASSING FAIR   •   •   •   •   •   32 NEW SIRENS   188
    DOUBTLESS THOU FEAREST TO MEET BALDERS VOICE   • 124 BALDER DEAD 3   392
    BUT THEY TOO DOUBTLESS WILL HAVE BREATHED THE BALM   126 BALDER DEAD 3   437
    YET DOUBTLESS WHEN THE DAY OF BATTLE COMES   • • • 127 BALDER DEAD 3   494
    DOUBTLESS THEY BEAR THEM TO MY FATHERS TOMB   • 331 MEROPE   55
    DOUBTLESS THOU RECKONEST ON THE HELP OF FRIENDS   • 341 MEROPE   356
    DOUBTLESS THOU RECKONEST ON THE HOPE OF FRIENDS   • 341 MEROPE   V 356
    AND I SHALL DOUBTLESS SEE THEM ALL AGAIN   •   •   • 428 EMPEDOCLES I 2   476

DOUBTS
    LET ALL DOUBTS BE DUMB   •   •   •   •   •   •   • 39 STAGIRIUS   53
    FROM DOUBTS WHERE ALL IS DOUBLE   •   •   •   •   • 39 STAGIRIUS   V 39
    MAZED WITH DOUBTS AND SICK WITH FEARS   •   •   • 44 QUESTION   13
    OF DOUBTS DISPUTES DISTRACTIONS FEARS   •   •   • 271 MEMORIAL VERSES 44
    NOT ABOVE ALL IN THE DOUBTS   •   •   •   •   • 370 MEROPE   1112
    MAY IT TURN HAPPIER THAN MY DOUBTS PORTEND   • • • 390 MEROPE   1583

DOWER
    IT SEEMD A CHILD OF LIGHT DID BRING THE DOWER   • • 446 WESTMIN ABBEY   74

DOWN
    ROSE-CROWND AND EVER WHEN THE SUN WENT DOWN   • • 11 MYCERINUS   93
    DOWN THE SAVOY VALLEYS SOUNDING   •   •   •   •   • 12 CHURCH BROU 1   1
    DOWN THE FOREST-RIDINGS LONE   •   •   •   •   •   • 13 CHURCH BROU 1   22
    DOWN THE LEAF-STREWN FOREST-ROAD   •   •   •   •   • 13 CHURCH BROU 1   30
    IN THE HALL THEY LAID HIM DOWN   •   •   •   •   •   14 CHURCH BROU 1   46
    DOWN THE MOUNTAIN-WAY   •   •   •   •   •   •   • 17 CHURCH BROU 2   27
    AND LOOKING DOWN ON THE WARM ROSY TINTS   •   • 18 CHURCH BROU 3   28
    OF DARK ELMS SHOOT ROUND DROPPING DOWN THE   19 MODERN SAPPHO   6
        PROUD STREAM
    SO TO WAIT BUT WHAT NOTES DOWN THE WIND HARK   20 MODERN SAPPHO   29
        ARE DRIVING
    OF DARK ELMS COME ROUND DROPPING DOWN THE PROUD STREAM   19 MODERN SAPPHO   V 6
    THEN TO WAIT BUT WHAT NOTES DOWN THE WIND HARK   20 MODERN SAPPHO   V 29
        ARE DRIVING
    MARTIN AND I DOWN A GREEN ALPINE STREAM   •   •   • 24 DREAM   2
    DOWN THE STATUED ALLEYS CAME   •   •   •   •   •   • 29 NEW SIRENS   102
    WHICH YOUR LOVERS WANDERD DOWN   •   •   •   •   • 30 NEW SIRENS   126
    IN SOME WINDLESS VALLEY FARTHER DOWN   •   •   •   31 NEW SIRENS   146
    IN A WINDLESS VALLEY FURTHER DOWN   •   •   •   •   31 NEW SIRENS   V 146
    SO MANY FIERY SPIRITS QUITE COOLD DOWN   •   •   • 37 WORLDS TRIUMPHS   6
    DOWN THE PALE CHEEK LONG LINES OF SHADOW SLOPE   • 43 GIPSY CHILD   37
    DOWN THY PALE CHEEK THOSE LINES OF SHADOW SLOPE   • 43 GIPSY CHILD   V 37
    ONCE ERE THY DAY GO DOWN THOU SHALT DISCERN   • • 44 GIPSY CHILD   V 65
    WEIGHS DOWN MY SOUL   •   •   •   •   •   •   •   • 50 CONSOLATION   5
    DOWN LYDIAN MOUNTAINS SO WHEN SNOWS   •   •   •   52 RESIGNATION   7
    WENT LURID DOWN OER FLOODED PLAINS   •   •   •   52 RESIGNATION   11
    THERE SPRINGS THE BROOK WILL GUIDE US DOWN   • • 54 RESIGNATION   76
    LINGERING WE FOLLOW DOWN WE GAIN   •   •   •   • 54 RESIGNATION   78
    HERE WHENCE THE EYE FIRST SEES FAR DOWN   •   • 55 RESIGNATION   92
    FROM SOME HIGH STATION HE LOOKS DOWN   •   •   • 57 RESIGNATION 164
    BUT WHERE THE FARTHER SIDE SLOPES DOWN   •   • 57 RESIGNATION 180
    BUT WHERE THE FURTHER SIDE SLOPES DOWN   •   • 57 RESIGNATION V 180
    WHAT NEWS BUT SIT DOWN FIRST AND EAT AND DRINK   • 67 SOHRAB RUSTUM   206
    COME DOWN AND HELP US RUSTUM OR WE LOSE   •   • 67 SOHRAB RUSTUM   219
    DOWN THROUGH THE MIDDLE OF A RICH MANS CORN   • 70 SOHRAB RUSTUM   294
    HIS SPEAR DOWN FROM THE SHOULDER DOWN IT CAME   • 73 SOHRAB RUSTUM   399
    HIS SPEAR DOWN FROM THE SHOULDER DOWN IT CAME   • 73 SOHRAB RUSTUM   399
    HISSD AND WENT QUIVERING DOWN INTO THE SAND   • 73 SOHRAB RUSTUM   404
    COME RUSHING DOWN TOGETHER FROM THE CLOUDS   • • 75 SOHRAB RUSTUM   473
    OR ELSE THAT THE GREAT RUSTUM WOULD COME DOWN   • 77 SOHRAB RUSTUM   531
    AND HIS HEAD SWAM AND HE SANK DOWN TO EARTH   • 81 SOHRAB RUSTUM   693
    THE DOOM WHICH AT MY BIRTH WAS WRITTEN DOWN   • 82 SOHRAB RUSTUM   709
    I KNOW IT BUT FATE TROD THOSE PROMPTINGS DOWN   • 82 SOHRAB RUSTUM   713
    THE BIG WARM TEARS ROLLD DOWN AND CAKED THE SAND   • 82 SOHRAB RUSTUM   736

DOWN   (CONTINUED)

```
FLOWD WITH THE STREAM ALL DOWN HIS COLD WHITE SIDE        86 SOHRAB RUSTUM     842
DOWN OER HIS FACE AND SATE BY HIS DEAD SON      . . . .   86 SOHRAB RUSTUM     859
LIE PRONE ENORMOUS DOWN THE MOUNTAIN SIDE    . ; . .      86 SOHRAB RUSTUM     863
AND NIGHT CAME DOWN OVER THE SOLEMN WASTE    . . . .      86 SOHRAB RUSTUM     865
AND HIS HEAD SWAM AND HE SUNK DOWN TO EARTH    . . .      81 SOHRAB RUSTUM   V 693
THE DOOM THAT AT MY BIRTH WAS WRITTEN DOWN   . . . .      82 SOHRAB RUSTUM   V 709
O VIZIER WITHOUT LYING DOWN    . . . . . . .              88 SICK KING BOKH     15
FROM YESTERDAY AND FALLING DOWN      . . . . . .          89 SICK KING BOKH     51
DOWN HAVING FEVER FOR A DRINK    . . . . . . .            90 SICK KING BOKH     76
THEIR LIPS STILL WET WHEN I CAME DOWN    . . . .          90 SICK KING BOKH     84
FROWNING GRIM DOWN THOU WICKED KING      . . . .          91 SICK KING BOKH     97
KNEELD DOWN AND CRIED NOT NEITHER RAN    . . . .          91 SICK KING BOKH    120
DOWN TO THE MARGIN OF THE ROARING SEA    . . . .          97 BALDER DEAD 1      77
THROUGH THE CLIFF-WALL AND A FRESH STREAM RUNS DOWN       97 BALDER DEAD 1      82
PAST MIDGARD FORTRESS DOWN TO EARTH AND MEN    . .        99 BALDER DEAD 1     142
AND STRAIGHT HE WILL COME DOWN TO OCEANS STRAND   . .     99 BALDER DEAD 1     159
AND CAME AGAIN DOWN TO THE ROARING WAVES   . . .        101 BALDER DEAD 1     199
BUT NIGHT CAME DOWN AND DARKEND ASGARD STREETS    .     101 BALDER DEAD 1     202
AND EACH BESPAKE HIM AS HE LAID HIM DOWN   . . .       101 BALDER DEAD 1     215
HOME AND LAY DOWN TO SLEEP IN HIS OWN HOUSE    . .      102 BALDER DEAD 1     247
AND ALL THE GODS LAY DOWN IN THEIR OWN HOMES   . .     102 BALDER DEAD 1     248
AND IN VALHALLA ODIN LAID HIM DOWN   . . . . .         102 BALDER DEAD 1     267
THEY WENT AND LAID THEM DOWN AND NANNA WENT    . .     103 BALDER DEAD 1     277
INTO AN UPPER CHAMBER AND LAY DOWN   . . . . .         103 BALDER DEAD 1     278
PAST MIDGARD FORTRESS DOWN TO EARTH THEY CAME    . .   105 BALDER DEAD 2      23
THERE ALL THE GODS IN SILENCE SATE THEM DOWN    . .    106 BALDER DEAD 2      39
BUT HERMOD THOU TAKE SLEIPNER AND RIDE DOWN    . .     106 BALDER DEAD 2      45
AND UP AND DOWN AND SIDE AND SLANT THEY ROAMD   . .    106 BALDER DEAD 2      53
MADE FAST THE WOVEN ROPES AND HALED THEM DOWN   . .    106 BALDER DEAD 2      58
WENT STRAINING THROUGH THE CRACKLING BRUSHWOOD DOWN    106 BALDER DEAD 2      62
AND HE CAME DOWN TO OCEANS NORTHERN STRAND   . .       108 BALDER DEAD 2     141
WHEREWITH THEY STAMPD THEM DOWN AND TROD THEM DEEP     109 BALDER DEAD 2     174
SHE SPAKE BUT DOWN OFF SLEIPNER HERMOD SPRANG   . .    110 BALDER DEAD 2     186
AND HERMOD CAME DOWN TOWRDS THEM FROM THE GATE   .     113 BALDER DEAD 3       3
AND HERMOD CAME AND LEAPT FROM SLEIPNER DOWN   . .     114 BALDER DEAD 3      33
AND CAME DOWN MOANING TO THE SEA FIRST SQUALLS   .     118 BALDER DEAD 3     182
AND WHILE THEY GAZED THE SUN WENT LURID DOWN   . .     119 BALDER DEAD 3     194
TO ASGARD AND SATE DOWN IN ODINS HALL    . . .         119 BALDER DEAD 3     208
THERE CAME THE GODS AND SATE THEM DOWN ON STONES   .   120 BALDER DEAD 3     223
AND FROM THE BOUGHS THE SNOWLOADS SHUFFLE DOWN   . .   122 BALDER DEAD 3     313
AND THEY GO LONG DAYS TOSSING UP AND DOWN    . .       124 BALDER DEAD 3     365
AND DOWN TO OCEAN GROPED AND CROSSD THE ICE            124 BALDER DEAD 3     376
THEIR SPEARS ARE DOWN THEIR STEEDS ARE BATHED IN FOAM  137 TRISTRAM 1        237
RIDE DOWN AND BATHE MY HOT BROW IN THE FLOOD           139 TRISTRAM 1        282
THE WIND IS DOWN BUT SHELL NOT COME TO-NIGHT           139 TRISTRAM 1        300
DOWN ON HIS WASTED FINGERS RAIND     . . . . .         140 TRISTRAM 1        318
DOWN ON HER SLENDER FINGERS RAIND    . . . . .         140 TRISTRAM 1      V 318
BEND BEND DOWN I YET HAVE MUCH TO SAY    . . .         145 TRISTRAM 2         76
HE GAZES DOWN INTO THE ROOM    . . . . . . .           148 TRISTRAM 2        161
MOVED UP AND DOWN UNDER THE GLOSSY TREES   . .         150 TRISTRAM 3         43
CAME KEEN AND CHILL DOWN ON THE HEATHER BRIGHT   .     151 TRISTRAM 3         57
IN A SLOPED SWARD DOWN TO A BRAWLING BROOK   . .       155 TRISTRAM 3        187
WHO COME AT NOON DOWN TO THE WATER HERE    . .         155 TRISTRAM 3        194
THEY SATE THEM DOWN TOGETHER AND A SLEEP   . .         155 TRISTRAM 3        213
DOWN IN THE MIDDLE OF THE HOLLOW STOOD   . .               TRISTRAM 3      V  19
MOVD UP AND DOWN UNDER THEIR GLOSSY TREES    . .           TRISTRAM 3      V  43
WHICH COME AT NOON DOWN TO THE WATER HERE    . .       155 TRISTRAM 3      V 194
AND BORE HER DOWN TO THE SEA-HALLS   . . . .           160 NECKAN             31
DOWN AND AWAY BELOW    . . . . . . . . .               161 FORSAKEN MERM       2
COME DEAR CHILDREN COME AWAY DOWN    . . . .           162 FORSAKEN MERM      23
THEN COME DOWN     . . . . . . . . . .                 162 FORSAKEN MERM      27
WHEN DOWN SWUNG THE SOUND OF A FAR-OFF BELL   .        163 FORSAKEN MERM      54
WE WENT UP THE BEACH BY THE SANDY DOWN   . .           163 FORSAKEN MERM      68
COME AWAY COME DOWN CALL NO MORE     . . . .           164 FORSAKEN MERM      84
DOWN DOWN DOWN     . . . . . . . . . .                 164 FORSAKEN MERM      85
DOWN DOWN DOWN     . . . . . . . . . .                 164 FORSAKEN MERM      85
DOWN DOWN DOWN     . . . . . . . . . .                 164 FORSAKEN MERM      85
DOWN TO THE DEPTHS OF THE SEA    . . . . .             164 FORSAKEN MERM      86
COME CHILDREN COME DOWN    . . . . . . . .             164 FORSAKEN MERM     109
AND THEN COME BACK DOWN    . . . . . . . .             165 FORSAKEN MERM     139
WHEN DOWN SWUNG THE SOUND OF THE FAR-OFF BELL    .     163 FORSAKEN MERM   V  54
THE WORLD SHALL BE THRUST DOWN AND WE UP-BORNE   .     172 IMMORTALITY         4
WHERE THE NICHED SNOW-BED SPRAYS DOWN    . .           176 PARTING            49
AND THROUGH THOSE FIELDS COMES DOWN THE AAR   .        184 TERRACE BERNE       8
AND FLITTED DOWN THE FLOWERY TRACK   . . . .           184 TERRACE BERNE      19
DOWN ON ME THY RIGHT ARM   . . . . . . .               186 STRAYED REVEL       8
CAME SWIFT DOWN TO JOIN    . . . . . . . .             186 STRAYED REVEL      35
DOWN THE DARK VALLEY I SAW     . . . . . .             187 STRAYED REVEL      42
AND SANK DOWN HERE SLEEPING    . . . . . .             187 STRAYED REVEL      51
HE TETHERS HIS BEAST DOWN AND MAKES HIS MEAL          191 STRAYED REVEL     165
MOWN THEM DOWN FAR FROM HOME     . . . . .             193 STRAYED REVEL     253
DOWN AT THE WATER-SIDE     . . . . . . . .             194 STRAYED REVEL     266
AND SUNK DOWN HERE SLEEPING    . . . . . .             187 STRAYED REVEL   V  51
OF THE NIGHT-WIND DOWN THE VAST EDGES DREAR           211 DOVER BEACH        27
AND DOWN HE LAYS HIS WEARY BONES     . . . .           213 PROGRESS POESY     12
HANGS DOWN HIS BEAUTIFUL HEAD    . . . . . .           214 NEW ROME            2
HANGS DOWN HIS HEAD AS BEFORE    . . . . . .           214 NEW ROME           18
OF THIS OR THAT DOWN-TRODDEN NAME    . . . .           219 BACCHANALIA 2      16
DOWN OER THE STATELY BRIDGE THE BREEZE   . . .         223 EPILOG LAOCOON     65
```

DOWN   (CONTINUED)
        HIS EYE MUST TRAVEL DOWN AT FULL   . . . . 225 EPILOG LAOCOON   145
        SILENT AND WHITE UNOPENING DOWN   . . . . 242 SUMMER NIGHT   4
        DOWN AT THE FAR HORIZONS RIM   . . . .   242 SUMMER NIGHT   9
        GLOOM SETTLES SLOWLY DOWN OVER THEIR BREAST   . . .   243 SUMMER NIGHT   46
        THE NIGHT COMES DOWN UPON THE GRASS   . . . . . .   249 KENSINGTON GARD   35
        AND HERE TILL SUN-DOWN SHEPHERD WILL I BE   . . . .   255 SCHOLAR-GIPSY   22
        THEIR SCENT AND RUSTLE DOWN THEIR PERFUMED SHOWERS   256 SCHOLAR-GIPSY   27
        AND THE EYE TRAVELS DOWN TO OXFORDS TOWERS   . . . .   256 SCHOLAR-GIPSY   30
        THERE WHERE DOWN CLOUDY CLIFFS THROUGH SHEETS OF FOAM   262 SCHOLAR-GIPSY   248
        ROSES THAT DOWN THE ALLEYS SHINE AFAR   . . . .   264 THYRSIS   67
        ABOVE BY ENSHAM DOWN BY SANDFORD YIELDS   . . . .   266 THYRSIS   109
        DOWN EACH GREEN BANK HATH GONE THE PLOUGHBOYS TEAM   266 THYRSIS   118
        I TAKE THE OMEN EVE LETS DOWN HER VEIL   . . . .   267 THYRSIS   161
        HIS EYE PLUNGED DOWN THE WELTERING STRIFE   . . . .   270 MEMORIAL VERSES   25
        HIS EYE PLUNGED DOWN THE SEETHING STRIFE   . . . .   270 MEMORIAL VERSES V 25
        DOWN TO THE BRIMMD MOON-CHARMED MAIN   . . . . .   279 SOUTHERN NIGHT   118
        POACH THE DEEP WAYS COMING DOWN   . . . . . .   282 HAWORTH CHURCH   59
        FAIN TO DROP DOWN AND TO DIE   . . . . . .   290 RUGBY CHAPEL   130
        WIDE GERMAN LAND GOING DOWN   . . . . . .   297 HEINES GRAVE   173
        OER THE GRACIOUS SPURS COMING DOWN   . . . .   297 HEINES GRAVE   179
        WHILE HARK FAR DOWN WITH STRANGLED SOUND   . . .   299 GRANDE CHARTR   9
        WHENCE DROPS THE PATH TO ALLIERE DOWN   . . .   313 OBERMANN MORE   23
        DOWN OVER HILL AND WOOD   . . . .   314 OBERMANN MORE   58
        AND LAID HER SCEPTRE DOWN   . . . . . .   316 OBERMANN MORE   126
        THE SYRIAN STARS LOOK DOWN   . . . . . .   318 OBERMANN MORE   176
        DOWN CAME THE STORM OER FRANCE IT PASSD   . . . .   319 OBERMANN MORE   201
        DOWN CAME THE STORM IN RUINS FELL   . . . .   319 OBERMANN MORE   205
        DOWN CAME THE STORM IN RUIN FELL   . . . .   319 OBERMANN MORE   V 205
        MY MOTHERS FAITHFUL SERVANT LAID ME DOWN   . . .   331 MEROPE   31
        SET DOWN YOUR PITCHERS MAIDENS AND FALL BACK   . .   332 MEROPE   76
        THROW HIM A PEALING WORD OF SUMMONS DOWN   . . .   349 MEROPE   576
        AND STRIKE OPPOSERS DOWN   . . . .   352 MEROPE   659
        WELL THIRST TO DRAG THE WRONGFUL RULER DOWN   . .   353 MEROPE   670
        WHERE AS LIFE EBBD HIS BEARERS LAID HIM DOWN   . .   357 MEROPE   783
        WE BOUNDED DOWN THE SWARDED SLOPE WE PLUNGED   . .   357 MEROPE   790
        NOW IN THE WOODS FAR DOWN I SAW THEM CROSS . . .   357 MEROPE   801
        PEERING TO SPY A GOAT-TRACK DOWN THE CLIFF . . .   357 MEROPE   804
        ALL THE STYMPHALIAN PLAIN ARE NOW SUCKD DOWN   . .   358 MEROPE   816
        SWEPT DOWN A CHASM RIFTED IN THE CLIFF   . . .   363 MEROPE   960
        BUT DOWN THOU FLEESTY HERE AND LEAVST OUR SCOURGE . . 367 MEROPE   1050
        WHICH STYXS AWFUL WATERS TRICKLE DOWN   . . .   368 MEROPE   1065
        FOR A GRAND CULPRIT SHORTLY COMING DOWN   . . .   373 MEROPE   1189
        AND I WHEN TO HIS RIGHTEOUS STANDARD DOWN   . . .   388 MEROPE   1502
        DOWN THOSE DISFIGURED   . . . .   393 MEROPE   1670
        AND HEW OPPOSERS DOWN   . . . .   352 MEROPE   V 659
        SWEPT DOWN A CHASM BROKEN IN THE CLIFF   . . .   363 MEROPE   V 960
        AND ON THE HIGHEST PINES BUT FARTHER DOWN   . . .   406 EMPEDOCLES I 1   11
        THE MULES MUST BE BELOW FAR DOWN I HEAR   . . .   407 EMPEDOCLES I 1   27
        BUT HIDE THEE IN THE ROCKS A GREAT WAY DOWN   . .   409 EMPEDOCLES I 1   96
        AND ON THE HIGHEST PINES BUT FURTHER DOWN   . . .   406 EMPEDOCLES I 1 V 11
        THE TRACK WINDS DOWN TO THE CLEAR STREAM   . . .   413 EMPEDOCLES I 2   36
        DOWN ITS STEEP VERDANT SIDES THE AIR   . . . . .   414 EMPEDOCLES I 2   45
        TO HAVE ADVANCED TRUE FRIENDS AND BEAT DOWN   425 EMPEDOCLES I 2   401
              BAFFLING FOES
        DOWN BY THE STREAM YES MASTER IN THE WOOD   . . . .   427 EMPEDOCLES I 2   462
        TAKE DOWN WITH THEE THE REST TO CATANA   . . . .   428 EMPEDOCLES I 2   466
        JUST SINCE DOWN AT THE STREAM HO CALLICLES . . . .   428 EMPEDOCLES I 2   486
        TO HAVE RAISD FAITHFUL FRIENDS AND CUT DOWN   425 EMPEDOCLES I 2 V 401
              SPITEFUL FOES
        WHERE ERST THE STRONG SEA-CURRENTS SUCKD THEE DOWN   430 EMPEDOCLES II   59
        GREAT QUALITIES ARE TRODDEN DOWN   . . . . .   431 EMPEDOCLES II   92
        LIVES AND THAT OTHER FAINTER SEA FAR DOWN   . . .   438 EMPEDOCLES II   311
        DOWN IN OUR MOTHER EARTHS MIRACULOUS WOMB   . . .   439 EMPEDOCLES II   340
        BUT WHERE HELICON BREAKS DOWN   . . . . . .   441 EMPEDOCLES II   423
        AND DOWN OVER THE THAMES THE DARKNESS DREW . . .   444 WESTMIN ABBEY   13
        PLUCKD FROM THE FIRE THE CHILD AND LAID HIM DOWN . . 447 WESTMIN ABBEY   95
        DOWN THE LONG AGE OF TRUTH THAT RIPENS SLOW   . . .   448 WESTMIN ABBEY   148
        AND HUMBLY LAY THEE DOWN TO DIE   . . . . .   450 GEISTS GRAVE   36
        WE STRIVE TO CARRY DOWN THY NAME   . . . . .   451 GEISTS GRAVE   63
        DOWN SHE SANK AMID HER FUR   . . . .   453 POOR MATTHIAS   36
        DRIVN INSHORE WE FOLLOW DOWN   . . . . . .   457 POOR MATTHIAS   181
        DOWN THE UNCOMPANIOND WAY   . . . . . .   458 POOR MATTHIAS   209
        SIX YEARS AGO I BROUGHT HIM DOWN   . . . . .   459 KAISER DEAD   13
        SLOPE STATELY DOWN AND MELT INTO THE PLAIN . . . .   473 CROMWELL   38
        GAZD SADLY DOWN ON HIS UNRESTFUL LOT   . . . . .   474 CROMWELL   86
        UNTIL ANOTHER ROSE AND SMOTE HIM DOWN   . . .   476 CROMWELL   144
        FAR DOWN THE TORRENT CLEAVES ITS WAY   . . . . .   479 HAYSWATER BOAT   10
        THE GRATING SHINGLE STRAGGLED DOWN   . . . . .   480 HAYSWATER BOAT   30
        OR DOT THE SLOPES TO VEVEY DOWN   . . . . .   483 ROME-SICKNESS   12
        HATH FRAYD AND SLIDDEN DOWN AND WE NO MORE . . . .   EVERLASTING SUB   2
        HATH FRAYD AND SLIDDEN DOWN AND THEY NO MORE   . .   EVERLASTING SUB V 2

DOWNCAST
        WHEN THAT WITH DOWNCAST LOOKS I HITHER CAME   . .   125 BALDER DEAD 3   409
        POOR MAX WITH DOWNCAST REVERENT HEAD . . . . . .   460 KAISER DEAD   67

DOWNS
        THE SIGNAL-ELM THAT LOOKS ON ILSLEY DOWNS   . . . .   263 THYRSIS   14

DOWNWARD
        THAT HE SITS BENDING DOWNWARD   . . . .   188 STRAYED REVEL   82

DOZED
    YOU DOZED EYELIDS SOUGHT AGAIN • • • • • • • • 31 NEW SIRENS 148

DOZING
    CAN YOUR EYES WHILE FOOLS ARE DOZING • • • • • • 33 NEW SIRENS 209

DRAG
    WELL THIRST TO DRAG THE WRONGFUL RULER DOWN • • 353 MEROPE 670
    ON NATIVE GROUND THAN DRAG THE TEDIOUS HOURS • • 383 MEROPE 1380

DRAGGD
    AND THE SOMBRE DAY DRAGGD ON • • • • • • • 30 NEW SIRENS 116
    WHICH HE THE SEED OF HERACLES DRAGGD ON • • • • 356 MEROPE 770

DRAGGING
    DRAGGING THEIR NETS THROUGH THE ROUGH WAVES AFAR • • 151 TRISTRAM 3 80
    MONTH AFTER MONTH THROUGH THE SLOW-DRAGGING YEAR • • 347 MEROPE V

DRAGON
    FROM THE DRAGON-WARDERD FOUNTAINS • • • • • • • 27 NEW SIRENS 33

DRAGS
    DRAGS TO HIS NURSE HIS BROKEN TOY • • • • • • KENSINGTON GARD V 10
    FATE SEALS MY LIPS AND DRAGS TO RUIN THEE • • • • 397 MEROPE 1779

DRAIND
    DRAIND ALL THE LIFE MY FULL HEART HAD TO SPILL • • 36 VOICE V 39
    AND DRAIND HIS MIGHTY BOWL • • • • • • • • 47 WORLD QUIETIST 32
    MOST SULTRY DRAIND THE PITCHER THERE • • • • • • 90 SICK KING BOKH 82

DRANK
    WAILING NO MORE IN SILENCE ATE AND DRANK • • • • 97 BALDER DEAD 1 70
    AND FROM THEIR HORNS WITH SILVER RIMMD DRANK MEAD • 119 BALDER DEAD 3 211
    I DRANK GODDESS • • • • • • • • • • • • 187 STRAYED REVEL 50
    TIRESIAS DRANK AND DIED • • • • • • • • • • 229 YOUTH OF NATURE 45
    HE MADE A FEAST DRANK FIERCE AND FAST • • • • 316 OBERMANN MORE 101

DRAUGHT
    WITH TRISTRAM THAT SPICED MAGIC DRAUGHT • • • • 132 TRISTRAM 1 64
    DOES THE LOVE-DRAUGHT WORK NO MORE • • • • • • 133 TRISTRAM 1 80
    CHILD TIS NO TRUE DRAUGHT THIS TIS POISOND WINE • • 133 TRISTRAM 1 103
    TO SEEK A DRAUGHT TO SLAKE THY THIRST • • • • 316 OBERMANN MORE 119

DRAUGHTS
    DRINKING DEEP DRAUGHTS OF JOY YE DWELL SERENE • • 10 MYCERINUS 48
    THE DEEP DRAUGHTS OF DEATH IN BEARING ME • • • • 145 TRISTRAM 2 84
    THE CUP ABOUT WHOSE DRAUGHTS BEGUILE • • • • • 431 EMPEDOCLES II 85

DRAVE
    FORTH WENDED THEY AND DRAVE THEIR STEEDS BEFORE • • 106 BALDER DEAD 2 50
    AND DRAVE THEM HOMEWARD AND THE SNORTING STEEDS • • 106 BALDER DEAD 2 61

DRAW
    SHALL DRAW TO SWELL THAT SHOULDERING HERD • • • • 48 HORATIAN ECHO 9
    THIS WORLD IN WHICH WE DRAW OUR BREATH • • • • 59 RESIGNATION 229
    DRAW HOMEWARD TO THE GENERAL LIFE • • • • • • 59 RESIGNATION 252
    DRAW HOMEWARDS TO THE GENERAL LIFE • • • • • • 59 RESIGNATION V 252
    AND WITH THESE SLAUGHTEROUS HANDS DRAW SWORD NO MORE 68 SOHRAB RUSTUM 241
    AND HE DESIRED TO DRAW FORTH THE STEEL • • • • 80 SOHRAB RUSTUM 651
    TO DRAW IT AND FOR EVER LET LIFE OUT • • • • • 82 SOHRAB RUSTUM 705
    WARNING THE GODS THAT FOES DRAW NIGH TO HEAVEN • • 105 BALDER DEAD 2 7
    AND BOUND THE LOGS BEHIND THEIR STEEDS TO DRAW • • 106 BALDER DEAD 2 60
    LIKE MEN WHO LIVE AND DRAW THE VITAL AIR • • • 108 BALDER DEAD 2 108
    WHEN I DRAW NIGH AND THE WAN TRIBES OF DEAD • • 126 BALDER DEAD 3 464
    OF PEBBLES WHICH THE WAVES DRAW BACK AND FLING • • 211 DOVER BEACH 10
    SOME AS PRISONERS DRAW BREATH • • • • • • • • 216 LORDS MESSENGER 15
    I SEE HER VEIL DRAW SOFT ACROSS THE DAY • • • • 266 THYRSIS 133
    HOW WITHOUT CHARM WILT THOU DRAW • • • • • • 295 HEINES GRAVE 106
    DRAW DRAW NEAR TO THE TOMB • • • • • • • • 342 MEROPE 385
    DRAW DRAW NEAR TO THE TOMB • • • • • • • • 342 MEROPE 385
    TO DRAW THE COVERTS ON CYLLENES SIDE • • • • • 356 MEROPE 750
    MIGHT FROM THE PEOPLE DRAW IF RIGHTLY USED • • • • 382 MEROPE 1336

DRAWBRIDGE
    FROM THE CASTLE PAST THE DRAWBRIDGE • • • • • • 13 CHURCH BROU 1 7
    TO THE CASTLE PAST THE DRAWBRIDGE • • • • • • 13 CHURCH BROU 1 31
    AND RIDE ACROSS THE DRAWBRIDGE WITH THY HOUNDS • • 18 CHURCH BROU 3 10
    THE DRAWBRIDGE AND THE MOAT APPEAR • • • • • • 148 TRISTRAM 2 171

DRAWING
    PARIS DRAWING-ROOMS AND LAMPS • • • • • • • • 296 HEINES GRAVE 141

DRAWN
    FALLS HEAVILY AWAY WITH LONG-DRAWN ROAR • • • • 40 HUMAN LIFE 21
    THE ARMIES ARE DRAWN OUT AND STAND AT GAZE • • • • 67 SOHRAB RUSTUM 210
    SHOULDERING THY HAMMER IN THY CHARIOT DRAWN • • • 115 BALDER DEAD 3 72
    DRAWN IN HIS CAR BESIDE ME AND MY SONS • • • • 120 BALDER DEAD 3 240
    AND HAVE DRAWN UPWARD TO THIS VERGE OF HELL • • 126 BALDER DEAD 3 439
    AND HAVE DRAWN UPWARDS TO THIS VERGE OF HELL • • 126 BALDER DEAD 3 V 439

DRAWN   (CONTINUED)

```
        HIS ROBE DRAWN OVER            . . . . . . . . . .   190 STRAYED REVEL      139
        WITH MUSIC TO HAVE DRAWN THE STARS FROM HEAVEN   . .   409 EMPEDOCLES I 1     81
```

DRAWS

```
        IT DRAWS THEM ON THEY CANNOT SAVE       . . . . . .   226 EPILOG LAOCOON     165
        AS IT DRAWS TO THE OCEAN MAY STRIKE     . . . . . .   254 FUTURE             81
        FRESH FROM THEIR FATHER DRAWS NEAR      . . . . . .   346 MEROPE            498
        THAT MURDER DRAWS THIS BREACH THAT THOU WOULDST CLOSE  335 MEROPE        V 187
        AND STILL I KNOW NOT HOW HE DRAWS ME TO HIM   . .   408 EMPEDOCLES I 1     58
        DRAWS IN THE ENAMOURD GAZER TO ITS SHINING BREAST   424 EMPEDOCLES I 2    356
```

DREAD

```
        FELL THIS DREAD VOICE FROM LIPS THAT CANNOT LIE   . .     8 MYCERINUS          5
        BEGIN THOU ART MORE VAST MORE DREAD THAN I   . . . .    72 SOHRAB RUSTUM    385
        FOR DREAD FOR LIKE A WHIRLWIND ODIN CAME     . . . .   102 BALDER DEAD 1    264
        AND SHE WHOSE CENSURE THOU DOST DREAD        . . . .   241 MORALITY          19
        DREAD THOUGH HIS ACTS TO WHOSE HAND          . . . .   361 MEROPE           906
        THAT STERN WORD MURDER HAD TOO DREAD A SOUND   . .    365 MEROPE           992
        AT THE DREAD ALTAR OF HER HUSBANDS TOMB      . . . .   385 MEROPE          1414
        TO MURDERS DREAD ARENA WHERE I SAW   . . . . . .    387 MEROPE          1462
        WHICH DOOMS DREAD ENDS TO DREADFUL DEEDS     . . . .   398 MEROPE          1808
        AND CLASP CONJECTURED JOYS OR DREAD CONJECTURED WOES   425 EMPEDOCLES I 2  V 406
        THE WHILE THERE SLEEPS WITHIN THY PRECINCTS DREAD   464 ALARIC AT ROME     51
        THRILLD WITH A DREAD NO SLUMBER COULD CONTROL   . .   477 CROMWELL         200
```

DREADED

```
        SHE WILL CRY IS THIS THE FOE I DREADED       . . . .   144 TRISTRAM 2         65
        SHE WILL SAY IS THIS THE FORM I DREADED      . . . .   144 TRISTRAM 2      V 65
```

DREADFUL

```
        WHO STOOD AT HAND UTTERD A DREADFUL CRY      . . . .    76 SOHRAB RUSTUM    502
        THEN RUSTUM RAISED HIS HEAD HIS DREADFUL EYES   . .    76 SOHRAB RUSTUM    514
        A LIFE OF BLOOD INDEED THOU DREADFUL MAN     . . . .    85 SOHRAB RUSTUM    828
        MOTHER A DREADFUL WAY IS THIS THOU SHOWST    . . . .   100 BALDER DEAD 1    185
        ALCMENAS DREADFUL SON       . . . . . . . . . .   192 STRAYED REVEL     231
        OF A DREADFUL PRESENCE OF FEAR   . . . . . . . .   346 MEROPE           494
        WHICH DOOMS DREAD ENDS TO DREADFUL DEEDS     . . . .   398 MEROPE          1808
        SO LOOKD HE IN THAT DREADFUL DAY OF DEATH    . . . .   404 MEROPE          1977
```

DREADING

```
        DREADING THINE OVER-WROUGHT MOOD     . . . . . .   371 MEROPE          1131
```

DREAM

```
        IT CHANCED I KNOW NOT HOW MY DREAM WAS FLED     . .       EMERSONS ESSAYS V  8
        SEEING THIS VALE THIS EARTH WHEREON WE DREAM    . .     7 REP FRIEND CONT    5
        OF ONE SHORT JOY ONE LUST ONE PLEASANT DREAM    . .    10 MYCERINUS         50
        WHERE IN ONE DREAM THE FEVERISH TIME OF YOUTH   . .    11 MYCERINUS         89
        WHO WRESTLES WITH HIS DREAM AS SOME PALE SHAPE  . .    11 MYCERINUS        103
        WAS IT A DREAM WE SAILD I THOUGHT WE SAILD   . . . .    24 DREAM              1
        O LET THE FALSE DREAM FLY     . . . . . . . .    39 STAGIRIUS         49
        NO EXILES DREAM WAS EVER HALF SO SAD     . . . .    42 GIPSY CHILD       27
        STAND MUTE SELF-CENTRED STERN AND DREAM NO MORE   . .    42 GIPSY CHILD       32
        ONLY BY THIS THOU CANST THE COLOURD DREAM    . . . .    45 IN UTRUMQUE PAR   13
        CHIEF DREAMER OWN THY DREAM       . . . . . . .    46 IN UTRUMQUE PAR   37
        AH SWEET ANGELS LET HIM DREAM     . . . . . . .   133 TRISTRAM 1       105
        LET A DREAM LIKE THIS RESTORE     . . . . . . .   135 TRISTRAM 1       159
        AH SWEET SAINTS HIS DREAM DOTH MOVE     . . . .   135 TRISTRAM 1       170
        MINGLE WITH HIS HURRYING DREAM    . . . . . . .   136 TRISTRAM 1       183
        ALL WHICH WE DID BEFORE SHADOW AND DREAM     . . . .   153 TRISTRAM 3       132
        ALL THAT WE DID BEFORE SHADOW AND DREAM      . . . .   153 TRISTRAM 3    V 132
        COME NOW AND LET ME DREAM IT TRUTH      . . . .   209 LONGING           10
        WE BUT DREAM WE HAVE OUR WISHD-FOR POWERS   . . . .   210 SELF-DECEPTION    25
        SUNK IN THY DREAM       . . . . . . . . . . .   220 BACCHANALIA 2     50
        LOVELY AND SOFT AS A DREAM    . . . . . . . .   228 YOUTH OF NATURE    3
        FABLE AND DREAM       . . . . . . . . . . .   252 FUTURE            20
        AND LEANING BACKWARD IN A PENSIVE DREAM      . . . .   257 SCHOLAR-GIPSY     77
        BUT WHAT I DREAM TWO HUNDRED YEARS ARE FLOWN    . .   259 SCHOLAR-GIPSY    131
        AND WISH THE LONG UNHAPPY DREAM WOULD END    . . . .   260 SCHOLAR-GIPSY    192
        AND LEANING BACKWARDS IN A PENSIVE DREAM     . . . .   257 SCHOLAR-GIPSY  V 77
        OF FITFUL DREAM AND FEVERISH POWER      . . . .   270 MEMORIAL VERSES   24
        SEEMD BUT A DREAM OF THE HEART    . . . . . . .   290 RUGBY CHAPEL     151
        BUT A DEAD TIMES EXPLODED DREAM   . . . . . . .   302 GRANDE CHARTR     98
        THE DREAM WHICH FILLD OUR BRAIN   . . . . . . .   323 OBERMANN MORE  V 314
        WHAT THOU I DREAM MAYST THOU DREAM EVER SO   . . . .   377 MEROPE          1219
        WHAT THOU I DREAM MAYST THOU DREAM EVER SO   . . . .   377 MEROPE          1219
        MELT LIKE A PASSING SMOKE A NIGHTLY DREAM    . . . .   402 MEROPE          1945
        AND WHILE WE DREAM ON THIS    . . . . . . . .   425 EMPEDOCLES I 2   404
        BECAUSE THOU MUST NOT DREAM THOU NEEDST NOT      426 EMPEDOCLES I 2   426
            THEN DESPAIR
        AND WHILE WE DREAM OF THIS    . . . . . . . .   425 EMPEDOCLES I 2 V 404
        AMBITIONS BOLDEST DREAM MIGHT SOBER AND APPAL   . .   463 ALARIC AT ROME    42
        OH IT IS BITTER THAT EACH FAIREST DREAM     . . . .   470 ALARIC AT ROME   211
        OF SLEEP UNSHADOWD BY A DREAM OF WOE    . . . .   474 CROMWELL         103
        THEN ALL HIS DREAM WAS TROUBLED AND HIS SOUL    . .   477 CROMWELL         199
        THERE HE FEELS IT WAS NO DREAM DECEIVING     . . . .   483 THEKLAS ANSWER    17
```

DREAMD

```
        FOR I DREAMD THEY WORE YOUR FORMS    . . . . . .    26 NEW SIRENS        10
        HAVE DREAMD TWO HUMAN HEARTS MIGHT BLEND     . . . .   181 ISOLATION MARG    38
        AH TIS NOT WHAT IN YOUTH WE DREAMD TWOULD BE    . .   212 GROWING OLD       12
```

DREAMD   (CONTINUED)
    HAVE DREAMD THAT I LIVED BUT FOR THEM   • • • •   232 YOUTH OF NATURE   131
    HAVE DREAMD THAT MY SECRET WAS THEIRS   • • • •   232 YOUTH OF NATURE V 130
    HOW OFTEN HAVE I DREAMD OF THEE LIKE THIS • • • •   372 MEROPE   1158

DREAMER
    CHIEF DREAMER OWN THY DREAM   • • • • • • •   46 IN UTRUMQUE PAR   37
    AND THE GENEROUS DREAMER INVESTS   • • • • • •   233 YOUTH OF MAN   33

DREAMERS
    SOME DREAMERS WHO FAR OFF A SUMMERS DAY   • • • •   42 GIPSY CHILD   V 22
    OH WHAT A SPASM SHAKES THE DREAMERS HEART • • • •   46 IN UTRUMQUE PAR   41

DREAMING
    ROSES FOR THAT DREAMING BROW   • • • • • • •   32 NEW SIRENS   174
    ROUND THY STILL DREAMING BROTHER-WORLD OUTSPREAD • • • 45 IN UTRUMQUE PAR   31
    DREAMING WOODS   • • • • • • • • • •   194 STRAYED REVEL   285
    DREAMING OF NOUGHT BEYOND THEIR PRISON-WALL • •   243 SUMMER NIGHT   41
    AND THAT SWEET CITY WITH HER DREAMING SPIRES • •   263 THYRSIS   19
    AND GROUPS UNDER THE DREAMING GARDEN-TREES • • • •   264 THYRSIS   69
    DARE O FRIEND BE WANDERING DARE BE DREAMING • •   483 THEKLAS ANSWER   23

DREAMS
    VAIN DREAMS WHICH QUENCH OUR PLEASURES THEN DEPART   9 MYCERINUS   27
    VAIN DREAMS THAT QUENCH OUR PLEASURES THEN DEPART   9 MYCERINUS   V 27
    AH NO THE BLISS YOUTH DREAMS IS ONE   • • • •   22 YOUTH AND CALM   16
    YOUTH DREAMS A BLISS ON THIS SIDE DEATH   • • • •   22 YOUTH AND CALM   19
    IT DREAMS A REST IF NOT MORE DEEP   • • • •   22 YOUTH AND CALM   20
    YOUTH DREAMS A JOY ON THIS SIDE DEATH   • • • •   22 YOUTH AND CALM   V 19
    DREAMS DAWN AND FLY FRIENDS SMILE AND DIE • • • •   44 QUESTION   8
    WE COUNT THE HOURS THESE DREAMS OF OURS   • • • •   44 QUESTION   15
    PLIES SOME LIGHT FEMALE TASK NOR DREAMS OF US • •   80 SOHRAB RUSTUM   647
    OF US SHE DREAMS NOT NOR OF WOUNDS NOR WAR • • • •   80 SOHRAB RUSTUM   648
    HAPLY IN HIS DREAMS THE WIND   • • • • • •   136 TRISTRAM 1   190
    FAR HENCE HER DREAMS ARE FAIR SMOOTH IS HER BROW •   139 TRISTRAM 1   302
    I HAVE HAD DREAMS I HAVE HAD DREAMS MY PAGE • •   140 TRISTRAM 1   304
    I HAVE HAD DREAMS I HAVE HAD DREAMS MY PAGE • •   140 TRISTRAM 1   304
    BUT YOU SEE FAIRER IN YOUR DREAMS   • • • •   141 TRISTRAM 1   371
    FAR HENCE HER DREAMS ARE FAIR HER SLEEP IS STILL • •   139 TRISTRAM 1   V 302
    COME TO ME IN MY DREAMS AND THEN   • • • • •   208 LONGING   1
    COME TO ME IN MY DREAMS AND THEN   • • • • •   209 LONGING   13
    TO LIE BEFORE US LIKE A LAND OF DREAMS   • •   211 DOVER BEACH   31
    SEEST OUR DREAMS ONE BY ONE   • • • • • •   232 YOUTH OF MAN   7
    AWAY THE DREAMS THAT BUT DECEIVE   • • • •   310 OBERMANN   129
    IN DREAMS I SAW THE FUTURE SHINE   • • • •   321 OBERMANN MORE   259
    O THOU LONG-LOST LONG SEEN IN DREAMS ALONE • •   381 MEROPE   1288
    HE ERRS BECAUSE HE DREAMS   • • • • • •   418 EMPEDOCLES I 2   175
    ARE DREAMS THIS ONLY IS   • • • • • • •   422 EMPEDOCLES I 2   305
    MAKE US NOT FLY TO DREAMS BUT MODERATE DESIRE • •   425 EMPEDOCLES I 2   386
    AND HIS YOUNG DREAMS OF CONQUEST HOW TO-DAY • •   468 ALARIC AT ROME   171
    NEW DREAMS OF WIDE DOMINION MIGHTIER HIGHER • •   469 ALARIC AT ROME   175
    SAY NOT SUCH DREAMS ARE IDLE FOR THE MAN • • •   473 CROMWELL   45
    LIKE DREAMS BETWEEN TWO SORROWS WENT AND CAME • •   474 CROMWELL   96
    OF TOILSOME MANHOOD IN THE DREAMS OF YOUTH • • •   474 CROMWELL   98
    DREAMS THAT WERE SWEET AT EVE AT MORN WERE SIN • •   475 CROMWELL   121
    NO LIFE OF DREAMS NO HOME BEYOND THE DEEP • • •   475 CROMWELL   124
    THE CREDULOUS COMPLEXION OF THY DREAMS   • • • •   RUDE ORATOR   12

DREAMY
    TILL FANCIFUL REGRET AND DREAMY WOE • • • • • •   467 ALARIC AT ROME   125

DREAR
    TO THE DREAR EUXINE SO PRAY ALL   • • • • • •   52 RESIGNATION   13
    AT THE DREAR ICE BEYOND THE GIANTS HOME   • • • •   108 BALDER DEAD 2   142
    CHILL BLOWS THE WIND THE PLEASAUNCE-WALKS ARE DREAR   135 TRISTRAM 1   161
    SO SHE SAID AND DIED IN THE DREAR FOREST • • •   145 TRISTRAM 2   87
    WHY STOPS SHE BY THIS EMPTY PLAY-HOUSE DREAR • •   167 RACHEL 1   11
    THE WORLD TO THEM WAS STERN AND DREAR   • • •   203 EUPHROSYNE   9
    OF THE NIGHT-WIND DOWN THE VAST EDGES DREAR • •   211 DOVER BEACH   27
    HIGH IN THE VALLEY WET AND DREAR   • • • • •   299 GRANDE CHARTR   17
    THY REALM OF THOUGHT IS DREAR AND COLD   • • • •   309 OBERMANN   107

DREARILY
    SO DREARILY AND DOUBTFULLY   • • • • • • • •   36 VOICE   26

DREARY
    COME YOU SAY THE HOURS WERE DREARY   • • • • •   28 NEW SIRENS   65
    WHEN A DREARY DAWN IS WADING   • • • • • •   33 NEW SIRENS   211
    COME YOU SAY THE HOURS ARE DREARY   • • • • •   28 NEW SIRENS   V 65
    WHEN A DREARY LIGHT IS WADING   • • • • • •   33 NEW SIRENS   V 211
    YET DREARY NANNA IS THE LIFE THEY LEAD   • • • •   104 BALDER DEAD 1   314
    OBLIVIONS DREARY FOUNTAIN WHERE ART THOU • • •   462 ALARIC AT ROME   2

DRENCHD
    PALE DEW-DRENCHD HALF-SHUT ROSES GLEAM   • • • •   57 RESIGNATION   179
    ALL DRENCHD IN DEW • • • • • • • • • •   186 STRAYED REVEL   34
    DARK BLUEBELLS DRENCHD WITH DEWS OF SUMMER EVES • •   257 SCHOLAR-GIPSY   88

DRESS
    A DARK GREEN FOREST-DRESS   • • • • • • • •   131 TRISTRAM 1   16

DRESS   (CONTINUED)
    I KNOW HIM BY HIS FOREST-DRESS • • • • • • •   131 TRISTRAM 1   21
    I KNOW HER BY HER RICH SILK DRESS • • • • • •   132 TRISTRAM 1   52
    SO SLIGHT A FORM IN SO RICH A DRESS • • • • •   131 TRISTRAM 1   V
    TO REST UNGLOVED ON HER GREEN RIDING-DRESS • • • •   154 TRISTRAM 3   175
    CLEAR AS THE PAINTERS ART CAN DRESS • • • • • •   225 EPILOG LAOCOON   134

DRESSD
    THE FLOWER-DRESSD VICTIM STOOD A MILK-WHITE BULL • • •   401 MEROPE   1910

DREST
    FROM THOSE STILL DEEPS IN FORM AND COLOUR DREST • •   45 IN UTRUMQUE PAR   4

DREW
    DREW A WARM SCENT ABROAD BEHIND THE PINES • • • •   25 DREAM   6
    BUT COURTEOUSLY DREW BACK AND SPOKE AND SAID • •   74 SOHRAB RUSTUM   426
    AND HE TOO DREW HIS SWORD AT ONCE THEY RUSHD • •   75 SOHRAB RUSTUM   471
    THE SPEAR AND DREW IT FROM HIS SIDE AND EASED • •   85 SOHRAB RUSTUM   839
    AND THE GREAT RUSTUM DREW HIS HORSEMANS CLOAK • •   86 SOHRAB RUSTUM   858
    BUT HE LOOKD ON AND SMILED NOR DREW HIS SWORD • •   74 SOHRAB RUSTUM V 425
    DREW CLOSE TOGETHER AND CONFERRD • • • • • •   91 SICK KING BOKH   106
    TO HER DREW HODER NEAR AND SPAKE AND SAID • • •   98 BALDER DEAD 1   94
    THEN BALDERS SPIRIT THROUGH THE GLOOM DREW NEAR • •   103 BALDER DEAD 1   282
    THEN HE DISMOUNTED AND DREW TIGHT THE GIRTHS • •   109 BALDER DEAD 2   146
    AND HE DREW NEAR AND HEARD NO LIVING VOICE • • •   113 BALDER DEAD 2   305
    DREW ISEULT FORTH HER CHILDREN WERE AT PLAY • •   TRISTRAM 3 V 5
    THE KNIGHTS DREW SWORD THE LADIES SCREAMD • • •   159 NECKAN   27
    SHUDDERING THEY DREW HER GARMENTS OFF AND FOUND • •   166 AUSTERITY POET   10
    SHE HER GOOD SHEPHERDS HASTY IMAGE DREW • • •   172 GOOD SHEPHERD   13
    THE CAUSE WHICH DREW HIM TO HIS DEED • • • • •   352 MEROPE   650
    FAR IN THE LIQUID LAKE WE SATE AND DREW • • •   356 MEROPE   752
    AT LAST THE CRY DREW TO THE WATERS EDGE • • •   357 MEROPE   806
    AS DREW OF OLD THE PEOPLE AFTER HIM • • • • •   408 EMPEDOCLES I 1   63
    AND DOWN OVER THE THAMES THE DARKNESS DREW • • •   444 WESTMIN ABBEY   13
    THEN FROM THOSE WHITENING LIPS AS DEATH DREW NEAR   478 CROMWELL   213

DRIED
    WONDER NOT DEAD AND THIRST NOT DRIED • • • • • •   59 RESIGNATION   226
    SPIRITS DRIED UP AND CLOSELY FURLD • • • • •   272 MEMORIAL VERSES   56
    SWEET CHESTNUTS BARLEY-CAKES AND BOARS-FLESH DRIED   356 MEROPE   754
    RIVERS ARE DRIED WINDS STAYD • • • • • • • •   416 EMPEDOCLES I 2   125
    AND DRIED ITS SELF-SUFFICING FOUNT OF JOY • • • •   429 EMPEDOCLES II   22
    WHOSE SPRING OF HOPE IS DRIED WHOSE SPIRIT HAS FAILD   438 EMPEDOCLES II   317

DRIES
    LIFE DRIES UP THE HEART DISSEMBLES • • • • • •   29 NEW SIRENS   83

DRIFT
    HALT THROUGH THE CLOUD-DRIFT SOMETHING SHINES • •   299 GRANDE CHARTR   16

DRIFTED
    SO FEATLY STREWN WITH DRIFTED SAND • • • • • •   480 HAYSWATER BOAT   22
    THE BOAT HATH DRIFTED IN THE BAY • • • • • • •   480 HAYSWATER BOAT   37

DRIFTING
    DRIFTING KNIFE IN HAND • • • • • • • • •   190 STRAYED REVEL   152
    DRIFTING DRIFTING ROUND HIM • • • • • • • •   190 STRAYED REVEL   158
    DRIFTING DRIFTING ROUND HIM • • • • • • • •   190 STRAYED REVEL   158

DRIFTS
    AS HE DRIFTS TO FATIGUE DISCONTENT AND DEJECTION • •   20 MODERN SAPPHO   19
    WITH CHERRIES SERVD IN DRIFTS OF SNOW • • • •   94 SICK KING BOKH   197
    STREWN WITH ITS DANK YELLOW DRIFTS • • • • • •   286 RUGBY CHAPEL   3

DRIFTWOOD
    LIKE DRIFTWOOD SPARS WHICH MEET AND PASS • • • •   185 TERRACE BERNE   45

DRINK
    LIGHT MEN AND ON LIGHT STEEDS WHO ONLY DRINK • •   64 SOHRAB RUSTUM   124
    WHAT NEWS BUT SIT DOWN FIRST AND EAT AND DRINK • •   67 SOHRAB RUSTUM   206
    NOT NOW A TIME WILL COME TO EAT AND DRINK • • •   67 SOHRAB RUSTUM   208
    UNSEEN AND HAVING DRINK TO SPARE • • • • •   90 SICK KING BOKH   71
    DOWN HAVING FEVER FOR A DRINK • • • • •   90 SICK KING BOKH   76
    AND I HAVE MEAT AND DRINK AT WILL • • • •   94 SICK KING BOKH   213
    AND ALL THESE GLADLY WHILE WE DRINK WE HEAR • •   117 BALDER DEAD 3   135
    MIGHT DRINK IT ON THEIR MARRIAGE-DAY • • • •   135 TRISTRAM 1   139
    LET THEM DRINK IT LET THEIR HANDS • • • • •   135 TRISTRAM 1   147
    DRINK THEN I CHIDE THEE NOT • • • • • •   187 STRAYED REVEL   59
    DRINK DRINK AGAIN • • • • • • • • • •   187 STRAYED REVEL   62
    DRINK DRINK AGAIN • • • • • • • • • •   187 STRAYED REVEL   62
    DRINK OF THE FEELING OF QUIET AGAIN • • • • •   253 FUTURE   68
    BUT MID THEIR DRINK AND CLATTER HE WOULD FLY • •   257 SCHOLAR-GIPSY   61
    HERE AND THERE EAT AND DRINK • • • • • • •   288 RUGBY CHAPEL   61

DRINKING
    DRINKING DEEP DRAUGHTS OF JOY YE DWELL SERENE • •   10 MYCERINUS   48

DRINKS
    DRINKS UP DELIGHTED ECSTASY • • • • • • • •   227 EPILOG LAOCOON   194
    AND COOL DRINKS AND AN EASED • • • • • • • •   293 HEINES GRAVE   19

DRINKS   (CONTINUED)
        PEISIANAX THOU KNOWST DRINKS LATE AND THEN . . . .   407 EMPEDOCLES I 1   39

DRINKST
        AND DRINKST UNTROUBLED SLUMBER TO SLEEP OFF   . .   373 MEROPE   1180

DRIPPING
        NEVER THE BLACK AND DRIPPING PRECIPICES   . . . .   78 SOHRAB RUSTUM   571
        AFTER AN HOUR A DRIPPING SOUND IS HEARD   . . . .   122 BALDER DEAD 3   310
        SO THROUGH THE WORLD WAS HEARD A DRIPPING NOISE . . 122 BALDER DEAD 3   317
        RAISED ARE THE DRIPPING OARS   . . . .   228 YOUTH OF NATURE   1
        UNDER THE DRIPPING BLACK TARTAREAN CLIFF   . . . .   368 MEROPE   1064

DRIVE
        AY WE WOULD EACH FAIN DRIVE   . . . .   40 HUMAN LIFE   13
        AND CLIP HIS BORDERS SHORT AND DRIVE HIS HERDS . . .   68 SOHRAB RUSTUM   234
        AND CLIP HIS BORDERS ROUND AND DRIVE HIS HERDS . . .   68 SOHRAB RUSTUM   V 234
        BUT AS WHEN COWHERDS IN OCTOBER DRIVE   . . . .   107 BALDER DEAD 2   91
        THERE THE TORRENTS DRIVE UPWARD   . . . . . .   175 PARTING   29
        OF THE GRIM LAPITHAE AND THESEUS DRIVE   . . . .   192 STRAYED REVEL   228
        DRIVE CRASHING THROUGH THEIR BONES THEY FEEL . . .   192 STRAYED REVEL   229
        THE AUTUMN STORM—WINDS DRIVE THE RACK   . . . .   306 OBERMANN   3
        A FOOL CAN DRIVE IT AND A FLY MAY SCARE   . . . .   382 MEROPE   1344
        TILL THE ROUGH COW—HERDS DRIVE THEM PAST   . . . .   413 EMPEDOCLES I 2   40
        AND HURRY WHERE THEY DRIVE   . . . .   415 EMPEDOCLES I 2   95

DRIVEN
        AS THE DRIVEN SNOW ARE WHITE   . . . .   131 TRISTRAM 1   31
        A FRENZIED WANDERER A GOD—DRIVEN MAN . . . . . .   385 MEROPE   1424

DRIVES
        CATCHES THEM AND DRIVES OUT AGAIN TO SEA   . . . .   124 BALDER DEAD 3   364
        WHERE THIS PLAGUE DRIVES THEM AND HAVE LITTLE EASE   153 TRISTRAM 3   141
        THE WIND IS UP AND DRIVES THE RAIN   . . . . . .   299 GRANDE CHARTR   8
        ONE DRIVES HIM TO THE WORLD WITHOUT   . . . . .   309 OBERMANN   95
        I GO FATE DRIVES ME BUT I LEAVE   . . . . . .   310 OBERMANN   131
        DRIVES THE AXE TO ITS GOAL   . . . .   400 MEROPE   1864
        LOOKS ONCE AND DRIVES ELSEWHERE AND LEAVES   415 EMPEDOCLES I 2   86
            ITS LAST EMPLOY
        THROUGH WHOSE HEART ETNA DRIVES HER ROOTS OF STONE   430 EMPEDOCLES II   43

DRIVING
        SO TO WAIT BUT WHAT NOTES DOWN THE WIND HARK   20 MODERN SAPPHO   29
            ARE DRIVING
        THEN TO WAIT BUT WHAT NOTES DOWN THE WIND HARK   20 MODERN SAPPHO   V 29
            ARE DRIVING
        ONLY A DRIVING WRECK   . . . .   244 SUMMER NIGHT   64
        THOUGH DRIVING ON WITH IT ETERNALLY   . . . . . .   246 BURIED LIFE   44
        STORMY THROUGH DRIVING MIST   . . . .   286 HAWORTH CHURCH   131

DRIVN
        DRIVN INSHORE WE FOLLOW DOWN   . . . .   457 POOR MATTHIAS   181

DRIZZLED
        SPRAY—DRIZZLED LONELY   . . . .   392 MEROPE   1647

DRIZZLING
        THROUGH POURING TIDE HE PULLS AND DRIZZLING HAZE . .   445 WESTMIN ABBEY   29

DROOP
        HE KNEW WHICH MADE HIM DROOP AND FILLD HIS HEAD   . .   264 THYRSIS   47

DROOPD
        DROOPD UNBRAIDED ON YOUR LISTLESS ARMS   . . . .   30 NEW SIRENS   122
        BUT YOU DROOPD IN EXPECTATION   . . . .   31 NEW SIRENS   141
        INDOORS FROM THE SUNS EYE HIS HEAD DROOPD LOW . .   86 SOHRAB RUSTUM   847
        FROM THE HOT FIELDS AT NOON HIS HEAD DROOPD LOW . .   86 SOHRAB RUSTUM   V 847
        FROM THE HOT FIELD AT NOON HIS HEAD DROOPD LOW . .   86 SOHRAB RUSTUM   V 847
        SERE WITH SEPTEMBER DROOPD THE CHESTNUT—TREES . .   167 RACHEL 1   3
        BROWN WITH SEPTEMBER DROOPD THE CHESTNUT—TREES . .   167 RACHEL 1   V   3
        THEY DROOPD THEY GREW BLIND THEY GREW OLD . . .   233 YOUTH OF MAN   48
        AND DROOPD AND SLOWLY DIED UPON THEIR THRONE . .   239 REVOLUTIONS   16
        THAT WAN NAILD FORM WITH HEAD DROOPD LOW   . . .   317 OBERMANN MORE   V 155
        THY HEAD DROOPD SOFTLY AND THE GOLDEN CURLS   . .   373 MEROPE   1161

DROOPING
        BUT HERMOD STOOD BESIDE HIS DROOPING HORSE   . . .   129 BALDER DEAD 3   554
        WANDERING THROUGH THEIR DROOPING SAILS   . . . .   135 TRISTRAM 1   157
        THE OTHER WARDED OFF THE DROOPING BOUGHS   . . .   154 TRISTRAM 3   176
        HIS DROOPING GARLAND   . . . .   194 STRAYED REVEL   268
        HIS DROOPING HEAD BOWED MEEKLY ON HIS BREAST . .   476 CROMWELL   167

DROOPS
        DROOPS ALL HIS SHEENY BROWN DEEP—FEATHERD NECK . .   431 EMPEDOCLES II   76

DROP
        THEN THEY DROP AWAY   . . . .   17 CHURCH BROU 2   38
        DROP WITH MINE ADOWN LIFES LATTER DAYS   . . . .   33 NEW SIRENS   210
        OF MAD DELIGHT THEY DROP THEIR SPOILS AND BOUND . .   150 TRISTRAM 3   27
        DROP BY AND LEAVE ITS SEEKER STILL UNTIRED   . . .   268 THYRSIS   207
        FAIN TO DROP DOWN AND TO DIE   . . . .   290 RUGBY CHAPEL   130
        INGLORIOUS AND SHOULD DROP AT LAST UNKNOWN   . . .   356 MEROPE   771

DROPPD

SO SAID HE AND DROPPD SOHRABS HAND AND LEFT   • •   63 SOHRAB RUSTUM   94
AND WITH A CRY SPRANG UP AND DROPPD THE BIRD   • •   67 SOHRAB RUSTUM   203
AND THEN HE STOOD BEWILDERD AND HE DROPPD   • • •   76 SOHRAB RUSTUM   519
HAVEN THE MURDERER HAD DROPPD   • • • • • • •   371 MEROPE   1128
I DROPPD THE BOOK AND OF MY CHILD I THOUGHT   • •   485 S S LUSITANIA   9

DROPPING

OF DARK ELMS SHOOT ROUND DROPPING DOWN THE   19 MODERN SAPPHO   6
     PROUD STREAM
OF DARK ELMS COME ROUND DROPPING DOWN THE PROUD STREAM   19 MODERN SAPPHO   V   6
AND OER HIS VISAGE SERPENTS DROPPING GALL   • • • •   111 BALDER DEAD 2   221
POWER DROPPING FROM THE HAND   • • • • • •   282 HAWORTH CHURCH   V
THE DROPPING PATTER OF A CHILDS SMALL FEET   • • •   FRAGMENT 7   1

DROPS

SIX YEARS SIX LITTLE YEARS SIX DROPS OF TIME   • •   10 MYCERINUS   61
DROPS LIKE A PLUMMET SOHRAB SAW IT COME   • • •   73 SOHRAB RUSTUM   402
ARE JEWELLD WITH BRIGHT DROPS OF RAIN   • • • •   141 TRISTRAM 1   360
TILL THE SPINDLE DROPS FROM HER HAND   • • • •   164 FORSAKEN MERM   96
AND ANON THERE DROPS A TEAR   • • • • •   164 FORSAKEN MERM   102
OF SILK-BALES AND OF BALSAM-DROPS   • • • •   191 STRAYED REVEL   193
STILL GLIDES THE STREAM SLOW DROPS THE BOAT   •   206 RIVER   1
AND SEES NOT THAT THE SACRED DROPS   • • •   213 PROGRESS POESY   7
THEIR DROPS OF BLOOD THEIR DEATH IN LIFE   • •   301 GRANDE CHARTR   54
WHENCE DROPS THE PATH TO ALLIERE DOWN   • •   313 OBERMANN MORE   23

DROPT

DROPT BY THE FAR AUSTRALIAN FOAM   • • • • •   451 GEISTS GRAVE   56

DROUGHT

AND FOR THIS DROUGHT ALL KINDS OF FRUITS   • • •   94 SICK KING BOKH   195

DROVE

A COLT BENEATH ITS DAM AND DROVE HIM HOME   • • •   69 SOHRAB RUSTUM   275
A COLT BESIDE ITS DAM AND DROVE HIM HOME   • •   69 SOHRAB RUSTUM   V 275
DAY DROVE HIS COURSER WITH THE SHINING MANE   •   105 BALDER DEAD 2   2
FORTH WENDED THEY AND DROVE THEIR STEEDS BEFORE   •   106 BALDER DEAD 2   V   50
AND DROVE THEM HOMEWARD AND THE SNORTING STEEDS   •   106 BALDER DEAD 2   V   61
FIRST DROVE HIM FROM ME INTO DISTANT LANDS   • •   116 BALDER DEAD 3   108
DROVE ON ABLAZE ABOVE HER HULL WITH FIRE   • •   119 BALDER DEAD 3   192
HE DROVE ABROAD IN FURIOUS GUISE   • • • •   315 OBERMANN MORE   99
WHICH TO THE WILDERNESS DROVE OUT   • • • •   323 OBERMANN MORE   317
UNQUIET DROVE HIM EVER TO PURSUE   • • • •   355 MEROPE   726
DROVE THEM SCREAMING FROM THEIR EYRIES   • •   399 MEROPE   1829
DROVE MY DAUGHTER SMALL AND ME   • • • •   457 POOR MATTHIAS   179
SO HE SPAKE AND DROVE WITH A CRY HIS STEEDS   HOMER TRANS   63
     INTO BATTLE

DROWN

WHICH THE CHARMD WINDS NEVER DROWN   • • • •   27 NEW SIRENS   28
BUT DEEP IF THOU DEVISEDST IT TO DROWN   • • •   114 BALDER DEAD 3   28
AND ALL THE RACE OF YMIR THOU DIDST DROWN   • •   121 BALDER DEAD 3   271
BEGIN TO ROLL AND ALMOST DROWN   • • • • •   431 EMPEDOCLES II   63

DROWND

THROUGH THE DARK UP THE DROWND SAND   • • •   137 TRISTRAM 1   218
WHICH HANGS OER THE STYMPHALIAN LAKE AND DROWND   •   363 MEROPE   961
THIS STRANGE UNLIKELY TALE THE PRINCE WAS DROWND   •   364 MEROPE   V
OR DROWND IN MISTS OF CHILDISH WONDERMENT   • • •   446 WESTMIN ABBEY   65

DROWNING

STILL HE REPEATS THE DROWNING STORY HERE   • • • •   365 MEROPE   987

DROWSY

HE SEES THE DROWSY NEW-WAKED CLOWN   • • • • •   57 RESIGNATION   181
THE DROWSY BEE AS OF OLD   • • • • • • • •   285 HAWORTH CHURCH   120

DRUDGE

EYES THROUGH HER SILKEN CURTAINS THE POOR DRUDGE   •   70 SOHRAB RUSTUM   303
OF THAT POOR DRUDGE MAY BE SO RUSTUM EYED   • •   70 SOHRAB RUSTUM   308
AND DRUDGE UNDER SOME FOOLISH MASTERS KEN   • •   169 WORLDLY PLACE   6

DRUGGING

THOU DRUGGING PAIN BY PATIENCE HALF AVERSE   • • •   42 GIPSY CHILD   13

DRUGS

BUT DRUGS TO CHARM WITH   • • • • • • • •   432 EMPEDOCLES II   116

DRUIDS

NO VICTIMS BLEED NO DRUIDS BOW   • • • • • •   274 STANZAS CARNAC   15

DRUNK

HATH IT DRUNK OF OUR LOVE-POTIONS   • • •   29 NEW SIRENS   87
AND THE BLACK TOORKMUN TENTS AND ONLY DRUNK   • •   83 SOHRAB RUSTUM   762

DRUNKEN

WITH FOLLY OR WHAT DRUNKEN SLAVE   • • • • •   89 SICK KING BOKH   41

DRY

ERE THE PARTING KISS BE DRY   • • • • • •   22 MEMORY-PICTURE   V
ON THE DRY NOON SHOOK THEIR DEW   • • • • •   29 NEW SIRENS   108

DRY   (CONTINUED)
        WITH COLD DRY EYES AND HEARTS COMPOSED AND STERN   • •   96 BALDER DEAD 1   35
        THOK WITH DRY EYES WILL WEEP OER BALDERS PYRE   • •   123 BALDER DEAD 3   352
        BUT STILL AS THEY PURSUED THEIR WARM DRY ROAD   • •   150 TRISTRAM 3   44
        THE GRASS WAS DRY AND MOSSD AND YOU SAW CLEAR   • •   155 TRISTRAM 3   206
        DRY THEIR MAIL AND BASK IN THE BRINE   • • • •   • •   162 FORSAKEN MERM   42
        THE EBB-TIDE LEAVES DRY   • • • • • • • •   • •   165 FORSAKEN MERM   135
        AND DRY UP MY TEARS   • • • • • • • • • •   177 PARTING   84
        THE MOUNT IS MUTE THE CHANNEL DRY   • • • •   • •   213 PROGRESS POESY   11
        WHICH HAS NOT FALLN ON THE DRY HEART LIKE RAIN   • •   238 PROGRESS   42
        RIVE ITS DRY BONES AND WITH NEW FORCE   • • • • •   319 OBERMANN MORE   199
        THE MOUNTAINS WHERE THE GLENS ARE DRY   • • • • •   414 EMPEDOCLES I 2   62

DRYING
        BY DRYING UP OUR JOY IN EVERYTHING   • • • • • •   153 TRISTRAM 3   125

DUBIOUS
        RUNS HIS OLD ROUND OF DUBIOUS CHEER   • • • • • •   56 RESIGNATION   129
        INFIRM PROTECTORS DUBIOUS ORACLES   • • • • • •   336 MEROPE   215
        THAT WAY IS DUBIOUS FOR A MOTHERS PRAYER   • • • •   349 MEROPE   583

DUCHESS
        SMILES THE DUCHESS MARGUERITE   • • • • • • • •   13 CHURCH BROU 1   12
        SATE THE DUCHESS MARGUERITE   • • • • • • • •   13 CHURCH BROU 1   36
        AND THE DUCHESS CLAPS HER HANDS   • • • • • • •   14 CHURCH BROU 1   40
        WAS THE DUCHESS MARGUERITE   • • • • • • • •   14 CHURCH BROU 1   56
        WHICH THE DUCHESS MAUD BEGAN   • • • • • • • •   14 CHURCH BROU 1   64
        OLD THAT DUCHESS STERN BEGAN IT   • • • • • • •   14 CHURCH BROU 1   65
        SAID THE DUCHESS MARGUERITE THEN   • • • • • • •   15 CHURCH BROU 1   74
        DEAD OUR DUKE AND GONE HIS DUCHESS   • • • • • •   15 CHURCH BROU 1   83
        ON HER PALFREY WHITE THE DUCHESS   • • • • • • •   15 CHURCH BROU 1   93
        ONE THE DUCHESS IN HER VEIL   • • • • • • • •   16 CHURCH BROU 1   108
        THEN THE DUCHESS CLOSED HER LABOURS   • • • • • •   16 CHURCH BROU 1   111
        FROM THE FRINGED MATTRESS WHERE THY DUCHESS LIES   • •   18 CHURCH BROU 3   8

DUE
        CALLD HISTORY KEEPS A SPLENDOUR DUE TO WIT   • • • •   5 DUKE WELLINGTON   13
        COLD HEARTS AND THANKLESS TONGUES WHERE THANKS ARE DUE   8 MYCERINUS   4
        COLD HEARTS AND THANKLESS TONGUES WHERE THANKS   8 MYCERINUS   V   4
            WERE DUE
        DUE TO PLEASURE AS TO PAIN   • • • • • • • •   28 NEW SIRENS   60
        ITS DUE REVERSAL   • • • • • • • • • • • •   51 CONSOLATION   54
        VENGEANCE O QUEEN IS HIS DUE   • • • • • • • •   343 MEROPE   408
        TO GIVE TO VIRTUE HER DOMINION DUE   • • • • • •   353 MEROPE   666
        SO MUCH IS DUE TO TRUTH EVEN TOWRDS OUR FOE   • • •   388 MEROPE   1493
        ARE NEVER FREE FROM DOUBT THOUGH SOMETIMES DUE   • •   388 MEROPE   1522
        BUT NOW HIS HEAD TO DEATH AGAIN IS DUE   • • • • •   447 WESTMIN ABBEY   106
        TRIBUTE DUE TO THEE A VERSE   • • • • • • • •   453 POOR MATTHIAS   18

DUES
        THEM AND THEIR DUES THIS DAY THE KING   • • • • •   87 SICK KING BOKH   3

DUKE
        SAVOYS DUKE HAD LEFT HIS BRIDE • • • • • • • •   13 CHURCH BROU 1   6
        GOD THE DUKE LIES STRETCHD BESIDE HIM • • • • • •   13 CHURCH BROU 1   27
        DEAD OUR DUKE AND GONE HIS DUCHESS   • • • • • •   15 CHURCH BROU 1   83
        ONE THE DUKE IN HELM AND ARMOUR   • • • • • • •   16 CHURCH BROU 1   107

DULL
        BUSINESS COULD NOT MAKE DULL NOR PASSION WILD   • •   2 TO A FRIEND   11
        ENNOBLING THIS DULL POMP THE LIFE OF KINGS   • • • •   9 MYCERINUS   11
        AND THE DULL GODS BEHOLD ERE THESE ARE FLOWN   • •   10 MYCERINUS   65
        AND WHEN THE MIRTH WAXD LOUDEST WITH DULL SOUND   • •   12 MYCERINUS   123
        IN THE DULL OCTOBER EVENING   • • • • • • • •   13 CHURCH BROU 1   29
        DULL DID LIFE IN TORPOR FADE   • • • • • • • •   28 NEW SIRENS   66
        GUESTS THE DULL SENSE NEVER KNEW   • • • • • • •   30 NEW SIRENS   136
        DULL WITHOUT LOVE LIFE DOTH FADE   • • • • • • •   28 NEW SIRENS   V   66
        NOT DAILY LABOURS DULL LETHAEAN SPRING   • • • • •   43 GIPSY CHILD   54
        YE GODS GOOD LACK IS IT SO DULL IN HEAVEN   • • • •   123 BALDER DEAD 3   337
        THEY CLOUD THE BRAIN THEY DULL THE BLOOD   • • • •   138 TRISTRAM 1   248
        WOULD NOT FADE WITH THE DULL YEARS AWAY   • • • • •   143 TRISTRAM 2   26
        FESTERS THE DULL REMEMBRANCE OF A CHANGE   • • • •   213 GROWING OLD   29
        FROM DULL OBLIVION NOR ALL   • • • • • • • • •   288 RUGBY CHAPEL   82
        HOLLOW AND DULL ARE THE GREAT   • • • • • • • •   295 HEINES GRAVE   113
        INTERPRET THEN FOR WE IT SEEMS ARE DULL   • • • • •   365 MEROPE   989
        A PEOPLE LIKE A COMMON MAN IS DULL   • • • • • •   382 MEROPE   1342
        DULL LOOK ON WHEN DEATH IS NIGH   • • • • • • •   455 POOR MATTHIAS   107
        DULL OF HEART AND HARD OF TOUCH   • • • • • • •   457 POOR MATTHIAS   168
        THAT WHILE WE FEEL THE WORLD IS DULL AND LOW   • •   470 ALARIC AT ROME   215
        DECKD THE DULL WASTE AND THE FAMILIAR FIELD   • •   472 CROMWELL   34
        THE COLD DULL SOIL OF HIS UNFRUITFUL YOUTH   • • • •   473 CROMWELL   54
        THE COLD DULL SHADOW OF THEIR ICY WING   • • • • •   474 CROMWELL   92

DULLD
        WAS DULLD FOR HE SLEPT LIGHT AN OLD MANS SLEEP   • •   62 SOHRAB RUSTUM   29

DULLEST
        NOR THE DULLEST BEEN DEAD TO THEM QUITE   • • • • •   230 YOUTH OF NATURE   83

DULLS
        THOUGH EASE DULLS GRACE AND WISDOM BE TOO PROUD   • •   44 GIPSY CHILD   63

DULLS   (CONTINUED)
        THOUGH EASE DULLS GRACE AND WISDOM IS TOO PROUD   .   .   44 GIPSY CHILD   V 63

DULY
        THE DEAD HATH NOW HIS OFFERINGS DULY PAID   .   .   .   .   350 MEROPE   596

DUMB
        DUMB JUDGES ANSWER TRUTH OR MOCKERY   .   .   .   .   .   4 EMERSONS ESSAYS   14
        BUT ELSE THE WOODS AND FIELDS ARE DUMB   .   .   .   .   17 CHURCH BROU 2   31
        ONLY THE BLESSED SAINTS ARE SMILING DUMB   .   .   .   .   17 CHURCH BROU 3   4
        I AM DUMB ALAS TOO SOON ALL   .   .   .   .   29 NEW SIRENS   89
        WITH THE DUMB WOODS AND THE NIGHT ALONE   .   .   .   .   32 NEW SIRENS   194
        LET ALL DOUBTS BE DUMB   .   .   .   .   39 STAGIRIUS   53
        THAT LIFE WHOSE DUMB WISH IS NOT MISSD   .   .   .   .   58 RESIGNATION   193
        OF HELL BEHELD THEM AND THE GHOSTS STOOD DUMB   .   .   112 BALDER DEAD 2   281
        IN ASGARD AND THE GOLDEN HALLS WERE DUMB   .   .   .   113 BALDER DEAD 2   306
        IN ASGARD BUT THE GOLDEN HALLS WERE DUMB   .   .   .   113 BALDER DEAD 2   V 306
        THE SURPLICED PRIEST STOOD DUMB   .   .   .   .   .   .   159 NECKAN   28
        BARING HIS DUMB REMORSE TO FUTURE DAYS   .   .   .   167 PICT NEWSTEAD   13
        THE HOARSE TORRENT DUMB   .   .   .   .   175 PARTING   32
        THE TOO CLEAR WEB AND THY DUMB SISTERS SHAME   .   .   201 PHILOMELA   21
        CHARGE ONCE MORE THEN AND BE DUMB   .   .   .   .   .   215 LAST WORD   13
        OUR HEARTS OUR VOICES MUST WE TOO BE DUMB   .   .   .   245 BURIED LIFE   25
        THE LAST POETIC VOICE IS DUMB   .   .   .   .   .   .   270 MEMORIAL VERSES   4
        THE KINGS OF MODERN THOUGHT ARE DUMB   .   .   .   .   303 GRANDE CHARTR   116
        REGARD HIS DEATH-PLACE DUMB   .   .   .   .   .   .   318 OBERMANN MORE   178
        SO CHARGD HE STOOD DUMB-FOUNDERD CYPSELUS   .   .   .   365 MEROPE   V
        LEND LIFE TO THE DUMB STONES   .   .   .   .   .   .   421 EMPEDOCLES I 2   274
        FOR EVER THROUGH THE GLENS PLACID AND DUMB   .   .   .   427 EMPEDOCLES I 2   460
        DUMB INSCRUTABLE AND GRAND   .   .   .   .   453 POOR MATTHIAS   40
        IN FRONT THE DUMB ROCK RISES STEEP   .   .   .   .   .   479 HAYSWATER BOAT   11
        WHERE TIME ELSE DUMB HATH SIGNIFIED HIS SWAY   .   .   FRAGMENT 2   2

DUMBLY
        DUMBLY SMILING AS YOU GO   .   .   .   .   31 NEW SIRENS   160

DUN
        THE DARKER ELMS STAND GRAVE AND DUN   .   .   .   .   .   248 KENSINGTON GARD   V
        THE MASSIER ELMS STAND GRAVE AND DUN   .   .   .   .   .   KENSINGTON GARD   V

DUNBAR
        FROM THEIR DEEP BASE THY BEETLING CLIFFS DUNBAR   .   .   476 CROMWELL   151

DUNGEON
        MY DUNGEON WHERE THE SERPENTS STUNG ME DEAD   .   .   117 BALDER DEAD 3   146

DUPED
        WHEN THE DUPED SOUL SELF-MASTERD CLAIMS ITS MEED   .   .   9 MYCERINUS   28
        TO MY MESSENIANS DUPED DISARMD DESPISED   .   .   .   366 MEROPE   1006

DURABILITY
        A SHADOWY DURABILITY   .   .   .   .   185 TERRACE BERNE   43

DUSK
        DUSK THE HALL WITH YEW   .   .   .   .   30 NEW SIRENS   114
        FROM THIS DUSK OF LEAF-STREWN PLACES   .   .   .   .   .   32 NEW SIRENS   193
        DUSK OH DUSK THE HALL WITH YEW   .   .   .   .   .   .   35 NEW SIRENS   270
        DUSK OH DUSK THE HALL WITH YEW   .   .   .   .   .   .   35 NEW SIRENS   270
        DUSK THE HALL WITH YEW   .   .   .   .   35 NEW SIRENS   276
        AND THERE IN THE DUSK BY THE WALLS   .   .   .   .   .   234 YOUTH OF MAN   83
        OF QUIET LOOK ADOWN THE DUSK HILL-SIDE   .   .   .   .   267 THYRSIS   152
        OF THAT DUSK SLOW-MOVING BAND   .   .   .   .   .   META CLOISTER   10

DUSKY
        GLIDING HALF HIDDEN THROUGH THE DUSKY STEMS   .   .   11 MYCERINUS   104
        THERE ITS DUSKY BLUE CLUSTERS   .   .   .   .   .   .   176 PARTING   51
        AND THE LONG DUSKY LINE OF ITALY   .   .   .   .   .   438 EMPEDOCLES II   314

DUST
        WHERE FAITHS ARE BUILT ON DUST   .   .   .   .   .   .   39 STAGIRIUS   45
        BE CRUMBLING BONES AND WINDY DUST   .   .   .   .   .   48 HORATIAN ECHO   32
        OF DUST WHICH WREATHED THEIR STRUGGLING FILES   .   .   52 RESIGNATION   6
        OF DUST THAT WREATHED THEIR STRUGGLING FILES   .   .   52 RESIGNATION   V 6
        THE BALEFUL SIGN OF FEVERS DUST HAD SOILD   .   .   .   74 SOHRAB RUSTUM   453
        NEVER TILL NOW DEFILED SANK TO THE DUST   .   .   .   76 SOHRAB RUSTUM   498
        IN BOTH HIS HANDS THE DUST WHICH LAY AROUND   .   .   81 SOHRAB RUSTUM   700
        SWEEPING THE DUST CAME NEAR AND IN MUTE WOE   .   .   82 SOHRAB RUSTUM   732
        NEVER DEFACD TILL NOW SHAMD TO THE DUST   .   .   .   76 SOHRAB RUSTUM   V 498
        NEVER TILL NOW DEFILED SUNK TO THE DUST   .   .   .   76 SOHRAB RUSTUM   V 498
        ALL RENT AND DUST UPON HIS HAIR   .   .   .   .   .   .   88 SICK KING BOKH   32
        AND BURNING DUST AGAIN I CREEP   .   .   .   .   .   .   90 SICK KING BOKH   75
        WHO SHUFFLES THROUGH THE DEEP DEW-MOISTEND DUST   .   101 BALDER DEAD 1   232
        MID DUST AND GROANS AND LIMBS LOPPD OFF AND BLOOD   .   105 BALDER DEAD 2   16
        HANGS QUIVERING OUT BETWEEN HIS DUST-SMEARD JAWS   .   .   114 BALDER DEAD 3   15
        ITS STORMS OF DUST WITH BURNING HEAT   .   .   .   .   157 SAINT BRANDAN   44
        BUT EACH DAY BRINGS ITS PETTY DUST   .   .   .   .   .   183 ABSENCE   9
        THEY ARE DUST THEY ARE CHANGED THEY ARE GONE   .   .   232 YOUTH OF NATURE   133
        AND THOUGH SO TASKD KEEP FREE FROM DUST AND SOIL   .   .   244 SUMMER NIGHT   82
        ALOFT ARE HURLD IN THE DUST   .   .   .   .   288 RUGBY CHAPEL   64
        IN AN EDDY OF PURPOSELESS DUST   .   .   .   .   .   .   288 RUGBY CHAPEL   77

DUST
 (CONTINUED)

THAT THE BLOOD RUSHES IN STREAMS TO THE DUST	• •	400 MEROPE	1865
THE WORLD IS WHAT IT IS FOR ALL OUR DUST AND DIN	• • •	419 EMPEDOCLES I 2	206
TREADS ON THE SLUMBERING DUST OF OTHER YEARS	• •	464 ALARIC AT ROME	50
GREEN TURF ABOVE AND CRUMBLING DUST BELOW	• • • •	464 ALARIC AT ROME	57
THY DEAD ARE KINGS THY DUST ARE PALACES	• • • •	464 ALARIC AT ROME	61
IN THE BLOODY DUST BENEATH THE FEET OF THEIR FOEMEN		HOMER TRANS	26

DUSTED
SOON SHALL WE HAVE GOLD-DUSTED SNAPDRAGON	• • • •	264 THYRSIS	64

DUSTY
AND MANY A MILE OF DUSTY WAY	• • • • • • • •	54 RESIGNATION	80
WHEN FROM THEIR DUSTY LIFE THEY PASS	• • • • •	277 SOUTHERN NIGHT	59
BETWEEN THE DUSTY VINEYARD-WALLS	• • • • • •	311 OBERMANN	169
BY THE STREAM-SIDE AFTER THE DUSTY LANES	• • • •	406 EMPEDOCLES I 1	3
WHILE OER THE DUSTY PLAIN THE MURMUROUS THRONG	• •	473 CROMWELL	43

DUTIES
ONE LESSON OF TWO DUTIES KEPT AT ONE	• • • • • •	1 QUIET WORK		3
TWO BLENDING DUTIES HARMONISD IN ONE	• • • • • •	1 QUIET WORK	V	3
ONE LESSON OF TWO DUTIES SERVD IN ONE	• • • •	1 QUIET WORK	V	3
ONE LESSON OF TWO DUTIES KEPT IN ONE	• • • • •	1 QUIET WORK	V	3

DUTY
HATE DUTY INTEREST PASSION CALL ONE WAY	• • • •	383 MEROPE	1382

DWARF
SMOKY DWARF HOUSES • • • • • • • • • • • •		50 CONSOLATION	2

DWELL
DRINKING DEEP DRAUGHTS OF JOY YE DWELL SERENE	• •	10 MYCERINUS		48
THOU WHO DOST DWELL ALONE	• • • • • • • •	38 STAGIRIUS		1
WHO DWELL IN KIPCHAK AND THE NORTHERN WASTE	• •	65 SOHRAB RUSTUM	V	131
LIKE THOSE WHICH MEN WHO DWELL IN TREELESS PLAINS	• •	73 SOHRAB RUSTUM	V	410
AND ON WHOSE MARGE THE ANCIENT GIANTS DWELL	• •	99 BALDER DEAD 1		161
THE PLAINS OF NIFLHEIM WHERE DWELL THE DEAD	• •	100 BALDER DEAD 1		172
WHICH HE IN ASGARD BUILT HIM THERE TO DWELL	• •	101 BALDER DEAD 1		224
THE PLAINS OF NIFLHEIM WHERE DWELL THE DEAD	• •	109 BALDER DEAD 2		150
WHO SEE THE LIGHT AND BLEST IN ASGARD DWELL	• •	112 BALDER DEAD 2		255
AND SET BY OCEANS UTMOST MARGE TO DWELL	• • • •	121 BALDER DEAD 3		275
AND ALONE DWELL FOR EVER	• • • • • • • •	165 FORSAKEN MERM		122
WHERE WE HAD LONG BEEN DOOMD TO DWELL	• • •	271 MEMORIAL VERSES	V	
WHO DWELL ON A FIRM BASIS OF CONTENT	• • • • •	436 EMPEDOCLES II		260
THOU WONDROUS CHAOS WHERE TOGETHER DWELL	• • •	463 ALARIC AT ROME		43

DWELLEST
BROTHER THOU DWELLEST IN THE DARKSOME LAND	• • •	115 BALDER DEAD 3	75

DWELLING
MAKING THE HEAVEN OF HEAVENS HIS DWELLING-PLACE	• •	3 SHAKESPEARE	6
OTHER FAVOURITES DWELLING HERE • • • • • • •		455 POOR MATTHIAS	87

DWELLS
MY MOTHER WHO IN ADER-BAIJAN DWELLS	• • • • •	78 SOHRAB RUSTUM		590
DWELLS ON LOUD TYNTAGELS HILL	• • • • • • •	134 TRISTRAM 1		134
DWELLS ON PROUD TYNTAGELS HILL	• • • • • • •	134 TRISTRAM 1	V	134
SINGING THERE DWELLS A LOVED ONE	• • • • •	165 FORSAKEN MERM		140
THE UNCONQUERD JOY IN WHICH HER SPIRIT DWELLS	• •	176 PARTING		40
AND NOW DWELLS ONLY IN THE GRAVE	• • • • •	KENSINGTON GARD	V	28
HERE THEN IT IS WHERE POLYPHONTES DWELLS	• • •	354 MEROPE		706
THERE FROM SIN DELIVERD DWELLS MY FATHER	• • •	482 THEKLAS ANSWER		15

DWELT
DWELT WITH MERE OUTWARD SEEMING HE WITHIN	• • • •	12 MYCERINUS	108
HE PERISHD IN ARCADIA WHERE HE DWELT	• • • • •	355 MEROPE	717
DWELT IT SEEMD IN SYMPATHY	• • • • • • •	454 POOR MATTHIAS	52

DWINDLING
A HOUSE ONCE GREAT NOW DWINDLING IN ITS SONS	• •	337 MEROPE	237
TO NURSE HIS DWINDLING FACULTY OF JOY	• • • •	437 EMPEDOCLES II	273

DYING
AND HEARD THEIR HOLLOW ROAR OF DYING MEN	• • • •	74 SOHRAB RUSTUM	435
LIES DYING WITH THE ARROW IN HER SIDE	• • • •	78 SOHRAB RUSTUM	567
OVER HIS DYING SON AND KNEW HIM NOT	• • • • •	78 SOHRAB RUSTUM	575
ON THE MOWN DYING GRASS SO SOHRAB LAY	• • • •	80 SOHRAB RUSTUM	638
TRUTH SITS UPON THE LIPS OF DYING MEN	• • • •	80 SOHRAB RUSTUM	656
NOT WOUNDS YET DYING THEY THEIR ARMOUR WORE	• •	109 BALDER DEAD 2	168
SOFT WHO IS THAT STANDS BY THE DYING FIRE	• • •	130 TRISTRAM 1	7
MIGHT THY DYING KNIGHT RESTORE • • • • • •		132 TRISTRAM 1	79
I AM DYING BUILD THOU MAYST MY GRAVE	• • • •	142 TRISTRAM 2	12
I AM DYING START NOT NOR LOOK WILDLY	• • • • •	145 TRISTRAM 2	89
SHE SEEMS ONE DYING IN A MASK OF YOUTH	• • • •	151 TRISTRAM 3	75
THE DYING RACHEL IN A CHAIR THEY BORE	• • • •	167 RACHEL 2	3
SOLE OBJECT OF HER DYING EYES REMAIN	• • • • •	168 RACHEL 2	13
EASTWARD THE OTHER FROM THE DYING DAY	• • • •	170 EAST AND WEST	7
TO THE DYING SPIRIT OF YOUTH	• • • • • •	234 YOUTH OF MAN	55
ONCE MORE BEFORE MY DYING EYES • • • • •		250 WISH	32
AND HOW THE DYING SPARK OF HOPE WAS FED	• • • •	260 SCHOLAR-GIPSY	188

DYING   (CONTINUED)
          HE LOOKD ON EUROPES DYING HOUR   . . . .   270 MEMORIAL VERSES   23
          HIS DYING STRAIN   . . . .   278 SOUTHERN NIGHT   100
          A DYING STRAIN   . . . .   278 SOUTHERN NIGHT   V 100
          OF THE EARLY-DYING ALAS   . . . .   283 HAWORTH CHURCH   67
          DYING TOO SOON YET GREEN   . . . .   283 HAWORTH CHURCH   71
          WHOSE TOO BOLD DYING SONG   . . . .   285 HAWORTH CHURCH   99
          OF ENEMIES AND COUNT THEIR DYING GROANS   . . . .   387 MEROPE   1469
          FALLN BENEATH HIS PERCH AND DYING   . . . . .   452 POOR MATTHIAS   2
          OUR COMPANIONS DYING SIGN   . . . .   456 POOR MATTHIAS   126
          FALLEN DYING OFF THY PERCH   . . . . . .   456 POOR MATTHIAS   130
          AND WITH ITS CLEAR CALM TONES THAT DYING PRAYER   . .   478 CROMWELL   217

DYNASTIES
          OF DYNASTIES LONG-FIXD AND HONOURD LONG   . . . .   390 MEROPE   1562

EAGER
          EVER IN THEIR OWN EAGER PASTIME BENT   . . . . .   8 RELIGIOUS ISOL   2
          EAGER TELL-TALES OF HER MIND   . . . .   24 MEMORY-PICTURE   42
          GLANCING FEET AND EAGER EYES   . . . .   32 NEW SIRENS   176
          AND HE GREW FOND AND EAGER TO OBEY   . . . . .   155 TRISTRAM 3   183
          THEN AS NOW THIS TREMULOUS EAGER BEING   . . . .   210 SELF-DECEPTION   9
          PASSIONATE EAGER HIS YOUTH   . . . .   298 HEINES GRAVE   194
          SAD EAGER EYES   . . . .   393 MEROPE   1664
          NOT EAGER NOR NOT SAD   . . . .   426 EMPEDOCLES I 2   V 410

EAGERLY
          THEIR LIPS MOVED THEIR WHITE ARMS WAVED EAGERLY   . .   25 DREAM   28
          WE MUST NOT SNATCH IT EAGERLY   . . . .   94 SICK KING BOKH   212
          EAGERLY ONCE HER GRACIOUS KEN   . . . .   202 URANIA   9

EAGLE
          SEALING HER EAGLE EYES   . . . .   38 STAGIRIUS   21
          A BREEDING EAGLE SITTING ON HER NEST   . . . . .   77 SOHRAB RUSTUM   557
          ALL KNOW HOW WEAK THE EAGLE HERACLES   . . . . .   336 MEROPE   212
          AND THE EAGLE AT THE BECK   . . . .   431 EMPEDOCLES II   74

EAGLES
          TOGETHER AS TWO EAGLES ON ONE PREY   . . . . .   75 SOHRAB RUSTUM   472
          ECHOING THE SCREAMS OF THE EAGLES   . . . . .   252 FUTURE   10
          SHE VEILD HER EAGLES SNAPPD HER SWORD   . . . .   316 OBERMANN MORE   125
          O CLIFFS LEFT BY THE EAGLES   . . . .   399 MEROPE   1825
          AND THE SEA-EAGLES BUILD THEIR NEST   . . . . .   414 EMPEDOCLES I 2   67
          THY DAZZLING LIGHT AN EAGLES GAZE SHOULD TIRE   . .   463 ALARIC AT ROME   32

EAGLETS
          HIS PUNY CALLOW EAGLETS AND WHAT TRIALS   . . . .   336 MEROPE   214

EAR
          AND IN THE SWEEPING OF THE WIND YOUR EAR   . . .   19 CHURCH BROU 3   43
          LEANS HER EAR TO YOUR MAD SALLIES   . . . . .   27 NEW SIRENS   27
          THEY BEAT UPON MINE EAR AGAIN   . . . .   36 VOICE   33
          DID STEAL INTO MINE EAR   . . . .   36 VOICE   36
          DO ADVERSE VOICES FALL ON THE WORLDS EAR   . . .   47 WORLD QUIETIST   19
          PIERCE FATES IMPENETRABLE EAR   . . . .   60 RESIGNATION   274
          HIM WILL I SEEK AND CARRY TO HIS EAR   . . . .   66 SOHRAB RUSTUM   180
          SURELY THE NEWS WILL ONE DAY REACH HIS EAR   . . .   78 SOHRAB RUSTUM   581
          FROM TRIBE TO TRIBE UNTIL IT REACH HER EAR   . . .   79 SOHRAB RUSTUM   597
          MOST DEAF WHERE THOU SHOULDST MOST GIVE EAR   . . .   91 SICK KING BOKH   98
          NOT SUFFERING WHICH SHUTS UP EYE AND EAR   . . .   152 TRISTRAM 3   113
          NOT SUFFERING THAT SHUTS UP EYE AND EAR   . . .   152 TRISTRAM 3   V 113
          CALL ONCE MORE TO A MOTHERS EAR   . . . . . .   161 FORSAKEN MERM   15
          SOMETIMES A SECONDS SPACE THEIR EAR   . . . . .   226 EPILOG LAOCOON   179
          FOR EVER MAKES THEIR EAR REJOICE   . . . . .   227 EPILOG LAOCOON   196
          AND THE CLANG OF ARMS IN HIS EAR   . . . . .   229 YOUTH OF NATURE   42
          WHEN OUR WORLD-DEAFEND EAR   . . . .   247 BURIED LIFE   82
          WHILE TO MY EAR FROM UPLANDS FAR AWAY   . . . .   255 SCHOLAR-GIPSY   17
          GAINS NOT AN EARTH-DEAFEND EAR   . . . . . .   281 HAWORTH CHURCH   36
          CONSOLE WE CANNOT HER EAR   . . . .   282 HAWORTH CHURCH   50
          THE ORGAN CARRIES TO OUR EAR   . . . .   306 GRANDE CHARTR   203
          THESE WORDS TO THINE INDULGENT EAR THY WIFE   . . .   350 MEROPE   594
          HIS TALE WAS MEETER FOR THAT EAR THAN THINE   . . .   362 MEROPE   929
          FOR THE KINGS PRIVATE EAR RESERVES LIKE THIS   . .   364 MEROPE   965
          AH WHO ARE THESE WHAT SHRILL EAR-PIERCING SCREAM   . .   375 MEROPE   1202
          THE ENFORCED LEISURE OF AN EXILES EAR   . . . .   387 MEROPE   1488
          AND KEEP THEIR FRIENDLY CHATTER AT HIS EAR   . . .   435 EMPEDOCLES II   224
          AY ME TIS DEAF THAT EAR   . . . .   449 WESTMIN ABBEY   161
          ASLEEP YET LENDING HALF AN EAR   . . . . . .   452 GEISTS GRAVE   69
          OF GOTHIC CLARION SMOTE THY STARTLED EAR   . . .   465 ALARIC AT ROME   80
          AND THE SAME WORLD HAS TONGUE AND EAR AND EYE   . .   470 ALARIC AT ROME   218
          HIGH FATE IS THEIRS YE SLEEPLESS WAVES WHOSE EAR   . .   471 CROMWELL   1
          FLASHD FROM THY SOUL UPON THINE INWARD EAR   . . .   472 CROMWELL   28
          LIKE SOUNDS FROM OTHER WORLDS THE SPARTANS EAR   . .   473 CROMWELL   42
          SMOTE LIKE THE RUSH OF WATERS ON HIS EAR   . . .   475 CROMWELL   136
          HIS LATEST LOFTIEST MUSIC SMOTE HIS EAR   . . .   478 CROMWELL   210

EARLIER
          GONE IS THE CALM OF ITS EARLIER SHORE   . . . .   253 FUTURE   52

EARLIEST
    THE COMING SPRING-TIMES EARLIEST STIR   . . . . 483 ROME-SICKNESS   6

EARLY
    FOR HE REMEMBERD HIS OWN EARLY YOUTH . . . . . .   79 SOHRAB RUSTUM   619
    AN EMPERORS GIFT AT EARLY MORN HE PAINTS   . . . .   81 SOHRAB RUSTUM   674
    TO THE DARK FORESTS IN THE EARLY DAWN . . . . .   106 BALDER DEAD 2   52
    AND AS A TRAVELLER IN THE EARLY DAWN . . . . .   113 BALDER DEAD 2   295
    LET THE EARLY SUMMER BE . . . .   135 TRISTRAM 1   153
    THE ROUT EARLY GATHERD . . . .   186 STRAYED REVEL   36
    BECKONS TOO EARLY THE GUEST . . . .   199 EARLY DEATH   9
    OF ITS EARLY MOUNTAINOUS SHORE . . . .   254 FUTURE   76
    CHILDREN WHO EARLY RANGE THESE SLOPES AND LATE   . 258 SCHOLAR-GIPSY   105
    FOR EARLY DIDST THOU LEAVE THE WORLD WITH POWERS . 260 SCHOLAR-GIPSY   161
    SO SOME TEMPESTUOUS MORN IN EARLY JUNE   . . . . 264 THYRSIS   51
    THE FRESHNESS OF THE EARLY WORLD   . . . . . 272 MEMORIAL VERSES   57
    MY BROTHER AND THINE EARLY LOT . . . . 276 SOUTHERN NIGHT   19
    OF THE EARLY-DYING ALAS . . . . 283 HAWORTH CHURCH   67
    EARLY SHE GOES ON THE PATH . . . . 283 HAWORTH CHURCH   68
    FENCED EARLY IN THIS CLOISTRAL ROUND . . . . . 306 GRANDE CHARTR   205
    THE EARLY PEASANT STILL RECALLS   . . . . . 311 OBERMANN   171
    EARLY-SLAIN INNOCENTS NEAR   . . . . 378 MEROPE   1239
    LOST IN DIM MEMORIES OF HIS EARLY HOME . . . . 468 ALARIC AT ROME   170
    THE VANISHT GLORIES OF THINE EARLY DAY   . . . . 471 ALARIC AT ROME   224

EARN
    THAT SCANTY GRACE SHALL EARN THEE THIS REPLY   . . 395 MEROPE   1732
    THOU WILT EARN MY THANKS SURE AND PERHAPS HIS   . . 409 EMPEDOCLES I 1   99

EARNEST
    YET THAT SEVERE THAT EARNEST AIR   . . . . . 241 MORALITY   29
    AND FILL THY LEISURE WITH AN EARNEST PRAYER   . . 332 MEROPE   72
    AND DEATHS COLD DEWS BEDIMMD HIS EARNEST BROW   . . 476 CROMWELL   170

EARNESTLY
    LAST NIGHT WE STOOD EARNESTLY TALKING TOGETHER   . .   19 MODERN SAPPHO   9
    CRIES OUT MOST EARNESTLY O KING   . . . . .   89 SICK KING BOKH   52
    BUT EARNESTLY I LONGD TO HOVER NEAR   . . . . . 125 BALDER DEAD 3   416
    FOR THE LAST TIME I ASK ASK EARNESTLY   . . . . 394 MEROPE   1717

EARNING
    EARNING SHE TOO HER PRAISE   . . . . 280 HAWORTH CHURCH   14

EARNS
    NO SMALL PROFIT THAT MAN EARNS . . . .   49 SECOND BEST   16

EARS
    DID STEAL INTO MINE EARS . . . . .   36 VOICE   V 36
    ARE IN HIS EYES AND IN HIS EARS   . . . . .   57 RESIGNATION   187
    WHEN THE DEW GLISTENS ON THE PEARLED EARS . . . .   65 SOHRAB RUSTUM   155
    FOR ALLAH SHUT MY EARS AND MIND   . . . . .   88 SICK KING BOKH   24
    WHAT FOOL IS THIS THAT HURTS OUR EARS   . . . .   89 SICK KING BOKH   40
    MINE EARS ARE STUNND WITH BLOWS AND SICK FOR CALM   128 BALDER DEAD 3   508
    ABOVE THE DIN HER VOICE IS IN MY EARS . . . . 137 TRISTRAM 1   240
    THEY SHINE UPON THE WORLD THEIR EARS . . . . . 203 EUPHROSYNE   21
    THEY SMILE UPON THE WORLD THEIR EARS . . . . . 203 EUPHROSYNE   V 21
    NOW STRIFES ARE HUSHD OUR EARS DOTH MEET . . . . 219 BACCHANALIA 2   14
    NOW STRIFE IS HUSHD OUR EARS DOTH MEET . . . . 219 BACCHANALIA 2   V 14
    WITH DEW OR LISTEN WITH ENCHANTED EARS   . . . 261 SCHOLAR-GIPSY   219
    EARS AND LABOUR-DIMMD EYES   . . . . 295 HEINES GRAVE   89
    THEIR VOICES WERE IN ALL MENS EARS   . . . . . 303 GRANDE CHARTR   123
    IN THESE EARS THEY THUNDER THEY RING   . . . . 346 MEROPE   500
    THESE POOR EARS STILL AND THESE EYES . . . . . 346 MEROPE   501
    A TALE MEANWHILE FORGED FOR HIS SUBJECTS EARS   . 366 MEROPE   1002
    TO SOUND THY TRIUMPH IN HIS WIDOWS EARS   . . . 395 MEROPE   1739
    AUTHENTIC PROOF OF WHAT THOU TELLST OUR EARS   . 403 MEROPE   1952
    WE SEE THE FLAPS OF THY LARGE EARS   . . . . . 451 GEISTS GRAVE   49
    PRINKING EARS AND DEWLAP THROAT . . . . . 454 POOR MATTHIAS   72
    MISS OUR EYES AND MISS OUR EARS   . . . . . 457 POOR MATTHIAS   166
    HE HATH PLEASED OUR EYES AND EARS   . . . . . 458 POOR MATTHIAS   203
    SET THINE EARS WITH SOUL-FRAUGHT MUSIC RINGING   . 482 THEKLAS ANSWER   7

EARTH
    YES WHILE ON EARTH A THOUSAND DISCORDS RING   . .   1 QUIET WORK   9
    DIDST TREAD ON EARTH UNGUESSD AT BETTER SO . . . .   3 SHAKESPEARE   11
    DIDST WALK ON EARTH UNGUESSD AT BETTER SO . . . .   3 SHAKESPEARE   V 11
    DIDST PASS ON EARTH UNGUESSD AT BETTER SO . . . .   3 SHAKESPEARE   V 11
    DIDST STAND ON EARTH UNGUESSD AT BETTER SO . . . .   3 SHAKESPEARE   V 11
    DIDST LIVE ON EARTH UNGUESSD AT BETTER SO   . . .   3 SHAKESPEARE   V 11
    SEEING THIS VALE THIS EARTH WHEREON WE DREAM   . .   7 REP FRIEND CONT   5
    MOULD NOT THE SOLID EARTH THOUGH NEVER WINDS   . .   8 RELIGIOUS ISOL   10
    LIVE BY THY LIGHT AND EARTH WILL LIVE BY HERS   . .   8 RELIGIOUS ISOL   14
    MOULDS NOT THE SOLID EARTH THOUGH NEVER WINDS   . .   8 RELIGIOUS ISOL   V 10
    SWEEPS EARTH AND HEAVEN AND MEN AND GODS ALONG   . .   9 MYCERINUS   39
    BEARS EARTH AND HEAVEN AND MEN AND GODS ALONG   . .   9 MYCERINUS   V 39
    WHIRLS EARTH AND HEAVEN AND MEN AND GODS ALONG   . .   9 MYCERINUS   V 39
    NOT IDLY EARTH AND OCEAN LABOUR ON   . . . .   42 GIPSY CHILD   7
    GLOOMS THAT ENHANCE AND GLORIFY THIS EARTH . . . .   42 GIPSY CHILD   20
    WHAT HEAVENS WHAT EARTH WHAT SUN SHALT THOU DISCERN   43 GIPSY CHILD   44
    AND GRIEF THAT HEALD AT EVERY SMILE OF EARTH   .   41 GIPSY CHILD   V 20
    WHAT HEAVENS WHAT EARTH WHAT SUNS SHALT THOU DISCERN   43 GIPSY CHILD   V 44

EARTH   (CONTINUED)
        IN THE BLANK ECHOING SOLITUDE IF EARTH   . . . .   45 IN UTRUMQUE PAR   24
        O MAN WHOM EARTH THY LONG-VEXT MOTHER BARE   . . . .   46 IN UTRUMQUE PAR   32
        THE WIDE EARTH IS STILL . . . .   50 CONSOLATION   V
        WHEN MORNING PURIFIES THE EARTH   . . . . . .   57 RESIGNATION   171
        RUKSH WHOSE RENOWN WAS NOISED THROUGH ALL THE EARTH   69 SOHRAB RUSTUM   272
        THUNDERING TO EARTH AND LEAPT FROM RUSTUMS HAND   . .   73 SOHRAB RUSTUM   419
        COME PLANT WE HERE IN EARTH OUR ANGRY SPEARS . . .   74 SOHRAB RUSTUM   439
        AND HIS HEAD SWAM AND HE SANK DOWN TO EARTH   . .   81 SOHRAB RUSTUM   693
        AND THOU MUST LAY ME IN THAT LOVELY EARTH   . .   84 SOHRAB RUSTUM   787
        AND I WILL LAY THEE IN THAT LOVELY EARTH   . . . .   84 SOHRAB RUSTUM   802
        AND HIS HEAD SWAM AND HE SUNK DOWN TO EARTH   .   81 SOHRAB RUSTUM   V 693
        THOUGH IT BE GREAT ALL THE EARTH ROUND   . . . .   92 SICK KING BOKH   158
        TO LOOK ON MIDGARD AND THE EARTH AND MEN   . .   96 BALDER DEAD 1   52
        PAST MIDGARD FORTRESS DOWN TO EARTH AND MEN   . .   99 BALDER DEAD 1   142
        TOWRD EARTH AND FIGHTS OF MEN AND AT THEIR SIDE   .   105 BALDER DEAD 2   20
        PAST MIDGARD FORTRESS DOWN TO EARTH THEY CAME   .   105 BALDER DEAD 2   23
        LET ALL THAT LIVES AND MOVES UPON THE EARTH   . .   111 BALDER DEAD 2   236
        WHO EVER HAVE BEEN KNOWN IN EARTH OR HEAVEN   . .   112 BALDER DEAD 2   258
        NAMES HATH SHE MANY VANADIS ON EARTH . . . . .   116 BALDER DEAD 3   96
        SUCH AS ON EARTH WE VALIANTLY HAVE WAGED   . .   117 BALDER DEAD 3   139
        IN HEAVEN AND EARTH AND WHO WOULD GRUDGE HIM TEARS   120 BALDER DEAD 3   233
        LORD OVER MEN ON EARTH AND GODS IN HEAVEN   . . .   120 BALDER DEAD 3   251
        THE EARTH AND OCEAN AND ABOVE THEM HEAVEN   . .   121 BALDER DEAD 3   261
        OF WOOD AND FRAMEDST MEN WHO TILL THE EARTH   .   121 BALDER DEAD 3   269
        MOURN FOR THE MEN ON EARTH THE GODS IN HEAVEN   127 BALDER DEAD 3   485
        THITHER WHEN OER THIS PRESENT EARTH AND HEAVENS   .   128 BALDER DEAD 3   522
        FROM THE BRIGHT OCEAN AT OUR FEET AN EARTH   . . .   128 BALDER DEAD 3   528
        AS ROOTED TO THE EARTH NOR SOUNDS   . . . . . .   148 TRISTRAM 2   V
        ON EARTH MY CRIME MY DEATH THEY KNEW   . . . .   157 SAINT BRANDAN   26
        ON EARTH THE CHRISTMAS-NIGHTS REPOSE   . . . .   158 SAINT BRANDAN   66
        OF EARTH OF EARTH THE NECKAN SINGS . . . . . .   159 NECKAN   11
        OF EARTH OF EARTH THE NECKAN SINGS . . . . . .   159 NECKAN   11
        OF ALL HE SAW AND FELT ON EARTH   . . . . . .   159 NECKAN   15
        HE ROSE TO EARTH AGAIN . . . .   160 NECKAN   38
        HE WEPT THE EARTH HATH KINDNESS   . . . . . .   161 NECKAN   61
        EARTH SEA AND SKY AND GOD ABOVE   . . . . . .   161 NECKAN   63
        HE SAID THE EARTH HATH KINDNESS   . . . . . .   161 NECKAN   V 61
        HE MUSED THE EARTH HATH KINDNESS . . . . . .   161 NECKAN   V 61
        ON THIS WILD EARTH OF HATE AND FEAR   . . . . .   180 FAREWELL   86
        THE EARTH AND MEN   . . . .   190 STRAYED REVEL   134
        OF TURQUOISE-EARTH AND AMETHYST   . . . . . .   191 STRAYED REVEL   195
        FITFUL EARTH-MURMUR   . . . .   194 STRAYED REVEL   284
        THE BROAD EARTH OPEND AND WHELMD THEM AND HIM   .   197 FRAG ANTIGONE   87
        WERE GORGEOUS UPON EARTH AGAIN . . . .   204 CALAIS SANDS   8
        SINCE MAN WOKE ON EARTH HE KNOWS HIS STORY . . .   209 SELF-DECEPTION   3
        BUT BEFORE WE WOKE ON EARTH WE WERE   . . . .   209 SELF-DECEPTION   4
        AND ON EARTH WE WANDER GROPING REELING   . . .   210 SELF-DECEPTION   21
        CARRY MY PEACE UPON EARTH   . . . .   216 LORDS MESSENGER   6
        EARTH WITH THEIR DEEDS THEY FILL   . . . . .   220 BACCHANALIA 2   43
        WHILE THROUGH THEIR EARTH-MOORD NAVE BELOW   . .   223 EPILOG LAOCOON   73
        WHILE THROUGH THE EARTH-MOORD NAVE BELOW   . .   223 EPILOG LAOCOON   V 73
        THOUGH SHE MOVE NOT EARTH TO-DAY   . . . . .   227 PERSIST POETRY   2
        THOUGH SHE RULE NOT EARTH TO-DAY   . . . . .   227 PERSIST POETRY   V   2
        OF HIS RACE IS PAST ON THE EARTH   . . . . .   229 YOUTH OF NATURE   57
        THERE ARE WORSE PLAGUES ON EARTH THAN TEARS   .   250 WISH   8
        WHO CAN SEE THE GREEN EARTH ANY MORE . . . . .   252 FUTURE   27
        FOR NATURE HATH LONG KEPT THIS INN THE EARTH . .   251 FUTURE   V
        AND THOU FROM EARTH ART GONE . . . .   259 SCHOLAR-GIPSY   136
        FOR THERE THINE EARTH-FORGETTING EYELIDS KEEP   .   267 THYRSIS   168
        ON THE COOL FLOWERY LAP OF EARTH   . . . . .   271 MEMORIAL VERSES   49
        ITS GOLDEN RAIN ON EARTH CONFERS   . . . . .   277 SOUTHERN NIGHT   54
        GAINS NOT AN EARTH-DEAFEND EAR . . . .   281 HAWORTH CHURCH   36
        OF YORKSHIRE A LITTLE EARTH   . . . .   282 HAWORTH CHURCH   53
        IN THE DARK FERMENTATION OF EARTH   . . . . .   286 HAWORTH CHURCH   135
        THIS WAS THY LIFE UPON EARTH . . . .   288 RUGBY CHAPEL   57
        OF MORTAL MEN ON THE EARTH   . . . .   288 RUGBY CHAPEL   59
        SON OF MANKIND TO THE EARTH   . . . .   293 HEINES GRAVE   30
        HAIL AS IT PASSES FROM EARTH . . . .   298 HEINES GRAVE   204
        LIKE THESE ON EARTH I WAIT FORLORN . . . . .   302 GRANDE CHARTR   88
        FOR THOU ART GONE AWAY FROM EARTH   . . . . .   310 OBERMANN   141
        EARTH HAPPIER THAN BEFORE   . . . .   314 OBERMANN MORE   56
        THOU FLEDST ME WHEN THE UNGENIAL EARTH   . .   315 OBERMANN MORE   77
        FILLD EARTH AND HEAVEN AND CAUGHT AWAY   . . .   317 OBERMANN MORE   143
        WHILE WE BELIEVED ON EARTH HE WENT . . . . .   318 OBERMANN MORE   169
        A GREEN NEW EARTH APPEARS   . . . .   322 OBERMANN MORE   286
        THOU FLEDDST ME WHEN THE UNGENIAL EARTH   . .   315 OBERMANN MORE   V 77
        SINCE LAST ON EARTH THERE LIVED AND WROUGHT   . .   315 OBERMANN MORE   V 83
        WHO UNDER EARTH WATCH GUILTY DEEDS OF MEN   . . .   332 MEROPE   74
        EVEN EARTH WHEREON HE TREADS . . . .   352 MEROPE   626
        FIRST CITY FOUNDED ON THE EARTH BY MEN . . . .   359 MEROPE   849
        FLED FOR YEARS AFTER OER THE FACE OF EARTH . . .   385 MEROPE   1423
        BUT THAT SINCE FIRST THE BLACK AND FRUITFUL EARTH   389 MEROPE   1536
        THIS AWE WHICH GUARDS OUR EARTH-SPRUNG LINEAL KINGS   389 MEROPE   1543
        WHICH FELLD HIM TO THE EARTH AND OER HIM STOOD . .   402 MEROPE   1922
        MIND IS THE SPELL WHICH GOVERNS EARTH AND HEAVEN . .   413 EMPEDOCLES I 2   27
        HEAVEN IS WITH EARTH AT STRIFE . . . .   416 EMPEDOCLES I 2   122
        OF EARTH AND AIR AND SEA . . . .   422 EMPEDOCLES I 2   292
        THAT SELF-HELPING SON OF EARTH . . . .   432 EMPEDOCLES II   103
        OUR BODIES TO EARTH   . . . .   439 EMPEDOCLES II   333

EARTH   (CONTINUED)
          OVER THE UNALLIED UNOPENING EARTH . . . . . .   439 EMPEDOCLES II   360
          WILL BLOW US FIERCELY BACK TO SEA AND EARTH   . . 439 EMPEDOCLES II   362
          THE SELF-HELPING SON OF EARTH . . . .   432 EMPEDOCLES II   V 103
          LONG SINCE HIS NAME IS HEARD ON EARTH NO MORE   . . 447 WESTMIN ABBEY   113
          THAT KNEW NOT EARTH SOARD UPWARDS TO THE SKY   . . 477 CROMWELL   178
          OF ALL LIVING THINGS THAT ON EARTH ARE BREATHING
                AND MOVING   HOMER TRANS   13
          BUT LET ME BE DEAD AND THE EARTH BE MOUNDED ABOVE ME   HOMER TRANS   37
          EARTH AND HEAVENS STAR-SPANGLED LOAD . . . . . .   PILLARS UNIVERS   4

EARTHEN
          HIS COAT HIS BASKET AND HIS EARTHEN CRUSE . . . . 255 SCHOLAR-GIPSY   13
          WE MINE THIS EARTHEN BALL   . . . .   423 EMPEDOCLES I 2   320

EARTHLY
          WHERE EARTHLY VOICE CLIMBS NEVER WING THEIR FLIGHT   10 MYCERINUS   44
          NO WEAK NURSLING OF AN EARTHLY SUN . . . . . .   30 NEW SIRENS   112
          FROM SOME TRANSIENT EARTHLY SUN   . . . . . .   31 NEW SIRENS   152
          SNATCHD AN EARTHLY INSPIRATION . . . .   31 NEW SIRENS   V 151
          OF THIS EARTHLY NATURE . . . .   39 STAGIRIUS   31
          BUT EARTHLY KNIGHTS HAVE HARDER HEARTS . . . .   159 NECKAN   19
          SINGS OF HIS EARTHLY BRIDAL   . . . .   159 NECKAN   21
          AND HE WHO FLAGGD NOT IN THE EARTHLY STRIFE   . . 172 IMMORTALITY   11
          AS HAND IN HAND FACE EARTHLY LIFE   . . . . .   179 FAREWELL   68
          HOW SWEET UNREACHD BY EARTHLY JARS . . . . .   180 FAREWELL   77
          ASKD AN OUTFIT FOR ITS EARTHLY ROAD   . . . . .   209 SELF-DECEPTION   8
          BEFORE MAN PARTED FOR THIS EARTHLY STRAND   . .   239 REVOLUTIONS   1
          AND STRANGE AND VAIN THE EARTHLY TURMOIL GROWS . . 267 THYRSIS   148
          THAT SMILE WAS HEINE FOR ITS EARTHLY HOUR . . . 298 HEINES GRAVE   210
          WHISPERING FROM ALL AROUND ALL EARTHLY THINGS MUST DIE 469 ALARIC AT ROME   180
          EVER AGAIN PUT EARTHLY LIKENESS ON . . . . . .   470 ALARIC AT ROME   206
          OF ALL THIRST OF EARTHLY THINGS   . . . . . .   META CLOISTER   2

EARTHS
          WHEREIN EARTHS GREAT ONES ARE DISQUIETED . . . .   7 REP FRIEND   10
          POINTING TO EARTHS CAREWORN CREATURES   . . . .   28 NEW SIRENS   61
          IN EARTHS THRONGD FIELDS WHERE WINNING COMES BY STRIFE 43 GIPSY CHILD   V 58
          COULD FROM EARTHS WAYS THAT FIGURE SLIGHT   . . . 184 TERRACE BERNE   29
          FAIL FROM EARTHS AIR AND I NOT KNOW   . . . . .   184 TERRACE BERNE   32
          WAS ONCE TOO AT THE FULL AND ROUND EARTHS SHORE   . . 211 DOVER BEACH   22
          DOWN IN OUR MOTHER EARTHS MIRACULOUS WOMB . . . 439 EMPEDOCLES II   340
          EARTHS OLD HEROIC FORMS IN PEACEFUL SLUMBERS DEEP   464 ALARIC AT ROME   60

EARTHWARD
          FROM THEIR EARTHWARD-BOUND DEVOTION . . . . . .   31 NEW SIRENS   157

EASE
          OR IN DEAF EASE ON THRONES OF DAZZLING SHEEN   . .   10 MYCERINUS   47
          AND EASE FROM SHAME AND REST FROM FEAR . . . .   21 YOUTH AND CALM   2
          THOUGH EASE DULLS GRACE AND WISDOM BE TOO PROUD   . . 44 GIPSY CHILD   63
          THOUGH EASE DULLS GRACE AND WISDOM IS TOO PROUD   . . 44 GIPSY CHILD   V 63
          WHO TREADS AT EASE LIFES UNCHEERD WAYS . . . .   59 RESIGNATION   237
          IS ILL AT EASE AND CALLS FOR THEE   . . . . .   87 SICK KING BOKH   4
          LONG THEY STAYD STILL THEN PACING AT THEIR EASE . . 150 TRISTRAM 3   42
          WHERE THIS PLAGUE DRIVES THEM AND HAVE LITTLE EASE   153 TRISTRAM 3   141
          THAT JOPPAN LEPERS EASE WAS PAIN . . . .   158 SAINT BRANDAN   72
          SMILES BROKE FROM US AND WE HAD EASE . . . . .   271 MEMORIAL VERSES   50
          HEALTH EASE A HEART ELATE   . . . .   273 EDW QUILLINAN   12
          BUT IF YOU CANNOT GIVE US EASE . . . .   302 GRANDE CHARTR   109
          THY FATHERS PASSION WAS THIS PEOPLES EASE   . . . 404 MEROPE   2000
          WHY ARE MEN ILL AT EASE   . . . .   417 EMPEDOCLES I 2   148
          ARE FOR THE HAPPY FOR THE SOULS AT EASE   . . .   436 EMPEDOCLES II   259
          THAT THEY SHOULD EASE GRAVE COUNSEL OF ITS CARE . .   RUDE ORATOR   10

EASED
          OF GRIEF AND EASED US WITH A THOUSAND SLEEPS   . .   43 GIPSY CHILD   52
          THE SPEAR AND DREW IT FROM HIS SIDE AND EASED   . . 85 SOHRAB RUSTUM   839
          SAW HIM LOOK EASED AND HURRIED BY   . . . . .   158 SAINT BRANDAN   52
          AND EASED OF BASKET AND OF ROD . . . .   248 KENSINGTON GARD   19
          AND COOL DRINKS AND AN EASED . . . .   293 HEINES GRAVE   19
          WE HAD THE POWER TO FEEL THE PRESSURE EASED   . . 436 EMPEDOCLES II   245

EASIER
          COULD LIFE RUN NO EASIER WAY . . . .   33 NEW SIRENS   V 200
          OR ARE WE EASIER TO HAVE READ   . . . .   304 GRANDE CHARTR   145
          NO EASIER NOR NO QUICKER PASSD . . . .   316 OBERMANN MORE   103
          BUT WE AN EASIER WAY TO CHEAT OUR PAINS HAVE FOUND   421 EMPEDOCLES I 2   271

EASILY
          EASILY QUELLD AND THE FINE . . . .   293 HEINES GRAVE   25
          WITH GOD AND FATE TO RAIL AT SUFFERING EASILY   . . 421 EMPEDOCLES I 2   281

EAST
          SEE THE WHITE EAST AND THE MORNING RAYS . . . .   34 NEW SIRENS   242
          THE LONG-MUSED THOUGHT TO NORTH SOUTH EAST AND WEST   45 IN UTRUMQUE PAR   6
          AND THE FIRST GREY OF MORNING FILLD THE EAST   . .   61 SOHRAB RUSTUM   1
          ONE FROM THE EAST ONE FROM THE WEST THEIR SHIELDS   75 SOHRAB RUSTUM   474

EAST   (CONTINUED)
        AND THE FIRST RAYS OF MORNING STREAKD THE EAST   • •   61 SOHRAB RUSTUM   V   1
        FORTH FROM THE EAST UP THE ASCENT OF HEAVEN   • •   105 BALDER DEAD 2   1
        BUT IN THE HILLS A STRONG EAST-WIND AROSE   • • • •   118 BALDER DEAD 3   181
        NORTH SOUTH EAST WEST THEY STRUCK AND ROAMD THE WORLD   122 BALDER DEAD 3   304
        OF JARNVID WHICH TO EAST OF MIDGARD LIES   • • • •   123 BALDER DEAD 3   330
        WHILE FROM THE EAST THE GIANT RYMER STEERS   • • • •   127 BALDER DEAD 3   478
        THE SEER FROM THE EAST WAS THEN IN LIGHT   • • • •   170 EAST AND WEST   10
        HE OF THE MYSTIC EAST IS TOUCHD WITH NIGHT   • • • •   170 EAST AND WEST   14
        THE NILE THE EAST   • • • • • • • • • • • •   277 SOUTHERN NIGHT   68
        THE BROODING EAST WITH AWE BEHELD   • • • • • •   316 OBERMANN MORE   105
        THE EAST BOWD LOW BEFORE THE BLAST   • • • • •   316 OBERMANN MORE   109

EASTER
        WAS AT EASTER-TIDE PUT ON   • • • • • • •   16 CHURCH BROU 1   110
        TWILL BE EASTER-TIME IN THE WORLD AH ME   • • • •   163 FORSAKEN MERM   58

EASTERN
        TROOPS LIKE EASTERN KINGS APPEARING   • • • • • • •   26 NEW SIRENS   V 23
        FOR ME NO EASTERN DESERT LONE   • • • • • • • •   317 OBERMANN MORE   151
        ALL IDLY FLUTTERD IN THE EASTERN GALE   • • • •   473 CROMWELL   68

EASTWARD
        EASTWARD THE OTHER FROM THE DYING DAY   • • • •   170 EAST AND WEST   7
        OR FAR EASTWARD WHERE UP-PILD   • • • • • • •   PILLARS UNIVERS   6
        THERE OR EASTWARD WHERE UP-PILD   • • • • • •   PILLARS UNIVERS   V   6

EASY
        SHOUTS GREETING FROM HIS EASY CHAIR   • • • • • •   53 RESIGNATION   43
        IN AN EASY OLD AGE IN A HAPPY HOME   • • • • • •   199 FRAG DEJANEIRA   23
        O EASY ACCESS TO THE HEARERS GRACE   • • • • •   265 THYRSIS   91
        ARE APT TO SNAP THE EASY-STRETCHD ENDURE   • • •   339 MEROPE   308
        OF DARING EASY AS IT SEEMS WHEN DONE   • • • • •   403 MEROPE   1949
        IS EASY AT NO MOMENT BUT THE RIGHT   • • • • • •   403 MEROPE   1950
        BUT I HAVE NOT GROWN EASY IN THESE BONDS   • • • •   440 EMPEDOCLES II   397

EAT
        WHAT NEWS BUT SIT DOWN FIRST AND EAT AND DRINK   • •   67 SOHRAB RUSTUM   206
        NOT NOW A TIME WILL COME TO EAT AND DRINK   • • • •   67 SOHRAB RUSTUM   208
        EAT NOT THE FRUIT OF THEIR OWN HANDS   • • • • • •   93 SICK KING BOKH   170
        HERE AND THERE EAT AND DRINK   • • • • • • • •   288 RUGBY CHAPEL   61

EAVES
        UNDER THE EAVES PEERD ROWS OF INDIAN CORN   • • • •   25 DREAM   19
        TO SEE THE SPARKLE ON THE EAVES   • • • • • •   141 TRISTRAM 1   357

EBB
        OF PASSIONS THAT FOR EVER EBB AND FLOW   • • • •   37 YOUTHS AGIT   4
        THE EBB-TIDE LEAVES DRY   • • • • • • • • • •   165 FORSAKEN MERM   135
        ABOVE THE HOWLING SENSES EBB AND FLOW   • • • •   169 EAST LONDON   11
        SELF-SWAYD OUR FEELINGS EBB AND SWELL   • • • •   180 ISOLATION MARG   11
        INTO HIS MIND THE TURBID EBB AND FLOW   • • • •   211 DOVER BEACH   17
        WHERE THE EBB MEETS THE MOON-BLANCHD SAND   • • • •   211 DOVER BEACH   V   8
        INTO HIS MIND THE TROUBLED EBB AND FLOW   • • • •   211 DOVER BEACH   V 17
        NEVER TO EBB THE ACCURST   • • • • • • • • •   378 MEROPE   1245
        EBB OF LIFE AND MORTAL PAIN   • • • • • • • •   456 POOR MATTHIAS   124

EBBD
        NOR PALLD WITH ITS OWN FULNESS EBBD AND DIED   • •   12 MYCERINUS   116
        TILL NOW ALL STRENGTH WAS EBBD AND FROM HIS LIMBS   • •   86 SOHRAB RUSTUM   853
        WHERE AS LIFE EBBD HIS BEARERS LAID HIM DOWN   • •   357 MEROPE   783

EBBS
        JOY COMES AND GOES HOPE EBBS AND FLOWS   • • • •   44 QUESTION   1

EBONY
        HER ROSARY-BEADS OF EBONY TIPPD WITH GOLD   • • • •   152 TRISTRAM 3   93

ECHEMUS
        SENT FORTH ECHEMUS THE VICTOR THE KING   • • • •   344 MEROPE   442

ECHO
        ECHO HER STORMY SCREAM AS SHE SAILS BY   • • • •   78 SOHRAB RUSTUM   572
        AND FROM THE GLENS ALL DAY AN ECHO CAME   • • • •   106 BALDER DEAD 2   54
        HOW LONELY RINGS THE ECHO OF MY FEET   • • • • •   242 SUMMER NIGHT   2
        ECHO THE BLAME OF HER FOES   • • • • • • •   294 HEINES GRAVE   75
        HERE IS NO ECHO TO THE SOUND OF HOME   • • • • •   468 ALARIC AT ROME   149

ECHOED
        TO HAVE ECHOED THE MOAN OF MY SEAS   • • • • • •   231 YOUTH OF NATURE   124
        ECHOED HER BACK BY THE CROWD   • • • • • • • •   281 HAWORTH CHURCH   43
        SEEMS STRANGELY ECHOED BACK BY TONES OF YESTERDAY   464 ALARIC AT ROME   48

ECHOES
        SOMETIMES FROM THE GROVES CENTRE ECHOES CAME   • •   12 MYCERINUS   124
        SENT ECHOES THROUGH THE NIGHT TO WAKE   • • • •   177 FAREWELL   3
        COME AIRS AND FLOATING ECHOES AND CONVEY   • • • •   247 BURIED LIFE   75

ECHOING
        ECHOING ROUND THIS CASTLE OLD   • • • • • • • • •   12 CHURCH BROU 1   2

ECHOING   (CONTINUED)
      IN THE BLANK ECHOING SOLITUDE IF EARTH   . . . .   45 IN UTRUMQUE PAR   24
      WITH ECHOING STRAITS BETWEEN US THROWN   . . . . 182 TO MARG CONT   2
      OR WHERE THE ECHOING OARS   . . . . 193 STRAYED REVEL   258
      ECHOING THE SCREAMS OF THE EAGLES   . . . . . . 252 FUTURE   10
      IN ECHOING UNNEARD SILENCE   . . . . 437 EMPEDOCLES II   295

ECSTASY
      HOURS IF NOT OF ECSTASY   . . . . 137 TRISTRAM 1   232
      DRINKS UP DELIGHTED ECSTASY   . . . . 227 EPILOG LAOCOON   194

EDDIES
      IN THE YELLOW EDDIES   . . . . 192 STRAYED REVEL   199

EDDY
      IN ACTIONS DIZZYING EDDY WHIRLD   . . . . . .   60 RESIGNATION   277
      MOST MEN EDDY ABOUT   . . . . 288 RUGBY CHAPEL   60
      IN AN EDDY OF PURPOSELESS DUST   . . . . 288 RUGBY CHAPEL   77

EDDYING
      ROUND ALPINE SUMMITS EDDYING ROSE   . . . . .   52 RESIGNATION   8
      WASHD EDDYING FROM THIS BANK THEIR HOME   . . .   58 RESIGNATION   202
      EDDYING AND MOANING ROUND AND SWEPT THE PLAIN   . .   75 SOHRAB RUSTUM   V 484
      WHO ALL WILL FLIT LIKE EDDYING LEAVES AROUND   . . 100 BALDER DEAD 1   177
      OF EDDYING FORMS   . . . . 185 STRAYED REVEL   5
      OF EDDYING FORMS   . . . . 194 STRAYED REVEL   296
      YES ALL THIS EDDYING MOTLEY THRONG   . . . . . 226 EPILOG LAOCOON   157
      EDDYING AT LARGE IN BLIND UNCERTAINTY   . . . . 246 BURIED LIFE   43
      EDDYING ABOUT IN BLIND UNCERTAINTY   . . . . . 246 BURIED LIFE   V 43

EDEN
      AIRS FROM THE EDEN OF YOUTH   . . . . 235 YOUTH OF MAN   91

EDGE
      UPON THE MOSSY ROCKS AT THE STREAMS EDGE   . . .   25 DREAM   14
      TO THE STEEP EDGE OF SOME GREAT VALLEY COMES   . . 113 BALDER DEAD 2   296
      THAT CITIES WILL CROWD TO ITS EDGE   . . . . . 253 FUTURE   60
      BY THE LAKE-EDGE BROKE THE SHARP CRY OF HOUNDS . . 357 MEROPE   787
      AT LAST THE CRY DREW TO THE WATERS EDGE   . . . 357 MEROPE   806
      THAT CLIMB FROM THE STREAMS EDGE THE LONG GREY TUFTS 406 EMPEDOCLES I 1   16

EDGED
      BEYOND THE HEATHS EDGED BY THE LONELY SEA   . . . 154 TRISTRAM 3   155
      WHERE MOST THE GIPSIES BY THE TURF-EDGED WAY   . . 258 SCHOLAR-GIPSY   112

EDGES
      OF THE NIGHT-WIND DOWN THE VAST EDGES DREAR   . . 211 DOVER BEACH   27

EEN
      AND YET EEN THERE THE CANVAS GLOWD   . . . . . 222 EPILOG LAOCOON   23
      HAVE TEMPERD ME EEN THUS AND IN SOME SOULS . . . 366 MEROPE   1024
      HOMES EEN NOW IS THERE WAIL   . . . . 369 MEROPE   1095

EFFACE
      TO EFFACE IN ME THE MEMORY OF HIS CRIME   . . . 387 MEROPE   1478
      THOUGH IT EFFACE NOT THAT YET MAKES ME WISH   . . 387 MEROPE   1479
      EFFACE THE ENDLESS   . . . . 398 MEROPE   1804
      EFFACE THE HUMBLER GRAVES OF SEBERTS LINE   . . . 445 WESTMIN ABBEY   54

EFFACED
      MAY BE BY MAN EFFACED MAN CAN CONTROL   . . . .   6 GEO CRUIKSHANK   12
      ME LET NO HALF-EFFACED MEMORIES CUMBER   . . . . 206 SEPARATION   9
      THE BOUNDS OF EFFACED STATES   . . . . 423 EMPEDOCLES I 2   324

EFFACING
      EXPERIENCE LIKE A SEA SOAKS ALL-EFFACING IN   . . 419 EMPEDOCLES I 2   201

EFFECT
      THAT DOOM OBTAIN EFFECT FROM GODS OR MEN   . . . 349 MEROPE   558

EFFIGY
      TO-DAYS EXACT REPEATED EFFIGY   . . . . 152 TRISTRAM 3   95

EFFLUENCE
      UPON OUR LIFE A RULING EFFLUENCE SEND   . . . . 236 PALLADIUM   22

EFFORT
      OUTLASTS EACH EFFORT INTEREST HOPE   . . . . .   58 RESIGNATION   217
      VAIN IS THE EFFORT TO FORGET   . . . . 207 ON THE RHINE   1
      THERE IS NO EFFORT ON MY BROW   . . . . 241 MORALITY   25
      EFFORT UNMEANING AND VAIN   . . . . 288 RUGBY CHAPEL   78
      WHAT THOUGH THERE STILL NEED EFFORT STRIFE . . . 322 OBERMANN MORE   289
      OR OUR OWN WANT OF EFFORT BE THE BAR   . . . . . 352 MEROPE   643
      TO GUIDE OUR EFFORT TO A PROSPEROUS CLOSE   . . . 332 MEROPE   V 75
      LEAVES HUMAN EFFORT SCOPE   . . . . 426 EMPEDOCLES I 2   423
      AND WE SHALL FEEL OUR POWERS OF EFFORT FLAG   . . 440 EMPEDOCLES II   387

EFFORTS
      THAT NATURAL CAUSES MAR THY EFFORTS AND NOT FATE . .   EMPEDOCLES I 2   V

EGREMONT
AND EGREMONT SLEEPS BY THE SEA • • • • • • • • 228 YOUTH OF NATURE 17

EGYPT
YE MEN OF EGYPT YE HAVE HEARD YOUR KING • • • • 11 MYCERINUS 73
WHICH VENICE SHIPS DO FROM SWART EGYPT BRING • • 150 TRISTRAM 3 41

EIGHT
EIGHT IN NUMBER NOW THE YEARS • • • • • • • 458 POOR MATTHIAS 202

EIGHTEEN
SO CHRIST SAID EIGHTEEN HUNDRED YEARS AGO • • • • 237 PROGRESS 13

ELASTIC
AND NUMB THE ELASTIC POWERS • • • • • • • • 259 SCHOLAR-GIPSY 146

ELATE
HEALTH EASE A HEART ELATE • • • • • • • • 273 EDW QUILLINAN 12
AND WHO CAN BE ALONE ELATE • • • • • • • • 321 OBERMANN MORE 247

ELATED
WHEN WITH ELATED HEARTS WE JOINED YOUR TRAIN • • 436 EMPEDOCLES II 238

ELATION
GAY RAIMENT SPARKLING GAUDS ELATION STRONG • • • • 166 AUSTERITY POET 7
COLD THE ELATION OF JOY • • • • • • • • • • 231 YOUTH OF NATURE 95

ELBRUIS
GREAT ELBRUIS WHITENS CLEAR • • • • • • • • PILLARS UNIVERS 10

ELBURZ
OF ELBURZ FROM THE ARALIAN ESTUARIES • • • • • • 64 SOHRAB RUSTUM 114

ELDER
AND FROM THE ELDER-BLOSSOM WHITE • • • • • 218 BACCHANALIA 1 11
BEHOLD THE ELDER TO-DAY • • • • • • • • • 281 HAWORTH CHURCH 30
OF MY TWO ELDER SONS SLAIN LONG AGO • • • • • 367 MEROPE 1038

ELDEST
THINE ELDEST AND OF ME THE GODS ARE SPRUNG • • • 121 BALDER DEAD 3 285
FELL THE ELDEST OF THE SONS OF HERACLES • • • • 344 MEROPE 445
THE ELDEST MIGHTIEST BROTHER TEMENUS TOOK • • • • 389 MEROPE 1550

ELECT
ELECT HIMSELF HEAVENS DESTINED ARM • • • • • • 353 MEROPE 691

ELECTRA
AH PYLADES AND ELECTRA • • • • • • • • • 344 MEROPE 459
HAD NOT ELECTRA TO HAUNT • • • • • • • • • 346 MEROPE 507

ELECTRIFY
ELECTRIFY THEIR HEARTS MAKE THEM NO MORE A MOB • • 383 MEROPE V1360

ELEGY
WHISPERS IN MOURNFUL TONES THY SILENT ELEGY • • 464 ALARIC AT ROME 66

ELEMENT
WHERE WILL THEY FIND THEIR PARENT ELEMENT • • • • 439 EMPEDOCLES II 347

ELEMENTAL
IT PASSD THAT ELEMENTAL SWELL • • • • • • • • 319 OBERMANN MORE 207

ELEMENTS
AND TURN THEE TO THE ELEMENTS THY FRIENDS • • • • 429 EMPEDOCLES II 25
TO THE ELEMENTS IT CAME FROM • • • • • • • 439 EMPEDOCLES II 331
AND THEREFORE O YE ELEMENTS I KNOW • • • • • • 441 EMPEDOCLES II 404

ELEUSINIAN
THE CHARMD BABE OF THE ELEUSINIAN KING • • • • 446 WESTMIN ABBEY 85

ELF
IS EVERYWHERE SUSTAINS THE WISE THE FOOLISH ELF • • 422 EMPEDOCLES I 2 306

ELLA
LIVING BUT ELLA CAPTURED HIM AND SLEW • • • • 117 BALDER DEAD 3 128

ELLAS
NOR ELLAS VICTORY ON THE ENGLISH COAST • • • • 117 BALDER DEAD 3 147

ELM
TO DANCE AROUND THE FYFIELD ELM IN MAY • • • • 257 SCHOLAR-GIPSY 83
PAST THE HIGH WOOD TO WHERE THE ELM-TREE CROWNS • • 263 THYRSIS 12
THE SIGNAL-ELM THAT LOOKS ON ILSLEY DOWNS • • • • 263 THYRSIS 14
THAT SINGLE ELM-TREE BRIGHT • • • • • • • 263 THYRSIS 26
UP PAST THE WOOD TO WHERE THE ELM-TREE CROWNS • • 263 THYRSIS V 12

ELMS
OF DARK ELMS SHOOT ROUND DROPPING DOWN THE 19 MODERN SAPPHO 6
    PROUD STREAM
OF DARK ELMS COME ROUND DROPPING DOWN THE PROUD STREAM 19 MODERN SAPPHO V 6
AND STILL THE UNBLACKEND ELMS WERE GAY • • • • 222 EPILOG LAOCOON 39

ELMS   (CONTINUED)
     THE GRASS THE ELMS THAT BLOSSOMD THORN   . . . .   222 EPILOG LAOCOON   52
     THE DARKER ELMS STAND GRAVE AND DUN   . . . . . .   248 KENSINGTON GARD   V
     THE MASSIER ELMS STAND GRAVE AND DUN   . . . . . .   KENSINGTON GARD   V
     OF WITHERD LEAVES AND THE ELMS   . . . .   286 RUGBY CHAPEL   4

ELOQUENCE
     OF HER OWN ELOQUENCE   . . . .   39 STAGIRIUS   27

ELOQUENT
     IS ELOQUENT IS WELL BUT TIS NOT TRUE   . . . . . .   247 BURIED LIFE   66
     UNHAPPY ELOQUENT THE CHILD   . . . .   285 HAWORTH CHURCH   105
     YES IN SUCH ELOQUENT SILENCE DIDST THOU LIE   . .   464 ALARIC AT ROME   67

ELSE
     BUT ELSE IT IS A LONELY TIME   . . . .   17 CHURCH BROU 2   23
     BUT ELSE THE WOODS AND FIELDS ARE DUMB   . . . .   17 CHURCH BROU 2   31
     HAVE KNOWN TOO MUCH OR ELSE FORGOTTEN ALL   . . .   43 GIPSY CHILD   48
     BLITHE ALL ELSE STIRS THOU STIRREST NOT AVERSE   . . 41 GIPSY CHILD   V 13
     OR ELSE TOO WEAK AND ALL EYES TURN TO THEE   . . .   67 SOHRAB RUSTUM   218
     OR ELSE THY BONES SHALL STREW THIS SAND TILL WINDS   72 SOHRAB RUSTUM   376
     OR ELSE THAT THE GREAT RUSTUM WOULD COME DOWN   .   77 SOHRAB RUSTUM   531
     YET HERE THOU ERREST SOHRAB OR ELSE MEN   . . . .   80 SOHRAB RUSTUM   643
     BUT ELSE THEY ARE SO STILL   . . . .   141 TRISTRAM 1   350
     OR ELSE SHE WILL FALL MUSING HER BLUE EYES   . . .   152 TRISTRAM 3   90
     UNTIL THEY CRUMBLE OR ELSE GROW LIKE STEEL   . . .   153 TRISTRAM 3   121
     ITS ELSE UNUTTERABLE SPELL   . . . .   223 EPILOG LAOCOON   86
     BRIGHT ELSE AND FAST THE STREAM OF LIFE MAY ROLL . 238 PROGRESS   29
     ELSE WERT THOU LONG SINCE NUMBERD WITH THE DEAD   . 259 SCHOLAR-GIPSY   153
     ELSE HADST THOU SPENT LIKE OTHER MEN THY FIRE   . . 259 SCHOLAR-GIPSY   154
     WHAT ELSE IS ALL THESE WATERS ARE   . . . . . .   279 SOUTHERN NIGHT   133
     WHAT ELSE IS STEEPD IN LUCID SHEEN   . . . . . .   279 SOUTHERN NIGHT   134
     WHAT ELSE IS BRIGHT WHAT ELSE IS FAIR   . . . .   279 SOUTHERN NIGHT   135
     WHAT ELSE IS BRIGHT WHAT ELSE IS FAIR   . . . .   279 SOUTHERN NIGHT   135
     WHAT ELSE SERENE   . . . .   279 SOUTHERN NIGHT   136
     BY FORMER AGES WHO ELSE   . . . .   290 RUGBY CHAPEL   148
     ELSE OF THE MYRIADS WHO FILL   . . . .   291 RUGBY CHAPEL   183
     HATE TO THEIR RULE WHICH ELSE WOULD DIE AWAY   . . 331 MEROPE   43
     A MOURNFUL FEUD ALIVE WHICH ELSE WOULD DIE   . . .   332 MEROPE   82
     CLAIMS EVER HOSTILE ELSE AND SET THY SON   . . .   335 MEROPE   168
     YET NOT FOR THIS ELSE MIGHT THY CRIME IN PART   . . 339 MEROPE   314
     WHILE ALL ELSE GRIEVES HIM THAT HIS GRANDCHILDS DEATH 359 MEROPE   851
     OR ELSE NOT LIVE AT ALL BUT HERE I HAUNT   . . .   366 MEROPE   1020
     IN ALL ELSE WILLING TO BE TAUGHT IN THIS   . . .   379 MEROPE   1258
     NOR ANY PLEADER ELSE SHALL BE INDULGED   . . . .   389 MEROPE   1527
     ALL ELSE BLACK WATER AND AFLOAT   . . . . . .   479 HAYSWATER BOAT   15
     WHERE TIME ELSE DUMB HATH SIGNIFIED HIS SWAY   . .   FRAGMENT 2   2

ELSEWHERE
     DISTRESS ELSEWHERE . . . .   51 CONSOLATION   60
     SHE SMILES ELSEWHERE WE MAKE A DIN   . . . . . .   204 EUPHROSYNE   V
     TO WORK OR WAIT ELSEWHERE OR HERE   . . . . . .   251 WISH   52
     LOOKS ONCE AND DRIVES ELSEWHERE AND LEAVES   415 EMPEDOCLES I 2   86
            ITS LAST EMPLOY
     TO ATTACH BLAME ELSEWHERE   . . . .   422 EMPEDOCLES I 2   308
     A LIKE EVENT ELSEWHERE   . . . .   425 EMPEDOCLES I 2   385

ELUSIVE
     THAT FLYING AND ELUSIVE SHADOW REST   . . . . .   247 BURIED LIFE   93

ELYSIAN
     BEFORE THEY REACH THE ELYSIAN PLACE   . . . . .   414 EMPEDOCLES I 2   74

EMBATTLED
     TWICE ERE THAT DAY OF SHAME THE EMBATTLED FOE   . . 465 ALARIC AT ROME   73
     OF HEAVENS EMBATTLED MYRIADS SWEPT ALONG   . . . .   473 CROMWELL   44

EMBERS
     BAKED ON THE EMBERS ALL AROUND   . . . .   191 STRAYED REVEL   167

EMBITTER
     TO EMBITTER HUMAN LIFE MALIGNANT DEITIES   . . .   422 EMPEDOCLES I 2   311

EMBLEMS
     EMBLEMS OF HOPE OVER THE GRAVE   . . . .   305 GRANDE CHARTR   201
     EMBLEMS OF LIGHT ABOVE THE GRAVE   . . . . . .   305 GRANDE CHARTR   V 201

EMBOLDEND
     EMBOLDEND BY MY LENIENCE THINK IT FEAR   . . . .   341 MEROPE   373

EMBOSSED
     PUT TIGHTNESS IN THY GOLD-EMBOSSED REIN   . . . .   349 MEROPE   574

EMBRACE
     HER LOOK WAS LIKE A SAD EMBRACE   . . . . . .   140 TRISTRAM 1   322
     WHICH THE LIGHTNINGS DOTH EMBRACE   . . . . . .   431 EMPEDOCLES II   72
     CAME FAINT AND FEEBLE IN THE EMBRACE OF DEATH   . . 478 CROMWELL   208

EMBRACED
     AND HE RAN FORWARD AND EMBRACED HIS KNEES   . . .   71 SOHRAB RUSTUM   341
     AND HE RAN FORWARDS AND EMBRACED HIS KNEES   . . .   71 SOHRAB RUSTUM   V 341

EMBRACES
    THE DELIGHT OF DEATH-EMBRACES · · · · · · · ·   27 NEW SIRENS   55
    THE DELIGHT OF FIERCE EMBRACES · · · · · · · ·   27 NEW SIRENS   V 55

EMBREATHED
    DEEP HAVE EMBREATHED AT ITS CORE   · · · · · · 299 HEINES GRAVE   230

EMBROIDERD
    IN HIS WHITE QUAINT-EMBROIDERD FROCK · · · · · ·   57 RESIGNATION   182

EMBROILD
    CAN HOUSES THUS ILL-SEATED THUS EMBROILD · · · · 390 MEROPE   1559
    AND JUDGMENT ALL EMBROILD   · · · · · · · · · 425 EMPEDOCLES I 2   394
    AND JUDGMENTS ALL EMBROILD   · · · · · · · · 425 EMPEDOCLES I 2 V 394

EMERGE
    EMERGE AND SHINE UPON THE ARAL SEA   · · · · ·   87 SOHRAB RUSTUM   892
    THERE RE-ASSEMBLING WE SHALL SEE EMERGE   · · · 128 BALDER DEAD 3   527
    EMERGE AND RESTING ON THE MOONLIT PALES   · · · · 261 SCHOLAR-GIPSY   217

EMERGING
    EMERGING ON THE GREEN HILL-SIDE   · · · · · ·   54 RESIGNATION   59
    DESCRIED AT SUNRISE AN EMERGING PROW · · · · · 262 SCHOLAR-GIPSY   233

EMINENT
    BUT PRIZED BUT LOVED BUT EMINENT IN YOU   · · · ·   6 REP FRIEND | 3
    SEE THE WIFE OF HECTOR THAT GREAT PRE-EMINENT CAPTAIN   HOMER TRANS   33

EMOTION
    CHANGING THE PURE EMOTION   · · · · · · · ·   39 STAGIRIUS   24
    FREEZING THE PURE EMOTION   · · · · · · · ·   39 STAGIRIUS   V 24
    GIVE HIM EMOTION THOUGH PAIN · · · · · · · · 200 EARLY DEATH   · 16
    BUT NO EMOTION NONE   · · · · · · · · · 213 GROWING OLD   30
    LIFE AND EMOTION AND I · · · · · · · · · · 230 YOUTH OF NATURE   90
    NOR LIFE NOR EMOTION NOR POWER · · · · · · 233 YOUTH OF MAN   31
    A STRONG EMOTION ON HER CHEEK   · · · · · · 241 MORALITY   22
    THE HEART LESS BOUNDING AT EMOTION NEW   · · · · 266 THYRSIS   139
    AH NOT THE EMOTION OF THAT PAST   · · · · · · 321 OBERMANN MORE   241

EMOTIONS
    HATH YOUR WISDOM FELT EMOTIONS · · · · · · ·   29 NEW SIRENS   85
    HATH YOUR WISDOM KNOWN EMOTIONS   · · · · · · ·   29 NEW SIRENS   V 85
    IN A TOO STRONG EMOTIONS SWAY · · · · · · · · 178 FAREWELL ·   30

EMPEDOCLES
    I KNOW NOT IN WHAT MIND EMPEDOCLES   · · · · · 407 EMPEDOCLES I 1   21
    AND IN THE LITTER SATE EMPEDOCLES   · · · · · · 407 EMPEDOCLES I 1   42
    THOU MUST BE VIEWLESS TO EMPEDOCLES   · · · · · 408 EMPEDOCLES I 1   52
    WOULD I BESTOW TO HELP EMPEDOCLES   · · · · · · 409 EMPEDOCLES I 1   102
    AND WHOM EMPEDOCLES CALLD BACK TO LIFE   · · · · 410 EMPEDOCLES I 1   111
    EMPEDOCLES WOULD SAY SO DID HE DEIGN · · · · · 410 EMPEDOCLES I 1   137
    I MUST REJOIN EMPEDOCLES DO THOU   · · · · · · 411 EMPEDOCLES I 1   165
    LET US REST HERE AND NOW EMPEDOCLES   · · · · · 412 EMPEDOCLES I 2   7
    NO THOU ART COME TOO LATE EMPEDOCLES · · · · · 429 EMPEDOCLES II   16
    AND SAY YE HELPERS HEAR EMPEDOCLES   · · · · · 429 EMPEDOCLES II   27
    A LIVING MAN NO MORE EMPEDOCLES   · · · · · · 438 EMPEDOCLES II   328
    AND SAY YE SERVANTS HEAR EMPEDOCLES · · · · · 429 EMPEDOCLES II   V 27

EMPEROR
    WITH THE ROMAN EMPEROR   · · · · · · · · · · 138 TRISTRAM 1   255

EMPERORS
    AN EMPERORS GIFT AT EARLY MORN HE PAINTS   · · · ·   81 SOHRAB RUSTUM   674

EMPIRE
    A QUEEN AND EMPIRE OVER ALL THE DEAD · · · · · · 121 BALDER DEAD 3   278
    THAT EMPIRE WILT THOU NOW INVADE LIGHT UP   · · · · 121 BALDER DEAD 3   279
    HIS MISTRESS USE HER EMPIRE AS SHE MAY   · · · · 155 TRISTRAM 3   184
    AND EMPIRE AFTER EMPIRE AT THEIR HEIGHT   · · · · 239 REVOLUTIONS   13
    AND EMPIRE AFTER EMPIRE AT THEIR HEIGHT   · · · · 239 REVOLUTIONS   13
    OF SOPHISTS HAS GOT EMPIRE IN OUR SCHOOLS   · · · · 410 EMPEDOCLES I 1   122
    SONOROUS WITNESS TO HIS EMPIRE GAVE   · · · · · · 476 CROMWELL   158
    THAT STREWD THE BLOOD-STAIND PATH WHERE EMPIRE LED   478 CROMWELL   226

EMPLOY
    SURELY THAN THOSE WHICH SHOULD THINE AGE EMPLOY   · ·   41 GIPSY CHILD   V 11
    FOR EVER LEAVES ITS VAIN EMPLOY   · · · · · · 206 RIVER   18
    DEEP IN HER UNKNOWN DAYS EMPLOY   · · · · · · 248 KENSINGTON GARD 12
    WE IN SOME UNKNOWN POWERS EMPLOY   · · · · · 310 OBERMANN   133
    AND JOY THAT SHOULD ALL HEARTS EMPLOY   · · · · 320 OBERMANN MORE   239
    WHAT STILL OF STRENGTH IS LEFT EMPLOY   · · · · 323 OBERMANN MORE   321
    LOOKS ONCE AND DRIVES ELSEWHERE AND LEAVES   415 EMPEDOCLES I 2   86
        ITS LAST EMPLOY
    AND SPEND OUR WIT TO NAME WHAT MOST EMPLOY UNNAMED   423 EMPEDOCLES I 2   331

EMPOWERD
    THOUGH TO HIS ACT EMPOWERD NAY IMPELLD   · · · · 385 MEROPE   1421

EMPRISE
    FOILING HER HIGH EMPRISE · · · · · · · · · ·   38 STAGIRIUS   20

EMPRIZE
        FOILING HER HIGH EMPRIZE . . . .   38 STAGIRIUS   V 20

EMPTY
        AND THROUGH THE EMPTY STREETS HE RODE AND PASSD . .   113 BALDER DEAD 2   308
        BUT EMPTY FOR HIS WIFE FOR NANNA CAME   . . .   125 BALDER DEAD 3   433
        WHY STOPS SHE BY THIS EMPTY PLAY-HOUSE DREAR   .   167 RACHEL 1   11
        SMOKELESS EMPTY   . . . .   187 STRAYED REVEL   45
        NO MORE AN EXILE FED ON EMPTY HOPES . . . . . .   335 MEROPE   169

EMULATE
        MAY THINK TO EMULATE   . . . .   308 OBERMANN   56

ENAMELLD
        HOUSES ARCADES ENAMELLD MOSQUES   . . . . . .   94 SICK KING BOKH   199

ENAMOURD
        DRAWS IN THE ENAMOURD GAZER TO ITS SHINING BREAST   424 EMPEDOCLES I 2   356

ENCHANTED
        STREAM ALL DAY THROUGH YOUR ENCHANTED LAWN . . .   26 NEW SIRENS   24
        WHERE MERLIN BY THE ENCHANTED THORN-TREE SLEEPS . .   154 TRISTRAM 3   158
        WITH DEW OR LISTEN WITH ENCHANTED EARS   . . .   261 SCHOLAR-GIPSY   219

ENCHANTER
        AS IF THE ENCHANTER MERLINS WILL   . . . . .   STANZAS CARNAC   V   7

ENCHANTMENTS
        THE ENCHANTMENTS THAT RECALL THE DEAD TO LIFE   . .   101 BALDER DEAD 1   209

ENCIRCLED
        HIS FLOWING LOCKS AND GOLD-ENCIRCLED BROW   . . . .   408 EMPEDOCLES I 1   60

ENCIRCLING
        FIRST MEETS THE ENCIRCLING HEATH AT ONCE ALL ROUND   TRISTRAM 3   V 14
        FIRST LEAVES THE ENCIRCLING HEATH AT ONCE ALL ROUND   TRISTRAM 3   V 14
        AT LAST THE ENCIRCLING TREES RETIRE   . . . . . .   300 GRANDE CHARTR   21

ENCLASPING
        THE ISLANDS FEEL THE ENCLASPING FLOW . . . . . .   182 TO MARG CONT   5

ENCOUNTER
        BUT WITH WHAT EYES SHOULD I ENCOUNTER THERE   . .   367 MEROPE   1032

ENCOURAGED
        OUR SOOTHED ENCOURAGED SOULS WILL DARE   . . . .   179 FAREWELL   62

ENCROACHING
        FROM THE ENCROACHING EUXINE SEA   . . . . . .   PILLARS UNIVERS   8

END
        THE CROWNING END OF LIFE AND YOUTH   . . . . .   21 YOUTH AND CALM   6
        TO GUIDE ME I HAVE STEERD BY TO THE END   . . . .   40 HUMAN LIFE   6
        HOPES BORN HERE AND BORN TO END   . . . . . .   44 QUESTION   20
        AND STILL EXPECTS AN END   . . . .   47 WORLD QUIETIST   16
        WELL PLEASED SEE END   . . . .   52 CONSOLATION   65
        FOR WILLINGLY I KNOW THOU METST THINE END   . . .   85 SOHRAB RUSTUM   823
        AND I SHALL NEVER END THIS LIFE OF BLOOD   . . .   85 SOHRAB RUSTUM   826
        AND FATE SET SEAL THAT SO HIS END MUST BE   . . .   96 BALDER DEAD 1   25
        IN THE STRAIT PASSAGE AT THE FARTHER END   . . .   107 BALDER DEAD 2   88
        NOT FOR SUCH END O QUEEN THOU HOLDST THY REALM   . .   110 BALDER DEAD 2   197
        IN THE STRAIT PASSAGE AT THE FURTHER END   . . .   107 BALDER DEAD 2   V 88
        TO THE WORLDS END AND BALDER NOW IS GONE   . . .   117 BALDER DEAD 3   121
        AT WINTERS END BEFORE THE SPRING BEGINS   . . .   122 BALDER DEAD 3   308
        HUSH TIS VAIN I FEEL MY END APPROACHING   . . .   145 TRISTRAM 2   81
        AND BROUGHT HER TALE TO AN END AND FOUND THE PATH   151 TRISTRAM 3   62
        ON HER WHITE PALFREY HERE HE MET HIS END   . . .   154 TRISTRAM 3   162
        CAN NEVER END THEIR TASKS ARE HARD TO PLEASE   . .   153 TRISTRAM 3   V 142
        HAD BEEN BUT AT THE END TO HER PURE SOUL   . . .   173 MONICAS PRAYER   9
        FROM ISOLATION WITHOUT END   . . . .   181 ISOLATION MARG   40
        SUCH END OERTOOK THAT LOVE   . . . .   197 FRAG ANTIGONE   70
        FROM HIS APPOINTED END   . . . .   197 FRAG ANTIGONE   83
        AND HIM ON WHOM AT THE END   . . . .   199 FRAG DEJANEIRA   18
        NO END BUT THIS YOU PRAISE   . . . .   199 FRAG DEJANEIRA   24
        SOME END IS THERE WE INDEED MAY GAIN . . . . .   210 SELF-DECEPTION   28
        REMEMBER EACH UNTO THE END   . . . .   217 NAMELESS EPIT   4
        FOLLOW ITS WINDINGS TO THE END   . . . . . .   227 EPILOG LAOCOON   192
        AND WHILE IT LASTS WE CANNOT WHOLLY END   . . .   236 PALLADIUM   24
        HERE LET THAT VOICE MAKE END THEN LET A STRAIN . .   238 PROGRESS   33
        CALM ME AH COMPOSE ME TO THE END   . . . . . .   240 SELF-DEPENDENCE   8
        AND AT ITS END TO STAY THE EYE   . . . . . .   248 KENSINGTON GARD   3
        AND WISH THE LONG UNHAPPY DREAM WOULD END   . . .   260 SCHOLAR-GIPSY   192
        HE SAID THE END IS EVERYWHERE   . . . . . .   271 MEMORIAL VERSES   27
        FOR FOOD TO KEEP HIM TILL HE END   . . . . . .   278 SOUTHERN NIGHT   83
        COME TO THE END OF OUR WAY   . . . .   289 RUGBY CHAPEL   108
        AND AT THE END OF THY DAY   . . . .   290 RUGBY CHAPEL   142
        THAT END TO HELP ATTAIN   . . . .   323 OBERMANN MORE   322
        THAT END TO HELP MEN GAIN   . . . .   323 OBERMANN MORE   V 322
        THIS END TO HELP ATTAIN   . . . .   323 OBERMANN MORE   V 322

END   (CONTINUED)
        THAT WILL I DO AND TO THIS END I CAME   • • • •   355 MEROPE   721
        TO THE STYMPHALIAN LAKE OUR JOURNEYS END   • • • •   356 MEROPE   749
        WHEREWITH FROM END TO END ARCADIA RINGS   • • • •   362 MEROPE   943
        WHEREWITH FROM END TO END ARCADIA RINGS   • • • •   362 MEROPE   943
        I ASK IF BLOODLESS MEANS MAY GAIN HIS END   • • • •   387 MEROPE   1465
        AS I HAVE PRAYD THEE THAT AND TO WHAT END   • • • •   412 EMPEDOCLES I 2   21
        END HERE ETNA BEYOND IN THE BROAD GLARE   • • • •   414 EMPEDOCLES I 2   53
        THEREFORE THEY DID NOT END THEIR DAYS   • • • •   427 EMPEDOCLES I 2   452
        WEEPING AT HIS MASTERS END   • • • •   434 EMPEDOCLES II   167
        WAIT FOR THE LEAVEN TO WORK THE LET TO END   • • • •   449 WESTMIN ABBEY   170
        ONE MORE GASP IT IS THE END   • • • • •   •   452 POOR MATTHIAS   13
        GEIST HAD VERSE TO MOURN HIS END   • • • •   454 POOR MATTHIAS   58
        POOR MATTHIAS SEE THY END   • • • • •   •   457 POOR MATTHIAS   173
        TO US DECLINING TOWRDS OUR END   • • • • •   • •   459 KAISER DEAD   35

ENDEARD
        AND TO MENS HEARTS THIS ANCIENT PLACE ENDEARD   • •   444 WESTMIN ABBEY   9

ENDEAVOUR
        ALL IT BEFORE ENDEAVOUR   • • • • • • • • •   320 OBERMANN MORE   214
        ALL THEY BEFORE ENDEAVOURD   • • • • • • • •   320 OBERMANN MORE   V 214

ENDED
        TOIL ENDED THROUGH THE SHINING STREETS   • • • •   57 RESIGNATION   167
        THE VISION ENDED I AWOKE   • • • • •   • • •   323 OBERMANN MORE   325
        SO HE PLAYD ON THEN ENDED WITH A SMILE   • • • •   357 MEROPE   784
        AM I NOT CONCLUDED NOW AND ENDED   • • •   • • •   482 THEKLAS ANSWER   3
        SHALL TRANSPORT THEE AWAY AND THE DAY OF THY   HOMER TRANS   28
              FREEDOM BE ENDED
        IN SOME OTHER SORT THAN YOUR LAST WHEN THE   HOMER TRANS   41
              BATTLE IS ENDED

ENDING
        AND TO WHAT GOAL WHAT ENDING BOUND   • • • • • • •   225 EPILOG LAOCOON   126

ENDLESS
        HERE MUST THOU LIE AND WAIT AN ENDLESS AGE   • • • •   126 BALDER DEAD 3   452
        OR HIS ENDLESS REVERIES   • • • • • • •   • • •   137 TRISTRAM 1   219
        TO RUE MY GUILT IN ENDLESS FLAME   • • • •   157 SAINT BRANDAN   32
        AND THEN THEIR ENDLESS BOUNDS THEY KNOW   • • • •   182 TO MARG CONT   6
        WHAT ENDLESS ACTIVE LIFE IS HERE   • • •   • • •   248 KENSINGTON GARD   14
        WHAT SWARMY ENDLESS LIFE IS HERE   • • •   • • •   KENSINGTON GARD V 14
        WHAT ACTIVE ENDLESS LIFE IS HERE   • • •   • • •   KENSINGTON GARD V 14
        ENDLESS EXTINCTION OF UNHAPPY HATES   • • •   • • •   333 MEROPE   102
        EFFACE THE ENDLESS   • • • • •   • • •   • • •   398 MEROPE   1804
        THEIR ENDLESS ABODE   • • • • •   • • •   • • •   442 EMPEDOCLES II   456
        THEY YOKD IN HIM FOR ENDLESS STRIFE   • • •   • • •   481 DESTINY   5

ENDOWD
        NOT WITHOUT JOY SO RADIANT SO ENDOWD • • • • • • •   46 IN UTRUMQUE PAR   33
        FOR ILL-ENDOWD FOR SUCH A WAY   • • • • • • • •   226 EPILOG LAOCOON   171

ENDS
        MAN MUST BEGIN KNOW THIS WHERE NATURE ENDS   • • • •   5 HARMONY NATURE   12
        ENDS WE SEEK WE NEVER SHALL ATTAIN   • • •   • • •   210 SELF-DECEPTION   26
        THE EPOCH ENDS THE WORLD IS STILL   • • •   • • •   219 BACCHANALIA 2   1
        THE EPOCH ENDS THE WORLD IS STILL   • • •   • • •   220 BACCHANALIA 2   28
        WHERE ENDS THE GLADE TO STAY THE EYE • • •   • • •   248 KENSINGTON GARD V 3
        WHICH DOOMS DREAD ENDS TO DREADFUL DEEDS   • • •   398 MEROPE   1808
        WE WANT ALL PLEASANT ENDS BUT WILL USE NO HARSH MEANS   420 EMPEDOCLES I 2   236

ENDURANCE
        OF CALM WISHES MILD ENDURANCE   • • • • • • • •   META CLOISTER   23

ENDURE
        ALL PAINS THE IMMORTAL SPIRIT MUST ENDURE   • • • •   3 SHAKESPEARE   12
        TILL THEN IF FATE SO WILLS LET ME ENDURE   • • • •   85 SOHRAB RUSTUM   837
        NOT DAILY TO ENDURE ABHORRING GODS   • • •   • • •   125 BALDER DEAD 3   398
        I REST THE THRALL OF HELA AND ENDURE • • •   • • •   129 BALDER DEAD 3   545
        RAISE ME MY PAGE THIS CANNOT LONG ENDURE   • • • •   130 TRISTRAM 1   3
        MUST EVERY DAY ENDURE   • • • • •   • • •   • • •   195 FRAG ANTIGONE   22
        SO BUT THY IMAGE ENDURE IN ITS PRIME • • •   • • •   206 SEPARATION   4
        ARE APT TO SNAP THE EASY-STRETCHD ENDURE   • • • •   339 MEROPE   308

ENDURED
        UNHAPPY HOW HAST THOU ENDURED TO LEAVE   • • • •   110 BALDER DEAD 2   180
        OF A MIGHTY OAK HAVE ENDURED   • • • •   • • •   287 RUGBY CHAPEL   33
        AY AGES LONG ENDURED HIS SPAN   • • • •   • • •   318 OBERMANN MORE   165
        BUT CALM BUT UNRESENTFUL I ENDURED   • • •   • • •   366 MEROPE   1014
        THAT ALL MAY BE ENDURED AND ALL FORGIVN   • • •   394 MEROPE   1710
        MIGHT ASK WHY WE ENDURED THEIR YOKE SO LONG   • •   402 MEROPE   1947

ENDURES
        I CHAFE NOT WITH THEE THAT THY HATE ENDURES   • •   398 MEROPE   1785

ENDURETH
        ITS WINTER WHICH ENDURETH STILL   • • • • • • •   136 TRISTRAM 1   176

ENDURING
        ARE THOSE FRAIL FORMS MORE ENDURING   • • • • • •   27 NEW SIRENS   43
        IS PERSISTENCE ALL-ENDURING   • • • • • • • •   SECOND BEST   V 22

ENDURING   (CONTINUED)
        AND THOU PROVED MUCH ENDURING   . . . .   194 STRAYED REVEL   287
        WHAT THINGS DARING WHAT ENDURING   . . . . . .   405 MEROPE   2023

ENDYMIONS
        TO HANG OVER ENDYMIONS SLEEP   . . . .   181 ISOLATION MARG   23

ENEMIES
        DIED IN HIS ENEMIES DAY   . . . .   229 YOUTH OF NATURE   35
        SLEW THEIR ENEMIES KING TISAMENUS   . . . . . .   344 MEROPE   451
        OF ENEMIES AND COUNT ·THEIR DYING GROANS   . .   387 MEROPE   1469
        SO RULE THAT EVEN THINE ENEMIES MAY FAIL   . . .   404 MEROPE   2005
        THE SOPHISTS ARE NO ENEMIES OF HIS   . . . . .   411 EMPEDOCLES I 1   146
        OF PITYING FRIENDS DERISIVE ENEMIES   . . . . .   LUCRETIUS 2   15

ENEMY
        ENEMY MOCKER WHOM THOUGH GODS WE HATE   . . .   114 BALDER DEAD 3   22
        AND YET NO ENEMY DID THIS O QUEEN   . . . . .   363 MEROPE   951
        NO ENEMY AND WHAT HAST THOU THEN HEARD   . . .   363 MEROPE   953
        THINE ENEMY THOU KNOWST NOT NOR HIS STRENGTH   .   381 MEROPE   1294
        THE STRICKEN KING A SECOND ENEMY   . . . . .   381 MEROPE   1297
        HER WELL-KNOWN ENEMY   . . . .   393 MEROPE   1666
        THINE ENEMY IS SLAIN THY SON IS KING   . . . .   403 MEROPE   1957
        THIS IRON MAN MY ENEMY AND THINE   . . . . .   403 MEROPE   1964

ENEMYS
        AT LARGE HIS ENEMYS SPEAR   . . . .   197 FRAG ANTIGONE   89
        BETTER FROM THINE THAN FROM AN ENEMYS TONGUE   . .   363 MEROPE   950
        THAT THOU MAYST READ THINE ENEMYS COUNSEL PLAIN   . .   380 MEROPE   1278
        TAKE THESE MY SON OVER THINE ENEMYS CORPSE   . . .   404 MEROPE   2010

ENERGIES
        ENERGIES WASTED UNIMPROVED HOURS   . . . . . .   470 ALARIC AT ROME   201

ENERGY
        SUBDUES THAT ENERGY TO SCAN   . . . .   56 RESIGNATION   146
        NO NO THE ENERGY OF LIFE MAY BE   . . . . . .   172 IMMORTALITY   9
        THAT WILL THAT ENERGY THOUGH RARE   . . . . .   178 FAREWELL   39
        EXHAUST THE ENERGY OF STRONGEST SOULS   . . . .   259 SCHOLAR-GIPSY   145
        FIND HENCEFORTH ENERGY AND HEART BUT I   . . . .   429 EMPEDOCLES II   10
        WHOSE WEARINESS NO ENERGY CAN REACH   . . . . .   429 EMPEDOCLES II   13

ENFOLDS
        OCEAN WHOSE WATERY RING ENFOLDS THE WORLD   . . .   99 BALDER DEAD 1   160
        AND NOW WITH GLEAMING RING ENFOLDS THE WORLD   . .   110 BALDER DEAD 2   211

ENFORCED
        TO OTHER GODS IT WERE IS MY ENFORCED   . . . . .   127 BALDER DEAD 3   501
        THE ENFORCED LEISURE OF AN EXILES EAR   . . . .   387 MEROPE   1488

ENFORCEMENT
        YES BUT THAT ENFORCEMENT STRONG   . . . .   454 POOR MATTHIAS   59

ENGAGED
        UNDER ITS IRON HEEL FATE FATE ENGAGED   . . . .   82 SOHRAB RUSTUM   714

ENGARLANDED
        THESE BRAMBLES PALE WITH MIST ENGARLANDED   . . .   267 THYRSIS   173

ENGINE
        OF ALL THE ENGINE-WORK OF STATE   . . . . . .   48 HORATIAN ECHO   14
        A PASSIVE ENGINE AT THEIR GENERALS WILL   . . . .   382 MEROPE   1340

ENGLAND
        GLEAMS AND IS GONE THE CLIFFS OF ENGLAND STAND   . .   210 DOVER BEACH   4
        SHINES AND IS GONE THE CLIFFS OF ENGLAND   . . .   210 DOVER BEACH   V   4
        ROME ENGLAND FRANCE YES NOR IN VAIN ESSAYD   . . .   239 REVOLUTIONS   6
        ENGLAND MY COUNTRY FOR WE   . . . .   294 HEINES GRAVE   72
        FROM ENGLAND GERMANY OR SPAIN   . . . .   301 GRANDE CHARTR   63
        NOT IN RICH ENGLAND BENT BUT TO MAKE POUR   . . .   480 HUNGARIAN NAT   2

ENGLANDS
        TO ENGLANDS CLIFFS MY GAZE IS TURND   . . . . . .   205 CALAIS SANDS   19
        TO ENGLANDS CLIFFS MY LOOK IS TURND   . . . . . .   205 CALAIS SANDS   V 19
        BY ENGLANDS LAKES IN GREY OLD AGE   . . . . . .   308 OBERMANN   49

ENGLISH
        NOR ELLAS VICTORY ON THE ENGLISH COAST   . . . .   117 BALDER DEAD 3   147
        SAY HAS SOME WET BIRD-HAUNTED ENGLISH LAWN   . . .   175 PARTING   19
        HERE THROUGH THE MOONLIGHT ON THIS ENGLISH GRASS   . .   201 PHILOMELA   17
        AH VAIN THESE ENGLISH FIELDS THIS UPLAND DIM   . .   267 THYRSIS   172
        NEATH THE MILD CANOPY OF ENGLISH AIR   . . . . .   268 THYRSIS   194
        NEATH THE SOFT CANOPY OF ENGLISH AIR   . . . . .   268 THYRSIS   V 194
        HOME ROUND INTO THE ENGLISH WAVE   . . . . . .   275 STANZAS CARNAC   37
        WHICH FOR TWO JADED ENGLISH SAVES   . . . . . .   277 SOUTHERN NIGHT   58
        IN CITIES SHOULD WE ENGLISH LIE   . . . .   277 SOUTHERN NIGHT   61
        WHO MOURN THEE IN THINE ENGLISH HOME   . . . . .   451 GEISTS GRAVE   54

ENGRAVE
        SILENT WHILE YEARS ENGRAVE THE BROW   . . . . . .   302 GRANDE CHARTR   113

ENGRAVES
    AND THOUGHTS THAT WERE BUT OUTLINES TIME ENGRAVES   473 CROMWELL   47

ENGULPHD
    THROUGH VALLEYS DEEP-ENGULPHD WITH ROARING STREAMS   99 BALDER DEAD 1   146
    THROUGH VALLEYS DEEP-ENGULPHD BY ROARING STREAMS . . 107 BALDER DEAD 2   84

ENHANCE
    GLOOMS THAT ENHANCE AND GLORIFY THIS EARTH . . . . 42 GIPSY CHILD   20

ENISLED
    YES IN THE SEA OF LIFE ENISLED . . . . 182 TO MARG CONT   1

ENJOIN
    THAT HOW TO ACCOMPLISH WHAT THE GODS ENJOIN   . . 379 MEROPE   1263

ENJOIND
    WHERE INTEREST SEEMS TO HAVE ENJOIND IT TOO   . . 341 MEROPE   364

ENJOINS
    ALL THE HEART ENJOINS BUT ONLY HERE . . . . . . META CLOISTER   24

ENJOY
    IN THY OWN HOUSE BREIDABLIK NOR ENJOY . . . 126 BALDER DEAD 3   449
    CAN NEITHER WHEN WE WILL ENJOY . . . . 310 OBERMANN   135
    THEN WE COULD STILL ENJOY THEN NEITHER THOUGHT . . 436 EMPEDOCLES II   240

ENJOYD
    THAT HE ENJOYD BUT PART BEING HEIR TO ALL . . . 394 MEROPE   1701
    TO HAVE ENJOYD THE SUN . . . . 425 EMPEDOCLES I 2   398

ENKERCHIEFD
    I KNOW THAT SOFT ENKERCHIEFD HAIR . . . . . . 174 MEETING   7

ENMITY
    THOUGH THE LOUD WORLD PROCLAIM THEIR ENMITY . . 1 QUIET WORK   4

ENNA
    SHE KNEW EACH LILY WHITE WHICH ENNA YIELDS . . . 265 THYRSIS   95

ENNERDALE
    WHICH BORDER ENNERDALE LAKE . . . . 228 YOUTH OF NATURE   16
    THAT BORDER ENNERDALE LAKE . . . . 228 YOUTH OF NATURE V 16

ENNOBLED
    WAS CALMD ENNOBLED COMFORTED SUSTAIND . . . . 12 MYCERINUS   111
    ENNOBLED BY A VAST REGRET . . . . 179 FAREWELL   71
    COMPOSED REFRESHD ENNOBLED CLEAR . . . . . 251 WISH   50

ENNOBLING
    ENNOBLING THIS DULL POMP THE LIFE OF KINGS . . . 9 MYCERINUS   11
    SEE AN ENNOBLING SIGHT . . . . 253 FUTURE   67

ENORMOUS
    LIE PRONE ENORMOUS DOWN THE MOUNTAIN SIDE . . . . 86 SOHRAB RUSTUM   863

ENOUGH
    ENOUGH WE LIVE AND IF A LIFE . . . . 60 RESIGNATION   261
    THERE ARE ENOUGH FOES IN THE PERSIAN HOST . . . 74 SOHRAB RUSTUM   443
    CHAMPIONS ENOUGH AFRASIAB HAS WHOM THOU . . . 74 SOHRAB RUSTUM   445
    ENOUGH OF TEARS YE GODS ENOUGH OF WAIL . . . 95 BALDER DEAD 1   18
    ENOUGH OF TEARS YE GODS ENOUGH OF WAIL . . . 95 BALDER DEAD 1   18
    WHEN YE ENOUGH HAVE WEPT THEN BUILD A PILE . . 115 BALDER DEAD 3   53
    BUT DEEP ENOUGH ALAS NONE EVER MINES . . . 246 BURIED LIFE   56
    ENOUGH THE BOAT WITH QUIET SHOCK . . . 276 SOUTHERN NIGHT   45
    ENOUGH OF THIS SINCE THAT I HAVE MAINTAIND . . . 334 MEROPE   134
    THIS WERE ENOUGH BUT LET ME TELL THEE TOO . . . 338 MEROPE   282
    ENOUGH OF THIS THOUGH NOT A FINGER STIR . . . 383 MEROPE   1375
    TELLS ME ENOUGH THOU KNOWST THE NEWS WHICH ALL . 393 MEROPE   1685
    THY CRIME THAT WERE ENOUGH TO MAKE ONE FEAR . . 396 MEROPE   1767
    ENOUGH ENOUGH I WILL NO LONGER HEAR . . . 397 MEROPE   1780
    ENOUGH ENOUGH I WILL NO LONGER HEAR . . . 397 MEROPE   1780
    ENOUGH OF THIS SINCE THEN I HAVE MAINTAIND . . 334 MEROPE V 134
    BLOOD I ASK NOT ENOUGH . . . . 348 MEROPE V
    SATED AND MORE THAN ENOUGH . . . . . . 348 MEROPE V
    ENOUGH OF THIS I SEE THE LITTER WIND . . . 411 EMPEDOCLES I 1   163
    IT IS ENOUGH THAT ALL MEN SPEAK OF IT . . . 413 EMPEDOCLES I 2   22
    THEY HAD STAYD LONG ENOUGH TO SEE . . . . 427 EMPEDOCLES I 2   444
    I HAVE BEEN ENOUGH ALONE . . . . 435 EMPEDOCLES II   219

ENQUIRE
    STILL TO ENQUIRE HOW PARTIES TEND . . . . . . 47 HORATIAN ECHO   2

ENQUIRED
    MET HIM AND OF HIS WAY OF LIFE ENQUIRED . . . . 256 SCHOLAR-GIPSY   43

ENQUIRERS
    NEW HEARTS WITH THE ENQUIRERS HOLY ROBE . . . . 198 FRAG DEJANEIRA   16

ENRAPTURE
    WHAT VOICES ENRAPTURE   • • • • • • • • • •   442 EMPEDOCLES II   443

ENSHAM
    ABOVE BY ENSHAM DOWN BY SANDFORD YIELDS   • • • •   266 THYRSIS   109

ENSIGN
    SCORNFUL APOLLOS ENSIGN LIE THOU THERE   • • • • •   434 EMPEDOCLES II   193

ENSIGNS
    THE CONQUERING TARTAR ENSIGNS THROUGH THE WORLD   • •   62 SOHRAB RUSTUM   47
    ASSUME THE ENSIGNS OF MY FATHERS POWER   • • • •   405 MEROPE   2020
    LIE THERE YE ENSIGNS   • • • • • • • • •   432 EMPEDOCLES II   109

ENSLAVE
    STRONG TO DECEIVE STRONG TO ENSLAVE   • • • • •   39 STAGIRIUS   28

ENSLAVED
    NOT TO DIE WHOLLY NOT TO BE ALL ENSLAVED   • • • •   441 EMPEDOCLES II   406

ENTANGLED
    HUMAN THINGS SO FAST ENTANGLED   • • • • • • • •   49 SECOND BEST   10
    HUMAN THINGS SO DEEP ENTANGLED   • • • • • • • •   SECOND BEST   V 10

ENTER
    HO ENTER YE WHO TARRY THERE   • • • • • • •   92 SICK KING BOKH   132
    RE-ENTER THEM WITH WONDER NEVER FILL   • • • • • •   128 BALDER DEAD 3   535
    AN UNKNOWN GUEST WILL ENTER BRINGING WORD   • • • •   331 MEROPE   48

ENTERD
    SLOW THEY ENTERD WITH THEIR MASTER   • • • •   14 CHURCH BROU 1   45
    SHE ENTERD THAT MOMENT HIS EYES TURND FROM ME   • •   19 MODERN SAPPHO   10
    AND GUDURZ ENTERD RUSTUMS TENT AND FOUND   • • •   67 SOHRAB RUSTUM   195
    AND A DEEP PITY ENTERD RUSTUMS SOUL   • • • • •   70 SOHRAB RUSTUM   319
    BUT AS HE ENTERD ON THE EXTREMEST BOUND   • • •   124 BALDER DEAD 3   381
    TREMBLING I ENTERD BEHELD   • • • • • • •   187 STRAYED REVEL   46

ENTEREST
    ENTEREST THE HOUSE OF THE GRAVE   • • • • • •   284 HAWORTH CHURCH   78

ENTERING
    ENTERING HEEDLESS KISSD BY THEE   • • • • • •   23 MEMORY-PICTURE   20
    HAD FOUND HIM SEATED AT THEIR ENTERING   • • • •   256 SCHOLAR-GIPSY   60
    MET THEM ENTERING THEIR HALLS   • • • • • • •   343 MEROPE   419

ENTERPRISING
    AT ONE BOLD WORD ONE ENTERPRISING BLOW   • • • •   402 MEROPE   1946

ENTERS
    HE ENTERS NOT THE ATLANTIC MAIN   • • • • • •   275 STANZAS CARNAC   40

ENTERTAINMENT
    FOR COURTEOUS ENTERTAINMENT WELCOME WARM   • • • •   356 MEROPE   760
    ALL ENTERTAINMENT WHICH A TRAVELLER NEEDS   • • • •   359 MEROPE   870

ENTERTAINST
    AND ENTERTAINST THOU CHILD SUCH DANGEROUS FRIENDS   380 MEROPE   1276

ENTHRALL
    WHOM LABOURS SELF-ORDAIND ENTHRALL   • • • • • •   52 RESIGNATION   14

ENTHROND
    ABIDES ENTHROND AMID THE MIST AND STORM   • • • •   472 CROMWELL   18

ENTHRONED
    NOR THOUGH ENTHRONED TOO HIGH   • • • • • • • •   197 FRAG ANTIGONE   80

ENTOMB
    THE JUST MAN NOT TO ENTOMB   • • • • • • • •   420 EMPEDOCLES I 2   253

ENTOMBD
    IN SPITE OF HOPES ENTOMBD   • • • • • •   424 EMPEDOCLES I 2   368
    THEY WERE WELL BORN THEY WILL BE WELL ENTOMBD   • •   439 EMPEDOCLES II   337

ENTRANCE
    DO THOU TILL FOR THINE ENTRANCE TO THIS HOUSE   • •   332 MEROPE   66

ENTREAT
    LET ME ENTREAT FOR THEM WHAT HAVE THEY DONE   • •   84 SOHRAB RUSTUM   780
    AND PAY HER HOMAGE AND ENTREAT WITH PRAYERS   • •   100 BALDER DEAD 1   179
    SEND THROUGH THE WORLD THY MESSENGERS ENTREAT   • •   122 BALDER DEAD 3   291

ENTREATED
    AND SPAKE AND MILD ENTREATED HER AND SAID   • • • •   110 BALDER DEAD 2   188

ENTREATING
    ENTREATING ALL THINGS TO WEEP BALDERS DEATH   • •   122 BALDER DEAD 3   305

ENVELOPED
    CLOUD-ENVELOPED OBSCURE   • • • • • • • • • • •   370 MEROPE   1106

ENVIES
    ENVIES THE ALL-REGARDED PLACE . . . . 57 RESIGNATION 159
    O HEAVEN-ABANDOND WRETCH THAT ENVIES THEE . . . . 397 MEROPE 1773

ENVIOUS
    TO FEAR ASSAULT OF ENVIOUS GODS . . . . . . 197 FRAG ANTIGONE 81
    AND ARTISTS ENVIOUS AND THE MOB PROFANE . . . . 295 HEINES GRAVE 114
    THIS ENVIOUS MISERABLE AGE . . . . 432 EMPEDOCLES II 107

ENVY
    LUST AVARICE ENVY LIBERATED MAN . . . . . . 7 REP FRIEND CONT 12
    SUCCUMBD TO THE ENVY OF UNKIND GODS . . . . . 197 FRAG ANTIGONE 77
    FAME AND HER LESS FAIR FOLLOWERS ENVY STRIFE . . 199 EARLY DEATH 4
    HATRED AND PASSIONATE ENVY BLIND THINE EYES . . 397 MEROPE 1772
    THE ILL-BODING NOTE WHICH FRANTIC ENVY SOUNDS . . 397 MEROPE V1781
    ENVY THEE AND OPPRESS . . . . 416 EMPEDOCLES I 2 118
    THEY ENVY NOT THIS TRANQUIL BROOD . . . . . . 484 ROME-SICKNESS 17

ENWOUND
    WHEN YOUR SHOWERING LOCKS ENWOUND YOU . . . . 29 NEW SIRENS 97
    THE KERCHIEF THAT ENWOUND THY HAIR . . . . . . 184 TERRACE BERNE 24

EPOCH
    THE EPOCH ENDS THE WORLD IS STILL . . . . . . 219 BACCHANALIA 2 1
    THE EPOCH ENDS THE WORLD IS STILL . . . . . . 220 BACCHANALIA 2 28

EQUAL
    YET HELEN HAD AN EQUAL GRACE . . . . 48 HORATIAN ECHO 28
    CHANGED GIFTS AND WENT ON EQUAL TERMS AWAY . . . 72 SOHRAB RUSTUM 361
    FAIR TERMS OF RECONCILEMENT EQUAL RULE . . . . 360 MEROPE 882
    NATURE WITH EQUAL MIND . . . . 421 EMPEDOCLES I 2 257

EQUALLY
    WHENCE EQUALLY THE SEAS OF LIFE AND DEATH ARE FED 60 RESIGNATION 260

ERASE
    WROUGHT TO ERASE FROM ITS DEPTH . . . . . . 281 HAWORTH CHURCH 39

ERASED
    ERASED THE RAVAGES OF TIME . . . . 147 TRISTRAM 2 140

ERE
    AND THE DULL GODS BEHOLD ERE THESE ARE FLOWN . . 10 MYCERINUS 65
    ERE HE COME ERE THE BOAT BY THE SHINING-BRANCHD BORDER 19 MODERN SAPPHO 5
    ERE HE COME ERE THE BOAT BY THE SHINING-BRANCHD BORDER 19 MODERN SAPPHO 5
    ERE THEIR BOAT-MUSIC SOUND ERE THEIR BROIDERD 19 MODERN SAPPHO 8
        FLAGS GLEAM
    ERE THEIR BOAT-MUSIC SOUND ERE THEIR BROIDERD 19 MODERN SAPPHO 8
        FLAGS GLEAM
    THEIR PASSION BURN MORE ERE IT CEASES TO BURN . . 19 MODERN SAPPHO 14
    ERE THE PARTING HOUR GO BY . . . . 22 MEMORY-PICTURE 7
    ERE THE PARTING HOUR GO BY . . . . 23 MEMORY-PICTURE 15
    ERE THE PARTING HOUR GO BY . . . . 23 MEMORY-PICTURE 23
    ERE THE PARTING HOUR GO BY . . . . 23 MEMORY-PICTURE 31
    ERE THE PARTING HOUR GO BY . . . . 23 MEMORY-PICTURE 39
    ERE THE PARTING HOUR GO BY . . . . 24 MEMORY-PICTURE 47
    ERE THE PARTING HOUR GO BY . . . . 24 MEMORY-PICTURE 63
    ERE THE PARTING KISS BE DRY . . . . 22 MEMORY-PICTURE V
    ERE THE LONG NIGHT WHOSE STILLNESS BROOKS NO STAR 43 GIPSY CHILD 45
    ONCE ERE THE DAY DECLINE THOU SHALT DISCERN . . 44 GIPSY CHILD 65
    OH ONCE ERE NIGHT IN THY SUCCESS THY CHAIN . . 44 GIPSY CHILD 66
    ERE THE LONG EVENING CLOSE THOU SHALT RETURN . . 44 GIPSY CHILD 67
    MUSINGS THAT ERE THEY COULD GROW RIPE WERE FLOWN . 41 GIPSY CHILD V 19
    ONCE ERE THY DAY GO DOWN THOU SHALT DISCERN . . 44 GIPSY CHILD V 65
    OR ERE THEY BROUGHT THY MASTER TO THIS FIELD . . 83 SOHRAB RUSTUM 740
    HOW CANST THOU ERE THOU HEAR DISCERN . . . . 89 SICK KING BOKH 54
    LO I AM OLD THREE KINGS ERE THEE . . . . . . 92 SICK KING BOKH 143
    MAY I ERE I DEPART BID BALDER HAIL . . . . . 111 BALDER DEAD 2 244
    IN THE BEGINNING ERE THE GODS WERE BORN . . . 121 BALDER DEAD 3 255
    ERE DANTE CAME THE TRUMP OF SACRED SONG . . . 166 AUSTERITY POET 2
    AND OTHERS ERE I WAS . . . . 176 PARTING 69
    AND SOME FIND DEATH ERE THEY FIND LOVE . . . 206 TOO LATE 2
    ROAMD ERE BIRTH THE TREASURIES OF GOD . . . 209 SELF-DECEPTION 6
    THE WORLD WHICH WAS ERE I WAS BORN . . . . 250 WISH 35
    HAD LEFT ERE HE WOKE ON ITS BREAST . . . . 252 FUTURE 22
    VOICE TO ITS CREED ERE THE CREED . . . . . 281 HAWORTH CHURCH 45
    ERE HE PLODS ON AGAIN . . . . 311 OBERMANN 174
    O THOU WHO ERE THY FLYING SPAN . . . . . 322 OBERMANN MORE 277
    SUCH AS ERE NOW HATH SPURRD TO FEARFUL DEEDS . 366 MEROPE 1012
    HERE BRING HIM ERE THE KING COME BACK FROM COUNCIL 379 MEROPE 1262
    WITH GLAD ACCLAIM ERE THEY FORESTALL MY NEWS . 401 MEROPE 1887
    ERE QUITE THE BEING OF MAN ERE QUITE THE WORLD . 429 EMPEDOCLES II 31
    ERE QUITE THE BEING OF MAN ERE QUITE THE WORLD . 429 EMPEDOCLES II 31
    ERE IT FLAG ERE THE MISTS . . . . 441 EMPEDOCLES II 413
    ERE IT FLAG ERE THE MISTS . . . . 441 EMPEDOCLES II 413
    TWICE ERE THAT DAY OF SHAME THE EMBATTLED FOE . 465 ALARIC AT ROME 73
    ERE I HEAR THY CRIES AND THY CAPTIVITY TOLD OF HOMER TRANS 38
    DIDST FORCE AN AUDIENCE ERE I STRUCK THE SCALE . . RUDE ORATOR 6

ERECT
    AND STOOD ERECT TREMBLING WITH RAGE HIS CLUB . . 74 SOHRAB RUSTUM 449

ERECT   (CONTINUED)
        COURTEOUS-EYED ERECT AND SLIM • • • • • • • • 458 POOR MATTHIAS   194

EREMITE
        AN EREMITE WITH THEE IN THOUGHT   • • • • • • 313 OBERMANN MORE   43

EREWHILE
        SOULS EREWHILE WHO CAUGHT HER WORD • • • • • • • 227 PERSIST POETRY   3

ERINNYS
        BEARING WITH IT TO ERINNYS   • • • • • • • • 400 MEROPE   1866

ERRAND
        EACH WITH SOME ERRAND OF ITS OWN   • • • • •   57 RESIGNATION   168
        THEY GO THE ERRAND AND THE WAY IS KNOWN   • • • • 110 BALDER DEAD 2   191
        A STRANGE UNLIKELY ERRAND SURE IS THINE   • • • • 110 BALDER DEAD 2   203
        HIS MASTERS ERRAND WELL DONE   • • • • • • • 217 LORDS MESSENGER   22
        LAIAS ALONE NO ERRAND MINE FOR CROWDS   • • • • 380 MEROPE   1285

ERRANDS
        HER OWN SWEET ERRANDS ALL FORGONE   • • • • •   53 RESIGNATION   36
        THEIR ERRANDS TO EACH OTHER OR THE WAYS   • • • • 110 BALDER DEAD 2   190
        THOU HADST THINE ERRANDS OFF AND ON • • • • • 460 KAISER DEAD   62

ERRD
        SON LOVED OF ZEUS HIS FATHER FOR HE ERRD   • • • • 398 MEROPE   V1814

ERREST
        YET HERE THOU ERREST SOHRAB OR ELSE MEN   • • • •   80 SOHRAB RUSTUM   643

ERRONEOUS
        UNJUST SUSPICION AND ERRONEOUS FEAR • • • • • • 342 MEROPE   384

ERROR
        BE ERROR DEEMD BUT THAT PRETENCE IS VAIN   • • • • 339 MEROPE   315
        ERROR ON ERROR AND BLOOD • • • • • • • • • 343 MEROPE   424
        ERROR ON ERROR AND BLOOD • • • • • • • • • 343 MEROPE   424

ERRORS
        SEEST OUR ERRORS DEPART   • • • • • • • • • 232 YOUTH OF MAN   8
        OUR WANTS HAVE ALL BEEN FELT OUR ERRORS MADE BEFORE 419 EMPEDOCLES I 2   211

ERRS
        ERRS STRANGELY FOR THE KING FOR KAI KHOSROO   • •   67 SOHRAB RUSTUM   223
        MAN ERRS NOT THAT HE DEEMS   • • • • • • • 418 EMPEDOCLES I 2   173
        HE ERRS BECAUSE HE DREAMS   • • • • • • • • 418 EMPEDOCLES I 2   175

ERST
        STANDS AS ERST THE BUILDERS LEFT IT • • • • • •   15 CHURCH BROU 1   69
        ERST ABODE AMBUSHD • • • • • • • • • • •   51 CONSOLATION   32
        TO LIVE AS ERST YOUR DAILY LIFE IN HEAVEN • • • •   96 BALDER DEAD 1   36
        AND LEAD AS ERST OUR DAILY LIFE IN HEAVEN • • • • 115 BALDER DEAD 3   56
        TO THAT FAIR YOUTH SHE ERST   • • • • • • 196 FRAG ANTIGONE   56
        TWO SCHOLARS WHOM AT COLLEGE ERST HE KNEW • • • • 256 SCHOLAR-GIPSY   42
        SINCE ERST AT MORN SOME WANDERING SHADE   • • • • 271 MEMORIAL VERSES   37
        ONCE MORE WE LAY AS ERST AT BIRTH   • • • • • 271 MEMORIAL VERSES V 48
        NO SOMETHING MUST BE DARED AND GREAT AS ERST   • • 367 MEROPE   1054
        THESE ARE NOT NOW THE SAVAGE BAND WHO ERST • • • 381 MEROPE   1299
        AS ERST THEY SHADOWD • • • • • • • • • 391 MEROPE   1600
        WHERE ERST THE STRONG SEA-CURRENTS SUCKD THEE DOWN 430 EMPEDOCLES II   59
        SOUNDS SUCH AS ERST THE LONE WAYFARING MAN • • • 473 CROMWELL   39

ERYMANTHUS
        O ERYMANTHUS FROM SIGHT • • • • • • • • • 347 MEROPE   V

ESCAPD
        THENCE HE ESCAPD AND NEXT I FIND HIM HERE • • • • 365 MEROPE   V

ESCAPE
        ESCAPE THEIR PRISON AND DEPART • • • • • • • 243 SUMMER NIGHT   52

ESCAPES
        HE ESCAPES THENCE BUT WE ABIDE • • • • • •   58 RESIGNATION   213
        SEIZED HE ESCAPES AND NEXT I FIND HIM HERE • • • 364 MEROPE   983
        WHAT YOU FEEL ESCAPES OUR KEN   • • • • • • 457 POOR MATTHIAS   161

ESCAPING
        STREAMD TO THE GROUND BY THE YOKE ESCAPING   HOMER TRANS   45
            FROM UNDER THE COLLAR

ESPY
        WHAT ONCE-FAMED WRETCH HE THERE DID ESPY HID   • • 396 MEROPE   1754

ESSAYD
        ROME ENGLAND FRANCE YES NOR IN VAIN ESSAYD • • • 239 REVOLUTIONS   6

ESTEEM
        ESTEEM AND FUNCTION AND SO FAR IS WELL   • • • • 127 BALDER DEAD 3   470
        DISTINCTIONS WE ESTEEM SO GRAVE   • • • • • • 311 OBERMANN   151

ESTEEMD
    IF MEN ESTEEMD THEE FEEBLE GAVE THEE POWER • • • •   269 THYRSIS   214
    AND NOW I LEAVE THEE TO THESE RITES ESTEEMD   • •   342 MEROPE   379

ESTRANGED
    THINE ATTITUDE OF COLD ESTRANGED REPROACH • • • •   332 MEROPE   85
    ESTRANGED LIKE MINE AND SAD • • • • • • • •   426 EMPEDOCLES I 2   410

ESTRANGEMENT
    NOT IN ABHORRD ESTRANGEMENT LET YOU STAND • • • •   339 MEROPE   300

ESTRANGING
    THE UNPLUMBD SALT ESTRANGING SEA • • • • •   182 TO MARG CONT   24
    GULFS OF ESTRANGING BLOOD ACROSS THAT CHASM   • •   336 MEROPE   194

ESTRELLE
    UP THE STEEP PINE-PLUMED PATHS OF THE ESTRELLE • •   167 RACHEL 2   4

ESTUARIES
    OF ELBURZ FROM THE ARALIAN ESTUARIES • • • • •   64 SOHRAB RUSTUM   114

ETERNAL
    THE RUSTLE OF THE ETERNAL RAIN OF LOVE • • •   19 CHURCH BROU 3   46
    RANGED DIAMOND-BRIGHT THE ETERNAL WALL OF SNOW • •   25 DREAM   13
    FAR REGIONS OF ETERNAL CHANGE • • • • • •   58 RESIGNATION   222
    ETERNAL MUNDANE SPECTACLE • • • • • • •   59 RESIGNATION   228
    MOUNTS AND THAT HARDLY TO ETERNAL LIFE • • •   172 IMMORTALITY   14
    THEN IN THE ETERNAL FATHERS SMILE • • • •   179 FAREWELL   61
    TO HIM POSTPONING AN ETERNAL LAW • • • •   197 FRAG ANTIGONE   75
    ETERNAL PASSION • • • • • • • •   201 PHILOMELA   31
    ETERNAL PAIN • • • • • • • • •   201 PHILOMELA   32
    AS IS THE ETERNAL MOONLIT SNOW • • • •   207 ON THE RHINE   3
    THE ETERNAL NOTE OF SADNESS IN • • • •   211 DOVER BEACH   14
    ETERNAL PASSION-FRAUGHT AND FREE • • •   224 EPILOG LAOCOON 105
    THE PURE ETERNAL COURSE OF LIFE • • •   251 WISH   47
    OF PASSION WITH ETERNAL LAW • • • •   270 MEMORIAL VERSES 11
    IN THE ETERNAL MOVEMENT • • • • •   286 HAWORTH CHURCH 137
    THE ETERNAL TRIFLER BREAKS YOUR SPELL • •   304 GRANDE CHARTR 155
    THE ETERNAL TRIFLER BREAKS THEIR SPELL • •   304 GRANDE CHARTR V 155
    HEARD ACCENTS OF THE ETERNAL TONGUE • •   310 OBERMANN   125
    ETERNAL SHOWERS OF SPRAY ON THE MOSSD ROOTS •   414 EMPEDOCLES I 2   47
    AND THE SOULS DEEP ETERNAL NIGHT COME ON • •   429 EMPEDOCLES II   35
    TWICE HAD THE ETERNAL CITY BOWED HER LOW • •   465 ALARIC AT ROME 75
    AND LO THE ETERNAL CITY AS THEY RISE • • •   468 ALARIC AT ROME 155
    THE ETERNAL HILLS THEIR GIANT SHADOWS FLUNG •   472 CROMWELL   14
    MAN ONLY WITH ETERNAL BENT • • • • • •   484 ROME-SICKNESS   21

ETERNALISE
    I WOULD ETERNALISE • • • • • • • • • •   52 CONSOLATION   63

ETERNALLY
    THOUGH DRIVING ON WITH IT ETERNALLY • • • •   246 BURIED LIFE   44
    BUT A NAKED ETERNALLY RESTLESS MIND • • • •   438 EMPEDOCLES II 330

ETERNE
    THE PROPHETESSES WHO BY RITE ETERNE • • • • •   97 BALDER DEAD 1   89

ETERNITY
    IN CLOUDY CIRCLES TO ETERNITY • • • • •   4 BUTLERS SERMONS 14
    HUSH YE WILL SAY IT IS ETERNITY • • • •   19 CHURCH BROU 3   40
    TRADE-WINDS WHICH CROSS IT FROM ETERNITY • • •   243 SUMMER NIGHT   58
    TRADE-WINDS THAT CROSS IT FROM ETERNITY • • •   243 SUMMER NIGHT V 58
    IT BEARS ETERNITY BE THOU • • • • •   321 OBERMANN MORE 271

ETHER
    YE AND THE PURE DARK ETHER WHERE YE RIDE • • •   438 EMPEDOCLES II 304

ETNA
    TO BRING THEE OUT WITH HIM ALONE ON ETNA • • • 409 EMPEDOCLES I 1 107
    ON ETNA HERE AND BE ALONE WITH HIM • • • •   410 EMPEDOCLES I 1 129
    ON ETNA AND THE BEAM • • • • • • •   414 EMPEDOCLES I 2 43
    END HERE ETNA BEYOND IN THE BROAD GLARE • • • 414 EMPEDOCLES I 2 53
    THROUGH WHOSE HEART ETNA DRIVES HER ROOTS OF STONE   430 EMPEDOCLES II   43
    ALL ETNA HEAVES FIERCELY • • • • • • •   441 EMPEDOCLES II 419

ETNAS
    SOMETIMES TO ETNAS TOP AND TO THE CONE • • • 409 EMPEDOCLES I 1 95
    CROWND BY THE AWFUL PEAK ETNAS GREAT MOUTH • • • 429 EMPEDOCLES II   3
    TO ETNAS LIPAREAN SISTER-FIRES • • • • •   438 EMPEDOCLES II 313

EUBOEA
    AND THE STRAND OF EUBOEA • • • • • • •   399 MEROPE   1815

EUGENIA
    BUT IS THY FAIR EUGENIA COLD • • • • • •   48 HORATIAN ECHO   27
    LISTEN EUGENIA • • • • • • • • •   201 PHILOMELA   28
    HARK HARK EUGENIA • • • • • • • •   201 PHILOMELA V 28

EUGENIAS
TO CROWN EUGENIAS HAIR . . . . 48 HORATIAN ECHO 24

EURIPUS
OF LOUD EURIPUS SAW . . . . 196 FRAG ANTIGONE 59

EUROPE
FILLD EUROPE ONCE WITH HIS LOVE-PAIN . . . . . . 278 SOUTHERN NIGHT 98
THROUGH EUROPE TO THE AETOLIAN SHORE . . . . . . 303 GRANDE CHARTR 135
AND EUROPE MADE HIS WOE HER OWN . . . . . . 303 GRANDE CHARTR 138
ALL EUROPE FELT THAT FIERY BLAST . . . . . . 319 OBERMANN MORE 203

EUROPES
SUNK THEN IS EUROPES SAGEST HEAD . . . . . . 270 MEMORIAL VERSES 16
HE LOOKD ON EUROPES DYING HOUR . . . . . . 270 MEMORIAL VERSES 23
BUT WHERE WILL EUROPES LATTER HOUR . . . . . . 272 MEMORIAL VERSES 62
BUT WHERE SHALL EUROPES LATTER HOUR . . . . . . 272 MEMORIAL VERSES V 62
OF EUROPES STORMIEST TIME . . . . 308 OBERMANN V 66

EUXINE
TO THE DREAR EUXINE SO PRAY ALL . . . . . . 52 RESIGNATION 13
FROM THE ENCROACHING EUXINE SEA . . . . . . PILLARS UNIVERS 8
FROM THE TYRANNOUS EUXINE SEA . . . . . . PILLARS UNIVERS V 8
FROM THE FIERCER EUXINE SEA . . . . . . PILLARS UNIVERS V 8

EVE
TO HUNT THE BOAR IN THE CRISP WOODS TILL EVE . . 18 CHURCH BROU 3 11
LATE AT EVE HAD LURED ME CREEPING . . . . . . 26 NEW SIRENS V 3
AT TWILIGHT ON A STORMY EVE IN MARCH . . . . . 69 SOHRAB RUSTUM V 286
AT EVE BY THE PALM-SHADED WELL . . . . . . 252 FUTURE 37
THIS WINTER-EVE IS WARM . . . . 263 THYRSIS 16
I TAKE THE OMEN EVE LETS DOWN HER VEIL . . . . 267 THYRSIS 161
ROUGH WAS THE WINTER EVE . . . . 444 WESTMIN ABBEY 11
DREAMS THAT WERE SWEET AT EVE AT MORN WERE SIN . . 475 CROMWELL 121

EVEN
MY SPECIAL THANKS WHOSE EVEN-BALANCED SOUL . . . . 2 TO A FRIEND 9
EVEN FOR YOURSELVES TO CONQUER OR BEGUILE . . . . 9 MYCERINUS 38
THE REST I IVE TO JOY EVEN WHILE I SPEAK . . . . 10 MYCERINUS 55
EVEN SO DO PAST AND FUTURE INTERTWINE . . . . 10 MYCERINUS 59
EVEN BY MOMENTS OF TO-DAY . . . . 33 NEW SIRENS 222
AND BREATHE MORE HAPPY IN AN EVEN CLIME . . . . 37 YOUTHS AGIT 6
EVEN SO WE LEAVE BEHIND . . . . 41 HUMAN LIFE 25
AND EVEN COULD THE INTEMPERATE PRAYER . . . . 60 RESIGNATION 271
OR RATHER WOULD THAT I EVEN I MYSELF . . . . . 85 SOHRAB RUSTUM 816
NOT EVEN WHAT THOU DOST O KING . . . . . . 88 SICK KING BOKH 25
EVEN THE GREAT HONOUR WHICH I HAVE . . . . . 94 SICK KING BOKH 217
BUT EVEN THERE O NANNA WE MIGHT FIND . . . . . 104 BALDER DEAD 1 326
EVEN IN THE ABODE OF DEATH O BALDER HAIL . . . . 112 BALDER DEAD 2 250
EVEN HERE THEY SEEK THEE OUT IN HELAS REALM . . 112 BALDER DEAD 2 256
THOU THREATENEST WHAT TRANSCENDS THY MIGHT EVEN THINE 120 BALDER DEAD 3 249
YET EVEN FROM THEE THYSELF HATH BEEN WITHHELD . . 120 BALDER DEAD 3 252
THE UNHAPPY WITH REPROACH EVEN IN THE GRAVE . . 124 BALDER DEAD 3 396
AND CANST THOU NOT EVEN HERE PASS PITYING BY . . 125 BALDER DEAD 3 400
BELOW AND DOST THOU HATE ME EVEN HERE . . . 125 BALDER DEAD 3 406
MY FORMER LIFE AND CHEERS ME EVEN HERE . . . 126 BALDER DEAD 3 462
DEATH AND THE GLOOM WHICH ROUND ME EVEN NOW . . 129 BALDER DEAD 3 546
BUT EVEN THAT COMES LANGUIDLY IN TRUTH . . . 151 TRISTRAM 3 74
EVEN IN A PALACE LIFE MAY BE LED WELL . . . . 168 WORLDLY PLACE 1
EVEN IN A PALACE ON HIS TRUTH SINCERE . . . . 169 WORLDLY PLACE 9
EVEN FOR A MOMENT DIDST DEPART . . . . . . 181 ISOLATION MARG 15
FOR TIS SO SURELY EVEN IN GREECE . . . . . . 221 EPILOG LAOCOON 13
EVEN IN THAT PHOEBUS-GUARDED GROUND . . . . 221 EPILOG LAOCOON 15
YET EVEN I AND NONE WILL BOW . . . . . . 222 EPILOG LAOCOON 30
ALAS IS EVEN LOVE TOO WEAK . . . . . . 245 BURIED LIFE 12
ARE EVEN LOVERS POWERLESS TO REVEAL . . . . 245 BURIED LIFE 14
AH WELL FOR US IF EVEN WE . . . . . . 245 BURIED LIFE 26
EVEN FOR A MOMENT CAN GET FREE . . . . . 245 BURIED LIFE 27
EVEN IN HIS OWN DESPITE HIS BEINGS LAW . . . 246 BURIED LIFE 37
OF THINE EVEN CHEERFULNESS CLEAR . . . . . 287 RUGBY CHAPEL V 22
EVEN OF ANGELS SOUNDS AMISS . . . . . . 295 HEINES GRAVE 102
EVEN NOW THEIR WHISPERS PIERCE THE GLOOM . . . 301 GRANDE CHARTR 71
THE KING I KNOW HIM EVEN THROUGH MANY YEARS . . 332 MEROPE 63
AND EVEN NOW IF TO BEHOLD ME HERE . . . . 333 MEROPE 104
EVEN FANCIED AND HIS DEATH THOU WROUGHTEST CHIEF . 339 MEROPE 328
EVEN EARTH WHEREON HE TREADS . . . . . 352 MEROPE 626
BUT EVEN OUR OWN HEART THAT NARROW WORLD . . 352 MEROPE 638
EVEN AS THOSE DEAD UNEPITAPHD WHO LIE . . . 356 MEROPE 772
AND EVEN NOW MY SON AH ME MY SON . . . . 366 MEROPE 1026
EVEN IN THE DEADLY PALACE OF MY FOE . . . . 375 MEROPE 1205
I HIDE NOT EVEN THIS THE REVERENCE DEEP . . . 387 MEROPE 1474
SO MUCH IS DUE TO TRUTH EVEN TOWRDS OUR FOE . . 388 MEROPE 1493
EVEN AFTER NEWS OF THIS SAD DEATH OUR LEAGUE . . 394 MEROPE 1689
EVEN IN DEATH THAT COUNTENANCE AUSTERE . . . 403 MEROPE 1970
SO RULE THAT EVEN THINE ENEMIES MAY FAIL . . . 404 MEROPE 2005
THAT EVEN IN THY VICTORY THOU SHOW . . . . 405 MEROPE 2012
YET EVEN WHEN MAN FORSAKES . . . . . . 420 EMPEDOCLES I 2 242
EVEN AS MY FATHER THOU . . . . 449 WESTMIN ABBEY 167
EVEN AS THAT LOVED THAT WELL-RECORDED FRIEND . . 449 WESTMIN ABBEY 168
EVEN TO A DATE BEYOND OUR OWN . . . . . 451 GEISTS GRAVE 62
EVEN IN THE GRAVE THEIR FRAGRANCE CANNOT FADE . . 462 ALARIC AT ROME 8

EVEN   (CONTINUED)
        EVEN IN THE LONENESS OF THY WIDOWED YEARS   . . . .   463 ALARIC AT ROME   22
        EVEN IN THE ACT TO BURST TWICE THREATENED TWICE   465 ALARIC AT ROME   84
            DELAYED
        AND THUS AMID THE GLORIOUS HUES OF EVEN   . . . . . 466 ALARIC AT ROME   105
        TO TOUCH WITH SORROW EVEN A VICTORS MIND   . . . . . 468 ALARIC AT ROME   166
        EVEN OF THAT ARDENT SPIRIT HOPES AND FEARS   . . . . 469 ALARIC AT ROME   178

EVENING
        IN THE DULL OCTOBER EVENING   . . . .   13 CHURCH BROU 1   29
        TILL AT EVENING WE DESCRY   . . . .   27 NEW SIRENS   46
        HEARD AT EVENING SOUNDS OF WARNING   . . . . . .   26 NEW SIRENS   V 7
        ERE THE LONG EVENING CLOSE THOU SHALT RETURN . .   44 GIPSY CHILD   67
        ON A MAY EVENING IN THE DARKEND LANES   . . . .   101 BALDER DEAD 1   233
        AND LATE AT EVENING SPENT AND PANTING FALLS . . .   114 BALDER DEAD 3   12
        AND TOWARDS EVENING SEE THE HEADLANDS RISE . . .   123 BALDER DEAD 3   359
        JOIND AT EVENING OF THEIR DAYS AGAIN   . . . .   143 TRISTRAM 2   32
        BOTH HAVE BROUGHT THEIR ANXIOUS DAY TO EVENING   144 TRISTRAM 2   55
        LOOKD STERNLY THROUGH THE FROSTY EVENING-AIR . .   151 TRISTRAM 3   60
        HE SINGS HOW ON AN EVENING   . . . .   160 NECKAN   41
        IS IT THEN EVENING   . . . .   186 STRAYED REVEL   14
        THE EVENING COMES THE FIELDS ARE STILL   . . . .   217 BACCHANALIA 1   1
        THE EVENING COMES THE FIELDS ARE STILL   . . . .   218 BACCHANALIA 1   19
        THE EVENING COMES THE FIELD IS STILL . . . .   217 BACCHANALIA 1   V 1
        THE EVENING COMES THE FIELD IS STILL . . . .   218 BACCHANALIA 1   V 19
        THE GLEAM OF THE EVENING STAR   . . . . . .   228 YOUTH OF NATURE   18
        PERFUMES THE EVENING AIR   . . . .   234 YOUTH OF MAN   69
        THEY GAZE AND THE EVENING WIND . . . .   235 YOUTH OF MAN   89
        AND THE FULL MOON AND THE WHITE EVENING-STAR .   264 THYRSIS   70
        THE ORANGE AND PALE VIOLET EVENING-SKY   . . .   267 THYRSIS   159
        IN THE MILD EVENING OF THE MAY   . . . . . .   274 STANZAS CARNAC   12
        EVENING A MEETING I SAW   . . . .   280 HAWORTH CHURCH   V
        THE AUTUMN-EVENING THE FIELD   . . . .   286 RUGBY CHAPEL   2
        OF THE AUTUMN EVENING BUT AH   . . . .   286 RUGBY CHAPEL   15
        IN THE AUTUMN EVENING AND THINK . . . . . .   287 RUGBY CHAPEL   24
        THE AUTUMNAL EVENING DARKENS ROUND   . . . . .   299 GRANDE CHARTR   7
        PLAY WHEN WE HALT AND WHEN THE EVENING COMES .   409 EMPEDOCLES I 1   90
        WHOM THE SUMMER EVENING SEES   . . . .   434 EMPEDOCLES II   181

EVENINGS
        ON WINTER-EVENINGS WHEN THE ROAR   . . . . . .   137 TRISTRAM 1   216

EVENT
        ONLY THE EVENT WILL TEACH US IN ITS HOUR   . . .   73 SOHRAB RUSTUM   397
        IF IN THE EVENT BE ANY PROOF   . . . .   354 MEROPE   701
        THE EVENT WILL QUICKLY SHOW   . . . .   354 MEROPE   702
        A LIKE EVENT ELSEWHERE   . . . .   425 EMPEDOCLES I 2   385

EVENTIDE
        MORN AND NOON AND EVENTIDE   . . . .   15 CHURCH BROU 1   100
        HER I LOVED AT EVENTIDE   . . . .   35 NEW SIRENS   272

EVER
        EVER IN THEIR OWN EAGER PASTIME BENT . . . . .   8 RELIGIOUS ISOL   2
        ROSE-CROWND AND EVER WHEN THE SUN WENT DOWN .   11 MYCERINUS   93
        SO REST FOR EVER REST O PRINCELY PAIR   . . .   17 CHURCH BROU 3   1
        SO SLEEP FOR EVER SLEEP O MARBLE PAIR   . . .   18 CHURCH BROU 3   16
        MOCKERY EVER AMBUSHD IN   . . . .   23 MEMORY-PICTURE   28
        OF PASSIONS THAT FOR EVER EBB AND FLOW   . . .   37 YOUTHS AGIT   4
        COULD EVER YET DARE TELL HIM FEARLESSLY . . .   40 HUMAN LIFE   3
        NO EXILES DREAM WAS EVER HALF SO SAD . . . .   42 GIPSY CHILD   27
        STILL SHARP AS EVER FREEZE AND PARCH   . . . .   56 RESIGNATION   131
        STILL GAZING ON THE EVER FULL   . . . . . .   59 RESIGNATION   227
        WHO LOVE THEE BUT MUST PRESS FOR EVER FIRST .   63 SOHRAB RUSTUM   68
        TO DRAW IT AND FOR EVER LET LIFE OUT   . . . .   82 SOHRAB RUSTUM   705
        FOR WOULD THAT ALL WHOM I HAVE EVER SLAIN . .   85 SOHRAB RUSTUM   809
        FOR WOULD THAT ALL THAT I HAVE EVER SLAIN . .   85 SOHRAB RUSTUM   V 809
        EVER SINCE PRAYER-TIME HE DOTH WAIT   . . . .   88 SICK KING BOKH   14
        BUT HE MUST EVER WATCH THE NORTHERN BEAR . .   99 BALDER DEAD 1   155
        WHO EVER HAVE BEEN KNOWN IN EARTH OR HEAVEN .   112 BALDER DEAD 2   258
        FOR DOUBLE-MINDED EVER WAS THE SEED   . . . .   112 BALDER DEAD 2   271
        HEARD NO ONE EVER AN INJURIOUS WORD   . . . .   116 BALDER DEAD 3   84
        THOU ONLY BALDER WAST FOR EVER KIND   . . . .   116 BALDER DEAD 3   112
        BUT THEY HARP EVER ON ONE STRING AND WAKE . .   117 BALDER DEAD 3   137
        TO LEAVE FOR EVER BALDER IN THE GRAVE   . . .   120 BALDER DEAD 3   228
        RUSTING FOR EVER AND THE YEARS ROLL ON   . . .   127 BALDER DEAD 3   472
        THOU ONLY BALDER WERT FOR EVER KIND   . . . .   116 BALDER DEAD 3   V 112
        WHICH SINCE THEN FOR EVER ROLLS   . . . . . .   132 TRISTRAM 1   65
        AND FOR EVER LOVE EACH OTHER   . . . .   135 TRISTRAM 1   140
        STAY PALE QUEEN FOR EVER BY MY SIDE   . . . .   144 TRISTRAM 2   68
        FLEW EVER TO THE DOOR   . . . .   146 TRISTRAM 2   122
        JOY HAS NOT FOUND HER YET NOR EVER WILL   . .   151 TRISTRAM 3   68
        ROUND THE WORLD FOR EVER AND AYE   . . . . .   162 FORSAKEN MERM   45
        AND ALONE DWELL FOR EVER   . . . .   165 FORSAKEN MERM   122
        SHE LEFT LONELY FOR EVER   . . . .   165 FORSAKEN MERM   142
        WHO SPOKE THESE WORDS NO SHADOW EVER CAME . .   169 WORLDLY PLACE   10
        A HEART EVER NEW   . . . .   177 PARTING   80
        WHERE THE WHITE MISTS FOR EVER   . . . . . .   177 PARTING   87
        EVER NEW MAGIC   . . . .   188 STRAYED REVEL   75
        OF THE CITY OF DEATH HAVE FOR EVER CLOSED . .   199 FRAG DEJANEIRA   30
        FOR EVER LEAVES ITS VAIN EMPLOY   . . . . . .   206 RIVER   18

228

EVER   (CONTINUED)
              AND NOT ONCE FEEL THAT WE WERE EVER YOUNG   •   •   •   •   •   212 GROWING OLD   22
              FOR EVER MAKES THEIR EAR REJOICE   •   •   •   •   •   •   227 EPILOG LAOCOON   196
              OF AN EVER-NARROWING WORLD   •   •   •   •   •   •   •   •   233 YOUTH OF MAN   47
              FOR EVER DOTH ACCOMPANY MANKIND   •   •   •   •   •   •   •   238 PROGRESS   38
              THAT MEN DID EVER FIND   •   •   •   •   •   •   •   •   •   •   238 PROGRESS   40
              EVER ACCOMPANIES THE MARCH OF MAN   •   •   •   •   •   •   •   238 PROGRESS   V   38
              HATH IN HIS EYE EVER BUT SERVD TO SHOW   •   •   •   •   •   238 PROGRESS   V
              THAT MAN DID EVER FIND   •   •   •   •   •   •   •   •   •   •   238 PROGRESS   V   40
              NOR EVER FEELS THE FIERY GLOW   •   •   •   •   •   •   •   •   243 SUMMER NIGHT   29
              BUT DEEP ENOUGH ALAS NONE EVER MINES   •   •   •   •   •   •   246 BURIED LIFE   56
              BUT THEY COURSE ON FOR EVER UNEXPRESSD   •   •   •   •   •   246 BURIED LIFE   63
              WHEREIN HE DOTH FOR EVER CHASE   •   •   •   •   •   •   •   247 BURIED LIFE   92
              YET HERE IS PEACE FOR EVER NEW   •   •   •   •   •   •   •   249 KENSINGTON GARD   29
              FOR EVER THE COURSE OF THE RIVER OF TIME   •   •   •   •   253 FUTURE   59
              IN EVER-NEARING CIRCLE WEAVES HER SHADE   •   •   •   •   266 THYRSIS   132
              WHERE CRIES ARE RISING EVER NEW   •   •   •   •   •   •   •   277 SOUTHERN NIGHT   62
              VESTED FOR EVER WITH GREEN   •   •   •   •   •   •   •   •   280 HAWORTH CHURCH   3
              STOPS IT FOR EVER TO PRAISE   •   •   •   •   •   •   •   •   282 HAWORTH CHURCH   54
              STAGGER FOR EVER IN VAIN   •   •   •   •   •   •   •   •   •   •   291 RUGBY CHAPEL   186
              LABOUR FOR EVER IN VAIN   •   •   •   •   •   •   •   •   •   •   291 RUGBY CHAPEL   V 186
              BATTER FOR EVER IN VAIN   •   •   •   •   •   •   •   •   •   •   291 RUGBY CHAPEL   V 186
              AS IF THE WORLD HAD EVER HAD   •   •   •   •   •   •   •   •   302 GRANDE CHARTR   101
              BY SILENCE EVER AFTER FOR BEHOLD   •   •   •   •   •   •   332 MEROPE   62
              AS I HAVE EVER FOUND THEE BENT TO KEEP   •   •   •   •   •   332 MEROPE   80
              CLAIMS EVER HOSTILE ELSE AND SET THY SON   •   •   •   •   335 MEROPE   168
              EVER FAITHFUL UNTIRED   •   •   •   •   •   •   •   •   •   •   344 MEROPE   460
              I PRAY THE FURIES EVER-RESTLESS BAND   •   •   •   •   •   •   349 MEROPE   569
              THE REIGN OF FOLLY USURPATION EVER   •   •   •   •   •   •   353 MEROPE   668
              WHO BLINDLY FOLLOW EVER   •   •   •   •   •   •   •   •   •   353 MEROPE   674
              UNQUIET DROVE HIM EVER TO PURSUE   •   •   •   •   •   •   355 MEROPE   726
              AND LOCKD MY SPEECH FOR EVER IN MY BREAST   •   •   •   •   362 MEROPE   941
              TO LIE IN GLOOM FOR EVER UNAPPEASED   •   •   •   •   •   •   367 MEROPE   1052
              WHAT THOU I DREAM MAYST THOU DREAM EVER SO   •   •   •   •   377 MEROPE   1219
              DID EVER BURN IS LONG BY TIME ALLAYD   •   •   •   •   •   •   387 MEROPE   1471
              THE BRAZEN-FOOTED FURY EVER STALKS   •   •   •   •   •   •   395 MEROPE   1734
              INSCRUTABLE AS EVER SEE IT KEEPS   •   •   •   •   •   •   403 MEROPE   1967
              AND KINGLY GAIT FOR EVER SUCH A SPELL   •   •   •   •   •   408 EMPEDOCLES I 1   61
              DARED ONE BUT TRY THOU WAST A KIND CHILD EVER   •   •   •   408 EMPEDOCLES I 1   76
              DARED ONE BUT TRY THOU WERT A KIND CHILD EVER   •   •   •   409 EMPEDOCLES I 1   V   76
              HE IS FOR EVER COMING ON THESE HILLS   •   •   •   •   •   •   412 EMPEDOCLES I 2   14
              BURNS EVER UNCONSUMED   •   •   •   •   •   •   •   •   •   424 EMPEDOCLES I 2   370
              FOR EVER THROUGH THE GLENS PLACID AND DUMB   •   •   •   •   427 EMPEDOCLES I 2   460
              HE EVER LOVED THE THEBAN STORY WELL   •   •   •   •   •   •   427 EMPEDOCLES I 2   463
              BAFFLED FOR EVER AND STILL THOUGHT AND MIND   •   •   •   439 EMPEDOCLES II   358
              AND BE ASTRAY FOR EVER SLAVE OF SENSE   •   •   •   •   •   440 EMPEDOCLES II   390
              LIVED EVER IN THE LIGHT OF MY OWN SOUL   •   •   •   •   •   440 EMPEDOCLES II   393
              FIERCE DISPUTATIOUS EVER AT WAR WITH MAN   •   •   •   •   440 EMPEDOCLES II   395
              WHAT WILL BE FOR EVER   •   •   •   •   •   •   •   •   •   •   443 EMPEDOCLES II   459
              AND THE ROUGH WAVES OF LIFE FOR EVER LAID   •   •   •   •   449 WESTMIN ABBEY   165
              CAN EVER QUITE REPEAT THE PAST   •   •   •   •   •   •   •   450 GEISTS GRAVE   27
              FARE FOR EVER WELL NOR FEAR   •   •   •   •   •   •   •   •   458 POOR MATTHIAS   207
              EVER AGAIN PUT EARTHLY LIKENESS ON   •   •   •   •   •   •   470 ALARIC AT ROME   206
              MORE CALM MORE DEEP THAN CHILDHOOD EVER KNEW   •   •   •   475 CROMWELL   116
              THERE WHERE WHAT IS JOIND IS JOIND FOR EVER   •   •   •   482 THEKLAS ANSWER   11
              THIS MORN AS EVER   •   •   •   •   •   •   •   •   •   •   •   •   EVERLASTING SUB   7

EVERLASTING
              SET UP A MARK OF EVERLASTING LIGHT   •   •   •   •   •   •   169 EAST LONDON   10
              CRISP EVERLASTING-FLOWERS   •   •   •   •   •   •   •   •   292 HEINES GRAVE   11
              BUT EVERLASTING HORROR TWIXT US TWO   •   •   •   •   •   •   336 MEROPE   193
              WITH THE GRAVES EVERLASTING   •   •   •   •   •   •   •   371 MEROPE   1140
              THE EVERLASTING SUBSTANCE OF THE HILLS   •   •   •   •   EVERLASTING SUB   1

EVERLASTINGLY
              TO SHINE THERE EVERLASTINGLY   •   •   •   •   •   •   •   220 BACCHANALIA 2   26

EVERMORE
              OF NEW CREATION EVERMORE   •   •   •   •   •   •   •   •   •   450 GEISTS GRAVE   26
              SILENT NOW FOR EVERMORE   •   •   •   •   •   •   •   •   •   453 POOR MATTHIAS   20

EVERY
              ONE LESSON WHICH IN EVERY WIND IS BLOWN   •   •   •   •   1 QUIET WORK   2
              TWO LESSONS THAT IN EVERY WIND ARE BLOWN   •   •   •   •   1 QUIET WORK   V   2
              TO ITS OWN IMPULSE EVERY CREATURE STIRS   •   •   •   •   8 RELIGIOUS ISOL   13
              AND GRIEF THAT HEALD AT EVERY SMILE OF EARTH   •   •   •   41 GIPSY CHILD   V 20
              THESE CLAIM NOT EVERY LAUGHING HOUR   •   •   •   •   •   53 RESIGNATION   30
              MAKES CLEAR OUR GOAL TO EVERY EYE   •   •   •   •   •   53 RESIGNATION   46
              THE LAW GREW STRONGER EVERY DAY   •   •   •   •   •   •   56 RESIGNATION   135
              AND BEAT THE PERSIANS BACK ON EVERY FIELD   •   •   •   •   62 SOHRAB RUSTUM   48
              WHEN RUSTUM WAS IN FRONT OF EVERY FRAY   •   •   •   •   63 SOHRAB RUSTUM   80
              WASTES AND RUNS THINNER EVERY DAY   •   •   •   •   •   89 SICK KING BOKH   64
              WHICH EVERY DAY THEY COME AND GO IN HEAVEN   •   •   •   99 BALDER DEAD 1   140
              AND EVERY GOD WENT HOME TO HIS OWN HOUSE   •   •   •   •   106 BALDER DEAD 2   69
              HE KNOWS EACH FRITH AND EVERY ROCKY CREEK   •   •   •   123 BALDER DEAD 3   326
              THEY TWO SCOURD EVERY COAST AND ALL THINGS WEPT   •   •   123 BALDER DEAD 3   328
              LIGHTENS EVERY OTHER BROW   •   •   •   •   •   •   •   138 TRISTRAM 1   262
              WHAT THAT EVERY OTHER BREAST   •   •   •   •   •   •   •   138 TRISTRAM 1   263
              AND UPON EVERY GIANT-BOUGH   •   •   •   •   •   •   •   141 TRISTRAM 1   358
              IN EVERY HUT ALONG THIS SEA-COAST WILD   •   •   •   •   152 TRISTRAM 3   109

EVERY   (CONTINUED)
        ONCE EVERY YEAR WHEN CAROLS WAKE   • • • • • •   158 SAINT BRANDAN   65
        TO EVERY THOUGHT THE MASS IGNORE   • • • • • •   179 FAREWELL   58
        MUST EVERY DAY ENDURE   • • • • • • • • • •   195 FRAG ANTIGONE   22
        FOR EVERY DAY MAN MAY BE LINKD AND LOOSED • • • •   196 FRAG ANTIGONE   34
        GROW STIFFER EVERY FUNCTION LESS EXACT   • • • •   212 GROWING OLD   9
        THEY FEEL RUNS OER IN EVERY LINE   • • • • • •   227 EPILOG LAOCOON   198
        THE SAME HEART BEATS IN EVERY HUMAN BREAST • • • •   245 BURIED LIFE   23
        HOW HE WOULD POUR HIMSELF IN EVERY STRIFE   • • • •   246 BURIED LIFE   33
        THERE BEATS ONE HEART IN EVERY HUMAN BREAST   • • •   245 BURIED LIFE   V 23
        PITCH THEIR SMOKED TENTS AND EVERY BUSH YOU SEE   • •   258 SCHOLAR-GIPSY   113
        AND EVERY DOUBT LONG BLOWN BY TIME AWAY   • • •   261 SCHOLAR-GIPSY   200
        SHAKES EVERY LEAF OF THE GROVE   • • • • • • •   293 HEINES GRAVE   43
        HAD EVERY OTHER GIFT BUT WANTED LOVE • • • • • •   295 HEINES GRAVE   100
        THAT THOUSANDS COUNTED EVERY GROAN   • • • • • •   303 GRANDE CHARTR   137
        BUT EVERY WORD WAS DEAD   • • • • • • • • • •   319 OBERMANN MORE   196
        BUT THAT WE KNOW HOW EVERY PERILOUS FEAT   • • • •   402 MEROPE   1948
        THOUGHTS SLAVES AND DEAD TO EVERY NATURAL JOY   • •   436 EMPEDOCLES II   249
        DEAR LITTLE FRIEND AT EVERY TURN   • • • • • •   450 GEISTS GRAVE   8
        STERN LAW OF EVERY MORTAL LOT   • • • • • • •   450 GEISTS GRAVE   29
        EVERY MORNING DID WE PAY • • • • • • • • • •   455 POOR MATTHIAS   111
        THOU SOLEMN GRAVE WHERE EVERY STEP WE TREAD   • •   464 ALARIC AT ROME   49
        WHILST EVERY CHORD THAT THRILLS AT THOUGHTS OF HOME   467 ALARIC AT ROME   131
        THOUGH EVERY HOLIEST FEELING EVERY TIE   • • • •   467 ALARIC AT ROME   145
        THOUGH EVERY HOLIEST FEELING EVERY TIE   • • • •   467 ALARIC AT ROME   145
        HOW EVERY BIRTH OF TIMES MIRACULOUS WOMB   • • • •   469 ALARIC AT ROME   191
        CHILLD EVERY BUOYANT HOPE THAT FLOATED BY   • • • •   474 CROMWELL   88
        ON EVERY BANK THE VIRGIN SAXIFRAGE   • • • • • •   EVERLASTING SUB   5

EVERYTHING
        BY DRYING UP OUR JOY IN EVERYTHING   • • • • • •   153 TRISTRAM 3   125
        EVERYTHING WILL RETURN   • • • • • • • • • •   439 EMPEDOCLES II   332

EVERYWHERE
        HEM ME ROUND EVERYWHERE   • • • • • • • • • •   50 CONSOLATION   3
        EVERYWHERE COUNTLESS   • • • • • • • • • •   50 CONSOLATION   7
        AND A FRESH BREATH OF SPRING STIRRD EVERYWHERE   • •   155 TRISTRAM 3   200
        EVERYWHERE HEARD WILL BE THE JUDGMENT-CALL • • •   173 MONICAS PRAYER   3
        FOR THESE IN TRUTH WERE EVERYWHERE   • • • • • •   222 EPILOG LAOCOON   19
        HE SAID THE END IS EVERYWHERE   • • • • • • •   271 MEMORIAL VERSES   27
        THE ORCHIS RED GLEAMS EVERYWHERE   • • • • • •   274 STANZAS CARNAC   18
        IS EVERYWHERE SUSTAINS THE WISE THE FOOLISH ELF • •   422 EMPEDOCLES I 2   306
        THE LYRES VOICE IS LOVELY EVERYWHERE • • • • • •   430 EMPEDOCLES II   37
        THE BRAVE IMPETUOUS HEART YIELDS EVERYWHERE   • • •   431 EMPEDOCLES II   90
        THE BRAVE IMPETUOUS HAND YIELDS EVERYWHERE • • • •   431 EMPEDOCLES II   V 90

EVES
        DARK BLUEBELLS DRENCHD WITH DEWS OF SUMMER EVES   • •   257 SCHOLAR-GIPSY   88

EVIDENCE
        THEN EVIDENCE CAME HIS COMRADES OF THE HUNT   • •   365 MEROPE   V

EVIL
        SWELLS WITH THE SWELLING EVIL OF THIS TIME • • • •   410 EMPEDOCLES I 1   113
        A MIGHTY NAME FOR EVIL OR FOR GOOD   • • • • • •   463 ALARIC AT ROME   21

EXACT
        TO TOO EXACT A STEERING OF OUR WAY   • • • • • •   40 HUMAN LIFE   9
        TO-DAYS EXACT REPEATED EFFIGY   • • • • • • •   152 TRISTRAM 3   95
        THE GODS EXACT FOR SONG   • • • • • • • • • •   193 STRAYED REVEL   233
        GROW STIFFER EVERY FUNCTION LESS EXACT   • • • •   212 GROWING OLD   9
        AND PATIENTLY EXACT   • • • • • • • • • •   422 EMPEDOCLES I 2   297
        AND PUNCTUALLY EXACT   • • • • • • • • • •   422 EMPEDOCLES I 2 V 297

EXACTER
        AM THE EXACTER LABOURER   • • • • • • • • • •   22 MEMORY-PICTURE   6

EXACTING
        JEALOUS BLOOD-EXACTING FRIENDS   • • • • • • •   344 MEROPE   461

EXALTED
        OH WHEN MOST SELF-EXALTED MOST ALONE • • • • • •   46 IN UTRUMQUE PAR   36

EXAMIND
        EXAMIND CLOSE HE OWND THIS STORY FALSE   • • • •   365 MEROPE   V

EXAMPLE
        BUT THE SIGNAL EXAMPLE   • • • • • • • • • •   398 MEROPE   1810

EXCEL
        CHILDREN OF MEN NOT THAT YOUR AGE EXCEL   • • • •   238 PROGRESS   45

EXCHANGE
        AND MAKE EXCHANGE AND GIVE MY LIFE FOR HIS • • • •   98 BALDER DEAD 1   110

EXCLAIMD
        THE WORLD OF MUSIC I EXCLAIMD   • • • • • • •   223 EPILOG LAOCOON   77

EXCULPATES
        WHO SELF-EXCULPATES LEND TO FOULEST DEEDS   • • • •   338 MEROPE   279

EXCULPATION
    NOT WELCOME EXCULPATION TO HER KIN • • • • • • 386 MEROPE   1453
    YET EXCULPATION NEEDS IT IF I SEEK • • • • • • 387 MEROPE   1454

EXCUSE
    ALBEIT WITH LIPS UNAPT TO SELF-EXCUSE • • • • 336 MEROPE   199

EXECUTION
    I SELF-DEFENCE AND RIGHTEOUS EXECUTION • • • • 338 MEROPE   277

EXEMPT
    AND WE IMAGINE THEE EXEMPT FROM AGE • • • • • 259 SCHOLAR-GIPSY   158
    AGAINST A POWER EXEMPT FROM COMMON CHECKS • • • • 336 MEROPE   206

EXERCISE
    SPARKLED WITH MOCKING GLEE AND EXERCISE • • • • 154 TRISTRAM 3   170

EXHAUST
    EXHAUST THE ENERGY OF STRONGEST SOULS • • • • 259 SCHOLAR-GIPSY   145

EXILE
    THEE A PINING EXILE IN THY FOREST • • • • • • 144 TRISTRAM 2   51
    THEE A WEEPING EXILE IN THY FOREST • • • • • 144 TRISTRAM 2   V 51
    NO MORE AN EXILE FED ON EMPTY HOPES • • • • • 335 MEROPE   169
    EXILE ABROAD MORE SAFE THAN HEIRSHIP HERE • • • 340 MEROPE   337
    OF A PROTECTED EXILE ANY MORE • • • • • • • 383 MEROPE   1381
    WITH EXILE AND WITH BROODING ON HIS WRONGS • • • 407 EMPEDOCLES I 1 24

EXILED
    IN HIS EXILED LONELINESS • • • • • • • • • 137 TRISTRAM 1   208
    EXILED REMEMBERS HIS HOME • • • • • • • • 347 MEROPE   533
    THE ANXIOUS MOTHER OF AN EXILED SON • • • • • 403 MEROPE   1956
    FROM THAT ON WHICH HIS EXILED AGE IS THROWN • • 436 EMPEDOCLES II 263

EXILES
    WE ARE EXILES WE ARE FALLING • • • • • • • 27 NEW SIRENS   37
    SOME EXILES MINDFUL HOW THE PAST WAS GLAD • • • • 42 GIPSY CHILD   25
    NO EXILES DREAM WAS EVER HALF SO SAD • • • • • 42 GIPSY CHILD   27
    WHAT EXILES CHANGING BITTER THOUGHTS WITH GLAD • • 42 GIPSY CHILD V 25
    SOME EXILES MINDFUL HOW HIS PAST WAS GLAD • • • 42 GIPSY CHILD   V 25
    NEVER WAS EXILES MEMORY HALF SO SAD • • • • • 42 GIPSY CHILD   V 27
    VOYAGES EXILES HATES DISSENSIONS WARS • • • • 195 FRAG ANTIGONE   23
    THE ENFORCED LEISURE OF AN EXILES EAR • • • • 387 MEROPE   1488

EXIST
    OF THE SPIRIT IN WHOM WE EXIST • • • • • • • 298 HEINES GRAVE   216
    OF THE BEING IN WHOM WE EXIST • • • • • • • 298 HEINES GRAVE   V 216
    THE WORLD DOES BUT EXIST THAT WELFARE TO BESTOW • • 418 EMPEDOCLES I 2 176
    AND MUCH MAY STILL EXIST • • • • • • • • • 421 EMPEDOCLES I 2   284

EXISTENCE
    OF HIS DEEPEST BEST EXISTENCE • • • • • • • 49 SECOND BEST   22
    STIR OF EXISTENCE • • • • • • • • • • • 233 YOUTH OF MAN   52

EXISTENCES
    OTHER EXISTENCES THERE ARE THAT CLASH WITH OURS • • 420 EMPEDOCLES I 2 246
    OTHER EXISTENCES THERE ARE WHICH CLASH WITH OURS • • 420 EMPEDOCLES I 2 V 246

EXISTS
    AH SOME POWER EXISTS THERE WHICH IS OURS • • • • 210 SELF-DECEPTION 27

EXPANSE
    OF THE GREY EXPANSE WHERE HE FLOATS • • • • • • 254 FUTURE   79

EXPECT
    HIM YOU EXPECT TO BEHOLD • • • • • • • • • 199 FRAG DEJANEIRA   22
    NO NOR EXPECT THEE TO ADMIT THE GROUNDS • • • • 340 MEROPE   339
    EXPECT NO WAVERING NO RETREAT NO CHANGE • • • • 342 MEROPE   378
    CANST THOU EXPECT WHEN THUS THY WIDOW FAILS • • 386 MEROPE   1433
    LIVE HAPPY THEN EXPECT YOUR PERFECT MEED • • • • 448 WESTMIN ABBEY 138

EXPECTANT
    AH ME THE WRONG EXPECTANT GOT HIS NEWS • • • • 361 MEROPE   922

EXPECTATION
    BUT YOU DROOPD IN EXPECTATION • • • • • • • 31 NEW SIRENS   141
    PAST EXPECTATION HATH THY MURDERER BUILT • • • • 386 MEROPE   1435
    SILENCE AND EXPECTATION HELD US ALL • • • • • • 401 MEROPE   1902

EXPECTEST
    OR HOW EXPECTEST NOT TO LOSE WHO COMST • • • • 381 MEROPE   1292

EXPECTING
    LIES EXPECTING FROM DEATH • • • • • • • • • 281 HAWORTH CHURCH   31

EXPECTS
    AND STILL EXPECTS AN END • • • • • • • • • • 47 WORLD QUIETIST   16

EXPENSE
    WHEN YOUTH HAS DONE ITS TEDIOUS VAIN EXPENSE   • •   37 YOUTHS AGIT   3

EXPERIENCE
    WHAT THROUGH EXPERIENCE OTHERS LEARN • • • • • •   59 RESIGNATION   234
    AND ALL HIS STORE OF SAD EXPERIENCE HE   • • • •   260 SCHOLAR-GIPSY   185
    WITH SAGE EXPERIENCE SHE SPEAKS AND THOU   • • • •   382 MEROPE   1331
    MAIDENS AND READS EXPERIENCE MUCH AMISS   • • • •   382 MEROPE   1334
    IN ALL BY THY EXPERIENCE TO BE RULED • • • • • •   405 MEROPE   2015
    EXPERIENCE LIKE A SEA SOAKS ALL-EFFACING IN   • • •   419 EMPEDOCLES I 2   201

EXPIATE
    WHO ARE NOT EXPIATE THE GENERAL SIN • • • • • •   341 MEROPE   366

EXPIATION
    BEHELD HIS EXPIATION FOR HE DIED   • • • • • •   399 MEROPE   1819

EXPIRE
    OF MERCY CAUGHT DID NOT EXPIRE • • • • • • • •   158 SAINT BRANDAN   62
    DO TWENTY YEARS WEAR OUT AND SEE EXPIRE   • • • •   335 MEROPE   180
    NO PASSING PAGEANT BORN BUT TO EXPIRE   • • • •   463 ALARIC AT ROME   34

EXPIRED
    AND PULSE BY PULSE EXPIRED   • • • • • • • •   319 OBERMANN MORE   192
    WHAT IS THE HAPPY GLOW SO SOON EXPIRED   • • • •   444 WESTMIN ABBEY   10

EXPIRING
    THE TURMOIL OF EXPIRING LIFE   • • • • • • • •   271 MEMORIAL VERSES   26

EXPLAIN
    TO THEE THAT NEEDS NO OEDIPUS TO EXPLAIN   • • • •   365 MEROPE   988

EXPLODED
    BUT A DEAD TIMES EXPLODED DREAM   • • • • • •   302 GRANDE CHARTR   98

EXPLOIT
    ON LAND RENEW THAT GREEK EXPLOIT WHOSE GLORIES   • •   481 HUNGARIAN NAT   12

EXPLORE
    THE FEELING NOT I GRANT EXPLORE   • • • • • •   225 EPILOG LAOCOON   135
    WITH SAFE UNWANDERING FEET EXPLORE   • • • • • •   226 EPILOG LAOCOON   190
    MY HUMBLE TOMB EXPLORE • • • • • • • • • •   321 OBERMANN MORE   270
    THE CENTAUR TAUGHT HIM TO EXPLORE   • • • • •   414 EMPEDOCLES I 2   61
    HOW MAN MAY HERE BEST LIVE NO CARE TOO GREAT   419 EMPEDOCLES I 2   216
        TO EXPLORE
    OF SECRETS YET TO EXPLORE   • • • • • • • •   423 EMPEDOCLES I 2   335

EXPLORED
    YEA AND NOT ONLY HAVE WE NOT EXPLORED   • • • •   352 MEROPE   636

EXPRESS
    SO PERFECTLY THE LINES EXPRESS • • • • • • •   147 TRISTRAM 2   144
    THE ASPECT NOT I GRANT EXPRESS • • • • • • • •   225 EPILOG LAOCOON   133
    YE EXPRESS NOT YOURSELVES CAN YOU MAKE   • • • •   231 YOUTH OF NATURE   107
    YE EXPRESS NOT YOURSELVES CAN YE MAKE   • • • •   231 YOUTH OF NATURE V 107

EXPRESSION
    THE SWEET EXPRESSION OF HER BROW   • • • • • •   147 TRISTRAM 2   138

EXPRESSIVE
    EYES TOO EXPRESSIVE TO BE BLUE • • • • • • • •   208 ON THE RHINE   19

EXQUISITE
    HOW EXQUISITE THY VOICE WOULD COME   • • • • • •   205 CALAIS SANDS   13

EXTEND
    WHO CAN EXTEND THEIR HANDS MAIDENS TAKE BACK   • •   336 MEROPE   195

EXTERNE
    AND PULLULATING RITES EXTERNE AND VAIN   • • • •   449 WESTMIN ABBEY   160

EXTINCT
    WITH HOPE EXTINCT AND BROW COMPOSED   • • • • • •   322 OBERMANN MORE   297

EXTINCTION
    ENDLESS EXTINCTION OF UNHAPPY HATES   • • • • • •   333 MEROPE   102

EXTINGUISHES
    EXTINGUISHES DISTRUST TWIXT HIM AND THEE   • • • •   359 MEROPE   852

EXTRACT
    OF MATTER AND HARD TO EXTRACT   • • • • • • • •   230 YOUTH OF NATURE   69

EXTRAVAGANT
    NURSE NO EXTRAVAGANT HOPE   • • • • • • • •   426 EMPEDOCLES I 2   425

EXTREME
    FROM FIRST YOUTH TESTED UP TO EXTREME OLD AGE   • •   2 TO A FRIEND   10

EXTREMEST
    BUT AS HE ENTERD ON THE EXTREMEST BOUND   • • • •   124 BALDER DEAD 3   381
    TO SUCCOUR ME IN MY EXTREMEST NEED   • • • • • •   383 MEROPE   1376

EXTREMITY
    LIKE WANDERERS FROM THE WORLDS EXTREMITY   • • • •   36 VOICE   30

EXULT
    ONE MERIT THEN THOU HAST EXULT IN THAT   • • • • 341 MEROPE   353

EXULTING
    THE EXULTING THUNDER OF YOUR RACE   • • • • • • 304 GRANDE CHARTR   164
    NEITHER EXULTING NOR ASHAMED I STAND • • • • 398 MEROPE   1788
    AROUND WHOSE FEET THE EXULTING WAVES HAVE SUNG • • 472 CROMWELL   13

EXULTS
    EXULTS YET FOR NO MOMENTS SPACE   • • • • • •   57 RESIGNATION   158

EYD
    THERE FALKLAND EYD THE STRIFE THAT WOULD NOT CEASE   477 CROMWELL   173

EYE
    BEND YE ON THESE INDEED AN UNMOVED EYE   • • •   9 MYCERINUS   35
    IT MAY BE ON THAT JOYLESS FEAST HIS EYE   • • •   11 MYCERINUS   107
    FOR COLD IS HIS EYE TO MERE BEAUTY WHO BREAKING • •   20 MODERN SAPPHO   21
    ITS STEP SO FIRM ITS EYE SO BRIGHT   • • • • •   21 YOUTH AND CALM   10
    ITS STEP SO GAY ITS EYE SO BRIGHT   • • • • •   21 YOUTH AND CALM V 10
    LOFTIER BEARING AND A PROUDER EYE   • • • • •   28 NEW SIRENS   64
    FOR THE EYE GROWS FILLD WITH GAZING   • • • • •   30 NEW SIRENS   119
    THE EYE WANDERS FAITH IS FAILING   • • • • •   34 NEW SIRENS   223
    FOR THE EYE WAS FILLD WITH GAZING   • • • • •   30 NEW SIRENS V 119
    MAKES CLEAR OUR GOAL TO EVERY EYE   • • • •   53 RESIGNATION   46
    HERE WHENCE THE EYE FIRST SEES FAR DOWN   • • •   55 RESIGNATION   92
    NOT FOOLISH FAUSTA IN HIS EYE   • • • • • •   59 RESIGNATION   256
    INDOORS FROM THE SUNS EYE HIS HEAD DROOPD LOW • •   86 SOHRAB RUSTUM   847
    THE MOUNT FROM WHENCE HIS EYE SURVEYS THE WORLD • •   96 BALDER DEAD 1   50
    SIGHTLESS IN SOUL AND EYE WHAT WORDS ARE THESE • •   98 BALDER DEAD 1   113
    WHO FROM HER FROZEN HEIGHT WITH JEALOUS EYE • •   99 BALDER DEAD 1   156
    THE THRONE FROM WHICH HIS EYE SURVEYS THE WORLD • • 102 BALDER DEAD 1   254
    FARTHER AND FARTHER LIKE AN EYE OF FIRE   • • • 119 BALDER DEAD 3   199
    AND HIS CLOSED EYE DOTH SWEEP   • • • • • • 133 TRISTRAM 1   90
    WHAT HIS EYE MUST SEE NO MORE   • • • • • • 135 TRISTRAM 1   160
    NOT SUFFERING WHICH SHUTS UP EYE AND EAR   • • • 152 TRISTRAM 3   113
    NOT SUFFERING THAT SHUTS UP EYE AND EAR   • • • 152 TRISTRAM 3 V 113
    THAT FURTIVE MIEN THAT SCOWLING EYE   • • • • 157 SAINT BRANDAN   17
    TEARS FILLD HIS MILD BLUE EYE   • • • • • • 160 NECKAN   46
    TEARS FILLD HIS COLD BLUE EYE   • • • • • • 160 NECKAN V 46
    TEARS FILLD HIS KIND BLUE EYE   • • • • • • 160 NECKAN V 46
    SAIL AND SAIL WITH UNSHUT EYE   • • • • • • 162 FORSAKEN MERM   44
    FROM A SORROW-CLOUDED EYE   • • • • • 164 FORSAKEN MERM   103
    WITH EYE SUFFUSED BUT HEART INSPIRED TRUE • • 172 GOOD SHEPHERD   10
    TEN YEARS AND TO MY WAKING EYE   • • • • • 183 TERRACE BERNE   1
    TO WOO THY SMILE TO SEEK THINE EYE   • • • • 205 CALAIS SANDS   26
    TO CATCH THY SMILE TO SEEK THINE EYE   • • • 205 CALAIS SANDS V 26
    THE LUSTRE OF THE EYE   • • • • • • • • 212 GROWING OLD   3
    HIS EYE MUST TRAVEL DOWN AT FULL   • • • • 225 EPILOG LAOCOON   145
    THEN FROM ITS BRIMMING WAVES THEIR EYE   • • • 227 EPILOG LAOCOON   193
    CLOUDED AND DIM GREW THEIR EYE   • • • • • 233 YOUTH OF MAN   43
    CHILDREN OF MEN THE UNSEEN POWER WHOSE EYE • • 238 PROGRESS   37
    HATH IN HIS EYE EVER BUT SERVD TO SHOW   • • • 238 PROGRESS V
    WHEN THOU DOST BASK IN NATURES EYE   • • • • 241 MORALITY   14
    WHOSE EYE THOU WAST AFRAID TO SEEK   • • • • 241 MORALITY   20
    WHOSE EYE THOU WERT AFRAID TO SEEK   • • • • 241 MORALITY V 20
    WHERE IN THE SUNS HOT EYE   • • • • • • • 243 SUMMER NIGHT   38
    THE EYE SINKS INWARD AND THE HEART LIES PLAIN • • 247 BURIED LIFE   86
    AND AT ITS END TO STAY THE EYE   • • • • • 248 KENSINGTON GARD   3
    AND AT ITS HEAD TO STAY THE EYE   • • • • 248 KENSINGTON GARD V   3
    WHERE ENDS THE GLADE TO STAY THE EYE   • • • 248 KENSINGTON GARD V   3
    AND THE EYE TRAVELS DOWN TO OXFORDS TOWERS • • 256 SCHOLAR-GIPSY   30
    TO THE LESS PRACTISED EYE OF SANGUINE YOUTH • • 267 THYRSIS   142
    TO THE UNPRACTISED EYE OF SANGUINE YOUTH   • • 267 THYRSIS V 142
    HIS EYE PLUNGED DOWN THE WELTERING STRIFE • • 270 MEMORIAL VERSES   25
    HIS EYE PLUNGED DOWN THE SEETHING STRIFE   • • 270 MEMORIAL VERSES V 25
    IS THIS THE EYE THE FOOTSTEP FAST   • • • • 276 SOUTHERN NIGHT   37
    IS THIS THE EYE THE FORM ALERT   • • • • • 276 SOUTHERN NIGHT V 37
    LUST OF THE EYE AND PRIDE OF LIFE   • • • • 317 OBERMANN MORE   133
    SIT AND EYE GRIMLY THE VICTIM UNSCOURGED   • • 347 MEROPE   531
    SAVE MINE HE MUST NOT MEET A HUMAN EYE   • • 408 EMPEDOCLES I 1   53
    NO EYE COULD BE TOO SOUND   • • • • • • 419 EMPEDOCLES I 2   212
    LOOK THE WORLD TEMPTS OUR EYE   • • • • • 423 EMPEDOCLES I 2   317
    WHILE OER HIS SOVRAN EYE   • • • • • • • 431 EMPEDOCLES II   78
    WHILE OER HIS SOVEREIGN EYE   • • • • • 431 EMPEDOCLES II V 78
    THAT LIQUID MELANCHOLY EYE   • • • • • • 450 GEISTS GRAVE   13
    PRAISED PERHAPS THY COURTEOUS EYE   • • • • 455 POOR MATTHIAS   117
    THINE EYE WAS BRIGHT THY COAT IT SHONE   • • 460 KAISER DEAD   61
    UPON ITS HEADLONG COURSE WITH SAD PROPHETIC EYE • 463 ALARIC AT ROME   24
    IT MAY BE IN THAT DESOLATE SIGHT HIS EYE   • • 469 ALARIC AT ROME   185
    YEA THOUGH HAND TOUCH THEE NOT NOR EYE SHOULD SEE   470 ALARIC AT ROME   209
    AND THE SAME WORLD HAS TONGUE AND EAR AND EYE   470 ALARIC AT ROME   218
    THESE HAD NO SOUND FOR THEE THAT COLD CALM EYE • • 472 CROMWELL   21
    ALL THESE HAD STIRRD THY SPIRIT AND THINE EYE • • 472 CROMWELL   31
    AND MEMORYS CALM CLEAR VOICE AND MOURNFUL EYE • • 474 CROMWELL   87
    ONE MOMENTS SPACE PERCHANCE MIGHT CHARM HIS EYE • • 475 CROMWELL   109

EYE   (CONTINUED)
          THEN HIS EYE SLUMBERD AND THE CHAIN WAS BROKE   •   •   475 CROMWELL   131
          AND HIS EYE KINDLED WITH THE KINDLING FRAY   •   •   •   •   475 CROMWELL   137
          THERE LAUD WITH NOISELESS STEPS AND GLITTERING EYE   476 CROMWELL   165
          FAIR BEYOND HUMAN BEAUTY AND HIS EYE   •   •   •   •   •   •   477 CROMWELL   177
          THAT CALM EYE FOLLOWD TURN HIM WHERE HE WILL   •   •   477 CROMWELL   196
          LURD HIM STARWARDS TO UPLIFT HIS EYE   •   •   •   •   •   •   483 THEKLAS ANSWER   18

EYEBALLS
          SEARD HIS KEEN EYEBALLS   •   •   •   •   •   •   •   •   •   •   51 CONSOLATION   37
          AND EYEBALLS STARING FOR REVENGE IN VAIN   •   •   •   •   373 MEROPE   1175

EYED
          SOHRAB COME FORTH AND EYED HIM AS HE CAME   •   •   •   •   70 SOHRAB RUSTUM   301
          OF THAT POOR DRUDGE MAY BE SO RUSTUM EYED   •   •   •   70 SOHRAB RUSTUM   308
          BUT RUSTUM EYED ASKANCE THE KNEELING YOUTH   •   •   •   71 SOHRAB RUSTUM   345
          THAT THE KNIGHTS EYED HER IN SURPRISE   •   •   •   •   146 TRISTRAM 2   123
          YOU SAW THE BRIGHT-EYED SQUIRRELS DART ALONG   •   •   •   155 TRISTRAM 3   195
          THE YOUNG LANGUID-EYED AMPELUS   •   •   •   •   •   •   •   188 STRAYED REVEL   78
          QUICK-EYED STRANGER   •   •   •   •   •   •   •   •   •   189 STRAYED REVEL   103
          HER SON HEART-STRICKEN EYED HER   •   •   •   •   •   •   393 MEROPE   1673
          EYED THEE WITH A SOUL RESIGND   •   •   •   •   •   •   •   453 POOR MATTHIAS   37
          COURTEOUS-EYED ERECT AND SLIM   •   •   •   •   •   •   •   458 POOR MATTHIAS   194

EYELIDS
          YOUR EYELIDS ON THE STONE WHERE YE REPOSE   •   •   •   18 CHURCH BROU 3   25
          YOU DOZED EYELIDS SOUGHT AGAIN   •   •   •   •   •   •   •   31 NEW SIRENS   148
          KEEP HIS EYELIDS LET HIM SEEM   •   •   •   •   •   •   •   133 TRISTRAM 1   106
          AH HIS EYELIDS SLOWLY BREAK   •   •   •   •   •   •   •   •   139 TRISTRAM 1   294
          FOR THERE THINE EARTH-FORGETTING EYELIDS KEEP   •   •   267 THYRSIS   168

EYES
          AND FOR SUCH DOING THEY REQUIRE NOT EYES   •   •   •   •   7 REP FRIEND   8
          AND FOR SUCH DOING HAVE NO NEED OF EYES   •   •   •   •   7 REP FRIEND   V   8
          AND FOR SUCH DOING THEY REQUIRE NO EYES   •   •   •   •   7 REP FRIEND   V   8
          SHE ENTERD THAT MOMENT HIS EYES TURND FROM ME   •   •   19 MODERN SAPPHO   10
          ITS STEP SO FIRM ITS EYES SO BRIGHT   •   •   •   •   •   21 YOUTH AND CALM   V   10
          PAINT THOSE EYES SO BLUE SO KIND   •   •   •   •   •   •   24 MEMORY-PICTURE   41
          THOSE FRANK EYES WHERE DEEP I SEE   •   •   •   •   •   24 MEMORY-PICTURE   45
          THOSE FRANK EYES WHERE DEEP DOTH LIE   •   •   •   •   •   24 MEMORY-PICTURE   V   45
          THOSE FRANK EYES WHERE DEEP DOTH BE   •   •   •   •   •   24 MEMORY-PICTURE   V   45
          THOSE FRANK EYES WHERE DEEP WILL BE   •   •   •   •   •   24 MEMORY-PICTURE   V   45
          AND MORE THAN MORTAL IMPULSE FILLD THEIR EYES   •   •   25 DREAM   27
          AND YOUR HEAVENLY EYES SHONE THROUGH   •   •   •   •   •   29 NEW SIRENS   98
          LIFTING UP YOUR LANGUID EYES   •   •   •   •   •   •   •   •   31 NEW SIRENS   158
          GLANCING FEET AND EAGER EYES   •   •   •   •   •   •   •   •   32 NEW SIRENS   176
          CAN YOUR EYES WHILE FOOLS ARE DOZING   •   •   •   •   •   33 NEW SIRENS   209
          ALL THE MEANING OF YOUR EYES   •   •   •   •   •   •   •   •   34 NEW SIRENS   238
          BUT WE TURN OUR EYES ARE FLITTING   •   •   •   •   •   •   34 NEW SIRENS   241
          THE SUNK EYES THE WAILING TONE   •   •   •   •   •   •   •   34 NEW SIRENS   248
          SEALING HER EAGLE EYES   •   •   •   •   •   •   •   •   •   38 STAGIRIUS   21
          WHO TAUGHT THIS PLEADING TO UNPRACTISED EYES   •   •   41 GIPSY CHILD   1
          WITH EYES WHICH SOUGHT THINE EYES THOU DIDST CONVERSE   42 GIPSY CHILD   15
          WITH EYES WHICH SOUGHT THINE EYES THOU DIDST CONVERSE   42 GIPSY CHILD   15
          WITH EYES WHICH SEEK THINE EYES THOU DOST CONVERSE   41 GIPSY CHILD   15
          WITH EYES WHICH SEEK THINE EYES THOU DOST CONVERSE   41 GIPSY CHILD   V   15
          WITH EYES THAT SOUGHT THINE EYES THOU DIDST CONVERSE   42 GIPSY CHILD   V   15
          WITH EYES THAT SOUGHT THINE EYES THOU DIDST CONVERSE   42 GIPSY CHILD   V   15
          O SCAN THY NATIVE WORLD WITH PIOUS EYES   •   •   •   •   46 IN UTRUMQUE PAR   V   40
          AND WITH EYES BRIMMING   •   •   •   •   •   •   •   •   •   •   51 CONSOLATION   47
          BEAUTIFUL EYES MEET HIS AND HE   •   •   •   •   •   •   •   57 RESIGNATION   160
          ARE IN HIS EYES AND IN HIS EARS   •   •   •   •   •   •   •   57 RESIGNATION   187
          YOUR EYES PURSUE THE BELLS OF FOAM   •   •   •   •   •   58 RESIGNATION   201
          WELCOME THESE EYES COULD SEE NO BETTER SIGHT   •   •   67 SOHRAB RUSTUM   205
          OR ELSE TOO WEAK AND ALL EYES TURN TO THEE   •   •   •   67 SOHRAB RUSTUM   218
          AND DEAR AS THE WET DIVER TO THE EYES   •   •   •   •   69 SOHRAB RUSTUM   284
          HIS EYES TOWARD THE TARTAR TENTS AND SAW   •   •   •   70 SOHRAB RUSTUM   300
          EYES THROUGH HER SILKEN CURTAINS THE POOR DRUDGE   •   •   70 SOHRAB RUSTUM   303
          BUT IN THE GLOOM THEY FOUGHT WITH BLOODSHOT EYES   •   •   75 SOHRAB RUSTUM   490
          THEN RUSTUM RAISED HIS HEAD HIS DREADFUL EYES   •   •   76 SOHRAB RUSTUM   514
          AND SCANND WITH BLINKING EYES THE ADVANCING FORM   •   •   76 SOHRAB RUSTUM   518
          AT THE FULL MOON TEARS GATHERD IN HIS EYES   •   •   •   79 SOHRAB RUSTUM   618
          AND HIMSELF SCANND IT LONG WITH MOURNFUL EYES   •   •   81 SOHRAB RUSTUM   685
          AND THEN A DARK CLOUD PASSD BEFORE HIS EYES   •   •   •   81 SOHRAB RUSTUM   692
          CAME BACK TO RUSTUM AND HE OPED HIS EYES   •   •   •   •   81 SOHRAB RUSTUM   698
          MIGHT MEAN AND FROM HIS DARK COMPASSIONATE EYES   •   •   82 SOHRAB RUSTUM   735
          WHITE WITH EYES CLOSED ONLY WHEN HEAVY GASPS   •   •   86 SOHRAB RUSTUM   849
          AND DEAR AS THE WET FISHER TO THE EYES   •   •   •   •   69 SOHRAB RUSTUM   V 284
          HIS EYES TOWARDS THE TARTAR TENTS AND SAW   •   •   •   70 SOHRAB RUSTUM   V 300
          TO FIND SUCH FAVOUR IN THINE EYES   •   •   •   •   •   •   92 SICK KING BOKH   136
          IN VAIN THEREFORE WITH WISTFUL EYES   •   •   •   •   •   93 SICK KING BOKH   189
          WITH COLD DRY EYES AND HEARTS COMPOSED AND STERN   •   •   96 BALDER DEAD 1   35
          SO THEY WITH PENT-UP HEARTS AND TEARLESS EYES   •   •   97 BALDER DEAD 1   69
          FOR FIRST THOU BAREST ME WITH BLINDED EYES   •   •   •   98 BALDER DEAD 1   96
          TEARS STAND UPON THE LASHES OF THINE EYES   •   •   •   103 BALDER DEAD 1   289
          TO FEAST THEIR EYES WITH LOOKING ON THE FRAY   •   •   105 BALDER DEAD 2   31
          AND PITEOUSLY HE EYES THE PASSERS BY   •   •   •   •   •   114 BALDER DEAD 3   16
          TEARS STARTED TO MINE EYES WITH YEARNING JOY   •   •   117 BALDER DEAD 3   151
          THOK WITH DRY EYES WILL WEEP OER BALDERS PYRE   •   •   123 BALDER DEAD 3   352
          HODER ILL-FATED BLIND IN HEART AND EYES   •   •   •   •   124 BALDER DEAD 3   387

EYES   (CONTINUED)

WHO LIVE AND WITH THEIR EYES SHALL SEE THAT DAY · · · 127 BALDER DEAD 3   486
MINE EYES ARE DIZZY WITH THE ARROWY HAIL · · · 128 BALDER DEAD 3   507
OUR EYES WITH GAZING AND REBUILD WITH TEARS · · · 128 BALDER DEAD 3   536
LET HER HAVE HER PROUD DARK EYES · · · · · · · 134 TRISTRAM 1   119
SHE RAISED HER EYES UPON HIS FACE · · · · · · · 140 TRISTRAM 1   319
SWEET FLOWER THY CHILDRENS EYES · · · · · · · 140 TRISTRAM 1   325
TURND TO EACH OTHER THE EYES CLOSED · · · · 141 TRISTRAM 1   338
BUT THY DARK EYES ARE NOT DIMMD PROUD ISEULT · · 142 TRISTRAM 2   19
CLOSE THINE EYES THIS FLOODING MOONLIGHT BLINDS THEM · 144 TRISTRAM 2   71
CLOSE MINE EYES THEN SEEK THE PRINCESS ISEULT · · 145 TRISTRAM 2   93
WITH HOT-FLUSHD CHEEKS AND BRILLIANT EYES · · · 146 TRISTRAM 2   117
AND STILL THE CHILDREN LISTEND THEIR BLUE EYES · · 150 TRISTRAM 3   46
HER FEATURES SO FATIGUED HER EYES THOUGH SWEET · · 151 TRISTRAM 3   70
OR ELSE SHE WILL FALL MUSING HER BLUE EYES · · · 152 TRISTRAM 3   90
WHICH PLAYD ON HER FLUSHD CHEEK AND HER BLUE EYES · 154 TRISTRAM 3   169
BUT STILL SHE CHATTED ON WITH HER BLUE EYES · · 154 TRISTRAM 3   177
TEARS STARTED TO SAINT BRANDANS EYES · · · · · 158 SAINT BRANDAN   73
FOR HER EYES WERE SEALD TO THE HOLY BOOK · · · 163 FORSAKEN MERM   81
AND HER EYES ARE SET IN A STARE · · · · · · 164 FORSAKEN MERM   100
FOR THE COLD STRANGE EYES OF A LITTLE MERMAIDEN · 164 FORSAKEN MERM   106
RACHEL WITH EYES NO GAZING CAN APPEASE · · · · 167 RACHEL 1   7
SOLE OBJECT OF HER DYING EYES REMAIN · · · · · 168 RACHEL 2   13
NO JUDGE EYES US FROM HEAVEN OUR SIN TO SCAN · · 170 BETTER PART   4
AND THOSE SWEET EYES OF BLUE · · · · · · · 174 MEETING   8
THE SWEET BLUE EYES THE SOFT ASH-COLOURD HAIR · · 175 PARTING   37
IN THIS FAIR STRANGERS EYES OF GREY · · · · · 183 ABSENCE   1
THINE EYES MY LOVE I SEE · · · · · · · · · 183 ABSENCE   2
THEIR SHINING EYES · · · · · · · · · · · 190 STRAYED REVEL   132
WITH HOT CHEEKS AND SEARD EYES · · · · · · · 201 PHILOMELA   20
YET SHE COULD LOVE THOSE EYES DECLARE · · · · 202 URANIA   7
HIS EYES BE LIKE THE STARRY LIGHTS · · · · · 202 URANIA   21
AND GAZING IN HIS EYES WILL STAND · · · · · · 202 URANIA   26
TILL THEN HER LOVELY EYES MAINTAIN · · · · · 202 URANIA   31
ON THE BLUE STRAIT MINE EYES I STRAIN · · · · 205 CALAIS SANDS   20
TO-NIGHT THOSE SOFT-FRINGED EYES SHALL CLOSE · · 205 CALAIS SANDS   35
NOT ONCE TO DAY THESE EYES HAVE STAYD · · · · 205 CALAIS SANDS   V 17
OER THE BLUE STRAIT MINE EYES I STRAIN · · · · 205 CALAIS SANDS   V 20
TO-NIGHT THOSE SOFT-VEILED EYES SHALL CLOSE · · 205 CALAIS SANDS   V 35
LET THOSE ARCH EYES NOW SOFTLY SHINE · · · · · 206 RIVER   5
AH LET THEM REST THOSE EYES ON MINE · · · · · 206 RIVER   7
WITH THE GREY AND THE LOVELY BROWN HAIR · · · 206 SEPARATION   16
THOSE EYES OF DEEP SOFT LUCENT HUE · · · · · 208 ON THE RHINE   18
EYES TOO EXPRESSIVE TO BE BLUE · · · · · · · 208 ON THE RHINE   19
AS FROM A HEIGHT WITH RAPT PROPHETIC EYES · · · 212 GROWING OLD   17
EYES FROM THE HEAVENLY HEIGHT · · · · · · · 216 LORDS MESSENGER V
MELT NOT THEIR EYES · · · · · · · · · · 219 BACCHANALIA 1   47
THEIR SHINING FLANKS THEIR LIQUID EYES · · · · 223 EPILOG LAOCOON   54
WHICH WE SAW WITH HIS EYES AND WERE GLAD · · · 229 YOUTH OF NATURE   55
AND DARKNESS RETURNS TO OUR EYES · · · · · · 229 YOUTH OF NATURE   58
OF HER EYES AS THEY RESTED ON THINE · · · · · 231 YOUTH OF NATURE   114
LIVES IN OUR EYES WHICH CAN PAINT · · · · · 233 YOUTH OF MAN   36
BEGIN TO STEAL TO THEIR EYES · · · · · · · 235 YOUTH OF MAN   98
FALL AWAY FROM THEIR EYES · · · · · · · · 235 YOUTH OF MAN   107
WHILE THE SOUL STILL LOOKS THROUGH THINE EYES · · 235 YOUTH OF MAN   113
HE SAW A FIRE IN HIS DISCIPLES EYES · · · · · 237 PROGRESS   2
BEHOLD WITH TEARS MINE EYES ARE WET · · · · · 245 BURIED LIFE   2
AND TURN THOSE LIMPID EYES ON MINE · · · · · 245 BURIED LIFE   10
OUR EYES CAN IN ANOTHERS EYES READ CLEAR · · · 247 BURIED LIFE   81
OUR EYES CAN IN ANOTHERS EYES READ CLEAR · · · 247 BURIED LIFE   81
BEHOLD WITH TEARS MY EYES ARE WET · · · · · 245 BURIED LIFE   V   2
ONCE MORE BEFORE MY DYING EYES · · · · · · 250 WISH   32
OR SHALL REACH WHEN HIS EYES HAVE BEEN CLOSED · · 252 FUTURE   23
AND THINE EYES RESTING ON THE MOONLIT STREAM · · 257 SCHOLAR-GIPSY   80
THY DARK VAGUE EYES AND SOFT ABSTRACTED AIR · · 258 SCHOLAR-GIPSY   99
HIS SHEEP HIS HAPLESS LOVE HIS BLINDED EYES · · 268 THYRSIS   187
WHEN BYRONS EYES WERE SHUT IN DEATH · · · · · 270 MEMORIAL VERSES   6
THE EYES ARE GLAZED THOU CANST NOT SPEAK · · · 276 SOUTHERN NIGHT   42
THOSE WHO WITH HALF-OPEN EYES · · · · · · · 288 RUGBY CHAPEL   53
LIGHTNINGS DAZZLE OUR EYES · · · · · · · · 289 RUGBY CHAPEL   93
EYES REKINDLING AND PRAYERS · · · · · · · 292 RUGBY CHAPEL   202
EARS AND LABOUR-DIMMD EYES · · · · · · · · 295 HEINES GRAVE   89
AND SECRET FROM THE EYES OF ALL · · · · · · 305 GRANDE CHARTR   172
MAKE THEIR BLOOD DANCE AND CHAIN THEIR EYES · · 305 GRANDE CHARTR   188
BUT WORDSWORTHS EYES AVERT THEIR KEN · · · · · 308 OBERMANN   53
HIS EYES ON NATURES PLAN · · · · · · · · · 308 OBERMANN   58
MY SOUL HIS EYES DID REST · · · · · · · · · 314 OBERMANN MORE   68
IN HIS COOL HALL WITH HAGGARD EYES · · · · · 315 OBERMANN MORE   97
AND ON HIS GRAVE WITH SHINING EYES · · · · · 318 OBERMANN MORE   175
BUT MEROPE THE EYES OF OTHER MEN · · · · · · 333 MEROPE   89
AND FUTURE KING LEFORE THIS PEOPLES EYES · · · 335 MEROPE   172
THESE POOR EARS STILL AND THESE EYES · · · · · 346 MEROPE   501
TURN WITH AVERTED EYES FROM DEEDS OF BLOOD · · · 354 MEROPE   695
HE BROUGHT REPORT THAT HIS OWN EYES HAD SEEN · · 363 MEROPE   958
BUT WITH WHAT EYES SHOULD I ENCOUNTER THERE · · 367 MEROPE   1032
WHEREWITH FATIGUE AND YOUTH HAD BOUND MINE EYES · 375 MEROPE   1204
NEER TO HAVE GONE FROM THESE EYES · · · · · 377 MEROPE   1230
PERISHD BEFORE THEIR EYES YET NO MAN STIRRD · · 381 MEROPE   1315
DEALT AT MY OWN SOLE RISK BEFORE THEIR EYES · · 383 MEROPE   1354
NOW THAT I FEED MINE EYES ON THAT YOUNG FACE · · 387 MEROPE   1459

EYES   (CONTINUED)

SAD EAGER EYES . . . . 393 MEROPE 1664
HATRED AND PASSIONATE ENVY BLIND THINE EYES . . 397 MEROPE 1772
AND SEEMD TO MUSE AWHILE THEN RAISED HIS EYES . . 402 MEROPE 1913
THAT MOMENT WHILE WITH UPTURND EYES HE PRAYD . . 402 MEROPE 1918
THOU SPEAKEST WELL BUT HERE TO GIVE OUR EYES . . 403 MEROPE 1951
ARE MINE EYES WITH BLOOD BUT IF THIS . . . . . . 348 MEROPE V
WE SHUT OUR EYES AND MUSE . . . . 423 EMPEDOCLES I 2 327
OUR HAIR GROWS GREY OUR EYES ARE DIMMD OUR . . 423 EMPEDOCLES I 2 336
    HEAT IS TAMED
AT ONCE OUR EYES GROW CLEAR . . . . 424 EMPEDOCLES I 2 362
WHO LOOK ON LIFE WITH EYES . . . . 426 EMPEDOCLES I 2 409
TILL MINE EYES ACHE WITH THE LONG SPECTACLE . . 428 EMPEDOCLES I 2 475
WHO STRIVE TO SEE WITH EYES . . . . 426 EMPEDOCLES I 2 V 409
TILL MY EYES ACHE WITH THE LONG SPECTACLE . . . 428 EMPEDOCLES I 2 V 475
DO THY BLOODSHOT EYES STILL WEEP . . . . . . 430 EMPEDOCLES II 55
HIS WHITE GARMENT TO HIS EYES . . . . 434 EMPEDOCLES II 188
DO THY BLOODSHOT EYES STILL SEE . . . . . . 430 EMPEDOCLES II V 55
DO THY BLOODSHOT EYES STILL FLEE . . . . . . 430 EMPEDOCLES II V 55
ONE STILL LAGS LAST AND TURNS AND EYES THE PILE . . 444 WESTMIN ABBEY 14
SOUL-FED EYES WITH SUFFERING WORN . . . . . . 454 POOR MATTHIAS 63
MISS OUR EYES AND MISS OUR EARS . . . . . . 457 POOR MATTHIAS 166
HE HATH PLEASED OUR EYES AND EARS . . . . . . 458 POOR MATTHIAS 203
THE EYES UNREST . . . . 459 KAISER DEAD 28
BY THEIR OWN CRIMES A LESSON TO ALL EYES . . 462 ALARIC AT ROME 11
AND AS THE PAGEANT SWEPT BEFORE THEIR EYES . . . 467 ALARIC AT ROME 122
BURSTS IN MAJESTIC BEAUTY ON HER CONQUERORS EYES . 468 ALARIC AT ROME 156
CROWNING HIS WILDEST HOPES PERCHANCE HIS EYES . . 468 ALARIC AT ROME 173
AND REST HIS WEARY EYES ON THE GREEN LAND AND THEE 470 ALARIC AT ROME 222
EYES THAT HE KNEW OLD FACES UNFORGOT . . . . . 474 CROMWELL 85
ON THAT DARK FORM HIS EYES HAD GAZD BEFORE . . . 477 CROMWELL 201
YOUR SWEET EYES ARE TURNED ON ME . . . . . . META CLOISTER 20

EYESIGHT
NO CLEARER EYESIGHT . . . . 51 CONSOLATION 34
AH AN HOUR OF HEALTH WOULD PURGE HIS EYESIGHT . . 144 TRISTRAM 2 67

EYING
HAVE KNOWN THEE EYING ALL AN APRIL-DAY . . . . 258 SCHOLAR-GIPSY 107

EYNE
DAZZLED NELLYS YOUTHFUL EYNE . . . . 458 POOR MATTHIAS 191

EYRIES
DROVE THEM SCREAMING FROM THEIR EYRIES . . . . 399 MEROPE 1829

EYRY
CIRCLES ABOVE HIS EYRY WITH LOUD SCREAMS . . . . 78 SOHRAB RUSTUM 565

FABLE
FABLE AND DREAM . . . . 252 FUTURE 20

FABLES
BUT CREDULOUS OF FABLES AS A GIRL . . . . . . 411 EMPEDOCLES I 1 160
HE FABLES YET SPEAKS TRUTH . . . . 431 EMPEDOCLES II 89

FABRIC
REACH THE VALLEY WHERE THE FABRIC . . . . . . 15 CHURCH BROU 1 87

FACE
SHALL BE LEFT STANDING FACE TO FACE WITH GOD . . 7 REP FRIEND CONT 14
SHALL BE LEFT STANDING FACE TO FACE WITH GOD . . 7 REP FRIEND CONT 14
ONCE I SAID A FACE IS GONE . . . . 23 MEMORY-PICTURE 9
MANY A FACE I SO LET FLEE . . . . 23 MEMORY-PICTURE 13
HER SOFT FACE HER HAIR AROUND . . . . 23 MEMORY-PICTURE 26
AS SHE TOWRD ME LEAND HER FACE . . . . 23 MEMORY-PICTURE 34
YOUNG I SAID A FACE IS GONE . . . . 23 MEMORY-PICTURE V 9
LONG I SAID A FACE IS GONE . . . . 23 MEMORY-PICTURE V 9
MANY A FACE I THEN LET BY . . . . 23 MEMORY-PICTURE V 13
MANY A FACE I THEN LET FLEE . . . . 23 MEMORY-PICTURE V 13
AS SHE TOWARDS ME LEAND HER FACE . . . . . 23 MEMORY-PICTURE V 34
AND JULIETS WAS AS FAIR A FACE . . . . . . 48 HORATIAN ECHO 29
THAN THE POOR FACE SHE SLIGHTS IN THEE . . . . 48 HORATIAN ECHO 35
HIDEST THY FACE TAKE HEED LEST MEN SHOULD SAY . . 68 SOHRAB RUSTUM 246
RASH BOY MEN LOOK ON RUSTUMS FACE AND FLEE . . . 72 SOHRAB RUSTUM 369
BEFORE THY FACE THIS DAY AND WERE REVEALD . . . 72 SOHRAB RUSTUM 371
HIS HAIR AND FACE AND BEARD AND GLITTERING ARMS . 82 SOHRAB RUSTUM 702
HAVE NEVER KNOWN MY GRANDSIRES FURROWD FACE . . 83 SOHRAB RUSTUM 756
AND RUSTUM GAZED IN SOHRABS FACE AND SAID . . 85 SOHRAB RUSTUM 835
AND FIXD THEM FEEBLY ON HIS FATHERS FACE . . . 86 SOHRAB RUSTUM 852
DOWN OER HIS FACE AND SATE BY HIS DEAD SON . . 86 SOHRAB RUSTUM 859
HIS FACE AND AIR AND WONDERD WHO HE WAS . . 70 SOHRAB RUSTUM V 312
AND RUSTUM GAZED ON SOHRABS FACE AND SAID . . 85 SOHRAB RUSTUM V 835
WITH A GREAT JOY UPON HIS FACE . . . . . . 91 SICK KING BOKH 119
MY LORD HAD COVERD UP HIS FACE . . . . 91 SICK KING BOKH 125
WHY FOR NO CAUSE MAKE SAD THY FACE . . . . 92 SICK KING BOKH 142
SHE SPOKE AND ON HER FACE LET FALL HER VEIL . . 100 BALDER DEAD 1 192
NOR YET COULD HERMOD SEE HIS BROTHERS FACE . . 101 BALDER DEAD 1 228
BRUSHES ACROSS A TIRED TRAVELLERS FACE . . . 101 BALDER DEAD 1 231
RAN BLACK OER THE SEAS FACE THEN STEADY RUSHD . . 118 BALDER DEAD 3 183
SHE SPAKE AND ON HER FACE LET FALL HER VEIL . . 122 BALDER DEAD 3 295

FACE   (CONTINUED)
        GOD TIS HER FACE PLAYS IN THE WATERS BRIGHT   •   •   139 TRISTRAM 1   284
        SHE RAISED HER EYES UPON HIS FACE   •   •   •   •   •   140 TRISTRAM 1   319
        AND THOUGH THE BED-CLOTHES HIDE HER FACE   •   •   •   147 TRISTRAM 2   136
        HE STARES AND STARES WITH TROUBLED FACE   •   •   •   148 TRISTRAM 2   157
        AND THOUGH THE CURTAINS HIDE HER FACE   •   •   •   147 TRISTRAM 2   V 136
        FIXD ON THEIR MOTHERS FACE IN WIDE SURPRISE   •   •   151 TRISTRAM 3   47
        FIXD FULL ON MERLINS FACE HER STATELY PRIZE   •   •   154 TRISTRAM 3   178
        THE SPIRIT OF THE WOODS WAS IN HER FACE   •   •   •   154 TRISTRAM 3   180
        FIXD ON THEIR MOTHERS FACE IN WIDE SURPRIZE   •   •   TRISTRAM 3   V   47
        TRICKD OUT WITH A PARISIAN SPEECH AND FACE •   •   •   •   168 RACHEL 3   4
        WHITEND HIS FACE FROM THE SUNS FRONTING RAY   •   •   170 EAST AND WEST   6
        AND HE WITH UNSUNND FACE DID ALWAYS GO   •   •   •   170 EAST AND WEST   8
        AS HAND IN HAND FACE EARTHLY LIFE   •   •   •   •   •   179 FAREWELL   68
        AND THEY THAT LOVELY FACE WHO VIEW •   •   •   •   •   203 EUPHROSYNE   3
        SCANNING MY FACE AND THE CHANGES WROUGHT THERE •   •   206 SEPARATION   14
        SEE ON HER FACE A GLOW IS SPREAD   •   •   •   •   •   241 MORALITY   21
        WITH ANGUISHD FACE AND FLYING HAIR •   •   •   •   •   244 SUMMER NIGHT   66
        AN AIR OF COOLNESS PLAYS UPON HIS FACE   •   •   •   247 BURIED LIFE   94
        THY FACE TOWRD HINKSEY AND ITS WINTRY RIDGE   •   •   258 SCHOLAR-GIPSY   125
        THY FACE TOWARDS HINKSEY AND ITS WINTRY RIDGE   •   •   258 SCHOLAR-GIPSY   V 125
        EACH ROSE WITH BLUSHING FACE   •   •   •   •   •   •   265 THYRSIS   96
        THAT COMELY FACE THAT CLUSTERD BROW   •   •   •   •   279 SOUTHERN NIGHT   125
        WITH VEILD FACE AND BOWD HEAD   •   •   •   •   •   •   283 HAWORTH CHURCH   V
        THE PENSIVE STRANGERS FACE •   •   •   •   •   •   311 OBERMANN   172
        BENT ON MY FACE WITH GAZE WHICH SCANND   •   •   •   314 OBERMANN MORE   67
        TEARS WASHD THE TROUBLE FROM HER FACE   •   •   •   317 OBERMANN MORE   137
        BENT ON MY FACE WITH GAZE THAT SCANND   •   •   •   314 OBERMANN MORE   V 67
        ALWAYS IN ARMS ALWAYS IN FACE OF FOES   •   •   •   334 MEROPE   153
        WITH PATIENCE ON THY FACE DEATH IN THY HEART   •   •   367 MEROPE   1045
        BUT NOW SEEN FACE TO FACE MY ONLY CHILD   •   •   •   381 MEROPE   1289
        BUT NOW SEEN FACE TO FACE MY ONLY CHILD   •   •   •   381 MEROPE   1289
        FLED FOR YEARS AFTER OER THE FACE OF EARTH •   •   •   385 MEROPE   1423
        NOW THAT I FEED MINE EYES ON THAT YOUNG FACE   •   •   387 MEROPE   1459
        O MEROPE THE TROUBLE ON THY FACE   •   •   •   •   •   393 MEROPE   1684
        AND I COULD WATCH HIM WITH HIS PROUD SAD FACE   •   •   408 EMPEDOCLES I 1   59
        SPREADING OER THE THUNDERERS FACE   •   •   •   •   •   431 EMPEDOCLES II   68
        BUT HE TURND HIS BEAUTEOUS FACE   •   •   •   •   •   433 EMPEDOCLES II   159
        THEN RAISED HER FACE AND GLORY ROUND HER STREAMD   •   447 WESTMIN ABBEY   96
        THEN RAISED HER FACE AND GLORY ROUND HER BEAMD •   •   447 WESTMIN ABBEY   V 96
        KAISER WITH HIS COLLIE FACE   •   •   •   •   •   •   454 POOR MATTHIAS   73
        OF OCEANS SLEEPING FACE OR HEAVENS UNBROKEN BLUE   •   463 ALARIC AT ROME   36
        STOOD LIKE A STATUE AND HIS FACE WAS FAIR   •   •   •   477 CROMWELL   176

FACES
        LOVE HAS FLUSHD THOSE CRUEL FACES   •   •   •   •   •   •   27 NEW SIRENS   53
        CAN I LOOK ON YOUR SWEET FACES •   •   •   •   •   •   •   32 NEW SIRENS   191
        IS THERE DOUBT ON DIVINE FACES •   •   •   •   •   •   •   34 NEW SIRENS   245
        FACES THAT SMILED AND FLED   •   •   •   •   •   •   •   •   44 QUESTION   19
        PLAYS ON THEIR FACES THEY GAZE •   •   •   •   •   •   •   235 YOUTH OF MAN   90
        FACES UNGREETING AND COLD   •   •   •   •   •   •   •   •   284 HAWORTH CHURCH   76
        AND WHITE UPLIFTED FACES STAND •   •   •   •   •   •   •   300 GRANDE CHARTR   41
        EYES THAT HE KNEW OLD FACES UNFORGOT   •   •   •   •   •   474 CROMWELL   85
        SAD FACES WATCHD AROUND HIM AND HIS BREATH •   •   •   •   478 CROMWELL   207
        TEARS HAVE WASHED THEIR AUSTERE FACES   •   •   •   •   •   META CLOISTER   7

FACING
        THE FRINGES OF A SOUTHWARD-FACING BROW   •   •   •   •   262 SCHOLAR-GIPSY   235

FACTION
        WAR-CRIES TO FACTION YEAR BY YEAR RENEWD   •   •   •   •   333 MEROPE   92
        OF THY DEAD HUSBANDS FACTION VIGOROUS ONCE •   •   •   •   334 MEROPE   139

FACTIONS
        OF PARALYTIC FACTIONS AND NO SOUL   •   •   •   •   •   •   282 HAWORTH CHURCH   V
        FACTIONS DIVIDE THEM THEIR HOST   •   •   •   •   •   •   291 RUGBY CHAPEL   180
        OUR FACTIONS WITH THE FRIENDSHIP OF THEIR CHIEFS   •   •   335 MEROPE   166

FACULTIES
        WE REST OUR FACULTIES   •   •   •   •   •   •   •   •   •   •   423 EMPEDOCLES I 2   337

FACULTY
        TO NURSE HIS DWINDLING FACULTY OF JOY   •   •   •   •   •   437 EMPEDOCLES II   273

FADE
        AND LANGUID PLEASURE FADE AND FLOWER AGAIN •   •   •   •   10 MYCERINUS   64
        MIGHT FADE IN SLUMBER AND THE FEET OF JOY   •   •   •   •   11 MYCERINUS   90
        DULL DID LIFE IN TORPOR FADE   •   •   •   •   •   •   •   28 NEW SIRENS   66
        LIFE IS LONG AND WILL NOT FADE •   •   •   •   •   •   •   28 NEW SIRENS   V 66
        LIFE WITHOUT LOVE DOES BUT FADE   •   •   •   •   •   •   28 NEW SIRENS   V 66
        DULL WITHOUT LOVE LIFE DOTH FADE   •   •   •   •   •   •   28 NEW SIRENS   V 66
        TO FADE AND NANNA IN HER SLEEP STRETCHD OUT   •   •   •   104 BALDER DEAD 1   332
        WOULD NOT FADE WITH THE DULL YEARS AWAY   •   •   •   •   143 TRISTRAM 2   26
        IN PARIS ALL LOOKD HOT AND LIKE TO FADE   •   •   •   •   167 RACHEL 1   1
        TILL THEY TOO FADE LIKE GRASS THEY CRAWL   •   •   •   •   193 STRAYED REVEL   242
        YE FADE YE SWIM YE WAVER BEFORE ME •   •   •   •   •   •   194 STRAYED REVEL   290
        MUST WHEN UNSEEN FROM THE SOUL FADE AWAY   •   •   •   •   206 SEPARATION   8
        AS THE BANKS FADE DIMMER AWAY   •   •   •   •   •   •   •   254 FUTURE   84
        AND THEN THY GLAD PERENNIAL YOUTH WOULD FADE   •   •   •   261 SCHOLAR-GIPSY   229
        FADE AND GROW OLD AT LAST AND DIE LIKE OURS   •   •   •   261 SCHOLAR-GIPSY   230

FADE   (CONTINUED)
        FADE INTO DIMNESS APACE . . . .   286 RUGBY CHAPEL   5
        FADE FROM THE DISTANT PEAKS OF SNOW . . . . .   310 OBERMANN   123
        I WATCHD THE CROCUS FADE AND FLOWER . . . . .   321 OBERMANN MORE   255
        FAIN WOULD I FADE AWAY AS I HAVE LIVED . . . .   366 MEROPE   1027
        EVEN IN THE GRAVE THEIR FRAGRANCE CANNOT FADE   462 ALARIC AT ROME   8
        AND SOONEST FADE IN THE BROAD GLARE OF DAY . . . 470 ALARIC AT ROME   214

FADED
        AH IS FADED UTTERLY   . . . .   23 MEMORY-PICTURE   14
        FADED THE MOSS THE ROCKS US BURNING PLAINS . . . . 25 DREAM   36
        SHALL I ASK WHAT FADED MOURNER . . . .   35 NEW SIRENS   273
        SO BALDER FADED IN THE NIGHT AWAY . . . . . .   104 BALDER DEAD 1   337
        FADED FROM SIGHT INTO THE INTERIOR GLOOM . . . 129 BALDER DEAD 3   553
        I A FADED WATCHER BY THY PILLOW . . . .   144 TRISTRAM 2   61
        THEIR FADED IGNOBLE LIVES . . . .   235 YOUTH OF MAN   111
        THEN ALL HIS VISION FADED AND HIS SOUL . . . . 479 CROMWELL   235

FADES
        THEN FADES BUT SPEAKS THE WHILE . . . .   445 WESTMIN ABBEY   47
        THEN FROM HIS ABBEY FADES . . . .   448 WESTMIN ABBEY   127
        AND FROM HIS ABBEY FADES . . . .   448 WESTMIN ABBEY   V 127

FADING
        WHEN THE FLUSHING HUES ARE FADING . . . . . .   33 NEW SIRENS   213
        WHEN THE FLASHING LIGHTS ARE FADING . . . . .   33 NEW SIRENS   V 213
        THE MOON AND LOST BEHIND HER FADING DIM . . . . 242 SUMMER NIGHT   7

FAIL
        LABOURERS THAT SHALL NOT FAIL WHEN MAN IS GONE . .   2 QUIET WORK   14
        NOR DO I JUDGE IF IT SHALL WIN OR FAIL . . . .   99 BALDER DEAD 1   129
        BUT MUCH MUST STILL BE TRIED WHICH SHALL BUT FAIL   99 BALDER DEAD 1   130
        BUT HOW YE SAY SHOULD THE FULFILMENT FAIL . . . 120 BALDER DEAD 3   230
        FAR OFF WHERE SOME UNWARND MIGHT FAIL TO WEEP . 122 BALDER DEAD 3   322
        TRISTRAM TRISTRAM LET THY HEART NOT FAIL . . . 145 TRISTRAM 2   78
        FAIL FROM EARTHS AIR AND I NOT KNOW . . . . . . 184 TERRACE BERNE   32
        SO RULE THAT EVEN THINE ENEMIES MAY FAIL . . . 404 MEROPE   2005
        FAIL TO MAKE BLEST THY STATE . . . .   426 EMPEDOCLES I 2   420
        AND RALLY THEM FOR ONE LAST FIGHT AND FAIL . . . 440 EMPEDOCLES II   388
        FAIL TO TRACK THEIR DEEP DISTRESS . . . . . .   455 POOR MATTHIAS   106

FAILD
        IT FLUTTERD AND FAILD FOR BREATH . . . .   21 REQUIESCAT   14
        RENT THE TOUGH PLATES BUT FAILD TO REACH THE SKIN   76 SOHRAB RUSTUM 493
        WHO FAILD UNDER THE HEAT OF THIS LIFES DAY . . . 172 IMMORTALITY   7
        FAILD TO PLACE THAT MASTER-FEELING CLEAR . . . 210 SELF-DECEPTION   24
        FAILD TO PLACE OUR MASTER-FEELING CLEAR . . . . 210 SELF-DECEPTION   V 24
        IT FAILD AND THOU WAST MUTE . . . .   269 THYRSIS   226
        IT FAILD AND THOU WERT MUTE . . . .   269 THYRSIS   V 226
        AT THE STRAITS FAILD THAT SPIRIT BRAVE . . . . 275 STANZAS CARNAC   46
        BY POLYPHONTES NEVER FAILD-IN ONCE . . . . . . 387 MEROPE   1476
        THE WORLD HATH FAILD TO IMPART . . . . 424 EMPEDOCLES I 2   374
        FAILD TO FILL UP THE VOID WHICH IN OUR BREASTS WE BEAR 424 EMPEDOCLES I 2 376
        TELL HIM I NEVER FAILD TO LOVE HIS LYRE . . . . 428 EMPEDOCLES I 2   468
        WHOSE SPRING OF HOPE IS DRIED WHOSE SPIRIT HAS FAILD 438 EMPEDOCLES II 317

FAILING
        THE EYE WANDERS FAITH IS FAILING . . . .   34 NEW SIRENS   223
        AND WITH A FAILING VOICE SOHRAB REPLIED . . . . 78 SOHRAB RUSTUM   579
        NOT WITH THE FAILING BREATH AND FOOT OF AGE . . 362 MEROPE   936
        CHEERD ALL THE FAILING HEARTS THAT SORROWD THERE . . 478 CROMWELL   218

FAILS
        FAILS BUT ONE THING TO GRIEVE HERE BALDER STOPS . 111 BALDER DEAD 2   235
        FAILS BUT ONE THING TO GRIEVE THERE BALDER STOPS . 114 BALDER DEAD 3   43
        AND WHEN IT FAILS FIGHT AS WE WILL WE DIE . . . 236 PALLADIUM   23
        POWER FAILS US TO TRY CLEARLY IF THAT CAUSE . . 352 MEROPE   647
        POWER FAILS THE MAN HIMSELF TO FIX DISTINCTLY . 352 MEROPE   649
        CANST THOU EXPECT WHEN THUS THY WIDOW FAILS . . 386 MEROPE   1433
        THE OCCASION IF OUR CHIEF CONFEDERATE FAILS . . 386 MEROPE   1447
        FAILS THEIR OWN WILL TO PLEASE . . . . 417 EMPEDOCLES I 2   150
        HE FAILS NOT TO JUDGE CLEAR IF THIS BE QUENCHD OR NO 418 EMPEDOCLES I 2 171
        FAIN WOULD DO ALL THINGS WELL BUT SOMETIMES . . 422 EMPEDOCLES I 2   296
                FAILS IN STRENGTH
        HE FAILS NOT TO JUDGE CLEAR IF THIS IS QUENCHD OR NO 418 EMPEDOCLES I 2 V 171

FAILURE
        AND STANDS A FAILURE THEN THEN HAPPENS OPPIUS . .   LUCRETIUS 2   12

FAIN
        NATURE IS STUBBORN MAN WOULD FAIN ADORE . . . .   5 HARMONY NATURE   8
        AND WHEN SHE FAIN WOULD SOAR . . . .   39 STAGIRIUS   22
        AY WE WOULD EACH FAIN DRIVE . . . .   40 HUMAN LIFE   13
        FAIN WOULD I KNOW THEE SAFE AND WELL THOUGH LOST . 63 SOHRAB RUSTUM   88
        TO US FAIN THEREFORE SEND THEE HENCE IN PEACE . . 63 SOHRAB RUSTUM   89
        YES AND I FAIN WOULD ALTOGETHER WARD . . . . . 104 BALDER DEAD 1   310
        MUTE GAZING AFTER THEM IN TEARS AND FAIN . . . 129 BALDER DEAD 3   555
        FAIN HAD HE FOLLOWD THEIR RECEDING STEPS . . . 129 BALDER DEAD 3   556
        AH MARGUERITE FAIN . . . .   176 PARTING   60
        AND FAIN WOULD ZEUS HAVE SAVED HIS TIRED SON . . 198 FRAG ANTIGONE   90
        FAIN WOULD HE HAVE RECALLD . . . . 198 FRAG ANTIGONE   94

FAIN   (CONTINUED)
    FAIN TO DROP DOWN AND TO DIE . . . . 290 RUGBY CHAPEL   130
    FAIN WOULD I FADE AWAY AS I HAVE LIVED . . . . . 366 MEROPE   1027
    I WOULD FAIN STAY AND HELP THEE TEND HIM ONCE . . 408 EMPEDOCLES I 1   56
    FAIN WOULD DO ALL THINGS WELL BUT SOMETIMES   422 EMPEDOCLES I 2   296
        FAILS IN STRENGTH
    FAIN WOULD WE DEEM THAT THOU HAST RISEN SO HIGH . . 463 ALARIC AT ROME   31
    FOND HEARTS THAT FAIN WOULD CLOTHE THE UNWELCOME TRUTH 474 CROMWELL   97
    AWE-STRUCK FAIN WOULD CEASE TO BE . . . .   META CLOISTER   18

FAINT
    BY FAINT MUSIC GUIDED RANGING . . . . 27 NEW SIRENS   29
    ONE FAINT FROWN OF DISTANT COLDNESS . . . . . . 31 NEW SIRENS   161
    AND FAINT THE CITY GLEAMS . . . .   45 IN UTRUMQUE PAR   16
    CAPPD WITH FAINT SMOKE THE NOISY TOWN . . . . . 55 RESIGNATION   93
    AND SHOWD A SIGN IN FAINT VERMILION POINTS . . . 81 SOHRAB RUSTUM   671
    THERE ARE THE POOR WHO FAINT ALWAY . . . . . 93 SICK KING BOKH   176
    SICK WITH GRIEF I AM AND FAINT WITH TRAVEL . . . 142 TRISTRAM 2   15
    WHEN SEMBLANCE OF IT FAINT LIKE MINE . . . . . 158 SAINT BRANDAN   V 55
    IF SEMBLANCE OF IT FAINT LIKE MINE . . . . . . 158 SAINT BRANDAN   V 55
    THE JUNGFRAU SNOWS LOOK FAINT AND FAR . . . . 184 TERRACE BERNE   6
    FAINT FAINT AH ME . . . . 187 STRAYED REVEL   68
    FAINT FAINT AH ME . . . . 187 STRAYED REVEL   68
    WE HEARD AFAR FAINT MUSIC PLAY . . . . 224 EPILOG LAOCOON   110
    THEY FAINT THEY STAGGER TO AND FRO . . . . . . 226 EPILOG LAOCOON   173
    TRIM MONTMARTRE THE FAINT . . . . 292 HEINES GRAVE   9
    FAINT BUGLE-NOTES FROM FAR ARE BORNE . . . . . 305 GRANDE CHARTR   182
    FOR FROM THE FIRST FAINT MORN . . . . 418 EMPEDOCLES I 2   167
    POETS FIRE GETS FAINT AND LOW . . . . 454 POOR MATTHIAS   78
    PALE PHANTOM HOSTS LIKE SHADOWS FAINT AND FAR . . 476 CROMWELL   141
    CAME FAINT AND FEEBLE IN THE EMBRACE OF DEATH . . 478 CROMWELL   208

FAINTED
    FAINTED AND FALLEN AND DIED . . . . 291 RUGBY CHAPEL   170

FAINTER
    BUT FAINTER AS THE STARS ROSE HIGH IT FLARED . . 119 BALDER DEAD 3   201
    BUT FAINTER AS THE STARS ROSE HIGH IT BURND . . 119 BALDER DEAD 3   V 201
    FAINTER AND FAINTER WRECK AND HELMSMAN LOOM . . 244 SUMMER NIGHT   72
    FAINTER AND FAINTER WRECK AND HELMSMAN LOOM . . 244 SUMMER NIGHT   72
    LIVES AND THAT OTHER FAINTER SEA FAR DOWN . . . . 438 EMPEDOCLES II   311

FAINTEST
    WHY FAINTEST THOU I WANDERD TILL I DIED . . . . 269 THYRSIS   237

FAINTING
    COME YOU SAY THE SOUL IS FAINTING . . . . . . 28 NEW SIRENS   73
    OF YOUR FAINTING DISPIRITED RACE . . . . 291 RUGBY CHAPEL   189

FAINTLY
    FAINTLY THE BARK OF A DOG . . . . 234 YOUTH OF MAN   73
    SELDOM AND FAINTLY THE DEPTH . . . . 282 HAWORTH CHURCH   V
    RISE FAINTLY TO ME NOW IT STOPS WHOS HERE . . . 407 EMPEDOCLES I 1   29

FAIR
    BUT ALL THINGS NOW ARE ORDERD FAIR . . . . . 16 CHURCH BROU 2   15
    OR IF YE WAKE LET IT BE THEN WHEN FAIR . . . . 18 CHURCH BROU 3   17
    AND IF YE WAKE LET IT BE THEN WHEN FAIR . . . . 18 CHURCH BROU 3   V 17
    DOUBTLESS YOU ARE PASSING FAIR . . . . 32 NEW SIRENS   188
    SYLVAN GODS OF THIS FAIR SHADE . . . . 34 NEW SIRENS   244
    IF SOME FAIR COAST HAVE LURED US TO MAKE STAY . . 40 HUMAN LIFE   11
    IF SOME FAIR COAST HAS LURED US TO MAKE STAY . . 40 HUMAN LIFE   V 11
    BUT IS THY FAIR EUGENIA COLD . . . . 48 HORATIAN ECHO   27
    AND JULIETS WAS AS FAIR A FACE . . . . 48 HORATIAN ECHO   29
    THEY STILL LOOK FAIR . . . . 50 CONSOLATION   20
    TWO YOUNG FAIR LOVERS . . . . 51 CONSOLATION   41
    HIS WANDERING GUEST AND GAVE HIM HIS FAIR CHILD . . 79 SOHRAB RUSTUM   626
    HATH SNATCHD A LITTLE FAIR-HAIRD SLAVE . . . . 93 SICK KING BOKH   165
    FAIR MEN WHO LIVE IN HOLES UNDER THE GROUND . . 97 BALDER DEAD 1   56
    DECEIVER FAIR IN FORM BUT FALSE IN HEART . . . 114 BALDER DEAD 3   21
    LEAVING HER SUNK AND PALE THOUGH FAIR . . . . 132 TRISTRAM 1   48
    IS THAT OTHER ISEULT FAIR . . . . 132 TRISTRAM 1   57
    OER SOME FAIR UNWINTRY SEA . . . . 133 TRISTRAM 1   91
    AND SHE TOO THAT PRINCESS FAIR . . . . 134 TRISTRAM 1   115
    FAIR LOVE SHE SAYS CANST THOU FORGET SO SOON . . 139 TRISTRAM 1   285
    FAR HENCE HER DREAMS ARE FAIR SMOOTH IS HER BROW . . 139 TRISTRAM 1   302
    FAR HENCE HER DREAMS ARE FAIR HER SLEEP IS STILL . . 139 TRISTRAM 1 V 302
    AND THY BEAUTY NEVER WAS MORE FAIR . . . . . 142 TRISTRAM 2   20
    AH HOW FAIR THOU STANDEST IN THE MOONLIGHT . . 143 TRISTRAM 2   27
    SPEAK HER FAIR SHE IS OF ROYAL BLOOD . . . . . 145 TRISTRAM 2   94
    WHO IS THAT KNEELING LADY FAIR . . . . 148 TRISTRAM 2   165
    THEN ISEULT TOOK BY THE HAND THOSE CHILDREN FAIR . . 151 TRISTRAM 3   61
    SHE LOOKD SO WITCHING FAIR THAT LEARNED WIGHT . . 154 TRISTRAM 3   181
    RANG LONELILY AND SHARP THE SKY WAS FAIR . . . 155 TRISTRAM 3   199
    FAIR WAS THE BRIDE AND ON HER FRONT DID GLOW . . 166 AUSTERITY POET   5
    THE LITTLE FAIR-HAIRD SON WITH VACANT GAZE . . . 167 PICT NEWSTEAD   10
    I KNOW THAT GRACEFUL FIGURE FAIR . . . . . . 174 MEETING   5
    IN THIS FAIR STRANGERS EYES OF GREY . . . . . 183 ABSENCE   1
    FLOWS BY THE TOWN THE CHURCHYARD FAIR . . . . 184 TERRACE BERNE   10
    TO THAT FAIR YOUTH SHE ERST . . . . 196 FRAG ANTIGONE   56
    HER FAIR YOUTH UNWILLINGLY GAVE . . . . 197 FRAG ANTIGONE   79

FAIR   (CONTINUED)
     FAME AND HER LESS FAIR FOLLOWERS ENVY STRIFE   • •   199 EARLY DEATH   4
     ON THIS FAIR WESTERN LAWN   • • • • • • • •   201 PHILOMELA   V 18
     YET LET ME SAY THAT THOU WAST FAIR   • • • • • •   203 EUPHROSYNE   2
     FAIR CHILD IT WAS THE BLISS WITHIN   • • • • • •   204 EUPHROSYNE   26
     YET LET ME SAY THAT THOU WERT FAIR   • • • • • •   203 EUPHROSYNE   V   2
     YET LET ME SAY THAT SHE WAS FAIR   • • • • • •   203 EUPHROSYNE   V   2
     THE TIDE IS FULL THE MOON LIES FAIR   • • • • • • 210 DOVER BEACH   2
     THE SOFT-COUCHD CATTLE WERE AS FAIR   • • • • •   222 EPILOG LAOCOON   43
     OF SUDDEN STIRS AND PAUSES FAIR   • • • • • • •   223 EPILOG LAOCOON   64
     THE YOUNG THE HAPPY AND THE FAIR   • • • • • •   224 EPILOG LAOCOON   117
     AND THEY FEEL HOW NATURE WAS FAIR   • • • • • •   235 YOUTH OF MAN   104
     THAT NIGHT WAS FAR MORE FAIR   • • • • • • • •   242 SUMMER NIGHT   22
     HOW FAIR A LOT TO FILL   • • • • • • • • •   244 SUMMER NIGHT   91
     THE NIGHT WAS FAR MORE FAIR   • • • • • • • •   242 SUMMER NIGHT   V 22
     AND WE SHOULD WIN THEE FROM THY OWN FAIR LIFE   • •   261 SCHOLAR-GIPSY   224
     HAVE FELT THIS BREATH HE LOVED OF FAIR   • • • •   275 STANZAS CARNAC   43
     WHAT ELSE IS BRIGHT WHAT ELSE IS FAIR   • • • • •   279 SOUTHERN NIGHT   135
     HOPE AT THAT MEETING SMILED FAIR   • • • • • •   281 HAWORTH CHURCH   26
     OF ITALIAN MILAN THE FAIR   • • • • • • • • •   296 HEINES GRAVE   130
     ROUND SOME FAIR FOREST-LODGE AT MORN   • • • • •   305 GRANDE CHARTR   184
     THE VALAIS OPENS FAIR   • • • • • • • • • •   324 OBERMANN MORE   340
     TOGETHER WON THIS FAIR MESSENIAN LAND   • • • •   334 MEROPE   126
     ALAS HOW FAIR A COLOUR CAN HIS TONGUE   • • • •   338 MEROPE   278
     ON THE FAIR CURLD HEADS OF MY SONS   • • • • •   346 MEROPE   504
     BY HIM SHOWN FAIR BUT I BELIEVE MOST FOUL   • • •   349 MEROPE   556
     FAIR TERMS OF RECONCILEMENT EQUAL RULE   • • • •   360 MEROPE   882
     LET HER COME FAIR PEACE LET HER COME   • • • • •   361 MEROPE   908
     AND THOU THOU FAIR-SKINND SERPENT THOU ART LAID   •   373 MEROPE   1177
     HEIRSHIP WITH FAIR INTENT AS I BELIEVE   • • • •   387 MEROPE   1484
     PROMISE NOT FAIR LET HIM A LITTLE WHILE   • • • •   388 MEROPE   1506
     BUT FAIR PROPOSAL MERITS FAIR REPLY   • • • • •   395 MEROPE   1728
     BUT FAIR PROPOSAL MERITS FAIR REPLY   • • • • •   395 MEROPE   1728
     BUT NEVER ON SO FAIR A MORN THE SUN   • • • • •   406 EMPEDOCLES I 1   9
     OF THIS FAIR SUMMER-WEATHER ON THESE HILLS   • • •   409 EMPEDOCLES I 1   101
     THE SUNSHINE IN THE HAPPY GLENS IS FAIR   • • • •   426 EMPEDOCLES I 2   430
     AND HEAVENLY ODOURS FAIR   • • • • • • • • •   445 WESTMIN ABBEY   37
     AND LIGHTS FAIR NURSLING STUPOR FIRST INVADES   •   448 WESTMIN ABBEY   129
     AND LIGHTS FAIR NURSLING LANGUOR FIRST INVADES   •   448 WESTMIN ABBEY   V 129
     HOME WE BROUGHT HIM YOUNG AND FAIR   • • • • •   458 POOR MATTHIAS   196
     ALL SHAPES THAT HAUNT REMEMBRANCE SOFT AND FAIR   •   474 CROMWELL   83
     STOOD LIKE A STATUE AND HIS FACE WAS FAIR   • • •   477 CROMWELL   176
     FAIR BEYOND HUMAN BEAUTY AND HIS EYE   • • • • •   477 CROMWELL   177

FAIRER
     BUT YOU SEE FAIRER IN YOUR DREAMS   • • • • •   141 TRISTRAM 1   371
     NO FAIRER RESTING-PLACE A MAN COULD FIND   • • • •   155 TRISTRAM 3   210

FAIREST
     THE YOUNGEST FAIREST CHATELAINE   • • • • • •   136 TRISTRAM 1   194
     GIVES THEN THE FIRST THE FAIREST PLACE   • • • •   227 EPILOG LAOCOON   208
     WILL LIE MY GRANDSIRE SAID OUR FAIREST CHANCE   • •   331 MEROPE   41
     THE LEADER IS FAIREST   • • • • • • • • •   442 EMPEDOCLES II   447
     OH IT IS BITTER THAT EACH FAIREST DREAM   • • • •   470 ALARIC AT ROME   211

FAIRFIELD
     RYDAL AND FAIRFIELD ARE THERE   • • • • • • •   228 YOUTH OF NATURE   8

FAIRLY
     MORE FORTUNATE THAN THEE MORE FAIRLY JUDGED   • •   350 MEROPE   590

FAIRY
     TO LOOK FORTH ON THE FAIRY SIGHT   • • • • • •   141 TRISTRAM 1   353
     SHE TOLD THEM OF THE FAIRY-HAUNTED LAND   • • • •   154 TRISTRAM 3   153
     ILSE THE FAIRY TRANSFORMD   • • • • • • • •   297 HEINES GRAVE   183
     WAVING HER MYRIADS OF WHITE FAIRY BLOOMS   • • • •   EVERLASTING SUB   6

FAITH
     THE EYE WANDERS FAITH IS FAILING   • • • • • •   34 NEW SIRENS   223
     ALL FRANK FAITH WHICH PASSION BREEDS   • • • • •   34 NEW SIRENS   230
     AND FAITH MAY OFT BE UNRETURND   • • • • • • •   180 ISOLATION MARG   10
     IN ONE AND WERE THROUGH FAITH RELEASED   • • • •   181 ISOLATION MARG   39
     AND FAITH IS OFTEN UNRETURND   • • • • • • •   180 ISOLATION MARG   V 10
     AND FAITH MAY WELL BE UNRETURND   • • • • • •   180 ISOLATION MARG   V 10
     AH LET THEM KEEP THEIR FAITH SINCERE   • • • • •   203 EUPHROSYNE   11
     THESE ASK NO LOVE THESE PLIGHT NO FAITH   • • • •   203 EUPHROSYNE   15
     THE SEA OF FAITH   • • • • • • • • • • •   211 DOVER BEACH   21
     AND PURGED ITS FAITH AND TRIMMD ITS FIRE   • • •   301 GRANDE CHARTR   68
     THEIR FAITH MY TEARS THE WORLD DERIDE   • • • •   302 GRANDE CHARTR   89
     FOR THE WORLD CRIES YOUR FAITH IS NOW   • • • •   302 GRANDE CHARTR   97
     A FAITH OR SCIOLISTS BEEN SAD   • • • • • • •   302 GRANDE CHARTR   102
     AND PRUND ITS FAITH AND QUENCHD ITS FIRE   • • •   301 GRANDE CHARTR   V 68
     HAVE FAITH AND TRUST THE FUTURE AND THE GODS   • •   388 MEROPE   1507

FAITHFUL
     FOLLOWD HIM LIKE A FAITHFUL HOUND AT HEEL   • • •   69 SOHRAB RUSTUM   271
     OR THOU WILT FIND HIM IN THY FAITHFUL SEARCH   • •   116 BALDER DEAD 3   116
     WITH FAITHFUL UNRELAXING FORCE   • • • • • • •   225 EPILOG LAOCOON   147
     O FAITHFUL SHEPHERD TO COME   • • • • • • • •   290 RUGBY CHAPEL   143
     MY MOTHERS FAITHFUL SERVANT LAID ME DOWN   • • • • 331 MEROPE   31

FAITHFUL   (CONTINUED)
   OF FAITHFUL FONDNESS FOR THEIR FORMER KING • • • • 331 MEROPE   39
   COURAGEOUS FAITHFUL ACTIONS NOBLY DARED • • • • • 333 MEROPE   88
   EVER FAITHFUL UNTIRED • • • • • • • • • • • 344 MEROPE   460
   MY FAITHFUL FOLLOWER COMES WELCOME OLD FRIEND • • 362 MEROPE   937
   FAITHFUL NOT WELCOME WHEN MY TALE IS TOLD • • • 362 MEROPE   938
   AND YE KEEP FAITHFUL SILENCE FRIENDS AND MARK • • 368 MEROPE   1073
   BUT THE FAITHFUL SERVANT AND NURSE • • • • • • 369 MEROPE   1090
   SINCE FROM THY FAITHFUL SUBJECTS WHAT REVENGE • • 386 MEROPE   1432
   O HONOURD QUEEN O FAITHFUL FOLLOWERS • • • • • 400 MEROPE   1882
   OF FAITHFUL FONDNESS TOWARDS THEIR FORMER KING • 331 MEROPE   V 39
   BUT THE FAITHFUL SERVANT AND GUARD • • • • • • 369 MEROPE   V1090
   WHO STILL WAS FAITHFUL WHAT MIGHT PROFIT ME • • 410 EMPEDOCLES I 1   131
   TO HAVE RAISD FAITHFUL FRIENDS AND CUT DOWN • • 425 EMPEDOCLES I 2   V 401
     SPITEFUL FOES
   FAITHFUL LOVE IN DEPTH DIVINE • • • • • • • • 454 POOR MATTHIAS   65
   WERE THINE IN STORE THOU FAITHFUL FRIEND • • • • 459 KAISER DEAD   33
   THIS FAITHFUL IMPULSE OF UNFAITHFUL WILLS • • • • FRAGMENT 8   4

FAITHFULLY
   MORE FAITHFULLY THAN THESE   • • • • • • • 237 PROGRESS   8

FAITHLESS
   BUT FAITHLESS WAS SHE • • • • • • • • • • • 165 FORSAKEN MERM   121
   THE FAITHLESS MURDERERS OWN NO OTHER TONGUE • • 364 MEROPE   V

FAITHLESSLY
   FAITHLESSLY MURDERD HIS FRIEND • • • • • • • • 371 MEROPE   1124

FAITHS
   WHERE FAITHS ARE BUILT ON DUST • • • • • • • • 39 STAGIRIUS   45
   AND WE MUST LEAVE THE OLD FAITHS AND WALK THEREIN 237 PROGRESS   26
   FOR BOTH WERE FAITHS AND BOTH ARE GONE • • • • 301 GRANDE CHARTR   84

FALCON
   LISTLESS AND HELD A FALCON ON HIS WRIST • • • • 67 SOHRAB RUSTUM   200

FALKLAND
   THERE FALKLAND EYD THE STRIFE THAT WOULD NOT CEASE 477 CROMWELL   173

FALL
   AND THE NIGHT WAXES AND THE SHADOWS FALL • • • • 10 MYCERINUS   72
   O LET FALL ONE TEAR AND SET US FREE • • • • • • 34 NEW SIRENS   226
   FALL ON THE THROBBING BROW FALL ON THE BURNING BREAST 36 VOICE   15
   FALL ON THE THROBBING BROW FALL ON THE BURNING BREAST 36 VOICE   15
   LIKE BRIGHT WAVES THAT FALL • • • • • • • • • 36 VOICE   17
   DO ADVERSE VOICES FALL ON THE WORLDS EAR • • • • 47 WORLD QUIETIST   19
   RUSTUM WILL SURELY HEAR IT IF I FALL • • • • • 62 SOHRAB RUSTUM   58
   WHICH HANGS UNCERTAIN TO WHICH SIDE TO FALL • • 72 SOHRAB RUSTUM   392
   FALL AND THY SPEAR TRANSFIXD AN UNARMD FOE • • • 77 SOHRAB RUSTUM   550
   SHE SPOKE AND ON HER FACE LET FALL HER VEIL • • 100 BALDER DEAD 1   192
   THERE THROUGH SOME BATTLE-FIELD WHERE MEN FALL FAST 105 BALDER DEAD 2   24
   SHE SPAKE AND ON HER FACE LET FALL HER VEIL • • 122 BALDER DEAD 3   295
   THE DAY WILL COME WHEN FALL SHALL ASGARDS TOWERS • 127 BALDER DEAD 3   487
   THE DAY WILL COME WHEN ASGARDS TOWERS SHALL FALL • 127 BALDER DEAD 3   V 487
   OR ELSE SHE WILL FALL MUSING HER BLUE EYES • • • 152 TRISTRAM 3   90
   CARE NOT FOR THAT AND LAY ME WHERE I FALL • • • 173 MONICAS PRAYER   2
   ITS POWDERY FALL • • • • • • • • • • • • • 176 PARTING   50
   WHEN THE FORTS OF FOLLY FALL • • • • • • • • 215 LAST WORD   15
   FALL AWAY FROM THEIR EYES • • • • • • • • • 235 YOUTH OF MAN   107
   ROUND TROY BUT WHILE THIS STOOD TROY COULD NOT FALL 236 PALLADIUM   8
   FRESH PRODUCTS OF THEIR BARREN LABOUR FALL • • • 243 SUMMER NIGHT   43
   AND WAITING FOR THE SPARK FROM HEAVEN TO FALL • 258 SCHOLAR-GIPSY   120
   TURND ONCE TO WATCH WHILE THICK THE SNOWFLAKES FALL 259 SCHOLAR-GIPSY   128
   AND NIGHT AS WELCOME AS A FRIEND WOULD FALL • • 267 THYRSIS   150
   BUT IF THE STROKE MUST FALL • • • • • • • • 282 HAWORTH CHURCH   V
   MIGHT FALL A FRESHENING STORM • • • • • • • • 319 OBERMANN MORE   198
   SET DOWN YOUR PITCHERS MAIDENS AND FALL BACK • • 332 MEROPE   76
   THE KING CRESPHONTES THY GREAT HUSBAND FALL • • 333 MEROPE   118
   THE SCEPTRE NOT REMISSLY LET IT FALL • • • • • 334 MEROPE   135
   NOW CRUSHD BUT NOT QUITE LIFELESS BY HIS FALL • • 334 MEROPE   140
   TO AVENGE THAT FALL AND BRING THEM BACK TO POWER • 334 MEROPE   146
   FOR IF THE OTHER LORDS DESIRED HIS FALL • • • • 339 MEROPE   329
   AND HAVE TO THANK THEE FOR A FALL BEWARE • • • 342 MEROPE   375
   TEARS FALL THICKLY THE WHILE • • • • • • • • 342 MEROPE   389
   NIGHT AND DAY SEE THEM FALL • • • • • • • • 346 MEROPE   502
   AND RIGHTEOUS IF HE FALLS I COUNT HIS FALL • • • 349 MEROPE   552
   HIS FATHER AND HIS ILL-STARRD BRETHREN FALL • • 387 MEROPE   1463
   HER SWORD WILL BE THE FIRST TO BID IT FALL • • • 388 MEROPE   1504
   NOT FROM MY LIPS SHOULD CONSOLATION FALL • • • • 393 MEROPE   1687
   AS IF THE SKY WAS IMPIOUS NOT TO FALL • • • • 411 EMPEDOCLES I 1   145
   SCRATCHD BY A FALL WITH MOANS • • • • • • • • 421 EMPEDOCLES I 2   272
   OR WHETHER WE WILL ONCE MORE FALL AWAY • • • • 440 EMPEDOCLES II   373
   AND THEN THAT MIGHTIEST CRASH THAT GIANT FALL • • 463 ALARIC AT ROME   41
   DID FALL LIKE RAIN IN THE FORSAKEN STREET • • • • FRAGMENT 7   2

FALLEN
   HAD FALLEN BACK HER ARMS OUTSPREAD • • • • • • 146 TRISTRAM 2   104
   MANY SPENT FAMES AND FALLEN MIGHTS • • • • • • 220 BACCHANALIA 2   23
   WITH BLOSSOMS RED AND WHITE OF FALLEN MAY • • • • 264 THYRSIS   55
   HAD FALLEN ON THIS IRON TIME • • • • • • • • 271 MEMORIAL VERSES   43

FALLEN   (CONTINUED)
        WAS FALLEN ON THE IRON TIME . . . . 271 MEMORIAL VERSES V 43
        FAINTED AND FALLEN AND DIED . . . . 291 RUGBY CHAPEL   170
        BEFORE SOME FALLEN RUNIC STONE . . . . 301 GRANDE CHARTR   83
        OH HAD HE FALLEN OF OLD. . . . . 345 MEROPE   478
        MY FIRST STROKE OF REVENGE HAD NEARLY FALLEN . . 377 MEROPE   1224
        FALLEN DYING OFF THY PERCH . . . . 456 POOR MATTHIAS   130

FALLEST
        STRAIGHTWAY THOU FALLEST TO ARRAIGN THE TIMES . . 411 EMPEDOCLES I 1   144

FALLING
        FLASHD ONCE LIKE FALLING STREAMS WE ROSE WE GAZED   25 DREAM   29
        WE ARE EXILES WE ARE FALLING . . . .   27 NEW SIRENS   37
        FROM YESTERDAY AND FALLING DOWN . . . .   89 SICK KING BOKH   51
        WITH THEIR THICK-FALLING TEARS SO GOOD A FRIEND   115 BALDER DEAD 3   63
        A CHARRD LOG FALLING MAKES A SHOWER OF SPARKS .   119 BALDER DEAD 3   204
        FALLING FORWARD MINGLING . . . .   188 STRAYED REVEL   87
        FALLING FORWARDS MINGLING . . . .   188 STRAYED REVEL   V 87
        AND SOME MAN MAY SAY AS HE LOOKS AND SEES THY   HOMER TRANS   32
                TEARS FALLING

FALLN
        WITH A CLAY FORT BUT THAT WAS FALLN AND NOW . .   61 SOHRAB RUSTUM   21
        AND NOW WOULD NIGHT HAVE FALLN AND FOUND THEM YET   95 BALDER DEAD 1   15
        WHICH HAS NOT FALLN ON THE DRY HEART LIKE RAIN . 238 PROGRESS   42
        THEIR MASTER FALLN THESE WILL NOT FLINCH BUT BAND 381 MEROPE   1306
        FALLN BENEATH HIS PERCH AND DYING . . . . . .   452 POOR MATTHIAS   2

FALLOW
        THROUGH LAST YEARS FERN OF THE SHY FALLOW-DEER . 155 TRISTRAM 3   193
        THROUGH THE GREEN FERN OF THE SHY FALLOW-DEER . 155 TRISTRAM 3   V 193

FALLS
        FALLS HEAVILY AWAY WITH LONG-DRAWN ROAR   . . . . 40 HUMAN LIFE   21
        THIS STREAM WHICH FALLS INCESSANTLY . . . . . .   60 RESIGNATION   267
        THIS STREAM THAT FALLS INCESSANTLY . . . . . .   60 RESIGNATION   V 267
        OF CRASHING FALLS FOR WITH HIS HAMMER THOR . . . 106 BALDER DEAD 2   55
        AND LATE AT EVENING SPENT AND PANTING FALLS . . 114 BALDER DEAD 3   12
        AND ON THE SNOWY PILLOW FALLS . . . .   141 TRISTRAM 1   336
        WHEN CLEAR FALLS THE MOONLIGHT . . . .   165 FORSAKEN MERM   126
        TILL THE SHUTTLE FALLS FROM HER HAND . . . . . 164 FORSAKEN MERM   V 96
        FIND THEN SUCH CAUSE THE CHARGE OF MURDER FALLS . 336 MEROPE   210
        AND RIGHTEOUS IF HE FALLS I COUNT HIS FALL . . . 349 MEROPE   552
        WHERE MY OWN YOUTH FALLS SHORT BUT LAIAS NOW . . 405 MEROPE   2016

FALSE
        O. YE FALSE ONES AT YOUR CALLING . . . .   27 NEW SIRENS   39
        FALSE WE WERE NOT NOR UNRULY . . . .   34 NEW SIRENS   233
        O LET THE FALSE DREAM FLY . . . .   39 STAGIRIUS   49
        FALSE AND HOLLOW . . . .   44 QUESTION   16
        FALSE WILY BOASTFUL ARE THESE TARTAR BOYS . . .   71 SOHRAB RUSTUM   348
        BY A FALSE BOAST THE STYLE OF RUSTUMS SON . . .   79 SOHRAB RUSTUM   613
        HAVE TOLD THEE FALSE THOU ART NOT RUSTUMS SON . .   80 SOHRAB RUSTUM 644
        DECEIVER FAIR IN FORM BUT FALSE IN HEART . . .   114 BALDER DEAD 3   21
        ART THOU COLD OR FALSE OR DEAD . . . .   133 TRISTRAM 1   81
        THOSE WERE FRIENDS TO MAKE ME FALSE TO THEE . . 144 TRISTRAM 2   48
        HE WAS ON FOOT AND THAT FALSE FAY HIS FRIEND . . 154 TRISTRAM 3   161
        FALSE NECKAN SHARES MY BED SHE WEEPS . . . . . 160 NECKAN   35
        OUR JANGLE OF FALSE WITS OUR CLIMATES FROWNS . . 168 RACHEL 2   11
        AWHILE HE HOLDS SOME FALSE WAY UNDEBARRD . . . 244 SUMMER NIGHT   59
        STILL STANDING FOR SOME FALSE IMPOSSIBLE SHORE . 244 SUMMER NIGHT   69
        FROM HER FALSE FRIENDS APPROACH IN HADES TURN . 261 SCHOLAR-GIPSY   209
        NOT CHAFED BY HOURLY FALSE CONTROL . . . . . . 302 GRANDE CHARTR   96
        NOT CHAFED BY HOURLY FALSE CONTROUL . . . . . . 302 GRANDE CHARTR V 96
        O FALSE FRIENDS INTO WHAT . . . .   371 MEROPE   1127
        SWORN TO OUR PLOT HE IS IF FALSE SURMISE . . . 379 MEROPE   1272
        FOR THAT HE PLOTS THY DEATH ACCOUNT IT FALSE . . 387 MEROPE   1485
        EXAMIND CLOSE HE OWND THIS STORY FALSE . . . . 365 MEROPE   V
        TO LEAD THOSE FALSE WHO TRUST IT HIST ONCE MORE . 413 EMPEDOCLES I 2   33
        AND DARES STAMP NOTHING FALSE WHERE HE FINDS   . 415 EMPEDOCLES I 2   91
                NOTHING SURE
        MAY WHAT IS FALSE HOLD DEAR . . . . 419 EMPEDOCLES I 2   203
        A FALSE COURSE FOR THE WORLD AND FOR OURSELVES   419 EMPEDOCLES I 2   226
                FALSE POWERS
        A FALSE COURSE FOR THE WORLD AND FOR OURSELVES   419 EMPEDOCLES I 2   226
                FALSE POWERS
        MAY WHAT IS FALSE MAINTAIN . . . .   419 EMPEDOCLES I 2 V 203
        FALSE WEAKNESS IN THE WORLD AND IN OURSELVES   419 EMPEDOCLES I 2 V 226
                FALSE POWERS
        FALSE WEAKNESS IN THE WORLD AND IN OURSELVES   419 EMPEDOCLES I 2 V 226
                FALSE POWERS
        FOND FANCIES HERE THERE FALSE PHILOSOPHY . . . 446 WESTMIN ABBEY   66
        NO SOFTENING RAY NO VISIONS FALSE AND WILD . . . 475 CROMWELL   125

FALSEHOOD
        AND FALSEHOOD WHILE I LIVED WAS FAR FROM MINE . .   80 SOHRAB RUSTUM 657
        SWIFT AS I CAME HATH FALSEHOOD BEEN BEFORE . . . . 363 MEROPE   954

FALTER
        WHO HESITATE AND FALTER LIFE AWAY . . . . . . 260 SCHOLAR-GIPSY   178
        FALTER ARE LOST IN THE STORM . . . . 289 RUGBY CHAPEL   103
        WHY DOST THOU FALTER AND MAKE HALF REPLY . . . 362 MEROPE   930

FALTERING
        AND WITH FOND FALTERING FINGERS STROKED HIS CHEEKS   81 SOHRAB RUSTUM   696

FALTERING   (CONTINUED)
          DEEP THRO HIS SOUL AND CHOKD HIS FALTERING TONGUE   478 CROMWELL   224
          IS WEAKNESS IS A FALTERING COURSE   . . . . . .   482 COURAGE   26

FALTERS
          FLUENT OF HORRORS FALTERS TO RELATE IT   . . . .   385 MEROPE   1419

FAMD
          TWO FRIENDS MET THERE TWO FAMD   . . . .   280 HAWORTH CHURCH   V   7
          XANTHUS AND BALIUS BOTH YE FAR-FAMD SEED OF PODARGA   HOMER TRANS   39

FAME
          NOT FROM HERSELF HER FAME OF STRENGTH SHE TOOK   . .   37 WORLDS TRIUMPHS   3
          BUT OF A SINGLE COMBAT FAME SPEAKS CLEAR   . . . .   62 SOHRAB RUSTUM   62
          FOR WHAT CARE I THOUGH ALL SPEAK SOHRABS FAME   . .   68 SOHRAB RUSTUM   228
          AND REST MY AGE AND HEAR OF SOHRABS FAME   . . . .   68 SOHRAB RUSTUM   239
          LIKE SOME OLD MISER RUSTUM HOARDS HIS FAME   . . .   68 SOHRAB RUSTUM   247
          COME THOU SHALT SEE HOW RUSTUM HOARDS HIS FAME   . .   68 SOHRAB RUSTUM   256
          AND PRAISE MY FAME AND PROFFER COURTEOUS GIFTS   . .   71 SOHRAB RUSTUM   353
          THY COURAGE OR THY CRAFT AND SPREAD THY FAME   . .   77 SOHRAB RUSTUM   535
          OR THAT MEN GAVE IT HIM TO SWELL HIS FAME   . . .   79 SOHRAB RUSTUM   614
          THEY FOLLOWD ME MY HOPE MY FAME MY STAR   . . . .   84 SOHRAB RUSTUM   781
          AND THROUGH WHOSE DEATH I WON THAT FAME I HAVE   . .   85 SOHRAB RUSTUM   812
          FOR WHAT CARE I THAT SOHRABS FAME QUENCH THEIRS   . .   68 SOHRAB RUSTUM   V 228
          SO HAVE I NEITHER JOY NOR FAME   . . . .   94 SICK KING BOKH   219
          TOO SOON FOR FAME WITH WHITE UNGRAVEN SHIELDS   . .   109 BALDER DEAD 2   165
          A KING WHOSE FAME THEN FILLD THE VAST OF HEAVEN   . .   117 BALDER DEAD 3   129
          ART THOU NOT HE WHOM FAME   . . . .   189 STRAYED REVEL   108
          FAME AND HER LESS FAIR FOLLOWERS ENVY STRIFE   . .   199 EARLY DEATH   4
          TRIPLE HIS PULSES WITH FAME   . . . .   200 EARLY DEATH   19
          QUICKEN HIS PULSES WITH FAME   . . . .   200 EARLY DEATH   V 19
          ASCENDING PURE THE BELL-LIKE FAME   . . . . .   219 BACCHANALIA 2   15
          SOME DOCTOR FULL OF PHRASE AND FAME   . . . . .   250 WISH   18
          AND WISHD HIM HEALTH SUCCESS AND FAME   . . . .   272 EDW QUILLINAN   3
          THE OTHER MATURER IN FAME   . . . .   280 HAWORTH CHURCH   13
          LAY BEFORE BOTH AND A FAME   . . . .   281 HAWORTH CHURCH   28
          SHORT BUT REDOUBLED BY FAME   . . . .   283 HAWORTH CHURCH   73
          INFERIOR ALL IN FAME   . . . .   284 HAWORTH CHURCH   83
          HEAR WITH DELIGHT OF THY FAME   . . . .   284 HAWORTH CHURCH   87
          SHORT YET REDOUBLED BY FAME   . . . .   283 HAWORTH CHURCH   V 73
          BROKE ON THE FIELD OF HIS FAME   . . . . . .   296 HEINES GRAVE   128
          ACTION I HAD NOT FOLLOWERS FAME   . . . . . .   321 OBERMANN MORE   261
          WHAT WE FOUND HERE WERE TRIBES OF FAME OBSCURE   . .   337 MEROPE   233
          YET FONDLY ZEALOUS FOR THY FAME   . . . . . .   451 GEISTS GRAVE   61
          BUSY FOR PRIAMS FAME AND MY OWN IN SPITE OF THE FUTURE   HOMER TRANS   19

FAMED
          FRANCE FAMED IN ALL GREAT ARTS IN NONE SUPREME   . .   7 REP FRIEND CONT   4
          A SON SO FAMED SO BRAVE TO SEND TO WAR   . . . .   68 SOHRAB RUSTUM   231
          WHAT IS ONE MORE ONE LESS OBSCURE OR FAMED   . . .   68 SOHRAB RUSTUM   252
          LIKE THAT BALD CAESAR THE FAMED ROMAN WIGHT   . .   153 TRISTRAM 3   143
          LIKE THAT BOLD CAESAR THE FAMED ROMAN WIGHT   . .   153 TRISTRAM 3   V 143
          OF LESSINGS FAMED LAOCOON   . . . .   221 EPILOG LAOCOON   3
          THIS BREEZE THAT RUSTLES BY THAT FAMED   . . . .   223 EPILOG LAOCOON   78
          THAT WORLD-FAMED SON OF FIRE SHE WHO SANK   . . .   285 HAWORTH CHURCH   97
          TO THE CARTHUSIANS WORLD-FAMED HOME   . . . .   300 GRANDE CHARTR   30
          THIS IS THAT FRUITFUL FAMED MESSENIAN LAND   . . .   330 MEROPE   4
          MATRICIDAL WORLD-FAMED   . . . .   344 MEROPE   440
          WHAT ONCE-FAMED WRETCH HE THERE DID ESPY HID   . .   396 MEROPE   1754
          WHAT ONCE-FAMED WRETCH HE HATH SEEN LURKING THERE   . .   396 MEROPE   V1754
          THE WORLD-FAMED ABBEY BY THE WESTERING THAMES   . .   444 WESTMIN ABBEY   20

FAMES
          MANY SPENT FAMES AND FALLEN MIGHTS   . . . . . .   220 BACCHANALIA 2   23

FAMILIAR
          THOUGH SLOWLY THE FAMILIAR WHOLE   . . . . .   55 RESIGNATION   95
          FAMILIAR HALLS WHERE WE HAVE SUPPD OF OLD   . . .   128 BALDER DEAD 3   534
          FAMILIAR MEANINGS IN YOUR MYSTIC TONE   . . . .   472 CROMWELL   4
          DECKD THE DULL WASTE AND THE FAMILIAR FIELD   . .   472 CROMWELL   34

FAMINE
          FAMINE AND SORROW ARE NO STRANGERS HERE   . . . .   465 ALARIC AT ROME   82

FAMOUS
          WHO IN THEIR LIVES WERE FAMOUS FOR THEIR SONG   . .   103 BALDER DEAD 1   272
          FAMOUS IN ARTHURS COURT OF OLD   . . . .   131 TRISTRAM 1   20
          THE FAMOUS TOWNS OF ITALY   . . . .   138 TRISTRAM 1   251
          OH THAT TO SHARE THIS FAMOUS SCENE   . . . . .   204 CALAIS SANDS   9
          OER CALAIS AND ITS FAMOUS PLAIN   . . . . . .   205 CALAIS SANDS   18
          THE FAMOUS ORATORS HAVE SHONE   . . . . . .   219 BACCHANALIA 2   3
          THE FAMOUS POETS SUNG AND GONE   . . . . . .   219 BACCHANALIA 2   4
          THE FAMOUS MEN OF WAR HAVE FOUGHT   . . . . .   219 BACCHANALIA 2   5
          THE FAMOUS SPECULATORS THOUGHT   . . . . . .   219 BACCHANALIA 2   6
          THE FAMOUS PLAYERS SCULPTORS WROUGHT   . . . . .   219 BACCHANALIA 2   7
          THE FAMOUS PAINTERS FILLD THEIR WALL   . . . . .   219 BACCHANALIA 2   8
          THE FAMOUS CRITICS JUDGED IT ALL   . . . . .   219 BACCHANALIA 2   9
          THE FAMOUS ORATORS HAVE DONE   . . . . . .   219 BACCHANALIA 2   V 3
          IN A BOOK WHICH OF WORLD-FAMOUS SOULS   . . . .   280 HAWORTH CHURCH   19
          SAW THE FAMOUS ALAS   . . . .   281 HAWORTH CHURCH   V

FAMOUS   (CONTINUED)
        FAMOUS OF WOMEN THE QUEENS   . . . .   296 HEINES GRAVE   144
        THAT FAMOUS FINAL VICTORY   . . . .   432 EMPEDOCLES II   127
        THERE WAS HELD THE FAMOUS STRIFE   . . . . . .   433 EMPEDOCLES II   140

FANCIED
        EVEN FANCIED AND HIS DEATH THOU WROUGHTEST CHIEF . . 339 MEROPE   328

FANCIES
        FOND FANCIES HERE THERE FALSE PHILOSOPHY   . . . .   446 WESTMIN ABBEY   66

FANCIFUL
        TILL FANCIFUL REGRET AND DREAMY WOE . . . . . .   467 ALARIC AT ROME   125

FANCY
        WHOSE MOOD SHALL FANCY LIKEN TO THY WOE   . . . .   42 GIPSY CHILD   V 21
        BEFORE THE CHILDRENS FANCY HIM AND HER   . . . .   154 TRISTRAM 3   166
        AND FANCY THAT WE PUT FORTH ALL OUR LIFE . . . .   236 PALLADIUM   19
        UNDUPED OF FANCY HENCEFORTH MAN   . . . . . .   319 OBERMANN MORE   185
        UNLED OF FANCY HENCEFORTH MAN   . . . .   319 OBERMANN MORE V 185
        OH YES IF FANCY FEELS BEYOND TO DAY . . . . . .   467 ALARIC AT ROME   127
        SWEPT OER THE FANCY OF THAT HEEDLESS CHILD . . . . 473 CROMWELL   52

FANCYS
        HERE SHOULD A THOUSAND FORMS ON FANCYS WINGS . . . 470 ALARIC AT ROME   207
        THEN FANCYS ROVING VISIONS BOLD AND FREE   . . . . 474 CROMWELL   93

FANE
        IACCHUS WHITE FANE . . . .   186 STRAYED REVEL   38
        BUT ONE VAST FANE WHERE ALL UNCONSCIOUS SLEEP . .   464 ALARIC AT ROME   59
        IN FRONT OF SOME GREAT FANE WHEREOF WE KNOW   . .   LUCRETIUS 5   7

FANTASTIC
        MOODS OF FANTASTIC SADNESS NOTHING WORTH . . . .   42 GIPSY CHILD   18
        SOME SLOUGH OF SENSE OR SOME FANTASTIC MAZE   . .   440 EMPEDOCLES II   375
        CUTS SHORT THE FEIGNINGS OF FANTASTIC GRIEF   . .   FRAGMENT 1   6

FANTASY
        CHRIST KEEP US FROM SUCH FANTASY   . . . .   147 TRISTRAM 2   130
        HEAVEN KEEP US FROM SUCH FANTASY   . . . .   147 TRISTRAM 2   V 130

FAR
        FAR NOISIER SCHEMES ACCOMPLISHD IN REPOSE . . . .   1 QUIET WORK   7
        OF LABOUR THAT IN FRUIT BY FAR OUTGOES   . . . .   1 QUIET WORK   V   6
        OF LABOUR THAT IN FRUIT BY FAR OUTGROWS   . . . .   1 QUIET WORK   V   6
        FAR FROM TOWN OR HAUNT OF MAN   . . . .   14 CHURCH BROU 1   62
        FAR UP SHINES THE HOUSE AND BENEATH FLOWS THE RIVER   19 MODERN SAPPHO   3
        FAR UP GLEAMS THE HOUSE AND BENEATH FLOWS THE RIVER   19 MODERN SAPPHO V   3
        FROM THE FAR GRAVE TO WHICH IT GOES . . . . . .   21 YOUTH AND CALM   13
        DEEP AND FAR A BROKEN GLEAMING   . . . .   32 NEW SIRENS   185
        THIS FAR-REACHING MAGIC CHAIN   . . . .   33 NEW SIRENS   204
        SO FAR AS I CONCEIVE THE WORLDS REBUKE   . . . .   37 WORLDS TRIUMPHS   1
        I THINK THOU WILT HAVE FATHOMD LIFE TOO FAR   . .   43 GIPSY CHILD   47
        SOME DREAMERS WHO FAR OFF A SUMMERS DAY   . . . .   42 GIPSY CHILD   V 22
        FAR HENCE IN ASIA . . . .   50 CONSOLATION   11
        THERE CLIMBING HANGS A FAR-SEEN SIGN . . . . . .   54 RESIGNATION   60
        HERE WHENCE THE EYE FIRST SEES FAR DOWN   . . . .   55 RESIGNATION   92
        IS IN THEIR FAR-OFF TRIUMPHS PROUD   . . . . . .   57 RESIGNATION   163
        FAR REGIONS OF ETERNAL CHANGE   . . . .   58 RESIGNATION   222
        THAT WERE FAR BEST MY SON TO STAY WITH US . . . .   63 SOHRAB RUSTUM   71
        BUT FAR HENCE SEEK HIM FOR HE IS NOT HERE . . . .   63 SOHRAB RUSTUM   78
        FROM FAR AND A MORE DOUBTFUL SERVICE OWND . . . .   64 SOHRAB RUSTUM   127
        BUT RUSTUM IS FAR HENCE AND WE STAND HERE . . . .   72 SOHRAB RUSTUM   384
        FAR OFF ANON HER MATE COMES WINGING BACK   . . . .   78 SOHRAB RUSTUM   561
        IN SOME FAR STONY GORGE OUT OF HIS KEN   . . . .   78 SOHRAB RUSTUM   568
        SOMEWHERE I KNOW NOT WHERE BUT FAR FROM HERE . .   78 SOHRAB RUSTUM   583
        BY THE FAR-DISTANT OXUS HE IS SLAIN . . . . . .   79 SOHRAB RUSTUM   601
        A FAR BRIGHT CITY SMITTEN BY THE SUN . . . . . .   79 SOHRAB RUSTUM   622
        AND FALSEHOOD WHILE I LIVED WAS FAR FROM MINE . .   80 SOHRAB RUSTUM   657
        AND PLANT A FAR-SEEN PILLAR OVER ALL . . . . . .   84 SOHRAB RUSTUM   789
        AND PLANT A FAR-SEEN PILLAR OVER ALL . . . . . .   84 SOHRAB RUSTUM   804
        WITH CURIOUS FRUIT-TREES BROUGHT FROM FAR . . . .   94 SICK KING BOKH   201
        WITH CURIOUS FRUIT TREES BOUGHT FROM FAR   . . . .   94 SICK KING BOKH V 201
        AND FAR FROM HEAVEN HE TURND HIS SHINING ORBS . .   96 BALDER DEAD 1   51
        UNTRODDEN LONELY FAR FROM LIGHT AND HEAVEN . . . . 99 BALDER DEAD 1   136
        FAR FAR BEYOND THE OUTMOST GIANTS HOME   . . . .   100 BALDER DEAD 1   163
        FAR FAR BEYOND THE OUTMOST GIANTS HOME   . . . .   100 BALDER DEAD 1   163
        AND FAR INTO THE NIGHT THEY WAILD THEIR DIRGE . . 103 BALDER DEAD 1   275
        ALIVE I KEPT NOT FAR FROM THEE DEAR SOUL   . . . . 103 BALDER DEAD 1   293
        FAR HENCE IN ASGARD IN THE CITY OF GODS   . . . .   108 BALDER DEAD 2   114
        AND SURE OF ALL THE HAPPIEST FAR ART THOU . . . . 112 BALDER DEAD 2   257
        BUT FEEBLY AS A VOICE FAR OFF HE SAID . . . . . . 112 BALDER DEAD 2   263
        FAR IN THE COUNTRY WONDERING WHERE HE IS   . . . . 114 BALDER DEAD 3   18
        AND LONG IN THE FAR DARK BLAZED BALDERS PILE . .   119 BALDER DEAD 3   200
        FOR OF ALL POWERS THE MIGHTIEST FAR ART THOU . .   120 BALDER DEAD 3   250
        BUT ALL THAT BROOD THOU HAST REMOVED FAR OFF . .   121 BALDER DEAD 3   274
        FAR OFF WHERE SOME UNWARND MIGHT FAIL TO WEEP . . 122 BALDER DEAD 3   322
        OF PORT THEY HAD MAKES BITTERER FAR THEIR TOIL . . 124 BALDER DEAD 3   367
        FAR FROM THE OTHER GHOSTS AND HELAS THRONE . . .   124 BALDER DEAD 3   391
        NOT TOO FAR OFF WHEN THAT THOU CAMEST BY   . . . . 125 BALDER DEAD 3   417

FAR   (CONTINUED)
               ESTEEM AND FUNCTION AND SO FAR IS WELL   • • • •   127 BALDER DEAD 3   470
               FAR TO THE SOUTH BEYOND THE BLUE THERE SPREADS • • •   128 BALDER DEAD 3   518
               OUT OF THE BLACK WASTE FOREST FAR BELOW   • • • •   119 BALDER DEAD 3   V
               SO FLARD IN THE FAR DARKNESS BALDERS PYRE   • • • •   119 BALDER DEAD 3   V 200
               SO SHOWED IN THE FAR DARKNESS BALDERS PYRE   • • • •   119 BALDER DEAD 3   V 200
               AS HE WANDERS FAR FROM HERE   • • • • • 133 TRISTRAM 1   88
               FAR HENCE HER DREAMS ARE FAIR SMOOTH IS HER BROW • •   139 TRISTRAM 1   302
               FAR LOVELIER THAN THEY ARE BY DAY   • • • •   141 TRISTRAM 1   356
               AND FAR BEYOND THE SPARKLING TREES   • • • •   141 TRISTRAM 1   362
               MOOR BEHIND MOOR FAR FAR AWAY   • • • •   141 TRISTRAM 1   365
               MOOR BEHIND MOOR FAR FAR AWAY   • • • •   141 TRISTRAM 1   365
               FAR HENCE HER DREAMS ARE FAIR HER SLEEP IS STILL • •   139 TRISTRAM 1   V 302
               GO NOT FAR O ISEULT FROM MY GRAVE   • • • •   145 TRISTRAM 2   92
               THE SUNKEN REEFS AND FAR AWAY   • • • •   148 TRISTRAM 2   173
               AND TO ONE STANDING ON THEM FAR AND NEAR   • • •   149 TRISTRAM 3   11
               FOR THEY HAD TRAVELLD FAR AND NOT STOPPD YET • • •   154 TRISTRAM 3   172
               BUT THEIR SLOPE WAS NOT DEEP AND FAR AND NEAR   TRISTRAM 3   V 11
               FAR FROM THE KIND SEA-WAVE   • • • •   159 NECKAN   16
               FAR FROM THE GREEN SEA WAVE   • • • •   159 NECKAN   V 16
               THE FAR-OFF SOUND OF A SILVER BELL   • • • •   162 FORSAKEN MERM   34
               WHEN DOWN SWUNG THE SOUND OF A FAR-OFF BELL   • • •   163 FORSAKEN MERM   54
               WHEN DOWN SWUNG THE SOUND OF THE FAR-OFF BELL • •   163 FORSAKEN MERM   V 54
               WAS WOE THAN BYRONS WOE MORE TRAGIC FAR   • • •   167 PICT NEWSTEAD   14
               FAR FAR FROM EACH OTHER   • • • • • • 177 PARTING   71
               FAR FAR FROM EACH OTHER   • • • • • • 177 PARTING   71
               ARE YET FAR FAR LESS RARE THAN LOVE   • • • •   178 FAREWELL   40
               ARE YET FAR FAR LESS RARE THAN LOVE   • • • •   178 FAREWELL   40
               WHAT FAR TOO SOON ALAS I LEARND   • • • •   180 ISOLATION MARG   8
               WANDERING IN HEAVEN FAR REMOVED   • • • •   181 ISOLATION MARG   27
               HAD BORNE ME FAR FROM THEE   • • • •   183 ABSENCE   4
               THE JUNGFRAU SNOWS LOOK FAINT AND FAR   • • •   184 TERRACE BERNE   6
               MOWN THEM DOWN FAR FROM HOME   • • • •   193 STRAYED REVEL   253
               ONE THAN CREON CRUELLER FAR   • • • •   196 FRAG ANTIGONE   47
               FAR FROM THE GODS WITH HERS   • • • •   197 FRAG ANTIGONE   74
               BUT I MAY STAND FAR OFF AND GAZE   • • • •   205 CALAIS SANDS   27
               SO FAR APART THEIR LIVES ARE THROWN   • • • •   206 TOO LATE   3
               AND THAT FAR PURPLE MOUNTAIN-LINE   • • • •   208 ON THE RHINE   13
               GIRT BY HIS FAR-SHINING TRAIN   • • • •   216 LORDS MESSENGER   V
               AND ON THE PURE HORIZON FAR   • • • •   218 BACCHANALIA 1   16
               AND FAR TO THE SOUTH THE HEATH   • • • •   228 YOUTH OF NATURE   22
               FAR OFF A GLORY OF DAY   • • • •   234 YOUTH OF MAN   81
               AND HECTOR WAS IN ILIUM FAR BELOW   • • • •   236 PALLADIUM   3
               FROM A FAR LONELIER DISTANCE LIKE THE WIND   • • • •   238 PROGRESS   34
               DOWN AT THE FAR HORIZONS RIM   • • • •   242 SUMMER NIGHT   9
               OF A PAST NIGHT AND A FAR DIFFERENT SCENE   • • • •   242 SUMMER NIGHT   13
               THAT NIGHT WAS FAR MORE FAIR   • • • •   242 SUMMER NIGHT   22
               THE NIGHT WAS FAR MORE FAIR   • • • •   242 SUMMER NIGHT   V 22
               WHILE TO MY EAR FROM UPLANDS FAR AWAY   • • • •   255 SCHOLAR-GIPSY   17
               FAR ON THE FOREST-SKIRTS WHERE NONE PURSUE   • • • •   261 SCHOLAR-GIPSY   215
               WHERE THICK THE COWSLIPS GREW AND FAR DESCRIED • •   266 THYRSIS   114
               CAUSES OF THINGS AND FAR BELOW   • • • •   271 MEMORIAL VERSES   30
               FAR ON ITS ROCKY KNOLL DESCRIED   • • • •   273 STANZAS CARNAC   1
               WHERE THAT FAR SAIL IS PASSING NOW   • • • •   274 STANZAS CARNAC   34
               FAR IN THE BAY   • • • •   275 SOUTHERN NIGHT   12
               AH ME GIBRALTARS STRAND IS FAR   • • • • • 277 SOUTHERN NIGHT   49
               IS DEAF FAR NORTHWARD FROM HERE   • • • •   282 HAWORTH CHURCH   51
               SPACE FOR THINGS FAR FROM THEMSELVES   • • • •   282 HAWORTH CHURCH   V
               YES IN SOME FAR-SHINING SPHERE   • • • •   287 RUGBY CHAPEL   44
               FAR GERMAN HOME OF HIS YOUTH   • • • •   296 HEINES GRAVE   151
               WHILE HARK FAR DOWN WITH STRANGLED SOUND   • • • •   299 GRANDE CHARTR   9
               BUT AS ON SOME FAR NORTHERN STRAND   • • • •   301 GRANDE CHARTR   80
               FAINT BUGLE-NOTES FROM FAR ARE BORNE   • • • •   305 GRANDE CHARTR   182
               GREATER BY FAR THAN THOU ARE DEAD   • • • •   309 OBERMANN   91
               LAKE LEMANS WATERS FAR BELOW   • • • •   310 OBERMANN   121
               HAD BEEN TOO FAR TO FLEE   • • • •   317 OBERMANN MORE   152
               NOW HE IS DEAD FAR HENCE HE LIES   • • • •   318 OBERMANN MORE   173
               THE SILENCE FAR BELOW   • • • •   323 OBERMANN MORE   328
               O POLICY TOO SUBTLE FAR FOR SENSE   • • • •   339 MEROPE   311
               FAR ON MARATHON PLAIN   • • • •   343 MEROPE   431
               FAR MID ARCADIAN HILLS   • • • •   346 MEROPE   512
               FAR IN THE LIQUID LAKE WE SATE AND DREW   • • • •   356 MEROPE   752
               FAR IN THE WOODS AHEAD THEIR MUSIC RANG   • • • •   357 MEROPE   792
               NOW IN THE WOODS FAR DOWN I SAW THEM CROSS   • • • •   357 MEROPE   801
               OF THIS FAR-SCHEMING TYRANT AND HIS BOON   • • • •   366 MEROPE   998
               WORSE FAR WORSE IF HIS FRIEND   • • • •   370 MEROPE   1120
               DIVULGE NOT TO THE FAR-OFF WORLD OF MEN   • • • •   396 MEROPE   1753
               WHAT FOR SO FAR FATE HATH NOT PROVED MY FOE   • • • •   397 MEROPE   1778
               WHAT FOR SO FAR SHE HATH NOT PROVED MY FOE   • • • •   397 MEROPE   V1778
               THE MULES MUST BE BELOW FAR DOWN I HEAR   • • • •   407 EMPEDOCLES I 1   27
               THEN WATCH HIM FOR HE RANGES SWIFT AND FAR   • • • •   409 EMPEDOCLES I 1   94
               THAT NEEDS NO THANKS ONE IS FAR BETTER HERE   • • •   409 EMPEDOCLES I 1   103
               AND WE WERE NOT SO FAR FROM HUMAN HAUNT   • • • •   412 EMPEDOCLES I 2   10
               SOMETIMES AND WANDERS FAR AMONG THE GLENS   • • • •   412 EMPEDOCLES I 2   17
               HE SHOWD HIM PHTHIA FAR AWAY   • • • •   414 EMPEDOCLES I 2   68
               SO EACH NEW MAN STRIKES ROOT INTO A FAR FORE-TIME • •   418 EMPEDOCLES I 2   191
               FAR FAR FROM HERE   • • • • • • 426 EMPEDOCLES I 2   427
               FAR FAR FROM HERE   • • • • • • 426 EMPEDOCLES I 2   427
               THERE THOSE TWO LIVE FAR IN THE ILLYRIAN BRAKES • •   427 EMPEDOCLES I 2   443
               IN SIGHT OF BLOOD BUT WERE RAPT FAR AWAY   • • • •   427 EMPEDOCLES I 2   453

FAR (CONTINUED)
I SAW HIM THROUGH THE CHESTNUTS FAR BELOW . . . . 428 EMPEDOCLES I 2 485
PAUSANIAS IS FAR HENCE AND THAT IS WELL . . . . . 429 EMPEDOCLES II 5
WHEN FROM FAR PARNASSUS SIDE . . . . 433 EMPEDOCLES II 129
LIVES AND THAT OTHER FAINTER SEA FAR DOWN . . . . 438 EMPEDOCLES II 311
FAR FROM MY OWN SOUL FAR FROM WARMTH AND LIGHT . . 440 EMPEDOCLES II 396
FAR FROM MY OWN SOUL FAR FROM WARMTH AND LIGHT . . 440 EMPEDOCLES II 396
SEND FAR THEIR LIGHT VOICE . . . . 442 EMPEDOCLES II 426
THOUGH MOVING INLY TO ONE FAR-SET GOAL . . . . 448 WESTMIN ABBEY 153
THOUGH MOVING INLY TO ONE FAR-OFF GOAL . . . . 448 WESTMIN ABBEY V 153
DROPT BY THE FAR AUSTRALIAN FOAM . . . . . 451 GEISTS GRAVE 56
BUT FAR IN OBSCURE THERE STIRRD . . . . . 458 POOR MATTHIAS 192
PERCHANCE HIS WANDERING HEART WAS FAR AWAY . . . . 468 ALARIC AT ROME 169
ALAS FAR OTHER THOUGHTS MIGHT WELL BE OURS . . . . 470 ALARIC AT ROME 199
FAR OER THE GLISTENING SHEETS OF WINDY CORN . . 473 CROMWELL 36
FROM A FAR LAND THE CHILDREN OF THE SNOW . . . . 474 CROMWELL 90
ONE MOMENTS SPACE MIGHT WAFT HIM FAR AWAY . . . . 475 CROMWELL 111
FAR OER THE PATHLESS WASTE OF LABOURING FOAM . . 475 CROMWELL 114
FAR ON THE DIM HORIZON WHEN THE SKY . . . . . 475 CROMWELL 129
PALE PHANTOM HOSTS LIKE SHADOWS FAINT AND FAR . . 476 CROMWELL 141
FAR DOWN THE TORRENT CLEAVES ITS WAY . . . . . 479 HAYSWATER BOAT 10
AT LAST IN AIR FAR OFF DIM ROSE A HEIGHT . . . . 484 S S LUSITANIA 6
XANTHUS AND BALIUS BOTH YE FAR-FAMD SEED OF PODARGA HOMER TRANS 39
THUS FAR HE AND HERE HIS VOICE WAS STOPPED HOMER TRANS 57
   BY THE FURIES
FAR FROM MY FATHER AND MOTHER DEAR FOR ALL HOMER TRANS 61
   THAT I WILL NOT
OR FAR EASTWARD WHERE UP-PILD . . . . PILLARS UNIVERS 6
SOFTLY GLEAM THE FAR BLUE MOUNTAINS . . . . . . META CLOISTER 13

FARE
OUR JOVIAL HOST AS FORTH WE FARE . . . . . 53 RESIGNATION 42
THROUGH THE DEEP NOONTIDE HEATS WE FARE . . . . 54 RESIGNATION 69
AND HE MUST FARE ACROSS THE DISMAL ICE . . . . 100 BALDER DEAD 1 165
AND HE WILL FARE ACROSS THE DISMAL ICE . . . . 100 BALDER DEAD 1 V 165
FARE FAREWELL THOU LONG THOU DEEPLY LOVD . . . . 145 TRISTRAM 2 V 98
ILL AND OERWORKD HOW FARE YOU IN THIS SCENE . . 169 EAST LONDON 6
HOW ANGRILY THOU SPURNST ALL SIMPLER FARE . . . 170 BETTER PART 2
FORTH TO THE WORLD THOSE SOLDIERS FARE . . . . 305 GRANDE CHARTR 179
FORTH TO THE MIGHTY WORLD THEY FARE . . . . . 305 GRANDE CHARTR V 179
FULL-FOAMING MILK-PAILS ALPINE FARE . . . . . 313 OBERMANN MORE 17
SUMPTUOUS ITS CLOTHING RICH ITS FARE . . . . . 315 OBERMANN MORE 87
CATES FROM OUR HUNTERS POUCH ARCADIAN FARE . . . . 356 MEROPE 753
FARE THEE WELL COMPANION DEAR . . . . 458 POOR MATTHIAS 206
FARE FOR EVER WELL NOR FEAR . . . . 458 POOR MATTHIAS 207

FARED
AND UP THE DEWY MOUNTAIN-TRACKS THEY FARED . . . . 106 BALDER DEAD 2 51
BUT HERMOD MOUNTED HIM AND SADLY FARED . . . . 107 BALDER DEAD 2 78
BUT BY THE BLOTTED LIGHT OF STARS HE FARED . . . . 108 BALDER DEAD 2 140
AND OER THE ICE HE FARED TO OCEANS STRAND . . . . 113 BALDER DEAD 2 288
BETTER MEN FARED THUS BEFORE THEE . . . . . 215 LAST WORD 10
FORWARD THE GRACIOUS HOURS HAVE FARED . . . . 322 OBERMANN MORE 283
ONE NIGHT AND THE NEXT DAY AT DAWN FARED ON . . 356 MEROPE 747

FARES
WITH SCARLET BERRIES GEMMD THE FELL-FARES FOOD . . 150 TRISTRAM 3 22
THE FELL-FARES AND THE SPECKLED MISSEL-THRUSH . . 150 TRISTRAM 3 30
THE FELL-FARES SETTLED ON THE THICKETS NEAR . . 151 TRISTRAM 3 55
AND NEVER KNOW HOW WITH THE SOUL IT FARES . . . . 236 PALLADIUM 20
YET ON HE FARES BY HIS OWN HEART INSPIRED . . . . 269 THYRSIS 210

FAREWELL
FAREWELL O BALDER BRIGHT AND LOVED MY SON . . . . 115 BALDER DEAD 3 67
HAIL AND FAREWELL FOR HERE THOU COMST NO MORE . . 126 BALDER DEAD 3 455
FAREWELL FOR LONGER SPEECH IS NOT ALLOWD . . . 129 BALDER DEAD 3 543
HE SPOKE AND WAVED FAREWELL AND GAVE HIS HAND . . 129 BALDER DEAD 3 549
FARE FAREWELL THOU LONG THOU DEEPLY LOVD . . . . 145 TRISTRAM 2 V 98
THOU LOVST NO MORE FAREWELL FAREWELL . . . . . 180 ISOLATION MARG 12
THOU LOVST NO MORE FAREWELL FAREWELL . . . . . 180 ISOLATION MARG 12
FAREWELL AND THOU THOU LONELY HEART . . . . . 181 ISOLATION MARG 13
UNSOILD AND SO FAREWELL . . . . 311 OBERMANN 160
FAREWELL WHETHER THOU NOW LIEST NEAR . . . . . 311 OBERMANN 161
FAREWELL UNDER THE SKY WE PART . . . . . . 312 OBERMANN 181
A LAST A LAST FAREWELL . . . . 312 OBERMANN 184
THEN PLAY THY KIND PART WELL FAREWELL TILL NIGHT . . 411 EMPEDOCLES I 1 167
MEANWHILE STAY ME NOT NOW FAREWELL PAUSANIAS . . 428 EMPEDOCLES I 2 478

FAREWELLS
NODS SMILES AND GREETINGS AND FAREWELLS . . . . 224 EPILOG LAOCOON 121

FARING
SANDALLD PALMERS FARING HOMEWARD . . . . . . 15 CHURCH BROU 1 77

FARM
BUT HOME HIS MASTER COMES TO HIS OWN FARM . . . 114 BALDER DEAD 3 17
FROM A DISTANT FARM IN THE HILLS . . . . . . 234 YOUTH OF MAN 74
RUNS IT NOT HERE THE TRACK BY CHILDSWORTH FARM . . 263 THYRSIS 11

FARMER
LIKE AS A FARMER WHO HATH LOST HIS DOG . . . . 113 BALDER DEAD 3 8

FARMS
    OF ITS DARK UPLAND FARMS IS PAST   • • • • • •   54 RESIGNATION   55
    COOL FARMS WITH OPEN-LYING STORES   • • • • • •   54 RESIGNATION   56
    O JOY AGAIN THE FARMS APPEAR   • • • • • • • •   54 RESIGNATION   74
    LONE FARMS WITH OPEN-LYING STORES   • • • • • •   54 RESIGNATION   V 56
    THIN-SPRINKLED WITH FARMS   • • • • • • • •   175 PARTING   6
    ALL HOUSED WITHIN THE SLEEPING FARMS   • • • •   218 BACCHANALIA 1   7
    AND IN THE SCATTERED FARMS THE LIGHTS COME OUT   • •   267 THYRSIS   164
    ITS FIR-TOPPED HURST ITS FARMS ITS QUIET FIELDS   • •   269 THYRSIS   217

FARRINGFORD
    FROM WHERE IN FARRINGFORD SHE BREWS   • • • • • •   458 KAISER DEAD   3

FARTHER
    IN SOME WINDLESS VALLEY FARTHER DOWN   • • • • •   31 NEW SIRENS   146
    BUT WHERE THE FARTHER SIDE SLOPES DOWN   • • • •   57 RESIGNATION   180
    IN THE STRAIT PASSAGE AT THE FARTHER END   • • • •   107 BALDER DEAD 2   88
    BUT OER THEM ON THE FARTHER SLOPE DESCRIES   • • •   113 BALDER DEAD 2   299
    FARTHER AND FARTHER LIKE AN EYE OF FIRE   • • • •   119 BALDER DEAD 3   199
    FARTHER AND FARTHER LIKE AN EYE OF FIRE   • • • •   119 BALDER DEAD 3   199
    ON THE BROOKS FARTHER SIDE WAS CLEAR BUT THEN   • •   155 TRISTRAM 3   189
    INTO YON FARTHER FIELD TIS DONE AND SEE   • • • •   267 THYRSIS   157
    BUT FARTHER YET ACROSS THE BRINE   • • • • • •   277 SOUTHERN NIGHT   50
    AND ON THE HIGHEST PINES BUT FARTHER DOWN   • • • •   406 EMPEDOCLES I 1   11

FARTHEST
    IS TO THEIR FARTHEST CAVERNS SENT   • • • • •   182 TO MARG CONT   14
    IN THE FARTHEST WESTERN WILD   • • • • • • • •   PILLARS UNIVERS   5

FASCINATES
    LIFES MOVEMENT FASCINATES CONTROLS   • • • • • •   226 EPILOG LAOCOON   164

FASHION
    FROM THE INGRAIND FASHION   • • • • • • • •   39 STAGIRIUS   30

FAST
    NATURE AND MAN CAN NEVER BE FAST FRIENDS   • • •   5 HARMONY NATURE   13
    FLITTING FAST ACROSS EACH MARBLE BROW   • • • •   31 NEW SIRENS   162
    HUMAN THINGS SO FAST ENTANGLED   • • • • • • •   49 SECOND BEST   10
    RUNNING FAST HOMEWARD WITH THE TURN OF TIDE   • •   69 SOHRAB RUSTUM   V 287
    THROUGH THE FAST-DARKENING STREETS TO HIS OWN HOUSE   101 BALDER DEAD 1   207
    THERE THROUGH SOME BATTLE-FIELD WHERE MEN FALL FAST   105 BALDER DEAD 2   24
    MADE FAST THE WOVEN ROPES AND HALED THEM DOWN   • •   106 BALDER DEAD 2   58
    MADE FAST TO THE BORED CRAG BY WILE NOT STRENGTH   • •   111 BALDER DEAD 2   215
    FAST BESIDE THE SOUNDING SEA   • • • • • • • •   134 TRISTRAM 1   V 135
    HARK FAST BY THE WINDOW   • • • • • • • • • •   175 PARTING   25
    FAST FAST BY MY WINDOW   • • • • • • • • •   PARTING   25
    FAST FAST BY MY WINDOW   • • • • • • • • •   PARTING   V 25
    UP THE STEEP STREET I HURRIED FAST   • • • • •   177 FAREWELL   7
    VAIN THY ONSET ALL STANDS FAST   • • • • • •   215 LAST WORD   3
    ALL CHANGES FAST AND HIES ALONG   • • • • • •   225 EPILOG LAOCOON   124
    DARKENING FAST BUT A LIGHT   • • • • • • •   234 YOUTH OF MAN   80
    BRIGHT ELSE AND FAST THE STREAM OF LIFE MAY ROLL   • •   238 PROGRESS   29
    IS THIS THE EYE THE FOOTSTEP FAST   • • • • •   276 SOUTHERN NIGHT   37
    FAST RUSH THE SPECTRAL VAPOURS WHITE   • • • •   299 GRANDE CHARTR   V 13
    TOO FAST WE LIVE TOO MUCH ARE TRIED   • • • •   308 OBERMANN   77
    HE MADE A FEAST DRANK FIERCE AND FAST   • • • •   316 OBERMANN MORE   101
    MILLIONS WHOSE LIFE IN ICE LAY FAST   • • • • •   322 OBERMANN MORE   287
    FOR I HAVE KEPT CONSPIRACY FAST-CHAIND   • • •   334 MEROPE   149
    FAST PERMANENCE TO AN ILL-GOTTEN THRONE   • • •   388 MEROPE   1509
    NOW DO WE SOON PERCEIVE HOW FAST OUR YOUTH IS SPENT   424 EMPEDOCLES I 2   361
    NOR DO WE SOON PERCEIVE HOW FAST OUR YOUTH IS SPENT   424 EMPEDOCLES I 2   V 361
    PRESSING FAST WITH BOTH HIS HANDS   • • • • •   434 EMPEDOCLES II   187

FASTEND
    FASTEND ON HER DARK HAIR AND HER WREATH OF   19 MODERN SAPPHO   11
        WHITE HEATHER

FASTENINGS
    BEHOLD THE FASTENINGS WITHDRAWN   • • • • • •   372 MEROPE   1149

FASTER
    FASTER SURELY THAN IT SHOULD   • • • • • • • •   135 TRISTRAM 1   171
    FASTER FASTER   • • • • • • • • • • • •   185 STRAYED REVEL   1
    FASTER FASTER   • • • • • • • • • • • •   185 STRAYED REVEL   1
    FASTER FASTER   • • • • • • • • • • • •   194 STRAYED REVEL   292
    FASTER FASTER   • • • • • • • • • • • •   194 STRAYED REVEL   292

FASTIDIOUS
    LOVERS OF CHANGE YE ARE FASTIDIOUS SPRITES   • • • •   123 BALDER DEAD 3   339

FASTNESS
    STILL DOTH THE SOUL FROM ITS LONE FASTNESS HIGH   • •   236 PALLADIUM   21
    AS FROM A FASTNESS IN THE ROCKS OUR SCANT   • • •   337 MEROPE   247

FAT
    THERE A BIRD HIGH-COLOURED FAT   • • • • • • • •   457 POOR MATTHIAS   188

FATAL
    AS OLD AGE YOUTHS FATAL MORROW   • • • • • • •   33 NEW SIRENS   217
    BUT IN HIS BREAST STOOD FIXT THE FATAL BOUGH   • •   95 BALDER DEAD 1   5

FATAL   (CONTINUED)
        AS THEY FEEL THE FATAL BANDS   • • • • • • •   135 TRISTRAM 1   149
        FATAL TO ALL THE RACE OF HERACLES   • • • • • •   382 MEROPE   1330

FATE
        FOR FATE DECREED IT SO   • • • • • • • •   46 WORLD QUIETIST   10
        FATE GAVE WHAT CHANCE SHALL NOT CONTROL   • • • •   58 RESIGNATION   197
        AND THOUGH FATE GRUDGE TO THEE AND ME   • • • •   59 RESIGNATION   245
        NO GIFTS FROM CHANCE HAVE CONQUERD FATE   • • • •   59 RESIGNATION   248
        POISED ON THE TOP OF A HUGE WAVE OF FATE • • • •   72 SOHRAB RUSTUM   391
        AND NOW THOU BOASTEST AND INSULTST MY FATE • • •   77 SOHRAB RUSTUM   551
        I KNOW IT BUT FATE TROD THOSE PROMPTINGS DOWN • •   82 SOHRAB RUSTUM   713
        UNDER ITS IRON HEEL FATE FATE ENGAGED   • • • •   82 SOHRAB RUSTUM   714
        UNDER ITS IRON HEEL FATE FATE ENGAGED   • • • •   82 SOHRAB RUSTUM   714
        TILL THEN IF FATE SO WILLS LET ME ENDURE • • • •   85 SOHRAB RUSTUM   837
        AND FATE SET SEAL THAT SO HIS END MUST BE • • •   96 BALDER DEAD 1   25
        BUT FATE WITHSTANDS AND LAWS FORBID THIS WAY • •   98 BALDER DEAD 1   127
        AND PERISH AGAINST FATE BEFORE THY DAY   • • • •   114 BALDER DEAD 3   29
        OF SHARERS IN A COMMON HUMAN FATE   • • • • •   170 WEST LONDON   11
        GO THEN TILL TIME AND FATE IMPRESS   • • • • •   179 FAREWELL   41
        NOR IF FATE BINDS NOT BEAR   • • • • • • •   196 FRAG ANTIGONE   38
        BUT HE PREFERRD FATE TO HIS STRONG DESIRE • • •   198 FRAG ANTIGONE   97
        YET OH THAT FATE WOULD LET HER SEE   • • • • •   202 URANIA   V   17
        AND SOMETIMES BY STILL HARDER FATE   • • • • •   207 TOO LATE   5
        FATE WHICH FORESAW • • • • • • • • •   246 BURIED LIFE   30
        PIPING A DITTY SAD FOR BIONS FATE   • • • • •   265 THYRSIS   84
        AND HEADLONG FATE BE HAPPINESS   • • • • • •   271 MEMORIAL VERSES   33
        STRANGE IRONY OF FATE ALAS   • • • • • • •   277 SOUTHERN NIGHT   57
        OF THE TOO VAST ORB OF HER FATE   • • • • • •   295 HEINES GRAVE   96
        FROM HALF OF HUMAN FATE   • • • • • • • •   308 OBERMANN   54
        I GO FATE DRIVES ME BUT I LEAVE   • • • • • •   310 OBERMANN   131
        OR WHETHER BY MALIGNER FATE   • • • • • • •   311 OBERMANN   175
        WITH FATE I MURMUR NOT NOR CHIDE • • • • • •   321 OBERMANN MORE   267
        ORDERD BY FATE TO THEIR HOME • • • • • • •   343 MEROPE   413
        AT THE FATE-DENIED STRAITS   • • • • • • •   344 MEROPE   444
        SAILD BY THE FATE-MEANT GULF TO THEIR CONQUEST •   344 MEROPE   450
        THOU TELLEST THE FATE OF THE LAST   • • • • •   345 MEROPE   469
        O THRICE UNHAPPY HOW I GROAN THY FATE   • • •   362 MEROPE   931
        BUT IS IT ONLY A FATE   • • • • • • • •   369 MEROPE   1099
        THOU FATE GIVES IT AH ME   • • • • • • •   370 MEROPE   1111
        TO-DAY I REIGN THE REST I LEAVE TO FATE   • • •   397 MEROPE   1776
        FOR FATE THOU WAITST NOT LONG SINCE IN THIS HOUR •   397 MEROPE   1777
        WHAT FOR SO FAR FATE HATH NOT PROVED MY FOE   • •   397 MEROPE   1778
        FATE SEALS MY LIPS AND DRAGS TO RUIN THEE • • •   397 MEROPE   1779
        IS FATE INDEED SO STRONG MANS STRENGTH INDEED SO POOR   415 EMPEDOCLES I 2   96
        WITH GOD AND FATE TO RAIL AT SUFFERING EASILY • •   421 EMPEDOCLES I 2   281
        MEN SCOFF AT HEAVEN AND FATE   • • • • • •   426 EMPEDOCLES I 2   418
        THAT NATURAL CAUSES MAR THY EFFORTS AND NOT FATE • •   EMPEDOCLES I 2   V
        THAT NATURAL CAUSES THWART THY WELFARE AND NOT FATE   EMPEDOCLES I 2   V
        OH THAT FATE HAD LET ME SEE   • • • • • • •   432 EMPEDOCLES II   125
        THINK YE IT STRIKES TOO SLOW THE SWORD OF FATE • •   466 ALARIC AT ROME   115
        HIGH FATE IS THEIRS YE SLEEPLESS WAVES WHOSE EAR •   471 CROMWELL   1
        HIGH FATE IS THEIRS WHO WHERE THE SILENT SKY   • •   472 CROMWELL   9
        WHEN FATE AND CIRCUMSTANCE ARE STRONG   • • • •   481 COURAGE   6

FATED
        HODER ILL-FATED CHILD OF BALE MY SON • • • • • •   98 BALDER DEAD 1   112
        HODER ILL-FATED BLIND IN HEART AND EYES   • • • •   124 BALDER DEAD 3   387
        LO THE ILL-FATED ONE   • • • • • • • • •   400 MEROPE   1876
        WHICH MEN SAY IS THE FLEETEST OF WINDS TIS   HOMER TRANS   55
                THOU WHO ART FATED

FATEFUL
        GIRD THEE AND ON UPON THY FATEFUL PATH   • • • •   465 ALARIC AT ROME   88

FATES
        PIERCE FATES IMPENETRABLE EAR   • • • • • • •   60 RESIGNATION   274
        OR FOR THOU KNOWST THE FATES AND THINGS ALLOWD • •   98 BALDER DEAD 1   108
        BIRTH-GODDESS AND THE AUSTERE FATES FIRST GAVE • •   195 FRAG ANTIGONE   10
        TILL THE FATES COME AGAIN THIS TIME WITH DEATH • •   195 FRAG ANTIGONE   16
        TILL THE FATES COME AGAIN ALONE WITH DEATH   • • •   195 FRAG ANTIGONE   V   16
        HARSH GODS AND HOSTILE FATES • • • • • • •   422 EMPEDOCLES I 2   304
        FATES THREATNINGS ARE NOT VAIN THE SPOILER   466 ALARIC AT ROME   120
                COMES NOT SLOW
        NO BUT THE WILL OF HEAVEN AND FATES INVINCIBLE POWER   HOMER TRANS   49

FATHER
        NOT BY THE JUSTICE THAT MY FATHER SPURND • • • •   8 MYCERINUS   1
        NOT FOR THE THOUSANDS WHOM MY FATHER SLEW   • • •   8 MYCERINUS   2
        MY FATHER LOVED INJUSTICE AND LIVED LONG   • • •   9 MYCERINUS   13
        RUSTUM MY FATHER WHO I HOPED SHOULD GREET   • • •   62 SOHRAB RUSTUM   50
        TO FIND A FATHER THOU HAST NEVER SEEN   • • • •   63 SOHRAB RUSTUM   70
        IN SEISTAN WITH ZAL HIS FATHER OLD   • • • •   63 SOHRAB RUSTUM   82
        TO SEEK THY FATHER NOT SEEK SINGLE FIGHTS   • • •   63 SOHRAB RUSTUM   90
        MY FATHER WHOM THE ROBBER AFGHANS VEX   • • • •   68 SOHRAB RUSTUM   233
        TO GLAD THY FATHER IN HIS WEAK OLD AGE   • • • •   77 SOHRAB RUSTUM   536
        THAN TO THY FRIENDS AND TO THY FATHER OLD   • • •   77 SOHRAB RUSTUM   539
        MY FATHER WHOM I SEEK THROUGH ALL THE WORLD • • •   77 SOHRAB RUSTUM   554
        WITH THAT OLD KING HER FATHER WHO GROWS GREY   • •   78 SOHRAB RUSTUM   591
        AND THAT OLD KING HER FATHER WHO LOVED WELL   • •   79 SOHRAB RUSTUM   625
        RUSTUMS GREAT FATHER WHOM THEY LEFT TO DIE   • • •   81 SOHRAB RUSTUM   680
        O BOY THY FATHER AND HIS VOICE CHOKED THERE • •   81 SOHRAB RUSTUM   691

FATHER   (CONTINUED)
    FATHER FORBEAR FOR I BUT MEET TO-DAY • • • • • 82 SOHRAB RUSTUM 708
    MY FATHER LET ME FEEL THAT I HAVE FOUND • • • • 82 SOHRAB RUSTUM 717
    DESIRE NOT THAT MY FATHER THOU MUST LIVE • • • • 84 SOHRAB RUSTUM 772
    THOU ART MY FATHER AND THY GAIN IS MINE • • • • 84 SOHRAB RUSTUM 777
    WHOM HIS GREAT FATHER DID IN IGNORANCE KILL • • 84 SOHRAB RUSTUM 793
    AND THUS THE FATHER OF THE AGES SPAKE • • • • 95 BALDER DEAD 1 17
    I MOST MIGHT WEEP HIS FATHER SUCH A SON • • • • 96 BALDER DEAD 1 21
    HEARING THE WRATHFUL FATHER COMING HOME • • • • 102 BALDER DEAD 1 263
    AND THUS THE FATHER OF THE AGES SPAKE • • • • 106 BALDER DEAD 2 40
    THREE MIGHTY CHILDREN TO MY FATHER LOK • • • 110 BALDER DEAD 2 206
    LOK STILL SUBSISTS IN HEAVEN OUR FATHER WISE • • 111 BALDER DEAD 2 217
    TO ODIN TO MY FATHER TAKE THIS RING • • • • 112 BALDER DEAD 2 274
    AND LOK THE FATHER OF THE SERPENT FIRST • • • 113 BALDER DEAD 3 4
    PEACE LEST OUR FATHER ODIN HEAR THEE GIBE • • 114 BALDER DEAD 3 23
    ODIN MY FATHER AND YE GODS OF HEAVEN • • • • 114 BALDER DEAD 3 36
    AND STRAIGHT THE FATHER OF THE AGES SAID • • 115 BALDER DEAD 3 48
    FOLLOWD IN TEARS THEIR FATHER AND THEIR KING • 115 BALDER DEAD 3 60
    BUT THEN THE FATHER OF THE AGES SAID • • • • 118 BALDER DEAD 3 156
    AND THUS THE FATHER OF THE AGES SAID • • • • 120 BALDER DEAD 3 224
    MY FATHER AND HIS PRIDE THE WARRIOR THOR • • 127 BALDER DEAD 3 491
    BEHOLD THE STERN MAILD FATHER STAFF IN HAND • 167 PICT NEWSTEAD 9
    METHINKS THE WOE WHICH MADE THAT FATHER STAND   167 PICT NEWSTEAD 12
    THE CHILDLESS FATHER ALAS • • • • • • 283 HAWORTH CHURCH V
    THOU MY FATHER ART LAID • • • • • • • • 286 RUGBY CHAPEL 13
    BE SAVED MY FATHER ALONE • • • • • • • 290 RUGBY CHAPEL 125
    ZEUS HATH HIS ALTAR WHERE THY FATHER FELL • • 330 MEROPE 15
    AND SECOND FATHER FROM THAT HOUR WHEN FIRST • 331 MEROPE 30
    BECAUSE THOU SLEWST HIS BROTHERS WITH THEIR FATHER 336 MEROPE 191
    WHY WITH THE OFFENDING FATHER DID YE SLAY • • 339 MEROPE 318
    SUCH CHANCE AS KILLD THE FATHER KILLD THE SONS • 340 MEROPE 347
    FRESH FROM THEIR FATHER DRAWS NEAR • • • • 346 MEROPE 498
    A RETURN O FATHER GIVE TO THY BOY • • • • 348 MEROPE 542
    THY KIND-SPEAKING FATHER STANDS • • • • 378 MEROPE 1240
    FOLLOWD THY FATHER FROM THEIR NORTHERN HILLS • 381 MEROPE 1300
    THY FATHER PERISHD IN THIS PEOPLES CAUSE • • 381 MEROPE 1314
    WHEN MY GREAT FATHER FELL THEY HAD REPLIED • 383 MEROPE 1366
    MY FATHER THEN AND HIS ARCADIAN CHIEFS • • 384 MEROPE 1395
    MY FATHER BY YOUR STROKES MY MOTHER SLAIN • 385 MEROPE 1412
    O HONOURD FATHER HIDE THEE IN THY GRAVE • • 386 MEROPE 1430
    HIS FATHER AND HIS ILL-STARRD BRETHREN FALL • 387 MEROPE 1463
    WITH CYPSELUS OUR FATHER WHERE WE SAW • • 388 MEROPE 1515
    SON LOVED OF ZEUS HIS FATHER FOR HE SINND • 398 MEROPE 1814
    SO RULE THAT AS THY FATHER THOU BE LOVED • 404 MEROPE 2008
    SON LOVED OF ZEUS HIS FATHER FOR HE ERRD • 398 MEROPE V1814
    FIRST HYMN THEY THE FATHER • • • • • 443 EMPEDOCLES II 461
    EVEN AS MY FATHER THOU • • • • • • • 449 WESTMIN ABBEY 167
    THERE FROM SIN DELIVERD DWELLS MY FATHER • • 482 THEKLAS ANSWER 15
    FAR FROM MY FATHER AND MOTHER DEAR FOR ALL   HOMER TRANS 61
       THAT I WILL NOT
    TOUCH HIS ROBE AND SAY MY FATHER • • • • • META CLOISTER 27
    SAY MY FATHER DOES THE TIRED • • • • • • META CLOISTER 29

FATHERS
    O BY THY FATHERS HEAD BY THINE OWN SOUL • • 71 SOHRAB RUSTUM 343
    WHAT PRATE IS THIS OF FATHERS AND REVENGE • 78 SOHRAB RUSTUM 577
    THE STRIFE AND HURLD ME ON MY FATHERS SPEAR • 82 SOHRAB RUSTUM 715
    MY TERRIBLE FATHERS TERRIBLE HORSE AND SAID • 83 SOHRAB RUSTUM 744
    AND SNUFFD THE BREEZES OF MY FATHERS HOME • • 83 SOHRAB RUSTUM 749
    BUT LODGED AMONG MY FATHERS FOES AND SEEN • • 83 SOHRAB RUSTUM 759
    AND FIXD THEM FEEBLY ON HIS FATHERS FACE • • 86 SOHRAB RUSTUM 852
    FATHERS WE MUST HAVE WIFE AND CHILD • • • • 92 SICK KING BOKH 149
    FEAST IN VALHALLA IN MY FATHERS HALL • • • • 104 BALDER DEAD 1 322
    AND IN HIS FATHERS HAND PUT SLEIPNERS REIN • 114 BALDER DEAD 3 34
    QUITTING AT HER FATHERS WILL • • • • • 134 TRISTRAM 1 129
    THEN IN THE ETERNAL FATHERS SMILE • • • • 179 FAREWELL 61
    YOUR FATHERS INNERMOST MIND • • • • • 291 RUGBY CHAPEL 165
    OUR FATHERS WATERD WITH THEIR TEARS • • • • 303 GRANDE CHARTR 121
    THEIR FATHERS WATERD WITH THEIR TEARS • • • 303 GRANDE CHARTR V 121
    BEHOLD THY HERITAGE THY FATHERS REALM • • • 330 MEROPE 3
    FELL TO THY FATHERS LOT THE SECOND PRIZE • • 330 MEROPE 8
    SNATCHD FROM THE SLAUGHTER OF THY FATHERS HOUSE • 330 MEROPE 22
    MEANWHILE WITHIN MY FATHERS PALACE I • • • 331 MEROPE 47
    DOUBTLESS THEY BEAR THEM TO MY FATHERS TOMB • 331 MEROPE 55
    BEHIND THE SHELTER OF THY FATHERS TOMB • • 332 MEROPE 68
    THEIR FATHERS REALM THIS ISLE FROM PELOPS NAMED • 336 MEROPE 219
    WERE BAR AND THIS TOO WAS THEIR FATHERS CRIME • 339 MEROPE 326
    HAD IN A FATHERS PLACE HE BASELY MURDERD • • 364 MEROPE 977
    FATHERS SONS GRANDSONS ARE ALL • • • • 379 MEROPE 1254
    THEIR LOYAL PASSION TOWRD MY FATHERS HOUSE • 383 MEROPE 1359
    THY KINSFOLK AND THY FATHERS FRIENDS FOR AID • 384 MEROPE 1389
    OUR FATHERS KINGDOM BECAUSE PURE IS SAFE • • 389 MEROPE 1533
    THY FATHERS MURDERER IN THE PUBLIC PLACE • • 391 MEROPE 1588
    THY FATHERS PASSION WAS THIS PEOPLES EASE • • 404 MEROPE 2000
    ASSUME THE ENSIGNS OF MY FATHERS POWER • • • 405 MEROPE 2020
    AND WENT WHERE ALL HIS FATHERS WENT BEFORE • • 447 WESTMIN ABBEY 116
    YEA ON YOUR FATHERS BONES THE AVENGERS TREAD • 467 ALARIC AT ROME 134
    MOVES ME SO MUCH NOT HECUBAS GRIEF NOR PRIAM   HOMER TRANS 24
       MY FATHERS
    TOUCH THE SAME SURFACE WHICH OUR FATHERS TROD • • EVERLASTING SUB 3
    HAVE THE SAME SURFACE WHICH OUR FATHERS TROD • • EVERLASTING SUB V 3
    HAVE THE SAME SURFACE WHICH OUR FATHERS FELT • • EVERLASTING SUB V 3

FATHERS   (CONTINUED)
        HAVE THE SAME SURFACE WHICH OUR FATHERS TOUCHD   • •   EVERLASTING SUB   V   3
        TOUCH THE SAME SURFACE WHICH OUR FATHERS FELT   • •   EVERLASTING SUB   V   3
        TOUCH THE SAME SURFACE WHICH OUR FATHERS TOUCHD   • •   EVERLASTING SUB   V   3

FATHOMD
        I THINK THOU WILT HAVE FATHOMD LIFE TOO FAR   • •   43 GIPSY CHILD   47

FATIGUE
        AS HE DRIFTS TO FATIGUE DISCONTENT AND DEJECTION   • •   20 MODERN SAPPHO   19
        IS IT THAT A DEEP FATIGUE   • • • • •   •   131 TRISTRAM 1   37
        FREE FROM THE SICK FATIGUE THE LANGUID DOUBT   • •   260 SCHOLAR-GIPSY   164
        TO CHASE FATIGUE AND FEAR   • •   269 THYRSIS   236
        WHEREWITH FATIGUE AND YOUTH HAD BOUND MINE EYES   • •   375 MEROPE   1204

FATIGUED
        HER FEATURES SO FATIGUED HER EYES THOUGH SWEET   • •   151 TRISTRAM 3   70

FAULT
        THE FAULT WAS GRAVE I MIGHT HAVE KNOWN   • • • •   180 ISOLATION MARG   7
        THAT THOU MIGHTST REIGN HE DIED NOT FOR HIS FAULT   339 MEROPE   327
        TO FIND IN THEE A FAULT WHEREON TO FOUND   • • • •   404 MEROPE   2006
        HOW DEEP A FAULT IS THIS • • • • • • • • •   •   417 EMPEDOCLES I 2   158

FAUN
        SOMETIMES A FAUN WITH TORCHES   • • • • • • • •   194 STRAYED REVEL   276
        MARSYAS THAT UNHAPPY FAUN   • • • • • • • • •   433 EMPEDOCLES II   149
        FOR THE FAUN HAD BEEN HIS FRIEND   • • • • • • •   434 EMPEDOCLES II   168
        AH POOR FAUN POOR FAUN AH POOR FAUN • • • • • • •   434 EMPEDOCLES II   190
        AH POOR FAUN POOR FAUN AH POOR FAUN • • • • • • •   434 EMPEDOCLES II   190
        AH POOR FAUN POOR FAUN AH POOR FAUN • • • • • • • •   434 EMPEDOCLES II   190

FAUNS
        SITTING BY ME WHILE HIS FAUNS   • • • • • • • • •   194 STRAYED REVEL   265

FAUSTA
        THESE FAUSTA ASK NOT THIS NOR THOU   • • • • • • •   53 RESIGNATION   38
        BUT FAUSTA I REMEMBER WELL   • • • • • • • • •   54 RESIGNATION   82
        FAUSTA WHICH TEN YEARS SINCE WE TROD • • • • • •   55 RESIGNATION   87
        FAUSTA TIMES PAST WITH TIMES THAT ARE   • • • •   56 RESIGNATION   137
        FAUSTA BETRAYS YOU COLD THE WHILE   • • • • • • •   58 RESIGNATION   200
        IN SOME SENSE FAUSTA OUTLASTS DEATH • • • • • • •   59 RESIGNATION   230
        HIM BLAME NOT FAUSTA RATHER PRAISE   • • • • • •   59 RESIGNATION   238
        NOT FOOLISH FAUSTA IN HIS EYE • • • • • • • •   59 RESIGNATION   256
        YET FAUSTA THE MUTE TURF WE TREAD   • • • • • •   60 RESIGNATION   265

FAVOUR
        TO FIND SUCH FAVOUR IN THINE EYES   • • • • • •   92 SICK KING BOKH   136
        WITH CERTAINTY OF FAVOUR • • • • • • • • • • •   391 MEROPE   1599

FAVOURD
        THE FAVOURD GUEST OF CIRCE BROUGHT BY THE WAVES   • •   189 STRAYED REVEL   110
        OF FORTUNES FAVOURD SONS NOT ME   • • • • • • •   249 WISH   4

FAVOURITE
        BY THE FAVOURITE WATERS OF RUTH   • • • • • •   229 YOUTH OF NATURE   24
        WOULD FIX OUR FAVOURITE ON THE SCENE • • • • • •   451 GEISTS GRAVE   38

FAVOURITES
        OTHER FAVOURITES DWELLING HERE   • • • • • • • •   455 POOR MATTHIAS   87
        OTHER FAVOURITES HE HATH KNOWN   • • • • • • • •   458 POOR MATTHIAS   204

FAWN
        MY DAPPLED FAWN-SKIN   • • • • • • • • • • •   186 STRAYED REVEL   30
        HIS FAWN-SKIN HALF UNTIED   • • • • • • • • •   188 STRAYED REVEL   89

FAY
        THE SOUTHERN WINTER-PARLOUR BY MY FAY   • • • •   135 TRISTRAM 1   164
        FOR HERE HE CAME WITH THE FAY VIVIAN • • • • •   154 TRISTRAM 3   159
        HE WAS ON FOOT AND THAT FALSE FAY HIS FRIEND   • •   154 TRISTRAM 3   161
        THIS TALE OF MERLIN AND THE LOVELY FAY   • • • •   154 TRISTRAM 3   164

FEAR
        AND EASE FROM SHAME AND REST FROM FEAR   • • • •   21 YOUTH AND CALM   2
        BUT AH THOUGH PEACE AND REST FROM FEAR   • • • •   21 YOUTH AND CALM   V   2
        AFTER SHORT COMMERCE WITH ME FEAR MY FROWN • • • •   37 WORLDS TRIUMPHS   8
        FEAR NO UNDOING • • • • • • • • • • • •   40 STAGIRIUS   60
        LET US NOT FRET AND FEAR TO MISS OUR AIM   • • •   40 HUMAN LIFE   10
        FOR FEAR THEY SHOULD DISLODGE THE OERHANGING SNOWS   66 SOHRAB RUSTUM   168
        SO THE PALE PERSIANS HELD THEIR BREATH WITH FEAR   • •   66 SOHRAB RUSTUM   169
        BACK QUICKLY THROUGH THE CAMP IN FEAR AND JOY   • •   69 SOHRAB RUSTUM   261
        FEAR AT HIS WRATH BUT JOY THAT RUSTUM CAME   • • •   69 SOHRAB RUSTUM   262
        THE TWO HOSTS HEARD THAT CRY AND QUAKED FOR FEAR   • •   76 SOHRAB RUSTUM   507
        SO THAT SAD MOTHER SENT HIM WORD FOR FEAR   • • •   79 SOHRAB RUSTUM   610
        FEAR NOT AS THOU HAST SAID SOHRAB MY SON   • • •   84 SOHRAB RUSTUM   796
        FEAR AT HIS WRATH AND JOY THAT RUSTUM CAME   • • •   69 SOHRAB RUSTUM   V 262
        FEAR NOTHING BUT THAT ALL SHALL BE FULFILLD   • •   112 BALDER DEAD 2   253
        HATH COME ON HER A CHILLY FEAR   • • • • • • •   131 TRISTRAM 1   38
        AND WITH A BLOOD LIKE MINE WILL LEAVE I FEAR   • •   140 TRISTRAM 1   306
        FEAR NOT NOW THAT MEN SHOULD TAX THINE HONOUR   • •   142 TRISTRAM 2   11

FEAR
                    (CONTINUED)
        FEAR ME NOT I WILL BE ALWAYS WITH THEE   .   .   .   .   143 TRISTRAM 2   29
        WHICH DOGGD BY FEAR AND FOUGHT BY SHAME   .   .   .   .   147 TRISTRAM 2   132
        O HUNTER AND WITHOUT A FEAR   .   .   .   .   149 TRISTRAM 2   187
        FEAR NOT NOW THAT MEN SHOULD TAX THY HONOUR   .   .   .   142 TRISTRAM 2   V 11
        WHICH KNOWS NO DOUBT WHICH FEELS NO FEAR   .   .   .   .   178 FAREWELL   36
        ON THIS WILD EARTH OF HATE AND FEAR   .   .   .   .   .   180 FAREWELL   86
        TO FEAR ASSAULT OF ENVIOUS GODS   .   .   .   .   .   .   197 FRAG ANTIGONE   81
        THEIR THOUGHTS FOR FEAR THAT IF REVEALD   .   .   .   .   245 BURIED LIFE   17
        FLY HENCE OUR CONTACT FEAR   .   .   .   .   261 SCHOLAR-GIPSY   206
        TO CHASE FATIGUE AND FEAR   .   .   .   .   269 THYRSIS   236
        AND AGAINST FEAR OUR BREAST TO STEEL   .   .   .   .   .   272 MEMORIAL VERSES   65
        MIST AND ILLUSION AND FEAR   .   .   .   .   281 HAWORTH CHURCH   40
        YES THE CROWD MUTTERS THAT REMORSEFUL FEAR   .   .   .   333 MEROPE   97
        IF THIS WAS FEAR OF THEM IT SHAMED THE KING   .   .   .   337 MEROPE   252
        EMBOLDENED BY MY LENIENCE THINK IT FEAR   .   .   .   .   341 MEROPE   373
        UNJUST SUSPICION AND ERRONEOUS FEAR   .   .   .   .   .   342 MEROPE   384
        OF A DREADFUL PRESENCE OF FEAR   .   .   .   .   .   .   346 MEROPE   494
        HIS GRANDSIRE AND HIS UNCLES FEAR THE RISK   .   .   .   350 MEROPE   603
        WITH ARMS THEY DARE NOT AND BY STEALTH THEY FEAR   .   .   351 MEROPE   607
        THE HEART OF YOUTH I KNOW THAT MOST I FEAR   .   .   .   351 MEROPE   609
        BUT WHO CAN SAY WITHOUT A FEAR   .   .   .   .   .   .   353 MEROPE   676
        YE KEPT SILENCE IN FEAR   .   .   .   .   371 MEROPE   1129
        O LOVED MISTRESS IN FEAR   .   .   .   .   371 MEROPE   1130
        I PROMISE BUT I FEAR   .   .   .   .   371 MEROPE   1136
        I FEAR NOT BUT I THINK ON MY DESIGN   .   .   .   .   .   378 MEROPE   1235
        WOMANLY PITY NOR MATERNAL FEAR   .   .   .   .   .   .   389 MEROPE   1526
        O BROTHER THOU HAST CONQUERD YET I FEAR   .   .   .   .   390 MEROPE   1581
        AS OUR JUST CAUSE DESERVES I DO NOT FEAR   .   .   .   391 MEROPE   1595
        THY CRIME THAT WERE ENOUGH TO MAKE ONE FEAR   .   .   396 MEROPE   1767
        HE IS NOW ALWAYS MOODY AND I FEAR HIM   .   .   .   .   408 EMPEDOCLES I 1   74
        TO WATCH MAN DOUBT AND FEAR   .   .   .   .   415 EMPEDOCLES I 2   88
        I THINK MIGHT MAKE US FEAR   .   .   .   .   425 EMPEDOCLES I 2   384
        I SAY FEAR NOT LIFE STILL   .   .   .   .   426 EMPEDOCLES I 2   422
        AND KISS CONJECTURED JOYS OR FEAR CONJECTURED WOES   425 EMPEDOCLES I 2   V 406
        ARE YOU TOO WHAT I FEAR TO BECOME   .   .   .   .   .   437 EMPEDOCLES II   281
        ALLOWD NO FEAR   .   .   .   .   441 EMPEDOCLES II   403
        AND MAJESTY AND SACRED FORM AND FEAR   .   .   .   .   .   445 WESTMIN ABBEY   58
        FEAR NOT BUT THY LIGHT ONCE MORE SHALL BURN   .   .   449 WESTMIN ABBEY   174
        FARE FOR EVER WELL NOR FEAR   .   .   .   .   458 POOR MATTHIAS   207
        LOOKS ON IN FEAR AND WHEN THE SEAL IS SET   .   .   .   465 ALARIC AT ROME   92
        NOR TONGUE OF MAN NOR FEAR NOR SHAME CAN PREACH   .   467 ALARIC AT ROME   141
        LEARNS FREEDOMS LESSON FROM YOUR VOICE OF FEAR   .   471 CROMWELL   2
        OR THAT MYSTERIOUS CRY THAT SMOTE WITH FEAR   .   .   473 CROMWELL   41
        THE SHOUT OF ONSET AND THE SHRIEK OF FEAR   .   .   .   475 CROMWELL   135
        THE GATHERING TEMPEST WITH ITS VOICE OF FEAR   .   .   478 CROMWELL   209
        ALL THESE WERE THINE OH THOUGHT OF FEAR AND THOU   .   479 CROMWELL   233
        AND WIN DELIBERATE REASON TO PUT ON FEAR   .   .   .   RUDE ORATOR   11
        NEITHER HATE HAVE THEY NOR FEAR NOR PRIDE   .   .   .   META CLOISTER   8
        SHARP SENSE OF DEEP SELF-IGNORANCE FEAR OF LOOKS   .   .   LUCRETIUS 2   14

FEARD
        NOR FEARD BUT THY LOVE LIKEWISE GREW   .   .   .   .   .   180 ISOLATION MARG   5
        THE FEARD AND BLACKEND RULER OF THEIR RACE   .   .   .   336 MEROPE   198
        AND WEAKNESS WARND HIM AND HE FEARD DECLINE   .   .   447 WESTMIN ABBEY   123

FEAREST
        DOUBTLESS THOU FEAREST TO MEET BALDERS VOICE   .   .   124 BALDER DEAD 3   392

FEARFUL
        TOO FEARFUL OR TOO FOND TO PLAY ALONE   .   .   .   .   .   8 RELIGIOUS ISOL   5
        FEARFUL AND WE IN OUR MARCH   .   .   .   .   290 RUGBY CHAPEL   129
        FEARFUL AND SAD FOR HER SONS   .   .   .   .   294 HEINES GRAVE   V 73
        SUCH AS ERE NOW HATH SPURRD TO FEARFUL DEEDS   .   .   366 MEROPE   1012

FEARING
        IN HER ROUGH FORM FEARING   .   .   .   .   392 MEROPE   1634

FEARLESS
        FOR QUIET AND A FEARLESS MIND   .   .   .   .   59 RESIGNATION   244
        AND WITH A FEARLESS MIEN SOHRAB REPLIED   .   .   .   .   77 SOHRAB RUSTUM   540

FEARLESSLY
        COULD EVER YET DARE TELL HIM FEARLESSLY   .   .   .   .   40 HUMAN LIFE   3
        OTHERS WILL FRONT IT FEARLESSLY   .   .   .   .   .   .   272 MEMORIAL VERSES   69
        STEMMD BY THE STRENGTH OF MANHOOD FEARLESSLY   .   .   473 CROMWELL   50

FEARS
        NATURE FORGIVES NO DEBT AND FEARS NO GRAVE .   .   .   .   5 HARMONY NATURE   10
        MAZED WITH DOUBTS AND SICK WITH FEARS   .   .   .   .   44 QUESTION   13
        SEES THEE NOR STOPS HIS MEAL NOR FEARS AT ALL   .   .   258 SCHOLAR-GIPSY   117
        OF DOUBTS DISPUTES DISTRACTIONS FEARS   .   .   .   .   .   271 MEMORIAL VERSES   44
        OF FESTERING THOUGHTS AND PERSONAL FEARS   .   .   .   .   271 MEMORIAL VERSES   V
        INTO A JEALOUS TYRANT SCOURGED WITH FEARS   .   .   .   335 MEROPE   159
        MOTHER THY FEARS ARE IDLE FOR I COME   .   .   .   .   .   379 MEROPE   1256
        BE NOT THEN FEARS BLIND SLAVE   .   .   .   .   415 EMPEDOCLES I 2   102
        AND THOU HAST DONE WITH FEARS   .   .   .   .   417 EMPEDOCLES I 2   143
        HUMAN LONGINGS HUMAN FEARS   .   .   .   .   457 POOR MATTHIAS   165
        WHAT ONCE HAD HUMAN PASSIONS HOPES AND FEARS   .   .   464 ALARIC AT ROME   52
        EVEN OF THAT ARDENT SPIRIT HOPES AND FEARS .   .   .   469 ALARIC AT ROME   178

FEARS   (CONTINUED)
          THE FEARS AND HOPES AND PASSIONS OF MANKIND   • •   479 CROMWELL   232

FEARST
          FEARST THOU NOW   • • • • • • • • • ▪ • • •   378 MEROPE   1234
          BECAUSE THE GODS THOU FEARST   • • ▪ • • • • • •   426 EMPEDOCLES I 2   419

FEAST
          HERE CAME THE KING HOLDING HIGH FEAST AT MORN   • •   11 MYCERINUS   92
          REVEALING ALL THE TUMULT OF THE FEAST   • • • •   11 MYCERINUS   96
          IT MAY BE ON THAT JOYLESS FEAST HIS EYE   • • • •   11 MYCERINUS   107
          FEAST AND DANCE HER YOUTH BEGUILED   • • • • • •   14 CHURCH BROU 1   58
          SO WHEN THE FEAST GREW LOUD   • • • • • •   47 WORLD QUIETIST   25
          AND ON A FEAST-TIDE IN AFRASIABS HALL   • • • •   71 SOHRAB RUSTUM   355
          AND ON A FEAST DAY IN AFRASIABS HALL   • • • • •   71 SOHRAB RUSTUM   V 355
          WHICH GODS AND HEROES LEAD IN FEAST AND FRAY   • •   98 BALDER DEAD 1   123
          THEN FROM THEIR LOATHED FEAST THE GODS AROSE   • •   101 BALDER DEAD 1   203
          FEAST IN VALHALLA IN MY FATHERS HALL   • • • • •   104 BALDER DEAD 1   322
          TO GLAD THE GODS AND FEAST IN ODINS HALL   • • •   105 BALDER DEAD 2   28
          TO FEAST THEIR EYES WITH LOOKING ON THE FRAY   •   105 BALDER DEAD 2   31
          AFTER THE FEAST IS DONE IN ODINS HALL   • • •   117 BALDER DEAD 3   136
          AT TABLE AND THE FUNERAL-FEAST BEGAN   • • • • •   119 BALDER DEAD 3   209
          THEN FROM THEIR LOATHED FEAST THE GODS AROSE   • •   119 BALDER DEAD 3   214
          WHEN THE FEAST WAS GAY AND THE LAUGHTER LOUD   •   146 TRISTRAM 2   114
          WHEN THE FEAST WAS LOUD AND THE LAUGHTER SHRILL   •   146 TRISTRAM 2   V 114
          HE MADE A FEAST DRANK FIERCE AND FAST   • • •   316 OBERMANN MORE   101
          AND THE FEAST PAST ITS PRIME SO WE SLIPPD OUT   •   407 EMPEDOCLES I 1   37

FEASTING
          BUT THE BLIND HODER LEFT THE FEASTING GODS   • • • •   97 BALDER DEAD 1   72

FEASTS
          MAR THE MUSIC OF YOUR FEASTS IN VAIN   • • • • •   32 NEW SIRENS   170
          BLAME THE MUSIC OF YOUR FEASTS IN VAIN   • • • •   32 NEW SIRENS   V 170
          YOUR MATE THOUGH LOATHED AND FEASTS IN ODINS HALL   111 BALDER DEAD 2   218
          AND WHEN HE COMES AMONG HIS FRIENDS AT FEASTS   • •   408 EMPEDOCLES I 1   70

FEAT
          BUT THAT WE KNOW HOW EVERY PERILOUS FEAT   • • • •   402 MEROPE   1948

FEATHERD
          UNDER THE FEATHERD HATS OF THE SWEET PAIR   • • • •   150 TRISTRAM 3   33
          DROOPS ALL HIS SHEENY BROWN DEEP-FEATHERD NECK   • •   431 EMPEDOCLES II   76
          STILL BENEATH THEIR FEATHERD BREAST   • • • • • •   455 POOR MATTHIAS   101

FEATHERS
          A HEAP OF FLUTTERING FEATHERS NEVER MORE   • • • •   78 SOHRAB RUSTUM   569
          CAUGHT THEM AS WIND TAKES FEATHERS WHIRLD THEM ROUND   358 MEROPE   824
          TILL THE SAND THY FEATHERS SMIRCH   • • • • • •   456 POOR MATTHIAS   129

FEATHERY
          POOR FUGITIVE THE FEATHERY CHANGE   • • • • • •   201 PHILOMELA   24
          ON SOME TALL SCAR FRINGED WITH DARK FEATHERY PINES   357 MEROPE   803

FEATLY
          SO FEATLY STREWN WITH DRIFTED SAND   • • • • • •   480 HAYSWATER BOAT   22

FEATS
          MANS NOISY FEATS ACCOMPLISHD IN REPOSE   • • • •   1 QUIET WORK   V   7
          THEIR VAUNTS THEIR FEATS LET A SARDONIC SMILE   • •   298 HEINES GRAVE   208

FEATURE ▪
          IN GARB IN FORM IN FEATURE AS HE WAS   • • • • •   103 BALDER DEAD 1   283
          IF THE LOVED▪FORM AND THE DEEP-CHERISHD FEATURE   • •   206 SEPARATION   7

FEATURED
          THIS SPARE DARK-FEATURED   • • • • • • • • •   189 STRAYED REVEL   102

FEATURES
          AH WE OWN DIVINER FEATURES   • • • • • • • • •   28 NEW SIRENS   63
          CAN MEN WORSHIP THE WAN FEATURES   • • • • • •   34 NEW SIRENS   247
          HER FEATURES SO FATIGUED HER EYES THOUGH SWEET   • •   151 TRISTRAM 3   70
          THOSE PENSIVE FEATURES WELL I KNEW   • • • • •   314 OBERMANN MORE   61
          BUT OH HOW CHANGD THOSE DEATHLIKE FEATURES WORE   • •   477 CROMWELL   181
          THAT FORM WAS HIS THOSE FEATURES WERE HIS OWN   • •   478 CROMWELL   204

FED
          AND THE HUNGRY THOUGHT THAT MUST BE FED   • • • •   30 NEW SIRENS   130
          NOR WEARINESS THE FULL-FED SOULS ANNOY   • • • •   42 GIPSY CHILD   11
          WHENCE EQUALLY THE SEAS OF LIFE AND DEATH ARE FED   60 RESIGNATION   260
          AND SLEW THE DOGS WHO AT HIS TABLE FED   • • • •   118 BALDER DEAD 3   170
          AND SLEW THE DOGS WHICH AT HIS TABLE FED   • • • •   118 BALDER DEAD 3   V 170
          WELL-FED WELL-CLOTHED WELL-FRIENDED I   • • • •   158 SAINT BRANDAN   57
          LONG FED ON BOUNDLESS HOPES O RACE OF MAN   • • • •   170 BETTER PART   1
          THE FLOWERS UPCLOSE THE BIRDS ARE FED   • • • •   249 KENSINGTON GARD   34
          THE FLOWERS CLOSE THE BIRDS ARE FED   • • • • •   249 KENSINGTON GARD   V 34
          AND HOW THE DYING SPARK OF HOPE WAS FED   • • • •   260 SCHOLAR-GIPSY   188
          WILLINGLY FED OR NO THEIR MOST VAIN HOPES   • • • •   334 MEROPE   148
          NO MORE AN EXILE FED ON EMPTY HOPES   • • • • •   335 MEROPE   169
          WHOSE MIND WAS FED ON OTHER FOOD WAS TRAIND   • •   436 EMPEDOCLES II   264

```
FED          ( CONTINUED )
       FROM WHOSE PATHETIC SOUL-FED SPRINGS  .  .  .  .  .  .   450 GEISTS GRAVE        14
       SOUL-FED EYES WITH SUFFERING WORN     .  .  .  .  .  .   454 POOR MATTHIAS       63

FEEBLE
       THE FEEBLE SONS OF PLEASURE SET THEIR HAND  .  .  .  .     5 DUKE WELLINGTON      7
       WHAT MY FRIENDS THESE FEEBLE LINES     .  .  .  .  .  .    24 MEMORY-PICTURE      49
       AND HE WILL SEE THE FEEBLE SHADOWY TRIBES   .  .  .  .   100 BALDER DEAD 1      174
       WHERE IDLY FLIT ABOUT THE FEEBLE SHADES     .  .  .  .   110 BALDER DEAD 2      182
       AND TALKEST WITH THE FEEBLE TRIBES OF GHOSTS   .  .  .   115 BALDER DEAD 3       76
       THEIR INEFFECTUAL FEUDS AND FEEBLE HATES   .  .  .  .    126 BALDER DEAD 3      466
       IF MEN ESTEEMD THEE FEEBLE GAVE THEE POWER  .  .  .  .   269 THYRSIS            214
       A FEEBLE WAVERING LINE   .  .  .  .  .  .  .  .  .  .    291 RUGBY CHAPEL       173
       SO FEEBLE IS HIS MARCH SO SLOW  .  .  .  .  .  .  .  .   352 MEROPE             627
       IF IN THIS FEEBLE BOSOM SUCH A FIRE   .  .  .  .  .  .   387 MEROPE            1470
       A HOLIER INCENSE THAN THIS FEEBLE LAY  .  .  .  .  .  .   471 ALARIC AT ROME     226
       CAME FAINT AND FEEBLE IN THE EMBRACE OF DEATH  .  .  .   478 CROMWELL           208
       FEEBLE HE RESTS IF FEEBLE HE WAS BORN  .  .  .  .  .        LUCRETIUS 3          7
       FEEBLE HE RESTS IF FEEBLE HE WAS BORN  .  .  .  .  .        LUCRETIUS 3          7

FEEBLER
       WE DO NOT AS SOME FEEBLER HATERS DO   .  .  .  .  .  .   111 BALDER DEAD 2      228
       TO A MUCH FEEBLER WIGHT THE HEROIC MAN  .  .  .  .  .    198 FRAG ANTIGONE       96

FEEBLY
       AND FIXD THEM FEEBLY ON HIS FATHERS FACE  .  .  .  .      86 SOHRAB RUSTUM      852
       BUT FEEBLY AS A VOICE FAR OFF HE SAID  .  .  .  .  .     112 BALDER DEAD 2      263
       WHERE FEEBLY COMES THE MOURNFUL ROAR  .  .  .  .  .      140 TRISTRAM 1         330
       AND FEEL BUT HALF AND FEEBLY WHAT WE FEEL  .  .  .  .    213 GROWING OLD         27
       AND FEEBLY RAKES AMONG THE STONES  .  .  .  .  .  .  .   213 PROGRESS POESY      10

FEED
       URGED AND TO FEED WHOSE MOVEMENT SPINNING SAND  .  .      5 DUKE WELLINGTON      6
       WHICH ON THE SWEETS THAT WOO IT DARES NOT FEED  .  .      9 MYCERINUS           26
       KOHIK AND WHERE THE KALMUKS FEED THEIR SHEEP  .  .       83 SOHRAB RUSTUM      764
       ON FREAS HEARTH FEED HIGH THE SACRED FIRE  .  .  .       97 BALDER DEAD 1       90
       FEED IN THE OOZE OF THEIR PASTURE-GROUND  .  .  .  .     162 FORSAKEN MERM       40
       NOT TO FEED PRIESTLY PRIDE ARE THERE  .  .  .  .  .      300 GRANDE CHARTR       50
       IS CHARGED AGAINST THIS STRIPLING AGENTS FEED  .  .     364 MEROPE             980
       NOW THAT I FEED MINE EYES ON THAT YOUNG FACE  .  .  .    387 MEROPE            1459
       NEVER AGAIN IN LIFE NEXT AGENTS FEED  .  .  .  .  .  .    365 MEROPE        V
       AND WHERE THE HILL-GOATS COME TO FEED  .  .  .  .  .     414 EMPEDOCLES I 2      66

FEEDEST
       BUT SO MANY WISHES FEEDEST     .  .  .  .  .  .  .  .     49 SECOND BEST          7
       BUT SO MANY PASSIONS FEEDEST   .  .  .  .  .  .  .  .  .     SECOND BEST     V    7
       BUT SUCH FURIOUS PASSIONS FEEDEST   .  .  .  .  .  .  .     SECOND BEST     V    7

FEEDING
       LONG WE WANDERD WITH YOU FEEDING  .  .  .  .  .  .  .     34 NEW SIRENS         235
       THE SPRINGING PASTURES AND THE FEEDING KINE  .  .  .    258 SCHOLAR-GIPSY      108

FEEDS
       THE WILD BOAR HARBOURS CLOSE AND FEEDS  .  .  .  .  .    148 TRISTRAM 2      V

FEEL
       THEN AM I YOURS AND WHAT YOU FEEL I SHARE  .  .  .  .      7 REP FRIEND          14
       ONLY WHAT WE FEEL WE KNOW  .  .  .  .  .  .  .  .  .      29 NEW SIRENS          84
       AND I FEEL THE COLD NIGHT-AIR  .  .  .  .  .  .  .  .     32 NEW SIRENS         190
       THEY FEEL NOT THOUGH THEY MOVE AND SEE  .  .  .  .  .     58 RESIGNATION        205
       WHOM I MAY MEET AND STRIKE AND FEEL NO PANG  .  .  .     74 SOHRAB RUSTUM      444
       MY FATHER LET ME FEEL THAT I HAVE FOUND  .  .  .  .  .    82 SOHRAB RUSTUM      717
       TO FEEL THE PRESENCE OF A BROTHER GOD  .  .  .  .  .     125 BALDER DEAD 3      418
       AS THEY FEEL THE FATAL BANDS  .  .  .  .  .  .  .  .     135 TRISTRAM 1         149
       CHIDE NOT WITH THE PAST BUT FEEL THE PRESENT  .  .  .    142 TRISTRAM 2           7
       I AM HAPPY YET I FEEL THERES SOMETHING  .  .  .  .  .    145 TRISTRAM 2          73
       HUSH TIS VAIN I FEEL MY END APPROACHING  .  .  .  .     145 TRISTRAM 2          81
       WHICH LEAVES THE FIERCE NECESSITY TO FEEL  .  .  .  .    153 TRISTRAM 3         123
       THEY WILL FOR THOU I FEEL NOT LESS  .  .  .  .  .  .     179 FAREWELL            43
       HOW SWEET TO FEEL ON THE BOON AIR  .  .  .  .  .  .      180 FAREWELL            81
       TO FEEL THAT NOTHING CAN IMPAIR  .  .  .  .  .  .  .     180 FAREWELL            83
       THEY WILL FOR THOU I FEEL NO LESS  .  .  .  .  .  .      179 FAREWELL     V      43
       THE ISLANDS FEEL THE ENCLASPING FLOW  .  .  .  .  .      182 TO MARG CONT         5
       FOR SURELY ONCE THEY FEEL WE WERE  .  .  .  .  .  .      182 TO MARG CONT        15
       BE LOST AND I NOT FEEL TWAS SO  .  .  .  .  .  .  .      184 TERRACE BERNE       30
       I FEEL IT STILL NOW YOUTH IS OER  .  .  .  .  .  .  .    185 TERRACE BERNE       50
       ON PELION THEN THEY FEEL  .  .  .  .  .  .  .  .  .      192 STRAYED REVEL      224
       THEY FEEL THE BITING SPEARS  .  .  .  .  .  .  .  .      192 STRAYED REVEL      227
       DRIVE CRASHING THROUGH THEIR BONES THEY FEEL  .  .      192 STRAYED REVEL      229
       LET HIM LIVE LET HIM FEEL I HAVE LIVED  .  .  .  .  .    200 EARLY DEATH         17
       THY FLIGHT AND FEEL COME OVER THEE  .  .  .  .  .  .     201 PHILOMELA           23
       AH QUIET ALL THINGS FEEL THY BALM  .  .  .  .  .  .      208 ON THE RHINE        21
       IS IT TO FEEL OUR STRENGTH  .  .  .  .  .  .  .  .  .     212 GROWING OLD          6
       IS IT TO FEEL EACH LIMB  .  .  .  .  .  .  .  .  .  .     212 GROWING OLD          8
       AND WEEP AND FEEL THE FULNESS OF THE PAST  .  .  .  .    212 GROWING OLD         19
       AND NOT ONCE FEEL THAT WE WERE EVER YOUNG  .  .  .  .    212 GROWING OLD         22
       AND FEEL BUT HALF AND FEEBLY WHAT WE FEEL  .  .  .  .    213 GROWING OLD         27
       AND FEEL BUT HALF AND FEEBLY WHAT WE FEEL  .  .  .  .    213 GROWING OLD         27
       THEY FEEL RUNS OER IN EVERY LINE  .  .  .  .  .  .  .    227 EPILOG LAOCOON     198
       WHAT POETS FEEL NOT WHEN THEY MAKE  .  .  .  .  .  .     228 CAUTION POETS        1
```

FEEL   (CONTINUED)

```
        CAN I FEEL THAT THEIR POET IS GONE          .  .  .  .  .  .      229 YOUTH OF NATURE      27
        O CHARM O ROMANCE THAT WE FEEL  .  .  .  .  .  .  .  .  .  .      230 YOUTH OF NATURE      64
        LIVES IN OUR HEARTS WHICH CAN FEEL    .  .  .  .  .  .  .         233 YOUTH OF MAN         37
        ONLY THE LIVING CAN FEEL YOU    .  .  .  .  .  .  .  .  .         234 YOUTH OF MAN         59
        WELL I KNOW WHAT THEY FEEL     .  .  .  .  .  .  .  .  .  .       235 YOUTH OF MAN         88
        THE PAST RETURNS THEY FEEL     .  .  .  .  .  .  .  .  .  .       235 YOUTH OF MAN         93
        WELL I KNOW WHAT THEY FEEL     .  .  .  .  .  .  .  .  .  .       235 YOUTH OF MAN         96
        AND THEY FEEL HOW NATURE WAS FAIR   .  .  .  .  .  .  .           235 YOUTH OF MAN        104
        BUT THAT YE THINK CLEAR FEEL DEEP BEAR FRUIT WELL                238 PROGRESS            47
        BUT THAT YOU TOO FEEL DEEPLY BEAR FRUIT WELL      .  .  .        238 PROGRESS          V 47
        BUT THAT YOU THINK CLEAR FEEL DEEP BEAR FRUIT WELL   .           238 PROGRESS          V 47
        FEEL MY SOUL BECOMING VAST LIKE YOU    .  .  .  .  .  .          240 SELF-DEPENDENCE      12
        I FEEL A NAMELESS SADNESS OER ME ROLL    .  .  .  .  .  .        245 BURIED LIFE           3
        TO ONE ANOTHER WHAT INDEED THEY FEEL   .  .  .  .  .  .          245 BURIED LIFE          15
        TO FEEL AMID THE CITYS JAR    .  .  .  .  .  .  .  .  .  .        249 KENSINGTON GARD      38
        THE POWER TO FEEL WITH OTHERS GIVE   .  .  .  .  .  .  .         249 KENSINGTON GARD      42
        TO FEEL THE UNIVERSE MY HOME    .  .  .  .  .  .  .  .  .         251 WISH                 43
        I FEEL HER SLOWLY CHILLING BREATH INVADE   .  .  .  .  .         266 THYRSIS             134
        I FEEL HER FINGER LIGHT   .  .  .  .  .  .  .  .  .  .  .         266 THYRSIS             136
        AH MAY YE FEEL HIS VOICE AS WE  .  .  .  .  .  .  .  .  .         271 MEMORIAL VERSES      41
        BUT WHO AH WHO WILL MAKE US FEEL    .  .  .  .  .  .  .  .        272 MEMORIAL VERSES      67
        I FEEL THEE NEAR ONCE MORE    .  .  .  .  .  .  .  .  .           306 OBERMANN             12
        I TURN THY LEAVES I FEEL THEIR BREATH    .  .  .  .  .  .        306 OBERMANN             13
        TO THEE WE FEEL THY SPELL    .  .  .  .  .  .  .  .  .  .         309 OBERMANN             82
        AGAIN I FEEL THE WORDS INSPIRE   .  .  .  .  .  .  .  .  .        314 OBERMANN MORE        49
        FOR WOES THEY WHOLLY FEEL    .  .  .  .  .  .  .  .  .  .         320 OBERMANN MORE       236
        AGAIN I FEEL ITS WORDS INSPIRE   .  .  .  .  .  .  .  .  .        314 OBERMANN MORE     V 49
        THE CARES WHICH MIGHT IN ME WITH TIME I FEEL  .  .  .            335 MEROPE              161
        THEY FEEL THE COOL WET TURF UNDER THEIR FEET   .  .  .           406 EMPEDOCLES I 1        2
        AND WE FEEL DAY AND NIGHT    .  .  .  .  .  .  .  .  .  .         416 EMPEDOCLES I 2      127
        WE HAD THE POWER TO FEEL THE PRESSURE EASED    .  .  .  .        436 EMPEDOCLES II       245
        AND NEVER LET US CLASP AND FEEL THE ALL   .  .  .  .  .          439 EMPEDOCLES II       353
        AND WE SHALL FEEL THE AGONY OF THIRST   .  .  .  .  .            439 EMPEDOCLES II       356
        AND WE SHALL FEEL OUR POWERS OF EFFORT FLAG    .  .  .           440 EMPEDOCLES II       387
        I FEEL IT IN THIS HOUR THE NUMBING CLOUD   .  .  .  .            441 EMPEDOCLES II       407
        MOUNTS OFF MY SOUL I FEEL IT I BREATHE FREE    .  .             441 EMPEDOCLES II       408
        SYMPATHY COULD FEEL AND SHOW    .  .  .  .  .  .  .  .           455 POOR MATTHIAS        93
        WHAT YOU FEEL ESCAPES OUR KEN    .  .  .  .  .  .  .  .          457 POOR MATTHIAS       161
        TO FLAG AND FEEL HIS NARROWING SPAN   .  .  .  .  .  .           459 KAISER DEAD          38
        THAT WHILE WE FEEL THE WORLD IS DULL AND LOW   .  .  .           470 ALARIC AT ROME      215
        OF WHAT WE SAY WE FEEL BELOW THE STREAM   .  .  .  .            483 BELOW SURFACE         2
        AS LIGHT OF WHAT WE THINK WE FEEL THERE FLOWS   .  .             483 BELOW SURFACE         3
        THE CENTRAL STREAM OF WHAT WE FEEL INDEED  .  .  .  .            483 BELOW SURFACE         5

FEELEST
        THOU FEELEST THY SOULS FRAME    .  .  .  .  .  .  .  .  .         416 EMPEDOCLES I 2      114

FEELING
        FOR FEELING NERVES AND LIVING BREATH  .  .  .  .  .               22 YOUTH AND CALM       18
        AH AND HE WHO PLACED OUR MASTER-FEELING    .  .  .  .            210 SELF-DECEPTION       23
        FAILD TO PLACE THAT MASTER-FEELING CLEAR   .  .  .  .            210 SELF-DECEPTION       24
        FAILD TO PLACE OUR MASTER-FEELING CLEAR    .  .  .  .            210 SELF-DECEPTION     V 24
        SOME SOURCE OF FEELING HE MUST CHOOSE   .  .  .  .  .            223 EPILOG LAOCOON       83
        THE FEELING OF THE MOMENT KNOW  .  .  .  .  .  .  .  .           225 EPILOG LAOCOON      132
        THE FEELING NOT I GRANT EXPLORE  .  .  .  .  .  .  .  .          225 EPILOG LAOCOON      135
        AND DEEP AS WORDS CAN FOLLOW FEELING   .  .  .  .  .  .          225 EPILOG LAOCOON      138
        SOME PULSE OF FEELING HE MUST CHOOSE  .  .  .  .  .  .           223 EPILOG LAOCOON    V 83
        AND A LOST PULSE OF FEELING STIRS AGAIN    .  .  .  .            247 BURIED LIFE          85
        THUS FEELING GAZING MIGHT I GROW    .  .  .  .  .  .  .          251 WISH                 49
        THUS FEELING GAZING LET ME GROW  .  .  .  .  .  .  .  .          251 WISH              V 49
        OF FEELING AS TRANQUIL AS SURE   .  .  .  .  .  .  .  .          252 FUTURE               40
        DRINK OF THE FEELING OF QUIET AGAIN   .  .  .  .  .  .           253 FUTURE               68
        AND WHAT BUT NOBLE FEELING WARM    .  .  .  .  .  .  .           279 SOUTHERN NIGHT      130
        THY HEAD IS CLEAR THY FEELING CHILL   .  .  .  .  .  .           309 OBERMANN             87
        OF PERSONAL FEELING TO THE PUBLIC WEAL   .  .  .  .  .           394 MEROPE             1712
        FULNESS OF LIFE AND POWER OF FEELING YE   .  .  .  .            436 EMPEDOCLES II       258
        THOUGH EVERY HOLIEST FEELING EVERY TIE   .  .  .  .  .           467 ALARIC AT ROME      145

FEELINGS
        SELF-SWAYD OUR FEELINGS EBB AND SWELL    .  .  .  .  .           180 ISOLATION MARG       11
        OF WISER THOUGHTS AND FEELINGS BLOT   .  .  .  .  .  .           183 ABSENCE               7
        THE NAMELESS FEELINGS THAT COURSE THROUGH OUR BREAST            246 BURIED LIFE          62
        HOW MANY PRECIOUS FEELINGS OF MANS HEART   .  .  .  .            335 MEROPE              178
        FEELINGS AND MOTIVES THERE    .  .  .  .  .  .  .  .  .          352 MEROPE              635
        WISHES THERE AND FEELINGS STRONG    .  .  .  .  .  .  .          455 POOR MATTHIAS       103

FEELS
        DEEPER THE POET FEELS BUT HE    .  .  .  .  .  .  .  .            58 RESIGNATION         206
        DEEPLY THE POET FEELS BUT HE    .  .  .  .  .  .  .  .            58 RESIGNATION       V 206
        FEELS THE ABHORRD APPROACHES OF OLD AGE   .  .  .  .             63 SOHRAB RUSTUM        84
        IS NOT MORE LIGHTEND WHICH HE FEELS   .  .  .  .  .              94 SICK KING BOKH      205
        WHICH KNOWS NO DOUBT WHICH FEELS NO FEAR   .  .  .              178 FAREWELL             36
        THE WORLD BUT FEELS THE PRESENTS SPELL   .  .  .  .             221 BACCHANALIA 2        65
        THE POET FEELS THE PAST AS WELL    .  .  .  .  .  .  .           221 BACCHANALIA 2        66
        NOR EVER FEELS THE FIERY GLOW   .  .  .  .  .  .  .  .           243 SUMMER NIGHT         29
        WHICH ONE WHO FEELS DEATHS WINNOWING WINGS   .  .  .            250 WISH                 27
        AND YET THE VILLAGE-CHURL FEELS THE TRUTH MORE                  426 EMPEDOCLES I 2      411
               THAN YOU
        OH YES IF FANCY FEELS BEYOND TO DAY   .  .  .  .  .  .           467 ALARIC AT ROME      127
        THERE HE FEELS IT WAS NO DREAM DECEIVING   .  .  .  .           483 THEKLAS ANSWER       17
```

FEET
OF YOUTH SELF-GOVERND AT THE FEET OF LAW . . . . . 9 MYCERINUS 10
THEIR PLEASURE TO THEIR FEET AND REAP THEIR PRAISE 11 MYCERINUS 77
MIGHT FADE IN SLUMBER AND THE FEET OF JOY . . . . 11 MYCERINUS 90
WHICH CHEQUER AT YOUR FEET THE ILLUMINED FLINTS . . 18 CHURCH BROU 3 29
THAT CHEQUER AT YOUR FEET THE ILLUMINED FLINTS . . 18 CHURCH BROU 3 V 29
GLANCING FEET AND EAGER EYES . . . . 32 NEW SIRENS 176
OF IMMORTAL FEET IS GONE . . . . 34 NEW SIRENS 252
THY BROTHER-WORLD STIRS AT THY FEET UNKNOWN . . 46 IN UTRUMQUE PAR 38
THY NATIVE WORLD STIRS AT THY FEET UNKNOWN . . . . 46 IN UTRUMQUE PAR V 36
HE PASSD AND TIED HIS SANDALS ON HIS FEET . . . . 64 SOHRAB RUSTUM 97
HE SPOKE AND SOHRAB ANSWERD ON HIS FEET . . . . 72 SOHRAB RUSTUM 379
GIRL NIMBLE WITH THY FEET NOT WITH THY HANDS . . 74 SOHRAB RUSTUM 457
UNDER THEIR FEET AND MOANING SWEPT THE PLAIN . . 75 SOHRAB RUSTUM 484
SAW RUSTUM STANDING SAFE UPON HIS FEET . . . . . 77 SOHRAB RUSTUM 525
RUKSH NOW THOU GRIEVEST BUT O RUKSH THY FEET . . 83 SOHRAB RUSTUM 738
AND FELL AT THE KINGS FEET AND CRIED . . . . 88 SICK KING BOKH 35
AND AT HIS HEAD AND FEET SHE STATIOND SCALDS . . 102 BALDER DEAD 1 271
O HERMOD RARELY DO THE FEET OF GODS . . . . . 108 BALDER DEAD 2 119
AND FELL BEFORE HER FEET AND CLASPD HER KNEES . . 110 BALDER DEAD 2 187
TO CHEW THE STRAW HER LITTER AT HER FEET . . . 123 BALDER DEAD 3 343
FROM THE BRIGHT OCEAN AT OUR FEET AN EARTH . . . 128 BALDER DEAD 3 528
OVER THE SICK MANS FEET IS SPREAD . . . . . 131 TRISTRAM 1 15
WERE FEET LIKE THOSE MADE FOR SO WILD A WAY . . 135 TRISTRAM 1 163
WHO LIES GUARDING HER FEET ALONG THE GROUND . . 152 TRISTRAM 3 89
AND THERE BELOW THE NECKANS FEET . . . . . 159 NECKAN 7
A GIRL THEIR CLOTHES WERE RAGS THEIR FEET WERE BARE 169 WEST LONDON 4
MY HORSES FEET BESIDE THE LAKE . . . . . . 177 FAREWELL 1
WHERE FEET LIKE THINE TOO LIGHTLY COME . . . 184 TERRACE BERNE 20
THEIR FEET FROM ITS ALLURING WAVE . . . . . 226 EPILOG LAOCOON 166
WITH SAFE UNWANDERING FEET EXPLORE . . . . . 226 EPILOG LAOCOON 190
WITH ACHING HANDS AND BLEEDING FEET . . . . . 241 MORALITY 7
HOW LONELY RINGS THE ECHO OF MY FEET . . . . . 242 SUMMER NIGHT 2
HERE AT MY FEET WHAT WONDERS PASS . . . . . 248 KENSINGTON GARD 13
HIS FEET TO SEE THE LURID FLOW . . . . . . 271 MEMORIAL VERSES 31
AT MY FEET FREE . . . . 275 SOUTHERN NIGHT 4
STONES MIGHT HAVE WOUNDED THY FEET . . . . . 290 RUGBY CHAPEL 135
BEFORE THY FEET THIS RECENT CITY SPREADS . . . 330 MEROPE 9
WE SPRANG UPON OUR FEET WE SNATCHD OUR SPEARS . . 357 MEROPE 789
THY BROTHERS PLAY AT MY FEET . . . . 378 MEROPE 1238
THIS POLITIC SOVEREIGN LYING AT OUR FEET . . . 403 MEROPE 1965
THEY FEEL THE COOL WET TURF UNDER THEIR FEET . . 406 EMPEDOCLES I 1 2
NESTLING NEARER TO JOVES FEET . . . . . . 431 EMPEDOCLES II 77
AND HER FLUSHD FEET GLOW ON THE MARBLE FLOOR . . 431 EMPEDOCLES II 88
KAIS BRACELET TAIL KAIS BUSY FEET . . . . . . 459 KAISER DEAD 7
UNHALLOWED FEET ARE TRAMPLING ON THIS HAUNTED GROUND 467 ALARIC AT ROME 144
AND THERE BENEATH HIS FEET HIS CONQUEST LAY . . 468 ALARIC AT ROME 158
AROUND WHOSE FEET THE EXULTING WAVES HAVE SUNG . 472 CROMWELL 13
WITH FEET THAT SPURND THE GROUND LO MILTON THERE . . 477 CROMWELL 175
IN THE BLOODY DUST BENEATH THE FEET OF THEIR FOEMEN HOMER TRANS 26
THE DROPPING PATTER OF A CHILDS SMALL FEET . . . FRAGMENT 7 1

FEIGN
BENEATH THE CALM THEY FEIGN . . . . 307 OBERMANN 22
AND CANST TEACH SIMPLE ONES TO PLOT AND FEIGN . . 367 MEROPE 1059
AND FEIGN KIND GODS WHO PERFECT WHAT MAN VAINLY TRIES 422 EMPEDOCLES I 2 316
THAT WE MUST FEIGN A BLISS . . . . 425 EMPEDOCLES I 2 402

FEIGND
WITH A MASTERS ACCENT HER FEIGND . . . . . 280 HAWORTH CHURCH 11
THOU HADST NO CAUSE AS FEIGND IN HIS MISRULE . . 338 MEROPE 283
TAKE THIS FOR TRUE THE OTHER TALE FOR FEIGND . . 364 MEROPE 984

FEIGNING
FROM MIRTH THAT IS BUT FEIGNING . . . . . . 39 STAGIRIUS 34

FEIGNINGS
CUTS SHORT THE FEIGNINGS OF FANTASTIC GRIEF . . FRAGMENT 1 6

FEINTS
REMEMBER ALL THY VALOUR TRY THY FEINTS . . . . 75 SOHRAB RUSTUM 466

FELL
FELL THIS DREAD VOICE FROM LIPS THAT CANNOT LIE . . 8 MYCERINUS 5
FELL THIS LATE VOICE FROM LIPS THAT CANNOT LIE . . 8 MYCERINUS V 5
FELL LIKE OSSA ON THE CLIMBING SOUL . . . . . 28 NEW SIRENS 72
AND THAT SOUL-SEARCHING VISION FELL ON ME . . . 42 GIPSY CHILD 16
THAT AS THE BALMY DARKNESS FELL . . . . . . 54 RESIGNATION 83
AND RUSTUM FOLLOWD HIS OWN BLOW AND FELL . . . 73 SOHRAB RUSTUM 420
AND THEN THE GLOOM DISPERSED AND THE WIND FELL . . 76 SOHRAB RUSTUM 522
AND FOLLOWD HER TO FIND HER WHERE SHE FELL . . . 78 SOHRAB RUSTUM 560
AND KISSD HIM AND AWE FELL ON BOTH THE HOSTS . . 82 SOHRAB RUSTUM 729
AND FELL AT THE KINGS FEET AND CRIED . . . . 88 SICK KING BOKH 35
WHILE TWILIGHT FELL AND SACRED NIGHT CAME ON . . 97 BALDER DEAD 1 71
HIS SWORD UPRIGHT AND FELL ON IT AND DIED . . 102 BALDER DEAD 1 252
AND FELL BEFORE HER FEET AND CLASPD HER KNEES . . 110 BALDER DEAD 2 187
THEN THE WIND FELL WITH NIGHT AND THERE WAS CALM . 119 BALDER DEAD 3 196
SO WITH A SHOWER OF SPARKS THE PILE FELL IN . . 119 BALDER DEAD 3 205
AND THERE FELL JOY UPON THE GODS TO HEAR . . . 122 BALDER DEAD 3 319

FELL   (CONTINUED)
        WITH SCARLET BERRIES GEMMD THE FELL-FARES FOOD   •   •   150 TRISTRAM 3   22
        THE FELL-FARES AND THE SPECKLED MISSEL-THRUSH   •   •   150 TRISTRAM 3   30
        THE FELL-FARES SETTLED ON THE THICKETS NEAR   •   •   151 TRISTRAM 3   55
        FELL UPON MERLIN MORE LIKE DEATH SO DEEP   •   •   •   •   155 TRISTRAM 3   214
        OF HAIR THAT RED AND TUFTED FELL   •   •   •   •   •   157 SAINT BRANDAN   18
        OF HAIR THAT BLACK AND TUFTED FELL   •   •   •   •   •   157 SAINT BRANDAN   V   18
        A PROP GAVE WAY CRASH FELL A PLATFORM LO   •   •   •   166 AUSTERITY POET   8
        AND LAID HER IN A STATELY ROOM WHERE FELL   •   •   168 RACHEL 2   5
        AND SECRET LOATHING FELL   •   •   •   •   •   •   •   •   315 OBERMANN MORE   94
        DOWN CAME THE STORM IN RUINS FELL   •   •   •   •   •   319 OBERMANN MORE   205
        DOWN CAME THE STORM IN RUIN FELL   •   •   •   •   •   319 OBERMANN MORE   V 205
        FELL TO THY FATHERS LOT THE SECOND PRIZE   •   •   •   330 MEROPE   8
        ZEUS HATH HIS ALTAR WHERE THY FATHER FELL   •   •   •   330 MEROPE   15
        HIM WHOM THOU HIDDEST WHEN THY HUSBAND FELL   •   •   334 MEROPE   145
        FELL THE ELDEST OF THE SONS OF HERACLES   •   •   •   •   344 MEROPE   445
        A BLOW A BLOW WAS STRUCK AND HE FELL   •   •   •   •   •   346 MEROPE   490
        WHEN MY GREAT FATHER FELL THEY HAD REPLIED   •   •   •   383 MEROPE   1366
        WORST OF THE THREE THE STONY SPARTA FELL   •   •   •   389 MEROPE   1553
        BUT HE WHOSE YOUTH FELL ON A DIFFERENT WORLD   •   •   436 EMPEDOCLES II   262
        FELL ON THE CHERISHD PAST WITH TEARFUL SMILE   •   •   474 CROMWELL   70
        THE IMPRISONING CHAINS FELL OFF AND ALL WAS CLEAR   •   478 CROMWELL   214

FELLD
        WHICH FELLD HIM TO THE EARTH AND OER HIM STOOD   •   •   402 MEROPE   1922

FELLFARES
        WITH SCARLET BERRIES BRIGHT THE FELLFARES FOOD   •   •   TRISTRAM 3   V 22

FELLOW
        ALL DIFFERENCE WITH HIS FELLOW-MORTAL CLOSED   •   •   7 REP FRIEND CONT   13
        ALL DIFFERENCE WITH HIS FELLOW MAN COMPOSD   •   •   •   •   7 REP FRIEND CONT V 13
        PRICK ME THE FELLOW FROM THE PATH   •   •   •   •   •   89 SICK KING BOKH   43
        BROTHER AND FELLOW-SPORT OF LOK WITH ME   •   •   •   •   125 BALDER DEAD 3   412
        FOILD BY OUR FELLOW-MEN DEPRESSD OUTWORN   •   •   •   172 IMMORTALITY   1
        KNEW NO FELLOW FOR MIGHT   •   •   •   •   •   •   •   284 HAWORTH CHURCH   94
        HER FELLOW-PEOPLE SIT   •   •   •   •   •   •   •   •   282 HAWORTH CHURCH   V
        WHO HAS NO FRIEND NO FELLOW LEFT NOT ONE   •   •   •   437 EMPEDOCLES II   271
        KNOW WE MORE OUR FELLOW MEN   •   •   •   •   •   •   457 POOR MATTHIAS   162

FELLOWS
        YOURSELVES AND YOUR FELLOWS YE KNOW NOT AND ME   •   •   231 YOUTH OF NATURE   117
        NOR LET THY BAWLING FELLOWS RACK THEIR THROATS   •   •   255 SCHOLAR-GIPSY   4

FELLOWSHIP
        BUT THOU WHOM FELLOWSHIP OF MOOD   •   •   •   •   •   •   322 OBERMANN MORE   273

FELLS
        THE CHEERFUL SILENCE OF THE FELLS   •   •   •   •   •   •   54 RESIGNATION   67

FELT
        HATH YOUR WISDOM FELT EMOTIONS   •   •   •   •   •   •   •   29 NEW SIRENS   85
        FELT THE SLOW-ROLLING WORD   •   •   •   •   •   •   •   •   47 WORLD QUIETIST   29
        FELT ALREADY SOME DEEPER SMART   •   •   •   •   •   •   •   131 TRISTRAM 1   46
        I FELT AS I IN TORMENT LAY   •   •   •   •   •   •   •   157 SAINT BRANDAN   33
        OF ALL HE SAW AND FELT ON EARTH   •   •   •   •   •   159 NECKAN   15
        THE INFANT CHURCH OF LOVE SHE FELT THE TIDE   •   •   172 GOOD SHEPHERD   7
        I TOO HAVE FELT THE LOAD I BORE   •   •   •   •   •   178 FAREWELL   29
        WHICH LUNA FELT THAT SUMMER-NIGHT   •   •   •   •   •   181 ISOLATION MARG   20
        FELT THE DISSOLVING THROES   •   •   •   •   •   •   •   229 YOUTH OF NATURE   31
        MAKE OH MAKE YOURSELVES FELT   •   •   •   •   •   •   234 YOUTH OF MAN   54
        OF SWAY HAVE FELT THIS BODING SENSE COME ON   •   •   239 REVOLUTIONS   14
        HAVE FELT THEIR HUGE FRAMES NOT CONSTRUCTED RIGHT   239 REVOLUTIONS   15
        I SAW I FELT IT ONCE BUT WHERE   •   •   •   •   •   •   241 MORALITY   30
        I FELT IT IN SOME OTHER CLIME   •   •   •   •   •   •   242 MORALITY   33
        AS FLASHING AS MOSES FELT   •   •   •   •   •   •   253 FUTURE   45
        NO NO THOU HAST NOT FELT THE LAPSE OF HOURS   •   •   259 SCHOLAR-GIPSY   141
        WHO NEVER DEEPLY FELT NOR CLEARLY WILLD   •   •   •   260 SCHOLAR-GIPSY   173
        HAD FELT HIM LIKE THE THUNDERS ROLL   •   •   •   •   •   270 MEMORIAL VERSES   9
        OUR FOREHEADS FELT THE WIND AND RAIN   •   •   •   •   271 MEMORIAL VERSES   53
        HAVE FELT THIS BREATH HE LOVED OF FAIR   •   •   •   •   275 STANZAS CARNAC   43
        LISTEND AND FELT THYSELF GROW YOUNG   •   •   •   •   310 OBERMANN   127
        SHE FELT THE VOID WHICH MINED HER BREAST   •   •   •   316 OBERMANN MORE   123
        ALL EUROPE FELT THAT FIERY BLAST   •   •   •   •   •   319 OBERMANN MORE   203
        I FELT THE SUN AND WIND   •   •   •   •   •   •   •   321 OBERMANN MORE   256
        WHEREOF THY YOUTH FELT ALL THE SPELL   •   •   •   •   •   323 OBERMANN MORE   309
        OUR WANTS HAVE ALL BEEN FELT OUR ERRORS MADE BEFORE   419 EMPEDOCLES I 2   211
        HAVE THE SAME SURFACE WHICH OUR FATHERS FELT   EVERLASTING SUB   V   3
        TOUCH THE SAME SURFACE WHICH OUR FATHERS FELT   •   •   EVERLASTING SUB   V   3

FELTS
        A DOME OF LATHS AND OER IT FELTS WERE SPREAD   •   •   61 SOHRAB RUSTUM   23
        OF RUGS AND FELTS AND NEAR HIM LAY HIS ARMS   •   •   61 SOHRAB RUSTUM   27

FEMALE
        PLIES SOME LIGHT FEMALE TASK NOR DREAMS OF US   •   •   80 SOHRAB RUSTUM   647

FEN
        SAW THE WIDE PROSPECT AND THE ASIAN FEN   •   •   •   •   2 TO A FRIEND   3
        AND THAT NEW MINSTER IN THE MATTED FEN   •   •   •   •   444 WESTMIN ABBEY   19

FENCE
    AND WITH MY GREAT NAME FENCE THAT WEAK OLD MAN   • •   68 SOHRAB RUSTUM   237
    TAKE ME COWLD FORMS AND FENCE ME ROUND   • • • •   302 GRANDE CHARTR   93
    WHO WILL FENCE HIM FROM HIMSELF   • • • • • •   435 EMPEDOCLES II   212

FENCED
    FENCED EARLY IN THIS CLOISTRAL ROUND   • • • •   306 GRANDE CHARTR   205
    THOUGH FENCED BY SANCTION OF A THOUSAND YEARS   • •   353 MEROPE   669

FENCEST
    THOU FENCEST HIM FROM THE MULTITUDE   • • • • •   435 EMPEDOCLES II   211

FENRIS
    FENRIS THE WOLF THE SERPENT HUGE AND ME   • •   110 BALDER DEAD 2   208
    SUBDUED WITH LIMBER CHAINS LIVES FENRIS BOUND   • •   111 BALDER DEAD 2   216
    AND FENRIS AT HIS HEEL WITH BROKEN CHAIN   • • •   127 BALDER DEAD 3   477

FENSALER
    THERE IN THE GLEN FENSALER STANDS THE HOUSE   • •   97 BALDER DEAD 1   84
    FENSALER WHOSE LIT WINDOWS LOOK TO SEA   • • •   100 BALDER DEAD 1   198

FERABURZ
    AND FERABURZ WHO RULED THE PERSIAN HOST   • • •   66 SOHRAB RUSTUM   172

FERDOUSIS
    FERDOUSIS AND THE OTHERS LEAD   • • • • • • •   88 SICK KING BOKH   12

FERDUSIS
    FERDUSIS AND THE OTHERS LEAD   • • • • • • •   88 SICK KING BOKH   V 12

FERGHANA
    THE TARTARS OF FERGHANA FROM THE BANKS   • • •   64 SOHRAB RUSTUM   128

FERMENT
    AND KHIVA AND FERMENT THE MILK OF MARES   • • •   64 SOHRAB RUSTUM   120
    OF THE THOUGHTS THAT FERMENT IN MY BREAST   • • •   231 YOUTH OF NATURE   120
    ALL IN FERMENT BUT HE   • • • • • • • •   298 HEINES GRAVE   195

FERMENTATION
    IN THE DARK FERMENTATION OF EARTH   • • • • •   286 HAWORTH CHURCH   135

FERMENTS
    YET STILL FOR I CONCEAL IT NOT FERMENTS   • • • •   334 MEROPE   137

FERN
    THROUGH LAST YEARS FERN OF THE SHY FALLOW-DEER   • •   155 TRISTRAM 3   193
    THROUGH THE GREEN FERN OF THE SHY FALLOW-DEER   • •   155 TRISTRAM 3   V 193
    WITH WHITENING HEDGES AND UNCRUMPLING FERN   • • •   265 THYRSIS   74

FEROOD
    AND WHEN FEROOD WHO LED THE PERSIANS SAW   • • •   65 SOHRAB RUSTUM   144
    FEROOD AND YE PERSIANS AND TARTARS HEAR   • • •   65 SOHRAB RUSTUM   150
    AND TO FEROOD HIS BROTHER CHIEFS CAME UP   • • •   66 SOHRAB RUSTUM   170
    FEROOD SHAME BIDS US TAKE THEIR CHALLENGE UP   • •   66 SOHRAB RUSTUM   175
    SO SPAKE HE AND FEROOD STOOD FORTH AND CRIED   • •   66 SOHRAB RUSTUM   184
    SO SPAKE HE AND FEROOD STOOD FORTH AND SAID   • •   66 SOHRAB RUSTUM   V 184

FERRY
    THEY SEE THE FERRY   • • • • • • • • • • •   191 STRAYED REVEL   181
    THE FERRY-BOAT WITH WOVEN ROPES   • • • • •   191 STRAYED REVEL   186
    THEE AT THE FERRY OXFORD RIDERS BLITHE   • • • •   257 SCHOLAR-GIPSY   72

FERRYS
    AND CROSS THE UNPERMITTED FERRYS FLOW   • • • •   265 THYRSIS   85

FERVENT
    YET FERVENT HAD HER LONGING BEEN THROUGH ALL   • •   173 MONICAS PRAYER   6
    FERVENT HEROIC AND GOOD   • • • • • • • • •   291 RUGBY CHAPEL   160

FERVOURS
    SUPPORT THE FERVOURS OF THE HEAVENLY MORN   • • •   172 IMMORTALITY   8
    RELIGIOUS FERVOURS ARDOUR MISAPPLIED   • • • • •   237 PROGRESS   17

FESTAL
    FROM YOUR HUMMING FESTAL ROOM   • • • • • • •   32 NEW SIRENS   184
    FROM THE HUMMING FESTAL ROOM   • • • • • • •   32 NEW SIRENS   V 184
    IN HIS LIGHT YOUTH AMID A FESTAL THRONG   • • •   166 AUSTERITY POET   3
    THE LINE OF FESTAL LIGHT IN CHRIST-CHURCH HALL   • •   259 SCHOLAR-GIPSY   129

FESTERING
    OF FESTERING THOUGHTS AND PERSONAL FEARS   • • • •   271 MEMORIAL VERSES   V

FESTERS
    FESTERS THE DULL REMEMBRANCE OF A CHANGE   • • • •   213 GROWING OLD   29

FESTIVALS
    IN SUMMER TO ALL COUNTRY-FESTIVALS   • • • • • •   412 EMPEDOCLES I 2   15

FESTIVE
        THE DANCERS AND THE FESTIVE HOST   . . . . . . 146 TRISTRAM 2   121

FETCH
        NOR FETCH TO TAKE THE ACCUSTOMD TOLL . . . . . . 250 WISH   21
        BUT STOP TO FETCH BACK THOUGHTS THAT STRAY . . . . 313 OBERMANN MORE   29
        FETCH ME THE SACRIFICE-AXE   . . . . 371 MEROPE   1138
        LET HIM FETCH SUCCOURS FROM ARCADIA GAIN   . . . . 388 MEROPE   1498
        WELL FETCH HIS GRAVEN COLLAR FINE   . . . . . . 461 KAISER DEAD   79

FETCHEDST
        THOU SENTST AND FETCHEDST FIRE AND MADEST LIGHTS . . 121 BALDER DEAD 3   263

FETLOCK
        THEIR HORSES FETLOCK-DEEP IN BLOOD THEY RIDE   . . 105 BALDER DEAD 2   25

FETTERD
        OF HIS OWN BREAST FETTERD TO WHAT HE GUARDS   . . 437 EMPEDOCLES II   269

FEUD
        A MOURNFUL FEUD ALIVE WHICH ELSE WOULD DIE . . . . 332 MEROPE   82

FEUDS
        THEIR INEFFECTUAL FEUDS AND FEEBLE HATES   . . . . 126 BALDER DEAD 3   466
        WERE NOT AMONG THE FEUDS OF WARRIOR-CHIEFS . . . . 388 MEROPE   1512
        WERT NOT AMONG THE FEUDS OF WARRIOR-CHIEFS . . . . 388 MEROPE   V1512

FEVER
        AND CALL THIS HURRYING FEVER GENEROUS FIRE . . . . . 37 YOUTHS AGIT   12
        DOWN HAVING FEVER FOR A DRINK   . . . . 90 SICK KING BOKH   76
        HE IS WEAK WITH FEVER AND PAIN   . . . . 133 TRISTRAM 1   85
        NOT THIS FEVER-WASTED WIGHT   . . . . 133 TRISTRAM 1   107
        FROM THE FEVER IN HIS BLOOD   . . . . 136 TRISTRAM 1   172
        AND HIS BURNING FEVER-PAIN   . . . . 136 TRISTRAM 1   182
        TENDED OF HIS FEVER HERE . . . . 136 TRISTRAM 1   205
        I THINK I HAVE A FEVER IN MY BLOOD . . . . . . 139 TRISTRAM 1   280
        TO BED AND SLEEP MY FEVER IS GONE BY . . . . . 140 TRISTRAM 1   309
        LONG IVE WAITED LONG IVE FOUGHT MY FEVER   . . . . 142 TRISTRAM 2   3
        SHIVERING WITH FEVER NAKED OLD . . . . 157 SAINT BRANDAN   46
        MINED BY THE FEVER OF THE SOUL . . . . 178 FAREWELL   22
        CRUSHD THEM WITH TOLLS OR FEVER-AIRS . . . . . 193 STRAYED REVEL   251
        ALL THE FEVER OF SOME DIFFERING SOUL . . . . . 240 SELF-DEPENDENCE   24
        A FEVER IN THESE PAGES BURNS   . . . . 307 OBERMANN   21
        IN ME THE FEVER OF REVENGEFUL HATE . . . . . . 387 MEROPE   1466

FEVERD
        NOW MARK I BEING FEVERD SICK   . . . . 90 SICK KING BOKH   85
        THE HOT WIND FEVERD HIM FIVE-FOLD   . . . . . . 157 SAINT BRANDAN   48

FEVERISH
        WHERE IN ONE DREAM THE FEVERISH TIME OF YOUTH   . . . 11 MYCERINUS   89
        THIS STARTING FEVERISH HEART AWAY   . . . . . . 178 FAREWELL   32
        BUT FLY OUR PATHS OUR FEVERISH CONTACT FLY . . . . 261 SCHOLAR-GIPSY   221
        OF FITFUL DREAM AND FEVERISH POWER . . . . . . 270 MEMORIAL VERSES   24
        THE POETS FEVERISH BLOOD . . . . 309 OBERMANN   94
        YET HAPPY SINCE HIS FEVERISH BLOOD   . . . . . . 484 ROME-SICKNESS   25
        THE USHERS RASH AND FEVERISH MELANCHOLY   . . . .   FRAGMENT 1   5

FEVERS
        THE BALEFUL SIGN OF FEVERS DUST HAD SOILD . . . . . 74 SOHRAB RUSTUM   453

FEW
        THOSE VIRTUES PRIZED AND PRACTISED BY TOO FEW . . . . 6 REP FRIEND   2
        A FEW SAD SMILES AND THEN   . . . . 44 QUESTION   5
        AND ROOMS OF TREASURES NOT A FEW . . . . 94 SICK KING BOKH   214
        AH HOW FEW OF THEM ALL   . . . . 216 LORDS MESSENGER   10
        ALAS HOW FEW OF THEM ALL   . . . . 216 LORDS MESSENGER   V 10
        BUT AH HOW FEW OF ALL THAT TRY . . . . 226 EPILOG LAOCOON   169
        ONLY A FEW THE LIFE-STREAMS SHORE   . . . . . . 226 EPILOG LAOCOON   189
        AND THE REST A FEW . . . . 243 SUMMER NIGHT   51
        SING HIM THY BEST FOR FEW OR NONE   . . . . . . 272 MEMORIAL VERSES   73
        FROM A FEW BOYS LATE AT THEIR PLAY   . . . . . . 286 RUGBY CHAPEL   7
        AND GOETHES COURSE FEW SONS OF MEN . . . . . . 308 OBERMANN   55
        SO WOULD HAVE BUILT YOU IN A FEW SHORT YEARS   . . . 339 MEROPE   304
        MOST MEN ARE LED BY INTEREST AND THE FEW   . . . . 341 MEROPE   365

FEWER
        FEWER FINE SUCCESSES CAN DISPLAY   . . . . . . 221 EPILOG LAOCOON   12
        FEWER REAL SUCCESSES CAN DISPLAY   . . . . . . 221 EPILOG LAOCOON   V 12

FICKLE
        NATURE IS FICKLE MAN HATH NEED OF REST   . . . .   5 HARMONY NATURE   9

FICTION
        FIRST IN FICTION HAD SINCE   . . . . 280 HAWORTH CHURCH   15

FIELD
        AND BEAT THE PERSIANS BACK ON EVERY FIELD   . . . . 62 SOHRAB RUSTUM   48
        SHOULD ONE DAY GREET UPON SOME WELL-FOUGHT FIELD . . 62 SOHRAB RUSTUM   51
        DANGER OR DEATH AWAITS THEE ON THIS FIELD   . . . . 63 SOHRAB RUSTUM   87
        AND TRIED AND I HAVE STOOD ON MANY A FIELD . . . . 71 SOHRAB RUSTUM   326

FIELD   (CONTINUED)
```
          NEVER WAS THAT FIELD LOST OR THAT FOE SAVED      .  .   71 SOHRAB RUSTUM      328
          HERE ON THIS FIELD THERE WERE NO FIGHTING THEN   .  .   72 SOHRAB RUSTUM      383
          AND SWIFT FOR LIKE THE LIGHTNING TO THIS FIELD   .  .   82 SOHRAB RUSTUM      722
          OR ERE THEY BROUGHT THY MASTER TO THIS FIELD     .  .   83 SOHRAB RUSTUM      740
          WHEN FIRST THEY BORE THY MASTER TO THIS FIELD    .  .   83 SOHRAB RUSTUM    V 740
          FROM THE HOT FIELD AT NOON HIS HEAD DROOPD LOW   .  .   86 SOHRAB RUSTUM    V 847
          ON BATTLE-FIELD HAVE MET THEIR DEATH AND NOW     .  .  104 BALDER DEAD 1      321
          THERE THROUGH SOME BATTLE-FIELD WHERE MEN FALL FAST .  105 BALDER DEAD 2       24
          OR ON THE SEA THE FIELD OF PIRATES SAIL          .  .  121 BALDER DEAD 3      270
          OUT OF A TILLD FIELD INLAND THEN THE WIND        .  .  124 BALDER DEAD 3      363
          BY CASTLE FIELD AND TOWN  .  .  .  .  .  .  .     .  .  159 NECKAN              18
          THE HUNTER OF THE TANAGRAEAN FIELD               .  .  197 FRAG ANTIGONE       64
          TO LOOK TOWRD ARDRES GOLDEN FIELD                .  .  204 CALAIS SANDS         5
          TO SEE TOWRD ARDRES GOLDEN FIELD                 .  .  204 CALAIS SANDS     V   5
          FILL WITH THEIR SPORTS THE FIELD                 .  .  218 BACCHANALIA 1       38
          THE EVENING COMES THE FIELD IS STILL             .  .  217 BACCHANALIA 1    V   1
          THE EVENING COMES THE FIELD IS STILL             .  .  218 BACCHANALIA 1    V  19
          CORN-FIELD AND HAMLET AND COPSE                  .  .  234 YOUTH OF MAN        79
          SCREEND IS THIS NOOK OER THE HIGH HALF-REAPD FIELD .  255 SCHOLAR-GIPSY       21
          SCREEND IN THIS NOOK OER THE HIGH HALF-REAPD FIELD .  255 SCHOLAR-GIPSY    V  21
          BUT ONCE I KNEW EACH FIELD EACH FLOWER EACH STICK .  263 THYRSIS             32
          FROM THE WET FIELD THROUGH THE VEXT GARDEN-TREES .  .  264 THYRSIS             58
          INTO YON FARTHER FIELD TIS DONE AND SEE          .  .  267 THYRSIS            157
          INTO YON FURTHER FIELD TIS DONE AND SEE          .  .  267 THYRSIS          V 157
          THE AUTUMN-EVENING THE FIELD  .  .  .  .  .      .  .  286 RUGBY CHAPEL         2
          BROKE ON THE FIELD OF HIS FAME  .  .  .  .  .    .  .  296 HEINES GRAVE       128
          THE BROAD RED SUN OVER FIELD  .  .  .  .  .      .  .  297 HEINES GRAVE       170
          THREE BROTHERS WON THE FIELD  .  .  .  .  .      .  .  344 MEROPE             454
          DECKD THE DULL WASTE AND THE FAMILIAR FIELD      .  .  472 CROMWELL            34
          BY LEAGUERD TOWER AND TENTED FIELD IT CAME  .  . .  .  476 CROMWELL           148
          BY WORCESTERS FIELD THE WARRIOR-VISION PASSD     .  .  476 CROMWELL           150
          AND HURLD HIM ON THE FIELD OF LIFE  .  .  .      .  .  481 DESTINY              7
          AND HE DIES FRUITLESS HAVING FOUND NO FIELD          LUCRETIUS 2            6
```

FIELDS
```
          MID BRIGHT GREEN FIELDS BELOW THE PINES     .  .  .  .   16 CHURCH BROU 2        5
          BUT ELSE THE WOODS AND FIELDS ARE DUMB      .  .  .  .   17 CHURCH BROU 2       31
          IN THE THRONGD FIELDS WHERE WINNING COMES BY STRIFE  .   43 GIPSY CHILD         58
          IN EARTHS THRONGD FIELDS WHERE WINNING COMES BY STRIFE  43 GIPSY CHILD      V  58
          FRESH FROM THE SUMMER FIELDS  .  .  .  .  .  .  .     .   51 CONSOLATION         43
          FROM THE HOT FIELDS AT NOON HIS HEAD DROOPD LOW  .  .   86 SOHRAB RUSTUM    V 847
          AT THE CHINKD FIELDS OF ICE THE WASTE OF SNOW   .  .  100 BALDER DEAD 1      164
          THENCE ON HE JOURNEYD OER THE FIELDS OF ICE     .  .  109 BALDER DEAD 2      143
          LIFTED AND ISSUED ON THE FIELDS OF ICE  .  .  .  .  .  113 BALDER DEAD 2      287
          AND SET THE FIELDS OF GLOOM ABLAZE WITH LIGHT   .  .  120 BALDER DEAD 3      243
          AND IN FIELDS SLOPING TO THE SOUTH DARK PLOTS   .  .  122 BALDER DEAD 3      314
          ABSENCE FROM FIELDS WHERE I COULD NOTHING AID   .  .  127 BALDER DEAD 3      502
          BEFORE US ARE THE SWEET GREEN FIELDS OF WALES   .  .  133 TRISTRAM 1          95
          AH WOULD I WERE IN THOSE GREEN FIELDS AT PLAY   .  .  133 TRISTRAM 1          97
          DIE ON THE GREEN FIELDS OF WALES  .  .  .  .     .  .  135 TRISTRAM 1         158
          CREEPS OVER IT FROM THE TILLD FIELDS BEHIND     .  .  149 TRISTRAM 3           9
          STEALS OVER IT FROM THE TILLD FIELDS BEHIND     .  .      TRISTRAM 3        V   9
          THE VAST FIELDS OF SNOW  .  .  .  .  .  .  .  .  .  .      PARTING          V  28
          BUT BRIGHT ARE THOSE GREEN FIELDS AT HAND   .  .  .  .  184 TERRACE BERNE        7
          AND THROUGH THOSE FIELDS COMES DOWN THE AAR     .  .  184 TERRACE BERNE        8
          TO-MORROW HURRY THROUGH THE FIELDS  .  .  .  .   .  .  205 CALAIS SANDS        33
          THE EVENING COMES THE FIELDS ARE STILL          .  .  217 BACCHANALIA 1        1
          THE EVENING COMES THE FIELDS ARE STILL          .  .  218 BACCHANALIA 1       19
          THE PILLAR STILL BROODS OER THE FIELDS          .  .  228 YOUTH OF NATURE     15
          WHO IMAGINES HER FIELDS AS THEY LAY    .  .  .   .  .  252 FUTURE              29
          BUT WHEN THE FIELDS ARE STILL  .  .  .  .  .     .  .  255 SCHOLAR-GIPSY        6
          IN THIS HIGH FIELDS DARK CORNER WHERE HE LEAVES .  .  255 SCHOLAR-GIPSY       12
          PLUCKD IN SHY FIELDS AND DISTANT WYCHWOOD BOWERS .  .  257 SCHOLAR-GIPSY       79
          OFT THROUGH THE DARKENING FIELDS HAVE SEEN THEE ROAM  257 SCHOLAR-GIPSY       84
          MEN WHO THROUGH THOSE WIDE FIELDS OF BREEZY GRASS .  257 SCHOLAR-GIPSY       93
          WHERE HOME THROUGH FLOODED FIELDS FOOT-TRAVELLERS GO  258 SCHOLAR-GIPSY      122
          THOU THROUGH THE FIELDS AND THROUGH THE WOODS   .  .  261 SCHOLAR-GIPSY      197
                  DOST STRAY
          PLUCKD IN SHY FIELDS AND DISTANT WOODLAND BOWERS  .  .  257 SCHOLAR-GIPSY    V  79
          WHILE THE TREE LIVED HE IN THESE FIELDS LIVED ON .  .  263 THYRSIS             30
          FOR THAT A SHADOW LOURD ON THE FIELDS   .  .  .  .  .  264 THYRSIS             44
          FOR SHE HERSELF HAD TROD SICILIAN FIELDS   .  .  .  .  265 THYRSIS             93
          THE GRASSY HARVEST OF THE RIVER-FIELDS  .  .  .  .  .  266 THYRSIS            108
          AH VAIN THESE ENGLISH FIELDS THIS UPLAND DIM    .  .  267 THYRSIS            172
          SOLE IN THESE FIELDS YET WILL I NOT DESPAIR     .  .  268 THYRSIS            192
          FIELDS WHERE SOFT SHEEP FROM CAGES PULL THE HAY .  .  268 THYRSIS            198
          ITS FIR-TOPPED HURST ITS FARMS ITS QUIET FIELDS .  .  269 THYRSIS            217
          FOR THAT A SHADOW LOWERD ON THE FIELDS  .  .  .  .  .  264 THYRSIS          V  44
          FIELDS WHERE THE SHEEP FROM CAGES PULL THE HAY  .  .  268 THYRSIS          V 198
          WENT OER THE SUN-LIT FIELDS AGAIN  .  .  .  .  .  .  .  271 MEMORIAL VERSES     52
          COOL NORTHERN FIELDS AND GRASS AND FLOWERS   .  .  .  .  275 STANZAS CARNAC      44
          DOTTING THE FIELDS OF CORN AND VINE  .  .  .  .  .   .  275 SOUTHERN NIGHT       5
          OF ROTHA SPARKLES THROUGH FIELDS  .  .  .  .  .   .  .  280 HAWORTH CHURCH       2
          OF ROTHA SPARKLES THE FIELDS  .  .  .  .  .  .    .  .  280 HAWORTH CHURCH   V   2
          LONGD HIMSELF BACK TO THE FIELDS  .  .  .  .  .   .  .  296 HEINES GRAVE       137
          HIS OFTEN-LABOURD FIELDS  .  .  .  .  .  .  .     .  .  426 EMPEDOCLES I 2     415
          AS OF OLD IN THE FIELDS OF HEAVEN  .  .  .  .  .  .  .  437 EMPEDOCLES II      278
```

FIEND
```
          BUT THE ARCH-FIEND PRIDE  .  .  .  .  .  .  .  .  .  .  .   38 STAGIRIUS          18
```

FIEND   (CONTINUED)
        WHAT FOUL FIEND RIDES THEE ON INTO THE FIGHT   • • 137 TRISTRAM 1   239
        THOU SMILING FIEND AND CLAIM THY GUERDON THERE   • • 373 MEROPE   1184

FIERCE
        THE DELIGHT OF FIERCE EMBRACES • • • • • • • •   27 NEW SIRENS   V 55
        FROM THAT FIERCE ANGUISH • • • • • • • • •   38 STAGIRIUS   8
        FIERCE WORK IT WERE TO DO AGAIN   • • • • •   52 RESIGNATION   2
        ART THOU SO FIERCE THOU WILT NOT FRIGHT ME SO   72 SOHRAB RUSTUM   380
        UNKNOWN THOU ART YET THY FIERCE VAUNT IS VAIN • • 77 SOHRAB RUSTUM   541
        BUT HEAR THOU THIS FIERCE MAN TREMBLE TO HEAR • • 77 SOHRAB RUSTUM   552
        FIERCE MAN BETHINK THEE FOR AN ONLY SON   • • • • 78 SOHRAB RUSTUM   586
        THE ANGUISH OF THE DEEP-FIXD SPEAR GREW FIERCE • • 80 SOHRAB RUSTUM   650
        WHEREFORE HEAR THOU THOU KNOWST HOW FIERCE   • • 89 SICK KING BOKH   58
        HE SPAKE AND HIS FIERCE SONS APPLAUDED LOUD   • • 120 BALDER DEAD 3   245
        THOU AND THY BRETHREN FIERCE THE SONS OF BOR   • • 121 BALDER DEAD 3   258
        NOT THIS FIERCE ATLANTIC DEEP • • • • • • • •   133 TRISTRAM 1   92
        WHEN THE FIERCE PAINS TOOK HER IN THE FOREST   • • 145 TRISTRAM 2   83
        THE FIERCE HOUNDS SNUFF THE TAINTED AIR   • • • • 149 TRISTRAM 2   184
        WHICH LEAVES THE FIERCE NECESSITY TO FEEL • • • • 153 TRISTRAM 3   123
        TWAS AUGUST AND THE FIERCE SUN OVERHEAD   • • • • 169 EAST LONDON   1
        SO SPAKE THE FIERCE TERTULLIAN BUT SHE SIGHD   • • 172 GOOD SHEPHERD   6
        FROM THE FIERCE TEMPEST OF THINE AGE   • • • • •   304 GRANDE CHARTR   148
        HE MADE A FEAST DRANK FIERCE AND FAST   • • • • 316 OBERMANN MORE   101
        WHO SHOOK THE FIERCE NELEIDAE ON THEIR THRONE • • 338 MEROPE   292
        IN THIS HIS PRESENT FIERCE MAN-HATING MOOD • • •   409 EMPEDOCLES I 1   106
        DOTH THY FIERCE SOUL STILL DEPLORE   • • • • •   430 EMPEDOCLES II   52
        FIERCE DISPUTATIOUS EVER AT WAR WITH MAN   • • • • 440 EMPEDOCLES II   395
        AND THE ARMADA FLUNG TO THE FIERCE MAIN   • • • • 481 HUNGARIAN NAT   14
        IF NOT THY FIERCE AND TURBID SONG   • • • • • •   482 COURAGE   18

FIERCELY
        BREASTS HER OWN GRIEFS AND URGED TOO FIERCELY SAYS   6 GEO CRUIKSHANK   10
        BUT FIERCELY ODIN GALLOPD MOVED IN HEART   • • • •• 102 BALDER DEAD 1   258
        FROM THE OAK-BUILT FIERCELY-BURNING PYRE   • • • • 399 MEROPE   1827
        THE FIERCELY-REQUIRED VICTIM   • • • • • • • •   400 MEROPE   1869
        WILL BLOW US FIERCELY BACK TO SEA AND EARTH   • • 439 EMPEDOCLES II   362
        ALL ETNA HEAVES FIERCELY • • • • • • • • • •   441 EMPEDOCLES II   419

FIERCER
        FIERCER THE SUN OVERHEAD • • • • • • • • • •   253 FUTURE   65
        FROM THE FIERCER EUXINE SEA   • • • • • • • •   PILLARS UNIVERS V   8

FIERY
        I SATE OBEDIENT IN THE FIERY PRIME   • • • • • •   9 MYCERINUS   9
        SO MANY FIERY SPIRITS QUITE COOLD DOWN   • • •   37 WORLDS TRIUMPHS   6
        SEES HIS STRONG THOUGHT IN FIERY FLOOD   • • •   56 RESIGNATION   156
        WHOSE FIERY POINT NOW IN HIS MAILD RIGHT-HAND • • 74 SOHRAB RUSTUM   451
        WHO ART THOU ON THY BLACK AND FIERY HORSE • • •   107 BALDER DEAD 2   101
        WHEN FROM THE SOUTH SHALL MARCH THE FIERY BAND • • 127 BALDER DEAD 3   475
        NOR EVER FEELS THE FIERY GLOW • • • • • • •   243 SUMMER NIGHT   29
        WE WATCHD THE FOUNT OF FIERY LIFE   • • • • •   270 MEMORIAL VERSES   13
        MANS PRUDENCE AND MANS FIERY MIGHT   • • • • •   272 MEMORIAL VERSES   59
        ALL EUROPE FELT THAT FIERY BLAST   • • • • •   319 OBERMANN MORE   203
        FIERY PHANTOMS OF DEATH • • • • • • • • • •   346 MEROPE   503
        AND CHECK THY FIERY STEEDS AND LEANING BACK   • • 349 MEROPE   575
        IT IS TEN THOUSAND FIERY WILLS IN ONE   • • •   382 MEROPE   1348
        AND STOOD SHOUTING FOR A FIERY TORCH • • • • •   399 MEROPE   1835
        BRILLIANT ABOVE ME AND THOU FIERY WORLD   • • •   438 EMPEDOCLES II   305
        LAY ON THE HEARTH AMID A FIERY RING • • • • •   446 WESTMIN ABBEY   84
        ALAS THAT FIERY SPIRIT LITTLE KNEW   • • • • •   469 ALARIC AT ROME   187
        THY FIERY COURAGE STILL WAS STRONG   • • • • •   482 COURAGE   20

FIFTEEN
        FIFTEEN YEARS HAVE GONE ROUND • • • • • • •   287 RUGBY CHAPEL   26
        SUDDEN FOR FIFTEEN YEARS • • • • • • • • • •   287 RUGBY CHAPEL   30

FIFTY
        THERE SATE FIFTY MEN IN THE RUDDY LIGHT OF THE FIRE   HOMER TRANS   4

FIGHT
        DIM IS THE RUMOUR OF A COMMON FIGHT • • • • •   62 SOHRAB RUSTUM   60
        IN SINGLE FIGHT INCURRING SINGLE RISK   • • •   63 SOHRAB RUSTUM   69
        TO SEEK OUT RUSTUM SEEK HIM NOT THROUGH FIGHT • • 63 SOHRAB RUSTUM   75
        TO FIGHT OUR CHAMPION SOHRAB MAN TO MAN   • • •   65 SOHRAB RUSTUM   153
        HAPLY HE WILL FORGET HIS WRATH AND FIGHT   • • •   66 SOHRAB RUSTUM   182
        TO FIGHT THEIR CHAMPION AND THOU KNOWST HIS NAME • • 67 SOHRAB RUSTUM   213
        BUT I WILL FIGHT UNKNOWN AND IN PLAIN ARMS • • •   68 SOHRAB RUSTUM   257
        IN SINGLE FIGHT WITH ANY MORTAL MAN • • • • •   69 SOHRAB RUSTUM   259
        AND FIGHT BENEATH MY BANNER TILL I DIE   • • •   71 SOHRAB RUSTUM   332
        BUT HE WILL FIND SOME PRETEXT NOT TO FIGHT • • •   71 SOHRAB RUSTUM   352
        TO COPE WITH ME IN SINGLE FIGHT BUT THEY   • • •   72 SOHRAB RUSTUM   359
        IS IT WITH RUSTUM ONLY THOU WOULDST FIGHT • • •   72 SOHRAB RUSTUM   368
        MAYST FIGHT FIGHT THEM WHEN THEY CONFRONT THY SPEAR 74 SOHRAB RUSTUM   446
        MAYST FIGHT FIGHT THEM WHEN THEY CONFRONT THY SPEAR 74 SOHRAB RUSTUM   446
        FIGHT LET ME HEAR THY HATEFUL VOICE NO MORE   • • 75 SOHRAB RUSTUM   459
        OF WAR I FIGHT IT OUT AND HAND TO HAND   • • •   75 SOHRAB RUSTUM   464
        HIMSELF TO FIGHT AND THAT THY WILES WOULD MOVE • • 77 SOHRAB RUSTUM   532
        THEN WILL HE FIND SOME PRETEXT NOT TO FIGHT   • • 71 SOHRAB RUSTUM   V 352
        LIFE ONE PERPETUAL FIGHT A BATH OF BLOOD   • • • • 128 BALDER DEAD 3   506

FIGHT   (CONTINUED)
         WHAT FOUL FIEND RIDES THEE ON INTO THE FIGHT   . .   137 TRISTRAM 1   239
         ON THE WAVES OF THE TOSSD FIGHT   . . . . . .   138 TRISTRAM 1   266
         IN THE WAVES OF THE TOSSD FIGHT   . . . . . .   138 TRISTRAM 1   V 266
         SAFE THROUGH THE SMOKE OF THE FIGHT   . . . . . .   217 LORDS MESSENGER   23
         FIGHT LIFES MANY-CHANCD FIGHT   . . . . . .   216 LORDS MESSENGER V
         FIGHT LIFES MANY-CHANCD FIGHT   . . . . . .   216 LORDS MESSENGER V
         BACKWARD AND FORWARD ROLLD THE WAVES OF FIGHT   . .   236 PALLADIUM   7
         AND WHEN IT FAILS FIGHT AS WE WILL WE DIE   . .   236 PALLADIUM   23
         WHEN THE FIGHT HUNG IN DOUBT BUT SHE NOW   . . . .   343 MEROPE   429
         AT THE ISTHMUS IN FIGHT WITH HIS FOES   . . . .   345 MEROPE   479
         A PEOPLE IS NO ARMY TRAIND TO FIGHT   . . . . .   382 MEROPE   1339
         TO FIGHT AS BEST HE CAN   . . . .   421 EMPEDOCLES I 2   V 269
         THE FIGHT WHICH CROWND THINE ILLS   . . . . . .   430 EMPEDOCLES II   56
         AND RALLY THEM FOR ONE LAST FIGHT AND FAIL   . . .   440 EMPEDOCLES II   388
         THE FIGHT THAT CROWND THY ILLS . . . .   430 EMPEDOCLES II   V 56
         STAY THIS HAND FROM FIGHT TILL THE TROJANS   HOMER TRANS   62
                    ARE UTTERLY ROUTED

FIGHTERS
         OVER THE FIGHTERS HEADS AND A WIND ROSE   . . . .   75 SOHRAB RUSTUM   483

FIGHTING
         THERE WOULD BE THEN NO TALK OF FIGHTING MORE   . .   72 SOHRAB RUSTUM   372
         HERE ON THIS FIELD THERE WERE NO FIGHTING THEN   . .   72 SOHRAB RUSTUM   383
         ALWAYS AND ALWAYS FIGHTING AMONG THE FIRST   HOMER TRANS   18
                    OF THE TROJANS
         SLEW HIM FIGHTING IN FRONT OF THE FRAY AND   HOMER TRANS   53
                    GLORIFIED HECTOR

FIGHTS
         TO SEEK THY FATHER NOT SEEK SINGLE FIGHTS   . . . .   63 SOHRAB RUSTUM   90
         TOWRD EARTH AND FIGHTS OF MEN AND AT THEIR SIDE   . .   105 BALDER DEAD 2   20
         OF SOME SHIP THAT FIGHTS THE GALE   . . . . . .   130 TRISTRAM 1   13
         AT ARTHURS SIDE HE FIGHTS ONCE MORE   . . . . . .   138 TRISTRAM 1   254
         MAN WITH HIS LOT THUS FIGHTS   . . . .   417 EMPEDOCLES I 2   153

FIGMENTS
         FIGMENTS OF PLOTS WHEREWITH INTRIGUERS FILL   . .   387 MEROPE   1487

FIGS
         GREEN BURSTING FIGS AND TUNNIES STEEPD IN BRINE   . .   262 SCHOLAR-GIPSY   239

FIGURE
         HIS GIANT FIGURE PLANTED ON THE SAND   . . . . .   71 SOHRAB RUSTUM   336
         AND SOHRAB BARED THAT FIGURE ON HIS ARM   . . . .   81 SOHRAB RUSTUM   V 684
         I KNOW THAT GRACEFUL FIGURE FAIR   . . . . .   174 MEETING   5
         WHOSE FIGURE CASTS A SHADOW ON THE FLOOR   . . . .   175 PARTING   36
         COULD FROM EARTHS WAYS THAT FIGURE SLIGHT   . . . .   184 TERRACE BERNE   29
         THAT SLIGHT SWEET FIGURE AT MY SIDE   . . . . .   204 CALAIS SANDS   V 11
         THE FIGURE THE BLOOM OF THY LOVE   . . . . . .   231 YOUTH OF NATURE   111
         MARKD THINE OUTLANDISH GARB THY FIGURE SPARE . . .   258 SCHOLAR-GIPSY   98
         MARKD THY OUTLANDISH GARB THY FIGURE SPARE   . . .   258 SCHOLAR-GIPSY   V 98
         THAT BLACK-ROBED SWOONING FIGURE MEROPE   . . . .   376 MEROPE   1212
         THY SMALL BLACK FIGURE ON THE SNOW   . . . . . .   451 GEISTS GRAVE   52
         STILL STILL I SEE THE FIGURE SMART   . . . . . .   460 KAISER DEAD   49
         SEE ONE FIGURE QUITS THE MAZES   . . . .   META CLOISTER   9

FIGURED
         AT THAT BRIGHT IRON-FIGURED DOOR   . . . . . .   148 TRISTRAM 2   159
         AT THE BRIGHT IRON-FIGURED DOOR   . . . . . .   148 TRISTRAM 2   V 159

FIGURES
         PAINT THAT FIGURES PLIANT GRACE   . . . . . .   23 MEMORY-PICTURE   33
         OUR STORM-BEAT FIGURES AND ASKS   . . . . . .   289 RUGBY CHAPEL   114
         OF FIGURES WITH HER FULNESS VAST   . . . . . .   450 GEISTS GRAVE   25

FILE
         IN SINGLE FILE THEY MOVE AND STOP THEIR BREATH   . .   66 SOHRAB RUSTUM   167
         IN SINGLE FILE THEY PASS AND STOP THEIR BREATH   . .   66 SOHRAB RUSTUM   V 167
         IN SINGLE FILE THEY WIND AND STOP THEIR BREATH   . .   66 SOHRAB RUSTUM   V 167

FILED
         AND FROM THEIR TENTS THE TARTAR HORSEMEN FILED   . .   64 SOHRAB RUSTUM   106
         THESE ALL FILED OUT FROM CAMP INTO THE PLAIN   . .   65 SOHRAB RUSTUM   135

FILES
         OF DUST WHICH WREATHED THEIR STRUGGLING FILES   . .   52 RESIGNATION   6
         OF DUST THAT WREATHED THEIR STRUGGLING FILES   . .   52 RESIGNATION   V   6
         FROM THEIR BLACK TENTS LONG FILES OF HORSE   64 SOHRAB RUSTUM   110
                    THEY STREAMD
         AS WHEN SOME GREY NOVEMBER MORN THE FILES   . . . .   64 SOHRAB RUSTUM   111
         IN FILES AND IN ROUNDS   . . . .   218 BACCHANALIA 1   23
         YE FILL UP THE GAPS IN OUR FILES   . . . . . .   292 RUGBY CHAPEL   204

FILIAL
         NO RUSTUM SLAYS ME AND THIS FILIAL HEART   . . . .   77 SOHRAB RUSTUM   543

FILL
         NOBLER THAN THIS TO FILL THE DAY   . . . . .   59 RESIGNATION   240
         SHOULD CHANGE HIS LOT AND FILL ANOTHERS LIFE   . .   98 BALDER DEAD 1   115
         CLOUDS OF WHITE ROLLING VAPOURS FILL THE VALE   . .   113 BALDER DEAD 2   298
         RE-ENTER THEM WITH WONDER NEVER FILL   . . . . .   128 BALDER DEAD 3   535
         AND SO SHE SINGS HER FILL   . . . .   164 FORSAKEN MERM   94

FILL   (CONTINUED)
         OUR SOON-CHOKED SOULS TO FILL . . . .   183 ABSENCE   10
         FILL WITH THEIR SPORTS THE FIELD   . . . . . .   218 BACCHANALIA 1   38
         FILL WITH THEIR CRIES   . . . . . .   218 BACCHANALIA 1   39
         THE AGE HAS TALKD AND WORKD ITS FILL . . . . . 219 BACCHANALIA 2   2
         EARTH WITH THEIR DEEDS THEY FILL   . . . . .   220 BACCHANALIA 2   43
         FILL WITH THEIR CRIES   . . . . . .   220 BACCHANALIA 2   44
         AND MOUNTAINS THAT FILL US WITH JOY . . . . .   230 YOUTH OF NATURE   61
         BE HEARD FLOATING THROUGH HEAVEN AND FILL AGAIN 238 PROGRESS   35
         HOW FAIR A LOT TO FILL   . . . .   244 SUMMER NIGHT   91
         HOW HIGH A LOT TO FILL   . . . .   244 SUMMER NIGHT   V 91
         ELSE OF THE MYRIADS WHO FILL   . . . .   291 RUGBY CHAPEL   183
         YE FILL UP THE GAPS IN OUR FILES   . . . . . .   292 RUGBY CHAPEL   204
         HELP IT TO FILL THAT DEEP DESIRE   . . . . .   323 OBERMANN MORE   313
         AND FILL THY LEISURE WITH AN EARNEST PRAYER . . 332 MEROPE   72
         FILL THE WEALTH-GIVING THRONES . . . . . .   343 MEROPE   415
         FIGMENTS OF PLOTS WHEREWITH INTRIGUERS FILL . . 387 MEROPE   1487
         FILL THEE TO SEE OUR TIME   . . . . . .   416 EMPEDOCLES I 2   113
         TYRANNY PRIDE AND LUST FILL SICILYS ABODES . . . 416 EMPEDOCLES I 2   121
         ALL THINGS THE WORLD WHICH FILL   . . . . . .   422 EMPEDOCLES I 2   287
         FAILD TO FILL UP THE VOID WHICH IN OUR BREASTS WE BEAR 424 EMPEDOCLES I 2 376
         FILL THEE TO SEE OUR DAY . . . .   416 EMPEDOCLES I 2   V 113
         FILL THEE TO SEE OUR WORLD . . . .   416 EMPEDOCLES I 2   V 113
         ALL THINGS THE WORLD THAT FILL . . . .   422 EMPEDOCLES I 2   V 287
         HERE MATTHIAS SANG HIS FILL   . . . .   458 POOR MATTHIAS   198
         THE CYCLAMENS WHOSE BLOSSOMS FILL   . . . . .   484 ROME-SICKNESS   18

FILLD
         AND MORE THAN MORTAL IMPULSE FILLD THEIR EYES . .   25 DREAM   27
         FOR THE EYE GROWS FILLD WITH GAZING . . . . . .   30 NEW SIRENS   119
         FOR THE EYE WAS FILLD WITH GAZING   . . . . .   30 NEW SIRENS   V 119
         AND THE FIRST GREY OF MORNING FILLD THE EAST   . .   61 SOHRAB RUSTUM   1
         I FILLD MY PITCHER AND STOLE HOME   . . . . .   90 SICK KING BOKH   70
         AND TO MAKE ORCHARD-CLOSES FILLD   . . . . .   94 SICK KING BOKH   200
         A KING WHOSE FAME THEN FILLD THE VAST OF HEAVEN . . 117 BALDER DEAD 3   129
         THE BREEZE AND FILLD THE SAILS AND BLEW THE FIRE . . 118 BALDER DEAD 3   184
         FILLD UP THE HOLLOW CHEEK AND BROUGHT   . . . .   147 TRISTRAM 2   141
         TEARS FILLD HIS MILD BLUE EYE . . . .   160 NECKAN   46
         TEARS FILLD HIS COLD BLUE EYE . . . .   160 NECKAN   V 46
         TEARS FILLD HIS KIND BLUE EYE . . . .   160 NECKAN   V 46
         THE FAMOUS PAINTERS FILLD THEIR WALL . . . . .   219 BACCHANALIA 2   8
         FILLD HIM AND MADE HIM DIVINE . . . .   231 YOUTH OF NATURE   98
         HE KNEW WHICH MADE HIM DROOP AND FILLD HIS HEAD . 264 THYRSIS   47
         TRAVERSE IN TROOPS WITH CARE-FILLD BREAST   . . .   277 SOUTHERN NIGHT   66
         FILLD EUROPE ONCE WITH HIS LOVE-PAIN . . . . .   278 SOUTHERN NIGHT   98
         AND FILLD HER LIFE WITH DAY . . . .   316 OBERMANN MORE   116
         FILLD EARTH AND HEAVEN AND CAUGHT AWAY   . . .   317 OBERMANN MORE   143
         THE DREAM WHICH FILLD OUR BRAIN   . . . . . .   323 OBERMANN MORE   V 314
         IN THE SNOW-FILLD HOLLOWS   . . . .   392 MEROPE   1623
         AND BEAUTY FILLD HER AND SHE SPAKE ALOUD   . . .   447 WESTMIN ABBEY   100

FILLED
         STREAKD WITH ITS FIRST GREY HAIRS HOPE FILLED HIS SOUL 71 SOHRAB RUSTUM 340

FILLEST
         SPIRIT WHO FILLEST US ALL   . . . .   298 HEINES GRAVE   218

FILLS
         TO RIGHT AND LEFT AND WARM STEAM FILLS THE AIR . . 107 BALDER DEAD 2   98
         AND THEIR QUICK TWITTERING FILLS THE BANKS AND SHORES 109 BALDER DEAD 2   162
         MID WIDE GRASS MEADOWS WHICH THE SUNSHINE FILLS . . 257 SCHOLAR-GIPSY   68
         HOW CHANGED IS HERE EACH SPOT MAN MAKES OR FILLS . 262 THYRSIS   1
         WHOSE FLOOR TO-NIGHT SWEET MOONSHINE FILLS . . . . 277 SOUTHERN NIGHT   75
         WHICH THE RHONES MURMUR FILLS   . . . .   324 OBERMANN MORE   344

FILM
         MOCKING LAUGHTER A FILM . . . .   293 HEINES GRAVE   38

FILMS
         THE CURTAINS OF THE BLUE FILMS SLOWLY MEET . . . . 431 EMPEDOCLES II   79

FINAL
         WAITING THE DARKNESS OF THE FINAL TIMES   . . . .   98 BALDER DEAD 1   124
         AND BRING US NEARER TO THE FINAL DAY . . . . .   127 BALDER DEAD 3   474
         NOT YET THOUGH SUCH NO DOUBT HIS FINAL AIM . . .   380 MEROPE   1283
         MY FINAL VICTORY PROVES THE GODS APPEASED   . . .   397 MEROPE   1770
         WHO ASKS THIS FINAL SERVICE AT YOUR HANDS   . . .   429 EMPEDOCLES II   28
         THAT FAMOUS FINAL VICTORY   . . . .   432 EMPEDOCLES II   127

FINALLY
         HATH FINALLY INCLINED   . . . .   46 WORLD QUIETIST   2
         AND FINALLY THIS LAND THEN HALF-SUBDUED   . . . .   337 MEROPE   245

FIND
         FIND THEIR SOLE SPEECH IN THAT VICTORIOUS BROW . .   3 SHAKESPEARE   14
         FIND THEIR SOLE VOICE IN THAT VICTORIOUS BROW   . .   3 SHAKESPEARE   V 14
         LET ME PAUSE LET ME STRIVE IN MYSELF FIND SOME ORDER 19 MODERN SAPPHO   V 7
         FIND ASSURANCE IN TO-MORROW   . . . .   31 NEW SIRENS   165
         SHALL YOU FIND THE RADIANT LOVER   . . . . .   33 NEW SIRENS   221
         AH NO FOR THEN I SHALL BEGIN TO FIND . . . . .   37 YOUTHS AGIT   7

FIND   (CONTINUED)

LIFE WELL AND FIND IT WANTING NOR DEPLORE	42 GIPSY CHILD	30
DO WE GO HENCE AND FIND THEY ARE NOT DEAD	44 QUESTION	17
SHALL WE GO HENCE AND FIND THEY ARE NOT DEAD	44 QUESTION V	17
SO I LONG HOPED BUT HIM I NEVER FIND	62 SOHRAB RUSTUM	53
TO FIND A FATHER THOU HAST NEVER SEEN	63 SOHRAB RUSTUM	70
LET SOHRAB ARM AND WE WILL FIND A MAN	66 SOHRAB RUSTUM	186
DID IN BOKHARA BY THE RIVER FIND	69 SOHRAB RUSTUM	274
BUT HE WILL FIND SOME PRETEXT NOT TO FIGHT	71 SOHRAB RUSTUM	352
AND FOLLOWD HER TO FIND HER WHERE SHE FELL	78 SOHRAB RUSTUM	560
BUT LET US SPEAK NO MORE OF THIS I FIND	82 SOHRAB RUSTUM	716
THAT I SHOULD ONE DAY FIND THY LORD AND THEE	83 SOHRAB RUSTUM	745
THEN WILL HE FIND SOME PRETEXT NOT TO FIGHT	71 SOHRAB RUSTUM V	352
TO FIND SUCH FAVOUR IN THINE EYES	92 SICK KING BOKH	136
BUT EVEN THERE O NANNA WE MIGHT FIND	104 BALDER DEAD 1	326
OR THOU WILT FIND HIM IN THY FAITHFUL SEARCH	116 BALDER DEAD 3	116
OF CARNAGE AND FIND HERMOD IN YOUR LIFE	127 BALDER DEAD 3	504
BUT WE IN HEAVEN SHALL FIND AGAIN WITH JOY	128 BALDER DEAD 3	532
OF IDA AND AMONG THE GRASS SHALL FIND	128 BALDER DEAD 3	538
WAFTS HIM HERE AND LETS HIM FIND	136 TRISTRAM 1	191
SHE WOULD FIND ILL TO BEAR WEAK AS SHE IS	152 TRISTRAM 3	101
NO FAIRER RESTING-PLACE A MAN COULD FIND	155 TRISTRAM 3	210
THEY SEEK TO FIND IN THOSE THEY LOVE	178 FAREWELL	23
IN SEEKING WHAT WE SHALL NOT FIND	179 FAREWELL	52
OR SHALL I FIND THEE STILL BUT CHANGED	184 TERRACE BERNE	33
AND SOME FIND DEATH ERE THEY FIND LOVE	206 TOO LATE	2
AND SOME FIND DEATH ERE THEY FIND LOVE	206 TOO LATE	2
FIND ALSO IN THE SOUND A THOUGHT	211 DOVER BEACH	19
TELL ME CAN YOU FIND INDEED	215 PIS-ALLER	6
FIND THY BODY BY THE WALL	215 LAST WORD	16
TOO KEEN TO REST TOO WEAK TO FIND	217 NAMELESS EPIT V	
THAT MEN DID EVER FIND	238 PROGRESS V	40
THAT MAN DID EVER FIND	238 PROGRESS V	40
I ASK BUT THAT MY DEATH MAY FIND	250 WISH	9
IN THE OLD HAUNT AND FIND OUR TREE-TOPPD HILL	265 THYRSIS	103
AGAIN FIND WORDSWORTHS HEALING POWER	272 MEMORIAL VERSES	63
YE SHALL FIND YOURSELVES AGAIN	286 HAWORTH CHURCH	138
THE WILDERNESS TO FIND	317 OBERMANN MORE	136
DIDST FIND THE SOLITARY MAN	322 OBERMANN MORE	279
I SOUGHT THEE MEROPE I FIND THEE THUS	332 MEROPE	79
FIND THEN SUCH CAUSE THE CHARGE OF MURDER FALLS	336 MEROPE	210
AND I CAME THINKING TO FIND ARCAS HERE	361 MEROPE	916
SEIZED HE ESCAPES AND NEXT I FIND HIM HERE	364 MEROPE	983
FLY FIND ME ON THE INSTANT WHERE CONFER	368 MEROPE	1071
TO KEEP THEIR MASTERS POWER THOU WILT FIND	381 MEROPE	1307
THAT I TO-DAY RETURNING FIND MYSELF	385 MEROPE	1410
CLAMOURS TO FIND FULFILLD WHICH GOOD MEN PRAISE	386 MEROPE	1428
THE KING RETURN AND FIND YOU PRATING HERE	386 MEROPE	1443
MORE DARING AND MORE GRAND OFFENDER FIND	390 MEROPE	1571
COULD FIND NO WAY TO FOUND THEM SURE AS THIS	403 MEROPE	1960
FOR I FIND WORTH IN THEE AND BADNESS TOO	404 MEROPE	1990
TO FIND IN THEE A FAULT WHEREON TO FOUND	404 MEROPE	2006
THENCE HE ESCAPD AND NEXT I FIND HIM HERE	365 MEROPE V	
TO FIND WITH YOU THE JOY WE IN VAIN HERE REQUIRE	425 EMPEDOCLES I 2	381
FIND HENCEFORTH ENERGY AND HEART BUT I	429 EMPEDOCLES II	10
AND HE WILL FIND ITS AIR TOO KEEN FOR HIM	435 EMPEDOCLES II	228
WHERE WILL THEY FIND THEIR PARENT ELEMENT	439 EMPEDOCLES II	347
GAZING ON THEE WE WAKE TO FIND IT IS NOT SO	470 ALARIC AT ROME	216
FIND I HIM FROM WHOM I HAD TO SEVER	482 THEKLAS ANSWER	9
BELIEVE AND THOU SHALT FIND THE HOLY NIGH	483 THEKLAS ANSWER	20
THERE SHALL FIND FULFILMENT IN ITS DAY	483 THEKLAS ANSWER	22

FINDING

NO THOU SHALT NOT SPEAK I SHOULD BE FINDING	143 TRISTRAM 2	33
FINDING NOT DO ALL THEY CAN	455 POOR MATTHIAS	97

FINDS

FINDS HIM WITH MANY AN UNSOLVED PLAN	58 RESIGNATION	224
AND STRIKES THE ROCK AND FINDS THE VEIN	213 PROGRESS POESY	2
WHERE MANY A SPLENDOUR FINDS ITS TOMB	220 BACCHANALIA 2	22
WHO FINDS HIMSELF LOSES HIS MISERY	240 SELF-DEPENDENCE	32
WE JUDGED THE BEST CHANCE FINDS NO BETTER WAY	331 MEROPE	36
AND DARES STAMP NOTHING FALSE WHERE HE FINDS NOTHING SURE	415 EMPEDOCLES I 2	91
WHICH MAN PROUD MAN FINDS HARD TO BEAR	450 GEISTS GRAVE	30

FINE

WIDE STREETS WITH FINE DOUBLE TROTTOIRS	214 NEW ROME	15
NEW STREETS WITH FINE DOUBLE TROTTOIRS	214 NEW ROME V	15
FEWER FINE SUCCESSES CAN DISPLAY	221 EPILOG LAOCOON	12
EASILY QUELLD AND THE FINE	293 HEINES GRAVE	25
SMOOTH HIS RUFFLED PLUMAGE FINE	452 POOR MATTHIAS	11
WELL FETCH HIS GRAVEN COLLAR FINE	461 KAISER DEAD	79
WHEN HIS FINE GENIUS FOAMS ITSELF AWAY	LUCRETIUS 2	4

FINER

ONLY THAT WITH NO FINER ART	48 HORATIAN ECHO	19

FINEST

THEY ABIDE AND THE FINEST OF SOULS	230 YOUTH OF NATURE	81

FINGER

HER FINGER ON HER LIPS THEN VIVIAN ROSE	• • •	156 TRISTRAM 3	215
I FEEL HER FINGER LIGHT • • • • • • • • •	• • •	266 THYRSIS	136
AND STRUCK HIS FINGER ON THE PLACE • • • • • •	• •	270 MEMORIAL VERSES	21
ENOUGH OF THIS THOUGH NOT A FINGER STIR	• • •	383 MEROPE	1375

FINGERS

WHO WITH NUMB BLACKEND FINGERS MAKES HER FIRE	•	70 SOHRAB RUSTUM	304
TO HIS KNEES AND WITH HIS FINGERS CLUTCHD THE SAND		73 SOHRAB RUSTUM	421
THEN WITH WEAK HASTY FINGERS SOHRAB LOOSED • • •	•	81 SOHRAB RUSTUM	669
AND WITH FOND FALTERING FINGERS STROKED HIS CHEEKS		81 SOHRAB RUSTUM	696
TO HIS KNEES AND WITH HIS FINGERS GRASPD THE SAND		73 SOHRAB RUSTUM	V 421
HER LOOKS ARE MILD HER FINGERS SLIGHT	• • •	131 TRISTRAM 1	30
DOWN ON HIS WASTED FINGERS RAIND • • • • •	• •	140 TRISTRAM 1	318
AND OFTEN THE FINGERS CLOSE IN HASTE • • • • •	•	141 TRISTRAM 1	346
DOWN ON HER SLENDER FINGERS RAIND • • • • •	• •	140 TRISTRAM 1	V 318
TAKE MY HAND AND TOUCH THESE WASTED FINGERS	•	143 TRISTRAM 2	23
HER WORK AWAY AND LET HER FINGERS ROVE	• •	152 TRISTRAM 3	87
TRAILING IN THE COOL STREAM THY FINGERS WET	•	257 SCHOLAR-GIPSY	75
UNCLOSED HIS ITCHING FINGERS FROM HIS SWORD	•	394 MEROPE	1705
YES THERE ARE STAINS TIMES FINGERS CANNOT BLOT	•	462 ALARIC AT ROME	14

FINISHD

FINISHD THEIR WORK AND THEN A MEED REQUIRED	• • •	448 WESTMIN ABBEY	136
HAD FINISHD AND A MEED OF PRICE REQUIRED • • •	•	448 WESTMIN ABBEY	V 136

FINISTERES

OF FINISTERES UNQUIET BROW • • • • • • • •	• •	274 STANZAS CARNAC	36

FINNS

AND ON THE FINNS THE GENTLEST OF MANKIND • • •	•	97 BALDER DEAD 1	55

FIR

THROUGH THE ROUGH FIR-PLANKS • • • • • •	• •	186 STRAYED REVEL	25
I SNATCHD UP MY VINE-CROWN MY FIR-STAFF • • •	•	186 STRAYED REVEL	33
ITS FIR-TOPPED HURST ITS FARMS ITS QUIET FIELDS •	•	269 THYRSIS	217
IN SOME DARK FIR-TREES SHADOW AMID ROCKS • • •	•	373 MEROPE	1167
HANGD UPON A BRANCHING FIR • • • • • •	• •	433 EMPEDOCLES II	148
IN MOSS AND GORSE AND SHINING FIR • • • • •	•	483 ROME-SICKNESS	8

FIRE

WILL THE FIRE JOY HATH WASTED • • • • • •	• •	30 NEW SIRENS	133
WATCHERS FOR A PURER FIRE • • • • • • • •	•	31 NEW SIRENS	140
AND CALL THIS HURRYING FEVER GENEROUS FIRE • • •	•	37 YOUTHS AGIT	12
WHO WITH NUMB BLACKEND FINGERS MAKES HER FIRE	•	70 SOHRAB RUSTUM	304
FIRE TO THE WOOD AND SEND HIM OUT TO SEA • • •	•	96 BALDER DEAD 1	44
ON FREAS HEARTH FEED HIGH THE SACRED FIRE • • •	•	97 BALDER DEAD 1	90
BEGAN AGAIN TO HEAP THE SACRED FIRE • • • •	•	100 BALDER DEAD 1	196
UPON MY SHIP AND BURN MY CORPSE WITH FIRE • •	•	103 BALDER DEAD 1	297
OF THE HEAPD WOOD AND BURN HIS CORPSE WITH FIRE	•	115 BALDER DEAD 3	54
THEN THEY PUT FIRE TO THE WOOD AND THOR • • •	•	118 BALDER DEAD 3	175
THE BREEZE AND FILLD THE SAILS AND BLEW THE FIRE	•	118 BALDER DEAD 3	184
SOON WITH A ROARING ROSE THE MIGHTY FIRE • • •	•	118 BALDER DEAD 3	186
DROVE ON ABLAZE ABOVE HER HULL WITH FIRE • • •	•	119 BALDER DEAD 3	192
FARTHER AND FARTHER LIKE AN EYE OF FIRE • • •	•	119 BALDER DEAD 3	199
AND AS IN A DECAYING WINTER-FIRE • • • • •	•	119 BALDER DEAD 3	203
THOU SENTST AND FETCHEDST FIRE AND MADEST LIGHTS	•	121 BALDER DEAD 3	263
A FIRE OF WITHERD FURZE WHICH BOYS HAVE LIT	•	124 BALDER DEAD 3	361
SOFT WHO IS THAT STANDS BY THE DYING FIRE • • •	•	130 TRISTRAM 1	7
GLEAMS SO RICH IN THE LIGHT OF THE FIRE • • •	•	131 TRISTRAM 1	25
WITH A FIRE IN HIS BRAIN • • • • • • •	•	136 TRISTRAM 1	187
IS MY PAGE HERE COME TURN ME TO THE FIRE • • •	•	139 TRISTRAM 1	298
AND FRIENDS ME IN THE PIT OF FIRE • • • • •	•	158 SAINT BRANDAN	64
WHO ORDERD THAT THEIR LONGINGS FIRE • • • •	•	182 TO MARG CONT	19
HE SAW A FIRE IN HIS DISCIPLES EYES • • • •	•	237 PROGRESS	2
BUT GUARD THE FIRE WITHIN • • • • • • •	•	237 PROGRESS	28
QUENCH NOT THE FIRE WITHIN • • • • • • •	•	237 PROGRESS	V 28
THE FIRE WHICH IN THE HEART RESIDES • • • •	•	241 MORALITY	2
THE FIRE THAT IN THE HEART RESIDES • • • •	•	241 MORALITY	V 2
A THIRST TO SPEND OUR FIRE AND RESTLESS FORCE	•	246 BURIED LIFE	49
ELSE HADST THOU SPENT LIKE OTHER MEN THY FIRE	•	259 SCHOLAR-GIPSY	154
THAT WORLD-FAMED SON OF FIRE SHE WHO SANK • • •	•	285 HAWORTH CHURCH	97
BUT SOULS TEMPERD WITH FIRE • • • • • •	•	291 RUGBY CHAPEL	159
AND PURGED ITS FAITH AND TRIMMD ITS FIRE • • •	•	301 GRANDE CHARTR	68
AND PRUND ITS FAITH AND QUENCHD ITS FIRE • • •	•	301 GRANDE CHARTR	V 68
IN SHEETS OF SCATHING FIRE • • • • • •	•	319 OBERMANN MORE	202
THAT GLOW OF CENTRAL FIRE IS DONE • • • • •	•	320 OBERMANN MORE	221
CONSUMED OUR HEART WITH THIRST LIKE FIRE • • •	•	323 OBERMANN MORE	315
THE GLOW OF CENTRAL FIRE IS DONE • • • • •	•	320 OBERMANN MORE	V 221
FIXED IN OUR SOUL A THIRST LIKE FIRE • • • •	•	323 OBERMANN MORE	V 315
CONSUMD OUR SOUL WITH THIRST LIKE FIRE • • •	•	323 OBERMANN MORE	V 315
ROSE AND WITH FIRE AND SWORD ASSAILED MY HOUSE	•	340 MEROPE	344
IF WITH NO RAGE NO FIRE OF RIGHTEOUS HATE • •	•	366 MEROPE	1011
COME LIGHTNING PASSION THAT WITH FOOT OF FIRE	•	367 MEROPE	1060
A CRAVEN MOB BUT A DEVOURING FIRE • • • •	•	383 MEROPE	1361
IF IN THIS FEEBLE BOSOM SUCH A FIRE • • • •	•	387 MEROPE	1470
AGLOW WITH ANGRY FIRE TO KEEP US TWAIN •	•	395 MEROPE	1736
IS THY FIRE-SCATHED ARM STILL RASH • • • •	•	430 EMPEDOCLES II	50
HEAT TO FIRE • • • • • • • • • • •	•	439 EMPEDOCLES II	335
OR WITH THE NIMBLE RADIANT LIFE OF FIRE • • •	•	439 EMPEDOCLES II	344

FIRE   (CONTINUED)
        AND FIRE REPEL US FROM ITS LIVING WAVES   .   .   .   .   439 EMPEDOCLES II   363
        LEAP AND ROAR THOU SEA OF FIRE   .   .   .   .   441 EMPEDOCLES II   411
        OR WITH THE ACTIVE RADIANT LIFE OF FIRE   .   .   .   .   439 EMPEDOCLES II   V 344
        WHILE TONGUES OF FIRE ON COIGN AND CARVING PLAY   .   .   445 WESTMIN ABBEY   36
        AND SAW HER BABE AMIDST THE FIRE AND SCREAMD   .   .   446 WESTMIN ABBEY   93
        PLUCKD FROM THE FIRE THE CHILD AND LAID HIM DOWN .   .   447 WESTMIN ABBEY   95
        POETS FIRE GETS FAINT AND LOW   .   .   .   .   454 POOR MATTHIAS   78
        PERCHANCE THAT SOLEMN SIGHT MIGHT QUENCH THE FIRE   .   469 ALARIC AT ROME   177
        THE SOLDIER KINDLED AT HIS WORDS OF FIRE   .   .   .   .   476 CROMWELL   153
        A HEART OF ICE A SOUL OF FIRE   .   .   .   .   481 DESTINY   6
        THERE SATE FIFTY MEN IN THE RUDDY LIGHT OF THE FIRE   HOMER TRANS   4
        WHILE THEIR MASTERS SATE BY THE FIRE AND WAITED   HOMER TRANS   6
            FOR MORNING

FIRED
        FIRED THEIR RINGING SHOT AND PASSD   .   .   .   .   .   .   215 LAST WORD   11

FIREPLACE
        SHE LEFT THE GLEAM-LIT FIREPLACE   .   .   .   .   .   .   140 TRISTRAM 1   315
        AT THIS HUGE GLEAM-LIT FIREPLACE   .   .   .   .   .   .   148 TRISTRAM 2   158
        AT THE HUGE GLEAM-LIT FIREPLACE   .   .   .   .   .   .   148 TRISTRAM 2   V 158

FIRES
        WHOSE YOUTH IN THE FIRES OF ANGUISH HATH DIED   .   .   20 MODERN SAPPHO   28
        THE DINGY TENTS ARE PITCHD THE FIRES   .   .   .   .   .   55 RESIGNATION   116
        AS OF A GREAT ASSEMBLY LOOSED AND FIRES   .   .   .   .   86 SOHRAB RUSTUM   869
        RUDDY IN THE FIRES LIGHT   .   .   .   .   131 TRISTRAM 1   316
        QUENCH THEN THE ALTAR FIRES OF YOUR OLD GODS   .   .   237 PROGRESS   V 27
        CATCHES THE WESTERING SUNS LAST FIRES   .   .   .   .   274 STANZAS CARNAC   24
        ARDENT UNQUENCHABLE FIRES   .   .   .   .   288 RUGBY CHAPEL   74
        LIKE US THE LIGHTNING-FIRES   .   .   .   .   420 EMPEDOCLES I 2   247
        TO ETNAS LIPAREAN SISTER-FIRES   .   .   .   .   .   .   438 EMPEDOCLES II   313
        IN FIRES UNDYING OER THE GUILTY HEAD   .   .   .   .   .   463 ALARIC AT ROME   28
        BETWEEN THAT AND THE SHIPS THE TROJANS NUMEROUS FIRES   HOMER TRANS   2
        IN THE PLAIN THERE WERE KINDLED A THOUSAND   HOMER TRANS   3
            FIRES BY EACH ONE

FIRM
        LABORIOUS PERSEVERING SERIOUS FIRM   .   .   .   .   .   5 DUKE WELLINGTON   10
        ITS STEP SO FIRM ITS EYE SO BRIGHT   .   .   .   .   .   21 YOUTH AND CALM   10
        ITS STEP SO FIRM ITS EYES SO BRIGHT .   .   .   .   .   21 YOUTH AND CALM   V 10
        LEAVES US FIRM TO NOTHING LONG   .   .   .   .   .   .   24 MEMORY-PICTURE   V 58
        AND WE PLEAD AS FIRM ADHERENCE   .   .   .   .   .   .   28 NEW SIRENS   V 59
        FIRM HARNESSD BY THE MANE A CHIEF   .   .   .   .   .   191 STRAYED REVEL   188
        FIRM TO THEIR MARK NOT SPENT ON OTHER THINGS   .   .   260 SCHOLAR-GIPSY   163
        ZEALOUS BENEFICENT FIRM   .   .   .   .   287 RUGBY CHAPEL   43
        CHEERFUL AND HELPFUL AND FIRM   .   .   .   .   .   .   290 RUGBY CHAPEL   139
        AND VALIANT HEART OF YOUTH OR MANHOODS FIRM   .   .   335 MEROPE   157
        GRASPING FIRM IN HIS HAND   .   .   .   .   342 MEROPE   397
        SUSPICION GRAVE I SEE BUT NO FIRM PROOF   .   .   .   365 MEROPE   994
        SAGACIOUS MEN OF IRON WATCHFUL FIRM   .   .   .   .   381 MEROPE   1304
        WHO DWELL ON A FIRM BASIS OF CONTENT   .   .   .   .   436 EMPEDOCLES II   260

FIRMER
        THOUGH ROUND THY FIRMER MANHOOD CAST   .   .   .   .   323 OBERMANN MORE   307

FIRS
        ITS FIRS AND AFAR ROSE THE PEAKS   .   .   .   .   .   229 YOUTH OF NATURE   39
        UP THROUGH THE TALL DARK FIRS   .   .   .   .   .   .   297 HEINES GRAVE   156
        ABOVE HIS SUN-WARMD FIRS   .   .   .   .   313 OBERMANN MORE   34
        FORTUNATE FIRS WHO NEVER THINK   .   .   .   .   .   .   483 ROME-SICKNESS   9
        HOW FIRS LESS CURST BY FORTUNES FROWN   .   .   .   .   483 ROME-SICKNESS   10

FIRST
        FROM FIRST YOUTH TESTED UP TO EXTREME OLD AGE   .   .   2 TO A FRIEND   10
        WHEN THE FIRST ROSE FLUSH WAS STEEPING   .   .   .   .   31 NEW SIRENS   143
        AT FIRST IMAGINED LAY   .   .   .   .   45 IN UTRUMQUE PAR   2
        HERE WHENCE THE EYE FIRST SEES FAR DOWN   .   .   .   55 RESIGNATION   92
        THEIR CHILDREN AS WHEN FIRST THEY CAME   .   .   .   .   55 RESIGNATION   119
        AND THE FIRST GREY OF MORNING FILLD THE EAST   .   .   61 SOHRAB RUSTUM   1
        FROM THE STREAMS BRINK THE SPOT WHERE FIRST A BOAT .   61 SOHRAB RUSTUM   18
        THOU KNOWST IF SINCE FROM ADER-BAIJAN FIRST   .   .   62 SOHRAB RUSTUM   42
        WHO LOVE THEE BUT MUST PRESS FOR EVER FIRST   .   .   63 SOHRAB RUSTUM   68
        FIRST WITH BLACK SHEEP-SKIN CAPS AND WITH LONG SPEARS   64 SOHRAB RUSTUM   118
        FIRST A LIGHT CLOUD OF HORSE TARTARS THEY SEEMD   .   .   65 SOHRAB RUSTUM   137
        WHAT NEWS BUT SIT DOWN FIRST AND EAT AND DRINK   .   .   67 SOHRAB RUSTUM   206
        STREAKD WITH ITS FIRST GREY HAIRS HOPE FILLED HIS SOUL   71 SOHRAB RUSTUM   340
        AND LABOURING BREATH FIRST RUSTUM STRUCK THE SHIELD   75 SOHRAB RUSTUM   491
        BUT FIRST HE WOULD CONVINCE HIS STUBBORN FOE   .   .   80 SOHRAB RUSTUM   653
        WHEN FIRST I SAW THEE AND THY HEART SPOKE TOO   .   .   82 SOHRAB RUSTUM   712
        FIRST TO THE ONE THEN TO THE OTHER MOVED   .   .   .   82 SOHRAB RUSTUM   733
        SHOULD FIRST HAVE ROTTED ON THEIR NIMBLE JOINTS   .   .   83 SOHRAB RUSTUM   739
        AND THE FIRST RAYS OF MORNING STREAKD THE EAST   .   .   61 SOHRAB RUSTUM   V 1
        THOU KNOWEST IF SINCE FROM ADER-BAIJAN FIRST   .   .   62 SOHRAB RUSTUM   V 42
        WHEN FIRST THEY BORE THY MASTER TO THIS FIELD   .   .   83 SOHRAB RUSTUM   V 740
        FOR FIRST THOU BAREST ME WITH BLINDED EYES .   .   .   98 BALDER DEAD 1   96
        BUT HE WHOM FIRST THOU MEETEST WHEN THOU COMST   .   .   100 BALDER DEAD 1   189
        BUT THERE WAS ONE THE FIRST OF ALL THE GODS   .   .   101 BALDER DEAD 1   220
        BUT THEY WENT ODIN FIRST THE REST BEHIND   .   .   .   105 BALDER DEAD 2   35
        AND THUS BESPAKE HIM FIRST THE SOLEMN QUEEN   .   .   110 BALDER DEAD 2   179

FIRST   (CONTINUED)
        AND LOK THE FATHER OF THE SERPENT FIRST   • • • •   113 BALDER DEAD 3   4
        FIRST DROVE HIM FROM ME INTO DISTANT LANDS • • • •   116 BALDER DEAD 3   108
        AND CAME DOWN MOANING TO THE SEA FIRST SQUALLS • •   118 BALDER DEAD 3   182
        ME AND MY WORDS THOUGH THOU BE FIRST IN HEAVEN • •   121 BALDER DEAD 3   283
        SHE GREETED THEM THE FIRST AND LAUGHD AND SAID • •   123 BALDER DEAD 3   336
        THAT PROUD FIRST ISEULT CORNWALLS QUEEN   • • • •   132 TRISTRAM 1   58
        BUT PLEDGE ME IN IT FIRST FOR COURTESY   • • • •   133 TRISTRAM 1   101
        THAT FIRST ISEULT PRINCESS BRIGHT   • • • •   134 TRISTRAM 1   126
        ONE LAST KISS FIRST TIS VAIN TO HORSE AWAY • • • •   135 TRISTRAM 1   169
        AND PLEDGE ME IN IT FIRST FOR COURTESY   • • • •   133 TRISTRAM 1   V 101
        ONE APRIL WHEN THE WARM DAYS FIRST BEGAN   • • • •   154 TRISTRAM 3   160
        FIRST MEETS THE FRINGING HEATH AT ONCE ALL ROUND • •   TRISTRAM 3   V 14
        FIRST LEAVES THE FRINGING HEATH AT ONCE ALL ROUND   TRISTRAM 3   V 14
        FIRST MEETS THE ENCIRCLING HEATH AT ONCE ALL ROUND   TRISTRAM 3   V 14
        FIRST LEAVES THE ENCIRCLING HEATH AT ONCE ALL ROUND   TRISTRAM 3   V 14
        IT WAS THE FIRST AFTER I CAME   • • • • • • • •   157 SAINT BRANDAN   30
        WHERE MORN FIRST APPEARS   • • • • • • • • • •   177 PARTING   86
        WHEN THE WHITE DAWN FIRST   • • • • • • • •   186 STRAYED REVEL   24
        MUST VISIT FIRST THEM TOO AND MAKE THEM PALE   • •   193 STRAYED REVEL   246
        OF ARGO FIRST   • • • • • • • • • • • •   193 STRAYED REVEL   259
        BIRTH-GODDESS AND THE AUSTERE FATES FIRST GAVE • •   195 FRAG ANTIGONE   10
        FIRST TO THE LIGHT AND MARK   • • • • • • • •   195 FRAG ANTIGONE   13
        SEE PULSING WITH THE FIRST-BORN STAR   • • • • •   218 BACCHANALIA 1   17
        GIVES THEN THE FIRST THE FAIREST PLACE   • • •   227 EPILOG LAOCOON   208
        SINCE FIRST THE WORLD BEGAN   • • • • • • •   238 PROGRESS   V 40
        WHETHER HE FIRST SEES LIGHT   • • • • • •   252 FUTURE   13
        SINCE FIRST THY STORY RAN THROUGH OXFORD HALLS • •   259 SCHOLAR-GIPSY   132
        HERE TOO OUR SHEPHERD-PIPES WE FIRST ASSAYD   • •   263 THYRSIS   35
        ARE FLOWERS FIRST OPEND ON SICILIAN AIR   • • •   265 THYRSIS   89
        FIRST IN FICTION HAD SINCE   • • • • • •   280 HAWORTH CHURCH   15
        FIRST TO THE LIVING WE PAY   • • • • • • •   281 HAWORTH CHURCH   34
        AND SECOND FATHER FROM THAT HOUR WHEN FIRST   • •   331 MEROPE   30
        AND THOU ART POLYPHONTES FIRST HIS FRIEND   • • • •   335 MEROPE   185
        FOR FROM THE DAY WHEN THE FIRST   • • • • •   343 MEROPE   420
        WHERE FIRST THE CHASE PLUNGED IN THE BAY IS SMOOTH   358 MEROPE   819
        WHERE FIRST THE STAG TOOK WATER FLOATED STILL   • •   358 MEROPE   844
        FIRST CITY FOUNDED ON THE EARTH BY MEN   • • •   359 MEROPE   849
        FIRST HEARD OR IN ITS FUTURE ISSUE SHOWN   • • •   359 MEROPE   865
        GO THOU THE FIRST AND USHER IN THY LORD   • • •   373 MEROPE   1190
        MY FIRST STROKE OF REVENGE HAD NEARLY FALLEN   • •   377 MEROPE   1224
        FROM THE FIRST-WROUGHT VENGEANCE IS BORN   • • • •   379 MEROPE   1251
        AT LEAST IF THOU WILT TRUST THEM TRY THEM FIRST • •   381 MEROPE   1319
        FIRST RALLY THE MESSENIANS TO THY CAUSE   • • •   382 MEROPE   1322
        AT THIS FIRST MEETING AFTER ABSENCE LONG   • • •   386 MEROPE   1452
        PASSIONS FIRST FURIOUS LONGING TO IMBRUE   • • •   387 MEROPE   1467
        HER SWORD WILL BE THE FIRST TO BID IT FALL • • •   388 MEROPE   1504
        BUT THAT SINCE FIRST THE BLACK AND FRUITFUL EARTH   389 MEROPE   1536
        BE THEIR FIRST-FOUNDED ORDER STRICT MAINTAIND   • •   390 MEROPE   1565
        FIRST FOR OUR UNION TRUST ME TWIXT US TWO   • • •   395 MEROPE   1733
        SO LOOKD HE WHEN TO STENYCLAROS FIRST   • • •   403 MEROPE   1971
        FIRST WORK AFTER SUCH VICTORY LET US GO   • • •   405 MEROPE   2017
        IF THEIR FIRST-FOUNDED ORDER BE MAINTAIND   • • •   390 MEROPE   V1565
        CROUCH IN THE WOOD FIRST TILL THE MULES HAVE PASSD   408 EMPEDOCLES I 1   50
        WHEN FIRST HE SOJOURND WITH PEISIANAX   • • • •   408 EMPEDOCLES I 1   73
        A CORD THE GODS FIRST SLUNG   • • • • • • •   415 EMPEDOCLES I 2   78
        FOR FROM THE FIRST FAINT MORN   • • • • • • •   418 EMPEDOCLES I 2   167
        WHOLLY FORGET THEIR FIRST SAD LIFE AND HOME   • •   427 EMPEDOCLES I 2   458
        FIRST HYMN THEY THE FATHER   • • • • • • • •   443 EMPEDOCLES II   461
        WHEREIN AT FIRST WAS DIGHT   • • • • • • • •   446 WESTMIN ABBEY   62
        AND LIGHTS FAIR NURSLING STUPOR FIRST INVADES   • •   448 WESTMIN ABBEY   129
        WHEREWITH AT FIRST WAS DIGHT   • • • • • • •   446 WESTMIN ABBEY   V 62
        AND LIGHTS FAIR NURSLING LANGUOR FIRST INVADES • •   448 WESTMIN ABBEY   V 129
        WHICH MAY BE THE FIRST TO DIE   • • • • • • •   454 POOR MATTHIAS   75
        FIRST THE INEVITABLE WAY   • • • • • • • • •   454 POOR MATTHIAS   80
        BIRDS WERE BORN THE FIRST OF THINGS   • • • • •   456 POOR MATTHIAS   132
        AND THE FIRST SORROW WHICH IS CHILDHOODS GRAVE • •   474 CROMWELL   82
        THEIR FIRST GREEN MUFFLE ON THE GROUND   • • • •   484 ROME-SICKNESS   16
        ALWAYS AND ALWAYS FIGHTING AMONG THE FIRST   HOMER TRANS   18
            OF THE TROJANS

FISH
        TO BUILD THEM BOATS FISH FROM THE FLOODED RIVERS • •   73 SOHRAB RUSTUM   411
        TO SAW THEM PLANKS FISH FROM THE FLOODED RIVERS • •   73 SOHRAB RUSTUM   V 411

FISHER
        AND DEAR AS THE WET FISHER TO THE EYES   • • • •   69 SOHRAB RUSTUM   V 284
        THE FISHER AWED OBEYS   • • • • • • • • • • •   445 WESTMIN ABBEY   27
        O SAXON FISHER THOU HAST HAD WITH THEE   • • • •   445 WESTMIN ABBEY   44
        THE FISHER FROM THE LAKE OF GALILEE   • • • • • •   445 WESTMIN ABBEY   45
        ONLY THAT PRIMAL GUEST THE FISHER SAW   • • • •   445 WESTMIN ABBEY   59

FISHERMEN
        SHELL LIGHT HER SILVER LAMP WHICH FISHERMEN   • •   151 TRISTRAM 3   79
        SCANND OF TRAMPS AND FISHERMEN • • • • • • • •   457 POOR MATTHIAS   187

FISHERS
        NIORD THE GOD OF STORMS WHOM FISHERS KNOW   • • • •   122 BALDER DEAD 3   323
        FISHERS WHO LIVE ON THE LAKE-SIDE TO LAUNCH   • •   358 MEROPE   837
        THEIR CRAFT THE FISHERS LEAVE   • • • • • • • •   444 WESTMIN ABBEY   12
        AND BY THE FISHERS BARK   • • • • • • • • •   445 WESTMIN ABBEY   42

FISHING
    THE LANTERNS OF THE FISHING-BOATS AT SEA   • • • •   130 TRISTRAM 1   6

FISTS
    AND BEND THEIR LITTLE FISTS AND RATE THE SENSELESS   421 EMPEDOCLES I 2   276
       GROUND

FIT
    THIS OR SOME TYRANNOUS SINGLE THOUGHT SOME FIT   • •   153 TRISTRAM 3   127
    MYRTLE AND ROSE FIT THE YOUNG • • • • • • •   282 HAWORTH CHURCH V
    FIT DENIZEN THE LAMPLESS UNDER-WORLD • • • • • •   367 MEROPE   1031
    A FIT ALLS OVER • • • • • • • • • • •   460 KAISER DEAD   64

FITFUL
    MANS FITFUL UPROAR MINGLING WITH HIS TOIL   • • • •   1 QUIET WORK   10
    FITFUL EARTH-MURMUR • • • • • • • •   194 STRAYED REVEL   284
    OF FITFUL DREAM AND FEVERISH POWER • • • • •   270 MEMORIAL VERSES   24

FITS
    IF THE FITS OF JOY WERE LONGER • • • • • • •   29 NEW SIRENS   109
    FITS OF JOY AND FITS OF PAIN • • • • • • •   33 NEW SIRENS   206
    FITS OF JOY AND FITS OF PAIN • • • • • • •   33 NEW SIRENS   206
    RATHER IT FITS YOU HAVING WEPT YOUR HOUR • • • •   96 BALDER DEAD 1   34
    THESE MUSING FITS IN THE GREEN WOOD • • • • •   138 TRISTRAM 1   247
    OUR LABOURD PUNY PASSION-FITS • • • • • • •   202 URANIA   14
    AND SUCH AS FITS A ROYAL HOUSE TO SHOW • • •   359 MEROPE   871
    SAYS IT FITS THAT I REHEARSE • • • • • • •   453 POOR MATTHIAS   17

FIVE
    BUT YESTERMORN FIVE TROOPS OF DEAD PASSD BY • •   107 BALDER DEAD 2   104
    TO DIE AT THIRTY-FIVE IN BABYLON • • • •   154 TRISTRAM 3   150
    THE HOT WIND FEVERD HIM FIVE-FOLD • • • • •   157 SAINT BRANDAN   48
    HE PARCELLD OUT IN FIVE CONFEDERATE STATES • • •   337 MEROPE   249

FIX
    OR WHAT WE FIX WITH FOREIGN POWERS • • • • •   47 HORATIAN ECHO   3
    POWER FAILS THE MAN HIMSELF TO FIX DISTINCTLY • •   352 MEROPE   649
    FIX HIM THE AUTHOR OF MY DEATH I KNOW NOT • • •   379 MEROPE   1273
    WHO BADE HIM LOOSE HIS BOAT AND FIX HIS OAR • •   444 WESTMIN ABBEY   24
    WOULD FIX OUR FAVOURITE ON THE SCENE • • • • •   451 GEISTS GRAVE   38
    AND I WHISPERD FIX ON HIM • • • • • • • •   458 POOR MATTHIAS   195

FIXD
    AND CHECKD HIS RANKS AND FIXD THEM WHERE THEY STOOD   65 SOHRAB RUSTUM   147
    THE ANGUISH OF THE DEEP-FIXD SPEAR GREW FIERCE • •   80 SOHRAB RUSTUM   650
    AND FIXD THEM FEEBLY ON HIS FATHERS FACE • • •   86 SOHRAB RUSTUM   852
    NOT KNEELING STERNLY FIXD HE STOOD • • • • •   90 SICK KING BOKH   95
    FIXD ON THEIR MOTHERS FACE IN WIDE SURPRISE • •   151 TRISTRAM 3   47
    FIXD FULL ON MERLINS FACE HER STATELY PRIZE • •   154 TRISTRAM 3   178
    FIXD ON THEIR MOTHERS FACE IN WIDE SURPRIZE • •   TRISTRAM 3   V 47
    FIXD YESTERDAY AND TEN TIMES CHANGED SINCE THEN • •   389 MEROPE   1547
    OF DYNASTIES LONG-FIXD AND HONOURD LONG • • •   390 MEROPE   1562
    HIS FIXD CONDITION AND PERPETUAL WALK • • • •   404 MEROPE   1993
    FIXD HIM THE AUTHOR OF MY DEATH I KNEW NOT • • •   379 MEROPE   V1273
    WHOSE HABIT OF THOUGHT IS FIXD WHO WILL NOT CHANGE   437 EMPEDOCLES II   266

FIXED
    FIXED IN OUR SOUL A THIRST LIKE FIRE • • • • • •   323 OBERMANN MORE V 315

FIXING
    FIXING WITH A MUTE REGARD • • • • • • • •   456 POOR MATTHIAS   121

FIXT
    LEAVES US FIXT TO NOTHING LONG • • • • • •   24 MEMORY-PICTURE   58
    BUT IN HIS BREAST STOOD FIXT THE FATAL BOUGH • •   95 BALDER DEAD 1   5
    AND HE WENT IN AND SHUT THE DOOR AND FIXT • • •   102 BALDER DEAD 1   251
    THE MAST THEY FIXT AND HOISTED UP THE SAILS • •   118 BALDER DEAD 3   174
    FOR ALL WHICH HATH BEEN FIXT WAS FIXT BY THEE • •   121 BALDER DEAD 3   254
    FOR ALL WHICH HATH BEEN FIXT WAS FIXT BY THEE • •   121 BALDER DEAD 3   254
    THEY FIXT THE MAST AND HOISTED UP THE SAILS • •   118 BALDER DEAD 3 V 174
    FIXT HER SLIGHT HANDS CLASPD ON HER LAP THEN RISE   152 TRISTRAM 3   91

FLAG
    TIS HE TIS THEIR FLAG SHOOTING ROUND BY THE TREES   20 MODERN SAPPHO   30
    AND FLAG-LEAVED IRIS-FLOWERS • • • • • • •   191 STRAYED REVEL   170
    AND WE SHALL FEEL OUR POWERS OF EFFORT FLAG • •   440 EMPEDOCLES II   387
    ERE IT FLAG ERE THE MISTS • • • • • • •   441 EMPEDOCLES II   413
    TO FLAG AND FEEL HIS NARROWING SPAN • • • • •   459 KAISER DEAD   38
    THE DOOM PRONOUNCED THE BATTLE-FLAG UNFURLED • •   465 ALARIC AT ROME   93

FLAGGD
    AND HE WHO FLAGGD NOT IN THE EARTHLY STRIFE • •   172 IMMORTALITY   11

FLAGGING
    INSPIRE THIS COWARD HEART THIS FLAGGING ARM • •   368 MEROPE   1066

FLAGS
    ERE THEIR BOAT-MUSIC SOUND ERE THEIR BROIDERD   19 MODERN SAPPHO   8
       FLAGS GLEAM
    AND PLUCKING UP THE MARBLE FLAGS • • • • • •   95 SICK KING BOKH   227
    AND TEARING UP THE MARBLE FLAGS • • • • • •   95 SICK KING BOKH V 227

FLAGS   (CONTINUED)
        WE TOO SIGH THAT SHE FLAGS . . . . 294 HEINES GRAVE   76

FLAME
        IN DARK KNOTS CROUCH ROUND THE WILD FLAME . . . . 55 RESIGNATION   118
        SHARP QUIVERING TONGUES OF FLAME SHOT OUT AND LEAPT 119 BALDER DEAD 3   188
        SEES SUDDENLY A SPIRE OF FLAME SHOOT UP . . . . 119 BALDER DEAD 3   V
        TREMBLE AND THEIR CHEEKS BE FLAME . . . . . . 135 TRISTRAM 1   148
        CONSUMED HER BEAUTY LIKE A FLAME . . . . 147 TRISTRAM 2   134
        TO RUE MY GUILT IN ENDLESS FLAME . . . . 157 SAINT BRANDAN   32
        WITH FURTIVE STEP AND CHEEK OF FLAME . . . . . 278 SOUTHERN NIGHT   102
        WHICH WITH ITS FUSING FLAME . . . . 320 OBERMANN MORE   222
        THAT THE FLAME TOWERD ON HIGH TO THE HEAVEN . . 399 MEROPE   1840
        ARE SHINING ON THOSE NAKED SLOPES LIKE FLAME . . 412 EMPEDOCLES I 2   6
        TYPHO SUCH RED JETS OF FLAME . . . . . . 430 EMPEDOCLES II   48
        NOTHING BUT A DEVOURING FLAME OF THOUGHT . . . 438 EMPEDOCLES II   329
        THICK BREAKS THE RED FLAME . . . . . . 441 EMPEDOCLES II   418
        QUICK BREAKS THE RED FLAME . . . . . . 441 EMPEDOCLES II   V 418
        AND THY TRANSFIGURED WALLS BE TOUCHD WITH FLAME . 449 WESTMIN ABBEY   178
        THREADED AND LIGHTEND BY A TRACK OF FLAME . . . 473 CROMWELL   60
        PYMS LOOK OF HATE AND STRAFFORDS GLANCE OF FLAME . 476 CROMWELL   164

FLAMES
        LO YON ORIENT HILL IN FLAMES . . . . 35 NEW SIRENS   260
        THEBES WAS BEHIND HIM IN FLAMES . . . . . . 229 YOUTH OF NATURE   41
        IN JUNE AND MANY A SCYTHE IN SUNSHINE FLAMES . . 257 SCHOLAR-GIPSY   92
        THE HILL BEHIND WHOSE RIDGE THE SUNSET FLAMES . . 263 THYRSIS   13
        BUT ALL NIGHT LONG AMID THE FLAMES HE LAY . . . 446 WESTMIN ABBEY   89

FLAMING
        AND FROM THE FLAMING WORLD WHERE MUSPEL REIGNS . . 121 BALDER DEAD 3   262
        AND ALL ARE MARSHALLD IN ONE FLAMING SQUARE . . 127 BALDER DEAD 3   480

FLANDERS
        OF FLANDERS TO THE STORIED RHINE . . . . . . 205 CALAIS SANDS   34
        OF FLANDERS TO THE ANCIENT RHINE . . . . . . 205 CALAIS SANDS   V 34

FLANKS
        WITH FLANKS A-TREMBLE AND HIS SLENDER TONGUE . . 114 BALDER DEAD 3   14
        HER PALFREYS FLANKS WERE MIRED AND BATHED IN SWEAT 154 TRISTRAM 3   171
        WITH STREAMING FLANKS AND HEADS . . . . . . 190 STRAYED REVEL   148
        THEIR SHINING FLANKS THEIR LIQUID EYES . . . . 223 EPILOG LAOCOON   54
        PAST SONCHAUDS PINY FLANKS I GAZE . . . . . . 324 OBERMANN MORE   337
        AND SONCHAUDS PINY FLANKS I GAZE . . . . . . 324 OBERMANN MORE   V 337

FLAPS
        FLAPS THE GHOSTLIKE TAPESTRY . . . . 147 TRISTRAM 2   151
        WE SEE THE FLAPS OF THY LARGE EARS . . . . . 451 GEISTS GRAVE   49

FLARD
        SO FLARD IN THE FAR DARKNESS BALDERS PYRE . . . 119 BALDER DEAD 3   V 200

FLARED
        BUT FAINTER AS THE STARS ROSE HIGH IT FLARED . . 119 BALDER DEAD 3   201

FLARES
        AGAINST THE WOLVES AND ALL NIGHT LONG IT FLARES . 119 BALDER DEAD 3   V

FLARING
        BLOODY NEATH THE FLARING SCONCES . . . . . . 14 CHURCH BROU 1   51

FLASH
        LET YOUR BROAD LAMPS FLASH THE BRIGHTNESS . . . 32 NEW SIRENS   177
        FREELY DID THEY FLASH THEIR SPLENDOUR . . . . 35 NEW SIRENS   257
        AND SPRANG ASIDE QUICK AS A FLASH THE SPEAR . . 73 SOHRAB RUSTUM   403
        FLASH ON HER WHITE ARMS STILL . . . . 146 TRISTRAM 2   111
        FLASH THROUGH HER PURE IMMORTAL FRAME . . . . 181 ISOLATION MARG   21
        WHEREFORE DO THY NOSTRILS FLASH . . . . . . 430 EMPEDOCLES II   46

FLASHD
        FLASHD ONCE LIKE FALLING STREAMS WE ROSE WE GAZED 25 DREAM   29
        FLASHD IN THE SILVER SCONCES LIGHT . . . . . 146 TRISTRAM 2   113
        WHERE THE SUNS RAYS STRUCK FULL AND FLASHD BACK KEEN   TRISTRAM 3   V 21
        FLASHD FROM THY SOUL UPON THINE INWARD EAR . . . 472 CROMWELL   28

FLASHING
        WHEN THE FLASHING LIGHTS ARE FADING . . . . . 33 NEW SIRENS   V 213
        AS FLASHING AS MOSES FELT . . . . 253 FUTURE   45
        PENNON AND PLUME AND FLASHING LANCE . . . . . 305 GRANDE CHARTR   178
        THE BANNERS FLASHING THROUGH THE TREES . . . . 305 GRANDE CHARTR   187
        NOW TOLD BUT IN ONE FLASHING INSTANT PASSD . . . 358 MEROPE   828
        WHEN THE FLASHING TORCHES APPEAR . . . . . . 360 MEROPE   896
        FLASHING IN THE DANCES WHIRLS . . . . 434 EMPEDOCLES II   182

FLASHT
        FLASHT ON THE RUDE BARBARIANS WILD ARRAY . . . 464 ALARIC AT ROME   70

FLAT
        CLUSTERING LIKE BEE-HIVES ON THE LOW FLAT STRAND . . 61 SOHRAB RUSTUM   13

FLATS
    IN THE STILL NIGHT ACROSS THE STEAMING FLATS • • 12 MYCERINUS 126
    UNMOORD OUR SKIFF WHEN THROUGH THE WYTHAM FLATS • • 266 THYRSIS 123

FLATTER
    FLATTER THE PLAIN WHERE IT FLOWS • • • • • • 253 FUTURE 64

FLATTERER
    AH HARSH FLATTERER LET ALONE MY BEAUTY • • • • 143 TRISTRAM 2 21

FLATTERING
    WITH PLACE WITH HONOUR AND A FLATTERING CREW • • 268 THYRSIS 204

FLECKD
    MY MAN COMES RUNNING FLECKD WITH BLOOD • • • • 89 SICK KING BOKH 50
    OR WAS IT FROM SOME SUN-FLECKD MOUNTAIN-BROOK • • 175 PARTING 21

FLED
    IT CHANCED I KNOW NOT HOW MY DREAM WAS FLED • • EMERSONS ESSAYS V 8
    IT CHANCED I KNOW NOT HOW MY JOY WAS FLED • • • • EMERSONS ESSAYS V 8
    AS THOUGH MEN SPAKE OF LIFE A JOY WAS FLED • • • • EMERSONS ESSAYS V 8
    AND HIS CLEAR LAUGH FLED RINGING THROUGH THE GLOOM 12 MYCERINUS 113
    FACES THAT SMILED AND FLED • • • • • • • • 44 QUESTION 19
    UNWILLINGLY THE SPIRIT FLED AWAY • • • • • • 86 SOHRAB RUSTUM 854
    SAVE ONE BERGELMER HE ON SHIPBOARD FLED • • • 121 BALDER DEAD 3 272
    SHE SPAKE AND TO THE CAVERNS DEPTH SHE FLED • • 123 BALDER DEAD 3 355
    FOR THIS I DIED AND FLED BENEATH THE GLOOM • • • 124 BALDER DEAD 3 397
    BUT ALL I LEFT OF MY OWN ACT AND FLED • • • • 125 BALDER DEAD 3 405
    SHE FOLLOWS THE GAY WORLD WHOSE SWARMS HAVE FLED • 167 RACHEL 1 9
    FLED FLED AT ONCE BE ALL VESTIGE OF THEE • • • 206 SEPARATION 10
    FLED FLED AT ONCE BE ALL VESTIGE OF THEE • • • 206 SEPARATION 10
    AND WE SAY THAT REPOSE HAS FLED • • • • • 253 FUTURE 58
    THE GENERATIONS OF THY PEERS ARE FLED • • • • 259 SCHOLAR-GIPSY 155
    TO A BOON SOUTHERN COUNTRY HE IS FLED • • • • 268 THYRSIS 175
    SHE FLED HER PALACES • • • • • • • • 316 OBERMANN MORE 132
    WHEN BLOOD AND WARMTH WERE FLED • • • • 319 OBERMANN MORE 194
    THEN TO THE WILDERNESS I FLED • • • • • • 321 OBERMANN MORE 249
    WERE HUNTED OUT AND TO ACHAIA FLED • • • • 338 MEROPE 286
    FLED FOR YEARS AFTER OER THE FACE OF EARTH • • • 385 MEROPE 1423

FLEDDST
    THOU FLEDDST ME WHEN THE UNGENIAL EARTH • • • 315 OBERMANN MORE V 77

FLEDST
    THOU FLEDST ME WHEN THE UNGENIAL EARTH • • • • 315 OBERMANN MORE 77

FLEE
    MANY A FACE I SO LET FLEE • • • • • • • 23 MEMORY-PICTURE 13
    MANY A FACE I THEN LET FLEE • • • • • • • 23 MEMORY-PICTURE V 13
    RASH BOY MEN LOOK ON RUSTUMS FACE AND FLEE • • 72 SOHRAB RUSTUM 369
    THAT WAS BLISS TO MAKE MY SORROWS FLEE • • • 144 TRISTRAM 2 46
    THE WORDS ARE UTTERD AND THEY FLEE • • • • 224 EPILOG LAOCOON 90
    PANIC DESPAIR FLEE AWAY • • • • • • • • 292 RUGBY CHAPEL 197
    HAD BEEN TOO FAR TO FLEE • • • • • • 317 OBERMANN MORE 152
    WHERE PHILOCTETES PINED TAKE SHIP AND FLEE • • • 395 MEROPE 1747
    DO THY BLOODSHOT EYES STILL FLEE • • • • • 430 EMPEDOCLES II V 55

FLEECE
    BLACK GLOSSY CURLD THE FLEECE OF KARA-KUL • • • • 64 SOHRAB RUSTUM 101

FLEEING
    HIS FLEEING MOTHER • • • • • • • • • • • 393 MEROPE 1658

FLEES
    AND FLEES THE COMMON LIFE OF MEN • • • • • • 58 RESIGNATION 212

FLEEST
    BUT DOWN THOU FLEEST HERE AND LEAVST OUR SCOURGE • • 367 MEROPE 1050

FLEET
    MOST FLEET HE WAS BUT NOW HE WENT THE LAST • • • 101 BALDER DEAD 1 222
    SO SPEAKING THE FLEET-FOOTED HERMOD CAME • • • 102 BALDER DEAD 1 246
    AND THE FLEET-FOOTED HERMOD ANSWERD HER • • • 108 BALDER DEAD 2 111
    AND THE FLEET-FOOTED HERMOD MADE REPLY • • • • 126 BALDER DEAD 3 468
    HE SPAKE AND THE FLEET HERMOD THUS REPLIED • • • 128 BALDER DEAD 3 514
    THE FLEET DESPERATE HUNTER • • • • • • 393 MEROPE 1656
    SHOULD FLEET BEFORE US BUT TO MELT AWAY • • • 470 ALARIC AT ROME 212
    THEN FROM BENEATH THE YOKE THE FLEET HORSE HOMER TRANS 43
        XANTHUS ADDRESSED HIM

FLEETEST
    WHICH MEN SAY IS THE FLEETEST OF WINDS TIS HOMER TRANS 55
        THOU WHO ART FATED

FLEETING
    AND FLEETING THOUGHTS THAT ON THE LONELY WILD • • 473 CROMWELL 51
    WHEN MY FLEETING SHADOW PASSD FROM THEE • • • • 482 THEKLAS ANSWER 2

FLEETNESS
    COME LOOSE HANDS THE WINGED FLEETNESS • • • • 34 NEW SIRENS 251

FLEETS
    SURVEYS EACH HAPPY GROUP WHICH FLEETS   . . . .   57 RESIGNATION   166
    SURVEYS EACH HAPPY GROUP THAT FLEETS . . . . . .   57 RESIGNATION   V 166
    REGNER WHO SWEPT THE NORTHERN SEA WITH FLEETS   . .   117 BALDER DEAD 3   126

FLEMISH
    FLEMISH CARVERS LOMBARD GILDERS   . . . . . .   15 CHURCH BROU 1   95

FLESH
    NEW MESSES OF THE BOAR SERIMNERS FLESH   . . . .   97 BALDER DEAD 1   67
    AND THOU HAST FLESH AND COLOUR ON THY CHEEKS   . .   108 BALDER DEAD 2   107
    ALL NIGHT THEY ATE THE BOAR SERIMNERS FLESH   . .   119 BALDER DEAD 3   210
    BUT OF HIS FLESH AND MEMBERS THOU DIDST BUILD   . .   121 BALDER DEAD 3   260
    SWEET CHESTNUTS BARLEY-CAKES AND BOARS-FLESH DRIED   356 MEROPE   754
    INTO SOME BONDAGE OF THE FLESH OR MIND   . . . .   440 EMPEDOCLES II   374

FLEW
    THAT THEY FLEW THICK AND BRUISED HIM SORE   . . . .   91 SICK KING BOKH   122
    OF HEAVEN AND MIGHTILY AS WINGD HE FLEW   . . . .   113 BALDER DEAD 2   303
    TO PUSH THE SHIP THROUGH THE THICK SAND SPARKS FLEW   118 BALDER DEAD 3   177
    FLEW EVER TO THE DOOR   . . . .   146 TRISTRAM 2   122
    DAYS FLEW AH SOON I COULD DISCERN   . . . . . .   178 FAREWELL   13
    MUTE AS OF OLD DAYS FLEW . . . .   233 YOUTH OF MAN   39
    IN JOY THY LAST MORN FLEW ANON . . . .   460 KAISER DEAD   63

FLICKERD
    AND HIS CHILDS REASON FLICKERD AND DID DIE . . . .   166 PICT NEWSTEAD   6
    AND THE CHILDS REASON FLICKERD AND DID DIE . . . .   166 PICT NEWSTEAD   V   6

FLICKERING
    FLICKERING AND CIRCLING   . . . .   218 BACCHANALIA 1   22

FLIES
    YET AS THE WHEEL FLIES ROUND   . . . .   47 WORLD QUIETIST   17
    EACH MOMENT AS IT FLIES TO WHOM   . . . .   59 RESIGNATION   V 257
    AS THAT POOR BIRD FLIES HOME NOR KNOWS HIS LOSS   . .   78 SOHRAB RUSTUM   573
    THE FLIES A SUMMER-MURMUR MADE . . . .   222 EPILOG LAOCOON   41
    FROM BUSH TO BUSH THE CUCKOO FLIES   . . . . . .   274 STANZAS CARNAC   17
    A WHISPER THROUGH THE PALACE FLIES OF ONE   . . . .   361 MEROPE   914
    FLIES VICTORY WINGD AND JUSTICE RAISES THEN   . .   388 MEROPE   1503

FLIGHT
    WHERE EARTHLY VOICE CLIMBS NEVER WING THEIR FLIGHT   10 MYCERINUS   44
    HE STRAINS TO JOIN THEIR FLIGHT AND FROM HIS SHED   129 BALDER DEAD 3   563
    FORGOT HIS CRAFT AND HIS BEST WITS TOOK FLIGHT   .   155 TRISTRAM 3   182
    THY FLIGHT AND FEEL COME OVER THEE   . . . . . .   201 PHILOMELA   23
    SWEPT WITH CONFUSED ALARMS OF STRUGGLE AND FLIGHT   212 DOVER BEACH   36
    IF PARIS THAT BRIEF FLIGHT ALLOW   . . . . . .   321 OBERMANN MORE   269

FLIGHTS
    HIS HOUSE NOW MID THEIR BROKEN FLIGHTS OF STEPS   . .   86 SOHRAB RUSTUM   862

FLINCH
    THEIR MASTER FALLN THESE WILL NOT FLINCH BUT BAND   381 MEROPE   1306

FLING
    OF PEBBLES WHICH THE WAVES DRAW BACK AND FLING   . .   211 DOVER BEACH   10
    OF PEBBLES WHICH THE WAVES SUCK BACK AND FLING   . .   211 DOVER BEACH   V   10
    FLING THE FRESH HEAPS ABOUT   . . . .   218 BACCHANALIA 1   34
    FLING THE PILED SHEAVES ABOUT   . . . .   218 BACCHANALIA 1   V   34
    FLING THEIR WAVERING LIGHTS   . . . .   253 FUTURE   73
    FLING OFF THY CROWN SUPPOSED AT LAST SECURE   . .   395 MEROPE   1743
    OER FLOWERING PLAIN AND BLOSSOMD MEADOW FLING   . .   474 CROMWELL   91

FLINGING
    FLINGING ON THE MOUNTAIN-SOD   . . . .   433 EMPEDOCLES II   156

FLINTS
    WHICH CHEQUER AT YOUR FEET THE ILLUMINED FLINTS   . .   18 CHURCH BROU 3   29
    THAT CHEQUER AT YOUR FEET THE ILLUMINED FLINTS   . .   18 CHURCH BROU 3   V   29

FLINTY
    ALONG THE FLINTY FLOOR OF ASGARD STREETS   . . . .   102 BALDER DEAD 1   261

FLIT
    WHO ALL WILL FLIT LIKE EDDYING LEAVES AROUND   . .   100 BALDER DEAD 1   177
    WHERE IDLY FLIT ABOUT THE FEEBLE SHADES   . . . .   110 BALDER DEAD 2   182
    SOMETIMES A THRUSH FLIT OVERHEAD   . . . . . .   248 KENSINGTON GARD   11

FLITTED
    AND FLITTED DOWN THE FLOWERY TRACK   . . . . . .   184 TERRACE BERNE   19

FLITTEST
    OF THE DEEP INNER GLOOM BUT FLITTEST HERE   . . . .   124 BALDER DEAD 3   389

FLITTING
    FLITTING FAST ACROSS EACH MARBLE BROW   . . . . .   31 NEW SIRENS   162
    BUT WE TURN OUR EYES ARE FLITTING   . . . . . .   34 NEW SIRENS   241
    IN THEIR FLITTING LUSTRE VYING . . . .   131 TRISTRAM 1   27

FLOAT

THOU STRIKST TOO HARD THAT CLUB OF THINE WILL FLOAT	74	SOHRAB RUSTUM	427
HE SEES FLOAT PAST AN ICEBERG WHITE	156	SAINT BRANDAN	15
HE SEES FLOAT NEAR AN ICEBERG WHITE	156	SAINT BRANDAN	V 15
SILENT THE SWANS BESIDE US FLOAT	206	RIVER	3
FLOAT ON A ROLLING SEA	319	OBERMANN MORE	212
FLOAT IN A ROLLING SEA	319	OBERMANN MORE	V 212
AND CAROLS FLOAT ALONG THE HAPPY AIR	445	WESTMIN ABBEY	39
FLOAT THERE NOT VOICES ON THE MURMURING WIND	468	ALARIC AT ROME	164
FLOAT UP TO TELL OF AGES THAT ARE GONE	470	ALARIC AT ROME	208

FLOATED

BUT THE MAJESTIC RIVER FLOATED ON	86	SOHRAB RUSTUM	875
AND THE SHIP FLOATED ON THE WAVES AND ROCKD	118	BALDER DEAD 3	180
WHERE FIRST THE STAG TOOK WATER FLOATED STILL	358	MEROPE	844
CHILLD EVERY BUOYANT HOPE THAT FLOATED BY	474	CROMWELL	88

FLOATING

A FLOATING ISLE THICK-MATTED	190	STRAYED REVEL	154
BE HEARD FLOATING THROUGH HEAVEN AND FILL AGAIN	238	PROGRESS	35
COME AIRS AND FLOATING ECHOES AND CONVEY	247	BURIED LIFE	75
AND FLOATING HAIR	278	SOUTHERN NIGHT	108
BALMS FLOATING ON THY MOUNTAIN-AIR	309	OBERMANN	111
COME FLOATING UP FROM THE ABYSS OF YEARS	469	ALARIC AT ROME	176

FLOATS

WHICH FLOATS BEFORE A VISITANT FROM HEAVEN	126	BALDER DEAD 3	438
FLOATS THE IMPERIAL STREAM	234	YOUTH OF MAN	87
OF THE GREY EXPANSE WHERE HE FLOATS	254	FUTURE	79
QUICK FROM DISTRESSFUL THOUGHT AND FLOATS IN JOY	351	MEROPE	615

FLOCK

MAKE WHISTLING TOWRD HIS MIST-WREATHED FLOCK	57	RESIGNATION	183
MAKE WHISTLING TOWARDS HIS MIST-WREATHED FLOCK	57	RESIGNATION	V 183
HER FLOCK ALONG THE WHITE NORWEGIAN BEACH	117	BALDER DEAD 3	150
WHEN HE LAY IN THE NIGHT BY HIS FLOCK	253	FUTURE	46
NO LONGER LEAVE THY WISTFUL FLOCK UNFED	255	SCHOLAR-GIPSY	3
SHEPHERDING HIS FLOCK OF GOLD	457	POOR MATTHIAS	185

FLOCKD

AND FROM THE DARK FLOCKD UP THE SHADOWY TRIBES	109	BALDER DEAD 2	156
BEHIND FLOCKD WRANGLING UP A PITEOUS CREW	109	BALDER DEAD 2	170

FLOCKS

LONG FLOCKS OF TRAVELLING BIRDS DEAD ON THE SNOW	66	SOHRAB RUSTUM	164
FLOCKS OF HIS KIND PASS FLYING OER HIS HEAD	129	BALDER DEAD 3	561
THE BLEATING OF THE FOLDED FLOCKS IS BORNE	255	SCHOLAR-GIPSY	18
WEALTHY IN CORN AND FLOCKS WHICH WHEN AT LAST	330	MEROPE	5
LIE STREWN THE WHITE FLOCKS	442	EMPEDOCLES II	430

FLOOD

ON THE CARVED WESTERN FRONT A FLOOD OF LIGHT	18	CHURCH BROU 3	18
SEES HIS STRONG THOUGHT IN FIERY FLOOD	56	RESIGNATION	156
RIDE DOWN AND BATHE MY HOT BROW IN THE FLOOD	139	TRISTRAM 1	282
SEE LOW ABOVE THE TIDE AT FLOOD	274	STANZAS CARNAC	26
THE WORLD A ROLLING FLOOD	424	EMPEDOCLES I 2	354
HIGH THOUGHTS WERE HIS WHEN BY THE GLEAMING FLOOD	473	CROMWELL	65
ONCE MORE ALONE BESIDE THE GLEAMING FLOOD	479	CROMWELL	240
THE FLOOD OF THE WORLDS COMMERCE ON HER SHORE	480	HUNGARIAN NAT	3

FLOODED

WENT LURID DOWN OER FLOODED PLAINS	52	RESIGNATION	11
TO BUILD THEM BOATS FISH FROM THE FLOODED RIVERS	73	SOHRAB RUSTUM	411
TO SAW THEM PLANKS FISH FROM THE FLOODED RIVERS	73	SOHRAB RUSTUM	V 411
BUT THE VALLEYS ARE FLOODED WITH HAZE	228	YOUTH OF NATURE	7
WHERE HOME THROUGH FLOODED FIELDS FOOT-TRAVELLERS GO	258	SCHOLAR-GIPSY	122

FLOODING

CLOSE THINE EYES THIS FLOODING MOONLIGHT BLINDS THEM	144	TRISTRAM 2	71
CAME FLOODING TO THY LANGUID CHEEK	178	FAREWELL	V 10
ALL-FLOODING OCEAN OF BLOOD	378	MEROPE	1246

FLOODS

OF OXUS WHERE THE SUMMER-FLOODS OERFLOW	61	SOHRAB RUSTUM	14
BLEACH THEM OR OXUS WITH HIS SUMMER-FLOODS	72	SOHRAB RUSTUM	377
UPON THE SUMMER-FLOODS AND NOT MY BONES	74	SOHRAB RUSTUM	428
OF STARTLED PLEASURE FLOODS THY BROW	184	TERRACE BERNE	14
COME STREAMING WITH THE FLOODS OF GLORY IN	445	WESTMIN ABBEY	38

FLOOR

ON THE RED PININGS OF THEIR FOREST-FLOOR	25	DREAM	5
AND TRANQUIL FROM WHOSE FLOOR THE NEW-BATHED STARS	87	SOHRAB RUSTUM	891
SO ON THE FLOOR LAY BALDER DEAD AND ROUND	95	BALDER DEAD 1	1
AND STOOD ROUND BALDER ON THE BLOODY FLOOR	95	BALDER DEAD 1	10
AND LEFT HIS BODY STRETCHD UPON THE FLOOR	97	BALDER DEAD 1	63
OF BALDER FROM THE FLOOR OF ODINS HALL	101	BALDER DEAD 1	205
ALONG THE FLINTY FLOOR OF ASGARD STREETS	102	BALDER DEAD 1	261
I A STATUE ON THY CHAPEL-FLOOR	144	TRISTRAM 2	62
AND A GLANCE WHICH OVER THE CROWDED FLOOR	146	TRISTRAM 2	120
AND THOSE BLOWN RUSHES ON THE FLOOR	148	TRISTRAM 2	160
AND A GLANCE THAT OVER THE CROWDED FLOOR	146	TRISTRAM 2	V 120

FLOOR (CONTINUED)
```
                AND THE BLOWN RUSHES ON THE FLOOR          • • • • •   148 TRISTRAM 2        V 160
                WHOSE FIGURE CASTS A SHADOW ON THE FLOOR     • • • •   175 PARTING             36
                WHEN GARDEN-WALKS AND ALL THE GRASSY FLOOR • • • •     264 THYRSIS             54
                WHOSE FLOOR TO-NIGHT SWEET MOONSHINE FILLS • • • •     277 SOUTHERN NIGHT      75
                UPON THE WALL THE KNEE-WORN FLOOR       • • • • •      300 GRANDE CHARTR       46
                NO CLOISTER-FLOOR OF HUMID STONE          • • • •      317 OBERMANN MORE      149
                AND HER FLUSHD FEET GLOW ON THE MARBLE FLOOR • •       431 EMPEDOCLES II       88
                OER WHOSE LIT FLOOR A ROAD OF MOONBEAMS LEADS  •       438 EMPEDOCLES II      312
                THAT MILD AND LUMINOUS FLOOR OF WATERS LIVES   •       438 EMPEDOCLES II      315
                ALONG THE HOLY FLOOR        • • • • • • • •            445 WESTMIN ABBEY       52
```

FLOUTS
```
                IT IS THE ACCUSER LOK WHO FLOUTS US ALL    • • • •     124 BALDER DEAD 3      370
```

FLOW
```
                IF THOUGHTS NOT IDLE WHILE BEFORE ME FLOW   • • • •      7 REP FRIEND          11
                ARE RARE AH MOST LOVES BUT FLOW ONCE AND RETURN • •     19 MODERN SAPPHO       16
                WHEN THE FLOWER THEY FLOW FOR      • • • • •            36 VOICE               13
                OF PASSIONS THAT FOR EVER EBB AND FLOW    • • • •       37 YOUTHS AGIT          4
                AND LET THE BLOOD FLOW FREE AND SO TO DIE    • • •      80 SOHRAB RUSTUM      652
                FREEZING AND RIDGING IN THEIR ONWARD FLOW   • • • •    108 BALDER DEAD 2      129
                THESE FLOW BY HELAS THRONE AND NEAR THEIR SPRING •     109 BALDER DEAD 2      155
                NOW THE SALT TIDES SEAWARD FLOW        • • • • •       161 FORSAKEN MERM        5
                NOW THE SALT TIDES SEAWARDS FLOW         • • • •       161 FORSAKEN MERM     V  5
                ABOVE THE HOWLING SENSES EBB AND FLOW       • • •      169 EAST LONDON         11
                TWO SAINTS MET OFTEN WHERE THOSE WATERS FLOW   •       170 EAST AND WEST        4
                THE ISLANDS FEEL THE ENCLASPING FLOW     • • • •       182 TO MARG CONT         5
                UPON TIMES BARREN STORMY FLOW      • • • • • •         183 ABSENCE             19
                FLOW THE COOL LAKE-WAVES       • • • • • • • •         190 STRAYED REVEL      160
                THOSE BLUE HILLS TOO THIS RIVERS FLOW       • • •      208 ON THE RHINE        22
                INTO HIS MIND THE TURBID EBB AND FLOW     • • • •      211 DOVER BEACH         17
                INTO HIS MIND THE TROUBLED EBB AND FLOW    • • • •     211 DOVER BEACH       V 17
                THE FOUNT WHICH SHALL NOT FLOW AGAIN    • • • •        213 PROGRESS POESY       4
                WITH ITS UNCONQUERABLE FLOW       • • • • • •          226 EPILOG LAOCOON     168
                SET WHERE THE UPPER STREAMS OF SIMOIS FLOW • • •       236 PALLADIUM            1
                THE SPRING-TIDES BRIMMING FLOW        • • • • •        242 SUMMER NIGHT        16
                PURSUE WITH INDISCERNIBLE FLOW ITS WAY     • • •       246 BURIED LIFE         40
                A MAN BECOMES AWARE OF HIS LIFES FLOW      • • •       247 BURIED LIFE         88
                AND CROSS THE UNPERMITTED FERRYS FLOW      • • •       265 THYRSIS             85
                HIS FEET TO SEE THE LURID FLOW     • • • • • •         271 MEMORIAL VERSES     31
                NURSED BY HIS PASTORAL FLOW        • • • • • •         313 OBERMANN MORE       28
                THE BROW UNBOUND THE THOUGHTS FLOW FREE AGAIN         436 EMPEDOCLES II      246
                AND GENTLY SHALL THE MURMURING RIPPLES FLOW    •      469 ALARIC AT ROME     197
                OF MANY A LAWNY HILL AND STREAMS WITH SILVER FLOW     474 CROMWELL           104
```

FLOWD
```
                FLOWD THE HUNTERS MERRY TIDE    • • • • • • • •         13 CHURCH BROU 1        8
                A GATE SWINGS TO OUR TIDE HATH FLOWD    • • • •         53 RESIGNATION         48
                FLOWD WITH THE STREAM ALL DOWN HIS COLD WHITE SIDE      86 SOHRAB RUSTUM      842
                UNDER THE SOLITARY MOON HE FLOWD      • • • • •         87 SOHRAB RUSTUM      879
                FROM ISEULTS LIPS THE UNBROKEN STORY FLOWD   • •       150 TRISTRAM 3          45
                WHICH FLOWD FOR THAT TITANIC STRIFE     • • • •        270 MEMORIAL VERSES  V 14
```

FLOWER
```
                AND LANGUID PLEASURE FADE AND FLOWER AGAIN  • • • •     10 MYCERINUS           64
                HAREBELLS FLOWER IN THE NAVE      • • • • • •           15 CHURCH BROU 1       72
                WHEN THE FLOWER THEY FLOW FOR      • • • • • •          36 VOICE               13
                NIPS TOO KEENLY THE SWEET FLOWER       • • • •         131 TRISTRAM 1          36
                BEHOLD HER HERE THE PATIENT FLOWER       • • • •       132 TRISTRAM 1          72
                SWEET FLOWER THY CHILDRENS EYES        • • • •         140 TRISTRAM 1         325
                BUT ONCE I KNEW EACH FIELD EACH FLOWER EACH STICK      263 THYRSIS             32
                WOODS WITH ANEMONIES IN FLOWER TILL MAY     • • •      268 THYRSIS            199
                TWIXT MYRTLE-HEDGES ALL IN FLOWER       • • • •        278 SOUTHERN NIGHT     103
                FLOWER OF MARBLE WHITE        • • • • • • • •          296 HEINES GRAVE       131
                HOW CAN WE FLOWER IN FOREIGN AIR       • • • •         306 GRANDE CHARTR      208
                HOW SHOULD WE FLOWER IN FOREIGN AIR      • • • •       306 GRANDE CHARTR    V 208
                A MOUNTAIN-FLOWER WAS IN HIS HAND      • • • •         314 OBERMANN MORE       65
                I WATCHD THE CROCUS FADE AND FLOWER     • • • • •      321 OBERMANN MORE      255
                THE FLOWER-DRESSD VICTIM STOOD A MILK-WHITE BULL • •   401 MEROPE            1910
                HOW EACH BRIGHT TINT OF TREE AND FLOWER AND HEATH      466 ALARIC AT ROME     101
```

FLOWERD
```
                THE WET FLOWERD GRASS HEAVES UP ITS HEAD    • • • •     57 RESIGNATION        185
                THE GENTIAN-FLOWERD PASS ITS CROWN      • • • •        313 OBERMANN MORE       21
                AND THE PINK-FLOWERD OLEANDER     • • • • • • •        391 MEROPE            1617
                THE GOLD-FLOWERD BROOM       • • • • • • • •           442 EMPEDOCLES II      440
                ITS SHADOWS OER THE FUTURE FLOWERD AND GREW    • •     473 CROMWELL            56
```

FLOWERED
```
                HOW BOTH WERE HASTENING AS THEY FLOWERED AND GREW      469 ALARIC AT ROME     189
```

FLOWERING
```
                TALL GRASSES AND WHITE FLOWERING NETTLES WAVE    • •   259 SCHOLAR-GIPSY      139
                SEE FRAGRANT HERBS ARE FLOWERING THERE     • • • •    301 GRANDE CHARTR       56
                THOSE FRAGRANT HERBS ARE FLOWERING THERE   • • • •    301 GRANDE CHARTR     V 56
                OER FLOWERING PLAIN AND BLOSSOMD MEADOW FLING   • •    474 CROMWELL            91
```

FLOWERS
```
                SEEMS THERE NO JOY IN DANCES CROWND WITH FLOWERS • •     9 MYCERINUS           33
```

FLOWERS   (CONTINUED)

BURYING THEIR UNSUNND STEMS IN GRASS AND FLOWERS	11	MYCERINUS	88
CLAD WERE THEY BOTH IN WHITE FLOWERS IN THEIR BREAST	25	DREAM	23
CLAD WERE THEY BOTH IN WHITE FLOWERS IN THEIR BREASTS	25	DREAM V	23
SCENT AND SONG AND LIGHT AND FLOWERS	32	NEW SIRENS	171
AND YOUR FLOWERS ARE OVERBLOWN	34	NEW SIRENS	254
LIKE SPRING FLOWERS	44	QUESTION	9
WHEN THE FROST FLOWERS THE WHITEND WINDOW-PANES	70	SOHRAB RUSTUM	306
AND AS A SPRAY OF HONEYSUCKLE FLOWERS	101	BALDER DEAD 1	230
AS PALE AND STILL AS WITHERD FLOWERS	147	TRISTRAM 2	127
AND FLAG-LEAVED IRIS-FLOWERS	191	STRAYED REVEL	170
IN THE WHITE ACACIA FLOWERS	201	PHILOMELA V	
SUCH LOVELY FLOWERS FOR CHEERING SOULS	227	EPILOG LAOCOON	204
THE FLOWERS UPCLOSE THE BIRDS ARE FED	249	KENSINGTON GARD	34
THE FLOWERS CLOSE THE BIRDS ARE FED	249	KENSINGTON GARD V	34
AND FOSTERING IN THY LAP A HEAP OF FLOWERS	257	SCHOLAR-GIPSY	78
OF FLOWERS THE FRAIL-LEAFD WHITE ANEMONY	257	SCHOLAR-GIPSY	87
FRESHEN THY FLOWERS AS IN FORMER YEARS	261	SCHOLAR-GIPSY	218
AND CHESTNUT-FLOWERS ARE STREWN	264	THYRSIS	56
ARE FLOWERS FIRST OPEND ON SICILIAN AIR	265	THYRSIS	89
COOL NORTHERN FIELDS AND GRASS AND FLOWERS	275	STANZAS CARNAC	44
CRISP EVERLASTING-FLOWERS	292	HEINES GRAVE	11
AND CROWND HIS HAIR WITH FLOWERS	316	OBERMANN MORE	102
WITH PITCHERS IN THEIR HANDS AND FRESH-PULLD FLOWERS	331	MEROPE	54
DECK IT WITH GARLANDS OF FLOWERS	342	MEROPE	388
FLOWERS BUT THOU IN THE GLOOM	342	MEROPE	403
GIVES FLOWERS AFTER FLOWERS	424	EMPEDOCLES I 2	358
GIVES FLOWERS AFTER FLOWERS	424	EMPEDOCLES I 2	358
BUOYANT AND FRESH THE MOUNTAIN FLOWERS	426	EMPEDOCLES I 2	433

FLOWERY

AND FLITTED DOWN THE FLOWERY TRACK	184	TERRACE BERNE	19
THROUGH THE SILENT FLOWERY LAND	234	YOUTH OF MAN	85
PRIMROSES ORPHANS OF THE FLOWERY PRIME	266	THYRSIS	120
UNDER THE FLOWERY OLEANDERS PALE	267	THYRSIS	170
ON THE COOL FLOWERY LAP OF EARTH	271	MEMORIAL VERSES	49
GREEN HAPPY PLACES LIKE A FLOWERY LEA	475	CROMWELL	117

FLOWING

OH THAT ITS WAVES WERE FLOWING OVER ME	83	SOHRAB RUSTUM	768
FLOWING-ROBED THE BELOVED	194	STRAYED REVEL	279
OF THE NEW-BORN CLEAR-FLOWING STREAM	252	FUTURE	12
WHERE CLEAR-FLOWING LADON	391	MEROPE	1608
HIS FLOWING LOCKS AND GOLD-ENCIRCLED BROW	408	EMPEDOCLES I 1	60
LEFT THEIR FRIEND AND WITH ROBES FLOWING	433	EMPEDOCLES II	152

FLOWN

AND THE DULL GODS BEHOLD ERE THESE ARE FLOWN	10	MYCERINUS	65
MUSINGS THAT ERE THEY COULD GROW RIPE WERE FLOWN	41	GIPSY CHILD V	19
A YEAR HAD FLOWN AND OER THE SEA AWAY	149	TRISTRAM 3	1
A YEAR HAD FLOWN AND IN THE CHAPEL OLD	149	TRISTRAM 3 V	1
BUT WHAT I DREAM TWO HUNDRED YEARS ARE FLOWN	259	SCHOLAR-GIPSY	131
HE HEARKENS NOT LIGHT COMER HE IS FLOWN	265	THYRSIS	71
THEN SLOWLY BRIGHTEND AS THE DAYS HAD FLOWN	474	CROMWELL	76

FLOWS

FAR UP SHINES THE HOUSE AND BENEATH FLOWS THE RIVER	19	MODERN SAPPHO	3
FAR UP GLEAMS THE HOUSE AND BENEATH FLOWS THE RIVER	19	MODERN SAPPHO V	3
JOY COMES AND GOES HOPE EBBS AND FLOWS	44	QUESTION	1
FOR NEAR THE WALL THE RIVER OF ROARING FLOWS	109	BALDER DEAD 2	152
THROUGH WHICH A RIVER FLOWS AND SEES BENEATH	113	BALDER DEAD 2	297
ALL RED WITH BLOOD THE WHIRLING RIVER FLOWS	137	TRISTRAM 1	234
FLOWS BY THE TOWN THE CHURCHYARD FAIR	184	TERRACE BERNE	10
WHERE GAILY FLOWS THE HUMAN TIDE	224	EPILOG LAOCOON	108
LIGHT FLOWS OUR WAR OF MOCKING WORDS AND YET	245	BURIED LIFE	1
NOW FLOWS THROUGH WITH US IS THE PLAIN	253	FUTURE	51
FLATTER THE PLAIN WHERE IT FLOWS	253	FUTURE	64
FRESH BLOOD FLOWS CALLING FOR BLOOD	379	MEROPE	1253
WHETHER BLOOD FLOWS OR NO CAN YET INVEST	389	MEROPE	1545
AS LIGHT OF WHAT WE THINK WE FEEL THERE FLOWS	483	BELOW SURFACE	3

FLUCTUATE

AND FLUCTUATE TWIXT BLIND HOPES AND BLIND DESPAIRS	236	PALLADIUM	18
WHO FLUCTUATE IDLY WITHOUT TERM OR SCOPE	260	SCHOLAR-GIPSY	167

FLUCTUATES

BUT FLUCTUATES TO AND FRO	243	SUMMER NIGHT	31

FLUENT

FLUENT OF HORRORS FALTERS TO RELATE IT	385	MEROPE	1419

FLUNG

FROM THE RANK LIFE OF TOWNS THIS LEAF AND FLUNG	6	GEO CRUIKSHANK	2
LONG SINCE HATH FLUNG HER WEEDS AWAY	304	GRANDE CHARTR	154
THE ETERNAL HILLS THEIR GIANT SHADOWS FLUNG	472	CROMWELL	14
AND THE ARMADA FLUNG TO THE FIERCE MAIN	481	HUNGARIAN NAT	14

FLURRIED

WITH HEATED CHEEKS AND FLURRIED AIR	148	TRISTRAM 2	162

FLUSH
```
      WHEN THE FIRST ROSE FLUSH WAS STEEPING      . . . .    31 NEW SIRENS          143
      AH SHALL I SEE THEE WHILE A FLUSH      . . . . . .   184 TERRACE BERNE          13
      LOVELY THE FLUSH      . . . . . . . . . . . .   219 BACCHANALIA 1          49
      HEAVENLY THE FLUSH      . . . . . . . . . . .   221 BACCHANALIA 2          62
```

FLUSHD
```
      FLUSHD GUESTS AND GOLDEN GOBLETS FOAMD WITH WINE  . .    11 MYCERINUS          97
      LOVE HAS FLUSHD THOSE CRUEL FACES      . . . . . .    27 NEW SIRENS          53
      WITH HOT-FLUSHD CHEEKS AND BRILLIANT EYES  . . . .   146 TRISTRAM 2          117
      THEIR CHEEKS WERE FLUSHD AND OVER EACH HOT BROW   .   150 TRISTRAM 3          32
      WHICH PLAYD ON HER FLUSHD CHEEK AND HER BLUE EYES    154 TRISTRAM 3          169
      THEIR CHEEKS GREW FLUSHD AND OVER EACH HOT BROW   .       TRISTRAM 3       V  32
      THROUGH THE DELICATE FLUSHD MARBLE      . . . . .   187 STRAYED REVEL          56
      AND COMING FLUSHD OVER THE STORMY FRITH    . . . .   196 FRAG ANTIGONE          58
      AND HER FLUSHD FEET GLOW ON THE MARBLE FLOOR   . .   431 EMPEDOCLES II          88
```

FLUSHING
```
      TROOP ACROSS THE FLUSHING SANDS      . . . . . .    26 NEW SIRENS          14
      WHEN THE FLUSHING HUES ARE FADING      . . . . . .    33 NEW SIRENS          213
      POURD FLUSHING TO THY LANGUID CHEEK      . . . . .   178 FAREWELL          10
      CAME FLUSHING TO THY LANGUID CHEEK      . . . . .   178 FAREWELL       V  10
```

FLUTE
```
      THAN PANS FLUTE-MUSIC      . . . . . . . .   187 STRAYED REVEL          67
      FORTH WITH THY FLUTE      . . . . . . . . . .   219 BACCHANALIA 1          43
      FORTH WITH THY FLUTE      . . . . . . . . . .   220 BACCHANALIA 2          48
      SOME GOOD SURVIVOR WITH HIS FLUTE WOULD GO  . . . .   265 THYRSIS          83
      AND FLUTE HIS FRIEND LIKE ORPHEUS FROM THE DEAD   . .   265 THYRSIS          90
      WHAT THOUGH THE MUSIC OF THY RUSTIC FLUTE   . . . .   269 THYRSIS          221
      AND HE TAUGHT HIM FLUTE-PLAYING      . . . . .   434 EMPEDOCLES II          170
      A FLUTE-NOTE FROM THE WOODS      . . . . . . .   436 EMPEDOCLES II          252
```

FLUTED
```
      AND FROM THE FLUTED SPINE ATOP A PLUME      . . . .    69 SOHRAB RUSTUM          268
```

FLUTES
```
      SHE BROKE HER FLUTES SHE STOPPD HER SPORTS   . . . .   316 OBERMANN MORE          129
      OF THE PHRYGIAN FLUTES TO TAME      . . . . . . .   433 EMPEDOCLES II          131
      THERE THE PHRYGIAN BROUGHT HIS FLUTES      . . . .   433 EMPEDOCLES II          141
      AND HAD CARVED THEM INTO FLUTES      . . . . . .   434 EMPEDOCLES II          176
```

FLUTTER
```
      FLUTTER CHIRP SHE NEVER STIRRD  . . . . . . . .   453 POOR MATTHIAS          34
```

FLUTTERD
```
      IT FLUTTERD AND FAILD FOR BREATH      . . . . . .    21 REQUIESCAT          14
      ALL IDLY FLUTTERD IN THE EASTERN GALE      . . . .   473 CROMWELL          68
```

FLUTTERING
```
      LET THE FLUTTERING FRINGES STREAK      . . . . . .    23 MEMORY-PICTURE          29
      WHICH DANCED AND ON THEIR SHOULDERS FLUTTERING PLAYD    25 DREAM          25
      WHICH WAVD AND ON THEIR SHOULDERS FLUTTERING PLAYD     25 DREAM       V  25
      WHICH STIRRD AND ON THEIR SHOULDERS FLUTTERING PLAYD    25 DREAM       V  25
      A HEAP OF FLUTTERING FEATHERS NEVER MORE   . . . .    78 SOHRAB RUSTUM          569
      NINE TIMES SHE WAVED THE FLUTTERING WIMPLE ROUND  . .   156 TRISTRAM 3          219
      THY CHEEKS SOFT HUE AND FLUTTERING LACE   . . . .   184 TERRACE BERNE          23
      ONCE MORE BENEATH HIM AND THE FLUTTERING SAIL   . .   479 CROMWELL          237
```

FLUX
```
      YET INDEED THIS FLUX OF GUESSES      . . . . . .    33 NEW SIRENS          195
      BUT INDEED THIS FLUX OF GUESSES      . . . . . .    33 NEW SIRENS       V 195
      THE FLUX OF MORTAL THINGS      . . . . . . . .   448 WESTMIN ABBEY          152
```

FLY
```
      O LET THE FALSE DREAM FLY      . . . . . . . .    39 STAGIRIUS          49
      DREAMS DAWN AND FLY FRIENDS SMILE AND DIE   . . . .    44 QUESTION           8
      YET IF HE SEEK TO FLY GIVE WAY  . . . . . . . .    91 SICK KING BOKH          115
      WHERE IN AND OUT THE SCREAMING SEAFOWL FLY   . . . .    97 BALDER DEAD 1          80
      NOW THEREFORE WHAT TO ATTEMPT OR WHITHER FLY   . .    98 BALDER DEAD 1          105
      FLY SAVE THYSELF SAVE ME I DARE NOT STAY   . . . .   135 TRISTRAM 1          168
      IT IS OH WHERE SHALL BRANDAN FLY      . . . . . .   157 SAINT BRANDAN          19
      BUT MID THEIR DRINK AND CLATTER HE WOULD FLY   . .   257 SCHOLAR-GIPSY          61
      FLY HENCE OUR CONTACT FEAR      . . . . . . . .   261 SCHOLAR-GIPSY          206
      STILL FLY PLUNGE DEEPER IN THE BOWERING WOOD   . .   261 SCHOLAR-GIPSY          207
      BUT FLY OUR PATHS OUR FEVERISH CONTACT FLY   . . . .   261 SCHOLAR-GIPSY          221
      BUT FLY OUR PATHS OUR FEVERISH CONTACT FLY   . . .   261 SCHOLAR-GIPSY          221
      THEN FLY OUR GREETINGS FLY OUR SPEECH AND SMILES  . .   262 SCHOLAR-GIPSY          231
      THEN FLY OUR GREETINGS FLY OUR SPEECH AND SMILES  . .   262 SCHOLAR-GIPSY          231
      QUICK LET ME FLY AND CROSS      . . . . . . .   267 THYRSIS          156
      FLY HENCE POOR WRETCH WHOEER THOU ART      . . . .   307 OBERMANN          17
      FLY FIND ME ON THE INSTANT WHERE CONFER   . . . .   368 MEROPE          1071
      FLY BACK MY CHILD AND THOU SEEMST      . . . . .   377 MEROPE          1229
      WHY WILT THOU FLY TO LOSE AS SOON AS FOUND   . . .   381 MEROPE          1290
      A FOOL CAN DRIVE IT AND A FLY MAY SCARE   . . . .   382 MEROPE          1344
      TO THIS THOU WOULDST HAVE ANSWER TAKE IT FLY   . .   395 MEROPE          1741
      LEAP AND FLY OPEN OF THEMSELVES FOR JOY   . . . .   401 MEROPE          1885
      MAKE US NOT FLY TO DREAMS BUT MODERATE DESIRE   . .   425 EMPEDOCLES I 2          386
      WHERE SHALL THY VOTARY FLY THEN BACK TO MEN   . .   435 EMPEDOCLES II          220
      AND HE WILL FLY TO SOLITUDE AGAIN      . . . . .   435 EMPEDOCLES II          227
```

FLY   (CONTINUED)
```
     AND WE SHALL FLY FOR REFUGE TO PAST TIMES    . . . .   440 EMPEDOCLES II      383
```

FLYING
```
     WHICH IT SENT FLYING WIDE THEN SOHRAB THREW      . .    73 SOHRAB RUSTUM      405
     SHALL THE LAKE GLASS HER FLYING OVER IT        . . .    78 SOHRAB RUSTUM      570
     FLOCKS OF HIS KIND PASS FLYING OER HIS HEAD    . . .   129 BALDER DEAD 3      561
     THE FLYING LEAVES THE STRAINING BLAST       . . . .    136 TRISTRAM 1         179
     FLYING OER THE STORMY MAIN      . . . . . . . .        136 TRISTRAM 1         188
     HIS FLYING STEEDS CAME NEAR    . . . . . . . .         197 FRAG ANTIGONE       85
     WITH ANGUISHD FACE AND FLYING HAIR    . . . . .        244 SUMMER NIGHT        66
     THAT FLYING AND ELUSIVE SHADOW REST    . . . . .       247 BURIED LIFE         93
     O THOU WHO ERE THY FLYING SPAN    . . . . . . .        322 OBERMANN MORE      277
```

FOAM
```
     FOR THIS THY TRACK ACROSS THE FRETFUL FOAM    . . . .    5 DUKE WELLINGTON     11
     THE SAILING FOAM THE SHINING POOL     . . . . . .       55 RESIGNATION        105
     YOUR EYES PURSUE THE BELLS OF FOAM     . . . . . .      58 RESIGNATION        201
     THEIR SPEARS ARE DOWN THEIR STEEDS ARE BATHED IN FOAM  137 TRISTRAM 1         237
     THE WILD WHITE HORSES FOAM AND FRET     . . . . .      162 FORSAKEN MERM       21
     FRESHENING ITS CURRENT AND SPOTTED WITH FOAM   . .     254 FUTURE              80
     THERE WHERE DOWN CLOUDY CLIFFS THROUGH SHEETS OF FOAM  262 SCHOLAR-GIPSY      248
     PAST THE LOIRES MOUTH AND BY THE FOAM    . . . .       274 STANZAS CARNAC      35
     THE SEETHING FOAM    . . . . . . . . . .               276 SOUTHERN NIGHT      32
     DROPT BY THE FAR AUSTRALIAN FOAM     . . . . . .       451 GEISTS GRAVE        56
     FAR OER THE PATHLESS WASTE OF LABOURING FOAM   . .     475 CROMWELL           114
```

FOAMD
```
     FLUSHD GUESTS AND GOLDEN GOBLETS FOAMD WITH WINE  . .   11 MYCERINUS           97
     LOUD THUNDERING BORE US BY SWIFT SWIFT IT FOAMD  . .    25 DREAM               33
     HIS BREAST HEAVED HIS LIPS FOAMD AND TWICE HIS VOICE    74 SOHRAB RUSTUM      455
     FOAMD FOR A MOMENT AND GONE     . . . . . . . .        288 RUGBY CHAPEL        72
```

FOAMING
```
     NO AS THE FOAMING SWATH    . . . . . . . . .           40 HUMAN LIFE           19
     NO AS THE FOAMING SWATHE     . . . . . . . . .         40 HUMAN LIFE        V  19
     FULL-FOAMING MILK-PAILS ALPINE FARE    . . . . .      313 OBERMANN MORE        17
     POUR FORTH THE FOAMING VIALS OF THY WRATH    . . .    465 ALARIC AT ROME       86
```

FOAMLESS
```
     ON THE FOAMLESS LONG-HEAVING    . . . . . . . .       192 STRAYED REVEL       203
```

FOAMS
```
     WHEN HIS FINE GENIUS FOAMS ITSELF AWAY      . . . .       LUCRETIUS 2           4
```

FOE
```
     THE WORLD SPEAKS WELL YET MIGHT HER FOE REPLY    . .    38 WORLDS TRIUMPHS     11
     THE SUN IS NOT YET RISEN AND THE FOE     . . . .       62 SOHRAB RUSTUM       35
     OF BLOOD AND I HAVE FOUGHT WITH MANY A FOE   . . .     71 SOHRAB RUSTUM      327
     NEVER WAS THAT FIELD LOST OR THAT FOE SAVED    . .     71 SOHRAB RUSTUM      328
     FALL AND THY SPEAR TRANSFIXD AN UNARMD FOE   . . .     77 SOHRAB RUSTUM      550
     BUT THAT IN BATTLE WITH A NAMELESS FOE     . . . .     79 SOHRAB RUSTUM      600
     BUT FIRST HE WOULD CONVINCE HIS STUBBORN FOE   . .     80 SOHRAB RUSTUM      653
     THE FOE THE ACCUSER WHOM THOUGH GODS WE HATE   . .     96 BALDER DEAD 1       38
     THE FOE THE ACCUSER WHOM THOUGH GODS WE HATE   . .     98 BALDER DEAD 1      101
     SHE WILL CRY IS THIS THE FOE I DREADED     . . .      144 TRISTRAM 2          65
     SO THOU ARRAIGNST HER HER FOE    . . . . . .          295 HEINES GRAVE        85
     I COME NOT HERE TO BE YOUR FOE     . . . . . . .      301 GRANDE CHARTR       76
     YOUR SONS LEAP UPON THE FOE OF YOUR KIN    . . .      344 MEROPE             462
     IN THE DETESTED PALACE OF THY FOE    . . . . .        367 MEROPE            1044
     EVEN IN THE DEADLY PALACE OF MY FOE    . . . . .      375 MEROPE            1205
     ON WHAT RELYING TO CRUSH SUCH A FOE    . . . . .      380 MEROPE            1286
     WITH SUCH SLIGHT MEANS TO COPE WITH SUCH A FOE   . .  381 MEROPE            1293
     ALAS OUR FOE ALONE STOOD FORWARD THEN      . . .      383 MEROPE            1367
     SO MUCH IS DUE TO TRUTH EVEN TOWRDS OUR FOE    . .    388 MEROPE            1493
     AND THANK THY BITTEREST FOE THAT HAVING LOST   . .    396 MEROPE            1756
     WHAT FOR SO FAR FATE HATH NOT PROVED MY FOE    . .    397 MEROPE            1778
     SO RULE THAT AS HIS FOE THOU BE OBEYD    . . . .      404 MEROPE            2009
     YE LIE WATCHING FOR THE FOE OF YOUR KIN    . . .      344 MEROPE           V 462
     WHAT FOR SO FAR SHE HATH NOT PROVED MY FOE   . . .    397 MEROPE           V1778
     SO RULE THAT AS THY FOE THOU BE OBEYD    . . . .      404 MEROPE           V2009
     TWICE ERE THAT DAY OF SHAME THE EMBATTLED FOE   . .   465 ALARIC AT ROME      73
```

FOEMEN
```
     IN THE BLOODY DUST BENEATH THE FEET OF THEIR FOEMEN       HOMER TRANS         26
```

FOES
```
     HE WILL NOT YIELD INDEED NOR QUIT OUR FOES   . . .     71 SOHRAB RUSTUM      351
     THERE ARE ENOUGH FOES IN THE PERSIAN HOST    . . .     74 SOHRAB RUSTUM      443
     BUT LODGED AMONG MY FATHERS FOES AND SEEN    . . .     83 SOHRAB RUSTUM      759
     MIGHT BE ONCE MORE ALIVE MY BITTEREST FOES   . . .     85 SOHRAB RUSTUM      810
     WARNING THE GODS THAT FOES DRAW NIGH TO HEAVEN   . .  105 BALDER DEAD 2        7
     BUT HIM TOO FOES AWAIT AND NETTED SNARES     . . .    111 BALDER DEAD 2      219
     SEEK TO AFFLICT OUR FOES WITH PETTY PANGS    . . .    111 BALDER DEAD 2      229
     ECHO THE BLAME OF HER FOES     . . . . . . .          294 HEINES GRAVE        75
     THEREFORE WITH BLOOD OF THY FOES     . . . . . .      296 HEINES GRAVE       125
     ALWAYS IN ARMS ALWAYS IN FACE OF FOES    . . . .      334 MEROPE             153
     MERE PRISONERS MEANT OR NOT AMONG OUR FOES   . . .    337 MEROPE             251
     WHAT HIS FOES DARED NOT I HIS LOVER DARED    . . .    338 MEROPE             271
     HE WOULD HAVE MIXD YOU WITH YOUR FRIENDLY FOES   . .  339 MEROPE             301
```

FOES   (CONTINUED)
        FOES DAZZLED WITH YOUR PROWESS WELL INCLINED   • •   339 MEROPE   302
        AT THE ISTHMUS IN FIGHT WITH HIS FOES   • • • •   345 MEROPE   479
        I OFFERD TO MY FOES AND THEY REFUSED   • • • • •   360 MEROPE   883
        LIVED FOR THE DEATH OF HIS FOES   • • • • • •   368 MEROPE   1085
        ORPHAND OF BOTH MY PARENTS BY HIS FOES   • • • •   385 MEROPE   1411
        NOT MEROPE AND POLYPHONTES FOES   • • • • • •   394 MEROPE   1719
        THIS PEOPLES ANARCHY THY FOES PRETENCE   • • • •   404 MEROPE   2001
        TO HAVE ADVANCED TRUE FRIENDS AND BEAT DOWN   425 EMPEDOCLES I 2   401
            BAFFLING FOES
        TO HAVE RAISD FAITHFUL FRIENDS AND CUT DOWN   425 EMPEDOCLES I 2   V 401
            SPITEFUL FOES

FOG
        AND THE FOG ROSE OUT OF THE OXUS STREAM   • • • •   61 SOHRAB RUSTUM   2
        AND WENT ABROAD INTO THE COLD WET FOG   • • • • •   61 SOHRAB RUSTUM   10
        THE SUN BY THIS HAD RISEN AND CLEARD THE FOG   • •   64 SOHRAB RUSTUM   104
        AND DARKEND ALL AND A COLD FOG WITH NIGHT   • • • •   86 SOHRAB RUSTUM   867
        BEGAN TO TWINKLE THROUGH THE FOG FOR NOW   • • • •   86 SOHRAB RUSTUM   870
        BY THIS THE SUN HAD RISEN AND CLEARD THE FOG   •   64 SOHRAB RUSTUM   V 104
        SO HERMOD OER THE FOG BETWEEN SAW HEAVEN   • • • •   113 BALDER DEAD 2   301
        THE WHITE FOG CREEPS FROM BUSH TO BUSH ABOUT   • •   267 THYRSIS   162

FOILD
        TO THE FOILD SEARCHING OF MORTALITY   • • • • • •   3 SHAKESPEARE   8
        A FOILD CIRCUITOUS WANDERER TILL AT LAST   • • • •   87 SOHRAB RUSTUM   888
        FOILD BY OUR FELLOW-MEN DEPRESSD OUTWORN   • • • •   172 IMMORTALITY   1
        BUT HE IS NOW BY FORTUNE FOILD   • • • • • • •   273 EDW QUILLINAN   13
        RARE STRAGGLING HUNTERS FOILD BY BRAKE AND CRAG • •   357 MEROPE   798

FOILING
        FOILING HER HIGH EMPRISE   • • • • • • • • • •   38 STAGIRIUS   20
        FOILING HER HIGH EMPRIZE   • • • • • • • • • •   38 STAGIRIUS   V 20

FOLD
        THE HOT WIND FEVERD HIM FIVE-FOLD   • • • • • •   157 SAINT BRANDAN   48
        FOLD CLOSELY O NATURE   • • • • • • • • • •   177 PARTING   77
        SINGS HIS SICILIAN FOLD   • • • • • • • • • •   268 THYRSIS   186
        SHEEP MAKE THE DAISIED AISLES THEIR FOLD   • • • •   274 STANZAS CARNAC   16
        SHEEP MAKE THE FURZE-GROWN AISLES THEIR FOLD • •   274 STANZAS CARNAC   V 16
        SHEEP MAKE THE FURZE-GROWN NAVE THEIR FOLD • • • •   STANZAS CARNAC   V 16
        INVEST ME STEEP ME FOLD ME ROUND   • • • • • •   302 GRANDE CHARTR   V 93
        FOLD LIKE A SHROUD AROUND THY WITHERED BONES   • •   464 ALARIC AT ROME   64

FOLDED
        STORMS UNSMOOTHD YOUR FOLDED VALLEYS • • • • •   30 NEW SIRENS   123
        AND TO-MORROW FOLDED PALMS   • • • • • • • •   33 NEW SIRENS   198
        WITH FOLDED HANDS REVOLVING THINGS TO COME • • • •   98 BALDER DEAD 1   93
        AND BOWD HER HEAD AND SATE WITH FOLDED HANDS • •   100 BALDER DEAD 1   193
        AND BOWD HER HEAD AND SATE WITH FOLDED HANDS • •   122 BALDER DEAD 3   296
        THE BLEATING OF THE FOLDED FLOCKS IS BORNE • • • •   255 SCHOLAR-GIPSY   18
        HIS HANDS WERE FOLDED LIKE A SAINT AT REST • • • •   476 CROMWELL   168

FOLDING
        WITHIN A FOLDING OF THE APENNINE   • • • • • •   268 THYRSIS   180

FOLDS
        FOLDS THE STILL VALLEY ALMOST ROUND   • • • • • •   57 RESIGNATION   175
        LAY LIKE THE FOLDS OF A BRIGHT GIRDLE FURLD   • •   211 DOVER BEACH   23
        LAY LIKE THE FOLDS OF A BRIGHT GARMENT FURLD • •   211 DOVER BEACH   V 23

FOLIAGD
        LIGHT THE GREEN-FOLIAGD CHESTNUTS PLAY   • • • •   248 KENSINGTON GARD   V

FOLIAGE
        WHILE THE DEEP-BURNISHD FOLIAGE OVERHEAD   • • • •   11 MYCERINUS   98

FOLIAGED
        THE FOLIAGED MARBLE FOREST WHERE YE LIE   • • • •   19 CHURCH BROU 3   39
        LIGHT THE CLEAR FOLIAGED CHESTNUTS PLAY   • • • •   KENSINGTON GARD   V

FOLK
        FROM THE CHURCH CAME A MURMUR OF FOLK AT THEIR PRAYERS 163 FORSAKEN MERM   72
        AND WITH THE COUNTRY-FOLK ACQUAINTANCE MADE   • •   263 THYRSIS   33
        INTO ONE PUISSANT FOLK AS HE DESIGND • • • • • •   338 MEROPE   290

FOLLIES
        YOUTH STAIND WITH FOLLIES AND THE THOUGHTS OF ILL   474 CROMWELL   79

FOLLOW
        AND ON RAPTURES FOLLOW CALMS   • • • • •   • • • •   30 NEW SIRENS   120
        SHALL WE FOLLOW   • • • • • • • • • • • •   44 QUESTION   21
        LINGERING WE FOLLOW DOWN WE GAIN   • • • • • •   54 RESIGNATION   78
        WHICH FOLLOW ME I PRAY THEE SLAY NOT THESE • • • •   84 SOHRAB RUSTUM   779
        AND DEEP AS WORDS CAN FOLLOW FEELING • • • •   225 EPILOG LAOCOON   138
        HIS THOUGHT MUST FOLLOW WHERE THEY PASS   • • • •   225 EPILOG LAOCOON   154
        HIS THOUGHT MUST FOLLOW THROUGH THE CROWD   • • • • 225 EPILOG LAOCOON   156
        FOLLOW ITS WINDINGS TO THE END   • • • • • •   227 EPILOG LAOCOON   192
        FOLLOW YOUR STEPS AS YE GO   • • • • • • •   292 RUGBY CHAPEL   203
        YE SHY RECLUSES FOLLOW TOO   • • • • • • •   305 GRANDE CHARTR   192
        WHO BLINDLY FOLLOW EVER   • • • • • • • • •   353 MEROPE   674
        BUT THOU MUST KEEP UNSEEN FOLLOW US ON   • • • •   409 EMPEDOCLES I 1   86

FOLLOW   (CONTINUED)
         BUT HE MUST FOLLOW ME NO MORE TO-NIGHT   • • • •   428 EMPEDOCLES I 2   469
         DRIVN INSHORE WE FOLLOW DOWN   • • • • • • •   457 POOR MATTHIAS   181

FOLLOWD
         WHICH SAW ONE CLUE TO LIFE AND FOLLOWD IT   • • • •   5 DUKE WELLINGTON   14
         FOLLOWD HIM LIKE A FAITHFUL HOUND AT HEEL   • • • •   69 SOHRAB RUSTUM   271
         SO FOLLOWD RUSTUM LEFT HIS TENTS AND CROSSD   • • •   69 SOHRAB RUSTUM   280
         AND RUSTUM FOLLOWD HIS OWN BLOW AND FELL   • • • •   73 SOHRAB RUSTUM   420
         AND FOLLOWD HER TO FIND HER WHERE SHE FELL   • • •   78 SOHRAB RUSTUM   560
         THEY FOLLOWD ME MY HOPE MY FAME MY STAR   • • • •   84 SOHRAB RUSTUM   781
         SO FOLLOWD RUSTUM ISSUED FORTH AND CROSSD   • • •   69 SOHRAB RUSTUM   V 280
         FOLLOWD AND ON THEIR SHOULDERS CARRIED BOUGHS   • • 106 BALDER DEAD 2   64
         FOLLOWD IN TEARS THEIR FATHER AND THEIR KING   • • 115 BALDER DEAD 3   60
         FAIN HAD HE FOLLOWD THEIR RECEDING STEPS   • • •   129 BALDER DEAD 3   556
         IT MAY BE THOU HAST FOLLOWD   • • • • •   189 STRAYED REVEL   117
         ON THE HEIGHT OF THEIR BOLD-FOLLOWD WAY   • • •   216 LORDS MESSENGER   V 17
         BROTHER FOLLOWD SISTER   • • • • • • •   344 MEROPE   447
         THRICE SON FOLLOWD SIRE   • • • • • • •   345 MEROPE   467
         FOLLOWD THY FATHER FROM THEIR NORTHERN HILLS   • • 381 MEROPE   1300
         IF FOLLOWD MAKE THEIR SUCCOUR SLACK AND NULL   • • 382 MEROPE   1338
         WHAT FOLLOWD HIS MOST TRUSTED KINSMAN SLEW   • • • 389 MEROPE   1555
         UNWITTING FOLLOWD   • • • • • • • • • •   393 MEROPE   1660
         GRANDSON FOLLOWD SIRE   • • • • • • • •   345 MEROPE   V 467
         WHOSE MULES I FOLLOWD MAY BE COMING UP   • • •   407 EMPEDOCLES I 1   22
         WHY HAST THOU FOLLOWD US THE NIGHT WAS HOT   • • 407 EMPEDOCLES I 1   36
         THROUGH THE COOL LOVELY COUNTRY FOLLOWD YOU   • • 407 EMPEDOCLES I 1   45
         THAT CALM EYE FOLLOWD TURN HIM WHERE HE WILL   • • 477 CROMWELL   196

FOLLOWER
         MY FAITHFUL FOLLOWER COMES WELCOME OLD FRIEND   • • 362 MEROPE   937

FOLLOWERS
         HIS FOLLOWERS IN AND BADE THEM BRING HIS ARMS   • •   69 SOHRAB RUSTUM   264
         FAME AND HER LESS FAIR FOLLOWERS ENVY STRIFE   • • 199 EARLY DEATH   4
         ACTION I HAD NOT FOLLOWERS FAME   • • • • •   321 OBERMANN MORE   261
         O HONOURD QUEEN O FAITHFUL FOLLOWERS   • • • • 400 MEROPE   1882

FOLLOWING
         QUICK I PASSD FOLLOWING   • • • • • • • •   187 STRAYED REVEL   40
         FOLLOWING THE SUN WE SET OUR VESSELS HEAD   • • • 484 S S LUSITANIA   3

FOLLOWS
         AND FOLLOWS THIS MAN AFTER THAT FOR HOURS   • • • 114 BALDER DEAD 3   11
         AND STILL THE ACCEPTANCE FOLLOWS ME WHICH CROWND   • 126 BALDER DEAD 3   461
         FOLLOWS THEM WITH A LONG COMPLAINING CRY   • • • 129 BALDER DEAD 3   564
         SHE FOLLOWS THE GAY WORLD WHOSE SWARMS HAVE FLED   • 167 RACHEL 1   9
         HE FOLLOWS HOME AND LIVES THEIR LIFE   • • • • 226 EPILOG LAOCOON   162
         FOLLOWS THE APPROACHING QUEEN WHO STOPS AS CALLD   • 332 MEROPE   64
         FOLLOWS THE ISSUING QUEEN WHO STOPS AS CALLD   • • 332 MEROPE   V 64

FOLLY
         WITH FOLLY OR WHAT DRUNKEN SLAVE   • • • • •   89 SICK KING BOKH   41
         IF I SPEAK FOLLY BUT A KING   • • • • • • •   89 SICK KING BOKH   55
         THY BROTHER WHOM THROUGH FOLLY THOU DIDST SLAY   • • 124 BALDER DEAD 3   393
         WHEN THE FORTS OF FOLLY FALL   • • • • • •   215 LAST WORD   15
         ASK BUT THE FOLLY OF MANKIND   • • • • • •   250 WISH   11
         FORGIVE MY FOLLY AND WORK   • • • • • • •   348 MEROPE   538
         THE REIGN OF FOLLY USURPATION EVER   • • • • 353 MEROPE   668
         FOLLY REVIVED RE-FURBISHD SOPHISTRIES   • • • • 449 WESTMIN ABBEY   159

FOMENT.
         BE TO FOMENT OLD MEMORIES OF WRATH   • • • • • 342 MEROPE   381

FOND
         TOO FEARFUL OR TOO FOND TO PLAY ALONE   • • • •   8 RELIGIOUS ISOL   5
         AND WITH FOND FALTERING FINGERS STROKED HIS CHEEKS   81 SOHRAB RUSTUM   696
         AND HE GREW FOND AND EAGER TO OBEY   • • • • • 155 TRISTRAM 3   183
         FOND FANCIES HERE THERE FALSE PHILOSOPHY   • • • • 446 WESTMIN ABBEY   66
         FOND HEARTS THAT FAIN WOULD CLOTHE THE UNWELCOME TRUTH 474 CROMWELL   97

FONDLY
         PLAYS FONDLY ROUND THEM   • • • • • • • • •   51 CONSOLATION   44
         AND SINCE HAS FONDLY WATCHD HIM NIGHT AND DAY   • • 351 MEROPE   618
         YET FONDLY ZEALOUS FOR THY FAME   • • • • • • 451 GEISTS GRAVE   61

FONDNESS
         OF FAITHFUL FONDNESS FOR THEIR FORMER KING   • • • 331 MEROPE   39
         OF FAITHFUL FONDNESS TOWARDS THEIR FORMER KING   • • 331 MEROPE   V 39

FONTAINEBLEAU
         IN THE LONE BRAKES OF FONTAINEBLEAU   • • • • • 304 GRANDE CHARTR   149

FOOD
         THE TABLE STOOD BEFORE HIM CHARGED WITH FOOD   • •   67 SOHRAB RUSTUM   197
         HAS OFTEN STROKED THY NECK AND GIVEN THEE FOOD   • •   83 SOHRAB RUSTUM   753
         THE TABLE STOOD BESIDE HIM CHARGED WITH FOOD   • •   67 SOHRAB RUSTUM   V 197
         WITH SCARLET BERRIES GEMMD THE FELL-FARES FOOD   • • 150 TRISTRAM 3   22
         WITH SCARLET BERRIES BRIGHT THE FELLFARES FOOD   • •   TRISTRAM 3   V 22
         THE BLACKBIRD PICKING FOOD   • • • • • • • •   258 SCHOLAR-GIPSY   116

FOOD   (CONTINUED)
```
        FOR FOOD TO KEEP HIM TILL HE END        . . . . . .   278  SOUTHERN NIGHT     83
        WHOSE MIND WAS FED ON OTHER FOOD WAS TRAIND   . .     436  EMPEDOCLES II     264

FOOL
        IN HARMONY WITH NATURE RESTLESS FOOL . . . . . .       5  HARMONY NATURE      1
        FOOL IF THOU CANST NOT PASS HER REST HER SLAVE  . .    5  HARMONY NATURE     14
        MAN CANNOT THOUGH HE WOULD LIVE CHANCES FOOL   . .    40  HUMAN LIFE         18
        FOOL THOU ART SLAIN AND BY AN UNKNOWN MAN  . . . .    77  SOHRAB RUSTUM     537
        WHAT FOOL IS THIS THAT HURTS OUR EARS      . . . .    89  SICK KING BOKH     40
        FOOL THOU MISSEST WE ARE BOTH UNMOVD . . . . . .    146  TRISTRAM 2      V 100
        HOW THIS FOOL PASSION GULLS MEN POTENTLY   . . . .  153  TRISTRAM 3        134
        A FOOL CAN DRIVE IT AND A FLY MAY SCARE    . . . .  382  MEROPE           1344
        THE SOPHIST SNEERS FOOL TAKE . . . . . . . .       416  EMPEDOCLES I 2    132
        OF WONDER TO THE FOOL OF WARNING TO THE WISE  . .   462  ALARIC AT ROME     12

FOOLISH
        THEY ARE GONE ALL IS STILL FOOLISH HEART DOST       19  MODERN SAPPHO       1
            THOU QUIVER
        TO THE WISE FOOLISH TO THE WORLD     . . . . . .    59  RESIGNATION       254
        NOT FOOLISH FAUSTA IN HIS EYE  . . . . . . . .      59  RESIGNATION       256
        AND DRUDGE UNDER SOME FOOLISH MASTERS KEN  . . .   169  WORLDLY PLACE       6
        FOOLISH BOY WHY TREMBLEST THOU  . . . . . . .      187  STRAYED REVEL      53
        TURN ON THE FOOLISH THE STROKE   . . . . . . .     281  HAWORTH CHURCH  V
        O GODS FOOLISH OLD MAN THOU SPOILST MY BLOW  .     374  MEROPE           1194
        WHICH FOOLISH INNOCENCE PLAYS WITH SUBTLE GUILT  . 366  MEROPE          V
        IS EVERYWHERE SUSTAINS THE WISE THE FOOLISH ELF  . 422  EMPEDOCLES I 2    306
        THOU WOULDST CHIRP THOU FOOLISH BIRD  . . . . .    453  POOR MATTHIAS      33

FOOLS
        CAN YOUR EYES WHILE FOOLS ARE DOZING . . . . .      33  NEW SIRENS        209
        GODS WISDOM AND GODS GOODNESS AY BUT FOOLS  . . .  171  DIVINITY            9
        FOOLS THAT THESE MYSTICS ARE   . . . . . . .      233  YOUTH OF MAN       28
        ITS GREATNESS NOR THE REIGN OF FOOLS PROLONGD  .   282  HAWORTH CHURCH  V
        BUT WE ARE ALL THE SAME THE FOOLS OF OUR OWN WOES  417  EMPEDOCLES I 2    166
        FOOLS THAT IN MANS BRIEF TERM  . . . . . . .      424  EMPEDOCLES I 2    347
        FOOLS THAT SO OFTEN HERE . . . . . . . . .        425  EMPEDOCLES I 2    382
        ALL THE FOOLS-ARMOURY OF MAGIC LIE THERE   . . .   432  EMPEDOCLES II     118

FOOT
        HARK THE GAMES ON FOOT THEY SCATTER  . . . . .      13  CHURCH BROU 1      21
        THE ROYAL TROOPS OF PERSIA HORSE AND FOOT  . . .    65  SOHRAB RUSTUM     139
        HE HAS THE WILD STAGS FOOT THE LIONS HEART  . . .   66  SOHRAB RUSTUM     177
        HE HAS THE WILD STAGS FOOT THE LIONS HEART  . . .   67  SOHRAB RUSTUM     216
        HE HATH THE WILD STAGS FOOT THE LIONS HEART  . .    67  SOHRAB RUSTUM   V 216
        THOR CAME ON FOOT THE REST ON HORSEBACK RODE  .    120  BALDER DEAD 3     218
        HE WAS ON FOOT AND THAT FALSE FAY HIS FRIEND  .    154  TRISTRAM 3        161
        ON FOOT BEHIND THEM GO AND COME  . . . . . .      224  EPILOG LAOCOON    114
        WHERE HOME THROUGH FLOODED FIELDS FOOT-TRAVELLERS GO 258 SCHOLAR-GIPSY   122
        SEE TIS NO FOOT OF UNFAMILIAR MEN  . . . . . .     263  THYRSIS            7
        HER FOOT THE CUMNER COWSLIPS NEVER STIRRD  . . .   265  THYRSIS           99
        THE FOOT LESS PROMPT TO MEET THE MORNING DEW  .    266  THYRSIS          138
        AND SOON THY FOOT RESUMED ITS WANDERING WAY  .     269  THYRSIS          229
        HER FOOT THE CUMNER COWSLIPS NEVER STIRRD  . . .   265  THYRSIS        V  99
        A YOUTH WITH THE FOOT OF YOUTH . . . . . . .      297  HEINES GRAVE      154
        TO FOOT OF MORTAL WHERE HIS ANCESTOR . . . . .     357  MEROPE           776
        NOT WITH THE FAILING BREATH AND FOOT OF AGE  . .   362  MEROPE           936
        AH ME WITH WHAT A FOOT DOTH TREASON POST   . .     363  MEROPE           962
        COME LIGHTNING PASSION THAT WITH FOOT OF FIRE  .   367  MEROPE          1060
        PAUSANIAS AND ON FOOT ALONE AND THOU THEN  . . .   407  EMPEDOCLES I 1     30

FOOTED
        SO SPEAKING THE FLEET-FOOTED HERMOD CAME   . . .   102  BALDER DEAD 1     246
        AND THE FLEET-FOOTED HERMOD ANSWERD HER    . . .   108  BALDER DEAD 2     111
        AND THE FLEET-FOOTED HERMOD MADE REPLY     . . .   126  BALDER DEAD 3     468
        THE BRAZEN-FOOTED FURY EVER STALKS   . . . . .     395  MEROPE          1734

FOOTPRINTS
        ONE SEES ONES FOOTPRINTS CRUSHD IN THE WET GRASS  . 406  EMPEDOCLES I 1    14

FOOTSTEP
        IS THIS THE EYE THE FOOTSTEP FAST      . . . . .   276  SOUTHERN NIGHT     37
        PLANTED HIS FOOTSTEP THE SPRAY . . . . . . . .     289  RUGBY CHAPEL       97

FOOTSTEPS
        PLANTING HIS STEADFAST FOOTSTEPS IN THE SEA   . .    3  SHAKESPEARE         5

FORAY
        THE HORSE WHOM RUSTUM ON A FORAY ONCE    . . . .    69  SOHRAB RUSTUM     273

FORBADE
        THE ORACLE FORBADE NOT ILL-INSPIRED  . . . . .     448  WESTMIN ABBEY     133

FORBEAR
        MAN ITERATES WHILE THESE FORBEAR   . . . . . .      60  RESIGNATION       272
        FATHER FORBEAR FOR I BUT MEET TO-DAY . . . . .      82  SOHRAB RUSTUM     708
        FROM SIN WHICH HEAVEN RECORDS NOT WHY FORBEAR  .   171  BETTER PART        7
        TIME PRESSES SO THAT THEME FORBEAR I NOW   . . .   389  MEROPE           1530

FORBID
        FORBID HIM NOT BUT LET HIM GO  . . . . . . . .      91  SICK KING BOKH  V 116
```

FORBID   (CONTINUED)
     BUT FATE WITHSTANDS AND LAWS FORBID THIS WAY   • •   98 BALDER DEAD 1   127
     THE MANTINEAN SANCTUARY FORBID • • • • • • •   357 MEROPE   775

FORBORNE
     FOR TWENTY YEARS FORBORNE TO INTERRUPT   • • • •   395 MEROPE   1730

FORCE
     OR IS IT THAT SOME FORCE TOO WISE TOO STRONG   • •   9 MYCERINUS   37
     OR IS IT THAT SOME FORCE TOO STERN TOO STRONG   • •   9 MYCERINUS   V 37
     AND NOT TO OFFEND THEE HERMOD NOR TO FORCE • • • •   125 BALDER DEAD 3   413
     I TOO HAVE LONGD FOR TRENCHANT FORCE • • • • •   178 FAREWELL   33
     WE SHALL NOT THEN CALL HARDNESS FORCE   • • • •   179 FAREWELL   59
     WITH FAITHFUL UNRELAXING FORCE • • • • • •   225 EPILOG LAOCOON   147
     HIS GENUINE SELF AND FORCE HIM TO OBEY   • • • •   246 BURIED LIFE   36
     A THIRST TO SPEND OUR FIRE AND RESTLESS FORCE   • •   246 BURIED LIFE   49
     GOETHES SAGE MIND AND BYRONS FORCE • • • • •   272 MEMORIAL VERSES   61
     TARRIEST THOU NOW FOR THAT FORCE • • • • •   287 RUGBY CHAPEL   38
     STILL STILL WENT FORTH THAT CHILDS DEAR FORCE   • •   318 OBERMANN MORE   163
     RIVE ITS DRY BONES AND WITH NEW FORCE   • • • •   319 OBERMANN MORE   199
     SURELY IF RIGHTS MAY BE BY FORCE ASSERTED   • • •   352 MEROPE   656
     MAINTAIND COURAGE AND FORCE AND IN MYSELF   • • •   438 EMPEDOCLES II   319
     AND DEADLY AIRS HIS FORCE DID UNDERMINE   • • • •   448 WESTMIN ABBEY   V 126
     JOIND TO ITS CLEARNESS OF THEIR FORCE   • • • •   482 COURAGE   28
     DIDST FORCE AN AUDIENCE ERE I STRUCK THE SCALE   • •   RUDE ORATOR   6

FORCES
     OUT OF THIS STUFF THESE FORCES THOU ART GROWN   • •   46 IN UTRUMQUE PAR   V 38
     IN THE STIR OF THE FORCES   • • • • • • •   177 PARTING   89

FORD
     OR AT A FORD OR SLEEPING BY A TREE   • • • • •   117 BALDER DEAD 3   118
     KNEE-DEEP IN THE COOL FORD FOR TIS THE LAST   • •   413 EMPEDOCLES I 2   41

FORDONE
     WITH INDIAN HEATS AT LAST FORDONE   • • • • • •   276 SOUTHERN NIGHT   26
     WITH INDIAN SUNS AT LAST FORDONE   • • • • • •   276 SOUTHERN NIGHT   V 26

FORE
     WHAT CLOUDS THY FOREHEAD AND FORE-DATES THY DOOM • •   41 GIPSY CHILD   V 4
     SO EACH NEW MAN STRIKES ROOT INTO A FAR FORE-TIME   418 EMPEDOCLES I 2   191

FOREBODED
     LET THY FOREBODED HOMAGE CHECK THY TONGUE   • • • •   38 WORLDS TRIUMPHS   10
     LET THY FOREBODED TREASON CHECK THY TONGUE   • • • •   38 WORLDS TRIUMPHS   V 10

FOREBODES
     THERE GO THOU WILT NOT YET MY HEART FOREBODES   • •   63 SOHRAB RUSTUM   86
     BUT I SHALL CONQUER THAT MY HEART FOREBODES   • •   62 SOHRAB RUSTUM   V
     THY JOY OUR YOUTH FOREBODES   • • • • • • •   424 EMPEDOCLES I 2   375

FOREBODING
     HIS DARK FOREBODING   • • • • • • • • •   192 STRAYED REVEL   218
     WITH UNUTTERABLE FOREBODING   • • • • • • • •   393 MEROPE   1672

FOREFATHER
     PELASGUS OUR FOREFATHER AND MANKINDS • • • • •   389 MEROPE   1538

FOREGO
     AND YOUR SLACKEND ARMS FOREGO   • • • • • •   27 NEW SIRENS   V 54
     IS IT FOR BEAUTY TO FOREGO HER WREATH   • • • •   212 GROWING OLD   4

FOREHEAD
     WHAT CLOUDS THY FOREHEAD AND FORE-DATES THY DOOM • •   41 GIPSY CHILD   V 4
     LIGHTS UP HIS STUDIOUS FOREHEAD AND THIN HANDS   • •   81 SOHRAB RUSTUM   676
     AND GARLANDS FOR THEIR FOREHEAD WEAVE   • • • •   203 EUPHROSYNE   18
     CLUSTERING OER THY WHITE FOREHEAD LIKE A GIRLS   • •   373 MEROPE   1162
     THE AXE AND ON THE FOREHEAD OF THE KING   • • • •   402 MEROPE   1920
     PLEADING GAZE THAT FOREHEAD CLEAR   • • • • • •   META CLOISTER   38

FOREHEADS
     OUR FOREHEADS FELT THE WIND AND RAIN • • • • •   271 MEMORIAL VERSES   53
     WITH FROWNING FOREHEADS WITH LIPS   • • • • • •   289 RUGBY CHAPEL   105

FOREIGN
     OR WHAT WE FIX WITH FOREIGN POWERS   • • • • • •   47 HORATIAN ECHO   3
     HOW CAN WE FLOWER IN FOREIGN AIR   • • • • • •   306 GRANDE CHARTR   208
     HOW SHOULD WE FLOWER IN FOREIGN AIR   • • • • •   306 GRANDE CHARTR   V 208
     PRECARIOUSLY RULED BY FOREIGN LORDS   • • • • •   337 MEROPE   235

FOREKNOWN
     THOU HAST FOREKNOWN THE VANITY OF HOPE   • • • •   43 GIPSY CHILD   39
     STILL LIFTED WELL WAS HIS RETURN FOREKNOWN   • • • •   124 BALDER DEAD 3   378

FOREMOST
     HAST LABOURD WITH THE FOREMOST HAST BECOME   • • • •   5 DUKE WELLINGTON   V 9
     AND WITH HIS STAFF KEPT BACK THE FOREMOST RANKS • •   65 SOHRAB RUSTUM   143
     HAVE WADED FOREMOST IN THEIR BLOODY WAVES   • • • •   74 SOHRAB RUSTUM   434

FORESAW
FATE WHICH FORESAW . . . . 246 BURIED LIFE   30

FORESAWST
BALDER TOO TRULY THOU FORESAWST A SNARE   . . . . 126 BALDER DEAD 3   446

FORESEEN
FORESEEN THY HARVEST YET PROCEEDST TO LIVE . . . . 43 GIPSY CHILD   40

FORESHOWN
FORESHOWN THEE IN THY CONSECRATION-HOUR   . . . . 446 WESTMIN ABBEY   75

FOREST
NOW THE AUTUMN CRISPS THE FOREST   . . . . . 13 CHURCH BROU 1   15
DOWN THE FOREST-RIDINGS LONE   . . . . 13 CHURCH BROU 1   22
DOWN THE LEAF-STREWN FOREST-ROAD   . . . . 13 CHURCH BROU 1   30
THE FOLIAGED MARBLE FOREST WHERE YE LIE   . . . . 19 CHURCH BROU 3   39
ON THE RED PININGS OF THEIR FOREST-FLOOR   . . . . 25 DREAM   5
LODGERS IN THE FOREST AND THE CAVE   . . . . . 34 NEW SIRENS   234
AND BY THE DARKLING FOREST-PATHS THE GODS . . . . 106 BALDER DEAD 2   63
BUT WHEN THE GODS WERE TO THE FOREST GONE . . . . 106 BALDER DEAD 2   70
WHO BIVOUACS IN A FOREST MID THE HILLS   . . . . 119 BALDER DEAD 3   V
OUT OF THE BLACK WASTE FOREST FAR BELOW   . . . . 119 BALDER DEAD 3   V
A DARK GREEN FOREST-DRESS   . . . . 131 TRISTRAM 1   16
I KNOW HIM BY HIS FOREST-DRESS . . . . 131 TRISTRAM 1   21
IN THE FOREST-DEPTHS ALONE   . . . . 137 TRISTRAM 1   224
ALL ROUND THE FOREST SWEEPS OFF BLACK IN SHADE . . 139 TRISTRAM 1   276
THE FOREST-CHAPEL AND THE FOUNTAIN NEAR   . . . . 139 TRISTRAM 1   279
THEE A PINING EXILE IN THY FOREST   . . . . . 144 TRISTRAM 2   51
WHEN THE FIERCE PAINS TOOK HER IN THE FOREST   . . 145 TRISTRAM 2   83
SO SHE SAID AND DIED IN THE DREAR FOREST   . . . . 145 TRISTRAM 2   87
AND ROUND HIM A FRESH FOREST-SCENE   . . . . . 147 TRISTRAM 2   154
ON THAT CLEAR FOREST-KNOLL HE STAYS   . . . . . 148 TRISTRAM 2   155
THEE A WEEPING EXILE IN THY FOREST   . . . . . 144 TRISTRAM 2   V 51
WHERE THE DEEP FOREST STREAM CREEPS SLOW   . . . . 148 TRISTRAM 2   V
OF THE DEEP FOREST-GLADES OF BROCE-LIANDE . . . . 154 TRISTRAM 3   156
BLOWING BETWEEN THE STEMS THE FOREST-AIR   . . . . 154 TRISTRAM 3   167
AS IF TO ITSELF THE QUIET FOREST SMILED   . . . . 155 TRISTRAM 3   204
FROM THE DEWY FOREST-COVERTS   . . . . 193 STRAYED REVEL   263
AN AIR-STIRRD FOREST FRESH AND CLEAR . . . . . 248 KENSINGTON GARD   16
ABOVE THE FOREST-GROUND CALLED THESSALY   . . . . 258 SCHOLAR-GIPSY   115
FAR ON THE FOREST-SKIRTS WHERE NONE PURSUE . . . . 261 SCHOLAR-GIPSY   215
AND BLUE-BELLS TREMBLING BY THE FOREST-WAYS   . . 265 THYRSIS   75
YET CHARMD IT FROM HIS FOREST-GRAVE   . . . . . 273 STANZAS CARNAC   8
YET BOUND IT FROM HIS FOREST GRAVE   STANZAS CARNAC   V 8
FOREST AND CITY AND SPIRE   . . . . 297 HEINES GRAVE   171
THROUGH FOREST UP THE MOUNTAIN-SIDE   . . . . . 299 GRANDE CHARTR   6
MOUNTS UP THE STONY FOREST-WAY . . . . 300 GRANDE CHARTR   20
FORGOTTEN IN A FOREST-GLADE   . . . . 304 GRANDE CHARTR   171
ROUND SOME FAIR FOREST-LODGE AT MORN . . . . . 305 GRANDE CHARTR   184
ROUND SOME OLD FOREST-LODGE AT MORN   . . . . . 305 GRANDE CHARTR   V 184
AND LEAVE OUR FOREST TO ITS PEACE   . . . . . 306 GRANDE CHARTR   V 210
HER FOREST-CLOTHED FRAME   . . . . 441 EMPEDOCLES II   420
THE SUNLESS FOREST AND THE SEALIKE PLAIN   . . . . 475 CROMWELL   106

FORESTALL
WITH GLAD ACCLAIM ERE THEY FORESTALL MY NEWS   . . 401 MEROPE   1887

FORESTS
OFF THEY SWEEP THE MARSHY FORESTS   . . . . . 13 CHURCH BROU 1   19
HATH MADE IN HIMALAYAN FORESTS WRACK . . . . . 73 SOHRAB RUSTUM   414
MAKE OFTEN IN THE FORESTS HEART AT MORN   . . . . 75 SOHRAB RUSTUM   477
HAS MADE IN HIMALAYAN FORESTS WRACK   . . . . . 73 SOHRAB RUSTUM   V 414
MAKE OFTEN IN THE FORESTS DEPTH AT MORN   . . . . 75 SOHRAB RUSTUM   V 477
TO THE DARK FORESTS IN THE EARLY DAWN . . . . . 106 BALDER DEAD 2   52
IN ALL THE FORESTS AND THE SOFT-STREWN SNOW   . . 122 BALDER DEAD 3   311
TO OUR FORESTS TELL THY PAIN . . . . 139 TRISTRAM 1   275
WHEN OER THE ARCADIAN FORESTS THOU ART COME   . . 349 MEROPE   572
THE FORESTS ROUND THAT BELT CYLLENES SIDE . . . . 357 MEROPE   794
AMONG THE FORESTS ON CYLLENES SIDE   . . . . . 364 MEROPE   974
IN THE PRIMEVAL MOUNTAIN-FORESTS BORE . . . . . 389 MEROPE   1537
THE FORESTS ROUND WHICH BELT CYLLENES SIDE . . . . 357 MEROPE   V 794

FORETOLD
THE BOON THY DEDICATION-SIGN FORETOLD . . . . . 444 WESTMIN ABBEY   5
THE BOON TO THY FOUNDATION-HOUR FORETOLD   . . . . 444 WESTMIN ABBEY   V 5

FORFEIT
WHY NOT ON THEM HAVE PLACED THE FORFEIT CROWN . . 339 MEROPE   320
ALL CLAIM TO SUCCOUR FORFEIT TO MYSELF   . . . . 366 MEROPE   1008

FORGE
THAT PAIR WHOSE HEAD DID PLAN WHOSE HANDS DID FORGE   448 WESTMIN ABBEY   134

FORGED
A TALE MEANWHILE FORGED FOR HIS SUBJECTS EARS . . 366 MEROPE   1002
FORGED BY THE IMPERIOUS LONELY THINKING-POWER . . 440 EMPEDOCLES II   376

FORGES
PAST THE DARK FORGES LONG DISUSED   . . . . . . 299 GRANDE CHARTR   3

FORGET
HAPLY HE WILL FORGET HIS WRATH AND FIGHT • • • • 66 SOHRAB RUSTUM 182
AND MEN SHALL NOT FORGET THEE IN THY GRAVE • • • • 84 SOHRAB RUSTUM 805
WILL HELP HIM TO FORGET HIS CARE • • • • • • 138 TRISTRAM 1 257
FAIR LOVE SHE SAYS CANST THOU FORGET SO SOON • • • 139 TRISTRAM 1 285
CAN FORGET ALL TO HEAR THEM AS OF OLD • • • • 152 TRISTRAM 3 111
AND WE FORGET BECAUSE WE MUST • • • • • • • 183 ABSENCE 11
VAIN IS THE EFFORT TO FORGET • • • • • • • • 207 ON THE RHINE 1
ALAS TO HELP US FORGET • • • • • • • • 296 HEINES GRAVE 118
YES I FORGET THE WORLDS WORK WROUGHT • • • • • 313 OBERMANN MORE 41
LET US FORGET OURSELVES FOR THOSE WE RULE • • • • 394 MEROPE 1721
WHOLLY FORGET THEIR FIRST SAD LIFE AND HOME • • • 427 EMPEDOCLES I 2 458

FORGETFULNESS
PROVES FORGETFULNESS BEGUN • • • • • • • • 24 MEMORY-PICTURE 52
AT LEAST TO HALF FORGETFULNESS • • • • • • • 200 PHILOMELA V

FORGETS
THE AFTER-WORLD FORGETS MY NAME • • • • • • 321 OBERMANN MORE 263

FORGETTING
OXUS FORGETTING THE BRIGHT SPEED HE HAD • • • 87 SOHRAB RUSTUM 886
FOR THERE THINE EARTH-FORGETTING EYELIDS KEEP • • 267 THYRSIS 168

FORGETTST
POOR LAMB THOU SLEEPEST AND FORGETTST THY WOE • • 103 BALDER DEAD 1 288

FORGIVE
CHILDREN AS SUCH FORGIVE THEM HAVE I KNOWN • • • • 8 RELIGIOUS ISOL 1
I FORGIVE THEE ISEULT THOU WILT STAY • • • • • 143 TRISTRAM 2 28
FORGIVE ME FORGIVE ME • • • • • • • • • 176 PARTING 59
FORGIVE ME FORGIVE ME • • • • • • • • • 176 PARTING 59
FORGIVE ME MASTERS OF THE MIND • • • • • • • 301 GRANDE CHARTR 73
SOMETHING TOO STUDIOUSLY FORGIVE ME SHOWN • • • 334 MEROPE 142
FORGIVE MY FOLLY AND WORK • • • • • • • • 348 MEROPE 538
FORGIVE ME MAIDENS IF I SEEM TOO SLACK • • • • 348 MEROPE 548
FORGIVE FORGIVE THE BRINGER OF SUCH NEWS • • • 363 MEROPE 949
FORGIVE FORGIVE THE BRINGER OF SUCH NEWS • • • 363 MEROPE 949

FORGIVEN
SAY WHAT IS THIS WE ARE IN BLISS FORGIVEN • • • • 18 CHURCH BROU 3 30

FORGIVENESS
HIM CAN NO FOUNT OF FRESH FORGIVENESS LAVE • • • 172 GOOD SHEPHERD 4
THOUGH INJURED PAST FORGIVENESS AS MEN DEEM • • 394 MEROPE 1707

FORGIVES
NATURE FORGIVES NO DEBT AND FEARS NO GRAVE • • • • 5 HARMONY NATURE 10
HUSH NO WORDS THAT SMILE I SEE FORGIVES ME • • • • 144 TRISTRAM 2 69

FORGIVING
SWEET AND FORGIVING AND GOOD • • • • • • • 232 YOUTH OF MAN 15

FORGIVN
THAT ALL MAY BE ENDURED AND ALL FORGIVN • • • • 394 MEROPE 1710

FORGO
AND THOSE SLACKEND ARMS FORGO • • • • • • • • 27 NEW SIRENS 54

FORGOES
THE PERFUME WHICH THE DAY FORGOES • • • • • • 218 BACCHANALIA 1 15

FORGONE
HER OWN SWEET ERRANDS ALL FORGONE • • • • • 53 RESIGNATION 36
OF YOUTH TIS LIKE HAD NEVER QUITE FORGONE • • • • 394 MEROPE 1703

FORGOT
BECAUSE OUR SPIRITS HAVE FORGOT • • • • • • 60 RESIGNATION 276
I FORGOT THOU COMEST FROM THY VOYAGE • • • • • • 142 TRISTRAM 2 17
FORGOT HIS CRAFT AND HIS BEST WITS TOOK FLIGHT • • 155 TRISTRAM 3 182
FORGOT MY GOOD AS SOON AS DONE • • • • • • • 158 SAINT BRANDAN 60
FORGOT MY DEED AS SOON AS DONE • • • • • • • 158 SAINT BRANDAN V 60
BUT NOW THAT TROUBLE IS FORGOT • • • • • • • 276 SOUTHERN NIGHT 17
THOU HAST FORGOT THEN WHO I AM WHO HEAR • • • 335 MEROPE 182
HAD THEY MISRULED HAD THEY FORGOT THEIR FRIENDS • • 339 MEROPE 322
THE BOY HIS NURSE FORGOT • • • • • • • • • 447 WESTMIN ABBEY 111
THINGS THAT MAY CEASE BUT NEVER BE FORGOT • • • 462 ALARIC AT ROME 16
STILL TURND TO WATCH THE BATTLE STILL FORGOT • • 476 CROMWELL 171

FORGOTTEN
HAVE KNOWN TOO MUCH OR ELSE FORGOTTEN ALL • • • 43 GIPSY CHILD 48
AND I BE NOT FORGOTTEN IN MY GRAVE • • • • • 84 SOHRAB RUSTUM 794
THE CORONALS OF THAT FORGOTTEN TIME • • • • 266 THYRSIS 117
FORGOTTEN IN A FOREST-GLADE • • • • • • • 304 GRANDE CHARTR 171
UNWELCOME SHROUD OF THE FORGOTTEN DEAD • • • • 462 ALARIC AT ROME 1
TO HEAR A DIM AND LONG FORGOTTEN TONE • • • • 467 ALARIC AT ROME 123
LIKE SOME FORGOTTEN STRAIN THAT HAUNTS US STILL • • 477 CROMWELL 195

FORLORN
NOT INNOCENT INDEED YET NOT FORLORN • • • • • • 6 GEO CRUIKSHANK 5

```
FORLORN      ( CONTINUED )
       NOR ANY ANGELS SORROW SO FORLORN         . . . . . .    42 GIPSY CHILD         28
       AND NEVER ANGELS SORROW SO FORLORN       . . . . . .    42 GIPSY CHILD      V  28
       GREETED OF NONE DISFEATURED AND FORLORN    . . . .     109 BALDER DEAD 2       171
       AS WHOLLY TO BE PITIED QUITE FORLORN     . . . . .     126 BALDER DEAD 3       458
       BOTH HAVE PASSD A YOUTH FORLORN AND SAD    . . . .     144 TRISTRAM 2      V   54
       THEN SOOTHING WITH THY CHRISTIAN STRAIN FORLORN  .     168 RACHEL 3             6
       YET STILL FROM TIME TO TIME VAGUE AND FORLORN    .     247 BURIED LIFE         72
       LIKE THESE ON EARTH I WAIT FORLORN       . . . . .     302 GRANDE CHARTR       88
       WHILE THE WORLD LIES FORLORN     . . . . . . . .       321 OBERMANN MORE      248
       HADST THOU FROM THY FORLORN AND CAPTIVE STATE    .     383 MEROPE            1369
       LAY FORLORN LAY OUTCAST  . . . . . . . . . . .        391 MEROPE            1604

FORM
       FROM THOSE STILL DEEPS IN FORM AND COLOUR DREST   .     45 IN UTRUMQUE PAR      4
       AND SCANND WITH BLINKING EYES THE ADVANCING FORM  .     76 SOHRAB RUSTUM      518
       IN GARB IN FORM IN FEATURE AS HE WAS . . . . .        103 BALDER DEAD 1       283
       DECEIVER FAIR IN FORM BUT FALSE IN HEART   . . .      114 BALDER DEAD 3        21
       I SEE HER FORM GLIDE THROUGH THE CROSSING SPEARS .     138 TRISTRAM 1         241
       SO SLIGHT A FORM IN SO RICH A DRESS      . . . .      131 TRISTRAM 1      V
       SHE WILL SAY IS THIS THE FORM I DREADED    . . .      144 TRISTRAM 2      V   65
       AND ON IT CHRIST A LIVING FORM   . . . . . . .        156 SAINT BRANDAN       16
       IF THE LOVED FORM AND THE DEEP-CHERISHD FEATURE  .     206 SEPARATION           7
       IS IT TO LOSE THE GLORY OF THE FORM      . . . .      212 GROWING OLD          2
       IS THIS THE EYE THE FORM ALERT   . . . . . . .        276 SOUTHERN NIGHT  V   37
       THAT WAN NAILD FORM WITH HEAD DROOPD LOW   . . .      317 OBERMANN MORE   V  155
       AND LOOK TO MEET THEM THAT ONE GRIEF-PLUNGED FORM     331 MEROPE              56
       WHILE STOOD OER HIM A FORM       . . . . . . .        346 MEROPE             492
       SOME FORM AH ME AH . . . . . . . . . . . . .          346 MEROPE             493
       AIR TO HIS UNWINGD FORM DENIES A WAY     . . . .      351 MEROPE             624
       IN HER ROUGH FORM FEARING        . . . . . . .        392 MEROPE            1634
       AND SEE TO MEET THEM THAT ONE GRIEF-PLUNGED FORM .     331 MEROPE          V   56
       AND MAJESTY AND SACRED FORM AND FEAR     . . . .      445 WESTMIN ABBEY       58
       MANTLED HER FORM NO MORE HER HEAD WAS BOWD   . .      447 WESTMIN ABBEY       98
       ON LIPS THAT RARELY FORM THEM NOW    . . . . .        451 GEISTS GRAVE        42
       WHERE OFT WE WATCHD THY COUCHANT FORM    . . . .      451 GEISTS GRAVE        68
       ALL CONVULSED HIS LITTLE FORM    . . . . . . .        452 POOR MATTHIAS        4
       REGARDS HIS BROTHERS FORM OUTSPREAD      . . . .      460 KAISER DEAD         68
       ONE FORM STANDS GAZING SILENTLY BELOW    . . . .      468 ALARIC AT ROME     153
       THINE WAS NO MOUNTAIN HOME WHERE FREEDOMS FORM   .     472 CROMWELL            17
       A FORM THAT TOWERD ABOVE HIS BROTHER MEN   . . .      476 CROMWELL           145
       A FORM HE KNEW BUT IT WAS SHROUDED THEN    . . .      476 CROMWELL           146
       ON THAT DARK FORM HIS EYES HAD GAZD BEFORE . . .      477 CROMWELL           201
       THAT FORM WAS HIS THOSE FEATURES WERE HIS OWN    .     478 CROMWELL           204

FORMD
       AND ON THE OTHER SIDE THE PERSIANS FORMD   . . . .     65 SOHRAB RUSTUM      136

FORMER
       THEY RECOGNISE A FORMER SCENE    . . . . . . .         55 RESIGNATION        115
       THE GHOST IN THEM OF FORMER DAYS         . . . .       56 RESIGNATION        123
       THE GHOSTS IN THEM OF FORMER DAYS        . . . .       56 RESIGNATION     V  123
       THE MEN OF FORMER TIMES HAD CROWND THE TOP . . .       61 SOHRAB RUSTUM       20
       HATH BUILDED ON THE WASTE IN FORMER YEARS  . . .       71 SOHRAB RUSTUM      338
       HAS BUILDED ON THE WASTE IN FORMER YEARS   . . .       71 SOHRAB RUSTUM   V  338
       HATH BUILDED ON THE WASTE IN FORMER DAYS   . . .       71 SOHRAB RUSTUM   V  338
       HAS BUILDED ON THE WASTE IN FORMER DAYS    . . .       71 SOHRAB RUSTUM   V  338
       MY FORMER LIFE AND CHEERS ME EVEN HERE   . . . .      126 BALDER DEAD 3      462
       AND THAT WILL BRING TO MIND THE FORMER LIFE  . .      128 BALDER DEAD 3      540
       THAT A FORMER RIVAL SHARES HER OFFICE    . . . .      144 TRISTRAM 2          59
       TO MAKE OUR FORMER PLEASURES ALL SEEM STALE  . .      153 TRISTRAM 3         126
       THEIR LIVES AND FORMER VIOLENT TOIL IN THEBES    .     193 STRAYED REVEL      256
       FRESHEN THY FLOWERS AS IN FORMER YEARS   . . . .      261 SCHOLAR-GIPSY      218
       BY FORMER AGES WHO ELSE   . . . . . . . . . .        290 RUGBY CHAPEL       148
       OF A FORMER AGE ANY MORE  . . . . . . . . . .        294 HEINES GRAVE        80
       AND OUTCRY OF THE FORMER MEN     . . . . . . .        303 GRANDE CHARTR      128
       OF FAITHFUL FONDNESS FOR THEIR FORMER KING . . .      331 MEROPE              39
       OF FAITHFUL FONDNESS TOWARDS THEIR FORMER KING   .     331 MEROPE          V   39

FORMS
       ON THE TOMB TWO FORMS THEY SCULPTURED    . . . .       16 CHURCH BROU 1      105
       AND MARVEL AT THE FORMS OF STONE         . . . .       17 CHURCH BROU 2       36
       ON THE BROWN RUDE-CARVED BALCONY TWO FORMS . . .       25 DREAM               21
       FOR I DREAMD THEY WORE YOUR FORMS    . . . . .         26 NEW SIRENS          10
       ARE THOSE FRAIL FORMS MORE ENDURING      . . . .       27 NEW SIRENS          43
       AND IMMORTAL FORMS TO MEET YOU   . . . . . . .         29 NEW SIRENS         101
       FORMS WHAT SHE FORMS ALONE       . . . . . . .         45 IN UTRUMQUE PAR     28
       FORMS WHAT SHE FORMS ALONE       . . . . . . .         45 IN UTRUMQUE PAR     28
       ROUND WHERE THEY STOOD AND THEY BEHELD TWO FORMS .     126 BALDER DEAD 3      442
       TO FORMS FROM ANTIQUE GREECE AND ROME UPTORN . .      168 RACHEL 3             3
       OF EDDYING FORMS  . . . . . . . . . . . . .          185 STRAYED REVEL        5
       OF EDDYING FORMS  . . . . . . . . . . . . .          194 STRAYED REVEL      296
       COWLD FORMS BRUSH BY IN GLEAMING WHITE   . . . .      300 GRANDE CHARTR       36
       TAKE ME COWLD FORMS AND FENCE ME ROUND   . . . .      302 GRANDE CHARTR       93
       PLACED SAFELY IN CHANGED FORMS THE PAIR    . . .      427 EMPEDOCLES I 2     457
       BUT THROUGH THEIR FORMS AND MODES AND STIFLING VEILS  439 EMPEDOCLES II      354
       WHAT FORMS ARE THESE COMING      . . . . . . .        442 EMPEDOCLES II      437
       EARTHS OLD HEROIC FORMS IN PEACEFUL SLUMBERS DEEP     464 ALARIC AT ROME      60
       PEOPLED NIGHTS VOICELESS SHADES WITH FORMS OF LONG AGO 467 ALARIC AT ROME    126
       HERE SHOULD A THOUSAND FORMS ON FANCYS WINGS     . .  470 ALARIC AT ROME     207
```

FORMS   (CONTINUED)
    WHAT FORMS ARE THESE THAT WITH COMPLAINING SOUND • •   476 CROMWELL   159
    FORMS THAT WITH HIM SHALL TREAD LIFES CHANGING STAGE   476 CROMWELL   161

FORSAKE
    FORSAKE THIS AMPLE PROUD MESSENIAN REALM   • • • •   395 MEROPE   1744
    THE PIOUS WAIL FORSAKE   • • • • • • • • • •   416 EMPEDOCLES I 2   134

FORSAKEN
    DID FALL LIKE RAIN IN THE FORSAKEN STREET   • • • •   FRAGMENT 7   2

FORSAKES
    NO WHEN I SEE THEE WRATH FORSAKES MY SOUL   • • • •   74 SOHRAB RUSTUM   430
    YET EVEN WHEN MAN FORSAKES   • • • • • • • •   420 EMPEDOCLES I 2   242

FORSET
    FORSET THY SON TO BE BELOVED LIKE THEE   • • • •   126 BALDER DEAD 3   451

FORSOOK
    WHEN SHE FORSOOK THE STARRY HEIGHT   • • • • • •   181 ISOLATION MARG   22
    ONE SUMMER-MORN FORSOOK   • • • • • • • • • •   256 SCHOLAR-GIPSY   36

FORSWEAR
    INVITEST REASON TO FORSWEAR HER STATE   • • • •   RUDE ORATOR   18

FORSWORN
    FORSWORN THEIR BLOOD UNGRATEFULLY HAD THEY   • • • •   339 MEROPE   323

FORT
    WITH A CLAY FORT BUT THAT WAS FALLN AND NOW   • •   61 SOHRAB RUSTUM   21
    AND ASGARD THOU DIDST BUILD AND MIDGARD FORT   • •   121 BALDER DEAD 3   266
    UNBREACHABLE THE FORT   • • • • • • • • • •   267 THYRSIS   146

FORTH
    I WILL GO FORTH THOUGH SOMETHING WOULD I SAY   • •   10 MYCERINUS   68
    I WILL GO FORTH BUT SOMETHING WOULD I SAY   • • • •   10 MYCERINUS   V 68
    CAME FORTH OLIVIAS MARGUERITE AND THINE   • • • •   25 DREAM   22
    FORTH AT NOON HAD LURED ME CREEPING   • • • • •   26 NEW SIRENS   3
    OUR JOVIAL HOST AS FORTH WE FARE   • • • • •   53 RESIGNATION   42
    WILL CHALLENGE FORTH THE BRAVEST PERSIAN LORDS   • •   62 SOHRAB RUSTUM   56
    STAND FORTH THE WHILE AND TAKE THEIR CHALLENGE UP   66 SOHRAB RUSTUM   183
    SO SPAKE HE AND FEROOD STOOD FORTH AND CRIED   • •   66 SOHRAB RUSTUM   184
    WHEN SOHRAB DARES OUR BRAVEST FORTH AND SEEKS   68 SOHRAB RUSTUM   244
    SO ARMD HE ISSUED FORTH AND RUKSH HIS HORSE   69 SOHRAB RUSTUM   270
    SOHRAB COME FORTH AND EYED HIM AS HE CAME   • •   70 SOHRAB RUSTUM   301
    CAME SEEKING RUSTUM AND DEFYING FORTH   • • • •   70 SOHRAB RUSTUM   310
    BY CHALLENGE FORTH MAKE GOOD THY VAUNT OR YIELD   •   72 SOHRAB RUSTUM   367
    AND THE BRIGHT SUN BROKE FORTH AND MELTED ALL   • •   76 SOHRAB RUSTUM   523
    AND HE DESIRED TO DRAW FORTH THE STEEL   • •   80 SOHRAB RUSTUM   651
    OF RUSTUM AND HIS TEARS BROKE FORTH HE CAST   • •   82 SOHRAB RUSTUM   727
    SO SPAKE HE AND FEROOD STOOD FORTH AND SAID   • •   66 SOHRAB RUSTUM   V 184
    SO FOLLOWD RUSTUM ISSUED FORTH AND CROSSD   • •   69 SOHRAB RUSTUM   V 280
    WENT SEEKING RUSTUM AND DEFYING FORTH   • • • •   70 SOHRAB RUSTUM   V 310
    WATCHD MY LORDS COMING FORTH AND PUSHD   • • •   88 SICK KING BOKH   33
    WENT FORTH AGAIN THE HOLY BOOK   • • • • • •   89 SICK KING BOKH   47
    NOW I AT NIGHTFALL HAD GONE FORTH   • • • •   90 SICK KING BOKH   65
    BRAKE FORTH AND CURSED THEM DOST THOU HEAR   • • •   90 SICK KING BOKH   87
    TILL THAT THE KING STOOD FORTH AND SAID   • • •   91 SICK KING BOKH   107
    TAKE SLEIPNER HERMOD AND SET FORTH WITH DAWN   • •   102 BALDER DEAD 1   236
    FORTH FROM THE EAST UP THE ASCENT OF HEAVEN   • •   105 BALDER DEAD 2   1
    AND THE VALKYRIES ON THEIR STEEDS WENT FORTH   • •   105 BALDER DEAD 2   19
    FORTH WENDED THEY AND DRAVE THEIR STEEDS BEFORE   •   106 BALDER DEAD 2   50
    HERMOD LED SLEIPNER FROM VALHALLA FORTH   • • •   106 BALDER DEAD 2   71
    DID ANGERBODE THE GIANTESS BRING FORTH   • • •   110 BALDER DEAD 2   207
    THEN MOUNTED SLEIPNER AND SET FORTH TO RIDE   • •   112 BALDER DEAD 2   284
    FORTH WENDED THEY AND DROVE THEIR STEEDS BEFORE   •   106 BALDER DEAD 2   V 50
    HIS MESSENGER AND HE STOOD FORTH AND CRIED   • • •   114 BALDER DEAD 3   32
    AND TOOK THEIR HORSES AND SET FORTH TO RIDE   • •   119 BALDER DEAD 3   215
    THE GIANT YMIR WHOM THE ABYSS BROUGHT FORTH   • •   121 BALDER DEAD 3   257
    GO QUICKLY FORTH THROUGH ALL THE WORLD AND PRAY   •   122 BALDER DEAD 3   299
    THEIR HORSES AND RODE FORTH THROUGH ALL THE WORLD   122 BALDER DEAD 3   303
    HE SPOKE AND NIORD SET FORTH BACK TO HEAVEN   • •   124 BALDER DEAD 3   373
    STRETCHD FORTH HIS HAND AND WITH BENIGNANT VOICE   •   125 BALDER DEAD 3   410
    AT LAST HE SIGHD AND SET FORTH BACK TO HEAVEN   • •   129 BALDER DEAD 3   566
    AH HE WANDERS FORTH AGAIN   • • • • • • • •   138 TRISTRAM 1   243
    TO LOOK FORTH ON THE FAIRY SIGHT   • • • • •   141 TRISTRAM 1   353
    HAD WANDERD FORTH HER CHILDREN WERE AT PLAY   • •   149 TRISTRAM 3   6
    DREW ISEULT FORTH HER CHILDREN WERE AT PLAY   • •   TRISTRAM 3   V   5
    COME STRETCH FORTH THY HAND THEN SO   • • • • •   187 STRAYED REVEL   61
    COME FORTH ULYSSES   • • • • • • • • • •   188 STRAYED REVEL   71
    WHO SPEAKS AH WHO COMES FORTH   • • • • • •   189 STRAYED REVEL   99
    LIKE SHADOWS FORTH IN SPRING   • • • • • • •   193 STRAYED REVEL   243
    FORTH FROM THE PALACE HITHERWARD COMES   • • •   196 FRAG ANTIGONE   44
    THAT TRAVAILS SORE AND BRINGS FORTH WIND   • • •   217 NAMELESS EPIT   V
    FORTH WITH THY JOYOUS SONG   • • • • • • •   219 BACCHANALIA 1   42
    FORTH WITH THY FLUTE   • • • • • • • • •   219 BACCHANALIA 1   43
    FORTH WITH THY PRAISING VOICE   • • • • • •   220 BACCHANALIA 2   47
    FORTH WITH THY FLUTE   • • • • • • • •   220 BACCHANALIA 2   48
    AND FANCY THAT WE PUT FORTH ALL OUR LIFE   • • •   236 PALLADIUM   19
    CHEERFUL WITH FRIENDS WE SET FORTH   • • • • •   289 RUGBY CHAPEL   89

FORTH (CONTINUED)
FRIENDS WHO SET FORTH AT OUR SIDE • • • • • • 289 RUGBY CHAPEL 102
FORTH TO THE WORLD THOSE SOLDIERS FARE • • • • 305 GRANDE CHARTR 179
FORTH TO THE MIGHTY WORLD THEY FARE • • • • • • 305 GRANDE CHARTR V 179
BUT WE BROUGHT FORTH AND REARD IN HOURS • • • • 308 OBERMANN 69
STILL STILL WENT FORTH THAT CHILDS DEAR FORCE • • • 318 OBERMANN MORE 163
SHALL I NOT GREET HER SHALL I NOT LEAP FORTH • • 331 MEROPE 60
SENT FORTH ECHEMUS THE VICTOR THE KING • • • • 344 MEROPE 442
SET FORTH FROM TEGEA THE ROYAL TOWN • • • • • 355 MEROPE 732
COME FORTH DENOUNCE THE TRAFFIC AND THE TRAITOR • • 364 MEROPE 982
HAPLY HAD BUT ONE DARING SOUL STOOD FORTH • • • • 383 MEROPE 1364
TILL PRESENTLY THE KING CAME FORTH IN ROBE • • • • 401 MEROPE 1903
SISTER FROM THIS DAY FORTH THOU ART NO MORE • • 403 MEROPE 1954
FORTH FROM HIS PARENTS STEM • • • 418 EMPEDOCLES I 2 188
POUR FORTH THE FOAMING VIALS OF THY WRATH • • • • 465 ALARIC AT ROME 86
ARISE AND ARM THEE SPREAD THY BANNERS FORTH • • • 465 ALARIC AT ROME 95
SMILINGLY FORTH UPON HER SUNNY BAY • • • • • • 468 ALARIC AT ROME 160
SO SHONE FORTH IN FRONT OF TROY BY THE BED OF XANTHUS HOMER TRANS 1
BUT SHE WITH PRODIGALITY BRINGS FORTH • • • • EVERLASTING SUB 4

FORTIETH
EACH FORTIETH WEB OF CLOTH TO ME • • • • • • 87 SICK KING BOKH 8

FORTRESS
PAST MIDGARD FORTRESS DOWN TO EARTH AND MEN • • 99 BALDER DEAD 1 142
PAST MIDGARD FORTRESS DOWN TO EARTH THEY CAME • • 105 BALDER DEAD 2 23

FORTS
WHEN THE FORTS OF FOLLY FALL • • • • • • • • 215 LAST WORD 15

FORTUNATE
O RUKSH THOU ART MORE FORTUNATE THAN I • • • • 83 SOHRAB RUSTUM 747
WITH ALL THE FORTUNATE HAVE NOT • • • • • • 273 EDW QUILLINAN 17
MORE FORTUNATE ALAS THAN WE • • • • • • 304 GRANDE CHARTR 158
MORE FORTUNATE THAN THEE MORE FAIRLY JUDGED • • 350 MEROPE 590
FORTUNATE FIRS WHO NEVER THINK • • • • • • • 483 ROME-SICKNESS 9

FORTUNE
VALLEYS AND MEN TO MIDDLE FORTUNE BORN • • • • 6 GEO CRUIKSHANK 4
FORTUNE PRESENTS UNPRAYD • • • • • • • • • 195 FRAG ANTIGONE 5
WOUNDED BY MEN BY FORTUNE TRIED • • • • • 203 EUPHROSYNE 6
FRIENDS COULD NOT GIVE WHAT FORTUNE CAN • • • • 273 EDW QUILLINAN 11
BUT HE IS NOW BY FORTUNE FOILD • • • • • • • 273 EDW QUILLINAN 13
RADIANT WITH FORTUNE AND JOY • • • • • • • 393 MEROPE 1683
TO AFFRIGHT A FORTUNE WHICH THE GODS SECURE • • 398 MEROPE 1782

FORTUNES
FORTUNES NOW LESS FREQUENT HEIR • • • • • • 22 MEMORY-PICTURE V
OF FORTUNES FAVOURD SONS NOT ME • • • • • • 249 WISH 4
HOW FIRS LESS CURST BY FORTUNES FROWN • • • • 483 ROME-SICKNESS 10

FORWARD
AND HE RAN FORWARD AND EMBRACED HIS KNEES • • • 71 SOHRAB RUSTUM 341
FALLING FORWARD MINGLING • • • • • • • • • 188 STRAYED REVEL 87
BACKWARD AND FORWARD ROLLD THE WAVES OF FIGHT • • 236 PALLADIUM 7
FORWARD THE GRACIOUS HOURS HAVE FARED • • • • 322 OBERMANN MORE 283
ALAS OUR FOE ALONE STOOD FORWARD THEN • • • • 383 MEROPE 1367
BROKE FROM THE DORIAN LORDS FORWARD THEY RUSHD • • 402 MEROPE 1931

FORWARDS
AND HE RAN FORWARDS AND EMBRACED HIS KNEES • • • 71 SOHRAB RUSTUM V 341
FALLING FORWARDS MINGLING • • • • • • • • 188 STRAYED REVEL V 87
FORWARDS FORWARDS OER THE STARLIT SEA • • • • 239 SELF-DEPENDENCE 4
FORWARDS FORWARDS OER THE STARLIT SEA • • • • 239 SELF-DEPENDENCE 4

FOSTERD
TO BE DELIVERD FROM THY FOSTERD HATE • • • • • 342 MEROPE 383

FOSTERING
AND FOSTERING IN THY LAP A HEAP OF FLOWERS • • • 257 SCHOLAR-GIPSY 78

FOUGHT
SHOULD ONE DAY GREET UPON SOME WELL-FOUGHT FIELD • • 62 SOHRAB RUSTUM 51
OF BLOOD AND I HAVE FOUGHT WITH MANY A FOE • • • • 71 SOHRAB RUSTUM 327
BUT IN THE GLOOM THEY FOUGHT WITH BLOODSHOT EYES • • 75 SOHRAB RUSTUM 490
INTO THE TILT-YARD WHERE THE HEROES FOUGHT • • • 105 BALDER DEAD 2 30
LONG IVE WAITED LONG IVE FOUGHT MY FEVER • • • • 142 TRISTRAM 2 3
WHICH DOGGD BY FEAR AND FOUGHT BY SHAME • • • • 147 TRISTRAM 2 132
THE FAMOUS MEN OF WAR HAVE FOUGHT • • • • • 219 BACCHANALIA 2 5
AND FOUGHT AND SAW IT NOT BUT THERE IT STOOD • • 236 PALLADIUM 4
HARDLY OURSELVES WE FOUGHT THROUGH • • • • • • 289 RUGBY CHAPEL 120
OF THE HORSEMEN OF TROY IN THE DAY THEY FOUGHT HOMER TRANS 34
FOR THEIR CITY

FOUL
WHAT FOUL FIEND RIDES THEE ON INTO THE FIGHT • • • 137 TRISTRAM 1 239
BY HIM SHOWN FAIR BUT I BELIEVE MOST FOUL • • • 349 MEROPE 556
THE TOILS OF THY FOUL SERVICE TILL THOU WAKE • • 373 MEROPE 1181

FOULER
SINCE POLICY BIDS THUS WHAT FOULER DEATH • • • • 390 MEROPE 1568

FOULEST
    WHO SELF-EXCULPATES LEND TO FOULEST DEEDS . . . . 338 MEROPE   279

FOUND
    THERE THEY FOUND HER IN THE MOUNTAINS   . . . . 15 CHURCH BROU 1   99
    SHEPHERDS SAY THEY FOUND YOU SLEEPING   . . . . 31 NEW SIRENS   145
    HATH MADE OR BIRTH HATH FOUND RESIGND   . . . . 53 RESIGNATION   27
    AND FOUND THE OLD MAN SLEEPING ON HIS BED   . . . . 61 SOHRAB RUSTUM   26
    AND GUDURZ ENTERD RUSTUMS TENT AND FOUND   . . . . 67 SOHRAB RUSTUM   195
    AS WHEN SOME HUNTER IN THE SPRING HATH FOUND . . . 77 SOHRAB RUSTUM   556
    HIM THAT KIND CREATURE FOUND AND REARD AND LOVED . . 81 SOHRAB RUSTUM   682
    MY FATHER LET ME FEEL THAT I HAVE FOUND   . . . . 82 SOHRAB RUSTUM   717
    UNDER SOME MULBERRY-TREES I FOUND   . . . . 90 SICK KING BOKH   67
    NOW MEANWHILE HAD MY BRETHREN FOUND   . . . . 90 SICK KING BOKH   77
    THINGS WHICH MIGHT VEX HIM SHALL BE FOUND   . . . . 92 SICK KING BOKH   160
    AND NOW WOULD NIGHT HAVE FALLN AND FOUND THEM YET   95 BALDER DEAD 1   15
    AND IN THE HALL HE FOUND THOSE WOMEN OLD   . . . 97 BALDER DEAD 1   88
    AND TO THE WALL HE CAME AND FOUND THE GRATE. . . . 113 BALDER DEAD 2   286
    UNDER THE GATE-HOUSE TO THE SANDS AND FOUND . . . 113 BALDER DEAD 2   309
    FOR IN THE PATHS OF HEAVEN HE IS NOT FOUND   . . . . 116 BALDER DEAD 3   102
    AND THEY FOUND MIMIR SITTING BY HIS FOUNT   . . . . 120 BALDER DEAD 3   219
    AND CAME BENEATH THE WALL AND FOUND THE GRATE . . . 124 BALDER DEAD 3   377
    AND BROUGHT HER TALE TO AN END AND FOUND THE PATH   151 TRISTRAM 3   62
    JOY HAS NOT FOUND HER YET NOR EVER WILL   . . . . 151 TRISTRAM 3   68
    ARE THERE THE SOLE COMPANIONS TO BE FOUND   . . . . 152 TRISTRAM 3   99
    SHUDDERING THEY DREW HER GARMENTS OFF AND FOUND .   166 AUSTERITY POET   10
    PAUSANIAS ON HIS TRAVELS FOUND . . . .   221 EPILOG LAOCOON   16
    ILL FOUND IN STRENGTH IN WITS ARE THEY   . . . . 226 EPILOG LAOCOON   V 172
    SAY YE THE SPIRIT OF MAN HAS FOUND NEW ROADS . . . 237 PROGRESS   25
    SINCE HE HAS NOT YET FOUND THE WORD GOD WOULD . . . 239 REVOLUTIONS   12
    HAD FOUND HIM SEATED AT THEIR ENTERING   . . . . 256 SCHOLAR-GIPSY   60
    HE FOUND US WHEN THE AGE HAD BOUND   . . . . 271 MEMORIAL VERSES   45
    OF MEN SHALL THEY BE FOUND   . . . .   309 OBERMANN   100
    AND SOUGHT AND FOUND REPOSE   . . . .   321 OBERMANN MORE   252
    AS I HAVE EVER FOUND THEE BENT TO KEEP   . . . . 332 MEROPE   80
    WHAT WE FOUND HERE WERE TRIBES OF FAME OBSCURE   .   337 MEROPE   233
    THOUGH FOUND PERVERSE THE BLOOD OF HERACLES . . 337 MEROPE   256
    WHY WILT THOU FLY TO LOSE AS SOON AS FOUND   . . . 381 MEROPE   1290
    WHO KNOWS BUT THAT AVENGERS THOU HADST FOUND . . 383 MEROPE   1372
    AND HARDLY YET SOME SAY HATH FOUND A GRAVE   . . 385 MEROPE   1425
    THIS HAVING KNOWN LET US A UNION FOUND   . . . 394 MEROPE   1716
    COULD FIND NO WAY TO FOUND THEM SURE AS THIS . . 403 MEROPE   1960
    AND FOUND HIM AT MY HUSBANDS SIDE HIS FRIEND . . 403 MEROPE   1973
    TO FIND IN THEE A FAULT WHEREON TO FOUND   . . . 404 MEROPE   2006
    THIS HAVING LEARND LET US A UNION FOUND   . . . 394 MEROPE   V1716
    BUT WE AN EASIER WAY TO CHEAT OUR PAINS HAVE FOUND   421 EMPEDOCLES I 2   271
    AND SERVED MEN NOBLY AND ACCEPTANCE FOUND   . . . 448 WESTMIN ABBEY   143
    POOR MATTHIAS FOUND HIM LYING   . . . .   452 POOR MATTHIAS   1
    FOUND HIM STIFF YOU SAY THOUGH WARM . . . . .   452 POOR MATTHIAS   3
    THIS BOAT THEY FOUND AGAINST THE SHORE   . . . 480 HAYSWATER BOAT   25
    THERE IN THE LEAF-STREWN COPSE I FOUND   . . . . 484 ROME-SICKNESS   14
    AND HE DIES FRUITLESS HAVING FOUND NO FIELD . .   LUCRETIUS 2   6

FOUNDATION
    AUGUST INDEED WAS THE FOUNDATION HERE   . . . . 389 MEROPE   1554
    THE BOON TO THY FOUNDATION-HOUR FORETOLD   . . . . 444 WESTMIN ABBEY   V 5

FOUNDATIONS
    SPRING THE FOUNDATIONS OF THAT SHADOWY THRONE   . .   4 BUTLERS SERMONS   6
    SPRING THE FOUNDATIONS OF THE SHADOWY THRONE   . .   4 BUTLERS SERMONS   V 6

FOUNDED
    FIRST CITY FOUNDED ON THE EARTH BY MEN   . . . . 359 MEROPE   849
    BLOOD-FOUNDED THRONES THOU SAYST ARE INSECURE   . . 389 MEROPE   1532
    THUS LITTLE FOUNDED IN THEIR SUBJECTS LOVE   . . . 390 MEROPE   1560
    BE THEIR FIRST-FOUNDED ORDER STRICT MAINTAIND   . . 390 MEROPE   1565
    WHOSE STRIPED SHELL FOUNDED   . . . .   392 MEROPE   1628
    IF THEIR FIRST-FOUNDED ORDER BE MAINTAIND   . . . 390 MEROPE   V1565

FOUNDER
    OUR GLORIOUS FOUNDER   . . . .   398 MEROPE   1812

FOUNDERD
    SO CHARGD HE STOOD DUMB-FOUNDERD CYPSELUS   . . . 365 MEROPE   V
    ALLOWS THE PROUDLY-RIDING AND THE FOUNDERD BARK . . 421 EMPEDOCLES I 2   V 261

FOUNDERING
    ALLOWS THE PROUDLY-RIDING AND THE FOUNDERING BARK   421 EMPEDOCLES I 2   261

FOUNDERS
    YOUR RACES FOUNDERS   . . . .   391 MEROPE   1601

FOUNDEST
    LAST WALKING BY THE SEA THOU FOUNDEST SPARS . . 121 BALDER DEAD 3   268
    THEN WALKING BY THE SEA THOU FOUNDEST SPARS . . 121 BALDER DEAD 3   V 268

FOUNDS
    A PRIVATE LOSS HERE FOUNDS A NATIONS PEACE   . . . . 360 MEROPE   889

FOUNT
A LIGHT THAT FROM SOME UPPER FOUNT DID BEAM   • •   9 MYCERINUS   21
BY LONELY PURENESS TO THE ALL-PURE FOUNT   • • •   45 IN UTRUMQUE PAR   12
AND THEY FOUND MIMIR SITTING BY HIS FOUNT   • • •   120 BALDER DEAD 3   219
HIM CAN NO FOUNT OF FRESH FORGIVENESS LAVE   • • •   172 GOOD SHEPHERD   4
AND BRINGS THE WATER FROM THE FOUNT   • • • •   213 PROGRESS POESY   3
THE FOUNT WHICH SHALL NOT FLOW AGAIN   • • • •   213 PROGRESS POESY   4
AND ITS LOCKD FOUNT OF BEAUTY USE   • • • •   223 EPILOG LAOCOON   84
WE WATCHD THE FOUNT OF FIERY LIFE   • • • •   270 MEMORIAL VERSES   13
FOR THERE WHERE MORNINGS SACRED FOUNT   • • •   277 SOUTHERN NIGHT   53
AT THE UNDRIED FOUNT OF THIS BREAST   • • • •   378 MEROPE   1236
AND DRIED ITS SELF-SUFFICING FOUNT OF JOY   • • •   429 EMPEDOCLES II   22

FOUNTAIN
WHICH FROM THE FOUNTAIN OF VERGELMER RUN   • • •   108 BALDER DEAD 2   130
THE FOREST-CHAPEL AND THE FOUNTAIN NEAR   • • •   139 TRISTRAM 1   279
AND HEAVENWARD FROM THE FOUNTAIN-BRINK HE SPRANG   • •   268 THYRSIS   189
LOVE IS THE FOUNTAIN OF CHARM   • • • •   295 HEINES GRAVE   105
OBLIVIONS DREARY FOUNTAIN WHERE ART THOU   • • •   462 ALARIC AT ROME   2

FOUNTAINS
FROM THE DRAGON-WARDERD FOUNTAINS   • • •   27 NEW SIRENS   33
BY MIDNIGHT TO A BUBBLING FOUNTAINS SOUND   • • •   70 SOHRAB RUSTUM   317
THE SPLASHING ICY FOUNTAINS PLAY   • • • •   300 GRANDE CHARTR   33
BY THE THREE FOUNTAINS AND THE ADDERS HILL   • • •   356 MEROPE   748
CALM THE MURMUR OF THE FOUNTAINS   • • • •   META CLOISTER   15
COOL THE MURMUR OF THE FOUNTAINS   • • • •   META CLOISTER   V   15

FOUR
FOUR YEARS SINCE IN THE HOUSE   • • • • •   280 HAWORTH CHURCH   4
FOUR YEARS SINCE ON A MARKD   • • • • •   280 HAWORTH CHURCH   V
FROM THE FOUR-TOWND MOUNTAIN-SHADOWD DORIS   • •   400 MEROPE   1852
FOUR YEARS AND DIDST THOU STAY ABOVE   • • •   449 GEISTS GRAVE   1
THE GROUND WHICH HIDES THEE NOW BUT FOUR   • •   449 GEISTS GRAVE   2
ONLY FOUR YEARS THOSE WINNING WAYS   • • •   450 GEISTS GRAVE   5
WHAT WAS FOUR YEARS THEIR WHOLE SHORT DAY   • •   450 GEISTS GRAVE   20
YES ONLY FOUR AND NOT THE COURSE   • • •   450 GEISTS GRAVE   21
WHAT WAS FOUR YEARS THEIR WHOLE SHORT STAY   • •   450 GEISTS GRAVE   V   20

FOURTH
HARDLY THE FOURTH WITH GRIEVOUS LOSS REGAIND   • •   336 MEROPE   218

FOWL
NOR TO THE SHINING SEA-FOWL THAT WITH SCREAMS   • •   151 TRISTRAM 3   52
AND THE SPRINGING BUSTARD-FOWL   • • • • •   191 STRAYED REVEL   174

FOX
AH ME I MUSE WHAT THIS YOUNG FOX MAY MEAN   • • •   71 SOHRAB RUSTUM   347

FOXGLOVE
THE TENDER FOXGLOVE-PLANTS DISPLAY   • • • •   484 ROME-SICKNESS   15

FRAGILE
AND HER FRAGILE LOVELINESS   • • • • •   132 TRISTRAM 1   53

FRAGMENT
WHEN FRAGMENT OF IT SMALL LIKE MINE   • • • •   158 SAINT BRANDAN   55
IF FRAGMENT OF IT SMALL LIKE MINE   • • • •   158 SAINT BRANDAN   V   55

FRAGMENTS
THEIR FRAGMENTS ON THE CUMBERD GRASS   • • •   55 RESIGNATION   111
POOR FRAGMENTS OF A BROKEN WORLD   • • • •   320 OBERMANN MORE   217

FRAGRANCE
HEAVY WITH FRAGRANCE THE BLOND   • • • •   296 HEINES GRAVE   135
EVEN IN THE GRAVE THEIR FRAGRANCE CANNOT FADE   • •   462 ALARIC AT ROME   8
WITH FRAGRANCE ALL FRASCATIS WOOD   • • • •   484 ROME-SICKNESS   19

FRAGRANT
WHERE COOL GRASS AND FRAGRANT GLOOMS   • •   26 NEW SIRENS   2
AND LIES A FRAGRANT TOWER OF PURPLE BLOOM   • •   80 SOHRAB RUSTUM   637
ABOVE THE FRAGRANT WARM PROVENCAL SHORE   • •   167 RACHEL 2   2
AND CAN THIS FRAGRANT LAWN   • • • •   200 PHILOMELA   10
OF THE FRAGRANT STOCK AND THE PINK   • • •   234 YOUTH OF MAN   68
WHAT BLOWING DAISIES FRAGRANT GRASS   • • •   248 KENSINGTON GARD   15
AND STOCKS IN FRAGRANT BLOW   • • • •   264 THYRSIS   66
SEE FRAGRANT HERBS ARE FLOWERING THERE   • •   301 GRANDE CHARTR   56
THOSE FRAGRANT HERBS ARE FLOWERING THERE   • •   301 GRANDE CHARTR   V   56
OF IVY-PLANTS AND FRAGRANT HANGING BELLS   • •   414 EMPEDOCLES I 2   49

FRAIL
AND THE FRAIL SCARLET-BERRIED ASH BEGAN   • •   25 DREAM   9
ARE THOSE FRAIL FORMS MORE ENDURING   • • •   27 NEW SIRENS   43
HIS FRAIL BOAT MOORD TO   • • • • •   190 STRAYED REVEL   153
AND THESE FRAIL ACACIA BOUGHS   • • • •   200 PHILOMELA   V
THROUGH WHOSE FRAIL LEAVES AND SHOWERS   • •   200 PHILOMELA   V
OF FLOWERS THE FRAIL-LEAFD WHITE ANEMONY   • •   257 SCHOLAR-GIPSY   87
INACCURATE AND FRAIL   • • • • •   352 MEROPE   633
IN PRIESTLY GARB A FRAIL OLD MAN WENT BY   • •   476 CROMWELL   166

FRAME
　　BLEW SUCH MUSIC AS A GOD MAY FRAME . . . . . . 29 NEW SIRENS 104
　　DEEP HEAVY GASPS QUIVERING THROUGH ALL HIS FRAME . 86 SOHRAB RUSTUM 850
　　AND TAKE HER BROIDERY-FRAME AND THERE SHELL SIT . 152 TRISTRAM 3 82
　　FLASH THROUGH HER PURE IMMORTAL FRAME . . . . 181 ISOLATION MARG 21
　　I SAW HIM SENSITIVE IN FRAME . . . . 272 EDW QUILLINAN 1
　　ITS FRAME YET STOOD WITHOUT A BREACH . . . . 319 OBERMANN MORE 193
　　THOU FEELEST THY SOULS FRAME . . . . 416 EMPEDOCLES I 2 114
　　STILL ALERT THY STONE-CRUSHD FRAME . . . . . 430 EMPEDOCLES II 51
　　HER FOREST-CLOTHED FRAME . . . . 441 EMPEDOCLES II 420
　　VAINLY RAISE HIS RIGID FRAME . . . . 452 POOR MATTHIAS 8
　　THAT FRAME OF VIGOUR SHALL BE CRUMBLING CLAY . 469 ALARIC AT ROME 194
　　ALL AIRY HOPES THAT IDLE HEARTS CAN FRAME . . . 474 CROMWELL 95

FRAMED
　　TO BE LONG LOVED WAS NEVER FRAMED . . . . . 178 FAREWELL 18
　　WHERE BEST THE POET FRAMED HIS PIECE . . . . 221 EPILOG LAOCOON 14
　　WERE THE MESSENIAN CHIEFS THE LAWS HE FRAMED . . 337 MEROPE 243

FRAMEDST
　　OF WOOD AND FRAMEDST MEN WHO TILL THE EARTH . . 121 BALDER DEAD 3 269

FRAMES
　　HAVE FELT THEIR HUGE FRAMES NOT CONSTRUCTED RIGHT 239 REVOLUTIONS 15

FRANCE
　　PROSPECT OF HOPE WHICH FRANCE PROCLAIMS SO LOUD . . 7 REP FRIEND CONT 3
　　FRANCE FAMED IN ALL GREAT ARTS IN NONE SUPREME . . 7 REP FRIEND CONT 4
　　WESTWARD ON THE SIDE OF FRANCE . . . . . . 13 CHURCH BROU 1 20
　　IF FRANCE AND WE ARE REALLY FRIENDS . . . . . 47 HORATIAN ECHO 4
　　WHOM THIS REALM OF FRANCE CAN BOAST . . . . . 136 TRISTRAM 1 195
　　THAT THIS REALM OF FRANCE CAN BOAST . . . . . 136 TRISTRAM 1 V 195
　　GERMANY FRANCE CHRIST MOSES ATHENS ROME . . . 168 RACHEL 3 12
　　DAUGHTER OF FRANCE TO FRANCE THY HOME . . . . 184 TERRACE BERNE 18
　　DAUGHTER OF FRANCE TO FRANCE THY HOME . . . . 184 TERRACE BERNE 18
　　ROME ENGLAND FRANCE YES NOR IN VAIN ESSAYD . . . 239 REVOLUTIONS 6
　　A PALACE OF THE KINGS OF FRANCE . . . . . 300 GRANDE CHARTR 24
　　DOWN CAME THE STORM OER FRANCE IT PASSD . . . 319 OBERMANN MORE 201
　　NOT IN THAT MADHOUSE FRANCE FROM WHENCE THE CRY . 480 HUNGARIAN NAT 4

FRANK
　　THOSE FRANK EYES WHERE DEEP I SEE . . . . . 24 MEMORY-PICTURE 45
　　THOSE FRANK EYES WHERE DEEP DOTH LIE . . . . . 24 MEMORY-PICTURE V 45
　　THOSE FRANK EYES WHERE DEEP DOTH BE . . . . . 24 MEMORY-PICTURE V 45
　　THOSE FRANK EYES WHERE DEEP WILL BE . . . . . 24 MEMORY-PICTURE V 45
　　ALL FRANK FAITH WHICH PASSION BREEDS . . . . . 34 NEW SIRENS 230

FRANTIC
　　THE ILL-BODING NOTE WHICH FRANTIC HATRED SOUNDS . 397 MEROPE 1781
　　THE ILL-BODING NOTE WHICH FRANTIC ENVY SOUNDS . 397 MEROPE V1781

FRASCATIS
　　WITH FRAGRANCE ALL FRASCATIS WOOD . . . . . . 484 ROME-SICKNESS 19

FRAUD
　　THESE TERMS AND I SUSPECT SOME HIDDEN FRAUD . . 120 BALDER DEAD 3 235

FRAUDULENT
　　THE FRAUDULENT OATH WHICH BOUND . . . . . . 198 FRAG ANTIGONE 95

FRAUGHT
　　ETERNAL PASSION-FRAUGHT AND FREE . . . . . 224 EPILOG LAOCOON 105
　　PERENNIAL PASSION-FRAUGHT AND FREE . . . . . 224 EPILOG LAOCOON V 105
　　IS FRAUGHT TOO DEEP WITH PAIN . . . . . . 307 OBERMANN 38
　　SET THINE EARS WITH SOUL-FRAUGHT MUSIC RINGING . 482 THEKLAS ANSWER 7
　　OER THOSE SAME SEAS DARK TENERIFFE ROSE FRAUGHT . 485 S S LUSITANIA 11

FRAY
　　AH THINE WAS NOT THE SHELTER BUT THE FRAY . . . 42 GIPSY CHILD 24
　　WHEN RUSTUM WAS IN FRONT OF EVERY FRAY . . . . 63 SOHRAB RUSTUM 80
　　WHICH GODS AND HEROES LEAD IN FEAST AND FRAY . . 98 BALDER DEAD 1 123
　　WERE RANGED AND THEN THE DAILY FRAY BEGAN . . . 105 BALDER DEAD 2 14
　　TO FEAST THEIR EYES WITH LOOKING ON THE FRAY . . 105 BALDER DEAD 2 31
　　AND HIS EYE KINDLED WITH THE KINDLING FRAY . . . 475 CROMWELL 137
　　SLEW HIM FIGHTING IN FRONT OF THE FRAY AND HOMER TRANS 53
　　　　GLORIFIED HECTOR

FRAYD
　　HATH FRAYD AND SLIDDEN DOWN AND WE NO MORE . . . EVERLASTING SUB 2
　　HATH FRAYD AND SLIDDEN DOWN AND THEY NO MORE . . EVERLASTING SUB V 2

FREA
　　OF FREA HONOURD MOTHER OF THE GODS . . . . . 97 BALDER DEAD 1 85
　　PONDERING ON THAT WHICH FREA SAID SHOULD BE . . 101 BALDER DEAD 1 201
　　AND FREA SEALD HER TIRED LIDS WITH SLEEP . . . 103 BALDER DEAD 1 279
　　BUT PAINLESS SHALL A STROKE FROM FREA COME . . . 103 BALDER DEAD 1 302
　　FREA THE MOTHER OF THE GODS WITH STROKE . . . 104 BALDER DEAD 1 339
　　MOST HONOURD AFTER FREA ODINS WIFE . . . . . 116 BALDER DEAD 3 92
　　BUT FREA MOTHER OF THE GODS AROSE . . . . . 120 BALDER DEAD 3 246

FREAS
    ON FREAS HEARTH FEED HIGH THE SACRED FIRE • • • •   97 BALDER DEAD 1   90

FREE
    OTHERS ABIDE OUR QUESTION THOU ART FREE • • • •   2 SHAKESPEARE   1
    OF BITTER KNOWLEDGE YET THE WILL IS FREE • • • •   4 EMERSONS ESSAYS   10
    LOVE FREE TO RANGE AND REGAL BANQUETINGS • • • •   9 MYCERINUS   34
    O LET FALL ONE TEAR AND SET US FREE • • • •   34 NEW SIRENS   226
    OH SET US FREE • • • • • • • •   39 STAGIRIUS   48
    BUT MILDER NATURES AND MORE FREE • • • •   53 RESIGNATION   22
    ASK NOT TO AMUSE BUT TO SET FREE • • • •   59 RESIGNATION   242
    AND LET THE BLOOD FLOW FREE AND SO TO DIE • • •   80 SOHRAB RUSTUM   652
    TO CUT THY THREAD OF LIFE AND FREE THY SOUL •   103 BALDER DEAD 1   303
    PAINLESS AND SWIFT SET FREE HER AIRY SOUL • •   104 BALDER DEAD 1   340
    RIDE ON PASS FREE BUT HE BY THIS IS THERE • •   108 BALDER DEAD 2   134
    AND WITH HIMSELF SET US HIS OFFSPRING FREE •   111 BALDER DEAD 2   223
    FROM VIOLENT ANGUISH SURELY FREE • • • •   137 TRISTRAM 1   233
    IF ONESELF CANNOT GET FREE • • • • •   138 TRISTRAM 1   267
    NOT IN THE FREE GREEN WOOD AT ALL • • • •   149 TRISTRAM 2   179
    TO SEEM AS FREE FROM PRIDE AND GUILE • • •   179 FAREWELL   63
    FREE TO THE SWEEP OF LIGHT AND WIND • • •   223 EPILOG LAOCOON   72
    ETERNAL PASSION-FRAUGHT AND FREE • • • •   224 EPILOG LAOCOON   105
    PERENNIAL PASSION-FRAUGHT AND FREE • • •   224 EPILOG LAOCOON V 105
    THE BAND WILL QUIT MANS HEART HE WILL BREATHE FREE   239 REVOLUTIONS   20
    NATURE WHOSE FREE LIGHT CHEERFUL AIR • •   241 MORALITY   17
    AND THOUGH SO TASKD KEEP FREE FROM DUST AND SOIL •   244 SUMMER NIGHT   82
    HOW IT WERE GOOD TO ABIDE THERE AND BREATHE FREE •   244 SUMMER NIGHT   90
    HOW IT WERE GOOD TO SINK THERE AND BREATHE FREE   244 SUMMER NIGHT V 90
    HOW IT WERE GOOD TO LIVE THERE AND BREATHE FREE   244 SUMMER NIGHT V 90
    EVEN FOR A MOMENT CAN GET FREE • • • •   245 BURIED LIFE   27
    FROM BANDS OF GREEDY HEIRS BE FREE • • •   249 WISH   2
    FREE FROM THE SICK FATIGUE THE LANGUID DOUBT •   260 SCHOLAR-GIPSY   164
    WITH A FREE ONWARD IMPULSE BRUSHING THROUGH •   261 SCHOLAR-GIPSY   213
    AT MY FEET FREE • • • • • • • •   275 SOUTHERN NIGHT   4
    THAT CORDIAL HAND THAT BEARING FREE • • •   279 SOUTHERN NIGHT   126
    TILL FREE MY THOUGHTS BEFORE ME ROLL • • •   302 GRANDE CHARTR   95
    STRONG WAS HE WITH A SPIRIT FREE • • • •   308 OBERMANN   61
    OLD AGE IS MORE SUSPICIOUS THAN THE FREE •   335 MEROPE   156
    NOT MUCH A TYRANT THY FREE SPEECH DISPLAYS ME •   340 MEROPE   350
    FREE FROM ALL GUILT OF LAWLESSNESS • • •   353 MEROPE   660
    BROWND WITH THINE OPEN-AIR FREE HUNTERS LIFE •   373 MEROPE 1164
    THOUGH ALL FREE SPIRITS IN THIS LAND WERE DEAD •   383 MEROPE 1377
    ARE NEVER FREE FROM DOUBT THOUGH SOMETIMES DUE •   388 MEROPE 1522
    THOUGH ALL FREE SPIRITS IN THIS LAND BE DEAD •   383 MEROPE V1377
    WERE TO LIVE FREE FROM TERROR SPELLS MISTRUST THEM   413 EMPEDOCLES I 2   26
    ALL SKILL I WIELD ARE FREE • • • • •   415 EMPEDOCLES I 2   105
    TAKE THY BOUGH SET ME FREE FROM MY SOLITUDE •   435 EMPEDOCLES II   218
    THE BROW UNBOUND THE THOUGHTS FLOW FREE AGAIN •   436 EMPEDOCLES II   246
    AND WHO CAN SAY I HAVE BEEN ALWAYS FREE • •   440 EMPEDOCLES II   392
    MOUNTS OFF MY SOUL I FEEL IT I BREATHE FREE •   441 EMPEDOCLES II   408
    WHO WOULD NOT BURST HIS BONDS AND IN HIS TURN BE FREE   465 ALARIC AT ROME   90
    TO YEARN WITH SPEECHLESS IMPULSE TO THE FREE •   472 CROMWELL   7
    THEN FANCYS ROVING VISIONS BOLD AND FREE • •   474 CROMWELL   93
    TO MAINTAIN THE CASPIAN FREE • • • • •   PILLARS UNIVERS   7

FREED
    HATH FREED FROM PASSIONS AND THE STATE • • •   53 RESIGNATION   24
    THERE THE FREED PRISONER WHEREER HIS HEART • •   243 SUMMER NIGHT   54
    WERE TO LIVE FREED FROM TERROR SPELLS MISTRUST THEM   413 EMPEDOCLES I 2 V 26

FREEDOM
    IMPULSE AND REASON FREEDOM AND CONTROL • • •   4 BUTLERS SERMONS   2
    OUR FREEDOM FOR A LITTLE BREAD WE SELL • • •   169 WORLDLY PLACE   5
    THE FREEDOM TO MY LIFE DENIED • • • • •   250 WISH   10
    THY SHAME SECURES MY FREEDOM NOT THY WILL • •   340 MEROPE   351
    SHALL TRANSPORT THEE AWAY AND THE DAY OF THY   HOMER TRANS   28
        FREEDOM BE ENDED

FREEDOMS
    LEARNS FREEDOMS LESSON FROM YOUR VOICE OF FEAR • •   471 CROMWELL   2
    THINE WAS NO MOUNTAIN HOME WHERE FREEDOMS FORM •   472 CROMWELL   17
    ALL FREEDOMS MYSTIC LANGUAGE STORMS THAT ROAR •   472 CROMWELL   29

FREELY
    FREELY DID THEY FLASH THEIR SPLENDOUR • • • •   35 NEW SIRENS   257
    FREELY GAVE IT BUT IT DIES AWAY • • • •   35 NEW SIRENS   258
    WOULD FREELY DIE TO PURCHASE BALDER BACK • •   98 BALDER DEAD 1   120
    THOUGH OPULENT FREELY GIVE • • • • •   195 FRAG ANTIGONE   3

FREEZE
    WOULD YOU FREEZE MY TOO LOUD BOLDNESS • • •   31 NEW SIRENS   159
    WOULD YOU FREEZE MY LOUDER BOLDNESS • • • •   31 NEW SIRENS V 159
    STILL SHARP AS EVER FREEZE AND PARCH • • • •   56 RESIGNATION   131

FREEZES
    FREEZES THE SWEET STRAIN ON THE PARTED LIPS • •   FRAGMENT 1   7

FREEZING
    FREEZING THE PURE EMOTION • • • • • •   39 STAGIRIUS V 24
    FREEZING AND RIDGING IN THEIR ONWARD FLOW • • • •   108 BALDER DEAD 2   129

FREIGHT
    THE JADED HUNTERS WITH THEIR BLOODY FREIGHT . . 18 CHURCH BROU 3 14
    AND SETS HIS FREIGHT ASHORE ON THORNEY STRAND . . 445 WESTMIN ABBEY 30
    AND IN THY COURTS HIS SHINING FREIGHT UNROLLD . . 446 WESTMIN ABBEY 76

FREIGHTED
    FREIGHTED WITH AMBER GRAPES AND CHIAN WINE . . . . 262 SCHOLAR-GIPSY 238

FRENCH
    OF THE FRENCH THEATRE WORN WITH DISEASE . . . 167 RACHEL 1 6
    UPON THE STRAITS ON THE FRENCH COAST THE LIGHT . . 210 DOVER BEACH 3
    UPON THE STRAIT ON THE FRENCH COAST THE LIGHT . . DOVER BEACH V 3
    FRENCH CANARY-MERCHANT OLD . . . . 457 POOR MATTHIAS 184

FRENZIED
    A FRENZIED WANDERER A GOD-DRIVEN MAN . . . . . . 385 MEROPE 1424

FRENZY
    BREATHING SELF-MURDER FRENZY SPITE . . . . . . 157 SAINT BRANDAN 31

FREQUENT
    FORTUNES NOW LESS FREQUENT HEIR . . . . . 22 MEMORY-PICTURE V
    FREQUENT THE STILL RECESSES OF THE REALM . . . . 126 BALDER DEAD 3 435

FRESH
    STRONG IS THE SOUL AND FRESH AND BEAUTIFUL . . . . EMERSONS ESSAYS V 11
    OF OPEN HILL-SWARD FRESH AND GREEN . . . . . . 16 CHURCH BROU 2 13
    FRESH GARLANDS OF THIS DEWY ROSE . . . . . . 48 HORATIAN ECHO 23
    FRESH FROM THE SUMMER FIELDS . . . . 51 CONSOLATION 43
    THROUGH THE CLIFF-WALL AND A FRESH STREAM RUNS DOWN 97 BALDER DEAD 1 82
    WOUNDLESS AND FRESH SUCH LOT IS THEIRS IN HEAVEN . . 105 BALDER DEAD 2 18
    WHOSE MANGER IS STUFFD FULL OF GOOD FRESH HAY . . 123 BALDER DEAD 3 341
    MORE FRESH MORE VERDANT THAN THE LAST WITH FRUITS 128 BALDER DEAD 3 529
    AND ROUND HIM A FRESH FOREST-SCENE . . . . . 147 TRISTRAM 2 154
    HER HAVIOUR HAD THE MORNINGS FRESH CLEAR GRACE . . 154 TRISTRAM 3 179
    AND A FRESH BREATH OF SPRING STIRRD EVERYWHERE . . 155 TRISTRAM 3 200
    HIM CAN NO FOUNT OF FRESH FORGIVENESS LAVE . . . . 172 GOOD SHEPHERD 4
    OF THAT FRESH VOICE THE GAY DELIGHT . . . . . 184 TERRACE BERNE 31
    HOW SWEETLY WOULD THE FRESH SEA-BREEZE . . . . 205 CALAIS SANDS 15
    HOW SWEETLY WOULD THE FRESH SEA-WIND . . . . . . 205 CALAIS SANDS V 15
    FRESH BE THE WOUND STILL-RENEWD BE ITS SMARTING . . 206 SEPARATION 3
    FLING THE FRESH HEAPS ABOUT . . . . 218 BACCHANALIA 1 34
    NATURE IS FRESH AS OF OLD . . . . 228 YOUTH OF NATURE 11
    FRESH PRODUCTS OF THEIR BARREN LABOUR FALL . . . . 243 SUMMER NIGHT 43
    AN AIR-STIRRD FOREST FRESH AND CLEAR . . . . . . 248 KENSINGTON GARD 16
    FRESH UNDIVERTED TO THE WORLD WITHOUT . . . . 260 SCHOLAR-GIPSY 162
    O BORN IN DAYS WHEN WITS WERE FRESH AND CLEAR . . 261 SCHOLAR-GIPSY 201
    KEEP FRESH THE GRASS UPON HIS GRAVE . . . . . . 272 MEMORIAL VERSES 71
    OER THE FRESH SHORT TURF OF THE HARTZ . . . . 297 HEINES GRAVE 153
    FRESH THROUGH THESE PAGES BLOWS . . . . . . 307 OBERMANN 26
    SWEET HEAPS OF FRESH-CUT GRASS . . . . 313 OBERMANN MORE 18
    OF HIS FRESH-CONQUERD REALM THE ROYAL SEAT . . . . 330 MEROPE 11
    WITH PITCHERS IN THEIR HANDS AND FRESH-PULLD FLOWERS 331 MEROPE 54
    PURE LIBATIONS AND FRESH . . . . 342 MEROPE 402
    FRESH FROM THEIR FATHER DRAWS NEAR . . . . . 346 MEROPE 498
    FRESH BLOOD FLOWS CALLING FOR BLOOD . . . . . 379 MEROPE 1253
    HEAR THAT FRESH VOICE AND CLASP THAT GOLD-LOCKD HEAD 387 MEROPE 1460
    BUOYANT AND FRESH THE MOUNTAIN FLOWERS . . . . 426 EMPEDOCLES I 2 433
    OF FRESH-PULLD VIOLETS WREATHED AND NODDING OER . . 431 EMPEDOCLES II 87
    AND MAKES THY VERY RUIN FRESH AND BEAUTIFUL . . . 464 ALARIC AT ROME 54
    SO MANIFOLD SO FRESH SO BRAVE A WORLD . . . . LUCRETIUS 1 2

FRESHEN
    FRESHEN THY FLOWERS AS IN FORMER YEARS . . . . 261 SCHOLAR-GIPSY 218

FRESHEND
    FRESHEND BY PLUNGING TIDES BY SHOWERS . . . . 275 STANZAS CARNAC 42
    FRESHEND AND LIGHT WITH THE MAY . . . . . . 297 HEINES GRAVE 178
    IS FRESHEND BY THE LEAPING STREAM WHICH THROWS . . 414 EMPEDOCLES I 2 46

FRESHENING
    THE FRESHENING WIND AND BLACKENING WAVES . . . 244 SUMMER NIGHT 61
    FRESHENING ITS CURRENT AND SPOTTED WITH FOAM . . 254 FUTURE 80
    MIGHT FALL A FRESHENING STORM . . . . 319 OBERMANN MORE 198

FRESHER
    SCARCE FRESHER IS THE MOUNTAIN-SOD . . . . . . 248 KENSINGTON GARD 17
    NOT FRESHER IS THE MOUNTAIN SOD . . . . . . KENSINGTON GARD V 17

FRESHEST
    HER YOUNGEST RIVALS FRESHEST GRACE . . . . . . 147 TRISTRAM 2 V 146

FRESHLY
    LEFT FRESHLY GATHERD ON THEIR NATIVE BANK . . . . 86 SOHRAB RUSTUM 845

FRESHNESS
    A FRESHNESS BACK AS OF HER PRIME . . . . . . 147 TRISTRAM 2 142
    THE FRESHNESS OF THE EARLY WORLD . . . . . . 272 MEMORIAL VERSES 57

FRET
    HORSES FRET AND BOAR-SPEARS GLANCE . . . . . . 13 CHURCH BROU 1 18

FRET   (CONTINUED)
        SCOOP THE SHELVES AND FRET THE STORMS   .   .   .   .   26 NEW SIRENS   12
        LET US NOT FRET AND FEAR TO MISS OUR AIM   .   .   .   .   40 HUMAN LIFE   10
        THE WILD WHITE HORSES FOAM AND FRET   .   .   .   .   .   . 162 FORSAKEN MERM   21
        THE FRET AND MISERY OF OUR NORTHERN TOWNS   .   .   .   .   168 RACHEL 2   9
        AH LEAVE US NOT THE FRET ALONE   .   .   .   .   302 GRANDE CHARTR   108
        IN VAIN OUR PENT WILLS FRET   .   .   .   .   418 EMPEDOCLES I 2   182
        WILL FRET OUR MINDS TO AN INTENSER PLAY   .   .   .   .   440 EMPEDOCLES II   380
        FOR ANY MAN TO FRET AGAINST HIS WEAKNESS   .   .   .   .   LUCRETIUS 3   2
        OF MENTAL NATURE AS FOR HIM TO FRET   .   .   .   .   .   LUCRETIUS 3   3

FRETFUL
        FOR THIS THY TRACK ACROSS THE FRETFUL FOAM .   .   .   .   5 DUKE WELLINGTON   11
        ARE FRETFUL WITH THEMSELVES AND HARD TO PLEASE   .   .   153 TRISTRAM 3   V 142

FRETTED
        I HAVE A FRETTED BRICK-WORK TOMB   .   .   .   .   .   .   94 SICK KING BOKH   221
        A FRETTED WALL OF BLUE AND GREY   .   .   .   .   .   .   479 HAYSWATER BOAT   12

FRETWORK
        ROUND THE TOMB THE CARVED STONE FRETWORK   .   .   .   .   16 CHURCH BROU 1   109

FREYA
        AND FREYA NEXT CAME NIGH WITH GOLDEN TEARS .   .   .   .   116 BALDER DEAD 3   90
        THEY CALL HER FREYA IS HER NAME IN HEAVEN   .   .   .   .   116 BALDER DEAD 3   97
        WEEP NOT O FREYA WEEP NO GOLDEN TEARS   .   .   .   .   116 BALDER DEAD 3   114

FRIEND
        LIFES VOYAGE DONE HIS HEAVENLY FRIEND   .   .   .   .   40 HUMAN LIFE   2
        OR SOME FRIEND HAILD US TO KEEP COMPANY   .   .   .   .   40 HUMAN LIFE   12
        OMIT OMIT MY SIMPLE FRIEND   .   .   .   .   47 HORATIAN ECHO   1
        IS HE THY FRIEND OR OF THY BLOOD   .   .   .   .   .   .   92 SICK KING BOKH   135
        WITH THEIR THICK-FALLING TEARS SO GOOD A FRIEND .   .   115 BALDER DEAD 3   63
        ME THY LIVING FRIEND THOU CANST NOT SAVE   .   .   .   .   145 TRISTRAM 2   90
        HE WAS ON FOOT AND THAT FALSE FAY HIS FRIEND   .   .   154 TRISTRAM 3   161
        WITHOUT FRIEND CITY OR HOME   .   .   .   .   195 FRAG ANTIGONE   26
        AND KNOW HER FRIEND AND WEEP FOR GLEE   .   .   .   .   202 URANIA   27
        AND SAY MY FRIEND WHY SUFFEREST THOU .   .   .   .   .   209 LONGING   V 12
        ASK NOT MY NAME O FRIEND   .   .   .   .   217 NAMELESS EPIT   1
        MY FRIEND AND I BY CHANCE WE TALKD   .   .   .   .   .   221 EPILOG LAOCOON   2
        AH CRIES MY FRIEND BUT WHO HATH TAUGHT   .   .   .   .   221 EPILOG LAOCOON   8
        WHILE THUS MY FRIEND DISCOURSED WE PASS   .   .   .   .   222 EPILOG LAOCOON   36
        THE FRIEND OF MAN DESIRES   .   .   .   .   238 PROGRESS   48
        WHICH NEVER WAS THE FRIEND OF ONE   .   .   .   .   .   251 WISH   37
        WITH CLOSE-LIPPD PATIENCE FOR OUR ONLY FRIEND   .   .   260 SCHOLAR-GIPSY   194
        OUR FRIEND THE GIPSY-SCHOLAR WAS NOT DEAD   .   .   .   263 THYRSIS   29
        AND FLUTE HIS FRIEND LIKE ORPHEUS FROM THE DEAD .   .   265 THYRSIS   90
        AND NIGHT AS WELCOME AS A FRIEND WOULD FALL .   .   .   267 THYRSIS   150
        OUR FRIEND THE SCHOLAR-GIPSY WAS NOT DEAD   .   .   .   263 THYRSIS   V 29
        WORDSWORTHS SON-IN-LAW FRIEND   .   .   .   .   280 HAWORTH CHURCH   6
        WELCOME THE SISTER THE FRIEND   .   .   .   .   284 HAWORTH CHURCH   86
        NOT AS THEIR FRIEND OR CHILD I SPEAK .   .   .   .   .   301 GRANDE CHARTR   79
        AND THOU ART POLYPHONTES FIRST HIS FRIEND   .   .   .   335 MEROPE   185
        KINSMAN THOU SLEWST THY KINSMAN FRIEND THY FRIEND   338 MEROPE   281
        KINSMAN THOU SLEWST THY KINSMAN FRIEND THY FRIEND   338 MEROPE   281
        MY FAITHFUL FOLLOWER COMES WELCOME OLD FRIEND   .   .   362 MEROPE   937
        OF AN ARCADIAN LORD OUR PRINCES FRIEND   .   .   .   363 MEROPE   956
        COME HERMES WHO DOST FRIEND THE UNJUSTLY KILLD   .   .   367 MEROPE   1058
        IN A LAND OF FRIENDS BY A FRIEND   .   .   .   . . .   369 MEROPE   1101
        WORSE FAR WORSE IF HIS FRIEND   .   .   .   .   370 MEROPE   1120
        FAITHLESSLY MURDERD HIS FRIEND   .   .   .   .   371 MEROPE   1124
        AND FOUND HIM AT MY HUSBANDS SIDE HIS FRIEND   .   .   403 MEROPE   1973
        PAUSANIAS HIS SAGE FRIEND WHO MOUNTS WITH HIM   .   .   407 EMPEDOCLES I 1   25
        AND HE WOULD TELL ME AS HIS OLD TRIED FRIEND   .   .   410 EMPEDOCLES I 1   130
        AND THEN THY FRIEND IS BANISHD AND ON THAT .   .   .   411 EMPEDOCLES I 1   143
        AS OF HIS GIFTED MASTER AND ONCE FRIEND   .   .   .   411 EMPEDOCLES I 1   148
        THOU ART MY FRIEND TO THEE   .   .   .   .   415 EMPEDOCLES I 2   103
        GOOD FRIEND I SHALL REVISIT CATANA   .   .   .   .   .   428 EMPEDOCLES I 2   473
        LEFT THEIR FRIEND AND WITH ROBES FLOWING   .   .   .   433 EMPEDOCLES II   152
        FOR THE FAUN HAD BEEN HIS FRIEND   .   .   .   .   .   434 EMPEDOCLES II   168
        WHO HAS NO FRIEND NO FELLOW LEFT NOT ONE   .   .   .   437 EMPEDOCLES II   271
        WITHOUT FRIEND AND WITHOUT HOME .   .   .   .   .   .   438 EMPEDOCLES II   298
        PETER HIS FRIEND WITH LIGHT DID CONSECRATE .   .   .   445 WESTMIN ABBEY   50
        EVEN AS THAT LOVED THAT WELL-RECORDED FRIEND   .   .   449 WESTMIN ABBEY   168
        DEAR LITTLE FRIEND AT EVERY TURN   .   .   .   .   .   450 GEISTS GRAVE   8
        THE DACHS-HOUND GEIST THEIR LITTLE FRIEND   .   .   .   452 GEISTS GRAVE   80
        DEAD AND MUTE OUR TINY FRIEND   .   .   .   .   .   .   452 POOR MATTHIAS   14
        GEIST CAME NEXT OUR LITTLE FRIEND   .   .   .   .   .   454 POOR MATTHIAS   57
        WE WITHOUT THEE LITTLE FRIEND   .   .   .   .   .   .   458 POOR MATTHIAS   210
        WERE THINE IN STORE THOU FAITHFUL FRIEND   .   .   .   459 KAISER DEAD   33
        FULL WELL MAX KNOWS THE FRIEND IS DEAD   .   .   .   460 KAISER DEAD   69
        DARE O FRIEND BE WANDERING DARE BE DREAMING   .   .   483 THEKLAS ANSWER   23

FRIENDED
        WELL-FED WELL-CLOTHED WELL-FRIENDED I   .   .   .   .   158 SAINT BRANDAN   57

FRIENDLESS
        AND NOT FRIENDLESS AND NOT   .   .   .   .   284 HAWORTH CHURCH   74
        AND NOT FRIENDLESS NOR YET   .   .   .   .   284 HAWORTH CHURCH   V 74
        SINGLE AND FRIENDLESS GIVE TO CERTAIN DEATH   .   .   382 MEROPE   1326

FRIENDLESS   (CONTINUED)
    SINGLE AND FRIENDLESS THROW TO CERTAIN DEATH   • • 382 MEROPE   V1326
    FRIENDLESS AND HOPELESS LIKE A LONELY TREE • • • • 477 CROMWELL   189

FRIENDLY
    FRIENDLY AND GENTLE NOW DEAD • • • • • • • • 280 HAWORTH CHURCH V 5
    HE WOULD HAVE MIXD YOU WITH YOUR FRIENDLY FOES • • 339 MEROPE   301
    AND NOW TO ME THOU TENDEREST FRIENDLY LEAGUE   • • 340 MEROPE   333
    AND THE GOOD LEARNED FRIENDLY QUIET MAN • • • • 429 EMPEDOCLES II   8
    AND KEEP THEIR FRIENDLY CHATTER AT HIS EAR • • • 435 EMPEDOCLES II   224
    THUS SLEEPING IN THINE ABBEYS FRIENDLY SHADE   • • 449 WESTMIN ABBEY 164
    HERE SLEEPING IN THINE ABBEYS FRIENDLY SHADE   • • 449 WESTMIN ABBEY V 164

FRIENDS
    NATURE AND MAN CAN NEVER BE FAST FRIENDS • • • •   5 HARMONY NATURE   13
    LAUGH MY FRIENDS AND WITHOUT BLAME • • • • • •   22 MEMORY-PICTURE   1
    WHAT MY FRIENDS THESE FEEBLE LINES • • • • • •   24 MEMORY-PICTURE   49
    THE FRIENDS TO WHOM WE HAD NO NATURAL RIGHT   • •   41 HUMAN LIFE   29
    DREAMS DAWN AND FLY FRIENDS SMILE AND DIE • • • •   44 QUESTION   8
    IF FRANCE AND WE ARE REALLY FRIENDS • • • • • •   47 HORATIAN ECHO   4
    AND PLEDGE EACH OTHER IN RED WINE LIKE FRIENDS • •   74 SOHRAB RUSTUM   441
    THAN TO THY FRIENDS AND TO THY FATHER OLD • • •   77 SOHRAB RUSTUM   539
    THOU AND THE SNOW-HAIRD ZAL AND ALL THY FRIENDS • •   84 SOHRAB RUSTUM   786
    WITH THE SNOW-HEADED ZAL AND ALL MY FRIENDS   • •   84 SOHRAB RUSTUM   801
    BESIDES TO EACH ARE HIS OWN FRIENDS • • • • • •   92 SICK KING BOKH 155
    THOSE WERE FRIENDS TO MAKE ME FALSE TO THEE   • • 144 TRISTRAM 2   48
    AND FRIENDS ME IN THE PIT OF FIRE • • • • • • 158 SAINT BRANDAN   64
    SHE WILL NOT ASK OF ALIENS BUT OF FRIENDS • • • • 170 WEST LONDON   10
    THEN WE SHALL KNOW OUR FRIENDS THOUGH MUCH   • • 179 FAREWELL   65
    THE FRIENDS WHO COME AND GAPE AND GO • • • • • 250 WISH   14
    HIS FRIENDS AND WENT TO LEARN THE GIPSY-LORE • • 256 SCHOLAR-GIPSY   37
    BUT CAME TO OXFORD AND HIS FRIENDS NO MORE • • • 256 SCHOLAR-GIPSY   40
    FROM HER FALSE FRIENDS APPROACH IN HADES TURN • • 261 SCHOLAR-GIPSY 209
    FRIENDS COULD NOT GIVE WHAT FORTUNE CAN • • • • 273 EDW QUILLINAN   11
    THEY LIKE FRIENDS SHALL RECEIVE • • • • • • • 284 HAWORTH CHURCH   84
    SLEEP O CLUSTER OF FRIENDS • • • • • • • • • 285 HAWORTH CHURCH 112
    TWO FRIENDS MET THERE TWO FAMD • • • • • • • 280 HAWORTH CHURCH V 7
    CHEERFUL WITH FRIENDS WE SET FORTH • • • • • • 289 RUGBY CHAPEL   89
    FRIENDS WHO SET FORTH AT OUR SIDE • • • • • • 289 RUGBY CHAPEL   102
    STRIPPD WITHOUT FRIENDS AS WE ARE • • • • • • 289 RUGBY CHAPEL   121
    FRIENDS COMPANIONS AND TRAIN • • • • • • • • 289 RUGBY CHAPEL   122
    HELPERS AND FRIENDS OF MANKIND • • • • • • • 291 RUGBY CHAPEL   161
    FOR WE WERE KINSMEN MORE THAN KINSMEN FRIENDS • • 334 MEROPE   122
    HE HAD HIS COUNSEL PARTY FRIENDS I MINE • • • • 334 MEROPE   128
    OUR HANDS IN SOLEMN UNION MAKING FRIENDS • • • 335 MEROPE   165
    TO HIS NEW SUBJECTS THAN TO US HIS FRIENDS • • • 337 MEROPE   242
    FOR DEATH HIS ANCIENT TO HIS NEW-MADE FRIENDS • • 338 MEROPE   265
    INJUSTICE TO HIS KIN AND DORIAN FRIENDS • • • • 339 MEROPE   317
    HAD THEY MISRULED HAD THEY FORGOT THEIR FRIENDS • 339 MEROPE   322
    I SAVED THEM MEANT THEM HONOUR BUT THY FRIENDS • 340 MEROPE   343
    DOUBTLESS THOU RECKONEST ON THE HELP OF FRIENDS • 341 MEROPE   356
    HAST ALL IMPUNITY YET LEST THY FRIENDS • • • • 341 MEROPE   372
    JEALOUS BLOOD-EXACTING FRIENDS • • • • • • • 344 MEROPE   461
    A WOMAN O MY FRIENDS HAS ONE DESIRE • • • • • 349 MEROPE   565
    TO FRIENDS STILL MORE AND LABOURERS IN OUR CAUSE • 359 MEROPE   872
    LOOK UP AND SEE THY FRIENDS WHO COMFORT THEE • • 363 MEROPE   947
    AND YE KEEP FAITHFUL SILENCE FRIENDS AND MARK • 368 MEROPE   1073
    THOU NOTHING PROFITEST THY FRIENDS BUT MAKST • • 368 MEROPE   1080
    IN A LAND OF FRIENDS BY A FRIEND • • • • • • 369 MEROPE   1101
    O FALSE FRIENDS INTO WHAT • • • • • • • • • 371 MEROPE   1127
    BUT WHO ARE THESE MESSENIAN MAIDENS FRIENDS • • 375 MEROPE   1210
    O KIND MESSENIAN MAIDENS O MY FRIENDS • • • • 377 MEROPE   1222
    CONFERRING IN THE CITY WITH OUR FRIENDS • • • • 379 MEROPE   1261
    AND ENTERTAINST THOU CHILD SUCH DANGEROUS FRIENDS 380 MEROPE   1276
    NEWS OF MY BUSINESS PASTIME TEMPER FRIENDS • • • 380 MEROPE   1281
    THY KINSFOLK AND THY FATHERS FRIENDS FOR AID • • 384 MEROPE   1389
    AND TO WHAT FRIENDS SHOULD I FOR AID APPLY • • • 384 MEROPE   1390
    THAN I TO HELP RAISE HIS MESSENIAN FRIENDS • • • 388 MEROPE   1497
    ALAS AGAINST MY BROTHER SON AND FRIENDS • • • • 390 MEROPE   1579
    NEPHEW THY FRIENDS ARE SOUNDED AND PROVE TRUE • 390 MEROPE   1587
    DOUBTLESS THOU RECKONEST ON THE HOPE OF FRIENDS • 341 MEROPE   V 356
    CONCERTING IN THE CITY WITH OUR FRIENDS • • • 379 MEROPE   V1261
    AND WHEN HE COMES AMONG HIS FRIENDS AT FEASTS • • 408 EMPEDOCLES I 1   70
    TO HAVE ADVANCED TRUE FRIENDS AND BEAT DOWN   425 EMPEDOCLES I 2 401
        BAFFLING FOES
    TO HAVE RAISD FAITHFUL FRIENDS AND CUT DOWN   425 EMPEDOCLES I 2 V 401
        SPITEFUL FOES
    AND TURN THEE TO THE ELEMENTS THY FRIENDS • • • 429 EMPEDOCLES II   25
    THY WELL-TRIED FRIENDS THY WILLING MINISTERS • • 429 EMPEDOCLES II   26
    WHEN WE WERE YOUNG WHEN WE COULD NUMBER FRIENDS • • 436 EMPEDOCLES II   236
    FRIENDS MORE NEAR US THAN A BIRD • • • • • • 453 POOR MATTHIAS   23
    OF PITYING FRIENDS DERISIVE ENEMIES • • • • • •   LUCRETIUS 2   15

FRIENDSHIP
    MUCH HE WHOSE FRIENDSHIP I NOT LONG SINCE WON • •   2 TO A FRIEND   5
    OUR FACTIONS WITH THE FRIENDSHIP OF THEIR CHIEFS • • 335 MEROPE   166
    ONCE MORE MY FRIENDSHIP THOU REJECTEST WELL • • 398 MEROPE   1783

FRIGHT
    ART THOU SO FIERCE THOU WILT NOT FRIGHT ME SO • •   72 SOHRAB RUSTUM   380
    A PALE UNMEANING GHOST POWERLESS TO FRIGHT • • • 366 MEROPE   1021

FRIGHTEND
    WITH A LOVELY FRIGHTEND MIEN   . . . .   433 EMPEDOCLES II   157

FRIGHTENEST
    THOU FRIGHTENEST AND CONFOUNDST ME BY THY WORDS . . 362 MEROPE   932

FRINGD
    FRINGD WITH DEAD LEAVES AND MOSSES RARE   . . . . 148 TRISTRAM 2   V

FRINGE
    WHERE RED-BERRIED ASHES FRINGE . . .   . 190 STRAYED REVEL   146
    WHICH FRINGE THY SOFT BLUE SPEZZIAN BAY   . . . . 303 GRANDE CHARTR   142
    THAT FRINGE THY SOFT BLUE SPEZZIAN BAY   . . . . 303 GRANDE CHARTR V 142
    THAT FRINGE THY DARK BLUE SPEZZIAN BAY   . . . . 303 GRANDE CHARTR V 142
    OER GLION FRINGE THE MOUNTAINS BRINK . . . . . . 483 ROME-SICKNESS   11

FRINGED
    FROM THE FRINGED MATTRESS WHERE THY DUCHESS LIES . . 18 CHURCH BROU 3   8
    IN ITS CLEAR SHALLOW TURF-FRINGED BED   . . . . 55 RESIGNATION   91
    FRINGED WITH DARK PINES AND SANDS WHERE SEAFOWL SCREAM 123 BALDER DEAD 3   327
    EACH GLISTENING STRAND EACH HEATH-FRINGED BAY   . . 177 FAREWELL   4
    TO-NIGHT THOSE SOFT-FRINGED EYES SHALL CLOSE   . . 205 CALAIS SANDS   35
    ON SOME TALL SCAR FRINGED WITH DARK FEATHERY PINES 357 MEROPE   803

FRINGES
    LET THE FLUTTERING FRINGES STREAK   . . . . . . 23 MEMORY-PICTURE   29
    THE FRINGES OF A SOUTHWARD-FACING BROW   . . . . 262 SCHOLAR-GIPSY   235

FRINGING
    FIRST MEETS THE FRINGING HEATH AT ONCE ALL ROUND . . TRISTRAM 3 V 14
    FIRST LEAVES THE FRINGING HEATH AT ONCE ALL ROUND TRISTRAM 3 V 14

FRITH
    HE KNOWS EACH FRITH AND EVERY ROCKY CREEK   . . . . 123 BALDER DEAD 3   326
    AND COMING FLUSHD OVER THE STORMY FRITH   . . . . 196 FRAG ANTIGONE   58

FRITILLARIES
    I KNOW WHAT WHITE WHAT PURPLE FRITILLARIES   . . . . 266 THYRSIS   107

FRIVOLITY
    AND GAY WITHOUT FRIVOLITY   . . . . 304 GRANDE CHARTR   160

FRIVOLOUS
    O FRIVOLOUS MIND OF MAN   . . . . 198 FRAG DEJANEIRA   1
    HOW FRIVOLOUS A BABY MAN WOULD BE   . . . . . . 246 BURIED LIFE   31

FRO
    ROCKING HER OBSCURE BODY TO AND FRO   . . . . . . 45 IN UTRUMQUE PAR   25
    THEY TOO HAVE LONG ROAMD TO AND FRO   . . . . . 55 RESIGNATION   109
    THEY FAINT THEY STAGGER TO AND FRO   . . . . . 226 EPILOG LAOCOON   173
    BUT THE SAME RESTLESS PACINGS TO AND FRO   . . . . 242 SUMMER NIGHT   23
    BUT FLUCTUATES TO AND FRO   . . . . 243 SUMMER NIGHT   31
    ON THE BLACK WAVE BORNE TO AND FRO   . . . . . 370 MEROPE   1119
    BE MISERABLY BANDIED TO AND FRO   . . . . . . 435 EMPEDOCLES II   230
    AND ALL THE TEDIOUS TOSSING TO AND FRO   . . . . 448 WESTMIN ABBEY   150

FROCK
    IN HIS WHITE QUAINT-EMBROIDERD FROCK . . . . . . 57 RESIGNATION   182

FROCKD
    ON THE WARM INGLE-BENCH THE SMOCK-FROCKD BOORS . . 256 SCHOLAR-GIPSY   59

FRONT
    ON THE CARVED WESTERN FRONT A FLOOD OF LIGHT   . . 18 CHURCH BROU 3   18
    AND NOW IN FRONT BEHOLD OUTSPREAD   . . . . . . 54 RESIGNATION   64
    WHEN RUSTUM WAS IN FRONT OF EVERY FRAY   . . . . 63 SOHRAB RUSTUM   80
    THREADING THE TARTAR SQUADRONS TO THE FRONT   . . 65 SOHRAB RUSTUM   142
    HE TOOK HIS SPEAR AND TO THE FRONT HE CAME . . . . 65 SOHRAB RUSTUM   146
    AND RUSTUM TO THE PERSIAN FRONT ADVANCED   . . . . 70 SOHRAB RUSTUM   291
    SWIFT THROUGH THE TARTAR SQUADRONS TO THE FRONT   . 65 SOHRAB RUSTUM V 142
    SLOW THROUGH THE TARTAR SQUADRONS TO THE FRONT   . . 65 SOHRAB RUSTUM V 142
    FAIR WAS THE BRIDE AND ON HER FRONT DID GLOW   . . 166 AUSTERITY POET   5
    NOTHING BESIDES IN FRONT . . . . 234 YOUTH OF MAN   75
    OTHERS WILL FRONT IT FEARLESSLY   . . . . . . 272 MEMORIAL VERSES   69
    HIS BOLT-SCATHED FRONT TO THE STARS   . . . . . 293 HEINES GRAVE   32
    IN FRONT THE AWFUL ALPINE TRACK   . . . . . . 306 OBERMANN   1
    MAY BRAVELIER FRONT HIS LIFE AND IN HIMSELF   . . 429 EMPEDOCLES II   9
    IN FRONT THE DUMB ROCK RISES STEEP   . . . . . . 479 HAYSWATER BOAT   11
    SO SHONE FORTH IN FRONT OF TROY BY THE BED OF XANTHUS HOMER TRANS   1
    SLEW HIM FIGHTING IN FRONT OF THE FRAY AND HOMER TRANS   53
        GLORIFIED HECTOR
    IN FRONT OF SOME GREAT FANE WHEREOF WE KNOW   . . LUCRETIUS 5   7

FRONTIER
    UPON THE RUSSIAN FRONTIER WHERE   . . . . . . 93 SICK KING BOKH   161
    UPON THE NORTHERN FRONTIER WHERE   . . . . . . 93 SICK KING BOKH V 161

FRONTING
    WHITEND HIS FACE FROM THE SUNS FRONTING RAY   . . 170 EAST AND WEST   6

FRORE
    ALL THE FRORE PEAKS AWFUL CROWN   • • • • • •   31 NEW SIRENS   144
    OR SOME FRORE CASPIAN REED-BED SOUTHWARD BOUND • •   64 SOHRAB RUSTUM   115
    THE FRORE MOUNTAIN-WALL • • • • • • • • • •   176 PARTING   48

FROST
    WHEN THE FROST FLOWERS THE WHITEND WINDOW-PANES • •   70 SOHRAB RUSTUM   306
    AND AS IN WINTER WHEN THE FROST BREAKS UP • • • •   122 BALDER DEAD 3   307

FROSTS
    THE SCYTHIAN BUT LONG FROSTS • • • • • • • •   193 STRAYED REVEL   240

FROSTY
    INTO THE FROSTY STARLIGHT AND THERE MOVED • • • •   87 SOHRAB RUSTUM   877
    LOOKD STERNLY THROUGH THE FROSTY EVENING-AIR • •   151 TRISTRAM 3   60
    THEN LOOKD AND LO THE FROSTY SKIES • • • • • •   158 SAINT BRANDAN   75
    THE ICEBERG IN THE FROSTY AIR • • • • • • •   158 SAINT BRANDAN V 76

FROWN
    ON HIS BROW AN ANGRY FROWN • • • • • • •   14 CHURCH BROU 1   48
    WHERE SOME MUSE WITH HALF-CURVED FROWN • • • •   27 NEW SIRENS   26
    AND MADE ALL YOUR CEDARS FROWN • • • • • • •   30 NEW SIRENS   124
    ONE FAINT FROWN OF DISTANT COLDNESS • • • •   31 NEW SIRENS   161
    AFTER SHORT COMMERCE WITH ME FEAR MY FROWN • • •   37 WORLDS TRIUMPHS   8
    THE IRON FROWN OF HELA IS RELAXD • • • • •   126 BALDER DEAD 3   463
    THOSE WINDOWS WHICH I GAZE AT FROWN • • • •   242 SUMMER NIGHT   3
    A SIGH THE GODDESS GAVE AND WITH A FROWN • • •   447 WESTMIN ABBEY   94
    HOW FIRS LESS CURST BY FORTUNES FROWN • • • •   483 ROME-SICKNESS   10

FROWND
    HE SPOKE AND FROWND AND GUDURZ TURND AND RAN • •   69 SOHRAB RUSTUM   260

FROWNING
    SHAKES HER HEAD FROWNING • • • • • • • •   51 CONSOLATION   52
    FROWNING GRIM DOWN THOU WICKED KING • • • • •   91 SICK KING BOKH   97
    WITH FROWNING FOREHEADS WITH LIPS • • • • •   289 RUGBY CHAPEL   105
    WHERE THE SPHINX LIVED AMONG THE FROWNING HILLS •   427 EMPEDOCLES I 2   440
    HORDE AFTER HORDE STREAMED UP THY FROWNING CAPITOL   464 ALARIC AT ROME   72

FROWNS
    OUR JANGLE OF FALSE WITS OUR CLIMATES FROWNS • •   168 RACHEL 2   11

FROZE
    AND THE SIGHT FROZE ALL HER LIFE • • • • • •   14 CHURCH BROU 1   52

FROZEN
    NOT GODS BUT GHOSTS IN FROZEN APATHY • • • • •   9 MYCERINUS   36
    MAD DELIGHT AND FROZEN CALMS • • • • • • •   33 NEW SIRENS   196
    LIES FROZEN AND DEAD • • • • • • • • •   36 VOICE   14
    WHO FROM HER FROZEN HEIGHT WITH JEALOUS EYE •   99 BALDER DEAD 1   156
    THE RICH SHE HAD LET PASS WITH FROZEN STARE •   170 WEST LONDON   8
    WHEN WE ARE FROZEN UP WITHIN AND QUITE • • • •   213 GROWING OLD   32
    TO THE FROZEN HARTZ WITH HIS SOUL • • • • •   298 HEINES GRAVE   193
    DEATHS FROZEN HOUR IS DONE • • • • • • •   322 OBERMANN MORE   292
    CROSSING THE FROZEN LAKE APPEARS • • • • •   451 GEISTS GRAVE   51
    LIKE FROZEN WINDS ON SOUTHERN VALES THAT BLOW •   474 CROMWELL   89
    AND PILLOWS ON HER FROZEN BREAST AND LOCKS • • •   FRAGMENT 1   3

FRUIT
    OF LABOUR THAT IN LASTING FRUIT OUTGROWS • • •   1 QUIET WORK   6
    OF LABOUR THAT IN FRUIT BY FAR OUTGOES • • •   1 QUIET WORK V 6
    OF LABOUR THAT IN FRUIT BY FAR OUTGROWS • • •   1 QUIET WORK V 6
    EAT NOT THE FRUIT OF THEIR OWN HANDS • • • • •   93 SICK KING BOKH   170
    WITH CURIOUS FRUIT-TREES BROUGHT FROM FAR • • •   94 SICK KING BOKH   201
    WITH CURIOUS FRUIT TREES BOUGHT FROM FAR • • •   94 SICK KING BOKH V 201
    HE IS DEAD AND THE FRUIT-BEARING DAY • • • • •   229 YOUTH OF NATURE   56
    HUSH FOR FRUIT • • • • • • • • • • • •   235 YOUTH OF MAN   99
    BUT THAT YE THINK CLEAR FEEL DEEP BEAR FRUIT WELL   238 PROGRESS   47
    BUT THAT YOU TOO FEEL DEEPLY BEAR FRUIT WELL •   238 PROGRESS V 47
    BUT THAT YOU THINK CLEAR FEEL DEEP BEAR FRUIT WELL   238 PROGRESS V 47
    WHOSE INSIGHT NEVER HAS BORNE FRUIT IN DEEDS •   260 SCHOLAR-GIPSY   174

FRUITED
    UNDER A DARK RED-FRUITED YEW-TREES SHADE • • •   259 SCHOLAR-GIPSY   140
    AND THAT GOLDEN-FRUITED STRAND • • • • • • •   PILLARS UNIVERS   1

FRUITFUL
    THIS IS THAT FRUITFUL FAMED MESSENIAN LAND • • •   330 MEROPE   4
    BUT THAT SINCE FIRST THE BLACK AND FRUITFUL EARTH   389 MEROPE   1536
    AND WE MIGHT GLADLY SHARE THE FRUITFUL STIR • •   439 EMPEDOCLES II   339

FRUITLESS
    AND PRAYERS AND GIFTS AND TEARS ARE FRUITLESS ALL   10 MYCERINUS   71
    PLEASED YOU MOCK THE FRUITLESS CRY • • • • •   24 MEMORY-PICTURE   55
    FRUITLESS BUT SOMETHING TO SNATCH • • • • •   288 RUGBY CHAPEL   81
    AND HE DIES FRUITLESS HAVING FOUND NO FIELD •   LUCRETIUS 2   6
    TO GLUE MY FRUITLESS GAZE ON AND TO PINE • • •   FRAGMENT 5   6

FRUITS
    AND FOR THIS DROUGHT ALL KINDS OF FRUITS • • •   94 SICK KING BOKH   195
    MORE FRESH MORE VERDANT THAN THE LAST WITH FRUITS   128 BALDER DEAD 3   529

FRUSTRATE
    AND LEARN MY FRUSTRATE LIFE . . . . 322 OBERMANN MORE   276

FUGITIVE
    THE PRESSD FUGITIVE AGAIN . . . . 136 TRISTRAM 1   185
    POOR FUGITIVE THE FEATHERY CHANGE . . . . . . 201 PHILOMELA   24
    A FUGITIVE AND GRACIOUS LIGHT HE SEEKS . . . . 268 THYRSIS   201

FULFIL
    ILL DEEDS ILL PASSIONS ZEALOUS TO FULFIL . . . . 11 MYCERINUS   76
    HE TO FULFIL AN ORDER RAISED HIS HAND . . . . 384 MEROPE   1399
    A DARING HAND THAT SHRUNK NOT TO FULFIL . . . . 478 CROMWELL   227

FULFILLD
    FEAR NOTHING BUT THAT ALL SHALL BE FULFILLD . . 112 BALDER DEAD 2   253
    TO BE FULFILLD NOR MY RETURN AS SURE . . . . 112 BALDER DEAD 2   269
    SMOOTH SOUND THE TERMS AND LIGHT TO BE FULFILLD . 120 BALDER DEAD 3   231
    TILL ALL HAVE BEEN FULFILLD . . . . 237 PROGRESS   12
    TILL ALL SHALL BE FULFILLD . . . . 237 PROGRESS   V 12
    TILL ALL HATH BEEN FULFILLD . . . . 237 PROGRESS   V 12
    CAN BE THROUGH HOURS OF GLOOM FULFILLD . . . 241 MORALITY   6
    WHOSE VAGUE RESOLVES NEVER HAVE BEEN FULFILLD . 260 SCHOLAR-GIPSY   175
    WHOSE WEAK RESOLVES NEVER HAVE BEEN FULFILLD . 260 SCHOLAR-GIPSY V 175
    CLAMOURS TO FIND FULFILLD WHICH GOOD MEN PRAISE . 386 MEROPE   1428

FULFILMENT
    BUT HOW YE SAY SHOULD THE FULFILMENT FAIL . . . 120 BALDER DEAD 3   230
    THERE SHALL FIND FULFILMENT IN ITS DAY . . . . 483 THEKLAS ANSWER   22

FULFILS
    RESTORE HIM FOR WHAT PART FULFILS HE HERE . . . . 110 BALDER DEAD 2   194

FULL
    SCORNFUL AND STRANGE AND SORROWFUL AND FULL . .   4 EMERSONS ESSAYS   9
    SO SCORNFUL SEEMED THAT SMILE SO STRANGE SO FULL .   EMERSONS ESSAYS V 9
    THE PRODIGY OF FULL-BLOWN CRIME AMONG . . . .   6 GEO CRUIKSHANK   3
    WISHES UNWORTHY OF A MAN FULL-GROWN . . . . . .   8 RELIGIOUS ISOL   8
    CROWND WITH GRAY HAIRS HE DIED AND FULL OF SWAY .   9 MYCERINUS   14
    HAST THOU YET DEALT HIM O LIFE THY FULL MEASURE . 20 MODERN SAPPHO   33
    DRAIND ALL THE LIFE MY FULL HEART HAD TO SPILL . 36 VOICE   V 39
    NOR WEARINESS THE FULL-FED SOULS ANNOY . . . . 42 GIPSY CHILD   11
    STILL GAZING ON THE EVER FULL . . . . . . 59 RESIGNATION   227
    IN TURN AND FULL STRUCK RUSTUMS SHIELD SHARP RANG 73 SOHRAB RUSTUM   406
    AT THE FULL MOON TEARS GATHERD IN HIS EYES . . . 79 SOHRAB RUSTUM   618
    AND FULL OF BLOOD AND BATTLES IS MY AGE . . . 85 SOHRAB RUSTUM   825
    FULL THE DECKS BREADTH AND LOFTY THEN THE CORPSE . 118 BALDER DEAD 3   162
    WHOSE MANGER IS STUFFD FULL OF GOOD FRESH HAY . 123 BALDER DEAD 3   341
    FULL ON THEIR WINDOW THE MOONS RAY . . . . 140 TRISTRAM 1   333
    RACING FULL SPEED AND STARTLING IN THEIR RUSH . 150 TRISTRAM 3   29
    HOW THEY ARE FULL OF LANGUOR AND DISTRESS . . . 153 TRISTRAM 3   137
    FIXD FULL ON MERLINS FACE HER STATELY PRIZE . 154 TRISTRAM 3   178
    WHERE THE SUNS RAYS STRUCK FULL AND FLASHD BACK KEEN   TRISTRAM 3   V 21
    WHAT BLESSING MUST FULL GOODNESS SHOWER . . 158 SAINT BRANDAN   54
    POLYMNIA FULL ON HER DEATH-BED TWAS WELL . . . 168 RACHEL 2   8
    IN TEARS WITH HEARTS TOO FULL TO SPEAK . . . 178 FAREWELL   12
    SHREDS OF GIFTS WHICH HE REFUSED IN FULL . . . 210 SELF-DECEPTION   18
    THE TIDE IS FULL THE MOON LIES FAIR . . . . . 210 DOVER BEACH   2
    WAS ONCE TOO AT THE FULL AND ROUND EARTHS SHORE . 211 DOVER BEACH   22
    OF BARDS FULL MANY A STROKE DIVINE . . . . . 222 EPILOG LAOCOON   20
    FULL OF SWEET BREATHINGS WAS THE AIR . . . . 223 EPILOG LAOCOON   63
    HIS EYE MUST TRAVEL DOWN AT FULL . . . . . 225 EPILOG LAOCOON 145
    SOME DOCTOR FULL OF PHRASE AND FAME . . . . 250 WISH   18
    AND THE FULL MOON AND THE WHITE EVENING-STAR . 264 THYRSIS   70
    GERMAN KAISER FULL OFT . . . . 296 HEINES GRAVE   136
    FULL-FOAMING MILK-PAILS ALPINE FARE . . . . . 313 OBERMANN MORE   17
    ORCHARD AND CROFT AND FULL-STORED GRANGE . . . 313 OBERMANN MORE   27
    HIS ACTS THE WIFE HE CHOSE WAS FULL OF VIRTUES . 337 MEROPE   240
    DOUBLE OF ISSUE FULL OF PITS AND SNARES . . . 349 MEROPE   581
    FULL ON THE SHARP-POINTED . . . . 400 MEROPE   1880
    WITH THY HEAD FULL OF WINE AND THY HAIR CROWND . . 407 EMPEDOCLES I 1   32
    GRANT THAT THE WORLD WERE FULL OF GODS WE CANNOT SEE 421 EMPEDOCLES I 2 286
    OH THAT MY SOUL WERE FULL OF LIGHT AS THE STARS . 438 EMPEDOCLES II   325
    FULL WELL MAX KNOWS THE FRIEND IS DEAD . . . . 460 KAISER DEAD   69
    OTHERS THERE ARE AS DEATHLESS FULL AS THEY . . 462 ALARIC AT ROME   9
    BUT FULL AND DEATHLESS AS THE DEEP DARK HUE . 463 ALARIC AT ROME   35
    AND MEMORYS GUSHING TIDE SWELLS DEEP AND FULL . 464 ALARIC AT ROME   53
    WHILE FULL AND CEASELESS AS THE OCEAN ROLL . . . 464 ALARIC AT ROME   71
    THAT BROW SO SAD SO PALE SO FULL OF CARE . . . 477 CROMWELL   183

FULLER
    FULLER FOR HIM BE THE HOURS . . . . 200 EARLY DEATH   15

FULLEST
    WHAT MADE MY HEART AT NEWSTEAD FULLEST SWELL . . 166 PICT NEWSTEAD   1

FULLY
    WHEN FULLY LEARND WILL TO THE WORLD IMPART . . . . 256 SCHOLAR-GIPSY   49

FULNESS
NOR PALLD WITH ITS OWN FULNESS EBBD AND DIED	• •	12 MYCERINUS	116
AND WEEP AND FEEL THE FULNESS OF THE PAST	• • • •	212 GROWING OLD	19
FULNESS OF LIFE AND POWER OF FEELING YE	• • • •	436 EMPEDOCLES II	258
OF FIGURES WITH HER FULNESS VAST	• • • • • •	450 GEISTS GRAVE	25

FUME
THEY STRAIGHTWAY ARE BURNT UP WITH FUME AND CARE	• •	153 TRISTRAM 3	139

FUMES
AH THE SWEET FUMES AGAIN	• • • • • • • • • •	187 STRAYED REVEL	64
BY FUMES OF WINE AND SLEEP	• • • • • • • •	188 STRAYED REVEL	92
OF DAZZLING CONVERSE FROM FUMES	• • • • •	296 HEINES GRAVE	145
OF PRAISE HOT HEADY FUMES TO THE POOR BRAIN	• •	296 HEINES GRAVE	146
OF DAZZLING CONVERSE AND FUMES	• • • • • • •	296 HEINES GRAVE	V 145

FUNCTION
ESTEEM AND FUNCTION AND SO FAR IS WELL	• • • •	127 BALDER DEAD 3	470
GROW STIFFER EVERY FUNCTION LESS EXACT	• • • •	212 GROWING OLD	9

FUNDAMENTAL
MANS FUNDAMENTAL LIFE IF TO DESPISE	• • • • • •	6 REP FRIEND	4

FUNERAL
STRAINS OF GLAD MUSIC AT A FUNERAL	• • • • •	36 VOICE	22
OUR VAUNTED LIFE IS ONE LONG FUNERAL	• • • • •	44 QUESTION	10
AND ON THE DECK BUILD HIGH A FUNERAL-PILE	• • • •	96 BALDER DEAD 1	42
TO GATHER WOOD AND BUILD A FUNERAL-PILE	• • • •	103 BALDER DEAD 1	296
AND MAKE A FUNERAL-PILE ON BALDERS SHIP	• • • •	106 BALDER DEAD 2	43
AT TABLE AND THE FUNERAL-FEAST BEGAN	• • • • •	119 BALDER DEAD 3	209
THESE PUNCTUAL FUNERAL HONOURS YEAR BY YEAR	• •	332 MEROPE	86
LIVING HIS OWN FUNERAL-PILE	• • • • • • •	399 MEROPE	1834

FUNEREAL
MATCH THAT FUNEREAL ASPECT WITH HER PALL	• • • •	43 GIPSY CHILD	46

FUR
DOWN SHE SANK AMID HER FUR	• • • • • • • •	453 POOR MATTHIAS	36

FURBISHD
FOLLY REVIVED RE-FURBISHD SOPHISTRIES	• • • •	449 WESTMIN ABBEY	159

FURIES
I PRAY THE FURIES EVER-RESTLESS BAND	• • • • • •	349 MEROPE	569
COME YE SWIFT FURIES WHO TO HIM YE HAUNT	• • • •	367 MEROPE	1056
AND THE STANCH FURIES NEVER-SILENT SCOURGE	• • • •	373 MEROPE	1187
THUS FAR HE AND HERE HIS VOICE WAS STOPPED		HOMER TRANS	57
BY THE FURIES			

FURIOUS
FURIOUS SINGLE HORSEMEN GALLOP	• • • • • • • •	13 CHURCH BROU 1	23
BUT SUCH FURIOUS PASSIONS FEEDEST	• • • • • •	SECOND BEST	V 7
ARE FURIOUS WITH THEMSELVES AND HARD TO PLEASE	• •	153 TRISTRAM 3	142
HE DROVE ABROAD IN FURIOUS GUISE	• • • • • •	315 OBERMANN MORE	99
HE WOULD HAVE SAVED YOU FROM YOUR FURIOUS SELVES	• •	339 MEROPE	299
PASSIONS FIRST FURIOUS LONGING TO IMBRUE	• • • •	387 MEROPE	1467

FURLD
THE STRONG BAND WHICH PASSION AROUND HIM HATH FURLD		20 MODERN SAPPHO	22
THE STRONG BAND WHICH BEAUTY AROUND HIM HATH FURLD		20 MODERN SAPPHO	V 22
LAY LIKE THE FOLDS OF A BRIGHT GIRDLE FURLD	• •	211 DOVER BEACH	23
LAY LIKE THE FOLDS OF A BRIGHT GARMENT FURLD	• •	211 DOVER BEACH	V 23
SPIRITS DRIED UP AND CLOSELY FURLD	• • • • • •	272 MEMORIAL VERSES	56
SPIRITS DEEP-CRUSHED AND CLOSELY FURLD	• • • •	272 MEMORIAL VERSES	V 56
THEN AT A PARDONING WORD RE-FURLD	• • • • •	460 KAISER DEAD	57

FURNACE
NO TIS THE GRADUAL FURNACE OF THE WORLD	• • • •	153 TRISTRAM 3	119

FURROWD
ON EITHER SIDE THE BLACK DEEP-FURROWD PATH	• • •	41 HUMAN LIFE	22
HAVE NEVER KNOWN MY GRANDSIRES FURROWD FACE	• •	83 SOHRAB RUSTUM	756
FURROWD IT AND THE WATER GURGLED IN	• • • • •	118 BALDER DEAD 3	179

FURROWS
FURROWS THE RICH SOIL HERE AND THERE	• • • • •	191 STRAYED REVEL	176

FURS
MANTLES WITH THOSE RICH FURS DEEP GLISTERING	• •	150 TRISTRAM 3	40

FURTHER
IN A WINDLESS VALLEY FURTHER DOWN	• • • • •	31 NEW SIRENS	V 146
BUT WHERE THE FURTHER SIDE SLOPES DOWN	• • • •	57 RESIGNATION	V 180
IN THE STRAIT PASSAGE AT THE FURTHER END	• • •	107 BALDER DEAD 2	V 88
ON THE BROOKS FURTHER SIDE WAS CLEAR BUT THEN	• •	155 TRISTRAM 3	V 189
INTO YON FURTHER FIELD TIS DONE AND SEE	• • • •	267 THYRSIS	V 157
REMOVE YET FURTHER OFF IF AUGHT COMES NEAR	• • •	332 MEROPE	69
AND ON THE HIGHEST PINES BUT FURTHER DOWN	• • • •	406 EMPEDOCLES I 1	V 11
I DARE NOT URGE HIM FURTHER HE MUST GO	• • • •	428 EMPEDOCLES I 2	479
AND ROW HIM STRAIGHTWAY TO THE FURTHER SHORE	• •	444 WESTMIN ABBEY	25

FURTHERD
    HAVING BEEN FURTHERD TO HIS VERY WISH   • • • •   LUCRETIUS 2   11

FURTIVE
    THAT FURTIVE MIEN THAT SCOWLING EYE • • • • • • 157 SAINT BRANDAN   17
    WITH FURTIVE STEP AND CHEEK OF FLAME • • • • • • 278 SOUTHERN NIGHT   102

FURY
    FROM THE CHILDREN THE FURY TO THEM   • • • • 346 MEROPE   497
    EITHER A VENGEFUL FURY I SHOULD STALK   • • • 366 MEROPE   1019
    THE BRAZEN-FOOTED FURY EVER STALKS • • • • • 395 MEROPE   1734

FURZE
    A FIRE OF WITHERD FURZE WHICH BOYS HAVE LIT • • • 124 BALDER DEAD 3   361
    GOLD FURZE WITH BROOM IN BLOSSOM VIES • • • • 274 STANZAS CARNAC   19
    SHEEP MAKE THE FURZE-GROWN AISLES THEIR FOLD • • • 274 STANZAS CARNAC V 16
    SHEEP MAKE THE FURZE-GROWN NAVE THEIR FOLD • • •   STANZAS CARNAC V 16
    GOLD BROOM WITH FURZE IN BLOSSOM VIES • • • • 274 STANZAS CARNAC V 19
    THE FURZE-SCENT PERFUMES ALL THE AIR • • • • • 274 STANZAS CARNAC V 20

FUSING
    WHICH WITH ITS FUSING FLAME   • • • • • • • 320 OBERMANN MORE   222

FUTURE
    EVEN SO DO PAST AND FUTURE INTERTWINE • • •   10 MYCERINUS   59
    SUCH FOR THE FUTURE IS MY HOPE MEANWHILE • • • 129 BALDER DEAD 3   544
    GAVE HER THAT HER FUTURE LORD • • • • • • 134 TRISTRAM 1   137
    BARING HIS DUMB REMORSE TO FUTURE DAYS • • • 167 PICT NEWSTEAD   13
    AND DEAD TO HOPES OF FUTURE JOY • • • • • 206 RIVER   20
    THE FUTURE AND ITS VIEWLESS THINGS • • • • 250 WISH   25
    AND WAIT TO SEE THE FUTURE COME • • • • 303 GRANDE CHARTR   118
    IN DREAMS I SAW THE FUTURE SHINE - • • • 321 OBERMANN MORE   259
    AH THERE OUR FUTURE LIES • • • • • • 315 OBERMANN MORE V
    THE FUTURE NOT YET BORN • • • • • • • 321 OBERMANN MORE V 246
    AND FUTURE KING BEFORE THIS PEOPLES EYES • • • 335 MEROPE   172
    FIRST HEARD OR IN ITS FUTURE ISSUE SHOWN • • • 359 MEROPE   865
    HAVE FAITH AND TRUST THE FUTURE AND THE GODS • • 388 MEROPE   1507
    I THINK ON WHAT THE FUTURE HATH IN STORE • • • • 397 MEROPE   1775
    OF DOUBTFUL FUTURE DATE • • • • • • • 425 EMPEDOCLES I 2   403
    TO NAME FOR FUTURE TIMES TO KNOW • • • • 452 GEISTS GRAVE   79
    THOUGHTS OF THE PAST AND OF THE FUTURE TIME • • 467 ALARIC AT ROME   128
    ITS SHADOWS OER THE FUTURE FLOWERD AND GREW • • 473 CROMWELL   56
    FROM THE STERN FUTURE AND THE YEARS GONE BY • • 475 CROMWELL   110
    THE FUTURE ROLLD ITS GATHERING TIDES ALONG • • • 475 CROMWELL   134
    BUSY FOR PRIAMS FAME AND MY OWN IN SPITE OF THE FUTURE   HOMER TRANS   19

FYFIELD
    TO DANCE AROUND THE FYFIELD ELM IN MAY • • • • 257 SCHOLAR-GIPSY   83
    I KNOW THE FYFIELD TREE • • • • • • • • 266 THYRSIS   106

GABLE
    AND IN VALHALLA FROM HIS GABLE-PERCH • • • • • 105 BALDER DEAD 2   3

GAILY
    BENDING GAILY OER THY HAND   • • • • • 134 TRISTRAM 1   113
    GAILY THEIR PINE-STAFF GREEN • • • • • • 218 BACCHANALIA 1   24
    WHERE GAILY FLOWS THE HUMAN TIDE • • • • 224 EPILOG LAOCOON   108
    AND LIFE RAN GAILY AS THE SPARKLING THAMES • • • 261 SCHOLAR-GIPSY   202

GAIN
    LINGERING WE FOLLOW DOWN WE GAIN • • • •   54 RESIGNATION   78
    THOU ART MY FATHER AND THY GAIN IS MINE • • •   84 SOHRAB RUSTUM   777
    IN THE GREAT DEEP FOR GAIN AT LAST COME HOME • • 123 BALDER DEAD 3   358
    THAT NECKAN HEAVEN MIGHT GAIN • • • • • 160 NECKAN   40
    YET WE SHALL ONE DAY GAIN LIFE PAST • • • • 179 FAREWELL   53
    SOME END IS THERE WE INDEED MAY GAIN • • • • 210 SELF-DECEPTION   28
    AND LUMINOUS VIEW TO GAIN • • • • • • 308 OBERMANN   80
    THAT END TO HELP MEN GAIN   • • • • • 323 OBERMANN MORE V 322
    FOR PRIVATE GAIN OR HATRED TAKES A LIFE • • • 336 MEROPE   202
    I ASK IF BLOODLESS MEANS MAY GAIN HIS END • • • 387 MEROPE   1465
    LET HIM FETCH SUCCOURS FROM ARCADIA GAIN • • • 388 MEROPE   1498

GAIND
    A GOAL WHICH GAIND MAY GIVE REPOSE • • • •   53 RESIGNATION   17
    AND GAIND THE WHITE BROW OF THE CUMNER RANGE • • 259 SCHOLAR-GIPSY   127
    WHAT HAD OUR ARTHUR GAIND TO STOP AND SEE • • • 448 WESTMIN ABBEY   154

GAINS
    GAINS NOT AN EARTH-DEAFEND EAR • • • • • • 281 HAWORTH CHURCH   36

GAINSAID
    AND BELIEVES NATURE OUTRAGED IF HIS WILLS GAINSAID   417 EMPEDOCLES I 2   156

GAINST
    GAINST THAT ALONE HAD BALDERS LIFE NO CHARM • •   95 BALDER DEAD 1   8
    GAINST THAT ALONE HAD BALDERS LIFE NO CHARM • •   98 BALDER DEAD 1   104
    GAINST THICK-CRASHING INSANE • • • • • • 293 HEINES GRAVE   34
    THOU COUNTEST ON TO BACK THEE GAINST HIS LORDS • • 382 MEROPE   1321
    SINCE GAINST THE CLASSES • • • • • • • 460 KAISER DEAD   40
    BUT THAT WHEN GAINST HIMSELF HE RAISD • • • • 481 COURAGE   15

GAIT
    AND KINGLY GAIT FOR EVER SUCH A SPELL • • • • 408 EMPEDOCLES I 1   61

GALATEA
    AND GALATEA FROM THE BAY • • • • • • • • • 222 EPILOG LAOCOON   47

GALE
    OF SOME SHIP THAT FIGHTS THE GALE • • • • • 130 TRISTRAM 1   13
    IS IT THAT THE BLEAK SEA-GALE • • • • • • 131 TRISTRAM 1   33
    IS IT THAT THE BLACK SEA-GALE • • • • • • 131 TRISTRAM 1 V 33
    OER THE BLUE MIDLAND WATERS WITH THE GALE • • • 262 SCHOLAR-GIPSY   244
    STRESS OF GALE AND SHOWERS OF SPRAY • • • • 457 POOR MATTHIAS   178
    ALL IDLY FLUTTERD IN THE EASTERN GALE • • • • 473 CROMWELL   68
    WHERE THE DARK SHIPS RODE PROUDLY WOOD THE GALE • • 479 CROMWELL   238

GALILEE
    THE FISHER FROM THE LAKE OF GALILEE • • • • • • 445 WESTMIN ABBEY   45

GALL
    STILL THEY GALL YOU THE LONG HOURS • • • • •   30 NEW SIRENS   129
    DO THEY GALL YOU THE LONG HOURS • • • • •   30 NEW SIRENS V 129
    AND OER HIS VISAGE SERPENTS DROPPING GALL • • • 111 BALDER DEAD 2   221

GALLANT
    POOR GALLANT BOY FOR SUCH THOU WAST • • • • 276 SOUTHERN NIGHT   39
    POOR GALLANT BOY FOR SUCH THOU WERT • • • • 276 SOUTHERN NIGHT V 39

GALLANTS
    STEEDS ARE NEIGHING GALLANTS GLITTERING • • • 13 CHURCH BROU 1   9
    KINGS HOLD REVEL GALLANTS MEET • • • • • 14 CHURCH BROU 1   54

GALLERY
    IN THEIR COOL GALLERY • • • • • • 50 CONSOLATION   18
    PAINTED HE WILLD IT IN THE GALLERY • • • • • 166 PICT NEWSTEAD   7

GALLEY
    IN A TYRIAN GALLEY STEERING • • • • • • • 26 NEW SIRENS V 21

GALLOP
    FURIOUS SINGLE HORSEMEN GALLOP • • • • • • 13 CHURCH BROU 1   23

GALLOPD
    BUT FIERCELY ODIN GALLOPD MOVED IN HEART • • • 102 BALDER DEAD 1   258
    AND HERMOD GREETED HER AND GALLOPD BY • • • • 108 BALDER DEAD 2   136

GAME
    MURDERS UNCERTAIN SECRET PERILOUS GAME • • • 388 MEROPE   1501
    TO CHUCKLE WITH HIS SENDER OER THE GAME • • • 366 MEROPE V

GAMES
    HARK THE GAMES ON FOOT THEY SCATTER • • • • • 13 CHURCH BROU 1   21

GAOLERS
    BUT SEE HIS BLACK-COATED GAOLERS • • • • • 214 NEW ROME V 5

GAPE
    THE FRIENDS WHO COME AND GAPE AND GO • • • • 250 WISH   14
    GAPE AND CRY WIZARD AT HIM IF THEY LIST • • • 410 EMPEDOCLES I 1   139

GAPS
    YE FILL UP THE GAPS IN OUR FILES • • • • • 292 RUGBY CHAPEL   204

GARB
    IN GARB IN FORM IN FEATURE AS HE WAS • • • 103 BALDER DEAD 1   283
    MARKD THINE OUTLANDISH GARB THY FIGURE SPARE • • 258 SCHOLAR-GIPSY   98
    MARKD THY OUTLANDISH GARB THY FIGURE SPARE • • • 258 SCHOLAR-GIPSY V 98
    A SHEPHERDS GARB HE WORE • • • • • • • 314 OBERMANN MORE   64
    JADED WITH TRAVEL CLAD IN HUNTERS GARB • • • 363 MEROPE   957
    IN PRIESTLY GARB A FRAIL OLD MAN WENT BY • • • 476 CROMWELL   166

GARD
    WAS LAÚNCELOTS GUEST AT JOYOUS GARD • • • • • 136 TRISTRAM 1   203

GARDEN
    WHICH IN A QUEENS SECLUDED GARDEN THROWS • • 70 SOHRAB RUSTUM   315
    MOWING THE GARDEN GRASS-PLOTS NEAR ITS BED • • • 80 SOHRAB RUSTUM   636
    SERE IN THE GARDEN OF THE TUILERIES • • • • 167 RACHEL 1   2
    BROWN IN THE GARDEN OF THE TUILERIES • • • • 167 RACHEL 1 V 2
    AND NEATH THE GARDEN-WALK IT HUMS • • • • • 184 TERRACE BERNE   11
    CAME RUSTLING FROM THE GARDEN-TREES • • • • 223 EPILOG LAOCOON   66
    IN THIS SELF-SAME GARDEN AND SAID • • • • 233 YOUTH OF MAN   25
    WHEN GARDEN-WALKS AND ALL THE GRASSY FLOOR • • 264 THYRSIS   54
    FROM THE WET FIELD THROUGH THE VEXT GARDEN-TREES • • 264 THYRSIS   58
    AND GROUPS UNDER THE DREAMING GARDEN-TREES • • • 264 THYRSIS   69
    THE GARDEN OVERGROWN YET MILD • • • • • 301 GRANDE CHARTR   55
    THEN SOME WHO THROUGH THIS GARDEN PASS • • • 452 GEISTS GRAVE   73

GARDENER
    OF AN UNSKILFUL GARDENER HAS BEEN CUT • • • 80 SOHRAB RUSTUM   635

GARDENS
     THOU ART NOT IN AFRASIABS GARDENS NOW   • • • • •   75 SOHRAB RUSTUM   460
     FROM THE GREY-WALLD GARDENS A BREATH • • • • •   234 YOUTH OF MAN   67

GARLAND
     HIS DROOPING GARLAND • • • • • • • •   194 STRAYED REVEL   268
     WHEN THE WHITE-ROBED GARLAND-CROWNED MONARCH • • 400 MEROPE   1857
     AS I WAS LIFTING MY SOILD GARLAND OFF • • • •   407 EMPEDOCLES I 1   40

GARLANDS
     HANGING GARLANDS ON YOUR ODOROUS PINES • • • •   29 NEW SIRENS   96
     HANGING GARLANDS ON THE ODOROUS PINES • • • •   29 NEW SIRENS V 96
     FRESH GARLANDS OF THIS DEWY ROSE • • • • •   48 HORATIAN ECHO   23
     AND GARLANDS FOR THEIR FOREHEAD WEAVE • • • •   203 EUPHROSYNE   18
     GARLANDS THEIR PRIZE • • • • • • • •   218 BACCHANALIA 1   37
     DECK IT WITH GARLANDS OF FLOWERS • • • • •   342 MEROPE   388

GARMENT
     LAY LIKE THE FOLDS OF A BRIGHT GARMENT FURLD • 211 DOVER BEACH V 23
     SULLYING HIS GARMENT WITH DARK-STREAMING BLOOD • 346 MEROPE   491
     HIS WHITE GARMENT TO HIS EYES • • • • • •   434 EMPEDOCLES II   188

GARMENTS
     SHUDDERING THEY DREW HER GARMENTS OFF AND FOUND • • 166 AUSTERITY POET   10
     WHAT GARMENTS OUT-GLISTENING • • • • • •   442 EMPEDOCLES II   439

GASH
     CAME WELLING FROM THE OPEN GASH AND LIFE • • •   85 SOHRAB RUSTUM   841

GASP
     AND WE SHALL STRUGGLE AWHILE GASP AND REBEL • • 440 EMPEDOCLES II   382
     ONE MORE GASP IT IS THE END • • • • • •   452 POOR MATTHIAS   13

GASPS
     WHITE WITH EYES CLOSED ONLY WHEN HEAVY GASPS • • 86 SOHRAB RUSTUM   849
     DEEP HEAVY GASPS QUIVERING THROUGH ALL HIS FRAME • • 86 SOHRAB RUSTUM   850

GATE
     FROM THE GATE THE WARDERS ANSWERD • • • • •   15 CHURCH BROU 1   81
     COMING BENIGHTED TO THE CASTLE-GATE • • • • •   18 CHURCH BROU 3   15
     A GATE SWINGS TO OUR TIDE HATH FLOWD • • • • •   53 RESIGNATION   48
     HE LEANS UPON A GATE AND SEES • • • • • •   57 RESIGNATION   172
     LEAND ON HIS GATE HE GAZES TEARS • • • • •   57 RESIGNATION   186
     IN THE GREAT WINDOW OF THE GATE • • • •   88 SICK KING BOKH   16
     THEIR SHIPS AND THROUGH THE GATE BEYOND THE WALL • • 97 BALDER DEAD 1   75
     AND SWIFT TO ASGARD TO THE GATE HE CAME • • • • 102 BALDER DEAD 1   259
     AND TO VALHALLAS GATE HE RODE AND LEFT • • • • 102 BALDER DEAD 1   265
     UNDER THE GATE-HOUSE TO THE SANDS AND FOUND • • 113 BALDER DEAD 2   309
     AND HERMOD CAME DOWN TOWRDS THEM FROM THE GATE • 113 BALDER DEAD 3   3
     THOU HAST BEEN SEEN OR HANGING ON A GATE • • • 258 SCHOLAR-GIPSY   103
     THEN CROSS THE SWARD AND REACH THAT GATE • • • 300 GRANDE CHARTR   28
     YE HAVE NOT LEFT THIS GATE WHICH HE MUST PASS • • 361 MEROPE   917
     AND GLORY STRETCHD AT BURWOOD GATE • • • • 461 KAISER DEAD   73
     THAT YOUR OWN HANDS MUST OPEN WIDE THE GATE • • 466 ALARIC AT ROME   117

GATED
     SEVEN-GATED THEBES OR TROY • • • • • •   193 STRAYED REVEL   257
     UP FROM THE CITY TOWRD THIS GATED HILL • • • • 362 MEROPE   935
     UP FROM THE CITY TOWRDS THIS GATED HILL • • • • 362 MEROPE V 935

GATES
     HARK BELOW THE GATES UNBARRING • • • • • •   14 CHURCH BROU 1   37
     MOURNFULLY GRATING THE GATES • • • • • • •   199 FRAG DEJANEIRA   29
     SOFTLY STAND BACK SEE TO THESE PALACE GATES • • 331 MEROPE   51
     TO MAKE THE GATES OF THIS LONG-MOURNFUL HOUSE • • 401 MEROPE   1884
     SOFTLY STAND BACK SEE TOWRD THE PALACE GATES • • 331 MEROPE V 51

GATHER
     HUNTERS GATHER BUGLES RING • • • • • • •   13 CHURCH BROU 1   16
     TO GATHER WOOD AND BUILD A FUNERAL-PILE • • • 103 BALDER DEAD 1   296
     GATHER AND SQUANDER ARE RAISED • • • • • •   288 RUGBY CHAPEL   63
     WHERE HUNTERS GATHER STAGHOUNDS BAY • • • • 305 GRANDE CHARTR   183
     THE CATTLE LOVE TO GATHER ON THEIR WAY • • • • 413 EMPEDOCLES I 2   38

GATHERD
     AT THE FULL MOON TEARS GATHERD IN HIS EYES • • • 79 SOHRAB RUSTUM   618
     LEFT FRESHLY GATHERD ON THEIR NATIVE BANK • • • 86 SOHRAB RUSTUM   845
     BRING NOW THE GATHERD WOOD TO BALDERS SHIP • • 118 BALDER DEAD 3   158
     THE ROUT EARLY GATHERD • • • • • • •   186 STRAYED REVEL   36
     AND GATHERD ON IMMORTAL KNOLLS • • • • • •   227 EPILOG LAOCOON   203
     WHEN WE WERE GATHERD WITH PEISIANAX • • • • 410 EMPEDOCLES I 1   127

GATHERING
     ARE BUSY GATHERING SPARS OF QUARTZ AND STREAMS • 150 TRISTRAM 3   25
     THROUGH THE GATHERING DARKNESS ARISE • • • • • 286 RUGBY CHAPEL   11
     THE FUTURE ROLLD ITS GATHERING TIDES ALONG • • • 475 CROMWELL   134
     AND SLOW RELUCTANT STEPS ARE GATHERING ROUND • 476 CROMWELL   160
     THE GATHERING TEMPEST WITH ITS VOICE OF FEAR • • 478 CROMWELL   209

GAUDS

AND YOUR JEWELLD GAUDS SURRENDER   . . . . . .   35 NEW SIRENS   255
GAY RAIMENT SPARKLING GAUDS ELATION STRONG . . . .   166 AUSTERITY POET   7

GAUGE

I KNEW NOT YET THE GAUGE OF TIME   . . . . . .   242 MORALITY   31

GAUNT

WHERE THE GAUNT AND TACITURN HOST   . . . . . .   289 RUGBY CHAPEL   110

GAVE

THESE WE HAD AND WE GAVE TRULY . . . .   34 NEW SIRENS   231
DOUBT NOT WHAT WE HAD WE GAVE   . . . .   34 NEW SIRENS   232
FREELY GAVE IT BUT IT DIES AWAY   . . . . . .   35 NEW SIRENS   258
FATE GAVE WHAT CHANCE SHALL NOT CONTROL   . . .   58 RESIGNATION   197
OR THAT MEN GAVE IT HIM TO SWELL HIS FAME   . .   79 SOHRAB RUSTUM   614
HIS WANDERING GUEST AND GAVE HIM HIS FAIR CHILD . .   79 SOHRAB RUSTUM   626
THAT SEAL WHICH RUSTUM TO MY MOTHER GAVE   . . .   80 SOHRAB RUSTUM   659
OF MISTLETOE WHICH LOK THE ACCUSER GAVE   . . .   95 BALDER DEAD 1   6
AND GAVE ME NINE UNLIGHTED REALMS TO RULE   . . .   110 BALDER DEAD 2   213
HE SPAKE AND RAISED HIS HAND AND GAVE THE RING   .   112 BALDER DEAD 2   279
HE SPOKE AND WAVED FAREWELL AND GAVE HIS HAND   .   129 BALDER DEAD 3   549
TO NANNA AND SHE GAVE THEIR BROTHER BLIND   . . .   129 BALDER DEAD 3   550
GAVE HER THAT HER FUTURE LORD   . . . . . .   134 TRISTRAM 1   137
GAVE HER THAT KING MARC AND SHE   . . . . . .   134 TRISTRAM 1   138
GAVE HER THAT HER LORD AND SHE . . . .   134 TRISTRAM 1   V 137
BUT AH SHE GAVE ME NEVER A LOOK   . . . . . .   163 FORSAKEN MERM   80
A PROP GAVE WAY CRASH FELL A PLATFORM LO   . . .   166 AUSTERITY POET   11
WHO GAVE THEM VISION   . . . .   192 STRAYED REVEL   V 214
BIRTH-GODDESS AND THE AUSTERE FATES FIRST GAVE   .   195 FRAG ANTIGONE   10
HER FAIR YOUTH UNWILLINGLY GAVE   . . . . . .   197 FRAG ANTIGONE   79
STAVED US BACK AND GAVE OUR CHOICE THE LAW   . . .   210 SELF-DECEPTION   12
MEN GAVE THEE NOTHING BUT THIS HAPPY QUEST   . . .   269 THYRSIS   213
IF MEN ESTEEMD THEE FEEBLE GAVE THEE POWER   . . .   269 THYRSIS   214
IF MEN PROCURED THEE TROUBLE GAVE THEE REST   . . .   269 THYRSIS   215
HAIL TO THE COURAGE WHICH GAVE   . . . . . .   281 HAWORTH CHURCH   44
MARSHALLD THEM GAVE THEM THEIR GOAL   . . . . .   291 RUGBY CHAPEL   175
GOD GAVE THE POET HIS SONG   . . . .   296 HEINES GRAVE   120
GRACE TO YOUR MOOD OF SADNESS GAVE   . . . . .   304 GRANDE CHARTR   153
GRACE TO THEIR MOOD OF SADNESS GAVE   . . . . .   304 GRANDE CHARTR   V 153
AEGIMIUS GAVE OUR OUTCAST HOUSE A HOME   . . . .   337 MEROPE   224
PAST ARNE SPRING WHERE RHEA GAVE THE BABE   . . .   355 MEROPE   736
ARGOS A JUGGLE TO CRESPHONTES GAVE   . . . . .   389 MEROPE   1551
HERACLES GAVE US   . . . .   398 MEROPE   1813
A SIGH THE GODDESS GAVE AND WITH A FROWN   . . .   447 WESTMIN ABBEY   94
WAS THE WILD SHOUT THOSE GOTHIC MYRIADS GAVE   .   466 ALARIC AT ROME   112
SONOROUS WITNESS TO HIS EMPIRE GAVE   . . . . .   476 CROMWELL   158

GAVEST

THE INLY-WRITTEN CHART THOU GAVEST ME   . . . .   40 HUMAN LIFE   5
GAVEST THE WEARY THY HAND   . . . .   290 RUGBY CHAPEL   133

GAVST

AND GAVST HER NINE UNLIGHTED WORLDS TO RULE   . .   121 BALDER DEAD 3   277
A MORE JUST STROKE THAN THAT THOU GAVST MY SON   . .   373 MEROPE   1191

GAY

GAY HER SMILING LORD TO GREET   . . . .   13 CHURCH BROU 1   10
GAY OF OLD AMID THE GAYEST   . . . .   14 CHURCH BROU 1   55
DIGHT WITH MANTLES GAY   . . . .   17 CHURCH BROU 2   22
ITS STEP SO GAY ITS EYE SO BRIGHT   . . . . .   21 YOUTH AND CALM   V 10
TIMES GAY MINIONS PLEASED YOU SEE   . . . . .   24 MEMORY-PICTURE   53
GAY SHINE THE WATERS AND THE CLUSTERD PIER   . . .   41 GIPSY CHILD   V 6
OF SCARLET CLOTH THEY WERE AND GLITTERING GAY   . .   66 SOHRAB RUSTUM   192
THERES MANY A GAY KNIGHT WHERE HE GOES   . . . .   138 TRISTRAM 1   256
WHEN THE FEAST WAS GAY AND THE LAUGHTER LOUD   .   146 TRISTRAM 2   114
PRIEST KNIGHTS AND LADIES GAY   . . . . . .   159 NECKAN   22
GAY RAIMENT SPARKLING GAUDS ELATION STRONG   . .   166 AUSTERITY POET   7
SUCH POETS IS YOUR BRIDE THE MUSE YOUNG GAY   . .   166 AUSTERITY POET   12
SHE FOLLOWS THE GAY WORLD WHOSE SWARMS HAVE FLED   .   167 RACHEL 1   9
OF THAT FRESH VOICE THE GAY DELIGHT   . . . . .   184 TERRACE BERNE   31
THEIR GAY UNWAVERING DEEP DISDAIN   . . . . .   202 URANIA   V 32
AND STILL THE UNBLACKEND ELMS WERE GAY   . . . .   222 EPILOG LAOCOON   39
GRAVE GAY CHILD PARENT HUSBAND WIFE   . . . . .   226 EPILOG LAOCOON   161
AND THY GAY SMILES NO ANODYNE   . . . .   245 BURIED LIFE   8
AND GAY WITHOUT FRIVOLITY   . . . .   304 GRANDE CHARTR   160
GAY DAMES ARE THERE IN SYLVAN GREEN   . . . . .   305 GRANDE CHARTR   185
WITH A GAY REVELLING BAND HE BREAKS FROM THEM   .   412 EMPEDOCLES I 2   16
BY SPIRITS GLORIOUSLY GAY   . . . .   450 GEISTS GRAVE   18
ALL THAT GAY COURAGEOUS CHEER   . . . .   454 POOR MATTHIAS   61
JOYD WITH THEM WHEN THEY WERE GAY   . . . . .   455 POOR MATTHIAS   91
STUPID SALUTATIONS GAY   . . . .   455 POOR MATTHIAS   112

GAYEST

GAY OF OLD AMID THE GAYEST   . . . .   14 CHURCH BROU 1   55

GAZD

GAZD SADLY DOWN ON HIS UNRESTFUL LOT . . . .   474 CROMWELL   86
STILL AS HE GAZD THE PHANTOMS MOURNFUL GLANCE   . .   477 CROMWELL   193
ON THAT DARK FORM HIS EYES HAD GAZD BEFORE   . . .   477 CROMWELL   201

GAZE

THE ARMIES ARE DRAWN OUT AND STAND AT GAZE • • • • 67 SOHRAB RUSTUM 210
AND ON THE CONJURING LAPPS HE BENT HIS GAZE • • • 96 BALDER DEAD 1 53
THE GAZE OF ONE WHO CAN DIVINE • • • • • • 140 TRISTRAM 1 323
TO GAZE ON THE LIGHT SEA OF LEAF AND BOUGH • • • • 155 TRISTRAM 3 202
TO GAZE ON THE GREEN SEA OF LEAF AND BOUGH • • • • 155 TRISTRAM 3 V 202
WE WILL GAZE FROM THE SAND-HILLS • • • • 165 FORSAKEN MERM 136
THE LITTLE FAIR-HAIRD SON WITH VACANT GAZE • • • 167 PICT NEWSTEAD 10
TO ENGLANDS CLIFFS MY GAZE IS TURND • • • • 205 CALAIS SANDS 19
BUT I MAY STAND FAR OFF AND GAZE • • • • 205 CALAIS SANDS 27
ON THE BLUE SEA MY GAZE I STRAIN • • • • 205 CALAIS SANDS V 20
THEY GAZE AND THE EVENING WIND • • • • • 235 YOUTH OF MAN 89
PLAYS ON THEIR FACES THEY GAZE • • • • • • 235 YOUTH OF MAN 90
STILL STILL LET ME AS I GAZE UPON YOU • • • 240 SELF-DEPENDENCE 11
THOSE WINDOWS WHICH I GAZE AT FROWN • • • • 242 SUMMER NIGHT 3
THERE LET ME GAZE TILL I BECOME • • • • 251 WISH 41
IN SOUL WITH WHAT I GAZE ON WED • • • • 251 WISH 42
RIVETS HIS GAZE ON THE BANKS OF THE STREAM • • • • 251 FUTURE 6
THERE BADE ME GAZE AND THERE ASPIRE • • • • 301 GRANDE CHARTR 70
BENT ON MY FACE WITH GAZE WHICH SCANND • • • • 314 OBERMANN MORE 67
PAST SONCHAUDS PINY FLANKS I GAZE • • • • • 324 OBERMANN MORE 337
BENT ON MY FACE THAT SCANND • • • • 314 OBERMANN MORE V 67
AND SONCHAUDS PINY FLANKS I GAZE • • • • 324 OBERMANN MORE V 337
THY DAZZLING LIGHT AN EAGLES GAZE SHOULD TIRE • • 463 ALARIC AT ROME 32
AND DASH OUR HOLIEST RAPTURES WHILE WE GAZE • • 470 ALARIC AT ROME 200
PLEADING GAZE THAT FOREHEAD CLEAR • • • • • META CLOISTER 38
TO GLUE MY FRUITLESS GAZE ON AND TO PINE • • , • • FRAGMENT 5 6

GAZED

FLASHD ONCE LIKE FALLING STREAMS WE ROSE WE GAZED • 25 DREAM 29
AND RUSTUM GAZED ON HIM WITH GRIEF AND SAID • • 80 SOHRAB RUSTUM 640
HE SPOKE BUT RUSTUM GAZED AND GAZED AND STOOD • • 81 SOHRAB RUSTUM 689
HE SPOKE BUT RUSTUM GAZED AND GAZED AND STOOD • • 81 SOHRAB RUSTUM 689
AND RUSTUM GAZED IN SOHRABS FACE AND SAID • • • 85 SOHRAB RUSTUM 835
AND RUSTUM GAZED ON SOHRABS FACE AND SAID • • • 85 SOHRAB RUSTUM V 835
AND HERMOD GAZED INTO THE NIGHT AND SAID • • 102 BALDER DEAD 1 240
AND GAZED ON NANNA AS SHE SLEPT AND SPAKE • • • 103 BALDER DEAD 1 287
AND THE GODS STOOD UPON THE BEACH AND GAZED • • 119 BALDER DEAD 3 193
AND WHILE THEY GAZED THE SUN WENT LURID DOWN • • 119 BALDER DEAD 3 194
SO HERMOD GAZED AND YEARND TO JOIN HIS KIN • • • 129 BALDER DEAD 3 565
HE GAZED UPON ME AS I PASSD • • • • • 158 SAINT BRANDAN 49
AND WE GAZED UP THE AISLE THROUGH THE SMALL 163 FORSAKEN MERM 75
   LEADED PANES
THOU THAT HAST GAZED AS THE WORLD HURRIED BY • • 463 ALARIC AT ROME 23
HAD GAZED IN WONDER ON THAT GLORIOUS SIGHT • • • • 465 ALARIC AT ROME 74
THERE AS HE GAZED A WONDROUS BAND THEY CAME • • 476 CROMWELL 163

GAZER

WOULD CHARM THE GAZER TILL HIS THOUGHT • • • • 147 TRISTRAM 2 139
DRAWS IN THE ENAMOURD GAZER TO ITS SHINING BREAST • 424 EMPEDOCLES I 2 356
THAT LONG GAZER LEANING NEAR • • • • • • • META CLOISTER 26

GAZES

LEAND ON HIS GATE HE GAZES TEARS • • • • • 57 RESIGNATION 186
HE GAZES DOWN INTO THE ROOM • • • • • • • 148 TRISTRAM 2 161
THIS WAY MOVES AND PAUSES GAZES • • • • • META CLOISTER 11

GAZING

THE GAZING UP MID THE DIM PILLARS HIGH • • • 18 CHURCH BROU 3 38
THEN GAZING UP THROUGH THE DIM PILLARS HIGH • • 18 CHURCH BROU 3 V 38
FOR THE EYE GROWS FILLD WITH GAZING • • • • 30 NEW SIRENS 119
HALF IN DOUBT THEY SAY AND GAZING • • • • 31 NEW SIRENS 149
FOR THE EYE WAS FILLD WITH GAZING • • • • 30 NEW SIRENS V 119
STILL GAZING ON THE EVER FULL • • • • • • 59 RESIGNATION 227
AND THE TWO GAZING HOSTS AND THAT SOLE PAIR • • 86 SOHRAB RUSTUM 866
GAZING UP HITHER THE POOR MAN • • • • • • 93 SICK KING BOKH 190
OUR EYES WITH GAZING AND REBUILD WITH TEARS • • 128 BALDER DEAD 3 536
MUTE GAZING AFTER THEM IN TEARS AND FAIN • • • 129 BALDER DEAD 3 555
GAZING SEAWARD FOR THE LIGHT • • • • • 130 TRISTRAM 1 12
GAZING SEAWARDS MANY A LEAGUE • • • • • 131 TRISTRAM 1 42
GAZING SEAWARDS FOR THE LIGHT • • • • • 130 TRISTRAM 1 V 12
RACHEL WITH EYES NO GAZING CAN APPEASE • • • 167 RACHEL 1 7
AND GAZING IN HIS EYES WILL STAND • • • • 202 URANIA 26
THUS FEELING GAZING MIGHT I GROW • • • • 251 WISH 49
THUS FEELING GAZING LET ME GROW • • • • • 251 WISH V 49
HELPLESSLY GAZING ON THEIR OWN DECLINE • • 282 HAWORTH CHURCH V
THOU STANDEST GAZING TO SEE • • • • • 297 HEINES GRAVE 169
BUT GAZING AT HIM FROM THE GROUND THE KING • • • 402 MEROPE 1927
ONE FORM STANDS GAZING SILENTLY BELOW • • • • 468 ALARIC AT ROME 153
UNLIKE THAT OCEAN-CITY GAZING STILL • • • • 468 ALARIC AT ROME 159
GAZING ON THEE WE WAKE TO FIND IT IS NOT SO • • 470 ALARIC AT ROME 216
THIS WAY MOVES AND PAUSES GAZING • • • • • META CLOISTER V 11

GEESE

GEESE ARE SWANS AND SWANS ARE GEESE • • • • • 215 LAST WORD 6
GEESE ARE SWANS AND SWANS ARE GEESE • • • • • 215 LAST WORD 6

GEIST

WERE CROWDED GEIST INTO NO MORE • • • • • 449 GEISTS GRAVE 4
THE DACHS-HOUND GEIST THEIR LITTLE FRIEND • • • • 452 GEISTS GRAVE 80
GEIST CAME NEXT OUR LITTLE FRIEND • • • • • 454 POOR MATTHIAS 57

GEIST   (CONTINUED)
         GEIST HAD VERSE TO MOURN HIS END   •   •   •   •   •   454 POOR MATTHIAS   58
         WHICH COMPELLD FOR GEIST A SONG   •   •   •   •   •   454 POOR MATTHIAS   60
         AND THOU ART GONE WHERE GEIST HATH GONE   •   •   •   •   460 KAISER DEAD   65

GEMMD
         WITH SCARLET BERRIES GEMMD THE FELL-FARES FOOD   •   •   150 TRISTRAM 3   22

GENERAL
         AND IN THIS VISION OF THE GENERAL LAW   •   •   •   •   5 DUKE WELLINGTON   8
         THAT GENERAL LIFE WHICH DOES NOT CEASE   •   •   •   •   58 RESIGNATION   191
         DRAW HOMEWARD TO THE GENERAL LIFE   •   •   •   •   •   59 RESIGNATION   252
         NOT MILDER IS THE GENERAL LOT   •   •   •   •   •   •   60 RESIGNATION   275
         DRAW HOMEWARDS TO THE GENERAL LIFE   •   •   •   •   •   59 RESIGNATION   V 252
         THOUGHTS OF THE GENERAL WEAL   •   •   •   •   •   •   282 HAWORTH CHURCH   V
         A GENERAL ASSEMBLAGE OF THE REALM   •   •   •   •   •   338 MEROPE   263
         WHO ARE NOT EXPIATE THE GENERAL SIN   •   •   •   •   •   341 MEROPE   366
         MAY BE NAY SHOULD IF FOR THE GENERAL WEAL   •   •   •   352 MEROPE   657
         ARMD FOR RIGHT ONLY AND THE GENERAL GOOD   •   •   •   353 MEROPE   685
         A DEED SO AWFUL THAT THE GENERAL TONGUE   •   •   •   •   385 MEROPE   1418

GENERALS
         A PASSIVE ENGINE AT THEIR GENERALS WILL   •   •   •   •   382 MEROPE   1340

GENERATION
         IN THE THIRD GENERATION THE WAY   •   •   •   •   •   •   343 MEROPE   412

GENERATIONS
         THE GENERATIONS PASS THE AGES GROW   •   •   •   •   •   127 BALDER DEAD 3   473
         THE GENERATIONS OF THY PEERS ARE FLED   •   •   •   •   259 SCHOLAR-GIPSY   155
         THREE GENERATIONS OF HIS OFFSPRING OUT   •   •   •   •   336 MEROPE   217
         TWO GENERATIONS OF HIS OFFSPRING UP   •   •   •   •   •   336 MEROPE   V 217

GENEROUS
         AND CALL THIS HURRYING FEVER GENEROUS FIRE   •   •   •   •   37 YOUTHS AGIT   12
         AS GOOD AS GENEROUS AS THEY ARE   •   •   •   •   •   179 FAREWELL   64
         AND THE GENEROUS DREAMER INVESTS   •   •   •   •   •   233 YOUTH OF MAN   33
         BUT LIT FOR ALL ITS GENEROUS SUN   •   •   •   •   •   251 WISH   39
         SWEET GENEROUS AND HUMANE   •   •   •   •   •   •   •   273 EDW QUILLINAN   16

GENIUS
         MOVED ONLY BUT BY GENIUS IN THE STRIFE   •   •   •   •   4 DUKE WELLINGTON   4
         HER GENIUS AND HER GLORY ARE HER OWN   •   •   •   •   •   168 RACHEL 3   14
         LOOK AH WHAT GENIUS   •   •   •   •   •   •   •   •   220 BACCHANALIA 2   53
         LARGE AND PROFOUND HATH GENIUS HERE   •   •   •   •   •   223 EPILOG LAOCOON   80
         TO THE JUST-PAUSING GENIUS WE REMIT   •   •   •   •   •   259 SCHOLAR-GIPSY   149
         SHE WHOSE GENIUS THOUGH NOT   •   •   •   •   •   •   284 HAWORTH CHURCH   90
         TEMPER OF GENIUS SO SOON   •   •   •   •   •   •   •   293 HEINES GRAVE   26
         GLORY AND GENIUS AND JOY   •   •   •   •   •   •   •   295 HEINES GRAVE   84
         TEMPER OF GENIUS ALIVE   •   •   •   •   •   •   •   •   293 HEINES GRAVE   V 26
         WHEN HIS FINE GENIUS FOAMS ITSELF AWAY   •   •   •   •   LUCRETIUS 2   4

GENTIAN
         THE GENTIAN-FLOWERD PASS ITS CROWN   •   •   •   •   •   313 OBERMANN MORE   21
         OF THE SUN-LOVING GENTIAN IN THE HEAT   •   •   •   •   412 EMPEDOCLES I 2   5

GENTIANS
         YOU CRUSH THEM THE BLUE GENTIANS GLEAM   •   •   •   •   55 RESIGNATION   103

GENTLE
         HE SEES THE GENTLE STIR OF BIRTH   •   •   •   •   •   •   57 RESIGNATION   170
         HIS GENTLE BEARING AT THE SIDE   •   •   •   •   •   •   137 TRISTRAM 1   213
         THE CHEEKS THAT STILL THEIR GENTLE PALENESS WEAR   •   •   175 PARTING   38
         THEY ASK NOT KINDNESS GENTLE WAYS   •   •   •   •   •   178 FAREWELL   25
         WAS TO BE GENTLE TRANQUIL TRUE   •   •   •   •   •   •   179 FAREWELL   48
         WITH GENTLE VOICE AND BROW   •   •   •   •   •   •   •   273 EDW QUILLINAN   18
         I THINK OF HER WHOSE GENTLE TONGUE   •   •   •   •   •   279 SOUTHERN NIGHT   121
         OF A GENTLE SPIRIT NOW DEAD   •   •   •   •   •   •   •   280 HAWORTH CHURCH   5
         FRIENDLY AND GENTLE NOW DEAD   •   •   •   •   •   •   280 HAWORTH CHURCH   V 5
         O GENTLE WISDOM LITTLE UNDERSTOOD   •   •   •   •   •   339 MEROPE   309
         IN YOUR GENTLE MELANCHOLY   •   •   •   •   •   •   •   META CLOISTER   35

GENTLENESS
         THE GENTLENESS THE THIRST FOR PEACE   •   •   •   •   •   180 FAREWELL   84
         THE GENTLENESS TOO RUDELY HURLD   •   •   •   •   •   •   180 FAREWELL   85
         AND WHAT BUT GENTLENESS UNTIRED   •   •   •   •   •   •   279 SOUTHERN NIGHT   129

GENTLER
         AND PEACEFUL JOYS AND GENTLER THOUGHTS SWEPT BY   •   •   474 CROMWELL   71

GENTLEST
         AND ON THE FINNS THE GENTLEST OF MANKIND   •   •   •   •   97 BALDER DEAD 1   55

GENTLY
         AH GENTLY PLACE HIM ON THE BENCH   •   •   •   •   •   •   276 SOUTHERN NIGHT   34
         GENTLY BY HIS YE WATERS GLIDE   •   •   •   •   •   •   •   279 SOUTHERN NIGHT   138
         WHILE THUS I MUSED NIGHT GENTLY RAN   •   •   •   •   •   314 OBERMANN MORE   57
         AND GENTLY SHALL THE MURMURING RIPPLES FLOW   •   •   469 ALARIC AT ROME   197

GENUINE
    HIS GENUINE SELF AND FORCE HIM TO OBEY   • • • •   246 BURIED LIFE   36
    SHAME RARELY CHECKS THE GENUINE TYRANTS WILL   • •   340 MEROPE   352

GEORGES
    I CROSSD ST GEORGES HILL TO-DAY   • • • • • •   484 ROME-SICKNESS   13

GERM
    THAT GERM OF KINDNESS IN THE WOMB   • • • • • •   158 SAINT BRANDAN   61

GERMAN
    GERMAN MASONS SMITHS FROM SPAIN   • • • • • •   15 CHURCH BROU 1   96
    AT A MEAN INN IN GERMAN AARAU BORN   • • • • • •   168 RACHEL 3   2
    GERMAN KAISER FULL OFT   • • • • • • • •   296 HEINES GRAVE   136
    FAR GERMAN HOME OF HIS YOUTH   • • • • • • •   296 HEINES GRAVE   151
    WIDE GERMAN LAND GOING DOWN   • • • • • • •   297 HEINES GRAVE   173
    IN GERMAN WEIMAR SLEEPS   • • • • • • • •   308 OBERMANN   52
    NOR WORDY GERMAN IMBECILITY   • • • • • • • •   480 HUNGARIAN NAT   7

GERMANY
    GERMANY FRANCE CHRIST MOSES ATHENS ROME   • • •   168 RACHEL 3   12
    OF HIS NATIVE GERMANY SO   • • • • • • • • •   296 HEINES GRAVE   139
    FROM ENGLAND GERMANY OR SPAIN   • • • • • • • •   301 GRANDE CHARTR   63

GERMS
    GERMS YOUR UNTRIMMD PASSION OVERGREW   • • • • • •   30 NEW SIRENS   138

GESTURE
    WITH ITS GESTURE OF COMMAND   • • • • • • • •   134 TRISTRAM 1   122
    A GESTURE ANYTHING RETAIND   • • • • • • • •   185 TERRACE BERNE   39
    AVERSE AS DIDO DID WITH GESTURE STERN   • • • •   261 SCHOLAR-GIPSY   208
    BUT THY GESTURE THY LOOK   • • • • • • • • •   372 MEROPE   1145

GET
    WHAT WILT THOU PRAY AND GET THEE GRACE   • • •   91 SICK KING BOKH   101
    IF ONESELF CANNOT GET FREE   • • • • • • •   138 TRISTRAM 1   267
    EVEN FOR A MOMENT CAN GET FREE   • • • • • • •   245 BURIED LIFE   27
    RICHES WE WISH TO GET   • • • • • • • •   420 EMPEDOCLES I 2   227

GETS
    MAN GETS NO SECOND DAY   • • • • • • • • • •   321 OBERMANN MORE   258
    AND ASKS WHAT AILS HIM SO AND GETS WHAT CURE HE CAN   416 EMPEDOCLES I 2   131
    MAN GETS NO OTHER LIGHT   • • • • • • • • •   417 EMPEDOCLES I 2   144
    POETS FIRE GETS FAINT AND LOW   • • • • • \• • • •   454 POOR MATTHIAS   78

GHASTLY
    IN BROAD CLEAR LIGHT THE GHASTLY VISION SHONE   • •   477 CROMWELL   203

GHOST
    THE GHOST IN THEM OF FORMER DAYS   • • • • •   56 RESIGNATION   123
    AND STARTS HIM THAT HE THINKS A GHOST WENT BY   • •   101 BALDER DEAD 1   234
    OF NIFLHEIM HE SAW ONE GHOST COME NEAR   • • •   124 BALDER DEAD 3   382
    AND HERMOD LOOKD AND KNEW HIS BROTHERS GHOST   •   124 BALDER DEAD 3   385
    BUT THEN THEY DECKD A RESTLESS GHOST   • • • •   146 TRISTRAM 2   116
    TO HEAR THE WORLD APPLAUD THE HOLLOW GHOST   • • •   213 GROWING OLD   34
    A PALE UNMEANING GHOST POWERLESS TO FRIGHT   • • •   366 MEROPE   1021

GHOSTLIKE
    FLAPS THE GHOSTLIKE TAPESTRY   • • • • • • •   147 TRISTRAM 2   151
    SHINES THE GHOSTLIKE TAPESTRY   • • • • • • •   147 TRISTRAM 2   V 151
    WHERE GHOSTLIKE IN THE DEEPENING NIGHT   • • • •   300 GRANDE CHARTR   35

GHOSTS
    NOT GODS BUT GHOSTS IN FROZEN APATHY   • • • • •   9 MYCERINUS   36
    GHOSTS OF THAT BOISTEROUS COMPANY   • • • • •   55 RESIGNATION   89
    THE GHOSTS IN THEM OF FORMER DAYS   • • • • •   56 RESIGNATION   V 123
    TO THE LOW SHORE OF GHOSTS AND HELAS REALM   • •   99 BALDER DEAD 1   151
    THEN MUST HE NOT REGARD THE WAILFUL GHOSTS   • •   100 BALDER DEAD 1   176
    AND DOLEFUL ARE THE GHOSTS THE TROOPS OF DEAD   •   104 BALDER DEAD 1   316
    THEN HE MUST NOT REGARD THE WAILFUL GHOSTS   • •   100 BALDER DEAD 1   V 176
    THERE ARE THE JOYLESS SEATS THE HAUNT OF GHOSTS   •   108 BALDER DEAD 2   132
    SO AROUND HERMOD SWARMD THE TWITTERING GHOSTS   •   109 BALDER DEAD 2   163
    AND TOUCH THE APATHETIC GHOSTS WITH JOY   • • •   110 BALDER DEAD 2   196
    OF HELL BEHELD THEM AND THE GHOSTS STOOD DUMB   •   112 BALDER DEAD 2   281
    OF GHOSTS AND COMMUNED WITH THEIR SOLEMN QUEEN   •   114 BALDER DEAD 3   40
    AND TALKEST WITH THE FEEBLE TRIBES OF GHOSTS   •   115 BALDER DEAD 3   76
    FAR FROM THE OTHER GHOSTS AND HELAS THRONE   • •   124 BALDER DEAD 3   391
    AND WORDSWORTH AH PALE GHOSTS REJOICE   • • •   271 MEMORIAL VERSES   34
    LIKE GHOSTS THE HUGE GNARLD OLIVES STAND   • • •   275 SOUTHERN NIGHT   6

GIALLS
    WHICH SPANS WITH GOLDEN ARCHES GIALLS STREAM   •   99 BALDER DEAD 1   148
    WHICH SPANS WITH GOLDEN ARCHES GIALLS STREAM   •   107 BALDER DEAD 2   86
    UNDER WHOSE HOOFS THE BRIDGE OER GIALLS STREAM   •   107 BALDER DEAD 2   102
    HOW DIDST THOU CROSS THE BRIDGE OER GIALLS STREAM   110 BALDER DEAD 2   183
    TO THE ARMD DAMSELS BRIDGE AND GIALLS STREAM   •   113 BALDER DEAD 2   290
    THE WAY HE KNEW AND TRAVERSED GIALLS STREAM   • •   124 BALDER DEAD 3   375

GIANT
    HIS GIANT FIGURE PLANTED ON THE SAND   • • • •   71 SOHRAB RUSTUM   336
    THE GIANT YMIR WHOM THE ABYSS BROUGHT FORTH   • •   121 BALDER DEAD 3   257

```
GIANT                    ( CONTINUED )
        WHILE FROM THE EAST THE GIANT RYMER STEERS  . . . .   127 BALDER DEAD 3        478
        AND UPON EVERY GIANT-BOUGH  . . . . . . . .          141 TRISTRAM 1           358
        THE GIANT STONES OF CARNAC SLEEP  . . . . . .        274 STANZAS CARNAC        11
        SEE HOW THE GIANT SPIRES OF YELLOW BLOOM  . .        412 EMPEDOCLES I 2         4
        AND THEN THAT MIGHTIEST CRASH THAT GIANT FALL  .     463 ALARIC AT ROME        41
        THE ETERNAL HILLS THEIR GIANT SHADOWS FLUNG  . .     472 CROMWELL              14
        OF GIANT MOUNTAINS BY THE WESTERN MAIN  . . . .      475 CROMWELL             105

GIANTESS
        DID ANGERBODE THE GIANTESS BRING FORTH  . . . .      110 BALDER DEAD 2        207

GIANTS
        AND ON WHOSE MARGE THE ANCIENT GIANTS DWELL  . .      99 BALDER DEAD 1        161
        FAR FAR BEYOND THE OUTMOST GIANTS HOME  . . . .      100 BALDER DEAD 1        163
        SHOULDERING HIS HAMMER WHICH THE GIANTS KNOW  .      106 BALDER DEAD 2         49
        AT THE DREAR ICE BEYOND THE GIANTS HOME  . . . .     108 BALDER DEAD 2        142
        THY DELUGE AND FROM HIM THE GIANTS SPRANG  . . .     121 BALDER DEAD 3        273
        BORDERING THE GIANTS WHERE THE TREES ARE IRON  .     123 BALDER DEAD 3        331
        MOCKD HER POOR LOVELORN GIANTS LAY  . . . . .        222 EPILOG LAOCOON        48

GIBE
        PEACE LEST OUR FATHER ODIN HEAR THEE GIBE  . . . .   114 BALDER DEAD 3         23

GIBES
        TOOTHLESS AND OLD SHE GIBES THE PASSERS BY  . . .    123 BALDER DEAD 3        334
        THOK NOT FOR GIBES WE COME WE COME FOR TEARS  . .    123 BALDER DEAD 3        346

GIBING
        GIBING OF SPIRITS IN SCORN  . . . . . . . . .        293 HEINES GRAVE         42

GIBRALTARS
        THERE WHERE GIBRALTARS CANNOND STEEP  . . . . . .    276 SOUTHERN NIGHT       23
        TOUCHES AND ON GIBRALTARS ROCK  . . . . . . . .      276 SOUTHERN NIGHT       47
        AH ME GIBRALTARS STRAND IS FAR  . . . . . . . .      277 SOUTHERN NIGHT       49

GIFT
        HIS HEART TO TAKE A GIFT AND LET THEE GO  . . .       77 SOHRAB RUSTUM       533
        AN EMPERORS GIFT AT EARLY MORN HE PAINTS  . . .       81 SOHRAB RUSTUM       674
        A LAST CHOICE GIFT THEREON HIS GOLDEN RING  . .      118 BALDER DEAD 3       173
        STRAIND AND LONGD AND GRASPD EACH GIFT IT SAW  .     210 SELF-DECEPTION       10
        WILL YE CLAIM FOR YOUR GREAT ONES THE GIFT  . .      231 YOUTH OF NATURE     122
        SOME IN ART SOME IN GIFT  . . . . . .                284 HAWORTH CHURCH       82
        SOME IN GIFT SOME IN ART  . . . . . . . . .          284 HAWORTH CHURCH     V 82
        HAD EVERY OTHER GIFT BUT WANTED LOVE  . . . . .      295 HEINES GRAVE        100
        A GIFTED MAN THE POWER TO SHEW HIS GIFT  . . .           LUCRETIUS 2           2

GIFTED
        GIFTED WOMEN THE ONE  . . . . .                      280 HAWORTH CHURCH        8
        THE ARDENT THE GIFTED HOW MOURN  . . . . . .         282 HAWORTH CHURCH       49
        OF ALL THAT GIFTED RACE  . . . . . . . . .           285 HAWORTH CHURCH      103
        NOT THE LEAST GIFTED YOUNG  . . . . . . . .          285 HAWORTH CHURCH      104
        OF ALL HIS GIFTED RACE  . . . . . . . . . .          285 HAWORTH CHURCH    V 103
        AS OF HIS GIFTED MASTER AND ONCE FRIEND  . . .       411 EMPEDOCLES I 1      148
        A GIFTED MAN THE POWER TO SHEW HIS GIFT  . . .           LUCRETIUS 2           2

GIFTS
        AND PRAYERS AND GIFTS AND TEARS ARE FRUITLESS ALL     10 MYCERINUS           71
        TROOPS WITH GOLD AND GIFTS APPEARING  . . . . .       26 NEW SIRENS          23
        NO GIFTS FROM CHANCE HAVE CONQUERD FATE  . . .        59 RESIGNATION        248
        AND PRAISE MY FAME AND PROFFER COURTEOUS GIFTS  .     71 SOHRAB RUSTUM      353
        CHANGED GIFTS AND WENT ON EQUAL TERMS AWAY  . .       72 SOHRAB RUSTUM      361
        OF LOK AND DOUBLE ARE THE GIFTS THEY GIVE  . .       112 BALDER DEAD 2      272
        SAW THE GIFTS THE POWERS IT MIGHT INHERIT  . .       209 SELF-DECEPTION       7
        WHAT OUR GIFTS AND WHAT OUR WANTS SHOULD BE  .       210 SELF-DECEPTION      16
        SHREDS OF GIFTS WHICH HE REFUSED IN FULL  . . .      210 SELF-DECEPTION      18
        BUT MAN HAS A THOUSAND GIFTS  . . . . . . .          233 YOUTH OF MAN        32
        GOD DOTH MATCH HIS GIFTS TO MANS BELIEVING  . .      483 THEKLAS ANSWER      19

GILD
        AND THOUGH THE JUST SUN GILD AS MORTALS PRAY  .       43 GIPSY CHILD         59
        AND THOUGH THE JUST SUN GILD AS ALL MEN PRAY  .       43 GIPSY CHILD       V 59
        HERMOD THE NIMBLE GILD ME NOT MY DEATH  . . . .      112 BALDER DEAD 2      264

GILDED
        SITTING IN THE GILDED BARGE  . . . . . . . .         134 TRISTRAM 1         111

GILDERS
        FLEMISH CARVERS LOMBARD GILDERS  . . . . . . .        15 CHURCH BROU 1       95

GILT
        ON THE GILT TERRACES  . . . . . . . . . . .           50 CONSOLATION         13

GIPSIES
        THE GIPSIES WHOM WE MET BELOW  . . . . . . .          55 RESIGNATION        108
        THOSE GIPSIES SO YOUR THOUGHTS I SCAN  . . . .        58 RESIGNATION        203
        THE SAME THE GIPSIES WORE  . . . . . . . .           256 SCHOLAR-GIPSY       56
        WHERE MOST THE GIPSIES BY THE TURF-EDGED WAY  . .    258 SCHOLAR-GIPSY      112
```

GIPSY

HIS FRIENDS AND WENT TO LEARN THE GIPSY-LORE   • •   256 SCHOLAR-GIPSY   37
WHEREAT HE ANSWERD THAT THE GIPSY-CREW   • • • •   256 SCHOLAR-GIPSY   44
TO LEARN STRANGE ARTS AND JOIN A GIPSY-TRIBE   • •   259 SCHOLAR-GIPSY   135
OUR FRIEND THE GIPSY-SCHOLAR WAS NOT DEAD   • • • •   263 THYRSIS   29
OUR GIPSY-SCHOLAR HAUNTS OUTLIVING THEE   • • • •   268 THYRSIS   197
OUR FRIEND THE SCHOLAR-GIPSY WAS NOT DEAD   • • • •   263 THYRSIS   V 29

GIRD

GIRD THEE AND ON UPON THY FATEFUL PATH   • • • •   465 ALARIC AT ROME   88

GIRDLE

LAY LIKE THE FOLDS OF A BRIGHT GIRDLE FURLD   • •   211 DOVER BEACH   23

GIRDLED

GIRDLED THE GLISTENING BAY   • • • • • • • •   242 SUMMER NIGHT   19

GIRDLING

ACROSS THE GIRDLING CITYS HUM   • • • • • • • •   248 KENSINGTON GARD   6

GIRL

AND NOT THAT ONE SLIGHT HELPLESS GIRL I HAVE   • •   68 SOHRAB RUSTUM   230
I AM NO GIRL TO BE MADE PALE BY WORDS   • • •   72 SOHRAB RUSTUM   381
GIRL NIMBLE WITH THY FEET NOT WITH THY HANDS   • •   74 SOHRAB RUSTUM   457
HAD BEEN A PUNY GIRL NO BOY AT ALL   • • • • •   79 SOHRAB RUSTUM   609
BUT ONE A GIRL WHO WITH HER MOTHER NOW   • • •   80 SOHRAB RUSTUM   646
A GIRL THEIR CLOTHES WERE RAGS THEIR FEET WERE BARE   169 WEST LONDON   4
PASSD OPPOSITE SHE TOUCHD HER GIRL WHO HIED   •   170 WEST LONDON   6
GIRL STATESMAN MERCHANT SOLDIER BOLD   • • • • •   226 EPILOG LAOCOON   159
WHAT GIRL   • • • • • • • • • • • • • •   252 FUTURE   34
WHERE IS THE GIRL WHO BY THE BOATMANS DOOR   • •   266 THYRSIS   121
SOME GIRL WHO HERE FROM CASTLE-BOWER   • • • • •   278 SOUTHERN NIGHT   101
SOME GIRL WHO HERE FROM PALACE-BOWER   • • • • •   278 SOUTHERN NIGHT   V 101
BUT YOU A GRAVE FOR GIRL OR SAGE   • • • • •   279 SOUTHERN NIGHT   V 113
ALMOST AS MUCH AS THE NEW DANCING-GIRL   • •   407 EMPEDOCLES I 1   35
WAS SUBJECT TO THESE TRANCES FROM A GIRL   • • •   410 EMPEDOCLES I 1   136
BUT CREDULOUS OF FABLES AS A GIRL   • • • • •   411 EMPEDOCLES I 1   160
THE VILLAGE-GIRL AT HER WHEEL   • • • • • • •   436 EMPEDOCLES II   257

GIRLS

WITH TARTAR GIRLS WITH WHOM THOU ART WONT TO DANCE   75 SOHRAB RUSTUM   461
WITH THY LIGHT SKIPPING TRICKS AND THY GIRLS WILES   75 SOHRAB RUSTUM   469
CLUSTERING OER THY WHITE FOREHEAD LIKE A GIRLS   • •   373 MEROPE   1162
THE RED-SNOODED PHRYGIAN GIRLS   • • • • • • •   434 EMPEDOCLES II   180

GIRT

GIRT WITH A THRONG OF REVELLERS BENT HIS WAY   • •   11 MYCERINUS   83
HE ROSE AND CLAD HIMSELF AND GIRT HIS SWORD   • •   61 SOHRAB RUSTUM   8
GIRT BY HIS FAR-SHINING TRAIN   • • • • • • •   216 LORDS MESSENGER   V
GIRT WITH HIS COAT FOR THE CHASE   • • • • • •   342 MEROPE   394

GIRTHS

TIGHTEN THE GIRTHS OF SLEIPNER ODINS HORSE   • • •   100 BALDER DEAD 1   169
THEN HE DISMOUNTED AND DREW TIGHT THE GIRTHS   • •   109 BALDER DEAD 2   146

GIVE

THE REST I GIVE TO JOY EVEN WHILE I SPEAK   • • •   10 MYCERINUS   55
WHICH YEARS AND CURIOUS THOUGHT AND SUFFERING GIVE   43 GIPSY CHILD   38
WHICH YEARS TO MOST AND CARE AND SUFFERING GIVE   • •   43 GIPSY CHILD   V 38
WHO STILL THEIR LABOUR GIVE   • • • • • • • •   47 WORLD QUIETIST   15
A GOAL WHICH GAIND MAY GIVE REPOSE   • • • • •   53 RESIGNATION   17
GIVE TO THE WIND THEIR WAVERING SPIRES   • • • •   55 RESIGNATION   117
MOST DEAF WHERE THOU SHOULDST MOST GIVE EAR   • •   91 SICK KING BOKH   98
YET IF HE SEEK TO FLY GIVE WAY   • • • • • •   91 SICK KING BOKH   115
AND MAKE EXCHANGE AND GIVE MY LIFE FOR HIS   • •   98 BALDER DEAD 1   110
AND MAKE HER YIELD AND GIVE HIM BALDER BACK   • •   100 BALDER DEAD 1   183
WHERE THEY HOLD COUNCIL AND GIVE LAWS FOR MEN   • •   105 BALDER DEAD 2   34
AND BEND MY HEART AND GIVE HIM BACK TO HEAVEN   • •   111 BALDER DEAD 2   240
OF LOK AND DOUBLE ARE THE GIFTS THEY GIVE   • • •   112 BALDER DEAD 2   272
AND BEND HER HEART AND GIVE YOU BALDER BACK   • •   115 BALDER DEAD 3   46
BUT WILL RESTORE IF ALL THINGS GIVE HIM TEARS   • •   123 BALDER DEAD 3   348
FOR WHICH THEY WERE NOT MEANT TO GIVE   • • •   185 TERRACE BERNE   44
WHO GIVE THEM VISION   • • • • • • • • • •   192 STRAYED REVEL   214
THOUGH OPULENT FREELY GIVE   • • • • • • • •   195 FRAG ANTIGONE   3
GIVE HIM EMOTION THOUGH PAIN   • • • • • • •   200 EARLY DEATH   16
AND WHAT THE WORLD CAN GIVE THEY TAKE   • • •   203 EUPHROSYNE   19
THEY WILL NOT GIVE US LOVE AND TEARS   • • • •   203 EUPHROSYNE   23
IN OUTWARD SEMBLANCE HE MUST GIVE   • • • • •   223 EPILOG LAOCOON   57
AH FROM THE OLD WORLD LET SOME ONE ANSWER GIVE   • •   237 PROGRESS   21
THEIR LIVES TO SOME UNMEANING TASKWORK GIVE   • •   243 SUMMER NIGHT   40
GIVE ME THY HAND AND HUSH AWHILE   • • • • • •   245 BURIED LIFE   9
THE POWER TO FEEL WITH OTHERS GIVE   • • • • •   249 KENSINGTON GARD   42
TO SHAKE HIS SAPIENT HEAD AND GIVE   • • • • •   250 WISH   19
NOR PROMISED LOVE IT COULD NOT GIVE   • • • •   251 WISH   38
YET THYRSIS LET ME GIVE MY GRIEF ITS HOUR   • • •   265 THYRSIS   102
FRIENDS COULD NOT GIVE WHAT FORTUNE CAN   • • •   273 EDW QUILLINAN   11
BUT IF YOU CANNOT GIVE US EASE   • • • • • •   302 GRANDE CHARTR   109
YOU GIVE THE UNIVERSE YOUR LAW   • • • • • •   304 GRANDE CHARTR   165
SEEK THIS REVIVE UNITE IT GIVE IT HOPE   • • • •   331 MEROPE   45
FOR THAT DESTROYD HIM GIVE THEM PEACE THOU CANST   • •   335 MEROPE   176
UPON A THRONE NOT THINE TO GIVE IS HEIR   • • •   336 MEROPE   190

GIVE   (CONTINUED)
```
        GIVE THE THRONES THAT THEY CONQUERD   . . . . . .  344 MEROPE            456
        GIVE NOT THY HEART TO DESPAIR   . . . . . . . . .  347 MEROPE            523
        ONLY TO ME GIVE MY CHILD   . . . . . . . . . . .   348 MEROPE            540
        A RETURN O FATHER GIVE TO THY BOY   . . . . . .    348 MEROPE            542
        CAN VENGEANCE GIVE ME BACK THE MURDERED NO  . . .  349 MEROPE            567
        TO GIVE TO VIRTUE HER DOMINION DUE   . . . . . .   353 MEROPE            666
        TO THE GUEST-CHAMBER LEAD HIM SOME ONE GIVE  . .   359 MEROPE            869
        GIVE THEM COHESION PURPOSE AND RESOLVE   . . . .   382 MEROPE           1323
        SINGLE AND FRIENDLESS GIVE TO CERTAIN DEATH   . .  382 MEROPE           1326
        DO I THEN GIVE TO USURPATION GRACE   . . . . . .   388 MEROPE           1494
        WITH THE GODS AID AND IF THEY GIVE BUT AID  . . .  391 MEROPE           1594
        THOU SPEAKEST WELL BUT HERE TO GIVE OUR EYES  . .  403 MEROPE           1951
        WHAT THEY WILL BUT TO ME GIVE MY SON   . . . . .   348 MEROPE          V
        TO GIVE HIS VIRTUES ROOM   . . . . . . . . . . .   420 EMPEDOCLES I 2    255
        THE SMALLEST THING COULD GIVE US PLEASURE THEN  .  436 EMPEDOCLES II     250
        PROOF THEY GIVE TOO PRIMAL POWERS   . . . . . .    456 POOR MATTHIAS     137
        YET SOME THERE ARE THEIR VERY LIVES WOULD GIVE  .  462 ALARIC AT ROME    .17
        YET NOW WHEN BOLDEST WILLS GIVE PLACE   . . . .    481 COURAGE             5
        OH THAT PAST TIMES COULD GIVE OUR DAY   . . . .    482 COURAGE            27
        AH UNHAPPY PAIR TO PELEUS WHY DID WE GIVE YOU   .  HOMER TRANS            9
```

GIVEN
```
        MANS JUSTICE FROM THE ALL-JUST GODS WAS GIVEN   . .   9 MYCERINUS          20
        TO DIE BE GIVEN US OR ATTAIN   . . . . . . . . .    52 RESIGNATION         1
        HAS OFTEN STROKED THY NECK AND GIVEN THEE FOOD  .   83 SOHRAB RUSTUM      753
        OFT THOU HAST GIVEN THEM STORE   . . . . . . . .   257 SCHOLAR-GIPSY       86
        THEREFORE TO THEE IT WAS GIVEN   . . . . . . . .   290 RUGBY CHAPEL       140
        THESE TO THE WORLD TOO ARE GIVEN   . . . . . . .   295 HEINES GRAVE       110
        BID IT RISE BOLDLY AT THE SIGNAL GIVEN   . . . .   331 MEROPE             46
        SUCH A BOON TO BRING HATH BEEN GIVEN  . . . . .    361 MEROPE            907
        O AEPYTUS WEIGH WELL HER COUNSEL GIVEN   . . . .   382 MEROPE           1332
        AND HE WAS GIVEN A VOICE BY THE WHITE-ARMD         HOMER TRANS           46
            GODDESS HERA
```

GIVES
```
        TIME GIVES HIS HOUR-GLASS   . . . . . . . . . .    51 CONSOLATION         53
        IT GIVES THEM PATHOS GIVES THEM POWER   . . . .   227 EPILOG LAOCOON     200
        IT GIVES THEM PATHOS GIVES THEM POWER   . . . .   227 EPILOG LAOCOON     200
        GIVES THEN THE FIRST THE FAIREST PLACE   . . . .  227 EPILOG LAOCOON     208
        GIVES US A SENSE OF THE AWE   . . . . . . . . .   231 YOUTH OF NATURE    100
        WHICH THOUGH IT GIVES NO BLISS YET SPOILS FOR REST 261 SCHOLAR-GIPSY     223
        GIVES HER NAME TO THE SPRING   . . . . . . . . .  343 MEROPE            432
        THOU FATE GIVES IT AH ME  . . . . . . . . . . .   37C MEROPE           1111
        ILL COUNSEL IN MY JUDGMENT GIVES SHE HERE   . .   382 MEROPE           1333
        TRUE BUT WHAT CAUSE TO OUR ARCADIA GIVES   . . .  389 MEROPE           1534
        GIVES FLOWERS AFTER FLOWERS   . . . . . . . . .   424 EMPEDOCLES I 2    358
```

GIVING
```
        FILL THE WEALTH-GIVING THRONES . . . . . . . . .  343 MEROPE            415
```

GLACIER
```
        AND TRANQUIL AS THE GLACIER-SNOWS   . . . . . .   278 SOUTHERN NIGHT     90
```

GLACIERS
```
        THOUGH TO THESE LEAVES THE GLACIERS SPARE   . . .  307 OBERMANN           27
```

GLAD
```
        STRAINS OF GLAD MUSIC AT A FUNERAL   . . . . .    36 VOICE              22
        SOME EXILES MINDFUL HOW THE PAST WAS GLAD  . . .   42 GIPSY CHILD        25
        WHAT EXILES CHANGING BITTER THOUGHTS WITH GLAD  .  42 GIPSY CHILD      V 25
        SOME EXILES MINDFUL HOW HIS PAST WAS GLAD  . . .   42 GIPSY CHILD      V 25
        TO GLAD THY FATHER IN HIS WEAK OLD AGE   . . .    77 SOHRAB RUSTUM      536
        TO GLAD THE GODS AND FEAST IN ODINS HALL   . .   105 BALDER DEAD 2       28
        ARCHING HIS NECK AND GLAD TO BE BESTRODE   . .   107 BALDER DEAD 2       76
        AND WIDEN AND THE PEASANTS HEART IS GLAD   . .   122 BALDER DEAD 3      316
        AND HAVE NOW SHORT SPACE FOR BEING GLAD   . . .  144 TRISTRAM 2         56
        THE BROTHERHOODS OF SAINTS ARE GLAD  . . . . .   156 SAINT BRANDAN       2
        WHICH WE SAW WITH HIS EYES AND WERE GLAD   . .   229 YOUTH OF NATURE    55
        AND THEN THY GLAD PERENNIAL YOUTH WOULD FADE  .  261 SCHOLAR-GIPSY      229
        HE TO THEE SENDS ME ON IN ONE THING GLAD   . .   359 MEROPE            850
        WITH GLAD ACCLAIM ERE THEY FORESTALL MY NEWS  .  401 MEROPE           1887
        WELL WE KNEW WHEN THEY WERE GLAD   . . . . . .   455 POOR MATTHIAS      89
        TEEMING WITH PLANS ALERT AND GLAD   . . . . .    460 KAISER DEAD        45
```

GLADDEST
```
        IN HIS GLADDEST AIRIEST SONG   . . . . . . . .   231 YOUTH OF NATURE    96
```

GLADE
```
        UP COLD AISLES OF BURIED GLADE  . . . . . . .     32 NEW SIRENS        180
        BUT IT IS MOONLIGHT IN THE OPEN GLADE   . . . .  139 TRISTRAM 1        277
        AND IN THE BOTTOM OF THE GLADE SHINE CLEAR  . .  139 TRISTRAM 1        278
        IN THIS LONE OPEN GLADE I LIE  . . . . . . . .   248 KENSINGTON GARD     1
        SOMETIMES A CHILD WILL CROSS THE GLADE   . . .   248 KENSINGTON GARD     9
        STILL ALL THINGS IN THIS GLADE GO THROUGH   . .  249 KENSINGTON GARD    31
        WHERE ENDS THE GLADE TO STAY THE EYE  . . . .    248 KENSINGTON GARD  V  3
        THAT CHILD WHO DARTS ACROSS THE GLADE              KENSINGTON GARD  V  9
        BY NIGHT THE SILVERD BRANCHES OF THE GLADE  . .  261 SCHOLAR-GIPSY     214
        FORGOTTEN IN A FOREST-GLADE   . . . . . . . .    304 GRANDE CHARTR     171
        AN OPEN GLADE NOW HE WAS HIGH ALOFT  . . . . .   357 MEROPE            802
        THAT MUFFLE ITS WET BANKS BUT GLADE   . . . .    414 EMPEDOCLES I 2     51
```

GLADES
SHALL BREATHLESS GLADES CHEERD BY SHY DIANS HORN   •   •   6 GEO CRUIKSHANK   8
TO SEE THE PARK-GLADES WHERE YOU PLAY   •   •   •   141 TRISTRAM 1   355
AND THROUGH THE GLADES THY PASTIME TAKE   •   •   •   149 TRISTRAM 2   189
OF THE DEEP FOREST-GLADES OF BROCE-LIANDE   •   •   154 TRISTRAM 3   156
IN THESE LONE SYLVAN GLADES THAT APRIL-DAY   •   •   154 TRISTRAM 3   163
OF HIS MOTHER WHICH OF THY GLADES   •   •   •   •   347 MEROPE   V

GLADHEIM
TO THE HALL GLADHEIM WHICH IS BUILT OF GOLD   •   •   106 BALDER DEAD 2   36

GLADLY
AND ALL THESE GLADLY WHILE WE DRINK WE HEAR   •   •   117 BALDER DEAD 3   135
LOVE ME AND GLADLY BRING FOR MY AWARD   •   •   •   126 BALDER DEAD 3   465
TRUST ME AND GLADLY BRING FOR MY AWARD   •   •   126 BALDER DEAD 3   V 465
GLADLY THEY RISE AT HIS CALL   •   •   •   •   •   216 LORDS MESSENGER   7
GLADLY OBEY HIS COMMAND   •   •   •   •   •   •   216 LORDS MESSENGER   8
GLADLY DESCEND TO THE PLAIN   •   •   •   •   •   216 LORDS MESSENGER   9
GLADLY THEY TAKE HIS COMMAND   •   •   •   •   216 LORDS MESSENGER   V   8
BUT THEY WILL GLADLY WELCOME HIM ONCE MORE   •   •   435 EMPEDOCLES II   221
AND WE MIGHT GLADLY SHARE THE FRUITFUL STIR   •   •   439 EMPEDOCLES II   339

GLADNESS
MOCKD AND BAFFLED BY YOUR GLADNESS   •   •   •   •   32 NEW SIRENS   169
SHAMD AND BAFFLED BY YOUR GLADNESS   •   •   •   32 NEW SIRENS   V 169

GLADSOME
FOR NOT SO GLADSOME IS THAT LIFE IN HEAVEN   •   •   98 BALDER DEAD 1   122
A GLADSOME HUNTER OF DEER   •   •   •   •   •   347 MEROPE   520
AND GLADSOME GREETINGS OF THE BUOYANT SEA   •   •   472 CROMWELL   8

GLAMOUR
WHAT HAS SOME GLAMOUR MADE ME SLEEP   •   •   •   •   148 TRISTRAM 2   175
HAS THEN SOME GLAMOUR MADE HIM SLEEP   •   •   •   148 TRISTRAM 2   V 175

GLANCE
HORSES FRET AND BOAR-SPEARS GLANCE   •   •   •   13 CHURCH BROU 1   18
AND A GLANCE WHICH OVER THE CROWDED FLOOR   •   •   146 TRISTRAM 2   120
AND A GLANCE THAT OVER THE CROWDED FLOOR   •   •   146 TRISTRAM 2   V 120
AND HARDLY YET A GLANCE A TONE   •   •   •   185 TERRACE BERNE   38
YET NOW MY GLANCE BUT ONCE HATH ROVED   •   •   205 CALAIS SANDS   17
BUT NOW MY GLANCE BUT ONCE HATH ROVED   •   •   205 CALAIS SANDS   V   17
AND GLANCE AND NOD AND BUSTLE BY   •   •   •   277 SOUTHERN NIGHT   70
OFT THROUGH THE TREES THEY CATCH A GLANCE   •   •   305 GRANDE CHARTR   176
A MEEK LAST GLANCE OF LOVE DIDST THROW   •   •   450 GEISTS GRAVE   35
THE CARELESS GLANCE THE COLD UNMEANING SMILE   •   470 ALARIC AT ROME   219
HIGH THOUGHTS WERE HIS BUT MEMORYS GLANCE THE WHILE   474 CROMWELL   69
THE STATESMAN QUAILD BEFORE HIS GLANCE OF IRE   •   476 CROMWELL   154
PYMS LOOK OF HATE AND STRAFFORDS GLANCE OF FLAME   •   476 CROMWELL   164
CHILDHOODS BRIGHT GLANCE AND SUNNY SMILE NO MORE   •   477 CROMWELL   182
STILL AS HE GAZD THE PHANTOMS MOURNFUL GLANCE   •   477 CROMWELL   193

GLANCES
AS THE KINDLING GLANCES   •   •   •   •   •   •   •   •   35 VOICE   1

GLANCING
GLANCING FEET AND EAGER EYES   •   •   •   •   •   32 NEW SIRENS   176
LITHE AS THE GLANCING SNAKE AND THE CLUB CAME   •   73 SOHRAB RUSTUM   418
OF THY CUP THE BRIGHT GLANCING VINE-LEAVES   •   •   188 STRAYED REVEL   85

GLANVIL
AND THE GRAVE GLANVIL DID THE TALE INSCRIBE   •   •   259 SCHOLAR-GIPSY   133

GLANVILS
AND NEAR ME ON THE GRASS LIES GLANVILS BOOK   •   •   256 SCHOLAR-GIPSY   31
AND LIVING AS THOU LIVST ON GLANVILS PAGE   •   •   259 SCHOLAR-GIPSY   159

GLARE
THY SMILE AND ROUGE WITH STONY GLARE   •   •   •   184 TERRACE BERNE   22
WHEN JADED WITH THE RUSH AND GLARE   •   •   •   247 BURIED LIFE   79
END HERE ETNA BEYOND IN THE BROAD GLARE   •   •   414 EMPEDOCLES I 2   53
AND SOONEST FADE IN THE BROAD GLARE OF DAY   •   •   470 ALARIC AT ROME   214

GLARED
GLARED AND HE SHOOK ON HIGH HIS MENACING SPEAR   •   76 SOHRAB RUSTUM   515

GLASS
TIME GIVES HIS HOUR-GLASS   •   •   •   •   •   51 CONSOLATION   53
HIS HEAD BUT THIS TIME ALL THE BLADE LIKE GLASS   •   76 SOHRAB RUSTUM   511
SHALL THE LAKE GLASS HER FLYING OVER IT   •   •   78 SOHRAB RUSTUM   570
WHICH ARISE ON THE GLASS OF THE SAGE   •   •   •   230 YOUTH OF NATURE   73
AND REACH THAT GLIMMERING SHEET OF GLASS   •   •   310 OBERMANN   119

GLASSD
HELICON GLASSD IN THE LAKE   •   •   •   •   •   229 YOUTH OF NATURE   38

GLAZED
THE EYES ARE GLAZED THOU CANST NOT SPEAK   •   •   276 SOUTHERN NIGHT   42

GLEAM
ERE THEIR BOAT-MUSIC SOUND ERE THEIR BROIDERD FLAGS GLEAM		19 MODERN SAPPHO	8
LO SAILS THAT GLEAM A MOMENT AND ARE GONE	• • • •	42 GIPSY CHILD	5
YOU CRUSH THEM THE BLUE GENTIANS GLEAM	• • • •	55 RESIGNATION	103
PALE DEW-DRENCHD HALF-SHUT ROSES GLEAM	• • • •	57 RESIGNATION	179
FOR THE GLEAM OF THY WHITE SAIL	• • • • •	138 TRISTRAM 1	272
SHE LEFT THE GLEAM-LIT FIREPLACE	• • • • •	140 TRISTRAM 1	315
AT THIS HUGE GLEAM-LIT FIREPLACE	• • • •	148 TRISTRAM 2	158
AT THE HUGE GLEAM-LIT FIREPLACE	• • • •	148 TRISTRAM 2	V 158
WHERE THE SPENT LIGHTS QUIVER AND GLEAM	• • • •	162 FORSAKEN MERM	37
AND THE GLEAM OF HER GOLDEN HAIR	• • • • •	164 FORSAKEN MERM	107
THE GLEAM-LIGHTED LAKE	• • • • • • • •	174 PARTING	4
ASOPUS GLEAM ROCK-HEMMD	• • • • • • • •	197 FRAG ANTIGONE	63
SOMETIMES A MOMENTARY GLEAM	• • • • •	226 EPILOG LAOCOON	177
THE GLEAM OF THE EVENING STAR	• • • • •	228 YOUTH OF NATURE	18
TO HAVE RENDERD THE GLEAM OF MY SKIES	• • •	231 YOUTH OF NATURE	123
AND ONLY IN THE HIDDEN BROOKSIDE GLEAM	• • •	266 THYRSIS	119
ONCE MORE THINE IMMEMORIAL GLEAM RETURN	• • •	449 WESTMIN ABBEY	175
ONE DAY THINE IMMEMORIAL GLEAM RETURN	• • •	449 WESTMIN ABBEY	V 175
LIT BY A WANDERING GLEAM WE KNOW NOT HOW	• • •	475 CROMWELL	128
SOFTLY GLEAM THE FAR BLUE MOUNTAINS	• • • • •	META CLOISTER	13

GLEAMD
THERE GLEAMD SOMETHING WHICH RECALLD	• • • • • •	136 TRISTRAM 1	201
THERE GLEAMD SOMETHING THAT RECALLD	• • • • • •	136 TRISTRAM 1	V 201

GLEAMING
DEEP AND FAR A BROKEN GLEAMING	• • • • • •	32 NEW SIRENS	185
AND NOW WITH GLEAMING RING ENFOLDS THE WORLD	•	110 BALDER DEAD 2	211
OF VEIND WHITE-GLEAMING QUARTZ AND HERE AND THERE		150 TRISTRAM 3	17
WHERE THE RIVER IN GLEAMING RINGS	• • • • •	252 FUTURE	14
COWLD FORMS BRUSH BY IN GLEAMING WHITE	• • •	300 GRANDE CHARTR	36
HIGH THOUGHTS WERE HIS WHEN BY THE GLEAMING FLOOD		473 CROMWELL	65
ONCE MORE ALONE BESIDE THE GLEAMING FLOOD	• • •	479 CROMWELL	240

GLEAMS
FAR UP GLEAMS THE HOUSE AND BENEATH FLOWS THE RIVER		19 MODERN SAPPHO	V 3
AND FAINT THE CITY GLEAMS	• • • • • • • • •	45 IN UTRUMQUE PAR	16
GLEAMS SO RICH IN THE LIGHT OF THE FIRE	• • •	131 TRISTRAM 1	25
IN THE WOODS WHERE THE GLEAMS PLAY	• • • • •	137 TRISTRAM 1	220
BORE UP FROM WHERE THE BRIGHT ATLANTIC GLEAMS	• •	151 TRISTRAM 3	53
CAME IN FROM WHERE THE BRIGHT ATLANTIC GLEAMS	• •	TRISTRAM 3	V 53
THOUGHTS LIGHT LIKE GLEAMS MY SPIRITS SKY	• • •	209 DESPONDENCY	5
GLEAMS AND IS GONE THE CLIFFS OF ENGLAND STAND	•	210 DOVER BEACH	4
THE ORCHIS RED GLEAMS EVERYWHERE	• • • • • •	274 STANZAS CARNAC	18
THAT FOR A MOMENT GLEAMS AND ALL AGAIN IS NIGHT	•	463 ALARIC AT ROME	30

GLEAN
AND THOUGH THOU GLEAN WHAT STRENUOUS GLEANERS MAY		43 GIPSY CHILD	57

GLEAND
YET THIS GLEAND WHEN GODS WERE SPEAKING	• • • •	28 NEW SIRENS	79

GLEANED
SHE GLEANED FROM BRETON GRANDAMES WHEN A CHILD	• •	152 TRISTRAM 3	108

GLEANER
THE LAST BELATED GLEANER GONE	• • • • • • •	218 BACCHANALIA 1	V 9

GLEANERS
AND THOUGH THOU GLEAN WHAT STRENUOUS GLEANERS MAY		43 GIPSY CHILD	57

GLEANS
ALL YOUR SPIRITS HISTORY GLEANS	• • • • • •	META CLOISTER	36

GLEE
SHE BATHED IT IN SMILES OF GLEE	• • • • •	21 REQUIESCAT	6
WE BATHED OUR HANDS WITH SPEECHLESS GLEE	• • • •	54 RESIGNATION	84
SPARKLED WITH MOCKING GLEE AND EXERCISE	• • • •	154 TRISTRAM 3	170
AND KNOW HER FRIEND AND WEEP FOR GLEE	• • •	202 URANIA	27

GLEN
PLAY THROUGH THIS GRASSY UPLAND GLEN	• • • •	55 RESIGNATION	99
THERE IN THE GLEN FENSALER STANDS THE HOUSE	• •	97 BALDER DEAD 1	84
INTO THE TANGLED GLEN BELOW	• • • • • • •	148 TRISTRAM 2	V
THIS OPEN GLEN WAS STUDDED THICK WITH THORNS	• •	155 TRISTRAM 3	191
TO CROSS THE STEEP ISMENIAN GLEN	• • • • • •	197 FRAG ANTIGONE	86
ON THE PURE COLUMNS OF ITS GLEN-BUILT HALL	• • • •	236 PALLADIUM	6
IN SUCH A GLEN ON SUCH A DAY	• • • • • •	414 EMPEDOCLES I 2	57
AND IN THE LONELY ROCK-STREWN MOUNTAIN-GLEN	• •	430 EMPEDOCLES II	39

GLENS
THE SCARED GLENS WE WANDERD ON	• • • • • • •	27 NEW SIRENS	30
HIS WHO IN MOUNTAIN GLENS AT NOON OF DAY	• • •	42 GIPSY CHILD	22
AND FROM THE GLENS ALL DAY AN ECHO CAME	• • •	106 BALDER DEAD 2	54
AND IN THEIR GLENS ON STARRY NIGHTS	• • • • •	182 TO MARG CONT	9
IN THE UPPER GLENS	• • • • • • • • • • •	190 STRAYED REVEL	144
VAINLY FOR HE IN THE GLENS	• • • • • • •	347 MEROPE	518
ASLEEP IN THE ARCADIAN GLENS AT NOON	• • • • •	372 MEROPE	1160
OR SURPRISED IN THE GLENS	• • • • • • • •	392 MEROPE	1626

GLENS   (CONTINUED)
        SOMETIMES AND WANDERS FAR AMONG THE GLENS   • • • •   412 EMPEDOCLES I 2   17
        THE MOUNTAINS WHERE THE GLENS ARE DRY   • • • •   414 EMPEDOCLES I 2   62
        THE SUNSHINE IN THE HAPPY GLENS IS FAIR   • • • •   426 EMPEDOCLES I 2   430
        BASK IN THE GLENS OR ON THE WARM SEA-SHORE   • • • •   427 EMPEDOCLES I 2   437
        FOR EVER THROUGH THE GLENS PLACID AND DUMB   • • • •   427 EMPEDOCLES I 2   460

GLIDE
        ALL PAST AND THROUGH THE TREES WE GLIDE   • • • •   54 RESIGNATION   58
        I SEE HER FORM GLIDE THROUGH THE CROSSING SPEARS • • •   138 TRISTRAM 1   241
        GENTLY BY HIS YE WATERS GLIDE • • • • • • • • •   279 SOUTHERN NIGHT   138
        OF THEIR CLOISTER SEE THEY GLIDE   • • • • • • •   META CLOISTER   6

GLIDES
        STILL GLIDES THE STREAM SLOW DROPS THE BOAT   • •   206 RIVER   1
        THE MEADOWS WHERE IT GLIDES THE SUN THE BREEZE • •   247 BURIED LIFE   90
        VAINLY DOES EACH AS HE GLIDES • • • • • • • •   252 FUTURE   19

GLIDING
        GLIDING HALF HIDDEN THROUGH THE DUSKY STEMS   • •   11 MYCERINUS   104

GLIMMERING
        THIS IS THE GLIMMERING VERGE OF HEAVEN AND THESE • •   19 CHURCH BROU 3   41
        THAT NIGHT IN THE WIDE-GLIMMERING SEA   • • • •   54 RESIGNATION   85
        AH GLIMMERING WATER • • • • • • • • • • • •   194 STRAYED REVEL   283
        GLIMMERING AND VAST OUT IN THE TRANQUIL BAY   • • •   210 DOVER BEACH   5
        AND REACH THAT GLIMMERING SHEET OF GLASS   • • •   310 OBERMANN   119
        ACROSS THE GLIMMERING LAKE   • • • • • • •   324 OBERMANN MORE   346
        TO THE GLIMMERING MOUNTAIN-LAKES   • • • • • •   434 EMPEDOCLES II   172

GLIMPSE
        OVER THE GREY SEA-RIDGES AND THE GLIMPSE   • • •   124 BALDER DEAD 3   366
        TO WIN ONE INSTANTS GLIMPSE OF THEE • • • • • •   205 CALAIS SANDS   24
        THAT TRANSIENT GLIMPSE IN SONG THEY SAY   • • •   226 EPILOG LAOCOON   181

GLIMPSES
        SEEN BY RARE GLIMPSES PENSIVE AND TONGUE-TIED   • •   256 SCHOLAR-GIPSY   54
        A THOUSAND GLIMPSES WINS • • • • • • • • •   415 EMPEDOCLES I 2   84

GLINTS
        AND ON THE PAVEMENT ROUND THE TOMB THERE GLINTS • •   18 CHURCH BROU 3   22

GLION
        GLION AH TWENTY YEARS IT CUTS   • • • • • • • •   312 OBERMANN MORE   1
        GLION BUT NOT THE SAME • • • • • • • • • • •   312 OBERMANN MORE   4
        OER GLION FRINGE THE MOUNTAINS BRINK • • • • •   483 ROME-SICKNESS   11

GLISTENING
        UPON THE GLISTENING LEADEN ROOF   • • • • • •   16 CHURCH BROU 2   1
        UP THE STILL GLISTENING BEACHES   • • • • • •   165 FORSAKEN MERM   132
        EACH GLISTENING STRAND EACH HEATH-FRINGED BAY   • •   177 FAREWELL   4
        GIRDLED THE GLISTENING BAY   • • • • • • • •   242 SUMMER NIGHT   19
        AND OER THE GLISTENING LONELY LAND   • • • • •   274 STANZAS CARNAC   21
        CETTE WITH ITS GLISTENING HOUSES WHITE   • • •   275 SOUTHERN NIGHT   9
        WHAT GARMENTS OUT-GLISTENING   • • • • • • • •   442 EMPEDOCLES II   439
        FAR OER THE GLISTENING SHEETS OF WINDY CORN   • •   473 CROMWELL   36

GLISTENS
        WHEN THE DEW GLISTENS ON THE PEARLED EARS   • • • •   65 SOHRAB RUSTUM   155

GLISTERING
        IF THE GLISTERING WINGS OF MORNING   • • • • • •   29 NEW SIRENS   107
        MANTLES WITH THOSE RICH FURS DEEP GLISTERING   • •   150 TRISTRAM 3   40
        WHICH GLISTERING PLAYS ALL ROUND THEM LONE AND MILD   155 TRISTRAM 3   203
        WHICH GLISTERING LAY ALL ROUND THEM LONE AND MILD   155 TRISTRAM 3   V 203

GLITTERD
        SWISS CHALETS GLITTERD ON THE DEWY SLOPES   • • • •   25 DREAM   10

GLITTERING
        STEEDS ARE NEIGHING GALLANTS GLITTERING   • • •   13 CHURCH BROU 1   9
        FROM THE BROAD OXUS AND THE GLITTERING SANDS   • •   64 SOHRAB RUSTUM   105
        OF SCARLET CLOTH THEY WERE AND GLITTERING GAY   • •   66 SOHRAB RUSTUM   192
        HIS STATELY CREST AND DIMMD HIS GLITTERING ARMS • •   74 SOHRAB RUSTUM   454
        HIS HAIR AND FACE AND BEARD AND GLITTERING ARMS • •   82 SOHRAB RUSTUM   702
        LONG INLETS OF SMOOTH GLITTERING SEA • • • • •   141 TRISTRAM 1   368
        UNDER THE GLITTERING HOLLIES ISEULT STANDS   • • •   150 TRISTRAM 3   23
        TO CALAIS GLITTERING IN THE SUN   • • • • • •   204 CALAIS SANDS   4
        WHERE BLACK-WINGD SWALLOWS HAUNT THE GLITTERING THAMES   257 SCHOLAR-GIPSY   94
        NO GLITTERING HOPES ON LIFES GREY DISTANCE SMILED   475 CROMWELL   126
        THERE LAUD WITH NOISELESS STEPS AND GLITTERING EYE   476 CROMWELL   165

GLOOM
        LOST LABOUR WHEN THE CIRCUMAMBIENT GLOOM   • • • •   10 MYCERINUS   53
        A HUNDRED LAMPS BEAMD IN THE TRANQUIL GLOOM   • • • •   11 MYCERINUS   94
        AND HIS CLEAR LAUGH FLED RINGING THROUGH THE GLOOM   12 MYCERINUS   113
        LOOKS LANGUIDLY ROUND ON A GLOOM-BURIED WORLD   • •   20 MODERN SAPPHO   24
        THROUGH THAT GLOOM HE WILL SEE BUT A SHADOW APPEARING   20 MODERN SAPPHO   25
        REELS AND SHIVERS ON THE RUFFLED GLOOM   • • • •   32 NEW SIRENS   186
        WHO HID SUCH IMPORT IN AN INFANTS GLOOM   • • • •   41 GIPSY CHILD   2

GLOOM   (CONTINUED)
        THROUGH THE COLD GLOOM WITH MEASURED RACE · · · ·   53 RESIGNATION   34
        IN GLOOM THEY TWAIN WERE WRAPPD AND THEY ALONE · ·   75 SOHRAB RUSTUM   486
        BUT IN THE GLOOM THEY FOUGHT WITH BLOODSHOT EYES · ·   75 SOHRAB RUSTUM   490
        AND RUSTUM BOWD HIS HEAD BUT THEN THE GLOOM   · ·   76 SOHRAB RUSTUM   499
        AND THEN THE GLOOM DISPERSED AND THE WIND FELL · ·   76 SOHRAB RUSTUM   522
        THEN BALDERS SPIRIT THROUGH THE GLOOM DREW NEAR · · 103 BALDER DEAD 1   282
        AND SET THE FIELDS OF GLOOM ABLAZE WITH LIGHT   · · 120 BALDER DEAD 3   243
        OF THE DEEP INNER GLOOM BUT FLITTEST HERE · · · · 124 BALDER DEAD 3   389
        FOR THIS I DIED AND FLED BENEATH THE GLOOM   · · · 124 BALDER DEAD 3   397
        FROM THE DEEP GLOOM WHERE I WILL NOW RETURN   · · · 125 BALDER DEAD 3   415
        HE SPAKE AND TURND TO GO TO THE INNER GLOOM   · · 125 BALDER DEAD 3   421
        INACTIVE THEREFORE LET ME LIE IN GLOOM   · · · · · 128 BALDER DEAD 3   509
        DEATH AND THE GLOOM WHICH ROUND ME EVEN NOW   · · · 129 BALDER DEAD 3   546
        FADED FROM SIGHT INTO THE INTERIOR GLOOM   · · · 129 BALDER DEAD 3   553
        SHE IS HERE WHO HAD HIS GLOOM · · · · · · · · · 132 TRISTRAM 1   76
        ON THE BLANCHD SANDS A GLOOM · · · · · · · · · 165 FORSAKEN MERM   131
        HATH CHARMD AT BIRTH FROM GLOOM AND CARE · · · · 203 EUPHROSYNE   14
        HAS CHARMD AT BIRTH FROM GLOOM AND CARE · · · · 203 EUPHROSYNE   V   14
        OER THAT WIDE PLAIN NOW WRAPT IN GLOOM · · · · · 220 BACCHANALIA 2   21
        THE VASTNESS THE GRANDEUR THE GLOOM · · · · · · 231 YOUTH OF NATURE   101
        CAN BE THROUGH HOURS OF GLOOM FULFILLD   · · · · · 241 MORALITY   6
        OFT MADE THEE IN THY GLOOM DESPAIR · · · · · · · 241 MORALITY   18
        GLOOM SETTLES SLOWLY DOWN OVER THEIR BREAST · · · 243 SUMMER NIGHT   46
        OF SEA AND WIND AND THROUGH THE DEEPENING GLOOM · · 244 SUMMER NIGHT   71
        THE CEREMONIOUS AIR OF GLOOM · · · · · · · · · 250 WISH   15
        THROUGH HADES AND THE MOURNFUL GLOOM · · · · · · 271 MEMORIAL VERSES   39
        THERE THOU DOST LIE IN THE GLOOM · · · · · · · · 286 RUGBY CHAPEL   14
        THAT WORD GLOOM TO MY MIND · · · · · · · · · · 286 RUGBY CHAPEL   16
        IN THE GLOOM OF NOVEMBER WE PASSD · · · · · · · 286 RUGBY CHAPEL   19
        DAYS NOT OF GLOOM AT THY SIDE · · · · · · · · · 287 RUGBY CHAPEL   V   20
        EVEN NOW THEIR WHISPERS PIERCE THE GLOOM · · · · 301 GRANDE CHARTR   71
        OH HIDE ME IN YOUR GLOOM PROFOUND · · · · · · · 302 GRANDE CHARTR   91
        MANS WORK-PLACE LAY IN GLOOM · · · · · · · · · 315 OBERMANN MORE   78
        NOR BE COLD GLOOM THY PRISON · · · · · · · · · 322 OBERMANN MORE   282
        THOU SOUGHTEST LAY IN GLOOM · · · · · · · · · · 315 OBERMANN MORE   V   78
        GLOOM-WRAPPED WITHIN I LIVED AND DIED · · · · · 321 OBERMANN MORE   V 265
        THY DEEP SECLUSION THINE UNYIELDING GLOOM   · · · 332 MEROPE   84
        CLOSING IN BLOOD AND GLOOM HIS SULLEN REIGN · · · 335 MEROPE   160
        FLOWERS BUT THOU IN THE GLOOM · · · · · · · · · 342 MEROPE   403
        INTO THE QUIET GLOOM WHERE THOU ART NOW   · · · · 350 MEROPE   593
        BUT STILL OVER HIS SPEECH A GLOOM THERE HUNG   · · 356 MEROPE   764
        TO LIE IN GLOOM FOR EVER UNAPPEASED · · · · · · 367 MEROPE   1052
        WAKE AMID GLOOM AND HOWLING AND THE NOISE   · · · 373 MEROPE   1185
        AND ALL WHICH MIGHT RELAX HIS SETTLED GLOOM · · · 409 EMPEDOCLES I 1   84
        AND LIVES A LONELY MAN IN TRIPLE GLOOM · · · · · 410 EMPEDOCLES I 1   124
        I CANNOT I HAVE LIVED IN WRATH AND GLOOM   · · · · 440 EMPEDOCLES II   394
        OF DESPONDENCY AND GLOOM · · · · · · · · · · · 441 EMPEDOCLES II   414
        SO WHITE THROUGH THE GLOOM · · · · · · · · · · 442 EMPEDOCLES II   438
        HUGE IN THE GLOOM ACROSS IN THORNEY ISLE   · · · · 444 WESTMIN ABBEY   15
        AND YEARS OF CRIME AND NOTHINGNESS AND GLOOM · · 463 ALARIC AT ROME   40

GLOOMING
        WITH GLOOMING CLOUDS BROODS DARK AND HEAVILY   · · 475 CROMWELL   130

GLOOMS
        WHERE COOL GRASS AND FRAGRANT GLOOMS · · · · · ·   26 NEW SIRENS   2
        GLOOMS THAT GO DEEP AS THINE I HAVE NOT KNOWN · ·   42 GIPSY CHILD   17
        GLOOMS THAT ENHANCE AND GLORIFY THIS EARTH · · · ·   42 GIPSY CHILD   20

GLOOMY
        AND WEND THEMSELVES TO HELAS GLOOMY REALM · · · ·   98 BALDER DEAD 1   121
        WANDERING TOGETHER THROUGH THAT GLOOMY WORLD   · · 104 BALDER DEAD 1   328

GLORIES
        HALF THEIR GLORIES TO THE DAY · · · · · · · · ·   35 NEW SIRENS   256
        AND THE DIM GLORIES OF DEPARTED DAYS · · · · · · 464 ALARIC AT ROME   63
        THE VANISHT GLORIES OF THINE EARLY DAY · · · · · 471 ALARIC AT ROME   224
        ON LAND RENEW THAT GREEK EXPLOIT WHOSE GLORIES · · 481 HUNGARIAN NAT   12

GLORIFIED
        THE GLORIFIED TRAIN · · · · · · · · · · · · · 442 EMPEDOCLES II   452
        NAVE CHOIR AND TRANSEPT GLORIFIED WITH LIGHT   · · 445 WESTMIN ABBEY   35
        SLEW HIM FIGHTING IN FRONT OF THE FRAY AND   HOMER TRANS   53
                GLORIFIED HECTOR

GLORIFY
        GLOOMS THAT ENHANCE AND GLORIFY THIS EARTH · · · ·   42 GIPSY CHILD   20
        BACKD BY THE SUNSET WHICH DOTH GLORIFY · · · · · 267 THYRSIS   158

GLORIOUS
        THEIR GLORIOUS TASKS IN SILENCE PERFECTING · · · ·   2 QUIET WORK   12
        THEIR GLORIOUS COURSE IN SILENCE PERFECTING · · ·   2 QUIET WORK   V   12
        THEN RUSTUM TOOK IT FOR HIS GLORIOUS SIGN · · · ·   81 SOHRAB RUSTUM   683
        WHICH WERE HIS GLORIOUS MARK IN HEAVEN HE STOOD · · 103 BALDER DEAD 1   285
        THE BEAUTY AND THE GLORIOUS ART OF GREECE · · · · 168 RACHEL 2   14
        BECOME LIKE GLORIOUS LONDON · · · · · · · · · · 214 NEW ROME   V   13
        IN A BOOK WHICH OF GLORIOUS SOULS · · · · · · · 280 HAWORTH CHURCH   V   19
        AND GLORIOUS THERE WITHOUT A SOUND · · · · · · · 324 OBERMANN MORE   345
        AND NOW GLORIOUS SECURE · · · · · · · · · · · 343 MEROPE   414
        OUR GLORIOUS FOUNDER · · · · · · · · · · · · 398 MEROPE   1812

GLORIOUS (CONTINUED)
```
        AND VOUCHD BY GLORIOUS RENOWN  . . . . . . . .   459 KAISER DEAD          17
        A GLORIOUS MANHOOD YET A DIM OLD AGE  . . . . .   463 ALARIC AT ROME       39
        THOU SHATTERED MASS WHOSE GLORIOUS RUINS TELL   463 ALARIC AT ROME       45
        HAD GAZED IN WONDER ON THAT GLORIOUS SIGHT  . .   465 ALARIC AT ROME       74
        AND THUS AMID THE GLORIOUS HUES OF EVEN  . . .   466 ALARIC AT ROME      105
        AND NOT BETHINK HER OF HER GLORIOUS PRIME  . . .   467 ALARIC AT ROME      130
```

GLORIOUSLY
```
        BY SPIRITS GLORIOUSLY GAY  . . . . . . . . . .   450 GEISTS GRAVE         18
```

GLORY
```
        THE MELLOW GLORY OF THE ATTIC STAGE  . . . . .     2 TO A FRIEND          13
        OF THE SOILD GLORY AND THE TRAILING WING  . . .    43 GIPSY CHILD          56
        AND REAP A SECOND GLORIN IN THINE AGE  . . . .    84 SOHRAB RUSTUM       776
        AND OLD MEN KNOWN TO GLORY BUT THEIR STAR  . .   109 BALDER DEAD 2       166
        IN THE GLORY OF HIS PRIME  . . . . . . . . . .   134 TRISTRAM 1          110
        HER GENIUS AND HER GLORY ARE HER OWN  . . . . .   168 RACHEL 3             14
        SAY WHAT BLINDS US THAT WE CLAIM THE GLORY  . .   209 SELF-DECEPTION        1
        IS IT TO LOSE THE GLORY OF THE FORM  . . . . .   212 GROWING OLD           2
        THAT THEY WERE MY GLORY AND JOY  . . . . . . .   232 YOUTH OF NATURE     132
        FAR OFF A GLORY OF DAY  . . . . . . . . . . .   234 YOUTH OF MAN         81
        THEIR NAMES CHIEF GLORY OF ALL  . . . . . . .   281 HAWORTH CHURCH       22
        GLORY AND GENIUS AND JOY  . . . . . . . . . .   295 HEINES GRAVE         84
        CHARM IS THE GLORY WHICH MAKES  . . . . . . .   295 HEINES GRAVE        103
        HOW HAD ITS GLORY NEW  . . . . . . . . . . .   317 OBERMANN MORE       142
        THE GLORY OF THE LYRE  . . . . . . . . . . .   392 MEROPE             1630
        COME STREAMING WITH THE FLOODS OF GLORY IN  . .   445 WESTMIN ABBEY        38
        THEN RAISED HER FACE AND GLORY ROUND HER STREAMD   447 WESTMIN ABBEY        96
        THEN RAISED HER FACE AND GLORY ROUND HER BEAMD   447 WESTMIN ABBEY      V  96
        AND GLORY STRETCHD AT BURWOOD GATE  . . . . .   461 KAISER DEAD          73
        THERE ARE WHOSE GLORY PASSETH NOT AWAY  . . .   462 ALARIC AT ROME        7
        AND THE WINDS TOLD HIS GLORY AND THE WAVE  . .   476 CROMWELL            157
```

GLORYS
```
        AND BRIGHTEST IS THEIR GLORYS SHEEN  . . . . .   227 EPILOG LAOCOON      209
        GREW USED TO THE APPROACH OF GLORYS WINGS  . .   445 WESTMIN ABBEY        56
```

GLOSSY
```
        ON THE WET UMBRAGE OF THEIR GLOSSY TOPS  . . .    24 DREAM                 4
        BLACK GLOSSY CURLD THE FLEECE OF KARA-KUL  . .    64 SOHRAB RUSTUM       101
        OUT OF THEIR GLOSSY COVERTS BUT WHEN NOW  . . .   150 TRISTRAM 3           31
        MOVED UP AND DOWN UNDER THE GLOSSY TREES  . . .   150 TRISTRAM 3           43
        MOVD UP AND DOWN UNDER THEIR GLOSSY TREES  . .       TRISTRAM 3         V  43
        THE GLOSSY RUSHES NODDED BY  . . . . . . . .   480 HAYSWATER BOAT       26
```

GLOW
```
        BUT WHEN THE RED GLOW ON THE SEA GREW COLD  . .   151 TRISTRAM 3           58
        FAIR WAS THE BRIDE AND ON HER FRONT DID GLOW   166 AUSTERITY POET        5
        ONE CAME FROM PENMON WESTWARD AND A GLOW  . . .   170 EAST AND WEST         5
        FOR SOMETHING IN ITS DEPTHS DOTH GLOW  . . . .   178 FAREWELL             19
        TAMED IS THEIR TURBULENT YOUTHFUL GLOW  . . .   208 ON THE RHINE         24
        THE THOUGHTS THAT RAIN THEIR STEADY GLOW  . . .   209 DESPONDENCY           1
        MELLOWD AND SOFTEND AS WITH SUNSET-GLOW  . . .   212 GROWING OLD          14
        GLOW NOT THEIR SHOULDERS SMOOTH  . . . . . . .   219 BACCHANALIA 1        46
        CAN THE IMAGE OF LIFE HAVE THE GLOW  . . . . .   231 YOUTH OF NATURE     115
        SEE ON HER FACE A GLOW IS SPREAD  . . . . . .   241 MORALITY             21
        I RUSH WITH THE SWIFT SPHERES AND GLOW  . . .   241 MORALITY             27
        NOR EVER FEELS THE FIERY GLOW  . . . . . . .   243 SUMMER NIGHT         29
        THE GLOW HE CRIES THE THRILL OF LIFE  . . . .   309 OBERMANN             97
        THE GLOW OF THOUGHT THE THRILL OF LIFE  . . .   309 OBERMANN           V  97
        THAT GLOW OF CENTRAL FIRE IS DONE  . . . . .   320 OBERMANN MORE       221
        THE GLOW OF CENTRAL FIRE IS DONE  . . . . . .   320 OBERMANN MORE      V 221
        AND HER FLUSHD FEET GLOW ON THE MARBLE FLOOR   431 EMPEDOCLES II        88
        OH THAT I COULD GLOW LIKE THIS MOUNTAIN  . . .   438 EMPEDOCLES II       323
        BUT NO THIS HEART WILL GLOW NO MORE THOU ART   438 EMPEDOCLES II       327
        WHAT IS THE HAPPY GLOW SO SOON EXPIRED  . . .   444 WESTMIN ABBEY        10
        HE HAD HIS GLOW AND THOU HADST THINE  . . . .   482 COURAGE              24
```

GLOWD
```
        AND YET EEN THERE THE CANVAS GLOWD  . . . . .   222 EPILOG LAOCOON       23
```

GLOWING
```
        A CHEQUER-WORK OF GLOWING SAPPHIRE-TINTS  . . .    18 CHURCH BROU 3        23
        WHERE I STAND THE GRASS IS GLOWING  . . . . .    32 NEW SIRENS          187
        SO GLOWING AND SO NEAR  . . . . . . . . . . .    47 WORLD QUIETIST       23
        SEE ON THEIR GLOWING CHEEKS  . . . . . . . .   221 BACCHANALIA 2        61
        ALMOST BEFORE TIS PLANND COME GLOWING HATE  . .   367 MEROPE             1062
```

GLOWS
```
        WOULDST MORE OF IT SEE HOW GLOWS  . . . . . .   187 STRAYED REVEL        55
        WHICH GLOWS AS IF THE MIDDLE AGE  . . . . . .   204 CALAIS SANDS          7
        MY SOUL GLOWS TO MEET YOU  . . . . . . . . .   441 EMPEDOCLES II       412
```

GLUE
```
        TO GLUE MY FRUITLESS GAZE ON AND TO PINE  . . .       FRAGMENT 5            6
```

GLUT
```
        GLUT THE DEVOURING GRAVE  . . . . . . . . . . .   288 RUGBY CHAPEL         83
```

GNARLD

    LIKE GHOSTS THE HUGE GNARLD OLIVES STAND • • • • 275 SOUTHERN NIGHT 6

GNATS

    AND DARTING SWALLOWS AND LIGHT WATER-GNATS • • • • 266 THYRSIS 125

GNAWD

    IN THE UNKIND SPRING HAVE GNAWD • • • • • • 193 STRAYED REVEL V 238

GNAWN

    IN THE UNKIND SPRING HAVE GNAWN • • • • • • 193 STRAYED REVEL 238

GO

    AND THOU WHOSE WIT TO HIGHEST HEAVEN DID GO • • 3 SHAKESPEARE V 9
    STAND NEVER IDLE BUT GO ALWAYS ROUND • • • • 4 DUKE WELLINGTON 2
    I WILL GO FORTH THOUGH SOMETHING WOULD I SAY • • 10 MYCERINUS 68
    I GO AND I RETURN NOT BUT THE WILL • • • • 11 MYCERINUS 74
    I WILL GO FORTH BUT SOMETHING WOULD I SAY • • • 10 MYCERINUS V 68
    ERE THE PARTING HOUR GO BY • • • • • • • 22 MEMORY-PICTURE 7
    ERE THE PARTING HOUR GO BY • • • • • • • 23 MEMORY-PICTURE 15
    ERE THE PARTING HOUR GO BY • • • • • • • 23 MEMORY-PICTURE 23
    ERE THE PARTING HOUR GO BY • • • • • • • 23 MEMORY-PICTURE 31
    ERE THE PARTING HOUR GO BY • • • • • • • 23 MEMORY-PICTURE 39
    ERE THE PARTING HOUR GO BY • • • • • • • 24 MEMORY-PICTURE 47
    ERE THE PARTING HOUR GO BY • • • • • • • 24 MEMORY-PICTURE 63
    JUDGMENT SHIFTS CONVICTIONS GO • • • • • • 29 NEW SIRENS 82
    DUMBLY SMILING AS YOU GO • • • • • • • 31 NEW SIRENS 160
    GLOOMS THAT GO DEEP AS THINE I HAVE NOT KNOWN • • 42 GIPSY CHILD 17
    ONCE ERE THY DAY GO DOWN THOU SHALT DISCERN • • 44 GIPSY CHILD V 65
    DO WE GO HENCE AND FIND THEY ARE NOT DEAD • • • 44 QUESTION 17
    SHALL WE GO HENCE AND FIND THEY ARE NOT DEAD • • 44 QUESTION V 17
    THERE GO THOU WILT NOT YET MY HEART FOREBODES • 63 SOHRAB RUSTUM 86
    GO I WILL GRANT THEE WHAT THY HEART DESIRES • • 63 SOHRAB RUSTUM 93
    GO TO IF IRANS CHIEFS ARE OLD THEN I • • • • 67 SOHRAB RUSTUM 221
    THERE WOULD I GO AND HANG MY ARMOUR UP • • • 68 SOHRAB RUSTUM 236
    A BELT OR SWORD PERHAPS AND GO HIS WAY • • • 71 SOHRAB RUSTUM 354
    HIS HEART TO TAKE A GIFT AND LET THEE GO • • • 77 SOHRAB RUSTUM 533
    I CAME AND LIKE THE WIND I GO AWAY • • • • 82 SOHRAB RUSTUM 723
    FOR THOU HAST GONE WHERE I SHALL NEVER GO • • 83 SOHRAB RUSTUM 748
    AND I WILL SPARE THY HOST YEA LET THEM GO • • 84 SOHRAB RUSTUM 806
    AS THE LAW IS AND GO YOUR WAY • • • • • 87 SICK KING BOKH 9
    HINDER HIM NOT BUT LET HIM GO • • • • • 91 SICK KING BOKH 116
    TURNING HIM QUICKLY TO GO IN • • • • • 91 SICK KING BOKH 127
    FORBID HIM NOT BUT LET HIM GO • • • • • 91 SICK KING BOKH V 116
    AND HELA YIELD TO THIS AND LET HIM GO • • • 98 BALDER DEAD 1 116
    WHICH EVERY DAY THEY COME AND GO IN HEAVEN • • • 99 BALDER DEAD 1 140
    NO JOURNEY FOR A SIGHTLESS GOD TO GO • • • • 100 BALDER DEAD 1 186
    THEREFORE THYSELF THOU SHALT NOT GO MY SON • • • 100 BALDER DEAD 1 188
    SHALL GO AND I WILL BE HIS GUIDE UNSEEN • • • 100 BALDER DEAD 1 191
    GO QUICKLY GODS BRING WOOD TO THE SEASHORE • • 106 BALDER DEAD 2 41
    THEY GO THE ERRAND AND THE WAY IS KNOWN • • • 110 BALDER DEAD 2 191
    WORSE WAS THAT WAY TO GO THAN TO RETURN • • • 113 BALDER DEAD 2 291
    NINE DAYS HE TOOK TO GO TWO TO RETURN • • • 113 BALDER DEAD 2 293
    GO QUICKLY FORTH THROUGH ALL THE WORLD AND PRAY • 122 BALDER DEAD 3 299
    AND THEY GO LONG DAYS TOSSING UP AND DOWN • • 124 BALDER DEAD 3 365
    HE SPAKE AND TURND TO GO TO THE INNER GLOOM • • 125 BALDER DEAD 3 421
    GO NOT FAR O ISEULT FROM MY GRAVE • • • • 145 TRISTRAM 2 92
    RISE GO HENCE AND SEEK THE PRINCESS ISEULT • • • 145 TRISTRAM 2 V 93
    AND NOW SHE WILL GO HOME AND SOFTLY LAY • • • 151 TRISTRAM 3 76
    GO HENCE AND COOL THYSELF AN HOUR • • • • 157 SAINT BRANDAN 36
    CALL HER ONCE BEFORE YOU GO • • • • • • 161 FORSAKEN MERM 10
    SHE SAID I MUST GO FOR MY KINSFOLK PRAY • • • 163 FORSAKEN MERM 56
    I SAID GO UP DEAR HEART THROUGH THE WAVES • • • 163 FORSAKEN MERM 60
    AND HE WITH UNSUNND FACE DID ALWAYS GO • • • 170 EAST AND WEST 8
    AH WITH YOU LET ME GO • • • • • • • 175 PARTING 10
    THE RUSHING WINDS GO • • • • • • • • 175 PARTING 26
    AH WITH THAT LET ME GO • • • • • • • 176 PARTING 44
    GO THEN TILL TIME AND FATE IMPRESS • • • • 179 FAREWELL 41
    OF THE HIGH ALPS TO WHICH I GO • • • • • 207 ON THE RHINE 4
    HASTE ARISE YE AND GO • • • • • • • • 216 LORDS MESSENGER 5
    ON FOOT BEHIND THEM GO AND COME • • • • 224 EPILOG LAOCOON 114
    THEY CANNOT LEAVE IT THEY MUST GO • • • • 226 EPILOG LAOCOON 167
    AND WANDERING FROM THE STREAM THEY GO • • • • 226 EPILOG LAOCOON 174
    WHENCE OUR LIVES COME AND WHERE THEY GO • • • 246 BURIED LIFE 54
    WHENCE OUR THOUGHTS COME AND WHERE THEY GO • • 246 BURIED LIFE V 54
    STILL ALL THINGS IN THIS GLADE GO THROUGH • • 249 KENSINGTON GARD 31
    THE FRIENDS WHO COME AND GAPE AND GO • • • • 250 WISH 14
    THEN WILLING LET MY SPIRIT GO • • • • • 251 WISH 51
    GO FOR THEY CALL YOU SHEPHERD FROM THE HILL • • 255 SCHOLAR-GIPSY 1
    GO SHEPHERD AND UNTIE THE WATTLED COTES • • • • 255 SCHOLAR-GIPSY 2
    WHERE HOME THROUGH FLOODED FIELDS FOOT-TRAVELLERS GO 258 SCHOLAR-GIPSY 122
    AND WE OURSELVES SHALL GO • • • • • • 259 SCHOLAR-GIPSY 156
    THE BLOOM IS GONE AND WITH THE BLOOM GO I • • • 264 THYRSIS 60
    TOO QUICK DESPAIRER WHEREFORE WILT THOU GO • • • 264 THYRSIS 61
    SOME GOOD SURVIVOR WITH HIS FLUTE WOULD GO • • • 265 THYRSIS 83
    NOT WITHOUT AIM TO GO ROUND • • • • • • 288 RUGBY CHAPEL 76
    FOLLOW YOUR STEPS AS YE GO • • • • • • 292 RUGBY CHAPEL 203
    I GO FATE DRIVES ME BUT I LEAVE • • • • • 310 OBERMANN 131
    GO SEEK IT IN THY SOUL • • • • • • • 316 OBERMANN MORE 120
    THEY COME AND GO THEY WORK AND PLAN • • • • • 320 OBERMANN MORE V 215

GO

(CONTINUED)

GO THOU INTO THE CITY AND SEEK OUT	• • • • •	331 MEROPE	37
GO AS IT WILL BUT IF THIS	• • • • • • •	348 MEROPE	536
I GO I GO THE KING HOLDS COUNCIL THERE	• • •	368 MEROPE	1077
I GO I GO THE KING HOLDS COUNCIL THERE	• • •	368 MEROPE	1077
GO THOU THE FIRST AND USHER IN THY LORD	• •	373 MEROPE	1190
IF PRUDENCE COUNSELS THEE TO GO UNARMD	• •	391 MEROPE	1591
SPEAK I GO HENCE TO OFFER SACRIFICE	• • • •	394 MEROPE	1722
FIRST WORK AFTER SUCH VICTORY LET US GO	•	405 MEROPE	2017
I GO I GO YET QUEEN TAKE THIS ONE WORD	• • •	368 MEROPE	V1077
I GO I GO YET QUEEN TAKE THIS ONE WORD	• • •	368 MEROPE	V1077
GO WITH HIM CHOOSE THE MOMENT STRIKE THY BLOW	• •	391 MEROPE	V1590
BUT WITH THE WINDS MUST GO	• • • • • •	415 EMPEDOCLES I 2	94
WHAT LIFE AND CHANCE GO HARD WITH THEE TOO AS WITH US	416 EMPEDOCLES I 2	116
NOR LIGHTNINGS GO ASIDE	• • • • • • •	420 EMPEDOCLES I 2	254
BUT THE DAY WEARS GO NOW PAUSANIAS	• • • •	427 EMPEDOCLES I 2	464
I DARE NOT URGE HIM FURTHER HE MUST GO	• • •	428 EMPEDOCLES I 2	479
WHAT LIFE AND TIME GO HARD WITH THEE TOO AS WITH US	416 EMPEDOCLES I 2	V 116
GO THROUGH THE SAD PROBATION ALL AGAIN	• • •	440 EMPEDOCLES II	368
BUT THOU WHEN STRUCK THINE HOUR TO GO	• • •	450 GEISTS GRAVE	33
QUICK RAISED TO ASK WHICH WAY WE GO	• • • •	451 GEISTS GRAVE	50
TEACH US WHILE THEY COME AND GO	• •• • •	456 POOR MATTHIAS	139
GO AND NOW HIMSELF IS GONE	• • • • • •	458 POOR MATTHIAS	205
TO COME AND GO TO SHIFT AND RANGE	• • • •	484 ROME-SICKNESS	22
IT WILL COME WHEN SACRED TROY SHALL GO TO DESTRUCTION	HOMER TRANS	21

GOAD

WITH GOAD AND SHOUTING URGE THEIR CATTLE PAST	• •	107 BALDER DEAD 2	96
DID CONSCIENCE GOAD HIM TO DENOUNCE HIMSELF	• •	364 MEROPE	V
WILL GOAD OUR SENSES WITH A SHARPER SPUR	• • • •	440 EMPEDOCLES II	379

GOAL

A GOAL WHICH GAIND MAY GIVE REPOSE	• • • • •	53 RESIGNATION	17
MAKES CLEAR OUR GOAL TO EVERY EYE	• • • • •	53 RESIGNATION	46
AND TO WHAW GOAL WHAT ENDING BOUND	• • • • •	225	
AND TO WHAT GOAL WHAT ENDING BOUND	• • • • •	225 EPILOG LAOCOON	126
AND THE PURE GOAL OF BEING REACH	• • • • •	278 SOUTHERN NIGHT	85
PATH TO A CLEAR-PURPOSED GOAL	• • • • •	288 RUGBY CHAPEL	85
CONQUER AND COME TO THY GOAL	• • • • •	290 RUGBY CHAPEL	126
MARSHALLD THEM GAVE THEM THEIR GOAL	• • •	291 RUGBY CHAPEL	175
STAGGERING ON TO HER GOAL	• • • • • •	295 HEINES GRAVE	92
SON OF CRESPHONTES WE HAVE REACHD THE GOAL	•	330 MEROPE	1
PERISHD IN SIGHT OF THE GOAL	• • • • •	345 MEROPE	466
O VICTOR VICTOR TRIP NOT AT THE GOAL	• • •	397 MEROPE	1771
DRIVES THE AXE TO ITS GOAL	• • • • • •	400 MEROPE	1864
THOUGH MOVING INLY TO ONE FAR-SET GOAL	• •	448 WESTMIN ABBEY	153
THOUGH MOVING INLY TO ONE FAR-OFF GOAL	• •	448 WESTMIN ABBEY	V 153
TO RUN THEIR COURSE AND REACH THEIR GOAL	• • •	450 GEISTS GRAVE	11
THERE LIES THY GOAL TO MISS OR TO ATTAIN	• • •	465 ALARIC AT ROME	87
WITH CARES TO CONQUER AND A GOAL TO WIN	• • •	475 CROMWELL	122

GOAT

PEERING TO SPY A GOAT-TRACK DOWN THE CLIFF	• • • •	357 MEROPE	804

GOATS

SWAYING THE LONG-HAIRD GOATS WITH SILVERD REIN	• •	115 BALDER DEAD 3	73
HE SAVES THE SHEEP THE GOATS HE DOTH NOT SAVE	• •	172 GOOD SHEPHERD	1
WHICH THE GOATS LOVE ARE JEWELLD THICK WITH DEW	• •	407 EMPEDOCLES I 1	17
AND WHERE THE HILL-GOATS COME TO FEED	• • • •	414 EMPEDOCLES I 2	66

GOBLETS

FLUSHD GUESTS AND GOLDEN GOBLETS FOAMD WITH WINE	• •	11 MYCERINUS	97

GOD

GOD KNOWS IT I AM WITH YOU IF TO PRIZE	• • •	6 REP FRIEND	1
SHALL BE LEFT STANDING FACE TO FACE WITH GOD	• •	7 REP FRIEND CONT	14
GOD THE DUKE LIES STRETCHD BESIDE HIM	• • •	13 CHURCH BROU 1	27
BLEW SUCH MUSIC AS A GOD MAY FRAME	• • • •	29 NEW SIRENS	104
SEES GOD NO NEARER	• • • • • • • • •	38 STAGIRIUS	15
TO GOD COMES NO NIGHER	• • • • • • • •	38 STAGIRIUS	17
WHEN THE SOUL RISING HIGHER TO GOD COMES NO NIGHER	•	38 STAGIRIUS	V 14
WHEN THE MIND WAXING CLEARER SEES GOD NO NEARER	• •	38 STAGIRIUS	V 16
THEY MUST LIVE STILL AND YET GOD KNOWS	• • •	56 RESIGNATION	132
THE KAFFIRS ALSO WHOM GOD CURSE	• • • •	93 SICK KING BOKH	173
I LOSE TO-DAY SO BRIGHT SO LOVED A GOD	• • •	96 BALDER DEAD 1	22
THOUGH SIGHTLESS YET HIS OWN MIND LED THE GOD	• •	97 BALDER DEAD 1	76
BALDER THEIR JOY SO BRIGHT SO LOVED A GOD	• • •	98 BALDER DEAD 1	126
IS IT A MATTER WHICH A GOD MIGHT TRY	• • • •	99 BALDER DEAD 1	133
NO JOURNEY FOR A SIGHTLESS GOD TO GO	• • •	100 BALDER DEAD 1	186
AND EVERY GOD WENT HOME TO HIS OWN HOUSE	• •	106 BALDER DEAD 2	69
KNOWING THE GOD THEY WENT TO SEEK HOW DEAR	• •	107 BALDER DEAD 2	77
THEY MOURND THAT DAY SO BRIGHT SO LOVED A GOD	•	115 BALDER DEAD 3	64
TO GOD OR HERO BUT THOU KEPTEST BACK	• • •	116 BALDER DEAD 3	85
BUT NEITHER GOD NOR MORTAL HEEDS MY PAIN	• •	116 BALDER DEAD 3	111
NO GOD BUT OF THE HERO-TROOP THE CHIEF	• • •	117 BALDER DEAD 3	125
FROM THE DEEP TRENCH SHE PLOUGHD SO STRONG A GOD	•	118 BALDER DEAD 3	178
NIORD THE GOD OF STORMS WHOM FISHERS KNOW	• • •	122 BALDER DEAD 3	323
TO FEEL THE PRESENCE OF A BROTHER GOD	• • •	125 BALDER DEAD 3	418
GOD TIS HER FACE PLAYS IN THE WATERS BRIGHT	•	139 TRISTRAM 1	284
CALL ON GOD AND ON THE HOLY ANGELS	• • • •	145 TRISTRAM 2	79
O RUTH OF GOD THE PRIEST CRIED OUT	• • • • •	160 NECKAN	55

GOD   (CONTINUED)
        EARTH SEA AND SKY AND GOD ABOVE   • • • • • • 161 NECKAN   63
        TIS GOD HIMSELF BECOMES APPARENT WHEN   • • • 171 DIVINITY   3
        FOR GOD OF THESE HIS ATTRIBUTES IS MADE   • • • • 171 DIVINITY   5
        MIS-DEFINE THESE TILL GOD KNOWS THEM NO MORE • • 171 DIVINITY   10
        WISDOM AND GOODNESS THEY ARE GOD WHAT SCHOOLS   • • 171 DIVINITY   11
        AND UNION BEFORE GOD THE ONLY CARE   • • • • 173 MONICAS PRAYER   11
        KEEP BY THIS LIFE IN GOD AND UNION THERE   • • • • 173 MONICAS PRAYER   14
        TO THEE ONLY GOD GRANTED   • • • • 177 PARTING   79
        A GOD A GOD THEIR SEVERANCE RULED   • • • • 182 TO MARG CONT   22
        A GOD A GOD THEIR SEVERANCE RULED   • • • • 182 TO MARG CONT   22
        ROAMD ERE BIRTH THE TREASURIES OF GOD   • • • • 209 SELF-DECEPTION   6
        GOD PUT A HEAP OF LETTERS IN HIS HAND   • • • • 239 REVOLUTIONS   3
        SINCE HE HAS NOT YET FOUND THE WORD GOD WOULD • • 239 REVOLUTIONS   12
        THE WORD THE ORDER WHICH GOD MEANT SHOULD BE • • 239 REVOLUTIONS   18
        AND LAY UPON THE BREAST OF GOD   • • • • 242 MORALITY   36
        OF GOD OF THE WORLD OF THE SOUL   • • • • 253 FUTURE   - 43
        THE SMOOTH TO-DAY OF GOD   • • • • 262 THYRSIS   V
        SERVANTS OF GOD OR SONS   • • • • 291 RUGBY CHAPEL   162
        WHERE ARE THEY TENDING A GOD   • • • • 291 RUGBY CHAPEL   174
        ON TO THE CITY OF GOD   • • • • 292 RUGBY CHAPEL   208
        GOD GAVE THE POET HIS SONG   • • • • 296 HEINES GRAVE   120
        NEITHER MADE MAN TOO MUCH A GOD   • • • • 308 OBERMANN   59
        NOR GOD TOO MUCH A MAN   • • • • 308 OBERMANN   60
        A FRENZIED WANDERER A GOD-DRIVEN MAN   • • • • 385 MEROPE   1424
        SOME GOD MEROPE NOW   • • • • 393 MEROPE   1680
        WITH GOD AND FATE TO RAIL AT SUFFERING EASILY • • 421 EMPEDOCLES I 2   281
        THIS UNIVERSAL GOD   • • • • 422 EMPEDOCLES I 2   298
        CAME ABOUT THE YOUTHFUL GOD   • • • • 433 EMPEDOCLES II   158
        THOU YOUNG IMPLACABLE GOD AND ONLY DEATH   • • • 436 EMPEDOCLES II   232
        SEVEN DAYS THE GOD REPLIED   • • • • 448 WESTMIN ABBEY   137
        GOD DOTH MATCH HIS GIFTS TO MANS BELIEVING • • • • 483 THEKLAS ANSWER   19
        TO LIE LOW IN DEATH BY THE HAND OF A GOD AND A MORTAL   HOMER TRANS   56
        WHERE BROODS THE UNCOMPANIONED LIFE OF GOD • • • •   FRAGMENT 6   3

GODDESS
        THE PROMPT STERN GODDESS   • • • • • • 51 CONSOLATION   51
        DID THE JUST GODDESS   • • • • • • 51 CONSOLATION   57
        THE LOVELIEST GODDESS SHE IN HEAVEN BY ALL • • • • 116 BALDER DEAD 3   91
        FOR I TOO AM A GODDESS BORN OF THEE   • • • • 121 BALDER DEAD 3   284
        O CIRCE GODDESS   • • • • 185 STRAYED REVEL   2
        STIRS THY HAIR GODDESS   • • • • 186 STRAYED REVEL   21
        CAME BREAKING GODDESS   • • • • 186 STRAYED REVEL   28
        THY PALACE GODDESS   • • • • 187 STRAYED REVEL   44
        I DRANK GODDESS   • • • • 187 STRAYED REVEL   50
        WONDERFUL GODDESS BY THY ART   • • • • 188 STRAYED REVEL   77
        WHAT YOUTH GODDESS WHAT GUEST   • • • • 188 STRAYED REVEL   94
        TO THY SIDE GODDESS FROM WITHIN   • • • • 189 STRAYED REVEL   100
        AH GOLDEN-HAIRD STRANGELY SMILING GODDESS • • • 194 STRAYED REVEL   286
        O CIRCE GODDESS   • • • • 194 STRAYED REVEL   293
        BIRTH-GODDESS AND THE AUSTERE FATES FIRST GAVE • • 195 FRAG ANTIGONE   10
        WHICH THE DAWN-GODDESS BORE   • • • • 196 FRAG ANTIGONE   55
        SHE THOUGH A GODDESS BORN   • • • • 197 FRAG ANTIGONE   68
        A SIGH THE GODDESS GAVE AND WITH A FROWN   • • • 447 WESTMIN ABBEY   94
        AND HE WAS GIVEN A VOICE BY THE WHITE-ARMD   HOMER TRANS   46
                GODDESS HERA

GODDESSES
        CAME WITH THE GODDESSES WHO WROUGHT HER WILL   • • 102 BALDER DEAD 1   269
        SHE SPAKE AND ALL THE GODDESSES BEWAILD   • • • • 117 BALDER DEAD 3   123

GODLIKE
        THE SEEDS OF GODLIKE POWER ARE IN US STILL • • • •   4 EMERSONS ESSAYS   12
        SOULS AS LITTLE GODLIKE AS THEIR OWN   • • • • • 34 NEW SIRENS   250

GODS
        GODS ARE WE BARDS SAINTS HEROES IF WE WILL • • • •   4 EMERSONS ESSAYS   13
        SO MEN UNRAVELLING GODS HARMONIOUS WHOLE   • • • •   4 BUTLERS SERMONS   3
        THE GODS DECLARE MY RECOMPENCE TO-DAY   • • • •   9 MYCERINUS   16
        MANS JUSTICE FROM THE ALL-JUST GODS WAS GIVEN   • •   9 MYCERINUS   20
        DID SHADOW SOMEWHAT OF THE LIFE OF GODS   • • • •   9 MYCERINUS   24
        NOT GODS BUT GHOSTS IN FROZEN APATHY   • • • • •   9 MYCERINUS   36
        SWEEPS EARTH AND HEAVEN AND MEN AND GODS ALONG • •   9 MYCERINUS   39
        BUT HIDES IF GODS GODS CARELESS OF OUR DOOM   • • 10 MYCERINUS   54
        BUT HIDES IF GODS GODS CARELESS OF OUR DOOM   • • 10 MYCERINUS   54
        AND THE DULL GODS BEHOLD ERE THESE ARE FLOWN • • 10 MYCERINUS   65
        SOMETHING YET WHAT I KNOW NOT FOR THE GODS • • • • 10 MYCERINUS   69
        OF THE GREAT GODS IS PLAIN AND YE MUST BRING • • 11 MYCERINUS   75
        THE PRAISE OF GODS RICH BOON AND LENGTH OF DAYS • • 11 MYCERINUS   78
        WHIRLS EARTH AND HEAVEN AND MEN AND GODS ALONG • •   9 MYCERINUS   V 39
        BEARS EARTH AND HEAVEN AND MEN AND GODS ALONG   • •   9 MYCERINUS   V 39
        YET THIS GLEAND WHEN GODS WERE SPEAKING   • • • • 28 NEW SIRENS   79
        YET I THINK AT GODS TRIBUNAL   • • • • • 29 NEW SIRENS   91
        SYLVAN GODS OF THIS FAIR SHADE   • • • • 34 NEW SIRENS   244
        ARE THE BLESSED GODS DISMAYD   • • • • 34 NEW SIRENS   246
        ARE THE HAPPY GODS DISMAYD   • • • • 34 NEW SIRENS   V 246
        WHICH ALL THE GODS IN SPORT HAD IDLY THROWN   • • 95 BALDER DEAD 1   3
        AND ALL THE GODS AND ALL THE HEROES CAME   • • • • 95 BALDER DEAD 1   9
        ENOUGH OF TEARS YE GODS ENOUGH OF WAIL   • • • • 95 BALDER DEAD 1   18
        FOR YE YOURSELVES YE GODS SHALL MEET YOUR DOOM • • 96 BALDER DEAD 1   28
        THE FOE THE ACCUSER WHOM THOUGH GODS WE HATE • • 96 BALDER DEAD 1   38

GODS   (CONTINUED)

SO SPAKE THE KING OF GODS AND STRAIGHTWAY ROSE   • •   96 BALDER DEAD 1   46
NOR TOWRD VALHALLA AND THE SORROWING GODS   • • • •   97 BALDER DEAD 1   58
FOR WELL HE KNEW THE GODS WOULD HEED HIS WORD   • •   97 BALDER DEAD 1   59
BUT IN VALHALLA ALL THE GODS WENT BACK   • • • •   97 BALDER DEAD 1   61
BUT THE BLIND HODER LEFT THE FEASTING GODS   • • • •   97 BALDER DEAD 1   72
AND PAST THE HAVEN WHERE THE GODS HAVE MOORD   • •   97 BALDER DEAD 1   74
OF FREA HONOURD MOTHER OF THE GODS   • • • • •   97 BALDER DEAD 1   85
THE FOE THE ACCUSER WHOM THOUGH GODS WE HATE   • •   98 BALDER DEAD 1   101
AT WHOM THE GODS IN SPORT THEIR WEAPONS THREW   • •   98 BALDER DEAD 1   103
HE SPOKE THE MOTHER OF THE GODS REPLIED   • • •   98 BALDER DEAD 1   111
FOR MANY GODS IN HEAVEN NOT THOU ALONE   • • • •   98 BALDER DEAD 1   119
WHICH GODS AND HEROES LEAD IN FEAST AND FRAY   • •   98 BALDER DEAD 1   123
AND STRAIGHT THE MOTHER OF THE GODS REPLIED   • •   99 BALDER DEAD 1   134
NOR MUST HE CHOOSE THAT COMMON PATH OF GODS   • •   99 BALDER DEAD 1   139
AND STRAIGHT THE MOTHER OF THE GODS REPLIED   • •   100 BALDER DEAD 1   187
THEN FROM THEIR LOATHED FEAST THE GODS AROSE   • •   101 BALDER DEAD 1   203
THERE TO HIS HALL THE GODS BROUGHT BALDER HOME   • •   101 BALDER DEAD 1   214
SO THOU MIGHTST LIVE AND STILL DELIGHT THE GODS   • •   101 BALDER DEAD 1   218
BUT THERE WAS ONE THE FIRST OF ALL THE GODS   • • •   101 BALDER DEAD 1   220
AND ALL THE GODS LAY DOWN IN THEIR OWN HOMES   • • •   102 BALDER DEAD 1   248
LOATHING TO MEET AT DAWN THE OTHER GODS   • • • •   102 BALDER DEAD 1   250
AND THE GODS TREMBLED ON THEIR GOLDEN BEDS   • • • •   102 BALDER DEAD 1   262
FOR WITH TO-MORROWS DAWN THE GODS PREPARE   • • •   103 BALDER DEAD 1   295
DEATH FROM THY HEAD AND WITH THE GODS IN HEAVEN   • •   104 BALDER DEAD 1   311
FOR OF THE RACE OF GODS IS NO ONE THERE   • • • •   104 BALDER DEAD 1   318
WHILE WE YET LIVED AMONG THE OTHER GODS   • • • •   104 BALDER DEAD 1   330
FREA THE MOTHER OF THE GODS WITH STROKE   • • • •   104 BALDER DEAD 1   339
FOR YOU YOURSELVES YE GODS SHALL MEET YOUR DOOM   • •   96 BALDER DEAD 1   V   28
SO HAVING SPOKE THE KING OF GODS AROSE   • • • •   96 BALDER DEAD 1   V   46
NOR TOWARDS VALHALLA AND THE SORROWING GODS   • •   97 BALDER DEAD 1   V   58
WARNING THE GODS THAT FOES DRAW NIGH TO HEAVEN   • •   105 BALDER DEAD 2   7
TO WAKE THE GODS AND HEROES TO THEIR TASKS   • • •   105 BALDER DEAD 2   9
AND ALL THE GODS AND ALL THE HEROES WOKE   • • •   105 BALDER DEAD 2   10
TO GLAD THE GODS AND FEAST IN ODINS HALL   • • •   105 BALDER DEAD 2   28
BUT THE GODS WENT NOT NOW AS OTHERWHILE   • • • •   105 BALDER DEAD 2   29
THERE ALL THE GODS IN SILENCE SATE THEM DOWN   • •   106 BALDER DEAD 2   39
GO QUICKLY GODS BRING WOOD TO THE SEASHORE   • • •   106 BALDER DEAD 2   41
ON THE TWELFTH DAY THE GODS SHALL BURN HIS CORPSE   • •   106 BALDER DEAD 2   44
SO SAID HE AND THE GODS AROSE AND TOOK   • • • •   106 BALDER DEAD 2   47
AND BURST THEIR ROOTS WHILE TO THEIR TOPS THE GODS   106 BALDER DEAD 2   57
AND BY THE DARKLING FOREST-PATHS THE GODS   • • •   106 BALDER DEAD 2   63
BUT WHEN THE GODS WERE TO THE FOREST GONE   • • •   106 BALDER DEAD 2   70
FAR HENCE IN ASGARD IN THE CITY OF GODS   • • • •   108 BALDER DEAD 2   114
O HERMOD RARELY DO THE FEET OF GODS   • • • • •   108 BALDER DEAD 2   119
OR OF THE HORSES OF THE GODS RESOUND   • • • • •   108 BALDER DEAD 2   120
O HELA WHEREFORE SHOULD THE GODS DECLARE   • • •   110 BALDER DEAD 2   189
FOR HEAVEN WAS BALDER BORN THE CITY OF GODS   • •   110 BALDER DEAD 2   198
DO THE GODS SEND TO ME TO MAKE THEM BLEST   • • •   110 BALDER DEAD 2   204
SMALL BLISS MY RACE HATH OF THE GODS OBTAINED   • •   110 BALDER DEAD 2   205
WROUGHT BY THE GODS AND ASK THE GODS OUR AID   • •   111 BALDER DEAD 2   226
WROUGHT BY THE GODS AND ASK THE GODS OUR AID   • •   111 BALDER DEAD 2   226
LET GODS MEN BRUTES BEWEEP HIM PLANTS AND STONES   • •   111 BALDER DEAD 2   238
FOR NOT UNMINDFUL OF THEE ARE THE GODS   • • •   112 BALDER DEAD 2   254
ALIVE THOU WAST OF GODS THE MOST BELOVED   • • •   112 BALDER DEAD 2   259
AND TELL THE HEAVEN-BORN GODS HOW THOU HAST SEEN   • •   112 BALDER DEAD 2   276
THEN HERMOD KNEW WHAT LABOUR HELD THE GODS   • • •   113 BALDER DEAD 2   307
THE GODS ON THE SEA-SHORE BY BALDERS SHIP   • • •   113 BALDER DEAD 2   310
ALIVE THOU WERT OF GODS THE MOST BELOVED   • • •   112 BALDER DEAD 2   V   259
THE GODS HELD TALK TOGETHER GROUPD IN KNOTS   • • •   113 BALDER DEAD 3   1
ENEMY MOCKER WHOM THOUGH GODS WE HATE   • • • •   114 BALDER DEAD 3   22
AND GREETED ODIN AND THE GODS AND SAID   • • • •   114 BALDER DEAD 3   35
ODIN MY FATHER AND YE GODS OF HEAVEN   • • • • •   114 BALDER DEAD 3   36
LET GODS MEN BRUTES BEWEEP HIM PLANTS AND STONES   • •   114 BALDER DEAD 3   44
HE SPOKE AND ALL THE GODS TO ODIN LOOKD   • • • •   115 BALDER DEAD 3   47
YE GODS THESE TERMS MAY KEEP ANOTHER DAY   • • •   115 BALDER DEAD 3   49
HE SPOKE AND THE GODS ARMD AND ODIN DONND   • • •   115 BALDER DEAD 3   57
IN THAT GREAT DAY THE TWILIGHT OF THE GODS   • • •   115 BALDER DEAD 3   68
AMONG THE GODS AND HEROES HERE IN HEAVEN   • • •   115 BALDER DEAD 3   80
HE SPOKE AND ALL THE GODS ASSENTING WAILD   • • •   116 BALDER DEAD 3   89
YE GODS THERE WELL MAY BE TOO MUCH OF WAIL   • • •   118 BALDER DEAD 3   157
BUT WHEN THE GODS AND HEROES HEARD THEY BROUGHT   • •   118 BALDER DEAD 3   160
AND THE GODS STOOD UPON THE BEACH AND GAZED   • •   119 BALDER DEAD 3   193
BUT THE GODS WENT BY STARLIGHT UP THE SHORE   • •   119 BALDER DEAD 3   207
THEN FROM THEIR LOATHED FEAST THE GODS AROSE   • •   119 BALDER DEAD 3   214
THERE CAME THE GODS AND SATE THEM DOWN ON STONES   • •   120 BALDER DEAD 3   223
YE GODS THE TERMS YE KNOW WHICH HERMOD BROUGHT   • •   120 BALDER DEAD 3   225
BETHINK YE GODS IS THERE NO OTHER WAY   • • • •   120 BALDER DEAD 3   236
SPEAK WERE NOT THIS A WAY THE WAY FOR GODS   • • •   120 BALDER DEAD 3   237
BUT FREA MOTHER OF THE GODS AROSE   • • • • •   120 BALDER DEAD 3   246
LORD OVER MEN ON EARTH AND GODS IN HEAVEN   • • •   120 BALDER DEAD 3   251
IN THE BEGINNING ERE THE GODS WERE BORN   • • • •   121 BALDER DEAD 3   255
THEN ME THOU MADST OF US THE GODS WERE BORN   • •   121 BALDER DEAD 3   267
THINE ELDEST AND OF ME THE GODS ARE SPRUNG   • • •   121 BALDER DEAD 3   285
STRAIGHTWAY HE SPAKE AND THUS ADDRESSD THE GODS   • •   122 BALDER DEAD 3   298
WHEN THE GODS HEARD THEY STRAIGHT AROSE AND TOOK   • •   122 BALDER DEAD 3   302
AND THERE FELL JOY UPON THE GODS TO HEAR   • • •   122 BALDER DEAD 3   319
WITH MEN BUT LIVES A HOSTAGE WITH THE GODS   • • •   123 BALDER DEAD 3   325
YE GODS GOOD LACK IS IT SO DULL IN HEAVEN   • • • •   123 BALDER DEAD 3   337
SO YE GROW SQUEAMISH GODS AND SNIFF AT HEAVEN   • •   123 BALDER DEAD 3   344

GODS

(CONTINUED)

SO THE GODS CROSS WAS BITTERER FOR THEIR JOY	124 BALDER DEAD 3	368
NOT DAILY TO ENDURE ABHORRING GODS	125 BALDER DEAD 3	398
BUT GODS ARE LIKE THE SONS OF MEN IN THIS	125 BALDER DEAD 3	426
IN HEAVEN NOR LET THE OTHER GODS LAMENT	126 BALDER DEAD 3	457
AGAINST THE GODS UPON THE PLAINS OF HEAVEN	127 BALDER DEAD 3	481
MOURN NOT FOR ME MOURN HERMOD FOR THE GODS	127 BALDER DEAD 3	484
MOURN FOR THE MEN ON EARTH THE GODS IN HEAVEN	127 BALDER DEAD 3	485
TO OTHER GODS IT WERE IS MY ENFORCED	127 BALDER DEAD 3	501
SHALL A SMALL REMNANT OF THE GODS REPAIR	128 BALDER DEAD 3	525
AND PASTIME OF THE GODS THE WISE DISCOURSE	129 BALDER DEAD 3	541
GODS WISDOM AND GODS GOODNESS ARE DISPLAYD	171 DIVINITY	4
GODS WISDOM AND GODS GOODNESS ARE DISPLAYD	171 DIVINITY	4
GODS WISDOM AND GODS GOODNESS AY BUT FOOLS	171 DIVINITY	9
GODS WISDOM AND GODS GOODNESS AY BUT FOOLS	171 DIVINITY	9
BUT AT GODS ALTAR OH REMEMBER ME	173 MONICAS PRAYER	4
I HEAR A GODS TREMENDOUS VOICE	174 MEETING	11
OF GODS OR MORTALS	188 STRAYED REVEL	95
OF GODS AND HEROES	189 STRAYED REVEL	124
THE GODS ARE HAPPY	190 STRAYED REVEL	130
THE GODS BEHOLD THEM	192 STRAYED REVEL	200
TIRESIAS BUT THE GODS	192 STRAYED REVEL	213
THE GODS EXACT FOR SONG	193 STRAYED REVEL	233
ARE TO THE GODS A CARE	196 FRAG ANTIGONE	32
FAR FROM THE GODS WITH HERS	197 FRAG ANTIGONE	74
SUCCUMBD TO THE ENVY OF UNKIND GODS	197 FRAG ANTIGONE	77
TO FEAR ASSAULT OF ENVIOUS GODS	197 FRAG ANTIGONE	81
DO YOU SEEK COUNSEL OF THE GODS	198 FRAG DEJANEIRA	6
THE GODS HAVE SAID THAT REPOSE	199 FRAG DEJANEIRA	20
FOR GODS SAKE BELIEVE IT THEN	215 PIS-ALLER	12
ARE GODS WORST PORTION TO MANKIND	217 NAMELESS EPIT	V
LEAVE THEN THE CROSS AS YE HAVE LEFT CARVED GODS	237 PROGRESS	27
QUENCH THEN THE ALTAR FIRES OF YOUR OLD GODS	237 PROGRESS	V 27
IN WHAT STATE GODS OTHER WORKS MAY BE	240 SELF-DEPENDENCE	26
PONDERING GODS MYSTERIES UNTOLD	278 SOUTHERN NIGHT	89
THINKING OF HIS OWN GODS A GREEK	301 GRANDE CHARTR	81
THE LATE-RELENTING GODS WITH VICTORY BROUGHT	330 MEROPE	6
TO HIS AVENGING SHADE AND TO THE GODS	332 MEROPE	73
NOT HELP OF MEN ALTHOUGH PERHAPS OF GODS	341 MEROPE	357
WHAT GODS THE GODS OF CONCORD CIVIL WEAL	341 MEROPE	358
WHAT GODS THE GODS OF CONCORD CIVIL WEAL	341 MEROPE	358
NO THE AVENGING GODS WHO PUNISH CRIME	341 MEROPE	359
CLASH WITH JUSTICE THE GODS	348 MEROPE	537
SEND AN AVENGER GODS OF THE DEAD	348 MEROPE	543
THAT DOOM OBTAIN EFFECT FROM GODS OR MEN	349 MEROPE	558
AND PRAY THE GODS AND PRAY THE ALL-SEEING SUN	349 MEROPE	570
THENCE BY THE SEA-GODS SANCTUARY AND THE TOMB	356 MEROPE	740
A HELPLESS ONE I KNOW IT BUT THE GODS	366 MEROPE	1023
O MISTRESS BY THE GODS DO NOTHING RASH	368 MEROPE	1075
SWEAR BY THE GODS HENCEFORTH TO OBEY ME	371 MEROPE	1133
HE SLEEPS SLEEPS CALM O YE ALL-SEEING GODS	372 MEROPE	1153
O GODS FOOLISH OLD MAN THOU SPOILST MY BLOW	374 MEROPE	1194
NO BY THE GODS THOU SLAYST STAND OFF THY SON	375 MEROPE	1201
NO BY THE GODS ALIVE AND LIKE TO LIVE	377 MEROPE	1218
WE SEE DEAR MISTRESS AND WE SAY THE GODS	377 MEROPE	1225
MOTHER SOMETIMES THE JUSTICE OF THE GODS	378 MEROPE	1247
THAT HOW TO ACCOMPLISH WHAT THE GODS ENJOIN	379 MEROPE	1263
THE GODS COMMAND NOT WHERE THE HEART SPEAKS CLEAR	385 MEROPE	1404
BY THE ORACULAR SENTENCE OF THE GODS	385 MEROPE	1422
HAVE FAITH AND TRUST THE FUTURE AND THE GODS	388 MEROPE	1507
HE MAY FOR NEVER DID THE GODS ALLOW	388 MEROPE	1508
THE GODS O MISTRESS DEAR THE HARD-SOULD MAN	390 MEROPE	1577
WITH THE GODS AID AND IF THEY GIVE BUT AID	391 MEROPE	1594
WHOM THE GODS OERSHADOW	391 MEROPE	1597
THE GODS HAD PITY MADE THEM STARS	393 MEROPE	1674
MOST HONOURABLY I MEANT I CALL THE GODS	394 MEROPE	1695
THERE NURSE A LATE REMORSE AND THANK THE GODS	396 MEROPE	1755
MY FINAL VICTORY PROVES THE GODS APPEASED	397 MEROPE	1770
TO AFFRIGHT A FORTUNE WHICH THE GODS SECURE	398 MEROPE	1782
THE GODS PERHAPS ALLOWD YOU	398 MEROPE	1799
TO THE GODS OF HADES	400 MEROPE	1867
GODS UNAPPEASABLE	400 MEROPE	1875
TO THE GODS GRATEFUL SACRIFICE AND THEN	405 MEROPE	2019
AND ALL THIS BY THE WILL OF THE GODS	405 MEROPE	2024
AMISS FROM JUSTICE THE GODS	348 MEROPE	V
BUT I WILL ALSO SAY THAT WHEN THE GODS	413 EMPEDOCLES I 2	23
MIND IS A LIGHT WHICH THE GODS MOCK US WITH	413 EMPEDOCLES I 2	32
HE TOLD HIM OF THE GODS THE STARS	414 EMPEDOCLES I 2	71
A CORD THE GODS FIRST SLUNG	415 EMPEDOCLES I 2	78
THE GODS LAUGH IN THEIR SLEEVE	415 EMPEDOCLES I 2	87
SCARCE CAN ONE THINK IN CALM SO THREATENING ARE THE GODS	416 EMPEDOCLES I 2	126
NO TITLE FROM THE GODS TO WELFARE AND REPOSE	417 EMPEDOCLES I 2	161
NOR THINK THE GODS WERE CRAZED	417 EMPEDOCLES I 2	164
MAKE GODS TO WHOM TO IMPUTE	421 EMPEDOCLES I 2	279
GRANT THAT THE WORLD WERE FULL OF GODS WE CANNOT SEE	421 EMPEDOCLES I 2	286
HARSH GODS AND HOSTILE FATES	422 EMPEDOCLES I 2	304
AND FEIGN KIND GODS WHO PERFECT WHAT MAN VAINLY TRIES	422 EMPEDOCLES I 2	316
AND THUS ADDRESS THE GODS	423 EMPEDOCLES I 2	338
THAT THERE ARE GODS WHO DO	424 EMPEDOCLES I 2	350
AND THUS ADDRESS THE GODS	424 EMPEDOCLES I 2	373

GODS   (CONTINUED)
        BECAUSE THE GODS THOU FEARST   . . . .   426 EMPEDOCLES I 2   419
        THE GODS HAD TO THEIR MARRIAGE COME   . . . . .   427 EMPEDOCLES I 2   450
        AND THEN ADDRESS THE GODS   . . . .   424 EMPEDOCLES I 2   V 373
        AT LEAST THAT GODS THY LOT   EMPEDOCLES I 2   V
        LEARN THAT MEN WILL NOT AND GODS CANNOT HELP THY STATE   EMPEDOCLES I 2   V
        IN THE COURT OF GODS IN THE CITY OF MEN   . . . . 430 EMPEDOCLES II   38
        GODS AND THE RACE OF MORTALS LOVE SO WELL   . . . 431 EMPEDOCLES II   65
        ROSILY BRIGHTEN AND THE SOOTHED GODS SMILE . . . 431 EMPEDOCLES II   81
        IN AN OLDER WORLD PEOPLED BY GODS   . . . . . . 437 EMPEDOCLES II   285
        BEFORE THE GODS BEFORE MANKIND   . . . . 456 POOR MATTHIAS   134
        BUT THAT PRINCE AMONG GODS THE SON OF THE LOVELY—HAIRD HOMER TRANS   52
              LETO

GODSTOW
        AND ABOVE GODSTOW BRIDGE WHEN HAY—TIMES HERE   . . 257 SCHOLAR—GIPSY   91

GOES
        THE STREAM GOES LEAPING BY   . . . .   16 CHURCH BROU 2   3
        FROM THE FAR GRAVE TO WHICH IT GOES . . . . . .   21 YOUTH AND CALM   13
        JOY COMES AND GOES HOPE EBBS AND FLOWS   . . . .   44 QUESTION   1
        WHO GOES THAT WAY MUST TAKE NO OTHER HORSE . . . 99 BALDER DEAD 1   137
        THERES MANY A GAY KNIGHT WHERE HE GOES   . . . . 138 TRISTRAM 1   256
        THE LONE UNBROKEN VIEW GOES SPREADING CLEAR   . .   TRISTRAM 3   V 12
        GOES SLOWLY BY AND THIS AT SPEED   . . . . . .   224 EPILOG LAOCOON   116
        AND THE SEA WHERE IT GOES   . . . . 247 BURIED LIFE   98
        AND MENS INCESSANT STREAM GOES BY   . . . . . . 277 SOUTHERN NIGHT   63
        EARLY SHE GOES ON THE PATH   . . . .   283 HAWORTH CHURCH   68
        NOR LEFT GOES PASSIVELY BY   . . . .   295 HEINES GRAVE   91
        THE MULE—TRACK FROM SAINT LAURENT GOES   . . . . 299 GRANDE CHARTR   4
        GOES AN UNREVERSED DECREE   . . . .   456 POOR MATTHIAS   149

GOETHE
        GOETHE IN WEIMAR SLEEPS AND GREECE   . . . . . . 270 MEMORIAL VERSES   1
        GOETHE HAS DONE HIS PILGRIMAGE   . . . . 270 MEMORIAL VERSES   18
        WHEN GOETHE PASSD AWAY WE SAID   . . . .   270 MEMORIAL VERSES   V 15
        UNNAMED WHO GOETHE SAID   . . . .   295 HEINES GRAVE   99
        GOETHE TOO HAD BEEN THERE   . . . . 298 HEINES GRAVE   191

GOETHES
        HATH RISEN GOETHES WORDSWORTHS SONG   . . . . . . 222 EPILOG LAOCOON   29
        WHEN GOETHES DEATH WAS TOLD WE SAID . . . . . . 270 MEMORIAL VERSES   15
        GOETHES SAGE MIND AND BYRONS FORCE   . . . . . . 272 MEMORIAL VERSES   61
        AND GOETHES COURSE FEW SONS OF MEN   . . . . . . 308 OBERMANN   55
        WORDSWORTHS SWEET CALM OR GOETHES WIDE   . . . . 308 OBERMANN   79

GOING
        A TROOP OF OXFORD HUNTERS GOING HOME . . . . . . 267 THYRSIS   153
        WIDE GERMAN LAND GOING DOWN   . . . . 297 HEINES GRAVE   173

GOINGS
        THESE MOURN NOT THAT THEIR GOINGS PAY   . . . . 53 RESIGNATION   28

GOLD
        SPANND BY AERIAL ARCHES ALL OF GOLD . . . . . .   4 BUTLERS SERMONS   12
        TROOPS WITH GOLD AND GIFTS APPEARING . . . . . .   26 NEW SIRENS   23
        ON THE GOLD TERRACES   . . . .   50 CONSOLATION   V 13
        ONLY HIS HELM WAS RICH INLAID WITH GOLD   . . . . 69 SOHRAB RUSTUM   267
        CRUSTED WITH GOLD AND ON THE GROUND WERE WORKD . 69 SOHRAB RUSTUM   278
        AND IN THE HORNS AND GOLD—RIMMD SKULLS THE WINE . 95 BALDER DEAD 1   14
        AND IN THE HORNS AND GOLD—RIMMD SCULLS THE WINE . 95 BALDER DEAD 1   V 14
        TO THE HALL GLADHEIM WHICH IS BUILT OF GOLD   . . 106 BALDER DEAD 2   36
        HIS DAZZLING CORSLET AND HIS HELM OF GOLD   . . . 115 BALDER DEAD 3   58
        SINCE THEN SHE SEEKS HIM AND WEEPS TEARS OF GOLD . 116 BALDER DEAD 3   95
        AND BROUGHT HIS ARMS AND GOLD AND ALL HIS STUFF . 118 BALDER DEAD 3   169
        A GOLD HARP LEANS AGAINST THE BED   . . . . . . 131 TRISTRAM 1   17
        I KNOW HIM BY HIS HARP OF GOLD   . . . .   131 TRISTRAM 1   19
        WITH THE CLASP OF BURNISHD GOLD . . . .   131 TRISTRAM 1   28
        CIRCLED TRISTRAM BY A BAND OF GOLD   . . . . . . 143 TRISTRAM 2   44
        HOUR AFTER HOUR HER GOLD CURLS SWEEPING IT . . . 152 TRISTRAM 3   83
        HER ROSARY—BEADS OF EBONY TIPPD WITH GOLD   . . . 152 TRISTRAM 3   93
        SITS NECKAN WITH HIS HARP OF GOLD   . . . . . . 159 NECKAN   3
        HE SATE AND PLAYD HIS HARP OF GOLD   . . . . . . 160 NECKAN   43
        AND PLAYST THY HARP OF GOLD   . . . .   160 NECKAN   50
        SITS NECKAN WITH HIS HARP OF GOLD   . . . . . . 161 NECKAN   67
        ON A RED GOLD THRONE IN THE HEART OF THE SEA . . 163 FORSAKEN MERM   51
        OF GOLD AND IVORY   . . . .   191 STRAYED REVEL   194
        SOON SHALL WE HAVE GOLD—DUSTED SNAPDRAGON   . . . 264 THYRSIS   64
        THIS DOES NOT COME WITH HOUSES OR WITH GOLD   . . 268 THYRSIS   203
        GOLD FURZE WITH BROOM IN BLOSSOM VIES   . . . . 274 STANZAS CARNAC   19
        GOLD BROOM WITH FURZE IN BLOSSOM VIES   . . . . 274 STANZAS CARNAC   V 19
        PUT TIGHTNESS IN THY GOLD—EMBOSSED REIN   . . . . 349 MEROPE   574
        TO AEPYTUS THE KING SEDUCED WITH GOLD   . . . . 364 MEROPE   970
        REFRESHD AND CLAIM THY MASTERS THANKS AND GOLD . 373 MEROPE   1182
        HEAR THAT FRESH VOICE AND CLASP THAT GOLD—LOCKD HEAD 387 MEROPE   1460
        HIS FLOWING LOCKS AND GOLD—ENCIRCLED BROW   . . . 408 EMPEDOCLES I 1   60
        THE GOLD—FLOWERD BROOM   . . . .   442 EMPEDOCLES II   440
        SHEPHERDING HIS FLOCK OF GOLD   . . . .   457 POOR MATTHIAS   185

GOLDEN
        OR IN MID—HEAVEN PERHAPS YOUR GOLDEN CARS   . . . 10 MYCERINUS   43

GOLDEN   (CONTINUED)
          FLUSHD GUESTS AND GOLDEN GOBLETS FOAMD WITH WINE • •   11 MYCERINUS   97
          LAY THE WARM GOLDEN GOURDS GOLDEN WITHIN   • • • •   25 DREAM   18
          LAY THE WARM GOLDEN GOURDS GOLDEN WITHIN   • • • •   25 DREAM   18
          AND THROUGH GOLDEN HORNS TO GREET YOU   • • • •   29 NEW SIRENS   103
          FROM THE GOLDEN SPRINGS OF DAWN   • • • • • •   26 NEW SIRENS   V 22
          CORN IN A GOLDEN PLATTER SOAKD WITH WINE   • • • •   83 SOHRAB RUSTUM   754
          THE GOLDEN MACE-BEARERS ASIDE   • • • • • •   88 SICK KING BOKH   34
          UP TO ITS GOLDEN ROOF WITH SOBS AND CRIES   • • • •   95 BALDER DEAD 1   12
          AND ON THEIR GOLDEN CHAIRS THEY SATE AGAIN • • • •   97 BALDER DEAD 1   64
          UPON HER GOLDEN CHAIR THE MOTHER SATE   • • • •   98 BALDER DEAD 1   92
          WHICH SPANS WITH GOLDEN ARCHES GIALLS STREAM • •   99 BALDER DEAD 1   148
          AND THE GODS TREMBLED ON THEIR GOLDEN BEDS • • •   102 BALDER DEAD 1   262
          THE GOLDEN-CRESTED COCK BEGAN TO CROW   • • •   105 BALDER DEAD 2   4
          WHERE ARE IN CIRCLE RANGED TWELVE GOLDEN CHAIRS •   106 BALDER DEAD 2   37
          WHICH SPANS WITH GOLDEN ARCHES GIALLS STREAM • •   107 BALDER DEAD 2   86
          IN ASGARD AND THE GOLDEN HALLS WERE DUMB   • • •   113 BALDER DEAD 2   306
          IN ASGARD BUT THE GOLDEN HALLS WERE DUMB   • • •   113 BALDER DEAD 2   V 306
          AND FREYA NEXT CAME NIGH WITH GOLDEN TEARS • • •   116 BALDER DEAD 3   90
          AND WEEP FROM SHORE TO SHORE MY GOLDEN TEARS • •   116 BALDER DEAD 3   110
          WEEP NOT O FREYA WEEP NO GOLDEN TEARS   • • •   116 BALDER DEAD 3   114
          A LAST CHOICE GIFT THEREON HIS GOLDEN RING • • •   118 BALDER DEAD 3   173
          AND SUBSTANCE AND A GOLDEN HOUSE IN HEAVEN • • •   125 BALDER DEAD 3   404
          THE GOLDEN-CRESTED COCK SHALL SOUND ALARM   • • •   127 BALDER DEAD 3   496
          THE GOLDEN DICE WHEREWITH WE PLAYD OF YORE • • •   128 BALDER DEAD 3   539
          THE GOLDEN DICE WITH WHICH WE PLAYD OF YORE • •   128 BALDER DEAD 3   V 539
          HER SNOW-WHITE HANDS HER GOLDEN HAIR • • •   132 TRISTRAM 1   51
          REACH ME MY GOLDEN PHIAL STANDS BY THEE   • • •   133 TRISTRAM 1   100
          PLEDGE ME IN MY GOLDEN CUP   • • • • • •   135 TRISTRAM 1   146
          HARDLY LETS PEEP THE GOLDEN-HAIR   • • • •   141 TRISTRAM 1   341
          I KNOW HER BY HER GOLDEN HAIR   • • • • •   132 TRISTRAM 1   V 50
          REACH ME MY GOLDEN CUP THAT STANDS BY THEE • •   133 TRISTRAM 1   V 100
          AND THAT GOLDEN CUP HER MOTHER   • • • • •   134 TRISTRAM 1   V 136
          AND THE GOLDEN BRACELETS HEAVY AND RARE   • • •   146 TRISTRAM 2   110
          THY GOLDEN-TASSELLD BUGLE BLOW   • • • • •   149 TRISTRAM 2   188
          IN BLINDING MASSES SHOWERD THE GOLDEN HAIR • • •   150 TRISTRAM 3   34
          THROUGH WHOSE GREEN BOUGHS THE GOLDEN SUNSHINE CREEPS   154 TRISTRAM 3   157
          AND THE GLEAM OF HER GOLDEN HAIR   • • • • •   164 FORSAKEN MERM   107
          AH GOLDEN-HAIRD STRANGELY SMILING GODDESS   • • •   194 STRAYED REVEL   286
          TO LOOK TOWRD ARDRES GOLDEN FIELD   • • • • •   204 CALAIS SANDS   5
          TO SEE TOWRD ARDRES GOLDEN FIELD   • • • • •   204 CALAIS SANDS   V   5
          A GOLDEN DAYS DECLINE   • • • • • • • •   212 GROWING OLD   15
          AND ALL THE MARVEL OF THE GOLDEN SKIES   • • •   268 THYRSIS   190
          HERE WAS THINE HEIGHT OF STRENGTH THY GOLDEN PRIME   269 THYRSIS   219
          ITS GOLDEN RAIN ON EARTH CONFERS   • • • • •   277 SOUTHERN NIGHT   54
          OF HER GREATEST GOLDEN-MOUTHD SONS • • • • •   294 HEINES GRAVE   79
          A GOLDEN CIRCLET ON HER QUEENLY BROW • • • •   331 MEROPE   58
          THY HEAD DROOPD SOFTLY AND THE GOLDEN CURLS • •   373 MEROPE   1161
          AT ONE ANOTHER FROM THEIR GOLDEN CHAIRS   • • •   431 EMPEDOCLES II   82
          MY GOLDEN CIRCLET   • • • • • • • • •   432 EMPEDOCLES II   119
          VAINLY KISS HIS GOLDEN CREST   • • • • •   452 POOR MATTHIAS   10
          PRAISED THY GOLDEN LIVERY   • • • • • • •   455 POOR MATTHIAS   118
          AND THAT GOLDEN-FRUITED STRAND   • • • • •   PILLARS UNIVERS   1

GONE
          LABOURERS THAT SHALL NOT FAIL WHEN MAN IS GONE • •   2 QUIET WORK   14
          EACH TO HIS LABOUR AND WHEN ALL WERE GONE   • • •   EMERSONS ESSAYS V   7
          GONE O KNIGHTS IS SHE YOU KNEW   • • • • •   • •   15 CHURCH BROU 1   82
          DEAD OUR DUKE AND GONE HIS DUCHESS • • • •   15 CHURCH BROU 1   83
          THEY ARE GONE ALL IS STILL FOOLISH HEART DOST   19 MODERN SAPPHO   1
                  THOU QUIVER
          ONCE I SAID A FACE IS GONE   • • • • • • • •   23 MEMORY-PICTURE   9
          YOUNG I SAID A FACE IS GONE • • • • • • • •   23 MEMORY-PICTURE   V   9
          LONG I SAID A FACE IS GONE   • • • • • • • •   23 MEMORY-PICTURE   V   9
          OF THAT PRIMAL AGE IS GONE   • • • • • • •   27 NEW SIRENS   50
          AND THE JOYFUL DAWN WERE GONE   • • • • •   30 NEW SIRENS   118
          OF IMMORTAL FEET IS GONE • • • • • • •   34 NEW SIRENS   252
          LO SAILS THAT GLEAM A MOMENT AND ARE GONE   • •   42 GIPSY CHILD   5
          THAT SEVERD THE WORLDS MARCH AND THINE BE GONE •   44 GIPSY CHILD   62
          THAT SEVERD THE WORLDS MARCH AND THINE IS GONE •   44 GIPSY CHILD   V 62
          THEIR HOUR IS GONE   • • • • • • • • •   51 CONSOLATION   55
          AND CUNNING ALL THE PITY I HAD IS GONE   • • •   75 SOHRAB RUSTUM   467
          FOR THOU HAST GONE WHERE I SHALL NEVER GO   • •   83 SOHRAB RUSTUM   748
          NOW I AT NIGHTFALL HAD GONE FORTH   • • • •   90 SICK KING BOKH   65
          BUT WHEN THE GODS WERE TO THE FOREST GONE   • •   106 BALDER DEAD 2   70
          BALDER HATH GONE THIS WAY AND TAEN THE ROAD •   108 BALDER DEAD 2   122
          BALDER MY BROTHER THOU ART GONE A ROAD   • •   116 BALDER DEAD 3   99
          TO THE WORLDS END AND BALDER NOW IS GONE   • •   117 BALDER DEAD 3   121
          WHOM WE MAY BID TO SING THOUGH THOU ART GONE •   117 BALDER DEAD 3   134
          TELL ME THAT I MAY PONDER IT WHEN GONE   • •   128 BALDER DEAD 3   516
          IS ALREADY GONE AND PAST   • • • • • • •   136 TRISTRAM 1   174
          TO BED AND SLEEP MY FEVER IS GONE BY • • • •   140 TRISTRAM 1   309
          GLEAMS AND IS GONE THE CLIFFS OF ENGLAND STAND •   210 DOVER BEACH   4
          SHINES AND IS GONE THE CLIFFS OF ENGLAND   • •   210 DOVER BEACH   V   4
          THE LAST-LEFT HAYMAKER IS GONE   • • • • •   218 BACCHANALIA 1   9
          THE LAST BELATED GLEANER GONE   • • • • •   218 BACCHANALIA 1   V   9
          THE FAMOUS POETS SUNG AND GONE   • • • • •   219 BACCHANALIA 2   4
          AND AFTER WE AWHILE HAD GONE • • • • • • •   221 EPILOG LAOCOON   4
          MIGHTY THEIR PATHOS BUT TIS GONE   • • • • •   224 EPILOG LAOCOON   92
          THOUGH THE MUSE BE GONE AWAY • • • • • •   227 PERSIST POETRY   1
          CAN I FEEL THAT THEIR POET IS GONE • • • • •   229 YOUTH OF NATURE   27

GONE   (CONTINUED)
          BUT ARE LOST WHEN THEIR WATCHER IS GONE   • • •   230 YOUTH OF NATURE   74
          THEY ARE DUST THEY ARE CHANGED THEY ARE GONE   • •   232 YOUTH OF NATURE   133
          GONE IS THE CALM OF ITS EARLIER SHORE   • • •   253 FUTURE   52
          AND THE TIRED MEN AND DOGS ALL GONE TO REST   • •   255 SCHOLAR-GIPSY   7
          BUT WHEN THEY CAME FROM BATHING THOU WAST GONE •   258 SCHOLAR-GIPSY   100
          AND THOU FROM EARTH ART GONE   • • • • • •   259 SCHOLAR-GIPSY   136
          BUT WHEN THEY CAME FROM BATHING THOU WERT GONE •   258 SCHOLAR-GIPSY   V 100
          AND FROM THE SIGN IS GONE SIBYLLAS NAME   • •   262 THYRSIS   4
          AGAINST THE WEST I MISS IT IS IT GONE   • • •   263 THYRSIS   27
          THE BLOOM IS GONE AND WITH THE BLOOM GO I   • •   264 THYRSIS   60
          DOWN EACH GREEN BANK HATH GONE THE PLOUGHBOYS TEAM   266 THYRSIS   118
          THEY ALL ARE GONE AND THOU ART GONE AS WELL   • •   266 THYRSIS   130
          THEY ALL ARE GONE AND THOU ART GONE AS WELL   • •   266 THYRSIS   130
          YES THOU ART GONE AND ROUND ME TOO THE NIGHT   •   266 THYRSIS   131
          THERE THOU ART GONE AND ME THOU LEAVEST HERE   •   268 THYRSIS   191
          OUT OF THE HEED OF MORTALS HE IS GONE   • • •   269 THYRSIS   208
          HE HEARKENS NOT LIGHT COMER HE IS GONE   • • •   265 THYRSIS   V 71
          OUT OF THE HEED OF MORTALS IS HE GONE   • • •   269 THYRSIS   V 208
          WORDSWORTH HAS GONE FROM US AND YE   • • • •   271 MEMORIAL VERSES   40
          HEARS THY VOICE RIGHT NOW HE IS GONE   • • •   272 MEMORIAL VERSES   74
          WORDSWORTH IS GONE FROM US AND YE   • • • •   271 MEMORIAL VERSES   V 40
          FIFTEEN YEARS HAVE GONE ROUND   • • • • • •   287 RUGBY CHAPEL   26
          FOAMD FOR A MOMENT AND GONE   • • • • • •   288 RUGBY CHAPEL   72
          IN THE NOBLE AND GREAT WHO ARE GONE   • • • •   290 RUGBY CHAPEL   146
          FOR BOTH WERE FAITHS AND BOTH ARE GONE   • •   301 GRANDE CHARTR   84
          THE NOBLENESS OF GRIEF IS GONE   • • • • • •   302 GRANDE CHARTR   107
          KNOWS HOW THE DAY HATH GONE   • • • • • •   309 OBERMANN   102
          FOR THOU ART GONE AWAY FROM EARTH   • • • •   310 OBERMANN   141
          THE PAST ITS MASK OF UNION GONE   • • • • • •   320 OBERMANN MORE   227
          THEIR LOAD AND GONE AWAY   • • • • • •   315 OBERMANN MORE   V 82
          NAMED AEPYTUS LIKE HIM HAVING GONE IN   • • •   357 MEROPE   777
          THE PRICKERS SHOUTED THAT THE STAG WAS GONE   •   357 MEROPE   788
          THERE THE LAKE-WATERS WHICH IN AGES GONE   • •   358 MEROPE   814
          AND TOOK THREE STRIDES QUARRY AND DOGS WERE GONE •   358 MEROPE   830
          THE YOUTH IS GONE WITHIN ALAS HE BEARS   • •   359 MEROPE   873
          O HONOURD QUEEN THY SON MY CHARGE IS GONE   • •   362 MEROPE   944
          NEER TO HAVE GONE FROM THESE EYES   • • • •   377 MEROPE   1230
          CONDEMND BY PRUDENCE HAVE SOMETIMES GONE WELL •   383 MEROPE   1385
          THE HOUR FOR WORDS IS GONE IS COME FOR DEEDS   •   386 MEROPE   1445
          SOMETIMES WHEN HE WAS GONE I WISHD HIM BACK   •   387 MEROPE   1457
          MANY A MORNING HAD THEY GONE   • • • •   434 EMPEDOCLES II   171
          HIS MATES ARE GONE AND HE   • • • • • •   444 WESTMIN ABBEY   21
          GO AND NOW HIMSELF IS GONE   • • • • • •   458 POOR MATTHIAS   205
          AND THOU ART GONE WHERE GEIST HATH GONE   • •   460 KAISER DEAD   65
          AND THOU ART GONE WHERE GEIST HATH GONE   • •   460 KAISER DEAD   65
          FLOAT UP TO TELL OF AGES THAT ARE GONE   • • •   470 ALARIC AT ROME   208
          FROM THE STERN FUTURE AND THE YEARS GONE BY   • •   475 CROMWELL   110

GOOD
          AND IN THAT MORE LIE ALL HIS HOPES OF GOOD   • • •   5 HARMONY NATURE   6
          I LOVED THE GOOD HE SCORND AND HATED WRONG   • • •   9 MYCERINUS   15
          WHERE GOOD MEN ARE NOT STRONG   • • • •   39 STAGIRIUS   V 40
          BY CHALLENGE FORTH MAKE GOOD THY VAUNT OR YIELD •   72 SOHRAB RUSTUM   367
          WITH THEIR THICK-FALLING TEARS SO GOOD A FRIEND •   115 BALDER DEAD 3   63
          YE GODS GOOD LACK IS IT SO DULL IN HEAVEN   • •   123 BALDER DEAD 3   337
          WHOSE MANGER IS STUFFD FULL OF GOOD FRESH HAY •   123 BALDER DEAD 3   341
          HIS SWORD IS SHARP HIS HORSE IS GOOD   • • • •   138 TRISTRAM 1   249
          TO BED GOOD NIGHT   • • • • • • •   140 TRISTRAM 1   314
          SHE WILL GRANT IT SHE IS KIND AND GOOD   • • •   145 TRISTRAM 2   96
          HER MOODS GOOD LACK THEY PASS LIKE SHOWERS   • •   146 TRISTRAM 2   125
          DID THAT CHANCE ACT OF GOOD THAT ONE   • • • •   158 SAINT BRANDAN   58
          FORGOT MY GOOD AS SOON AS DONE   • • • • •   158 SAINT BRANDAN   60
          SHE HER GOOD SHEPHERDS HASTY IMAGE DREW   •   172 GOOD SHEPHERD   13
          AS GOOD AS GENEROUS AS THEY ARE   • • • •   179 FAREWELL   64
          TO SELF-SELECTED GOOD   • • • • • •   196 FRAG ANTIGONE   29
          GOOD POEMS IF HE LOOKD MORE RARE   • • • •   221 EPILOG LAOCOON   17
          THOUGH MANY THAN GOOD STATUES WERE   • • • •   221 EPILOG LAOCOON   18
          SWEET AND FORGIVING AND GOOD   • • • •   232 YOUTH OF MAN   15
          RALLY THE GOOD IN THE DEPTHS OF THYSELF   • •   235 YOUTH OF MAN   118
          HOW IT WERE GOOD TO ABIDE THERE AND BREATHE FREE   244 SUMMER NIGHT   90
          HOW IT WERE GOOD TO SINK THERE AND BREATHE FREE   244 SUMMER NIGHT   V 90
          HOW IT WERE GOOD TO LIVE THERE AND BREATHE FREE   244 SUMMER NIGHT   V 90
          AND CAME AS MOST MEN DEEMD TO LITTLE GOOD   • • •   256 SCHOLAR-GIPSY   39
          SOME GOOD SURVIVOR WITH HIS FLUTE WOULD GO   •   265 THYRSIS   83
          AND LEAVE NO GOOD BEHIND   • • • • • •   273 EDW QUILLINAN   6
          THE HUMBLE GOOD FROM THE GROUND   • • • •   287 RUGBY CHAPEL   50
          FERVENT HEROIC AND GOOD   • • • • • •   291 RUGBY CHAPEL   160
          MY GRANDFATHER THE GOOD ARCADIAN KING   331 MEROPE   33
          FOR TYRANTS MAKE MAN GOOD BEYOND HIMSELF   331 MEROPE   42
          THIS GOOD HE MEANT YOU AND FOR THIS HE DIED   •   339 MEROPE   313
          IN REASON GOOD WHICH JUSTIFIED MY DEED   • • •   340 MEROPE   340
          AND STAMP HIMSELF THEREAFTER BAD OR GOOD   • •   352 MEROPE   651
          WELL SOMETIMES MAY THE GOOD DESIRE   • • •   353 MEROPE   665
          ARMD FOR RIGHT ONLY AND THE GENERAL GOOD   • •   353 MEROPE   685
          ACCEPT THEM IN ONE WORD FOR GOOD OR BAD   • •   355 MEROPE   713
          PERFORMD GOOD SERVICE FOR HIS BLOODY WAGE   • •   364 MEROPE   975
          OUR PRINCE AND THE GOOD LAIAS WHOM HIS WARD   •   364 MEROPE   976
          WHILE THE GOOD SLEEP THE WORKERS HAVE THE DAY •   366 MEROPE   996
          GOOD TO OBEY WITHOUT A LEADER NOUGHT   • • • •   381 MEROPE   1302

GOOD (CONTINUED)
```
CLAMOURS TO FIND FULFILLD WHICH GOOD MEN PRAISE    . .   386 MEROPE              1428
ZEAL MAKES HIM MOST UNJUST BUT IN GOOD TIME        . .   386 MEROPE              1438
NOT MENS GOOD WORD HATH MADE ME WHAT I AM      . .  .    398 MEROPE              1791
BUT OUR OWN ACTS FOR GOOD OR ILL ARE MIGHTIER POWERS    420 EMPEDOCLES I 2       241
NOR IS THAT WIND LESS ROUGH WHICH BLOWS A GOOD          420 EMPEDOCLES I 2       256
     MANS BARGE
GOOD FRIEND I SHALL REVISIT CATANA     . . . . .        428 EMPEDOCLES I 2       473
NOR IS THE WIND LESS ROUGH THAT BLOWS A GOOD           420 EMPEDOCLES I 2      V 256
     MANS BARGE
AND THE GOOD LEARNED FRIENDLY QUIET MAN    . . . .      429 EMPEDOCLES II          8
ACHIEVE YOUR GOOD WHO CAN    . .  . . .  .  .  .        447 WESTMIN ABBEY        102
IF YOUR OWN HANDS THE GOOD BEGUN UNDO     .  . .  .     447 WESTMIN ABBEY        103
ROVER WITH THE GOOD BROWN HEAD   .  . .  .  .  .  .     453 POOR MATTHIAS         25
A MIGHTY NAME FOR EVIL OR FOR GOOD   .  .  .  .  . .    463 ALARIC AT ROME        21
WHEN RESTLESSNESS IS RESTLESS GOOD   .  .  .  . . .     484 ROME-SICKNESS         27
MANYS THE GOOD   . . . . . . . .  .  .  .  .  .         LUCRETIUS 7               1
```

GOODLY
```
AND SPEND THE GOODLY TREASUURES I HAVE GOT    . . .  .   68 SOHRAB RUSTUM        238
WHEREON THOU BUILDEST SUCH A GOODLY PRIDE    .  .  .     RUDE ORATOR              8
```

GOODNESS
```
WHAT BLESSING MUST FULL GOODNESS SHOWER    .  .  .  .   158 SAINT BRANDAN         54
WHAT BLESSING MUST TRUE GOODNESS SHOWER    .  .  .  .   158 SAINT BRANDAN       V 54
GODS WISDOM AND GODS GOODNESS ARE DISPLAYD   .  .  .    171 DIVINITY               4
GODS WISDOM AND GODS GOODNESS AY BUT FOOLS   .  .  .    171 DIVINITY               9
WISDOM AND GOODNESS THEY ARE GOD WHAT SCHOOLS   .  .    171 DIVINITY              11
THY GOODNESS NO MEN AID   .  .  .  .  .  .  .  .        416 EMPEDOCLES I 2       119
AND GOODNESS WARM AND TRUTH WITHOUT ALLOY    .  .  .    446 WESTMIN ABBEY         78
```

GOOSEBERRIES
```
WILD GOOSEBERRIES SCARED HER    .  .  .  .  .  .  .     392 MEROPE              1639
```

GORE
```
SENSELESS WELTERING IN HIS GORE     .  .  .  .  .  .     13 CHURCH BROU 1         28
STRETCHD AMONG BRIARS AND STONES THE SLOW BLACK GORE   373 MEROPE              1172
AND THAT CURST TREACHERY ON THE MOUNT OF GORE    .  .  430 EMPEDOCLES II         54
```

GORGE
```
IN SOME FAR STONY GORGE OUT OF HIS KEN    .  .  .  .     78 SOHRAB RUSTUM        568
IN THE TEMPLE-BUILT GORGE    .  .  .  .  .  .  .  .     345 MEROPE               464
OF THE GORGE OF DELPHI    .  .  .  .  .  .  .  .  .     435 EMPEDOCLES II        202
THE TEMPLE IN THE PURE PARNASSIAN GORGE    .  .  .  .   448 WESTMIN ABBEY        135
```

GORGED
```
THEN GORGED AND HELPLESS BE ASSAILD AND SLAIN    .  .  339 MEROPE               298
```

GORGEOUS
```
WERE GORGEOUS UPON EARTH AGAIN  .  .  .  .  .  .  .     204 CALAIS SANDS           8
```

GORGES
```
TO THE ICE-CUMBERD GORGES    .  .  .  .  .  .  .  .     175 PARTING               27
TOWARDS THE ICE-CUMBERD GORGES   .  .  .  .  .  .  .        PARTING             V 27
AMONG THEIR SAVAGE GORGES AND COLD SPRINGS   .  .  .    198 FRAG DEJANEIRA         9
HEMS IN ITS GORGES THE BED   .  .  .  .  .  .  .  .     252 FUTURE                11
GORGES OER MOUNTAINS IN SNOW    .  .  .  .  .  .  .     289 RUGBY CHAPEL          88
ONCE MID THOSE GORGES    .  .  .  .  .  .  .  .  .      392 MEROPE              1646
ONCE MID THE GORGES    .  .  .  .  .  .  .  .  .  .     392 MEROPE             V1646
```

GORGIAS
```
I HEAR GORGIAS THEIR CHIEF SPEAKS NOBLY OF HIM    .  .  411 EMPEDOCLES I 1       147
```

GORSE
```
IN MOSS AND GORSE AND SHINING FIR    .  .  .  .  .  .   483 ROME-SICKNESS          8
```

GOST
```
BUT WHITHER GOST THOU HENCE O QUEEN AWAY    .  .  .  .  350 MEROPE               597
```

GOT
```
AND SPEND THE GOODLY TREASUURES I HAVE GOT    .  .  .    68 SOHRAB RUSTUM        238
FOR THE PRIESTS HAVE GOT HIM IN PRISON    .  .  .  .    214 NEW ROME               3
AH ME THE WRONG EXPECTANT GOT HIS NEWS    .  .  .  .    361 MEROPE               922
OF SOPHISTS HAS GOT EMPIRE IN OUR SCHOOLS    .  .  .    410 EMPEDOCLES I 1       122
```

GOTH
```
THE GOTH BOUND ROME-WARDS SO THE HUN  .  .  .  .  .      52 RESIGNATION            9
WHEN THE GOTH STOOPED UPON HIS STRICKEN PREY    .  .    464 ALARIC AT ROME        68
JARRD WITH THE BURSTING SHOUT THEY COME THE            467 ALARIC AT ROME       132
     GOTH THEY COME
```

GOTHIC
```
OF GOTHIC CLARION SMOTE THY STARTLED EAR    .  .  .  .  465 ALARIC AT ROME        80
WAS THE WILD SHOUT THOSE GOTHIC MYRIADS GAVE    .  .    466 ALARIC AT ROME       112
```

GOTHLAND
```
BUT I HEARD THORA LAUGH IN GOTHLAND ISLE    .  .  .  .  117 BALDER DEAD 3        148
```

GOTTEN
```
FAST PERMANENCE TO AN ILL-GOTTEN THRONE    .  .  .  .   388 MEROPE              1509
```

GOURD
```
BRIGHT IN THE SUN THE CLIMBING GOURD-PLANTS LEAVES      25 DREAM                 16
```

GOURD   (CONTINUED)
     WITH STAFF AND GOURD HIS WAY DID BEND   . . . .   278 SOUTHERN NIGHT   81

GOURDS
     LAY THE WARM GOLDEN GOURDS GOLDEN WITHIN   . . . .   25 DREAM   18

GOVERN
     FROM RAVENING AND WHO GOVERN RUSTUMS SON   . . . .   63 SOHRAB RUSTUM   92

GOVERND
     OF YOUTH SELF-GOVERND AT THE FEET OF LAW   . . . .   9 MYCERINUS   10
     BE GOVERND QUIT THE TARTAR HOST AND COME   . . . .   71 SOHRAB RUSTUM   330

GOVERNING
     WHOSE MIND HATH KNOWN ALL ARTS OF GOVERNING   . .   43 GIPSY CHILD   35

GOVERNS
     TIME YOUR MASTER GOVERNS ME   . . . .   24 MEMORY-PICTURE   54
     MIND IS THE SPELL WHICH GOVERNS EARTH AND HEAVEN . . 413 EMPEDOCLES I 2   27

GRACE
     PAINT THAT FIGURES PLIANT GRACE   . . . .   23 MEMORY-PICTURE   33
     THOUGH EASE DULLS GRACE AND WISDOM BE TOO PROUD . .   44 GIPSY CHILD   63
     THOUGH EASE DULLS GRACE AND WISDOM IS TOO PROUD . .   44 GIPSY CHILD   V 63
     LOVE LENDS LIFE A LITTLE GRACE . . . .   44 QUESTION   4
     YET HELEN HAD AN EQUAL GRACE   . . . .   48 HORATIAN ECHO   28
     WHAT WILT THOU PRAY AND GET THEE GRACE   . . . .   91 SICK KING BOKH   101
     AND ALL GRACE SHALL TO ME BE GRUDGED . . . . . .   91 SICK KING BOKH   102
     HER YOUNGER RIVALS PUREST GRACE   . . . . . .   147 TRISTRAM 2   146
     HER YOUNGEST RIVALS FRESHEST GRACE   . . . . . .   147 TRISTRAM 2   V 146
     HER YOUNGER RIVALS CALMEST GRACE   . . . . . .   147 TRISTRAM 2   V 146
     HER HAVIOUR HAD THE MORNINGS FRESH CLEAR GRACE . . 154 TRISTRAM 3   179
     OH BRANDAN THINK WHAT GRACE DIVINE   . . . . . .   158 SAINT BRANDAN   53
     IMPARTING LIFE RENEWD OLD CLASSIC GRACE   . . . .   168 RACHEL 3   5
     IS IT YOU O BEAUTY O GRACE   . . . .   230 YOUTH OF NATURE   63
     LOVELINESS MAGIC AND GRACE   . . . .   230 YOUTH OF NATURE   79
     LOVELINESS MAGIC GRACE   . . . .   230 YOUTH OF NATURE V 79
     O EASY ACCESS TO THE HEARERS GRACE   . . . . . .   265 THYRSIS   91
     IS GRACE IS CHARM   . . . .   279 SOUTHERN NIGHT   132
     GRACE TO YOUR MOOD OF SADNESS GAVE   . . . . . .   304 GRANDE CHARTR   153
     GRACE TO THEIR MOOD OF SADNESS GAVE . . . . . .   304 GRANDE CHARTR V 153
     YES YES NOW I CONCEIVE THE LIBERAL GRACE . . . .   366 MEROPE   997
     DO I THEN GIVE TO USURPATION GRACE   . . . . . .   388 MEROPE   1494
     THAT SCANTY GRACE SHALL EARN THEE THIS REPLY   . .   395 MEROPE   1732
     AH NOW I COMPREHEND THE LIBERAL GRACE   . . . .   366 MEROPE   V 997

GRACEFUL
     I KNOW THAT GRACEFUL FIGURE FAIR   . . . . . .   174 MEETING   5
     SWEET AND GRACEFUL AND SHE   . . . .   284 HAWORTH CHURCH   92

GRACES
     WHO ARE THEY O PENSIVE GRACES   . . . .   26 NEW SIRENS   9
     AND YOU TOO O WORSHIPPD GRACES   . . . .   34 NEW SIRENS   243
     AND YOU TOO O WEEPING GRACES   . . . .   34 NEW SIRENS   V 243

GRACIOUS
     SLOPES GRACIOUS UP THE WESTERN RIDGE . . . . . .   54 RESIGNATION   53
     LOW WOODY HILL WITH GRACIOUS BOUND   . . . . . .   57 RESIGNATION   174
     THANKS GRACIOUS ONE   . . . .   187 STRAYED REVEL   63
     EAGERLY ONCE HER GRACIOUS KEN   . . . .   202 URANIA   9
     A FUGITIVE AND GRACIOUS LIGHT HE SEEKS   . . . .   268 THYRSIS   201
     NOT BY THIS GRACIOUS MIDLAND SEA   . . . . . .   277 SOUTHERN NIGHT   74
     OER THE GRACIOUS SPURS COMING DOWN   . . . . . .   297 HEINES GRAVE   179
     AND IN THAT GRACIOUS REGION BLAND   . . . . . .   311 OBERMANN   165
     BEYOND THIS GRACIOUS BOUND   . . . .   313 OBERMANN MORE   30
     THAT GRACIOUS CHILD THAT THORN-CROWND MAN . . .   318 OBERMANN MORE   167
     FORWARD THE GRACIOUS HOURS HAVE FARED   . . . .   322 OBERMANN MORE   283
     THAT DEAR-BELOVED THAT YOUNG THAT GRACIOUS HEAD . . 382 MEROPE   1327
     HOW GRACIOUS IS THE MOUNTAIN AT THIS HOUR . . . .   406 EMPEDOCLES I 1   6
     OF THE APPEASING GRACIOUS HARMONY   . . . . . .   431 EMPEDOCLES II   75
     THE PRESENCE OF THAT GRACIOUS INMATE LIGHT . . .   444 WESTMIN ABBEY   6
     THOUGH SUNK BE NOW THIS BRIGHT THIS GRACIOUS HEAD   449 WESTMIN ABBEY   176
     THOUGH SUNK IS NOW THIS BRIGHT THIS GRACIOUS HEAD   449 WESTMIN ABBEY V 176
     ALONG THE GRACIOUS ALBAN HILL   . . . .   484 ROME-SICKNESS   20

GRADUAL
     NO TIS THE GRADUAL FURNACE OF THE WORLD   . . . .   153 TRISTRAM 3   119

GRAIN
     DESERTED IS THE NEW-REAPD GRAIN   . . . . . .   217 BACCHANALIA 1   V 4
     PUTTING HIS SICKLE TO THE PERILOUS GRAIN . . . .   268 THYRSIS   182

GRAINS
     OH THAT I SAW ITS GRAINS OF YELLOW SILT   . . . .   83 SOHRAB RUSTUM   769

GRAND
     OF THE NEAR WAVES CAME SADLY GRAND   . . . . . .   137 TRISTRAM 1   217
     FOR THE BRIGHT STREAM A CHANNEL GRAND   . . . .   213 PROGRESS POESY   6
     FOR A GRAND CULPRIT SHORTLY COMING DOWN   . . . .   373 MEROPE   1189
     MORE DARING AND MORE GRAND OFFENDER FIND . . . .   390 MEROPE   1571

GRAND   (CONTINUED)
      DUMB INSCRUTABLE AND GRAND   • • • • • • • • •   453 POOR MATTHIAS   40
      HE HEARD OF LATE THE GRAND OLD MAN   • • • • • • •   460 KAISER DEAD   41

GRANDAMES
      SHE GLEANED FROM BRETON GRANDAMES WHEN A CHILD   • •   152 TRISTRAM 3   108

GRANDCHILDS
      WHILE ALL ELSE GRIEVES HIM THAT HIS GRANDCHILDS DEATH   359 MEROPE   851

GRANDEUR
      THE VASTNESS THE GRANDEUR THE GLOOM   • • • • • • •   231 YOUTH OF NATURE   101

GRANDEURS
      MATERIAL GRANDEURS DO IN HEAVEN DECAY   • • • •   FRAGMENT 2   4

GRANDFATHER
      MY GRANDFATHER THE GOOD ARCADIAN KING   • • • •   331 MEROPE   33

GRANDSIRE
      WILL LIE MY GRANDSIRE SAID OUR FAIREST CHANCE   • •   331 MEROPE   41
      HIS GRANDSIRE AND HIS UNCLES FEAR THE RISK • • • •   350 MEROPE   603
      SUSPICION FROM THY GRANDSIRE OF THY DEATH   • • • •   379 MEROPE   1270

GRANDSIRES
      HAVE NEVER KNOWN MY GRANDSIRES FURROWD FACE   • •   83 SOHRAB RUSTUM   756

GRANDSON
      GRANDSON FOLLOWD SIRE   • • • • • • • • • • •   345 MEROPE   V 467

GRANDSONS
      FATHERS SONS GRANDSONS ARE ALL • • • • • • • • •   379 MEROPE   1254

GRANGE
      THEN SOUGHT THY STRAW IN SOME SEQUESTERD GRANGE   • •   259 SCHOLAR-GIPSY   130
      ORCHARD AND CROFT AND FULL-STORED GRANGE   • • • •   313 OBERMANN MORE   27

GRANITE
      AS THOSE BLACK GRANITE PILLARS ONCE HIGH-REARD   • •   86 SOHRAB RUSTUM   860
      WHERE BETWEEN GRANITE TERRACES • • • • • • • • •   312 OBERMANN   177

GRANT
      COME THEN HEAR NOW AND GRANT ME WHAT I ASK   • • • •   62 SOHRAB RUSTUM   54
      GO I WILL GRANT THEE WHAT THY HEART DESIRES   • •   63 SOHRAB RUSTUM   93
      SHE WILL GRANT IT SHE IS KIND AND GOOD   • • • •   145 TRISTRAM 2   96
      THE ASPECT NOT I GRANT EXPRESS • • • • • • • •   225 EPILOG LAOCOON   133
      THE FEELING NOT I GRANT EXPLORE   • • • • • •   225 EPILOG LAOCOON   135
      GRANT HIM TO REIGN THERE WISE AND JUST LIKE THEE   • •   350 MEROPE   589
      YET GRANT THAT IT SUCCEEDS THOU HAST BEHIND   • •   381 MEROPE   1296
      AND GRANT HENCEFORTH TO THE MESSENIANS PEACE   • •   402 MEROPE   1917
      YET GRANT AS SENSE LONG MISSD • • • • • • • •   421 EMPEDOCLES I 2   282
      GRANT THAT THE WORLD WERE FULL OF GODS WE CANNOT SEE   421 EMPEDOCLES I 2   286

GRANTED
      TO THEE ONLY GOD GRANTED • • • • • • • • • • •   177 PARTING   79
      YE KNOW IT TOO IT HATH BEEN GRANTED ME   • • • •   441 EMPEDOCLES II   405
      HAVE NOT LIFE AND LOVE BEEN GRANTED ME   • • • •   482 THEKLAS ANSWER   4

GRAPE
      GRAPE-SYRUP SQUARES OF COLOURD ICE   • • • • • •   94 SICK KING BOKH   196

GRAPES
      FREIGHTED WITH AMBER GRAPES AND CHIAN WINE   • • • •   262 SCHOLAR-GIPSY   238

GRASMERE
      TWINKLES ON GRASMERE NO MORE   • • • • • • • •   228 YOUTH OF NATURE   19

GRASP
      HER DARKNESS FROM HER GRASP A SUBJECT TEAR   • • • •   121 BALDER DEAD 3   280
      I MUST NOT SPRING TO GRASP THY HAND   • • • • • •   205 CALAIS SANDS   25
      PLEASURE TO OUR HOT GRASP   • • • • • • • •   424 EMPEDOCLES I 2   357

GRASPD
      TO HIS KNEES AND WITH HIS FINGERS GRASPD THE SAND   73 SOHRAB RUSTUM   V 421
      STRAIND AND LONGD AND GRASPD EACH GIFT IT SAW   • •   210 SELF-DECEPTION   10

GRASPING
      GRASPING THE RUDDER HARD • • • • • • • • • • •   244 SUMMER NIGHT   67
      GRASPING FIRM IN HIS HAND   • • • • • • • •   342 MEROPE   397

GRASPS
      HE GRASPS THE VERY REINS OF LIFE AND DEATH   • • • •   410 EMPEDOCLES I 1   125

GRASS
      BURYING THEIR UNSUNND STEMS IN GRASS AND FLOWERS   • •   11 MYCERINUS   88
      WHERE COOL GRASS AND FRAGRANT GLOOMS   • • • • • •   26 NEW SIRENS   2
      WHERE I STAND THE GRASS IS GLOWING   • • • • • •   32 NEW SIRENS   187
      THEIR FRAGMENTS ON THE CUMBERD GRASS • • • • • •   55 RESIGNATION   111
      THE WET FLOWERD GRASS HEAVES UP ITS HEAD   • • • •   57 RESIGNATION   185
      MOWING THE GARDEN GRASS-PLOTS NEAR ITS BED • • • •   80 SOHRAB RUSTUM   636

GRASS   (CONTINUED)
        ON THE MOWN DYING GRASS SO SOHRAB LAY   • • • •   80 SOHRAB RUSTUM   638
        OF GRASS PEEP OUT AMID SURROUNDING SNOW   • • • •   122 BALDER DEAD 3   315
        OF IDA AND AMONG THE GRASS SHALL FIND   • • • •   128 BALDER DEAD 3   538
        ON THE GRASS UNDER THE TREES   • • • • • • •   137 TRISTRAM 1   221
        CREEPS THICKLY GROWS NOT HERE BUT THE PALE GRASS • • 150 TRISTRAM 3   15
        THE GRASS WAS DRY AND MOSSD AND YOU SAW CLEAR   • •   155 TRISTRAM 3   206
        THE HEATHER DISAPPEARS AND THE PALE GRASS   • • • •   TRISTRAM 3   V 15
        THE BOUNDLESS WAVING GRASS-PLAINS STRETCH THICK-STARRD 191 STRAYED REVEL   168
        TILL THEY TOO FADE LIKE GRASS THEY CRAWL   • • • • 193 STRAYED REVEL   242
        HERE THROUGH THE MOONLIGHT ON THIS ENGLISH GRASS • • 201 PHILOMELA   17
        TRAMPLE THE GRASS   • • • • • • • • • •   218 BACCHANALIA 1   35
        OUT OF THE PATH AND TAKE THE GRASS   • • • • 222 EPILOG LAOCOON   37
        THE GRASS HAD STILL THE GREEN OF MAY   • • • • 222 EPILOG LAOCOON   38
        THE GRASS THE ELMS THAT BLOSSOMD THORN   • • • • 222 EPILOG LAOCOON   52
        THE CATTLE RISING FROM THE GRASS   • • • • 225 EPILOG LAOCOON   153
        WHAT BLOWING DAISIES FRAGRANT GRASS   • • • • 248 KENSINGTON GARD   15
        THE NIGHT COMES DOWN UPON THE GRASS   • • • • 249 KENSINGTON GARD   35
        BUTTERCUPS CLOVER DAISIES GRASS   • • • •   KENSINGTON GARD   V 15
        OF BLOOM ON THE BENT GRASS WHERE I AM LAID   • • • • 256 SCHOLAR-GIPSY   28
        AND NEAR ME ON THE GRASS LIES GLANVILS BOOK • • • • 256 SCHOLAR-GIPSY   31
        MID WIDE GRASS MEADOWS WHICH THE SUNSHINE FILLS • • 257 SCHOLAR-GIPSY   68
        MEN WHO THROUGH THOSE WIDE FIELDS OF BREEZY GRASS   257 SCHOLAR-GIPSY   93
        THROUGH THE LONG DEWY GRASS MOVE SLOW AWAY   • • • • 258 SCHOLAR-GIPSY   110
        OF OUR BOAT PASSING HEAVED THE RIVER-GRASS   • • • • 266 THYRSIS   128
        KEEP FRESH THE GRASS UPON HIS GRAVE   • • • •   272 MEMORIAL VERSES   71
        COOL NORTHERN FIELDS AND GRASS AND FLOWERS   • • • • 275 STANZAS CARNAC   44
        ROUND THEE THEY LIE THE GRASS   • • • • • •   284 HAWORTH CHURCH   88
        CHEQUERING THE GRASS WITH THEIR SHADE   • • • • 297 HEINES GRAVE   158
        AND DARKNESS STEAL OER THE WET GRASS • • • • •   310 OBERMANN   117
        SWEET HEAPS OF FRESH-CUT GRASS   • • • • • •   313 OBERMANN MORE   18
        ON THE GRASS NEAR ME STOOD   • • • • • • •   314 OBERMANN MORE   60
        OF SHORT GRASS BEADED WITH DEW   • • • • • •   399 MEROPE   1823
        ONE SEES ONES FOOTPRINTS CRUSHD IN THE WET GRASS • 406 EMPEDOCLES I 1   14
        THE GRASS IS COOL THE SEA-SIDE AIR   • • • • •   426 EMPEDOCLES I 2   432
        HERE WHERE THE GRASS IS SMOOTH AND WARM   • • • • 451 GEISTS GRAVE   66
        SHALL SEE THY GRAVE UPON THE GRASS   • • • • •   452 GEISTS GRAVE   75

GRASSD
        WHAT DEEP-GRASSD MEADOW   • • • • • • • • • •   391 MEROPE   1606

GRASSES
        TALL GRASSES AND WHITE FLOWERING NETTLES WAVE   • • 259 SCHOLAR-GIPSY   139
        NOR THE CROPPD GRASSES SHOOT ANOTHER HEAD   • • • • 255 SCHOLAR-GIPSY   V   5

GRASSY
        WITH THEIR MILD DARK HIS GRASSY BANQUET-HALL   • •   12 MYCERINUS   119
        PLAY THROUGH THIS GRASSY UPLAND GLEN   • • • • •   55 RESIGNATION   99
        THE HOLLOWS GRASSY BANKS ARE SOFT-INCLINED   • • • • 149 TRISTRAM 3   10
        THE OPENINGS GRASSY BANKS ARE SOFT INCLINED   • •   TRISTRAM 3   V 10
        THE OPENINGS GRASSY BANKS WERE SOFT INCLINED   • •   TRISTRAM 3   V 10
        ON THE WARM GRASSY   • • • • • • • • • •   190 STRAYED REVEL   137
        WHEN GARDEN-WALKS AND ALL THE GRASSY FLOOR   • • • • 264 THYRSIS   54
        THE GRASSY HARVEST OF THE RIVER-FIELDS   • • • • 266 THYRSIS   108
        BEHIND ME ON THEIR GRASSY SWEEP   • • • • • •   274 STANZAS CARNAC   9
        THERE ON A GRASSY SPUR WHICH BATHES ITS ROOT   • •   356 MEROPE   V 751
        ON PELION ON THE GRASSY GROUND   • • • • • • •   414 EMPEDOCLES I 2   58
        FROM THE GRASSY SUN-WARMD PLACE   • • • • • •   433 EMPEDOCLES II   161

GRATE
        BARRING HIS WAY AND IN THE WALL A GRATE   • • • • 100 BALDER DEAD 1   167
        AND MAKE HIM LEAP THE GRATE AND COME WITHIN   • •   100 BALDER DEAD 1   170
        BARRING HIS WAY AND IN THE WALL A GRATE   • • • • 109 BALDER DEAD 2   145
        AND MADE HIM LEAP THE GRATE AND CAME WITHIN   • •   109 BALDER DEAD 2   148
        OR HOW OERLEAP THE GRATE THAT BARS THE WALL   • •   110 BALDER DEAD 2   185
        AND TO THE WALL HE CAME AND FOUND THE GRATE   • •   113 BALDER DEAD 2   286
        AND CAME BENEATH THE WALL AND FOUND THE GRATE   • • 124 BALDER DEAD 3   377

GRATEFUL
        MORE GRATEFUL THAN THIS MARBLE SLEEP   • • • • •   22 YOUTH AND CALM   21
        THEREFORE WITH GRATEFUL HEART I MOURN THEE DEAD   • • 117 BALDER DEAD 3   152
        MOST LIKELY GRATEFUL BUT IN ALL CASE SURE   • • • • 354 MEROPE   711
        ALL WHICH HE OWND AND PRAISED WITH GRATEFUL MIND • • 356 MEROPE   763
        TO THE GODS GRATEFUL SACRIFICE AND THEN   • • • • 405 MEROPE   2019

GRATEFULLY
        GRATEFULLY COLD ON THIS BROW   • • • • • • •   283 HAWORTH CHURCH   V

GRATING
        MOURNFULLY GRATING THE GATES   • • • • • • • •   199 FRAG DEJANEIRA   29
        LISTEN YOU HEAR THE GRATING ROAR   • • • • • •   211 DOVER BEACH   9
        THE GRATING SHINGLE STRAGGLED DOWN   • • • • • •   480 HAYSWATER BOAT   30

GRATITUDE
        THAT NEITHER GRATITUDE NOR TIE OF RACE   • • • • 389 MEROPE   1525

GRATITUDES
        HOW MANY LOVES HOW MANY GRATITUDES   • • • • • •   335 MEROPE   179

GRAVE

NATURE FORGIVES NO DEBT AND FEARS NO GRAVE	5	HARMONY NATURE	10
WHEN SHE SANK INTO HER GRAVE	15	CHURCH BROU 1	70
WHEN SHE SUNK INTO HER GRAVE	15	CHURCH BROU 1	V 70
ON AISLE AND TRANSEPT AND YOUR MARBLE GRAVE	17	CHURCH BROU 3	6
FROM THE FAR GRAVE TO WHICH IT GOES	21	YOUTH AND CALM	13
MANS GRAVE REASONS DISAPPEAR	29	NEW SIRENS	90
FROM THE CRADLE TO THE GRAVE	38	STAGIRIUS	4
HEAVY AS DEATH COLD AS THE GRAVE	38	STAGIRIUS	12
FROM THE CRADLE TO THE GRAVE	40	STAGIRIUS	61
IN THE GRAVE	44	QUESTION	7
AND WARM AND PLEASANT BUT THE GRAVE IS COLD	71	SOHRAB RUSTUM	323
HEAVENS AIR IS BETTER THAN THE COLD DEAD GRAVE	71	SOHRAB RUSTUM	324
BUT WITH A GRAVE MILD VOICE SOHRAB REPLIED	84	SOHRAB RUSTUM	771
AND I BE NOT FORGOTTEN IN MY GRAVE	84	SOHRAB RUSTUM	794
AND MEN SHALL NOT FORGET THEE IN THY GRAVE	84	SOHRAB RUSTUM	805
AND ZAL MIGHT WEEP ABOVE MY GRAVE NOT THINE	85	SOHRAB RUSTUM	821
FROM LAYING THY DEAR MASTER IN HIS GRAVE	85	SOHRAB RUSTUM	834
AND WITH A GRAVE MILD VOICE SOHRAB REPLIED	84	SOHRAB RUSTUM	V 771
THERE LAY HIS BODY IN MY GRAVE	95	SICK KING BOKH	228
HE SPOKE AND GRAVE REPLIED THE SOLEMN QUEEN	110	BALDER DEAD 2	201
TO LEAVE FOR EVER BALDER IN THE GRAVE	120	BALDER DEAD 3	228
THE UNHAPPY WITH REPROACH EVEN IN THE GRAVE	124	BALDER DEAD 3	396
HODER AND I SHALL JOIN THEM FROM THE GRAVE	128	BALDER DEAD 3	526
I AM DYING BUILD THOU MAYST MY GRAVE	142	TRISTRAM 2	12
GO NOT FAR O ISEULT FROM MY GRAVE	145	TRISTRAM 2	92
GRAVE IT ON BRASS WITH ADAMANTINE PEN	171	DIVINITY	2
KEPT ON AFTER THE GRAVE BUT NOT BEGUN	172	IMMORTALITY	10
STREAM ON HER FROM HER LORDS YET RECENT GRAVE	172	GOOD SHEPHERD	8
AH COULD THY GRAVE AT HOME AT CARTHAGE BE	173	MONICAS PRAYER	1
OH COULD THY GRAVE AT HOME AT CARTHAGE BE	173	MONICAS PRAYER	V 1
THY CHEEK WAS GRAVE THY SPEECH GREW RARE	178	FAREWELL	16
THE FAULT WAS GRAVE I MIGHT HAVE KNOWN	180	ISOLATION MARG	7
GRAVE GAY CHILD PARENT HUSBAND WIFE	226	EPILOG LAOCOON	161
NATURE IS HID IN THEIR GRAVE	232	YOUTH OF NATURE	128
AND NOW KEEPS ONLY IN THE GRAVE	249	KENSINGTON GARD	28
THE DARKER ELMS STAND GRAVE AND DUN	248	KENSINGTON GARD	V
THE MASSIER ELMS STAND GRAVE AND DUN		KENSINGTON GARD	V
AND NOW DWELLS ONLY IN THE GRAVE		KENSINGTON GARD	V 28
AND THE GRAVE GLANVIL DID THE TALE INSCRIBE	259	SCHOLAR-GIPSY	133
SOME COUNTRY-NOOK WHERE OER THY UNKNOWN GRAVE	259	SCHOLAR-GIPSY	138
AS SOME GRAVE TYRIAN TRADER FROM THE SEA	262	SCHOLAR-GIPSY	232
KEEP FRESH THE GRASS UPON HIS GRAVE	272	MEMORIAL VERSES	71
YET CHARMD IT FROM HIS FOREST-GRAVE	273	STANZAS CARNAC	8
THE SOUTH IS MISTRESS OF HIS GRAVE	275	STANZAS CARNAC	48
YET BOUND IT FROM HIS FOREST GRAVE		STANZAS CARNAC	V 8
IS HEARD TO-NIGHT AROUND THY GRAVE	276	SOUTHERN NIGHT	22
BUT YOU A GRAVE FOR KNIGHT OR SAGE	279	SOUTHERN NIGHT	113
MILD OER HER GRAVE YE MOUNTAINS SHINE	279	SOUTHERN NIGHT	137
BUT YOU A GRAVE FOR GIRL OR SAGE	279	SOUTHERN NIGHT	V 113
STREW WITH LAUREL THE GRAVE	283	HAWORTH CHURCH	66
ENTEREST THE HOUSE OF THE GRAVE	284	HAWORTH CHURCH	78
LASHES THE NEWLY-MADE GRAVE	286	HAWORTH CHURCH	133
STREW WITH ROSES THE GRAVE	283	HAWORTH CHURCH	V 66
GLUT THE DEVOURING GRAVE	288	RUGBY CHAPEL	83
AUSTERE DANTE NO GRAVE	294	HEINES GRAVE	62
POISONS THE PEACE OF THY GRAVE	294	HEINES GRAVE	69
SPEAK THE LAST WORD AT HIS GRAVE	298	HEINES GRAVE	201
YE SLUMBER IN YOUR SILENT GRAVE	304	GRANDE CHARTR	151
EMBLEMS OF HOPE OVER THE GRAVE	305	GRANDE CHARTR	201
THEY SLUMBER IN THEIR SILENT GRAVE	304	GRANDE CHARTR	V 151
EMBLEMS OF LIGHT ABOVE THE GRAVE	305	GRANDE CHARTR	V 201
DISTINCTIONS WE ESTEEM SO GRAVE	311	OBERMANN	151
STAND DARK ROUND THY GREEN GRAVE	311	OBERMANN	168
THE HARDLY-HEARD-OF GRAVE	312	OBERMANN	180
THY HARDLY HEARD OF GRAVE	312	OBERMANN	V 180
FROM CHRISTS THEN OPEN GRAVE	317	OBERMANN MORE	148
AND OPEN STOOD HIS GRAVE	318	OBERMANN MORE	170
AND ON HIS GRAVE WITH SHINING EYES	318	OBERMANN MORE	175
HOUSE OF THE GRAVE WHAT WE DO	342	MEROPE	391
HUSBAND AND KING TO THY GRAVE	342	MEROPE	401
AND THE GRAVE OF ORESTES	344	MEROPE	436
PRISONERS OF DEATH FROM THE GRAVE	347	MEROPE	525
SUSPICION GRAVE I SEE BUT NO FIRM PROOF	365	MEROPE	994
AND HARDLY YET SOME SAY HATH FOUND A GRAVE	385	MEROPE	1425
O HONOURD FATHER HIDE THEE IN THY GRAVE	386	MEROPE	1430
LAY IN THY SON IS BURIED IN HIS GRAVE	394	MEROPE	1694
SUSPICION GRAVE I SEE BUT NO CLEAR PROOF	365	MEROPE	V 994
OVER THE GRAVE OF THE SLAIN PYTHO	435	EMPEDOCLES II	205
AND IN THE GRAVE HE LAID A CHERISHD WIFE	447	WESTMIN ABBEY	124
AND TO THE GRAVE HE BORE A CHERISHD WIFE	447	WESTMIN ABBEY	V 124
SHALL SEE THY GRAVE UPON THE GRASS	452	GEISTS GRAVE	75
DIRGE FROM ME TO CROWN THEIR GRAVE	454	POOR MATTHIAS	82
DIRGE OF MINE TO CROWN THEIR GRAVE	454	POOR MATTHIAS	V 82
KAI IN THY GRAVE	461	KAISER DEAD	82
EVEN IN THE GRAVE THEIR FRAGRANCE CANNOT FADE	462	ALARIC AT ROME	8
THOU SOLEMN GRAVE WHERE EVERY STEP WE TREAD	464	ALARIC AT ROME	49
THEY SHALL NOT DECK YOUR LIFE BUT SANCTIFY YOUR GRAVE	467	ALARIC AT ROME	138
AND THE FIRST SORROW WHICH IS CHILDHOODS GRAVE	474	CROMWELL	82
AFFLICTS GRAVE HEAVEN WITH ITS LONG SENSELESS ROAR	480	HUNGARIAN NAT	5
THAT THEY SHOULD EASE GRAVE COUNSEL OF ITS CARE		RUDE ORATOR	10

GRAVED
BREIDABLIK ON WHOSE COLUMNS BALDER GRAVED • • • • 101 BALDER DEAD 1 208

GRAVELY
AND ME BELIEVE IT WISE MEN GRAVELY BLAME • • • • 333 MEROPE 94
GRAVELY THOU THE WHILE POOR DEAR • • • • • 455 POOR MATTHIAS 119

GRAVEN
BY MOUNDED TURF AND GRAVEN STONE • • • • • 451 GEISTS GRAVE 64
WELL FETCH HIS GRAVEN COLLAR FINE • • • • • 461 KAISER DEAD 79

GRAVER
WAFTS NOT FROM THINE OWN THOUGHTS OF GRAVER STRAIN 41 GIPSY CHILD V 10

GRAVES
MEN DIG GRAVES WITH BITTER TEARS • • • • • 44 QUESTION 11
AND LETS THE AGED MOULDER TO THEIR GRAVES • • • • 67 SOHRAB RUSTUM 225
WE CLIMBD ON THE GRAVES ON THE STONES WORN WITH RAINS 163 FORSAKEN MERM 74
OVER TOMBS AMID GRAVES • • • • • • • • • 220 BACCHANALIA 2 32
SUCH PEACEFUL GRAVES • • • • • • • • • 277 SOUTHERN NIGHT 60
SHOULD OUR GRAVES BE • • • • • • • • • 277 SOUTHERN NIGHT 76
THE PARSONAGE-HOUSE AND THE GRAVES • • • • • 283 HAWORTH CHURCH 65
BLOWS FROM THEIR GRAVES TO THY OWN • • • • • 284 HAWORTH CHURCH 89
BLOW FROM THEIR GRAVES TOWARD THINE • • • • • 284 HAWORTH CHURCH V 89
YELLOW AND BLACK ON THE GRAVES • • • • 292 HEINES GRAVE 12
THEIR ABBEY AND ITS CLOSE OF GRAVES • • • • • 305 GRANDE CHARTR 174
WITH THE GRAVES EVERLASTING • • • • • • 371 MEROPE 1140
EFFACE THE HUMBLER GRAVES OF SEBERTS LINE • • • • 445 WESTMIN ABBEY 54
BUT AS ONE VOICELESS BLANK A PLACE OF GRAVES • 469 ALARIC AT ROME 182

GRAVITY
AN ANGELIC GRAVITY • • • • • • • • • • • 24 MEMORY-PICTURE 46

GRAY
CROWND WITH GRAY HAIRS HE DIED AND FULL OF SWAY • • 9 MYCERINUS 14
IN GRAY AGE WITH PALSIED HANDS • • • • • • 14 CHURCH BROU 1 66
OR DO I WAIT TO HEAR SOME GRAY-HAIRD KING • • • 43 GIPSY CHILD 33
WHOSE SURENESS GRAY-HAIRD SCHOLARS HARDLY LEARN • • 43 GIPSY CHILD 42
MOVE BROWSING UP THE GRAY-WALLD LANE • • • • • 55 RESIGNATION 121

GREAT
TOO GREAT FOR HASTE TOO HIGH FOR RIVALRY • • • • 1 QUIET WORK 8
WHEREIN EARTHS GREAT ONES ARE DISQUIETED • • • 7 REP FRIEND 10
FRANCE FAMED IN ALL GREAT ARTS IN NONE SUPREME • • 7 REP FRIEND CONT 4
NATURES GREAT LAW AND LAW OF ALL MENS MINDS • • • 8 RELIGIOUS ISOL 12
AND THE GREAT POWERS WE SERVE THEMSELVES MAY BE • • 10 MYCERINUS 41
OF THE GREAT GODS IS PLAIN AND YE MUST BRING • • • 11 MYCERINUS 75
SPRING THE GREAT STREAMS • • • • • • • • 45 IN UTRUMQUE PAR 21
WHY WHEN THE WORLDS GREAT MIND • • • • • • 46 WORLD QUIETIST 1
A WHITE-ROBED SLAVE STOLE TO THE GREAT KINGS SIDE • 47 WORLD QUIETIST 27
HE SPAKE THE GREAT KING HEARD • • • • • • 47 WORLD QUIETIST 28
HE SPOKE THE GREAT KING HEARD • • • • • • 47 WORLD QUIETIST V 28
HE SEES IN SOME GREAT-HISTORIED LAND • • • • • 56 RESIGNATION 154
AND WITH MY GREAT NAME FENCE THAT WEAK OLD MAN • • 68 SOHRAB RUSTUM 237
BUT WHO FOR MEN OF NOUGHT WOULD DO GREAT DEEDS • • 68 SOHRAB RUSTUM 255
FOR WELL I KNOW THAT DID GREAT RUSTUM STAND • • • 72 SOHRAB RUSTUM 370
OR ELSE THAT THE GREAT RUSTUM WOULD COME DOWN • • 77 SOHRAB RUSTUM 531
FROM HUNTING AND A GREAT WAY OFF DESCRIES • • • • 78 SOHRAB RUSTUM 562
RUSTUMS GREAT FATHER WHOM THEY LEFT TO DIE • • • • 81 SOHRAB RUSTUM 680
THE NORTHERN SIR AND THIS GREAT OXUS STREAM • • • 83 SOHRAB RUSTUM 765
FOR SOME ARE BORN TO DO GREAT DEEDS AND LIVE • • • 84 SOHRAB RUSTUM 773
BUT COME THOU SEEST THIS GREAT HOST OF MEN • • • • 84 SOHRAB RUSTUM 778
MAY SEE MY TOMB A GREAT WAY OFF AND CRY • • • • 84 SOHRAB RUSTUM 791
WHOM HIS GREAT FATHER DID IN IGNORANCE KILL • • • 84 SOHRAB RUSTUM 793
AND THE GREAT RUSTUM DREW HIS HORSEMANS CLOAK • • 86 SOHRAB RUSTUM 858
AS OF A GREAT ASSEMBLY LOOSED AND FIRES • • • • 86 SOHRAB RUSTUM 869
MAY SEE MY TOMB A GREAT WAY OFF AND SAY • • • • 84 SOHRAB RUSTUM V 791
IN THE GREAT WINDOW OF THE GATE • • • • • 88 SICK KING BOKH 16
ON THIS GREAT SINNER WHO DID BREAK • • • • • 89 SICK KING BOKH 37
WHETHER A THING BE GREAT OR SMALL • • • • • 89 SICK KING BOKH 56
WITH A GREAT JOY UPON HIS FACE • • • • • • 91 SICK KING BOKH 119
THOUGH IT BE GREAT ALL THE EARTH ROUND • • • • 92 SICK KING BOKH 158
EVEN THE GREAT HONOUR WHICH I HAVE • • • • • 94 SICK KING BOKH 217
ON THIS GREAT SINNER WHO HATH BROKE • • • • • 89 SICK KING BOKH V 37
TO THE STEEP EDGE OF SOME GREAT VALLEY COMES • • 113 BALDER DEAD 2 296
IN THAT GREAT DAY THE TWILIGHT OF THE GODS • • • 115 BALDER DEAD 3 68
ON SOME GREAT ROAD OR RESTING IN AN INN • • • 116 BALDER DEAD 3 117
IN THE GREAT DEEP FOR GAIN AT LAST COME HOME • • 123 BALDER DEAD 3 358
HIS SHIP AND THE GREAT SERPENT MAKES TO LAND • • 127 BALDER DEAD 3 479
WHO CARRIED THE GREAT WAR FROM MACEDON • • • 154 TRISTRAM 3 148
NOW THE GREAT WINDS SHOREWARD BLOW • • • • • 161 FORSAKEN MERM 4
WHERE GREAT WHALES COME SAILING BY • • • • • 162 FORSAKEN MERM 43
NOW THE GREAT WINDS SHOREWARDS BLOW • • • • • 161 FORSAKEN MERM V 4
THE UNKNOWN LITTLE FROM THE UNKNOWING GREAT • • 170 WEST LONDON 13
ON SOME GREAT RIVERS MARGE • • • • • • 193 STRAYED REVEL 252
THE GREAT ORACULAR SHRINES • • • • • 198 FRAG DEJANEIRA 11
WILL YE CLAIM FOR YOUR GREAT ONES THE GIFT • • • 231 YOUTH OF NATURE 122
WHEN YOUR GREAT ONES DEPART WILL YE SAY • • • 231 YOUTH OF NATURE 126
OF LANGUOR THOUGH SO CALM AND THOUGH SO GREAT • • 244 SUMMER NIGHT 79

GREAT   (CONTINUED)
          WANDERING WITH THE GREAT MOTHERS TRAIN DIVINE   • •   268 THYRSIS   177
          THEN THROUGH THE GREAT TOWNS HARSH HEART-WEARYING ROAR 269 THYRSIS   234
          IN THE NOBLE AND GREAT WHO ARE GONE   • • • • • •   290 RUGBY CHAPEL   146
          HOLLOW AND DULL ARE THE GREAT   • • • • • • •   295 HEINES GRAVE   113
          OH HAD I LIVED IN THAT GREAT DAY   • • • • • •   317 OBERMANN MORE   141
          THE WORLDS GREAT ORDER DAWNS IN SHEEN   • • • •   322 OBERMANN MORE   293
          GREAT HERACLES AND IN THAT PUBLIC PLACE   • • • • 330 MEROPE   14
          THE KING CRESPHONTES THY GREAT HUSBAND FALL   • • 333 MEROPE   118
          BUT WHEN FOR SOME GREAT PUBLIC CAUSE AN ARM   • • 336 MEROPE   204
          A HOUSE ONCE GREAT NOW DWINDLING IN ITS SONS   • • 337 MEROPE   237
          FROM ALL FOR HIS GREAT LINEAGE AND HIS WOES   • • 356 MEROPE   762
          STRANGER THIS NEWS THOU BRINGEST IS TOO GREAT   • • 359 MEROPE   859
          NO SOMETHING MUST BE DARED AND GREAT AS ERST   • • 367 MEROPE   1054
          WHEN MY GREAT FATHER FELL THEY HAD REPLIED   • • •   383 MEROPE   1366
          STRANGER THE NEWS THOU BRINGEST IS TOO GREAT   • • 359 MEROPE   V 859
          BUT HIDE THEE IN THE ROCKS A GREAT WAY DOWN   • • 409 EMPEDOCLES I 1   96
          HOW MAN MAY HERE BEST LIVE NO CARE TOO GREAT   419 EMPEDOCLES I 2 216
              TO EXPLORE
          CROWND BY THE AWFUL PEAK ETNAS GREAT MOUTH   • • • • 429 EMPEDOCLES II   3
          GREAT QUALITIES ARE TRODDEN DOWN   • • • • • •   431 EMPEDOCLES II   92
          GREAT ATOSSA THEY ARE DEAD   • • • • • • • •   453 POOR MATTHIAS   26
          TO THE GREAT MAIN PASSD SEVILLE ON THE RIGHT   • • 484 S S LUSITANIA   4
          SEE THE WIFE OF HECTOR THAT GREAT PRE-EMINENT CAPTAIN   HOMER TRANS   33
          GREAT ELBRUIS WHITENS CLEAR   • • • • • • •   PILLARS UNIVERS 10
          IN FRONT OF SOME GREAT FANE WHEREOF WE KNOW   • •   LUCRETIUS 5   7
          SOONER THAN THOSE TWIN REACHES OF GREAT TIME   • •   FRAGMENT 5   7

GREATER
          THESE OR MUCH GREATER THINGS BUT CAUGHT   • • • •   223 EPILOG LAOCOON   55
          GREATER BY FAR THAN THOU ARE DEAD   • • • • • •   309 OBERMANN   91

GREATEST
          FOR GREATEST HATH THEIR LABOUR BEEN   • • • • •   227 EPILOG LAOCOON 210
          FOR GREATEST HAS THEIR LABOUR BEEN   • • • • • •   227 EPILOG LAOCOON V 210
          WHICH MAKES MANS GREATEST WOE   • • • • • •   238 PROGRESS   V
          OF HER GREATEST GOLDEN-MOUTHD SONS   • • • • •   294 HEINES GRAVE   79
          WHOSE BANISHMENT IS NOT HIS GREATEST ILL   • • •   429 EMPEDOCLES II   12

GREATLY
          AND GREATLY MOVED THEN RUSTUM MADE REPLY   • • • •   68 SOHRAB RUSTUM   249

GREATNESS
          YEARN TO THE GREATNESS OF NATURE   • • • • •   235 YOUTH OF MAN   117
          ITS GREATNESS NOR THE REIGN OF FOOLS PROLONGD   • • 282 HAWORTH CHURCH V
          WHAT ANGUISH OF GREATNESS   • • • • • • • •   432 EMPEDOCLES II 104
          THEIR SOUL OF UNWORN YOUTH THEIR BREATH OF GREATNESS 440 EMPEDOCLES II 384
          IN GREATNESS ONCE IN SACKCLOTH NOW AND TEARS   • • 463 ALARIC AT ROME   20
          IS THINE THE LAUREL-CROWN THAT GREATNESS WREATHES   463 ALARIC AT ROME   25

GRECIAN
          WHO WEPT AT READING OF A GRECIAN KNIGHT   • • • •   153 TRISTRAM 3   144
          O WANDERER FROM A GRECIAN SHORE   • • • • • •   200 PHILOMELA   5
          AND SAW THE MERRY GRECIAN COASTER COME   • • • •   262 SCHOLAR-GIPSY   237
          WAS IT AS THE GRECIAN SINGS   • • • • • • • •   456 POOR MATTHIAS   131

GREECE
          THE BEAUTY AND THE GLORIOUS ART OF GREECE   • • •   168 RACHEL 2   14
          TO FORMS FROM ANTIQUE GREECE AND ROME UPTORN   • • 168 RACHEL 3   3
          AH NOT THE RADIANT SPIRIT OF GREECE ALONE   • • •   168 RACHEL 3   9
          FOR TIS SO SURELY EVEN IN GREECE   • • • • •   221 EPILOG LAOCOON   13
          AND MAN HAS TURND THEM MANY TIMES MADE GREECE   • • 239 REVOLUTIONS   5
          GOETHE IN WEIMAR SLEEPS AND GREECE   • • • • •   270 MEMORIAL VERSES   1

GREEDY
          UPON THEIR CARAVAN OR GREEDY KINGS   • • • • • •   193 STRAYED REVEL   249
          FROM BANDS OF GREEDY HEIRS BE FREE   • • • • • •   249 WISH   2

GREEK
          DO FOR THIS RADIANT GREEK-SOULD ARTIST CEASE   • • 168 RACHEL 2   12
          THINKING OF HIS OWN GODS A GREEK   • • • • • •   301 GRANDE CHARTR   81
          ON LAND RENEW THAT GREEK EXPLOIT WHOSE GLORIES   • • 481 HUNGARIAN NAT   12

GREEKS
          WHO LED THE GREEKS TO ILIUM AGAMEMNON   • • • •   367 MEROPE   1035

GREEN
          MID BRIGHT GREEN FIELDS BELOW THE PINES   • • •   16 CHURCH BROU 2   5
          OF OPEN HILL-SWARD FRESH AND GREEN   • • • • •   16 CHURCH BROU 2   13
          OF SHAVEN HILL-SWARD TRIM AND GREEN   • • • • •   16 CHURCH BROU 2 V 13
          MARTIN AND I DOWN A GREEN ALPINE STREAM   • • •   24 DREAM   2
          EMERGING ON THE GREEN HILL-SIDE   • • • • • •   54 RESIGNATION   59
          THE LOOSE DARK STONES ON THE GREEN WAY   • • •   55 RESIGNATION   100
          AND DARK GREEN MELONS AND THERE RUSTUM SATE   • •   67 SOHRAB RUSTUM   199
          DIGHT WITH A SADDLE-CLOTH OF BROIDERD GREEN   • •   69 SOHRAB RUSTUM   277
          THAT THE GREEN WATER IN THE TANKS   • • • • •   89 SICK KING BOKH   60
          A DARK GREEN FOREST-DRESS   • • • • • • • •   131 TRISTRAM 1   16
          BEFORE US ARE THE SWEET GREEN FIELDS OF WALES   • • 133 TRISTRAM 1   95
          AH WOULD I WERE IN THOSE GREEN FIELDS AT PLAY   • • 133 TRISTRAM 1   97
          THE GREEN ISLE WHERE SHE WAS BRED   • • • • •   134 TRISTRAM 1   130
          DIE ON THE GREEN FIELDS OF WALES   • • • • • •   135 TRISTRAM 1   158

GREEN   (CONTINUED)
        THESE MUSING FITS IN THE GREEN WOOD   • • • • • •   138 TRISTRAM 1   247
        THE SOLITUDES OF THE GREEN WOOD   • • • • • •   139 TRISTRAM 1   290
        IN THE GREEN WOOD ALL OUR LIVES ALONE   • • • •   143 TRISTRAM 2   36
        A STATELY HUNTSMAN CLAD IN GREEN   • • • • • •   147 TRISTRAM 2   153
        NOT IN THE FREE GREEN WOOD AT ALL   • • • • • •   149 TRISTRAM 2   179
        IN A GREEN CIRCULAR HOLLOW IN THE HEATH   • • • •   149 TRISTRAM 3   7
        IS LIGHT AND GREEN THE HEATHER WHICH ALL ROUND   • • 150 TRISTRAM 3   14
        WARM WITH THE WINTER-SUN OF BURNISHD GREEN   • • • • 150 TRISTRAM 3   21
        THROUGH WHOSE GREEN BOUGHS THE GOLDEN SUNSHINE CREEPS 154 TRISTRAM 3   157
        TO REST UNGLOVED ON HER GREEN RIDING-DRESS   • • • • 154 TRISTRAM 3   175
        UNDER THE THORNS ON THE GREEN SWARD AND STRONG   • • 155 TRISTRAM 3   196
        IN THAT GREEN CIRCULAR OPENING IN THE HEATH   • •   TRISTRAM 3   V   7
        IN A GREEN CIRCULAR OPENING IN THE HEATH   • • • •   TRISTRAM 3   V   7
        IS GREEN AND CLEAR THE HEATHER WHICH ALL ROUND   • •   TRISTRAM 3   V   14
        IS LIGHT AND GREEN THE HEATHER WHICH ALL ROUND   TRISTRAM 3   V   14
        THROUGH THE GREEN FERN OF THE SHY FALLOW-DEER   • •   155 TRISTRAM 3   V 193
        TO GAZE ON THE GREEN SEA OF LEAF AND BOUGH   • • • • 155 TRISTRAM 3   V 202
        GREEN ROLLS BENEATH THE HEADLANDS   • • • • • •   159 NECKAN   5
        GREEN ROLLS THE BALTIC SEA   • • • • • • • •   159 NECKAN   6
        FAR FROM THE GREEN SEA WAVE   • • • • • • • •   159 NECKAN   V   16
        SHE SIGHD SHE LOOKD UP THROUGH THE CLEAR GREEN SEA   163 FORSAKEN MERM   55
        SMOTE ON THE SQUALID STREETS OF BETHNAL GREEN   • • 169 EAST LONDON   2
        BUT BRIGHT ARE THOSE GREEN FIELDS AT HAND   • • • •   184 TERRACE BERNE   7
        ROUND HIS GREEN HARVEST-PLOT   • • • • • • • •   190 STRAYED REVEL   159
        ALIVE WITH BRIGHT GREEN LIZARDS   • • • • • •   191 STRAYED REVEL   173
        GAILY THEIR PINE-STAFF GREEN   • • • • • • • •   218 BACCHANALIA 1   24
        THE GRASS HAD STILL THE GREEN OF MAY   • • • • • •   222 EPILOG LAOCOON   38
        HOW GREEN UNDER THE BOUGHS IT IS   • • • • • •   248 KENSINGTON GARD   7
        LIGHT THE GREEN-FOLIAGD CHESTNUTS PLAY   • • • •   248 KENSINGTON GARD V
        HOW GREEN AMONG THE BOUGHS IT IS   • • • • • •   KENSINGTON GARD V   7
        HOW GREEN BETWEEN THE STEMS IT IS   • • • • • •   KENSINGTON GARD V   7
        WHO CAN SEE THE GREEN EARTH ANY MORE   • • • • • •   252 FUTURE   27
        CROSS AND RECROSS THE STRIPS OF MOON-BLANCHD GREEN   255 SCHOLAR-GIPSY   9
        AND ROUND GREEN ROOTS AND YELLOWING STALKS I SEE   • 255 SCHOLAR-GIPSY   24
        AND WATCH THE WARM GREEN-MUFFLED CUMNER HILLS   • • 257 SCHOLAR-GIPSY   69
        GREEN BURSTING FIGS AND TUNNIES STEEPD IN BRINE   • 262 SCHOLAR-GIPSY   239
        DOWN EACH GREEN BANK HATH GONE THE PLOUGHBOYS TEAM   266 THYRSIS   118
        VESTED FOR EVER WITH GREEN   • • • • • • • •   280 HAWORTH CHURCH   3
        DYING TOO SOON YET GREEN • • • • • • • • • • • •   283 HAWORTH CHURCH   71
        ARE GREEN IN THE HOUSE OF ONE   • • • • • • • •   280 HAWORTH CHURCH V   4
        OF HAZELS GREEN IN WHOSE DEPTH   • • • • • • • •   297 HEINES GRAVE   182
        GAY DAMES ARE THERE IN SYLVAN GREEN   • • • • • •   305 GRANDE CHARTR   185
        HOW OFTEN WHERE THE SLOPES ARE GREEN   • • • • • •   310 OBERMANN   113
        STAND DARK ROUND THY GREEN GRAVE   • • • • • •   311 OBERMANN   168
        ISSUING ON THAT GREEN PLACE   • • • • • • • •   311 OBERMANN   170
        BY THEIR GREEN RIVER WHO DOTH CHANGE   • • • • • •   313 OBERMANN MORE   25
        A GREEN NEW EARTH APPEARS   • • • • • • • • • •   322 OBERMANN MORE   286
        THERE ON A HIGH GREEN SPUR WHICH BATHES ITS POINT   356 MEROPE   751
        AND THE GREEN AGNUS-CASTUS   • • • • • • • • • •   391 MEROPE   1618
        AMONG THE GREEN ILLYRIAN HILLS AND THERE   • • • •   426 EMPEDOCLES I 2   429
        WHERE THE LONG GREEN REED-BEDS SWAY   • • • • • • •   433 EMPEDOCLES II   133
        GREEN TURF ABOVE AND CRUMBLING DUST BELOW   • • • •   464 ALARIC AT ROME   57
        AND REST HIS WEARY EYES ON THE GREEN LAND AND THEE   470 ALARIC AT ROME   222
        LIKE A GREEN LAND AT SUNSET ALL WERE THERE   • • • • 474 CROMWELL   84
        GREEN HAPPY PLACES LIKE A FLOWERY LEA   • • • • • •   475 CROMWELL   117
        FROM THOSE WEIRD DOMES OF MOUNDED GREEN   • • • •   480 HAYSWATER BOAT   23
        THEIR FIRST GREEN MUFFLE ON THE GROUND   • • • •   484 ROME-SICKNESS   16

GREEND
        IT GREEND IT BRANCHD IT WAVED • • • • • • • • • •   160 NECKAN   54

GREENS
        THROUGH THIS WASTE OF SUNLESS GREENS • • • • • •   33 NEW SIRENS   212

GREENSWARD
        MOUNTAIN GREENSWARD PAVES THE CHANCEL   • • • •   15 CHURCH BROU 1   71

GREENWOOD
        DEEP DEEP THE GREENWOOD ROUND THEM WAVES   • • • •   305 GRANDE CHARTR   173

GREET
        GAY HER SMILING LORD TO GREET   • • • • • • • • •   13 CHURCH BROU 1   10
        AND THROUGH GOLDEN HORNS TO GREET YOU   • • • • • •   29 NEW SIRENS   103
        RUSTUM MY FATHER WHO I HOPED SHOULD GREET   • • • •   62 SOHRAB RUSTUM   50
        SHOULD ONE DAY GREET UPON SOME WELL-FOUGHT FIELD • • 62 SOHRAB RUSTUM   51
        OR IS IT HERE WITHHELD TO GREET THE DEAD   • • • •   111 BALDER DEAD 2   245
        HERMOD GREET BALDER IF THOU WILT AND HOLD   • • • •   111 BALDER DEAD 2   247
        AND GREET ACROSS INFINITY   • • • • • • • • • •   180 FAREWELL   76
        THIS COMER GREET HER WITH JOY   • • • • • • • • •   284 HAWORTH CHURCH   85
        SHALL I NOT GREET HER SHALL I NOT LEAP FORTH   • •   331 MEROPE   60
        WE GREET THEE BY THE WINDOW-PANE   • • • • • • • •   451 GEISTS GRAVE   47
        GREET UPON THE LAWN AT PLAY   • • • • • • • • • •   454 POOR MATTHIAS   68
        LAUD THEIR PLUMAGE GREET THEIR LAYS   • • • • • • •   455 POOR MATTHIAS   100

GREETED
        AND GREETED GUDURZ WITH BOTH HANDS AND SAID   • •   67 SOHRAB RUSTUM   204
        AND HERMOD GREETED HER AND GALLOPD BY   • • • • •   108 BALDER DEAD 2   136
        GREETED OF NONE DISFEATURED AND FORLORN   • • • •   109 BALDER DEAD 2   171
        AND GREETED ODIN AND THE GODS AND SAID • • • • •   114 BALDER DEAD 3   35

GREETED   (CONTINUED)
    SHE GREETED THEM THE FIRST AND LAUGHD AND SAID . . 123 BALDER DEAD 3   336

GREETING
    SHOUTS GREETING FROM HIS EASY CHAIR . . . . . . 53 RESIGNATION   43

GREETINGS
    AND THE BURST OF JOYFUL GREETINGS . . . . . . 30 NEW SIRENS   117
    NODS SMILES AND GREETINGS AND FAREWELLS . . . . 224 EPILOG LAOCOON   121
    THEN FLY OUR GREETINGS FLY OUR SPEECH AND SMILES . . 262 SCHOLAR-GIPSY   231
    A TIME WILL COME FOR GREETINGS BUT TO-DAY . . . 386 MEROPE   1444
    AND GLADSOME GREETINGS OF THE BUOYANT SEA . . . 472 CROMWELL   8

GREETS
    HE GREETS THEM ONCE HE SAILS AGAIN . . . . . . 156 SAINT BRANDAN   3

GREW
    NO NOR GREW DARK WHEN AUTUMN BROUGHT THE CLOUDS . . 12 MYCERINUS   121
    TIME IS LAME AND WE GREW WEARY . . . . 28 NEW SIRENS   67
    INTO DAYLIGHT NEVER GREW . . . . 29 NEW SIRENS   106
    VAIN IT WASTES AND WE GREW WEARY . . . . . . 28 NEW SIRENS   V 67
    VAIN IT WORE AND WE GREW WEARY . . . . 28 NEW SIRENS   V 67
    SO WHEN THE FEAST GREW LOUD . . . . 47 WORLD QUIETIST   25
    THE LAW GREW STRONGER EVERY DAY . . . . . . 56 RESIGNATION   135
    GREW SUDDENLY IN HEAVEN AND DARKD THE SUN . . . 75 SOHRAB RUSTUM   482
    GREW BLACKER THUNDER RUMBLED IN THE AIR . . . . 76 SOHRAB RUSTUM   500
    THE ANGUISH OF THE DEEP-FIXD SPEAR GREW FIERCE . . 80 SOHRAB RUSTUM   650
    HIS LIMBS GREW SLACK MOTIONLESS WHITE HE LAY . . 86 SOHRAB RUSTUM   848
    GREW DEEPER THUNDER CRASHD ALONG THE SKY . . . 76 SOHRAB RUSTUM   V 500
    FOR IT GREW DARK BUT HODER TOUCHD HIS ARM . . . 101 BALDER DEAD 1   229
    BUT WHEN THE RED GLOW ON THE SEA GREW COLD . . . 151 TRISTRAM 3   58
    AND HE GREW FOND AND EAGER TO OBEY . . . . . 155 TRISTRAM 3   183
    UPON THE BROW-TOP GREW A THORN AND HERE . . . . 155 TRISTRAM 3   205
    THEIR CHEEKS GREW FLUSHD AND OVER EACH HOT BROW . . TRISTRAM 3   V 32
    THY CHEEK WAS GRAVE THY SPEECH GREW RARE . . . 178 FAREWELL   16
    NOR FEARD BUT THY LOVE LIKEWISE GREW . . . . . 180 ISOLATION MARG   5
    BUT LIGHT THE SERIOUS VISAGE GREW . . . . . . 202 URANIA   11
    HE GREW OLD IN AN AGE HE CONDEMND . . . . . . 229 YOUTH OF NATURE   28
    CLOUDED AND DIM GREW THEIR EYE . . . . 233 YOUTH OF MAN   43
    THEY DROOPD THEY GREW BLIND THEY GREW OLD . . . 233 YOUTH OF MAN   48
    THEY DROOPD THEY GREW BLIND THEY GREW OLD . . . 233 YOUTH OF MAN   48
    WHERE THICK THE COWSLIPS GREW AND FAR DESCRIED . . 266 THYRSIS   114
    COUNTING TILL I GREW UP THE LAGGARD YEARS . . . 367 MEROPE   1046
    GREW USED TO THE APPROACH OF GLORYS WINGS . . . 445 WESTMIN ABBEY   56
    AND HARSH THE TEMPER GREW . . . . 446 WESTMIN ABBEY   67
    YES MAX AND WE GREW SLOW AND SAD . . . . . . 460 KAISER DEAD   43
    HOW BOTH WERE HASTENING AS THEY FLOWERED AND GREW . 469 ALARIC AT ROME   189
    ITS SHADOWS OER THE FUTURE FLOWERD AND GREW . . 473 CROMWELL   56

GREY
    GREY TIME-WORN MARBLES . . . . 50 CONSOLATION   16
    AND THE FIRST GREY OF MORNING FILLD THE EAST . . 61 SOHRAB RUSTUM   1
    BUT WHEN THE GREY DAWN STOLE INTO HIS TENT . . . 61 SOHRAB RUSTUM   7
    AS WHEN SOME GREY NOVEMBER MORN THE FILES . . . 64 SOHRAB RUSTUM   111
    STREAKD WITH ITS FIRST GREY HAIRS HOPE FILLED HIS SOUL 71 SOHRAB RUSTUM   340
    WITH THAT OLD KING HER FATHER WHO GROWS GREY . . 78 SOHRAB RUSTUM   591
    OVER THE GREY SEA-RIDGES AND THE GLIMPSE . . . 124 BALDER DEAD 3   366
    BY THE GREY ATLANTIC SEA . . . . 137 TRISTRAM 1   231
    AND THE GREY TURRETS OF THE CASTLE OLD . . . . 151 TRISTRAM 3   59
    THE CHILDREN AND THE GREY-HAIRD SENESCHAL . . . 152 TRISTRAM 3   97
    BUT NECKAN IN THE TWILIGHT GREY . . . . . . 161 NECKAN   59
    AND NECKAN IN THE TWILIGHT GREY . . . . . . 161 NECKAN   V 59
    AND THE LITTLE GREY CHURCH ON THE WINDY SHORE . . 162 FORSAKEN MERM   26
    IN THE LITTLE GREY CHURCH ON THE SHORE TO-DAY . . 163 FORSAKEN MERM   57
    TO THE LITTLE GREY CHURCH ON THE WINDY HILL . . 163 FORSAKEN MERM   71
    IN THIS FAIR STRANGERS EYES OF GREY . . . . . 183 ABSENCE   1
    BY THE GREY SEA IF SO THEN HAIL . . . . . . 189 STRAYED REVEL   128
    GREY RAIN-BLEARD STATUES OVERPEER . . . . . . 191 STRAYED REVEL   179
    WITH THE GREY EYES AND THE LOVELY BROWN HAIR . . 206 SEPARATION   16
    TOO LOVELY TO BE GREY . . . . 208 ON THE RHINE   20
    BUT RUIND AND SOLEMN AND GREY . . . . 228 YOUTH OF NATURE   20
    HERE WHERE THIS GREY BALUSTRADE . . . . . . 234 YOUTH OF MAN   62
    FROM THE GREY-WALLD GARDENS A BREATH . . . . . 234 YOUTH OF MAN   67
    WITH THE GREY MIST MARKING ITS COURSE . . . . 234 YOUTH OF MAN   84
    THE CLOUDED SKY IS STILL AND GREY . . . . . . 248 KENSINGTON GARD V
    OF THE GREY EXPANSE WHERE HE FLOATS . . . . . 254 FUTURE   79
    IN HAT OF ANTIQUE SHAPE AND CLOAK OF GREY . . . 256 SCHOLAR-GIPSY   55
    WITH SCARLET PATCHES TAGGD AND SHREDS OF GREY . . 258 SCHOLAR-GIPSY   114
    THE CHEEK GROWN THIN THE BROWN HAIR SPRENT WITH GREY 266 THYRSIS   135
    BEARDED WITH LICHEN SCRAWLD AND GREY . . . . . 274 STANZAS CARNAC   10
    BEARDED WITH LICHEN OLD AND GREY . . . . . . 274 STANZAS CARNAC   V 10
    SLOW TO A STOP AT MORNING GREY . . . . 276 SOUTHERN NIGHT   29
    SOME GREY CRUSADING KNIGHT AUSTERE . . . . . 278 SOUTHERN NIGHT   93
    GREY-HEADED WRINKLED CLAD IN WHITE . . . . . 278 SOUTHERN NIGHT   V 86
    LONG ON THE GREY HILL-SIDE . . . . 297 HEINES GRAVE   165
    LOOK THROUGH THE SHOWERY TWILIGHT GREY . . . . 300 GRANDE CHARTR   22
    BY ENGLANDS LAKES IN GREY OLD AGE . . . . . . 308 OBERMANN   49
    THE CONE OF JAMAN PALE AND GREY . . . . . . 313 OBERMANN MORE   31
    ACROSS HER SPIRIT GREY . . . . 316 OBERMANN MORE   114
    THAT CLIMB FROM THE STREAMS EDGE THE LONG GREY TUFTS 406 EMPEDOCLES I 1   16

GREY   (CONTINUED)
    OUR HAIR GROWS GREY OUR EYES ARE DIMMD OUR   423 EMPEDOCLES I 2   336
        HEAT IS TAMED
    A GREY OLD MAN AND WOMAN YET OF OLD . . . . . .   427 EMPEDOCLES I 2   449
    IN THE RIPPLED WATERS GREY . . . .   433 EMPEDOCLES II   134
    AND THOU O ABBEY GREY . . . .   449 WESTMIN ABBEY   171
    THOU DIDST KNOW THEM OLD AND GREY . . . . . .   453 POOR MATTHIAS   29
    NO GLITTERING HOPES ON LIFES GREY DISTANCE SMILED   475 CROMWELL   126
    A FRETTED WALL OF BLUE AND GREY . . . .   479 HAYSWATER BOAT   12
    THE GREY-STREAKD WATERS LABOUR STILL . . . . .   479 HAYSWATER BOAT   18

GRIEF
    AND ONE LOUD CRY OF GRIEF AND OF AMAZE . . . .   11 MYCERINUS   80
    FROM GRIEF THAT IS BUT PASSION . . . .   39 STAGIRIUS   33
    OF GRIEF AND EASED US WITH A THOUSAND SLEEPS . .   43 GIPSY CHILD   52
    AND WEAR THIS MAJESTY OF GRIEF AGAIN . . . . . .   44 GIPSY CHILD   68
    AND GRIEF THAT HEALD AT EVERY SMILE OF EARTH . .   41 GIPSY CHILD   V 20
    REMORSE GRIEF JOY AND WERE THE SCOPE . . . . .   58 RESIGNATION   218
    WHAT WILL THAT GRIEF WHAT WILL THAT VENGEANCE BE   78 SOHRAB RUSTUM   587
    OH COULD I LIVE TILL I THAT GRIEF HAD SEEN . . .   78 SOHRAB RUSTUM   588
    AND HIS SOUL SET TO GRIEF AS THE VAST TIDE . .   79 SOHRAB RUSTUM   616
    AND RUSTUM GAZED ON HIM WITH GRIEF AND SAID . .   80 SOHRAB RUSTUM   640
    WHEN THEY SAW RUSTUMS GRIEF AND RUKSH THE HORSE .   82 SOHRAB RUSTUM   730
    HIS HEAD AS IF INQUIRING WHAT THEIR GRIEF . .   82 SOHRAB RUSTUM   734
    NOW MUST I CALL THY GRIEF NOT WISE . . . . . .   92 SICK KING BOKH   134
    AND GRIEVOUS IS THE GRIEF FOR THESE . . . . .   92 SICK KING BOKH   150
    WEEP HIM AN HOUR BUT WHAT CAN GRIEF AVAIL . . .   96 BALDER DEAD 1   27
    TELLING HER ALL THAT GRIEF THEY HAVE IN HEAVEN .   100 BALDER DEAD 1   180
    AND HODER TOO CAME HOME DISTRAUGHT WITH GRIEF .   102 BALDER DEAD 1   249
    THOU KNOWST THOU KNOWST WHAT GRIEF WE HAVE IN HEAVEN 110 BALDER DEAD 2   192
    SHOW ME THROUGH ALL THE WORLD THE SIGNS OF GRIEF . 111 BALDER DEAD 2   234
    SHOW HER THROUGH ALL THE WORLD THE SIGNS OF GRIEF 114 BALDER DEAD 3   42
    OUT OF OUR SIGHT THAT WE MAY TURN FROM GRIEF . .   115 BALDER DEAD 3   55
    A GRIEF AND SYMPATHISE . . . .   140 TRISTRAM 1   324
    SICK WITH GRIEF I AM AND FAINT WITH TRAVEL . . .   142 TRISTRAM 2   15
    GRIEF SINCE THEN HIS HOME WITH ME DOTH MAKE . .   145 TRISTRAM 2   88
    POURD IN GRIEF BEFORE THE VIRGIN—MOTHER . . . .   144 TRISTRAM 2   V 63
    VAIN IS THE AGONY OF GRIEF . . . .   208 ON THE RHINE   6
    YET THYRSIS LET ME GIVE MY GRIEF ITS HOUR . . .   265 THYRSIS   102
    PASSION VEHEMENCE GRIEF . . . .   284 HAWORTH CHURCH   95
    SHUT OUT THE GRIEF THE DESPAIR . . . .   283 HAWORTH CHURCH   V
    ANOTHER GRIEF I SEE . . . .   283 HAWORTH CHURCH   V
    THE NOBLENESS OF GRIEF IS GONE . . . .   302 GRANDE CHARTR   107
    THEY HAVE THE GRIEF MEN HAD OF YORE . . . . . .   303 GRANDE CHARTR   119
    AND LOOK TO MEET THEM THAT ONE GRIEF—PLUNGED FORM 331 MEROPE   56
    BY SAD OBSERVANCES AND PUBLIC GRIEF . . . . .   332 MEROPE   81
    I WILL NOT VIOLATE THY NOBLE GRIEF . . . . . .   333 MEROPE   108
    AND THESE MEN LOOK TO THEE AND FROM THY GRIEF .   334 MEROPE   141
    UNADULATING GRIEF CONSPIRACY . . . .   338 MEROPE   261
    DEMANDEST VENGEANCE NOT GRIEF . . . .   343 MEROPE   405
    O THAT MY OVER—SPEED AND BURSTING GRIEF . . .   362 MEROPE   939
    WHERESOEER MEN ARE THERE IS GRIEF . . . . .   369 MEROPE   1093
    WHAT MAD BEWILDERMENT OF GRIEF IS THIS . . . .   396 MEROPE   1758
    AND SEE TO MEET THEM THAT ONE GRIEF—PLUNGED FORM . 331 MEROPE   V 56
    AND YET NOT THAT GRIEF WHICH THEN WILL BE OF   HOMER TRANS   23
        THE TROJANS
    MOVES ME SO MUCH NOT HECUBAS GRIEF NOR PRIAM   HOMER TRANS   24
        MY FATHERS
    AS THY GRIEF WHEN IN TEARS SOME BRAZEN—COATED ACHAIAN HOMER TRANS   27
    SO SOME MAN WILL SAY AND THEN THY GRIEF WILL REDOUBLE HOMER TRANS   35
    CUTS SHORT THE FEIGNINGS OF FANTASTIC GRIEF . .   FRAGMENT 1   6

GRIEFS
    ALL WEAKNESS WHICH IMPAIRS ALL GRIEFS WHICH BOW . .   3 SHAKESPEARE   13
    ALL WEAKNESS THAT IMPAIRS ALL GRIEFS THAT BOW . .   3 SHAKESPEARE   V 13
    BREASTS HER OWN GRIEFS AND URGED TOO FIERCELY SAYS   6 GEO CRUIKSHANK   10

GRIEVE
    FAILS BUT ONE THING TO GRIEVE HERE BALDER STOPS .   111 BALDER DEAD 2   235
    FAILS BUT ONE THING TO GRIEVE THERE BALDER STOPS . 114 BALDER DEAD 3   43
    LAST OF THE RACE OF THEM WHO GRIEVE . . . . .   302 GRANDE CHARTR   110
    THE MILLIONS SUFFER STILL AND GRIEVE . . . . .   320 OBERMANN MORE   233
    MORE FOR THIS LANDS SAKE GRIEVE I THAN MINE OWN .   398 MEROPE   1784

GRIEVES
    WHILE ALL ELSE GRIEVES HIM THAT HIS GRANDCHILDS DEATH 359 MEROPE   851

GRIEVEST
    RUKSH NOW THOU GRIEVEST BUT O RUKSH THY FEET . .   83 SOHRAB RUSTUM   738

GRIEVOUS
    AND GRIEVOUS IS THE GRIEF FOR THESE . . . . . .   92 SICK KING BOKH   150
    BUT NOT TO ME SO GRIEVOUS AS I KNOW . . . . .   127 BALDER DEAD 3   500
    WITH GRIEVOUS DEEDS PERHAPS WITH MURDER NO . . .   336 MEROPE   209
    HARDLY THE FOURTH WITH GRIEVOUS LOSS REGAIND . .   336 MEROPE   218
    HARDLY THE THIRD WITH GRIEVOUS LOSS REGAIND . .   336 MEROPE   V 218

GRIFFIN
    IT WAS THAT GRIFFIN WHICH OF OLD REARD ZAL . . .   81 SOHRAB RUSTUM   679

GRIM
    FROWNING GRIM DOWN THOU WICKED KING . . . . .   91 SICK KING BOKH   97
    OF THE GRIM LAPITHAE AND THESEUS DRIVE . . . .   192 STRAYED REVEL   228

GRIM   (CONTINUED)
        SERRIED AND GRIM THE RING OF DORIAN LORDS   . . . .   401 MEROPE   1900

GRIMED
        AND A ROUGH GRIMED RACE HAVE THEIR HOMES   . . . .   283 HAWORTH CHURCH   60

GRIMLY
        SIT AND EYE GRIMLY THE VICTIM UNSCOURGED   . . . .   347 MEROPE   531

GROAN
        HARK A SHOUT A CRASH A GROAN   . . . .   13 CHURCH BROU 1   24
        CEASES NOT FROM ALL TIME TO HEAVE AND GROAN . . .   45 IN UTRUMQUE PAR   26
        AND RUSTUM PLUCKD IT BACK WITH ANGRY GROAN   . . .   76 SOHRAB RUSTUM   494
        THEN WITH A HEAVY GROAN RUSTUM BEWAILD   . . .   83 SOHRAB RUSTUM   767
        AND WITH A HEAVY GROAN RUSTUM REPLIED   . . .   83 SOHRAB RUSTUM   V 767
        TOO LONG LET WE THEM GROAN   . . . .   216 LORDS MESSENGER   4
        OF MEN CONTENTION-TOST OF MEN WHO GROAN   . . .   269 THYRSIS   224
        THAT THOUSANDS COUNTED EVERY GROAN   . . . . .   303 GRANDE CHARTR   137
        O THRICE UNHAPPY HOW I GROAN THY FATE   . . .   362 MEROPE   931
        WHEREFORE DOST THOU GROAN SO LOUD   . . . . .   430 EMPEDOCLES II   45

GROAND
        SO REGNER SPAKE AND ALL THE HEROES GROAND   . . .   117 BALDER DEAD 3   153
        HE BOWD HIS HEAD AND DEEPLY GROAND AND DIED . .   402 MEROPE   1929

GROANING
        THROUGH WHICH THE GROANING DANUBE STRAINS   . . . .   52 RESIGNATION   12
        THE LOADED BOAT SWINGS GROANING   . . . . . .   192 STRAYED REVEL   198

GROANINGS
        AND STRONG CONVULSIVE GROANINGS SHOOK HIS BREAST . .   82 SOHRAB RUSTUM   703

GROANS
        MID DUST AND GROANS AND LIMBS LOPPD OFF AND BLOOD   105 BALDER DEAD 2   16
        AND THE SPERCHEIOS VALE SHAKEN WITH GROANS   . . . . 198 FRAG ANTIGONE   100
        OF ENEMIES AND COUNT THEIR DYING GROANS   . . .   387 MEROPE   1469
        THAT THY GROANS LIKE THUNDER PREST   . . . . .   430 EMPEDOCLES II   62
        THESE RUMBLINGS ARE NOT TYPHOS GROANS I KNOW . . .   431 EMPEDOCLES II   95
        THAT THY GROANS LIKE THUNDER DEEP   . . . . .   430 EMPEDOCLES II   V 62

GROPED
        AND DOWN TO OCEAN GROPED AND CROSSD THE ICE   . . 124 BALDER DEAD 3   376

GROPING
        HIS GROPING BLINDNESS   . . . .   192 STRAYED REVEL   217
        AND ON EARTH WE WANDER GROPING REELING   . . . . 210 SELF-DECEPTION   21

GROUND
        NOT BY THEIR HANDS WHO VEX THE PATIENT GROUND   . .   4 DUKE WELLINGTON   3
        SKIMS NOW AND THEN THE SHINING GROUND   . . . .   54 RESIGNATION   71
        CRUSTED WITH GOLD AND ON THE GROUND WERE WORKD . .   69 SOHRAB RUSTUM   278
        HE REELD AND STAGGERING BACK SANK TO THE GROUND . .   76 SOHRAB RUSTUM   521
        WITH HIS HEAD BOWING TO THE GROUND AND MANE . . .   82 SOHRAB RUSTUM   731
        HE REELD AND STAGGERING BACK SUNK TO THE GROUND . .   76 SOHRAB RUSTUM   V 521
        BEHIND THE DOOR UPON THE GROUND   . . . . .   90 SICK KING BOKH   79
        FAIR MEN WHO LIVE IN HOLES UNDER THE GROUND . . .   97 BALDER DEAD 1   56
        COUCHD BESIDE HIM ON THE GROUND   . . . . .   137 TRISTRAM 1   226
        SHE SINKS UPON THE GROUND HER HOOD   . . . . .   146 TRISTRAM 2   103
        OVER THE WASTE THIS CIRQUE OF OPEN GROUND   . . .   150 TRISTRAM 3   13
        AMONG THE HOLLY-CLUMPS AND BROKEN GROUND   . . .   150 TRISTRAM 3   28
        WHO LIES GUARDING HER FEET ALONG THE GROUND . . .   152 TRISTRAM 3   89
        PEERD TWIXT THE STEMS AND THE GROUND BROKE AWAY . . 155 TRISTRAM 3   186
        AND MADE A LITTLE PLOT OF MAGIC GROUND   . . .   156 TRISTRAM 3   220
        OVER THE WASTE THIS RING OF OPEN GROUND   . . .   150 TRISTRAM 3   V 13
        OVER THE WASTE BUT WHERE THIS OPEN GROUND   . . .   TRISTRAM 3   V 13
        OVER THE WASTE ALL THE HOLLOW GROUND   . . .   TRISTRAM 3   V 13
        FEED IN THE OOZE OF THEIR PASTURE-GROUND   . . .   162 FORSAKEN MERM   40
        RADIANT ADORND OUTSIDE A HIDDEN GROUND   . . .   166 AUSTERITY POET   13
        EVEN IN THAT PHOEBUS-GUARDED GROUND   . . .   221 EPILOG LAOCOON   15
        HIES AH FROM WHENCE WHAT NATIVE GROUND   . . .   225 EPILOG LAOCOON   125
        FOR MOST I KNOW THOU LOVST RETIRED GROUND   . . .   257 SCHOLAR-GIPSY   71
        ABOVE THE FOREST-GROUND CALLED THESSALY   . . .   258 SCHOLAR-GIPSY   115
        AND LOSE TO-MORROW THE GROUND WON TO-DAY   . . .   260 SCHOLAR-GIPSY   179
        OF STORMS THAT RAGE OUTSIDE OUR HAPPY GROUND . . .   264 THYRSIS   49
        AND THIS RUDE CUMNOR GROUND . . . . . .   269 THYRSIS   216
        AND THIS RUDE CUMNOR GROUND . . . . . .   269 THYRSIS   V 216
        THE HUMBLE GOOD FROM THE GROUND . . . . .   287 RUGBY CHAPEL   50
        HOW SHOULD WE GROW IN OTHER GROUND   . . . . .   306 GRANDE CHARTR   207
        THERE SOBS I KNOW NOT WHAT GROUND-TONE   . . .   307 OBERMANN   35
        ON NATIVE GROUND THAN DRAG THE TEDIOUS HOURS . . .   383 MEROPE   1380
        BUT GAZING AT HIM FROM THE GROUND THE KING   . . .   402 MEROPE   1927
        ON PELION ON THE GRASSY GROUND   . . . . . .   414 EMPEDOCLES I 2   58
        AND BEND THEIR LITTLE FISTS AND RATE THE SENSELESS   421 EMPEDOCLES I 2   276
            GROUND
        AFFORDS NO GROUND TO AFFIRM . . . .   424 EMPEDOCLES I 2   349
        THE GROUND WHICH HIDES THEE NOW BUT FOUR   . . .   449 GEISTS GRAVE   2
        UNHALLOWED FEET ARE TRAMPLING ON THIS HAUNTED GROUND 467 ALARIC AT ROME   144
        WITH FEET THAT SPURND THE GROUND LO MILTON THERE . . 477 CROMWELL   175
        THEIR FIRST GREEN MUFFLE ON THE GROUND   . . .   484 ROME-SICKNESS   16
        STREAMD TO THE GROUND BY THE YOKE ESCAPING   HOMER TRANS   45
            FROM UNDER THE COLLAR

GROUNDS
        ACCEPT THEM OR REJECT THEM BOTH HAVE GROUNDS   • •   120 BALDER DEAD 3   226
        BUT JOY WHOSE GROUNDS ARE TRUE • • • • • • • •   320 OBERMANN MORE   238
        AND JOY WHOSE GROUNDS ARE TRUE • • • • • • • •   320 OBERMANN MORE   V 238
        NO NOR EXPECT THEE TO ADMIT THE GROUNDS   • • • •   340 MEROPE   339
        HIS GROUNDS HOWEVER SPECIOUS SHOWN   • • • • • •   354 MEROPE   694

GROUP
        SURVEYS EACH HAPPY GROUP WHICH FLEETS   • • • •   57 RESIGNATION   166
        SURVEYS EACH HAPPY GROUP THAT FLEETS • • • • • •   57 RESIGNATION   V 166
        THE PASSING GROUP THE SUMMER-MORN   • • • • • •   222 EPILOG LAOCOON   51

GROUPD
        THE GODS HELD TALK TOGETHER GROUPD IN KNOTS   • •   113 BALDER DEAD 3   1
        BY CITY AND HOUSEHOLD GROUPD WE LIVE AND MANY SHOCKS   195 FRAG ANTIGONE   20
        GROUPD AROUND ZEUSS ALTAR ALL IN ARMS   • • • •   401 MEROPE   1899

GROUPS
        AND GROUPS UNDER THE DREAMING GARDEN-TREES   • • • •   264 THYRSIS   69

GROUSE
        THE RED-GROUSE SPRINGING AT OUR SOUND   • • • •   54 RESIGNATION   70
        HUM OER THE THYME THE GROUSE   • • • • • • • •   285 HAWORTH CHURCH   121

GROVE
        FROM PALM-GROVE ON TO PALM-GROVE HAPPY TREES   • •   11 MYCERINUS   86
        FROM PALM-GROVE ON TO PALM-GROVE HAPPY TREES   • •   11 MYCERINUS   86
        FROM TREE TO TREE ALL THROUGH THE TWINKLING GROVE   11 MYCERINUS   95
        SHAKES EVERY LEAF OF THE GROVE   • • • • • • •   293 HEINES GRAVE   43

GROVES
        INTO THE SILENCE OF THE GROVES AND WOODS   • • • •   10 MYCERINUS   67
        TO THE COOL REGION OF THE GROVES HE LOVED   • • • •   11 MYCERINUS   84
        SOMETIMES FROM THE GROVES CENTRE ECHOES CAME   • •   12 MYCERINUS   124

GROW
        THEIR LOVE LET ME KNOW MUST GROW STRONG AND   19 MODERN SAPPHO   13
            YET STRONGER
        AND YON WHITENING BONE-MOUNDS DO NOT GROW   • • • •   27 NEW SIRENS   56
        AND THOSE WHITENING BONE-MOUNDS DO NOT GROW   • •   27 NEW SIRENS   V 56
        TIME IS LAME AND WE GROW WEARY   • • • • • • •   28 NEW SIRENS   V 67
        MUSINGS THAT ERE THEY COULD GROW RIPE WERE FLOWN • •   41 GIPSY CHILD   V 19
        THIN THIN THE PLEASANT HUMAN NOISES GROW   • • • •   45 IN UTRUMQUE PAR   15
        THEIR JOINTS GROW STIFFER BUT THE YEAR   • • • •   56 RESIGNATION   128
        CHILLY THEY GROW YET WINDS IN MARCH   • • • • • •   56 RESIGNATION   130
        WHEN I AM DEAD WILL SOON GROW STILL   • • • • • •   94 SICK KING BOKH   218
        SO YE GROW SQUEAMISH GODS AND SNIFF AT HEAVEN   • •   123 BALDER DEAD 3   344
        THE GENERATIONS PASS THE AGES GROW   • • • • • •   127 BALDER DEAD 3   473
        UNTIL THEY CRUMBLE OR ELSE GROW LIKE STEEL • • • •   153 TRISTRAM 3   121
        AND GROW A HOME FOR ONLY THEE   • • • • • • •   180 ISOLATION MARG   4
        THAT MOCKING MOUTH GROW SWEETLY BLAND   • • • •   206 RIVER   6
        WHAT IS IT TO GROW OLD   • • • • • • • • • •   212 GROWING OLD   1
        GROW STIFFER EVERY FUNCTION LESS EXACT   • • • •   212 GROWING OLD   9
        TO GROW OLD IN DARKNESS AND PAIN   • • • • • •   234 YOUTH OF MAN   58
        THUS FEELING GAZING MIGHT I GROW   • • • • • •   251 WISH   49
        THUS FEELING GAZING LET ME GROW • • • • • • •   251 WISH   V 49
        THY HOPES GROW TIMOROUS AND UNFIXD THY POWERS   • •   261 SCHOLAR-GIPSY   227
        FADE AND GROW OLD AT LAST AND DIE LIKE OURS • • • •   261 SCHOLAR-GIPSY   230
        TOO RARE TOO RARE GROW NOW MY VISITS HERE   • • • •   263 THYRSIS   31
        THE WEST UNFLUSHES THE HIGH STARS GROW BRIGHT   • •   267 THYRSIS   163
        TOO RARE TOO RARE GROW NOW MY VISITS HERE   • • • •   269 THYRSIS   231
        HOW SHOULD WE GROW IN OTHER GROUND   • • • • • •   306 GRANDE CHARTR   207
        WHAT SHELTER TO GROW RIPE IS OURS   • • • • • •   308 OBERMANN   71
        WHAT LEISURE TO GROW WISE   • • • • • • • • •   308 OBERMANN   72
        THE SUMMER-DAY GROW LATE   • • • • • • • • •   310 OBERMANN   116
        LISTEND AND FELT THYSELF GROW YOUNG   • • • • • •   310 OBERMANN   127
        AND THE STRAIGHT ASHES GROW FOR SPEARS   • • • •   414 EMPEDOCLES I 2   65
        AT ONCE OUR EYES GROW CLEAR   • • • • • • •   424 EMPEDOCLES I 2   362
        STILL HUNGRIER FOR DELIGHT AS DELIGHTS GROW MORE RARE   424 EMPEDOCLES I 2   371
        THAT OTHER TORMENT GROW UNBEARABLE   • • • • • •   435 EMPEDOCLES II   226

GROWING
        WHEN THE SOUL GROWING CLEARER   • • • • • • • •   38 STAGIRIUS   14

GROWN
        WISHES UNWORTHY OF A MAN FULL-GROWN   • • • • • •   8 RELIGIOUS ISOL   8
        AH I HUSBAND WHATS GROWN RARE   • • • • • • • •   22 MEMORY-PICTURE   V
        OUT OF THIS STUFF THESE FORCES THOU ART GROWN   • •   46 IN UTRUMQUE PAR   V 38
        OUR SPIRITS HAVE GROWN   • • • • • • • • • •   177 PARTING   72
        UPON THE PINE-GROWN LATMIAN STEEP   • • • • • •   181 ISOLATION MARG   24
        THE CHEEK GROWN THIN THE BROWN HAIR SPRENT WITH GREY   266 THYRSIS   135
        SHEEP MAKE THE FURZE-GROWN AISLES THEIR FOLD   • •   274 STANZAS CARNAC   V 16
        SHEEP MAKE THE FURZE-GROWN NAVE THEIR FOLD • • • •   STANZAS CARNAC   V 16
        AND STOOPS TO CLEAR THY MOSS-GROWN DATE   • • • •   311 OBERMANN   173
        TOGETHER WE HAD GROWN TOGETHER LIVED • • • • • •   334 MEROPE   123
        WE HAD NOT LOST OUR BALANCE THEN NOR GROWN • • • •   436 EMPEDOCLES II   248
        BUT I HAVE NOT GROWN EASY IN THESE BONDS   • • • •   440 EMPEDOCLES II   397
        A CHURCH ONCE LARGE AND THEN GROWN STRAIT IN SOUL   449 WESTMIN ABBEY   156

GROWS
        BUT DEEPER THEIR VOICE GROWS AND NOBLER THEIR BEARING   20 MODERN SAPPHO   27

GROWS   (CONTINUED)
          FOR THE EYE GROWS FILLD WITH GAZING   . . . . . .   30 NEW SIRENS   119
          CROWDED AND KEEN THE COUNTRY GROWS   . . . . . .   56 RESIGNATION   133
          WITH THAT OLD KING HER FATHER WHO GROWS GREY   . .   78 SOHRAB RUSTUM   591
          THY LOVELY YOUTHFUL WIFE GROWS PALE . . . . . .   138 TRISTRAM 1   269
          THE LOVELY YOUTHFUL WIFE GROWS PALE . . . . . .   138 TRISTRAM 1   V 269
          CREEPS THICKLY GROWS NOT HERE BUT THE PALE GRASS . .   150 TRISTRAM 3   15
          BLOOMS THICKLY GROWS NOT HERE   . . . .   TRISTRAM 3   V 15
          CREEPS THICKLY GROWS NOT HERE   . . . .   TRISTRAM 3   V 15
          THE SEA GROWS STORMY THE LITTLE ONES MOAN   . . . .   163 FORSAKEN MERM   65
          THE SEA GROWS STORMY THE LITTLE ONES MOAN   . . . .   163 FORSAKEN MERM   79
          GROWS FROM SUCH SORROW AS THEIRS   . . . . . .   235 YOUTH OF MAN   100
          AS IT GROWS AS THE TOWNS ON ITS MARGE   . . . .   253 FUTURE   72
          AND STRANGE AND VAIN THE EARTHLY TURMOIL GROWS   . .   267 THYRSIS   148
          CLOUDS AND GROWS DAILY WORSE IN SICILY   . . . .   410 EMPEDOCLES I 1   120
          BORN INTO LIFE MAN GROWS . . . .   418 EMPEDOCLES I 2   187
          OUR HAIR GROWS GREY OUR EYES ARE DIMMD OUR   423 EMPEDOCLES I 2   336
               HEAT IS TAMED
          STILL WOULD BE TRUE YET STILL GROWS COLD   . . . .   481 DESTINY   3

GROWTH
          TELLS US HIS MISERYS BIRTH AND GROWTH AND SIGNS   . .   260 SCHOLAR-GIPSY   187
          HAS REACHD THE LIMIT OF HIS UTMOST GROWTH   . . . .   LUCRETIUS 2   9

GRUDGE
          AND THOUGH FATE GRUDGE TO THEE AND ME   . . . .   59 RESIGNATION   245
          THAT ONE SHOULD GRUDGE ITS LOSS FOR BALDERS SAKE . .   98 BALDER DEAD 1   125
          IN HEAVEN AND EARTH AND WHO WOULD GRUDGE HIM TEARS   120 BALDER DEAD 3   233

GRUDGED
          AND ALL GRACE SHALL TO ME BE GRUDGED . . . . . .   91 SICK KING BOKH   102

GUARD
          THE TARTARS OF THE OXUS THE KINGS GUARD   . . . .   64 SOHRAB RUSTUM   117
          AND HE HAS NONE TO GUARD HIS WEAK OLD AGE   . . . .   68 SOHRAB RUSTUM   235
          THE TARTARS OF BOKHARA THE KINGS GUARD   . . . .   64 SOHRAB RUSTUM   V 117
          BUT GUARD THE FIRE WITHIN   . . . .   237 PROGRESS   28
          THE CAPTAIN OF HIS SQUIRES AND HIS GUARD   . . . .   355 MEROPE   729
          THIS YOUNG ARCADIAN NOBLE GUARD AND MATE   . . . .   364 MEROPE   969
          THE GUARD ARCTURUS . . . .   393 MEROPE   1677
          THE GUARD-WATCHD BEAR   . . . .   393 MEROPE   1678
          BUT THE FAITHFUL SERVANT AND GUARD   . . . . . .   369 MEROPE   V1090
          IN CEASELESS OPPOSITION BE THE GUARD . . . . . .   437 EMPEDOCLES II   268

GUARDED
          EVEN IN THAT PHOEBUS-GUARDED GROUND   . . . . . .   221 EPILOG LAOCOON   15
          WHICH FROM ONE CENTRAL CITYS GUARDED SEAT   . . . .   337 MEROPE   246

GUARDEST
          THOU GUARDEST THEM APOLLO   . . . .   435 EMPEDOCLES II   204

GUARDIAN
          O BROTHER OF MY MOTHER GUARDIAN TRUE . . . . . .   330 MEROPE   29
          THE SPARTAN BROTHERS WITH THEIR GUARDIAN STRIVE   . .   390 MEROPE   1558
          THERE BUILD WE THEE O GUARDIAN DEAR   . . . . . .   452 GEISTS GRAVE   71
          THERE CHOOSE WE THEE O GUARDIAN DEAR . . . . . .   452 GEISTS GRAVE   V 71

GUARDIANS
          HIS YOUNG GUARDIANS HEART WITH LOVE   . . . . . .   137 TRISTRAM 1   207

GUARDING
          WHO LIES GUARDING HER FEET ALONG THE GROUND   . .   152 TRISTRAM 3   89

GUARDS
          MY GUARDS WHAT PRICK HIM WITH YOUR SPEARS   . . . .   89 SICK KING BOKH   42
          WHO GUARDS IN HER BREAST   . . . .   252 FUTURE   38
          THIS AWE WHICH GUARDS OUR EARTH-SPRUNG LINEAL KINGS   389 MEROPE   1543
          OF SACRIFICE HIS GUARDS CLEARING THE WAY   . . . .   401 MEROPE   1904
          OF HIS OWN BREAST FETTERD TO WHAT HE GUARDS   . .   437 EMPEDOCLES II   269

GUDURZ
          TO COUNSEL GUDURZ AND ZOARRAH CAME   . . . . . .   66 SOHRAB RUSTUM   171
          THESE CAME AND COUNSELLD AND THEN GUDURZ SAID   . .   66 SOHRAB RUSTUM   174
          BUT THROUGH THE ANXIOUS PERSIANS GUDURZ RAN   . .   66 SOHRAB RUSTUM   189
          AND GUDURZ ENTERD RUSTUMS TENT AND FOUND   . . .   67 SOHRAB RUSTUM   195
          AND PLAYD WITH IT BUT GUDURZ CAME AND STOOD   . .   67 SOHRAB RUSTUM   201
          AND GREETED GUDURZ WITH BOTH HANDS AND SAID   . .   67 SOHRAB RUSTUM   204
          BUT GUDURZ STOOD IN THE TENT-DOOR AND SAID   . . .   67 SOHRAB RUSTUM   207
          HE SPOKE AND SMILED AND GUDURZ MADE REPLY   . . .   68 SOHRAB RUSTUM   242
          O GUDURZ WHEREFORE DOST THOU SAY SUCH WORDS   . .   68 SOHRAB RUSTUM   250
          HE SPOKE AND FROWND AND GUDURZ TURND AND RAN . .   69 SOHRAB RUSTUM   260

GUERDON
          THOU SMILING FIEND AND CLAIM THY GUERDON THERE   . .   373 MEROPE   1184

GUESS
          AND SPELL THY LOOKS AND GUESS THY THOUGHTS . . . .   205 CALAIS SANDS   29
          AND WATCH THY AIR AND GUESS THY THOUGHTS   . . . .   205 CALAIS SANDS   V 29
          HERE AS I GUESS THE NOBLE LAIAS COMES   . . . . .   386 MEROPE   1439
          WHAT THEY WANT WE CANNOT GUESS . . . .   455 POOR MATTHIAS   105

GUESSES
    YET INDEED THIS FLUX OF GUESSES   . . . . . .   33 NEW SIRENS   195
    BUT INDEED THIS FLUX OF GUESSES   . . . . . .   33 NEW SIRENS   V 195

GUEST
    HIS WANDERING GUEST AND GAVE HIM HIS FAIR CHILD   . .   79 SOHRAB RUSTUM   626
    WAS LAUNCELOTS GUEST AT JOYOUS GARD . . . . . .   136 TRISTRAM 1   203
    WHAT YOUTH GODDESS WHAT GUEST . . . .   188 STRAYED REVEL   94
    THE FAVOURD GUEST OF CIRCE BROUGHT BY THE WAVES   . .   189 STRAYED REVEL   110
    BECKONS TOO EARLY THE GUEST   . . . .   199 EARLY DEATH   9
    AND MANY A GUEST HATH SHE THEREIN RECEIVD   . . .   251 FUTURE   V
    THE STRANGE GUEST SPARKLED NOW TIS PASSD AWAY   . .   298 HEINES GRAVE   211
    AN UNKNOWN GUEST WILL ENTER BRINGING WORD   . . .   331 MEROPE   48
    TO THE GUEST-CHAMBER LEAD HIM SOME ONE GIVE   . . .   359 MEROPE   869
    HE IN THE GUEST-CHAMBER NOW   . . . . . .   371 MEROPE   1123
    OF THE GUEST-CHAMBER DOOR   . . . .   372 MEROPE   1150
    BUT WE AS SOME RUDE GUEST   . . . .   419 EMPEDOCLES I 2   217
    ONLY THAT PRIMAL GUEST THE FISHER SAW   . . . .   445 WESTMIN ABBEY   59
    THEREFORE OUR HAPPY GUEST   . . . .   447 WESTMIN ABBEY   121
    BY THIS DEAR GUEST OVER THY PRECINCT SHED   . . . .   449 WESTMIN ABBEY   173

GUESTS
    SAY WHAT SHALL CALM US WHEN SUCH GUESTS INTRUDE   . .   6 GEO CRUIKSHANK   6
    FLUSHD GUESTS AND GOLDEN GOBLETS FOAMD WITH WINE   . .   11 MYCERINUS   97
    GUESTS THE DULL SENSE NEVER KNEW   . . . . .   30 NEW SIRENS   136
    AND PRAISED AND SPOILD BY MASTER AND BY GUESTS   . .   407 EMPEDOCLES I 1   34

GUIDANCE
    HER HAND IN TURN FOR GUIDANCE AND THE THREE   . .   129 BALDER DEAD 3   551

GUIDE
    GUIDE ME SOME ONE TO THE MOUNTAIN   . . . . .   15 CHURCH BROU 1   75
    GUIDE ME VASSALS TO THE MOUNTAIN   . . . . . .   15 CHURCH BROU 1   V 75
    TO GUIDE ME I HAVE STEERD BY TO THE END   . . . .   40 HUMAN LIFE   6
    THE GUIDE OF OUR DARK STEPS A TRIPLE VEIL   . . . .   43 GIPSY CHILD   49
    THERE SPRINGS THE BROOK WILL GUIDE US DOWN   . . . .   54 RESIGNATION   76
    SHALL GO AND I WILL BE HIS GUIDE UNSEEN   . . . .   100 BALDER DEAD 1   191
    AND CROSS THE BRIDGE OF HEAVEN WITH LOK FOR GUIDE   .   127 BALDER DEAD 3   476
    STRIKE LEFTWARD CRIES OUR GUIDE AND HIGHER   . . . .   300 GRANDE CHARTR   19
    AND THOU SAD GUIDE ADIEU   . . . .   310 OBERMANN   130
    TO GUIDE OUR VENGEANCE TO A PROSPEROUS CLOSE   . . .   332 MEROPE   75
    TO GUIDE OUR EFFORT TO A PROSPEROUS CLOSE   . . . .   332 MEROPE   V 75
    AND YOUR OWN VOICE GUIDE HIM TO HIS PREY   . . . .   466 ALARIC AT ROME   118

GUIDED
    BY FAINT MUSIC GUIDED RANGING   . . . .   27 NEW SIRENS   29
    AH WHOSE HAND THAT DAY THROUGH HEAVEN GUIDED   . . .   210 SELF-DECEPTION   13
    BE GUIDED O MY SON SPURN COUNSEL NOT   . . . . .   382 MEROPE   1328
    COMST THOU GUIDED SAFE TO THY HOME   . . . . . .   405 MEROPE   2022

GUIDES
    CHANCE GUIDES THE MIGRATORY RACE   . . . . .   55 RESIGNATION   113
    AND THEY SHALL BE THY GUIDES WHO HAVE THE POWER   . .   102 BALDER DEAD 1   238
    WHEN HE GUIDES MUSPELS CHILDREN TO THEIR BOURNE   . .   111 BALDER DEAD 2   224
    STANDS AT THE PROW AND GUIDES THEM BUT ASTERN   . .   191 STRAYED REVEL   190

GUIDING
    YE GUIDING POWERS WHO JOIN AND PART   . . . . . .   174 MEETING   13

GUIERS
    DOTH THE DEAD GUIERS STREAM COMPLAIN   . . . . . .   299 GRANDE CHARTR   10

GUILE
    TO SEEM AS FREE FROM PRIDE AND GUILE   . . . . . .   179 FAREWELL   63

GUILT
    TO RUE MY GUILT IN ENDLESS FLAME   . . . . . .   157 SAINT BRANDAN   32
    OUTLIVES MY GUILT OUTLIVES MY DOOM   . . . . . .   158 SAINT BRANDAN   63
    FREE FROM ALL GUILT OF LAWLESSNESS   . . . . . .   353 MEROPE   660
    WHICH FOOLISH INNOCENCE PLAYS WITH SUBTLE GUILT   . .   366 MEROPE   V
    AGREES TO DEEM SOME DEEDS SO DARK IN GUILT   . . . .   389 MEROPE   1524

GUILTINESS
    AND CRIED O ZEUS LET WHAT BLOOD-GUILTINESS   . . . .   402 MEROPE   1915

GUILTLESS
    THE HAND THAT DOES THEM GUILTLESS IN A WORD   . .   394 MEROPE   1714

GUILTY
    MIGHT SHRINK HALF STARTLED LIKE A GUILTY MAN   . .   11 MYCERINUS   102
    TRULY THOU SAYST THE PLANNING GUILTY MIND   . . .   125 BALDER DEAD 3   424
    WHO UNDER EARTH WATCH GUILTY DEEDS OF MEN   . . . .   332 MEROPE   74
    THIS PURE THAT GUILTY MAY HAVE EACH IMPELLD   . . .   352 MEROPE   646
    COMMITS ALL DEEDS THE GUILTY OFTENEST DO   . . . .   353 MEROPE   683
    WITHOUT A SINGLE GUILTY THOUGHT   . . . . . .   353 MEROPE   684
    THE WILLING SHARER OF HIS GUILTY RULE   . . . . .   366 MEROPE   1007
    FOR THIS IS THE TRUE STRENGTH OF GUILTY KINGS   . .   386 MEROPE   1436
    HAVE LEARND THAT THERE ARE GUILTY DEEDS WHICH LEAVE   394 MEROPE   1713
    IN FIRES UNDYING OER THE GUILTY HEAD   . . . . . .   463 ALARIC AT ROME   28

GUISE
    WHO LENT THEE CHILD THIS MEDITATIVE GUISE · · · · 41 GIPSY CHILD   3
    HE DROVE ABROAD IN FURIOUS GUISE · · · · · · 315 OBERMANN MORE   99

GULF
    BY SANDY BAHREIN IN THE PERSIAN GULF · · · · · · 69 SOHRAB RUSTUM   286
    OF THE UNLIT GULF OF HIMSELF · · · · · · · · 231 YOUTH OF NATURE V 102
    SAILD BY THE FATE-MEANT GULF TO THEIR CONQUEST · · 344 MEROPE   450
    OF EITHER GULF AND REMAIND · · · · · · · · 345 MEROPE   483
    RAKED FROM THE SWARMING GULF OF SORROWS HELL · · RUDE ORATOR   16

GULFS
    OR CLUSTERD PEAKS WITH PLUNGING GULFS BETWEEN · ·   4 BUTLERS SERMONS   11
    GULFS OF ESTRANGING BLOOD ACROSS THAT CHASM · · 336 MEROPE   194
    RAKED FROM THE SWARMING GULFS OF SORROWS HELL · · RUDE ORATOR   V 16

GULLIES
    IN THE THORN-CHOKED GULLIES · · · · · · · · 392 MEROPE   1638

GULLS
    HOW THIS FOOL PASSION GULLS MEN POTENTLY · · · · 153 TRISTRAM 3   134

GULLY
    UNTIL HE CAME TO WHERE A GULLY BREAKS · · · · 97 BALDER DEAD 1   81

GULPH
    WHY TARRIEST THOU TO PLUNGE THEE IN THE GULPH · · 124 BALDER DEAD 3 388
    THICKENS AND TO ITS INNER GULPH RECALLS · · · 129 BALDER DEAD 3 547
    AND THE ROUSED MALIAC GULPH · · · · · · 198 FRAG ANTIGONE 101
    OF THE UNLIT GULPH OF HIMSELF · · · · · · 231 YOUTH OF NATURE 102
    STAG DOGS AND HUNTER TO THE YAWNING GULPH · · · · 358 MEROPE   826

GURGLED
    FURROWD IT AND THE WATER GURGLED IN · · · · · 118 BALDER DEAD 3 179

GUSH
    A GUSH OF SUNBEAMS THROUGH A RUIND HALL · · · · 36 VOICE   21
    SHE KNEW THE DORIAN WATERS GUSH DIVINE · · · · 265 THYRSIS   94

GUSHES
    THY VOICE IN GUSHES COMES · · · · · · · · · 200 PHILOMELA   V
    THY VOICE BY GUSHES COMES · · · · · · · · · 200 PHILOMELA   V

GUSHING
    AND MEMORYS GUSHING TIDE SWELLS DEEP AND FULL · · 464 ALARIC AT ROME 53

GUST
    GUST ON GUST THE HARSH WINDS BLOW · · · · · · 32 NEW SIRENS   172
    GUST ON GUST THE HARSH WINDS BLOW · · · · · · 32 NEW SIRENS   172
    GUST ON GUST THE HOARSE WINDS BLOW · · · · · · 32 NEW SIRENS V 172
    GUST ON GUST THE HOARSE WINDS BLOW · · · · · · 32 NEW SIRENS V 172

GUSTS
    WHEN GUSTS SHAKE THE DOOR · · · · · · · · 164 FORSAKEN MERM 113
    WITH THE BLIND GUSTS THAT SHAKE THEIR OWN · · · · 178 FAREWELL   28
    WITH THE BLIND GUSTS WHICH SHAKE THEIR OWN · · · · 178 FAREWELL   V 28

GUSTY
    AND BADE THE WINDS THROUGH SPACE IMPEL THE GUSTY TOY 415 EMPEDOCLES I 2 81

HA
    HA DOST THOU START ARE THY LIPS BLANCHD LIKE MINE 133 TRISTRAM 1   102

HABIT
    DISENCHANTED BY HABIT AND NEWLY AWAKING · · · · 20 MODERN SAPPHO   23
    AND THE SCALES OF HABIT · · · · · · · · · · 235 YOUTH OF MAN   106
    WHOSE HABIT OF THOUGHT IS FIXD WHO WILL NOT CHANGE 437 EMPEDOCLES II 266

HABITATION
    NO HABITATION FOR THE NAMELESS DEAD · · · · · 464 ALARIC AT ROME 56

HABITS
    ONLY METHINKS SOME LOSS OF HABITS POWER · · · · 263 THYRSIS   22

HABITUAL
    DEAD TO ITS DEEP HABITUAL SMART · · · · · · 206 RIVER   19

HACKD
    AND ALL DAY LONG THEY THERE ARE HACKD AND HEWN · · 105 BALDER DEAD 2 15

HADES
    FROM HER FALSE FRIENDS APPROACH IN HADES TURN · · 261 SCHOLAR-GIPSY 209
    THROUGH HADES AND THE MOURNFUL GLOOM · · · · · · 271 MEMORIAL VERSES 39
    TO THE GODS OF HADES · · · · · · · · · · 400 MEROPE   1867

HAEMON
    BUT HUSH HAEMON WHOM ANTIGONE · · · · · · · · 196 FRAG ANTIGONE 39

HAG
    WHERE SATE IN THE CAVES MOUTH A SKINNY HAG · · · · 123 BALDER DEAD 3 333

HAG　　　　　　(CONTINUED)
  THEN WITH A LOUDER LAUGH THE HAG REPLIED •　•　•　• 123 BALDER DEAD 3 350
  BUT WITH A LOUDER LAUGH THE HAG REPLIED •　•　•　• 123 BALDER DEAD 3 V 350

HAGGARD
  AND FOR THROUGH THE HAGGARD AIR •　•　•　•　•　• 136 TRISTRAM 1 198
  IN HIS COOL HALL WITH HAGGARD EYES •　•　•　•　• 315 OBERMANN MORE 97

HAIL
  MAY I ERE I DEPART BID BALDER HAIL •　•　•　•　• 111 BALDER DEAD 2 244
  EVEN IN THE ABODE OF DEATH O BALDER HAIL •　•　• 112 BALDER DEAD 2 250
  THEREFORE FOR THE LAST TIME O BALDER HAIL •　•　• 126 BALDER DEAD 3 453
  HAIL AND FAREWELL FOR HERE THOU COMST NO MORE • 126 BALDER DEAD 3 455
  MINE EYES ARE DIZZY WITH THE ARROWY HAIL •　•　• 128 BALDER DEAD 3 507
  BY THE GREY SEA IF SO THEN HAIL •　•　•　•　• 189 STRAYED REVEL 128
  YET HAPPY OMEN HAIL •　•　•　•　•　•　•　• 267 THYRSIS 166
  ALL ROUND NO SOUL NO BOAT NO HAIL •　•　•　•　• 274 STANZAS CARNAC 30
  HAIL TO THE STEADFAST SOUL •　•　•　•　•　•　• 281 HAWORTH CHURCH 37
  HAIL TO THE SPIRIT WHICH DARED •　•　•　•　•　• 281 HAWORTH CHURCH 41
  HAIL TO THE COURAGE WHICH GAVE •　•　•　•　•　• 281 HAWORTH CHURCH 44
  HAIL AS IT PASSES FROM EARTH •　•　•　•　•　• 298 HEINES GRAVE 204
  WHO PASSD WITHIN THEIR PUISSANT HAIL •　•　•　• 303 GRANDE CHARTR 124
  O KING ALL HAIL I COME WITH WEIGHTY NEWS •　•　• 354 MEROPE 710

HAILD
  OR SOME FRIEND HAILD US TO KEEP COMPANY •　•　•　• 40 HUMAN LIFE 12
  HAILD BUT THE TARTARS KNEW NOT WHO HE WAS •　•　• 69 SOHRAB RUSTUM 283
  RUSTUM AND SOHRAB ON EACH OTHER HAILD •　•　•　• 75 SOHRAB RUSTUM 479
  HE IS AND BY THE PEOPLE HAILD FOR KING •　•　•　• 401 MEROPE 1890
  THE DORIANS LYING DEAD THY SON HAILD KING •　•　• 402 MEROPE 1942
  THAT DAY THAT HAILD HIS TRIUMPHS SAW HIM DIE •　• 478 CROMWELL 212

HAIR
  FASTEND ON HER DARK HAIR AND HER WREATH OF 19 MODERN SAPPHO 11
   WHITE HEATHER
  HER SOFT FACE HER HAIR AROUND •　•　•　•　•　• 23 MEMORY-PICTURE 26
  TO CROWN EUGENIAS HAIR •　•　•　•　•　•　•　•　• 48 HORATIAN ECHO 24
  AND THREW IT ON HIS HEAD AND SMIRCHD HIS HAIR • 81 SOHRAB RUSTUM 701
  HIS HAIR AND FACE AND BEARD AND GLITTERING ARMS • 82 SOHRAB RUSTUM 702
  ALL RENT AND DUST UPON HIS HAIR •　•　•　•　• 88 SICK KING BOKH 32
  HER SNOW-WHITE HANDS HER GOLDEN HAIR •　•　•　• 132 TRISTRAM 1 51
  AND SHAKE BACK HER RAVEN HAIR •　•　•　•　•　• 134 TRISTRAM 1 123
  THE STAIND ARMS THE MATTED HAIR •　•　•　•　• 136 TRISTRAM 1 199
  HARDLY LETS PEEP THE GOLDEN HAIR •　•　•　•　• 141 TRISTRAM 1 341
  I KNOW HER BY HER GOLDEN HAIR •　•　•　•　•　• 132 TRISTRAM 1 V 50
  YES THE SPRAY IS ON THY CLOAK AND HAIR •　•　• 142 TRISTRAM 2 18
  OER THE BLANCHD SHEET HER RAVEN HAIR •　•　•　• 146 TRISTRAM 2 107
  IN BLINDING MASSES SHOWERD THE GOLDEN HAIR •　• 150 TRISTRAM 3 34
  HAD LOOSEND THE BROWN HAIR OF VIVIANS HAIR •　• 154 TRISTRAM 3 168
  HAD LOOSEND THE BROWN CURLS OF VIVIANS HAIR • 154 TRISTRAM 3 V 168
  OF HAIR THAT RED AND TUFTED FELL •　•　•　•　• 157 SAINT BRANDAN 18
  OF HAIR THAT BLACK AND TUFTED FELL •　•　•　•　• 157 SAINT BRANDAN V 18
  SHE COMBD ITS BRIGHT HAIR AND SHE TENDED IT WELL • 163 FORSAKEN MERM 53
  AND THE GLEAM OF HER GOLDEN HAIR •　•　•　•　• 164 FORSAKEN MERM 107
  I KNOW THAT SOFT ENKERCHIEFD HAIR •　•　•　•　• 174 MEETING 7
  THE SWEET BLUE EYES THE SOFT ASH-COLOURD HAIR • 175 PARTING 37
  THE KERCHIEF THAT ENWOUND THY HAIR •　•　•　•　• 184 TERRACE BERNE 24
  STIRS THY HAIR GODDESS •　•　•　•　•　•　•　• 186 STRAYED REVEL 21
  THAT CROWN HIS HAIR •　•　•　•　•　•　•　•　• 188 STRAYED REVEL 86
  SHAKE LOOSE SOME BAND OF SOFT BROWN HAIR •　•　• 205 CALAIS SANDS 16
  SHAKE BACK THY BANDS OF SOFT BROWN HAIR •　•　• 205 CALAIS SANDS V 16
  SHAKE LOOSE SOME LOCK OF SOFT BROWN HAIR •　•　• 205 CALAIS SANDS V 16
  WITH THE GREY EYES AND THE LOVELY BROWN HAIR • 206 SEPARATION 16
  AND PART MY HAIR AND KISS MY BROW •　•　•　•　• 209 LONGING 11
  SHOWERING THEIR HAIR •　•　•　•　•　•　•　•　• 218 BACCHANALIA 1 27
  WITH ANGUISHD FACE AND FLYING HAIR •　•　•　•　• 244 SUMMER NIGHT 66
  OF PROSERPINE AMONG WHOSE CROWNED HAIR •　•　• 265 THYRSIS 88
  THE CHEEK GROWN THIN THE BROWN HAIR SPRENT WITH GREY 266 THYRSIS 135
  AND FLOATING HAIR •　•　•　•　•　•　•　•　•　• 278 SOUTHERN NIGHT 108
  AND UNBOUND HAIR •　•　•　•　•　•　•　•　•　• 278 SOUTHERN NIGHT V 108
  AND CROWND HIS HAIR WITH FLOWERS •　•　•　•　• 316 OBERMANN MORE 102
  WITH THY HEAD FULL OF WINE AND THY HAIR CROWND •　• 407 EMPEDOCLES I 1 32
  OUR HAIR GROWS GREY OUR EYES ARE DIMMD OUR 423 EMPEDOCLES I 2 336
   HEAT IS TAMED
  LETTING THE SEA-STREAM WANDER THROUGH THY HAIR •　• 430 EMPEDOCLES II 61
  IN THE WIND AND LOOSE DARK HAIR •　•　•　•　• 433 EMPEDOCLES II 153
  THE COLLIE HAIR THE COLLIE SWING •　•　•　•　• 459 KAISER DEAD 26

HAIRD
  OR DO I WAIT TO HEAR SOME GRAY-HAIRD KING •　•　• 43 GIPSY CHILD 33
  WHOSE SURENESS GRAY-HAIRD SCHOLARS HARDLY LEARN •　• 43 GIPSY CHILD 42
  AND I TO TARRY WITH THE SNOW-HAIRD ZAL •　•　• 68 SOHRAB RUSTUM 232
  THOU AND THE SNOW-HAIRD ZAL AND ALL THY FRIENDS •　• 84 SOHRAB RUSTUM 786
  AND I TO TARRY WITH THE WHITE-HAIRD ZAL •　•　• 68 SOHRAB RUSTUM V 232
  HATH SNATCHD A LITTLE FAIR-HAIRD SLAVE •　•　• 93 SICK KING BOKH 165
  SWAYING THE LONG-HAIRD GOATS WITH SILVERD REIN • 115 BALDER DEAD 3 73
  THE CHILDREN AND THE GREY-HAIRD SENESCHAL •　•　• 152 TRISTRAM 3 97
  THE LITTLE FAIR-HAIRD SON WITH VACANT GAZE •　•　• 167 PICT NEWSTEAD 10
  SOMETIMES A WILD-HAIRD MAENAD •　•　•　•　•　• 194 STRAYED REVEL 275
  AH GOLDEN-HAIRD STRANGELY SMILING GODDESS •　•　• 194 STRAYED REVEL 286
  LIFTING THE COOL-HAIRD CREEPERS STEALTHILY •　•　• 262 SCHOLAR-GIPSY 234
  BUT THAT PRINCE AMONG GODS THE SON OF THE LOVELY-HAIRD HOMER TRANS 52
   LETO

HAIRS
     CROWND WITH GRAY HAIRS HE DIED AND FULL OF SWAY • • •   9 MYCERINUS   14
     STREAKD WITH ITS FIRST GREY HAIRS HOPE FILLED HIS SOUL   71 SOHRAB RUSTUM   340
     HIS SCORND WHITE HAIRS   • • • • • • • • • • • •   192 STRAYED REVEL   219
     SHAKING HIS THIN WHITE HAIRS   • • • • • • • •   289 RUGBY CHAPEL   112

HALED
     MADE FAST THE WOVEN ROPES AND HALED THEM DOWN   • •   106 BALDER DEAD 2   58

HALF
     SO SPAKE HE HALF IN ANGER HALF IN SCORN • • • •   11 MYCERINUS   79
     SO SPAKE HE HALF IN ANGER HALF IN SCORN • • • •   11 MYCERINUS   79
     MIGHT SHRINK HALF STARTLED LIKE A GUILTY MAN • • •   11 MYCERINUS   102
     GLIDING HALF HIDDEN THROUGH THE DUSKY STEMS   • • •   11 MYCERINUS   104
     HALF REFUSED AND HALF RESIGND   • • • • • • •   23 MEMORY-PICTURE   35
     HALF REFUSED AND HALF RESIGND   • • • • • • •   23 MEMORY-PICTURE   35
     WHERE SOME MUSE WITH HALF-CURVED FROWN   • • •   27 NEW SIRENS   26
     LEAVES HER RIDDLE HALF UNKNOWN • • • • • •   28 NEW SIRENS   76
     HALF IN DOUBT THEY SAY AND GAZING • • • • •   31 NEW SIRENS   149
     HALF THEIR GLORIES TO THE DAY   • • • • • • •   35 NEW SIRENS   256
     WHERE LOVE IS HALF MISTRUST • • • • • •   39 STAGIRIUS   46
     THOU DRUGGING PAIN BY PATIENCE HALF AVERSE • • •   42 GIPSY CHILD   13
     NO EXILES DREAM WAS EVER HALF SO SAD • • • • •   42 GIPSY CHILD   27
     NEVER WAS EXILES MEMORY HALF SO SAD • • • •   42 GIPSY CHILD   V 27
     PALE DEW-DRENCHD HALF-SHUT ROSES GLEAM   • • • •   57 RESIGNATION   179
     IS BOWD HALF-BURIED ON THE BED • • • • • • •   146 TRISTRAM 2   106
     BUT WHO IS THIS BY THE HALF-OPEND DOOR   • • • •   175 PARTING   35
     HIS FAWN-SKIN HALF UNTIED   • • • • • • • •   188 STRAYED REVEL   89
     FROM THE HALF-TRIED BANQUET OF LIFE • • • •   199 EARLY DEATH   10
     AT LEAST TO HALF FORGETFULNESS • • • • • •   200 PHILOMELA   V
     ME LET NO HALF-EFFACED MEMORIES CUMBER   • • • •   206 SEPARATION   9
     AND FEEL BUT HALF AND FEEBLY WHAT WE FEEL • • •   213 GROWING OLD   27
     NOT YET HALF THROUGH THE DAY • • • • • • •   216 LORDS MESSENGER   17
     DESERTED IS THE HALF-MOWN PLAIN • • • • • •   217 BACCHANALIA 1   4
     OF HASTE HALF-WORK AND DISARRAY   • • • • •   222 EPILOG LAOCOON   27
     SCREEND IS THIS NOOK OER THE HIGH HALF-REAPD FIELD   255 SCHOLAR-GIPSY   21
     AND I MYSELF SEEM HALF TO KNOW THY LOOKS • • •   257 SCHOLAR-GIPSY   62
     AND EACH HALF LIVES A HUNDRED DIFFERENT LIVES • •   260 SCHOLAR-GIPSY   169
     LIGHT HALF-BELIEVERS OF OUR CASUAL CREEDS   • • •   260 SCHOLAR-GIPSY   172
     SCREEND IN THIS NOOK OER THE HIGH HALF-REAPD FIELD   255 SCHOLAR-GIPSY V 21
     VAGUE HALF-BELIEVERS OF OUR CASUAL CREEDS   • •   260 SCHOLAR-GIPSY V 172
     HALF HER LAURELS UNWON   • • • • • • • •   283 HAWORTH CHURCH   70
     THOSE WHO WITH HALF-OPEN EYES   • • • • • •   288 RUGBY CHAPEL   53
     HALF BLIND PALSIED IN PAIN • • • • • • •   292 HEINES GRAVE   13
     MUSICAL WATER HALF-HID   • • • • • • • •   297 HEINES GRAVE   161
     WITH HALF CENSURE WITH AWE • • • • • • •   298 HEINES GRAVE   203
     FROM HALF OF HUMAN FATE • • • • • • • •   308 OBERMANN   54
     HALF OF MY LIFE WITH YOU • • • • • • •   310 OBERMANN   132
     WITH OLD-WORLD CURES MEN HALF BELIEVE • • •   320 OBERMANN MORE   235
     THOUGH MORE THAN HALF THY YEARS BE PAST • • •   323 OBERMANN MORE   305
     AND FINALLY THIS LAND THEN HALF-SUBDUED • • •   337 MEROPE   245
     AND HALF-BESTOWD HALF YIELDED UP THEIR SOIL • •   339 MEROPE   294
     AND HALF-BESTOWD HALF YIELDED UP THEIR SOIL • •   339 MEROPE   294
     WHY DOST THOU FALTER AND MAKE HALF REPLY • • •   362 MEROPE   930
     LOW MOANS HALF UTTERD   • • • • • • • •   393 MEROPE   1667
     APPROVE NOT TOO I HAVE BUT HALF MY JOY   • • •   403 MEROPE   1962
     BUT IF AS MOST MEN SAY HE IS HALF MAD • • • •   407 EMPEDOCLES I 1   23
     ASLEEP YET LENDING HALF AN EAR • • • • • •   452 GEISTS GRAVE   69
     AND WITHER HALF THE LAURELS ON THY TOMB • • •   463 ALARIC AT ROME   38
     AND OER THY TOWERS THE WINDS HALF UTTERED SIGH • •   464 ALARIC AT ROME   65
     JOYS THAT HAD COME AND VANISHD HALF UNKNOWN   • •   474 CROMWELL   75

HALL
     WITH THEIR MILD DARK HIS GRASSY BANQUET-HALL   • •   12 MYCERINUS   119
     IN THE HALL WITH SCONCES BLAZING   • • • • •   13 CHURCH BROU 1   33
     TO THE HALL WHAT SPORT WHAT SPORT • • • • •   14 CHURCH BROU 1   44
     IN THE HALL THEY LAID HIM DOWN • • • • • •   14 CHURCH BROU 1   46
     THOU AND THY LADIES IN THE HALL OF STATE • • •   18 CHURCH BROU 3   13
     THE VASTY HALL OF DEATH • • • • • • • •   21 REQUIESCAT   16
     SEEKING CEILED CHAMBERS AND A PALACE-HALL   • •   27 NEW SIRENS   40
     DUSK THE HALL WITH YEW • • • • • • • •   30 NEW SIRENS   114
     DUSK OH DUSK THE HALL WITH YEW • • • • • •   35 NEW SIRENS   270
     DUSK THE HALL WITH YEW • • • • • • • •   35 NEW SIRENS   276
     A GUSH OF SUNBEAMS THROUGH A RUIND HALL • • •   36 VOICE   21
     AND ON A FEAST-TIDE IN AFRASIABS HALL • • •   71 SOHRAB RUSTUM   355
     AND ON A FEAST DAY IN AFRASIABS HALL • • • •   71 SOHRAB RUSTUM V 355
     AND FROM THE HALL OF HEAVEN HE RODE AWAY • • •   96 BALDER DEAD 1   48
     BESIDE THE TABLES IN THE HALL OF HEAVEN • • •   97 BALDER DEAD 1   65
     IN ODINS HALL AND WENT THROUGH ASGARD STREETS • •   97 BALDER DEAD 1   73
     AND IN THE HALL HE FOUND THOSE WOMEN OLD • • •   97 BALDER DEAD 1   88
     OF BALDER FROM THE FLOOR OF HEAVEN • • • •   101 BALDER DEAD 1   205
     THERE TO HIS HALL THE GODS BROUGHT BALDER HOME • •   101 BALDER DEAD 1   214
     FEAST IN VALHALLA IN MY FATHERS HALL • • • •   104 BALDER DEAD 1   322
     BUT ALL AT NIGHT RETURN TO ODINS HALL • • •   105 BALDER DEAD 2   17
     TO GLAD THE GODS AND FEAST IN ODINS HALL • • •   105 BALDER DEAD 2   28
     TO THE HALL GLADHEIM WHICH IS BUILT OF GOLD • •   106 BALDER DEAD 2   36
     YOUR MATE THOUGH LOATHED AND FEASTS IN ODINS HALL   111 BALDER DEAD 2   218
     WHO SCATTERS RUSHES IN A MASTERS HALL • • •   112 BALDER DEAD 2   266
     AFTER THE FEAST IS DONE IN ODINS HALL • • •   117 BALDER DEAD 3   136

HALL   (CONTINUED)
        TO ASGARD AND SATE DOWN IN ODINS HALL   • • • •   119 BALDER DEAD 3   208
        THROUGH SOME OLD SEA-SIDE KNIGHTLY HALL   • • • •   148 TRISTRAM 2   178
        IN THE BANQUET-HALL OF TYNTAGIL   • • • • •   146 TRISTRAM 2   V 115
        YES IT IS LONELY FOR HER IN HER HALL   • • • • • •   152 TRISTRAM 3   96
        ON THE PURE COLUMNS OF ITS GLEN-BUILT HALL   • • • •   236 PALLADIUM   6
        THE LINE OF FESTAL LIGHT IN CHRIST-CHURCH HALL • •   259 SCHOLAR-GIPSY   129
        IN HIS COOL HALL WITH HAGGARD EYES   • • • • • •   315 OBERMANN MORE   97

HALLOW
        HALLOW THE SALAMINIAN PROMONTORIES   • • • • • •   481 HUNGARIAN NAT   13

HALLOWED
        ROUND THE WAN TEMPLES OF THE HALLOWED DEAD • • • •   463 ALARIC AT ROME   26

HALLS
        HOME TO OUR HALLS WITH TORCHLIGHT BY OUR KIN • •   101 BALDER DEAD 1   217
        IN ASGARD AND THE GOLDEN HALLS WERE DUMB   • • •   113 BALDER DEAD 2   306
        IN ASGARD BUT THE GOLDEN HALLS WERE DUMB   • • •   113 BALDER DEAD 2   V 306
        FAMILIAR HALLS WHERE WE HAVE SUPPD OF OLD   • • •   128 BALDER DEAD 3   534
        HOME TRISTRAM TO THY HALLS AGAIN   • • • • • •   138 TRISTRAM 1   273
        AND BORE HER DOWN TO THE SEA-HALLS   • • • • •   160 NECKAN   31
        SINCE FIRST THY STORY RAN THROUGH OXFORD HALLS •   259 SCHOLAR-GIPSY   132
        THOSE HALLS TOO DESTINED TO CONTAIN   • • • • •   301 GRANDE CHARTR   61
        MET THEM ENTERING THEIR HALLS • • • • • • • •   343 MEROPE   419
        TO HAVE ANOTHER MURDER IN THESE HALLS   • • • •   349 MEROPE   562
        WHO SAVED HIM FROM THESE MURDEROUS HALLS A BABE •   351 MEROPE   617
        IN THIS BLOOD-DELUGED PALACE IN WHOSE HALLS   • •   366 MEROPE   1018
        OF WIDOWHOOD IN THESE POLLUTED HALLS • • • • • •   383 MEROPE   1370

HALO
        NOT WITH THE HALO OF YOUTH   • • • • • • • •   232 YOUTH OF MAN   19

HALT
        HERE LET US HALT SAID MERLIN THEN AND SHE   • • •   155 TRISTRAM 3   211
        HALT AT THE WHITE AND SILENT COLONNADE   • • • •   167 RACHEL 1   5
        HALT THROUGH THE CLOUD-DRIFT SOMETHING SHINES • •   299 GRANDE CHARTR   16
        TILL I THROWN OUT AND TIRED CAME TO HALT   • • •   357 MEROPE   795
        THEY DO BUT HALT THEY WILL BE HERE ANON   • • •   408 EMPEDOCLES I 1   51
        PLAY WHEN WE HALT AND WHEN THE EVENING COMES   • •   409 EMPEDOCLES I 1   90

HALTING
        THAT HALTING SLAVE WHO IN NICOPOLIS • • • • • •   2 TO A FRIEND   6

HALVE
        TO HALVE A LODGING THAT WAS ALL HER OWN   • • • •   44 GIPSY CHILD   64
        TO HALVE A HOUSE THAT SHOULD BE ALL HER OWN   • •   44 GIPSY CHILD   V 64

HALVES
        FROM THE TWIN SOUL WHICH HALVES THEIR OWN   • • • •   206 TOO LATE   4
        FROM THE TWIN SOUL THAT HALVES THEIR OWN   • • • •   206 TOO LATE   V 4

HAMAN
        INTO THE OPEN PLAIN SO HAMAN BADE   • • • • • •   64 SOHRAB RUSTUM   107
        HAMAN WHO NEXT TO PERAN-WISA RULED   • • • • • •   64 SOHRAB RUSTUM   108

HAMANS
        AND SOHRAB ARMD IN HAMANS TENT AND CAME   • • • •   70 SOHRAB RUSTUM   292

HAMLET
        CORN-FIELD AND HAMLET AND COPSE   • • • • • •   234 YOUTH OF MAN   79

HAMLETS
        MAIDENS WHO FROM THE DISTANT HAMLETS COME   • • • •   257 SCHOLAR-GIPSY   82

HAMMER
        SHOULDERING HIS HAMMER WHICH THE GIANTS KNOW   • •   106 BALDER DEAD 2   49
        OF CRASHING FALLS FOR WITH HIS HAMMER THOR • • • •   106 BALDER DEAD 2   55
        SHOULDERING THY HAMMER IN THY CHARIOT DRAWN   • •   115 BALDER DEAD 3   72

HAMMERS
        STONES ARE SAWING HAMMERS RINGING   • • • • • •   15 CHURCH BROU 1   89

HAMPDEN
        THERE HAMPDEN BENT HIM OER HIS SADDLE BOW   • • • •   476 CROMWELL   169

HAND
        THE FEEBLE SONS OF PLEASURE SET THEIR HAND • • • •   5 DUKE WELLINGTON   7
        ARTIST WHOSE HAND WITH HORROR WINGD HATH TORN • •   6 GEO CRUIKSHANK   1
        WOULD THRUST A HAND BEFORE THE LIFTED BOWL   • • •   11 MYCERINUS   105
        HEART QUITS HEART AND HAND QUITS HAND   • • • •   35 NEW SIRENS   264
        HEART QUITS HEART AND HAND QUITS HAND   • • • •   35 NEW SIRENS   264
        NOR WITH A LIGHTER HAND DISPOSE • • • • • •   48 HORATIAN ECHO   22
        HE SPOKE AND PERAN-WISA TOOK THE HAND   • • • •   63 SOHRAB RUSTUM   63
        SO SAID HE AND DROPPD SOHRABS HAND AND LEFT   • •   63 SOHRAB RUSTUM   94
        IN HIS RIGHT HAND A RULERS STAFF NO SWORD   • • •   64 SOHRAB RUSTUM   99
        AND BECKOND TO HIM WITH HIS HAND AND SAID   • • • •   70 SOHRAB RUSTUM   321
        AND CLASPD HIS HAND WITHIN HIS OWN AND SAID   • •   71 SOHRAB RUSTUM   342
        THUNDERING TO EARTH AND LEAPT FROM RUSTUMS HAND • •   73 SOHRAB RUSTUM   419
        WHOSE FIERY POINT NOW IN HIS MAILD RIGHT-HAND • •   74 SOHRAB RUSTUM   451

HAND   (CONTINUED)

OF WAR I FIGHT IT OUT AND HAND TO HAND   •   •   •   75 SOHRAB RUSTUM   464
OF WAR I FIGHT IT OUT AND HAND TO HAND   •   •   •   75 SOHRAB RUSTUM   464
FOR BOTH THE ON-LOOKING HOSTS ON EITHER HAND   •   •   75 SOHRAB RUSTUM   487
WHO STOOD AT HAND UTTERD A DREADFUL CRY   •   •   •   76 SOHRAB RUSTUM   502
AND IN THE HAND THE HILT REMAINT ALONE   •   •   •   76 SOHRAB RUSTUM   513
AND HIS KNEES TOTTERD AND HE SMOTE HIS HAND   •   •   80 SOHRAB RUSTUM   662
AGAINST HIS BREAST HIS HEAVY MAILED HAND   •   •   80 SOHRAB RUSTUM   663
AND TO HIS HEART HE PRESSD THE OTHER HAND   •   •   •   80 SOHRAB RUSTUM   665
AND THEN HE TOUCHD IT WITH HIS HAND AND SAID   •   •   81 SOHRAB RUSTUM   686
IN HEAVEN AND THOU ART HEAVENS UNCONSCIOUS HAND •   •   82 SOHRAB RUSTUM   710
COME LET ME LAY MY HAND UPON THY MANE   •   •   •   83 SOHRAB RUSTUM   746
AND IN HIS HAND THE HILT REMAINT ALONE   •   •   •   76 SOHRAB RUSTUM   V 513
SEEKING A PREY UNTO HIS HAND   •   •   •   •   •   •   93 SICK KING BOKH   164
UPON A HILL ON THE RIGHT HAND   •   •   •   •   •   94 SICK KING BOKH   222
ON BALDER DEATH HATH LAID HER HAND NOT THEE   •   •   98 BALDER DEAD 1   117
NO MEANER HAND THAN ODINS ON HIS MANE   •   •   •   107 BALDER DEAD 2   73
HE SPAKE AND RAISED HIS HAND AND GAVE THE RING •   •   112 BALDER DEAD 2   279
WOULD I MIGHT SEE HIM SNATCH THEE IN HIS HAND   •   •   114 BALDER DEAD 3   24
AND IN HIS FATHERS HAND PUT SLEIPNERS REIN   •   •   •   114 BALDER DEAD 3   34
TO TAKE MY HAND AND WIPE MY TEARS AND SAY   •   •   116 BALDER DEAD 3   113
HODER WHOM HIS BROTHER WHOM HIS OWN HAND SLEW   •   •   118 BALDER DEAD 3   165
HODER THE UNHAPPY WHOM HIS OWN HAND SLEW   •   •   •   124 BALDER DEAD 3   384
STRETCHD FORTH HIS HAND AND WITH BENIGNANT VOICE • •   125 BALDER DEAD 3   410
WAS LOKS THE UNWITTING HAND ALONE WAS THINE   •   •   125 BALDER DEAD 3   425
HE SPOKE AND WAVED FAREWELL AND GAVE HIS HAND   •   •   129 BALDER DEAD 3   549
HER HAND IN TURN FOR GUIDANCE AND THE THREE   •   •   129 BALDER DEAD 3   551
ISEULT OF THE SNOW-WHITE HAND   •   •   •   •   •   •   132 TRISTRAM 1   74
BENDING GAILY OER THY HAND   •   •   •   •   •   •   •   134 TRISTRAM 1   113
LET HER SWEEP HER DAZZLING HAND •   •   •   •   •   134 TRISTRAM 1   121
TRISTRAM NAY NAY THOU MUST NOT TAKE MY HAND   •   •   135 TRISTRAM 1   166
I AM HERE WE MEET I HOLD THY HAND   •   •   •   •   142 TRISTRAM 2   8
TAKE MY HAND DEAR TRISTRAM LOOK ON ME   •   •   •   142 TRISTRAM 2   16
TAKE MY HAND AND TOUCH THESE WASTED FINGERS   •   •   143 TRISTRAM 2   23
STILL HOLD HER LOVERS HAND HER HEAD •   •   •   •   146 TRISTRAM 2   105
THEN ISEULT TOOK BY THE HAND THOSE CHILDREN FAIR • •   151 TRISTRAM 3   61
HAD SCORED HER WHITE RIGHT HAND WHICH SHE ALLOWS • •   154 TRISTRAM 3   174
AND TAKES IT IN HER HAND AND WAVES IT OVER   •   •   156 TRISTRAM 3   217
TILL THE SPINDLE DROPS FROM HER HAND •   •   •   •   164 FORSAKEN MERM   96
TILL THE SHUTTLE FALLS FROM HER HAND •   •   •   •   164 FORSAKEN MERM   V 96
BEHOLD THE STERN MAILD FATHER STAFF IN HAND   •   •   167 PICT NEWSTEAD   9
AGAIN I SEE MY BLISS AT HAND   •   •   •   •   •   •   174 MEETING   1
THY HAND LAY LANGUIDLY IN MINE   •   •   •   •   •   •   178 FAREWELL   15
AS HAND IN HAND FACE EARTHLY LIFE   •   •   •   •   179 FAREWELL   68
AS HAND IN HAND FACE EARTHLY LIFE   •   •   •   •   179 FAREWELL   68
BUT BRIGHT ARE THOSE GREEN FIELDS AT HAND   •   •   •   184 TERRACE BERNE   7
COME STRETCH FORTH THY HAND THEN SO •   •   •   •   187 STRAYED REVEL   61
SITTING STAFF IN HAND   •   •   •   •   •   •   •   •   190 STRAYED REVEL   136
DRIFTING KNIFE IN HAND   •   •   •   •   •   •   •   190 STRAYED REVEL   152
AND SHE TO HIM WILL REACH HER HAND   •   •   •   •   202 URANIA   25
THY SHAWL THY LOOK THY SMILE THY HAND   •   •   •   204 CALAIS SANDS   12
I MUST NOT SPRING TO GRASP THY HAND •   •   •   •   205 CALAIS SANDS   25
THAT SHAWL THAT STEP THAT LOOK THAT HAND   •   •   204 CALAIS SANDS   V 12
I MUST NOT SPRING TO TOUCH THY HAND •   •   •   •   205 CALAIS SANDS   V 25
ON MINE LET REST THAT LOVELY HAND   •   •   •   •   206 RIVER   8
THEN LOVE THY HAND AH NO ADIEU   •   •   •   •   •   207 TOO LATE   8
AH WHOSE HAND THAT DAY THROUGH HEAVEN GUIDED   •   •   210 SELF-DECEPTION   13
RAN OFF AND VANISHD OUT OF HAND •   •   •   •   •   213 PROGRESS POESY   8
PROCLAIMS SALVATION AT HAND   •   •   •   •   •   214 NEW ROME   8
INSTILLS SALVATION AT HAND   •   •   •   •   •   •   214 NEW ROME   V 8
GOD PUT A HEAP OF LETTERS IN HIS HAND   •   •   •   239 REVOLUTIONS   3
GIVE ME THY HAND AND HUSH AWHILE •   •   •   •   •   245 BURIED LIFE   9
WHEN A BELOVED HAND IS LAID IN OURS •   •   •   •   247 BURIED LIFE   78
SCREEND BY DEEP BOUGHS ON EITHER HAND   •   •   •   248 KENSINGTON GARD   2
SCREEND BY DARK TREES ON EITHER HAND •   •   •   •   248 KENSINGTON GARD   V 2
RAPT TWIRLING IN THY HAND A WITHERD SPRAY   •   •   258 SCHOLAR-GIPSY   119
THAT CORDIAL HAND THAT BEARING FREE •   •   •   •   279 SOUTHERN NIGHT   126
TOTTERING A DEATH-STRICKEN HAND •   •   •   •   •   281 HAWORTH CHURCH   25
POWER DROPPING FROM THE HAND   •   •   •   •   •   282 HAWORTH CHURCH   V
LAY THY BENUMBING HAND   •   •   •   •   •   •   •   283 HAWORTH CHURCH   V
GAVEST THE WEARY THY HAND   •   •   •   •   •   •   290 RUGBY CHAPEL   133
BRINGING THY SHEEP IN THY HAND   •   •   •   •   •   290 RUGBY CHAPEL   144
PASSING THE HOST FROM HAND TO HAND   •   •   •   •   300 GRANDE CHARTR   42
PASSING THE HOST FROM HAND TO HAND   •   •   •   •   300 GRANDE CHARTR   42
A MOUNTAIN-FLOWER WAS IN HIS HAND   •   •   •   •   314 OBERMANN MORE   65
WHO TO THE INVADING DORIANS STRETCHD A HAND   •   •   338 MEROPE   293
GRASPING FIRM IN HIS HAND   •   •   •   •   •   •   342 MEROPE   397
BY WHOSE HAND AT THE ISTHMUS   •   •   •   •   •   •   344 MEROPE   443
SWAYING THE SCEPTRE WITH PREDESTINED HAND   •   •   345 MEROPE   473
DEAD AND WHEN DIED HE WHERE AND BY WHAT HAND   •   •   355 MEROPE   715
CHEERING WITH HAND AND VOICE AND HORN HIS DOGS •   •   357 MEROPE   805
DREAD THOUGH HIS ACTS TO WHOSE HAND •   •   •   •   361 MEROPE   906
BUT THE WIT-BAFFLING WILL AND HAND OF HEAVEN   •   •   363 MEROPE   952
HERE HERE THOU HAST HIM SLAUGHTERD BY THIS HAND • •   376 MEROPE   1217
HE TO FULFIL AN ORDER RAISED HIS HAND   •   •   •   384 MEROPE   1399
OUR OWN RIGHT HAND IN THE DETESTED BLOOD   •   •   387 MEROPE   1468
IN THE HAND OF HERMES   •   •   •   •   •   •   •   •   392 MEROPE   1629
IN DANGEROUS HOUR STRETCHES HIS HAND •   •   •   •   393 MEROPE   1681
THE HAND THAT DOES THEM GUILTLESS IN A WORD   •   •   394 MEROPE   1714
TO HEAVEN AND LAID HIS HAND UPON THE STEER   •   •   •   402 MEROPE   1914

HAND   (CONTINUED)

THE PRINCE SNATCHD FROM THE SACRIFICERS HAND   • • 402 MEROPE   1919
WHAT HAND TO STRIKE THEE MEET AS MINE THE HAND   • • 402 MEROPE   1925
WHAT HAND TO STRIKE THEE MEET AS MINE THE HAND   • • 402 MEROPE   1925
HIS KINSMAN HIS RIGHT HAND IN PEACE AND WAR   • • 403 MEROPE   1974
AND TALK TO HIM OF THINGS AT HAND AND COMMON   • • 411 EMPEDOCLES I 1   158
TO KNOW THOSE SPELLS OF THINE WHICH STAY THEIR HAND   413 EMPEDOCLES I 2   25
HAND AFTER HAND IN OURS • • • • • • • • • • •   424 EMPEDOCLES I 2   360
HAND AFTER HAND IN OURS • • • • • • • • • • •   424 EMPEDOCLES I 2   360
TO KNOW THOSE SPELLS OF TIME THAT STAY THEIR HAND   413 EMPEDOCLES I 2   V   25
TO KNOW THOSE SPELLS OF THINE THAT STAY THEIR HAND   413 EMPEDOCLES I 2   V   25
AS HE LETS HIS LAX RIGHT HAND • • • • • • •   431 EMPEDOCLES II   71
KNEAD US IN ITS HOT HAND AND CHANGE OUR NATURE   • • 440 EMPEDOCLES II   386
THE BRAVE IMPETUOUS HAND YIELDS EVERYWHERE   • • 431 EMPEDOCLES II   V   90
OR TIMES STERN HAND WHY BLOTS IT NOT AWAY   • • • 462 ALARIC AT ROME   5
YEA THOUGH HAND TOUCH THEE NOT NOR EYE SHOULD SEE   470 ALARIC AT ROME   209
AND TWINE WITH BOLDER HAND THY LAST MEMORIAL WREATH   471 ALARIC AT ROME   228
A DARING HAND THAT SHRUNK NOT TO FULFIL   • • • 478 CROMWELL   227
WHAT LIVING HAND HATH BROUGHT IT HERE   • • • • 480 HAYSWATER BOAT   40
TO DAILY TASKS WE SET OUR HAND • • • • • • •   483 ROME-SICKNESS   1
TO HOLD THE LIGHT AND REACH THE HAND • • • • •   484 ROME-SICKNESS   31
BUT THY DAY OF DEATH IS AT HAND NOR SHALL WE   HOMER TRANS   48
     BE THE REASON
TO LIE LOW IN DEATH BY THE HAND OF A GOD AND A MORTAL   HOMER TRANS   56
STAY THIS HAND FROM FIGHT TILL THE TROJANS   HOMER TRANS   62
     ARE UTTERLY ROUTED
NIGHT COMES WITH NIGHT COMES SILENCE HAND IN HAND   FRAGMENT 1   1
NIGHT COMES WITH NIGHT COMES SILENCE HAND IN HAND   FRAGMENT 1   1

HANDFUL
HANDFUL OF DORIAN CONQUERORS MIGHT HAVE CURBD   • • 337 MEROPE   248

HANDMAID
FOR HANDMAID TO THEIR STRIDING POWER • • • • • • •   53 RESIGNATION   31

HANDS
NOT BY THEIR HANDS WHO VEX THE PATIENT GROUND   • •   4 DUKE WELLINGTON   3
AND THE DUCHESS CLAPS HER HANDS • • • • • • •   14 CHURCH BROU 1   40
IN GRAY AGE WITH PALSIED HANDS • • • • • • •   14 CHURCH BROU 1   66
WITH BLOWN TRESSES AND WITH BECKONING HANDS   • •   26 NEW SIRENS   16
THE HANDS PROPPING THE SUNK HEAD • • • • • •   30 NEW SIRENS   128
O LOOSE HANDS AND LET IT BE • • • • • • •   34 NEW SIRENS   224
COME LOOSE HANDS THE WINGED FLEETNESS • • • • •   34 NEW SIRENS   251
WE BATHED OUR HANDS WITH SPEECHLESS GLEE • • • •   54 RESIGNATION   84
AND GREETED GUDURZ WITH BOTH HANDS AND SAID • •   67 SOHRAB RUSTUM   204
AND WITH THESE SLAUGHTEROUS HANDS DRAW SWORD NO MORE   68 SOHRAB RUSTUM   241
GIRL NIMBLE WITH THY FEET NOT WITH THY HANDS   • •   74 SOHRAB RUSTUM   457
LIGHTS UP HIS STUDIOUS FOREHEAD AND THIN HANDS   • •   81 SOHRAB RUSTUM   676
IN BOTH HIS HANDS THE DUST WHICH LAY AROUND   • •   81 SOHRAB RUSTUM   700
BUT SOHRAB SAW HIS THOUGHT AND HELD HIS HANDS   • •   82 SOHRAB RUSTUM   706
MY HEAD BETWIXT THY HANDS AND KISS MY CHEEKS   • •   82 SOHRAB RUSTUM   719
THE SWORD WERE BROKEN IN THY HANDS • • • • • •   92 SICK KING BOKH   140
EAT NOT THE FRUIT OF THEIR OWN HANDS • • • • •   93 SICK KING BOKH   170
WITH FOLDED HANDS REVOLVING THINGS TO COME • • •   98 BALDER DEAD 1   93
AND BOWD HER HEAD AND SATE WITH FOLDED HANDS   • • 100 BALDER DEAD 1   193
AND ODIN CAME AND LAID HIS KINGLY HANDS • • • •   115 BALDER DEAD 3   65
SHE IN HER HANDS TOOK BALDERS HEAD AND SPAKE   • • 116 BALDER DEAD 3   98
AND BOWD HER HEAD AND SATE WITH FOLDED HANDS   • • 122 BALDER DEAD 3   296
HER SNOW-WHITE HANDS HER GOLDEN HAIR • • • • • •   132 TRISTRAM 1   51
LET THEM DRINK IT LET THEIR HANDS • • • • • •   135 TRISTRAM 1   147
SHE TOOK HIS HANDS IN HERS HER TEARS • • • • •   140 TRISTRAM 1   317
STILL HOLD HER LOVERS HANDS HER HEAD • • • • •   146 TRISTRAM 2   V   105
STILL HOLDS HER LOVERS HANDS HER HEAD • • • •   146 TRISTRAM 2   V   105
WATCHING HER CHILDREN PLAY THEIR LITTLE HANDS   • • 150 TRISTRAM 3   24
FIXT HER SLIGHT HANDS CLASPD ON HER LAP THEN RISE   152 TRISTRAM 3   91
AND CLAP THY HANDS AND CRY TIS THOU • • • • •   184 TERRACE BERNE   16
WITH ACHING HANDS AND BLEEDING FEET • • • • •   241 MORALITY   7
FROM THEIR TIRED HANDS AND REST • • • • • •   243 SUMMER NIGHT   44
WITH PITCHERS IN THEIR HANDS AND FRESH-PULLD FLOWERS   331 MEROPE   54
OUR HANDS IN SOLEMN UNION MAKING FRIENDS • • •   335 MEROPE   165
WHO CAN EXTEND THEIR HANDS MAIDENS TAKE BACK   • • 336 MEROPE   195
THAT OUR JOINT HANDS MIGHT THEN TOGETHER PAY   • • 367 MEROPE   1047
YET STARK FROM THE DEATH-STRUGGLE TIGHT-CLENCHD HANDS   373 MEROPE   1174
WHAT HELP WHAT VENGEANCE AT THEIR HANDS HAVE I   • • 381 MEROPE   1318
THAT SPOTLESS HANDS UNSHAKEN SCEPTRES HOLD   • • 388 MEROPE   1519
WAVING HER HUNDRED HANDS A TORCH IN EACH   • • • • 395 MEROPE   1735
WE SEARCH OUT DEAD MENS WORDS AND WORKS OF   423 EMPEDOCLES I 2   326
     DEAD MENS HANDS
WHO ASKS THIS FINAL SERVICE AT YOUR HANDS • • • • 429 EMPEDOCLES II   28
PRESSING FAST WITH BOTH HIS HANDS • • • • • •   434 EMPEDOCLES II   187
SO SAITH HE BLESSING HIM WITH OUTSPREAD HANDS   • • 445 WESTMIN ABBEY   46
IF YOUR OWN HANDS THE GOOD BEGUN UNDO   • • • 447 WESTMIN ABBEY   103
THAT PAIR WHOSE HEAD DID PLAN WHOSE HANDS DID FORGE   448 WESTMIN ABBEY   134
HANDS HAD STROKED THEM WHICH ARE COLD • • • •   453 POOR MATTHIAS   47
THAT YOUR OWN HANDS MUST OPEN WIDE THE GATE   • • 466 ALARIC AT ROME   117
HIS HANDS WERE FOLDED LIKE A SAINT AT REST • • • • 476 CROMWELL   168

HANG
THERE WOULD I GO AND HANG MY ARMOUR UP   • • • •   68 SOHRAB RUSTUM   236
THERE WOULD I STAY AND HANG MY ARMOUR UP   • • • •   68 SOHRAB RUSTUM   V   236
HANG IN THE AIR AFIELD AND DISAPPEAR • • • • • •   104 BALDER DEAD 1   336
THE CALM SEA SHINES LOOSE HANG THE VESSELS SAILS   • • 133 TRISTRAM 1   94
THEY HANG THE PICTURE DOTH THE STORY TELL   • • • • 166 PICT NEWSTEAD   8

HANG   (CONTINUED)
        TO HANG OVER ENDYMIONS SLEEP . . . .   181 ISOLATION MARG   23
        SOME HANG UPON THE RAILS AND SOME . . . . . .   224 EPILOG LAOCOON   113
        HANG WEEDS OF OUR SAD TIME . . . .   323 OBERMANN MORE   308
        DOUBLE AND CLASHING THAT HANG . . . .   370 MEROPE   1113

HANGD
        HANGD UPON A BRANCHING FIR . . . .   433 EMPEDOCLES II   148

HANGING
        LEFT OUR AWFUL LAURELS HANGING . . . .   27 NEW SIRENS   31
        HANGING GARLANDS ON YOUR ODOROUS PINES . . . .   29 NEW SIRENS   96
        HANGING GARLANDS ON THE ODOROUS PINES . . . .   29 NEW SIRENS   V 96
        THY LEFT HOLDS HANGING LOOSELY . . . .   186 STRAYED REVEL   11
        THOU HAST BEEN SEEN OR HANGING ON A GATE . . .   258 SCHOLAR-GIPSY   103
        HANGING NOW OER A HEAD . . . .   281 HAWORTH CHURCH   V
        THEIR HANGING RUIN ALAS . . . .   289 RUGBY CHAPEL   100
        OF IVY-PLANTS AND FRAGRANT HANGING BELLS . . .   414 EMPEDOCLES I 2   49

HANGS
        THERE CLIMBING HANGS A FAR-SEEN SIGN . . . . .   54 RESIGNATION   60
        WHICH HANGS UNCERTAIN TO WHICH SIDE TO FALL . .   72 SOHRAB RUSTUM   392
        WHICH HANGS OVER THE ICE WHERE LIES THE ROAD .   108 BALDER DEAD 2   127
        AND TO EACH BULRUSH-CREST A SWALLOW HANGS . . .   109 BALDER DEAD 2   160
        HANGS QUIVERING OUT BETWEEN HIS DUST-SMEARD JAWS   114 BALDER DEAD 3   15
        HANGS DARK UPON THE ROLLING SEA . . . . . .   205 CALAIS SANDS   22
        HANGS DOWN HIS BEAUTIFUL HEAD . . . .   214 NEW ROME   2
        HANGS DOWN HIS HEAD AS BEFORE . . . .   214 NEW ROME   18
        HANGS TOUCHD WITH LIGHT ONE SNOWY SAIL . . .   274 STANZAS CARNAC   32
        HANGS TOUCHD WITH LIGHT ONE DISTANT SAIL . . .   274 STANZAS CARNAC   V 32
        WHICH HANGS OER THE STYMPHALIAN LAKE AND DROWND   363 MEROPE   961
        IS DARK AND ON THE STREAM THE MIST STILL HANGS   406 EMPEDOCLES I 1   13

HAPLESS
        HIS SHEEP HIS HAPLESS LOVE HIS BLINDED EYES . .   268 THYRSIS   187
        THERE THERE THOU LIEST NOW MY HAPLESS CHILD . .   373 MEROPE   1171

HAPLY
        HAPLY HE WILL FORGET HIS WRATH AND FIGHT . . .   66 SOHRAB RUSTUM   182
        IF HAPLY HE MAY MELT HER HEART WITH WORDS . . .   100 BALDER DEAD 1   182
        UNKNOWN AND LONG AND HAPLY ON THAT WAY . . . .   116 BALDER DEAD 3   100
        FOR BALDER IF THOU HAPLY THUS MAYST MELT . . .   122 BALDER DEAD 3   293
        BALDER IF HAPLY HE MAY THUS BE WON . . . . .   122 BALDER DEAD 3   301
        HAPLY IN HIS DREAMS THE WIND . . . .   136 TRISTRAM 1   190
        HAPLY HE SEEMS AGAIN TO MOVE . . . .   136 TRISTRAM 1   206
        HAPLY THE RIVER OF TIME . . . .   253 FUTURE   71
        HAPLY HAD BUT ONE DARING SOUL STOOD FORTH . . .   383 MEROPE   1364
        IF HAPLY AT THIS MOMENT SUCH ATTEMPT . . . . .   388 MEROPE   1505

HAPPENS
        AND STANDS A FAILURE THEN THEN HAPPENS OPPIUS . .   LUCRETIUS 2   12

HAPPIER
        COULD LIFE RUN NO HAPPIER WAY . . . .   33 NEW SIRENS   200
        IN NEW-RECOVERD SEATS THE HAPPIER DAY . . . .   128 BALDER DEAD 3   513
        BROTHER WHAT SEATS ARE THESE WHAT HAPPIER DAY .   128 BALDER DEAD 3   515
        A HAPPIER WORSE IT CANNOT BE . . . .   139 TRISTRAM 1   297
        AND LOVE IF LOVE OF HAPPIER MEN . . . . . .   181 ISOLATION MARG   36
        OF HAPPIER MEN FOR THEY AT LEAST . . . . . .   181 ISOLATION MARG   37
        AND NOW IN HAPPIER AIR . . . .   268 THYRSIS   176
        HAPPIER HAVE UTTERD IN MINE . . . .   299 HEINES GRAVE   228
        EARTH HAPPIER THAN BEFORE . . . .   314 OBERMANN MORE   56
        WITH HAPPIER ZEAL PURSUED . . . .   322 OBERMANN MORE   296
        WHEREFORE ACCEPT THAT HAPPIER OMEN . . . . .   344 MEROPE   452
        MAY IT TURN HAPPIER THAN MY DOUBTS PORTEND . . .   390 MEROPE   1583
        THAT WE WERE DESTIND TO A HAPPIER STATE . . . .   LUCRETIUS 3   11

HAPPIEST
        UNFRUITFUL OFT AND AT HER HAPPIEST THROE . . .   45 IN UTRUMQUE PAR   27
        AND SURE OF ALL THE HAPPIEST FAR ART THOU . . .   112 BALDER DEAD 2   257

HAPPINESS
        LENGTHEN THEIR HAPPINESS . . . .   51 CONSOLATION   58
        WELL HATH HE DONE WHO HATH SEIZED HAPPINESS . .   195 FRAG ANTIGONE   1
        THEY SPEAK THE HAPPINESS DIVINE . . . .   227 EPILOG LAOCOON   197
        AND HEADLONG FATE BE HAPPINESS . . . .   271 MEMORIAL VERSES   33
        HAPPINESS MOCKD OUR PRAYER . . . .   425 EMPEDOCLES I 2   383
        THE CLUE TO HAPPINESS . . . .   EMPEDOCLES I 2   V

HAPPY
        FROM PALM-GROVE ON TO PALM-GROVE HAPPY TREES . .   11 MYCERINUS   86
        MAY BRING ONE OF THE OLD HAPPY MOMENTS AGAIN . .   19 MODERN SAPPHO   V
        HAPPY AT THE NOON OF PLEASURE . . . .   33 NEW SIRENS   V 201
        ARE THE HAPPY GODS DISMAYD . . . .   34 NEW SIRENS   V 246
        AND BREATHE MORE HAPPY IN AN EVEN CLIME . . .   37 YOUTHS AGIT   6
        SUCH HAPPY ISSUE CROWND HER PAINFUL CARE . . .   46 IN UTRUMQUE PAR   34
        THE HOUR WHOSE HAPPY . . . .   52 CONSOLATION   61
        SURVEYS EACH HAPPY GROUP WHICH FLEETS . . . .   57 RESIGNATION   166
        SURVEYS EACH HAPPY GROUP THAT FLEETS . . . . .   57 RESIGNATION   V 166
        SAYS HAPPY HE WHO LODGES THERE . . . .   94 SICK KING BOKH   193

HAPPY   (CONTINUED)
    I AM HAPPY YET I FEEL THERES SOMETHING   • • • • 145 TRISTRAM 2   73
    AND IS SHE HAPPY DOES SHE SEE UNMOVED   • • • • 151 TRISTRAM 3   64
    THE GODS ARE HAPPY • • • • • • • • • • •   • • • • 190 STRAYED REVEL   130
    THE HAPPY ISLANDS • • • • • • • • • • • •   • • • • 192 STRAYED REVEL   206
    AND BLEND HIS HAPPY LIFE • • • • • • • •   • • • • 197 FRAG ANTIGONE   73
    IN AN EASY OLD AGE IN A HAPPY HOME   • • • • • • • • 199 FRAG DEJANEIRA   23
    FOR THEY ARE HAPPY AS THEY ARE • • • •   • • • • 203 EUPHROSYNE   16
    THE YOUNG THE HAPPY AND THE FAIR • • • •   • • • • 224 EPILOG LAOCOON   117
    BE OTHERS HAPPY IF THEY CAN • • • • • •   • • • • 249 KENSINGTON GARD   22
    THEN TO THEIR HAPPY REST THEY PASS • • •   • • • • 249 KENSINGTON GARD   33
    BUT IT NEEDS HAPPY MOMENTS FOR THIS SKILL   • • • • 256 SCHOLAR-GIPSY   V   50
    OF STORMS THAT RAGE OUTSIDE OUR HAPPY GROUND   • • • • 264 THYRSIS   49
    YET HAPPY OMEN HAIL • • • • • • • • • •   • • • • 267 THYRSIS   166
    MEN GAVE THEE NOTHING BUT THIS HAPPY QUEST   • • • • 269 THYRSIS   213
    KEPT NOT FOR LONG ITS HAPPY COUNTRY TONE   • • • • 269 THYRSIS   222
    AND HE WAS HAPPY IF TO KNOW • • • • • •   • • • • 271 MEMORIAL VERSES   29
    AND LIVED SOME MOONS IN HAPPY TRANCE • •   • • • • 279 SOUTHERN NIGHT   109
    THE HAPPY MOMENT COMES LURK HERE UNSEEN   • • • • 332 MEROPE   67
    THIS REGION IS NOT HAPPY FOR MY RACE • •   • • • • 357 MEROPE   785
    IN A RICH CHAMBER ON A HAPPY BED • • • •   • • • • 373 MEROPE   1178
    THE HAPPY HUNTER HE BASKS • • • • • •   • • • • 347 MEROPE   V
    THE SUNSHINE IN THE HAPPY GLENS IS FAIR   • • • • 426 EMPEDOCLES I 2   430
    ARE FOR THE HAPPY FOR THE SOULS AT EASE   • • • • 436 EMPEDOCLES II   259
    WHAT IS THE HAPPY GLOW SO SOON EXPIRED   • • • • 444 WESTMIN ABBEY   10
    AND CAROLS FLOAT ALONG THE HAPPY AIR • •   • • • • 445 WESTMIN ABBEY   39
    THE SAVIOURS HAPPY LIGHT • • • • • • •   • • • • 446 WESTMIN ABBEY   61
    THEREFORE OUR HAPPY GUEST • • • • • •   • • • • 447 WESTMIN ABBEY   121
    LIVE HAPPY THEN EXPECT YOUR PERFECT MEED   • • • • 448 WESTMIN ABBEY   138
    GREEN HAPPY PLACES LIKE A FLOWERY LEA   • • • • 475 CROMWELL   117
    O HAPPY SLUMBER IF THE DAY WERE DONE • • • •   • • • • 475 CROMWELL   120
    QUICKENED AND MOVED A HAPPY BREATH • • • •   • • • • 483 ROME-SICKNESS   7
    YET HAPPY SINCE HIS FEVERISH BLOOD • • • •   • • • • 484 ROME-SICKNESS   25
    AND DARED PRONOUNCE IT HAPPY WHAT ARE THESE   • •   RUDE ORATOR   7
    AND DARED PRONOUNCE THEM HAPPY WHAT ARE THESE   • •   RUDE ORATOR   V   7

HARASSD
    TOO HARASSD TO ATTAIN • • • • • • • • •   • • • • 308 OBERMANN   78
    AND MEN IGNOBLE HARASSD HIM WITH STRIFE   • • • • 447 WESTMIN ABBEY   125

HARBOUR
    ONE DAY TO HARBOUR IN THE TOMB • • • • •   • • • • 22 YOUTH AND CALM   15
    AGAINST THE HARBOUR BY THE CITY-WALL • • • •   • • • • 101 BALDER DEAD 1   225
    NEAR HARBOUR BUT THEY SHARE • • • • • •   • • • • 193 STRAYED REVEL   255
    STANDING FOR HARBOUR • • • • • • • • •   • • • • 400 MEROPE   1877
    RIGHT AT THE HARBOUR-MOUTH • • • • • •   • • • • 400 MEROPE   1878

HARBOURING
    BUT HERE WHILE HARBOURING ON ITS MARGIN LAY   • • 332 MEROPE   70

HARBOURS
    THE WILD BOAR HARBOURS CLOSE AND FEEDS   • • • • 148 TRISTRAM 2   V

HARD
    THOU STRIKST TOO HARD THAT CLUB OF THINE WILL FLOAT   74 SOHRAB RUSTUM   427
    THAT THE HARD IRON CORSLET CLANKD ALOUD   • • • • 80 SOHRAB RUSTUM   664
    HARD BY A CLOSE OF APRICOTS • • • • • • • •   • • • • 94 SICK KING BOKH   223
    AND TWAS WHEN NIGHT IS BORDERING HARD ON DAWN   • • • • 103 BALDER DEAD 1   280
    SET HIS STOUT SHOULDER HARD AGAINST THE STERN   • • • • 118 BALDER DEAD 3   176
    ARE FURIOUS WITH THEMSELVES AND HARD TO PLEASE • • • • 153 TRISTRAM 3   142
    CAN NEVER END THEIR TASKS ARE HARD TO PLEASE   • • • • 153 TRISTRAM 3   V 142
    ARE FRETFUL WITH THEMSELVES AND HARD TO PLEASE • • • • 153 TRISTRAM 3   V 142
    OF MATTER AND HARD TO EXTRACT • • • • • • •   • • • • 230 YOUTH OF NATURE   69
    GRASPING THE RUDDER HARD • • • • • •   • • • • 244 SUMMER NIGHT   67
    IN THE HUGE WORLD WHICH ROARS HARD BY   • • • • 249 KENSINGTON GARD   21
    THEY TRY US OFTENEST MAKE US HARD • • • • •   • • • • 273 EDW QUILLINAN   7
    ON THAT HARD PAGAN WORLD DISGUST • • • • •   • • • • 315 OBERMANN MORE   93
    I KNOW I KNOW HOW HARD IT IS TO THINK • • •   • • • • 341 MEROPE   362
    THE GODS O MISTRESS DEAR THE HARD-SOULD MAN   • • 390 MEROPE   1577
    WHAT LIFE AND CHANCE GO HARD WITH THEE TOO AS WITH US 416 EMPEDOCLES I 2   116
    WHEN THY OWN LOT WENT HARD • • • • • •   • • • • 417 EMPEDOCLES I 2   165
    HIS HARD-TASKD SUNBURNT WIFE • • • • • •   • • • • 426 EMPEDOCLES I 2   414
    WHAT LIFE AND TIME GO HARD WITH THEE TOO AS WITH US 416 EMPEDOCLES I 2   V   116
    WHICH MAN PROUD MAN FINDS HARD TO BEAR   • • • • 450 GEISTS GRAVE   30
    US THY HUMAN KEEPERS HARD • • • • • • • •   • • • • 456 POOR MATTHIAS   122
    DULL OF HEART AND HARD OF TOUCH • • • • •   • • • • 457 POOR MATTHIAS   168
    ALAS IT NEEDS NOT IS IT HARD TO KNOW • • • •   • • • • 466 ALARIC AT ROME   119

HARDER
    BUT EARTHLY KNIGHTS HAVE HARDER HEARTS   • • • • 159 NECKAN   19
    AND SOMETIMES BY STILL HARDER FATE • • • • •   • • • • 207 TOO LATE   5
    WILL MAKE OURSELVES HARDER TO BE DISCERND   • • • • 440 EMPEDOCLES II   381

HARDIHOOD
    WITH SUCH A PEEVISH HARDIHOOD OF SCORN   • • • •   RUDE ORATOR   20

HARDLY
    WHOSE SURENESS GRAY-HAIRD SCHOLARS HARDLY LEARN • • 43 GIPSY CHILD   42
    THOUGH BEARABLE SEEM HARDLY WORTH • • • • • • • • • 60 RESIGNATION   263
    HARDLY LETS PEEP THE GOLDEN HAIR • • • • • •   • • • 141 TRISTRAM 1   341

HARDLY   (CONTINUED)
        MOUNTS AND THAT HARDLY TO ETERNAL LIFE . . . . 172 IMMORTALITY   14
        AND HARDLY YET A GLANCE A TONE . . . . 185 TERRACE BERNE   38
        HARDLY HARDLY SHALL ONE . . . . 217 LORDS MESSENGER   19
        HARDLY HARDLY SHALL ONE . . . . 217 L'ORDS MESSENGER   19
        HARDLY HIS VOICE AT ITS BEST . . . . . . 231 YOUTH OF NATURE   99
        BUT HARDLY HAVE WE FOR ONE LITTLE HOUR . . . . 246 BURIED LIFE   59
        HARDLY HAD SKILL TO UTTER ONE OF ALL . . . . . 246 BURIED LIFE   61
        SILENT HARDLY A SHOUT . . . . 286 RUGBY CHAPEL   6
        HARDLY OURSELVES WE FOUGHT THROUGH . . . . . . 289 RUGBY CHAPEL   120
        THE HARDLY-HEARD-OF GRAVE . . . . 312 OBERMANN   180
        THY HARDLY HEARD OF GRAVE . . . . 312 OBERMANN   V 180
        HARDLY THE FOURTH WITH GRIEVOUS LOSS REGAIND . . 336 MEROPE   218
        BOUNDED IN OUR OWN BREAST WE HARDLY KNOW . . . 352 MEROPE   639
        AND HARDLY YET SOME SAY HATH FOUND A GRAVE . . . 385 MEROPE   1425
        HARDLY THE THIRD WITH GRIEVOUS LOSS REGAIND . . 336 MEROPE   V 218
        FOR MIST CAN HARDLY SEE . . . . 444 WESTMIN ABBEY   V 22
        WHAT ARE LEFT WILL HARDLY BE . . . . 458 POOR MATTHIAS   212

HARDNESS
        WE SHALL NOT THEN CALL HARDNESS FORCE . . . . 179 FAREWELL   59
        WHICH WITHOUT HARDNESS WILL BE SAGE . . . . . 304 GRANDE CHARTR   159

HAREBELLS
        HAREBELLS FLOWER IN THE NAVE . . . . 15 CHURCH BROU 1   72

HARK
        HARK WHAT BELL FOR CHURCH IS TOLLD . . . . . . 12 CHURCH BROU 1   4
        HARK THE GAMES ON FOOT THEY SCATTER . . . . . . 13 CHURCH BROU 1   21
        HARK A SHOUT A CRASH A GROAN . . . . 13 CHURCH BROU 1   24
        HARK BELOW THE GATES UNBARRING . . . . 14 CHURCH BROU 1   37
        SO TO WAIT BUT WHAT NOTES DOWN THE WIND HARK   20 MODERN SAPPHO   29
            ARE DRIVING
        THEN TO WAIT BUT WHAT NOTES DOWN THE WIND HARK   20 MODERN SAPPHO   V 29
            ARE DRIVING
        HARK HE MUTTERS IN HIS SLEEP . . . . 133 TRISTRAM 1   87
        HARK WHAT SHE SINGS O JOY O JOY . . . . . . 164 FORSAKEN MERM   89
        HARK FAST BY THE WINDOW . . . . . . 175 PARTING   25
        HARK THE WIND RUSHES PAST US . . . . . 176 PARTING   43
        HARK AH THE NIGHTINGALE . . . . 200 PHILOMELA   1
        HARK FROM THAT MOONLIT CEDAR WHAT A BURST . . . 200 PHILOMELA   3
        WHAT TRIUMPH HARK WHAT PAIN . . . . 200 PHILOMELA   4
        HARK HARK EUGENIA . . . . 201 PHILOMELA   V 28
        HARK HARK EUGENIA . . . . 201 PHILOMELA   V 28
        HARK THROUGH THE ALLEY RESOUNDS . . . . . . 293 HEINES GRAVE   37
        WHILE HARK FAR DOWN WITH STRANGLED SOUND . . . 299 GRANDE CHARTR   9
        HARK HOW THE SHOUTING CROWDS TRAMP HITHERWARD . 401 MEROPE   1886
        PANTHEIAS HISTORY HARK WHAT SOUND WAS THAT . . 412 EMPEDOCLES I 2   8
        HARK THERE AGAIN TIS THE BOY CALLICLES . . . . 412 EMPEDOCLES I 2   12
        I KNOW THESE NOTES AMONG A THOUSAND HARK . . . 413 EMPEDOCLES I 2   35
        I KNOW THOSE NOTES AMONG A THOUSAND HARK . . . 413 EMPEDOCLES I 2   V 35

HARM
        VAINLY YOU HEDGE HIM FROM THE ASSAULT OF HARM . 359 MEROPE   855
        OR HARM AND NURSE MY LONGING FOR MY SON . . . 366 MEROPE   1022
        OF NATURE HARM US NOT . . . . 421 EMPEDOCLES I 2   265

HARMONIA
        WHO ONCE WERE CADMUS AND HARMONIA . . . . . . 427 EMPEDOCLES I 2   436

HARMONIOUS
        SO MEN UNRAVELLING GODS HARMONIOUS WHOLE . . . . 4 BUTLERS SERMONS   3

HARMONISD
        TWO BLENDING DUTIES HARMONISD IN ONE . . . . . . 1 QUIET WORK   V 3

HARMONY
        IN HARMONY WITH NATURE RESTLESS FOOL . . . . . . 5 HARMONY NATURE   1
        THE HARMONY FROM WHICH MAN SWERVED . . . . . . 314 OBERMANN MORE   53
        WITH THE SWEET NIGHT TO HELP THY HARMONY . . . 409 EMPEDOCLES I 1   98
        OF THE APPEASING GRACIOUS HARMONY . . . . . . 431 EMPEDOCLES II   75

HARNESSD
        FIRM HARNESSD BY THE MANE A CHIEF . . . . . . 191 STRAYED REVEL   188

HARP
        BUT THEY HARP EVER ON ONE STRING AND WAKE . . . 117 BALDER DEAD 3   137
        A GOLD HARP LEANS AGAINST THE BED . . . . . . 131 TRISTRAM 1   17
        I KNOW HIM BY HIS HARP OF GOLD . . . . . . 131 TRISTRAM 1   19
        SITS NECKAN WITH HIS HARP OF GOLD . . . . . . 159 NECKAN   3
        HE SATE AND PLAYD HIS HARP OF GOLD . . . . . . 160 NECKAN   43
        AND PLAYST THY HARP OF GOLD . . . . . . 160 NECKAN   50
        SITS NECKAN WITH HIS HARP OF GOLD . . . . . . 161 NECKAN   67
        AH STILL HARP ON WHAT THEY HEARD . . . . . . 227 PERSIST POETRY   4
        SHAKING HER HEAD TOOK THE HARP . . . . . . 285 HAWORTH CHURCH   126
        OF THE HARP BE HEARD WITH THE PIPE . . . . . . 360 MEROPE   895
        I HAVE MY HARP TOO THAT IS WELL APOLLO . . . . 407 EMPEDOCLES I 1   19
        TOUCHING THY HARP AS THE WHIM CAME ON THEE . . 407 EMPEDOCLES I 1   33
        THOU KNOWST OF OLD HE LOVED THIS HARP OF MINE . 408 EMPEDOCLES I 1   72
        THOU HAST INDEED A RARE TOUCH ON THY HARP . . . 409 EMPEDOCLES I 1   78
        HE HATH HIS HARP AND LAUREL WITH HIM STILL . . 409 EMPEDOCLES I 1   82
        HE HAS HIS HARP AND LAUREL WITH HIM STILL . . 409 EMPEDOCLES I 1   V 82

HARP   (CONTINUED)
        I SHOULD HAVE SAID THAT SOME ONE TOUCHD A HARP   . . .   412 EMPEDOCLES I 2   11
        THE SWEETEST HARP-PLAYER IN CATANA   . . . . . .   412 EMPEDOCLES I 2   13
        THAT WAS MY HARP-PLAYER AGAIN WHERE IS HE   . . . .   427 EMPEDOCLES I 2   461
        SO PASS WE ON BUT OH TO HARP ARIGHT   . . . . . .   471 ALARIC AT ROME   223

HARPER
        THE PEERLESS HUNTER HARPER KNIGHT   . . . . . .   131 TRISTRAM 1   22

HARSH
        GUST ON GUST THE HARSH WINDS BLOW   . . . . . .   32 NEW SIRENS   172
        AH HARSH FLATTERER LET ALONE MY BEAUTY   . . . .   143 TRISTRAM 2   21
        THEN THROUGH THE GREAT TOWNS HARSH HEART-WEARYING ROAR   269 THYRSIS   234
        WHAT THEN SO HARSH AND MALIGN   . . . .   294 HEINES GRAVE   67
        WHAT SO HARSH AND MALIGN   . . . .   294 HEINES GRAVE   V 67
        WE WANT ALL PLEASANT ENDS BUT WILL USE NO HARSH MEANS   420 EMPEDOCLES I 2   236
        HARSH GODS AND HOSTILE FATES   . . . .   422 EMPEDOCLES I 2   304
        AND HARSH THE TEMPER GREW   . . . .   446 WESTMIN ABBEY   67

HARSHNESS
        OF TYRANNOUS HARSHNESS OR REMISSNESS WEAK   . . . .   404 MEROPE   2007

HARTZ
        OER THE FRESH SHORT TURF OF THE HARTZ   . . . .   297 HEINES GRAVE   153
        OF THE LOWER HARTZ AMONG OAKS   . . . .   297 HEINES GRAVE   180
        TO THE FROZEN HARTZ WITH HIS SOUL   . . . . . .   298 HEINES GRAVE   193

HARVEST
        FORESEEN THY HARVEST YET PROCEEDST TO LIVE   . . . .   43 GIPSY CHILD   40
        ROUND HIS GREEN HARVEST-PLOT   . . . .   190 STRAYED REVEL   159
        THEIR MELON-HARVEST TO THE HEART THEY SEE   . . . .   193 STRAYED REVEL   239
        THE GRASSY HARVEST OF THE RIVER-FIELDS   . . . .   266 THYRSIS   108
        SEED-TIME AND HARVEST   . . . .   436 EMPEDOCLES II   254

HASTE
        TOO GREAT FOR HASTE TOO HIGH FOR RIVALRY   . . . .   1 QUIET WORK   8
        BY CHILDREN WHOM THEIR NURSES CALL WITH HASTE   . .   86 SOHRAB RUSTUM   846
        LET HUSSEIN IF THOU WILT MAKE HASTE   . . . . . .   88 SICK KING BOKH   27
        AND OFTEN THE FINGERS CLOSE IN HASTE   . . . . .   141 TRISTRAM 1   346
        HASTE ARISE YE AND GO   . . . .   216 LORDS MESSENGER   5
        OF HASTE HALF-WORK AND DISARRAY   . . . . . .   222 EPILOG LAOCOON   27
        SONS OF THE WORLD OH HASTE THOSE YEARS   . . . .   304 GRANDE CHARTR   V 161
        HASTE AND ADVISE FOR DAY COMES ON APACE   . . . .   330 MEROPE   28
        AND I ACROSS THE MOUNTAINS BROUGHT WITH HASTE   . .   358 MEROPE   845
        POST-HASTE TO COBHAM CALLS THE MUSE   . . . . .   458 KAISER DEAD   2

HASTENING
        HOW BOTH WERE HASTENING AS THEY FLOWERED AND GREW   469 ALARIC AT ROME   189

HASTINGS
        ANCIENT STREETS OF HASTINGS TOWN   . . . . . .   457 POOR MATTHIAS   182

HASTY
        THEN WITH WEAK HASTY FINGERS SOHRAB LOOSED   . . . .   81 SOHRAB RUSTUM   669
        SHE HER GOOD SHEPHERDS HASTY IMAGE DREW   . . . .   172 GOOD SHEPHERD   13
        TOO HASTY HEADS FOR ORDERING WORLDS ALAS   . . . .   237 PROGRESS   9

HAT
        IN HAT OF ANTIQUE SHAPE AND CLOAK OF GREY   . . . .   256 SCHOLAR-GIPSY   55
        WITH THE LOW BROAD HAT OF THE TANND   . . . . .   342 MEROPE   395
        HIS BROAD-BRIMMD HUNTERS HAT WHICH IN THE BAY   . .   358 MEROPE   843

HATE
        THE FOE THE ACCUSER WHOM THOUGH GODS WE HATE   . .   96 BALDER DEAD 1   38
        THE FOE THE ACCUSER WHOM THOUGH GODS WE HATE   . .   98 BALDER DEAD 1   101
        ENEMY MOCKER WHOM THOUGH GODS WE HATE   . . . .   114 BALDER DEAD 3   22
        BELOW AND DOST HATE ME EVEN HERE   . . . . . .   125 BALDER DEAD 3   406
        ON THIS WILD EARTH OF HATE AND FEAR   . . . . .   180 FAREWELL   86
        WITH LOVE AND HATE TRIUMPH AND AGONY   . . . .   201 PHILOMELA   26
        CHATTER AND LOVE AND HATE   . . . .   288 RUGBY CHAPEL   62
        HATE TO THEIR RULE WHICH ELSE WOULD DIE AWAY   . .   331 MEROPE   43
        IS WITHOUT LOVE OR HATE AUSTERELY RAISED   . . . .   336 MEROPE   205
        DEEMING AS TYRANTS DEEM OUR SILENCE HATE   . . . .   338 MEROPE   260
        TO BE DELIVERD FROM THY FOSTERD HATE   . . . . .   342 MEROPE   383
        OF PEACE AND BEEN REPULSED WITH HATE AND SCORN   . .   360 MEROPE   881
        MURDER DISCORD AND HATE   . . . .   361 MEROPE   910
        IF WITH NO RAGE NO FIRE OF RIGHTEOUS HATE   . . . .   366 MEROPE   1011
        ALMOST BEFORE TIS PLANND COME GLOWING HATE   . . .   367 MEROPE   1062
        HATE DUTY INTEREST PASSION CALL ONE WAY   . . . .   383 MEROPE   1382
        IN ME THE FEVER OF REVENGEFUL HATE   . . . . .   387 MEROPE   1466
        I CHAFE NOT WITH THEE THAT THY HATE ENDURES   . .   398 MEROPE   1785
        WHAT HATE AND AWE AND SHAME   . . . .   416 EMPEDOCLES I 2   112
        AND JEALOUS JOCK THY ONLY HATE   . . . .   461 KAISER DEAD   75
        PYMS LOOK OF HATE AND STRAFFORDS GLANCE OF FLAME   . .   476 CROMWELL   164
        NEITHER HATE HAVE THEY NOR FEAR NOR PRIDE   . . . .   META CLOISTER   8

HATED
        I LOVED THE GOOD HE SCORND AND HATED WRONG   . . . .   9 MYCERINUS   15

HATED   (CONTINUED)
    A THOUSAND VIRTUES IN THIS HATED TIME   • • • •   37 YOUTHS AGIT   8
    MY HATED CONVERSE ON THEE CAME I UP • • • • • • 125 BALDER DEAD 3 414
    THE ALL-HATED ORDER-BREAKING • • • • • • • 195 FRAG ANTIGONE 25

HATEFUL
    FIGHT LET ME HEAR THY HATEFUL VOICE NO MORE • •   75 SOHRAB RUSTUM 459
    FOR WHO WILL BEAR MY HATEFUL SIGHT IN HEAVEN • •   98 BALDER DEAD 1 106
    NOR WITH A HATEFUL PRESENCE CUMBER HEAVEN • • • • 125 BALDER DEAD 3 399
    HATEFUL BY EACH MESSENIAN HEART ABHORRD • • • • 366 MEROPE 1009

HATEFULLY
    ONLY TO TYPHO IT SOUNDS HATEFULLY • • • • • • 430 EMPEDOCLES II 41

HATERS
    WE DO NOT AS SOME FEEBLER HATERS DO • • • • • • 111 BALDER DEAD 2 228

HATES
    BALDER UPBRAIDS ME NOT NOR HATES AT ALL • • • • 125 BALDER DEAD 3 407
    THEIR INEFFECTUAL FEUDS AND FEEBLE HATES • • • • 126 BALDER DEAD 3 466
    SHADOWS OF HATES BUT THEY DISTRESS THEM STILL • 126 BALDER DEAD 3 467
    VOYAGES EXILES HATES DISSENSIONS WARS • • • • 195 FRAG ANTIGONE 23
    ENDLESS EXTINCTION OF UNHAPPY HATES • • • • • • 333 MEROPE 102
    CONSIDER HIM CONSIDER NOT OLD HATES • • • • • • 335 MEROPE 173
    THIS IS NOT WHAT MAN HATES • • • • • • • 422 EMPEDOCLES I 2 302

HATING
    IN THIS HIS PRESENT FIERCE MAN-HATING MOOD • • • 409 EMPEDOCLES I 1 106

HATRED
    OR HATRED TO THEIR PRESENT IN THIS LAST • • • 331 MEROPE 40
    SHALL THEY NOT WEAR ONE HATRED OUT AS WELL • • • 335 MEROPE 181
    FOR PRIVATE GAIN OR HATRED TAKES A LIFE • • • 336 MEROPE 202
    MARCHD WITH THEM HATRED AND STRIFE • • • • • 343 MEROPE 418
    HATRED AND PASSIONATE ENVY BLIND THINE EYES • • 397 MEROPE 1772
    THE ILL-BODING NOTE WHICH FRANTIC HATRED SOUNDS • 397 MEROPE 1781
    POSSESSD IN HATRED LOST IN BLOOD • • • • • 399 MEROPE 1849

HATS
    STRAW HATS BEDECKD THEIR HEADS WITH RIBBONS BLUE • 25 DREAM 24
    OF STAGSHORN FOR THEIR HATS ANON WITH SCREAMS • 150 TRISTRAM 3 26
    UNDER THE FEATHERD HATS OF THE SWEET PAIR • • • 150 TRISTRAM 3 33

HAUGHTILY
    HAUGHTILY ANOTHER WAY • • • • • • • • • 433 EMPEDOCLES II 160

HAUGHTY
    FOR HAUGHTY SPIRITS AND HIGH WRATHS ARE RIFE • 115 BALDER DEAD 3 79
    THOU ART COME AT LAST THEN HAUGHTY QUEEN • • • 142 TRISTRAM 2 2
    WITH HAUGHTY SCORN WHICH MOCKD THE SMART • • • 303 GRANDE CHARTR 134

HAUNT
    FAR FROM TOWN OR HAUNT OF MAN • • • • • • • 14 CHURCH BROU 1 62
    THERE ARE THE JOYLESS SEATS THE HAUNT OF GHOSTS • 108 BALDER DEAD 2 132
    TO HAUNT THE PLACE WHERE PASSIONS REIGN • • • • 181 ISOLATION MARG 17
    WHERE BLACK-WINGD SWALLOWS HAUNT THE GLITTERING THAMES 257 SCHOLAR-GIPSY 94
    IN THE OLD HAUNT AND FIND OUR TREE-TOPPD HILL • 265 THYRSIS 103
    AND STILL THE HAUNT BELOVED A VIRTUE YIELDS • 269 THYRSIS 220
    LEFT HUMAN HAUNT AND ON ALONE TILL NIGHT • • • 269 THYRSIS 230
    HAD NOT ELECTRA TO HAUNT • • • • • • • • 346 MEROPE 507
    OF BEASTS OF CHASE THAT HAUNT THE ARCADIAN HILLS • 356 MEROPE 757
    OR ELSE NOT LIVE AT ALL BUT HERE I HAUNT • • • 366 MEROPE 1020
    COME YE SWIFT FURIES WHO TO HIM YE HAUNT • • • 367 MEROPE 1056
    AND WE WERE NOT SO FAR FROM HUMAN HAUNT • • • 412 EMPEDOCLES I 2 10
    AND HAUNT HIM TILL THE ABSENCE FROM HIMSELF • 435 EMPEDOCLES II 225
    ALL SHAPES THAT HAUNT REMEMBRANCE SOFT AND FAIR • 474 CROMWELL 83

HAUNTED
    SHE TOLD THEM OF THE FAIRY-HAUNTED LAND • • • 154 TRISTRAM 3 153
    SAY HAS SOME WET BIRD-HAUNTED ENGLISH LAWN • • • 175 PARTING 19
    THE VILLAGE STREET ITS HAUNTED MANSION LACKS • 262 THYRSIS 3
    UNHALLOWED FEET ARE TRAMPLING ON THIS HAUNTED GROUND 467 ALARIC AT ROME 144

HAUNTING
    HAVE KNOWN THEE HAUNTING ALL AN APRIL-DAY • • • 258 SCHOLAR-GIPSY V 107
    HAUNTING THE SHROUDED CHAMBERS OF HIS HEART • • 473 CROMWELL 58

HAUNTS
    OF YOUR ILLUMINED HAUNTS BY NIGHT • • • • • 141 TRISTRAM 1 354
    HAUNTS HIM THAT HE HAS NOT MADE WHAT HE SHOULD • • 239 REVOLUTIONS 10
    OUR GIPSY-SCHOLAR HAUNTS OUTLIVING THEE • • • 268 THYRSIS 197
    TO VILLAGES AND HAUNTS OF MAN • • • • • • • 278 SOUTHERN NIGHT V 82
    DID MAKE FROM HAUNTS OF STRIFE • • • • • • • 322 OBERMANN MORE 274
    ARE HAUNTS MEET FOR THEE • • • • • • • • 441 EMPEDOCLES II 422
    SOMETHING HAUNTS MY CONSCIENCE BRINGS • • • 455 POOR MATTHIAS 85
    LIKE SOME FORGOTTEN STRAIN THAT HAUNTS US STILL • 477 CROMWELL 195

HAUNTST
    AND WONDER IF THOU HAUNTST THEIR SHY RETREATS • • 257 SCHOLAR-GIPSY 70

HAVEN
    AND PAST THE HAVEN WHERE THE GODS HAVE MOORD • • 97 BALDER DEAD 1 74
    AND MIMIC BOATS THEIR HAVEN NEARD • • • • • 223 EPILOG LAOCOON 69
    UNTO ITS HAVEN COMING NIGH • • • • • • • 276 SOUTHERN NIGHT 46
    HAVEN THE MURDERER HAD DROPPD • • • • • • • 371 MEROPE 1128

HAVING
    HAVING MADE UP HIS TALE OF PRECIOUS PEARLS • • • 69 SOHRAB RUSTUM 288
    UNSEEN AND HAVING DRINK TO SPARE • • • • • 90 SICK KING BOKH 71
    DOWN HAVING FEVER FOR A DRINK • • • • • 90 SICK KING BOKH 76
    RATHER IT FITS YOU HAVING WEPT YOUR HOUR • • • 96 BALDER DEAD 1 34
    SO HAVING SPOKE THE KING OF GODS AROSE • • • 96 BALDER DEAD 1 V 46
    CROWND HAVING HONOUR AMONG ALL THE DEAD • • • 112 BALDER DEAD 2 278
    LO HOME HAVING PERFORMD YOUR WILL I COME • • • 114 BALDER DEAD 3 37
    NOT HAVING IT WHICH WHEN THEY DO POSSESS • • • 153 TRISTRAM 3 138
    UNFREED HAVING SEEN NOTHING STILL UNBLEST • • • 243 SUMMER NIGHT 50
    TILL HAVING USED OUR NERVES WITH BLISS AND TEEN • 259 SCHOLAR-GIPSY 147
    SOON HAVING ONCE BEHELD HIM TO DESCEND • • • 350 MEROPE 592
    OR HAVING LEARNT THEM WELL APPLY • • • • • 354 MEROPE 699
    NAMED AEPYTUS LIKE HIM HAVING GONE IN • • • 357 MEROPE 777
    FOR INSTANT COMMENT HAVING MANY SIDES • • • 359 MEROPE 860
    HAVING LEARNT THIS THEN USE THY KNOWLEDGE NOW • • 388 MEROPE 1520
    THIS HAVING KNOWN LET US A UNION FOUND • • • 394 MEROPE 1716
    AND THANK THY BITTEREST FOE THAT HAVING LOST • • 396 MEROPE 1756
    THIS HAVING LEARND LET US A UNION FOUND • • • 394 MEROPE V1716
    AND HE DIES FRUITLESS HAVING FOUND NO FIELD • • LUCRETIUS 2 6
    HAVING BEEN FURTHERD TO HIS VERY WISH • • • LUCRETIUS 2 11
    AND WHEREFORE THEN HAVING NO CLAIM TO MORE • • • LUCRETIUS 3 8

HAVIOUR
    HER HAVIOUR HAD THE MORNINGS FRESH CLEAR GRACE • • 154 TRISTRAM 3 179

HAVOC
    HAVOC IS MADE IN OUR TRAIN • • • • • • • 289 RUGBY CHAPEL 101

HAWK
    AS ON SOME PARTRIDGE IN THE CORN A HAWK • • • 73 SOHRAB RUSTUM 400

HAY
    WHOSE MANGER IS STUFFD FULL OF GOOD FRESH HAY • • 123 BALDER DEAD 3 341
    AND ABOVE GODSTOW BRIDGE WHEN HAY-TIMES HERE • • 257 SCHOLAR-GIPSY 91
    AND SCENT OF HAY NEW-MOWN • • • • • • • 265 THYRSIS 76
    FIELDS WHERE SOFT SHEEP FROM CAGES PULL THE HAY • • 268 THYRSIS 198
    FIELDS WHERE THE SHEEP FROM CAGES PULL THE HAY • • 268 THYRSIS V 198

HAYMAKER
    THE LAST-LEFT HAYMAKER IS GONE • • • • • • • 218 BACCHANALIA 1 9

HAZE
    BUT THE VALLEYS ARE FLOODED WITH HAZE • • • • 228 YOUTH OF NATURE 7
    THE BLUE HAZE-CRADLED MOUNTAINS SPREAD AWAY • • • 242 SUMMER NIGHT 21
    OF MALATRAIT TO WHERE IN HAZE • • • • • • 324 OBERMANN MORE 339
    THROUGH POURING TIDE HE PULLS AND DRIZZLING HAZE • • 445 WESTMIN ABBEY 29

HAZELS
    OF HAZELS GREEN IN WHOSE DEPTH • • • • • • • 297 HEINES GRAVE 182

HEAD
    AND THOU WHOSE HEAD DID STARS AND SUNBEAMS KNOW • • 3 SHAKESPEARE V 9
    HERE LEAN MY HEAD ON THIS COLD BALUSTRADE • • • 19 MODERN SAPPHO 4
    HERE LEAN MY HEAD ON THIS COOL BALUSTRADE • • • 19 MODERN SAPPHO V 4
    RARER SECRETS THAN THE TOILING HEAD • • • • • 28 NEW SIRENS 80
    THE HANDS PROPPING THE SUNK HEAD • • • • • • 30 NEW SIRENS 128
    O SEEMING SOLE TO AWAKE THY SUN-BATHED HEAD • • 45 IN UTRUMQUE PAR 29
    THAT THY POOR HEAD ALMOST TURNS • • • • • • 49 SECOND BEST 8
    SHAKES HER HEAD FROWNING • • • • • • • • • 51 CONSOLATION 52
    HERE WHERE THE BROOK SHINES NEAR ITS HEAD • • • 55 RESIGNATION 90
    THE WET FLOWERD GRASS HEAVES UP ITS HEAD • • • 57 RESIGNATION 185
    AND ON HIS HEAD HE SET HIS SHEEP-SKIN CAP • • • 64 SOHRAB RUSTUM 100
    AGAINST THE ROBBERS AND HE SAW THAT HEAD • • • 71 SOHRAB RUSTUM 339
    O BY THY FATHERS HEAD BY THINE OWN SOUL • • • 71 SOHRAB RUSTUM 343
    AND RUSTUM BOWD HIS HEAD BUT THEN THE GLOOM • • 76 SOHRAB RUSTUM 499
    HIS HEAD BUT THIS TIME ALL THE BLADE LIKE GLASS • • 76 SOHRAB RUSTUM 511
    THEN RUSTUM RAISED HIS HEAD HIS DREADFUL EYES • • 76 SOHRAB RUSTUM 514
    AND HIS HEAD SWAM AND HE SANK DOWN TO EARTH • • 81 SOHRAB RUSTUM 693
    AND THREW IT ON HIS HEAD AND SMIRCHD HIS HAIR • • 81 SOHRAB RUSTUM 701
    MY HEAD BETWIXT THY HANDS AND KISS MY CHEEKS • • 82 SOHRAB RUSTUM 719
    WITH HIS HEAD BOWING TO THE GROUND AND MANE • • 82 SOHRAB RUSTUM 731
    HIS HEAD AS IF INQUIRING WHAT THEIR GRIEF • • • 82 SOHRAB RUSTUM 734
    ROLL TUMBLING IN THE CURRENT OER MY HEAD • • • • 83 SOHRAB RUSTUM 770
    INDOORS FROM THE SUNS EYE HIS HEAD DROOPD LOW • • 86 SOHRAB RUSTUM 847
    AND ON HIS HEAD HE PLACD HIS SHEEP-SKIN CAP • • 64 SOHRAB RUSTUM V 100
    AND HIS HEAD SWAM AND HE SUNK DOWN TO EARTH • • 81 SOHRAB RUSTUM V 693
    FROM THE HOT FIELDS AT NOON HIS HEAD DROOPD LOW • • 86 SOHRAB RUSTUM V 847
    FROM THE HOT FIELD AT NOON HIS HEAD DROOPD LOW • • 86 SOHRAB RUSTUM V 847
    MAKES THE HEAD WHITE AND BOWS THE KNEES • • • • 92 SICK KING BOKH 152
    MY HEAD IS BURNING AND A HEAT • • • • • • • 93 SICK KING BOKH 183
    AND BOWD HER HEAD AND SATE WITH FOLDED HANDS • • 100 BALDER DEAD 1 193
    AND AT HIS HEAD AND FEET SHE STATIOND SCALDS • • 102 BALDER DEAD 1 271
    ALIVE AND STILL THE RAYS WERE ROUND HIS HEAD • • 103 BALDER DEAD 1 284

HEAD   (CONTINUED)
          DEATH FROM THY HEAD AND WITH THE GODS IN HEAVEN   • • 104 BALDER DEAD 1   311
          MOURNFULLY SHOOK HIS HEAD AND DISAPPEARD   • • • • 104 BALDER DEAD 1   334
          AXES AND ROPES AND AT THEIR HEAD CAME THOR   • • • 106 BALDER DEAD 2   48
          SHE IN HER HANDS TOOK BALDERS HEAD AND SPAKE   • • 116 BALDER DEAD 3   98
          AND BOWD HER HEAD AND SATE WITH FOLDED HANDS   • • 122 BALDER DEAD 3   296
          SNUFFS AT IT DAINTILY AND STOOPS HER HEAD   • • • 123 BALDER DEAD 3   342
          FLOCKS OF HIS KIND PASS FLYING OER HIS HEAD   • • 129 BALDER DEAD 3   561
          THOUGH THE LOCKS ARE YET BROWN ON HIS NOBLE HEAD   • 130 TRISTRAM 1   10
          HEAVEN HIS HEAD SINKS BACK UPON THE PILLOW   • • 145 TRISTRAM 2   77
          STILL HOLD HER LOVERS HAND HER HEAD   • • • • 146 TRISTRAM 2   105
          STILL HOLD HER LOVERS HANDS HER HEAD   • • • • 146 TRISTRAM 2   V 105
          STILL HOLDS HER LOVERS HANDS HER HEAD   • • • • 146 TRISTRAM 2   V 105
          LIFTING HER SOFT-BENT HEAD ONLY TO MIND   • • • 152 TRISTRAM 3   84
          AND FROM HER BROWN-LOCKD HEAD THE WIMPLE THROWS   • 156 TRISTRAM 3   216
          HE BOWD HIS HEAD HE BREATHED A PRAYER   • • • • 158 SAINT BRANDAN   74
          HER HEAD MID IGNOMINY DEATH AND TOMBS   • • • • 172 GOOD SHEPHERD   12
          HER HEAD IN IGNOMINY DEATH AND TOMBS   • • • • 172 GOOD SHEPHERD   V 12
          UP AT THE VALLEY-HEAD   • • • • • • • • • 186 STRAYED REVEL   27
          HIS OLD SIGHTLESS HEAD   • • • • • • • • • 190 STRAYED REVEL   140
          NONE SPEAKS NONE HEEDS AH TURN THY HEAD   • • • 206 RIVER   4
          AND ON THY SHOULDER REST MY HEAD   • • • • • 206 RIVER   12
          HANGS DOWN HIS BEAUTIFUL HEAD   • • • • • • 214 NEW ROME   2
          HANGS DOWN HIS HEAD AS BEFORE   • • • • • • 214 NEW ROME   18
          THE MOUNTAINS STAND AT ITS HEAD   • • • • • 228 YOUTH OF NATURE   5
          WELL MAY WE MOURN WHEN THE HEAD   • • • • • 229 YOUTH OF NATURE   48
          WHILE THE LOCKS ARE YET BROWN ON THY HEAD   • • 235 YOUTH OF MAN   112
          A WORLD ABOVE MANS HEAD TO LET HIM SEE   • • • 244 SUMMER NIGHT   87
          AND AT ITS HEAD TO STAY THE EYE   • • • • • 248 KENSINGTON GARD V 3
          TO SHAKE HIS SAPIENT HEAD AND GIVE   • • • • 250 WISH   19
          NOR THE CROPPD HERBAGE SHOOT ANOTHER HEAD   • • 255 SCHOLAR-GIPSY   5
          AND HOW THE BREAST WAS SOOTHED AND HOW THE HEAD   • 260 SCHOLAR-GIPSY   189
          NOR THE CROPPD GRASSES SHOOT ANOTHER HEAD   • • 255 SCHOLAR-GIPSY   V 5
          HE KNEW WHICH MADE HIM DROOP AND FILLD HIS HEAD   • 264 THYRSIS   47
          AND MADE LEAP UP WITH JOY THE BEAUTEOUS HEAD   • 265 THYRSIS   87
          WE BOWD OUR HEAD AND HELD OUR BREATH   • • • • 270 MEMORIAL VERSES   7
          SUNK THEN IS EUROPES SAGEST HEAD   • • • • • 270 MEMORIAL VERSES   16
          SHAKING HER HEAD TOOK THE HARP   • • • • • • 285 HAWORTH CHURCH   126
          HANGING NOW OER A HEAD   • • • • • • • • 281 HAWORTH CHURCH   V
          WITH VEILD FACE AND BOWD HEAD   • • • • • • 283 HAWORTH CHURCH   V
          WITH NOWHERE YET TO REST MY HEAD   • • • • • 302 GRANDE CHARTR   87
          WHICH TELLS US HOW THOU HIDDST THY HEAD   • • • 304 GRANDE CHARTR   147
          THY HEAD IS CLEAR THY FEELING CHILL   • • • • 309 OBERMANN   87
          ITS HEAD WAS CLEAR AND TRUE   • • • • • • 315 OBERMANN MORE   86
          AND ON HER HEAD WAS HURLD   • • • • • • • 316 OBERMANN MORE   108
          UPON HIS CROSS WITH HEAD SUNK LOW   • • • • • 317 OBERMANN MORE   155
          AND PASTORAL HUTS I HID MY HEAD   • • • • • 321 OBERMANN MORE   251
          THAT WAN NAILD FORM WITH HEAD DROOPD LOW   • • 317 OBERMANN MORE   V 155
          SOLE OFFERING THAT THOU HAST LOCKS FROM THY HEAD   • 332 MEROPE   71
          IN CALLING VENGEANCE ON A MURDERERS HEAD   • • 348 MEROPE   549
          THY HEAD DROOPD SOFTLY AND THE GOLDEN CURLS   • 373 MEROPE   1161
          BEAR WITNESS SEE MARK WELL ON WHAT A HEAD   • • 377 MEROPE   1223
          THAT DEAR-BELOVED THAT YOUNG THAT GRACIOUS HEAD   • 382 MEROPE   1327
          HEAR THAT FRESH VOICE AND CLASP THAT GOLD-LOCKD HEAD 387 MEROPE   1460
          THOU ART BEWILDERD THE SANE HEAD IS MINE   • • 396 MEROPE   1759
          SWAYING FROM SIDE TO SIDE HIS MASSY HEAD   • • 401 MEROPE   1911
          HE BOWD HIS HEAD AND DEEPLY GROAND AND DIED   • 402 MEROPE   1929
          WITH THY HEAD FULL OF WINE AND THY HAIR CROWND   • 407 EMPEDOCLES I 1   32
          TO THE SUBTLE CONTRIVING HEAD   • • • • • • 431 EMPEDOCLES II   91
          WITH ONE ARM OVER HIS HEAD   • • • • • • • 434 EMPEDOCLES II   163
          MANTLED HER FORM NO MORE HER HEAD WAS BOWD   • • 447 WESTMIN ABBEY   98
          BUT NOW HIS HEAD TO DEATH AGAIN IS DUE   • • • 447 WESTMIN ABBEY   106
          THAT PAIR WHOSE HEAD DID PLAN WHOSE HANDS DID FORGE   448 WESTMIN ABBEY   134
          THOUGH SUNK BE NOW THIS BRIGHT THIS GRACIOUS HEAD   449 WESTMIN ABBEY   176
          THOUGH SUNK IS NOW THIS BRIGHT THIS GRACIOUS HEAD   449 WESTMIN ABBEY   V 176
          ROVER WITH THE GOOD BROWN HEAD   • • • • • • 453 POOR MATTHIAS   25
          POOR MAX WITH DOWNCAST REVERENT HEAD   • • • • 460 KAISER DEAD   67
          IN FIRES UNDYING OER THE GUILTY HEAD   • • • • 463 ALARIC AT ROME   28
          THE VANISHT MIGHT OF THAT DISCROWNED HEAD   • • 464 ALARIC AT ROME   46
          PERCHANCE SOME MUTE MEMORIAL AT THEIR HEAD   • 464 ALARIC AT ROME   58
          HIDE HIS TORN HEAD BENEATH HIS SUNLESS CAVE   • 472 CROMWELL   24
          HIS DROOPING HEAD BOWED MEEKLY ON HIS BREAST   • 476 CROMWELL   167
          FOLLOWING THE SUN WE SET OUR VESSELS HEAD   • • 484 S S LUSITANIA   3
          AND HE SHOOK HIS HEAD AND THUS ADDRESSD HIS OWN BOSOM   HOMER TRANS   8
          SUDDEN HE BOWD HIS HEAD AND ALL HIS MANE AS HE BOWD IT   HOMER TRANS   44

HEADED
          WITH THE SNOW-HEADED ZAL AND ALL MY FRIENDS   • •   84 SOHRAB RUSTUM   801
          HOAR-HEADED WRINKLED CLAD IN WHITE   • • • • • 278 SOUTHERN NIGHT   86
          GREY-HEADED WRINKLED CLAD IN WHITE   • • • • • 278 SOUTHERN NIGHT   V 86

HEADLAND
          A HEADLAND WITH ONE AGED PLANE-TREE CROWND   • • • 358 MEROPE   817
          ON SOME BARE HEADLAND STRAINING MOURNFULLY   • • • 477 CROMWELL   190

HEADLANDS
          BLACK UNDER CLIFFS IT RACED ROUND HEADLANDS SHONE   25 DREAM   34
          AND TOWARDS EVENING SEE THE HEADLANDS RISE   • • • 123 BALDER DEAD 3   359
          IN SUMMER ON THE HEADLANDS   • • • • • • • 159 NECKAN   1
          GREEN ROLLS BENEATH THE HEADLANDS   • • • • • 159 NECKAN   5

HEADLANDS   (CONTINUED)
        HE SITS UPON THE HEADLANDS . . . . 159 NECKAN   13
        IN SUMMER ON THE HEADLANDS . . . . 161 NECKAN   65
        HEADLANDS STOOD OUT INTO THE MOONLIT DEEP . . . . 242 SUMMER NIGHT   14
        BUT ROUND THE HEADLANDS POINT A CURRENT SETS . . 358 MEROPE   820
        STOUTLY UNDER THE HEADLANDS LEE THEY SWAM . . . . 358 MEROPE   822

HEADLONG
        LAID PAUSEFULLY UPON LIFES HEADLONG TRAIN . . . . 266 THYRSIS   137
        AND HEADLONG FATE BE HAPPINESS . . . . 271 MEMORIAL VERSES 33
        THE IGNORANT HEADLONG MULTITUDE . . . . . . 353 MEROPE   673
        UPON ITS HEADLONG COURSE WITH SAD PROPHETIC EYE . . 463 ALARIC AT ROME 24

HEADS
        AND FROM YOUR BROIDERD PILLOWS LIFT YOUR HEADS . . 18 CHURCH BROU 3   26
        DOTH RUSTLINGLY ABOVE YOUR HEADS COMPLAIN . . . . 18 CHURCH BROU 3   33
        STRAW HATS BEDECKD THEIR HEADS WITH RIBBONS BLUE . . 25 DREAM   24
        AND YOUR PROUD HEADS BACKWARD THROWN . . . . . . 32 NEW SIRENS   192
        BY WELL-HEADS IN SUMMER DAYS . . . . 34 NEW SIRENS   240
        OVER THE FIGHTERS HEADS AND A WIND ROSE . . . . 75 SOHRAB RUSTUM   483
        AND ON TWO ANGEL-HEADS DOTH PLAY . . . . . . 141 TRISTRAM 1   337
        HUNG SOFT IN THEIR HEADS . . . . 176 PARTING   54
        WITH STREAMING FLANKS AND HEADS . . . . . . 190 STRAYED REVEL   148
        TOO HASTY HEADS FOR ORDERING WORLDS ALAS . . . . 237 PROGRESS   9
        WITH HEADS BENT OER THEIR TOIL THEY LANGUIDLY . . 243 SUMMER NIGHT   39
        ITS HEADS OERTAXD ITS PALSIED HEARTS WAS RIFE . . 261 SCHOLAR-GIPSY   205
        WE BOWD OUR HEADS AND HELD OUR BREATH . . . . 270 MEMORIAL VERSES V 7
        WARMING THEIR HEADS IN THE SUN . . . . . . 297 HEINES GRAVE   157
        ON THE FAIR CURLD HEADS OF MY SONS . . . . . . 346 MEROPE   504

HEADSTRONG
        BUT THOU TOO-BOLD HEADSTRONG PITILESS . . . . 196 FRAG ANTIGONE   50

HEADY
        OF PRAISE HOT HEADY FUMES TO THE POOR BRAIN . . 296 HEINES GRAVE   146
        OF HEADY MASTERFUL INJURIOUS MEN . . . . . . 339 MEROPE   312

HEAL
        SAY WILL IT NEVER HEAL . . . . 200 PHILOMELA   9
        AND WHAT CAN HELPERS HEAL . . . . 320 OBERMANN MORE   234

HEALD
        AND GRIEF THAT HEALD AT EVERY SMILE OF EARTH . . 41 GIPSY CHILD   V 20

HEALING
        FROM TEARS THAT BRING NO HEALING . . . . . 39 STAGIRIUS   35
        POSTURES OF RUNES AND HEALING HERBS HE KNEW . . 101 BALDER DEAD 1   211
        SO HEALING IS HER QUIET NOW . . . . 147 TRISTRAM 2   143
        I JOURNEY TO THESE HEALING SNOWS . . . . . 158 SAINT BRANDAN   68
        AGAIN FIND WORDSWORTHS HEALING POWER . . . . 272 MEMORIAL VERSES   63
        AND HEALING SIGHTS TO SEE . . . . 309 OBERMANN   112

HEALTH
        AH AN HOUR OF HEALTH WOULD PURGE HIS EYESIGHT . . 144 TRISTRAM 2   67
        AND WISHD HIM HEALTH SUCCESS AND FAME . . . . 272 EDW QUILLINAN   3
        HEALTH EASE A HEART ELATE . . . . 273 EDW QUILLINAN   12
        THAT MY SON STILL SURVIVES IN HEALTH IN BLOOM . . 351 MEROPE   612
        WE WOULD HAVE HEALTH AND YET . . . . 420 EMPEDOCLES I 2   229
        HEALTH SAPPD BY LIVING ILL . . . . 425 EMPEDOCLES I 2   393
        SUITED WELL TO HEALTH BUT HOW . . . . 455 POOR MATTHIAS   113

HEAP
        A HEAP OF FLUTTERING FEATHERS NEVER MORE . . . . 78 SOHRAB RUSTUM   569
        AND HEAP A STATELY MOUND ABOVE MY BONES . . . . 84 SOHRAB RUSTUM   788
        AND HEAP A STATELY MOUND ABOVE THY BONES . . . . 84 SOHRAB RUSTUM   803
        BEGAN AGAIN TO HEAP THE SACRED FIRE . . . . 100 BALDER DEAD 1   196
        HEAP ON THE DECK THE LOGS AND BUILD THE PYRE . . 118 BALDER DEAD 3   159
        HEAP UP HIS MOMENTS WITH LIFE . . . . 200 EARLY DEATH   18
        GOD PUT A HEAP OF LETTERS IN HIS HAND . . . . 239 REVOLUTIONS   3
        WE DIG AND HEAP LAY STONE ON STONE . . . . . 241 MORALITY   8
        AND FOSTERING IN THY LAP A HEAP OF FLOWERS . . . 257 SCHOLAR-GIPSY   78

HEAPD
        AND CAME HEAPD WITH MYRTLES TO YOUR THRONE . . . . 27 NEW SIRENS   32
        WHO LOITERS BY THE HIGH-HEAPD BOOTHS . . . . . . 93 SICK KING BOKH   191
        OF THE HEAPD WOOD AND BURN HIS CORPSE WITH FIRE . . 115 BALDER DEAD 3 54

HEAPS
        FLING THE FRESH HEAPS ABOUT . . . . 218 BACCHANALIA 1   34
        THE CRACKLING HUSK-HEAPS BURN AS IF . . . . . 312 OBERMANN MORE   11
        SWEET HEAPS OF FRESH-CUT GRASS . . . . 313 OBERMANN MORE   18
        THEIR CRACKLING HUSK-HEAPS BURN AS IF . . . . 312 OBERMANN MORE   V 11

HEAR
        THAT THOU CANST HEAR AND HEARING HOLD THY WAY . .   3 EMERSONS ESSAYS 2
        AND THEN YOU HEAR THE ORGANS HUM . . . . . . 17 CHURCH BROU 2   28
        YOU HEAR THE WHITE-ROBED PRIEST SAY MASS . . . . 17 CHURCH BROU 2   29
        THE PASSAGE OF THE ANGELS WINGS WILL HEAR . . . . 19 CHURCH BROU 3   44
        SOME LARGE ANSWER YOU SHALL HEAR . . . . . . 29 NEW SIRENS   92
        BUT I HEAR THE NORTH WIND BLOWING . . . . . . 32 NEW SIRENS   189

HEAR   (CONTINUED)
```
OR DO I WAIT TO HEAR SOME GRAY-HAIRD KING  . . . .  .   43 GIPSY CHILD          33
THEY WINNING ROOM TO SEE AND HEAR  . . . . . .  .   59 RESIGNATION         249
COME THEN HEAR NOW AND GRANT ME WHAT I ASK  . . . .   62 SOHRAB RUSTUM        54
RUSTUM WILL SURELY HEAR IT IF I FALL  . . . . . .   62 SOHRAB RUSTUM        58
FEROOD AND YE PERSIANS AND TARTARS HEAR  . . . .  .   65 SOHRAB RUSTUM       150
AND REST MY AGE AND HEAR OF SOHRABS FAME  . . . .  .   68 SOHRAB RUSTUM       239
FIGHT LET ME HEAR THY HATEFUL VOICE NO MORE  . . .   75 SOHRAB RUSTUM       459
BUT HEAR THOU THIS FIERCE MAN TREMBLE TO HEAR  . .   77 SOHRAB RUSTUM       552
BUT HEAR THOU THIS FIERCE MAN TREMBLE TO HEAR  . .   77 SOHRAB RUSTUM       552
HOW CANST THOU ERE THOU HEAR DISCERN  . . . . . .   89 SICK KING BOKH       54
WHEREFORE HEAR THOU THOU KNOWST HOW FIERCE  . . .   89 SICK KING BOKH       58
BRAKE FORTH AND CURSED THEM DOST THOU HEAR  . . .   90 SICK KING BOKH       87
I HEAR THE BEARERS ON THE STAIR  . . . . . .  .   92 SICK KING BOKH      130
BUT HEAR YE THIS YE SONS OF MEN  . . . . . .  .   93 SICK KING BOKH      185
ALL YE WHO HEAR ME AND INHABIT HEAVEN  . . . .  .   96 BALDER DEAD 1        29
AND HEAR THE ROARING OF THE STREAMS OF HELL  . .  100 BALDER DEAD 1       173
HEAR HOW TO HEAVEN MAY BALDER BE RESTORED  . . .  111 BALDER DEAD 2       233
PEACE LEST OUR FATHER ODIN HEAR THEE GIBE  . . .  114 BALDER DEAD 3        23
AND WRING HIS HEART WITH SHAME TO HEAR THY WORD  .  116 BALDER DEAD 3       105
AND ALL THESE GLADLY WHILE WE DRINK WE HEAR  . .  117 BALDER DEAD 3       135
AND THERE FELL JOY UPON THE GODS TO HEAR  . . .  .  122 BALDER DEAD 3       319
AND HEAR THE PASSAGE OF A HORSE OF HEAVEN  . . .  .  125 BALDER DEAD 3       419
WHAT I HEAR THESE BITTER WORDS FROM THEE  . . .  142 TRISTRAM 2           14
CAN FORGET ALL TO HEAR THEM AS OF OLD  . . . .  152 TRISTRAM 3          111
DEAR SAINTS IT IS NOT SORROW AS I HEAR  . . . .  152 TRISTRAM 3          112
SHE WILL HEAR THE WINDS HOWLING  . . . . .  .  164 FORSAKEN MERM       114
WILL HEAR THE WAVES ROAR  . . . . . . . . .  164 FORSAKEN MERM       115
I HEAR A GODS TREMENDOUS VOICE  . . . . .  .  174 MEETING              11
BUT ON THE STAIRS WHAT VOICE IS THIS I HEAR  . .  175 PARTING              17
BUT STRANGELY MISINTERPRET ALL YOU HEAR  . . .  .  198 FRAG DEJANEIRA       14
LISTEN YOU HEAR THE GRATING ROAR  . . . . . .  211 DOVER BEACH           9
BUT NOW I ONLY HEAR  . . . . . . . . .  211 DOVER BEACH          24
BUT NOW WE ONLY HEAR  . . . . . . . . .  211 DOVER BEACH      V   24
TO HEAR THE WORLD APPLAUD THE HOLLOW GHOST  . .  213 GROWING OLD          34
THE MURMUR OF ITS WAVES DOTH HEAR  . . . . .  226 EPILOG LAOCOON      180
THEY STAND AND LISTEN THEY HEAR  . . . . .  .  234 YOUTH OF MAN         71
A CRY LIKE THINE IN MINE OWN HEART I HEAR  . .  .  240 SELF-DEPENDENCE      30
A CRY LIKE THINE IN MY OWN HEART I HEAR  . . .  240 SELF-DEPENDENCE  V   30
THINK OFTEN AS I HEAR THEM RAVE  . . . . .  .  249 KENSINGTON GARD      26
THINK SOMETIMES AS I HEAR THEM RAVE  . . . .  249 KENSINGTON GARD  V   26
THINK SADLY AS I HEAR THEM RAVE  . . . . .  .      KENSINGTON GARD  V   26
ARE CONFUSED AS THE CRIES WHICH WE HEAR  . . .  .  253 FUTURE               56
HEAR IT FROM THY BROAD LUCENT ARNO-VALE  . . .  267 THYRSIS             167
HEAR IT O THYRSIS STILL OUR TREE IS THERE  . .  267 THYRSIS             171
HEAR WITH DELIGHT OF THY FAME  . . . . . .  .  284 HAWORTH CHURCH       87
THE SHINING MOORLAND TO HEAR  . . . . . . .  285 HAWORTH CHURCH      119
I HEAR THE TORRENTS ROAR  . . . . . . .  .  306 OBERMANN             10
THOUGH AS YOU READ YOU HEAR THE BELLS  . . .  307 OBERMANN             31
I HEAR THEE SAYING NOW  . . . . . . . .  .  309 OBERMANN             90
AND HEAR THE WILD BEES ALPINE HUM  . . . .  .  313 OBERMANN MORE        47
HEAR ME THEN SPEAK AND LET THIS MOURNFUL DAY  .  333 MEROPE              114
THOU HAST FORGOT THEN WHO I AM WHO HEAR  . . .  335 MEROPE              182
TRULY I HEAR OF A MAID  . . . . . . . .  .  343 MEROPE              425
HEAR US AND HELP US SHADE OF OUR KING  . . .  .  348 MEROPE              541
TO HEAR ANOTHER TUMULT IN THESE STREETS  . . .  349 MEROPE              561
MY WORDS BELOW TO THEE AND MAKE THEE HEAR  . .  .  350 MEROPE              586
I AUGUR THOU WILT HEAR SOME BOLD RESOLVE  . . .  351 MEROPE              610
I DARE NOT WISH IT BUT AT LEAST TO HEAR  . . .  .  351 MEROPE              611
TO HEAR THAT STILL HE LOVES STILL LONGS FOR ME  .  351 MEROPE              613
SAVE FOR THIS ANNUAL CHARGE I HOPE TO HEAR  . .  .  351 MEROPE              619
HEAR THAT FRESH VOICE AND CLASP THAT GOLD-LOCKD HEAD  387 MEROPE             1460
ENOUGH ENOUGH I WILL NO LONGER HEAR  . . . .  .  397 MEROPE             1780
THE MULES MUST BE BELOW FAR DOWN I HEAR  . . .  407 EMPEDOCLES I 1       27
I HEAR GORGIAS THEIR CHIEF SPEAKS NOBLY OF HIM  .  411 EMPEDOCLES I 1      147
AND SAY YE HELPERS HEAR EMPEDOCLES  . . . .  .  429 EMPEDOCLES II        27
AND SAY YE SERVANTS HEAR EMPEDOCLES  . . . .  429 EMPEDOCLES II    V   27
WHICH JOYD MY VOICE TO HEAR  . . . . . .  .  449 WESTMIN ABBEY       162
WE HEAR THY SCUFFLE ON THE STAIR  . . . . .  .  451 GEISTS GRAVE         48
SATST UPON THY PERCH TO HEAR  . . . . . .  .  455 POOR MATTHIAS       120
WHERE ALL WE SEE OR DO OR HEAR OR SAY  . . .  .  464 ALARIC AT ROME       47
TO HEAR A DIM AND LONG FORGOTTEN TONE  . . .  467 ALARIC AT ROME      123
OR HEAR MID CIRCLING CRAGS THE IMPATIENT CRY  .  472 CROMWELL             25
YET ALL HIGH SOUNDS THAT MOUNTAIN CHILDREN HEAR  . .  472 CROMWELL          27
ERE I HEAR THY CRIES AND THY CAPTIVITY TOLD OF  . .      HOMER TRANS         38
```

HEARD
```
YE MEN OF EGYPT YE HAVE HEARD YOUR KING  . . . .  .   11 MYCERINUS            73
HEARD IN SLUMBER SOUNDS OF WARNING  . . . . .  .   26 NEW SIRENS            7
HEARD THE HOARSE BOUGHS LABOUR IN THE WIND  . . .   26 NEW SIRENS            8
HEARD AT EVENING SOUNDS OF WARNING  . . . . .  .   26 NEW SIRENS       V    7
HE SPAKE THE GREAT KING HEARD  . . . . . .  .   47 WORLD QUIETIST       28
HE SPOKE THE MONARCH HEARD  . . . . . . .  .   47 WORLD QUIETIST   V   28
HE SPOKE THE GREAT KING HEARD  . . . . . .  .   47 WORLD QUIETIST   V   28
AND PERAN-WISA HEARD HIM THOUGH THE STEP  . . .  .   62 SOHRAB RUSTUM        28
SO WHEN THEY HEARD WHAT PERAN-WISA SAID  . . .  .   65 SOHRAB RUSTUM       157
SO HE SPAKE MILDLY SOHRAB HEARD HIS VOICE  . . .  .   71 SOHRAB RUSTUM       334
AND HEARD THEIR HOLLOW ROAR OF DYING MEN  . . .  .   74 SOHRAB RUSTUM       435
THE TWO HOSTS HEARD THAT CRY AND QUAKED FOR FEAR  .   76 SOHRAB RUSTUM       507
BUT SOHRAB HEARD AND QUAILD NOT BUT RUSHD ON  . .   76 SOHRAB RUSTUM       509
```

HEARD   (CONTINUED)

AND SHOUTED RUSTUM SOHRAB HEARD THAT SHOUT • • • •   76 SOHRAB RUSTUM   516
THE LONGD-FOR DASH OF WAVES IS HEARD AND WIDE   • •   87 SOHRAB RUSTUM   889
BUT SOHRAB HEARD AND QUAILD NOT BUT SPRANG ON   • •   76 SOHRAB RUSTUM   V 509
THESE MANY DAYS AND HEARD NO THING • • • • •   88 SICK KING BOKH   23
BEFORE THE PRIESTS THOU SHALT BE HEARD   • • • •   91 SICK KING BOKH   108
AND THE THING HEARD THEY DOUBTED NOT • • • • • •   91 SICK KING BOKH   110
AND HEARD THE THUNDER OF THE STREAMS OF HELL   •   109 BALDER DEAD 2   151
AND HE DREW NEAR AND HEARD NO LIVING VOICE • • • •   113 BALDER DEAD 2   305
HEARD NO ONE EVER AN INJURIOUS WORD • • • • •   116 BALDER DEAD 3   84
BUT I HEARD THORA LAUGH IN GOTHLAND ISLE   • • •   117 BALDER DEAD 3   148
BUT WHEN THE GODS AND HEROES HEARD THEY BROUGHT •   118 BALDER DEAD 3   160
WHEN THE GODS HEARD THEY STRAIGHT AROSE AND TOOK •   122 BALDER DEAD 3   302
AFTER AN HOUR A DRIPPING SOUND IS HEARD • • • •   122 BALDER DEAD 3   310
SO THROUGH THE WORLD WAS HEARD A DRIPPING NOISE •   122 BALDER DEAD 3   317
THE JOYLESS PLAINS AND HEARD THE STREAMS OF HELL •   124 BALDER DEAD 3   380
HE HEARD ACROSS THE HOWLING SEAS   • • • • •   156 SAINT BRANDAN   5
WE HEARD THE SWEET BELLS OVER THE BAY   • • • •   162 FORSAKEN MERM   31
HAVE YET SO MUCH AS HEARD THIS SIMPLER LORE • •   171 DIVINITY   12
EVERYWHERE HEARD WILL BE THE JUDGMENT-CALL   • • •   173 MONICAS PRAYER   3
AND HEARD HIM DELIGHTING • • • • • • • •   189 STRAYED REVEL   121
HEARD IT ON THE AEGEAN AND IT BROUGHT   • • •   211 DOVER BEACH   16
WE HEARD AFAR FAINT MUSIC PLAY • • • • • • •   224 EPILOG LAOCOON   110
AH STILL HARP ON WHAT THEY HEARD   • • • • •   227 PERSIST POETRY   4
THEY ARE HERE I HEARD AS MEN HEARD   • • • • •   230 YOUTH OF NATURE   75
THEY ARE HERE I HEARD AS MEN HEARD   • • • • •   230 YOUTH OF NATURE   75
BE HEARD FLOATING THROUGH HEAVEN AND FILL AGAIN •   238 PROGRESS   35
SO HAVE I HEARD THE CUCKOOS PARTING CRY   • • •   264 THYRSIS   57
BUT AH OF OUR POOR THAMES SHE NEVER HEARD   • •   265 THYRSIS   98
HEARD THE CLEAR SONG OF ORPHEUS COME • • • • •   271 MEMORIAL VERSES   38
IS HEARD TO-NIGHT AROUND THY GRAVE   • • • • •   276 SOUTHERN NIGHT   22
OF ONE TOO I HAVE HEARD   • • • • • • • •   285 HAWORTH CHURCH   101
AND THE PLOVER IS HEARD ON THE MOORS • • • • •   285 HAWORTH CHURCH   116
HEARD ACCENTS OF THE ETERNAL TONGUE   • • • • •   310 OBERMANN   125
THE HARDLY-HEARD-OF GRAVE   • • • • • •   312 OBERMANN   180
THY HARDLY HEARD OF GRAVE   • • • • • •   312 OBERMANN   V 180
SHE HEARD IT THE VICTORIOUS WEST   • • • • •   316 OBERMANN MORE   121
STILL IN MY SOUL THE VOICE I HEARD   • • • • •   324 OBERMANN MORE   333
FIRST HEARD OR IN ITS FUTURE ISSUE SHOWN   • • •   359 MEROPE   865
OF THE HARP BE HEARD WITH THE PIPE   • • • • •   360 MEROPE   895
NO ENEMY AND WHAT HAST THOU THEN HEARD   • • •   363 MEROPE   953
THE YOUTH THOU SAYST WE SAW AND HEARD BUT NOW •   365 MEROPE   985
HIS OFFERS COLDLY HEARD THEM COLD REPELLD   • •   366 MEROPE   1015
I HAVE HEARD O QUEEN HOW A PRINCE   • • • • •   368 MEROPE   1082
MUST FROM SOME MOUTH BE HEARD RELATE IT THOU •   401 MEROPE   1892
TO ARMED WARRIORS I HEARD VENGEFUL CRIES   • • •   402 MEROPE   1940
I HEARD THE CLASH OF WEAPONS THEN I SAW • • •   402 MEROPE   1941
THOU HAST HEARD ALL MEN SPEAKING OF PANTHEIA •   410 EMPEDOCLES I 1   108
LONG SINCE HIS NAME IS HEARD ON EARTH NO MORE •   447 WESTMIN ABBEY   113
HEARD THE MURMUR OF THE MOLE   • • • • • •   458 POOR MATTHIAS   201
HE HEARD OF LATE THE GRAND OLD MAN   • • • • •   460 KAISER DEAD   41

HEARERS
O EASY ACCESS TO THE HEARERS GRACE   • • • • • •   265 THYRSIS   91

HEAREST
AGAIN THOU HEAREST • • • • • • • • • • •   201 PHILOMELA   30
ONCE MORE THOU HEAREST   • • • • • • • •   201 PHILOMELA   V 30
THOU HEAREST THE IMMORTAL CHANTS OF OLD   • • •   268 THYRSIS   181
THOU HEAREST THE IMMORTAL STRAINS OF OLD   • • •   268 THYRSIS   V 181
WHEN THROUGH THY CAVES THOU HEAREST MUSIC SWELL • •   431 EMPEDOCLES II   66

HEARING
THAT THOU CANST HEAR AND HEARING HOLD THY WAY   • •   3 EMERSONS ESSAYS   2
HEARING THE WRATHFUL FATHER COMING HOME   • • • •   102 BALDER DEAD 1   263
THOU HEARST IF HEARING LIKE AS SPEECH IS THINE   • •   112 BALDER DEAD 2   251
HEARING IT BY THIS DISTANT NORTHERN SEA   • • • •   211 DOVER BEACH   20

HEARKENS
HE HEARKENS NOT LIGHT COMER HE IS FLOWN   • • • •   265 THYRSIS   71
HE HEARKENS NOT LIGHT COMER HE IS GONE   • • • •   265 THYRSIS   V 71

HEARS
IT HEARS A VOICE WITHIN IT TELL   • • • •   22 YOUTH AND CALM   22
SITS RAPT AND HEARS THE BATTLE BREAK BELOW • • • •   42 GIPSY CHILD   23
LIKE ALLAH HEARS AND JUDGES ALL   • • • • • •   89 SICK KING BOKH   57
HE HEARS A VOICE SIGH HUMBLY WAIT   • • • • •   157 SAINT BRANDAN   23
AND HEARS ITS WINDING MURMUR AND HE SEES • • • •   247 BURIED LIFE   89
TEARLESS WHEN OF MY DEATH HE HEARS   • • • • •   250 WISH   6
HEARS THY VOICE RIGHT NOW HE IS GONE • • • • •   272 MEMORIAL VERSES   74
ONE HEARS THEE SAYING NOW   • • • • • • • •   309 OBERMANN   V 90
HE HEARS NOTHING BUT THE CRY OF THE TORRENTS • •   435 EMPEDOCLES II   213

HEARST
THOU HEARST IF HEARING LIKE AS SPEECH IS THINE • •   112 BALDER DEAD 2   251
BUT THOU BECAUSE THOU HEARST   • • • • • • •   426 EMPEDOCLES I 2   417

HEART
IF SADNESS AT THE LONG HEART-WASTING SHOW   • • • •   7 REP FRIEND   9
MERE PHANTOMS OF MANS SELF-TORMENTING HEART   • •   9 MYCERINUS   25

HEART   (CONTINUED)

THEY ARE GONE ALL IS STILL FOOLISH HEART DOST   19 MODERN SAPPHO   1
    THOU QUIVER
WILL BE BROUGHT THOU POOR HEART HOW MUCH NEARER   20 MODERN SAPPHO   20
    TO THEE
BUT HER HEART WAS TIRED TIRED   . . . . .   21 REQUIESCAT   7
AND IS THE HEART OF YOUTH SO LIGHT   . . . . .   21 YOUTH AND CALM   9
SCREENS NOT NOW A HEART OF STONE   . . . . .   27 NEW SIRENS   52
WHILE THE SOVRAN HEART IS DEAD   . . . . .   28 NEW SIRENS   78
LIFE DRIES UP THE HEART DISSEMBLES   . . . .   29 NEW SIRENS   83
MUSED ON WARM THE HEART ANEW   . . . . .   30 NEW SIRENS   134
ALL MANS HEART WHICH BROOKS BESTOWAL   . . . .   34 NEW SIRENS   229
HEART QUITS HEART AND HAND QUITS HAND   . . .   35 NEW SIRENS   264
HEART QUITS HEART AND HAND QUITS HAND   . . .   35 NEW SIRENS   264
WHEN THE PRINCELY HEART IS DEAD   . . . . .   28 NEW SIRENS   V 78
WHILE THE PRINCELY HEART IS DEAD   . . . . .   28 NEW SIRENS   V 78
TO THIS DEEP-SOBERD HEART   . . . . .   36 VOICE   24
MADE MY TOST HEART ITS VERY LIFE-BLOOD SPILL   36 VOICE   39
TO THIS LONG SOBERD HEART   . . . . . .   36 VOICE   V 24
DRAIND ALL THE LIFE MY FULL HEART HAD TO SPILL   36 VOICE   V 39
OH WHAT A SPASM SHAKES THE DREAMERS HEART . . .   46 IN UTRUMQUE PAR   41
LONG SINCE THE WORLD HATH SET ITS HEART TO LIVE   46 WORLD QUIETIST   11
THEY CLOAK THE TROUBLES OF THE HEART   . . . .   48 HORATIAN ECHO   20
THE POET TO WHOSE MIGHTY HEART   . . . . . .   56 RESIGNATION   144
RATHER THAT HEART WHICH BURNS IN THEE   . . . .   59 RESIGNATION   241
AND I WILL TELL THEE WHAT MY HEART DESIRES   .   62 SOHRAB RUSTUM   41
O SOHRAB AN UNQUIET HEART IS THINE   . . . . .   63 SOHRAB RUSTUM   65
THERE GO THOU WILT NOT YET MY HEART FOREBODES .   63 SOHRAB RUSTUM   86
GO I WILL GRANT THEE WHAT THY HEART DESIRES .   63 SOHRAB RUSTUM   93
HE HAS THE WILD STAGS FOOT THE LIONS HEART . . .   66 SOHRAB RUSTUM   177
HE HAS THE WILD STAGS FOOT THE LIONS HEART . . .   67 SOHRAB RUSTUM   216
BUT NEVER WAS MY HEART THUS TOUCHD BEFORE . . .   74 SOHRAB RUSTUM   436
ARE THEY FROM HEAVEN THESE SOFTENINGS OF THE HEART 74 SOHRAB RUSTUM   437
MAKE OFTEN IN THE FORESTS HEART AT MORN . . .   75 SOHRAB RUSTUM   477
HIS HEART TO TAKE A GIFT AND LET THEE GO   . . .   77 SOHRAB RUSTUM   533
NO RUSTUM SLAYS ME AND THIS FILIAL HEART   . .   77 SOHRAB RUSTUM   543
WHICH TROUBLES ALL MY HEART AND MADE MY SHIELD .   77 SOHRAB RUSTUM   549
AND TO HIS HEART HE PRESSD THE OTHER HAND . .   80 SOHRAB RUSTUM   665
SURELY MY HEART CRIED OUT THAT IT WAS THOU . .   82 SOHRAB RUSTUM   711
WHEN FIRST I SAW THEE AND THY HEART SPOKE TOO .   82 SOHRAB RUSTUM   712
SO SAID HE AND HIS VOICE RELEASED THE HEART   .   82 SOHRAB RUSTUM   726
BUT I SHALL CONQUER THAT MY HEART FOREBODES . .   62 SOHRAB RUSTUM   V
HE HATH THE WILD STAGS FOOT THE LIONS HEART .   67 SOHRAB RUSTUM   V 216
IF HE FOR STRANGERS PAIND HIS HEART   . . . .   92 SICK KING BOKH   147
IF HAPLY HE MAY MELT HER HEART WITH WORDS   . .   100 BALDER DEAD 1   182
HEAVY IN HEART FOR BALDER TO HIS HOUSE   . . .   101 BALDER DEAD 1   223
BUT FIERCELY ODIN GALLOPD MOVED IN HEART   . .   102 BALDER DEAD 1   258
AND BEND MY HEART AND GIVE HIM BACK TO HEAVEN .   111 BALDER DEAD 2   240
DECEIVER FAIR IN FORM BUT FALSE IN HEART   . .   114 BALDER DEAD 3   21
AND BEND HER HEART AND GIVE YOU BALDER BACK   .   115 BALDER DEAD 3   46
AND WRING HIS HEART WITH SHAME TO HEAR THY WORD   116 BALDER DEAD 3   105
NOT LONG A WIFE WHEN HIS UNQUIET HEART   . . .   116 BALDER DEAD 3   107
THEREFORE WITH GRATEFUL HEART I MOURN THEE DEAD   117 BALDER DEAD 3   152
AND WIDEN AND THE PEASANTS HEART IS GLAD   . .   122 BALDER DEAD 3   316
THEN SAD AT HEART TO NIORD HERMOD SPAKE   . .   124 BALDER DEAD 3   369
HODER ILL-FATED BLIND IN HEART AND EYES   . .   124 BALDER DEAD 3   387
OR PERHAPS HAS HER YOUNG HEART   . . . . . .   131 TRISTRAM 1   45
OF THOSE THAT IN SECRET THE HEART-STRINGS RIVE . 132 TRISTRAM 1   47
HIS YOUNG GUARDIANS HEART WITH LOVE   . . . .   137 TRISTRAM 1   207
IF ONES OWN HEART BEATS NOT LIGHT   . . . . .   138 TRISTRAM 1   265
A LOOK AS IF THE HEART COMPLAINED   . . . . .   140 TRISTRAM 1   321
INTO THE HEART OF BRITTANY   . . . . . .   141 TRISTRAM 1   366
SWELLS MY HEART AND TAKES MY BREATH AWAY   . .   145 TRISTRAM 2   74
TRISTRAM TRISTRAM LET THY HEART NOT FAIL   . .   145 TRISTRAM 2   78
ON A RED GOLD THRONE IN THE HEART OF THE SEA .   163 FORSAKEN MERM   51
I SAID GO UP DEAR HEART THROUGH THE WAVES . .   163 FORSAKEN MERM   60
DEAR HEART I SAID WE ARE LONG ALONE   . . . .   163 FORSAKEN MERM   78
AND A HEART SORROW-LADEN   . . . .   164 FORSAKEN MERM   104
WHAT MADE MY HEART AT NEWSTEAD FULLEST SWELL .   166 PICT NEWSTEAD   1
WITH EYE SUFFUSED BUT HEART INSPIRED TRUE . .   172 GOOD SHEPHERD   10
AH WARN SOME MORE AMBITIOUS HEART   . . . . .   174 MEETING   15
AND WHAT HEART KNOWS ANOTHER   . . . .   177 PARTING   73
A HEART EVER NEW   . . . .   177 PARTING   80
I BLAME THEE NOT THIS HEART I KNOW   . . . .   178 FAREWELL   17
THIS STARTING FEVERISH HEART AWAY   . . . . .   178 FAREWELL   32
I BADE MY HEART MORE CONSTANT BE   . . . . .   180 ISOLATION MARG   2
THE HEART CAN BIND ITSELF ALONE   . . . . .   180 ISOLATION MARG   9
FAREWELL AND THOU THOU LONELY HEART   . . . .   181 ISOLATION MARG   13
ACROSS MY HEART TO SAY THY THREAD   . . . . .   184 TERRACE BERNE   27
THEIR MELON-HARVEST TO THE HEART THEY SEE   .   193 STRAYED REVEL   239
TO THY RACKD HEART AND BRAIN   . . . . . .   200 PHILOMELA   14
TO THY TORN HEART AND BRAIN   . . . . . .   200 PHILOMELA   V 14
MY HEART IS SWOLN WITH LOVE UNSAID   . . . . .   206 RIVER   10
BEFORE THIS TEASED OERLABOURD HEART   . . . . .   206 RIVER   17
THY HEART IS MINE TRUE TRUE AH TRUE   . . . . .   207 TOO LATE   7
AND HEART PROFOUNDLY STIRRD   . . . .   212 GROWING OLD   18
DEEP IN OUR HIDDEN HEART   . . . .   213 GROWING OLD   28
AND PRESS INTO ITS INMOST HEART   . . . . .   224 EPILOG LAOCOON   88
LANGUID THEIR HEART FOR YOUTH   . . . . . .   233 YOUTH OF MAN   44
WHILE THE HEART STILL POURS   . . . . . .   235 YOUTH OF MAN   114
WHICH HAS NOT FALLN ON THE DRY HEART LIKE RAIN . 238 PROGRESS   42
THE BAND WILL QUIT MANS HEART HE WILL BREATHE FREE 239 REVOLUTIONS   20

HEART   (CONTINUED)

ON MY HEART YOUR MIGHTY CHARM RENEW	240 SELF-DEPENDENCE	10
A CRY LIKE THINE IN MINE OWN HEART I HEAR	240 SELF-DEPENDENCE	30
A CRY LIKE THINE IN MY OWN HEART I HEAR	240 SELF-DEPENDENCE V	30
THE FIRE WHICH IN THE HEART RESIDES	241 MORALITY	2
THE FIRE THAT IN THE HEART RESIDES	241 MORALITY V	2
AND THE SAME VAINLY THROBBING HEART WAS THERE	242 SUMMER NIGHT	24
THERE THE FREED PRISONER WHEREER HIS HEART	243 SUMMER NIGHT	54
AND THE SAME AGITATED HEART WAS THERE	242 SUMMER NIGHT V	24
TO UNLOCK THE HEART AND LET IT SPEAK	245 BURIED LIFE	13
THE SAME HEART BEATS IN EVERY HUMAN BREAST	245 BURIED LIFE	23
OUR HEART AND HAVE OUR LIPS UNCHAIND	245 BURIED LIFE	28
INTO THE MYSTERY OF THIS HEART WHICH BEATS	246 BURIED LIFE	52
THE EYE SINKS INWARD AND THE HEART LIES PLAIN	247 BURIED LIFE	86
THERE BEATS ONE HEART IN EVERY HUMAN BREAST	245 BURIED LIFE V	23
INTO THE MYSTERY OF THIS HEART THAT BEATS	246 BURIED LIFE V	52
NEEDS MUST I LOSE THEM NEEDS WITH HEAVY HEART	264 THYRSIS	38
THE HEART LESS BOUNDING AT EMOTION NEW	266 THYRSIS	139
YET ON HE FARES BY HIS OWN HEART INSPIRED	269 THYRSIS	210
THEN THROUGH THE GREAT TOWNS HARSH HEART-WEARYING ROAR	269 THYRSIS	234
WITH SHIVERING HEART THE STRIFE WE SAW	270 MEMORIAL VERSES	10
HE SPOKE AND LOOSED OUR HEART IN TEARS	271 MEMORIAL VERSES	47
HEALTH EASE A HEART ELATE	273 EDW QUILLINAN	12
VEXT HEART DEPLORE	275 SOUTHERN NIGHT	16
IN HEART HIGH-SOULD	279 SOUTHERN NIGHT	124
UP TO THE HEART OF THE MOORS	282 HAWORTH CHURCH	56
ONLY TO LIVE BY THE HEART	282 HAWORTH CHURCH V	
SEEMD BUT A DREAM OF THE HEART	290 RUGBY CHAPEL	151
LANGUOR IS NOT IN YOUR HEART	292 RUGBY CHAPEL	193
THEREFORE THE VICTORS HEART	296 HEINES GRAVE	127
RESTED BY SLUMBER AND HEART	297 HEINES GRAVE	177
THE PAGEANT OF HIS BLEEDING HEART	303 GRANDE CHARTR	136
ALL SHIPWRECK IN THY OWN WEAK HEART	307 OBERMANN	19
O UNSTRUNG WILL O BROKEN HEART	312 OBERMANN	183
AND FROM THY WORLD WITH HEART OPPREST	314 OBERMANN MORE	73
BUT AH ITS HEART ITS HEART WAS STONE	315 OBERMANN MORE	91
BUT AH ITS HEART ITS HEART WAS STONE	315 OBERMANN MORE	91
CONSUMED OUR HEART WITH THIRST LIKE FIRE	323 OBERMANN MORE	315
O LAIAS LAIAS LET THE HEART SPEAK HERE	331 MEROPE	59
NOT SO THY HEART WOULD PAY ITS MOMENTS SPEECH	332 MEROPE	61
I BLAME THEE NOT I DO THY HEART NO WRONG	332 MEROPE	83
WAKENS O QUEEN REMEMBRANCE IN THY HEART	333 MEROPE	106
TO KEEP ALIVE THAT MEMORY IN MY HEART	334 MEROPE	120
AND VALIANT HEART OF YOUTH OR MANHOODS FIRM	335 MEROPE	157
HOW MANY PRECIOUS FEELINGS OF MANS HEART	335 MEROPE	178
HE SACRIFICED OUR RUIN IN HIS HEART	338 MEROPE	273
WITH WOMEN THE HEART ARGUES NOT THE MIND	340 MEROPE	341
FOR YEARS IN SILENCE DEVOURING HER HEART	346 MEROPE	509
GIVE NOT THY HEART TO DESPAIR	347 MEROPE	523
TO THE CHAFED HEART OF JUSTICE THAN TO MINE	349 MEROPE	560
THE HEART OF YOUTH I KNOW THAT MOST I FEAR	351 MEROPE	609
UNSCALED UNTRODDEN IS THE HEART OF MAN	352 MEROPE	630
THAT WIDE AND VARIOUS WORLD THE HEART OF OTHERS	352 MEROPE	637
BUT EVEN OUR OWN HEART THAT NARROW WORLD	352 MEROPE	638
AND KNOWING WELL MANS INMOST HEART INFIRM	353 MEROPE	692
AND ON THE HUNTING-RAMBLES WHICH HIS HEART	355 MEROPE	725
HATEFUL BY EACH MESSENIAN HEART ABHORRD	366 MEROPE	1009
HOW MUCH MEN THINK ME ABJECT VOID OF HEART	366 MEROPE	1016
WITH PATIENCE ON THY FACE DEATH IN THY HEART	367 MEROPE	1045
INSPIRE THIS COWARD HEART THIS FLAGGING ARM	368 MEROPE	1066
MOTHER MY HEART RUNS OVER BUT THE TIME	378 MEROPE	1232
FOR KNOW THOU THIS A VIOLENT HEART HATH BEEN	382 MEROPE	1329
IS LIFELESS WHILE ITS HEART REMAINS UNTOUCHD	382 MEROPE	1343
WHEN IT ADMIRES AND LOVES ITS HEART AWAKES	382 MEROPE	1345
BUT MUTE THOU SATST AND EACH MESSENIAN HEART	383 MEROPE	1373
THE GODS COMMAND NOT WHERE THE HEART SPEAKS CLEAR	385 MEROPE	1404
O MEROPE THE COMMON HEART OF MAN	389 MEROPE	1523
SON WITH A DOUBTING HEART THY MOTHER YIELDS	390 MEROPE	1582
HER SON HEART-STRICKEN EYED HER	393 MEROPE	1673
AND HE HIMSELF WITH THE IMPETUOUS HEART	394 MEROPE	1702
WHY SHOULD THIS HEART OF MINE SET MIGHTY STORE	398 MEROPE	1789
ASCENDED WITH UNDAUNTED HEART	399 MEROPE	1833
APPROACHES WITH UNDOUBTING HEART	400 MEROPE	1858
DEEP IN MANS HEART IS BORN	418 EMPEDOCLES I 2	169
OUR SHIVERING HEART IS MINED BY SECRET DISCONTENT	424 EMPEDOCLES I 2	366
WE PAUSE WE HUSH OUR HEART	424 EMPEDOCLES I 2	372
FIND HENCEFORTH ENERGY AND HEART BUT I	429 EMPEDOCLES II	10
THROUGH WHOSE HEART ETNA DRIVES HER ROOTS OF STONE	430 EMPEDOCLES II	43
IS THY TORTURED HEART STILL PROUD	430 EMPEDOCLES II	49
THE BRAVE IMPETUOUS HEART YIELDS EVERYWHERE	431 EMPEDOCLES II	90
AND THE BEATING OF HIS OWN HEART	435 EMPEDOCLES II	214
WITH HELD-IN JOY SWELLING ITS HEART I ONLY	438 EMPEDOCLES II	316
OH THAT MY HEART BOUNDED WITH THE SWELL OF THE SEA	438 EMPEDOCLES II	324
BUT NO THIS HEART WILL GLOW NO MORE THOU ART	438 EMPEDOCLES II	327
AND BREAK HIS HEART WITH ALL THE BAFFLING CHANGE	448 WESTMIN ABBEY	149
THAT LOVING HEART THAT PATIENT SOUL	450 GEISTS GRAVE	9
YET WOULD WE KEEP THEE IN OUR HEART	451 GEISTS GRAVE	37
DULL OF HEART AND HARD OF TOUCH	457 POOR MATTHIAS	168
AGAINST THY MISTRESS LOVING HEART	460 KAISER DEAD	53
THAT BINDS THE HEART OF MAN WITH MIGHTIEST POWER	467 ALARIC AT ROME	146

HEART   (CONTINUED)
        PERCHANCE HIS WANDERING HEART WAS FAR AWAY . .   . . 468 ALARIC AT ROME   169
        HAUNTING THE SHROUDED CHAMBERS OF HIS HEART   . . . 473 CROMWELL   58
        WITH HEART NEW STRUNG AND STERN RESOLVE HE STOOD . . 473 CROMWELL   66
        THAT BOUND HIS SPIRIT AND HIS HEART AWOKE   . . . . 475 CROMWELL   132
        A HEART THAT RECKD NOT OF THE COUNTLESS DEAD   . . . 478 CROMWELL   225
        A HEART OF ICE A SOUL OF FIRE . . . . 481 DESTINY   6
        NOR WOULD MY OWN HEART LET ME MY HEART WHICH   HOMER TRANS   17
              HAS BID ME BE VALIANT
        NOR WOULD MY OWN HEART LET ME MY HEART WHICH   HOMER TRANS   17
              HAS BID ME BE VALIANT
        THEN WITH A TROUBLED HEART THE SWIFT ACHILLES   HOMER TRANS   58
              ADDRESSD HIM
        NO LACK OF ANSWER HAST THOU O MY HEART   . . . . .   RUDE ORATOR   13
        ALL THE HEART ENJOINS BUT ONLY HERE . . . . . .   META CLOISTER   24
        RESTLESS HEART IN THIS RETREAT . . . .   META CLOISTER   30
        THE TRUE HEART-BREAKING BAFFLED HOPE AND SHAME   . .   LUCRETIUS 2   13
        AND REND HIS HEART WHO SEES THEM . . . .   LUCRETIUS 2   17

HEARTED
        THE YOUNG LIGHT-HEARTED MASTERS OF THE WAVES   . . 262 SCHOLAR-GIPSY   241

HEARTH
        ON FREAS HEARTH FEED HIGH THE SACRED FIRE   . . . .   97 BALDER DEAD 1   90
        BUT AT THE CENTRAL HEARTH THOSE WOMEN OLD   . . . . 100 BALDER DEAD 1   194
        AN INFANT AT THE HEARTH OF CYPSELUS . . . . . . 331 MEROPE   32
        LAY ON THE HEARTH AMID A FIERY RING . . . . . . 446 WESTMIN ABBEY   84
        UPON THE HEARTH AND PLAYD WITH THEM AND SMILED   . . 446 WESTMIN ABBEY   90

HEARTS
        COLD HEARTS AND THANKLESS TONGUES WHERE THANKS ARE DUE   8 MYCERINUS   4
        COLD HEARTS AND THANKLESS TONGUES WHERE THANKS   8 MYCERINUS   V   4
              WERE DUE
        THEY MUST LOVE WHILE THEY MUST BUT THE HEARTS   19 MODERN SAPPHO   15
              THAT LOVE LONGER
        ROUND OUR HEARTS WITH LONG CARESSES . . . . . .   28 NEW SIRENS   69
        WITH COLD DRY EYES AND HEARTS COMPOSED AND STERN   . . 96 BALDER DEAD 1   35
        SO THEY WITH PENT-UP HEARTS AND TEARLESS EYES   . .   97 BALDER DEAD 1   69
        TWINE ABOUT THEIR HEARTS AGAIN . . . . 135 TRISTRAM 1   152
        BUT EARTHLY KNIGHTS HAVE HARDER HEARTS   . . . . . 159 NECKAN   19
        IN TEARS WITH HEARTS TOO FULL TO SPEAK   . . . . . 178 FAREWELL   12
        KNOWS THAT THE BENT OF BOTH OUR HEARTS   . . . . . 179 FAREWELL   47
        HAVE DREAMD TWO HUMAN HEARTS MIGHT BLEND   . . . . 181 ISOLATION MARG   38
        NEW HEARTS WITH THE ENQUIRERS HOLY ROBE   . . . . 198 FRAG DEJANEIRA   16
        TRUTH WHAT IS TRUTH TWO BLEEDING HEARTS   . . . . 203 EUPHROSYNE   5
        LIVES IN OUR HEARTS WHICH CAN FEEL   . . . . . . 233 YOUTH OF MAN   37
        OUR HEARTS OUR VOICES MUST WE TOO BE DUMB   . . . . 245 BURIED LIFE   25
        ITS HEADS OERTAXD ITS PALSIED HEARTS WAS RIFE   . . 261 SCHOLAR-GIPSY   205
        LONG SINCE DEEP IN OUR HEARTS . . . . 294 HEINES GRAVE   74
        HAVE RESTLESS HEARTS ONE THROB THE LESS   . . . . 303 GRANDE CHARTR   144
        OF HOPES AND HEARTS IN BLOOM   . . . . 315 OBERMANN MORE   80
        SO MANY WOUNDED HEARTS . . . . 317 OBERMANN MORE   160
        AND JOY THAT SHOULD ALL HEARTS EMPLOY   . . . . . 320 OBERMANN MORE   239
        FOR THE MESSENIAN HEARTS WHO LOVED THE PRINCE   . . 365 MEROPE   993
        KINDLE THEIR HEARTS MAKE THEM NO MORE A MOB   . . . 383 MEROPE   1360
        ELECTRIFY THEIR HEARTS MAKE THEM NO MORE A MOB   . . 383 MEROPE   V1360
        WHEN WITH ELATED HEARTS WE JOIND YOUR TRAIN   . . . 436 EMPEDOCLES II   238
        AND TO MENS HEARTS THIS ANCIENT PLACE ENDEARD   . . 444 WESTMIN ABBEY   9
        ALL AIRY HOPES THAT IDLE HEARTS CAN FRAME   . . . . 474 CROMWELL   95
        FOND HEARTS THAT FAIN WOULD CLOTHE THE UNWELCOME TRUTH 474 CROMWELL   97
        THOSE LINGERING HOPES OF COWARD HEARTS THAT STILL   . 475 CROMWELL   107
        CHEERD ALL THE FAILING HEARTS THAT SORROWD THERE   . 478 CROMWELL   218
        THRO THE DARK CHAMBERS OF THE HEARTS OF MEN   . . 478 CROMWELL   230

HEAT
        WHO WITH SUCH HEAT DOST PREACH WHAT WERE TO THEE   . .   5 HARMONY NATURE   2
        IN MAZES OF HEAT AND SOUND . . . .   21 REQUIESCAT   10
        THEN I SHALL PRAISE THE HEAT WHICH THEN I LACK   . .   37 YOUTHS AGIT   11
        MY HEAD IS BURNING AND A HEAT   . . . .   93 SICK KING BOKH   183
        ITS STORMS OF DUST WITH BURNING HEAT   . . . . . 157 SAINT BRANDAN   44
        WHO STRUCK IN HEAT HIS CHILD HE LOVED SO WELL   . . 166 PICT NEWSTEAD   5
        WHO STRUCK IN HEAT THE CHILD HE LOVED SO WELL   . . 166 PICT NEWSTEAD   V   5
        WHO FAILD UNDER THE HEAT OF THIS LIFES DAY   . . . 172 IMMORTALITY   7
        WE BEAR THE BURDEN AND THE HEAT   . . . . 241 MORALITY   9
        OF THE SUN-LOVING GENTIAN IN THE HEAT   . . . . 412 EMPEDOCLES I 2   5
        OUR HAIR GROWS GREY OUR EYES ARE DIMMD OUR   423 EMPEDOCLES I 2   336
              HEAT IS TAMED
        THOUGH THOU HAST BEEN MY SHADE IN THE WORLDS HEAT   434 EMPEDOCLES II   194
        HEAT TO FIRE . . . . 439 EMPEDOCLES II   335

HEATED
        WITH HEATED CHEEKS AND FLURRIED AIR . . . . . . 148 TRISTRAM 2   162

HEATH
        IN A GREEN CIRCULAR HOLLOW IN THE HEATH   . . . . 149 TRISTRAM 3   7
        FROM THE OPEN HEATH STILL BY THE HEDGEROWS LAY   . . 151 TRISTRAM 3   51
        AND LED THEM HOME OVER THE DARKENING HEATH   . . . 151 TRISTRAM 3   63
        IN THAT GREEN CIRCULAR OPENING IN THE HEATH   . .   TRISTRAM 3   V   7
        IN A GREEN CIRCULAR OPENING IN THE HEATH   . . .   TRISTRAM 3   V   7
        FIRST MEETS THE FRINGING HEATH AT ONCE ALL ROUND   . .   TRISTRAM 3   V   14
        FIRST LEAVES THE FRINGING HEATH AT ONCE ALL ROUND   TRISTRAM 3   V   14
        FIRST MEETS THE ENCIRCLING HEATH AT ONCE ALL ROUND   TRISTRAM 3   V   14
        FIRST LEAVES THE ENCIRCLING HEATH AT ONCE ALL ROUND   TRISTRAM 3   V   14
        EACH GLISTENING STRAND EACH HEATH-FRINGED BAY   . . 177 FAREWELL   4
        AND FAR TO THE SOUTH THE HEATH . . . . 228 YOUTH OF NATURE   22
        BETWEEN HEATH-CLAD SHOWERY HILLS   . . . . . . 282 HAWORTH CHURCH   57

HEATH   (CONTINUED)
        HOW EACH BRIGHT TINT OF TREE AND FLOWER AND HEATH   466 ALARIC AT ROME   101
        I PASSD TO-DAY OER WALTON HEATH   • • • • • •   483 ROME-SICKNESS   5

HEATHEN
        THE HEATHEN SAXONS ON THE RHINE   • • • • • • •   138 TRISTRAM 1   253

HEATHER
        FASTEND ON HER DARK HAIR AND HER WREATH OF   19 MODERN SAPPHO   11
                WHITE HEATHER
        IS LIGHT AND GREEN THE HEATHER WHICH ALL ROUND   • •   150 TRISTRAM 3   14
        CAME KEEN AND CHILL DOWN ON THE HEATHER BRIGHT   • •   151 TRISTRAM 3   57
        IS GREEN AND CLEAR THE HEATHER WHICH ALL ROUND   • •   TRISTRAM 3   V   14
        IS LIGHT AND GREEN THE HEATHER WHICH ALL ROUND   • •   TRISTRAM 3   V   14
        THE HEATHER DISAPPEARS AND THE PALE GRASS   • • • •   TRISTRAM 3   V   15
        CALL FROM THE HEATHER IN BLOOM • • • • • • • •   285 HAWORTH CHURCH   122

HEATHS
        PASSD AMONG THESE HEATHS OF OURS   • • • • •   137 TRISTRAM 1   230
        THE BARE HEATHS SPREADING CLEAR AS DAY   • • •   141 TRISTRAM 1   364
        NOR TO THE BROWN HEATHS ROUND THEM BRIGHT AND WIDE   151 TRISTRAM 3   49
        IS WITH THEM AND THE WIDE HEATHS WHERE THEY PLAY • • 152 TRISTRAM 3   103
        BEYOND THE HEATHS EDGED BY THE LONELY SEA   • • • •   154 TRISTRAM 3   155
        NOR TO THE BROWN HEATHS ROUND THEM WARM AND WIDE • •   TRISTRAM 3   V   49
        FROM HEATHS STARRD WITH BROOM   • • • • • • • •   165 FORSAKEN MERM   129
        BACK TO YOUR NATIVE HEATHS   • • • • • • • •   285 HAWORTH CHURCH   115

HEATHY
        MILD HOLLOWS AND CLEAR HEATHY SWELLS • • • • • •   54 RESIGNATION   66
        THE SOLEMN WASTES OF HEATHY HILL   • • • • • •   55 RESIGNATION   96
        AND RULED OER DENMARK AND THE HEATHY ISLES   • • • • 117 BALDER DEAD 3   127
        BY NASEBYS HILL OER MARSTONS HEATHY WASTE   • • • •   476 CROMWELL   149

HEATS
        SHALL I NOT JOY YOUTHS HEATS ARE LEFT BEHIND   • •   37 YOUTHS AGIT   5
        THROUGH THE DEEP NOONTIDE HEATS WE FARE   • • •   54 RESIGNATION   69
        MOORD TO THE COOL BANK IN THE SUMMER-HEATS • • • •   257 SCHOLAR-GIPSY   67
        WITH INDIAN HEATS AT LAST FORDONE   • • • • • •   276 SOUTHERN NIGHT   26
        THAN IN THE BROILING CITY IN THESE HEATS   • • • •   409 EMPEDOCLES I 1   104

HEAVE
        CEASES NOT FROM ALL TIME TO HEAVE AND GROAN   • •   45 IN UTRUMQUE PAR   26
        AND WHETHER IT WILL HEAVE US UP TO LAND   • • • •   73 SOHRAB RUSTUM   393

HEAVED
        THEY SAW US THEY CONFERRD THEIR BOSOMS HEAVED   • •   25 DREAM   26
        HIS BREAST HEAVED HIS LIPS FOAMD AND TWICE HIS VOICE 74 SOHRAB RUSTUM   455
        IT WAS NOT LOVE WHICH HEAVED THY BREAST   • • • •   204 EUPHROSYNE   25
        IT WAS NOT LOVE THAT HEAVED THY BREAST   • • • •   204 EUPHROSYNE   V   25
        BUT TWAS NOT LOVE WHICH HEAVED HER BREAST   • • • •   204 EUPHROSYNE   V   25
        HEAVED DAZZLINGLY BETWEEN   • • • • • • • •   242 SUMMER NIGHT   17
        OF OUR BOAT PASSING HEAVED THE RIVER-GRASS • • • •   266 THYRSIS   128

HEAVEN
        MAKING THE HEAVEN OF HEAVENS HIS DWELLING-PLACE • •   3 SHAKESPEARE   6
        AND THOU WHOSE WIT TO HIGHEST HEAVEN DID GO   • •   3 SHAKESPEARE   V   9
        SOME BETTER ARCHETYPE WHOSE SEAT WAS HEAVEN   • •   9 MYCERINUS   22
        WHEN ON THE STRENUOUS JUST MAN HEAVEN BESTOWS   • •   9 MYCERINUS   29
        SWEEPS EARTH AND HEAVEN AND MEN AND GODS ALONG   • •   9 MYCERINUS   39
        OR IN MID-HEAVEN PERHAPS YOUR GOLDEN CARS   • • • •   10 MYCERINUS   43
        WHIRLS EARTH AND HEAVEN AND MEN AND GODS ALONG   • •   9 MYCERINUS   V   39
        BEARS EARTH AND HEAVEN AND MEN AND GODS ALONG   • •   9 MYCERINUS   V   39
        BEHOLD THE PAVEMENT OF THE COURTS OF HEAVEN   • •   18 CHURCH BROU 3   31
        THIS IS THE GLIMMERING VERGE OF HEAVEN AND THESE • •   19 CHURCH BROU 3   41
        HEAVEN DOTH A QUICKER PULSE IMPART   • • • • •   56 RESIGNATION   145
        O THOU YOUNG MAN THE AIR OF HEAVEN IS SOFT • • • •   70 SOHRAB RUSTUM   322
        BUT SUCCESS SWAYS WITH THE BREATH OF HEAVEN   • •   72 SOHRAB RUSTUM   387
        ARE THEY FROM HEAVEN THESE SOFTENINGS OF THE HEART   74 SOHRAB RUSTUM   437
        O THOU OLD WARRIOR LET US YIELD TO HEAVEN   • • • •   74 SOHRAB RUSTUM   438
        GREW SUDDENLY IN HEAVEN AND DARKD THE SUN   • • • •   75 SOHRAB RUSTUM   482
        IN HEAVEN AND THOU ART HEAVENS UNCONSCIOUS HAND • •   82 SOHRAB RUSTUM   710
        BUT IT WAS WRIT IN HEAVEN THAT THIS SHOULD BE   • •   82 SOHRAB RUSTUM   725
        ALL YE WHO HEAR ME AND INHABIT HEAVEN   • • •   96 BALDER DEAD 1   29
        TO LIVE AS ERST YOUR DAILY LIFE IN HEAVEN   • • • •   96 BALDER DEAD 1   36
        AND FROM THE HALL OF HEAVEN HE RODE AWAY   • • • •   96 BALDER DEAD 1   48
        AND FAR FROM HEAVEN HE TURND HIS SHINING ORBS   • •   96 BALDER DEAD 1   51
        BESIDE THE TABLES IN THE HALL OF HEAVEN   • • •   97 BALDER DEAD 1   65
        SIGHTLESS AND HELPLESS WANDERING WEAK IN HEAVEN • •   98 BALDER DEAD 1   97
        FOR WHO WILL BEAR MY HATEFUL SIGHT IN HEAVEN   • •   98 BALDER DEAD 1   106
        FOR MANY GODS IN HEAVEN NOT THOU ALONE   • • •   98 BALDER DEAD 1   119
        FOR NOT SO GLADSOME IS THAT LIFE IN HEAVEN • • • •   98 BALDER DEAD 1   122
        UNTRODDEN LONELY FAR FROM LIGHT AND HEAVEN • • • •   99 BALDER DEAD 1   136
        WHICH EVERY DAY THEY COME AND GO IN HEAVEN • • •   99 BALDER DEAD 1   140
        WHICH BRANCHES FROM THE NORTH OF HEAVEN AND RIDE • •   99 BALDER DEAD 1   144
        TELLING HER ALL THAT GRIEF THEY HAVE IN HEAVEN   • • 100 BALDER DEAD 1   180
        FOR SPEED AND HERMOD WAS HIS NAME IN HEAVEN   • • 101 BALDER DEAD 1   221
        TO ASGARD AND THE STARS CAME OUT IN HEAVEN • • •   102 BALDER DEAD 1   256
        WHICH WERE HIS GLORIOUS MARK IN HEAVEN HE STOOD • • 103 BALDER DEAD 1   285
        DEATH FROM THY HEAD AND WITH THE GODS IN HEAVEN • • 104 BALDER DEAD 1   311
        AND TALKING OF THE LIFE WE LED IN HEAVEN   • • • • 104 BALDER DEAD 1   329
        FORTH FROM THE EAST UP THE ASCENT OF HEAVEN   • • 105 BALDER DEAD 2   1

HEAVEN   (CONTINUED)

WARNING THE GODS THAT FOES DRAW NIGH TO HEAVEN • • 105 BALDER DEAD 2 7
WOUNDLESS AND FRESH SUCH LOT IS THEIRS IN HEAVEN • • 105 BALDER DEAD 2 18
WHOM THEY BRING BACK WITH THEM AT NIGHT TO HEAVEN • 105 BALDER DEAD 2 27
WHICH BRANCHES FROM THE NORTH OF HEAVEN AND WENT • • 107 BALDER DEAD 2 80
THOU KNOWST THOU KNOWST WHAT GRIEF WE HAVE IN HEAVEN 110 BALDER DEAD 2 192
FOR HEAVEN WAS BALDER BORN THE CITY OF GODS • 110 BALDER DEAD 2 198
HERMOD FOR HE THOU ART THOU SON OF HEAVEN • • • 110 BALDER DEAD 2 202
LOK STILL SUBSISTS IN HEAVEN OUR FATHER WISE • 111 BALDER DEAD 2 217
HEAR HOW TO HEAVEN MAY BALDER BE RESTORED • • • 111 BALDER DEAD 2 233
AND BEND MY HEART AND GIVE HIM BACK TO HEAVEN • 111 BALDER DEAD 2 240
THE TERMS OF THY RELEASEMENT HENCE TO HEAVEN • 112 BALDER DEAD 2 252
WHO EVER HAVE BEEN KNOWN IN EARTH OR HEAVEN • 112 BALDER DEAD 2 258
AND TELL THE HEAVEN-BORN GODS HOW THOU HAST SEEN • 112 BALDER DEAD 2 276
BACK THROUGH THE ASTONISHD TRIBES OF DEAD TO HEAVEN 112 BALDER DEAD 2 285
AND ON THE TWELFTH MORN SAW THE LIGHT OF HEAVEN • 113 BALDER DEAD 2 294
SO HERMOD OER THE FOG BETWEEN SAW HEAVEN • 113 BALDER DEAD 2 301
OF HEAVEN AND MIGHTILY AS WINGD HE FLEW • 113 BALDER DEAD 2 303
ODIN MY FATHER AND YE GODS OF HEAVEN • • • 114 BALDER DEAD 3 36
AND LEAD AS ERST OUR DAILY LIFE IN HEAVEN • • • 115 BALDER DEAD 3 56
WHEN MUSPELS CHILDREN SHALL BELEAGUER HEAVEN • 115 BALDER DEAD 3 69
AMONG THE GODS AND HEROES HERE IN HEAVEN • • • 115 BALDER DEAD 3 80
FOR WE LOSE HIM WHO SMOOTHED ALL STRIFE IN HEAVEN 116 BALDER DEAD 3 88
THE LOVELIEST GODDESS SHE IN HEAVEN BY ALL • 116 BALDER DEAD 3 91
THEY CALL HER FREYA IS HER NAME IN HEAVEN • 116 BALDER DEAD 3 97
FOR IN THE PATHS OF HEAVEN HE IS NOT FOUND • 116 BALDER DEAD 3 102
AND I AM LEFT UNCOMFORTED IN HEAVEN • • • • 117 BALDER DEAD 3 122
A KING WHOSE FAME THEN FILLD THE VAST OF HEAVEN • 117 BALDER DEAD 3 129
BALDER THERE YET ARE MANY SCALDS IN HEAVEN • • 117 BALDER DEAD 3 132
BUT NOW THE SUN HAD PASSD THE HEIGHT OF HEAVEN • 118 BALDER DEAD 3 154
IN HEAVEN AND EARTH AND WHO WOULD GRUDGE HIM TEARS 120 BALDER DEAD 3 233
ALL THE STRONG BROOD OF HEAVEN TO SWELL MY TRAIN • 120 BALDER DEAD 3 241
AND BRING IN TRIUMPH BALDER BACK TO HEAVEN • 120 BALDER DEAD 3 244
LORD OVER MEN ON EARTH AND GODS IN HEAVEN • • • 120 BALDER DEAD 3 251
THE EARTH AND OCEAN AND ABOVE THEM HEAVEN • 121 BALDER DEAD 3 261
SUN MOON AND STARS WHICH THOU HAST HUNG IN HEAVEN 121 BALDER DEAD 3 264
ME AND MY WORDS THOUGH THOU BE FIRST IN HEAVEN • 121 BALDER DEAD 3 283
BUT OFFERS TERMS FOR HIS RELEASE TO HEAVEN • 122 BALDER DEAD 3 289
HELA AND WIN THE LOVED ONE BACK TO HEAVEN • 122 BALDER DEAD 3 294
NOT BORN IN HEAVEN HE WAS IN VANHEIM REARD • 122 BALDER DEAD 3 324
YE GODS GOOD LACK IS IT SO DULL IN HEAVEN • • 123 BALDER DEAD 3 337
SO YE GROW SQUEAMISH GODS AND SNIFF AT HEAVEN • 123 BALDER DEAD 3 344
RIDE BACK AND TELL IN HEAVEN THIS HEAVY NEWS • 124 BALDER DEAD 3 371
HE SPOKE AND NIORD SET FORTH BACK TO HEAVEN • 124 BALDER DEAD 3 373
NOR WITH A HATEFUL PRESENCE CUMBER HEAVEN • 125 BALDER DEAD 3 399
OF HEAVEN AND COMMUNION WITH MY KIN • • • 125 BALDER DEAD 3 402
AND SUBSTANCE AND A GOLDEN HOUSE IN HEAVEN • 125 BALDER DEAD 3 404
AND HEAR THE PASSAGE OF A HORSE OF HEAVEN • 125 BALDER DEAD 3 419
WHICH FLOATS BEFORE A VISITANT FROM HEAVEN • • 126 BALDER DEAD 3 438
IN HEAVEN NOR LET THE OTHER GODS LAMENT • • • 126 BALDER DEAD 3 457
IN HEAVEN WAS SELDOM PARTED FROM MY SIDE • 126 BALDER DEAD 3 460
AND CROSS THE BRIDGE OF HEAVEN WITH LOK FOR GUIDE 127 BALDER DEAD 3 476
AGAINST THE GODS UPON THE PLAINS OF HEAVEN • • • 127 BALDER DEAD 3 481
MOURN FOR THE MEN ON EARTH THE GODS IN HEAVEN • 127 BALDER DEAD 3 485
AND ODIN AND HIS SONS THE SEED OF HEAVEN • 127 BALDER DEAD 3 488
AND THE TWO HOSTS ARE MARSHALLD AND IN HEAVEN • 127 BALDER DEAD 3 495
ANOTHER HEAVEN THE BOUNDLESS NO ONE YET • • • 128 BALDER DEAD 3 519
BUT WE IN HEAVEN SHALL FIND AGAIN WITH JOY • 128 BALDER DEAD 3 532
THOUGH THEY TO DEATH WERE BOUND AND HE TO HEAVEN • 129 BALDER DEAD 3 557
AT LAST HE SIGHD AND SET FORTH BACK TO HEAVEN • 129 BALDER DEAD 3 566
BUT OFFER TERMS FOR HIS RELEASE TO HEAVEN • 122 BALDER DEAD 3 V 289
TRISTRAM AH FOR LOVE OF HEAVEN SPEAK KINDLY • 142 TRISTRAM 2 13
HEAVEN HIS HEAD SINKS BACK UPON THE PILLOW • 145 TRISTRAM 2 77
TRISTRAM FOR THE LOVE OF HEAVEN SPEAK KINDLY • 142 TRISTRAM 2 V 13
HEAVEN KEEP US FROM SUCH FANTASY • • • • 147 TRISTRAM 2 V 130
THAT NECKAN HEAVEN MIGHT GAIN • • • • • 160 NECKAN 40
THAN THOU SHALT HEAVEN BEHOLD • • • • 160 NECKAN 52
THOU MAKST THE HEAVEN THOU HOPST INDEED THY HOME • 169 EAST LONDON 14
NO JUDGE EYES US FROM HEAVEN OUR SIN TO SCAN • 170 BETTER PART 4
FROM SIN WHICH HEAVEN RECORDS NOT WHY FORBEAR • 171 BETTER PART 7
SITS THERE NO JUDGE IN HEAVEN OUR SIN TO SEE • 171 BETTER PART 11
WANDERING IN HEAVEN FAR REMOVED • • • • 181 ISOLATION MARG 27
OUR ORDER HEAVEN-ORDAIND • • • • • 195 FRAG ANTIGONE 21
AH WHOSE HAND THAT DAY THROUGH HEAVEN GUIDED • 210 SELF-DECEPTION 13
BE HEARD FLOATING THROUGH HEAVEN AND FILL AGAIN • 238 PROGRESS 35
WHILE YET UPON THE VERGE OF HEAVEN HE STOOD • 239 REVOLUTIONS 2
FROM THE INTENSE CLEAR STAR-SOWN VAULT OF HEAVEN • 240 SELF-DEPENDENCE 13
DOTH A WHOLE TRACT OF HEAVEN DISCLOSE • • • 242 SUMMER NIGHT 10
BUT IT NEEDS HEAVEN-SENT MOMENTS FOR THIS SKILL • 256 SCHOLAR-GIPSY 50
AND WAITING FOR THE SPARK FROM HEAVEN TO FALL • 258 SCHOLAR-GIPSY 120
THOU WAITEST FOR THE SPARK FROM HEAVEN AND WE • 260 SCHOLAR-GIPSY 171
CAMST THOU FROM HEAVEN O CHILD • • • • 295 HEINES GRAVE 116
FILLD EARTH AND HEAVEN AND CAUGHT AWAY • • • 317 OBERMANN MORE 143
AND WHAT FROM HEAVEN SAW HE • • • • 319 OBERMANN MORE 210
SUN WHO CAREEREST THROUGH THE HEIGHT OF HEAVEN • 349 MEROPE 571
WORSE TERMS THAN MINE THEY HAVE OBTAIND FROM HEAVEN 360 MEROPE 884
NOT UNFAVOURD BY HEAVEN • • • • • • 360 MEROPE 904
BUT THE WIT-BAFFLING WILL AND HAND OF HEAVEN • 363 MEROPE 952
IN THE NORTHERN HEAVEN • • • • • • 393 MEROPE 1676
O HEAVEN-ABANDOND WRETCH THAT ENVIES THEE • • • 397 MEROPE 1773

HEAVEN   (CONTINUED)
DECREES OF HEAVEN . . . .   398 MEROPE   1805
THAT THE FLAME TOWERD ON HIGH TO THE HEAVEN   . . 399 MEROPE   1840
TO HEAVEN AND LAID HIS HAND UPON THE STEER . . .   402 MEROPE   1914
AND MAKE IT STAND INDEED THE WILL OF HEAVEN   404 MEROPE   1999
WITH MUSIC TO HAVE DRAWN THE STARS FROM HEAVEN . .   409 EMPEDOCLES I 1   81
MIND IS THE SPELL WHICH GOVERNS EARTH AND HEAVEN . . 413 EMPEDOCLES I 2   27
HEAVEN IS WITH EARTH AT STRIFE . . . . . .   416 EMPEDOCLES I 2   122
MEN SCOFF AT HEAVEN AND FATE . . . .   426 EMPEDOCLES I 2   418
NOR DOES HEAVEN TOIL THEREAT   EMPEDOCLES I 2   V
AS OF OLD IN THE FIELDS OF HEAVEN . . . .   437 EMPEDOCLES II   278
THE RADIANT REJOICING INTELLIGENT SONS OF HEAVEN . . 437 EMPEDOCLES II   287
AND THUS BENEATH THE CLEAR CALM VAULT OF HEAVEN . .   466 ALARIC AT ROME   103
AFFLICTS GRAVE HEAVEN WITH ITS LONG SENSELESS ROAR   480 HUNGARIAN NAT   5
NO BUT THE WILL OF HEAVEN AND FATES INVINCIBLE POWER   HOMER TRANS   49
MATERIAL GRANDEURS DO IN HEAVEN DECAY . . . .   FRAGMENT 2   4

HEAVENLY
LIKE COMETS ON THE HEAVENLY SOLITUDE . . . . .   6 GEO CRUIKSHANK   7
THE COLUMNS OF THE HEAVENLY PALACES . . . . .   19 CHURCH BROU 3   42
AND YOUR HEAVENLY EYES SHONE THROUGH . . . . .   29 NEW SIRENS   98
LIFES VOYAGE DONE HIS HEAVENLY FRIEND . . . . .   40 HUMAN LIFE   2
MID THE SOULS PLAGUED BY HEAVENLY POWER . . . .   157 SAINT BRANDAN   34
SUPPORT THE FERVOURS OF THE HEAVENLY MORN . . .   172 IMMORTALITY   8
YET SHOW HER ONCE YE HEAVENLY POWERS . . . . .   202 URANIA   17
EYES FROM THE HEAVENLY HEIGHT . . . . . .   216 LORDS MESSENGER   V
HEAVENLY THE FLUSH . . . .   221 BACCHANALIA 2   62
SUCH MULTITUDE OF HEAVENLY STRAINS . . . . .   222 EPILOG LAOCOON   33
TWAS WHEN THE HEAVENLY HOUSE I TROD . . . . .   242 MORALITY   35
DOTH ALL THE HEAVENLY OPENING CLOSE . . . . .   324 OBERMANN MORE   343
IN THE HEAVENLY WILDERNESS . . . .   437 EMPEDOCLES II   291
AND HEAVENLY ODOURS FAIR . . . .   445 WESTMIN ABBEY   37
BRINGER OF HEAVENLY LIGHT A HUMAN HOUR . . . .   447 WESTMIN ABBEY   120

HEAVENS
MAKING THE HEAVEN OF HEAVENS HIS DWELLING-PLACE . .   3 SHAKESPEARE   6
WHAT HEAVENS WHAT EARTH WHAT SUN SHALT THOU DISCERN   43 GIPSY CHILD   44
WHAT HEAVENS WHAT EARTH WHAT SUNS SHALT THOU DISCERN   43 GIPSY CHILD   V 44
HEAVENS AIR IS BETTER THAN THE COLD DEAD GRAVE . .   71 SOHRAB RUSTUM   324
IN HEAVEN AND THOU ART HEAVENS UNCONSCIOUS HAND . .   82 SOHRAB RUSTUM   710
AND THIS IS TRUE AND SUCH A LOSS IS HEAVENS . .   111 BALDER DEAD 2   232
BEFORE THE HEAVENS WERE BUILDED THOU DIDST SLAY . .   121 BALDER DEAD 3   256
THITHER WHEN OER THIS PRESENT EARTH AND HEAVENS . .   128 BALDER DEAD 3   522
THE MARCH THE LEAGUER HEAVENS BLITHE AIR . . .   138 TRISTRAM 1   258
YE HEAVENS WHOSE PURE DARK REGIONS HAVE NO SIGN . .   244 SUMMER NIGHT   78
ELECT HIMSELF HEAVENS DESTINED ARM . . . . .   353 MEROPE   691
CROWND WITH SUCCESS NOT IN MY WAY BUT HEAVENS . .   360 MEROPE   878
OF OCEANS SLEEPING FACE OR HEAVENS UNBROKEN BLUE . . 463 ALARIC AT ROME   36
OF HEAVENS EMBATTLED MYRIADS SWEPT ALONG . . .   473 CROMWELL   44
EARTH AND HEAVENS STAR-SPANGLED LOAD . . . . .   PILLARS UNIVERS   4

HEAVENWARD
AND HEAVENWARD FROM THE FOUNTAIN-BRINK HE SPRANG . . 268 THYRSIS   189

HEAVES
THE WET FLOWERD GRASS HEAVES UP ITS HEAD . . . .   57 RESIGNATION   185
THAT HEAVES ITS WHITE AND BILLOWY VAPOURS UP . .   438 EMPEDOCLES II   309
ALL ETNA HEAVES FIERCELY . . . .   441 EMPEDOCLES II   419

HEAVIEST
WHICH IS THE HEAVIEST OF ALL PLAGUES . . . . .   93 SICK KING BOKH   171
WAS INDEED THE HEAVIEST BURDEN THROWN . . . .   144 TRISTRAM 2   50

HEAVILY
FALLS HEAVILY AWAY WITH LONG-DRAWN ROAR . . . .   40 HUMAN LIFE   21
ROLLD HEAVILY THE LEADEN MIST ASIDE . . . . .   126 BALDER DEAD 3   441
WITH GLOOMING CLOUDS BROODS DARK AND HEAVILY . .   475 CROMWELL   130

HEAVING
ROLL THROUGH THE HEAVING MULTITUDE . . . . .   57 RESIGNATION   157
ON THE FOAMLESS LONG-HEAVING . . . .   192 STRAYED REVEL   203

HEAVY
HEAVY AS DEATH COLD AS THE GRAVE . . . . .   38 STAGIRIUS   12
SLOWLY BEHIND HIS HEAVY TREAD . . . . . .   57 RESIGNATION   184
SLOWLY BEHIND THE HEAVY TREAD . . . . . .   57 RESIGNATION   V 184
AGAINST HIS BREAST HIS HEAVY MAILED HAND . . .   80 SOHRAB RUSTUM   663
THEN WITH A HEAVY GROAN RUSTUM BEWAILD . . .   83 SOHRAB RUSTUM   767
WHITE WITH EYES CLOSED ONLY WHEN HEAVY GASPS . .   86 SOHRAB RUSTUM   849
DEEP HEAVY GASPS QUIVERING THROUGH ALL HIS FRAME . .   86 SOHRAB RUSTUM   850
AND WITH A HEAVY GROAN RUSTUM REPLIED . . .   83 SOHRAB RUSTUM   V 767
HEAVY IN HEART FOR BALDER TO HIS HOUSE . . .   101 BALDER DEAD 1   223
RIDE BACK AND TELL IN HEAVEN THIS HEAVY NEWS . .   124 BALDER DEAD 3   371
WHICH HER HEAVY ROBE DOTH HOLD . . . . . .   131 TRISTRAM 1   29
AND THE GOLDEN BRACELETS HEAVY AND RARE . . .   146 TRISTRAM 2   110
NEEDS MUST I LOSE THEM NEEDS WITH HEAVY HEART . .   264 THYRSIS   38
HEAVY AND SAD FOR HER SONS . . . .   294 HEINES GRAVE   73
HEAVY WITH FRAGRANCE THE BLOND . . . .   296 HEINES GRAVE   135
WHO SHALL TELL MEROPE THIS HEAVY NEWS . . .   359 MEROPE   858
WHAT KAISER DEAD THE HEAVY NEWS . . . . .   458 KAISER DEAD   1

HEBE
        TO THE SIDE OF HEBE   . . . .   399 MEROPE   1842
        ONLY THE LOVED HEBE BEARS   . . . .   431 EMPEDOCLES II   84

HEBREW
        WHILE BY HER BEDSIDE HEBREW RITES HAVE PLACE   . .   168 RACHEL 3   8

HEBRIDES
        HE SAW ON SPRAY-SWEPT HEBRIDES . . . .   156 SAINT BRANDAN   7

HECTOR
        AND HECTOR WAS IN ILIUM FAR BELOW   . . . . . .   236 PALLADIUM   3
        HECTOR AND AJAX WILL BE THERE AGAIN   . . . . . .   236 PALLADIUM   15
        SEE THE WIFE OF HECTOR THAT GREAT PRE-EMINENT CAPTAIN   HOMER TRANS   33
        SLEW HIM FIGHTING IN FRONT OF THE FRAY AND   HOMER TRANS   53
            GLORIFIED HECTOR

HECUBAS
        MOVES ME SO MUCH NOT HECUBAS GRIEF NOR PRIAM   HOMER TRANS   24
            MY FATHERS

HEDGE
        IN THE HEDGE STRAGGLING TO THE STREAM   . . . .   57 RESIGNATION   178
        AND PALE DOG-ROSES IN THE HEDGE   . . . . . .   218 BACCHANALIA 1   12
        TEAR FROM THE RIFLED HEDGE   . . . .   218 BACCHANALIA 1   36
        VAINLY YOU HEDGE HIM FROM THE ASSAULT OF HARM   . .   359 MEROPE   855
        BEHIND HIS CORPSE THEIR HEDGE OF SERRIED SPEARS   . .   381 MEROPE   1308
        STARLINGS SWIRLING FROM THE HEDGE   . . . . . .   456 POOR MATTHIAS   144

HEDGEROWS
        FROM THE OPEN HEATH STILL BY THE HEDGEROWS LAY   . .   151 TRISTRAM 3   51
        FROM THE OPEN WASTE WHITE BY THE HEDGEROWS LAY   . .   TRISTRAM 3   V 51

HEDGES
        WITH WHITENING HEDGES AND UNCRUMPLING FERN   . . . .   265 THYRSIS   74
        TWIXT MYRTLE-HEDGES ALL IN FLOWER   . . . . . .   278 SOUTHERN NIGHT   103
        WITH HEDGES OF THE WILD ROSE   . . . .   399 MEROPE   1821

HEED
        THY COUNSEL AND TO HEED THEE AS THY SON   . . .   62 SOHRAB RUSTUM   39
        HIDEST THY FACE TAKE HEED LEST MEN SHOULD SAY   . .   68 SOHRAB RUSTUM   246
        BUT I AM SICK NOR HEED I THESE . . . .   94 SICK KING BOKH   215
        FOR WELL HE KNEW THE GODS WOULD HEED HIS WORD   . .   97 BALDER DEAD 1   59
        AND BLOW A STRAIN THE WORLD AT LAST SHALL HEED   . .   265 THYRSIS   79
        OUT OF THE HEED OF MORTALS HE IS GONE   . . . .   269 THYRSIS   208
        OUT OF THE HEED OF MORTALS IS HE GONE   . . . .   269 THYRSIS   V 208
        BUT HEED HIM NOT HE WILL NOT MOUNT TO US   . . .   412 EMPEDOCLES I 2   18

HEEDLESS
        ENTERING HEEDLESS KISSD BY THEE   . . . . . .   23 MEMORY-PICTURE   20
        SWEPT OER THE FANCY OF THAT HEEDLESS CHILD   . . . .   473 CROMWELL   52

HEEDS
        BUT NEITHER GOD NOR MORTAL HEEDS MY PAIN   . . . .   116 BALDER DEAD 3   111
        NONE SPEAKS NONE HEEDS AH TURN THY HEAD   . . . .   206 RIVER   4

HEEL
        FOLLOWD HIM LIKE A FAITHFUL HOUND AT HEEL   . . . .   69 SOHRAB RUSTUM   271
        UNDER ITS IRON HEEL FATE FATE ENGAGED   . . . .   82 SOHRAB RUSTUM   714
        AND FENRIS AT HIS HEEL WITH BROKEN CHAIN   . . . .   127 BALDER DEAD 3   477
        SAND RAKED HIS SORES FROM HEEL TO PATE   . . . .   157 SAINT BRANDAN   47

HEIGHT
        JOYOUS AT THE HEIGHT OF PLEASURE   . . . . . .   33 NEW SIRENS   201
        WHO FROM HER FROZEN HEIGHT WITH JEALOUS EYE   . .   99 BALDER DEAD 1   156
        BUT NOW THE SUN HAD PASSD THE HEIGHT OF HEAVEN   . .   118 BALDER DEAD 3   154
        WHEN SHE FORSOOK THE STARRY HEIGHT   . . . . .   181 ISOLATION MARG   22
        AS FROM A HEIGHT WITH RAPT PROPHETIC EYES   . . . .   212 GROWING OLD   17
        EYES FROM THE HEAVENLY HEIGHT   . . . .   216 LORDS MESSENGER   V
        ON THE HEIGHT OF THEIR BOLD-FOLLOWD WAY   . . . .   216 LORDS MESSENGER   V 17
        AND FROM THE THYME UPON THE HEIGHT   . . . . .   218 BACCHANALIA 1   10
        AND EMPIRE AFTER EMPIRE AT THEIR HEIGHT   . . . .   239 REVOLUTIONS   13
        AT THE HEIGHT OF HIS VISION CAN DEEM . . . . . .   253 FUTURE   42
        HERE WAS THINE HEIGHT OF STRENGTH THY GOLDEN PRIME   269 THYRSIS   219
        THEN ON THE HEIGHT COMES THE STORM   . . . . .   289 RUGBY CHAPEL   90
        SUN WHO CAREEREST THROUGH THE HEIGHT OF HEAVEN   . .   349 MEROPE   571
        CUT SHORT THY TRIUMPH SEEMING AT ITS HEIGHT   . . .   395 MEROPE   1742
        WHO SCALE THE CLOUD-CAPT HEIGHT OR SINK TO REST   . .   472 CROMWELL   11
        AT LAST IN AIR FAR OFF DIM ROSE A HEIGHT   . . . .   484 S S LUSITANIA   6

HEIGHTEND
        HEIGHTEND AND MULTIPLIED POWER . . . .   281 HAWORTH CHURCH   29

HEIGHTENING
        SHE NEEDS NOT JUNE FOR BEAUTYS HEIGHTENING   . . . .   263 THYRSIS   20

HEIGHTS
        BE PASSD ON THE PROUD HEIGHTS OF SWAY   . . . .   56 RESIGNATION   149

HEIMDALLS
        OER THE BRIDGE BIFROST WHERE IS HEIMDALLS WATCH   . .   99 BALDER DEAD 1   141

HEIMDALLS   (CONTINUED)
          AND OVER BIFROST WHERE IS HEIMDALLS WATCH . . . .   105 BALDER DEAD 2   22
          OER THE BRIDGE BIFROST WHERE IS HEIMDALLS WATCH . .   119 BALDER DEAD 3   216

HEINE
          HENRI HEINE TIS HERE . . . .   292 HEINES GRAVE   1
          WAST THOU HEINE TO LIE . . . .   293 HEINES GRAVE   16
          HEINE ALAS HE IS YOURS . . . .   293 HEINES GRAVE   47
          HEINE DISTILS FROM THY LIFE . . . .   294 HEINES GRAVE   68
          HEINE THOU CLIMBEST AGAIN . . . .   297 HEINES GRAVE   155
          TAKE LEAVE OF HEINE NOT THUS . . . .   298 HEINES GRAVE   200
          THAT SMILE WAS HEINE FOR ITS EARTHLY HOUR . . .   298 HEINES GRAVE   210
          THAT WAS HEINE AND WE . . . .   298 HEINES GRAVE   212
          OF HEINE HIS STRANGE ALAS . . . .   299 HEINES GRAVE   224

HEINES
          HEINES SPIRIT OUTWORN . . . .   296 HEINES GRAVE   148

HEIR
          FORTUNES NOW LESS FREQUENT HEIR . . . . . .   22 MEMORY-PICTURE   V
          AND TO AN UNSUBSTANTIAL TITLE HEIR . . . . .   335 MEROPE   170
          UPON A THRONE NOT THINE TO GIVE IS HEIR . . . .   336 MEROPE   190
          THAT HE ENJOYD BUT PART BEING HEIR TO ALL . . . . 394 MEROPE   1701

HEIRS
          FROM BANDS OF GREEDY HEIRS BE FREE . . . . . .   249 WISH   2
          ILL-KEPT BY HIS INFIRM HEIRS . . . .   399 MEROPE   1846
          BORN REASONS HEIRS AND OF THAT HERITAGE . . . .   RUDE ORATOR   3

HEIRSHIP
          EXILE ABROAD MORE SAFE THAN HEIRSHIP HERE . . . . 340 MEROPE   337
          OF HEIRSHIP TO HIS KINGDOM FOR MY SON . . . .   366 MEROPE   999
          LIFTED AND THAT UNWISHD-FOR HEIRSHIP VOID . . . . 366 MEROPE   1001
          HEIRSHIP WITH FAIR INTENT AS I BELIEVE . . . .   387 MEROPE   1484

HELA
          AND HELA YIELD TO THIS AND LET HIM GO . . . .   98 BALDER DEAD 1   116
          WHOM HELA WITH AUSTERE CONTROL PRESIDES . . . .   104 BALDER DEAD 1   317
          SAVE ME ALONE AND HELA SOLEMN QUEEN . . . . .   104 BALDER DEAD 1   319
          OF HELA AND SAW NEAR IT BALDER CROWND . . . .   109 BALDER DEAD 2   177
          AND HELA SET THEREON WITH COUNTENANCE STERN . .   110 BALDER DEAD 2   178
          O HELA WHEREFORE SHOULD THE GODS DECLARE . . .   110 BALDER DEAD 2   189
          HELA SUCH AS THOU SAYST THE TERMS SHALL BE . . .   111 BALDER DEAD 2   242
          HE SPAKE AND STRAIGHTWAY HELA ANSWERED HIM . .   111 BALDER DEAD 2   246
          AND HELA SAT THEREON WITH COUNTENANCE STERN . .   110 BALDER DEAD 2   V 178
          BUT HELA INTO NIFLHEIM THOU THREWST . . . .   121 BALDER DEAD 3   276
          COME THEN SINCE HELA HOLDS BY RIGHT HER PREY . .   121 BALDER DEAD 3   288
          HELA AND WIN THE LOVED ONE BACK TO HEAVEN . . .   122 BALDER DEAD 3   294
          BALDER IS DEAD AND HELA HOLDS HER PREY . . . .   123 BALDER DEAD 3   347
          I WEEP HIM NOT LET HELA KEEP HER PREY . . . .   123 BALDER DEAD 3   354
          OF HELA AND HOLD CONVERSE UNDISTURBD . . . .   126 BALDER DEAD 3   436
          LOK TRIUMPHS STILL AND HELA KEEPS HER PREY . . .   126 BALDER DEAD 3   447
          THE IRON FROWN OF HELA IS RELAXD . . . . . .   126 BALDER DEAD 3   463
          I REST THE THRALL OF HELA AND ENDURE . . . .   129 BALDER DEAD 3   545

HELAS
          CAN I WITH HELAS POWER A COMPACT STRIKE . . . .   98 BALDER DEAD 1   109
          AND WEND THEMSELVES TO HELAS GLOOMY REALM . . .   98 BALDER DEAD 1   121
          THERE IS A ROAD WHICH LEADS TO HELAS REALM . . .   99 BALDER DEAD 1   135
          TO THE LOW SHORE OF GHOSTS AND HELAS REALM . . .   99 BALDER DEAD 1   151
          AND HE WILL SEE STRETCH ROUND HIM HELAS REALM . .   100 BALDER DEAD 1   171
          AND BALDER SITTING CROWND AND HELAS THRONE . . .   100 BALDER DEAD 1   175
          TO HELAS KINGDOM TO ASK BALDER BACK . . . . .   102 BALDER DEAD 1   237
          IN THAT DIM WORLD IN HELAS MOULDERING REALM . .   104 BALDER DEAD 1   315
          THERE IS A WAY WHICH LEADS TO HELAS REALM . . .   99 BALDER DEAD 1   V 135
          TO HELAS KINGDOM TO ASK BALDER BACK . . . . .   106 BALDER DEAD 2   46
          BOUND ON THEIR WAY BELOW TO HELAS REALM . . . .   107 BALDER DEAD 2   105
          BELOW THERE TO THE NORTH TOWRD HELAS REALM . . .   108 BALDER DEAD 2   123
          THE SPRING THAT BUBBLES UP BY HELAS THRONE . . .   108 BALDER DEAD 2   131
          HELAS PALE SWARMS AND THERE WAS BALDER BOUND . .   108 BALDER DEAD 2   133
          AND HE BEHELD SPREAD ROUND HIM HELAS REALM . . .   109 BALDER DEAD 2   149
          THESE FLOW BY HELAS THRONE AND NEAR THEIR SPRING . 109 BALDER DEAD 2   155
          AND NOW HAVE CHIEF REGARD IN HELAS REALM . . .   109 BALDER DEAD 2   169
          EVEN HERE THEY SEEK THEE OUT IN HELAS REALM . .   112 BALDER DEAD 2   256
          AND NOW THOU SITTEST CROWND BY HELAS SIDE . . .   112 BALDER DEAD 2   260
          ME SITTING HERE BELOW BY HELAS SIDE . . . . .   112 BALDER DEAD 2   277
          SHOULD MAKE IRRUPTION INTO HELAS REALM . . . .   120 BALDER DEAD 3   242
          I MUST AGAIN BELOW TO HELAS REALM . . . . .   124 BALDER DEAD 3   372
          FAR FROM THE OTHER GHOSTS AND HELAS THRONE . . .   124 BALDER DEAD 3   391
          SITS BALDER STILL IN POMP BY HELAS SIDE . . . .   125 BALDER DEAD 3   429
          HIS PLACE OF STATE REMAINS BY HELAS SIDE . . . . 125 BALDER DEAD 3   432

HELD
          SO THE PALE PERSIANS HELD THEIR BREATH WITH FEAR . . 66 SOHRAB RUSTUM   169
          LISTLESS AND HELD A FALCON ON HIS WRIST . . . . . 67 SOHRAB RUSTUM   200
          WHICH SOHRAB HELD STIFF OUT THE STEEL-SPIKED SPEAR .   75 SOHRAB RUSTUM   492
          BUT SOHRAB SAW HIS THOUGHT AND HELD HIS HANDS . .   82 SOHRAB RUSTUM   706
          WHICH SOHRAB HELD ADVANCD THE STEEL-SPIKED SPEAR . . 75 SOHRAB RUSTUM   V 492
          THEN HERMOD KNEW WHAT LABOUR HELD THE GODS . . .   113 BALDER DEAD 2   307
          THE GODS HELD TALK TOGETHER GROUPD IN KNOTS . .   113 BALDER DEAD 3   1

HELD   (CONTINUED)
```
    I HELD BUT NOW   . . . . . . . . . .   186 STRAYED REVEL        13
    AND DAY AND NIGHT HELD ON INDIGNANTLY      . . . .  262 SCHOLAR-GIPSY       243
    WE BOWD OUR HEAD AND HELD OUR BREATH  . . . . .  270 MEMORIAL VERSES       7
    WE BOWD OUR HEADS AND HELD OUR BREATH     . . .  270 MEMORIAL VERSES  V    7
    THE TWO HELD CONVERSE THEY WROTE    . . . . . .  280 HAWORTH CHURCH       18
    THEY MET HELD CONVERSE THEY WROTE      . . . .  280 HAWORTH CHURCH   V   18
    HELD MEMORIAL BARD  . . . . . . . . . .   281 HAWORTH CHURCH   V   20
    HELD BY THE WORLD WHICH WE    . . . . . . .  314 OBERMANN MORE        70
    AS DEAD WE HELD THEE MOURND FOR THEE AS DEAD   . .  375 MEROPE             1208
    SILENCE AND EXPECTATION HELD US ALL    . . . . .  401 MEROPE             1902
    THERE WAS HELD THE FAMOUS STRIFE    . . . . .  433 EMPEDOCLES II       140
    WITH HELD-IN JOY SWELLING ITS HEART I ONLY   . . .  438 EMPEDOCLES II       316
    MADE VOID AND HELD THE SORROW AND THE JOY   . . . .    RUDE ORATOR           4

HELEN
    YET HELEN HAD AN EQUAL GRACE    . . . . . . .   48 HORATIAN ECHO        28
    HELEN WILL COME UPON THE WALL TO SEE  . . . . . .  236 PALLADIUM            16

HELICON
    YET NOT ON HELICON  . . . . . . . . . .   50 CONSOLATION          23
    HELICON GLASSD IN THE LAKE    . . . . . . . .  229 YOUTH OF NATURE      38
    BUT WHERE HELICON BREAKS DOWN    . . . . . . .  441 EMPEDOCLES II       423

HELL
    AND HEAR THE ROARING OF THE STREAMS OF HELL   . .  100 BALDER DEAD 1       173
    AND HEARD THE THUNDER OF THE STREAMS OF HELL   . .  109 BALDER DEAD 2       151
    OF HELL BEHELD THEM AND THE GHOSTS STOOD DUMB   . .  112 BALDER DEAD 2       281
    FROM HELL AND SHALL I TELL THEE HOW HE SEEMS   . .  113 BALDER DEAD 3         7
    THE JOYLESS PLAINS AND HEARD THE STREAMS OF HELL . .  124 BALDER DEAD 3       380
    IN TWILIGHT ON THE LONELY VERGE OF HELL    . .  124 BALDER DEAD 3       390
    AND HAVE DRAWN UPWARD TO THIS VERGE OF HELL   . .  126 BALDER DEAD 3       439
    AND HAVE DRAWN UPWARDS TO THIS VERGE OF HELL   . .  126 BALDER DEAD 3  V 439
    THE TRAITOR JUDAS OUT OF HELL    . . . . . .  157 SAINT BRANDAN        20
    MATCHD WITH A PALACE IS NOT THIS A HELL    . .  169 WORLDLY PLACE         8
    MADE HUMAN LIFE A HELL    . . . . . . . .  315 OBERMANN MORE        96
    WAKE UP IN HELL FROM THINE UNHALLOWED SLEEP   . .  373 MEROPE             1183
    RAKED FROM THE SWARMING GULF OF SORROWS HELL   . .    RUDE ORATOR          16
    RAKED FROM THE SWARMING GULFS OF SORROWS HELL   . .    RUDE ORATOR      V  16
    THESE THESE ARE PANGS WHICH MAKE THE MIND A HELL . .    LUCRETIUS 2          16

HELM
    ONE THE DUKE IN HELM AND ARMOUR    . . . . .   16 CHURCH BROU 1       107
    ONLY HIS HELM WAS RICH INLAID WITH GOLD   . . . .   69 SOHRAB RUSTUM       267
    THEN SOHRAB WITH HIS SWORD SMOTE RUSTUMS HELM   . .   76 SOHRAB RUSTUM       495
    SPRANG IN A THOUSAND SHIVERS ON THE HELM   . .   76 SOHRAB RUSTUM       512
    HIS DAZZLING CORSLET AND HIS HELM OF GOLD   . . . .  115 BALDER DEAD 3        58

HELMSMAN
    FAINTER AND FAINTER WRECK AND HELMSMAN LOOM   . .  244 SUMMER NIGHT         72

HELMUND
    AND SEEN THE RIVER OF HELMUND AND THE LAKE  . . . .   83 SOHRAB RUSTUM       751
    NOR SLAKED MY THIRST AT THE CLEAR HELMUND STREAM  . .   83 SOHRAB RUSTUM       758

HELP
    COME DOWN AND HELP US RUSTUM OR WE LOSE   . . . .   67 SOHRAB RUSTUM       219
    I MOURN THEE THAT THOU CANST NOT HELP US THEN   . .  127 BALDER DEAD 3    -  482
    WILL HELP HIM TO FORGET HIS CARE    . . . . .  138 TRISTRAM 1          257
    AND MURMURD HELP ME OR I DIE   . . . . . . .  158 SAINT BRANDAN        50
    WILL HAVE BEEN LOST THE HELP IN STRIFE   . . . .  179 FAREWELL             66
    NOR CERTITUDE NOR PEACE NOR HELP FOR PAIN   . .  212 DOVER BEACH          34
    ALAS TO HELP US FORGET   . . . . . . . .  296 HEINES GRAVE        118
    HELP IT TO FILL THAT DEEP DESIRE    . . . . .  323 OBERMANN MORE       313
    THAT END TO HELP ATTAIN   . . . . . . . .  323 OBERMANN MORE       322
    HELP IT TO REACH OUR DEEP DESIRE    . . . . .  323 OBERMANN MORE    V 313
    THAT END TO HELP MEN GAIN    . . . . . . .  323 OBERMANN MORE    V 322
    THIS END TO HELP ATTAIN   . . . . . . . .  323 OBERMANN MORE    V 322
    BEGET A CRUEL TEMPER HELP ME QUELL    . . . .  335 MEROPE              162
    THE BREACH BETWEEN OUR PARTIES HELP ME CLOSE   . .  335 MEROPE              163
    DOUBTLESS THOU RECKONEST ON THE HELP OF FRIENDS   . .  341 MEROPE              356
    NOT HELP OF MEN ALTHOUGH PERHAPS OF GODS   . . .  341 MEROPE              357
    HEAR US AND HELP US SHADE OF OUR KING    . . .  348 MEROPE              541
    AN ARM ALOFT FOR HELP THEN SWEEP BENEATH   . .  358 MEROPE              833
    FOR WHOSE HELP DARE I COUNT ON IF NOT THINE   . .  379 MEROPE             1266
    WHAT HELP WHAT VENGEANCE AT THEIR HANDS HAVE I   . .  381 MEROPE             1318
    WAIT THEN UNTIL SUFFICIENT HELP APPEARS   . . .  384 MEROPE             1397
    THAN I TO HELP RAISE HIS MESSENIAN FRIENDS   . .  388 MEROPE             1497
    ONE ARM ALOFT FOR HELP THEN SWEEP BENEATH   . . .  358 MEROPE           V 833
    I WOULD FAIN STAY AND HELP THEE TEND HIM ONCE   . .  408 EMPEDOCLES I 1       56
    WITH THE SWEET NIGHT TO HELP THY HARMONY   . . .  409 EMPEDOCLES I 1       98
    WOULD I BESTOW TO HELP EMPEDOCLES    . . . . .  409 EMPEDOCLES I 1      102
    KNOW THAT AND HELP THYSELF BUT THINE OWN WORDS   . .  413 EMPEDOCLES I 2       29
    KNOW THAT AND HELP THYSELF BUT THY OWN WORDS   . .  413 EMPEDOCLES I 2  V  29
    LEARN THAT MEN WILL NOT AND GODS CANNOT HELP THY STATE    EMPEDOCLES I 2  V
    AND HELP HIM TO UNBEND HIS TOO TENSE THOUGHT   . .  435 EMPEDOCLES II       222

HELPD
    BEEN HELPD BY SLIPPING YEARS    . . . . . . .  200 PHILOMELA           V
```

HELPERS
    HELPERS AND FRIENDS OF MANKIND • • • • • • • • 291 RUGBY CHAPEL 161
    AND WHAT CAN HELPERS HEAL • • • • • • • • • 320 OBERMANN MORE 234
    AND WHAT ARCADIAN HELPERS BRINGST THOU HERE • • 380 MEROPE 1284
    AND SAY YE HELPERS HEAR EMPEDOCLES • • • • • • 429 EMPEDOCLES II 27

HELPFUL
    CHEERFUL AND HELPFUL AND FIRM • • • • • • • • 290 RUGBY CHAPEL 139

HELPING
    THAT SELF-HELPING SON OF EARTH • • • • • • • • 432 EMPEDOCLES II 103
    THE SELF-HELPING SON OF EARTH • • • • • • • • 432 EMPEDOCLES II V 103
    LITTLE HELPING WOUNDING MUCH • • • • • • • • 457 POOR MATTHIAS 167

HELPLESS
    AND NOT THAT ONE SLIGHT HELPLESS GIRL I HAVE • • 68 SOHRAB RUSTUM 230
    A HELPLESS BABE AMONG THE MOUNTAIN-ROCKS • • • • 81 SOHRAB RUSTUM 681
    SIGHTLESS AND HELPLESS WANDERING WEAK IN HEAVEN • • 98 BALDER DEAD 1 97
    HELPLESS TO BETTER US OR RUIN THEM • • • • • • 111 BALDER DEAD 2 230
    LIKE HELPLESS BIRDS IN THE WARM NEST • • • • • 140 TRISTRAM 1 328
    BUT IN MY HELPLESS CRADLE I • • • • • • • • 249 KENSINGTON GARD 23
    THEN GORGED AND HELPLESS BE ASSAILD AND SLAIN • • 339 MEROPE 298
    A HELPLESS ONE I KNOW IT BUT THE GODS • • • • 366 MEROPE 1023
    MESSENIA TO THOSE HELPLESS BOYS THE LOT • • • • 389 MEROPE 1552
    FOR YEARS THEY SITTING HELPLESS IN THEIR HOME • • 427 EMPEDOCLES I 2 448

HELPLESSLY
    HELPLESSLY GAZING ON THEIR OWN DECLINE • • • • 282 HAWORTH CHURCH V

HELPS
    WHAT HELPS IT NOW THAT BYRON BORE • • • • • • 303 GRANDE CHARTR 133
    ASK WHAT MOST HELPS WHEN KNOWN THOU SON OF ANCHITUS 416 EMPEDOCLES I 2 111

HEM
    HEM ME ROUND EVERYWHERE • • • • • • • • • • 50 CONSOLATION 3
    TO HEM HIS WATERY MARCH AND DAM HIS STREAMS • • 87 SOHRAB RUSTUM 882

HEMMD
    HEMMD BY TWO BANKS OF CLOUD PEERS PALE AND WEAK • • 10 MYCERINUS 57
    IN A LONE SAND-HEMMD • • • • • • • • • • • 51 CONSOLATION 27
    ASOPUS GLEAM ROCK-HEMMD • • • • • • • • • • 197 FRAG ANTIGONE 63

HEMS
    HEMS US ALL IN HE IS NOT BOUND • • • • • • • 58 RESIGNATION 210
    HEMS IN ITS GORGES THE BED • • • • • • • • • 252 FUTURE 11

HENCE
    WHEN I SHALL BE DIVORCED SOME TEN YEARS HENCE • • 37 YOUTHS AGIT 1
    DO WE GO HENCE AND FIND THEY ARE NOT DEAD • • • 44 QUESTION 17
    SHALL WE GO HENCE AND FIND THEY ARE NOT DEAD • • 44 QUESTION V 17
    FAR HENCE IN ASIA • • • • • • • • • • • • 50 CONSOLATION 11
    BUT FAR HENCE SEEK HIM FOR HE IS NOT HERE • • • 63 SOHRAB RUSTUM 78
    TO US FAIN THEREFORE SEND THEE HENCE IN PEACE • • 63 SOHRAB RUSTUM 89
    BUT RUSTUM IS FAR HENCE AND WE STAND HERE • • • 72 SOHRAB RUSTUM 384
    BUT ME THOU MUST BEAR HENCE NOT SEND WITH THEM • • 84 SOHRAB RUSTUM 783
    AND QUIT THE HOST AND BEAR THEE HENCE WITH ME • • 84 SOHRAB RUSTUM 798
    FAR HENCE IN ASGARD IN THE CITY OF GODS • • • 108 BALDER DEAD 2 114
    THE TERMS OF THY RELEASEMENT HENCE TO HEAVEN • • 112 BALDER DEAD 2 252
    AND HIS BLACK BROTHER-BIRD FROM HENCE REPLY • • 127 BALDER DEAD 3 497
    FAR HENCE HER DREAMS ARE FAIR SMOOTH IS HER BROW • • 139 TRISTRAM 1 302
    FAR HENCE HER DREAMS ARE FAIR HER SLEEP IS STILL • • 139 TRISTRAM 1 V 302
    RISE GO HENCE AND SEEK THE PRINCESS ISEULT • • • 145 TRISTRAM 2 V 93
    GO HENCE AND COOL THYSELF AN HOUR • • • • • • 157 SAINT BRANDAN 36
    HENCE HENCE THEY CRY YE DO BUT KEEP MAN BLIND • • 237 PROGRESS 18
    HENCE HENCE THEY CRY YE DO BUT KEEP MAN BLIND • • 237 PROGRESS 18
    FLY HENCE OUR CONTACT FEAR • • • • • • • • 261 SCHOLAR-GIPSY 206
    YEARS HENCE PERHAPS MAY DAWN AN AGE • • • • • 304 GRANDE CHARTR 157
    FLY HENCE POOR WRETCH WHOEER THOU ART • • • • 307 OBERMANN 17
    NOW HE IS DEAD FAR HENCE HE LIES • • • • • • 318 OBERMANN MORE 173
    BUT WHITHER GOST THOU HENCE O QUEEN AWAY • • • 350 MEROPE 597
    DEEP AS THOU CANST FOR HENCE NO SUCCOUR COMES • • 386 MEROPE 1431
    SPEAK I GO HENCE TO OFFER SACRIFICE • • • • • 394 MEROPE 1722
    PAUSANIAS IS FAR HENCE AND THAT IS WELL • • • • 429 EMPEDOCLES II 5

HENCEFORTH
    JOIND WE ARE HENCEFORTH NOR WILL THY PEOPLE • • 144 TRISTRAM 2 57
    VOW TO BEAT HENCEFORTH SIDE BY SIDE • • • • • 203 EUPHROSYNE 8
    BE MAN HENCEFORTH NO MORE A PREY • • • • • • 302 GRANDE CHARTR 105
    UNDUPED OF FANCY HENCEFORTH MAN • • • • • • • 319 OBERMANN MORE 185
    UNLED OF FANCY HENCEFORTH MAN • • • • • • • 319 OBERMANN MORE V 185
    SELF-POISED CLEAR-MINDED HENCEFORTH MAN • • • • 319 OBERMANN MORE V 185
    HENCEFORTH BE HONOURD AS THE DATE OF PEACE • • • 333 MEROPE 116
    AND ME HENCEFORTH SOLE RIVAL WITH HIMSELF • • • 366 MEROPE 1003
    SWEAR BY THE GODS HENCEFORTH TO OBEY ME • • • 371 MEROPE 1133
    HENCEFORTH IF WHAT I URGE DISPLEASE I MAY • • • 395 MEROPE 1727
    AND GRANT HENCEFORTH TO THE MESSENIANS PEACE • • 402 MEROPE 1917
    WHICH HENCEFORTH WE RESIGN • • • • • • • • 423 EMPEDOCLES I 2 345
    HENCEFORTH LOOK ON TO YOU • • • • • • • • • 425 EMPEDOCLES I 2 380
    FOR I MUST HENCEFORTH SPEAK NO MORE WITH MAN • • 429 EMPEDOCLES II 6
    FIND HENCEFORTH ENERGY AND HEART BUT I • • • • 429 EMPEDOCLES II 10

HENCEFORWARD
    ALONE SELF-POISED HENCEFORWARD MAN   • • • • • • • 319 OBERMANN MORE   V 185

HENRI
    HENRI HEINE TIS HERE   • • • • • • • • • 292 HEINES GRAVE   1

HERA
    AND HE WAS GIVEN A VOICE BY THE WHITE-ARMD   HOMER TRANS   46
        GODDESS HERA

HERACLEIDAE
    THE HERACLEIDAE BACK TO PELOPS ISLE   • • • • • 330 MEROPE   7
    OF HERACLES SCARCE HERACLEIDAE LESS • • • • • 337 MEROPE   222
    WHOSE PEOPLE WHEN THE HERACLEIDAE CAME   • • • 338 MEROPE   285
    HERACLEIDAE RECEIVED   • • • • • • • • • 343 MEROPE   421
    OF THE THREE HERACLEIDAE • • • • • • • 345 MEROPE   470

HERACLEIDAN
    HOW CAN YOUR HERACLEIDAN CHIEFS INSPIRE   • • • • 389 MEROPE   1542
    OF THE HERACLEIDAN CONQUERORS AS THOU SAIDST   • • 404 MEROPE   1982

HERACLES
    GREAT HERACLES AND IN THAT PUBLIC PLACE   • • • 330 MEROPE   14
    TO TAKE THE INHERITANCE OF HERACLES   • • • • • 334 MEROPE   125
    ALL KNOW HOW WEAK THE EAGLE HERACLES   • • • • 336 MEROPE   212
    OF HERACLES SCARCE HERACLEIDAE LESS   • • • • • 337 MEROPE   222
    THOUGH FOUND PERVERSE THE BLOOD OF HERACLES   • 337 MEROPE   256
    OF MEN THE LINE OF HERACLES PREFERRD   • • • • 338 MEROPE   269
    FELL THE ELDEST OF THE SONS OF HERACLES   • • • 344 MEROPE   445
    WHICH HE THE SEED OF HERACLES DRAGGD ON   • • • 356 MEROPE   770
    FATAL TO ALL THE RACE OF HERACLES   • • • • • 382 MEROPE   1330
    THE UNDEGENERATE BLOOD OF HERACLES   • • • • 383 MEROPE   1356
    HERACLES GAVE US   • • • • • • • • 398 MEROPE   1813
    FOR THEIR HERACLES-ISSUED PRINCES   • • • • • 400 MEROPE   1853

HERALD
    HIS HERALD TO HIS SIDE AND WENT ABROAD   • • • • 64 SOHRAB RUSTUM   103
    BUT PERAN-WISA WITH HIS HERALD CAME   • • • • • 65 SOHRAB RUSTUM   141
    MAY HERMES HERALD OF THE DEAD CONVEY   • • • • 349 MEROPE   585

HERAS
    BEAR HERAS ANGER   • • • • • • • • • • • 192 STRAYED REVEL   220

HERBAGE
    NOR THE CROPPD HERBAGE SHOOT ANOTHER HEAD   • • • 255 SCHOLAR-GIPSY   5

HERBS
    POSTURES OF RUNES AND HEALING HERBS HE KNEW   • • 101 BALDER DEAD 1   211
    SEE FRAGRANT HERBS ARE FLOWERING THERE   • • • • 301 GRANDE CHARTR   56
    THOSE FRAGRANT HERBS ARE FLOWERING THERE   • • • • 301 GRANDE CHARTR   V 56

HERD
    SHALL DRAW TO SWELL THAT SHOULDERING HERD   • • • 48 HORATIAN ECHO   9

HERDS
    AND CLIP HIS BORDERS SHORT AND DRIVE HIS HERDS   • • 68 SOHRAB RUSTUM   234
    AND CLIP HIS BORDERS ROUND AND DRIVE HIS HERDS   • • 68 SOHRAB RUSTUM   V 234
    TILL THE ROUGH COW-HERDS DRIVE THEM PAST   • • • • 413 EMPEDOCLES I 2   40

HEREAFTER
    HEREAFTER IN THE BLACKEST DEAD OF NIGHT   • • • • 105 BALDER DEAD 2   5
    HATH REACHD IT THERE HEREAFTER SHALL ARISE   • • • • 128 BALDER DEAD 3   520

HEREDITARY
    IN THEIR HEREDITARY WAY   • • • • • • • • • • 56 RESIGNATION   139

HERETOFORE
    TIS IN THE DESERT NOW AND HERETOFORE   • • • • • • 171 DIVINITY   14

HERITAGE
    BEHOLD THY HERITAGE THY FATHERS REALM   • • • • 330 MEROPE   3
    OF THEIR HERITAGE PELOPS ISLE   • • • • • • • 343 MEROPE   416
    IN A KINGS HOUSE THY VICTIMS HERITAGE   • • • • 373 MEROPE   1179
    O HERITAGE OF NELEUS   • • • • • • • • • 399 MEROPE   1845
    BORN REASONS HEIRS AND OF THAT HERITAGE   • • • • RUDE ORATOR   3

HERMES
    MAY HERMES HERALD OF THE DEAD CONVEY   • • • • • • 349 MEROPE   585
    COME HERMES WHO DOST FRIEND THE UNJUSTLY KILLD   • • 367 MEROPE   1058
    IN THE HAND OF HERMES   • • • • • • • • • • 392 MEROPE   1629
    COME HERMES WHO DOST WATCH THE UNJUSTLY KILLD   • • 367 MEROPE   V1058

HERMOD
    FOR SPEED AND HERMOD WAS HIS NAME IN HEAVEN   • • 101 BALDER DEAD 1   221
    NOR YET COULD HERMOD SEE HIS BROTHERS FACE   • • • 101 BALDER DEAD 1   228
    TAKE SLEIPNER HERMOD AND SET FORTH WITH DAWN   • • 102 BALDER DEAD 1   236
    AND HERMOD GAZED INTO THE NIGHT AND SAID   • • • 102 BALDER DEAD 1   240
    SO SPEAKING THE FLEET-FOOTED HERMOD CAME   • • • 102 BALDER DEAD 1   246
    BUT HERMOD THOU TAKE SLEIPNER AND RIDE DOWN   • • 106 BALDER DEAD 2   45
    HERMOD LED SLEIPNER FROM VALHALLA FORTH   • • • • 106 BALDER DEAD 2   71

HERMOD   (CONTINUED)
        BUT HERMOD MOUNTED HIM AND SADLY FARED   • • • •   107 BALDER DEAD 2   78
        AND QUESTIOND HERMOD AS HE CAME AND SAID   • • • •   107 BALDER DEAD 2   100
        AND THE FLEET-FOOTED HERMOD ANSWERD HER   • • • •   108 BALDER DEAD 2   111
        O DAMSEL HERMOD AM I CALLD THE SON   • • • •   108 BALDER DEAD 2   112
        O HERMOD RARELY DO THE FEET OF GODS   • • • •   108 BALDER DEAD 2   119
        AND HERMOD GREETED HER AND GALLOPD BY   • • • •   108 BALDER DEAD 2   136
        BUT NORTHWARD HERMOD RODE THE WAY BELOW   • • • •   108 BALDER DEAD 2   138
        SO AROUND HERMOD SWARMD THE TWITTERING GHOSTS • • •   109 BALDER DEAD 2   163
        SHE SPAKE BUT DOWN OFF SLEIPNER HERMOD SPRANG • • •   110 BALDER DEAD 2   186
        HERMOD FOR HE THOU ART THOU SON OF HEAVEN   • • • •   110 BALDER DEAD 2   202
        SHE SPAKE AND HERMOD ANSWERD HER AND SAID   • • • •   111 BALDER DEAD 2   241
        HERMOD GREET BALDER IF THOU WILT AND HOLD   • • • •   111 BALDER DEAD 2   247
        AND STRAIGHT TO BALDER HERMOD TURND AND SPAKE • • •   111 BALDER DEAD 2   249
        HERMOD THE NIMBLE GILD ME NOT MY DEATH   • • • •   112 BALDER DEAD 2   264
        BUT HERMOD TOOK THE RING AND YET ONCE MORE • • • •   112 BALDER DEAD 2   282
        SO HERMOD OER THE FOG BETWEEN SAW HEAVEN   • • • •   113 BALDER DEAD 2   301
        AND HERMOD SAW THE TOWERS OF ASGARD RISE   • • • •   113 BALDER DEAD 2   304
        THEN HERMOD KNEW WHAT LABOUR HELD THE GODS • • • •   113 BALDER DEAD 2   307
        AND HERMOD CAME DOWN TOWRDS THEM FROM THE GATE • •   113 BALDER DEAD 3   3
        SEE HERE IS HERMOD WHO COMES SINGLE BACK   • • • •   113 BALDER DEAD 3   6
        SO HERMOD COMES TO-DAY UNFOLLOWD HOME   • • • •   114 BALDER DEAD 3   19
        AND HERMOD CAME AND LEAPT FROM SLEIPNER DOWN • • •   114 BALDER DEAD 3   33
        YE GODS THE TERMS YE KNOW WHICH HERMOD BROUGHT • •   120 BALDER DEAD 3   225
        BUT HERMOD RODE WITH NIORD WHOM HE TOOK   • • • •   122 BALDER DEAD 3   320
        SHE SPAKE BUT HERMOD ANSWERD HER AND SAID   • • • •   123 BALDER DEAD 3   345
        MOCKING AND HERMOD KNEW THEIR TOIL WAS VAIN • • •   123 BALDER DEAD 3   356
        THEN SAD AT HEART TO NIORD HERMOD SPAKE   • • • •   124 BALDER DEAD 3   369
        BUT NORTHWARD HERMOD RODE THE WAY BELOW   • • • •   124 BALDER DEAD 3   374
        AND ONCE MORE HERMOD SAW AROUND HIM SPREAD • • • •   124 BALDER DEAD 3   379
        AND HERMOD LOOKD AND KNEW HIS BROTHERS GHOST • • •   124 BALDER DEAD 3   385
        HERMOD THE NIMBLE DOST THOU STILL PURSUE   • • • •   124 BALDER DEAD 3   395
        AND NOT TO OFFEND THEE HERMOD NOR TO FORCE • • • •   125 BALDER DEAD 3   413
        BUT HERMOD STAYD HIM WITH MILD WORDS AND SAID • • •   125 BALDER DEAD 3   422
        AND HERMOD STRAIGHT PERCEIVED THEM WHO THEY WERE • • 126 BALDER DEAD 3   444
        YET MOURN NOT FOR ME HERMOD WHEN THOU SITTST • • •   126 BALDER DEAD 3   456
        AND THE FLEET-FOOTED HERMOD MADE REPLY   • • • •   126 BALDER DEAD 3   468
        MOURN NOT FOR ME MOURN HERMOD FOR THE GODS • • • •   127 BALDER DEAD 3   484
        OF CARNAGE AND FIND HERMOD IN YOUR LIFE   • • • •   127 BALDER DEAD 3   504
        HE SPAKE AND THE FLEET HERMOD THUS REPLIED • • • •   128 BALDER DEAD 3   514
        O HERMOD PRAY THAT THOU MAYST JOIN US THEN • • • •   129 BALDER DEAD 3   543
        BUT HERMOD STOOD BESIDE HIS DROOPING HORSE • • • •   129 BALDER DEAD 3   554
        SO HERMOD GAZED AND YEARND TO JOIN HIS KIN • • • •   129 BALDER DEAD 3   565

HERMODS
        SO HODER BRUSHD BY HERMODS SIDE AND SAID   • • • •   101 BALDER DEAD 1   235
        YET DOCILE NOW HE STOOD AT HERMODS SIDE   • • • •   107 BALDER DEAD 2   75

HERO
        TO GOD OR HERO BUT THOU KEPTEST BACK   • • • •   116 BALDER DEAD 3   85
        NO GOD BUT OF THE HERO-TROOP THE CHIEF   • • • •   117 BALDER DEAD 3   125
        WHEN THE SHIRT-WRAPT POISON-BLISTERD HERO   • • • •   399 MEROPE   1832
        THE LABOUR-RELEASED HERO   • • • •   399 MEROPE   1844
        THAT HOLDS THE ASHES OF YOUR HERO-DEAD   • • • •   467 ALARIC AT ROME   136

HEROES
        GODS ARE WE BARDS SAINTS HEROES IF WE WILL • • • •   4 EMERSONS ESSAYS   13
        AND ALL THE GODS AND ALL THE HEROES CAME   • • • •   95 BALDER DEAD 1   9
        FROM AROUND BALDER ALL THE HEROES WENT   • • • •   97 BALDER DEAD 1   62
        WHICH GODS AND HEROES LEAD IN FEAST AND FRAY • • •   98 BALDER DEAD 1   123
        TO WAKE THE GODS AND HEROES TO THEIR TASKS • • • •   105 BALDER DEAD 2   9
        AND ALL THE GODS AND ALL THE HEROES WOKE   • • • •   105 BALDER DEAD 2   10
        AND FROM THEIR BEDS THE HEROES ROSE AND DONND • • •   105 BALDER DEAD 2   11
        INTO THE TILT-YARD WHERE THE HEROES FOUGHT • • • •   105 BALDER DEAD 2   30
        AND HEROES WHERE THEY LIVE IN LIGHT AND JOY • • •   110 BALDER DEAD 2   199
        AMONG THE GODS AND HEROES HERE IN HEAVEN   • • • •   115 BALDER DEAD 3   80
        LAST FROM AMONG THE HEROES ONE CAME NEAR   • • • •   117 BALDER DEAD 3   124
        SO REGNER SPAKE AND ALL THE HEROES GROAND   • • • •   117 BALDER DEAD 3   153
        BUT WHEN THE GODS AND HEROES HEARD THEY BROUGHT • •   118 BALDER DEAD 3   160
        OF GODS AND HEROES   • • • • • • • • • 189 STRAYED REVEL   124
        THEY SEE THE HEROES   • • • • • • • • • 192 STRAYED REVEL   201
        THEY SEE THE HEROES   • • • • • • • • • 193 STRAYED REVEL   254
        AND OF THE LIFE WHICH HEROES LEAD   • • • • 414 EMPEDOCLES I 2   73
        AND OF THE LIFE THAT HEROES LEAD   • • • • 414 EMPEDOCLES I 2   V 73

HEROIC
        TO A MUCH FEEBLER WIGHT THE HEROIC MAN   • • • •   198 FRAG ANTIGONE   96
        FERVENT HEROIC AND GOOD   • • • • • • • • • 291 RUGBY CHAPEL   160
        AND TEMPER OF HEROIC MOULD   • • • • • • • • • 450 GEISTS GRAVE   19
        EARTHS OLD HEROIC FORMS IN PEACEFUL SLUMBERS DEEP   464 ALARIC AT ROME   60

HEROICALLY
        PAIN HEROICALLY BORNE   • • • • • • • • • • 454 POOR MATTHIAS   64

HEROISM
        LIES ANY HOPE OF HEROISM MORE   • • • • • • • • 480 HUNGARIAN NAT   8

HEROS
        TO-DAY A HEROS BANNER IS UNFURLD   • • • • • •   3 EMERSONS ESSAYS   4

HESITATE
 WHO HESITATE AND FALTER LIFE AWAY • • • • • • 260 SCHOLAR-GIPSY 178

HEST
 WHO IS IT UTTERS THROUGH THE DARK HIS HEST • • • • 102 BALDER DEAD 1 241
 HOWBEIT I WILL SEE AND DO HIS HEST • • • • • • 102 BALDER DEAD 1 244
 THAT DELPHIC HEST TO RETURN • • • • • • • 343 MEROPE 422
 A MOTHERS MURDER NEEDED HEST DIVINE • • • • • 385 MEROPE 1402
 HE HAD A HEST AT LEAST AND THOU HAST NONE • • • • 385 MEROPE 1403

HEW
 AND HEW OPPOSERS DOWN • • • • • • • • • 352 MEROPE V 659

HEWING
 OF HEWING AXES CRASHING TREES SUCH BLOWS • • • • 75 SOHRAB RUSTUM 478

HEWN
 AND ALL DAY LONG THEY THERE ARE HACKD AND HEWN • • 105 BALDER DEAD 2 15
 TOPPD WITH ROUGH-HEWN • • • • • • • • • 191 STRAYED REVEL 178

HID
 WHO HID SUCH IMPORT IN AN INFANTS GLOOM • • • • 41 GIPSY CHILD 2
 SOHRAB MEN CALL HIM BUT HIS BIRTH IS HID • • • • 67 SOHRAB RUSTUM 214
 I HID THE CAN BEHIND THE DOOR • • • • • • • 90 SICK KING BOKH 72
 ON THOSE WALLS SUBTERRANEAN WHERE SHE HID • • • 172 GOOD SHEPHERD 11
 NATURE IS HID IN THEIR GRAVE • • • • • • • 232 YOUTH OF NATURE 128
 MUSICAL WATER HALF-HID • • • • • • • • 297 HEINES GRAVE 161
 AND PASTORAL HUTS I HID MY HEAD • • • • • • 321 OBERMANN MORE 251
 MORE THAN ALL SECRETS HID THE WAY IT KEEPS • • • 352 MEROPE 631
 HID THE BABE HID ARCAS • • • • • • • • 391 MEROPE 1614
 HID THE BABE HID ARCAS • • • • • • • • 391 MEROPE 1614
 WHAT ONCE-FAMED WRETCH HE THERE DID ESPY HID • • 396 MEROPE 1754
 WHICH HID ULYSSES WAVED ITSELF AND SAID • • • • 484 S S LUSITANIA 2

HIDDEN
 GLIDING HALF HIDDEN THROUGH THE DUSKY STEMS • • 11 MYCERINUS 104
 TO ASGARD AND DECLARST THIS HIDDEN WAY • • • 100 BALDER DEAD 1 190
 THESE TERMS AND I SUSPECT SOME HIDDEN FRAUD • • 120 BALDER DEAD 3 235
 RADIANT ADORND OUTSIDE A HIDDEN GROUND • • • 166 AUSTERITY POET 13
 DEEP IN OUR HIDDEN HEART • • • • • • • 213 GROWING OLD 28
 OUR HIDDEN SELF AND WHAT WE SAY AND DO • • • 247 BURIED LIFE 65
 AND ONLY IN THE HIDDEN BROOKSIDE GLEAM • • • • 266 THYRSIS 119

HIDDEST
 HIM WHOM THOU HIDDEST WHEN THY HUSBAND FELL • • 334 MEROPE 145

HIDDST
 WHICH TELLS US HOW THOU HIDDST THY HEAD • • • • 304 GRANDE CHARTR 147

HIDE
 AND HIDE IT NOT BUT SAY RUSTUM IS HERE • • • • 71 SOHRAB RUSTUM 350
 TO HIDE THEIR SHAMEFUL MEMORY FROM MEN • • • 109 BALDER DEAD 2 175
 AND THOUGH THE BED-CLOTHES HIDE HER FACE • • • 147 TRISTRAM 2 136
 AND THOUGH THE CURTAINS HIDE HER FACE • • • • 147 TRISTRAM 2 V 136
 OH HIDE ME IN YOUR GLOOM PROFOUND • • • 302 GRANDE CHARTR 91
 SEND US THE YOUTH WHOM YE HIDE • • • • • • 342 MEROPE 393
 POSEIDON TO THE SHEPHERD-BOYS TO HIDE • • • • 355 MEROPE 737
 O HONOURD FATHER HIDE THEE IN THY GRAVE • • • 386 MEROPE 1430
 I HIDE NOT EVEN THIS THE REVERENCE DEEP • • • 387 MEROPE 1474
 THERE IN UNVOICED OBLIVION HIDE THY NAME • • • 395 MEROPE V1751
 BUT HIDE THEE IN THE ROCKS A GREAT WAY DOWN • • 409 EMPEDOCLES I 1 96
 RECEIVE ME HIDE ME QUENCH ME TAKE ME HOME • • • 429 EMPEDOCLES II 36
 SWEPT OFF THE WITHERED LEAVES THAT HIDE THE NAKED TOMB 469 ALARIC AT ROME 192
 HIDE HIS TORN HEAD BENEATH HIS SUNLESS CAVE • • 472 CROMWELL 24

HIDEOUS
 ALL WHICH MAKES DEATH A HIDEOUS SHOW • • • • • 250 WISH 16
 ALL THAT MAKES DEATH A HIDEOUS SHOW • • • • • 250 WISH V 16
 HIDEOUS AND ARID AND VILE • • • • • • • 290 RUGBY CHAPEL 158

HIDES
 BUT HIDES IF GODS GODS CARELESS OF OUR DOOM • • 10 MYCERINUS 54
 I KNOW THE WOOD WHICH HIDES THE DAFFODIL • • • 266 THYRSIS 105
 THE GROUND WHICH HIDES THEE NOW BUT FOUR • • • 449 GEISTS GRAVE 2

HIDEST
 HIDEST THY FACE TAKE HEED LEST MEN SHOULD SAY • • 68 SOHRAB RUSTUM 246

HIDING
 WHETHER A NATURAL OBSCURENESS HIDING • • • • • 352 MEROPE 641
 IN HER HIDING-PLACE OF THE THICKETS • • • • • 392 MEROPE 1632

HIE
 UP THE CREEKS WE WILL HIE • • • • • • • • 165 FORSAKEN MERM 133

HIED
 PASSD OPPOSITE SHE TOUCHD HER GIRL WHO HIED • • 170 WEST LONDON 6

HIES
 ALL CHANGES FAST AND HIES ALONG • • • • • • 225 EPILOG LAOCOON 124

HIES   (CONTINUED)
        HIES AH FROM WHENCE WHAT NATIVE GROUND   • • • •   225 EPILOG LAOCOON   125

HIGH
        TOO GREAT FOR HASTE TOO HIGH FOR RIVALRY   • • • •   1 QUIET WORK   8
        IS ON ALL SIDES OERSHADOWD BY THE HIGH   • • • •   7 REP FRIEND CONT   6
        I LOOKD FOR LIFE MORE LASTING RULE MORE HIGH   • •   9 MYCERINUS   17
        HERE CAME THE KING HOLDING HIGH FEAST AT MORN • •   11 MYCERINUS   92
        STANDS THE CHURCH ON HIGH   • • • • • • •   16 CHURCH BROU 2   6
        IN YOUR HIGH CHURCH MID THE STILL MOUNTAIN-AIR • •   17 CHURCH BROU 3   2
        THE GAZING UP MID THE DIM PILLARS HIGH   • • • •   18 CHURCH BROU 3   38
        THEN GAZING UP THROUGH THE DIM PILLARS HIGH   • •   18 CHURCH BROU 3   V 38
        AND FROM SOME SWARDED SHELF HIGH UP THERE CAME • •   25 DREAM   11
        FOILING HER HIGH EMPRISE   • • • • • • • • •   38 STAGIRIUS   20
        OF HER HIGH DEVOTION   • • • • • • • • •   39 STAGIRIUS   25
        FOILING HER HIGH EMPRIZE   • • • • • • • • •   38 STAGIRIUS   V 20
        HIGH AS THY LIFE BE RISEN TIS FROM THESE   46 IN UTRUMQUE PAR   V 41
        HIGH ON A BANK OUR LEADER STANDS   • • • • •   53 RESIGNATION   44
        FROM SOME HIGH STATION HE LOOKS DOWN   • • • •   57 RESIGNATION   164
        THE CUCKOO LOUD ON SOME HIGH LAWN   • • • • •   57 RESIGNATION   176
        WHEN THE SUN MELTS THE SNOWS IN HIGH PAMERE   •   61 SOHRAB RUSTUM   15
        CROSSING SO HIGH THAT AS THEY MOUNT THEY PASS   66 SOHRAB RUSTUM   163
        JUST PITCHD THE HIGH PAVILION IN THE MIDST   •   67 SOHRAB RUSTUM   193
        HYPHASIS OR HYDASPES WHEN HIGH UP   • • • •   73 SOHRAB RUSTUM   412
        GLARED AND HE SHOOK ON HIGH HIS MENACING SPEAR •   76 SOHRAB RUSTUM   515
        WHEN THOU SHALT SAIL IN A HIGH-MASTED SHIP • •   85 SOHRAB RUSTUM   831
        AS THOSE BLACK GRANITE PILLARS ONCE HIGH-REARD •   86 SOHRAB RUSTUM   860
        IN HIS HIGH MOUNTAIN-CRADLE IN PAMERE   • • •   87 SOHRAB RUSTUM   887
        WINDING SO HIGH THAT AS THEY MOUNT THEY PASS   66 SOHRAB RUSTUM   V 163
        NEW PITCHD THE HIGH PAVILION IN THE MIDST   • •   67 SOHRAB RUSTUM   V 193
        WHO LOITERS BY THE HIGH-HEAPD BOOTHS   • • • •   93 SICK KING BOKH   191
        AND ON THE DECK BUILD HIGH A FUNERAL-PILE   • •   96 BALDER DEAD 1   42
        FROM THE HIGH MOORS BEHIND AND MEETS THE SEA   •   97 BALDER DEAD 1   83
        ON FREAS HEARTH FEED HIGH THE SACRED FIRE   • •   97 BALDER DEAD 1   90
        HIGH OVER ASGARD TO LIGHT HOME THE KING   • • •   102 BALDER DEAD 1   257
        OF ODIN AND MY HIGH-ROOFD HOUSE IS BUILT   • •   108 BALDER DEAD 2   113
        FOR HAUGHTY SPIRITS AND HIGH WRATHS ARE RIFE   •   115 BALDER DEAD 3   79
        BUT FAINTER AS THE STARS ROSE HIGH IT FLARED   119 BALDER DEAD 3   201
        BUT FAINTER AS THE STARS ROSE HIGH IT BURND   119 BALDER DEAD 3   V 201
        HIGH ABOVE THE SOUNDING SEA   • • • • • • •   134 TRISTRAM 1   135
        AND UP AS HIGH AS WHERE THEY STOOD TO LOOK   • •   155 TRISTRAM 3   188
        BY HIGH PERMISSION I AM HERE   • • • • • •   157 SAINT BRANDAN   24
        AND HIGH ROCKS THROW MILDLY   • • • • • • •   165 FORSAKEN MERM   130
        HATH MAN NO SECOND LIFE PITCH THIS ONE HIGH   •   171 BETTER PART   10
        WHERE THE HIGH WOODS STRIP SADLY   • • • • •   175 PARTING   7
        ON THY HIGH MOUNTAIN-PLATFORMS   • • • • • •   177 PARTING   85
        THE ROCKY BANKS THE TERRACE HIGH   • • • • •   183 TERRACE BERNE   3
        HIGH ON A JUTTING ROCK IN THE RED STREAM   • •   192 STRAYED REVEL   230
        NOR THOUGH ENTHRONED TOO HIGH   • • • • • •   197 FRAG ANTIGONE   80
        LONE DAULIS AND THE HIGH CEPHISSIAN VALE   • •   201 PHILOMELA   27
        OF THE HIGH ALPS TO WHICH I GO   • • • • • •   207 ON THE RHINE   4
        AT THEIR RETURN UP THE HIGH STRAND   • • • •   211 DOVER BEACH   11
        WAS THE PALLADIUM HIGH MID ROCK AND WOOD   • •   236 PALLADIUM   2
        STILL DOTH THE SOUL FROM ITS LONE FASTNESS HIGH   236 PALLADIUM   21
        HOW HIGH A LOT TO FILL   • • • • • • • • •   244 SUMMER NIGHT   V 91
        IN THIS HIGH FIELDS DARK CORNER WHERE HE LEAVES   255 SCHOLAR-GIPSY   12
        SCREEND IS THIS NOOK OER THE HIGH HALF-REAPD FIELD 255 SCHOLAR-GIPSY   21
        SCREEND IN THIS NOOK OER THE HIGH HALF-REAPD FIELD 255 SCHOLAR-GIPSY   V 21
        PAST THE HIGH WOOD TO WHERE THE ELM-TREE CROWNS • 263 THYRSIS   12
        SOON WILL THE HIGH MIDSUMMER POMPS COME ON   • •   264 THYRSIS   62
        HIGH TOWERD THE SPIKES OF PURPLE ORCHISES   • •   266 THYRSIS   115
        AND HIGH THE MOUNTAIN-TOPS IN CLOUDY AIR   • •   267 THYRSIS   143
        THE WEST UNFLUSHES THE HIGH STARS GROW BRIGHT   267 THYRSIS   163
        IN HEART HIGH-SOULD   • • • • • • • • • • •   279 SOUTHERN NIGHT   124
        IN A CHURCHYARD HIGH MID THE MOORS   • • • •   282 HAWORTH CHURCH   52
        OF RAVENNA PINES FOR A HIGH   • • • • • •   294 HEINES GRAVE   61
        RIVERS AND HIGH-ROOFD TOWNS   • • • • • • •   296 HEINES GRAVE   138
        HIGH IN THE VALLEY WET AND DREAR   • • • •   299 GRANDE CHARTR   17
        SHOWD ME THE HIGH WHITE STAR OF TRUTH   • • •   301 GRANDE CHARTR   69
        IN THE HIGH ALTARS DEPTH DIVINE   • • • • •   306 GRANDE CHARTR   202
        OF THE HIGH-PASTURING KINE   • • • • • • •   307 OBERMANN   32
        BY SOME HIGH CHALET-DOOR AND SEEN   • • • •   310 OBERMANN   115
        BLOCKS OF THE PAST LIKE ICEBERGS HIGH   • • •   319 OBERMANN MORE   211
        HIGH IN THE VALAIS-DEPTH PROFOUND   • • • •   324 OBERMANN MORE   347
        ON THE HIGH SEA-BANK IN THE SIGHT   • • • •   345 MEROPE   482
        HIM IF HIGH-RULING ZEUS   • • • • • • • •   347 MEROPE   534
        THERE ON A HIGH GREEN SPUR WHICH BATHES ITS POINT 356 MEROPE   751
        AN OPEN GLADE NOW HE WAS HIGH ALOFT   • • • •   357 MEROPE   802
        OF HIGH CYLLENE   • • • • • • • • • •   392 MEROPE   1624
        THAT THE FLAME TOWERD ON HIGH TO THE HEAVEN   •   399 MEROPE   1840
        O TOWN HIGH STENYCLAROS   • • • • • • • •   399 MEROPE   1850
        IN THE HIGH UNFREQUENTED MOUNTAIN-SPOTS   • •   409 EMPEDOCLES I 1   93
        HE IS TOO SCORNFUL TOO HIGH-WROUGHT TOO BITTER   411 EMPEDOCLES I 1   149
        TO THE HIGH MOUNTAIN-PASTURES AND TO STAY   • •   413 EMPEDOCLES I 2   39
        OF ALL THE WOODY HIGH WELL-WATERD DELLS   • •   414 EMPEDOCLES I 2   42
        SHALL WE JUDGE WHAT FOR MAN IS NOT HIGH BLISS OR IS 425 EMPEDOCLES I 2 V 396
        MOUNTING WESTWARD HIGH AND HIGHER   • • • •   433 EMPEDOCLES II   139
        SHONE OFT SO HIGH A LIGHT   • • • • • • •   446 WESTMIN ABBEY   82
        AND BORNE TO LIGHT AND RIGHT HIS WITNESS HIGH   448 WESTMIN ABBEY   144
        THERE A BIRD HIGH-COLOURED FAT   • • • • •   457 POOR MATTHIAS   188

HIGH (CONTINUED)
YES THERE ARE STORIES REGISTERED ON HIGH • • • 462 ALARIC AT ROME 13
FAIN WOULD WE DEEM THAT THOU HAST RISEN SO HIGH • • 463 ALARIC AT ROME 31
AS TOWERED ON HIGH ABOVE THEIR MOONLIT ROAD • • 466 ALARIC AT ROME 113
HIGH FATE IS THEIRS YE SLEEPLESS WAVES WHOSE EAR • • 471 CROMWELL 1
HIGH FATE IS THEIRS WHO WHERE THE SILENT SKY • • 472 CROMWELL 9
YET ALL HIGH SOUNDS THAT MOUNTAIN CHILDREN HEAR • • 472 CROMWELL 27
HIGH THOUGHTS WERE HIS WHEN BY THE GLEAMING FLOOD • 473 CROMWELL 65
HIGH THOUGHTS WERE HIS BUT MEMORYS GLANCE THE WHILE • 474 CROMWELL 69
THAT DAY OF BOUNDLESS HOPE AND PROMISE HIGH • • 478 CROMWELL 211

HIGHER
RISES HIGHER DAY BY DAY • • • • • • • • • • 15 CHURCH BROU 1 88
WHEN THE SOUL MOUNTING HIGHER • • • • • • • • 38 STAGIRIUS 16
WHEN THE SOUL RISING HIGHER TO GOD COMES NO NIGHER • 38 STAGIRIUS V 14
AND IN THE MIDST ONE HIGHER ODINS THRONE • • • • 106 BALDER DEAD 2 38
CURLING AND DARTING HIGHER UNTIL THEY LICKD • • 119 BALDER DEAD 3 189
STRIKE LEFTWARD CRIES OUR GUIDE AND HIGHER • • • • 300 GRANDE CHARTR 19
MOUNTING WESTWARD HIGH AND HIGHER • • • • • 433 EMPEDOCLES II 139
NO LINEAGE HIGHER • • • • • • • • • • • 459 KAISER DEAD 22
NEW DREAMS OF WIDE DOMINION MIGHTIER HIGHER • • 469 ALARIC AT ROME 175

HIGHEST
AND THOU WHOSE WIT TO HIGHEST HEAVEN DID GO • • • 3 SHAKESPEARE V 9
OF BALDER ON THE HIGHEST TOP THEY LAID • • • • 118 BALDER DEAD 3 163
AH WHERE THE SPIRIT ITS HIGHEST LIFE HATH LED • • 167 RACHEL 1 12
AND ON THE HIGHEST PINES BUT FARTHER DOWN • • • • 406 EMPEDOCLES I 1 11
AND ON THE HIGHEST PINES BUT FURTHER DOWN • • • • 406 EMPEDOCLES I 1 V 11

HIGHLAND
LETS FROM HIS SHAGGY HIGHLAND PATE • • • • • • 461 KAISER DEAD 77

HIGHLANDS
TO THE PHRYGIAN HIGHLANDS CAME • • • • • • • 433 EMPEDOCLES II 132

HIGHWAY
THE TOWN THE HIGHWAY AND THE PLAIN • • • • • • 54 RESIGNATION 79

HILL
AND TMOLUS HILL AND SMYRNA BAY THOUGH BLIND • • 2 TO A FRIEND 4
AND TMOLUS HILL AND SMYRNAS BAY THOUGH BLIND • • 2 TO A FRIEND V 4
OUT-TOPPING KNOWLEDGE FOR THE LOFTIEST HILL • • 2 SHAKESPEARE 3
OUT-TOPPING KNOWLEDGE SO SOME SOVRAN HILL • • • 2 SHAKESPEARE V 3
OF OPEN HILL-SWARD FRESH AND GREEN • • • • 16 CHURCH BROU 2 13
OF SHAVEN HILL-SWARD TRIM AND GREEN • • • • 16 CHURCH BROU 2 V 13
LO YON ORIENT HILL IN FLAMES • • • • • • 35 NEW SIRENS 260
EMERGING ON THE GREEN HILL-SIDE • • • • • 54 RESIGNATION 59
OVER THE SUMMIT OF THE HILL • • • • • • 54 RESIGNATION 63
THE SOLEMN WASTES OF HEATHY HILL • • • • 55 RESIGNATION 96
LOW WOODY HILL WITH GRACIOUS BOUND • • • • 57 RESIGNATION 174
UPON THE CRAGGY ISLE OF A HILL-LAKE • • • • 78 SOHRAB RUSTUM 558
UPON A HILL ON THE RIGHT HAND • • • • • 94 SICK KING BOKH 222
BUT FROM THE HILL OF LIDSKIALF ODIN ROSE • • 102 BALDER DEAD 1 253
DWELLS ON LOUD TYNTAGELS HILL • • • • • 134 TRISTRAM 1 134
TYNTAGEL ON ITS SURGE-BEAT HILL • • • • • 136 TRISTRAM 1 177
DWELLS ON PROUD TYNTAGELS HILL • • • • • 134 TRISTRAM 1 V 134
SITS ON PROUD TYNTAGELS HILL • • • • • 134 TRISTRAM 1 V 134
TO THE LITTLE GREY CHURCH ON THE WINDY HILL • • 163 FORSAKEN MERM 71
AT THE CHURCH ON THE HILL-SIDE • • • • • • 165 FORSAKEN MERM 138
WHO CROSS TO THE HILL-SIDE • • • • • • • 175 PARTING 5
TO THE CLEAR WANING HILL-SIDE • • • • • • 176 PARTING 45
ON YONDER HILL • • • • • • • • • • • 186 STRAYED REVEL 39
THE LIQUID SKY ABOVE THE HILL • • • • • • 218 BACCHANALIA 1 18
LIKE STARS OVER THE BOUNDING HILL • • • • • 220 BACCHANALIA 2 27
GO FOR THEY CALL YOU SHEPHERD FROM THE HILL • • 255 SCHOLAR-GIPSY 1
AND THOU HAST CLIMBD THE HILL • • • • • • 258 SCHOLAR-GIPSY 126
THE HILL BEHIND WHOSE RIDGE THE SUNSET FLAMES • • 263 THYRSIS 13
IN THE OLD HAUNT AND FIND OUR TREE-TOPPD HILL • • 265 THYRSIS 103
BUT MANY A DINGLE ON THE LOVED HILL-SIDE • • • 266 THYRSIS 112
OF QUIET LOOK ADOWN THE DUSK HILL-SIDE • • • 267 THYRSIS 152
DOST THOU ASK PROOF OUR TREE YET CROWNS THE HILL • 269 THYRSIS 239
OUR SCHOLAR TRAVELS YET THE LOVED HILL-SIDE • • 269 THYRSIS 240
STANDS ON THE CREST OF THE HILL • • • • • 283 HAWORTH CHURCH 63
LONG ON THE GREY HILL-SIDE • • • • • • • 297 HEINES GRAVE 165
DOWN OVER HILL AND WOOD • • • • • • • • 314 OBERMANN MORE 58
THERE WITH THE CHIEF OF THAT HILL-TOWN WE LODGED • 356 MEROPE 746
BY THE THREE FOUNTAINS AND THE ADDERS HILL • • 356 MEROPE 748
THEN TURNING WESTWARD TO THE ADDERS HILL • • 357 MEROPE 779
UP FROM THE CITY TOWRD THIS GATED HILL • • • 362 MEROPE 935
UP FROM THE CITY TOWRDS THIS GATED HILL • • • 362 MEROPE V 935
UPON THE OPEN SHOULDER OF THE HILL • • • • 412 EMPEDOCLES I 2 3
AND WHERE THE HILL-GOATS COME TO FEED • • • 414 EMPEDOCLES I 2 66
CUCKOO CALLING FROM THE HILL • • • • • • 456 POOR MATTHIAS 141
SAW THE CEDARS OF PAINS HILL • • • • • • 458 POOR MATTHIAS 199
OF THY STERN HILL THOU MIGHTY CAPITOL • • • 468 ALARIC AT ROME 152
YES THERE HE STOOD UPON THAT SILENT HILL • • 468 ALARIC AT ROME 157
BY HILL OR WAVE THE MOUNTAIN OR THE SHORE • • • 472 CROMWELL 30
OF MANY A LAWNY HILL AND STREAMS WITH SILVER FLOW • 474 CROMWELL 104
BY NASEBYS HILL OER MARSTONS HEATHY WASTE • • 476 CROMWELL 149
FROM THAT MILD HOLLOW IN THE HILL • • • • • 479 HAYSWATER BOAT 20

HILL   (CONTINUED)
        I CROSSD ST GEORGES HILL TO-DAY   • • • • • •   484 ROME-SICKNESS   13
        ALONG THE GRACIOUS ALBAN HILL • • • • • • • •   484 ROME-SICKNESS   20

HILLOCK
        AND TO A HILLOCK CAME A LITTLE BACK   • • • • • •   61 SOHRAB RUSTUM   17

HILLS
        THE HILLS ARE CLOTHED WITH PINES SUN-PROOF • • • •   16 CHURCH BROU 2   4
        THE SOLEMN HILLS AROUND US SPREAD   • • • • • •   60 RESIGNATION   266
        AND HOUND AND MORN ON THOSE DELIGHTFUL HILLS • • •   80 SOHRAB RUSTUM   630
        BUT IN THE HILLS A STRONG EAST-WIND AROSE   • • • •   118 BALDER DEAD 3   181
        WHO BIVOUACS IN A FOREST MID THE HILLS   • • • •   119 BALDER DEAD 3   V
        WE WILL GAZE FROM THE SAND-HILLS   • • • • • •   165 FORSAKEN MERM   136
        TO WATCH THIS LINE OF SAND-HILLS RUN • • • • • •   204 CALAIS SANDS   2
        TO SEE THIS LINE OF SAND-HILLS RUN   • • • • • •   204 CALAIS SANDS   V   2
        THOSE BLUE HILLS TOO THIS RIVERS FLOW   • • • •   208 ON THE RHINE   22
        FOR HE LENT A NEW LIFE TO THESE HILLS   • • • •   228 YOUTH OF NATURE   14
        UTTERD THE VOICE OF MY HILLS   • • • • • •   231 YOUTH OF NATURE   125
        FROM A DISTANT FARM IN THE HILLS   • • • • • •   234 YOUTH OF MAN   74
        THE HILLS WHERE HIS LIFE ROSE   • • • • • •   247 BURIED LIFE   97
        AND WATCH THE WARM GREEN-MUFFLED CUMNER HILLS • •   257 SCHOLAR-GIPSY   69
        AT SOME LONE HOMESTEAD IN THE CUMNER HILLS • • • • 258 SCHOLAR-GIPSY   101
        ARE YE TOO CHANGED YE HILLS   • • • • •   263 THYRSIS   6
        THE HILLS WERE ROUND US AND THE BREEZE   • • • •   271 MEMORIAL VERSES   51
        NOT BY THOSE HOARY INDIAN HILLS   • • • • • •   277 SOUTHERN NIGHT   73
        BETWEEN HEATH-CLAD SHOWERY HILLS   • • • • • •   282 HAWORTH CHURCH   57
        LOOM THE BLURRD HILLS THE RAIN • • • • • • •   286 HAWORTH CHURCH   132
        THE HILLS IN THEIR OLD ORDER RANGED   • • • • •   312 OBERMANN MORE   7
        BEHIND THE UPCROWDING HILLS   • • • • • •   324 OBERMANN MORE   342
        THEN TO THE NORTH LYCAEUS AND THE HILLS   • • • •   330 MEROPE   20
        O ARCADIAN HILLS • • • • • • • • • • • •   342 MEROPE   392
        FAR MID ARCADIAN HILLS • • • • • • • • • •   346 MEROPE   512
        OF BEASTS OF CHASE THAT HAUNT THE ARCADIAN HILLS • • 356 MEROPE   757
        WASHD AS THE MARKS UPON THE HILLS STILL SHOW • •   358 MEROPE   815
        FOLLOWD THY FATHER FROM THEIR NORTHERN HILLS • •   381 MEROPE   1300
        OF THIS FAIR SUMMER-WEATHER ON THESE HILLS • • • • 409 EMPEDOCLES I 1   101
        HE IS FOR EVER COMING ON THESE HILLS • • • • •   412 EMPEDOCLES I 2   14
        AMONG THE GREEN ILLYRIAN HILLS AND THERE   • • • •   426 EMPEDOCLES I 2   429
        WHERE THE SPHINX LIVED AMONG THE FROWNING HILLS • • 427 EMPEDOCLES I 2   440
        THINE ANCIENT ROUT BY THE CILICIAN HILLS   • • • •   430 EMPEDOCLES II   53
        TOUCHD THE HILLS THE STRIFE WAS DONE • • • • •   433 EMPEDOCLES II   144
        ASLEEP ON THE HILLS   • • • • • • • • • • •   442 EMPEDOCLES II   436
        THY ANCIENT ROUT BY THE CILICIAN HILLS   • • • •   430 EMPEDOCLES II   V   53
        THE ANCIENT ROUT BY THE CILICIAN HILLS   • • • •   430 EMPEDOCLES II   V   53
        POUR FROM A THOUSAND HILLS THY WARRIORS OF THE NORTH 465 ALARIC AT ROME   96
        THE ETERNAL HILLS THEIR GIANT SHADOWS FLUNG   • •   472 CROMWELL   14
        TILL ALL BRIGHT THOUGHTS THAT HILLS OR WAVES CAN YIELD 472 CROMWELL   33
        THE EVERLASTING SUBSTANCE OF THE HILLS   • • • •   EVERLASTING SUB   1
        HER VALLIES AND BLUE HILLS   • • • • , • • • •   FRAGMENT 8   2

HILT
        AND IN THE HAND THE HILT REMAIND ALONE   • • • •   76 SOHRAB RUSTUM   513
        AND IN HIS HAND THE HILT REMAIND ALONE   • • • •   76 SOHRAB RUSTUM   V 513

HIMALAYAN
        HATH MADE IN HIMALAYAN FORESTS WRACK   • • • • •   73 SOHRAB RUSTUM   414
        HAS MADE IN HIMALAYAN FORESTS WRACK   • • • • •   73 SOHRAB RUSTUM   V 414
        THE SNOWY HIMALAYAN MOUNT   • • • • • • • •   277 SOUTHERN NIGHT   55

HINDER
        HINDER HIM NOT BUT LET HIM GO   • • • • • • • •   91 SICK KING BOKH   116

HINDS
        WEDGED IN THE SNOW THEN PAINFULLY THE HINDS   • •   107 BALDER DEAD 2   95

HINKSEY
        THY FACE TOWRD HINKSEY AND ITS WINTRY RIDGE   • •   258 SCHOLAR-GIPSY   125
        THY FACE TOWARDS HINKSEY AND ITS WINTRY RIDGE • •   258 SCHOLAR-GIPSY   V 125

HINKSEYS
        IN THE TWO HINKSEYS NOTHING KEEPS THE SAME • • • • 262 THYRSIS   2

HISSD
        HISSD AND WENT QUIVERING DOWN INTO THE SAND   • •   73 SOHRAB RUSTUM   404
        THEY OUT-TALKD THEE HISSD THEE TORE THEE   • • • •   215 LAST WORD   9

HIST
        MARGARET HIST COME QUICK WE ARE HERE   • • • • • •   163 FORSAKEN MERM   77
        HIST THOU WITHIN THERE   • • • • • • • • • •   188 STRAYED REVEL   70
        HIST HE WAKES   • • • • • • • • • • • •   188 STRAYED REVEL   96
        TO LEAD THOSE FALSE WHO TRUST IT HIST ONCE MORE   • • 413 EMPEDOCLES I 2   33

HISTORIED
        HE SEES IN SOME GREAT-HISTORIED LAND • • • • • •   56 RESIGNATION   154

HISTORY
        CALLD HISTORY KEEPS A SPLENDOUR DUE TO WIT • • • •   5 DUKE WELLINGTON   13
        TOLD THEM AN OLD-WORLD BRETON HISTORY   • • • •   150 TRISTRAM 3   37

HISTORY   (CONTINUED)
     HISTORY POLITICS MIND • • • • • • • •   280 HAWORTH CHURCH   17
     HISTORY OF PASSIONATE LIFE   • • • • • •   280 HAWORTH CHURCH   V 12
     PANTHEIAS HISTORY HARK WHAT SOUND WAS THAT • • • •   412 EMPEDOCLES I 2   8
     STIRS A HISTORY UNEXPRESSD • • • • • • •   455 POOR MATTHIAS   102
     ALL YOUR SPIRITS HISTORY GLEANS   • • • • • •   META CLOISTER   36

HISTORYS
     WHO FROM HISTORYS VAGUE NARRATIONS • • • • • •   SECOND BEST   V 17

HITHE
     CROSSING THE STRIPLING THAMES AT BAB-LOCK-HITHE • • • 257 SCHOLAR-GIPSY   74

HITHER
     GAZING UP HITHER THE POOR MAN • • • • • • • •   93 SICK KING BOKH   190
     WHEN THAT WITH DOWNCAST LOOKS I HITHER CAME • •   125 BALDER DEAD 3   409
     HITHER LET HIM WANDER NOW • • • • • • • •   137 TRISTRAM 1   228
     HITHER TO THE QUIET HOURS • • • • • • • •   137 TRISTRAM 1   229
     HAST THOU THEN LURED HITHER • • • • • • •   188 STRAYED REVEL   76
     I LURED HIM NOT HITHER ULYSSES • • • • • • • 188 STRAYED REVEL   97
     HITHER TO COME FROM THE STREETS   • • • • • 292 HEINES GRAVE   14
     HITHER TO COME AND TO SLEEP • • • • • • •   293 HEINES GRAVE   21
     HITHER AND THITHER SPINS • • • • • • • •   415 EMPEDOCLES I 2   82
     HITHER HE CAME LATE-BORN AND LONG-DESIRED • • • • 444 WESTMIN ABBEY   8

HITHERTO
     AS HITHERTO THEY KEPT HIM KEEP HIM NOW • • • •   377 MEROPE   1226

HITHERWARD
     FORTH FROM THE PALACE HITHERWARD COMES   • • •   196 FRAG ANTIGONE   44
     HARK HOW THE SHOUTING CROWDS TRAMP HITHERWARD • • 401 MEROPE   1886

HIVES
     CLUSTERING LIKE BEE-HIVES ON THE LOW FLAT STRAND • •   61 SOHRAB RUSTUM   13

HO
     HO THIS WAY YE LAGGARD HUNTERS • • • • • •   14 CHURCH BROU 1   43
     HO ENTER YE WHO TARRY THERE   • • • • • • •   92 SICK KING BOKH   132
     JUST SINCE DOWN AT THE STREAM HO CALLICLES • • •   428 EMPEDOCLES I 2   486

HOAR
     HOAR-HEADED WRINKLED CLAD IN WHITE • • • • • •   278 SOUTHERN NIGHT   86

HOARDS
     LIKE SOME OLD MISER RUSTUM HOARDS HIS FAME • • • •   68 SOHRAB RUSTUM   247
     COME THOU SHALT SEE HOW RUSTUM HOARDS HIS FAME • •   68 SOHRAB RUSTUM   256

HOARSE
     HEARD THE HOARSE BOUGHS LABOUR IN THE WIND • • • •   26 NEW SIRENS   8
     SAW THE HOARSE BOUGHS LABOUR IN THE WIND • • •   26 NEW SIRENS   V 8
     GUST ON GUST THE HOARSE WINDS BLOW • • • • •   32 NEW SIRENS   V 172
     THE HOARSE WIND BLOWS COLDLY • • • • • •   164 FORSAKEN MERM   110
     THE HOARSE WIND BLOWS COLDER • • • • • •   164 FORSAKEN MERM   V 110
     THE HOARSE TORRENT DUMB • • • • • • • •   175 PARTING   32
     BORDERD BY CITIES AND HOARSE • • • • • •   253 FUTURE   53
     OF THE HOARSE ONSET OF THE SURGING WAVE   • • •   466 ALARIC AT ROME   110

HOARY
     NOT BY THOSE HOARY INDIAN HILLS   • • • • • 277 SOUTHERN NIGHT   73
     YE TOO WHO STAND BESIDE THE HOARY THRONE   • • • •   FRAGMENT 2   1

HODER
     TO HODER AND UNWITTING HODER THREW • • • •   95 BALDER DEAD 1   7
     TO HODER AND UNWITTING HODER THREW • • • • •   95 BALDER DEAD 1   7
     BUT THE BLIND HODER LEFT THE FEASTING GODS • • •   97 BALDER DEAD 1   72
     TO HER DREW HODER NEAR AND SPAKE AND SAID • •   98 BALDER DEAD 1   94
     HODER ILL-FATED CHILD OF BALE MY SON • • •   98 BALDER DEAD 1   112
     AND THE BLIND HODER ANSWERD HER AND SAID • •   99 BALDER DEAD 1   131
     SHE SPOKE BUT HODER ANSWERD HER AND SAID • •   100 BALDER DEAD 1   184
     AND HODER TURND AND LEFT HIS MOTHERS HOUSE • •   100 BALDER DEAD 1   197
     HIM THE BLIND HODER MET AS HE CAME UP   • •   101 BALDER DEAD 1   226
     FOR IT GREW DARK BUT HODER TOUCHD HIS ARM • •   101 BALDER DEAD 1   229
     SO HODER BRUSHD BY HERMODS SIDE AND SAID •   101 BALDER DEAD 1   235
     AND HODER TOO CAME HOME DISTRAUGHT WITH GRIEF • • 102 BALDER DEAD 1   249
     HODER HIS BROTHER WHOM HIS OWN HAND SLEW • •   118 BALDER DEAD 3   165
     HODER THE UNHAPPY WHOM HIS OWN HAND SLEW • •   124 BALDER DEAD 3   384
     HODER ILL-FATED BLIND IN HEART AND EYES   • •   124 BALDER DEAD 3   387
     HE SPOKE BUT HODER ANSWERD HIM AND SAID   • •   124 BALDER DEAD 3   394
     THOU DOEST WELL TO CHIDE ME HODER BLIND   • •   125 BALDER DEAD 3   423
     AND THE BLIND HODER ANSWERD HIM AND SPAKE • •   125 BALDER DEAD 3   431
     HODER AND I SHALL JOIN THEM FROM THE GRAVE • •   128 BALDER DEAD 3   526

HODERS
     THE VOICE WAS LIKE THE UNHAPPY HODERS VOICE • •   102 BALDER DEAD 1   243

HOG
     WILD HOG AND BEAR AND MOUNTAIN-DEER AND ROE • •   356 MEROPE   758

HOISTED
     THE MAST THEY FIXT AND HOISTED UP THE SAILS • •   118 BALDER DEAD 3   174

HOISTED   (CONTINUED)
        THEY FIXT THE MAST AND HOISTED UP THE SAILS   • • 118 BALDER DEAD 3   V 174

HOLD
        THAT THOU CANST HEAR AND HEARING HOLD THY WAY   • •   3 EMERSONS ESSAYS   2
        KINGS HOLD REVEL GALLANTS MEET • • • • • • • •   14 CHURCH BROU 1   54
        HOLD THE PURE MUSES   • • • • • • • • • •   50 CONSOLATION   17
        WHERE THEY HOLD COUNCIL AND GIVE LAWS FOR MEN   • • 105 BALDER DEAD 2   34
        HERMOD GREET BALDER IF THOU WILT AND HOLD   • • • 111 BALDER DEAD 2   247
        OF HELA AND HOLD CONVERSE UNDISTURBD • • • • • 126 BALDER DEAD 3   436
        WHICH HER HEAVY ROBE DOTH HOLD • • • • • • • 131 TRISTRAM 1   29
        I AM HERE WE MEET I HOLD THY HAND   • • • • • • 142 TRISTRAM 2   8
        STILL HOLD HER LOVERS HAND HER HEAD   • • • • • 146 TRISTRAM 2   105
        STILL HOLD HER LOVERS HANDS HER HEAD • • • • • 146 TRISTRAM 2   V 105
        STAND AND LET VENGEANCE PASS HOLD O QUEEN HOLD   • • 374 MEROPE   1198
        STAND AND LET VENGEANCE PASS HOLD O QUEEN HOLD   • • 374 MEROPE   1198
        THAT SPOTLESS HANDS UNSHAKEN SCEPTRES HOLD • • • 388 MEROPE   1519
        MAY WHAT IS FALSE HOLD DEAR   • • • • • • ’ • 419 EMPEDOCLES I 2   203
        THE SUNNY WATERS HOLD THEIR JOYOUS WAY   • • • • 469 ALARIC AT ROME   196
        STILL SHOULD THE SPIRIT HOLD COMMUNION ROME WITH THEE   • 470 ALARIC AT ROME   210
        TO HOLD THE LIGHT AND REACH THE HAND • • • • • 484 ROME-SICKNESS   31

HOLDING
        HERE CAME THE KING HOLDING HIGH FEAST AT MORN   • •   11 MYCERINUS   92

HOLDS
        HOLDS ONLY PAIN   • • • • • • • • • • • •   51 CONSOLATION   40
        FOR BALDER WHOM SHE HOLDS BY RIGHT BELOW   • • • 100 BALDER DEAD 1   181
        COME THEN SINCE HELA HOLDS BY RIGHT HER PREY   • • 121 BALDER DEAD 3   288
        BALDER IS DEAD AND HELA HOLDS HER PREY   • • • • 123 BALDER DEAD 3   347
        STILL HOLDS HER LOVERS HANDS HER HEAD   • • • • 146 TRISTRAM 2   V 105
        THY LEFT HOLDS HANGING LOOSELY • • • • • • • 186 STRAYED REVEL   11
        AWHILE HE HOLDS SOME FALSE WAY UNDEBARRD • • • • 244 SUMMER NIGHT   59
        HOLDS HIS LANTERN TO SCAN • • • • • • • • • 289 RUGBY CHAPEL   113
        HOLDS RULE AH ME AH • • • • • • • • • • 345 MEROPE   475
        HOLDS COUNTLESS TRACTS UNTROD • • • • • • • 352 MEROPE   628
        I GO I GO THE KING HOLDS COUNCIL THERE   • • • • 368 MEROPE   1077
        AND HOLDS MEN MUTE TO SEE WHERE IT WILL RISE   • • 410 EMPEDOCLES I 1   114
        THAT HOLDS THE ASHES OF YOUR HERO-DEAD   • • • • 467 ALARIC AT ROME   136

HOLDST
        FOR BALDER WHOM THOU HOLDST BY RIGHT BELOW • • • 110 BALDER DEAD 2   193
        NOT FOR SUCH END O QUEEN THOU HOLDST THY REALM   • • 110 BALDER DEAD 2   197
        THOU HOLDST SO CHEAP THEN THE MESSENIAN CROWN   • • 397 MEROPE   1774

HOLES
        FAIR MEN WHO LIVE IN HOLES UNDER THE GROUND   • •   97 BALDER DEAD 1   56
        UNDER THE TREES IS DIBBLED THICK WITH HOLES   • • 122 BALDER DEAD 3   312

HOLIDAY
        MY PIPE IS LOST MY SHEPHERDS HOLIDAY • • • • • • 264 THYRSIS   37
        OF CITIZENS IN HOLIDAY ATTIRE   • • • • • • • 401 MEROPE   1897
        OF HOLIDAY-CLAD CITIZENS TRANSFORMD   • • • • • • 402 MEROPE   1939
        KEEP ALL O KEEP CONTINUAL HOLIDAY   • • • • • •   FRAGMENT 2   5

HOLIER
        A HOLIER INCENSE THAN THIS FEEBLE LAY   • • • • 471 ALARIC AT ROME   226

HOLIEST
        TELL OF OLD TIMES AND HOLIEST MEMORIES   • • • • 467 ALARIC AT ROME   124
        THOUGH EVERY HOLIEST FEELING EVERY TIE   • • • • 467 ALARIC AT ROME   145
        AND DASH OUR HOLIEST RAPTURES WHILE WE GAZE   • • 470 ALARIC AT ROME   200

HOLLIES
        THREE HOLLIES SIDE BY SIDE AND MADE A SCREEN   • • 150 TRISTRAM 3   20
        UNDER THE GLITTERING HOLLIES ISEULT STANDS • • • 150 TRISTRAM 3   23
        UNDER THE HOLLIES IN THE CLEAR STILL AIR • • • • 150 TRISTRAM 3   39
        THE HOLLIES AND THE CLIFF AND THE SEA-SHORE   • • 152 TRISTRAM 3   104
        UNDER THE HOLLIES THAT BRIGHT WINTERS DAY   • • • 154 TRISTRAM 3   152
        UNDER THE BURNISHD HOLLIES ISEULT STANDS • • • •   TRISTRAM 3   V 23

HOLLOW
        FALSE AND HOLLOW   • • • • • • • • • • •   44 QUESTION   16
        AND HEARD THEIR HOLLOW ROAR OF DYING MEN   • • •   74 SOHRAB RUSTUM   435
        AND IN A HOLLOW VOICE HE SPAKE AND SAID   • • • •   80 SOHRAB RUSTUM   666
        FILLD UP THE HOLLOW CHEEK AND BROUGHT   • • • • 147 TRISTRAM 2   141
        IN A GREEN CIRCULAR HOLLOW IN THE HEATH   • • • • 149 TRISTRAM 3   7
        ACROSS THE HOLLOW WHITE ANEMONIES   • • • • • 155 TRISTRAM 3   207
        OVER THE WASTE ALL THE HOLLOW GROUND   • • • • •   TRISTRAM 3   V 13
        DOWN IN THE MIDDLE OF THE HOLLOW STOOD   • • , •   TRISTRAM 3   V 19
        IN THE SMOOTH CENTRE OF THE HOLLOW STOOD • • • •   TRISTRAM 3   V 19
        TO HEAR THE WORLD APPLAUD THE HOLLOW GHOST • • • 213 GROWING OLD   34
        HOLLOW AND DULL ARE THE GREAT   • • • • • • • 295 HEINES GRAVE   113
        FROM THAT MILD HOLLOW IN THE HILL   • • • • • • 479 HAYSWATER BOAT   20

HOLLOWS
        MILD HOLLOWS AND CLEAR HEATHY SWELLS • • • • • •   54 RESIGNATION   66
        THE HOLLOWS GRASSY BANKS ARE SOFT-INCLINED • • • 149 TRISTRAM 3   10
        BUT WHEN THE MOON THEIR HOLLOWS LIGHTS   • • • • 182 TO MARG CONT   7

HOLLOWS   (CONTINUED)
        IN THE SNOW-FILLD HOLLOWS   . . . .   392 MEROPE   1623
        THEY ARE LOST IN THE HOLLOWS   . . . .   442 EMPEDOCLES II   449

HOLLY
        DOTTED WITH HOLLY-TREES AND JUNIPER   . . . . .   150 TRISTRAM 3   18
        AMONG THE HOLLY-CLUMPS AND BROKEN GROUND   . . .   150 TRISTRAM 3   28
        CLUSTERD UNDER THE HOLLY-SCREEN AND SHE   . . .   150 TRISTRAM 3   36
        SPRINKLED WITH HOLLY TREES AND JUNIPER   . . .   TRISTRAM 3   V 18
        BETWEEN THE HOLLY AND THE BEECH . . . .   451 GEISTS GRAVE   67

HOLLYHOCK
        WITH SAFFRON AND THE YELLOW HOLLYHOCK . . . .   191 STRAYED REVEL   169

HOLY
        WHAT THOUGH THE HOLY SECRET WHICH MOULDS THEE . .   8 RELIGIOUS ISOL   9
        OF HOLY LASSA   . . . .   50 CONSOLATION   14
        WENT FORTH AGAIN THE HOLY BOOK   . . . .   89 SICK KING BOKH   47
        CALL ON GOD AND ON THE HOLY ANGELS   . . . . .   145 TRISTRAM 2   79
        ONE MOMENT WAIT THOU HOLY MAN . . . .   157 SAINT BRANDAN   25
        FOR HER EYES WERE SEALD TO THE HOLY BOOK   . . .   163 FORSAKEN MERM   81
        FOR THE PRIEST AND THE BELL AND THE HOLY WELL . . 164 FORSAKEN MERM   91
        NEW HEARTS WITH THE ENQUIRERS HOLY ROBE   . . .   198 FRAG DEJANEIRA   16
        YE SOLEMN SEATS OF HOLY PAIN   . . . .   302 GRANDE CHARTR   92
        ALONG THE HOLY FLOOR   . . . .   445 WESTMIN ABBEY   52
        BELIEVE AND THOU SHALT FIND THE HOLY NIGH . . .   483 THEKLAS ANSWER   20

HOLYHOCK
        WITH SAFFRON AND THE YELLOW HOLYHOCK . . . . .   191 STRAYED REVEL   V 169

HOMAGE
        HOMAGE TO YOUR AUSTRIAN DAME   . . . .   15 CHURCH BROU 1   80
        LET THY FOREBODED HOMAGE CHECK THY TONGUE . . .   38 WORLDS TRIUMPHS   10
        AND PAY HER HOMAGE AND ENTREAT WITH PRAYERS . .   100 BALDER DEAD 1   179
        KNEELD AND DID HOMAGE TO THE SOLEMN QUEEN . . .   112 BALDER DEAD 2   283
        THE WORLD TO THEM MAY HOMAGE MAKE . . . . . .   203 EUPHROSYNE   17
        MOURNFUL HOMAGE THE MUSE   . . . .   281 HAWORTH CHURCH   35
        SAD REVERENTIAL HOMAGE HAD OUR PRINCE . . . .   356 MEROPE   761
        IN SULLEN HOMAGE TO THE INVADERS MIGHT   . . .   465 ALARIC AT ROME   76

HOME
        UNTO THEIR ANCIENT HOME   . . . .   36 VOICE   31
        WASHD EDDYING FROM THIS BANK THEIR HOME   . . .   58 RESIGNATION   202
        BUT NOW HE KEEPS APART AND SITS AT HOME   . . .   63 SOHRAB RUSTUM   81
        A COLT BENEATH ITS DAM AND DROVE HIM HOME . . .   69 SOHRAB RUSTUM   275
        AS THAT POOR BIRD FLIES HOME NOR KNOWS HIS LOSS   78 SOHRAB RUSTUM   573
        AND SNUFFD THE BREEZES OF MY FATHERS HOME . . .   83 SOHRAB RUSTUM   749
        RETURNING HOME OVER THE SALT BLUE SEA . . . .   85 SOHRAB RUSTUM   833
        HIS LUMINOUS HOME OF WATERS OPENS BRIGHT   . . .   87 SOHRAB RUSTUM   890
        A COLT BESIDE ITS DAM AND DROVE HIM HOME   . . .   69 SOHRAB RUSTUM   V 275
        I FILLD MY PITCHER AND STOLE HOME . . . . .   90 SICK KING BOKH   70
        FAR FAR BEYOND THE OUTMOST GIANTS HOME   . . .   100 BALDER DEAD 1   163
        AND LAID IT ON A BIER AND BARE HIM HOME   . . .   101 BALDER DEAD 1   206
        THERE TO HIS HALL THE GODS BROUGHT BALDER HOME   101 BALDER DEAD 1   214
        HOME TO OUR HALLS WITH TORCHLIGHT BY OUR KIN .   101 BALDER DEAD 1   217
        THEY SPAKE AND EACH WENT HOME TO HIS OWN HOUSE   101 BALDER DEAD 1   219
        HOME AND LAY DOWN TO SLEEP IN HIS OWN HOUSE .   102 BALDER DEAD 1   247
        AND HODER TOO CAME HOME DISTRAUGHT WITH GRIEF   102 BALDER DEAD 1   249
        HIGH OVER ASGARD TO LIGHT HOME THE KING   . . .   102 BALDER DEAD 1   257
        HEARING THE WRATHFUL FATHER COMING HOME   . . .   102 BALDER DEAD 1   263
        AND EVERY GOD WENT HOME TO HIS OWN HOUSE   . . .   106 BALDER DEAD 2   69
        RUMBLES AND SHAKES TELL ME THY RACE AND HOME   107 BALDER DEAD 2   103
        AT THE DREAR ICE BEYOND THE GIANTS HOME   . . .   108 BALDER DEAD 2   142
        BEFORE A STRANGERS THRESHOLD NOT HIS HOME . . .   114 BALDER DEAD 3   15
        BUT HOME HIS MASTER COMES TO HIS OWN FARM . . .   114 BALDER DEAD 3   17
        SO HERMOD COMES TO-DAY UNFOLLOWD HOME . . . .   114 BALDER DEAD 3   19
        LO HOME HAVING PERFORMD YOUR WILL I COME   . . .   114 BALDER DEAD 3   37
        AND WIFE AND CHILDREN AND OUR ANCIENT HOME . .   117 BALDER DEAD 3   144
        AND THEY RODE HOME TOGETHER THROUGH THE WOOD   123 BALDER DEAD 3   329
        IN THE GREAT DEEP FOR GAIN AT LAST COME HOME   123 BALDER DEAD 3   358
        HOME TRISTRAM TO THY HALLS AGAIN   . . . . .   138 TRISTRAM 1   273
        GRIEF SINCE THEN HIS HOME WITH ME DOTH MAKE .   145 TRISTRAM 2   88
        AND LED THEM HOME OVER THE DARKENING HEATH . .   151 TRISTRAM 3   63
        AND NOW SHE WILL GO HOME AND SOFTLY LAY   . . .   151 TRISTRAM 3   76
        SHE HAD ONE POWER WHICH MADE HER BREAST ITS HOME . 168 RACHEL 3   10
        THOU MAKST THE HEAVEN THOU HOPST INDEED THY HOME . 169 EAST LONDON   14
        AH COULD THY GRAVE AT HOME AT CARTHAGE BE . . .   173 MONICAS PRAYER   1
        HER COURSE FOR HOME AT LAST AND BURIAL   . . .   173 MONICAS PRAYER   7
        OH COULD THY GRAVE AT HOME AT CARTHAGE BE . . .   173 MONICAS PRAYER   V 1
        AND GROW A HOME FOR ONLY THEE . . . . . .   180 ISOLATION MARG   4
        DAUGHTER OF FRANCE TO FRANCE THY HOME . . . .   184 TERRACE BERNE   18
        MOWN THEM DOWN FAR FROM HOME   . . . .   193 STRAYED REVEL   253
        A COUNTRY FOR HIM KINSFOLK AND A HOME . . . .   195 FRAG ANTIGONE   14
        WITHOUT FRIEND CITY OR HOME . . . .   195 FRAG ANTIGONE   26
        IN AN EASY OLD AGE IN A HAPPY HOME   . . . . .   199 FRAG DEJANEIRA   23
        HE FOLLOWS HOME AND LIVES THEIR LIFE   . . . .   226 EPILOG LAOCOON   162
        TO FEEL THE UNIVERSE MY HOME   . . . .   251 WISH   43
        RETURNING HOME ON SUMMER-NIGHTS HAVE MET   . . .   257 SCHOLAR-GIPSY   73
        WHERE HOME THROUGH FLOODED FIELDS FOOT-TRAVELLERS GO 258 SCHOLAR-GIPSY   122
        AND KNEW THE INTRUDERS ON HIS ANCIENT HOME . .   262 SCHOLAR-GIPSY   240

HOME   (CONTINUED)
        A TROOP OF OXFORD HUNTERS GOING HOME   . . . . . .   267 THYRSIS   153
        THYRSIS IN REACH OF SHEEP-BELLS IS MY HOME . . . .   269 THYRSIS   233
        HOME ROUND INTO THE ENGLISH WAVE   . . . . . .   275 STANZAS CARNAC   37
        AND CAME HOME HURT TO DEATH AND HERE . . . . . .   278 SOUTHERN NIGHT   95
        OF THIS AMIABLE HOME OF THE DEAD   . . . . . .   293 HEINES GRAVE   45
        FAR GERMAN HOME OF HIS YOUTH   . . . . . .   296 HEINES GRAVE   151
        TO THE CARTHUSIANS WORLD-FAMED HOME   . . . . . .   300 GRANDE CHARTR   30
        HIS QUIET HOME ONE KEEPS   . . . .   308 OBERMANN   50
        OF OUR NIGHT-JOURNEY AND THOU SEEST THY HOME .   330 MEROPE   2
        BUT LET US KEEP THAT PURPOSE WHICH AT HOME . . .   331 MEROPE   35
        THESE OFFERINGS HOME OUR RITES ARE SPOILD TO-DAY . . 336 MEROPE   196
        AEGIMIUS GAVE OUR OUTCAST HOUSE A HOME   . . .   337 MEROPE   224
        ORDERD BY FATE TO THEIR HOME   . . . . . .   343 MEROPE   413
        SOON SOON SHALL ZEUS BRING HIM HOME   . . . . .   347 MEROPE   514
        SPARES NOT A THOUGHT TO HIS HOME   . . . . .   347 MEROPE   522
        EXILED REMEMBERS HIS HOME   . . . . . .   347 MEROPE   533
        CAN IT BRING HOME MY CHILD AH IF IT CAN   . . .   349 MEROPE   568
        WHEN THE YOUTHS BRING HOME THE BRIDE   . . . . .   360 MEROPE   901
        WITHOUT HOME WITHOUT MOTHER   . . . . . .   391 MEROPE   1613
        COMST THOU GUIDED SAFE TO THY HOME   . . . . .   405 MEROPE   2022
        YET YET SHALL ZEUS BRING HIM HOME   . . . . .   347 MEROPE   V 514
        ON THE BLOOD-STAIND HOME OF HIS BIRTH   . . . .   347 MEROPE   V
        THOU TOO WAST WITH HIM STRAIGHTWAY I SPED HOME   .   407 EMPEDOCLES I 1   43
        THOU TOO WERT WITH HIM STRAIGHTWAY I SPED HOME   .   407 EMPEDOCLES I 1   V 43
        TO THOSE HE BRINGS FROM HOME   . . . . . .   419 EMPEDOCLES I 2   220
        FOR YEARS THEY SITTING HELPLESS IN THEIR HOME   .   427 EMPEDOCLES I 2   448
        WHOLLY FORGET THEIR FIRST SAD LIFE AND HOME   .   427 EMPEDOCLES I 2   458
        RECEIVE ME HIDE ME QUENCH ME TAKE ME HOME   . . .   429 EMPEDOCLES II   36
        WITHOUT FRIEND AND WITHOUT HOME   . . . . .   438 EMPEDOCLES II   298
        WHAT WILL RECEIVE THEM WHO WILL CALL THEM HOME .   439 EMPEDOCLES II   348
        WHO MOURN THEE IN THINE ENGLISH HOME . . . . .   451 GEISTS GRAVE   54
        HOME WE BROUGHT HIM YOUNG AND FAIR   . . . . .   458 POOR MATTHIAS   196
        THEN HOME RETURND ONCE MORE DEPART   . . . . .   460 KAISER DEAD   51
        WHILST EVERY CHORD THAT THRILLS AT THOUGHTS OF HOME   467 ALARIC AT ROME   131
        HERE IS NO ECHO TO THE SOUND OF HOME . . . . .   468 ALARIC AT ROME   149
        LOST IN DIM MEMORIES OF HIS EARLY HOME   . . .   468 ALARIC AT ROME   170
        THINE WAS NO MOUNTAIN HOME WHERE FREEDOMS FORM .   472 CROMWELL   17
        LIKE LOVING SHADOWS ROUND THAT CHILDHOODS HOME .   474 CROMWELL   74
        MIGHT PAINT THE CALM SWEET PEACE THE REST OF HOME   475 CROMWELL   113
        NO LIFE OF DREAMS NO HOME BEYOND THE DEEP   . . .   475 CROMWELL   124
        AND OFT THE SPIRIT PENT AT HOME   . . . . . .   483 ROME-SICKNESS   2
        SEE THAT YE BRING YOUR MASTER HOME TO THE HOST   HOMER TRANS   40
                OF THE ARGIVES

HOMELESS
        THE ARMIES OF THE HOMELESS AND UNFED . . . . .   7 REP FRIEND   12
        DISTRACTED AS A HOMELESS WIND   . . . .   179 FAREWELL   50
        WILL HURRY US WITH THEM ON THEIR HOMELESS MARCH . . 439 EMPEDOCLES II   359

HOMELY
        SWEET-WILLIAM WITH HIS HOMELY COTTAGE-SMELL   . . 264 THYRSIS   65

HOMER
        WHERE ORPHEUS AND WHERE HOMER ARE   . . . . .   58 RESIGNATION   208
        THE CHARM WHICH HOMER SHAKESPEARE TEACH   . . . .   227 EPILOG LAOCOON   206

HOMES
        THE HOMES THAT WERE NOT DESTINED TO BE OURS   . .   41 HUMAN LIFE   30
        AND ALL THE GODS LAY DOWN IN THEIR OWN HOMES   .   102 BALDER DEAD 1   248
        TO VILLAGES AND HOMES OF MAN   . . . . . .   278 SOUTHERN NIGHT   82
        AND A ROUGH GRIMED RACE HAVE THEIR HOMES   . . .   283 HAWORTH CHURCH   60
        HOMES EEN NOW IS THERE WAIL   . . . .   369 MEROPE   1095

HOMESTEAD
        AT SOME LONE HOMESTEAD IN THE CUMNER HILLS . . . .   258 SCHOLAR-GIPSY   101

HOMEWARD
        SANDALLD PALMERS FARING HOMEWARD   . . . . .   15 CHURCH BROU 1   77
        DRAW HOMEWARD TO THE GENERAL LIFE   . . . . .   59 RESIGNATION   252
        RUNNING FAST HOMEWARD WITH THE TURN OF TIDE   .   69 SOHRAB RUSTUM   V 287
        AND DRAVE THEM HOMEWARD AND THE SNORTING STEEDS .   106 BALDER DEAD 2   61
        AND DROVE THEM HOMEWARD AND THE SNORTING STEEDS .   106 BALDER DEAD 2   V 61

HOMEWARDS
        DRAW HOMEWARDS TO THE GENERAL LIFE   . . . . . .   59 RESIGNATION   V 252

HOMILY
        AND READ THEIR HOMILY TO MAN   . . . .   450 GEISTS GRAVE   12

HONEY
        OF THAT WORLD-SHADOWING TREE WITH HONEY-DEW   . . 120 BALDER DEAD 3   222
        LAY HONEY-CAKES ON ITS MARGE   . . . .   342 MEROPE   386

HONEYSUCKLE
        AND AS A SPRAY OF HONEYSUCKLE FLOWERS   . . . . 101 BALDER DEAD 1   230

HONIED
        SILKEN COURTIERS WHISPERING HONIED NOTHINGS   . . 144 TRISTRAM 2   47
        AND STEALS THE HONIED MUSIC OF HIS TONGUE   . . . .   FRAGMENT 1   8

HONOUR

WITH SPOILS AND HONOUR WHEN THE WAR IS DONE	• •	79 SOHRAB RUSTUM	595
EVEN THE GREAT HONOUR WHICH I HAVE • • • • • •		94 SICK KING BOKH	217
THAT SAD SOLE HONOUR OF THE DEAD AND THEE • • • •		103 BALDER DEAD 1	298
HERE AND HAST HONOUR AMONG ALL THE DEAD • • • •		112 BALDER DEAD 2	261
CROWND HAVING HONOUR AMONG ALL THE DEAD • • • •		112 BALDER DEAD 2	278
FEAR NOT NOW THAT MEN SHOULD TAX THINE HONOUR • •		142 TRISTRAM 2	11
FEAR NOT NOW THAT MEN SHOULD TAX THY HONOUR • •		142 TRISTRAM 2	V 11
I HONOUR AND WELCOME THEE • • • • •		189 STRAYED REVEL	129
WITH PLACE WITH HONOUR AND A FLATTERING CREW • •		268 THYRSIS	204
HOW SHALL WE HONOUR THE YOUNG • • • • • • •		282 HAWORTH CHURCH	48
I SAVED THEM MEANT THEM HONOUR BUT THY FRIENDS • •		340 MEROPE	343

HONOURABLY

MOST HONOURABLY I MEANT I CALL THE GODS • • • •		394 MEROPE	1695

HONOURD

SELF-SCHOOLD SELF-SCANND SELF-HONOURD SELF-SECURE		3 SHAKESPEARE	10
OF FREA HONOURD MOTHER OF THE GODS • • • • • •		97 BALDER DEAD 1	85
MOST HONOURD AFTER FREA ODINS WIFE • • • • •		116 BALDER DEAD 3	92
PURE SOULS HONOURD AND BLEST • • • • • •		290 RUGBY CHAPEL	147
HENCEFORTH BE HONOURD AS THE DATE OF PEACE • • •		333 MEROPE	116
BUT WHILE I SMOTE HIM QUEEN I HONOURD HIM • • •		334 MEROPE	132
HONOURD AND SUNG OF BY ALL • • • • •		343 MEROPE	430
O HONOUR QUEEN THY SON MY CHARGE IS GONE • • •		362 MEROPE	944
O HONOURD FATHER HIDE THEE IN THY GRAVE • • • •		386 MEROPE	1430
OF DYNASTIES LONG-FIXD AND HONOURD LONG • • • •		390 MEROPE	1562
O HONOURD QUEEN O FAITHFUL FOLLOWERS • • • • • •		400 MEROPE	1882

HONOUREST

AH ME HONOUREST MORE THAN THY LOVER • • • • • •		196 FRAG ANTIGONE	51

HONOURING

AND CHAMPION TO THE THRONE I HONOURING MOST • •		338 MEROPE	268
THOUGH I HAVE LOVED THEE LIVED IN HONOURING THEE • •		434 EMPEDOCLES II	195

HONOURS

HIMSELF IS YOUNG AND HONOURS YOUNGER MEN • • • •		67 SOHRAB RUSTUM	224
THESE PUNCTUAL FUNERAL HONOURS YEAR BY YEAR • •		332 MEROPE	86
I KNOW SHE HONOURS NOT THE DEAD SO ILL • • • •		386 MEROPE	1450

HOOD

SHE SINKS UPON THE GROUND HER HOOD • • • • • •		146 TRISTRAM 2	103

HOOFS

AND TERRIBLY THE HOOFS OF SLEIPNER RANG • • • •		102 BALDER DEAD 1	260
UNDER WHOSE HOOFS THE BRIDGE OER GIALLS STREAM • •		107 BALDER DEAD 2	102

HOPE

PROSPECT OF HOPE WHICH FRANCE PROCLAIMS SO LOUD • •		7 REP FRIEND CONT	3
AH HOPE CANNOT LONG LIGHTEN TORMENTS LIKE THESE • •		20 MODERN SAPPHO	32
IS IT HOPE MAKES ME LINGER THE DIM THOUGHT THAT SORROW		19 MODERN SAPPHO	V
BECAUSE IT HATH THE HOPE TO COME • • • • •		21 YOUTH AND CALM	14
BECAUSE IT HAS THE HOPE TO COME • • • • •		21 YOUTH AND CALM	V 14
AH I HOPE YET ONCE AWAY • • • • • • • •		23 MEMORY-PICTURE	21
OR PERHAPS IF HOPE WERE STRONGER • • • • • •		29 NEW SIRENS	111
THOU HAST FOREKNOWN THE VANITY OF HOPE • • • •		43 GIPSY CHILD	39
JOY COMES AND GOES HOPE EBBS AND FLOWS • • • •		44 QUESTION	1
TO THE WORDS HOPE LIGHT PERSISTENCE • • • • • •		49 SECOND BEST	23
OUTLASTS EACH EFFORT INTEREST HOPE • • • • •		58 RESIGNATION	217
OF PRIDE AND HOPE FOR SOHRAB WHOM THEY LOVED • •		65 SOHRAB RUSTUM	159
STREAKD WITH ITS FIRST GREY HAIRS HOPE FILLED HIS SOUL		71 SOHRAB RUSTUM	340
THEY FOLLOWD ME MY HOPE MY FAME MY STAR • • • •		84 SOHRAB RUSTUM	781
SUCH FOR THE FUTURE IS MY HOPE MEANWHILE • • • •		129 BALDER DEAD 3	544
NOT WITH THE SUNSHINE OF HOPE • • • • • •		233 YOUTH OF MAN	21
WHO WAIT LIKE THEE BUT NOT LIKE THEE IN HOPE • •		260 SCHOLAR-GIPSY	170
AND HOW THE DYING SPARK OF HOPE WAS FED • • • •		260 SCHOLAR-GIPSY	188
BUT NONE HAS HOPE LIKE THINE • • • • • •		261 SCHOLAR-GIPSY	196
STILL NURSING THE UNCONQUERABLE HOPE • • • • •		261 SCHOLAR-GIPSY	211
AND HOPE ONCE CRUSHD LESS QUICK TO SPRING AGAIN • •		266 THYRSIS	140
HOPE AT THAT MEETING SMILED FAIR • • • • •		281 HAWORTH CHURCH	26
BEACONS OF HOPE YE APPEAR • • • • • • •		292 RUGBY CHAPEL	192
EMBLEMS OF HOPE OVER THE GRAVE • • • • • •		305 GRANDE CHARTR	201
ITS COMMON HOPE WERE VAIN • • • • • • •		321 OBERMANN MORE	242
SOME NEW SUCH HOPE MUST DAWN AT LAST • • • • •		321 OBERMANN MORE	243
WITH HOPE EXTINCT AND BROW COMPOSED • • • • •		322 OBERMANN MORE	297
HOPE TO A WORLD NEW-MADE • • • • • • •		323 OBERMANN MORE	312
A NEW SUCH HOPE MUST DAWN AT LAST • • • • •		321 OBERMANN MORE	V 243
HOPE TO A WORLD RE-MADE • • • • • • •		323 OBERMANN MORE	V 312
SEEK THIS REVIVE UNITE IT GIVE IT HOPE • • • •		331 MEROPE	45
OF MY OWN DEATH BUT LAIAS WELL I HOPE • • • •		331 MEROPE	49
PERPETUAL PROMPTINGS TO REBELLIOUS HOPE • • • •		333 MEROPE	91
BUT HER NURSLING HER HOPE CAME AT LAST • • • •		346 MEROPE	510
THOU TOO REAREST IN HOPE • • • • • • •		346 MEROPE	511
SAVE FOR THIS ANNUAL CHARGE I HOPE TO HEAR • • •		351 MEROPE	619
WHISPERING HOPE OF A LIFE • • • • • • •		369 MEROPE	1088
DOUBTLESS THOU RECKONEST ON THE HOPE OF FRIENDS • •		341 MEROPE	V 356
NURSE NO EXTRAVAGANT HOPE • • • • • • •		426 EMPEDOCLES I 2	425
AND AWE BE DEAD AND HOPE IMPOSSIBLE • • • • • •		429 EMPEDOCLES II	34
WHOSE SPRING OF HOPE IS DRIED WHOSE SPIRIT HAS FAILD		438 EMPEDOCLES II	317

HOPE   (CONTINUED)
        CHILLD EVERY BUOYANT HOPE THAT FLOATED BY   •   •   •   474 CROMWELL   88
        THAT DAY OF BOUNDLESS HOPE AND PROMISE HIGH   •   •   478 CROMWELL   211
        LIES ANY HOPE OF HEROISM MORE   •   •   •   •   •   •   480 HUNGARIAN NAT   8
        OF MEN WHO AGAINST HOPE REPELLD THE CHAIN   •   •   •   480 HUNGARIAN NAT   10
        THE TRUE HEART-BREAKING BAFFLED HOPE AND SHAME   •   •   LUCRETIUS 2   13

HOPED
        RUSTUM MY FATHER WHO I HOPED SHOULD GREET   •   •   •   •   62 SOHRAB RUSTUM   50
        SO I LONG HOPED BUT HIM I NEVER FIND   •   •   •   •   •   62 SOHRAB RUSTUM   53

HOPELESS
        WHILE WE FOR HOPELESS PASSION DIE   •   •   •   •   •   •   202 URANIA   6
        THE HOPELESS LONGING OF THE DAY   •   •   •   •   •   •   208 LONGING   4
        THE HOPELESS LONGING OF THE DAY   •   •   •   •   •   •   209 LONGING   16
        STILL THESE WASTE US WITH THEIR HOPELESS STRAINING   210 SELF-DECEPTION   19
        THE HOPELESS TANGLE OF OUR AGE   •   •   •   •   •   •   •   309 OBERMANN   83
        FRIENDLESS AND HOPELESS LIKE A LONELY TREE   •   •   •   •   477 CROMWELL   189

HOPES
        AND IN THAT MORE LIE ALL HIS HOPES OF GOOD   •   •   •   •   5 HARMONY NATURE   6
        FOR THEIR DEAD HOPES AND ALL   •   •   •   •   •   •   •   44 QUESTION   12
        HOPES BORN HERE AND BORN TO END   •   •   •   •   •   •   44 QUESTION   20
        BE PASSIONATE HOPES NOT ILL RESIGND   •   •   •   •   •   59 RESIGNATION   243
        LONG FED ON BOUNDLESS HOPES O RACE OF MAN   •   •   •   •   170 BETTER PART   1
        AND DEAD TO HOPES OF FUTURE JOY   •   •   •   •   •   •   206 RIVER   20
        AND FLUCTUATE TWIXT BLIND HOPES AND BLIND DESPAIRS   236 PALLADIUM   18
        THY HOPES GROW TIMOROUS AND UNFIXD THY POWERS   •   •   261 SCHOLAR-GIPSY   227
        OF MANY HOPES OF MANY TEARS   •   •   •   •   •   •   •   285 HAWORTH CHURCH   106
        OF HOPES AND HEARTS IN BLOOM   •   •   •   •   •   •   •   315 OBERMANN MORE   80
        SUCH ARE THEIR HOPES I ASK NOT IF BY THEE   •   •   •   •   334 MEROPE   147
        WILLINGLY FED OR NO THEIR MOST VAIN HOPES   •   •   •   •   334 MEROPE   148
        NO MORE AN EXILE FED ON EMPTY HOPES   •   •   •   •   •   335 MEROPE   169
        IN SPITE OF HOPES ENTOMBD   •   •   •   •   •   •   •   •   424 EMPEDOCLES I 2   368
        WHAT ONCE HAD HUMAN PASSIONS HOPES AND FEARS   •   •   464 ALARIC AT ROME   52
        CROWNING HIS WILDEST HOPES PERCHANCE HIS EYES   •   •   468 ALARIC AT ROME   173
        EVEN OF THAT ARDENT SPIRIT HOPES AND FEARS   •   •   •   469 ALARIC AT ROME   178
        ALL AIRY HOPES THAT IDLE HEARTS CAN FRAME   •   •   •   474 CROMWELL   95
        THOSE LINGERING HOPES OF COWARD HEARTS THAT STILL   •   475 CROMWELL   107
        NO GLITTERING HOPES ON LIFES GREY DISTANCE SMILED   475 CROMWELL   126
        THE FEARS AND HOPES AND PASSIONS OF MANKIND   •   •   479 CROMWELL   232

HOPING
        IN VAIN MEN STILL WITH HOPING NEW   •   •   •   •   •   •   318 OBERMANN MORE   177

HOPST
        THOU MAKST THE HEAVEN THOU HOPST INDEED THY HOME   •   •   169 EAST LONDON   14

HORDE
        HORDE AFTER HORDE STREAMED UP THY FROWNING CAPITOL   464 ALARIC AT ROME   72
        HORDE AFTER HORDE STREAMED UP THY FROWNING CAPITOL   464 ALARIC AT ROME   72

HORDES
        AND CLOSE-SET SKULL-CAPS AND THOSE WILDER HORDES   •   •   64 SOHRAB RUSTUM   130

HORIZON
        AND ON THE PURE HORIZON FAR   •   •   •   •   •   •   •   218 BACCHANALIA 1   16
        TO THE DIM HORIZON REPOSED   •   •   •   •   •   •   •   •   234 YOUTH OF MAN   77
        FAR ON THE DIM HORIZON WHEN THE SKY   •   •   •   •   •   475 CROMWELL   129

HORIZONS
        DOWN AT THE FAR HORIZONS RIM   •   •   •   •   •   •   •   242 SUMMER NIGHT   9
        HOW BOUNDLESS MIGHT HIS SOULS HORIZONS BE   •   •   •   •   244 SUMMER NIGHT   88
        BUT ON THE HORIZONS VERGE DESCRIED   •   •   •   •   •   •   274 STANZAS CARNAC   31

HORN
        SHALL BREATHLESS GLADES CHEERD BY SHY DIANS HORN   •   •   6 GEO CRUIKSHANK   8
        WHERE HORN AND HOUND AND VASSALS NEVER COME   •   •   17 CHURCH BROU 3   3
        HIS LIFTED HORN NOR CHEERS HIS HOUNDS   •   •   •   •   148 TRISTRAM 2   V
        CHEERING WITH HAND AND VOICE AND HORN HIS DOGS   •   •   357 MEROPE   805

HORNED
        I READ IN DANTE HOW THAT HORNED LIGHT   •   •   •   •   484 S S LUSITANIA   1

HORNS
        AND THROUGH GOLDEN HORNS TO GREET YOU   •   •   •   •   29 NEW SIRENS   103
        AND IN THE HORNS AND GOLD-RIMMD SKULLS THE WINE •   •   95 BALDER DEAD 1   14
        AND THE VALKYRIES CROWND THEIR HORNS WITH MEAD   •   •   97 BALDER DEAD 1   68
        AND IN THE HORNS AND GOLD-RIMMD SCULLS THE WINE •   •   95 BALDER DEAD 1   V 14
        AND FROM THEIR HORNS WITH SILVER RIMMD DRANK MEAD   119 BALDER DEAD 3   211
        THEN WHITE WITH BLOSSOM AND YOU SAW THE HORNS   •   •   155 TRISTRAM 3   192

HORRIBLE
        AGREES TO DEEM SOME DEEDS SO HORRIBLE   •   •   •   •   389 MEROPE   V1524

HORROR
        ARTIST WHOSE HAND WITH HORROR WINGD HATH TORN   •   •   6 GEO CRUIKSHANK   1
        AND THEY STOOD WIDE WITH HORROR AND HE SEIZED   •   •   81 SOHRAB RUSTUM   699
        WITH HORROR FROM THY TREE   •   •   •   •   •   •   •   PHILOMELA   V
        BUT EVERLASTING HORROR TWIXT US TWO   •   •   •   •   •   336 MEROPE   193

HORRORS
    FLUENT OF HORRORS FALTERS TO RELATE IT   • • • • 385 MEROPE   1419

HORSE
    FROM THEIR BLACK TENTS LONG FILES OF HORSE   64 SOHRAB RUSTUM   110
        THEY STREAMD
    AND THEN A SWARM OF WANDERING HORSE WHO CAM • • 64 SOHRAB RUSTUM   126
    FIRST A LIGHT CLOUD OF HORSE TARTARS THEY SEEMD • • 65 SOHRAB RUSTUM   137
    THE ROYAL TROOPS OF PERSIA HORSE AND FOOT • • • 65 SOHRAB RUSTUM   139
    SO ARMD HE ISSUED FORTH AND RUKSH HIS HORSE • • 69 SOHRAB RUSTUM   270
    THE HORSE WHOM RUSTUM ON A FORAY ONCE • • • 69 SOHRAB RUSTUM   273
    AND LIGHTNINGS RENT THE CLOUD AND RUKSH THE HORSE   76 SOHRAB RUSTUM   501
    WHEN THEY SAW RUSTUMS GRIEF AND RUKSH THE HORSE • • 82 SOHRAB RUSTUM   730
    BUT SOHRAB LOOKD UPON THE HORSE AND SAID • • • 83 SOHRAB RUSTUM   741
    MY TERRIBLE FATHERS TERRIBLE HORSE AND SAID • • 83 SOHRAB RUSTUM   744
    AND MOUNTED HIS HORSE SLEIPNER WHOM HE RODE • • 96 BALDER DEAD 1   47
    WHO GOES THAT WAY MUST TAKE NO OTHER HORSE • • • 99 BALDER DEAD 1   137
    TO RIDE BUT SLEIPNER ODINS HORSE ALONE • • • 99 BALDER DEAD 1   138
    TIGHTEN THE GIRTHS OF SLEIPNER ODINS HORSE • • • 100 BALDER DEAD 1   169
    WHO ART THOU ON THY BLACK AND FIERY HORSE • • • 107 BALDER DEAD 2   101
    AND SLEIPNER ODINS HORSE IS THIS I RIDE • • • 108 BALDER DEAD 2   115
    ON THE SMOOTH ICE OF SLEIPNER ODINS HORSE • • • 109 BALDER DEAD 2   147
    AND HIS HORSE BALDERS HORSE WHOM MOST HE LOVED • 118 BALDER DEAD 3   171
    AND HIS HORSE BALDERS HORSE WHOM MOST HE LOVED • 118 BALDER DEAD 3   171
    AND HEAR THE PASSAGE OF A HORSE OF HEAVEN • • • 125 BALDER DEAD 3   419
    BUT HERMOD STOOD BESIDE HIS DROOPING HORSE • • 129 BALDER DEAD 3   554
    ONE LAST KISS FIRST TIS VAIN TO HORSE AWAY • • • 135 TRISTRAM 1   169
    HIS SWORD IS SHARP HIS HORSE IS GOOD • • • • 138 TRISTRAM 1   249
    A CLOUD OF DESERT ROBBER—HORSE HAVE BURST • • • 193 STRAYED REVEL   248
    A CLOUD OF DESERT ROBBER—HORSE HAS BURST • • • 193 STRAYED REVEL   V 248
    THEN FROM BENEATH THE YOKE THE FLEET HORSE   HOMER TRANS   43
        XANTHUS ADDRESSED HIM

HORSEBACK
    THOR CAME ON FOOT THE REST ON HORSEBACK RODE • • 120 BALDER DEAD 3   218

HORSEHAIR
    OF HORSEHAIR WAVED A SCARLET HORSEHAIR PLUME • • 69 SOHRAB RUSTUM   269
    OF HORSEHAIR WAVED A SCARLET HORSEHAIR PLUME • • 69 SOHRAB RUSTUM   269
    HE SHORE AWAY AND THAT PROUD HORSEHAIR PLUME • • 76 SOHRAB RUSTUM   497

HORSEMAN
    THAT SO THE PASSING HORSEMAN ON THE WASTE • • • 84 SOHRAB RUSTUM   790

HORSEMANS
    AND TOOK HIS HORSEMANS CLOAK AND LEFT HIS TENT • • 61 SOHRAB RUSTUM   9
    AND THE GREAT RUSTUM DREW HIS HORSEMANS CLOAK • • 86 SOHRAB RUSTUM   858

HORSEMEN
    FURIOUS SINGLE HORSEMEN GALLOP • • • • • 13 CHURCH BROU 1   23
    AND FROM THEIR TENTS THE TARTAR HORSEMEN FILED • • 64 SOHRAB RUSTUM   106
    OF THE HORSEMEN OF TROY IN THE DAY THEY FOUGHT   HOMER TRANS   34
        FOR THEIR CITY

HORSES
    HORSES FRET AND BOAR—SPEARS GLANCE • • • • • 13 CHURCH BROU 1   18
    NO HORSES CRY WAS THAT MOST LIKE THE ROAR • • • 76 SOHRAB RUSTUM   503
    THEIR ARMS AND LED THEIR HORSES FROM THE STALL • 105 BALDER DEAD 2   12
    THEIR HORSES FETLOCK—DEEP IN BLOOD THEY RIDE • • 105 BALDER DEAD 2   25
    ASGARD AND LED THEIR HORSES TO THE BEACH • • • 106 BALDER DEAD 2   66
    OR OF THE HORSES OF THE GODS RESOUND • • • • 108 BALDER DEAD 2   120
    AND TOOK THEIR HORSES AND SET FORTH TO RIDE • • 119 BALDER DEAD 3   215
    THEIR HORSES AND RODE FORTH THROUGH ALL THE WORLD 122 BALDER DEAD 3   303
    NOW THE WILD WHITE HORSES PLAY • • • • • 161 FORSAKEN MERM   6
    THE WILD WHITE HORSES FOAM AND FRET • • • • 162 FORSAKEN MERM   21
    MY HORSES FEET BESIDE THE LAKE • • • • • 177 FAREWELL   1
    TWO HORSES STRONGLY SWIMMING TOW • • • • • 191 STRAYED REVEL   185

HOST
    OUR JOVIAL HOST AS FORTH WE FARE • • • • • 53 RESIGNATION   42
    WHERE HOST MEETS HOST AND MANY NAMES ARE SUNK • • 62 SOHRAB RUSTUM   61
    WHERE HOST MEETS HOST AND MANY NAMES ARE SUNK • • 62 SOHRAB RUSTUM   61
    THE HOST AND STILL WAS IN HIS LUSTY PRIME • • • 64 SOHRAB RUSTUM   109
    AND FERABURZ WHO RULED THE PERSIAN HOST • • • 66 SOHRAB RUSTUM   172
    THE CAMP AND TO THE PERSIAN HOST APPEARD • • • 69 SOHRAB RUSTUM   281
    BE GOVERND QUIT THE TARTAR HOST AND COME • • • 71 SOHRAB RUSTUM   330
    THERE ARE ENOUGH FOES IN THE PERSIAN HOST • • • 74 SOHRAB RUSTUM   443
    AND THEN THAT ALL THE TARTAR HOST WOULD PRAISE • 77 SOHRAB RUSTUM   534
    BUT COME THOU SEEST THIS GREAT HOST OF MEN • • 84 SOHRAB RUSTUM   778
    AND QUIT THE HOST AND BEAR THEE HENCE WITH ME • 84 SOHRAB RUSTUM   798
    AND I WILL SPARE THY HOST YEA LET THEM GO • • • 84 SOHRAB RUSTUM   806
    THE DANCERS AND THE FESTIVE HOST • • • • 146 TRISTRAM 2   121
    WHERE THE GAUNT AND TACITURN HOST • • • • 289 RUGBY CHAPEL   110
    MARCHES THE HOST OF MANKIND • • • • • • 291 RUGBY CHAPEL   172
    FACTIONS DIVIDE THEM THEIR HOST • • • • 291 RUGBY CHAPEL   180
    PASSING THE HOST FROM HAND TO HAND • • • • 300 GRANDE CHARTR   42
    EACH ITS OWN PILGRIM—HOST OF OLD • • • • 301 GRANDE CHARTR   62
    AGAINST THE KING HIMSELF ARRAY THE HOST • • 382 MEROPE   1320
    SEE THAT YE BRING YOUR MASTER HOME TO THE HOST   HOMER TRANS   40
        OF THE ARGIVES

HOSTAGE
    WITH MEN BUT LIVES A HOSTAGE WITH THE GODS • • • 123 BALDER DEAD 3   325

HOSTILE

WHEN IT SHOULD PLUCK THEE FROM THY HOSTILE WAY • • • 333 MEROPE 99
CLAIMS EVER HOSTILE ELSE AND SET THY SON • • • • 335 MEROPE 168
REMORSEFUL TOWRD MY HOSTILE SOLITUDE • • • • • • 387 MEROPE 1475
HARSH GODS AND HOSTILE FATES • • • • • • • • 422 EMPEDOCLES I 2 304

HOSTS

BETWIXT THE SILENT HOSTS AND SPAKE AND SAID • • 65 SOHRAB RUSTUM 149
LET THERE BE TRUCE BETWEEN THE HOSTS TO-DAY • • 65 SOHRAB RUSTUM 151
AND LEAVE TO DEATH THE HOSTS OF THANKLESS KINGS • • 68 SOHRAB RUSTUM 240
BECAUSE THOU HAST SHAMED ME BEFORE BOTH THE HOSTS • • 75 SOHRAB RUSTUM 468
FOR BOTH THE ON-LOOKING HOSTS ON EITHER HAND • • 75 SOHRAB RUSTUM 487
THE TWO HOSTS HEARD THAT CRY AND QUAKED FOR FEAR • • 76 SOHRAB RUSTUM 507
AND KISSD HIM AND AWE FELL ON BOTH THE HOSTS • • 82 SOHRAB RUSTUM 729
AND THE TWO GAZING HOSTS AND THAT SOLE PAIR • • 86 SOHRAB RUSTUM 866
BETWIXT THE SILENT HOSTS AND SPOKE AND SAID • • 65 SOHRAB RUSTUM V 149
AND THE TWO HOSTS ARE MARSHALLD AND IN HEAVEN • • 127 BALDER DEAD 3 495
PALE PHANTOM HOSTS LIKE SHADOWS FAINT AND FAR • • 476 CROMWELL 141

HOT

BECAUSE ON ITS HOT BROW THERE BLOWS • • • • • 21 YOUTH AND CALM 11
BECAUSE ON ITS HOT HOUR THERE BLOWS • • • • • 21 YOUTH AND CALM V 11
FROM THE HOT FIELDS AT NOON HIS HEAD DROOPD LOW • • 86 SOHRAB RUSTUM V 847
FROM THE HOT FIELD AT NOON HIS HEAD DROOPD LOW • • 86 SOHRAB RUSTUM V 847
RIDE DOWN AND BATHE MY HOT BROW IN THE FLOOD • • 139 TRISTRAM 1 282
THEIR HOT SEALS AND LET HIM WAKE • • • • • 139 TRISTRAM 1 295
WITH HOT-FLUSHD CHEEKS AND BRILLIANT EYES • • • 146 TRISTRAM 2 117
THEIR CHEEKS WERE FLUSHD AND OVER EACH HOT BROW • • 150 TRISTRAM 3 32
IN WHOSE HOT AIR OUR SPIRITS ARE UPCURLD • • • 153 TRISTRAM 3 120
THEIR CHEEKS GREW FLUSHD AND OVER EACH HOT BROW • • TRISTRAM 3 V 32
THE HOT WIND FEVERD HIM FIVE-FOLD • • • • • • 157 SAINT BRANDAN 48
IN PARIS ALL LOOKD HOT AND LIKE TO FADE • • • • 167 RACHEL 1 1
WITH HOT CHEEKS AND SEARD EYES • • • • • • 201 PHILOMELA 20
IN THE HOT PRISON OF THE PRESENT MONTH • • • • 212 GROWING OLD 24
IN THE HOT PRESS OF THE NOON-DAY • • • • • • 219 BACCHANALIA 2 18
WHERE IN THE SUNS HOT EYE • • • • • • • 243 SUMMER NIGHT 38
AND THERE ARRIVES A LULL IN THE HOT RACE • • • 247 BURIED LIFE 91
IN THE HOT CORNFIELD OF THE PHRYGIAN KING • • • 268 THYRSIS 183
TOUCHD WITH YELLOW BY HOT • • • • • • • 292 HEINES GRAVE 5
SO HOW OFTEN FROM HOT • • • • • • • • 296 HEINES GRAVE 140
OF PRAISE HOT HEADY FUMES TO THE POOR BRAIN • • 296 HEINES GRAVE 146
WHY HAST THOU FOLLOWD US THE NIGHT WAS HOT • • • 407 EMPEDOCLES I 1 36
THE NOON IS HOT WHEN WE HAVE CROSSD THE STREAM • • 412 EMPEDOCLES I 2 1
OF THE HOT NOON WITHOUT A SHADE • • • • • 414 EMPEDOCLES I 2 54
PLEASURE TO OUR HOT GRASP • • • • • • • 424 EMPEDOCLES I 2 357
KNEAD US IN ITS HOT HAND AND CHANGE OUR NATURE • • 440 EMPEDOCLES II 386

HOTELS

AND THEN THE LONDON HOTELS • • • • • • • • 214 NEW ROME 16

HOTLIER

HOTLIER THAN THOU AND WERE BY THEE KEPT BACK • • 339 MEROPE 330

HOTLY

IF TOO HOTLY MUSED UPON • • • • • • • • • 23 MEMORY-PICTURE 10
HOTLY CHARGED AND SANK AT LAST • • • • • • • 215 LAST WORD 12
HOTLY CHARGED AND BROKE AT LAST • • • • • • 215 LAST WORD V 12

HOTNESS

THE DAY IN HIS HOTNESS • • • • • • • • • • 443 EMPEDOCLES II 465
THE DAY IN ITS HOTNESS • • • • • • • • • • 443 EMPEDOCLES II V 465

HOUND

WHERE HORN AND HOUND AND VASSALS NEVER COME • • 17 CHURCH BROU 3 3
FOLLOWD HIM LIKE A FAITHFUL HOUND AT HEEL • • • 69 SOHRAB RUSTUM 271
AND HOUND AND MORN ON THOSE DELIGHTFUL HILLS • • 80 SOHRAB RUSTUM 630
THE CHASE NEGLECTED AND HIS HOUND • • • • • 137 TRISTRAM 1 225
ACROSS THE SHAGGY BROWS OF TRISTRAMS HOUND • • • 152 TRISTRAM 3 88
HER WOMEN AND SIR TRISTRAMS AGED HOUND • • • • 152 TRISTRAM 3 98
THE DACHS-HOUND GEIST THEIR LITTLE FRIEND • • • 452 GEISTS GRAVE 80

HOUNDS

HOUNDS ARE PULLING PRICKERS SWEARING • • • • • 13 CHURCH BROU 1 17
AND RIDE ACROSS THE DRAWBRIDGE WITH THY HOUNDS • • 18 CHURCH BROU 3 10
THE FIERCE HOUNDS SNUFF THE TAINTED AIR • • • • 149 TRISTRAM 2 184
BUT LORD AND HOUNDS KEEP ROOTED THERE • • • • 149 TRISTRAM 2 185
HIS LIFTED HORN NOR CHEERS HIS HOUNDS • • • • 148 TRISTRAM 2 V
FROM HUNTING WITH THE BERKSHIRE HOUNDS THEY COME • • 267 THYRSIS 155
WITH BEATERS HOUNDS AND HUNTSMEN HE AND I • • • 355 MEROPE 731
BY THE LAKE-EDGE BROKE THE SHARP CRY OF HOUNDS • • 357 MEROPE 787
OF THAT UNFLAGGING QUARRY AND THE HOUNDS • • • 357 MEROPE 800
AND TOOK THE LAKE TWO HOUNDS ALONE PURSUED • • • 357 MEROPE 809

HOUR

OF LABOUR THAT IN ONE SHORT HOUR OUTGROWS • • • 1 QUIET WORK V 6
TILL THAT HOUR SHE NEVER SORROWD • • • • • • 14 CHURCH BROU 1 59
BECAUSE ON ITS HOT HOUR THERE BLOWS • • • • • 21 YOUTH AND CALM V 11
ERE THE PARTING HOUR GO BY • • • • • • • 22 MEMORY-PICTURE 7
ERE THE PARTING HOUR GO BY • • • • • • • 23 MEMORY-PICTURE 15
ERE THE PARTING HOUR GO BY • • • • • • • 23 MEMORY-PICTURE 23
ERE THE PARTING HOUR GO BY • • • • • • • 23 MEMORY-PICTURE 31

HOUR   (CONTINUED)
          ERE THE PARTING HOUR GO BY   . . . .   23 MEMORY-PICTURE   39
          ERE THE PARTING HOUR GO BY   . . . .   24 MEMORY-PICTURE   47
          ERE THE PARTING HOUR GO BY   . . . .   24 MEMORY-PICTURE   63
          MOURN WILL WE NOT YOUR CLOSING HOUR   . . . . . .   48 HORATIAN ECHO   10
          TIME GIVES HIS HOUR-GLASS   . . . .   51 CONSOLATION   53
          THEIR HOUR IS GONE . . . .   51 CONSOLATION   55
          THE HOUR WHOSE HAPPY   . . . .   52 CONSOLATION   61
          THE BLEAK STERN HOUR   . . . .   52 CONSOLATION   66
          THESE CLAIM NOT EVERY LAUGHING HOUR   . . . . . .   53 RESIGNATION   30
          ONLY THE EVENT WILL TEACH US IN ITS HOUR   . . . .   73 SOHRAB RUSTUM   397
          THE MORROW AT THE SELF-SAME HOUR   . . . . .   90 SICK KING BOKH   93
          WEEP HIM AN HOUR BUT WHAT CAN GRIEF AVAIL . . . .   96 BALDER DEAD 1   27
          RATHER IT FITS YOU HAVING WEPT YOUR HOUR   . . . .   96 BALDER DEAD 1   34
          AFTER AN HOUR A DRIPPING SOUND IS HEARD   . . . .   122 BALDER DEAD 3   310
          BUT WHAT WERE I TO SAVE THEM IN THAT HOUR . . . .   127 BALDER DEAD 3   489
          PASSING ALL HER YOUTHFUL HOUR   . . . . . .   131 TRISTRAM 1   39
          EACH HER HOUR OF TRISTRAMS DAY . . . . . .   132 TRISTRAM 1   69
          WHO POSSESSD HIS DARKER HOUR   . . . . . .   132 TRISTRAM 1   73
          AT THIS SOFT HOUR UNDER THIS SWEET MOON   . . . .   139 TRISTRAM 1   286
          AH AN HOUR OF HEALTH WOULD PURGE HIS EYESIGHT . .   144 TRISTRAM 2   67
          HOUR AFTER HOUR HER GOLD CURLS SWEEPING IT . . .   152 TRISTRAM 3   83
          HOUR AFTER HOUR HER GOLD CURLS SWEEPING IT . . .   152 TRISTRAM 3   83
          GO HENCE AND COOL THYSELF AN HOUR   . . . . .   157 SAINT BRANDAN   36
          O BRANDAN TO THIS HOUR OF REST . . . . . .   158 SAINT BRANDAN   71
          BUT HARDLY HAVE WE FOR ONE LITTLE HOUR   . . . .   246 BURIED LIFE   59
          OF ALL THE THOUSAND NOTHINGS OF THE HOUR   . . . .   247 BURIED LIFE   69
          ONCE PASSD I BLINDFOLD HERE AT ANY HOUR   . . . .   263 THYRSIS   24
          YET THYRSIS LET ME GIVE MY GRIEF ITS HOUR . . . .   265 THYRSIS   102
          THOU WANDEREDST WITH ME FOR A LITTLE HOUR . . . .   269 THYRSIS   212
          HE LOOKD ON EUROPES DYING HOUR . . . . . .   270 MEMORIAL VERSES   23
          BUT WHERE WILL EUROPES LATTER HOUR   . . . . .   272 MEMORIAL VERSES   62
          BUT WHERE SHALL EUROPES LATTER HOUR . . . . .   272 MEMORIAL VERSES   V 62
          THEN IN SUCH HOUR OF NEED . . . .   291 RUGBY CHAPEL   188
          THAT SMILE WAS HEAVEN FOR ITS EARTHLY HOUR . . .   298 HEINES GRAVE   210
          RETURNST THOU IN HER HOUR OF BIRTH   . . . . .   315 OBERMANN MORE   79
          IT WAS NOT YET THE APPOINTED HOUR   . . . . .   321 OBERMANN MORE   253
          YET WARM IT MOUNTS THE HOUR OF LIFE . . . . .   322 OBERMANN MORE   291
          DEATHS FROZEN HOUR IS DONE   . . . .   322 OBERMANN MORE   292
          BUT THOU THOUGH TO THE WORLDS NEW HOUR   . . . .   322 OBERMANN MORE   301
          AND SECOND FATHER FROM THAT HOUR WHEN FIRST . .   331 MEROPE   30
          ADMIRE THEN MAIDENS HOW IN ONE SHORT HOUR . . .   360 MEROPE   875
          IN THEIR ALLEGIANCE ME IN MY SONS DEATH-HOUR . .   366 MEROPE   1004
          THE HOUR FOR WORDS IS GONE IS COME FOR DEEDS . .   386 MEROPE   1445
          EACH SOVEREIGN FOR HIS DEAR-BOUGHT HOUR BORN . .   388 MEROPE   1513
          IN DANGEROUS HOUR STRETCHES HIS HAND   . . . .   393 MEROPE   1681
          FOR FATE THOU WAITST NOT LONG SINCE IN THIS HOUR .   397 MEROPE   1777
          THE MULES I THINK WILL NOT BE HERE THIS HOUR . .   406 EMPEDOCLES I 1   1
          HOW GRACIOUS IS THE MOUNTAIN AT THIS HOUR . . .   406 EMPEDOCLES I 1   6
          AND HAVE THIS HOUR SATE BY THE TORRENT HERE . .   408 EMPEDOCLES I 1   47
          I FEEL IT IN THIS HOUR THE NUMBING CLOUD   . . .   441 EMPEDOCLES II   407
          FORESHOWN THEE IN THY CONSECRATION-HOUR . . .   446 WESTMIN ABBEY   75
          THEIR KINDNESS SHOWN ME IN MY WANDERING HOUR . .   447 WESTMIN ABBEY   109
          BRINGER OF HEAVENLY LIGHT A HUMAN HOUR   . . . .   447 WESTMIN ABBEY   120
          THE BOON TO THY FOUNDATION-HOUR FORETOLD   . . .   444 WESTMIN ABBEY   V 5
          BUT THOU WHEN STRUCK THINE HOUR TO GO . . . .   450 GEISTS GRAVE   33
          TILL WHAT AT MORNINGS HOUR LOOKT WARM AND BRIGHT .   466 ALARIC AT ROME   107
          BE CRUSHT AND OUTRAGED IN THIS BITTER HOUR . . .   468 ALARIC AT ROME   148
          NEARER AND NEARER TO THEIR CLOSING HOUR . . . .   469 ALARIC AT ROME   190
          WHOSE SPELL-BOUND SENSE FROM CHILDHOODS HOUR   471 CROMWELL   3
               HATH KNOWN

HOURLY
          AND ALL HIS HOURLY VARIED ANODYNES   . . . . .   260 SCHOLAR-GIPSY   190
          NOT CHAFED BY HOURLY FALSE CONTROL   . . . . .   302 GRANDE CHARTR   96
          NOT CHAFED BY HOURLY FALSE CONTROUL . . . . .   302 GRANDE CHARTR   V 96
          WHEN I COULD HOURLY SCAN . . . .   317 OBERMANN MORE   154
          WHEN I COULD HOURLY SEE   . . . .   315 OBERMANN MORE   V 154

HOURS
          COME YOU SAY THE HOURS WERE DREARY   . . . . .   28 NEW SIRENS   65
          STILL THEY GALL YOU THE LONG HOURS   . . . . .   30 NEW SIRENS   129
          COME YOU SAY THE HOURS ARE DREARY   . . . . .   28 NEW SIRENS   V 65
          DO THEY GALL YOU THE LONG HOURS . . . . . .   30 NEW SIRENS   V 129
          COUNT THE HOURS . . . .   44 QUESTION   14
          WE COUNT THE HOURS THESE DREAMS OF OURS . . . .   44 QUESTION   15
          AGES OR HOURS O WAKING ON LIFES STREAM   . . . .   45 IN UTRUMQUE PAR   11
          SOME UNDIMMD HOURS . . . .   52 CONSOLATION   75
          SOME TWO HOURS MARCH WITH SERIOUS AIR   . . . .   54 RESIGNATION   68
          AND FOLLOWS THIS MAN AFTER THAT FOR HOURS . . .   114 BALDER DEAD 3   11
          HITHER TO THE QUIET HOURS   . . . .   137 TRISTRAM 1   229
          HOURS IF NOT OF ECSTASY   . . . .   137 TRISTRAM 1   232
          FOR LITTLE DO THE ALL-CONTAINING HOURS   . . . .   195 FRAG ANTIGONE   2
          FULLER FOR HIM BE THE HOURS   . . . . . .   200 EARLY DEATH   15
          BUT TASKS IN HOURS OF INSIGHT WILLD . . . .   241 MORALITY   5
          CAN BE THROUGH HOURS OF GLOOM FULFILLD   . . . .   241 MORALITY   6
          NOT TILL THE HOURS OF LIGHT RETURN   . . . . .   241 MORALITY   11
          OF THE INTERMINABLE HOURS   . . . .   247 BURIED LIFE   80
          NO NO THOU HAST NOT FELT THE LAPSE OF HOURS . .   259 SCHOLAR-GIPSY   141
          BUT WE BROUGHT FORTH AND REARD IN HOURS . . . .   308 OBERMANN   69
          THE IMPRACTICABLE HOURS   . . . .   316 OBERMANN MORE   104

HOURS   (CONTINUED)
        FORWARD THE GRACIOUS HOURS HAVE FARED   • • • •   322 OBERMANN MORE   283
        STILL RULES STILL WATCHES AND NUMBRETH THE HOURS • •   347 MEROPE   527
        ON NATIVE GROUND THAN DRAG THE TEDIOUS HOURS   • •   383 MEROPE   1380
        STILL RULES STILL WATCHES AND NUMBERS THE HOURS   • • 347 MEROPE   V 527
        SIT FOR HOURS BESIDE THY CAGE • • • • • • • • • •   453 POOR MATTHIAS   32
        ENERGIES WASTED UNIMPROVED HOURS • • • • • • • •   470 ALARIC AT ROME   201
        PEACE THAT RECALLD HIS CHILDISH HOURS ANEW • • • •   475 CROMWELL   115

HOUSE
        FAR UP SHINES THE HOUSE AND BENEATH FLOWS THE RIVER   19 MODERN SAPPHO   3
        FAR UP GLEAMS THE HOUSE AND BENEATH FLOWS THE RIVER   19 MODERN SAPPHO   V 3
        TO HALVE A HOUSE THAT SHOULD BE ALL HER OWN   • •   44 GIPSY CHILD   V 64
        NOR SEEN HIS LOFTY HOUSE IN SEISTAN • • • • • •   83 SOHRAB RUSTUM   757
        HIS HOUSE NOW MID THEIR BROKEN FLIGHTS OF STEPS   • •   86 SOHRAB RUSTUM   862
        THERE IN THE GLEN FENSALER STANDS THE HOUSE   •   97 BALDER DEAD 1   84
        AND HODER TURND AND LEFT HIS MOTHERS HOUSE • • • •   100 BALDER DEAD 1   197
        THROUGH THE FAST-DARKENING STREETS TO HIS OWN HOUSE   101 BALDER DEAD 1   207
        THEY SPAKE AND EACH WENT HOME TO HIS OWN HOUSE   • • 101 BALDER DEAD 1   219
        HEAVY IN HEART FOR BALDER TO HIS HOUSE   • • • • •   101 BALDER DEAD 1   223
        HOME AND LAY DOWN TO SLEEP IN HIS OWN HOUSE   • •   102 BALDER DEAD 1   247
        AND EVERY GOD WENT HOME TO HIS OWN HOUSE   • • • •   106 BALDER DEAD 2   69
        OF ODIN AND MY HIGH-ROOFD HOUSE IS BUILT   • • • •   108 BALDER DEAD 2   113
        UNDER THE GATE-HOUSE TO THE SANDS AND FOUND   • •   113 BALDER DEAD 2   309
        AND SUBSTANCE AND A GOLDEN HOUSE IN HEAVEN • • • •   125 BALDER DEAD 3   404
        IN THY OWN HOUSE BREIDABLIK NOR ENJOY   • • • •   126 BALDER DEAD 3   449
        WHY STOPS SHE BY THIS EMPTY PLAY-HOUSE DREAR • •   167 RACHEL 1   11
        THE HOUSE AND IS MY MARGUERITE THERE • • • • • •   184 TERRACE BERNE   12
        HIS WHEELD HOUSE AT NOON • • • • • • • •   191 STRAYED REVEL   164
        IS THE CASTLED HOUSE WITH ITS WOODS • • • • •   234 YOUTH OF MAN   64
        IN THE CASTLED HOUSE WITH ITS WOODS • • • • • •   234 YOUTH OF MAN   V 64
        TWAS WHEN THE HEAVENLY HOUSE I TROD   • • • • • •   242 MORALITY   35
        HE WENDS UNFOLLOWD HE MUST HOUSE ALONE   • • • •   269 THYRSIS   209
        FOUR YEARS SINCE IN THE HOUSE   • • • • • • • •   280 HAWORTH CHURCH   4
        THE PARSONAGE-HOUSE AND THE GRAVES   • • • • •   283 HAWORTH CHURCH   65
        ENTEREST THE HOUSE OF THE GRAVE   • • • • • •   284 HAWORTH CHURCH   78
        ARE GREEN IN THE HOUSE OF ONE • • • • • • • •   280 HAWORTH CHURCH   V 4
        SEE IN THE DESOLATE HOUSE   • • • • • • • •   283 HAWORTH CHURCH   V
        IN THE SOUNDING LABOUR-HOUSE VAST • • • • • •   287 RUGBY CHAPEL   41
        THE HOUSE THE BROTHERHOOD AUSTERE   • • • • • •   301 GRANDE CHARTR   65
        SNATCHD FROM THE SLAUGHTER OF THY FATHERS HOUSE • • 330 MEROPE   22
        DO THOU TILL FOR THINE ENTRANCE TO THIS HOUSE   •   332 MEROPE   66
        AEGIMIUS GAVE OUR OUTCAST HOUSE A HOME   • • • •   337 MEROPE   224
        A HOUSE ONCE GREAT NOW DWINDLING IN ITS SONS   • •   337 MEROPE   237
        ROSE AND WITH FIRE AND SWORD ASSAILED MY HOUSE   •   340 MEROPE   344
        HOUSE OF THE GRAVE WHAT WE DO • • • • • • • •   342 MEROPE   391
        LIGHT TO SPRING UP TO THY HOUSE   • • • • • • •   343 MEROPE   407
        HIS MOST JUST PRAYER YET HIS HOUSE   • • • • • •   343 MEROPE   409
        HYLLUS THE CHIEF OF HIS HOUSE • • • • • • •   344 MEROPE   446
        TO WHAT HATH IN THIS HOUSE BEFALLN   • • • • •   354 MEROPE   700
        WHO TOLD ME THAT THE ROYAL HOUSE WAS HERE • • •   354 MEROPE   704
        HE DOTH THOU HAST BOTH HOUSE AND MASTER RIGHT •   354 MEROPE   707
        AND SUCH AS FITS A ROYAL HOUSE TO SHOW   • • •   359 MEROPE   871
        TO OUR UNHAPPY HOUSE THE DEBT WE OWE • • • • •   367 MEROPE   1048
        IN A KINGS HOUSE THY VICTIMS HERITAGE   • • • •   373 MEROPE   1179
        ONCE MORE ROLL BACK ON MY HOUSE   • • • • •   378 MEROPE   1244
        TOO DEAR HIS SECRET WILES HAVE COST OUR HOUSE •   380 MEROPE   1279
        THEIR LOYAL PASSION TOWRD MY FATHERS HOUSE   •   383 MEROPE   1359
        THY PRISON-HOUSE RAISED ONE IMPLORING CRY   • •   383 MEROPE   1371
        THAT HOUSE LIKE OURS INTESTINE MURDER MAIMS   •   384 MEROPE   1392
        TO ANNOUNCE THE RUIN OF MY HUSBANDS HOUSE   • • • 395 MEROPE   1738
        TO MAKE THE GATES OF THIS LONG-MOURNFUL HOUSE • 401 MEROPE   1884
        TO ONE UNHAPPY HOUSE THE DEBT WE OWE • • • • •   367 MEROPE   V1048

HOUSED
        ALL HOUSED WITHIN THE SLEEPING FARMS • • • • • •   218 BACCHANALIA 1   7

HOUSEHOLD
        BY CITY AND HOUSEHOLD GROUPD WE LIVE AND MANY SHOCKS 195 FRAG ANTIGONE   20
        UNTO THIS PIOUS HOUSEHOLD TO REPAY   • • • • • •   447 WESTMIN ABBEY   108

HOUSES
        SMOKY DWARF HOUSES • • • • • • • • • • • •   50 CONSOLATION   2
        HOUSES ARCADES ENAMELLD MOSQUES   • • • • • • •   94 SICK KING BOKH   199
        HOUSES WITH LONG WHITE SWEEP   • • • • • • •   242 SUMMER NIGHT   18
        THIS DOES NOT COME WITH HOUSES OR WITH GOLD   •   268 THYRSIS   203
        CETTE WITH ITS GLISTENING HOUSES WHITE   • • • • 275 SOUTHERN NIGHT   9
        WHITE HOUSES PRANK WHERE ONCE WERE HUTS   • • •   312 OBERMANN MORE   3
        CAN HOUSES THUS ILL-SEATED THUS EMBROILD   • • •   390 MEROPE   1559
        WHO WORSHIPPD ME IN THEIR HOUSES   • • • • • •   432 EMPEDOCLES II   114

HOUSETOPS
        A BREAK BETWEEN THE HOUSETOPS SHOWS   • • • • • •   242 SUMMER NIGHT   6

HOUSEWIFE
        WHERE AT HER OPEN DOOR THE HOUSEWIFE DARNS • • • • 258 SCHOLAR-GIPSY   102

HOVER
        NOR IDLY DO THESE SEA-BIRDS HOVER NEAR   • • • •   42 GIPSY CHILD   8
        AND BLITHELY DO THESE SEA-BIRDS HOVER NEAR • • • • 41 GIPSY CHILD   V 8

HOVER   (CONTINUED)
        BUT EARNESTLY I LONGD TO HOVER NEAR   • • • • •   125 BALDER DEAD 3   416

HOVERING
        HOVERING AND STOPPING OFT AS IF AFRAID   • • • •   124 BALDER DEAD 3   383

HOWBEIT
        HOWBEIT I WILL SEE AND DO HIS HEST   • • • • •   102 BALDER DEAD 1   244
        HOWBEIT WE ABIDE OUR DAY TILL THEN   • • • • •   111 BALDER DEAD 2   227
        HOWBEIT REPORT THY MESSAGE AND THEREWITH   • • • • 112 BALDER DEAD 2   273
        HOWBEIT STAY AND BE APPEASED AND TELL   • • • •   125 BALDER DEAD 3   428
        HOWBEIT I JUDGE AS LOST   • • • • • • •   415 EMPEDOCLES I 2   98

HOWL
        WHAT MUST I HOWL IN THE NEXT WORLD   • • • • • •   91 SICK KING BOKH   99

HOWLING
        YET I SEE THE HOWLING LEVELS   • • • • • •   26 NEW SIRENS   17
        THESE VEXT BRANCHES AND THIS HOWLING SKY   • • • •   27 NEW SIRENS   48
        THE STORM THE ABYSS THE HOWLING AND THE PAIN   • • 109 BALDER DEAD 2   154
        HE HEARD ACROSS THE HOWLING SEAS   • • • • • •   156 SAINT BRANDAN   5
        SHE WILL HEAR THE WINDS HOWLING   • • • • •   164 FORSAKEN MERM   114
        ABOVE THE HOWLING SENSES EBB AND FLOW   • • •   169 EAST LONDON   11
        OR THE HOWLING OUTERMOST MAIN   • • • • •   361 MEROPE   913
        WAKE AMID GLOOM AND HOWLING AND THE NOISE   • • •   373 MEROPE   1185
        THE HOWLING VOID TO SPAN   • • • • • • • •   415 EMPEDOCLES I 2   V 77

HOWLS
        LOUD HOWLS THE WIND SHARP PATTERS THE RAIN   • • • • 133 TRISTRAM 1   83

HUDDLING
        HIS HUDDLING YOUNG LEFT SOLE AT THAT HE CHECKS   • • 78 SOHRAB RUSTUM   563
        ARE SWEPT LIKE HUDDLING SHEEP ALONG   • • • • •   481 COURAGE   8

HUE
        THAT CHEEK OF LANGUID HUE   • • • • • • •   174 MEETING   6
        THY CHEEKS SOFT HUE AND FLUTTERING LACE   • • • • 184 TERRACE BERNE   23
        THOSE EYES OF DEEP SOFT LUCENT HUE   • • • • •   208 ON THE RHINE   18
        ONE COLOUR IN THY LIFE THE HUE OF TRUTH   • • • • 404 MEROPE   1996
        BUT FULL AND DEATHLESS AS THE DEEP DARK HUE   • •   463 ALARIC AT ROME   35

HUES
        WHEN THE FLUSHING HUES ARE FADING   • • • • •   33 NEW SIRENS   213
        AND THE DEEP HUES OF AN ITALIAN SKY   • • • • •   464 ALARIC AT ROME   69
        WERE MINGLING WITH THE SERE AND WITHERED HUES OF DEATH   466 ALARIC AT ROME 102
        AND THUS AMID THE GLORIOUS HUES OF EVEN   • • • • 466 ALARIC AT ROME   105

HUGE
        POISED ON THE TOP OF A HUGE WAVE OF FATE   • • •   72 SOHRAB RUSTUM   391
        COULD WIELD AN UNLOPPD TRUNK IT WAS AND HUGE   • •   73 SOHRAB RUSTUM   409
        AND STREWN THE CHANNELS WITH TORN BOUGHS SO HUGE   • • 73 SOHRAB RUSTUM   415
        FENRIS THE WOLF THE SERPENT HUGE AND ME   • • • • 110 BALDER DEAD 2   208
        AT THIS HUGE GLEAM-LIT FIREPLACE   • • • • • •   148 TRISTRAM 2   158
        AT THE HUGE GLEAM-LIT FIREPLACE   • • • • •   148 TRISTRAM 2   V 158
        HAVE FELT THEIR HUGE FRAMES NOT CONSTRUCTED RIGHT   239 REVOLUTIONS   15
        IN THE HUGE WORLD WHICH ROARS HARD BY   • • • •   249 KENSINGTON GARD   21
        IN THE HUGE WORLD THAT RUMBLES NIGH   • • • • •   KENSINGTON GARD V 21
        LIKE GHOSTS THE HUGE GNARLD OLIVES STAND   • • • • 275 SOUTHERN NIGHT   6
        UP BY THE STREAM WITH ITS HUGE   • • • • •   297 HEINES GRAVE   159
        HUGE IN THE GLOOM ACROSS IN THORNEY ISLE   • • • • 444 WESTMIN ABBEY   15

HULL
        DROVE ON ABLAZE ABOVE HER HULL WITH FIRE   • • • • 119 BALDER DEAD 3   192

HUM
        AND THEN YOU HEAR THE ORGANS HUM   • • • • • •   17 CHURCH BROU 2   28
        CREPT FROM THE OXUS SOON A HUM AROSE   • • • • •   86 SOHRAB RUSTUM   868
        OUT OF THE MIST AND HUM OF THAT LOW LAND   • • • •   87 SOHRAB RUSTUM   876
        THEIR ROCK-STRANGLED HUM   • • • • • • •   175 PARTING   30
        THE MOUNTAIN-BEES HUM   • • • • • • • •   176 PARTING   56
        ACROSS THE GIRDLING CITYS HUM   • • • • • •   248 KENSINGTON GARD   6
        HUM OER THE THYME THE GROUSE   • • • • • •   285 HAWORTH CHURCH   121
        YET THROUGH THE HUM OF TORRENT LONE   • • • • •   307 OBERMANN   33
        AND HEAR THE WILD BEES ALPINE HUM   • • • • •   313 OBERMANN MORE   47

HUMAN
        NOR WILL THAT DAY DAWN AT A HUMAN NOD   • • • •   7 REP FRIEND CONT   9
        FROM SOME TRANSIENT HUMAN SUN   • • • • •   31 NEW SIRENS   V 152
        THIN THIN THE PLEASANT HUMAN NOISES GROW   • • •   45 IN UTRUMQUE PAR   15
        HUMAN THINGS SO FAST ENTANGLED   • • • • •   49 SECOND BEST   10
        HUMAN THINGS SO DEEP ENTANGLED   • • • • •   SECOND BEST   V 10
        JUDGE VAIN BEFOREHAND HUMAN CARES   • • • • • •   59 RESIGNATION   232
        THE SEA WITHOUT A HUMAN SHORE   • • • • • •   156 SAINT BRANDAN   12
        BUT AH NOT HUMAN SOULS   • • • • • • •   161 NECKAN   64
        O HUMAN SOUL AS LONG AS THOU CANST SO   • • • •   169 EAST LONDON   9
        OF SHARERS IN A COMMON HUMAN FATE   • • • • •   170 WEST LONDON   11
        CHRIST SOME ONE SAYS WAS HUMAN AS WE ARE   • • •   170 BETTER PART   3
        HAVE DREAMD TWO HUMAN HEARTS MIGHT BLEND   • • •   181 ISOLATION MARG   38
        OF HUMAN MISERY WE   • • • • • • • •   211 DOVER BEACH   18
        IN LAWS BY HUMAN ARTISTS BOUND   • • • • • •   223 EPILOG LAOCOON   76

HUMAN   (CONTINUED)
        WHERE GAILY FLOWS THE HUMAN TIDE   • •   • • •   224 EPILOG LAOCOON   108
        LEAVE NOT A HUMAN SOUL   • • • • • • • • •   234 YOUTH OF MAN   57
        THE SAME HEART BEATS IN EVERY HUMAN BREAST • • • •   245 BURIED LIFE   23
        THERE BEATS ONE HEART IN EVERY HUMAN BREAST • • •   245 BURIED LIFE   V 23
        NOT HUMAN COMBATINGS WITH DEATH   • • • • •   251 WISH   48
        LEFT HUMAN HAUNT AND ON ALONE TILL NIGHT • • • •   269 THYRSIS   230
        HE TOOK THE SUFFERING HUMAN RACE   • • • • •   270 MEMORIAL VERSES   19
        OF HUMAN TASKS THEIR ONLY ONE   • • • • • •   301 GRANDE CHARTR   59
        A WOUNDED HUMAN SPIRIT TURNS   • • • • • •   307 OBERMANN   23
        OF HUMAN AGONY   • • • • • • • •   307 OBERMANN   36
        FROM HALF OF HUMAN FATE   • • • • • • •   308 OBERMANN   54
        MADE HUMAN LIFE A HELL   • • • • • • •   315 OBERMANN MORE   96
        HIS ALL TOO HUMAN CREEDS AND SCAN   • • • •   319 OBERMANN MORE   187
        HOW OF ALL HUMAN RULES THE OVER-TENSE   • • •   339 MEROPE   307
        TEARS COURSED TEARS HUMAN   • • • • • •   393 MEROPE   1669
        ONCE HUMAN CHEEKS   • • • • • • • •   393 MEROPE   1671
        SAVE MINE HE MUST NOT MEET A HUMAN EYE   • • •   408 EMPEDOCLES I 1   53
        AND WE WERE NOT SO FAR FROM HUMAN HAUNT   • • •   412 EMPEDOCLES I 2   10
        THOUGH THE NON-HUMAN POWERS   • • • • • •   421 EMPEDOCLES I 2   264
        TO EMBITTER HUMAN LIFE MALIGNANT DEITIES   • • •   422 EMPEDOCLES I 2   311
        OF LONG-PAST HUMAN THINGS   • • • • • •   423 EMPEDOCLES I 2   323
        LEAVES HUMAN EFFORT SCOPE   • • • • • •   426 EMPEDOCLES I 2   423
        THIS UNCONGENIAL PLACE THIS HUMAN LIFE   • • •   440 EMPEDOCLES II   366
        AND IN OUR INDIVIDUAL HUMAN STATE   • • • •   440 EMPEDOCLES II   367
        HAD HUMAN CRY NOT MARRD THE WORK DIVINE   • • •   447 WESTMIN ABBEY   104
        BRINGER OF HEAVENLY LIGHT A HUMAN HOUR   • • •   447 WESTMIN ABBEY   120
        NEARER HUMAN WERE THEIR POWERS   • • • • •   453 POOR MATTHIAS   45
        ALL THAT HUMAN PATHOS DEAR   • • • • • •   454 POOR MATTHIAS   62
        US THY HUMAN KEEPERS HARD   • • • • • •   456 POOR MATTHIAS   122
        HUMAN SUFFERING AT OUR SIDE   • • • • • •   457 POOR MATTHIAS   163
        HUMAN LONGINGS HUMAN FEARS   • • • • • •   457 POOR MATTHIAS   165
        HUMAN LONGINGS HUMAN FEARS   • • • • • •   457 POOR MATTHIAS   165
        WHAT ONCE HAD HUMAN PASSIONS HOPES AND FEARS   •   464 ALARIC AT ROME   52
        ALL NATURAL LOVE ALL HUMAN SYMPATHY   • • • •   467 ALARIC AT ROME   147
        FAIR BEYOND HUMAN BEAUTY AND HIS EYE   • • •   477 CROMWELL   177
        A LIFE WHOSE WAYS NO HUMAN THOUGHT COULD SCAN   •   478 CROMWELL   219
        AND WELTERS LIKE A HUMAN THING • • • • • •   479 HAYSWATER BOAT   7
        AND IN THEIR RUSH THE HUMAN RACE   • • • • •   481 COURAGE   7
        STILL MENDING LESSENING HUMAN ILL   • • • •   484 ROME-SICKNESS   28

HUMANE
        SWEET GENEROUS AND HUMANE   • • • • • • •   273 EDW QUILLINAN   16

HUMBLE
        THE HUMBLE GOOD FROM THE GROUND   • • • • •   287 RUGBY CHAPEL   50
        MY HUMBLE TOMB EXPLORE   • • • • • • • •   321 OBERMANN MORE   270
        TO SOME SMALL HUMBLE AND UNNOTED STRAND   • • •   395 MEROPE   1745

HUMBLED
        WHEN SHE SEES HER HUMBLED PALE AND STILL   • • •   144 TRISTRAM 2   60
        OER HUMBLED PRIDE AND SELF-REPROACHING WOE   • • •   462 ALARIC AT ROME   4
        BUT OER HER VANISHT MIGHT AND HUMBLED PRIDE   • •   468 ALARIC AT ROME   161

HUMBLER
        EFFACE THE HUMBLER GRAVES OF SEBERTS LINE   • • •   445 WESTMIN ABBEY   54
        THE HUMBLER SORT WHO SERVE AND TEND   • • • • •   459 KAISER DEAD   32

HUMBLY
        HE HEARS A VOICE SIGH HUMBLY WAIT   • • • • •   157 SAINT BRANDAN   23
        AND HUMBLY LAY THEE DOWN TO DIE   • • • • • •   450 GEISTS GRAVE   36

HUMID
        HUMID THE AIR LEAFLESS YET SOFT AS SPRING   • • •   263 THYRSIS   17
        THE HUMID CORRIDORS BEHOLD   • • • • • • •   300 GRANDE CHARTR   34
        NO CLOISTER-FLOOR OF HUMID STONE   • • • • • •   317 OBERMANN MORE   149

HUMMING
        FROM YOUR HUMMING FESTAL ROOM   • • • • • •   32 NEW SIRENS   184
        FROM THE HUMMING FESTAL ROOM   • • • • • • •   32 NEW SIRENS   V 184
        SHE SITS AT HER WHEEL IN THE HUMMING TOWN   • • • •   164 FORSAKEN MERM   87
        FOR THE HUMMING STREET AND THE CHILD WITH ITS TOY   164 FORSAKEN MERM   90

HUMS
        AND NEATH THE GARDEN-WALK IT HUMS   • • • • • •   184 TERRACE BERNE   11

HUN
        THE GOTH BOUND ROME-WARDS SO THE HUN • • • • • •   52 RESIGNATION   9

HUNDRED
        A HUNDRED LAMPS BEAMD IN THE TRANQUIL GLOOM   • •   11 MYCERINUS   94
        AND THIRTEEN HUNDRED YEARS AGONE THEY SAY   • • •   170 EAST AND WEST   3
        SO CHRIST SAID EIGHTEEN HUNDRED YEARS AGO   • • •   237 PROGRESS   13
        BUT WHAT I DREAM TWO HUNDRED YEARS ARE FLOWN   • •   259 SCHOLAR-GIPSY   131
        AND EACH HALF LIVES A HUNDRED DIFFERENT LIVES   • •   260 SCHOLAR-GIPSY   169
        WAVING HER HUNDRED HANDS A TORCH IN EACH   • • •   395 MEROPE   1735
        THESE HUNDRED DOCTORS TRY   • • • • • • •   417 EMPEDOCLES I 2   137
        TWELVE HUNDRED YEARS AND MORE   • • • • • • •   445 WESTMIN ABBEY   -51
        IN SOOTH IT SEEMS A HUNDRED YEAR   • • • • • •   480 HAYSWATER BOAT   35

HUNG
HUNG POISED AND THEN THE DARTING RIVER OF LIFE • • 25 DREAM 31
AND ROUND THEM STILL THE WATTLED HURDLES HUNG • • 109 BALDER DEAD 2 173
SUN MOON AND STARS WHICH THOU HAST HUNG IN HEAVEN 121 BALDER DEAD 3 264
HUNG SOFT IN THEIR HEADS • • • • • • 176 PARTING 54
THE MISTS ARE ON THE MOUNTAIN HUNG • • • • • 185 TERRACE BERNE 51
THE MISTS ARE ON THE MOUNTAINS HUNG • • • • • 185 TERRACE BERNE V 51
THROUGH CENTURIES PAST IT HAS HUNG SO • • • • 214 NEW ROME 19
ALL THE CENTURIES PAST IT HAS HUNG SO • • • • 214 NEW ROME V 19
BUT RUMOURS HUNG ABOUT THE COUNTRY-SIDE • • • 256 SCHOLAR-GIPSY 52
MOSS-HUNG BOULDERS AND THIN • • • • • • • 297 HEINES GRAVE 160
WHEN THE FIGHT HUNG IN DOUBT BUT SHE NOW • • • 343 MEROPE 429
BUT STILL OVER HIS SPEECH A GLOOM THERE HUNG • • 356 MEROPE 764
THERE LIKE A MIRROR HUNG • • • • • • • • 415 EMPEDOCLES I 2 80
TWICE HATH THE CLOUD HUNG OER THEE TWICE BEEN STAYED 465 ALARIC AT ROME 83

HUNGARIANS
HUNGARIANS SAVE THE WORLD RENEW THE STORIES • • 480 HUNGARIAN NAT 9

HUNGER
REMAINING IN THY HUNGER AND THY PAIN • • • • • • 42 GIPSY CHILD 12

HUNGRIER
STILL HUNGRIER FOR DELIGHT AS DELIGHTS GROW MORE RARE 424 EMPEDOCLES I 2 371

HUNGRY
AND THE HUNGRY THOUGHT THAT MUST BE FED • • • • 30 NEW SIRENS 130
HUNGRY AND BARREN AND SHARP AS THE SEA • • • • 39 STAGIRIUS 47

HUNT
AND IN WILD HUNT THROUGH MAZY TRACTS OF STARS • • 10 MYCERINUS 45
TO HUNT THE BOAR IN THE CRISP WOODS TILL EVE • • 18 CHURCH BROU 3 11
THE CASTLE AND THE DEWY WOODS AND HUNT • • • • 79 SOHRAB RUSTUM 629
THEN EVIDENCE CAME HIS COMRADES OF THE HUNT • • 365 MEROPE V

HUNTED
WERE HUNTED OUT AND TO ACHAIA FLED • • • • • • 338 MEROPE 286
RAILD AND HUNTED FROM THE WORLD • • • • • • 432 EMPEDOCLES II 105

HUNTER
AS WHEN SOME HUNTER IN THE SPRING HATH FOUND • • 77 SOHRAB RUSTUM 556
CONFRONTS THE DOG AND HUNTER IN THE SOUTH • • • • 99 BALDER DEAD 1 157
THE PEERLESS HUNTER HARPER KNIGHT • • • • • • 131 TRISTRAM 1 22
O HUNTER AND WITHOUT A FEAR • • • • • • • 149 TRISTRAM 2 187
THE HUNTER OF THE TANAGRAEAN FIELD • • • • • 197 FRAG ANTIGONE 64
HUNTER OERSHADOWING HIS BROW • • • • • • • 342 MEROPE 396
A GLADSOME HUNTER OF DEER • • • • • • • 347 MEROPE 520
AND SEEST MY STRIPLING HUNTER THERE AFIELD • • • 349 MEROPE 573
STAG DOGS AND HUNTER TO THE YAWNING GULPH • • • 358 MEROPE 826
THE HUNTER ON THE OUTLOOK • • • • • • • 392 MEROPE 1635
THE FLEET DESPERATE HUNTER • • • • • • • 393 MEROPE 1656
THE HAPPY HUNTER HE BASKS • • • • • • • 347 MEROPE V

HUNTERS
FLOWD THE HUNTERS MERRY TIDE • • • • • • • • 13 CHURCH BROU 1 8
HUNTERS GATHER BUGLES RING • • • • • • • • 13 CHURCH BROU 1 16
PALE AND BREATHLESS CAME THE HUNTERS • • • • • • 13 CHURCH BROU 1 25
CAME THE HUNTERS WITH THEIR LOAD • • • • • • 13 CHURCH BROU 1 32
SLOW AND TIRED CAME THE HUNTERS • • • • • • 14 CHURCH BROU 1 41
HO THIS WAY YE LAGGARD HUNTERS • • • • • • • 14 CHURCH BROU 1 43
THE JADED HUNTERS WITH THEIR BLOODY FREIGHT • • 18 CHURCH BROU 3 14
ALL BEASTS OF CHASE ALL BEASTS WHICH HUNTERS KNOW 69 SOHRAB RUSTUM 279
HATH TRAILD THE HUNTERS JAVELIN IN HIS SIDE • • 76 SOHRAB RUSTUM 505
HAS TRAILD THE HUNTERS JAVELIN IN HIS SIDE • • • 76 SOHRAB RUSTUM V 505
A TROOP OF OXFORD HUNTERS GOING HOME • • • • 267 THYRSIS 153
WHERE HUNTERS GATHER STAGHOUNDS BAY • • • • • 305 GRANDE CHARTR 183
CATES FROM OUR HUNTERS POUCH ARCADIAN FARE • • • 356 MEROPE 753
RARE STRAGGLING HUNTERS FOILD BY BRAKE AND CRAG • 357 MEROPE 798
SOME STRAGGLING HUNTERS TO MY AID TO ROUSE • • • 358 MEROPE 836
HIS BROAD-BRIMMD HUNTERS HAT WHICH IN THE BAY • • 358 MEROPE 843
JADED WITH TRAVEL CLAD IN HUNTERS GARB • • • • 363 MEROPE 957
BROWND WITH THINE OPEN-AIR FREE HUNTERS LIFE • • 373 MEROPE 1164

HUNTING
TIS MY LORD COME BACK FROM HUNTING • • • • • 14 CHURCH BROU 1 39
FROM HUNTING AND A GREAT WAY OFF DESCRIES • • • 78 SOHRAB RUSTUM 562
ART TIRED WITH HUNTING • • • • • • • • 188 STRAYED REVEL 72
FROM HUNTING WITH THE BERKSHIRE HOUNDS THEY COME • 267 THYRSIS 155
AND ON THE HUNTING-RAMBLES WHICH HIS HEART • • • 355 MEROPE 725
ON SUCH A HUNTING-JOURNEY THREE MORNS SINCE • • 355 MEROPE 730
HE ON A HUNTING PARTY TWO DAYS SINCE • • • • • 364 MEROPE 973
WITH THY SOILD HUNTING-COAT AND SANDALS TORN • • 372 MEROPE 1159
OOZING THROUGH THY SOAKD HUNTING-SHIRT WITH LIMBS 373 MEROPE 1173
HE ON A HUNTING PARTY THREE DAYS SINCE • • • • 364 MEROPE V 973

HUNTSMAN
A STATELY HUNTSMAN CLAD IN GREEN • • • • • • 147 TRISTRAM 2 153

HUNTSMEN
WITH BEATERS HOUNDS AND HUNTSMEN HE AND I • • • 355 MEROPE 731

HURDLES

AND ROUND THEM STILL THE WATTLED HURDLES HUNG   • •   109 BALDER DEAD 2   173

HURL

AND HURL THEE IN A LAKE TO SINK OR SWIM   • • • •   114 BALDER DEAD 3   26

HURLD

THE STRONG SPELL WHICH PASSION UPON HIM HATH HURLD   20 MODERN SAPPHO   V   22
HE SPOKE AND RUSTUM ANSWERD NOT BUT HURLD • • • •   73 SOHRAB RUSTUM   398
THE STRIFE AND HURLD ME ON MY FATHERS SPEAR • • •   82 SOHRAB RUSTUM   715
THE GENTLENESS TOO RUDELY HURLD • • • • •   180 FAREWELL   85
I ON MENS IMPIOUS UPROAR HURLD • • • • • •   249 KENSINGTON GARD   25
BUT I ON MENS IMPIOUS TUMULT HURLD • • • • • •   KENSINGTON GARD   V   25
I ON MENS IMPIOUS TUMULT HURLD • • • • • • •   KENSINGTON GARD   V   25
ALOFT ARE HURLD IN THE DUST • • • • • • •   288 RUGBY CHAPEL   64
WHO WAS ON ACTION HURLD • • • • • • • •   311 OBERMANN   154
AND ON HER HEAD WAS HURLD • • • • • •   316 OBERMANN MORE   108
WHY WERE YE TOO TO DEATH NOT HURLD • • • • •   320 OBERMANN MORE   219
SHAKEN AND RUDELY HURLD • • • • • •   416 EMPEDOCLES I 2   V 115
AND HURLD HIM ON THE FIELD OF LIFE • • • • •   481 DESTINY   7

HURRIED

SAW HIM LOOK EASED AND HURRIED BY • • • • •   158 SAINT BRANDAN   52
UP THE STEEP STREET I HURRIED FAST • • • • •   177 FAREWELL   7
AND HURRIED TORN WITH INWARD STRIFE • • • • •   317 OBERMANN MORE   135
THOU THAT HAST GAZED AS THE WORLD HURRIED BY • •   463 ALARIC AT ROME   23

HURRY

TO-MORROW HURRY THROUGH THE FIELDS • • • • •   205 CALAIS SANDS   33
THEY LIGHT ME ONCE THEY HURRY BY • • • • • •   209 DESPONDENCY   7
WITH ITS SICK HURRY ITS DIVIDED AIMS • • • • •   261 SCHOLAR-GIPSY   204
AND HURRY WHERE THEY DRIVE • • • • • • •   415 EMPEDOCLES I 2   95
WILL HURRY US WITH THEM ON THEIR HOMELESS MARCH • •   439 EMPEDOCLES II   359
BUT TRAVELLERS IN A HURRY TO ARRIVE • • • • •   LUCRETIUS 6   2

HURRYING

AND CALL THIS HURRYING FEVER GENEROUS FIRE • • • •   37 YOUTHS AGIT   12
MINGLE WITH HIS HURRYING DREAM • • • • • • •   136 TRISTRAM 1   183
LIGHT IGNORANCE AND HURRYING UNSURE THOUGHTS • •   198 FRAG DEJANEIRA   2

HURST

SHEPHERDS HAD MET HIM ON THE HURST IN SPRING • • •   256 SCHOLAR-GIPSY   57
ITS FIR-TOPPED HURST ITS FARMS ITS QUIET FIELDS • •   269 THYRSIS   217

HURT

MID STRUGGLING SUFFERERS HURT TO DEATH SHE LAY • •   166 AUSTERITY POET   9
AND NO MAN MAY THE OTHERS HURT BEHOLD • • • •   238 PROGRESS   30
AND CAME HOME HURT TO DEATH AND HERE • • • • •   278 SOUTHERN NIGHT   95
AND FOR WHOSE HURT COURAGE IS NOT THE CURE • • • •   429 EMPEDOCLES II   14

HURTLING

THE HURTLING POLAR LIGHTS ARE NEARD • • • • • •   156 SAINT BRANDAN   11

HURTS

WHAT FOOL IS THIS THAT HURTS OUR EARS • • • •   89 SICK KING BOKH   40

HUSBAND

DEAD HER PRINCELY YOUTHFUL HUSBAND • • • • • •   14 CHURCH BROU 1   49
AH I HUSBAND WHATS GROWN RARE • • • • • • •   22 MEMORY-PICTURE   V
FOR HE MY HUSBAND LEFT ME HERE TO PINE • • • •   116 BALDER DEAD 3   106
ROYAL STATE WITH MARC MY DEEP-WRONGD HUSBAND • •   144 TRISTRAM 2   45
WITH HER OWN HUSBAND BY THE LIBYAN SEA • • • •   173 MONICAS PRAYER   8
THY HUSBAND WEAK AVENGER THROUGH THYSELF • • • •   201 PHILOMELA   V
GRAVE GAY CHILD PARENT HUSBAND WIFE • • • • •   226 EPILOG LAOCOON   161
THE KING CRESPHONTES THY GREAT HUSBAND FALL • • •   333 MEROPE   118
HIM WHOM THOU HIDDEST WHEN THY HUSBAND FELL • • •   334 MEROPE   145
TO THEIR DEAD KING THY HUSBAND YEA TOO DEAR • • •   335 MEROPE   175
WHO TO MESSENIA WITH THY HUSBAND CAME • • • •   337 MEROPE   230
HUSBAND AND KING TO THY GRAVE • • • • • • •   342 MEROPE   401
RATHER ON THEE I CALL HUSBAND BELOVED • • • •   349 MEROPE   584
MY HUSBAND WANDERING WITH HIS STERN COMPEERS • •   367 MEROPE   1033
O HUSBAND O CLOTHED • • • • • • • •   371 MEROPE   1139
THE WIDOW OF A HUSBAND UNAVENGED • • • • • •   403 MEROPE   1955

HUSBANDS

OF THY DEAD HUSBANDS FACTION VIGOROUS ONCE • • • •   334 MEROPE   139
HAD MOST THY HUSBANDS CONFIDENCE CONSULT • • • •   337 MEROPE   239
I ASK THEE NOT TO APPROVE THY HUSBANDS DEATH • •   340 MEROPE   338
AT THE DREAD ALTAR OF HER HUSBANDS TOMB • • • •   385 MEROPE   1414
THAN THINE ILLUSTRIOUS HUSBANDS TO AVENGE • • • •   390 MEROPE   1569
TO ANNOUNCE THE RUIN OF MY HUSBANDS HOUSE • • • •   395 MEROPE   1738
AT THY DEAD HUSBANDS NAME THE PEOPLE SHOW • • • •   401 MEROPE   1894
AND FOUND HIM AT MY HUSBANDS SIDE HIS FRIEND • •   403 MEROPE   1973

HUSH

HUSH YE WILL SAY IT IS ETERNITY • • • • • •   19 CHURCH BROU 3   40
HUSH NO WORDS THAT SMILE I SEE FORGIVES ME • • • •   144 TRISTRAM 2   69
HUSH TIS VAIN I FEEL MY END APPROACHING • • • •   145 TRISTRAM 2   81
THEN HUSH THOU BOISTEROUS BUGLE-PEAL • • • • • •   149 TRISTRAM 2   182

HUSH   (CONTINUED)
        THE HUSH AMONG THE SHINING STARS   • • • • • •   180 FAREWELL   79
        BUT HUSH HAEMON WHOM ANTIGONE   • • • • • • •   196 FRAG ANTIGONE   39
        SO WAS THE HUSH   • • • • • • • • • • •   219 BACCHANALIA 1   51
        SO WAS THE HUSH   • • • • • • • • • • •   221 BACCHANALIA 2   64
        HUSH FOR TEARS   • • • • • • • • • • •   235 YOUTH OF MAN   97
        HUSH FOR FRUIT   • • • • • • • • • • •   235 YOUTH OF MAN   99
        GIVE ME THY HAND AND HUSH AWHILE   • • • • •   245 BURIED LIFE   9
        AND THE WIDTH OF THE WATERS THE HUSH • • • • •   254 FUTURE   78
        BUT HUSH THE UPLAND HATH A SUDDEN LOSS   • • •   267 THYRSIS   151
        WE PAUSE WE HUSH OUR HEART   • • • • • •   424 EMPEDOCLES I 2   372
        BUT HUSH THIS MOURNFUL STRAIN   • • • • • •   448 WESTMIN ABBEY   131

HUSHD
        WAS HUSHD AND STILL THE MEN WERE PLUNGED IN SLEEP   61 SOHRAB RUSTUM   4
        REJOICING THROUGH THE HUSHD CHORASMIAN WASTE   • •   87 SOHRAB RUSTUM   878
        THROUGH THE HUSHD CAMP TO PERAN-WISAS TENT   • •   61 SOHRAB RUSTUM   V 11
        COME TO THE WINDOW HUSHD IS THE NIGHT-AIR   • • •   210 DOVER BEACH   V   6
        NOW STRIFES ARE HUSHD OUR EARS DOTH MEET   • • •   219 BACCHANALIA 2   14
        NOW STRIFE IS HUSHD OUR EARS DOTH MEET   • • •   219 BACCHANALIA 2   V 14

HUSK
        THE CRACKLING HUSK-HEAPS BURN AS IF   • • • • •   312 OBERMANN MORE   11
        THEIR CRACKLING HUSK-HEAPS BURN AS IF   • • • •   312 OBERMANN MORE   V 11

HUSSEIN
        O HUSSEIN LEAD ME TO THE KING   • • • • • • •   87 SICK KING BOKH   10
        LET HUSSEIN IF THOU WILT MAKE HASTE   • • • • •   88 SICK KING BOKH   27

HUSTLE
        THEY HUSTLE ONE ANOTHER AND THEY PASS   • • • •   262 THYRSIS   V

HUSTLING
        BUT ALL OUR HUSTLING MORROWS ONLY MAKE   • • • •   262 THYRSIS   V

HUT
        REJOINS HER IN THEIR HUT UPON THE SANDS   • • • •   70 SOHRAB RUSTUM   289
        IN EVERY HUT ALONG THIS SEA-COAST WILD   • • • •   152 TRISTRAM 3   109
        OF MY HUT BY THE CHESTNUTS   • • • • • • •   186 STRAYED REVEL   26
        WHERE THEY LAY BY THE HUT DOOR   • • • • • •   186 STRAYED REVEL   32
        TO THE STONE-ROOFD HUT AT THE TOP   • • • • •   297 HEINES GRAVE   166
        SOLEMN OER HUT AND WOOD   • • • • • • • •   323 OBERMANN MORE   330

HUTS
        RARE THE LONE PASTORAL HUTS MARVEL NOT THOU   • •   45 IN UTRUMQUE PAR   17
        THE HUTS OF COURRERIE APPEAR   • • • • • • •   299 GRANDE CHARTR   18
        WHITE HOUSES PRANK WHERE ONCE WERE HUTS   • • •   312 OBERMANN MORE   3
        THE HUTS OF AVANT SHINE   • • • • • • • •   312 OBERMANN MORE   14
        AND PASTORAL HUTS I HID MY HEAD   • • • • • •   321 OBERMANN MORE   251

HYACINTH
        LIKE SOME RICH HYACINTH WHICH BY THE SCYTHE   • •   80 SOHRAB RUSTUM   634

HYACINTHS
        OF HYACINTHS AND ON LATE ANEMONIES   • • • • • •   414 EMPEDOCLES I 2   50
        OF HYACINTHS AND ON LATE ANEMONES   • • • • • •   414 EMPEDOCLES I 2   V 50

HYDASPES
        HYPHASIS OR HYDASPES WHEN HIGH UP   • • • • • •   73 SOHRAB RUSTUM   412

HYDE
        ONE MORN AS THROUGH HYDE PARK WE WALKD   • • • •   221 EPILOG LAOCOON   1

HYLLUS
        HYLLUS THE CHIEF OF HIS HOUSE   • • • • • • • •   344 MEROPE   446

HYMN
        TO HYMN THE CONQUERING MARCH OF ROME   • • • • •   300 GRANDE CHARTR   51
        FIRST HYMN THEY THE FATHER   • • • • • • •   443 EMPEDOCLES II   461

HYPEREIA
        OR BEAR PAILS TO THE WELL OF MESSEIS OR HYPEREIA • •   HOMER TRANS   30

HYPHASIS
        HYPHASIS OR HYDASPES WHEN HIGH UP   • • • • • •   73 SOHRAB RUSTUM   412

I
        MUCH HE WHOSE FRIENDSHIP I NOT LONG SINCE WON   • •   2 TO A FRIEND   5
        HAST THOU NO LIP FOR WELCOME SO I SAID   • • • •   3 EMERSONS ESSAYS   5
        IT CHANCED I KNOW NOT HOW MY DREAM WAS FLED   • •   EMERSONS ESSAYS   V   8
        IT CHANCED I KNOW NOT HOW MY JOY WAS FLED   • • •   EMERSONS ESSAYS   V   8
        GOD KNOWS IT I AM WITH YOU IF TO PRIZE   • • • •   6 REP FRIEND   1
        THEN AM I YOURS AND WHAT YOU FEEL I SHARE   • • •   7 REP FRIEND   14
        THEN AM I YOURS AND WHAT YOU FEEL I SHARE   • • •   7 REP FRIEND   14
        YET WHEN I MUSE ON WHAT LIFE IS I SEEM   • • • •   7 REP FRIEND CONT   1
        YET WHEN I MUSE ON WHAT LIFE IS I SEEM   • • • •   7 REP FRIEND CONT   1
        CHILDREN AS SUCH FORGIVE THEM HAVE I KNOWN   • • •   8 RELIGIOUS ISOL   1
        I WILL UNFOLD MY SENTENCE AND MY CRIME   • • • •   9 MYCERINUS   7
        I SATE OBEDIENT IN THE FIERY PRIME   • • • • •   9 MYCERINUS   9
        I LOVED THE GOOD HE SCORND AND HATED WRONG   • • •   9 MYCERINUS   15

I

(CONTINUED)

I LOOKD FOR LIFE MORE LASTING RULE MORE HIGH	9	MYCERINUS	17
AND WHEN SIX YEARS ARE MEASURED LO I DIE	9	MYCERINUS	18
YET SURELY O MY PEOPLE DID I DEEM	9	MYCERINUS	19
THE REST I GIVE TO JOY EVEN WHILE I SPEAK	10	MYCERINUS	55
THE REST I GIVE TO JOY EVEN WHILE I SPEAK	10	MYCERINUS	55
I WILL GO FORTH THOUGH SOMETHING WOULD I SAY	10	MYCERINUS	68
I WILL GO FORTH THOUGH SOMETHING WOULD I SAY	10	MYCERINUS	68
SOMETHING YET WHAT I KNOW NOT FOR THE GODS	10	MYCERINUS	69
I GO AND I RETURN NOT BUT THE WILL	11	MYCERINUS	74
I GO AND I RETURN NOT BUT THE WILL	11	MYCERINUS	74
I WILL GO FORTH BUT SOMETHING WOULD I SAY	10	MYCERINUS V	68
I WILL GO FORTH BUT SOMETHING WOULD I SAY	10	MYCERINUS V	68
I SHALL SUFFER BUT THEY WILL OUTLIVE THEIR AFFECTION	20	MODERN SAPPHO	17
I SHALL WEEP BUT THEIR LOVE WILL BE COOLING AND HE	20	MODERN SAPPHO	18
PERCEIVE BUT A VOICE AS I COME TO HIS SIDE	20	MODERN SAPPHO	26
IT WAS WELL WITH ME ONCE IF I SAW HIM TO-MORROW	19	MODERN SAPPHO V	
AH WOULD THAT I DID TOO	20	REQUIESCAT	4
I WITH LITTLE LAND TO STIR	22	MEMORY-PICTURE	5
ONCE I SAID A FACE IS GONE	23	MEMORY-PICTURE	9
MANY A FACE I SO LET FLEE	23	MEMORY-PICTURE	13
SOME DAY NEXT YEAR I SHALL BE	23	MEMORY-PICTURE	19
AH I HOPE YET ONCE AWAY	23	MEMORY-PICTURE	21
THOSE FRANK EYES WHERE DEEP I SEE	24	MEMORY-PICTURE	45
TO PAINT ILL AS I HAVE DONE	24	MEMORY-PICTURE	51
AH I HUSBAND WHATS GROWN RARE	22	MEMORY-PICTURE V	
YOUNG I SAID A FACE IS GONE	23	MEMORY-PICTURE V	9
LONG I SAID A FACE IS GONE	23	MEMORY-PICTURE V	9
MANY A FACE I THEN LET BY	23	MEMORY-PICTURE V	13
MANY A FACE I THEN LET FLEE	23	MEMORY-PICTURE V	13
WAS IT A DREAM WE SAILD I THOUGHT WE SAILD	24	DREAM	1
MARTIN AND I DOWN A GREEN ALPINE STREAM	24	DREAM	2
I WHO IN YOUR TRAIN AT MORNING	26	NEW SIRENS	5
FOR I DREAMD THEY WORE YOUR FORMS	26	NEW SIRENS	10
YET I SEE THE HOWLING LEVELS	26	NEW SIRENS	17
I AM DUMB ALAS TOO SOON ALL	29	NEW SIRENS	89
YET I THINK AT GODS TRIBUNAL	29	NEW SIRENS	91
ON THESE LAWNS I SAW YOU PLAYING	29	NEW SIRENS	95
YES I MUSE AND IF THE DAWNING	29	NEW SIRENS	105
DO I BRIGHTEN AT YOUR SORROW	31	NEW SIRENS	163
WHERE I STAND THE GRASS IS GLOWING	32	NEW SIRENS	187
BUT I HEAR THE NORTH WIND BLOWING	32	NEW SIRENS	189
AND I FEEL THE COLD NIGHT-AIR	32	NEW SIRENS	190
CAN I LOOK ON YOUR SWEET FACES	32	NEW SIRENS	191
SHALL I SEEK THAT I MAY SCORN HER	35	NEW SIRENS	271
SHALL I SEEK THAT I MAY SCORN HER	35	NEW SIRENS	271
HER I LOVED AT EVENTIDE	35	NEW SIRENS	272
SHALL I ASK WHAT FADED MOURNER	35	NEW SIRENS	273
WHEN I SHALL BE DIVORCED SOME TEN YEARS HENCE	37	YOUTHS AGIT	1
FROM THIS POOR PRESENT SELF WHICH I AM NOW	37	YOUTHS AGIT	2
SHALL I NOT JOY YOUTHS HEATS ARE LEFT BEHIND	37	YOUTHS AGIT	5
AH NO FOR THEN I SHALL BEGIN TO FIND	37	YOUTHS AGIT	7
THEN I SHALL WISH ITS AGITATIONS BACK	37	YOUTHS AGIT	9
THEN I SHALL PRAISE THE HEAT WHICH THEN I LACK	37	YOUTHS AGIT	11
THEN I SHALL PRAISE THE HEAT WHICH THEN I LACK	37	YOUTHS AGIT	11
SO FAR AS I CONCEIVE THE WORLDS REBUKE	37	WORLDS TRIUMPHS	1
I HAVE KEPT UNINFRINGED MY NATURES LAW	40	HUMAN LIFE	4
TO GUIDE ME I HAVE STEERD BY TO THE END	40	HUMAN LIFE	6
GLOOMS THAT GO DEEP AS THINE I HAVE NOT KNOWN	42	GIPSY CHILD	17
OR DO I WAIT TO HEAR SOME GRAY-HAIRD KING	43	GIPSY CHILD	33
I THINK THOU WILT HAVE FATHOMD LIFE TOO FAR	43	GIPSY CHILD	47
I TOO BUT SEEM	46	IN UTRUMQUE PAR	42
CRITIAS LONG SINCE I KNOW	46	WORLD QUIETIST	9
YET WHILE I LANGUISH	50	CONSOLATION	6
I WOULD ETERNALISE	52	CONSOLATION	63
I WOULD ANNIHILATE	52	CONSOLATION	68
BUT FAUSTA I REMEMBER WELL	54	RESIGNATION	82
ALONE WE TREAD IT YOU AND I	55	RESIGNATION	88
AND DOES NOT SAY I AM ALONE	57	RESIGNATION	169
THOSE GIPSIES SO YOUR THOUGHTS I SCAN	58	RESIGNATION	203
WEAK YET NOT WEAK I MIGHT REPLY	59	RESIGNATION	255
IF I MIGHT LEND THEIR LIFE A VOICE	60	RESIGNATION	269
THOU KNOWST ME PERAN-WISA IT IS I	62	SOHRAB RUSTUM	34
SLEEP BUT I SLEEP NOT ALL NIGHT LONG I LIE	62	SOHRAB RUSTUM	36
SLEEP BUT I SLEEP NOT ALL NIGHT LONG I LIE	62	SOHRAB RUSTUM	36
TOSSING AND WAKEFUL AND I COME TO THEE	62	SOHRAB RUSTUM	37
AND I WILL TELL THEE WHAT MY HEART DESIRES	62	SOHRAB RUSTUM	41
I CAME AMONG THE TARTARS AND BORE ARMS	62	SOHRAB RUSTUM	43
I HAVE STILL SERVED AFRASIAB WELL AND SHOWN	62	SOHRAB RUSTUM	44
THIS TOO THOU KNOWST THAT WHILE I STILL BEAR ON	62	SOHRAB RUSTUM	46
I SEEK ONE MAN ONE MAN AND ONE ALONE	62	SOHRAB RUSTUM	49
RUSTUM MY FATHER WHO I HOPED SHOULD GREET	62	SOHRAB RUSTUM	50
SO I LONG HOPED BUT HIM I NEVER FIND	62	SOHRAB RUSTUM	53
SO I LONG HOPED BUT HIM I NEVER FIND	62	SOHRAB RUSTUM	53
COME THEN HEAR NOW AND GRANT ME WHAT I ASK	62	SOHRAB RUSTUM	54
LET THE TWO ARMIES REST TO-DAY BUT I	62	SOHRAB RUSTUM	55
TO MEET ME MAN TO MAN IF I PREVAIL	62	SOHRAB RUSTUM	57
RUSTUM WILL SURELY HEAR IT IF I FALL	62	SOHRAB RUSTUM	58
FOR NOW IT IS NOT AS WHEN I WAS YOUNG	63	SOHRAB RUSTUM	79
FAIN WOULD I KNOW THEE SAFE AND WELL THOUGH LOST	63	SOHRAB RUSTUM	88

I

(CONTINUED)

GO I WILL GRANT THEE WHAT THY HEART DESIRES	• •	63 SOHRAB RUSTUM	93
HIM WILL I SEEK AND CARRY TO HIS EAR • • •	• •	66 SOHRAB RUSTUM	180
GO TO IF IRANS CHIEFS ARE OLD THEN I • • •	• •	67 SOHRAB RUSTUM	221
THE YOUNG MAY RISE AT SOHRABS VAUNTS NOT I •	• •	68 SOHRAB RUSTUM	227
FOR WHAT CARE I THOUGH ALL SPEAK SOHRABS FAME	• •	68 SOHRAB RUSTUM	228
FOR WOULD THAT I MYSELF HAD SUCH A SON •	• •	68 SOHRAB RUSTUM	229
AND NOT THAT ONE SLIGHT HELPLESS GIRL I HAVE	• •	68 SOHRAB RUSTUM	230
AND I TO TARRY WITH THE SNOW-HAIRD ZAL • •	• •	68 SOHRAB RUSTUM	232
THERE WOULD I GO AND HANG MY ARMOUR UP •	• •	68 SOHRAB RUSTUM	236
AND SPEND THE GOODLY TREASUURES I HAVE GOT •	• •	68 SOHRAB RUSTUM	238
ARE NOT THEY MORTAL AM NOT I MYSELF • • •	• •	68 SOHRAB RUSTUM	254
BUT I WILL FIGHT UNKNOWN AND IN PLAIN ARMS •	• •	68 SOHRAB RUSTUM	257
BEHOLD ME I AM VAST AND CLAD IN IRON • •	• •	71 SOHRAB RUSTUM	325
AND TRIED AND I HAVE STOOD ON MANY A FIELD •	• •	71 SOHRAB RUSTUM	326
OF BLOOD AND I HAVE FOUGHT WITH MANY A FOE •	• •	71 SOHRAB RUSTUM	327
AND FIGHT BENEATH MY BANNER TILL I DIE • •	• •	71 SOHRAB RUSTUM	332
AH ME I MUSE WHAT THIS YOUNG FOX MAY MEAN •	• •	71 SOHRAB RUSTUM	347
FOR IF I NOW CONFESS THIS THING HE ASKS •	• •	71 SOHRAB RUSTUM	349
I CHALLENGED ONCE WHEN THE TWO ARMIES CAMPD •	• •	72 SOHRAB RUSTUM	357
SHRANK ONLY RUSTUM DARED THEN HE AND I • •	• •	72 SOHRAB RUSTUM	360
OF RUSTUM I AM HERE WHOM THOU HAST CALLD •	• •	72 SOHRAB RUSTUM	366
FOR WELL I KNOW THAT DID GREAT RUSTUM STAND •	• •	72 SOHRAB RUSTUM	370
BUT BEING WHAT I AM I TELL THEE THIS • •	• •	72 SOHRAB RUSTUM	373
BUT BEING WHAT I AM I TELL THEE THIS • •	• •	72 SOHRAB RUSTUM	373
I AM NO GIRL TO BE MADE PALE BY WORDS • •	• •	72 SOHRAB RUSTUM	381
BEGIN THOU ART MORE VAST MORE DREAD THAN I •	• •	72 SOHRAB RUSTUM	385
AND THOU ART PROVED I KNOW AND I AM YOUNG •	• •	72 SOHRAB RUSTUM	386
AND THOU ART PROVED I KNOW AND I AM YOUNG •	• •	72 SOHRAB RUSTUM	386
BUT RISE AND BE NOT WROTH NOT WROTH AM I •	• •	74 SOHRAB RUSTUM	429
NO WHEN I SEE THEE WRATH FORSAKES MY SOUL •	• •	74 SOHRAB RUSTUM	430
BOY AS I AM I HAVE SEEN BATTLES TOO • •	• •	74 SOHRAB RUSTUM	433
BOY AS I AM I HAVE SEEN BATTLES TOO • •	• •	74 SOHRAB RUSTUM	433
WHOM I MAY MEET AND STRIKE AND FEEL NO PANG •	• •	74 SOHRAB RUSTUM	444
OF WAR I FIGHT IT OUT AND HAND TO HAND • •	• •	75 SOHRAB RUSTUM	464
AND CUNNING ALL THE PITY I HAD IS GONE •	• •	75 SOHRAB RUSTUM	467
FOR WERE I MATCHD WITH TEN SUCH MEN AS THEE •	• •	77 SOHRAB RUSTUM	544
AND I WERE THAT WHICH TILL TO-DAY I WAS • •	• •	77 SOHRAB RUSTUM	545
AND I WERE THAT WHICH TILL TO-DAY I WAS • •	• •	77 SOHRAB RUSTUM	545
THEY SHOULD BE LYING HERE I STANDING THERE •	• •	77 SOHRAB RUSTUM	546
THAT NAME AND SOMETHING I CONFESS IN THEE •	• •	77 SOHRAB RUSTUM	548
MY FATHER WHOM I SEEK THROUGH ALL THE WORLD •	• •	77 SOHRAB RUSTUM	554
AH YES HE HAD AND THAT LOST SON AM I • •	• •	78 SOHRAB RUSTUM	580
SOMEWHERE I KNOW NOT WHERE BUT FAR FROM HERE •	• •	78 SOHRAB RUSTUM	583
OH COULD I LIVE TILL I THAT GRIEF HAD SEEN •	• •	78 SOHRAB RUSTUM	588
OH COULD I LIVE TILL I THAT GRIEF HAD SEEN •	• •	78 SOHRAB RUSTUM	588
YET HIM I PITY NOT SO MUCH BUT HER • • •	• •	78 SOHRAB RUSTUM	589
HER MOST I PITY WHO NO MORE WILL SEE • •	• •	78 SOHRAB RUSTUM	593
AND FALSEHOOD WHILE I LIVED WAS FAR FROM MINE •	• •	80 SOHRAB RUSTUM	657
I TELL THEE PRICKD UPON THIS ARM I BEAR •	• •	80 SOHRAB RUSTUM	658
I TELL THEE PRICKD UPON THIS ARM I BEAR •	• •	80 SOHRAB RUSTUM	658
FATHER FORBEAR FOR I BUT MEET TO-DAY • • •	• •	82 SOHRAB RUSTUM	708
WHEN FIRST I SAW THEE AND THY HEART SPOKE TOO	• •	82 SOHRAB RUSTUM	712
I KNOW IT BUT FATE TROD THOSE PROMPTINGS DOWN	• •	82 SOHRAB RUSTUM	713
BUT LET US SPEAK NO MORE OF THIS I FIND •	• •	82 SOHRAB RUSTUM	716
MY FATHER LET ME FEEL THAT I HAVE FOUND •	• •	82 SOHRAB RUSTUM	717
I CAME AND LIKE THE WIND I GO AWAY • •	• •	82 SOHRAB RUSTUM	723
I CAME AND LIKE THE WIND I GO AWAY • •	• •	82 SOHRAB RUSTUM	723
THAT I SHOULD ONE DAY FIND THY LORD AND THEE	• •	83 SOHRAB RUSTUM	745
O RUKSH THOU ART MORE FORTUNATE THAN I •	• •	83 SOHRAB RUSTUM	747
FOR THOU HAST GONE WHERE I SHALL NEVER GO •	• •	83 SOHRAB RUSTUM	748
AND SAID O RUKSH BEAR RUSTUM WELL BUT I •	• •	83 SOHRAB RUSTUM	755
THE YELLOW OXUS BY WHOSE BRINK I DIE • •	• •	83 SOHRAB RUSTUM	766
OH THAT I SAW ITS GRAINS OF YELLOW SILT •	• •	83 SOHRAB RUSTUM	769
DO THOU THE DEEDS I DIE TOO YOUNG TO DO •	• •	84 SOHRAB RUSTUM	775
WHICH FOLLOW ME I PRAY THEE SLAY NOT THESE •	• •	84 SOHRAB RUSTUM	779
AND I BE NOT FORGOTTEN IN MY GRAVE • •	• •	84 SOHRAB RUSTUM	794
SO SHALL IT BE FOR I WILL BURN MY TENTS •	• •	84 SOHRAB RUSTUM	797
AND I WILL LAY THEE IN THAT LOVELY EARTH •	• •	84 SOHRAB RUSTUM	802
AND I WILL SPARE THY HOST YEA LET THEM GO •	• •	84 SOHRAB RUSTUM	806
WHAT SHOULD I DO WITH SLAYING ANY MORE •	• •	85 SOHRAB RUSTUM	808
FOR WOULD THAT ALL WHOM I HAVE EVER SLAIN •	• •	85 SOHRAB RUSTUM	809
AND THROUGH WHOSE DEATH I WON THAT FAME I HAVE	• •	85 SOHRAB RUSTUM	812
AND THROUGH WHOSE DEATH I WON THAT FAME I HAVE	• •	85 SOHRAB RUSTUM	812
AND I WERE NOTHING BUT A COMMON MAN • •	• •	85 SOHRAB RUSTUM	813
OR RATHER WOULD THAT I EVEN I MYSELF • •	• •	85 SOHRAB RUSTUM	816
OR RATHER WOULD THAT I EVEN I MYSELF • •	• •	85 SOHRAB RUSTUM	816
NOT THOU OF MINE AND I MIGHT DIE NOT THOU •	• •	85 SOHRAB RUSTUM	819
AND I NOT THOU BE BORNE TO SEISTAN • •	• •	85 SOHRAB RUSTUM	820
AND SAY O SON I WEEP THEE NOT TOO SORE •	• •	85 SOHRAB RUSTUM	822
FOR WILLINGLY I KNOW THOU METST THINE END •	• •	85 SOHRAB RUSTUM	823
AND I SHALL NEVER END THIS LIFE OF BLOOD •	• •	85 SOHRAB RUSTUM	826
BUT I SHALL CONQUER THAT MY HEART FOREBODES •	• •	62 SOHRAB RUSTUM	V
I AM NOT WRONGD WHEN MEN SPEAK SOHRABS PRAISE	• •	68 SOHRAB RUSTUM	V 228
FOR WHAT CARE I THAT SOHRABS FAME QUENCH THEIRS	• •	68 SOHRAB RUSTUM	V 228
AND I TO TARRY WITH THE WHITE-HAIRD ZAL • •	• •	68 SOHRAB RUSTUM	V 232
THERE WOULD I STAY AND HANG MY ARMOUR UP •	• •	68 SOHRAB RUSTUM	V 236
FOR WERE I MATCHD WITH TEN SUCH MEN AS THOU •	• •	77 SOHRAB RUSTUM	V 544
AND I WERE HE WHO TILL TO-DAY I WAS • • •	• •	77 SOHRAB RUSTUM	V 545
AND I WERE HE WHO TILL TO-DAY I WAS • • •	• •	77 SOHRAB RUSTUM	V 545

I

(CONTINUED)

```
FOR WOULD THAT ALL THAT I HAVE EVER SLAIN        85 SOHRAB RUSTUM     V 809
O VIZIER I MAY BURY HIM                          88 SICK KING BOKH       21
O KING THOU KNOWST I HAVE BEEN SICK              88 SICK KING BOKH       22
WHEREFORE THAT I MAY COUNSEL THEE                88 SICK KING BOKH       26
MY LORD O KING DO RIGHT I PRAY                   89 SICK KING BOKH       53
IF I SPEAK FOLLY BUT A KING                      89 SICK KING BOKH       55
NOW I AT NIGHTFALL HAD GONE FORTH                90 SICK KING BOKH       65
UNDER SOME MULBERRY-TREES I FOUND                90 SICK KING BOKH       67
I FILLD MY PITCHER AND STOLE HOME                90 SICK KING BOKH       70
I HID THE CAN BEHIND THE DOOR                    90 SICK KING BOKH       72
AND BURNING DUST AGAIN I CREEP                   90 SICK KING BOKH       75
THEIR LIPS STILL WET WHEN I CAME DOWN            90 SICK KING BOKH       84
NOW MARK I BEING FEVERD SICK                     90 SICK KING BOKH       85
WHAT MUST I HOWL IN THE NEXT WORLD               91 SICK KING BOKH       99
NAY BUT I SWEAR FROM THIS MY PATH                91 SICK KING BOKH      103
I WILL NOT STIR TILL I BE JUDGED                 91 SICK KING BOKH      104
I WILL NOT STIR TILL I BE JUDGED                 91 SICK KING BOKH      104
AND TRULY WHILE I SPEAK O KING                   92 SICK KING BOKH      129
I HEAR THE BEARERS ON THE STAIR                  92 SICK KING BOKH      130
O KING IN THIS I PRAISE THEE NOT                 92 SICK KING BOKH      133
NOW MUST I CALL THY GRIEF NOT WISE               92 SICK KING BOKH      134
LO I AM OLD THREE KINGS ERE THEE                 92 SICK KING BOKH      143
HAVE I SEEN REIGNING IN THIS PLACE               92 SICK KING BOKH      144
O VIZIER THOU ART OLD I YOUNG                    93 SICK KING BOKH      181
CLEAR IN THESE THINGS I CANNOT SEE               93 SICK KING BOKH      182
AND I HAVE MEAT AND DRINK AT WILL                94 SICK KING BOKH      213
BUT I AM SICK NOR HEED I THESE                   94 SICK KING BOKH      215
BUT I AM SICK NOR HEED I THESE                   94 SICK KING BOKH      215
AND WHAT I WOULD I CANNOT DO                     94 SICK KING BOKH      216
AND WHAT I WOULD I CANNOT DO                     94 SICK KING BOKH      216
EVEN THE GREAT HONOUR WHICH I HAVE               94 SICK KING BOKH      217
WHEN I AM DEAD WILL SOON GROW STILL              94 SICK KING BOKH      218
SO HAVE I NEITHER JOY NOR FAME                   94 SICK KING BOKH      219
BUT WHAT I CAN DO THAT I WILL                    94 SICK KING BOKH      220
BUT WHAT I CAN DO THAT I WILL                    94 SICK KING BOKH      220
I HAVE A FRETTED BRICK-WORK TOMB                 94 SICK KING BOKH      221
THITHER O VIZIER WILL I BEAR                     95 SICK KING BOKH      225
I MOST MIGHT WEEP HIS FATHER SUCH A SON          96 BALDER DEAD 1        21
I LOSE TO-DAY SO BRIGHT SO LOVED A GOD           96 BALDER DEAD 1        22
AND I TOO ODIN TOO THE LORD OF ALL               96 BALDER DEAD 1        30
THAT I ALONE MUST TAKE THE BRANCH FROM LOK       98 BALDER DEAD 1       100
CAN I O MOTHER BRING THEM BALDER BACK            98 BALDER DEAD 1       107
CAN I WITH HELAS POWER A COMPACT STRIKE          98 BALDER DEAD 1       109
YET IN MY SECRET MIND ONE WAY I KNOW             99 BALDER DEAD 1       128
NOR DO I JUDGE IF IT SHALL WIN OR FAIL           99 BALDER DEAD 1       129
SHALL GO AND I WILL BE HIS GUIDE UNSEEN         100 BALDER DEAD 1       191
HOWBEIT I WILL SEE AND DO HIS HEST              102 BALDER DEAD 1       244
SLEEP ON I WATCH THEE AND AM HERE TO AID        103 BALDER DEAD 1       292
ALIVE I KEPT NOT FAR FROM THEE DEAR SOUL        103 BALDER DEAD 1       293
NEITHER DO I NEGLECT THEE NOW THOUGH DEAD       103 BALDER DEAD 1       294
AND WELL I KNOW THAT BY NO STROKE OF DEATH      103 BALDER DEAD 1       305
WHOM THOU SO WELL HAST LOVED BUT I CAN SMOOTH   103 BALDER DEAD 1       308
YES AND I FAIN WOULD ALTOGETHER WARD            104 BALDER DEAD 1       310
O DAMSEL HERMOD AM I CALLD THE SON              108 BALDER DEAD 2       112
AND SLEIPNER ODINS HORSE IS THIS I RIDE         108 BALDER DEAD 2       115
AND I COME SENT THIS ROAD ON BALDERS TRACK      108 BALDER DEAD 2       116
UPON MY BRIDGE AND WHEN THEY CROSS I KNOW       108 BALDER DEAD 2       121
SO SHALL I KNOW THE LOST WAS DEAR INDEED        111 BALDER DEAD 2       239
MAY I ERE I DEPART BID BALDER HAIL              111 BALDER DEAD 2       244
MAY I ERE I DEPART BID BALDER HAIL              111 BALDER DEAD 2       244
AND NOW I COUNT NOT OF THESE TERMS AS SAFE      112 BALDER DEAD 2       268
THOUGH I BE LOVED AND MANY MOURN MY DEATH       112 BALDER DEAD 2       270
FROM HELL AND SHALL I TELL THEE HOW HE SEEMS    113 BALDER DEAD 3         7
WOULD I MIGHT SEE HIM SNATCH THEE IN HIS HAND   114 BALDER DEAD 3        24
LO HOME HAVING PERFORMD YOUR WILL I COME        114 BALDER DEAD 3        37
INTO THE JOYLESS KINGDOM HAVE I BEEN            114 BALDER DEAD 3        38
NOW AND I KNOW NOT HOW THEY PRIZE THEE THERE    115 BALDER DEAD 3        77
BUT HERE I KNOW THOU WILT BE MISSD AND MOURND   115 BALDER DEAD 3        78
SINCE THEN I VAINLY SEEK HIM THROUGH THE WORLD  116 BALDER DEAD 3       109
SO BALDER SAID BUT ODER WELL I KNOW             117 BALDER DEAD 3       119
MY TRUANT ODER I SHALL SEE NO MORE              117 BALDER DEAD 3       120
AND I AM LEFT UNCOMFORTED IN HEAVEN             117 BALDER DEAD 3       122
YES AND I TOO REMEMBERD THEN NO MORE            117 BALDER DEAD 3       145
BUT I HEARD THORA LAUGH IN GOTHLAND ISLE        117 BALDER DEAD 3       148
THEREFORE WITH GRATEFUL HEART I MOURN THEE DEAD 117 BALDER DEAD 3       152
THESE TERMS AND I SUSPECT SOME HIDDEN FRAUD     120 BALDER DEAD 3       235
IF I IF ODIN CLAD IN RADIANT ARMS               120 BALDER DEAD 3       238
TRY IT BUT I FOR ONE WILL NOT APPLAUD           121 BALDER DEAD 3       281
NOR DO I MERIT ODIN THOU SHOULDST SLIGHT        121 BALDER DEAD 3       282
FOR I TOO AM A GODDESS BORN OF THEE             121 BALDER DEAD 3       284
AND ALL THAT IS TO COME I KNOW BUT LOCK         121 BALDER DEAD 3       286
I WEEP HIM NOT LET HELA KEEP HER PREY           123 BALDER DEAD 3       354
I MUST AGAIN BELOW TO HELAS REALM               124 BALDER DEAD 3       372
FOR THIS I DIED AND FLED BENEATH THE GLOOM      124 BALDER DEAD 3       397
NO LESS THAN BALDER HAVE I LOST THE LIGHT       125 BALDER DEAD 3       401
I TOO HAD ONCE A WIFE AND ONCE A CHILD          125 BALDER DEAD 3       403
BUT ALL I LEFT OF MY OWN ACT AND FLED           125 BALDER DEAD 3       405
WHEN THAT WITH DOWNCAST LOOKS I HITHER CAME     125 BALDER DEAD 3       409
MY HATED CONVERSE ON THEE CAME I UP             125 BALDER DEAD 3       414
```

I   (CONTINUED)
FROM THE DEEP GLOOM WHERE I WILL NOW RETURN   • •   125 BALDER DEAD 3   415
BUT EARNESTLY I LONGD TO HOVER NEAR   • • • • •   125 BALDER DEAD 3   416
WHEN I DRAW NIGH AND THE WAN TRIBES OF DEAD   • •   126 BALDER DEAD 3   464
I MOURN THEE THAT THOU CANST NOT HELP US THEN   • •   127 BALDER DEAD 3   482
BUT WHAT WERE I TO SAVE THEM IN THAT HOUR   • • •   127 BALDER DEAD 3   489
I WHAT WERE I WHEN THESE CAN NOUGHT AVAIL   • • •   127 BALDER DEAD 3   493
I WHAT WERE I WHEN THESE CAN NOUGHT AVAIL   • • •   127 BALDER DEAD 3   493
BUT NOT TO ME SO GRIEVOUS AS I KNOW   • • • •   127 BALDER DEAD 3   500
ABSENCE FROM FIELDS WHERE I COULD NOTHING AID   • •   127 BALDER DEAD 3   502
FOR I AM LONG SINCE WEARY OF YOUR STORM   • • •   127 BALDER DEAD 3   503
UNARMD INGLORIOUS I ATTEND THE COURSE   • • • •   128 BALDER DEAD 3   510
TELL ME THAT I MAY PONDER IT WHEN GONE   • • •   128 BALDER DEAD 3   516
HODER AND I SHALL JOIN THEM FROM THE GRAVE   • •   128 BALDER DEAD 3   526
I REST THE THRALL OF HELA AND ENDURE   • • • •   129 BALDER DEAD 3   545
ISEULT AH NOT THE ISEULT I DESIRE   • • • • •   130 TRISTRAM 1   8
I KNOW HIM BY HIS HARP OF GOLD   • • • • • •   131 TRISTRAM 1   19
I KNOW HIM BY HIS FOREST—DRESS   • • • • • •   131 TRISTRAM 1   21
I KNOW HER BY HER MILDNESS RARE   • • • • •   132 TRISTRAM 1   50
I KNOW HER BY HER RICH SILK DRESS   • • • • •   132 TRISTRAM 1   52
AH WOULD I WERE IN THOSE GREEN FIELDS AT PLAY   • •   133 TRISTRAM 1   97
TRISTRAM I PRAY THEE OF THY COURTESY   • • • • •   133 TRISTRAM 1   99
FLY SAVE THYSELF SAVE ME I DARE NOT STAY   • •   135 TRISTRAM 1   168
I SEE HER FORM GLIDE THROUGH THE CROSSING SPEARS   • •   138 TRISTRAM 1   241
I THINK I HAVE A FEVER IN MY BLOOD   • • • •   139 TRISTRAM 1   280
I THINK I HAVE A FEVER IN MY BLOOD   • • • •   139 TRISTRAM 1   280
I HAVE HAD DREAMS I HAVE HAD DREAMS MY PAGE   • •   140 TRISTRAM 1   304
I HAVE HAD DREAMS I HAVE HAD DREAMS MY PAGE   • •   140 TRISTRAM 1   304
AND WITH A BLOOD LIKE MINE WILL LEAVE I FEAR   • •   140 TRISTRAM 1   306
POOR CHILD THOU ART ALMOST AS PALE AS I   • • •   140 TRISTRAM 1   312
I KNOW HER BY HER GOLDEN HAIR   • • • • •   132 TRISTRAM 1   V   50
RAISE THE LIGHT MY PAGE THAT I MAY SEE HER   • •   142 TRISTRAM 2   1
BLAME ME NOT POOR SUFFERER THAT I TARRIED   • •   142 TRISTRAM 2   5
BOUND I WAS I COULD NOT BREAK THE BAND   • • •   142 TRISTRAM 2   6
BOUND I WAS I COULD NOT BREAK THE BAND   • • •   142 TRISTRAM 2   6
I AM HERE WE MEET I HOLD THY HAND   • • • •   142 TRISTRAM 2   8
I AM HERE WE MEET I HOLD THY HAND   • • • •   142 TRISTRAM 2   8
I AM DYING BUILD THOU MAYST MY GRAVE   • • •   142 TRISTRAM 2   12
WHAT I HEAR THESE BITTER WORDS FROM THEE   • •   142 TRISTRAM 2   14
SICK WITH GRIEF I AM AND FAINT WITH TRAVEL   • •   142 TRISTRAM 2   15
I FORGOT THOU COMEST FROM THY VOYAGE   • • •   142 TRISTRAM 2   17
I LIKE THEE HAVE LEFT MY YOUTH AFAR   • • •   143 TRISTRAM 2   22
I FORGIVE THEE ISEULT THOU WILT STAY   • • •   143 TRISTRAM 2   28
FEAR ME NOT I WILL BE ALWAYS WITH THEE   • •   143 TRISTRAM 2   29
I WILL WATCH THEE TEND THEE SOOTHE THY PAIN   • •   143 TRISTRAM 2   30
NO THOU SHALT NOT SPEAK I SHOULD BE FINDING   • •   143 TRISTRAM 2   33
SIT SIT BY ME I WILL THINK WEVE LIVED SO   • •   143 TRISTRAM 2   35
I A FADED WATCHER BY THY PILLOW   • • • •   144 TRISTRAM 2   61
I A STATUE ON THY CHAPEL—FLOOR   • • • • •   144 TRISTRAM 2   62
SHE WILL CRY IS THIS THE FOE I DREADED   • • •   144 TRISTRAM 2   65
HUSH NO WORDS THAT SMILE I SEE FORGIVES ME   • •   144 TRISTRAM 2   69
I AM NOW THY NURSE I BID THEE SLEEP   • • •   144 TRISTRAM 2   70
I AM NOW THY NURSE I BID THEE SLEEP   • • •   144 TRISTRAM 2   70
I AM HAPPY YET I FEEL THERES SOMETHING   • •   145 TRISTRAM 2   73
I AM HAPPY YET I FEEL THERES SOMETHING   • •   145 TRISTRAM 2   73
THROUGH A MIST I SEE THEE NEAR COME NEARER   • •   145 TRISTRAM 2   75
BEND BEND DOWN I YET HAVE MUCH TO SAY   • •   145 TRISTRAM 2   76
HUSH TIS VAIN I FEEL MY END APPROACHING   • •   145 TRISTRAM 2   81
I AM DYING START NOT NOR LOOK WILDLY   • •   145 TRISTRAM 2   89
SAY I WILLD SO THAT THOU STAY BESIDE ME   • •   145 TRISTRAM 2   95
NOW TO SAIL THE SEAS OF DEATH I LEAVE THEE   • •   145 TRISTRAM 2   97
I WAS BOUND I COULD NOT BREAK THE BAND   • • •   142 TRISTRAM 2   V   6
I WAS BOUND I COULD NOT BREAK THE BAND   • • •   142 TRISTRAM 2   V   6
SHE WILL SAY IS THIS THE FORM I DREADED   • • •   144 TRISTRAM 2   V   65
SAY I CHARGD HER THAT YE LIVE TOGETHER   • •   145 TRISTRAM 2   V   95
SAY I CHARGD HER THAT THOU STAY BESIDE ME   • •   145 TRISTRAM 2   V   95
SAY I CHARGD THEE THAT THOU STAY BESIDE HER   • •   145 TRISTRAM 2   V   95
TRISTRAM TRISTRAM STAY I COME AH SORROW   • •   146 TRISTRAM 2   V   99
DEAR SAINTS IT IS NOT SORROW AS I HEAR   • • •   152 TRISTRAM 3   112
AND YET I SWEAR IT ANGERS ME TO SEE   • • • •   153 TRISTRAM 3   133
BY HIGH PERMISSION I AM HERE   • • • • • •   157 SAINT BRANDAN   24
IT WAS THE FIRST AFTER I CAME   • • • • • •   157 SAINT BRANDAN   30
I FELT AS I IN TORMENT LAY   • • • • • • •   157 SAINT BRANDAN   33
I FELT AS I IN TORMENT LAY   • • • • • • •   157 SAINT BRANDAN   33
AH WHENCE THIS MERCY LORD I SAID   • • • • •   157 SAINT BRANDAN   37
THEN I REMEMBERD HOW I WENT   • • • • • •   157 SAINT BRANDAN   41
THEN I REMEMBERD HOW I WENT   • • • • • •   157 SAINT BRANDAN   41
HE GAZED UPON ME AS I PASSD   • • • • • •   158 SAINT BRANDAN   49
AND MURMURD HELP ME OR I DIE   • • • • • •   158 SAINT BRANDAN   50
TO THE POOR WRETCH MY CLOAK I CAST   • • • •   158 SAINT BRANDAN   51
WELL—FED WELL—CLOTHED WELL—FRIENDED I   • •   158 SAINT BRANDAN   57
I JOURNEY TO THESE HEALING SNOWS   • • • • •   158 SAINT BRANDAN   68
I STANCH WITH ICE MY BURNING BREAST   • • • •   158 SAINT BRANDAN   69
I AM NO KNIGHT HE ANSWERED   • • • • • • •   159 NECKAN   25
FROM THE SEA—WAVES I COME   • • • • • • •   159 NECKAN   26
NO CHRISTIAN MATE HAVE I   • • • • • • • •   160 NECKAN   36
SHE SAID I MUST GO FOR MY KINSFOLK PRAY   • •   163 FORSAKEN MERM   56
AND I LOSE MY POOR SOUL MERMAN HERE WITH THEE   • •   163 FORSAKEN MERM   59
I SAID GO UP DEAR HEART THROUGH THE WAVES   • •   163 FORSAKEN MERM   60
LONG PRAYERS I SAID IN THE WORLD THEY SAY   • •   163 FORSAKEN MERM   66

I

(CONTINUED)

COME I SAID AND WE ROSE THROUGH THE SURF IN THE BAY   163 FORSAKEN MERM   67
DEAR HEART I SAID WE ARE LONG ALONE   • • • • •   163 FORSAKEN MERM   78
FOR THE WHEEL WHERE I SPUN   • • • • • • •   164 FORSAKEN MERM   92
I MET A PREACHER THERE I KNEW AND SAID   • • •   169 EAST LONDON   5
I MET A PREACHER THERE I KNEW AND SAID   • • •   169 EAST LONDON   5
BRAVELY SAID HE FOR I OF LATE HAVE BEEN   • • •   169 EAST LONDON   7
A TRAMP I SAW ILL MOODY AND TONGUE-TIED   • •   169 WEST LONDON   2
THOUGHT I ABOVE HER STATE THIS SPIRIT TOWERS   •   170 WEST LONDON   9
CARE NOT FOR THAT AND LAY ME WHERE I FALL   • •   173 MONICAS PRAYER   2
AGAIN I SEE MY BLISS AT HAND   • • • • • •   174 MEETING   1
I KNOW THAT GRACEFUL FIGURE FAIR   • • • •   174 MEETING   5
I KNOW THAT SOFT ENKERCHIEFD HAIR   • • • •   174 MEETING   7
AGAIN I SPRING TO MAKE MY CHOICE   • • • •   174 MEETING   9
I HEAR A GODS TREMENDOUS VOICE   • • • • •   174 MEETING   11
AH WOULD I WERE THERE   • • • • • • • •   175 PARTING   16
BUT ON THE STAIRS WHAT VOICE IS THIS I HEAR   • •   175 PARTING   17
I COME O YE MOUNTAINS   • • • • • • • •   175 PARTING   33
YE TORRENTS I COME   • • • • • • • • •   175 PARTING   34
I COME O YE MOUNTAINS   • • • • • • • •   176 PARTING   57
YE PINE-WOODS I COME   • • • • • • • •   176 PARTING   58
AND OTHERS ERE I WAS   • • • • • • • •   176 PARTING   69
I COME TO THE WILD   • • • • • • • • •   177 PARTING   76
UP THE STEEP STREET I HURRIED FAST   • • • •   177 FAREWELL   7
I CAME I SAW THEE RISE THE BLOOD   • • • •   178 FAREWELL   9
I CAME I SAW THEE RISE THE BLOOD   • • • •   178 FAREWELL   9
DAYS FLEW AH SOON I COULD DISCERN   • • • •   178 FAREWELL   13
I BLAME THEE NOT THIS HEART I KNOW   • • • •   178 FAREWELL   17
I BLAME THEE NOT THIS HEART I KNOW   • • • •   178 FAREWELL   17
I TOO HAVE FELT THE LOAD I BORE   • • • • •   178 FAREWELL   29
I TOO HAVE FELT THE LOAD I BORE   • • • • •   178 FAREWELL   29
I TOO HAVE WISHD NO WOMAN MORE   • • • •   178 FAREWELL   31
I TOO HAVE LONGD FOR TRENCHANT FORCE   • • •   178 FAREWELL   33
BUT IN THE WORLD I LEARNT WHAT THERE   • • •   178 FAREWELL   37
THEY WILL FOR THOU I FEEL NOT LESS   • • • •   179 FAREWELL   43
THAN I WAST DESTINED TO THIS LORE   • • • •   179 FAREWELL   44
THEY WILL FOR THOU I FEEL NO LESS   • • • •   179 FAREWELL   V   43
THAN I WERT DESTIND TO THIS LORE   • • • •   179 FAREWELL   V   44
I BADE MY HEART MORE CONSTANT BE   • • • •   180 ISOLATION MARG   2
I BADE IT KEEP THE WORLD AWAY   • • • •   180 ISOLATION MARG   3
THE FAULT WAS GRAVE I MIGHT HAVE KNOWN   • •   180 ISOLATION MARG   7
WHAT FAR TOO SOON ALAS I LEARND   • • • •   180 ISOLATION MARG   8
THINE EYES MY LOVE I SEE   • • • • •   183 ABSENCE   2
I SHIVER FOR THE PASSING DAY   • • • • •   183 ABSENCE   3
I STRUGGLE TOWARDS THE LIGHT AND YE   • • •   183 ABSENCE   13
I BEAR THAT YE REMOVE   • • • • • • •   183 ABSENCE   16
I STRUGGLE TOWARDS THE LIGHT BUT OH   • • •   183 ABSENCE   17
I SHUDDER FOR THE PASSING DAY   • • • •   183 ABSENCE   V   3
THE STREAM AND DO I LINGER HERE   • • • •   183 TERRACE BERNE   4
AH SHALL I SEE THEE WHILE A FLUSH   • • •   184 TERRACE BERNE   13
BE LOST AND I NOT FEEL TWAS SO   • • • •   184 TERRACE BERNE   30
FAIL FROM EARTHS AIR AND I NOT KNOW   • • •   184 TERRACE BERNE   32
OR SHALL I FIND THEE STILL BUT CHANGED   • •   184 TERRACE BERNE   33
I WILL NOT KNOW FOR WHEREFORE TRY   • • •   185 TERRACE BERNE   41
I KNEW IT WHEN MY LIFE WAS YOUNG   • • • •   185 TERRACE BERNE   49
I FEEL IT STILL NOW YOUTH IS OER   • • • •   185 TERRACE BERNE   50
AND MARGUERITE I SHALL SEE NO MORE   • • •   185 TERRACE BERNE   52
I HELD BUT NOW   • • • • • • • • •   186 STRAYED REVEL   13
SO SOON I SEE THE NIGHT-DEWS   • • • •   186 STRAYED REVEL   15
I SPRANG UP I THREW ROUND ME   • • • •   186 STRAYED REVEL   29
I SPRANG UP I THREW ROUND ME   • • • •   186 STRAYED REVEL   29
I SNATCHD UP MY VINE-CROWN MY FIR-STAFF   •   186 STRAYED REVEL   33
QUICK I PASSD FOLLOWING   • • • • • •   187 STRAYED REVEL   40
DOWN THE DARK VALLEY I SAW   • • • • •   187 STRAYED REVEL   42
TREMBLING I ENTERD BEHELD   • • • • •   187 STRAYED REVEL   46
I DRANK GODDESS   • • • • • • •   187 STRAYED REVEL   50
DRINK THEN I CHIDE THEE NOT   • • • • •   187 STRAYED REVEL   59
I LURED HIM NOT HITHER ULYSSES   • • • •   188 STRAYED REVEL   97
HOW SHALL I NAME HIM   • • • • • • •   189 STRAYED REVEL   101
AH AND I SEE TOO   • • • • • • • •   189 STRAYED REVEL   104
I AM ULYSSES   • • • • • • • • •   189 STRAYED REVEL   114
I HONOUR AND WELCOME THEE   • • • • •   189 STRAYED REVEL   129
BUT I ULYSSES   • • • • • • • •   194 STRAYED REVEL   270
HIM THEN I PRAISE WHO DARES   • • • • •   196 FRAG ANTIGONE   28
NO NO OLD MEN CREON I CURSE NOT   • • • •   196 FRAG ANTIGONE   45
I WEEP THEBANS   • • • • • • • • •   196 FRAG ANTIGONE   46
HOW I BEWAIL YOU   • • • • • • • •   198 FRAG DEJANEIRA   4
HIM I COUNT HIM WELL-STARRD   • • • •   199 FRAG DEJANEIRA   31
I PRAISE THE LIFE WHICH SLIPS AWAY   • • •   199 EARLY DEATH   2
LET HIM LIVE LET HIM FEEL I HAVE LIVED   • • •   200 EARLY DEATH   17
I TOO HAVE SUFFERD YET I KNOW   • • • • •   201 URANIA   1
I TOO HAVE SUFFERD YET I KNOW   • • • • •   201 URANIA   1
I TOO HAVE SUFFERD BUT I KNOW   • • • •   201 URANIA   V   1
I TOO HAVE SUFFERD BUT I KNOW   • • • •   201 URANIA   V   1
I MUST NOT SAY THAT THOU WAST TRUE   • • •   203 EUPHROSYNE   1
I MUST NOT SAY THAT THOU WERT TRUE   • • •   203 EUPHROSYNE   V   1
I WILL NOT SAY THAT THOU WAST TRUE   • • •   203 EUPHROSYNE   V   1
I MUST NOT SAY THAT SHE WAS TRUE   • • • •   203 EUPHROSYNE   V   1
I SAW UPON THE OPEN SAND   • • • • •   204 CALAIS SANDS   10
ON THE BLUE STRAIT MINE EYES I STRAIN   • • •   205 CALAIS SANDS   20

I

(CONTINUED)

Line	Page	Title		Num
I MUST NOT SPRING TO GRASP THY HAND	205	CALAIS SANDS		25
BUT I MAY STAND FAR OFF AND GAZE	205	CALAIS SANDS		27
AH MIGHT I ALWAYS REST UNSEEN	205	CALAIS SANDS		31
SO I MIGHT HAVE THEE ALWAYS NEAR	205	CALAIS SANDS		32
OH WERT THOU HERE THAT I MIGHT TURN	204	CALAIS SANDS	V	9
ON THE BLUE SEA MY GAZE I STRAIN	205	CALAIS SANDS	V	20
OER THE BLUE STRAIT MINE EYES I STRAIN	205	CALAIS SANDS	V	20
I MUST NOT SPRING TO TOUCH THY HAND	205	CALAIS SANDS	V	25
OH MIGHT I ALWAYS REST UNSEEN	205	CALAIS SANDS	V	31
BEFORE I DIE BEFORE THE SOUL	206	RIVER		13
SOME DAY I SHALL BE COLD I KNOW	207	ON THE RHINE		2
SOME DAY I SHALL BE COLD I KNOW	207	ON THE RHINE		2
OF THE HIGH ALPS TO WHICH I GO	207	ON THE RHINE		4
BY DAY I SHALL BE WELL AGAIN	208	LONGING		2
BY DAY I SHALL BE WELL AGAIN	209	LONGING		14
BUT NOW I ONLY HEAR	211	DOVER BEACH		24
NO I NOTHING CAN PERCEIVE	215	PIS-ALLER		9
THAT OR NOTHING I BELIEVE	215	PIS-ALLER		11
THIS SENTENCE HAVE I LEFT BEHIND	217	NAMELESS EPIT	V	
MY FRIEND AND I BY CHANCE WE TALKD	221	EPILOG LAOCOON		2
YET EVEN I AND NONE WILL BOW	222	EPILOG LAOCOON		30
BEHOLD I SAID THE PAINTERS SPHERE	222	EPILOG LAOCOON		49
THE WORLD OF MUSIC I EXCLAIMD	223	EPILOG LAOCOON		77
BUT WHO I SAID SUFFICES HERE	225	EPILOG LAOCOON		128
THE ASPECT NOT I GRANT EXPRESS	225	EPILOG LAOCOON		133
THE FEELING NOT I GRANT EXPLORE	225	EPILOG LAOCOON		135
CAN I FEEL THAT THEIR POET IS GONE	229	YOUTH OF NATURE		27
THEY ARE HERE I HEARD AS MEN HEARD	230	YOUTH OF NATURE		75
LIFE AND EMOTION AND I	230	YOUTH OF NATURE		90
HAVE DREAMD THAT I LIVED BUT FOR THEM	232	YOUTH OF NATURE		131
I REMAIN	232	YOUTH OF NATURE		134
HAVE THOUGHT THAT I LIVED BUT FOR THEM	232	YOUTH OF NATURE	V	131
THIS I KNOW IS THE LAW	232	YOUTH OF MAN		3
WELL I KNOW WHAT THEY FEEL	235	YOUTH OF MAN		88
WELL I KNOW WHAT THEY FEEL	235	YOUTH OF MAN		96
I SAY UNTO YOU SEE YE KEEP THAT LAW	237	PROGRESS		7
THINK NOT THAT I TO ANNUL THE LAW HAVE WILLD	237	PROGRESS		10
I SAY UNTO YOU SEE THAT YOUR SOULS LIVE	237	PROGRESS		23
WHAT I AM AND WHAT I OUGHT TO BE	239	SELF-DEPENDENCE		2
WHAT I AM AND WHAT I OUGHT TO BE	239	SELF-DEPENDENCE		2
AT THIS VESSELS PROW I STAND WHICH BEARS ME	239	SELF-DEPENDENCE		3
OER THE SEA AND TO THE STARS I SEND	240	SELF-DEPENDENCE		6
AH ONCE MORE I CRIED YE STARS YE WATERS	240	SELF-DEPENDENCE		9
STILL STILL LET ME AS I GAZE UPON YOU	240	SELF-DEPENDENCE		11
A CRY LIKE THINE IN MINE OWN HEART I HEAR	240	SELF-DEPENDENCE		30
AT THE VESSELS PROW I STAND WHICH BEARS ME	239	SELF-DEPENDENCE	V	3
A CRY LIKE THINE IN MY OWN HEART I HEAR	240	SELF-DEPENDENCE	V	30
I DO NOT STRIVE I DO NOT WEEP	241	MORALITY		26
I DO NOT STRIVE I DO NOT WEEP	241	MORALITY		26
I RUSH WITH THE SWIFT SPHERES AND GLOW	241	MORALITY		27
IN JOY AND WHEN I WILL I SLEEP	241	MORALITY		28
IN JOY AND WHEN I WILL I SLEEP	241	MORALITY		28
I SAW I FELT IT ONCE BUT WHERE	241	MORALITY		30
I SAW I FELT IT ONCE BUT WHERE	241	MORALITY		30
I KNEW NOT YET THE GAUGE OF TIME	242	MORALITY		31
I FELT IT IN SOME OTHER CLIME	242	MORALITY		33
I SAW IT IN SOME OTHER PLACE	242	MORALITY		34
TWAS WHEN THE HEAVENLY HOUSE I TROD	242	MORALITY		35
THOSE WINDOWS WHICH I GAZE AT FROWN	242	SUMMER NIGHT		3
AND I I KNOW NOT IF TO PRAY	243	SUMMER NIGHT		34
AND I I KNOW NOT IF TO PRAY	243	SUMMER NIGHT		34
STILL TO BE WHAT I AM OR YIELD AND BE	243	SUMMER NIGHT		35
LIKE ALL THE OTHER MEN I SEE	243	SUMMER NIGHT		36
I WILL NOT SAY THAT YOUR MILD DEEPS RETAIN	244	SUMMER NIGHT		83
BUT I WILL RATHER SAY THAT YOU REMAIN	244	SUMMER NIGHT		86
I FEEL A NAMELESS SADNESS OER ME ROLL	245	BURIED LIFE		3
I KNEW THE MASS OF MEN CONCEALD	245	BURIED LIFE		16
I KNEW THEY LIVED AND MOVED	245	BURIED LIFE		20
IN THIS LONE OPEN GLADE I LIE	248	KENSINGTON GARD		1
BUT IN MY HELPLESS CRADLE I	249	KENSINGTON GARD		23
I ON MENS IMPIOUS UPROAR HURLD	249	KENSINGTON GARD		25
THINK OFTEN AS I HEAR THEM RAVE	249	KENSINGTON GARD		26
WHEN I WHO WATCH THEM AM AWAY	249	KENSINGTON GARD		30
BEFORE I HAVE BEGUN TO LIVE	249	KENSINGTON GARD		44
HERE WHERE I LIE WHAT MARVELS PASS		KENSINGTON GARD	V	13
BUT I ON MENS IMPIOUS TUMULT HURLD		KENSINGTON GARD	V	25
I ON MENS IMPIOUS TUMULT HURLD		KENSINGTON GARD	V	25
THINK SOMETIMES AS I HEAR THEM RAVE	249	KENSINGTON GARD	V	26
THINK SADLY AS I HEAR THEM RAVE		KENSINGTON GARD	V	26
I ASK NOT THAT MY BED OF DEATH	249	WISH		1
I ASK NOT EACH KIND SOUL TO KEEP	250	WISH		5
I ASK BUT THAT MY DEATH MAY FIND	250	WISH		9
THE WORLD WHICH WAS ERE I WAS BORN	250	WISH		35
THE WORLD WHICH LASTS WHEN I AM DEAD	250	WISH		36
THERE LET ME GAZE TILL I BECOME	251	WISH		41
IN SOUL WITH WHAT I GAZE ON WED	251	WISH		42
THUS FEELING GAZING MIGHT I GROW	251	WISH		49
HERE WILL I SIT AND WAIT	255	SCHOLAR-GIPSY		16
AND HERE TILL SUN-DOWN SHEPHERD WILL I BE	255	SCHOLAR-GIPSY		22

I

(CONTINUED)

AND ROUND GREEN ROOTS AND YELLOWING STALKS I SEE	255	SCHOLAR-GIPSY	24
OF BLOOM ON THE BENT GRASS WHERE I AM LAID	256	SCHOLAR-GIPSY	28
AND I HE SAID THE SECRET OF THEIR ART	256	SCHOLAR-GIPSY	48
AND I MYSELF SEEM HALF TO KNOW THY LOOKS	257	SCHOLAR-GIPSY	62
I ASK IF THOU HAST PASSD THEIR QUIET PLACE	257	SCHOLAR-GIPSY	65
OR IN MY BOAT I LIE	257	SCHOLAR-GIPSY	66
FOR MOST I KNOW THOU LOVST RETIRED GROUND	257	SCHOLAR-GIPSY	71
HAVE I NOT PASSD THEE ON THE WOODEN BRIDGE	258	SCHOLAR-GIPSY	123
BUT WHAT I DREAM TWO HUNDRED YEARS ARE FLOWN	259	SCHOLAR-GIPSY	131
HERE CAME I OFTEN OFTEN IN OLD DAYS	263	THYRSIS	9
THYRSIS AND I WE STILL HAD THYRSIS THEN	263	THYRSIS	10
ONCE PASSD I BLINDFOLD HERE AT ANY HOUR	263	THYRSIS	24
NOW SELDOM COME I SINCE I CAME WITH HIM	263	THYRSIS	25
NOW SELDOM COME I SINCE I CAME WITH HIM	263	THYRSIS	25
AGAINST THE WEST I MISS IT IS IT GONE	263	THYRSIS	27
BUT ONCE I KNEW EACH FIELD EACH FLOWER EACH STICK	263	THYRSIS	32
NEEDS MUST I LOSE THEM NEEDS WITH HEAVY HEART	264	THYRSIS	38
SO HAVE I HEARD THE CUCKOOS PARTING CRY	264	THYRSIS	57
THE BLOOM IS GONE AND WITH THE BLOOM GO I	264	THYRSIS	60
WHO IF NOT I FOR QUESTING HERE HATH POWER	265	THYRSIS	104
I KNOW THE WOOD WHICH HIDES THE DAFFODIL	266	THYRSIS	105
I KNOW THE FYFIELD TREE	266	THYRSIS	106
I KNOW WHAT WHITE WHAT PURPLE FRITILLARIES	266	THYRSIS	107
I KNOW THESE SLOPES WHO KNOWS THEM IF NOT I	266	THYRSIS	111
I KNOW THESE SLOPES WHO KNOWS THEM IF NOT I	266	THYRSIS	111
I SEE HER VEIL DRAW SOFT ACROSS THE DAY	266	THYRSIS	133
I FEEL HER SLOWLY CHILLING BREATH INVADE	266	THYRSIS	134
I FEEL HER FINGER LIGHT	266	THYRSIS	136
I TAKE THE OMEN EVE LETS DOWN HER VEIL	267	THYRSIS	161
I CANNOT REACH THE SIGNAL-TREE TO-NIGHT	267	THYRSIS	165
I TROW THE MIGHTY MOTHER DOTH NOT SEE	268	THYRSIS	179
SOLE IN THESE FIELDS YET WILL I NOT DESPAIR	268	THYRSIS	192
DESPAIR I WILL NOT WHILE I YET DESCRY	268	THYRSIS	193
DESPAIR I WILL NOT WHILE I YET DESCRY	268	THYRSIS	193
SHY TO ILLUMINE AND I SEEK IT TOO	268	THYRSIS	202
WHY FAINTEST THOU I WANDERD TILL I DIED	269	THYRSIS	237
WHY FAINTEST THOU I WANDERD TILL I DIED	269	THYRSIS	237
I SAW HIM SENSITIVE IN FRAME	272	EDW QUILLINAN	1
I KNEW HIS SPIRITS LOW	272	EDW QUILLINAN	2
I DO NOT WISH IT NOW	272	EDW QUILLINAN	4
I CLIMBD BENEATH ME BRIGHT AND WIDE	273	STANZAS CARNAC	3
I SEE THE SMOKE-CROWND VESSEL COME	276	SOUTHERN NIGHT	30
SO SANG I BUT THE MIDNIGHT BREEZE	279	SOUTHERN NIGHT	117
I THINK OF HER WHOSE GENTLE TONGUE	279	SOUTHERN NIGHT	121
OF THEE I THINK MY BROTHER YOUNG	279	SOUTHERN NIGHT	123
I SEE THEM STILL I SEE THEM NOW	279	SOUTHERN NIGHT	127
I SEE THEM STILL I SEE THEM NOW	279	SOUTHERN NIGHT	127
I SAW THE MEETING OF TWO	280	HAWORTH CHURCH	7
HOW SHALL I SING HER WHOSE SOUL	284	HAWORTH CHURCH	93
OF ONE TOO I HAVE HEARD	285	HAWORTH CHURCH	101
I KNOW NOT WHAT AND INTERPOSED	285	HAWORTH CHURCH	111
SO I SANG BUT THE MUSE	285	HAWORTH CHURCH	125
EVENING A MEETING I SAW	280	HAWORTH CHURCH	V
I BEHELD THE OBSCURE	281	HAWORTH CHURCH	V
ANOTHER GRIEF I SEE	283	HAWORTH CHURCH	V
SUCH THOU WAST AND I STAND	287	RUGBY CHAPEL	23
AND THROUGH THEE I BELIEVE	290	RUGBY CHAPEL	145
IS THE RACE OF MEN WHOM I SEE	290	RUGBY CHAPEL	150
YES I BELIEVE THAT THERE LIVED	290	RUGBY CHAPEL	153
SHALL I NOT CALL YOU BECAUSE	291	RUGBY CHAPEL	163
ONLY A MOMENT I LONGD	294	HEINES GRAVE	48
ONLY A MOMENT I KNEW	294	HEINES GRAVE	52
BURIED I KNEW HE WAS YOURS	294	HEINES GRAVE	54
AH I KNEW THAT I SAW	294	HEINES GRAVE	55
AH I KNEW THAT I SAW	294	HEINES GRAVE	55
I CHIDE WITH THEE NOT THAT THY SHARP	294	HEINES GRAVE	70
BUT WAS IT THOU I THINK	295	HEINES GRAVE	97
ALL ARE BEFORE ME I BEHOLD	301	GRANDE CHARTR	64
AND WHAT AM I THAT I AM HERE	301	GRANDE CHARTR	66
AND WHAT AM I THAT I AM HERE	301	GRANDE CHARTR	66
AT WHOSE BEHEST I LONG AGO	301	GRANDE CHARTR	74
I COME NOT HERE TO BE YOUR FOE	301	GRANDE CHARTR	76
I SEEK THESE ANCHORITES NOT IN RUTH	301	GRANDE CHARTR	77
NOT AS THEIR FRIEND OR CHILD I SPEAK	301	GRANDE CHARTR	79
LIKE THESE ON EARTH I WAIT FORLORN	302	GRANDE CHARTR	88
I COME TO SHED THEM AT THEIR SIDE	302	GRANDE CHARTR	90
TILL I POSSESS MY SOUL AGAIN	302	GRANDE CHARTR	94
I HEAR THE TORRENTS ROAR	306	OBERMANN	10
I FEEL THEE NEAR ONCE MORE	306	OBERMANN	12
I TURN THY LEAVES I FEEL THEIR BREATH	306	OBERMANN	13
I TURN THY LEAVES I FEEL THEIR BREATH	306	OBERMANN	13
THERE SOBS I KNOW NOT WHAT GROUND-TONE	307	OBERMANN	35
I KNOW BUT TWO WHO HAVE ATTAIND	307	OBERMANN	47
I HEAR THEE SAYING NOW	309	OBERMANN	90
I GO FATE DRIVES ME BUT I LEAVE	310	OBERMANN	131
I GO FATE DRIVES ME BUT I LEAVE	310	OBERMANN	131
I IN THE WORLD MUST LIVE BUT THOU	310	OBERMANN	137
AND YET I KNOW NOT ALL UNCHANGED	312	OBERMANN MORE	5
I LEFT THEM YESTERDAY	312	OBERMANN MORE	12

I

(CONTINUED)

YES I FORGET THE WORLDS WORK WROUGHT	313	OBERMANN MORE	41
ONCE MORE I SLIP MY CHAIN	313	OBERMANN MORE	44
AGAIN I FEEL THE WORDS INSPIRE	314	OBERMANN MORE	49
WHILE THUS I MUSED NIGHT GENTLY RAN	314	OBERMANN MORE	57
THOSE PENSIVE FEATURES WELL I KNEW	314	OBERMANN MORE	61
OH HAD I LIVED IN THAT GREAT DAY	317	OBERMANN MORE	141
WHEN I COULD HOURLY SCAN	317	OBERMANN MORE	154
YE LIVE I CRIED YE WORK AND PLAN	320	OBERMANN MORE	215
SEE I MAKE ALL THINGS NEW	320	OBERMANN MORE	232
THEN TO THE WILDERNESS I FLED	321	OBERMANN MORE	249
AND PASTORAL HUTS I HID MY HEAD	321	OBERMANN MORE	251
I WATCHD THE CROCUS FADE AND FLOWER	321	OBERMANN MORE	255
I FELT THE SUN AND WIND	321	OBERMANN MORE	256
THE DAY I LIVED IN WAS NOT MINE	321	OBERMANN MORE	257
IN DREAMS I SAW THE FUTURE SHINE	321	OBERMANN MORE	259
BUT AH I COULD NOT STAY	321	OBERMANN MORE	260
ACTION I HAD NOT FOLLOWERS FAME	321	OBERMANN MORE	261
I PASSD OBSCURE ALONE	321	OBERMANN MORE	262
NOR DO I WISH IT KNOWN	321	OBERMANN MORE	264
COMPOSED TO BEAR I LIVED AND DIED	321	OBERMANN MORE	265
WITH FATE I MURMUR NOT NOR CHIDE	321	OBERMANN MORE	267
DESPAIR NOT THOU AS I DESPAIRD	322	OBERMANN MORE	281
I MARKD THE PRESENT DIE	322	OBERMANN MORE	298
YET IT HAD MORE THAN I	322	OBERMANN MORE	300
THE VISION ENDED I AWOKE	323	OBERMANN MORE	325
STILL IN MY SOUL THE VOICE I HEARD	324	OBERMANN MORE	333
I TURNED BY SOME VAGUE IMPULSE STIRRD	324	OBERMANN MORE	335
PAST SONCHAUDS PINY FLANKS I GAZE	324	OBERMANN MORE	337
I SAW THE MORNING BREAK	324	OBERMANN MORE	348
AGAIN I FEEL ITS WORDS INSPIRE	314	OBERMANN MORE	V 49
WHEN I COULD HOURLY SEE	315	OBERMANN MORE	V 154
GLOOM-WRAPPED WITHIN I LIVED AND DIED	321	OBERMANN MORE	V 265
AND SONCHAUDS PINY FLANKS I GAZE	324	OBERMANN MORE	V 337
MEANWHILE WITHIN MY FATHERS PALACE I	331	MEROPE	47
OF MY OWN DEATH BUT LAIAS WELL I HOPE	331	MEROPE	49
SHALL I NOT GREET HER SHALL I NOT LEAP FORTH	331	MEROPE	60
SHALL I NOT GREET HER SHALL I NOT LEAP FORTH	331	MEROPE	60
THE KING I KNOW HIM EVEN THROUGH MANY YEARS	332	MEROPE	63
NO LINGERING NOW STRAIGHT TO THE CITY I	332	MEROPE	65
I SOUGHT THEE MEROPE I FIND THEE THUS	332	MEROPE	79
I SOUGHT THEE MEROPE I FIND THEE THUS	332	MEROPE	79
AS I HAVE EVER FOUND THEE BENT TO KEEP	332	MEROPE	80
I BLAME THEE NOT I DO THY HEART NO WRONG	332	MEROPE	83
I BLAME THEE NOT I DO THY HEART NO WRONG	332	MEROPE	83
REPEATED ARE IN THEE I WELL BELIEVE	333	MEROPE	87
AND IGNORANT MEN DESPISE ME THAT I STAND	333	MEROPE	95
ALL THIS I BEAR FOR WHAT I SEEK I KNOW	333	MEROPE	100
ALL THIS I BEAR FOR WHAT I SEEK I KNOW	333	MEROPE	100
ALL THIS I BEAR FOR WHAT I SEEK I KNOW	333	MEROPE	100
PEACE PEACE IS WHAT I SEEK AND PUBLIC CALM	333	MEROPE	101
TOO WIDE AT VARIANCE WITH THE PEACE I SEEK	333	MEROPE	107
I WILL NOT VIOLATE THY NOBLE GRIEF	333	MEROPE	108
THE PRAYER I CAME TO URGE I WILL DEFER	333	MEROPE	109
THE PRAYER I CAME TO URGE I WILL DEFER	333	MEROPE	109
I AM I SHALL BE HAVE BEEN IN MY MIND	333	MEROPE	111
I AM I SHALL BE HAVE BEEN IN MY MIND	333	MEROPE	111
IT LIVES AND WHILE I SEE THE LIGHT WILL LIVE	334	MEROPE	121
HE HAD HIS COUNSEL PARTY FRIENDS I MINE	334	MEROPE	128
HE STOOD BY WHAT HE WISHD FOR I THE SAME	334	MEROPE	129
I SMOTE HIM WHEN OUR WISHES CLASHD IN ARMS	334	MEROPE	130
HE HAD SMIT ME HAD HE BEEN SWIFT AS I	334	MEROPE	131
BUT WHILE I SMOTE HIM QUEEN I HONOURD HIM	334	MEROPE	132
BUT WHILE I SMOTE HIM QUEEN I HONOURD HIM	334	MEROPE	132
ENOUGH OF THIS SINCE THAT I HAVE MAINTAIND	334	MEROPE	134
AND I AM SEATED ON A PROSPEROUS THRONE	334	MEROPE	136
YET STILL FOR I CONCEAL IT NOT FERMENTS	334	MEROPE	137
SUCH ARE THEIR HOPES I ASK NOT IF BY THEE	334	MEROPE	147
FOR I HAVE KEPT CONSPIRACY FAST-CHAIND	334	MEROPE	149
TILL NOW AND I HAVE STRENGTH TO CHAIN IT STILL	334	MEROPE	150
BUT MEROPE THE YEARS ADVANCE I STAND	334	MEROPE	151
LEAVES ME AUSTERER STERNER THAN I WOULD	335	MEROPE	155
UNCLOUDED REASON I WOULD NOT DECLINE	335	MEROPE	158
THE CARES WHICH MIGHT IN ME WITH TIME I FEEL	335	MEROPE	161
THOU HAST FORGOT THEN WHO I AM WHO HEAR	335	MEROPE	182
AND WHO THOU ART WHO SPEAKEST TO ME I	335	MEROPE	183
WERE THEY WE DISPOSSESSED OF US I SPEAK	337	MEROPE	229
I SPEAK NOT NOW OF ARGOS WHERE HIS BROTHER	337	MEROPE	231
PATIENCE WAS THENCEFORTH SELF DESTRUCTION I	338	MEROPE	266
I HIS CHIEF KINSMAN I HIS PIONEER	338	MEROPE	267
I HIS CHIEF KINSMAN I HIS PIONEER	338	MEROPE	267
AND CHAMPION TO THE THRONE I HONOURING MOST	338	MEROPE	268
WHAT HIS FOES DARED NOT I HIS LOVER DARED	338	MEROPE	271
I AT THAT ALTAR WHERE MID SHOUTING CROWDS	338	MEROPE	272
I SELF-DEFENCE AND RIGHTEOUS EXECUTION	338	MEROPE	277
FOR ME I DEEM SUCH IMPIOUS AND FOR HIM	340	MEROPE	336
I ASK THEE NOT TO APPROVE THY HUSBANDS DEATH	340	MEROPE	338
BUT FOR THY CHILDRENS DEATH I STAND ASSOILD	340	MEROPE	342
I SAVED THEM MEANT THEM HONOUR BUT THY FRIENDS	340	MEROPE	343
ONE SON AT LEAST I SPARED FOR STILL HE LIVES	340	MEROPE	348

I

(CONTINUED)

THOU STANDEST OUT I SEE REPELLEST PEACE   341 MEROPE   354
THY SWORD REPELLD IT LONG AGO NOT I   341 MEROPE   355
BEWARE FROM THEE UPBRAIDINGS I RECEIVE   341 MEROPE   360
I KNOW I KNOW HOW HARD IT IS TO THINK   341 MEROPE   362
I KNOW I KNOW HOW HARD IT IS TO THINK   341 MEROPE   362
TO RULE THIS KINGDOM I INTEND WITH SWAY   342 MEROPE   376
AND NOW I LEAVE THEE TO THESE RITES ESTEEMD   342 MEROPE   379
WHAT SHALL I BEAR O LOST   342 MEROPE   400
TRULY I HEAR OF A MAID   343 MEROPE   425
MONTH AFTER MONTH I AWAIT   347 MEROPE   517
AN AVENGER I ASK NOT SEND ME MY SON   348 MEROPE   544
THINKING THAT SO I PRAYD ARIGHT I PRAYD   348 MEROPE   546
THINKING THAT SO I PRAYD ARIGHT I PRAYD   348 MEROPE   546
IF I PRAYD WRONGLY I REVOKE THE PRAYER   348 MEROPE   547
IF I PRAYD WRONGLY I REVOKE THE PRAYER   348 MEROPE   547
FORGIVE ME MAIDENS IF I SEEM TOO SLACK   348 MEROPE   548
IMPIOUS I DEEM THE ALLIANCE WHICH HE ASKS   348 MEROPE   550
AND RIGHTEOUS IF HE FALLS I COUNT HIS FALL   349 MEROPE   552
THE TRUE AVENGERS THESE I LEAVE HIS DEED   349 MEROPE   555
BY HIM SHOWN FAIR BUT I BELIEVE MOST FOUL   349 MEROPE   556
I PRAY THE FURIES EVER-RESTLESS BAND   349 MEROPE   569
RATHER ON THEE I CALL HUSBAND BELOVED   349 MEROPE   584
THIS FOR OUR SON AND FOR MYSELF I PRAY   350 MEROPE   591
I SEND AND THESE LIBATIONS POUR THE WHILE   350 MEROPE   595
I DOUBT THEIR CAUTION LITTLE SUITS THEIR WARD   351 MEROPE   608
THE HEART OF YOUTH I KNOW THAT MOST I FEAR   351 MEROPE   609
THE HEART OF YOUTH I KNOW THAT MOST I FEAR   351 MEROPE   609
I AUGUR THOU WILT HEAR SOME BOLD RESOLVE   351 MEROPE   610
I DARE NOT WISH IT BUT AT LEAST TO HEAR   351 MEROPE   611
SAVE FOR THIS ANNUAL CHARGE I HOPE TO HEAR   351 MEROPE   619
IF THIS BE ALL I KNOW NOT BUT I KNOW   351 MEROPE   620
IF THIS BE ALL I KNOW NOT BUT I KNOW   351 MEROPE   620
THESE MANY YEARS I LIVE FOR THIS ALONE   351 MEROPE   621
THAT BEST WHO OUGHT TO RULE AM I   353 MEROPE   677
I THE ONE RIGHTEOUS THEY THE MANY BAD   353 MEROPE   679
THUS THOUGH A WOMAN I WAS SCHOOLD   354 MEROPE   696
BY THOSE WHOM I REVERE   354 MEROPE   697
WHETHER I LEARNT THEIR LESSONS WELL   354 MEROPE   698
O KING ALL HAIL I COME WITH WEIGHTY NEWS   354 MEROPE   710
SPEAK THEM THAT I MAY JUDGE THEIR KIND MYSELF   354 MEROPE   712
ONE OF THE TRAIN OF CYPSELUS AM I   355 MEROPE   719
THAT WILL I DO AND TO THIS END I CAME   355 MEROPE   721
THAT WILL I DO AND TO THIS END I CAME   355 MEROPE   721
THE SON OF AN ARCADIAN NOBLE I   355 MEROPE   723
FROM CHIEF TO CHIEF I WANDERD AT HIS SIDE   355 MEROPE   728
WITH BEATERS HOUNDS AND HUNTSMEN HE AND I   355 MEROPE   731
TILL I THROWN OUT AND TIRED CAME TO HALT   357 MEROPE   795
AND RESTING THERE TO BREATHE I WATCHD THE CHASE   357 MEROPE   797
NOW IN THE WOODS FAR DOWN I SAW THEM CROSS   357 MEROPE   801
WHILE FROM THE TURF WHEREON I LAY I SPRANG   358 MEROPE   829
WHILE FROM THE TURF WHEREON I LAY I SPRANG   358 MEROPE   829
A MOMENT MORE I SAW THE PRINCE TURN ROUND   358 MEROPE   831
AND WHAT I COULD I DID TO CALL BY CRIES   358 MEROPE   835
AND WHAT I COULD I DID TO CALL BY CRIES   358 MEROPE   835
AND I ACROSS THE MOUNTAINS BROUGHT WITH HASTE   358 MEROPE   845
BUT I FROM OUR DEPLORED MISCHANCE LEARN THIS   359 MEROPE   853
REFRESHMENT NEEDED BY THEE AS I JUDGE   359 MEROPE   867
THIS AT A MOMENT TOO WHEN I HAD URGED   360 MEROPE   879
I OFFERD TO MY FOES AND THEY REFUSED   360 MEROPE   883
DIRE IS THIS BLOW FOR MEROPE AND I   360 MEROPE   885
I SPEAK NO WORD OF BOAST BUT THIS I SAY   360 MEROPE   888
I SPEAK NO WORD OF BOAST BUT THIS I SAY   360 MEROPE   888
AND I CAME THINKING TO FIND ARCAS HERE   361 MEROPE   916
O THRICE UNHAPPY HOW I GROAN THY FATE   362 MEROPE   931
AH AH AH ME AND I TOO SAY AH ME   363 MEROPE   948
SWIFT AS I CAME HATH FALSEHOOD BEEN BEFORE   363 MEROPE   954
ANOTHER TALE I TROW THY MESSENGER   364 MEROPE   964
SEIZED HE ESCAPES AND NEXT I FIND HIM HERE   364 MEROPE   983
SUSPICION GRAVE I SEE BUT NO FIRM PROOF   365 MEROPE   994
YES YES NOW I CONCEIVE THE LIBERAL GRACE   366 MEROPE   997
HIS OFFERS I REPELLD BUT WHAT OF THAT   366 MEROPE   1010
BUT CALM BUT UNRESENTFUL I ENDURED   366 MEROPE   1014
WHILE ALL THIS TIME I BEAR TO LINGER ON   366 MEROPE   1017
EITHER A VENGEFUL FURY I SHOULD STALK   366 MEROPE   1019
OR ELSE NOT LIVE AT ALL BUT HERE I HAUNT   366 MEROPE   1020
A HELPLESS ONE I KNOW IT BUT THE GODS   366 MEROPE   1023
FAIN WOULD I FADE AWAY AS I HAVE LIVED   366 MEROPE   1027
FAIN WOULD I FADE AWAY AS I HAVE LIVED   366 MEROPE   1027
BUT WITH WHAT EYES SHOULD I ENCOUNTER THERE   367 MEROPE   1032
OR WITH WHAT VOICE SHALL I THE QUESTIONS MEET   367 MEROPE   1037
MOTHER I WELL BELIEVED THOU LIVEDST ON   367 MEROPE   1043
COUNTING TILL I GREW UP THE LAGGARD YEARS   367 MEROPE   1046
WHAT SHALL I HAVE TO ANSWER TO SUCH WORDS   367 MEROPE   1053
I GO I GO THE KING HOLDS COUNCIL THERE   368 MEROPE   1077
I GO I GO THE KING HOLDS COUNCIL THERE   368 MEROPE   1077
WILL I SEEK TIDINGS TAKE THE WHILE THIS WORD   368 MEROPE   1078
I HAVE HEARD O QUEEN HOW A PRINCE   368 MEROPE   1082
WHAT I KNEW I CONCEALD   371 MEROPE   1132
WHAT I KNEW I CONCEALD   371 MEROPE   1132

I   (CONTINUED)

I PROMISE BUT I FEAR . . . .   371 MEROPE   1136
I PROMISE BUT I FEAR . . . .   371 MEROPE   1136
AH I BESEECH THEE WITH TEARS . . . . . .   372 MEROPE   1151
WHAT SWEETER SLEEP THAN THIS COULD I DESIRE 372 MEROPE   1156
HOW OFTEN HAVE I DREAMD OF THEE LIKE THIS . . 372 MEROPE   1158
WHAT DO I SEE A MURDERER AT DEATHS DOOR   374 MEROPE   1195
THOU KNOWST NOT WHOM THOU STRIKST I KNOW HIS CRIME 374 MEROPE 1199
IN WORD I DIED THAT I IN DEED MIGHT LIVE . . . 375 MEROPE   1209
IN WORD I DIED THAT I IN DEED MIGHT LIVE . . . 375 MEROPE   1209
AND ARCAS BUT I TREMBLE BOLDLY ASK . . . .   375 MEROPE   1211
WHAT THOU I DREAM MAYST THOU DREAM EVER SO . . 377 MEROPE   1219
I HAVE I HAVE THEE THE YEARS . . . . . .   377 MEROPE   1228
I HAVE I HAVE THEE THE YEARS . . . . . .   377 MEROPE   1228
I FEAR NOT BUT I THINK ON MY DESIGN . . . .   378 MEROPE   1235
I FEAR NOT BUT I THINK ON MY DESIGN . . . .   378 MEROPE   1235
REMEMBER TO REVENGE HIS DEATH I COME . . .   378 MEROPE   1241
THAT WORD IT KILLS ME I SEE . . . .   378 MEROPE   1243
MOTHER THY FEARS ARE IDLE FOR I COME . . .   379 MEROPE   1256
INSTRUCT ME NOT I HAVE MY LESSON CLEAR . . . 379 MEROPE   1259
FOR WHOSE HELP DARE I COUNT ON IF NOT THINE . 379 MEROPE   1266
FOR WHOM AS I SUPPOSE THOU PASSEST HERE . .   379 MEROPE   1271
FIX HIM THE AUTHOR OF MY DEATH I KNOW NOT . . 379 MEROPE   1273
WITH THIS MESSENIAN TYRANT THAT I KNOW . . . 380 MEROPE   1275
FOR YEARS HIS WIDOW IN THEIR SIGHT I STAND . 381 MEROPE   1316
WHAT HELP WHAT VENGEANCE AT THEIR HANDS HAVE I 381 MEROPE   1318
NOW I IF I INVITE THEM TO RUN RISK . . . .   382 MEROPE   1349
NOW I IF I INVITE THEM TO RUN RISK . . . .   382 MEROPE   1349
HOW SHALL I ROUSE THEIR LOVE THEIR ARDOUR SO 382 MEROPE   1352
THEN MIGHT I USE THEM THEN FOR ONE WHO THUS . 383 MEROPE   1362
YET FOR ME MOTHER I HAD LIEFER DIE . . . .   383 MEROPE   1379
HERE STAND I NOW AND THE ATTEMPT SHALL BE . . 383 MEROPE   1383
AND TO WHAT FRIENDS SHOULD I FOR AID APPLY . 384 MEROPE   1390
WHAT ORDER MORE PRECISE HAD HE THAN I . . .   384 MEROPE   1400
THOU WILT DESTROY I SEE THYSELF AND US . .   385 MEROPE   1405
THAT I TO-DAY RETURNING FIND MYSELF . . . .   385 MEROPE   1410
HERE AS I GUESS THE NOBLE LAIAS COMES . .   386 MEROPE   1439
I KNOW SHE HONOURS NOT THE DEAD SO ILL . .   386 MEROPE   1450
YET EXCULPATION NEEDS IT IF I SEEK . . . .   387 MEROPE   1454
SOMETIMES WHEN HE WAS GONE I WISHD HIM BACK . 387 MEROPE   1457
RISK WHAT HE MIGHT NOW THAT I HAVE HIM HERE . 387 MEROPE   1458
NOW THAT I FEED MINE EYES ON THAT YOUNG FACE 387 MEROPE   1459
I SHUDDER LAIAS TO COMMIT MY CHILD . . . .   387 MEROPE   1461
TO MURDERS DREAD ARENA WHERE I SAW . . . .   387 MEROPE   1462
I LOATHE FOR HIM THE SLIPPERY WAY OF BLOOD . 387 MEROPE   1464
I ASK IF BLOODLESS MEANS MAY GAIN HIS END .   387 MEROPE   1465
AND I WOULD NOW HAVE JUSTICE STRIKE NOT ME . 387 MEROPE   1472
I HIDE NOT EVEN THIS THE REVERENCE DEEP . .   387 MEROPE   1474
HEIRSHIP WITH FAIR INTENT AS I BELIEVE . .   387 MEROPE   1484
DO I THEN GIVE TO USURPATION GRACE . . . .   388 MEROPE   1494
THAN I TO HELP RAISE HIS MESSENIAN FRIENDS . 388 MEROPE   1497
AND I WHEN TO HIS RIGHTEOUS STANDARD DOWN .   388 MEROPE   1502
DESPISE THEM NOT FOR BROTHER THOU AND I . .   388 MEROPE   1511
WHICH WAY TO LEAN I KNOW NOT BLOODY STROKES . 388 MEROPE   1521
TIME PRESSES SO THAT THEME FORBEAR I NOW . . 389 MEROPE   1530
DIRECT TO THY DISSUASIONS I REPLY . . . .   389 MEROPE   1531
ONE AND A WOMAN HOW CAN I PREVAIL . . . .   390 MEROPE   1580
O BROTHER THOU HAST CONQUERD YET I FEAR . .   390 MEROPE   1581
AS OUR JUST CAUSE DESERVES I DO NOT FEAR . . 391 MEROPE   1595
TO OFFER THAT I COME NOT BUT TO URGE . . .   394 MEROPE   1688
YES ONCE AGAIN I COME I WILL NOT TAKE . . .   394 MEROPE   1690
YES ONCE AGAIN I COME I WILL NOT TAKE . . .   394 MEROPE   1690
TO THE MESSENIAN KINGDOM THOU AND I . . .   394 MEROPE   1692
MOST HONOURABLY I MEANT I CALL THE GODS . .   394 MEROPE   1695
MOST HONOURABLY I MEANT I CALL THE GODS . .   394 MEROPE   1695
TWIXT THEE AND ME SUSPICION THAT I NURSED .   394 MEROPE   1699
FOR THE LAST TIME I ASK ASK EARNESTLY . .   394 MEROPE   1717
SPEAK I GO HENCE TO OFFER SACRIFICE . . . .   394 MEROPE   1722
HENCEFORTH IF WHAT I URGE DISPLEASE I MAY .   395 MEROPE   1727
HENCEFORTH IF WHAT I URGE DISPLEASE I MAY .   395 MEROPE   1727
I PITY THEE AND WISH THEE CALMER MIND . . .   396 MEROPE   1760
AND IN MY TURN I WISH THE SAME FOR THEE . .   396 MEROPE   1763
ALL I COULD DO TO SOOTHE THEE HAS BEEN TRIED 396 MEROPE   1764
I THINK ON WHAT THE FUTURE HATH IN STORE . . 397 MEROPE   1775
TO-DAY I REIGN THE REST I LEAVE TO FATE . .   397 MEROPE   1776
TO-DAY I REIGN THE REST I LEAVE TO FATE . .   397 MEROPE   1776
ENOUGH ENOUGH I WILL NO LONGER HEAR . . . .   397 MEROPE   1780
MORE FOR THIS LANDS SAKE GRIEVE I THAN MINE OWN 398 MEROPE   1784
I CHAFE NOT WITH THEE THAT THY HATE ENDURES . 398 MEROPE   1785
WHAT I HAVE DONE IS DONE BY MY OWN DEED . .   398 MEROPE   1787
NEITHER EXULTING NOR ASHAMED I STAND . . .   398 MEROPE   1788
NOT MENS GOOD WORD HATH MADE ME WHAT I AM .   398 MEROPE   1791
ALONE I MASTERD POWER AND ALONE . . . .   398 MEROPE   1792
SINCE SO THOU WILT I DARE MAINTAIN IT STILL . 398 MEROPE   1793
DID I THEN WAVER . . . .   398 MEROPE   1794
OF YOUR DEAD MASTERS LINE I BRING YOU NEWS . 400 MEROPE   1883
I TOOK MY STAND AND SAW THE UNARMD CROWDS .   401 MEROPE   1896
I TREMBLED FOR OUR PRINCE AND HIS ATTEMPT .   401 MEROPE   1901
AND FROM THAT MOMENT I SAW NOTHING CLEAR . . 402 MEROPE   1936
TO ARMED WARRIORS I HEARD VENGEFUL CRIES . . 402 MEROPE   1940

I   (CONTINUED)

I HEARD THE CLASH OF WEAPONS THEN I SAW	• • • •	402	MEROPE	1941
I HEARD THE CLASH OF WEAPONS THEN I SAW	• • • •	402	MEROPE	1941
APPROVE NOT TOO I HAVE BUT HALF MY JOY	• • • •	403	MEROPE	1962
A NEW-MADE WIFE I FROM ARCADIA CAME	• • • • •	403	MEROPE	1972
HIS BLOOD TO ME FOR I CONFESS IT KIND	• • • •	404	MEROPE	1976
I KNOW NOT JUST IN EITHER CASE THE STROKE	• • • •	404	MEROPE	1986
BUT YET NOT KNOWING THIS I TRIUMPH NOT	• • • •	404	MEROPE	1988
FOR I FIND WORTH IN THEE AND BADNESS TOO	• • • •	404	MEROPE	1990
ENOUGH OF THIS SINCE THEN I HAVE MAINTAIND	• • • •	334	MEROPE	V 134
LONGING LISTENING I WAIT I IMPLORE	• • • •	347	MEROPE	V
LONGING LISTENING I WAIT I IMPLORE	• • • •	347	MEROPE	V
BRING TO HIS MOTHER THE REST I COMMIT	• • • •	348	MEROPE	V
BLOOD I ASK NOT ENOUGH	• • • •	348	MEROPE	V
AND RESTING THERE TO BREATHE I SAW BELOW	• • • •	357	MEROPE	V 797
THENCE HE ESCAPD AND NEXT I FIND HIM HERE	• • • •	365	MEROPE	V
SUSPICION GRAVE I SEE BUT NO CLEAR PROOF	• • • •	365	MEROPE	V 994
AH NOW I COMPREHEND THE LIBERAL GRACE	• • • •	366	MEROPE	V 997
I GO I GO YET QUEEN TAKE THIS ONE WORD	• • • •	368	MEROPE	V1077
I GO I GO YET QUEEN TAKE THIS ONE WORD	• • • •	368	MEROPE	V1077
FIXD HIM THE AUTHOR OF MY DEATH I KNEW NOT	• • • •	379	MEROPE	V1273
TO OFFER THAT I CAME NOT BUT TO URGE	• • •	394	MEROPE	V1688
SINCE SO THOU WILT I WILL MAINTAIN IT STILL	• • • •	398	MEROPE	V1793
THE MULES I THINK WILL NOT BE HERE THIS HOUR	• •	406	EMPEDOCLES I 1	1
A THOUSAND TIMES HAVE I BEEN HERE ALONE	• • •	406	EMPEDOCLES I 1	7
HERE WILL I STAY TILL THE SLOW LITTER COMES	• •	407	EMPEDOCLES I 1	18
I HAVE MY HARP TOO THAT IS WELL APOLLO	• • •	407	EMPEDOCLES I 1	19
I KNOW NOT IN WHAT MIND EMPEDOCLES	• • •	407	EMPEDOCLES I 1	21
WHOSE MULES I FOLLOWD MAY BE COMING UP	• • •	407	EMPEDOCLES I 1	22
THE MULES MUST BE BELOW FAR DOWN I HEAR	• • •	407	EMPEDOCLES I 1	27
I LEFT THEE SUPPING WITH PEISIANAX	• • • •	407	EMPEDOCLES I 1	31
AS I WAS LIFTING MY SOILD GARLAND OFF	• • •	407	EMPEDOCLES I 1	40
I SAW THE MULES AND LITTER IN THE COURT	• • •	407	EMPEDOCLES I 1	41
THOU TOO WAST WITH HIM STRAIGHTWAY I SPED HOME	• •	407	EMPEDOCLES I 1	43
I SADDLED MY WHITE MULE AND ALL NIGHT LONG	• •	407	EMPEDOCLES I 1	44
I THINK THOU WOULDST NOT VEX HIM NO AND YET	• •	408	EMPEDOCLES I 1	55
I WOULD FAIN STAY AND HELP THEE TEND HIM ONCE	•	408	EMPEDOCLES I 1	56
AND STILL I KNOW NOT HOW HE DRAWS ME TO HIM	• •	408	EMPEDOCLES I 1	58
AND I COULD WATCH HIM WITH HIS PROUD SAD FACE	•	408	EMPEDOCLES I 1	59
HE IS NOW ALWAYS MOODY AND I FEAR HIM	• • •	408	EMPEDOCLES I 1	74
BUT I WOULD SERVE HIM SOOTHE HIM IF I COULD	• •	408	EMPEDOCLES I 1	75
BUT I WOULD SERVE HIM SOOTHE HIM IF I COULD	• •	408	EMPEDOCLES I 1	75
AND I MUST LEAVE HIM FOR HIS PLEASURE IS	• • •	409	EMPEDOCLES I 1	91
WOULD I BESTOW TO HELP EMPEDOCLES	• • • •	409	EMPEDOCLES I 1	102
I ASKD HIM OF PANTHEIA YESTERDAY	• • • •	410	EMPEDOCLES I 1	126
AND HE MADE ANSWER I SHOULD COME AT NIGHT	• •	410	EMPEDOCLES I 1	128
PANTHEIA FOR I KNOW HER KINSMEN WELL	• • •	410	EMPEDOCLES I 1	135
I HEAR GORGIAS THEIR CHIEF SPEAKS NOBLY OF HIM	•	411	EMPEDOCLES I 1	147
ENOUGH OF THIS I SEE THE LITTER WIND	• • •	411	EMPEDOCLES I 1	163
I MUST REJOIN EMPEDOCLES DO THOU	• • • •	411	EMPEDOCLES I 1	165
THOU TOO WERT WITH HIM STRAIGHTWAY I SPED HOME	• •	407	EMPEDOCLES I 1	V 43
I SHOULD HAVE SAID THAT SOME ONE TOUCHD A HARP	• •	412	EMPEDOCLES I 2	11
I SPOKE WITH HIM THIS MORNING ONCE MORE THEREFORE		412	EMPEDOCLES I 2	19
AS I HAVE PRAYD THEE THAT AND TO WHAT END	• •	412	EMPEDOCLES I 2	21
BUT I WILL ALSO SAY THAT WHEN THE GODS	• • •	413	EMPEDOCLES I 2	23
I KNOW THESE NOTES AMONG A THOUSAND HARK	• • •	413	EMPEDOCLES I 2	35
AND SAID O BOY I TAUGHT THIS LORE	• • • •	414	EMPEDOCLES I 2	69
I WILL NOT JUDGE THAT MAN	• • • • • •	415	EMPEDOCLES I 2	97
HOWBEIT I JUDGE AS LOST	• • • • •	415	EMPEDOCLES I 2	98
ALL KNOWLEDGE THAT I HAVE	• • • • • •	415	EMPEDOCLES I 2	104
ALL SKILL I WIELD ARE FREE	• • • • •	415	EMPEDOCLES I 2	105
I THINK MIGHT MAKE US FEAR	• • • • • •	425	EMPEDOCLES I 2	384
WHY SHOULD I SAY THAT LIFE NEED YIELD BUT MODERATE		425	EMPEDOCLES I 2	391
BLISS				
NOT MUCH I KNOW YOU PRIZE	• • • • •	426	EMPEDOCLES I 2	407
I SAY FEAR NOT LIFE STILL	• • • • • •	426	EMPEDOCLES I 2	422
FOR I MUST BE ALONE LEAVE ME ONE MULE	• • •	428	EMPEDOCLES I 2	465
TELL HIM I NEVER FAILD TO LOVE HIS LYRE	• • •	428	EMPEDOCLES I 2	468
GOOD FRIEND I SHALL REVISIT CATANA	• • • •	428	EMPEDOCLES I 2	473
I HAVE SEEN MANY CITIES IN MY TIME	• • •	428	EMPEDOCLES I 2	474
AND I SHALL DOUBTLESS SEE THEM ALL AGAIN	• • •	428	EMPEDOCLES I 2	476
I DARE NOT URGE HIM FURTHER HE MUST GO	• • •	428	EMPEDOCLES I 2	479
BUT HE IS STRANGELY WROUGHT I WILL SPEED BACK	•	428	EMPEDOCLES I 2	480
I SAW HIM THROUGH THE CHESTNUTS FAR BELOW	• •	428	EMPEDOCLES I 2	485
I KNOW THOSE NOTES AMONG A THOUSAND HARK	• •	413	EMPEDOCLES I 2	V 35
NOT MUCH THOU KNOWST I PRIZE	• • • • •	426	EMPEDOCLES I 2	V 407
NOT OVERMUCH I PRIZE	• • • • • •	426	EMPEDOCLES I 2	V 407
FOR I MUST HENCEFORTH SPEAK NO MORE WITH MAN	•	429	EMPEDOCLES II	6
FIND HENCEFORTH ENERGY AND HEART BUT I	• • •	429	EMPEDOCLES II	10
WHAT SHOULD I DO WITH LIFE AND LIVING MORE	• •	429	EMPEDOCLES II	15
THESE RUMBLINGS ARE NOT TYPHOS GROANS I KNOW	•	431	EMPEDOCLES II	95
I AM WEARY OF IT	• • • • • • •	432	EMPEDOCLES II	108
THOUGH I HAVE LOVED THEE LIVED IN HONOURING THEE	•	434	EMPEDOCLES II	195
I AM WEARY OF THEE	• • • • • •	435	EMPEDOCLES II	198
I AM WEARY OF THE SOLITUDE	• • • • •	435	EMPEDOCLES II	199
I HAVE BEEN ENOUGH ALONE	• • • • •	435	EMPEDOCLES II	219
ARE YOU TOO WHAT I FEAR TO BECOME	• • • •	437	EMPEDOCLES II	281
UPON WHOSE CHARRD AND QUAKING CRUST I STAND	•	438	EMPEDOCLES II	307
WITH HELD-IN JOY SWELLING ITS HEART I ONLY	• •	438	EMPEDOCLES II	316
I WHO HAVE NOT LIKE THESE IN SOLITUDE	• • •	438	EMPEDOCLES II	318
NURSED AN IMMORTAL VIGOUR I ALONE	• • • •	438	EMPEDOCLES II	320

I (CONTINUED)

AM DEAD TO LIFE AND JOY THEREFORE I READ   • • • •   438 EMPEDOCLES II   321
OH THAT I COULD GLOW LIKE THIS MOUNTAIN   • • • •   438 EMPEDOCLES II   323
I HAVE IN NO WISE BEEN BUT SLAVE OF THOUGHT   • •   440 EMPEDOCLES II   391
AND WHO CAN SAY I HAVE BEEN ALWAYS FREE   • • •   440 EMPEDOCLES II   392
I CANNOT I HAVE LIVED IN WRATH AND GLOOM   • • • •   440 EMPEDOCLES II   394
I CANNOT I HAVE LIVED IN WRATH AND GLOOM   • • • •   440 EMPEDOCLES II   394
BUT I HAVE NOT GROWN EASY IN THESE BONDS   • • •   440 EMPEDOCLES II   397
BUT I HAVE NOT DENIED WHAT BONDS THESE WERE   •   440 EMPEDOCLES II   398
YEA I TAKE MYSELF TO WITNESS   • • • • • •   441 EMPEDOCLES II   399
THAT I HAVE LOVED NO DARKNESS   • • • • • •   441 EMPEDOCLES II   400
AND THEREFORE O YE ELEMENTS I KNOW   • • • •   441 EMPEDOCLES II   404
I FEEL IT IN THIS HOUR THE NUMBING CLOUD   • • •   441 EMPEDOCLES II   407
MOUNTS OFF MY SOUL I FEEL IT I BREATHE FREE   •   441 EMPEDOCLES II   408
MOUNTS OFF MY SOUL I FEEL IT I BREATHE FREE   •   441 EMPEDOCLES II   408
IMMORTAL HAD I MADE THIS BOY OF MINE   • • • •   447 WESTMIN ABBEY   105
AND I HAVE NOW NO POWER   • • • • • • •   447 WESTMIN ABBEY   107
YET WOULD I NOT DISTURB THEE FROM THY TOMB   •   449 WESTMIN ABBEY   163
I WOULD NOT BREAK THY REST NOR CHANGE THY DOOM   • •   449 WESTMIN ABBEY   166
AND BUILDS HIMSELF I KNOW NOT WHAT   • • • •   450 GEISTS GRAVE   31
OF SECOND LIFE I KNOW NOT WHERE   • • • • •   450 GEISTS GRAVE   32
SAYS IT FITS THAT I REHEARSE   • • • • • •   453 POOR MATTHIAS   17
VAIN TO AUGUR THEY OR I   • • • • • • •   454 POOR MATTHIAS   76
BUT AS AGE COMES ON I KNOW   • • • • • •   454 POOR MATTHIAS   77
MUCH I DOUBT IF THEY SHALL HAVE   • • • •   454 POOR MATTHIAS   81
AND I WHISPERD FIX ON HIM   • • • • •   458 POOR MATTHIAS   195
WHAT POOR KAI DEAD SAY ALL I MEET   • • • •   459 KAISER DEAD   9
SIX YEARS AGO I BROUGHT HIM DOWN   • • • •   459 KAISER DEAD   13
STILL STILL I SEE THE FIGURE SMART   • • • •   460 KAISER DEAD   49
I SEE THE TAIL LIKE BRACELET TWIRLD   • • •   460 KAISER DEAD   55
LAST NIGHT I LOOKD THE SKY WAS CLEAR   • • •   480 HAYSWATER BOAT   33
WHERE I AM THOU ASKST AND WHERE I WENDED   • •   482 THEKLAS ANSWER   1
WHERE I AM THOU ASKST AND WHERE I WENDED   • •   482 THEKLAS ANSWER   1
AM I NOT CONCLUDED NOW AND ENDED   • • • •   482 THEKLAS ANSWER   3
FIND I HIM FROM WHOM I HAD TO SEVER   • • •   482 THEKLAS ANSWER   9
FIND I HIM FROM WHOM I HAD TO SEVER   • • •   482 THEKLAS ANSWER   9
I PASSD TO-DAY OER WALTON HEATH   • • • •   483 ROME-SICKNESS   5
I CROSSD ST GEORGES HILL TO-DAY   • • •   484 ROME-SICKNESS   13
THERE IN THE LEAF-STREWN COPSE I FOUND   • • •   484 ROME-SICKNESS   14
I READ IN DANTE HOW THAT HORNED LIGHT   • • •   484 S S LUSITANIA   1
I DROPPD THE BOOK AND OF MY CHILD I THOUGHT   •   485 S S LUSITANIA   9
I DROPPD THE BOOK AND OF MY CHILD I THOUGHT   •   485 S S LUSITANIA   9
WITH OMEN OH WERE THAT MOUNT PASSD I SAY   • • •   485 S S LUSITANIA   12
WOMAN I TOO TAKE THOUGHT FOR THIS BUT THEN   HOMER TRANS   14
      I BETHINK ME
WOMAN I TOO TAKE THOUGHT FOR THIS BUT THEN   HOMER TRANS   14
      I BETHINK ME
IF LIKE A COWARD I SKULKD BEHIND APART FROM THE BATTLE   HOMER TRANS   16
ERE I HEAR THY CRIES AND THY CAPTIVITY TOLD OF   • •   HOMER TRANS   38
I OF MYSELF KNOW WELL THAT HERE I AM DESTIND TO PERISH   HOMER TRANS   60
I OF MYSELF KNOW WELL THAT HERE I AM DESTIND TO PERISH   HOMER TRANS   60
FAR FROM MY FATHER AND MOTHER DEAR FOR ALL   HOMER TRANS   61
      THAT I WILL NOT
WHO WHILE I PONDERED ON THE LOT OF SOULS   • • •   RUDE ORATOR   2
DIDST FORCE AN AUDIENCE ERE I STRUCK THE SCALE   • •   RUDE ORATOR   6
THOU WILT BE MOST UNLOVELY SHALL I CHUSE   • • •   FRAGMENT 5   3
I BELIEVE   • • • • • • • • • • •   FRAGMENT 6   1

IACCHUS

IACCHUS WHITE FANE   • • • • • • •   186 STRAYED REVEL   38
IACCHUS DARLING   • • • • • • • • •   188 STRAYED REVEL   79
BELOVED IACCHUS   • • • • • • • • •   194 STRAYED REVEL   281
YOUTH AND IACCHUS   • • • • • • • •   218 BACCHANALIA 1   30

IBERIANS

SHY TRAFFICKERS THE DARK IBERIANS COME   • • •   262 SCHOLAR-GIPSY   249

ICE

GRAPE-SYRUP SQUARES OF COLOURD ICE   • • • •   94 SICK KING BOKH   196
NINE DAYS NINE NIGHTS TOWARD THE NORTHERN ICE   •   99 BALDER DEAD 1   145
AT THE CHINKD FIELDS OF ICE THE WASTE OF SNOW   •   100 BALDER DEAD 1   164
AND HE MUST FARE ACROSS THE DISMAL ICE   • • •   100 BALDER DEAD 1   165
BUT THEN HE MUST DISMOUNT AND ON THE ICE   • • •   100 BALDER DEAD 1   168
NINE DAYS NINE NIGHTS TOWARDS THE NORTHERN ICE   •   99 BALDER DEAD 1   V 145
AND HE WILL FARE ACROSS THE DISMAL ICE   • •   100 BALDER DEAD 1   V 165
NINE DAYS NINE NIGHTS TOWARD THE NORTHERN ICE   •   107 BALDER DEAD 2   83
WHICH HANGS OVER THE ICE WHERE LIES THE ROAD   •   108 BALDER DEAD 2   127
FOR IN THAT ICE ARE LOST THOSE NORTHERN STREAMS   •   108 BALDER DEAD 2   128
AT THE DREAR ICE BEYOND THE GIANTS HOME   • •   108 BALDER DEAD 2   142
THENCE ON HE JOURNEYD OER THE FIELDS OF ICE   •   109 BALDER DEAD 2   143
ON THE SMOOTH ICE OF SLEIPNER ODINS HORSE   • •   109 BALDER DEAD 2   147
LIFTED AND ISSUED ON THE FIELDS OF ICE   • • •   113 BALDER DEAD 2   287
AND OER THE ICE HE FARED TO OCEANS STRAND   • •   113 BALDER DEAD 2   288
NINE DAYS NINE NIGHTS TOWARDS THE NORTHERN ICE   •   107 BALDER DEAD 2   V 83
AND DOWN TO OCEAN GROPED AND CROSSD THE ICE   •   124 BALDER DEAD 3   376
I STANCH WITH ICE MY BURNING BREAST   • • •   158 SAINT BRANDAN   69
TO THE ICE-CUMBERD GORGES   • • • • • •   175 PARTING   27
TOWARDS THE ICE-CUMBERD GORGES   • • • • •   PARTING   V 27
MILLIONS WHOSE LIFE IN ICE LAY FAST   • • • •   322 OBERMANN MORE   287
THAN THE ICE-BASTIOND CAUCASIAN MOUNT   • • •   395 MEROPE   1749
IN DESERT ICE OF SUBTLETIES WAS SPENT   • • •   446 WESTMIN ABBEY   64
A HEART OF ICE A SOUL OF FIRE   • • • • • •   481 DESTINY   6

ICEBERG
        HE SEES FLOAT PAST AN ICEBERG WHITE   • • • • •   156 SAINT BRANDAN   15
        THE MOON WAS BRIGHT THE ICEBERG NEAR   • • • • •   157 SAINT BRANDAN   22
        THE ICEBERG AND NO JUDAS THERE   • •   • • • • • 158 SAINT BRANDAN   76
        HE SEES FLOAT NEAR AN ICEBERG WHITE   • • • • •   156 SAINT BRANDAN   V 15
        THE ICEBERG IN THE FROSTY AIR   • •   • • • • • 158 SAINT BRANDAN   V 76
        THE ICEBERG AND NO TENANT THERE   • • • • •   158 SAINT BRANDAN   V 76

ICEBERGS
        BLOCKS OF THE PAST LIKE ICEBERGS HIGH   • • • • 319 OBERMANN MORE   211
        HE MELTS THE ICEBERGS OF THE PAST   • • • • • • 322 OBERMANN MORE   V 285

ICY
        THE SPLASHING ICY FOUNTAINS PLAY   • • • • •   300 GRANDE CHARTR   33
        AND ICY THY DESPAIR   • • • • •   • • • • •   309 OBERMANN   88
        THE COLD DULL SHADOW OF THEIR ICY WING   • • • • 474 CROMWELL   92

IDA
        OF IDA AND AMONG THE GRASS SHALL FIND   • • • • 128 BALDER DEAD 3   538
        IN MYSIAN IDA THE VOICE   • • • • • • • • • • 230 YOUTH OF NATURE   76

IDAS
        NOR DID HE LOOK ONCE MORE TO IDAS PLAIN   • • • • 97 BALDER DEAD 1   57
        BY THE ASH IGDRASIL IN IDAS PLAIN   • • • • • • 105 BALDER DEAD 2   33
        TO THE ASH IGDRASIL AND IDAS PLAIN   • • • • • • 120 BALDER DEAD 3   217

IDENTITY
        AND WELL-NIGH CHANGE HIS OWN IDENTITY   • • • • 246 BURIED LIFE   34

IDLE
        STAND NEVER IDLE BUT GO ALWAYS ROUND   • • • • •   4 DUKE WELLINGTON   2
        IF THOUGHTS NOT IDLE WHILE BEFORE ME FLOW   • • • •   7 REP FRIEND   11
        AND AS A STORK WHICH IDLE BOYS HAVE TRAPPD • • • • 129 BALDER DEAD 3   559
        IDLE AS A MOSSY STONE   • • • • •   • • • • 137 TRISTRAM 1   223
        IN THE NEVER IDLE WORKSHOP OF NATURE   • • • • •   286 HAWORTH CHURCH   136
        THE WORLD WHICH FOR AN IDLE DAY   • •   • • • • • 304 GRANDE CHARTR   152
        MOTHER THY FEARS ARE IDLE FOR I COME   • • • • •   379 MEROPE   1256
        WITH QUESTIONINGS ABOUT AN IDLE TALE   • • • • •   411 EMPEDOCLES I 1   155
        SAY NOT SUCH DREAMS ARE IDLE FOR THE MAN   • • • • 473 CROMWELL   45
        ALL AIRY HOPES THAT IDLE HEARTS CAN FRAME   • • • • 474 CROMWELL   95
        IT SEEMS AN IDLE THING WHICH COULD NOT LIVE   • •   FRAGMENT 9   1

IDLERS
        MIXT WITH THE IDLERS ON THE PIER   • • • • •   205 CALAIS SANDS   30

IDLY
        NOT IDLY EARTH AND OCEAN LABOUR ON   • • • • •   42 GIPSY CHILD   7
        NOR IDLY DO THESE SEA-BIRDS HOVER NEAR   • • • • 42 GIPSY CHILD   8
        WHICH ALL THE GODS IN SPORT HAD IDLY THROWN   • •   95 BALDER DEAD 1   3
        WHERE IDLY FLIT ABOUT THE FEEBLE SHADES   • • • • 110 BALDER DEAD 2   182
        WHO FLUCTUATE IDLY WITHOUT TERM OR SCOPE   • • • • 260 SCHOLAR-GIPSY   167
        ALL IDLY FLUTTERD IN THE EASTERN GALE   • • • • 473 CROMWELL   68

IDOL
        THIS HIS IDOL THIS THAT ROYAL BRIDE   • • • • •   144 TRISTRAM 2   66
        TO BEND IN RAPTURE AT SOME IDOL THRONE   • • • • 474 CROMWELL   99

IDOLS
        MAKES IDOLS TO ADORE   • • • • • • • • • • •   39 STAGIRIUS   23

IGDRASIL
        BY THE ASH IGDRASIL IN IDAS PLAIN   • • • • • • 105 BALDER DEAD 2   33
        TO THE ASH IGDRASIL AND IDAS PLAIN   • • • • • • 120 BALDER DEAD 3   217

IGNOBLE
        BUT OUR IGNOBLE SOULS LACK MIGHT   • • • • •   201 URANIA   4
        THEIR FADED IGNOBLE LIVES   • • •   • • • • • • 235 YOUTH OF MAN   111
        FOR A YOUNGER IGNOBLE WORLD • • •   • • • • • • 437 EMPEDOCLES II   292
        AND MEN IGNOBLE HARASSD HIM WITH STRIFE   • • • • 447 WESTMIN ABBEY   125

IGNOMINIOUS
        THIS IGNOMINIOUS SPECTACLE   • • • • • • • • • 282 HAWORTH CHURCH   V

IGNOMINY
        HER HEAD MID IGNOMINY DEATH AND TOMBS   • • • • 172 GOOD SHEPHERD   12
        HER HEAD IN IGNOMINY DEATH AND TOMBS   • • • • •   172 GOOD SHEPHERD   V 12

IGNORANCE
        WHOM HIS GREAT FATHER DID IN IGNORANCE KILL   • •   84 SOHRAB RUSTUM   793
        LIGHT IGNORANCE AND HURRYING UNSURE THOUGHTS   • •   198 FRAG DEJANEIRA   2
        SHARP SENSE OF DEEP SELF-IGNORANCE FEAR OF LOOKS • •   LUCRETIUS 2   14

IGNORANT
        NEAR DEATH AND BY AN IGNORANT STROKE OF THINE • •   85 SOHRAB RUSTUM   818
        AND AFTER THAT OF IGNORANT WITLESS MIND   • • • • 98 BALDER DEAD 1   98
        IGNORANT WHERE TO STAND OR WHOM TO AVOID   • • • • 195 FRAG ANTIGONE   19
        A DEAD IGNORANT THANKLESS CORPSE • •   • • • •   196 FRAG ANTIGONE   53
        PROUD IGNORANT SELF-ADORED YOU LIVE ALONE   • • • • 198 FRAG DEJANEIRA   7
        WHERE IGNORANT ARMIES CLASH BY NIGHT   • • • • •   212 DOVER BEACH   37
        AND IGNORANT MEN DESPISE ME THAT I STAND   • • •   333 MEROPE   95

IGNORANT   (CONTINUED)
    THE IGNORANT HEADLONG MULTITUDE • • • • • 353 MEROPE   673
    ARE LIKE THE MOB VICIOUS AND IGNORANT • • • • 404 MEROPE   2004
    O IGNORANT RACE OF MAN • • • • • • • • • 447 WESTMIN ABBEY   101

IGNORE
    TO EVERY THOUGHT THE MASS IGNORE • • • • • 179 FAREWELL   58

ILEX
    THROUGH THE DENSE ILEX-THICKETS TO THE DOGS • • 357 MEROPE   791
    OF THE LENTISK AND ILEX • • • • • • • • • 392 MEROPE   1633

ILIUM
    AND HECTOR WAS IN ILIUM FAR BELOW • • • • • 236 PALLADIUM   3
    WHO LED THE GREEKS TO ILIUM AGAMEMNON • • • • 367 MEROPE   1035

ILL
    ILL DEEDS ILL PASSIONS ZEALOUS TO FULFIL • • • • 11 MYCERINUS   76
    ILL DEEDS ILL PASSIONS ZEALOUS TO FULFIL • • • • 11 MYCERINUS   76
    TO PAINT ILL AS I HAVE DONE • • • • • • 24 MEMORY-PICTURE   51
    AND HE SPINS ILL WHO MISSES ONE • • • • • 48 HORATIAN ECHO   26
    BE PASSIONATE HOPES NOT ILL RESIGND • • • • 59 RESIGNATION   243
    IS ILL AT EASE AND CALLS FOR THEE • • • • • 87 SICK KING BOKH   4
    HODER ILL-FATED CHILD OF BALE MY SON • • • • • 98 BALDER DEAD 1   112
    HODER ILL-FATED BLIND IN HEART AND EYES • • 124 BALDER DEAD 3   387
    OF THAT STRANGER-KNIGHT ILL-STARRD • • • • 136 TRISTRAM 1   200
    NOR THY YOUNGER ISEULT TAKE IT ILL • • • • 144 TRISTRAM 2   58
    SHE WOULD FIND ILL TO BEAR WEAK AS SHE IS • • 152 TRISTRAM 3   101
    AND WHEN MY ILL-SCHOOLD SPIRIT IS AFLAME • • • 169 WORLDLY PLACE   11
    ILL STOP AND SAY THERE WERE NO SUCCOUR HERE • 169 WORLDLY PLACE   13
    ILL AND OERWORKD HOW FARE YOU IN THIS SCENE • 169 EAST LONDON   6
    A TRAMP I SAW ILL MOODY AND TONGUE-TIED • • 169 WEST LONDON   2
    FOR ILL-ENDOWD FOR SUCH A WAY • • • • • 226 EPILOG LAOCOON   171
    ILL-STORED IN STRENGTH IN WITS ARE THEY • • 226 EPILOG LAOCOON   172
    FOR ILL PREPARED FOR SUCH A WAY • • • • • 226 EPILOG LAOCOON V 171
    ILL FOUND IN STRENGTH IN WITS ARE THEY • • 226 EPILOG LAOCOON V 172
    THE ILL HE CANNOT CURE A NAME • • • • • • 250 WISH   20
    BEFITS YOU ILL • • • • • • • • • 279 SOUTHERN NIGHT   116
    QUICKEST TO ILL IS THE PRAISE • • • • • • 293 HEINES GRAVE V 27
    AND TRULY IN THIS ILL-RULED WORLD • • • • 353 MEROPE   664
    WELL-MOURND BUT ILL-AVENGED • • • • • • 372 MEROPE   1142
    ILL COUNSEL IN MY JUDGMENT GIVES SHE HERE • • • 382 MEROPE   1333
    I KNOW SHE HONOURS NOT THE DEAD SO ILL • • • 386 MEROPE   1450
    HIS FATHER AND HIS ILL-STARRD BRETHREN FALL • 387 MEROPE   1463
    FAST PERMANENCE TO AN ILL-GOTTEN THRONE • • 388 MEROPE   1509
    CAN HOUSES THUS ILL-SEATED THUS EMBROILD • • • 390 MEROPE   1559
    SOME ILL DESIGN AGAINST HIM JEALOUSY • • • • 394 MEROPE   1700
    THE ILL-BODING NOTE WHICH FRANTIC HATRED SOUNDS • • 397 MEROPE   1781
    ILL-KEPT BY HIS INFIRM HEIRS • • • • • • 399 MEROPE   1846
    LO THE ILL-FATED ONE • • • • • • • • 400 MEROPE   1876
    THE ILL-BODING NOTE WHICH FRANTIC ENVY SOUNDS • • 397 MEROPE V1781
    AND HE TREATS DOUBT THE BEST WHO TRIES TO SEE 415 EMPEDOCLES I 2   101
        LEAST ILL
    WHY ARE MEN ILL AT EASE • • • • • • • • 417 EMPEDOCLES I 2   148
    STILL USE OUR BODIES ILL • • • • • • • • 420 EMPEDOCLES I 2   230
    BUT OUR OWN ACTS FOR GOOD OR ILL ARE MIGHTIER POWERS 420 EMPEDOCLES I 2   241
    THE ILL DEEDS OF OTHER MEN MAKE OFTEN OUR LIFE DARK 421 EMPEDOCLES I 2   266
    HEALTH SAPPD BY LIVING ILL • • • • • • • 425 EMPEDOCLES I 2   393
    BUT SINCE LIFE TEEMS WITH ILL • • • • • • 426 EMPEDOCLES I 2   424
    WHOSE BANISHMENT IS NOT HIS GREATEST ILL • • • 429 EMPEDOCLES II   12
    THE ORACLE FORBADE NOT ILL-INSPIRED • • • • • 448 WESTMIN ABBEY   133
    YOUTH STAIND WITH FOLLIES AND THE THOUGHTS OF ILL 474 CROMWELL   79
    MUST BEAR IN SILENCE MANY AN ILL • • • • • 481 COURAGE   3
    STILL MENDING LESSENING HUMAN ILL • • • • • 484 ROME-SICKNESS   28

ILLIMITABLE
    MANS MEASURES CANNOT SPAN THE ILLIMITABLE ALL • • 423 EMPEDOCLES I 2 V 341

ILLS
    THOU TOUCHEST THE WORST OF MY ILLS • • • • • • 345 MEROPE   477
    THE ILLS WE OUGHT TO BEAR • • • • • • • 421 EMPEDOCLES I 2   280
    IN BREATHLESS QUIET AFTER ALL THEIR ILLS • • • 427 EMPEDOCLES I 2   438
    THE FIGHT WHICH CROWND THINE ILLS • • • • • 430 EMPEDOCLES II   56
    THE FIGHT THAT CROWND THY ILLS • • • • • • 430 EMPEDOCLES II V 56
    FOR SUCH A DAMNING CATALOGUE OF ILLS • • • • • RUDE ORATOR   14

ILLUMINATES
    NOT LESS THY BOAST ILLUMINATES CONTROL • • • • 8 RELIGIOUS ISOL   7

ILLUMINE
    SHY TO ILLUMINE AND I SEEK IT TOO • • • • • • 268 THYRSIS   202

ILLUMINED
    WHICH CHEQUER AT YOUR FEET THE ILLUMINED FLINTS • • 18 CHURCH BROU 3   29
    THAT CHEQUER AT YOUR FEET THE ILLUMINED FLINTS • • 18 CHURCH BROU 3 V 29
    OF YOUR ILLUMINED HAUNTS BY NIGHT • • • • • 141 TRISTRAM 1   354

ILLUSION
    MIST AND ILLUSION AND FEAR • • • • • • • • 281 HAWORTH CHURCH   40

ILLUSTRIOUS
    THAN THINE ILLUSTRIOUS HUSBANDS TO AVENGE • • • • 390 MEROPE   1569

ILLYRIAN
    AMONG THE GREEN ILLYRIAN HILLS AND THERE • • • • 426 EMPEDOCLES I 2   429
    THERE THOSE TWO LIVE FAR IN THE ILLYRIAN BRAKES • • 427 EMPEDOCLES I 2   443

ILSE
    ILSE THE FAIRY TRANSFORMD • • • • • • • • • 297 HEINES GRAVE   183

ILSLEY
    THE SIGNAL-ELM THAT LOOKS ON ILSLEY DOWNS • • • • 263 THYRSIS   14

ILYATS
    THE ILYATS OF KHORASSAN AND BEHIND • • • • • • 65 SOHRAB RUSTUM   138

IMAGE
    AND SOHRAB BARED THAT IMAGE ON HIS ARM • • • • 81 SOHRAB RUSTUM   684
    SHE HER GOOD SHEPHERDS HASTY IMAGE DREW • • • • 172 GOOD SHEPHERD   13
    SO BUT THY IMAGE ENDURE IN ITS PRIME • • • • • 206 SEPARATION   4
    CAN THE IMAGE OF LIFE HAVE THE GLOW • • • • • 231 YOUTH OF NATURE 115
    THE IMAGE OF A MAN UNSPOILD • • • • • • 273 EDW QUILLINAN V 15
    OURS IS THE REFLEX IMAGE OF THE WORLD • • • •   LUCRETIUS 5   1

IMAGED
    IMAGED SO OFT IMAGED SO TRUE • • • • • • 314 OBERMANN MORE   63
    IMAGED SO OFT IMAGED SO TRUE • • • • • • 314 OBERMANN MORE   63
    DIVINELIER IMAGED CLEARER SEEN • • • • • • • 322 OBERMANN MORE 295

IMAGINE
    AND WE IMAGINE THEE EXEMPT FROM AGE • • • • • 259 SCHOLAR-GIPSY   158

IMAGINED
    AT FIRST IMAGINED LAY • • • • • • • • • 45 IN UTRUMQUE PAR   2

IMAGINES
    WHO IMAGINES HER FIELDS AS THEY LAY • • • • • 252 FUTURE   29

IMBECILES
    YE IMBECILES IN PRESENT POWER • • • • • • • 48 HORATIAN ECHO   11

IMBECILITY
    NOR WORDY GERMAN IMBECILITY • • • • • • • 480 HUNGARIAN NAT   7

IMBED
    TO IMBED THEM IN THE SEA • • • • • • • • • • 430 EMPEDOCLES II   44

IMBRUE
    PASSIONS FIRST FURIOUS LONGING TO IMBRUE • • • • 387 MEROPE   1467

IMMATURE
    BY SEVERANCE IMMATURE • • • • • • • • • 197 FRAG ANTIGONE   66
    BUT WHEN IMMATURE DEATH • • • • • • • • • 199 EARLY DEATH   8

IMMEASURABLE
    MANS MEASURES CANNOT METE THE IMMEASURABLE ALL • • 423 EMPEDOCLES I 2   341

IMMEDICABLE
    IMMEDICABLE PAIN • • • • • • • • • • • 323 OBERMANN MORE 316

IMMEMORIAL
    ONCE MORE THINE IMMEMORIAL GLEAM RETURN • • • • 449 WESTMIN ABBEY   175
    ONE DAY THINE IMMEMORIAL GLEAM RETURN • • • • 449 WESTMIN ABBEY V 175

IMMENSE
    BEARING ON SHOULDERS IMMENSE • • • • • • • 295 HEINES GRAVE   93
    THE WORLDS IMMENSE DESIGN • • • • • • • • 423 EMPEDOCLES I 2   343

IMMERSED
    OR ARE YE IMMERSED IN THE MASS • • • • • • 230 YOUTH OF NATURE   68
    BUT KEEP HIM SELF-IMMERSED PREOCCUPIED • • • 237 PROGRESS   19
    IMMERSED IN SERIOUS STATE-CRAFT IS THE KING • • 387 MEROPE   1489

IMMORTAL
    ALL PAINS THE IMMORTAL SPIRIT MUST ENDURE • • • •   3 SHAKESPEARE   12
    AND IMMORTAL FORMS TO MEET YOU • • • • • • 29 NEW SIRENS   101
    OF IMMORTAL FEET IS GONE • • • • • • • • 34 NEW SIRENS   252
    THOUGH HE HATH BORNE IMMORTAL PAINS • • • • 56 RESIGNATION   151
    BREATHES WHEN HE WILL IMMORTAL AIR • • • • 58 RESIGNATION   207
    AND WILL NOT THEN THE IMMORTAL ARMIES SCORN • • • 172 IMMORTALITY   5
    FLASH THROUGH HER PURE IMMORTAL FRAME • • • 181 ISOLATION MARG   21
    IMMORTAL MORTAL MAN • • • • • • • • 197 FRAG ANTIGONE   72
    THE ONE OR TWO IMMORTAL LIGHTS • • • • • 220 BACCHANALIA 2   24
    AND GATHERD ON IMMORTAL KNOLLS • • • • • 227 EPILOG LAOCOON 203
    BUT THEY ARE IMMORTAL AND LIVE • • • • • 230 YOUTH OF NATURE   85
    BUT THOU POSSESSEST AN IMMORTAL LOT • • • • 259 SCHOLAR-GIPSY   157
    THOU HEAREST THE IMMORTAL CHANTS OF OLD • • • 268 THYRSIS   181
    THOU HEAREST THE IMMORTAL STRAINS OF OLD • • • 268 THYRSIS   V 181
    TO IMMORTAL DELIGHT • • • • • • • • • 399 MEROPE   1843
    AND REST IN THE IMMORTAL MEAD • • • • • • 414 EMPEDOCLES I 2   75
    NURSED AN IMMORTAL VIGOUR I ALONE • • • • • 438 EMPEDOCLES II   320

IMMORTAL   (CONTINUED)
        IMMORTAL HAD I MADE THIS BOY OF MINE . . . . . .   447 WESTMIN ABBEY   105
        TO A MORTAL BUT YE ARE WITHOUT OLD AGE AND IMMORTAL   HOMER TRANS   10

IMMORTALITY
        HIS BOON OF LIFE AND IMMORTALITY   . . . . . .   446 WESTMIN ABBEY   63

IMMORTALS
        THE REST OF IMMORTALS . . . .   443 EMPEDOCLES II   463

IMMOVEABLE
        IMMOVEABLE THOU SITTEST STILL . . . .   309 OBERMANN   85

IMMUNITY
        IMMUNITY FROM MY CONTROL . . . .   206 RIVER   15
        ITS PRIVILEGED IMMUNITY FROM BLOOD . . . . . .   389 MEROPE   1535

IMMURED
        IT IS TO ADD IMMURED   . . . .   212 GROWING OLD   23

IMPAIR
        TO FEEL THAT NOTHING CAN IMPAIR   . . . . . .   180 FAREWELL   83

IMPAIRD
        SEASONS IMPAIRD NOT THE RAY   . . . .   287 RUGBY CHAPEL   21
        FOR SOMETHING HAS IMPAIRD THY SPIRITS STRENGTH . . 429 EMPEDOCLES II   21

IMPAIRS
        ALL WEAKNESS WHICH IMPAIRS ALL GRIEFS WHICH BOW . .   3 SHAKESPEARE   13
        ALL WEAKNESS THAT IMPAIRS ALL GRIEFS THAT BOW   . .   3 SHAKESPEARE   V   13

IMPART
        HEAVEN DOTH A QUICKER PULSE IMPART   . . . . . .   56 RESIGNATION   145
        WHEN FULLY LEARND WILL TO THE WORLD IMPART . . . . 256 SCHOLAR-GIPSY   49
        THE WORLD HATH FAILD TO IMPART . . . .   424 EMPEDOCLES I 2   374

IMPARTING
        IMPARTING LIFE RENEWD OLD CLASSIC GRACE   . . . .   168 RACHEL 3   5

IMPATIENT
        WITH SHORT IMPATIENT LOWINGS THERE HE STOPPD   . . 402 MEROPE   1912
        OR HEAR MID CIRCLING CRAGS THE IMPATIENT CRY   . . 472 CROMWELL   25

IMPEL
        AND BADE THE WINDS THROUGH SPACE IMPEL THE GUSTY TOY 415 EMPEDOCLES I 2   81

IMPELLD
        THIS PURE THAT GUILTY MAY HAVE EACH IMPELLD   . .   352 MEROPE   646
        THOUGH TO HIS ACT EMPOWERD NAY IMPELLD   . . . .   385 MEROPE   1421

IMPENDING
        AS OF ONE SHADOWD BY IMPENDING DEATH . . . . . .   356 MEROPE   765

IMPENETRABLE
        PIERCE FATES IMPENETRABLE EAR   . . . .   60 RESIGNATION   274

IMPERIAL
        SO SPAKE THE IMPERIAL SAGE PUREST OF MEN   . . .   168 WORLDLY PLACE   2
        SO SPOKE THE IMPERIAL SAGE PUREST OF MEN   . . .   168 WORLDLY PLACE   V   2
        FLOATS THE IMPERIAL STREAM   . . . .   234 YOUTH OF MAN   87
        AND HER IMPERIAL CROWN   . . . .   316 OBERMANN MORE   128
        AND SO HE BORE THE IMPERIAL NAME   . . . . . .   459 KAISER DEAD   23
        BUT THOU IMPERIAL CITY THAT HAST STOOD   . . . .   463 ALARIC AT ROME   19
        BEHELD HIM MASTER OF IMPERIAL ROME . . . . . .   468 ALARIC AT ROME   172

IMPERIOUS
        THE TOO IMPERIOUS TRAVELLER ON . . . .   53 RESIGNATION   37
        HIS WOUNDS IMPERIOUS ANGUISH BUT THE BLOOD . . .   85 SOHRAB RUSTUM   840
        WITH THE OLD IMPERIOUS AIR   . . . .   134 TRISTRAM 1   124
        IMPERIOUS SELF-ASSERTING VIOLENCE   . . . . . .   353 MEROPE   689
        FORGED BY THE IMPERIOUS LONELY THINKING-POWER   . . 440 EMPEDOCLES II   376

IMPETUOUS
        PAINT WITH THEIR IMPETUOUS STRESS   . . . . . .   24 MEMORY-PICTURE   43
        VIDAR THE SILENT THE IMPETUOUS TYR   . . . . . .   127 BALDER DEAD 3   492
        WELL SPAKE THE IMPETUOUS SAINT AND BORE OF MEN . . 171 DIVINITY   6
        AND HE HIMSELF WITH THE IMPETUOUS HEART   . . . .   394 MEROPE   1702
        THE BRAVE IMPETUOUS HEART YIELDS EVERYWHERE   . .   431 EMPEDOCLES II   90
        THE BRAVE IMPETUOUS HAND YIELDS EVERYWHERE . . .   431 EMPEDOCLES II   V   90

IMPIOUS
        I ON MENS IMPIOUS UPROAR HURLD . . . .   249 KENSINGTON GARD   25
        BUT I ON MENS IMPIOUS TUMULT HURLD   . . . . . .   KENSINGTON GARD V   25
        I ON MENS IMPIOUS TUMULT HURLD . . . .   KENSINGTON GARD V   25
        HER IMPIOUS YOUNGER WORLD   . . . .   316 OBERMANN MORE   106
        FOR ME I DEEM SUCH IMPIOUS AND FOR HIM   . . . .   340 MEROPE   336
        PIOUS BUT IMPIOUS SURELY IF THEIR SCOPE   . . . .   342 MEROPE   380
        IMPIOUS I DEEM THE ALLIANCE WHICH HE ASKS   . . .   348 MEROPE   550
        THE MURDERER AND HIS IMPIOUS SETTER-ON   . . . .   368 MEROPE   1072
        AS IF THE SKY WAS IMPIOUS NOT TO FALL   . . . .   411 EMPEDOCLES I 1   145

IMPLACABLE
 THOU YOUNG IMPLACABLE GOD AND ONLY DEATH   • • • •   436 EMPEDOCLES II   232

IMPLIES
 HIS PRESENCE WITH THE KING THOU MEANST IMPLIES   • •   365 MEROPE   V

IMPLORE
 LONGING LISTENING I WAIT I IMPLORE   • • • • •   347 MEROPE   V

IMPLORING
 ROBS OF A LOVED BRIDE PALE IMPLORING • • • • •   196 FRAG ANTIGONE   42
 THY PRISON-HOUSE RAISED ONE IMPLORING CRY   • • • •   383 MEROPE   1371

IMPORT
 WHO HID SUCH IMPORT IN AN INFANTS GLOOM   • • • •   41 GIPSY CHILD   2
 OF IMPORT AND IN SILENCE BEST RECEIVED   • • • •   359 MEROPE   861
 SOUNDS OF DEEP IMPORT VOICES THAT BEGUILE   • • • •   472 CROMWELL   5

IMPOSED
 SHALL BE IMPOSED TO US SHALL BE THE DEED   • • • •   390 MEROPE   1585

IMPOSSIBILITY
 WHEN TRUE THE LAST IMPOSSIBILITY   • • • • •   5 HARMONY NATURE   3

IMPOSSIBLE
 STILL STANDING FOR SOME FALSE IMPOSSIBLE SHORE   • •   244 SUMMER NIGHT   69
 AND AWE BE DEAD AND HOPE IMPOSSIBLE   • • • •   429 EMPEDOCLES II   34
 AND WE SHALL SINK IN THE IMPOSSIBLE STRIFE • • • •   440 EMPEDOCLES II   389

IMPOTENCE
 AND NEXT THE CROWNING IMPOTENCE OF DEATH   • • • •   448 WESTMIN ABBEY   130
 AND THEN THE CROWNING IMPOTENCE OF DEATH   • • • •   448 WESTMIN ABBEY   V 130

IMPRACTICABLE
 THE IMPRACTICABLE HOURS • • • • • • • • •   316 OBERMANN MORE   104

IMPRESS
 GO THEN TILL TIME AND FATE IMPRESS   • • • • •   179 FAREWELL   41

IMPRESSION
 IF THE CLEAR IMPRESSION DIES   • • • • • • •   24 MEMORY-PICTURE   61

IMPRESSIONS
 AND OUR BEST IMPRESSIONS ARE   • • • • • • •   23 MEMORY-PICTURE   11

IMPRISONING
 THE IMPRISONING CHAINS FELL OFF AND ALL WAS CLEAR   478 CROMWELL   214

IMPRISONS
 SHEDS BLOOD IMPRISONS BANISHES ATTAINTS   • • • •   353 MEROPE   682

IMPULSE
 IMPULSE AND REASON FREEDOM AND CONTROL   • • • •   4 BUTLERS SERMONS   2
 TO ITS OWN IMPULSE EVERY CREATURE STIRS   • • •   8 RELIGIOUS ISOL   13
 AND MORE THAN MORTAL IMPULSE FILLD THEIR EYES   • •   25 DREAM   27
 THAT AN IMPULSE FROM THE DISTANCE   • •   • •   49 SECOND BEST   21
 WITH A FREE ONWARD IMPULSE BRUSHING THROUGH   • •   261 SCHOLAR-GIPSY   213
 I TURNED BY SOME VAGUE IMPULSE STIRRD   • • •   324 OBERMANN MORE   335
 TO YEARN WITH SPEECHLESS IMPULSE TO THE FREE   • •   472 CROMWELL   7
 THIS FAITHFUL IMPULSE OF UNFAITHFUL WILLS • • • •   FRAGMENT 8   4

IMPUNITY
 HAST ALL IMPUNITY YET LEST THY FRIENDS   • • • •   341 MEROPE   372
 AND COUNT ON LIKE IMPUNITY AND RISE   • • • • •   342 MEROPE   374

IMPUTE
 TO CHANCE IMPUTE THEIR DEATHS THEN NOT TO ME   • •   340 MEROPE   346
 MAKE GODS TO WHOM TO IMPUTE   • • • • • • •   421 EMPEDOCLES I 2   279

INACCESSIBLE
 SOME SOLITUDE MORE INACCESSIBLE   • • • • • •   395 MEROPE   1748

INACCURATE
 INACCURATE AND FRAIL   • • • • • • • • •   352 MEROPE   633

INACTIVE
 INACTIVE THEREFORE LET ME LIE IN GLOOM   • • • •   128 BALDER DEAD 3   509

INALIENABLE
 HATH SUCH INALIENABLE POWER   • • • • • • •   158 SAINT BRANDAN   V 56

INCENSE
 A HOLIER INCENSE THAN THIS FEEBLE LAY   • • • •   471 ALARIC AT ROME   226

INCESSANT
 AND MENS INCESSANT STREAM GOES BY   • • • • • •   277 SOUTHERN NIGHT   63
 THE INCESSANT WANDERER TAKES HIS WAY • • • • • •   484 ROME-SICKNESS   30

INCESSANTER
    IN A BLACKER INCESSANTER LINE • • • • • • • • 253 FUTURE   61

INCESSANTLY
    THIS STREAM WHICH FALLS INCESSANTLY • • • • • • 60 RESIGNATION   267
    THIS STREAM THAT FALLS INCESSANTLY • • • • • • 60 RESIGNATION   V 267

INCITE
    INCITE THE MASSES • • • • • • • • • • 460 KAISER DEAD   42

INCLINED
    HATH FINALLY INCLINED • • • • • • • 46 WORLD QUIETIST   2
    THE HOLLOWS GRASSY BANKS ARE SOFT-INCLINED • • • • 149 TRISTRAM 3   10
    THE OPENINGS GRASSY BANKS ARE SOFT INCLINED • • TRISTRAM 3   V 10
    THE OPENINGS GRASSY BANKS WERE SOFT INCLINED • • TRISTRAM 3   V 10
    FOES DAZZLED WITH YOUR PROWESS WELL INCLINED • • 339 MEROPE   302

INCOGNISABLE
    ON LIFES INCOGNISABLE SEA • • • • • • • • 40 HUMAN LIFE   8

INCOMMUNICABLY
    INCOMMUNICABLY THRONG • • • • • • • • • • 455 POOR MATTHIAS   104

INCONGRUOUS
    MOCKING HOW INCONGRUOUS NOW • • • • • • • 455 POOR MATTHIAS   114

INCREDULITY
    A SMILE OF WISTFUL INCREDULITY • • • • • • • 3 EMERSONS ESSAYS   7
    A SMILE OF MOURNFUL INCREDULITY • • • • • • EMERSONS ESSAYS V   7

INCREDULOUS
    BUT WITH A COLD INCREDULOUS VOICE HE SAID • • • 78 SOHRAB RUSTUM   576
    AND WITH A COLD INCREDULOUS VOICE HE SAID • • • • 78 SOHRAB RUSTUM   V 576

INCURIOUS
    TO MAKE THE INCURIOUS BYSTANDER INTENT • • • • 8 RELIGIOUS ISOL   3

INCURRING
    IN SINGLE FIGHT INCURRING SINGLE RISK • • • • 63 SOHRAB RUSTUM   69

INDEED
    NOT INNOCENT INDEED YET NOT FORLORN • • • • • 6 GEO CRUIKSHANK   5
    BEND YE ON THESE INDEED AN UNMOVED EYE • • • • 9 MYCERINUS   35
    TIS DEATH AND PEACE INDEED IS HERE • • • • • 21 YOUTH AND CALM   1
    YET INDEED THIS FLUX OF GUESSES • • • • • 33 NEW SIRENS   195
    BUT INDEED THIS PROUD POSSESSION • • • • • 33 NEW SIRENS   203
    BUT INDEED THIS FLUX OF GUESSES • • • • • 33 NEW SIRENS   V 195
    BUT IF THIS ONE DESIRE INDEED RULES ALL • • • • 63 SOHRAB RUSTUM   74
    HE WILL NOT YIELD INDEED NOR QUIT OUR FOES • • • 71 SOHRAB RUSTUM   351
    O SOHRAB THOU INDEED ART SUCH A SON • • • • 80 SOHRAB RUSTUM   641
    A LIFE OF BLOOD INDEED THOU DREADFUL MAN • • • 85 SOHRAB RUSTUM   828
    OR IF INDEED THIS ONE DESIRE RULES ALL • • • • 63 SOHRAB RUSTUM   V 74
    SO SHALL I KNOW THE LOST WAS DEAR INDEED • • • 111 BALDER DEAD 2   239
    SO SHALL SHE KNOW YOUR LOSS WAS DEAR INDEED • • 115 BALDER DEAD 3   45
    THOU ART COME INDEED THOU HAST REJOIND ME • • • 142 TRISTRAM 2   9
    WAS INDEED THE HEAVIEST BURDEN THROWN • • • • 144 TRISTRAM 2   50
    THOU MAKST THE HEAVEN THOU HOPST INDEED THY HOME • • 169 EAST LONDON   14
    WHICH CONSECRATES THE TIES OF BLOOD FOR THESE INDEED 196 FRAG ANTIGONE   31
    TIS TRUE INDEED AN IRON KNOT • • • • • 208 ON THE RHINE   7
    SOME END IS THERE WE INDEED MAY GAIN • • • • 210 SELF-DECEPTION   28
    TELL ME CAN YOU FIND INDEED • • • • • • 215 PIS-ALLER   6
    TO ONE ANOTHER WHAT INDEED THEY FEEL • • • • 245 BURIED LIFE   15
    IF STILL INDEED HE LIVES WHOM THOU WOULDST SEAT • • 336 MEROPE   189
    ADVISING US A COURSE WHICH WOULD INDEED • • • 382 MEROPE   1337
    A PEOPLE THEN IS AN ALLY INDEED • • • • • 382 MEROPE   1347
    ALAS AN ADAMANTINE STRENGTH INDEED • • • • 386 MEROPE   1434
    AUGUST INDEED WAS THE FOUNDATION HERE • • • 389 MEROPE   1554
    INDEED THY LIFELONG PASSION AND SOLE AIM • • • 404 MEROPE   1983
    AND MAKE IT STAND INDEED THE WILL OF HEAVEN • • 404 MEROPE   1999
    AS THE CHIEFS RULE INDEED THE PEOPLE ARE • • • 404 MEROPE   V2002
    THOU HAST INDEED A RARE TOUCH ON THY HARP • • • 409 EMPEDOCLES I 1   78
    IS FATE INDEED SO STRONG MANS STRENGTH INDEED SO POOR 415 EMPEDOCLES I 2   96
    IS FATE INDEED SO STRONG MANS STRENGTH INDEED SO POOR 415 EMPEDOCLES I 2   96
    DEATH DEATH WAS JUDGED THE BOON SUPREME INDEED • 448 WESTMIN ABBEY   140
    HAD THEY INDEED NO LONGER SPAN • • • • • • 450 GEISTS GRAVE   10
    A LOSS INDEED • • • • • • • • • • 459 KAISER DEAD   10
    THE CENTRAL STREAM OF WHAT WE FEEL INDEED • • • 483 BELOW SURFACE   5
    FOR THAN MAN INDEED THERE BREATHES NO WRETCHEDER   HOMER TRANS   12
        CREATURE

INDEX
    A NEVER-CHANGING INDEX TO REVENGE • • • • • • 381 MEROPE   1317

INDIAN
    UNDER THE EAVES PEERD ROWS OF INDIAN CORN • • • • 25 DREAM   19
    CROSS UNDERNEATH THE INDIAN CAUCASUS • • • • • 65 SOHRAB RUSTUM   161
    WIND UNDERNEATH THE INDIAN CAUCASUS • • • • • 66 SOHRAB RUSTUM   V 161
    CLIMB UNDERNEATH THE INDIAN CAUCASUS • • • • • 66 SOHRAB RUSTUM   V 161
    THEY SEE THE INDIAN • • • • • • • • • • 190 STRAYED REVEL   151
    THEY SEE THE INDIAN • • • • • • • • • • 193 STRAYED REVEL   235
    WITH INDIAN HEATS AT LAST FORDONE • • • • • 276 SOUTHERN NIGHT   26
    NOT BY THOSE HOARY INDIAN HILLS • • • • • • 277 SOUTHERN NIGHT   73

INDIAN   (CONTINUED)
        HE BY THOSE INDIAN MOUNTAINS OLD   . . . . . .   278 SOUTHERN NIGHT   91
        WITH INDIAN SUNS AT LAST FORDONE   . . . . . .   276 SOUTHERN NIGHT   V 26

INDIFFERENCE
        WITH BLANK INDIFFERENCE OR WITH BLAME REPROVED   . .   245 BURIED LIFE   19

INDIGNANTLY
        AND DAY AND NIGHT HELD ON INDIGNANTLY   . . . .   262 SCHOLAR-GIPSY   243

INDISCERNIBLE
        PURSUE WITH INDISCERNIBLE FLOW ITS WAY   . . . .   246 BURIED LIFE   40
        INDISCERNIBLE BY MAN   . . . .   456 POOR MATTHIAS   152

INDISTINCT
        AND RECOLLECTIONS INDISTINCT AND DIM . . . . . .   469 ALARIC AT ROME   183

INDIVIDUAL
        THROUGH CLOUDS OF INDIVIDUAL STRIFE   . . . . . .   59 RESIGNATION   251
        AND IN OUR INDIVIDUAL HUMAN STATE   . . . . . .   440 EMPEDOCLES II   367

INDOMITABLE
        THE TAILS INDOMITABLE RING   . . . .   459 KAISER DEAD   27

INDOORS
        INDOORS FROM THE SUNS EYE HIS HEAD DROOPD LOW   . .   86 SOHRAB RUSTUM   847

INDULGED
        NOR ANY PLEADER ELSE SHALL BE INDULGED   . . . .   389 MEROPE   1527
        O SELF-WILL RECKLESSLY INDULGED   . . . . . .   398 MEROPE   1801

INDULGENCE
        WITH WEAK INDULGENCE   . . . .   51 CONSOLATION   56

INDULGENT
        THESE WORDS TO THINE INDULGENT EAR THY WIFE   . .   350 MEROPE   594
        PRACTISE THE INDULGENT BLOODLESS POLICY   . . . .   390 MEROPE   1561

INDULGENTLY
        CONSTRUED HIS ACTS INDULGENTLY REVERED   . . . .   337 MEROPE   255

INEFFABLE
        CANST THOU PAINT THE INEFFABLE SMILE . . . . . .   231 YOUTH OF NATURE   113
        THE INEFFABLE LONGING FOR THE LIFE OF LIFE . . . .   439 EMPEDOCLES II   357

INEFFECTUAL
        THEIR INEFFECTUAL FEUDS AND FEEBLE HATES   . . . .   126 BALDER DEAD 3   466

INESTIMABLE
        HATH SUCH INESTIMABLE POWER   . . . .   158 SAINT BRANDAN   56

INEVITABLE
        FIRST THE INEVITABLE WAY . . . .   454 POOR MATTHIAS   80

INEVITABLY
        INEVITABLY HAD SURGED UP PERHAPS   . . . . . .   394 MEROPE   1698

INEXTINGUISHABLE
        BUT AH AN INEXTINGUISHABLE SENSE   . . . . . .   239 REVOLUTIONS   9

INFANT
        THE INFANT CHURCH OF LOVE SHE FELT THE TIDE   . .   172 GOOD SHEPHERD   7
        AN INFANT AT THE HEARTH OF CYPSELUS . . . . . .   331 MEROPE   32

INFANTINE
        HATH YET AN INFANTINE AND SILVER TONE   . . . .   151 TRISTRAM 3   73
        HAS YET AN INFANTINE AND SILVER TONE . . . . . .   151 TRISTRAM 3   V 73

INFANTS
        WHO HID SUCH IMPORT IN AN INFANTS GLOOM   . . . .   41 GIPSY CHILD   2
        WOMEN AND INFANTS AND YOUNG MEN WHO DIED   . . . .   109 BALDER DEAD 2   164

INFECTION
        FOR STRONG THE INFECTION OF OUR MENTAL STRIFE   . .   261 SCHOLAR-GIPSY   222

INFECTIOUS
        SUCH PREGNANT AND INFECTIOUS QUALITY . . . . . .   50 CONSOLATION   V

INFECTS
        THE SOMETHING THAT INFECTS THE WORLD . . . . . .   60 RESIGNATION   278

INFER
        INFER THEE THEIR ACCOMPLICE AND THEY SAY   . . . .   334 MEROPE   143

INFERIOR
        INFERIOR ALL IN FAME   . . . .   284 HAWORTH CHURCH   83

INFINITE
        INFINITE MAKES THEM MAKES THEM YOUNG . . . . . .   224 EPILOG LAOCOON   97
        MURMURS AND SCENTS OF THE INFINITE SEA   . . . .   254 FUTURE   87

INFINITE   (CONTINUED)
        DEADEN THE INFINITE PAIN . . . . 283 HAWORTH CHURCH   V
        YET TINGED WITH INFINITE DESIRE . . . . . . 314 OBERMANN MORE   51
        AND NOT THE INFINITE RESOURCE . . . . 450 GEISTS GRAVE   23

INFINITELY
        AS FROM AN INFINITELY DISTANT LAND . . . . . . 247 BURIED LIFE   74

INFINITY
        AND GREET ACROSS INFINITY . . . . 180 FAREWELL   76

INFIRM
        INFIRM PROTECTORS DUBIOUS ORACLES . . . . . . 336 MEROPE   215
        AND KNOWING WELL MANS INMOST HEART INFIRM . . . . 353 MEROPE   692
        ILL-KEPT BY HIS INFIRM HEIRS . . . . 399 MEROPE   1846

INFORM
        A NEW-SPRUNG WORLD INFORM . . . . 319 OBERMANN MORE   200
        MIGHT SOME ONE STRAIGHT INFORM HIM HE IS SOUGHT . . 354 MEROPE   708
        INFORM HIM THAT THYSELF FOR HERE HE COMES . . . . 354 MEROPE   709

INFRINGED
        AND JUSTICE NOT INFRINGED . . . . 195 FRAG ANTIGONE   7

INFUSE
        OBLIVION IN LOST ANGELS CAN INFUSE . . . . . .   43 GIPSY CHILD   55
        OBLIVION IN LORN ANGELS CAN INFUSE . . . . . .   43 GIPSY CHILD   V 55

INGLE
        ON THE WARM INGLE-BENCH THE SMOCK-FROCKD BOORS . . 256 SCHOLAR-GIPSY   59

INGLORIOUS
        HIS NOT UNWORTHY NOT INGLORIOUS SON . . . . .   62 SOHRAB RUSTUM   52
        ONLY THE INGLORIOUS SORT ARE THERE BELOW . . . . 104 BALDER DEAD 1   323
        UNARMD INGLORIOUS I ATTEND THE COURSE . . . . . 128 BALDER DEAD 3   510
        INGLORIOUS AND SHOULD DROP AT LAST UNKNOWN . . . 356 MEROPE   771

INGRAIND
        FROM THE INGRAIND FASHION . . . .   39 STAGIRIUS   30

INHABIT
        ALL YE WHO HEAR ME AND INHABIT HEAVEN . . . . .   96 BALDER DEAD 1   29

INHERIT
        TO-NIGHT IT DOTH INHERIT . . . .   21 REQUIESCAT   15
        SAW THE GIFTS THE POWERS IT MIGHT INHERIT . . . . 209 SELF-DECEPTION   7

INHERITANCE
        TO TAKE THE INHERITANCE OF HERACLES . . . . . . 334 MEROPE   125

INHERITOR
        THE INHERITOR OF THE BOW . . . . 399 MEROPE   1837
        THE INHERITOR OF THE REALM . . . . 400 MEROPE   1862

INHERITORS
        INHERITORS OF THY DISTRESS . . . . 303 GRANDE CHARTR   143

INJURED
        THOUGH INJURED PAST FORGIVENESS AS MEN DEEM . . 394 MEROPE   1707

INJURIOUS
        HEARD NO ONE EVER AN INJURIOUS WORD . . . . . . 116 BALDER DEAD 3   84
        OF HEADY MASTERFUL INJURIOUS MEN . . . . 339 MEROPE   312

INJUSTICE
        MY FATHER LOVED INJUSTICE AND LIVED LONG . . . .   9 MYCERINUS   13
        INJUSTICE TO HIS KIN AND DORIAN FRIENDS . . . . 339 MEROPE   317

INKEN
        THE INKEN THROATED . . . . 200 PHILOMELA   V   2

INLAID
        ONLY HIS HELM WAS RICH INLAID WITH GOLD . . . .   69 SOHRAB RUSTUM   267

INLAND
        OUT OF A TILLD FIELD INLAND THEN THE WIND . . . . 124 BALDER DEAD 3   363
        INLAND OR BUILT . . . . 189 STRAYED REVEL   127
        THAT MUCH-LOVED INLAND SEA . . . . 311 OBERMANN   162
        INLAND FROM THE ROCKS AND SEA . . . . 457 POOR MATTHIAS   180

INLETS
        LONG INLETS OF SMOOTH GLITTERING SEA . . . . . 141 TRISTRAM 1   368
        WHERE THE MOON-SILVERD INLETS . . . . 442 EMPEDOCLES II   425

INLY
        STARS SET DEEP YET INLY BURNING . . . .   30 NEW SIRENS   137
        THE INLY-WRITTEN CHART THOU GAVEST ME . . . . .   40 HUMAN LIFE   5
        REVOLVING INLY . . . . 190 STRAYED REVEL   141
        THOUGH MOVING INLY TO ONE FAR-SET GOAL . . . . . 448 WESTMIN ABBEY   153
        THOUGH MOVING INLY TO ONE FAR-OFF GOAL . . . . . 448 WESTMIN ABBEY V 153

INMATE
    THE PRESENCE OF THAT GRACIOUS INMATE LIGHT • • • • 444 WESTMIN ABBEY 6

INMATES
    ITS INMATES ON THEIR DAILY TASKS ABROAD • • • • 330 MEROPE 27

INMOST
    DO THOU WHOM LIGHT IN THINE OWN INMOST SOUL • • 8 RELIGIOUS ISOL 6
    YET DOTH THINE INMOST SOUL WITH YEARNING TEEM • • 46 IN UTRUMQUE PAR 40
    DO THOU RECORD IT IN THINE INMOST SOUL • • • • 72 SOHRAB RUSTUM 374
    AND PRESS INTO ITS INMOST HEART • • • • 224 EPILOG LAOCOON 88
    AND LET ME READ THERE LOVE THY INMOST SOUL • • • • 245 BURIED LIFE 11
    WHO IN MANS INMOST BOSOM SIT AND JUDGE • • • • 349 MEROPE 554
    AND KNOWING WELL MANS INMOST HEART INFIRM • • • • 353 MEROPE 692

INN
    THAT WAYSIDE INN WE LEFT TO-DAY • • • • • 53 RESIGNATION 41
    ON SOME GREAT ROAD OR RESTING IN AN INN • • • • 116 BALDER DEAD 3 117
    AT A MEAN INN IN GERMAN AARAU BORN • • • • • 168 RACHEL 3 2
    FOR NATURE HATH LONG KEPT THIS INN THE EARTH • • 251 FUTURE V
    TO THE LONELY INN MID THE ROCKS • • • • • 289 RUGBY CHAPEL 109

INNER
    BOTH NIGHT AND DAY AND BY THE INNER WALL • • • • 98 BALDER DEAD 1 91
    OF THE DEEP INNER GLOOM BUT FLITTEST HERE • • • • 124 BALDER DEAD 3 389
    HE SPAKE AND TURND TO GO TO THE INNER GLOOM • • 125 BALDER DEAD 3 421
    THICKENS AND TO ITS INNER GULPH RECALLS • • • • 129 BALDER DEAD 3 547
    THEY PAINT OF SOULS THE INNER STRIFE • • • • • 301 GRANDE CHARTR 53

INNERMOST
    YOUR FATHERS INNERMOST MIND • • • • • • • 291 RUGBY CHAPEL 165

INNOCENCE
    WHICH FOOLISH INNOCENCE PLAYS WITH SUBTLE GUILT • • 366 MEROPE V

INNOCENT
    NOT INNOCENT INDEED YET NOT FORLORN • • • • • 6 GEO CRUIKSHANK 5
    ARE NOT MORE INNOCENT THAN THINE • • • • • 140 TRISTRAM 1 326
    READ IN THESE ACTIONS INNOCENT IN THEE • • • 333 MEROPE 90
    TWO UNOFFENDING BABES HIS INNOCENT SONS • • • 339 MEROPE 319
    AND WHERE DOST THOU SLEEP NOW MY INNOCENT BOY • • 373 MEROPE 1166
    WHICH NATURE SANCTIONS WHICH THE INNOCENT BLOOD • • 386 MEROPE 1427

INNOCENTS
    WHILE TROUBLED INNOCENTS TOSS AND LIE AWAKE • • 372 MEROPE 1155
    EARLY-SLAIN INNOCENTS NEAR • • • • • • • 378 MEROPE 1239

INNS
    AND IN THE DESERT SPACIOUS INNS • • • • • • 94 SICK KING BOKH 203
    WHAT INNS YOUR STREETS TOO HOW NARROW • • • • 214 NEW ROME 11

INQUIRE
    A LONGING TO INQUIRE • • • • • • • • • 246 BURIED LIFE 51

INQUIRING
    OF INQUIRING TENDERNESS • • • • • • • • • 24 MEMORY-PICTURE 44
    HIS HEAD AS IF INQUIRING WHAT THEIR GRIEF • • • • 82 SOHRAB RUSTUM 734

INQUISITORS
    WITH THIS TO THOSE UNBRIBED INQUISITORS • • • • 349 MEROPE 553

INSANE
    OF TERROR AND INSANE DISTRESS • • • • • • • 271 MEMORIAL VERSES 32
    GAINST THICK-CRASHING INSANE • • • • • • • 293 HEINES GRAVE 34

INSCRIBE
    AND THE GRAVE GLANVIL DID THE TALE INSCRIBE • • 259 SCHOLAR-GIPSY 133

INSCRUTABLE
    AND WITH INSCRUTABLE REGARD THE QUEEN • • • • 112 BALDER DEAD 2 280
    INSCRUTABLE AS EVER SEE IT KEEPS • • • • • 403 MEROPE 1967
    DUMB INSCRUTABLE AND GRAND • • • • • • • 453 POOR MATTHIAS 40

INSCRUTABLY
    MILD AND INSCRUTABLY CALM • • • • • • • • 232 YOUTH OF MAN 10

INSECURE
    BLOOD-FOUNDED THRONES THOU SAYST ARE INSECURE • • 389 MEROPE 1532
    HIS WELFARE INSECURE • • • • • • • • • 420 EMPEDOCLES I 2 245

INSHORE
    DRIVN INSHORE WE FOLLOW DOWN • • • • • • • 457 POOR MATTHIAS 181

INSIGHT
    WHOSE NATURAL INSIGHT CAN DISCERN • • • • • 59 RESIGNATION 233
    BUT TASKS IN HOURS OF INSIGHT WILLD • • • • • 241 MORALITY 5
    WHOSE INSIGHT NEVER HAS BORNE FRUIT IN DEEDS • • 260 SCHOLAR-GIPSY 174

INSINCERE
        INSINCERE PRAISES WHICH DESCENDS   • • • • • •   199 EARLY DEATH   6

INSPIRATION
        SNATCHD A TURBID INSPIRATION   • • • • • • • •   31 NEW SIRENS   151
        SNATCHD AN EARTHLY INSPIRATION • • • • • • • •   31 NEW SIRENS   V 151

INSPIRE
        PRAISE RE-INSPIRE THE BRAVE   • • • • • • • •   292 RUGBY CHAPEL   200
        AGAIN I FEEL THE WORDS INSPIRE • • • • • • • •   314 OBERMANN MORE   49
        AGAIN I FEEL ITS WORDS INSPIRE • • • • • • • •   314 OBERMANN MORE   V 49
        INSPIRE THIS COWARD HEART THIS FLAGGING ARM   • • •   368 MEROPE   1066
        HOW CAN YOUR HERACLEIDAN CHIEFS INSPIRE   • • • •   389 MEROPE   1542

INSPIRED
        WITH EYE SUFFUSED BUT HEART INSPIRED TRUE • • • •   172 GOOD SHEPHERD   10
        THE INSPIRED MUSICIAN WHAT A RANGE   • •   • • • •   223 EPILOG LAOCOON   81
        YET ON HE FARES BY HIS OWN HEART INSPIRED • • • •   269 THYRSIS   210
        WHEREVER SHOWN HOWEER INSPIRED • • • • • • • •   279 SOUTHERN NIGHT   131
        THE ORACLE FORBADE NOT ILL-INSPIRED • • • • • •   448 WESTMIN ABBEY   133

INSTALL
        INSTALL HIM IN THY THRONE STILL WITHOUT BLOOD • •   350 MEROPE   588

INSTALLD
        WELCOMED HERE AND HERE INSTALLD   • • • • • •   136 TRISTRAM 1   204

INSTANCES
        THOU DOST ALLEDGE FOR PROOF SUCH INSTANCES • • • •   RUDE ORATOR   15

INSTANT
        NOW TOLD BUT IN ONE FLASHING INSTANT PASSD • • • •   358 MEROPE   828
        FOR INSTANT COMMENT HAVING MANY SIDES   • • • •   359 MEROPE   860
        FLY FIND ME ON THE INSTANT WHERE CONFER   • • • •   368 MEROPE   1071

INSTANTLY
        AND INSTANTLY THE SACRED MORN APPEARD   • • • •   104 BALDER DEAD 1   342

INSTANTS
        TO WIN ONE INSTANTS GLIMPSE OF THEE   • • • • • •   205 CALAIS SANDS   24

INSTEAD
        AND INSTEAD THEREOF IS SEEN   • • • • • • • •   136 TRISTRAM 1   175
        TO HAVE BEFORE MY MIND INSTEAD • • • • • • • •   251 WISH   44

INSTILLS
        INSTILLS SALVATION AT HAND   • • • • • • • •   214 NEW ROME   V   8

INSTINCT
        BRIGHT WITS AND INSTINCT SURE   • • • • • • • •   446 WESTMIN ABBEY   V 77

INSTINCTS
        AFFECTIONS INSTINCTS PRINCIPLES AND POWERS • • • •   4 BUTLERS SERMONS   1
        BRIGHT WITS AND INSTINCTS SURE • • • • • • • •   446 WESTMIN ABBEY   77

INSTRUCT
        INSTRUCT ME OF THE MANNER OF HIS DEATH   • • • •   355 MEROPE   720
        INSTRUCT ME NOT I HAVE MY LESSON CLEAR   • • • •   379 MEROPE   1259
        INSTRUCT ME OF PANTHEIAS STORY MASTER   • • • •   412 EMPEDOCLES I 2   20

INSULTST
        AND NOW THOU BOASTEST AND INSULTST MY FATE • • • •   77 SOHRAB RUSTUM   551

INSURGED
        LIKE THE BROAD RUSHING OF THE INSURGED NILE   • •   10 MYCERINUS   V 40

INSURGENT
        LIKE THE BROAD VOLUME OF THE INSURGENT NILE • •   10 MYCERINUS   40
        LIKE THE BROAD RUSHING OF THE INSURGENT NILE • •   10 MYCERINUS   V 40

INTELLECTUAL
        HIS SEAT UPON THE INTELLECTUAL THRONE   • • • •   260 SCHOLAR-GIPSY   184

INTELLIGENT
        THE RADIANT REJOICING INTELLIGENT SONS OF HEAVEN • •   437 EMPEDOCLES II   287

INTEMPERATE
        AND EVEN COULD THE INTEMPERATE PRAYER   • • • •   60 RESIGNATION   271

INTEND
        TO RULE THIS KINGDOM I INTEND WITH SWAY   • • • •   342 MEROPE   376
        DID BY THIS STONE IT SEEMS INTEND   • • • • • •   452 GEISTS GRAVE   78

INTENDS
        AND WHAT THE RUSSIAN CZAR INTENDS   • • • • • •   47 HORATIAN ECHO   5

INTENSE
        FROM THE INTENSE CLEAR STAR-SOWN VAULT OF HEAVEN • •   240 SELF-DEPENDENCE   13

INTENSER
        WILL FRET OUR MINDS TO AN INTENSER PLAY   • • • •   440 EMPEDOCLES II   380

INTENT
    TO MAKE THE INCURIOUS BYSTANDER INTENT   • • • •   8 RELIGIOUS ISOL   3
    APPROVES MY BROTHER LAIAS THIS INTENT   • • • • 379 MEROPE   1267
    HEIRSHIP WITH FAIR INTENT AS I BELIEVE   • • • • 387 MEROPE   1484
    NOR ONLY IN THE INTENT • • • • • • • • 422 EMPEDOCLES I 2   307

INTER
    AND IN THE MOUNTAIN-CHINKS INTER THE WINDS • • • • 410 EMPEDOCLES I 1   118

INTERCEPTED
    COME BUT BEEN INTERCEPTED BY THE KING   • • • • 361 MEROPE   919

INTEREST
    ON HIS OWN SWARMING THOUGHTS AN INTEREST OWN   • •   8 RELIGIOUS ISOL   4
    OUTLASTS EACH EFFORT INTEREST HOPE • • • • • 58 RESIGNATION   217
    WHERE INTEREST SEEMS TO HAVE ENJOIND IT TOO   • • 341 MEROPE   364
    MOST MEN ARE LED BY INTEREST AND THE FEW • • • 341 MEROPE   365
    HATE DUTY INTEREST PASSION CALL ONE WAY   • • • 383 MEROPE   1382

INTERIOR
    FADED FROM SIGHT INTO THE INTERIOR GLOOM   • • • • 129 BALDER DEAD 3   553

INTERMINABLE
    OF THE INTERMINABLE HOURS   • • • • • • • • 247 BURIED LIFE   80

INTERMIXD
    WOMEN AND CHILDREN INTERMIXD AND THEN   • • • 401 MEROPE   1898

INTERPOSED
    I KNOW NOT WHAT AND INTERPOSED • • • • • • • 285 HAWORTH CHURCH   111

INTERPRET
    INTERPRET THEN FOR WE IT SEEMS ARE DULL   • • • • 365 MEROPE   989

INTERRD
    COWARDS WHO WERE IN SLOUGHS INTERRD ALIVE • • • • 109 BALDER DEAD 2   172

INTERRUPT
    WELL MAY HE LONG TO INTERRUPT • • • • • • • 353 MEROPE   667
    FOR TWENTY YEARS FORBORNE TO INTERRUPT   • • • • 395 MEROPE   1730
    WELL MAY THEY LONG TO INTERRUPT • • • • • • 353 MEROPE   V 667

INTERRUPTED
    STERN INTERRUPTED MY STRAIN • • • • • • • 285 HAWORTH CHURCH   127

INTERTWINE
    EVEN SO DO PAST AND FUTURE INTERTWINE   • • • • 10 MYCERINUS   59

INTERVALS
    SHEDDING HER PENSIVE LIGHT AT INTERVALS   • • • • 18 CHURCH BROU 3   35

INTERVENE
    WHERE THOUGH LONG WANDERINGS INTERVENE   • • • • 55 RESIGNATION   114

INTESTINE
    THAT HOUSE LIKE OURS INTESTINE MURDER MAIMS   • • 384 MEROPE   1392

INTOLERABLE
    AND OH WITH SUCH INTOLERABLE CHANGE • • • • • • 36 VOICE   27

INTOLERABLY
    THOUGH YOUNG INTOLERABLY SEVERE   • • • • • 435 EMPEDOCLES II   206

INTONED
    THESE OER THE CORPSE INTONED A PLAINTIVE STRAIN • • 103 BALDER DEAD 1   273

INTRACTABLE
    OF THE MOUNTAIN-CRUSHD TORTURED INTRACTABLE TITAN KING 432 EMPEDOCLES II   98

INTRIGUERS
    FIGMENTS OF PLOTS WHEREWITH INTRIGUERS FILL   • • 387 MEROPE   1487

INTRUDE
    SAY WHAT SHALL CALM US WHEN SUCH GUESTS INTRUDE • • 6 GEO CRUIKSHANK   6

INTRUDERS
    AND KNEW THE INTRUDERS ON HIS ANCIENT HOME • • • • 262 SCHOLAR-GIPSY   240

INTRUDES
    NO LIFE SAVE HIS AND OURS INTRUDES   • • • • • • 54 RESIGNATION   72

INVADE
    THAT EMPIRE WILT THOU NOW INVADE LIGHT UP • • • • 121 BALDER DEAD 3   279
    I FEEL HER SLOWLY CHILLING BREATH INVADE • • • • 266 THYRSIS   134

INVADERS
    IN SULLEN HOMAGE TO THE INVADERS MIGHT   • • • • 465 ALARIC AT ROME   76

INVADES
      AND LIGHTS FAIR NURSLING STUPOR FIRST INVADES   • • 448 WESTMIN ABBEY   129
      AND LIGHTS FAIR NURSLING LANGUOR FIRST INVADES   • • 448 WESTMIN ABBEY   V 129

INVADING
      OF THE INVADING POPULACE • • • • • • • • • • • 48 HORATIAN ECHO   8
      WHO TO THE INVADING DORIANS STRETCHD A HAND   • • 338 MEROPE   293

INVARIABLENESS
      OF INVARIABLENESS OF JUSTICE • • • • • • • • • 398 MEROPE   1811

INVASIONS
      CONSTRUED AWRY MISPLANND INVASIONS WORE   • • • • 336 MEROPE   216
      CONSTRUED AWRY MISPLANND INVASIONS USD   • • • • 336 MEROPE   V 216

INVENT
      WE SPURN IT AND INVENT   • • • • • • • • • • • 419 EMPEDOCLES I 2   225
      DO WE AT WILL INVENT   • • • • • • • • • • • 422 EMPEDOCLES I 2   309
      WE SPURN THEM AND INVENT • • • • • • • • • • • 419 EMPEDOCLES I 2   V 225

INVENTIVE
      OF PREGNANT PARTS AND QUICK INVENTIVE BRAIN   • • 256 SCHOLAR-GIPSY   34
      OF SHINING PARTS AND QUICK INVENTIVE BRAIN • • • • 256 SCHOLAR-GIPSY   V 34

INVEST
      INVEST ME STEEP ME FOLD ME ROUND   • • • • • • 302 GRANDE CHARTR   V 93
      WHETHER BLOOD FLOWS OR NO CAN YET INVEST   • • • • 389 MEROPE   1545

INVESTS
      AND THE GENEROUS DREAMER INVESTS   • • • • • • 233 YOUTH OF MAN   33
      INVESTS THE STERN AND NAKED PRAYER • • • • • • 300 GRANDE CHARTR   38

INVINCIBLE
      IS BECOME INVINCIBLE   • • • • • • • • • • • 431 EMPEDOCLES II   94
      NO BUT THE WILL OF HEAVEN AND FATES INVINCIBLE POWER   HOMER TRANS   49

INVIOLABLE
      STILL CLUTCHING THE INVIOLABLE SHADE • • • • • • 261 SCHOLAR-GIPSY   212

INVISIBLE
      TO THE INVISIBLE PLAINS TO ROAM WITH THEE • • • • 367 MEROPE   1030

INVITE
      INVITE TO REST THE TRAVELLER THERE   • • • • • • 313 OBERMANN MORE   19
      NOW I IF I INVITE THEM TO RUN RISK   • • • • • • 382 MEROPE   1349

INVITEST
      INVITEST REASON TO FORSWEAR HER STATE   • • • •   RUDE ORATOR   18

INVOLVED
      INVOLVED IN ONE SUSPICION WITH THE BASE   • • • • 341 MEROPE   367
      WHAT HATH INVOLVED THEM BUT BLIND   • • • • • • 343 MEROPE   423

INWARD
      MORE STRICTLY THEN THE INWARD JUDGE OBEY   • • • • 171 BETTER PART   12
      LET BEAM UPON MY INWARD VIEW • • • • • • • • 208 ON THE RHINE   17
      SCORN YE THIS WORLD THEIR TEARS THEIR INWARD CARES • • 237 PROGRESS   22
      WITH INWARD STRIVING AND DEMAND • • • • • • 247 BURIED LIFE   68
      THE EYE SINKS INWARD AND THE HEART LIES PLAIN   • • 247 BURIED LIFE   86
      AND HURRIED TORN WITH INWARD STRIFE • • • • • • 317 OBERMANN MORE   135
      BUT OF THAT INWARD PRIZE • • • • • • • • • • 315 OBERMANN MORE   V
      WE WOULD HAVE INWARD PEACE   • • • • • • • • 420 EMPEDOCLES I 2   232
      FLASHD FROM THY SOUL UPON THINE INWARD EAR • • • • 472 CROMWELL   28
      AN INWARD LIGHT THAT WITH ITS STREAMING RAY   • • 473 CROMWELL   61

INWOUND
      ORIGINAL DEEP-INWOUND   • • • • • • • • • • • 196 FRAG ANTIGONE   36

IRAN
      TO IRAN AND BE AS MY SON TO ME • • • • • • • • 71 SOHRAB RUSTUM   331
      THERE ARE NO YOUTHS IN IRAN BRAVE AS THOU • • • • 71 SOHRAB RUSTUM   333
      THEN WERE THE CHIEFS OF IRAN SHAMED THROUGH ME • • 72 SOHRAB RUSTUM   363

IRANS
      AND HE IS YOUNG AND IRANS CHIEFS ARE OLD   • • • • 67 SOHRAB RUSTUM   217
      GO TO IF IRANS CHIEFS ARE OLD THEN I • • • • • • 67 SOHRAB RUSTUM   221

IRE
      AGAIN IN TONES OF IRE • • • • • • • • • • • 174 MEETING   10
      THE STATESMAN QUAILD BEFORE HIS GLANCE OF IRE   • • 476 CROMWELL   154

IRELAND
      FROM IRELAND TO CORNWALL BORE • • • • • • • • 132 TRISTRAM 1   60
      ISEULT OF IRELAND • • • • • • • • • • • • 133 TRISTRAM 1   82
      ISEULT OF IRELAND • • • • • • • • • • • • 134 TRISTRAM 1   114
      AND HER BOWER IN IRELAND • • • • • • • • • • 134 TRISTRAM 1   131
      TO TYNTAGIL FROM IRELAND BORE • • • • • • • • 132 TRISTRAM 1   V 60

IRIS
      AND FLAG-LEAVED IRIS-FLOWERS   • • • • • • • • 191 STRAYED REVEL   170

IRKD

IT IRKD HIM TO BE HERE HE COULD NOT REST   • • • •   264 THYRSIS   41

IRKS

WHAT IRKS IT ME THAT MEN SPEAK SOHRABS PRAISE   • •   68 SOHRAB RUSTUM   V 228

IRON

IN THE DAYS LIFE WHOSE IRON ROUND   • • • • •   58 RESIGNATION   209
BEHOLD ME I AM VAST AND CLAD IN IRON   • • • •   71 SOHRAB RUSTUM   325
THE IRON PLATES RANG SHARP BUT TURND THE SPEAR   •   73 SOHRAB RUSTUM   407
THAT THE HARD IRON CORSLET CLANKD ALOUD   • • •   80 SOHRAB RUSTUM   664
UNDER ITS IRON HEEL FATE. FATE ENGAGED   • • •   82 SOHRAB RUSTUM   714
BORDERING THE GIANTS WHERE THE TREES ARE IRON   • •   123 BALDER DEAD 3   331
THAT YE COME PLEASURING TO THOKS IRON WOOD   • • •   123 BALDER DEAD 3   338
THE IRON FROWN OF HELA IS RELAXD   • • • • •   126 BALDER DEAD 3   463
AT THAT BRIGHT IRON-FIGURED DOOR   • • • • •   148 TRISTRAM 2   159
AT THE BRIGHT IRON-FIGURED DOOR   • • • • •   148 TRISTRAM 2   V 159
ALONG THIS IRON COAST KNOW LIKE A STAR   • • •   151 TRISTRAM 3   81
TIS TRUE INDEED AN IRON KNOT   • • • • • •   208 ON THE RHINE   7
PHYSICIAN OF THE IRON AGE   • • • • • • •   270 MEMORIAL VERSES   17
HAD FALLEN ON THIS IRON TIME   • • • • •   271 MEMORIAL VERSES   43
WAS FALLEN ON THE IRON TIME   • • • • •   271 MEMORIAL VERSES   V 43
ROCK TO ITS IRON CROSS   • • • • • •   298 HEINES GRAVE   188
SAGACIOUS MEN OF IRON WATCHFUL FIRM   • • •   381 MEROPE   1304
THIS IRON MAN MY ENEMY AND THINE   • • • • •   403 MEROPE   1964

IRONY

STRANGE IRONY OF FATE ALAS   • • • • • • •   277 SOUTHERN NIGHT   57

IRRESISTIBLY

THEN IRRESISTIBLY IT LIVES IT WORKS   • • • • • •   382 MEROPE   1346

IRRETRIEVABLE

FROM IRRETRIEVABLE WOE   • • • • • • • • •   391 MEROPE   1602

IRRUPTION

SHOULD MAKE IRRUPTION INTO HELAS REALM   • • • •   120 BALDER DEAD 3   242

ISEULT

ISEULT AH NOT THE ISEULT I DESIRE   • • • • •   130 TRISTRAM 1   8
ISEULT AH NOT THE ISEULT I DESIRE   • • • • •   130 TRISTRAM 1   8
ISEULT OF BRITTANY   • • • • • • • • •   132 TRISTRAM 1   55
ISEULT OF BRITTANY BUT WHERE   • • • • • •   132 TRISTRAM 1   56
IS THAT OTHER ISEULT FAIR   • • • • • • •   132 TRISTRAM 1   57
THAT PROUD FIRST ISEULT CORNWALLS QUEEN   • • •   132 TRISTRAM 1   58
ISEULT OF THE SNOW-WHITE HAND   • • • • •   132 TRISTRAM 1   74
ISEULT OF IRELAND   • • • • • • • • •   133 TRISTRAM 1   82
ISEULT   • • • • • • • • • • •   133 TRISTRAM 1   104
ISEULT OF IRELAND   • • • • • • • • •   134 TRISTRAM 1   114
THAT FIRST ISEULT PRINCESS BRIGHT   • • • •   134 TRISTRAM 1   126
ISEULT OF BRITTANY   • • • • • • • •   136 TRISTRAM 1   197
ISEULT   • • • • • • • • • • •   138 TRISTRAM 1   242
ISEULT   • • • • • • • • • • •   139 TRISTRAM 1   287
BUT THY DARK EYES ARE NOT DIMMD PROUD ISEULT   •   142 TRISTRAM 2   19
THOU ART PALER BUT THY SWEET CHARM ISEULT   • • •   143 TRISTRAM 2   25
I FORGIVE THEE ISEULT THOU WILT STAY   • • • •   143 TRISTRAM 2   28
NOR THY YOUNGER ISEULT TAKE IT ILL   • • • •   144 TRISTRAM 2   58
GO NOT FAR O ISEULT FROM MY GRAVE   • • • •   145 TRISTRAM 2   92
CLOSE MINE EYES THEN SEEK THE PRINCESS ISEULT   •   145 TRISTRAM 2   93
ISEULT LEAVES THEE TRISTRAM NEVER MORE   • • •   146 TRISTRAM 2   100
RISE GO HENCE AND SEEK THE PRINCESS ISEULT   • • •   145 TRISTRAM 2   V 93
IN CORNWALL TRISTRAM AND QUEEN ISEULT LAY   • •   149 TRISTRAM 3   2
THE YOUNG SURVIVING ISEULT ONE BRIGHT DAY   • •   149 TRISTRAM 3   5
UNDER THE GLITTERING HOLLIES ISEULT STANDS   • • •   150 TRISTRAM 3   23
THEN ISEULT CALLD THEM TO HER AND THE THREE   • •   150 TRISTRAM 3   35
THEN ISEULT TOOK BY THE HAND THOSE CHILDREN FAIR   •   151 TRISTRAM 3   61
WHAT TALE DID ISEULT TO THE CHILDREN SAY   • • •   154 TRISTRAM 3   151
WAS THE ONE ISEULT CHOSE AND SHE BROUGHT CLEAR   •   154 TRISTRAM 3   165
LAY TRISTRAM AND QUEEN ISEULT DEAD AND COLD   • •   149 TRISTRAM 3   V 2
DREW ISEULT FORTH HER CHILDREN WERE AT PLAY   • •   TRISTRAM 3   V 5
UNDER THE BURNISHD HOLLIES ISEULT STANDS   • • • •   TRISTRAM 3   V 23

ISEULTS

THERE WERE TWO ISEULTS WHO DID SWAY   • • • • •   132 TRISTRAM 1   68
FROM ISEULTS LIPS THE UNBROKEN STORY FLOWD   • • • •   150 TRISTRAM 3   45

ISLAND

WHILE ON HIS ISLAND IN THE LAKE AFAR   • • • • • •   111 BALDER DEAD 2   214

ISLANDS

AND RAYS HER POWERS LIKE SISTER-ISLANDS SEEN   • •   4 BUTLERS SERMONS   9
THE ISLANDS FEEL THE ENCLASPING FLOW   • • • • •   182 TO MARG CONT   5
THROUGH THE ISLANDS SOME DIVINE BARD   • • • • •   189 STRAYED REVEL   118
THE HAPPY ISLANDS   • • • • • • • • •   192 STRAYED REVEL   206
REACHD CAPE VERDE ISLANDS LUSITANIA   • • • • •   485 S S LUSITANIA   14

ISLE

UPON THE CRAGGY ISLE OF A HILL-LAKE   • • • • • •   78 SOHRAB RUSTUM   558
BUT I HEARD THORA LAUGH IN GOTHLAND ISLE   • • • •   117 BALDER DEAD 3   148
THE GREEN ISLE WHERE SHE WAS BRED   • • • • • •   134 TRISTRAM 1   130

ISLE   (CONTINUED)
        A FLOATING ISLE THICK-MATTED • • • • • • • •   190 STRAYED REVEL   154
        SAW IN THE ROCKY ISLE OF DELOS DIE • • • • • •   197 FRAG ANTIGONE   69
        THE HERACLEIDAE BACK TO PELOPS ISLE • • • • •   330 MEROPE   7
        TOGETHER TO THIS ISLE OF PELOPS CAME • • • • •   334 MEROPE   124
        THEIR FATHERS REALM THIS ISLE FROM PELOPS NAMED • • 336 MEROPE   219
        OF THEIR HERITAGE PELOPS ISLE • • • • • • •   343 MEROPE   416
        FOR THE THREE CONQUERD KINGDOMS OF THIS ISLE • •   389 MEROPE   1549
        SOME ROCK MORE LONELY THAN THAT LEMNIAN ISLE • •   395 MEROPE   1746
        TO MOAT THIS ISLE OF ASHES FROM THE WORLD • • •   438 EMPEDOCLES II   310
        HUGE IN THE GLOOM ACROSS IN THORNEY ISLE • • • • 444 WESTMIN ABBEY   15
        HOW HIS ST PETERS CHURCH IN THORNEY ISLE • • • • 445 WESTMIN ABBEY   49

ISLES
        THROUGH BEDS OF SAND AND MATTED RUSHY ISLES • •   87 SOHRAB RUSTUM   885
        AND RULED OER DENMARK AND THE HEATHY ISLES • • • 117 BALDER DEAD 3   127
        AMONG THE AEGAEAN ISLES • • • • • • • • •   262 SCHOLAR-GIPSY   236
        LIKE ISLES OF SUNLIGHT ON A MOUNTAINS BROW • • • 475 CROMWELL   127

ISMENIAN
        TO CROSS THE STEEP ISMENIAN GLEN • • • • • • • 197 FRAG ANTIGONE   86

ISMENUS
        NOR THEBES NOR THE ISMENUS ANY MORE • • • • • • 427 EMPEDOCLES I 2   442

ISOLATION
        FROM ISOLATION WITHOUT END • • • • • • • • • 181 ISOLATION MARG   40

ISRAELS
        SPRUNG FROM THE BLOOD OF ISRAELS SCATTERD RACE • • 168 RACHEL 3   1

ISSUE
        SUCH HAPPY ISSUE CROWND HER PAINFUL CARE • • • • 46 IN UTRUMQUE PAR   34
        DOUBLE OF ISSUE FULL OF PITS AND SNARES • • • • 349 MEROPE   581
        FIRST HEARD OR IN ITS FUTURE ISSUE SHOWN • • • • 359 MEROPE   865
        THEN TRY THE ISSUE AND NOT RUSHING ON • • • • • 382 MEROPE   1325
        AND WAIT THE ISSUE SLEEPING UNDERGROUND • • • • 448 WESTMIN ABBEY   146

ISSUED
        SO ARMD HE ISSUED FORTH AND RUKSH HIS HORSE • •   69 SOHRAB RUSTUM   270
        SO FOLLOWD RUSTUM ISSUED FORTH AND CROSSD • • • • 69 SOHRAB RUSTUM V 280
        LIFTED AND ISSUED ON THE FIELDS OF ICE • • • •   113 BALDER DEAD 2   287
        WHENCE ISSUED THE WORLD • • • • • • • • •   177 PARTING   90
        THRICE ISSUED WITH US FROM THEIR PASTORAL VALES • • 337 MEROPE   226
        FOR THEIR HERACLES-ISSUED PRINCES • • • • • • 400 MEROPE   1853

ISSUES
        WHERE THE ROAD ISSUES BETWEEN WALLING ROCKS • •   107 BALDER DEAD 2   89

ISSUING
        OF SOME CLEAR RIVER ISSUING FROM A LAKE • • • • 109 BALDER DEAD 2   158
        ISSUING ON THAT GREEN PLACE • • • • • • • • 311 OBERMANN   170
        FOLLOWS THE ISSUING QUEEN WHO STOPS AS CALLD • • 332 MEROPE   V 64

ISTER
        WHERE YOUNG ARCHESTES DOTH WITH ISTER JOIN • • • •   FRAGMENT 4   1
        ISTER TETHYS AND OCEANS SIXTH-BORN SON • • • •   FRAGMENT 4   2

ISTHMUS
        BY WHOSE HAND AT THE ISTHMUS • • • • • • • • 344 MEROPE   443
        AT THE ISTHMUS IN FIGHT WITH HIS FOES • • • • • 345 MEROPE   479

ITALIAN
        OF ITALIAN MILAN THE FAIR • • • • • • • • • 296 HEINES GRAVE   130
        MUSICAL THROUGH ITALIAN TREES • • • • • • •   303 GRANDE CHARTR   141
        IN ALL THE ITALIAN CITIES LIKE OURSELVES • • • • 436 EMPEDOCLES II   237
        AND THE DEEP HUES OF AN ITALIAN SKY • • • • •   464 ALARIC AT ROME   69

ITALY
        THE FAMOUS TOWNS OF ITALY • • • • • • • • • 138 TRISTRAM 1   251
        THAT SON OF ITALY WHO TRIED TO BLOW • • • • •   166 AUSTERITY POET   1
        THUS MONICA AND DIED IN ITALY • • • • • • •   173 MONICAS PRAYER   5
        AND THE LONG DUSKY LINE OF ITALY • • • • • •   438 EMPEDOCLES II   314

ITCHING
        UNCLOSED HIS ITCHING FINGERS FROM HIS SWORD • •   394 MEROPE   1705

ITERATES
        MAN ITERATES WHILE THESE FORBEAR • • • • • •   60 RESIGNATION   272

IVE
        LONG IVE WAITED LONG IVE FOUGHT MY FEVER • • • • 142 TRISTRAM 2   3
        LONG IVE WAITED LONG IVE FOUGHT MY FEVER • • • • 142 TRISTRAM 2   3
        AND CRY LONG LONG IVE LOOKD FOR THEE • • • • • 202 URANIA   28

IVIED
        ON ITS IVIED WINDOWS A SCENT • • • • • • • • 234 YOUTH OF MAN   66

IVORY
 OF GOLD AND IVORY • • • • • • • • • • • • 191 STRAYED REVEL 194

IVY
 THE DEEP CUP IVY-CINCTURED • • • • • • • • 186 STRAYED REVEL 12
 TO THE IVY-WREATHED MARGE • • • • • • • • 188 STRAYED REVEL 84
 WITH THE DARK IVY-PLANTS • • • • • • • • 188 STRAYED REVEL 88
 OF IVY-PLANTS AND FRAGRANT HANGING BELLS • • • • 414 EMPEDOCLES I 2 49

JACKALS
 DEARER TO THE RED JACKALS SHALT THOU BE • • • • 77 SOHRAB RUSTUM 538

JADED
 THE JADED HUNTERS WITH THEIR BLOODY FREIGHT • • 18 CHURCH BROU 3 14
 WHEN JADED WITH THE RUSH AND GLARE • • • • • 247 BURIED LIFE 79
 WHICH FOR TWO JADED ENGLISH SAVES • • • • • • 277 SOUTHERN NIGHT 58
 JADED WITH TRAVEL CLAD IN HUNTERS GARB • • • • 363 MEROPE 957

JAGGD
 MY CHILD LIES IN HIS JAGGD • • • • • • 370 MEROPE 1117
 MY CHILD LIES IN A JAGGD • • • • • • • • • 370 MEROPE V1117

JAMAN
 ON JAMAN HAST THOU SATE • • • • • • • • • 310 OBERMANN 114
 THE CONE OF JAMAN PALE AND GREY • • • • • • 313 OBERMANN MORE 31
 AH JAMAN DELICATELY TALL • • • • • • • • • 313 OBERMANN MORE 33
 THE PEAK OF JAMAN STOOD • • • • • • • • • 323 OBERMANN MORE 332

JANGLE
 OUR JANGLE OF FALSE WITS OUR CLIMATES FROWNS • • 168 RACHEL 2 11

JANGLED
 AND THE WORLDS SO MADLY JANGLED • • • • • • 49 SECOND BEST 9

JAR
 TO FEEL AMID THE CITYS JAR • • • • • • • • 249 KENSINGTON GARD 38

JARNVID
 OF JARNVID WHICH TO EAST OF MIDGARD LIES • • • • 123 BALDER DEAD 3 330

JARRD
 JARRD WITH THE BURSTING SHOUT THEY COME THE 467 ALARIC AT ROME 132
  GOTH THEY COME

JARS
 AND THEY SET JARS OF WINE AND OIL TO LEAN • • • • 118 BALDER DEAD 3 166
 HOW SWEET UNREACHD BY EARTHLY JARS • • • • • 180 FAREWELL 77
 THE JARS OF MEN REACH HIM NOT IN THY VALLEY • • 435 EMPEDOCLES II 209

JASMINE
 AND OPEN JASMINE-MUFFLED LATTICES • • • • • • 264 THYRSIS 68

JASPER
 JASPER AND CHALCEDONY • • • • • • • • • • 191 STRAYED REVEL 196

JAVELIN
 HATH TRAILD THE HUNTERS JAVELIN IN HIS SIDE • • 76 SOHRAB RUSTUM 505
 HAS TRAILD THE HUNTERS JAVELIN IN HIS SIDE • • • • 76 SOHRAB RUSTUM V 505

JAVELINS
 ADVANCED TWO JAVELINS NOT NOW • • • • • • • 342 MEROPE 398

JAWS
 HANGS QUIVERING OUT BETWEEN HIS DUST-SMEARD JAWS • • 114 BALDER DEAD 3 15

JAXARTES
 OF THE JAXARTES MEN WITH SCANTY BEARDS • • • • 64 SOHRAB RUSTUM 129

JEALOUS
 WHICH THE JEALOUS SOUL CONCEDES • • • • • • 34 NEW SIRENS 228
 WHO FROM HER FROZEN HEIGHT WITH JEALOUS EYE • • 99 BALDER DEAD 1 156
 INTO A JEALOUS TYRANT SCOURGED WITH FEARS • • • 335 MEROPE 159
 JEALOUS BLOOD-EXACTING FRIENDS • • • • • • 344 MEROPE 461
 PERISHD IN ARGOS BY HIS JEALOUS SONS • • • 389 MEROPE 1557
 WHEN JEALOUS PAN WITH MARSYAS DID CONSPIRE • • • • 432 EMPEDOCLES II 128
 AND JEALOUS JOCK THY ONLY HATE • • • • • • 461 KAISER DEAD 75

JEALOUSY
 STUPID DETRACTION JEALOUSY CABAL • • • • • • 199 EARLY DEATH 5
 IF JEALOUSY OF US IT SHAMED THE MAN • • • • • 337 MEROPE 253
 YET HAD HE LIVED SUSPICION JEALOUSY • • • • • 394 MEROPE 1697
 SOME ILL DESIGN AGAINST HIM JEALOUSY • • • • • 394 MEROPE 1700

JEMSHID
 BY JEMSHID IN PERSEPOLIS TO BEAR • • • • • • 86 SOHRAB RUSTUM 861

JEST
 MADCAP WHAT JEST WAS THIS TO MEET ME HERE • • • • 135 TRISTRAM 1 162

JEST   (CONTINUED)
        AH WHAT BOOTS IT THAT THE JEST • • • • • • • •   138 TRISTRAM 1   261
        YES YES WE KNOW THAT WE CAN JEST • • • • • •   245 BURIED LIFE   4

JETS
        TYPHO SUCH RED JETS OF FLAME • • • • • • • •   430 EMPEDOCLES II   48

JEWELLD
        FROM THE JEWELLD LANDS OF DAWN • • • • • • •   26 NEW SIRENS   22
        AND YOUR JEWELLD GAUDS SURRENDER   • • • • • •   35 NEW SIRENS   255
        ARE JEWELLD WITH BRIGHT DROPS OF RAIN • • • •   141 TRISTRAM 1   360
        STARRD AND JEWELLD OF MEN • • • • • • • •   296 HEINES GRAVE   143
        WHICH THE GOATS LOVE ARE JEWELLD THICK WITH DEW • • 407 EMPEDOCLES I 1   17

JOCK
        AND JEALOUS JOCK THY ONLY HATE • • • • • • • •   461 KAISER DEAD   75

JOCUND
        HERE CAMST THOU IN THY JOCUND YOUTHFUL TIME • • 269 THYRSIS   218
        COMING SWIFTLY THROUGH THE JOCUND DORIANS • • • 400 MEROPE   1863

JOHN
        AND SHE DIED AT THE ST JOHN   • • • • • • •   16 CHURCH BROU 1   112

JOIN
        HODER AND I SHALL JOIN THEM FROM THE GRAVE • • • 128 BALDER DEAD 3   526
        O HERMOD PRAY THAT THOU MAYST JOIN US THEN • • • 129 BALDER DEAD 3   543
        HE STRAINS TO JOIN THEIR FLIGHT AND FROM HIS SHED   129 BALDER DEAD 3   563
        SO HERMOD GAZED AND YEARND TO JOIN HIS KIN • • • 129 BALDER DEAD 3   565
        YE GUIDING POWERS WHO JOIN AND PART • • • • •   174 MEETING   13
        CAME SWIFT DOWN TO JOIN   • • • • • • • •   186 STRAYED REVEL   35
        TO LEARN STRANGE ARTS AND JOIN A GIPSY-TRIBE   259 SCHOLAR-GIPSY   135
        ASSIST ME TO RULE MILDLY LET US JOIN • • • • •   335 MEROPE   164
        YE TOO YE TOO JOIN TO BETRAY THEN   • • • • •   371 MEROPE   1125
        WHERE YOUNG ARCHESTES DOTH WITH ISTER JOIN • • •   FRAGMENT 4   1

JOIND
        LEAVES US JOIND TO NOTHING LONG   • • • • • •   24 MEMORY-PICTURE   V 58
        WITH SWEET JOIND VOICES • • • • • • • • • •   51 CONSOLATION   46
        LATELY BELOW AND JOIND HIM AND THE PAIR • • • • 125 BALDER DEAD 3   434
        JOIND AT EVENING OF THEIR DAYS AGAIN • • • • •   143 TRISTRAM 2   32
        JOIND WE ARE HENCEFORTH NOR WILL THY PEOPLE • • 144 TRISTRAM 2   57
        WHEN WITH ELATED HEARTS WE JOIND YOUR TRAIN • • 436 EMPEDOCLES II   238
        JOIND TO ITS CLEARNESS OF THEIR FORCE • • • •   482 COURAGE   28
        THERE WHERE WHAT IS JOIND IS JOIND FOR EVER • • 482 THEKLAS ANSWER   11
        THERE WHERE WHAT IS JOIND IS JOIND FOR EVER • • 482 THEKLAS ANSWER   11

JOINT
        THAT OUR JOINT HANDS MIGHT THEN TOGETHER PAY • • 367 MEROPE   1047

JOINTS
        THEIR JOINTS GROW STIFFER BUT THE YEAR   • • •   56 RESIGNATION   128
        SHOULD FIRST HAVE ROTTED ON THEIR NIMBLE JOINTS • • 83 SOHRAB RUSTUM   739
        SHOULD THEN HAVE ROTTED ON THY NIMBLE JOINTS • • 83 SOHRAB RUSTUM   V 739
        SHOULD THEN HAVE ROTTED ON THEIR NIMBLE JOINTS • • 83 SOHRAB RUSTUM   V 739

JOKES
        AND JOKES IN DOGGISH LANGUAGE SAID   • • • • •   460 KAISER DEAD   71

JOPPA
        IN JOPPA AND THY CHARITY • • • • • • • • •   157 SAINT BRANDAN   40
        IN JOPPA THROUGH THE PUBLIC STREET   • • • • •   157 SAINT BRANDAN   42

JOPPAN
        THAT JOPPAN LEPERS EASE WAS PAIN   • • • • • •   158 SAINT BRANDAN   72

JOT
        NO JOT NO TITTLE FROM THE LAW SHALL PASS • • •   237 PROGRESS   11

JOURNEY
        THEN HE WILL JOURNEY THROUGH NO LIGHTED LAND • • 99 BALDER DEAD 1   153
        NO JOURNEY FOR A SIGHTLESS GOD TO GO • • • • •   100 BALDER DEAD 1   186
        THE LIGHT AND JOURNEY TO THE CHEERLESS LAND • • 110 BALDER DEAD 2   181
        I JOURNEY TO THESE HEALING SNOWS   • • • • •   158 SAINT BRANDAN   68
        A LONG STEEP JOURNEY THROUGH SUNK   • • • • •   288 RUGBY CHAPEL   87
        OF OUR NIGHT-JOURNEY AND THOU SEEST THY HOME • • 330 MEROPE   2
        OUR JOURNEY IS WELL MADE THE WORK REMAINS • •   330 MEROPE   24
        ON SUCH A HUNTING-JOURNEY THREE MORNS SINCE • • 355 MEROPE   730
        HAD ON THE JOURNEY CHOKED MY LABOURING BREATH • • 362 MEROPE   940

JOURNEYD
        AND ALL THAT NIGHT HE RODE AND JOURNEYD SO • • • 107 BALDER DEAD 2   82
        THENCE ON HE JOURNEYD OER THE FIELDS OF ICE • • 109 BALDER DEAD 2   143

JOURNEYED
        CAUGHT AS HE JOURNEYED FROM THE LIPS OF PAN • • 473 CROMWELL   40

JOURNEYS
        TO THE STYMPHALIAN LAKE OUR JOURNEYS END • • • • 356 MEROPE   749

JOVES
    NESTLING NEARER TO JOVES FEET • • • • • • • • 431 EMPEDOCLES II   77

JOVIAL
    OUR JOVIAL HOST AS FORTH WE FARE   • • • • • • 53 RESIGNATION   42
    AS IN OLD DAYS JOVIAL AND TALKING RIDE   • • • • 267 THYRSIS   154

JOY
    IT CHANCED I KNOW NOT HOW MY JOY WAS FLED • • • •   EMERSONS ESSAYS V   8
    AS THOUGH MEN SPAKE OF LIFE A JOY WAS FLED • • • •   EMERSONS ESSAYS V   8
    SEEMS THERE NO JOY IN DANCES CROWND WITH FLOWERS • •   9 MYCERINUS   33
    DRINKING DEEP DRAUGHTS OF JOY YE DWELL SERENE • • • 10 MYCERINUS   48
    OF ONE SHORT JOY ONE LUST ONE PLEASANT DREAM • • • 10 MYCERINUS   50
    THE REST I GIVE TO JOY EVEN WHILE I SPEAK • • • • 10 MYCERINUS   55
    REVELS MORE DEEP JOY KEENER THAN THEIR OWN • • • • 10 MYCERINUS   66
    MIGHT FADE IN SLUMBER AND THE FEET OF JOY • • • • 11 MYCERINUS   90
    YOUTH DREAMS A JOY ON THIS SIDE DEATH • • • • 22 YOUTH AND CALM V   19
    IF THE FITS OF JOY WERE LONGER • • • • • • • 29 NEW SIRENS   109
    WILL THE FIRE JOY HATH WASTED • • • • • • • 30 NEW SIRENS   133
    OF ONE JOY WHICH YOU HAVE NOT • • • • • • • 31 NEW SIRENS   166
    FITS OF JOY AND FITS OF PAIN • • • • • • • 33 NEW SIRENS   206
    SHALL I NOT JOY YOUTHS HEATS ARE LEFT BEHIND • • • 37 YOUTHS AGIT   5
    WHERE SORROW TREADS ON JOY • • • • • • 39 STAGIRIUS   43
    WHERE SORROW PUTS OUT JOY • • • • • • 39 STAGIRIUS V   43
    BUT THOU WHOM SUPERFLUITY OF JOY • • • • • 42 GIPSY CHILD   9
    POOR CHILD WHOM THE LIGHT AIR OF CHILDISH JOY • • • 41 GIPSY CHILD V   9
    JOY COMES AND GOES HOPE EBBS AND FLOWS • • • • 44 QUESTION   1
    NOT WITHOUT JOY SO RADIANT SO ENDOWD • • • • • 46 IN UTRUMQUE PAR   33
    STAND TRANCED IN JOY • • • • • • • 51 CONSOLATION   45
    IN WARMTH LIGHT JOY • • • • • • • 52 CONSOLATION   70
    O JOY AGAIN THE FARMS APPEAR • • • • • • 54 RESIGNATION   74
    WHOSE SECRET IS NOT JOY BUT PEACE • • • • • 58 RESIGNATION   192
    REMORSE GRIEF JOY AND WERE THE SCOPE • • • • • 58 RESIGNATION   218
    A SHIVER RUNS THROUGH THE DEEP CORN FOR JOY • • • 65 SOHRAB RUSTUM   156
    BACK QUICKLY THROUGH THE CAMP IN FEAR AND JOY • • • 69 SOHRAB RUSTUM   261
    FEAR AT HIS WRATH BUT JOY THAT RUSTUM CAME • • • • 69 SOHRAB RUSTUM   262
    WITH JOY AND ALL THE PLEASANT LIFE THEY LED • • • 79 SOHRAB RUSTUM   627
    FEAR AT HIS WRATH AND JOY THAT RUSTUM CAME • • • 69 SOHRAB RUSTUM V 262
    WITH A GREAT JOY UPON HIS FACE • • • • • 91 SICK KING BOKH   119
    SO HAVE I NEITHER JOY NOR FAME • • • • • 94 SICK KING BOKH   219
    BALDER THEIR JOY SO BRIGHT SO LOVED A GOD • • • 98 BALDER DEAD 1   126
    AND TOUCH THE APATHETIC GHOSTS WITH JOY • • • 110 BALDER DEAD 2   196
    AND HEROES WHERE THEY LIVE IN LIGHT AND JOY • • • 110 BALDER DEAD 2   199
    AS AMONG THOSE WHOSE JOY AND WORK IS WAR • • • • 115 BALDER DEAD 3   81
    TEARS STARTED TO MINE EYES WITH YEARNING JOY • • • 117 BALDER DEAD 3   151
    AND THERE FELL JOY UPON THE GODS TO HEAR • • • 122 BALDER DEAD 3   319
    SO THE GODS CROSS WAS BITTERER FOR THEIR JOY • • • 124 BALDER DEAD 3   368
    BUT WE IN HEAVEN SHALL FIND AGAIN WITH JOY • • • 128 BALDER DEAD 3   532
    JOY HAS NOT FOUND HER YET NOR EVER WILL • • • 151 TRISTRAM 3   68
    BY DRYING UP OUR JOY IN EVERYTHING • • • • 153 TRISTRAM 3   125
    HARK WHAT SHE SINGS O JOY O JOY • • • • 164 FORSAKEN MERM   89
    HARK WHAT SHE SINGS O JOY O JOY • • • • 164 FORSAKEN MERM   89
    THE UNCONQUERD JOY IN WHICH HER SPIRIT DWELLS • • 176 PARTING   40
    AND LIFE AND OTHERS JOY AND PAIN • • • • • 181 ISOLATION MARG   35
    THEY BRING US LIGHT AND WARMTH AND JOY • • • 203 EUPHROSYNE   24
    AND DEAD TO HOPES OF FUTURE JOY • • • • 206 RIVER   20
    THEIR JOY IS IN THEIR CALM • • • • • • 208 ON THE RHINE   25
    HATH REALLY NEITHER JOY NOR LOVE NOR LIGHT • • • 211 DOVER BEACH   33
    AND MOUNTAINS THAT FILL US WITH JOY • • • • 230 YOUTH OF NATURE   61
    COLD THE ELATION OF JOY • • • • • • • 231 YOUTH OF NATURE   95
    MY LONGING MY SADNESS MY JOY • • • • • 231 YOUTH OF NATURE   121
    THAT THEY WERE MY GLORY AND JOY • • • • • 232 YOUTH OF NATURE   132
    AND WITH JOY THE STARS PERFORM THEIR SHINING • • 240 SELF-DEPENDENCE   21
    IN JOY AND WHEN I WILL I SLEEP • • • • • • 241 MORALITY   28
    BRIMMING WITH WONDER AND JOY • • • • • 251 FUTURE   4
    NURSING THY PROJECT IN UNCLOUDED JOY • • • • 261 SCHOLAR-GIPSY   199
    HE LOVED EACH SIMPLE JOY THE COUNTRY YIELDS • • 264 THYRSIS   42
    AND MAKE LEAP UP WITH JOY THE BEAUTEOUS HEAD • • 265 THYRSIS   87
    THIS COMER GREET HER WITH JOY • • • • • 284 HAWORTH CHURCH   85
    PEERLESS IN RADIANCE IN JOY • • • • • • 294 HEINES GRAVE   66
    GLORY AND GENIUS AND JOY • • • • • • 295 HEINES GRAVE   84
    MADE IT A BEAT OF THY JOY • • • • • • 299 HEINES GRAVE   232
    A CONQUERING NEW-BORN JOY AWOKE • • • • • 316 OBERMANN MORE   115
    AND YET MEN HAVE SUCH NEED OF JOY • • • • 320 OBERMANN MORE   237
    BUT JOY WHOSE GROUNDS ARE TRUE • • • • • 320 OBERMANN MORE   238
    AND JOY THAT SHOULD ALL HEARTS EMPLOY • • • 320 OBERMANN MORE   239
    SHORN OF THE JOY THE BLOOM THE POWER • • • • 322 OBERMANN MORE   303
    ONE COMMON WAVE OF THOUGHT AND JOY • • • • 323 OBERMANN MORE   323
    AND YET THEY HAVE SUCH NEED OF JOY • • • • 320 OBERMANN MORE V 237
    AND JOY WHOSE GROUNDS ARE TRUE • • • • 320 OBERMANN MORE V 238
    ONE MIGHTY WAVE OF THOUGHT AND JOY • • • • 323 OBERMANN MORE V 323
    QUICK FROM DISTRESSFUL THOUGHT AND FLOATS IN JOY • • 351 MEROPE   615
    WHETHER IT TURN AT LAST TO JOY OR WOE • • • • 359 MEROPE   862
    MY CHILD UNHURT ONLY BY OVER JOY • • • • 377 MEROPE   1220
    AND ONLY BAD MEN JOY TO SEE UNDONE • • • • 386 MEROPE   1429
    RADIANT WITH FORTUNE AND JOY • • • • • • 393 MEROPE   1683
    NOW FOR THYSELF THOU COMST WITH WELL-CLOAKD JOY • • 395 MEROPE   1737

JOY   (CONTINUED)
        LEAP AND FLY OPEN OF THEMSELVES FOR JOY   • • • •   401 MEROPE   1885
        APPROVE NOT TOO I HAVE BUT HALF MY JOY   • • • •   403 MEROPE   1962
        THOU TOO REAREST IN JOY • • • • • • • • •   346 MEROPE   V 511
        THY JOY OUR YOUTH FOREBODES   • • • • • • •   424 EMPEDOCLES I 2   375
        TO FIND WITH YOU THE JOY WE IN VAIN HERE REQUIRE • • 425 EMPEDOCLES I 2   381
        AND DRIED ITS SELF-SUFFICING FOUNT OF JOY   • • • •   429 EMPEDOCLES II   22
        ON SIMPLE MINDS WITH A PURE NATURAL JOY   • • • •   436 EMPEDOCLES II   243
        THOUGHTS SLAVES AND DEAD TO EVERY NATURAL JOY • •   436 EMPEDOCLES II   249
        TO NURSE HIS DWINDLING FACULTY OF JOY   • • • •   437 EMPEDOCLES II   273
        JOY AND THE OUTWARD WORLD MUST DIE TO HIM   • • • •   437 EMPEDOCLES II   274
        WITH HELD-IN JOY SWELLING ITS HEART I ONLY • • • •   438 EMPEDOCLES II   316
        AM DEAD TO LIFE AND JOY THEREFORE I READ   • • • •   438 EMPEDOCLES II   321
        WE MIGHT HAVE JOY BLENT WITH THE ALL-BATHING AIR • • 439 EMPEDOCLES II   343
        WE SHOULD HAVE JOY BLENT WITH THE ALL-BATHING AIR • • 439 EMPEDOCLES II   V 343
        AS IF THE REIGN OF JOY DID NOW BEGIN • • • • •   445 WESTMIN ABBEY   40
        AND JOY IN LIGHT AND POWER TO SPREAD THE JOY • •   446 WESTMIN ABBEY   80
        AND JOY IN LIGHT AND POWER TO SPREAD THE JOY • •   446 WESTMIN ABBEY   80
        IN JOY THY LAST MORN FLEW ANON • • • • • • •   460 KAISER DEAD   63
        AND WREST ONE TEAR FROM JOY OH WHO SHALL PEN •   468 ALARIC AT ROME   167
        THE CHILD-COMPANION OF HIS CHILDISH JOY   • • • •   477 CROMWELL   180
        MADE VOID AND HELD THE SORROW AND THE JOY   • • • •   RUDE ORATOR   4

JOYANCE
        THY VOICE OF JOYANCE MINDED US AND YOUTH   • • • •   117 BALDER DEAD 3   143

JOYD
        WHICH JOYD MY VOICE TO HEAR   • • • • • • • •   449 WESTMIN ABBEY   162
        JOYD WITH THEM WHEN THEY WERE GAY • • • • • •   455 POOR MATTHIAS   91

JOYFUL
        FROM THE LOUD JOYFUL LAUGHTER OF HIS LIPS   • • • •   11 MYCERINUS   101
        STROLLD AND SANG WITH JOYFUL MIND • • • • • •   26 NEW SIRENS   6
        AND THE BURST OF JOYFUL GREETINGS • • • • • •   30 NEW SIRENS   117
        AND THE JOYFUL DAWN WERE GONE • • • • • • • •   30 NEW SIRENS   118

JOYFULLY
        SINGING MOST JOYFULLY   • • • • • • • • • •   164 FORSAKEN MERM   88
        SINGING MOST JOYFULLY   • • • • • • • • • •   164 FORSAKEN MERM   95
        YOU TOO MOVED JOYFULLY   • • • • • • • • • •   437 EMPEDOCLES II   283

JOYLESS
        O BARREN BOAST O JOYLESS MOCKERY   • • • • •   EMERSONS ESSAYS V 14
        IT MAY BE ON THAT JOYLESS FEAST HIS EYE   • • • •   11 MYCERINUS   107
        LOVELESS RAYLESS JOYLESS YOU SHALL STAND   • •   35 NEW SIRENS   266
        THERE ARE THE JOYLESS SEATS THE HAUNT OF GHOSTS • • 108 BALDER DEAD 2   132
        INTO THE JOYLESS KINGDOM HAVE I BEEN • • • • •   114 BALDER DEAD 3   38
        THE JOYLESS PLAINS AND HEARD THE STREAMS OF HELL • •124 BALDER DEAD 3   380

JOYOUS
        JOYOUS AT THE HEIGHT OF PLEASURE   • • • • • •   33 NEW SIRENS   201
        WAS LAUNCELOTS GUEST AT JOYOUS GARD • • • • •   136 TRISTRAM 1   203
        FORTH WITH THY JOYOUS SONG   • • • • • • •   219 BACCHANALIA 1   42
        THE SUNNY WATERS HOLD THEIR JOYOUS WAY   • • • • 469 ALARIC AT ROME   196

JOYS
        THE JOYS WHICH WERE NOT FOR OUR USE DESIGND • •   41 HUMAN LIFE   28
        JOYS WE DIMLY APPREHEND • • • • • • • • • •   44 QUESTION   18
        THE THOUSAND SWEET STILL JOYS OF SUCH • • • •   179 FAREWELL   67
        SAY HAVE THEIR SONS ACHIEVED MORE JOYS • • • •   303 GRANDE CHARTR   129
        SAY HAVE THEIR SONS OBTAIN MORE JOYS   • • • •   303 GRANDE CHARTR   V 129
        TREMBLEST AND WILT NOT DARE TO TRUST THE JOYS   426 EMPEDOCLES I 2   421
                THERE ARE
        AND CLASP CONJECTURED JOYS OR DREAD CONJECTURED WOES 425 EMPEDOCLES I 2   V 406
        AND KISS CONJECTURED JOYS OR FEAR CONJECTURED WOES   425 EMPEDOCLES I 2   V 406
        BEFORE THE SOUL LOSE ALL HER SOLEMN JOYS   • • •   429 EMPEDOCLES II   33
        AND PEACEFUL JOYS AND GENTLER THOUGHTS SWEPT BY • • 474 CROMWELL   71
        JOYS THAT HAD COME AND VANISHD HALF UNKNOWN • •   474 CROMWELL   75
        OF JOYS UNCLOUDED YEARS UNSTIRRD BY STRIFE • • •   474 CROMWELL   102

JUDAS
        THE TRAITOR JUDAS OUT OF HELL • • • • • • •   157 SAINT BRANDAN   20
        THE ICEBERG AND NO JUDAS THERE • • • • • • •   158 SAINT BRANDAN   76

JUDGE
        JUDGE VAIN BEFOREHAND HUMAN CARES • • • • •   59 RESIGNATION   232
        NOR DO I JUDGE IF IT SHALL WIN OR FAIL • • • •   99 BALDER DEAD 1   129
        NO JUDGE EYES US FROM HEAVEN OUR SIN TO SCAN • •   170 BETTER PART   4
        SITS THERE NO JUDGE IN HEAVEN OUR SIN TO SEE •   171 BETTER PART   11
        MORE STRICTLY THEN THE INWARD JUDGE OBEY   • • •   171 BETTER PART   12
        BE JUDGE THYSELF IF IT ABOUND NOT HERE • • • •   336 MEROPE   211
        WHO IN MANS INMOST BOSOM SIT AND JUDGE • • • •   349 MEROPE   554
        SPEAK THEM THAT I MAY JUDGE THEIR KIND MYSELF •   354 MEROPE   712
        REFRESHMENT NEEDED BY THEE AS I JUDGE   • • • •   359 MEROPE   867
        I WILL NOT JUDGE THAT MAN   • • • • • • • •   415 EMPEDOCLES I 2   97
        HOWBEIT I JUDGE AS LOST • • • • • • • • • •   415 EMPEDOCLES I 2   98
        HE FAILS NOT TO JUDGE CLEAR IF THIS BE QUENCHD OR NO 418 EMPEDOCLES I 2   171

JUDGE   (CONTINUED)
        SHALL WE JUDGE WHAT FOR MAN IS NOT TRUE BLISS OR IS   425 EMPEDOCLES I 2   396
        HE FAILS NOT TO JUDGE CLEAR IF THIS IS QUENCHD OR NO   418 EMPEDOCLES I 2   V 171
        SHALL WE JUDGE WHAT FOR MAN IS NOT HIGH BLISS OR IS   425 EMPEDOCLES I 2   V 396

JUDGED
        I WILL NOT STIR TILL I BE JUDGED   .   .   .   .   .   .   91 SICK KING BOKH   104
        THE FAMOUS CRITICS JUDGED IT ALL   .   .   .   .   .   .   219 BACCHANALIA 2   9
        WE JUDGED THE BEST CHANCE FINDS NO BETTER WAY   .   .   331 MEROPE   36
        MORE FORTUNATE THAN THEE MORE FAIRLY JUDGED   .   .   350 MEROPE   590
        THEREFORE WHILE ACTS ARE FROM THEIR MOTIVES JUDGED   352 MEROPE   644
        DEATH DEATH WAS JUDGED THE BOON SUPREME INDEED   .   .   448 WESTMIN ABBEY   140

JUDGES
        DUMB JUDGES ANSWER TRUTH OR MOCKERY   .   .   .   .   .   .   4 EMERSONS ESSAYS   14
        LIKE ALLAH HEARS AND JUDGES ALL   .   .   .   .   .   .   89 SICK KING BOKH   57

JUDGMENT
        JUDGMENT SHIFTS CONVICTIONS GO   .   .   .   .   29 NEW SIRENS   82
        NOR DID THEY TO THEIR JUDGMENT-PLACE REPAIR   .   .   105 BALDER DEAD 2   32
        IS MERLIN PRISONER TILL THE JUDGMENT-DAY   .   .   .   156 TRISTRAM 3   222
        EVERYWHERE HEARD WILL BE THE JUDGMENT-CALL   .   .   .   173 MONICAS PRAYER   3
        ILL COUNSEL IN MY JUDGMENT GIVES SHE HERE   .   .   .   382 MEROPE   1333
        O WOMANS JUDGMENT   .   .   .   .   398 MEROPE   1795
        AND JUDGMENT ALL EMBROILD   .   .   .   .   425 EMPEDOCLES I 2   394

JUDGMENTS
        AND JUDGMENTS ALL EMBROILD   .   .   .   .   425 EMPEDOCLES I 2   V 394

JUGGLE
        ARGOS A JUGGLE TO CRESPHONTES GAVE   .   .   .   .   .   .   389 MEROPE   1551

JULIETS
        AND JULIETS WAS AS FAIR A FACE   .   .   .   .   48 HORATIAN ECHO   29

JULY
        SLEEP IN THE JULY SUNSHINE STILL   .   .   .   .   .   .   55 RESIGNATION   97

JUNE
        WHERE THE WARM JUNE-WIND   .   .   .   .   51 CONSOLATION   42
        AS IN THE COUNTRY ON A MORN IN JUNE   .   .   .   .   .   .   65 SOHRAB RUSTUM   154
        CLEAR IN THE PURE JUNE-NIGHT   .   .   .   .   228 YOUTH OF NATURE   6
        IN JUNE AND MANY A SCYTHE IN SUNSHINE FLAMES   .   .   257 SCHOLAR-GIPSY   92
        SHE NEEDS NOT JUNE FOR BEAUTYS HEIGHTENING   .   .   .   263 THYRSIS   20
        SO SOME TEMPESTUOUS MORN IN EARLY JUNE   .   .   .   264 THYRSIS   51

JUNGFRAU
        THE JUNGFRAU SNOWS LOOK FAINT AND FAR   .   .   .   .   184 TERRACE BERNE   6

JUNIPER
        DOTTED WITH HOLLY-TREES AND JUNIPER   .   .   .   .   .   .   150 TRISTRAM 3   18
        SPRINKLED WITH HOLLY TREES AND JUNIPER   .   .   .   .   TRISTRAM 3   V 18

JUST
        TEACHES THE LIMIT OF THE JUST AND TRUE   .   .   .   .   7 REP FRIEND   7
        MANS JUSTICE FROM THE ALL-JUST GODS WAS GIVEN   .   .   9 MYCERINUS   20
        WHEN ON THE STRENUOUS JUST MAN HEAVEN BESTOWS   .   .   9 MYCERINUS   29
        WHERE JUST MEN SUFFER WRONG   .   .   .   .   39 STAGIRIUS   42
        AND THOUGH THE JUST SUN GILD AS MORTALS PRAY   .   .   43 GIPSY CHILD   59
        AND THOUGH THE JUST SUN GILD AS ALL MEN PRAY   .   .   43 GIPSY CHILD   V 59
        DID THE JUST GODDESS   .   .   .   .   51 CONSOLATION   57
        WE LEFT JUST TEN YEARS SINCE YOU SAY   .   .   .   .   .   53 RESIGNATION   40
        JUST PITCHD THE HIGH PAVILION IN THE MIDST   .   .   .   67 SOHRAB RUSTUM   193
        O MOST JUST VIZIER SEND AWAY   .   .   .   .   87 SICK KING BOKH   1
        WAS JUST TO WHAT HE DID NOT WIN   .   .   .   .   .   .   204 EUPHROSYNE   28
        TO THE JUST-PAUSING GENIUS WE REMIT   .   .   .   .   .   259 SCHOLAR-GIPSY   149
        HIS BIRTH-NAME JUST BELOW   .   .   .   .   313 OBERMANN MORE   26
        A JUST THEREFORE A SAFE SUPREMACY   .   .   .   .   .   339 MEROPE   305
        WHICH IN A DEED LIKE MINE A JUST MAN TREADS   .   .   341 MEROPE   369
        HIS MOST JUST PRAYER YET HIS HOUSE   .   .   .   .   .   343 MEROPE   409
        GRANT HIM TO REIGN THERE WISE AND JUST LIKE THEE   .   .   350 MEROPE   589
        A MORE JUST STROKE THAN THAT THOU GAVST MY SON   .   .   373 MEROPE   1191
        UNHAPPY ONE THOU STRIKST A MOST JUST BLOW   .   .   374 MEROPE   1200
        HIS JUST REVENGE TO AN UNNATURAL DEED   .   .   .   385 MEROPE   1417
        AS OUR JUST CAUSE DESERVES I DO NOT FEAR   .   .   .   391 MEROPE   1595
        UNARMD AND TRAVEL-SOILD JUST AS HE WAS   .   .   .   401 MEROPE   1906
        I KNOW NOT JUST IN EITHER CASE THE STROKE   .   .   .   404 MEROPE   1986
        HIS MOST JUST PRAYER YET HIS RACE   .   .   .   .   .   343 MEROPE   V 409
        ALL SIN IS JUST IS PURE   .   .   .   .   420 EMPEDOCLES I 2   243
        THE JUST MAN NOT TO ENTOMB   .   .   .   .   420 EMPEDOCLES I 2   253
        JUST SINCE DOWN AT THE STREAM HO CALLICLES   .   .   428 EMPEDOCLES I 2   486
        OR JUST THY LITTLE SELF RESTORE   .   .   .   .   .   .   450 GEISTS GRAVE   28

JUSTICE
        NOT BY THE JUSTICE THAT MY FATHER SPURND   .   .   .   8 MYCERINUS   1
        MANS JUSTICE FROM THE ALL-JUST GODS WAS GIVEN   .   .   9 MYCERINUS   20
        JUSTICE O KING AND ON MYSELF   .   .   .   .   89 SICK KING BOKH   36

JUSTICE   (CONTINUED)
    AND JUSTICE NOT INFRINGED   • • • • • • •   195 FRAG ANTIGONE   7
    CLASH WITH JUSTICE THE GODS   • • • • • • •   348 MEROPE   537
    TO THE CHAFED HEART OF JUSTICE THAN TO MINE   • •   349 MEROPE   560
    ZEUS AND PURE-THOUGHTED JUSTICE BRAND   • • • • •   353 MEROPE   688
    MOTHER SOMETIMES THE JUSTICE OF THE GODS • • • •   378 MEROPE   1247
    AND I WOULD NOW HAVE JUSTICE STRIKE NOT ME • • •   387 MEROPE   1472
    FLIES VICTORY WINGD AND JUSTICE RAISES THEN   • •   388 MEROPE   1503
    JUSTICE MY SISTER LONG DEMANDS THIS BLOW   • • •   390 MEROPE   1572
    JUSTICE AND WISDOM IS NO LIFE AT ALL • • • • • •   390 MEROPE   1576
    MAKE JUSTICE ALTER   • • • • • • • • • • •   398 MEROPE   1806
    OF INVARIABLENESS OF JUSTICE   • • • • • • • •   398 MEROPE   1811
    THAT JUSTICE THAT SAGE ORDER NOT ALONE   • • • •   404 MEROPE   1997
    AMISS FROM JUSTICE THE GODS   • • • • • • •   348 MEROPE   V

JUSTIFIED
    IN REASON GOOD WHICH JUSTIFIED MY DEED   • • • •   340 MEROPE   340

JUTS
    CLIMBING THE ROCK WHICH JUTS   • • • • • • •   297 HEINES GRAVE   186

JUTTING
    HIGH ON A JUTTING ROCK IN THE RED STREAM   • • • •   192 STRAYED REVEL   230

KAFFIRS
    THE KAFFIRS ALSO WHOM GOD CURSE   • • • • • •   93 SICK KING BOKH   173

KAI
    ERRS STRANGELY FOR THE KING FOR KAI KHOSROO   • •   67 SOHRAB RUSTUM   223
    THOU AND THE OTHER PEERS OF KAI KHOSROO   • • • •   85 SOHRAB RUSTUM   832
    WHAT POOR KAI DEAD SAY ALL I MEET   • • • • • •   459 KAISER DEAD   9
    KAI STOOD CONFEST   • • • • • • • • • • • •   459 KAISER DEAD   30
    BUT KAI A TIRELESS SHEPHERD-LAD   • • • • • •   460 KAISER DEAD   44
    KAI IN THY GRAVE   • • • • • • • • • • •   461 KAISER DEAD   82

KAIS
    KAIS BRACELET TAIL KAIS BUSY FEET   • • • • • •   459 KAISER DEAD   7
    KAIS BRACELET TAIL KAIS BUSY FEET   • • • • • •   459 KAISER DEAD   7

KAISER
    GERMAN KAISER FULL OFT   • • • • • • • • •   296 HEINES GRAVE   136
    MAX AND KAISER WE TO-DAY   • • • • • • • • • •   454 POOR MATTHIAS   67
    KAISER SHOULD BE BUT IS NOT   • • • • • • • •   454 POOR MATTHIAS   70
    KAISER WITH HIS COLLIE FACE   • • • • • • • •   454 POOR MATTHIAS   73
    WHAT KAISER DEAD THE HEAVY NEWS   • • • • • •   458 KAISER DEAD   1

KAISERS
    AND KAISERS RACE WE DEEMD THE SAME   • • • • • •   459 KAISER DEAD   21

KALMUCKS
    KALMUCKS AND UNKEMPT KUZZAKS TRIBES WHO STRAY   • •   65 SOHRAB RUSTUM   132
    KALMUCKS AND UNKEMPD KUZZAKS TRIBES WHO STRAY   • •   65 SOHRAB RUSTUM   V 132

KALMUKS
    KOHIK AND WHERE THE KALMUKS FEED THEIR SHEEP   • •   83 SOHRAB RUSTUM   764

KARA
    BLACK GLOSSY CURLD THE FLEECE OF KARA-KUL   • • • •   64 SOHRAB RUSTUM   101

KEEN
    SEARD HIS KEEN EYEBALLS   • • • • • • • • • •   51 CONSOLATION   37
    CROWDED AND KEEN THE COUNTRY GROWS   • • • • • •   56 RESIGNATION   133
    CAME KEEN AND CHILL DOWN ON THE HEATHER BRIGHT   • • 151 TRISTRAM 3   57
    WHERE THE SUNS RAYS STRUCK FULL AND FLASHD BACK KEEN   TRISTRAM 3   V 21
    HAVE PRAISED THE KEEN UNSCRUPULOUS COURSE   • • • •   178 FAREWELL   35
    TOO KEEN TO REST TOO WEAK TO FIND   • • • • • •   217 NAMELESS EPIT   V
    FOR THERE WITH BODILY ANGUISH KEEN   • • • • • •   276 SOUTHERN NIGHT   25
    WHICH UNFLINCHING AND KEEN   • • • • • • • •   281 HAWORTH CHURCH   38
    AND HE WILL FIND ITS AIR TOO KEEN FOR HIM   • • • •   435 EMPEDOCLES II   228

KEENER
    REVELS MORE DEEP JOY KEENER THAN THEIR OWN • • • •   10 MYCERINUS   66
    KEENER TO SLAY THEE LEST THOU POISON ME   • • • •   38 WORLDS TRIUMPHS   14

KEENLY
    NIPS TOO KEENLY THE SWEET FLOWER   • • • • • •   131 TRISTRAM 1   36

KEEP
    OR SOME FRIEND HAILD US TO KEEP COMPANY   • • • •   40 HUMAN LIFE   12
    IN VAIN BUT WHO CAN KEEP THE LIONS CUB   • • • •   63 SOHRAB RUSTUM   91
    ALL THESE HAVE SORROW AND KEEP STILL • • • • • •   93 SICK KING BOKH   177
    TO KEEP HIS OWN LIFE SAFE AND SEE THE SUN   • • • •   101 BALDER DEAD 3   213
    YE GODS THESE TERMS MAY KEEP ANOTHER DAY   • • • •   115 BALDER DEAD 3   49
    I WEEP HIM NOT LET HELA KEEP HER PREY   • • • • •   123 BALDER DEAD 3   354
    TO WARMER LANDS AND COASTS THAT KEEP THE SUN • • •   129 BALDER DEAD 3   562
    KEEP HIS EYELIDS LET HIM SEEM • • • • • • • •   133 TRISTRAM 1   106
    WE CANNOT KEEP HIM NOW AS THEN • • • • • • • •   138 TRISTRAM 1   244

KEEP   (CONTINUED)
        TO-NIGHT MY PAGE SHALL KEEP ME COMPANY   • • • •   140 TRISTRAM 1   310
        CHRIST KEEP US FROM SUCH FANTASY   • • • • •   147 TRISTRAM 2   130
        BUT LORD AND HOUNDS KEEP ROOTED THERE   • • • •   149 TRISTRAM 2   185
        HEAVEN KEEP US FROM SUCH FANTASY   • • • • •   147 TRISTRAM 2   V 130
        YET WE HER MEMORY AS SHE PRAYD WILL KEEP   • • • •   173 MONICAS PRAYER   13
        KEEP BY THIS LIFE IN GOD AND UNION THERE   • • • •   173 MONICAS PRAYER   14
        I BADE IT KEEP THE WORLD AWAY   • • • • • •   180 ISOLATION MARG   3
        AH LET THEM KEEP THEIR FAITH SINCERE   • • • • •   203 EUPHROSYNE   11
        I SAY UNTO YOU SEE YE KEEP THAT LAW   • • • • •   237 PROGRESS   7
        HENCE HENCE THEY CRY YE DO BUT KEEP MAN BLIND   • • •   237 PROGRESS   18
        BUT KEEP HIM SELF-IMMERSED PREOCCUPIED   • • • •   237 PROGRESS   19
        AND THOUGH SO TASKD KEEP FREE FROM DUST AND SOIL   • •   244 SUMMER NIGHT   82
        THAT IT MIGHT KEEP FROM HIS CAPRICIOUS PLAY   • • •   246 BURIED LIFE   35
        I ASK NOT EACH KIND SOUL TO KEEP   • • • • •   250 WISH   5
        WAVE US AWAY AND KEEP THY SOLITUDE   • • • • •   261 SCHOLAR-GIPSY   210
        HE LOVED HIS MATES BUT YET HE COULD NOT KEEP   • •   264 THYRSIS   43
        FOR THERE THINE EARTH-FORGETTING EYELIDS KEEP   • •   267 THYRSIS   168
        KEEP FRESH THE GRASS UPON HIS GRAVE   • • • • •   272 MEMORIAL VERSES   71
        FOR FOOD TO KEEP HIM TILL HE END   • • • • •   278 SOUTHERN NIGHT   83
        AH KEEP KEEP THEM COMBINED   • • • • • •   291 RUGBY CHAPEL   182
        AH KEEP KEEP THEM COMBINED   • • • • • •   291 RUGBY CHAPEL   182
        BUT LET US KEEP THAT PURPOSE WHICH AT HOME   • • •   331 MEROPE   35
        THEIR DAILY-PRACTISED CHAFINGS KEEP ALIVE   • • •   331 MEROPE   44
        AS I HAVE EVER FOUND THEE BENT TO KEEP   • • •   332 MEROPE   80
        SPEAK THEREFORE OR KEEP SILENCE WHICH THOU WILT   • •   333 MEROPE   113
        TO KEEP ALIVE THAT MEMORY IN MY HEART   • • • •   334 MEROPE   120
        AND YE KEEP FAITHFUL SILENCE FRIENDS AND MARK   • •   368 MEROPE   1073
        AS HITHERTO THEY KEPT HIM KEEP HIM NOW   • • • •   377 MEROPE   1226
        TO KEEP THEIR MASTERS POWER THOU WILT FIND   • • •   381 MEROPE   1307
        MEAN STILL TO KEEP ALOOF FROM DORIAN BROIL   • • •   384 MEROPE   1396
        AGLOW WITH ANGRY FIRE TO KEEP US TWAIN   • • •   395 MEROPE   1736
        BUT THOU MUST KEEP UNSEEN FOLLOW US ON   • • •   409 EMPEDOCLES I 1   86
        AND KEEP HIS MIND FROM PREYING ON ITSELF   • • •   411 EMPEDOCLES I 1   157
        TO TUNES WE DID NOT CALL OUR BEING MUST KEEP CHIME •   418 EMPEDOCLES I 2   196
        WHICH HE CAN WIN OR KEEP   • • • • • • • •   EMPEDOCLES I 2   V
        AND KEEP THEIR FRIENDLY CHATTER AT HIS EAR   • • •   435 EMPEDOCLES II   224
        AND KEEP US PRISONERS OF OUR CONSCIOUSNESS   • • •   439 EMPEDOCLES II   352
        COULDST THOU NO BETTER KEEP O ABBEY OLD   • • •   444 WESTMIN ABBEY   4
        YET WOULD WE KEEP THEE IN OUR HEART   • • • •   451 GEISTS GRAVE   37
        THERE OF THY MASTER KEEP THAT SIGN   • • • •   461 KAISER DEAD   83
        BOTH HE MUST KEEP TORMENT HIM HOW THEY MAY   • • •   LUCRETIUS 3   V   7
        BOTH HE MUST KEEP TORMENT HIM AS THEY MAY   • • •   LUCRETIUS 3   V   7
        KEEP ALL O KEEP CONTINUAL HOLIDAY   • • • • •   FRAGMENT 2   5
        KEEP ALL O KEEP CONTINUAL HOLIDAY   • • • • •   FRAGMENT 2   5

KEEPERS
        US THY HUMAN KEEPERS HARD   • • • • • • • •   456 POOR MATTHIAS   122

KEEPEST
        THOU KEEPEST ALOOF THE PROFANE   • • • • • • • •   435 EMPEDOCLES II   207

KEEPS
        CALLD HISTORY KEEPS A SPLENDOUR DUE TO WIT   • • • •   5 DUKE WELLINGTON   13
        BETWIXT OUR SENSES AND OUR SORROW KEEPS   • • • •   43 GIPSY CHILD   50
        BUT NOW HE KEEPS APART AND SITS AT HOME   • • • •   63 SOHRAB RUSTUM   81
        NOT BIFROST BUT THAT BRIDGE A DAMSEL KEEPS   • • • •   99 BALDER DEAD 1   149
        LOK TRIUMPHS STILL AND HELA KEEPS HER PREY   • • • •   126 BALDER DEAD 3   447
        KEEPS HIS COURT IN TYNTAGIL   • • • • • • • •   134 TRISTRAM 1   V 134
        HE DOES WELL TOO WHO KEEPS THAT CLUE THE MILD   • •   195 FRAG ANTIGONE   9
        AND NOW KEEPS ONLY IN THE GRAVE   • • • • •   249 KENSINGTON GARD   28
        IN THE TWO HINKSEYS NOTHING KEEPS THE SAME   • • •   262 THYRSIS   2
        HIS QUIET HOME ONE KEEPS   • • • • • • • •   308 OBERMANN   50
        WHAT KEEPS HIM IN ARCADIA FROM RETURN   • • • •   350 MEROPE   602
        AND KEEPS ITS LIQUID SOLITUDES UNSCALED   • • •   351 MEROPE   625
        MORE THAN ALL SECRETS HID THE WAY IT KEEPS   • • •   352 MEROPE   631
        INSCRUTABLE AS EVER SEE IT KEEPS   • • • • •   403 MEROPE   1967

KEIGHLEY
        WHERE BEHIND KEIGHLEY THE ROAD   • • • • • • • •   282 HAWORTH CHURCH   55

KEMPIS
        A-KEMPIS HER DEPARTING SOUL OUTWORN   • • • • • •   168 RACHEL 3   7

KEN
        IN SOME FAR STONY GORGE OUT OF HIS KEN   • • • •   78 SOHRAB RUSTUM   568
        AND DRUDGE UNDER SOME FOOLISH MASTERS KEN   • • • •   169 WORLDLY PLACE   6
        EAGERLY ONCE HER GRACIOUS KEN   • • • • • • •   202 URANIA   9
        BUT WORDSWORTHS EYES AVERT THEIR KEN   • • • • •   308 OBERMANN   53
        AH CARRY BACK THY KEN   • • • • • • • • •   315 OBERMANN MORE   82
        WHAT YOU FEEL ESCAPES OUR KEN   • • • • • •   457 POOR MATTHIAS   161
        BOLD ACTIONS PARENT AND A PIERCING KEN   • • • •   478 CROMWELL   229

KEPT
        ONE LESSON OF TWO DUTIES KEPT AT ONE   • • • • • •   1 QUIET WORK   3
        ONE LESSON OF TWO DUTIES KEPT IN ONE   • • • • • •   1 QUIET WORK   V   3
        I HAVE KEPT UNINFRINGED MY NATURES LAW   • • • •   40 HUMAN LIFE   4
        QUIET LIVING STRICT-KEPT MEASURE   • • • • •   49 SECOND BEST   2

KEPT   (CONTINUED)

KEPT THEY MORE CLOUDLESS	50	CONSOLATION	24
AND WITH HIS STAFF KEPT BACK THE FOREMOST RANKS	65	SOHRAB RUSTUM	143
THAT PERAN-WISA KEPT THE TARTARS BACK	65	SOHRAB RUSTUM	145
ALIVE I KEPT NOT FAR FROM THEE DEAR SOUL	103	BALDER DEAD 1	293
KEPT ON AFTER THE GRAVE BUT NOT BEGUN	172	IMMORTALITY	10
FOR NATURE HATH LONG KEPT THIS INN THE EARTH	251	FUTURE	V
KEPT NOT FOR LONG ITS HAPPY COUNTRY TONE	269	THYRSIS	222
KEPT THE MEMORIAL BARD	281	HAWORTH CHURCH	20
KNIT ALL YOUR PARTS AND KEPT YOU ONE	320	OBERMANN MORE	223
FOR I HAVE KEPT CONSPIRACY FAST-CHAIND	334	MEROPE	149
HOTLIER THAN THOU AND WERE BY THEE KEPT BACK	339	MEROPE	330
HE KEPT HIS TALE THEN FOR THE KING ALONE	362	MEROPE	928
KEPT ME THEIR MOTHER FROM THEIR SIDE SO LONG	367	MEROPE	1040
YE KEPT SILENCE IN FEAR	371	MEROPE	1129
AS HITHERTO THEY KEPT HIM KEEP HIM NOW	377	MEROPE	1226
OH HADST THOU POLYPHONTES STILL BUT KEPT	395	MEROPE	1725
THE SILENCE THOU HAST KEPT FOR TWENTY YEARS	395	MEROPE	1726
ILL-KEPT BY HIS INFIRM HEIRS	399	MEROPE	1846
KEPT MORE THAN US THEIR STRENGTH OF SOUL	481	COURAGE	12

KEPTEST

TO GOD OR HERO BUT THOU KEPTEST BACK	116	BALDER DEAD 3	85

KERCHIEF

PAINT THAT LILAC KERCHIEF BOUND	23	MEMORY-PICTURE	25
THE KERCHIEF THAT ENWOUND THY HAIR	184	TERRACE BERNE	24

KHELMOS

BY THE PRECIPICES OF KHELMOS	393	MEROPE	1655

KHIVA

AND KHIVA AND FERMENT THE MILK OF MARES	64	SOHRAB RUSTUM	120
BOKHARA AND LONE KHIVA IN THE WASTE	83	SOHRAB RUSTUM	761

KHORASSAN

THE ILYATS OF KHORASSAN AND BEHIND	65	SOHRAB RUSTUM	138

KHOSROO

ERRS STRANGELY FOR THE KING FOR KAI KHOSROO	67	SOHRAB RUSTUM	223
THOU AND THE OTHER PEERS OF KAI KHOSROO	85	SOHRAB RUSTUM	832

KID

AND ON HIS SHOULDERS NOT A LAMB A KID	172	GOOD SHEPHERD	14

KILL

SOHRAB THOU THOUGHTEST IN THY MIND TO KILL	77	SOHRAB RUSTUM	528
WHOM HIS GREAT FATHER DID IN IGNORANCE KILL	84	SOHRAB RUSTUM	793
THEN WENT MY WAY TO KILL AND LIE	158	SAINT BRANDAN	59
NOT ONLY WOUND THE SENSE BUT KILL THE SOUL	385	MEROPE	1408

KILLD

SUCH CHANCE AS KILLD THE FATHER KILLD THE SONS	340	MEROPE	347
SUCH CHANCE AS KILLD THE FATHER KILLD THE SONS	340	MEROPE	347
COME HERMES WHO DOST FRIEND THE UNJUSTLY KILLD	367	MEROPE	1058
COME HERMES WHO DOST WATCH THE UNJUSTLY KILLD	367	MEROPE	V1058

KILLS

WHICH KILLS IN US THE BLOOM THE YOUTH THE SPRING	153	TRISTRAM 3	122
THAT WORD IT KILLS ME I SEE	378	MEROPE	1243

KIN

OLD MAN THE DEAD NEED NO ONE CLAIM NO KIN	62	SOHRAB RUSTUM	59
HOME TO OUR HALLS WITH TORCHLIGHT BY OUR KIN	101	BALDER DEAD 1	217
OF HEAVEN AND COMMUNION WITH MY KIN	125	BALDER DEAD 3	402
SO HERMOD GAZED AND YEARND TO JOIN HIS KIN	129	BALDER DEAD 3	565
THY MOTHERS KIN RECEIVED THEE AND REARD UP	330	MEROPE	23
INJUSTICE TO HIS KIN AND DORIAN FRIENDS	339	MEROPE	317
YOUR SONS LEAP UPON THE FOE OF YOUR KIN	344	MEROPE	462
TO THE DEAR NEXT-OF-KIN OF HIM HE MURDERD	374	MEROPE	1197
NOT WELCOME EXCULPATION TO HER KIN	386	MEROPE	1453
YE LIE WATCHING FOR THE FOE OF YOUR KIN	344	MEROPE	V 462

KIND

PAINT THOSE EYES SO BLUE SO KIND	24	MEMORY-PICTURE	41
HE LEAVES HIS KIND OERLEAPS THEIR PEN	58	RESIGNATION	211
HIM THAT KIND CREATURE FOUND AND REARD AND LOVED	81	SOHRAB RUSTUM	682
BE YE THEN KIND AS BALDER TOO WAS KIND	116	BALDER DEAD 3	87
BE YE THEN KIND AS BALDER TOO WAS KIND	116	BALDER DEAD 3	87
THOU ONLY BALDER WAST FOR EVER KIND	116	BALDER DEAD 3	112
FLOCKS OF HIS KIND PASS FLYING OER HIS HEAD	129	BALDER DEAD 3	561
THOU ONLY BALDER WERT FOR EVER KIND	116	BALDER DEAD 3	V 112
BLUE AND OER ITS MIRROR KIND	135	TRISTRAM 1	155
SHE WILL GRANT IT SHE IS KIND AND GOOD	145	TRISTRAM 2	96
FAR FROM THE KIND SEA-WAVE	159	NECKAN	16
TEARS FILLD HIS KIND BLUE EYE	160	NECKAN	V 46
SAY THY PRAYER AND COME BACK TO THE KIND SEA-CAVES	163	FORSAKEN MERM	61
AS KIND TO OTHERS AS TO ME	208	LONGING	8

```
KIND            ( CONTINUED )
        AS KIND TO ALL THE REST AS ME  . . . . . . .  208 LONGING          V   8
        I ASK NOT EACH KIND SOUL TO KEEP   . . . . . .  250 WISH                 5
        LESS MODEST PURE AND KIND  . . . . . . . .  273 EDW QUILLINAN            8
        REQUITE HIM WORDS SEVERE FOR SEEMING KIND   . . .  349 MEROPE           551
        SPEAK THEM THAT I MAY JUDGE THEIR KIND MYSELF  . .  354 MEROPE           712
        O KIND MESSENIAN MAIDENS O MY FRIENDS  . . . .  377 MEROPE          1222
        THY KIND-SPEAKING FATHER STANDS  . . . . . .  378 MEROPE          1240
        AND THE KIND CHANCE-ARRIVED WANDERER  . . . . .  399 MEROPE          1836
        HIS BLOOD TO ME FOR I CONFESS IT KIND  . . . .  404 MEROPE          1976
        DARED ONE BUT TRY THOU WAST A KIND CHILD EVER  . .  408 EMPEDOCLES I 1    76
        THEN PLAY THY KIND PART WELL FAREWELL TILL NIGHT  .  411 EMPEDOCLES I 1   167
        DARED ONE BUT TRY THOU WERT A KIND CHILD EVER  . .  409 EMPEDOCLES I 1  V  76
        AND FEIGN KIND GODS WHO PERFECT WHAT MAN VAINLY TRIES  422 EMPEDOCLES I 2  316
        AND THOU DEEMEDST CATS WERE KIND  . . . . . .  453 POOR MATTHIAS     38
        PROVE US SO REMOTE IN KIND  . . . . . . . .  457 POOR MATTHIAS    156

KINDLE
        WE CANNOT KINDLE WHEN WE WILL  . . . . . . .  241 MORALITY             1
        KINDLE THEIR HEARTS MAKE THEM NO MORE A MOB  . .  383 MEROPE          1360
        BUT NOW YE KINDLE  . . . . . . . . . . .  437 EMPEDOCLES II    288
        BUT NOW YOU KINDLE  . . . . . . . . . . .  437 EMPEDOCLES II  V 288

KINDLED
        HE SPOKE AND SOHRAB KINDLED AT HIS TAUNTS  . . .   75 SOHRAB RUSTUM    470
        SHOULD BE AS SOON AS KINDLED COOLD  . . . . .  182 TO MARG CONT      20
        AND HIS EYE KINDLED WITH THE KINDLING FRAY  . . .  475 CROMWELL         137
        THE SOLDIER KINDLED AT HIS WORDS OF FIRE  . . .  476 CROMWELL         153
        IN THE PLAIN THERE WERE KINDLED A THOUSAND          HOMER TRANS        3
            FIRES BY EACH ONE

KINDLING
        AS THE KINDLING GLANCES  . . . . . . . . .   35 VOICE                1
        AND HIS EYE KINDLED WITH THE KINDLING FRAY  . . .  475 CROMWELL         137

KINDLY
        AND OFTEN TO SOME KINDLY PLACE  . . . . . . .   55 RESIGNATION      112
        TRISTRAM AH FOR LOVE OF HEAVEN SPEAK KINDLY   . .  142 TRISTRAM 2        13
        TRISTRAM FOR THE LOVE OF HEAVEN SPEAK KINDLY  . .  142 TRISTRAM 2     V  13
        WAKES ME THUS KINDLY FROM THE PERILOUS SLEEP  . .  375 MEROPE          1203

KINDNESS
        THAT GERM OF KINDNESS IN THE WOMB  . . . . . .  158 SAINT BRANDAN     61
        HE WEPT THE EARTH HATH KINDNESS  . . . . . .  161 NECKAN            61
        HE SAID THE EARTH HATH KINDNESS  . . . . . .  161 NECKAN         V  61
        HE MUSED THE EARTH HATH KINDNESS  . . . . . .  161 NECKAN         V  61
        THEY ASK NOT KINDNESS GENTLE WAYS  . . . . . .  178 FAREWELL          25
        THEIR KINDNESS SHOWN ME IN MY WANDERING HOUR  . .  447 WESTMIN ABBEY    109
        KINDNESS WE BESTOW AND PRAISE  . . . . . . .  455 POOR MATTHIAS     99

KINDS
        AND FOR THIS DROUGHT ALL KINDS OF FRUITS  . . . .   94 SICK KING BOKH   195

KINE
        CROSSING THE STREAM THE KINE ARE SEEN  . . . .   16 CHURCH BROU 2     10
        WHERE THE LOOMING KINE ARE LAID  . . . . . .   32 NEW SIRENS       182
        THEIR KINE ACROSS A SNOWY MOUNTAIN-PASS  . . . .  107 BALDER DEAD 2     92
        THE KINE WERE RESTING IN THE SHADE  . . . . .  222 EPILOG LAOCOON    40
        THE SPRINGING PASTURES AND THE FEEDING KINE  . .  258 SCHOLAR-GIPSY    108
        OF THE HIGH-PASTURING KINE  . . . . . . . .  307 OBERMANN          32
        WAYS FOR THE PASTURING KINE  . . . . . . . .  312 OBERMANN MORE     16
        WAYS FOR THE TINKLING KINE  . . . . . . . .  312 OBERMANN MORE  V  16

KING
        YE MEN OF EGYPT YE HAVE HEARD YOUR KING  . . .   11 MYCERINUS         73
        HERE CAME THE KING HOLDING HIGH FEAST AT MORN  . .   11 MYCERINUS         92
        TO TELL HIS WONDERING PEOPLE OF THEIR KING  . . .   12 MYCERINUS        125
        PROUDLY LIKE A KING BEWAILING  . . . . . . .   34 NEW SIRENS       225
        OR DO I WAIT TO HEAR SOME GRAY-HAIRD KING  . . .   43 GIPSY CHILD       33
        HE SPAKE THE GREAT KING HEARD  . . . . . . .   47 WORLD QUIETIST    28
        HE SPOKE THE GREAT KING HEARD  . . . . . . .   47 WORLD QUIETIST  V 28
        FOR SO DID KING AFRASIAB BID ME SEEK  . . . . .   62 SOHRAB RUSTUM     38
        OR IN SOME QUARREL WITH THE PERSIAN KING  . . .   63 SOHRAB RUSTUM     85
        SECOND AND WAS THE UNCLE OF THE KING  . . . . .   66 SOHRAB RUSTUM    173
        AM OLDER IF THE YOUNG ARE WEAK THE KING  . . . .   67 SOHRAB RUSTUM    222
        ERRS STRANGELY FOR THE KING FOR KAI KHOSROO  . .   67 SOHRAB RUSTUM    223
        WITH THAT OLD KING HER FATHER WHO GROWS GREY  . .   78 SOHRAB RUSTUM    591
        AND THAT OLD KING HER FATHER WHO LOVED WELL  . .   79 SOHRAB RUSTUM    625
        THEM AND THEIR DUES THIS DAY THE KING  . . . .   87 SICK KING BOKH     3
        O HUSSEIN LEAD ME TO THE KING  . . . . . . .   87 SICK KING BOKH    10
        O KING THOU KNOWST I HAVE BEEN SICK  . . . . .   88 SICK KING BOKH    22
        NOT EVEN WHAT THOU DOST O KING  . . . . . . .   88 SICK KING BOKH    25
        JUSTICE O KING AND ON MYSELF  . . . . . . .   89 SICK KING BOKH    36
        VENGEANCE O KING BUT THE KING SPAKE  . . . . .   89 SICK KING BOKH    39
        VENGEANCE O KING BUT THE KING SPAKE  . . . . .   89 SICK KING BOKH    39
        AS THE KING SAID SO IT WAS DONE  . . . . . .   89 SICK KING BOKH    44
        BUT ON THE MORROW WHEN THE KING  . . . . . .   89 SICK KING BOKH    46
        CRIES OUT MOST EARNESTLY O KING  . . . . . .   89 SICK KING BOKH    52
        MY LORD O KING DO RIGHT I PRAY  . . . . . . .   89 SICK KING BOKH    53
        IF I SPEAK FOLLY BUT A KING  . . . . . . . .   89 SICK KING BOKH    55
        IT IS SOME MADMAN THE KING SAID  . . . . . .   90 SICK KING BOKH    91
```

KING (CONTINUED)

AS THE KING BADE SO WAS IT DONE	90 SICK KING BOKH	92
FROWNING GRIM DOWN THOU WICKED KING	91 SICK KING BOKH	97
THEN THEY WHO STOOD ABOUT THE KING	91 SICK KING BOKH	105
TILL THAT THE KING STOOD FORTH AND SAID	91 SICK KING BOKH	107
NOW THE KING CHARGED US SECRETLY	91 SICK KING BOKH	113
SO SAYING THE KING TOOK A STONE	91 SICK KING BOKH	117
AND TRULY WHILE I SPEAK O KING	92 SICK KING BOKH	129
O KING IN THIS I PRAISE THEE NOT	92 SICK KING BOKH	133
STILL THOU ART KING AND THE LAW STANDS	92 SICK KING BOKH	138
NO NOR ON THIS DEAD DOG O KING	93 SICK KING BOKH	180
IN VAIN HATH A KING POWER TO BUILD	94 SICK KING BOKH	198
BECAUSE A KING SHALL BURY HIM	95 SICK KING BOKH	232
VENGEANCE O KING BUT THE KING SPOKE	89 SICK KING BOKH V	39
VENGEANCE O KING BUT THE KING SPOKE	89 SICK KING BOKH V	39
AS THE KING SAID SO WAS IT DONE	89 SICK KING BOKH V	44
AS THE KING SAID SO WAS IT DONE	90 SICK KING BOKH V	92
SO SPAKE THE KING OF GODS AND STRAIGHTWAY ROSE	96 BALDER DEAD 1	46
HIGH OVER ASGARD TO LIGHT HOME THE KING	102 BALDER DEAD 1	257
SO HAVING SPOKE THE KING OF GODS AROSE	96 BALDER DEAD 1 V	46
THAN BE A CROWND KING HERE AND RULE THE DEAD	112 BALDER DEAD 2	267
FOLLOWD IN TEARS THEIR FATHER AND THEIR KING	115 BALDER DEAD 3	60
A KING WHOSE FAME THEN FILLD THE VAST OF HEAVEN	117 BALDER DEAD 3	129
OF KING MARC TO BE HIS BRIDE	132 TRISTRAM 1	62
GAVE HER THAT KING MARC AND SHE	134 TRISTRAM 1	138
IN KING MARCS CHAPEL IN TYNTAGEL OLD	149 TRISTRAM 3	3
AT TYNTAGIL IN KING MARCS CHAPEL OLD	149 TRISTRAM 3 V	3
MAN MAN IS THE KING OF THE WORLD	233 YOUTH OF MAN	27
FOR MAN IS THE KING OF THE WORLD	233 YOUTH OF MAN V	27
IN THE HOT CORNFIELD OF THE PHRYGIAN KING	268 THYRSIS	183
CHRISTIAN AND PAGAN KING AND SLAVE	311 OBERMANN	149
MY GRANDFATHER THE GOOD ARCADIAN KING	331 MEROPE	33
OF FAITHFUL FONDNESS FOR THEIR FORMER KING	331 MEROPE	39
THE KING I KNOW HIM EVEN THROUGH MANY YEARS	332 MEROPE	63
THE KING CRESPHONTES THY GREAT HUSBAND FALL	333 MEROPE	118
LET US IN MARRIAGE KING AND QUEEN UNITE	335 MEROPE	167
AND FUTURE KING BEFORE THIS PEOPLES EYES	335 MEROPE	172
TO THEIR DEAD KING THY HUSBAND YEA TOO DEAR	335 MEROPE	175
THAN THEY THESE AND THE DORIAN LORDS WHOSE KING	337 MEROPE	223
IF THIS WAS FEAR OF THEM IT SHAMED THE KING	337 MEROPE	252
BEHOLD O KING FROM THE DARK	342 MEROPE	390
HUSBAND AND KING TO THY GRAVE	342 MEROPE	401
SENT FORTH ECHEMUS THE VICTOR THE KING	344 MEROPE	442
SLEW THEIR ENEMIES KING TISAMENUS	344 MEROPE	451
A KING A KING WAS HE WHILE HE LIVED	345 MEROPE	472
A KING A KING WAS HE WHILE HE LIVED	345 MEROPE	472
HEAR US AND HELP US SHADE OF OUR KING	348 MEROPE	541
O KING ALL HAIL I COME WITH WEIGHTY NEWS	354 MEROPE	710
ALL THIS O KING NOT PIECEMEAL AS TO THEE	358 MEROPE	827
COME BUT BEEN INTERCEPTED BY THE KING	361 MEROPE	919
ARRIVED AND OF THE KING HAD SPEECH BUT NOW	361 MEROPE	921
THE MESSAGE BROUGHT WAS FOR THE KING DESIGND	361 MEROPE	923
HE KEPT HIS TALE THEN FOR THE KING ALONE	362 MEROPE	928
TO AEPYTUS THE KING SEDUCED WITH GOLD	364 MEROPE	970
TO PLY TWIXT THE MESSENIAN KING AND HIM	364 MEROPE	981
YOUR KING DESIRED THE PROFIT OF HIS DEATH	365 MEROPE	990
AMPHIARAOS OR MYCENAES KING	367 MEROPE	1034
I GO I GO THE KING HOLDS COUNCIL THERE	368 MEROPE	1077
ALL-COVERING DARKNESS O KING	372 MEROPE	1141
TAKE NOT WITH HIM TO COUNCIL DID THE KING	373 MEROPE	1192
HERE BRING HIM ERE THE KING COME BACK FROM COUNCIL	379 MEROPE	1262
THE STRICKEN KING A SECOND ENEMY	381 MEROPE	1297
AGAINST THE KING HIMSELF ARRAY THE HOST	382 MEROPE	1320
THE KING RETURN AND FIND YOU PRATING HERE	386 MEROPE	1443
IMMERSED IN SERIOUS STATE-CRAFT IS THE KING	387 MEROPE	1489
BLOOD-SEVERD BUT MESSENIAS KING AND QUEEN	394 MEROPE	1720
HE IS AND BY THE PEOPLE HAILD FOR KING	401 MEROPE	1890
TILL PRESENTLY THE KING CAME FORTH IN ROBE	401 MEROPE	1903
WITH HIM CONFERRING THE KING SLOWLY REACHD	401 MEROPE	1907
THE AXE AND ON THE FOREHEAD OF THE KING	402 MEROPE	1920
BUT GAZING AT HIM FROM THE GROUND THE KING	402 MEROPE	1927
THE DORIANS LYING DEAD THY SON HAILD KING	402 MEROPE	1942
THINE ENEMY IS SLAIN THY SON IS KING	403 MEROPE	1957
OF FAITHFUL FONDNESS TOWARDS THEIR FORMER KING	331 MEROPE V	39
HIS PRESENCE WITH THE KING THOU MEANST IMPLIES	365 MEROPE V	
OF THE MOUNTAIN-CRUSHD TORTURED INTRACTABLE TITAN KING	432 EMPEDOCLES II	98
KING SEBERTS WORK THE WONDROUS MINSTER NEW	444 WESTMIN ABBEY	16
AT DAWN THOU TO KING SEBERT SHALT RELATE	445 WESTMIN ABBEY	48
THE CHARMD BABE OF THE ELEUSINIAN KING	446 WESTMIN ABBEY	85

KINGDOM

TO HELAS KINGDOM TO ASK BALDER BACK	102 BALDER DEAD 1	237
TO HELAS KINGDOM TO ASK BALDER BACK	106 BALDER DEAD 2	46
INTO THE JOYLESS KINGDOM HAVE I BEEN	114 BALDER DEAD 3	38
TO RULE THIS KINGDOM I INTEND WITH SWAY	342 MEROPE	376
OF HEIRSHIP TO HIS KINGDOM FOR MY SON	366 MEROPE	999
TREATY AND TO THIS KINGDOM FOR MY SON	387 MEROPE	1483
OUR FATHERS KINGDOM BECAUSE PURE IS SAFE	389 MEROPE	1533
TO THE MESSENIAN KINGDOM THOU AND I	394 MEROPE	1692
O KINGDOM OF MESSENE	399 MEROPE	1847

KINGDOMS
    FOR THE THREE CONQUERD KINGDOMS OF THIS ISLE   • •   389 MEROPE   1549

KINGLY
    AND ODIN CAME AND LAID HIS KINGLY HANDS   • • • •   115 BALDER DEAD 3   65
    AND KINGLY GAIT FOR EVER SUCH A SPELL   • • • •   408 EMPEDOCLES I 1   61
    THEN LIKE A KINGLY RIVER SWIFT AND STRONG   • • • •   475 CROMWELL   133
    AND ONE SWAYD ALL WHO WORE A KINGLY CROWN   • • • •   476 CROMWELL   143
    SO SADLY CALM SO KINGLY SO SERENE   • • • • • •   477 CROMWELL   186

KINGS
    ENNOBLING THIS DULL POMP THE LIFE OF KINGS • • • •   9 MYCERINUS   11
    KINGS HOLD REVEL GALLANTS MEET • • • • • • • •   14 CHURCH BROU 1   54
    LIKE THOSE KINGS WITH TREASURE STEERING   • • • •   26 NEW SIRENS   21
    TROOPS LIKE EASTERN KINGS APPEARING   • • • • •   26 NEW SIRENS   V 23
    A WHITE-ROBED SLAVE STOLE TO THE GREAT KINGS SIDE   •   47 WORLD QUIETIST   27
    THE TARTARS OF THE OXUS THE KINGS GUARD   • • • •   64 SOHRAB RUSTUM   117
    AND LEAVE TO DEATH THE HOSTS OF THANKLESS KINGS   •   68 SOHRAB RUSTUM   240
    THE TARTARS OF BOKHARA THE KINGS GUARD   • • • •   64 SOHRAB RUSTUM   V 117
    O VIZIER HERE IS THE KINGS DOOR   • • • • • •   88 SICK KING BOKH   20
    AND FELL AT THE KINGS FEET AND CRIED   • • • • •   88 SICK KING BOKH   35
    IN THE KINGS PATH BEHOLD THE MAN   • • • • • •   90 SICK KING BOKH   94
    LO I AM OLD THREE KINGS ERE THEE   • • • • •   92 SICK KING BOKH   143
    THE KINGS OF THE SEA   • • • • • • • • • •   165 FORSAKEN MERM   123
    THE KINGS OF THE SEA   • • • • • • • • • •   165 FORSAKEN MERM   143
    UPON THEIR CARAVAN OR GREEDY KINGS   • • • • •   193 STRAYED REVEL   249
    AS FROM THE KINGS OF SOUND ARE BLOWN   • • • • •   222 EPILOG LAOCOON   34
    A PALACE OF THE KINGS OF FRANCE   • • • • • •   300 GRANDE CHARTR   24
    THE KINGS OF MODERN THOUGHT ARE DUMB   • • • • •   303 GRANDE CHARTR   116
    FOR THE KINGS PRIVATE EAR RESERVES LIKE THIS   • •   364 MEROPE   965
    AS MUCH TO THE KINGS WISH MORE TO HIS SHAME   • •   364 MEROPE   968
    IN A KINGS HOUSE THY VICTIMS HERITAGE   • • •   373 MEROPE   1179
    FOR THIS IS THE TRUE STRENGTH OF GUILTY KINGS   • •   386 MEROPE   1436
    THE SIMPLE PATRIARCHAL STATE OF KINGS   • • •   388 MEROPE   1516
    THIS AWE WHICH GUARDS OUR EARTH-SPRUNG LINEAL KINGS   389 MEROPE   1543
    THAT KINGS LIVE FOR THEIR PEOPLES NOT THEMSELVES   •   394 MEROPE   1715
    THE CONQUERORS WITH THE KINGS DEAD BODY COME   • •   403 MEROPE   1953
    WE MORTALS ARE NO KINGS   • • • • • • • •   418 EMPEDOCLES I 2   177
    THE LINES OF DECEASED KINGS   • • • • • • •   423 EMPEDOCLES I 2   325
    PAGEANTS HAVE PASSD AND TOMBS OF MIGHTY KINGS   • •   445 WESTMIN ABBEY   53
    THY DEAD ARE KINGS THY DUST ARE PALACES   • • •   464 ALARIC AT ROME   61
    LIKE STONE-SCULPTURED ANTIQUE KINGS   • • • • •   META CLOISTER   4

KINSFOLK
    SHE SAID I MUST GO FOR MY KINSFOLK PRAY   • • • •   163 FORSAKEN MERM   56
    A COUNTRY FOR HIM KINSFOLK AND A HOME   • • • •   195 FRAG ANTIGONE   14
    THY KINSFOLK AND THY FATHERS FRIENDS FOR AID   • •   384 MEROPE   1389

KINSMAN
    I HIS CHIEF KINSMAN I HIS PIONEER   • • • • • •   338 MEROPE   267
    KINSMAN THOU SLEWST THY KINSMAN FRIEND THY FRIEND   338 MEROPE   281
    KINSMAN THOU SLEWST THY KINSMAN FRIEND THY FRIEND   338 MEROPE   281
    WHAT FOLLOWD HIS MOST TRUSTED KINSMAN SLEW • • • •   389 MEROPE   1555
    HIS KINSMAN HIS RIGHT HAND IN PEACE AND WAR   • •   403 MEROPE   1974

KINSMEN
    FOR WE WERE KINSMEN MORE THAN KINSMEN FRIENDS   • •   334 MEROPE   122
    FOR WE WERE KINSMEN MORE THAN KINSMEN FRIENDS   • •   334 MEROPE   122
    WHO BUT THE KINSMEN OF THE ROYAL BROOD   • • •   336 MEROPE   221
    PANTHEIA FOR I KNOW HER KINSMEN WELL   • • • • •   410 EMPEDOCLES I 1   135

KIPCHAK
    WHO ROAM OER KIPCHAK AND THE NORTHERN WASTE   • •   65 SOHRAB RUSTUM   131
    WHO COME FROM KIPCHAK AND THE NORTHERN WASTE   • •   65 SOHRAB RUSTUM   V 131
    WHO DWELL IN KIPCHAK AND THE NORTHERN WASTE   • •   65 SOHRAB RUSTUM   V 131
    WHO ROVE OER KIPCHAK AND THE NORTHERN WASTE   • •   65 SOHRAB RUSTUM   V 131

KIRGHIZZES
    NEAREST THE POLE AND WANDERING KIRGHIZZES   • • • •   65 SOHRAB RUSTUM   133

KISS
    ERE THE PARTING KISS BE DRY   • • • • • • •   22 MEMORY-PICTURE   V
    MY HEAD BETWIXT THY HANDS AND KISS MY CHEEKS   • •   82 SOHRAB RUSTUM   719
    ONE SUCH KISS AS THOSE OF YORE • • • • • • •   132 TRISTRAM 1   78
    ONE LAST KISS FIRST TIS VAIN TO HORSE AWAY • • •   135 TRISTRAM 1   169
    AND THAT LONG WILD KISS THEIR LAST • • • • •   136 TRISTRAM 1   180
    WHERE DO THE CHILDREN SLEEP KISS THEM FOR ME   • •   140 TRISTRAM 1   311
    ONE LAST KISS UPON THE LIVING SHORE   • • • • •   145 TRISTRAM 2   98
    AND PART MY HAIR AND KISS MY BROW   • • • • • •   209 LONGING   11
    AND KISS CONJECTURED JOYS OR FEAR CONJECTURED WOES   425 EMPEDOCLES I 2   V 406
    VAINLY KISS HIS GOLDEN CREST   • • • • • • •   452 POOR MATTHIAS   10

KISSD
    ENTERING HEEDLESS KISSD BY THEE   • • • • • •   23 MEMORY-PICTURE   20
    HIS ARMS ABOUT HIS NECK AND KISSD HIS LIPS • • •   81 SOHRAB RUSTUM   695
    AND KISSD HIM AND AWE FELL ON BOTH THE HOSTS   • •   82 SOHRAB RUSTUM   729
    AND FROM THE WAVE-KISSD MARBLE STAIR   • • • • •   278 SOUTHERN NIGHT   106

KNEAD
    KNEAD US IN ITS HOT HAND AND CHANGE OUR NATURE   440 EMPEDOCLES II   386

KNEE
    WORLD HAVE THY CHILDREN YET BOWD AT HIS KNEE   20 MODERN SAPPHO   34
    AND THE YOUNGEST SATE ON HER KNEE   163 FORSAKEN MERM   52
    UPON THE WALL THE KNEE-WORN FLOOR   300 GRANDE CHARTR   46
    KNEE-DEEP IN THE COOL FORD FOR TIS THE LAST   413 EMPEDOCLES I 2   41

KNEEL
    THAT LADY BY THE BED DOTH KNEEL   149 TRISTRAM 2   181
    AND AT HER PRIE-DIEU KNEEL UNTIL SHE HAVE TOLD   152 TRISTRAM 3   92
    WITH PENITENTIAL CRIES THEY KNEEL   300 GRANDE CHARTR   39

KNEELD
    KNEELD DOWN AND CRIED NOT NEITHER RAN   91 SICK KING BOKH   120
    KNEELD AND DID HOMAGE TO THE SOLEMN QUEEN   112 BALDER DEAD 2   283

KNEELING
    BUT RUSTUM EYED ASKANCE THE KNEELING YOUTH   71 SOHRAB RUSTUM   345
    NOT KNEELING STERNLY FIXD HE STOOD   90 SICK KING BOKH   95
    AND REMAIND KNEELING AS BEFORE   91 SICK KING BOKH   124
    WHO IS THAT KNEELING LADY FAIR   148 TRISTRAM 2   165

KNEES
    AND HE RAN FORWARD AND EMBRACED HIS KNEES   71 SOHRAB RUSTUM   341
    TO HIS KNEES AND WITH HIS FINGERS CLUTCHD THE SAND   73 SOHRAB RUSTUM   421
    DIZZY AND ON HIS KNEES AND CHOKED WITH SAND   74 SOHRAB RUSTUM   424
    AND HIS KNEES TOTTERD AND HE SMOTE HIS HAND   80 SOHRAB RUSTUM   662
    AND HE RAN FORWARDS AND EMBRACED HIS KNEES   71 SOHRAB RUSTUM   V 341
    TO HIS KNEES AND WITH HIS FINGERS GRASPD THE SAND   73 SOHRAB RUSTUM   V 421
    MAKES THE HEAD WHITE AND BOWS THE KNEES   92 SICK KING BOKH   152
    AND FELL BEFORE HER FEET AND CLASPD HER KNEES   110 BALDER DEAD 2   187
    SINK UPON HIS MIGHTY KNEES   431 EMPEDOCLES II   73

KNEW
    TOOK MEASURE OF HIS SOUL AND KNEW ITS STRENGTH   12 MYCERINUS   109
    GONE O KNIGHTS IS SHE YOU KNEW   15 CHURCH BROU 1   82
    GUESTS THE DULL SENSE NEVER KNEW   30 NEW SIRENS   136
    AND ALL THE PERSIANS KNEW HIM AND WITH SHOUTS   69 SOHRAB RUSTUM   282
    HAILD BUT THE TARTARS KNEW NOT WHO HE WAS   69 SOHRAB RUSTUM   283
    SO RUSTUM KNEW NOT HIS OWN LOSS BUT STOOD   78 SOHRAB RUSTUM   574
    OVER HIS DYING SON AND KNEW HIM NOT   78 SOHRAB RUSTUM   575
    WHO SPOKE ALTHOUGH HE CALLD BACK NAMES HE KNEW   79 SOHRAB RUSTUM   606
    FOR WELL HE KNEW THE GODS WOULD HEED HIS WORD   97 BALDER DEAD 1   59
    POSTURES OF RUNES AND HEALING HERBS HE KNEW   101 BALDER DEAD 1   211
    FROM THE SEA CITYWARD AND KNEW HIS STEP   101 BALDER DEAD 1   227
    THEN HERMOD KNEW WHAT LABOUR HELD THE GODS   113 BALDER DEAD 2   307
    MOCKING AND HERMOD KNEW THEIR TOIL WAS VAIN   123 BALDER DEAD 3   356
    THE WAY HE KNEW AND TRAVERSED GIALLS STREAM   124 BALDER DEAD 3   375
    AND HERMOD LOOKD AND KNEW HIS BROTHERS GHOST   124 BALDER DEAD 3   385
    ON EARTH MY CRIME MY DEATH THEY KNEW   157 SAINT BRANDAN   26
    I MET A PREACHER THERE I KNEW AND SAID   169 EAST LONDON   5
    PROLONGD NOR KNEW ALTHOUGH NOT LESS   181 ISOLATION MARG   41
    I KNEW IT WHEN MY LIFE WAS YOUNG   185 TERRACE BERNE   49
    I KNEW NOT YET THE GAUGE OF TIME   242 MORALITY   31
    I KNEW THE MASS OF MEN CONCEALD   245 BURIED LIFE   16
    I KNEW THEY LIVED AND MOVED   245 BURIED LIFE   20
    TWO SCHOLARS WHOM AT COLLEGE ERST HE KNEW   256 SCHOLAR-GIPSY   42
    AND KNEW THE INTRUDERS ON HIS ANCIENT HOME   262 SCHOLAR-GIPSY   240
    BUT ONCE I KNEW EACH FIELD EACH FLOWER EACH STICK   263 THYRSIS   32
    HE KNEW WHICH MADE HIM DROOP AND FILLD HIS HEAD   264 THYRSIS   47
    SHE KNEW THE DORIAN WATERS GUSH DIVINE   265 THYRSIS   94
    SHE KNEW EACH LILY WHITE WHICH ENNA YIELDS   265 THYRSIS   95
    I KNEW HIS SPIRITS LOW   272 EDW QUILLINAN   2
    KNEW NO FELLOW FOR MIGHT   284 HAWORTH CHURCH   94
    NOT AS SERVANTS YE KNEW   291 RUGBY CHAPEL   164
    ONLY A MOMENT I KNEW   294 HEINES GRAVE   52
    BURIED I KNEW HE WAS YOURS   294 HEINES GRAVE   54
    AH I KNEW THAT I SAW   294 HEINES GRAVE   55
    THOSE PENSIVE FEATURES WELL I KNEW   314 OBERMANN MORE   61
    NO PAUSE ITS ACTION KNEW   315 OBERMANN MORE   88
    THE WORN-OUT WORLD WE KNEW   319 OBERMANN MORE   206
    AND KNEW MY LIFE WAS VAIN   321 OBERMANN MORE   266
    AH ME WE ANCHORITES KNEW IT BEST   314 OBERMANN MORE   V 75
    THE OUT-WORN WORLD WE KNEW   319 OBERMANN MORE   V 206
    FOR WELL HE KNEW WHAT YOU HIS CHIEFS DID NOT   339 MEROPE   306
    YOUR QUEEN WHAT IS THIS YE KNEW   371 MEROPE   1126
    WHAT I KNEW I CONCEALD   371 MEROPE   1132
    FIXD HIM THE AUTHOR OF MY DEATH I KNEW NOT   379 MEROPE   V1273
    HE KNEW ME WELL AND WOULD OFT NOTICE ME   408 EMPEDOCLES I 1   57
    THE BOORS WITH WHOM HE TALKD THE COUNTRY-SPOTS HE KNEW   426 EMPEDOCLES I 2   416
    KNEW CARE AND KNEW UNREST   447 WESTMIN ABBEY   122
    KNEW CARE AND KNEW UNREST   447 WESTMIN ABBEY   122
    WELL HE KNEW HIS MISTRESS DEAR   452 POOR MATTHIAS   6
    WELL WE KNEW WHEN THEY WERE GLAD   455 POOR MATTHIAS   89
    ALAS THAT FIERY SPIRIT LITTLE KNEW   469 ALARIC AT ROME   187
    EYES THAT HE KNEW OLD FACES UNFORGOT   474 CROMWELL   85
    MORE CALM MORE DEEP THAN CHILDHOOD EVER KNEW   475 CROMWELL   116
    A FORM HE KNEW BUT IT WAS SHROUDED THEN   476 CROMWELL   146
    THAT KNEW NOT EARTH SOARD UPWARDS TO THE SKY   477 CROMWELL   178

KNIFE
    DRIFTING KNIFE IN HAND   • • • • • • • • • • 190 STRAYED REVEL   152
    AND BEGAN TO WHET HIS KNIFE   • • • • • • • • 433 EMPEDOCLES II   150

KNIGHT
    WHAT KNIGHT IS THIS SO WEAK AND PALE • • • • • • 130 TRISTRAM 1   9
    THE PEERLESS HUNTER HARPER KNIGHT • • • • • • 131 TRISTRAM 1   22
    MIGHT THY DYING KNIGHT RESTORE • • • • • • • 132 TRISTRAM 1   79
    AND THE KNIGHT SINKS BACK ON HIS PILLOWS AGAIN   • 133 TRISTRAM 1   84
    BUT THE BRILLIANT YOUTHFUL KNIGHT • • • • • • 134 TRISTRAM 1   109
    CHATTING WITH HER YOUTHFUL KNIGHT   • • • • • 134 TRISTRAM 1   127
    THE LOVE-DESPERATE BANISHD KNIGHT   • • • • • 136 TRISTRAM 1   186
    OF THAT STRANGER-KNIGHT ILL-STARRD • • • • • 136 TRISTRAM 1   200
    UP TRISTRAM UP MEN CRY THOU MOONSTRUCK KNIGHT   • 137 TRISTRAM 1   238
    THERES MANY A GAY KNIGHT WHERE HE GOES • • • • 138 TRISTRAM 1   256
    AND ON HIS PILLOWS THAT PALE KNIGHT • • • • • 148 TRISTRAM 2   166
    WHO WEPT AT READING OF A GRECIAN KNIGHT • • • 153 TRISTRAM 3   144
    SINGS HOW A KNIGHT HE WANDERD • • • • • • 159 NECKAN   17
    SIR KNIGHT WHO WEDDST TO-DAY • • • • • • • 159 NECKAN   24
    I AM NO KNIGHT HE ANSWERED • • • • • • • 159 NECKAN   25
    SOME GREY CRUSADING KNIGHT AUSTERE • • • • 278 SOUTHERN NIGHT   93
    BUT YOU A GRAVE FOR KNIGHT OR SAGE • • • • 279 SOUTHERN NIGHT 113

KNIGHTLY
    THROUGH SOME OLD SEA-SIDE KNIGHTLY HALL   • • • • 148 TRISTRAM 2   178

KNIGHTS
    AUSTRIAN KNIGHTS FROM SYRIA CAME   • • • • • 15 CHURCH BROU 1   78
    GONE O KNIGHTS IS SHE YOU KNEW • • • • • • • 15 CHURCH BROU 1   82
    AUSTRIAN KNIGHTS AND MARCH-WORN PALMERS • • • 15 CHURCH BROU 1   85
    WHILE THE KNIGHTS ARE AT THE WARS • • • • • 131 TRISTRAM 1   44
    THAT THE KNIGHTS EYED HER IN SURPRISE • • • • 146 TRISTRAM 2   123
    THAT KNIGHTS ASLEEP AND AT HER PRAYER • • • • 149 TRISTRAM 2   180
    BUT EARTHLY KNIGHTS HAVE HARDER HEARTS • • • 159 NECKAN   19
    PRIEST KNIGHTS AND LADIES GAY • • • • • • • 159 NECKAN   22
    THE KNIGHTS DREW SWORD THE LADIES SCREAMD • • 159 NECKAN   27
    A THOUSAND KNIGHTS HAVE REIND THEIR STEEDS • • • 204 CALAIS SANDS   1

KNIT
    HIS SOUL WELL-KNIT AND ALL HIS BATTLES WON • • • 172 IMMORTALITY   13
    KNIT ALL YOUR PARTS AND KEPT YOU ONE • • • • • 320 OBERMANN MORE   223
    CLOSER KNIT THEIR LIFE WITH OURS • • • • • • 453 POOR MATTHIAS   46

KNOCK
    ◢KNOCK PASS THE WICKET THOU ART COME • • • • • 300 GRANDE CHARTR   29

KNOCKING
    WHO TIRED OF KNOCKING AT PREFERMENTS DOOR • • • • 256 SCHOLAR-GIPSY   35

KNOLL
    ON THAT CLEAR FOREST-KNOLL HE STAYS • • • • • 148 TRISTRAM 2   155
    FAR ON ITS ROCKY KNOLL DESCRIED • • • • • • 273 STANZAS CARNAC   1

KNOLLS
    AND GATHERD ON IMMORTAL KNOLLS • • • • • • • • 227 EPILOG LAOCOON 203

KNOT
    TIS TRUE INDEED AN IRON KNOT • • • • • • • • 208 ON THE RHINE   7

KNOTS
    SCORES OF TRUE LOVE KNOTS ARE BREAKING • • • 35 NEW SIRENS   261
    IN DARK KNOTS CROUCH ROUND THE WILD FLAME • • • 55 RESIGNATION   118
    THE GODS HELD TALK TOGETHER GROUPD IN KNOTS • • 113 BALDER DEAD 3   1

KNOW
    AND THOU WHO DIDST THE STARS AND SUNBEAMS KNOW • • 3 SHAKESPEARE   9
    AND THOU WHOSE HEAD DID STARS AND SUNBEAMS KNOW • • 3 SHAKESPEARE V   9
    IT CHANCED I KNOW NOT HOW MY DREAM WAS FLED   EMERSONS ESSAYS V   8
    IT CHANCED I KNOW NOT HOW MY JOY WAS FLED • • • EMERSONS ESSAYS V   8
    KNOW MAN HATH ALL WHICH NATURE HATH BUT MORE • • 5 HARMONY NATURE   5
    MAN MUST BEGIN KNOW THIS WHERE NATURE ENDS • • • 5 HARMONY NATURE   12
    KNOW THOU THE WORST SO MUCH NOT MORE HE CAN • • 6 GEO CRUIKSHANK   14
    SOMETHING YET WHAT I KNOW NOT FOR THE GODS • • • 10 MYCERINUS   69
    THEIR LOVE LET ME KNOW MUST GROW STRONG AND   19 MODERN SAPPHO   13
        YET STRONGER
    ONLY WHAT WE FEEL WE KNOW • • • • • • • 29 NEW SIRENS   84
    THOU WHO DOST KNOW THINE OWN • • • • • • • 38 STAGIRIUS   2
    CRITIAS LONG SINCE I KNOW • • • • • • • 46 WORLD QUIETIST   9
    ACTION AND SUFFERING THOUGH HE KNOW • • • • 56 RESIGNATION   152
    WHO NEEDS NOT LOVE AND POWER TO KNOW • • • • 59 RESIGNATION   235
    FAIN WOULD I KNOW THEE SAFE AND WELL THOUGH LOST • • 63 SOHRAB RUSTUM   88
    ALL BEASTS OF CHASE ALL BEASTS WHICH HUNTERS KNOW   69 SOHRAB RUSTUM 279
    FOR WELL I KNOW THAT DID GREAT RUSTUM STAND • • 72 SOHRAB RUSTUM 370
    AND THOU ART PROVED I KNOW AND I AM YOUNG • • • 72 SOHRAB RUSTUM 386
    THY VICTORY YET THOU CANST NOT SURELY KNOW • • 72 SOHRAB RUSTUM 389
    WE KNOW NOT AND NO SEARCH WILL MAKE US KNOW • • 73 SOHRAB RUSTUM 396
    WE KNOW NOT AND NO SEARCH WILL MAKE US KNOW • • 73 SOHRAB RUSTUM 396
    SOMEWHERE I KNOW NOT WHERE BUT FAR FROM HERE • • 78 SOHRAB RUSTUM 583
    I KNOW IT BUT FATE TROD THOSE PROMPTINGS DOWN • • 82 SOHRAB RUSTUM 713
    FOR WILLINGLY I KNOW THOU METST THINE END • • • 85 SOHRAB RUSTUM 823

KNOW   (CONTINUED)

YET IN MY SECRET MIND ONE WAY I KNOW • • • • • •   99 BALDER DEAD 1   128
UNHAPPY BUT THAT ART HE DID NOT KNOW • • • •   101 BALDER DEAD 1   212
AND WELL I KNOW THAT BY NO STROKE OF DEATH • • • •   103 BALDER DEAD 1   305
SHOULDERING HIS HAMMER WHICH THE GIANTS KNOW • •   106 BALDER DEAD 2   49
UPON MY BRIDGE AND WHEN THEY CROSS I KNOW • • •   108 BALDER DEAD 2   121
SO SHALL I KNOW THE LOST WAS DEAR INDEED • • •   111 BALDER DEAD 2   239
SO SHALL SHE KNOW YOUR LOSS WAS DEAR INDEED • •   115 BALDER DEAD 3   45
NOW AND I KNOW NOT HOW THEY PRIZE THEE THERE • •   115 BALDER DEAD 3   77
BUT HERE I KNOW THOU WILT BE MISSD AND MOURND • •   115 BALDER DEAD 3   78
SO BALDER SAID BUT ODER WELL I KNOW • • • • •   117 BALDER DEAD 3   119
YE GODS THE TERMS YE KNOW WHICH HERMOD BROUGHT • •   120 BALDER DEAD 3   225
AND ALL THAT IS TO COME I KNOW BUT LOCK • • • •   121 BALDER DEAD 3   286
NIORD THE GOD OF STORMS WHOM FISHERS KNOW • • •   122 BALDER DEAD 3   323
BUT NOT TO ME SO GRIEVOUS AS I KNOW • • • • •   127 BALDER DEAD 3   500
I KNOW HIM BY HIS HARP OF GOLD • • • • • •   131 TRISTRAM 1   19
I KNOW HIM BY HIS FOREST-DRESS • • • • • •   131 TRISTRAM 1   21
I KNOW HER BY HER MILDNESS RARE • • • • •   132 TRISTRAM 1   50
I KNOW HER BY HER RICH SILK DRESS • • • • •   132 TRISTRAM 1   52
I KNOW HER BY HER GOLDEN HAIR • • • • •   132 TRISTRAM 1   V   50
ALONG THIS IRON COAST KNOW LIKE A STAR • • •   151 TRISTRAM 3   81
IN A VOICE THAT SHE WILL KNOW • • • •   161 FORSAKEN MERM   12
I KNOW THAT GRACEFUL FIGURE FAIR • • • • •   174 MEETING   5
I KNOW THAT SOFT ENKERCHIEFD HAIR • • • • •   174 MEETING   7
I BLAME THEE NOT THIS HEART I KNOW • • • •   178 FAREWELL   17
THEN WE SHALL KNOW OUR FRIENDS THOUGH MUCH • •   179 FAREWELL   65
AND THEN THEIR ENDLESS BOUNDS THEY KNOW • •   182 TO MARG CONT   6
FAIL FROM EARTHS AIR AND I NOT KNOW • • • •   184 TERRACE BERNE   32
I WILL NOT KNOW FOR WHEREFORE TRY • • • •   185 TERRACE BERNE   41
I TOO HAVE SUFFERD YET I KNOW • • • • •   201 URANIA   1
AND KNOW HER FRIEND AND WEEP FOR GLEE • •   202 URANIA   27
I TOO HAVE SUFFERD BUT I KNOW • • • • •   201 URANIA   V   1
SOME DAY I SHALL BE COLD I KNOW • • • •   207 ON THE RHINE   2
WHICH OTHERS KNOW OR SAY THEY KNOW • • •   209 DESPONDENCY   3
WHICH OTHERS KNOW OR SAY THEY KNOW • • •   209 DESPONDENCY   3
THE FEELING OF THE MOMENT KNOW • • • • •   225 EPILOG LAOCOON   132
WILL YE NOT LEARN IT AND KNOW • • • • • •   230 YOUTH OF NATURE   87
YE KNOW NOT YOURSELVES AND YOUR BARDS • •   231 YOUTH OF NATURE   103
YOURSELVES AND YOUR FELLOWS YE KNOW NOT AND ME • •   231 YOUTH OF NATURE   117
THE MATELESS THE ONE WILL YE KNOW • • • •   231 YOUTH OF NATURE   118
THIS I KNOW IS THE LAW • • • • •   232 YOUTH OF MAN   3
WELL I KNOW WHAT THEY FEEL • • • • • •   235 YOUTH OF MAN   88
WELL I KNOW WHAT THEY FEEL • • • • • •   235 YOUTH OF MAN   96
AND NEVER KNOW HOW WITH THE SOUL IT FARES • • •   236 PALLADIUM   20
AH WE SHALL KNOW THAT WELL WHEN IT COMES NEAR   239 REVOLUTIONS   19
RESOLVE TO BE THYSELF AND KNOW THAT HE • • •   240 SELF-DEPENDENCE   31
AND I I KNOW NOT IF TO PRAY • • • • • •   243 SUMMER NIGHT   34
NOR DOTH HE KNOW HOW THERE PREVAIL • • •   243 SUMMER NIGHT   56
NOR DOES HE KNOW HOW THERE PREVAIL • • •   243 SUMMER NIGHT   V   56
YES YES WE KNOW THAT WE CAN JEST • • • •   245 BURIED LIFE   4
WE KNOW WE KNOW THAT WE CAN SMILE • • • •   245 BURIED LIFE   5
WE KNOW WHAT WE KNOW THAT WE CAN SMILE • • •   245 BURIED LIFE   5
SO WILD SO DEEP IN US TO KNOW • • • • • •   246 BURIED LIFE   53
AND WHAT WE MEAN WE SAY AND WHAT WE WOULD WE KNOW   247 BURIED LIFE   87
BUT WHAT WAS BEFORE US WE KNOW NOT • • • •   253 FUTURE   69
AND WE KNOW NOT WHAT SHALL SUCCEED • • • •   253 FUTURE   70
AND I MYSELF SEEM HALF TO KNOW THY LOOKS • •   257 SCHOLAR-GIPSY   62
FOR MOST I KNOW THOU LOVST RETIRED GROUND • •   257 SCHOLAR-GIPSY   71
I KNOW THE WOOD WHICH HIDES THE DAFFODIL • •   266 THYRSIS   105
I KNOW THE FYFIELD TREE • • • • • •   266 THYRSIS   106
I KNOW WHAT WHITE WHAT PURPLE FRITILLARIES • •   266 THYRSIS   107
I KNOW THESE SLOPES WHO KNOWS THEM IF NOT I •   266 THYRSIS   111
KNOW HIM A WANDERER STILL THEN WHY NOT ME • •   268 THYRSIS   200
AND HE WAS HAPPY IF TO KNOW • • • • •   271 MEMORIAL VERSES   29
I KNOW NOT WHAT AND INTERPOSED • • • • •   285 HAWORTH CHURCH   111
WE KNOW ALL THIS WE KNOW • • • • • •   295 HEINES GRAVE   115
WE KNOW ALL THIS WE KNOW • • • • • •   295 HEINES GRAVE   115
THERE SOBS I KNOW NOT WHAT GROUND-TONE • •   307 OBERMANN   35
I KNOW BUT TWO WHO HAVE ATTAIND • • • •   307 OBERMANN   47
AND YET I KNOW NOT ALL UNCHANGED • • •   312 OBERMANN MORE   5
AND KNOW NOT YE ARE SEVERD • • • • •   320 OBERMANN MORE   216
AND KNOW NOT THEY ARE SEVERD • • • •   320 OBERMANN MORE V   216
THE KING I KNOW HIM EVEN THROUGH MANY YEARS •   332 MEROPE   63
ALL THIS I BEAR FOR WHAT I SEEK I KNOW • • •   333 MEROPE   100
ALL THIS I KNOW HOW WEAK THE EAGLE HERACLES •   336 MEROPE   212
I KNOW I KNOW HOW HARD IT IS TO THINK • •   341 MEROPE   362
I KNOW I KNOW HOW HARD IT IS TO THINK • •   341 MEROPE   362
THE HEART OF YOUTH I KNOW THAT MOST I FEAR •   351 MEROPE   609
IF THIS BE ALL I KNOW NOT BUT I KNOW • • •   351 MEROPE   620
IF THIS BE ALL I KNOW NOT BUT I KNOW • • •   351 MEROPE   620
BOUNDED IN OUR OWN BREAST WE HARDLY KNOW • •   352 MEROPE   639
A HELPLESS ONE I KNOW IT BUT THE GODS • • •   366 MEROPE   1023
HOW SAY YE MAIDENS DO YE KNOW THESE PRAYERS •   368 MEROPE   1067
THOU KNOWST NOT WHOM THOU STRIKST I KNOW HIS CRIME   374 MEROPE   1199
FIX HIM THE AUTHOR OF MY DEATH I KNOW NOT • •   379 MEROPE   1273
WITH THIS MESSENIAN TYRANT THAT I KNOW • • •   380 MEROPE   1275
FOR KNOW THOU THIS A VIOLENT HEART HATH BEEN •   382 MEROPE   1329
I KNOW SHE HONOURS NOT THE DEAD SO ILL • • •   386 MEROPE   1450
WHICH WAY TO LEAN I KNOW NOT BLOODY STROKES •   388 MEROPE   1521
BUT THAT WE KNOW HOW EVERY PERILOUS FEAT • • •   402 MEROPE   1948

KNOW   (CONTINUED)

I KNOW NOT JUST IN EITHER CASE THE STROKE	404	MEROPE	1986
I KNOW NOT IN WHAT MIND EMPEDOCLES	407	EMPEDOCLES I 1	21
AND STILL I KNOW NOT HOW HE DRAWS ME TO HIM	408	EMPEDOCLES I 1	58
PANTHEIA FOR I KNOW HER KINSMEN WELL	410	EMPEDOCLES I 1	135
TO KNOW THOSE SPELLS OF THINE WHICH STAY THEIR HAND	413	EMPEDOCLES I 2	25
KNOW THAT AND HELP THYSELF BUT THINE OWN WORDS	413	EMPEDOCLES I 2	29
I KNOW THESE NOTES AMONG A THOUSAND HARK	413	EMPEDOCLES I 2	35
AND WE WOULD KNOW IT ALL	423	EMPEDOCLES I 2	318
AND YET FOR THOSE WHO KNOW	425	EMPEDOCLES I 2	387
NOT MUCH I KNOW YOU PRIZE	426	EMPEDOCLES I 2	407
TO KNOW THOSE SPELLS OF TIME THAT STAY THEIR HAND	413	EMPEDOCLES I 2 V	25
TO KNOW THOSE SPELLS OF THINE THAT STAY THEIR HAND	413	EMPEDOCLES I 2 V	25
KNOW THAT AND HELP THYSELF BUT THY OWN WORDS	413	EMPEDOCLES I 2 V	29
I KNOW THOSE NOTES AMONG A THOUSAND HARK	413	EMPEDOCLES I 2 V	35
THESE RUMBLINGS ARE NOT TYPHOS GROANS I KNOW	431	EMPEDOCLES II	95
ABOVE A RACE YOU KNOW NOT	437	EMPEDOCLES II	296
AND THEREFORE O YE ELEMENTS I KNOW	441	EMPEDOCLES II	404
YE KNOW IT TOO IT HATH BEEN GRANTED ME	441	EMPEDOCLES II	405
AND BUILDS HIMSELF I KNOW NOT WHAT	450	GEISTS GRAVE	31
OF SECOND LIFE I KNOW NOT WHERE	450	GEISTS GRAVE	32
TO NAME FOR FUTURE TIMES TO KNOW	452	GEISTS GRAVE	79
THOU DIDST KNOW THEM OLD AND GREY	453	POOR MATTHIAS	29
KNOW THEM IN THEIR SAD DECAY	453	POOR MATTHIAS	30
BUT AS AGE COMES ON I KNOW	454	POOR MATTHIAS	77
KNOW WE MORE OUR FELLOW MEN	457	POOR MATTHIAS	162
ALAS IT NEEDS NOT IS IT HARD TO KNOW	466	ALARIC AT ROME	119
LIT BY A WANDERING GLEAM WE KNOW NOT HOW	475	CROMWELL	128
I OF MYSELF KNOW WELL THAT HERE I AM DESTIND TO PERISH		HOMER TRANS	60
LEARN TO KNOW WHAT IT DESIRED		META CLOISTER	31
IN FRONT OF SOME GREAT FANE WHEREOF WE KNOW		LUCRETIUS 5	7

KNOWEST

THOU KNOWEST BETTER WORDS THAN THIS TO SAY	68	SOHRAB RUSTUM	251
AND THOUGH THOU THINKEST THAT THOU KNOWEST SURE	72	SOHRAB RUSTUM	388
THOU KNOWEST IF SINCE FROM ADER-BAIJAN FIRST	62	SOHRAB RUSTUM V	42
YES THOU KNOWEST IT THIS	369	MEROPE	1097
KNOWEST THOU NOT HOW TIMOROUS HOW UNSURE	381	MEROPE	1311

KNOWING

KNOWING THE GOD THEY WENT TO SEEK HOW DEAR	107	BALDER DEAD 2	77
AND KNOWING WELL MANS INMOST HEART INFIRM	353	MEROPE	692
KNOWING HE DID IT UNKNOWING PAYS FOR IT	400	MEROPE	1870
BUT YET NOT KNOWING THIS I TRIUMPH NOT	404	MEROPE	1988
KNOWING CLASP IT AND SERENELY BEAT		META CLOISTER	32

KNOWLEDGE

OUT-TOPPING KNOWLEDGE FOR THE LOFTIEST HILL	2	SHAKESPEARE	3
OUT-TOPPING KNOWLEDGE SO SOME SOVRAN HILL	2	SHAKESPEARE V	3
OF BITTER KNOWLEDGE YET THE WILL IS FREE	4	EMERSONS ESSAYS	10
AND BY THAT SILENT KNOWLEDGE DAY BY DAY	12	MYCERINUS	110
WHERE THE SPRINGS OF KNOWLEDGE ARE	27	NEW SIRENS	34
KNOWLEDGE NO RUIN	40	STAGIRIUS	59
WHERE NO MORE LIGHTS OF SENSE OR KNOWLEDGE ARE	167	PICT NEWSTEAD	11
AFTER THE KNOWLEDGE OF OUR BURIED LIFE	246	BURIED LIFE	48
SUCH BARREN KNOWLEDGE AWHILE	296	HEINES GRAVE	119
HAVING LEARNT THIS THEN USE THY KNOWLEDGE NOW	388	MEROPE	1520
AND THOU A BOY WHOSE TONGUE OUTRUNS HIS KNOWLEDGE	411	EMPEDOCLES I 1	161
ALL KNOWLEDGE THAT I HAVE	415	EMPEDOCLES I 2	104

KNOWN

CHILDREN AS SUCH FORGIVE THEM HAVE I KNOWN	8	RELIGIOUS ISOL	1
HATH YOUR WISDOM KNOWN EMOTIONS	29	NEW SIRENS V	85
THOU TO WHOM ALL ARE KNOWN	38	STAGIRIUS	3
GLOOMS THAT GO DEEP AS THINE I HAVE NOT KNOWN	42	GIPSY CHILD	17
WHOSE MIND HATH KNOWN ALL ARTS OF GOVERNING	43	GIPSY CHILD	35
HAVE KNOWN TOO MUCH OR ELSE FORGOTTEN ALL	43	GIPSY CHILD	48
THE SOLEMN PEAKS BUT TO THE STARS ARE KNOWN	45	IN UTRUMQUE PAR	18
IN DIVINE SEATS HATH KNOWN	45	IN UTRUMQUE PAR	23
HAVE NEVER KNOWN MY GRANDSIRES FURROWD FACE	83	SOHRAB RUSTUM	756
AND OLD MEN KNOWN TO GLORY BUT THEIR STAR	109	BALDER DEAD 2	166
THEY GO THE ERRAND AND THE WAY IS KNOWN	110	BALDER DEAD 2	191
WHO EVER HAVE BEEN KNOWN IN EARTH OR HEAVEN	112	BALDER DEAD 2	258
AND WE SHALL TREAD ONCE MORE THE WELL-KNOWN PLAIN	128	BALDER DEAD 3	537
THESE THEY THEMSELVES HAVE TRIED AND KNOWN	178	FAREWELL	26
THE FAULT WAS GRAVE I MIGHT HAVE KNOWN	180	ISOLATION MARG	7
THAT BEING ONLY WHICH HATH KNOWN EACH MAN	217	NAMELESS EPIT	2
HAVE KNOWN THEE EYING ALL AN APRIL-DAY	258	SCHOLAR-GIPSY	107
SO OFTEN HAS HE KNOWN THEE PAST HIM STRAY	258	SCHOLAR-GIPSY	118
HAVE KNOWN THEE WATCHING ALL AN APRIL-DAY	258	SCHOLAR-GIPSY V	107
HAVE KNOWN THEE HAUNTING ALL AN APRIL-DAY	258	SCHOLAR-GIPSY V	107
NOR DO I WISH IT KNOWN	321	OBERMANN MORE	264
HER WELL-KNOWN ENEMY	393	MEROPE	1666
THIS HAVING KNOWN LET US A UNION FOUND	394	MEROPE	1716
ASK WHAT MOST HELPS WHEN KNOWN THOU SON OF ANCHITUS	416	EMPEDOCLES I 2	111
OTHER FAVOURITES HE HATH KNOWN	458	POOR MATTHIAS	204
WERE KNOWN TO ALL THE VILLAGE-STREET	459	KAISER DEAD	8
WHOSE SPELL-BOUND SENSE FROM CHILDHOODS HOUR HATH KNOWN	471	CROMWELL	3
NOR KNOWN IT THEN BUT IT WAS VEILD NO MORE	477	CROMWELL	202
TO THE BLIND SLAVES OF POWER TO MAKE IT KNOWN		FRAGMENT 2	3

KNOWS
GOD KNOWS IT I AM WITH YOU IF TO PRIZE   • • •   6 REP FRIEND   1
FROM THINE OWN MOTHERS BREAST THAT KNOWS NOT THEE   42 GIPSY CHILD   14
THEY MUST LIVE STILL AND YET GOD KNOWS • • •   56 RESIGNATION 132
AS THAT POOR BIRD FLIES HOME NOR KNOWS HIS LOSS • •   78 SOHRAB RUSTUM 573
AND OER A DARKSOME TRACT WHICH KNOWS NO SUN • • • 108 BALDER DEAD 2 139
HE KNOWS EACH FRITH AND EVERY ROCKY CREEK • • • • 123 BALDER DEAD 3 326
MIS-DEFINE THESE TILL GOD KNOWS THEM NO MORE • • 171 DIVINITY   10
AND WHAT HEART KNOWS ANOTHER • • • • • • • • 177 PARTING   73
AH WHO KNOWS HIS OWN • • • • • • • • • • 177 PARTING   74
WHICH KNOWS NO DOUBT WHICH FEELS NO FEAR • • • • 178 FAREWELL   36
KNOWS THAT THE BENT OF BOTH OUR HEARTS • • • • • 179 FAREWELL   47
SINCE MAN WOKE ON EARTH HE KNOWS HIS STORY • • • 209 SELF-DECEPTION   3
STILL BENT TO MAKE SOME PORT HE KNOWS NOT WHERE • • 244 SUMMER NIGHT   68
AND THEN HE THINKS HE KNOWS • • • • • • • 247 BURIED LIFE   96
OF WHOM EACH STRIVES NOR KNOWS FOR WHAT HE STRIVES 260 SCHOLAR-GIPSY 168
I KNOW THESE SLOPES WHO KNOWS THEM IF NOT I • • 266 THYRSIS 111
IT KNOWS NOT WHAT HE SAYS • • • • • • • 307 OBERMANN   44
KNOWS HOW THE DAY HATH GONE • • • • • • • 309 OBERMANN 102
WHO KNOWS BUT THAT AVENGERS THOU HADST FOUND • • 383 MEROPE 1372
WHO KNOWS NOT WHAT TO BELIEVE • • • • • • 415 EMPEDOCLES I 2   89
FULL WELL MAX KNOWS THE FRIEND IS DEAD • • • • 460 KAISER DEAD   69

KNOWST
THOU KNOWST ME PERAN-WISA IT IS I • • • • •   62 SOHRAB RUSTUM   34
THOU KNOWST IF SINCE FROM ADER-BAIJAN FIRST • •   62 SOHRAB RUSTUM   42
THIS TOO THOU KNOWST THAT WHILE I STILL BEAR ON • •   62 SOHRAB RUSTUM   46
TO FIGHT THEIR CHAMPION AND THOU KNOWST HIS NAME • •   67 SOHRAB RUSTUM 213
O KING THOU KNOWST I HAVE BEEN SICK • • • • •   88 SICK KING BOKH   22
WHEREFORE HEAR THOU THOU KNOWST HOW FIERCE • • •   89 SICK KING BOKH   58
OR FOR THOU KNOWST THE FATES AND THINGS ALLOWD • •   98 BALDER DEAD 1 108
THOU KNOWST THOU KNOWST WHAT GRIEF WE HAVE IN HEAVEN 110 BALDER DEAD 2 192
THOU KNOWST THOU KNOWST WHAT GRIEF WE HAVE IN HEAVEN 110 BALDER DEAD 2 192
THOU KNOWST NOT WHOM THOU STRIKST I KNOW HIS CRIME   374 MEROPE 1199
THINE ENEMY THOU KNOWST NOT NOR HIS STRENGTH • • 381 MEROPE 1294
TELLS ME ENOUGH THOU KNOWST THE NEWS WHICH ALL • • 393 MEROPE 1685
KNOWST THOU THEN AUGHT THAT THUS THOU SOUNDST   396 MEROPE 1766
    THE ALARM
PEISIANAX THOU KNOWST DRINKS LATE AND THEN • • • • 407 EMPEDOCLES I 1   39
ONE OF HIS MOODS IS ON HIM THAT THOU KNOWST • • 408 EMPEDOCLES I 1   54
THOU KNOWST OF OLD HE LOVED THIS HARP OF MINE • • 408 EMPEDOCLES I 1   72
THOU KNOWST ME FOR A WANDERER FROM OF OLD • • • 428 EMPEDOCLES I 2 477
NOT MUCH THOU KNOWST I PRIZE • • • • • • • 426 EMPEDOCLES I 2 V 407

KOHIK
KOHIK AND WHERE THE KALMUKS FEED THEIR SHEEP • •   83 SOHRAB RUSTUM 764

KOORDS
WITH AGE AND RULES OVER THE VALIANT KOORDS • • • •   78 SOHRAB RUSTUM 592

KUL
BLACK GLOSSY CURLD THE FLEECE OF KARA-KUL • • • •   64 SOHRAB RUSTUM 101

KUZZAKS
KALMUCKS AND UNKEMPT KUZZAKS TRIBES WHO STRAY • •   65 SOHRAB RUSTUM 132
KALMUCKS AND UNKEMPD KUZZAKS TRIBES WHO STRAY • •   65 SOHRAB RUSTUM V 132

KYBI
SEIRIOL THE BRIGHT KYBI THE DARK MEN SAID • • • • 170 EAST AND WEST   9

LABEL
AND LABEL WITH THE BLESSED SIGN • • • • • • • 138 TRISTRAM 1 252

LABORIOUS
LABORIOUS PERSEVERING SERIOUS FIRM • • • • • •   5 DUKE WELLINGTON   10

LABOUR
OF LABOUR THAT IN LASTING FRUIT OUTGROWS • • • •   1 QUIET WORK   6
OF LABOUR THAT IN ONE SHORT HOUR OUTGROWS • • •   1 QUIET WORK V 6
OF LABOUR THAT IN STILL ADVANCE OUTGROWS • • •   1 QUIET WORK V 6
OF LABOUR THAT IN FRUIT BY FAR OUTGOES • • •   1 QUIET WORK V 6
OF LABOUR THAT IN FRUIT BY FAR OUTGROWS • • •   1 QUIET WORK V 6
OF LABOUR THAT WITH MUTE ADVANCE OUTGOES • • •   1 QUIET WORK V 6
EACH TO HIS LABOUR AND WHEN ALL WERE GONE • • •   EMERSONS ESSAYS V 7
VAIN LABOUR DEEP AND BROAD WHERE NONE MAY SEE • •   4 BUTLERS SERMONS   5
LOST LABOUR WHEN THE CIRCUMAMBIENT GLOOM • • •   10 MYCERINUS   53
HEARD THE HOARSE BOUGHS LABOUR IN THE WIND • • •   26 NEW SIRENS   8
OF MANS LABOUR IS BUT VAIN • • • • • • •   28 NEW SIRENS   58
SAW THE HOARSE BOUGHS LABOUR IN THE WIND • • •   26 NEW SIRENS V 8
NOT IDLY EARTH AND OCEAN LABOUR ON • • • • •   42 GIPSY CHILD   7
WHO STILL THEIR LABOUR GIVE • • • • • • •   47 WORLD QUIETIST   15
THEN HERMOD KNEW WHAT LABOUR HELD THE GODS • • • 113 BALDER DEAD 2 307
BUT OH WHAT LABOUR • • • • • • • • • • 192 STRAYED REVEL 210
WITHOUT PAIN WITHOUT LABOUR • • • • • • 194 STRAYED REVEL 274
THE MAN MATURE WITH LABOUR CHOPS • • • • • 213 PROGRESS POESY   5
FOR GREATEST HATH THEIR LABOUR BEEN • • • • • 227 EPILOG LAOCOON 210
FOR GREATEST HAS THEIR LABOUR BEEN • • • • • 227 EPILOG LAOCOON V 210

LABOUR   (CONTINUED)
```
DARKEN IN LABOUR AND PAIN                            •  •  •  •  •  •  •  •  229 YOUTH OF NATURE      52
FRESH PRODUCTS OF THEIR BARREN LABOUR FALL          •  •  •  •  243 SUMMER NIGHT          43
IN THE SOUNDING LABOUR-HOUSE VAST                   •  •  •  •  •  287 RUGBY CHAPEL          41
LABOUR FOR EVER IN VAIN                             •  •  •  •  •  •  •  •  291 RUGBY CHAPEL       V 186
EARS AND LABOUR-DIMMD EYES                          •  •  •  •  •  •  •  295 HEINES GRAVE          89
MUST LABOUR MUST RESIGN                             •  •  •  •  •  •  319 OBERMANN MORE        186
THOU FOR THY LABOUR HAST DESERVED OUR BEST          •  •  •  •  359 MEROPE               866
THE LABOUR-RELEASED HERO  •  •  •  •  •  •  •  •     •  •  •  399 MEROPE              1844
THE GREY-STREAKD WATERS LABOUR STILL    •  •  •  •  •  •  479 HAYSWATER BOAT        18
```

LABOURD
```
HAST LABOURD BUT WITH PURPOSE HAST BECOME           •  •  •  •    5 DUKE WELLINGTON        9
HAST LABOURD WITH THE FOREMOST HAST BECOME          •  •  •  •    5 DUKE WELLINGTON      V  9
OUR LABOURD PUNY PASSION-FITS   •  •  •  •  •  •  •  •  •  202 URANIA               14
HIS OFTEN-LABOURD FIELDS  •  •  •  •  •  •  •  •  •  •  •  426 EMPEDOCLES I 2       415
```

LABOURER
```
AM THE EXACTER LABOURER    •  •  •  •  •  •  •  •  •  •   22 MEMORY-PICTURE         6
THE RUGGED LABOURER        •  •  •  •  •  •  •  •  •  •   47 WORLD QUIETIST        21
```

LABOURERS
```
LABOURERS THAT SHALL NOT FAIL WHEN MAN IS GONE      •  •    2 QUIET WORK            14
STILL DOTH FOR LABOURERS SEND   •  •  •  •  •  •  •  •   47 WORLD QUIETIST        14
TO FRIENDS STILL MORE AND LABOURERS IN OUR CAUSE   •  •  359 MEROPE               872
```

LABOUREST
```
NOT WITH LOST TOIL THOU LABOUREST THROUGH THE NIGHT     169 EAST LONDON           13
```

LABOURING
```
CUT BY AN ONWARD-LABOURING VESSELS PRORE           •  •  •  •   41 HUMAN LIFE            23
AND LABOURING BREATH FIRST RUSTUM STRUCK THE SHIELD    75 SOHRAB RUSTUM        491
AND THESE ALL LABOURING FOR A LORD  •  •  •  •  •  •   93 SICK KING BOKH       169
THE OTHERS LABOURING TO COMPOSE THEIR BRAWLS       •  •  116 BALDER DEAD 3         86
SOME LABOURING MEN WHOSE WORK LAY SOMEWHERE THERE      170 WEST LONDON            5
HAD ON THE JOURNEY CHOKED MY LABOURING BREATH      •  •  362 MEROPE               940
FAR OER THE PATHLESS WASTE OF LABOURING FOAM       •  •  475 CROMWELL             114
```

LABOURS
```
THEN THE DUCHESS CLOSED HER LABOURS    •  •  •  •  •   16 CHURCH BROU 1        111
NOT DAILY LABOURS DULL LETHAEAN SPRING   •  •  •  •  •   43 GIPSY CHILD           54
WHOM LABOURS SELF-ORDAIND ENTHRALL    •  •  •  •  •   52 RESIGNATION           14
```

LACE
```
THY CHEEKS SOFT HUE AND FLUTTERING LACE     •  •  •  •  184 TERRACE BERNE         23
```

LACEDAEMON
```
FOR ASK AT ARGOS ASK IN LACEDAEMON    •  •  •  •  •  •  338 MEROPE               284
```

LACK
```
THEN I SHALL PRAISE THE HEAT WHICH THEN I LACK     •  •   37 YOUTHS AGIT           11
YE GODS GOOD LACK IS IT SO DULL IN HEAVEN     •  •  •  123 BALDER DEAD 3        337
HER MOODS GOOD LACK THEY PASS LIKE SHOWERS     •  •  •  146 TRISTRAM 2           125
BUT OUR IGNOBLE SOULS LACK MIGHT       •  •  •  •   201 URANIA                4
FOR LACK OF LIGHT WHICH SHOULD THE BOON CONVEY     •  •  446 WESTMIN ABBEY      V  70
THE THOUGHTLESS WORD THE LACK OF SYMPATHY     •  •  •  470 ALARIC AT ROME       220
NO LACK OF ANSWER HAST THOU O MY HEART     •  •  •  •      RUDE ORATOR           13
```

LACKING
```
LACKING THE SHELTER OF THEE    •  •  •  •  •  •  •  •  287 RUGBY CHAPEL          36
```

LACKS
```
THE VILLAGE STREET ITS HAUNTED MANSION LACKS       •  •  262 THYRSIS                3
```

LACONIAS
```
TAYGETUS LACONIAS BORDER-WALL    •  •  •  •  •  •  •  330 MEROPE               17
```

LAD
```
BUT KAI A TIRELESS SHEPHERD-LAD      •  •  •  •  •  •  460 KAISER DEAD           44
```

LADEN
```
AND A HEART SORROW-LADEN  •  •  •  •  •  •  •  •  •  •  164 FORSAKEN MERM        104
ON THE BROAD CLAY-LADEN   •  •  •  •  •  •  •  •  •  •  191 STRAYED REVEL        182
```

LADIES
```
LADIES WAITING ROUND HER SEAT   •  •  •  •  •  •  •  •   13 CHURCH BROU 1         34
THOU AND THY LADIES IN THE HALL OF STATE    •  •  •  •   18 CHURCH BROU 3         13
PRIEST KNIGHTS AND LADIES GAY   •  •  •  •  •  •  •  159 NECKAN                22
THE KNIGHTS DREW SWORD THE LADIES SCREAMD     •  •  •  •  159 NECKAN                27
```

LADON
```
WHERE CLEAR-FLOWING LADON    •  •  •  •  •  •  •  •  •  391 MEROPE              1608
```

LADY
```
AS SOME RICH LADY ON A WINTERS MORN    •  •  •  •  •   70 SOHRAB RUSTUM      V 302
WHAT LADY IS THIS WHOSE SILK ATTIRE   •  •  •  •  •  •  131 TRISTRAM 1            24
WHO IS THAT KNEELING LADY FAIR  •  •  •  •  •  •  •  •  148 TRISTRAM 2           165
THAT LADY BY THE BED DOTH KNEEL   •  •  •  •  •  •  •  149 TRISTRAM 2           181
```

LAERTES
    LAERTES SON • • • • • • • • • • • • • • 189 STRAYED REVEL 113

LAGGARD
    HO THIS WAY YE LAGGARD HUNTERS • • • • • • • • 14 CHURCH BROU 1 43
    COUNTING TILL I GREW UP THE LAGGARD YEARS • • • • 367 MEROPE 1046

LAGS
    ONE STILL LAGS LAST AND TURNS AND EYES THE PILE • • 444 WESTMIN ABBEY 14

LAIAS
    OF MY OWN DEATH BUT LAIAS WELL I HOPE • • • • 331 MEROPE 49
    O LAIAS LAIAS LET THE HEART SPEAK HERE • • • • 331 MEROPE 59
    O LAIAS LAIAS LET THE HEART SPEAK HERE • • • • 331 MEROPE 59
    OUR PRINCE AND THE GOOD LAIAS WHOM HIS WARD • • 364 MEROPE 976
    ARCAS SEEK OUT MY UNCLE LAIAS NOW • • • • • 379 MEROPE 1260
    APPROVES MY BROTHER LAIAS THIS INTENT • • • • 379 MEROPE 1267
    LAIAS ALONE NO ERRAND MINE FOR CROWDS • • • • 380 MEROPE 1285
    HERE AS I GUESS THE NOBLE LAIAS COMES • • • • 386 MEROPE 1439
    O PRINCELY LAIAS TO WHAT PURPOSE CALLS • • • • 386 MEROPE 1446
    I SHUDDER LAIAS TO COMMIT MY CHILD • • • • 387 MEROPE 1461
    THESE ARE BUT WOMANS WORDS YET LAIAS THOU • • 388 MEROPE 1510
    LAIAS IN ARMS SPRANG TO HIS NEPHEWS SIDE • • 402 MEROPE 1933
    WHERE MY OWN YOUTH FALLS SHORT BUT LAIAS NOW • 405 MEROPE 2016
    THE PRINCE HIS UNCLE LAIAS WHOM HIS WARD • • 364 MEROPE V 976
    WHO SAW THE PRINCE AND LAIAS LAST WITH HIM • 365 MEROPE V
    APPROVES MY BROTHER LAIAS THIS DESIGN • • • • 379 MEROPE V1267

LAID
    IN THE HALL THEY LAID HIM DOWN • • • • • 14 CHURCH BROU 1 46
    WHERE THE LOOMING KINE ARE LAID • • • • • 32 NEW SIRENS 182
    WHERE THE LOOMING DEER ARE LAID • • • • • 32 NEW SIRENS V 182
    BOTH ARE LAID IN ONE COLD PLACE • • • • • 44 QUESTION 6
    ON BALDER DEATH HATH LAID HER HAND NOT THEE • 98 BALDER DEAD 1 117
    AND LAID IT ON A BIER AND BARE HIM HOME • • 101 BALDER DEAD 1 206
    AND EACH BESPAKE HIM AS HE LAID HIM DOWN • • 101 BALDER DEAD 1 215
    AND IN VALHALLA ODIN LAID HIM DOWN • • • 102 BALDER DEAD 1 267
    THEY WENT AND LAID THEM DOWN AND NANNA WENT • 103 BALDER DEAD 1 277
    AND ODIN CAME AND LAID HIS KINGLY HANDS • • 115 BALDER DEAD 3 65
    OF BALDER ON THE HIGHEST TOP THEY LAID • • 118 BALDER DEAD 3 163
    AND LAID HER IN A STATELY ROOM WHERE FELL • 168 RACHEL 2 5
    THE PUISSANT CROWND THE WEAK LAID LOW • • 219 BACCHANALIA 2 12
    WHEN A BELOVED HAND IS LAID IN OURS • • • 247 BURIED LIFE 78
    OF BLOOM ON THE BENT GRASS WHERE I AM LAID • 256 SCHOLAR-GIPSY 28
    LONG SINCE AND IN SOME QUIET CHURCHYARD LAID • 259 SCHOLAR-GIPSY 137
    LAID PAUSEFULLY UPON LIFES HEADLONG TRAIN • 266 THYRSIS 137
    HE LAID US AS WE LAY AT BIRTH • • • • • 271 MEMORIAL VERSES 48
    THOU MY FATHER ART LAID • • • • • • • 286 RUGBY CHAPEL 13
    AND LAID HER SCEPTRE DOWN • • • • • • 316 OBERMANN MORE 126
    MY MOTHERS FAITHFUL SERVANT LAID ME DOWN • • 331 MEROPE 31
    WHERE AS LIFE EBBD HIS BEARERS LAID HIM DOWN • 357 MEROPE 783
    AND THOU THOU FAIR-SKINND SERPENT THOU ART LAID • 373 MEROPE 1177
    TO HEAVEN AND LAID HIS HAND UPON THE STEER • 402 MEROPE 1914
    WHICH LAID THEE LOW FOR BLOOD REQUIRES BLOOD • 404 MEROPE 1987
    BUT HE HAS LAID THE USE OF MUSIC BY • • • 409 EMPEDOCLES I 1 83
    PLUCKD FROM THE FIRE THE CHILD AND LAID HIM DOWN • 447 WESTMIN ABBEY 95
    AND IN THE GRAVE HE LAID A CHERISHD WIFE • 447 WESTMIN ABBEY 124
    AND THE ROUGH WAVES OF LIFE FOR EVER LAID • 449 WESTMIN ABBEY 165

LAIN
    HE HAD LAIN WAKEFUL TOSSING ON HIS BED • • • • 61 SOHRAB RUSTUM 6

LAIR
    AT SUNRISE FROM THEIR DEWY LAIR • • • • 16 CHURCH BROU 2 9
    OF THE DEEP ARE NOT YOUR LAIR • • • • • 26 NEW SIRENS 18
    THE WILD BOAR RUSTLES IN HIS LAIR • • • • 149 TRISTRAM 2 183
    HAST THOU SWORN IN THY SAD LAIR • • • • 430 EMPEDOCLES II 58

LAKE
    UPON THE CRAGGY ISLE OF A HILL-LAKE • • • 78 SOHRAB RUSTUM 558
    SHALL THE LAKE GLASS HER FLYING OVER IT • • 78 SOHRAB RUSTUM 570
    AND SEEN THE RIVER OF HELMUND AND THE LAKE • 83 SOHRAB RUSTUM 751
    OF SOME CLEAR RIVER ISSUING FROM A LAKE • 109 BALDER DEAD 2 158
    WHILE ON HIS ISLAND IN THE LAKE AFAR • • • 111 BALDER DEAD 2 214
    AND HURL THEE IN A LAKE TO SINK OR SWIM • • 114 BALDER DEAD 3 26
    ARISING FROM THE SINNERS LAKE • • • • • 158 SAINT BRANDAN 67
    THE TOWN THE LAKE ARE HERE • • • • • 174 MEETING 2
    THE GLEAM-LIGHTED LAKE • • • • • • • 174 PARTING 4
    MY HORSES FEET BESIDE THE LAKE • • • • 177 FAREWELL 1
    FLOW THE COOL LAKE-WAVES • • • • • • 190 STRAYED REVEL 160
    ON HIS MOUNTAIN LAKE BUT SQUALLS • • • • 193 STRAYED REVEL 236
    SILENT THE BOAT THE LAKE • • • • • • 228 YOUTH OF NATURE 2
    WHICH BORDER ENNERDALE LAKE • • • • • 228 YOUTH OF NATURE 16
    HELICON GLASSD IN THE LAKE • • • • • 229 YOUTH OF NATURE 38
    MOONLIGHT AND SHADOW AND LAKE • • • • 230 YOUTH OF NATURE 60
    THAT BORDER ENNERDALE LAKE • • • • • 228 YOUTH OF NATURE V 16
    LAKE LEMANS WATERS FAR BELOW • • • • • 310 OBERMANN 121
    THE LAKE WITH CHILLON BY • • • • • • 312 OBERMANN MORE 8
    ACROSS THE GLIMMERING LAKE • • • • • 324 OBERMANN MORE 346
    TO THE STYMPHALIAN LAKE OUR JOURNEYS END • • 356 MEROPE 749
    FAR IN THE LIQUID LAKE WE SATE AND DREW • • 356 MEROPE 752

LAKE   (CONTINUED)
        BY THE LAKE-EDGE BROKE THE SHARP CRY OF HOUNDS   • •   357 MEROPE   787
        AND TOOK THE LAKE TWO HOUNDS ALONE PURSUED • • • •   357 MEROPE   809
        WALLS ON ONE SIDE THE DEEP STYMPHALIAN LAKE   • •   358 MEROPE   813
        THERE THE LAKE-WATERS WHICH IN AGES GONE   • • • •   358 MEROPE   814
        FISHERS WHO LIVE ON THE LAKE-SIDE TO LAUNCH   • •   358 MEROPE   837
        HIS BOAR-SPEARS BROKEN SHAFT BACK ON THE LAKE   • •   358 MEROPE   840
        WHICH HANGS OER THE STYMPHALIAN LAKE AND DROWND • •   363 MEROPE   961
        OF THAT SOLITARY LAKE   • • • • • • • •   433 EMPEDOCLES II   135
        BUT ALOOF ON THE LAKE-STRAND • • • • • •   434 EMPEDOCLES II   165
        THE FISHER FROM THE LAKE OF GALILEE   • • • • •   445 WESTMIN ABBEY   45
        CROSSING THE FROZEN LAKE APPEARS   • • • • •   451 GEISTS GRAVE   51
        TO THE VEXD WATERS OF A MOUNTAIN LAKE   • • • •   477 CROMWELL   192

LAKES
        AND FROM THE BLUE TWIN-LAKES IT COMES   • • •   184 TERRACE BERNE   9
        THE SANDY SPITS THE SHORE-LOCKD LAKES   • • •   275 SOUTHERN NIGHT   1
        BY ENGLANDS LAKES IN GREY OLD AGE   • • • • • •   308 OBERMANN   49
        TO THE GLIMMERING MOUNTAIN-LAKES   • • • • • •   434 EMPEDOCLES II   172

LAMB
        POOR LAMB THOU SLEEPEST AND FORGETTST THY WOE   • •   103 BALDER DEAD 1   288
        AND ON HIS SHOULDERS NOT A LAMB A KID   • • •   172 GOOD SHEPHERD   14

LAMBETH
        TIS LAMBETH NOW WHERE THEN   • • • • • • • •   444 WESTMIN ABBEY   17

LAMBS
        FROM SATURNS SEARCH AMONG THE NEW-YEAND LAMBS   • •   355 MEROPE   738

LAME
        OF THAT LAME SLAVE WHO IN NICOPOLIS   • • • • • •   2 TO A FRIEND   V   6
        TIME IS LAME AND WE GREW WEARY • • • • • • • •   28 NEW SIRENS   67
        TIME IS LAME AND WE GROW WEARY • • • • • • • •   28 NEW SIRENS   V 67
        AND LAME THE ACTIVE MIND • • • • • • • •   237 PROGRESS   20

LAMENT
        NOT TO LAMENT IN WAS VALHALLA MADE   • • • • • •   95 BALDER DEAD 1   19
        IN HEAVEN NOR LET THE OTHER GODS LAMENT   • • •   126 BALDER DEAD 3   457

LAMENTATION
        NO LAMENTATION CAN LOOSE • • • • • • • • •   347 MEROPE   524

LAMENTING
        MOTHERS LAMENTING THEIR SONS   • • • • • • •   369 MEROPE   1096

LAMP
        AND ALL DAY LONG AND WHEN NIGHT COMES THE LAMP   • •   81 SOHRAB RUSTUM   675
        SHELL LIGHT HER SILVER LAMP WHICH FISHERMEN   • •   151 TRISTRAM 3   79

LAMPLESS
        FIT DENIZEN THE LAMPLESS UNDER-WORLD • • • • • •   367 MEROPE   1031

LAMPS
        A HUNDRED LAMPS BEAMD IN THE TRANQUIL GLOOM   • •   11 MYCERINUS   94
        LET YOUR BROAD LAMPS FLASH THE BRIGHTNESS • • • •   32 NEW SIRENS   177
        WHEN THE LAMPS ARE PALED AT MORNING   • • • • • •   35 NEW SIRENS   263
        PARIS DRAWING-ROOMS AND LAMPS   • • • • • • •   296 HEINES GRAVE   141

LANCE
        PENNON AND PLUME AND FLASHING LANCE   • • • • • •   305 GRANDE CHARTR   178

LANCES
        WHICH THE BRIGHT MOON LANCES   • • • • • • • •   35 VOICE   3
        THE TUKAS AND THE LANCES OF SALORE   • • • • • •   64 SOHRAB RUSTUM   122

LAND
        I WITH LITTLE LAND TO STIR   • • • • • • •   22 MEMORY-PICTURE   5
        HE SEES IN SOME GREAT-HISTORIED LAND • • • • • •   56 RESIGNATION   154
        CROSSING THE STREAM IN SUMMER SCRAPES THE LAND   • •   61 SOHRAB RUSTUM   19
        AND WHETHER IT WILL HEAVE US UP TO LAND   • • •   73 SOHRAB RUSTUM   393
        OUT OF THE MIST AND HUM OF THAT LOW LAND   • • •   87 SOHRAB RUSTUM   876
        CROSSING THE STREAM IN SUMMER MEETS THE LAND   • •   61 SOHRAB RUSTUM   V 19
        THEN HE WILL JOURNEY THROUGH NO LIGHTED LAND   • •   99 BALDER DEAD 1   153
        THE LIGHT AND JOURNEY TO THE CHEERLESS LAND   • •   110 BALDER DEAD 2   181
        BUT ODIN LOOKD TOWARD THE LAND AND SAW   • • •   114 BALDER DEAD 3   31
        BROTHER THOU DWELLEST IN THE DARKSOME LAND • • •   115 BALDER DEAD 3   75
        HIS SHIP AND THE GREAT SERPENT MAKES TO LAND   • •   127 BALDER DEAD 3   479
        AND HERE AND THERE LOCKD BY THE LAND • • • • •   141 TRISTRAM 1   367
        SHE TOLD THEM OF THE FAIRY-HAUNTED LAND   • • •   154 TRISTRAM 3   153
        CREEPS OVER IT FROM THE TILLD LAND BEHIND • • •   TRISTRAM 3   V   9
        STEALS OVER IT FROM THE TILLD LAND BEHIND • • •   TRISTRAM 3   V   9
        WHERE THE SEA MEETS THE MOON-BLANCHD LAND • • •   211 DOVER BEACH   8
        TO LIE BEFORE US LIKE A LAND OF DREAMS   • • •   211 DOVER BEACH   31
        SEE THROUGH THE QUIET LAND   • • • • • • •   218 BACCHANALIA 1   32
        THE LAND OF ARIOSTO SHOWD   • • • • • • •   222 EPILOG LAOCOON   22
        THROUGH THE SILENT FLOWERY LAND   • • • • • •   234 YOUTH OF MAN   85
        AS FROM AN INFINITELY DISTANT LAND   • • • • • •   247 BURIED LIFE   74
        AND THEN THEY LAND AND THOU ART SEEN NO MORE   • •   257 SCHOLAR-GIPSY   81
        AND OER THE GLISTENING LONELY LAND   • • • • • •   274 STANZAS CARNAC   21

LAND   (CONTINUED)
        TREAD THE BORDER-LAND DIM . . . .   288 RUGBY CHAPEL   54
        WIDE GERMAN LAND GOING DOWN . . . .   297 HEINES GRAVE   173
        CONDUCTED TO THEIR COMMON LAND . . . . 311 OBERMANN   147
        AH OER THAT SILENT SACRED LAND . . . . 318 OBERMANN MORE   181
        AH FROM THAT SILENT SACRED LAND . . . . . .   318 OBERMANN MORE   V 181
        THIS IS THAT FRUITFUL FAMED MESSENIAN LAND . 330 MEROPE   4
        TOGETHER WON THIS FAIR MESSENIAN LAND . . .   334 MEROPE   126
        AND FINALLY THIS LAND THEN HALF-SUBDUED . .   337 MEROPE   245
        SOON SHALL HE DAWN ON THIS LAND . . . . . .   347 MEROPE   515
        IN A LAND OF FRIENDS BY A FRIEND . . . . .   369 MEROPE   1101
        THOUGH ALL FREE SPIRITS IN THIS LAND WERE DEAD . 383 MEROPE   1377
        YET STAINS OUR LAND BE BY THIS BLOOD WASHD OUT . 402 MEROPE   1916
        YET SHALL HE DAWN ON THIS LAND . . . . . .   347 MEROPE   V 515
        THOUGH ALL FREE SPIRITS IN THIS LAND BE DEAD . 383 MEROPE   V1377
        AND REST HIS WEARY EYES ON THE GREEN LAND AND THEE 470 ALARIC AT ROME 222
        LIKE A GREEN LAND AT SUNSET ALL WERE THERE . . 474 CROMWELL   84
        FROM A FAR LAND THE CHILDREN OF THE SNOW . . 474 CROMWELL   90
        ONE ROOD FROM LAND THEY PUSHD NO MORE . . .   480 HAYSWATER BOAT   27
        ON LAND RENEW THAT GREEK EXPLOIT WHOSE GLORIES . 481 HUNGARIAN NAT   12
        UNWEARIED AS FROM LAND TO LAND . . . . 484 ROME-SICKNESS   29
        UNWEARIED AS FROM LAND TO LAND . . . . 484 ROME-SICKNESS   29
        ON THE SWEET AND MOON-BATHED LAND . . . . .   META CLOISTER   12

LANDED
        LANDED TO DIE . . . .   278 SOUTHERN NIGHT   96

LANDING
        AND THIS AT LANDING SPIED BY US AND SAVED . . . 358 MEROPE   842

LANDS
        FROM THE JEWELLD LANDS OF DAWN . . . . . .   26 NEW SIRENS   22
        TO MATE BUT LEFT HER TO ROAM DISTANT LANDS . . 116 BALDER DEAD 3   94
        FIRST DROVE HIM FROM ME INTO DISTANT LANDS . . 116 BALDER DEAD 3   108
        TO WARMER LANDS AND COASTS THAT KEEP THE SUN . 129 BALDER DEAD 3   562
        STILL AFTER MANY YEARS IN DISTANT LANDS . . . 200 PHILOMELA   6
        OF THE LANDS WHICH THE RIVER OF TIME . . . .   252 FUTURE   21
        LANDS THEE TO DIE . . . .   276 SOUTHERN NIGHT   48
        MORE FOR THIS LANDS SAKE GRIEVE I THAN MINE OWN . 398 MEROPE   1784

LANDSCAPE
        THE WIDE AERIAL LANDSCAPE SPREAD . . . . .   250 WISH   34
        WHAT DEATHLIKE STILLNESS OER THE LANDSCAPE LAY . 466 ALARIC AT ROME 99

LANDWARD
        SWOOPING TO LANDWARD NOR TO WHERE QUITE CLEAR . . 151 TRISTRAM 3   54

LANE
        MOVE BROWSING UP THE GRAY-WALLD LANE . . . . . 55 RESIGNATION   121

LANES
        ON A MAY EVENING IN THE DARKEND LANES . . . . 101 BALDER DEAD 1   233
        BUT ONCE YEARS AFTER IN THE COUNTRY-LANES . . 256 SCHOLAR-GIPSY   41
        BY THE STREAM-SIDE AFTER THE DUSTY LANES . . . 406 EMPEDOCLES I 1   3

LANGUAGE
        AND JOKES IN DOGGISH LANGUAGE SAID . . . . .   460 KAISER DEAD   71
        ALL FREEDOMS MYSTIC LANGUAGE STORMS THAT ROAR . 472 CROMWELL   29

LANGUID
        AND LANGUID PLEASURE FADE AND FLOWER AGAIN . . 10 MYCERINUS   64
        LIFTING UP YOUR LANGUID EYES . . . .   31 NEW SIRENS   158
        LEARND IN MORE LANGUID CLIMES . . . .   46 WORLD QUIETIST   5
        THAT CHEEK OF LANGUID HUE . . . .   174 MEETING   6
        POURD FLUSHING TO THY LANGUID CHEEK . . . .   178 FAREWELL   10
        CAME FLOODING TO THY LANGUID CHEEK . . . .   178 FAREWELL   V 10
        CAME FLUSHING TO THY LANGUID CHEEK . . . .   178 FAREWELL   V 10
        THE YOUNG LANGUID-EYED AMPELUS . . . . . .   188 STRAYED REVEL   78
        LANGUID THEIR HEART FOR YOUTH . . . .   233 YOUTH OF MAN   44
        FREE FROM THE SICK FATIGUE THE LANGUID DOUBT . 260 SCHOLAR-GIPSY   164
        HIS WERE NO TRANQUIL YEARS NO LANGUID SLEEP . 475 CROMWELL   123

LANGUIDLY
        LOOKS LANGUIDLY ROUND ON A GLOOM-BURIED WORLD . 20 MODERN SAPPHO   24
        BUT EVEN THAT COMES LANGUIDLY IN TRUTH . . . 151 TRISTRAM 3   74
        THY HAND LAY LANGUIDLY IN MINE . . . . . .   178 FAREWELL   15
        WITH HEADS BENT OER THEIR TOIL THEY LANGUIDLY . 243 SUMMER NIGHT   39

LANGUISH
        WHEREIN WE LANGUISH . . . .   38 STAGIRIUS   9
        YET WHILE I LANGUISH . . . .   50 CONSOLATION   6

LANGUOR
        IN THE RICH LANGUOR OF LONG SUMMER-DAYS . . . 12 MYCERINUS   117
        HOW THEY ARE FULL OF LANGUOR AND DISTRESS . . 153 TRISTRAM 3   137
        OF LANGUOR THOUGH SO CALM AND THOUGH SO GREAT . 244 SUMMER NIGHT   79
        LANGUOR IS NOT IN YOUR HEART . . . .   292 RUGBY CHAPEL   193
        THAT AIR OF LANGUOR COLD AND DEATH . . . . . 306 OBERMANN   15
        NO LANGUOR NO DECAY LANGUOR AND DEATH . . . . 438 EMPEDOCLES II   302
        NO LANGUOR NO DECAY LANGUOR AND DEATH . . . . 438 EMPEDOCLES II   302

LANGUOR   (CONTINUED)
        AND LIGHTS FAIR NURSLING LANGUOR FIRST INVADES   •   •   448 WESTMIN ABBEY   V 129
        THAT CITY TOLD OF LANGUOR AND DECAY •   •   •   •   •   •   466 ALARIC AT ROME   106

LANTERN
        HOLDS HIS LANTERN TO SCAN   •   •   •   •   •   •   •   •   289 RUGBY CHAPEL   113

LANTERNS
        THE LANTERNS OF THE FISHING-BOATS AT SEA   •   •   •   •   130 TRISTRAM 1   6

LAOCOON
        OF LESSINGS FAMED LAOCOON   •   •   •   •   •   •   •   •   221 EPILOG LAOCOON   3

LAP
        FIXT HER SLIGHT HANDS CLASPD ON HER LAP THEN RISE   152 TRISTRAM 3   91
        AND FOSTERING IN THY LAP A HEAP OF FLOWERS •   •   •   •   257 SCHOLAR-GIPSY   78
        ON THE COOL FLOWERY LAP OF EARTH   •   •   •   •   •   •   271 MEMORIAL VERSES   49

LAPITHAE
        OF THE GRIM LAPITHAE AND THESEUS DRIVE   •   •   •   •   192 STRAYED REVEL   228

LAPPS
        AND ON THE CONJURING LAPPS HE BENT HIS GAZE   •   •   96 BALDER DEAD 1   53

LAPS
        AND NOW PEACE LAPS HER ROUND   •   •   •   •   •   •   •   21 REQUIESCAT   12

LAPSE
        NO NO THOU HAST NOT FELT THE LAPSE OF HOURS   •   •   259 SCHOLAR-GIPSY   141

LARGE
        AH YOU SAY THE LARGE APPEARANCE   •   •   •   •   •   28 NEW SIRENS   57
        SOME LARGE ANSWER YOU SHALL HEAR   •   •   •   •   •   29 NEW SIRENS   92
        ALL TRUE SPEECH AND LARGE AVOWAL   •   •   •   •   •   34 NEW SIRENS   227
        COME YOU SAY THE LARGE APPEARANCE   •   •   •   •   •   28 NEW SIRENS   V 57
        WITH LARGE RESULTS SO LITTLE RIFE   •   •   •   •   •   60 RESIGNATION   262
        LARGE MEN LARGE STEEDS WHO FROM BOKHARA COME   •   •   64 SOHRAB RUSTUM   119
        LARGE MEN LARGE STEEDS WHO FROM BOKHARA COME   •   •   64 SOHRAB RUSTUM   119
        BRIMMING AND BRIGHT AND LARGE THEN SANDS BEGIN •   •   87 SOHRAB RUSTUM   881
        WITH LARGE-LEAVED LOW-CREEPING MELON-PLANTS   •   190 STRAYED REVEL   155
        SWELL THEIR LARGE VEINS TO BURSTING IN WILD PAIN •   •   192 STRAYED REVEL   226
        AT LARGE HIS ENEMYS SPEAR   •   •   •   •   •   •   •   197 FRAG ANTIGONE   89
        LARGE AND PROFOUND HATH GENIUS HERE   •   •   •   •   223 EPILOG LAOCOON   80
        AND ROLL ADOWN A CHANNEL LARGE   •   •   •   •   •   •   224 EPILOG LAOCOON   101
        EDDYING AT LARGE IN BLIND UNCERTAINTY   •   •   •   •   246 BURIED LIFE   43
        LIKE US THE LIBYAN WIND DELIGHTS TO ROAM AT LARGE   420 EMPEDOCLES I 2   251
        A CHURCH ONCE LARGE AND THEN GROWN STRAIT IN SOUL   449 WESTMIN ABBEY   156
        WE SEE THE FLAPS OF THY LARGE EARS   •   •   •   •   •   451 GEISTS GRAVE   49

LASHD
        THE LOUD RAINS LASHD THE MOUNTAINS CROWN   •   •   •   480 HAYSWATER BOAT   29

LASHER
        TO BATHE IN THE ABANDOND LASHER PASS •   •   •   •   •   258 SCHOLAR-GIPSY   95

LASHES
        TEARS STAND UPON THE LASHES OF THINE EYES   •   •   •   103 BALDER DEAD 1   289
        THE LASHES ON THE CHEEKS REPOSED   •   •   •   •   •   •   141 TRISTRAM 1   339
        LASHES THE NEWLY-MADE GRAVE   •   •   •   •   •   •   •   286 HAWORTH CHURCH   133

LASSA
        OF HOLY LASSA   •   •   •   •   •   •   •   •   •   •   •   •   50 CONSOLATION   14

LAST
        WHEN TRUE THE LAST IMPOSSIBILITY   •   •   •   •   •   •   5 HARMONY NATURE   3
        LAST OF ALL THE BUILDERS REARD HER •   •   •   •   •   16 CHURCH BROU 1   103
        WHERE LAST YEAR THEY LAY   •   •   •   •   •   •   •   16 CHURCH BROU 1   14
        LAST NIGHT WE STOOD EARNESTLY TALKING TOGETHER •   •   19 MODERN SAPPHO   9
        MARGUERITE SAYS AS LAST YEAR WENT   •   •   •   •   •   23 MEMORY-PICTURE   17
        ITS WOODY BORDER AND THE LAST   •   •   •   •   •   •   54 RESIGNATION   54
        WHETHER THAT HIS OWN MIGHTY STRENGTH AT LAST   •   •   63 SOHRAB RUSTUM   83
        BUT RUSTUM CAME LAST NIGHT ALOOF HE SITS   •   •   •   66 SOHRAB RUSTUM   178
        WAS CHOKED WITH RAGE AT LAST THESE WORDS BROKE WAY   74 SOHRAB RUSTUM   456
        A FOILD CIRCUITOUS WANDERER TILL AT LAST   •   •   •   87 SOHRAB RUSTUM   888
        IN THESE LAST DAYS THE SUN HATH BURND   •   •   •   •   89 SICK KING BOKH   59
        MOST FLEET HE WAS BUT NOW HE WENT THE LAST •   •   •   101 BALDER DEAD 1   222
        LAST FROM AMONG THE HEROES ONE CAME NEAR   •   •   •   117 BALDER DEAD 3   124
        HE LAST APPROACHD THE CORPSE AND SPAKE AND SAID •   •   117 BALDER DEAD 3   131
        A LAST CHOICE GIFT THEREON HIS GOLDEN RING •   •   •   118 BALDER DEAD 3   173
        LAST WALKING BY THE SEA THOU FOUNDEST SPARS •   •   •   121 BALDER DEAD 3   268
        IN THE GREAT DEEP FOR GAIN AT LAST COME HOME   •   •   123 BALDER DEAD 3   358
        FOR THE LAST TIME FOR HERE THOU COMST NO MORE   •   •   125 BALDER DEAD 3   420
        THEREFORE FOR THE LAST TIME O BALDER HAIL   •   •   •   126 BALDER DEAD 3   453
        MORE FRESH MORE VERDANT THAN THE LAST WITH FRUITS   128 BALDER DEAD 3   529
        AT LAST HE SIGHD AND SET FORTH BACK TO HEAVEN   •   •   129 BALDER DEAD 3   566
        ONE LAST KISS FIRST TIS VAIN TO HORSE AWAY •   •   •   135 TRISTRAM 1   169
        AND THAT LONG WILD KISS THEIR LAST •   •   •   •   •   136 TRISTRAM 1   180
        THOU ART COME AT LAST THEN HAUGHTY QUEEN   •   •   •   142 TRISTRAM 2   2
        ONE LAST KISS UPON THE LIVING SHORE •   •   •   •   •   145 TRISTRAM 2   98
        THROUGH LAST YEARS FERN OF THE SHY FALLOW-DEER   155 TRISTRAM 3   193

LAST   (CONTINUED)
    AT LAST IT WAS THE CHRISTMAS NIGHT • • • •   • 156 SAINT BRANDAN   13
    ONE LAST LOOK AT THE WHITE-WALLD TOWN • • • • • 162 FORSAKEN MERM   25
    IN THIS HER LIFES LAST DAY OUR POOR OUR PAIN • • 168 RACHEL 2   10
    HER COURSE FOR HOME AT LAST AND BURIAL • • • • 173 MONICAS PRAYER   7
    SHALL SEE OURSELVES AND LEARN AT LAST • • • • 179 FAREWELL   55
    AT LAST SHALL DESCEND UNDISTURBD • • • • • • 199 FRAG DEJANEIRA   21
    IT IS LAST STAGE OF ALL • • • • • • • • • • 213 GROWING OLD   31
    THOU THYSELF MUST BREAK AT LAST • • • • • 215 LAST WORD   4
    HOTLY CHARGED AND SANK AT LAST • • • • • 215 LAST WORD   12
    HOTLY CHARGED AND BROKE AT LAST • • • • • 215 LAST WORD   V 12
    THE LAST-LEFT HAYMAKER IS GONE • • • • • 218 BACCHANALIA 1   9
    THE LAST BELATED GLEANER GONE • • • • • 218 BACCHANALIA 1   V   9
    BEHOLD AT LAST THE POETS SPHERE • • • • • 225 EPILOG LAOCOON   127
    ATTEND IT TO THE LAST REPOSE • • • • • 225 EPILOG LAOCOON   151
    AND WHEN AT LAST THEIR SNATCHES CEASE • • • 226 EPILOG LAOCOON   185
    AND WHEN AT LAST THESE SNATCHES CEASE • • • 226 EPILOG LAOCOON   V 185
    ONE DAY THOU SAYST THERE WILL AT LAST APPEAR • 239 REVOLUTIONS   17
    THEN THEN AT LAST TO QUIT MY SIDE • • • • • 250 WISH   12
    FADE AND GROW OLD AT LAST AND DIE LIKE OURS • 261 SCHOLAR-GIPSY   230
    AND BLOW A STRAIN THE WORLD AT LAST SHALL HEED • 265 THYRSIS   79
    THE LAST POETIC VOICE IS DUMB • • • • • • 270 MEMORIAL VERSES   4
    CATCHES THE WESTERING SUNS LAST FIRES • • • 274 STANZAS CARNAC   24
    WITH INDIAN HEATS AT LAST FORDONE • • • • • 276 SOUTHERN NIGHT   26
    WITH INDIAN SUNS AT LAST FORDONE • • • • • 276 SOUTHERN NIGHT   V 26
    SCOTT HAD BESTOWD THERE HIS LAST • • • • • 281 HAWORTH CHURCH   23
    IN MORTAL WEAKNESS A LAST • • • • • 281 HAWORTH CHURCH   32
    SCOTT HAD CONSIGND THERE HIS LAST • • • • • 281 HAWORTH CHURCH   V 23
    ON AND AT NIGHTFALL AT LAST • • • • • 289 RUGBY CHAPEL   107
    SPEAK THE LAST WORD AT HIS GRAVE • • • • • 298 HEINES GRAVE   201
    AT LAST THE ENCIRCLING TREES RETIRE • • • • 300 GRANDE CHARTR   21
    LAST OF THE RACE OF THEM WHO GRIEVE • • • • 302 GRANDE CHARTR   110
    LAST OF THE PEOPLE WHO BELIEVE • • • • • 302 GRANDE CHARTR   112
    A LAST A LAST FAREWELL • • • • • 312 OBERMANN   184
    A LAST A LAST FAREWELL • • • • • 312 OBERMANN   184
    SOME NEW SUCH HOPE MUST DAWN AT LAST • • • • 321 OBERMANN MORE   243
    SINCE LAST ON EARTH THERE LIVED AND WROUGHT • 315 OBERMANN MORE   V 83
    A NEW SUCH HOPE MUST DAWN AT LAST • • • • • 321 OBERMANN MORE   V 243
    WEALTHY IN CORN AND FLOCKS WHICH WHEN AT LAST • 330 MEROPE   5
    OR HATRED TO THEIR PRESENT IN THIS LAST • • • 331 MEROPE   40
    AT LAST IT REACHD US THAT HE STILL MISTRUSTFUL • 338 MEROPE   259
    THOU TELLEST THE FATE OF THE LAST • • • • • 345 MEROPE   469
    BUT HER NURSLING HER HOPE CAME AT LAST • • • 346 MEROPE   510
    LAST OF OUR QUARTERS WITH THE ARCADIAN CHIEFS • 356 MEROPE   759
    INGLORIOUS AND SHOULD DROP AT LAST UNKNOWN • • 356 MEROPE   771
    AT LAST THE CRY DREW TO THE WATERS EDGE • • • 357 MEROPE   806
    SO DIES THE LAST SHOOT OF OUR ROYAL TREE •.• • 359 MEROPE   857
    WHETHER IT TURN AT LAST TO JOY OR WOE • • • 359 MEROPE   862
    A LAST LONG-CHERISHD PROJECT IN MY AIM • • • 360 MEROPE   880
    OR HOW REPLY TO THEE MY CHILD LAST-BORN • • • 367 MEROPE   1041
    LAST-MURDERD WHO REPROACHFULLY WILT SAY • • • 367 MEROPE   1042
    ONE LAST MURDER-SAVED CHILD • • • • • 369 MEROPE   1102
    AND THE SLOW-RIPENING TIME AT LAST PREPARES • 379 MEROPE   1264
    THIS MORNINGS ANGRY ANSWER FOR THY LAST • • • 394 MEROPE   1691
    FOR THE LAST TIME I ASK ASK EARNESTLY • • • 394 MEROPE   1717
    FLING OFF THY CROWN SUPPOSED AT LAST SECURE • 395 MEROPE   1743
    THY MOTHERS PRAYERS AND THIS PRAYER LAST OF ALL • 405 MEROPE   2011
    WHO SAW THE PRINCE AND LAIAS LAST WITH HIM • • • 365 MEROPE   V
    KNEE-DEEP IN THE COOL FORD FOR TIS THE LAST • 413 EMPEDOCLES I 2   41
    LOOKS ONCE AND DRIVES ELSEWHERE AND LEAVES • 415 EMPEDOCLES I 2   86
        ITS LAST EMPLOY
    ASK NOT THE LATEST NEWS OF THE LAST MIRACLE • • 415 EMPEDOCLES I 2   106
    BAFFLERS OF OUR OWN PRAYERS FROM YOUTH TO LIFES • 420 EMPEDOCLES I 2   231
        LAST SCENES
    THE LAST SPARK OF MANS CONSCIOUSNESS WITH WORDS • 429 EMPEDOCLES II   30
    THY LAST MISCHANCE ON THIS SICILIAN DEEP • • • 430 EMPEDOCLES II   57
    TO SEE IF WE WILL POISE OUR LIFE AT LAST • • • 440 EMPEDOCLES II   369
    TO SEE IF WE WILL NOW AT LAST BE TRUE • • • 440 EMPEDOCLES II   370
    WILL HAVE MORE PERIL FOR US THAN THE LAST • • • 440 EMPEDOCLES II   378
    AND RALLY THEM FOR ONE LAST FIGHT AND FAIL • • • 440 EMPEDOCLES II   388
    THY LAST DEFEAT IN THIS SICILIAN SEA • • • • 430 EMPEDOCLES II   V 57
    ONE STILL LAGS LAST AND TURNS AND EYES THE PILE • 444 WESTMIN ABBEY   14
    SEEMD TO COME TRUE AT LAST O ABBEY OLD • • • 446 WESTMIN ABBEY   73
    A MEEK LAST GLANCE OF LOVE DIDST THROW • • • 450 GEISTS GRAVE   35
    MARKD WITH A STONE THY LAST ABODE • • • • • 452 GEISTS GRAVE   72
    SOOTHED THEM IN THEIR LAST DECAY • • • • • 455 POOR MATTHIAS   92
    WHAT A TALE OF THY LAST WEEK • • • • • 455 POOR MATTHIAS   110
    IN JOY THY LAST MORN FLEW ANON • • • • • 460 KAISER DEAD   63
    AND TWINE WITH BOLDER HAND THY LAST MEMORIAL WREATH • 471 ALARIC AT ROME   228
    LAST NIGHT THE WIND WAS UP AND STRONG • • • 479 HAYSWATER BOAT   17
    LAST NIGHT I LOOKD THE SKY WAS CLEAR • • • • 480 HAYSWATER BOAT   33
    AT LAST IN AIR FAR OFF DIM ROSE A HEIGHT • • • 484 S S LUSITANIA   6
    IN SOME OTHER SORT THAN YOUR LAST WHEN THE • •   HOMER TRANS   41
        BATTLE IS ENDED

LASTED
    ONLY WHILE THEIR LOVE LIVD LASTED THEY • • • • • 482 THEKLAS ANSWER   8

LASTING
    OF LABOUR THAT IN LASTING FRUIT OUTGROWS • • • • 1 QUIET WORK   6
    I LOOKD FOR LIFE MORE LASTING RULE MORE HIGH • • 9 MYCERINUS   17

LASTLY
    AND LASTLY THOUGH OF OURS • • • • • • • • • 421 EMPEDOCLES I 2   262

LASTS
 AND WHILE IT LASTS WE CANNOT WHOLLY END • • • • 236 PALLADIUM   24
 THE WORLD WHICH LASTS WHEN I AM DEAD • • • • • 250 WISH   36
 THY MEMORY LASTS BOTH HERE AND THERE • • • • • • 451 GEISTS GRAVE   57

LATE
 FELL THIS LATE VOICE FROM LIPS THAT CANNOT LIE • • 8 MYCERINUS V 5
 LATE AT EVE HAD LURED ME CREEPING • • • • 26 NEW SIRENS V 3
 AND LATE AT EVENING SPENT AND PANTING FALLS • • 114 BALDER DEAD 3   12
 OF AGES AND MY LATE RETURN TO LIGHT • • • • 128 BALDER DEAD 3   511
 THIS COMES OF NURSING LONG AND WATCHING LATE • • 140 TRISTRAM 1   313
 MY PRINCESS ART THOU THERE SWEET TIS TOO LATE • • 140 TRISTRAM 1 V 308
 LATE THOU COMEST CRUEL THOU HAST BEEN • • • • 142 TRISTRAM 2   4
 THOU HAST DARED IT BUT TOO LATE TO SAVE • • • • 142 TRISTRAM 2   10
 SO LATE SUCH STORMS THE SAINT IS MAD • • • • 156 SAINT BRANDAN   4
 BRAVELY SAID HE FOR I OF LATE HAVE BEEN • • • • 169 EAST LONDON   7
 SO LATE IN THY PORTICO • • • • • • • 188 STRAYED REVEL   93
 THE LOVERS MEET BUT MEET TOO LATE • • • • 207 TOO LATE   6
 HERE WHERE THE REAPER WAS AT WORK OF LATE • • 255 SCHOLAR-GIPSY   11
 CHILDREN WHO EARLY RANGE THESE SLOPES AND LATE • 258 SCHOLAR-GIPSY   105
 FROM A FEW BOYS LATE AT THEIR PLAY • • • • 286 RUGBY CHAPEL   7
 AND CALL US BUT TOO LATE YE COME • • • • 305 GRANDE CHARTR   196
 TOO LATE FOR US YOUR CALL YE BLOW • • • • 305 GRANDE CHARTR   197
 THE SUMMER-DAY GROW LATE • • • • • 310 OBERMANN   116
 THOUGH LATE THOUGH DIMMD THOUGH WEAK YET TELL • 323 OBERMANN MORE   311
 THE LATE-RELENTING GODS WITH VICTORY BROUGHT • 330 MEROPE   6
 TO COME A LATE AVENGER TO THE AID • • • • 349 MEROPE   577
 THERE NURSE A LATE REMORSE AND THANK THE GODS • 396 MEROPE   1755
 PEISIANAX THOU KNOWST DRINKS LATE AND THEN • • 407 EMPEDOCLES I 1   39
 BUT OH PAUSANIAS HE IS CHANGED OF LATE • • • 408 EMPEDOCLES I 1   67
 OF HYACINTHS AND ON LATE ANEMONIES • • • • 414 EMPEDOCLES I 2   50
 OF HYACINTHS AND ON LATE ANEMONES • • • • 414 EMPEDOCLES I 2 V 50
 NO THOU ART COME TOO LATE EMPEDOCLES • • • • 429 EMPEDOCLES II   16
 HITHER HE CAME LATE-BORN AND LONG-DESIRED • • 444 WESTMIN ABBEY   8
 HE HEARD OF LATE THE GRAND OLD MAN • • • • 460 KAISER DEAD   41
 WHO OF LATE ON THE SOFT NIGHTS OF MAY • • • • 482 THEKLAS ANSWER   6

LATELY
 LATELY BELOW AND JOIND HIM AND THE PAIR • • • • 125 BALDER DEAD 3   434

LATER
 NOW TIME OBSCURES IT AND MENS LATER DEEDS • • • • 117 BALDER DEAD 3   130
 OR YET LATER IN WATCH • • • • • • • • • 297 HEINES GRAVE   167

LATEST
 FOR THESE BESIEGE THE LATEST BREATH • • • • • • 249 WISH   3
 ASK NOT THE LATEST NEWS OF THE LAST MIRACLE • • 415 EMPEDOCLES I 2   106
 HIS LATEST LOFTIEST MUSIC SMOTE HIS EAR • • • • 478 CROMWELL   210

LATHS
 A DOME OF LATHS AND OER IT FELTS WERE SPREAD • • 61 SOHRAB RUSTUM   23

LATMIAN
 UPON THE PINE-GROWN LATMIAN STEEP • • • • • • 181 ISOLATION MARG   24

LATTER
 DROP WITH MINE ADOWN LIFES LATTER DAYS • • • • 33 NEW SIRENS   210
 THE TEMPEST OF THE LATTER DAYS HATH SWEPT • • • • 128 BALDER DEAD 3   523
 BUT WHERE WILL EUROPES LATTER HOUR • • • • • 272 MEMORIAL VERSES   62
 BUT WHERE SHALL EUROPES LATTER HOUR • • • • • 272 MEMORIAL VERSES V 62
 YET IN THIS LATTER TIME • • • • • • • • • 446 WESTMIN ABBEY   71

LATTICES
 AND OPEN JASMINE-MUFFLED LATTICES • • • • • • 264 THYRSIS   68

LAUD
 WE LAUD THEM BUT THEY ARE NOT OURS • • • • • 304 GRANDE CHARTR   168
 LAUD THEIR PLUMAGE GREET THEIR LAYS • • • • • 455 POOR MATTHIAS   100
 THERE LAUD WITH NOISELESS STEPS AND GLITTERING EYE 476 CROMWELL   165

LAUGH
 AND HIS CLEAR LAUGH FLED RINGING THROUGH THE GLOOM 12 MYCERINUS   113
 LAUGH MY FRIENDS AND WITHOUT BLAME • • • • • 22 MEMORY-PICTURE   1
 BUT I HEARD THORA LAUGH IN GOTHLAND ISLE • • • 117 BALDER DEAD 3   148
 THEN WITH A LOUDER LAUGH THE HAG REPLIED • • • 123 BALDER DEAD 3   350
 BUT WITH A LOUDER LAUGH THE HAG REPLIED • • • 123 BALDER DEAD 3 V 350
 ONLY TO LAUGH AND TO DIE • • • \• • • • • 298 HEINES GRAVE   198
 THE GODS LAUGH IN THEIR SLEEVE • • • • • • 415 EMPEDOCLES I 2   87
 TO MAKE HIM LAUGH OR WEEP • • • • • • • EMPEDOCLES I 2 V

LAUGHD
 SHE GREETED THEM THE FIRST AND LAUGHD AND SAID • • 123 BALDER DEAD 3   336

LAUGHING
 THESE CLAIM NOT EVERY LAUGHING HOUR • • • • • • 53 RESIGNATION   30
 AND TO TRISTRAM LAUGHING SAY • • • • • • • 135 TRISTRAM 1   144
 HER LAUGHING CHILDREN IN THEIR BEDS AND PLAY • • 151 TRISTRAM 3   77

LAUGHS
    AND NOW TO-NIGHT SHE LAUGHS AND SPEAKS   •   •   •   •   147 TRISTRAM 2   128

LAUGHTER
    FROM THE LOUD JOYFUL LAUGHTER OF HIS LIPS   •   •   •   11 MYCERINUS   101
    WHEN THE FEAST WAS GAY AND THE LAUGHTER LOUD   •   •   146 TRISTRAM 2   114
    WHEN THE FEAST WAS LOUD AND THE LAUGHTER SHRILL   •   •   146 TRISTRAM 2   V 114
    DOTH RIOTOUS LAUGHTER NOW REPLACE   •   •   •   •   184 TERRACE BERNE   21
    MOCKING LAUGHTER A FILM   •   •   •   •   •   •   293 HEINES GRAVE   38
    LAUGHTER AND CRIES THOSE NOTES BETWEEN   •   •   •   305 GRANDE CHARTR   186

LAUNCELOTS
    WAS LAUNCELOTS GUEST AT JOYOUS GARD   •   •   •   •   136 TRISTRAM 1   203

LAUNCH
    FISHERS WHO LIVE ON THE LAKE-SIDE TO LAUNCH   •   •   358 MEROPE   837

LAUREL
    STREW WITH LAUREL THE GRAVE   •   •   •   •   •   283 HAWORTH CHURCH   66
    LAUREL AND OAK THE MATURE   •   •   •   •   •   282 HAWORTH CHURCH   V
    HE HATH HIS HARP AND LAUREL WITH HIM STILL   •   •   409 EMPEDOCLES I 1   82
    HE HAS HIS HARP AND LAUREL WITH HIM STILL   •   •   409 EMPEDOCLES I 1   V 82
    MY LAUREL BOUGH   •   •   •   •   •   •   •   •   434 EMPEDOCLES II   192
    MY LAUREL BOUGH   •   •   •   •   •   •   •   •   435 EMPEDOCLES II   197
    IS THINE THE LAUREL-CROWN THAT GREATNESS WREATHES   463 ALARIC AT ROME   25

LAURELLD
    IN THE LAURELLD ROCK OER THE BLUE   •   •   •   •   294 HEINES GRAVE   57

LAURELS
    LEFT OUR AWFUL LAURELS HANGING   •   •   •   •   •   27 NEW SIRENS   31
    HALF HER LAURELS UNWON   •   •   •   •   •   •   283 HAWORTH CHURCH   70
    LAURELS SHE HAD AND A COURSE   •   •   •   •   283 HAWORTH CHURCH   72
    AND WITHER HALF THE LAURELS ON THY TOMB   •   •   463 ALARIC AT ROME   38
    IF WREATHS MAY TWINE FOR YOU OR LAURELS WAVE   •   467 ALARIC AT ROME   137

LAURENT
    THE MULE-TRACK FROM SAINT LAURENT GOES   •   •   •   299 GRANDE CHARTR   4

LAVE
    HIM CAN NO FOUNT OF FRESH FORGIVENESS LAVE   •   •   ‚   •   172 GOOD SHEPHERD   4
    MEDITERRANEAN WATERS LAVE   •   •   •   •   •   •   275 STANZAS CARNAC   39

LAVENDER
    WITH PALE-SPIKED LAVENDER   •   •   •   •   •   •   392 MEROPE   1642

LAW
    AND IN THIS VISION OF THE GENERAL LAW   •   •   •   5 DUKE WELLINGTON   8
    NATURES GREAT LAW AND LAW OF ALL MENS MINDS   •   •   8 RELIGIOUS ISOL   12
    OF YOUTH SELF-GOVERND AT THE FEET OF LAW   •   •   9 MYCERINUS   10
    NATURES GREAT LAW AND LAW OF ALL MENS MINDS   •   •   8 RELIGIOUS ISOL   12
    I HAVE KEPT UNINFRINGED MY NATURES LAW   •   •   •   40 HUMAN LIFE   4
    THE LAW GREW STRONGER EVERY DAY   •   •   •   •   56 RESIGNATION   135
    AS THE LAW IS AND GO YOUR WAY   •   •   •   •   87 SICK KING BOKH   9
    THE LAW AND BY THE LAW MUST DIE   •   •   •   •   89 SICK KING BOKH   38
    THE LAW AND BY THE LAW MUST DIE   •   •   •   •   89 SICK KING BOKH   38
    BUT SENTENCED HIM AS THE LAW IS   •   •   •   •   91 SICK KING BOKH   111
    STONED MUST HE BE THE LAW STANDS SO   •   •   •   91 SICK KING BOKH   114
    STILL THOU ART KING AND THE LAW STANDS   •   •   92 SICK KING BOKH   138
    THE LAW IS PLANTED TO ABIDE   •   •   •   •   •   94 SICK KING BOKH   208
    ADDED THIS LAW   •   •   •   •   •   •   •   •   192 STRAYED REVEL   215
    MAKES HIS OWN WELFARE HIS UNSWERVED-FROM LAW   •   195 FRAG ANTIGONE   8
    PREFER OBEDIENCE TO THE PRIMAL LAW   •   •   •   196 FRAG ANTIGONE   30
    AGAINST CREONS LAW POLYNICES   •   •   •   •   196 FRAG ANTIGONE   41
    TO HIM POSTPONING AN ETERNAL LAW   •   •   •   197 FRAG ANTIGONE   75
    STAVED US BACK AND GAVE OUR CHOICE THE LAW   •   •   210 SELF-DECEPTION   12
    THIS I KNOW IS THE LAW   •   •   •   •   •   •   232 YOUTH OF MAN   3
    THE OLD LAW THEY CRIED IS WHOLLY COME TO NOUGHT   •   237 PROGRESS   3
    THE OLD LAW OBSERVED BY SCRIBES AND PHARISEES   •   237 PROGRESS   6
    I SAY UNTO YOU SEE YE KEEP THAT LAW   •   •   •   237 PROGRESS   7
    THINK NOT THAT I TO ANNUL THE LAW HAVE WILLD   •   237 PROGRESS   10
    NO JOT NO TITTLE FROM THE LAW SHALL PASS   •   •   237 PROGRESS   11
    THE OLD LAW THEY SAID IS WHOLLY COME TO NOUGHT   •   237 PROGRESS   V 3
    EVEN IN HIS OWN DESPITE HIS BEINGS LAW   •   •   246 BURIED LIFE   37
    OF PASSION WITH ETERNAL LAW   •   •   •   •   •   270 MEMORIAL VERSES   11
    WORDSWORTHS SON-IN-LAW FRIEND   •   •   •   •   280 HAWORTH CHURCH   6
    YOU GIVE THE UNIVERSE YOUR LAW   •   •   •   •   304 GRANDE CHARTR   165
    ARTS CAME AND ARMS AND LAW   •   •   •   •   •   445 WESTMIN ABBEY   57
    STERN LAW OF EVERY MORTAL LOT   •   •   •   •   450 GEISTS GRAVE   29
    TRUE WE MUST BOW TO NATURES LAW   •   •   •   •   481 COURAGE   2

LAWLESS
    O LAWLESS DARING OF THE STRONG   •   •   •   •   •   •   398 MEROPE   1800

LAWLESSNESS
    FREE FROM ALL GUILT OF LAWLESSNESS   •   •   •   •   353 MEROPE   660

LAWN
    NOTHING STIRS ON THE LAWN BUT THE QUICK LILAC-SHADE   19 MODERN SAPPHO   2
    NOTHING MOVES ON THE LAWN BUT THE QUICK LILAC-SHADE   19 MODERN SAPPHO   V 2
    STREAM ALL DAY THROUGH YOUR ENCHANTED LAWN   •   •   26 NEW SIRENS   24

LAWN   (CONTINUED)
        THE CUCKOO LOUD ON SOME HIGH LAWN   .   .   .   .   .   .   57 RESIGNATION   176
        SAY HAS SOME WET BIRD=HAUNTED ENGLISH LAWN   .   .   .   .   175 PARTING   19
        AND CAN THIS FRAGRANT LAWN   .   .   .   .   200 PHILOMELA   10
        ON THIS FAIR WESTERN LAWN   .   .   .   .   201 PHILOMELA   V 18
        GREET UPON THE LAWN AT PLAY   .   .   .   .   454 POOR MATTHIAS   68

LAWNS
        ON THESE LAWNS I SAW YOU PLAYING   .   .   .   .   .   .   29 NEW SIRENS   95
        THEIR CHILDREN PLAY ON THE LAWNS   .   .   .   .   .   .   234 YOUTH OF MAN   70
        YE WITNESSD YE MOUNTAIN LAWNS   .   .   .   .   399 MEROPE   1831
        TO THOSE UNTRODDEN MOUNTAIN-LAWNS AND THERE   .   .   .   427 EMPEDOCLES I 2   456

LAWNY
        OF MANY A LAWNY HILL AND STREAMS WITH SILVER FLOW   474 CROMWELL   104

LAWS
        OF COMMERCE LAWS AND POLICY   .   .   .   .   48 HORATIAN ECHO   15
        BUT FATE WITHSTANDS AND LAWS FORBID THIS WAY   .   .   .   98 BALDER DEAD 1   127
        WHERE THEY HOLD COUNCIL AND GIVE LAWS FOR MEN   .   .   .   105 BALDER DEAD 2   34
        AUGUST LAWS DOTH MIGHTILY VINDICATE   .   .   .   .   .   196 FRAG ANTIGONE   49
        IN LAWS BY HUMAN ARTISTS BOUND   .   .   .   .   223 EPILOG LAOCOON   76
        WERE THE MESSENIAN CHIEFS THE LAWS HE FRAMED   .   .   .   337 MEROPE   243

LAX
        AS HE LETS HIS LAX RIGHT HAND   .   .   .   .   431 EMPEDOCLES II   71

LAY
        LAY BEFORE HIS YOUTHFUL WIFE   .   .   .   .   14 CHURCH BROU 1   50
        WHERE LAST YEAR THEY LAY   .   .   .   .   16 CHURCH BROU 2   14
        LAY THE WARM GOLDEN GOURDS GOLDEN WITHIN   .   .   .   .   25 DREAM   18
        AT FIRST IMAGINED LAY   .   .   .   .   45 IN UTRUMQUE PAR   2
        LIE STREWN IT SEEMS WHERE THEN THEY LAY   .   .   .   . .   55 RESIGNATION   101
        OF RUGS AND FELTS AND NEAR HIM LAY HIS ARMS   .   .   .   61 SOHRAB RUSTUM   27
        HIS BED AND THE WARM RUGS WHEREON HE LAY   .   .   .   .   63 SOHRAB RUSTUM   95
        AND CROSSD THE CAMP WHICH LAY BEHIND AND REACHD   .   .   66 SOHRAB RUSTUM   190
        WAS RUSTUMS AND HIS MEN LAY CAMPD AROUND   .   .   .   .   67 SOHRAB RUSTUM   194
        AND PIERCED THE MIGHTY RUSTUM WHILE HE LAY   .   .   .   73 SOHRAB RUSTUM   423
        ON THE MOWN DYING GRASS SO SOHRAB LAY   .   .   .   .   80 SOHRAB RUSTUM   638
        BUT SOHRAB CRAWLD TO WHERE HE LAY AND CAST   .   .   .   81 SOHRAB RUSTUM   694
        IN BOTH HIS HANDS THE DUST WHICH LAY AROUND   .   .   .   81 SOHRAB RUSTUM   700
        COME LET ME LAY MY HAND UPON THY MANE   .   .   .   .   83 SOHRAB RUSTUM   746
        AND THOU MUST LAY ME IN THAT LOVELY EARTH   .   .   .   84 SOHRAB RUSTUM   787
        AND I WILL LAY THEE IN THAT LOVELY EARTH   .   .   .   .   84 SOHRAB RUSTUM   802
        HIS LIMBS GREW SLACK MOTIONLESS WHITE HE LAY   .   .   .   86 SOHRAB RUSTUM   848
        SO ON THE BLOODY SAND SOHRAB LAY DEAD   .   .   .   .   86 SOHRAB RUSTUM   857
        SO IN THE SAND LAY RUSTUM BY HIS SON   .   .   .   .   .   86 SOHRAB RUSTUM   864
        THERE LAY HIS BODY IN MY GRAVE   .   .   .   .   .   .   95 SICK KING BOKH   228
        SO ON THE FLOOR LAY BALDER DEAD AND ROUND   .   .   .   95 BALDER DEAD 1   1
        LAY THICKLY STREWN SWORDS AXES DARTS AND SPEARS   .   .   95 BALDER DEAD 1   2
        AND ON THE TOP LAY BALDERS CORPSE AND PUT   .   .   .   .   96 BALDER DEAD 1   43
        HOME AND LAY DOWN TO SLEEP IN HIS OWN HOUSE   .   .   .   102 BALDER DEAD 1   247
        AND ALL THE GODS LAY DOWN IN THEIR OWN HOMES   .   .   .   102 BALDER DEAD 1   248
        INTO AN UPPER CHAMBER AND LAY DOWN   .   .   .   .   .   103 BALDER DEAD 1   278
        IN CORNWALL TRISTRAM AND QUEEN ISEULT LAY   .   .   .   .   149 TRISTRAM 3   2
        FROM THE OPEN HEATH STILL BY THE HEDGEROWS LAY   .   .   151 TRISTRAM 3   51
        AND NOW SHE WILL GO HOME AND SOFTLY LAY   .   .   .   .   151 TRISTRAM 3   76
        LAY TRISTRAM AND QUEEN ISEULT DEAD AND COLD   .   .   .   149 TRISTRAM 3   V   2
        FROM THE OPEN WASTE WHITE BY THE HEDGEROWS LAY   .   .   TRISTRAM 3   V 51
        WHICH GLISTERING LAY ALL ROUND THEM LONE AND MILD   .   .   155 TRISTRAM 3   V 203
        I FELT AS I IN TORMENT LAY   .   .   .   .   157 SAINT BRANDAN   33
        IN THE CAVERNS WHERE WE LAY   .   .   .   .   162 FORSAKEN MERM   32
        MID STRUGGLING SUFFERERS HURT TO DEATH SHE LAY   .   .   166 AUSTERITY POET   9
        SOME LABOURING MEN WHOSE WORK LAY SOMEWHERE THERE   170 WEST LONDON   5
        CARE NOT FOR THAT AND LAY ME WHERE I FALL   .   .   .   173 MONICAS PRAYER   2
        WHERE SWEET THE UNBROKEN MOONBEAMS LAY   .   .   .   .   177 FAREWELL   2
        THY HAND LAY LANGUIDLY IN MINE   .   .   .   .   178 FAREWELL   15
        WHERE THEY LAY BY THE HUT DOOR   .   .   .   .   .   .   186 STRAYED REVEL   32
        LAY LIKE THE FOLDS OF A BRIGHT GIRDLE FURLD   .   .   .   211 DOVER BEACH   23
        LAY LIKE THE FOLDS OF A BRIGHT GARMENT FURLD   .   .   .   211 DOVER BEACH   V 23
        WHEN ON THE BEACH THE CYCLOPS LAY   .   .   .   .   .   .   222 EPILOG LAOCOON   46
        MOCKD HER POOR LOVELORN GIANTS LAY   .   .   .   .   .   222 EPILOG LAOCOON   48
        AFAR IN REST THE CATTLE LAY   .   .   .   .   224 EPILOG LAOCOON   109
        COPAIS LAY BRIGHT IN THE MOON   .   .   .   .   229 YOUTH OF NATURE   37
        WHO CRY ALOUD TO LAY THE OLD WORLD LOW   .   .   .   .   237 PROGRESS   15
        WE DIG AND HEAP LAY STONE ON STONE   .   .   .   .   .   241 MORALITY   8
        AND LAY UPON THE BREAST OF GOD   .   .   .   .   .   .   242 MORALITY   36
        WHO IMAGINES HER FIELDS AS THEY LAY   .   .   .   .   .   252 FUTURE   29
        WHEN HE LAY IN THE NIGHT BY HIS FLOCK   .   .   .   .   253 FUTURE   46
        HE LAID US AS WE LAY AT BIRTH   .   .   .   .   .   .   271 MEMORIAL VERSES   48
        ONCE MORE WE LAY AS ERST AT BIRTH   .   .   .   .   .   .   271 MEMORIAL VERSES V 48
        LAY THE LONE COAST OF BRITTANY   .   .   .   .   273 STANZAS CARNAC   4
        IT LAY BESIDE THE ATLANTIC WAVE   .   .   .   .   .   .   273 STANZAS CARNAC   6
        TWAS MEET TO LAY   .   .   .   .   279 SOUTHERN NIGHT   112
        LAY BEFORE BOTH AND A FAME   .   .   .   .   281 HAWORTH CHURCH   28
        LAY THY BENUMBING HAND   .   .   .   .   283 HAWORTH CHURCH   V
        MANS WORK-PLACE LAY IN GLOOM   .   .   .   .   315 OBERMANN MORE   78
        THE ROMAN NOBLE LAY   .   .   .   .   315 OBERMANN MORE   98
        MILLIONS WHOSE LIFE IN ICE LAY FAST   .   .   .   .   .   322 OBERMANN MORE   287
        THOU SOUGHTEST LAY IN GLOOM   .   .   .   .   315 OBERMANN MORE   V 78

LAY   (CONTINUED)
        BUT HERE WHILE HARBOURING ON ITS MARGIN LAY   •   •   332 MEROPE   70
        LAY HONEY-CAKES ON ITS MARGE   • • • • • • •   342 MEROPE   386
        WHILE FROM THE TURF WHEREON I LAY I SPRANG • • • •   358 MEROPE   829
        LAY FORLORN LAY OUTCAST   • • • • • • • • •   391 MEROPE   1604
        LAY FORLORN LAY OUTCAST   • • • • • • • • ꞏ⁴ • 391 MEROPE   1604
        LAY IN THY SON IS BURIED IN HIS GRAVE   • • • •   394 MEROPE   1694
        THE WOMAN WHO AT AGRIGENTUM LAY   • • • • •   410 EMPEDOCLES I 1   109
        CHIRON THE AGED CENTAUR LAY   • • • • • • •   414 EMPEDOCLES I 2   59
        IN TRANCE PANTHEIA LAY   • • • • • • • •   416 EMPEDOCLES I 2   108
        WHERE IN PROUD REPOSE HE LAY   • • • • • •   433 EMPEDOCLES II   162
        LAY ON THE HEARTH AMID A FIERY RING   • • • •   446 WESTMIN ABBEY   84
        BUT ALL NIGHT LONG AMID THE FLAMES HE LAY   • • •   446 WESTMIN ABBEY   89
        AND HUMBLY LAY THEE DOWN TO DIE   • • • • •   450 GEISTS GRAVE   36
        WE LAY THEE CLOSE WITHIN OUR REACH   • • • •   451 GEISTS GRAVE   65
        WHAT DEATHLIKE STILLNESS OER THE LANDSCAPE LAY   •   466 ALARIC AT ROME   99
        IN MOURNFUL LOVELINESS THAT CITY LAY   • • • •   466 ALARIC AT ROME   104
        AND THERE BENEATH HIS FEET HIS CONQUEST LAY   • •   468 ALARIC AT ROME   158
        A HOLIER INCENSE THAN THIS FEEBLE LAY   • • • •   471 ALARIC AT ROME   226
        THE OARS HAVE MOULDERD AS THEY LAY   • • • •   480 HAYSWATER BOAT   38
        IN WHOSE CAPACIOUS SPIRIT LAY HIS PLAN   • • • •   LUCRETIUS 5   4
        IN WHOSE PROPHETIC SPIRIT LAY THE PLAN   • • • •   LUCRETIUS 5   V   4

LAYING
        FROM LAYING THY DEAR MASTER IN HIS GRAVE   •   •   •   •   85 SOHRAB RUSTUM   834

LAYS
        AND DOWN HE LAYS HIS WEARY BONES   • • • • • •   213 PROGRESS POESY   12
        LAYS BARE OF WRETCHED DAYS   • • • • • • •   260 SCHOLAR-GIPSY   186
        LAUD THEIR PLUMAGE GREET THEIR LAYS   • • • • •   455 POOR MATTHIAS   100

LEA
        GREEN HAPPY PLACES LIKE A FLOWERY LEA   •   •   •   •   475 CROMWELL   117

LEAD
        O HUSSEIN LEAD ME TO THE KING   • • • • • • •   87 SICK KING BOKH   10
        FERDOUSIS AND THE OTHERS LEAD   • • • • • • •   88 SICK KING BOKH   12
        FERDUSIS AND THE OTHERS LEAD   • • • • • • •   88 SICK KING BOKH   V   12
        WHICH GODS AND HEROES LEAD IN FEAST AND FRAY   • •   98 BALDER DEAD 1   123
        YET DREARY NANNA IS THE LIFE THEY LEAD   • • • •   104 BALDER DEAD 1   314
        AND LEAD AS ERST OUR DAILY LIFE IN HEAVEN   • • •   115 BALDER DEAD 3   56
        TO THE GUEST-CHAMBER LEAD HIM SOME ONE GIVE   • •   359 MEROPE   869
        TO RALLY THEM AND LEAD THEM TO REVENGE   • • • •   383 MEROPE   1365
        BUT LEAD HIM THROUGH THE LOVELY MOUNTAIN-PATHS   •   411 EMPEDOCLES I 1   156
        TO LEAD THOSE FALSE WHO TRUST IT HIST ONCE MORE   •   413 EMPEDOCLES I 2   33
        AND OF THE LIFE WHICH HEROES LEAD   • • • • •   414 EMPEDOCLES I 2   73
        AND OF THE LIFE THAT HEROES LEAD   • • • • • •   414 EMPEDOCLES I 2   V   73

LEADED
        AND WE GAZED UP THE AISLE THROUGH THE SMALL   163 FORSAKEN MERM   75
            LEADED PANES

LEADEN
        UPON THE GLISTENING LEADEN ROOF   • • • • • •   16 CHURCH BROU 2   1
        ON THE SMOOTH LEADEN ROOF AND ON THE WALLS   • • •   18 CHURCH BROU 3   34
        ROLLD HEAVILY THE LEADEN MIST ASIDE   • • • • •   126 BALDER DEAD 3   441

LEADER
        HIGH ON A BANK OUR LEADER STANDS   • • • • • •   53 RESIGNATION   44
        GOOD TO OBEY WITHOUT A LEADER NOUGHT   • • • • •   381 MEROPE   1302
        THE LEADER IS FAIREST   • • • • • • • • •   442 EMPEDOCLES II   447

LEADERS
        BLIND LEADERS TO THEIR BANE   • • • • • • •   353 MEROPE   675

LEADING
        SO IT MUST BE YET WHILE LEADING   • • • • • •   49 SECOND BEST   13
        TIS APOLLO COMES LEADING • • • • • • • • •   442 EMPEDOCLES II   445

LEADS
        AND ON THE LICHEN-CRUSTED LEADS ABOVE   • • • •   19 CHURCH BROU 3   45
        THERE IS A ROAD WHICH LEADS TO HELAS REALM   • • •   99 BALDER DEAD 1   135
        THERE IS A WAY WHICH LEADS TO HELAS REALM   • • •   99 BALDER DEAD 1   V 135
        PATH OF ADVANCE BUT IT LEADS   • • • • • • •   288 RUGBY CHAPEL   86
        OER WHOSE LIT FLOOR A ROAD OF MOONBEAMS LEADS   • •   438 EMPEDOCLES II   312

LEAF
        FROM THE RANK LIFE OF TOWNS THIS LEAF AND FLUNG   • •   6 GEO CRUIKSHANK   2
        DOWN THE LEAF-STREWN FOREST-ROAD   • • • • • •   13 CHURCH BROU 1   30
        HAST THOU WITH MYRTLE-LEAF CROWND HIM O PLEASURE   • •   20 MODERN SAPPHO   35
        FROM THIS DUSK OF LEAF-STREWN PLACES   • • • • •   32 NEW SIRENS   193
        TO GAZE ON THE LIGHT SEA OF LEAF AND BOUGH   • • •   155 TRISTRAM 3   202
        TO GAZE ON THE GREEN SEA OF LEAF AND BOUGH   • • •   155 TRISTRAM 3   V 202
        SHAKES EVERY LEAF OF THE GROVE   • • • • • •   293 HEINES GRAVE   43
        THERE IN THE LEAF-STREWN COPSE I FOUND   • • • •   484 ROME-SICKNESS   14

LEAFD
        OF BRIGHT-LEAFD CHESTNUTS AND MOSSD WALNUT-TREES   • •   25 DREAM   8
        OF FLOWERS THE FRAIL-LEAFD WHITE ANEMONY   • • • •   257 SCHOLAR-GIPSY   87

LEAFLESS
    HUMID THE AIR LEAFLESS YET SOFT AS SPRING • • • • 263 THYRSIS   17

LEAGUE
    AND SPLIT HIS CURRENTS THAT FOR MANY A LEAGUE • •   87 SOHRAB RUSTUM   883
    GAZING SEAWARDS MANY A LEAGUE • • • • • • • 131 TRISTRAM 1   42
    AND NOW TO ME THOU TENDEREST FRIENDLY LEAGUE • • 340 MEROPE   333
    SHORT ANSWER IS SUFFICIENT LEAGUE WITH THEE • • 340 MEROPE   335
    EVEN AFTER NEWS OF THIS SAD DEATH OUR LEAGUE • • 394 MEROPE   1689
    SO WHEN HE PLEADED FOR OUR LEAGUE BUT NOW • • • • 404 MEROPE   1978

LEAGUER
    THE MARCH THE LEAGUER HEAVENS BLITHE AIR • • • • 138 TRISTRAM 1   258

LEAGUERD
    BY LEAGUERD TOWER AND TENTED FIELD IT CAME • • • • 476 CROMWELL   148

LEAN
    HERE LEAN MY HEAD ON THIS COLD BALUSTRADE • • • •   19 MODERN SAPPHO   4
    HERE LEAN MY HEAD ON THIS COOL BALUSTRADE • • • •   19 MODERN SAPPHO V   4
    AND THEY SET JARS OF WINE AND OIL TO LEAN • • • • 118 BALDER DEAD 3   166
    WHICH WAY TO LEAN I KNOW NOT BLOODY STROKES • • 388 MEROPE   1521
    AND LEAN UPON THE THOUGHT • • • • • • • 420 EMPEDOCLES I 2   239
    WE NOW WOULD LEAN UPON • • • • • • • • 422 EMPEDOCLES I 2   315

LEAND
    AS SHE TOWRD ME LEAND HER FACE • • • • • • •   23 MEMORY-PICTURE   34
    AS SHE TOWARDS ME LEAND HER FACE • • • • • •   23 MEMORY-PICTURE V 34
    LEAND ON HIS GATE HE GAZES TEARS • • • • • •   57 RESIGNATION   186
    LEAND UP AGAINST THE COLUMN THERE • • • • • 186 STRAYED REVEL   9

LEANEST
    ON WHAT A REED MY CHILD THOU LEANEST THERE • • • • 381 MEROPE   1310

LEANING
    AND LEANING BACKWARD IN A PENSIVE DREAM • • • • 257 SCHOLAR-GIPSY   77
    AND LEANING BACKWARDS IN A PENSIVE DREAM • • • • 257 SCHOLAR-GIPSY V 77
    AND CHECK THY FIERY STEEDS AND LEANING BACK • • 349 MEROPE   575
    THAT LONG GAZER LEANING NEAR • • • • • • •   META CLOISTER   26

LEANS
    LEANS HER EAR TO YOUR MAD SALLIES • • • • • •   27 NEW SIRENS   27
    HE LEANS UPON A GATE AND SEES • • • • • • •   57 RESIGNATION   172
    A GOLD HARP LEANS AGAINST THE BED • • • • • • 131 TRISTRAM 1   17
    FROM THE PILLAR WHERE HE LEANS • • • • • •   META CLOISTER   34

LEAP
    AND PIERCE HIM LIKE A STAB AND MAKE HIM LEAP • •   78 SOHRAB RUSTUM   584
    AND MAKE HIM LEAP THE GRATE AND COME WITHIN • • 100 BALDER DEAD 1   170
    AND MADE HIM LEAP THE GRATE AND CAME WITHIN • • 109 BALDER DEAD 2   148
    AND MAKE LEAP UP WITH JOY THE BEAUTEOUS HEAD • • 265 THYRSIS   87
    SHALL I NOT GREET HER SHALL I NOT LEAP FORTH • 331 MEROPE   60
    YOUR SONS LEAP UPON THE FOE OF YOUR KIN • • • • 344 MEROPE   462
    LEAP AND FLY OPEN OF THEMSELVES FOR JOY • • • • 401 MEROPE   1885
    LEAP AND ROAR THOU SEA OF FIRE • • • • • • • 441 EMPEDOCLES II   411
    AND MAKE THE WORLDS DEAD SPIRIT LEAP AGAIN • • • • 481 HUNGARIAN NAT   11

LEAPEST
    THOU LEAPEST TO THY DEED AND HAST NOT ASKD • • • • 384 MEROPE   1388

LEAPING
    THE STREAM GOES LEAPING BY • • • • • • •   16 CHURCH BROU 2   3
    LOITERING AND LEAPING • • • • • • • • • 218 BACCHANALIA 1   20
    IS FRESHEND BY THE LEAPING STREAM WHICH THROWS • • 414 EMPEDOCLES I 2   46

LEAPT
    THUNDERING TO EARTH AND LEAPT FROM RUSTUMS HAND • •   73 SOHRAB RUSTUM   419
    AND HERMOD CAME AND LEAPT FROM SLEIPNER DOWN • • 114 BALDER DEAD 3   33
    SHARP QUIVERING TONGUES OF FLAME SHOT OUT AND LEAPT 119 BALDER DEAD 3   188

LEARN
    ONE LESSON NATURE LET ME LEARN OF THEE • • • •   1 QUIET WORK   1
    TWO LESSONS NATURE LET ME LEARN OF THEE • • • •   1 QUIET WORK V   1
    TILL SHE SEARCH AND LEARN HER OWN • • • • •   28 NEW SIRENS   74
    WHOSE SURENESS GRAY-HAIRD SCHOLARS HARDLY LEARN • •   43 GIPSY CHILD   42
    WHAT THROUGH EXPERIENCE OTHERS LEARN • • • •   59 RESIGNATION   234
    AND THEN WILL THAT DEFENCELESS WOMAN LEARN • • •   79 SOHRAB RUSTUM   598
    SHALL SEE OURSELVES AND LEARN AT LAST • • • • 179 FAREWELL   55
    O LEARN OF LONDON WHOSE PAUPERS • • • • • 214 NEW ROME   13
    WILL YE NOT LEARN IT AND KNOW • • • • • • • 230 YOUTH OF NATURE   87
    HIS FRIENDS AND WENT TO LEARN THE GIPSY-LORE • • 256 SCHOLAR-GIPSY   37
    TO LEARN STRANGE ARTS AND JOIN A GIPSY-TRIBE • • 259 SCHOLAR-GIPSY 135
    AND LEARN MY FRUSTRATE LIFE • • • • • • • 322 OBERMANN MORE   276
    BUT I FROM OUR DEPLORED MISCHANCE LEARN THIS • • 359 MEROPE   853
    LEARN THAT FROM OTHER LIPS O QUEEN THAN MINE • • 362 MEROPE   927
    COULDST THOU PAUSANIAS LEARN • • • • • • 417 EMPEDOCLES I 2   157
    WE MARK NOT THE WORLDS WAYS BUT WOULD HAVE   419 EMPEDOCLES I 2 V 221
        IT LEARN OURS
    THEN WILT THOU LEARN IF NOT • • • • • • •   EMPEDOCLES I 2 V
    LEARN THAT MEN WILL NOT AND GODS CANNOT HELP THY STATE   EMPEDOCLES I 2 V
    MUST LEARN TO WAIT RENOUNCE WITHDRAW • • • • • 481 COURAGE   4
    LEARN TO KNOW WHAT IT DESIRED • • • • • • •   META CLOISTER   31

LEARND

LEARND IN MORE LANGUID CLIMES	• • • •	46 WORLD QUIETIST	5
WHAT FAR TOO SOON ALAS I LEARND	• • • • •	180 ISOLATION MARG	8
IN THE BANQUET AND LEARND HIS SONGS	• • • • •	189 STRAYED REVEL	123
WHEN FULLY LEARND WILL TO THE WORLD IMPART	• • • •	256 SCHOLAR-GIPSY	49
AND FROM THAT TEACHER MAYST HAVE LEARND LIKE ME	• •	394 MEROPE	1709
HAVE LEARND THAT WE MUST SACRIFICE THE BENT	• •	394 MEROPE	1711
HAVE LEARND THAT THERE ARE GUILTY DEEDS WHICH LEAVE		394 MEROPE	1713
HAVE LEARND THAT WE MUST SACRIFICE THE THIRST	• •	394 MEROPE	V1711
THIS HAVING LEARND LET US A UNION FOUND	• • •	394 MEROPE	V1716

LEARNED

SHE LOOKD SO WITCHING FAIR THAT LEARNED WIGHT	• •	154 TRISTRAM 3	181
NOT MIRACLES THOU ART A LEARNED MAN	• • • •	411 EMPEDOCLES I 1	159
AND THE GOOD LEARNED FRIENDLY QUIET MAN	• • •	429 EMPEDOCLES II	8

LEARNS

WHO EACH DAY MORE SURELY LEARNS	• • • • •	49 SECOND BEST	20
TURNING SICK AND BAFFLED LEARNS	• • • • •	SECOND BEST	V 20
LEARNS FREEDOMS LESSON FROM YOUR VOICE OF FEAR	• •	471 CROMWELL	2

LEARNST

THOU LEARNST TO THINK AS THEY	• • • • • • •	311 OBERMANN	148

LEARNT

BUT IN THE WORLD I LEARNT WHAT THERE	• • • • •	178 FAREWELL	37
LOST IT TOO SOON AND LEARNT A STORMY NOTE	• • •	269 THYRSIS	223
THEN LEARNT HIS DEATH AND PINED AWAY	• • • •	279 SOUTHERN NIGHT	110
BUT WE WE LEARNT YOUR LORE TOO WELL	• • • •	304 GRANDE CHARTR	156
BUT WE WE LEARNT THEIR LORE TOO WELL	• • • •	304 GRANDE CHARTR	V 156
WHETHER I LEARNT THEIR LESSONS WELL	• • • •	354 MEROPE	698
OR HAVING LEARNT THEM WELL APPLY	• • • •	354 MEROPE	699
UNHACKD UNSMIRCHD UNBLOODIED AND HAVE LEARNT	• •	388 MEROPE	1518
HAVING LEARNT THIS THEN USE THY KNOWLEDGE NOW	• •	388 MEROPE	1520
UNHACKD UNSMIRCHD UNBLOODIED AND HAST LEARNT	• •	388 MEROPE	V1518

LEASH

AND HAD HIM AT THE PRINCES SIDE IN LEASH	• • • •	364 MEROPE	971

LEAST

THY WAY AND THIS AT LEAST MY PRAYERS AVAIL	• • •	104 BALDER DEAD 1	309
OF HAPPIER MEN FOR THEY AT LEAST	• • • •	181 ISOLATION MARG	37
FOR HE HE AT LEAST BY SLAYING HER	• • • •	196 FRAG ANTIGONE	48
AT LEAST TO HALF FORGETFULNESS	• • • • •	200 PHILOMELA	V
ADIEU AND SAY THAT ONE AT LEAST	• • • • '•	204 EUPHROSYNE	27
NOT THE LEAST GIFTED YOUNG	• • • • • •	285 HAWORTH CHURCH	104
AT LEAST THE RESTLESSNESS THE PAIN	• • • •	302 GRANDE CHARTR	104
ONE SON AT LEAST I SPARED FOR STILL HE LIVES	• •	340 MEROPE	348
I DARE NOT WISH IT BUT AT LEAST TO HEAR	• • •	351 MEROPE	611
AT LEAST IF THOU WILT TRUST THEM TRY THEM FIRST	• •	381 MEROPE	1319
HE HAD A HEST AT LEAST AND THOU HAST NONE	• • •	385 MEROPE	1403
AND HE TREATS DOUBT THE BEST WHO TRIES TO SEE		415 EMPEDOCLES I 2	101
LEAST ILL			
AT LEAST THAT GODS THY LOT	• • • • • • •	EMPEDOCLES I 2	V

LEAVE

CROWN CROWN HIM QUICKLY AND LEAVE HIM FOR ME	• •	20 MODERN SAPPHO	36
LEAVE THE LILIES IN THEIR DEW	• • • • • •	35 NEW SIRENS	268
EVEN SO WE LEAVE BEHIND	• • • • • • • •	41 HUMAN LIFE	25
AND LEAVE TO DEATH THE HOSTS OF THANKLESS KINGS	• •	68 SOHRAB RUSTUM	240
UNHAPPY HOW HAST THOU ENDURED TO LEAVE	• • •	110 BALDER DEAD 2	180
TO LEAVE FOR EVER BALDER IN THE GRAVE	• • •	120 BALDER DEAD 3	228
COME LET ME LEAVE THE SHADOW OF THIS WOOD	• •	139 TRISTRAM 1	281
AND WITH A BLOOD LIKE MINE WILL LEAVE I FEAR	• •	140 TRISTRAM 1	306
NOW TO SAIL THE SEAS OF DEATH I LEAVE THEE	• • •	145 TRISTRAM 2	97
WE LEAVE THE BRUTAL WORLD TO TAKE ITS WAY	• • •	172 IMMORTALITY	2
THEY CANNOT LEAVE IT THEY MUST GO	• • • •	226 EPILOG LAOCOON	167
LEAVE NOT A HUMAN SOUL	• • • • • • •	234 YOUTH OF MAN	57
BUT LEAVE US NOT WHILE WE LIVE	• • • • •	234 YOUTH OF MAN	60
AND WE MUST LEAVE THE OLD FAITHS AND WALK THEREIN		237 PROGRESS	26
LEAVE THEN THE CROSS AS YE HAVE LEFT CARVED GODS	• •	237 PROGRESS	27
NO LONGER LEAVE THY WISTFUL FLOCK UNFED	• • •	255 SCHOLAR-GIPSY	3
FOR EARLY DIDST THOU LEAVE THE WORLD WITH POWERS	• •	260 SCHOLAR-GIPSY	161
DROP BY AND LEAVE ITS SEEKER STILL UNTIRED	• • •	268 THYRSIS	207
AND LEAVE NO GOOD BEHIND	• • • • • • •	273 EDW QUILLINAN	6
AND LEAVE NO TRACE BEHIND	• • • • • •	273 EDW QUILLINAN	V 6
TAKE LEAVE OF HEINES GRAVE NOT THUS	• • • •	298 HEINES GRAVE	200
AH LEAVE US NOT THE FRET ALONE	• • • •	302 GRANDE CHARTR	108
HERE LEAVE US TO DIE OUT WITH THESE	• • • •	302 GRANDE CHARTR	111
AND LEAVE OUR DESERT TO ITS PEACE	• • • •	306 GRANDE CHARTR	210
AH LEAVE US NOT THE PANG ALONE	• • • • •	302 GRANDE CHARTR	V 108
AND LEAVE OUR FOREST TO ITS PEACE	• • • •	306 GRANDE CHARTR	V 210
I GO FATE DRIVES ME BUT I LEAVE	• • • • •	310 OBERMANN	131
AND NOW I LEAVE THEE TO THESE RITES ESTEEMD	• •	342 MEROPE	379
THE TRUE AVENGERS THESE I LEAVE HIS DEED	• • •	349 MEROPE	555
OF THE THRACIAN SEA LET HER LEAVE	• • • •	361 MEROPE	912
TO ME AND THE MESSENIANS LEAVE THE REST	• • •	391 MEROPE	1593
HAVE LEARND THAT THERE ARE GUILTY DEEDS WHICH LEAVE		394 MEROPE	1713
TO-DAY I REIGN THE REST I LEAVE TO FATE	• • •	397 MEROPE	1776
CRYING O YE MESSENIANS WILL YE LEAVE	• • • •	402 MEROPE	1934

LEAVE   (CONTINUED)
        AND I MUST LEAVE HIM FOR HIS PLEASURE IS   . . . .   409 EMPEDOCLES I 1   91
        WHOS LOATH TO LEAVE THIS LIFE . . . .   426 EMPEDOCLES I 2   412
        FOR I MUST BE ALONE LEAVE ME ONE MULE   . . . .   428 EMPEDOCLES I 2   465
        TO LEAVE HIS VIRTUES ROOM   . . . .   420 EMPEDOCLES I 2   V 255
        THEIR CRAFT THE FISHERS LEAVE . . . .   444 WESTMIN ABBEY   12
        AND LEAVE IT ROUND THY NECK TO TWINE . . . . . .   461 KAISER DEAD   81
        AND NOT LEAVE HIM BEHIND A CORPSE ON THE PLAIN   HOMER TRANS   42
            LIKE PATROCLUS

LEAVED
        WITH LARGE-LEAVED LOW-CREEPING MELON-PLANTS   . .   190 STRAYED REVEL   155
        AND FLAG-LEAVED IRIS-FLOWERS . . . .   191 STRAYED REVEL   170

LEAVEN
        WAIT FOR THE LEAVEN TO WORK THE LET TO END . . .   449 WESTMIN ABBEY   170

LEAVES
        ON HIS COAT WERE LEAVES AND BLOOD-STAINS   . . . .   14 CHURCH BROU 1   47
        LEAVES US FIXT TO NOTHING LONG . . . .   24 MEMORY-PICTURE   58
        LEAVES US TRUE TO NOTHING LONG . . . .   24 MEMORY-PICTURE   V 58
        LEAVES US FIRM TO NOTHING LONG . . . .   24 MEMORY-PICTURE   V 58
        LEAVES US JOIND TO NOTHING LONG   . . . .   24 MEMORY-PICTURE   V 58
        BRIGHT IN THE SUN THE CLIMBING GOURD-PLANTS LEAVES   25 DREAM   16
        LEAVES HER RIDDLE HALF UNKNOWN . . . .   28 NEW SIRENS   76
        LEAVES WERE WHIRLING IN THE ALLEYS   . . . . . .   30 NEW SIRENS   125
        LEAVES ARE WHIRLING IN THE ALLEYS   . . . . . .   30 NEW SIRENS   V 125
        HE LEAVES HIS KIND OERLEAPS THEIR PEN   . . . .   58 RESIGNATION   211
        LIKE LEAVES BY SUNS NOT YET UNCURLD . . . . . .   59 RESIGNATION   253
        WHO ALL WILL FLIT LIKE EDDYING LEAVES AROUND   . .   100 BALDER DEAD 1   177
        THE FLYING LEAVES THE STRAINING BLAST   . . . .   136 TRISTRAM 1   179
        OF THOSE OLD OAKS WHOSE WET RED LEAVES   . . . .   141 TRISTRAM 1   359
        ISEULT LEAVES THEE TRISTRAM NEVER MORE   . . . .   146 TRISTRAM 2   100
        FRINGD WITH DEAD LEAVES AND MOSSES RARE   . . .   148 TRISTRAM 2   V
        WHICH LEAVES THE FIERCE NECESSITY TO FEEL . . . .   153 TRISTRAM 3   123
        FIRST LEAVES THE FRINGING HEATH AT ONCE ALL ROUND   TRISTRAM 3   V 14
        FIRST LEAVES THE ENCIRCLING HEATH AT ONCE ALL ROUND   TRISTRAM 3   V 14
        SOONER SHALL THIS MY STAFF BEAR LEAVES   . . . .   160 NECKAN   51
        THE EBB-TIDE LEAVES DRY . . . .   165 FORSAKEN MERM   135
        MAN NEARS MAN MEETS AND LEAVES AGAIN . . . . . .   185 TERRACE BERNE   V 48
        OF THY CUP THE BRIGHT GLANCING VINE-LEAVES . . . .   188 STRAYED REVEL   85
        LEAVES NO LEISURE TO PRESS . . . .   199 EARLY DEATH   12
        HOW THICK THE BURSTS COME CROWDING THROUGH THE LEAVES   201 PHILOMELA   29
        THROUGH WHOSE FRAIL LEAVES AND SHOWERS   . . . .   200 PHILOMELA   V
        THROUGH WHOSE LIGHT LEAVES AND SHOWERS   . . . .   200 PHILOMELA   V
        FOR EVER LEAVES ITS VAIN EMPLOY   . . . .   206 RIVER   18
        IN THIS HIGH FIELDS DARK CORNER WHERE HE LEAVES   . .   255 SCHOLAR-GIPSY   12
        AND PURPLE ORCHISES WITH SPOTTED LEAVES   . . . .   257 SCHOLAR-GIPSY   89
        TO THE SILENT COUNTRY AND LEAVES   . . . . . .   283 HAWORTH CHURCH   69
        OF WITHERD LEAVES AND THE ELMS . . . .   286 RUGBY CHAPEL   4
        THE LEAVES ARE ON THE VALLEY-PATHS   . . . . . .   306 OBERMANN   7
        I TURN THY LEAVES I FEEL THEIR BREATH   . . . .   306 OBERMANN   13
        THOUGH TO THESE LEAVES THE GLACIERS SPARE   . . .   307 OBERMANN   27
        LEAVES ME AUSTERER STERNER THAN I WOULD   . . . .   335 MEROPE   155
        LOOKS ONCE AND DRIVES ELSEWHERE AND LEAVES . .   415 EMPEDOCLES I 2   86
            ITS LAST EMPLOY
        LEAVES HUMAN EFFORT SCOPE   . . . .   426 EMPEDOCLES I 2   423
        SWEPT OFF THE WITHERED LEAVES THAT HIDE THE NAKED TOMB   469 ALARIC AT ROME   192
        LEAVES HIM NO REST AND CHANGE HE WILL   . . . .   484 ROME-SICKNESS   26

LEAVEST
        THERE THOU ART GONE AND ME THOU LEAVEST HERE   . .   268 THYRSIS   191

LEAVING
        THEY RAMBLE LEAVING WHERE THEY PASS   . . . . . .   55 RESIGNATION   110
        LEAVING HER SUNK AND PALE THOUGH FAIR   . . . .   132 TRISTRAM 1   48
        LEAVING THE SALT SEA-BEDS   . . . .   196 FRAG ANTIGONE   57
        LEAVING THE REST IN THE WILD . . . .   290 RUGBY CHAPEL   127

LEAVINGS
        THE WORLDS POOR ROUTED LEAVINGS OR WILL THEY   . .   172 IMMORTALITY   6

LEAVST
        BUT DOWN THOU FLEEST HERE AND LEAVST OUR SCOURGE . .   367 MEROPE   1050

LED
        A BLIND LED BEGGAR . . . .   51 CONSOLATION   29
        AND WHEN FEROOD WHO LED THE PERSIANS SAW   . . . .   65 SOHRAB RUSTUM   144
        WITH JOY AND ALL THE PLEASANT LIFE THEY LED   . .   79 SOHRAB RUSTUM   627
        THOUGH SIGHTLESS YET HIS OWN MIND LED THE GOD   . .   97 BALDER DEAD 1   76
        AND TALKING OF THE LIFE WE LED IN HEAVEN   . . .   104 BALDER DEAD 1   329
        THEIR ARMS AND LED THEIR HORSES FROM THE STALL . .   105 BALDER DEAD 2   12
        ASGARD AND LED THEIR HORSES TO THE BEACH   . . .   106 BALDER DEAD 2   66
        HERMOD LED SLEIPNER FROM VALHALLA FORTH   . . . .   106 BALDER DEAD 2   71
        AND LED THE WAY ON SLEIPNER AND THE REST   . . .   115 BALDER DEAD 3   59
        AND LED THEM HOME OVER THE DARKENING HEATH . . .   151 TRISTRAM 3   63
        AH WHERE THE SPIRIT ITS HIGHEST LIFE HATH LED   . .   167 RACHEL 1   12
        EVEN IN A PALACE LIFE MAY BE LED WELL   . . . .   168 WORLDLY PLACE   1
        LED BY THY TAPERS STARLIKE BEAM   . . . . . .   177 FAREWELL   8
        WHEN HIS AWE-STRUCK CAPTORS LED   . . . . . .   229 YOUTH OF NATURE   43
        MOST MEN ARE LED BY INTEREST AND THE FEW   . . .   341 MEROPE   365
        SHE LED THE WAY OF DEATH . . . .   344 MEROPE   434

LED   (CONTINUED)
          WHO LED THE GREEKS TO ILIUM AGAMEMNON   • • • •   367 MEROPE   1035
          BE NEITHER SAINT NOR SOPHIST-LED BUT BE A MAN • •   416 EMPEDOCLES I 2   136
          THAT STREWD THE BLOOD-STAIND PATH WHERE EMPIRE LED   478 CROMWELL   226

LEE
          STOUTLY UNDER THE HEADLANDS LEE THEY SWAM   • • •   358 MEROPE   822

LEFT
          SHALL BE LEFT STANDING FACE TO FACE WITH GOD   • •   7 REP FRIEND CONT   14
          AND TURNING LEFT THEM THERE AND WITH BRIEF PAUSE   • •   11 MYCERINUS   82
          SAVOYS DUKE HAD LEFT HIS BRIDE • • • • • •   13 CHURCH BROU 1   6
          STANDS AS ERST THE BUILDERS LEFT IT   • • • • •   15 CHURCH BROU 1   69
          THE PRINCELY PAIR ARE LEFT ALONE   • • • • • •   17 CHURCH BROU 2   39
          LEFT OUR AWFUL LAURELS HANGING   • • • • • •   27 NEW SIRENS   31
          SHALL I NOT JOY YOUTHS HEATS ARE LEFT BEHIND   • •   37 YOUTHS AGIT   5
          WE LEFT JUST TEN YEARS SINCE YOU SAY   • • • •   53 RESIGNATION   40
          THAT WAYSIDE INN WE LEFT TO-DAY   • • • • • •   53 RESIGNATION   41
          AND TOOK HIS HORSEMANS CLOAK AND LEFT HIS TENT   • •   61 SOHRAB RUSTUM   9
          SO SAID HE AND DROPPD SOHRABS HAND AND LEFT   • •   63 SOHRAB RUSTUM   94
          SO FOLLOWD RUSTUM LEFT HIS TENTS AND CROSSD   • •   69 SOHRAB RUSTUM   280
          HE LEFT TO LIE BUT HAD REGAIND HIS SPEAR   • • •   74 SOHRAB RUSTUM   450
          HIS HUDDLING YOUNG LEFT SOLE AT THAT HE CHECKS   • •   78 SOHRAB RUSTUM   563
          THINKING OF HER HE LEFT AND HIS OWN DEATH   • • •   79 SOHRAB RUSTUM   603
          HE SPOKE AND ALL THE BLOOD LEFT RUSTUMS CHEEKS   •   80 SOHRAB RUSTUM   661
          RUSTUMS GREAT FATHER WHOM THEY LEFT TO DIE   • • •   81 SOHRAB RUSTUM   680
          LEFT FRESHLY GATHERD ON THEIR NATIVE BANK   • • •   86 SOHRAB RUSTUM   845
          REGRETTING THE WARM MANSION WHICH IT LEFT   • • •   86 SOHRAB RUSTUM   855
          AND RUSTUM AND HIS SON WERE LEFT ALONE   • • • •   86 SOHRAB RUSTUM   874
          AND LEFT HIS BODY STRETCHD UPON THE FLOOR   • • •   97 BALDER DEAD 1   63
          BUT THE BLIND HODER LEFT THE FEASTING GODS   • • •   97 BALDER DEAD 1   72
          AND HODER TURND AND LEFT HIS MOTHERS HOUSE   • • •   100 BALDER DEAD 1   197
          AND TO VALHALLAS GATE HE RODE AND LEFT   • • • •   102 BALDER DEAD 1   265
          SCANT SPACE THAT WARDER LEFT FOR PASSERS BY   • •   107 BALDER DEAD 2   90
          TO RIGHT AND LEFT AND WARM STEAM FILLS THE AIR   •   107 BALDER DEAD 2   98
          SHE SPAKE AND STEPPD ASIDE AND LEFT HIM ROOM   • •   108 BALDER DEAD 2   135
          TO MATE BUT LEFT HER TO ROAM DISTANT LANDS   • • •   116 BALDER DEAD 3   94
          FOR HE MY HUSBAND LEFT ME HERE TO PINE   • • • •   116 BALDER DEAD 3   106
          AND I AM LEFT UNCOMFORTED IN HEAVEN   • • • • •   117 BALDER DEAD 3   122
          STILL LEFT AND THAT CHIEF SCALD THY BROTHER BRAGE   117 BALDER DEAD 3   133
          WITH NANNA ON HIS RIGHT AND ON HIS LEFT   • • •   118 BALDER DEAD 3   164
          BUT ALL I LEFT OF MY OWN ACT AND FLED   • • • •   125 BALDER DEAD 3   405
          SHE LEFT THE GLEAM-LIT FIREPLACE   • • • • •   140 TRISTRAM 1   315
          I LIKE THEE HAVE LEFT MY YOUTH AFAR   • • • • •   143 TRISTRAM 2   22
          SHE LEFT LONELY FOR EVER   • • • • • • •   165 FORSAKEN MERM   142
          THY LEFT HOLDS HANGING LOOSELY   • • • • • •   186 STRAYED REVEL   11
          ON MY LEFT THROUGH THE BEECHES   • • • • • •   187 STRAYED REVEL   43
          AND OUR OWN PLACE ONCE LEFT   • • • • • • •   195 FRAG ANTIGONE   18
          FOR ALAS HE LEFT US EACH RETAINING   • • • • •   210 SELF-DECEPTION   17
          THIS SENTENCE HAVE I LEFT BEHIND   • • • • • •   217 NAMELESS EPIT   V
          THE LAST-LEFT HAYMAKER IS GONE   • • • • • •   218 BACCHANALIA 1   9
          LESS THAN THEY LEFT UNREVEALD   • • • • • •   231 YOUTH OF NATURE   106
          LEAVE THEN THE CROSS AS YE HAVE LEFT CARVED GODS   •   237 PROGRESS   27
          IS LEFT TO EACH MAN STILL   • • • • • • •   244 SUMMER NIGHT   92
          THAT PEACE HAS LEFT THE UPPER WORLD   • • • •   249 KENSINGTON GARD   27
          HAD LEFT ERE HE WOKE ON ITS BREAST   • • • • •   252 FUTURE   22
          THIS SAID HE LEFT THEM AND RETURND NO MORE   • • •   256 SCHOLAR-GIPSY   51
          LEFT HUMAN HAUNT AND ON ALONE TILL NIGHT   • • •   269 THYRSIS   230
          WARRIOR STATESMAN HAD LEFT   • • • • • • •   281 HAWORTH CHURCH   V 21
          HAVE RUN THEIR CIRCLE AND LEFT   • • • • • •   282 HAWORTH CHURCH   V
          SURELY HAS NOT BEEN LEFT VAIN   • • • • • •   287 RUGBY CHAPEL   39
          WE WE ONLY ARE LEFT   • • • •   289 RUGBY CHAPEL   104
          WHOM WE HAVE LEFT IN THE SNOW   • • • • • •   289 RUGBY CHAPEL   116
          NOR LEFT GOES PASSIVELY BY   • • • • • • •   295 HEINES GRAVE   91
          LEFT IT AND THOU ALAS   • • • • • • •   298 HEINES GRAVE   197
          THE SUFFERERS DIED THEY LEFT THEIR PAIN   • • •   303 GRANDE CHARTR   131
          I LEFT THEM YESTERDAY   • • • • • • •   312 OBERMANN MORE   12
          BUT LEFT THIS MANY A YEAR   • • • • • • •   313 OBERMANN MORE   40
          SHE LEFT IT ALL BEHIND   • • • • • • •   317 OBERMANN MORE   134
          WHAT STILL OF STRENGTH IS LEFT EMPLOY   • • •   323 OBERMANN MORE   321
          SOARING FROM HIS DEATH-PILE ON OETA LEFT   • •   336 MEROPE   213
          YE HAVE NOT LEFT THIS GATE WHICH HE MUST PASS   •   361 MEROPE   917
          CARRY HIS MESSENGER BUT LEFT HIM HERE   • • •   374 MEROPE   1193
          AND ONLY SLAVES AND TYRANTS LEFT ALIVE   • • •   383 MEROPE   1378
          ARE THE SOLE CLAIMANTS LEFT WHAT CAUSE OF STRIFE   •   394 MEROPE   1693
          O CLIFFS LEFT BY THE EAGLES   • • • • • •   399 MEROPE   1825
          THE SON TO PERISH AS YE LEFT THE SIRE   • • •   402 MEROPE   1935
          I LEFT THEE SUPPING WITH PEISIANAX   • • • •   407 EMPEDOCLES I 1   31
          TO BE LEFT MUSING THESE SOFT NIGHTS ALONE   • •   409 EMPEDOCLES I 1   92
          WE SHALL HAVE LEFT THE WOODY TRACT AND COME   •   412 EMPEDOCLES I 2   2
          O SAGE O SAGE TAKE THEN THE ONE WAY LEFT   • •   429 EMPEDOCLES II   24
          LEFT THEIR FRIEND AND WITH ROBES FLOWING   • • •   433 EMPEDOCLES II   152
          WHO HAS NO FRIEND NO FELLOW LEFT NOT ONE   • • •   437 EMPEDOCLES II   271
          WHAT ARE LEFT WILL HARDLY BE   • • • • • •   458 POOR MATTHIAS   212
          AND LEFT IT ROCKING IN THE BAY   • • • • • •   480 HAYSWATER BOAT   32
          AND CEUTA ON THE LEFT THEN SOUTHWARD SPED   • •   484 S S LUSITANIA   5

LEFTWARD
          STRIKE LEFTWARD CRIES OUR GUIDE AND HIGHER   • • • •   300 GRANDE CHARTR   19

LEGENDARY
THE ROSE-CROWND QUEEN OF LEGENDARY LORE • • • • • 168 RACHEL 2 7

LEGIONS
SHE LET THE LEGIONS THUNDER PAST • • • • • • • 316 OBERMANN MORE 111

LEGITIMATELY
LEGITIMATELY SIRE TO SON WITH US • • • • • • • 389 MEROPE 1539

LEISURE
MODERATE TASKS AND MODERATE LEISURE • • • • • • 49 SECOND BEST 1
SCANT LEISURE FOR A SECOND MESSENGER • • • • • • 140 TRISTRAM 1 307
LEAVES NO LEISURE TO PRESS • • • • • • • 199 EARLY DEATH 12
WHAT LEISURE TO GROW WISE • • • • • • • • 308 OBERMANN 72
AND FILL THY LEISURE WITH AN EARNEST PRAYER • • 332 MEROPE 72
THE ENFORCED LEISURE OF AN EXILES EAR • • • • 387 MEROPE 1488

LEMANS
LAKE LEMANS WATERS FAR BELOW • • • • • • • • • 310 OBERMANN 121

LEMNIAN
SOME ROCK MORE LONELY THAN THAT LEMNIAN ISLE • • 395 MEROPE 1746

LEND
IF I MIGHT LEND THEIR LIFE A VOICE • • • • • 60 RESIGNATION 269
WHO SELF-EXCULPATES LEND TO FOULEST DEEDS • • • • 338 MEROPE 279
LEND LIFE TO THE DUMB STONES • • • • • • • 421 EMPEDOCLES I 2 274
WHAT A LESSON DOTH IT LEND • • • • • • • 457 POOR MATTHIAS 174

LENDING
ASLEEP YET LENDING HALF AN EAR • • • • • • • 452 GEISTS GRAVE 69

LENDS
LOVE LENDS LIFE A LITTLE GRACE • • • • • • • • 44 QUESTION 4

LENGTH
THE PRAISE OF GODS RICH BOON AND LENGTH OF DAYS • • 11 MYCERINUS 78
AT SUCH DESPOTIC LENGTH TO PROVE • • • • • HORATIAN ECHO V
BUT WHO THROUGH ALL THIS LENGTH OF TIME • • • • 92 SICK KING BOKH 145
IN ITS WEARY UNPROFITABLE LENGTH • • • • • • 235 YOUTH OF MAN 110
ONE WITH THE OERLABOURD POWER THAT THROUGH 422 EMPEDOCLES I 2 291
   THE BREADTH AND LENGTH

LENGTHEN
LENGTHEN THEIR HAPPINESS • • • • • • • • • • 51 CONSOLATION 58

LENGTHEND
SHE LENGTHEND ALSO • • • • • • • • • • 51 CONSOLATION 59
THROUGH A LIFE LENGTHEND • • • • • • • • • • 192 STRAYED REVEL 221

LENIENCE
EMBOLDEND BY MY LENIENCE THINK IT FEAR • • • • 341 MEROPE 373

LENT
AND SIGH THAT ONE THING ONLY HAS BEEN LENT • • • • 37 YOUTHS AGIT 13
WHO LENT THEE CHILD THIS MEDITATIVE GUISE • • • • 41 GIPSY CHILD 3
LENT IT THE MUSIC OF ITS TREES AT DAWN • • • • 175 PARTING 20
FOR HE LENT A NEW LIFE TO THESE HILLS • • • • 228 YOUTH OF NATURE 14

LENTISK
OF THE LENTISK AND ILEX • • • • • • • • • • 392 MEROPE 1633

LEPER
THE LEPER RECOLLECT SAID HE • • • • • • • • 157 SAINT BRANDAN ' 38
AND IN THE STREET A LEPER SATE • • • • • • • 157 SAINT BRANDAN 45

LEPERS
THERE ARE THE LEPERS AND ALL SICK • • • • • • 93 SICK KING BOKH 175
THAT JOPPAN LEPERS EASE WAS PAIN • • • • • • 158 SAINT BRANDAN 72

LESS
NOT LESS THY BOAST ILLUMINATES CONTROL • • • • 8 RELIGIOUS ISOL 7
IT MAY BE BUT NOT LESS HIS BROW WAS SMOOTH • • • • 12 MYCERINUS 112
FORTUNES NOW LESS FREQUENT HEIR • • • • • 22 MEMORY-PICTURE V
ARE LESS LONELY THAN THEY WERE • • • • • • 26 NEW SIRENS 20
ARE LESS THE POET MORE THAN MAN • • • • • 58 RESIGNATION 204
WHAT IS ONE MORE ONE LESS OBSCURE OR FAMED • • • 68 SOHRAB RUSTUM 252
NOT LESS THAN THOSE WHO MERIT TEARS • • • • • 92 SICK KING BOKH 148
NO LESS THAN BALDER HAVE I LOST THE LIGHT • • • 125 BALDER DEAD 3 401
IN TIMES LESS ALIEN TO A SPIRIT MILD • • • • 128 BALDER DEAD 3 512
IF HER BLOOM BE NOW LESS RARE • • • • • • • 134 TRISTRAM 1 116
ALL SPOTS MATCHD WITH THAT SPOT ARE LESS DIVINE • • 167 RACHEL 1 13
ARE YET FAR FAR LESS RARE THAN LOVE • • • • 178 FAREWELL 40
THEY WILL FOR THOU I FEEL NOT LESS • • • • • 179 FAREWELL 43
THEY WILL FOR THOU I FEEL NO LESS • • • • • 179 FAREWELL V 43
PROLONGD NOR KNEW ALTHOUGH NOT LESS • • • • • 181 ISOLATION MARG 41
NOR DID THERE NEED LESS THAN THE BURNING PILE • • 198 FRAG ANTIGONE 98
FAME AND HER LESS FAIR FOLLOWERS ENVY STRIFE • • 199 EARLY DEATH 4
GROW STIFFER EVERY FUNCTION LESS EXACT • • • • 212 GROWING OLD 9
THAT THE SINGER WAS LESS THAN HIS THEMES • • • • 230 YOUTH OF NATURE 89
LESS THAN THEY LEFT UNREVEALD • • • • • • 231 YOUTH OF NATURE 106
THE FOOT LESS PROMPT TO MEET THE MORNING DEW • • 266 THYRSIS 138

LESS   (CONTINUED)
         THE HEART LESS BOUNDING AT EMOTION NEW   •   •   •   266 THYRSIS   139
         AND HOPE ONCE CRUSHD LESS QUICK TO SPRING AGAIN   •   •   266 THYRSIS   140
         TO THE LESS PRACTISED EYE OF SANGUINE YOUTH   •   •   •   267 THYRSIS   142
         LESS MODEST PURE AND KIND   •   •   •   •   •   •   273 EDW QUILLINAN   8
         HAVE RESTLESS HEARTS ONE THROB THE LESS   •   •   •   •   303 GRANDE CHARTR   144
         OF HERACLES SCARCE HERACLEIDAE LESS   •   •   •   •   •   337 MEROPE   222
         SCARCE DANGEROUS LESS THAN HIM THE DORIAN LORDS   •   •   381 MEROPE   1298
         ALL STRIVE TO MAKE IT LESS   •   •   •   •   •   •   •   416 EMPEDOCLES I 2   120
         THEN THOU WOULDST LOOK LESS MAZED   •   •   •   •   •   417 EMPEDOCLES I 2   162
         THROUGH WHICH TO SEE LESS CLEAR   •   •   •   •   •   •   419 EMPEDOCLES I 2   205
         NOR IS THAT WIND LESS ROUGH WHICH BLOWS A GOOD   •   •   420 EMPEDOCLES I 2   256
             MANS BARGE
         THROUGH WHICH TO SEE LESS PLAIN   •   •   •   •   •   •   419 EMPEDOCLES I 2   V 205
         NOR IS THE WIND LESS ROUGH THAT BLOWS A GOOD   420 EMPEDOCLES I 2   V 256
             MANS BARGE
         LESS THAN THEY TO US ARE YOU   •   •   •   •   •   •   •   453 POOR MATTHIAS   44
         SOMEWHAT MORE OR SOMEWHAT LESS   •   •   •   •   •   •   457 POOR MATTHIAS   159
         THEY LESS THAN US MIGHT RECOGNIZE   •   •   •   •   •   481 COURAGE   11
         HOW FIRS LESS CURST BY FORTUNES FROWN   •   •   •   •   483 ROME-SICKNESS   10

LESSENING
         STILL MENDING LESSENING HUMAN ILL   •   •   •   •   •   •   484 ROME-SICKNESS   28

LESSER
         ON HIS BROAD BACK NO LESSER RIDER BORE   •   •   •   •   107 BALDER DEAD 2   74

LESSINGS
         OF LESSINGS FAMED LAOCOON   •   •   •   •   •   •   •   •   221 EPILOG LAOCOON   3
         IN LESSINGS TRACK AND TRIED TO SEE   •   •   •   •   •   221 EPILOG LAOCOON   5

LESSON
         ONE LESSON NATURE LET ME LEARN OF THEE   •   •   •   •   1 QUIET WORK   1
         ONE LESSON WHICH IN EVERY WIND IS BLOWN   •   •   •   •   1 QUIET WORK   2
         ONE LESSON OF TWO DUTIES KEPT AT ONE   •   •   •   •   •   1 QUIET WORK   3
         ONE LESSON OF TWO DUTIES SERVD IN ONE   •   •   •   •   •   1 QUIET WORK   V   3
         ONE LESSON OF TWO DUTIES KEPT IN ONE   •   •   •   •   •   1 QUIET WORK   V   3
         INSTRUCT ME NOT I HAVE MY LESSON CLEAR   •   •   •   •   379 MEROPE   1259
         HE HATH HIS LESSON TOO AND THAT DEBTS PAID   •   •   •   429 EMPEDOCLES II   7
         HE HAS HIS LESSON TOO AND THAT DEBTS PAID   •   •   •   429 EMPEDOCLES II   V   7
         WHAT A LESSON DOTH IT LEND   •   •   •   •   •   •   •   457 POOR MATTHIAS   174
         FOR THAT LESSON THOU SHALT HAVE   •   •   •   •   •   •   457 POOR MATTHIAS   175
         BY THEIR OWN CRIMES A LESSON TO ALL EYES   •   •   •   462 ALARIC AT ROME   11
         SO STERN A LESSON AS NECESSITY   •   •   •   •   •   •   467 ALARIC AT ROME   142
         LEARNS FREEDOMS LESSON FROM YOUR VOICE OF FEAR   •   471 CROMWELL   2

LESSONS
         TWO LESSONS NATURE LET ME LEARN OF THEE   •   •   •   •   1 QUIET WORK   V   1
         TWO LESSONS THAT IN EVERY WIND ARE BLOWN   •   •   •   •   1 QUIET WORK   V   2
         WHETHER I LEARNT THEIR LESSONS WELL   •   •   •   •   •   354 MEROPE   698

LEST
         KEENER TO SLAY THEE LEST THOU POISON ME   •   •   •   •   38 WORLDS TRIUMPHS   14
         HIDEST THY FACE TAKE HEED LEST MEN SHOULD SAY   •   •   68 SOHRAB RUSTUM   246
         PEACE LEST OUR FATHER ODIN HEAR THEE GIBE   •   •   •   114 BALDER DEAD 3   23
         HAST ALL IMPUNITY YET LEST THY FRIENDS   •   •   •   •   341 MEROPE   372
         LEST FROM THE COUNCIL-CHAMBER PRESENTLY   •   •   •   •   386 MEROPE   1442

LET
         ONE LESSON NATURE LET ME LEARN OF THEE   •   •   •   •   1 QUIET WORK   1
         TWO LESSONS NATURE LET ME LEARN OF THEE   •   •   •   •   1 QUIET WORK   V   1
         OR IF YE WAKE LET IT BE THEN WHEN FAIR   •   •   •   •   18 CHURCH BROU 3   17
         OR LET IT BE ON AUTUMN NIGHTS WHEN RAIN   •   •   •   •   18 CHURCH BROU 3   32
         AND IF YE WAKE LET IT BE THEN WHEN FAIR   •   •   •   •   18 CHURCH BROU 3   V   17
         LET ME PAUSE LET ME STRIVE IN MYSELF MAKE SOME ORDER   19 MODERN SAPPHO   7
         LET ME PAUSE LET ME STRIVE IN MYSELF MAKE SOME ORDER   19 MODERN SAPPHO   7
         THEIR LOVE LET ME KNOW MUST GROW STRONG AND   19 MODERN SAPPHO   13
             YET STRONGER
         LET MY TURN IF IT WILL COME BE SWIFT IN ARRIVING   •   •   20 MODERN SAPPHO   31
         LET ME PAUSE LET ME STRIVE IN MYSELF FIND SOME ORDER   19 MODERN SAPPHO   V   7
         LET ME PAUSE LET ME STRIVE IN MYSELF FIND SOME ORDER   19 MODERN SAPPHO   V   7
         AND NOW THEY LET HER BE   •   •   •   •   •   •   •   •   21 REQUIESCAT   8
         MANY A FACE I SO LET FLEE   •   •   •   •   •   •   •   •   23 MEMORY-PICTURE   13
         LET THE FLUTTERING FRINGES STREAK   •   •   •   •   •   •   23 MEMORY-PICTURE   29
         MANY A FACE I THEN LET BY   •   •   •   •   •   •   •   •   23 MEMORY-PICTURE   V 13
         MANY A FACE I THEN LET FLEE   •   •   •   •   •   •   •   23 MEMORY-PICTURE   V 13
         LET THIS SOBBING PHRYGIAN STRAIN   •   •   •   •   •   •   32 NEW SIRENS   168
         LET YOUR BROAD LAMPS FLASH THE BRIGHTNESS   •   •   •   •   32 NEW SIRENS   177
         O LOOSE HANDS AND LET IT BE   •   •   •   •   •   •   •   34 NEW SIRENS   224
         O LET FALL ONE TEAR AND SET US FREE   •   •   •   •   •   34 NEW SIRENS   226
         O SPEAK ONCE AND LET MY SADNESS   •   •   •   •   •   •   32 NEW SIRENS   V 167
         LET THIS THROBBING PHRYGIAN STRAIN   •   •   •   •   •   32 NEW SIRENS   V 168
         LET THY FOREBODED HOMAGE CHECK THY TONGUE   •   •   •   38 WORLDS TRIUMPHS   10
         ARE WILLS SO WEAK THEN LET NOT MINE WAIT LONG   •   •   38 WORLDS TRIUMPHS   12
         HAST THOU SO RARE A POISON LET ME BE   •   •   •   •   •   38 WORLDS TRIUMPHS   13
         LET THY FOREBODED TREASON CHECK THY TONGUE   •   •   •   38 WORLDS TRIUMPHS   V 10
         O LET THE FALSE DREAM FLY   •   •   •   •   •   •   •   •   39 STAGIRIUS   49
         LET ALL DOUBTS BE DUMB   •   •   •   •   •   •   •   •   39 STAGIRIUS   53
         LET ALL WORDS BE MILD   •   •   •   •   •   •   •   •   •   40 STAGIRIUS   54
         AH LET US MAKE NO CLAIM   •   •   •   •   •   •   •   •   40 HUMAN LIFE   7
         LET US NOT FRET AND FEAR TO MISS OUR AIM   •   •   •   •   40 HUMAN LIFE   16
         AND LET US BEAR THAT THEY DEBATE   •   •   •   •   •   •   48 HORATIAN ECHO   13
         WITH PLEASANT SMILE LET US TAKE CARE   •   •   •   •   •   48 HORATIAN ECHO   21

LET   (CONTINUED)

LET THE TWO ARMIES REST TO-DAY BUT I • • •   • •   62 SOHRAB RUSTUM   55
LET THERE BE TRUCE BETWEEN THE HOSTS TO-DAY   • •   65 SOHRAB RUSTUM   151
LET SOHRAB ARM AND WE WILL FIND A MAN   • • • • •   66 SOHRAB RUSTUM   186
LET NOT MEN SAY OF RUSTUM HE WAS MATCHD • • • • •   69 SOHRAB RUSTUM   258
O THOU OLD WARRIOR LET US YIELD TO HEAVEN • • • •   74 SOHRAB RUSTUM   438
BUT OH LET THERE BE PEACE TWIXT THEE AND ME   • •   74 SOHRAB RUSTUM   447
FIGHT LET ME HEAR THY HATEFUL VOICE NO MORE   • •   75 SOHRAB RUSTUM   459
HIS HEART TO TAKE A GIFT AND LET THEE GO   • • • •   77 SOHRAB RUSTUM   533
AND LET THE BLOOD FLOW FREE AND SO TO DIE   • •   80 SOHRAB RUSTUM   652
TO DRAW IT AND FOR EVER LET LIFE OUT • • •   • •   82 SOHRAB RUSTUM   705
BUT LET US SPEAK NO MORE OF THIS I FIND   • •   82 SOHRAB RUSTUM   716
MY FATHER LET ME FEEL THAT I HAVE FOUND   • •   82 SOHRAB RUSTUM   717
COME LET ME LAY MY HAND UPON THY MANE   • •   83 SOHRAB RUSTUM   746
LET ME ENTREAT FOR THEM WHAT HAVE THEY DONE   • •   84 SOHRAB RUSTUM   780
LET THEM ALL CROSS THE OXUS BACK IN PEACE   • •   84 SOHRAB RUSTUM   782
AND I WILL SPARE THY HOST YEA LET THEM GO   • •   84 SOHRAB RUSTUM   806
LET THEM ALL CROSS THE OXUS BACK IN PEACE   • •   85 SOHRAB RUSTUM   807
TILL THEN IF FATE SO WILLS LET ME ENDURE   • •   85 SOHRAB RUSTUM   837
THE CLOTH-MERCHANTS AND LET THEM BE   • • • • • •   87 SICK KING BOKH   2
LET HUSSEIN IF THOU WILT MAKE HASTE   • • •   • •   88 SICK KING BOKH   27
HINDER HIM NOT BUT LET HIM GO • • • • • •   • •   91 SICK KING BOKH   116
FORBID HIM NOT BUT LET HIM GO • • • •   • •   91 SICK KING BOKH V 116
AND HELA YIELD TO THIS AND LET HIM GO • • •   • •   98 BALDER DEAD 1   116
SHE SPOKE AND ON HER FACE LET FALL HER VEIL   • •   100 BALDER DEAD 1   192
LET ALL THAT LIVES AND MOVES UPON THE EARTH   • •   111 BALDER DEAD 2   236
LET GODS MEN BRUTES BEWEEP HIM PLANTS AND STONES •   111 BALDER DEAD 2   238
LET GODS MEN BRUTES BEWEEP HIM PLANTS AND STONES •   114 BALDER DEAD 3   44
SHE SPAKE AND ON HER FACE LET FALL HER VEIL   • •   122 BALDER DEAD 3   295
I WEEP HIM NOT LET HELA KEEP HER PREY   • • •   • •   123 BALDER DEAD 3   354
IN HEAVEN NOR LET THE OTHER GODS LAMENT   • •   126 BALDER DEAD 3   457
INACTIVE THEREFORE LET ME LIE IN GLOOM   • •   128 BALDER DEAD 3   509
AH SWEET ANGELS LET HIM DREAM • • • • • •   • •   133 TRISTRAM 1   105
KEEP HIS EYELIDS LET HIM SEEM • • • • • •   • •   133 TRISTRAM 1   106
LET HER HAVE HER YOUTH AGAIN   • • • • • •   • •   134 TRISTRAM 1   117
LET HER BE AS SHE WAS THEN • • • • • •   • •   134 TRISTRAM 1   118
LET HER HAVE HER PROUD DARK EYES   • • •   • •   134 TRISTRAM 1   119
LET HER SWEEP HER DAZZLING HAND   • •   • •   134 TRISTRAM 1   121
AS OF OLD SO LET HER BE • • • • • •   • •   134 TRISTRAM 1   125
LET HER AS SHE SITS ON BOARD   • • • • •   • •   135 TRISTRAM 1   141
LET THEM DRINK IT LET THEIR HANDS • •   • •   135 TRISTRAM 1   147
LET THEM DRINK IT LET THEIR HANDS • •   • •   135 TRISTRAM 1   147
LET THE EARLY SUMMER BE • • • • • •   • •   135 TRISTRAM 1   153
LET THE BREATH OF THE MAY-WIND   • •   • •   135 TRISTRAM 1   156
LET A DREAM LIKE THIS RESTORE • • • •   • •   135 TRISTRAM 1   159
HITHER LET HIM WANDER NOW   • • • • • •   • •   137 TRISTRAM 1   228
WHICH WILL NEVER LET HIM REST • • • • • •   • •   138 TRISTRAM 1   246
COME LET ME LEAVE THE SHADOW OF THIS WOOD • • • •   139 TRISTRAM 1   281
THEIR HOT SEALS AND LET HIM WAKE   • •   • •   139 TRISTRAM 1   295
THAT WILL NEVER LET HIM REST   • • • • •   • •   138 TRISTRAM 1   V 246
AH HARSH FLATTERER LET ALONE MY BEAUTY   • •   143 TRISTRAM 2   21
TRISTRAM TRISTRAM LET THY HEART NOT FAIL   • •   145 TRISTRAM 2   78
HER WORK AWAY AND LET HER FINGERS ROVE   • •   152 TRISTRAM 3   87
HERE LET US HALT SAID MERLIN THEN AND SHE   • •   155 TRISTRAM 3   211
COME DEAR CHILDREN LET US AWAY   • • • • •   • •   161 FORSAKEN MERM   1
CHILDREN DEAR LET US AWAY   • • • • • •   • •   161 FORSAKEN MERM   8
THE RICH SHE HAD LET PASS WITH FROZEN STARE   • •   170 WEST LONDON   8
WAS CHRIST A MAN LIKE US AH LET US TRY   • •   • •   171 BETTER PART   13
AND LET THE PEACEFUL BE • • • • • •   • •   174 MEETING   16
AH WITH YOU LET ME GO • • • • • •   • •   175 PARTING   10
AH WITH THAT LET ME GO   • • • • • •   • •   176 PARTING   44
WOULD NEVER LET US SATIATE HERE   • •   • •   180 FAREWELL   88
LET THE WILD THRONGING TRAIN   • • • • • •   • •   185 STRAYED REVEL   3
LET THE WILD THRONGING TRAIN   • • • •   • •   194 STRAYED REVEL   294
LET HIM LIVE LET HIM FEEL I HAVE LIVED   • •   200 EARLY DEATH   17
LET HIM LIVE LET HIM FEEL I HAVE LIVED   • •   200 EARLY DEATH   17
IN ALL HIS LOVELY MIEN LET PIERCE • •   • •   202 URANIA   23
YET OH THAT FATE WOULD LET HER SEE • • •   • •   202 URANIA   V 17
YET LET ME SAY THAT THOU WAST FAIR   • •   • •   203 EUPHROSYNE   2
AH LET THEM KEEP THEIR FAITH SINCERE   • •   • •   203 EUPHROSYNE   11
YET LET ME SAY THAT THOU WERT FAIR   • • •   • •   203 EUPHROSYNE   V   2
YET LET ME SAY THAT SHE WAS FAIR   • •   • •   203 EUPHROSYNE   V   2
LET THOSE ARCH EYES NOW SOFTLY SHINE   • •   206 RIVER   5
AH LET THEM REST THOSE EYES ON MINE   • •   • •   206 RIVER   7
ON MINE LET REST THAT LOVELY HAND • •   • •   206 RIVER   8
AH LET ME WEEP AND TELL MY PAIN   • •   • •   206 RIVER   11
ME LET ME NO HALF-EFFACED MEMORIES CUMBER • • • •   206 SEPARATION   9
WHO LET ME SAY IS THIS STRANGER REGARDS ME • • •   206 SEPARATION   15
AWHILE LET ME WITH THOUGHT HAVE DONE   • •   • •   208 ON THE RHINE   11
SO LET ME LIE AND CALM AS THEY   • • • • •   • •   208 ON THE RHINE   16
LET BEAM UPON MY INWARD VIEW   • • • •   • •   208 ON THE RHINE   17
COME NOW AND LET ME DREAM IT TRUTH   • •   • •   209 LONGING   10
COME NOW AND LET ME DEEM IT TRUTH • •   • •   209 LONGING   V 10
AH LOVE LET US BE TRUE • • • • • •   • •   211 DOVER BEACH   29
CREEP AND LET NO MORE BE SAID • • • • • •   • •   215 LAST WORD   2
LET THE LONG CONTENTION CEASE • • • • • •   • •   215 LAST WORD   5
LET THEM HAVE IT HOW THEY WILL   • • • •   • •   215 LAST WORD   7
LET THE VICTORS WHEN THEY COME   • • • •   • •   215 LAST WORD   14
TOO LONG LET WE THEM GROAN • • • • • •   • •   216 LORDS MESSENGER   4
THEN LET HIM CHOOSE HIS MOMENT WELL   • • •   • •   223 EPILOG LAOCOON   59

LET

(CONTINUED)

AH FROM THE OLD WORLD LET SOME ONE ANSWER GIVE	• •	237 PROGRESS	21
HERE LET THAT VOICE MAKE END THEN LET A STRAIN	• •	238 PROGRESS	33
HERE LET THAT VOICE MAKE END THEN LET A STRAIN	• •	238 PROGRESS	33
STILL STILL LET ME AS I GAZE UPON YOU	• • •	240 SELF-DEPENDENCE	11
A WORLD ABOVE MANS HEAD TO LET HIM SEE	• • •	244 SUMMER NIGHT	87
AND LET ME READ THERE LOVE THY INMOST SOUL	• •	245 BURIED LIFE	11
TO UNLOCK THE HEART AND LET IT SPEAK	• • •	245 BURIED LIFE	13
CALM CALM ME MORE NOR LET ME DIE	• • •	249 KENSINGTON GARD	43
LET THOSE WHO WILL IF ANY WEEP	•	250 WISH	7
BRING NONE OF THESE BUT LET ME BE	• • •	250 WISH	29
THERE LET ME GAZE TILL I BECOME	• • •	251 WISH	41
THEN WILLING LET MY SPIRIT GO	• • •	251 WISH	51
THUS FEELING GAZING LET ME GROW	• • •	251 WISH V	49
NOR LET THY BAWLING FELLOWS RACK THEIR THROATS	• •	255 SCHOLAR-GIPSY	4
COME LET ME READ THE OFT-READ TALE AGAIN	• •	256 SCHOLAR-GIPSY	32
YET THYRSIS LET ME GIVE MY GRIEF ITS HOUR	• •	265 THYRSIS	102
QUICK LET ME FLY AND CROSS	• • • •	267 THYRSIS	156
LET IN THY VOICE A WHISPER OFTEN COME	• •	269 THYRSIS	235
THEIR VAUNTS THEIR FEATS LET A SARDONIC SMILE	• •	298 HEINES GRAVE	208
SHE LET THE LEGIONS THUNDER PAST	• • •	316 OBERMANN MORE	111
LET US CONSULT BEFORE THIS PALACE SENDS	• •	330 MEROPE	26
BUT LET US KEEP THAT PURPOSE WHICH AT HOME	• •	331 MEROPE	35
O LAIAS LAIAS LET THE HEART SPEAK HERE	• •	331 MEROPE	59
BEACONS OF VENGEANCE NOT TO BE LET DIE	• •	333 MEROPE	93
HEAR ME THEN SPEAK AND LET THIS MOURNFUL DAY	• •	333 MEROPE	114
THE SCEPTRE NOT REMISSLY LET IT FALL	• •	334 MEROPE	135
ASSIST ME TO RULE MILDLY LET US JOIN	• • •	335 MEROPE	164
LET US IN MARRIAGE KING AND QUEEN UNITE	• •	335 MEROPE	167
NOT SO LET THESE MESSENIAN MAIDENS MARK	• •	336 MEROPE	197
MURDER LET OTHERS CALL THIS IF THEY WILL	• •	338 MEROPE	276
THIS WERE ENOUGH BUT LET ME TELL THEE TOO	• •	338 MEROPE	282
HE WOULD NOT LET HIS SAVAGE CHIEFS ALIGHT	• •	339 MEROPE	295
NOT IN ABHORRD ESTRANGEMENT LET YOU STAND	• •	339 MEROPE	300
BRING TO ME SAFE LET THE REST	• • • •	348 MEROPE	535
IF THESE CONDEMN HIM LET THEM PASS HIS DOOM	• •	349 MEROPE	557
LET THE BEST RULE THEY SAY AGAIN	• • •	352 MEROPE	653
LET HER COME FAIR PEACE LET HER COME	• • •	361 MEROPE	908
LET HER COME FAIR PEACE LET HER COME	• • •	361 MEROPE	908
OF THE THRACIAN SEA LET HER LEAVE	• • •	361 MEROPE	912
THUS PEACEFULLY DO YE LET SINNERS SLEEP	• •	372 MEROPE	1154
STAND AND LET VENGEANCE PASS HOLD O QUEEN HOLD	•	374 MEROPE	1198
PRESSES ME CHIDES ME WILL NOT LET ME WEEP	• •	378 MEROPE	1233
NOT SO LET HIM AND NONE SHALL BE MORE PROMPT	• •	388 MEROPE	1496
LET HIM FETCH SUCCOURS FROM ARCADIA GAIN	• •	388 MEROPE	1498
LET HIM DO THIS DO AUGHT BUT RECOMMENCE	• •	388 MEROPE	1500
PROMISE NOT FAIR LET HIM A LITTLE WHILE	• •	388 MEROPE	1506
THIS HAVING KNOWN LET US A UNION FOUND	• •	394 MEROPE	1716
BASED ON PURE PUBLIC WELFARE LET US BE	• •	394 MEROPE	1718
LET US FORGET OURSELVES FOR THOSE WE RULE	• •	394 MEROPE	1721
TO THE PRESERVER ZEUS LET ME RETURN	• • •	395 MEROPE	1723
AND CRIED O ZEUS LET WHAT BLOOD-GUILTINESS	• •	402 MEROPE	1915
FIRST WORK AFTER SUCH VICTORY LET US GO	• •	405 MEROPE	2017
THIS HAVING LEARND LET US A UNION FOUND	• •	394 MEROPE	V1716
LET US REST HERE AND NOW EMPEDOCLES	• •	412 EMPEDOCLES I 2	7
LET US WITH CHANGELESS WILL	• • • •	425 EMPEDOCLES I 2	379
OH THAT FATE HAD LET ME SEE	• • • •	432 EMPEDOCLES II	125
AND NEVER LET US CLASP AND FEEL THE ALL	• •	439 EMPEDOCLES II	353
WAIT FOR THE LEAVEN TO WORK THE LET TO END	• •	449 WESTMIN ABBEY	170
LET BUT THE LIGHT APPEAR	• • • • •	449 WESTMIN ABBEY	177
NOR LET THEE UTTERLY DEPART	• • • •	451 GEISTS GRAVE	39
NOTE NO CHANGE AND LET THEM DIE	• • •	455 POOR MATTHIAS	108
THOSE STERNER SPIRITS LET ME PRIZE	• • •	481 COURAGE	9
AND BYRON LET US DARE ADMIRE	• • • •	482 COURAGE	17
NOR WOULD MY OWN HEART LET ME MY HEART WHICH		HOMER TRANS	17
HAS BID ME BE VALIANT			
BUT LET ME BE DEAD AND THE EARTH BE MOUNDED ABOVE ME		HOMER TRANS	37
AND LET • • • • • • • • • • • • •	•	FRAGMENT 2	6

LETHAEAN

NOT DAILY LABOURS DULL LETHAEAN SPRING	• • • •	43 GIPSY CHILD	54

LETO

BUT THAT PRINCE AMONG GODS THE SON OF THE LOVELY-HAIRD		HOMER TRANS	52
LETO			

LETS

AND LETS THE AGED MOULDER TO THEIR GRAVES	• • • •	67 SOHRAB RUSTUM	225
WAFTS HIM HERE AND LETS HIM FIND	• • • •	136 TRISTRAM 1	191
HARDLY LETS PEEP THE GOLDEN HAIR	• • • •	141 TRISTRAM 1	341
AND LETS US BE WHAT WE WERE ONCE NO MORE	• •	153 TRISTRAM 3	115
I TAKE THE OMEN EVE LETS DOWN HER VEIL	• •	267 THYRSIS	161
OF MECHANIC BUSINESS AND LETS	• • • • •	295 HEINES GRAVE	82
BUT HE STILL LETS THE PEOPLE WHOM HE SCORNS	• •	410 EMPEDOCLES I 1	138
AS HE LETS HIS LAX RIGHT HAND	• • • •	431 EMPEDOCLES II	71
LETS FROM HIS SHAGGY HIGHLAND PATE	• • • •	461 KAISER DEAD	77

LETTERS

GOD PUT A HEAP OF LETTERS IN HIS HAND	• • •	239 REVOLUTIONS	3
THE LETTERS HAVE COMBINED SOMETHING WAS MADE	• •	239 REVOLUTIONS	8

LETTING
    LETTING THE SEA-STREAM WANDER THROUGH THY HAIR   •   •   430 EMPEDOCLES II   61

LEVELS
    YET I SEE THE HOWLING LEVELS   •   •   •   •   •   •   •   26 NEW SIRENS   17

LIANDE
    OF THE DEEP FOREST-GLADES OF BROCE-LIANDE   •   •   •   154 TRISTRAM 3   156

LIBATION
    POUR THE LIBATION OF MILK   •   •   •   •   •   •   •   342 MEROPE   387

LIBATIONS
    PRAY AS THOU POURST LIBATIONS ON THIS TOMB   •   •   •   342 MEROPE   382
    PURE LIBATIONS AND FRESH   •   •   •   •   •   •   342 MEROPE   402
    I SEND AND THESE LIBATIONS POUR THE WHILE   •   •   •   350 MEROPE   595

LIBERAL
    YES YES NOW I CONCEIVE THE LIBERAL GRACE   •   •   •   366 MEROPE   997
    AH NOW I COMPREHEND THE LIBERAL GRACE   •   •   •   366 MEROPE   V 997

LIBERATED
    LUST AVARICE ENVY LIBERATED MAN   •   •   •   •   •   7 REP FRIEND CONT   12

LIBERTY
    DID THE WAVES CHAUNT THEIR SONG OF LIBERTY   •   •   •   472 CROMWELL   16

LIBRARY
    THE LIBRARY WHERE TRACT AND TOME   •   •   •   •   •   300 GRANDE CHARTR   49

LIBYAN
    WITH HER OWN HUSBAND BY THE LIBYAN SEA   •   •   •   173 MONICAS PRAYER   8
    LIKE US THE LIBYAN WIND DELIGHTS TO ROAM AT LARGE   420 EMPEDOCLES I 2   251

LICHEN
    AND ON THE LICHEN-CRUSTED LEADS ABOVE   •   •   •   19 CHURCH BROU 3   45
    SMOTE MID THE ROCKS THE LICHEN-BEARDED PINES   •   •   106 BALDER DEAD 2   56
    BEARDED WITH LICHEN SCRAWLD AND GREY   •   •   •   274 STANZAS CARNAC   10
    BEARDED WITH LICHEN OLD AND GREY   •   •   •   •   274 STANZAS CARNAC   V 10

LICKD
    CURLING AND DARTING HIGHER UNTIL THEY LICKD   •   •   119 BALDER DEAD 3   189

LIDS
    AND FREA SEALD HER TIRED LIDS WITH SLEEP   •   •   •   103 BALDER DEAD 1   279

LIDSKIALF
    TO LIDSKIALF AND SATE UPON HIS THRONE   •   •   •   96 BALDER DEAD 1   49
    BUT FROM THE HILL OF LIDSKIALF ODIN ROSE   •   •   •   102 BALDER DEAD 1   253

LIE
    AND IN THAT MORE LIE ALL HIS HOPES OF GOOD   •   •   •   5 HARMONY NATURE   6
    FELL THIS DREAD VOICE FROM LIPS THAT CANNOT LIE   •   •   8 MYCERINUS   5
    FELL THIS LATE VOICE FROM LIPS THAT CANNOT LIE   •   •   8 MYCERINUS   V 5
    THE FOLIAGED MARBLE FOREST WHERE YE LIE   •   •   •   19 CHURCH BROU 3   39
    THOSE FRANK EYES WHERE DEEP DOTH LIE   •   •   •   24 MEMORY-PICTURE   V 45
    WHEREIN WE LIE ASLEEP   •   •   •   •   •   •   •   38 STAGIRIUS   11
    WHERE OUR SICK SOULS DO LIE   •   •   •   •   •   39 STAGIRIUS   50
    LIE STREWN IT SEEMS WHERE THEN THEY LAY   •   •   •   55 RESIGNATION   101
    SLEEP BUT I SLEEP NOT ALL NIGHT LONG I LIE   •   •   62 SOHRAB RUSTUM   36
    HE LEFT TO LIE BUT HAD REGAIND HIS SPEAR   •   •   •   74 SOHRAB RUSTUM   450
    SOHRAB THAT WERE A PROOF WHICH COULD NOT LIE   •   •   81 SOHRAB RUSTUM   667
    LIE PRONE ENORMOUS DOWN THE MOUNTAIN SIDE   •   •   •   86 SOHRAB RUSTUM   863
    HERE MUST THOU LIE AND WAIT AN ENDLESS AGE   •   •   •   126 BALDER DEAD 3   452
    INACTIVE THEREFORE LET ME LIE IN GLOOM   •   •   •   128 BALDER DEAD 3   509
    AH TIRED MADCAPS YOU LIE STILL   •   •   •   •   141 TRISTRAM 1   351
    THEN WENT MY WAY TO KILL AND LIE   •   •   •   •   158 SAINT BRANDAN   59
    MID SHELLS THAT ROUND HER LIE   •   •   •   •   160 NECKAN   34
    LIE SWEETLY IN THE LOOK DIVINE   •   •   •   •   •   208 ON THE RHINE   14
    SO LET ME LIE AND CALM AS THEY   •   •   •   •   208 ON THE RHINE   16
    TO LIE BEFORE US LIKE A LAND OF DREAMS   •   •   •   211 DOVER BEACH   31
    IN THIS LONE OPEN GLADE I LIE   •   •   •   •   •   248 KENSINGTON GARD   1
    HERE WHERE I LIE WHAT MARVELS PASS   •   •   •   KENSINGTON GARD   V 13
    OR IN MY BOAT I LIE   •   •   •   •   •   •   257 SCHOLAR-GIPSY   66
    IN CITIES SHOULD WE ENGLISH LIE   •   •   •   •   277 SOUTHERN NIGHT   61
    ROUND THEE THEY LIE THE GRASS   •   •   •   •   284 HAWORTH CHURCH   88
    THERE THOU DOST LIE IN THE GLOOM   •   •   •   286 RUGBY CHAPEL   14
    WAST THOU HEINE TO LIE   •   •   •   •   •   •   293 HEINES GRAVE   16
    AND LIE BESIDE ITS DOOR   •   •   •   •   •   •   313 OBERMANN MORE   46
    SOFT DARKNESS ON THE TURF DID LIE   •   •   •   •   323 OBERMANN MORE   329
    WILL LIE MY GRANDSIRE SAID OUR FAIREST CHANCE   •   331 MEROPE   41
    EVEN AS THOSE DEAD UNEPITAPHD WHO LIE   •   •   •   356 MEROPE   772
    TO LIE IN GLOOM FOR EVER UNAPPEASED   •   •   •   367 MEROPE   1052
    WHILE TROUBLED INNOCENTS TOSS AND LIE AWAKE   •   372 MEROPE   1155
    YE LIE WATCHING FOR THE FOE OF YOUR KIN   •   •   •   344 MEROPE   V 462
    LIE THERE YE ENSIGNS   •   •   •   •   •   •   432 EMPEDOCLES II   109
    ALL THE FOOLS-ARMOURY OF MAGIC LIE THERE   •   •   432 EMPEDOCLES II   118
    AND LIE THOU THERE   •   •   •   •   •   •   434 EMPEDOCLES II   191
    SCORNFUL APOLLOS ENSIGN LIE THOU THERE   •   •   •   434 EMPEDOCLES II   193
    YET LIE THOU THERE   •   •   •   •   •   •   435 EMPEDOCLES II   196
    LIE STREWN THE WHITE FLOCKS   •   •   •   •   •   442 EMPEDOCLES II   430

LIE   (CONTINUED)
          LIE WRAPT IN THEIR BLANKETS   • • • • • •   442 EMPEDOCLES II   435
          YES IN SUCH ELOQUENT SILENCE DIDST THOU LIE   • •   464 ALARIC AT ROME   67
          TO LIE LOW IN DEATH BY THE HAND OF A GOD AND A MORTAL   HOMER TRANS   56

LIEF
          WE RUSH BY COASTS WHERE WE HAD LIEF REMAIN • • • •   40 HUMAN LIFE   17

LIEFER
          YET FOR ME MOTHER I HAD LIEFER DIE   • • • • • •   383 MEROPE   379

LIES
          GOD THE DUKE LIES STRETCHD BESIDE HIM   • • • •   13 CHURCH BROU 1   27
          ON THE TURF DEAD LIES THE BOAR   • • • • • • •   13 CHURCH BROU 1   26
          FROM THE FRINGED MATTRESS WHERE THY DUCHESS LIES • •   18 CHURCH BROU 3   8
          MEANS PARTING THAT ONLY IN ABSENCE LIES PAIN   • • •   19 MODERN SAPPHO   V
          LIES FROZEN AND DEAD   • • • • • • • • • •   36 VOICE   14
          THE PORT LIES BRIGHT UNDER THE AUGUST SUN • • • •   41 GIPSY CHILD   V   5
          YET THERE THY SECRET LIES   • • • • • • • • •   46 IN UTRUMQUE PAR V 37
          LIES DYING WITH THE ARROW IN HER SIDE   • • • • •   78 SOHRAB RUSTUM   567
          AND LIES A FRAGRANT TOWER OF PURPLE BLOOM   • • • •   80 SOHRAB RUSTUM   637
          SOHRAB THE MIGHTY RUSTUMS SON LIES THERE   • • • •   84 SOHRAB RUSTUM   792
          WHICH HANGS OVER THE ICE WHERE LIES THE ROAD • • •   108 BALDER DEAD 2   127
          OF JARNVID WHICH TO EAST OF MIDGARD LIES   • • • •   123 BALDER DEAD 3   330
          LIES IN DISORDERD STREAMS AND THERE   • • • • •   146 TRISTRAM 2   108
          WHO LIES GUARDING HER FEET ALONG THE GROUND   • • •   152 TRISTRAM 3   89
          WHEN HE LOOKD UP TENANTLESS LIES   • • • • • •   158 SAINT BRANDAN   V 75
          THE TIDE IS FULL THE MOON LIES FAIR   • • • • •   210 DOVER BEACH   2
          IN THE SHADOW WORDSWORTH LIES DEAD   • • • • •   228 YOUTH OF NATURE   9
          OF A SACRED POET LIES LOW   • • • • • • • •   229 YOUTH OF NATURE   49
          THE EYE SINKS INWARD AND THE HEART LIES PLAIN • •   247 BURIED LIFE   86
          WHERE THE TIRED ANGLER LIES STRETCHD OUT   • • •   248 KENSINGTON GARD   18
          WHERE THE LONE ANGLER LIES STRETCHD OUT   • • •   KENSINGTON GARD V 18
          WHILE ALL AROUND IN SILENCE LIES   • • • • •   250 WISH   30
          AND NEAR ME ON THE GRASS LIES GLANVILS BOOK   • •   256 SCHOLAR-GIPSY   31
          LOVELY ALL TIMES SHE LIES LOVELY TO-NIGHT • • •   263 THYRSIS   21
          LIES EXPECTING FROM DEATH   • • • • • • • •   281 HAWORTH CHURCH   31
          NOW HE IS DEAD FAR HENCE HE LIES   • • • • •   318 OBERMANN MORE   173
          WHILE THE WORLD LIES FORLORN   • • • • • • •   321 OBERMANN MORE   248
          AH THERE OUR FUTURE LIES   • • • • • • • •   315 OBERMANN MORE   V
          OF WHAT IT LIES WITH THEM TO MAKE RISK NONE   • •   350 MEROPE   604
          MY CHILD LIES IN HIS JAGGD   • • • • • • •   370 MEROPE   1117
          MY CHILD LIES IN A JAGGD   • • • • • • • •   370 MEROPE   V1117
          SLOPE BEHIND SLOPE UP TO THE PEAK LIES BARE   • •   414 EMPEDOCLES I 2   55
          THERE LIES THY GOAL TO MISS OR TO ATTAIN   • • •   465 ALARIC AT ROME   87
          LIES ANY HOPE OF HEROISM MORE • • • • • • •   480 HUNGARIAN NAT   8
          LOFTY THOUGHT LIES OFT IN CHILDISH PLAY   • • • •   483 THEKLAS ANSWER   24

LIEST
          YET HERE THOU LIEST BALDER UNDERGROUND   • • • •   127 BALDER DEAD 3   471
          FAREWELL WHETHER THOU NOW LIEST NEAR • • • • •   311 OBERMANN   161
          THERE THERE THOU LIEST NOW MY HAPLESS CHILD   • •   373 MEROPE   1171

LIFE
          WHO SAW LIFE STEADILY AND SAW IT WHOLE   • • • •   2 TO A FRIEND   12
          AS THOUGH ONE SPAKE OF LIFE UNTO THE DEAD • • •   3 EMERSONS ESSAYS   8
          AS THOUGH MEN SPAKE OF LIFE A JOY WAS FLED • • •   EMERSONS ESSAYS V   8
          REND IN A THOUSAND SHREDS THIS LIFE OF OURS • • •   4 BUTLERS SERMONS   4
          WHEREOER THE CHARIOT WHEELS OF LIFE ARE ROLLD • •   4 BUTLERS SERMONS   13
          BECAUSE THOU HAST BELIEVED THE WHEELS OF LIFE • •   4 DUKE WELLINGTON   1
          WHICH SAW ONE CLUE TO LIFE AND FOLLOWD IT   • • •   5 DUKE WELLINGTON   14
          FROM THE RANK LIFE OF TOWNS THIS LEAF AND FLUNG • •   6 GEO CRUIKSHANK   2
          MANS FUNDAMENTAL LIFE IF TO DESPISE   • • • • •   6 REP FRIEND   4
          YET WHEN I MUSE ON WHAT LIFE IS I SEEM   • • • •   7 REP FRIEND CONT   1
          ENNOBLING THIS DULL POMP THE LIFE OF KINGS • • •   9 MYCERINUS   11
          I LOOKD FOR LIFE MORE LASTING RULE MORE HIGH • •   9 MYCERINUS   17
          DID SHADOW SOMEWHAT OF THE LIFE OF GODS   • • •   9 MYCERINUS   24
          CROWN OF HIS STRUGGLING LIFE AN UNJUST CLOSE • •   9 MYCERINUS   30
          AND THE SIGHT FROZE ALL HER LIFE   • • • • •   14 CHURCH BROU 1   52
          HAST THOU YET DEALT HIM O LIFE THY FULL MEASURE •   20 MODERN SAPPHO   33
          HER LIFE WAS TURNING TURNING   • • • • • • •   21 REQUIESCAT   9
          THE CROWNING END OF LIFE AND YOUTH   • • • • •   21 YOUTH AND CALM   6
          HUNG POISED AND THEN THE DARTING RIVER OF LIFE • •   25 DREAM   31
          SUCH NOW METHOUGHT IT WAS THE RIVER OF LIFE • • •   25 DREAM   32
          DULL DID LIFE IN TORPOR FADE   • • • • • • •   28 NEW SIRENS   66
          LIFE DRIES UP THE HEART DISSEMBLES   • • • • •   29 NEW SIRENS   83
          COULD LIFE RUN NO HAPPIER WAY • • • • • • •   33 NEW SIRENS   200
          LIFE IS LONG AND WILL NOT FADE   • • • • • •   28 NEW SIRENS   V 66
          LIFE WITHOUT LOVE DOES BUT FADE   • • • • • •   28 NEW SIRENS   V 66
          DULL WITHOUT LOVE LIFE DOTH FADE   • • • • • •   28 NEW SIRENS   V 66
          COULD LIFE RUN NO EASIER WAY   • • • • • • •   33 NEW SIRENS   V 200
          MADE MY TOST HEART ITS VERY LIFE-BLOOD SPILL • •   36 VOICE   39
          DRAIND ALL THE LIFE MY FULL HEART HAD TO SPILL • •   36 VOICE   V 39
          WE STEM ACROSS THE SEA OF LIFE BY NIGHT   • • •   41 HUMAN LIFE   27
          LIFE WELL AND FIND IT WANTING NOR DEPLORE • • •   42 GIPSY CHILD   30
          MUSED MUCH LOVED LIFE A LITTLE LOATHED IT MORE • •   43 GIPSY CHILD   36
          I THINK THOU WILT HAVE FATHOMD LIFE TOO FAR • •   43 GIPSY CHILD   47
          SOME REACHES OF THY STORM-VEXT STREAM OF LIFE • •   43 GIPSY CHILD   60
          LOVE LENDS LIFE A LITTLE GRACE   • • • • • •   44 QUESTION   4
          OUR VAUNTED LIFE IS ONE LONG FUNERAL   • • • • •   44 QUESTION   10

LIFE   (CONTINUED)

OF LIFE REMOUNT	• • • • • • • • • •	45	IN UTRUMQUE PAR	14
HIGH AS THY LIFE BE RISEN TIS FROM THESE	• • •	46	IN UTRUMQUE PAR V	41
OF LITTLE THREADS OUR LIFE IS SPUN	• • • •	48	HORATIAN ECHO	25
A STRAIND LIFE WHILE OVERFEEDING	• • • •	49	SECOND BEST	14
NO LIFE SAVE HIS AND OURS INTRUDES	• • • •	54	RESIGNATION	72
BEFORE HIM HE SEES LIFE UNROLL	• • • • •	57	RESIGNATION	189
THAT GENERAL LIFE WHICH DOES NOT CEASE	• • •	58	RESIGNATION	191
THAT LIFE WHOSE DUMB WISH IS NOT MISSD	• • •	58	RESIGNATION	193
THE LIFE OF PLANTS AND STONES AND RAIN	• • •	58	RESIGNATION	195
THE LIFE HE CRAVES IF NOT IN VAIN	• • • •	58	RESIGNATION	196
IN THE DAYS LIFE WHOSE IRON ROUND	• • • •	58	RESIGNATION	209
AND FLEES THE COMMON LIFE OF MEN	• • • •	58	RESIGNATION	212
DRAW HOMEWARD TO THE GENERAL LIFE	• • •	59	RESIGNATION	252
WHENCE EQUALLY THE SEAS OF LIFE AND DEATH ARE FED		60	RESIGNATION	260
ENOUGH WE LIVE AND IF A LIFE	• • • • •	60	RESIGNATION	261
IF I MIGHT LEND THEIR LIFE A VOICE	• • • •	60	RESIGNATION	269
DRAW HOMEWARDS TO THE GENERAL LIFE	• • •	59	RESIGNATION V	252
WITH JOY AND ALL THE PLEASANT LIFE THEY LED	• •	79	SOHRAB RUSTUM	627
TRYING TO CALL HIM BACK TO LIFE AND LIFE	• •	81	SOHRAB RUSTUM	697
TRYING TO CALL HIM BACK TO LIFE AND LIFE	• •	81	SOHRAB RUSTUM	697
TO DRAW IT AND FOR EVER LET LIFE OUT	• • •	82	SOHRAB RUSTUM	705
QUICK QUICK FOR NUMBERD ARE MY SANDS OF LIFE	•	82	SOHRAB RUSTUM	721
AND I SHALL NEVER END THIS LIFE OF BLOOD	• •	85	SOHRAB RUSTUM	826
A LIFE OF BLOOD INDEED THOU DREADFUL MAN	• •	85	SOHRAB RUSTUM	828
CAME WELLING FROM THE OPEN GASH AND LIFE	• •	85	SOHRAB RUSTUM	841
CONVULSED HIM BACK TO LIFE HE OPEND THEM	• •	86	SOHRAB RUSTUM	851
GAINST THAT ALONE HAD BALDERS LIFE NO CHARM	• ~ •	95	BALDER DEAD 1	8
TO LIVE AS ERST YOUR DAILY LIFE IN HEAVEN	• • •	96	BALDER DEAD 1	36
GAINST THAT ALONE HAD BALDERS LIFE NO CHARM	• •	98	BALDER DEAD 1	104
AND MAKE EXCHANGE AND GIVE MY LIFE FOR HIS	• •	98	BALDER DEAD 1	110
SHOULD CHANGE HIS LOT AND FILL ANOTHERS LIFE	•	98	BALDER DEAD 1	115
NOR DOTH SHE COUNT THIS LIFE A PRICE FOR THAT	•	98	BALDER DEAD 1	118
FOR NOT SO GLADSOME IS THAT LIFE IN HEAVEN	• • •	98	BALDER DEAD 1	122
THE ENCHANTMENTS THAT RECALL THE DEAD TO LIFE	•	101	BALDER DEAD 1	209
TO KEEP HIS OWN LIFE SAFE AND SEE THE SUN	• •	101	BALDER DEAD 1	213
TO CUT THY THREAD OF LIFE AND FREE THY SOUL	•	103	BALDER DEAD 1	303
PROLONG THY LIFE THOUGH NOT BY THEE DESIRED	•	104	BALDER DEAD 1	312
YET DREARY NANNA IS THE LIFE THEY LEAD	• • •	104	BALDER DEAD 1	314
AND TALKING OF THE LIFE WE LED IN HEAVEN	• •	104	BALDER DEAD 1	329
WEEP HIM AND ALL THAT IS WITHOUT LIFE WEEP	• •	111	BALDER DEAD 2	237
AND LEAD AS ERST OUR DAILY LIFE IN HEAVEN	• •	115	BALDER DEAD 3	56
AND ALL THAT LIVED AND ALL WITHOUT LIFE WEPT	•	122	BALDER DEAD 3	306
MY FORMER LIFE AND CHEERS ME EVEN HERE	• • •	126	BALDER DEAD 3	462
OF CARNAGE AND FIND HERMOD IN YOUR LIFE	• •	127	BALDER DEAD 3	504
LIFE ONE PERPETUAL FIGHT A BATH OF BLOOD	• •	128	BALDER DEAD 3	506
AND THAT WILL BRING TO MIND THE FORMER LIFE	•	128	BALDER DEAD 3	540
HIS TRANQUIL LIFE IN THIS LONE PLACE	• • • •	137	TRISTRAM 1	212
COURTLY LIFE IS LIGHT AND CANNOT REACH IT	• •	143	TRISTRAM 2	39
BUT THESE SHE LOVES AND NOISIER LIFE THAN THIS	•	152	TRISTRAM 3	100
AH WHERE THE SPIRIT ITS HIGHEST LIFE HATH LED	•	167	RACHEL 1	12
IMPARTING LIFE RENEWD OLD CLASSIC GRACE	• • •	168	RACHEL 3	5
EVEN IN A PALACE LIFE MAY BE LED WELL	• • •	168	WORLDLY PLACE	1
OF COMMON LIFE WHERE CROWDED UP PELL-MELL	• •	168	WORLDLY PLACE	4
SOME NOBLER AMPLER STAGE OF LIFE TO WIN	• • •	169	WORLDLY PLACE	12
THE AIDS TO NOBLE LIFE ARE ALL WITHIN	• • •	169	WORLDLY PLACE	14
LIVE WE LIKE BRUTES OUR LIFE WITHOUT A PLAN	•	171	BETTER PART	8
HATH MAN NO SECOND LIFE PITCH THIS ONE HIGH	•	171	BETTER PART	10
AND PATIENCE IN ANOTHER LIFE WE SAY	• • •	172	IMMORTALITY	3
NO NO THE ENERGY OF LIFE MAY BE	• • • •	172	IMMORTALITY	9
MOUNTS AND THAT HARDLY TO ETERNAL LIFE	• • •	172	IMMORTALITY	14
KEEP BY THIS LIFE IN GOD AND UNION THERE	• •	173	MONICAS PRAYER	14
NO LIFE BUT AT MOMENTS	• • • • • • • •	176	PARTING	55
AND THOUGH WE WEAR OUT LIFE ALAS	• • • •	179	FAREWELL	49
YET WE SHALL ONE DAY GAIN LIFE PAST	• • •	179	FAREWELL	53
AS HAND IN HAND FACE EARTHLY LIFE	• • • •	179	FAREWELL	68
AND LIFE AND OTHERS JOY AND PAIN	• • • •	181	ISOLATION MARG	35
YES IN THE SEA OF LIFE ENISLED	• • • • •	182	TO MARG CONT	1
THIS IS THE CURSE OF LIFE THAT NOT	• • • •	183	ABSENCE	5
OF LIFE WAS CUT AND CLOSED THY SPAN	• • •	184	TERRACE BERNE	28
SO ON THE SEA OF LIFE ALAS	• • • •	185	TERRACE BERNE	47
I KNEW IT WHEN MY LIFE WAS YOUNG	• • • •	185	TERRACE BERNE	49
THROUGH A LIFE LENGTHEND	• • • • • •	192	STRAYED REVEL	221
WHO WEIGHING THAT LIFE WELL	• • •	195	FRAG ANTIGONE	4
ROBBING HERSELF OF LIFE IN BURYING	• • • •	196	FRAG ANTIGONE	40
AND BLEND HIS HAPPY LIFE	• • • • •	197	FRAG ANTIGONE	73
OF LIFE WITH VIGOUR UNDIMMD	• • • •	199	FRAG DEJANEIRA	26
I PRAISE THE LIFE WHICH SLIPS AWAY	• • •	199	EARLY DEATH	2
FROM THE HALF-TRIED BANQUET OF LIFE	• • •	199	EARLY DEATH	10
OF A TRANQUIL LIFE IN THE SHADE	• • • •	199	EARLY DEATH	14
HEAP UP HIS MOMENTS WITH LIFE	• • • •	200	EARLY DEATH	18
THAT LIFE IS BEST WHICH SLIPS AWAY	• • • •	199	EARLY DEATH V	2
TIS NOT TO HAVE OUR LIFE	• • • • •	212	GROWING OLD	13
LIFE IS THEIR PRIZE	• • • •	220	BACCHANALIA 2	42
A MOMENTS LIFE OF THINGS THAT LIVE	• • •	223	EPILOG LAOCOON	58
MEN WITH THEIR STREAM OF LIFE WERE HERE	• •	224	EPILOG LAOCOON	112
THE MOVEMENT HE MUST TELL OF LIFE	• • •	225	EPILOG LAOCOON	143
HE FOLLOWS HOME AND LIVES THEIR LIFE	• • •	226	EPILOG LAOCOON	162
ONLY A FEW THE LIFE-STREAMS SHORE	• • • •	226	EPILOG LAOCOON	189
FOR HE LENT A NEW LIFE TO THESE HILLS	• • •	228	YOUTH OF NATURE	14

LIFE   (CONTINUED)
    FOR THEY ARE THE LIFE OF THE WORLD • • • • •   230 YOUTH OF NATURE   86
    LIFE AND EMOTION AND I • • • • • • • • •   230 YOUTH OF NATURE   90
    CAN THE IMAGE OF LIFE HAVE THE GLOW • • • • •   231 YOUTH OF NATURE   115
    THE MOTION OF LIFE ITSELF • • • • • • • •   231 YOUTH OF NATURE   116
    NOR LIFE NOR EMOTION NOR POWER • • • • • •   233 YOUTH OF MAN   31
    AND FANCY THAT WE PUT FORTH ALL OUR LIFE • • •   236 PALLADIUM   19
    UPON OUR LIFE A RULING EFFLUENCE SEND • • • •   236 PALLADIUM   22
    A DEEPER LIFE THAN THEIRS • • • • • • • •   237 PROGRESS   24
    BRIGHT ELSE AND FAST THE STREAM OF LIFE MAY ROLL • 238 PROGRESS   29
    IN PRIDE OF LIFE THE AGES OF YOUR SIRES • • • • 238 PROGRESS   46
    THESE ATTAIN THE MIGHTY LIFE YOU SEE • • • • • 240 SELF-DEPENDENCE   28
    ON THE WIDE OCEAN OF LIFE ANEW • • • • • •   243 SUMMER NIGHT   53
    IS THERE NO LIFE BUT THESE ALONE • • • • • •   244 SUMMER NIGHT   74
    THE UNREGARDED RIVER OF OUR LIFE • • • • • •   246 BURIED LIFE   39
    AFTER THE KNOWLEDGE OF OUR BURIED LIFE • • • •   246 BURIED LIFE   48
    THE HILLS WHERE HIS LIFE ROSE • • • • • • •   247 BURIED LIFE   97
    WHAT ENDLESS ACTIVE LIFE IS HERE • • • • • •   248 KENSINGTON GARD   14
    WHAT SWARMY ENDLESS LIFE IS HERE • • • • • •   KENSINGTON GARD   V   14
    WHAT ACTIVE ENDLESS LIFE IS HERE • • • • • •   KENSINGTON GARD   V   14
    THE FREEDOM TO MY LIFE DENIED • • • • • • •   250 WISH   10
    THE PURE ETERNAL COURSE OF LIFE • • • • • •   251 WISH   47
    MET HIM AND OF HIS WAY OF LIFE ENQUIRED • • • • 256 SCHOLAR-GIPSY   43
    FOR WHAT WEARS OUT THE LIFE OF MORTAL MEN • • •   259 SCHOLAR-GIPSY   142
    OUR WORN-OUT LIFE AND ARE WHAT WE HAVE BEEN • •   259 SCHOLAR-GIPSY   150
    O LIFE UNLIKE TO OURS • • • • • • • • •   260 SCHOLAR-GIPSY   166
    WHO HESITATE AND FALTER LIFE AWAY • • • • •   260 SCHOLAR-GIPSY   178
    AND LIFE RAN GAILY AS THE SPARKLING THAMES • •   261 SCHOLAR-GIPSY   202
    BEFORE THIS STRANGE DISEASE OF MODERN LIFE • •   261 SCHOLAR-GIPSY   203
    AND WE SHOULD WIN THEE FROM THY OWN FAIR LIFE •   261 SCHOLAR-GIPSY   224
    OUR WELL-WORN LIFE AND ARE WHAT WE HAVE BEEN •   259 SCHOLAR-GIPSY   V 150
    SOME LIFE OF MEN UNBLEST • • • • • • • •   264 THYRSIS   46
    WE WATCHD THE FOUNT OF FIERY LIFE • • • • •   270 MEMORIAL VERSES   13
    THE TURMOIL OF EXPIRING LIFE • • • • • • •   271 MEMORIAL VERSES   26
    WHEN FROM THEIR DUSTY LIFE THEY PASS • • • •   277 SOUTHERN NIGHT   59
    AND MEN WERE SPECKS AND LIFE A PLAY • • • • •   277 SOUTHERN NIGHT   78
    STORY OF PASSIONATE LIFE • • • • • • • •   280 HAWORTH CHURCH   12
    HISTORY OF PASSIONATE LIFE • • • • • • • •   280 HAWORTH CHURCH   V   12
    THIS WAS THY LIFE UPON EARTH • • • • • • •   288 RUGBY CHAPEL   57
    WHAT IS THE COURSE OF THE LIFE • • • • • • • 288 RUGBY CHAPEL   58
    BLUSTER OR CRINGE AND MAKE LIFE • • • • • •   290 RUGBY CHAPEL   157
    HEINE DISTILS FROM THY LIFE • • • • • • • • 294 HEINES GRAVE   68
    SLOW DIE OUT OF HER LIFE • • • • • • • •   295 HEINES GRAVE   83
    A SINGLE MOOD OF THE LIFE • • • • • • • •   298 HEINES GRAVE   215
    BITTER AND STRANGE WAS THE LIFE • • • • • •   299 HEINES GRAVE   223
    HIS BITTER LIFE MAY A LIFE • • • • • • • •   299 HEINES GRAVE   225
    HIS BITTER LIFE MAY A LIFE • • • • • • • •   299 HEINES GRAVE   225
    THEIR DROPS OF BLOOD THEIR DEATH IN LIFE • • •   301 GRANDE CHARTR   54
    SAY IS LIFE LIGHTER NOW THAN THEN • • • • •   303 GRANDE CHARTR   130
    YOUR PRIDE OF LIFE YOUR TIRELESS POWERS • • •   304 GRANDE CHARTR   167
    TO LIFE TO CITIES AND TO WAR • • • • • • •   305 GRANDE CHARTR   180
    THE GLOW HE CRIES THE THRILL OF LIFE • • • •   309 OBERMANN   97
    HE ONLY LIVES WITH THE WORLDS LIFE • • • • •   309 OBERMANN   103
    HALF OF MY LIFE WITH YOU • • • • • • • •   310 OBERMANN   132
    THE GLOW OF THOUGHT THE THRILL OF LIFE • • •   309 OBERMANN   V   97
    MADE HUMAN LIFE A HELL • • • • • • • • •   315 OBERMANN MORE   96
    AND FILLD HER LIFE WITH DAY • • • • • • •   316 OBERMANN MORE   116
    LUST OF THE EYE AND PRIDE OF LIFE • • • • •   317 OBERMANN MORE   133
    NO LONELY LIFE HAD PASSD TOO SLOW • • • • •   317 OBERMANN MORE   153
    OF LIFE TIS TRUE RECEIVED • • • • • • • •   318 OBERMANN MORE   166
    WHICH BATHED OUR LIFE RETIRED • • • • • • •   319 OBERMANN MORE   190
    AND KNEW MY LIFE WAS VAIN • • • • • • • •   321 OBERMANN MORE   266
    AND LEARN MY FRUSTRATE LIFE • • • • • • •   322 OBERMANN MORE   276
    MILLIONS WHOSE LIFE IN ICE LAY FAST • • • • • 322 OBERMANN MORE   287
    YET WARM IT MOUNTS THE HOUR OF LIFE • • • • • 322 OBERMANN MORE   291
    ITS TERM OF LIFE WAS NEARLY CLOSED • • • • •   322 OBERMANN MORE   299
    OUR LIFE TO ALPINE SNOW • • • • • • • • •   323 OBERMANN MORE   318
    FOR PRIVATE GAIN OR HATRED TAKES A LIFE • • •   336 MEROPE   202
    WAS SAVED A BABE BUT TO A LIFE OBSCURE • • • • 356 MEROPE   769
    WHERE AS LIFE EBBD HIS BEARERS LAID HIM DOWN •   357 MEROPE   783
    WHISPERING HOPE OF A LIFE • • • • • • • •   369 MEROPE   1088
    BROWND WITH THINE OPEN-AIR FREE HUNTERS LIFE •   373 MEROPE   1164
    MY CHILD MY CHARGE BELOVED WELCOME TO LIFE • •   375 MEROPE   1207
    MY NEW-WON TREASURE THY BELOVED LIFE • • • •   381 MEROPE   1291
    OF LIFE FOR MY ADVANTAGE AND MYSELF • • • • • 382 MEROPE   1350
    JUSTICE AND WISDOM IS NO LIFE AT ALL • • • •   390 MEROPE   1576
    ALL THINGS BUT LIFE THOU LOSE NOT LIFE AS WELL • 396 MEROPE   1757
    ALL THINGS BUT LIFE THOU LOSE NOT LIFE AS WELL • 396 MEROPE   1757
    THE TRUE ONE OF A MAN WHAT WAY OF LIFE • • •   404 MEROPE   1992
    ONE COLOUR IN THY LIFE THE HUE OF TRUTH • • •   404 MEROPE   1996
    NEVER AGAIN IN LIFE NEXT AGENTS FEED • • • •   365 MEROPE   V
    AND WHOM EMPEDOCLES CALLD BACK TO LIFE • • •   410 EMPEDOCLES I 1   111
    HE GRASPS THE VERY REINS OF LIFE AND DEATH • •   410 EMPEDOCLES I 1   125
    AND OF THE LIFE WHICH HEROES LEAD • • • • •   414 EMPEDOCLES I 2   73
    WHAT LIFE AND CHANCE GO HARD WITH THEE TOO AS WITH US 416 EMPEDOCLES I 2   116
    THE DEAD RETURN TO LIFE • • • • • • • • •   416 EMPEDOCLES I 2   124
    OF LIFE THE THIRST FOR BLISS • • • • • • •   418 EMPEDOCLES I 2   168
    BORN INTO LIFE WE ARE AND LIFE MUST BE OUR MOULD • 418 EMPEDOCLES I 2   186
    BORN INTO LIFE WE ARE AND LIFE MUST BE OUR MOULD • 418 EMPEDOCLES I 2   186
    BORN INTO LIFE MAN GROWS • • • • • • • • • 418 EMPEDOCLES I 2   187

LIFE   (CONTINUED)
        BORN INTO LIFE WE BRING   418 EMPEDOCLES I 2   192
        BORN INTO LIFE IN VAIN   419 EMPEDOCLES I 2   197
        BORN INTO LIFE WHO LISTS   419 EMPEDOCLES I 2   202
        BORN INTO LIFE TIS WE   419 EMPEDOCLES I 2   207
        THE ILL DEEDS OF OTHER MEN MAKE OFTEN OUR LIFE DARK   421 EMPEDOCLES I 2   266
        THROUGH THIS SHARP TOIL-SET LIFE   421 EMPEDOCLES I 2   268
        LEND LIFE TO THE DUMB STONES   421 EMPEDOCLES I 2   274
        TO EMBITTER HUMAN LIFE MALIGNANT DEITIES   422 EMPEDOCLES I 2   311
        THEIR WAY THROUGH LIFE AND BOW   425 EMPEDOCLES I 2   389
        WHY SHOULD I SAY THAT LIFE NEED YIELD BUT MODERATE   425 EMPEDOCLES I 2   391
            BLISS
        WHO LOOK ON LIFE WITH EYES   426 EMPEDOCLES I 2   409
        WHOS LOATH TO LEAVE THIS LIFE   426 EMPEDOCLES I 2   412
        I SAY FEAR NOT LIFE STILL   426 EMPEDOCLES I 2   422
        BUT SINCE LIFE TEEMS WITH ILL   426 EMPEDOCLES I 2   424
        WHOLLY FORGET THEIR FIRST SAD LIFE AND HOME   427 EMPEDOCLES I 2   458
        AND OF THE LIFE THAT HEROES LEAD   414 EMPEDOCLES I 2   V 73
        WHAT LIFE AND TIME GO HARD WITH THEE TOO AS WITH US   416 EMPEDOCLES I 2 V 116
        MAY BRAVELIER FRONT HIS LIFE AND IN HIMSELF   429 EMPEDOCLES II   9
        WHAT SHOULD I DO WITH LIFE AND LIVING MORE   429 EMPEDOCLES II   15
        BUT CAN LIFE REACH HIM   435 EMPEDOCLES II   210
        FULNESS OF LIFE AND POWER OF FEELING YE   436 EMPEDOCLES II   258
        THOU TOO BRIMMEST WITH LIFE THE SEA OF CLOUD   438 EMPEDOCLES II   308
        AM DEAD TO LIFE AND JOY THEREFORE I READ   438 EMPEDOCLES II   321
        OR WITH THE NIMBLE RADIANT LIFE OF FIRE   439 EMPEDOCLES II   344
        THE INEFFABLE LONGING FOR THE LIFE OF LIFE   439 EMPEDOCLES II   357
        THE INEFFABLE LONGING FOR THE LIFE OF LIFE   439 EMPEDOCLES II   357
        THIS UNCONGENIAL PLACE THIS HUMAN LIFE   440 EMPEDOCLES II   366
        TO SEE IF WE WILL POISE OUR LIFE AT LAST   440 EMPEDOCLES II   369
        OR WITH THE ACTIVE RADIANT LIFE OF FIRE   439 EMPEDOCLES II   V 344
        HIS BOON OF LIFE AND IMMORTALITY   446 WESTMIN ABBEY   63
        AND SCARCE THE BOON OF LIFE COULD STRUGGLE THROUGH   446 WESTMIN ABBEY   69
        AND THE ROUGH WAVES OF LIFE FOR EVER LAID   449 WESTMIN ABBEY   165
        AND ALL THAT LIFE AND ALL THAT LOVE   449 GEISTS GRAVE   3
        OF SECOND LIFE I KNOW NOT WHERE   450 GEISTS GRAVE   32
        CLOSER KNIT THEIR LIFE WITH OURS   453 POOR MATTHIAS   46
        EBB OF LIFE AND MORTAL PAIN   456 POOR MATTHIAS   124
        THEY SHALL NOT DECK YOUR LIFE BUT SANCTIFY YOUR GRAVE   467 ALARIC AT ROME 138
        THE CHANGE OF LIFE THE NOTHINGNESS OF POWER   469 ALARIC AT ROME   188
        DEEP ON HIS LIFE AND CHILDHOODS BABY WAVES   473 CROMWELL   48
        TILL WITH HIS DAILY LIFE A LIFE THAT THREW   473 CROMWELL   55
        TILL WITH HIS DAILY LIFE A LIFE THAT THREW   473 CROMWELL   55
        TILL LIFE UNSTIRRD BY ACTION LIFE BECAME   473 CROMWELL   59
        TILL LIFE UNSTIRRD BY ACTION LIFE BECAME   473 CROMWELL   59
        SOME SHADOWY VISION OF A TRANQUIL LIFE   474 CROMWELL   101
        NO LIFE OF DREAMS NO HOME BEYOND THE DEEP   475 CROMWELL   124
        A LIFE WHOSE WAYS NO HUMAN THOUGHT COULD SCAN   478 CROMWELL   219
        A LIFE THAT WAS NOT AS THE LIFE OF MAN   478 CROMWELL   220
        A LIFE THAT WAS NOT AS THE LIFE OF MAN   478 CROMWELL   220
        A LIFE THAT WROTE ITS PURPOSE WITH A SWORD   478 CROMWELL   221
        AND HURLD HIM ON THE FIELD OF LIFE   481 DESTINY   7
        HAVE NOT LIFE AND LOVE BEEN GRANTED ME   482 THEKLAS ANSWER   4
        AT LIFE AND LIVING NOT CONTENT   484 ROME-SICKNESS   23
        HERE WHERE LIFE AND ALL THINGS LIVING   META CLOISTER   17
        THY LITTLE MOMENT LIFE OF LOVELINESS   FRAGMENT 5   4
        WHERE BROODS THE UNCOMPANIONED LIFE OF GOD   FRAGMENT 6   3

LIFELESS
        ON THE LIFELESS MARGIN OF THE SPARKLING OCEAN   36 VOICE   19
        WHERE THOSE LIFELESS LOVERS BE   147 TRISTRAM 2   149
        NOW CRUSHD BUT NOT QUITE LIFELESS BY HIS FALL   334 MEROPE   140
        IS LIFELESS WHILE ITS HEART REMAINS UNTOUCHD   382 MEROPE   1343
        SOME LIFELESS SOULLESS PHANTOM OF THEIR OWN   474 CROMWELL   100

LIFELIKE
        LIFELIKE IN THE MARBLE PALE   16 CHURCH BROU 1   106
        WITH A LIFELIKE MOTION   36 VOICE   18

LIFELONG
        INDEED THY LIFELONG PASSION AND SOLE AIM   404 MEROPE   1983

LIFES
        TO SPURN MANS COMMON LURE LIFES PLEASANT THINGS   9 MYCERINUS   32
        CALMS NOT LIFES CROWN THOUGH CALM IS WELL   22 YOUTH AND CALM   23
        DROP WITH MINE ADOWN LIFES LATTER DAYS   33 NEW SIRENS   210
        LIFES VOYAGE DONE HIS HEAVENLY FRIEND   40 HUMAN LIFE   2
        ON LIFES INCOGNISABLE SEA   40 HUMAN LIFE   8
        AGES OR HOURS O WAKING ON LIFES STREAM   45 IN UTRUMQUE PAR   11
        IT TURNS LIFES MIGHTY WHEEL   47 WORLD QUIETIST   13
        WHO TREADS AT EASE LIFES UNCHEERD WAYS   59 RESIGNATION   237
        IN THIS HER LIFES LAST DAY OUR POOR OUR PAIN   168 RACHEL 2   10
        WHO FAILD UNDER THE HEAT OF THIS LIFES DAY   172 IMMORTALITY   7
        LIKE STARS ON LIFES COLD SEA   209 DESPONDENCY   2
        YOUTH RAMBLES ON LIFES ARID MOUNT   213 PROGRESS POESY   1
        FIGHT LIFES MANY-CHANCD FIGHT   216 LORDS MESSENGER   V
        OF TOIL HE MUST LIFES MOVEMENT TELL   225 EPILOG LAOCOON   140
        LIFES MOVEMENT FASCINATES CONTROLS   226 EPILOG LAOCOON   164
        THE STREAM OF LIFES MAJESTIC WHOLE   226 EPILOG LAOCOON   187
        DESPOTIC ON LIFES SEA   243 SUMMER NIGHT   V 57
        A MAN BECOMES AWARE OF HIS LIFES FLOW   247 BURIED LIFE   88

LIFES   (CONTINUED)
          LAID PAUSEFULLY UPON LIFES HEADLONG TRAIN   •   •   •   266 THYRSIS   137
          TOPS IN LIFES MORNING-SUN SO BRIGHT AND BARE   •   •   267 THYRSIS   145
          MADE HIS LIFES RULE ONCE MORE   •   •   •   •   •   •   314 OBERMANN MORE   54
          BAFFLERS OF OUR OWN PRAYERS FROM YOUTH TO LIFES   420 EMPEDOCLES I 2   231
               LAST SCENES
          ON LIFES WILD WAVES THE LIVING AND THE LOST   •   474 CROMWELL   78
          NO GLITTERING HOPES ON LIFES GREY DISTANCE SMILED   475 CROMWELL   126
          FORMS THAT WITH HIM SHALL TREAD LIFES CHANGING STAGE   476 CROMWELL   161

LIFT
          AND FROM YOUR BROIDERD PILLOWS LIFT YOUR HEADS   •   •   18 CHURCH BROU 3   26
          BLOW YE WINDS LIFT ME WITH YOU   •   •   •   •   •   •   177 PARTING   75

LIFTED
          WOULD THRUST A HAND BEFORE THE LIFTED BOWL   •   •   •   11 MYCERINUS   105
          THE CLUB WHICH RUSTUM LIFTED NOW AND STRUCK   •   •   73 SOHRAB RUSTUM   416
          LIFTED AND ISSUED ON THE FIELDS OF ICE   •   •   •   113 BALDER DEAD 2   287
          STILL LIFTED WELL WAS HIS RETURN FOREKNOWN   •   •   124 BALDER DEAD 3   378
          YET WERE IT LIFTED TO THE LIGHT   •   •   •   •   •   147 TRISTRAM 2   137
          HIS LIFTED HORN NOR CHEERS HIS HOUNDS   •   •   •   148 TRISTRAM 2   V
          SO SUNK SO RARELY LIFTED SAVE TO MEET   •   •   •   •   151 TRISTRAM 3   71
          LIFTED AND THAT UNWISHD-FOR HEIRSHIP VOID   •   •   •   366 MEROPE   1001
          BEFORE A STONE WAS LIFTED AND WE MEMMIUS   •   •   •   LUCRETIUS 5   5

LIFTING
          LIFTING UP YOUR LANGUID EYES   •   •   •   •   •   •   •   31 NEW SIRENS   158
          LIFTING HER SOFT-BENT HEAD ONLY TO MIND   •   •   •   152 TRISTRAM 3   84
          LIFTING THE COOL-HAIRD CREEPERS STEALTHILY   •   •   •   262 SCHOLAR-GIPSY   234
          LIFTING MANKIND AGAIN   •   •   •   •   •   •   •   •   323 OBERMANN MORE   324
          LIFTING MANKIND AMAIN   •   •   •   •   •   •   •   •   323 OBERMANN MORE   V 324
          AS I WAS LIFTING MY SOILD GARLAND OFF   •   •   •   •   407 EMPEDOCLES I 1   40

LIFTS
          THROUGH THE LOOSE CLOUDS LIFTS DIMLY   •   •   •   •   •   175 PARTING   13

LIGHT
          DO THOU WHOM LIGHT IN THINE OWN INMOST SOUL   •   •   8 RELIGIOUS ISOL   6
          LIVE BY THY LIGHT AND EARTH WILL LIVE BY HERS   •   •   8 RELIGIOUS ISOL   14
          A LIGHT THAT FROM SOME UPPER FOUNT DID BEAM   •   •   9 MYCERINUS   21
          A LIGHT THAT SHINING FROM THE BLEST ABODES   •   •   •   9 MYCERINUS   23
          SEEMS IT SO LIGHT A THING THEN AUSTERE POWERS   •   •   9 MYCERINUS   31
          ON THE CARVED WESTERN FRONT A FLOOD OF LIGHT   •   •   18 CHURCH BROU 3   18
          SHEDDING HER PENSIVE LIGHT AT INTERVALS   •   •   •   •   18 CHURCH BROU 3   35
          AND IS THE HEART OF YOUTH SO LIGHT   •   •   •   •   •   21 YOUTH AND CALM   9
          HAST LIVD LIGHT AS THESE LIVE NOW   •   •   •   •   •   22 MEMORY-PICTURE   V
          SCENT AND SONG AND LIGHT AND FLOWERS   •   •   •   •   32 NEW SIRENS   171
          SPREADS ITS COLD LIGHT WIDER ALL THAT WHILE   •   •   33 NEW SIRENS   218
          WHEN A DREARY LIGHT IS WADING   •   •   •   •   •   •   33 NEW SIRENS   V 211
          LIGHT BRING NO BLINDNESS   •   •   •   •   •   •   •   •   40 STAGIRIUS   57
          POOR CHILD WHOM THE LIGHT AIR OF CHILDISH JOY   •   •   41 GIPSY CHILD   V   9
          TO THE WORDS HOPE LIGHT PERSISTENCE   •   •   •   •   •   49 SECOND BEST   23
          IN WARMTH LIGHT JOY   •   •   •   •   •   •   •   •   •   52 CONSOLATION   70
          WAS DULLD FOR HE SLEPT LIGHT AN OLD MANS SLEEP   •   •   62 SOHRAB RUSTUM   29
          LIGHT MEN AND ON LIGHT STEEDS WHO ONLY DRINK   •   64 SOHRAB RUSTUM   124
          LIGHT MEN AND ON LIGHT STEEDS WHO ONLY DRINK   •   64 SOHRAB RUSTUM   124
          FIRST A LIGHT CLOUD OF HORSE TARTARS THEY SEEMD   •   •   65 SOHRAB RUSTUM   137
          WITH THY LIGHT SKIPPING TRICKS AND THY GIRLS WILES   75 SOHRAB RUSTUM   469
          PLIES SOME LIGHT FEMALE TASK NOR DREAMS OF US   •   •   80 SOHRAB RUSTUM   647
          UNTRODDEN LONELY FAR FROM LIGHT AND HEAVEN   •   •   •   99 BALDER DEAD 1   136
          HIGH OVER ASGARD TO LIGHT HOME THE KING   •   •   •   102 BALDER DEAD 1   257
          BY THE DIM VAPOUR-BLOTTED LIGHT OF STARS   •   •   •   108 BALDER DEAD 2   126
          BUT BY THE BLOTTED LIGHT OF STARS HE FARED   •   •   108 BALDER DEAD 2   140
          THE LIGHT AND JOURNEY TO THE CHEERLESS LAND   •   •   110 BALDER DEAD 2   181
          AND HEROES WHERE THEY LIVE IN LIGHT AND JOY   •   •   110 BALDER DEAD 2   199
          WHO SEE THE LIGHT AND BLEST IN ASGARD DWELL   •   •   112 BALDER DEAD 2   255
          AND ON THE TWELFTH MORN SAW THE LIGHT OF HEAVEN   •   113 BALDER DEAD 2   294
          SMOOTH SOUND THE TERMS AND LIGHT TO BE FULFILLD   •   120 BALDER DEAD 3   231
          AND SET THE FIELDS OF GLOOM ABLAZE WITH LIGHT   •   120 BALDER DEAD 3   243
          THAT EMPIRE WILT THOU NOW INVADE LIGHT UP   •   •   •   121 BALDER DEAD 3   279
          NO LESS THAN BALDER HAVE I LOST THE LIGHT   •   •   •   125 BALDER DEAD 3   401
          OF AGES AND MY LATE RETURN TO LIGHT   •   •   •   •   128 BALDER DEAD 3   511
          GAZING SEAWARD FOR THE LIGHT   •   •   •   •   •   •   130 TRISTRAM 1   12
          RUDDY IN THE FIRES LIGHT   •   •   •   •   •   •   •   •   131 TRISTRAM 1   18
          GLEAMS SO RICH IN THE LIGHT OF THE FIRE   •   •   •   131 TRISTRAM 1   25
          IF ONES OWN HEART BEATS NOT LIGHT   •   •   •   •   •   138 TRISTRAM 1   265
          MILD SHINES THE COLD SPRING IN THE MOONS CLEAR LIGHT   139 TRISTRAM 1   283
          GAZING SEAWARDS FOR THE LIGHT   •   •   •   •   •   •   130 TRISTRAM 1   V 12
          RAISE THE LIGHT MY PAGE THAT I MAY SEE HER   •   •   •   142 TRISTRAM 2   1
          COURTLY LIFE IS LIGHT AND CANNOT REACH IT   •   •   •   143 TRISTRAM 2   39
          FLASHD IN THE SILVER SCONCES LIGHT   •   •   •   •   •   146 TRISTRAM 2   113
          YET WERE IT LIFTED TO THE LIGHT   •   •   •   •   •   147 TRISTRAM 2   137
          SWINGING WITH IT IN THE LIGHT   •   •   •   •   •   •   147 TRISTRAM 2   150
          IS LIGHT AND GREEN THE HEATHER WHICH ALL ROUND   •   150 TRISTRAM 3   14
          SHELL LIGHT HER SILVER LAMP WHICH FISHERMEN   •   •   151 TRISTRAM 3   79
          TO GAZE ON THE SEA OF LEAF AND BOUGH   •   •   •   155 TRISTRAM 3   202
          IS LIGHT AND GREEN THE HEATHER WHICH ALL ROUND   •   •   TRISTRAM 3   V 14
          AND THE LIGHT CHIPPING OF THE WOODPECKER   •   •   •   155 TRISTRAM 3   V 198
          AND THE BLESSED LIGHT OF THE SUN   •   •   •   •   •   164 FORSAKEN MERM   93
          IN HIS LIGHT YOUTH AMID A FESTAL THRONG   •   •   •   166 AUSTERITY POET   3
          SET UP A MARK OF EVERLASTING LIGHT   •   •   •   •   •   169 EAST LONDON   10

LIGHT   (CONTINUED)
THE SEER FROM THE EAST WAS THEN IN LIGHT • • • • 170 EAST AND WEST   10
I STRUGGLE TOWARDS THE LIGHT AND YE • • • • • 183 ABSENCE   13
IF WITH THE LIGHT YE CANNOT BE • • • • • • 183 ABSENCE   15
I STRUGGLE TOWARDS THE LIGHT BUT OH • • • • • 183 ABSENCE   17
FIRST TO THE LIGHT AND MARK • • • • • • • 195 FRAG ANTIGONE   13
LIGHT IGNORANCE AND HURRYING UNSURE THOUGHTS • • 198 FRAG DEJANEIRA   2
DO YOU BETAKE YOURSELVES FOR LIGHT • • • • • 198 FRAG DEJANEIRA   13
OUT OF THE LIGHT AND MUTELY WHICH AVOIDS • • • 199 EARLY DEATH   3
THROUGH WHOSE LIGHT LEAVES AND SHOWERS • • • 200 PHILOMELA   V
SHE IS NOT COLD SHE IS NOT LIGHT • • • • • 201 URANIA   3
BUT LIGHT THE SERIOUS VISAGE GREW • • • • • 202 URANIA   11
THEY BRING US LIGHT AND WARMTH AND JOY • • • 203 EUPHROSYNE   24
THOUGHTS LIGHT LIKE GLEAMS MY SPIRITS SKY • • • 209 DESPONDENCY   5
THEY LIGHT ME ONCE THEY HURRY BY • • • • • 209 DESPONDENCY   7
UPON THE STRAITS ON THE FRENCH COAST THE LIGHT • 210 DOVER BEACH   3
HATH REALLY NEITHER JOY NOR LOVE NOR LIGHT • • 211 DOVER BEACH   33
UPON THE STRAIT ON THE FRENCH COAST THE LIGHT •   DOVER BEACH   V
LIGHT-PLASHING WAVES AN ANSWER MADE • • • • 223 EPILOG LAOCOON   68
FREE TO THE SWEEP OF LIGHT AND WIND • • • • • 223 EPILOG LAOCOON   72
CROWNING THEIR BROWS WITH ITS LIGHT • • • • • 232 YOUTH OF MAN   20
DARKENING FAST BUT A LIGHT • • • • • • • 234 YOUTH OF MAN   80
IT STOOD AND SUN AND MOONSHINE RAIND THEIR LIGHT • 236 PALLADIUM   5
NOT TILL THE HOURS OF LIGHT RETURN • • • • • 241 MORALITY   11
NATURE WHOSE FREE LIGHT CHEERFUL AIR • • • • 241 MORALITY   17
LIGHT FLOWS OUR WAR OF MOCKING WORDS AND YET • 245 BURIED LIFE   1
TO WHICH THY LIGHT WORDS BRING NO REST • • • 245 BURIED LIFE   7
LIGHT THE GREEN-FOLIAGD CHESTNUTS PLAY • • • 248 KENSINGTON GARD   V
LIGHT THE CLEAR FOLIAGED CHESTNUTS PLAY • • •   KENSINGTON GARD   V
HE SPREADS OUT HIS ARMS TO THE LIGHT • • • • 251 FUTURE   5
WHETHER HE FIRST SEES LIGHT • • • • • • • 252 FUTURE   13
THE LINE OF FESTAL LIGHT IN CHRIST-CHURCH HALL • 259 SCHOLAR-GIPSY   129
LIGHT HALF-BELIEVERS OF OUR CASUAL CREEDS • • 260 SCHOLAR-GIPSY   172
THE YOUNG LIGHT-HEARTED MASTERS OF THE WAVES • 262 SCHOLAR-GIPSY   241
HE HEARKENS NOT LIGHT COMER HE IS FLOWN • • • 265 THYRSIS   71
AND DARTING SWALLOWS AND LIGHT WATER-GNATS • • 266 THYRSIS   125
I FEEL HER FINGER LIGHT • • • • • • • • 266 THYRSIS   136
A FUGITIVE AND GRACIOUS LIGHT HE SEEKS • • • • 268 THYRSIS   201
YET HADST THOU ALWAY VISIONS OF OUR LIGHT • • • 269 THYRSIS   227
ROAM ON THE LIGHT WE SOUGHT IS SHINING STILL • 269 THYRSIS   238
HE HEARKENS NOT LIGHT COMER HE IS GONE • • • 265 THYRSIS   V 71
AH SINCE DARK DAYS STILL BRING TO LIGHT • • • 272 MEMORIAL VERSES   58
HANGS TOUCHD WITH LIGHT ONE SNOWY SAIL • • • 274 STANZAS CARNAC   32
HANGS TOUCHD WITH LIGHT ONE DISTANT SAIL • • • 274 STANZAS CARNAC   V 32
BRINGS THEE BACK IN THE LIGHT • • • • • • 286 RUGBY CHAPEL   17
OF LIGHT BUT THIS TO DECLARE • • • • • • • 296 HEINES GRAVE   117
FRESHEND AND LIGHT WITH THE MAY • • • • • 297 HEINES GRAVE   178
IN A THOUSAND WATER-BREAKS LIGHT • • • • • 297 HEINES GRAVE   184
EMBLEMS OF LIGHT ABOVE THE GRAVE • • • • • 305 GRANDE CHARTR   V 201
AND WATCHD THE ROSY LIGHT • • • • • • • 310 OBERMANN   122
IT LIVES AND WHILE I SEE THE LIGHT WILL LIVE • • 334 MEROPE   121
LIGHT TO SPRING UP TO THY HOUSE • • • • • • 343 MEROPE   407
SOMEWHERE FOR VENGEANCE A CHAMPION A LIGHT • • 346 MEROPE   513
YET WITH A LIGHT UNCAREWORN SPIRIT TURNS • • • 351 MEROPE   614
LIGHT TO SPRING UP TO THY RACE • • • • • • 343 MEROPE   V 407
SOMEWHERE IN SAFETY A NURSLING A LIGHT • • • 346 MEROPE   V 513
MIND IS A LIGHT WHICH THE GODS MOCK US WITH • 413 EMPEDOCLES I 2   32
MAN GETS NO OTHER LIGHT • • • • • • • • 417 EMPEDOCLES I 2   144
TO HAVE LIVED LIGHT IN THE SPRING • • • • • 425 EMPEDOCLES I 2   399
OH THAT MY SOUL WERE FULL OF LIGHT AS THE STARS • 438 EMPEDOCLES II   325
LIVED EVER IN THE LIGHT OF MY OWN SOUL • • • 440 EMPEDOCLES II   393
FAR FROM MY OWN SOUL FAR FROM WARMTH AND LIGHT • 440 EMPEDOCLES II   396
SEND FAR THEIR LIGHT VOICE • • • • • • • 442 EMPEDOCLES II   426
THE PRESENCE OF THAT GRACIOUS INMATE LIGHT • • 444 WESTMIN ABBEY   6
A CHILD OF LIGHT APPEARD • • • • • • • • 444 WESTMIN ABBEY   7
NAVE CHOIR AND TRANSEPT GLORIFIED WITH LIGHT • • 445 WESTMIN ABBEY   35
PETER HIS FRIEND WITH LIGHT DID CONSECRATE • • • 445 WESTMIN ABBEY   50
LIGHT ONLY LIGHT WAS SLOW TO REAPPEAR • • • 445 WESTMIN ABBEY   60
LIGHT ONLY LIGHT WAS SLOW TO REAPPEAR • • • 445 WESTMIN ABBEY   60
THE SAVIOURS HAPPY LIGHT • • • • • • • 446 WESTMIN ABBEY   61
FOR WANT OF LIGHT WHICH SHOULD THE BOON CONVEY • 446 WESTMIN ABBEY   70
IT SEEMD A CHILD OF LIGHT DID BRING THE DOWER • 446 WESTMIN ABBEY   74
AND JOY IN LIGHT AND POWER TO SPREAD THE JOY • 446 WESTMIN ABBEY   80
SHONE OFT SO HIGH A LIGHT • • • • • • • 446 WESTMIN ABBEY   82
BRINGER OF HEAVENLY LIGHT A HUMAN HOUR • • • 447 WESTMIN ABBEY   120
AND BORNE TO LIGHT AND RIGHT HIS WITNESS HIGH • 448 WESTMIN ABBEY   144
FEAR NOT BUT THAT THY LIGHT ONCE MORE SHALL BURN • 449 WESTMIN ABBEY   174
LET BUT THE LIGHT APPEAR • • • • • • • 449 WESTMIN ABBEY   177
FOR LACK OF LIGHT WHICH SHOULD THE BOON CONVEY • 446 WESTMIN ABBEY   V 70
OR THE BRIEF SPLENDOUR OF THAT METEOR LIGHT • • 463 ALARIC AT ROME   29
THY DAZZLING LIGHT AN EAGLES GAZE SHOULD TIRE • 463 ALARIC AT ROME   32
NO SHAME THAT SUNS SHOULD RISE TO LIGHT A CONQUERD 468 ALARIC AT ROME   150
    ROME
AN INWARD LIGHT THAT WITH ·ITS STREAMING RAY • • 473 CROMWELL   61
IN BROAD CLEAR LIGHT THE GHASTLY VISION SHONE • • 477 CROMWELL   203
BELOW THE SURFACE-STREAM SHALLOW AND LIGHT • • • 483 BELOW SURFACE   1
AS LIGHT OF WHAT WE THINK WE FEEL THERE FLOWS • • 483 BELOW SURFACE   3
TO HOLD THE LIGHT AND REACH THE HAND • • • • • 484 ROME-SICKNESS   31
I READ IN DANTE HOW THAT HORNED LIGHT • • • • 484 S S LUSITANIA   1
THERE SATE FIFTY MEN IN THE RUDDY LIGHT OF THE FIRE   HOMER TRANS   4
IN HIS SNOWY LIGHT AUSTERE • • • • • • • •   PILLARS UNIVERS   9

LIGHT   (CONTINUED)
    IN HIS ROSEATE LIGHT AUSTERE   • • • • • • • •   PILLARS UNIVERS V   9
    IN HIS WINTRY LIGHT AUSTERE   • • • • • • • •   PILLARS UNIVERS V   9

LIGHTED
    AND SHOWS ITS LIGHTED WINDOWS TO THE MAIN • • • •   97 BALDER DEAD 1   86
    THEN HE WILL JOURNEY THROUGH NO LIGHTED LAND   • •   99 BALDER DEAD 1   153
    AND LIGHTED TORCHES AND TOOK UP THE CORPSE • • • •   101 BALDER DEAD 1   204
    WHICH WOODCUTTERS HAVE LIGHTED NEAR THEIR LODGE • • 119 BALDER DEAD 3 V
    THE GLEAM-LIGHTED LAKE • • • • • • • •   174 PARTING   4
    COULD SCARCE HAVE LIGHTED ON A LOVELIER CURE   • •   407 EMPEDOCLES I 1   26
    IN A LOW DIM-LIGHTED PEN • • • • • • • • •   457 POOR MATTHIAS   186

LIGHTEN
    AH HOPE CANNOT LONG LIGHTEN TORMENTS LIKE THESE • •   20 MODERN SAPPHO   32

LIGHTEND
    IS NOT MORE LIGHTEND WHICH HE FEELS • • • • •   94 SICK KING BOKH   205
    HOW HIS BROW LIGHTEND AS THE MUSIC ROSE   • • • •   428 EMPEDOCLES I 2   483
    THREADED AND LIGHTEND BY A TRACK OF FLAME • • • •   473 CROMWELL   60

LIGHTENS
    LIGHTENS EVERY OTHER BROW   • • • • • • • • •   138 TRISTRAM 1   262

LIGHTER
    NOR WITH A LIGHTER HAND DISPOSE   • • • • • •   48 HORATIAN ECHO   22
    SAY IS LIFE LIGHTER NOW THAN THEN   • • • • • •   303 GRANDE CHARTR   130
    SEEMS IT LIGHTER MY LOSS • • • • • • • • • •   370 MEROPE   1115

LIGHTHOUSE
    TO WHERE THE LIGHTHOUSE BEACONS BRIGHT   • • • •   275 SOUTHERN NIGHT   11

LIGHTLY
    LIGHTLY QUIT WHAT LIGHTLY CAME • • • • • • • •-   22 MEMORY-PICTURE   2
    LIGHTLY QUIT WHAT LIGHTLY CAME • • • • • • • •   22 MEMORY-PICTURE   2
    WHERE FEET LIKE THINE TOO LIGHTLY COME   • • • •   184 TERRACE BERNE   20

LIGHTNESS
    COME ONCE MORE THAT ANCIENT LIGHTNESS   • • • •   32 NEW SIRENS   175
    NOR LIGHTNESS WISDOM ANY MORE • • • • • • •   179 FAREWELL   60
    AND ON WHOSE LIGHTNESS BLAME IS THROWN AWAY   • •   411 EMPEDOCLES I 1   162

LIGHTNING
    AND SWIFT FOR LIKE THE LIGHTNING TO THIS FIELD • •   82 SOHRAB RUSTUM   722
    THE LIGHTNING-BURSTS IS SEEN   • • • • • • • •   244 SUMMER NIGHT   63
    COME LIGHTNING PASSION THAT WITH FOOT OF FIRE • •   367 MEROPE   1060
    NOT TIME NOT LIGHTNING • • • • • • • • • •   398 MEROPE   1802
    LIKE US THE LIGHTNING-FIRES   • • • • • • • •   420 EMPEDOCLES I 2   247

LIGHTNINGS
    AND LIGHTNINGS RENT THE CLOUD AND RUKSH THE HORSE   76 SOHRAB RUSTUM   501
    LIGHTNINGS DAZZLE OUR EYES • • • • • • • • •   289 RUGBY CHAPEL   93
    ARROWY LIGHTNINGS OF SOUL • • • • • • • • •   293 HEINES GRAVE   36
    NOT BY THE LIGHTNINGS OF WIT   • • • • • • • •   295 HEINES GRAVE   108
    SCATTERING LIGHTNINGS THAT SOUL   • • • • • •   298 HEINES GRAVE   205
    NOR LIGHTNINGS GO ASIDE • • • • • • • • • •   420 EMPEDOCLES I 2   254
    WHICH THE LIGHTNINGS DOTH EMBRACE • • • • • •   431 EMPEDOCLES II   72
    LIKE SUMMER LIGHTNINGS OER A DARKEND SKY   • • •   474 CROMWELL   72

LIGHTS
    WHEN THE FLASHING LIGHTS ARE FADING • • • • •   33 NEW SIRENS   V 213
    LIGHTS UP HIS STUDIOUS FOREHEAD AND THIN HANDS • •   81 SOHRAB RUSTUM   676
    THOU SENTST AND FETCHEDST FIRE AND MADEST LIGHTS • • 121 BALDER DEAD 3   263
    WHAT LIGHTS WILL THOSE OUT TO THE NORTHWARD BE • • 130 TRISTRAM 1   5
    WHAT LIGHTS IN THE COURT WHAT STEPS ON THE STAIR • • 142 TRISTRAM 1   373
    TWINKLE THE MONASTERY-LIGHTS   • • • • • • •   156 SAINT BRANDAN   8
    THE HURTLING POLAR LIGHTS ARE NEARD • • • • •   156 SAINT BRANDAN   11
    WHERE THE SPENT LIGHTS QUIVER AND GLEAM   • • •   162 FORSAKEN MERM   37
    LIGHTS SHINE IN THE TOWN • • • • • • • • • •   164 FORSAKEN MERM   111
    WHERE NO MORE LIGHTS OF SENSE OR KNOWLEDGE ARE • • 167 PICT NEWSTEAD   11
    BUT WHEN THE MOON THEIR HOLLOWS LIGHTS   • • •   182 TO MARG CONT   7
    HIS EYES BE LIKE THE STARRY LIGHTS   • • • • •   202 URANIA   21
    THE ONE OR TWO IMMORTAL LIGHTS   • • • • • •   220 BACCHANALIA 2   24
    FLING THEIR WAVERING LIGHTS   • • • • • • •   253 FUTURE   73
    AND IN THE SCATTERED FARMS THE LIGHTS COME OUT • • 267 THYRSIS   164
    THE LIGHTS COME OUT IN THE STREET   • • • • •   286 RUGBY CHAPEL   8
    YOUR LONELY COLD-SHINING LIGHTS   • • • • •   437 EMPEDOCLES II   289
    AND LIGHTS FAIR NURSLING STUPOR FIRST INVADES • •   448 WESTMIN ABBEY   129
    AFTER LIGHTS TERM A TERM OF CECITY   • • • •   448 WESTMIN ABBEY   155
    AND LIGHTS FAIR NURSLING LANGUOR FIRST INVADES • • 448 WESTMIN ABBEY   V 129

LIKE
    WHERE MANS ONE NATURE QUEEN-LIKE SITS ALONE   • •   4 BUTLERS SERMONS   7
    AND RAYS HER POWERS LIKE SISTER-ISLANDS SEEN   • •   4 BUTLERS SERMONS   9
    TO BE LIKE NATURE STRONG LIKE NATURE COOL • • •   5 HARMONY NATURE   4
    TO BE LIKE NATURE STRONG LIKE NATURE COOL • • •   5 HARMONY NATURE   4
    LIKE COMETS ON THE HEAVENLY SOLITUDE • • • • •   6 GEO CRUIKSHANK   7
    LIKE THE BROAD VOLUME OF THE INSURGENT NILE   • •   10 MYCERINUS   40
    MIGHT SHRINK HALF STARTLED LIKE A GUILTY MAN   • •   11 MYCERINUS   102
    LIKE THE BROAD RUSHING OF THE INSURGENT NILE   • •   10 MYCERINUS   V   40

LIKE   (CONTINUED)

LIKE THE BROAD RUSHING OF THE COLUMND NILE • • • •   10 MYCERINUS   V 40
LIKE THE BROAD RUSHING OF THE INSURGED NILE   • •   10 MYCERINUS   V 40
AH HOPE CANNOT LONG LIGHTEN TORMENTS LIKE THESE • •   20 MODERN SAPPHO   32
BUT IS A CALM LIKE THIS IN TRUTH   • • • • •   21 YOUTH AND CALM   5
YET IS A CALM LIKE THIS IN TRUTH   • • • • • •   21 YOUTH AND CALM   V   5
FLASHD ONCE LIKE FALLING STREAMS WE ROSE WE GAZED   25 DREAM   29
LIKE THOSE KINGS WITH TREASURE STEERING • • • •   26 NEW SIRENS   21
FELL LIKE OSSA ON THE CLIMBING SOUL • • • • • •   28 NEW SIRENS   72
ONCE LIKE US YOU TOOK YOUR STATION   • • • • •   31 NEW SIRENS   139
PROUDLY LIKE A KING BEWAILING • • • • • • • •   34 NEW SIRENS   225
TROOPS LIKE EASTERN KINGS APPEARING • • • • •   26 NEW SIRENS   V 23
WEIGHS LIKE OSSA ON THE AERY SOUL   • • • • •   28 NEW SIRENS   V 72
WEIGHD LIKE OSSA ON THE AERY SOUL   • • • • •   28 NEW SIRENS   V 72
ONCE LIKE ME YOU TOOK YOUR STATION   • • • • •   31 NEW SIRENS   V 139
QUEEN—LIKE AND CLEAR • • • • • • • • • •   35 VOICE   2
LIKE BRIGHT WAVES THAT FALL   • • • • • •   36 VOICE   17
LIKE WANDERERS FROM THE WORLDS EXTREMITY • • •   36 VOICE   30
THOSE LUTE—LIKE TONES WHICH IN THE BYGONE YEAR   36 VOICE   35
THOSE LUTE—LIKE TONES WHICH IN LONG DISTANT YEARS   36 VOICE   V 35
WHAT MOOD WEARS LIKE COMPLEXION TO THY WOE • • •   42 GIPSY CHILD   21
LIKE THE WAVE   • • • • • • • • • • •   44 QUESTION   2
LIKE SPRING FLOWERS   • • • • • • • • •   44 QUESTION   9
LIKE THE REST HIS WIT WITH READING • • • •   49 SECOND BEST   15
LIKE LEAVES BY SUNS NOT YET UNCURLD • • • • •   59 RESIGNATION   253
CLUSTERING LIKE BEE—HIVES ON THE LOW FLAT STRAND • •   61 SOHRAB RUSTUM   13
O RUSTUM LIKE THY MIGHT IS THIS YOUNG MANS • •   67 SOHRAB RUSTUM   215
LIKE SOME OLD MISER RUSTUM HOARDS HIS FAME • • •   68 SOHRAB RUSTUM   247
FOLLOWD HIM LIKE A FAITHFUL HOUND AT HEEL • • •   69 SOHRAB RUSTUM   271
LIKE SOME YOUNG CYPRESS TALL AND DARK AND STRAIGHT   70 SOHRAB RUSTUM   314
SOLE LIKE SOME SINGLE TOWER WHICH A CHIEF • •   71 SOHRAB RUSTUM   337
FOR WE ARE ALL LIKE SWIMMERS IN THE SEA • • •   72 SOHRAB RUSTUM   390
DROPS LIKE A PLUMMET SOHRAB SAW IT COME • • •   73 SOHRAB RUSTUM   402
STILL ROUGH LIKE THOSE WHICH MEN IN TREELESS PLAINS   73 SOHRAB RUSTUM   410
AND PLEDGE EACH OTHER IN RED WINE LIKE FRIENDS • •   74 SOHRAB RUSTUM   441
BLAZED BRIGHT AND BALEFUL LIKE THAT AUTUMN—STAR • •   74 SOHRAB RUSTUM   452
NO HORSES CRY WAS THAT MOST LIKE THE ROAR • • •   76 SOHRAB RUSTUM   503
HIS HEAD BUT THIS TIME ALL THE BLADE LIKE GLASS   76 SOHRAB RUSTUM   511
AND PIERCE HIM LIKE A STAB AND MAKE HIM LEAP • •   78 SOHRAB RUSTUM   584
LIKE SOME RICH HYACINTH WHICH BY THE SCYTHE • •   80 SOHRAB RUSTUM   634
AND SWIFT FOR LIKE THE LIGHTNING TO THIS FIELD • •   82 SOHRAB RUSTUM   722
I CAME AND LIKE THE WIND I GO AWAY   • • • •   82 SOHRAB RUSTUM   723
SUDDEN AND SWIFT AND LIKE A PASSING WIND • • •   82 SOHRAB RUSTUM   724
LIKE THE SOILD TISSUE OF WHITE VIOLETS • • •   86 SOHRAB RUSTUM   844
LIKE THOSE WHICH MEN WHO DWELL IN TREELESS PLAINS   73 SOHRAB RUSTUM   V 410
LIKE ALLAH HEARS AND JUDGES ALL   • • • • •   89 SICK KING BOKH   57
WHO ALL WILL FLIT LIKE EDDYING LEAVES AROUND   100 BALDER DEAD 1   177
THE VOICE WAS LIKE THE UNHAPPY HODERS VOICE • •   102 BALDER DEAD 1   243
FOR DREAD FOR LIKE A WHIRLWIND ODIN CAME • • •   102 BALDER DEAD 1   264
LIKE A YOUNG CHILD HAST CRIED THYSELF TO SLEEP   103 BALDER DEAD 1   291
LIKE MEN WHO LIVE AND DRAW THE VITAL AIR • • •   108 BALDER DEAD 2   108
NOR LOOKST THOU PALE AND WAN LIKE MEN DECEASED   108 BALDER DEAD 2   109
THOU HEARST IF HEARING LIKE AS SPEECH IS THINE • • 112 BALDER DEAD 2   251
LIKE AS A FARMER WHO HATH LOST HIS DOG • • •   113 BALDER DEAD 3   8
AND BIND THY CARCASE LIKE A BALE WITH CORDS • •   114 BALDER DEAD 3   25
ANOTHER NOTE AND LIKE A BIRD IN SPRING • • •   117 BALDER DEAD 3   142
FARTHER AND FARTHER LIKE AN EYE OF FIRE • • •   119 BALDER DEAD 3   199
BUT GODS ARE LIKE THE SONS OF MEN IN THIS • • •   125 BALDER DEAD 3   426
FORSET THY SON TO BE BELOVED LIKE THEE • • •   126 BALDER DEAD 3   451
HA DOST THOU START ARE THY LIPS BLANCHD LIKE MINE   133 TRISTRAM 1   102
LET A DREAM LIKE THIS RESTORE   • • • • •   135 TRISTRAM 1   159
WERE FEET LIKE THOSE MADE FOR SO WILD A WAY • •   135 TRISTRAM 1   163
AND WITH A BLOOD LIKE MINE WILL LEAVE I FEAR • •   140 TRISTRAM 1   306
HER LOOK WAS LIKE A SAD EMBRACE   • • • •   140 TRISTRAM 1   322
LIKE HELPLESS BIRDS IN THE WARM NEST • • • •   140 TRISTRAM 1   328
I LIKE THEE HAVE LEFT MY YOUTH AFAR • • • •   143 TRISTRAM 2   22
LOVE LIKE MINE IS ALTERD IN THE BREAST • • •   143 TRISTRAM 2   38
STRUNG LIKE WHITE STARS THE PEARLS STILL ARE • •   146 TRISTRAM 2   109
HER MOODS GOOD LACK THEY PASS LIKE SHOWERS • • •   146 TRISTRAM 2   125
CONSUMED HER BEAUTY LIKE A FLAME   • • • •   147 TRISTRAM 2   134
AND DIMMD IT LIKE THE DESERT—BLAST • • • •   147 TRISTRAM 2   135
AND DIMMD HER LIKE THE DESERT—BLAST • • • •   147 TRISTRAM 2   V 135
ONE AFTER ONE TO—MORROW LIKE TO—DAY • • • •   151 TRISTRAM 3   67
ALONG THIS IRON COAST KNOW LIKE A STAR • • •   151 TRISTRAM 3   81
UNTIL THEY CRUMBLE OR ELSE GROW LIKE STEEL • •   153 TRISTRAM 3   121
LIKE THAT BALD CAESAR THE FAMED ROMAN WIGHT • •   153 TRISTRAM 3   143
FELL UPON MERLIN MORE LIKE DEATH SO DEEP • • •   155 TRISTRAM 3   214
LIKE THAT BOLD CAESAR THE FAMED ROMAN WIGHT • •   153 TRISTRAM 3   V 143
WHEN FRAGMENT OF IT SMALL LIKE MINE • • • •   158 SAINT BRANDAN   55
WHEN SEMBLANCE OF IT FAINT LIKE MINE • • • •   158 SAINT BRANDAN   V 55
IF SEMBLANCE OF IT FAINT LIKE MINE   • • •   158 SAINT BRANDAN   V 55
IF FRAGMENT OF IT SMALL LIKE MINE   • • • •   158 SAINT BRANDAN   V 55
YOUTH LIKE A STAR AND WHAT TO YOUTH BELONG • •   166 AUSTERITY POET   6
IN PARIS ALL LOOKD HOT AND LIKE TO FADE • • •   167 RACHEL 1   1
IN HER LIKE US THERE CLASHD CONTENDING POWERS • •   168 RACHEL 3   11
LIVE WE LIKE BRUTES OUR LIFE WITHOUT A PLAN • •   171 BETTER PART   8
WAS CHRIST A MAN LIKE US AH LET US TRY • • •   171 BETTER PART   13
AND WILL LIKE A DIVIDING SPEAR   • • • • •   178 FAREWELL   34
LIKE MINE EACH DAY MORE TRIED MORE TRUE • • •   180 ISOLATION MARG   6
OH THEN A LONGING LIKE DESPAIR • • • • • • •   182 TO MARG CONT   13

LIKE   (CONTINUED)

WHERE FEET LIKE THINE TOO LIGHTLY COME   184 TERRACE BERNE   20
LIKE DRIFTWOOD SPARS WHICH MEET AND PASS   185 TERRACE BERNE   45
LIKE SHIPS THAT MEET AND SPEAK AND PASS   185 TERRACE BERNE   V   45
TILL THEY TOO FADE LIKE GRASS THEY CRAWL   193 STRAYED REVEL   242
LIKE SHADOWS FORTH IN SPRING   193 STRAYED REVEL   243
BUT LIKE ME SHE WROTH COMPLAINING   197 FRAG ANTIGONE   76
HIS EYES BE LIKE THE STARRY LIGHTS   202 URANIA   21
HIS VOICE LIKE SOUNDS OF SUMMER NIGHTS   202 URANIA   22
LIKE STARS ON LIFES COLD SEA   209 DESPONDENCY   2
THOUGHTS LIGHT LIKE GLEAMS MY SPIRITS SKY   209 DESPONDENCY   5
LAY LIKE THE FOLDS OF A BRIGHT GIRDLE FURLD   211 DOVER BEACH   23
TO LIE BEFORE US LIKE A LAND OF DREAMS   211 DOVER BEACH   31
LAY LIKE THE FOLDS OF A BRIGHT GARMENT FURLD   211 DOVER BEACH   V   23
BECOME LIKE GLORIOUS LONDON   214 NEW ROME   V.   13
BE MADE LIKE LONDON WHERE PAUPERS   214 NEW ROME   V   13
WHERE POOR HAVE PLACE LIKE THE SWELLS   214 NEW ROME   V   14
IS NOT ON CHEEKS LIKE THOSE   219 BACCHANALIA 1   48
ASCENDING PURE THE BELL-LIKE FAME   219 BACCHANALIA 2   15
LIKE STARS OVER THE BOUNDING HILL   220 BACCHANALIA 2   27
SOLDIERS LIKE CAESAR   220 BACCHANALIA 2   55
STATESMEN LIKE PITT   220 BACCHANALIA 2   56
SCULPTORS LIKE PHIDIAS   221 BACCHANALIA 2   57
POETS LIKE SHAKESPEARE   221 BACCHANALIA 2   59
LIKE THESE AND IN ONE ASPECT BROUGHT   223 EPILOG LAOCOON   56
ITS SPELL IS ROUND THEM LIKE A SHOWER   227 EPILOG LAOCOON   199
AND LIKE THE THEBAN SEER   229 YOUTH OF NATURE   34
ARE YE LIKE DAYLIGHT AND SUN   230 YOUTH OF NATURE   66
LIKE STARS IN THE DEEP OF THE SKY   230 YOUTH OF NATURE   72
COME LIKE THE BREATH OF THE SPRING   234 YOUTH OF MAN   56
STRETCHING OUT LIKE THE DESERT   235 YOUTH OF MAN   109
FROM A FAR LONELIER DISTANCE LIKE THE WIND   238 PROGRESS   34
WHICH HAS NOT FALLN ON THE DRY HEART LIKE RAIN   238 PROGRESS   42
FEEL MY SOUL BECOMING VAST LIKE YOU   240 SELF-DEPENDENCE   12
A CRY LIKE THINE IN MINE OWN HEART I HEAR   240 SELF-DEPENDENCE   30
A CRY LIKE THINE IN MY OWN HEART I HEAR   240 SELF-DEPENDENCE   V   30
LIKE ALL THE OTHER MEN I SEE   243 SUMMER NIGHT   36
BUT WE MY LOVE DOTH A LIKE SPELL BENUMB   245 BURIED LIFE   24
BUT WE MY LOVE DOES A LIKE SPELL BENUMB   245 BURIED LIFE   V   24
THE BECK OF THE SPIRIT LIKE HIM   253 FUTURE   49
ELSE HADST THOU SPENT LIKE OTHER MEN THY FIRE   259 SCHOLAR-GIPSY   154
WHO WAIT LIKE THEE BUT NOT LIKE THEE IN HOPE   260 SCHOLAR-GIPSY   170
WHO WAIT LIKE THEE BUT NOT LIKE THEE IN HOPE   260 SCHOLAR-GIPSY   170
BUT NONE HAS HOPE LIKE THINE   261 SCHOLAR-GIPSY   196
LIKE US DISTRACTED AND LIKE US UNBLEST   261 SCHOLAR-GIPSY   225
LIKE US DISTRACTED AND LIKE US UNBLEST   261 SCHOLAR-GIPSY   225
FADE AND GROW OLD AT LAST AND DIE LIKE OURS   261 SCHOLAR-GIPSY   230
AND FLUTE HIS FRIEND LIKE ORPHEUS FROM THE DEAD   265 THYRSIS   90
THOU TOO O THYRSIS ON LIKE QUEST WAST BOUND   269 THYRSIS   211
THOU TOO O THYRSIS ON LIKE QUEST WERT BOUND   269 THYRSIS   V   211
HAD FELT HIM LIKE THE THUNDERS ROLL   270 MEMORIAL VERSES   9
BUT WHO LIKE HIM WILL PUT IT BY   272 MEMORIAL VERSES   70
LIKE GHOSTS THE HUGE GNARLD OLIVES STAND   275 SOUTHERN NIGHT   6
THEY LIKE FRIENDS SHALL RECEIVE   284 HAWORTH CHURCH   84
PUISSANT LIKE THINE WAS YET   284 HAWORTH CHURCH   91
STIRRD LIKE A CLARION-BLAST MY SOUL   285 HAWORTH CHURCH   100
SHOOK LIKE A CLARION-BLAST MY SOUL   284 HAWORTH CHURCH   V 100
STILL LIKE A TRUMPET DOST ROUSE   287 RUGBY CHAPEL   52
OTHERS LIKE THEE IN THE PAST   290 RUGBY CHAPEL   154
NOT LIKE THE MEN OF THE CROWD   290 RUGBY CHAPEL   155
YE LIKE ANGELS APPEAR   291 RUGBY CHAPEL   190
LIKE THESE ON EARTH I WAIT FORLORN   302 GRANDE CHARTR   88
WE ARE LIKE CHILDREN REARD IN SHADE   304 GRANDE CHARTR   169
THE WHITE MISTS ROLLING LIKE A SEA   306 OBERMANN   9
LIKE CHILDREN BATHING ON THE SHORE   308 OBERMANN   73
NO MORE SO HE BUT REST LIKE THEE   311 OBERMANN   159
LIKE OURS IT LOOKD IN OUTWARD AIR   315 OBERMANN MORE   85
BLOCKS OF THE PAST LIKE ICEBERGS HIGH   319 OBERMANN MORE   211
CONSUMED OUR HEART WITH THIRST LIKE FIRE   323 OBERMANN MORE   315
A WORLD LIKE OURS TO-DAY   315 OBERMANN MORE   V   84
FIXED IN OUR SOUL A THIRST LIKE FIRE   323 OBERMANN MORE   V 315
CONSUMD OUR SOUL WITH THIRST LIKE FIRE   323 OBERMANN MORE   V 315
AND SHED THEIR BLOOD LIKE WATER IN OUR CAUSE   337 MEROPE   227
WHICH IN A DEED LIKE MINE A JUST MAN TREADS   341 MEROPE   369
AND COUNT ON LIKE IMPUNITY AND RISE   342 MEROPE   374
GRANT HIM TO REIGN THERE WISE AND JUST LIKE THEE   350 MEROPE   589
NO CERTAIN NEWS IF LIKE THE REST IT RUN   350 MEROPE   600
FOR BEING OF LIKE AGE OF BIRTH NOT MEAN   355 MEROPE   722
NAMED AEPYTUS LIKE HIM HAVING GONE IN   357 MEROPE   777
ANOTHER ANCESTOR NAMED TOO LIKE ME   357 MEROPE   780
FOR THE KINGS PRIVATE EAR RESERVES LIKE THIS   364 MEROPE   965
BETRAYD LIKE HIM BUT NOT LIKE HIM AVENGED   367 MEROPE   1036
BETRAYD LIKE HIM BUT NOT LIKE HIM AVENGED   367 MEROPE   1036
HOW OFTEN HAVE I DREAMD OF THEE LIKE THIS   372 MEROPE   1158
CLUSTERING OER THY WHITE FOREHEAD LIKE A GIRLS   373 MEROPE   1162
NO BY THE GODS ALIVE AND LIKE TO LIVE   377 MEROPE   1218
THEIR CHIEF HATH TRAIND THEM MADE THEM LIKE HIMSELF   381 MEROPE   1303
A PEOPLE LIKE A COMMON MAN IS DULL   382 MEROPE   1342
THAT HOUSE LIKE OURS INTESTINE MURDER MAIMS   384 MEROPE   1392
WHAT PERMANENCE WHAT STABILITY LIKE OURS   389 MEROPE   1544

LIKE   (CONTINUED)

SO LIKE A STAR DAWNS THY SON	393	MEROPE	1682
OF YOUTH TIS LIKE HAD NEVER QUITE FORGONE	394	MEROPE	1703
AND FROM THAT TEACHER MAYST HAVE LEARND LIKE ME	394	MEROPE	1709
MELT LIKE A PASSING SMOKE A NIGHTLY DREAM	402	MEROPE	1945
ARE LIKE THE MOB VICIOUS AND IGNORANT	404	MEROPE	2004
DESPISE THEM NOT FOR BROTHER THOU LIKE ME	388	MEROPE	V1511
ARE SHINING ON THOSE NAKED SLOPES LIKE FLAME	412	EMPEDOCLES I 2	6
THERE LIKE A MIRROR HUNG	415	EMPEDOCLES I 2	80
EXPERIENCE LIKE A SEA SOAKS ALL-EFFACING IN	419	EMPEDOCLES I 2	201
LIKE US THE LIGHTNING-FIRES	420	EMPEDOCLES I 2	247
THE STREAM LIKE US DESIRES	420	EMPEDOCLES I 2	249
LIKE US THE LIBYAN WIND DELIGHTS TO ROAM AT LARGE	420	EMPEDOCLES I 2	251
A LIKE EVENT ELSEWHERE	425	EMPEDOCLES I 2	385
ESTRANGED LIKE MINE AND SAD	426	EMPEDOCLES I 2	410
THAT THY GROANS LIKE THUNDER PREST	430	EMPEDOCLES II	62
IN AN AGE LIKE THIS	432	EMPEDOCLES II	111
LIKE A SEA-WAVE BETWIXT THE WORLD AND THEE	436	EMPEDOCLES II	231
IN ALL THE ITALIAN CITIES LIKE OURSELVES	436	EMPEDOCLES II	237
WEARY LIKE US THOUGH NOT	438	EMPEDOCLES II	299
I WHO HAVE NOT LIKE THESE IN SOLITUDE	438	EMPEDOCLES II	318
OH THAT I COULD GLOW LIKE THIS MOUNTAIN	438	EMPEDOCLES II	323
OH THAT IT BROODED OVER THE WORLD LIKE THE AIR	438	EMPEDOCLES II	326
THAT THY GROANS LIKE THUNDER DEEP	430	EMPEDOCLES II	V 62
WHEN WE TOO LIKE THYSELF ARE CLAY	452	GEISTS GRAVE	74
NO AWAY WITH TALES LIKE THESE	456	POOR MATTHIAS	153
AH LIKE YOURS IS UNDESCRIED	457	POOR MATTHIAS	164
LIKE SUNSHINE WENT AND CAME AND BADE	460	KAISER DEAD	47
I SEE THE TAIL LIKE BRACELET TWIRLD	460	KAISER DEAD	55
FOLD LIKE A SHROUD AROUND THY WITHERED BONES	464	ALARIC AT ROME	64
SOON WAS THAT STILLNESS BROKEN LIKE THE CRY	466	ALARIC AT ROME	109
LIKE SOUNDS FROM OTHER WORLDS THE SPARTANS EAR	473	CROMWELL	42
LIKE A SWIFT RIVER THRO A SILENT PLAIN	473	CROMWELL	64
LIKE SUMMER LIGHTNINGS OER A DARKEND SKY	474	CROMWELL	72
LIKE LOVING SHADOWS ROUND THAT CHILDHOODS HOME	474	CROMWELL	74
LIKE A GREEN LAND AT SUNSET ALL WERE THERE	474	CROMWELL	84
LIKE FROZEN WINDS ON SOUTHERN VALES THAT BLOW	474	CROMWELL	89
LIKE DREAMS BETWEEN TWO SORROWS WENT AND CAME	474	CROMWELL	96
GREEN HAPPY PLACES LIKE A FLOWERY LEA	475	CROMWELL	117
LIKE ISLES OF SUNLIGHT ON A MOUNTAINS BROW	475	CROMWELL	127
THEN LIKE A KINGLY RIVER SWIFT AND STRONG	475	CROMWELL	133
SMOTE LIKE THE RUSH OF WATERS ON HIS EAR	475	CROMWELL	136
PALE PHANTOM HOSTS LIKE SHADOWS FAINT AND FAR	476	CROMWELL	141
HIS HANDS WERE FOLDED LIKE A SAINT AT REST	476	CROMWELL	168
STOOD LIKE A STATUE AND HIS FACE WAS FAIR	477	CROMWELL	176
FRIENDLESS AND HOPELESS LIKE A LONELY TREE	477	CROMWELL	189
LIKE SOME FORGOTTEN STRAIN THAT HAUNTS US STILL	477	CROMWELL	195
PASSD LIKE A MORNING MIST IN TEARS AWAY	477	CROMWELL	198
LIKE LOWERING CLOUDS THAT AT THE CLOSE OF DAY	478	CROMWELL	215
AND WELTERS LIKE A HUMAN THING	479	HAYSWATER BOAT	7
ARE SWEPT LIKE HUDDLING SHEEP ALONG	481	COURAGE	8
IF LIKE A COWARD I SKULKD BEHIND APART FROM THE BATTLE		HOMER TRANS	16
AT THY WANT OF A MAN LIKE ME TO SAVE THEE FROM BONDAGE		HOMER TRANS	36
AND NOT LEAVE HIM BEHIND A CORPSE ON THE PLAIN		HOMER TRANS	42
LIKE PATROCLUS			
LIKE STONE-SCULPTURED ANTIQUE KINGS		META CLOISTER	4
DID FALL LIKE RAIN IN THE FORSAKEN STREET		FRAGMENT 7	2

LIKELIEST

HAD BEEN THE LIKELIEST TRYSTING-PLACE TO-DAY	135	TRISTRAM 1	165

LIKELY

MOST LIKELY GRATEFUL BUT IN ALL CASE SURE	354	MEROPE	711

LIKEN

WHOSE MOOD SHALL FANCY LIKEN TO THY WOE	42	GIPSY CHILD	V 21

LIKENESS

EVER AGAIN PUT EARTHLY LIKENESS ON	470	ALARIC AT ROME	206
OF LIKENESS OR COMPARISON CAN BE		LUCRETIUS 5	9

LIKEWISE

NOR FEARD BUT THY LOVE LIKEWISE GREW	180	ISOLATION MARG	5

LILAC

NOTHING STIRS ON THE LAWN BUT THE QUICK LILAC-SHADE	19	MODERN SAPPHO	2
NOTHING MOVES ON THE LAWN BUT THE QUICK LILAC-SHADE	19	MODERN SAPPHO	V 2
PAINT THAT LILAC KERCHIEF BOUND	23	MEMORY-PICTURE	25

LILIES

LEAVE THE LILIES IN THEIR DEW	35	NEW SIRENS	268

LILY

SHE KNEW EACH LILY WHITE WHICH ENNA YIELDS	265	THYRSIS	95

LIMB

WASH OFF ALL BLOOD SET SMOOTH EACH LIMB	95	SICK KING BOKH	230
IS IT TO FEEL EACH LIMB	212	GROWING OLD	8

LIMBER

SUBDUED WITH LIMBER CHAINS LIVES FENRIS BOUND	111	BALDER DEAD 2	216

LIMBS
AND OER HIS CHILLY LIMBS HIS WOOLLEN COAT • • • • • 63 SOHRAB RUSTUM 96
HIS LIMBS GREW SLACK MOTIONLESS WHITE HE LAY • • 86 SOHRAB RUSTUM 848
TILL NOW ALL STRENGTH WAS EBBD AND FROM HIS LIMBS 86 SOHRAB RUSTUM 853
MID DUST AND GROANS AND LIMBS LOPPD OFF AND BLOOD 105 BALDER DEAD 2 16
THE LIMBS THEIR WONTED TASKS REFUSE • • • • • • 276 SOUTHERN NIGHT 41
OR NEXT MORNING WITH LIMBS • • • • • • • • 297 HEINES GRAVE 176
OOZING THROUGH THY SOAKD HUNTING-SHIRT WITH LIMBS 373 MEROPE 1173

LIMES
SWARDED ALLEYS THE LIMES • • • • • • • • • 292 HEINES GRAVE 4

LIMESTONE
PAST LIMESTONE SCARS WITH RAGGED PINES • • • • 299 GRANDE CHARTR 14

LIMIT
TEACHES THE LIMIT OF THE JUST AND TRUE • • • • 7 REP FRIEND 7
HAS REACHD THE LIMIT OF HIS UTMOST GROWTH • • • • LUCRETIUS 2 9

LIMITS
THE LIMITS OF HIS ART APPEAR • • • • • • • 222 EPILOG LAOCOON 50
LIMITS WE DID NOT SET • • • • • • • • • 418 EMPEDOCLES I 2 184

LIMPID
THE SMOOTHNESS OF THAT LIMPID BROW • • • • • • 21 YOUTH AND CALM 4
AND TURN THOSE LIMPID EYES ON MINE • • • • • • 245 BURIED LIFE 10

LINDENS
AND AIR-SWEPT LINDENS YIELD • • • • • • • • 255 SCHOLAR-GIPSY 26

LINE
OUR WAVERING MANY-COLOURED LINE • • • • • • 54 RESIGNATION 61
THE TRACK A STRAIGHT BLACK LINE • • • • • • 191 STRAYED REVEL 175
TO WATCH THIS LINE OF SAND-HILLS RUN • • • • • 204 CALAIS SANDS 2
TO SEE THIS LINE OF SAND-HILLS RUN • • • • • 204 CALAIS SANDS V 2
EACH ON HIS OWN STRICT LINE WE MOVE • • • • • 206 TOO LATE 1
AND THAT FAR PURPLE MOUNTAIN-LINE • • • • • 208 ON THE RHINE 13
ONLY FROM THE LONG LINE OF SPRAY • • • • • 211 DOVER BEACH 7
IN DANTES PETRARCHS TASSOS LINE • • • • • 222 EPILOG LAOCOON 21
THEY FEEL RUNS OER IN EVERY LINE • • • • • 227 EPILOG LAOCOON 198
BEEN ON OUR OWN LINE HAVE WE BEEN OURSELVES • 246 BURIED LIFE 60
IN A BLACKER INCESSANTER LINE • • • • • • 253 FUTURE 61
THE LINE OF FESTAL LIGHT IN CHRIST-CHURCH HALL • 259 SCHOLAR-GIPSY 129
BEHIND THAT LOVELY MOUNTAIN-LINE • • • • • 275 SOUTHERN NIGHT 7
A FEEBLE WAVERING LINE • • • • • • • • 291 RUGBY CHAPEL 173
STRENGTHEN THE WAVERING LINE • • • • • • 292 RUGBY CHAPEL 205
MOVE ON A RIGOROUS LINE • • • • • • • • 310 OBERMANN 134
OF MEN THE LINE OF HERACLES PREFERRD • • • • 338 MEROPE 269
MORE LOYAL AS OUR LINE CONTINUES MORE • • • 389 MEROPE 1541
OF YOUR DEAD MASTERS LINE I BRING YOU NEWS • • • 400 MEROPE 1883
AND THE LONG DUSKY LINE OF ITALY • • • • 438 EMPEDOCLES II 314
EFFACE THE HUMBLER GRAVES OF SEBERTS LINE • • • 445 WESTMIN ABBEY 54

LINEAGE
THE MANY OF THAT LINEAGE TO THE ONE • • • • • 338 MEROPE 270
TO REVERENCE YOUR LINEAGE MORE TO OBEY • • • • 339 MEROPE 303
FROM ALL FOR HIS GREAT LINEAGE AND HIS WOES • • 356 MEROPE 762
NO LINEAGE HIGHER • • • • • • • • • • 459 KAISER DEAD 22

LINEAL
THIS AWE WHICH GUARDS OUR EARTH-SPRUNG LINEAL KINGS 389 MEROPE 1543

LINEAMENTS
HE SPAKE AND STRAIGHT HIS LINEAMENTS BEGAN • • • • 104 BALDER DEAD 1 331

LINEN
BRING WATER NARD AND LINEN ROLLS • • • • • • 95 SICK KING BOKH 229

LINES
WHAT MY FRIENDS THESE FEEBLE LINES • • • • • • 24 MEMORY-PICTURE 49
DOWN THE PALE CHEEK LONG LINES OF SHADOW SLOPE • • 43 GIPSY CHILD 37
DOWN THY PALE CHEEK THOSE LINES OF SHADOW SLOPE • • 43 GIPSY CHILD V 37
SO PERFECTLY THE LINES EXPRESS • • • • • • • 147 TRISTRAM 2 144
AND WE HAVE BEEN ON MANY THOUSAND LINES • • • • 246 BURIED LIFE 57
POPULAR REVERENCE TO THESE RECENT LINES • • • • 390 MEROPE 1564
THE LINES OF DECEASED KINGS • • • • • • • 423 EMPEDOCLES I 2 325
YOUR DISTANT MELANCHOLY LINES • • • • • • • 437 EMPEDOCLES II 279
AND SO THERE RISE THESE LINES OF VERSE • • • • 451 GEISTS GRAVE 41

LINGER
IS IT HOPE MAKES ME LINGER THE DIM THOUGHT THAT SORROW 19 MODERN SAPPHO V
THE STREAM AND DO I LINGER HERE • • • • • • 183 TERRACE BERNE 4
WHILE ALL THIS TIME I BEAR TO LINGER ON • • • • 366 MEROPE 1017
SCOURGE OF THE NATIONS WOULDEST THOU LINGER YET • • 465 ALARIC AT ROME 94

LINGERD
WHAT TRACE OF CARELESS CHILDHOOD LINGERD THERE • • 477 CROMWELL 184

LINGERERS
    UNWILLING LINGERERS   • • • • • • • • • •   437 EMPEDOCLES II   290

LINGERING
    LINGERING WE FOLLOW DOWN WE GAIN   • • • • • •   54 RESIGNATION   78
    NO LINGERING NOW STRAIGHT TO THE CITY I   • • • •   332 MEROPE   65
    THOSE LINGERING HOPES OF COWARD HEARTS THAT STILL   475 CROMWELL   107

LINGERS
    HE LINGERS WHERE THE ROCK OF SPAIN   • • • • • •   275 STANZAS CARNAC   V 38

LINKD
    FOR EVERY DAY MAN MAY BE LINKD AND LOOSED   • • • •   196 FRAG ANTIGONE   34

LINKING
    LINKING THEIR CORAL ARMS UNDER THE SEA   • • • •   4 BUTLERS SERMONS   10
    LINKING IN A MAD SUCCESSION   • • • • • • • •   33 NEW SIRENS   205

LION
    OF SOME PAIND DESERT-LION WHO ALL DAY   • • • •   76 SOHRAB RUSTUM   504

LIONS
    IN VAIN BUT WHO CAN KEEP THE LIONS CUB   • • • •   63 SOHRAB RUSTUM   91
    HE HAS THE WILD STAGS FOOT THE LIONS HEART   • • • •   66 SOHRAB RUSTUM   177
    HE HAS THE WILD STAGS FOOT THE LIONS HEART   • • • •   67 SOHRAB RUSTUM   216
    HE HATH THE WILD STAGS FOOT THE LIONS HEART   • •   67 SOHRAB RUSTUM   V 216
    THE LIONS SLEEPING   • • • • • • • • • •   187 STRAYED REVEL   48

LIP
    HAST THOU NO LIP FOR WELCOME SO I SAID   • • • •   3 EMERSONS ESSAYS   5
    BECKOND HIM ON WITH QUIVERING LIP   • • • • •   278 SOUTHERN NIGHT   107
    THE SHORT PROUD LIP SHOWING THY RACE THY CHEEKS   • •   373 MEROPE   1163
    AGAIN FROM LIP TO LIP WILL PASS HIS NAME   • • • •   449 WESTMIN ABBEY   180
    AGAIN FROM LIP TO LIP WILL PASS HIS NAME   • • • •   449 WESTMIN ABBEY   180

LIPAREAN
    TO ETNAS LIPAREAN SISTER-FIRES   • • • • • • • •   438 EMPEDOCLES II   313

LIPPD
    WITH CLOSE-LIPPD PATIENCE FOR OUR ONLY FRIEND   • •   260 SCHOLAR-GIPSY   194

LIPS
    FELL THIS DREAD VOICE FROM LIPS THAT CANNOT LIE   • •   8 MYCERINUS   5
    FROM THE LOUD JOYFUL LAUGHTER OF HIS LIPS   • • •   11 MYCERINUS   101
    FELL THIS LATE VOICE FROM LIPS THAT CANNOT LIE   • •   8 MYCERINUS   V 5
    THEIR LIPS MOVED THEIR WHITE ARMS WAVED EAGERLY   • •   25 DREAM   28
    HIS BREAST HEAVED HIS LIPS FOAMD AND TWICE HIS VOICE   74 SOHRAB RUSTUM   455
    TRUTH SITS UPON THE LIPS OF DYING MEN   • • • •   80 SOHRAB RUSTUM   656
    HIS ARMS ABOUT HIS NECK AND KISSD HIS LIPS   • • • •   81 SOHRAB RUSTUM   695
    THEIR LIPS STILL WET WHEN I CAME DOWN   • • • •   90 SICK KING BOKH   84
    BUT FROM THY LIPS O BALDER NIGHT OR DAY   • • • •   116 BALDER DEAD 3   83
    HA DOST THOU START ARE THY LIPS BLANCHD LIKE MINE   133 TRISTRAM 1   102
    THROUGH THE SOFT-OPEND LIPS THE AIR   • • • • •   141 TRISTRAM 1   342
    SEE MY CHEEK AND LIPS HOW WHITE THEY ARE   • • • •   143 TRISTRAM 2   24
    AND QUIVERING LIPS ON WHICH THE TIDE   • • • • •   146 TRISTRAM 2   118
    FROM ISEULTS LIPS THE UNBROKEN STORY FLOWD   • • • •   150 TRISTRAM 3   45
    HER FINGER ON HER LIPS THEN VIVIAN ROSE   • • •   156 TRISTRAM 3   215
    THE LOVELY LIPS WITH THEIR ARCH SMILE THAT TELLS   • •   176 PARTING   39
    SWEET LIPS THIS WAY   • • • • • • • • • •   176 PARTING   42
    TO THE LIPS AH OF OTHERS   • • • • • • • •   176 PARTING   67
    THOSE LIPS HAVE BEEN PREST   • • • • • • • •   176 PARTING   68
    OUR HEART AND HAVE OUR LIPS UNCHAIND   • • • • •   245 BURIED LIFE   28
    WITH FROWNING FOREHEADS WITH LIPS   • • • • •   289 RUGBY CHAPEL   105
    FOR ONE SHORT MOMENT WANDER OER HIS LIPS   • • • •   298 HEINES GRAVE   209
    FROM DAVIDS LIPS THIS WORD DID ROLL   • • • •   318 OBERMANN MORE   V
    FROM DAVIDS LIPS THAT WORD DID ROLL   • • • •   318 OBERMANN MORE   V
    ALBEIT WITH LIPS UNAPT TO SELF-EXCUSE   • • • •   336 MEROPE   199
    LEARN THAT FROM OTHER LIPS O QUEEN THAN MINE   • •   362 MEROPE   927
    NOT FROM MY LIPS SHOULD CONSOLATION FALL   • • •   393 MEROPE   1687
    FATE SEALS MY LIPS AND DRAGS TO RUIN THEE   • • •   397 MEROPE   1779
    ON LIPS THAT RARELY FORM THEM NOW   • • • •   451 GEISTS GRAVE   42
    CAUGHT AS HE JOURNEYED FROM THE LIPS OF PAN   • •   473 CROMWELL   40
    THEN FROM THOSE WHITENING LIPS AS DEATH DREW NEAR   478 CROMWELL   213
    SCANS THOSE PARTED LIPS THAT PURELY   • • • • • •   META CLOISTER   37
    FREEZES THE SWEET STRAIN ON THE PARTED LIPS   • •   FRAGMENT 1   7

LIQUID
    THE LIQUID SKY ABOVE THE HILL   • • • • • • • •   218 BACCHANALIA 1   18
    THEIR SHINING FLANKS THEIR LIQUID EYES   • • • •   223 EPILOG LAOCOON   54
    AND KEEPS ITS LIQUID SOLITUDES UNSCALED   • • •   351 MEROPE   625
    FAR IN THE LIQUID LAKE WE SATE AND DREW   • • •   356 MEROPE   752
    THAT LIQUID MELANCHOLY EYE   • • • • • • •   450 GEISTS GRAVE   13

LIQUOR
    THE RED CREAMING LIQUOR   • • • • • • • • • •   187 STRAYED REVEL   57

LIST
    GAPE AND CRY WIZARD AT HIM IF THEY LIST   • • • •   410 EMPEDOCLES I 1   139

LISTEN
    YOU LISTEN BUT THAT WANDERING SMILE   • • • • • •   58 RESIGNATION   199

LISTEN   (CONTINUED)
    BECAUSE THOU WILT NOT LISTEN HERE   • • • • • • 91 SICK KING BOKH   100
    HER CHILDREN OR TO LISTEN TO THE WIND   • • • • • 152 TRISTRAM 3   85
    LISTEN EUGENIA • • • • • • • • • • 201 PHILOMELA   28
    LISTEN YOU HEAR THE GRATING ROAR   • • • • • 211 DOVER BEACH   9
    THEY STAND AND LISTEN THEY HEAR   • • • • • 234 YOUTH OF MAN   71
    WITH DEW OR LISTEN WITH ENCHANTED EARS   • • • 261 SCHOLAR-GIPSY   219
    LISTEN PAUSANIUS AY TIS CALLICLES   • • • • 413 EMPEDOCLES I 2   34

LISTEND
    HE SPOKE BUT RUSTUM LISTEND PLUNGED IN THOUGHT   • • 79 SOHRAB RUSTUM   604
    SO DEEMD HE YET HE LISTEND PLUNGED IN THOUGHT   • • 79 SOHRAB RUSTUM   615
    AND STILL THE CHILDREN LISTEND THEIR BLUE EYES   • • 150 TRISTRAM 3   46
    AND THEY WOULD STILL HAVE LISTEND TILL DARK NIGHT   • 151 TRISTRAM 3   56
    LISTEND AND FELT THYSELF GROW YOUNG   • • • • 310 OBERMANN   127
    LISTEND AND WEPT AWAY • • • • • • • • 310 OBERMANN   128

LISTENING
    LONGING LISTENING I WAIT I IMPLORE • • • • • 347 MEROPE   V
    AND WHISPERS TO THE LISTENING WINDS THAT SWELL   • • 472 CROMWELL   19
    THEN RESTED LISTENING SILENTLY • • • • • • 480 HAYSWATER BOAT   28

LISTETH
    LISTETH WILL SAIL • • • • • • • • • • 243 SUMMER NIGHT   55

LISTLESS
    DROOPD UNBRAIDED ON YOUR LISTLESS ARMS   • • • 30 NEW SIRENS   122
    LISTLESS AND HELD A FALCON ON HIS WRIST   • • • 67 SOHRAB RUSTUM   200

LISTLESSLY
    LISTLESSLY THROUGH THE WINDOW-BARS   • • • • • 131 TRISTRAM 1   41

LISTS
    BORN INTO LIFE WHO LISTS • • • • • • • • • 419 EMPEDOCLES I 2   202

LIT
    FENSALER WHOSE LIT WINDOWS LOOK TO SEA   • • • 100 BALDER DEAD 1   198
    NOR LIT WITH SUN BUT THROUGH THE DARKSOME AIR   • • 108 BALDER DEAD 2   125
    NOT LIT WITH SUN BUT THROUGH THE DARKSOME AIR   • 108 BALDER DEAD 2 V 125
    A FIRE OF WITHERD FURZE WHICH BOYS HAVE LIT   • 124 BALDER DEAD 3   361
    SHE LEFT THE GLEAM-LIT FIREPLACE   • • • • 140 TRISTRAM 1   315
    AT THIS HUGE GLEAM-LIT FIREPLACE   • • • • 148 TRISTRAM 2   158
    AT THE HUGE GLEAM-LIT FIREPLACE   • • • • 148 TRISTRAM 2 V 158
    LIT BY THY TAPERS STARLIKE BEAM   • • • • 177 FAREWELL   V 8
    OVER THE LIT SEAS UNQUIET WAY • • • • 240 SELF-DEPENDENCE 14
    BUT LIT FOR ALL ITS GENEROUS SUN   • • • • 251 WISH   39
    WENT OER THE SUN-LIT FIELDS AGAIN   • • • • 271 MEMORIAL VERSES 52
    OER WHOSE LIT FLOOR A ROAD OF MOONBEAMS LEADS   • 438 EMPEDOCLES II   312
    LIT WITH NO RAPTURE AS THE STORM SWEPT BY   • • • 472 CROMWELL   22
    LIT BY A WANDERING GLEAM WE KNOW NOT HOW   • • • 475 CROMWELL   128

LITHE
    LITHE AS THE GLANCING SNAKE AND THE CLUB CAME   • • 73 SOHRAB RUSTUM   418

LITTER
    TO CHEW THE STRAW HER LITTER AT HER FEET   • • • 123 BALDER DEAD 3   343
    HERE WILL I STAY TILL THE SLOW LITTER COMES • • 407 EMPEDOCLES I 1   18
    I SAW THE MULES AND LITTER IN THE COURT   • • • 407 EMPEDOCLES I 1   41
    AND IN THE LITTER SATE EMPEDOCLES • • • • 407 EMPEDOCLES I 1   42
    ENOUGH OF THIS I SEE THE LITTER WIND • • • • 411 EMPEDOCLES I 1   163

LITTLE
    SIX YEARS SIX LITTLE YEARS SIX DROPS OF TIME   • • 10 MYCERINUS   61
    WHISPERING A LITTLE SPACE AND THOU ART MINE   • • 11 MYCERINUS   106
    I WITH LITTLE LAND TO STIR   • • • • • • 22 MEMORY-PICTURE   5
    YET IF LITTLE STAYS WITH MAN • • • • • 24 MEMORY-PICTURE 59
    SOULS AS LITTLE GODLIKE AS THEIR OWN • • • • 34 NEW SIRENS   250
    MUSED MUCH LOVED LIFE A LITTLE LOATHED IT MORE   • • 43 GIPSY CHILD   36
    LOVE LENDS LIFE A LITTLE GRACE • • • • • 44 QUESTION   4
    OF LITTLE THREADS OUR LIFE IS SPUN • • • • 48 HORATIAN ECHO   25
    WHILE IT MENDS LITTLE TROUBLES MUCH   • • • 56 RESIGNATION   127
    WITH LARGE RESULTS SO LITTLE RIFE   • • • 60 RESIGNATION   262
    AND TO A HILLOCK CAME A LITTLE BACK   • • • 61 SOHRAB RUSTUM   17
    A LITTLE POOL AND IN SHORT SPACE   • • • • 90 SICK KING BOKH   68
    HATH SNATCHD A LITTLE FAIR-HAIRD SLAVE   • • 93 SICK KING BOKH 165
    A LITTLE POOL AND IN BRIEF SPACE   • • • 90 SICK KING BOKH V 68
    AND AS THE WOODMAN SEES A LITTLE SMOKE   • • • 104 BALDER DEAD 1   335
    AS LITTLE AS DID SOLITUDE • • • • • • 139 TRISTRAM 1   293
    ONE LITTLE WANDERING ARM IS THROWN   • • • 141 TRISTRAM 1   344
    WATCHING HER CHILDREN PLAY THEIR LITTLE HANDS   • 150 TRISTRAM 3   24
    WHERE THIS PLAGUE DRIVES THEM AND HAVE LITTLE EASE   153 TRISTRAM 3   141
    AND MADE A LITTLE PLOT OF MAGIC GROUND   • • • 156 TRISTRAM 3   220
    AND THE LITTLE GREY CHURCH ON THE WINDY SHORE   • 162 FORSAKEN MERM   26
    IN THE LITTLE GREY CHURCH ON THE SHORE TO-DAY   • 163 FORSAKEN MERM   57
    THE SEA GROWS STORMY THE LITTLE ONES MOAN • • 163 FORSAKEN MERM   65
    TO THE LITTLE GREY CHURCH ON THE WINDY HILL   • 163 FORSAKEN MERM   71
    THE SEA GROWS STORMY THE LITTLE ONES MOAN • • 163 FORSAKEN MERM   79
    FOR THE COLD STRANGE EYES OF A LITTLE MERMAIDEN   • 164 FORSAKEN MERM   106
    THE LITTLE FAIR-HAIRD SON WITH VACANT GAZE • • • 167 PICT NEWSTEAD   10
    OUR FREEDOM FOR A LITTLE BREAD WE SELL   • • • 169 WORLDLY PLACE   5

LITTLE   (CONTINUED)
      THE UNKNOWN LITTLE FROM THE UNKNOWING GREAT   • •   170 WEST LONDON   13
      FOR LITTLE DO THE ALL-CONTAINING HOURS   • • • 195 FRAG ANTIGONE   2
      IN LITTLE COMPANIES   • • • • • • • • • 195 FRAG ANTIGONE   17
      LITTLE IN YOUR PROSPERITY   • • • • • • • • 198 FRAG DEJANEIRA   5
      BUT HARDLY HAVE WE FOR ONE LITTLE HOUR   • • • 246 BURIED LIFE   59
      THE TURMOIL FOR A LITTLE BREATH   • • • • • • 251 WISH   46
      A TURMOIL FOR A LITTLE BREATH   • • • • • • • 251 WISH   V 46
      AND CAME AS MOST MEN DEEMD TO LITTLE GOOD   • • • 256 SCHOLAR-GIPSY   39
      THOU WANDEREDST WITH ME FOR A LITTLE HOUR   • • 269 THYRSIS   212
      HE TAUGHT US LITTLE BUT OUR SOUL   • • • • • • 270 MEMORIAL VERSES   8
      OF YORKSHIRE A LITTLE EARTH   • • • • • • • 282 HAWORTH CHURCH   53
      ONE OF HIS LITTLE ONES LOST   • • • • • • • 291 RUGBY CHAPEL   167
      AH NOT LITTLE WHEN PAIN   • • • • • • • • 293 HEINES GRAVE   23
      SO LITTLE LOVES THY STRAIN   • • • • • • • 307 OBERMANN   40
      HAVE TO HIS LITTLE ARMS BEGUILED   • • • • • 317 OBERMANN MORE   159
      MUCH TURBULENCE AND LITTLE CONSTANCY   • • • • 337 MEROPE   234
      RAVIN A LITTLE WHILE IN SPOIL AND BLOOD   • • • 339 MEROPE   297
      O GENTLE WISDOM LITTLE UNDERSTOOD   • • • • 339 MEROPE   309
      I DOUBT THEIR CAUTION LITTLE SUITS THEIR WARD   • • 351 MEROPE   608
      PROMISE NOT FAIR LET HIM A LITTLE WHILE   • • • 388 MEROPE   1506
      THUS LITTLE FOUNDED IN THEIR SUBJECTS LOVE   • • • 390 MEROPE   1560
      THE REST TO ME IS LITTLE YET SINCE THAT   • • • 401 MEROPE   1891
      NOT LITTLE IF THOU SAWST WHAT LOVE WHAT ZEAL   • • 401 MEROPE   1893
      PASSD YOU A LITTLE SINCE AS MORNING DAWND   • • • 408 EMPEDOCLES I 1   46
      TROUBLES CONFOUND THE LITTLE WIT HE HAS   • • • 413 EMPEDOCLES I 2   31
      AND BEND THEIR LITTLE FISTS AND RATE THE SENSELESS   421 EMPEDOCLES I 2   276
         GROUND
      WHICH TO HIM LITTLE YIELDS   • • • • • • 426 EMPEDOCLES I 2   413
      TROUBLES CONFUSE THE LITTLE WIT HE HAS   • • • 413 EMPEDOCLES I 2   V   31
      DEAR LITTLE FRIEND AT EVERY TURN   • • • • 450 GEISTS GRAVE   8
      OR JUST THY LITTLE SELF RESTORE   • • • • • 450 GEISTS GRAVE   28
      THE DACHS-HOUND GEIST THEIR LITTLE FRIEND   • • • 452 GEISTS GRAVE   80
      ALL CONVULSED HIS LITTLE FORM   • • • • • 452 POOR MATTHIAS   4
      GEIST CAME NEXT OUR LITTLE FRIEND   • • • • • 454 POOR MATTHIAS   57
      LITTLE HELPING WOUNDING MUCH   • • • • • • 457 POOR MATTHIAS   167
      HERE HE POURD HIS LITTLE SOUL   • • • • • • 458 POOR MATTHIAS   200
      WE WITHOUT THEE LITTLE FRIEND   • • • • • • 458 POOR MATTHIAS   210
      ALAS THAT FIERY SPIRIT LITTLE KNEW   • • • • 469 ALARIC AT ROME   187
      ONE LITTLE YEAR THAT RESTLESS SOUL SHALL REST   • • 469 ALARIC AT ROME   193
      A LITTLE WHILE ALAS A LITTLE WHILE   • • • • 470 ALARIC AT ROME   217
      A LITTLE WHILE ALAS A LITTLE WHILE   • • • • 470 ALARIC AT ROME   217
      RETAIND SO LITTLE IN THY CARELESS DEPTHS   • • •   LUCRETIUS 1   4
      THIS LITTLE WHICH WE ARE   • • • • • • • •   FRAGMENT 3   1
      THY LITTLE MOMENT LIFE OF LOVELINESS   • • • •   FRAGMENT 5   4

LITTLENESS
      AND LITTLENESS UNITED   • • • • • • • • • • 431 EMPEDOCLES II   93

LITYERSES
      FOR THEE THE LITYERSES-SONG AGAIN   • • • • • 268 THYRSIS   184

LIVD
      HAST LIVD LIGHT AS THESE LIVE NOW   • • • • •   22 MEMORY-PICTURE   V
      THE TRIBES WHO THEN LIVD ON HER BREAST   • • • 252 FUTURE   V 32
      HE PERISHD IN ARCADIA WHERE HE LIVD   • • • • 355 MEROPE   V 717
      ONLY WHILE THEIR LOVE LIVD LASTED THEY   • • • 482 THEKLAS ANSWER   8

LIVE
      DIDST LIVE ON EARTH UNGUESSD AT BETTER SO   • • •   3 SHAKESPEARE   V 11
      LIVE BY THY LIGHT AND EARTH WILL LIVE BY HERS   • •   8 RELIGIOUS ISOL   14
      LIVE BY THY LIGHT AND EARTH WILL LIVE BY HERS   • •   8 RELIGIOUS ISOL   14
      HAST LIVD LIGHT AS THESE LIVE NOW   • • • •   22 MEMORY-PICTURE   V
      MAN CANNOT THOUGH HE WOULD LIVE CHANCES FOOL   • •   40 HUMAN LIFE   18
      FORESEEN THY HARVEST YET PROCEEDST TO LIVE   • •   43 GIPSY CHILD   40
      LONG SINCE THE WORLD HATH SET ITS HEART TO LIVE   • •   46 WORLD QUIETIST   11
      THEY MUST LIVE STILL AND YET GOD KNOWS   • • •   56 RESIGNATION   132
      THE WORLD IN WHICH WE LIVE AND MOVE   • • • •   58 RESIGNATION   215
      ENOUGH WE LIVE AND IF A LIFE   • • • • • •   60 RESIGNATION   261
      OH COULD I LIVE TILL I THAT GRIEF HAD SEEN   • •   78 SOHRAB RUSTUM   588
      DESIRE NOT THAT MY FATHER THOU MUST LIVE   • • •   84 SOHRAB RUSTUM   772
      FOR SOME ARE BORN TO DO GREAT DEEDS AND LIVE   • •   84 SOHRAB RUSTUM   773
      SO THOU MIGHTEST LIVE TOO MY SON MY SON   • • •   85 SOHRAB RUSTUM   815
      TO LIVE AS ERST YOUR DAILY LIFE IN HEAVEN   • •   96 BALDER DEAD 1   36
      FAIR MEN WHO LIVE IN HOLES UNDER THE GROUND   • •   97 BALDER DEAD 1   56
      SO THOU MIGHTST LIVE AND STILL DELIGHT THE GODS   • • 101 BALDER DEAD 1   218
      LIKE MEN WHO LIVE AND DRAW THE VITAL AIR   • • 108 BALDER DEAD 2   108
      AND HEROES WHERE THEY LIVE IN LIGHT AND JOY   • • 110 BALDER DEAD 2   199
      TILL THEN IN PERIL OR IN PAIN WE LIVE   • • • 111 BALDER DEAD 2   225
      BETTER TO LIVE A SERF A CAPTURED MAN   • • • 112 BALDER DEAD 2   265
      BETTER TO LIVE A SLAVE A CAPTURED MAN   • • • 112 BALDER DEAD 2   V 265
      WHO LIVE AND WITH THEIR EYES SHALL SEE THAT DAY   • • 127 BALDER DEAD 3   486
      WHO THEN SHALL LIVE IN PEACE AS NOW IN WAR   • • 128 BALDER DEAD 3   531
      SAY I CHARGD HER THAT YE LIVE TOGETHER   • • • 145 TRISTRAM 2   V 95
      TILL FOR ITS SAKE ALONE WE LIVE AND MOVE   • • • 153 TRISTRAM 3   129
      WE LIVE NO MORE WHEN WE HAVE DONE OUR SPAN   • • 171 BETTER PART   5
      LIVE WE LIKE BRUTES OUR LIFE WITHOUT A PLAN   • • 171 BETTER PART   8
      AND WOMEN THINGS THAT LIVE AND MOVE   • • • • • 178 FAREWELL   21
      WE MORTAL MILLIONS LIVE ALONE   • • • • • • 182 TO MARG CONT   4
      TO THINGS BY MORTAL COURSE THAT LIVE   • • • • • 185 TERRACE BERNE   42
      BY CITY AND HOUSEHOLD GROUPD WE LIVE AND MANY SHOCKS   195 FRAG ANTIGONE   20

LIVE   (CONTINUED)
    PROUD IGNORANT SELF-ADORED YOU LIVE ALONE   • • •   198 FRAG DEJANEIRA   7
    LET HIM LIVE LET HIM FEEL I HAVE LIVED   • • •   200 EARLY DEATH   17
    FOR HIM WHO MUST LIVE MANY YEARS   • • • • • 199 EARLY DEATH   V 1
    A MOMENTS LIFE OF THINGS THAT LIVE   • • • • • 223 EPILOG LAOCOON   58
    AND STILL THEY LIVE AND STILL THEY BURN   • • •   224 EPILOG LAOCOON   104
    BUT THEY ARE IMMORTAL AND LIVE   • • • • • • •   230 YOUTH OF NATURE   85
    WHAT CHARMD YOU IN OTHERS RE-LIVE   • • • • •   231 YOUTH OF NATURE   109
    SEEST US CHANGE WHILE WE LIVE   • • • • • • •   232 YOUTH OF MAN   6
    BUT LEAVE US NOT WHILE WE LIVE   • • • • • •   234 YOUTH OF MAN   60
    I SAY UNTO YOU SEE THAT YOUR SOULS LIVE   • • •   237 PROGRESS   23
    WOULDST THOU BE AS THESE ARE LIVE AS THEY   • • •   240 SELF-DEPENDENCE   16
    FOR SELF-POISED THEY LIVE NOR PINE WITH NOTING   • •   240 SELF-DEPENDENCE   23
    FOR ALONE THEY LIVE NOR PINE WITH NOTING   • •   240 SELF-DEPENDENCE   23
    WHY SELF-POISED THEY LIVE NOR PINE WITH NOTING   •   240 SELF-DEPENDENCE   V 23
    FOR MOST MEN IN A BRAZEN PRISON LIVE   • • • • •   243 SUMMER NIGHT   37
    HOW IT WERE GOOD TO LIVE THERE AND BREATHE FREE •   244 SUMMER NIGHT   V 90
    BEFORE I HAVE BEGUN TO LIVE   • • • • • • •   249 KENSINGTON GARD   44
    NOR BRING TO SEE ME CEASE TO LIVE   • • • • •   250 WISH   17
    AND LIVED ITSELF AND MADE US LIVE   • • • • •   251 WISH   40
    ALL THE LIVE MURMUR OF A SUMMERS DAY   • • • • •   255 SCHOLAR-GIPSY   20
    ONLY TO LIVE BY THE HEART   • • • • • •   282 HAWORTH CHURCH   V
    OF THE SPIRIT IN WHOM THOU DOST LIVE   • • -• • •   287 RUGBY CHAPEL   47
    DESTINED TO WORK AND TO LIVE   • • • • • • •   298 HEINES GRAVE   196
    MYRIADS WHO LIVE WHO HAVE LIVED   • • • • •   298 HEINES GRAVE   213
    TOO FAST WE LIVE TOO MUCH ARE TRIED   • • • • •   308 OBERMANN   77
    I IN THE WORLD MUST LIVE BUT THOU   • • • •   310 OBERMANN   137
    YE LIVE I CRIED YE WORK AND PLAN   • • • • •   320 OBERMANN MORE   215
    HAD CEASED TO LIVE AND THRIVE   • • • • • •   320 OBERMANN MORE   226
    THROUGH THAT PRETENDED DEATH TO LIVE AND REIGN   •   331 MEROPE   50
    IT LIVES AND WHILE I SEE THE LIGHT WILL LIVE   •   334 MEROPE   121
    TO SEE SECURE TO LIVE WITH THOSE SHE LOVES   • •   349 MEROPE   566
    THESE MANY YEARS I LIVE FOR THIS ALONE   • • •   351 MEROPE   621
    FISHERS WHO LIVE ON THE LAKE-SIDE TO LAUNCH .   358 MEROPE   837
    OR ELSE NOT LIVE AT ALL BUT HERE I HAUNT   • • •   366 MEROPE   1020
    IN WORD I DIED THAT I IN DEED MIGHT LIVE   • • •   375 MEROPE   1209
    NO BY THE GODS ALIVE AND LIKE TO LIVE   • • •   377 MEROPE   1218
    FOR TO LIVE DISOBEDIENT TO THESE TWO   • • • •   390 MEROPE   1575
    THAT KINGS LIVE FOR THEIR PEOPLES NOT THEMSELVES •   394 MEROPE   1715
    WERE TO LIVE FREE FROM TERROR SPELLS MISTRUST THEM   413 EMPEDOCLES I 2   26
    HOW MAN MAY HERE BEST LIVE NO CARE TOO GREAT   419 EMPEDOCLES I 2   216
          TO EXPLORE
    THERE THOSE TWO LIVE FAR IN THE ILLYRIAN BRAKES • • 427 EMPEDOCLES I 2   443
    WERE TO LIVE FREED FROM TERROR SPELLS MISTRUST THEM   413 EMPEDOCLES I 2   V 26
    NOT THOU THE WORLD WITH MEN THOU CANST NOT LIVE   •   429 EMPEDOCLES II   18
    THOU CANST NOT LIVE WITH MEN NOR WITH THYSELF   •   429 EMPEDOCLES II   23
    LIVE HAPPY THEN EXPECT YOUR PERFECT MEED   • • •   448 WESTMIN ABBEY   138
    TO LIVE AND SEE ARISE   • • • • • • •   449 WESTMIN ABBEY   157
    AND THOU SHALT LIVE AS LONG AS WE   • • • • •   451 GEISTS GRAVE   58
    LIVE BESIDE US BUT ALONE   • • • • • • •   455 POOR MATTHIAS   96
    LIVE OUT THE DAY   • • • • • • • • •   460 KAISER DEAD   48
    DEEDS THAT SHALL LIVE WHEN THEY WHO DID THEM DIE •   462 ALARIC AT ROME   15
    TO BE REMEMBERED THUS AND YET THEY CANNOT LIVE   •   462 ALARIC AT ROME   18
    STOOPS TO THE SOARING MOUNTAINS LIVE AND DIE   •   472 CROMWELL   10
    THERE THOU TOO SHALT LIVE WITH US TOGETHER   • • •   482 THEKLAS ANSWER   13
    IT SEEMS AN IDLE THING WHICH COULD NOT LIVE   • •   FRAGMENT 9   1

LIVED
    MY FATHER LOVED INJUSTICE AND LIVED LONG   • • • •   9 MYCERINUS   13
    HE HATH NOT LIVED IF HE LIVES SO   • • •   56 RESIGNATION   153
    AND FALSEHOOD WHILE I LIVED WAS FAR FROM MINE • •   80 SOHRAB RUSTUM   657
    WHILE WE YET LIVED AMONG THE OTHER GODS   • • •   104 BALDER DEAD 1   330
    FOR DEAR-BELOVED WAS BALDER WHILE HE LIVED   • •   120 BALDER DEAD 3   232
    AND ALL THAT LIVED AND ALL WITHOUT LIFE WEPT   •   122 BALDER DEAD 3   306
    SIT SIT BY ME I WILL THINK WEVE LIVED SO   • • •   143 TRISTRAM 2   35
    COLD COLD AS THOSE WHO LIVED AND LOVED   • • •   149 TRISTRAM 2   192
    THE DAYS IN WHICH SHE MIGHT HAVE LIVED AND LOVED • 151 TRISTRAM 3   65
    LET HIM LIVE LET HIM FEEL I HAVE LIVED   • • •   200 EARLY DEATH   17
    HAVE DREAMD THAT I LIVED BUT FOR THEM   • • •   232 YOUTH OF NATURE   131
    HAVE THOUGHT THAT I LIVED BUT FOR THEM   • • •   232 YOUTH OF NATURE V 131
    I KNEW THEY LIVED AND MOVED   • • • • • •   245 BURIED LIFE   20
    AND LIVED ITSELF AND MADE US LIVE   • • • •   251 WISH   40
    THOU HAST NOT LIVED WHY SHOULDST THOU PERISH SO • 259 SCHOLAR-GIPSY   151
    WHILE THE TREE LIVED HE IN THESE FIELDS LIVED ON • 263 THYRSIS   30
    WHILE THE TREE LIVED HE IN THESE FIELDS LIVED ON • 263 THYRSIS   30
    AND LIVED SOME MOONS IN HAPPY TRANCE   • • • •   279 SOUTHERN NIGHT   109
    YES I BELIEVE THAT THERE LIVED   • • • • •   290 RUGBY CHAPEL   153
    MYRIADS WHO LIVE WHO HAVE LIVED   • • • • •   298 HEINES GRAVE   213
    OH HAD I LIVED IN THAT GREAT DAY   • • • • •   317 OBERMANN MORE   141
    HE LIVED WHILE WE BELIEVED   • • • • •   318 OBERMANN MORE   168
    THE DAY I LIVED IN WAS NOT MINE   • • • •   321 OBERMANN MORE   257
    COMPOSED TO BEAR I LIVED AND DIED   • • • •   321 OBERMANN MORE   265
    SINCE LAST ON EARTH THERE LIVED AND WROUGHT   •   315 OBERMANN MORE   V 83
    GLOOM-WRAPPED WITHIN I LIVED AND DIED   • •   321 OBERMANN MORE   V 265
    TOGETHER WE HAD GROWN TOGETHER LIVED   • • •   334 MEROPE   123
    A KING A KING WAS HE WHILE HE LIVED   • • • •   345 MEROPE   472
    FAIN WOULD I FADE AWAY AS I HAVE LIVED   • • •   366 MEROPE   1027
    LIVED FOR THE DEATH OF HIS FOES   • • • • •   368 MEROPE   1085
    YET HAD HE LIVED SUSPICION JEALOUSY   • • • • •   394 MEROPE   1697
    TOGETHER WE HAD SPRUNG TOGETHER LIVED   • • •   334 MEROPE   V 123
    TO HAVE LIVED LIGHT IN THE SPRING   • • • • •   425 EMPEDOCLES I 2   399

LIVED   (CONTINUED)
          WHERE THE SPHINX LIVED AMONG THE FROWNING HILLS   • • 427 EMPEDOCLES I 2   440
          THOUGH I HAVE LOVED THEE LIVED IN HONOURING THEE • • 434 EMPEDOCLES II   195
          YOU TOO ONCE LIVED • • • • • • • • • • 437 EMPEDOCLES II   282
          LIVED EVER IN THE LIGHT OF MY OWN SOUL • • • • 440 EMPEDOCLES II   393
          I CANNOT I HAVE LIVED IN WRATH AND GLOOM • • • • 440 EMPEDOCLES II   394
          PEOPLE WHO LIVED HERE LONG AGO • • • • • • • 452 GEISTS GRAVE   77
          OPEN LIVED TO US AND NEAR • • • • • • • • • 455 POOR MATTHIAS   88

LIVEDST
          MOTHER I WELL BELIEVED THOU LIVEDST ON • • • • 367 MEROPE   1043

LIVERY
          PRAISED THY GOLDEN LIVERY • • • • • • • • • 455 POOR MATTHIAS   118

LIVES
          HE HATH NOT LIVED IF HE LIVES SO • • • • • •   56 RESIGNATION   153
          AND WONDERS HOW SHE LIVES AND WHAT THE THOUGHTS • •   70 SOHRAB RUSTUM   307
          WHO IN THEIR LIVES WERE FAMOUS FOR THEIR SONG • • 103 BALDER DEAD 1   272
          SUBDUED WITH LIMBER CHAINS LIVES FENRIS BOUND • • 111 BALDER DEAD 2   216
          LET ALL THAT LIVES AND MOVES UPON THE EARTH • • • 111 BALDER DEAD 2   236
          WITH MEN BUT LIVES A HOSTAGE WITH THE GODS • • • 123 BALDER DEAD 3   325
          IN THE GREEN WOOD ALL OUR LIVES ALONE • • • • 143 TRISTRAM 2   36
          AH IT LIVES BECAUSE SO DEEP-SUPPRESSD • • • • 143 TRISTRAM 2   40
          AND SPEND THEIR LIVES IN POSTING HERE AND THERE • • 153 TRISTRAM 3   140
          THEIR LIVES AND FORMER VIOLENT TOIL IN THEBES • • 193 STRAYED REVEL   256
          SO FAR APART THEIR LIVES ARE THROWN • • • • • 206 TOO LATE   3
          HE FOLLOWS HOME AND LIVES THEIR LIFE • • • • • 226 EPILOG LAOCOON   162
          LIVES IN OUR EYES WHICH CAN PAINT • • • • • • 233 YOUTH OF MAN   36
          LIVES IN OUR HEARTS WHICH CAN FEEL • • • • • • 233 YOUTH OF MAN   37
          THEIR FADED IGNOBLE LIVES • • • • • • • • 235 YOUTH OF MAN   111
          SO IN ITS LOVELY MOONLIGHT LIVES THE SOUL • • • 236 PALLADIUM   9
          THEIR LIVES TO SOME UNMEANING TASKWORK GIVE • • • 243 SUMMER NIGHT   40
          WHENCE OUR LIVES COME AND WHERE THEY GO • • • • 246 BURIED LIFE   54
          AND EACH HALF LIVES A HUNDRED DIFFERENT LIVES • • 260 SCHOLAR-GIPSY   169
          AND EACH HALF LIVES A HUNDRED DIFFERENT LIVES • • 260 SCHOLAR-GIPSY   169
          HE ONLY LIVES WITH THE WORLDS LIFE • • • • • 309 OBERMANN   103
          IT LIVES AND WHILE I SEE THE LIGHT WILL LIVE • • 334 MEROPE   121
          IF STILL INDEED HE LIVES WHOM THOU WOULDST SEAT • • 336 MEROPE   189
          NO BUT TO THY AMBITION THEIR POOR LIVES • • • • 339 MEROPE   325
          ONE SON AT LEAST I SPARED FOR STILL HE LIVES • • 340 MEROPE   348
          WHO LIVES WITNESSES TRUE • • • • • • • • 369 MEROPE   1098
          THEN IRRESISTIBLY IT LIVES IT WORKS • • • • • 382 MEROPE   1346
          AND LIVES A LONELY MAN IN TRIPLE GLOOM • • • • 410 EMPEDOCLES I 1   124
          LIVES AND THAT OTHER FAINTER SEA FAR DOWN • • • 438 EMPEDOCLES II   311
          THAT MILD AND LUMINOUS FLOOR OF WATERS LIVES • • 438 EMPEDOCLES II   315
          YET SOME THERE ARE THEIR VERY LIVES WOULD GIVE • • 462 ALARIC AT ROME   17

LIVING
          FOR FEELING NERVES AND LIVING BREATH • • • • •   22 YOUTH AND CALM   18
          QUIET LIVING STRICT-KEPT MEASURE • • • • • •   49 SECOND BEST   2
          AND HE DREW NEAR AND HEARD NO LIVING VOICE • • • 113 BALDER DEAD 2   305
          LIVING BUT ELLA CAPTURED HIM AND SLEW • • • • 117 BALDER DEAD 3   128
          ALL LIVING AND UNLIVING THINGS TO WEEP • • • • 122 BALDER DEAD 3   292
          ALL LIVING AND UNLIVING THINGS TO WEEP • • • • 122 BALDER DEAD 3   300
          ME THY LIVING FRIEND THOU CANST NOT SAVE • • • 145 TRISTRAM 2   90
          BUT SINCE LIVING WE WERE UNUNITED • • • • • • 145 TRISTRAM 2   91
          ONE LAST KISS UPON THE LIVING SHORE • • • • • 145 TRISTRAM 2   98
          AND ON IT CHRIST A LIVING FORM • • • • • • • 156 SAINT BRANDAN   16
          MUCH CHEERD WITH THOUGHTS OF CHRIST THE LIVING BREAD • 169 EAST LONDON   8
          WHICH BLAMED THE LIVING MAN • • • • • • • • 213 GROWING OLD   35
          MURMUR OF LIVING • • • • • • • • • • • 233 YOUTH OF MAN   51
          ONLY THE LIVING CAN FEEL YOU • • • • • • • 234 YOUTH OF MAN   59
          AND LIVING AS THOU LIVST ON GLANVILS PAGE • • • 259 SCHOLAR-GIPSY   159
          O ROTHA WITH THY LIVING WAVE • • • • • • • 272 MEMORIAL VERSES   72
          IN THIS HIS LIVING STATE • • • • • • • • • 273 EDW QUILLINAN   V 10
          FIRST TO THE LIVING WE PAY • • • • • • • • 281 HAWORTH CHURCH   34
          WHAT DOST THOU IN THIS LIVING TOMB • • • • • 301 GRANDE CHARTR   72
          TIS TRUE AND LIVING YET • • • • • • • • • 318 OBERMANN MORE   V
          LIVING HIS OWN FUNERAL-PILE • • • • • • • • 399 MEROPE   1834
          LIVING HIS OWN SACRIFICE-BLOCK • • • • • • • 400 MEROPE   1859
          HEALTH SAPPD BY LIVING ILL • • • • • • • • 425 EMPEDOCLES I 2   393
          WHAT SHOULD I DO WITH LIFE AND LIVING MORE • • • 429 EMPEDOCLES II   15
          A LIVING MAN NO MORE EMPEDOCLES • • • • • • 438 EMPEDOCLES II   328
          AND FIRE REPEL US FROM ITS LIVING WAVES • • • • 439 EMPEDOCLES II   363
          PRESENT AND PAST THE LIVING AND THE DEAD • • • • 463 ALARIC AT ROME   44
          PERCHANCE HAD QUICKEND WITH A LIVING TRUTH • • • 473 CROMWELL   53
          ON LIFES WILD WAVES THE LIVING AND THE LOST • • • 474 CROMWELL   78
          WHAT LIVING HAND HATH BROUGHT IT HERE • • • • 480 HAYSWATER BOAT   40
          AT LIFE AND LIVING NOT CONTENT • • • • • • • 484 ROME-SICKNESS   23
          OF ALL LIVING THINGS THAT ON EARTH ARE BREATHING   HOMER TRANS   13
                  AND MOVING
          HERE WHERE LIFE AND ALL THINGS LIVING • • • •   META CLOISTER   17

LIVST
          AND LIVING AS THOU LIVST ON GLANVILS PAGE • • • • 259 SCHOLAR-GIPSY   159

LIZARDS
          ALIVE WITH BRIGHT GREEN LIZARDS • • • • • • • 191 STRAYED REVEL   173

LO

AND WHEN SIX YEARS ARE MEASURED LO I DIE   • • • •   9 MYCERINUS   18
LO YON ORIENT HILL IN FLAMES   • • • • •   35 NEW SIRENS   260
LO SAILS THAT GLEAM A MOMENT AND ARE GONE   • • • •   42 GIPSY CHILD   5
LO I AM OLD THREE KINGS ERE THEE   • • • •   92 SICK KING BOKH   143
LO HOME HAVING PERFORMD YOUR WILL I COME   • • •   114 BALDER DEAD 3   37
THEN LOOKD AND LO THE FROSTY SKIES   • • • • •   158 SAINT BRANDAN   75
BUT LO THE STAFF IT BUDDED   • • • • • • •   160 NECKAN   53
A PROP GAVE WAY CRASH FELL A PLATFORM LO   • • • •   166 AUSTERITY POET   8
LO THE ILL-FATED ONE   • • • • • •   400 MEROPE   1876
LO ON A SUDDEN ALL THE PILE IS BRIGHT   • • • •   445 WESTMIN ABBEY   34
THEREFORE ARISE AND ARM THEE LO THE WORLD   • • •   465 ALARIC AT ROME   91
AND LO THE ETERNAL CITY AS THEY RISE   • • • •   468 ALARIC AT ROME   155
WITH FEET THAT SPURND THE GROUND LO MILTON THERE   •   477 CROMWELL   175
SPRANG FROM ITS SLEEP AND LO THE WATERS ROLL   • •   479 CROMWELL   236

LOAD

CAME THE HUNTERS WITH THEIR LOAD   • • • • •   13 CHURCH BROU 1   32
AND HER LOAD OF STEAMING TRESSES   • • • • •   28 NEW SIRENS   71
I TOO HAVE FELT THE LOAD I BORE   • • • • •   178 FAREWELL   29
SORE LOAD AND WORDS CAN DO NO MORE   • • • •   224 EPILOG LAOCOON   94
ATLANTEAN THE LOAD   • • • • • • • •   295 HEINES GRAVE   94
THEIR LOAD AND GONE AWAY   • • • • • • • •   315 OBERMANN MORE   V 82
AND IF THE SACRED LOAD OPPRESSD OUR BRAIN   • • •   436 EMPEDOCLES II   244
EARTH AND HEAVENS STAR-SPANGLED LOAD   • • • • •   PILLARS UNIVERS   4

LOADED

THE LOADED BOAT SWINGS GROANING   • • • • • •   192 STRAYED REVEL   198

LOADS

BUT OTHER LOADS THAN THIS HIS OWN   • • • • •   92 SICK KING BOKH   153
AND LOOSED THEM OF THEIR LOADS ON THE SEASHORE   • •   106 BALDER DEAD 2   67

LOATH

TARDY OR SWIFT WOULDST THOU BE LOATH TO DIE   • •   103 BALDER DEAD 1   306
UPROAR SURELY NOT LOATH   • • • • • • • • • •   293 HEINES GRAVE   15
SO LOATH TO SUFFER MUTE   • • • • • • • • • •   421 EMPEDOCLES I 2   277
WHOS LOATH TO LEAVE THIS LIFE   • • • • • • •   426 EMPEDOCLES I 2   412

LOATHE

I LOATHE FOR HIM THE SLIPPERY WAY OF BLOOD   • • • •   387 MEROPE   1464

LOATHED

MUSED MUCH LOVED LIFE A LITTLE LOATHED IT MORE   • •   43 GIPSY CHILD   36
THEN FROM THEIR LOATHED FEAST THE GODS AROSE   • •   101 BALDER DEAD 1   203
YOUR MATE THOUGH LOATHED AND FEASTS IN ODINS HALL   •   111 BALDER DEAD 2   218
THEN FROM THEIR LOATHED FEAST THE GODS AROSE   • •   119 BALDER DEAD 3   214

LOATHING

LOATHING TO MEET AT DAWN THE OTHER GODS   • • • •   102 BALDER DEAD 1   250
AND SECRET LOATHING FELL   • • • • • • • • •   315 OBERMANN MORE   94

LOAVES

A SIDE OF ROASTED SHEEP AND LOAVES OF BREAD   • •   67 SOHRAB RUSTUM   V 198

LOCK

AND ALL THAT IS TO COME I KNOW BUT LOCK   • • • •   121 BALDER DEAD 3   286
SHAKE LOOSE SOME LOCK OF SOFT BROWN HAIR   • • • •   205 CALAIS SANDS   V 16
CROSSING THE STRIPLING THAMES AT BAB-LOCK-HITHE   • •   257 SCHOLAR-GIPSY   74

LOCKD

AND HERE AND THERE LOCKD BY THE LAND   • • • • •   141 TRISTRAM 1   367
AND FROM HER BROWN-LOCKD HEAD THE WIMPLE THROWS   • •   156 TRISTRAM 3   216
LOCKD IN EACH OTHERS ARMS WE STOOD   • • • • • •   178 FAREWELL   11
AND ITS LOCKD FOUNT OF BEAUTY USE   • • • • • •   223 EPILOG LAOCOON   84
THE SANDY SPITS THE SHORE-LOCKD LAKES   • • • • •   275 SOUTHERN NIGHT   1
AND LOCKD MY SPEECH FOR EVER IN MY BREAST   • • • •   362 MEROPE   941
HEAR THAT FRESH VOICE AND CLASP THAT GOLD-LOCKD HEAD   387 MEROPE   1460

LOCKS

WHEN YOUR SHOWERING LOCKS ENWOUND YOU   • • • •   29 NEW SIRENS   97
AND THOSE WARM LOCKS MEN WERE PRAISING   • • • •   30 NEW SIRENS   121
THOUGH THE LOCKS ARE YET BROWN ON HIS NOBLE HEAD   •   130 TRISTRAM 1   10
HAD LOOSEND THE BROWN LOCKS OF VIVIANS HAIR   • •   154 TRISTRAM 3   168
WHILE THE LOCKS ARE YET BROWN ON THY HEAD   • • •   235 YOUTH OF MAN   112
ABOVE THE LOCKS ABOVE THE BOATING THRONG   • • • •   266 THYRSIS   122
SOLE OFFERING THAT THOU HAST LOCKS FROM THY HEAD   • •   332 MEROPE   71
HIS FLOWING LOCKS AND GOLD-ENCIRCLED BROW   • • •   408 EMPEDOCLES I 1   60
SHOOK BACK HIS TANGLED LOCKS AND MURMURD PEACE   • •   477 CROMWELL   174
AND PILLOWS ON HER FROZEN BREAST AND LOCKS   • • •   FRAGMENT 1   3

LODGE

THE SHEPHERD FROM HIS MOUNTAIN-LODGE DESCRIES   • •   79 SOHRAB RUSTUM   621
NO MORE TO ASGARD SHALT THOU COME NOR LODGE   • •   126 BALDER DEAD 3   448
WHICH WOODCUTTERS HAVE LIGHTED NEAR THEIR LODGE   • •   119 BALDER DEAD 3   V
ROUND SOME FAIR FOREST-LODGE AT MORN   • • • • •   305 GRANDE CHARTR   184
ROUND SOME OLD FOREST-LODGE AT MORN   • • • • •   305 GRANDE CHARTR   V 184

LODGED

BUT LODGED AMONG MY FATHERS FOES AND SEEN   • • •   83 SOHRAB RUSTUM   759
THERE WITH THE CHIEF OF THAT HILL-TOWN WE LODGED   • •   356 MEROPE   746

LODGERS
    LODGERS IN THE FOREST AND THE CAVE   • • • • • •   34 NEW SIRENS   234

LODGES
    SAYS HAPPY HE WHO LODGES THERE • • • • • • • •   94 SICK KING BOKH   193

LODGING
    TO HALVE A LODGING THAT WAS ALL HER OWN   • • • •   44 GIPSY CHILD   64

LOFTIER
    LOFTIER BEARING AND A PROUDER EYE   • • • • • •   28 NEW SIRENS   64
    HIS STEP WAS LOFTIER THAN THE STEPS OF MAN • • • •   476 CROMWELL   156

LOFTIEST
    OUT-TOPPING KNOWLEDGE FOR THE LOFTIEST HILL   • •   2 SHAKESPEARE   3
    HIS LATEST LOFTIEST MUSIC SMOTE HIS EAR   • • • •   478 CROMWELL   210

LOFTY
    AND REARD HIM A BRIGHT BAY WITH LOFTY CREST   • •   69 SOHRAB RUSTUM   276
    NOR SEEN HIS LOFTY HOUSE IN SEISTAN • • • • • •   83 SOHRAB RUSTUM   757
    AND TRAIND HIM A BRIGHT BAY WITH LOFTY CREST   •   69 SOHRAB RUSTUM   V 276
    FULL THE DECKS BREADTH AND LOFTY THEN THE CORPSE •   118 BALDER DEAD 3   162
    LOFTY THOUGHT LIES OFT IN CHILDISH PLAY   • • •   483 THEKLAS ANSWER   24

LOG
    A CHARRD LOG FALLING MAKES A SHOWER OF SPARKS   • •   119 BALDER DEAD 3   204

LOGS
    AND BOUND THE LOGS BEHIND THEIR STEEDS TO DRAW   • •   106 BALDER DEAD 2   60
    HEAP ON THE DECK THE LOGS AND BUILD THE PYRE   • •   118 BALDER DEAD 3   159
    AND THE PILE CRACKLED AND BETWEEN THE LOGS • • • •   118 BALDER DEAD 3   187

LOIRES
    PAST THE LOIRES MOUTH AND BY THE FOAM   • • • •   274 STANZAS CARNAC   35

LOITERER
    LOITERER WHY SITTEST THOU   • • • • • • • •   220 BACCHANALIA 2   49

LOITERING
    LOITERING AND LEAPING   • • • • • • • • • •   218 BACCHANALIA 1   20

LOITERS
    WHO LOITERS BY THE HIGH-HEAPD BOOTHS • • • • • •   93 SICK KING BOKH   191
    THINK YE THE AVENGER LOITERS ON HIS WAY   • • • •   466 ALARIC AT ROME   116

LOK
    OF MISTLETOE WHICH LOK THE ACCUSER GAVE   • • •   95 BALDER DEAD 1   6
    BY ME SHALL VENGEANCE ON THE MURDERER LOK   • • •   96 BALDER DEAD 1   37
    THAT I ALONE MUST TAKE THE BRANCH FROM LOK • • • •   98 BALDER DEAD 1   100
    THREE MIGHTY CHILDREN TO MY FATHER LOK   • • • •   110 BALDER DEAD 2   206
    LOK STILL SUBSISTS IN HEAVEN OUR FATHER WISE   • •   111 BALDER DEAD 2   217
    OF LOK AND DOUBLE ARE THE GIFTS THEY GIVE   • • •   112 BALDER DEAD 2   272
    AND LOK THE FATHER OF THE SERPENT FIRST   • • •   113 BALDER DEAD 3   4
    BUT FROM THE TRAITOROUS SEED OF LOK THEY COME   •   120 BALDER DEAD 3   234
    THOK IS SHE CALLD BUT NOW LOK WORE HER SHAPE   •   123 BALDER DEAD 3   335
    IT IS THE ACCUSER LOK WHO FLOUTS US ALL   • • •   124 BALDER DEAD 3   370
    BROTHER AND FELLOW-SPORT OF LOK WITH ME   • • •   125 BALDER DEAD 3   412
    LOK TRIUMPHS STILL AND HELA KEEPS HER PREY • • • •   126 BALDER DEAD 3   447
    AND CROSS THE BRIDGE OF HEAVEN WITH LOK FOR GUIDE   127 BALDER DEAD 3   476

LOKS
    WAS LOKS THE UNWITTING HAND ALONE WAS THINE   • •   125 BALDER DEAD 3   425

LOLLING
    CAME LOLLING IN THE SUNSHINE   • • • • • • • •   193 STRAYED REVEL   262

LOMBARD
    FLEMISH CARVERS LOMBARD GILDERS   • • • • • •   15 CHURCH BROU 1   95

LONDON
    O LEARN OF LONDON WHOSE PAUPERS   • • • • • •   214 NEW ROME   13
    AND THEN THE LONDON HOTELS   • • • • • • • •   214 NEW ROME   16
    BECOME LIKE GLORIOUS LONDON   • • • • • • • •   214 NEW ROME   V   13
    BE MADE LIKE LONDON WHERE PAUPERS   • • • • • •   214 NEW ROME   V   13
    A BABY DOG FROM LONDON TOWN   • • • • • • • •   459 KAISER DEAD   14

LONE
    DOWN THE FOREST-RIDINGS LONE   • • • • • •   13 CHURCH BROU 1   22
    RARE THE LONE PASTORAL HUTS MARVEL NOT THOU   • •   45 IN UTRUMQUE PAR   17
    IN A LONE SAND-HEMMD   • • • • • • • • • •   51 CONSOLATION   27
    LONE FARMS WITH OPEN-LYING STORES   • • • • •   54 RESIGNATION   V   56
    BOKHARA AND LONE KHIVA IN THE WASTE   • • • • •   83 SOHRAB RUSTUM   761
    HIS TRANQUIL LIFE IN THIS LONE PLACE • • • • • •   137 TRISTRAM 1   212
    THE LONE UNBROKEN VIEW SPREADS BRIGHT AND CLEAR   •   150 TRISTRAM 3   12
    IN THESE LONE SYLVAN GLADES THAT APRIL-DAY • • • •   154 TRISTRAM 3   163
    WHICH GLISTERING PLAYS ALL ROUND THEM LONE AND MILD   155 TRISTRAM 3   203
    THE LONE UNBROKEN VIEW STRETCHD BRIGHT AND CLEAR • •   TRISTRAM 3   V   12
    THE LONE UNBROKEN VIEW GOES SPREADING CLEAR   • • •   TRISTRAM 3   V   12
    WHICH GLISTERING LAY ALL ROUND THEM LONE AND MILD   155 TRISTRAM 3   V 203

LONE   (CONTINUED)
    LONE CHORASMIAN STREAM THEREON . . . .   191 STRAYED REVEL   183
    LONE DAULIS AND THE HIGH CEPHISSIAN VALE . . . .   201 PHILOMELA   27
    STILL DOTH THE SOUL FROM ITS LONE FASTNESS HIGH . .   236 PALLADIUM   21
    IN THIS LONE OPEN GLADE I LIE . . . .   248 KENSINGTON GARD   1
    WHERE THE LONE ANGLER LIES STRETCHD OUT . . . .   KENSINGTON GARD   V 18
    AT SOME LONE ALEHOUSE IN THE BERKSHIRE MOORS . . .   256 SCHOLAR-GIPSY   58
    AND BOYS WHO IN LONE WHEATFIELDS SCARE THE ROOKS . .   257 SCHOLAR-GIPSY   64
    AT SOME LONE HOMESTEAD IN THE CUMNER HILLS . . . .   258 SCHOLAR-GIPSY   101
    THE VALE THE THREE LONE WEIRS THE YOUTHFUL THAMES .   263 THYRSIS   15
    THAT LONE SKY-POINTING TREE ARE NOT FOR HIM . . .   267 THYRSIS   174
    LAY THE LONE COAST OF BRITTANY . . . .   273 STANZAS CARNAC   4
    AH SUCH A NIGHT SO SOFT SO LONE . . . .   275 SOUTHERN NIGHT   13
    IN THE LONE BRAKES OF FONTAINEBLEAU . . . . .   304 GRANDE CHARTR   149
    MUTE IN THEIR MEADOWS LONE . . . . . .   306 OBERMANN   6
    YET THROUGH THE HUM OF TORRENT LONE . . . . .   307 OBERMANN   33
    FOR ME NO EASTERN DESERT LONE . . . . . .   317 OBERMANN MORE   151
    SOUNDS SUCH AS ERST THE LONE WAYFARING MAN . . .   473 CROMWELL   39
    CROSS HIS LONE PATH OR SHARE HIS PILGRIMAGE . .   476 CROMWELL   162

LONELIER
    FROM A FAR LONELIER DISTANCE LIKE THE WIND . . . .   238 PROGRESS   34

LONELILY
    RANG LONELILY AND SHARP THE SKY WAS FAIR   . . . .   155 TRISTRAM 3   199

LONELINESS
    IN HIS EXILED LONELINESS . . . .   137 TRISTRAM 1   208
    ALONE THAN THOU THEIR LONELINESS   . . . . . .   181 ISOLATION MARG   42

LONELY
    STANDS A LONELY CHURCH UNFINISHD   . . . . .   14 CHURCH BROU 1   63
    BUT ELSE IT IS A LONELY TIME . . . .   17 CHURCH BROU 2   23
    ARE LESS LONELY THAN THEY WERE . . . .   26 NEW SIRENS   20
    OF A LONELY MERE . . . .   35 VOICE   6
    BY LONELY PURENESS TO THE ALL-PURE FOUNT . . .   45 IN UTRUMQUE PAR   12
    THE STRANGE-SCRAWLD ROCKS THE LONELY SKY . . .   60 RESIGNATION   268
    UNTRODDEN LONELY FAR FROM LIGHT AND HEAVEN . . .   99 BALDER DEAD 1   136
    IN TWILIGHT ON THE LONELY VERGE OF HELL . . . .   124 BALDER DEAD 3   390
    FROM HER LONELY SHORE-BUILT TOWER . . . . .   131 TRISTRAM 1   43
    TO OUR LONELY SEA COMPLAIN . . . .   139 TRISTRAM 1   274
    YES IT IS LONELY FOR HER IN HER HALL . . . .   152 TRISTRAM 3   96
    BEYOND THE HEATHS EDGED BY THE LONELY SEA . . .   154 TRISTRAM 3   155
    SHE LEFT LONELY FOR EVER . . . .   165 FORSAKEN MERM   142
    UNTO A LONELY VILLA IN A DELL . . . .   167 RACHEL 2   1
    FAREWELL AND THOU THOU LONELY HEART . . . . .   181 ISOLATION MARG   13
    CLUSTERS OF LONELY MOUNDS . . . .   191 STRAYED REVEL   177
    OUTWEARIED WITH THEIR LONELY PARTS . . . . .   203 EUPHROSYNE   7
    MY DARLING ON THIS LONELY AIR . . . .   205 CALAIS SANDS   14
    HOW LONELY RINGS THE ECHO OF MY FEET . . . .   242 SUMMER NIGHT   2
    BARE ON ITS LONELY RIDGE THE TREE THE TREE . .   267 THYRSIS   160
    THAT LONELY TREE AGAINST THE WESTERN SKY . . .   268 THYRSIS   195
    AND OER THE GLISTENING LONELY LAND . . . . .   274 STANZAS CARNAC   21
    LONELY AND BLEAK AT ITS SIDE . . . .   283 HAWORTH CHURCH   64
    TO THE LONELY INN MID THE ROCKS . . . . . .   289 RUGBY CHAPEL   109
    FOR HE PURSUED A LONELY ROAD . . . .   308 OBERMANN   57
    NO LONELY LIFE HAD PASSD TOO SLOW . . . . .   317 OBERMANN MORE   153
    SPRAY-DRIZZLED LONELY . . . .   392 MEROPE   1647
    SOME ROCK MORE LONELY THAN THAT LEMNIAN ISLE . .   395 MEROPE   1746
    AND LIVES A LONELY MAN IN TRIPLE GLOOM . . . .   410 EMPEDOCLES I 1   124
    AND BEING LONELY THOU ART MISERABLE . . . . .   429 EMPEDOCLES II   20
    AND IN THE LONELY ROCK-STREWN MOUNTAIN-GLEN . .   430 EMPEDOCLES II   39
    YOUR LONELY COLD-SHINING LIGHTS . . . . . .   437 EMPEDOCLES II   289
    FORGED BY THE IMPERIOUS LONELY THINKING-POWER . .   440 EMPEDOCLES II   376
    THE THOUGHTS THAT TOUCHT THY BREAST THOU LONELY   468 ALARIC AT ROME   168
            CONQUEROR THEN
    AND FLEETING THOUGHTS THAT ON THE LONELY WILD . .   473 CROMWELL   51
    FRIENDLESS AND HOPELESS LIKE A LONELY TREE . . .   477 CROMWELL   189
    AND LONELY AS A TRUANT CHILD . . . .   479 HAYSWATER BOAT   3

LONENESS
    EVEN IN THE LONENESS OF THY WIDOWED YEARS . . .   463 ALARIC AT ROME   22

LONG
    MUCH HE WHOSE FRIENDSHIP I NOT LONG SINCE WON . .   2 TO A FRIEND   5
    IF SADNESS AT THE LONG HEART-WASTING SHOW . . .   7 REP FRIEND   9
    MY FATHER LOVED INJUSTICE AND LIVED LONG . . .   9 MYCERINUS   13
    MIGHT WANDER ALL DAY LONG AND NEVER TIRE . . .   11 MYCERINUS   91
    IN THE RICH LANGUOR OF LONG SUMMER-DAYS . . . .   12 MYCERINUS   117
    SO SIX LONG YEARS HE REVELLD NIGHT AND DAY . . .   12 MYCERINUS   122
    AH HOPE CANNOT LONG LIGHTEN TORMENTS LIKE THESE .   20 MODERN SAPPHO   32
    LEAVES US FIXT TO NOTHING LONG . . . .   24 MEMORY-PICTURE   56
    LONG I SAID A FACE IS GONE . . . .   23 MEMORY-PICTURE   V 9
    LEAVES US TRUE TO NOTHING LONG . . . .   24 MEMORY-PICTURE   V 58
    LEAVES US FIRM TO NOTHING LONG . . . .   24 MEMORY-PICTURE   V 58
    LEAVES US JOIND TO NOTHING LONG . . . . . .   24 MEMORY-PICTURE   V 58
    ROUND OUR HEARTS WITH LONG CARESSES . . . . .   28 NEW SIRENS   69
    STILL THEY GALL YOU THE LONG HOURS . . . . .   30 NEW SIRENS   129
    PATIENT OF A LONG REVIEW . . . .   30 NEW SIRENS   132
    LONG WE WANDERD WITH YOU FEEDING . . . . .   34 NEW SIRENS   235
    LIFE IS LONG AND WILL NOT FADE . . . . . .   28 NEW SIRENS   V 66

LONG   (CONTINUED)

DO THEY GALL YOU THE LONG HOURS   • • • • • •   30 NEW SIRENS   V 129
TO THIS LONG SOBERD HEART   • • • • • • •   36 VOICE   V 24
THOSE LUTE-LIKE TONES WHICH IN LONG DISTANT YEARS   36 VOICE   V 35
LOOK HOW SO MANY VALOURS LONG UNDULLD   • • •   37 WORLDS TRIUMPHS   7
ARE WILLS SO WEAK THEN LET NOT MINE WAIT LONG • •   38 WORLDS TRIUMPHS   12
FALLS HEAVILY AWAY WITH LONG-DRAWN ROAR • • •   40 HUMAN LIFE   21
DOWN THE PALE CHEEK LONG LINES OF SHADOW SLOPE • •   43 GIPSY CHILD   37
ERE THE LONG NIGHT WHOSE STILLNESS BROOKS NO STAR   43 GIPSY CHILD   45
ERE THE LONG EVENING CLOSE THOU SHALT RETURN • •   44 GIPSY CHILD   67
OUR VAUNTED LIFE IS ONE LONG FUNERAL • • • • •   44 QUESTION   10
THE LONG-MUSED THOUGHT TO NORTH SOUTH EAST AND WEST   45 IN UTRUMQUE PAR   6
O MAN WHOM EARTH THY LONG-VEXT MOTHER BARE • • •   46 IN UTRUMQUE PAR   32
CRITIAS LONG SINCE I KNOW   • • • • • •   46 WORLD QUIETIST   9
LONG SINCE THE WORLD HATH SET ITS HEART TO LIVE • •   46 WORLD QUIETIST   11
LONG SINCE WITH CREDULOUS ZEAL   • • • • • •   46 WORLD QUIETIST   12
MOUNTING TO POWER LONG DENIED   • • • • • • •   HORATIAN ECHO   V
PAST STRAITS AND CURRENTS LONG STEERD THROUGH • •   53 RESIGNATION   21
THEY TOO HAVE LONG ROAMD TO AND FRO   • • • •   55 RESIGNATION   109
WHERE THOUGH LONG WANDERINGS INTERVENE   • • •   55 RESIGNATION   114
SOHRAB ALONE HE SLEPT NOT ALL NIGHT LONG • • •   61 SOHRAB RUSTUM   5
SLEEP BUT I SLEEP NOT ALL NIGHT LONG I LIE • • •   62 SOHRAB RUSTUM   36
SO I LONG HOPED BUT HIM I NEVER FIND   • • • •   62 SOHRAB RUSTUM   53
FROM THEIR BLACK TENTS LONG FILES OF HORSE
      THEY STREAMD   64 SOHRAB RUSTUM   110
IN MARCHING ORDER SPREAD OF LONG-NECKD CRANES • •   64 SOHRAB RUSTUM   112
FIRST WITH BLACK SHEEP-SKIN CAPS AND WITH LONG SPEARS   64 SOHRAB RUSTUM   118
LONG FLOCKS OF TRAVELLING BIRDS DEAD ON THE SNOW • •   66 SOHRAB RUSTUM   164
ALL THE MOST VALIANT CHIEFS LONG HE PERUSED • •   70 SOHRAB RUSTUM   311
THAT LONG HAS TOWERD IN THE AIRY CLOUDS • • •   73 SOHRAB RUSTUM   401
REACH RUSTUM WHERE HE SITS AND TARRIES LONG • •   78 SOHRAB RUSTUM   582
THEY THREE IN THAT LONG-DISTANT SUMMER-TIME • •   79 SOHRAB RUSTUM   628
AND ALL DAY LONG AND WHEN NIGHT COMES THE LAMP • •   81 SOHRAB RUSTUM   675
AND HIMSELF SCANND IT LONG WITH MOURNFUL EYES • •   81 SOHRAB RUSTUM   685
BUT HE HAS MET THAT DOOM WHICH LONG AGO • • •   96 BALDER DEAD 1   23
THAT ONE LONG PORTION WITH HIS DOOM OF DEATH • •   98 BALDER DEAD 1   114
AND ALL DAY LONG THEY THERE ARE HACKD AND HEWN • • 105 BALDER DEAD 2   15
SWAYING THE LONG-HAIRD GOATS WITH SILVERD REIN • • 115 BALDER DEAD 3   73
HER LONG AGO THE WANDERING ODER TOOK   • • • • 116 BALDER DEAD 3   93
UNKNOWN AND LONG AND HAPLY ON THAT WAY   • • • 116 BALDER DEAD 3   100
MY LONG-LOST WANDERING ODER THOU HAST MET • • 116 BALDER DEAD 3   101
NOT LONG A WIFE WHEN HIS UNQUIET HEART   • • • 116 BALDER DEAD 3   107
AND LONG IN THE FAR DARK BLAZED BALDERS PILE • • 119 BALDER DEAD 3   200
AND AS SEAFARING MEN WHO LONG HAVE WROUGHT • • 123 BALDER DEAD 3   357
AND THEY GO LONG DAYS TOSSING UP AND DOWN • • • 124 BALDER DEAD 3   365
FOR I AM LONG SINCE WEARY OF YOUR STORM • • • 127 BALDER DEAD 3   503
FOLLOWS THEM WITH A LONG COMPLAINING CRY • • • 129 BALDER DEAD 3   564
AGAINST THE WOLVES AND ALL NIGHT LONG IT FLARES • • 119 BALDER DEAD 3   V
RAISE ME MY PAGE THIS CANNOT LONG ENDURE • • • 130 TRISTRAM 1   3
AND THAT LONG WILD KISS THEIR LAST   • • • • 136 TRISTRAM 1   180
HIS LONG RAMBLES BY THE SHORE   • • • • • 137 TRISTRAM 1   215
PASSING THE LONG SUMMERS DAY   • • • • 137 TRISTRAM 1   222
THIS COMES OF NURSING LONG AND WATCHING LATE • 140 TRISTRAM 1   313
LONG INLETS OF SMOOTH GLITTERING SEA • • • • 141 TRISTRAM 1   368
LONG IVE WAITED LONG IVE FOUGHT MY FEVER • • 142 TRISTRAM 2   3
LONG IVE WAITED LONG IVE FOUGHT MY FEVER • • 142 TRISTRAM 2   3
SING THEE TALES OF TRUE LONG-PARTED LOVERS • • 143 TRISTRAM 2   31
FARE FAREWELL THOU LONG THOU DEEPLY LOVD • • 145 TRISTRAM 2   V 98
LONG THEY STAYD STILL THEN PACING AT THEIR EASE • 150 TRISTRAM 3   42
CHILDREN DEAR WERE WE LONG ALONE   • • • • 163 FORSAKEN MERM   64
LONG PRAYERS I SAID IN THE WORLD THEY SAY • • 163 FORSAKEN MERM   66
DEAR HEART I SAID WE ARE LONG ALONE   • • • 163 FORSAKEN MERM   78
A LONG LONG SIGH   • • • • • • • • • 164 FORSAKEN MERM 105
A LONG LONG SIGH   • • • • • • • • • 164 FORSAKEN MERM 105
O HUMAN SOUL AS LONG AS THOU CANST SO   • • • 169 EAST LONDON   9
LONG FED ON BOUNDLESS HOPES O RACE OF MAN • • 170 BETTER PART   1
TO BE LONG LOVED WAS NEVER FRAMED   • • • • 178 FAREWELL   18
BUT THOU HAST LONG HAD PLACE TO PROVE   • • • 181 ISOLATION MARG   28
OR HAST THOU LONG SINCE WANDERD BACK • • • • 184 TERRACE BERNE   17
THIS LONG TIME RUMOURS   • • • • • • • 189 STRAYED REVEL   109
HE MAKES HIS MEAL BEFORE HIM FOR LONG MILES • 191 STRAYED REVEL   172
THE COWERING MERCHANTS IN LONG ROBES • • • 191 STRAYED REVEL   191
ON THE FOAMLESS LONG-HEAVING   • • • • 192 STRAYED REVEL   203
THE SCYTHIAN BUT LONG FROSTS   • • • • • 193 STRAYED REVEL   240
ALL DAY LONG HAVE SEEN   • • • • • • 194 STRAYED REVEL   273
AND CRY LONG LONG IVE LOOKD FOR THEE   • • • 202 URANIA   28
AND CRY LONG LONG IVE LOOKD FOR THEE   • • • 202 URANIA   28
WERE RESTLESS ONCE BUT LONG AGO   • • • • 208 ON THE RHINE   23
LONG LONG SINCE UNDOWERD YET OUR SPIRIT • • • 209 SELF-DECEPTION   5
LONG LONG SINCE UNDOWERD YET OUR SPIRIT • • • 209 SELF-DECEPTION   5
ONLY FROM THE LONG LINE OF SPRAY   • • • • 211 DOVER BEACH   7
SOPHOCLES LONG AGO   • • • • • • • • 211 DOVER BEACH   15
ITS MELANCHOLY LONG WITHDRAWING ROAR • • • 211 DOVER BEACH   25
IT IS TO SPEND LONG DAYS • • • • • • 212 GROWING OLD   21
AND PSYCHE LONG HAS BEEN DEAD   • • • • • 214 NEW ROME   4
LET THE LONG CONTENTION CEASE   • • • • • 215 LAST WORD   5
TOO LONG LET WE THEM GROAN   • • • • • • 216 LORDS MESSENGER 4
THE LONG UNPAUSING SPECTACLE   • • • • • 225 EPILOG LAOCOON 146
AND THE SEA ITS LONG MOON-SILVERD ROLL • • • 240 SELF-DEPENDENCE 22
O AIR-BORN VOICE LONG SINCE SEVERELY CLEAR • • 240 SELF-DEPENDENCE 29
OF THE LONG DAY AND WISH TWERE DONE   • • • • • 241 MORALITY   10

460

LONG   (CONTINUED)
HOUSES WITH LONG WHITE SWEEP . . . .   242 SUMMER NIGHT   18
AND LONG WE TRY IN VAIN TO SPEAK AND ACT . . . .   247 BURIED LIFE   64
FOR NATURE HATH LONG KEPT THIS INN THE EARTH .   251 FUTURE   V
THAT THE LOST SCHOLAR LONG WAS SEEN TO STRAY .   256 SCHOLAR-GIPSY   53
THROUGH THE LONG DEWY GRASS MOVE SLOW AWAY . .   258 SCHOLAR-GIPSY   110
LONG SINCE AND IN SOME QUIET CHURCHYARD LAID .   259 SCHOLAR-GIPSY   137
ELSE WERT THOU LONG SINCE NUMBERD WITH THE DEAD .   259 SCHOLAR-GIPSY   153
AND WISH THE LONG UNHAPPY DREAM WOULD END . . .   260 SCHOLAR-GIPSY   192
AND EVERY DOUBT LONG BLOWN BY TIME AWAY . . .   261 SCHOLAR-GIPSY   200
AND LONG THE WAY APPEARS WHICH SEEMD SO SHORT .   267 THYRSIS   141
OF THE LONG-BATTERD WORLD UPLIFTS ITS WALL . . .   267 THYRSIS   147
KEPT NOT FOR LONG ITS HAPPY COUNTRY TONE . . .   269 THYRSIS   222
AND LONG WITH MEN OF CARE THOU COULDST NOT STAY .   269 THYRSIS   228
LONG SINCE SAW BYRONS STRUGGLE CEASE . . . . .   270 MEMORIAL VERSES   2
ON SPIRITS THAT HAD LONG BEEN DEAD . . . . . .   272 MEMORIAL VERSES   55
WHERE WE HAD LONG BEEN DOOMD TO DWELL . . . .   271 MEMORIAL VERSES   V
A LONG STEEP JOURNEY THROUGH SUNK . . . . . .   288 RUGBY CHAPEL   87
AH BUT THE WAY IS SO LONG . . . .   291 RUGBY CHAPEL   176
LONG SINCE DEEP IN OUR HEARTS . . . .   294 HEINES GRAVE   74
LONG ON THE GREY HILL-SIDE . . . .   297 HEINES GRAVE   165
IN THE LONG-PAST WINTER HE CAME . . . .   298 HEINES GRAVE   192
PAST THE DARK FORGES LONG DISUSED . . . . . .   299 GRANDE CHARTR   3
AT WHOSE BEHEST I LONG AGO . . . .   301 GRANDE CHARTR   74
LONG SINCE HATH FLUNG HER WEEDS AWAY . . . . .   304 GRANDE CHARTR   154
WHOSE BENT WAS TAKEN LONG AGO . . . .   305 GRANDE CHARTR   198
LONG SINCE WE PACE THIS SHADOWD NAVE . . . . .   305 GRANDE CHARTR   199
LONG SINCE HATH THROWN HER WEEDS AWAY . . . .   304 GRANDE CHARTR   V 154
AND IS IT THOU HE CRIED SO LONG . . . . . .   314 OBERMANN MORE   69
AY AGES LONG ENDURED HIS SPAN . . . .   318 OBERMANN MORE   165
AFTER LONG DARKNESS RUDE . . . .   322 OBERMANN MORE   294
THE LONG REPRESSIVE ATTITUDE OF RULE . . . . .   334 MEROPE   154
LONG WE REFRAIND OURSELVES SUBMITTED LONG . . .   337 MEROPE   254
LONG WE REFRAIND OURSELVES SUBMITTED LONG . . .   337 MEROPE   254
THY SWORD REPELLD IT LONG AGO NOT I . . . . .   341 MEROPE   355
WELL MAY HE LONG TO INTERRUPT . . . .   353 MEROPE   667
A LAST LONG-CHERISHD PROJECT IN MY AIM . . . .   360 MEROPE   880
PEACE WHO TARRIEST TOO LONG . . . .   360 MEROPE   890
BUT THE DEMONS LONG NOURISHD HERE . . . . . .   361 MEROPE   909
OF MY TWO ELDER SONS SLAIN LONG AGO . . . . .   367 MEROPE   1038
KEPT ME THEIR MOTHER FROM THEIR SIDE SO LONG .   367 MEROPE   1040
A LONG SUCCESSION OF CRIMES . . . .   379 MEROPE   1252
O THOU LONG-LOST LONG SEEN IN DREAMS ALONE . .   381 MEROPE   1288
O THOU LONG-LOST LONG SEEN IN DREAMS ALONE . .   381 MEROPE   1288
AT THIS FIRST MEETING AFTER ABSENCE LONG . . .   386 MEROPE   1452
DID EVER BURN IS LONG BY TIME ALLAYD . . . . .   387 MEROPE   1471
OF DYNASTIES LONG-FIXD AND HONOURD LONG . . .   390 MEROPE   1562
OF DYNASTIES LONG-FIXD AND HONOURD LONG . . .   390 MEROPE   1562
JUSTICE MY SISTER LONG DEMANDS THIS BLOW . . .   390 MEROPE   1572
YET HAST BEEN LONG AT SCHOOL WITH THOUGHTFUL TIME   394 MEROPE   1708
MY DEED IS OF OLD DATE AND LONG ATONED . . .   396 MEROPE   1768
FOR FATE THOU WAITST NOT LONG SINCE IN THIS HOUR .   397 MEROPE   1777
TO MAKE THE GATES OF THIS LONG-MOURNFUL HOUSE .   401 MEROPE   1884
MIGHT ASK WHY WE ENDURED THEIR YOKE SO LONG .   402 MEROPE   1947
WELL MAY THEY LONG TO INTERRUPT . . . . . .   353 MEROPE   V 667
THAT CLIMB FROM THE STREAMS EDGE THE LONG GREY TUFTS 406 EMPEDOCLES I 1   16
I SADDLED MY WHITE MULE AND ALL NIGHT LONG . . .   407 EMPEDOCLES I 1   44
THIRTY LONG DAYS IN A COLD TRANCE OF DEATH . .   410 EMPEDOCLES I 1   110
OF TREES AND VEINS OF TURF AND LONG DARK SHOOTS .   414 EMPEDOCLES I 2   48
TO PELEUS IN LONG DISTANT YEARS . . . . . .   414 EMPEDOCLES I 2   70
YET GRANT AS SENSE LONG MISSD . . . .   421 EMPEDOCLES I 2   282
OF LONG-PAST HUMAN THINGS . . . .   423 EMPEDOCLES I 2   323
THEY HAD STAYD LONG ENOUGH TO SEE . . . . .   427 EMPEDOCLES I 2   444
TILL MINE EYES ACHE WITH THE LONG SPECTACLE .   428 EMPEDOCLES I 2   475
TILL MY EYES ACHE WITH THE LONG SPECTACLE . .   428 EMPEDOCLES I 2   V 475
WHERE THE LONG GREEN REED-BEDS SWAY . . . . .   433 EMPEDOCLES II   133
WITH LONG PLUMES AND SOFT BROWN SEEDS . . . .   434 EMPEDOCLES II   175
AND THE LONG DUSKY LINE OF ITALY . . . . . .   438 EMPEDOCLES II   314
HITHER HE CAME LATE-BORN AND LONG-DESIRED . .   444 WESTMIN ABBEY   8
THAT TO MY MIND THERE CAME HOW LONG AGO . .   446 WESTMIN ABBEY   83
BUT ALL NIGHT LONG AMID THE FLAMES HE LAY . .   446 WESTMIN ABBEY   89
LONG SINCE HIS NAME IS HEARD ON EARTH NO MORE .   447 WESTMIN ABBEY   113
DOWN THE LONG AGE OF TRUTH THAT RIPENS SLOW .   448 WESTMIN ABBEY   148
AND THOU SHALT LIVE AS LONG AS WE . . . . .   451 GEISTS GRAVE   58
PEOPLE WHO LIVED HERE LONG AGO . . . . . .   452 GEISTS GRAVE   77
TO HEAR A DIM AND LONG FORGOTTEN TONE . . . .   467 ALARIC AT ROME   123
PEOPLED NIGHTS VOICELESS SHADES WITH FORMS OF LONG AGO 467 ALARIC AT ROME   126
AND THE LONG VISION OF THE YEARS TO BE . . .   475 CROMWELL   140
THAT ALL NIGHT LONG ITS WEARY MOAN DOTH MAKE .   477 CROMWELL   191
TILL THE PALE MONARCH AND THE LONG ARRAY . .   477 CROMWELL   197
AFFLICTS GRAVE HEAVEN WITH ITS LONG SENSELESS ROAR   480 HUNGARIAN NAT   5
IN HIS LONG BLACK SHIP SPEEDING NIGHT AND DAY .   485 S S LUSITANIA   10
THAT LONG GAZER LEANING NEAR . . . .   META CLOISTER   26

LONGD
THE LONGD-FOR DASH OF WAVES IS HEARD AND WIDE .   87 SOHRAB RUSTUM   889
BUT EARNESTLY I LONGD TO HOVER NEAR . . . . .   125 BALDER DEAD 3   416
I TOO HAVE LONGD FOR TRENCHANT FORCE . . . .   178 FAREWELL   33
ONCE-LONGD-FOR STORMS OF LOVE . . . .   183 ABSENCE   14
STRAIND AND LONGD AND GRASPD EACH GIFT IT SAW .   210 SELF-DECEPTION   10

LONGD   (CONTINUED)
    WHO HAVE LONGD DEEPLY ONCE AND LONGD IN VAIN   • •   244 SUMMER NIGHT   85
    WHO HAVE LONGD DEEPLY ONCE AND LONGD IN VAIN   • •   244 SUMMER NIGHT   85
    HE LONGD FOR IT PRESSD ON IN VAIN   • • • • •   275 STANZAS CARNAC   45
    HE LONGD IT HE PRESSD ON IN VAIN   • • • • •   275 STANZAS CARNAC   V   45
    ONLY A MOMENT I LONGD   • • • • •   • • • •   294 HEINES GRAVE   48
    LONGD HIMSELF BACK TO THE FIELDS   • • • • •   296 HEINES GRAVE   137
    LONGD ITSELF OUT OF THE DIN   • • • • • • • •   296 HEINES GRAVE   149

LONGER
    THEY MUST LOVE WHILE THEY MUST BUT THE HEARTS   19 MODERN SAPPHO   15
        THAT LOVE LONGER
    IF THE FITS OF JOY WERE LONGER   • • • • • • •   29 NEW SIRENS   109
    FAREWELL FOR LONGER SPEECH IS NOT ALLOWD   • • • •   129 BALDER DEAD 3   548
    NO LONGER LEAVE THY WISTFUL FLOCK UNFED   • • • •   255 SCHOLAR-GIPSY   3
    ENOUGH ENOUGH I WILL NO LONGER HEAR   • • • • •   397 MEROPE   1780
    HAD THEY INDEED NO LONGER SPAN   • • • • • • •   450 GEISTS GRAVE   10

LONGEST
    BEFORE THE ROSES AND THE LONGEST DAY • • • • •   264 THYRSIS   53

LONGING
    LONGING WILL STIR WITHIN MY BREAST THOUGH VAIN   • •   127 BALDER DEAD 3   499
    YES NOW THE LONGING IS OERPAST   • • • • • •   • •   147 TRISTRAM 2   131
    YET FERVENT HAD HER LONGING BEEN THROUGH ALL   • •   173 MONICAS PRAYER   6
    OH THEN A LONGING LIKE DESPAIR   • • • • • •   • •   182 TO MARG CONT   13
    THE HOPELESS LONGING OF THE DAY   • • • • •   • •   208 LONGING   4
    THE HOPELESS LONGING OF THE DAY   • • • • •   • •   209 LONGING   16
    MY LONGING MY SADNESS MY JOY   • • • • •   • •   231 YOUTH OF NATURE   121
    A LONGING TO INQUIRE   • • • • • •   • •   246 BURIED LIFE   51
    OR HARM AND NURSE MY LONGING FOR MY SON   • •   366 MEROPE   1022
    PASSIONS FIRST FURIOUS LONGING TO IMBRUE   • •   387 MEROPE   1467
    DISTRESSFUL LONGING   • • • • • • •   • •   393 MEROPE   1663
    LONGING LISTENING I WAIT I IMPLORE   • • • •   • •   347 MEROPE   V
    THAT LONGING OF OUR YOUTH   • • • • •   • •   424 EMPEDOCLES I 2   369
    THE INEFFABLE LONGING FOR THE LIFE OF LIFE • • • • •   439 EMPEDOCLES II   357

LONGINGS
    WAFTS NOT FROM THINE OWN THOUGHTS NOR LONGINGS VAIN   42 GIPSY CHILD   10
    WHO ORDERD THAT THEIR LONGINGS FIRE   • • • • • •   182 TO MARG CONT   19
    HUMAN LONGINGS HUMAN FEARS   • • • • • •   • •   457 POOR MATTHIAS   165

LONGS
    TO HEAR THAT STILL HE LOVES STILL LONGS FOR ME   • •   351 MEROPE   613
    BREAKS OUT AND LONGS FOR SWITZERLAND   • • • • •   • •   483 ROME-SICKNESS   3
    LONGS OFTENER YET AND PINES FOR ROME   • • • • •   • •   483 ROME-SICKNESS   4

LOOK
    CAN I LOOK ON YOUR SWEET FACES   • • •   • •   32 NEW SIRENS   191
    LOOK HOW SO MANY VALOURS LONG UNDULLD   • •   • •   37 WORLDS TRIUMPHS   7
    THEY STILL LOOK FAIR   • • • • • •   • •   50 CONSOLATION   20
    RASH BOY MEN LOOK ON RUSTUMS FACE AND FLEE   • •   72 SOHRAB RUSTUM   369
    LOOK THIS IS BUT ONE SINGLE PLACE   • •   • •   92 SICK KING BOKH   157
    TO LOOK ON MIDGARD AND THE EARTH AND MEN   • •   96 BALDER DEAD 1   52
    NOR DID HE LOOK ONCE MORE TO IDAS PLAIN   • •   97 BALDER DEAD 1   57
    FENSALER WHOSE LIT WINDOWS LOOK TO SEA   • •   100 BALDER DEAD 1   198
    SOME SOLACE IN EACH OTHERS LOOK AND SPEECH • • •   • •   104 BALDER DEAD 1   327
    LOOK AS IN SOME BOORS YARD A SWEET-BREATHD COW   123 BALDER DEAD 3   340
    NOT WITH A LOOK OF WOUNDED PRIDE   • • • • •   • •   140 TRISTRAM 1   320
    A LOOK AS IF THE HEART COMPLAINED   • • • • •   • •   140 TRISTRAM 1   321
    HER LOOK WAS LIKE A SAD EMBRACE   • • • • •   • •   140 TRISTRAM 1   322
    TO LOOK FORTH ON THE FAIRY SIGHT   • • • • •   • •   141 TRISTRAM 1   353
    TAKE MY HAND DEAR TRISTRAM LOOK ON ME • • • •   • •   142 TRISTRAM 2   16
    I AM DYING START NOT NOR LOOK WILDLY • •   • • •   • •   145 TRISTRAM 2   89
    AND UP AS HIGH AS WHERE THEY STOOD TO LOOK • • •   • •   155 TRISTRAM 3   188
    SAW HIM LOOK EASED AND HURRIED BY   • • • •   • •   158 SAINT BRANDAN   52
    ONE LAST LOOK AT THE WHITE-WALLD TOWN • • • •   • •   162 FORSAKEN MERM   25
    BUT AH SHE GAVE ME NEVER A LOOK   • • • • •   • •   163 FORSAKEN MERM   80
    THE JUNGFRAU SNOWS LOOK FAINT AND FAR • • • •   • •   184 TERRACE BERNE   6
    TO LOOK TOWRD ARDRES GOLDEN FIELD   • • • •   • •   204 CALAIS SANDS   5
    THY SHAWL THY LOOK THY SMILE THY HAND • • • •   • •   204 CALAIS SANDS   12
    THAT SHAWL THAT STEP THAT LOOK THAT HAND   • • •   • •   204 CALAIS SANDS   V   12
    TO ENGLANDS CLIFFS MY LOOK IS TURND   • • • • •   • •   205 CALAIS SANDS   V   19
    THEN WHEN WE MEET AND THY LOOK STRAYS TOWARD ME   • •   206 SEPARATION   13
    THEN WHEN WE MEET AND THY LOOK STRAYS TOWARDS ME • •   206 SEPARATION   V   13
    LIE SWEETLY IN THE LOOK DIVINE   • • • • •   • •   208 ON THE RHINE   14
    NAY LOOK CLOSER INTO MAN • • • • • •   • •   215 PIS-ALLER   5
    LOOK AH WHAT GENIUS   • • • • • • •   • •   220 BACCHANALIA 2   53
    AND A LOOK OF PASSIONATE DESIRE   • • • • •   • •   240 SELF-DEPENDENCE   5
    OF QUIET LOOK ADOWN THE DUSK HILL-SIDE   • • •   • •   267 THYRSIS   152
    LOOK THROUGH THE SHOWERY TWILIGHT GREY   • • •   • •   300 GRANDE CHARTR   22
    THE SYRIAN STARS LOOK DOWN   • • • • • •   • •   318 OBERMANN MORE   176
    AND LOOK TO MEET THEM THAT ONE GRIEF-PLUNGED FORM   331 MEROPE   56
    AND THESE MEN LOOK TO THEE AND FROM THY GRIEF   • •   334 MEROPE   141
    IF SO ALLS WELL FOR LOOK THE OLD MAN SPEEDS   • •   362 MEROPE   934
    LOOK UP O QUEEN LOOK UP O MISTRESS DEAR   • • •   • •   363 MEROPE   946
    LOOK UP O QUEEN LOOK UP O MISTRESS DEAR   • • •   • •   363 MEROPE   946
    LOOK UP AND SEE THY FRIENDS WHO COMFORT THEE   • •   363 MEROPE   947
    BUT THY GESTURE THY LOOK • • • • • •   • • •   • •   372 MEROPE   1145
    WHICH MAKES THE TIME LOOK BLACK AND SAD TO HIM   • •   411 EMPEDOCLES I 1   153
    WHICH MAKES THE TIMES LOOK BLACK AND SAD TO HIM   • •   411 EMPEDOCLES I 1   V 153

LOOK   (CONTINUED)
  THEN THOU WOULDST LOOK LESS MAZED   • • • • •   417 EMPEDOCLES I 2   162
  YET WILL NOT LOOK WITHIN • • • • • • • • •   420 EMPEDOCLES I 2   233
  LOOK THE WORLD TEMPTS OUR EYE   • • • • • •   423 EMPEDOCLES I 2   317
  HENCEFORTH LOOK ON TO YOU   • • • • • • • •   425 EMPEDOCLES I 2   380
  WHO LOOK ON LIFE WITH EYES   • • • • • • •   426 EMPEDOCLES I 2   409
  DULL LOOK ON WHEN DEATH IS NIGH   • • • • •   455 POOR MATTHIAS   107
  PYMS LOOK OF HATE AND STRAFFORDS GLANCE OF FLAME • • 476 CROMWELL   164

LOOKD
  I LOOKD FOR LIFE MORE LASTING RULE MORE HIGH   • •   9 MYCERINUS   17
  BEFORE HIM AND HE LOOKD AND SAW HIM STAND • • • •   67 SOHRAB RUSTUM   202
  BUT HE LOOKD ON AND SMILED NOR BARED HIS SWORD • •   74 SOHRAB RUSTUM   425
  BUT SOHRAB LOOKD UPON THE HORSE AND SAID   • • • •   83 SOHRAB RUSTUM   741
  BUT HE LOOKD ON AND SMILED NOR DREW HIS SWORD • •   74 SOHRAB RUSTUM   V 425
  BUT ODIN LOOKD TOWARD THE LAND AND SAW   • • • •   114 BALDER DEAD 3   31
  BELOW AND LOOKD UPON THE SHADOWY TRIBES   • • • •   114 BALDER DEAD 3   39
  HE SPOKE AND ALL THE GODS TO ODIN LOOKD   • • • •   115 BALDER DEAD 3   47
  AND HERMOD LOOKD AND KNEW HIS BROTHERS GHOST   • •   124 BALDER DEAD 3   385
  LOOKD STERNLY THROUGH THE FROSTY EVENING-AIR   • •   151 TRISTRAM 3   60
  SHE LOOKD SO WITCHING FAIR THAT LEARNED WIGHT • •   154 TRISTRAM 3   181
  THEN LOOKD AND LO THE FROSTY SKIES   • • • • • •   158 SAINT BRANDAN   75
  WHEN HE LOOKD UP TENANTLESS LIES   • • • • • •   158 SAINT BRANDAN   V 75
  SHE SIGHD SHE LOOKD UP THROUGH THE CLEAR GREEN SEA   163 FORSAKEN MERM   55
  IN PARIS ALL LOOKD HOT AND LIKE TO FADE   • • • •   167 RACHEL 1   1
  IN SPITALFIELDS LOOKD THRICE DISPIRITED   • • • •   169 EAST LONDON   4
  SHE LOOKD AND SMILED AND SAW THEM THROUGH • • • •   202 URANIA   12
  AND CRY LONG LONG IVE LOOKD FOR THEE   • • • • •   202 URANIA   28
  GOOD POEMS IF HE LOOKD MORE RARE   • • • • • •   221 EPILOG LAOCOON   17
  HE LOOKD ON THE RUSHING DECAY   • • • • • •   229 YOUTH OF NATURE   29
  HATH LOOKD ON NO RELIGION SCORNFULLY   • • • • •   238 PROGRESS   39
  HE LOOKD ON EUROPES DYING HOUR   • • • • • • • •   270 MEMORIAL VERSES   23
  LIKE OURS IT LOOKD IN OUTWARD AIR   • • • • • •   315 OBERMANN MORE   85
  SO LOOKD HE WHEN TO STENYCLAROS FIRST   • • • •   403 MEROPE   1971
  SO LOOKD HE IN THAT DREADFUL DAY OF DEATH • • • •   404 MEROPE   1977
  LOOKD ON TO SOMETHING NEW   • • • • • • • •   425 EMPEDOCLES I 2   378
  LAST NIGHT I LOOKD THE SKY WAS CLEAR • • • • •   480 HAYSWATER BOAT   33

LOOKED
  WAS LOOKED ON BY THE RURAL PAN • • • • • • •   KENSINGTON GARD V 24
  AS THEY LOOKED STERNLY ON BEHELD NEW VICTORIES • •   468 ALARIC AT ROME   174

LOOKING
  AND LOOKING DOWN ON THE WARM ROSY TINTS   • • • •   18 CHURCH BROU 3   28
  FOR BOTH THE ON-LOOKING HOSTS ON EITHER HAND   • •   75 SOHRAB RUSTUM   487
  LOOKING INTO THE REGISTAN   • • • • • •   88 SICK KING BOKH   17
  TO FEAST THEIR EYES WITH LOOKING ON THE FRAY   • •   105 BALDER DEAD 2   31
  LOOKING OVER THE VALLEY   • • • • • • • • • •   194 STRAYED REVEL   272

LOOKS
  LOOKS LANGUIDLY ROUND ON A GLOOM-BURIED WORLD • •   20 MODERN SAPPHO   24
  FROM SOME HIGH STATION HE LOOKS DOWN • • • • •   57 RESIGNATION   164
  OF AGE AND LOOKS TO BE HIS OWN DEAR SON   • • • •   80 SOHRAB RUSTUM   632
  WHEN THAT WITH DOWNCAST LOOKS I HITHER CAME   • •   125 BALDER DEAD 3   409
  HER LOOKS ARE MILD HER FINGERS SLIGHT   • • • •   131 TRISTRAM 1   30
  NOR DID THEIR LOOKS STRAY ONCE TO THE SEA-SIDE • •   151 TRISTRAM 3   48
  SHE STEALS TO THE WINDOW AND LOOKS AT THE SAND • •   164 FORSAKEN MERM   98
  AND SPELL THY LOOKS AND GUESS THY THOUGHTS • • • •   205 CALAIS SANDS   29
  WITHOUT THAT WHO LOOKS WITHIN • • • • • • • •   215 PIS-ALLER   3
  LOOKS IN VAIN FOR ALLS OBSCURE   • • • • • • •   215 PIS-ALLER   4
  WHILE THE SOUL STILL LOOKS THROUGH THINE EYES • •   235 YOUTH OF MAN   113
  AND I MYSELF SEEM HALF TO KNOW THY LOOKS   • • • •   257 SCHOLAR-GIPSY   62
  THE SIGNAL-ELM THAT LOOKS ON ILSLEY DOWNS • • • •   263 THYRSIS   14
  IN HIS SEVERE LOOKS SUCH A MAJESTY   • • • • • •   408 EMPEDOCLES I 1   62
  LOOKS ONCE AND DRIVES ELSEWHERE AND LEAVES   • •   415 EMPEDOCLES I 2   86
      ITS LAST EMPLOY
  SUCH WAYS SUCH ARTS SUCH LOOKS HADST THOU • • • •   451 GEISTS GRAVE   44
  LOOKS ON IN FEAR AND WHEN THE SEAL IS SET • • • •   465 ALARIC AT ROME   92
  AND SOME MAN MAY SAY AS HE LOOKS AND SEES THY   HOMER TRANS   32
      TEARS FALLING
  SHARP SENSE OF DEEP SELF-IGNORANCE FEAR OF LOOKS • •   LUCRETIUS 2   14

LOOKST
  NOR LOOKST THOU PALE AND WAN LIKE MEN DECEASED   • • 108 BALDER DEAD 2   109

LOOKT
  TILL WHAT AT MORNINGS HOUR LOOKT WARM AND BRIGHT • • 466 ALARIC AT ROME   107

LOOM
  FAINTER AND FAINTER WRECK AND HELMSMAN LOOM   • •   244 SUMMER NIGHT   72
  LOOM THE BLURRD HILLS THE RAIN • • • • • • • •   286 HAWORTH CHURCH   132
  THEN PERHAPS THOU SHALT WORK AT THE LOOM OF   HOMER TRANS   29
      ANOTHER IN ARGOS

LOOMING
  WHERE THE LOOMING KINE ARE LAID   • • • • • •   32 NEW SIRENS   182
  WHERE THE LOOMING DEER ARE LAID   • • • • • •   32 NEW SIRENS   V 182

LOOSE
  O LOOSE HANDS AND LET IT BE   • • • • • • • •   34 NEW SIRENS   224
  COME LOOSE HANDS THE WINGED FLEETNESS   • • • •   34 NEW SIRENS   251
  THE LOOSE DARK STONES ON THE GREEN WAY   • • • •   55 RESIGNATION   100
  THE CALM SEA SHINES LOOSE HANG THE VESSELS SAILS • • 133 TRISTRAM 1   94

LOOSE   (CONTINUED)
```
        THROUGH THE LOOSE CLOUDS LIFTS DIMLY  . . . . . .   175  PARTING              13
        SHAKE LOOSE SOME BAND OF SOFT BROWN HAIR    . . . .   205  CALAIS SANDS         16
        SHAKE LOOSE SOME LOCK OF SOFT BROWN HAIR    . . . .   205  CALAIS SANDS     V   16
        LOOSE OER THEIR SHOULDERS WHITE        . . . . . .   218  BACCHANALIA 1        26
        NO LAMENTATION CAN LOOSE  . . . . . . . . . .   347  MEROPE              524
        IN THE WIND AND LOOSE DARK HAIR        . . . . . .   433  EMPEDOCLES II       153
        WHO BADE HIM LOOSE HIS BOAT AND FIX HIS OAR    . .   444  WESTMIN ABBEY        24
```

LOOSED
```
        THOUGH HE HATH LOOSED A THOUSAND CHAINS    . . . .    56  RESIGNATION         150
        THEN WITH WEAK HASTY FINGERS SOHRAB LOOSED   . . .    81  SOHRAB RUSTUM       669
        AS OF A GREAT ASSEMBLY LOOSED AND FIRES    . . . .    86  SOHRAB RUSTUM       869
        AND LOOSED THEM OF THEIR LOADS ON THE SEASHORE   .   106  BALDER DEAD 2        67
        FOR EVERY DAY MAN MAY BE LINKD AND LOOSED    . . .   196  FRAG ANTIGONE        34
        HE SPOKE AND LOOSED OUR HEART IN TEARS     . . . .   271  MEMORIAL VERSES      47
```

LOOSELY
```
        THY LEFT HOLDS HANGING LOOSELY    . . . . . . .   186  STRAYED REVEL        11
        EACH NERVE MORE LOOSELY STRUNG    . . . . . . .   212  GROWING OLD          10
```

LOOSEND
```
        HAD LOOSEND THE BROWN LOCKS OF VIVIANS HAIR    . .   154  TRISTRAM 3          168
        HAD LOOSEND THE BROWN CURLS OF VIVIANS HAIR    . .   154  TRISTRAM 3       V  168
        WHERE RODE THE TALL DARK SHIPS WHOSE LOOSEND SAIL    473  CROMWELL             67
```

LOOSESTRIFE
```
        RED LOOSESTRIFE AND BLOND MEADOW-SWEET AMONG   . .   266  THYRSIS             124
```

LOPPD
```
        MID DUST AND GROANS AND LIMBS LOPPD OFF AND BLOOD    105  BALDER DEAD 2        16
        AND LOPPD THEIR BOUGHS AND CLOVE THEM ON THE SWARD   106  BALDER DEAD 2        59
```

LORD
```
        GAY HER SMILING LORD TO GREET    . . . . . . .    13  CHURCH BROU 1        10
        TIS MY LORD COME BACK FROM HUNTING    . . . . . .    14  CHURCH BROU 1        39
        A PERSIAN LORD THIS DAY AND STRIP HIS CORPSE   . .    77  SOHRAB RUSTUM       529
        THAT I SHOULD ONE DAY FIND THY LORD AND THEE   . .    83  SOHRAB RUSTUM       745
        HOW IS IT WITH MY LORD ALONE    . . . . . . .    88  SICK KING BOKH       13
        AND TO THE MOSQUE MY LORD PASSD ON    . . . . . .    89  SICK KING BOKH       45
        MY LORD O KING DO RIGHT I PRAY   . . . . . . .    89  SICK KING BOKH       53
        BUT MY LORD MUSED A SPACE AND SAID    . . . . . .    90  SICK KING BOKH       89
        MY LORD HAD COVERD UP HIS FACE   . . . . . . .    91  SICK KING BOKH      125
        AND THESE ALL LABOURING FOR A LORD    . . . . . .    93  SICK KING BOKH      169
        AND I TOO ODIN TOO THE LORD OF ALL    . . . . . .    96  BALDER DEAD 1        30
        LORD OVER MEN ON EARTH AND GODS IN HEAVEN    . . .   120  BALDER DEAD 3       251
        GAVE HER THAT HER FUTURE LORD    . . . . . . .   134  TRISTRAM 1          137
        GAVE HER THAT HER LORD AND SHE   . . . . . . .   134  TRISTRAM 1       V  137
        BUT LORD AND HOUNDS KEEP ROOTED THERE      . . . .   149  TRISTRAM 2          185
        AH WHENCE THIS MERCY LORD I SAID    . . . . . .   157  SAINT BRANDAN        37
        IT WAS THE SIGHT OF THAT LORD ARUNDEL      . . . .   166  PICT NEWSTEAD         4
        THUS SAITH THE LORD TO HIS OWN   . . . . . . .   216  LORDS MESSENGER       1
        SILENT THE LORD OF THE WORLD    . . . . . . .   216  LORDS MESSENGER   V
        THEN SAITH THE LORD TO HIS OWN   . . . . . . .   216  LORDS MESSENGER   V   1
        WAS IT THE LORD THEN SAID WITH SCORN YE SAW    . .   237  PROGRESS             5
        THY TRUSTING LORD DIDST THOU HIS SERVANT SLAY   .   338  MEROPE              280
        OF AN ARCADIAN LORD OUR PRINCES FRIEND     . . . .   363  MEROPE              956
        GO THOU THE FIRST AND USHER IN THY LORD    . . . .   373  MEROPE             1190
```

LORDS
```
        WILL CHALLENGE FORTH THE BRAVEST PERSIAN LORDS  . .    62  SOHRAB RUSTUM        56
        BUT CHOOSE A CHAMPION FROM THE PERSIAN LORDS    . .    65  SOHRAB RUSTUM       152
        TO PICK A CHAMPION FROM THE PERSIAN LORDS   . . . .    67  SOHRAB RUSTUM       212
        BESIDE THE OXUS ALL THE PERSIAN LORDS      . . . .    72  SOHRAB RUSTUM       358
        WATCHD MY LORDS COMING FORTH AND PUSHD     . . . .    88  SICK KING BOKH       33
        STREAM ON HER FROM HER LORDS YET RECENT GRAVE  . .   172  GOOD SHEPHERD         8
        THAN THEY THESE AND THE DORIAN LORDS WHOSE KING . .   337  MEROPE              223
        PRECARIOUSLY RULED BY FOREIGN LORDS   . . . . . .   337  MEROPE              235
        PREFERRD MESSENIAN SERFS TO DORIAN LORDS   . . . .   339  MEROPE              324
        FOR IF THE OTHER LORDS DESIRED HIS FALL    . . . .   339  MEROPE              329
        SCARCE DANGEROUS LESS THAN HIM THE DORIAN LORDS .   381  MEROPE             1298
        THOU COUNTEST ON TO BACK THEE GAINST HIS LORDS  .   382  MEROPE             1321
        SERRIED AND GRIM THE RING OF DORIAN LORDS   . . .   401  MEROPE             1900
        BROKE FROM THE DORIAN LORDS FORWARD THEY RUSHD  .   402  MEROPE             1931
        BURST OER THE ALTAR AND THE DORIAN LORDS   . . . .   402  MEROPE             1938
        THE POWER OF THIS TYRANT AND HIS LORDS     . . . .   402  MEROPE             1944
        AND THEY WILL BE OUR LORDS AS THEY ARE NOW   . . .   439  EMPEDOCLES II       351
```

LORDSHIPS
```
        THROUGH ALL THE LORDSHIPS OF THE ARCADIAN DALES  . .   355  MEROPE              727
```

LORE
```
        UNRAVEL ALL HIS MANY-COLOURED LORE    . . . . . .    43  GIPSY CHILD          34
        THAT THE ONE LORE THATS ASSURING      . . . . . .        SECOND BEST      V   21
        THE ROSE-CROWND QUEEN OF LEGENDARY LORE    . . . .   168  RACHEL 2             7
        HAVE YET SO MUCH AS HEARD THIS SIMPLER LORE    . .   171  DIVINITY            12
        THAN I WAST DESTINED TO THIS LORE     . . . . . .   179  FAREWELL            44
        THAN I WERT DESTIND TO THIS LORE      . . . . . .   179  FAREWELL         V   44
        SO DEEP AS THE MUSICIANS LORE    . . . . . . .   225  EPILOG LAOCOON      136
        HIS FRIENDS AND WENT TO LEARN THE GIPSY-LORE    . .   256  SCHOLAR-GIPSY        37
```

LORE (CONTINUED)
```
BUT WE WE LEARNT YOUR LORE TOO WELL    • • • • • •   304 GRANDE CHARTR     156
BUT WE WE LEARNT THEIR LORE TOO WELL   • • • • • •   304 GRANDE CHARTR   V 156
AND THY SAD TRANQUIL LORE      • • • • • • •         313 OBERMANN MORE      48
AND SAID O BOY I TAUGHT THIS LORE    • • • • • •     414 EMPEDOCLES I 2     69
```

LORN
```
OBLIVION IN LORN ANGELS CAN INFUSE   • • • • • •      43 GIPSY CHILD     V  55
LORN AUTUMNS AND TRIUMPHANT SPRINGS  • • • • • •     181 ISOLATION MARG    34
IN THE LORN SYRIAN TOWN   • • • • • • • • •          318 OBERMANN MORE    174
```

LOSE
```
COME DOWN AND HELP US RUSTUM OR WE LOSE   • • • •     67 SOHRAB RUSTUM    219
I LOSE TO-DAY SO BRIGHT SO LOVED A GOD   • • • •      96 BALDER DEAD 1     22
FOR WE LOSE HIM WHO SMOOTHED ALL STRIFE IN HEAVEN    116 BALDER DEAD 3     88
AND I LOSE MY POOR SOUL MERMAN HERE WITH THEE  • •   163 FORSAKEN MERM     59
IS IT TO LOSE THE GLORY OF THE FORM   • • • • •      212 GROWING OLD        2
AND LOSE TO-MORROW THE GROUND WON TO-DAY   • • •     260 SCHOLAR-GIPSY    179
NEEDS MUST I LOSE THEM NEEDS WITH HEAVY HEART  • •   264 THYRSIS           38
SHE WILL NOT SEE HER COUNTRY LOSE   • • • • •        282 HAWORTH CHURCH   V
SURE ALL-COMMON TO LOSE   • • • • • • • •            369 MEROPE          1100
WHY WILT THOU FLY TO LOSE AS SOON AS FOUND  • • •    381 MEROPE          1290
OR HOW EXPECTEST NOT TO LOSE WHO COMST   • • •       381 MEROPE          1292
ALL THINGS BUT LIFE THOU LOSE NOT LIFE AS WELL  •    396 MEROPE          1757
LOSE ALL OUR PRESENT STATE   • • • • • • •           425 EMPEDOCLES I 2   405
BEFORE THE SOUL LOSE ALL HER SOLEMN JOYS   • • • •   429 EMPEDOCLES II     33
```

LOSES
```
WHO FINDS HIMSELF LOSES HIS MISERY   • • • • • •     240 SELF-DEPENDENCE   32
```

LOSS
```
AS THAT POOR BIRD FLIES HOME NOR KNOWS HIS LOSS  • •  78 SOHRAB RUSTUM    573
SO RUSTUM KNEW NOT HIS OWN LOSS BUT STOOD   • • • •   78 SOHRAB RUSTUM    574
THAT ONE SHOULD GRUDGE ITS LOSS FOR BALDERS SAKE  •   98 BALDER DEAD 1    125
AND THIS IS TRUE AND SUCH A LOSS IS HEAVENS    • •   111 BALDER DEAD 2    232
SO SHALL SHE KNOW YOUR LOSS WAS DEAR INDEED    • •   115 BALDER DEAD 3     45
ALL THINGS HAVE SUFFERD A LOSS   • • • • • •         232 YOUTH OF NATURE  127
ONLY METHINKS SOME LOSS OF HABITS POWER   • • •      263 THYRSIS           22
BUT HUSH THE UPLAND HATH A SUDDEN LOSS   • • •       267 THYRSIS          151
WEAKEN THE SENSE OF HIS LOSS   • • • • • •           283 HAWORTH CHURCH   V
HARDLY THE FOURTH WITH GRIEVOUS LOSS REGAIND   •     336 MEROPE           218
A PRIVATE LOSS HERE FOUNDS A NATIONS PEACE  • • •    360 MEROPE           889
TOO SUDDENLY THOU TELLEST SUCH A LOSS   • • • •      363 MEROPE           945
SEEMS IT LIGHTER MY LOSS   • • • • • • • •           370 MEROPE          1115
HARDLY THE THIRD WITH GRIEVOUS LOSS REGAIND    •     336 MEROPE          V 218
A LOSS INDEED   • • • • • • • • • • • •              459 KAISER DEAD       10
```

LOST
```
LOST LABOUR WHEN THE CIRCUMAMBIENT GLOOM   • • • •    10 MYCERINUS         53
WE HAVE LOST THEM AT YOUR CALL   • • • • • •          27 NEW SIRENS        38
OBLIVION IN LOST ANGELS CAN INFUSE   • • • • •        43 GIPSY CHILD       55
FAIN WOULD I KNOW THEE SAFE AND WELL THOUGH LOST  •   63 SOHRAB RUSTUM     88
NEVER WAS THAT FIELD LOST OR THAT FOE SAVED    • •    71 SOHRAB RUSTUM    328
AH YES HE HAD AND THAT LOST SON AM I   • • • •        78 SOHRAB RUSTUM    580
FOR IN THAT ICE ARE LOST THOSE NORTHERN STREAMS  •   108 BALDER DEAD 2    128
SO SHALL I KNOW THE LOST WAS DEAR INDEED   • • •     111 BALDER DEAD 2    239
LIKE AS A FARMER WHO HATH LOST HIS DOG   • • •       113 BALDER DEAD 3      8
MY LONG-LOST WANDERING ODER THOU HAST MET  • • •     116 BALDER DEAD 3    101
NO LESS THAN BALDER HAVE I LOST THE LIGHT   • • •    125 BALDER DEAD 3    401
THIS LOST SEA-CREATURE SAVED   • • • • • • •         160 NECKAN            56
NOT WITH LOST TOIL THOU LABOUREST THROUGH THE NIGHT  169 EAST LONDON       13
WILL HAVE BEEN LOST THE HELP IN STRIFE   • • • •     179 FAREWELL          66
THOUGH THESE BE LOST THERE WILL BE YET   • • • •     179 FAREWELL          69
BE LOST AND I NOT FEEL TWAS SO   • • • • • •         184 TERRACE BERNE     30
SOME IN THE TUMULT ARE LOST   • • • • • •            216 LORDS MESSENGER   13
BUT ARE LOST WHEN THEIR WATCHER IS GONE   • • •      230 YOUTH OF NATURE   74
THE MOON AND LOST BEHIND HER FADING DIM   • • •      242 SUMMER NIGHT       7
AND A LOST PULSE OF FEELING STIRS AGAIN   • • •      247 BURIED LIFE       85
THAT THE LOST SCHOLAR LONG WAS SEEN TO STRAY   •     256 SCHOLAR-GIPSY     53
MY PIPE IS LOST MY SHEPHERDS HOLIDAY   • • • • •     264 THYRSIS           37
BUT WHEN SICILIAN SHEPHERDS LOST A MATE   • • •      265 THYRSIS           82
LOST IT TOO SOON AND LEARNT A STORMY NOTE  • • •     269 THYRSIS          223
FALTER ARE LOST IN THE STORM   • • • • • •           289 RUGBY CHAPEL     103
ONLY OURSELVES WE LOST   • • • • • • •               289 RUGBY CHAPEL     118
ONE OF HIS LITTLE ONES LOST   • • • • • • •          291 RUGBY CHAPEL     167
WHAT SHALL I BEAR O LOST   • • • • • • •             342 MEROPE           400
AND HE IS LOST AND THOU HAST THAT TO ATONE  • • •    368 MEROPE          1070
BEARS SAD WITNESS IS LOST   • • • • • •              369 MEROPE          1092
O THOU LONG-LOST LONG SEEN IN DREAMS ALONE  • •      381 MEROPE          1288
AND THANK THY BITTEREST FOE THAT HAVING LOST   •     396 MEROPE          1756
POSSESSD IN HATRED LOST IN BLOOD   • • • • •         399 MEROPE          1849
HOWBEIT I JUDGE AS LOST   • • • • • • • •            415 EMPEDOCLES I 2    98
WE HAD NOT LOST OUR BALANCE THEN NOR GROWN  • • •    436 EMPEDOCLES II    248
THEY ARE LOST IN THE HOLLOWS   • • • • •             442 EMPEDOCLES II    449
OF THE LOVED THE LOST THE YOUNG   • • • •            454 POOR MATTHIAS     55
LOST IN DIM MEMORIES OF HIS EARLY HOME   • • •       468 ALARIC AT ROME   170
ON LIFES WILD WAVES THE LIVING AND THE LOST   • •    474 CROMWELL          78
WE PRIZE NOT WHEN TIS PRESENT BUT WHEN LOST   • •        LUCRETIUS 7        2
```

LOT

```
O SWEET PLEADERS DOTH MY LOT                • • • • • • • •   31 NEW SIRENS        164
NOT MILDER IS THE GENERAL LOT               • • • • • • • •   60 RESIGNATION       275
SO THEY WHOSE LOT IT WAS CAST STONES        • • • • • • • •   91 SICK KING BOKH    121
SHOULD CHANGE HIS LOT AND FILL ANOTHERS LIFE       • • • •   98 BALDER DEAD 1      115
WOUNDLESS AND FRESH SUCH LOT IS THEIRS IN HEAVEN   • • •    105 BALDER DEAD 2       18
THEIR LOT WAS BUT TO WEEP AND MOAN          • • • • • •     203 EUPHROSYNE          10
TIES STRAITLY UP FROM MINE THY LOT          • • • • • • •   208 ON THE RHINE         8
HOW FAIR A LOT TO FILL                      • • • • • • • • 244 SUMMER NIGHT        91
HOW HIGH A LOT TO FILL                      • • • • • • • • 244 SUMMER NIGHT      V 91
BUT THOU POSSESSEST AN IMMORTAL LOT         • • • • • •     259 SCHOLAR-GIPSY      157
ALIVE WE WOULD HAVE CHANGED HIS LOT         • • • • • •     273 EDW QUILLINAN       19
MY BROTHER AND THINE EARLY LOT              • • • • • • •   276 SOUTHERN NIGHT      19
FELL TO THY FATHERS LOT THE SECOND PRIZE    • • • • • •     330 MEROPE               8
NOT OF HIM OF CRESPHONTES THOU SHAREDST THE LOT    • •      345 MEROPE             471
MESSENIA TO THOSE HELPLESS BOYS THE LOT     • • • •         389 MEROPE            1552
TIS THAT THE LOT THEY HAVE                  • • • • • • •   417 EMPEDOCLES I 2     149
MAN WITH HIS LOT THUS FIGHTS                • • • • • • •   417 EMPEDOCLES I 2     153
WHEN THY OWN LOT WENT HARD                  • • • • • • •   417 EMPEDOCLES I 2     165
NO WEAKNESS SPOIL OUR LOT                   • • • • • • •   421 EMPEDOCLES I 2     263
AT LEAST THAT GODS THY LOT                  • • • • • • •       EMPEDOCLES I 2   V
THAT EACH MANS LOT IS THAT                  • • • • • • •       EMPEDOCLES I 2   V
AND BORE A MORTAL LOT          • • • • • • • • •           447 WESTMIN ABBEY      112
STERN LAW OF EVERY MORTAL LOT  • • • • • • • • •           450 GEISTS GRAVE        29
GAZD SADLY DOWN ON HIS UNRESTFUL LOT        • • • • •       474 CROMWELL            86
HIMSELF HIS SUFFERINGS IN HIS COUNTRYS LOT  • • • •        477 CROMWELL           172
WHO WHILE I PONDERED ON THE LOT OF SOULS    • • • •            RUDE ORATC           2
```

LOTS

```
AH ON WHICH IF BOTH OUR LOTS WERE BALANCED  • • • •        144 TRISTRAM ?          49
```

LOUD

```
THOUGH THE LOUD WORLD PROCLAIM THEIR ENMITY        • •      1 QUIET WORK           4
PROSPECT OF HOPE WHICH FRANCE PROCLAIMS SO LOUD    • •      7 REP FRIEND CONT      3
AND ONE LOUD CRY OF GRIEF AND OF AMAZE      • • • • •      11 MYCERINUS           80
FROM THE LOUD JOYFUL LAUGHTER OF HIS LIPS   • • • •        11 MYCERINUS          101
LOUD THUNDERING BORE US BY SWIFT SWIFT IT FOAMD    •       25 DREAM               33
WOULD YOU FREEZE MY TOO LOUD BOLDNESS       • • • •        31 NEW SIRENS         159
SO WHEN THE FEAST GREW LOUD     • • • • • •               47 WORLD QUIETIST      25
THE CUCKOO LOUD ON SOME HIGH LAWN           • • • •        57 RESIGNATION        176
CIRCLES ABOVE HIS EYRY WITH LOUD SCREAMS    • • • •        78 SOHRAB RUSTUM      565
BUT HE PRAISED ALLAH WITH LOUD VOICE        • • • •        91 SICK KING BOKH     123
HE SPAKE AND HIS FIERCE SONS APPLAUDED LOUD        •      120 BALDER DEAD 3      245
LOUD HOWLS THE WIND SHARP PATTERS THE RAIN  • • • •       133 TRISTRAM 1          83
DWELLS ON LOUD TYNTAGELS HILL               • • • • •     134 TRISTRAM 1         134
WHEN THE FEAST WAS GAY AND THE LAUGHTER LOUD       •      146 TRISTRAM 2         114
WHEN THE FEAST WAS LOUD AND THE LAUGHTER SHRILL    •      146 TRISTRAM 2       V 114
LOUD PRAYS THE PRIEST SHUT STANDS THE DOOR  • • • •       163 FORSAKEN MERM       82
OF LOUD EURIPUS SAW             • • • • • • • • •         196 FRAG ANTIGONE       59
WHEREFORE DOST THOU GROAN SO LOUD           • • • •       430 EMPEDOCLES II       45
THE LOUD RAINS LASHD THE MOUNTAINS CROWN    • • • •       480 HAYSWATER BOAT      29
```

LOUDER

```
WOULD YOU FREEZE MY LOUDER BOLDNESS         • • • • •      31 NEW SIRENS       V 159
THEN WITH A LOUDER LAUGH THE HAG REPLIED    • • • •       123 BALDER DEAD 3      350
BUT WITH A LOUDER LAUGH THE HAG REPLIED     • • • •       123 BALDER DEAD 3    V 350
OR LOUDER RUSH OF WHIRLWINDS SWEEPING BY    • • • •       466 ALARIC AT ROME     111
THE TRUMPET SWELLS YET LOUDER THEY ARE HERE        •      467 ALARIC AT ROME     133
```

LOUDEST

```
AND WHEN THE MIRTH WAXD LOUDEST WITH DULL SOUND    • •     12 MYCERINUS          123
```

LOUGHRIGG

```
WHERE UNDER LOUGHRIGG THE STREAM            • • • • • • •  280 HAWORTH CHURCH       1
```

LOUIS

```
WHO BORE SAINT LOUIS COMPANY    • • • • • • • •           278 SOUTHERN NIGHT      94
```

LOURD

```
FOR THAT A SHADOW LOURD ON THE FIELDS       • • • •       264 THYRSIS             44
```

LOVD

```
FARE FAREWELL THOU LONG THOU DEEPLY LOVD    • • • •       145 TRISTRAM 2       V 98
ONLY TO LOVE AND BE LOVD  • • • • • • • • • •             282 HAWORTH CHURCH   V
```

LOVDST

```
THOSE OF THY BLOOD WHOM THOU LOVDST    • • • • • •        284 HAWORTH CHURCH      79
```

LOVE

```
LOVE FREE TO RANGE AND REGAL BANQUETINGS    • • • •         9 MYCERINUS           34
THE RUSTLE OF THE ETERNAL RAIN OF LOVE      • • • •        19 CHURCH BROU 3       46
THEIR LOVE LET ME KNOW MUST GROW STRONG AND               19 MODERN SAPPHO       13
   YET STRONGER
THEY MUST LOVE WHILE THEY MUST BUT THE HEARTS             19 MODERN SAPPHO       15
   THAT LOVE LONGER
THEY MUST LOVE WHILE THEY MUST BUT THE HEARTS             19 MODERN SAPPHO       15
   THAT LOVE LONGER
I SHALL WEEP BUT THEIR LOVE WILL BE COOLING AND HE        20 MODERN SAPPHO       18
SHOW YOU SAY MY LOVE DECLINES   • • • • • • •             24 MEMORY-PICTURE      50
LOVE HAS FLUSHD THOSE CRUEL FACES           • • • •       27 NEW SIRENS          53
HATH IT DRUNK OF OUR LOVE-POTIONS           • • • •       29 NEW SIRENS          87
SCORES OF TRUE LOVE KNOTS ARE BREAKING      • • • •       35 NEW SIRENS         261
LIFE WITHOUT LOVE DOES BUT FADE             • • • • •     28 NEW SIRENS       V 66
DULL WITHOUT LOVE LIFE DOTH FADE            • • • • •     28 NEW SIRENS       V 66
```

LOVE   (CONTINUED)
WHERE LOVE IS HALF MISTRUST   39 STAGIRIUS   46
LOVE NO UNKINDNESS   40 STAGIRIUS   58
LOVE LENDS LIFE A LITTLE GRACE   44 QUESTION   4
WHO WILL NOT MOUNT IN PEACE BUT LOVE   HORATIAN ECHO   V
OUTLASTS AVERSION OUTLASTS LOVE   58 RESIGNATION   216
WHO NEEDS NOT LOVE AND POWER TO KNOW   59 RESIGNATION   235
LOVE TRANSIENT POWER AN UNREAL SHOW   59 RESIGNATION   236
WHO LOVE THEE BUT MUST PRESS FOR EVER FIRST   63 SOHRAB RUSTUM   68
THE LOVE ALL BEAR TOWARD THEE NOR TRAIN UP   126 BALDER DEAD 3   450
LOVE ME AND GLADLY BRING FOR MY AWARD   126 BALDER DEAD 3   465
THE LOVE ALL BEAR TOWARDS THEE NOR TRAIN UP   126 BALDER DEAD 3   V 450
WORKING LOVE BUT WORKING TEEN   132 TRISTRAM 1   67
DOES THE LOVE-DRAUGHT WORK NO MORE   133 TRISTRAM 1   80
AND FOR EVER LOVE EACH OTHER   135 TRISTRAM 1   140
OF A LOVE THEY DARE NOT NAME   135 TRISTRAM 1   150
TRISTRAM SWEET LOVE WE ARE BETRAYD OUT-PLANND   135 TRISTRAM 1   167
ALL THE SPRING-TIME OF HIS LOVE   136 TRISTRAM 1   173
THE LOVE-DESPERATE BANISHD KNIGHT   136 TRISTRAM 1   186
HIS YOUNG GUARDIANS HEART WITH LOVE   137 TRISTRAM 1   207
FAIR LOVE SHE SAYS CANST THOU FORGET SO SOON   139 TRISTRAM 1   285
TRISTRAM AH FOR LOVE OF HEAVEN SPEAK KINDLY   142 TRISTRAM 2   13
LOVE LIKE MINE IS ALTERD IN THE BREAST   143 TRISTRAM 2   38
WHAT LOVE COURAGE CHRIST HE IS SO PALE   145 TRISTRAM 2   80
TRISTRAM FOR THE LOVE OF HEAVEN SPEAK KINDLY   142 TRISTRAM 2   V 13
CALL IT AMBITION OR REMORSE OR LOVE   153 TRISTRAM 3   130
FOR SHE WAS PASSING WEARY OF HIS LOVE   156 TRISTRAM 3   224
THE INFANT CHURCH OF LOVE SHE FELT THE TIDE   172 GOOD SHEPHERD   7
THEY SEEK TO FIND IN THOSE THEY LOVE   178 FAREWELL   23
ARE YET FAR FAR LESS RARE THAN LOVE   178 FAREWELL   40
NOR FEARD BUT THY LOVE LIKEWISE GREW   180 ISOLATION MARG   5
HOW VAIN A THING IS MORTAL LOVE   181 ISOLATION MARG   26
AND LOVE IF LOVE OF HAPPIER MEN   181 ISOLATION MARG   36
AND LOVE IF LOVE OF HAPPIER MEN   181 ISOLATION MARG   36
THINE EYES MY LOVE I SEE   183 ABSENCE   2
ONCE-LONGD-FOR STORMS OF LOVE   183 ABSENCE   14
NOR WAS THE LOVE UNTRUE   196 FRAG ANTIGONE   54
SAW AND SNATCHD WILD WITH LOVE   196 FRAG ANTIGONE   60
SUCH END OERTOOK THAT LOVE   197 FRAG ANTIGONE   70
WITH LOVE AND HATE TRIUMPH AND AGONY   201 PHILOMELA   26
YET SHE COULD LOVE THOSE EYES DECLARE   202 URANIA   7
HOW DEEPLY SHE WHO SCORNS CAN LOVE   202 URANIA   20
THESE ASK NO LOVE THESE PLIGHT NO FAITH   203 EUPHROSYNE   15
THEY WILL NOT GIVE US LOVE AND TEARS   203 EUPHROSYNE   23
IT WAS NOT LOVE WHICH HEAVED THY BREAST   204 EUPHROSYNE   25
IT WAS NOT LOVE THAT HEAVED THY BREAST   204 EUPHROSYNE   V 25
BUT TWAS NOT LOVE WHICH HEAVED HER BREAST   204 EUPHROSYNE   V 25
MY HEART IS SWOLN WITH LOVE UNSAID   206 RIVER   10
AND SOME FIND DEATH ERE THEY FIND LOVE   206 TOO LATE   2
THEN LOVE THY HAND AH NO ADIEU   207 TOO LATE   8
AND SAY MY LOVE WHY SUFFEREST THOU   209 LONGING   12
AH LOVE LET US BE TRUE   211 DOVER BEACH   29
HATH REALLY NEITHER JOY NOR LOVE NOR LIGHT   211 DOVER BEACH   33
THE FIGURE THE BLOOM OF THY LOVE   231 YOUTH OF NATURE   111
YIELD THEM LOVE AMUSEMENT SYMPATHY   240 SELF-DEPENDENCE   20
AND LET ME READ THERE LOVE THY INMOST SOUL   245 BURIED LIFE   11
ALAS IS EVEN LOVE TOO WEAK   245 BURIED LIFE   12
BUT WE MY LOVE DOTH A LIKE SPELL BENUMB   245 BURIED LIFE   24
BUT WE MY LOVE DOES A LIKE SPELL BENUMB   245 BURIED LIFE   V 24
NOR PROMISED LOVE IT COULD NOT GIVE   251 WISH   38
HIS SHEEP HIS HAPLESS LOVE HIS BLINDED EYES   268 THYRSIS   187
FILLD EUROPE ONCE WITH HIS LOVE-PAIN   278 SOUTHERN NIGHT   98
ONLY TO LOVE AND BE LOVD   282 HAWORTH CHURCH   V
CHATTER AND LOVE AND HATE   288 RUGBY CHAPEL   62
HAD EVERY OTHER GIFT BUT WANTED LOVE   295 HEINES GRAVE   100
LOVE WITHOUT WHICH THE TONGUE   295 HEINES GRAVE   101
LOVE IS THE FOUNTAIN OF CHARM   295 HEINES GRAVE   105
OF LOVE WHICH SET SO DEEP AND STRONG   317 OBERMANN MORE   147
AND LOVE HIS CHEERLESS TRUTH   322 OBERMANN MORE   280
IS WITHOUT LOVE OR HATE AUSTERELY RAISED   336 MEROPE   205
ONE SUDDEN STROKE AND THE MESSENIANS LOVE   381 MEROPE   1287
BUT TO MATCH THESE THOU HAST THE PEOPLES LOVE   381 MEROPE   1309
HOW SHALL I ROUSE THEIR LOVE THEIR ARDOUR SO   382 MEROPE   1352
LOVE A WON CAUSE BUT NOT A CAUSE TO WIN   384 MEROPE   1394
THUS LITTLE FOUNDED IN THEIR SUBJECTS LOVE   390 MEROPE   1560
NOT LITTLE IF THOU SAWST WHAT LOVE WHAT ZEAL   401 MEROPE   1893
WHICH THE GOATS LOVE ARE JEWELLD THICK WITH DEW   407 EMPEDOCLES I 1   17
THE CATTLE LOVE TO GATHER ON THEIR WAY   413 EMPEDOCLES I 2   38
LOVE TO HAVE SCOPE AND PLAY   420 EMPEDOCLES I 2   248
TELL HIM I NEVER FAILD TO LOVE HIS LYRE   428 EMPEDOCLES I 2   468
GODS AND THE RACE OF MORTALS LOVE SO WELL   431 EMPEDOCLES II   65
AND TEMPER SWEET AND LOVE OF ALL THINGS PURE   446 WESTMIN ABBEY   79
AND ALL THAT LIFE AND ALL THAT LOVE   449 GEISTS GRAVE   3
A MEEK LAST GLANCE OF LOVE DIDST THROW   450 GEISTS GRAVE   35
FAITHFUL LOVE IN DEPTH DIVINE   454 POOR MATTHIAS   65
ALL NATURAL LOVE ALL HUMAN SYMPATHY   467 ALARIC AT ROME   147
TO LOVE MORE DEEPLY THAN HE CAN   481 DESTINY   2
HAVE NOT LIFE AND LOVE BEEN GRANTED ME   482 THEKLAS ANSWER   4
ONLY WHILE THEIR LOVE LIVD LASTED THEY   482 THEKLAS ANSWER   8
WHEN THOU TOO HAST BORNE THE LOVE WE BORE   482 THEKLAS ANSWER   14

LOVED

BUT PRIZED BUT LOVED BUT EMINENT IN YOU	• • • •	6 REP FRIEND	3
MY FATHER LOVED INJUSTICE AND LIVED LONG	• • • •	9 MYCERINUS	13
I LOVED THE GOOD HE SCORND AND HATED WRONG	• • • •	9 MYCERINUS	15
TO THE COOL REGION OF THE GROVES HE LOVED	• • • •	11 MYCERINUS	84
HER I LOVED AT EVENTIDE	• • • • • •	35 NEW SIRENS	272
MUSED MUCH LOVED LIFE A LITTLE LOATHED IT MORE	• •	43 GIPSY CHILD	36
OF PRIDE AND HOPE FOR SOHRAB WHOM THEY LOVED	•	65 SOHRAB RUSTUM	159
AND THAT OLD KING HER FATHER WHO LOVED WELL	•	79 SOHRAB RUSTUM	625
WHOM RUSTUM WERT THOU HIS MIGHT WELL HAVE LOVED	•	80 SOHRAB RUSTUM	642
HIM THAT KIND CREATURE FOUND AND REARD AND LOVED	• •	81 SOHRAB RUSTUM	682
I LOSE TO-DAY SO BRIGHT SO LOVED A GOD	• •	96 BALDER DEAD 1	22
AND CAST IT AT THE DEAR-LOVED BALDERS BREAST	•	98 BALDER DEAD 1	102
BALDER THEIR JOY SO BRIGHT SO LOVED A GOD	•	98 BALDER DEAD 1	126
WHOM THOU SO WELL HAST LOVED BUT I CAN SMOOTH	•	103 BALDER DEAD 1	308
THOUGH I BE LOVED AND MANY MOURN MY DEATH	•	112 BALDER DEAD 2	270
THEY MOURND THAT DAY SO BRIGHT SO LOVED A GOD	•	115 BALDER DEAD 3	64
FAREWELL O BALDER BRIGHT AND LOVED MY SON	•	115 BALDER DEAD 3	67
AND HIS HORSE BALDERS HORSE WHOM MOST HE LOVED	•	118 BALDER DEAD 3	171
HELA AND WIN THE LOVED ONE BACK TO HEAVEN	• •	122 BALDER DEAD 3	294
COLD COLD AS THOSE WHO LIVED AND LOVED	•	149 TRISTRAM 2	192
THE DAYS IN WHICH SHE MIGHT HAVE LIVED AND LOVED	•	151 TRISTRAM 3	65
SINGING THERE DWELLS A LOVED ONE	• •	165 FORSAKEN MERM	140
WHO STRUCK IN HEAT HIS CHILD HE LOVED SO WELL	•	166 PICT NEWSTEAD	5
WHO STRUCK IN HEAT THE CHILD HE LOVED SO WELL	•	166 PICT NEWSTEAD V	5
TO BE LONG LOVED WAS NEVER FRAMED	•	178 FAREWELL	18
ROBS OF A LOVED BRIDE PALE IMPLORING	• • • •	196 FRAG ANTIGONE	42
IF THE LOVED FORM AND THE DEEP-CHERISHD FEATURE	•	206 SEPARATION	7
OF A SOCIAL ORDER HE LOVED	• • • •	229 YOUTH OF NATURE	32
IS BY THE TONES OF A LOVED VOICE CARESSD	•	247 BURIED LIFE	83
HE LOVED EACH SIMPLE JOY THE COUNTRY YIELDS	•	264 THYRSIS	42
HE LOVED HIS MATES BUT YET HE COULD NOT KEEP	•	264 THYRSIS	43
SHE LOVED THE DORIAN PIPE THE DORIAN STRAIN	•	265 THYRSIS	97
BUT MANY A DINGLE ON THE LOVED HILL-SIDE	• • •	266 THYRSIS	112
OUR SCHOLAR TRAVELS YET THE LOVED HILL-SIDE	•	269 THYRSIS	240
HAVE FELT THIS BREATH HE LOVED OF FAIR	• • •	275 STANZAS CARNAC	43
THAT MUCH-LOVED INLAND SEA	• • • • •	311 OBERMANN	162
LOVED NOT WHO TURNEST FROM THE THRONG	•	314 OBERMANN MORE	71
AND NOW MINISTER LOVED	• • • • • •	345 MEROPE	474
FOR THE MESSENIAN HEARTS WHO LOVED THE PRINCE	•	365 MEROPE	993
O LOVED MISTRESS IN FEAR	• • • • • •	371 MEROPE	1130
SON LOVED OF ZEUS HIS FATHER FOR HE SINND	•	398 MEROPE	1814
SO RULE THAT AS THY FATHER THOU BE LOVED	• •	404 MEROPE	2008
SON LOVED OF ZEUS HIS FATHER FOR HE ERRD	•	398 MEROPE	V1814
THOU KNOWST OF OLD HE LOVED THIS HARP OF MINE	•	408 EMPEDOCLES I 1	72
TO HAVE LOVED TO HAVE THOUGHT TO HAVE DONE	•	425 EMPEDOCLES I 2	400
HE EVER LOVED THE THEBAN STORY WELL	• • •	427 EMPEDOCLES I 2	463
ONLY THE LOVED HEBE BEARS	• • • • •	431 EMPEDOCLES II	84
THOUGH I HAVE LOVED THEE LIVED IN HONOURING THEE	•	434 EMPEDOCLES II	195
THAT I HAVE LOVED NO DARKNESS	• • • •	441 EMPEDOCLES II	400
EVEN AS THAT LOVED THAT WELL-RECORDED FRIEND	•	449 WESTMIN ABBEY	168
OF THE LOVED THE LOST THE YOUNG	• • • •	454 POOR MATTHIAS	55
WHEN THOU ART EITHER NOUGHT AND SO NOT LOVED	• •	FRAGMENT 5	8

LOVELESS

LOVELESS RAYLESS JOYLESS YOU SHALL STAND	• • • •	35 NEW SIRENS	266

LOVELIER

FAR LOVELIER THAN THEY ARE BY DAY	• • • •	141 TRISTRAM 1	356
COULD SCARCE HAVE LIGHTED ON A LOVELIER CURE	• •	407 EMPEDOCLES I 1	26

LOVELIEST

THE LOVELIEST GODDESS SHE IN HEAVEN BY ALL	• • •	116 BALDER DEAD 3	91
SHAKESPEARE LOVELIEST OF SOULS	• • • • •	294 HEINES GRAVE	65
THAT WILDEST VISIONS STILL SHOULD LOVELIEST SEEM	• •	470 ALARIC AT ROME	213

LOVELINESS

AND HER FRAGILE LOVELINESS	• • • • • • •	132 TRISTRAM 1	53
A TRANQUIL SETTLED LOVELINESS	• • • • • •	147 TRISTRAM 2	145
A PLACID SETTLED LOVELINESS	• • • • • •	147 TRISTRAM 2	V 145
LOVELINESS MAGIC AND GRACE	• • • • • •	230 YOUTH OF NATURE	79
LOVELINESS MAGIC GRACE	• • • • • •	230 YOUTH OF NATURE	V 79
IN MOURNFUL LOVELINESS THAT CITY LAY	• • • •	466 ALARIC AT ROME	104
THY LITTLE MOMENT LIFE OF LOVELINESS	• • • • •	FRAGMENT 5	4

LOVELORN

MOCKD HER POOR LOVELORN GIANTS LAY	• • • •	222 EPILOG LAOCOON	48

LOVELY

PITEOUS AND LOVELY LYING ON THE SAND	• • •	80 SOHRAB RUSTUM	633
LOVELY IN DEATH UPON THE COMMON SAND	• • • •	80 SOHRAB RUSTUM	639
AND THOU MUST LAY ME IN THAT LOVELY EARTH	• • •	84 SOHRAB RUSTUM	787
AND I WILL LAY THEE IN THAT LOVELY EARTH	• • •	84 SOHRAB RUSTUM	802
AT THY SIDE THOU LOVELY CHARGE	• • • • •	134 TRISTRAM 1	112
THE LOVELY ORPHAN CHILD AGAIN	• • • • •	136 TRISTRAM 1	192
THY LOVELY YOUTHFUL WIFE GROWS PALE	• • • •	138 TRISTRAM 1	269
THE LOVELY YOUTHFUL WIFE GROWS PALE	• • • • •	138 TRISTRAM 1	V 269
THIS TALE OF MERLIN AND THE LOVELY FAY	• • •	154 TRISTRAM 3	164
THE LOVELY LIPS WITH THEIR ARCH SMILE THAT TELLS	• •	176 PARTING	39

LOVELY (CONTINUED)

AND LOVELY NOTES FROM SHORE TO SHORE • • • • • • 182 TO MARG CONT   11
IN ALL HIS LOVELY MIEN LET PIERCE • • • • • • 202 URANIA   23
TILL THEN HER LOVELY EYES MAINTAIN • • • • • • 202 URANIA   31
AND THEY THAT LOVELY FACE WHO VIEW • • • • • • 203 EUPHROSYNE   3
THY LOVELY PRESENCE AT MY SIDE • • • • • • • 204 CALAIS SANDS   11
AND SEE UPON THE LOVELY SAND • • • • • • • 204 CALAIS SANDS   V 10
ON MINE LET REST THAT LOVELY HAND • • • • • • 206 RIVER   8
WITH THE GREY EYES AND THE LOVELY BROWN HAIR • • 206 SEPARATION   16
TOO LOVELY TO BE GREY • • • • • • • • • 208 ON THE RHINE   20
LOVELY THE FLUSH • • • • • • • • • • • 219 BACCHANALIA 1   49
SUCH LOVELY FLOWERS FOR CHEERING SOULS • • • • 227 EPILOG LAOCOON   204
LOVELY AND SOFT AS A DREAM • • • • • • • 228 YOUTH OF NATURE   3
IS LOVELY A MORTAL IS DEAD • • • • • • • 228 YOUTH OF NATURE   12
SO IN ITS LOVELY MOONLIGHT LIVES THE SOUL • • • • 236 PALLADIUM   9
LOVELY ALL TIMES SHE LIES LOVELY TO-NIGHT • • • 263 THYRSIS   21
LOVELY ALL TIMES SHE LIES LOVELY TO-NIGHT • • • 263 THYRSIS   21
BEHIND THAT LOVELY MOUNTAIN-LINE • • • • • • 275 SOUTHERN NIGHT   7
CARRIED THY LOVELY WAIL AWAY • • • • • • • 303 GRANDE CHARTR   140
THROUGH THE COOL LOVELY COUNTRY FOLLOWD YOU • • • 407 EMPEDOCLES I 1   45
BUT LEAD HIM THROUGH THE LOVELY MOUNTAIN-PATHS • • 411 EMPEDOCLES I 1   156
THE LYRES VOICE IS LOVELY EVERYWHERE • • • • • 430 EMPEDOCLES II   37
WITH A LOVELY FRIGHTEND MIEN • • • • • • • 433 EMPEDOCLES II   157
ALL THOU AUGUREST HERE OF LOVELY SEEMING • • • • 483 THEKLAS ANSWER   21
BUT THAT PRINCE AMONG GODS THE SON OF THE LOVELY-HAIRD   HOMER TRANS   52
     LETO

LOVER

SHALL YOU FIND THE RADIANT LOVER • • • • • • 33 NEW SIRENS   221
THE BLOSSOMD THORN-TREE AND HER SLEEPING LOVER • • 156 TRISTRAM 3   218
AH ME HONOUREST MORE THAN THY LOVER • • • • • 196 FRAG ANTIGONE   51
WHAT HIS FOES DARED NOT I HIS LOVER DARED • • • • 338 MEROPE   271

LOVERS

WHICH YOUR LOVERS WANDERD DOWN • • • • • • • 30 NEW SIRENS   126
AH NOT THE NECTAROUS POPPY LOVERS USE • • • • 43 GIPSY CHILD   53
TWO YOUNG FAIR LOVERS • • • • • • • • • 51 CONSOLATION   41
LOVERS OF CHANGE YE ARE FASTIDIOUS SPRITES • • • 123 BALDER DEAD 3   339
SING THEE TALES OF TRUE LONG-PARTED LOVERS • • • 143 TRISTRAM 2   31
STILL HOLD HER LOVERS HAND HER HEAD • • • • • 146 TRISTRAM 2   105
WHERE THOSE LIFELESS LOVERS BE • • • • • • • 147 TRISTRAM 2   149
STILL HOLD HER LOVERS HANDS HER HEAD • • • • 146 TRISTRAM 2   V 105
STILL HOLDS HER LOVERS HANDS HER HEAD • • • • 146 TRISTRAM 2   V 105
THERE IN A SHIP THEY BORE THOSE LOVERS COLD • • 149 TRISTRAM 3   4
THE LOVERS MEET BUT MEET TOO LATE • • • • • 207 TOO LATE   6
ARE EVEN LOVERS POWERLESS TO REVEAL • • • • • 245 BURIED LIFE   14
TO MEET HER PIRATE-LOVERS SHIP • • • • • • • 278 SOUTHERN NIGHT   105

LOVES

ARE RARE AH MOST LOVES BUT FLOW ONCE AND RETURN • • 19 MODERN SAPPHO   16
RUSTUM HE LOVES NO MORE BUT LOVES THE YOUNG • • • 67 SOHRAB RUSTUM   226
RUSTUM HE LOVES NO MORE BUT LOVES THE YOUNG • • • 67 SOHRAB RUSTUM   226
BUT THESE SHE LOVES AND NOISIER LIFE THAN THIS • • 152 TRISTRAM 3   100
SHE HERSELF LOVES THEM STILL AND WHEN THEY ARE TOLD 152 TRISTRAM 3   110
SO LITTLE LOVES THY STRAIN • • • • • • • 307 OBERMANN   40
FOR THE WORLD LOVES NEW WAYS • • • • • • • 307 OBERMANN   42
HOW MANY LOVES HOW MANY GRATITUDES • • • • • 335 MEROPE   179
TO SEE SECURE TO LIVE WITH THOSE SHE LOVES • • • 349 MEROPE   566
TO HEAR THAT STILL HE LOVES STILL LONGS FOR ME • • 351 MEROPE   613
WHEN IT ADMIRES AND LOVES ITS HEART AWAKES • • 382 MEROPE   1345
HE LOVES THEE BUT HE MUST NOT SEE THEE NOW • • • 409 EMPEDOCLES I 1   77
HE LOVES THAT IN THEE TOO THERE WAS A TIME • • • 409 EMPEDOCLES I 1   79
BUT IN A WORLD HE LOVES NOT MUST SUBSIST • • • 437 EMPEDOCLES II   267

LOVEST

THOU LOVEST IT THEN MY WINE • • • • • • • • 187 STRAYED REVEL   54

LOVING

LOVING A SISTERLY BAND • • • • • • • • • 284 HAWORTH CHURCH   81
OF THE SUN-LOVING GENTIAN IN THE HEAT • • • • 412 EMPEDOCLES I 2   5
THAT LOVING HEART THAT PATIENT SOUL • • • • • 450 GEISTS GRAVE   9
AGAINST THY MISTRESS LOVING HEART • • • • • 460 KAISER DEAD   53
LIKE LOVING SHADOWS ROUND THAT CHILDHOODS HOME • • 474 CROMWELL   74

LOVST

THOU LOVST NO MORE FAREWELL FAREWELL • • • • • 180 ISOLATION MARG   12
AND WERE IT SNAPT THOU LOVST ME NOT • • • • • 208 ON THE RHINE   9
FOR MOST I KNOW THOU LOVST RETIRED GROUND • • • 257 SCHOLAR-GIPSY   71

LOW

WITH LOW SIGHINGS SILENCE STOLE • • • • • • 28 NEW SIRENS   70
WITH LOW SIGHS HATH SILENCE STOLE • • • • • 28 NEW SIRENS   V 70
LOW WOODY HILL WITH GRACIOUS BOUND • • • • • 57 RESIGNATION   174
CLUSTERING LIKE BEE-HIVES ON THE LOW FLAT STRAND • • 61 SOHRAB RUSTUM   13
THROUGH THE BLACK TENTS HE PASSD OER THAT LOW STRAND 61 SOHRAB RUSTUM   16
INDOORS FROM THE SUNS EYE HIS HEAD DROOPD LOW • • 86 SOHRAB RUSTUM   847
OUT OF THE MIST AND HUM OF THAT LOW LAND • • • 87 SOHRAB RUSTUM   876
FROM THE HOT FIELDS AT NOON HIS HEAD DROOPD LOW • • 86 SOHRAB RUSTUM V 847
FROM THE HOT FIELD AT NOON HIS HEAD DROOPD LOW • • 86 SOHRAB RUSTUM V 847
TO THE LOW SHORE OF GHOSTS AND HELAS REALM • • • 99 BALDER DEAD 1   151
WHEN AIR IS CHILLIEST AND THE STARS SUNK LOW • • 103 BALDER DEAD 1   281

LOW   (CONTINUED)
       YET LOW AND FROM THE BOTTOM YET TO ONE STANDING IN IT   TRISTRAM 3   V   11
       WHEN SPRING-TIDES ARE LOW   • • • • • • • •   165 FORSAKEN MERM   127
       WITH LARGE-LEAVED LOW-CREEPING MELON-PLANTS   • •   190 STRAYED REVEL   155
       THE PUISSANT CROWND THE WEAK LAID LOW   • • • •   219 BACCHANALIA 2   12
       OF A SACRED POET LIES LOW   • • • • • • • •   229 YOUTH OF NATURE   49
       WHO CRY ALOUD TO LAY THE OLD WORLD LOW   • • • •   237 PROGRESS   15
       I KNEW HIS SPIRITS LOW   • • • • • •   272 EDW QUILLINAN   2
       SEE LOW ABOVE THE TIDE AT FLOOD   • • • • •   274 STANZAS CARNAC   26
       THE EAST BOWD LOW BEFORE THE BLAST   • • • •   316 OBERMANN MORE   109
       UPON HIS CROSS WITH HEAD SUNK LOW   • • • • •   317 OBERMANN MORE   155
       THAT WAN NAILD FORM WITH HEAD DROOPD LOW   • • •   317 OBERMANN MORE   V 155
       WITH THE LOW BROAD HAT OF THE TANND   • • • •   342 MEROPE   395
       THE LOW-BROWD CAVERN-ARCH AND DISAPPEAR   • • •   358 MEROPE   834
       LOW MOANS HALF UTTERD   • • • • • • • • •   393 MEROPE   1667
       NOR BEND MYSELF TOO LOW TO MAKE IT YIELD   • • •   398 MEROPE   1786
       WHICH LAID THEE LOW FOR BLOOD REQUIRES BLOOD   •   404 MEROPE   1987
       POETS FIRE GETS FAINT AND LOW   • • • • • •   454 POOR MATTHIAS   78
       IN A LOW DIM-LIGHTED PEN   • • • • • • • •   457 POOR MATTHIAS   186
       TWICE HAD THE ETERNAL CITY BOWED HER LOW   • • •   465 ALARIC AT ROME   75
       THAT WHILE WE FEEL THE WORLD IS DULL AND LOW   • •   470 ALARIC AT ROME   215
       TO LIE LOW IN DEATH BY THE HAND OF A GOD AND A MORTAL   HOMER TRANS   56

LOWER
       OR AT HIS WORK IN THAT DIM LOWER WORLD   • • • •   198 FRAG ANTIGONE   93
       OF THE LOWER HARTZ AMONG OAKS   • • • • • • •   297 HEINES GRAVE   180

LOWERD
       FOR THAT A SHADOW LOWERD ON THE FIELDS   • • • •   264 THYRSIS   V 44
       A BOAT IS LOWERD FROM HER SIDE   • • • • • • •   276 SOUTHERN NIGHT   33

LOWERING
       LIKE LOWERING CLOUDS THAT AT THE CLOSE OF DAY   • •   478 CROMWELL   215

LOWINGS
       WITH SHORT IMPATIENT LOWINGS THERE HE STOPPD   • •   402 MEROPE   1912

LOYAL
       WHOSE BEACH ONCE RAN WITH LOYAL BLOOD   • • • •   274 STANZAS CARNAC   28
       THEIR LOYAL PASSION TOWRD MY FATHERS HOUSE   • • •   383 MEROPE   1359
       MORE LOYAL AS OUR LINE CONTINUES MORE   • • • •   389 MEROPE   1541

LOYALTY
       WHILE LOYALTY WITH ALL HER SPEED IS SLOW   • • • •   363 MEROPE   963

LUCENT
       THOSE EYES OF DEEP SOFT LUCENT HUE   • • • • •   208 ON THE RHINE   18
       HEAR IT FROM THY BROAD LUCENT ARNO-VALE   • • • •   267 THYRSIS   167

LUCID
       WHAT ELSE IS STEEPD IN LUCID SHEEN   • • • • •   279 SOUTHERN NIGHT   134

LUCIDITY
       HIS SAD LUCIDITY OF SOUL   • • • • • • • • •   58 RESIGNATION   198

LUCRETIUS
       TO ME IT SEEMS AS VAIN LUCRETIUS   • • • • • •   LUCRETIUS 3   1

LULL
       AND THERE ARRIVES A LULL IN THE HOT RACE   • • • •   247 BURIED LIFE   91
       WHEN THE WIND SLUMBERETH IN A SUDDEN LULL   • • •   466 ALARIC AT ROME   98

LULLD
       BEHOLD SHE CRIES SO MANY RAGES LULLD   • • • • •   37 WORLDS TRIUMPHS   5
       SOFT LULLD BY THE RILLS   • • • • • • • • • •   442 EMPEDOCLES II   434

LULLING
       THE SWEET NOTES WHOSE LULLING SPELL   • • • • •   431 EMPEDOCLES II   64

LUMINOUS
       HIS LUMINOUS HOME OF WATERS OPENS BRIGHT   • • • •   87 SOHRAB RUSTUM   890
       SPREAD WIDE AWAY THE LUMINOUS PLAIN   • • • • •   204 CALAIS SANDS   V   6
       AND LUMINOUS VIEW TO GAIN   • • • • • • •   308 OBERMANN   80
       THAT MILD AND LUMINOUS FLOOR OF WATERS LIVES   • •   438 EMPEDOCLES II   315

LUNA
       WHICH LUNA FELT THAT SUMMER-NIGHT   • • • • •   181 ISOLATION MARG   20

LUNAR
       BUT TO THE STARS AND THE COLD LUNAR BEAMS   • • • •   45 IN UTRUMQUE PAR   19

LURD
       LURD HIM STARWARDS TO UPLIFT HIS EYE   • • • • •   483 THEKLAS ANSWER   18

LURE
       TO SPURN MANS COMMON LURE LIFES PLEASANT THINGS   • •   9 MYCERINUS   32
       LURE NOT THEIR CRIES   • • • • • • • • • •   219 BACCHANALIA 1   45

LURED
       FORTH AT NOON HAD LURED ME CREEPING   • • • • • •   26 NEW SIRENS   3

LURED   (CONTINUED)
        OFT AT NOON HAVE LURED ME CREEPING   . . . . . .   26 NEW SIRENS   V   3
        LATE AT EVE HAD LURED ME CREEPING   . . . . . .   26 NEW SIRENS   V   3
        IF SOME FAIR COAST HAVE LURED US TO MAKE STAY   . .   40 HUMAN LIFE   11
        IF SOME FAIR COAST HAS LURED US TO MAKE STAY   . .   40 HUMAN LIFE   V 11
        HAST THOU THEN LURED HITHER   . . . .   188 STRAYED REVEL   76
        I LURED HIM NOT HITHER ULYSSES . . . .   188 STRAYED REVEL   97

LURID
        WENT LURID DOWN OER FLOODED PLAINS   . . . . . .   52 RESIGNATION   11
        AND WHILE THEY GAZED THE SUN WENT LURID DOWN   . .   119 BALDER DEAD 3   194
        HIS FEET TO SEE THE LURID FLOW . . . .   271 MEMORIAL VERSES   31

LURING
        ARE THE ACCENTS OF YOUR LURING . . . .   27 NEW SIRENS   41
        THAT MANS SPIRIT AT ITS LURING . . . .   SECOND BEST   V 23

LURK
        THE HAPPY MOMENT COMES LURK HERE UNSEEN   . . . .   332 MEROPE   67

LURKING
        WHAT ONCE-FAMED WRETCH HE HATH SEEN LURKING THERE   396 MEROPE   V1754

LUSITANIA
        REACHD CAPE VERDE ISLANDS LUSITANIA   . . . . . .   485 S S LUSITANIA   14

LUST
        LUST AVARICE ENVY LIBERATED MAN   . . . . . .   7 REP FRIEND CONT   12
        OF ONE SHORT JOY ONE LUST ONE PLEASANT DREAM   . .   10 MYCERINUS   50
        DEEP WEARINESS AND SATED LUST   . . . .   315 OBERMANN MORE   95
        LUST OF THE EYE AND PRIDE OF LIFE   . . . . . .   317 OBERMANN MORE   133
        OR SELFISH LUST OF PERSONAL POWER   . . . . . .   353 MEROPE   661
        TYRANNY PRIDE AND LUST FILL SICILYS ABODES . . . .   416 EMPEDOCLES I 2   121

LUSTRE
        IN THEIR FLITTING LUSTRE VYING . . . .   131 TRISTRAM 1   27
        THE LUSTRE OF THE EYE   . . . .   212 GROWING OLD   3

LUSTY
        THE HOST AND STILL WAS IN HIS LUSTY PRIME   . . . .   64 SOHRAB RUSTUM   109

LUTE
        THOSE LUTE-LIKE TONES WHICH IN THE BYGONE YEAR   . .   36 VOICE   35
        THOSE LUTE-LIKE TONES WHICH IN LONG DISTANT YEARS   36 VOICE   V 35

LYCAEUS
        THEN TO THE NORTH LYCAEUS AND THE HILLS   . . . .   330 MEROPE   20
        OF LYCAEUS AFAR . . . .   347 MEROPE   519
        O LYCAEUS CONCEALS . . . .   347 MEROPE   V

LYCAON
        WHEN THE SEED OF LYCAON . . . .   391 MEROPE   1603

LYCAONS
        NEAR LYCOSURA BUILDS LYCAONS TOWN   . . . . . .   359 MEROPE   848

LYCOSURA
        NEAR LYCOSURA BUILDS LYCAONS TOWN   . . . . . .   359 MEROPE   848

LYDIAN
        DOWN LYDIAN MOUNTAINS SO WHEN SNOWS   . . . . . .   52 RESIGNATION   7

LYING
        COOL FARMS WITH OPEN-LYING STORES   . . . . . .   54 RESIGNATION   56
        LONE FARMS WITH OPEN-LYING STORES   . . . . . .   54 RESIGNATION   V 56
        THEY SHOULD BE LYING HERE I STANDING THERE . . . .   77 SOHRAB RUSTUM   546
        PITEOUS AND LOVELY LYING ON THE SAND   . . . . . .   80 SOHRAB RUSTUM   633
        MIGHT NOW BE LYING ON THIS BLOODY SAND   . . . .   85 SOHRAB RUSTUM   817
        O VIZIER WITHOUT LYING DOWN   . . . .   88 SICK KING BOKH   15
        AND STOOD BY BALDER LYING ON HIS BIER   . . . . . .   102 BALDER DEAD 1   270
        AND STOOD ROUND BALDER LYING ON HIS BIER   . . . .   102 BALDER DEAD 1   V 270
        THE RINGLETS ON HER SHOULDERS LYING   . . . . . .   131 TRISTRAM 1   26
        THE DORIANS LYING DEAD THY SON HAILD KING   . . . .   402 MEROPE   1942
        THIS POLITIC SOVEREIGN LYING AT OUR FEET   . . . .   403 MEROPE   1965
        POOR MATTHIAS FOUND HIM LYING   . . . .   452 POOR MATTHIAS   1
        NOR MY BRETHRENS MANY AND BRAVE WHO THEN WILL BE LYING   HOMER TRANS   25

LYONESS
        TRISTRAM OF LYONESS   . . . .   131 TRISTRAM 1   23

LYRE
        THE GLORY OF THE LYRE   . . . .   392 MEROPE   1690
        CHAIN MADMEN BY THE MUSIC OF HIS LYRE   . . . .   410 EMPEDOCLES I 1   116
        TELL HIM I NEVER FAILD TO LOVE HIS LYRE   . . . .   428 EMPEDOCLES I 2   468
        THE MUSIC OF THE LYRE BLOWS AWAY   . . . . . .   432 EMPEDOCLES II   123
        THAT TRIUMPH OF THE SWEET PERSUASIVE LYRE   . . . .   432 EMPEDOCLES II   126
        AND APOLLO BROUGHT HIS LYRE   . . . .   433 EMPEDOCLES II   142

LYRES
        THE LYRES VOICE IS LOVELY EVERYWHERE   . . . . . .   430 EMPEDOCLES II   37

MACARIA
    MACARIA BLESSED CHILD • • • • • • • • • • 343 MEROPE   433

MACE
    THE GOLDEN MACE-BEARERS ASIDE • • • • • • • • 88 SICK KING BOKH   34

MACEDON
    WHO CARRIED THE GREAT WAR FROM MACEDON • • • • 154 TRISTRAM 3   148

MACHINE
    THE SECRETS OF THE WORLDS MACHINE • • • • • • 48 HORATIAN ECHO   16

MAD
    LEANS HER EAR TO YOUR MAD SALLIES • • • • • • 27 NEW SIRENS   27
    MAD DELIGHT AND FROZEN CALMS • • • • • • • 33 NEW SIRENS   196
    LINKING IN A MAD SUCCESSION • • • • • • • • 33 NEW SIRENS   205
    OF MAD DELIGHT THEY DROP THEIR SPOILS AND BOUND • • 150 TRISTRAM 3   27
    SO LATE SUCH STORMS THE SAINT IS MAD • • • • 156 SAINT BRANDAN   4
    IN THE RUSHING THUNDERING MAD • • • • • • 370 MEROPE   1105
    THAT MAD BEWILDERMENT OF GRIEF IS THIS • • • • 396 MEROPE   1758
    BUT IF AS MOST MEN SAY HE IS HALF MAD • • • • 407 EMPEDOCLES I 1   23

M CAP
    MADCAP WHAT JEST WAS THIS TO MEET ME HERE • • • • 135 TRISTRAM 1   162

MADCAPS
    AH TIRED MADCAPS YOU LIE STILL • • • • • • • • 141 TRISTRAM 1   351

MADDEN
    THAT MOUNT THAT MADDEN HOW OFT • • • • • • • 296 HEINES GRAVE   147

MADDENING
    THEY TOO THE MADDENING WINE • • • • • • • 192 STRAYED REVEL   225
    MADDENING THEIR BLOOD • • • • • • • • • 218 BACCHANALIA 1   31

MADE
    WAS NEW MADE TO BREAK AGAIN • • • • • • • 23 MEMORY-PICTURE   38
    AND MADE ALL YOUR CEDARS FROWN • • • • • • • 30 NEW SIRENS   124
    MADE MY TOST HEART ITS VERY LIFE-BLOOD SPILL • • 36 VOICE   39
    HATH MADE OR BIRTH HATH FOUND RESIGND • • • • 53 RESIGNATION   27
    PARCHD AND ROAD-WORN WE MADE THAT DAY • • • • 54 RESIGNATION   81
    OF THESE AFFECTIONS WIDER MADE • • • • • • • 58 RESIGNATION   219
    HE SPOKE AND SMILED AND GUDURZ MADE REPLY • • • 68 SOHRAB RUSTUM   242
    AND GREATLY MOVED THEN RUSTUM MADE REPLY • • • 68 SOHRAB RUSTUM   249
    HAVING MADE UP HIS TALE OF PRECIOUS PEARLS • • • 69 SOHRAB RUSTUM   288
    I AM NO GIRL TO BE MADE PALE BY WORDS • • • • 72 SOHRAB RUSTUM   381
    HATH MADE IN HIMALAYAN FORESTS WRACK • • • • • 73 SOHRAB RUSTUM   414
    WHICH TROUBLES ALL MY HEART AND MADE MY SHIELD • • 77 SOHRAB RUSTUM   549
    HAS MADE IN HIMALAYAN FORESTS WRACK • • • • • 73 SOHRAB RUSTUM V 414
    ONE MAN IS NOT WELL MADE TO BEAR • • • • • 92 SICK KING BOKH   154
    ARE IN THEIR TURN OBEDIENT MADE • • • • • • 93 SICK KING BOKH   188
    NOT TO LAMENT IN WAS VALHALLA MADE • • • • • 95 BALDER DEAD 1   19
    MADE FAST THE WOVEN ROPES AND HALED THEM DOWN • • 106 BALDER DEAD 2   58
    AND MADE HIM LEAP THE GRATE AND CAME WITHIN • • 109 BALDER DEAD 2   148
    MADE FAST TO THE BORED CRAG BY WILE NOT STRENGTH • • 111 BALDER DEAD 2   215
    AND THE FLEET-FOOTED HERMOD MADE REPLY • • • 126 BALDER DEAD 3   468
    WERE FEET LIKE THOSE MADE FOR SO WILD A WAY • • 135 TRISTRAM 1   163
    WHAT HAS SOME GLAMOUR MADE ME SLEEP • • • • 148 TRISTRAM 2   175
    HAS THEN SOME GLAMOUR MADE HIM SLEEP • • • • 148 TRISTRAM 2 V 175
    THREE HOLLIES SIDE BY SIDE AND MADE A SCREEN • • 150 TRISTRAM 3   20
    WHO MADE A NAME AT YOUNGER YEARS THAN HE • • 153 TRISTRAM 3   145
    AND MADE A LITTLE PLOT OF MAGIC GROUND • • • 156 TRISTRAM 3   220
    WHAT MADE MY HEART AT NEWSTEAD FULLEST SWELL • • 166 PICT NEWSTEAD   1
    METHINKS THE WOE WHICH MADE THAT FATHER STAND • • 167 PICT NEWSTEAD   12
    TWAS DAWN A BROUGHAM ROLLD THROUGH THE STREETS 167 RACHEL 1   4
          AND MADE
    SHE HAD ONE POWER WHICH MADE HER BREAST ITS HOME • • 168 RACHEL 3   10
    FOR GOD OF THESE HIS ATTRIBUTES IS MADE • • • 171 DIVINITY   5
    BE MADE LIKE LONDON WHERE PAUPERS • • • • • 214 NEW ROME V 13
    THE FLIES A SUMMER-MURMUR MADE • • • • • • • 222 EPILOG LAOCOON   41
    LIGHT-PLASHING WAVES AN ANSWER MADE • • • • • 223 EPILOG LAOCOON   68
    NOR NO MUSICIAN MADE AS THEY • • • • • • • 227 EPILOG LAOCOON   202
    FILLD HIM AND MADE HIM DIVINE • • • • • • • 231 YOUTH OF NATURE   98
    AND MAN HAS TURND THEM MANY TIMES MADE GREECE • • 239 REVOLUTIONS   5
    THE LETTERS HAVE COMBINED SOMETHING WAS MADE • • 239 REVOLUTIONS   8
    HAUNTS HIM THAT HE HAS NOT MADE WHAT HE SHOULD • • 239 REVOLUTIONS   10
    OFT MADE THEE IN THY GLOOM DESPAIR • • • • • 241 MORALITY   18
    AND LIVED ITSELF AND MADE US LIVE • • • • • 251 WISH   40
    AND THY CLEAR AIMS BE CROSS AND SHIFTING MADE • • 261 SCHOLAR-GIPSY   228
    AND WITH THE COUNTRY-FOLK ACQUAINTANCE MADE • • 263 THYRSIS   33
    HE KNEW WHICH MADE HIM DROOP AND FILLD HIS HEAD • • 264 THYRSIS   47
    WHO MADE THE ROOTS OF TREES HIS BED • • • • 277 SOUTHERN NIGHT   79
    LASHES THE NEWLY-MADE GRAVE • • • • • • • 286 HAWORTH CHURCH   133
    HAVOC IS MADE IN OUR TRAIN • • • • • • • 289 RUGBY CHAPEL   101
    MADE IT A RAY OF THY THOUGHT • • • • • • • 299 HEINES GRAVE   231
    MADE IT A BEAT OF THY JOY • • • • • • • 299 HEINES GRAVE   232
    AND EUROPE MADE HIS WOE HER OWN • • • • • • 303 GRANDE CHARTR   138
    NEITHER MADE MAN TOO MUCH A GOD • • • • • • 308 OBERMANN   59
    MADE HIS LIFES RULE ONCE MORE • • • • • • • 314 OBERMANN MORE   54
    MADE HUMAN LIFE A HELL • • • • • • • • 315 OBERMANN MORE   96

MADE   (CONTINUED)
        HE MADE A FEAST DRANK FIERCE AND FAST   •   •   •   •   316 OBERMANN MORE   101
        HOPE TO A WORLD NEW-MADE •   •   •   •   •   •   •   •   323 OBERMANN MORE   312
        HOPE TO A WORLD RE-MADE •   •   •   •   •   •   •   • V 323 OBERMANN MORE   V 312
        O STENYCLAROS WHICH HE BUILT AND MADE   •   •   •   •   330 MEROPE   10
        OUR JOURNEY IS WELL MADE THE WORK REMAINS   •   •   •   •   330 MEROPE   24
        WHICH TO PERFORM WE MADE IT MEANS FOR THAT   •   •   •   330 MEROPE   25
        WHO MADE THAT TRIUMPH THOUGH DEFERRD SECURE   •   •   336 MEROPE   220
        FOR DEATH HIS ANCIENT TO HIS NEW-MADE FRIENDS   •   •   •   338 MEROPE   265
        DISCOVERY OF A VISIT MADE BY STEALTH   •   •   •   •   351 MEROPE   605
        THEIR CHIEF HATH TRAIND THEM MADE THEM LIKE HIMSELF   •   381 MEROPE   1303
        AND THOU MY MOTHER HADST THOU MADE A SIGN   •   •   •   383 MEROPE   1368
        THE GODS HAD PITY MADE THEM STARS   •   •   •   •   393 MEROPE   1674
        NOT MENS GOOD WORD HATH MADE ME WHAT I AM   •   •   •   398 MEROPE   1791
        A NEW-MADE WIFE I FROM ARCADIA CAME   •   •   •   •   403 MEROPE   1972
        AND HE MADE ANSWER I SHOULD COME AT NIGHT   •   •   •   410 EMPEDOCLES I 1   128
        A NEW-MADE WORLD UP-SPRINGS   •   •   •   •   •   •   418 EMPEDOCLES I 2   179
        OUR WANTS HAVE ALL BEEN FELT OUR ERRORS MADE BEFORE   419 EMPEDOCLES I 2   211
        AND WHAT WE MADE TO CURSE   •   •   •   •   •   •   •   422 EMPEDOCLES I 2   314
        HOW OUR OWN MINDS ARE MADE   •   •   •   •   •   •   423 EMPEDOCLES I 2   328
        IMMORTAL HAD I MADE THIS BOY OF MINE   •   •   •   •   447 WESTMIN ABBEY   105
        WHO FOR THEMSELVES A MONUMENT HAVE MADE   •   •   •   462 ALARIC AT ROME   10
        MADE ROUGH WITH CARE BECOME THE CHANGEFUL SEA   •   •   473 CROMWELL   49
        MADE VOID AND HELD THE SORROW AND THE JOY   •   •   •   RUDE ORATOR   4

MADEST
        THOU SENTST AND FETCHEDST FIRE AND MADEST LIGHTS   •   •   121 BALDER DEAD 3   263

MADHOUSE
        NOT IN THAT MADHOUSE FRANCE FROM WHENCE THE CRY   •   •   480 HUNGARIAN NAT   4

MADLY
        SPEND AS MADLY AS YOU MAY   •   •   •   •   •   •   22 MEMORY-PICTURE   4
        AND THE WORLDS SO MADLY JANGLED   •   •   •   •   •   49 SECOND BEST   9
        MADLY BELOW IN THE PLAIN •   •   •   •   •   •   •   •   216 LORDS MESSENGER   V

MADMAN
        IT IS SOME MADMAN THE KING SAID   •   •   •   •   •   90 SICK KING BOKH   91
        MADMAN OR SLAVE MUST MAN BE ONE   •   •   •   •   •   244 SUMMER NIGHT   75

MADMEN
        CHAIN MADMEN BY THE MUSIC OF HIS LYRE   •   •   •   •   410 EMPEDOCLES I 1   116

MADST
        THEN ME THOU MADST OF US THE GODS WERE BORN   •   •   121 BALDER DEAD 3   267

MAEANDERS
        WHERE MAEANDERS SPRINGS ARE BORN   •   •   •   •   •   433 EMPEDOCLES II   136

MAENAD
        SOMETIMES A WILD-HAIRD MAENAD   •   •   •   •   •   •   194 STRAYED REVEL   275

MAENADS
        SEE THE WILD MAENADS   •   •   •   •   •   •   •   •   218 BACCHANALIA 1   28
        BUT THE MAENADS WHO WERE THERE   •   •   •   •   •   •   433 EMPEDOCLES II   151

MAENALUS
        WHITHER FROM WINTRY MAENALUS WERE BROUGHT   •   •   •   356 MEROPE   741

MAGIC
        THIS FAR-REACHING MAGIC CHAIN   •   •   •   •   •   •   33 NEW SIRENS   204
        WITH TRISTRAM THAT SPICED MAGIC DRAUGHT   •   •   •   132 TRISTRAM 1   64
        AND MADE A LITTLE PLOT OF MAGIC GROUND   •   •   •   156 TRISTRAM 3   220
        EVER NEW MAGIC   •   •   •   •   •   •   •   •   •   188 STRAYED REVEL   75
        THE MAGIC OF THE UNIVERSE   •   •   •   •   •   •   202 URANIA   24
        LOVELINESS MAGIC AND GRACE   •   •   •   •   •   •   230 YOUTH OF NATURE   79
        LOVELINESS MAGIC GRACE   •   •   •   •   •   •   •   230 YOUTH OF NATURE   V 79
        ALL THE FOOLS-ARMOURY OF MAGIC LIE THERE   •   •   •   432 EMPEDOCLES II   118

MAIA
        AND MAIA REARD HIM •   •   •   •   •   •   •   •   •   •   •   392 MEROPE   1621

MAID
        TRULY I HEAR OF A MAID   •   •   •   •   •   •   •   •   •   343 MEROPE   425

MAIDENS
        PLUCK PLUCK CYPRESS O PALE MAIDENS   •   •   •   •   30 NEW SIRENS   113
        PLUCK NO MORE RED ROSES MAIDENS   •   •   •   •   •   35 NEW SIRENS   267
        PLUCK PLUCK CYPRESS O PALE MAIDENS   •   •   •   •   35 NEW SIRENS   269
        PLUCK PLUCK CYPRESS O PALE MAIDENS   •   •   •   •   35 NEW SIRENS   275
        STREW NO MORE RED ROSES MAIDENS   •   •   •   •   •   35 NEW SIRENS   V 267
        SPINNING WITH HER MAIDENS HERE •   •   •   •   •   •   131 TRISTRAM 1   40
        MAIDENS WHO FROM THE DISTANT HAMLETS COME   •   •   •   257 SCHOLAR-GIPSY   82
        SAD-CHANTING MAIDENS CLAD IN MOURNING ROBES   •   •   331 MEROPE   53
        SET DOWN YOUR PITCHERS MAIDENS AND FALL BACK   •   •   332 MEROPE   76
        WHO CAN EXTEND THEIR HANDS MAIDENS TAKE BACK   •   •   336 MEROPE   195
        NOT SO LET THESE MESSENIAN MAIDENS MARK   •   •   •   336 MEROPE   197
        FORGIVE ME MAIDENS IF I SEEM TOO SLACK   •   •   •   348 MEROPE   548
        MAIDENS ASSURE ME IF THEY TOLD ME TRUE   •   •   •   •   354 MEROPE   703
        ADMIRE THEN MAIDENS HOW IN ONE SHORT HOUR   •   •   •   360 MEROPE   875

MAIDENS   (CONTINUED)
        WITH DANCING MAIDENS AND BOYS . . . .   360 MEROPE   898
        HOW SAY YE MAIDENS DO YE KNOW THESE PRAYERS   . .   368 MEROPE   1067
        BUT WHO ARE THESE MESSENIAN MAIDENS FRIENDS   . .   375 MEROPE   1210
        O KIND MESSENIAN MAIDENS O MY FRIENDS   . . . .   377 MEROPE   1222
        MAIDENS AND READS EXPERIENCE MUCH AMISS . . . .   382 MEROPE   1334

MAIL
        DRY THEIR MAIL AND BASK IN THE BRINE . . . . . .   162 FORSAKEN MERM   42

MAILD
        WHOSE FIERY POINT NOW IN HIS MAILD RIGHT-HAND   . .   74 SOHRAB RUSTUM   451
        BEHOLD THE STERN MAILD FATHER STAFF IN HAND   . .   167 PICT NEWSTEAD   9
        THE SURGING BATTLE AND THE MAILD ARRAY   . . . .   475 CROMWELL   138

MAILED
        AGAINST HIS BREAST HIS HEAVY MAILED HAND   . . . .   80 SOHRAB RUSTUM   663

MAIMS
        THAT HOUSE LIKE OURS INTESTINE MURDER MAIMS   . .   384 MEROPE   1392

MAIN
        OF TORN-UP WATER ON THE MAIN   . . . .   40 HUMAN LIFE   20
        AND SHOWS ITS LIGHTED WINDOWS TO THE MAIN . . . .   97 BALDER DEAD 1   86
        FLYING OER THE STORMY MAIN   . . . .   136 TRISTRAM 1   188
        SAINT BRANDAN SAILS THE NORTHERN MAIN   . . . .   156 SAINT BRANDAN   1
        HE ENTERS NOT THE ATLANTIC MAIN   . . . . . .   275 STANZAS CARNAC   40
        DOWN TO THE BRIMMD MOON-CHARMED MAIN   . . . . .   279 SOUTHERN NIGHT   118
        OR THE HOWLING OUTERMOST MAIN . . . .   361 MEROPE   913
        WITH WHAT ROLLD OF US IN THE STORMY MAIN   . . . .   439 EMPEDOCLES II   342
        OF GIANT MOUNTAINS BY THE WESTERN MAIN   . . . .   475 CROMWELL   105
        AND THE ARMADA FLUNG TO THE FIERCE MAIN   . . . .   481 HUNGARIAN NAT   14
        TO THE GREAT MAIN PASSD SEVILLE ON THE RIGHT   . .   484 S S LUSITANIA   4

MAINTAIN
        MY SISTER TO MAINTAIN WITH THEE   . . . . . .   180 FAREWELL   78
        TILL THEN HER LOVELY EYES MAINTAIN   . . . . . .   202 URANIA   31
        SINCE SO THOU WILT I DARE MAINTAIN IT STILL   . .   398 MEROPE   1793
        NATURAL VENGEANCE MAY MAINTAIN THINE ACT   . . . .   404 MEROPE   1998
        SINCE SO THOU WILT I WILL MAINTAIN IT STILL   . .   398 MEROPE   V1793
        MAY WHAT IS FALSE MAINTAIN   . . . .   419 EMPEDOCLES I 2   V 203
        TO MAINTAIN THE CASPIAN FREE   . . . .   PILLARS UNIVERS   7

MAINTAIND
        ENOUGH OF THIS SINCE THAT I HAVE MAINTAIND   . . . .   334 MEROPE   134
        BE THEIR FIRST-FOUNDED ORDER STRICT MAINTAIND   . .   390 MEROPE   1565
        ENOUGH OF THIS SINCE THEN I HAVE MAINTAIND   . . . .   334 MEROPE   V 134
        IF THEIR FIRST-FOUNDED ORDER BE MAINTAIND   . . . .   390 MEROPE   V1565
        MAINTAIND COURAGE AND FORCE AND IN MYSELF   . . . .   438 EMPEDOCLES II   319

MAJESTIC
        CENTRED IN A MAJESTIC UNITY   . . . .   4 BUTLERS SERMONS   8
        WITH A SAD MAJESTIC MOTION   . . . .   31 NEW SIRENS   155
        BUT THE MAJESTIC RIVER FLOATED ON   . . . . . .   86 SOHRAB RUSTUM   875
        THE STREAM OF LIFES MAJESTIC WHOLE   . . . . . .   226 EPILOG LAOCOON   187
        ITS SOMBRE ASPECT OF MAJESTIC CARE   . . . . . .   403 MEROPE   1968
        HIS MOTHER MOST MAJESTIC DAME . . . .   459 KAISER DEAD   19
        BURSTS IN MAJESTIC BEAUTY ON HER CONQUERORS EYES . .   468 ALARIC AT ROME   156
        WHAT SPRING OF YOUTH IN THAT MAJESTIC MIEN   . . . .   477 CROMWELL   185

MAJESTY
        WHO TO THE STARS UNCROWNS HIS MAJESTY   . . . .   2 SHAKESPEARE   4
        THAT TO THE STARS UNCROWNS HIS MAJESTY   . . . .   2 SHAKESPEARE   V   4
        AND WEAR THIS MAJESTY OF GRIEF AGAIN . . . . . .   44 GIPSY CHILD   68
        IN HIS SEVERE LOOKS SUCH A MAJESTY   . . . . . .   408 EMPEDOCLES I 1   62
        AND MAJESTY AND SACRED FORM AND FEAR   . . . . .   445 WESTMIN ABBEY   58

MAKE
        BUSINESS COULD NOT MAKE DULL NOR PASSION WILD   . .   2 TO A FRIEND   11
        TO MAKE THE INCURIOUS BYSTANDER INTENT   . . . .   8 RELIGIOUS ISOL   3
        LET ME PAUSE LET ME STRIVE IN MYSELF MAKE SOME ORDER   19 MODERN SAPPHO   7
        AH LET US MAKE NO CLAIM   . . . .   40 HUMAN LIFE   7
        IF SOME FAIR COAST HAVE LURED US TO MAKE STAY   . .   40 HUMAN LIFE   11
        IF SOME FAIR COAST HAS LURED US TO MAKE STAY   . .   40 HUMAN LIFE   V   11
        MAKE WHISTLING TOWRD HIS MIST-WREATHED FLOCK   . .   57 RESIGNATION   183
        MAKE WHISTLING TOWARDS HIS MIST-WREATHED FLOCK   . .   57 RESIGNATION   V 183
        BY CHALLENGE FORTH MAKE GOOD THY VAUNT OR YIELD . .   72 SOHRAB RUSTUM   367
        WE KNOW NOT AND NO SEARCH WILL MAKE US KNOW   . .   73 SOHRAB RUSTUM   396
        AND MAKE A TRUCE AND SIT UPON THIS SAND . . . .   74 SOHRAB RUSTUM   440
        OF BATTLE AND WITH ME WHO MAKE NO PLAY   . . . .   75 SOHRAB RUSTUM   463
        MAKE OFTEN IN THE FORESTS HEART AT MORN . . . .   75 SOHRAB RUSTUM   477
        AND PIERCE HIM LIKE A STAB AND MAKE HIM LEAP   . .   78 SOHRAB RUSTUM   584
        MAKE OFTEN IN THE FORESTS DEPTH AT MORN . . . .   75 SOHRAB RUSTUM   V 477
        LET HUSSEIN IF THOU WILT MAKE HASTE . . . . . .   88 SICK KING BOKH   27
        SEND HIM AWAY SIRS AND MAKE ON . . . .   90 SICK KING BOKH   90
        WHY FOR NO CAUSE MAKE SAD THY FACE   . . . . . .   92 SICK KING BOKH   142
        WHILST OTHER MEN MAKE CHEER AND SING . . . . . .   93 SICK KING BOKH   178
        AND TO MAKE ORCHARD-CLOSES FILLD   . . . . . .   94 SICK KING BOKH   200
        AND MAKE EXCHANGE AND GIVE MY LIFE FOR HIS   . . .   98 BALDER DEAD 1   110
        AND MAKE HIM LEAP THE GRATE AND COME WITHIN   . .   100 BALDER DEAD 1   170

MAKE   (CONTINUED)

AND MAKE HER YIELD AND GIVE HIM BALDER BACK		100 BALDER DEAD 1	183
AND MAKE A FUNERAL-PILE ON BALDERS SHIP	• • • •	106 BALDER DEAD 2	43
DO THE GODS SEND TO ME TO MAKE THEM BLEST	• • • •	110 BALDER DEAD 2	204
SHOULD MAKE IRRUPTION INTO HELAS REALM	• •	120 BALDER DEAD 3	242
MAKE TOWARD THEM OER THE STRETCHING CLOUDY PLAIN	• •	126 BALDER DEAD 3	443
SOMETHING TOO MUCH OF WAR AND BROILS WHICH MAKE	• •	128 BALDER DEAD 3	505
MAKE TOWARDS THEM OER THE STRETCHING CLOUDY PLAIN		126 BALDER DEAD 3	V 443
THAT WAS BLISS TO MAKE MY SORROWS FLEE	• • •	144 TRISTRAM 2	46
THOSE WERE FRIENDS TO MAKE ME FALSE TO THEE	• •	144 TRISTRAM 2	48
ROUSE NO ANGER MAKE NO RIVALS MORE	• • • •	144 TRISTRAM 2	64
GRIEF SINCE THEN HIS HOME WITH ME DOTH MAKE	• •	145 TRISTRAM 2	88
TO MAKE OUR FORMER PLEASURES ALL SEEM STALE	• •	153 TRISTRAM 3	126
THIS TOO CAN CHANGE US WHOLLY AND MAKE SEEM	• •	153 TRISTRAM 3	131
AGAIN I SPRING TO MAKE MY CHOICE	• • • •	174 MEETING	9
THIS TRUTH TO PROVE AND MAKE THINE OWN	• • •	181 ISOLATION MARG	29
MAKE THEIR SKIFF REEL AND WORMS	• • • •	193 STRAYED REVEL	237
MUST VISIT FIRST THEM TOO AND MAKE THEM PALE	• •	193 STRAYED REVEL	246
FOR SHE DESIRED TO MAKE		197 FRAG ANTIGONE	71
ONCE MORE AND ONCE MORE SEEM TO MAKE RESOUND	• •	201 PHILOMELA	25
THE WORLD TO THEM MAY HOMAGE MAKE	• • • •	203 EUPHROSYNE	17
SHE SMILES ELSEWHERE WE MAKE A DIN	• • •	204 EUPHROSYNE	V
BARDS MAKE NEW POEMS	• • • •	220 BACCHANALIA 2	37
BUT CLEAR AS WORDS CAN MAKE REVEALING	• • •	225 EPILOG LAOCOON	137
WHAT POETS FEEL NOT WHEN THEY MAKE	• • •	228 CAUTION POETS	1
YE EXPRESS NOT YOURSELVES CAN YOU MAKE	• • •	231 YOUTH OF NATURE	107
YE EXPRESS NOT YOURSELVES CAN YE MAKE	• • •	231 YOUTH OF NATURE	V 107
MAKE OH MAKE YOURSELVES FELT	• • • • •	234 YOUTH OF MAN	54
MAKE OH MAKE YOURSELVES FELT	• • • • •	234 YOUTH OF MAN	54
HERE LET THAT VOICE MAKE END THEN LET A STRAIN	•	238 PROGRESS	33
AND BADE HIM MAKE WITH THEM WHAT WORD HE COULD	•	239 REVOLUTIONS	4
STILL BENT TO MAKE SOME PORT HE KNOWS NOT WHERE	•	244 SUMMER NIGHT	68
BIRDS HERE MAKE SONG EACH BIRD HAS HIS	• • •	248 KENSINGTON GARD	5
CALM SOUL OF ALL THINGS MAKE IT MINE	• • •	249 KENSINGTON GARD	37
MAN DID NOT MAKE AND CANNOT MAR	• • • •	249 KENSINGTON GARD	40
AND MAKE LEAP UP WITH JOY THE BEAUTEOUS HEAD	• •	265 THYRSIS	87
BUT ALL OUR HUSTLING MORROWS ONLY MAKE	• • •	262 THYRSIS	V
BUT WHO AH WHO WILL MAKE US FEEL	• • •	272 MEMORIAL VERSES	67
THEY TRY US OFTENEST MAKE US HARD	• • • •	273 EDW QUILLINAN	7
SHEEP MAKE THE DAISIED AISLES THEIR FOLD	• • •	274 STANZAS CARNAC	16
SHEEP MAKE THE FURZE-GROWN AISLES THEIR FOLD	•	274 STANZAS CARNAC	V 16
SHEEP MAKE THE FURZE-GROWN NAVE THEIR FOLD	• •	STANZAS CARNAC	V 16
BLUSTER OR CRINGE AND MAKE LIFE	• • • •	290 RUGBY CHAPEL	157
MAKE THEIR BLOOD DANCE AND CHAIN THEIR EYES	• •	305 GRANDE CHARTR	188
SEE I MAKE ALL THINGS NEW	• • • • •	320 OBERMANN MORE	232
DID MAKE FROM HAUNTS OF STRIFE	• • • •	322 OBERMANN MORE	274
AND ON THIS SIDE THOSE CONFLUENT STREAMS WHICH MAKE		330 MEROPE	18
FOR TYRANTS MAKE MAN GOOD BEYOND HIMSELF	• •	331 MEROPE	42
HER BLOOD THAT SO SHE MIGHT MAKE	• • • •	343 MEROPE	427
MY WORDS BELOW TO THEE AND MAKE THEE HEAR	• •	350 MEROPE	586
OF WHAT IT LIES WITH THEM TO MAKE RISK NONE	• •	350 MEROPE	604
WHY DOST THOU FALTER AND MAKE HALF REPLY	• • •	362 MEROPE	930
IF FOLLOWD MAKE THEIR SUCCOUR SLACK AND NULL	• •	382 MEROPE	1338
KINDLE THEIR HEARTS MAKE THEM NO MORE A MOB	• •	383 MEROPE	1360
THY CRIME THAT WERE ENOUGH TO MAKE ONE FEAR	• •	396 MEROPE	1767
NOR BEND MYSELF TOO LOW TO MAKE IT YIELD	• • •	398 MEROPE	1786
MAKE JUSTICE ALTER	• • • • • • •	398 MEROPE	1806
TO MAKE THE GATES OF THIS LONG-MOURNFUL HOUSE	•	401 MEROPE	1884
BUT THOU MY SON STUDY TO MAKE PREVAIL	• • •	404 MEROPE	1995
AND MAKE IT STAND INDEED THE WILL OF HEAVEN	• •	404 MEROPE	1999
SIT AND MAKE READY THE SERPENT THE SCOURGE	• •	347 MEROPE	V 531
ELECTRIFY THEIR HEARTS MAKE THEM NO MORE A MOB	•	383 MEROPE	V1360
ALL STRIVE TO MAKE IT LESS	• • • • • •	416 EMPEDOCLES I 2	120
SIGNS MAKE THY SOUL AFRAID	• • • • •	416 EMPEDOCLES I 2	123
FOR MAN WOULD MAKE NO MURMURING WERE HIS WILL OBEYD		417 EMPEDOCLES I 2	151
AND FOR HIMSELF MAKE MISTS	• • • • •	419 EMPEDOCLES I 2	204
THE ILL DEEDS OF OTHER MEN MAKE OFTEN OUR LIFE DARK		421 EMPEDOCLES I 2	266
MAKE GODS TO WHOM TO IMPUTE	• • • • •	421 EMPEDOCLES I 2	279
STERN POWERS WHO MAKE THEIR CARE	• • • •	422 EMPEDOCLES I 2	310
I THINK MIGHT MAKE US FEAR	• • • • •	425 EMPEDOCLES I 2	384
MAKE US NOT FLY TO DREAMS BUT MODERATE DESIRE	•	425 EMPEDOCLES I 2	386
FAIL TO MAKE BLEST THY STATE	• • • • •	426 EMPEDOCLES I 2	420
TO MAKE HIM LAUGH OR WEEP	•	EMPEDOCLES I 2	V
WILL MAKE OURSELVES HARDER TO BE DISCERND	• • •	440 EMPEDOCLES II	381
WHICH MAKE ME FOR THY PRESENCE YEARN	• • •	450 GEISTS GRAVE	6
AND RUB THE STEEL AND MAKE IT SHINE	• • •	461 KAISER DEAD	80
THAT ALL NIGHT LONG ITS WEARY MOAN DOTH MAKE	•	477 CROMWELL	191
NOT IN RICH ENGLAND BENT BUT TO MAKE POUR	• •	480 HUNGARIAN NAT	2
AND MAKE THE WORLDS DEAD SPIRIT LEAP AGAIN	• •	481 HUNGARIAN NAT	11
MAKE CESSION OF HER SCEPTRE DOOM HERSELF	• •	RUDE ORATOR	19
THESE THESE ARE PANGS WHICH MAKE THE MIND A HELL	•	LUCRETIUS 2	16
NEITHER HIS MIND NOR BODY DID HE MAKE	• •	LUCRETIUS 3	5
TO THE BLIND SLAVES OF POWER TO MAKE IT KNOWN	• •	FRAGMENT 2	3

MAKES

IS IT HOPE MAKES ME LINGER THE DIM THOUGHT THAT SORROW		19 MODERN SAPPHO	V
MAKES IDOLS TO ADORE	• • • • • • • • •	39 STAGIRIUS	23
MAKES CLEAR OUR GOAL TO EVERY EYE	• • • • •	53 RESIGNATION	46
WHO WITH NUMB BLACKEND FINGERS MAKES HER FIRE	• •	70 SOHRAB RUSTUM	304
MAKES THE HEAD WHITE AND BOWS THE KNEES	• • • •	92 SICK KING BOKH	152

MAKES   (CONTINUED)
          A CHARRD LOG FALLING MAKES A SHOWER OF SPARKS   • • 119 BALDER DEAD 3   204
          OF PORT THEY HAD MAKES BITTERER FAR THEIR TOIL   • • 124 BALDER DEAD 3   367
          HIS SHIP AND THE GREAT SERPENT MAKES TO LAND   • • 127 BALDER DEAD 3   479
          MAKES THEIR CHAMBER AS BRIGHT AS DAY • • • •   • • 140 TRISTRAM 1   334
          IS IT THIS THOUGHT WHICH MAKES HER MIEN SO STILL   • • 151 TRISTRAM 3   69
          IS IT THIS THOUGHT THAT MAKES HER MIEN SO STILL   • • 151 TRISTRAM 3   V   69
          HE TETHERS HIS BEAST DOWN AND MAKES HIS MEAL   • • 191 STRAYED REVEL   165
          HE MAKES HIS MEAL BEFORE HIM FOR LONG MILES   • • 191 STRAYED REVEL   172
          MAKES HIS OWN WELFARE HIS UNSWERVED—FROM LAW   • • 195 FRAG ANTIGONE   8
          BESIDES WHAT WASTE HE MAKES   • • • • • •   • • 195 FRAG ANTIGONE   24
          REVELATION MAKES HIM SURE   • • • • • • •   • • 215 PIS—ALLER   2
          POOR BOUNDED WORDS AND MAKES THEM NEW   • • •   • • 224 EPILOG LAOCOON   96
          INFINITE MAKES THEM MAKES THEM YOUNG • • • •   • • 224 EPILOG LAOCOON   97
          INFINITE MAKES THEM MAKES THEM YOUNG • • • •   • • 224 EPILOG LAOCOON   97
          FOR EVER MAKES THEIR EAR REJOICE   • • • • •   • • 227 EPILOG LAOCOON   196
          WHICH MAKES MANS GREATEST WOE   • • • • • •   • • 238 PROGRESS   V
          ALL WHICH MAKES DEATH A HIDEOUS SHOW • • • •   • • 250 WISH   16
          ALL THAT MAKES DEATH A HIDEOUS SHOW   • • • •   • • 250 WISH   V 16
          HOW CHANGED IS HERE EACH SPOT MAN MAKES OR FILLS   • • 262 THYRSIS   1
          CHARM IS THE GLORY WHICH MAKES • • • • • •   • • 295 HEINES GRAVE   103
          WHAT BLACK PROCESSION SLOWLY MAKES APPROACH   • • 331 MEROPE   52
          THAT HE TO POWER MAKES WAY BY ARMS   • • • •   • • 353 MEROPE   681
          MY DEATH MAKES MY DEBT VOID AND DOUBLES THINE   • • 367 MEROPE   1049
          ZEAL MAKES HIM MOST UNJUST BUT IN GOOD TIME   • • 386 MEROPE   1438
          THOUGH IT EFFACE NOT THAT YET MAKES ME WISH   • • 387 MEROPE   1479
          WHICH MAKES THE TIME LOOK BLACK AND SAD TO HIM   • • 411 EMPEDOCLES I 1   153
          WHICH MAKES THE TIMES LOOK BLACK AND SAD TO HIM   • • 411 EMPEDOCLES I 1 V 153
          WHAT MAKES THEE STRUGGLE AND RAVE • • • • •   • • 417 EMPEDOCLES I 2   147
          TIS THAT HE MAKES THIS WILL   • • • • • •   • • 417 EMPEDOCLES I 2   154
          ABANDONS ALL WHICH MAKES • • • • • • • •   • • 420 EMPEDOCLES I 2   244
          ABANDONS ALL THAT MAKES   • • • • • • • •   • • 420 EMPEDOCLES I 2 V 244
          AND MAKES THE MASSD CLOUDS ROLL   • • • • •   • • 432 EMPEDOCLES II   122
          AND MAKES THY VERY RUIN FRESH AND BEAUTIFUL   • • 464 ALARIC AT ROME   54

MAKING
          MAKING THE HEAVEN OF HEAVENS HIS DWELLING—PLACE   • •   3 SHAKESPEARE   6
          OUR HANDS IN SOLEMN UNION MAKING FRIENDS   • • • • 335 MEROPE   165
          MAKING WANT OF THEIRS AND PLAN • • • • • •   • • 456 POOR MATTHIAS   151

MAKST
          THOU MAKST THE HEAVEN THOU HOPST INDEED THY HOME   • • 169 EAST LONDON   14
          THOU NOTHING PROFITEST THY FRIENDS BUT MAKST   • • 368 MEROPE   1080

MALATRAIT
          OF MALATRAIT TO WHERE IN HAZE • • • • • •   • • 324 OBERMANN MORE   339

MALIAC
          AND THE ROUSED MALIAC GULPH   • • • • • •   • • 198 FRAG ANTIGONE   101

MALIGN
          WHAT THEN SO HARSH AND MALIGN • • • • • •   • • 294 HEINES GRAVE   67
          WHAT SO HARSH AND MALIGN • • • • • • • •   • • 294 HEINES GRAVE   V   67

MALIGNANT
          TO EMBITTER HUMAN LIFE MALIGNANT DEITIES   • • • • 422 EMPEDOCLES I 2   311

MALIGNER
          OR WHETHER BY MALIGNER FATE   • • • • • •   • • 311 OBERMANN   175

MAN
          LABOURERS THAT SHALL NOT FAIL WHEN MAN IS GONE   • •   2 QUIET WORK   14
          HE MUCH THE OLD MAN WHO CLEAREST—SOULD OF MEN   • •   2 TO A FRIEND   2
          MAN AFTER MAN THE WORLD SMILED AND PASSD BY   • •   3 EMERSONS ESSAYS   6
          MAN AFTER MAN THE WORLD SMILED AND PASSD BY   • •   3 EMERSONS ESSAYS   6
          MAN AFTER MAN THEY SMILED AND PASSED ON   • • • •   EMERSONS ESSAYS V   6
          MAN AFTER MAN THEY SMILED AND PASSED ON   • • • •   EMERSONS ESSAYS V   6
          KNOW MAN HATH ALL WHICH NATURE HATH BUT MORE   • •   5 HARMONY NATURE   5
          NATURE IS CRUEL MAN IS SICK OF BLOOD • • • •   • •   5 HARMONY NATURE   7
          NATURE IS STUBBORN MAN WOULD FAIN ADORE   • • • •   5 HARMONY NATURE   8
          NATURE IS FICKLE MAN HATH NEED OF REST   • • •   • •   5 HARMONY NATURE   9
          MAN WOULD BE MILD AND WITH SAFE CONSCIENCE BLEST   • •   5 HARMONY NATURE   11
          MAN MUST BEGIN KNOW THIS WHERE NATURE ENDS • • • •   5 HARMONY NATURE   12
          NATURE AND MAN CAN NEVER BE FAST FRIENDS   • • • •   5 HARMONY NATURE   13
          WHY TREMBLE TRUE THE NOBLENESS OF MAN   • • •   • •   6 GEO CRUIKSHANK   11
          MAY BE BY MAN EFFACED MAN CAN CONTROL   • • •   • •   6 GEO CRUIKSHANK   12
          MAY BE BY MAN EFFACED MAN CAN CONTROL   • • •   • •   6 GEO CRUIKSHANK   12
          LUST AVARICE ENVY LIBERATED MAN   • • • • •   • •   7 REP FRIEND CONT   12
          ALL DIFFERENCE WITH HIS FELLOW MAN COMPOSD • • • •   7 REP FRIEND CONT V 13
          WISHES UNWORTHY OF A MAN FULL—GROWN   • • • •   • •   8 RELIGIOUS ISOL   8
          WHEN ON THE STRENUOUS JUST MAN HEAVEN BESTOWS   • •   9 MYCERINUS   29
          MIGHT SHRINK HALF STARTLED LIKE A GUILTY MAN   • •   11 MYCERINUS   102
          FAR FROM TOWN OR HAUNT OF MAN • • • • • •   • •   14 CHURCH BROU 1   62
          TIS ALL PERHAPS WHICH MAN ACQUIRES   • • • •   • •   22 YOUTH AND CALM   24
          TIS ALL PERHAPS THAT MAN ACQUIRES • • • • •   • •   22 YOUTH AND CALM   V 24
          YET IF LITTLE STAYS WITH MAN   • • • • • •   • •   24 MEMORY—PICTURE   59
          MAN CANNOT THOUGH HE WOULD LIVE CHANCES FOOL   • •   40 HUMAN LIFE   18
          O MAN WHOM EARTH THY LONG—VEXT MOTHER BARE • •   • •   46 IN UTRUMQUE PAR   32
          AND WHAT THE RIGHTS OF MAN MAY MEAN   • • • •   • •   48 HORATIAN ECHO   17
          NO SMALL PROFIT THAT MAN EARNS • • • • • •   • •   49 SECOND BEST   16

MAN　　　　　　(CONTINUED)

WHO TO NO ONE MAN	52	CONSOLATION	72
NOT HIS OWN COURSE BUT THAT OF MAN	56	RESIGNATION	147
ARE LESS THE POET MORE THAN MAN	58	RESIGNATION	204
MAN STILL WOULD SEE AND SEE DISMAYD	58	RESIGNATION	220
NAY AND SINCE DEATH WHICH WIPES OUT MAN	58	RESIGNATION	223
MAN ITERATES WHILE THESE FORBEAR	60	RESIGNATION	272
AND FOUND THE OLD MAN SLEEPING ON HIS BED	61	SOHRAB RUSTUM	26
AT MY BOYS YEARS THE COURAGE OF A MAN	62	SOHRAB RUSTUM	45
I SEEK ONE MAN ONE MAN AND ONE ALONE	62	SOHRAB RUSTUM	49
I SEEK ONE MAN ONE MAN AND ONE ALONE	62	SOHRAB RUSTUM	49
TO MEET ME MAN TO MAN IF I PREVAIL	62	SOHRAB RUSTUM	57
TO MEET ME MAN TO MAN IF I PREVAIL	62	SOHRAB RUSTUM	57
OLD MAN THE DEAD NEED NO ONE CLAIM NO KIN	62	SOHRAB RUSTUM	59
OF THE YOUNG MAN IN HIS AND SIGHD AND SAID	63	SOHRAB RUSTUM	64
TO FIGHT OUR CHAMPION SOHRAB MAN TO MAN	65	SOHRAB RUSTUM	153
TO FIGHT OUR CHAMPION SOHRAB MAN TO MAN	65	SOHRAB RUSTUM	153
OLD MAN BE IT AGREED AS THOU HAST SAID	66	SOHRAB RUSTUM	185
LET SOHRAB ARM AND WE WILL FIND A MAN	66	SOHRAB RUSTUM	186
AND WITH MY GREAT NAME FENCE THAT WEAK OLD MAN	68	SOHRAB RUSTUM	237
IN SINGLE FIGHT WITH ANY MORTAL MAN	69	SOHRAB RUSTUM	259
O THOU YOUNG MAN THE AIR OF HEAVEN IS SOFT	70	SOHRAB RUSTUM	322
FOOL THOU ART SLAIN AND BY AN UNKNOWN MAN	77	SOHRAB RUSTUM	537
THOU DOST NOT SLAY ME PROUD AND BOASTFUL MAN	77	SOHRAB RUSTUM	542
BUT HEAR THOU THIS FIERCE MAN TREMBLE TO HEAR	77	SOHRAB RUSTUM	552
FIERCE MAN BETHINK THEE FOR AN ONLY SON	78	SOHRAB RUSTUM	586
MAN WHO ART THOU WHO DOST DENY MY WORDS	80	SOHRAB RUSTUM	655
AND I WERE NOTHING BUT A COMMON MAN	85	SOHRAB RUSTUM	813
A LIFE OF BLOOD INDEED THOU DREADFUL MAN	85	SOHRAB RUSTUM	828
ARE THIS WAY BRINGING THE DEAD MAN	88	SICK KING BOKH	19
MY MAN COMES RUNNING FLECKD WITH BLOOD	89	SICK KING BOKH	50
IN THE KINGS PATH BEHOLD THE MAN	90	SICK KING BOKH	94
AND CAST IT SOFTLY BUT THE MAN	91	SICK KING BOKH	118
ONE MAN IS NOT WELL MADE TO BEAR	92	SICK KING BOKH	154
IF A MAN BEAR TO HAVE IT SO	92	SICK KING BOKH	159
NEAR ONE ANOTHER MANY A MAN	93	SICK KING BOKH	163
GAZING UP HITHER THE POOR MAN	93	SICK KING BOKH	190
THOU WAST A SINNER THOU POOR MAN	94	SICK KING BOKH	209
THIS MAN MY PITY COULD NOT SAVE	95	SICK KING BOKH	226
THOU WERT A SINNER THOU POOR MAN	94	SICK KING BOKH	V 209
BETTER TO LIVE A SERF A CAPTURED MAN	112	BALDER DEAD 2	265
BETTER TO LIVE A SLAVE A CAPTURED MAN	112	BALDER DEAD 2	V 265
AND FOLLOWS THIS MAN AFTER THAT FOR HOURS	114	BALDER DEAD 3	11
SELF-SPRINGING A SEED OF MAN PRESERVED	128	BALDER DEAD 3	530
AND AS IN THE DARK NIGHT A TRAVELLING MAN	119	BALDER DEAD 3	V
NO FAIRER RESTING-PLACE A MAN COULD FIND	155	TRISTRAM 3	210
ONE MOMENT WAIT THOU HOLY MAN	157	SAINT BRANDAN	25
THE MAN OF THE BOLD WEST NOW COMES ARRAYD	170	EAST AND WEST	13
LONG FED ON BOUNDLESS HOPES O RACE OF MAN	170	BETTER PART	1
HATH MAN NO SECOND LIFE PITCH THIS ONE HIGH	171	BETTER PART	10
WAS CHRIST A MAN LIKE US AH LET US TRY	171	BETTER PART	13
MAN MEETS MAN MEETS AND QUITS AGAIN	185	TERRACE BERNE	48
MAN MEETS MAN MEETS AND QUITS AGAIN	185	TERRACE BERNE	48
MAN NEARS MAN MEETS AND LEAVES AGAIN	185	TERRACE BERNE	V 48
MAN NEARS MAN MEETS AND LEAVES AGAIN	185	TERRACE BERNE	V 48
FOR EVERY DAY MAN MAY BE LINKD AND LOOSED	196	FRAG ANTIGONE	34
IMMORTAL MORTAL MAN	197	FRAG ANTIGONE	72
TO A MUCH FEEBLER WIGHT THE HEROIC MAN	198	FRAG ANTIGONE	96
O FRIVOLOUS MIND OF MAN	198	FRAG DEJANEIRA	1
THOUGH MAN BEWAILS YOU NOT	198	FRAG DEJANEIRA	3
SINCE MAN WOKE ON EARTH HE KNOWS HIS STORY	209	SELF-DECEPTION	3
WHICH BLAMED THE LIVING MAN	213	GROWING OLD	35
THE MAN MATURE WITH LABOUR CHOPS	213	PROGRESS POESY	5
AND THEN THE OLD MAN TOTTERS NIGH	213	PROGRESS POESY	9
MAN IS BLIND BECAUSE OF SIN	215	PIS-ALLER	1
NAY LOOK CLOSER INTO MAN	215	PIS-ALLER	5
WARFARE OF MAN FROM HIS BIRTH	216	LORDS MESSENGER	3
THAT BEING ONLY WHICH HATH KNOWN EACH MAN	217	NAMELESS EPIT	2
RACE AFTER RACE MAN AFTER MAN	232	YOUTH OF NATURE	129
RACE AFTER RACE MAN AFTER MAN	232	YOUTH OF NATURE	129
MAN MAN IS THE KING OF THE WORLD	233	YOUTH OF MAN	27
MAN MAN IS THE KING OF THE WORLD	233	YOUTH OF MAN	27
BUT MAN HAS A THOUSAND GIFTS	233	YOUTH OF MAN	32
FOR MAN IS THE KING OF THE WORLD	233	YOUTH OF MAN	V 27
HENCE HENCE THEY CRY YE DO BUT KEEP MAN BLIND	237	PROGRESS	18
SAY YE THE SPIRIT OF MAN HAS FOUND NEW ROADS	237	PROGRESS	25
AND NO MAN MAY THE OTHERS HURT BEHOLD	238	PROGRESS	30
WHICH HAS NOT CRIED TO SUNK SELF-WEARY MAN	238	PROGRESS	43
THE FRIEND OF MAN DESIRES	238	PROGRESS	48
EVER ACCOMPANIES THE MARCH OF MAN	238	PROGRESS	V 38
THAT MAN MUST STILL TO SOME NEW WORSHIP PRESS	238	PROGRESS	V
THAT MAN DID EVER FIND	238	PROGRESS	V 40
BEFORE MAN PARTED FOR THIS EARTHLY STRAND	239	REVOLUTIONS	1
AND MAN HAS TURND THEM MANY TIMES MADE GREECE	239	REVOLUTIONS	5
MADMAN OR SLAVE MUST MAN BE ONE	244	SUMMER NIGHT	75
IS LEFT TO EACH MAN STILL	244	SUMMER NIGHT	92
HOW FRIVOLOUS A BABY MAN WOULD BE	246	BURIED LIFE	31
AND MANY A MAN IN HIS OWN BREAST THEN DELVES	246	BURIED LIFE	55
A MAN BECOMES AWARE OF HIS LIFES FLOW	247	BURIED LIFE	88
MAN DID NOT MAKE AND CANNOT MAR	249	KENSINGTON GARD	40

MAN   (CONTINUED)
  A WANDERER IS MAN FROM HIS BIRTH   251 FUTURE   1
  SO IS THE MIND OF THE MAN   252 FUTURE   18
  PEACE TO THE SOUL OF THE MAN ON ITS BREAST   254 FUTURE   82
  HOW CHANGED IS HERE EACH SPOT MAN MAKES OR FILLS   262 THYRSIS   1
  ALAS YET TO THE SUFFERING MAN   273 EDW QUILLINAN   9
  THE MEMORY OF A MAN UNSPOILD   273 EDW QUILLINAN   15
  THE IMAGE OF A MAN UNSPOILD   273 EDW QUILLINAN   V 15
  TO VILLAGES AND HOMES OF MAN   278 SOUTHERN NIGHT   82
  TO VILLAGES AND HAUNTS OF MAN   278 SOUTHERN NIGHT   V 82
  IS MOST QUELLING AND MAN   293 HEINES GRAVE   24
  THE CELLS THE SUFFERING SON OF MAN   300 GRANDE CHARTR   45
  BE MAN HENCEFORTH NO MORE A PREY   302 GRANDE CHARTR   105
  NEITHER MADE MAN TOO MUCH A GOD   308 OBERMANN   59
  NOR GOD TOO MUCH A MAN   308 OBERMANN   60
  THE HARMONY FROM WHICH MAN SWERVED   314 OBERMANN MORE   53
  THAT NAILD THORN-CROWNED MAN   317 OBERMANN MORE   156
  THAT GRACIOUS CHILD THAT THORN-CROWND MAN   318 OBERMANN MORE   167
  UNDUPED OF FANCY HENCEFORTH MAN   319 OBERMANN MORE   185
  UPON THEM PLIES THE RACE OF MAN   320 OBERMANN MORE   213
  OR MAN MUST TOSS IN PAIN   321 OBERMANN MORE   244
  MAN GETS NO SECOND DAY   321 OBERMANN MORE   258
  DIDST FIND THE SOLITARY MAN   322 OBERMANN MORE   279
  NO MAN CAN SAVE HIS BROTHERS SOUL   318 OBERMANN MORE   V
  ALONE SELF-POISED HENCEFORWARD MAN   319 OBERMANN MORE   V 185
  UNLED OF FANCY HENCEFORTH MAN   319 OBERMANN MORE   V 185
  SELF-POISED CLEAR-MINDED HENCEFORTH MAN   319 OBERMANN MORE   V 185
  UPON THEM PLY THE RACE OF MAN   320 OBERMANN MORE   V 213
  DIDST SEEK THE SOLITARY MAN   322 OBERMANN MORE   V 279
  FOR TYRANTS MAKE MAN GOOD BEYOND HIMSELF   331 MEROPE   42
  RANKS ANY MAN WITH MURDER SUCH AN ACT   336 MEROPE   208
  IF JEALOUSY OF US IT SHAMED THE MAN   337 MEROPE   253
  WHICH IN A DEED LIKE MINE A JUST MAN TREADS   341 MEROPE   369
  STERNLY REQUIREST A MAN   343 MEROPE   406
  CONCEALS FROM MAN WHO CANNOT PLUMB ITS DEPTHS   351 MEROPE   623
  UNSCALED UNTRODDEN IS THE HEART OF MAN   352 MEROPE   630
  POWER FAILS THE MAN HIMSELF TO FIX DISTINCTLY   352 MEROPE   649
  STERNLY CONDEMN THE TOO BOLD MAN WHO DARES   353 MEROPE   690
  THE MAN WHO TO UNTIMELY DEATH IS DOOMD   359 MEROPE   854
  SURELY NO SINNER THE MAN   361 MEROPE   905
  A YOUNGER MAN AND OF A DIFFERENT NAME   361 MEROPE   925
  IF SO ALLS WELL FOR LOOK THE OLD MAN SPEEDS   362 MEROPE   934
  YET THEN ANOTHER MAN WOULD BRING THIS NEWS   362 MEROPE   942
  OLD MAN OLD MAN THOU HADST MY BOY IN CHARGE   368 MEROPE   1069
  OLD MAN OLD MAN THOU HADST MY BOY IN CHARGE   368 MEROPE   1069
  O GODS FOOLISH OLD MAN THOU SPOILST MY BLOW   374 MEROPE   1194
  PERISHD BEFORE THEIR EYES YET NO MAN STIRRD   381 MEROPE   1315
  A PEOPLE LIKE A COMMON MAN IS DULL   382 MEROPE   1342
  THE NOBLE THOUGHT WHICH IS ALONE THE MAN   385 MEROPE   1409
  A FRENZIED WANDERER A GOD-DRIVEN MAN   385 MEROPE   1424
  O MEROPE THE COMMON HEART OF MAN   389 MEROPE   1523
  THE GODS O MISTRESS DEAR THE HARD-SOULD MAN   390 MEROPE   1577
  UNCLIMBD OF MAN   392 MEROPE   1648
  THIS IRON MAN MY ENEMY AND THINE   403 MEROPE   1964
  THE TRUE ONE OF A MAN WHAT WAY OF LIFE   404 MEROPE   1992
  MORTAL THE MODERATION OF A MAN   405 MEROPE   2013
  UNCLIMBD BY MAN   392 MEROPE   V1648
  IN THIS HIS PRESENT FIERCE MAN-HATING MOOD   409 EMPEDOCLES I 1   106
  AND LIVES A LONELY MAN IN TRIPLE GLOOM   410 EMPEDOCLES I 1   124
  NOT MIRACLES THOU ART A LEARNED MAN   411 EMPEDOCLES I 1   159
  MAN HAS A MIND WITH WHICH TO PLAN HIS SAFETY   413 EMPEDOCLES I 2   28
  THE WIT AND COUNSEL OF MAN WAS NEVER CLEAR   413 EMPEDOCLES I 2   30
  AND THEN THE SOUL OF MAN   415 EMPEDOCLES I 2   79
  TO WATCH MAN DOUBT AND FEAR   415 EMPEDOCLES I 2   88
  I WILL NOT JUDGE THAT MAN   415 EMPEDOCLES I 2   97
  BE NEITHER SAINT NOR SOPHIST-LED BUT BE A MAN   416 EMPEDOCLES I 2   136
  MAN GETS NO OTHER LIGHT   417 EMPEDOCLES I 2   144
  FOR MAN WOULD MAKE NO MURMURING WERE HIS WILL OBEYD   417 EMPEDOCLES I 2   151
  MAN WITH HIS LOT THUS FIGHTS   417 EMPEDOCLES I 2   153
  MAN ERRS NOT THAT HE DEEMS   418 EMPEDOCLES I 2   173
  BORN INTO LIFE MAN GROWS   418 EMPEDOCLES I 2   187
  SO EACH NEW MAN STRIKES ROOT INTO A FAR FORE-TIME   418 EMPEDOCLES I 2   191
  HOW MAN MAY HERE BEST LIVE NO CARE TOO GREAT   419 EMPEDOCLES I 2   216
     TO EXPLORE
  ON WHICH MAN WINS CONTENT   419 EMPEDOCLES I 2   223
  YET EVEN WHEN MAN FORSAKES   420 EMPEDOCLES I 2   242
  THE JUST MAN NOT TO ENTOMB   420 EMPEDOCLES I 2   253
  SEES MAN CONTROL THE WIND   421 EMPEDOCLES I 2   259
  THE WIND SWEEP MAN AWAY   421 EMPEDOCLES I 2   260
  THIS IS NOT WHAT MAN HATES   422 EMPEDOCLES I 2   302
  AND FEIGN KIND GODS WHO PERFECT WHAT MAN VAINLY TRIES   422 EMPEDOCLES I 2   316
  SHALL WE JUDGE WHAT FOR MAN IS NOT TRUE BLISS OR IS   425 EMPEDOCLES I 2   396
  A GREY OLD MAN AND WOMAN YET OF OLD   427 EMPEDOCLES I 2   449
  SHALL WE JUDGE WHAT FOR MAN IS NOT HIGH BLISS OR IS   425 EMPEDOCLES I 2 V 396
  FOR I MUST HENCEFORTH SPEAK NO MORE WITH MAN   429 EMPEDOCLES II   6
  AND THE GOOD LEARNED FRIENDLY QUIET MAN   429 EMPEDOCLES II   8
  THE WEARY MAN THE BANISHD CITIZEN   429 EMPEDOCLES II   11
  ERE QUITE THE BEING OF MAN ERE QUITE THE WORLD   429 EMPEDOCLES II   31
  A LIVING MAN NO MORE EMPEDOCLES   438 EMPEDOCLES II   328
  FIERCE DISPUTATIOUS EVER AT WAR WITH MAN   440 EMPEDOCLES II   395
  O IGNORANT RACE OF MAN   447 WESTMIN ABBEY   101

MAN   (CONTINUED)
        AND READ THEIR HOMILY TO MAN   • • • • •   • •   450 GEISTS GRAVE   12
        WHICH MAN PROUD MAN FINDS HARD TO BEAR   • • • •   450 GEISTS GRAVE   30
        WHICH MAN PROUD MAN FINDS HARD TO BEAR   • • • •   450 GEISTS GRAVE   30
        PASSAGE FROM THEIR SOULS TO MAN   • • • • •   •   455 POOR MATTHIAS   98
        INDISCERNIBLE BY MAN   • • • • • •   • • • •   •   •   456 POOR MATTHIAS   152
        HE HEARD OF LATE THE GRAND OLD MAN   • • •   460 KAISER DEAD   41
        NOR TONGUE OF MAN NOR FEAR NOR SHAME CAN PREACH   • •   467 ALARIC AT ROME   141
        THAT BINDS THE HEART OF MAN WITH MIGHTIEST POWER • •   467 ALARIC AT ROME   146
        SOUNDS SUCH AS ERST THE LONE WAYFARING MAN   • • •   473 CROMWELL   39
        SAY NOT SUCH DREAMS ARE IDLE FOR THE MAN   • • • •   473 CROMWELL   45
        HIS STEP WAS LOFTIER THAN THE STEPS OF MAN   • • • •   476 CROMWELL   156
        IN PRIESTLY GARB A FRAIL OLD MAN WENT BY   • • • •   476 CROMWELL   166
        A LIFE THAT WAS NOT AS THE LIFE OF MAN   • • • •   478 CROMWELL   220
        ASK OF THE POWERS THAT SPORT WITH MAN   • • • •   481 DESTINY   4
        MAN ONLY WITH ETERNAL BENT   • • • • • • •   • •   •   484 ROME-SICKNESS   21
        WAS IT THAT YE WITH MAN MIGHT HAVE YOUR THOUSANDS   HOMER TRANS   11
               OF SORROWS
        FOR THAN MAN INDEED THERE BREATHES NO WRETCHEDER   HOMER TRANS   12
               CREATURE
        AND SOME MAN MAY SAY AS HE LOOKS AND SEES THY   HOMER TRANS   32
               TEARS FALLING
        SO SOME MAN WILL SAY AND THEN THY GRIEF WILL REDOUBLE HOMER TRANS   35
        AT THY WANT OF A MAN LIKE ME TO SAVE THEE FROM BONDAGE HOMER TRANS   36
        A GIFTED MAN THE POWER TO SHEW HIS GIFT   • • • •   LUCRETIUS 2   2
        HAS BEEN PERFORMD WHICH CAN BE WHEN THE MAN   • • LUCRETIUS 2   8
        FOR ANY MAN TO FRET AGAINST HIS WEAKNESS   • • • •   LUCRETIUS 3   2

MANACLES
        NOR WORE THE MANACLES OF SPACE • • • • • • • •   •   242 MORALITY   32

MANE
        WITH HIS HEAD BOWING TO THE GROUND AND MANE   • •   82 SOHRAB RUSTUM   731
        COME LET ME LAY MY HAND UPON THY MANE   • • • •   83 SOHRAB RUSTUM   746
        DAY DROVE HIS COURSER WITH THE SHINING MANE   • • •   105 BALDER DEAD 2   2
        NO MEANER HAND THAN ODINS ON HIS MANE   • • • • 107 BALDER DEAD 2   73
        FIRM HARNESSD BY THE MANE A CHIEF   • • • • • •   •   191 STRAYED REVEL   188
        SUDDEN HE BOWD HIS HEAD AND ALL HIS MANE AS HE BOWD IT HOMER TRANS   44

MANGER
        WHOSE MANGER IS STUFFD FULL OF GOOD FRESH HAY   • •   123 BALDER DEAD 3   341

MANHOOD
        FOR THOUGH HIS MANHOOD BORE THE BLAST   • • • • 308 OBERMANN   65
        THOUGH ROUND THY FIRMER MANHOOD CAST   • • • • •   •   323 OBERMANN MORE   307
        A GLORIOUS MANHOOD YET A DIM OLD AGE   • • • • •   •   463 ALARIC AT ROME   39
        STEMMD BY THE STRENGTH OF MANHOOD FEARLESSLY   • •   473 CROMWELL   50
        OF TOILSOME MANHOOD IN THE DREAMS OF YOUTH   • • •   474 CROMWELL   98

MANHOODS
        AND VALIANT HEART OF YOUTH OR MANHOODS FIRM   • •   335 MEROPE   157
        CRUSHD AS THEY ROSE BY MANHOODS STERNER WILL   • •   474 CROMWELL   80

MANIFOLD
        SO MANIFOLD SO FRESH SO BRAVE A WORLD   • • • • LUCRETIUS 1   2

MANKIND
        AND ON THE FINNS THE GENTLEST OF MANKIND   • • • •   97 BALDER DEAD 1   55
        ARE GODS WORST PORTION TO MANKIND   • • • • • •   •   217 NAMELESS EPIT   V
        FOR EVER DOTH ACCOMPANY MANKIND   • • • • • •   •   238 PROGRESS   38
        ASK BUT THE FOLLY OF MANKIND   • • • • • • •   • •   250 WISH   11
        HELPERS AND FRIENDS OF MANKIND • • • • • • •   • •   291 RUGBY CHAPEL   161
        YOURS IS THE PRAISE IF MANKIND • • • • • • •   • •   291 RUGBY CHAPEL   168
        MARCHES THE HOST OF MANKIND   • • • • • • •   • •   291 RUGBY CHAPEL   172
        SON OF MANKIND TO THE EARTH   • • • • • • •   • •   293 HEINES GRAVE   30
        NEW-COMING SON OF MANKIND   • • • • • • •   • •   298 HEINES GRAVE   220
        LIFTING MANKIND AGAIN   • • • • •   • • •   • •   323 OBERMANN MORE   324
        LIFTING MANKIND AMAIN   • • • • • • •   • • •   • •   323 OBERMANN MORE   V 324
        SORROW O QUEEN OF MANKIND   • • • • •   • • •   •   346 MEROPE   506
        BEFORE THE GODS BEFORE MANKIND • • • • • •   • • •   456 POOR MATTHIAS   134
        THE FEARS AND HOPES AND PASSIONS OF MANKIND   • •   479 CROMWELL   232

MANKINDS
        PELASGUS OUR FOREFATHER AND MANKINDS   • • • • •   • 389 MEROPE   1538

MANNER
        INSTRUCT ME OF THE MANNER OF HIS DEATH   • • • • 355 MEROPE   720

MANNERS
        WE SCHOOL OUR MANNERS ACT OUR PARTS   • • • • •   •   179 FAREWELL   45
        THE MANNERS THERE PROFESSD   • • • • • • •   • •   419 EMPEDOCLES I 2   219

MANS
        MANS FITFUL UPROAR MINGLING WITH HIS TOIL   • • • •   1 QUIET WORK   10
        MANS NOISY SCHEMES ACCOMPLISHD IN REPOSE   • • •   1 QUIET WORK   V   7
        MANS NOISY FEATS ACCOMPLISHD IN REPOSE   • • • •   1 QUIET WORK   V   7
        MANS NOISY WORK ACCOMPLISHD IN REPOSE   • • • •   1 QUIET WORK   V   7
        MANS WEAK COMPLAININGS MINGLING WITH HIS TOIL   • •   1 QUIET WORK   V 10
        MANS SENSELESS UPROAR MINGLING WITH HIS TOIL   • •   1 QUIET WORK   V 10
        WHERE MANS ONE NATURE QUEEN-LIKE SITS ALONE   • • •   4 BUTLERS SERMONS   7
        MANS FUNDAMENTAL LIFE IF TO DESPISE   • • • • •   •   6 REP FRIEND   4
        MANS JUSTICE FROM THE ALL-JUST GODS WAS GIVEN   • •   9 MYCERINUS   20
        MERE PHANTOMS OF MANS SELF-TORMENTING HEART   • •   9 MYCERINUS   25

MANS   (CONTINUED)
        TO SPURN MANS COMMON LURE LIFES PLEASANT THINGS   • •   9 MYCERINUS   32
        OF MANS LABOUR IS BUT VAIN   • • • • • • • •   28 NEW SIRENS   58
        AND THE WISDOM OF MANS PAINTING   • • • • • • •   28 NEW SIRENS   75
        MANS GRAVE REASONS DISAPPEAR   • • • • • • • • •   29 NEW SIRENS   90
        ALL MANS HEART WHICH BROOKS BESTOWAL   • • • • • •   34 NEW SIRENS   229
        OF MANS MENTAL OPERATIONS   • • • • • • •   SECOND BEST   V 19
        THAT MANS SPIRIT AT ITS LURING   • • • • • •   SECOND BEST   V 23
        WIDER THAN ONE MANS PASSION THERES NO MOOD • • • • 50 CONSOLATION   V
        CASD IN ONE MANS DIMENSIONS CAN DISTIL   • • • •   50 CONSOLATION   V
        WAS DULLD FOR HE SLEPT LIGHT AN OLD MANS SLEEP •   62 SOHRAB RUSTUM   29
        THE TARTAR CHALLENGE AND THIS YOUNG MANS NAME   •   66 SOHRAB RUSTUM   181
        O RUSTUM LIKE THY MIGHT IS THIS YOUNG MANS • • •   67 SOHRAB RUSTUM   215
        DOWN THROUGH THE MIDDLE OF A RICH MANS CORN   • •   70 SOHRAB RUSTUM   294
        OF RUSTUMS SON OR OF SOME OTHER MANS   • • • • •   81 SOHRAB RUSTUM   688
        TO THAT MANS MIND WHO UNDERSTANDS   • • • • • •   93 SICK KING BOKH   172
        OVER THE SICK MANS FEET IS SPREAD   • • • • • •   131 TRISTRAM 1   15
        WOULD TAKE A SCORE YEARS FROM A STRONG MANS AGE • 140 TRISTRAM 1   305
        MANS NEW SPIRIT SINCE IT WAS NOT WE   • • • • •   210 SELF-DECEPTION   14
        MANS BLANK SPIRIT SINCE IT WAS NOT WE   • • • •   210 SELF-DECEPTION   V 14
        WHICH MAKES MANS GREATEST WOE   • • • • • • • •   238 PROGRESS   V
        THE BAND WILL QUIT MANS HEART HE WILL BREATHE FREE 239 REVOLUTIONS   20
        A WORLD ABOVE MANS HEAD TO LET HIM SEE   • • • •   244 SUMMER NIGHT   87
        MANS PRUDENCE AND MANS FIERY MIGHT   • • • • • •   272 MEMORIAL VERSES   59
        MANS PRUDENCE AND MANS FIERY MIGHT   • • • • • •   272 MEMORIAL VERSES   59
        MANS WORK-PLACE LAY IN GLOOM   • • • • • • •   315 OBERMANN MORE   78
        HOW MANY PRECIOUS FEELINGS OF MANS HEART   • • •   335 MEROPE   178
        WHO IN MANS INMOST BOSOM SIT AND JUDGE   • • •   349 MEROPE   554
        AND KNOWING WELL MANS INMOST HEART INFIRM   • • •   353 MEROPE   692
        IS FATE INDEED SO STRONG MANS STRENGTH INDEED SO POOR 415 EMPEDOCLES I 2   96
        DEEP IN MANS HEART IS BORN   • • • • • • • • •   418 EMPEDOCLES I 2   169
        NOR IS THAT WIND LESS ROUGH WHICH BLOWS A GOOD   420 EMPEDOCLES I 2   256
            MANS BARGE
        WHAT WERE THE WISE MANS PLAN   • • • • • • • • •   421 EMPEDOCLES I 2   267
        MANS MEASURES CANNOT METE THE IMMEASURABLE ALL • • 423 EMPEDOCLES I 2   341
        FOOLS THAT IN MANS BRIEF TERM   • • • • • • •   424 EMPEDOCLES I 2   347
        NOR IS THE WIND LESS ROUGH THAT BLOWS A GOOD   420 EMPEDOCLES I 2   V 256
            MANS BARGE
        MANS MEASURES CANNOT SPAN THE ILLIMITABLE ALL   • • 423 EMPEDOCLES I 2   V 341
        THAT EACH MANS LOT IS THAT   • • • • • • • •   EMPEDOCLES I 2   V
        THE LAST SPARK OF MANS CONSCIOUSNESS WITH WORDS • 429 EMPEDOCLES II   30
        BROTHER MANS DESPAIRING SIGN   • • • • • • • •   457 POOR MATTHIAS   169
        GOD DOTH MATCH HIS GIFTS TO MANS BELIEVING   • • • 483 THEKLAS ANSWER   19

MANSION
        REGRETTING THE WARM MANSION WHICH IT LEFT   • • • • 86 SOHRAB RUSTUM   855
        THE VILLAGE STREET ITS HAUNTED MANSION LACKS   • • 262 THYRSIS   3

MANTINEA
        TO MANTINEA WITH ITS UNBAKED WALLS   • • • • • • • 355 MEROPE   V 739

MANTINEAN
        THE MANTINEAN SANCTUARY FORBID   • • • • • • • • • 357 MEROPE   775

MANTINEIA
        TO MANTINEIA WITH ITS UNBAKED WALLS   • • • • • •   355 MEROPE   739

MANTLED
        MANTLED HER FORM NO MORE HER HEAD WAS BOWD   • • • 447 WESTMIN ABBEY   98

MANTLES
        DIGHT WITH MANTLES GAY   • • • • • • • • • • •   17 CHURCH BROU 2   22
        WARM IN THEIR MANTLES WRAPT THE THREE STOOD THERE   150 TRISTRAM 3   38
        MANTLES WITH THOSE RICH FURS DEEP GLISTERING   • • 150 TRISTRAM 3   40
        WARM IN THEIR MANTLES WRAPT THE THREE STAYD THERE   TRISTRAM 3   V 38

MANTLING
        THE MANTLING BLOOD TO THY CHEEK   • • • • • •   235 YOUTH OF MAN   115

MANY
        YET SUNS SHALL RISE AND MANY MOONS SHALL WANE   • • 10 MYCERINUS   62
        MANY A FACE I SO LET FLEE   • • • • • • • •   23 MEMORY-PICTURE   13
        MANY A BROKEN PROMISE THEN   • • • • • • • •   23 MEMORY-PICTURE   37
        MANY A FACE I THEN LET BY   • • • • • • • •   23 MEMORY-PICTURE   V 13
        MANY A FACE I THEN LET FLEE   • • • • • • •   23 MEMORY-PICTURE   V 13
        BEHOLD SHE CRIES SO MANY RAGES LULLD   • • • • •   37 WORLDS TRIUMPHS   5
        SO MANY FIERY SPIRITS QUITE COOLD DOWN   • • • •   37 WORLDS TRIUMPHS   6
        LOOK HOW SO MANY VALOURS LONG UNDULLD   • • • •   37 WORLDS TRIUMPHS   7
        UNRAVEL ALL HIS MANY-COLOURD LORE   • • • • • •   43 GIPSY CHILD   34
        BUT SO MANY BOOKS THOU READEST   • • • • • • •   49 SECOND BEST   5
        BUT SO MANY SCHEMES THOU BREEDEST   • • • • • •   49 SECOND BEST   6
        BUT SO MANY WISHES FEEDEST   • • • • • • • •   49 SECOND BEST   7
        BUT SO MANY PASSIONS FEEDEST   • • • • • • • •   SECOND BEST   V   7
        OUR WAVERING MANY-COLOURD LINE   • • • • • • •   54 RESIGNATION   61
        AND MANY A MILE OF DUSTY WAY   • • • • • • •   54 RESIGNATION   80
        FINDS HIM WITH MANY AN UNSOLVED PLAN   • • • •   58 RESIGNATION   224
        WHERE HOST MEETS HOST AND MANY NAMES ARE SUNK   •   62 SOHRAB RUSTUM   61
        AND TRIED AND I HAVE STOOD ON MANY A FIELD   • • •   71 SOHRAB RUSTUM   326
        OF BLOOD AND I HAVE FOUGHT WITH MANY A FOE   • • •   71 SOHRAB RUSTUM   327
        THROUGH MANY ROLLING CLOUDS SO RUSTUM SAW   • • •   87 SOHRAB RUSTUM   623
        AND SPLIT HIS CURRENTS THAT FOR MANY A LEAGUE   •   87 SOHRAB RUSTUM   883
        THESE MANY DAYS AND HEARD NO THING   • • • • •   88 SICK KING BOKH   23

MANY   (CONTINUED)
        NEAR ONE ANOTHER MANY A MAN   . . . .   93 SICK KING BOKH   163
        FOR MANY GODS IN HEAVEN NOT THOU ALONE   . . . .   98 BALDER DEAD 1   119
        FOR WISE HE WAS AND MANY CURIOUS ARTS   . . . .   101 BALDER DEAD 1   210
        THOUGH I BE LOVED AND MANY MOURN MY DEATH   . . . .   112 BALDER DEAD 2   270
        THROUGH MANY STREETS THE POOR BEAST RUNS IN VAIN . .   114 BALDER DEAD 3   10
        NAMES HATH SHE MANY VANADIS ON EARTH   . . . . .   116 BALDER DEAD 3   96
        BALDER THERE YET ARE MANY SCALDS IN HEAVEN . . . . .   117 BALDER DEAD 3   132
        GAZING SEAWARDS MANY A LEAGUE   . . . .   131 TRISTRAM 1   42
        THERES MANY A GAY KNIGHT WHERE HE GOES   . . . .   138 TRISTRAM 1   256
        THROUGH MANY A ROOM AND CORRIDOR   . . . . . .   140 TRISTRAM 1   332
        AND MANY A STRETCH OF WATERY SAND   . . . . . .   141 TRISTRAM 1   369
        IS STREWN WITH ROCKS AND MANY A SHIVERD MASS   . .   150 TRISTRAM 3   16
        BY AGE TAUGHT MANY THINGS   . . . .   189 STRAYED REVEL   119
        BY CITY AND HOUSEHOLD GROUPD WE LIVE AND MANY SHOCKS   195 FRAG ANTIGONE   20
        FOR HIM WHO MUST SEE MANY YEARS   . . . . . .   199 EARLY DEATH   1
        FOR HIM WHO MUST LIVE MANY YEARS   . . . . . .   199 EARLY DEATH   V   1
        STILL AFTER MANY YEARS IN DISTANT LANDS   . . . .   200 PHILOMELA   6
        FIGHT LIFES MANY-CHANCD FIGHT   . . . .   216 LORDS MESSENGER   V
        WHERE MANY A SPLENDOUR FINDS ITS TOMB   . . . .   220 BACCHANALIA 2   22
        MANY SPENT FAMES AND FALLEN MIGHTS   '. . . . . .   220 BACCHANALIA 2   23
        THOUGH MANY THAN GOOD STATUES WERE   . . . . .   221 EPILOG LAOCOON   18
        OF BARDS FULL MANY A STROKE DIVINE   . . . . .   222 EPILOG LAOCOON   20
        AND MANY MANY ARE THE SOULS   . . . .   226 EPILOG LAOCOON   163
        AND MANY MANY ARE THE SOULS   . . . .   226 EPILOG LAOCOON   163
        AND MAN HAS TURND THEM MANY TIMES MADE GREECE . .   239 REVOLUTIONS   5
        AND MANY A MAN IN HIS OWN BREAST THEN DELVES   . .   246 BURIED LIFE   55
        AND WE HAVE BEEN ON MANY THOUSAND LINES   . . . .   246 BURIED LIFE   57
        AND MANY A GUEST HATH SHE THEREIN RECEIVD   . . . .   251 FUTURE   V
        IN JUNE AND MANY A SCYTHE IN SUNSHINE FLAMES   . .   257 SCHOLAR-GIPSY   92
        AH ME THIS MANY A YEAR   . . . .   263 THYRSIS   36
        BUT MANY A DINGLE ON THE LOVED HILL-SIDE   . . .   266 THYRSIS   112
        OF MANY HOPES OF MANY TEARS   . . . .   285 HAWORTH CHURCH   106
        OF MANY HOPES OF MANY TEARS   . . . .   285 HAWORTH CHURCH   106
        MANY TO SAVE WITH THYSELF   . . . .   290 RUGBY CHAPEL   141
        OF MANY A DARK-BOUGHD PINE   . . . .   307 OBERMANN   30
        WHOM MANY A DIFFERENT WAY   . . . .   311 OBERMANN   146
        BUT LEFT THIS MANY A YEAR   . . . .   313 OBERMANN MORE   40
        SO MANY WOUNDED HEARTS   . . . .   317 OBERMANN MORE   160
        THE KING I KNOW HIM EVEN THROUGH MANY YEARS   . .   332 MEROPE   63
        O MEROPE HOW MANY NOBLE THOUGHTS   . . . . .   335 MEROPE   177
        HOW MANY PRECIOUS FEELINGS OF MANS HEART   . . .   335 MEROPE   178
        HOW MANY LOVES HOW MANY GRATITUDES   . . . .   335 MEROPE   179
        HOW MANY LOVES HOW MANY GRATITUDES   . . . .   335 MEROPE   179
        THE MANY OF THAT LINEAGE TO THE ONE   . . . .   338 MEROPE   270
        THESE MANY YEARS I LIVE FOR THIS ALONE   . . .   351 MEROPE   621
        AND TO ONE ACT MANY MOST UNLIKE MOTIVES   . . .   352 MEROPE   645
        I THE ONE RIGHTEOUS THEY THE MANY BAD   . . .   353 MEROPE   679
        AND MANY TIMES THAT MORN WE COURSED IN RING   . .   357 MEROPE   793
        FOR INSTANT COMMENT HAVING MANY SIDES   . . .   359 MEROPE   860
        I HAVE SEEN MANY CITIES IN MY TIME   . . . . .   428 EMPEDOCLES I 2   474
        MANY A MORNING HAD THEY GONE   . . . . . .   434 EMPEDOCLES II   171
        AND SO CHANGE BACK AND MANY THOUSAND TIMES   . .   435 EMPEDOCLES II   229
        POOR CANARY MANY A YEAR   . . . .   452 POOR MATTHIAS   5
        SONGSTER THOU OF MANY A YEAR   . . . .   452 POOR MATTHIAS   15
        MANY YEARS HAVE NOT TO SPEND   . . . .   458 POOR MATTHIAS   211
        OF MANY A LAWNY HILL AND STREAMS WITH SILVER FLOW   474 CROMWELL   104
        WITH MANY A WILD WEED OVERGROWN   . . . . . .   479 HAYSWATER BOAT   14
        MUST BEAR IN SILENCE MANY AN ILL   . . . . . .   481 COURAGE   3
        NOR MY BRETHRENS MANY AND BRAVE WHO THEN WILL BE LYING   HOMER TRANS   25

MANYS
        MANYS THE GOOD   . . . .   LUCRETIUS 7   1

MAP
        WE MAP THE STARRY SKY   . . . .   423 EMPEDOCLES I 2   319
        MARK THE SEASONS MAP OUR YEAR   . . . .   456 POOR MATTHIAS   145

MAR
        MAR THE MUSIC OF YOUR FEASTS IN VAIN . . . . . .   32 NEW SIRENS   170
        MAN DID NOT MAKE AND CANNOT MAR   . . . . . .   249 KENSINGTON GARD   40
        THAT NATURAL CAUSES MAR THY EFFORTS AND NOT FATE . .   EMPEDOCLES I 2   V

MARATHON
        FAR ON MARATHON PLAIN   . . . .   343 MEROPE   431

MARBLE
        LIFELIKE IN THE MARBLE PALE   . . . .   16 CHURCH BROU 1   106
        ON AISLE AND TRANSEPT AND YOUR MARBLE GRAVE   . .   17 CHURCH BROU 3   6
        SO SLEEP FOR EVER SLEEP O MARBLE PAIR   . . .   18 CHURCH BROU 3   16
        AND RISE UPON YOUR COLD WHITE MARBLE BEDS   . .   18 CHURCH BROU 3   27
        THE FOLIAGED MARBLE FOREST WHERE YE LIE   . .   19 CHURCH BROU 3   39
        AND RAISE YOU ON YOUR COLD WHITE MARBLE BEDS . .   18 CHURCH BROU 3   V   27
        MORE GRATEFUL THAN THIS MARBLE SLEEP . . . . .   22 YOUTH AND CALM   21
        FLITTING FAST ACROSS EACH MARBLE BROW   . . .   31 NEW SIRENS   162
        AND PLUCKING UP THE MARBLE FLAGS   . . . . .   95 SICK KING BOKH   227
        AND TEARING UP THE MARBLE FLAGS   . . . . . .   95 SICK KING BOKH   V 227
        WHO SEEMS OF MARBLE ON A TOMB   . . . . . .   148 TRISTRAM 2   167
        THE SHADOW OF A MARBLE MUSE OF YORE   . . . .   168 RACHEL 2   6
        THROUGH THE DELICATE FLUSHD MARBLE   . . . . .   187 STRAYED REVEL   56

```
MARBLE         ( CONTINUED )
        WITH MARBLE WITH COLOUR WITH WORD      •  •  •  •  •  •    231 YOUTH OF NATURE    108
        AND FROM THE WAVE-KISSD MARBLE STAIR   •  •  •  •  •  •    278 SOUTHERN NIGHT     106
        FLOWER OF MARBLE OF WHITE       •  •  •  •  •  •  •  •     296 HEINES GRAVE       131
        AND HER FLUSHD FEET GLOW ON THE MARBLE FLOOR    •  •      431 EMPEDOCLES II       88
        WITHIN THE MARBLE PRISON OF HER ARMS  •  •  •  •  •  •        FRAGMENT 1           4

MARBLES
        GREY TIME-WORN MARBLES   •  •  •  •  •  •  •  •  •  •       50 CONSOLATION         16

MARC
        OF KING MARC TO BE HIS BRIDE    •  •  •  •  •  •  •  •     132 TRISTRAM 1          62
        GAVE HER THAT KING MARC AND SHE     •  •  •  •  •  •       134 TRISTRAM 1         138
        ROYAL STATE WITH MARC MY DEEP-WRONGD HUSBAND    •  •      144 TRISTRAM 2          45

MARCH
        AUSTRIAN KNIGHTS AND MARCH-WORN PALMERS     •  •  •  •     15 CHURCH BROU 1       85
        THAT SEVERD THE WORLDS MARCH AND THINE BE GONE   •  •     44 GIPSY CHILD         62
        THAT SEVERD THE WORLDS MARCH AND THINE IS GONE   •  •     44 GIPSY CHILD       V 62
        TO AWAIT THEIR MARCH AND WHEN APPEARD       •  •  •  •     53 RESIGNATION         33
        SOME TWO HOURS MARCH WITH SERIOUS AIR       •  •  •  •     54 RESIGNATION         68
        CHILLY THEY GROW YET WINDS IN MARCH   •  •  •  •  •        56 RESIGNATION        130
        TO HEM HIS WATERY MARCH AND DAM HIS STREAMS     •  •      87 SOHRAB RUSTUM       882
        AT TWILIGHT ON A STORMY EVE IN MARCH  •  •  •  •  •        69 SOHRAB RUSTUM     V 286
        WHEN FROM THE SOUTH SHALL MARCH THE FIERY BAND   •  •    127 BALDER DEAD 3       475
        THE MARCH THE LEAGUER HEAVENS BLITHE AIR    •  •  •  •    138 TRISTRAM 1         258
        THIS MIGHTY MARCH DO AUGHT BUT DIE    •  •  •  •  •       226 EPILOG LAOCOON      170
        EVER ACCOMPANIES THE MARCH OF MAN     •  •  •  •  •       238 PROGRESS          V 38
        FEARFUL AND WE IN OUR MARCH•    •  •  •  •  •  •  •       290 RUGBY CHAPEL        129
        HATH NOT AS YET IN ITS MARCH    •  •  •  •  •  •  •       291 RUGBY CHAPEL        169
        STABLISH CONTINUE OUR MARCH     •  •  •  •  •  •  •       292 RUGBY CHAPEL        206
        TO HYMN THE CONQUERING MARCH OF ROME  •  •  •  •  •       300 GRANDE CHARTR       51
        SO FEEBLE IS HIS MARCH SO SLOW  •  •  •  •  •  •  •       352 MEROPE             627
        WILL HURRY US WITH THEM ON THEIR HOMELESS MARCH  •  •    439 EMPEDOCLES II       359

MARCHD
        IN SAMARCAND BEFORE THE ARMY MARCHD   •  •  •  •  •        62 SOHRAB RUSTUM        40
        MARCHD WITH THEM HATRED AND STRIFE    •  •  •  •  •       343 MEROPE             418

MARCHES
        MARCHES THE HOST OF MANKIND     •  •  •  •  •  •  •       291 RUGBY CHAPEL        172

MARCHING
        IN MARCHING ORDER SPREAD OF LONG-NECKD CRANES     •  •     64 SOHRAB RUSTUM       112

MARCS
        IN KING MARCS CHAPEL IN TYNTAGEL OLD  •  •  •  •  •  •    149 TRISTRAM 3           3
        AT TYNTAGIL IN KING MARCS CHAPEL OLD  •  •  •  •  •  •    149 TRISTRAM 3        V  3

MARCUS
        MARCUS AURELIUS BUT THE STIFLING DEN  •  •  •  •  •  •    168 WORLDLY PLACE        3

MARES
        AND KHIVA AND FERMENT THE MILK OF MARES     •  •  •  •     64 SOHRAB RUSTUM       120
        MARES MILK AND BREAD     •  •  •  •  •  •  •  •  •  •     191 STRAYED REVEL       166

MARGARET
        MARGARET MARGARET   •  •  •  •  •  •  •  •  •  •  •  •     161 FORSAKEN MERM        13
        MARGARET MARGARET   •  •  •  •  •  •  •  •  •  •  •  •     161 FORSAKEN MERM        13
        MARGARET MARGARET   •  •  •  •  •  •  •  •  •  •  •  •     162 FORSAKEN MERM        22
        MARGARET MARGARET   •  •  •  •  •  •  •  •  •  •  •  •     162 FORSAKEN MERM        22
        MARGARET HIST COME QUICK WE ARE HERE  •  •  •  •  •  •    163 FORSAKEN MERM        77

MARGE
        SOUTHWARD THE TARTARS BY THE RIVER MARGE    •  •  •  •     86 SOHRAB RUSTUM       873
        AND ON WHOSE MARGE THE ANCIENT GIANTS DWELL     •  •      99 BALDER DEAD 1       161
        AND SET BY OCEANS UTMOST MARGE TO DWELL     •  •  •  •    121 BALDER DEAD 3       275
        TO THE IVY-WREATHED MARGE       •  •  •  •  •  •  •       188 STRAYED REVEL        84
        ON SOME GREAT RIVERS MARGE      •  •  •  •  •  •  •       193 STRAYED REVEL       252
        AS IT GROWS AS THE TOWNS ON ITS MARGE       •  •  •  •    253 FUTURE              72
        LAY HONEY-CAKES ON ITS MARGE    •  •  •  •  •  •  •       342 MEROPE             386

MARGES
        OH MIGHT OUR MARGES MEET AGAIN  •  •  •  •  •  ,  •  •    182 TO MARG CONT         18

MARGIN
        SPARING US NARROWER MARGIN THAN WE DEEM     •  •  •  •      7 REP FRIEND CONT      8
        ON THE LIFELESS MARGIN OF THE SPARKLING OCEAN     •  •     36 VOICE               19
        DOWN TO THE MARGIN OF THE ROARING SEA       •  •  •  •     97 BALDER DEAD 1       77
        BUT HERE WHILE HARBOURING ON ITS MARGIN LAY     •  •      332 MEROPE              70

MARGUERITE
        SMILES THE DUCHESS MARGUERITE   •  •  •  •  •  •  •  •     13 CHURCH BROU 1        12
        SATE THE DUCHESS MARGUERITE     •  •  •  •  •  •  •  •     13 CHURCH BROU 1        36
        WAS THE DUCHESS MARGUERITE      •  •  •  •  •  •  •  •     14 CHURCH BROU 1        56
        SAID THE DUCHESS MARGUERITE THEN      •  •  •  •  •  •     15 CHURCH BROU 1        74
        MARGUERITE SAYS AS LAST YEAR WENT     •  •  •  •  •  •     23 MEMORY-PICTURE      17
        CAME FORTH OLIVIAS MARGUERITE AND THINE     •  •  •  •     25 DREAM               22
        MY MARGUERITE SMILES UPON THE STRAND  •  •  •  •  •  •    174 MEETING              3
        AH MARGUERITE FAIN  •  •  •  •  •  •  •  •  •  •  •  •    176 PARTING             60
```

MARGUERITE   (CONTINUED)
          STAY WITH ME MARGUERITE STILL   183 ABSENCE   20
          THE HOUSE AND IS MY MARGUERITE THERE   184 TERRACE BERNE   12
          BUT NOT THE MARGUERITE OF THY PRIME   184 TERRACE BERNE   34
          AND MARGUERITE I SHALL SEE NO MORE   185 TERRACE BERNE   52

MARGUERITES
          OF ALL THAT WAS MY MARGUERITES OWN   185 TERRACE BERNE   40

MARK
          NOW MARK I BEING FEVERD SICK   90 SICK KING BOKH   85
          WHICH WERE HIS GLORIOUS MARK IN HEAVEN HE STOOD   103 BALDER DEAD 1   285
          SET UP A MARK OF EVERLASTING LIGHT   169 EAST LONDON   10
          FIRST TO THE LIGHT AND MARK   195 FRAG ANTIGONE   13
          FIRM TO THEIR MARK NOT SPENT ON OTHER THINGS   260 SCHOLAR-GIPSY   163
          WE MARK THEM BUT THEY ARE NOT OURS   304 GRANDE CHARTR   V 168
          NOT SO LET THESE MESSENIAN MAIDENS MARK   336 MEROPE   197
          AND YE KEEP FAITHFUL SILENCE FRIENDS AND MARK   368 MEROPE   1073
          BEAR WITNESS SEE MARK WELL ON WHAT A HEAD   377 MEROPE   1223
          WE MARK NOT THE WORLDS COURSE BUT WOULD HAVE   419 EMPEDOCLES I 2   221
               IT TAKE OURS
          WE MARK NOT THE WORLDS WAYS BUT WOULD HAVE   419 EMPEDOCLES I 2   V 221
               IT LEARN OURS
          MARK THE SEASONS MAP OUR YEAR   456 POOR MATTHIAS   145
          TO MARK WITH SHIVERD CREST THE REELING WAVE   472 CROMWELL   23

MARKD
          AND THEN THE BEACH AND MARKD WITH SPRAY   148 TRISTRAM 2   172
          MARKD THINE OUTLANDISH GARB THY FIGURE SPARE   258 SCHOLAR-GIPSY   98
          AND MARKD THEE WHEN THE STARS COME OUT AND SHINE   258 SCHOLAR-GIPSY   109
          MARKD THY OUTLANDISH GARB THY FIGURE SPARE   258 SCHOLAR-GIPSY   V 98
          FOUR YEARS SINCE ON A MARKD   280 HAWORTH CHURCH   V
          I MARKD THE PRESENT DIE   322 OBERMANN MORE   298
          MARKD WITH A STONE THY LAST ABODE   452 GEISTS GRAVE   72

MARKED
          HAST THOU NOT MARKED ON A WILD AUTUMN DAY   466 ALARIC AT ROME   97

MARKET
          SOME MORN AT MARKET IN A CROWDED TOWN   114 BALDER DEAD 3   9
          ONE MORN AT MARKET IN A CROWDED TOWN   114 BALDER DEAD 3   V   9
          TIS NOT IN THE WORLDS MARKET BOUGHT AND SOLD   268 THYRSIS   205

MARKING
          WITH THE GREY MIST MARKING ITS COURSE   234 YOUTH OF MAN   84

MARKS
          WASHD AS THE MARKS UPON THE HILLS STILL SHOW   358 MEROPE   815

MARRD
          THOU COME WITH ASPECT MARRD   322 OBERMANN MORE   302
          HAD HUMAN CRY NOT MARRD THE WORK DIVINE   447 WESTMIN ABBEY   104

MARRIAGE
          MIGHT DRINK IT ON THEIR MARRIAGE-DAY   135 TRISTRAM 1   139
          LET US IN MARRIAGE KING AND QUEEN UNITE   335 MEROPE   167
          IN THE MARRIAGE-TRAIN COMING ON   360 MEROPE   897
          THE GODS HAD TO THEIR MARRIAGE COME   427 EMPEDOCLES I 2   450

MARS
          THAT MARS THY CREATURE   39 STAGIRIUS   32
          MARS THE BENIGNANT REPOSE   293 HEINES GRAVE   44

MARSHAL
          MARSHAL THEM TO AN ARMY THEN ADVANCE   382 MEROPE   1324
          WHO SLOWLY BEGIN TO MARSHAL   437 EMPEDOCLES II   277

MARSHALLD
          MARSHALLD BATTALIONS BRIGHT IN BURNISHD STEEL   65 SOHRAB RUSTUM   140
          AND ALL ARE MARSHALLD IN ONE FLAMING SQUARE   127 BALDER DEAD 3   480
          AND THE TWO HOSTS ARE MARSHALLD AND IN HEAVEN   127 BALDER DEAD 3   495
          MARSHALLD THEM GAVE THEM THEIR GOAL   291 RUGBY CHAPEL   175

MARSHY
          OFF THEY SWEEP THE MARSHY FORESTS   13 CHURCH BROU 1   19
          ON TO THE MARSHY ORCHOMENIAN PLAIN   356 MEROPE   743

MARSTONS
          BY NASEBYS HILL OER MARSTONS HEATHY WASTE   476 CROMWELL   149

MARSYAS
          WHEN JEALOUS PAN WITH MARSYAS DID CONSPIRE   432 EMPEDOCLES II   128
          MARSYAS THOU ART VANQUISHED   433 EMPEDOCLES II   146
          MARSYAS THAT UNHAPPY FAUN   433 EMPEDOCLES II   149

MARTIN
          MARTIN AND I DOWN A GREEN ALPINE STREAM   24 DREAM   2

MARTYRS
          PROPHETS TRANSFIGURED SAINTS AND MARTYRS BRAVE   18 CHURCH BROU 3   20

MARVEL
    AND MARVEL AT THE FORMS OF STONE   • • • • •   17 CHURCH BROU 2   36
    RARE THE LONE PASTORAL HUTS MARVEL NOT THOU   • •   45 IN UTRUMQUE PAR   17
    AND ALL THE MARVEL OF THE GOLDEN SKIES   • • • •   268 THYRSIS   190
    STILL AT HIS MOUNTAIN-TOMB MEN MARVEL BUILT   • •   357 MEROPE   782

MARVELS
    HERE WHERE I LIE WHAT MARVELS PASS   • • • • • •   KENSINGTON GARD V 13

MASK
    SHE SEEMS ONE DYING IN A MASK OF YOUTH   • • • •   151 TRISTRAM 3   75
    THE PAST ITS MASK OF UNION ON • • • • • • •   320 OBERMANN MORE   225
    THE PAST ITS MASK OF UNION GONE • • • • • •   320 OBERMANN MORE   227

MASONS
    GERMAN MASONS SMITHS FROM SPAIN   • • • • • •   15 CHURCH BROU 1   96

MASS
    YOU HEAR THE WHITE-ROBED PRIEST SAY MASS   • • • •   17 CHURCH BROU 2   29
    AND AFTER CHURCH WHEN MASS IS DONE • • • • •   17 CHURCH BROU 2   33
    BUT IF THE WILD UNFATHERD MASS NO BIRTH • • •   45 IN UTRUMQUE PAR   22
    IS STREWN WITH ROCKS AND MANY A SHIVERD MASS •   150 TRISTRAM 3   16
    TO EVERY THOUGHT THE MASS IGNORE • • • • •   179 FAREWELL   58
    OR ARE YE IMMERSED IN THE MASS • • • • • •   230 YOUTH OF NATURE   68
    I KNEW THE MASS OF MEN CONCEALD • • • • •   245 BURIED LIFE   16
    THE MASS SWELLS MORE AND MORE • • • • •   423 EMPEDOCLES I 2   333
    THE MINSTERS OUTLINED MASS • • • • • •   445 WESTMIN ABBEY   31
    THOU SHATTERED MASS WHOSE GLORIOUS RUINS TELL •   463 ALARIC AT ROME   45

MASSD
    WHO MASSD ROUND THAT SLIGHT BROW THESE CLOUDS OF DOOM   41 GIPSY CHILD   4
    AND MAKES THE MASSD CLOUDS ROLL • • • • •   432 EMPEDOCLES II   122

MASSES
    IN BLINDING MASSES SHOWERD THE GOLDEN HAIR • • •   150 TRISTRAM 3   34
    INCITE THE MASSES • • • • • • • •   460 KAISER DEAD   42

MASSIER
    THE MASSIER ELMS STAND GRAVE AND DUN • • • • •   KENSINGTON GARD V

MASSY
    SWAYING FROM SIDE TO SIDE HIS MASSY HEAD • • • •   401 MEROPE   1911

MAST
    THE MAST THEY FIXT AND HOISTED UP THE SAILS • •   118 BALDER DEAD 3   174
    THE SUMMIT OF THE PILE THE DEAD THE MAST • • •   119 BALDER DEAD 3   190
    THEY FIXT THE MAST AND HOISTED UP THE SAILS •   118 BALDER DEAD 3 V 174
    NO MAST NO SAILS ARE SET THEREON • • • •   479 HAYSWATER BOAT   5

MASTED
    WHEN THOU SHALT SAIL IN A HIGH-MASTED SHIP • • •   85 SOHRAB RUSTUM   831

MASTER
    SLOW THEY ENTERD WITH THEIR MASTER • • • • •   14 CHURCH BROU 1   45
    TIME YOUR MASTER GOVERNS ME • • • • • •   24 MEMORY-PICTURE   54
    OR ERE THEY BROUGHT THY MASTER TO THIS FIELD •   83 SOHRAB RUSTUM   740
    FROM LAYING THY DEAR MASTER IN HIS GRAVE • •   85 SOHRAB RUSTUM   834
    WHEN FIRST THEY BORE THY MASTER TO THIS FIELD   83 SOHRAB RUSTUM V 740
    BUT HOME HIS MASTER COMES TO HIS OWN FARM • •   114 BALDER DEAD 3   17
    AH AND HE WHO PLACED OUR MASTER-FEELING • •   210 SELF-DECEPTION   23
    FAILD TO PLACE THAT MASTER-FEELING CLEAR • •   210 SELF-DECEPTION   24
    FAILD TO PLACE OUR MASTER-FEELING CLEAR • •   210 SELF-DECEPTION V 24
    BACK TO HIS MASTER AGAIN • • • • • •   217 LORDS MESSENGER   24
    MASTER AND SERVANT YOUNG AND OLD • • • •   226 EPILOG LAOCOON   160
    THE MASTER STOOD UPON THE MOUNT AND TAUGHT • •   237 PROGRESS   1
    AND THE PALE MASTER ON HIS SPAR-STREWN DECK •   244 SUMMER NIGHT   65
    THOU MASTER OF MY WANDERING YOUTH • • •   313 OBERMANN MORE   39
    HE DOTH THOU HAST BOTH HOUSE AND MASTER RIGHT •   354 MEROPE   707
    ARCAS THOU HERE O MY DEAR MASTER O • • • •   375 MEROPE   1206
    THEIR MASTER FALLN THESE WILL NOT FLINCH BUT BAND   381 MEROPE   1306
    AND PRAISED AND SPOILD BY MASTER AND BY GUESTS •   407 EMPEDOCLES I 1   34
    AS OF HIS GIFTED MASTER AND ONCE FRIEND • •   411 EMPEDOCLES I 1   148
    INSTRUCT ME OF PANTHEIAS STORY MASTER • • •   412 EMPEDOCLES I 2   20
    DOWN BY THE STREAM YES MASTER IN THE WOOD • •   427 EMPEDOCLES I 2   462
    IF THESE HAVE BEEN THE MASTER PART OF US • •   439 EMPEDOCLES II   346
    THERE OF THY MASTER KEEP THAT SIGN • • • •   461 KAISER DEAD   83
    BEHELD HIM MASTER OF IMPERIAL ROME • • •   468 ALARIC AT ROME   172
    TO READ EACH THOUGHT AND TEACH THAT MASTER MIND •   478 CROMWELL   231
    SEE THAT YE BRING YOUR MASTER HOME TO THE HOST   HOMER TRANS   40
        OF THE ARGIVES

MASTERD
    WHEN THE DUPED SOUL SELF-MASTERD CLAIMS ITS MEED •   9 MYCERINUS   28
    ALONE I MASTERD POWER AND ALONE • • • • •   398 MEROPE   1792

MASTERFUL
    OF HEADY MASTERFUL INJURIOUS MEN • • • • •   339 MEROPE   312

MASTERS
    WHO SCATTERS RUSHES IN A MASTERS HALL • • • •   112 BALDER DEAD 2   266
    AND DRUDGE UNDER SOME FOOLISH MASTERS KEN • • •   169 WORLDLY PLACE   6
    IN THE MASTERS PRESENCE AGAIN • • • • • •   216 LORDS MESSENGER   12

MASTERS   (CONTINUED)
        HIS MASTERS ERRAND WELL DONE • • • • • • • •   217 LORDS MESSENGER   22
        IN THEIR MASTERS PRESENCE AGAIN   • • • • • •   216 LORDS MESSENGER V 12
        THE YOUNG LIGHT-HEARTED MASTERS OF THE WAVES   • •   262 SCHOLAR-GIPSY   241
        WITH A MASTERS ACCENT HER FEIGND   • • • • •   280 HAWORTH CHURCH   11
        FORGIVE ME MASTERS OF THE MIND • • • • • • • •   301 GRANDE CHARTR   73
        AM MEROPE THY MURDERD MASTERS WIFE   • • • • • •   335 MEROPE   184
        REFRESHD AND CLAIM THY MASTERS THANKS AND GOLD   • •   373 MEROPE   1182
        TO KEEP THEIR MASTERS POWER THOU WILT FIND   • • • •   381 MEROPE   1307
        OF YOUR DEAD MASTERS LINE I BRING YOU NEWS   • • • •   400 MEROPE   1883
        OF AEPYTUS THY MURDERD MASTERS SON   • • • • • •   402 MEROPE   1926
        WEEPING AT HIS MASTERS END   • • • • • • • •   434 EMPEDOCLES II   167
        AT HIS MASTERS PITEOUS CRIES   • • • • • • • •   434 EMPEDOCLES II   186
        THOU HAST THINE ABSENT MASTERS TEAR   • • • • • •   451 GEISTS GRAVE   55
        WHILE THEIR MASTERS SATE BY THE FIRE AND WAITED
                FOR MORNING   HOMER TRANS   6

MASTERY
        THAT THE WORLD WIN NO MASTERY OVER HIM   • • • •   437 EMPEDOCLES II   270

MATCH
        MATCH THAT FUNEREAL ASPECT WITH HER PALL   • • • •   43 GIPSY CHILD   46
        YET CHAMPION HAVE WE NONE TO MATCH THIS YOUTH   • •   66 SOHRAB RUSTUM   176
        BUT TO MATCH THESE THOU HAST THE PEOPLES LOVE   • •   381 MEROPE   1309
        GOD DOTH MATCH HIS GIFTS TO MANS BELIEVING • • • •   483 THEKLAS ANSWER   19

MATCHD
        LET NOT MEN SAY OF RUSTUM HE WAS MATCHD   • • • •   69 SOHRAB RUSTUM   258
        FOR WERE I MATCHD WITH TEN SUCH MEN AS THEE   • •   77 SOHRAB RUSTUM   544
        FOR WERE I MATCHD WITH TEN SUCH MEN AS THOU   • •   77 SOHRAB RUSTUM V 544
        ALL SPOTS MATCHD WITH THAT SPOT ARE LESS DIVINE   •   167 RACHEL 1   13
        MATCHD WITH A PALACE IS NOT THIS A HELL   • • • •   169 WORLDLY PLACE   8

MATCHEST
        WITH SUCH A DEED AS THIS THOU MATCHEST MINE   • •   385 MEROPE   1426

MATE
        FAR OFF ANON HER MATE COMES WINGING BACK   • • • •   78 SOHRAB RUSTUM   561
        CHIDING HIS MATE BACK TO HER NEST BUT SHE   • • • •   78 SOHRAB RUSTUM   566
        YOUR MATE THOUGH LOATHED AND FEASTS IN ODINS HALL   111 BALDER DEAD 2   218
        TO MATE BUT LEFT HER TO ROAM DISTANT LANDS • • • •   116 BALDER DEAD 3   94
        NO CHRISTIAN MATE HAVE I   • • • • • • • • •   160 NECKAN   36
        BUT WHEN SICILIAN SHEPHERDS LOST A MATE   • • • •   265 THYRSIS   82
        THIS YOUNG ARCADIAN NOBLE GUARD AND MATE   • • • •   364 MEROPE   969
        AND WHAT OF THINE ARCADIAN MATE WHO BEARS   • • • •   379 MEROPE   1269
        A MATE HOW DEAR   • • • • • • • • • • •   459 KAISER DEAD   36

MATELESS
        THE MATELESS THE ONE WILL YE KNOW   • • • • • •   231 YOUTH OF NATURE   118

MATERIAL
        MATERIAL GRANDEURS DO IN HEAVEN DECAY   • • • •   FRAGMENT 2   4

MATERNAL
        WOMANLY PITY NOR MATERNAL FEAR • • • • • • • •   389 MEROPE   1526

MATES
        HIS MATES HAD ARTS TO RULE AS THEY DESIRED • • • •   256 SCHOLAR-GIPSY   45
        HE LOVED HIS MATES BUT YET HE COULD NOT KEEP   • •   264 THYRSIS   43
        FROM SUCH MATES THE OUTWORN   • • • • • • • •   294 HEINES GRAVE   50
        HIS MATES ARE GONE AND HE   • • • • • • • •   444 WESTMIN ABBEY   21

MATIN
        ON SUNDAYS AT THE MATIN-CHIME • • • • • • • •   17 CHURCH BROU 2   17

MATRICIDAL
        MATRICIDAL WORLD-FAMED   • • • • • • • • • • •   344 MEROPE   440

MATRONS
        WHILE THE MATRONS COME TO THE DOORS   • • • • • •   360 MEROPE   899

MATTED
        THROUGH BEDS OF SAND AND MATTED RUSHY ISLES   • •   87 SOHRAB RUSTUM   885
        THE STAIND ARMS THE MATTED HAIR   • • • • • • •   136 TRISTRAM 1   199
        A FLOATING ISLE THICK-MATTED   • • • • • • • •   190 STRAYED REVEL   154
        AND THAT NEW MINSTER IN THE MATTED FEN   • • • •   444 WESTMIN ABBEY   19

MATTER
        IS IT A MATTER WHICH A GOD MIGHT TRY   • • • • • •   99 BALDER DEAD 1   133
        OF MATTER AND HARD TO EXTRACT • • • • • • • •   230 YOUTH OF NATURE   69

MATTERS
        WHAT MATTERS IT NEXT YEAR HE WILL RETURN   • • • •   265 THYRSIS   72

MATTHIAS
        POOR MATTHIAS FOUND HIM LYING • • • • • • • •   452 POOR MATTHIAS   1
        POOR MATTHIAS WOULDST THOU HAVE   • • • • • • •   453 POOR MATTHIAS   21
        POOR MATTHIAS WERE THEY THINE • • • • • • • •   454 POOR MATTHIAS   66
        POOR MATTHIAS COULDST THOU SPEAK   • • • • • • •   455 POOR MATTHIAS   109
        POOR MATTHIAS SEE THY END   • • • • • • • •   457 POOR MATTHIAS   173
        HERE MATTHIAS SANG HIS FILL   • • • • • • • •   458 POOR MATTHIAS   198

MATTRESS
FROM THE FRINGED MATTRESS WHERE THY DUCHESS LIES • • 18 CHURCH BROU 3 8

MATURE
THE MAN MATURE WITH LABOUR CHOPS • • • • • • • 213 PROGRESS POESY 5
LAUREL AND OAK THE MATURE • • • • • • • • 282 HAWORTH CHURCH V

MATURER
THE OTHER MATURER IN FAME • • • • • • • • 280 HAWORTH CHURCH 13

MAUD
WHICH THE DUCHESS MAUD BEGAN • • • • • • • • 14 CHURCH BROU 1 64

MAX
MAX AND KAISER WE TO-DAY • • • • • • • • • 454 POOR MATTHIAS 67
MAX A DACHSHOUND WITHOUT BLOT • • • • • • • 454 POOR MATTHIAS 69
MAX WITH SHINING YELLOW COAT • • • • • • • • 454 POOR MATTHIAS 71
FOR MAX THY BROTHER-DOG BEGAN • • • • • • • • 459 KAISER DEAD 37
YES MAX AND WE GREW SLOW AND SAD • • • • • • 460 KAISER DEAD 43
POOR MAX WITH DOWNCAST REVERENT HEAD • • • • • 460 KAISER DEAD 67
FULL WELL MAX KNOWS THE FRIEND IS DEAD • • • 460 KAISER DEAD 69

MAY   (FOR THE MONTH, SEE PREFACE)

MAZE
SOME SLOUGH OF SENSE OR SOME FANTASTIC MAZE • • 440 EMPEDOCLES II 375

MAZED
MAZED WITH DOUBTS AND SICK WITH FEARS • • • • 44 QUESTION 13
THEN THOU WOULDST LOOK LESS MAZED • • • • • 417 EMPEDOCLES I 2 162

MAZES
IN MAZES OF HEAT AND SOUND • • • • • • • • 21 REQUIESCAT 10
SEE ONE FIGURE QUITS THE MAZES • • • • • • • META CLOISTER 9

MAZY
AND IN WILD HUNT THROUGH MAZY TRACTS OF STARS • • 10 MYCERINUS 45

ME
ONE LESSON NATURE LET ME LEARN OF THEE • • • • 1 QUIET WORK 1
TWO LESSONS NATURE LET ME LEARN OF THEE • • • • 1 QUIET WORK V 1
IF THOUGHTS NOT IDLE WHILE BEFORE ME FLOW • • • • 7 REP FRIEND 11
GUIDE ME SOME ONE TO THE MOUNTAIN • • • • • 15 CHURCH BROU 1 75
GUIDE ME VASSALS TO THE MOUNTAIN • • • • • • 15 CHURCH BROU 1 V 75
LET ME PAUSE LET ME STRIVE IN MYSELF MAKE SOME ORDER 19 MODERN SAPPHO 7
LET ME PAUSE LET ME STRIVE IN MYSELF MAKE SOME ORDER 19 MODERN SAPPHO 7
SHE ENTERD THAT MOMENT HIS EYES TURND FROM ME • • 19 MODERN SAPPHO 10
THEIR LOVE LET ME KNOW MUST GROW STRONG AND 19 MODERN SAPPHO 13
   YET STRONGER
CROWN CROWN HIM QUICKLY AND LEAVE HIM FOR ME • • 20 MODERN SAPPHO 36
LET ME PAUSE LET ME STRIVE IN MYSELF FIND SOME ORDER 19 MODERN SAPPHO V 7
LET ME PAUSE LET ME STRIVE IN MYSELF FIND SOME ORDER 19 MODERN SAPPHO V 7
IS IT HOPE MAKES ME LINGER THE DIM THOUGHT THAT SORROW 19 MODERN SAPPHO V
IT WAS WELL WITH ME ONCE IF I SAW HIM TO-MORROW • • 19 MODERN SAPPHO V
AS SHE TOWRD ME LEAND HER FACE • • • • • • • 23 MEMORY-PICTURE 34
TIME YOUR MASTER GOVERNS ME • • • • • • • 24 MEMORY-PICTURE 54
BUT MY YOUTH REMINDS ME THOU • • • • • • • 22 MEMORY-PICTURE V
AS SHE TOWARDS ME LEAND HER FACE • • • • • • 23 MEMORY-PICTURE V 34
FORTH AT NOON HAD LURED ME CREEPING • • • • • 26 NEW SIRENS 3
BUT FOR ME MY THOUGHTS ARE STRAYING • • • • • 29 NEW SIRENS 93
OFT AT NOON HAVE LURED ME CREEPING • • • • • 26 NEW SIRENS V 3
LATE AT EVE HAD LURED ME CREEPING • • • • • 26 NEW SIRENS V 3
ONCE LIKE ME YOU TOOK YOUR STATION • • • • • 31 NEW SIRENS V 139
AFTER SHORT COMMERCE WITH ME FEAR MY FROWN • • • 37 WORLDS TRIUMPHS 8
HAST THOU SO RARE A POISON LET ME BE • • • • • 38 WORLDS TRIUMPHS 13
KEENER TO SLAY THEE LEST THOU POISON ME • • • • 38 WORLDS TRIUMPHS 14
THE INLY-WRITTEN CHART THOU GAVEST ME • • • • 40 HUMAN LIFE 5
TO GUIDE ME I HAVE STEERD BY TO THE END • • • • 40 HUMAN LIFE 6
AND THAT SOUL-SEARCHING VISION FELL ON ME • • • 42 GIPSY CHILD 16
AND THY DARK MOURNFUL VISION RESTS ON ME • • • 41 GIPSY CHILD V 16
HEM ME ROUND EVERYWHERE • • • • • • • • 50 CONSOLATION 3
AND THOUGH FATE GRUDGE TO THEE AND ME • • • • 59 RESIGNATION 245
YET THEY BELIEVE ME WHO AWAIT • • • • • • • 59 RESIGNATION 247
THOU KNOWST ME PERAN-WISA IT IS I • • • • • 62 SOHRAB RUSTUM 34
FOR SO DID KING AFRASIAB BID ME SEEK • • • • • 62 SOHRAB RUSTUM 38
COME THEN HEAR NOW AND GRANT ME WHAT I ASK • • • 62 SOHRAB RUSTUM 54
TO MEET ME MAN TO MAN IF I PREVAIL • • • • • 62 SOHRAB RUSTUM 57
VALIANT OR CRAVEN YOUNG OR OLD TO ME • • • • • 68 SOHRAB RUSTUM 253
BEHOLD ME I AM VAST AND CLAD IN IRON • • • • • 71 SOHRAB RUSTUM 325
TO IRAN AND BE AS MY SON TO ME • • • • • • 71 SOHRAB RUSTUM 331
AH ME I MUSE WHAT THIS YOUNG FOX MAY MEAN • • • 71 SOHRAB RUSTUM 347
TO COPE WITH ME IN SINGLE FIGHT BUT THEY • • • 72 SOHRAB RUSTUM 359
THEN WERE THE CHIEFS OF IRAN SHAMED THROUGH ME • • 72 SOHRAB RUSTUM 363
ART THOU SO FIERCE THOU WILT NOT FRIGHT ME SO • • 72 SOHRAB RUSTUM 380
AND THOU SHALT TALK TO ME OF RUSTUMS DEEDS • • • 74 SOHRAB RUSTUM 442
BUT OH LET THERE BE PEACE TWIXT THEE AND ME • • 74 SOHRAB RUSTUM 447
FIGHT LET ME HEAR THY HATEFUL VOICE NO MORE • • 75 SOHRAB RUSTUM 459
OF BATTLE AND WITH ME WHO MAKE NO PLAY • • • 75 SOHRAB RUSTUM 463
SPEAK NOT TO ME OF TRUCE AND PLEDGE AND WINE • • 75 SOHRAB RUSTUM 465
BECAUSE THOU HAST SHAMED ME BEFORE BOTH THE HOSTS 75 SOHRAB RUSTUM 468
THOU DOST NOT SLAY ME PROUD AND BOASTFUL MAN • • 77 SOHRAB RUSTUM 542
NO RUSTUM SLAYS ME AND THIS FILIAL HEART • • • 77 SOHRAB RUSTUM 543

ME   (CONTINUED)

THE STRIFE AND HURLD ME ON MY FATHERS SPEAR	82 SOHRAB RUSTUM	715
MY FATHER LET ME FEEL THAT I HAVE FOUND	82 SOHRAB RUSTUM	717
COME SIT BESIDE ME ON THIS SAND AND TAKE	82 SOHRAB RUSTUM	718
MY MOTHER TOLD ME OF THEE THOU BRAVE STEED	83 SOHRAB RUSTUM	743
COME LET ME LAY MY HAND UPON THY MANE	83 SOHRAB RUSTUM	746
OH THAT ITS WAVES WERE FLOWING OVER ME	83 SOHRAB RUSTUM	768
WHICH FOLLOW ME I PRAY THEE SLAY NOT THESE	84 SOHRAB RUSTUM	779
LET ME ENTREAT FOR THEM WHAT HAVE THEY DONE	84 SOHRAB RUSTUM	780
THEY FOLLOWD ME MY HOPE MY FAME MY STAR	84 SOHRAB RUSTUM	781
BUT ME THOU MUST BEAR HENCE NOT SEND WITH THEM	84 SOHRAB RUSTUM	783
BUT CARRY ME WITH THEE TO SEISTAN	84 SOHRAB RUSTUM	784
AND PLACE ME ON A BED AND MOURN FOR ME	84 SOHRAB RUSTUM	785
AND PLACE ME ON A BED AND MOURN FOR ME	84 SOHRAB RUSTUM	785
AND THOU MUST LAY ME IN THAT LOVELY EARTH	84 SOHRAB RUSTUM	787
AND QUIT THE HOST AND BEAR THEE HENCE WITH ME	84 SOHRAB RUSTUM	798
TILL THEN IF FATE SO WILLS LET ME ENDURE	85 SOHRAB RUSTUM	837
WHAT IRKS IT ME THAT MEN SPEAK SOHRABS PRAISE	68 SOHRAB RUSTUM	V 228
EACH FORTIETH WEB OF CLOTH TO ME	87 SICK KING BOKH	8
O HUSSEIN LEAD ME TO THE KING	87 SICK KING BOKH	10
PRICK ME THE FELLOW FROM THE PATH	89 SICK KING BOKH	43
AND ALL GRACE SHALL TO ME BE GRUDGED	91 SICK KING BOKH	102
BRING THOU TO ME HIS CORPSE HE SAID	91 SICK KING BOKH	128
IS IN MY SKIN WHICH ANGERS ME	93 SICK KING BOKH	184
ALL YE WHO HEAR ME AND INHABIT HEAVEN	96 BALDER DEAD 1	29
BY ME SHALL VENGEANCE ON THE MURDERER LOK	96 BALDER DEAD 1	37
MOTHER A CHILD OF BALE THOU BARST IN ME	98 BALDER DEAD 1	95
FOR FIRST THOU BAREST ME WITH BLINDED EYES	98 BALDER DEAD 1	96
THOU BAREST ME AND UNFORESEEING SOUL	98 BALDER DEAD 1	99
WITH ME FOR THUS ORDAINS THE COMMON RITE	103 BALDER DEAD 1	300
SAVE ME ALONE AND HELA SOLEMN QUEEN	104 BALDER DEAD 1	319
RUMBLES AND SHAKES TELL ME THY RACE AND HOME	107 BALDER DEAD 2	103
DO THE GODS SEND TO ME TO MAKE THEM BLEST	110 BALDER DEAD 2	204
FENRIS THE WOLF THE SERPENT HUGE AND ME	110 BALDER DEAD 2	208
ME ON THIS CHEERLESS NETHER WORLD YE THREW	110 BALDER DEAD 2	212
AND GAVE ME NINE UNLIGHTED REALMS TO RULE	110 BALDER DEAD 2	213
SHOW ME THROUGH ALL THE WORLD THE SIGNS OF GRIEF	111 BALDER DEAD 2	234
BUT COME DECLARE ME THIS AND TRULY TELL	111 BALDER DEAD 2	243
HERMOD THE NIMBLE GILD ME NOT MY DEATH	112 BALDER DEAD 2	264
MEMORIAL OF ME WHETHER SAVED OR NO	112 BALDER DEAD 2	275
ME SITTING HERE BELOW BY HELAS SIDE	112 BALDER DEAD 2	277
FOR HE MY HUSBAND LEFT ME HERE TO PINE	116 BALDER DEAD 3	106
FIRST DROVE HIM FROM ME INTO DISTANT LANDS	116 BALDER DEAD 3	108
MY DUNGEON WHERE THE SERPENTS STUNG ME DEAD	117 BALDER DEAD 3	146
DRAWN IN HIS CAR BESIDE ME AND MY SONS	120 BALDER DEAD 3	240
THEN ME THOU MADST OF US THE GODS WERE BORN	121 BALDER DEAD 3	267
ME AND MY WORDS THOUGH THOU BE FIRST IN HEAVEN	121 BALDER DEAD 3	283
THINE ELDEST AND OF ME THE GODS ARE SPRUNG	121 BALDER DEAD 3	285
BELOW AND DOST THOU HATE ME EVEN HERE	125 BALDER DEAD 3	406
BALDER UPBRAIDS ME NOT NOR HATES AT ALL	125 BALDER DEAD 3	407
BROTHER AND FELLOW-SPORT OF LOK WITH ME	125 BALDER DEAD 3	412
THOU DOEST WELL TO CHIDE ME HODER BLIND	125 BALDER DEAD 3	423
YET MOURN NOT FOR ME HERMOD WHEN THOU SITTST	126 BALDER DEAD 3	456
FOR NANNA HATH REJOIND ME WHO OF OLD	126 BALDER DEAD 3	459
AND STILL THE ACCEPTANCE FOLLOWS ME WHICH CROWND	126 BALDER DEAD 3	461
MY FORMER LIFE AND CHEERS ME EVEN HERE	126 BALDER DEAD 3	462
LOVE ME AND GLADLY BRING FOR MY AWARD	126 BALDER DEAD 3	465
MOURN NOT FOR ME MOURN HERMOD FOR THE GODS	127 BALDER DEAD 3	484
BUT NOT TO ME SO GRIEVOUS AS I KNOW	127 BALDER DEAD 3	500
INACTIVE THEREFORE LET ME LIE IN GLOOM	128 BALDER DEAD 3	509
TELL ME THAT I MAY PONDER IT WHEN GONE	128 BALDER DEAD 3	516
DEATH AND THE GLOOM WHICH ROUND ME EVEN NOW	129 BALDER DEAD 3	546
TRUST ME AND GLADLY BRING FOR MY AWARD	126 BALDER DEAD 3	V 465
PROP ME UPON THE PILLOWS ONCE AGAIN	130 TRISTRAM 1	2
RAISE ME MY PAGE THIS CANNOT LONG ENDURE	130 TRISTRAM 1	3
REACH ME MY GOLDEN PHIAL STANDS BY THEE	133 TRISTRAM 1	100
BUT PLEDGE ME IN IT FIRST FOR COURTESY	133 TRISTRAM 1	101
PLEDGE ME IN MY GOLDEN CUP	135 TRISTRAM 1	146
MADCAP WHAT JEST WAS THIS TO MEET ME HERE	135 TRISTRAM 1	162
FLY SAVE THYSELF SAVE ME I DARE NOT STAY	135 TRISTRAM 1	168
COME LET ME LEAVE THE SHADOW OF THIS WOOD	139 TRISTRAM 1	281
IS MY PAGE HERE COME TURN ME TO THE FIRE	139 TRISTRAM 1	298
OF ME SHE RECKS NOT NOR MY VAIN DESIRE	140 TRISTRAM 1	303
TO-NIGHT MY PAGE SHALL KEEP ME COMPANY	140 TRISTRAM 1	310
WHERE DO THE CHILDREN SLEEP KISS THEM FOR ME	140 TRISTRAM 1	311
REACH ME MY GOLDEN CUP THAT STANDS BY THEE	133 TRISTRAM 1	V 100
AND PLEDGE ME IN IT FIRST FOR COURTESY	133 TRISTRAM 1	V 101
OF ME SHE RECKS NOT NOR OF MY DESIRE	140 TRISTRAM 1	V 303
BLAME ME NOT POOR SUFFERER THAT I TARRIED	142 TRISTRAM 2	5
THOU ART COME INDEED THOU HAST REJOIND ME	142 TRISTRAM 2	9
TAKE MY HAND DEAR TRISTRAM LOOK ON ME	142 TRISTRAM 2	16
FEAR ME NOT I WILL BE ALWAYS WITH THEE	143 TRISTRAM 2	29
SIT SIT BY ME I WILL THINK WEVE LIVED SO	143 TRISTRAM 2	35
ALTERD TRISTRAM NOT IN COURTS BELIEVE ME	143 TRISTRAM 2	37
THOSE WERE FRIENDS TO MAKE ME FALSE TO THEE	144 TRISTRAM 2	48
ME A SMILING QUEEN UPON MY THRONE	144 TRISTRAM 2	52
HUSH NO WORDS THAT SMILE I SEE FORGIVES ME	144 TRISTRAM 2	69
THE DEEP DRAUGHTS OF DEATH IN BEARING ME	145 TRISTRAM 2	84
GRIEF SINCE THEN HIS HOME WITH ME DOTH MAKE	145 TRISTRAM 2	88
ME THY LIVING FRIEND THOU CANST NOT SAVE	145 TRISTRAM 2	90

ME

(CONTINUED)

SAY I WILLD SO THAT THOU STAY BESIDE ME • • • 145 TRISTRAM 2 95
TRISTRAM TRISTRAM STAY RECEIVE ME WITH THEE • • 146 TRISTRAM 2 99
WHAT HAS SOME GLAMOUR MADE ME SLEEP • • • • • 148 TRISTRAM 2 175
AND SENT ME WITH MY DOGS TO SWEEP • • • • • • 148 TRISTRAM 2 176
SAY I CHARGD HER THAT THOU STAY BESIDE ME • • • 145 TRISTRAM 2 V 95
NOW STAND CLEAR BEFORE ME IN THE MOONLIGHT • • • 145 TRISTRAM 2 V 97
AND YET I SWEAR IT ANGERS ME TO SEE • • • • • 153 TRISTRAM 3 133
HE GAZED UPON ME AS I PASSD • • • • • • • • 158 SAINT BRANDAN 49
AND MURMURD HELP ME OR I DIE • • • • • • • • 158 SAINT BRANDAN 50
AND FRIENDS ME IN THE PIT OF FIRE • • • • • • 158 SAINT BRANDAN 64
ONCE SHE SATE WITH YOU AND ME • • • • • • • 163 FORSAKEN MERM 50
TWILL BE EASTER-TIME IN THE WORLD AH ME • • • • 163 FORSAKEN MERM 58
BUT AH SHE GAVE ME NEVER A LOOK • • • • • 163 FORSAKEN MERM 80
CARE NOT FOR THAT AND LAY ME WHERE I FALL • • • 173 MONICAS PRAYER 2
BUT AT GODS ALTAR OH REMEMBER ME • • • • • • 173 MONICAS PRAYER 4
WHAT WOULD YE HAVE WITH ME • • • • • • • 174 MEETING 14
AH WITH YOU LET ME GO • • • • • • • • • 175 PARTING 10
AH WITH THAT LET ME GO • • • • • • • • • 176 PARTING 44
FORGIVE ME FORGIVE ME • • • • • • • • • 176 PARTING 59
FORGIVE ME FORGIVE ME • • • • • • • • • 176 PARTING 59
BLOW YE WINDS LIFT ME WITH YOU • • • • • • • 177 PARTING 75
AH CALM ME RESTORE ME • • • • • • • • • 177 PARTING 83
AH CALM ME RESTORE ME • • • • • • • • • 177 PARTING 83
HAD BORNE ME FAR FROM THEE • • • • • • • • 183 ABSENCE 4
STAY WITH ME MARGUERITE STILL • • • • • • • 183 ABSENCE 20
DOWN ON ME THY RIGHT ARM • • • • • • • • • 186 STRAYED REVEL 8
I SPRANG UP I THREW ROUND ME • • • • • • • 186 STRAYED REVEL 29
MORE SOFT AH ME • • • • • • • • • • • 187 STRAYED REVEL 65
FAINT FAINT AH ME • • • • • • • • • • • 187 STRAYED REVEL 68
SITTING BY ME WHILE HIS FAUNS • • • • • • • 194 STRAYED REVEL 265
HE TOLD ME THESE THINGS • • • • • • • • • 194 STRAYED REVEL 269
YE FADE YE SWIM YE WAVER BEFORE ME • • • • • 194 STRAYED REVEL 290
AH ME HONOUREST MORE THAN THY LOVER • • • • • 196 FRAG ANTIGONE 51
BUT LIKE ME SHE WROTH COMPLAINING • • • • • • 197 FRAG ANTIGONE 76
YET LET ME SAY THAT THOU WAST FAIR • • • • • 203 EUPHROSYNE 2
YET LET ME SAY THAT THOU WERT FAIR • • • • • 203 EUPHROSYNE V 2
YET LET ME SAY THAT SHE WAS FAIR • • • • • • 203 EUPHROSYNE V 2
AH LET ME WEEP AND TELL MY PAIN • • • • • • 206 RIVER 11
STOP NOT TO ME AT THIS BITTER DEPARTING • • • 206 SEPARATION 1
ME LET NO HALF-EFFACED MEMORIES CUMBER • • • • 206 SEPARATION 9
DEAD BE THE PAST AND ITS PHANTOMS TO ME • • • • 206 SEPARATION 12
THEN WHEN WE MEET AND THY LOOK STRAYS TOWARD ME • 206 SEPARATION 13
WHO LET ME SAY IS THIS STRANGER REGARDS ME • • • 206 SEPARATION 15
WHO LET ME SAY IS THIS STRANGER REGARDS ME • • • 206 SEPARATION 15
THEN WHEN WE MEET AND THY LOOK STRAYS TOWARDS ME • 206 SEPARATION V 13
AND WERE IT SNAPT THOU LOVST ME NOT • • • • • 208 ON THE RHINE 9
AWHILE LET ME WITH THOUGHT HAVE DONE • • • • • 208 ON THE RHINE 11
SO LET ME LIE AND CALM AS THEY • • • • • • • 208 ON THE RHINE 16
COME TO ME IN MY DREAMS AND THEN • • • • • • 208 LONGING 1
AS KIND TO OTHERS AS TO ME • • • • • • • • 208 LONGING 8
COME NOW AND LET ME DREAM IT TRUTH • • • • • 209 LONGING 10
COME TO ME IN MY DREAMS AND THEN • • • • • • 209 LONGING 13
AS KIND TO ALL THE REST AS ME • • • • • • • 208 LONGING V 8
COME NOW AND LET ME DEEM IT TRUTH • • • • • • 209 LONGING V 10
THEY NEVER SHONE FOR ME • • • • • • • • • 209 DESPONDENCY 4
THEY LIGHT ME ONCE THEY HURRY BY • • • • • • 209 DESPONDENCY 7
TELL ME CAN YOU FIND INDEED • • • • • • • • 215 PIS-ALLER 6
YOURSELVES AND YOUR FELLOWS YE KNOW NOT AND ME • • 231 YOUTH OF NATURE 117
WILL YE SCAN ME AND READ ME AND TELL • • • • • 231 YOUTH OF NATURE 119
WILL YE SCAN ME AND READ ME AND TELL • • • • • 231 YOUTH OF NATURE 119
AT THIS VESSELS PROW I STAND WHICH BEARS ME • • 239 SELF-DEPENDENCE 3
YE WHO FROM MY CHILDHOOD UP HAVE CALMD ME • • • 240 SELF-DEPENDENCE 7
CALM ME AH COMPOSE ME TO THE END • • • • • • 240 SELF-DEPENDENCE 8
CALM ME AH COMPOSE ME TO THE END • • • • • • 240 SELF-DEPENDENCE 8
STILL STILL LET ME AS I GAZE UPON YOU • • • • 240 SELF-DEPENDENCE 11
AT THE VESSELS PROW I STAND WHICH BEARS ME • • • 239 SELF-DEPENDENCE V 3
I FEEL A NAMELESS SADNESS OER ME ROLL • • • • 245 BURIED LIFE 3
GIVE ME THY HAND AND HUSH AWHILE • • • • • • 245 BURIED LIFE 9
AND LET ME READ THERE LOVE THY INMOST SOUL • • • 245 BURIED LIFE 11
CALM CALM ME MORE NOR LET ME DIE • • • • • • 249 KENSINGTON GARD 43
CALM CALM ME MORE NOR LET ME DIE • • • • • • 249 KENSINGTON GARD 43
OF FORTUNES FAVOUR SONS NOT ME • • • • • • • 249 WISH 4
SPARE ME THE WHISPERING CROWDED ROOM • • • • • 250 WISH 13
NOR BRING TO SEE ME CEASE TO LIVE • • • • • • 250 WISH 17
BRING NONE OF THESE BUT LET ME BE • • • • • • 250 WISH 29
THERE LET ME GAZE TILL I BECOME • • • • • • 251 WISH 41
THUS FEELING GAZING LET ME GROW • • • • • • 251 WISH V 49
AND BOWER ME FROM THE AUGUST SUN WITH SHADE • • 256 SCHOLAR-GIPSY 29
AND NEAR ME ON THE GRASS LIES GLANVILS BOOK • • 256 SCHOLAR-GIPSY 31
COME LET ME READ THE OFT-READ TALE AGAIN • • • 256 SCHOLAR-GIPSY 32
BEFALLS ME WANDERING THROUGH THIS UPLAND DIM • • 263 THYRSIS 23
AH ME THIS MANY A YEAR • • • • • • • • • 263 THYRSIS 36
YET THYRSIS LET ME GIVE MY GRIEF ITS HOUR • • • 265 THYRSIS 102
YES THOU ART GONE AND ROUND ME TOO THE NIGHT • • 266 THYRSIS 131
QUICK LET ME FLY AND CROSS • • • • • • • • 267 THYRSIS 156
THERE THOU ART GONE AND ME THOU LEAVEST HERE • • 268 THYRSIS 191
KNOW HIM A WANDERER STILL THEN WHY NOT ME • • • 268 THYRSIS 200
THOU WANDEREDST WITH ME FOR A LITTLE HOUR • • • 269 THYRSIS 212
I CLIMBD BENEATH ME BRIGHT AND WIDE • • • • • 273 STANZAS CARNAC 3

ME   (CONTINUED)

BEHIND ME ON THEIR GRASSY SWEEP . . . . 274 STANZAS CARNAC   9
SO MOONLIT SAW ME ONCE OF YORE . . . . 275 SOUTHERN NIGHT   14
POSSESS ME QUITE . . . . 276 SOUTHERN NIGHT   20
STILL ART TO ME . . . . 276 SOUTHERN NIGHT   40
AH ME GIBRALTARS STRAND IS FAR . . . . 277 SOUTHERN NIGHT   49
WHO ALL ROUND ME TO-DAY . . . . 290 RUGBY CHAPEL   156
BUT SOMETHING PROMPTS ME NOT THUS . . . . . . 298 HEINES GRAVE   199
ALL ARE BEFORE ME I BEHOLD . . . . . . 301 GRANDE CHARTR   64
SHOWD ME THE HIGH WHITE STAR OF TRUTH . . . . 301 GRANDE CHARTR   69
THERE BADE ME GAZE AND THERE ASPIRE . . . . . 301 GRANDE CHARTR   70
FORGIVE ME MASTERS OF THE MIND . . . . . 301 GRANDE CHARTR   73
OH HIDE ME IN YOUR GLOOM PROFOUND . . . . . 302 GRANDE CHARTR   91
TAKE ME COWLD FORMS AND FENCE ME ROUND . . . 302 GRANDE CHARTR   93
TAKE ME COWLD FORMS AND FENCE ME ROUND . . . 302 GRANDE CHARTR   93
TILL FREE MY THOUGHTS BEFORE ME ROLL . . . . 302 GRANDE CHARTR   95
SHOWD ME THE PALE COLD STAR OF TRUTH . . . . 301 GRANDE CHARTR   V 69
INVEST ME STEEP ME FOLD ME ROUND . . . . . 302 GRANDE CHARTR   V 93
INVEST ME STEEP ME FOLD ME ROUND . . . . . 302 GRANDE CHARTR   V 93
INVEST ME STEEP ME FOLD ME ROUND . . . . . 302 GRANDE CHARTR   V 93
ONCE MORE UPON ME ROLL . . . . . . 306 OBERMANN   14
I GO FATE DRIVES ME BUT I LEAVE . . . . . . 310 OBERMANN   131
WILT NOT IF THOU CANST SEE ME NOW . . . . . 310 OBERMANN   139
CONDEMN ME NOR UPBRAID . . . . 310 OBERMANN   140
WHAT THOUGHTS TO ME HIS ROCKS RECALL . . . . 313 OBERMANN MORE   35
OBERMANN WITH ME HERE . . . . 313 OBERMANN MORE   38
ON THE GRASS NEAR ME STOOD . . . . . 314 OBERMANN MORE   60
BACK TO THY YOUTH AND ME . . . . . . 314 OBERMANN MORE   72
AH ME WE ANCHORITES READ THINGS BEST . . . . 314 OBERMANN MORE   75
THOU FLEDST ME WHEN THE UNGENIAL EARTH . . . 315 OBERMANN MORE   77
HAD BEEN TOO COLD FOR ME . . . . . . 317 OBERMANN MORE   150
FOR ME NO EASTERN DESERT LONE . . . . . 317 OBERMANN MORE   151
AH ME WE ANCHORITES KNEW IT BEST . . . . 314 OBERMANN MORE   V 75
THOU FLEDDST ME WHEN THE UNGENIAL EARTH . . 315 OBERMANN MORE   V 77
MY MOTHERS FAITHFUL SERVANT LAID ME DOWN . . . 331 MEROPE   31
AND ME BELIEVE IT WISE MEN GRAVELY BLAME . . . 333 MEROPE   94
AND IGNORANT MEN DESPISE ME THAT I STAND . . . 333 MEROPE   95
AND EVEN NOW IF TO BEHOLD ME HERE . . . . . 333 MEROPE   104
HEAR ME THEN SPEAK AND LET THIS MOURNFUL DAY . 333 MEROPE   114
HE HAD SMIT ME HAD HE BEEN SWIFT AS I . . . 334 MEROPE   131
ME TOO HAD HE PREVAILD HE HAD NOT SCORND . . 334 MEROPE   133
SOMETHING TOO STUDIOUSLY FORGIVE ME SHOWN . . 334 MEROPE   142
LEAVES ME AUSTERER STERNER THAN I WOULD . . . 335 MEROPE   155
THE CARES WHICH MIGHT IN ME WITH TIME I FEEL . 335 MEROPE   161
BEGET A CRUEL TEMPER HELP ME QUELL . . . . 335 MEROPE   162
THE BREACH BETWEEN OUR PARTIES HELP ME CLOSE . 335 MEROPE   163
ASSIST ME TO RULE MILDLY LET US JOIN . . . 335 MEROPE   164
AND WHO THOU ART WHO SPEAKEST TO ME I . . 335 MEROPE   183
THIS WERE ENOUGH BUT LET ME TELL THEE TOO . . 338 MEROPE   282
AND NOW TO ME THOU TENDEREST FRIENDLY LEAGUE . 340 MEROPE   333
FOR ME I DEEM SUCH IMPIOUS AND FOR HIM . . 340 MEROPE   336
TO CHANCE IMPUTE THEIR DEATHS THEN NOT TO ME . 340 MEROPE   346
NOT MUCH A TYRANT THY FREE SPEECH DISPLAYS ME . 340 MEROPE   350
HOLDS RULE AH ME AH . . . . . . 345 MEROPE   475
SOME FORM AH ME AH . . . . 346 MEROPE   493
BRING TO ME SAFE LET THE REST . . . . 348 MEROPE   535
ONLY TO ME GIVE MY CHILD . . . . 348 MEROPE   540
AN AVENGER I ASK NOT SEND ME MY SON . . . 348 MEROPE   544
FORGIVE ME MAIDENS IF I SEEM TOO SLACK . . . 348 MEROPE   548
CAN VENGEANCE GIVE ME BACK THE MURDERED NO . . 349 MEROPE   567
BRINGING ME OF MY BOY THE ANNUAL NEWS . . 350 MEROPE   599
TO HEAR THAT STILL HE LOVES STILL LONGS FOR ME 351 MEROPE   613
MAIDENS ASSURE ME IF THEY TOLD ME TRUE . . . 354 MEROPE   703
MAIDENS ASSURE ME IF THEY TOLD ME TRUE . . . 354 MEROPE   703
WHO TOLD ME THAT THE ROYAL HOUSE WAS HERE . . 354 MEROPE   704
AND WHO ART THOU WHO BRINGEST ME SUCH NEWS . . 355 MEROPE   716
INSTRUCT ME OF THE MANNER OF HIS DEATH . . . 355 MEROPE   720
ANOTHER ANCESTOR NAMED TOO LIKE ME . . . 357 MEROPE   780
HE TO THEE SENDS ME ON IN ONE THING GLAD . . 359 MEROPE   850
TELL ME HATH ONE NOT COME OR WORSE MISCHANCE . 361 MEROPE   918
AH ME THE WRONG EXPECTANT GOT HIS NEWS . . . 361 MEROPE   922
THOU FRIGHTENEST AND CONFOUNDST ME BY THY WORDS 362 MEROPE   932
AH AH AH ME AND I TOO SAY AH ME . . . 363 MEROPE   948
AH AH AH ME AND I TOO SAY AH ME . . . 363 MEROPE   948
AH ME WITH WHAT A FOOT DOTH TREASON POST . . 363 MEROPE   962
AND ME HENCEFORTH SOLE RIVAL WITH HIMSELF . . 366 MEROPE   1003
IN THEIR ALLEGIANCE ME IN MY SONS DEATH-HOUR . 366 MEROPE   1004
WHEN ALL TURND TOWRDS ME ME HE WOULD HAVE SHOWN 366 MEROPE   1005
WHEN ALL TURND TOWRDS ME ME HE WOULD HAVE SHOWN 366 MEROPE   1005
HOW MUCH MEN THINK ME ABJECT VOID OF HEART . . 366 MEROPE   1016
HAVE TEMPERD ME EEN THUS AND IN SOME SOULS . . 366 MEROPE   1024
AND EVEN NOW MY SON AH ME MY SON . . . 366 MEROPE   1026
WHO SADLY ASK ME WHAT IF NOT REVENGE . . . 367 MEROPE   1039
KEPT ME THEIR MOTHER FROM THEIR SIDE SO LONG . 367 MEROPE   1040
FLY FIND ME ON THE INSTANT WHERE CONFER . . 368 MEROPE   1071
UNFAITHFUL SERVANT DOST THOU TOO DESERT ME . . 368 MEROPE   1076
THOU DESTROYEST ME HOW . . . . . . 369 MEROPE   1087
AH ME . . . . 370 MEROPE   1103
THOU FATE GIVES IT AH ME . . . . . . 370 MEROPE   1111
SWEAR BY THE GODS HENCEFORTH TO OBEY ME . . . 371 MEROPE   1133

ME   (CONTINUED)
          FETCH ME THE SACRIFICE-AXE . . . . 371 MEROPE   1138
          APPALS ME SHAKES ME WITH AWE . . . . 372 MEROPE   1146
          APPALS ME SHAKES ME WITH AWE . . . . 372 MEROPE   1146
          AH ME . . . . 373 MEROPE   1165
          WAKES ME THUS KINDLY FROM THE PERILOUS SLEEP . . 375 MEROPE   1203
          O MOTHER MOTHER WHO UPBRAIDS ME AH . . . . . 376 MEROPE   1213
          PRESSES ME CHIDES ME WILL NOT LET ME WEEP . . . 378 MEROPE   1233
          PRESSES ME CHIDES ME WILL NOT LET ME WEEP . . . 378 MEROPE   1233
          PRESSES ME CHIDES ME WILL NOT LET ME WEEP . . . 378 MEROPE   1233
          THAT WORD IT KILLS ME I SEE . . . . 378 MEROPE   1243
          INSTRUCT ME NOT I HAVE MY LESSON CLEAR . . . . 379 MEROPE   1259
          YES AND ALONE IS WITH ME HERE TO SHARE . . . . 379 MEROPE   1268
          ANNOUNCES ME THEIR RIGHTFUL PRINCE RETURND . . . 383 MEROPE   1355
          TO SUCCOUR ME IN MY EXTREMEST NEED . . . . . 383 MEROPE   1376
          YET FOR ME MOTHER I HAD LIEFER DIE . . . . . 383 MEROPE   1379
          IN ME THE FEVER OF REVENGEFUL HATE . . . . . 387 MEROPE   1466
          AND I WOULD NOW HAVE JUSTICE STRIKE NOT ME . . . 387 MEROPE   1472
          TO EFFACE IN ME THE MEMORY OF HIS CRIME . . . . 387 MEROPE   1478
          THOUGH IT EFFACE NOT THAT YET MAKES ME WISH . . 387 MEROPE   1479
          TREACHEROUSLY PLOTTED TWIXT MY SON AND ME . . . 387 MEROPE   1481
          TO ME AND THE MESSENIANS LEAVE THE REST . . . 391 MEROPE   1593
          TELLS ME ENOUGH THOU KNOWST THE NEWS WHICH ALL . 393 MEROPE   1685
          TWIXT THEE AND ME SUSPICION THAT I NURSED . . . 394 MEROPE   1699
          THE THOUGHT OF VENGEANCE ON ME NEVER QUITE . . . 394 MEROPE   1704
          AND FROM THAT TEACHER MAYST HAVE LEARND LIKE ME . 394 MEROPE   1709
          TO THE PRESERVER ZEUS LET ME RETURN . . . . . 395 MEROPE   1723
          FIRST FOR OUR UNION TRUST ME TWIXT US TWO . . . 395 MEROPE   1733
          NOT MENS GOOD WORD HATH MADE ME WHAT I AM . . . 398 MEROPE   1791
          THE REST TO ME IS LITTLE YET SINCE THAT . . . . 401 MEROPE   1891
          REJOICE WITH US AND TRUST ME HE WHO WISHD . . . 403 MEROPE   1958
          MOTHER ALL THESE APPROVE ME BUT IF THOU . . . . 403 MEROPE   1961
          HIS BLOOD TO ME FOR I CONFESS IT KIND . . . . 404 MEROPE   1976
          WHAT THEY WILL BUT TO ME GIVE MY SON . . . . 348 MEROPE   V
          DESPISE THEM NOT FOR BROTHER THOU LIKE ME . . . 388 MEROPE   V1511
          RISE FAINTLY TO ME NOW IT STOPS WHOS HERE . . . 407 EMPEDOCLES I 1   29
          HE KNEW ME WELL AND WOULD OFT NOTICE ME . . . . 408 EMPEDOCLES I 1   57
          HE KNEW ME WELL AND WOULD OFT NOTICE ME . . . . 408 EMPEDOCLES I 1   57
          AND STILL I KNOW NOT HOW HE DRAWS ME TO HIM . . 408 EMPEDOCLES I 1   58
          IS POTENT STILL ON ME IN HIS DECLINE . . . . . 408 EMPEDOCLES I 1   66
          BUT TELL ME HOW HAST THOU PERSUADED HIM . . . . 409 EMPEDOCLES I 1   105
          AND HE WOULD TELL ME AS HIS OLD TRIED FRIEND . . 410 EMPEDOCLES I 1   130
          WHO STILL WAS FAITHFUL WHAT MIGHT PROFIT ME . . 410 EMPEDOCLES I 1   131
          INSTRUCT ME OF PANTHEIAS STORY MASTER . . . . 412 EMPEDOCLES I 2   20
          FOR I MUST BE ALONE LEAVE ME ONE MULE . . . . 428 EMPEDOCLES I 2   465
          AND FOR YOUNG CALLICLES THANK HIM FROM ME . . . 428 EMPEDOCLES I 2   467
          BUT HE MUST FOLLOW ME NO MORE TO-NIGHT . . . . 428 EMPEDOCLES I 2   469
          THOU KNOWST ME FOR A WANDERER FRO4 OF OLD . . . 428 EMPEDOCLES I 2   477
          MEANWHILE STAY ME NOT NOW FAREWELL PAUSANIAS . . 428 EMPEDOCLES I 2   478
          RECEIVE ME HIDE ME QUENCH ME TAKE ME HOME . . . 429 EMPEDOCLES II   36
          RECEIVE ME HIDE ME QUENCH ME TAKE ME HOME . . . 429 EMPEDOCLES II   36
          RECEIVE ME HIDE ME QUENCH ME TAKE ME HOME . . . 429 EMPEDOCLES II   36
          RECEIVE ME HIDE ME QUENCH ME TAKE ME HOME . . . 429 EMPEDOCLES II   36
          WHO THRONGD ME IN THEIR CITIES . . . . 432 EMPEDOCLES II   113
          WHO WORSHIPPD ME IN THEIR HOUSES . . . . . . 432 EMPEDOCLES II   114
          OH THAT FATE HAD LET ME SEE . . . . 432 EMPEDOCLES II   125
          TAKE THY BOUGH SET ME FREE FROM MY SOLITUDE . . 435 EMPEDOCLES II   218
          AS THEY ARE DEAD TO ME . . . . 437 EMPEDOCLES II   275
          THEY ARE WITH ME NOT YOU YE ARE ALIVE . . . . 438 EMPEDOCLES II   303
          BRILLIANT ABOVE ME AND THOU FIERY WORLD . . . . 438 EMPEDOCLES II   305
          YE KNOW IT TOO IT HATH BEEN GRANTED ME . . . . 441 EMPEDOCLES II   405
          RECEIVE ME SAVE ME . . . . 441 EMPEDOCLES II   416
          RECEIVE ME SAVE ME . . . . 441 EMPEDOCLES II   416
          THEIR KINDNESS SHOWN ME IN MY WANDERING HOUR . . 447 WESTMIN ABBEY   109
          AY ME TIS DEAF THAT EAR . . . . 449 WESTMIN ABBEY   161
          WHICH MAKE ME FOR THY PRESENCE YEARN . . . . 450 GEISTS GRAVE   6
          DIRGE FROM ME TO CROWN THEIR GRAVE . . . . . 454 POOR MATTHIAS   82
          MOVES ME SOMEHOW TO REMORSE . . . . 454 POOR MATTHIAS   84
          DROVE MY DAUGHTER SMALL AND ME . . . . . . 457 POOR MATTHIAS   179
          THOSE STERNER SPIRITS LET ME PRIZE . . . . . 481 COURAGE   9
          HAVE NOT LIFE AND LOVE BEEN GRANTED ME . . . . 482 THEKLAS ANSWER   4
          WOMAN I TOO TAKE THOUGHT FOR THIS BUT THEN   HOMER TRANS   14
               I BETHINK ME
          NOR WOULD MY OWN HEART LET ME MY HEART WHICH   HOMER TRANS   17
               HAS BID ME BE VALIANT
          NOR WOULD MY OWN HEART LET ME MY HEART WHICH   HOMER TRANS   17
               HAS BID ME BE VALIANT
          MOVES ME SO MUCH NOT HECUBAS GRIEF NOR PRIAM   HOMER TRANS   24
               MY FATHERS
          AT THY WANT OF A MAN LIKE ME TO SAVE THEE FROM BONDAGE HOMER TRANS   36
          BUT LET ME BE DEAD AND THE EARTH BE MOUNDED ABOVE ME   HOMER TRANS   37
          BUT LET ME BE DEAD AND THE EARTH BE MOUNDED ABOVE ME   HOMER TRANS   37
          WHY DOST THOU PROPHESY SO MY DEATH TO ME XANTHUS   HOMER TRANS   59
               IT NEEDS NOT
          YOUR SWEET EYES ARE TURNED ON ME . . . . . .   META CLOISTER   20
          SPARE ME META QUESTION RATHER . . . .   META CLOISTER   25
          TELL ME IS IT QUIET HERE . . . .   META CLOISTER   28
          TO ME IT SEEMS AS VAIN LUCRETIUS . . . . . .   LUCRETIUS 3   1

MEAD
          AND THE VALKYRIES CROWND THEIR HORNS WITH MEAD .   97 BALDER DEAD 1   68
          AND FROM THEIR HORNS WITH SILVER RIMMD DRANK MEAD 119 BALDER DEAD 3   211
          AND REST IN THE IMMORTAL MEAD . . . . 414 EMPEDOCLES I 2   75

MEADOW

RED LOOSESTRIFE AND BLOND MEADOW-SWEET AMONG • • 266 THYRSIS 124
WHAT DEEP-GRASSD MEADOW • • • • • • • • • • 391 MEROPE 1606
BACK TO THIS MEADOW OF CALAMITY • • • • • 440 EMPEDOCLES II 365
OER FLOWERING PLAIN AND BLOSSOMD MEADOW FLING • • 474 CROMWELL 91

MEADOWS

IN THE SAVOY MOUNTAIN-MEADOWS • • • • • • • 15 CHURCH BROU 1 91
IN THE MIDST OF RIVER-MEADOWS • • • • • • • 32 NEW SIRENS 181
IN THE MIST OF RIVER MEADOWS • • • • • • • 32 NEW SIRENS V 181
THE MEADOWS WHERE IT GLIDES THE SUN THE BREEZE • • 247 BURIED LIFE 90
MID WIDE GRASS MEADOWS WHICH THE SUNSHINE FILLS • 257 SCHOLAR-GIPSY 68
STRATFORD MEADOWS FOR THEE • • • • • • • 294 HEINES GRAVE 64
THROUGH ALPINE MEADOWS SOFT-SUFFUSED • • • • • 299 GRANDE CHARTR 1
MUTE IN THEIR MEADOWS LONE • • • • • • • • 306 OBERMANN 6

MEAL

RUSTUM HIS MORNING MEAL WAS DONE BUT STILL • • • 67 SOHRAB RUSTUM 196
BOTH ARMIES MOVED TO CAMP AND TOOK THEIR MEAL • • 86 SOHRAB RUSTUM 871
HE TETHERS HIS BEAST DOWN AND MAKES HIS MEAL • • 191 STRAYED REVEL 165
HE MAKES HIS MEAL BEFORE HIM FOR LONG MILES • • 191 STRAYED REVEL 172
SEES THEE NOR STOPS HIS MEAL NOR FEARS AT ALL • • 258 SCHOLAR-GIPSY 117

MEAN

WHEN THE MEAN SHALL NO MORE SORROW • • • • • 33 NEW SIRENS 215
ARE WHAT WE MEAN TO BE • • • • • • • • • 46 WORLD QUIETIST 8
AND WHAT THE RIGHTS OF MAN MAY MEAN • • • • • 48 HORATIAN ECHO 17
AH ME I MUSE WHAT THIS YOUNG FOX MAY MEAN • • • 71 SOHRAB RUSTUM 347
MIGHT MEAN AND FROM HIS DARK COMPASSIONATE EYES • • 82 SOHRAB RUSTUM 735
A POOR MEAN SOLDIER AND WITHOUT RENOWN • • • • 85 SOHRAB RUSTUM 814
AT A MEAN INN IN GERMAN AARAU BORN • • • • • 168 RACHEL 3 2
AND WHAT WE MEAN WE SAY AND WHAT WE WOULD WE KNOW 247 BURIED LIFE 87
FOR BEING OF LIKE AGE OF BIRTH NOT MEAN • • • 355 MEROPE 722
MEAN STILL TO KEEP ALOOF FROM DORIAN BROIL • • • 384 MEROPE 1396

MEANER

NO MEANER HAND THAN ODINS ON HIS MANE • • • • 107 BALDER DEAD 2 73

MEANING

ALL THE MEANING OF YOUR EYES • • • • • • • 34 NEW SIRENS 238
ALL MEANING FROM A NAME • • • • • • • • • 312 OBERMANN MORE 2

MEANINGS

FAMILIAR MEANINGS IN YOUR MYSTIC TONE • • • • 472 CROMWELL 4

MEANS

MEANS PARTING THAT ONLY IN ABSENCE LIES PAIN • • 19 MODERN SAPPHO V
WHICH TO PERFORM WE MADE IT MEANS FOR THAT • • • 330 MEROPE 25
WITH SUCH SLIGHT MEANS TO COPE WITH SUCH A FOE • • 381 MEROPE 1293
I ASK IF BLOODLESS MEANS MAY GAIN HIS END • • • 387 MEROPE 1465
WE WANT ALL PLEASANT ENDS BUT WILL USE NO HARSH MEANS 420 EMPEDOCLES I 2 236

MEANST

HIS PRESENCE WITH THE KING THOU MEANST IMPLIES • • 365 MEROPE V

MEANT

FOR WHICH THEY WERE NOT MEANT TO GIVE • • • • 185 TERRACE BERNE 44
THE WORD THE ORDER WHICH GOD MEANT SHOULD BE • • 239 REVOLUTIONS 18
MERE PRISONERS MEANT OR NOT AMONG OUR FOES • • • 337 MEROPE 251
THIS GOOD HE MEANT YOU AND FOR THIS HE DIED • • 339 MEROPE 313
I SAVED THEM MEANT THEM HONOUR BUT THY FRIENDS • • 340 MEROPE 343
SAILD BY THE FATE-MEANT GULF TO THEIR CONQUEST • • 344 MEROPE 450
MOST HONOURABLY I MEANT I CALL THE GODS • • • 394 MEROPE 1695
MEANT MERELY FOR HIS PLAY • • • • • • • • 418 EMPEDOCLES I 2 180

MEANTEST

WHAT MEANTEST THOU O POLYPHONTES WHAT • • • • 404 MEROPE 1979

MEANTIME

MEANTIME ON THEE THE TASK OF SILENCE ONLY • • • 390 MEROPE 1584

MEANWHILE

NOW MEANWHILE HAD MY BRETHREN FOUND • • • • • 90 SICK KING BOKH 77
MEANWHILE TO-MORROW WHEN THE MORNING DAWNS • • • 96 BALDER DEAD 1 40
SUCH FOR THE FUTURE IS MY HOPE MEANWHILE • • • 129 BALDER DEAD 3 544
MEANWHILE WITHIN MY FATHERS PALACE I • • • • 331 MEROPE 47
A TALE MEANWHILE FORGED FOR HIS SUBJECTS EARS • • 366 MEROPE 1002
MEANWHILE STAY ME NOT NOW FAREWELL PAUSANIAS • • 428 EMPEDOCLES I 2 478

MEASURE

TOOK MEASURE OF HIS SOUL AND KNEW ITS STRENGTH • • 12 MYCERINUS 109
HAST THOU YET DEALT HIM O LIFE THY FULL MEASURE • • 20 MODERN SAPPHO 33
IS THIS ALL THIS BALANCED MEASURE • • • • • 33 NEW SIRENS 199
QUIET LIVING STRICT-KEPT MEASURE • • • • • 49 SECOND BEST 2
THE MEASURE OF HIS RIGHTS • • • • • • • • 417 EMPEDOCLES I 2 155
WE MEASURE THE SEA-TIDES WE NUMBER THE SEA-SANDS • • 423 EMPEDOCLES I 2 321

MEASURED

AND WHEN SIX YEARS ARE MEASURED LO I DIE • • • • 9 MYCERINUS 18
THROUGH THE COLD GLOOM WITH MEASURED RACE • • • • 53 RESIGNATION 34

MEASURES
    MANS MEASURES CANNOT METE THE IMMEASURABLE ALL • • 423 EMPEDOCLES I 2   341
    MANS MEASURES CANNOT SPAN THE ILLIMITABLE ALL • • 423 EMPEDOCLES I 2 V 341

MEAT
    AND I HAVE MEAT AND DRINK AT WILL • • • • • • 94 SICK KING BOKH   213

MEATS
    AND ON THE TABLES STOOD THE UNTASTED MEATS • • • • 95 BALDER DEAD 1   13

MECCA
    SO PILGRIMS BOUND FOR MECCA PRAYD • • • • • • 52 RESIGNATION   3

MECHANIC
    OF MECHANIC BUSINESS AND LETS • • • • • • • • 295 HEINES GRAVE   82

MEDICINE
    HAD NO MEDICINE FOR THY MOOD • • • • • • • 139 TRISTRAM 1   291

MEDITATION
    A WEIGHT OF MEDITATION MIXD WITH PAIN • • • • 41 GIPSY CHILD V 12
    NO MEDITATION NO DELIGHT NO SORROW • • • • • 50 CONSOLATION V
    WHERE MEDITATION WAS • • • • • • • • • FRAGMENT 9   2

MEDITATIVE
    WHO LENT THEE CHILD THIS MEDITATIVE GUISE • • • • 41 GIPSY CHILD   3

MEDITERRANEAN
    MEDITERRANEAN WATERS LAVE • • • • • • 275 STANZAS CARNAC   39
    THE SOFT MEDITERRANEAN BREAKS • • • • • • • 275 SOUTHERN NIGHT   3
    THE SOFT MEDITERRANEAN SIDE • • • • • • • 277 SOUTHERN NIGHT   67

MEED
    WHEN THE DUPED SOUL SELF-MASTERD CLAIMS ITS MEED • • 9 MYCERINUS   28
    FINISHD THEIR WORK AND THEN A MEED REQUIRED • • 448 WESTMIN ABBEY   136
    LIVE HAPPY THEN EXPECT YOUR PERFECT MEED • • • 448 WESTMIN ABBEY   138
    HAD FINISHD AND A MEED OF PRICE REQUIRED • • • 448 WESTMIN ABBEY V 136
    MEED FOR DAILY SONG OF YORE • • • • • • 453 POOR MATTHIAS   19

MEEK
    O MEEK ANTICIPANT OF THAT SURE PAIN • • • • 43 GIPSY CHILD   41
    A MEEK LAST GLANCE OF LOVE DIDST THROW • • • 450 GEISTS GRAVE   35

MEEKLY
    HIS DROOPING HEAD BOWED MEEKLY ON HIS BREAST • • 476 CROMWELL   167

MEET
    KINGS HOLD REVEL GALLANTS MEET • • • • • • • 14 CHURCH BROU 1   54
    AND IMMORTAL FORMS TO MEET YOU • • • • • • • 29 NEW SIRENS   101
    BEAUTIFUL EYES MEET HIS AND HE • • • • • • • 57 RESIGNATION   160
    TO MEET ME MAN TO MAN IF I PREVAIL • • • • 62 SOHRAB RUSTUM   57
    WHOM I MAY MEET AND STRIKE AND FEEL NO PANG • • 74 SOHRAB RUSTUM   444
    FATHER FORBEAR FOR I BUT MEET TO-DAY • • • 82 SOHRAB RUSTUM   708
    IT WERE NOT MEET THE BALANCE SWERVED • • • 92 SICK KING BOKH   139
    FOR YE YOURSELVES YE GODS SHALL MEET YOUR DOOM • • 96 BALDER DEAD 1   28
    BUT OURS WE SHALL NOT MEET WHEN THAT DAY COMES • • 96 BALDER DEAD 1   31
    WHY SHOULD WE MEET ANOTHERS PORTION SO • • 96 BALDER DEAD 1   33
    LOATHING TO MEET AT DAWN THE OTHER GODS • • 102 BALDER DEAD 1   250
    FOR YOU YOURSELVES YE GODS SHALL MEET YOUR DOOM • • 96 BALDER DEAD 1 V 28
    DOUBTLESS THOU FEAREST TO MEET BALDERS VOICE • • 124 BALDER DEAD 3   392
    MADCAP WHAT JEST WAS THIS TO MEET ME HERE • • 135 TRISTRAM 1   162
    I AM HERE WE MEET I HOLD THY HAND • • • 142 TRISTRAM 2   8
    SO SUNK SO RARELY LIFTED SAVE TO MEET • • 151 TRISTRAM 3   71
    OH MIGHT OUR MARGES MEET AGAIN • • • • • 182 TO MARG CONT   18
    LIKE DRIFTWOOD SPARS WHICH MEET AND PASS • • 185 TERRACE BERNE   45
    LIKE SHIPS THAT MEET AND SPEAK AND PASS • • 185 TERRACE BERNE V 45
    THE LOVERS MEET BUT MEET TOO LATE • • • 207 TOO LATE   6
    THE LOVERS MEET BUT MEET TOO LATE • • • 207 TOO LATE   6
    THEN WHEN WE MEET AND THY LOOK STRAYS TOWARD ME • 206 SEPARATION   13
    THEN WHEN WE MEET AND THY LOOK STRAYS TOWARDS ME • 206 SEPARATION V 13
    NOW STRIFES ARE HUSHD OUR EARS DOTH MEET • • 219 BACCHANALIA 2   14
    NOW STRIFE IS HUSHD OUR EARS DOTH MEET • • 219 BACCHANALIA 2 V 14
    THE FOOT LESS PROMPT TO MEET THE MORNING DEW • 266 THYRSIS   138
    TO MEET HER PIRATE-LOVERS SHIP • • • • • 278 SOUTHERN NIGHT   105
    TWAS MEET TO LAY • • • • • • • 279 SOUTHERN NIGHT   112
    ONLY WITH STRANGERS TO MEET • • • • • 284 HAWORTH CHURCH   75
    AND LOOK TO MEET THEM THAT ONE GRIEF-PLUNGED FORM • 331 MEROPE   56
    OR WITH WHAT VOICE SHALL I THE QUESTIONS MEET • 367 MEROPE   1037
    WHAT BLOOD SO MEET AS THINE TO WASH IT OUT • • 402 MEROPE   1924
    WHAT HAND TO STRIKE THEE MEET AS MINE THE HAND • 402 MEROPE   1925
    AND SEE TO MEET THEM THAT ONE GRIEF-PLUNGED FORM • 331 MEROPE V 56
    SAVE MINE HE MUST NOT MEET A HUMAN EYE • • 408 EMPEDOCLES I 1   53
    THE CURTAINS OF THE BLUE FILMS SLOWLY MEET • • 431 EMPEDOCLES II   79
    MY SOUL GLOWS TO MEET YOU • • • • 441 EMPEDOCLES II   412
    ARE HAUNTS MEET FOR THEE • • • • • • 441 EMPEDOCLES II   422
    WHAT POOR KAI DEAD SAY ALL I MEET • • • 459 KAISER DEAD   9

MEETER
    HIS TALE WAS MEETER FOR THAT EAR THAN THINE • • 362 MEROPE   929

MEETEST
    BUT HE WHOM FIRST THOU MEETEST WHEN THOU COMST   • •   100 BALDER DEAD 1   189

MEETING
    I SAW THE MEETING OF TWO • • • • • • • • • • 280 HAWORTH CHURCH   7
    HOPE AT THAT MEETING SMILED FAIR   • • • • • • 281 HAWORTH CHURCH   26
    EVENING A MEETING I SAW • • • • • • • • • 280 HAWORTH CHURCH   V
    AT THIS FIRST MEETING AFTER ABSENCE LONG • • • • 386 MEROPE   1452
    AT THE MEETING VALLEYS • • • • • • • • • • 391 MEROPE   1607

MEETINGS
    FOR A BOUND WAS SET TO MEETINGS   • • • • • • • 30 NEW SIRENS   115
    BUT A BOUND WAS SET TO MEETINGS   • • • • • • 30 NEW SIRENS   V 115

MEETS
    WHO THROUGH ALL HE MEETS CAN STEER HIM   • • • 49 SECOND BEST   17
    WHERE HOST MEETS HOST AND MANY NAMES ARE SUNK • • 62 SOHRAB RUSTUM   61
    CROSSING THE STREAM IN SUMMER MEETS THE LAND • • 61 SOHRAB RUSTUM V 19
    FROM THE HIGH MOORS BEHIND AND MEETS THE SEA • • 97 BALDER DEAD 1   83
    NORTHWARD UNTIL HE MEETS A STRETCHING WALL • • • 100 BALDER DEAD 1   166
    FIRST MEETS THE FRINGING HEATH AT ONCE ALL ROUND • • TRISTRAM 3 V 14
    FIRST MEETS THE ENCIRCLING HEATH AT ONCE ALL ROUND   TRISTRAM 3 V 14
    MAN MEETS MAN MEETS AND QUITS AGAIN • • • • • 185 TERRACE BERNE   48
    MAN MEETS MAN MEETS AND QUITS AGAIN • • • • • 185 TERRACE BERNE   48
    MAN NEARS MAN MEETS AND LEAVES AGAIN • • • • • 185 TERRACE BERNE V 48
    WHERE THE SEA MEETS THE MOON-BLANCHD LAND • • • • 211 DOVER BEACH   8
    WHERE THE EBB MEETS THE MOON-BLANCHD SAND • • • • 211 DOVER BEACH V 8
    WHERE THE SEA MEETS THE MOON-BLANCHD SAND • • • • 211 DOVER BEACH V 8

MEILLERIE
    VEVEY AND MEILLERIE   • • • • • • • • • • 311 OBERMANN   164

MELANCHOLY
    THOSE MELANCHOLY TONES SO SWEET AND STILL • • • • 36 VOICE   34
    ITS MELANCHOLY LONG WITHDRAWING ROAR • • • • • 211 DOVER BEACH   25
    A MELANCHOLY INTO ALL OUR DAY • • • • • 247 BURIED LIFE   76
    MY MELANCHOLY SCIOLISTS SAY • • • • • • 302 GRANDE CHARTR   99
    THOU MELANCHOLY SHADE • • • • • • • 310 OBERMANN   138
    SUSPEND YOUR MELANCHOLY RITES AWHILE • • • • 332 MEROPE   77
    ON THIS CHARRD BLACKEND MELANCHOLY WASTE • • • 428 EMPEDOCLES II   2
    YOUR DISTANT MELANCHOLY LINES • • • • • 437 EMPEDOCLES II   279
    THAT LIQUID MELANCHOLY EYE • • • • • • 450 GEISTS GRAVE   13
    IN YOUR GENTLE MELANCHOLY   • • • • • • META CLOISTER   35
    THE USHERS RASH AND FEVERISH MELANCHOLY • • • FRAGMENT 1   5

MELL
    OF COMMON LIFE WHERE CROWDED UP PELL-MELL • • • • 168 WORLDLY PLACE   4

MELLOW
    THE MELLOW GLORY OF THE ATTIC STAGE • • • • • • 2 TO A FRIEND   13

MELLOWD
    MELLOWD AND SOFTEND AS WITH SUNSET-GLOW • • • • 212 GROWING OLD   14

MELODIOUS
    MORE MELODIOUS THAN OF YORE • • • • • • • 27 NEW SIRENS   42
    AND ITS DEEP-TONED MELODIOUS VOICE • • • • • • 227 EPILOG LAOCOON   195

MELON
    WITH LARGE-LEAVED LOW-CREEPING MELON-PLANTS • • 190 STRAYED REVEL   155
    THEIR MELON-HARVEST TO THE HEART THEY SEE • • • • 193 STRAYED REVEL   239

MELONS
    AND DARK GREEN MELONS AND THERE RUSTUM SATE • • 67 SOHRAB RUSTUM   199

MELT
    IF HAPLY HE MAY MELT HER HEART WITH WORDS • • • 100 BALDER DEAD 1   182
    FOR BALDER IF THOU HAPLY THUS MAYST MELT • • • 122 BALDER DEAD 3   293
    MELT NOT THEIR EYES • • • • • • • • 219 BACCHANALIA 1   47
    MELT INTO OPEN MOONLIT SEA • • • • • • 275 SOUTHERN NIGHT   2
    MELT LIKE A PASSING SMOKE A NIGHTLY DREAM • • • 402 MEROPE   1945
    SHOULD FLEET BEFORE US BUT TO MELT AWAY • • • • 470 ALARIC AT ROME   212
    SLOPE STATELY DOWN AND MELT INTO THE PLAIN • • • 473 CROMWELL   38
    BATHD IN A BLAZE OF SUNSET MELT AWAY • • • • • 478 CROMWELL   216

MELTED
    AND THE BRIGHT SUN BROKE FORTH AND MELTED ALL • • 76 SOHRAB RUSTUM   523

MELTS
    WHEN THE SUN MELTS THE SNOWS IN HIGH PAMERE • • 61 SOHRAB RUSTUM   15
    HE MELTS THE ICEBERGS OF THE PAST • • • • • • 322 OBERMANN MORE V 285

MEMBERS
    BUT OF HIS FLESH AND MEMBERS THOU DIDST BUILD • • 121 BALDER DEAD 3   260

MEMMIUS
    BEFORE A STONE WAS LIFTED AND WE MEMMIUS • • • • LUCRETIUS 5   5

MEMORIAL
    MEMORIAL OF ME WHETHER SAVED OR NO • • • • • • 112 BALDER DEAD 2   275

MEMORIAL   (CONTINUED)
        KEPT THE MEMORIAL BARD   . . . .   281 HAWORTH CHURCH   20
        HELD MEMORIAL BARD   . . . .   281 HAWORTH CHURCH   V 20
        NOBLE MEMORIAL OF WORTH   . . . .   345 MEROPE   485
        PERCHANCE SOME MUTE MEMORIAL AT THEIR HEAD   . . . .   464 ALARIC AT ROME   58
        RELICS OF NATIONS THY MEMORIAL-STONES   . . . . .   464 ALARIC AT ROME   62
        AND TWINE WITH BOLDER HAND THY LAST MEMORIAL WREATH   471 ALARIC AT ROME   228

MEMORIES
        ME LET NO HALF-EFFACED MEMORIES CUMBER   . . . . .   206 SEPARATION   9
        WHAT MEMORIES HE STIRS   . . . .   313 OBERMANN MORE   36
        BE TO FOMENT OLD MEMORIES OF WRATH   . . . . . .   342 MEROPE   381
        TELL OF OLD TIMES AND HOLIEST MEMORIES   . . . . .   467 ALARIC AT ROME   124
        LOST IN DIM MEMORIES OF HIS EARLY HOME   . . . . .   468 ALARIC AT ROME   170

MEMORY
        QUICK THY TABLETS MEMORY   . . . .   22 MEMORY-PICTURE   8
        QUICK THY TABLETS MEMORY   . . . .   23 MEMORY-PICTURE   16
        QUICK THY TABLETS MEMORY   . . . .   23 MEMORY-PICTURE   24
        QUICK THY TABLETS MEMORY   . . . .   23 MEMORY-PICTURE   32
        QUICK THY TABLETS MEMORY   . . . .   23 MEMORY-PICTURE   40
        QUICK THY TABLETS MEMORY   . . . .   24 MEMORY-PICTURE   48
        QUICK THY TABLETS MEMORY   . . . .   24 MEMORY-PICTURE   56
        QUICK THY TABLETS MEMORY   . . . .   24 MEMORY-PICTURE   64
        NEVER WAS EXILES MEMORY HALF SO SAD   . . . . . .   42 GIPSY CHILD   V 27
        TO HIDE THEIR SHAMEFUL MEMORY FROM MEN   . . . .   109 BALDER DEAD 2   175
        YET WE HER MEMORY AS SHE PRAYD WILL KEEP   . . .   173 MONICAS PRAYER   13
        THE MEMORY OF A MAN UNSPOILD   . . . .   273 EDW QUILLINAN   15
        THY MEMORY THY PAIN TO-NIGHT   . . . .   276 SOUTHERN NIGHT   18
        TO KEEP ALIVE THAT MEMORY IN MY HEART   . . . .   334 MEROPE   120
        TO EFFACE IN ME THE MEMORY OF HIS CRIME   . . .   387 MEROPE   1478
        THY MEMORY LASTS BOTH HERE AND THERE   . . . .   451 GEISTS GRAVE   57
        THY MEMORY DIE   . . . .   461 KAISER DEAD   78

MEMORYS
        AND MEMORYS GUSHING TIDE SWELLS DEEP AND FULL   . .   464 ALARIC AT ROME   53
        HIGH THOUGHTS WERE HIS BUT MEMORYS GLANCE THE WHILE   474 CROMWELL   69
        AND MEMORYS CALM CLEAR VOICE AND MOURNFUL EYE   . .   474 CROMWELL   87

MEN
        HE MUCH THE OLD MAN WHO CLEAREST-SOULD OF MEN   . .   2 TO A FRIEND   2
        AS THOUGH MEN SPAKE OF LIFE A JOY WAS FLED   . . .   EMERSONS ESSAYS   V 8
        SO MEN UNRAVELLING GODS HARMONIOUS WHOLE   . . .   4 BUTLERS SERMONS   3
        VALLEYS AND MEN TO MIDDLE FORTUNE BORN   . . . .   6 GEO CRUIKSHANK   4
        SWEEPS EARTH AND HEAVEN AND MEN AND GODS ALONG   . .   9 MYCERINUS   39
        AND OLD MEN DIE AND YOUNG MEN PASS THEIR PRIME   . .   10 MYCERINUS   63
        AND OLD MEN DIE AND YOUNG MEN PASS THEIR PRIME   . .   10 MYCERINUS   63
        YE MEN OF EGYPT YE HAVE HEARD YOUR KING   . . . .   11 MYCERINUS   73
        WHIRLS EARTH AND HEAVEN AND MEN AND GODS ALONG   . .   9 MYCERINUS   ∨ 39
        BEARS EARTH AND HEAVEN AND MEN AND GODS ALONG   . .   9 MYCERINUS   V 39
        TRAMP OF MEN AND QUICK COMMANDS   . . . . . .   14 CHURCH BROU 1   38
        WHAT CHURCH IS THIS FROM MEN ALOOF   . . . . .   16 CHURCH BROU 2   7
        AND THOSE WARM LOCKS MEN WERE PRAISING   . . . .   30 NEW SIRENS   121
        SADLY BACK THE SEATS OF MEN   . . . .   31 NEW SIRENS   150
        CAN MEN WORSHIP THE WAN FEATURES   . . . . . .   34 NEW SIRENS   247
        WHERE WISE MEN ARE NOT STRONG   . . . .   39 STAGIRIUS   40
        WHERE JUST MEN SUFFER WRONG   . . . .   39 STAGIRIUS   42
        WHERE GOOD MEN ARE NOT STRONG   . . . .   39 STAGIRIUS   V 40
        AND THOUGH THE JUST SUN GILD AS ALL MEN PRAY   . .   43 GIPSY CHILD   V 59
        CHANGE DOTH UNKNIT THE TRANQUIL STRENGTH OF MEN   . .   44 QUESTION   3
        MEN DIG GRAVES WITH BITTER TEARS   . . . . . .   44 QUESTION   11
        BRINGS ROUND TO ALL MEN   . . . .   52 CONSOLATION   74
        AND FLEES THE COMMON LIFE OF MEN   . . . . . .   58 RESIGNATION   212
        WAS HUSHD AND STILL THE MEN WERE PLUNGED IN SLEEP   .   61 SOHRAB RUSTUM   4
        THE MEN OF FORMER TIMES HAD CROWND THE TOP   . . .   61 SOHRAB RUSTUM   20
        LARGE MEN LARGE STEEDS WHO FROM BOKHARA COME   . .   64 SOHRAB RUSTUM   119
        LIGHT MEN AND ON LIGHT STEEDS WHO ONLY DRINK   . .   64 SOHRAB RUSTUM   124
        OF THE JAXARTES MEN WITH SCANTY BEARDS   . . . .   64 SOHRAB RUSTUM   129
        WAS RUSTUMS AND HIS MEN LAY CAMPD AROUND   . . .   67 SOHRAB RUSTUM   194
        SOHRAB MEN CALL HIM BUT HIS BIRTH IS HID   . . .   67 SOHRAB RUSTUM   214
        HIMSELF IS YOUNG AND HONOURS YOUNGER MEN   . . .   67 SOHRAB RUSTUM   224
        WHAT THEN O RUSTUM WILL MEN SAY TO THIS   . . . .   68 SOHRAB RUSTUM   243
        HIDEST THY FACE TAKE HEED LEST MEN SHOULD SAY   . .   68 SOHRAB RUSTUM   246
        AND SHUNS TO PERIL IT WITH YOUNGER MEN   . . . .   68 SOHRAB RUSTUM   248
        BUT WHO FOR MEN OF NOUGHT WOULD DO GREAT DEEDS   . .   68 SOHRAB RUSTUM   255
        LET NOT MEN SAY OF RUSTUM HE WAS MATCHD   . . . .   69 SOHRAB RUSTUM   258
        SO ON EACH SIDE WERE SQUARES OF MEN WITH SPEARS   . .   70 SOHRAB RUSTUM   297
        SO WILL HE SPEAK PERHAPS WHILE MEN APPLAUD   . . .   72 SOHRAB RUSTUM   362
        RASH BOY MEN LOOK ON RUSTUMS FACE AND FLEE   . . .   72 SOHRAB RUSTUM   369
        STILL ROUGH LIKE THOSE WHICH MEN IN TREELESS PLAINS   .   73 SOHRAB RUSTUM   410
        AND HEARD THEIR HOLLOW ROAR OF DYING MEN   . . . .   74 SOHRAB RUSTUM   435
        FOR WERE I MATCHD WITH TEN SUCH MEN AS THEE   . . .   77 SOHRAB RUSTUM   544
        OR THAT MEN GAVE IT HIM TO SWELL HIS FAME   . . .   79 SOHRAB RUSTUM   614
        YET HERE THOU ERREST SOHRAB OR ELSE MEN   . . . .   80 SOHRAB RUSTUM   643
        TRUTH SITS UPON THE LIPS OF DYING MEN   . . . . .   80 SOHRAB RUSTUM   656
        BUT COME THOU SEEST THIS GREAT HOST OF MEN   . . .   84 SOHRAB RUSTUM   778
        AND MEN SHALL NOT FORGET THEE IN THY GRAVE   . . .   84 SOHRAB RUSTUM   805
        WHAT IRKS IT ME THAT MEN SPEAK SOHRABS PRAISE   . .   68 SOHRAB RUSTUM   V 228
        I AM NOT WRONGD WHEN MEN SPEAK SOHRABS PRAISE   . .   68 SOHRAB RUSTUM   V 228
        LIKE THOSE WHICH MEN WHO DWELL IN TREELESS PLAINS   .   73 SOHRAB RUSTUM   V 410

MEN   (CONTINUED)

FOR WERE I MATCHD WITH TEN SUCH MEN AS THOU • •	77 SOHRAB RUSTUM	V 544
WHILST OTHER MEN MAKE CHEER AND SING • • • • • •	93 SICK KING BOKH	178
BUT HEAR YE THIS YE SONS OF MEN • • • • • • •	93 SICK KING BOKH	185
TO LOOK ON MIDGARD AND THE EARTH AND MEN • • • •	96 BALDER DEAD 1	52
FAIR MEN WHO LIVE IN HOLES UNDER THE GROUND • •	97 BALDER DEAD 1	56
PAST MIDGARD FORTRESS DOWN TO EARTH AND MEN • •	99 BALDER DEAD 1	142
AND ALL THE NOBLER SOULS OF MORTAL MEN • • • •	104 BALDER DEAD 1	320
MEN SPENT BY SICKNESS OR OBSCURE DECAY • • • •	104 BALDER DEAD 1	325
FOR ALL THE NOBLER SOULS OF MORTAL MEN • • • •	104 BALDER DEAD 1	V 320
TOWRD EARTH AND FIGHTS OF MEN AND AT THEIR SIDE •	105 BALDER DEAD 2	20
THERE THROUGH SOME BATTLE-FIELD WHERE MEN FALL FAST	105 BALDER DEAD 2	24
WHERE THEY HOLD COUNCIL AND GIVE LAWS FOR MEN • •	105 BALDER DEAD 2	34
LIKE MEN WHO LIVE AND DRAW THE VITAL AIR • • •	108 BALDER DEAD 2	108
NOR LOOKST THOU PALE AND WAN LIKE MEN DECEASED • •	108 BALDER DEAD 2	109
WOMEN AND INFANTS AND YOUNG MEN WHO DIED • • • •	109 BALDER DEAD 2	164
AND OLD MEN KNOWN TO GLORY BUT THEIR STAR • • •	109 BALDER DEAD 2	166
TO HIDE THEIR SHAMEFUL MEMORY FROM MEN • • • •	109 BALDER DEAD 2	175
LET GODS MEN BRUTES BEWEEP HIM PLANTS AND STONES •	111 BALDER DEAD 2	238
LET GODS MEN BRUTES BEWEEP HIM PLANTS AND STONES •	114 BALDER DEAD 3	44
LORD OVER MEN ON EARTH AND GODS IN HEAVEN • • •	120 BALDER DEAD 3	251
OF WOOD AND FRAMEDST MEN WHO TILL THE EARTH • •	121 BALDER DEAD 3	269
WITH MEN BUT LIVES A HOSTAGE WITH THE GODS • • •	123 BALDER DEAD 3	325
AND AS SEAFARING MEN WHO LONG HAVE WROUGHT • • •	123 BALDER DEAD 3	357
BUT GODS ARE LIKE THE SONS OF MEN IN THIS • • •	125 BALDER DEAD 3	426
MOURN FOR THE MEN ON EARTH THE GODS IN HEAVEN • •	127 BALDER DEAD 3	485
UP TRISTRAM UP MEN CRY THOU MOONSTRUCK KNIGHT • •	137 TRISTRAM 1	238
FEAR NOT NOW THAT MEN SHOULD TAX THINE HONOUR • •	142 TRISTRAM 2	11
WHAT THOU THINKST MEN SPEAK IN COURTLY CHAMBERS • •	143 TRISTRAM 2	41
FEAR NOT NOW THAT MEN SHOULD TAX THY HONOUR • • •	142 TRISTRAM 2	V 11
HOW THIS FOOL PASSION GULLS MEN POTENTLY • • • •	153 TRISTRAM 3	134
AND IN THAT DAISIED CIRCLE AS MEN SAY • • • •	156 TRISTRAM 3	221
SO SPAKE THE IMPERIAL SAGE PUREST OF MEN • • • •	168 WORLDLY PLACE	2
SO SPOKE THE IMPERIAL SAGE PUREST OF MEN • • • •	168 WORLDLY PLACE	V 2
SOME LABOURING MEN WHOSE WORK LAY SOMEWHERE THERE	170 WEST LONDON	5
SEIRIOL THE BRIGHT KYBI THE DARK MEN SAID • • • •	170 EAST AND WEST	9
IF WE THEN TOO CAN BE SUCH MEN AS HE • • • •	171 BETTER PART	14
WELL SPAKE THE IMPETUOUS SAINT AND BORE OF MEN • •	171 DIVINITY	6
FOILD BY OUR FELLOW-MEN DEPRESSD OUTWORN • • • •	172 IMMORTALITY	1
AND LOVE IF LOVE OF HAPPIER MEN • • • • • • •	181 ISOLATION MARG	36
OF HAPPIER MEN FOR THEY AT LEAST • • • • • •	181 ISOLATION MARG	37
THE EARTH AND MEN • • • • • • • • • • •	190 STRAYED REVEL	134
NO NO OLD MEN CREON I CURSE NOT • • • • • •	196 FRAG ANTIGONE	45
WERE BUT MEN NOBLER THAN THEY ARE • • • • • •	202 URANIA	8
WAS TURND UPON THE SONS OF MEN • • • • • • •	202 URANIA	10
COLDLY SHE MOCKS THE SONS OF MEN • • • • • •	202 URANIA	30
WOUNDED BY MEN BY FORTUNE TRIED • • • • • •	203 EUPHROSYNE	6
WITHOUT THAT ALLS DARK FOR MEN • • • • • • •	215 PIS-ALLER	10
BETTER MEN FARED THUS BEFORE THEE • • • • • •	215 LAST WORD	10
THE FAMOUS MEN OF WAR HAVE FOUGHT • • • • • •	219 BACCHANALIA 2	5
WHATEVER MEN HAVE DONE MIGHT DO • • • • • •	221 BACCHANALIA 2	67
MEN WITH THEIR STREAM OF LIFE WERE HERE • • • •	224 EPILOG LAOCOON	112
THE COMPLAINING MILLIONS OF MEN • • • • • •	229 YOUTH OF NATURE	51
THEY ARE HERE I HEARD AS MEN HEARD • • • • •	230 YOUTH OF NATURE	75
MEN WILL RENEW THE BATTLE IN THE PLAIN • • • •	236 PALLADIUM	V 13
CHILDREN OF MEN THE UNSEEN POWER WHOSE EYE • • •	238 PROGRESS	37
THAT MEN DID EVER FIND • • • • • • • • •	238 PROGRESS	40
CHILDREN OF MEN NOT THAT YOUR AGE EXCEL • • • •	238 PROGRESS	45
LIKE ALL THE OTHER MEN I SEE • • • • • • •	243 SUMMER NIGHT	36
FOR MOST MEN IN A BRAZEN PRISON LIVE • • • • •	243 SUMMER NIGHT	37
I KNEW THE MASS OF MEN CONCEALD • • • • • •	245 BURIED LIFE	16
THEY WOULD BY OTHER MEN BE MET • • • • • •	245 BURIED LIFE	18
OF MEN AND ALIEN TO THEMSELVES AND YET • • • •	245 BURIED LIFE	22
AND THE TIRED MEN AND DOGS ALL GONE TO REST • •	255 SCHOLAR-GIPSY	7
AND CAME AS MOST MEN DEEMD TO LITTLE GOOD • • •	256 SCHOLAR-GIPSY	39
MEN WHO THROUGH THOSE WIDE FIELDS OF BREEZY GRASS	257 SCHOLAR-GIPSY	93
FOR WHAT WEARS OUT THE LIFE OF MORTAL MEN • • •	259 SCHOLAR-GIPSY	142
ELSE HADST THOU SPENT LIKE OTHER MEN THY FIRE • •	259 SCHOLAR-GIPSY	154
SEE TIS NO FOOT OF UNFAMILIAR MEN • • • • •	263 THYRSIS	7
INTO THE WORLD AND WAVE OF MEN DEPART • • • •	264 THYRSIS	39
SOME LIFE OF MEN UNBLEST • • • • • • • •	264 THYRSIS	46
MEN GAVE THEE NOTHING BUT THIS HAPPY QUEST • • •	269 THYRSIS	213
IF MEN ESTEEMD THEE FEEBLE GAVE THEE POWER • • •	269 THYRSIS	214
IF MEN PROCURED THEE TROUBLE GAVE THEE REST • • •	269 THYRSIS	215
OF MEN CONTENTION-TOST OF MEN WHO GROAN • • • •	269 THYRSIS	224
OF MEN CONTENTION-TOST OF MEN WHO GROAN • • • •	269 THYRSIS	224
AND LONG WITH MEN OF CARE THOU COULDST NOT STAY •	269 THYRSIS	228
AND MEN WERE SPECKS AND LIFE A PLAY • • • • •	277 SOUTHERN NIGHT	78
OF MORTAL MEN ON THE EARTH • • • • • • • •	288 RUGBY CHAPEL	59
MOST MEN EDDY ABOUT • • • • • • • • •	288 RUGBY CHAPEL	60
IS THE RACE OF MEN WHOM I SEE • • • • • • •	290 RUGBY CHAPEL	150
NOT LIKE THE MEN OF THE CROWD • • • • • • •	290 RUGBY CHAPEL	155
STARRD AND JEWELLD OF MEN • • • • • • • •	296 HEINES GRAVE	143
BEHOLDING THE ABSURDITY OF MEN • • • • • • •	298 HEINES GRAVE	207
THEY HAVE THE GRIEF MEN HAD OF YORE • • • • •	303 GRANDE CHARTR	119
AND OUTCRY OF THE FORMER MEN • • • • • • •	303 GRANDE CHARTR	128
AND GOETHES COURSE FEW SONS OF MEN • • • • •	308 OBERMANN	55
OF MEN SHALL THEY BE FOUND • • • • • • • •	309 OBERMANN	100
AMONG THE SWARMS OF MEN • • • • • • • • •	311 OBERMANN	176
MEN CALLD FROM CHAMBER CHURCH AND TENT • • • •	318 OBERMANN MORE	171

MEN (CONTINUED)
IN VAIN MEN STILL WITH HOPING NEW . . . . 318 OBERMANN MORE 177
WHEREON MEN PITCH THEIR TENT . . . . . . 320 OBERMANN MORE 218
WITH OLD-WORLD CURES MEN HALF BELIEVE . . . . 320 OBERMANN MORE 235
AND YET MEN HAVE SUCH NEED OF JOY . . . . . 320 OBERMANN MORE 237
THAT END TO HELP MEN GAIN . . . . 323 OBERMANN MORE V 322
WHO UNDER EARTH WATCH GUILTY DEEDS OF MEN . . . . 332 MEROPE 74
BUT MEROPE THE EYES OF OTHER MEN . . . . . 333 MEROPE 89
AND ME BELIEVE IT WISE MEN GRAVELY BLAME . . . 333 MEROPE 94
AND IGNORANT MEN DESPISE ME THAT I STAND . . . 333 MEROPE 95
AND THESE MEN LOOK TO THEE AND FROM THY GRIEF . . 334 MEROPE 141
OF MEN THE LINE OF HERACLES PREFERRD . . . . 338 MEROPE 269
OF HEADY MASTERFUL INJURIOUS MEN . . . . 339 MEROPE 312
NOT HELP OF MEN ALTHOUGH PERHAPS OF GODS . . . 341 MEROPE 357
MOST MEN ARE LED BY INTEREST AND THE FEW . . . 341 MEROPE 365
THAT DOOM OBTAIN EFFECT FROM GODS OR MEN . . . 349 MEROPE 558
THE MOST ARE BAD WISE MEN HAVE SAID . . . . 352 MEROPE 652
STILL AT HIS MOUNTAIN-TOMB MEN MARVEL BUILT . . 357 MEROPE 782
FIRST CITY FOUNDED ON THE EARTH BY MEN . . . 359 MEROPE 849
AND THE OLD MEN RISE FROM THEIR BENCH . . . 360 MEROPE 900
HOW MUCH MEN THINK ME ABJECT VOID OF HEART . . . 366 MEROPE 1016
WHERESOEER MEN ARE THERE IS GRIEF . . . . 369 MEROPE 1093
SAGACIOUS MEN OF IRON WATCHFUL FIRM . . . 381 MEROPE 1304
CLAMOURS TO FIND FULFILLD WHICH GOOD MEN PRAISE . 386 MEROPE 1428
AND ONLY BAD MEN JOY TO SEE UNDONE . . . . 386 MEROPE 1429
THOUGH INJURED PAST FORGIVENESS AS MEN DEEM . . 394 MEROPE 1707
DIVULGE NOT TO THE FAR-OFF WORLD OF MEN . . . 396 MEROPE 1753
BY THE CONSTRUCTION AND REPORT OF MEN . . . 398 MEROPE 1790
AND VIOLENT DEATHS TO VIOLENT MEN . . . . 398 MEROPE 1809
BUT IF AS MOST MEN SAY HE IS HALF MAD . . . 407 EMPEDOCLES I 1 23
THOU HAST HEARD ALL MEN SPEAKING OF PANTHEIA . . 410 EMPEDOCLES I 1 108
AND HOLDS MEN MUTE TO SEE WHERE IT WILL RISE . . 410 EMPEDOCLES I 1 114
IT IS ENOUGH THAT ALL MEN SPEAK OF IT . . . 413 EMPEDOCLES I 2 22
THY GOODNESS NO MEN AID . . . . 416 EMPEDOCLES I 2 119
WHY ARE MEN ILL AT EASE . . . . 417 EMPEDOCLES I 2 148
THE ILL DEEDS OF OTHER MEN MAKE OFTEN OUR LIFE DARK 421 EMPEDOCLES I 2 266
IN MEN AND PLANTS AND STONES . . . . . . 422 EMPEDOCLES I 2 293
MEN SCOFF AT HEAVEN AND FATE . . . . . . 426 EMPEDOCLES I 2 418
LEARN THAT MEN WILL NOT AND GODS CANNOT HELP THY STATE EMPEDOCLES I 2 V
NOT THOU THE WORLD WITH MEN THOU CANST NOT LIVE . . 429 EMPEDOCLES II 18
THOU CANST NOT LIVE WITH MEN NOR WITH THYSELF . . 429 EMPEDOCLES II 23
IN THE COURT OF GODS IN THE CITY OF MEN . . . . 430 EMPEDOCLES II 38
THE JARS OF MEN REACH HIM NOT IN THY VALLEY . . 435 EMPEDOCLES II 209
WHERE SHALL THY VOTARY FLY THEN BACK TO MEN . . 435 EMPEDOCLES II 220
THE ACTION OF MEN . . . . 443 EMPEDOCLES II 464
OF MEN WITH MIND THUS DARKEND AND ASTRAY . . . 446 WESTMIN ABBEY 68
AND MEN IGNOBLE HARASSD HIM WITH STRIFE . . . 447 WESTMIN ABBEY 125
AND SERVED MEN NOBLY AND ACCEPTANCE FOUND . . . 448 WESTMIN ABBEY 143
OF MEN WHOSE MINDS WERE DARKEND AND ASTRAY . . . 446 WESTMIN ABBEY V 68
KNOW WE MORE OUR FELLOW MEN . . . . . . 457 POOR MATTHIAS 162
A FORM THAT TOWERD ABOVE HIS BROTHER MEN . . . 476 CROMWELL 145
THRO THE DARK CHAMBERS OF THE HEARTS OF MEN . . 478 CROMWELL 230
OF MEN WHO AGAINST HOPE REPELLD THE CHAIN . . . 480 HUNGARIAN NAT 10
THERE SATE FIFTY MEN IN THE RUDDY LIGHT OF THE FIRE HOMER TRANS 4
WHAT THE TROJAN MEN AND TROJAN WOMEN MIGHT MURMUR HOMER TRANS 15
WHICH MEN SAY IS THE FLEETEST OF WINDS TIS HOMER TRANS 55
     THOU WHO ART FATED

MENACING
     GLARED AND HE SHOOK ON HIGH HIS MENACING SPEAR . . 76 SOHRAB RUSTUM 515

MENDELSSOHN
     MOZART BEETHOVEN MENDELSSOHN . . . . 222 EPILOG LAOCOON 35

MENDING
     STILL MENDING LESSENING HUMAN ILL . . . . . . 484 ROME-SICKNESS 28

MENDS
     WHILE IT MENDS LITTLE TROUBLES MUCH . . . . . 56 RESIGNATION 127

MENS
     NATURES GREAT LAW AND LAW OF ALL MENS MINDS . . 8 RELIGIOUS ISOL 12
     AND TO MENS BUSINESS NOT TOO NEAR . . . . . 59 RESIGNATION 250
     NOW TIME OBSCURES IT AND MENS LATER DEEDS . . . 117 BALDER DEAD 3 130
     MY NAME IS UNDER ALL MENS BAN . . . . . . 157 SAINT BRANDAN 27
     THESE MENS PROFOUNDEST MIND . . . . . . 238 PROGRESS 36
     I ON MENS IMPIOUS UPROAR HURLD . . . . . 249 KENSINGTON GARD 25
     BUT I ON MENS IMPIOUS TUMULT HURLD . . . . . KENSINGTON GARD V 25
     I ON MENS IMPIOUS TUMULT HURLD . . . . . KENSINGTON GARD V 25
     THE WORKINGS OF MENS BRAINS . . . . . . 256 SCHOLAR-GIPSY 46
     AND MENS INCESSANT STREAM GOES BY . . . . . 277 SOUTHERN NIGHT 63
     THEIR VOICES WERE IN ALL MENS EARS . . . . . 303 GRANDE CHARTR 123
     NOT MENS GOOD WORD HATH MADE ME WHAT I AM . . . 398 MEROPE 1791
     WE SEARCH OUT DEAD MENS WORDS AND WORKS OF 423 EMPEDOCLES I 2 326
          DEAD MENS HANDS
     WE SEARCH OUT DEAD MENS WORDS AND WORKS OF 423 EMPEDOCLES I 2 326
          DEAD MENS HANDS
     AND TO MENS HEARTS THIS ANCIENT PLACE ENDEARD . . 444 WESTMIN ABBEY 9

MENTAL
     OF MANS MENTAL OPERATIONS . . . . SECOND BEST V 19
     FOR STRONG THE INFECTION OF OUR MENTAL STRIFE . . 261 SCHOLAR-GIPSY 222
     OF MENTAL NATURE AS FOR HIM TO FRET . . . . . LUCRETIUS 3 3

MENTION
        WHOSE PRAISE DO THEY MENTION   • • • • • • • •   443 EMPEDOCLES II   457

MENTIOND
        THE STORY OF SPOTS MENTIOND TO HIS OWN   • • • •   356 MEROPE   767

MERCHANT
        GIRL STATESMAN MERCHANT SOLDIER BOLD • • • • • •   226 EPILOG LAOCOON   159
        FRENCH CANARY-MERCHANT OLD   • • • • • • • •   457 POOR MATTHIAS   184

MERCHANTS
        THE CLOTH-MERCHANTS AND LET THEM BE   • • • • • •   87 SICK KING BOKH   2
        O MERCHANTS TARRY YET A DAY   • • • • • • •   87 SICK KING BOKH   5
        THE COWERING MERCHANTS IN LONG ROBES • • • • • •   191 STRAYED REVEL   191
        THEY SEE THE MERCHANTS   • • • • • • • • •   193 STRAYED REVEL   244

MERCY
        AH WHENCE THIS MERCY LORD I SAID   • • • • • •   157 SAINT BRANDAN   37
        OF MERCY CAUGHT DID NOT EXPIRE • • • • • • •   158 SAINT BRANDAN   62

MERE
        MERE PHANTOMS OF MANS SELF-TORMENTING HEART   • •   9 MYCERINUS   25
        DWELT WITH MERE OUTWARD SEEMING HE WITHIN   • • • •   12 MYCERINUS   108
        FOR COLD IS HIS EYE TO MERE BEAUTY WHO BREAKING   • •   20 MODERN SAPPHO   21
        OF A LONELY MERE   • • • • • • • • • •   35 VOICE   6
        MERE PRISONERS MEANT OR NOT AMONG OUR FOES   • • • •   337 MEROPE   251
        MERE RUTHLESS AND UNCOUNSELLD WOLVES OF WAR   • •   381 MEROPE   1301
        MERE RUTHLESS AND UNCOUNSELLD TOOLS OF WAR • • • •   381 MEROPE   V1301

MERELY
        MEANT MERELY FOR HIS PLAY   • • • • • • • •   418 EMPEDOCLES I 2   180

MERIT
        NOT LESS THAN THOSE WHO MERIT TEARS   • • • • • •   92 SICK KING BOKH   148
        NOR DO I MERIT ODIN THOU SHOULDST SLIGHT   • • • •   121 BALDER DEAD 3   282
        ONE MERIT THEN THOU HAST EXULT IN THAT   • • • •   341 MEROPE   353

MERITS
        BUT FAIR PROPOSAL MERITS FAIR REPLY • • • • • •   395 MEROPE   1728

MERLIN
        WHERE MERLIN BY THE ENCHANTED THORN-TREE SLEEPS   • •   154 TRISTRAM 3   158
        THIS TALE OF MERLIN AND THE LOVELY FAY   • • • •   154 TRISTRAM 3   164
        MERLIN AND VIVIAN STOPPD ON THE SLOPES BROW   • •   155 TRISTRAM 3   201
        HERE LET US HALT SAID MERLIN THEN AND SHE   • • •   155 TRISTRAM 3   211
        FELL UPON MERLIN MORE LIKE DEATH SO DEEP   • • •   155 TRISTRAM 3   214
        IS MERLIN PRISONER TILL THE JUDGMENT-DAY   • • • •   156 TRISTRAM 3   222

MERLINS
        FIXD FULL ON MERLINS FACE HER STATELY PRIZE   • •   154 TRISTRAM 3   178
        AS THOUGH THE WIZARD MERLINS WILL   • • • • •   273 STANZAS CARNAC   7
        AS IF THE WIZARD MERLINS WILL   • • • • • • •   273 STANZAS CARNAC   V   7
        AS IF THE ENCHANTER MERLINS WILL   • • • • •   STANZAS CARNAC   V   7

MERMAIDEN
        FOR THE COLD STRANGE EYES OF A LITTLE MERMAIDEN   • •   164 FORSAKEN MERM   106

MERMAN
        AND I LOSE MY POOR SOUL MERMAN HERE WITH THEE   • •   163 FORSAKEN MERM   59

MEROPE
        I SOUGHT THEE MEROPE I FIND THEE THUS   • • • •   332 MEROPE   79
        BUT MEROPE THE EYES OF OTHER MEN   • • • • •   333 MEROPE   89
        BUT MEROPE THE YEARS ADVANCE I STAND • • • • •   334 MEROPE   151
        O MEROPE HOW MANY NOBLE THOUGHTS   • • • • •   335 MEROPE   177
        AM MEROPE THY MURDERD MASTERS WIFE   • • • • •   335 MEROPE   184
        WHO SHALL TELL MEROPE THIS HEAVY NEWS   • • • •   359 MEROPE   858
        DIRE IS THIS BLOW FOR MEROPE AND I   • • • •   360 MEROPE   885
        THAT BLACK-ROBED SWOONING FIGURE MEROPE   • • •   376 MEROPE   1212
        O MEROPE THE COMMON HEART OF MAN   • • • •   389 MEROPE   1523
        SOME GOD MEROPE NOW   • • • • • • • •   393 MEROPE   1680
        O MEROPE THE TROUBLE ON THY FACE   • • • •   393 MEROPE   1684
        BUT THOU O MEROPE THOUGH DEEPLY WRONGD   • • •   394 MEROPE   1706
        NOT MEROPE AND POLYPHONTES FOES   • • • • •   394 MEROPE   1719

MEROPES
        ARE THESE WORDS MEROPES IS THIS VOICE MINE • • • •   368 MEROPE   1068

MERRIMENT
        AND SOME IN TALK AND MERRIMENT • • • • • • • •   224 EPILOG LAOCOON   120

MERRY
        FLOWD THE HUNTERS MERRY TIDE   • • • • • • •   13 CHURCH BROU 1   8
        AND SAW THE MERRY GRECIAN COASTER COME   • • • •   262 SCHOLAR-GIPSY   237

MERVE
        THEY SNATCH ALSO TOWARDS MERVE • • • • • • • •   93 SICK KING BOKH   166

MESSAGE
    HOWBEIT REPORT THY MESSAGE AND THEREWITH • • • •   112 BALDER DEAD 2   273
    THE MESSAGE BROUGHT WAS FOR THE KING DESIGND • •   361 MEROPE   923

MESSAGES
    HIS MESSAGES THEN POINT NOT TO THY MURDER • • • •   380 MEROPE   1282

MESSEIS
    OR BEAR PAILS TO THE WELL OF MESSEIS OR HYPEREIA • •   HOMER TRANS   30

MESSENE
    O KINGDOM OF MESSENE • • • • • • • • •   399 MEROPE   1847

MESSENGER
    HIS MESSENGER AND HE STOOD FORTH AND CRIED • • •   114 BALDER DEAD 3   32
    IS SHE NOT COME THE MESSENGER WAS SURE • • • •   130 TRISTRAM 1   1
    SCANT LEISURE FOR A SECOND MESSENGER • • • •   140 TRISTRAM 1   307
    A MESSENGER FROM RADIANT CLIMES • • • • •   208 LONGING   6
    A MESSENGER SENT FROM ARCADIA HERE • • • • •   361 MEROPE   920
    HOW SO WAS ARCAS NOT THE MESSENGER • • • • •   361 MEROPE   924
    ANOTHER TALE I TROW THY MESSENGER • • • •   364 MEROPE   964
    CARRY HIS MESSENGER BUT LEFT HIM HERE • • • •   374 MEROPE   1193

MESSENGERS
    SEND THROUGH THE WORLD THY MESSENGERS ENTREAT • •   122 BALDER DEAD 3   291

MESSENIA
    WHO TO MESSENIA WITH THY HUSBAND CAME • • •   337 MEROPE   230
    MESSENIA TO THOSE HELPLESS BOYS THE LOT • • •   389 MEROPE   1552
    CRESPHONTES IN MESSENIA TEMENUS • • •   389 MEROPE   1556
    MESSENIA SPEAKS THE PRINCE THY SON IS DEAD • • •   393 MEROPE   1686

MESSENIAN
    THIS IS THAT FRUITFUL FAMED MESSENIAN LAND • • •   330 MEROPE   4
    PAMISUS WATERING THE MESSENIAN PLAIN • • •   330 MEROPE   19
    WHATEER IN THE MESSENIAN PEOPLE STIRS • • •   331 MEROPE   38
    TOGETHER WON THIS FAIR MESSENIAN LAND • • •   334 MEROPE   126
    IN THE MESSENIAN PEOPLE WHAT REMAINS • • • •   334 MEROPE   138
    NOT SO LET THESE MESSENIAN MAIDENS MARK • • •   336 MEROPE   197
    WERE THE MESSENIAN CHIEFS THE LAWS HE FRAMED • •   337 MEROPE   243
    THESE STURDY AND UNWORN MESSENIAN TRIBES • • •   338 MEROPE   291
    PREFERRD MESSENIAN SERFS TO DORIAN LORDS • • •   339 MEROPE   324
    AEPYTUS THE MESSENIAN PRINCE IS DEAD • • • •   355 MEROPE   714
    TO PLY TWIXT THE MESSENIAN KING AND HIM • • •   364 MEROPE   981
    FOR THE MESSENIAN HEARTS WHO LOVED THE PRINCE • •   365 MEROPE   993
    HATEFUL BY EACH MESSENIAN HEART ABHORRD • • •   366 MEROPE   1009
    BUT WHO ARE THESE MESSENIAN MAIDENS FRIENDS • •   375 MEROPE   1210
    O KIND MESSENIAN MAIDENS O MY FRIENDS • • •   377 MEROPE   1222
    WITH THIS MESSENIAN TYRANT THAT I KNOW • • •   380 MEROPE   1275
    BUT MUTE THOU SATST AND EACH MESSENIAN HEART • •   383 MEROPE   1373
    THAN I TO HELP RAISE HIS MESSENIAN FRIENDS • • •   388 MEROPE   1497
    TO THE MESSENIAN KINGDOM THOU AND I • • •   394 MEROPE   1692
    FORSAKE THIS AMPLE PROUD MESSENIAN REALM • •   395 MEROPE   1744
    THOU HOLDST SO CHEAP THEN THE MESSENIAN CROWN • •   397 MEROPE   1774
    WELFARE TO THE MESSENIAN STATE AND CALM • • •   403 MEROPE   1959
    WHATEER IN THE MESSENIAN CITY STIRS • • • •   331 MEROPE   V 38

MESSENIANS
    TO MY MESSENIANS DUPED DISARMD DESPISED • • •   366 MEROPE   1006
    ONE SUDDEN STROKE AND THE MESSENIANS LOVE • • •   381 MEROPE   1287
    FIRST RALLY THE MESSENIANS TO THY CAUSE • • •   382 MEROPE   1322
    TO ME AND THE MESSENIANS LEAVE THE REST • • •   391 MEROPE   1593
    AND GRANT HENCEFORTH TO THE MESSENIANS PEACE • •   402 MEROPE   1917
    CRYING O YE MESSENIANS WILL YE LEAVE • • • •   402 MEROPE   1934
    TO RENDER TO MY TRUE MESSENIANS THANKS • • •   405 MEROPE   2018

MESSENIAS
    BLOOD-SEVERD BUT MESSENIAS KING AND QUEEN • • •   394 MEROPE   1720

MESSES
    NEW MESSES OF THE BOAR SERIMNERS FLESH • • • •   97 BALDER DEAD 1   67

MESSOGIS
    OF MESSOGIS WESTWARD BREAK • • • • • • • •   433 EMPEDOCLES II   138

MET
    THE GIPSIES WHOM WE MET BELOW • • • • • • •   55 RESIGNATION   108
    BUT WHEN THE ULEMAS WERE MET • • • • • • •   91 SICK KING BOKH   109
    BUT WHEN THE ULEMA WERE MET • • • • • • •   91 SICK KING BOKH   V 109
    BUT HE HAS MET THAT DOOM WHICH LONG AGO • • •   96 BALDER DEAD 1   23
    BALDER HAS MET HIS DEATH AND YE SURVIVE • • •   96 BALDER DEAD 1   26
    HIM THE BLIND HODER MET AS HE CAME UP • • •   101 BALDER DEAD 1   226
    ON BATTLE-FIELD HAVE MET THEIR DEATH AND NOW • •   104 BALDER DEAD 1   321
    STILL NORTH UNTIL HE MET A STRETCHING WALL • • •   109 BALDER DEAD 2   144
    MY LONG-LOST WANDERING ODER THOU HAST MET • • •   116 BALDER DEAD 3   101
    ON HER WHITE PALFREY HERE HE MET HIS END • • •   154 TRISTRAM 3   162
    I MET A PREACHER THERE I KNEW AND SAID • • •   169 EAST LONDON   5
    TWO SAINTS MET OFTEN WHERE THOSE WATERS FLOW • •   170 EAST AND WEST   4
    THEY WOULD BY OTHER MEN BE MET • • • • • •   245 BURIED LIFE   18
    MET HIM AND OF HIS WAY OF LIFE ENQUIRED • • •   256 SCHOLAR-GIPSY   43
    SHEPHERDS HAD MET HIM ON THE HURST IN SPRING • •   256 SCHOLAR-GIPSY   57

MET   (CONTINUED)
        RETURNING HOME ON SUMMER-NIGHTS HAVE MET   •   •   •   •   257 SCHOLAR-GIPSY   73
        TWO FRIENDS MET THERE TWO FAMD   •   •   •   •   •   •   •   280 HAWORTH CHURCH   V 7
        THEY MET HELD CONVERSE THEY WROTE   •   •   •   •   •   280 HAWORTH CHURCH   V 18
        MET THEM ENTERING THEIR HALLS   •   •   •   •   •   •   •   343 MEROPE   419
        DOUBT IT NOT WE MET AND WE ARE ONE   •   •   •   •   •   • 482 THEKLAS ANSWER   10

META
        META WITH A VAGUE MISGIVING   •   •   •   •   •   •   •   META CLOISTER   19
        SPARE ME META QUESTION RATHER   •   •   •   •   •   •   •   META CLOISTER   25

METE
        MANS MEASURES CANNOT METE THE IMMEASURABLE ALL   •   •   423 EMPEDOCLES I 2   341

METEOR
        OR THE BRIEF SPLENDOUR OF THAT METEOR LIGHT   •   •   463 ALARIC AT ROME   29
        NO METEOR BRIGHTNESS TO BE SEEN AND DIE   •   •   •   •   463 ALARIC AT ROME   33

METHINKS
        METHINKS THE WOE WHICH MADE THAT FATHER STAND   •   •   167 PICT NEWSTEAD   12
        ONLY METHINKS SOME LOSS OF HABITS POWER   •   •   •   •   263 THYRSIS   22

METHOUGHT
        SUCH NOW METHOUGHT IT WAS THE RIVER OF LIFE   •   •   25 DREAM   32

METST
        FOR WILLINGLY I KNOW THOU METST THINE END   •   •   •   • 85 SOHRAB RUSTUM   823

MICHAEL
        THE SHEEPFOLD OF MICHAEL SURVIVES   •   •   •   •   •   • 228 YOUTH OF NATURE   21

MICHAELS
        SAINT MICHAELS CHAPEL CUTS THE SKY   •   •   •   •   •   • 273 STANZAS CARNAC   2

MID
        OR IN MID-HEAVEN PERHAPS YOUR GOLDEN CARS   •   •   •   10 MYCERINUS   43
        MID THE DISTANT MOUNTAIN-CHALETS   •   •   •   •   •   •   12 CHURCH BROU 1   3
        MID THE SAVOY MOUNTAIN VALLEYS   •   •   •   •   •   •   •   14 CHURCH BROU 1   61
        MID BRIGHT GREEN FIELDS BELOW THE PINES   •   •   •   •   16 CHURCH BROU 2   5
        IN YOUR HIGH CHURCH MID THE STILL MOUNTAIN-AIR   •   •   17 CHURCH BROU 3   2
        THE GAZING UP MID THE DIM PILLARS HIGH   •   •   •   •   18 CHURCH BROU 3   38
        AND THE WIND WASHES MID THE MOUNTAIN PINES   •   •   •   18 CHURCH BROU 3   V 37
        SOON THE PLANKD COTTAGE MID THE SUN-WARMD PINES   •   •   25 DREAM   V 35
        HIS HOUSE NOW MID THEIR BROKEN FLIGHTS OF STEPS   •   •   86 SOHRAB RUSTUM   862
        MID DUST AND GROANS AND LIMBS LOPPD OFF AND BLOOD   •   105 BALDER DEAD 2   16
        SMOTE THE ROCKS THE LICHEN-BEARDED PINES   •   •   •   106 BALDER DEAD 2   56
        WHO BIVOUACS IN A FOREST MID THE HILLS   •   •   •   •   119 BALDER DEAD 3   V
        MID THE SOULS PLAGUED BY HEAVENLY POWER   •   •   •   •   157 SAINT BRANDAN   34
        MID SHELLS THAT ROUND HER LIE   •   •   •   •   •   •   • 160 NECKAN   34
        MID STRUGGLING SUFFERERS HURT TO DEATH SHE LAY   •   166 AUSTERITY POET   9
        HER HEAD MID IGNOMINY DEATH AND TOMBS   •   •   •   •   172 GOOD SHEPHERD   12
        ATTEND IT OF ITS MID CAREER   •   •   •   •   •   •   • 225 EPILOG LAOCOON   150
        WAS THE PALLADIUM HIGH MID ROCK AND WOOD   •   •   •   • 236 PALLADIUM   2
        BUT MID THEIR DRINK AND CLATTER HE WOULD FLY   •   •   257 SCHOLAR-GIPSY   61
        MID WIDE GRASS MEADOWS WHICH THE SUNSHINE FILLS   •   •   257 SCHOLAR-GIPSY   68
        MID CITY-NOISE NOT AS WITH THEE OF YORE   •   •   •   •   269 THYRSIS   232
        IN A CHURCHYARD HIGH MID THE MOORS   •   •   •   •   •   282 HAWORTH CHURCH   52
        TO THE LONELY INN MID THE ROCKS   •   •   •   •   •   •   289 RUGBY CHAPEL   109
        MID WEEDS AND WRECKS SHE STOOD A PLACE   •   •   •   •   317 OBERMANN MORE   139
        I AT THAT ALTAR WHERE MID SHOUTING CROWDS   •   •   •   • 338 MEROPE   272
        FAR MID ARCADIAN HILLS   •   •   •   •   •   •   •   •   • 346 MEROPE   512
        ONCE MID THOSE GORGES   •   •   •   •   •   •   •   •   • 392 MEROPE   1646
        ONCE MID THE GORGES   •   •   •   •   •   •   •   •   •   •392 MEROPE   V1646
        OR HEAR MID CIRCLING CRAGS THE IMPATIENT CRY   •   •   472 CROMWELL   25

MIDDLE
        VALLEYS AND MEN TO MIDDLE FORTUNE BORN   •   •   •   •   6 GEO CRUIKSHANK   4
        DOWN THROUGH THE MIDDLE OF A RICH MANS CORN   •   •   70 SOHRAB RUSTUM   294
        DOWN IN THE MIDDLE OF THE HOLLOW STOOD   •   •   •   •   TRISTRAM 3   V 19
        WHICH GLOWS AS IF THE MIDDLE AGE   •   •   •   •   •   •   204 CALAIS SANDS   7
        ADVANCEST TO THE MIDDLE OF A DEED   •   •   •   •   •   • 367 MEROPE   1061
        THE ALTAR IN THE MIDDLE OF THE SQUARE   •   •   •   •   • 401 MEROPE   1908

MIDGARD
        TO LOOK ON MIDGARD AND THE EARTH AND MEN   •   •   •   96 BALDER DEAD 1   52
        PAST MIDGARD FORTRESS DOWN TO EARTH AND MEN   •   •   99 BALDER DEAD 1   142
        PAST MIDGARD FORTRESS DOWN TO EARTH THEY CAME   •   •   105 BALDER DEAD 2   23
        AND ASGARD THOU DIDST BUILD AND MIDGARD FORT   •   •   121 BALDER DEAD 3   266
        OF JARNVID WHICH TO EAST OF MIDGARD LIES   •   •   •   • 123 BALDER DEAD 3   330

MIDLAND
        OER THE BLUE MIDLAND WATERS WITH THE GALE   •   •   •   • 262 SCHOLAR-GIPSY   244
        THE MURMUR OF THIS MIDLAND DEEP   •   •   •   •   •   •   276 SOUTHERN NIGHT   21
        NOT BY THIS GRACIOUS MIDLAND SEA   •   •   •   •   •   • 277 SOUTHERN NIGHT   74

MIDMOST
        OF THE MIDMOST OCEAN HAVE SWELLD   •   •   •   •   •   • 288 RUGBY CHAPEL   71

MIDNIGHT
        PASSIVE AT THE MIDNIGHT OF DESPAIR   •   •   •   •   •   • 33 NEW SIRENS   V 202

MIDNIGHT   (CONTINUED)
    BY MIDNIGHT TO A BUBBLING FOUNTAINS SOUND   •   •   •   70 SOHRAB RUSTUM   317
    AND WHEN THE CLOCK PEALS MIDNIGHT SHE WILL MOVE •   •   •   152 TRISTRAM 3   86
    BUT CHILDREN AT MIDNIGHT • • • • • • • • •   165 FORSAKEN MERM   124
    SO SANG I BUT THE MIDNIGHT BREEZE   •   •   •   •   •   •   279 SOUTHERN NIGHT   117
    BUT ONCE AT MIDNIGHT DEEP   •   •   •   •   •   •   •   446 WESTMIN ABBEY   91

MIDST
    IN THE MIDST OF RIVER-MEADOWS   •   •   •   •   32 NEW SIRENS   181
    JUST PITCHD THE HIGH PAVILION IN THE MIDST   •   •   •   67 SOHRAB RUSTUM   193
    AND IN THE MIDST A STUBBLE SHORT AND BARE   •   •   •   70 SOHRAB RUSTUM   296
    BRISTLING AND IN THE MIDST THE OPEN SAND   •   •   •   70 SOHRAB RUSTUM   298
    NEW PITCHD THE HIGH PAVILION IN THE MIDST   •   •   •   67 SOHRAB RUSTUM   V 193
    AND IN THE MIDST ONE HIGHER ODINS THRONE   •   •   •   106 BALDER DEAD 2   38
    IN THE BARE MIDST OF ANGLESEY THEY SHOW   •   •   •   170 EAST AND WEST   1

MIDSUMMER
    SOON WILL THE HIGH MIDSUMMER POMPS COME ON   •   •   •   264 THYRSIS   62

MIEN
    AND WITH A FEARLESS MIEN SOHRAB REPLIED   •   •   •   •   77 SOHRAB RUSTUM   540
    IS IT THIS THOUGHT WHICH MAKES HER MIEN SO STILL   •   •   151 TRISTRAM 3   69
    IS IT THIS THOUGHT THAT MAKES HER MIEN SO STILL   •   •   151 TRISTRAM 3   V 69
    THAT FURTIVE MIEN THAT SCOWLING EYE   •   •   •   •   157 SAINT BRANDAN   17
    IN ALL HIS LOVELY MIEN LET PIERCE   •   •   •   •   •   202 URANIA   23
    THE MIEN OF YOUTH WE USED TO SEE   •   •   •   •   •   276 SOUTHERN NIGHT   38
    WITH A LOVELY FRIGHTEND MIEN   •   •   •   •   •   •   433 EMPEDOCLES II   157
    WHAT SPRING OF YOUTH IN THAT MAJESTIC MIEN   •   •   •   477 CROMWELL   185

MIGHT
    MIGHT FADE IN SLUMBER AND THE FEET OF JOY   •   •   •   •   11 MYCERINUS   90
    MIGHT WANDER ALL DAY LONG AND NEVER TIRE   •   •   •   •   11 MYCERINUS   91
    MIGHT SHRINK HALF STARTLED LIKE A GUILTY MAN   •   •   •   11 MYCERINUS   102
    THE WORLD SPEAKS WELL YET MIGHT HER FOE REPLY   •   •   38 WORLDS TRIUMPHS   11
    SIGNS ARE NOT WANTING WHICH MIGHT RAISE   •   •   •   •   56 RESIGNATION   122
    SO MIGHT THEY REASON SO COMPARE   •   •   •   •   •   •   56 RESIGNATION   136
    WEAK YET NOT WEAK I MIGHT REPLY   •   •   •   •   •   •   59 RESIGNATION   255
    IF I MIGHT LEND THEIR LIFE A VOICE   •   •   •   •   •   60 RESIGNATION   269
    O RUSTUM LIKE THY MIGHT IS THIS YOUNG MANS   •   •   •   67 SOHRAB RUSTUM   215
    AND NOW MIGHT SOHRAB HAVE UNSHEATHED HIS SWORD   •   •   73 SOHRAB RUSTUM   422
    WHOM RUSTUM WERT THOU HIS MIGHT WELL HAVE LOVED   •   •   80 SOHRAB RUSTUM   642
    THAT SHE MIGHT PRICK IT ON THE BABE SHE BORE   •   •   •   80 SOHRAB RUSTUM   660
    MIGHT MEAN AND FROM HIS DARK COMPASSIONATE EYES   •   •   82 SOHRAB RUSTUM   735
    MIGHT BE ONCE MORE ALIVE MY BITTEREST FOES   •   •   •   85 SOHRAB RUSTUM   810
    MIGHT NOW BE LYING ON THIS BLOODY SAND   •   •   •   •   85 SOHRAB RUSTUM   817
    NOT THOU OF MINE AND I MIGHT DIE NOT THOU   •   •   •   85 SOHRAB RUSTUM   819
    AND ZAL MIGHT WEEP ABOVE MY GRAVE NOT THINE   •   •   85 SOHRAB RUSTUM   821
    THINGS WHICH MIGHT VEX HIM SHALL BE FOUND   •   •   •   92 SICK KING BOKH   160
    IF ANY HERE MIGHT WEEP FOR BALDERS DEATH   •   •   •   96 BALDER DEAD 1   20
    I MOST MIGHT WEEP HIS FATHER SUCH A SON   •   •   •   96 BALDER DEAD 1   21
    IS IT A MATTER WHICH A GOD MIGHT TRY   •   •   •   •   99 BALDER DEAD 1   133
    BUT EVEN THERE O NANNA WE MIGHT FIND   •   •   •   •   104 BALDER DEAD 1   326
    WOULD I MIGHT SEE HIM SNATCH THEE IN HIS HAND   •   •   114 BALDER DEAD 3   24
    THOU THREATENEST WHAT TRANSCENDS THY MIGHT EVEN THINE   120 BALDER DEAD 3   249
    FAR OFF WHERE SOME UNWARND MIGHT FAIL TO WEEP   •   •   122 BALDER DEAD 3   322
    IF STRENGTH MIGHT SAVE THEM COULD NOT ODIN SAVE   •   •   127 BALDER DEAD 3   490
    MIGHT THY DYING KNIGHT RESTORE   •   •   •   •   •   132 TRISTRAM 1   79
    MIGHT DRINK IT ON THEIR MARRIAGE-DAY   •   •   •   •   135 TRISTRAM 1   139
    THE DAYS IN WHICH SHE MIGHT HAVE LIVED AND LOVED   •   •   151 TRISTRAM 3   65
    THAT NECKAN HEAVEN MIGHT GAIN   •   •   •   •   •   •   160 NECKAN   40
    THE FAULT WAS GRAVE I MIGHT HAVE KNOWN   •   •   •   •   180 ISOLATION MARG   7
    HAVE DREAMD TWO HUMAN HEARTS MIGHT BLEND   •   •   •   181 ISOLATION MARG   38
    OH MIGHT OUR MARGES MEET AGAIN   •   •   •   •   •   •   182 TO MARG CONT   18
    BUT OUR IGNOBLE SOULS LACK MIGHT   •   •   •   •   •   201 URANIA   4
    ONE FOR WHOSE SAKE SHE ONCE MIGHT PROVE   •   •   •   202 URANIA   19
    AH MIGHT I ALWAYS REST UNSEEN   •   •   •   •   •   •   205 CALAIS SANDS   31
    SO I MIGHT HAVE THEE ALWAYS NEAR   •   •   •   •   •   205 CALAIS SANDS   32
    OH WERT THOU HERE THAT I MIGHT TURN   •   •   •   •   204 CALAIS SANDS   V   9
    OH MIGHT I ALWAYS REST UNSEEN   •   •   •   •   •   •   205 CALAIS SANDS   V 31
    SAW THE GIFTS THE POWERS IT MIGHT INHERIT   •   •   •   209 SELF-DECEPTION   7
    WHATEVER MEN HAVE DONE MIGHT DO   •   •   •   •   •   221 BACCHANALIA 2   67
    WHATEVER THOUGHT MIGHT THINK IT TOO   •   •   •   •   221 BACCHANALIA 2   68
    HOW BOUNDLESS MIGHT HIS SOULS HORIZONS BE   •   •   •   244 SUMMER NIGHT   88
    THAT IT MIGHT KEEP FREE FROM HIS CAPRICIOUS PLAY   •   •   246 BURIED LIFE   35
    THUS FEELING GAZING MIGHT I GROW   •   •   •   •   •   251 WISH   49
    MANS PRUDENCE AND MANS FIERY MIGHT   •   •   •   •   •   272 MEMORIAL VERSES   59
    A BREATH MIGHT QUENCH   •   •   •   •   •   •   •   •   276 SOUTHERN NIGHT   36
    MIGHT WELL REPOSE   •   •   •   •   •   •   •   •   278 SOUTHERN NIGHT   92
    KNEW NO FELLOW FOR MIGHT   •   •   •   •   •   •   •   284 HAWORTH CHURCH   94
    WHAT MIGHT WE SAY TO CONSOLE   •   •   •   •   •   •   282 HAWORTH CHURCH   V
    SUNSHINE AND RAIN AS WE MIGHT   •   •   •   •   •   •   287 RUGBY CHAPEL   34
    STONES MIGHT HAVE WOUNDED THY FEET   •   •   •   •   •   290 RUGBY CHAPEL   135
    IN PITY AND MOURNFUL AWE MIGHT STAND   •   •   •   •   301 GRANDE CHARTR   82
    FOR ALL THAT MIGHT HAVE BEEN   •   •   •   •   •   •   314 OBERMANN MORE   52
    MIGHT FALL A FRESHENING STORM   •   •   •   •   •   319 OBERMANN MORE   198
    THE CARES WHICH MIGHT IN ME WITH TIME I FEEL   •   •   335 MEROPE   161
    HANDFUL OF DORIAN CONQUERORS MIGHT HAVE CURBD   •   •   337 MEROPE   248
    YET NOT FOR THIS ELSE MIGHT THY CRIME IN PART   •   •   339 MEROPE   314
    IF THAT MIGHT SOOTHE HIM BELOW   •   •   •   •   •   •   343 MEROPE   410
    HER BLOOD THAT SO SHE MIGHT MAKE   •   •   •   •   •   343 MEROPE   427

MIGHT   (CONTINUED)
        MIGHT SOME ONE STRAIGHT INFORM HIM HE IS SOUGHT   • •   354 MEROPE   708
        THAT OUR JOINT HANDS MIGHT THEN TOGETHER PAY   • •   367 MEROPE   1047
        IN WORD I DIED THAT I IN DEED MIGHT LIVE   • • • • 375 MEROPE   1209
        MIGHT FROM THE PEOPLE DRAW IF RIGHTLY USED   • •   382 MEROPE   1336
        HOW MIGHT NOT SUCH A SIGHT AS THIS REVIVE   • • • • 383 MEROPE   1358
        THEN MIGHT I USE THEM THEN FOR ONE WHO THUS   • •   383 MEROPE   1362
        RISK WHAT HE MIGHT NOW THAT I HAVE HIM HERE   • •   387 MEROPE   1458
        MIGHT ASK WHY WE ENDURED THEIR YOKE SO LONG   • •   402 MEROPE   1947
        AND ALL WHICH MIGHT RELAX HIS SETTLED GLOOM   • •   409 EMPEDOCLES I 1   84
        WHO STILL WAS FAITHFUL WHAT MIGHT PROFIT ME   • •   410 EMPEDOCLES I 1   131
        I THINK MIGHT MAKE US FEAR   • • • • • • •   425 EMPEDOCLES I 2   384
        AND WE MIGHT GLADLY SHARE THE FRUITFUL STIR   • •   439 EMPEDOCLES II   339
        WE MIGHT HAVE JOY BLENT WITH THE ALL—BATHING AIR   • •   439 EMPEDOCLES II   343
        WELL MIGHT IT BE   • • • • • • • • • •   439 EMPEDOCLES II   V 341
        SO TIBERIUS MIGHT HAVE SAT   • •   453 POOR MATTHIAS   41
        AMBITIONS BOLDEST DREAM MIGHT SOBER AND APPAL   • •   463 ALARIC AT ROME   42
        THE VANISHT MIGHT OF THAT DISCROWNED HEAD   • • •   464 ALARIC AT ROME   46
        IN SULLEN HOMAGE TO THE INVADERS MIGHT   • • •   465 ALARIC AT ROME   76
        BUT OER HER VANISHT MIGHT AND HUMBLED PRIDE   • •   468 ALARIC AT ROME   161
        PERCHANCE THAT SOLEMN SIGHT MIGHT QUENCH THE FIRE • •   469 ALARIC AT ROME   177
        MIGHT WELL BE MINGLING AT THAT MURMURED SIGH   • •   469 ALARIC AT ROME   179
        ALAS FAR OTHER THOUGHTS MIGHT WELL BE OURS   • • •   470 ALARIC AT ROME   199
        AND WHILE THEY RISE HERE MIGHT WE STAND ALONE   • •   470 ALARIC AT ROME   203
        THERE NEEDS A MINSTREL OF DIVINER MIGHT   • •   471 ALARIC AT ROME   225
        ONE MOMENTS SPACE PERCHANCE MIGHT CHARM HIS EYE   • •   475 CROMWELL   109
        ONE MOMENTS SPACE MIGHT WAFT HIM FAR AWAY   • •   475 CROMWELL   111
        MIGHT PAINT THE CALM SWEET PEACE THE REST OF HOME   475 CROMWELL   113
        THEY LESS THAN US MIGHT RECOGNIZE   • • • • •   • •   481 COURAGE   11
        WE CHEERD BUT FROM IT RUSHD A BLAST OF MIGHT   • •   484 S S LUSITANIA   7
        WAS IT THAT YE WITH MAN MIGHT HAVE YOUR THOUSANDS   HOMER TRANS   11
            OF SORROWS
        WHAT THE TROJAN MEN AND TROJAN WOMEN MIGHT MURMUR   HOMER TRANS   15
        SWIMS ON AN OBSCURE MUCH WE MIGHT HAVE BEEN   • •   FRAGMENT 3   2

MIGHTEST
        SO THOU MIGHTEST LIVE TOO MY SON MY SON   • • • •   85 SOHRAB RUSTUM   815

MIGHTIER
        BUT OUR OWN ACTS FOR GOOD OR ILL ARE MIGHTIER POWERS   420 EMPEDOCLES I 2   241
        IN A MIGHTIER ORDER   • • • • • • • • • •   437 EMPEDOCLES II   286
        NEW DREAMS OF WIDE DOMINION MIGHTIER HIGHER   • •   469 ALARIC AT ROME   175

MIGHTIEST
        FOR OF ALL POWERS THE MIGHTIEST FAR ART THOU   • •   120 BALDER DEAD 3   250
        THE ELDEST MIGHTIEST BROTHER TEMENUS TOOK   • • •   389 MEROPE   1550
        AND THEN THAT MIGHTIEST CRASH THAT GIANT FALL   • •   463 ALARIC AT ROME   41
        HOW SHOULD THAT MIGHTIEST CITY PASS AWAY   • • •, 467 ALARIC AT ROME   129
        THAT BINDS THE HEART OF MAN WITH MIGHTIEST POWER   • •   467 ALARIC AT ROME   146

MIGHTILY
        OF HEAVEN AND MIGHTILY AS WINGD HE FLEW   • • • • 113 BALDER DEAD 2   303
        AUGUST LAWS DOTH MIGHTILY VINDICATE   • • • • • •   196 FRAG ANTIGONE   49

MIGHTS
        MANY SPENT FAMES AND FALLEN MIGHTS   • • • • • •   220 BACCHANALIA 2   23

MIGHTY
        IT TURNS LIFES MIGHTY WHEEL   • • • • • • • •   47 WORLD QUIETIST   13
        AND DRAIND HIS MIGHTY BOWL   • • • • • • • •   47 WORLD QUIETIST   32
        THE POET TO WHOSE MIGHTY HEART   • • • • • • •   56 RESIGNATION   144
        WHETHER THAT HIS OWN MIGHTY STRENGTH AT LAST   • •   63 SOHRAB RUSTUM   83
        THE MIGHTY VOICE OF RUSTUM AND HE SAW   • • •   71 SOHRAB RUSTUM   335
        AND PIERCED THE MIGHTY RUSTUM WHILE HE LAY   • • •   73 SOHRAB RUSTUM   423
        THE MIGHTY RUSTUM SHALL AVENGE MY DEATH   • • •   77 SOHRAB RUSTUM   553
        THE MIGHTY RUSTUM NEVER HAD A SON   • • • •   78 SOHRAB RUSTUM   578
        SOHRAB THE MIGHTY RUSTUMS SON LIES THERE   • • •   84 SOHRAB RUSTUM   792
        THREE MIGHTY CHILDREN TO MY FATHER LOK   • • •   110 BALDER DEAD 2   206
        SOON WITH A ROARING ROSE THE MIGHTY FIRE   • • •   118 BALDER DEAD 3   186
        MIGHTY THEIR PATHOS BUT TIS GONE   • • • •   224 EPILOG LAOCOON   92
        THIS MIGHTY MARCH DO AUGHT BUT DIE   • • • •   226 EPILOG LAOCOON   170
        OF THE MIGHTY MOTHER OR CRETE   • • • • • •   230 YOUTH OF NATURE   77
        ON MY HEART YOUR MIGHTY CHARM RENEW   • • • •   240 SELF-DEPENDENCE   10
        THESE ATTAIN THE MIGHTY LIFE YOU SEE   • • • •   240 SELF-DEPENDENCE   28
        I TROW THE MIGHTY MOTHER DOTH NOT SEE • • • •   268 THYRSIS   179
        OF A MIGHTY OAK HAVE ENDURED   • • • • •   287 RUGBY CHAPEL   33
        FORTH TO THE MIGHTY WORLD THEY FARE   • • • • •   305 GRANDE CHARTR   V 179
        ONE MIGHTY WAVE OF THOUGHT AND JOY   • • • •   323 OBERMANN MORE   V 323
        PROSPEROUS MIGHTY CAME BACK   • • • • •   343 MEROPE   411
        TO SEE ANOTHER MIGHTY VICTIM BLEED   • • • •   349 MEROPE   563
        WHY SHOULD THIS HEART OF MINE SET MIGHTY STORE   • •   398 MEROPE   1789
        WHERE TWINES THE CHAPLET DEALT A MIGHTY BLOW   • •   402 MEROPE   1921
        SINK UPON HIS MIGHTY KNEES   • • • • • • •   431 EMPEDOCLES II   73
        BUT WE RECEIVED THE SHOCK OF MIGHTY THOUGHTS   • •   436 EMPEDOCLES II   242
        PAGEANTS HAVE PASSD AND TOMBS OF MIGHTY KINGS   • •   445 WESTMIN ABBEY   53
        HIS NURSE THE MIGHTY MOTHER WILLD IT SO   • • •   446 WESTMIN ABBEY   86
        THE NURSLING OF THE MIGHTY MOTHER DIED   • • •   447 WESTMIN ABBEY   115
        A MIGHTY NAME FOR EVIL OR FOR GOOD   • • • •   463 ALARIC AT ROME   21
        OF THY STERN HILL THOU MIGHTY CAPITOL • • • •   468 ALARIC AT ROME   152
        TRULY YET THIS TIME WILL WE SAVE THEE MIGHTY ACHILLES   HOMER TRANS   47

MIGRATORY
        CHANCE GUIDES THE MIGRATORY RACE   • • • • • •   55 RESIGNATION   113

MILAN
        OF ITALIAN MILAN THE FAIR   • • • • • • • •   296 HEINES GRAVE   130

MILD
        MAN WOULD BE MILD AND WITH SAFE CONSCIENCE BLEST   • •   5 HARMONY NATURE   11
        AND HIS MIRTH QUAILD NOT AT THE MILD REPROOF   • •   12 MYCERINUS   114
        WITH THEIR MILD DARK HIS GRASSY BANQUET-HALL   • •   12 MYCERINUS   119
        LET ALL WORDS BE MILD   • • • • • • • • •   40 STAGIRIUS   54
        MILD HOLLOWS AND CLEAR HEATHY SWELLS   • • • • • •   54 RESIGNATION   66
        ON THIS MILD BANK ABOVE THE STREAM   • • • • •   55 RESIGNATION   102
        BUT WITH A GRAVE MILD VOICE SOHRAB REPLIED   • • • •   84 SOHRAB RUSTUM   771
        AND WITH A GRAVE MILD VOICE SOHRAB REPLIED   • • • •   84 SOHRAB RUSTUM   V 771
        BUT IT SHALL NOT BE SO BUT MILD BUT SWIFT   • • • •   103 BALDER DEAD 1   301
        AND SPAKE AND MILD ENTREATED HER AND SAID   • •   110 BALDER DEAD 2   188
        BUT HERMOD STAYD HIM WITH MILD WORDS AND SAID   • •   125 BALDER DEAD 3   422
        IN TIMES LESS ALIEN TO A SPIRIT MILD   • • • • •   128 BALDER DEAD 3   512
        HER LOOKS ARE MILD HER FINGERS SLIGHT   • • • •   131 TRISTRAM 1   30
        MILD SHINES THE COLD SPRING IN THE MOONS CLEAR LIGHT   139 TRISTRAM 1   283
        WHICH GLISTERING PLAYS ALL ROUND THEM LONE AND MILD   155 TRISTRAM 3   203
        WHICH GLISTERING LAY ALL ROUND THEM LONE AND MILD   155 TRISTRAM 3   V 203
        TEARS FILLD HIS MILD BLUE EYE   • • • • • • •   160 NECKAN   46
        HE DOES WELL TOO WHO KEEPS THAT CLUE THE MILD   • •   195 FRAG ANTIGONE   9
        MILD AND INSCRUTABLY CALM   • • • • • • • •   232 YOUTH OF MAN   10
        I WILL NOT SAY THAT YOUR MILD DEEPS RETAIN   • • • •   244 SUMMER NIGHT   83
        ON SOME MILD PASTORAL SLOPE   • • • • • • •   261 SCHOLAR-GIPSY   216
        NEATH THE MILD CANOPY OF ENGLISH AIR   • • • • •   268 THYRSIS   194
        IN THE MILD EVENING OF THE MAY   • • • • • • •   274 STANZAS CARNAC   12
        MILD OER HER GRAVE YE MOUNTAINS SHINE   • • • •   279 SOUTHERN NIGHT   137
        IN THE MOONLIT SOLITUDES MILD   • • • • • • •   288 RUGBY CHAPEL   70
        THE GARDEN OVERGROWN YET MILD   • • • • • • •   301 GRANDE CHARTR   55
        THAT MILD AND LUMINOUS FLOOR OF WATERS LIVES   • •   438 EMPEDOCLES II   315
        FROM THAT MILD HOLLOW IN THE HILL   • • • • •   479 HAYSWATER BOAT   20
        OF CALM WISHES MILD ENDURANCE   • • • • • • •   META CLOISTER   23

MILDER
        BUT MILDER NATURES AND MORE FREE   • • • • • •   53 RESIGNATION   22
        NOT MILDER IS THE GENERAL LOT   • • • • • • • •   60 RESIGNATION   275
        OTHER AND MILDER BE MINE   • • • • • • • • •   299 HEINES GRAVE   226

MILDLY
        SO HE SPAKE MILDLY SOHRAB HEARD HIS VOICE   • • • •   71 SOHRAB RUSTUM   334
        AND HIGH ROCKS THROW MILDLY   • • • • • • •   165 FORSAKEN MERM   130
        ASSIST ME TO RULE MILDLY LET US JOIN   • • • • •   335 MEROPE   164

MILDNESS
        I KNOW HER BY HER MILDNESS RARE   • • • • • •   132 TRISTRAM 1   50

MILE
        AND MANY A MILE OF DUSTY WAY   • • • • • • •   54 RESIGNATION   80

MILES
        SCARFD WITH THE CROSS WHO WATCHD THE MILES   • • • •   52 RESIGNATION   5
        HE MAKES HIS MEAL BEFORE HIM FOR LONG MILES   • •   191 STRAYED REVEL   172

MILK
        AND KHIVA AND FERMENT THE MILK OF MARES   • • • •   64 SOHRAB RUSTUM   120
        THE ACRID MILK OF CAMELS AND THEIR WELLS   • • • •   64 SOHRAB RUSTUM   125
        THAT VAST SKY-NEIGHBOURING MOUNTAIN OF MILK SNOW   • •   66 SOHRAB RUSTUM   162
        MARES MILK AND BREAD   • • • • • • • • •   191 STRAYED REVEL   166
        AND MILK-BARRD ONYX-STONES   • • • • • • • •   192 STRAYED REVEL   197
        FULL-FOAMING MILK-PAILS ALPINE FARE   • • • • •   313 OBERMANN MORE   17
        POUR THE LIBATION OF MILK   • • • • • • • •   342 MEROPE   387
        THE FLOWER-DRESSD VICTIM STOOD A MILK-WHITE BULL   • •   401 MEROPE   1910

MILL
        SWALLOW SKIMMING BY THE MILL   • • • • • • • •   456 POOR MATTHIAS   142

MILLIONS
        WE MORTAL MILLIONS LIVE ALONE   • • • • • • •   182 TO MARG CONT   4
        THE COMPLAINING MILLIONS OF MEN   • • • • • •   229 YOUTH OF NATURE   51
        THE MILLIONS SUFFER STILL AND GRIEVE   • • • • •   320 OBERMANN MORE   233
        MILLIONS WHOSE LIFE IN ICE LAY FAST   • • • • •   322 OBERMANN MORE   287

MILTON
        WITH FEET THAT SPURND THE GROUND LO MILTON THERE   • •   477 CROMWELL   175

MIMIC
        FOR THOSE MIMIC RAPTURES YOU HAD WON   • • • • •   31 NEW SIRENS   154
        FOR THE MIMIC RAPTURES YOU HAD WON   • • • • •   31 NEW SIRENS   V 154
        AND MIMIC BOATS THEIR HAVEN NEARD   • • • • •   223 EPILOG LAOCOON   69

MIMIR
        AND THEY FOUND MIMIR SITTING BY HIS FOUNT   • • • •   120 BALDER DEAD 3   219

MIND
        WHO PROP THOU ASKST IN THESE BAD DAYS MY MIND   • •   2 TO A FRIEND   1
        EAGER TELL-TALES OF HER MIND   • • • • • • •   24 MEMORY-PICTURE   42

MIND   (CONTINUED)
        STROLLD AND SANG WITH JOYFUL MIND . . . . . .   26 NEW SIRENS   6
        WHEN THE MIND WAXING CLEARER SEES GOD NO NEARER . . 38 STAGIRIUS   V 16
        WHOSE MIND HATH KNOWN ALL ARTS OF GOVERNING . .   43 GIPSY CHILD   35
        IF IN THE SILENT MIND OF ONE ALL-PURE . . . .   45 IN UTRUMQUE PAR   1
        WHY WHEN THE WORLDS GREAT MIND . . . .   46 WORLD QUIETIST   1
        WHOM SCHOOLING OF THE STUBBORN MIND . . . . .   53 RESIGNATION   26
        FOR QUIET AND A FEARLESS MIND . . . .   59 RESIGNATION   244
        SOHRAB THOU THOUGHTEST IN THY MIND TO KILL . . .   77 SOHRAB RUSTUM   528
        FOR ALLAH SHUT MY EARS AND MIND . . . . .   88 SICK KING BOKH   24
        TO THAT MANS MIND WHO UNDERSTANDS . . . . .   93 SICK KING BOKH   172
        THOUGH SIGHTLESS YET HIS OWN MIND LED THE GOD . . 97 BALDER DEAD 1   76
        AND AFTER THAT OF IGNORANT WITLESS MIND . . .   98 BALDER DEAD 1   98
        YET IN MY SECRET MIND ONE WAY I KNOW . . . .   99 BALDER DEAD 1   128
        TRULY THOU SAYST THE PLANNING GUILTY MIND . . .   125 BALDER DEAD 3   424
        AND THAT WILL BRING TO MIND THE FORMER LIFE . .   128 BALDER DEAD 3   540
        LIFTING HER SOFT-BENT HEAD ONLY TO MIND . . . .   152 TRISTRAM 3   84
        O FRIVOLOUS MIND OF MAN . . . .   198 FRAG DEJANEIRA   1
        WITH UNSPENT MIND AND A SOUL . . . .   199 FRAG DEJANEIRA   27
        INTO HIS MIND THE TURBID EBB AND FLOW . . . .   211 DOVER BEACH   17
        INTO HIS MIND THE TROUBLED EBB AND FLOW . . . .   211 DOVER BEACH   V 17
        AN ACHING BODY AND A MIND . . . .   217 NAMELESS EPIT   V
        AND LAME THE ACTIVE MIND . . . .   237 PROGRESS   20
        THESE MENS PROFOUNDEST MIND . . . .   238 PROGRESS   36
        AND TO MY MIND THE THOUGHT . . . .   242 SUMMER NIGHT   11
        TO HAVE BEFORE MY MIND INSTEAD . . . .   251 WISH   44
        SO IS THE MIND OF THE MAN . . . .   252 FUTURE   18
        GOETHES SAGE MIND AND BYRONS FORCE . . . . .   272 MEMORIAL VERSES   61
        HISTORY POLITICS MIND . . . .   280 HAWORTH CHURCH   17
        THAT WORD GLOOM TO MY MIND . . . .   286 RUGBY CHAPEL   16
        YOUR FATHERS INNERMOST MIND . . . .   291 RUGBY CHAPEL   165
        FORGIVE ME MASTERS OF THE MIND . . . .   301 GRANDE CHARTR   73
        ON MY MIND YEARS BEFORE . . . .   314 OBERMANN MORE   62
        I AM I SHALL BE HAVE BEEN IN MY MIND . . . . .   333 MEROPE   111
        WITH WOMEN THE HEART ARGUES NOT THE MIND . . .   340 MEROPE   341
        ALL WHICH HE OWND AND PRAISED WITH GRATEFUL MIND . 356 MEROPE   763
        I PITY THEE AND WISH THEE CALMER MIND . . . .   396 MEROPE   1760
        I KNOW NOT IN WHAT MIND EMPEDOCLES . . . . .   407 EMPEDOCLES I 1   21
        AND KEEP HIS MIND FROM PREYING ON ITSELF . . .   411 EMPEDOCLES I 1   157
        MIND IS THE SPELL WHICH GOVERNS EARTH AND HEAVEN . 413 EMPEDOCLES I 2   27
        MAN HAS A MIND WITH WHICH TO PLAN HIS SAFETY . .   413 EMPEDOCLES I 2   28
        MIND IS A LIGHT WHICH THE GODS MOCK US WITH . .   413 EMPEDOCLES I 2   32
        WHOSE MIND ALLOWS A PLAN . . . .   415 EMPEDOCLES I 2   99
        THE OBSTINATE MIND DECREES . . . .   419 EMPEDOCLES I 2   200
        NATURE WITH EQUAL MIND . . . .   421 EMPEDOCLES I 2   257
        SURE ONLY THAT YOUR MIND SEES ALL THINGS WHICH BEFAL 423 EMPEDOCLES I 2   346
        WHOSE MIND WAS FED ON OTHER FOOD WAS TRAIND . .   436 EMPEDOCLES II   264
        BUT A NAKED ETERNALLY RESTLESS MIND . . . .   438 EMPEDOCLES II   330
        BUT MIND . . . .   439 EMPEDOCLES II   338
        BUT MIND BUT THOUGHT . . . .   439 EMPEDOCLES II   345
        BAFFLED FOR EVER AND STILL THOUGHT AND MIND . .   439 EMPEDOCLES II   358
        INTO SOME BONDAGE OF THE FLESH OR MIND . . .   440 EMPEDOCLES II   374
        OF MEN WITH MIND THUS DARKEND AND ASTRAY . . .   446 WESTMIN ABBEY   68
        THAT TO MY MIND THERE CAME HOW LONG AGO . . .   446 WESTMIN ABBEY   83
        DOES IT IF WE MISS YOUR MIND . . . . .   457 POOR MATTHIAS   155
        TO TOUCH WITH SORROW EVEN A VICTORS MIND . . .   468 ALARIC AT ROME   166
        TO READ EACH THOUGHT AND TEACH THAT MASTER MIND . 478 CROMWELL   231
        THESE THESE ARE PANGS WHICH MAKE THE MIND A HELL .   LUCRETIUS 2   16
        NEITHER HIS MIND NOR BODY DID HE MAKE . . . .   LUCRETIUS 3   5
        NEITHER HIS MIND NOR BODY CAN HE CHANGE . . .   LUCRETIUS 3   6

MINDED
        FOR DOUBLE-MINDED EVER WAS THE SEED . . . .   112 BALDER DEAD 2   271
        THY VOICE OF JOYANCE MINDED US AND YOUTH . . .   117 BALDER DEAD 3   143
        SELF-POISED CLEAR-MINDED HENCEFORTH MAN . . .   319 OBERMANN MORE   V 185
        TELLING US ARNE MINDED HIM HE TOO . . . . .   356 MEROPE   768

MINDFUL
        SOME EXILES MINDFUL HOW THE PAST WAS GLAD . . .   42 GIPSY CHILD   25
        SOME EXILES MINDFUL HOW HIS PAST WAS GLAD . . .   42 GIPSY CHILD   V 25

MINDS
        NATURES GREAT LAW AND LAW OF ALL MENS MINDS . .   8 RELIGIOUS ISOL   12
        AND PURGED CONSIDERATE MINDS . . . .   198 FRAG DEJANEIRA   17
        AND WE ON ITS BREAST OUR MINDS . . . . . .   253 FUTURE   55
        HOW OUR OWN MINDS ARE MADE . . . .   423 EMPEDOCLES I 2   328
        ON SIMPLE MINDS WITH A PURE NATURAL JOY . . .   436 EMPEDOCLES II   243
        WILL FRET OUR MINDS TO AN INTENSER PLAY . . .   440 EMPEDOCLES II   380
        OF MEN WHOSE MINDS WERE DARKEND AND ASTRAY . . . 446 WESTMIN ABBEY   V 68

MINE
        BLOTTING THIS SIX YEARS SPACE WHICH YET IS MINE . 10 MYCERINUS   60
        WHISPERING A LITTLE SPACE AND THOU ART MINE . .   11 MYCERINUS   106
        DROP WITH MINE ADOWN LIFES LATTER DAYS . . .   33 NEW SIRENS   210
        THEY BEAT UPON MINE EAR AGAIN . . . . . .   36 VOICE   33
        DID STEAL INTO MINE EAR . . . .   36 VOICE   36
        DID STEAL INTO MINE EARS . . . .   36 VOICE   V 36
        ARE WILLS SO WEAK THEN LET NOT MINE WAIT LONG . . 38 WORLDS TRIUMPHS   12
        AND FALSEHOOD WHILE I LIVED WAS FAR FROM MINE . . 80 SOHRAB RUSTUM   657
        THOU ART MY FATHER AND THY GAIN IS MINE . . .   84 SOHRAB RUSTUM   777

MINE   (CONTINUED)
        NOT THOU OF MINE AND I MIGHT DIE NOT THOU   • • •   85 SOHRAB RUSTUM   819
        AND THEY SHALL BURN THY CORPSE WITH MINE NOT THEE   103 BALDER DEAD 1   304
        TEARS STARTED TO MINE EYES WITH YEARNING JOY   • •   117 BALDER DEAD 3   151
        IN MINE OWN BREAST AND HAVE TO NONE REVEALD   • •   121 BALDER DEAD 3   287
        MINE EYES ARE DIZZY WITH THE ARROWY HAIL   • • •   128 BALDER DEAD 3   507
        MINE EARS ARE STUNND WITH BLOWS AND SICK FOR CALM   128 BALDER DEAD 3   508
        HA DOST THOU START ARE THY LIPS BLANCHD LIKE MINE   133 TRISTRAM 1   102
        AND WITH A BLOOD LIKE MINE WILL LEAVE I FEAR   • •   140 TRISTRAM 1   306
        LOVE LIKE MINE IS ALTERD IN THE BREAST   • • •   143 TRISTRAM 2   38
        CLOSE MINE EYES THEN SEEK THE PRINCESS ISEULT   • • 145 TRISTRAM 2   93
        AN ANGEL TOUCH MINE ARM AND SAY   • • • • • •   157 SAINT BRANDAN   35
        WHEN FRAGMENT OF IT SMALL LIKE MINE   • • • • •   158 SAINT BRANDAN   55
        WHEN SEMBLANCE OF IT FAINT LIKE MINE   • • • • •   158 SAINT BRANDAN   V   55
        IF SEMBLANCE OF IT FAINT LIKE MINE   • • • • •   158 SAINT BRANDAN   V   55
        IF FRAGMENT OF IT SMALL LIKE MINE   • • • • •   158 SAINT BRANDAN   V   55
        THY HAND LAY LANGUIDLY IN MINE   • • • • • • •   178 FAREWELL   15
        THIS TRUTH ON THEE BE MINE NO MORE   • • • • • •   179 FAREWELL   42
        LIKE MINE EACH DAY MORE TRIED MORE TRUE   • •   180 ISOLATION MARG   6
        ON THE BLUE STRAIT MINE EYES I STRAIN   • • • •   205 CALAIS SANDS   20
        OH THAT YON SEA-BIRDS WINGS WERE MINE   • • • •   205 CALAIS SANDS   23
        BENEATH ONE ROOF MY QUEEN WITH MINE   • • • • •   205 CALAIS SANDS   36
        OER THE BLUE STRAIT MINE EYES I STRAIN   • • • •   205 CALAIS SANDS   V   20
        OH THAT THAT SEA-BIRDS WINGS WERE MINE   • • • •   205 CALAIS SANDS   V   23
        AH LET THEM REST THOSE EYES ON MINE   • • • • •   206 RIVER   7
        ON MINE LET REST THAT LOVELY HAND   • • • • •   206 RIVER   8
        WHICH NOW IS MINE MUST RE-ATTAIN   • • • • •   206 RIVER   14
        THY HEART IS MINE TRUE TRUE AH TRUE   • • • • •   207 TOO LATE   7
        TIES STRAITLY UP FROM MINE THY LOT   • • • • •   208 ON THE RHINE   8
        A CRY LIKE THINE IN MINE OWN HEART I HEAR   • • •   240 SELF-DEPENDENCE   30
        WHENCE WAS IT FOR IT IS NOT MINE   • • • • • •   241 MORALITY   24
        BEHOLD WITH TEARS MINE EYES ARE WET   • • • • •   245 BURIED LIFE   2
        AND TURN THOSE LIMPID EYES ON MINE   • • • • •   245 BURIED LIFE   10
        CALM SOUL OF ALL THINGS MAKE IT MINE   • • • • •   249 KENSINGTON GARD   37
        OTHER AND MILDER BE MINE • • • • • • • •   299 HEINES GRAVE   226
        HAPPIER HAVE UTTERD IN MINE   • • • • • • •   299 HEINES GRAVE   228
        THE DAY I LIVED IN WAS NOT MINE   • • • • •   321 OBERMANN MORE   257
        THY PART IT WERE TO ADVISE AND MINE TO OBEY   • •   331 MEROPE   34
        HE HAD HIS COUNSEL PARTY FRIENDS I MINE   • • •   334 MEROPE   128
        ONE VOICE PREACHD PATIENCE AND THAT VOICE WAS MINE   337 MEROPE   258
        TO ZEUS BEFORE HE STRUCK HIS BLOW STRUCK MINE   • • 338 MEROPE   274
        WHICH IN A DEED LIKE MINE A JUST MAN TREADS   • •   341 MEROPE   369
        TO THE CHAFED HEART OF JUSTICE THAN TO MINE   • •   349 MEROPE   560
        WORSE TERMS THAN MINE THEY HAVE OBTAIND FROM HEAVEN 360 MEROPE   884
        LEARN THAT FROM OTHER LIPS O QUEEN THAN MINE   • •   362 MEROPE   927
        ARE THESE WORDS MEROPES IS THIS VOICE MINE   • • • 368 MEROPE   1068
        RACE OF CALAMITY MINE   • • • • • • • •   370 MEROPE   1108
        WHEREWITH FATIGUE AND YOUTH HAD BOUND MINE EYES • 375 MEROPE   1204
        LAIAS ALONE NO ERRAND MINE FOR CROWDS   • • • •   380 MEROPE   1285
        WITH SUCH A DEED AS THIS THOU MATCHEST MINE   • •   385 MEROPE   1426
        NOW THAT I FEED MINE EYES ON THAT YOUNG FACE   • •   387 MEROPE   1459
        THOU ART BEWILDERD THE SANE HEAD IS MINE   • • •   396 MEROPE   1759
        MORE FOR THIS LANDS SAKE GRIEVE I THAN MINE OWN • 398 MEROPE   1784
        WHY SHOULD THIS HEART OF MINE SET MIGHTY STORE   • 398 MEROPE   1789
        WHAT HAND TO STRIKE THEE MEET AS MINE THE HAND   • 402 MEROPE   1925
        ARE MINE EYES WITH BLOOD BUT IF THIS   • • • •   348 MEROPE   V
        SAVE MINE HE MUST NOT MEET A HUMAN EYE   • • • •   408 EMPEDOCLES I 1   53
        THOU KNOWST OF OLD HE LOVED THIS HARP OF MINE   • • 408 EMPEDOCLES I 1   72
        WE MINE THIS EARTHEN BALL   • • • • • • •   423 EMPEDOCLES I 2   320
        ESTRANGED LIKE MINE AND SAD   • • • • • • •   426 EMPEDOCLES I 2   410
        TILL MINE EYES ACHE WITH THE LONG SPECTACLE   • •   428 EMPEDOCLES I 2   475
        IMMORTAL HAD I MADE THIS BOY OF MINE   • • • • •   447 WESTMIN ABBEY   105
        DIRGE OF MINE TO CROWN THEIR GRAVE   • • • • •   454 POOR MATTHIAS   V   82

MINED
        MINED BY THE FEVER OF THE SOUL   • • • • • •   178 FAREWELL   22
        SHE FELT THE VOID WHICH MINED HER BREAST   • • •   316 OBERMANN MORE   123
        OUR SHIVERING HEART IS MINED BY SECRET DISCONTENT   424 EMPEDOCLES I 2   366

MINES
        BUT DEEP ENOUGH ALAS NONE EVER MINES   • • • • •   246 BURIED LIFE   56

MINGLE
        MINGLE WITH HIS HURRYING DREAM   • • • • • •   136 TRISTRAM 1   183
        AND MINGLE WITH THY RUINS SOMEWHAT OF OUR OWN   • • 470 ALARIC AT ROME   204

MINGLED
        THEY PASS HE MINGLED WITH THE CROWD   • • • • •   57 RESIGNATION   162
        OR IS HE MINGLED WITH THE UNNUMBERD DEAD   • • •   125 BALDER DEAD 3   430

MINGLING
        MANS FITFUL UPROAR MINGLING WITH HIS TOIL   • • •   1 QUIET WORK   10
        MANS WEAK COMPLAININGS MINGLING WITH HIS TOIL   • •   1 QUIET WORK   V   10
        MANS SENSELESS UPROAR MINGLING WITH HIS TOIL   • •   1 QUIET WORK   V   10
        OUR SENSELESS UPROAR MINGLING WITH OUR TOIL   • •   1 QUIET WORK   V   10
        FALLING FORWARD MINGLING • • • • • • • • •   188 STRAYED REVEL   87
        FALLING FORWARDS MINGLING   • • • • • • • •   188 STRAYED REVEL   V   87
        WERE MINGLING WITH THE SERE AND WITHERED HUES OF DEATH 466 ALARIC AT ROME   102
        MIGHT WELL BE MINGLING AT THAT MURMURED SIGH   • •   469 ALARIC AT ROME   179

MINION
      CURLD MINION DANCER COINER OF SWEET WORDS   •   •   •   •   74 SOHRAB RUSTUM   458

MINIONS
      TIMES GAY MINIONS PLEASED YOU SEE   •   •   •   •   •   •   24 MEMORY-PICTURE   53

MINISTER
      AND NOW MINISTER LOVED   •   •   •   •   •   •   •   •   •   345 MEROPE   474
      WHERE BY THE SACRIFICING MINISTER   •   •   •   •   •   •   401 MEROPE   1909
      THEN APOLLOS MINISTER   •   •   •   •   •   •   •   •   •   433 EMPEDOCLES II   147

MINISTERS
      STILL DO THY SLEEPLESS MINISTERS MOVE ON   •   •   •   •   1 QUIET WORK   11
      STILL DO THY QUIET MINISTERS MOVE ON   •   •   •   •   •   1 QUIET WORK   V   11
      THY WELL-TRIED FRIENDS THY WILLING MINISTERS   •   •   429 EMPEDOCLES II   26

MINISTRY
      DECLINES HER MINISTRY AND CARVES HIS OWN   •   •   •   •   195 FRAG ANTIGONE   6

MINSTER
      KING SEBERTS WORK THE WONDROUS MINSTER NEW   •   •   •   •   444 WESTMIN ABBEY   16
      AND THAT NEW MINSTER IN THE MATTED FEN   •   •   •   •   444 WESTMIN ABBEY   19
      AND AS YEARS SPED THE MINSTER-AISLES DIVINE   •   •   445 WESTMIN ABBEY   55

MINSTERS
      THE MINSTERS OUTLINED MASS   •   •   •   •   •   •   •   •   445 WESTMIN ABBEY   31

MINSTREL
      THERE NEEDS A MINSTREL OF DIVINER MIGHT   •   •   •   •   471 ALARIC AT ROME   225

MINT
      AND FROM THE MINT-PLANT IN THE SEDGE   •   •   •   •   •   •   218 BACCHANALIA 1   13

MINUTES
      WHO HAS NO MINUTES BREATHING SPACE ALLOWD   •   •   •   •   437 EMPEDOCLES II   272

MIRACLE
      THAT IS THE SECRET OF THIS MIRACLE   •   •   •   •   •   410 EMPEDOCLES I 1   132
      SIMPLE PAUSANIAS TWAS NO MIRACLE   •   •   •   •   •   •   410 EMPEDOCLES I 1   134
      ASK NOT THE LATEST NEWS OF THE LAST MIRACLE   •   •   415 EMPEDOCLES I 2   106

MIRACLES
      NOT MIRACLES THOU ART A LEARNED MAN   •   •   •   •   •   •   411 EMPEDOCLES I 1   159

MIRACULOUS
      DOWN IN OUR MOTHER EARTHS MIRACULOUS WOMB   •   •   •   •   439 EMPEDOCLES II   340
      HOW EVERY BIRTH OF TIMES MIRACULOUS WOMB   •   •   •   •   469 ALARIC AT ROME   191

MIRED
      HER PALFREYS FLANKS WERE MIRED AND BATHED IN SWEAT   154 TRISTRAM 3   171

MIRROR
      BLUE AND OER ITS MIRROR KIND   •   •   •   •   •   •   •   •   135 TRISTRAM 1   155
      OR THAT RENOWND MIRROR OF CHIVALRY   •   •   •   •   •   153 TRISTRAM 1   146
      THERE LIKE A MIRROR HUNG   •   •   •   •   •   •   •   •   415 EMPEDOCLES I 2   80
      THOU MIRROR THAT HAST DANCD THROUGH SUCH A WORLD   •   •   LUCRETIUS 1   1

MIRRORD
      HATH NEER BEEN MIRRORD ON THEIR SOUL   •   •   •   •   •   •   226 EPILOG LAOCOON   188

MIRRORING
      THE WIND-BORNE MIRRORING SOUL   •   •   •   •   •   •   •   •   415 EMPEDOCLES I 2   83

MIRTH
      AND HIS MIRTH QUAILD NOT AT THE MILD REPROOF   •   •   12 MYCERINUS   114
      AND WHEN THE MIRTH WAXD LOUDEST WITH DULL SOUND   •   •   12 MYCERINUS   123
      HER MIRTH THE WORLD REQUIRED   •   •   •   •   •   •   •   21 REQUIESCAT   5
      MIRTH TO-DAY AND VINE-BOUND TRESSES   •   •   •   •   •   33 NEW SIRENS   197
      FROM MIRTH THAT IS BUT FEIGNING   •   •   •   •   •   •   39 STAGIRIUS   34

MIS
      MIS-DEFINE THESE TILL GOD KNOWS THEM NO MORE   •   •   171 DIVINITY   10

MISAPPLIED
      RELIGIOUS FERVOURS ARDOUR MISAPPLIED   •   •   •   •   •   237 PROGRESS   17

MISCHANCE
      BUT I FROM OUR DEPLORED MISCHANCE LEARN THIS   •   •   359 MEROPE   853
      TELL ME HATH ONE NOT COME OR WORSE MISCHANCE   •   •   361 MEROPE   918
      THY LAST MISCHANCE ON THIS SICILIAN DEEP   •   •   •   •   430 EMPEDOCLES II   57

MISCHIEF
      COME BANEFUL MISCHIEF FROM THY MURKY DEN   •   •   •   •   367 MEROPE   1063

MISER
      LIKE SOME OLD MISER RUSTUM HOARDS HIS FAME   •   •   •   •   68 SOHRAB RUSTUM   247

MISERABLE
      AH MISERABLE   •   •   •   •   •   •   •   •   •   •   •   •   •   •   373 MEROPE   1176
      AND BEING LONELY THOU ART MISERABLE   •   •   •   •   •   429 EMPEDOCLES II   20

MISERABLE   (CONTINUED)
    THIS ENVIOUS MISERABLE AGE   • • • • • • • • •   432 EMPEDOCLES II   107

MISERABLY
    BE MISERABLY BANDIED TO AND FRO   • • • • • •   435 EMPEDOCLES II   230

MISERERE
    MISERERE DOMINE   • • • • • • • • • • •   224 EPILOG LAOCOON   89
    MISERERE DOMINE   • • • • • • • • • • •   224 EPILOG LAOCOON   106

MISERY
    FROM THE CLOG OF MISERY   • • • • • • • •   138 TRISTRAM 1   268
    THE FRET AND MISERY OF OUR NORTHERN TOWNS   • • •   168 RACHEL 2   9
    OF HUMAN MISERY WE   • • • • • • • • •   211 DOVER BEACH   18
    WHO FINDS HIMSELF LOSES HIS MISERY   • • • •   240 SELF-DEPENDENCE   32
    MISERY WHICH ROUSES OTHERS BREAKS THE SPRING   • •   366 MEROPE   1025
    OUR MISERY MORE AND THINE OWN RUIN SURE   • • •   368 MEROPE   1081
    WE WOULD HAVE MISERY CEASE   • • • • • •   420 EMPEDOCLES I 2   234

MISERYS
    TELLS US HIS MISERYS BIRTH AND GROWTH AND SIGNS   • •   260 SCHOLAR-GIPSY   187

MISGIVING
    META WITH A VAGUE MISGIVING   • • • • • • •   META CLOISTER   19

MISINTERPRET
    BUT STRANGELY MISINTERPRET ALL YOU HEAR   • • • •   198 FRAG DEJANEIRA   14

MISLED
    MISLED BY SEEMING   • • • • • • • • • • • •   398 MEROPE   1796

MISPLANND
    CONSTRUED AWRY MISPLANND INVASIONS WORE   • • • •   336 MEROPE   216
    CONSTRUED AWRY MISPLANND INVASIONS USD   • • • •   336 MEROPE   V 216

MISRULE
    THOU HADST NO CAUSE AS FEIGND IN HIS MISRULE   • •   338 MEROPE   283
    FOR IF YE SLEW HIM FOR SUPPOSED MISRULE   • • • •   339 MEROPE   316

MISRULED
    HAD THEY MISRULED HAD THEY FORGOT THEIR FRIENDS   • •   339 MEROPE   322

MISS
    LET US NOT FRET AND FEAR TO MISS OUR AIM   • • •   40 HUMAN LIFE   10
    THEN WE SHALL MISS THY COUNSEL AND THY ARM   • • •   115 BALDER DEAD 3   70
    AGAINST THE WEST I MISS IT IS IT GONE   • • •   263 THYRSIS   27
    DOES IT IF WE MISS YOUR MIND   • • • • • •   457 POOR MATTHIAS   155
    MISS OUR EYES AND MISS OUR EARS   • • • • •   457 POOR MATTHIAS   166
    MISS OUR EYES AND MISS OUR EARS   • • • • •   457 POOR MATTHIAS   166
    THERE LIES THY GOAL TO MISS OR TO ATTAIN   • • • •   465 ALARIC AT ROME   87

MISSD
    THAT LIFE WHOSE DUMB WISH IS NOT MISSD   • • • •   58 RESIGNATION   193
    RENT THE TOUGH PLATES BUT MISSD TO REACH THE SKIN   •   76 SOHRAB RUSTUM   V 493
    BUT HERE I KNOW THOU WILT BE MISSD AND MOURND   • •   115 BALDER DEAD 3   78
    YET GRANT AS SENSE LONG MISSD   • • • • • • •   421 EMPEDOCLES I 2   282

MISSEL
    THE FELL-FARES AND THE SPECKLED MISSEL-THRUSH   • •   150 TRISTRAM 3   30

MISSES
    AND HE SPINS ILL WHO MISSES ONE   • • • • • •   48 HORATIAN ECHO   26

MISSEST
    FOOL THOU MISSEST WE ARE BOTH UNMOVD   • • • • •   146 TRISTRAM 2   V 100

MISSILE
    BY THE SWIFT-RUSHING MISSILE OF DEATH   • • • •   216 LORDS MESSENGER   V 18

MIST
    IN THE MIST OF RIVER MEADOWS   • • • • • • •   32 NEW SIRENS   V 181
    MIST CLOGS THE SUNSHINE   • • • • • • • • •   50 CONSOLATION   1
    MAKE WHISTLING TOWRD HIS MIST-WREATHED FLOCK   • •   57 RESIGNATION   183
    MAKE WHISTLING TOWARDS HIS MIST-WREATHED FLOCK   • •   57 RESIGNATION   V 183
    OUT OF THE MIST AND HUM OF THAT LOW LAND   • • •   87 SOHRAB RUSTUM   876
    FROM HERE THE COLD WHITE MIST CAN BE DISCERND   • •   108 BALDER DEAD 2   124
    ROLLD HEAVILY THE LEADEN MIST ASIDE   • • • • •   126 BALDER DEAD 3   441
    THROUGH A MIST I SEE THEE NEAR COME NEARER   • • •   145 TRISTRAM 2   75
    BY MIST AND CHIMNEYS UNCONFINED   • • • • •   223 EPILOG LAOCOON   71
    WITH THE GREY MIST MARKING ITS COURSE   • • • •   234 YOUTH OF MAN   84
    THESE BRAMBLES PALE WITH MIST ENGARLANDED   • • •   267 THYRSIS   173
    MIST AND ILLUSION AND FEAR   • • • • • • •   281 HAWORTH CHURCH   40
    STORMY THROUGH DRIVING MIST   • • • • • • •   286 HAWORTH CHURCH   131
    AND MIST-TRACKD STREAM OF THE WIDE   • • • • •   297 HEINES GRAVE   172
    IS DARK AND ON THE STREAM THE MIST STILL HANGS   •   406 EMPEDOCLES I 1   13
    FOR MIST CAN SCARCELY SEE   • • • • • • • •   444 WESTMIN ABBEY   22
    FOR MIST CAN HARDLY SEE   • • • • • • • • •   444 WESTMIN ABBEY   V 22
    ABIDES ENTHROND AMID THE MIST AND STORM   • • •   472 CROMWELL   18
    PASSD LIKE A MORNING MIST IN TEARS AWAY   • • • •   477 CROMWELL   198

MISTAKES
        SAW THE MISTAKES OF OUR YOUTH • • • • • • • •   232 YOUTH OF MAN   14

MISTLETOE
        OF MISTLETOE WHICH LOK THE ACCUSER GAVE   • • • •   95 BALDER DEAD 1   6

MISTRESS
        AND SCORN US AS OUR MISTRESS MAY   • • • • • •   48 HORATIAN ECHO   33
        HIS MISTRESS USE HER EMPIRE AS SHE MAY   • • • • 155 TRISTRAM 3   184
        THE SOUTH IS MISTRESS OF HIS GRAVE • • • • • •   275 STANZAS CARNAC   48
        LOOK UP O QUEEN LOOK UP O MISTRESS DEAR   • • • • 363 MEROPE   946
        O MISTRESS BY THE GODS DO NOTHING RASH   • • • • 368 MEROPE   1075
        O LOVED MISTRESS IN FEAR • • • • • • •   371 MEROPE   1130
        WE SEE DEAR MISTRESS AND WE SAY THE GODS   • • • • 377 MEROPE   1225
        THE GODS O MISTRESS DEAR THE HARD-SOULD MAN • •   390 MEROPE   1577
        WELL HE KNEW HIS MISTRESS DEAR • • • • • •   452 POOR MATTHIAS   6
        NOW THY MISTRESS BRINGS THEE HERE   • • • • • •   452 POOR MATTHIAS   16
        AGAINST THY MISTRESS LOVING HEART   • • • • • •   460 KAISER DEAD   53

MISTRUST
        WHERE LOVE IS HALF MISTRUST   • • • • • • •   39 STAGIRIUS   46
        WERE TO LIVE FREE FROM TERROR SPELLS MISTRUST THEM   413 EMPEDOCLES I 2   26
        WERE TO LIVE FREED FROM TERROR SPELLS MISTRUST THEM 413 EMPEDOCLES I 2 V 26

MISTRUSTFUL
        AT LAST IT REACHD US THAT HE STILL MISTRUSTFUL   • • 338 MEROPE   259

MISTS
        WHERE THE WHITE MISTS FOR EVER • • • • • • •   177 PARTING   87
        THE MISTS ARE ON THE MOUNTAIN HUNG • • • • • •   185 TERRACE BERNE   51
        THE MISTS ARE ON THE MOUNTAINS HUNG • • • • • •   185 TERRACE BERNE   V 51
        AND THE MISTS OF DELUSION • • • • • • •   235 YOUTH OF MAN   105
        THE MISTS ARE ON THE RHONE • • • • • • •   306 OBERMANN   8
        THE WHITE MISTS ROLLING LIKE A SEA • • • • • •   306 OBERMANN   9
        FROM MISTS AND SANE AND CLEAR   • • • • • • •   308 OBERMANN   62
        AND FOR HIMSELF MAKE MISTS • • • • • • •   419 EMPEDOCLES I 2   204
        ERE IT FLAG ERE THE MISTS   • • • • • • •   441 EMPEDOCLES II   413
        OR DROWND IN MISTS OF CHILDISH WONDERMENT • • • • 446 WESTMIN ABBEY   65
        THE MORNING MISTS FROM TOWER AND TEMPLE ROLL   • • 468 ALARIC AT ROME   154

MISTY
        AND UP FROM THENCE A WET AND MISTY ROAD   • • • • 113 BALDER DEAD 2   289

MIXD
        MIXD WITH THE MURMUR OF THE MOVING NILE   • • •   12 MYCERINUS   127
        A WEIGHT OF MEDITATION MIXD WITH PAIN   • • • •   41 GIPSY CHILD   V 12
        HE WOULD HAVE MIXD YOU WITH YOUR FRIENDLY FOES • • 339 MEROPE   301
        THEIR TINKLING BELLS MIXD WITH THE SONG OF BIRDS • • 407 EMPEDOCLES I 1   28

MIXT
        MIXT WITH THE IDLERS ON THE PIER   • • • • • •   205 CALAIS SANDS   30

MIXTURE
        THE STRIFE THE MIXTURE IN HER SOUL ARE OURS   • • 168 RACHEL 3   13

MOAN
        THE SEA GROWS STORMY THE LITTLE ONES MOAN • • • • 163 FORSAKEN MERM   65
        THE SEA GROWS STORMY THE LITTLE ONES MOAN • • • • 163 FORSAKEN MERM   79
        THEIR LOT WAS BUT TO WEEP AND MOAN • • • • •   203 EUPHROSYNE   10
        DEEP IS THEIR PENITENTIAL MOAN • • • • • • •   224 EPILOG LAOCOON   91
        TO HAVE ECHOED THE MOAN OF MY SEAS • • • • •   231 YOUTH OF NATURE 124
        THAT ALL NIGHT LONG ITS WEARY MOAN DOTH MAKE   • • 477 CROMWELL   191

MOANING
        UNDER THEIR FEET AND MOANING SWEPT THE PLAIN   • •   75 SOHRAB RUSTUM   484
        EDDYING AND MOANING ROUND AND SWEPT THE PLAIN • •   75 SOHRAB RUSTUM V 484
        AND CAME DOWN MOANING TO THE SEA FIRST SQUALLS • • 118 BALDER DEAD 3   182

MOANS
        LOW MOANS HALF UTTERD • • • • • • • • •   393 MEROPE   1667
        SCRATCHD BY A FALL WITH MOANS   • • • • • • • •   421 EMPEDOCLES I 2   272
        AND TRAVAILS PANTS AND MOANS   • • • • • • • •   422 EMPEDOCLES I 2   295
        AND STRUGGLES PANTS AND MOANS   • • • • • • • •   422 EMPEDOCLES I 2 V 295
        AND TRAVAILS STRIVES AND MOANS • • • • • • • •   422 EMPEDOCLES I 2 V 295

MOAT
        THE DRAWBRIDGE AND THE MOAT APPEAR • • • • • •   148 TRISTRAM 2   171
        TO MOAT THIS ISLE OF ASHES FROM THE WORLD • • • • 438 EMPEDOCLES II   310

MOB
        AND ARTISTS ENVIOUS AND THE MOB PROFANE   • • • • 295 HEINES GRAVE   114
        STRUCK ONCE AND AWED HIS MOB AND SAVED THIS REALM   338 MEROPE   275
        THE MOB WHO OUGHT TO OBEY ARE THESE • • • • •   353 MEROPE   678
        KINDLE THEIR HEARTS MAKE THEM NO MORE A MOB   • • 383 MEROPE   1360
        A CRAVEN MOB BUT A DEVOURING FIRE   • • • • •   383 MEROPE   1361
        ARE LIKE THE MOB VICIOUS AND IGNORANT   • • • •   404 MEROPE   2004
        ELECTRIFY THEIR HEARTS MAKE THEM NO MORE A MOB • • 383 MEROPE   V1360

MOCK
        PLEASED YOU MOCK THE FRUITLESS CRY • • • • • •   24 MEMORY-PICTURE   55

MOCK   (CONTINUED)
        MIND IS A LIGHT WHICH THE GODS MOCK US WITH   • •   413 EMPEDOCLES I 2   32

MOCKD
        MOCKD AND BAFFLED BY YOUR GLADNESS   • • • • • •   32 NEW SIRENS   169
        MOCKD HER POOR LOVELORN GIANTS LAY   • • • • • •   222 EPILOG LAOCOON   48
        WITH HAUGHTY SCORN WHICH MOCKD THE SMART   • • • • 303 GRANDE CHARTR   134
        HAPPINESS MOCKD OUR PRAYER   • • • • • • • • •   425 EMPEDOCLES I 2   383

MOCKER
        ENEMY MOCKER WHOM THOUGH GODS WE HATE   • • • •   114 BALDER DEAD 3   22

MOCKERY
        DUMB JUDGES ANSWER TRUTH OR MOCKERY   • • • • • •   4 EMERSONS ESSAYS   14
        O BARREN BOAST O JOYLESS MOCKERY   • • • • • •   EMERSONS ESSAYS   V 14
        MOCKERY EVER AMBUSHD IN   • • • • • • • • • •   23 MEMORY-PICTURE   28

MOCKING
        MOCKING AND HERMOD KNEW THEIR TOIL WAS VAIN   • •   123 BALDER DEAD 3   356
        SPARKLED WITH MOCKING GLEE AND EXERCISE   • • • •   154 TRISTRAM 3   170
        THAT MOCKING MOUTH GROW SWEETLY BLAND   • • • •   206 RIVER   6
        LIGHT FLOWS OUR WAR OF MOCKING WORDS AND YET   • • 245 BURIED LIFE   1
        MOCKING LAUGHTER A FILM   • • • • • • • • •   293 HEINES GRAVE   38
        MOCKING HOW INCONGRUOUS NOW   • • • • • • •   455 POOR MATTHIAS   114

MOCKS
        COLDLY SHE MOCKS THE SONS OF MEN   • • • • • •   202 URANIA   30

MODE
        IS A PASSD MODE AN OUTWORN THEME   • • • • • •   302 GRANDE CHARTR   100

MODERATE
        MODERATE TASKS AND MODERATE LEISURE   • • • • •   49 SECOND BEST   1
        MODERATE TASKS AND MODERATE LEISURE   • • • •   49 SECOND BEST   1
        MAKE US NOT FLY TO DREAMS BUT MODERATE DESIRE   • 425 EMPEDOCLES I 2   386
        WHY SHOULD I SAY THAT LIFE NEED YIELD BUT MODERATE 425 EMPEDOCLES I 2   391
            BLISS

MODERATION
        MORTAL THE MODERATION OF A MAN   • • • • • • • •   405 MEROPE   2013

MODERN
        BEFORE THIS STRANGE DISEASE OF MODERN LIFE   • • • •   261 SCHOLAR-GIPSY   203
        THE KINGS OF MODERN THOUGHT ARE DUMB   • • • • • • 303 GRANDE CHARTR   116

MODERNISE
        SAYS APOLLO MODERNISE ROME   • • • • • • • •   214 NEW ROME   10

MODERNISED
        SAYS APOLLO MODERNISED ROME   • • • • • • • •   214 NEW ROME   V 10

MODES
        BUT THROUGH THEIR FORMS AND MODES AND STIFLING VEILS   439 EMPEDOCLES II   354

MODEST
        LESS MODEST PURE AND KIND   • • • • • • • •   273 EDW QUILLINAN   8

MOISTEND
        WHO SHUFFLES THROUGH THE DEEP DEW-MOISTEND DUST   • •   101 BALDER DEAD 1   232

MOLE
        HEARD THE MURMUR OF THE MOLE   • • • • • • • •   458 POOR MATTHIAS   201

MOLES
        OF COMFORTABLE MOLES WHOM WHAT THEY DO   • • • •   7 REP FRIEND   6

MOMENT
        SHE ENTERD THAT MOMENT HIS EYES TURND FROM ME   • • 19 MODERN SAPPHO   10
        ONE MOMENT ON THE RAPIDS TOP OUR BOAT   • • • •   25 DREAM   30
        LO SAILS THAT GLEAM A MOMENT AND ARE GONE   • • •   42 GIPSY CHILD   5
        TO WHOM EACH MOMENT IN ITS RACE   • • • • •   59 RESIGNATION   257
        EACH MOMENT AS IT FLIES TO WHOM   • • • • •   59 RESIGNATION   V 257
        ONE MOMENT WAIT THOU HOLY MAN   • • • • •   157 SAINT BRANDAN   25
        EVEN FOR A MOMENT DIDST DEPART   • • • • • •   181 ISOLATION MARG   15
        AND SOMETIMES FOR A MOMENT   • • • • • • •   194 STRAYED REVEL   277
        THEN LET HIM CHOOSE HIS MOMENT WELL   • • • •   223 EPILOG LAOCOON   59
        THE ASPECT OF THE MOMENT SHOW   • • • • • •   225 EPILOG LAOCOON   131
        THE FEELING OF THE MOMENT KNOW   • • • • • •   225 EPILOG LAOCOON   132
        AND THEY SEE FOR A MOMENT   • • • • • • •   235 YOUTH OF MAN   108
        EVEN FOR A MOMENT CAN GET FREE   • • • • • •   245 BURIED LIFE   27
        FOAMD FOR A MOMENT AND GONE   • • • • • • •   288 RUGBY CHAPEL   72
        ONLY A MOMENT I LONGD   • • • • • • • •   294 HEINES GRAVE   48
        ONLY A MOMENT I KNEW   • • • • • • • •   294 HEINES GRAVE   52
        FOR ONE SHORT MOMENT WANDER OER HIS LIPS   • • •   298 HEINES GRAVE   209
        THE HAPPY MOMENT COMES LURK HERE UNSEEN   • • •   332 MEROPE   67
        WE CHEERED HIM BUT THAT MOMENT FROM THE COPSE   • •   357 MEROPE   786
        A MOMENT MORE I SAW THE PRINCE TURN ROUND   • • • 358 MEROPE   831
        THIS AT A MOMENT TOO WHEN I HAD URGED   • • •   360 MEROPE   879
        IF HAPLY AT THIS MOMENT SUCH ATTEMPT   • • • •   388 MEROPE   1505
        BE WITH HIM CHOOSE THE MOMENT STRIKE THY BLOW   • •   391 MEROPE   1590
        THAT MOMENT WHILE WITH UPTURND EYES HE PRAYD   • • 402 MEROPE   1918

MOMENT   (CONTINUED)
```
        AND FROM THAT MOMENT I SAW NOTHING CLEAR     .  .  .  .     402 MEROPE            1936
        IS EASY AT NO MOMENT BUT THE RIGHT     .  .  .  .  .        403 MEROPE            1950
        GO WITH HIM CHOOSE THE MOMENT STRIKE THY BLOW      .  .     391 MEROPE           V1590
        IS IT BUT FOR A MOMENT     .  .  .  .  .  .  .  .  .        441 EMPEDOCLES II      409
        THAT FOR A MOMENT GLEAMS AND ALL AGAIN IS NIGHT    .  .     463 ALARIC AT ROME      30
        A MOMENT DISPOSSESSD REALITY     .  .  .  .  .  .  .  .     474 CROMWELL            94
        THY LITTLE MOMENT LIFE OF LOVELINESS     .  .  .  .  .  .       FRAGMENT 5           4
```

MOMENTARY
```
        SOMETIMES A MOMENTARY GLEAM     .  .  .  .  .  .  .  .      226 EPILOG LAOCOON     177
        ADMITS NO MOMENTARY BRIGHTENING NOW     .  .  .  .  .  .    408 EMPEDOCLES I 1      69
```

MOMENTS
```
        MAY BRING ONE OF THE OLD HAPPY MOMENTS AGAIN      .  .       19 MODERN SAPPHO      V
        CROWNING MOMENTS WITH THE WEALTH OF YEARS     .  .  .  .     29 NEW SIRENS          88
        EVEN BY MOMENTS OF TO-DAY     .  .  .  .  .  .  .  .  .       33 NEW SIRENS         222
        CROWNING MOMENTS WITH THE WEIGHT OF YEARS     .  .  .  .     29 NEW SIRENS       V  88
        UNALLOYD MOMENTS     .  .  .  .  .  .  .  .  .  .  .  .       52 CONSOLATION         62
        WHOSE SEVERE MOMENTS     .  .  .  .  .  .  .  .  .  .         52 CONSOLATION         67
        EXULTS YET FOR NO MOMENTS SPACE     .  .  .  .  .  .         57 RESIGNATION        158
        NO LIFE BUT AT MOMENTS     .  .  .  .  .  .  .  .  .        176 PARTING             55
        HEAP UP HIS MOMENTS WITH LIFE     .  .  .  .  .  .  .       200 EARLY DEATH         18
        A MOMENTS LIFE OF THINGS THAT LIVE     .  .  .  .  .        223 EPILOG LAOCOON      58
        WE VISIT IT BY MOMENTS AH TOO RARE     .  .  .  .  .        236 PALLADIUM           12
        BUT IT NEEDS HEAVEN-SENT MOMENTS FOR THIS SKILL    .  .     256 SCHOLAR-GIPSY       50
        BUT IT NEEDS HAPPY MOMENTS FOR THIS SKILL     .  .  .       256 SCHOLAR-GIPSY    V  50
        NOT SO THY HEART WOULD PAY ITS MOMENTS SPEECH      .  .     332 MEROPE              61
        IN MOMENTS OF DISGRACE UNCURLD     .  .  .  .  .  .  .      460 KAISER DEAD         56
        ONE MOMENTS SPACE PERCHANCE MIGHT CHARM HIS EYE    .  .     475 CROMWELL           109
        ONE MOMENTS SPACE MIGHT WAFT HIM FAR AWAY     .  .  .  .    475 CROMWELL           111
```

MONARCH
```
        HE SPOKE THE MONARCH HEARD     .  .  .  .  .  .  .  .        47 WORLD QUIETIST   V  28
        WHEN THE WHITE-ROBED GARLAND-CROWNED MONARCH      .  .      400 MEROPE            1857
        NO ALL WAS CHANGD THE MONARCH WEPT ALONE     .  .  .  .     477 CROMWELL           187
        TILL THE PALE MONARCH AND THE LONG ARRAY     .  .  .  .     477 CROMWELL           197
```

MONARCHS
```
        WHO HATH A MONARCHS HATH NO BROTHERS PART     .  .  .  .     46 IN UTRUMQUE PAR     39
        A WHITE-ROBED SLAVE STOLE TO THE MONARCHS SIDE    .  .       47 WORLD QUIETIST   V  27
        FOR THE AWFUL MONARCHS BELOW     .  .  .  .  .  .  .  .     345 MEROPE             476
```

MONASTERY
```
        TWINKLE THE MONASTERY-LIGHTS     .  .  .  .  .  .  .  .     156 SAINT BRANDAN        8
```

MONGREL
```
        THE CASE WAS CLEAR A MONGREL THING     .  .  .  .  .  .     459 KAISER DEAD         29
```

MONICA
```
        THUS MONICA AND DIED IN ITALY     .  .  .  .  .  .  .  .    173 MONICAS PRAYER       5
```

MONSTROUS
```
        O MONSTROUS DEAD UNPROFITABLE WORLD     .  .  .  .  .  .      3 EMERSONS ESSAYS      1
```

MONTH
```
        IN THE HOT PRISON OF THE PRESENT MONTH     .  .  .  .      212 GROWING OLD         24
        TO MONTH WITH WEARY PAIN     .  .  .  .  .  .  .  .  .      212 GROWING OLD         25
        MONTH AFTER MONTH I AWAIT     .  .  .  .  .  .  .  .  .     347 MEROPE             517
        MONTH AFTER MONTH I AWAIT     .  .  .  .  .  .  .  .  .     347 MEROPE             517
        MONTH AFTER MONTH THROUGH THE SLOW-DRAGGING YEAR   .  .     347 MEROPE            V
        MONTH AFTER MONTH THROUGH THE SLOW-DRAGGING YEAR   .  .     347 MEROPE            V
```

MONTMARTRE
```
        TRIM MONTMARTRE THE FAINT     .  .  .  .  .  .  .  .  .     292 HEINES GRAVE         9
```

MONUMENT
```
        WHO FOR THEMSELVES A MONUMENT HAVE MADE      .  .  .  .     462 ALARIC AT ROME      10
```

MOOD
```
        WHAT MOOD WEARS LIKE COMPLEXION TO THY WOE    .  .  .  .     42 GIPSY CHILD         21
        WHOSE MOOD SHALL FANCY LIKEN TO THY WOE     .  .  .  .       42 GIPSY CHILD      V  21
        WIDER THAN ONE MANS PASSION THERES NO MOOD    .  .  .  .     50 CONSOLATION      V
        HAD NO MEDICINE FOR THY MOOD     .  .  .  .  .             139 TRISTRAM 1         291
        STILL WE WALKD ON IN THOUGHTFUL MOOD     .  .  .  .  .      223 EPILOG LAOCOON      61
        WHAT ARE WE ALL BUT A MOOD     .  .  .  .  .  .  .  .       298 HEINES GRAVE       214
        A SINGLE MOOD OF THE LIFE     .  .  .  .  .  .  .  .  .     298 HEINES GRAVE       215
        MAYST THOU A MOOD MORE SERENE     .  .  .  .  .  .  .       299 HEINES GRAVE       227
        GRACE TO YOUR MOOD OF SADNESS GAVE     .  .  .  .  .        304 GRANDE CHARTR      153
        GRACE TO THEIR MOOD OF SADNESS GAVE     .  .  .  .  .       304 GRANDE CHARTR    V 153
        BUT THOU WHOM FELLOWSHIP OF MOOD     .  .  .  .  .  .       322 OBERMANN MORE      273
        DREADING THINE OVER-WROUGHT MOOD     .  .  .  .  .  .       371 MEROPE            1131
        WHAT MOOD OF SPIRIT THEREFORE SHALL WE CALL       .  .      404 MEROPE            1991
        IN THIS HIS PRESENT FIERCE MAN-HATING MOOD    .  .  .      409 EMPEDOCLES I 1     106
        PESTER HIM NOT IN THIS HIS SOMBRE MOOD     .  .  .  .      411 EMPEDOCLES I 1     154
```

MOODS
```
        MOODS OF FANTASTIC SADNESS NOTHING WORTH      .  .  .  .     42 GIPSY CHILD         18
        PASS COUNTLESS MOODS     .  .  .  .  .  .  .  .  .  .  .     50 CONSOLATION         10
        HER MOODS GOOD LACK THEY PASS LIKE SHOWERS    .  .  .  .    146 TRISTRAM 2         125
```

MOODS   (CONTINUED)
        O THOU ONE OF WHOSE MOODS • • • • • • • • • 299 HEINES GRAVE   222
        ONE OF HIS MOODS IS ON HIM THAT THOU KNOWST • • 408 EMPEDOCLES I 1   54

MOODY
        A TRAMP I SAW ILL MOODY AND TONGUE-TIED • • • • • 169 WEST LONDON   2
        HE IS NOW ALWAYS MOODY AND I FEAR HIM   • • • • 408 EMPEDOCLES I 1   74

MOOLLAH
        A CERTAIN MOOLLAH WITH HIS ROBE   • • • • • • •   88 SICK KING BOKH   31

MOON
        SPLINTERD THE SILVER ARROWS OF THE MOON • • • • •   11 MYCERINUS   99
        THE MOON THROUGH THE CLERE-STORY WINDOWS SHINES • •   18 CHURCH BROU 3   36
        WHICH THE BRIGHT MOON LANCES • • • • • • • •   35 VOICE   3
        AT THE FULL MOON TEARS GATHERD IN HIS EYES • • • •   79 SOHRAB RUSTUM   618
        UNDER THE SOLITARY MOON HE FLOWD   • • • • • •   87 SOHRAB RUSTUM   879
        SUN MOON AND STARS WHICH THOU HAST HUNG IN HEAVEN 121 BALDER DEAD 3   264
        AT THIS SOFT HOUR UNDER THIS SWEET MOON • • • • 139 TRISTRAM 1   286
        UPON THE WINDOW-PANES THE MOON SHINES BRIGHT • • 139 TRISTRAM 1   299
        ALL SHINING IN THE WHITE MOON-BEAMS • • • • • 141 TRISTRAM 1   370
        YOU SEE THEM CLEAR THE MOON SHINES BRIGHT • • • 146 TRISTRAM 2   101
        THE MOON WAS BRIGHT THE ICEBERG NEAR • • • • • 157 SAINT BRANDAN   22
        BUT WHEN THE MOON THEIR HOLLOWS LIGHTS • • • • 182 TO MARG CONT   7
        THE TIDE IS FULL THE MOON LIES FAIR • • • • 210 DOVER BEACH   2
        WHERE THE SEA MEETS THE MOON-BLANCHD LAND • • • 211 DOVER BEACH   8
        WHERE THE EBB MEETS THE MOON-BLANCHD SAND • • • 211 DOVER BEACH   V 8
        WHERE THE SEA MEETS THE MOON-BLANCHD SAND • • • 211 DOVER BEACH   V 8
        SWIMS IN THE SHEEN OF THE MOON • • • • • • • 228 YOUTH OF NATURE   4
        COPAIS LAY BRIGHT IN THE MOON • • • • • • • 229 YOUTH OF NATURE   37
        AND THE SEA ITS LONG MOON-SILVERD ROLL • • • • 240 SELF-DEPENDENCE   22
        IN THE DESERTED MOON-BLANCHD STREET   • • • • • 242 SUMMER NIGHT   1
        THE MOON AND LOST BEHIND HER FADING DIM • • • • 242 SUMMER NIGHT   7
        AND THE SAME BRIGHT CALM MOON • • • • • • • 242 SUMMER NIGHT   25
        CROSS AND RECROSS THE STRIPS OF MOON-BLANCHD GREEN 255 SCHOLAR-GIPSY   9
        AND THE FULL MOON AND THE WHITE EVENING-STAR • • 264 THYRSIS   70
        DOWN TO THE BRIMMD MOON-CHARMED MAIN • • • • • • 279 SOUTHERN NIGHT   118
        WHERE THE MOON-SILVERD INLETS • • • • • • • • 442 EMPEDOCLES II   425
        ON THE SWEET AND MOON-BATHED LAND   • • • • •   META CLOISTER   12

MOONBEAMS
        WHERE SWEET THE UNBROKEN MOONBEAMS LAY • • • • 177 FAREWELL   2
        OER WHOSE LIT FLOOR A ROAD OF MOONBEAMS LEADS • • 438 EMPEDOCLES II   312

MOONLIGHT
        BUT IT IS MOONLIGHT IN THE OPEN GLADE • • • • • 139 TRISTRAM 1   277
        AH HOW FAIR THOU STANDEST IN THE MOONLIGHT • • • 143 TRISTRAM 2   27
        CLOSE THINE EYES THIS FLOODING MOONLIGHT BLINDS THEM 144 TRISTRAM 2   71
        NOW STAND CLEAR BEFORE ME IN THE MOONLIGHT • • • 145 TRISTRAM 2   V 97
        WHEN CLEAR FALLS THE MOONLIGHT • • • • • • • 165 FORSAKEN MERM   126
        HERE THROUGH THE MOONLIGHT ON THIS ENGLISH GRASS • 201 PHILOMELA   17
        AND MOONLIGHT AND THE DEW   • • • • • • • • 200 PHILOMELA   V
        MOONLIGHT AND SHADOW AND LAKE • • • • • • • 230 YOUTH OF NATURE   60
        SO IN ITS LOVELY MOONLIGHT LIVES THE SOUL • • • 236 PALLADIUM   9
        AND THE CALM MOONLIGHT SEEMS TO SAY • • • • • 243 SUMMER NIGHT   26
        BY MOONLIGHT CAME • • • • • • • • • • 278 SOUTHERN NIGHT   104
        IN THE MOONLIGHT THE SHEPHERDS • • • • • • • 442 EMPEDOCLES II   433

MOONLIT
        ITS SLIGHT DARK SHADOW ON THE MOONLIT TURF • • • •   70 SOHRAB RUSTUM   316
        THE CALM UPON THE MOONLIT SEA • • • • • • • 180 FAREWELL   80
        HARK FROM THAT MOONLIT CEDAR WHAT A BURST • • • 200 PHILOMELA   3
        AS IS THE ETERNAL MOONLIT SNOW • • • • • • • 207 ON THE RHINE   3
        HEADLANDS STOOD OUT INTO THE MOONLIT DEEP • • • 242 SUMMER NIGHT   14
        AND THEIR EYES RESTING ON THE MOONLIT STREAM • • 257 SCHOLAR-GIPSY   80
        EMERGE AND RESTING ON THE MOONLIT PALES • • • • 261 SCHOLAR-GIPSY   217
        MELT INTO OPEN MOONLIT SEA • • • • • • • • 275 SOUTHERN NIGHT   2
        SO MOONLIT SAW ME ONCE OF YORE • • • • • • • 275 SOUTHERN NIGHT   14
        IN THE MOONLIT SOLITUDES MILD • • • • • • • 288 RUGBY CHAPEL   70
        OF THE MOONLIT PEAKS AND THE CAVES • • • • • 435 EMPEDOCLES II   203
        AS TOWERED ON HIGH ABOVE THEIR MOONLIT ROAD • • 466 ALARIC AT ROME   113

MOONS
        YET SUNS SHALL RISE AND MANY MOONS SHALL WANE • •   10 MYCERINUS   62
        MILD SHINES THE COLD SPRING IN THE MOONS CLEAR LIGHT 139 TRISTRAM 1   283
        FULL ON THEIR WINDOW THE MOONS RAY • • • • • 140 TRISTRAM 1   333
        AND LIVED SOME MOONS IN HAPPY TRANCE • • • • • 279 SOUTHERN NIGHT   109

MOONSHINE
        AND MOONSHINE AND THE DEW • • • • • • • • 200 PHILOMELA   13
        IT STOOD AND SUN AND MOONSHINE RAIND THEIR LIGHT • • 236 PALLADIUM   5
        WHOSE FLOOR TO-NIGHT SWEET MOONSHINE FILLS • • • 277 SOUTHERN NIGHT   75

MOONSTRUCK
        UP TRISTRAM UP MEN CRY THOU MOONSTRUCK KNIGHT • • 137 TRISTRAM 1   238

MOOR
        MOOR BEHIND MOOR FAR FAR AWAY • • • • • • • • 141 TRISTRAM 1   365
        MOOR BEHIND MOOR FAR FAR AWAY • • • • • • • • 141 TRISTRAM 1   365

MOORD
    AND PAST THE HAVEN WHERE THE GODS HAVE MOORD   •   97 BALDER DEAD 1   74
    HIS FRAIL BOAT MOORD TO • • • • • • • •   190 STRAYED REVEL   153
    WHILE THROUGH THEIR EARTH-MOORD NAVE BELOW • • • •   223 EPILOG LAOCOON   73
    WHILE THROUGH THE EARTH-MOORD NAVE BELOW • • • •   223 EPILOG LAOCOON V 73
    MOORD TO THE COOL BANK IN THE SUMMER-HEATS • • • •   257 SCHOLAR-GIPSY   67
    THEY MOORD THEIR BOATS AMONG THE BULRUSH STEMS • •   444 WESTMIN ABBEY   18

MOORGHAB
    THE DESERT RIVERS MOORGHAB AND TEJEND   • • • • •   83 SOHRAB RUSTUM   763

MOORLAND
    THE MOORLAND TOWN BUT THE CHURCH   • • • • • •   283 HAWORTH CHURCH   62
    THE SHINING MOORLAND TO HEAR   • • • • • • • •   285 HAWORTH CHURCH 119
    THE MOORLAND PLACE BUT THE CHURCH   • • • • •   283 HAWORTH CHURCH V 62

MOORS
    FROM THE HIGH MOORS BEHIND AND MEETS THE SEA   • •   97 BALDER DEAD 1   83
    AT SOME LONE ALEHOUSE IN THE BERKSHIRE MOORS   • •   256 SCHOLAR-GIPSY   58
    IN A CHURCHYARD HIGH MID THE MOORS   • • • • • •   282 HAWORTH CHURCH   52
    UP TO THE HEART OF THE MOORS   • • • • • • •   282 HAWORTH CHURCH   56
    AND THE PLOVER IS HEARD ON THE MOORS • • • • • •   285 HAWORTH CHURCH 116
    RUSH OER THE YORKSHIRE MOORS   • • • • • •   286 HAWORTH CHURCH 130

MORAL
    NOTHING SURE NO MORAL PLAN   • • • • • • • •   215 PIS-ALLER   7

MORALITY
    THY STRUGGLING TASKD MORALITY   • • • • • • •   241 MORALITY   16

MORASS
    ROSE DIM FROM THE MORASS   • • • • • • • • •   445 WESTMIN ABBEY   32

MORE
    KNOW MAN HATH ALL WHICH NATURE HATH BUT MORE   • •   5 HARMONY NATURE   5
    AND IN THAT MORE LIE ALL HIS HOPES OF GOOD • • • •   5 HARMONY NATURE   6
    KNOW THOU THE WORST SO MUCH NOT MORE HE CAN   • •   6 GEO CRUIKSHANK   14
    I LOOKD FOR LIFE MORE LASTING RULE MORE HIGH   • •   9 MYCERINUS   17
    I LOOKD FOR LIFE MORE LASTING RULE MORE HIGH   • •   9 MYCERINUS   17
    REVELS MORE DEEP JOY KEENER THAN THEIR OWN • • • •   10 MYCERINUS   66
    WHERE THOU YOUNG PRINCE SHALT NEVER MORE ARISE   • •   18 CHURCH BROU 3   7
    AND THOU O PRINCESS SHALT NO MORE RECEIVE   • • • •   18 CHURCH BROU 3   12
    THEIR PASSION BURN MORE ERE IT CEASES TO BURN   • •   19 MODERN SAPPHO   14
    IT DREAMS A REST IF NOT MORE DEEP   • • • • • •   22 YOUTH AND CALM   20
    MORE GRATEFUL THAN THIS MARBLE SLEEP   • • • • •   22 YOUTH AND CALM   21
    IT ASKS A REST IF NOT MORE DEEP   • • • • • •   22 YOUTH AND CALM V 20
    AND MORE THAN MORTAL IMPULSE FILLD THEIR EYES   • •   25 DREAM   27
    MORE MELODIOUS THAN OF YORE   • • • • • • •   27 NEW SIRENS   42
    ARE THOSE FRAIL FORMS MORE ENDURING   • • • • •   27 NEW SIRENS   43
    COME ONCE MORE THAT ANCIENT LIGHTNESS   • • • •   32 NEW SIRENS 175
    WHEN THE MEAN SHALL NO MORE SORROW   • • • • •   33 NEW SIRENS 215
    AND THE PROUDEST NO MORE SMILE • • • • • •   33 NEW SIRENS 216
    PLUCK NO MORE RED ROSES MAIDENS   • • • • •   35 NEW SIRENS 267
    STREW NO MORE RED ROSES MAIDENS   • • • • •   35 NEW SIRENS V 267
    AND BREATHE MORE HAPPY IN AN EVEN CLIME   • • • •   37 YOUTHS AGIT   6
    STAND MUTE SELF-CENTRED STERN AND DREAM NO MORE   • •   42 GIPSY CHILD   32
    MUSED MUCH LOVED LIFE A LITTLE LOATHED IT MORE   • •   43 GIPSY CHILD   36
    LEARND IN MORE LANGUID CLIMES   • • • • • • •   46 WORLD QUIETIST   5
    WHO EACH DAY MORE SURELY LEARNS   • • • • •   49 SECOND BEST   20
    KEPT THEY MORE CLOUDLESS • • • • • • • •   50 CONSOLATION   24
    BUT MILDER NATURES AND MORE FREE   • • • • •   53 RESIGNATION   22
    ONCE MORE WE TREAD THIS SELF-SAME ROAD   • • • •   55 RESIGNATION   86
    ARE SCARCE MORE CHANGED IN TRUTH THAN THEY • • • •   55 RESIGNATION 107
    ARE LESS THE POET MORE THAN MAN   • • • • • •   58 RESIGNATION 204
    NEXT THE MORE TEMPERATE TOORKMUNS OF THE SOUTH   • •   64 SOHRAB RUSTUM 121
    FROM FAR AND A MORE DOUBTFUL SERVICE OWND   • • •   64 SOHRAB RUSTUM 127
    RUSTUM HE LOVES NO MORE BUT LOVES THE YOUNG   • •   67 SOHRAB RUSTUM 226
    AND WITH THESE SLAUGHTEROUS HANDS DRAW SWORD NO MORE   68 SOHRAB RUSTUM 241
    WHAT IS ONE MORE ONE LESS OBSCURE OR FAMED • • • •   68 SOHRAB RUSTUM 252
    THERE WOULD BE THEN NO TALK OF FIGHTING MORE   • •   72 SOHRAB RUSTUM 372
    BEGIN THOU ART MORE VAST MORE DREAD THAN I   • • •   72 SOHRAB RUSTUM 385
    BEGIN THOU ART MORE VAST MORE DREAD THAN I   • • •   72 SOHRAB RUSTUM 385
    FIGHT LET ME HEAR THY HATEFUL VOICE NO MORE   • •   75 SOHRAB RUSTUM 459
    A HEAP OF FLUTTERING FEATHERS NEVER MORE   • • •   78 SOHRAB RUSTUM 569
    HER MOST I PITY WHO NO MORE WILL SEE   • • •   78 SOHRAB RUSTUM 593
    THAT SOHRAB WILL REJOICE HER SIGHT NO MORE   • • •   79 SOHRAB RUSTUM 599
    BUT LET US SPEAK NO MORE OF THIS I FIND   • • •   82 SOHRAB RUSTUM 716
    O RUKSH THOU ART MORE FORTUNATE THAN I   • • • •   83 SOHRAB RUSTUM 747
    WHAT SHOULD I DO WITH SLAYING ANY MORE   • • • •   85 SOHRAB RUSTUM 808
    MIGHT BE ONCE MORE ALIVE MY BITTEREST FOES   • • •   85 SOHRAB RUSTUM 810
    UNTO A RULE MORE STRONG THAN THEIRS   • • • • •   93 SICK KING BOKH 187
    IS NOT MORE LIGHTEND WHICH HE FEELS   • • • •   94 SICK KING BOKH 205
    NOR DID HE LOOK ONCE MORE TO IDAS PLAIN   • • • •   97 BALDER DEAD 1   57
    WAILING NO MORE IN SILENCE ATE AND DRANK   • • •   97 BALDER DEAD 1   70
    BUT HERMOD TOOK THE RING AND YET ONCE MORE   • • •   112 BALDER DEAD 2 282
    MY TRUANT ODER I SHALL SEE NO MORE   • • • • •   117 BALDER DEAD 3 120
    YES AND I TOO REMEMBERD THEN NO MORE   • • • •   117 BALDER DEAD 3 145
    ACCEPT THE CHANCE THOU CANST NO MORE OBTAIN   • • •   122 BALDER DEAD 3 290
    AND ONCE MORE HERMOD SAW AROUND HIM SPREAD   • • •   124 BALDER DEAD 3 379

MORE   (CONTINUED)

FOR THE LAST TIME FOR HERE THOU COMST NO MORE   • • 125 BALDER DEAD 3   420
NO MORE TO ASGARD SHALT THOU COME NOR LODGE   • • 126 BALDER DEAD 3   448
HAIL AND FAREWELL FOR HERE THOU COMST NO MORE   • • 126 BALDER DEAD 3   455
MORE FRESH MORE VERDANT THAN THE LAST WITH FRUITS   128 BALDER DEAD 3   529
MORE FRESH MORE VERDANT THAN THE LAST WITH FRUITS   128 BALDER DEAD 3   529
AND WE SHALL TREAD ONCE MORE THE WELL-KNOWN PLAIN   128 BALDER DEAD 3   537
DOES THE LOVE-DRAUGHT WORK NO MORE   • • • • • • •   133 TRISTRAM 1   80
ONCE MORE ROUND THEM AND THE SEA   • • • • • • •   135 TRISTRAM 1   154
WHAT HIS EYE MUST SEE NO MORE   • • • • • • • •   135 TRISTRAM 1   160
AT ARTHURS SIDE HE FIGHTS ONCE MORE   • • • • •   138 TRISTRAM 1   254
ARE NOT MORE INNOCENT THAN THINE   • • • • • •   140 TRISTRAM 1   326
AND THY BEAUTY NEVER WAS MORE FAIR   • • • • • •   142 TRISTRAM 2   20
ROUSE NO ANGER MAKE NO RIVALS MORE   • • • • • •   144 TRISTRAM 2   64
ISEULT LEAVES THEE TRISTRAM NEVER MORE   • • • •   146 TRISTRAM 2   100
AND LETS US BE WHAT WE WERE ONCE NO MORE   • •   153 TRISTRAM 3   115
FELL UPON MERLIN MORE LIKE DEATH SO DEEP   • •   155 TRISTRAM 3   214
AND NOW NO BELLS NO CONVENTS MORE   • • • • •   156 SAINT BRANDAN   10
CALL ONCE MORE TO A MOTHERS EAR   • • • • •   161 FORSAKEN MERM   15
CALL NO MORE   • • • • • • • • • • •   162 FORSAKEN MERM   24
COME AWAY CHILDREN CALL NO MORE   • • • • •   164 FORSAKEN MERM   83
COME AWAY COME DOWN CALL NO MORE   • • • • •   164 FORSAKEN MERM   84
WHERE NO MORE LIGHTS OF SENSE OR KNOWLEDGE ARE • •   167 PICT NEWSTEAD   11
WAS WOE THAN BYRONS WOE MORE TRAGIC FAR   • •   167 PICT NEWSTEAD   14
WE LIVE NO MORE WHEN WE HAVE DONE OUR SPAN   • •   171 BETTER PART   5
MORE STRICTLY THEN THE INWARD JUDGE OBEY   • •   171 BETTER PART   12
MIS-DEFINE THESE TILL GOD KNOWS THEM NO MORE   171 DIVINITY   10
AH WARN SOME MORE AMBITIOUS HEART   • • • • •   174 MEETING   15
I TOO HAVE WISHD NO WOMAN MORE   • • • • • • •   178 FAREWELL   31
THIS TRUTH ON THEE BE MINE NO MORE   • • • •   179 FAREWELL   42
NOR LIGHTNESS WISDOM ANY MORE   • • • • • • •   179 FAREWELL   60
MAY THEN MORE NEIGHBOURING COURSES PLY   • • •   180 FAREWELL   74
I BADE MY HEART MORE CONSTANT BE   • • • • •   180 ISOLATION MARG   2
LIKE MINE EACH DAY MORE TRIED MORE TRUE   • •   180 ISOLATION MARG   6
LIKE MINE EACH DAY MORE TRIED MORE TRUE   • •   180 ISOLATION MARG   6
THOU LOVST NO MORE FAREWELL FAREWELL   • • •   180 ISOLATION MARG   12
ONCE MORE THE ROOFS OF BERNE APPEAR   • • •   183 TERRACE BERNE   2
AND MARGUERITE I SHALL SEE NO MORE   • • • • •   185 TERRACE BERNE   52
WOULDST MORE OF IT SEE HOW GLOWS   • • • • •   187 STRAYED REVEL   55
MORE SOFT AH ME   • • • • • • • • • •   187 STRAYED REVEL   65
MORE SUBTLE-WINDING   • • • • • • • • •   187 STRAYED REVEL   66
AH ME HONOUREST MORE THAN THY LOVER • • • •   196 FRAG ANTIGONE   51
DOST THOU ONCE MORE ASSAY   • • • • • • •   201 PHILOMELA   22
ONCE MORE AND ONCE MORE SEEM TO MAKE RESOUND • •   201 PHILOMELA   25
ONCE MORE AND ONCE MORE SEEM TO MAKE RESOUND • •   201 PHILOMELA   25
ONCE MORE THOU HEAREST   • • • • • • • •   201 PHILOMELA   V 30
BUT THEY BRING MORE THAN THEY RECEIVE   • • •   203 EUPHROSYNE   20
FOR THEN THE NIGHT WILL MORE THAN PAY   • • •   208 LONGING   3
FOR THEN THE NIGHT WILL MORE THAN PAY   • • •   209 LONGING   15
FOR SO THE NIGHT WILL MORE THAN PAY • • •   208 LONGING   V
EACH NERVE MORE LOOSELY STRUNG   • • • • • •   212 GROWING OLD   10
YES THIS AND MORE BUT NOT   • • • • • • •   212 GROWING OLD   11
THE YEARS THAT ARE NO MORE   • • • • • • •   212 GROWING OLD   20
EACH NERVE MORE WEAKLY STRUNG   • • • • •   212 GROWING OLD   V 10
AND WILL THROUGH CENTURIES MORE • • • • •   214 NEW ROME   20
AND WILL FOR CENTURIES MORE • • • • • •   214 NEW ROME   V 20
CREEP AND LET NO MORE BE SAID   • • • • •   215 LAST WORD   2
CHARGE ONCE MORE THEN AND BE DUMB   • • • •   215 LAST WORD   13
GOOD POEMS IF HE LOOKD MORE RARE   • • • •   221 EPILOG LAOCOON   17
SORE LOAD AND WORDS CAN DO NO MORE   • • • •   224 EPILOG LAOCOON   94
TWINKLES ON GRASMERE NO MORE   • • • •   228 YOUTH OF NATURE   19
IN AN AGE WHICH CAN REAR THEM NO MORE   • • •   229 YOUTH OF NATURE   50
MORE THAN THE SINGER ARE THESE   • • • • •   230 YOUTH OF NATURE   91
YES BUT MORE THAN THIS   • • • • • • •   232 YOUTH OF MAN   4
QUICKEND ITS PULSES NO MORE • • • • • •   233 YOUTH OF MAN   45
NATURE THEY SAW NO MORE • • • • • • •   233 YOUTH OF MAN   50
MORE FAITHFULLY THAN THESE   • • • • • •   237 PROGRESS   8
AH ONCE MORE I CRIED YE STARS YE WATERS • • •   240 SELF-DEPENDENCE   9
THAT NIGHT WAS FAR MORE FAIR   • • • •   242 SUMMER NIGHT   22
NEVER YET COMES MORE NEAR   • • • • • •   243 SUMMER NIGHT   45
AND HE TOO DISAPPEARS AND COMES NO MORE • • •   244 SUMMER NIGHT   73
THE NIGHT WAS FAR MORE FAIR • • • • • •   242 SUMMER NIGHT   V 22
AND THEN WE WILL NO MORE BE RACKD   • • • •   247 BURIED LIFE   67
CALM CALM ME MORE NOR LET ME DIE   • • • •   249 KENSINGTON GARD   43
ONCE MORE BEFORE MY DYING EYES   • • • • •   250 WISH   32
WHO CAN SEE THE GREEN EARTH ANY MORE   • • •   252 FUTURE   27
THAT THE DIN WILL BE MORE ON ITS BANKS   • • •   253 FUTURE   62
BUT CAME TO OXFORD AND HIS FRIENDS NO MORE • • •   256 SCHOLAR-GIPSY   40
THIS SAID HE LEFT THEM AND RETURND NO MORE • • •   256 SCHOLAR-GIPSY   51
AND THEN THEY LAND AND THOU ART SEEN NO MORE • •   257 SCHOLAR-GIPSY   81
AND SNATCHD HIS RUDDER AND SHOOK OUT MORE SAIL •   262 SCHOLAR-GIPSY   242
BUT THYRSIS NEVER MORE WE SWAINS SHALL SEE • • •   265 THYRSIS   77
AND PURER OR MORE SUBTLE SOUL THAN THEE • • •   268 THYRSIS   178
ONCE MORE WE LAY AS ERST AT BIRTH   • • • •   271 MEMORIAL VERSES   V 48
NO MORE AND WE RETAIN   • • • • • • •   273 EDW QUILLINAN   14
SHE WILL BEHOLD NO MORE • • • • • • •   282 HAWORTH CHURCH   V
MORE THAN HE ASKS WHAT WAVES   • • • •   288 RUGBY CHAPEL   69
CARVED THERE NO MORE AND THE SMOOTH • • • •   292 HEINES GRAVE   3
POSTURE AND OPIUM NO MORE   • • • • • •   293 HEINES GRAVE   20
OF A FORMER AGE ANY MORE   • • • • • • •   294 HEINES GRAVE   80

MORE   (CONTINUED)
ONCE MORE THOU CLINGST TO THE CROSS   298 HEINES GRAVE   189
MAYST THOU A MOOD MORE SERENE   299 HEINES GRAVE   227
IS BURIED IN HIS COWL ONCE MORE   300 GRANDE CHARTR   44
BE MAN HENCEFORTH NO MORE A PREY   302 GRANDE CHARTR   105
BUT THEY CONTEND AND CRY NO MORE   303 GRANDE CHARTR   120
SAY HAVE THEIR SONS ACHIEVED MORE JOYS   303 GRANDE CHARTR   129
MORE FORTUNATE ALAS THAN WE   304 GRANDE CHARTR   158
SAY HAVE THEIR SONS OBTAIND MORE JOYS   303 GRANDE CHARTR   V 129
I FEEL THEE NEAR ONCE MORE   306 OBERMANN   12
ONCE MORE UPON ME ROLL   306 OBERMANN   14
NO MORE SO HE BUT REST LIKE THEE   311 OBERMANN   159
ONCE MORE I SLIP MY CHAIN   313 OBERMANN MORE   44
MADE HIS LIFES RULE ONCE MORE   314 OBERMANN MORE   54
SAY IS IT MORE ALIVE   320 OBERMANN MORE   228
MY REFUGE AND NO MORE   321 OBERMANN MORE   272
YET IT HAD MORE THAN I   322 OBERMANN MORE   300
THOUGH MORE THAN HALF THY YEARS BE PAST   323 OBERMANN MORE   305
SOUL THAT THAN THEY WE TAKE MORE CARE   315 OBERMANN MORE   V
SOUL THAT WE TAKE MORE COUNT AND CARE   315 OBERMANN MORE   V
FOR WE WERE KINSMEN MORE THAN KINSMEN FRIENDS   334 MEROPE   122
OLD AGE IS MORE SUSPICIOUS THAN THE FREE   335 MEROPE   156
NO MORE AN EXILE FED ON EMPTY HOPES   335 MEROPE   169
BUT AN ARCADIAN PRINCESS MORE AKIN   337 MEROPE   241
TO REVERENCE YOUR LINEAGE MORE TO OBEY   339 MEROPE   303
EXILE ABROAD MORE SAFE THAN HEIRSHIP HERE   340 MEROPE   337
MORE PIERCING THE SECOND CRY RANG   346 MEROPE   495
SO BE IT YET WILL THAT MORE SOLACE BRING   349 MEROPE   559
MORE FORTUNATE THAN THEE MORE FAIRLY JUDGED 350 MEROPE   590
MORE FORTUNATE THAN THEE MORE FAIRLY JUDGED 350 MEROPE   590
BUT MORE THAN ALL UNPLUMBD   352 MEROPE   629
MORE THAN ALL SECRETS HID THE WAY IT KEEPS   352 MEROPE   631
A MOMENT MORE I SAW THE PRINCE TURN ROUND   358 MEROPE   831
TO FRIENDS STILL MORE AND LABOURERS IN OUR CAUSE 359 MEROPE   872
AS MUCH TO THE KINGS WISH MORE TO HIS SHAME 364 MEROPE   968
OUR MISERY MORE AND THINE OWN RUIN SURE   368 MEROPE   1081
A MORE JUST STROKE THAN THAT THOU GAVST MY SON 373 MEROPE   1191
ONCE MORE ROLL BACK ON MY HOUSE   378 MEROPE   1244
WHO CHIEFLY PROFIT RUN NO MORE THAN THEY   382 MEROPE   1351
KINDLE THEIR HEARTS MAKE THEM NO MORE A MOB 383 MEROPE   1360
OF A PROTECTED EXILE ANY MORE   383 MEROPE   1381
ORESTES IN MYCENAE HAD NO MORE   384 MEROPE   1398
WHAT ORDER MORE PRECISE HAD HE THAN I   384 MEROPE   1400
NOT SO LET HIM AND NONE SHALL BE MORE PROMPT 388 MEROPE   1496
MORE LOYAL AS OUR LINE CONTINUES MORE   389 MEROPE   1541
MORE LOYAL AS OUR LINE CONTINUES MORE   389 MEROPE   1541
MORE DARING AND MORE GRAND OFFENDER FIND   390 MEROPE   1571
MORE DARING AND MORE GRAND OFFENDER FIND   390 MEROPE   1571
TO STRIKE IT THEN DISSUADE THY SON NO MORE   390 MEROPE   1574
SOME ROCK MORE LONELY THAN THAT LEMNIAN ISLE 395 MEROPE   1746
SOME SOLITUDE MORE INACCESSIBLE   395 MEROPE   1748
PITY THYSELF NONE NEEDS COMPASSION MORE   396 MEROPE   1761
ONCE MORE MY FRIENDSHIP THOU REJECTEST WELL 398 MEROPE   1783
MORE FOR THIS LANDS SAKE GRIEVE I THAN MINE OWN 398 MEROPE   1784
ACCEPT IT POLYPHONTES IS NO MORE   401 MEROPE   1888
SISTER FROM THIS DAY FORTH THOU ART NO MORE 403 MEROPE   1954
SATED AND MORE THAN ENOUGH   348 MEROPE   V
ELECTRIFY THEIR HEARTS MAKE THEM NO MORE A MOB 383 MEROPE   V1360
MORE THAN A DAY AND NIGHT PAUSANIAS   409 EMPEDOCLES I 1   100
I SPOKE WITH HIM THIS MORNING ONCE MORE THEREFORE 412 EMPEDOCLES I 2 19
TO LEAD THOSE FALSE WHO TRUST IT HIST ONCE MORE 413 EMPEDOCLES I 2   33
THE MASS SWELLS MORE AND MORE   423 EMPEDOCLES I 2 333
THE MASS SWELLS MORE AND MORE   423 EMPEDOCLES I 2 333
STILL HUNGRIER FOR DELIGHT AS DELIGHTS GROW MORE RARE 424 EMPEDOCLES I 2 371
AND YET THE VILLAGE-CHURL FEELS THE TRUTH MORE   426 EMPEDOCLES I 2 411
        THAN YOU
MORE VIRGINAL AND SWEET THAN OURS   426 EMPEDOCLES I 2 434
NOR THEBES NOR THE ISMENUS ANY MORE   427 EMPEDOCLES I 2 442
BUT HE MUST FOLLOW ME NO MORE TO-NIGHT   428 EMPEDOCLES I 2 469
FOR I MUST HENCEFORTH SPEAK NO MORE WITH MAN 429 EMPEDOCLES II   6
WHAT SHOULD I DO WITH LIFE AND LIVING MORE   429 EMPEDOCLES II   15
BUT THEY WILL GLADLY WELCOME HIM ONCE MORE   435 EMPEDOCLES II   221
BUT NO THIS HEART WILL GLOW NO MORE THOU ART 438 EMPEDOCLES II   327
A LIVING MAN NO MORE EMPEDOCLES   438 EMPEDOCLES II   328
OR WHETHER WE WILL ONCE MORE FALL AWAY   440 EMPEDOCLES II   373
WILL HAVE MORE PERIL FOR US THAN THE LAST   440 EMPEDOCLES II   378
TWELVE HUNDRED YEARS AND MORE   445 WESTMIN ABBEY   51
THE MOURNING-STOLE NO MORE   447 WESTMIN ABBEY   97
MANTLED HER FORM NO MORE HER HEAD WAS BOWD   447 WESTMIN ABBEY   98
LONG SINCE HIS NAME IS HEARD ON EARTH NO MORE 447 WESTMIN ABBEY 113
FEAR NOT BUT THAT THY LIGHT ONCE MORE SHALL BURN 449 WESTMIN ABBEY 174
ONCE MORE THINE IMMEMORIAL GLEAM RETURN   449 WESTMIN ABBEY   175
WERE CROWDED GEIST INTO NO MORE   449 GEISTS GRAVE   4
ONE MORE GASP IT IS THE END   452 POOR MATTHIAS   13
MORE THAN PITY CLAIMST A STAVE   453 POOR MATTHIAS   22
FRIENDS MORE NEAR US THAN A BIRD   453 POOR MATTHIAS   23
BIRDS COMPANIONS MORE UNKNOWN   455 POOR MATTHIAS   95
OF A PRESCIENCE MORE THAN OURS   456 POOR MATTHIAS   138
SOMEWHAT MORE OR SOMEWHAT LESS   457 POOR MATTHIAS   159
KNOW WE MORE OUR FELLOW MEN   457 POOR MATTHIAS   162
THEN HOME RETURND ONCE MORE DEPART   460 KAISER DEAD   51

MORE   (CONTINUED)
        TO CHANT THY REQUIEM WITH MORE PASSIONATE BREATH   • • 471 ALARIC AT ROME   227
        MORE CALM MORE DEEP THAN CHILDHOOD EVER KNEW   • • 475 CROMWELL   116
        MORE CALM MORE DEEP THAN CHILDHOOD EVER KNEW   • • 475 CROMWELL   116
        CHILDHOODS BRIGHT GLANCE AND SUNNY SMILE NO MORE   • • 477 CROMWELL   182
        NOR KNOWN IT THEN BUT IT WAS VEILD NO MORE   • • • • 477 CROMWELL   202
        ONCE MORE BENEATH HIM AND THE FLUTTERING SAIL   • • 479 CROMWELL   237
        ONCE MORE ALONE BESIDE THE GLEAMING FLOOD   • • 479 CROMWELL   240
        ONE ROOD FROM LAND THEY PUSHD NO MORE   • • • • 480 HAYSWATER BOAT   27
        LIES ANY HOPE OF HEROISM MORE   • • • • • • 480 HUNGARIAN NAT   8
        TO LOVE MORE DEEPLY THAN HE CAN   • • • • • • 481 DESTINY   2
        KEPT MORE THAN US THEIR STRENGTH OF SOUL   • • 481 COURAGE   12
        THERE WHERE TEARS ARE NEVER MORE TO RUN   • • • 482 THEKLAS ANSWER   12
        TRACKD BY MURDERS BLOODY SWORD NO MORE   • • • 482 THEKLAS ANSWER   16
        THERE IS A SIGHT MORE SADDENING YET WHEN ALL   • •   LUCRETIUS 2   7
        AND WHEREFORE THEN HAVING NO CLAIM TO MORE   • • •   LUCRETIUS 3   8
        HATH FRAYD AND SLIDDEN DOWN AND WE NO MORE   • •   EVERLASTING SUB   2
        HATH FRAYD AND SLIDDEN DOWN AND THEY NO MORE   • •   EVERLASTING SUB V   2

MORN
        HERE CAME THE KING HOLDING HIGH FEAST AT MORN   • •   11 MYCERINUS   92
        MORN AND NOON AND EVENTIDE   • • • • • • • •   15 CHURCH BROU 1   100
        BLITHELY THIS MORN OLD OCEANS WORK IS DONE   • • •   41 GIPSY CHILD   V   7
        AS WHEN SOME GREY NOVEMBER MORN THE FILES   • • •   64 SOHRAB RUSTUM   111
        AS IN THE COUNTRY ON A MORN IN JUNE   • • • • •   65 SOHRAB RUSTUM   154
        AS SOME RICH WOMAN ON A WINTERS MORN   • • • • •   70 SOHRAB RUSTUM   302
        AT COCK-CROW ON A STARLIT WINTERS MORN   • • •   70 SOHRAB RUSTUM   305
        MAKE OFTEN IN THE FORESTS HEART AT MORN   • • •   75 SOHRAB RUSTUM   477
        AND HOUND AND MORN ON THOSE DELIGHTFUL HILLS   • •   80 SOHRAB RUSTUM   630
        AN EMPERORS GIFT AT EARLY MORN HE PAINTS   • • •   81 SOHRAB RUSTUM   674
        AS SOME RICH LADY ON A WINTERS MORN   • • • • •   70 SOHRAB RUSTUM   V 302
        MAKE OFTEN IN THE FORESTS DEPTH AT MORN   • • •   75 SOHRAB RUSTUM   V 477
        AND HE WILL REACH ON THE TENTH MORN A BRIDGE   • •   99 BALDER DEAD 1   147
        AND INSTANTLY THE SACRED MORN APPEARD   • • • 104 BALDER DEAD 1   342
        AND ON THE TENTH MORN HE BEHELD THE BRIDGE   • • • 107 BALDER DEAD 2   85
        AND ON THE TWELFTH MORN SAW THE LIGHT OF HEAVEN   • • 113 BALDER DEAD 2   294
        SOME MORN AT MARKET IN A CROWDED TOWN   • • • • 114 BALDER DEAD 3   9
        SILENT AND WAITED FOR THE SACRED MORN   • • • • 119 BALDER DEAD 3   212
        ONE MORN AT MARKET IN A CROWDED TOWN   • • • • • 114 BALDER DEAD 3   V   9
        ONE MORN WHEN THE SIROCCO SPENT   • • • • • 157 SAINT BRANDAN   43
        SUPPORT THE FERVOURS OF THE HEAVENLY MORN   • • • 172 IMMORTALITY   8
        WHERE MORN FIRST APPEARS   • • • • • • • • • 177 PARTING   86
        ONE MORN AS THROUGH HYDE PARK WE WALKD   • • • 221 EPILOG LAOCOON   1
        BRIGHT WAS THE MORN AND SOUTH THE AIR   • • • • 222 EPILOG LAOCOON   42
        THAT OLD-WORLD MORN IN SICILY   • • • • • • 222 EPILOG LAOCOON   45
        THE PASSING GROUP THE SUMMER-MORN   • • • • • 222 EPILOG LAOCOON   51
        BATHED IN THE SACRED DEWS OF MORN   • • • • • 250 WISH   33
        ONE SUMMER-MORN FORSOOK   • • • • • • • • • 256 SCHOLAR-GIPSY   36
        SO SOME TEMPESTUOUS MORN IN EARLY JUNE   • • • • 264 THYRSIS   51
        SINCE ERST AT MORN SOME WANDERING SHADE   • • • 271 MEMORIAL VERSES   37
        ROUND SOME FAIR FOREST-LODGE AT MORN   • • • • • 305 GRANDE CHARTR   184
        ROUND SOME OLD FOREST-LODGE AT MORN   • • • • • 305 GRANDE CHARTR   V 184
        AND MANY TIMES THAT MORN WE COURSED IN RING   • • • 357 MEROPE   793
        ON THAT SAME SPUR WHERE WE HAD SATE AT MORN   • • • 357 MEROPE   796
        ON THAT MORN WHEN THE SMOKE-CLOUD   • • • • • 399 MEROPE   1826
        ON THE SAME SPUR WHERE WE HAD SATE AT MORN   • • • 357 MEROPE   V 796
        BUT NEVER ON SO FAIR A MORN THE SUN   • • • • • 406 EMPEDOCLES I 1   9
        FOR FROM THE FIRST FAINT MORN   • • • • • • 418 EMPEDOCLES I 2   167
        IN JOY THY LAST MORN FLEW ANON   • • • • • • 460 KAISER DEAD   63
        DREAMS THAT WERE SWEET AT EVE AT MORN WERE SIN   • • 475 CROMWELL   121
        THIS MORN AS EVER   • • • • • • • • • • •   EVERLASTING SUB   7

MORNING
        IN THE BRIGHT OCTOBER MORNING   • • • • • •   13 CHURCH BROU 1   5
        BORDERD EACH BANK WITH PINES THE MORNING SUN   • •   24 DREAM   3
        UNDER OERHANGING PINES THE MORNING SUN   • • • •   24 DREAM   V   3
        I WHO IN YOUR TRAIN AT MORNING   • • • • • •   26 NEW SIRENS   5
        AND THE BRIGHT AND MORNING STAR   • • • • • •   27 NEW SIRENS   36
        IF THE GLISTERING WINGS OF MORNING   • • • • •   29 NEW SIRENS   107
        SEE THE WHITE EAST AND THE MORNING RAYS   • • •   34 NEW SIRENS   242
        WHEN THE LAMPS ARE PALED AT MORNING   • • • • •   35 NEW SIRENS   263
        WHEN MORNING PURIFIES THE EARTH   • • • • • •   57 RESIGNATION   171
        AND THE FIRST GREY OF MORNING FILLD THE EAST   • •   61 SOHRAB RUSTUM   1
        RUSTUM HIS MORNING MEAL WAS DONE BUT STILL   • • •   67 SOHRAB RUSTUM   196
        AND THE FIRST RAYS OF MORNING STREAKD THE EAST   • •   61 SOHRAB RUSTUM   V   1
        MEANWHILE TO-MORROW WHEN THE MORNING DAWNS   • • •   96 BALDER DEAD 1   40
        AND MORNING OVER ALL THE WORLD WAS SPREAD   • • • 119 BALDER DEAD 3   213
        BUOYANT AS MORNING AND AS MORNING CLEAR   • • • 175 PARTING   18
        BUOYANT AS MORNING AND AS MORNING CLEAR   • • • 175 PARTING   18
        AS SHE WAS IN HER MORNING OF SPRING   • • • • • 231 YOUTH OF NATURE   112
        WHICH IN OUR MORNING-PRIME   • • • • • • • 232 YOUTH OF MAN   13
        AND IN THE SUN ALL MORNING BINDS THE SHEAVES   • • 255 SCHOLAR-GIPSY   14
        THE FOOT LESS PROMPT TO MEET THE MORNING DEW   • • 266 THYRSIS   138
        TOPS IN LIFES MORNING-SUN SO BRIGHT AND BARE   • • 267 THYRSIS   145
        SLOW TO A STOP AT MORNING GREY   • • • • • • 276 SOUTHERN NIGHT   29
        IN THE SUMMER-MORNING THE ROAD   • • • • • • 287 RUGBY CHAPEL   28
        OR NEXT MORNING WITH LIMBS   • • • • • • • 297 HEINES GRAVE   176
        SO WELL SHE MUSED A MORNING BROKE   • • • • • 316 OBERMANN MORE   113
        I SAW THE MORNING BREAK   • • • • • • • • • 324 OBERMANN MORE   348
        BASKS IN HIS MORNING OF YOUTH   • • • • • • 347 MEROPE   521

MORNING   (CONTINUED)
        CLEARD WITH BLITHE TRAVEL AND THE MORNING AIR   • • • 355 MEROPE   734
        FOR WHEN THIS MORNING IN THE PUBLIC SQUARE   • • • • 401 MEROPE   1895
        IN YOUTHS PURE MORNING NOR THINKS   • • • • • 347 MEROPE   V
        PASSD YOU A LITTLE SINCE AS MORNING DAWND   • • • 408 EMPEDOCLES I 1   46
        I SPOKE WITH HIM THIS MORNING ONCE MORE THEREFORE • 412 EMPEDOCLES I 2   19
        MANY A MORNING HAD THEY GONE   • • • • • • • 434 EMPEDOCLES II   171
        EVERY MORNING DID WE PAY   • • • • • • • • 455 POOR MATTHIAS   111
        THE MORNING MISTS FROM TOWER AND TEMPLE ROLL   • • 468 ALARIC AT ROME   154
        PASSD LIKE A MORNING MIST IN TEARS AWAY   • • • 477 CROMWELL   198
        WHILE THEIR MASTERS SATE BY THE FIRE AND WAITED   HOMER TRANS   6
            FOR MORNING

MORNINGLESS
        THE MORNINGLESS AND UNAWAKENING SLEEP   • • • • 267 THYRSIS   169

MORNINGS
        ON AUTUMN-MORNINGS WHEN THE BUGLE SOUNDS   • • • • 18 CHURCH BROU 3   9
        HER HAVIOUR HAD THE MORNINGS FRESH CLEAR GRACE • • 154 TRISTRAM 3   179
        FOR THERE WHERE MORNINGS SACRED FOUNT   • • • • 277 SOUTHERN NIGHT   53
        THIS MORNINGS ANGRY ANSWER FOR THY LAST   • • • 394 MEROPE   1691
        TILL WHAT AT MORNINGS HOUR LOOKT WARM AND BRIGHT • 466 ALARIC AT ROME   107

MORNS
        ON SUCH A HUNTING-JOURNEY THREE MORNS SINCE   • • 355 MEROPE   730

MORROW
        AS YESTERDAY WAS SO TO-MORROW WILL BE   • • • • 19 MODERN SAPPHO   12
        IT WAS WELL WITH ME ONCE IF I SAW HIM TO-MORROW • • 19 MODERN SAPPHO   V
        RICH TO-MORROW AS TO-DAY   • • • • • • • • 22 MEMORY-PICTURE   3
        FIND ASSURANCE TO-MORROW   • • • • • • • • 31 NEW SIRENS   165
        AND TO-MORROW FOLDED PALMS   • • • • • • • 33 NEW SIRENS   198
        AS OLD AGE YOUTHS FATAL MORROW   • • • • • • 33 NEW SIRENS   217
        WHILE THE DAWNING OF THE MORROW   • • • • • • 33 NEW SIRENS   V 217
        PRAYERS THAT TO-MORROW   • • • • • • • • • 36 VOICE   11
        TO-MORROW ON THE SELF-SAME PLAN   • • • • • • 56 RESIGNATION   141
        TO-MORROW COME AND YE SHALL PAY   • • • • • • 87 SICK KING BOKH   7
        BUT ON THE MORROW WHEN THE KING   • • • • • • 89 SICK KING BOKH   46
        THE MORROW AT THE SELF-SAME HOUR   • • • • • 90 SICK KING BOKH   93
        MEANWHILE TO-MORROW WHEN THE MORNING DAWNS • • • 96 BALDER DEAD 1   40
        ONE AFTER ONE TO-MORROW LIKE TO-DAY   • • • • 151 TRISTRAM 3   67
        TO-MORROW HURRY THROUGH THE FIELDS   • • • • 205 CALAIS SANDS   33
        TO-MORROW RED WITH BLOOD WILL XANTHUS BE   • • • 236 PALLADIUM   14
        AND LOSE TO-MORROW THE GROUND WON TO-DAY   • • • 260 SCHOLAR-GIPSY   179
        THUS YESTERDAY TO-DAY TO-MORROW COME   • • • • 262 THYRSIS   V
        THIS DAY TO-MORROW YESTERDAY ALIKE   • • • • 333 MEROPE   110
        THOU WILT RETURN TO-MORROW TO THE CITY   • • • • 428 EMPEDOCLES I 2   470
        EITHER TO-MORROW OR SOME OTHER DAY   • • • • • 428 EMPEDOCLES I 2   471

MORROWLL
        THEN TO HER SOFT SLEEP AND TO-MORROWLL BE   • • • 152 TRISTRAM 3   94

MORROWS
        FOR WITH TO-MORROWS DAWN THE GODS PREPARE   • • • • 103 BALDER DEAD 1   295
        BUT ALL OUR HUSTLING MORROWS ONLY MAKE   • • • • 262 THYRSIS   V

MORTAL
        ALL DIFFERENCE WITH HIS FELLOW-MORTAL CLOSED   • •   7 REP FRIEND CONT   13
        AND MORE THAN MORTAL IMPULSE FILLD THEIR EYES • • 25 DREAM   27
        WHAT MORTAL WHEN HE SAW   • • • • • • • • • 40 HUMAN LIFE   1
        ARE NOT THEY MORTAL AM NOT I MYSELF   • • • • • 68 SOHRAB RUSTUM   254
        IN SINGLE FIGHT WITH ANY MORTAL MAN   • • • • • 69 SOHRAB RUSTUM   259
        AND ALL THE NOBLER SOULS OF MORTAL MEN   • • • 104 BALDER DEAD 1   320
        FOR ALL THE NOBLER SOULS OF MORTAL MEN   • • • 104 BALDER DEAD 1   V 320
        BUT NEITHER GOD NOR MORTAL HEEDS MY PAIN   • • • 116 BALDER DEAD 3   111
        SINGING HERE CAME A MORTAL   • • • • • • • 165 FORSAKEN MERM   120
        HOW VAIN A THING IS MORTAL LOVE   • • • • • 181 ISOLATION MARG   26
        WE MORTAL MILLIONS LIVE ALONE • • • • • • • 182 TO MARG CONT   4
        TO THINGS BY MORTAL COURSE THAT LIVE   • • • • 185 TERRACE BERNE   42
        IMMORTAL MORTAL MAN • • • • • • • • • • 197 FRAG ANTIGONE   72
        IS LOVELY A MORTAL IS DEAD   • • • • • • • 228 YOUTH OF NATURE   12
        OF THE SICK ROOM THE MORTAL STRIFE   • • • • 251 WISH   45
        OF A SICK ROOM A MORTAL STRIFE   • • • • • • 251 WISH   V 45
        FOR WHAT WEARS OUT THE LIFE OF MORTAL MEN • • • 259 SCHOLAR-GIPSY   142
        THE CLOUD OF MORTAL DESTINY   • • • • • • • 272 MEMORIAL VERSES   68
        IN THIS HIS MORTAL STATE   • • • • • • • • 273 EDW QUILLINAN   10
        HIS MORTAL SPAN • • • • • • • • • • • 278 SOUTHERN NIGHT   84
        IN MORTAL WEAKNESS A LAST • • • • • • • • 281 HAWORTH CHURCH   32
        OF MORTAL MEN ON THE EARTH   • • • • • • • 288 RUGBY CHAPEL   59
        TO FOOT OF MORTAL WHERE HIS ANCESTOR   • • • • 357 MEROPE   776
        MORTAL THE MODERATION OF A MAN   • • • • • • 405 MEROPE   2013
        WHAT MORTAL COULD BE SICK OR SORRY HERE   • • • 407 EMPEDOCLES I 1   20
        THE TIDES AND THEN OF MORTAL WARS   • • • • • 414 EMPEDOCLES I 2   72
        AND BORE A MORTAL LOT   • • • • • • • • 447 WESTMIN ABBEY   112
        THE FLUX OF MORTAL THINGS   • • • • • • • 448 WESTMIN ABBEY   152
        THE SENSE OF TEARS IN MORTAL THINGS   • • • • 450 GEISTS GRAVE   16
        STERN LAW OF EVERY MORTAL LOT   • • • • • • 450 GEISTS GRAVE   29
        EBB OF LIFE AND MORTAL PAIN   • • • • • • • 456 POOR MATTHIAS   124
        TO A MORTAL BUT YE ARE WITHOUT OLD AGE AND IMMORTAL   HOMER TRANS   10
        TO LIE LOW IN DEATH BY THE HAND OF A GOD AND A MORTAL   HOMER TRANS   56

MORTALITY
    TO THE FOILD SEARCHING OF MORTALITY • • • • • •   3 SHAKESPEARE   8

MORTALS
    AND THOUGH THE JUST SUN GILD AS MORTALS PRAY   • •   43 GIPSY CHILD   59
    OF GODS OR MORTALS • • • • • • • • • • 188 STRAYED REVEL   95
    OUT OF THE HEED OF MORTALS HE IS GONE   • • • • 269 THYRSIS   208
    OUT OF THE HEED OF MORTALS IS HE GONE   • • • • 269 THYRSIS   V 208
    WE MORTALS ARE NO KINGS • • • • • • • • 418 EMPEDOCLES I 2 177
    GODS AND THE RACE OF MORTALS LOVE SO WELL • • • 431 EMPEDOCLES II   65

MOSES
    GERMANY FRANCE CHRIST MOSES ATHENS ROME • • • 168 RACHEL 3   12
    AS FLASHING AS MOSES FELT   • • • • • • • 253 FUTURE   45

MOSQUE
    AND TO THE MOSQUE MY LORD PASSD ON   • • • • •   89 SICK KING BOKH   45

MOSQUES
    HOUSES ARCADES ENAMELLD MOSQUES   • • • • •   94 SICK KING BOKH 199

MOSS
    FADED THE MOSS THE ROCKS US BURNING PLAINS • • •   25 DREAM   36
    BY MOSS-BORDERD STATUES SITTING   • • • • •   34 NEW SIRENS   239
    MOSS-HUNG BOULDERS AND THIN   • • • • • • 297 HEINES GRAVE 160
    AND STOOPS TO CLEAR THY MOSS-GROWN DATE   • • • 311 OBERMANN   173
    IN MOSS AND GORSE AND SHINING FIR   • • • • • 483 ROME-SICKNESS   8

MOSSD
    OF BRIGHT-LEAFD CHESTNUTS AND MOSSD WALNUT-TREES • •   25 DREAM   8
    THE GRASS WAS DRY AND MOSSD AND YOU SAW CLEAR • • 155 TRISTRAM 3   206
    ETERNAL SHOWERS OF SPRAY ON THE MOSSD ROOTS • • 414 EMPEDOCLES I 2 47

MOSSES
    FRINGD WITH DEAD LEAVES AND MOSSES RARE   • • • • 148 TRISTRAM 2   V

MOSSY
    UPON THE MOSSY ROCKS AT THE STREAMS EDGE   • • • •   25 DREAM   14
    IDLE AS A MOSSY STONE • • • • • • • • • 137 TRISTRAM 1   223
    THE QUIET MOSSY TRACK TO AGE • • • • • • • 199 EARLY DEATH   7
    THE MOSSY QUIET TRACK TO AGE • • • • • • • 199 EARLY DEATH   V 7
    TO WATCH THE THRESHERS IN THE MOSSY BARNS • • • 258 SCHOLAR-GIPSY 104

MOST
    CLEARD ROME OF WHAT MOST SHAMED HIM BUT BE HIS • •   2 TO A FRIEND   8
    ARE RARE AH MOST LOVES BUT FLOW ONCE AND RETURN • •   19 MODERN SAPPHO   16
    WHICH YEARS TO MOST AND CARE AND SUFFERING GIVE • •   43 GIPSY CHILD   V 38
    OH WHEN MOST SELF-EXALTED MOST ALONE • • • •   46 IN UTRUMQUE PAR 36
    OH WHEN MOST SELF-EXALTED MOST ALONE • • • •   46 IN UTRUMQUE PAR 36
    THEE MOST OF ALL AND THOU WHOM MOST HE SEEKS • •   68 SOHRAB RUSTUM 245
    THEE MOST OF ALL AND THOU WHOM MOST HE SEEKS • •   68 SOHRAB RUSTUM 245
    ALL THE MOST VALIANT CHIEFS LONG HE PERUSED • •   70 SOHRAB RUSTUM 311
    NO HORSES CRY WAS THAT MOST LIKE THE ROAR • • •   76 SOHRAB RUSTUM 503
    HER MOST I PITY WHO NO MORE WILL SEE • • • •   78 SOHRAB RUSTUM 593
    O MOST JUST VIZIER SEND AWAY • • • • • •   87 SICK KING BOKH   1
    CRIES OUT MOST EARNESTLY O KING • • • • •   89 SICK KING BOKH   52
    MOST SULTRY DRAIND THE PITCHER THERE • • • •   90 SICK KING BOKH   82
    MOST UNBLEST ALSO AT THAT SIGHT • • • • •   90 SICK KING BOKH   86
    MOST DEAF WHERE THOU SHOULDST MOST GIVE EAR • •   91 SICK KING BOKH   98
    MOST DEAF WHERE THOU SHOULDST MOST GIVE EAR • •   91 SICK KING BOKH   98
    I MOST MIGHT WEEP HIS FATHER SUCH A SON • • •   96 BALDER DEAD 1   21
    MOST FLEET HE WAS BUT NOW HE WENT THE LAST • • • 101 BALDER DEAD 1   222
    ALIVE THOU WAST OF GODS THE MOST BELOVED • • • 112 BALDER DEAD 2   259
    ALIVE THOU WERT OF GODS THE MOST BELOVED • • • 112 BALDER DEAD 2 V 259
    MOST HONOURD AFTER FREA ODINS WIFE • • • • • 116 BALDER DEAD 3   92
    AND HIS HORSE BALDERS HORSE WHOM MOST HE LOVED • • 118 BALDER DEAD 3   171
    SINGING MOST JOYFULLY • • • • • • • • • 164 FORSAKEN MERM   88
    SINGING MOST JOYFULLY • • • • • • • • • 164 FORSAKEN MERM   95
    TOO DEEP FOR THE MOST TO DISCERN • • • • • 230 YOUTH OF NATURE   71
    MOST IN THEMSELVES HAVE BEHELD • • • • • 231 YOUTH OF NATURE 105
    FOR MOST MEN IN A BRAZEN PRISON LIVE • • • • 243 SUMMER NIGHT   37
    BUT OFTEN IN THE WORLDS MOST CROWDED STREETS • • 246 BURIED LIFE   45
    AND CAME AS MOST MEN DEEMD TO LITTLE GOOD • • • 256 SCHOLAR-GIPSY   39
    FOR MOST I KNOW THOU LOVST RETIRED GROUND • • • 257 SCHOLAR-GIPSY   71
    WHERE MOST THE GIPSIES BY THE TURF-EDGED WAY • • 258 SCHOLAR-GIPSY 112
    WHO MOST HAS SUFFERD TAKES DEJECTEDLY • • • • 260 SCHOLAR-GIPSY 183
    AGE WHOM THE MOST OF US CHIDE • • • • • 283 HAWORTH CHURCH   V
    MOST MEN EDDY ABOUT • • • • • • • • 288 RUGBY CHAPEL   60
    IS MOST QUELLING AND MAN • • • • • • • • 293 HEINES GRAVE   24
    WILLINGLY FED OR NO THEIR MOST VAIN HOPES • • • 334 MEROPE   148
    HAD MOST THY HUSBANDS CONFIDENCE CONSULT • • • 337 MEROPE   239
    AND CHAMPION TO THE THRONE I HONOURING MOST • • 338 MEROPE   268
    MOST MEN ARE LED BY INTEREST AND THE FEW • • • 341 MEROPE   365
    HIS MOST JUST PRAYER YET HIS HOUSE • • • • • 343 MEROPE   409
    BY HIM SHOWN FAIR BUT I BELIEVE MOST FOUL • • • 349 MEROPE   556
    THE HEART OF YOUTH I KNOW THAT MOST I FEAR • • • 351 MEROPE   609
    AND TO ONE ACT MANY MOST UNLIKE MOTIVES • • • 352 MEROPE   645
    THE MOST ARE BAD WISE MEN HAVE SAID • • • • • 352 MEROPE   652
    MOST LIKELY GRATEFUL BUT IN ALL CASE SURE • • • 354 MEROPE   711
    UNHAPPY ONE THOU STRIKST A MOST JUST BLOW • • • 374 MEROPE   1200

MOST   (CONTINUED)
        ZEAL MAKES HIM MOST UNJUST BUT IN GOOD TIME   •   •   386 MEROPE   1438
        WHAT FOLLOWD HIS MOST TRUSTED KINSMAN SLEW • • • •   389 MEROPE   1555
        MOST BEAUTIFUL OF WATERS • • • • • •   •   •   391 MEROPE   1609
        MOST HONOURABLY I MEANT I CALL THE GODS   •   •   394 MEROPE   1695
        HIS MOST JUST PRAYER YET HIS RACE   • • • •   •   343 MEROPE   V 409
        BUT IF AS MOST MEN SAY HE IS HALF MAD   • • • •   407 EMPEDOCLES I 1   23
        WHICH WOULD DEGRADE IT MOST   • • • •   • •   415 EMPEDOCLES I 2   100
        ASK WHAT MOST HELPS WHEN KNOWN THOU SON OF ANCHITUS   416 EMPEDOCLES I 2   111
        AND SPEND OUR WIT TO NAME WHAT MOST EMPLOY UNNAMED   423 EMPEDOCLES I 2   331
        HIS MOTHER MOST MAJESTIC DAME   • • • • • •   459 KAISER DEAD   19
        THOU WILT BE MOST UNLOVELY SHALL I CHUSE   • •   •   FRAGMENT 5   3
        OR SOMEWHAT BUT THAT MOST UNLOVEABLE • • • • •   FRAGMENT 5   9

MOTHER
        O MAN WHOM EARTH THY LONG-VEXT MOTHER BARE   • • • •   46 IN UTRUMQUE PAR   32
        MY MOTHER WHO IN ADER-BAIJAN DWELLS • •   • • •   78 SOHRAB RUSTUM   590
        SO THAT SAD MOTHER SENT HIM WORD FOR FEAR   • •   •   79 SOHRAB RUSTUM   610
        HIS YOUTH SAW SOHRABS MOTHER IN HER BLOOM   • •   •   79 SOHRAB RUSTUM   624
        BUT ONE A GIRL WHO WITH HER MOTHER NOW   • • •   •   80 SOHRAB RUSTUM   646
        THAT SEAL WHICH RUSTUM TO MY MOTHER GAVE   • •   •   80 SOHRAB RUSTUM   659
        MY MOTHER TOLD ME OF THEE THOU BRAVE STEED • • •   83 SOHRAB RUSTUM   743
        AND CALLD MY MOTHER AND THEY ALL   • • • •   •   90 SICK KING BOKH   80
        ONE WAS MY MOTHER NOW DO RIGHT   • • • •   90 SICK KING BOKH   88
        THE NORNIES WHEN HIS MOTHER BARE HIM SPUN   • •   •   96 BALDER DEAD 1   24
        OF FREA HONOURD MOTHER OF THE GODS   • •   • •   97 BALDER DEAD 1   85
        UPON HER GOLDEN CHAIR THE MOTHER SATE   • • •   •   98 BALDER DEAD 1   92
        MOTHER A CHILD OF BALE THOU BARST IN ME   • •   •   98 BALDER DEAD 1   95
        CAN I O MOTHER BRING THEM BALDER BACK   • • •   •   98 BALDER DEAD 1   107
        HE SPOKE THE MOTHER OF THE GODS REPLIED   • •   •   98 BALDER DEAD 1   111
        WHAT WAY IS THIS O MOTHER THAT THOU SHOWST • • •   99 BALDER DEAD 1   132
        AND STRAIGHT THE MOTHER OF THE GODS REPLIED   •   •   99 BALDER DEAD 1   134
        MOTHER A DREADFUL WAY IS THIS THOU SHOWST   • • •   100 BALDER DEAD 1   185
        AND STRAIGHT THE MOTHER OF THE GODS REPLIED   •   •   100 BALDER DEAD 1   187
        WHO WHILE THE MOTHER SPAKE HAD CEASED THEIR TOIL   •   100 BALDER DEAD 1   195
        FREA THE MOTHER OF THE GODS WITH STROKE   • •   •   104 BALDER DEAD 1   339
        BUT FREA MOTHER OF THE GODS AROSE   • • • •   •   120 BALDER DEAD 3   246
        AND THAT POTION RARE HER MOTHER • • • • •   •   134 TRISTRAM 1   136
        AND THAT GOLDEN CUP HER MOTHER   • • • • •   •   134 TRISTRAM 1   V 136
        AND THAT PHIAL RARE HER MOTHER   • • • • •   •   134 TRISTRAM 1   V 136
        POURD IN PRAYER BEFORE THE VIRGIN-MOTHER   • • •   144 TRISTRAM 2   63
        THIS IS WHAT MY MOTHER SAID SHOULD BE   • • •   •   145 TRISTRAM 2   82
        POURD IN GRIEF BEFORE THE VIRGIN-MOTHER   • • •   144 TRISTRAM 2   V 63
        MOTHER DEAR WE CANNOT STAY   • • • • • •   •   162 FORSAKEN MERM   20
        OF THE MIGHTY MOTHER OR CRETE   • • • • •   •   230 YOUTH OF NATURE   77
        I TROW THE MIGHTY MOTHER DOTH NOT SEE   • • •   •   268 THYRSIS   179
        COULD SEE THE MOTHER WITH HER CHILD • • • •   •   317 OBERMANN MORE   157
        COULD SEE THE MOTHER WITH THE CHILD • • • •   •   317 OBERMANN MORE   V 157
        O BROTHER OF MY MOTHER GUARDIAN TRUE   • • •   •   330 MEROPE   29
        KEPT ME THEIR MOTHER FROM THEIR SIDE SO LONG   • •   367 MEROPE   1040
        MOTHER I WELL BELIEVED THOU LIVEDST ON   • • • •   367 MEROPE   1043
        O MOTHER MOTHER WHO UPBRAIDS ME AH   • • • •   •   376 MEROPE   1213
        O MOTHER MOTHER WHO UPBRAIDS ME AH   • • • •   •   376 MEROPE   1213
        MOTHER MY HEART RUNS OVER BUT THE TIME   • • •   •   378 MEROPE   1232
        MOTHER SOMETIMES THE JUSTICE OF THE GODS   • • •   378 MEROPE   1247
        MOTHER THY FEARS ARE IDLE FOR I COME   • • •   •   379 MEROPE   1256
        WE TWO WITH THEE MY MOTHER MAY CONSULT   • • •   •   379 MEROPE   1265
        AND THOU MY MOTHER HADST THOU MADE A SIGN   • • •   383 MEROPE   1368
        YET FOR ME MOTHER I HAD LIEFER DIE   • • • •   •   383 MEROPE   1379
        MY FATHER BY YOUR STROKES MY MOTHER SLAIN   • • •   385 MEROPE   1412
        FOR THIS IS NOT MY MOTHER WHO DISSUADES   • • •   385 MEROPE   1413
        MY MOTHER STANDS ALOOF AND BLAMES OUR DEED • • •   386 MEROPE   1448
        A WOMAN AND A MOTHER TO AVERT   • • • •   •   387 MEROPE   1455
        SON WITH A DOUBTING HEART THY MOTHER YIELDS   •   •   390 MEROPE   1582
        O SON AND MOTHER   • • • • • • • •   •   391 MEROPE   1596
        WITHOUT HOME WITHOUT MOTHER   • • • • •   •   391 MEROPE   1613
        BUT HIS MOTHER CALLISTO • • • • • • •   •   392 MEROPE   1631
        HIS FLEEING MOTHER   • • • • • • • •   •   393 MEROPE   1658
        THE ANXIOUS MOTHER OF AN EXILED SON • • • •   •   403 MEROPE   1956
        MOTHER ALL THESE APPROVE ME BUT IF THOU • • •   •   403 MEROPE   1961
        O MOTHER MY BEST DILIGENCE SHALL BE • • • •   •   405 MEROPE   2014
        OF HIS MOTHER WHICH OF THY GLADES   • • • •   •   347 MEROPE   V
        BRING TO HIS MOTHER THE REST I COMMIT   • • •   •   348 MEROPE   V
        DOWN IN OUR MOTHER EARTHS MIRACULOUS WOMB   • • •   439 EMPEDOCLES II   340
        HIS NURSE THE MIGHTY MOTHER WILLD IT SO   • • •   446 WESTMIN ABBEY   86
        HIS MOTHER WOKE FROM SLEEP   • • • • •   • •   446 WESTMIN ABBEY   92
        THE NURSLING OF THE MIGHTY MOTHER DIED   • • •   •   447 WESTMIN ABBEY   115
        HIS MOTHER MOST MAJESTIC DAME   • • • • •   • •   459 KAISER DEAD   19
        FAR FROM MY FATHER AND MOTHER DEAR FOR ALL   HOMER TRANS   61
                THAT I WILL NOT

MOTHERS
        MOTHERS HAVE SHED   • • • • • • • • • • • •   36 VOICE   10
        FROM THINE OWN MOTHERS BREAST THAT KNOWS NOT THEE •   42 GIPSY CHILD   14
        NAY WERE HE THINE OWN MOTHERS SON   • • • • •   92 SICK KING BOKH   137
        AND HODER TURND AND LEFT HIS MOTHERS HOUSE • • •   100 BALDER DEAD 1   197
        FIXD ON THEIR MOTHERS FACE IN WIDE SURPRISE   • •   151 TRISTRAM 3   47
        FIXD ON THEIR MOTHERS FACE IN WIDE SURPRIZE   • •   TRISTRAM 3   V 47
        CALL ONCE MORE TO A MOTHERS EAR   • • • • •   161 FORSAKEN MERM   15
        WANDERING WITH THE GREAT MOTHERS TRAIN DIVINE   • •   268 THYRSIS   177
        THY MOTHERS KIN RECEIVED THEE AND REARD UP • • •   330 MEROPE   23

MOTHERS   (CONTINUED)
    MY MOTHERS FAITHFUL SERVANT LAID ME DOWN   • • • •   331 MEROPE   31
    THAT WAY IS DUBIOUS FOR A MOTHERS PRAYER   • • • •   349 MEROPE   583
    MOTHERS LAMENTING THEIR SONS • • • • • • •   369 MEROPE   1096
    A MOTHERS MURDER NEEDED HEST DIVINE • • • •   385 MEROPE   1402
    THY MOTHERS PRAYERS AND THIS PRAYER LAST OF ALL • •   405 MEROPE   2011

MOTION
    WITH A SAD MAJESTIC MOTION • • • • • • • •   31 NEW SIRENS   155
    WITH A LIFELIKE MOTION • • • • • • • •   36 VOICE   18
    THE MOTION OF LIFE ITSELF • • • • • • •   231 YOUTH OF NATURE   116

MOTIONLESS
    HIS LIMBS GREW SLACK MOTIONLESS WHITE HE LAY • •   86 SOHRAB RUSTUM   848

MOTIVES
    FEELINGS AND MOTIVES THERE • • • • • •   352 MEROPE   635
    THEREFORE WHILE ACTS ARE FROM THEIR MOTIVES JUDGED   352 MEROPE   644
    AND TO ONE ACT MANY MOST UNLIKE MOTIVES • • • •   352 MEROPE   645

MOTLEY
    REVIEWS AND RANKS HIS MOTLEY BANDS • • • • • •   53 RESIGNATION   45
    YES ALL THIS EDDYING MOTLEY THRONG • • • • • •   226 EPILOG LAOCOON   157

MOULD
    MOULD NOT THE SOLID EARTH THOUGH NEVER WINDS • •   8 RELIGIOUS ISOL   10
    BORN INTO LIFE WE ARE AND LIFE MUST BE OUR MOULD • •   418 EMPEDOCLES I 2   186
    AND TEMPER OF HEROIC MOULD • • • • • •   450 GEISTS GRAVE   19
    NOW FOR YEARS IN CHURCHYARD MOULD • • • • •   453 POOR MATTHIAS   48

MOULDER
    AND LETS THE AGED MOULDER TO THEIR GRAVES • • • •   67 SOHRAB RUSTUM   225

MOULDERD
    THE OARS HAVE MOULDERD AS THEY LAY • • • • • •   480 HAYSWATER BOAT   38

MOULDERING
    A WILD ROSE CLIMBING UP A MOULDERING WALL • • • •   36 VOICE   20
    IN THAT DIM WORLD IN HELAS MOULDERING REALM • •   104 BALDER DEAD 1   315

MOULDING
    MOULDING ITSELF IN ACTION NOT IN WORD • • • •   478 CROMWELL   222

MOULDS
    WHAT THOUGH THE HOLY SECRET WHICH MOULDS THEE • •   8 RELIGIOUS ISOL   9
    MOULDS NOT THE SOLID EARTH THOUGH NEVER WINDS • •   8 RELIGIOUS ISOL V 10

MOUND
    AND HEAP A STATELY MOUND ABOVE MY BONES • • • •   84 SOHRAB RUSTUM . 788
    AND HEAP A STATELY MOUND ABOVE THY BONES • • • •   84 SOHRAB RUSTUM . 803

MOUNDED
    BY MOUNDED TURF AND GRAVEN STONE • • • • •   451 GEISTS GRAVE   64
    FROM THOSE WEIRD DOMES OF MOUNDED GREEN • • • •   480 HAYSWATER BOAT   23
    BUT LET ME BE DEAD AND THE EARTH BE MOUNDED ABOVE ME   HOMER TRANS   37

MOUNDS
    AND YON WHITENING BONE-MOUNDS DO NOT GROW • • •   27 NEW SIRENS   56
    AND THOSE WHITENING BONE-MOUNDS DO NOT GROW • •   27 NEW SIRENS V 56
    CLUSTERS OF LONELY MOUNDS • • • • • • •   191 STRAYED REVEL   177

MOUNT
    WHO WILL NOT MOUNT IN PEACE BUT LOVE • • • • •   HORATIAN ECHO V
    CROSSING SO HIGH THAT AS THEY MOUNT THEY PASS • •   66 SOHRAB RUSTUM   163
    WINDING SO HIGH THAT AS THEY MOUNT THEY PASS • •   66 SOHRAB RUSTUM V 163
    THE MOUNT FROM WHENCE HIS EYE SURVEYS THE WORLD • •   96 BALDER DEAD 1   50
    BUT NOW PUT ON YOUR ARMS AND MOUNT YOUR STEEDS • •   115 BALDER DEAD 3   50
    YOUTH RAMBLES ON LIFES ARID MOUNT • • • • •   213 PROGRESS POESY   1
    THE MOUNT IS MUTE THE CHANNEL DRY • • • •   213 PROGRESS POESY   11
    THE MASTER STOOD UPON THE MOUNT AND TAUGHT • • •   237 PROGRESS   1
    THE SNOWY HIMALAYAN MOUNT • • • • • •   277 SOUTHERN NIGHT   55
    THAT MOUNT THAT MADDEN HOW OFT • • • • •   296 HEINES GRAVE   147
    THAN THE ICE-BASTIOND CAUCASIAN MOUNT • • •   395 MEROPE   1749
    BUT HEED HIM NOT HE WILL NOT MOUNT TO US • •   412 EMPEDOCLES I 2   18
    AND THAT CURST TREACHERY ON THE MOUNT OF GORE •   430 EMPEDOCLES II   54
    THAT SAPPST THE VITALS OF THIS TERRIBLE MOUNT •   438 EMPEDOCLES II   306
    WITH OMEN OH WERE THAT MOUNT PASSD I SAY • • •   485 S S LUSITANIA   12

MOUNTAIN
    MID THE DISTANT MOUNTAIN-CHALETS • • • • •   12 CHURCH BROU 1   3
    MID THE SAVOY MOUNTAIN VALLEYS • • • • •   14 CHURCH BROU 1   61
    MOUNTAIN GREENSWARD PAVES THE CHANCEL • • •   15 CHURCH BROU 1   71
    GUIDE ME SOME ONE TO THE MOUNTAIN • • • •   15 CHURCH BROU 1   75
    CLIMB THE WINDING MOUNTAIN-WAY • • • • •   15 CHURCH BROU 1   86
    IN THE SAVOY MOUNTAIN-MEADOWS • • • • • •   15 CHURCH BROU 1   91
    GUIDE ME VASSALS TO THE MOUNTAIN • • • •   15 CHURCH BROU 1 V 75
    DOWN THE MOUNTAIN-WAY • • • • • • •   17 CHURCH BROU 2   27
    IN YOUR HIGH CHURCH MID THE STILL MOUNTAIN-AIR • •   17 CHURCH BROU 3   2
    AND THE WIND WASHES THROUGH THE MOUNTAIN-PINES • •   18 CHURCH BROU 3   37
    AND THE WIND WASHES IN THE MOUNTAIN PINES • • •   18 CHURCH BROU 3 V 37

MOUNTAIN   (CONTINUED)

AND THE WIND WAILS AMONG THE MOUNTAIN PINES	18 CHURCH BROU 3	V 37
AND THE WIND WASHES MID THE MOUNTAIN PINES	18 CHURCH BROU 3	V 37
THE MOUNTAIN-SKIRTS WITH ALL THEIR SYLVAN CHANGE	25 DREAM	7
HIS WHO IN MOUNTAIN GLENS AT NOON OF DAY	42 GIPSY CHILD	22
THAT VAST SKY-NEIGHBOURING MOUNTAIN OF MILK SNOW	66 SOHRAB RUSTUM	162
THE SHEPHERD FROM HIS MOUNTAIN-LODGE DESCRIES	79 SOHRAB RUSTUM	621
A HELPLESS BABE AMONG THE MOUNTAIN-ROCKS	81 SOHRAB RUSTUM	681
LIE PRONE ENORMOUS DOWN THE MOUNTAIN SIDE	86 SOHRAB RUSTUM	863
IN HIS HIGH MOUNTAIN-CRADLE IN PAMERE	87 SOHRAB RUSTUM	887
AND UP THE DEWY MOUNTAIN-TRACKS THEY FARED	106 BALDER DEAD 2	51
THEIR KINE ACROSS A SNOWY MOUNTAIN-PASS	107 BALDER DEAD 2	92
OR WAS IT FROM SOME SUN-FLECKD MOUNTAIN-BROOK	175 PARTING	21
THE FRORE MOUNTAIN-WALL	176 PARTING	48
THE MOUNTAIN-BEES HUM	176 PARTING	56
ON THY HIGH MOUNTAIN-PLATFORMS	177 PARTING	85
THE MISTS ARE ON THE MOUNTAIN HUNG	185 TERRACE BERNE	51
THE MOUNTAIN WIND	190 STRAYED REVEL	150
ON HIS MOUNTAIN LAKE BUT SQUALLS	193 STRAYED REVEL	236
AND THAT FAR PURPLE MOUNTAIN-LINE	208 ON THE RHINE	13
SCARCE FRESHER IS THE MOUNTAIN-SOD	248 KENSINGTON GARD	17
NOT FRESHER IS THE MOUNTAIN SOD	KENSINGTON GARD	V 17
AND HIGH THE MOUNTAIN-TOPS IN CLOUDY AIR	267 THYRSIS	143
THE MOUNTAIN-TOPS WHERE IS THE THRONE OF TRUTH	267 THYRSIS	144
BEHIND THAT LOVELY MOUNTAIN-LINE	275 SOUTHERN NIGHT	7
THROUGH FOREST UP THE MOUNTAIN-SIDE	299 GRANDE CHARTR	6
YES THOUGH THE VIRGIN MOUNTAIN-AIR	307 OBERMANN	25
THOUGH HERE A MOUNTAIN-MURMUR SWELLS	307 OBERMANN	29
AND BROODING MOUNTAIN-BEE	307 OBERMANN	34
BALMS FLOATING ON THY MOUNTAIN-AIR	309 OBERMANN	111
AND TO THY MOUNTAIN-CHALET COME	313 OBERMANN MORE	45
A MOUNTAIN-FLOWER WAS IN HIS HAND	314 OBERMANN MORE	65
COME TO MY MOUNTAIN-SOLITUDE	322 OBERMANN MORE	275
WILD HOG AND BEAR AND MOUNTAIN-DEER AND ROE	356 MEROPE	758
STILL AT HIS MOUNTAIN-TOMB MEN MARVEL BUILT	357 MEROPE	782
BROKE BLACK WITH SWEAT THE ANTLERD MOUNTAIN-STAG	357 MEROPE	808
WITH MOUNTAIN-TRAVEL AND NIGHT-WATCHING SPENT	359 MEROPE	868
IN THE PRIMEVAL MOUNTAIN-FORESTS BORE	389 MEROPE	1537
THE WHITE MOUNTAIN-BIRDS	392 MEROPE	1625
THE SHY MOUNTAIN-BEAR	392 MEROPE	1640
O PASTURES OF THE MOUNTAIN	399 MEROPE	1822
YE WITNESSD YE MOUNTAIN LAWNS	399 MEROPE	1831
FROM THE FOUR-TOWND MOUNTAIN-SHADOWD DORIS	400 MEROPE	1852
HOW GRACIOUS IS THE MOUNTAIN AT THIS HOUR	406 EMPEDOCLES I 1	6
OR WITH THE REVELLERS FROM THE MOUNTAIN-TOWNS	406 EMPEDOCLES I 1	8
IS SHINING ON THE BRILLIANT MOUNTAIN-CRESTS	406 EMPEDOCLES I 1	10
IN THIS CLEAR MOUNTAIN-AIR A VOICE WILL RISE	409 EMPEDOCLES I 1	88
IN THE HIGH UNFREQUENTED MOUNTAIN-SPOTS	409 EMPEDOCLES I 1	93
AND IN THE MOUNTAIN-CHINKS INTER THE WINDS	410 EMPEDOCLES I 1	118
BUT LEAD HIM THROUGH THE LOVELY MOUNTAIN-PATHS	411 EMPEDOCLES I 1	156
TO THE HIGH MOUNTAIN-PASTURES AND TO STAY	413 EMPEDOCLES I 2	39
BUOYANT AND FRESH THE MOUNTAIN FLOWERS	426 EMPEDOCLES I 2	433
TO THOSE UNTRODDEN MOUNTAIN-LAWNS AND THERE	427 EMPEDOCLES I 2	456
AND IN THE LONELY ROCK-STREWN MOUNTAIN-GLEN	430 EMPEDOCLES II	39
IN THE STILL MOUNTAIN AIR	430 EMPEDOCLES II	40
OF THE MOUNTAIN-CRUSHD TORTURED INTRACTABLE TITAN KING	432 EMPEDOCLES II	98
FLINGING ON THE MOUNTAIN-SOD	433 EMPEDOCLES II	156
TO THE GLIMMERING MOUNTAIN-LAKES	434 EMPEDOCLES II	172
IN THE MOUNTAIN-VILLAGES	434 EMPEDOCLES II	184
OH THAT I COULD GLOW LIKE THIS MOUNTAIN	438 EMPEDOCLES II	323
WHAT SEEKS ON THIS MOUNTAIN	442 EMPEDOCLES II	451
THEY BATHE ON THIS MOUNTAIN	442 EMPEDOCLES II	453
THINE WAS NO MOUNTAIN HOME WHERE FREEDOMS FORM	472 CROMWELL	17
YET ALL HIGH SOUNDS THAT MOUNTAIN CHILDREN HEAR	472 CROMWELL	27
BY HILL OR WAVE THE MOUNTAIN OR THE SHORE	472 CROMWELL	30
SKIES THAT UNBOUND BY CLASP OF MOUNTAIN CHAIN	473 CROMWELL	37
TO THE VEXD WATERS OF A MOUNTAIN LAKE	477 CROMWELL	192

MOUNTAINOUS

WHERE THE SNOWY MOUNTAINOUS PASS	252 FUTURE	9
OF ITS EARLY MOUNTAINOUS SHORE	254 FUTURE	76

MOUNTAINS

UNOERLEAPD MOUNTAINS OF NECESSITY	7 REP FRIEND CONT	7
THERE THEY FOUND HER IN THE MOUNTAINS	15 CHURCH BROU 1	99
FROM THE WATCHERS ON THE MOUNTAINS	27 NEW SIRENS	35
DOWN LYDIAN MOUNTAINS SO WHEN SNOWS	52 RESIGNATION	7
THOUGH HE MOVE MOUNTAINS THOUGH HIS DAY	56 RESIGNATION	148
BEYOND THE MOUNTAINS WILL HE SEE	138 TRISTRAM 1	250
YE ARE BOUND FOR THE MOUNTAINS	175 PARTING	9
I COME O YE MOUNTAINS	175 PARTING	33
I COME O YE MOUNTAINS	176 PARTING	57
THE MISTS ARE ON THE MOUNTAINS HUNG	185 TERRACE BERNE	V 51
THE MOUNTAINS RING THEM	190 STRAYED REVEL	161
THE MOUNTAINS STAND AT ITS HEAD	228 YOUTH OF NATURE	5
AND MOUNTAINS THAT FILL US WITH JOY	230 YOUTH OF NATURE	61
MOUNTAINS SURROUND IT AND SWEET VIRGIN AIR	236 PALLADIUM	10
THE BLUE HAZE-CRADLED MOUNTAINS SPREAD AWAY	242 SUMMER NIGHT	21
HE BY THOSE INDIAN MOUNTAINS OLD	278 SOUTHERN NIGHT	91
MILD OER HER GRAVE YE MOUNTAINS SHINE	279 SOUTHERN NIGHT	137

MOUNTAINS   (CONTINUED)
    GORGES OER MOUNTAINS IN SNOW   • • • • • • • • •   289 RUGBY CHAPEL   88
    AND I ACROSS THE MOUNTAINS BROUGHT WITH HASTE   • •   358 MEROPE   845
    THE MOUNTAINS WHERE THE GLENS ARE DRY   • • • •   414 EMPEDOCLES I 2   62
    STOOPS TO THE SOARING MOUNTAINS LIVE AND DIE   • •   472 CROMWELL   10
    OF GIANT MOUNTAINS BY THE WESTERN MAIN   • • • •   475 CROMWELL   105
    BETWEEN THE BARREN MOUNTAINS AND THE STORMY SEA   • •   475 CROMWELL   118
    LIKE ISLES OF SUNLIGHT ON A MOUNTAINS BROW   • • • •   475 CROMWELL   127
    THE LOUD RAINS LASHD THE MOUNTAINS CROWN   • • • •   480 HAYSWATER BOAT   29
    OER GLION FRINGE THE MOUNTAINS BRINK   • • • • • •   483 ROME-SICKNESS   11
    SOFTLY GLEAM THE FAR BLUE MOUNTAINS   • • • • • •   META CLOISTER   13

MOUNTED
    AND MOUNTED HIS HORSE SLEIPNER WHOM HE RODE   • •   96 BALDER DEAD 1   47
    AND MOUNTED SLEIPNER AND IN DARKNESS RODE   • • • •   102 BALDER DEAD 1   255
    AND MOUNTED THEM AND IN VALHALLAS COURT   • • • •   105 BALDER DEAD 2   13
    BUT HERMOD MOUNTED HIM AND SADLY FARED   • • • •   107 BALDER DEAD 2   78
    THEN MOUNTED SLEIPNER AND SET FORTH TO RIDE   • •   112 BALDER DEAD 2   284
    MOUNTED ON SLEIPNER WITH THE WARRIOR THOR   • • • •   120 BALDER DEAD 3   239

MOUNTING
    WHEN THE SOUL MOUNTING HIGHER   • • • • • • •   38 STAGIRIUS   16
    MOUNTING TO POWER LONG DENIED   • • • • • • • •   HORATIAN ECHO   V
    MOUNTING WESTWARD HIGH AND HIGHER   • • • • • •   433 EMPEDOCLES II   139

MOUNTS
    MOUNTS AT HER SIDE   • • • • • • • • • •   38 STAGIRIUS   19
    MOUNTS AND THAT HARDLY TO ETERNAL LIFE   • • •   172 IMMORTALITY   14
    MOUNTS UP THE STONY FOREST-WAY   • • • • • •   300 GRANDE CHARTR   20
    AND STONY MOUNTS THE WAY   • • • • • • • •   312 OBERMANN MORE   10
    YET WARM IT MOUNTS THE HOUR OF LIFE   • • • •   322 OBERMANN MORE   291
    PAUSANIAS HIS SAGE FRIEND WHO MOUNTS WITH HIM   • •   407 EMPEDOCLES I 1   25
    MOUNTS OFF MY SOUL I FEEL IT I BREATHE FREE   • •   441 EMPEDOCLES II   408

MOURN
    MOURN WILL WE NOT YOUR CLOSING HOUR   • • • • • •   48 HORATIAN ECHO   10
    THESE MOURN NOT THAT THEIR GOINGS PAY   • • • •   53 RESIGNATION   28
    AND PLACE ME ON A BED AND MOURN FOR ME   • • •   84 SOHRAB RUSTUM   785
    AND PLACE THEE ON A BED AND MOURN FOR THEE   • • • •   84 SOHRAB RUSTUM   800
    TO MOURN WITH HIM AND SHOW HIM CARE   • • • • •   92 SICK KING BOKH   156
    AND CEASE TO MOURN AND THINK OF BALDERS PYRE   • •   97 BALDER DEAD 1   60
    THOUGH I BE LOVED AND MANY MOURN MY DEATH   • • •   112 BALDER DEAD 2   270
    THEREFORE WITH GRATEFUL HEART I MOURN THEE DEAD • •   117 BALDER DEAD 3   152
    YET MOURN NOT FOR ME HERMOD WHEN THOU SITTST   • •   126 BALDER DEAD 3   456
    I MOURN THEE THAT THOU CANST NOT HELP US THEN   • •   127 BALDER DEAD 3   482
    MOURN NOT FOR ME MOURN HERMOD FOR THE GODS   • • •   127 BALDER DEAD 3   484
    MOURN NOT FOR ME MOURN HERMOD FOR THE GODS   • • •   127 BALDER DEAD 3   484
    MOURN FOR THE MEN ON EARTH THE GODS IN HEAVEN   • •   127 BALDER DEAD 3   485
    WELL MAY WE MOURN WHEN THE HEAD   • • • • •   229 YOUTH OF NATURE   48
    WHEN YE MOURN THAT A POET IS DEAD   • • • •   230 YOUTH OF NATURE   88
    THE ARDENT THE GIFTED HOW MOURN   • • • • •   282 HAWORTH CHURCH   49
    OVER THY CORPSE TRIUMPH NOT NEITHER MOURN   • • •   404 MEROPE   1989
    WHO MOURN THEE IN THINE ENGLISH HOME   • • • • •   451 GEISTS GRAVE   54
    GEIST HAD VERSE TO MOURN HIS END   • • • • • •   454 POOR MATTHIAS   58

MOURND
    THEY MOURND THAT DAY SO BRIGHT SO LOVED A GOD   • •   115 BALDER DEAD 3   64
    BUT HERE I KNOW THOU WILT BE MISSD AND MOURND   • •   115 BALDER DEAD 3   78
    THOU O MOURND ONE TO-DAY   • • • • • • • •   284 HAWORTH CHURCH   77
    WELL-MOURND BUT ILL-AVENGED   • • • • • • •   372 MEROPE   1142
    AS DEAD WE HELD THEE MOURND FOR THEE AS DEAD   • •   375 MEROPE   1208

MOURNER
    SHALL I ASK WHAT FADED MOURNER   • • • • • • • •   35 NEW SIRENS   273

MOURNERS
    TEN THOUSAND MOURNERS   • • • • • • • • • • •   52 CONSOLATION   64

MOURNFUL
    A SMILE OF MOURNFUL INCREDULITY   • • • • •   EMERSONS ESSAYS   V   7
    AND THY DARK MOURNFUL VISION RESTS ON ME   • • • •   41 GIPSY CHILD   V 16
    WHY WITH THESE MOURNFUL RHYMES   • • • • • •   46 WORLD QUIETIST   4
    AND HIMSELF SCANND IT LONG WITH MOURNFUL EYES   • •   81 SOHRAB RUSTUM   685
    AND WITH A MOURNFUL VOICE RUSTUM REPLIED   • • •   84 SOHRAB RUSTUM   795
    WHERE FEEBLY COMES THE MOURNFUL ROAR   • • • • •   140 TRISTRAM 1   330
    AND SINGS A MOURNFUL STAVE   • • • • •   159 NECKAN   14
    WITH MOURNFUL CADENCE SLOW AND BRING   • • • • •   211 DOVER BEACH   V 13
    THE WAVES OF MOURNFUL THOUGHT BY WHICH THEY ARE PREST   243 SUMMER NIGHT   48
    THROUGH HADES AND THE MOURNFUL GLOOM   • • • • •   271 MEMORIAL VERSES   39
    MOURNFUL HOMAGE THE MUSE   • • • • • • • •   281 HAWORTH CHURCH   35
    IN PITY AND MOURNFUL AWE MIGHT STAND   • • • • •   301 GRANDE CHARTR   82
    THEIR MOURNFUL CALM SERENE   • • • • • • •   314 OBERMANN MORE   50
    A MOURNFUL FEUD ALIVE WHICH ELSE WOULD DIE   • • •   332 MEROPE   82
    HEAR ME THEN SPEAK AND LET THIS MOURNFUL DAY   •   333 MEROPE   114
    MOURNFUL PREEMINENCE NOT   • • • • • • • • • •   370 MEROPE   1110
    THROUGH TWENTY YEARS HIS MOURNFUL ANXIOUS ZEAL   • •   387 MEROPE   1477
    TO MAKE THE GATES OF THIS LONG-MOURNFUL HOUSE   • •   401 MEROPE   1884
    BUT HUSH THIS MOURNFUL STRAIN   • • • • • • •   448 WESTMIN ABBEY   131
    THAT STEADFAST MOURNFUL STRAIN CONSOLED   • • •   450 GEISTS GRAVE   17
    WHISPERS IN MOURNFUL TONES THY SILENT ELEGY   • •   464 ALARIC AT ROME   66

MOURNFUL   (CONTINUED)
        IN MOURNFUL LOVELINESS THAT CITY LAY • • • • • • • 466 ALARIC AT ROME   104
        AND MEMORYS CALM CLEAR VOICE AND MOURNFUL EYE   • • 474 CROMWELL   87
        STILL AS HE GAZD THE PHANTOMS MOURNFUL GLANCE   • • 477 CROMWELL   193

MOURNFULLEST
        THAT THRILLS IN HIS MOURNFULLEST CHORD   • • • • 231 YOUTH OF NATURE   93

MOURNFULLY
        ON THE WILD WHIRLING WAVES MOURNFULLY MOURNFULLY • • 35 VOICE   7
        ON THE WILD WHIRLING WAVES MOURNFULLY MOURNFULLY • • 35 VOICE   7
        MOURNFULLY SHOOK HIS HEAD AND DISAPPEARD   • • • • 104 BALDER DEAD 1   334
        MOURNFULLY GRATING THE GATES   • • • • • • • 199 FRAG DEJANEIRA   29
        ON SOME BARE HEADLAND STRAINING MOURNFULLY • • • • 477 CROMWELL   190

MOURNING
        SAD-CHANTING MAIDENS CLAD IN MOURNING ROBES   • • 331 MEROPE   53
        THE MOURNING-STOLE NO MORE   • • • • • • • • • 447 WESTMIN ABBEY   97
        MOURNING AS WIDOWED VENICE OER HER ADRIAN TIDE   • • 468 ALARIC AT ROME   162

MOUTH
        WHERE SATE IN THE CAVES MOUTH A SKINNY HAG • • • • 123 BALDER DEAD 3   333
        THAT MOCKING MOUTH GROW SWEETLY BLAND   • • • • 206 RIVER   6
        PAST THE LOIRES MOUTH AND BY THE FOAM   • • • 274 STANZAS CARNAC   35
        STRONG BLACK TEMPESTUOUS TO THE CAVERN-MOUTH   • • 358 MEROPE   821
        RIGHT AT THE HARBOUR-MOUTH   • • • • • • • • • 400 MEROPE   1878
        MUST FROM SOME MOUTH BE HEARD RELATE IT THOU   • • 401 MEROPE   1892
        CROWND BY THE AWFUL PEAK ETNAS GREAT MOUTH • • • • 429 EMPEDOCLES II   3
        TROPHY IN MOUTH AGOG TO START   • • • • • • • 460 KAISER DEAD   50

MOUTHD
        OF HER GREATEST GOLDEN-MOUTHD SONS   • • • • • • 294 HEINES GRAVE   79

MOVD
        MOVD UP AND DOWN UNDER THEIR GLOSSY TREES   • • • •   TRISTRAM 3   V 43

MOVE
        STILL DO THY SLEEPLESS MINISTERS MOVE ON   • • • •   1 QUIET WORK   11
        STILL DO THY QUIET MINISTERS MOVE ON • • • • • • •   1 QUIET WORK   V 11
        MOVE BROWSING UP THE GRAY-WALLD LANE • • • • • • 55 RESIGNATION   121
        THOUGH HE MOVE MOUNTAINS THOUGH HIS DAY   • • • • 56 RESIGNATION   148
        THEY FEEL NOT THOUGH THEY MOVE AND SEE   • • • • 58 RESIGNATION   205
        THE WORLD IN WHICH WE LIVE AND MOVE   • • • • • • 58 RESIGNATION   215
        IN SINGLE FILE THEY MOVE AND STOP THEIR BREATH   • • 66 SOHRAB RUSTUM   167
        HIMSELF TO FIGHT AND THAT THY WILES WOULD MOVE   • • 77 SOHRAB RUSTUM   532
        AH SWEET SAINTS HIS DREAM DOTH MOVE   • • • • • • 135 TRISTRAM 1   170
        HAPLY HE SEEMS AGAIN TO MOVE   • • • • • • • 136 TRISTRAM 1   206
        AND WHEN THE CLOCK PEALS MIDNIGHT SHE WILL MOVE   • • 152 TRISTRAM 3   86
        TILL FOR ITS SAKE ALONE WE LIVE AND MOVE   • • • 153 TRISTRAM 3   129
        AND WOMEN THINGS THAT LIVE AND MOVE   • • • • • • 178 FAREWELL   21
        EACH ON HIS OWN STRICT LINE WE MOVE   • • • • • • 206 TOO LATE   1
        THOUGH SHE MOVE NOT EARTH TO-DAY   • • • • • • 227 PERSIST POETRY   2
        THROUGH THE LONG DEWY GRASS MOVE SLOW AWAY • • • • 258 SCHOLAR-GIPSY   110
        PUBLIC CARES WHICH MOVE • • • • • • • • • • 282 HAWORTH CHURCH   V
        YE MOVE THROUGH THE RANKS RECALL   • • • • • • 292 RUGBY CHAPEL   198
        MOVE ON A RIGOROUS LINE • • • • • • • • • • 310 OBERMANN   134

MOVED
        MOVED ONLY BUT BY GENIUS IN THE STRIFE   • • • •   4 DUKE WELLINGTON   4
        THEIR LIPS MOVED THEIR WHITE ARMS WAVED EAGERLY   • • 25 DREAM   28
        AND GREATLY MOVED THEN RUSTUM MADE REPLY   • • • • 68 SOHRAB RUSTUM   249
        FIRST TO THE ONE THEN TO THE OTHER MOVED   • • • • 82 SOHRAB RUSTUM   733
        BOTH ARMIES MOVED TO CAMP AND TOOK THEIR MEAL   • • 86 SOHRAB RUSTUM   871
        INTO THE FROSTY STARLIGHT AND THERE MOVED   • • • • 87 SOHRAB RUSTUM   877
        BUT FIERCELY ODIN GALLOPD MOVED IN HEART   • • • • 102 BALDER DEAD 1   258
        AND STRAIGHT HIS NEIGHBOUR MOVED WITH WRATH REPLIED   114 BALDER DEAD 3   20
        MOVED UP AND DOWN UNDER THE GLOSSY TREES   • • • • 150 TRISTRAM 3   43
        POWER TO BE MOVED AND SOOTHED FOR ALL OUR PAIN   • • 153 TRISTRAM 3   117
        ONWARD WE MOVED AND REACHD THE RIDE   • • • • • 224 EPILOG LAOCOON   107
        I KNEW THEY LIVED AND MOVED   • • • • • • • • 245 BURIED LIFE   20
        MOVED TO THE WINDOW NEAR AND SEE   • • • • • • 250 WISH   31
        VOICE MOVED ONLY THE TORRENT BROKE   • • • • • • 323 OBERMANN MORE   327
        YOU TOO MOVED JOYFULLY   • • • • • • • • • 437 EMPEDOCLES II   283
        QUICKENED AND MOVED A HAPPY BREATH   • • • • • • 483 ROME-SICKNESS   7

MOVEMENT
        URGED AND TO FEED WHOSE MOVEMENT SPINNING SAND   • •   5 DUKE WELLINGTON   6
        FOR MOVEMENT FOR AN AMPLER SPHERE   • • • • • • • 60 RESIGNATION   273
        OF TOIL HE MUST LIFES MOVEMENT TELL   • • • • • • 225 EPILOG LAOCOON   140
        THE MOVEMENT HE MUST TELL OF LIFE   • • • • • • 225 EPILOG LAOCOON   143
        LIFES MOVEMENT FASCINATES CONTROLS   • • • • • • 226 EPILOG LAOCOON   164
        UNTIRED ITS MOVEMENT BRIGHT ATTEND   • • • • • • 227 EPILOG LAOCOON   191
        IN THE ETERNAL MOVEMENT • • • • • • • • • • 286 HAWORTH CHURCH   137

MOVES
        NOTHING MOVES ON THE LAWN BUT THE QUICK LILAC-SHADE   19 MODERN SAPPHO   V 2
        LET ALL THAT LIVES AND MOVES UPON THE EARTH   • • 111 BALDER DEAD 2   236
        SCARCELY MOVES THE COVERLET   • • • • • • • 141 TRISTRAM 1   343
        HER CHILDRENS SHE MOVES SLOW HER VOICE ALONE   • • 151 TRISTRAM 3   72
        MOVES THROUGH THEIR ROWS OF PILLARS OLD   • • • • 274 STANZAS CARNAC   14

MOVES   (CONTINUED)
    THAT MURDER MOVES THIS BREACH THAT THOU WOULDST CLOSE   335 MEROPE   187
    MOVES ME SOMEHOW TO REMORSE   • • • • • • • •   454 POOR MATTHIAS   84
    IT MOVES BUT NEVER MOVETH ON   • • • • • • • • •   479 HAYSWATER BOAT   6
    MOVES ME SO MUCH NOT HECUBAS GRIEF NOR PRIAM   HOMER TRANS   24
        MY FATHERS
    THIS WAY MOVES AND PAUSES GAZES   • • • • • •   META CLOISTER   11
    THIS WAY MOVES AND PAUSES GAZING   • • • • • •   META CLOISTER   V 11

MOVETH
    IT MOVES BUT NEVER MOVETH ON   • • • • • • • •   479 HAYSWATER BOAT   6

MOVING
    MIXD WITH THE MURMUR OF THE MOVING NILE   • • • •   12 MYCERINUS   127
    THOUGH MOVING INLY TO ONE FAR-SET GOAL   • • • •   448 WESTMIN ABBEY   153
    THOUGH MOVING INLY TO ONE FAR-OFF GOAL   • • • •   448 WESTMIN ABBEY   V 153
    OF ALL LIVING THINGS THAT ON EARTH ARE BREATHING   HOMER TRANS   13
        AND MOVING
    OF THAT DUSK SLOW-MOVING BAND   • • • • • • • •   META CLOISTER   10

MOWERS
    THE MOWERS CRY THE DOGS ALARMS   • • • • • • •   218 BACCHANALIA 1   6
    WHERE ARE THE MOWERS WHO AS THE TINY SWELL   • • • •   266 THYRSIS   127

MOWING
    MOWING THE GARDEN GRASS-PLOTS NEAR ITS BED   • • • •   80 SOHRAB RUSTUM   636

MOWN
    ON THE MOWN DYING GRASS SO SOHRAB LAY   • • • •   80 SOHRAB RUSTUM   638
    MOWN THEM DOWN FAR FROM HOME   • • • • • • • •   193 STRAYED REVEL   253
    DESERTED IS THE HALF-MOWN PLAIN   • • • • • • •   217 BACCHANALIA 1   4
    AND SCENT OF HAY NEW-MOWN   • • • • • • • •   265 THYRSIS   76

MOZART
    MOZART BEETHOVEN MENDELSSOHN   • • • • • • • •   222 EPILOG LAOCOON   35

MUCH
    MUCH NOISIER WORK ACCOMPLISHD IN REPOSE   • • • •   1 QUIET WORK   V   7
    HE MUCH THE OLD MAN WHO CLEAREST-SOULD OF MEN   • •   2 TO A FRIEND   2
    MUCH HE WHOSE FRIENDSHIP I NOT LONG SINCE WON   • •   2 TO A FRIEND   5
    KNOW THOU THE WORST SO MUCH NOT MORE HE CAN   • •   6 GEO CRUIKSHANK   14
    WILL BE BROUGHT THOU POOR HEART HOW MUCH NEARER   20 MODERN SAPPHO   20
        TO THEE
    MUCH HAST HAD HAST SQUANDERD MUCH   • • • • • •   22 MEMORY-PICTURE   V
    MUCH HAST HAD HAST SQUANDERD MUCH   • • • • • •   22 MEMORY-PICTURE   V
    MUSED MUCH LOVED LIFE A LITTLE LOATHED IT MORE   • •   43 GIPSY CHILD   36
    HAVE KNOWN TOO MUCH OR ELSE FORGOTTEN ALL   • • • •   43 GIPSY CHILD   48
    WHILE IT MENDS LITTLE TROUBLES MUCH   • • • • •   56 RESIGNATION   127
    WITH MUCH UNKNOWN AND MUCH UNTRIED   • • • • •   59 RESIGNATION   225
    WITH MUCH UNKNOWN AND MUCH UNTRIED   • • • • •   59 RESIGNATION   225
    YET HIM I PITY NOT SO MUCH BUT HER   • • • • •   78 SOHRAB RUSTUM   589
    BUT MUCH MUST STILL BE TRIED WHICH SHALL BUT FAIL   99 BALDER DEAD 1   130
    NOR SHOOK THE BRIDGE SO MUCH AS THOU ALONE   • • •   107 BALDER DEAD 2   106
    YE GODS THERE WELL MAY BE TOO MUCH OF WAIL   • • • •   118 BALDER DEAD 3   157
    SOMETHING TOO MUCH OF WAR AND BROILS WHICH MAKE   • •   128 BALDER DEAD 3   505
    BEND BEND DOWN I YET HAVE MUCH TO SAY   • • • •   145 TRISTRAM 2   76
    MUCH CHEERD WITH THOUGHTS OF CHRIST THE LIVING BREAD   169 EAST LONDON   8
    HAVE YET SO MUCH AS HEARD THIS SIMPLER LORE   • •   171 DIVINITY   12
    THEN WE SHALL KNOW OUR FRIENDS THOUGH MUCH   • • • •   179 FAREWELL   65
    AND THOU PROVED MUCH ENDURING   • • • • • • • •   194 STRAYED REVEL   287
    TO A MUCH FEEBLER WIGHT THE HEROIC MAN   • • • •   198 FRAG ANTIGONE   96
    TOO MUCH OF PALACE AND DOME   • • • • • • • •   214 NEW ROME   12
    THESE OR MUCH GREATER THINGS BUT CAUGHT   • • • •   223 EPILOG LAOCOON   55
    FOR AH SO MUCH HE HAS TO DO   • • • • • • • •   225 EPILOG LAOCOON   129
    WHICH HAS NOT TAUGHT WEAK WILLS HOW MUCH THEY CAN   238 PROGRESS   41
    WHICH MUCH TO HAVE TRIED IN MUCH BEEN BAFFLED BRINGS   260 SCHOLAR-GIPSY   165
    WHICH MUCH TO HAVE TRIED IN MUCH BEEN BAFFLED BRINGS   260 SCHOLAR-GIPSY   165
    SO MUCH UNLEARNT SO MUCH RESIGND   • • • • • •   301 GRANDE CHARTR   75
    SO MUCH UNLEARNT SO MUCH RESIGND   • • • • • •   301 GRANDE CHARTR   75
    AND ONE THE STRONG MUCH-TOILING SAGE   • • • •   308 OBERMANN   51
    NEITHER MADE MAN TOO MUCH A GOD   • • • • • •   308 OBERMANN   59
    NOR GOD TOO MUCH A MAN   • • • • • • •   308 OBERMANN   60
    CLEARER HOW MUCH THAN OURS YET WE   • • • •   308 OBERMANN   63
    TOO FAST WE LIVE TOO MUCH ARE TRIED   • • • •   308 OBERMANN   77
    THAT MUCH-LOVED INLAND SEA   • • • • • •   311 OBERMANN   162
    THOUGH MUCH BE STILL UNWON   • • • • • • • •   322 OBERMANN MORE   290
    MUCH TURBULENCE AND LITTLE CONSTANCY   • • • •   337 MEROPE   234
    NOT MUCH A TYRANT THY FREE SPEECH DISPLAYS ME   • •   340 MEROPE   350
    THUS MUCH FROM ARCAS MY OLD SERVANT TRUE   • • •   351 MEROPE   616
    MUCH IS THERE WHICH THE SEA   • • • • • • •   351 MEROPE   622
    AS MUCH TO THE KINGS WISH MORE TO HIS SHAME   • •   364 MEROPE   968
    HOW MUCH MEN THINK ME ABJECT VOID OF HEART   • •   366 MEROPE   1016
    MAIDENS AND READS EXPERIENCE MUCH AMISS   • • • •   382 MEROPE   1334
    SO MUCH IS DUE TO TRUTH EVEN TOWRDS OUR FOE   • •   388 MEROPE   1493
    ALMOST AS MUCH AS THE NEW DANCING-GIRL   • • • •   407 EMPEDOCLES I 1   35
    AND MUCH MAY STILL EXIST   • • • • • • • •   421 EMPEDOCLES I 2   284
    NOT MUCH I KNOW YOU PRIZE   • • • • • • •   426 EMPEDOCLES I 2   407
    NOT MUCH THOU KNOWST I PRIZE   • • • • • •   426 EMPEDOCLES I 2   V 407
    MUCH I DOUBT IF THEY SHALL HAVE   • • • • •   454 POOR MATTHIAS   81
    LITTLE HELPING WOUNDING MUCH   • • • • • • •   457 POOR MATTHIAS   167
    MOVES ME SO MUCH NOT HECUBAS GRIEF NOR PRIAM   HOMER TRANS   24
        MY FATHERS
    THAT HAST SO MUCH REFLECTED BUT ALAS • • • • • •   LUCRETIUS 1   3
    SWIMS ON AN OBSCURE MUCH WE MIGHT HAVE BEEN   • •   FRAGMENT 3   2

MUFFLE
    THAT MUFFLE ITS WET BANKS BUT GLADE • • • • • •   414 EMPEDOCLES I 2   51
    THEIR FIRST GREEN MUFFLE ON THE GROUND • • • •   484 ROME-SICKNESS   16

MUFFLED
    MUFFLED ITS WALLS AND ON THE STONE-STREWN ROOF • •   25 DREAM   17
    AND WATCH THE WARM GREEN-MUFFLED CUMNER HILLS • •   257 SCHOLAR-GIPSY   69
    AND OPEN JASMINE-MUFFLED LATTICES • • • • • •   264 THYRSIS   68
    WHENCE THE RIDGD PINE-MUFFLED ROOTS • • • • • •   433 EMPEDOCLES II   V 137

MULBERRIES
    SLAKE THEIR PARCHD THROATS WITH SUGARD MULBERRIES   66 SOHRAB RUSTUM   166

MULBERRY
    UNDER SOME MULBERRY-TREES I FOUND • • • • • •   90 SICK KING BOKH   67

MULE
    ON HIS WHITE MULE ACROSS THE BRIDGE • • • • • •   160 NECKAN   47
    AND VANISHED WITH HIS MULE • • • • • •   161 NECKAN   58
    THE MULE-TRACK FROM SAINT LAURENT GOES • • •   299 GRANDE CHARTR   4
    I SADDLED MY WHITE MULE AND ALL NIGHT LONG • • •   407 EMPEDOCLES I 1   44
    FOR I MUST BE ALONE LEAVE ME ONE MULE • • • •   428 EMPEDOCLES I 2   465

MULES
    THE MULES I THINK WILL NOT BE HERE THIS HOUR • •   406 EMPEDOCLES I 1   1
    WHOSE MULES I FOLLOWD MAY BE COMING UP • • •   407 EMPEDOCLES I 1   22
    THE MULES MUST BE BELOW FAR DOWN I HEAR • • •   407 EMPEDOCLES I 1   27
    I SAW THE MULES AND LITTER IN THE COURT • • •   407 EMPEDOCLES I 1   41
    TILL THE SLOW MULES SHOULD CLIMB IN SIGHT AGAIN •   408 EMPEDOCLES I 1   48
    CROUCH IN THE WOOD FIRST TILL THE MULES HAVE PASSD   408 EMPEDOCLES I 1   50
    CROUCH IN THE BRUSHWOOD TILL THE MULES HAVE PASSD   411 EMPEDOCLES I 1   166

MULLIOND
    FROM HER MULLIOND CHAMBER-CASEMENT • • • • • •   13 CHURCH BROU 1   11
    THROUGH WHOSE MULLIOND WINDOWS CLEAR • • • • • •   148 TRISTRAM 2   169

MULTIPLIED
    HEIGHTEND AND MULTIPLIED POWER • • • • • • • •   281 HAWORTH CHURCH   29

MULTITUDE
    ROLL THROUGH THE HEAVING MULTITUDE • • • • • •   57 RESIGNATION   157
    SUCH MULTITUDE OF HEAVENLY STRAINS • • • • • •   222 EPILOG LAOCOON   33
    THE IGNORANT HEADLONG MULTITUDE • • • • • •   353 MEROPE   673
    THOU FENCEST HIM FROM THE MULTITUDE • • • • • •   435 EMPEDOCLES II   211

MUNDANE
    ETERNAL MUNDANE SPECTACLE • • • • • • •   59 RESIGNATION   228
    AIRY ANTE-MUNDANE THRONG • • • • • • • •   456 POOR MATTHIAS   135

MURDER
    BREATHING SELF-MURDER FRENZY SPITE • • • • • •   157 SAINT BRANDAN   31
    THAT MURDER MOVES THIS BREACH THAT THOU WOULDST CLOSE   335 MEROPE   187
    WAS BY THAT MURDER OPEND THAT ONE CHILD • • •   335 MEROPE   188
    BLOW OFF THE SPOT OF MURDER FROM HIS NAME • • •   336 MEROPE   200
    MURDER BUT WHAT IS MURDER WHEN A WRETCH • • •   336 MEROPE   201
    MURDER BUT WHAT IS MURDER WHEN A WRETCH • • •   336 MEROPE   201
    WE CALL IT MURDER CRUSH HIM BRAND HIS NAME • • •   336 MEROPE   203
    RANKS ANY MAN WITH MURDER SUCH AN ACT • • • •   336 MEROPE   208
    WITH GRIEVOUS DEEDS PERHAPS WITH MURDER NO • • •   336 MEROPE   209
    FIND THEN SUCH CAUSE THE CHARGE OF MURDER FALLS •   336 MEROPE   210
    MURDER LET OTHERS CALL THIS IF THEY WILL • • •   338 MEROPE   276
    TYRANTS THINK HIM THEY MURDER NOT THEY SPARE • •   340 MEROPE   349
    TO HAVE ANOTHER MURDER IN THESE HALLS • • • •   349 MEROPE   562
    MURDER DISCORD AND HATE • • • • • • • •   361 MEROPE   910
    THAT STERN WORD MURDER HAD TOO DREAD A SOUND • •   365 MEROPE   992
    ONE LAST MURDER-SAVED CHILD • • • • • • •   369 MEROPE   1102
    HIS MESSAGES THEN POINT NOT TO THY MURDER • • •   380 MEROPE   1282
    THAT HOUSE LIKE OURS INTESTINE MURDER MAIMS • •   384 MEROPE   1392
    A MOTHERS MURDER NEEDED HEST DIVINE • • • • •   385 MEROPE   1402
    THAT MURDER DRAWS THIS BREACH THAT THOU WOULDST CLOSE   335 MEROPE   V 187
    AND THIS PERFIDIOUS MURDER WHO REVEALD • • • •   364 MEROPE   V
    BUT NOT A WORD APPEARS OF MURDER HERE • • • •   364 MEROPE   V

MURDERD
    AM MEROPE THY MURDERD MASTERS WIFE • • • • • •   335 MEROPE   184
    HAD IN A FATHERS PLACE HE BASELY MURDERD • • •   364 MEROPE   977
    LAST-MURDERD WHO REPROACHFULLY WILT SAY • • •   367 MEROPE   1042
    FAITHLESSLY MURDERD HIS FRIEND • • • • • •   371 MEROPE   1124
    TO THE DEAR NEXT-OF-KIN OF HIM HE MURDERD • • •   374 MEROPE   1197
    THEIR MURDERD RULERS TERRIBLY AVENGED • • • •   390 MEROPE   1566
    OF AEPYTUS THY MURDERD MASTERS SON • • • • •   402 MEROPE   1926

MURDERED
    CAN VENGEANCE GIVE ME BACK THE MURDERED NO • • • •   349 MEROPE   567

MURDERER
    BY ME SHALL VENGEANCE ON THE MURDERER LOK • • •   96 BALDER DEAD 1   37
    AND THEN HIS MURDERER THESE OFFENDING TEARS • •   335 MEROPE   186
    NOT THE BLACK CREDIT OF HIS MURDERER • • • • • •   365 MEROPE   991

MURDERER   (CONTINUED)
    HE HAD HIS MURDERER READY AND THE SWORD   • • • • 366 MEROPE   1000
    THE MURDERER AND HIS IMPIOUS SETTER-ON   • • • • 368 MEROPE   1072
    HAVEN THE MURDERER HAD DROPPD • • • • • • 371 MEROPE   1128
    WHAT DO I SEE A MURDERER AT DEATHS DOOR • • • • 374 MEROPE   1195
    THEREFORE NO WORDS A MURDERER AND A CAPTIVE   • • 374 MEROPE   1196
    HIS SON FROM VENGEANCE ON HIS MURDERER   • • • • 385 MEROPE   1415
    PAST EXPECTATION HATH THY MURDERER BUILT   • • • 386 MEROPE   1435
    THY FATHERS MURDERER IN THE PUBLIC PLACE   • • • 391 MEROPE   1588

MURDERERS
    IN CALLING VENGEANCE ON A MURDERERS HEAD   • • • 348 MEROPE   549
    THE FAITHLESS MURDERERS OWN NO OTHER TONGUE   • • 364 MEROPE   V

MURDEROUS
    WHO SAVED HIM FROM THESE MURDEROUS HALLS A BABE • • 351 MEROPE   617
    WHAT WAVST THOU OFF THAT MURDEROUS AXE AWAY   • • 376 MEROPE   1215

MURDERS
    TO MURDERS DREAD ARENA WHERE I SAW   • • • • • 387 MEROPE   1462
    MURDERS UNCERTAIN SECRET PERILOUS GAME   • • • • 388 MEROPE   1501
    TRACKD BY MURDERS BLOODY SWORD NO MORE   • • • • 482 THEKLAS ANSWER   16

MURKY
    COME BANEFUL MISCHIEF FROM THY MURKY DEN   • • • • 367 MEROPE   1063

MURMUR
    MIXD WITH THE MURMUR OF THE MOVING NILE   • • • • 12 MYCERINUS   127
    COME YOU MURMUR WITH A SIGH • • • • • • • 28 NEW SIRENS   62
    THE MURMUR OF A THOUSAND YEARS • • • • • • 57 RESIGNATION   188
    FROM THE CHURCH CAME A MURMUR OF FOLK AT THEIR PRAYERS 163 FORSAKEN MERM   72
    FITFUL EARTH-MURMUR • • • • • • • • 194 STRAYED REVEL   284
    THE FLIES A SUMMER-MURMUR MADE • • • • • • 222 EPILOG LAOCOON   41
    THE MURMUR OF ITS WAVES DOTH HEAR   • • • • • 226 EPILOG LAOCOON   180
    THE MURMUR OF NATURE REPLY • • • • • • 230 YOUTH OF NATURE 78
    MURMUR OF LIVING • • • • • • • • 233 YOUTH OF MAN   51
    AND HEARS ITS WINDING MURMUR AND HE SEES   • • • 247 BURIED LIFE   89
    ALL THE LIVE MURMUR OF A SUMMERS DAY   • • • • 255 SCHOLAR-GIPSY   20
    THE MURMUR OF THIS MIDLAND DEEP • • • • • 276 SOUTHERN NIGHT 21
    MURMUR OF PARIS OUTSIDE • • • • • • 292 HEINES GRAVE   10
    THOUGH HERE A MOUNTAIN-MURMUR SWELLS • • • • 307 OBERMANN   29
    WITH FATE I MURMUR NOT NOR CHIDE   • • • • • 321 OBERMANN MORE 267
    WHICH THE RHONES MURMUR FILLS • • • • • • 324 OBERMANN MORE 344
    TO THE WEST-WINDS MURMUR • • • • • • • 391 MEROPE   1619
    HEARD THE MURMUR OF THE MOLE • • • • • • 458 POOR MATTHIAS   201
    WHAT THE TROJAN MEN AND TROJAN WOMEN MIGHT MURMUR   HOMER TRANS   15
    CALM THE MURMUR OF THE FOUNTAINS • • • • • META CLOISTER   15
    COOL THE MURMUR OF THE FOUNTAINS • • • • • META CLOISTER   V 15

MURMURD
    AND MURMURD HELP ME OR I DIE • • • • • • 158 SAINT BRANDAN   50
    IS IT THEN THOU HE MURMURD AND WITH THAT   • • • 402 MEROPE   1928
    SHOOK BACK HIS TANGLED LOCKS AND MURMURD PEACE • • 477 CROMWELL   174
    AND THE WIND MURMURD ROUND HIM AND HE STOOD   • • 479 CROMWELL   239

MURMURED
    MIGHT WELL BE MINGLING AT THAT MURMURED SIGH   • • 469 ALARIC AT ROME   179

MURMURING
    MURMURING ART THOU STILL UNKIND • • • • • • 23 MEMORY-PICTURE 36
    FOR MAN WOULD MAKE NO MURMURING WERE HIS WILL OBEYD 417 EMPEDOCLES I 2 151
    FLOAT THERE NOT VOICES ON THE MURMURING WIND   • • 468 ALARIC AT ROME   164
    AND GENTLY SHALL THE MURMURING RIPPLES FLOW   • • 469 ALARIC AT ROME   197

MURMUROUS
    WHILE OER THE DUSTY PLAIN THE MURMUROUS THRONG • • 473 CROMWELL   43

MURMURS
    MURMURS AND SCENTS OF THE INFINITE SEA   • • • • 254 FUTURE   87
    AND MURMURS OF THE ADRIATIC COME   • • • • • 427 EMPEDOCLES I 2 455

MUSE
    YET WHEN I MUSE ON WHAT LIFE IS I SEEM   • • • • 7 REP FRIEND CONT   1
    WHERE SOME MUSE WITH HALF-CURVED FROWN   • • • • 27 NEW SIRENS   26
    YES I MUSE AND IF THE DAWNING • • • • • • 29 NEW SIRENS   105
    AH ME I MUSE WHAT THIS YOUNG FOX MAY MEAN   • • • 71 SOHRAB RUSTUM   347
    SUCH POETS IS YOUR BRIDE THE MUSE YOUNG GAY   • 166 AUSTERITY POET   12
    THE SHADOW OF A MARBLE MUSE OF YORE   • • • • 168 RACHEL 2   6
    THOUGH THE MUSE BE GONE AWAY • • • • • • 227 PERSIST POETRY   1
    MOURNFUL HOMAGE THE MUSE • • • • • • • 281 HAWORTH CHURCH 35
    ON THEE TOO DID THE MUSE • • • • • • • 285 HAWORTH CHURCH 108
    SO I SANG BUT THE MUSE • • • • • • • • 285 HAWORTH CHURCH 125
    YOUNGER BUT THIS THE MUSE • • • • • • • 283 HAWORTH CHURCH V
    AND SEEMD TO MUSE AWHILE THEN RAISED HIS EYES   • 402 MEROPE   1913
    WE SHUT OUR EYES AND MUSE • • • • • • 423 EMPEDOCLES I 2 327
    POST-HASTE TO COBHAM CALLS THE MUSE • • • • • 458 KAISER DEAD   2

MUSED
    IF TOO HOTLY MUSED UPON • • • • • • • • 23 MEMORY-PICTURE 10
    MUSED ON WARM THE HEART ANEW • • • • • • 30 NEW SIRENS   134

MUSED   (CONTINUED)
        MUSED MUCH LOVED LIFE A LITTLE LOATHED IT MORE   . .   43 GIPSY CHILD   36
        THE LONG-MUSED THOUGHT TO NORTH SOUTH EAST AND WEST   45 IN UTRUMQUE PAR   6
        BUT MY LORD MUSED A SPACE AND SAID   . . . . . .   90 SICK KING BOKH   89
        HE MUSED THE EARTH HATH KINDNESS   . . . . . .   161 NECKAN   V 61
        WHILE THUS I MUSED NIGHT GENTLY RAN   . . . . . .   314 OBERMANN MORE   57
        SO WELL SHE MUSED A MORNING BROKE   . . . . . .   316 OBERMANN MORE   113

MUSES
        HOLD THE PURE MUSES   . . . .   50 CONSOLATION   17
        AGE AND THE MUSES   . . . .   189 STRAYED REVEL   120
        AND AT THE BANQUET ALL THE MUSES SANG   . . . .   427 EMPEDOCLES I 2   451
        AND THE ATTENTIVE MUSES SAID   . . . .   433 EMPEDOCLES II   145

MUSIC
        ERE THEIR BOAT-MUSIC SOUND ERE THEIR BROIDERD   19 MODERN SAPPHO   8
               FLAGS GLEAM
        NOTES OF WILD PASTORAL MUSIC OVER ALL   . . . .   25 DREAM   12
        BY FAINT MUSIC GUIDED RANGING   . . . .   27 NEW SIRENS   29
        BLEW SUCH MUSIC AS A GOD MAY FRAME   . . . . . .   29 NEW SIRENS   104
        MAR THE MUSIC OF YOUR FEASTS IN VAIN   . . . . .   32 NEW SIRENS   170
        BLAME THE MUSIC OF YOUR FEASTS IN VAIN . . . . .   32 NEW SIRENS   V 170
        STRAINS OF GLAD MUSIC AT A FUNERAL   . . . . . .   36 VOICE   22
        WHEN DID MUSIC COME THIS WAY   . . . . . .   162 FORSAKEN MERM   46
        LENT IT THE MUSIC OF ITS TREES AT DAWN . . . . .   175 PARTING   20
        THAN PANS FLUTE-MUSIC   . . . .   187 STRAYED REVEL   67
        WHY MUSIC AND THE OTHER ARTS   . . . .   221 EPILOG LAOCOON   9
        THE WORLD OF MUSIC I EXCLAIMD . . . .   223 EPILOG LAOCOON   77
        AND THROUGH THE STREAM OF MUSIC TELL   . . . . .   223 EPILOG LAOCOON   85
        PAGE AFTER PAGE OF MUSIC TURN . . . .   224 EPILOG LAOCOON   103
        WE HEARD AFAR FAINT MUSIC PLAY . . . .   224 EPILOG LAOCOON   110
        WHAT THOUGH THE MUSIC OF THY RUSTIC FLUTE . . .   269 THYRSIS   221
        THAT BUGLE-MUSIC ON THE BREEZE . . . .   305 GRANDE CHARTR   189
        FAR IN THE WOODS AHEAD THEIR MUSIC RANG   . . .   357 MEROPE   792
        WITH MUSIC TO HAVE DRAWN THE STARS FROM HEAVEN   .   409 EMPEDOCLES I 1   81
        BUT HE HAS LAID THE USE OF MUSIC BY   . . . . .   409 EMPEDOCLES I 1   83
        CHAIN MADMEN BY THE MUSIC OF HIS LYRE . . . . .   410 EMPEDOCLES I 1   116
        HOW HIS BROW LIGHTEND AS THE MUSIC ROSE   . . .   428 EMPEDOCLES I 2   483
        WHEN THROUGH THY CAVES THOU HEAREST MUSIC SWELL .   431 EMPEDOCLES II   66
        THE MUSIC OF THE LYRE BLOWS AWAY   . . . . .   432 EMPEDOCLES II   123
        HIS LATEST LOFTIEST MUSIC SMOTE HIS EAR   . . .   478 CROMWELL   210
        SET THINE EARS WITH SOUL-FRAUGHT MUSIC RINGING .   482 THEKLAS ANSWER   7
        AND STEALS THE HONIED MUSIC OF HIS TONGUE . . .   FRAGMENT 1   8

MUSICAL
        MUSICAL WATER HALF-HID   . . . .   297 HEINES GRAVE   161
        MUSICAL THROUGH ITALIAN TREES . . . .   303 GRANDE CHARTR   141

MUSICIAN
        THE INSPIRED MUSICIAN WHAT A RANGE   . . . . .   223 EPILOG LAOCOON   81
        BE PAINTER AND MUSICIAN TOO   . . . .   225 EPILOG LAOCOON   130
        BUT NOT AS THE MUSICIAN WELL   . . . .   226 EPILOG LAOCOON   184
        NOR NO MUSICIAN MADE AS THEY   . . . .   227 EPILOG LAOCOON   202

MUSICIANS
        SO DEEP AS THE MUSICIANS LORE . . . .   225 EPILOG LAOCOON   136

MUSING
        THESE MUSING FITS IN THE GREEN WOOD   . . . . .   138 TRISTRAM 1   247
        OR ELSE SHE WILL FALL MUSING HER BLUE EYES . . .   152 TRISTRAM 3   90
        SOME VACANT AND SOME MUSING WENT   . . . . .   224 EPILOG LAOCOON   119
        TO BE LEFT MUSING THESE SOFT NIGHTS ALONE . . .   409 EMPEDOCLES I 1   92

MUSINGS
        MUSINGS THAT ERE THEY COULD GROW RIPE WERE FLOWN . . 41 GIPSY CHILD   V 19
        AH THEY WALK IN STARRY MUSINGS . . . .   META CLOISTER   3

MUSK
        SOON WILL THE MUSK CARNATIONS BREAK AND SWELL   . . 264 THYRSIS   63

MUSPEL
        AND FROM THE FLAMING WORLD WHERE MUSPEL REIGNS   . . 121 BALDER DEAD 3   262

MUSPELS
        WHEN HE GUIDES MUSPELS CHILDREN TO THEIR BOURNE   . . 111 BALDER DEAD 2   224
        WHEN MUSPELS CHILDREN SHALL BELEAGUER HEAVEN   . . 115 BALDER DEAD 3   69

MUTE
        OF LABOUR THAT WITH MUTE ADVANCE OUTGOES   . . . .   1 QUIET WORK   V 6
        STAND MUTE SELF-CENTRED STERN AND DREAM NO MORE . . 42 GIPSY CHILD   32
        YET FAUSTA THE MUTE TURF WE TREAD   . . . . .   60 RESIGNATION   265
        SWEEPING THE DUST CAME NEAR AND IN MUTE WOE . .   82 SOHRAB RUSTUM   732
        MUTE GAZING AFTER THEM IN TEARS AND FAIN   . . .   129 BALDER DEAD 3   555
        THE MOUNT IS MUTE THE CHANNEL DRY . . . . .   213 PROGRESS POESY   11
        SHEPHERD WHY MUTE . . . .   219 BACCHANALIA 1   41
        SAY WHY SO MUTE   . . . .   220 BACCHANALIA 2   46
        THOU O NATURE WAST MUTE   . . . .   233 YOUTH OF MAN   38
        MUTE AS OF OLD DAYS FLEW   . . . .   233 YOUTH OF MAN   39
        THOU O NATURE WERT MUTE   . . . .   233 YOUTH OF MAN   V 38
        IT FAILD AND THOU WAST MUTE   . . . .   269 THYRSIS   226
        IT FAILD AND THOU WERT MUTE   . . . .   269 THYRSIS   V 226

MUTE   (CONTINUED)
        BUT WE STAND MUTE AND WATCH THE WAVES   • • • •   303 GRANDE CHARTR   126
        BUT THEY STAND MUTE AND WATCH THE WAVES   • • • •   303 GRANDE CHARTR   V 126
        MUTE IN THEIR MEADOWS LONE   • • • • • •   306 OBERMANN   6
        THE SOUL OF THEIR MUTE SNOWS   • • • • • •   307 OBERMANN   V 28
        BUT MUTE THOU SATST AND EACH MESSENIAN HEART   • •   383 MEROPE   1373
        AND HOLDS MEN MUTE TO SEE WHERE IT WILL RISE   • •   410 EMPEDOCLES I 1   114
        SO LOATH TO SUFFER MUTE   • • • • • • • •   421 EMPEDOCLES I 2   277
        DEAD AND MUTE OUR TINY FRIEND   • • • • • •   452 POOR MATTHIAS   14
        FIXING WITH A MUTE REGARD   • • • • • • • •   456 POOR MATTHIAS   121
        PERCHANCE SOME MUTE MEMORIAL AT THEIR HEAD   • • •   464 ALARIC AT ROME   58

MUTELY
        OUT OF THE LIGHT AND MUTELY WHICH AVOIDS   • • • • 199 EARLY DEATH   3
        MUTELY SHE REGARDED   • • • • • • • • •   393 MEROPE   1665

MUTTER
        BUT SPELLS TO MUTTER   • • • • • • • • • •   432 EMPEDOCLES II   117

MUTTERS
        HARK HE MUTTERS IN HIS SLEEP   • • • • • • •   133 TRISTRAM 1   87
        WHILE HE MUTTERS BROKENLY   • • • • • • • •   133 TRISTRAM 1   93
        AS HE MUTTERS BROKENLY   • • • • • • • • •   133 TRISTRAM 1   V 93
        YES THE CROWD MUTTERS THAT REMORSEFUL FEAR   • • • • 333 MEROPE   97

MY
        WHO PROP THOU ASKST IN THESE BAD DAYS MY MIND   • •   2 TO A FRIEND   1
        MY SPECIAL THANKS WHOSE EVEN-BALANCED SOUL   • • • •   2 TO A FRIEND   9
        IT CHANCED I KNOW NOT HOW MY DREAM WAS FLED   • •   EMERSONS ESSAYS   V 8
        IT CHANCED I KNOW NOT HOW MY JOY WAS FLED   • • •   EMERSONS ESSAYS   V 8
        NOT BY THE JUSTICE THAT MY FATHER SPURND   • • •   8 MYCERINUS   1
        NOT FOR THE THOUSANDS WHOM MY FATHER SLEW   • • •   8 MYCERINUS   2
        I WILL UNFOLD MY SENTENCE AND MY CRIME   • • • •   9 MYCERINUS   7
        I WILL UNFOLD MY SENTENCE AND MY CRIME   • • • •   9 MYCERINUS   7
        MY CRIME THAT RAPT IN REVERENTIAL AWE   • • • •   9 MYCERINUS   8
        MY FATHER LOVED INJUSTICE AND LIVED LONG   • • • •   9 MYCERINUS   13
        THE GODS DECLARE MY RECOMPENCE TO-DAY   • • • •   9 MYCERINUS   16
        YET SURELY O MY PEOPLE DID I DEEM   • • • • •   9 MYCERINUS   19
        MY SAND RUNS SHORT AND AS YON STAR-SHOT RAY   • • •   10 MYCERINUS   56
        TIS MY LORD COME BACK FROM HUNTING   • • • • •   14 CHURCH BROU 1   39
        IN MY CASTLE ALL IS SORROW   • • • • • • •   15 CHURCH BROU 1   73
        HERE LEAN MY HEAD ON THIS COLD BALUSTRADE   • • •   19 MODERN SAPPHO   4
        LET MY TURN IF IT WILL COME BE SWIFT IN ARRIVING • • 20 MODERN SAPPHO   31
        HERE LEAN MY HEAD ON THIS COOL BALUSTRADE   • • •   19 MODERN SAPPHO   V 4
        LAUGH MY FRIENDS AND WITHOUT BLAME   • • • •   22 MEMORY-PICTURE   1
        WHAT MY FRIENDS THESE FEEBLE LINES   • • • •   24 MEMORY-PICTURE   49
        SHOW YOU SAY MY LOVE DECLINES   • • • • • •   24 MEMORY-PICTURE   50
        BUT MY YOUTH REMINDS ME THOU   • • • • • •   22 MEMORY-PICTURE V
        BUT FOR ME MY THOUGHTS ARE STRAYING   • • • •   29 NEW SIRENS   93
        WOULD YOU FREEZE MY TOO LOUD BOLDNESS   • • •   31 NEW SIRENS   159
        O SWEET PLEADERS DOTH MY LOT   • • • • • •   31 NEW SIRENS   164
        O SPEAK ONCE AND SHAME MY SADNESS   • • • • •   32 NEW SIRENS   167
        STANDS AT DAYBREAK WEEPING BY MY SIDE   • • •   35 NEW SIRENS   274
        WOULD YOU FREEZE MY LOUDER BOLDNESS   • • • •   31 NEW SIRENS   V 159
        O SPEAK ONCE AND LET MY SADNESS   • • • • •   32 NEW SIRENS   V 167
        BLEW SUCH A THRILLING SUMMONS TO MY WILL   • • •   36 VOICE   37
        MADE MY TOST HEART ITS VERY LIFE-BLOOD SPILL   • •   36 VOICE   39
        DRAIND ALL THE LIFE MY FULL HEART HAD TO SPILL   • • 36 VOICE   V 39
        AFTER SHORT COMMERCE WITH ME FEAR MY FROWN   • • •   37 WORLDS TRIUMPHS   8
        THOU TOO WHEN THOU AGAINST MY CRIMES WOULDST CRY •   38 WORLDS TRIUMPHS   9
        THUS THOU WHEN THOU AGAINST MY CRIMES WOULDST CRY   38 WORLDS TRIUMPHS V 9
        I HAVE KEPT UNINFRINGED MY NATURES LAW   • • •   40 HUMAN LIFE   4
        OMIT OMIT MY SIMPLE FRIEND   • • • • • • •   47 HORATIAN ECHO   1
        WEIGHS DOWN MY SOUL   • • • • • • • •   50 CONSOLATION   5
        AND I WILL TELL THEE WHAT MY HEART DESIRES   • • •   62 SOHRAB RUSTUM   41
        AT MY BOYS YEARS THE COURAGE OF A MAN   • • •   62 SOHRAB RUSTUM   45
        RUSTUM MY FATHER WHO I HOPED SHOULD GREET   • • •   62 SOHRAB RUSTUM   50
        THAT WERE FAR BEST MY SON TO STAY WITH US   • • •   63 SOHRAB RUSTUM   71
        THERE GO THOU WILT NOT YET MY HEART FOREBODES   • •   63 SOHRAB RUSTUM   86
        MY FATHER WHOM THE ROBBER AFGHANS VEX   • • •   68 SOHRAB RUSTUM   233
        THERE WOULD I GO AND HANG MY ARMOUR UP   • • •   68 SOHRAB RUSTUM   236
        AND WITH MY GREAT NAME FENCE THAT WEAK OLD MAN   •   68 SOHRAB RUSTUM   237
        AND REST MY AGE AND HEAR OF SOHRABS FAME   • • •   68 SOHRAB RUSTUM   239
        TO IRAN AND BE AS MY SON TO ME   • • • • •   71 SOHRAB RUSTUM   331
        AND FIGHT BENEATH MY BANNER TILL I DIE   • • •   71 SOHRAB RUSTUM   332
        AND PRAISE MY FAME AND PROFFER COURTEOUS GIFTS   •   71 SOHRAB RUSTUM   353
        UPON THE SUMMER-FLOODS AND NOT MY BONES   • • •   74 SOHRAB RUSTUM   428
        NO WHEN I SEE THEE WRATH FORSAKES MY SOUL   • • •   74 SOHRAB RUSTUM   430
        WHO ART THOU THEN THAT CANST SO TOUCH MY SOUL   • •   74 SOHRAB RUSTUM   432
        BUT NEVER WAS MY HEART THUS TOUCHD BEFORE   • • •   74 SOHRAB RUSTUM   436
        BUT THAT BELOVED NAME UNNERVED MY ARM   • • •   77 SOHRAB RUSTUM   547
        WHICH TROUBLES ALL MY HEART AND MADE MY SHIELD   •   77 SOHRAB RUSTUM   549
        WHICH TROUBLES ALL MY HEART AND MADE MY SHIELD   •   77 SOHRAB RUSTUM   549
        AND NOW THOU BOASTEST AND INSULTST MY-FATE   • • •   77 SOHRAB RUSTUM   551
        THE MIGHTY RUSTUM SHALL AVENGE MY DEATH   • • •   77 SOHRAB RUSTUM   553
        MY FATHER WHOM I SEEK THROUGH ALL THE WORLD   • • •   77 SOHRAB RUSTUM   554
        HE SHALL AVENGE MY DEATH AND PUNISH THEE   • • •   77 SOHRAB RUSTUM   555
        MY MOTHER WHO IN ADER-BAIJAN DWELLS   • • • •   78 SOHRAB RUSTUM   590
        MAN WHO ART THOU WHO DOST DENY MY WORDS   • • •   80 SOHRAB RUSTUM   655
        THAT SEAL WHICH RUSTUM TO MY MOTHER GAVE   • • •   80 SOHRAB RUSTUM   659

MY   (CONTINUED)

THE DOOM WHICH AT MY BIRTH WAS WRITTEN DOWN   • • 82 SOHRAB RUSTUM 709
SURELY MY HEART CRIED OUT THAT IT WAS THOU • • • • 82 SOHRAB RUSTUM 711
THE STRIFE AND HURLD ME ON MY FATHERS SPEAR • • • 82 SOHRAB RUSTUM 715
MY FATHER LET ME FEEL THAT I HAVE FOUND • • • • 82 SOHRAB RUSTUM 717
MY HEAD BETWIXT THY HANDS AND KISS MY CHEEKS • • 82 SOHRAB RUSTUM 719
MY HEAD BETWIXT THY HANDS AND KISS MY CHEEKS • • 82 SOHRAB RUSTUM 719
AND WASH THEM WITH THY TEARS AND SAY MY SON • • 82 SOHRAB RUSTUM 720
QUICK QUICK FOR NUMBERD ARE MY SANDS OF LIFE • • 82 SOHRAB RUSTUM 721
MY MOTHER TOLD ME OF THEE THOU BRAVE STEED • • • 83 SOHRAB RUSTUM 743
MY TERRIBLE FATHERS TERRIBLE HORSE AND SAID • • 83 SOHRAB RUSTUM 744
COME LET ME LAY MY HAND UPON THY MANE • • • • 83 SOHRAB RUSTUM 746
AND SNUFFD THE BREEZES OF MY FATHERS HOME • • • 83 SOHRAB RUSTUM 749
HAVE NEVER KNOWN MY GRANDSIRES FURROWD FACE • • 83 SOHRAB RUSTUM 756
NOR SLAKED MY THIRST AT THE CLEAR HELMUND STREAM • 83 SOHRAB RUSTUM 758
BUT LODGED AMONG MY FATHERS FOES AND SEEN • • • 83 SOHRAB RUSTUM 759
ROLL TUMBLING IN THE CURRENT OER MY HEAD • • • 83 SOHRAB RUSTUM 770
DESIRE NOT THAT MY FATHER THOU MUST LIVE • • • 84 SOHRAB RUSTUM 772
THOU ART MY FATHER AND THY GAIN IS MINE • • • 84 SOHRAB RUSTUM 777
THEY FOLLOWD ME MY HOPE MY FAME MY STAR • • • 84 SOHRAB RUSTUM 781
THEY FOLLOWD ME MY HOPE MY FAME MY STAR • • • 84 SOHRAB RUSTUM 781
THEY FOLLOWD ME MY HOPE MY FAME MY STAR • • • 84 SOHRAB RUSTUM 781
AND HEAP A STATELY MOUND ABOVE MY BONES • • • 84 SOHRAB RUSTUM 788
MAY SEE MY TOMB A GREAT WAY OFF AND CRY • • • 84 SOHRAB RUSTUM 791
AND I BE NOT FORGOTTEN IN MY GRAVE • • • 84 SOHRAB RUSTUM 794
FEAR NOT AS THOU HAST SAID SOHRAB MY SON • • • 84 SOHRAB RUSTUM 796
SO SHALL IT BE FOR I WILL BURN MY TENTS • • • 84 SOHRAB RUSTUM 797
WITH THE SNOW-HEADED ZAL AND ALL MY FRIENDS • • 84 SOHRAB RUSTUM 801
MIGHT BE ONCE MORE ALIVE MY BITTEREST FOES • • 85 SOHRAB RUSTUM 810
SO THOU MIGHTEST LIVE TOO MY SON MY SON • • • 85 SOHRAB RUSTUM 815
SO THOU MIGHTEST LIVE TOO MY SON MY SON • • • 85 SOHRAB RUSTUM 815
AND ZAL MIGHT WEEP ABOVE MY GRAVE NOT THINE • • 85 SOHRAB RUSTUM 821
BUT NOW IN BLOOD AND BATTLES WAS MY YOUTH • • 85 SOHRAB RUSTUM 824
AND FULL OF BLOOD AND BATTLES IS MY AGE • • • 85 SOHRAB RUSTUM 825
SOON BE THAT DAY MY SON AND DEEP THAT SEA • • 85 SOHRAB RUSTUM 836
BUT I SHALL CONQUER THAT MY HEART FOREBODES • • 62 SOHRAB RUSTUM V
THERE WOULD I STAY AND HANG MY ARMOUR UP • • • 68 SOHRAB RUSTUM V 236
THE DOOM THAT AT MY BIRTH WAS WRITTEN DOWN • • 82 SOHRAB RUSTUM V 709
MAY SEE MY TOMB A GREAT WAY OFF AND SAY • • • 84 SOHRAB RUSTUM V 791
HOW IS IT WITH MY LORD ALONE • • • • • • 88 SICK KING BOKH 13
FOR ALLAH SHUT MY EARS AND MIND • • • • • 88 SICK KING BOKH 24
WATCHD MY LORDS COMING FORTH AND PUSHD • • • 88 SICK KING BOKH 33
MY GUARDS WHAT PRICK HIM WITH YOUR SPEARS • • 89 SICK KING BOKH 42
AND TO THE MOSQUE MY LORD PASSD ON • • • • 89 SICK KING BOKH 45
MY MAN COMES RUNNING FLECKD WITH BLOOD • • • 89 SICK KING BOKH 50
MY LORD O KING DO RIGHT I PRAY • • • • • 89 SICK KING BOKH 53
I FILLD MY PITCHER AND STOLE HOME • • • • 90 SICK KING BOKH 70
NOW MEANWHILE HAD MY BRETHREN FOUND • • • 90 SICK KING BOKH 77
AND CALLD MY MOTHER AND THEY ALL • • • • 90 SICK KING BOKH 80
THAT THEY SATE WITH IT IN MY SIGHT • • • • 90 SICK KING BOKH 83
ONE WAS MY MOTHER NOW DO RIGHT • • • • • 90 SICK KING BOKH 88
BUT MY LORD MUSED A SPACE AND SAID • • • • 90 SICK KING BOKH 89
MY LORD HAD COVERD UP HIS FACE • • • • • 91 SICK KING BOKH 125
MY HEAD IS BURNING AND A HEAT • • • • • 93 SICK KING BOKH 183
IS IN MY SKIN WHICH ANGERS ME • • • • • 93 SICK KING BOKH 184
THIS MAN MY PITY COULD NOT SAVE • • • • • 95 SICK KING BOKH 226
THERE LAY HIS BODY IN MY GRAVE • • • • • 95 SICK KING BOKH 228
FOR WHO WILL BEAR MY HATEFUL SIGHT IN HEAVEN • • 98 BALDER DEAD 1 106
AND MAKE EXCHANGE AND GIVE MY LIFE FOR HIS • • 98 BALDER DEAD 1 110
HODER ILL-FATED CHILD OF BALE MY SON • • • 98 BALDER DEAD 1 112
YET IN MY SECRET MIND ONE WAY I KNOW • • • 99 BALDER DEAD 1 128
THEREFORE THYSELF THOU SHALT NOT GO MY SON • • 100 BALDER DEAD 1 188
UPON MY SHIP AND BURN MY CORPSE WITH FIRE • • 103 BALDER DEAD 1 297
UPON MY SHIP AND BURN MY CORPSE WITH FIRE • • 103 BALDER DEAD 1 297
THEY THINK TO BURN AND ALL MY CHOICEST WEALTH • 103 BALDER DEAD 1 299
SO IT RESTORED THEE NANNA TO MY SIDE • • • 103 BALDER DEAD 1 307
THY WAY AND THIS AT LEAST MY PRAYERS AVAIL • • 104 BALDER DEAD 1 309
FEAST IN VALHALLA IN MY FATHERS HALL • • • 104 BALDER DEAD 1 322
SOULS BOUND BELOW MY DAILY PASSERS HERE • • 108 BALDER DEAD 2 110
OF ODIN AND MY HIGH-ROOFD HOUSE IS BUILT • • 108 BALDER DEAD 2 113
UPON MY BRIDGE AND WHEN THEY CROSS I KNOW • • 108 BALDER DEAD 2 121
SMALL BLISS MY RACE HATH OF THE GODS OBTAINED • 110 BALDER DEAD 2 205
THREE MIGHTY CHILDREN TO MY FATHER LOK • • 110 BALDER DEAD 2 206
AND BEND MY HEART AND GIVE HIM BACK TO HEAVEN • 111 BALDER DEAD 2 240
HERMOD THE NIMBLE GILD ME NOT MY DEATH • • 112 BALDER DEAD 2 264
TO BE FULFILLD NOR MY RETURN AS SURE • • • 112 BALDER DEAD 2 269
THOUGH I BE LOVED AND MANY MOURN MY DEATH • • 112 BALDER DEAD 2 270
TO ODIN TO MY FATHER TAKE THIS RING • • • 112 BALDER DEAD 2 274
ODIN MY FATHER AND YE GODS OF HEAVEN • • • 114 BALDER DEAD 3 36
FAREWELL O BALDER BRIGHT AND LOVED MY SON • • 115 BALDER DEAD 3 67
BALDER MY BROTHER THOU ART GONE A ROAD • • 116 BALDER DEAD 3 99
MY LONG-LOST WANDERING ODER THOU HAST MET • • 116 BALDER DEAD 3 101
FOR HE MY HUSBAND LEFT ME HERE TO PINE • • 116 BALDER DEAD 3 106
AND WEEP FROM SHORE TO SHORE MY GOLDEN TEARS • 116 BALDER DEAD 3 110
BUT NEITHER GOD NOR MORTAL HEEDS MY PAIN • • 116 BALDER DEAD 3 111
TO TAKE MY HAND AND WIPE MY TEARS AND SAY • • 116 BALDER DEAD 3 113
TO TAKE MY HAND AND WIPE MY TEARS AND SAY • • 116 BALDER DEAD 3 113
MY TRUANT ODER I SHALL SEE NO MORE • • • 117 BALDER DEAD 3 120
MY DUNGEON WHERE THE SERPENTS STUNG ME DEAD • 117 BALDER DEAD 3 146
AND SAW MY SHEPHERDESS ASLAUGA TEND • • • 117 BALDER DEAD 3 149

MY   (CONTINUED)

```
DRAWN IN HIS CAR BESIDE ME AND MY SONS          120 BALDER DEAD 3      240
ALL THE STRONG BROOD OF HEAVEN TO SWELL MY TRAIN 120 BALDER DEAD 3      241
ME AND MY WORDS THOUGH THOU BE FIRST IN HEAVEN  121 BALDER DEAD 3      283
OF HEAVEN AND COMMUNION WITH MY KIN             125 BALDER DEAD 3      402
BUT ALL I LEFT OF MY OWN ACT AND FLED           125 BALDER DEAD 3      405
MY HATED CONVERSE ON THEE CAME I UP             125 BALDER DEAD 3      414
IN HEAVEN WAS SELDOM PARTED FROM MY SIDE        126 BALDER DEAD 3      460
MY FORMER LIFE AND CHEERS ME EVEN HERE          126 BALDER DEAD 3      462
LOVE ME AND GLADLY BRING FOR MY AWARD           126 BALDER DEAD 3      465
MY FATHER AND HIS PRIDE THE WARRIOR THOR        127 BALDER DEAD 3      491
LONGING WILL STIR WITHIN MY BREAST THOUGH VAIN  127 BALDER DEAD 3      499
TO OTHER GODS IT WERE IS MY ENFORCED            127 BALDER DEAD 3      501
OF AGES AND MY LATE RETURN TO LIGHT             128 BALDER DEAD 3      511
SUCH FOR THE FUTURE IS MY HOPE MEANWHILE        129 BALDER DEAD 3      544
IN MY OWN BREAST AND HAVE TO NONE REVEALD       121 BALDER DEAD 3    V 287
TRUST ME AND GLADLY BRING FOR MY AWARD          126 BALDER DEAD 3    V 465
RAISE ME MY PAGE THIS CANNOT LONG ENDURE        130 TRISTRAM 1          3
REACH ME MY GOLDEN PHIAL STANDS BY THEE         133 TRISTRAM 1        100
PLEDGE ME IN MY GOLDEN CUP                      135 TRISTRAM 1        146
THE SOUTHERN WINTER-PARLOUR BY MY FAY           135 TRISTRAM 1        164
TRISTRAM NAY NAY THOU MUST NOT TAKE MY HAND     135 TRISTRAM 1        166
ABOVE THE DIN HER VOICE IS IN MY EARS           137 TRISTRAM 1        240
I THINK I HAVE A FEVER IN MY BLOOD              139 TRISTRAM 1        280
RIDE DOWN AND BATHE MY HOT BROW IN THE FLOOD    139 TRISTRAM 1        282
IS MY PAGE HERE COME TURN ME TO THE FIRE        139 TRISTRAM 1        298
OF ME SHE RECKS NOT NOR MY VAIN DESIRE          140 TRISTRAM 1        303
I HAVE HAD DREAMS I HAVE HAD DREAMS MY PAGE     140 TRISTRAM 1        304
MY PRINCESS ART THOU THERE SWEET DO NOT WAIT    140 TRISTRAM 1        308
TO BED AND SLEEP MY FEVER IS GONE BY            140 TRISTRAM 1        309
TO-NIGHT MY PAGE SHALL KEEP ME COMPANY          140 TRISTRAM 1        310
REACH ME MY GOLDEN CUP THAT STANDS BY THEE      133 TRISTRAM 1      V 100
OF ME SHE RECKS NOT NOR OF MY DESIRE            140 TRISTRAM 1      V 303
MY PRINCESS ART THOU THERE SWEET TIS TOO LATE   140 TRISTRAM 1      V 308
RAISE THE LIGHT MY PAGE THAT I MAY SEE HER      142 TRISTRAM 2          1
LONG IVE WAITED LONG IVE FOUGHT MY FEVER        142 TRISTRAM 2          3
I AM DYING BUILD THOU MAYST MY GRAVE            142 TRISTRAM 2         12
TAKE MY HAND DEAR TRISTRAM LOOK ON ME           142 TRISTRAM 2         16
AH HARSH FLATTERER LET ALONE MY BEAUTY          143 TRISTRAM 2         21
I LIKE THEE HAVE LEFT MY YOUTH AFAR             143 TRISTRAM 2         22
TAKE MY HAND AND TOUCH THESE WASTED FINGERS     143 TRISTRAM 2         23
SEE MY CHEEK AND LIPS HOW WHITE THEY ARE        143 TRISTRAM 2         24
ROYAL STATE WITH MARC MY DEEP-WRONGD HUSBAND    144 TRISTRAM 2         45
THAT WAS BLISS TO MAKE MY SORROWS FLEE          144 TRISTRAM 2         46
ME A SMILING QUEEN UPON MY THRONE               144 TRISTRAM 2         52
STAY PALE QUEEN FOR EVER BY MY SIDE             144 TRISTRAM 2         68
SWELLS MY HEART AND TAKES MY BREATH AWAY        145 TRISTRAM 2         74
SWELLS MY HEART AND TAKES MY BREATH AWAY        145 TRISTRAM 2         74
HUSH TIS VAIN I FEEL MY END APPROACHING         145 TRISTRAM 2         81
THIS IS WHAT MY MOTHER SAID SHOULD BE           145 TRISTRAM 2         82
TRISTRAM ART THOU CALLD FOR MY DEATHS SAKE      145 TRISTRAM 2         86
GO NOT FAR O ISEULT FROM MY GRAVE               145 TRISTRAM 2         92
AND SENT ME WITH MY DOGS TO SWEEP               148 TRISTRAM 2        176
ON EARTH MY CRIME MY DEATH THEY KNEW            157 SAINT BRANDAN      26
ON EARTH MY CRIME MY DEATH THEY KNEW            157 SAINT BRANDAN      26
MY NAME IS UNDER ALL MENS BAN                   157 SAINT BRANDAN      27
AH TELL THEM OF MY RESPITE TOO                  157 SAINT BRANDAN      28
TO RUE MY GUILT IN ENDLESS FLAME                157 SAINT BRANDAN      32
TO THE POOR WRETCH MY CLOAK I CAST              158 SAINT BRANDAN      51
THEN WENT MY WAY TO KILL AND LIE                158 SAINT BRANDAN      59
FORGOT MY GOOD AS SOON AS DONE                  158 SAINT BRANDAN      60
OUTLIVES MY GUILT OUTLIVES MY DOOM              158 SAINT BRANDAN      63
OUTLIVES MY GUILT OUTLIVES MY DOOM              158 SAINT BRANDAN      63
I STANCH WITH ICE MY BURNING BREAST             158 SAINT BRANDAN      69
WITH SILENCE BALM MY WHIRLING BRAIN             158 SAINT BRANDAN      70
FORGOT MY DEED AS SOON AS DONE                  158 SAINT BRANDAN    V 60
FALSE NECKAN SHARES MY BED SHE WEEPS            160 NECKAN             35
SOONER SHALL THIS MY STAFF BEAR LEAVES          160 NECKAN             51
NOW MY BROTHERS CALL FROM THE BAY               161 FORSAKEN MERM       3
SHE SAID I MUST GO FOR MY KINSFOLK PRAY         163 FORSAKEN MERM      56
AND I LOSE MY POOR SOUL MERMAN HERE WITH THEE   163 FORSAKEN MERM      59
WHAT MADE MY HEART AT NEWSTEAD FULLEST SWELL    166 PICT NEWSTEAD       1
AND WHEN MY ILL-SCHOOLD SPIRIT IS AFLAME        169 WORLDLY PLACE      11
AGAIN I SEE MY BLISS AT HAND                    174 MEETING             1
MY MARGUERITE SMILES UPON THE STRAND            174 MEETING             3
AGAIN I SPRING TO MAKE MY CHOICE                174 MEETING             9
MY STRETCHD ARMS ARE CAST                       176 PARTING            64
AND DRY UP MY TEARS                             177 PARTING            84
FAST FAST BY MY WINDOW                              PARTING          V 25
MY STRAIND ARMS ARE CAST                        176 PARTING          V 64
MY HORSES FEET BESIDE THE LAKE                  177 FAREWELL            1
MY SISTER TO MAINTAIN WITH THEE                 180 FAREWELL           78
MY SISTER TO BEHOLD WITH THEE                   180 FAREWELL         V 78
I BADE MY HEART MORE CONSTANT BE                180 ISOLATION MARG      2
THINE EYES MY LOVE I SEE                        183 ABSENCE             2
TEN YEARS AND TO MY WAKING EYE                  183 TERRACE BERNE       1
THE HOUSE AND IS MY MARGUERITE THERE            184 TERRACE BERNE      12
ACROSS MY HEART TO SAY THY THREAD               184 TERRACE BERNE      27
OF ALL THAT WAS MY MARGUERITES OWN              185 TERRACE BERNE      40
I KNEW IT WHEN MY LIFE WAS YOUNG                185 TERRACE BERNE      49
```

MY   (CONTINUED)

SWEEP THROUGH MY SOUL	185	STRAYED REVEL	6
OF MY HUT BY THE CHESTNUTS	186	STRAYED REVEL	26
MY DAPPLED FAWN-SKIN	186	STRAYED REVEL	30
I SNATCHD UP MY VINE-CROWN MY FIR-STAFF	186	STRAYED REVEL	33
I SNATCHD UP MY VINE-CROWN MY FIR-STAFF	186	STRAYED REVEL	33
ON MY LEFT THROUGH THE BEECHES	187	STRAYED REVEL	43
THOU LOVEST IT THEN MY WINE	187	STRAYED REVEL	54
DENY THEE NOT MY BOWL	187	STRAYED REVEL	60
SWEEP THROUGH MY SOUL	194	STRAYED REVEL	297
TO ACHIEVE HIS SONS DELIVERANCE O MY CHILD	198	FRAG ANTIGONE	103
THY LOVELY PRESENCE AT MY SIDE	204	CALAIS SANDS	11
MY DARLING ON THIS LONELY AIR	205	CALAIS SANDS	14
YET NOW MY GLANCE BUT ONCE HATH ROVED	205	CALAIS SANDS	17
TO ENGLANDS CLIFFS MY GAZE IS TURND	205	CALAIS SANDS	19
BENEATH ONE ROOF MY QUEEN WITH MINE	205	CALAIS SANDS	36
THAT SLIGHT SWEET FIGURE AT MY SIDE	204	CALAIS SANDS	V 11
MY DARLING ON THIS QUIET AIR	205	CALAIS SANDS	V 14
BUT NOW MY GLANCE BUT ONCE HATH ROVED	205	CALAIS SANDS	V 17
TO ENGLANDS CLIFFS MY LOOK IS TURND	205	CALAIS SANDS	V 19
ON THE BLUE SEA MY GAZE I STRAIN	205	CALAIS SANDS	V 20
MY PENT-UP TEARS OPPRESS MY BRAIN	206	RIVER	9
MY PENT-UP TEARS OPPRESS MY BRAIN	206	RIVER	9
MY HEART IS SWOLN WITH LOVE UNSAID	206	RIVER	10
AH LET ME WEEP AND TELL MY PAIN	206	RIVER	11
AND ON THY SHOULDER REST MY HEAD	206	RIVER	12
IMMUNITY FROM MY CONTROL	206	RIVER	15
SCANNING MY FACE AND THE CHANGES WROUGHT THERE	206	SEPARATION	14
LET BEAM UPON MY INWARD VIEW	208	ON THE RHINE	17
COME TO ME IN MY DREAMS AND THEN	208	LONGING	1
AND PART MY HAIR AND KISS MY BROW	209	LONGING	11
AND PART MY HAIR AND KISS MY BROW	209	LONGING	11
AND SAY MY LOVE WHY SUFFEREST THOU	209	LONGING	12
COME TO ME IN MY DREAMS AND THEN	209	LONGING	13
AND SAY MY FRIEND WHY SUFFEREST THOU	209	LONGING	V 12
THOUGHTS LIGHT LIKE GLEAMS MY SPIRITS SKY	209	DESPONDENCY	5
CARRY MY PEACE UPON EARTH	216	LORDS MESSENGER	6
ASK NOT MY NAME O FRIEND	217	NAMELESS EPIT	1
MY FRIEND AND I BY CHANCE WE TALKD	221	EPILOG LAOCOON	2
AH CRIES MY FRIEND BUT WHO HATH TAUGHT	221	EPILOG LAOCOON	8
WHILE THUS MY FRIEND DISCOURSED WE PASS	222	EPILOG LAOCOON	36
OF THE THOUGHTS THAT FERMENT IN MY BREAST	231	YOUTH OF NATURE	120
MY LONGING MY SADNESS MY JOY	231	YOUTH OF NATURE	121
MY LONGING MY SADNESS MY JOY	231	YOUTH OF NATURE	121
MY LONGING MY SADNESS MY JOY	231	YOUTH OF NATURE	121
TO HAVE RENDERD THE GLEAM OF MY SKIES	231	YOUTH OF NATURE	123
TO HAVE ECHOED THE MOAN OF MY SEAS	231	YOUTH OF NATURE	124
UTTERD THE VOICE OF MY HILLS	231	YOUTH OF NATURE	125
HAVE THOUGHT THAT MY SECRET WAS THEIRS	232	YOUTH OF NATURE	130
THAT THEY WERE MY GLORY AND JOY	232	YOUTH OF NATURE	132
HAVE DREAMD THAT MY SECRET WAS THEIRS	232	YOUTH OF NATURE	V 130
YEARS AGO AT MY SIDE	233	YOUTH OF MAN	24
YE WHO FROM MY CHILDHOOD UP HAVE CALMD ME	240	SELF-DEPENDENCE	7
ON MY HEART YOUR MIGHTY CHARM RENEW	240	SELF-DEPENDENCE	10
FEEL MY SOUL BECOMING VAST LIKE YOU	240	SELF-DEPENDENCE	12
A CRY LIKE THINE IN MY OWN HEART I HEAR	240	SELF-DEPENDENCE	V 30
THERE IS NO EFFORT ON MY BROW	241	MORALITY	25
HOW LONELY RINGS THE ECHO OF MY FEET	242	SUMMER NIGHT	2
AND TO MY MIND THE THOUGHT	242	SUMMER NIGHT	11
BUT WE MY LOVE DOTH A LIKE SPELL BENUMB	245	BURIED LIFE	24
BEHOLD WITH TEARS MY EYES ARE WET	245	BURIED LIFE	V 2
BUT WE MY LOVE DOES A LIKE SPELL BENUMB	245	BURIED LIFE	V 24
HERE AT MY FEET WHAT WONDERS PASS	248	KENSINGTON GARD	13
BUT IN MY HELPLESS CRADLE I	249	KENSINGTON GARD	23
I ASK NOT THAT MY BED OF DEATH	249	WISH	1
TEARLESS WHEN OF MY DEATH HE HEARS	250	WISH	6
I ASK BUT THAT MY DEATH MAY FIND	250	WISH	9
THE FREEDOM TO MY LIFE DENIED	250	WISH	10
THEN THEN AT LAST TO QUIT MY SIDE	250	WISH	12
ONCE MORE BEFORE MY DYING EYES	250	WISH	32
TO FEEL THE UNIVERSE MY HOME	251	WISH	43
TO HAVE BEFORE MY MIND INSTEAD	251	WISH	44
THEN WILLING LET MY SPIRIT GO	251	WISH	51
WHILE TO MY EAR FROM UPLANDS FAR AWAY	255	SCHOLAR-GIPSY	17
OR IN MY BOAT I LIE	257	SCHOLAR-GIPSY	66
TOO RARE TOO RARE GROW NOW MY VISITS HERE	263	THYRSIS	31
MY PIPE IS LOST MY SHEPHERDS HOLIDAY	264	THYRSIS	37
MY PIPE IS LOST MY SHEPHERDS HOLIDAY	264	THYRSIS	37
YET THYRSIS LET ME GIVE MY GRIEF ITS HOUR	265	THYRSIS	102
TOO RARE TOO RARE GROW NOW MY VISITS HERE	269	THYRSIS	231
THYRSIS IN REACH OF SHEEP-BELLS IS MY HOME	269	THYRSIS	233
AT MY FEET FREE	275	SOUTHERN NIGHT	4
WANDER UNQUIET AND MY OWN	275	SOUTHERN NIGHT	15
MY BROTHER AND THINE EARLY LOT	276	SOUTHERN NIGHT	19
AND CHECKS MY STRAIN	279	SOUTHERN NIGHT	120
OF THEE I THINK MY BROTHER YOUNG	279	SOUTHERN NIGHT	123
STIRRD LIKE A CLARION-BLAST MY SOUL	285	HAWORTH CHURCH	100
STERN INTERRUPTED MY STRAIN	285	HAWORTH CHURCH	127
SHOOK LIKE A CLARION-BLAST MY SOUL	284	HAWORTH CHURCH	V 100
THOU MY FATHER ART LAID	286	RUGBY CHAPEL	13

MY   (CONTINUED)

THAT WORD GLOOM TO MY MIND	286 RUGBY CHAPEL	16
BE SAVED MY FATHER ALONE	290 RUGBY CHAPEL	125
SADDENS MY SOUL WITH ITS CHILL	293 HEINES GRAVE	41
ENGLAND MY COUNTRY FOR WE	294 HEINES GRAVE	72
FOR RIGOROUS TEACHERS SEIZED MY YOUTH	301 GRANDE CHARTR	67
WITH NOWHERE YET TO REST MY HEAD	302 GRANDE CHARTR	87
THEIR FAITH MY TEARS THE WORLD DERIDE	302 GRANDE CHARTR	89
TILL I POSSESS MY SOUL AGAIN	302 GRANDE CHARTR	94
TILL FREE MY THOUGHTS BEFORE ME ROLL	302 GRANDE CHARTR	95
MY MELANCHOLY SCIOLISTS SAY	302 GRANDE CHARTR	99
HALF OF MY LIFE WITH YOU	310 OBERMANN	132
THOU MASTER OF MY WANDERING YOUTH	313 OBERMANN MORE	39
ONCE MORE I SLIP MY CHAIN	313 OBERMANN MORE	44
ON MY MIND YEARS BEFORE	314 OBERMANN MORE	62
BENT ON MY FACE WITH GAZE WHICH SCANND	314 OBERMANN MORE	67
MY SOUL HIS EYES DID REST	314 OBERMANN MORE	68
MY RAVISHD SPIRIT TOO	317 OBERMANN MORE	144
AND PASTORAL HUTS I HID MY HEAD	321 OBERMANN MORE	251
THE AFTER-WORLD FORGETS MY NAME	321 OBERMANN MORE	263
AND KNEW MY LIFE WAS VAIN	321 OBERMANN MORE	266
MY HUMBLE TOMB EXPLORE	321 OBERMANN MORE	270
MY REFUGE AND NO MORE	321 OBERMANN MORE	272
COME TO MY MOUNTAIN-SOLITUDE	322 OBERMANN MORE	275
AND LEARN MY FRUSTRATE LIFE	322 OBERMANN MORE	276
STILL IN MY SOUL THE VOICE I HEARD	324 OBERMANN MORE	333
BENT ON MY FACE WITH GAZE THAT SCANND	314 OBERMANN MORE V	67
O BROTHER OF MY MOTHER GUARDIAN TRUE	330 MEROPE	29
MY MOTHERS FAITHFUL SERVANT LAID ME DOWN	331 MEROPE	31
MY GRANDFATHER THE GOOD ARCADIAN KING	331 MEROPE	33
WILL LIE MY GRANDSIRE SAID OUR FAIREST CHANCE	331 MEROPE	41
MEANWHILE WITHIN MY FATHERS PALACE I	331 MEROPE	47
OF MY OWN DEATH BUT LAIAS WELL I HOPE	331 MEROPE	49
DOUBTLESS THEY BEAR THEM TO MY FATHERS TOMB	331 MEROPE	55
AND PARALYSING CONSCIENCE STOP MY ARM	333 MEROPE	98
I AM I SHALL BE HAVE BEEN IN MY MIND	333 MEROPE	111
TO KEEP ALIVE THAT MEMORY IN MY HEART	334 MEROPE	120
AND TO MY SON REVERSION TO THY THRONE	340 MEROPE	334
IN REASON GOOD WHICH JUSTIFIED MY DEED	340 MEROPE	340
ROSE AND WITH FIRE AND SWORD ASSAILED MY HOUSE	340 MEROPE	344
THY SHAME SECURES MY FREEDOM NOT THY WILL	340 MEROPE	351
EMBOLDEND BY MY LENIENCE THINK IT FEAR	341 MEROPE	373
THOU TOUCHEST THE WORST OF MY ILLS	345 MEROPE	477
ON THE FAIR CURLD HEADS OF MY SONS	346 MEROPE	504
FORGIVE MY FOLLY AND WORK	348 MEROPE	538
ONLY TO ME GIVE MY CHILD	348 MEROPE	540
AN AVENGER I ASK NOT SEND ME MY SON	348 MEROPE	544
A WOMAN O MY FRIENDS HAS ONE DESIRE	349 MEROPE	565
CAN IT BRING HOME MY CHILD AH IF IT CAN	349 MEROPE	568
AND SEEST MY STRIPLING HUNTER THERE AFIELD	349 MEROPE	573
IF THIS WILL BRING HIM BACK BE THIS MY PRAYER	349 MEROPE	579
MY WORDS BELOW TO THEE AND MAKE THEE HEAR	350 MEROPE	586
BRINGING ME OF MY BOY THE ANNUAL NEWS	350 MEROPE	599
THAT MY SON STILL SURVIVES IN HEALTH IN BLOOM	351 MEROPE	612
THUS MUCH FROM ARCAS MY OLD SERVANT TRUE	351 MEROPE	616
THIS REGION IS NOT HAPPY FOR MY RACE	357 MEROPE	785
SOME STRAGGLING HUNTERS TO MY AID TO ROUSE	358 MEROPE	836
CROWND WITH SUCCESS NOT IN MY WAY BUT HEAVENS	360 MEROPE	878
A LAST LONG-CHERISHD PROJECT IN MY AIM	360 MEROPE	880
I OFFERD TO MY FOES AND THEY REFUSED	360 MEROPE	883
NOT CONDEMND BY MY VOICE	360 MEROPE	902
MY FAITHFUL FOLLOWER COMES WELCOME OLD FRIEND	362 MEROPE	937
FAITHFUL NOT WELCOME WHEN MY TALE IS TOLD	362 MEROPE	938
O THAT MY OVER-SPEED AND BURSTING GRIEF	362 MEROPE	939
HAD ON THE JOURNEY CHOKED MY LABOURING BREATH	362 MEROPE	940
AND LOCKD MY SPEECH FOR EVER IN MY BREAST	362 MEROPE	941
AND LOCKD MY SPEECH FOR EVER IN MY BREAST	362 MEROPE	941
O HONOURD QUEEN THY SON MY CHARGE IS GONE	362 MEROPE	944
OF HEIRSHIP TO HIS KINGDOM FOR MY SON	366 MEROPE	999
IN THEIR ALLEGIANCE ME IN MY SONS DEATH-HOUR	366 MEROPE	1004
TO MY MESSENIANS DUPED DISARMD DESPISED	366 MEROPE	1006
WEAK WOMEN WITH A THOUSANDTH PART MY WRONGS	366 MEROPE	1013
OR HARM AND NURSE MY LONGING FOR MY SON	366 MEROPE	1022
OR HARM AND NURSE MY LONGING FOR MY SON	366 MEROPE	1022
AND EVEN NOW MY SON AH ME MY SON	366 MEROPE	1026
AND EVEN NOW MY SON AH ME MY SON	366 MEROPE	1026
MY HUSBAND WANDERING WITH HIS STERN COMPEERS	367 MEROPE	1033
OF MY TWO ELDER SONS SLAIN LONG AGO	367 MEROPE	1038
OR HOW REPLY TO THEE MY CHILD LAST-BORN	367 MEROPE	1041
MY DEATH MAKES MY DEBT VOID AND DOUBLES THINE	367 MEROPE	1049
MY DEATH MAKES MY DEBT VOID AND DOUBLES THINE	367 MEROPE	1049
OLD MAN OLD MAN THOU HADST MY BOY IN CHARGE	368 MEROPE	1069
SEEMS IT LIGHTER MY LOSS	370 MEROPE	1115
MY CHILD LIES IN HIS JAGGD	370 MEROPE	1117
FOR THEE MY CHILD IF THOU WERT YET ALIVE	372 MEROPE	1157
AND WHERE DOST THOU SLEEP NOW MY INNOCENT BOY	373 MEROPE	1166
THERE THERE THOU LIEST NOW MY HAPLESS CHILD	373 MEROPE	1171
A MORE JUST STROKE THAN THAT THOU GAVST MY SON	373 MEROPE	1191
O GODS FOOLISH OLD MAN THOU SPOILST MY BLOW	374 MEROPE	1194
EVEN IN THE DEADLY PALACE OF MY FOE	375 MEROPE	1205

MY   (CONTINUED)

ARCAS THOU HERE O MY DEAR MASTER O   • •   •   •   •   375 MEROPE   1206
MY CHILD MY CHARGE BELOVED WELCOME TO LIFE •   •   •   •   375 MEROPE   1207
MY CHILD MY CHARGE BELOVED WELCOME TO LIFE •   •   •   •   375 MEROPE   1207
MY CHILD UNHURT ONLY BY OVER JOY   • •   •   •   •   •   377 MEROPE   1220
O KIND MESSENIAN MAIDENS O MY FRIENDS   •   •   •   •   377 MEROPE   1222
MY FIRST STROKE OF REVENGE HAD NEARLY FALLEN   •   •   •   377 MEROPE   1224
O MY SON   •   •   •   •   •   •   •   •   •   •   •   377 MEROPE   1227
FLY BACK MY CHILD AND THOU SEEMST   •   •   •   •   377 MEROPE   1229
MOTHER MY HEART RUNS OVER BUT THE TIME   •   •   •   378 MEROPE   1232
I FEAR NOT BUT I THINK ON MY DESIGN   •   •   •   •   378 MEROPE   1235
THY BROTHERS PLAY AT MY FEET   •   •   •   •   •   378 MEROPE   1238
ONCE MORE ROLL BACK ON MY HOUSE   •   •   • •   •   378 MEROPE   1244
INSTRUCT ME NOT I HAVE MY LESSON CLEAR   •   •   •   379 MEROPE   1259
ARCAS SEEK OUT MY UNCLE LAIAS NOW   •   •   •   •   379 MEROPE   1260
WE TWO WITH THEE MY MOTHER MAY CONSULT   •   •   •   379 MEROPE   1265
APPROVES MY BROTHER LAIAS THIS INTENT   •   •   •   •   379 MEROPE   1267
FIX HIM THE AUTHOR OF MY DEATH I KNOW NOT   •   •   •   379 MEROPE   1273
THIS COMMERCE FOR MY BEST BEHOOF HE PLIES   •   •   •   380 MEROPE   1277
NEWS OF MY BUSINESS PASTIME TEMPER FRIENDS   •   •   •   380 MEROPE   1281
BUT NOW SEEN FACE TO FACE MY ONLY CHILD   •   •   •   381 MEROPE   1289
MY NEW-WON TREASURE THY BELOVED LIFE   •   •   •   381 MEROPE   1291
ON WHAT A REED MY CHILD THOU LEANEST THERE   •   •   •   381 MEROPE   1310
BE GUIDED O MY SON SPURN COUNSEL NOT   •   •   •   382 MEROPE   1328
ILL COUNSEL IN MY JUDGMENT GIVES SHE HERE   •   •   •   382 MEROPE   1333
OF LIFE FOR MY ADVANTAGE AND MYSELF   • •   •   •   382 MEROPE   1350
DEALT AT MY OWN SOLE RISK BEFORE THEIR EYES   •   •   •   383 MEROPE   1354
THEIR LOYAL PASSION TOWRD MY FATHERS HOUSE   •   •   •   383 MEROPE   1359
WHEN MY GREAT FATHER FELL THEY HAD REPLIED   •   •   •   383 MEROPE   1366
AND THOU MY MOTHER HADST THOU MADE A SIGN   •   •   •   383 MEROPE   1368
TO SUCCOUR ME IN MY EXTREMEST NEED   •   •   •   •   383 MEROPE   1376
MY FATHER THEN AND HIS ARCADIAN CHIEFS   •   •   •   384 MEROPE   1395
ORPHAND OF BOTH MY PARENTS BY HIS FOES   •   •   •   385 MEROPE   1411
MY FATHER BY YOUR STROKES MY MOTHER SLAIN   •   •   •   385 MEROPE   1412
MY FATHER BY YOUR STROKES MY MOTHER SLAIN   •   •   •   385 MEROPE   1412
FOR THIS IS NOT MY MOTHER WHO DISSUADES   •   •   •   385 MEROPE   1413
MY MOTHER STANDS ALOOF AND BLAMES OUR DEED   •   •   •   386 MEROPE   1448
MY ROYAL SISTER BUT WITHOUT SOME CAUSE   •   •   •   386 MEROPE   1449
RISK FROM MY NEW-RESTORED MY ONLY SON   •   •   •   387 MEROPE   1456
RISK FROM MY NEW-RESTORED MY ONLY SON   •   •   •   387 MEROPE   1456
I SHUDDER LAIAS TO COMMIT MY CHILD   • •   •   •   387 MEROPE   1461
BESIDES FOR FROM MY BROTHER AND MY SON   •   •   •   387 MEROPE   1473
BESIDES FOR FROM MY BROTHER AND MY SON   •   •   •   387 MEROPE   1473
REMORSEFUL TOWRD MY HOSTILE SOLITUDE   • •   •   •   387 MEROPE   1475
TREACHEROUSLY PLOTTED TWIXT MY SON AND ME   •   •   •   387 MEROPE   1481
TREATY AND TO THIS KINGDOM FOR MY SON   •   •   •   387 MEROPE   1483
AND FROM HIS NATURAL RIGHTS MY SON DEBAR   •   •   •   388 MEROPE   1495
JUSTICE MY SISTER LONG DEMANDS THIS BLOW   •   •   •   390 MEROPE   1572
ALAS AGAINST MY BROTHER SON AND FRIENDS   •   •   •   390 MEROPE   1579
MAY IT TURN HAPPIER THAN MY DOUBTS PORTEND   •   •   •   390 MEROPE   1583
NOT FROM MY LIPS SHOULD CONSOLATION FALL   •   •   •   393 MEROPE   1687
TO ANNOUNCE THE RUIN OF MY HUSBANDS HOUSE   •   •   •   395 MEROPE   1738
AND IN MY TURN I WISH THE SAME FOR THEE   •   •   •   396 MEROPE   1763
FOR THAT IN THIS MY WARNING THOU ART PAID   •   •   •   396 MEROPE   1765
MY DEED IS OF OLD DATE AND LONG ATONED   •   •   •   396 MEROPE   1768
MY FINAL VICTORY PROVES THE GODS APPEASED   •   •   •   397 MEROPE   1770
WHAT FOR SO FAR FATE HATH NOT PROVED MY FOE   •   •   397 MEROPE   1778
FATE SEALS MY LIPS AND DRAGS TO RUIN THEE   •   •   •   397 MEROPE   1779
ONCE MORE MY FRIENDSHIP THOU REJECTEST WELL   •   •   398 MEROPE   1783
WHAT I HAVE DONE IS DONE BY MY OWN DEED   •   •   •   398 MEROPE   1787
WITH GLAD ACCLAIM ERE THEY FORESTALL MY NEWS   •   •   401 MEROPE   1887
IS MY SON SAFE THAT QUESTION BOUNDS MY CARE   •   •   401 MEROPE   1889
IS MY SON SAFE THAT QUESTION BOUNDS MY CARE   •   •   401 MEROPE   1889
I TOOK MY STAND AND SAW THE UNARMD CROWDS   •   •   401 MEROPE   1896
APPROVE NOT TOO I HAVE BUT HALF MY JOY   •   •   •   403 MEROPE   1962
O AEPYTUS MY SON BEHOLD BEHOLD   • •   •   •   403 MEROPE   1963
THIS IRON MAN MY ENEMY AND THINE   •   •   •   •   403 MEROPE   1964
AND FOUND HIM AT MY HUSBANDS SIDE HIS FRIEND   •   •   403 MEROPE   1973
BUT THOU MY SON STUDY TO MAKE PREVAIL   •   •   •   404 MEROPE   1995
AS THE CHIEFS RULE MY SON THE PEOPLE ARE   •   •   •   404 MEROPE   2002
TAKE THESE MY SON OVER THINE ENEMYS CORPSE   •   •   404 MEROPE   2010
O MOTHER MY BEST DILIGENCE SHALL BE   • •   •   •   405 MEROPE   2014
WHERE MY OWN YOUTH FALLS SHORT BUT LAIAS NOW   •   •   405 MEROPE   2016
TO RENDER TO MY TRUE MESSENIANS THANKS   •   •   •   405 MEROPE   2018
ASSUME THE ENSIGNS OF MY FATHERS POWER   •   •   •   405 MEROPE   2020
O MY COMFORTERS STRAYS   •   •   •   •   •   •   •   348 MEROPE   V
WHAT THEY WILL BUT TO ME GIVE MY SON   •   •   •   348 MEROPE   V
NOT DECRIED BY MY VOICE   •   •   •   •   •   •   360 MEROPE   V 902
MY CHILD LIES IN A JAGGD   •   •   •   •   •   370 MEROPE   V1117
APPROVES MY BROTHER LAIAS THIS DESIGN   •   •   •   379 MEROPE   V1267
FIXD HIM THE AUTHOR OF MY DEATH I KNEW NOT   •   •   379 MEROPE   V1273
WHAT FOR SO FAR SHE HATH NOT PROVED MY FOE   •   •   397 MEROPE   V1778
I HAVE MY HARP TOO THAT IS WELL APOLLO   •   •   •   407 EMPEDOCLES I 1   19
AS I WAS LIFTING MY SOILD GARLAND OFF   •   •   •   407 EMPEDOCLES I 1   40
I SADDLED MY WHITE MULE AND ALL NIGHT LONG   •   •   407 EMPEDOCLES I 1   44
AND TRY THY NOBLEST STRAINS MY CALLICLES   •   •   409 EMPEDOCLES I 1   97
THOU WILT EARN MY THANKS SURE AND PERHAPS HIS   •   409 EMPEDOCLES I 1   99
THOU ART MY FRIEND TO THEE   •   •   •   •   •   415 EMPEDOCLES I 2   103
THAT WAS MY HARP-PLAYER AGAIN WHERE IS HE   •   •   427 EMPEDOCLES I 2   461
I HAVE SEEN MANY CITIES IN MY TIME   •   •   •   •   428 EMPEDOCLES I 2   474

MY　　　　　　　(CONTINUED)

TILL MY EYES ACHE WITH THE LONG SPECTACLE • • • • 428 EMPEDOCLES I 2   V 475
OF MY UNLOVED PREEMINENCE • • • • • • • • 432 EMPEDOCLES II   110
MY GOLDEN CIRCLET • • • • • • • • • 432 EMPEDOCLES II   119
MY PURPLE ROBE • • • • • • • • • • 432 EMPEDOCLES II   120
MY LAUREL BOUGH • • • • • • • • • • 434 EMPEDOCLES II   192
THOUGH THOU HAST BEEN MY SHADE IN THE WORLDS HEAT 434 EMPEDOCLES II   194
MY LAUREL BOUGH • • • • • • • • • • 435 EMPEDOCLES II   197
TAKE THY BOUGH SET ME FREE FROM MY SOLITUDE • • 435 EMPEDOCLES II   218
IN ALL THINGS MY OWN DEADNESS • • • • • • 438 EMPEDOCLES II   322
OH THAT MY HEART BOUNDED WITH THE SWELL OF THE SEA 438 EMPEDOCLES II   324
OH THAT MY SOUL WERE FULL OF LIGHT AS THE STARS • 438 EMPEDOCLES II   325
LIVED EVER IN THE LIGHT OF MY OWN SOUL • • • 440 EMPEDOCLES II   393
FAR FROM MY OWN SOUL FAR FROM WARMTH AND LIGHT • 440 EMPEDOCLES II   396
MOUNTS OFF MY SOUL I FEEL IT I BREATHE FREE • • 441 EMPEDOCLES II   408
MY SOUL GLOWS TO MEET YOU • • • • • • • 441 EMPEDOCLES II   412
THAT TO MY MIND THERE CAME HOW LONG AGO • • • 446 WESTMIN ABBEY   83
THEIR KINDNESS SHOWN ME IN MY WANDERING HOUR • • 447 WESTMIN ABBEY   109
WHICH JOYD MY VOICE TO HEAR • • • • • • 449 WESTMIN ABBEY   162
EVEN AS MY FATHER THOU • • • • • • • • 449 WESTMIN ABBEY   167
SOMETHING HAUNTS MY CONSCIENCE BRINGS • • • 455 POOR MATTHIAS   85
DROVE MY DAUGHTER SMALL AND ME • • • • • • 457 POOR MATTHIAS   179
WHEN MY FLEETING SHADOW PASSD FROM THEE • • • 482 THEKLAS ANSWER   2
THERE FROM SIN DELIVERD DWELLS MY FATHER • • • 482 THEKLAS ANSWER   15
I DROPPD THE BOOK AND OF MY CHILD I THOUGHT • • 485 S S LUSITANIA   9
NOR WOULD MY OWN HEART LET ME MY HEART WHICH   HOMER TRANS   17
    HAS BID ME BE VALIANT
NOR WOULD MY OWN HEART LET ME MY HEART WHICH   HOMER TRANS   17
    HAS BID ME BE VALIANT
BUSY FOR PRIAMS FAME AND MY OWN IN SPITE OF THE FUTURE HOMER TRANS   19
FOR THAT DAY WILL COME MY SOUL IS ASSURD OF ITS COMING HOMER TRANS   20
MOVES ME SO MUCH NOT HECUBAS GRIEF NOR PRIAM   HOMER TRANS   24
    MY FATHERS
NOR MY BRETHRENS MANY AND BRAVE WHO THEN WILL BE LYING HOMER TRANS   25
WHY DOST THOU PROPHESY SO MY DEATH TO ME XANTHUS   HOMER TRANS   59
    IT NEEDS NOT
FAR FROM MY FATHER AND MOTHER DEAR FOR ALL   HOMER TRANS   61
    THAT I WILL NOT
NO LACK OF ANSWER HAST THOU O MY HEART • • • • RUDE ORATOR   13
TOUCH HIS ROBE AND SAY MY FATHER • • • • • • META CLOISTER   27
SAY MY FATHER DOES THE TIRED • • • • • • META CLOISTER   29
YOU SAY TRUE MY DAUGHTER PEACE IS HERE • • • • META CLOISTER   40
TO GLUE MY FRUITLESS GAZE ON AND TO PINE • • • FRAGMENT 5   6

MYCENAE
AGAMEMNONS SON IN MYCENAE • • • • • • • • 368 MEROPE   1083
ORESTES IN MYCENAE HAD NO MORE • • • • • • • 384 MEROPE   1398

MYCENAES
AMPHIARAOS OR MYCENAES KING • • • • • • • • 367 MEROPE   1034

MYRIADS
ELSE OF THE MYRIADS WHO FILL • • • • • • • 291 RUGBY CHAPEL   183
MYRIADS WHO LIVE WHO HAVE LIVED • • • • • • 298 HEINES GRAVE   213
WAS THE WILD SHOUT THOSE GOTHIC MYRIADS GAVE • • 466 ALARIC AT ROME   112
OF HEAVENS EMBATTLED MYRIADS SWEPT ALONG • • • • 473 CROMWELL   44
WAVING HER MYRIADS OF WHITE FAIRY BLOOMS • • • • EVERLASTING SUB   6

MYRTLE
HAST THOU WITH MYRTLE-LEAF CROWND HIM O PLEASURE • • 20 MODERN SAPPHO   35
TWIXT MYRTLE-HEDGES ALL IN FLOWER • • • • • • 278 SOUTHERN NIGHT   103
MYRTLE AND ROSE FIT THE YOUNG • • • • • • • 282 HAWORTH CHURCH   V
BUT THE SWEET-SMELLING MYRTLE • • • • • • • 391 MEROPE   1616

MYRTLES
AND CAME HEAPD WITH MYRTLES TO YOUR THRONE • • • • 27 NEW SIRENS   32

MYSELF
LET ME PAUSE LET ME STRIVE IN MYSELF MAKE SOME ORDER 19 MODERN SAPPHO   7
LET ME PAUSE LET ME STRIVE IN MYSELF FIND SOME ORDER 19 MODERN SAPPHO   V   7
FOR WOULD THAT I MYSELF HAD SUCH A SON • • • • 68 SOHRAB RUSTUM   229
ARE NOT THEY MORTAL AM NOT I MYSELF • • • • • 68 SOHRAB RUSTUM   254
OR RATHER WOULD THAT I EVEN I MYSELF • • • • • 85 SOHRAB RUSTUM   816
JUSTICE O KING AND ON MYSELF • • • • • • 89 SICK KING BOKH   36
WEARY OF MYSELF AND SICK OF ASKING • • • • • 239 SELF-DEPENDENCE   1
AND I MYSELF SEEM HALF TO KNOW THY LOOKS • • • 257 SCHOLAR-GIPSY   62
THIS FOR OUR SON AND FOR MYSELF I PRAY • • • • 350 MEROPE   591
SPEAK THEM THAT I MAY JUDGE THEIR KIND MYSELF • • 354 MEROPE   712
ALL CLAIM TO SUCCOUR FORFEIT TO MYSELF • • • • 366 MEROPE   1008
OF LIFE FOR MY ADVANTAGE AND MYSELF • • • • • 382 MEROPE   1350
THAT I TO-DAY RETURNING FIND MYSELF • • • • • 385 MEROPE   1410
NOR BEND MYSELF TOO LOW TO MAKE IT YIELD • • • • 398 MEROPE   1786
MAINTAIND COURAGE AND FORCE AND IN MYSELF • • • • 438 EMPEDOCLES II   319
YEA I TAKE MYSELF TO WITNESS • • • • • • • 441 EMPEDOCLES II   399
I OF MYSELF KNOW WELL THAT HERE I AM DESTIND TO PERISH HOMER TRANS   60

MYSIAN
IN MYSIAN IDA THE VOICE • • • • • • • • • 230 YOUTH OF NATURE   76

MYSTERIES
PONDERING GODS MYSTERIES UNTOLD • • • • • • 278 SOUTHERN NIGHT   89

MYSTERIOUS
THEY CATCH OF THE MYSTERIOUS STREAM • • • • • 226 EPILOG LAOCOON   178
OR THAT MYSTERIOUS CRY THAT SMOTE WITH FEAR • • 473 CROMWELL   41

MYSTERY
    IN MYSTERY OUR SOUL ABIDES • • • • • • • • •   241 MORALITY   4
    INTO THE MYSTERY OF THIS HEART WHICH BEATS • • • •   246 BURIED LIFE   52
    INTO THE MYSTERY OF THIS HEART THAT BEATS • • • •   246 BURIED LIFE   V 52
    THAT UNDISCOVERD MYSTERY • • • • • • • • •   250 WISH   26

MYSTIC
    HE OF THE MYSTIC EAST IS TOUCHD WITH NIGHT • • • •   170 EAST AND WEST   14
    FAMILIAR MEANINGS IN YOUR MYSTIC TONE • • • •   472 CROMWELL   4
    ALL FREEDOMS MYSTIC LANGUAGE STORMS THAT ROAR • •   472 CROMWELL   29

MYSTICS
    FOOLS THAT THESE MYSTICS ARE • • • • • • • •   233 YOUTH OF MAN   28

NADIR
    PASSIVE AT THE NADIR OF DISMAY • • • • • • •   33 NEW SIRENS   202

NAILD
    THAT NAILD THORN-CROWNED MAN • • • • • •   317 OBERMANN MORE   156
    THAT WAN NAILD FORM WITH HEAD DROOPD LOW • • •   317 OBERMANN MORE   V 155

NAKED
    SHIVERING WITH FEVER NAKED OLD • • • • • •   157 SAINT BRANDAN   46
    AND NAKED SHINGLES OF THE WORLD • • • • •   211 DOVER BEACH   28
    INVESTS THE STERN AND NAKED PRAYER • • • •   300 GRANDE CHARTR   38
    ARE SHINING ON THOSE NAKED SLOPES LIKE FLAME • •   412 EMPEDOCLES I 2   6
    BUT A NAKED ETERNALLY RESTLESS MIND • • • •   438 EMPEDOCLES II   330
    SWEPT OFF THE WITHERED LEAVES THAT HIDE THE NAKED TOMB   469 ALARIC AT ROME   192

NAME
    THE TARTAR CHALLENGE AND THIS YOUNG MANS NAME • •   66 SOHRAB RUSTUM   181
    TO FIGHT THEIR CHAMPION AND THOU KNOWST HIS NAME • •   67 SOHRAB RUSTUM   213
    AND WITH MY GREAT NAME FENCE THAT WEAK OLD MAN • •   68 SOHRAB RUSTUM   237
    BUT THAT BELOVED NAME UNNERVED MY ARM • • •   77 SOHRAB RUSTUM   547
    THAT NAME AND SOMETHING I CONFESS IN THEE • • •   77 SOHRAB RUSTUM   548
    FOR SPEED AND HERMOD WAS HIS NAME IN HEAVEN •   101 BALDER DEAD 1   221
    THEY CALL HER FREYA IS HER NAME IN HEAVEN • •   116 BALDER DEAD 3   97
    AND CALLD HIM BY HIS NAME AND STERNLY SAID • •   124 BALDER DEAD 3   386
    THE SECOND ASGARD WITH ANOTHER NAME • • •   128 BALDER DEAD 3   521
    OF A LOVE THEY DARE NOT NAME • • • • •   135 TRISTRAM 1   150
    SON SHE SAID THY NAME SHALL BE OF SORROW • •   145 TRISTRAM 2   85
    WHO MADE A NAME AT YOUNGER YEARS THAN HE • •   153 TRISTRAM 3   145
    MY NAME IS UNDER ALL MENS BAN • • • • •   157 SAINT BRANDAN   27
    HOW SHALL I NAME HIM • • • • • • •   189 STRAYED REVEL   101
    ASK NOT MY NAME O FRIEND • • • • • •   217 NAMELESS EPIT   1
    OF THIS OR THAT DOWN-TRODDEN NAME • • •   219 BACCHANALIA 2   16
    THE ILL HE CANNOT CURE A NAME • • • • •   250 WISH   20
    AND FROM THE SIGN IS GONE SIBYLLAS NAME • • •   262 THYRSIS   4
    THAT BLACK TOMBSTONE THE NAME • • • • •   292 HEINES GRAVE   2
    THE BLACK TOMBSTONE THE NAME • • • • •   292 HEINES GRAVE   V 2
    ALL MEANING FROM A NAME • • • • • •   312 OBERMANN MORE   2
    HIS BIRTH-NAME JUST BELOW • • • • • •   313 OBERMANN MORE   26
    THE AFTER-WORLD FORGETS MY NAME • • • •   321 OBERMANN MORE   263
    BLOW OFF THE SPOT OF MURDER FROM HIS NAME • • •   336 MEROPE   200
    WE CALL IT MURDER CRUSH HIM BRAND HIS NAME • • •   336 MEROPE   203
    RULED IN THEIR NAME AND TRAIND THEM TO YOUR WILL • •   339 MEROPE   321
    GIVES HER NAME TO THE SPRING • • • • •   343 MEROPE   432
    A YOUNGER MAN AND OF A DIFFERENT NAME • • •   361 MEROPE   925
    ORESTES DIED BUT IN NAME • • • • • •   368 MEROPE   1084
    THERE IN UNVOICED OBLIVION SINK THY NAME • • •   395 MEROPE   1751
    AT THY DEAD HUSBANDS NAME THE PEOPLE SHOW • • •   401 MEROPE   1894
    THERE IN UNVOICED OBLIVION HIDE THY NAME • • •   395 MEROPE   V1751
    AND SPEND OUR WIT TO NAME WHAT MOST EMPLOY UNNAMED   423 EMPEDOCLES I 2   331
    LONG SINCE HIS NAME IS HEARD ON EARTH NO MORE • •   447 WESTMIN ABBEY   113
    AGAIN FROM LIP TO LIP WILL PASS HIS NAME • • •   449 WESTMIN ABBEY   180
    WE STRIVE TO CARRY DOWN THY NAME • • • •   451 GEISTS GRAVE   63
    TO NAME FOR FUTURE TIMES TO KNOW • • • •   452 GEISTS GRAVE   79
    NOW IN VAIN YOU CALL HIS NAME • • • • •   452 POOR MATTHIAS   7
    AND SO HE BORE THE IMPERIAL NAME • • • •   459 KAISER DEAD   23
    A MIGHTY NAME FOR EVIL OR FOR GOOD • • • •   463 ALARIC AT ROME   21

NAMED
    THEIR FATHERS REALM THIS ISLE FROM PELOPS NAMED • •   336 MEROPE   219
    THE BONES OF ARCAS WHENCE OUR RACE IS NAMED • •   356 MEROPE   742
    NAMED AEPYTUS LIKE HIM HAVING GONE IN • • •   357 MEROPE   777
    ANOTHER ANCESTOR NAMED TOO LIKE ME • • • •   357 MEROPE   780

NAMELESS
    BUT THAT IN BATTLE WITH A NAMELESS FOE • • •   79 SOHRAB RUSTUM   600
    I FEEL A NAMELESS SADNESS OER ME ROLL • • •   245 BURIED LIFE   3
    THE NAMELESS FEELINGS THAT COURSE THROUGH OUR BREAST   246 BURIED LIFE   62
    NO HABITATION FOR THE NAMELESS DEAD • • • •   464 ALARIC AT ROME   56

NAMES
    WHERE HOST MEETS HOST AND MANY NAMES ARE SUNK • •   62 SOHRAB RUSTUM   61
    WHO SPOKE ALTHOUGH HE CALLD BACK NAMES HE KNEW • •   79 SOHRAB RUSTUM   606
    NAMES HATH SHE MANY VANADIS ON EARTH • • •   116 BALDER DEAD 3   96
    THEIR NAMES CHIEF GLORY OF ALL • • • • •   281 HAWORTH CHURCH   22
    THEIR NAMES CHIEF TREASURE OF ALL • • • •   281 HAWORTH CHURCH V 22

NANNA

BUT IN BREIDABLIK NANNA BALDERS WIFE	• • • • •	102 BALDER DEAD 1	268
A DIRGE AND NANNA AND HER TRAIN REPLIED	• • • •	103 BALDER DEAD 1	274
THEY WENT AND LAID THEM DOWN AND NANNA WENT	• •	103 BALDER DEAD 1	277
AND GAZED ON NANNA AS SHE SLEPT AND SPAKE	• • • •	103 BALDER DEAD 1	287
SO IT RESTORED THEE NANNA TO MY SIDE	• • • • •	103 BALDER DEAD 1	307
YET DREARY NANNA IS THE LIFE THEY LEAD	• • • •	104 BALDER DEAD 1	314
BUT EVEN THERE O NANNA WE MIGHT FIND	• • • •	104 BALDER DEAD 1	326
TO FADE AND NANNA IN HER SLEEP STRETCHD OUT	• •	104 BALDER DEAD 1	332
AND NANNA ON HER BED SANK BACK BUT THEN	• • • •	104 BALDER DEAD 1	338
AND NANNA ON HER BED SUNK BACK BUT THEN	• • • •	104 BALDER DEAD 1	V 338
WITH NANNA ON HIS RIGHT AND ON HIS LEFT	• • • •	118 BALDER DEAD 3	164
BUT EMPTY FOR HIS WIFE FOR NANNA CAME	• • • •	125 BALDER DEAD 3	433
BALDER AND NANNA AND TO BALDER SAID	• • • • •	126 BALDER DEAD 3	445
FOR NANNA HATH REJOIND ME WHO OF OLD	• • • •	126 BALDER DEAD 3	459
TO NANNA AND SHE GAVE THEIR BROTHER BLIND	• • • •	129 BALDER DEAD 3	550

NAPLES

NAPLES BAY FOR A SWEET	• • • • • • • • • •	294 HEINES GRAVE	58

NARD

BRING WATER NARD AND LINEN ROLLS	• • • • • •	95 SICK KING BOKH	229

NARRATIONS

WHO FROM HISTORYS VAGUE NARRATIONS	• • • • •	SECOND BEST	V 17

NARROW

THROUGH THE NARROW PAVED STREETS WHERE ALL WAS STILL	163 FORSAKEN MERM	70
WHAT INNS YOUR STREETS TOO HOW NARROW	• • • •	214 NEW ROME	11
YOUR STREETS ARE ANCIENT AND NARROW	• • • • •	214 NEW ROME	V 11
YOUR STREETS HOW ANCIENT AND NARROW	• • • • •	214 NEW ROME	V 11
CREEP INTO THY NARROW BED	• • • • • •	215 LAST WORD	1
BUT EVEN OUR OWN HEART THAT NARROW WORLD	• • • •	352 MEROPE	638
INTO THE NARROW PATH OF RIGHT	• • • • • • •	353 MEROPE	672

NARROWER

SPARING US NARROWER MARGIN THAN WE DEEM	• • • •	7 REP FRIEND CONT	8

NARROWING

OF AN EVER-NARROWING WORLD	• • • • • • • •	233 YOUTH OF MAN	47
TO FLAG AND FEEL HIS NARROWING SPAN	• • • • •	459 KAISER DEAD	38

NARROWS

TO ALL REEFS AND NARROWS WENDING	• • • • • •	26 NEW SIRENS	15

NASEBYS

BY NASEBYS HILL OER MARSTONS HEATHY WASTE	• • • •	476 CROMWELL	149

NATIONS

UNION CEMENTED FOR THIS NATIONS WEAL	• • • •	333 MEROPE	103
A PRIVATE LOSS HERE FOUNDS A NATIONS PEACE	• • • •	360 MEROPE	889
RELICS OF NATIONS THY MEMORIAL-STONES	• • • •	464 ALARIC AT ROME	62
SCOURGE OF THE NATIONS WOULDEST THOU LINGER YET	• •	465 ALARIC AT ROME	94

NATIVE

THY NATIVE WORLD STIRS AT THY FEET UNKNOWN	• • • •	46 IN UTRUMQUE PAR	V 36
O SCAN THY NATIVE WORLD WITH PIOUS EYES	• • • •	46 IN UTRUMQUE PAR	V 40
LEFT FRESHLY GATHERD ON THEIR NATIVE BANK	• • • •	86 SOHRAB RUSTUM	845
HIES AH FROM WHENCE WHAT NATIVE GROUND	• • • •	225 EPILOG LAOCOON	125
BACK TO YOUR NATIVE HEATHS	• • • • • • •	285 HAWORTH CHURCH	115
OF HIS NATIVE GERMANY SO	• • • • • • • •	296 HEINES GRAVE	139
ON NATIVE GROUND THAN DRAG THE TEDIOUS HOURS	• •	383 MEROPE	1380

NATURAL

THE FRIENDS TO WHOM WE HAD NO NATURAL RIGHT	• •	41 HUMAN LIFE	29
WHOSE NATURAL INSIGHT CAN DISCERN	• • • • •	59 RESIGNATION	233
WHETHER A NATURAL OBSCURENESS HIDING	• • • • •	352 MEROPE	641
AND FROM HIS NATURAL RIGHTS MY SON DEBAR	• • •	388 MEROPE	1495
NATURAL VENGEANCE MAY MAINTAIN THINE ACT	• • •	404 MEROPE	1998
THAT NATURAL CAUSES MAR THY EFFORTS AND NOT FATE	• •	EMPEDOCLES I 2	V
THAT NATURAL CAUSES THWART THY WELFARE AND NOT FATE		EMPEDOCLES I 2	V
ON SIMPLE MINDS WITH A PURE NATURAL JOY	• • • •	436 EMPEDOCLES II	243
THOUGHTS SLAVES AND DEAD TO EVERY NATURAL JOY	• •	436 EMPEDOCLES II	249
ALL NATURAL LOVE ALL HUMAN SYMPATHY	• • • • •	467 ALARIC AT ROME	147

NATURE

ONE LESSON NATURE LET ME LEARN OF THEE	• • • •	1 QUIET WORK	1
TWO LESSONS NATURE LET ME LEARN OF THEE	• • • •	1 QUIET WORK	V 1
WHERE MANS ONE NATURE QUEEN-LIKE SITS ALONE	• •	4 BUTLERS SERMONS	7
IN HARMONY WITH NATURE RESTLESS FOOL	• • • •	5 HARMONY NATURE	1
TO BE LIKE NATURE STRONG LIKE NATURE COOL	• •	5 HARMONY NATURE	4
TO BE LIKE NATURE STRONG LIKE NATURE COOL	• • • •	5 HARMONY NATURE	4
KNOW MAN HATH ALL WHICH NATURE HATH BUT MORE	• •	5 HARMONY NATURE	5
NATURE IS CRUEL MAN IS SICK OF BLOOD	• • • •	5 HARMONY NATURE	7
NATURE IS STUBBORN MAN WOULD FAIN ADORE	• • •	5 HARMONY NATURE	8
NATURE IS FICKLE MAN HATH NEED OF REST	• • •	5 HARMONY NATURE	9
NATURE FORGIVES NO DEBT AND FEARS NO GRAVE	• • •	5 HARMONY NATURE	10
MAN MUST BEGIN KNOW THIS WHERE NATURE ENDS	• • •	5 HARMONY NATURE	12
NATURE AND MAN CAN NEVER BE FAST FRIENDS	• • •	5 HARMONY NATURE	13

NATURE   (CONTINUED)
          OF THIS EARTHLY NATURE . . . .   39 STAGIRIUS   31
          TIS FOR THIS THY NATURE YEARNS . . . . . .   49 SECOND BEST   4
          FOLD CLOSELY O NATURE . . . .   177 PARTING   77
          BUT IF THE STEDFAST COMMANDMENT OF NATURE . . .   206 SEPARATION   5
          NATURE IS FRESH AS OF OLD . . . .   228 YOUTH OF NATURE   11
          THE MURMUR OF NATURE REPLY . . . .   230 YOUTH OF NATURE   78
          NATURE IS HID IN THEIR GRAVE . . . . . .   232 YOUTH OF NATURE   128
          WE O NATURE DEPART . . . .   232 YOUTH OF MAN   1
          WATCHEST US NATURE THROUGHOUT . . . . . .   232 YOUTH OF MAN   9
          BEHOLD O NATURE THIS PAIR . . . .   232 YOUTH OF MAN   17
          WHO PRATE OF NATURE FOR SHE . . . . . .   233 YOUTH OF MAN   29
          NATURE IS NOTHING HER CHARM . . . . . .   233 YOUTH OF MAN   35
          THOU O NATURE WAST MUTE . . . .   233 YOUTH OF MAN   38
          NATURE THEY SAW NO MORE . . . .   233 YOUTH OF MAN   50
          THEY NOT NATURE ARE CHANGED . . . . . .   235 YOUTH OF MAN   95
          AND THEY FEEL HOW NATURE WAS FAIR . . . .   235 YOUTH OF MAN   104
          YEARN TO THE GREATNESS OF NATURE . . . .   235 YOUTH OF MAN   117
          WHO PRATE OF NATURE BUT SHE . . . . . .   233 YOUTH OF MAN   V 29
          THOU O NATURE WERT MUTE . . . .   233 YOUTH OF MAN   V 38
          NATURE WHOSE FREE LIGHT CHEERFUL AIR . . . .   241 MORALITY   17
          FOR NATURE HATH LONG KEPT THIS INN THE EARTH . .   251 FUTURE   V
          IN THE NEVER IDLE WORKSHOP OF NATURE . . . .   286 HAWORTH CHURCH   136
          WHICH NATURE SANCTIONS WHICH THE INNOCENT BLOOD .   386 MEROPE   1427
          AND BELIEVES NATURE OUTRAGED IF HIS WILLS GAINSAID   417 EMPEDOCLES I 2   156
          NATURE WITH EQUAL MIND . . . .   421 EMPEDOCLES I 2   257
          OF NATURE HARM US NOT . . . .   421 EMPEDOCLES I 2   265
          KNEAD US IN ITS HOT HAND AND CHANGE OUR NATURE .   440 EMPEDOCLES II   386
          OF NATURE WITH HER COUNTLESS SUM . . . .   450 GEISTS GRAVE   24
          OF MENTAL NATURE AS FOR HIM TO FRET . . . .   LUCRETIUS 3   3

NATURES
          NATURES GREAT LAW AND LAW OF ALL MENS MINDS . .   8 RELIGIOUS ISOL   12
          I HAVE KEPT UNINFRINGED MY NATURES LAW . . . .   40 HUMAN LIFE   4
          NATURES WISH MUST NOW BE STRANGLED . . . . .   49 SECOND BEST   11
          BUT MILDER NATURES AND MORE FREE . . . . .   53 RESIGNATION   22
          WHEN THOU DOST BASK IN NATURES EYE . . . . .   241 MORALITY   14
          HIS EYES ON NATURES PLAN . . . .   308 OBERMANN   58
          TRUE WE MUST BOW TO NATURES LAW . . . . . .   481 COURAGE   2

NAVE
          HAREBELLS FLOWER IN THE NAVE . . . .   15 CHURCH BROU 1   72
          IN THE NAVE A TOMB OF STONE . . . .   16 CHURCH BROU 1   104
          THE PEOPLE TO THE NAVE REPAIR . . . . . .   17 CHURCH BROU 2   34
          FROM THE RICH PAINTED WINDOWS OF THE NAVE . . .   17 CHURCH BROU 3   5
          IN THE VAST WESTERN WINDOW OF THE NAVE . . . .   18 CHURCH BROU 3   21
          WHILE THROUGH THEIR EARTH-MOORD NAVE BELOW . . .   223 EPILOG LAOCOON   73
          WHILE THROUGH THE EARTH-MOORD NAVE BELOW . . .   223 EPILOG LAOCOON   V 73
          SHEEP MAKE THE FURZE-GROWN NAVE THEIR FOLD . . .   STANZAS CARNAC   V 16
          LONG SINCE WE PACE THIS SHADOWD NAVE . . . .   305 GRANDE CHARTR   199
          NAVE CHOIR AND TRANSEPT GLORIFIED WITH LIGHT . .   445 WESTMIN ABBEY   35

NAY
          NAY AND SINCE DEATH WHICH WIPES OUT MAN . . . .   58 RESIGNATION   223
          NAY BUT I SWEAR FROM THIS THY PATH . . . . .   91 SICK KING BOKH   103
          NAY WERE HE THINE OWN MOTHERS SON . . . . .   92 SICK KING BOKH   137
          TRISTRAM NAY NAY THOU MUST NOT TAKE MY HAND . .   135 TRISTRAM 1   166
          TRISTRAM NAY NAY THOU MUST NOT TAKE MY HAND . .   135 TRISTRAM 1   166
          NAY ALLS WELL AGAIN THOU MUST NOT WEEP . . . .   144 TRISTRAM 2   72
          NAY ASK HIM . . . .   188 STRAYED REVEL   98
          NAY LOOK CLOSER INTO MAN . . . .   215 PIS-ALLER   5
          WITH PITY NAY WITH REVERENCE YET BEWARE . . . .   341 MEROPE   361
          MAY BE NAY SHOULD IF FOR THE GENERAL WEAL . . .   352 MEROPE   657
          THOUGH TO HIS ACT EMPOWERD NAY IMPELLD . . . .   385 MEROPE   1421

NAYE
          ALONG THE ROCKS OF NAYE . . . .   324 OBERMANN MORE   336

NEAR
          NOR IDLY DO THESE SEA-BIRDS HOVER NEAR . . . .   42 GIPSY CHILD   8
          AND BLITHELY DO THESE SEA-BIRDS HOVER NEAR . . .   41 GIPSY CHILD   V   8
          SO GLOWING AND SO NEAR . . . .   47 WORLD QUIETIST   23
          HERE WHERE THE BROOK SHINES NEAR ITS HEAD . . .   55 RESIGNATION   90
          AND TO MENS BUSINESS NOT TOO NEAR . . . . .   59 RESIGNATION   250
          OF RUGS AND FELTS AND NEAR HIM LAY HIS ARMS . .   61 SOHRAB RUSTUM   27
          MOWING THE GARDEN GRASS-PLOTS NEAR ITS BED . . .   80 SOHRAB RUSTUM   636
          HIS BELT AND NEAR THE SHOULDER BARED HIS ARM . .   81 SOHRAB RUSTUM   670
          SWEEPING THE DUST CAME NEAR AND IN MUTE WOE . .   82 SOHRAB RUSTUM   732
          NEAR DEATH AND BY AN IGNORANT STROKE OF THINE . .   85 SOHRAB RUSTUM   818
          NEAR ONE ANOTHER MANY A MAN . . . .   93 SICK KING BOKH   163
          TO HER DREW HODER NEAR AND SPAKE AND SAID . . .   98 BALDER DEAD 1   94
          THEN BALDERS SPIRIT THROUGH THE GLOOM DREW NEAR .   103 BALDER DEAD 1   282
          FOR NEAR THE WALL THE RIVER OF ROARING FLOWS . .   109 BALDER DEAD 2   152
          OUTMOST THE OTHERS NEAR THE CENTRE RUN . . . .   109 BALDER DEAD 2   153
          THESE FLOW BY HELAS THRONE AND NEAR THEIR SPRING .   109 BALDER DEAD 2   155
          OF HELA AND SAW NEAR IT BALDER CROWND . . . .   109 BALDER DEAD 2   177
          AND HE DREW NEAR AND HEARD NO LIVING VOICE . . .   113 BALDER DEAD 2   305
          AND IN PROCESSION ALL COME NEAR AND WEEP . . .   115 BALDER DEAD 3   51
          THOU CAMEST NEAR THE NEXT O WARRIOR THOR . . .   115 BALDER DEAD 3   71
          LAST FROM AMONG THE HEROES ONE CAME NEAR . . .   117 BALDER DEAD 3   124

NEAR   (CONTINUED)
```
        AGAINST THE BODIES AND STUCK TORCHES NEAR    •  •  •  •    118 BALDER DEAD 3      167
        OF NIFLHEIM HE SAW ONE GHOST COME NEAR        •  •  •  •    124 BALDER DEAD 3      382
        BUT EARNESTLY I LONGD TO HOVER NEAR  •  •  •  •  •  •      125 BALDER DEAD 3      416
        WHICH WOODCUTTERS HAVE LIGHTED NEAR THEIR LODGE  •  •      119 BALDER DEAD 3      V
        OF THE NEAR WAVES CAME SADLY GRAND  •  •  •  •  •  •       137 TRISTRAM 1         217
        THE FOREST-CHAPEL AND THE FOUNTAIN NEAR  •  •  •  •        139 TRISTRAM 1         279
        THROUGH A MIST I SEE THEE NEAR COME NEARER  •  •  •       145 TRISTRAM 2          75
        AND TO ONE STANDING ON THEM FAR AND NEAR  •  •  •  •      149 TRISTRAM 3          11
        THE FELL-FARES SETTLED ON THE THICKETS NEAR   •  •       151 TRISTRAM 3          55
        THE BLACKBIRD WHISTLED FROM THE DINGLES NEAR  •  •       155 TRISTRAM 3         197
        BUT THEIR SLOPE WAS NOT DEEP AND FAR AND NEAR   •            TRISTRAM 3       V  11
        THE MOON WAS BRIGHT THE ICEBERG NEAR  •  •  •  •  •       157 SAINT BRANDAN       22
        HE SEES FLOAT NEAR AN ICEBERG WHITE   •  •  •  •  •       156 SAINT BRANDAN    V  15
        MAY TO EACH OTHER BE BROUGHT NEAR    •  •  •  •  •        180 FAREWELL            75
        NEAR HARBOUR BUT THEY SHARE   •  •  •  •  •  •            193 STRAYED REVEL      255
        HIS FLYING STEEDS CAME NEAR   •  •  •  •  •  •  •         197 FRAG ANTIGONE       85
        SO I MIGHT HAVE THEE ALWAYS NEAR   •  •  •  •  •  •       205 CALAIS SANDS        32
        BUT AGITATED BRISK AND NEAR   •  •  •  •  •  •  •         224 EPILOG LAOCOON     111
        AH WE SHALL KNOW THAT WELL WHEN IT COMES NEAR   •        239 REVOLUTIONS         19
        NEVER YET COMES MORE NEAR  •  •  •  •  •  •  •  •         243 SUMMER NIGHT        45
        MOVED TO THE WINDOW NEAR AND SEE   •  •  •  •  •          250 WISH                31
        WITH A PLAINNESS AS NEAR  •  •  •  •  •  •  •  •          253 FUTURE              44
        AND NEAR ME ON THE GRASS LIES GLANVILS BOOK    •  •      256 SCHOLAR-GIPSY       31
        HAVE OFTEN PASSD THEE NEAR  •  •  •  •  •  •  •           258 SCHOLAR-GIPSY       96
        SAD PATIENCE TOO NEAR NEIGHBOUR TO DESPAIR  •  •  •      261 SCHOLAR-GIPSY      195
        AND NEAR AND REAL THE CHARM OF THY REPOSE  •  •  •       267 THYRSIS            149
        HE SCANND EACH WOUND EACH WEAKNESS NEAR    •  •  •       270 MEMORIAL VERSES  V  20
        FOR REST IN THIS OUTBUILDING NEAR   •  •  •  •  •        300 GRANDE CHARTR       27
        OR CHALETS NEAR THE ALPINE SNOW   •  •  •  •  •  •       304 GRANDE CHARTR      150
        BUT WHERE THE ROAD RUNS NEAR THE STREAM   •  •  •       305 GRANDE CHARTR      175
        I FEEL THEE NEAR ONCE MORE    •  •  •  •  •  •           306 OBERMANN            12
        FAREWELL WHETHER THOU NOW LIEST NEAR  •  •  •  •         311 OBERMANN           161
        ON THE GRASS NEAR ME STOOD    •  •  •  •  •  •           314 OBERMANN MORE       60
        REMOVE YET FURTHER OFF IF AUGHT COMES NEAR   •  •       332 MEROPE              69
        DRAW DRAW NEAR TO THE TOMB    •  •  •  •  •  •  •        342 MEROPE             385
        FRESH FROM THEIR FATHER DRAWS NEAR   •  •  •  •          346 MEROPE             498
        BOATS AND APPROACH NEAR AS WE DARED THE CHASM   •       358 MEROPE             838
        NEAR LYCOSURA BUILDS LYCAONS TOWN  •  •  •  •  •         359 MEROPE             848
        EARLY-SLAIN INNOCENTS NEAR    •  •  •  •  •  •           378 MEROPE            1239
        AFFECTS US WE COME NEAR   •  •  •  •  •  •  •            418 EMPEDOCLES I 2     195
        WHEN THE SOUND CLIMBS NEAR HIS SEAT  •  •  •  •          431 EMPEDOCLES II       69
        FRIENDS MORE NEAR US THAN A BIRD   •  •  •  •  •         453 POOR MATTHIAS       23
        OPEN LIVED TO US AND NEAR  •  •  •  •  •  •  •           455 POOR MATTHIAS       88
        THEN FROM THOSE WHITENING LIPS AS DEATH DREW NEAR       478 CROMWELL           213
        NEAR WHERE ATLAS HATH HIS STAND   •  •  •  •  •  •           PILLARS UNIVERS      2
        THAT LONG GAZER LEANING NEAR  •  •  •  •  •  •  •            META CLOISTER       26

NEARD
        THE HURTLING POLAR LIGHTS ARE NEARD   •  •  •  •  •       156 SAINT BRANDAN       11
        AND MIMIC BOATS THEIR HAVEN NEARD    •  •  •  •  •       223 EPILOG LAOCOON      69

NEARER
        WILL BE BROUGHT THOU POOR HEART HOW MUCH NEARER           20 MODERN SAPPHO       20
            TO THEE
        SEES GOD NO NEARER  •  •  •  •  •  •  •  •  •  •           38 STAGIRIUS           15
        WHEN THE MIND WAXING CLEARER SEES GOD NO NEARER  •  •     38 STAGIRIUS        V  16
        AND BRING US NEARER TO THE FINAL DAY  •  •  •  •         127 BALDER DEAD 3      474
        THROUGH A MIST I SEE THEE NEAR COME NEARER  •  •  •      145 TRISTRAM 2          75
        AH IT COMES NEARER  •  •  •  •  •  •  •  •  •  •          175 PARTING             23
        AH THEY BEND NEARER    •  •  •  •  •  •  •  •  •          176 PARTING             41
        NESTLING NEARER TO JOVES FEET   •  •  •  •  •  •         431 EMPEDOCLES II       77
        NEARER HUMAN WERE THEIR POWERS   •  •  •  •  •  •        453 POOR MATTHIAS       45
        NEARER AND NEARER TO THEIR CLOSING HOUR   •  •  •        469 ALARIC AT ROME     190
        NEARER AND NEARER TO THEIR CLOSING HOUR   •  •  •        469 ALARIC AT ROME     190

NEAREST
        NEAREST THE POLE AND WANDERING KIRGHIZZES   •  •  •       65 SOHRAB RUSTUM      133
        WHEN THEY HAVE WOE THEY BLAME THE NEAREST CAUSE  •  •    125 BALDER DEAD 3      427

NEARING
        AT SUNSET NEARING   •  •  •  •  •  •  •  •  •  •          192 STRAYED REVEL      205
        IN EVER-NEARING CIRCLE WEAVES HER SHADE   •  •  •  •     266 THYRSIS            132

NEARLY
        ITS TERM OF LIFE WAS NEARLY CLOSED   •  •  •  •  •       322 OBERMANN MORE      299
        MY FIRST STROKE OF REVENGE HAD NEARLY FALLEN   •  •      377 MEROPE            1224

NEARS
        MAN NEARS MAN MEETS AND LEAVES AGAIN  •  •  •  •  •  •    185 TERRACE BERNE    V  48

NEATH
        BLOODY NEATH THE FLARING SCONCES   •  •  •  •  •  •        14 CHURCH BROU 1       51
        AND NEATH THE GARDEN-WALK IT HUMS   •  •  •  •  •        184 TERRACE BERNE       11
        NEATH THE MILD CANOPY OF ENGLISH AIR  •  •  •  •         268 THYRSIS            194
        NEATH THE SOFT CANOPY OF ENGLISH AIR  •  •  •  •  •      268 THYRSIS          V 194
        AND NEATH THOSE CHESTNUT-TREES WHERE STIFF   •  •  •     312 OBERMANN MORE        9

NECESSITATE
        OF STRUGGLE THESE NECESSITATE   •  •  •  •  •  •  •        53 RESIGNATION         25
```

NECESSITY
 UNOERLEAPD MOUNTAINS OF NECESSITY   • • • • • •   7 REP FRIEND CONT   7
 SLAVES OF A TYRANNOUS NECESSITY   • • • • • •   10 MYCERINUS   42
 WHICH LEAVES THE FIERCE NECESSITY TO FEEL   • • •   153 TRISTRAM 3   123
 AND RENEW BY NECESSITY   • • • • • • •   437 EMPEDOCLES II   293
 SO STERN A LESSON AS NECESSITY   • • • • • • •   467 ALARIC AT ROME   142

NECESSITYS
 SORELY AGAINST THY WILL BY STRONG NECESSITYS ORDER   HOMER TRANS   31

NECK
 HIS ARMS ABOUT HIS NECK AND KISSD HIS LIPS   • • • •   81 SOHRAB RUSTUM   695
 HIS ARMS ROUND HIS SONS NECK AND WEPT ALOUD   • •   82 SOHRAB RUSTUM   728
 HAS OFTEN STROKED THY NECK AND GIVEN THEE FOOD   • •   83 SOHRAB RUSTUM   753
 ARCHING HIS NECK AND GLAD TO BE BESTRODE   • • • •   107 BALDER DEAD 2   76
 HIS WHITE DELICATE NECK   • • • • • • • •   188 STRAYED REVEL   83
 DROOPS ALL HIS SHEENY BROWN DEEP-FEATHERD NECK   • •   431 EMPEDOCLES II   76
 AND LEAVE IT ROUND THY NECK TO TWINE   • • • • • •   461 KAISER DEAD   81

NECKAN
 SITS NECKAN WITH HIS HARP OF GOLD   • • • • • •   159 NECKAN   3
 OF EARTH OF EARTH THE NECKAN SINGS   • • • • • •   159 NECKAN   11
 FALSE NECKAN SHARES MY BED SHE WEEPS   • • • • • •   160 NECKAN   35
 THAT NECKAN HEAVEN MIGHT GAIN   • • • • • • •   160 NECKAN   40
 BESIDE THE POOL SATE NECKAN   • • • • • • • •   160 NECKAN   45
 WHY SITTST THOU THERE O NECKAN   • • • • • • •   160 NECKAN   49
 BUT NECKAN IN THE TWILIGHT GREY   • • • • • • •   161 NECKAN   59
 SITS NECKAN WITH HIS HARP OF GOLD   • • • • • •   161 NECKAN   67
 AND NECKAN IN THE TWILIGHT GREY   • • • • • • •   161 NECKAN   V 59

NECKANS
 AND THERE BELOW THE NECKANS FEET   • • • • • •   159 NECKAN   7

NECKD
 IN MARCHING ORDER SPREAD OF LONG-NECKD CRANES   • •   64 SOHRAB RUSTUM   112

NECTAROUS
 AH NOT THE NECTAROUS POPPY LOVERS USE   • • • •   43 GIPSY CHILD   53

NEED
 NATURE IS FICKLE MAN HATH NEED OF REST   • • • •   5 HARMONY NATURE   9
 AND FOR SUCH DOING HAVE NO NEED OF EYES   • • • •   7 REP FRIEND   V 8
 FOR THEM VICISSITUDE AND NEED   • • • • • • •   56 RESIGNATION   143
 OLD MAN THE DEAD NEED NO ONE CLAIM NO KIN   • • •   62 SOHRAB RUSTUM   59
 NOR DID THERE NEED LESS THAN THE BURNING PILE   • •   198 FRAG ANTIGONE   98
 THEN IN SUCH HOUR OF NEED   • • • • • • • •   291 RUGBY CHAPEL   188
 AND YET MEN HAVE SUCH NEED OF JOY   • • • • • •   320 OBERMANN MORE   237
 WHAT THOUGH THERE STILL NEED EFFORT STRIFE   • • • •   322 OBERMANN MORE   289
 AND YET THEY HAVE SUCH NEED OF JOY   • • • • •   320 OBERMANN MORE   V 237
 TO SUCCOUR ME IN MY EXTREMEST NEED   • • • • • •   383 MEROPE   1376
 WHY SHOULD I SAY THAT LIFE NEED YIELD BUT MODERATE   425 EMPEDOCLES I 2   391
  BLISS
 NEVER DOUBTFUL OF THY NEED   • • • • • • • •   455 POOR MATTHIAS   116

NEEDED
 REFRESHMENT NEEDED BY THEE AS I JUDGE   • • • •   359 MEROPE   867
 A MOTHERS MURDER NEEDED HEST DIVINE   • • • • • •   385 MEROPE   1402

NEEDLE
 AND IN A CAVE A BED OF NEEDLE-ROCKS   • • • • • •   111 BALDER DEAD 2   220
 NEEDLE OF RUIN   • • • • • • • • • • •   400 MEROPE   1881

NEEDS
 WHETHER IT NEEDS THEE COUNT   • • • • • • • •   45 IN UTRUMQUE PAR   9
 WHO NEEDS NOT LOVE AND POWER TO KNOW   • • • • •   59 RESIGNATION   235
 BUT NOT TO-DAY TO-DAY HAS OTHER NEEDS   • • • •   67 SOHRAB RUSTUM   209
 DEEPER TO THESE MUST NEEDS ALLOW   • • • • • •   222 EPILOG LAOCOON   31
 MUST NEEDS READ CLEARER SURE THAN HE   • • • • •   250 WISH   28
 BUT IT NEEDS HEAVEN-SENT MOMENTS FOR THIS SKILL   •   256 SCHOLAR-GIPSY   50
 BUT IT NEEDS HAPPY MOMENTS FOR THIS SKILL   • • • •   256 SCHOLAR-GIPSY   V 50
 SHE NEEDS NOT JUNE FOR BEAUTYS HEIGHTENING   • • •   263 THYRSIS   20
 NEEDS MUST I LOSE THEM NEEDS WITH HEAVY HEART   • •   264 THYRSIS   38
 NEEDS MUST I LOSE THEM NEEDS WITH HEAVY HEART   • •   264 THYRSIS   38
 IT NEEDS NO YEARLY OFFERINGS AT HIS TOMB   • • • •   334 MEROPE   119
 ALL ENTERTAINMENT WHICH A TRAVELLER NEEDS   • • • •   359 MEROPE   870
 TO THEE THAT NEEDS NO OEDIPUS TO EXPLAIN   • • • •   365 MEROPE   988
 YET EXCULPATION NEEDS IT IF I SEEK   • • • • • •   387 MEROPE   1454
 PITY THYSELF NONE NEEDS COMPASSION MORE   • • • •   396 MEROPE   1761
 THAT NEEDS NO THANKS ONE IS FAR BETTER HERE   • • •   409 EMPEDOCLES I 1   103
 ALAS IT NEEDS NOT IS IT HARD TO KNOW   • • • • •   466 ALARIC AT ROME   119
 THERE NEEDS A MINSTREL OF DIVINER MIGHT   • • • •   471 ALARIC AT ROME   225
 WHY DOST THOU PROPHESY SO MY DEATH TO ME XANTHUS   HOMER TRANS   59
  IT NEEDS NOT

NEEDST
 BECAUSE THOU MUST NOT DREAM THOU NEEDST NOT   426 EMPEDOCLES I 2   426
  THEN DESPAIR

NEER
 HATH NEER BEEN MIRRORD ON THEIR SOUL   • • • • • •   226 EPILOG LAOCOON   188
 NEER TO HAVE GONE FROM THESE EYES   • • • • • •   377 MEROPE   1230
 AND BE AS IF THOU NEER HADST BEEN   • • • • • •   451 GEISTS GRAVE   40

NEGLECT
    NEITHER DO I NEGLECT THEE NOW THOUGH DEAD • • • • •   103 BALDER DEAD 1   294

NEGLECTED
    TO HIS NEGLECTED WIFE AND WHAT HE IS • • • • • •   116 BALDER DEAD 3   104
    THE CHASE NEGLECTED AND HIS HOUND • • • • • •   137 TRISTRAM 1   225

NEIGHBOUR
    BEHELD HIM COME AND TO HIS NEIGHBOUR SPAKE • • •   113 BALDER DEAD 3   5
    AND STRAIGHT HIS NEIGHBOUR MOVED WITH WRATH REPLIED   114 BALDER DEAD 3   20
    SAD PATIENCE TOO NEAR NEIGHBOUR TO DESPAIR • • • •   261 SCHOLAR-GIPSY   195

NEIGHBOURING
    THAT VAST SKY-NEIGHBOURING MOUNTAIN OF MILK SNOW • •   66 SOHRAB RUSTUM   162
    MAY THEN MORE NEIGHBOURING COURSES PLY • • • •   180 FAREWELL   74

NEIGHING
    STEEDS ARE NEIGHING GALLANTS GLITTERING • • • •   13 CHURCH BROU 1   9
    THE NEIGHING STEEDS THE RINGING BLOWS • • • •   138 TRISTRAM 1   259

NELEIDAE
    WHO SHOOK THE FIERCE NELEIDAE ON THEIR THRONE • •   338 MEROPE   292

NELEUS
    FROM THE AEOLIAN STOCK OF NELEUS SPRUNG • • • •   337 MEROPE   236
    O HERITAGE OF NELEUS • • • • • • • •   399 MEROPE   1845

NELLYS
    DAZZLED NELLYS YOUTHFUL EYNE • • • • • • •   458 POOR MATTHIAS   191

NEPHEW
    UNCLE AND NEPHEW DISAPPEAR THEIR DEATH • •   364 MEROPE   979
    NEPHEW THY FRIENDS ARE SOUNDED AND PROVE TRUE • •   390 MEROPE   1587

NEPHEWS
    NOT NOW OF SPARTA WHERE HIS NEPHEWS REIGND • • •   337 MEROPE   232
    TWO BROTHERS AND THEIR ORPHAN NEPHEWS STROVE • •   389 MEROPE   1548
    LAIAS IN ARMS SPRANG TO HIS NEPHEWS SIDE • • •   402 MEROPE   1933

NERVE
    EACH NERVE MORE LOOSELY STRUNG • • • • • • •   212 GROWING OLD   10
    EACH NERVE MORE WEAKLY STRUNG • • • • • • •   212 GROWING OLD   V 10

NERVES
    FOR FEELING NERVES AND LIVING BREATH • • • • •   22 YOUTH AND CALM   18
    TILL HAVING USED OUR NERVES WITH BLISS AND TEEN • •   259 SCHOLAR-GIPSY   147

NEST
    A BREEDING EAGLE SITTING ON HER NEST • • • • •   77 SOHRAB RUSTUM   557
    CHIDING HIS MATE BACK TO HER NEST BUT SHE • • • •   78 SOHRAB RUSTUM   566
    LIKE HELPLESS BIRDS IN THE WARM NEST • • • • •   140 TRISTRAM 1   328
    AND THE SEA-EAGLES BUILD THEIR NEST • • • • •   414 EMPEDOCLES I 2   67

NESTLING
    NESTLING NEARER TO JOVES FEET • • • • • • • •   431 EMPEDOCLES II   77

NETHER
    ME ON THIS CHEERLESS NETHER WORLD YE THREW • • • •   110 BALDER DEAD 2   212

NETS
    DRAGGING THEIR NETS THROUGH THE ROUGH WAVES AFAR • •   151 TRISTRAM 3   80

NETTED
    BUT HIM TOO FOES AWAIT AND NETTED SNARES • • • •   111 BALDER DEAD 2   219

NETTLES
    TALL GRASSES AND WHITE FLOWERING NETTLES WAVE • •   259 SCHOLAR-GIPSY   139

NETWORK
    WHEN BURSTING THROUGH THE NETWORK SUPERPOSED • •   7 REP FRIEND CONT   10

NEUTRAL
    CROWD AS WE WILL ITS NEUTRAL SPACE • • • • • •   59 RESIGNATION   258
    CROWD AS WE WILL ITS NEUTRAL ROOM • • • • • •   59 RESIGNATION   V 258

NEVER
    STAND NEVER IDLE BUT GO ALWAYS ROUND • • • • •   4 DUKE WELLINGTON   2
    NATURE AND MAN CAN NEVER BE FAST FRIENDS • • •   5 HARMONY NATURE   13
    MOULD NOT THE SOLID EARTH THOUGH NEVER WINDS • • •   8 RELIGIOUS ISOL   10
    MOULDS NOT THE SOLID EARTH THOUGH NEVER WINDS • •   8 RELIGIOUS ISOL   V 10
    WHERE EARTHLY VOICE CLIMBS NEVER WING THEIR FLIGHT   10 MYCERINUS   44
    MIGHT WANDER ALL DAY LONG AND NEVER TIRE • • • •   11 MYCERINUS   91
    TILL THAT HOUR SHE NEVER SORROWD • • • • •   14 CHURCH BROU 1   59
    BUT FROM THEN SHE NEVER SMILED • • • • • •   14 CHURCH BROU 1   60
    WHERE HORN AND HOUND AND VASSALS NEVER COME • •   17 CHURCH BROU 3   3
    WHERE THOU YOUNG PRINCE SHALT NEVER MORE ARISE • •   18 CHURCH BROU 3   7
    AND NEVER A SPRAY OF YEW • • • • • • • •   20 REQUIESCAT   2
    WHICH THE CHARMD WINDS NEVER DROWN • • • • •   27 NEW SIRENS   28
    INTO DAYLIGHT NEVER GREW • • • • • • • •   29 NEW SIRENS   106
    GUESTS THE DULL SENSE NEVER KNEW • • • • •   30 NEW SIRENS   136

NEVER   (CONTINUED)
AND NEVER TOUCHES THE SHIP-SIDE AGAIN   41 HUMAN LIFE   24
NEVER WAS EXILES MEMORY HALF SO SAD   42 GIPSY CHILD   V   27
AND NEVER ANGELS SORROW SO FORLORN   42 GIPSY CHILD   V   28
SO I LONG HOPED BUT HIM I NEVER FIND   62 SOHRAB RUSTUM   53
TO FIND A FATHER THOU HAST NEVER SEEN   63 SOHRAB RUSTUM   70
NEVER WAS THAT FIELD LOST OR THAT FOE SAVED   71 SOHRAB RUSTUM   328
BUT NEVER WAS MY HEART THUS TOUCHD BEFORE   74 SOHRAB RUSTUM   436
NEVER TILL NOW DEFILED SANK TO THE DUST   76 SOHRAB RUSTUM   498
A HEAP OF FLUTTERING FEATHERS NEVER MORE   78 SOHRAB RUSTUM   569
NEVER THE BLACK AND DRIPPING PRECIPICES   78 SOHRAB RUSTUM   571
THE MIGHTY RUSTUM NEVER HAD A SON   78 SOHRAB RUSTUM   578
FOR THOU HAST GONE WHERE I SHALL NEVER GO   83 SOHRAB RUSTUM   748
HAVE NEVER KNOWN MY GRANDSIRES FURROWD FACE   83 SOHRAB RUSTUM   756
AND I SHALL NEVER END THIS LIFE OF BLOOD   85 SOHRAB RUSTUM   826
NEVER DEFACD TILL NOW SHAMD TO THE DUST   76 SOHRAB RUSTUM   V 498
NEVER TILL NOW DEFILED SUNK TO THE DUST   76 SOHRAB RUSTUM   V 498
RE-ENTER THEM WITH WONDER NEVER FILL   128 BALDER DEAD 3   535
WHICH WILL NEVER LET HIM REST   138 TRISTRAM 1   246
NEVER SURELY HAS BEEN SEEN   131 TRISTRAM 1   V
THAT WILL NEVER LET HIM REST   138 TRISTRAM 1   V 246
AND THY BEAUTY NEVER WAS MORE FAIR   142 TRISTRAM 2   20
ISEULT LEAVES THEE TRISTRAM NEVER MORE   146 TRISTRAM 2   100
CAN NEVER END THEIR TASKS ARE HARD TO PLEASE   153 TRISTRAM 3   V 142
BUT AH SHE GAVE ME NEVER A LOOK   163 FORSAKEN MERM   80
TO BE LONG LOVED WAS NEVER FRAMED   178 FAREWELL   18
THEY ASK A SOUL WHICH NEVER SWAYS   178 FAREWELL   27
WOULD NEVER LET US SATIATE HERE   180 FAREWELL   88
THEY ASK A SOUL THAT NEVER SWAYS   178 FAREWELL   V   27
WHICH NEVER YET WITHOUT REMORSE   181 ISOLATION MARG   14
YET SHE CHASTE QUEEN HAD NEVER PROVED   181 ISOLATION MARG   25
SAY WILL IT NEVER HEAL   200 PHILOMELA   9
ALONG THE NEVER-SILENT STRAIT   204 CALAIS SANDS   3
ALONG THE NEVER-SILENT BEACH   204 CALAIS SANDS   V   3
OR AS THOU NEVER CAMST IN SOOTH   209 LONGING   9
THEY NEVER SHONE FOR ME   209 DESPONDENCY   4
AND NEVER COME AGAIN   209 DESPONDENCY   8
ENDS WE SEEK WE NEVER SHALL ATTAIN   210 SELF-DECEPTION   26
AND NEVER KNOW HOW WITH THE SOUL IT FARES   236 PALLADIUM   20
WAY AFTER WAY CHANGES THAT NEVER CEASE   239 REVOLUTIONS   7
NEVER BY PASSION QUITE POSSESSD   243 SUMMER NIGHT   32
AND NEVER QUITE BENUMBD BY THE WORLDS SWAY   243 SUMMER NIGHT   33
NEVER YET COMES MORE NEAR   243 SUMMER NIGHT   45
WHICH NEVER DEADENS INTO REST   243 SUMMER NIGHT   V 28
WHICH NEVER WAS THE FRIEND OF ONE   251 WISH   37
THAT NEVER WILL THOSE ON ITS BREAST   253 FUTURE   66
WHO NEVER DEEPLY FELT NOR CLEARLY WILLD   260 SCHOLAR-GIPSY   173
WHOSE INSIGHT NEVER HAS BORNE FRUIT IN DEEDS   260 SCHOLAR-GIPSY   174
WHOSE VAGUE RESOLVES NEVER HAVE BEEN FULFILLD   260 SCHOLAR-GIPSY   175
WHOSE WEAK RESOLVES NEVER HAVE BEEN FULFILLD   260 SCHOLAR-GIPSY   V 175
BUT THYRSIS NEVER MORE WE SWAINS SHALL SEE   265 THYRSIS   77
BUT AH OF OUR POOR THAMES SHE NEVER HEARD   265 THYRSIS   98
HER FOOT THE CUMNER COWSLIPS NEVER STIRRD   265 THYRSIS   99
HER FOOT THE CUMNOR COWSLIPS NEVER STIRRD   265 THYRSIS   V 99
FOR NEVER HAS SUCH SOOTHING VOICE   271 MEMORIAL VERSES   35
AND NEVER ONCE POSSESS OUR SOUL   277 SOUTHERN NIGHT   71
IN THE NEVER IDLE WORKSHOP OF NATURE   286 HAWORTH CHURCH   136
WHERE TRAVELLERS NEVER PASS WHERE ONLY COME   373 MEROPE   1169
AND THE STANCH FURIES NEVER-SILENT SCOURGE   373 MEROPE   1187
ART THOU THEN COME NEVER TO PART AGAIN   377 MEROPE   1221
NEVER BEEN TORN FROM THIS BREAST   377 MEROPE   1231
NEVER TO EBB THE ACCURST   378 MEROPE   1245
A NEVER-CHANGING INDEX TO REVENGE   381 MEROPE   1317
BY POLYPHONTES NEVER FAILD-IN ONCE   387 MEROPE   1476
HE MAY FOR NEVER DID THE GODS ALLOW   388 MEROPE   1508
ARE NEVER FREE FROM DOUBT THOUGH SOMETIMES DUE   388 MEROPE   1522
OF YOUTH TIS LIKE HAD NEVER QUITE FORGONE   394 MEROPE   1703
THE THOUGHT OF VENGEANCE ON ME NEVER QUITE   394 MEROPE   1704
NEVER AGAIN IN LIFE NEXT AGENTS FEED   365 MEROPE   V
BUT NEVER ON SO FAIR A MORN THE SUN   406 EMPEDOCLES I 1   9
THE WIT AND COUNSEL OF MAN WAS NEVER CLEAR   413 EMPEDOCLES I 2   30
AND NEVER SEES A WHOLE   415 EMPEDOCLES I 2   85
TELL HIM I NEVER FAILD TO LOVE HIS LYRE   428 EMPEDOCLES I 2   468
NEVER TO CEASE TO WRITHE AND TRY TO REST   430 EMPEDOCLES II   60
AND NEVER LET US CLASP AND FEEL THE ALL   439 EMPEDOCLES II   353
NEVER TO CEASE TO WRITHE AND TRY TO SLEEP   430 EMPEDOCLES II   V 60
FLUTTER CHIRP SHE NEVER STIRRD   453 POOR MATTHIAS   34
NEVER DOUBTFUL OF THY NEED   455 POOR MATTHIAS   116
AND NEVER PINE   460 KAISER DEAD   60
THINGS THAT MAY CEASE BUT NEVER BE FORGOT   462 ALARIC AT ROME   16
IT MOVES BUT NEVER MOVETH ON   479 HAYSWATER BOAT   6
THERE WHERE TEARS ARE NEVER MORE TO RUN   482 THEKLAS ANSWER   12
FORTUNATE FIRS WHO NEVER THINK   483 ROME-SICKNESS   9
AND WHEREFORE THEN IF HE CAN NEVER CHANGE   LUCRETIUS 3   V   8
THE DOUBT THAT ASSAILS ALL THINGS NEVER WON   FRAGMENT 8   3

NEW

OF THE NEW PILE THE SUNLIGHT SHINES   16 CHURCH BROU 2   2
WAS NEW MADE TO BREAK AGAIN   23 MEMORY-PICTURE   38
TO HIM ADDRESSD WHO WOULD RECAST HER NEW   37 WORLDS TRIUMPHS   2

NEW   (CONTINUED)

TO HIM ADDRESSD WHO WOULD RECAST IT NEW . . . .   37 WORLDS TRIUMPHS V   2
HE SEES THE DROWSY NEW-WAKED CLOWN . . . . . .   57 RESIGNATION   181
AND TRANQUIL FROM WHOSE FLOOR THE NEW-BATHED STARS 87 SOHRAB RUSTUM   891
NEW PITCHD THE HIGH PAVILION IN THE MIDST . . .   67 SOHRAB RUSTUM   V 193
NEW MESSES OF THE BOAR SERIMNERS FLESH . . . .   97 BALDER DEAD 1   67
IN NEW-RECOVERD SEATS THE HAPPIER DAY . . . .   128 BALDER DEAD 3   513
WHAT NEW CHANGE SHALL WE NOW SEE . . . . . .   139 TRISTRAM 1   296
A HEART EVER NEW . . . .   177 PARTING   80
EVER NEW MAGIC . . . .   188 STRAYED REVEL   75
NEW HEARTS WITH THE ENQUIRERS HOLY ROBE . . .   198 FRAG DEJANEIRA   16
AND SMILE ON THY NEW WORLD AND BE . . . . . .   208 LONGING   7
MANS NEW SPIRIT SINCE IT WAS NOT WE . . . . .   210 SELF-DECEPTION   14
SO VARIOUS SO BEAUTIFUL SO NEW . . . .   211 DOVER BEACH   32
NEW STREETS WITH FINE DOUBLE TROTTOIRS . . . .   214 NEW ROME   V 15
DESERTED IS THE NEW-REAPD GRAIN . . . .   217 BACCHANALIA 1   V   4
COMES THE NEW AGE . . . .   220 BACCHANALIA 2   36
BARDS MAKE NEW POEMS . . . .   220 BACCHANALIA 2   37
THINKERS NEW SCHOOLS . . . .   220 BACCHANALIA 2   38
STATESMEN NEW SYSTEMS . . . .   220 BACCHANALIA 2   39
CRITICS NEW RULES . . . .   220 BACCHANALIA 2   40
TEMPTS NOT THE BRIGHT NEW AGE . . . .   220 BACCHANALIA 2   51
POOR BOUNDED WORDS AND MAKES THEM NEW . . . .   224 EPILOG LAOCOON   96
FOR HE LENT A NEW LIFE TO THESE HILLS . . . .   228 YOUTH OF NATURE   14
BEHOLD THE NEW WORLD RISE . . . .   237 PROGRESS   4
TO CLEAR THE NEW WORLDS WAY . . . .   237 PROGRESS   16
SAY YE THE SPIRIT OF MAN HAS FOUND NEW ROADS .   237 PROGRESS   25
THAT MAN MUST STILL TO SOME NEW WORSHIP PRESS   238 PROGRESS   V
YET HERE IS PEACE FOR EVER NEW . . . .   249 KENSINGTON GARD   29
BUT HERE THIS CALM IS NOTHING NEW . . . . . .   KENSINGTON GARD V 29
OF THE NEW-BORN CLEAR-FLOWING STREAM . . . .   252 FUTURE   12
BREEDS NEW BEGINNINGS DISAPPOINTMENTS NEW . .   260 SCHOLAR-GIPSY   177
BREEDS NEW BEGINNINGS DISAPPOINTMENTS NEW . .   260 SCHOLAR-GIPSY   177
BY BARN IN THRESHING-TIME BY NEW-BUILT RICK .   263 THYRSIS   34
AND SCENT OF HAY NEW-MOWN . . . .   265 THYRSIS   76
THE HEART LESS BOUNDING AT EMOTION NEW . . .   266 THYRSIS   139
WHERE CRIES ARE RISING EVER NEW . . . . . .   277 SOUTHERN NIGHT   62
NEW-COMING SON OF MANKIND . . . .   298 HEINES GRAVE   220
FOR THE WORLD LOVES NEW WAYS . . . .   307 OBERMANN   42
A CONQUERING NEW-BORN JOY AWOKE . . . . . .   316 OBERMANN MORE   115
HOW HAD ITS GLORY NEW . . . .   317 OBERMANN MORE   142
IN VAIN MEN STILL WITH HOPING NEW . . . . .   318 OBERMANN MORE   177
RIVE ITS DRY BONES AND WITH NEW FORCE . . . .   319 OBERMANN MORE   199
A NEW-SPRUNG WORLD INFORM . . . .   319 OBERMANN MORE   200
THE SUN SHONE IN THE NEW-WASHD SKY . . . . .   319 OBERMANN MORE   209
SEE I MAKE ALL THINGS NEW . . . .   320 OBERMANN MORE   232
AS WHEN THE PAST WAS NEW . . . .   320 OBERMANN MORE   240
SOME NEW SUCH HOPE MUST DAWN AT LAST . . . .   321 OBERMANN MORE   243
THE NEW IS NOT YET BORN . . . .   321 OBERMANN MORE   246
A GREEN NEW EARTH APPEARS . . . .   322 OBERMANN MORE   286
BUT THOU THOUGH TO THE WORLDS NEW HOUR . . .   322 OBERMANN MORE   301
HOPE TO A WORLD NEW-MADE . . . .   323 OBERMANN MORE   312
A NEW SUCH HOPE MUST DAWN AT LAST . . . . .   321 OBERMANN MORE   V 243
TO HIS NEW SUBJECTS THAN TO US HIS FRIENDS .   337 MEROPE   242
FOR DEATH HIS ANCIENT TO HIS NEW-MADE FRIENDS   338 MEROPE   265
FROM SATURNS SEARCH AMONG THE NEW-YEAND LAMBS   355 MEROPE   738
BASILIS HIS NEW CITY WHICH HE NOW . . . . .   359 MEROPE   847
TO CLOSE AN OLD WOUND NOT TO OPEN NEW . . .   379 MEROPE   1257
MY NEW-WON TREASURE THY BELOVED LIFE . . . .   381 MEROPE   1291
RISK FROM MY NEW-RESTORED MY ONLY SON . . .   387 MEROPE   1456
WITH NEW WALLS WHICH THE VICTORS . . . . .   400 MEROPE   1851
YE WITNESS YE NEW-BUILT TOWERS . . . . . .   400 MEROPE   1856
A NEW-MADE WIFE I FROM ARCADIA CAME . . . .   403 MEROPE   1972
ALMOST AS MUCH AS THE NEW DANCING-GIRL . . .   407 EMPEDOCLES I 1   35
SINCE BROILS TEAR US IN TWAIN SINCE THIS NEW SWARM 410 EMPEDOCLES I 1   121
A NEW-MADE WORLD UP-SPRINGS . . . .   418 EMPEDOCLES I 2   179
SO EACH NEW MAN STRIKES ROOT INTO A FAR FORE-TIME 418 EMPEDOCLES I 2   191
AND WHEN HERE EACH NEW THING . . . . . .   418 EMPEDOCLES I 2   194
AND NOT THE WORLD ARE NEW . . . .   419 EMPEDOCLES I 2   208
LOOKD ON TO SOMETHING NEW . . . .   425 EMPEDOCLES I 2   378
KING SEBERTS WORK THE WONDROUS MINSTER NEW . .   444 WESTMIN ABBEY   16
AND THAT NEW MINSTER IN THE MATTED FEN . .   444 WESTMIN ABBEY   19
OF NEW CREATION EVERMORE . . . .   450 GEISTS GRAVE   26
AS THEY LOOKED STERNLY ON BEHELD NEW VICTORIES   468 ALARIC AT ROME   174
NEW DREAMS OF WIDE DOMINION MIGHTIER HIGHER .   469 ALARIC AT ROME   175
WITH HEART NEW STRUNG AND STERN RESOLVE HE STOOD 473 CROMWELL   66

NEWLY
DISENCHANTED BY HABIT AND NEWLY AWAKING . . .   20 MODERN SAPPHO   23
LASHES THE NEWLY-MADE GRAVE . . . .   286 HAWORTH CHURCH   133

NEWNESS
OF NEWNESS AND DELIGHT . . . .   424 EMPEDOCLES I 2   355

NEWS
SPEAK IS THERE NEWS OR ANY NIGHT ALARM . . .   62 SOHRAB RUSTUM   32
WHAT NEWS BUT SIT DOWN FIRST AND EAT AND DRINK   67 SOHRAB RUSTUM   206
SURELY THE NEWS WILL ONE DAY REACH HIS EAR . .   78 SOHRAB RUSTUM   581
RIDE BACK AND TELL IN HEAVEN THIS HEAVY NEWS   124 BALDER DEAD 3   371
BRINGING ME OF MY BOY THE ANNUAL NEWS . . .   350 MEROPE   599

NEWS   (CONTINUED)
            NO CERTAIN NEWS IF LIKE THE REST IT RUN   • • • •   350 MEROPE   600
            O KING ALL HAIL I COME WITH WEIGHTY NEWS   • • • •   354 MEROPE   710
            AND WHO ART THOU WHO BRINGEST ME SUCH NEWS   • • • •   355 MEROPE   716
            TO CYPSELUS AT BASILIS THIS NEWS   • • • • • • • •   359 MEROPE   846
            WHO SHALL TELL MEROPE THIS HEAVY NEWS   • • • •   359 MEROPE   858
            STRANGER THIS NEWS THOU BRINGEST IS TOO GREAT   • • • •   359 MEROPE   859
            ARRIVED FROM TEGEA WITH WEIGHTY NEWS   • • • • • •   361 MEROPE   915
            AH ME THE WRONG EXPECTANT GOT HIS NEWS   • • • •   361 MEROPE   922
            AND WHAT ARCADIAN NEWS HAD HE TO TELL   • • • •   361 MEROPE   926
            YET THEN ANOTHER MAN WOULD BRING THIS NEWS   • • • •   362 MEROPE   942
            FORGIVE FORGIVE THE BRINGER OF SUCH NEWS   • • • •   363 MEROPE   949
            NEWS OF MY BUSINESS PASTIME TEMPER FRIENDS • • • •   380 MEROPE   1281
            TELLS ME ENOUGH THOU KNOWST THE NEWS WHICH ALL   • • • •   393 MEROPE   1685
            EVEN AFTER NEWS OF THIS SAD DEATH OUR LEAGUE   • • • •   394 MEROPE   1689
            OF YOUR DEAD MASTERS LINE I BRING YOU NEWS • • • •   400 MEROPE   1883
            WITH GLAD ACCLAIM ERE THEY FORESTALL MY NEWS   • • • •   401 MEROPE   1887
            STRANGER THE NEWS THOU BRINGEST IS TOO GREAT   • • •   359 MEROPE   V 859
            ASK NOT THE LATEST NEWS OF THE LAST MIRACLE   • • • •   415 EMPEDOCLES I 2   106
            WHAT KAISER DEAD THE HEAVY NEWS   • • • • • •   458 KAISER DEAD   1

NEWSTEAD
            WHAT MADE MY HEART AT NEWSTEAD FULLEST SWELL   • •   166 PICT NEWSTEAD   1

NEXT
            SOME DAY NEXT YEAR I SHALL BE   • • • • • • •   23 MEMORY-PICTURE   19
            HAMAN WHO NEXT TO PERAN-WISA RULED   • • • • • • •   64 SOHRAB RUSTUM   108
            NEXT THE MORE TEMPERATE TOORKMUNS OF THE SOUTH   • • •   64 SOHRAB RUSTUM   121
            WHAT MUST I HOWL IN THE NEXT WORLD   • • • • • •   91 SICK KING BOKH   99
            THOU CAMEST NEAR THE NEXT O WARRIOR THOR   • • •   115 BALDER DEAD 3   71
            AND FREYA NEXT CAME NIGH WITH GOLDEN TEARS • • • •   116 BALDER DEAD 3   90
            A ROBE OF SACKCLOTH NEXT THE SMOOTH WHITE SKIN   • •   166 AUSTERITY POET   11
            WHAT MATTERS IT NEXT YEAR HE WILL RETURN   • • •   265 THYRSIS   72
            TURN WE NEXT TO THE DEAD   • • • • • • • • •   282 HAWORTH CHURCH   47
            OR NEXT MORNING WITH LIMBS   • • • • • • •   297 HEINES GRAVE   176
            ONE NIGHT AND THE NEXT DAY AT DAWN FARED ON   • • •   356 MEROPE   747
            SEIZED HE ESCAPES AND NEXT I FIND HIM HERE • • • •   364 MEROPE   983
            TO THE DEAR NEXT-OF-KIN OF HIM HE MURDERD   • • • •   374 MEROPE   1197
            NEVER AGAIN IN LIFE NEXT AGENTS FEED • • • • •   365 MEROPE   V
            THENCE HE ESCAPD AND NEXT I FIND HIM HERE   • • •   365 MEROPE   V
            BUT NEXT WE WOULD REVERSE   • • • • • •   422 EMPEDOCLES I 2   312
            AND NEXT THE CROWNING IMPOTENCE OF DEATH   • • •   448 WESTMIN ABBEY   130
            GEIST CAME NEXT OUR LITTLE FRIEND   • • • • • •   454 POOR MATTHIAS   57

NICHED
            WHERE THE NICHED SNOW-BED SPRAYS DOWN   • • • •   176 PARTING   49

NICOPOLIS
            THAT HALTING SLAVE WHO IN NICOPOLIS   • • • • • • •   2 TO A FRIEND   6
            OF THAT LAME SLAVE WHO IN NICOPOLIS   • • • • • • •   2 TO A FRIEND   V 6

NIFLHEIM
            THE PLAINS OF NIFLHEIM WHERE DWELL THE DEAD   • •   100 BALDER DEAD 1   172
            THE PLAINS OF NIFLHEIM WHERE DWELL THE DEAD   • •   109 BALDER DEAD 2   150
            BUT HELA INTO NIFLHEIM THOU THREWST   • • • • •   121 BALDER DEAD 3   276
            OF NIFLHEIM HE SAW ONE GHOST COME NEAR   • • • •   124 BALDER DEAD 3   382

NIGH
            WARNING THE GODS THAT FOES DRAW NIGH TO HEAVEN   • •   105 BALDER DEAD 2   7
            AND FREYA NEXT CAME NIGH WITH GOLDEN TEARS • • • •   116 BALDER DEAD 3   90
            WHEN I DRAW NIGH AND THE WAN TRIBES OF DEAD   • •   126 BALDER DEAD 3   464
            AND THEN THE OLD MAN TOTTERS NIGH   • • • • • •   213 PROGRESS POESY   9
            AND WELL-NIGH CHANGE HIS OWN IDENTITY   • • •   246 BURIED LIFE   34
            IN THE QUICK WORLD THAT RUMBLES NIGH • • • • •   KENSINGTON GARD   V 21
            IN THE HUGE WORLD THAT RUMBLES NIGH   • • • • • •   KENSINGTON GARD   V 21
            UNTO ITS HAVEN COMING NIGH   • • • • • •   276 SOUTHERN NIGHT   46
            DULL LOOK ON WHEN DEATH IS NIGH   • • • • • •   455 POOR MATTHIAS   107
            BELIEVE AND THOU SHALT FIND THE HOLY NIGH   • • • •   483 THEKLAS ANSWER   20

NIGHER
            TO GOD COMES NO NIGHER   • • • • • • • • • • •   38 STAGIRIUS   17
            WHEN THE SOUL RISING HIGHER TO GOD COMES NO NIGHER   38 STAGIRIUS   V 14

NIGHT
            SWEEP IN THE SOUNDING STILLNESS OF THE NIGHT   • •   10 MYCERINUS   46
            AND THE NIGHT WAXES AND THE SHADOWS FALL   • • •   10 MYCERINUS   72
            SO SIX LONG YEARS HE REVELLD NIGHT AND DAY • • • •   12 MYCERINUS   122
            IN THE STILL NIGHT ACROSS THE STEAMING FLATS   • •   12 MYCERINUS   126
            LAST NIGHT WE STOOD EARNESTLY TALKING TOGETHER   • •   19 MODERN SAPPHO   9
            TO-NIGHT IT DOTH INHERIT   • • • • • • • • • •   21 REQUIESCAT   15
            AND I FEEL THE COLD NIGHT-AIR   • • • • • • •   32 NEW SIRENS   190
            WITH THE DUMB WOODS AND THE NIGHT ALONE   • • •   32 NEW SIRENS   194
            WE STEM ACROSS THE SEA OF LIFE BY NIGHT   • • •   41 HUMAN LIFE   27
            WE STEM ACROSS THE SEA BY NIGHT   • • • • • •   41 HUMAN LIFE   V 27
            ERE THE LONG NIGHT WHOSE STILLNESS BROOKS NO STAR   • •   43 GIPSY CHILD   45
            OH ONCE ERE NIGHT IN THY SUCCESS THY CHAIN • • • •   44 GIPSY CHILD   66
            SEASONS ALTERNATING AND NIGHT AND DAY   • • •   45 IN UTRUMQUE PAR   5
            THAT NIGHT IN THE WIDE-GLIMMERING SEA   • • •   54 RESIGNATION   85
            SOHRAB ALONE HE SLEPT NOT ALL NIGHT LONG   • • • •   61 SOHRAB RUSTUM   5
            SPEAK IS THERE NEWS OR ANY NIGHT ALARM   • • • •   62 SOHRAB RUSTUM   32

NIGHT   (CONTINUED)

SLEEP BUT I SLEEP NOT ALL NIGHT LONG I LIE	62	SOHRAB RUSTUM	36
BUT RUSTUM CAME LAST NIGHT ALOOF HE SITS	66	SOHRAB RUSTUM	178
PLUNGING ALL DAY IN THE BLUE WAVES AT NIGHT	69	SOHRAB RUSTUM	287
AND COMES AT NIGHT TO DIE UPON THE SAND	76	SOHRAB RUSTUM	506
AND ALL DAY LONG AND WHEN NIGHT COMES THE LAMP	81	SOHRAB RUSTUM	675
AND NIGHT CAME DOWN OVER THE SOLEMN WASTE	86	SOHRAB RUSTUM	865
AND DARKEND ALL AND A COLD FOG WITH NIGHT	86	SOHRAB RUSTUM	867
BUT IN THE NIGHT WHICH WAS WITH WIND	90	SICK KING BOKH	74
AS THEY WERE THIRSTY AND THE NIGHT	90	SICK KING BOKH	81
VEX ONE ANOTHER NIGHT AND DAY	93	SICK KING BOKH	174
AND NOW WOULD NIGHT HAVE FALLN AND FOUND THEM YET	95	BALDER DEAD 1	15
WHILE TWILIGHT FELL AND SACRED NIGHT CAME ON	97	BALDER DEAD 1	71
BOTH NIGHT AND DAY AND BY THE INNER WALL	98	BALDER DEAD 1	91
BUT NIGHT CAME DOWN AND DARKEND ASGARD STREETS	101	BALDER DEAD 1	202
AND HERMOD GAZED INTO THE NIGHT AND SAID	102	BALDER DEAD 1	240
AND FAR INTO THE NIGHT THEY WAILD THEIR DIRGE	103	BALDER DEAD 1	275
AND TWAS WHEN NIGHT IS BORDERING HARD ON DAWN	103	BALDER DEAD 1	280
SO BALDER FADED IN THE NIGHT AWAY	104	BALDER DEAD 1	337
HEREAFTER IN THE BLACKEST DEAD OF NIGHT	105	BALDER DEAD 2	5
BUT ALL AT NIGHT RETURN TO ODINS HALL	105	BALDER DEAD 2	17
WHOM THEY BRING BACK WITH THEM AT NIGHT TO HEAVEN	105	BALDER DEAD 2	27
ALL DAY AND DAYLIGHT WANED AND NIGHT CAME ON	107	BALDER DEAD 2	81
AND ALL THAT NIGHT HE RODE AND JOURNEYD SO	107	BALDER DEAD 2	82
BUT FROM THY LIPS O BALDER NIGHT OR DAY	116	BALDER DEAD 3	83
INTO THE SMOKE-WRAPT SEA AND NIGHT CAME ON	119	BALDER DEAD 3	195
THEN THE WIND FELL WITH NIGHT AND THERE WAS CALM	119	BALDER DEAD 3	196
ALL NIGHT THEY ATE THE BOAR SERIMNERS FLESH	119	BALDER DEAD 3	210
DIVIDING CLEAR THE PATHS OF NIGHT AND DAY	121	BALDER DEAD 3	265
AND AS IN THE DARK NIGHT A TRAVELLING MAN	119	BALDER DEAD 3	V
AGAINST THE WOLVES AND ALL NIGHT LONG IT FLARES	119	BALDER DEAD 3	V
CHRIST WHAT A NIGHT HOW THE SLEET WHIPS THE PANE	130	TRISTRAM 1	4
ON THIS WILD DECEMBER NIGHT	130	TRISTRAM 1	14
AND THIS ROUGH DECEMBER-NIGHT	136	TRISTRAM 1	181
THE WIND IS DOWN BUT SHELL NOT COME TO-NIGHT	139	TRISTRAM 1	300
TO-NIGHT MY PAGE SHALL KEEP ME COMPANY	140	TRISTRAM 1	310
TO BED GOOD NIGHT	140	TRISTRAM 1	314
OF YOUR ILLUMINED HAUNTS BY NIGHT	141	TRISTRAM 1	354
WHAT VOICES ARE THESE ON THE CLEAR NIGHT-AIR	142	TRISTRAM 1	372
AND NOW TO-NIGHT SHE LAUGHS AND SPEAKS	147	TRISTRAM 2	128
SHOOK HER WEAK BOSOM DAY AND NIGHT	147	TRISTRAM 2	133
THE AIR OF THE DECEMBER-NIGHT	147	TRISTRAM 2	147
BY NIGHT WITH BOISTEROUS BUGLE-PEAL	148	TRISTRAM 2	177
AND THEY WOULD STILL HAVE LISTEND TILL DARK NIGHT	151	TRISTRAM 3	56
SHE HAS HER CHILDREN TOO AND NIGHT AND DAY	152	TRISTRAM 3	102
AT LAST IT WAS THE CHRISTMAS NIGHT	156	SAINT BRANDAN	13
TELL THEM ONE BLESSED CHRISTMAS-NIGHT	157	SAINT BRANDAN	29
NOT WITH LOST TOIL THOU LABOUREST THROUGH THE NIGHT	169	EAST LONDON	13
HE OF THE MYSTIC EAST IS TOUCHD WITH NIGHT	170	EAST AND WEST	14
SENT ECHOES THROUGH THE NIGHT TO WAKE	177	FAREWELL	3
WHICH LUNA FELT THAT SUMMER-NIGHT	181	ISOLATION MARG	20
OCEAN AND CLOUDS AND NIGHT AND DAY	181	ISOLATION MARG	33
WHILE YET THE NIGHT IS CHILL	183	ABSENCE	18
SO SOON I SEE THE NIGHT-DEWS	186	STRAYED REVEL	15
THE COOL NIGHT-WIND TOO	186	STRAYED REVEL	19
AH COOL NIGHT-WIND TREMULOUS STARS	194	STRAYED REVEL	282
WITH ITS COOL TREES AND NIGHT	200	PHILOMELA	11
DOST THOU TO-NIGHT BEHOLD	201	PHILOMELA	16
CAN CHANGE OF SCENE AND NIGHT	200	PHILOMELA	V
TO-NIGHT THOSE SOFT-FRINGED EYES SHALL CLOSE	205	CALAIS SANDS	35
TO-NIGHT THOSE SOFT-VEILED EYES SHALL CLOSE	205	CALAIS SANDS	V 35
FOR THEN THE NIGHT WILL MORE THAN PAY	208	LONGING	3
FOR THEN THE NIGHT WILL MORE THAN PAY	209	LONGING	15
FOR SO THE NIGHT WILL MORE THAN PAY	208	LONGING	V
THE SEA IS CALM TO-NIGHT	210	DOVER BEACH	1
COME TO THE WINDOW SWEET IS THE NIGHT-AIR	210	DOVER BEACH	6
OF THE NIGHT-WIND DOWN THE VAST EDGES DREAR	211	DOVER BEACH	27
WHERE IGNORANT ARMIES CLASH BY NIGHT	212	DOVER BEACH	37
COME TO THE WINDOW HUSHD IS THE NIGHT-AIR	210	DOVER BEACH	V 6
IN PUFFS OF BALM THE NIGHT-AIR BLOWS	218	BACCHANALIA 1	14
CLEAR IN THE PURE JUNE-NIGHT	228	YOUTH OF NATURE	6
PAIN AND DEJECTION TO-NIGHT	229	YOUTH OF NATURE	26
SEE THEM TO-NIGHT WHERE THEY STAND	232	YOUTH OF MAN	18
HERE THEY STAND TO-NIGHT	234	YOUTH OF MAN	61
IN THE RUSTLING NIGHT-AIR CAME THE ANSWER	240	SELF-DEPENDENCE	15
OF A PAST NIGHT AND A FAR DIFFERENT SCENE	242	SUMMER NIGHT	13
THAT NIGHT WAS FAR MORE FAIR	242	SUMMER NIGHT	22
THE NIGHT WAS FAR MORE FAIR	242	SUMMER NIGHT	V 22
THE NIGHT COMES DOWN UPON THE GRASS	249	KENSINGTON GARD	35
WHEN HE LAY IN THE NIGHT BY HIS FLOCK	253	FUTURE	46
AS THE STARS COME OUT AND THE NIGHT-WIND	254	FUTURE	85
BY NIGHT THE SILVERD BRANCHES OF THE GLADE	261	SCHOLAR-GIPSY	214
AND DAY AND NIGHT HELD ON INDIGNANTLY	262	SCHOLAR-GIPSY	243
TO-NIGHT FROM OXFORD UP YOUR PATHWAY STRAYS	263	THYRSIS	8
LOVELY ALL TIMES SHE LIES LOVELY TO-NIGHT	263	THYRSIS	21
YES THOU ART GONE AND ROUND ME TOO THE NIGHT	266	THYRSIS	131
AND NIGHT AS WELCOME AS A FRIEND WOULD FALL	267	THYRSIS	150
I CANNOT REACH THE SIGNAL-TREE TO-NIGHT	267	THYRSIS	165
LEFT HUMAN HAUNT AND ON ALONE TILL NIGHT	269	THYRSIS	230
AH SUCH A NIGHT SO SOFT SO LONE	275	SOUTHERN NIGHT	13

NIGHT   (CONTINUED)
    THY MEMORY THY PAIN TO-NIGHT · · · · · · ·   276 SOUTHERN NIGHT   18
    IS HEARD TO-NIGHT AROUND THY GRAVE · · · · ·   276 SOUTHERN NIGHT   22
    WHOSE FLOOR TO-NIGHT SWEET MOONSHINE FILLS · · · · 277 SOUTHERN NIGHT   75
    BY DAY AND NIGHT · · · · · · · · · · ·   278 SOUTHERN NIGHT   88
    THE SILENT COURTS WHERE NIGHT AND DAY · · · ·   300 GRANDE CHARTR   31
    WHERE GHOSTLIKE IN THE DEEPENING NIGHT · · · ·   300 GRANDE CHARTR   35
    AND ON THE AIR OF NIGHT · · · · · · · ·   310 OBERMANN   124
    WHILE THUS I MUSED NIGHT GENTLY RAN · · · ·   314 OBERMANN MORE   57
    OF OUR NIGHT-JOURNEY AND THOU SEEST THY HOME · ·   330 MEROPE   2
    BY NIGHT IN THAT BLIND TUMULT THEY WERE SLAIN · ·   340 MEROPE   345
    NIGHT AND DAY SEE THEM FALL · · · · · · ·   346 MEROPE   502
    AND SINCE HAS FONDLY WATCHD HIM NIGHT AND DAY · ·   351 MEROPE   618
    ONE NIGHT AND THE NEXT DAY AT DAWN FARED ON · ·   356 MEROPE   747
    WITH MOUNTAIN-TRAVEL AND NIGHT-WATCHING SPENT · ·   359 MEROPE   868
    IN WHICH THEY HAVE TOILD ALL NIGHT FROM CATANA · · 406 EMPEDOCLES I 1   4
    WHY HAST THOU FOLLOWD US THE NIGHT WAS HOT · ·   407 EMPEDOCLES I 1   36
    I SADDLED MY WHITE MULE AND ALL NIGHT LONG · · ·   407 EMPEDOCLES I 1   44
    WITH THE SWEET NIGHT TO HELP THY HARMONY · · · ·   409 EMPEDOCLES I 1   98
    MORE THAN A DAY AND NIGHT PAUSANIAS · · · · ·   409 EMPEDOCLES I 1   100
    AND HE MADE ANSWER I SHOULD COME AT NIGHT · · ·   410 EMPEDOCLES I 1   128
    THEN PLAY THY KIND PART WELL FAREWELL TILL NIGHT · 411 EMPEDOCLES I 1   167
    AND WE FEEL DAY AND NIGHT · · · · · · · ·   416 EMPEDOCLES I 2   127
    BUT HE MUST FOLLOW ME NO MORE TO-NIGHT · · ·   428 EMPEDOCLES I 2   469
    AND THE SOULS DEEP ETERNAL NIGHT COME ON · · ·   429 EMPEDOCLES II   35
    THROUGH THE DARK NIGHT SUDDENLY · · · · · ·   430 EMPEDOCLES II   47
    NIGHT AFTER NIGHT YOUR COURSES · · · · · ·   437 EMPEDOCLES II   294
    NIGHT AFTER NIGHT YOUR COURSES · · · · · ·   437 EMPEDOCLES II   294
    THE NIGHT IN HER SILENCE · · · · · · · ·   443 EMPEDOCLES II   467
    THE NIGHT IN ITS SILENCE · · · · · · · ·   443 EMPEDOCLES II   V 467
    CHEERD US AND NOW IS PASSD INTO THE NIGHT · · ·   444 WESTMIN ABBEY   3
    BUT ALL NIGHT LONG AMID THE FLAMES HE LAY · · ·   446 WESTMIN ABBEY   89
    QUIET IN SLEEP THE SEVENTH NIGHT THEY DIED · · ·   448 WESTMIN ABBEY   139
    THAT FOR A MOMENT GLEAMS AND ALL AGAIN IS NIGHT ·   463 ALARIC AT ROME   30
    WAS COLD AND SAD BENEATH THAT BREATHLESS VOICELESS 466 ALARIC AT ROME   108
            NIGHT
    THAT TROUBLOUS NIGHT IS OVER ON THE BROW · · ·   468 ALARIC AT ROME   151
    THAT ALL NIGHT LONG ITS WEARY MOAN DOTH MAKE · ·   477 CROMWELL   191
    THE NIGHT OF TERRORS AND THE DAY OF CARE · · ·   478 CROMWELL   205
    LAST NIGHT THE WIND WAS UP AND STRONG · · · ·   479 HAYSWATER BOAT   17
    ALL NIGHT THEY SATE THEN STOLE AWAY · · · · ·   480 HAYSWATER BOAT   31
    LAST NIGHT I LOOKD THE SKY WAS CLEAR · · · ·   480 HAYSWATER BOAT   33
    IN HIS LONG BLACK SHIP SPEEDING NIGHT AND DAY · ·   485 S S LUSITANIA   10
    NIGHT COMES WITH NIGHT COMES SILENCE HAND IN HAND   FRAGMENT 1   1
    NIGHT COMES WITH NIGHT COMES SILENCE HAND IN HAND   FRAGMENT 1   1
    WITH NIGHT COMES SILENCE AND WITH THAT REPOSE · ·   FRAGMENT 1   2

NIGHTFALL
    NOW I AT NIGHTFALL HAD GONE FORTH · · · · · ·   90 SICK KING BOKH   65
    ON AND AT NIGHTFALL AT LAST · · · · · · · ·   289 RUGBY CHAPEL   107
    STANDEST AT NIGHTFALL ALONE · · · · · · · ·   297 HEINES GRAVE   175

NIGHTINGALE
    HARK AH THE NIGHTINGALE · · · · · · · · ·   200 PHILOMELA   1

NIGHTINGALES
    THE NIGHTINGALES DIVINELY SING · · · · · · · ·   182 TO MARG CONT   10
    FROM THE DARK DINGLES TO THE NIGHTINGALES · · · ·   261 SCHOLAR-GIPSY   220
    ASK WHERE NOW THOSE NIGHTINGALES ARE SINGING · ·   482 THEKLAS ANSWER   5

NIGHTLY
    IN THE YET STAR-SOWN NIGHTLY SKY · · · · · ·   323 OBERMANN MORE   331
    MELT LIKE A PASSING SMOKE A NIGHTLY DREAM · · · ·   402 MEROPE   1945

NIGHTS
    OR LET IT BE ON AUTUMN NIGHTS WHEN RAIN · · ·   18 CHURCH BROU 3   32
    NINE DAYS NINE NIGHTS TOWARDS THE NORTHERN ICE · ·   99 BALDER DEAD 1   145
    NINE DAYS NINE NIGHTS TOWARDS THE NORTHERN ICE · ·   99 BALDER DEAD 1   V 145
    NINE DAYS NINE NIGHTS TOWARDS THE NORTHERN ICE · · 107 BALDER DEAD 2   83
    NINE DAYS NINE NIGHTS TOWARDS THE NORTHERN ICE · · 107 BALDER DEAD 2   V 83
    CHIME CONVENT-BELLS ON WINTRY NIGHTS · · · · ·   156 SAINT BRANDAN   6
    ON EARTH THE CHRISTMAS-NIGHTS REPOSE · · · · ·   158 SAINT BRANDAN   66
    AND IN THEIR GLENS ON STARRY NIGHTS · · · · ·   182 TO MARG CONT   9
    HIS VOICE LIKE SOUNDS OF SUMMER NIGHTS · · · ·   202 URANIA   22
    RETURNING HOME ON SUMMER-NIGHTS HAVE MET · · · ·   257 SCHOLAR-GIPSY   73
    TO BE LEFT MUSING THESE SOFT NIGHTS ALONE · · ·   409 EMPEDOCLES I 1   92
    ASK NOT WHAT DAYS AND NIGHTS · · · · · · · ·   416 EMPEDOCLES I 2   107
    THE NIGHTS BALMY PRIME · · · · · · · · · ·   442 EMPEDOCLES II   444
    PEOPLED NIGHTS VOICELESS SHADES WITH FORMS OF LONG AGO 467 ALARIC AT ROME 126
    WHO OF LATE ON THE SOFT NIGHTS OF MAY · · · ·   482 THEKLAS ANSWER   6

NILE
    LIKE THE BROAD VOLUME OF THE INSURGENT NILE · ·   10 MYCERINUS   40
    MIXD WITH THE MURMUR OF THE MOVING NILE · · · ·   12 MYCERINUS   127
    LIKE THE BROAD RUSHING OF THE INSURGENT NILE · ·   10 MYCERINUS   V 40
    LIKE THE BROAD RUSHING OF THE COLUMND NILE · · ·   10 MYCERINUS   V 40
    LIKE THE BROAD RUSHING OF THE INSURGED NILE · ·   10 MYCERINUS   V 40
    THE NILE THE EAST · · · · · · · · · · · ·   277 SOUTHERN NIGHT   68

NIMBLE
    GIRL NIMBLE WITH THY FEET NOT WITH THY HANDS · ·   74 SOHRAB RUSTUM   457

```
NIMBLE             ( CONTINUED )
        SHOULD FIRST HAVE ROTTED ON THEIR NIMBLE JOINTS    • •     83 SOHRAB RUSTUM      739
        SHOULD THEN HAVE ROTTED ON THY NIMBLE JOINTS       • •     83 SOHRAB RUSTUM    V 739
        SHOULD THEN HAVE ROTTED ON THEIR NIMBLE JOINTS     • •     83 SOHRAB RUSTUM    V 739
        HERMOD THE NIMBLE GILD ME NOT MY DEATH         • • •      112 BALDER DEAD 2      264
        HERMOD THE NIMBLE DOST THOU STILL PURSUE       • • •      124 BALDER DEAD 2      395
        OR WITH THE NIMBLE RADIANT LIFE OF FIRE      • • • •      439 EMPEDOCLES II      344

NINE
        NINE DAYS NINE NIGHTS TOWARD THE NORTHERN ICE      • •     99 BALDER DEAD 1      145
        NINE DAYS NINE NIGHTS TOWARD THE NORTHERN ICE      • •     99 BALDER DEAD 1      145
        NINE DAYS NINE NIGHTS TOWARDS THE NORTHERN ICE     • •     99 BALDER DEAD 1    V 145
        NINE DAYS NINE NIGHTS TOWARD THE NORTHERN ICE      • •     99 BALDER DEAD 1    V 145
        NINE DAYS NINE NIGHTS TOWARD THE NORTHERN ICE      • •    107 BALDER DEAD 2       83
        NINE DAYS NINE NIGHTS TOWARD THE NORTHERN ICE      • •    107 BALDER DEAD 2       83
        AND GAVE ME NINE UNLIGHTED REALMS TO RULE    • • •       110 BALDER DEAD 2      213
        NINE DAYS HE TOOK TO GO TWO TO RETURN          • • •      113 BALDER DEAD 2      293
        NINE DAYS NINE NIGHTS TOWARDS THE NORTHERN ICE     • •    107 BALDER DEAD 2    V  83
        NINE DAYS NINE NIGHTS TOWARDS THE NORTHERN ICE     • •    107 BALDER DEAD 2    V  83
        AND GAVST HER NINE UNLIGHTED WORLDS TO RULE        • •    121 BALDER DEAD 3      277
        NINE TIMES SHE WAVED THE FLUTTERING WIMPLE ROUND   • •    156 TRISTRAM 3         219
        HIS CHOIR THE NINE • • • • • • • • • • •     • •    442 EMPEDOCLES II      446

NIORD
        BUT HERMOD RODE WITH NIORD WHOM HE TOOK      • • • •      122 BALDER DEAD 3      320
        NIORD THE GOD OF STORMS WHOM FISHERS KNOW    • • • •      122 BALDER DEAD 3      323
        THEN SAD AT HEART TO NIORD HERMOD SPAKE      • • • •      124 BALDER DEAD 3      369
        HE SPOKE AND NIORD SET FORTH BACK TO HEAVEN      • •     124 BALDER DEAD 3      373

NIPS
        NIPS TOO KEENLY THE SWEET FLOWER         • • • • • •      131 TRISTRAM 1          36

NOBLE
        THEIR NOBLE CALM   • • • • • • • • • • •     • •     50 CONSOLATION         25
        THOUGH THE LOCKS ARE YET BROWN ON HIS NOBLE HEAD  • •    130 TRISTRAM 1          10
        THE AIDS TO NOBLE LIFE ARE ALL WITHIN        • • • •     169 WORLDLY PLACE       14
        WHO THOUGH SO NOBLE SHARE IN THE WORLDS TOIL      • •    244 SUMMER NIGHT        81
        AND WHAT BUT NOBLE FEELING WARM        • • • • •         279 SOUTHERN NIGHT     130
        IN THE NOBLE AND GREAT WHO ARE GONE     • • • • •        290 RUGBY CHAPEL       146
        THE ROMAN NOBLE LAY       • • • • • • •      • •         315 OBERMANN MORE       98
        I WILL NOT VIOLATE THY NOBLE GRIEF      • • • • •        333 MEROPE             108
        O MEROPE HOW MANY NOBLE THOUGHTS        • • • • •        335 MEROPE             177
        NOBLE MEMORIAL OF WORTH     • • • • • •      • •         345 MEROPE             485
        HOWEVER NOBLE THE COMMITTER BE    • • • • •     •        353 MEROPE             693
        THE SON OF AN ARCADIAN NOBLE I    • • • • •     •        355 MEROPE             723
        THIS YOUNG ARCADIAN NOBLE GUARD AND MATE    • • •        364 MEROPE             969
        THE NOBLE THOUGHT WHICH IS ALONE THE MAN    • • •        385 MEROPE            1409
        HERE AS I GUESS THE NOBLE LAIAS COMES     • • •         386 MEROPE            1439

NOBLENESS
        WHY TREMBLE TRUE THE NOBLENESS OF MAN      • • • •        6 GEO CRUIKSHANK      11
        THE NOBLENESS OF GRIEF IS GONE  • • • • • • •          302 GRANDE CHARTR      107

NOBLER
        BUT DEEPER THEIR VOICE GROWS AND NOBLER THEIR BEARING    20 MODERN SAPPHO       27
        NOBLER THAN THIS TO FILL THE DAY      • • • • •          59 RESIGNATION        240
        AND ALL THE NOBLER SOULS OF MORTAL MEN     • • •        104 BALDER DEAD 1      320
        FOR ALL THE NOBLER SOULS OF MORTAL MEN     • • •        104 BALDER DEAD 1    V 320
        SOME NOBLER AMPLER STAGE OF LIFE TO WIN    • • •        169 WORLDLY PLACE       12
        A NOBLER CALMER TRAIN      • • • • • •      • •         183 ABSENCE              6
        WERE BUT MEN NOBLER THAN THEY ARE     • • • • •         202 URANIA               8

NOBLEST
        AND TRY THY NOBLEST STRAINS MY CALLICLES    • • • •     409 EMPEDOCLES I 1      97

NOBLY
        AND NOBLY PERFECT IN OUR DAY     • • • • • • •          222 EPILOG LAOCOON      26
        COURAGEOUS FAITHFUL ACTIONS NOBLY DARED     • • •       333 MEROPE              88
        I HEAR GORGIAS THEIR CHIEF SPEAKS NOBLY OF HIM    • •   411 EMPEDOCLES I 1     147
        AND SERVED MEN NOBLY AND ACCEPTANCE FOUND    • • •      448 WESTMIN ABBEY      143

NOD
        NOR WILL THAT DAY DAWN AT A HUMAN NOD      • • • •        7 REP FRIEND CONT      9
        AND GLANCE AND NOD AND BUSTLE BY      • • • • • •       277 SOUTHERN NIGHT      70
        PROCEEDS AT ANY NOD      • • • • • • • •     •, • •     422 EMPEDOCLES I 2     300

NODDED
        NODDED AND TIED HER PALFREY TO A TREE      • • • •      155 TRISTRAM 3         212
        THE GLOSSY RUSHES NODDED BY     • • • '• • • •         480 HAYSWATER BOAT      26

NODDING
        OF FRESH=PULLD VIOLETS WREATHED AND NODDING OER   • •   431 EMPEDOCLES II       87

NODS
        NODS SMILES AND GREETINGS AND FAREWELLS    • • • •      224 EPILOG LAOCOON     121

NOISE
        AS THOUGH ONE SPAKE OF NOISE UNTO THE DEAD  • • • •       3 EMERSONS ESSAYS  V   8
        SO THROUGH THE WORLD WAS HEARD A DRIPPING NOISE   • •   122 BALDER DEAD 3      317
        MID CITY=NOISE NOT AS WITH THEE OF YORE     • • • •     269 THYRSIS            232
```

NOISE   (CONTINUED)

FOR WHAT AVAILD IT ALL THE NOISE	• • • • •	303 GRANDE CHARTR	127
WAKE AMID GLOOM AND HOWLING AND THE NOISE	• • • •	373 MEROPE	1185

NOISED

RUKSH WHOSE RENOWN WAS NOISED THROUGH ALL THE EARTH		69 SOHRAB RUSTUM	**272**

NOISELESS

THERE LAUD WITH NOISELESS STEPS AND GLITTERING EYE		476 CROMWELL	165
WITH NOISELESS CURRENT STRONG OBSCURE AND DEEP	• •	483 BELOW SURFACE	4

NOISES

THIN THIN THE PLEASANT HUMAN NOISES GROW	• • • •	45 IN UTRUMQUE PAR	15

NOISIER

FAR NOISIER SCHEMES ACCOMPLISHD IN REPOSE	• • • •	1 QUIET WORK	7
MUCH NOISIER WORK ACCOMPLISHD IN REPOSE	• • • •	1 QUIET WORK	V 7
BUT THESE SHE LOVES AND NOISIER LIFE THAN THIS	• •	152 TRISTRAM 3	100

NOISY

MANS NOISY SCHEMES ACCOMPLISHD IN REPOSE	• • • •	1 QUIET WORK	V 7
MANS NOISY FEATS ACCOMPLISHD IN REPOSE	• • • •	1 QUIET WORK	V 7
MANS NOISY WORK ACCOMPLISHD IN REPOSE	• • • •	1 QUIET WORK	V 7
HIM NOT THE NOISY SWARMING RACE	• • • •	HORATIAN ECHO	V 7
BRIGHT COMRADE TO THE NOISY TOWN	• • • • • •	54 RESIGNATION	77
CAPPD WITH FAINT SMOKE THE NOISY TOWN	• • • •	55 RESIGNATION	93

NON

THOUGH THE NON-HUMAN POWERS	• • • • • • •	421 EMPEDOCLES I 2	264

NONACRIS

OF CRAG-PERCHD NONACRIS	• • • • • • • •	392 MEROPE	1650

NONE

VAIN LABOUR DEEP AND BROAD WHERE NONE MAY SEE	• •	4 BUTLERS SERMONS	5
FRANCE FAMED IN ALL GREAT ARTS IN NONE SUPREME	• •	7 REP FRIEND CONT	4
YET CHAMPION HAVE WE NONE TO MATCH THIS YOUTH	• •	66 SOHRAB RUSTUM	176
AND HE HAS NONE TO GUARD HIS WEAK OLD AGE	• • •	68 SOHRAB RUSTUM	235
AND RUSTUM SEIZED HIS CLUB WHICH NONE BUT HE	• •	73 SOHRAB RUSTUM	408
THEN RUSTUM SEIZED HIS CLUB WHICH NONE BUT HE	• •	73 SOHRAB RUSTUM	V 408
GREETED OF NONE DISFEATURED AND FORLORN	• • •	109 BALDER DEAD 2	171
IN MINE OWN BREAST AND HAVE TO NONE REVEALD	• •	121 BALDER DEAD 3	287
IN MY OWN BREAST AND HAVE TO NONE REVEALD	• • •	121 BALDER DEAD 3	V 287
NONE SPEAKS NONE HEEDS AH TURN THY HEAD	• •	206 RIVER	4
NONE SPEAKS NONE HEEDS AH TURN THY HEAD	• •	206 RIVER	4
BUT NO EMOTION NONE	• • • • • •	213 GROWING OLD	30
YET EVEN I AND NONE WILL BOW	• • • •	222 EPILOG LAOCOON	30
BUT DEEP ENOUGH ALAS NONE EVER MINES	• • •	246 BURIED LIFE	56
BRING NONE OF THESE BUT LET ME BE	• • • •	250 WISH	29
BUT NONE HATH WORDS SHE CAN REPORT OF THEE	• •	257 SCHOLAR-GIPSY	90
BUT NONE HAS HOPE LIKE THINE	• • • • •	261 SCHOLAR-GIPSY	196
FAR ON THE FOREST-SKIRTS WHERE NONE PURSUE	• •	261 SCHOLAR-GIPSY	215
BUT NONE HAS WORDS SHE CAN REPORT OF THEE	• •	257 SCHOLAR-GIPSY	V 90
SING HIM THY BEST FOR FEW OR NONE	• • • •	272 MEMORIAL VERSES	73
OF WHAT IT LIES WITH THEM TO MAKE RISK NONE	• •	350 MEROPE	604
NONE CAN TRULY CLAIM THAT	• • • • •	370 MEROPE	1109
HE HAD A HEST AT LEAST AND THOU HAST NONE	• •	385 MEROPE	1403
NOT SO LET HIM AND NONE SHALL BE MORE PROMPT	• •	388 MEROPE	1496
PITY THYSELF NONE NEEDS COMPASSION MORE	• • •	396 MEROPE	1761
NONE SINCE A TWOFOLD COLOUR REIGNS IN ALL	• • •	404 MEROPE	1994
AND WERE THERE NONE TO STAND AND WEEP ALONE	• •	467 ALARIC AT ROME	121
THE RUDDER SWINGS YET NONE DOTH STEER	• • •	480 HAYSWATER BOAT	39

NOOK

SCREEND IS THIS NOOK OER THE HIGH HALF-REAPD FIELD		255 SCHOLAR-GIPSY	21
SOME COUNTRY-NOOK WHERE OER THY UNKNOWN GRAVE	• •	259 SCHOLAR-GIPSY	138
SCREEND IN THIS NOOK OER THE HIGH HALF-REAPD FIELD		255 SCHOLAR-GIPSY	V 21

NOON

MORN AND NOON AND EVENTIDE	• • • • • • •	15 CHURCH BROU 1	100
FORTH AT NOON HAD LURED ME CREEPING	• • • • •	26 NEW SIRENS	3
ON THE DRY NOON SHOOK THEIR DEW	• • • • • •	29 NEW SIRENS	108
OFT AT NOON HAVE LURED ME CREEPING	• • • •	26 NEW SIRENS	V 3
HAPPY AT THE NOON OF PLEASURE	• • • • •	33 NEW SIRENS	V 201
HIS WHO IN MOUNTAIN GLENS AT NOON OF DAY	• • •	42 GIPSY CHILD	22
AT BURNING NOON SO WARRIORS SAID	• • • • •	52 RESIGNATION	4
FROM THE HOT FIELDS AT NOON HIS HEAD DROOPD LOW	• •	86 SOHRAB RUSTUM	V 847
FROM THE HOT FIELD AT NOON HIS HEAD DROOPD LOW	• •	86 SOHRAB RUSTUM	V 847
HERE IN BOKHARA BUT AT NOON	• • • • • •	87 SICK KING BOKH	6
TIS NOON WITH HIM AND YET HE STAYS	• • • •	148 TRISTRAM 2	V 155
WHO COME AT NOON DOWN TO THE WATER HERE	• •	155 TRISTRAM 3	194
WHICH COME AT NOON DOWN TO THE WATER HERE	• •	155 TRISTRAM 3	V 194
HIS WHEELD HOUSE AT NOON	• • • • • •	191 STRAYED REVEL	164
THIS WAY AT NOON	• • • • • • •	193 STRAYED REVEL	264
IN THE HOT PRESS OF THE NOON-DAY	• • • •	219 BACCHANALIA 2	18
AS CLEARLY AS AT NOON	• • • • • • •	242 SUMMER NIGHT	15
THEN HERE AT NOON COMES BACK HIS STORES TO USE	• •	255 SCHOLAR-GIPSY	15
ASLEEP IN THE ARCADIAN GLENS AT NOON	• • • •	372 MEROPE	1160
PERFORMS THIS NOON A SOLEMN SACRIFICE	• • •	391 MEROPE	1589
THE NOON IS HOT WHEN WE HAVE CROSSD THE STREAM	• •	412 EMPEDOCLES I 2	1

NOON   (CONTINUED)
      OF NOON IS BROKEN THERE BY CHESTNUT-BOUGHS . . . . .   414 EMPEDOCLES I 2   44
      OF THE HOT NOON WITHOUT A SHADE   . . . .   414 EMPEDOCLES I 2   54

NOONTIDE
      THROUGH THE DEEP NOONTIDE HEATS WE FARE . . . . .   54 RESIGNATION   69

NORNIES
      THE NORNIES WHEN HIS MOTHER BARE HIM SPUN . . . . .   96 BALDER DEAD 1   24
      SKULDA THE YOUNGEST OF THE NORNIES RODE   . . . . . 105 BALDER DEAD 2   21
      AND SAW THE NORNIES WATERING THE ROOTS   . . . . . 120 BALDER DEAD 3   221

NORTH
      BUT I HEAR THE NORTH WIND BLOWING   . . . . . .   32 NEW SIRENS   189
      THE LONG-MUSED THOUGHT TO NORTH SOUTH EAST AND WEST   45 IN UTRUMQUE PAR   6
      WHICH BRANCHES FROM THE NORTH OF HEAVEN AND RIDE .   99 BALDER DEAD 1   144
      WHICH BRANCHES FROM THE NORTH OF HEAVEN AND WENT . 107 BALDER DEAD 2   80
      BELOW THERE TO THE NORTH TOWRD HELAS REALM . . . . 108 BALDER DEAD 2   123
      STILL NORTH UNTIL HE MET A STRETCHING WALL . . . . 109 BALDER DEAD 2   144
      NORTH SOUTH EAST WEST THEY STRUCK AND ROAMD THE WORLD 122 BALDER DEAD 3   304
      BUT NORTH STILL NORTH SAINT BRANDAN STEERD . . . . 156 SAINT BRANDAN   9
      BUT NORTH STILL NORTH SAINT BRANDAN STEERD . . . . 156 SAINT BRANDAN   9
      THEN TO THE NORTH LYCAEUS AND THE HILLS   . . . . . 330 MEROPE   20
      POUR FROM A THOUSAND HILLS THY WARRIORS OF THE NORTH 465 ALARIC AT ROME   96

NORTHERN
      WHO ROAM OER KIPCHAK AND THE NORTHERN WASTE . .   65 SOHRAB RUSTUM   131
      THE NORTHERN SIR AND THIS GREAT OXUS STREAM . .   83 SOHRAB RUSTUM   765
      WHO COME FROM KIPCHAK AND THE NORTHERN WASTE . .   65 SOHRAB RUSTUM   V 131
      WHO DWELL IN KIPCHAK AND THE NORTHERN WASTE . .   65 SOHRAB RUSTUM   V 131
      WHO ROVE OER KIPCHAK AND THE NORTHERN WASTE . .   65 SOHRAB RUSTUM   V 131
      UPON THE NORTHERN FRONTIER WHERE   . . . . .   93 SICK KING BOKH   V 161
      NINE DAYS NINE NIGHTS TOWARD THE NORTHERN ICE .   99 BALDER DEAD 1   145
      BUT HE MUST EVER WATCH THE NORTHERN BEAR . . .   99 BALDER DEAD 1   155
      BUT HE WILL REACH ITS UNKNOWN NORTHERN SHORE .   99 BALDER DEAD 1   162
      NINE DAYS NINE NIGHTS TOWARDS THE NORTHERN ICE .   99 BALDER DEAD 1   V 145
      NINE DAYS NINE NIGHTS TOWARD THE NORTHERN ICE .   107 BALDER DEAD 2   83
      FOR IN THAT ICE ARE LOST THOSE NORTHERN STREAMS . 108 BALDER DEAD 2   128
      AND HE CAME DOWN TO OCEANS NORTHERN STRAND . .   108 BALDER DEAD 2   141
      NINE DAYS NINE NIGHTS TOWARDS THE NORTHERN ICE .   107 BALDER DEAD 2   V 83
      REGNER WHO SWEPT THE NORTHERN SEA WITH FLEETS .   117 BALDER DEAD 3   126
      SAINT BRANDAN SAILS THE NORTHERN MAIN   . . . .   156 SAINT BRANDAN   1
      THE FRET AND MISERY OF OUR NORTHERN TOWNS . . .   168 RACHEL 2   9
      HEARING IT BY THIS DISTANT NORTHERN SEA . . . .   211 DOVER BEACH   20
      COOL NORTHERN FIELDS AND GRASS AND FLOWERS . . .   275 STANZAS CARNAC   44
      BUT AS ON SOME FAR NORTHERN STRAND   . . . . .   301 GRANDE CHARTR   80
      FOLLOWD THY FATHER FROM THEIR NORTHERN HILLS .   381 MEROPE   1300
      IN THE NORTHERN HEAVEN . . . .   393 MEROPE   1676

NORTHWARD
      AND SHE WILL BID HIM NORTHWARD STEER HIS COURSE .   99 BALDER DEAD 1   152
      NORTHWARD UNTIL HE MEETS A STRETCHING WALL . .   100 BALDER DEAD 1   166
      BUT NORTHWARD HERMOD RODE THE WAY BELOW   . . .   108 BALDER DEAD 2   138
      BUT NORTHWARD HERMOD RODE THE WAY BELOW   . . .   124 BALDER DEAD 3   374
      WHAT LIGHTS WILL THOSE OUT TO THE NORTHWARD BE .   130 TRISTRAM 1   5
      IS DEAF FAR NORTHWARD FROM HERE   . . . . . .   282 HAWORTH CHURCH   51

NORWEGIAN
      HER FLOCK ALONG THE WHITE NORWEGIAN BEACH . . . . 117 BALDER DEAD 3   150

NOSTRILS
      WHEREFORE DO THY NOSTRILS FLASH   . . . . 430 EMPEDOCLES II   46

NOTE
      FOR THERE RANG NOTE DIVINE IN THAT COMMAND . . .   102 BALDER DEAD 1   245
      BUT NOW HE CREW AT DAWN A CHEERFUL NOTE   . . . .   105 BALDER DEAD 2   8
      ANOTHER NOTE AND LIKE A BIRD IN SPRING   . . . .   117 BALDER DEAD 3   142
      THE ETERNAL NOTE OF SADNESS IN   . . . . . .   211 DOVER BEACH   14
      LOST IT TOO SOON AND LEARNT A STORMY NOTE . . .   269 THYRSIS   223
      THE ILL-BODING NOTE WHICH FRANTIC HATRED SOUNDS . 397 MEROPE   1781
      THE ILL-BODING NOTE WHICH FRANTIC ENVY SOUNDS .   397 MEROPE   V1781
      THOU ART TOO YOUNG TO NOTE IT BUT HIS POWER . .   410 EMPEDOCLES I 1   112
      A FLUTE-NOTE FROM THE WOODS   . . . . . .   436 EMPEDOCLES II   252
      THAT VOICE HAD NOTE SO CLEAR OF SWEET COMMAND .   445 WESTMIN ABBEY   28
      NOTE NO CHANGE AND LET THEM DIE   . . . . . .   455 POOR MATTHIAS   108

NOTES
      SO TO WAIT BUT WHAT NOTES DOWN THE WIND HARK   20 MODERN SAPPHO   29
            ARE DRIVING
      THEN TO WAIT BUT WHAT NOTES DOWN THE WIND HARK   20 MODERN SAPPHO   V 29
            ARE DRIVING
      NOTES OF WILD PASTORAL MUSIC OVER ALL   . . . .   25 DREAM   12
      SWEET NOTES THIS WAY   . . . .   175 PARTING   24
      AND LOVELY NOTES FROM SHORE TO SHORE . . . . .   182 TO MARG CONT   11
      FAINT BUGLE-NOTES FROM FAR ARE BORNE . . . . .   305 GRANDE CHARTR   182
      LAUGHTER AND CRIES THOSE NOTES BETWEEN   . . . .   305 GRANDE CHARTR   186
      I KNOW THESE NOTES AMONG A THOUSAND HARK . . .   413 EMPEDOCLES I 2   35
      I KNOW THOSE NOTES AMONG A THOUSAND HARK . . .   413 EMPEDOCLES I 2   V 35
      THE SWEET NOTES WHOSE LULLING SPELL   . . . . . .   431 EMPEDOCLES II   64

NOTHING
      NOTHING STIRS ON THE LAWN BUT THE QUICK LILAC-SHADE 19 MODERN SAPPHO   2

NOTHING   (CONTINUED)
        NOTHING MOVES ON THE LAWN BUT THE QUICK LILAC-SHADE   19 MODERN SAPPHO   V   2
        THERES NOTHING CAN DISMARBLE NOW   . . . . . .   21 YOUTH AND CALM   3
        THOUGH NOTHING CAN DISMARBLE NOW   . . . . . .   21 YOUTH AND CALM   V   3
        LEAVES US FIXT TO NOTHING LONG . . . .   24 MEMORY-PICTURE   58
        LEAVES US TRUE TO NOTHING LONG . . . .   24 MEMORY-PICTURE   V   58
        LEAVES US FIRM TO NOTHING LONG . . . .   24 MEMORY-PICTURE   V   58
        LEAVES US JOIND TO NOTHING LONG   . . . . . .   24 MEMORY-PICTURE   V   58
        MOODS OF FANTASTIC SADNESS NOTHING WORTH   . . . .   42 GIPSY CHILD   18
        AND I WERE NOTHING BUT A COMMON MAN . . . . . .   85 SOHRAB RUSTUM   813
        BUT BEING NOTHING AS HE IS . . . .   92 SICK KING BOKH   141
        FEAR NOTHING BUT THAT ALL SHALL BE FULFILLD . .   112 BALDER DEAD 2   253
        ABSENCE FROM FIELDS WHERE I COULD NOTHING AID . .   127 BALDER DEAD 3   502
        TO FEEL THAT NOTHING CAN IMPAIR   . . . . . .   180 FAREWELL   83
        NOTHING SURE NO MORAL PLAN . . . .   215 PIS-ALLER   7
        NO I NOTHING CAN PERCEIVE . . . .   215 PIS-ALLER   9
        THAT OR NOTHING I BELIEVE . . . .   215 PIS-ALLER   11
        NATURE IS NOTHING HER CHARM . . . .   233 YOUTH OF MAN   35
        NOTHING BESIDES IN FRONT . . . .   234 YOUTH OF MAN   75
        UNFREED HAVING SEEN NOTHING STILL UNBLEST   . . . .   243 SUMMER NIGHT   50
        BUT HERE THIS CALM IS NOTHING NEW   . . . .   KENSINGTON GARD   V   29
        IN THE TWO HINKSEYS NOTHING KEEPS THE SAME   . . . .   262 THYRSIS   2
        MEN GAVE THEE NOTHING BUT THIS HAPPY QUEST   . . . .   269 THYRSIS   213
        NOTHING AND THEN THEY DIE . . . .   288 RUGBY CHAPEL   66
        NOTHING TO US THOU WAST STILL . . . . . .   290 RUGBY CHAPEL   138
        NOTHING TO US THOU WERT STILL . . . . . .   290 RUGBY CHAPEL   V 138
        ARE NOTHING IN THEIR SIGHT . . . .   311 OBERMANN   152
        BUT OF THE PRINCE NOTHING REMAIN SAVE THIS   . .   358 MEROPE   839
        O MISTRESS BY THE GODS DO NOTHING RASH   . . . .   368 MEROPE   1075
        THOU NOTHING PROFITEST THY FRIENDS BUT MAKST . . .   368 MEROPE   1080
        AND FROM THAT MOMENT I SAW NOTHING CLEAR   . . . .   402 MEROPE   1936
        SINCE HE SEES NOTHING CLEAR . . . . . .   415 EMPEDOCLES I 2   90
        AND DARES STAMP NOTHING FALSE WHERE HE FINDS   415 EMPEDOCLES I 2   91
            NOTHING SURE
        AND DARES STAMP NOTHING FALSE WHERE HE FINDS   415 EMPEDOCLES I 2   91
            NOTHING SURE
        WHERE HE SEES NOTHING CLEAR . . . . . .   415 EMPEDOCLES I 2   V   90
        HE HEARS NOTHING BUT THE CRY OF THE TORRENTS . .   435 EMPEDOCLES II   213
        NOTHING BUT A DEVOURING FLAME OF THOUGHT   . . .   438 EMPEDOCLES II   329
        STRETCHD ON THAT BED OF DEATH ART NOTHING NOW . .   479 CROMWELL   234
        NOTHING BUT THAT WE SEE IT WHAT RESPECT   . . . .   LUCRETIUS 5   8
        BETWIXT BLANK NOTHING AND ABHORRED DECAY   . . . .   FRAGMENT 5   5

NOTHINGNESS
        AND YEARS OF CRIME AND NOTHINGNESS AND GLOOM . .   463 ALARIC AT ROME   40
        THE CHANGE OF LIFE THE NOTHINGNESS OF POWER . .   469 ALARIC AT ROME   188

NOTHINGS
        SILKEN COURTIERS WHISPERING HONIED NOTHINGS . .   144 TRISTRAM 2   47
        OF ALL THE THOUSAND NOTHINGS OF THE HOUR   . . . .   247 BURIED LIFE   69

NOTICE
        HE KNEW ME WELL AND WOULD OFT NOTICE ME   . . . .   408 EMPEDOCLES I 1   57

NOTING
        FOR SELF-POISED THEY LIVE NOR PINE WITH NOTING . .   240 SELF-DEPENDENCE   23
        FOR ALONE THEY LIVE NOR PINE WITH NOTING   . . . .   240 SELF-DEPENDENCE   V   23
        WHY SELF-POISED THEY LIVE NOR PINE WITH NOTING . .   240 SELF-DEPENDENCE   V   23

NOUGHT
        BUT WHO FOR MEN OF NOUGHT WOULD DO GREAT DEEDS . .   68 SOHRAB RUSTUM   255
        I WHAT WERE I WHEN THESE CAN NOUGHT AVAIL . .   127 BALDER DEAD 3   493
        THE OLD LAW THEY CRIED IS WHOLLY COME TO NOUGHT . .   237 PROGRESS   3
        THE OLD LAW THEY SAID IS WHOLLY COME TO NOUGHT . .   237 PROGRESS   V   3
        DREAMING OF NOUGHT BEYOND THEIR PRISON-WALL . .   243 SUMMER NIGHT   41
        SLOW SLOW THE OLD WORLD WORE TO NOUGHT   . . .   319 OBERMANN MORE   191
        GOOD TO OBEY WITHOUT A LEADER NOUGHT . . . .   381 MEROPE   1302
        WHEN THOU ART EITHER NOUGHT AND SO NOT LOVED . .   FRAGMENT 5   8

NOURISHD
        BUT THE DEMONS LONG NOURISHD HERE   . . . . . .   361 MEROPE   909

NOURISHING
        STILL NOURISHING IN THY BEWILDERD BRAIN   . . . .   200 PHILOMELA   7

NOVEMBER
        AS WHEN SOME GREY NOVEMBER MORN THE FILES   . . . .   64 SOHRAB RUSTUM   111
        IN THE GLOOM OF NOVEMBER WE PASSD   . . . . . .   286 RUGBY CHAPEL   19

NOWHERE
        WITH NOWHERE YET TO REST MY HEAD   . . . . . .   302 GRANDE CHARTR   87

NULL
        STILL THE ATTEMPT TO USE THEM PROVES THEM NULL . .   210 SELF-DECEPTION   20
        IF FOLLOWD MAKE THEIR SUCCOUR SLACK AND NULL . .   382 MEROPE   1338

NUMB
        WHO WITH NUMB BLACKEND FINGERS MAKES HER FIRE . .   70 SOHRAB RUSTUM   304
        AND NUMB THE ELASTIC POWERS . . . .   259 SCHOLAR-GIPSY   146

NUMBER
        YEARS IN NUMBER IT SEEMD . . . .   281 HAWORTH CHURCH   27

NUMBER   (CONTINUED)
        NUMBER IT WITH THE THOUSAND RUMOURS VAIN   • •   • • 387 MEROPE   1486
        WE MEASURE THE SEA-TIDES WE NUMBER THE SEA-SANDS • • 423 EMPEDOCLES I 2   321
        WHEN WE WERE YOUNG WHEN WE COULD NUMBER FRIENDS • • 436 EMPEDOCLES II   236
        EIGHT IN NUMBER NOW THE YEARS   • • • • • • 458 POOR MATTHIAS   202

NUMBERD
        QUICK QUICK FOR NUMBERD ARE MY SANDS OF LIFE   • •   82 SOHRAB RUSTUM   721
        ELSE WERT THOU LONG SINCE NUMBERD WITH THE DEAD • • 259 SCHOLAR-GIPSY   153

NUMBERS
        STILL RULES STILL WATCHES AND NUMBERS THE HOURS • • 347 MEROPE   V 527

NUMBING
        I FEEL IT IN THIS HOUR THE NUMBING CLOUD   • • • • 441 EMPEDOCLES II   407

NUMBRETH
        STILL RULES STILL WATCHES AND NUMBRETH THE HOURS • • 347 MEROPE   527

NUMEROUS
        BETWEEN THAT AND THE SHIPS THE TROJANS NUMEROUS FIRES   HOMER TRANS   2

NURSD
        NO WONDERS NURSD THY CHILDHOOD NOT FOR THEE   • • 472 CROMWELL   15

NURSE
        I AM NOW THY NURSE I BID THEE SLEEP   • • • • • 144 TRISTRAM 2   70
        TO TAKE HIS NURSE HIS BROKEN TOY   • • • • • 248 KENSINGTON GARD   10
        DRAGS TO HIS NURSE HIS BROKEN TOY   • • • • •   KENSINGTON GARD V 10
        OR HARM AND NURSE MY LONGING FOR MY SON   • • • 366 MEROPE   1022
        BUT THE FAITHFUL SERVANT AND NURSE   • • • • 369 MEROPE   1090
        THERE NURSE A LATE REMORSE AND THANK THE GODS   • • 396 MEROPE   1755
        NURSE NO EXTRAVAGANT HOPE   • • • • • • • 426 EMPEDOCLES I 2   425
        TO NURSE HIS DWINDLING FACULTY OF JOY   • • • 437 EMPEDOCLES II   273
        HIS NURSE THE MIGHTY MOTHER WILLD IT SO   • • • 446 WESTMIN ABBEY   86
        THE BOY HIS NURSE FORGOT   • • • • • • • 447 WESTMIN ABBEY   111

NURSED
        NURSED BY HIS PASTORAL FLOW   • • • • • 313 OBERMANN MORE   28
        TWIXT THEE AND ME SUSPICION THAT I NURSED   • • 394 MEROPE   1699
        NURSED AN IMMORTAL VIGOUR I ALONE   • • • • • 438 EMPEDOCLES II   320
        NURSED NO DELUSION   • • • • • • • • • 441 EMPEDOCLES II   402

NURSES
        BY CHILDREN WHOM THEIR NURSES CALL WITH HASTE   • •   86 SOHRAB RUSTUM   846
        BY ROMPING CHILDREN WHOM THEIR NURSES CALL   • • •   86 SOHRAB RUSTUM   V 846

NURSING
        THIS COMES OF NURSING LONG AND WATCHING LATE   • • 140 TRISTRAM 1   313
        NURSING THY PROJECT IN UNCLOUDED JOY   • • • • • 261 SCHOLAR-GIPSY   199
        STILL NURSING THE UNCONQUERABLE HOPE   • • • • • 261 SCHOLAR-GIPSY   211

NURSLING
        NO WEAK NURSLING OF AN EARTHLY SUN   • • • • •   30 NEW SIRENS   112
        BUT HER NURSLING HER HOPE CAME AT LAST   • • • 346 MEROPE   510
        THE NURSLING OF THE DELLS   • • • • • • 391 MEROPE   1615
        SOMEWHERE IN SAFETY A NURSLING A LIGHT   • • • 346 MEROPE   V 513
        THE NURSLING OF THE MIGHTY MOTHER DIED   • • • 447 WESTMIN ABBEY   115
        AND LIGHTS FAIR NURSLING STUPOR FIRST INVADES   • • 448 WESTMIN ABBEY   129
        AND LIGHTS FAIR NURSLING LANGUOR FIRST INVADES   • • 448 WESTMIN ABBEY V 129

NURTUREST
        THAT THOU IN SECRET NURTUREST UP THY SON   • • • • 334 MEROPE   144

NYMPHS
        OF PAN AND THE NYMPHS   • • • • • • • • • • 188 STRAYED REVEL   81

O
        O MONSTROUS DEAD UNPROFITABLE WORLD   • • • • •   3 EMERSONS ESSAYS   1
        O BARREN BOAST O JOYLESS MOCKERY   • • • • •   EMERSONS ESSAYS V 14
        O BARREN BOAST O JOYLESS MOCKERY   • • • • •   EMERSONS ESSAYS V 14
        YET SURELY O MY PEOPLE DID I DEEM   • • • • •   9 MYCERINUS   19
        AUSTRIAN WANDERERS BRING O WARDERS   • • • • •   15 CHURCH BROU 1   79
        GONE O KNIGHTS IS SHE YOU KNEW   • • • • • •   15 CHURCH BROU 1   82
        SO REST FOR EVER REST O PRINCELY PAIR   • • • •   17 CHURCH BROU 3   1
        AND THOU O PRINCESS SHALT NO MORE RECEIVE   • • •   18 CHURCH BROU 3   12
        SO SLEEP FOR EVER SLEEP O MARBLE PAIR   • • • •   18 CHURCH BROU 3   16
        HAST THOU YET DEALT HIM O LIFE THY FULL MEASURE   • •   20 MODERN SAPPHO   33
        HAST THOU WITH MYRTLE-LEAF CROWND HIM O PLEASURE   • •   20 MODERN SAPPHO   35
        WHO ARE THEY O PENSIVE GRACES   • • • • • •   26 NEW SIRENS   9
        O YE FALSE ONES AT YOUR CALLING   • • • • • •   27 NEW SIRENS   39
        PLUCK PLUCK CYPRESS O PALE MAIDENS   • • • • •   30 NEW SIRENS   113
        O SWEET PLEADERS DOTH MY LOT   • • • • • •   31 NEW SIRENS   164
        O SPEAK ONCE AND SHAME MY SADNESS   • • • • •   32 NEW SIRENS   167
        O LOOSE HANDS AND LET IT BE   • • • • • •   34 NEW SIRENS   224
        O LET FALL ONE TEAR AND SET US FREE   • • • • •   34 NEW SIRENS   226
        AND YOU TOO O WORSHIPPD GRACES   • • • • • •   34 NEW SIRENS   243
        PLUCK PLUCK CYPRESS O PALE MAIDENS   • • • • •   35 NEW SIRENS   269
        PLUCK PLUCK CYPRESS O PALE MAIDENS   • • • • •   35 NEW SIRENS   275
        O SPEAK ONCE AND LET MY SADNESS   • • • • • •   32 NEW SIRENS   V 167

(CONTINUED)

AND YOU TOO O WEEPING GRACES	34	NEW SIRENS	V 243
O UNFORGOTTEN VOICE THY ACCENTS COME	36	VOICE	29
O UNFORGOTTEN VOICE THY WHISPERS COME	36	VOICE	V 29
O LET THE FALSE DREAM FLY	39	STAGIRIUS	49
O WHERE THY VOICE DOTH COME	39	STAGIRIUS	52
O MEEK ANTICIPANT OF THAT SURE PAIN	43	GIPSY CHILD	41
O WAKING ON A WORLD WHICH THUS-WISE SPRINGS	45	IN UTRUMQUE PAR	8
AGES OR HOURS O WAKING ON LIFES STREAM	45	IN UTRUMQUE PAR	11
O SEEMING SOLE TO AWAKE THY SUN-BATHED HEAD	45	IN UTRUMQUE PAR	29
O MAN WHOM EARTH THY LONG-VEXT MOTHER BARE	46	IN UTRUMQUE PAR	32
O SCAN THY NATIVE WORLD WITH PIOUS EYES	46	IN UTRUMQUE PAR	V 40
O JOY AGAIN THE FARMS APPEAR	54	RESIGNATION	74
O SOHRAB AN UNQUIET HEART IS THINE	63	SOHRAB RUSTUM	65
O SOHRAB CARRY AN UNWOUNDED SON	63	SOHRAB RUSTUM	77
O RUSTUM LIKE THY MIGHT IS THIS YOUNG MANS	67	SOHRAB RUSTUM	215
WHAT THEN O RUSTUM WILL MEN SAY TO THIS	68	SOHRAB RUSTUM	243
O GUDURZ WHEREFORE DOST THOU SAY SUCH WORDS	68	SOHRAB RUSTUM	250
O THOU YOUNG MAN THE AIR OF HEAVEN IS SOFT	70	SOHRAB RUSTUM	322
O SOHRAB WHEREFORE WILT THOU RUSH ON DEATH	71	SOHRAB RUSTUM	329
O BY THY FATHERS HEAD BY THINE OWN SOUL	71	SOHRAB RUSTUM	343
O THOU OLD WARRIOR LET US YIELD TO HEAVEN	74	SOHRAB RUSTUM	438
O SOHRAB THOU INDEED ART SUCH A SON	80	SOHRAB RUSTUM	641
O BOY THY FATHER AND HIS VOICE CHOKED THERE	81	SOHRAB RUSTUM	691
RUKSH NOW THOU GRIEVEST BUT O RUKSH THY FEET	83	SOHRAB RUSTUM	738
O RUKSH THOU ART MORE FORTUNATE THAN I	83	SOHRAB RUSTUM	747
AND SAID O RUKSH BEAR RUSTUM WELL BUT I	83	SOHRAB RUSTUM	755
AND SAY O SON I WEEP THEE NOT TOO SORE	85	SOHRAB RUSTUM	822
O MOST JUST VIZIER SEND AWAY	87	SICK KING BOKH	1
O MERCHANTS TARRY YET A DAY	87	SICK KING BOKH	5
O HUSSEIN LEAD ME TO THE KING	87	SICK KING BOKH	10
O VIZIER WITHOUT LYING DOWN	88	SICK KING BOKH	15
O VIZIER HERE IS THE KINGS DOOR	88	SICK KING BOKH	20
O VIZIER I MAY BURY HIM	88	SICK KING BOKH	21
O KING THOU KNOWST I HAVE BEEN SICK	88	SICK KING BOKH	22
NOT EVEN WHAT THOU DOST O KING	88	SICK KING BOKH	25
O VIZIER BE IT AS THOU SAYST	88	SICK KING BOKH	29
JUSTICE O KING AND ON MYSELF	89	SICK KING BOKH	36
VENGEANCE O KING BUT THE KING SPAKE	89	SICK KING BOKH	39
CRIES OUT MOST EARNESTLY O KING	89	SICK KING BOKH	52
MY LORD O KING DO RIGHT I PRAY	89	SICK KING BOKH	53
AND TRULY WHILE I SPEAK O KING	92	SICK KING BOKH	129
O KING IN THIS I PRAISE THEE NOT	92	SICK KING BOKH	133
NO NOR ON THIS DEAD DOG O KING	93	SICK KING BOKH	180
O VIZIER THOU ART OLD I YOUNG	93	SICK KING BOKH	181
THITHER O VIZIER WILL I BEAR	95	SICK KING BOKH	225
VENGEANCE O KING BUT THE KING SPOKE	89	SICK KING BOKH	V 39
CAN I O MOTHER BRING THEM BALDER BACK	98	BALDER DEAD 1	107
WHAT WAY IS THIS O MOTHER THAT THOU SHOWST	99	BALDER DEAD 1	132
WOULD THAT OURSELVES O BALDER WE WERE BORNE	101	BALDER DEAD 1	216
BUT EVEN THERE O NANNA WE MIGHT FIND	104	BALDER DEAD 1	326
O DAMSEL HERMOD AM I CALLD THE SON	108	BALDER DEAD 2	112
O HERMOD RARELY DO THE FEET OF GODS	108	BALDER DEAD 2	119
O HELA WHEREFORE SHOULD THE GODS DECLARE	110	BALDER DEAD 2	189
NOT FOR SUCH END O QUEEN THOU HOLDST THY REALM	110	BALDER DEAD 2	197
EVEN IN THE ABODE OF DEATH O BALDER HAIL	112	BALDER DEAD 2	250
FAREWELL O BALDER BRIGHT AND LOVED MY SON	115	BALDER DEAD 3	67
THOU CAMEST NEAR THE NEXT O WARRIOR THOR	115	BALDER DEAD 3	71
BUT FROM THY LIPS O BALDER NIGHT OR DAY	116	BALDER DEAD 3	83
WEEP NOT O FREYA WEEP NO GOLDEN TEARS	116	BALDER DEAD 3	114
THEREFORE FOR THE LAST TIME O BALDER HAIL	126	BALDER DEAD 3	453
O HERMOD PRAY THAT THOU MAYST JOIN US THEN	129	BALDER DEAD 3	543
GO NOT FAR O ISEULT FROM THY GRAVE	145	TRISTRAM 2	92
O HUNTER AND WITHOUT A FEAR	149	TRISTRAM 2	187
O BRANDAN TO THIS HOUR OF REST	158	SAINT BRANDAN	71
WHY SITTST THOU THERE O NECKAN	160	NECKAN	49
O RUTH OF GOD THE PRIEST CRIED OUT	160	NECKAN	55
HARK WHAT SHE SINGS O JOY O JOY	164	FORSAKEN MERM	89
HARK WHAT SHE SINGS O JOY O JOY	164	FORSAKEN MERM	89
O HUMAN SOUL AS LONG AS THOU CANST SO	169	EAST LONDON	9
LONG FED ON BOUNDLESS HOPES O RACE OF MAN	170	BETTER PART	1
I COME O YE MOUNTAINS	175	PARTING	33
I COME O YE MOUNTAINS	176	PARTING	57
FOLD CLOSELY O NATURE	177	PARTING	77
O CIRCE GODDESS	185	STRAYED REVEL	2
O PRINCE WHAT PAIN	192	STRAYED REVEL	211
O CIRCE GODDESS	194	STRAYED REVEL	293
O ANTIGONE	196	FRAG ANTIGONE	52
TO ACHIEVE HIS SONS DELIVERANCE O MY CHILD	198	FRAG ANTIGONE	103
O FRIVOLOUS MIND OF MAN	198	FRAG DEJANEIRA	1
O WANDERER FROM A GRECIAN SHORE	200	PHILOMELA	5
O LEARN OF LONDON WHOSE PAUPERS	214	NEW ROME	13
ASK NOT MY NAME O FRIEND	217	NAMELESS EPIT	1
IS IT YOU O BEAUTY O GRACE	230	YOUTH OF NATURE	63
IS IT YOU O BEAUTY O GRACE	230	YOUTH OF NATURE	63
O CHARM O ROMANCE THAT WE FEEL	230	YOUTH OF NATURE	64
O CHARM O ROMANCE THAT WE FEEL	230	YOUTH OF NATURE	64
CAN THY PENCIL O ARTIST RESTORE	231	YOUTH OF NATURE	110
WE O NATURE DEPART	232	YOUTH OF MAN	1
BEHOLD O NATURE THIS PAIR	232	YOUTH OF MAN	17

(CONTINUED)

THOU O NATURE WAST MUTE	233	YOUTH OF MAN		38
SINK O YOUTH IN THY SOUL	235	YOUTH OF MAN		116
THOU O NATURE WERT MUTE	233	YOUTH OF MAN	V	38
O AIR-BORN VOICE LONG SINCE SEVERELY CLEAR	240	SELF-DEPENDENCE		29
O LIFE UNLIKE TO OURS	260	SCHOLAR-GIPSY		166
O BORN IN DAYS WHEN WITS WERE FRESH AND CLEAR	261	SCHOLAR-GIPSY		201
O EASY ACCESS TO THE HEARERS GRACE	265	THYRSIS		91
HEAR IT O THYRSIS STILL OUR TREE IS THERE	267	THYRSIS		171
THOU TOO O THYRSIS ON LIKE QUEST WAST BOUND	269	THYRSIS		211
THOU TOO O THYRSIS ON LIKE QUEST WERT BOUND	269	THYRSIS	V	211
O ROTHA WITH THY LIVING WAVE	272	MEMORIAL VERSES		72
O SPENT ONES OF A WORK-DAY AGE	279	SOUTHERN NIGHT		115
THOU O MOURND ONE TO-DAY	284	HAWORTH CHURCH		77
O BOY IF HERE THOU SLEEPST SLEEP WELL	285	HAWORTH CHURCH		107
SLEEP O CLUSTER OF FRIENDS	285	HAWORTH CHURCH		112
TURN O DEATH ON THE VILE	281	HAWORTH CHURCH	V	
O STRONG SOUL BY WHAT SHORE	287	RUGBY CHAPEL		37
O FAITHFUL SHEPHERD TO COME	290	RUGBY CHAPEL		143
CAMST THOU FROM HEAVEN O CHILD	295	HEINES GRAVE		116
O THOU ONE OF WHOSE MOODS	299	HEINES GRAVE		222
O OBERMANN THE SAD STERN PAGE	304	GRANDE CHARTR		146
O CHILDREN WHAT DO YE REPLY	305	GRANDE CHARTR		193
WHERE THOU O SEER ART SET	309	OBERMANN		106
O UNSTRUNG WILL O BROKEN HEART	312	OBERMANN		183
O UNSTRUNG WILL O BROKEN HEART	312	OBERMANN		183
O THOU WHO ERE THY FLYING SPAN	322	OBERMANN MORE		277
O STENYCLAROS WHICH HE BUILT AND MADE	330	MEROPE		10
O BROTHER OF MY MOTHER GUARDIAN TRUE	330	MEROPE		29
O LAIAS LAIAS LET THE HEART SPEAK HERE	331	MEROPE		59
WAKENS O QUEEN REMEMBRANCE IN THY HEART	333	MEROPE		106
O MEROPE HOW MANY NOBLE THOUGHTS	335	MEROPE		177
O GENTLE WISDOM LITTLE UNDERSTOOD	339	MEROPE		309
O ARTS ABOVE THE VULGAR TYRANTS REACH	339	MEROPE		310
O POLICY TOO SUBTLE FAR FOR SENSE	339	MEROPE		311
BEHOLD O KING FROM THE DARK	342	MEROPE		390
O ARCADIAN HILLS	342	MEROPE		392
WHAT SHALL I BEAR O LOST	342	MEROPE		400
VENGEANCE O QUEEN IS HIS DUE	343	MEROPE		408
SORROW O QUEEN OF MANKIND	346	MEROPE		506
A RETURN O FATHER GIVE TO THY BOY	348	MEROPE		542
O QUEEN FOR AN AVENGER TO APPEAR	348	MEROPE		545
A WOMAN O MY FRIENDS HAS ONE DESIRE	349	MEROPE		565
BUT WHITHER GOST THOU HENCE O QUEEN AWAY	350	MEROPE		597
O KING ALL HAIL I COME WITH WEIGHTY NEWS	354	MEROPE		710
ALL THIS O KING NOT PIECEMEAL AS TO THEE	358	MEROPE		827
LEARN THAT FROM OTHER LIPS O QUEEN THAN MINE	362	MEROPE		927
O THRICE UNHAPPY HOW I GROAN THY FATE	362	MEROPE		931
O WERE BUT ARCAS COME ALL WOULD BE WELL	362	MEROPE		933
O THAT MY OVER-SPEED AND BURSTING GRIEF	362	MEROPE		939
O HONOURD QUEEN THY SON MY CHARGE IS GONE	362	MEROPE		944
LOOK UP O QUEEN LOOK UP O MISTRESS DEAR	363	MEROPE		946
LOOK UP O QUEEN LOOK UP O MISTRESS DEAR	363	MEROPE		946
AND YET NO ENEMY DID THIS O QUEEN	363	MEROPE		951
O MISTRESS BY THE GODS DO NOTHING RASH	368	MEROPE		1075
I HAVE HEARD O QUEEN HOW A PRINCE	368	MEROPE		1082
O FALSE FRIENDS INTO WHAT	371	MEROPE		1127
O LOVED MISTRESS IN FEAR	371	MEROPE		1130
O HUSBAND O CLOTHED	371	MEROPE		1139
O HUSBAND O CLOTHED	371	MEROPE		1139
ALL-COVERING DARKNESS O KING	372	MEROPE		1141
HE SLEEPS SLEEPS CALM O YE ALL-SEEING GODS	372	MEROPE		1153
O GODS FOOLISH OLD MAN THOU SPOILST MY BLOW	374	MEROPE		1194
STAND AND LET VENGEANCE PASS HOLD O QUEEN HOLD	374	MEROPE		1198
ARCAS THOU HERE O MY DEAR MASTER O	375	MEROPE		1206
ARCAS THOU HERE O MY DEAR MASTER O	375	MEROPE		1206
O MOTHER MOTHER WHO UPBRAIDS ME AH	376	MEROPE		1213
O KIND MESSENIAN MAIDENS O MY FRIENDS	377	MEROPE		1222
O KIND MESSENIAN MAIDENS O MY FRIENDS	377	MEROPE		1222
O MY SON	377	MEROPE		1227
O THOU LONG-LOST LONG SEEN IN DREAMS ALONE	381	MEROPE		1288
BE GUIDED O MY SON SPURN COUNSEL NOT	382	MEROPE		1328
O AEPYTUS WEIGH WELL HER COUNSEL GIVEN	382	MEROPE		1332
O SUFFERING O CALAMITY HOW TEN	385	MEROPE		1406
O SUFFERING O CALAMITY HOW TEN	385	MEROPE		1406
O HONOURD FATHER HIDE THEE IN THY GRAVE	386	MEROPE		1430
O PRINCELY LAIAS TO WHAT PURPOSE CALLS	386	MEROPE		1446
O MEROPE THE COMMON HEART OF MAN	389	MEROPE		1523
THE GODS O MISTRESS DEAR THE HARD-SOULD MAN	390	MEROPE		1577
O BROTHER THOU HAST CONQUERD YET I FEAR	390	MEROPE		1581
O SON AND MOTHER	391	MEROPE		1596
O MEROPE THE TROUBLE ON THY FACE	393	MEROPE		1684
BUT THOU O MEROPE THOUGH DEEPLY WRONGD	394	MEROPE		1706
O VICTOR VICTOR TRIP NOT AT THE GOAL	397	MEROPE		1771
O HEAVEN-ABANDOND WRETCH THAT ENVIES THEE	397	MEROPE		1773
O WOMANS JUDGMENT	398	MEROPE		1795
O LAWLESS DARING OF THE STRONG	398	MEROPE		1800
O SELF-WILL RECKLESSLY INDULGED	398	MEROPE		1801
O VILLAGES OF OETA	399	MEROPE		1820
O PASTURES OF THE MOUNTAIN	399	MEROPE		1822

O   (CONTINUED)
        O CLIFFS LEFT BY THE EAGLES   • • • • • • • •   399 MEROPE   1825
        O HERITAGE OF NELEUS   • • • • • • • • •   399 MEROPE   1845
        O KINGDOM OF MESSENE   • • • • • • • •   399 MEROPE   1847
        O TOWN HIGH STENYCLAROS   • • • • • • •   399 MEROPE   1850
        O HONOURD QUEEN O FAITHFUL FOLLOWERS • • • •   400 MEROPE   1882
        O HONOURD QUEEN O FAITHFUL FOLLOWERS • • • •   400 MEROPE   1882
        AND CRIED O ZEUS LET WHAT BLOOD-GUILTINESS • • •   402 MEROPE   1915
        CRYING O YE MESSENIANS WILL YE LEAVE • • • •   402 MEROPE   1934
        O AEPYTUS MY SON BEHOLD BEHOLD • • • • •   403 MEROPE   1963
        WHAT MEANTEST THOU O POLYPHONTES WHAT • • •   404 MEROPE   1979
        O MOTHER MY BEST DILIGENCE SHALL BE • • • •   405 MEROPE   2014
        O ERYMANTHUS FROM SIGHT   • • • • • • • •   347 MEROPE   V
        O LYCAEUS CONCEALS   • • • • • • • • •   347 MEROPE   V
        O MY COMFORTERS STRAYS   • • • • • • • •   348 MEROPE   V
        AND SCARCELY WILL THEY BUDGE A YARD O PAN • • •   406 EMPEDOCLES I 1   5
        AND SAID O BOY I TAUGHT THIS LORE • • • • •   414 EMPEDOCLES I 2   69
        O SAGE O SAGE TAKE THEN THE ONE WAY LEFT • • •   429 EMPEDOCLES II   24
        O SAGE O SAGE TAKE THEN THE ONE WAY LEFT • • •   429 EMPEDOCLES II   24
        AND THEREFORE O YE ELEMENTS I KNOW • • • •   441 EMPEDOCLES II   404
        NOT HERE O APOLLO   • • • • • • • • •   441 EMPEDOCLES II   421
        O SPEED AND REJOICE   • • • • • • • • •   442 EMPEDOCLES II   428
        COULDST THOU NO BETTER KEEP O ABBEY OLD • • •   444 WESTMIN ABBEY   4
        O SAXON FISHER THOU HAST HAD WITH THEE • • •   445 WESTMIN ABBEY   44
        SEEMD TO COME TRUE AT LAST O ABBEY OLD • • •   446 WESTMIN ABBEY   73
        O IGNORANT RACE OF MAN   • • • • • • •   447 WESTMIN ABBEY   101
        AND THOU O ABBEY GREY   • • • • • • • •   449 WESTMIN ABBEY   171
        THERE BUILD WE THEE O GUARDIAN DEAR • • • •   452 GEISTS GRAVE   71
        THERE CHOOSE WE THEE O GUARDIAN DEAR • • • •   452 GEISTS GRAVE   V 71
        O FOR THE CROON PATHETIC SWEET • • • • • •   459 KAISER DEAD   11
        SWEPT FROM THY WALLS O ROME ON ITS TRIUMPHANT WAY   465 ALARIC AT ROME   78
        O PLEASANT REST IF ONCE THE RACE WERE RUN • • •   475 CROMWELL   119
        O HAPPY SLUMBER IF THE DAY WERE DONE • • • •   475 CROMWELL   120
        DARE O FRIEND BE WANDERING DARE BE DREAMING • •   483 THEKLAS ANSWER   23
        NO LACK OF ANSWER HAST THOU O MY HEART • • • •   RUDE ORATOR   13
        KEEP ALL O KEEP CONTINUAL HOLIDAY • • • • •   FRAGMENT 2   5

OAK
        LAUREL AND OAK THE MATURE • • • • • • • •   282 HAWORTH CHURCH   V
        OF A MIGHTY OAK HAVE ENDURED • • • • • • •   287 RUGBY CHAPEL   33
        FROM THE OAK-BUILT FIERCELY-BURNING PYRE • • • •   399 MEROPE   1827

OAKS
        OF THOSE OLD OAKS WHOSE WET RED LEAVES • • •   141 TRISTRAM 1   359
        OF THE LOWER HARTZ AMONG OAKS • • • • • • •   297 HEINES GRAVE   180
        WE RODE FROM TEGEA THROUGH THE WOODS OF OAKS • •   355 MEROPE   735

OAR
        WHO BADE HIM LOOSE HIS BOAT AND FIX HIS OAR • •   444 WESTMIN ABBEY   24

OARS
        OR WHERE THE ECHOING OARS • • • • • • • •   193 STRAYED REVEL   258
        RAISED ARE THE DRIPPING OARS • • • • • • • •   228 YOUTH OF NATURE   1
        THE OARS HAVE MOULDERD AS THEY LAY • • • • • •   480 HAYSWATER BOAT   38

OATH
        THE FRAUDULENT OATH WHICH BOUND • • • • • •   198 FRAG ANTIGONE   95

OBEDIENCE
        OBEDIENCE TO THE PASSING DAY • • • • • • •   53 RESIGNATION   29
        PREFER OBEDIENCE TO THE PRIMAL LAW • • • • • •   196 FRAG ANTIGONE   30

OBEDIENT
        I SATE OBEDIENT IN THE FIERY PRIME • • • • • •   9 MYCERINUS   9
        ARE IN THEIR TURN OBEDIENT MADE • • • • • •   93 SICK KING BOKH   188

OBERLAND
        THE CLOUDS ARE ON THE OBERLAND • • • • • • • •   184 TERRACE BERNE   5

OBERMANN
        O OBERMANN THE SAD STERN PAGE • • • • • • •   304 GRANDE CHARTR   146
        YES OBERMANN ALL SPEAKS OF THEE • • • • • •   306 OBERMANN   11
        THAT OBERMANN THE WORLD AROUND • • • • • •   307 OBERMANN   39
        OBERMANN WITH ME HERE   • • • • • • • •   313 OBERMANN MORE   38
        THEN STILL AND SUDDEN OBERMANN • • • • • • •   314 OBERMANN MORE   59
        OF OBERMANN AWAY   • • • • • • • • • •   324 OBERMANN MORE   334

OBEY
        AND HE GREW FOND AND EAGER TO OBEY • • • • •   155 TRISTRAM 3   183
        MORE STRICTLY THEN THE INWARD JUDGE OBEY • • •   171 BETTER PART   12
        GLADLY OBEY HIS COMMAND   • • • • • • • •   216 LORDS MESSENGER   8
        HIS GENUINE SELF AND FORCE HIM TO OBEY • • •   246 BURIED LIFE   36
        CAN RISE AND OBEY   • • • • • • • • • •   253 FUTURE   48
        THY PART IT WERE TO ADVISE AND MINE TO OBEY • •   331 MEROPE   34
        TO REVERENCE YOUR LINEAGE MORE TO OBEY • • •   339 MEROPE   303
        THE MOB WHO OUGHT TO OBEY ARE THESE • • • •   353 MEROPE   678
        SWEAR BY THE GODS HENCEFORTH TO OBEY ME • • •   371 MEROPE   1133
        GOOD TO OBEY WITHOUT A LEADER NOUGHT • • • • •   381 MEROPE   1302

OBEYD
    THEY THAT BEAR RULE AND ARE OBEYD   • • • • • •   93 SICK KING BOKH   186
    SHE SHIVERD AND OBEYD • • • • • • • • • 316 OBERMANN MORE   124
    SO RULE THAT AS HIS FOE THOU BE OBEYD   • • • • 404 MEROPE   2009
    SO RULE THAT AS THY FOE THOU BE OBEYD   • • • • 404 MEROPE   V2009
    FOR MAN WOULD MAKE NO MURMURING WERE HIS WILL OBEYD 417 EMPEDOCLES I 2   · 151

OBEYS
    HIM WHO OBEYS THY SPELL • • • • • • • • • • 311 OBERMANN   158
    THE FISHER AWED OBEYS • • • • • • • • • • 445 WESTMIN ABBEY   27

OBJECT
    SOLE OBJECT OF HER DYING EYES REMAIN • • • • • 168 RACHEL 2   13

OBJECTS
    RAISED BY THE OBJECTS HE PASSES ARE HIS   • • • • 252 FUTURE   26

OBLIVION
    OBLIVION IN LOST ANGELS CAN INFUSE   • • • • • •   43 GIPSY CHILD   55
    OBLIVION IN LORN ANGELS CAN INFUSE   • • • • • •   43 GIPSY CHILD   V 55
    FROM DULL OBLIVION NOR ALL   • • • • • • 288 RUGBY CHAPEL   82
    THERE IN UNVOICED OBLIVION SINK THY NAME • • • • 395 MEROPE   1751
    THERE IN UNVOICED OBLIVION HIDE THY NAME • • • • 395 MEROPE   V1751

OBLIVIONS
    OBLIVIONS DREARY FOUNTAIN WHERE ART THOU • • • • 462 ALARIC AT ROME   2

OBSCURE
    ROCKING HER OBSCURE BODY TO AND FRO • • • • •   45 IN UTRUMQUE PAR   25
    WHAT IS ONE MORE ONE LESS OBSCURE OR FAMED • • •   68 SOHRAB RUSTUM   252
    MEN SPENT BY SICKNESS OR OBSCURE DECAY   • • • • 104 BALDER DEAD 1   325
    RECALLS THE OBSCURE OPPOSER HE OUTWEIGHD • • • • 171 DIVINITY   8
    LOOKS IN VAIN FOR ALLS OBSCURE • • • • • • 215 PIS-ALLER   4
    I BEHELD THE OBSCURE • • • • • • • • 281 HAWORTH CHURCH V
    I PASSD OBSCURE ALONE • • • • • • • • 321 OBERMANN MORE   262
    WHAT WE FOUND HERE WERE TRIBES OF FAME OBSCURE • • 337 MEROPE   233
    WAS SAVED A BABE BUT TO A LIFE OBSCURE • • • • 356 MEROPE   769
    CLOUD-ENVELOPED OBSCURE • • • • • • • • 370 MEROPE   1106
    BUT FAR IN OBSCURE THERE STIRRD • • • • • 458 POOR MATTHIAS   192
    WITH NOISELESS CURRENT STRONG OBSCURE AND DEEP • • 483 BELOW SURFACE   4
    SWIMS ON AN OBSCURE MUCH WE MIGHT HAVE BEEN • •   FRAGMENT 3   2

OBSCURED
    AS SOME ARE BORN TO BE OBSCURED AND DIE • • • •   84 SOHRAB RUSTUM   774

OBSCURENESS
    WHETHER A NATURAL OBSCURENESS HIDING • • • • • 352 MEROPE   641

OBSCURES
    NOW TIME OBSCURES IT AND MENS LATER DEEDS • • • • 117 BALDER DEAD 3   130

OBSCURITY
    INTO THE DEWY DARK OBSCURITY • • • • • • • • 242 SUMMER NIGHT   8

OBSERVANCES
    BY SAD OBSERVANCES AND PUBLIC GRIEF • • • • • • 332 MEROPE   81

OBSERVE
    TO OBSERVE A WORLD SO VAST • • • • • • • • 419 EMPEDOCLES I 2   213

OBSERVED
    THE OLD LAW OBSERVED BY SCRIBES AND PHARISEES • • 237 PROGRESS   6

OBSTINATE
    THE OBSTINATE MIND DECREES • • • • • • • • 419 EMPEDOCLES I 2   200

OBTAIN
    ACCEPT THE CHANCE THOU CANST NO MORE OBTAIN • • 122 BALDER DEAD 3   290
    THAT DOOM OBTAIN EFFECT FROM GODS OR MEN • • • • 349 MEROPE   558
    DID THE TROJANS OBTAIN TO STRIP THE ARMS FROM   HOMER TRANS   51
        PATROCLUS

OBTAIND
    SAY HAVE THEIR SONS OBTAIND MORE JOYS • • • 303 GRANDE CHARTR V 129
    WORSE TERMS THAN MINE THEY HAVE OBTAIND FROM HEAVEN 360 MEROPE   884

OBTAINED
    SMALL BLISS MY RACE HATH OF THE GODS OBTAINED • • 110 BALDER DEAD 2   205

OBTUSE
    NOR ANY OF OUR ORGANS SO OBTUSE • • • • • • 352 MEROPE   632

OCCASION
    EACH TO HIS POST WHERE THE OCCASION CALLS • • • • 386 MEROPE   1441
    THE OCCASION IF OUR CHIEF CONFEDERATE FAILS • • 386 MEROPE   1447

OCCUPATION
    BY SELFISH OCCUPATION PLOT AND PLAN • • • • • •   7 REP FRIEND CONT   11

OCEAN
    ON THE LIFELESS MARGIN OF THE SPARKLING OCEAN • •   36 VOICE   19
    NOT IDLY EARTH AND OCEAN LABOUR ON • • • • •   42 GIPSY CHILD   7

OCEAN   (CONTINUED)
     OF THE BRIGHT ROCKING OCEAN SETS TO SHORE . . . .   79 SOHRAB RUSTUM   617
     OCEAN WHOSE WATERY RING ENFOLDS THE WORLD . . . .   99 BALDER DEAD 1   160
     THE EARTH AND OCEAN AND ABOVE THEM HEAVEN . . . .   121 BALDER DEAD 3   261
     AND DOWN TO OCEAN GROPED AND CROSSD THE ICE   . .   124 BALDER DEAD 3   376
     FROM THE BRIGHT OCEAN AT OUR FEET AN EARTH . . . . 128 BALDER DEAD 3   528
     HE SINGS NOT OF THE OCEAN . . . .   159 NECKAN   9
     OCEAN AND CLOUDS AND NIGHT AND DAY . . . . . .   181 ISOLATION MARG   33
     UPON THE BOUNDLESS OCEAN-PLAIN . . . .   185 TERRACE BERNE   46
     ON THE WIDE OCEAN OF LIFE ANEW . . . .   243 SUMMER NIGHT   53
     AS IT DRAWS TO THE OCEAN MAY STRIKE . . . . .   254 FUTURE   81
     OF THE MIDMOST OCEAN HAVE SWELLD . . . . . .   288 RUGBY CHAPEL   71
     STILL THE SAME OCEAN ROUND US RAVES . . . . .   303 GRANDE CHARTR   125
     ALL-FLOODING OCEAN OF BLOOD   . . . .   378 MEROPE   1246
     WHILE FULL AND CEASELESS AS THE OCEAN ROLL . . . . 464 ALARIC AT ROME   71
     UNLIKE THAT OCEAN-CITY GAZING STILL . . . . .   468 ALARIC AT ROME   159

OCEANS
     BLITHELY THIS MORN OLD OCEANS WORK IS DONE . . . .   41 GIPSY CHILD   V   7
     AND IS ALONE NOT DIPT IN OCEANS STREAM . . . .   99 BALDER DEAD 1   158
     AND STRAIGHT HE WILL COME DOWN TO OCEANS STRAND . . 99 BALDER DEAD 1   159
     AND HE CAME DOWN TO OCEANS NORTHERN STRAND . . .   108 BALDER DEAD 2   141
     BEING ALIVE AND COME TO OCEANS SHORE . . . . .   110 BALDER DEAD 2   184
     AND OER THE ICE HE FARED TO OCEANS STRAND . . .   113 BALDER DEAD 2   288
     AND SET BY OCEANS UTMOST MARGE TO DWELL . . . .   121 BALDER DEAD 3   275
     OF OCEANS SLEEPING FACE OR HEAVENS UNBROKEN BLUE . 463 ALARIC AT ROME   36
     ISTER TETHYS AND OCEANS SIXTH-BORN SON . . . .   FRAGMENT 4   2

OCTOBER
     IN THE BRIGHT OCTOBER MORNING . . . .   13 CHURCH BROU 1   5
     IN THE DULL OCTOBER EVENING . . . .   13 CHURCH BROU 1   29
     BUT AS WHEN COWHERDS IN OCTOBER DRIVE . . . .   107 BALDER DEAD 2   91

ODE
     THE ODE SUBLIME   . . . .   458 KAISER DEAD   4

ODER
     HER LONG AGO THE WANDERING ODER TOOK . . . . .   116 BALDER DEAD 3   93
     MY LONG-LOST WANDERING ODER THOU HAST MET . . .   116 BALDER DEAD 3   101
     ONE DAY THE WANDERING ODER WILL RETURN . . . .   116 BALDER DEAD 3   115
     SO BALDER SAID BUT ODER WELL I KNOW . . . . .   117 BALDER DEAD 3   119
     MY TRUANT ODER I SHALL SEE NO MORE . . . . .   117 BALDER DEAD 3   120

ODIN
     AND I TOO ODIN TOO THE LORD OF ALL   . . . . .   96 BALDER DEAD 1   30
     BUT FROM THE HILL OF LIDSKIALF ODIN ROSE . . .   102 BALDER DEAD 1   253
     BUT FIERCELY ODIN GALLOPD MOVED IN HEART . . .   102 BALDER DEAD 1   258
     FOR DREAD FOR LIKE A WHIRLWIND ODIN CAME . . .   102 BALDER DEAD 1   264
     AND IN VALHALLA ODIN LAID HIM DOWN . . . . .   102 BALDER DEAD 1   267
     BUT THEY WENT ODIN FIRST THE REST BEHIND . . .   105 BALDER DEAD 2   35
     OF ODIN AND MY HIGH-ROOFD HOUSE IS BUILT . . .   108 BALDER DEAD 2   113
     TO ODIN TO MY FATHER TAKE THIS RING   . . . .   112 BALDER DEAD 2   274
     PEACE LEST OUR FATHER ODIN HEAR THEE GIBE . . .   114 BALDER DEAD 3   23
     BUT ODIN LOOKD TOWARD THE LAND AND SAW . . . .   114 BALDER DEAD 3   31
     AND GREETED ODIN AND THE GODS AND SAID . . . .   114 BALDER DEAD 3   35
     ODIN MY FATHER AND YE GODS OF HEAVEN . . . . .   114 BALDER DEAD 3   36
     HE SPOKE AND ALL THE GODS TO ODIN LOOKD . . .   115 BALDER DEAD 3   47
     HE SPOKE AND THE GODS ARMD AND ODIN DONND . . .   115 BALDER DEAD 3   57
     AND ODIN CAME AND LAID HIS KINGLY HANDS . . .   115 BALDER DEAD 3   65
     AND PLACED THEM ON THE PYRE AND ODIN THREW . . .   118 BALDER DEAD 3   172
     IF I IF ODIN CLAD IN RADIANT ARMS   . . . . .   120 BALDER DEAD 3   238
     DAUGHTER AND WIFE OF ODIN THUS SHE SAID . . . .   120 BALDER DEAD 3   247
     ODIN THOU WHIRLWIND WHAT A THREAT IS THIS . . .   120 BALDER DEAD 3   248
     NOR DO I MERIT ODIN THOU SHOULDST SLIGHT . . .   121 BALDER DEAD 3   282
     NOR DID THE ALL-RULING ODIN SLIGHT HER WORD . .   122 BALDER DEAD 3   297
     AND ODIN AND HIS SONS THE SEED OF HEAVEN . . .   127 BALDER DEAD 3   488
     IF STRENGTH MIGHT SAVE THEM COULD NOT ODIN SAVE   127 BALDER DEAD 3   490
     THE RUIND PALACES OF ODIN SEATS   . . . . .   128 BALDER DEAD 3   533
     OF ODIN THE DELIGHTS OF OTHER DAYS . . . . .   129 BALDER DEAD 3   542
     AND THREW THEM ON THE PYRE AND ODIN THREW . . .   118 BALDER DEAD 3   V 172
     IF STRENGTH COULD SAVE THEM COULD NOT ODIN SAVE . 127 BALDER DEAD 3   V 490

ODINS
     WAILING BUT OTHERWISE WAS ODINS WILL . . . . .   95 BALDER DEAD 1   16
     IN ODINS HALL AND WENT THROUGH ASGARD STREETS . . 97 BALDER DEAD 1   73
     TO RIDE BUT SLEIPNER ODINS HORSE ALONE . . . .   99 BALDER DEAD 1   138
     TIGHTEN THE GIRTHS OF SLEIPNER ODINS HORSE . . .   100 BALDER DEAD 1   169
     OF BALDER FROM THE FLOOR OF ODINS HALL . . . .   101 BALDER DEAD 1   205
     BUT ALL AT NIGHT RETURN TO ODINS HALL . . . .   105 BALDER DEAD 2   17
     TO GLAD THE GODS AND FEAST IN ODINS HALL . . .   105 BALDER DEAD 2   28
     AND IN THE MIDST ONE HIGHER ODINS THRONE . . .   106 BALDER DEAD 2   38
     NO MEANER HAND THAN ODINS ON HIS MANE . . . .   107 BALDER DEAD 2   73
     AND SLEIPNER ODINS HORSE IS THIS I RIDE . . .   108 BALDER DEAD 2   115
     ON THE SMOOTH ICE OF SLEIPNER ODINS HORSE . . .   109 BALDER DEAD 2   147
     YOUR MATE THOUGH LOATHED AND FEASTS IN ODINS HALL 111 BALDER DEAD 2   218
     MOST HONOURD AFTER FREA ODINS WIFE . . . . .   116 BALDER DEAD 3   92
     AFTER THE FEAST IS DONE IN ODINS HALL   . . . .   117 BALDER DEAD 3   136
     TO ASGARD AND SATE DOWN IN ODINS HALL . . . .   119 BALDER DEAD 3   208

ODOROUS
HANGING GARLANDS ON YOUR ODOROUS PINES • • • • 29 NEW SIRENS 96
HANGING GARLANDS ON THE ODOROUS PINES • • • • 29 NEW SIRENS V 96

ODOURS
AND HEAVENLY ODOURS FAIR • • • • • • • • • • 445 WESTMIN ABBEY 37

OEDIPUS
TO THEE THAT NEEDS NO OEDIPUS TO EXPLAIN • • • • 365 MEROPE 988

OER
WENT LURID DOWN OER FLOODED PLAINS • • • • • • 52 RESIGNATION 11
THROUGH THE BLACK TENTS HE PASSD OER THAT LOW STRAND 61 SOHRAB RUSTUM 16
A DOME OF LATHS AND OER IT FELTS WERE SPREAD • • 61 SOHRAB RUSTUM 23
AND OER HIS CHILLY LIMBS HIS WOOLLEN COAT • • • • 63 SOHRAB RUSTUM 96
WHO ROAM OER KIPCHAK AND THE NORTHERN WASTE • • 65 SOHRAB RUSTUM 131
ROLL TUMBLING IN THE CURRENT OER MY HEAD • • • • 83 SOHRAB RUSTUM 770
DOWN OER HIS FACE AND SATE BY HIS DEAD SON • • • 86 SOHRAB RUSTUM 859
WHO ROVE OER KIPCHAK AND THE NORTHERN WASTE • • 65 SOHRAB RUSTUM V 131
OER THE BRIDGE BIFROST WHERE IS HEIMDALLS WATCH • • 99 BALDER DEAD 1 141
THESE OER THE CORPSE INTONED A PLAINTIVE STRAIN • • 103 BALDER DEAD 1 273
UNDER WHOSE HOOFS THE BRIDGE OER GIALLS STREAM • • 107 BALDER DEAD 2 102
AND OER A DARKSOME TRACT WHICH KNOWS NO SUN • • 108 BALDER DEAD 2 139
THENCE ON HE JOURNEYD OER THE FIELDS OF ICE • • 109 BALDER DEAD 2 143
HOW DIDST THOU CROSS THE BRIDGE OER GIALLS STREAM • 110 BALDER DEAD 2 183
AND OER HIS VISAGE SERPENTS DROPPING GALL • • • • 111 BALDER DEAD 2 221
AND OER THE ICE HE FARED TO OCEANS STRAND • • • 113 BALDER DEAD 2 288
BUT OER THEM ON THE FARTHER SLOPE DESCRIES • • • 113 BALDER DEAD 2 299
SO HERMOD OER THE FOG BETWEEN SAW HEAVEN • • • 113 BALDER DEAD 2 301
AND RULED OER DENMARK AND THE HEATHY ISLES • • • 117 BALDER DEAD 3 127
RAN BLACK OER THE SEAS FACE THEN STEADY RUSHD • • 118 BALDER DEAD 3 183
STILL CARRIED OER THE DISTANT WATERS ON • • • • 119 BALDER DEAD 3 198
OER THE BRIDGE BIFROST WHERE IS HEIMDALLS WATCH • • 119 BALDER DEAD 3 216
THOK WITH DRY EYES WILL WEEP OER BALDERS PYRE • • 123 BALDER DEAD 3 352
MAKE TOWARD THEM OER THE STRETCHING CLOUDY PLAIN • 126 BALDER DEAD 3 443
THITHER WHEN OER THIS PRESENT EARTH AND HEAVENS • • 128 BALDER DEAD 3 522
DEPARTED OER THE CLOUDY PLAIN AND SOON • • • • 129 BALDER DEAD 3 552
FLOCKS OF HIS KIND PASS FLYING OER HIS HEAD • • 129 BALDER DEAD 3 561
MAKE TOWARDS THEM OER THE STRETCHING CLOUDY PLAIN • 126 BALDER DEAD 3 V 443
OER SOME FAIR UNWINTRY SEA • • • • • • • • 133 TRISTRAM 1 91
BENDING GAILY OER THY HAND • • • • • • • • 134 TRISTRAM 1 113
AS HE STEERS HER OER THE SEA • • • • • • • • 134 TRISTRAM 1 128
BLUE AND OER ITS MIRROR KIND • • • • • • • • 135 TRISTRAM 1 155
FLYING OER THE STORMY MAIN • • • • • • • • 136 TRISTRAM 1 188
OER THE BLANCHD SHEET HER RAVEN HAIR • • • • • 146 TRISTRAM 2 107
A YEAR HAD FLOWN AND OER THE SEA AWAY • • • • 149 TRISTRAM 3 1
THERE TO WATCH OER THE SUNK VALE • • • • • • 176 PARTING 47
CLEAR PROSPECT OER OUR BEINGS WHOLE • • • • • 179 FAREWELL 54
I FEEL IT STILL NOW YOUTH IS OER • • • • • • 185 TERRACE BERNE 50
OER THE SUN-REDDEND WESTERN STRAITS • • • • • 198 FRAG ANTIGONE 92
OER CALAIS AND ITS FAMOUS PLAIN • • • • • • 205 CALAIS SANDS 18
OER THE BLUE STRAIT MINE EYES I STRAIN • • • • 205 CALAIS SANDS V 20
OER THE CLOUD-WRAPT PERILOUS PLAIN • • • • • 217 LORDS MESSENGER V 21
LOOSE OER THEIR SHOULDERS WHITE • • • • • • 218 BACCHANALIA 1 26
AND OER THE PLAIN WHERE THE DEAD AGE • • • • 219 BACCHANALIA 2 19
OER THAT WIDE PLAIN NOW WRAPT IN GLOOM • • • • 220 BACCHANALIA 2 21
DOWN OER THE STATELY BRIDGE THE BREEZE • • • • 223 EPILOG LAOCOON 65
THEY FEEL RUNS OER IN EVERY LINE • • • • • • 227 EPILOG LAOCOON 198
THE PILLAR STILL BROODS OER THE FIELDS • • • • 228 YOUTH OF NATURE 15
FORWARDS FORWARDS OER THE STARLIT SEA • • • • 239 SELF-DEPENDENCE 4
OER THE SEA AND TO THE STARS I SEND • • • • • 240 SELF-DEPENDENCE 6
WITH HEADS BENT OER THEIR TOIL THEY LANGUIDLY • • 243 SUMMER NIGHT 39
I FEEL A NAMELESS SADNESS OER ME ROLL • • • • 245 BURIED LIFE 3
SCREEND IS THIS NOOK OER THE HIGH HALF-REAPD FIELD 255 SCHOLAR-GIPSY 21
SOME COUNTRY-NOOK WHERE OER THY UNKNOWN GRAVE • • 259 SCHOLAR-GIPSY 138
OER THE BLUE MIDLAND WATERS WITH THE GALE • • • • 262 SCHOLAR-GIPSY 244
SCREEND IN THIS NOOK OER THE HIGH HALF-REAPD FIELD 255 SCHOLAR-GIPSY V 21
WHEN THE YEARS PRIMAL BURST OF BLOOM IS OER • • 264 THYRSIS 52
WENT OER THE SUN-LIT FIELDS AGAIN • • • • • 271 MEMORIAL VERSES 52
WHAT SHALL BE SAID OER WORDSWORTHS TOMB • • • 270 MEMORIAL VERSES V 5
AND OER THE GLISTENING LONELY LAND • • • • • 274 STANZAS CARNAC 21
MILD OER HER GRAVE YE MOUNTAINS SHINE • • • • 279 SOUTHERN NIGHT 137
HUM OER THE THYME THE GROUSE • • • • • • • 285 HAWORTH CHURCH 121
RUSH OER THE YORKSHIRE MOORS • • • • • • • 286 HAWORTH CHURCH 130
HANGING NOW OER A HEAD • • • • • • • • 281 HAWORTH CHURCH V
GORGES OER MOUNTAINS IN SNOW • • • • • • • 289 RUGBY CHAPEL 88
BOILS OER ITS BORDERS ALOFT • • • • • • • 289 RUGBY CHAPEL 98
CREEPS OER THE SUNSHINE A BREEZE • • • • • • 293 HEINES GRAVE 39
IN THE LAURELLD ROCK OER THE BLUE • • • • • 294 HEINES GRAVE 57
OER THE FRESH SHORT TURF OF THE HARTZ • • • • 297 HEINES GRAVE 153
UP OER THE ROCK-STREWN SLOPE • • • • • • 297 HEINES GRAVE 162
OER THE GRACIOUS SPURS COMING DOWN • • • • • 297 HEINES GRAVE 179
OER THE VALLEY THE DIZZILY PERCHD • • • • • 297 HEINES GRAVE 187
FOR ONE SHORT MOMENT WANDER OER HIS LIPS • • • 298 HEINES GRAVE 209
CLOSE OER IT IN THE AIR • • • • • • • • 306 OBERMANN 4
WHICH BROODED OER THY SOUL • • • • • • • 306 OBERMANN 16
AND DARKNESS STEAL OER THE WET GRASS • • • • 310 OBERMANN 117
AH OER THAT SILENT SACRED LAND • • • • • • • 318 OBERMANN MORE 181
DOWN CAME THE STORM OER FRANCE IT PASSD • • • • 319 OBERMANN MORE 201
SOLEMN OER HUT AND WOOD • • • • • • • • 323 OBERMANN MORE 330
WHILE STOOD OER HIM A FORM • • • • • • • 346 MEROPE 492

OER   (CONTINUED)
          WHEN OER THE ARCADIAN FORESTS THOU ART COME   • •   349 MEROPE   572
          WHICH HANGS OER THE STYMPHALIAN LAKE AND DROWND • •   363 MEROPE   961
          CLUSTERING OER THY WHITE FOREHEAD LIKE A GIRLS   • •   373 MEROPE   1162
          FLED FOR YEARS AFTER OER THE FACE OF EARTH • • • •   385 MEROPE   1423
          OER WHOSE CLIFFS THE TOWNSMEN • • • • • •   392 MEROPE   1649
          SO OER THEE AND THY CHILD   • • • • • •   393 MEROPE   1679
          WHICH FELLD HIM TO THE EARTH AND OER HIM STOOD   • •   402 MEROPE   1922
          BURST OER THE ALTAR AND THE DORIAN LORDS   • • • •   402 MEROPE   1938
          TO CHUCKLE WITH HIS SENDER OER THE GAME   • • • •   366 MEROPE   V
          SPREADING OER THE THUNDERERS FACE   • • • • •   431 EMPEDOCLES II   68
          WHILE OER HIS SOVRAN EYE • • • • • • • • •   431 EMPEDOCLES II   78
          OF FRESH-PULLD VIOLETS WREATHED AND NODDING OER • •   431 EMPEDOCLES II   87
          OER THEIR POLISHD BOSOMS BLOWING   • • • • •   433 EMPEDOCLES II   154
          OER WHOSE LIT FLOOR A ROAD OF MOONBEAMS LEADS   • •   438 EMPEDOCLES II   312
          WHILE OER HIS SOVEREIGN EYE   • • • • • • •   431 EMPEDOCLES II V 78
          OER HUMBLED PRIDE AND SELF-REPROACHING WOE • • • •   462 ALARIC AT ROME   4
          IN FIRES UNDYING OER THE GUILTY HEAD • • • • •   463 ALARIC AT ROME   28
          AND OER THY TOWERS THE WINDS HALF UTTERED SIGH   • •   464 ALARIC AT ROME   65
          TWICE HATH THE CLOUD HUNG OER THEE TWICE BEEN STAYED   465 ALARIC AT ROME   83
          WHAT DEATHLIKE STILLNESS OER THE LANDSCAPE LAY   • •   466 ALARIC AT ROME   99
          BUT OER HER VANISH MIGHT AND HUMBLED PRIDE • • •   468 ALARIC AT ROME   161
          MOURNING AS WIDOWED VENICE OER HER ADRIAN TIDE   • •   468 ALARIC AT ROME   162
          FAR OER THE GLISTENING SHEETS OF WINDY CORN • • •   473 CROMWELL   36
          WHILE OER THE DUSTY PLAIN THE MURMUROUS THRONG   • •   473 CROMWELL   43
          SWEPT OER THE FANCY OF THAT HEEDLESS CHILD • • • •   473 CROMWELL   52
          ITS SHADOWS OER THE FUTURE FLOWERD AND GREW • • •   473 CROMWELL   56
          LIKE SUMMER LIGHTNINGS OER A DARKEND SKY   • • •   474 CROMWELL   72
          OER FLOWERING PLAIN AND BLOSSOMD MEADOW FLING   • •   474 CROMWELL   91
          FAR OER THE PATHLESS WASTE OF LABOURING FOAM   • •   475 CROMWELL   114
          BY NASEBYS HILL OER MARSTONS HEATHY WASTE   • • •   476 CROMWELL   149
          THERE HAMPDEN BENT HIM OER HIS SADDLE BOW   • • •   476 CROMWELL   169
          I PASSD TO-DAY OER WALTON HEATH   • • • • • •   483 ROME-SICKNESS   5
          OER GLION FRINGE THE MOUNTAINS BRINK • • • • •   483 ROME-SICKNESS   11
          AND STRUCK AND OER US THE SEA-WATERS SPREAD • •   484 S S LUSITANIA   8
          OER THOSE SAME SEAS DARK TENERIFFE ROSE FRAUGHT • •   485 S S LUSITANIA   11

OERFLOW
          OF OXUS WHERE THE SUMMER-FLOODS OERFLOW   • • • •   61 SOHRAB RUSTUM   14

OERFROWNS
          OERFROWNS THE WAVE • • • • • • • • • • •   276 SOUTHERN NIGHT   24

OERGROWN
          SITTING UPON THE RIVER BANK OERGROWN   • • • • • • 258 SCHOLAR-GIPSY   97

OERHANGING
          UNDER OERHANGING PINES THE MORNING SUN   • • • •   24 DREAM   V   3
          FOR FEAR THEY SHOULD DISLODGE THE OERHANGING SNOWS   66 SOHRAB RUSTUM   168
          BETWEEN THE WAVES AND BLACK OERHANGING CLIFFS   • •   97 BALDER DEAD 1   79

OERLABOURD
          BEFORE THIS TEASED OERLABOURD HEART   • • • • • •   206 RIVER   17
          ONE WITH THE OERLABOURD POWER THAT THROUGH   422 EMPEDOCLES I 2   291
                  THE BREADTH AND LENGTH

OERLEAP
          OR HOW OERLEAP THE GRATE THAT BARS THE WALL   • •   110 BALDER DEAD 2   185

OERLEAPS
          HE LEAVES HIS KIND OERLEAPS THEIR PEN   • • • •   58 RESIGNATION   211

OERPASS
          OR OERPASS THE SEVERING SEA   • • • • • • • •   456 POOR MATTHIAS   127

OERPAST
          YES NOW THE LONGING IS OERPAST • • • • • • • •   147 TRISTRAM 2   131

OERSHADOW
          WHOM THE GODS OERSHADOW   • • • • • • • • • •   391 MEROPE   1597

OERSHADOWD
          IS ON ALL SIDES OERSHADOWD BY THE HIGH   • • • •   7 REP FRIEND CONT   6

OERSHADOWING
          HUNTER OERSHADOWING HIS BROW • • • • • • • •   342 MEROPE   396

OERSHADOWS
          OERSHADOWS HERS   • • • • • • • • • • •   277 SOUTHERN NIGHT   56

OERTAXD
          ITS HEADS OERTAXD ITS PALSIED HEARTS WAS RIFE   • •   261 SCHOLAR-GIPSY   205

OERTHROWN
          TO TYPHO ONLY THE REBEL OERTHROWN   • • • • • •   430 EMPEDOCLES II   42
          ONLY TO TYPHO THE REBEL OERTHROWN   • • • • • •   430 EMPEDOCLES II V 42

OERTOOK
          SUCH END OERTOOK THAT LOVE   • • • • • • • •   197 FRAG ANTIGONE   70

OERWORKD
    ILL AND OERWORKD HOW FARE YOU IN THIS SCENE   • • 169 EAST LONDON   6

OETA
    SOARING FROM HIS DEATH-PILE ON OETA LEFT   • • • • 336 MEROPE   213
    O VILLAGES OF OETA • • • • • • • • • • • 399 MEROPE   1820

OETAEAN
    AND SCARED OETAEAN SNOWS • • • • • • • • • • 198 FRAG ANTIGONE   102

OFF
    OFF THEY SWEEP THE MARSHY FORESTS   • • • • • • 13 CHURCH BROU 1   19
    SOME DREAMERS WHO FAR OFF A SUMMERS DAY   • • • 42 GIPSY CHILD   V 22
    IS IN THEIR FAR-OFF TRIUMPHS PROUD   • • • • • 57 RESIGNATION   163
    FAR OFF ANON HER MATE COMES WINGING BACK   • • • 78 SOHRAB RUSTUM   561
    FROM HUNTING AND A GREAT WAY OFF DESCRIES   • • • 78 SOHRAB RUSTUM   562
    MAY SEE MY TOMB A GREAT WAY OFF AND CRY   • • • 84 SOHRAB RUSTUM   791
    MAY SEE MY TOMB A GREAT WAY OFF AND SAY   • • • 84 SOHRAB RUSTUM   V 791
    WASH OFF ALL BLOOD SET SMOOTH EACH LIMB   • • • 95 SICK KING BOKH   230
    MID DUST AND GROANS AND LIMBS LOPPD OFF AND BLOOD   • 105 BALDER DEAD 2   16
    SHE SPAKE BUT DOWN OFF SLEIPNER HERMOD SPRANG   • 110 BALDER DEAD 2   186
    BUT FEEBLY AS A VOICE FAR OFF HE SAID   • • • 112 BALDER DEAD 2   263
    BUT ALL THAT BROOD THOU HAST REMOVED FAR OFF   • 121 BALDER DEAD 3   274
    FAR OFF WHERE SOME UNWARND MIGHT FAIL TO WEEP   • 122 BALDER DEAD 3   322
    NOT TOO FAR OFF WHEN THAT THOU CAMEST BY   • • • 125 BALDER DEAD 3   417
    ALL ROUND THE FOREST SWEEPS OFF BLACK IN SHADE   • 139 TRISTRAM 1   276
    THE OTHER WARDED OFF THE DROOPING BOUGHS   • • • 154 TRISTRAM 3   176
    THE FAR-OFF SOUND OF A SILVER BELL   • • • • 162 FORSAKEN MERM   34
    WHEN DOWN SWUNG THE SOUND OF A FAR-OFF BELL   • 163 FORSAKEN MERM   54
    WHEN DOWN SWUNG THE SOUND OF THE FAR-OFF BELL   • 163 FORSAKEN MERM   V 54
    SHUDDERING THEY DREW HER GARMENTS OFF AND FOUND   • 166 AUSTERITY POET   10
    BUT I MAY STAND FAR OFF AND GAZE   • • • • • 205 CALAIS SANDS   27
    RAN OFF AND VANISHD OUT OF HAND   • • • • • 213 PROGRESS POESY   8
    BRUSHD OFF THE BLOOM FROM THEIR SOUL   • • • • 233 YOUTH OF MAN   42
    FAR OFF A GLORY OF DAY   • • • • • • • 234 YOUTH OF MAN   81
    THEN WHEN THE CLOUDS ARE OFF THE SOUL   • • • • 241 MORALITY   13
    REMOVE YET FURTHER OFF IF AUGHT COMES NEAR   • • • 332 MEROPE   69
    BLOW OFF THE SPOT OF MURDER FROM HIS NAME   • • • 336 MEROPE   200
    AND DRINKST UNTROUBLED SLUMBER TO SLEEP OFF   • 373 MEROPE   1180
    NO BY THE GODS THOU SLAYST STAND OFF THY SON   • 375 MEROPE   1201
    WHAT WAVST THOU OFF THAT MURDEROUS AXE AWAY   • 376 MEROPE   1215
    BREAK OFF BREAK OFF YOUR TALKING AND DEPART   • 386 MEROPE   1440
    BREAK OFF BREAK OFF YOUR TALKING AND DEPART   • 386 MEROPE   1440
    FLING OFF THY CROWN SUPPOSED AT LAST SECURE   • 395 MEROPE   1743
    DIVULGE NOT TO THE FAR-OFF WORLD OF MEN   • • • 396 MEROPE   1753
    AS I WAS LIFTING MY SOILD GARLAND OFF   • • • 407 EMPEDOCLES I 1   40
    MOUNTS OFF MY SOUL I FEEL IT I BREATHE FREE   • 441 EMPEDOCLES II   408
    THOUGH MOVING INLY TO ONE FAR-OFF GOAL   • • • 448 WESTMIN ABBEY   V 153
    FALLEN DYING OFF THY PERCH   • • • • • • 456 POOR MATTHIAS   130
    THOU HADST THINE ERRANDS OFF AND ON   • • • • 460 KAISER DEAD   62
    SWEPT OFF THE WITHERED LEAVES THAT HIDE THE NAKED TOMB 469 ALARIC AT ROME   192
    THE IMPRISONING CHAINS FELL OFF AND ALL WAS CLEAR   478 CROMWELL   214
    AT LAST IN AIR FAR OFF DIM ROSE A HEIGHT   • • • 484 S S LUSITANIA   6

OFFEND
    AND NOT TO OFFEND THEE HERMOD NOR TO FORCE • • • • 125 BALDER DEAD 3   413

OFFENDER
    MORE DARING AND MORE GRAND OFFENDER FIND   • • • • 390 MEROPE   1571

OFFENDING
    AND THEN HIS MURDERER THESE OFFENDING TEARS   • • 335 MEROPE   186
    WHY WITH THE OFFENDING FATHER DID YE SLAY   • • • 339 MEROPE   318

OFFER
    BUT OFFER TERMS FOR HIS RELEASE TO HEAVEN   • • • 122 BALDER DEAD 3   V 289
    TO OFFER THAT I COME NOT BUT TO URGE • • • • • • 394 MEROPE   1688
    SPEAK I GO HENCE TO OFFER SACRIFICE   • • • • • 394 MEROPE   1722
    TO OFFER THAT I CAME NOT BUT TO URGE   • • • • • 394 MEROPE   V1688

OFFERD
    I OFFERD TO MY FOES AND THEY REFUSED • • • • • • 360 MEROPE   883
    CAKE WE OFFERD SUGAR SEED   • • • • • • • 455 POOR MATTHIAS   115

OFFERING
    SOLE OFFERING THAT THOU HAST LOCKS FROM THY HEAD • • 332 MEROPE   71
    TO WITNESS OFFERING HIM RETURN AND POWER   • • • 394 MEROPE   1696

OFFERINGS
    IT NEEDS NO YEARLY OFFERINGS AT HIS TOMB   • • • 334 MEROPE   119
    THESE OFFERINGS HOME OUR RITES ARE SPOILD TO-DAY • • 336 MEROPE   196
    THE DEAD HATH NOW HIS OFFERINGS DULY PAID   • • • 350 MEROPE   596

OFFERS
    BUT OFFERS TERMS FOR HIS RELEASE TO HEAVEN   • • • 122 BALDER DEAD 3   289
    SMALL COMFORT OFFERS FOR A WOMAN THERE   • • • 349 MEROPE   564
    HIS OFFERS I REPELLD BUT WHAT OF THAT   • • • • 366 MEROPE   1010
    HIS OFFERS COLDLY HEARD THEM COLD REPELLD   • • • 366 MEROPE   1015

OFFICE
    THAT A FORMER RIVAL SHARES HER OFFICE   • • • • 144 TRISTRAM 2   59

OFFICE   (CONTINUED)
        THAT AN ANCIENT RIVAL SHARES HER OFFICE   •   •   •   •   144 TRISTRAM 2   V 59

OFFICIAL
        TO CANVASS WITH OFFICIAL BREATH   •   •   •   •   •   250 WISH   24

OFFSPRING
        AND WITH HIMSELF SET US HIS OFFSPRING FREE   •   •   •   •   111 BALDER DEAD 2   223
        THREE GENERATIONS OF HIS OFFSPRING OUT   •   •   •   •   336 MEROPE   217
        TWO GENERATIONS OF HIS OFFSPRING UP   •   •   •   •   •   336 MEROPE   V 217

OFT
        OFT AT NOON HAVE LURED ME CREEPING   •   •   •   •   26 NEW SIRENS   V   3
        UNFRUITFUL OFT AND AT HER HAPPIEST THROE   •   •   •   •   45 IN UTRUMQUE PAR   27
        HOVERING AND STOPPING OFT AS IF AFRAID   •   •   •   •   124 BALDER DEAD 3   383
        AND FAITH MAY OFT BE UNRETURND   •   •   •   •   •   •   180 ISOLATION MARG   10
        OFT MADE THEE IN THY GLOOM DESPAIR   •   •   •   •   •   241 MORALITY   18
        COME LET ME READ THE OFT-READ TALE AGAIN   •   •   •   •   256 SCHOLAR-GIPSY   32
        OFT THROUGH THE DARKENING FIELDS HAVE SEEN THEE ROAM   •   •   257 SCHOLAR-GIPSY   84
        OFT THOU HAST GIVEN THEM STORE   •   •   •   •   •   •   257 SCHOLAR-GIPSY   86
        GERMAN KAISER FULL OFT   •   •   •   •   •   •   •   296 HEINES GRAVE   136
        THAT MOUNT THAT MADDEN HOW OFT   •   •   •   •   •   296 HEINES GRAVE   147
        OFT THROUGH THE TREES THEY CATCH A GLANCE   •   •   •   305 GRANDE CHARTR   176
        IMAGED SO OFT IMAGED SO TRUE   •   •   •   •   •   314 OBERMANN MORE   63
        HE KNEW ME WELL AND WOULD OFT NOTICE ME   •   •   •   408 EMPEDOCLES I 1   57
        SHONE OFT SO HIGH A LIGHT   •   •   •   •   •   •   446 WESTMIN ABBEY   82
        WHERE OFT WE WATCHD THY COUCHANT FORM   •   •   •   •   451 GEISTS GRAVE   68
        LOFTY THOUGHT LIES OFT IN CHILDISH PLAY   •   •   •   •   483 THEKLAS ANSWER   24
        AND OFT THE SPIRIT PENT AT HOME   •   •   •   •   •   483 ROME-SICKNESS   2

OFTEN
        SPARES OFTEN BUT THE BORDER OF HIS BASE   •   •   •   •   3 SHAKESPEARE   V   7
        SPARES BUT THE BORDER OFTEN OF HIS BASE   •   •   •   •   3 SHAKESPEARE   V   7
        AND OFTEN TO SOME KINDLY PLACE   •   •   •   •   •   55 RESIGNATION   112
        MAKE OFTEN IN THE FORESTS HEART AT MORN   •   •   •   •   75 SOHRAB RUSTUM   477
        IS THIS THEN RUKSH HOW OFTEN IN PAST DAYS   •   •   •   83 SOHRAB RUSTUM   742
        HAS OFTEN STROKED THY NECK AND GIVEN THEE FOOD   •   •   83 SOHRAB RUSTUM   753
        MAKE OFTEN IN THE FORESTS DEPTH AT MORN   •   •   •   •   75 SOHRAB RUSTUM   V 477
        AND OFTEN THE FINGERS CLOSE IN HASTE   •   •   •   •   141 TRISTRAM 1   346
        TWO SAINTS MET OFTEN WHERE THOSE WATERS FLOW   •   •   170 EAST AND WEST   4
        AND FAITH IS OFTEN UNRETURND   •   •   •   •   •   •   180 ISOLATION MARG   V 10
        BUT OFTEN IN THE WORLDS MOST CROWDED STREETS   •   •   246 BURIED LIFE   45
        BUT OFTEN IN THE DIN OF STRIFE   •   •   •   •   •   246 BURIED LIFE   46
        THINK OFTEN AS I HEAR THEM RAVE   •   •   •   •   •   249 KENSINGTON GARD   26
        HAVE OFTEN PASSD THEE NEAR   •   •   •   •   •   •   258 SCHOLAR-GIPSY   96
        SO OFTEN HAS HE KNOWN THEE PAST HIM STRAY   •   •   •   258 SCHOLAR-GIPSY   118
        HERE CAME I OFTEN OFTEN IN OLD DAYS   •   •   •   •   263 THYRSIS   9
        HERE CAME I OFTEN OFTEN IN OLD DAYS   •   •   •   •   263 THYRSIS   9
        LET IN THY VOICE A WHISPER OFTEN COME   •   •   •   •   269 THYRSIS   235
        UPBRAIDINGS OFTEN ASSAILD   •   •   •   •   •   •   294 HEINES GRAVE   71
        SO HOW OFTEN FROM HOT   •   •   •   •   •   •   •   296 HEINES GRAVE   140
        HOW OFTEN WHERE THE SLOPES ARE GREEN   •   •   •   •   310 OBERMANN   113
        HOW OFTEN HAVE I DREAMD OF THEE LIKE THIS   •   •   •   372 MEROPE   1158
        THE ILL DEEDS OF OTHER MEN MAKE OFTEN OUR LIFE DARK   •   421 EMPEDOCLES I 2   266
        FOOLS THAT SO OFTEN HERE   •   •   •   •   •   •   •   425 EMPEDOCLES I 2   382
        HIS OFTEN-LABOURD FIELDS   •   •   •   •   •   •   •   426 EMPEDOCLES I 2   415

OFTENER
        OFTENER PERFORM ARIGHT THEIR PARTS   •   •   •   •   •   221 EPILOG LAOCOON   10
        LONGS OFTENER YET AND PINES FOR ROME   •   •   •   •   •   483 ROME-SICKNESS   4

OFTENEST
        THEY TRY US OFTENEST MAKE US HARD   •   •   •   •   273 EDW QUILLINAN   7
        COMMITS ALL DEEDS THE GUILTY OFTENEST DO   •   •   •   353 MEROPE   683

OIL
        AND THEY SET JARS OF WINE AND OIL TO LEAN   •   •   •   118 BALDER DEAD 3   166

OLD
        HE MUCH THE OLD MAN WHO CLEAREST-SOULD OF MEN   •   •   2 TO A FRIEND   2
        FROM FIRST YOUTH TESTED UP TO EXTREME OLD AGE   •   •   2 TO A FRIEND   10
        AND OLD MEN DIE AND YOUNG MEN PASS THEIR PRIME   •   •   10 MYCERINUS   63
        ECHOING ROUND THIS CASTLE OLD   •   •   •   •   •   •   12 CHURCH BROU 1   2
        GAY OF OLD AMID THE GAYEST   •   •   •   •   •   •   •   14 CHURCH BROU 1   55
        OLD THAT DUCHESS STERN BEGAN IT   •   •   •   •   •   14 CHURCH BROU 1   65
        HER OLD ARCHITECT BESIDE   •   •   •   •   •   •   •   15 CHURCH BROU 1   98
        MAY BRING ONE OF THE OLD HAPPY MOMENTS AGAIN   •   •   19 MODERN SAPPHO   V
        OR ARE THOSE OLD THOUGHTS RETURNING   •   •   •   •   30 NEW SIRENS   135
        AS OLD AGE YOUTHS FATAL MORROW   •   •   •   •   •   •   33 NEW SIRENS   217
        THINE OLD STRENGTH REVEALING   •   •   •   •   •   •   39 STAGIRIUS   37
        BLITHELY THIS MORN OLD OCEANS WORK IS DONE   •   •   •   41 GIPSY CHILD   V   7
        RUNS HIS OLD ROUND OF DUBIOUS CHEER   •   •   •   •   56 RESIGNATION   129
        AND FOUND THE OLD MAN SLEEPING ON HIS BED   •   •   •   61 SOHRAB RUSTUM   26
        WAS DULLD FOR HE SLEPT LIGHT AN OLD MANS SLEEP   •   •   62 SOHRAB RUSTUM   29
        OLD MAN THE DEAD NEED NO ONE CLAIM NO KIN   •   •   •   62 SOHRAB RUSTUM   59
        IN SEISTAN WITH ZAL HIS FATHER OLD   •   •   •   •   •   63 SOHRAB RUSTUM   82
        FEELS THE ABHORRD APPROACHES OF OLD AGE   •   •   •   •   63 SOHRAB RUSTUM   84
        AND THE OLD TARTAR CAME UPON THE SAND   •   •   •   •   65 SOHRAB RUSTUM   148
        OLD MAN BE IT AGREED AS THOU HAST SAID   •   •   •   •   66 SOHRAB RUSTUM   185
        AND HE IS YOUNG AND IRANS CHIEFS ARE OLD   •   •   •   67 SOHRAB RUSTUM   217

OLD   (CONTINUED)

GO TO IF IRANS CHIEFS ARE OLD THEN I • • • • • • 67 SOHRAB RUSTUM 221
AND HE HAS NONE TO GUARD HIS WEAK OLD AGE • • • • 68 SOHRAB RUSTUM 235
AND WITH MY GREAT NAME FENCE THAT WEAK OLD MAN • • 68 SOHRAB RUSTUM 237
LIKE SOME OLD MISER RUSTUM HOARDS HIS FAME • • • • 68 SOHRAB RUSTUM 247
VALIANT OR CRAVEN YOUNG OR OLD TO ME • • • • • 68 SOHRAB RUSTUM 253
O THOU OLD WARRIOR LET US YIELD TO HEAVEN • • • • 74 SOHRAB RUSTUM 438
TO GLAD THY FATHER IN HIS WEAK OLD AGE • • • • 77 SOHRAB RUSTUM 536
THAN TO THY FRIENDS AND TO THY FATHER OLD • • • • 77 SOHRAB RUSTUM 539
WITH THAT OLD KING HER FATHER WHO GROWS GREY • • 78 SOHRAB RUSTUM 591
AND THAT OLD KING HER FATHER WHO LOVED WELL • • • 79 SOHRAB RUSTUM 625
IT WAS THAT GRIFFIN WHICH OF OLD REARD ZAL • • • • 81 SOHRAB RUSTUM 679
LO I AM OLD THREE KINGS ERE THEE • • • • • 92 SICK KING BOKH 143
O VIZIER THOU ART OLD I YOUNG • • • • • • • 93 SICK KING BOKH 181
AND IN THE HALL HE FOUND THOSE WOMEN OLD • • • • 97 BALDER DEAD 1 88
BUT AT THE CENTRAL HEARTH THOSE WOMEN OLD • • • • 100 BALDER DEAD 1 194
THE OLD THE COWARDS AND THE WEAK ARE THERE • • • • 104 BALDER DEAD 1 324
AND OLD MEN KNOWN TO GLORY BUT THEIR STAR • • • • 109 BALDER DEAD 2 166
TOOTHLESS AND OLD SHE GIBES THE PASSERS BY • • • • 123 BALDER DEAD 3 334
FOR NANNA HATH REJOIND ME WHO OF OLD • • • 126 BALDER DEAD 3 459
FAMILIAR HALLS WHERE WE HAVE SUPPD OF OLD • • • • 128 BALDER DEAD 3 534
FAMOUS IN ARTHURS COURT OF OLD • • • • • • 131 TRISTRAM 1 20
WITH THE OLD IMPERIOUS AIR • • • • • • • • 134 TRISTRAM 1 124
AS OF OLD SO LET HER BE • • • • • • • • 134 TRISTRAM 1 125
OF THOSE OLD OAKS WHOSE WET RED LEAVES • • • • 141 TRISTRAM 1 359
THROUGH SOME OLD SEA-SIDE KNIGHTLY HALL • • • • 148 TRISTRAM 2 178
IN KING MARCS CHAPEL IN TYNTAGEL OLD • • • • 149 TRISTRAM 3 3
TOLD THEM AN OLD-WORLD BRETON HISTORY • • • • 150 TRISTRAM 3 37
AND THE GREY TURRETS OF THE CASTLE OLD • • • • 151 TRISTRAM 3 59
CAN FORGET ALL TO HEAR THEM AS OF OLD • • • • 152 TRISTRAM 3 111
BY WHAT OF OLD PLEASED US AND WILL AGAIN • • • • 153 TRISTRAM 3 118
A YEAR HAD FLOWN AND IN THE CHAPEL OLD • • • • 149 TRISTRAM 3 V 1
AT TYNTAGIL IN KING MARCS CHAPEL OLD • • • • • 149 TRISTRAM 3 V 3
SHIVERING WITH FEVER NAKED OLD • • • • 157 SAINT BRANDAN 46
IMPARTING LIFE RENEWD OLD CLASSIC GRACE • • • • 168 RACHEL 3 5
HIS OLD SIGHTLESS HEAD • • • • • • • • 190 STRAYED REVEL 140
THE OLD SILENUS • • • • • • • • • • 193 STRAYED REVEL 261
NO NO OLD MEN CREON I CURSE NOT • • • • • • 196 FRAG ANTIGONE 45
IN AN EASY OLD AGE IN A HAPPY HOME • • • • • 199 FRAG DEJANEIRA 23
THAT WILD UNQUENCHD DEEP-SUNKEN OLD-WORLD PAIN • 200 PHILOMELA 8
OF THAT OLD PAIN • • • • • • • • • 200 PHILOMELA V
WHAT IS IT TO GROW OLD • • • • • • • • 212 GROWING OLD 1
AND THEN THE OLD MAN TOTTERS NIGH • • • • • 213 PROGRESS POESY 9
THAT OLD-WORLD MORN IN SICILY • • • • • • 222 EPILOG LAOCOON 45
THE OLD THE SAD THE WORN WERE THERE • • • • • 224 EPILOG LAOCOON 118
MASTER AND SERVANT YOUNG AND OLD • • • • • 226 EPILOG LAOCOON 160
NATURE IS FRESH AS OF OLD • • • • • 228 YOUTH OF NATURE 11
HE GREW OLD IN AN AGE HE CONDEMND • • • • • 229 YOUTH OF NATURE 28
TO THAT WHICH OF OLD IN HIS YOUTH • • • • • 231 YOUTH OF NATURE 97
WHICH THEY HAD OF OLD WHEN THEY STOOD • • • • 233 YOUTH OF MAN 23
MUTE AS OF OLD DAYS FLEW • • • • • • • 233 YOUTH OF MAN 39
THEY DROOPD THEY GREW BLIND THEY GREW OLD • • • • 233 YOUTH OF MAN 48
TO GROW OLD IN DARKNESS AND PAIN • • • • • 234 YOUTH OF MAN 58
THE OLD LAW THEY CRIED IS WHOLLY COME TO NOUGHT • • 237 PROGRESS 3
THE OLD LAW OBSERVED BY SCRIBES AND PHARISEES • • 237 PROGRESS 6
WHO CRY ALOUD TO LAY THE OLD WORLD LOW • • • • 237 PROGRESS 15
AH FROM THE OLD WORLD LET SOME ONE ANSWER GIVE • • 237 PROGRESS 21
AND WE MUST LEAVE THE OLD FAITHS AND WALK THEREIN • 237 PROGRESS 26
THE OLD LAW THEY SAID IS WHOLLY COME TO NOUGHT • • 237 PROGRESS V 3
QUENCH THEN THE ALTAR FIRES OF YOUR OLD GODS • • • 237 PROGRESS V 27
THAT HE HAS STILL THOUGH OLD TO RECOMMENCE • • • 239 REVOLUTIONS 11
HAST THOU THEN STILL THE OLD UNQUIET BREAST • • 243 SUMMER NIGHT 27
FADE AND GROW.OLD AT LAST AND DIE LIKE OURS • • 261 SCHOLAR-GIPSY 230
HERE CAME I OFTEN OFTEN IN OLD DAYS • • • • • 263 THYRSIS 9
IN THE OLD HAUNT AND FIND OUR TREE-TOPPD HILL • • 265 THYRSIS 103
WITH THORNS ONCE STUDDED OLD WHITE-BLOSSOMD TREES • 266 THYRSIS 113
AS IN OLD DAYS JOVIAL AND TALKING RIDE • • • • 267 THYRSIS 154
THOU HEAREST THE IMMORTAL CHANTS OF OLD • • • • 268 THYRSIS 181
THOU HEAREST THE IMMORTAL STRAINS OF OLD • • • • 268 THYRSIS V 181
MOVES THROUGH THEIR ROWS OF PILLARS OLD • • • • 274 STANZAS CARNAC 14
BEARDED WITH LICHEN OLD AND GREY • • • • 274 STANZAS CARNAC V 10
STREAMS THROUGH THEIR ROWS OF PILLARS OLD • • • • 274 STANZAS CARNAC V 14
HE BY THOSE INDIAN MOUNTAINS OLD • • • • • 278 SOUTHERN NIGHT 91
THE DROWSY BEE AS OF OLD • • • • • • • 285 HAWORTH CHURCH 120
AH AS OF OLD FROM THE POMP • • • • • • 296 HEINES GRAVE 129
EACH ITS OWN PILGRIM-HOST OF OLD • • • • • 301 GRANDE CHARTR 62
BENEATH SOME OLD-WORLD ABBEY WALL • • • • • 304 GRANDE CHARTR 170
ROUND SOME OLD FOREST-LODGE AT MORN • • • • 305 GRANDE CHARTR V 184
BY ENGLANDS LAKES IN GREY OLD AGE • • • • • 308 OBERMANN 49
THE HILLS IN THEIR OLD ORDER RANGED • • • • 312 OBERMANN MORE 7
SLOW SLOW THE OLD WORLD WORE TO NOUGHT • • • • 319 OBERMANN MORE 191
WITH OLD-WORLD CURES MEN HALF BELIEVE • • • • 320 OBERMANN MORE 235
BUT NOW THE OLD IS OUT OF DATE • • • • 321 OBERMANN MORE 245
UPON THE THRESHOLD OF OLD AGE ALONE • • • • 334 MEROPE 152
OLD AGE IS MORE SUSPICIOUS THAN THE FREE • • • 335 MEROPE 156
CONSIDER HIM CONSIDER NOT OLD HATES • • • • • 335 MEROPE 173
BE TO FOMENT OLD MEMORIES OF WRATH • • • • • 342 MEROPE 381
OH HAD HE FALLEN OF OLD • • • • • • 345 MEROPE 478
THUS MUCH FROM ARCAS MY OLD SERVANT TRUE • • • 351 MEROPE 616
AND THE OLD MEN RISE FROM THEIR BENCH • • • 360 MEROPE 900

OLD   (CONTINUED)
         IF SO ALLS WELL FOR LOOK THE OLD MAN SPEEDS   . .   362 MEROPE   934
         MY FAITHFUL FOLLOWER COMES WELCOME OLD FRIEND   . .   362 MEROPE   937
         OLD MAN OLD MAN THOU HADST MY BOY IN CHARGE   . .   368 MEROPE   1069
         OLD MAN OLD MAN THOU HADST MY BOY IN CHARGE   . .   368 MEROPE   1069
         O GODS FOOLISH OLD MAN THOU SPOILST MY BLOW   . .   374 MEROPE   1194
         TO CLOSE AN OLD WOUND NOT TO OPEN NEW   . . . .   379 MEROPE   1257
         MY DEED IS OF OLD DATE AND LONG ATONED   . . . . 396 MEROPE   1768
         AS DREW OF OLD THE PEOPLE AFTER HIM   . . . . .   408 EMPEDOCLES I 1   63
         THOU KNOWST OF OLD HE LOVED THIS HARP OF MINE   . .   408 EMPEDOCLES I 1   72
         HE COULD STAY SWIFT DISEASES IN OLD DAYS   . . . . 410 EMPEDOCLES I 1   115
         THIS HE COULD DO OF OLD BUT NOW SINCE ALL   . . . . 410 EMPEDOCLES I 1   119
         AND HE WOULD TELL ME AS HIS OLD TRIED FRIEND   . .   410 EMPEDOCLES I 1   130
         NO WE ARE STRANGERS HERE THE WORLD IS FROM OF OLD   418 EMPEDOCLES I 2   181
         A GREY OLD MAN AND WOMAN YET OF OLD   . . . . .   427 EMPEDOCLES I 2   449
         A GREY OLD MAN AND WOMAN YET OF OLD   . . . . .   427 EMPEDOCLES I 2   449
         THOU KNOWST ME FOR A WANDERER FROM OF OLD   . . .   428 EMPEDOCLES I 2   477
         AS OF OLD IN THE FIELDS OF HEAVEN   . . . . .   437 EMPEDOCLES II   278
         WHAT WAS FROM OF OLD   . . . .   443 EMPEDOCLES II   460
         COULDST THOU NO BETTER KEEP O ABBEY OLD   . . .   444 WESTMIN ABBEY   4
         SEEMD TO COME TRUE AT LAST O ABBEY OLD   . . .   446 WESTMIN ABBEY   73
         THOU DIDST KNOW THEM OLD AND GREY   . . . . .   453 POOR MATTHIAS   29
         FRENCH CANARY-MERCHANT OLD   . . . .   457 POOR MATTHIAS   184
         HE HEARD OF LATE THE GRAND OLD MAN   . . . . . 460 KAISER DEAD   41
         A GLORIOUS MANHOOD YET A DIM OLD AGE   . . . . . 463 ALARIC AT ROME   39
         EARTHS OLD HEROIC FORMS IN PEACEFUL SLUMBERS DEEP   464 ALARIC AT ROME   60
         TELL OF OLD TIMES AND HOLIEST MEMORIES   . . .   467 ALARIC AT ROME   124
         EYES THAT HE KNEW OLD FACES UNFORGOT   . . . . . 474 CROMWELL   85
         IN PRIESTLY GARB A FRAIL OLD MAN WENT BY   . . .   476 CROMWELL   166
         THE BOAT WAS OLD A BATTERD BOAT   . . . . . . 480 HAYSWATER BOAT   34
         WHY EACH IS STRIVING FROM OF OLD   . . . . .   481 DESTINY   1
         TO A MORTAL BUT YE ARE WITHOUT OLD AGE AND IMMORTAL   HOMER TRANS   10

OLDER
         AM OLDER IF THE YOUNG ARE WEAK THE KING   . . .   67 SOHRAB RUSTUM   222
         IN AN OLDER WORLD PEOPLED BY GODS   . . . . .   437 EMPEDOCLES II   285

OLEANDER
         AND THE PINK-FLOWERD OLEANDER   . . . .   391 MEROPE   1617

OLEANDERS
         QUICK THROUGH THE OLEANDERS BRUSH   . . . . .   184 TERRACE BERNE   15
         UNDER THE FLOWERY OLEANDERS PALE   . . . . .   267 THYRSIS   170

OLIVE
         COMES SOFTLY THROUGH THE OLIVE-TREES   . . . . . 279 SOUTHERN NIGHT   119

OLIVES
         LIKE GHOSTS THE HUGE GNARLD OLIVES STAND   . . .   275 SOUTHERN NIGHT   6

OLIVIAS
         CAME FORTH OLIVIAS MARGUERITE AND THINE   . . .   25 DREAM   22

OLYMPIA
         IN AGRIGENTUM AND OLYMPIA   . . . . 408 EMPEDOCLES I 1   64

OLYMPIAN
         THE OLYMPIAN COUNCIL SEES   . . . . 431 EMPEDOCLES II   70

OLYMPUS
         BEARING WITH IT TO OLYMPUS   . . . . 399 MEROPE   1841
         AND THE WHITE OLYMPUS-PEAKS   . . . . 431 EMPEDOCLES II   80
         DID THE YOUNG OLYMPUS STAND   . . . . 434 EMPEDOCLES II   166
         THEREFORE NOW OLYMPUS STANDS   . . . . 434 EMPEDOCLES II   185
         THEN ON TO OLYMPUS   . . . . 442 EMPEDOCLES II   455

OMEN
         I TAKE THE OMEN EVE LETS DOWN HER VEIL   . . .   267 THYRSIS   161
         YET HAPPY OMEN HAIL   . . . . 267 THYRSIS   166
         WHEREFORE ACCEPT THAT HAPPIER OMEN   . . . . .   344 MEROPE   452
         WITH OMEN OH WERE THAT MOUNT PASSD I SAY   . . .   485 S S LUSITANIA   12

OMIT
         OMIT OMIT MY SIMPLE FRIEND   . . . . 47 HORATIAN ECHO   1
         OMIT OMIT MY SIMPLE FRIEND   . . . . 47 HORATIAN ECHO   1

OMNIPOTENCE
         OF HIS OMNIPOTENCE   . . . .   47 WORLD QUIETIST   24

ONCE
         ARE RARE AH MOST LOVES BUT FLOW ONCE AND RETURN   . . 19 MODERN SAPPHO   16
         IT WAS WELL WITH ME ONCE IF I SAW HIM TO-MORROW   . . 19 MODERN SAPPHO   V
         ONCE I SAID A FACE IS GONE   . . . .   23 MEMORY-PICTURE   9
         AH I HOPE YET ONCE AWAY   . . . .   23 MEMORY-PICTURE   21
         FLASHD ONCE LIKE FALLING STREAMS WE ROSE WE GAZED   25 DREAM   29
         ONCE LIKE US YOU TOOK YOUR STATION   . . . . .   31 NEW SIRENS   139
         O SPEAK ONCE AND SHAME MY SADNESS   . . . . .   32 NEW SIRENS   167
         COME ONCE MORE THAT ANCIENT LIGHTNESS   . . . .   32 NEW SIRENS   175
         ONCE LIKE ME YOU TOOK YOUR STATION   . . . . .   31 NEW SIRENS   V 139
         O SPEAK ONCE AND LET MY SADNESS   . . . . . .   32 NEW SIRENS   V 167

ONCE   (CONTINUED)

ONCE ERE THE DAY DECLINE THOU SHALT DISCERN	• •	44 GIPSY CHILD	65
OH ONCE ERE NIGHT IN THY SUCCESS THY CHAIN • • • •		44 GIPSY CHILD	66
ONCE ERE THY DAY GO DOWN THOU SHALT DISCERN	• •	44 GIPSY CHILD	V 65
WHERE THEY STOOD ONCE TO THEM WERE PAIN	• • • •	53 RESIGNATION	19
ONCE MORE WE TREAD THIS SELF-SAME ROAD	• • • •	55 RESIGNATION	86
THE HORSE WHOM RUSTUM ON A FORAY ONCE	• • • •	69 SOHRAB RUSTUM	273
I CHALLENGED ONCE WHEN THE TWO ARMIES CAMPD	• •	72 SOHRAB RUSTUM	357
AND HE TOO DREW HIS SWORD AT ONCE THEY RUSHD	• •	75 SOHRAB RUSTUM	471
MIGHT BE ONCE MORE ALIVE MY BITTEREST FOES • • • •		85 SOHRAB RUSTUM	810
AS THOSE BLACK GRANITE PILLARS ONCE HIGH-REARD •		86 SOHRAB RUSTUM	860
NOR DID HE LOOK ONCE MORE TO IDAS PLAIN	• • • •	97 BALDER DEAD 1	57
BUT HERMOD TOOK THE RING AND YET ONCE MORE • • • •		112 BALDER DEAD 2	282
AND ONCE MORE HERMOD SAW AROUND HIM SPREAD • • • •		124 BALDER DEAD 3	379
I TOO HAD ONCE A WIFE AND ONCE A CHILD	• • • •	125 BALDER DEAD 3	403
I TOO HAD ONCE A WIFE AND ONCE A CHILD	• • • •	125 BALDER DEAD 3	403
AND WE SHALL TREAD ONCE MORE THE WELL-KNOWN PLAIN		128 BALDER DEAD 3	537
PROP ME UPON THE PILLOWS ONCE AGAIN	• • • • • •	130 TRISTRAM 1	2
ONCE MORE ROUND THEM AND THE SEA	• • • • • •	135 TRISTRAM 1	154
AT ARTHURS SIDE HE FIGHTS ONCE MORE • • • •		138 TRISTRAM 1	254
NOR DID THEIR LOOKS STRAY ONCE TO THE SEA-SIDE	• •	151 TRISTRAM 3	48
AND LETS US BE WHAT WE WERE ONCE NO MORE	• •	153 TRISTRAM 3	115
FIRST MEETS THE FRINGING HEATH AT ONCE ALL ROUND	• •	TRISTRAM 3	V 14
FIRST LEAVES THE FRINGING HEATH AT ONCE ALL ROUND		TRISTRAM 3	V 14
FIRST MEETS THE ENCIRCLING HEATH AT ONCE ALL ROUND		TRISTRAM 3	V 14
FIRST LEAVES THE ENCIRCLING HEATH AT ONCE ALL ROUND		TRISTRAM 3	V 14
HE GREETS THEM ONCE HE SAILS AGAIN	• • • • •	156 SAINT BRANDAN	3
ONCE EVERY YEAR WHEN CAROLS WAKE	• • • • •	158 SAINT BRANDAN	65
CALL HER ONCE BEFORE YOU GO	• • • • • •	161 FORSAKEN MERM	10
CALL ONCE YET	• • • • •	161 FORSAKEN MERM	11
CALL ONCE MORE TO A MOTHERS EAR	• • • • •	161 FORSAKEN MERM	15
CALL HER ONCE AND COME AWAY	• • • • • •	162 FORSAKEN MERM	18
CALL YET ONCE THAT SHE WENT AWAY	• • • • •	162 FORSAKEN MERM	49
ONCE SHE SATE WITH YOU AND ME	• • • • •	163 FORSAKEN MERM	50
WHO SINS ONCE WASHD BY THE BAPTISMAL WAVE	• •	172 GOOD SHEPHERD	5
FOR SURELY ONCE THEY FEEL WE WERE	• • • • •	182 TO MARG CONT	15
ONCE-LONGD-FOR STORMS OF LOVE • • • • •		183 ABSENCE	14
ONCE MORE THE ROOFS OF BERNE APPEAR	• • • •	183 TERRACE BERNE	2
AND OUR OWN PLACE ONCE LEFT	• • • • •	195 FRAG ANTIGONE	18
DOST THOU ONCE MORE ASSAY	• • • • • •	201 PHILOMELA	22
ONCE MORE AND ONCE MORE SEEM TO MAKE RESOUND	• •	201 PHILOMELA	25
ONCE MORE AND ONCE MORE SEEM TO MAKE RESOUND	• •	201 PHILOMELA	25
ONCE MORE THOU HEAREST	• • • • •	201 PHILOMELA	V 30
EAGERLY ONCE HER GRACIOUS KEN • • • •		202 URANIA	9
YET SHOW HER ONCE YE HEAVENLY POWERS • • • •		202 URANIA	17
ONE FOR WHOSE SAKE SHE ONCE MIGHT PROVE	• • •	202 URANIA	19
YET NOW MY GLANCE BUT ONCE HATH ROVED	• • •	205 CALAIS SANDS	17
NOT ONCE TO DAY THESE EYES HAVE STAYD	• • •	205 CALAIS SANDS	V 17
BUT NOW MY GLANCE BUT ONCE HATH ROVED	• • •	205 CALAIS SANDS	V 17
FLED FLED AT ONCE BE ALL VESTIGE OF THEE	• • •	206 SEPARATION	10
WERE RESTLESS ONCE BUT LONG AGO	• • • • •	208 ON THE RHINE	23
THEY LIGHT ME ONCE THEY HURRY BY	• • • • •	209 DESPONDENCY	7
WAS ONCE TOO AT THE FULL AND ROUND EARTHS SHORE	• •	211 DOVER BEACH	22
AND NOT ONCE FEEL THAT WE WERE EVER YOUNG	• • •	212 GROWING OLD	22
CHARGE ONCE MORE THEN AND BE DUMB	• • • •	215 LAST WORD	13
TO THAT WHICH ONCE RAN THROUGH HIS SOUL	• • •	231 YOUTH OF NATURE	94
AH ONCE MORE I CRIED YE STARS YE WATERS	• • •	240 SELF-DEPENDENCE	9
I SAW I FELT IT ONCE BUT WHERE	• • • • •	241 MORALITY	30
WHO HAVE LONGD DEEPLY ONCE AND LONGD IN VAIN	•	244 SUMMER NIGHT	85
ONCE MORE BEFORE MY DYING EYES • • • •		250 WISH	32
BUT ONCE YEARS AFTER IN THE COUNTRY-LANES	• • •	256 SCHOLAR-GIPSY	41
AND ONCE IN WINTER ON THE CAUSEWAY CHILL	• • •	258 SCHOLAR-GIPSY	121
TURND ONCE TO WATCH WHILE THICK THE SNOWFLAKES FALL		259 SCHOLAR-GIPSY	128
ONCE PASSD I BLINDFOLD HERE AT ANY HOUR	• • •	263 THYRSIS	24
BUT ONCE I KNEW EACH FIELD EACH FLOWER EACH STICK		263 THYRSIS	32
WITH THORNS ONCE STUDDED OLD WHITE-BLOSSOMD TREES		266 THYRSIS	113
AND HOPE ONCE CRUSHD LESS QUICK TO SPRING AGAIN	• •	266 THYRSIS	140
ONCE MORE WE LAY AS ERST AT BIRTH • • • •		271 MEMORIAL VERSES	V 48
WHOSE BEACH ONCE RAN WITH LOYAL BLOOD	• • •	274 STANZAS CARNAC	28
OH COULD HE ONCE HAVE REACHD THIS AIR	• • •	275 STANZAS CARNAC	41
SO MOONLIT SAW ME ONCE OF YORE • • • •		275 SOUTHERN NIGHT	14
AND NEVER ONCE POSSESS OUR SOUL	• • • • •	277 SOUTHERN NIGHT	71
AND ONCE A DAY • • • • •		277 SOUTHERN NIGHT	80
FILLD EUROPE ONCE WITH HIS LOVE-PAIN • • • •		278 SOUTHERN NIGHT	98
COME UNUPBRAIDED FOR ONCE • • • •		283 HAWORTH CHURCH	V
IN THE PLACE WHERE THE WAYFARER ONCE • • • • •		289 RUGBY CHAPEL	96
ONCE MORE THOU CLINGST TO THE CROSS	• • •	298 HEINES GRAVE	189
IS BURIED IN HIS COWL ONCE MORE	• • • • •	300 GRANDE CHARTR	44
I FEEL THEE NEAR ONCE MORE	• • • • •	306 OBERMANN	12
ONCE MORE UPON ME ROLL • • • • •		306 OBERMANN	14
WHITE HOUSES PRANK WHERE ONCE WERE HUTS	• • •	312 OBERMANN MORE	3
ONCE MORE I SLIP MY CHAIN • • • • •		313 OBERMANN MORE	44
MADE HIS LIFES RULE ONCE MORE • • • •		314 OBERMANN MORE	54
OF THY DEAD HUSBANDS FACTION VIGOROUS ONCE	• • •	334 MEROPE	139
A HOUSE ONCE GREAT NOW DWINDLING IN ITS SONS	• •	337 MEROPE	237
STRUCK ONCE AND AWED HIS MOB AND SAVED THIS REALM		338 MEROPE	275
SOON HAVING ONCE BEHELD HIM TO DESCEND	• • •	350 MEROPE	592
ONCE IN THE BLACK AND ARROWY RACE AND CAST	• • •	358 MEROPE	832
ONCE MORE ROLL BACK ON MY HOUSE	• • • • •	378 MEROPE	1244
BY POLYPHONTES NEVER FAILD-IN ONCE	• • • • •	387 MEROPE	1476

ONCE   (CONTINUED)

ONCE MID THOSE GORGES	392 MEROPE	1646
ONCE HUMAN CHEEKS	393 MEROPE	1671
YES ONCE AGAIN I COME I WILL NOT TAKE	394 MEROPE	1690
WHAT ONCE-FAMED WRETCH HE THERE DID ESPY HID	396 MEROPE	1754
ONCE MORE MY FRIENDSHIP THOU REJECTEST WELL	398 MEROPE	1783
ONCE MID THE GORGES	392 MEROPE	V1646
WHAT ONCE-FAMED WRETCH HE HATH SEEN LURKING THERE	396 MEROPE	V1754
I WOULD FAIN STAY AND HELP THEE TEND HIM ONCE	408 EMPEDOCLES I 1	56
AS OF HIS GIFTED MASTER AND ONCE FRIEND	411 EMPEDOCLES I 1	148
I SPOKE WITH HIM THIS MORNING ONCE MORE THEREFORE	412 EMPEDOCLES I 2	19
TO LEAD THOSE FALSE WHO TRUST IT HIST ONCE MORE	413 EMPEDOCLES I 2	33
LOOKS ONCE AND DRIVES ELSEWHERE AND LEAVES	415 EMPEDOCLES I 2	86
ITS LAST EMPLOY		
ONCE READ THY OWN BREAST RIGHT	417 EMPEDOCLES I 2	142
COULDST THOU BUT ONCE DISCERN	417 EMPEDOCLES I 2	159
AT ONCE OUR EYES GROW CLEAR	424 EMPEDOCLES I 2	362
WHO ONCE WERE CADMUS AND HARMONIA	427 EMPEDOCLES I 2	436
HIS COUNSEL COULD ONCE SOOTHE HIM BUT APOLLO	428 EMPEDOCLES I 2	482
BUT THEY WILL GLADLY WELCOME HIM ONCE MORE	435 EMPEDOCLES II	221
YOU TOO ONCE LIVED	437 EMPEDOCLES II	282
OR WHETHER WE WILL ONCE MORE FALL AWAY	440 EMPEDOCLES II	373
BUT ONCE AT MIDNIGHT DEEP	446 WESTMIN ABBEY	91
A CHURCH ONCE LARGE AND THEN GROWN STRAIT IN SOUL	449 WESTMIN ABBEY	156
FEAR NOT BUT THAT THY LIGHT ONCE MORE SHALL BURN	449 WESTMIN ABBEY	174
ONCE MORE THINE IMMEMORIAL GLEAM RETURN	449 WESTMIN ABBEY	175
THEN HOME RETURND ONCE MORE DEPART	460 KAISER DEAD	51
IN GREATNESS ONCE IN SACKCLOTH NOW AND TEARS	463 ALARIC AT ROME	20
WHAT ONCE HAD HUMAN PASSIONS HOPES AND FEARS	464 ALARIC AT ROME	52
YET ONCE AGAIN STERN CHIEF YET ONCE AGAIN	465 ALARIC AT ROME	85
YET ONCE AGAIN STERN CHIEF YET ONCE AGAIN	465 ALARIC AT ROME	85
WHOSE SONS WERE CONQUERORS ONCE AND NOW WERE SLAVES	469 ALARIC AT ROME	184
O PLEASANT REST IF ONCE THE RACE WERE RUN	475 CROMWELL	119
ONCE MORE BENEATH HIM AND THE FLUTTERING SAIL	479 CROMWELL	237
ONCE MORE ALONE BESIDE THE GLEAMING FLOOD	479 CROMWELL	240

ONE

ONE LESSON NATURE LET ME LEARN OF THEE	1 QUIET WORK	1
ONE LESSON WHICH IN EVERY WIND IS BLOWN	1 QUIET WORK	2
ONE LESSON OF TWO DUTIES KEPT AT ONE	1 QUIET WORK	3
ONE LESSON OF TWO DUTIES KEPT AT ONE	1 QUIET WORK	3
TWO BLENDING DUTIES HARMONISD IN ONE	1 QUIET WORK	V 3
ONE LESSON OF TWO DUTIES SERVD IN ONE	1 QUIET WORK	V 3
ONE LESSON OF TWO DUTIES SERVD IN ONE	1 QUIET WORK	V 3
ONE LESSON OF TWO DUTIES KEPT IN ONE	1 QUIET WORK	V 3
ONE LESSON OF TWO DUTIES KEPT IN ONE	1 QUIET WORK	V 3
OF LABOUR THAT IN ONE SHORT HOUR OUTGROWS	1 QUIET WORK	V 6
AS THOUGH ONE SPAKE OF LIFE UNTO THE DEAD	3 EMERSONS ESSAYS	8
AS THOUGH ONE SPAKE OF NOISE UNTO THE DEAD	3 EMERSONS ESSAYS	V 8
WHERE MANS ONE NATURE QUEEN-LIKE SITS ALONE	4 BUTLERS SERMONS	7
WHICH SAW ONE CLUE TO LIFE AND FOLLOWD IT	5 DUKE WELLINGTON	14
OF ONE SHORT JOY ONE LUST ONE PLEASANT DREAM	10 MYCERINUS	50
OF ONE SHORT JOY ONE LUST ONE PLEASANT DREAM	10 MYCERINUS	50
OF ONE SHORT JOY ONE LUST ONE PLEASANT DREAM	10 MYCERINUS	50
AND ONE LOUD CRY OF GRIEF AND OF AMAZE	11 MYCERINUS	80
WHERE IN ONE DREAM THE FEVERISH TIME OF YOUTH	11 MYCERINUS	89
GUIDE ME SOME ONE TO THE MOUNTAIN	15 CHURCH BROU 1	75
ONE THE DUKE IN HELM AND ARMOUR	16 CHURCH BROU 1	107
ONE THE DUCHESS IN HER VEIL	16 CHURCH BROU 1	108
MAY BRING ONE OF THE OLD HAPPY MOMENTS AGAIN	19 MODERN SAPPHO	V
ONE DAY TO HARBOUR IN THE TOMB	22 YOUTH AND CALM	15
AH NO THE BLISS YOUTH DREAMS IS ONE	22 YOUTH AND CALM	16
ONE MOMENT ON THE RAPIDS TOP OUR BOAT	25 DREAM	30
ONE FAINT FROWN OF DISTANT COLDNESS	31 NEW SIRENS	161
OF ONE JOY WHICH YOU HAVE NOT	31 NEW SIRENS	166
WHEN THE SLOW TIDE SETS ONE WAY	33 NEW SIRENS	220
O LET FALL ONE TEAR AND SET US FREE	34 NEW SIRENS	226
AND SIGH THAT ONE THING ONLY HAS BEEN LENT	37 YOUTHS AGIT	13
BOTH ARE LAID IN ONE COLD PLACE	44 QUESTION	6
OUR VAUNTED LIFE IS ONE LONG FUNERAL	44 QUESTION	10
IF IN THE SILENT MIND OF ONE ALL-PURE	45 IN UTRUMQUE PAR	1
AND HE SPINS ILL WHO MISSES ONE	48 HORATIAN ECHO	26
THAT THE ONE LORE THATS ASSURING	SECOND BEST	V 21
WHO TO NO ONE MAN	52 CONSOLATION	72
WIDER THAN ONE MANS PASSION THERES NO MOOD	50 CONSOLATION	V
CASD IN ONE MANS DIMENSIONS CAN DISTIL	50 CONSOLATION	V
THE VALLEY-PASTURES ONE BY ONE	53 RESIGNATION	50
THE VALLEY-PASTURES ONE BY ONE	53 RESIGNATION	50
AND HE ROSE QUICKLY ON ONE ARM AND SAID	62 SOHRAB RUSTUM	30
I SEEK ONE MAN ONE MAN AND ONE ALONE	62 SOHRAB RUSTUM	49
I SEEK ONE MAN ONE MAN AND ONE ALONE	62 SOHRAB RUSTUM	49
I SEEK ONE MAN ONE MAN AND ONE ALONE	62 SOHRAB RUSTUM	49
SHOULD ONE DAY GREET UPON SOME WELL-FOUGHT FIELD	62 SOHRAB RUSTUM	51
OLD MAN THE DEAD NEED NO ONE CLAIM NO KIN	62 SOHRAB RUSTUM	59
BUT IF THIS ONE DESIRE INDEED RULES ALL	63 SOHRAB RUSTUM	74
AND NOT THAT ONE SLIGHT HELPLESS GIRL I HAVE	68 SOHRAB RUSTUM	230
WHAT IS ONE MORE ONE LESS OBSCURE OR FAMED	68 SOHRAB RUSTUM	252
WHAT IS ONE MORE ONE LESS OBSCURE OR FAMED	68 SOHRAB RUSTUM	252
ONE STROKE BUT AGAIN SOHRAB SPRANG ASIDE	73 SOHRAB RUSTUM	417
TOGETHER AS TWO EAGLES ON ONE PREY	75 SOHRAB RUSTUM	472
ONE FROM THE EAST ONE FROM THE WEST THEIR SHIELDS	75 SOHRAB RUSTUM	474

ONE   (CONTINUED)

ONE FROM THE EAST ONE FROM THE WEST THEIR SHIELDS	75	SOHRAB RUSTUM	474
AND SHRANK AMAZED BACK HE RECOILD ONE STEP	76	SOHRAB RUSTUM	517
SURELY THE NEWS WILL ONE DAY REACH HIS EAR	78	SOHRAB RUSTUM	581
FOR RUSTUM HAD NO SON ONE CHILD HE HAD	80	SOHRAB RUSTUM	645
BUT ONE A GIRL WHO WITH HER MOTHER NOW	80	SOHRAB RUSTUM	646
AND RISING STERNLY ON ONE ARM HE SAID	80	SOHRAB RUSTUM	654
SPEECHLESS AND THEN HE UTTERD ONE SHARP CRY	81	SOHRAB RUSTUM	690
FIRST TO THE ONE THEN TO THE OTHER MOVED	82	SOHRAB RUSTUM	733
THAT I SHOULD ONE DAY FIND THY LORD AND THEE	83	SOHRAB RUSTUM	745
OR IF INDEED THIS ONE DESIRE RULES ALL	63	SOHRAB RUSTUM V	74
AND SHRANK AMAZED BACK HE RECOILD ONE PACE	76	SOHRAB RUSTUM V	517
ONE WAS MY MOTHER NOW DO RIGHT	90	SICK KING BOKH	88
BUT WHEN ONE TOLD HIM HE IS DEAD	91	SICK KING BOKH	126
ONE MAN IS NOT WELL MADE TO BEAR	92	SICK KING BOKH	154
LOOK THIS IS BUT ONE SINGLE PLACE	92	SICK KING BOKH	157
NEAR ONE ANOTHER MANY A MAN	93	SICK KING BOKH	163
VEX ONE ANOTHER NIGHT AND DAY	93	SICK KING BOKH	174
THAT ONE LONG PORTIOND WITH HIS DOOM OF DEATH	98	BALDER DEAD 1	114
THAT ONE SHOULD GRUDGE ITS LOSS FOR BALDERS SAKE	98	BALDER DEAD 1	125
YET IN MY SECRET MIND ONE WAY I KNOW	99	BALDER DEAD 1	128
BUT THERE WAS ONE THE FIRST OF ALL THE GODS	101	BALDER DEAD 1	220
FOR OF THE RACE OF GODS IS NO ONE THERE	104	BALDER DEAD 1	318
AND IN THE MIDST ONE HIGHER ODINS THRONE	106	BALDER DEAD 2	38
YET HE SHALL ONE DAY RISE AND BURST HIS BONDS	111	BALDER DEAD 2	222
FAILS BUT ONE THING TO GRIEVE HERE BALDER STOPS	111	BALDER DEAD 2	235
SO THEY TWO SOFT TO ONE ANOTHER SPAKE	114	BALDER DEAD 3	30
FAILS BUT ONE THING TO GRIEVE THERE BALDER STOPS	114	BALDER DEAD 3	43
HEARD NO ONE EVER AN INJURIOUS WORD	116	BALDER DEAD 3	84
ONE DAY THE WANDERING ODER WILL RETURN	116	BALDER DEAD 3	115
LAST FROM AMONG THE HEROES ONE CAME NEAR	117	BALDER DEAD 3	124
BUT THEY HARP EVER ON ONE STRING AND WAKE	117	BALDER DEAD 3	137
ONE THING TO UNDO WHAT THOU THYSELF HAST RULED	120	BALDER DEAD 3	253
SAVE ONE BERGELMER HE ON SHIPBOARD FLED	121	BALDER DEAD 3	272
TRY IT BUT I FOR ONE WILL NOT APPLAUD	121	BALDER DEAD 3	281
HELA AND WIN THE LOVED ONE BACK TO HEAVEN	122	BALDER DEAD 3	294
OF NIFLHEIM HE SAW ONE GHOST COME NEAR	124	BALDER DEAD 3	382
AND ALL ARE MARSHALLD IN ONE FLAMING SQUARE	127	BALDER DEAD 3	480
LIFE ONE PERPETUAL FIGHT A BATH OF BLOOD	128	BALDER DEAD 3	506
ANOTHER HEAVEN THE BOUNDLESS NO ONE YET	128	BALDER DEAD 3	519
ONE MORN AT MARKET IN A CROWDED TOWN	114	BALDER DEAD 3 V	9
BUT ONE POSSESSD HIS WANING TIME	132	TRISTRAM 1	70
ONE SUCH KISS AS THOSE OF YORE	132	TRISTRAM 1	78
ONE LAST KISS FIRST TIS VAIN TO HORSE AWAY	135	TRISTRAM 1	169
THE GAZE OF ONE WHO CAN DIVINE	140	TRISTRAM 1	323
ONE LITTLE WANDERING ARM IS THROWN	141	TRISTRAM 1	344
OF THE CASTLE-PARK ONE SEES	141	TRISTRAM 1	363
ONE LAST KISS UPON THE LIVING SHORE	145	TRISTRAM 2	98
THE YOUNG SURVIVING ISEULT ONE BRIGHT DAY	149	TRISTRAM 3	5
AND TO ONE STANDING ON THEM FAR AND NEAR	149	TRISTRAM 3	11
ONE AFTER ONE TO-MORROW LIKE TO-DAY	151	TRISTRAM 3	67
ONE AFTER ONE TO-MORROW LIKE TO-DAY	151	TRISTRAM 3	67
SHE SEEMS ONE DYING IN A MASK OF YOUTH	151	TRISTRAM 3	75
ONE APRIL WHEN THE WARM DAYS FIRST BEGAN	154	TRISTRAM 3	160
WAS THE ONE ISEULT CHOSE AND SHE BROUGHT CLEAR	154	TRISTRAM 3	165
THE YEAR HAD TRAVELLD ROUND AND ONE BRIGHT DAY		TRISTRAM 3 V	1
YET LOW AND FROM THE BOTTOM YET TO ONE STANDING IN IT		TRISTRAM 3 V	11
ONE MOMENT WAIT THOU HOLY MAN	157	SAINT BRANDAN	25
TELL THEM ONE BLESSED CHRISTMAS-NIGHT	157	SAINT BRANDAN	29
ONE MORN WHEN THE SIROCCO SPENT	157	SAINT BRANDAN	43
DID THAT CHANCE ACT OF GOOD THAT ONE	158	SAINT BRANDAN	58
ONE LAST LOOK AT THE WHITE-WALLD TOWN	162	FORSAKEN MERM	25
SINGING THERE DWELLS A LOVED ONE	165	FORSAKEN MERM	140
SHE HAD ONE POWER WHICH MADE HER BREAST ITS HOME	168	RACHEL 3	10
TWO SPRINGS WHICH CLOSE BY ONE ANOTHER PLAY	170	EAST AND WEST	2
ONE CAME FROM PENMON WESTWARD AND A GLOW	170	EAST AND WEST	5
CHRIST SOME ONE SAYS WAS HUMAN AS WE ARE	170	BETTER PART	3
HATH MAN NO SECOND LIFE PITCH THIS ONE HIGH	171	BETTER PART	10
THE SUFFRAGE CAPTIVE NOW NOT ONE IN TEN	171	DIVINITY	7
THOU TOO WILT SURELY ONE DAY PROVE	178	FAREWELL	38
YET WE SHALL ONE DAY GAIN LIFE PAST	179	FAREWELL	53
IN ONE AND WERE THROUGH FAITH RELEASED	181	ISOLATION MARG	39
THANKS GRACIOUS ONE	187	STRAYED REVEL	63
WITH ONE ARM BARE	189	STRAYED REVEL	107
ONE THAN CREON CRUELLER FAR	196	FRAG ANTIGONE	47
ONE OF SOME WORTHIER RACE THAN OURS	202	URANIA	18
ONE FOR WHOSE SAKE SHE ONCE MIGHT PROVE	202	URANIA	19
ONE OF SOME BETTER RACE THAN WE	202	URANIA V	18
ONE OF SOME WORTHIER RACE THAN WE	202	URANIA V	18
TO ONE DEMAND ALONE ARE COY	203	EUPHROSYNE	22
ADIEU AND SAY THAT ONE AT LEAST	204	EUPHROSYNE	27
ON ONE SHE SMILED AND HE WAS BLEST	204	EUPHROSYNE V	
TO WIN ONE INSTANTS GLIMPSE OF THEE	205	CALAIS SANDS	24
BENEATH ONE ROOF MY QUEEN WITH MINE	205	CALAIS SANDS	36
TO ONE ANOTHER FOR THE WORLD WHICH SEEMS	211	DOVER BEACH	30
HARDLY HARDLY SHALL ONE	217	LORDS MESSENGER	19
THE ONE OR TWO IMMORTAL LIGHTS	220	BACCHANALIA 2	24
ONE MORN AS THROUGH HYDE PARK WE WALKD	221	EPILOG LAOCOON	1
LIKE THESE AND IN ONE ASPECT BROUGHT	223	EPILOG LAOCOON	56
THE THREAD WHICH BINDS IT ALL IN ONE	225	EPILOG LAOCOON	141

ONE   (CONTINUED)
THE MATELESS THE ONE WILL YE KNOW . . . . 231 YOUTH OF NATURE   118
SEEST OUR DREAMS ONE BY ONE . . . . 232 YOUTH OF MAN   7
SEEST OUR DREAMS ONE BY ONE . . . . 232 YOUTH OF MAN   7
AH FROM THE OLD WORLD LET SOME ONE ANSWER GIVE . . 237 PROGRESS   21
YET EACH WILL HAVE ONE ANGUISH HIS OWN SOUL . . 238 PROGRESS   31
ONE DAY THOU SAYST THERE WILL AT LAST APPEAR . . 239 REVOLUTIONS   17
MADMAN OR SLAVE MUST MAN BE ONE . . . . 244 SUMMER NIGHT   75
TO ONE ANOTHER WHAT INDEED THEY FEEL . . . . . 245 BURIED LIFE   15
BUT HARDLY HAVE WE FOR ONE LITTLE HOUR . . . . 246 BURIED LIFE   59
HARDLY HAD SKILL TO UTTER ONE OF ALL . . . . . 246 BURIED LIFE   61
THERE BEATS ONE HEART IN EVERY HUMAN BREAST . . 245 BURIED LIFE   V 23
WHICH ONE WHO FEELS DEATHS WINNOWING WINGS . . . 250 WISH   27
WHICH NEVER WAS THE FRIEND OF ONE . . . . . . 251 WISH   37
ONE SUMMER-MORN FORSOOK . . . . 256 SCHOLAR-GIPSY   36
THOU HADST ONE AIM ONE BUSINESS ONE DESIRE . . . 259 SCHOLAR-GIPSY 152
THOU HADST ONE AIM ONE BUSINESS ONE DESIRE . . . 259 SCHOLAR-GIPSY 152
THOU HADST ONE AIM ONE BUSINESS ONE DESIRE . . . 259 SCHOLAR-GIPSY 152
AND THEN WE SUFFER AND AMONGST US ONE . . . . 260 SCHOLAR-GIPSY   182
THEY HUSTLE ONE ANOTHER AND THEY PASS . . . . 262 THYRSIS   V
BUT ONE SUCH DEATH REMAIN TO COME . . . . . . 270 MEMORIAL VERSES   3
HANGS TOUCHD WITH LIGHT ONE SNOWY SAIL . . . . 274 STANZAS CARNAC   32
HANGS TOUCHD WITH LIGHT ONE DISTANT SAIL . . . 274 STANZAS CARNAC V 32
GIFTED WOMEN THE ONE . . . . 280 HAWORTH CHURCH   8
THOU O MOURND ONE TO-DAY . . . . 284 HAWORTH CHURCH   77
OF ONE TOO I HAVE HEARD . . . . 285 HAWORTH CHURCH   101
ARE GREEN IN THE HOUSE OF ONE . . . . 280 HAWORTH CHURCH   V   4
PERISH AND NO ONE ASKS . . . . 288 RUGBY CHAPEL   67
ONE OF HIS LITTLE ONES LOST . . . . 291 RUGBY CHAPEL   167
THAT ARMY NOT ONE SHALL ARRIVE . . . . 291 RUGBY CHAPEL   184
DIE ONE BY ONE IN THE WASTE . . . . 291 RUGBY CHAPEL   187
DIE ONE BY ONE IN THE WASTE . . . . 291 RUGBY CHAPEL   187
FOR ONE SHORT MOMENT WANDER OER HIS LIPS . . . . 298 HEINES GRAVE   209
WHO ALONE IS ALL THINGS IN ONE . . . . 298 HEINES GRAVE   217
O THOU ONE OF WHOSE MOODS . . . . 299 HEINES GRAVE   222
OF HUMAN TASKS THEIR ONLY ONE . . . . 301 GRANDE CHARTR   59
WANDERING BETWEEN TWO WORLDS ONE DEAD . . . . 302 GRANDE CHARTR   85
HAVE RESTLESS HEARTS ONE THROB THE LESS . . . . 303 GRANDE CHARTR   144
HIS QUIET HOME ONE KEEPS . . . . 308 OBERMANN   50
AND ONE THE STRONG MUCH-TOILING SAGE . . . . . 308 OBERMANN   51
ONE DRIVES HIM TO THE WORLD WITHOUT . . . . . 309 OBERMANN   95
AND ONE TO SOLITUDE . . . . 309 OBERMANN   96
WHOSE ONE BOND IS THAT ALL HAVE BEEN . . . . . 311 OBERMANN   155
ONE HEARS THEE SAYING NOW . . . . 309 OBERMANN   V 90
SOUNDS NOW ONE WORD ALONE . . . . 318 OBERMANN MORE   184
KNIT ALL YOUR PARTS AND KEPT YOU ONE . . . . . 320 OBERMANN MORE   223
ONE COMMON WAVE OF THOUGHT AND JOY . . . . . 323 OBERMANN MORE   323
COMES NOW ONE WORD ALONE . . . . 318 OBERMANN MORE   V 184
ONE MIGHTY WAVE OF THOUGHT AND JOY . . . . . 323 OBERMANN MORE   V 323
AND LOOK TO MEET THEM THAT ONE GRIEF-PLUNGED FORM   331 MEROPE   56
SHALL THEY NOT WEAR ONE HATRED OUT AS WELL . . . 335 MEROPE   181
WAS BY THAT MURDER OPEND THAT ONE CHILD . . . . 335 MEROPE   188
WHICH FROM ONE CENTRAL CITYS GUARDED SEAT . . . 337 MEROPE   246
ONE VOICE PREACHD PATIENCE AND THAT VOICE WAS MINE 337 MEROPE   258
THE MANY OF THAT LINEAGE TO THE ONE . . . . . 338 MEROPE   270
INTO ONE PUISSANT FOLK AS HE DESIGND . . . . . 338 MEROPE   290
ONE SON AT LEAST I SPARED FOR STILL HE LIVES . . 340 MEROPE   348
ONE MERIT THEN THOU HAST EXULT IN THAT . . . . 341 MEROPE   353
INVOLVED IN ONE SUSPICION WITH THE BASE . . . . 341 MEROPE   367
A WOMAN O MY FRIENDS HAS ONE DESIRE . . . . . 349 MEROPE   565
AND TO ONE ACT MANY MOST UNLIKE MOTIVES . . . . 352 MEROPE   645
ASSIGND US BY THE ACTOR BE THE TRUE ONE . . . . 352 MEROPE   648
I THE ONE RIGHTEOUS THEY THE MANY BAD . . . . 353 MEROPE   679
MIGHT SOME ONE STRAIGHT INFORM HIM HE IS SOUGHT . . 354 MEROPE   708
ACCEPT THEM IN ONE WORD FOR GOOD OR BAD . . . . 355 MEROPE   713
ONE OF THE TRAIN OF CYPSELUS AM I . . . . . . 355 MEROPE   719
ONE NIGHT AND THE NEXT DAY AT DAWN FARED ON . . 356 MEROPE   747
AS OF ONE SHADOWD BY IMPENDING DEATH . . . . . 356 MEROPE   765
WALLS ON ONE SIDE THE DEEP STYMPHALIAN LAKE . . 358 MEROPE   813
A HEADLAND WITH ONE AGED PLANE-TREE CROWND . . . 358 MEROPE   817
NOW TOLD BUT IN ONE FLASHING INSTANT PASSD . . . 358 MEROPE   828
HE TO THEE SENDS ME ON IN ONE THING GLAD . . . 359 MEROPE   850
TO THE GUEST-CHAMBER LEAD HIM SOME ONE GIVE . . 359 MEROPE   869
A PRESENCE SAD FOR SOME ONE THROUGH THOSE DOORS . . 359 MEROPE   874
ADMIRE THEN MAIDENS HOW IN ONE SHORT HOUR . . . 360 MEROPE   875
A WHISPER THROUGH THE PALACE FLIES OF ONE . . . 361 MEROPE   914
TELL ME HATH ONE NOT COME OR WORSE MISCHANCE . . 361 MEROPE   918
IN ONE THING ONLY THAT THE PRINCE IS DEAD . . . 364 MEROPE   966
A HELPLESS ONE I KNOW IT BUT THE GODS . . . . 366 MEROPE   1023
WHAT ONE WEAK WOMAN CAN ACHIEVE ALONE . . . . 368 MEROPE   1074
ONE LAST MURDER-SAVED CHILD . . . . 369 MEROPE   1102
UNHAPPY ONE WHAT DEED . . . . 371 MEROPE   1134
UNHAPPY ONE THOU STRIKST A MOST JUST BLOW . . . 374 MEROPE   1200
UPBRAIDS THEE NO ONE THOU DOST WELL BUT TAKE . . 376 MEROPE   1214
THY SON IS HERE ONE SAID SO SURE BUT NOW . . . 376 MEROPE   1216
ONE DEATH-DEALING VENGEFUL TRAIN . . . . . . 379 MEROPE   1255
ONE SUDDEN STROKE AND THE MESSENIANS LOVE . . . 381 MEROPE   1287
AGAINST THE ONE AND CERTAIN ARM OF POWER . . . 381 MEROPE   1313
IT IS TEN THOUSAND FIERY WILLS IN ONE . . . . 382 MEROPE   1348
THEN MIGHT I USE THEM THEN FOR ONE WHO THUS . . 383 MEROPE   1362

ONE
 (CONTINUED)
HAPLY HAD BUT ONE DARING SOUL STOOD FORTH • • • • 383 MEROPE 1364
THY PRISON-HOUSE RAISED ONE IMPLORING CRY • • • • 383 MEROPE 1371
HATE DUTY INTEREST PASSION CALL ONE WAY • • • • 383 MEROPE 1382
ONE AND A WOMAN HOW CAN I PREVAIL • • • • • 390 MEROPE 1580
THY CRIME THAT WERE ENOUGH TO MAKE ONE FEAR • • 396 MEROPE 1767
LO THE ILL-FATED ONE • • • • • • • • 400 MEROPE 1876
AND TRULY ONE WHO SEES WHAT SEEMD SO STRONG • • 402 MEROPE 1943
AT ONE BOLD WORD ONE ENTERPRISING BLOW • • • • 402 MEROPE 1946
AT ONE BOLD WORD ONE ENTERPRISING BLOW • • • • 402 MEROPE 1946
THE TRUE ONE OF A MAN WHAT WAY OF LIFE • • • • 404 MEROPE 1992
ONE COLOUR IN THY LIFE THE HUE OF TRUTH • • • 404 MEROPE 1996
AND SEE TO MEET THEM THAT ONE GRIEF-PLUNGED FORM • • 331 MEROPE V 56
ONE ARM ALOFT FOR HELP THEN SWEEP BENEATH • • • 358 MEROPE V 833
TO ONE UNHAPPY HOUSE THE DEBT WE OWE • • • • 367 MEROPE V1048
I GO I GO YET QUEEN TAKE THIS ONE WORD • • • 368 MEROPE V1077
ONE SEES ONES FOOTPRINTS CRUSHD IN THE WET GRASS • • 406 EMPEDOCLES I 1 14
ONE OF HIS MOODS IS ON HIM THAT THOU KNOWST • • 408 EMPEDOCLES I 1 54
DARED ONE BUT TRY THOU WAST A KIND CHILD EVER • • 408 EMPEDOCLES I 1 76
THAT NEEDS NO THANKS ONE IS FAR BETTER HERE • • 409 EMPEDOCLES I 1 103
DARED ONE BUT TRY THOU WERT A KIND CHILD EVER • • 409 EMPEDOCLES I 1 V 76
I SHOULD HAVE SAID THAT SOME ONE TOUCHD A HARP • • 412 EMPEDOCLES I 2 11
SCARCE CAN ONE THINK IN CALM SO THREATENING • • 416 EMPEDOCLES I 2 126
 ARE THE GODS
OF BUT ONE STUFF ARE SPUN • • • • • • • 422 EMPEDOCLES I 2 288
WITH WHAT WE RAIL AT ONE • • • • • • • • 422 EMPEDOCLES I 2 290
ONE WITH THE OERLABOURD POWER THAT THROUGH • • 422 EMPEDOCLES I 2 291
 THE BREADTH AND LENGTH
FOR I MUST BE ALONE LEAVE ME ONE MULE • • • • 428 EMPEDOCLES I 2 465
O SAGE O SAGE TAKE THEN THE ONE WAY LEFT • • • 429 EMPEDOCLES II 24
AT ONE ANOTHER FROM THEIR GOLDEN CHAIRS • • • • 431 EMPEDOCLES II 82
AND NO ONE ROUND THE CHARMED CIRCLE SPEAKS • • • 431 EMPEDOCLES II 83
WITH ONE ARM OVER HIS HEAD • • • • • • • 434 EMPEDOCLES II 163
WHO HAS NO FRIEND NO FELLOW LEFT NOT ONE • • • • 437 EMPEDOCLES II 271
BEING ONE WITH WHICH WE ARE ONE WITH THE WHOLE WORLD • • 440 EMPEDOCLES II 372
BEING ONE WITH WHICH WE ARE ONE WITH THE WHOLE WORLD • • 440 EMPEDOCLES II 372
AND RALLY THEM FOR ONE LAST FIGHT AND FAIL • • • • 440 EMPEDOCLES II 308
ONE STILL LAGS LAST AND TURNS AND EYES THE PILE • • 444 WESTMIN ABBEY 14
THOUGH MOVING INLY TO ONE FAR-SET GOAL • • • • 448 WESTMIN ABBEY 153
THOUGH MOVING INLY TO ONE FAR-OFF GOAL • • • • 448 WESTMIN ABBEY V 153
ONE DAY THINE IMMEMORIAL GLEAM RETURN • • • • 449 WESTMIN ABBEY V 175
ONE MORE GASP IT IS THE END • • • • • • • 452 POOR MATTHIAS 13
TELLING HOW ONE STORMY DAY • • • • • • • 457 POOR MATTHIAS 177
BUT ONE VAST FANE WHERE ALL UNCONSCIOUS SLEEP • • 464 ALARIC AT ROME 59
ONE FORM STANDS GAZING SILENTLY BELOW • • • • 468 ALARIC AT ROME 153
AND WREST ONE TEAR FROM JOY OH WHO SHALL PEN • • 468 ALARIC AT ROME 167
BUT AS ONE VOICELESS BLANK A PLACE OF GRAVES • • 469 ALARIC AT ROME 182
ONE LITTLE YEAR THAT RESTLESS SOUL SHALL REST • • 469 ALARIC AT ROME 193
ONE MOMENTS SPACE PERCHANCE MIGHT CHARM HIS EYE • • 475 CROMWELL 109
ONE MOMENTS SPACE MIGHT WAFT HIM FAR AWAY • • • • 475 CROMWELL 111
AND ONE SWAYD ALL WHO WORE A KINGLY CROWN • • • • 476 CROMWELL 143
ONE ROOD FROM SHORE THAT SINGLE BOAT • • • • • 479 HAYSWATER BOAT 16
ONE ROOD FROM LAND THEY PUSHD NO MORE • • • • 480 HAYSWATER BOAT 27
DOUBT IT NOT WE MET AND WE ARE ONE • • • • • 482 THEKLAS ANSWER 10
IN THE PLAIN THERE WERE KINDLED A THOUSAND   HOMER TRANS 3
 FIRES BY EACH ONE
SEE ONE FIGURE QUITS THE MAZES • • • • • • • META CLOISTER 9

ONES
WHEREIN EARTHS GREAT ONES ARE DISQUIETED • • • • 7 REP FRIEND 10
O YE FALSE ONES AT YOUR CALLING • • • • • 27 NEW SIRENS 39
IF ONES OWN HEART BEATS NOT LIGHT • • • • 138 TRISTRAM 1 265
THE SEA GROWS STORMY THE LITTLE ONES MOAN • • • • 163 FORSAKEN MERM 65
THE SEA GROWS STORMY THE LITTLE ONES MOAN • • • 163 FORSAKEN MERM 79
WILL YE CLAIM FOR YOUR GREAT ONES THE GIFT • • • 231 YOUTH OF NATURE 122
WHEN YOUR GREAT ONES DEPART WILL YE SAY • • • 231 YOUTH OF NATURE 126
O SPENT ONES OF A WORK-DAY AGE • • • • • • 279 SOUTHERN NIGHT 115
ONE OF HIS LITTLE ONES LOST • • • • • • • 291 RUGBY CHAPEL 167
TO TELL TOO DEEP ONES IS NOT WELL • • • • • 307 OBERMANN 43
AND CANST TEACH SIMPLE ONES TO PLOT AND FEIGN • • 367 MEROPE 1059
ONE SEES ONES FOOTPRINTS CRUSHD IN THE WET GRASS • • 406 EMPEDOCLES I 1 14
ONES BREATH CURLS IN THE AIR AND ON THESE PINES • • 406 EMPEDOCLES I 1 15

ONESELF
IF ONESELF CANNOT GET FREE • • • • • • • 138 TRISTRAM 1 267

ONLY
MOVED ONLY BUT BY GENIUS IN THE STRIFE • • • • 4 DUKE WELLINGTON 4
ONLY THE BLESSED SAINTS ARE SMILING DUMB • • • • 17 CHURCH BROU 3 4
MEANS PARTING THAT ONLY IN ABSENCE LIES PAIN • • 19 MODERN SAPPHO V
ONLY WHAT WE FEEL WE KNOW • • • • • • • 29 NEW SIRENS 84
AND SIGH THAT ONE THING ONLY HAS BEEN LENT • • • 37 YOUTHS AGIT 13
ONLY BY THIS THOU CANST THE COLOURD DREAM • • • • 45 IN UTRUMQUE PAR 13
ONLY THAT WITH NO FINER ART • • • • • • • 48 HORATIAN ECHO 19
HOLDS ONLY PAIN • • • • • • • • • 51 CONSOLATION 40
LIGHT MEN AND ON LIGHT STEEDS WHO ONLY DRINK • • 64 SOHRAB RUSTUM 124
ONLY HIS HELM WAS RICH INLAID WITH GOLD • • • • 69 SOHRAB RUSTUM 267
SHRANK ONLY RUSTUM DARED THEN HE AND I • • • • 72 SOHRAB RUSTUM 360
IS IT WITH RUSTUM ONLY THOU WOULDST FIGHT • • • 72 SOHRAB RUSTUM 368
ONLY THE EVENT WILL TEACH US IN ITS HOUR • • • • 73 SOHRAB RUSTUM 397
FIERCE MAN BETHINK THEE FOR AN ONLY SON • • • • 78 SOHRAB RUSTUM 586
AFRASIABS CITIES ONLY SAMARCAND • • • • • 83 SOHRAB RUSTUM 760
AND THE BLACK TOORKMUN TENTS AND ONLY DRUNK • • 83 SOHRAB RUSTUM 762

ONLY   (CONTINUED)

BUT THOU SHALT YET HAVE PEACE ONLY NOT NOW	85 SOHRAB RUSTUM	829
WHITE WITH EYES CLOSED ONLY WHEN HEAVY GASPS	86 SOHRAB RUSTUM	849
BUT RIGHT BARS THIS NOT ONLY THY DESIRE	104 BALDER DEAD 1	313
ONLY THE INGLORIOUS SORT ARE THERE BELOW	104 BALDER DEAD 1	323
THOU ONLY BALDER WAST FOR EVER KIND	116 BALDER DEAD 3	112
THOU ONLY BALDER WERT FOR EVER KIND	116 BALDER DEAD 3	V 112
ONLY DEATH CAN BALM THY WOE	139 TRISTRAM 1	289
LIFTING HER SOFT-BENT HEAD ONLY TO MIND	152 TRISTRAM 3	84
FROM STRENGTH TO STRENGTH ADVANCING ONLY HE	172 IMMORTALITY	12
AND UNION BEFORE GOD THE ONLY CARE	173 MONICAS PRAYER	11
TO THEE ONLY GOD GRANTED	177 PARTING	79
AND GROW A HOME FOR ONLY THEE	180 ISOLATION MARG	4
ONLY FROM THE LONG LINE OF SPRAY	211 DOVER BEACH	7
BUT NOW I ONLY HEAR	211 DOVER BEACH	24
BUT NOW WE ONLY HEAR	211 DOVER BEACH	V 24
NOT OUR BLOOM ONLY BUT OUR STRENGTH DECAY	212 GROWING OLD	7
THAT BEING ONLY WHICH HATH KNOWN EACH MAN	217 NAMELESS EPIT	2
ONLY A FEW THE LIFE-STREAMS SHORE	226 EPILOG LAOCOON	189
ONLY THE LIVING CAN FEEL YOU	234 YOUTH OF MAN	59
ONLY A DRIVING WRECK	244 SUMMER NIGHT	64
ONLY BUT THIS IS RARE	247 BURIED LIFE	77
AND NOW KEEPS ONLY IN THE GRAVE	249 KENSINGTON GARD	28
AND NOW DWELLS ONLY IN THE GRAVE	KENSINGTON GARD	V 28
ONLY THE TRACT WHERE HE SAILS	252 FUTURE	24
HE WOTS OF ONLY THE THOUGHTS	252 FUTURE	25
AND ONLY THE WHITE SHEEP ARE SOMETIMES SEEN	255 SCHOLAR-GIPSY	8
WITH CLOSE-LIPPD PATIENCE FOR OUR ONLY FRIEND	260 SCHOLAR-GIPSY	194
ONLY METHINKS SOME LOSS OF HABITS POWER	263 THYRSIS	22
AND ONLY IN THE HIDDEN BROOKSIDE GLEAM	266 THYRSIS	119
BUT ALL OUR HUSTLING MORROWS ONLY MAKE	262 THYRSIS	V
ONLY WITH STRANGERS TO MEET	284 HAWORTH CHURCH	75
SLEEP OR ONLY WHEN MAY	285 HAWORTH CHURCH	113
SLEEP OR ONLY FOR THIS	285 HAWORTH CHURCH	123
ONLY TO LIVE BY THE HEART	282 HAWORTH CHURCH	V
ONLY TO LOVE AND BE LOVD	282 HAWORTH CHURCH	V
WE WE ONLY ARE LEFT	289 RUGBY CHAPEL	104
ONLY OURSELVES WE LOST	289 RUGBY CHAPEL	118
ONLY A MOMENT I LONGD	294 HEINES GRAVE	48
ONLY A MOMENT I KNEW	294 HEINES GRAVE	52
ONLY TO LAUGH AND TO DIE	298 HEINES GRAVE	198
OF HUMAN TASKS THEIR ONLY ONE	301 GRANDE CHARTR	59
HE ONLY LIVES WITH THE WORLDS LIFE	309 OBERMANN	103
VOICE MOVED ONLY THE TORRENT BROKE	323 OBERMANN MORE	327
WHY DOST THOU ONLY PROFIT BY HIS DEATH	340 MEROPE	331
NOT TO THEE ONLY HATH COME	346 MEROPE	505
ONLY TO ME GIVE MY CHILD	348 MEROPE	540
YEA AND NOT ONLY HAVE WE NOT EXPLORED	352 MEROPE	636
BENT ONLY TO SERVE VIRTUE	353 MEROPE	662
ARMD FOR RIGHT ONLY AND THE GENERAL GOOD	353 MEROPE	685
IN ONE THING ONLY THAT THE PRINCE IS DEAD	364 MEROPE	966
BUT IS IT ONLY A FATE	369 MEROPE	1099
WHERE TRAVELLERS NEVER PASS WHERE ONLY COME	373 MEROPE	1169
MY CHILD UNHURT ONLY BY OVER JOY	377 MEROPE	1220
AND YET THE ONLY PEACE TO US ALLOWD	378 MEROPE	1250
BUT NOW SEEN FACE TO FACE MY ONLY CHILD	381 MEROPE	1289
AND ONLY SLAVES AND TYRANTS LEFT ALIVE	383 MEROPE	1378
NOT ONLY WOUND THE SENSE BUT KILL THE SOUL	385 MEROPE	1408
AND ONLY BAD MEN JOY TO SEE UNDONE	386 MEROPE	1429
RISK FROM MY NEW-RESTORED MY ONLY SON	387 MEROPE	1456
MEANTIME ON THEE THE TASK OF SILENCE ONLY	390 MEROPE	1584
AND BID THE SUN THINE ONLY VISITANT	395 MEROPE	1752
ARE DREAMS THIS ONLY IS	422 EMPEDOCLES I 2	305
NOR ONLY IN THE INTENT	422 EMPEDOCLES I 2	307
YOU ONLY CAN TAKE IN	423 EMPEDOCLES I 2	342
SURE ONLY THAT YOUR MIND SEES ALL THINGS WHICH BEFAL	423 EMPEDOCLES I 2	346
ONLY TO TYPHO IT SOUNDS HATEFULLY	430 EMPEDOCLES II	41
TO TYPHO ONLY THE REBEL OERTHROWN	430 EMPEDOCLES II	42
ONLY THE LOVED HEBE BEARS	431 EMPEDOCLES II	84
THOU YOUNG IMPLACABLE GOD AND ONLY DEATH	436 EMPEDOCLES II	232
WITH HELD-IN JOY SWELLING ITS HEART I ONLY	438 EMPEDOCLES II	316
TO OUR OWN ONLY TRUE DEEP-BURIED SELVES	440 EMPEDOCLES II	371
ONLY TO TYPHO THE REBEL OERTHROWN	430 EMPEDOCLES II	V 42
ONLY THAT PRIMAL GUEST THE FISHER SAW	445 WESTMIN ABBEY	59
LIGHT ONLY LIGHT WAS SLOW TO REAPPEAR	445 WESTMIN ABBEY	60
ONLY FOUR YEARS THOSE WINNING WAYS	450 GEISTS GRAVE	5
YES ONLY FOUR AND NOT THE COURSE	450 GEISTS GRAVE	21
NOR TO US ONLY ART THOU DEAR	451 GEISTS GRAVE	53
AND JEALOUS JOCK THY ONLY HATE	461 KAISER DEAD	75
ONLY WHILE THEIR LOVE LIVD LASTED THEY	482 THEKLAS ANSWER	8
MAN ONLY WITH ETERNAL BENT	484 ROME-SICKNESS	21
ALL THE HEART ENJOINS BUT ONLY HERE	META CLOISTER	24

ONSET

VAIN THY ONSET ALL STANDS FAST	215 LAST WORD	3
OF THE HOARSE ONSET OF THE SURGING WAVE	466 ALARIC AT ROME	110
THE SHOUT OF ONSET AND THE SHRIEK OF FEAR	475 CROMWELL	135

ONWARD

CUT BY AN ONWARD-LABOURING VESSELS PRORE	41 HUMAN LIFE	23

ONWARD   (CONTINUED)
        FREEZING AND RIDGING IN THEIR ONWARD FLOW . . . .   108 BALDER DEAD 2   129
        ONWARD WE MOVED AND REACHD THE RIDE . . . . . .   224 EPILOG LAOCOON   107
        WITH A FREE ONWARD IMPULSE BRUSHING THROUGH   . .   261 SCHOLAR-GIPSY   213

ONWARDS
        THE CASSOCKD PRIEST RODE ONWARDS . . . .   161 NECKAN   57

ONYX
        AND MILK-BARRD ONYX-STONES . . . .   192 STRAYED REVEL   197

OOZE
        FEED IN THE OOZE OF THEIR PASTURE-GROUND . . . .   162 FORSAKEN MERM   40

OOZING
        OOZING THROUGH THY SOAKD HUNTING-SHIRT WITH LIMBS   373 MEROPE   1173

OPE
        ITS PINES UNDER THEIR BRANCHES OPE . . . . . .   312 OBERMANN MORE   15

OPED
        CAME BACK TO RUSTUM AND HE OPED HIS EYES . . . .   81 SOHRAB RUSTUM   698

OPEN
        OF OPEN HILL-SWARD FRESH AND GREEN . . . . . .   16 CHURCH BROU 2   13
        COOL FARMS WITH OPEN-LYING STORES . . . . . .   54 RESIGNATION   56
        LONE FARMS WITH OPEN-LYING STORES . . . . . .   54 RESIGNATION   V 56
        INTO THE OPEN PLAIN SO HAMAN BADE . . . . . .   64 SOHRAB RUSTUM   107
        BRISTLING AND IN THE MIDST THE OPEN SAND . . .   70 SOHRAB RUSTUM   298
        CAME WELLING FROM THE OPEN GASH AND LIFE . . .   85 SOHRAB RUSTUM   841
        THE PERSIANS TOOK IT ON THE OPEN SANDS . . . .   86 SOHRAB RUSTUM   872
        THERE HE WENT UP AND PASSD THE OPEN DOORS . . .   97 BALDER DEAD 1   87
        BUT IT IS MOONLIGHT IN THE OPEN GLADE . . . .   139 TRISTRAM 1   277
        OVER THE WASTE THIS CIRQUE OF OPEN GROUND . . .   150 TRISTRAM 3   13
        FROM THE OPEN HEATH STILL BY THE HEDGEROWS LAY .   151 TRISTRAM 3   51
        THIS OPEN GLEN WAS STUDDED THICK WITH THORNS   .   155 TRISTRAM 3   191
        OVER THE WASTE THIS RING OF OPEN GROUND . . .   150 TRISTRAM 3   V 13
        OVER THE WASTE BUT WHERE THIS OPEN GROUND . . .   TRISTRAM 3   V 13
        FROM THE OPEN WASTE WHITE BY THE HEDGEROWS LAY .   TRISTRAM 3   V 51
        TO ALL ALWAYS OPEN . . . .   177 PARTING   81
        I SAW UPON THE OPEN SAND . . . .   204 CALAIS SANDS   10
        IN THIS LONE OPEN GLADE I LIE . . . .   248 KENSINGTON GARD   1
        WHERE AT HER OPEN DOOR THE HOUSEWIFE DARNS . . .   258 SCHOLAR-GIPSY   102
        AND OPEN JASMINE-MUFFLED LATTICES . . . . . .   264 THYRSIS   68
        MELT INTO OPEN MOONLIT SEA . . . .   275 SOUTHERN NIGHT   2
        THOSE WHO WITH HALF-OPEN EYES . . . .   288 RUGBY CHAPEL   53
        FROM CHRISTS THEN OPEN GRAVE . . . .   317 OBERMANN MORE   148
        AND OPEN STOOD HIS GRAVE . . . .   318 OBERMANN MORE   170
        AN OPEN GLADE NOW HE WAS HIGH ALOFT . . . . .   357 MEROPE   802
        THROW THE DOOR OPEN TIS DONE . . . .   372 MEROPE   1152
        BROWND WITH THINE OPEN-AIR FREE HUNTERS LIFE   .   373 MEROPE   1164
        TO CLOSE AN OLD WOUND NOT TO OPEN NEW . . . .   379 MEROPE   1257
        LEAP AND FLY OPEN OF THEMSELVES FOR JOY . . . .   401 MEROPE   1885
        UPON THE OPEN SHOULDER OF THE HILL . . . . .   412 EMPEDOCLES I 2   3
        OPEN LIVED TO US AND NEAR . . . .   455 POOR MATTHIAS   88
        THAT YOUR OWN HANDS MUST OPEN WIDE THE GATE   . .   466 ALARIC AT ROME   117
        SLOWLY PAST THE OPEN SPACES . . . .   META CLOISTER   5

OPEND
        CONVULSED HIM BACK TO LIFE HE OPEND THEM . . .   86 SOHRAB RUSTUM   851
        THROUGH THE SOFT-OPEND LIPS THE AIR . . . . .   141 TRISTRAM 1   342
        BUT WHO IS THIS BY THE HALF-OPEND DOOR . . . .   175 PARTING   35
        THE BROAD EARTH OPEND AND WHELMD THEM AND HIM . .   197 FRAG ANTIGONE   87
        ARE FLOWERS FIRST OPEND ON SICILIAN AIR . . . .   265 THYRSIS   89
        WAS BY THAT MURDER OPEND THAT ONE CHILD . . . .   335 MEROPE   188

OPENING
        BACK THROUGH THE OPENING SQUADRONS TO HIS TENT   .   66 SOHRAB RUSTUM   188
        IN THE SMOOTH CENTRE OF THE OPENING STOOD . . .   150 TRISTRAM 3   19
        IN THAT GREEN CIRCULAR OPENING IN THE HEATH   . .   TRISTRAM 3   V   7
        IN A GREEN CIRCULAR OPENING IN THE HEATH . . .   TRISTRAM 3   V   7
        THE OPENING SUMMER THE SKY . . . . . .   285 HAWORTH CHURCH   118
        DOTH ALL THE HEAVENLY OPENING CLOSE . . . . .   324 OBERMANN MORE   343

OPENINGS
        THE OPENINGS GRASSY BANKS ARE SOFT INCLINED   . .   TRISTRAM 3   V 10
        THE OPENINGS GRASSY BANKS WERE SOFT INCLINED   . .   TRISTRAM 3   V 10

OPENS
        HIS LUMINOUS HOME OF WATERS OPENS BRIGHT . . . .   87 SOHRAB RUSTUM   890
        THE VALAIS OPENS FAIR . . . .   324 OBERMANN MORE   340
        THEN THE DOOR OPENS AND THIS CARD IS BROUGHT   . .   485 S S LUSITANIA   13

OPERATIONS
        OF MANS MENTAL OPERATIONS . . . .   SECOND BEST   V 19

OPINION
        COME YOU SAY OPINION TREMBLES . . . .   29 NEW SIRENS   81

OPINIONS
    OPINIONS THOSE OR THESE • • • • • • • • • 419 EMPEDOCLES I 2 198

OPIUM
    POSTURE AND OPIUM NO MORE • • • • • • • • 293 HEINES GRAVE 20

OPPIUS
    AND STANDS A FAILURE THEN THEN HAPPENS OPPIUS • • LUCRETIUS 2 12

OPPOSER
    RECALLS THE OBSCURE OPPOSER HE OUTWEIGHD • • • • 171 DIVINITY 8

OPPOSERS
    AND STRIKE OPPOSERS DOWN • • • • • • • • • 352 MEROPE 659
    AND HEW OPPOSERS DOWN • • • • • • • • • 352 MEROPE V 659

OPPOSITE
    RIGHT OPPOSITE AND THUS BEGAN • • • • • • • 90 SICK KING BOKH 96
    PASSD OPPOSITE SHE TOUCHD HER GIRL WHO HIED • • 170 WEST LONDON 6

OPPOSITION
    IN CEASELESS OPPOSITION BE THE GUARD • • • • • 437 EMPEDOCLES II 268

OPPRESS
    MY PENT-UP TEARS OPPRESS MY BRAIN • • • • • 206 RIVER 9
    ENVY THEE AND OPPRESS • • • • • • • • • 416 EMPEDOCLES I 2 118

OPPRESSD
    OF PLAINNESS OPPRESSD BY CUNNING • • • • • 432 EMPEDOCLES II 101
    AS THE WELL-COUNSELLD ZEUS OPPRESSD • • • • • 432 EMPEDOCLES II 102
    AND IF THE SACRED LOAD OPPRESSD OUR BRAIN • • • • 436 EMPEDOCLES II 244

OPPRESSES
    BUT THE SOLITUDE OPPRESSES THY VOTARY • • • • 435 EMPEDOCLES II 208

OPPRESSORS
    BUT SEE HIS SHAVEN OPPRESSORS • • • • • • • 214 NEW ROME 5

OPPREST
    AND FROM THY WORLD WITH HEART OPPREST • • • • 314 OBERMANN MORE 73

OPTIMISTIC
    THE BARREN OPTIMISTIC SOPHISTRIES • • • • • • 7 REP FRIEND 5

OPULENT
    THOUGH OPULENT FREELY GIVE • • • • • • • 195 FRAG ANTIGONE 3

ORACLE
    AND YET THEIR ORACLE • • • • • • • • • • 417 EMPEDOCLES I 2 140
    THE ORACLE FORBADE NOT ILL-INSPIRED • • • • • • 448 WESTMIN ABBEY 133

ORACLES
    INFIRM PROTECTORS DUBIOUS ORACLES • • • • • • 336 MEROPE 215

ORACULAR
    A VOICE ORACULAR HATH PEALD TO-DAY • • • • • • 3 EMERSONS ESSAYS 3
    THE GREAT ORACULAR SHRINES • • • • • • • 198 FRAG DEJANEIRA 11
    BY THE ORACULAR SENTENCE OF THE GODS • • • • • • 385 MEROPE 1422

ORANGE
    THE ORANGE AND PALE VIOLET EVENING-SKY • • • • 267 THYRSIS 159
    TERRACED AND ORANGE-BOWERS • • • • • • • • 296 HEINES GRAVE 134

ORATOR
    RUDE ORATOR • • • • • • • • • • • • • • RUDE ORATOR 1

ORATORS
    THE FAMOUS ORATORS HAVE SHONE • • • • • • • 219 BACCHANALIA 2 3
    THE FAMOUS ORATORS HAVE DONE • • • • • • • 219 BACCHANALIA 2 V 3

ORB
    OF THE TOO VAST ORB OF HER FATE • • • • • • 295 HEINES GRAVE 96

ORBS
    AND FAR FROM HEAVEN HE TURND HIS SHINING ORBS • • 96 BALDER DEAD 1 51

ORCHARD
    AND TO MAKE ORCHARD-CLOSES FILLD • • • • • • 94 SICK KING BOKH 200
    ORCHARD AND CROFT AND FULL-STORED GRANGE • • • • 313 OBERMANN MORE 27

ORCHIS
    THE ORCHIS RED GLEAMS EVERYWHERE • • • • • • 274 STANZAS CARNAC 18

ORCHISES
    AND PURPLE ORCHISES WITH SPOTTED LEAVES • • • • 257 SCHOLAR-GIPSY 89
    HIGH TOWERD THE SPIKES OF PURPLE ORCHISES • • • • 266 THYRSIS 115

ORCHOMENIAN
    ON TO THE MARSHY ORCHOMENIAN PLAIN • • • • • • 356 MEROPE 743

ORCHOMENUS
    IN THE STONE COFFINS AT ORCHOMENUS • • • • • • 356 MEROPE   773

ORDAIND
    WHOM LABOURS SELF-ORDAIND ENTHRALL • • • • • • 52 RESIGNATION   14
    OUR ORDER HEAVEN-ORDAIND • • • • • • • • 195 FRAG ANTIGONE   21
    FOR THAT WHICH SEALS THEM HATH BEEN DEEP-ORDAIND • • 245 BURIED LIFE   29

ORDAINS
    WITH ME FOR THUS ORDAINS THE COMMON RITE • • • • 103 BALDER DEAD 1   300

ORDER
    LET ME PAUSE LET ME STRIVE IN MYSELF MAKE SOME ORDER   19 MODERN SAPPHO   7
    LET ME PAUSE LET ME STRIVE IN MYSELF FIND SOME ORDER   19 MODERN SAPPHO V 7
    IN MARCHING ORDER SPREAD OF LONG-NECKD CRANES • • 64 SOHRAB RUSTUM   112
    TO SPEAK IN ORDER WHAT HATH CHANCED • • • • • 88 SICK KING BOKH   28
    OUR ORDER HEAVEN-ORDAIND • • • • • • • • 195 FRAG ANTIGONE   21
    THE ALL-HATED ORDER-BREAKING • • • • • • • 195 FRAG ANTIGONE   25
    OF A SOCIAL ORDER HE LOVED • • • • • • • 229 YOUTH OF NATURE 32
    THE WORD THE ORDER WHICH GOD MEANT SHOULD BE • 239 REVOLUTIONS   18
    ORDER COURAGE RETURN • • • • • • • • 292 RUGBY CHAPEL   201
    THE HILLS IN THEIR OLD ORDER RANGED • • • • 312 OBERMANN MORE   7
    THE UNIVERSAL ORDER SERVED • • • • • • 314 OBERMANN MORE   55
    YOUR SOCIAL ORDER TOO • • • • • • • 320 OBERMANN MORE 230
    THE WORLDS GREAT ORDER DAWNS IN SHEEN • • • 322 OBERMANN MORE 293
    HE TO FULFIL AN ORDER RAISED HIS HAND • • • 384 MEROPE   1399
    WHAT ORDER MORE PRECISE HAD HE THAN I • • • 384 MEROPE   1400
    THE BROKEN ORDER OF YOUR DORIAN THRONES • • • 389 MEROPE   1546
    BE THEIR FIRST-FOUNDED ORDER STRICT MAINTAIND • 390 MEROPE   1565
    THAT JUSTICE THAT SAGE ORDER NOT ALONE • • 404 MEROPE   1997
    IF THEIR FIRST-FOUNDED ORDER BE MAINTAIND • • • 390 MEROPE   V1565
    IN A MIGHTIER ORDER • • • • • • • • 437 EMPEDOCLES II 286
    SORELY AGAINST THY WILL BY STRONG NECESSITYS ORDER   HOMER TRANS   31

ORDERD
    BUT ALL THINGS NOW ARE ORDERD FAIR • • • • • 16 CHURCH BROU 2   15
    WHO ORDERD THAT THEIR LONGINGS FIRE • • • • 182 TO MARG CONT   19
    ORDERD BY FATE TO THEIR HOME • • • • • • 343 MEROPE   413

ORDERING
    TOO HASTY HEADS FOR ORDERING WORLDS ALAS • • • 237 PROGRESS   9

ORESTES
    AND THE GRAVE OF ORESTES • • • • • • • • 344 MEROPE   436
    ORESTES DIED BUT IN NAME • • • • • • • • 368 MEROPE   1084
    ORESTES IN MYCENAE HAD NO MORE • • • • 384 MEROPE   1398

ORGAN
    THE ORGAN CARRIES TO OUR EAR • • • • • • 306 GRANDE CHARTR 203

ORGANS
    AND THEN YOU HEAR THE ORGANS HUM • • • • • 17 CHURCH BROU 2   28
    THE CHAPEL WHERE NO ORGANS PEAL • • • • 300 GRANDE CHARTR   37
    NOR ANY OF OUR ORGANS SO OBTUSE • • • • 352 MEROPE   632

ORGUNJE
    RIGHT FOR THE POLAR STAR PAST ORGUNJE • • • 87 SOHRAB RUSTUM   880
    AND UP FROM THENCE TO ORGUNJE • • • • • 93 SICK KING BOKH 168

ORIENT
    LO YON ORIENT HILL IN FLAMES • • • • • • 35 NEW SIRENS   260

ORIGINAL
    ORIGINAL DEEP-INWOUND • • • • • • • 196 FRAG ANTIGONE   36
    IN TRACKING OUT OUR TRUE ORIGINAL COURSE • • • 246 BURIED LIFE   50

ORPHAN
    THE LOVELY ORPHAN CHILD AGAIN • • • • • • 136 TRISTRAM 1   192
    TWO BROTHERS AND THEIR ORPHAN NEPHEWS STROVE • • 389 MEROPE   1548
    TIS AS AN ORPHAN AMONG PROSPEROUS BOYS • • • 408 EMPEDOCLES I 1 71

ORPHAND
    ORPHAND OF BOTH MY PARENTS BY HIS FOES • • • 385 MEROPE   1411

ORPHANS
    PRIMROSES ORPHANS OF THE FLOWERY PRIME • • • 266 THYRSIS   120

ORPHEUS
    WHERE ORPHEUS AND WHERE HOMER ARE • • • • • 58 RESIGNATION   208
    AND FLUTE HIS FRIEND LIKE ORPHEUS FROM THE DEAD • • 265 THYRSIS   90
    HEARD THE CLEAR SONG OF ORPHEUS COME • • • • 271 MEMORIAL VERSES 38

OSCILLATIONS
    CAN CUT HIS OSCILLATIONS SHORT AND SO • • • 436 EMPEDOCLES II 233
    SHALL CUT HIS OSCILLATIONS SHORT AND SO • • • 436 EMPEDOCLES II V 233

OSSA
    FELL LIKE OSSA ON THE CLIMBING SOUL • • • • 28 NEW SIRENS   72
    WEIGHS LIKE OSSA ON THE AERY SOUL • • • • • 28 NEW SIRENS V 72
    WEIGHD LIKE OSSA ON THE AERY SOUL • • • • • 28 NEW SIRENS V 72

OTHERWHILE
    BUT THE GODS WENT NOT NOW AS OTHERWHILE • • • • 105 BALDER DEAD 2   29

OTHERWISE
    WAILING BUT OTHERWISE WAS ODINS WILL • • • • • 95 BALDER DEAD 1   16

OUGHT
    WHAT I AM AND WHAT I OUGHT TO BE • • • • • 239 SELF-DEPENDENCE   2
    THAT BEST WHO OUGHT TO RULE AM I • • • • • 353 MEROPE   677
    THE MOB WHO OUGHT TO OBEY ARE THESE • • • • • 353 MEROPE   678
    WE DO NOT WHAT WE OUGHT • • • • • • • 420 EMPEDOCLES I 2   237
    WHAT WE OUGHT NOT WE DO • • • • • • • • 420 EMPEDOCLES I 2   238
    THE ILLS WE OUGHT TO BEAR • • • • • • 421 EMPEDOCLES I 2   280

OUR
    STILL WORKING BLAMING STILL OUR VAIN TURMOIL • • 2 QUIET WORK   13
    OUR SENSELESS UPROAR MINGLING WITH OUR TOIL • • 1 QUIET WORK V 10
    OUR SENSELESS UPROAR MINGLING WITH OUR TOIL • • 1 QUIET WORK V 10
    STILL WORKING CHIDING STILL OUR VAIN TURMOIL • • 2 QUIET WORK V 13
    OTHERS ABIDE OUR QUESTION THOU ART FREE • • • • 2 SHAKESPEARE   1
    VAIN DREAMS WHICH QUENCH OUR PLEASURES THEN DEPART 9 MYCERINUS   27
    OH WHEREFORE CHEAT OUR YOUTH IF THUS IT BE • • • 10 MYCERINUS   49
    BUT HIDES IF GODS GODS CARELESS OF OUR DOOM • • 10 MYCERINUS   54
    VAIN DREAMS THAT QUENCH OUR PLEASURES THEN DEPART 9 MYCERINUS V 27
    DEAD OUR DUKE AND GONE HIS DUCHESS • • • • • 15 CHURCH BROU 1   83
    BUT TIS NOT WHAT OUR YOUTH'DESIRES • • • • • 22 YOUTH AND CALM   25
    AND OUR BEST IMPRESSIONS ARE • • • • • 23 MEMORY-PICTURE   11
    ONE MOMENT ON THE RAPIDS TOP OUR BOAT • • • • 25 DREAM   30
    LEFT OUR AWFUL LAURELS HANGING • • • • • 27 NEW SIRENS   31
    ROUND OUR HEARTS WITH LONG CARESSES • • • • 28 NEW SIRENS   69
    WILL IT WEEP OUR BURNING TEARS • • • • • 29 NEW SIRENS   86
    HATH IT DRUNK OF OUR LOVE-POTIONS • • • • 29 NEW SIRENS   87
    OUR RAPT SOULS ON YOUR REPLIES • • • • • 34 NEW SIRENS   236
    BUT WE TURN OUR EYES ARE FLITTING • • • • 34 NEW SIRENS   241
    OUR SAD SOULS ON YOUR REPLIES • • • • • 34 NEW SIRENS V 236
    WHERE OUR SICK SOULS DO LIE • • • • • 39 STAGIRIUS   50
    TO TOO EXACT A STEERING OF OUR WAY • • • • 40 HUMAN LIFE   9
    LET US NOT FRET AND FEAR TO MISS OUR AIM • • 40 HUMAN LIFE   10
    WINDS FROM OUR SIDE THE UNSUITING CONSORT RIVE • • 40 HUMAN LIFE   16
    THE JOYS WHICH WERE NOT FOR OUR USE DESIGND • • 41 HUMAN LIFE   28
    THE GUIDE OF OUR DARK STEPS A TRIPLE VEIL • • 43 GIPSY CHILD   49
    BETWIXT OUR SENSES AND OUR SORROW KEEPS • • 43 GIPSY CHILD   50
    BETWIXT OUR SENSES AND OUR SORROW KEEPS • • 43 GIPSY CHILD   50
    OUR VAUNTED LIFE IS ONE LONG FUNERAL • • • 44 QUESTION   10
    BLAME OUR ACTIVITY • • • • • • • • • 46 WORLD QUIETIST   6
    OF LITTLE THREADS OUR LIFE IS SPUN • • • • 48 HORATIAN ECHO   25
    AND SCORN US AS OUR MISTRESS MAY • • • • 48 HORATIAN ECHO   33
    OUR JOVIAL HOST AS FORTH WE FARE • • • • 53 RESIGNATION   42
    HIGH ON A BANK OUR LEADER STANDS • • • • 53 RESIGNATION   44
    MAKES CLEAR OUR GOAL TO EVERY EYE • • • • 53 RESIGNATION   46
    A GATE SWINGS TO OUR TIDE HATH FLOWD • • • 53 RESIGNATION   48
    OUR WAVERING MANY-COLOURD LINE • • • • 54 RESIGNATION   61
    THE RED-GROUSE SPRINGING AT OUR SOUND • • • 54 RESIGNATION   70
    WE BATHED OUR HANDS WITH SPEECHLESS GLEE • • 54 RESIGNATION   84
    THIS WORLD IN WHICH WE DRAW OUR BREATH • • 59 RESIGNATION   229
    BECAUSE OUR SPIRITS HAVE FORGOT • • • • 60 RESIGNATION   276
    UNMURMURING IN OUR TENTS WHILE IT IS WAR • • 63 SOHRAB RUSTUM   72
    TO FIGHT OUR CHAMPION SOHRAB MAN TO MAN • • 65 SOHRAB RUSTUM   153
    WHEN SOHRAB DARES OUR BRAVEST FORTH AND SEEKS • 68 SOHRAB RUSTUM   244
    HE WILL NOT YIELD INDEED NOR QUIT OUR FOES • • 71 SOHRAB RUSTUM   351
    COME PLANT WE HERE IN EARTH OUR ANGRY SPEARS • 74 SOHRAB RUSTUM   439
    WHAT FOOL IS THIS THAT HURTS OUR EARS • • • 89 SICK KING BOKH   40
    HOME TO OUR HALLS WITH TORCHLIGHT BY OUR KIN • 101 BALDER DEAD 1   217
    HOME TO OUR HALLS WITH TORCHLIGHT BY OUR KIN • 101 BALDER DEAD 1   217
    LOK STILL SUBSISTS IN HEAVEN OUR FATHER WISE • 111 BALDER DEAD 2   217
    WROUGHT BY THE GODS AND ASK THE GODS OUR AID • 111 BALDER DEAD 2   226
    HOWBEIT WE ABIDE OUR DAY TILL THEN • • • 111 BALDER DEAD 2   227
    SEEK TO AFFLICT OUR FOES WITH PETTY PANGS • • 111 BALDER DEAD 2   229
    PEACE LEST OUR FATHER ODIN HEAR THEE GIBE • • 114 BALDER DEAD 3   23
    OUT OF OUR SIGHT THAT WE MAY TURN FROM GRIEF • 115 BALDER DEAD 3   55
    AND LEAD AS ERST OUR DAILY LIFE IN HEAVEN • • 115 BALDER DEAD 3   56
    REMEMBRANCE IN OUR SOUL OF WARS ALONE • • 117 BALDER DEAD 3   138
    AND WIFE AND CHILDREN AND OUR ANCIENT HOME • 117 BALDER DEAD 3   144
    FROM THE BRIGHT OCEAN AT OUR FEET AN EARTH • 128 BALDER DEAD 3   528
    OUR EYES WITH GAZING AND REBUILD WITH TEARS • 128 BALDER DEAD 3   536
    OUR SNOWDROP BY THE ATLANTIC SEA • • • • 136 TRISTRAM 1   196
    TO OUR LONELY SEA COMPLAIN • • • • • 139 TRISTRAM 1   274
    TO OUR FORESTS TELL THY PAIN • • • • • 139 TRISTRAM 1   275
    IN THE GREEN WOOD ALL OUR LIVES ALONE • • • 143 TRISTRAM 2   36
    AH ON WHICH IF BOTH OUR LOTS WERE BALANCED • 144 TRISTRAM 2   49
    POWER TO BE MOVED AND SOOTHED FOR ALL OUR PAIN • 153 TRISTRAM 3   117
    IN WHOSE HOT AIR OUR SPIRITS ARE UPCURLD • • 153 TRISTRAM 3   120
    BY DRYING UP OUR JOY IN EVERYTHING • • • 153 TRISTRAM 3   125
    TO MAKE OUR FORMER PLEASURES ALL SEEM STALE • 153 TRISTRAM 3   126
    OF PASSION WHICH SUBDUES OUR SOULS TO IT • • 153 TRISTRAM 3   128
    THE FRET AND MISERY OF OUR NORTHERN TOWNS • • 168 RACHEL 2   9
    IN THIS HER LIFES LAST DAY OUR POOR OUR PAIN • • 168 RACHEL 2   10
    IN THIS HER LIFES LAST DAY OUR POOR OUR PAIN • • 168 RACHEL 2   10
    OUR JANGLE OF FALSE WITS OUR CLIMATES FROWNS • • 168 RACHEL 2   11

OUR   (CONTINUED)

OUR JANGLE OF FALSE WITS OUR CLIMATES FROWNS   • •   168 RACHEL 2   11
OUR FREEDOM FOR A LITTLE BREAD WE SELL   • • • •   169 WORLDLY PLACE   5
WHO RATES US IF WE PEER OUTSIDE OUR PEN   • • •   169 WORLDLY PLACE   7
NO JUDGE EYES US FROM HEAVEN OUR SIN TO SCAN   • •   170 BETTER PART   4
WE LIVE NO MORE WHEN WE HAVE DONE OUR SPAN   • • •   171 BETTER PART   5
LIVE WE LIKE BRUTES OUR LIFE WITHOUT A PLAN   • •   171 BETTER PART   8
SITS THERE NO JUDGE IN HEAVEN OUR SIN TO SEE   • •   171 BETTER PART   11
FOILD BY OUR FELLOW-MEN DEPRESSD OUTWORN   • • • •   172 IMMORTALITY   1
OUR DIFFERENT PAST • • • • • • • • •   •   176 PARTING   66
OUR SPIRITS HAVE GROWN   • • • • • • • • •   177 PARTING   72
WE SCHOOL OUR MANNERS ACT OUR PARTS   • • • • •   179 FAREWELL   45
WE SCHOOL OUR MANNERS ACT OUR PARTS   • • • • •   179 FAREWELL   45
KNOWS THAT THE BENT OF BOTH OUR HEARTS   • • • •   179 FAREWELL   47
CLEAR PROSPECT OER OUR BEINGS WHOLE   • • • • •   179 FAREWELL   54
OUR TRUE AFFINITIES OF SOUL   • • • • • • • •   179 FAREWELL   56
OUR SOOTHED ENCOURAGED SOULS WILL DARE   • • • •   179 FAREWELL   62
THEN WE SHALL KNOW OUR FRIENDS THOUGH MUCH   • •   179 FAREWELL   65
ALL OUR UNQUIET PULSES CEASE   • • • • • •   •   180 FAREWELL   82
SELF-SWAYD OUR FEELINGS EBB AND SWELL   • • • •   180 ISOLATION MARG   11
OH MIGHT OUR MARGES MEET AGAIN   • • • • • • •   182 TO MARG CONT   18
OUR PASSIONS FROM OUR BRAIN   • • • • • • • •   183 ABSENCE   8
OUR PASSIONS FROM OUR BRAIN   • • • • • • • •   183 ABSENCE   8
OUR SOON-CHOKED SOULS TO FILL   • • • • • • •   183 ABSENCE   10
AND OUR OWN PLACE ONCE LEFT   • • • • • • • •   195 FRAG ANTIGONE   18
OUR ORDER HEAVEN-ORDAIND   • • • • • • • • •   195 FRAG ANTIGONE   21
IN THIS OUR THEBES BUT WHEN   • • • • • • •   •   197 FRAG ANTIGONE   84
BUT OUR IGNOBLE SOULS LACK MIGHT   • • • • • •   201 URANIA   4
OUR PETTY SOULS OUR STRUTTING WITS   • • • • •   202 URANIA   13
OUR PETTY SOULS OUR STRUTTING WITS   • • • • •   202 URANIA   13
OUR LABOURD PUNY PASSION-FITS   • • • • • • •   202 URANIA   14
OF POSSESSING POWERS NOT OUR SHARE   • • • • •   209 SELF-DECEPTION   2
LONG LONG SINCE UNDOWERD YET OUR SPIRIT   • • •   209 SELF-DECEPTION   5
THEN AS NOW A POWER BEYOND OUR SEEING   • • • •   210 SELF-DECEPTION   11
STAVED US BACK AND GAVE OUR CHOICE THE LAW   • •   210 SELF-DECEPTION   12
AH WHO SWAYD OUR CHOICE AND WHO DECIDED   • • •   210 SELF-DECEPTION   15
WHAT OUR GIFTS AND WHAT OUR WANTS SHOULD BE   •   210 SELF-DECEPTION   16
WHAT OUR GIFTS AND WHAT OUR WANTS SHOULD BE   •   210 SELF-DECEPTION   16
AH AND HE WHO PLACED OUR MASTER-FEELING   • • •   210 SELF-DECEPTION   23
WE BUT DREAM WE HAVE OUR WISHD-FOR POWERS   • •   210 SELF-DECEPTION   25
FAILD TO PLACE OUR MASTER-FEELING CLEAR   • • •   210 SELF-DECEPTION   V 24
IS IT TO FEEL OUR STRENGTH   • • • • • •   •   212 GROWING OLD   6
NOT OUR BLOOM ONLY BUT OUR STRENGTH DECAY   • •   212 GROWING OLD   7
NOT OUR BLOOM ONLY BUT OUR STRENGTH DECAY   • •   212 GROWING OLD   7
TIS NOT TO HAVE OUR LIFE   • • • • • • •   •   212 GROWING OLD   13
DEEP IN OUR HIDDEN HEART   • • • • • • • •   213 GROWING OLD   28
NOW STRIFES ARE HUSHD OUR EARS DOTH MEET   • • •   219 BACCHANALIA 2   14
NOW STRIFE IS HUSHD OUR EARS DOTH MEET   • • •   219 BACCHANALIA 2   V 14
AND NOBLY PERFECT IN OUR DAY   • • • • • • •   222 EPILOG LAOCOON   26
THEY YIELD US NOT TO SOOTHE OUR PAINS   • • • •   222 EPILOG LAOCOON   32
AND DARKNESS RETURNS TO OUR EYES   • • • • •   229 YOUTH OF NATURE   58
SEEST OUR DREAMS ONE BY ONE   • • • • • • •   232 YOUTH OF MAN   7
SEEST OUR ERRORS DEPART   • • • • • • • •   232 YOUTH OF MAN   8
WHICH IN OUR MORNING-PRIME   • • • • • • • •   232 YOUTH OF MAN   13
SAW THE MISTAKES OF OUR YOUTH   • • • • • • •   232 YOUTH OF MAN   14
LIVES IN OUR EYES WHICH CAN PAINT   • • • • •   233 YOUTH OF MAN   36
LIVES IN OUR HEARTS WHICH CAN FEEL   • • • • •   233 YOUTH OF MAN   37
AND FANCY THAT WE PUT FORTH ALL OUR LIFE   • • •   236 PALLADIUM   19
UPON OUR LIFE A RULING EFFLUENCE SEND   • • • •   236 PALLADIUM   22
IN MYSTERY OUR SOUL ABIDES   • • • • • • • •   241 MORALITY   4
LIGHT FLOWS OUR WAR OF MOCKING WORDS AND YET   •   245 BURIED LIFE   1
OUR HEARTS OUR VOICES MUST WE TOO BE DUMB   • • •   245 BURIED LIFE   25
OUR HEARTS OUR VOICES MUST WE TOO BE DUMB   • • •   245 BURIED LIFE   25
OUR HEART AND HAVE OUR LIPS UNCHAIND   • • • •   245 BURIED LIFE   28
OUR HEART AND HAVE OUR LIPS UNCHAIND   • • • •   245 BURIED LIFE   28
BADE THROUGH THE DEEP RECESSES OF OUR BREAST   •   246 BURIED LIFE   38
THE UNREGARDED RIVER OF OUR LIFE   • • • • •   246 BURIED LIFE   39
AFTER THE KNOWLEDGE OF OUR BURIED LIFE   • • •   246 BURIED LIFE   48
A THIRST TO SPEND OUR FIRE AND RESTLESS FORCE •   246 BURIED LIFE   49
IN TRACKING OUT OUR TRUE ORIGINAL COURSE   • • •   246 BURIED LIFE   50
WHENCE OUR LIVES COME AND WHERE THEY GO   • • •   246 BURIED LIFE   54
BEEN ON OUR OWN LINE HAVE WE BEEN OURSELVES • •   246 BURIED LIFE   60
THE NAMELESS FEELINGS THAT COURSE THROUGH OUR BREAST 246 BURIED LIFE   62
OUR HIDDEN SELF AND WHAT WE SAY AND DO   • • •   247 BURIED LIFE   65
AH YES AND THEY BENUMB US AT OUR CALL   • • • •   247 BURIED LIFE   71
A MELANCHOLY INTO ALL OUR DAY   • • • • • •   247 BURIED LIFE   76
OUR EYES CAN IN ANOTHERS EYES READ CLEAR   • • •   247 BURIED LIFE   81
WHEN OUR WORLD-DEAFEND EAR   • • • • • • •   247 BURIED LIFE   82
A BOLT IS SHOT BACK SOMEWHERE IN OUR BREAST • •   247 BURIED LIFE   84
WHENCE OUR THOUGHTS COME AND WHERE THEY GO • •   246 BURIED LIFE   V 54
AND WE ON ITS BREAST OUR MINDS   • • • • • •   253 FUTURE   55
TILL HAVING USED OUR NERVES WITH BLISS AND TEEN   259 SCHOLAR-GIPSY   147
AND TIRED UPON A THOUSAND SCHEMES OUR WIT   • •   259 SCHOLAR-GIPSY   148
OUR WORN-OUT LIFE AND ARE WHAT WE HAVE BEEN   •   259 SCHOLAR-GIPSY   150
LIGHT HALF-BELIEVERS OF OUR CASUAL CREEDS   • • •   260 SCHOLAR-GIPSY   172
THIS FOR OUR WISEST AND WE OTHERS PINE   • • •   260 SCHOLAR-GIPSY   191
WITH CLOSE-LIPPD PATIENCE FOR OUR ONLY FRIEND •   260 SCHOLAR-GIPSY   194
FLY HENCE OUR CONTACT FEAR   • • • • • •   •   261 SCHOLAR-GIPSY   206
BUT FLY OUR PATHS OUR FEVERISH CONTACT FLY   • •   261 SCHOLAR-GIPSY   221
BUT FLY OUR PATHS OUR FEVERISH CONTACT FLY   • •   261 SCHOLAR-GIPSY   221

OUR   (CONTINUED)

```
FOR STRONG THE INFECTION OF OUR MENTAL STRIFE      261 SCHOLAR-GIPSY      222
THEN FLY OUR GREETINGS FLY OUR SPEECH AND SMILES   262 SCHOLAR-GIPSY      231
THEN FLY OUR GREETINGS FLY OUR SPEECH AND SMILES   262 SCHOLAR-GIPSY      231
OUR WELL-WORN LIFE AND ARE WHAT WE HAVE BEEN       259 SCHOLAR-GIPSY    V 150
VAGUE HALF-BELIEVERS OF OUR CASUAL CREEDS          260 SCHOLAR-GIPSY    V 172
OUR FRIEND THE GIPSY-SCHOLAR WAS NOT DEAD          263 THYRSIS             29
HERE TOO OUR SHEPHERD-PIPES WE FIRST ASSAYD        263 THYRSIS             35
OF STORMS THAT RAGE OUTSIDE OUR HAPPY GROUND       264 THYRSIS             49
BUT AH OF OUR POOR THAMES SHE NEVER HEARD          265 THYRSIS             98
AND WE SHOULD TEASE HER WITH OUR PLAINT IN VAIN    265 THYRSIS            100
IN THE OLD HAUNT AND FIND OUR TREE-TOPPD HILL      265 THYRSIS            103
HATH SINCE OUR DAY PUT BY                          266 THYRSIS            116
UNMOORD OUR SKIFF WHEN THROUGH THE WYTHAM FLATS    266 THYRSIS            123
OF OUR BOAT PASSING HEAVED THE RIVER-GRASS         266 THYRSIS            128
HEAR IT O THYRSIS STILL OUR TREE IS THERE          267 THYRSIS            171
OUR GIPSY-SCHOLAR HAUNTS OUTLIVING THEE            268 THYRSIS            197
YET HADST THOU ALWAY VISIONS OF OUR LIGHT          269 THYRSIS            227
DOST THOU ASK PROOF OUR TREE YET CROWNS THE HILL   269 THYRSIS            239
OUR SCHOLAR TRAVELS YET THE LOVED HILL-SIDE        269 THYRSIS            240
BUT ALL OUR HUSTLING MORROWS ONLY MAKE             262 THYRSIS          V
OUR FRIEND THE SCHOLAR-GIPSY WAS NOT DEAD          263 THYRSIS          V  29
WE BOWD OUR HEAD AND HELD OUR BREATH               270 MEMORIAL VERSES      7
WE BOWD OUR HEAD AND HELD OUR BREATH               270 MEMORIAL VERSES      7
HE TAUGHT US LITTLE BUT OUR SOUL                   270 MEMORIAL VERSES      8
OUR SOULS IN ITS BENUMBING ROUND                   271 MEMORIAL VERSES     46
HE SPOKE AND LOOSED OUR HEART IN TEARS             271 MEMORIAL VERSES     47
OUR FOREHEADS FELT THE WIND AND RAIN               271 MEMORIAL VERSES     53
OUR YOUTH RETURND FOR THERE WAS SHED               271 MEMORIAL VERSES     54
AND AGAINST FEAR OUR BREAST TO STEEL               272 MEMORIAL VERSES     65
WE BOWD OUR HEADS AND HELD OUR BREATH              270 MEMORIAL VERSES  V   7
WE BOWD OUR HEADS AND HELD OUR BREATH              270 MEMORIAL VERSES  V   7
OUR SPIRITS IN A BRAZEN ROUND                      271 MEMORIAL VERSES  V  46
OUR YOUTH CAME BACK FOR THERE WAS SHED             271 MEMORIAL VERSES  V  54
OUR BUSINESS WITH UNSLACKENING STRIDE              277 SOUTHERN NIGHT      65
AND NEVER ONCE POSSESS OUR SOUL                    277 SOUTHERN NIGHT      71
SHOULD OUR GRAVES BE                               277 SOUTHERN NIGHT      76
WE WE HAVE CHOSEN OUR PATH                         288 RUGBY CHAPEL        84
LIGHTNINGS DAZZLE OUR EYES                         289 RUGBY CHAPEL        93
HAVOC IS MADE IN OUR TRAIN                         289 RUGBY CHAPEL       101
FRIENDS WHO SET FORTH AT OUR SIDE                  289 RUGBY CHAPEL       102
COME TO THE END OF OUR WAY                         289 RUGBY CHAPEL       108
OUR STORM-BEAT FIGURES AND ASKS                    289 RUGBY CHAPEL       114
WHOM IN OUR PARTY WE BRING                         289 RUGBY CHAPEL       115
THE AVALANCHE SWEPT FROM OUR SIDE                  289 RUGBY CHAPEL       123
FEARFUL AND WE IN OUR MARCH                        290 RUGBY CHAPEL       129
YE ALIGHT IN OUR VAN AT YOUR VOICE                 292 RUGBY CHAPEL       196
YE FILL UP THE GAPS IN OUR FILES                   292 RUGBY CHAPEL       204
STABLISH CONTINUE OUR MARCH                        292 RUGBY CHAPEL       206
LONG SINCE DEEP IN OUR HEARTS                      294 HEINES GRAVE        74
SHOWING THEN BLOTTING FROM OUR SIGHT               299 GRANDE CHARTR       15
STRIKE LEFTWARD CRIES OUR GUIDE AND HIGHER         300 GRANDE CHARTR       19
OUR FATHERS WATERD WITH THEIR TEARS                303 GRANDE CHARTR      121
BUT WHILE WE WAIT ALLOW OUR TEARS                  304 GRANDE CHARTR      162
THE ORGAN CARRIES TO OUR EAR                       306 GRANDE CHARTR      203
AND LEAVE OUR DESERT TO ITS PEACE                  306 GRANDE CHARTR      210
BUT TILL THEY RISE ALLOW OUR TEARS                 304 GRANDE CHARTR    V 162
AND LEAVE OUR FOREST TO ITS PEACE                  306 GRANDE CHARTR    V 210
IN THIS OUR TROUBLED DAY                           307 OBERMANN            46
THE HOPELESS TANGLE OF OUR AGE                     309 OBERMANN            83
WHICH BATHED OUR LIFE RETIRED                      319 OBERMANN MORE      190
HANG WEEDS OF OUR SAD TIME                         323 OBERMANN MORE      308
THE WANT WHICH RACKD OUR BRAIN                     323 OBERMANN MORE      314
CONSUMED OUR HEART WITH THIRST LIKE FIRE           323 OBERMANN MORE      315
OUR LIFE TO ALPINE SNOW                            323 OBERMANN MORE      318
AND PALSIED ALL OUR WORD WITH DOUBT                323 OBERMANN MORE      319
AND ALL OUR WORK WITH WOE                          323 OBERMANN MORE      320
AH THERE OUR FUTURE LIES                           315 OBERMANN MORE    V
WHEREON WE PITCH OUR TENT                          320 OBERMANN MORE    V 218
HELP IT TO REACH OUR DEEP DESIRE                   323 OBERMANN MORE    V 313
THE DREAM WHICH FILLD OUR BRAIN                    323 OBERMANN MORE    V 314
THE WANT WHICH CRAZED OUR BRAIN                    323 OBERMANN MORE    V 314
THE WANT WHICH WORE OUR BRAIN                      323 OBERMANN MORE    V 314
FIXED IN OUR SOUL A THIRST LIKE FIRE               323 OBERMANN MORE    V 315
CONSUMD OUR SOUL WITH THIRST LIKE FIRE             323 OBERMANN MORE    V 315
AND PALSIED ALL OUR DEED WITH DOUBT                323 OBERMANN MORE    V 319
AND ALL OUR WORD WITH WOE                          323 OBERMANN MORE    V 320
OF OUR NIGHT-JOURNEY AND THOU SEEST THY HOME       330 MEROPE               2
OUR JOURNEY IS WELL MADE THE WORK REMAINS          330 MEROPE              24
WILL LIE MY GRANDSIRE SAID OUR FAIREST CHANCE      331 MEROPE              41
TO GUIDE OUR VENGEANCE TO A PROSPEROUS CLOSE       332 MEROPE              75
ALAS THAT HOW TO RULE IT WAS OUR BROIL             334 MEROPE             127
I SMOTE HIM WHEN OUR WISHES CLASHD IN ARMS         334 MEROPE             130
THE BREACH BETWEEN OUR PARTIES HELP ME CLOSE       335 MEROPE             163
OUR HANDS IN SOLEMN UNION MAKING FRIENDS           335 MEROPE             165
OUR FACTIONS WITH THE FRIENDSHIP OF THEIR CHIEFS   335 MEROPE             166
THESE OFFERINGS HOME OUR RITES ARE SPOILD TO-DAY   336 MEROPE             196
AEGIMIUS GAVE OUR OUTCAST HOUSE A HOME             337 MEROPE             224
AND SHED THEIR BLOOD LIKE WATER IN OUR CAUSE       337 MEROPE             227
WERE AIMD AT THEIR PROMOTION OUR DECLINE           337 MEROPE             244
```

OUR   (CONTINUED)
            AS FROM A FASTNESS IN THE ROCKS OUR SCANT   •   •   •   •   337 MEROPE   247
            MERE PRISONERS MEANT OR NOT AMONG OUR FOES   •   •   •   •   337 MEROPE   251
            DEEMING AS TYRANTS DEEM OUR SILENCE HATE   •   •   •   •   338 MEROPE   260
            HE SACRIFICED OUR RUIN IN HIS HEART   •   •   •   •   •   338 MEROPE   273
            HEAR US AND HELP US SHADE OF OUR KING   •   •   •   •   348 MEROPE   541
            BRING BACK OUR SON IF MAY BE WITHOUT BLOOD   •   •   •   350 MEROPE   587
            THIS FOR OUR SON AND FOR MYSELF I PRAY   •   •   •   •   350 MEROPE   591
            NOR ANY OF OUR ORGANS SO OBTUSE   •   •   •   •   •   •   352 MEROPE   632
            BUT EVEN OUR OWN HEART THAT NARROW WORLD   •   •   •   •   352 MEROPE   638
            BOUNDED IN OUR OWN BREAST WE HARDLY KNOW   •   •   •   •   352 MEROPE   639
            OF OUR OWN ACTIONS DIMLY TRACE THE CAUSES   •   •   •   •   352 MEROPE   640
            OR OUR OWN WANT OF EFFORT BE THE BAR   •   •   •   •   352 MEROPE   643
            THE BONES OF ARCAS WHENCE OUR RACE IS NAMED   •   •   •   356 MEROPE   742
            TO THE STYMPHALIAN LAKE OUR JOURNEYS END   •   •   •   •   356 MEROPE   749
            CATES FROM OUR HUNTERS POUCH ARCADIAN FARE   •   •   •   •   356 MEROPE   753
            LAST OF OUR QUARTERS WITH THE ARCADIAN CHIEFS   •   •   •   356 MEROPE   759
            SAD REVERENTIAL HOMAGE HAD OUR PRINCE   •   •   •   •   356 MEROPE   761
            WE SPRANG UPON OUR FEET WE SNATCHD OUR SPEARS   •   •   •   357 MEROPE   789
            WE SPRANG UPON OUR FEET WE SNATCHD OUR SPEARS   •   •   •   357 MEROPE   789
            BUT I FROM OUR DEPLORED MISCHANCE LEARN THIS   •   •   •   359 MEROPE   853
            SO DIES THE LAST SHOOT OF OUR ROYAL TREE   •   •   •   •   359 MEROPE   857
            THOU FOR THY LABOUR HAST DESERVED OUR BEST   •   •   •   •   359 MEROPE   866
            TO FRIENDS STILL MORE AND LABOURERS IN OUR CAUSE   •   •   359 MEROPE   872
            WISHD TRULY WISHD SOLUTION TO OUR BROIL   •   •   •   •   360 MEROPE   886
            COME COME BACK TO OUR PRAYER   •   •   •   •   •   •   •   360 MEROPE   892
            VISIT OUR STREETS AND THE SOUND   •   •   •   •   •   •   360 MEROPE   894
            OF AN ARCADIAN LORD OUR PRINCES FRIEND   •   •   •   •   363 MEROPE   956
            OUR PRINCE AND THE GOOD LAIAS WHOM HIS WARD   •   •   •   364 MEROPE   976
            THAT OUR JOINT HANDS MIGHT THEN TOGETHER PAY   •   •   •   367 MEROPE   1047
            TO OUR UNHAPPY HOUSE THE DEBT WE OWE   •   •   •   •   •   367 MEROPE   1048
            BUT DOWN THOU FLEEST HERE AND LEAVST OUR SCOURGE   •   •   367 MEROPE   1050
            TRIUMPHANT AND CONDEMNEST ALL OUR RACE   •   •   •   •   367 MEROPE   1051
            OUR DASTARD PATIENCE BE OUR DARING NOW   •   •   •   •   367 MEROPE   1055
            OUR DASTARD PATIENCE BE OUR DARING NOW   •   •   •   •   367 MEROPE   1055
            OUR MISERY MORE AND THINE OWN RUIN SURE   •   •   •   •   368 MEROPE   1081
            CONFERRING IN THE CITY WITH OUR FRIENDS   •   •   •   •   379 MEROPE   1261
            SWORN TO OUR PLOT HE IS IF FALSE SURMISE   •   •   •   •   379 MEROPE   1272
            TOO DEAR HIS SECRET WILES HAVE COST OUR HOUSE   •   •   •   380 MEROPE   1279
            DISCREDITING THE SUCCOUR WHICH OUR CAUSE   •   •   •   •   382 MEROPE   1335
            ALAS OUR FOE ALONE STOOD FORWARD THEN   •   •   •   •   383 MEROPE   1367
            THE OCCASION IF OUR CHIEF CONFEDERATE FAILS   •   •   •   386 MEROPE   1447
            MY MOTHER STANDS ALOOF AND BLAMES OUR DEED   •   •   •   •   386 MEROPE   1448
            OUR OWN RIGHT HAND IN THE DETESTED BLOOD   •   •   •   •   387 MEROPE   1468
            SO MUCH IS DUE TO TRUTH EVEN TOWRDS OUR FOE   •   •   •   388 MEROPE   1493
            WITH CYPSELUS OUR FATHER WHERE WE SAW   •   •   •   •   388 MEROPE   1515
            OUR FATHERS KINGDOM BECAUSE PURE IS SAFE   •   •   •   •   389 MEROPE   1533
            TRUE BUT WHAT CAUSE TO OUR ARCADIA GIVES   •   •   •   •   389 MEROPE   1534
            PELASGUS OUR FOREFATHER AND MANKINDS   •   •   •   •   •   389 MEROPE   1538
            BEQUEATHS THE ALLEGIANCE OF OUR SHEPHERD-TRIBES   •   •   389 MEROPE   1540
            MORE LOYAL AS OUR LINE CONTINUES MORE   •   •   •   •   389 MEROPE   1541
            THIS AWE WHICH GUARDS OUR EARTH-SPRUNG LINEAL KINGS   389 MEROPE   1543
            NOW NOT ANOTHER WORD BUT TO OUR ACT   •   •   •   •   •   390 MEROPE   1586
            AS OUR JUST CAUSE DESERVES I DO NOT FEAR   •   •   •   •   391 MEROPE   1595
            EVEN AFTER NEWS OF THIS SAD DEATH OUR LEAGUE   •   •   •   394 MEROPE   1689
            THANKS TO HIM FOR OUR AMITY AS WELL   •   •   •   •   •   395 MEROPE   1724
            FIRST FOR OUR UNION TRUST ME TWIXT US TWO   •   •   •   •   395 MEROPE   1733
            OUR GLORIOUS FOUNDER   •   •   •   •   •   •   •   •   •   398 MEROPE   1812
            I TREMBLED FOR OUR PRINCE AND HIS ATTEMPT   •   •   •   401 MEROPE   1901
            YET STAINS OUR LAND BE BY THIS BLOOD WASHD OUT   •   •   402 MEROPE   1916
            THOU SPEAKEST WELL BUT HERE TO GIVE OUR EYES   •   •   •   403 MEROPE   1951
            AUTHENTIC PROOF OF WHAT THOU TELLST OUR EARS   •   •   •   403 MEROPE   1952
            THIS POLITIC SOVEREIGN LYING AT OUR FEET   •   •   •   •   403 MEROPE   1965
            SO WHEN HE PLEADED FOR OUR LEAGUE BUT NOW   •   •   •   •   404 MEROPE   1978
            TO GUIDE OUR EFFORT TO A PROSPEROUS CLOSE   •   •   •   •   332 MEROPE   V 75
            CONCERTING IN THE CITY WITH OUR FRIENDS   •   •   •   •   379 MEROPE   V1261
            SWORN TO OUR PLOT HE IS BUT THAT SURMISE   •   •   •   •   379 MEROPE   V1272
            OF SOPHISTS HAS GOT EMPIRE IN OUR SCHOOLS   •   •   •   •   410 EMPEDOCLES I 1   122
            AND CAN OUR SOULS NOT STRIVE   •   •   •   •   •   •   •   415 EMPEDOCLES I 2   93
            FILL THEE TO SEE OUR TIME   •   •   •   •   •   •   •   •   416 EMPEDOCLES I 2   113
            BUT WE ARE ALL THE SAME THE FOOLS OF OUR OWN WOES   •   417 EMPEDOCLES I 2   166
            IN VAIN OUR PENT WILLS FRET   •   •   •   •   •   •   •   418 EMPEDOCLES I 2   182
            BORN INTO LIFE WE ARE AND LIFE MUST BE OUR MOULD   •   •   418 EMPEDOCLES I 2   186
            TO TUNES WE DID NOT CALL OUR BEING MUST KEEP CHIME   418 EMPEDOCLES I 2   196
            THE WORLD IS WHAT IT IS FOR ALL OUR DUST AND DIN   •   •   419 EMPEDOCLES I 2   206
            OUR CRY FOR BLISS OUR PLEA   •   •   •   •   •   •   •   419 EMPEDOCLES I 2   209
            OUR CRY FOR BLISS OUR PLEA   •   •   •   •   •   •   •   419 EMPEDOCLES I 2   209
            OUR WANTS HAVE ALL BEEN FELT OUR ERRORS MADE BEFORE   419 EMPEDOCLES I 2   211
            OUR WANTS HAVE ALL BEEN FELT OUR ERRORS MADE BEFORE   419 EMPEDOCLES I 2   211
            STILL USE OUR BODIES ILL   •   •   •   •   •   •   •   •   420 EMPEDOCLES I 2   230
            BAFFLERS OF OUR OWN PRAYERS FROM YOUTH TO LIFES   420 EMPEDOCLES I 2   231
                LAST SCENES
            BUT OUR OWN ACTS FOR GOOD OR ILL ARE MIGHTIER POWERS   420 EMPEDOCLES I 2   241
            NO WEAKNESS SPOIL OUR LOT   •   •   •   •   •   •   •   421 EMPEDOCLES I 2   263
            THE ILL DEEDS OF OTHER MEN MAKE OFTEN OUR LIFE DARK   421 EMPEDOCLES I 2   266
            BUT WE AN EASIER WAY TO CHEAT OUR PAINS HAVE FOUND   421 EMPEDOCLES I 2   271
            LOOK THE WORLD TEMPTS OUR EYE   •   •   •   •   •   •   •   423 EMPEDOCLES I 2   317
            WE SHUT OUR EYES AND MUSE   •   •   •   •   •   •   •   423 EMPEDOCLES I 2   327
            HOW OUR OWN MINDS ARE MADE   •   •   •   •   •   •   •   423 EMPEDOCLES I 2   328
            AND SPEND OUR WIT TO NAME WHAT MOST EMPLOY UNNAMED   423 EMPEDOCLES I 2   331
            OUR HAIR GROWS GREY OUR EYES ARE DIMMD OUR   423 EMPEDOCLES I 2   336
                HEAT IS TAMED

OUR   (CONTINUED)
         OUR HAIR GROWS GREY OUR EYES ARE DIMMD OUR   423 EMPEDOCLES I 2   336
              HEAT IS TAMED
         OUR HAIR GROWS GREY OUR EYES ARE DIMMD OUR   423 EMPEDOCLES I 2   336
              HEAT IS TAMED
         WE REST OUR FACULTIES . . . .   423 EMPEDOCLES I 2   337
         OUR DESPERATE SEARCH WAS SIN . . . .   423 EMPEDOCLES I 2   344
         AGAIN OUR YOUTHFUL BLOOD . . . .   424 EMPEDOCLES I 2   352
         PLEASURE TO OUR HOT GRASP . . . .   424 EMPEDOCLES I 2   357
         NOW DO WE SOON PERCEIVE HOW FAST OUR YOUTH IS SPENT 424 EMPEDOCLES I 2   361
         AT ONCE OUR EYES GROW CLEAR . . . .   424 EMPEDOCLES I 2   362
         OUR SHIVERING HEART IS MINED BY SECRET DISCONTENT 424 EMPEDOCLES I 2   366
         THAT LONGING OF OUR YOUTH . . . .   424 EMPEDOCLES I 2   369
         WE PAUSE WE HUSH OUR HEART . . . .   424 EMPEDOCLES I 2   372
         THY JOY OUR YOUTH FOREBODES . . . .   424 EMPEDOCLES I 2   375
         FAILD TO FILL UP THE VOID WHICH IN OUR BREASTS WE BEAR 424 EMPEDOCLES I 2   376
         HAPPINESS MOCKD OUR PRAYER . . . .   425 EMPEDOCLES I 2   383
         LOSE ALL OUR PRESENT STATE . . . .   425 EMPEDOCLES I 2   405
         AND RELEGATE TO WORLDS YET DISTANT OUR REPOSE .   425 EMPEDOCLES I 2   406
         FILL THEE TO SEE OUR DAY . . . .   416 EMPEDOCLES I 2   V 113
         FILL THEE TO SEE OUR WORLD . . . .   416 EMPEDOCLES I 2   V 113
         NOR DO WE SOON PERCEIVE HOW FAST OUR YOUTH IS SPENT 424 EMPEDOCLES I 2   V 361
         AND IF THE SACRED LOAD OPPRESSD OUR BRAIN . . .   436 EMPEDOCLES II   244
         WE HAD NOT LOST OUR BALANCE THEN NOR GROWN . .   436 EMPEDOCLES II   248
         WEARY WITH OUR WEARINESS . . . .   438 EMPEDOCLES II   300
         OUR BODIES TO EARTH . . . .   439 EMPEDOCLES II   333
         OUR BLOOD TO WATER . . . .   439 EMPEDOCLES II   334
         DOWN IN OUR MOTHER EARTHS MIRACULOUS WOMB . . .   439 EMPEDOCLES II   340
         AND THEY WILL BE OUR LORDS AS THEY ARE NOW . .   439 EMPEDOCLES II   351
         AND KEEP US PRISONERS OF OUR CONSCIOUSNESS . .   439 EMPEDOCLES II   352
         AND IN OUR INDIVIDUAL HUMAN STATE . . . . .   440 EMPEDOCLES II   367
         TO SEE IF WE WILL POISE OUR LIFE AT LAST . . .   440 EMPEDOCLES II   369
         TO OUR OWN ONLY TRUE DEEP-BURIED SELVES . . .   440 EMPEDOCLES II   371
         WILL GOAD OUR SENSES WITH A SHARPER SPUR . . .   440 EMPEDOCLES II   379
         WILL FRET OUR MINDS TO AN INTENSER PLAY . . .   440 EMPEDOCLES II   380
         KNEAD US IN ITS HOT HAND AND CHANGE OUR NATURE .   440 EMPEDOCLES II   386
         AND WE SHALL FEEL OUR POWERS OF EFFORT FLAG . .   440 EMPEDOCLES II   387
         OUR SHINING VISITANT . . . .   444 WESTMIN ABBEY   2
         THEREFORE OUR HAPPY GUEST . . . .   447 WESTMIN ABBEY   121
         WHAT HAD OUR ARTHUR GAIND TO STOP AND SEE . . .   448 WESTMIN ABBEY   154
         OUR ARTHUR WILL AGAIN BE PRESENT HERE . . .   449 WESTMIN ABBEY   179
         YET WOULD WE KEEP THEE IN OUR HEART . . . .   451 GEISTS GRAVE   37
         WOULD FIX OUR FAVOURITE ON THE SCENE . . . .   451 GEISTS GRAVE   38
         EVEN TO A DATE BEYOND OUR OWN . . . .   451 GEISTS GRAVE   62
         WE LAY THEE CLOSE WITHIN OUR REACH . . . . .   451 GEISTS GRAVE   65
         DEAD AND MUTE OUR TINY FRIEND . . . .   452 POOR MATTHIAS   14
         COMRADES OF OUR PAST WERE THEY . . . . . .   453 POOR MATTHIAS   49
         GEIST CAME NEXT OUR LITTLE FRIEND . . . . .   454 POOR MATTHIAS   57
         TROUBLING WITH OUR CHATTER VAIN . . . . . .   456 POOR MATTHIAS   123
         OUR COMPANIONS DYING SIGN . . . .   456 POOR MATTHIAS   126
         MARK THE SEASONS MAP OUR YEAR . . . .   456 POOR MATTHIAS   145
         WHAT YOU FEEL ESCAPES OUR KEN . . . .   457 POOR MATTHIAS   161
         KNOW WE MORE OUR FELLOW MEN . . . .   457 POOR MATTHIAS   162
         HUMAN SUFFERING AT OUR SIDE . . . .   457 POOR MATTHIAS   163
         MISS OUR EYES AND MISS OUR EARS . . . . . .   457 POOR MATTHIAS   166
         MISS OUR EYES AND MISS OUR EARS . . . . . .   457 POOR MATTHIAS   166
         HE HATH PLEASED OUR EYES AND EARS . . . . .   458 POOR MATTHIAS   203
         TO US DECLINING TOWRDS OUR END . . . . . .   459 KAISER DEAD   35
         AND DASH OUR HOLIEST RAPTURES WHILE WE GAZE .   470 ALARIC AT ROME   200
         AND MINGLE WITH THY RUINS SOMEWHAT OF OUR OWN .   470 ALARIC AT ROME   204
         TRUE WE MUST TAME OUR REBEL WILL . . . . .   481 COURAGE   1
         OUR BANE DISGUISE IT AS WE MAY . . . . . .   482 COURAGE   25
         OH THAT PAST TIMES COULD GIVE OUR DAY . . .   482 COURAGE   27
         TO DAILY TASKS WE SET OUR HAND . . . . . .   483 ROME-SICKNESS   1
         FOLLOWING THE SUN WE SET OUR VESSELS HEAD . . .   484 S S LUSITANIA   3
         OUR DISCONTENT ITSELF IS ARGUMENT . . . . .   LUCRETIUS 3   10
         TOUCH THE SAME SURFACE WHICH OUR FATHERS TROD .   EVERLASTING SUB   3
         HAVE THE SAME SURFACE WHICH OUR FATHERS TROD .   EVERLASTING SUB   V   3
         HAVE THE SAME SURFACE WHICH OUR FATHERS FELT .   EVERLASTING SUB   V   3
         HAVE THE SAME SURFACE WHICH OUR FATHERS TOUCHD .   EVERLASTING SUB   V   3
         TOUCH THE SAME SURFACE WHICH OUR FATHERS FELT .   EVERLASTING SUB   V   3
         TOUCH THE SAME SURFACE WHICH OUR FATHERS TOUCHD .   EVERLASTING SUB   V   3

OURS
         REND IN A THOUSAND SHREDS THIS LIFE OF OURS . .   4 BUTLERS SERMONS   4
         THE HOMES THAT WERE NOT DESTINED TO BE OURS . .   41 HUMAN LIFE   30
         WE COUNT THE HOURS THESE DREAMS OF OURS . . .   44 QUESTION   15
         IS NO CONCERN OF OURS . . . .   47 HORATIAN ECHO   6
         NO LIFE SAVE HIS AND OURS INTRUDES . . . . .   54 RESIGNATION   72
         BUT OURS WE SHALL NOT MEET WHEN THAT DAY COMES .   96 BALDER DEAD 1   31
         PASSD AMONG THESE HEATHS OF OURS . . . . .   137 TRISTRAM 1   230
         THE STRIFE THE MIXTURE IN HER SOUL ARE OURS . .   168 RACHEL 3   13
         AND POINTS US TO A BETTER TIME THAN OURS . . .   170 WEST LONDON   14
         ONE OF SOME WORTHIER RACE THAN OURS . . . .   202 URANIA   18
         AH SOME POWER EXISTS THERE WHICH IS OURS . . .   210 SELF-DECEPTION   27
         WE ARE YOUNG AND THE WORLD IS OURS . . . . .   233 YOUTH OF MAN   26
         WHEN A BELOVED HAND IS LAID IN OURS . . . .   247 BURIED LIFE   78
         O LIFE UNLIKE TO OURS . . . .   260 SCHOLAR-GIPSY   166
         FADE AND GROW OLD AT LAST AND DIE LIKE OURS . .   261 SCHOLAR-GIPSY   230
         NOR YET TO AMUSE AS OURS ARE . . . .   300 GRANDE CHARTR   52
         WE LAUD THEM BUT THEY ARE NOT OURS . . . . .   304 GRANDE CHARTR   168
         THEY AWE US BUT THEY ARE NOT OURS . . . . .   304 GRANDE CHARTR   V 168

OURS   (CONTINUED)
          WE MARK THEM BUT THEY ARE NOT OURS   • • • • •   304 GRANDE CHARTR   V 168
          WE PRAISE THEM BUT THEY ARE NOT OURS   • • • • •   304 GRANDE CHARTR   V 168
          CLEARER HOW MUCH THAN OURS YET WE   • • • • •   308 OBERMANN   63
          WHAT SHELTER TO GROW RIPE IS OURS   • • • • •   308 OBERMANN   71
          LIKE OURS IT LOOKD IN OUTWARD AIR   • • • • •   315 OBERMANN MORE   85
          A WORLD LIKE OURS TO-DAY   • • • • • •   315 OBERMANN MORE   V 84
          THAT HOUSE LIKE OURS INTESTINE MURDER MAIMS   •   384 MEROPE   1392
          WHAT PERMANENCE WHAT STABILITY LIKE OURS   • •   389 MEROPE   1544
          WE MARK NOT THE WORLDS COURSE BUT WOULD HAVE   419 EMPEDOCLES I 2   221
               IT TAKE OURS
          OTHER EXISTENCES THERE ARE THAT CLASH WITH OURS   • •   420 EMPEDOCLES I 2   246
          AND LASTLY THOUGH OF OURS   • • • • • • •   421 EMPEDOCLES I 2   262
          HAND AFTER HAND IN OURS   • • • • •   424 EMPEDOCLES I 2   360
          MORE VIRGINAL AND SWEET THAN OURS   • • •   426 EMPEDOCLES I 2   434
          WE MARK NOT THE WORLDS WAYS BUT WOULD HAVE   419 EMPEDOCLES I 2   V 221
               IT LEARN OURS
          OTHER EXISTENCES THERE ARE WHICH CLASH WITH OURS   • •   420 EMPEDOCLES I 2   V 246
          AS VIRGINAL AND SWEET AS OURS   • • • • •   426 EMPEDOCLES I 2   V 434
          CLOSER KNIT THEIR LIFE WITH OURS   • • • •   453 POOR MATTHIAS   46
          OF A PRESCIENCE MORE THAN OURS   • • • •   456 POOR MATTHIAS   138
          STAND NOT TWIXT HIS SOUL AND OURS   • • •   457 POOR MATTHIAS   172
          ALAS FAR OTHER THOUGHTS MIGHT WELL BE OURS   • • •   470 ALARIC AT ROME   199
          FOR BY NO SLOW PACE OR WANT OF SWIFTNESS OF OURS   • •   HOMER TRANS   50
          OURS IS THE REFLEX IMAGE OF THE WORLD   • • • •   LUCRETIUS 5   1

OURSELVES
          WOULD THAT OURSELVES O BALDER WE WERE BORNE   • •   101 BALDER DEAD 1   216
          SHALL SEE OURSELVES AND LEARN AT LAST   • • • •   179 FAREWELL   55
          THE PHANTOM OF OURSELVES   • • • • • • • •   213 GROWING OLD   33
          BEEN ON OUR OWN LINE HAVE WE BEEN OURSELVES   • •   246 BURIED LIFE   60
          AND WE OURSELVES SHALL GO   • • • • • • •   259 SCHOLAR-GIPSY   156
          ONLY OURSELVES WE LOST   • • • • • • • •   289 RUGBY CHAPEL   118
          HARDLY OURSELVES WE FOUGHT THROUGH   • • • •   289 RUGBY CHAPEL   120
          LONG WE REFRAIND OURSELVES SUBMITTED LONG   • • • •   337 MEROPE   254
          LET US FORGET OURSELVES FOR THOSE WE RULE   • • • •   394 MEROPE   1721
          THE BURDEN OF OURSELVES   • • • • • • • •   416 EMPEDOCLES I 2   128
          A FALSE COURSE FOR THE WORLD AND FOR OURSELVES   419 EMPEDOCLES I 2   226
               FALSE POWERS
          THE SCHEME OURSELVES HAVE SPUN   • • • • •   422 EMPEDOCLES I 2   313
          FALSE WEAKNESS IN THE WORLD AND IN OURSELVES   419 EMPEDOCLES I 2   V 226
               FALSE POWERS
          IN ALL THE ITALIAN CITIES LIKE OURSELVES   • • • •   436 EMPEDOCLES II   237
          WILL MAKE OURSELVES HARDER TO BE DISCERND   • • •   440 EMPEDOCLES II   381
          SET BETWIXT OURSELVES AND THEE   • • • • •   456 POOR MATTHIAS   128
          WHAT AMONGST OURSELVES WE DO   • • • • • • •   457 POOR MATTHIAS   158

OUT
          OUT-TOPPING KNOWLEDGE FOR THE LOFTIEST HILL   • •   2 SHAKESPEARE   3
          OUT-TOPPING KNOWLEDGE SO SOME SOVRAN HILL   • • • •   2 SHAKESPEARE   V 3
          SIGHD OUT BY WINTERS SAD TRANQUILLITY   • • • •   12 MYCERINUS   115
          RIDE OUT TO CHURCH FROM CHAMBERY   • • • • •   17 CHURCH BROU 2   21
          WHERE SORROW PUTS OUT JOY   • • • • • • •   39 STAGIRIUS   V 43
          OUT OF THIS STUFF THESE FORCES THOU ART GROWN   • •   46 IN UTRUMQUE PAR   V 38
          NAY AND SINCE DEATH WHICH WIPES OUT MAN   • • •   58 RESIGNATION   223
          AND THE FOG ROSE OUT OF THE OXUS STREAM   • • •   61 SOHRAB RUSTUM   2
          TO SEEK OUT RUSTUM SEEK HIM NOT THROUGH FIGHT   • •   63 SOHRAB RUSTUM   75
          THESE ALL FILED OUT FROM CAMP INTO THE PLAIN   • •   65 SOHRAB RUSTUM   135
          OUT ON THE SANDS BEYOND IT RUSTUMS TENTS   • • •   66 SOHRAB RUSTUM   191
          THE ARMIES ARE DRAWN OUT AND STAND AT GAZE   • • •   67 SOHRAB RUSTUM   210
          OR WHETHER IT WILL ROLL US OUT TO SEA   • • •   73 SOHRAB RUSTUM   394
          BACK OUT TO SEA TO THE DEEP WAVES OF DEATH   • • •   73 SOHRAB RUSTUM   395
          OF WAR I FIGHT IT OUT AND HAND TO HAND   • • •   75 SOHRAB RUSTUM   464
          WHICH SOHRAB HELD STIFF OUT THE STEEL-SPIKED SPEAR   75 SOHRAB RUSTUM   492
          IN SOME FAR STONY GORGE OUT OF HIS KEN   • • • •   78 SOHRAB RUSTUM   568
          TO DRAW IT AND FOR EVER LET LIFE OUT   • • • •   82 SOHRAB RUSTUM   705
          SURELY MY HEART CRIED OUT THAT IT WAS THOU   • • •   82 SOHRAB RUSTUM   711
          OUT OF THE MIST AND HUM OF THAT LOW LAND   • • •   87 SOHRAB RUSTUM   876
          CRIES OUT MOST EARNESTLY O KING   • • • •   89 SICK KING BOKH   52
          FIRE TO THE WOOD AND SEND HIM OUT TO SEA   • • •   96 BALDER DEAD 1   44
          WHERE IN AND OUT THE SCREAMING SEAFOWL FLY   • •   97 BALDER DEAD 1   80
          TO ASGARD AND THE STARS CAME OUT IN HEAVEN   • •   102 BALDER DEAD 1   256
          TO FADE AND NANNA IN HER SLEEP STRETCHD OUT   • •   104 BALDER DEAD 1   332
          AND PICK THE BRAVEST WARRIORS OUT FOR DEATH   •   105 BALDER DEAD 2   26
          AND THEY CAME OUT UPON THE PLAIN AND PASSD   • • •   106 BALDER DEAD 2   65
          EVEN HERE THEY SEEK THEE OUT IN HELAS REALM   • •   112 BALDER DEAD 2   256
          HANGS QUIVERING OUT BETWEEN HIS DUST-SMEARD JAWS   •   114 BALDER DEAD 3   15
          OUT OF OUR SIGHT THAT WE MAY TURN FROM GRIEF   • •   115 BALDER DEAD 3   55
          AND WREATHED IN SMOKE THE SHIP STOOD OUT TO SEA   •   118 BALDER DEAD 3   185
          SHARP QUIVERING TONGUES OF FLAME SHOT OUT AND LEAPT   119 BALDER DEAD 3   188
          OF GRASS PEEP OUT AMID SURROUNDING SNOW   • • •   122 BALDER DEAD 3   315
          OUT OF A TILLD FIELD INLAND THEN THE WIND   • • •   124 BALDER DEAD 3   363
          CATCHES THEM AND DRIVES OUT AGAIN TO SEA   • • •   124 BALDER DEAD 3   364
          OUT OF THE BLACK WASTE FOREST FAR BELOW   • • • •   119 BALDER DEAD 3   V
          WHAT LIGHTS WILL THOSE OUT TO THE NORTHWARD BE   •   130 TRISTRAM 1   5
          TRISTRAM SWEET LOVE WE ARE BETRAYD OUT-PLANND   •   135 TRISTRAM 1   167
          OUT OF THEIR GLOSSY COVERTS BUT WHEN NOW   • • •   150 TRISTRAM 3   31
          RAN OUT FROM THE DARK UNDERWOOD BEHIND   • • • •   155 TRISTRAM 3   209
          THE TRAITOR JUDAS OUT OF HELL   • • • • • •   157 SAINT BRANDAN   20
          O RUTH OF GOD THE PRIEST CRIED OUT   • • • •   160 NECKAN   55
          TRICKD OUT WITH A PARISIAN SPEECH AND FACE   • • •   168 RACHEL 3   4
          AND THOUGH WE WEAR OUT LIFE ALAS   • • • •   179 FAREWELL   49
          PASSING OUT FROM THE WET TURF   • • • • • • •   186 STRAYED REVEL   31
          OUT OF THE LIGHT AND MUTELY WHICH AVOIDS   • • • •   199 EARLY DEATH   3

OUT   (CONTINUED)
        GLIMMERING AND VAST OUT IN THE TRANQUIL BAY   • •   210 DOVER BEACH   5
        RAN OFF AND VANISHD OUT OF HAND   • • • • •   213 PROGRESS POESY   8
        ARE NOT PUSHED OUT BY THE SWELLS   • • • • •   214 NEW ROME   14
        THEY OUT-TALKD THEE HISSD THEE TORE THEE   • •   215 LAST WORD   9
        OUT OF THE PATH AND TAKE THE GRASS   • • •   222 EPILOG LAOCOON   37
        STRETCHING OUT LIKE THE DESERT   • • • • •   235 YOUTH OF MAN   109
        HEADLANDS STOOD OUT INTO THE MOONLIT DEEP   • • • 242 SUMMER NIGHT   14
        IN TRACKING OUT OUR TRUE ORIGINAL COURSE   • •   246 BURIED LIFE   50
        WHERE THE TIRED ANGLER LIES STRETCHD OUT   • •   248 KENSINGTON GARD   18
        WHERE THE LONE ANGLER LIES STRETCHD OUT   • •   KENSINGTON GARD   V 18
        HE SPREADS OUT HIS ARMS TO THE LIGHT   • • •   251 FUTURE   5
        AS THE STARS COME OUT AND THE NIGHT-WIND   • •   254 FUTURE   85
        AND MARKD THEE WHEN THE STARS COME OUT AND SHINE   258 SCHOLAR-GIPSY   109
        FOR WHAT WEARS OUT THE LIFE OF MORTAL MEN   • •   259 SCHOLAR-GIPSY   142
        OUR WORN-OUT LIFE AND ARE WHAT WE HAVE BEEN   •   259 SCHOLAR-GIPSY   150
        AND SNATCHD HIS RUDDER AND SHOOK OUT MORE SAIL •   262 SCHOLAR-GIPSY   242
        AND IN THE SCATTERD FARMS THE LIGHTS COME OUT •   267 THYRSIS   164
        OUT OF THE HEED OF MORTALS HE IS GONE   • • •   269 THYRSIS   208
        OUT OF THE HEED OF MORTALS IS HE GONE   • • •   269 THYRSIS   V 208
        SHUT OUT THE GRIEF THE DESPAIR • • • • • •   283 HAWORTH CHURCH   V
        THE LIGHTS COME OUT IN THE STREET   • • • • •   286 RUGBY CHAPEL   8
        SLOW DIE OUT OF HER LIFE • • • • • • •   295 HEINES GRAVE   83
        LONGD ITSELF OUT OF THE DIN   • • • • • •   296 HEINES GRAVE   149
        TO THESE OUT-DATED STINGS AGAIN   • • • • •   302 GRANDE CHARTR   106
        HERE LEAVE US TO DIE OUT WITH THESE   • • • •   302 GRANDE CHARTR   111
        THE WORN-OUT WORLD WE KNEW   • • • • • •   319 OBERMANN MORE   206
        BUT NOW THE OLD IS OUT OF DATE   • • • • •   321 OBERMANN MORE   245
        WHICH TO THE WILDERNESS DROVE OUT   • • • •   323 OBERMANN MORE   317
        AS OUT OF SLEEP AND NO   • • • • • • •   323 OBERMANN MORE   326
        THE OUT-WORN WORLD WE KNEW   • • • • • •   319 OBERMANN MORE   V 206
        BUT NOW THE PAST IS OUT OF DATE • • • • •   321 OBERMANN MORE   V 245
        GO THOU INTO THE CITY AND SEEK OUT   • • • •   331 MEROPE   37
        DO TWENTY YEARS WEAR OUT AND SEE EXPIRE • •   335 MEROPE   180
        SHALL THEY NOT WEAR ONE HATRED OUT AS WELL   • •   335 MEROPE   181
        THREE GENERATIONS OF HIS OFFSPRING OUT   • • •   336 MEROPE   217
        HE PARCELLD OUT IN FIVE CONFEDERATE STATES   • •   337 MEROPE   249
        WERE HUNTED OUT AND TO ACHAIA FLED   • • • •   338 MEROPE   286
        THOU STANDEST OUT I SEE REPELLEST PEACE • • •   341 MEROPE   354
        TILL I THROWN OUT AND TIRED CAME TO HALT   • •   357 MEROPE   795
        ARCAS SEEK OUT MY UNCLE LAIAS NOW   • • • •   379 MEROPE   1260
        YET STAINS OUR LAND BE BY THIS BLOOD WASHD OUT   402 MEROPE   1916
        WHAT BLOOD SO MEET AS THINE TO WASH IT OUT • •   402 MEROPE   1924
        AND THE FEAST PAST ITS PRIME SO WE SLIPPD OUT   407 EMPEDOCLES I 1   37
        TO BRING THEE OUT WITH HIM ALONE ON ETNA   • •   409 EMPEDOCLES I 1   107
        THE OUT-SPREAD WORLD TO SPAN   • • • • • •   415 EMPEDOCLES I 2   77
        SHAKEN AND OUT OF CHIME   • • • • • • •   416 EMPEDOCLES I 2   115
        WE SEARCH OUT DEAD MENS WORDS AND WORKS OF   423 EMPEDOCLES I 2   326
            DEAD MENS HANDS
        WHAT GARMENTS OUT-GLISTENING   • • • • • • •   442 EMPEDOCLES II   439
        OUT-PERFUMES THE THYME   • • • • • • •   442 EMPEDOCLES II   442
        PURSY PLAYD-OUT PHILISTINE   • • • • • •   457 POOR MATTHIAS   190
        LIVE OUT THE DAY   • • • • • •   460 KAISER DEAD   48
        BREAKS OUT AND LONGS FOR SWITZERLAND   • • • •   483 ROME-SICKNESS   3

OUTBUILDING
        FOR REST IN THIS OUTBUILDING NEAR   • • • • •   300 GRANDE CHARTR   27

OUTCAST
        AEGIMIUS GAVE OUR OUTCAST HOUSE A HOME   • • •   337 MEROPE   224
        LAY FORLORN LAY OUTCAST   • • • • • • • •   391 MEROPE   1604

OUTCRY
        AND OUTCRY OF THE FORMER MEN   • • • • • • •   303 GRANDE CHARTR   128

OUTERMOST
        OR THE HOWLING OUTERMOST MAIN • • • • • • •   361 MEROPE   913

OUTFIT
        ASKD AN OUTFIT FOR ITS EARTHLY ROAD • • • • •   209 SELF-DECEPTION   8

OUTGOES
        OF LABOUR THAT IN FRUIT BY FAR OUTGOES   • • •   1 QUIET WORK   V   6
        OF LABOUR THAT WITH MUTE ADVANCE OUTGOES   • • •   1 QUIET WORK   V   6

OUTGROWS
        OF LABOUR THAT IN LASTING FRUIT OUTGROWS   • •   1 QUIET WORK   6
        OF LABOUR THAT IN ONE SHORT HOUR OUTGROWS • • •   1 QUIET WORK   V   6
        OF LABOUR THAT IN STILL ADVANCE OUTGROWS   • •   1 QUIET WORK   V   6
        OF LABOUR THAT IN FRUIT BY FAR OUTGROWS   • • •   1 QUIET WORK   V   6

OUTGUSHING
        WAS BLINDED BY THE OUTGUSHING SPRINGS OF BRINE • • 357 MEROPE   778

OUTLANDISH
        MARKD THINE OUTLANDISH GARB THY FIGURE SPARE   • • 258 SCHOLAR-GIPSY   98
        MARKD THY OUTLANDISH GARB THY FIGURE SPARE • • • • 258 SCHOLAR-GIPSY   V 98

OUTLASTS
        OUTLASTS AVERSION OUTLASTS LOVE   • • • • • •   58 RESIGNATION   216
        OUTLASTS AVERSION OUTLASTS LOVE   • • • • • •   58 RESIGNATION   216

OUTLASTS   (CONTINUED)
          OUTLASTS EACH EFFORT INTEREST HOPE . . . . . .   58 RESIGNATION   217
          IN SOME SENSE FAUSTA OUTLASTS DEATH . . . . . .   59 RESIGNATION   230

OUTLINED
          THE MINSTERS OUTLINED MASS   . . . . 445 WESTMIN ABBEY   31

OUTLINES
          AND THOUGHTS THAT WERE BUT OUTLINES TIME ENGRAVES 473 CROMWELL   47

OUTLIVE
          I SHALL SUFFER BUT THEY WILL OUTLIVE THEIR AFFECTION   20 MODERN SAPPHO   17

OUTLIVED
          OUTLIVED HIS BRETHREN HIS PEERS   . . . . . .   229 YOUTH OF NATURE   33
          BUT HE WHO HAS OUTLIVED HIS PROSPEROUS DAYS   . . 436 EMPEDOCLES II   261

OUTLIVES
          OUTLIVES MY GUILT OUTLIVES MY DOOM . . . . . .   158 SAINT BRANDAN   63
          OUTLIVES MY GUILT OUTLIVES MY DOOM . . . . . .   158 SAINT BRANDAN   63

OUTLIVING
          OUR GIPSY-SCHOLAR HAUNTS OUTLIVING THEE   . . . . 268 THYRSIS   197

OUTLOOK
          THE HUNTER ON THE OUTLOOK   . . . .   392 MEROPE   1635

OUTMOST
          FAR FAR BEYOND THE OUTMOST GIANTS HOME   . . . . 100 BALDER DEAD 1   163
          OUTMOST THE OTHERS NEAR THE CENTRE RUN   . . . . 109 BALDER DEAD 2   153

OUTRAGED
          AND BELIEVES NATURE OUTRAGED IF HIS WILLS GAINSAID 417 EMPEDOCLES I 2   156
          BE CRUSHT AND OUTRAGED IN THIS BITTER HOUR . . . 468 ALARIC AT ROME   148

OUTRUNS
          AND THOU A BOY WHOSE TONGUE OUTRUNS HIS KNOWLEDGE 411 EMPEDOCLES I 1   161

OUTSIDE
          RADIANT ADORND OUTSIDE A HIDDEN GROUND   . . . . 166 AUSTERITY POET   13
          WHO RATES US IF WE PEER OUTSIDE OUR PEN . . . . 169 WORLDLY PLACE   7
          OUTSIDE THE WESTERN STRAITS AND UNBENT SAILS . . 262 SCHOLAR-GIPSY   247
          OF STORMS THAT RAGE OUTSIDE OUR HAPPY GROUND . . 264 THYRSIS   49
          MURMUR OF PARIS OUTSIDE . . . .   292 HEINES GRAVE   10

OUTSPREAD
          ROUND THY STILL DREAMING BROTHER-WORLD OUTSPREAD . .   45 IN UTRUMQUE PAR   31
          AND NOW IN FRONT BEHOLD OUTSPREAD . . . . . .   54 RESIGNATION   64
          HAD FALLEN BACK HER ARMS OUTSPREAD   . . . . .   146 TRISTRAM 2   104
          SO SAITH HE BLESSING HIM WITH OUTSPREAD HANDS . . 445 WESTMIN ABBEY   46
          REGARDS HIS BROTHERS FORM OUTSPREAD . . . . .   460 KAISER DEAD   68

OUTSPREADS
          THE WIDE WIDE VALLEY OUTSPREADS   . . . . . .   234 YOUTH OF MAN   76

OUTWARD
          DWELT WITH MERE OUTWARD SEEMING HE WITHIN   . . .   12 MYCERINUS   108
          IN OUTWARD SEMBLANCE HE MUST GIVE . . . . . .   223 EPILOG LAOCOON   57
          LIKE OURS IT LOOKD IN OUTWARD AIR   . . . . .   315 OBERMANN MORE   85
          NOR OUTWARD THINGS WERE CLOSED AND DEAD TO US . . 436 EMPEDOCLES II   241
          JOY AND THE OUTWARD WORLD MUST DIE TO HIM   . . . 437 EMPEDOCLES II   274

OUTWEARIED
          OUTWEARIED WITH THEIR LONELY PARTS   . . . . .   203 EUPHROSYNE   7
          WHO HERE OUTWEARIED SUNK AND SUNG   . . . . .   278 SOUTHERN NIGHT   V 99

OUTWEIGHD
          RECALLS THE OBSCURE OPPOSER HE OUTWEIGHD . . . . 171 DIVINITY   8

OUTWORN
          A-KEMPIS HER DEPARTING SOUL OUTWORN . . . . .   168 RACHEL 3   7
          FOILD BY OUR FELLOW-MEN DEPRESSD OUTWORN . . . . 172 IMMORTALITY   1
          WHO HERE OUTWORN HAD SUNK AND SUNG   . . . . .   278 SOUTHERN NIGHT   99
          THE STRAGGLERS REFRESH THE OUTWORN   . . . . .   292 RUGBY CHAPEL   199
          FROM SUCH MATES THE OUTWORN   . . . .   294 HEINES GRAVE   50
          HEINES SPIRIT OUTWORN   . . . .   296 HEINES GRAVE   148
          IS A PASSD MODE AN OUTWORN THEME   . . . . . .   302 GRANDE CHARTR   100

OVATION
          AND PROCLAIMD YOUR VAIN OVATION   . . . . . .   31 NEW SIRENS   153

OVER
          NOTES OF WILD PASTORAL MUSIC OVER ALL   . . . .   25 DREAM   12
          THEN WHEN CHANGE ITSELF IS OVER   . . . . . .   33 NEW SIRENS   219
          OVER THE SUMMIT OF THE HILL   . . . . . .   54 RESIGNATION   63
          STREAM OVER CASBIN AND THE SOUTHERN SLOPES . . .   64 SOHRAB RUSTUM   113
          OVER THE FIGHTERS HEADS AND A WIND ROSE . . . .   75 SOHRAB RUSTUM   483
          SHALL THE LAKE GLASS HER FLYING OVER IT . . . .   73 SOHRAB RUSTUM   570
          OVER HIS DYING SON AND KNEW HIM NOT . . . . .   78 SOHRAB RUSTUM   575
          WITH AGE AND RULES OVER THE VALIANT KOORDS . . .   78 SOHRAB RUSTUM   592

OVER (CONTINUED)
    OH THAT ITS WAVES WERE FLOWING OVER ME   • • • • • •   83 SOHRAB RUSTUM   768
    AND PLANT A FAR-SEEN PILLAR OVER ALL • • • • • •   84 SOHRAB RUSTUM   789
    AND PLANT A FAR-SEEN PILLAR OVER ALL • • • • • •   84 SOHRAB RUSTUM   804
    RETURNING HOME OVER THE SALT BLUE SEA   • • • • •   85 SOHRAB RUSTUM   833
    AND NIGHT CAME DOWN OVER THE SOLEMN WASTE   • •   86 SOHRAB RUSTUM   865
    WHOM ANTLERD REINDEER PULL OVER THE SNOW   • •   96 BALDER DEAD 1   54
    HIGH OVER ASGARD TO LIGHT HOME THE KING   • • •   102 BALDER DEAD 1   257
    OVER AGAINST THE CURTAIN OF THE BED   • • • •   103 BALDER DEAD 1   286
    AND OVER BIFROST WHERE IS HEIMDALLS WATCH   •   105 BALDER DEAD 2   22
    WHICH HANGS OVER THE ICE WHERE LIES THE ROAD   •   108 BALDER DEAD 2   127
    SHALL HE SHED CHEER OVER THE CHEERLESS SEATS   •   110 BALDER DEAD 2   195
    AND OVER BALDERS CORPSE THESE WORDS DIDST SAY   •   115 BALDER DEAD 3   74
    AND MORNING OVER ALL THE WORLD WAS SPREAD   • •   119 BALDER DEAD 3   213
    LORD OVER MEN ON EARTH AND GODS IN HEAVEN   • •   120 BALDER DEAD 3   251
    A QUEEN AND EMPIRE OVER ALL THE DEAD   • • •   121 BALDER DEAD 3   278
    OVER THE GREY SEA-RIDGES AND THE GLIMPSE   • •   124 BALDER DEAD 3   366
    OVER THE SICK MANS FEET IS SPREAD • • • •   131 TRISTRAM 1   15
    AND A GLANCE WHICH OVER THE CROWDED FLOOR   • •   146 TRISTRAM 2   120
    AND A GLANCE THAT OVER THE CROWDED FLOOR   • •   146 TRISTRAM 2   V 120
    CREEPS OVER IT FROM THE TILLD FIELDS BEHIND   •   149 TRISTRAM 3   9
    OVER THE WASTE THIS CIRQUE OF OPEN GROUND   • •   150 TRISTRAM 3   13
    THEIR CHEEKS WERE FLUSHD AND OVER EACH HOT BROW   •   150 TRISTRAM 3   32
    AND LED THEM HOME OVER THE DARKENING HEATH   • •   151 TRISTRAM 3   63
    AND TAKES IT IN HER HAND AND WAVES IT OVER   • •   156 TRISTRAM 3   217
    CREEPS OVER IT FROM THE TILLD LAND BEHIND   • •   TRISTRAM 3   V   9
    STEALS OVER IT FROM THE TILLD LAND BEHIND   • •   TRISTRAM 3   V   9
    STEALS OVER IT FROM THE TILLD FIELDS BEHIND   •   TRISTRAM 3   V   9
    OVER THE WASTE THIS RING OF OPEN GROUND   • •   150 TRISTRAM 3   V 13
    OVER THE WASTE BUT WHERE THIS OPEN GROUND   • •   TRISTRAM 3   V 13
    OVER THE WASTE ALL THE HOLLOW GROUND   • • •   TRISTRAM 3   V 13
    THEIR CHEEKS GREW FLUSHD AND OVER EACH HOT BROW   •   TRISTRAM 3   V 32
    WE HEARD THE SWEET BELLS OVER THE BAY   • • •   162 FORSAKEN MERM   31
    AND OVER THE SAND AT THE SEA • • • • •   164 FORSAKEN MERM   99
    OVER BANKS OF BRIGHT SEAWEED • • • • •   165 FORSAKEN MERM   134
    TO HANG OVER ENDYMIONS SLEEP • • • • •   181 ISOLATION MARG   23
    OR IS IT OVER ART THOU DEAD • • • • •   184 TERRACE BERNE   25
    HIS ROBE DRAWN OVER   • • • • • •   190 STRAYED REVEL   139
    LOOKING OVER THE VALLEY   • • • • •   194 STRAYED REVEL   272
    AND COMING FLUSHD OVER THE STORMY FRITH   • •   196 FRAG ANTIGONE   58
    THY FLIGHT AND FEEL COME OVER THEE   • • •   201 PHILOMELA   23
    LIKE STARS OVER THE BOUNDING HILL   • • •   220 BACCHANALIA 2   27
    OVER TOMBS AMID GRAVES   • • • • •   220 BACCHANALIA 2   32
    OVER THE LIT SEAS UNQUIET WAY   • • • •   240 SELF-DEPENDENCE   14
    GLOOM SETTLES SLOWLY DOWN OVER THEIR BREAST   •   243 SUMMER NIGHT   46
    THE BROAD RED SUN OVER FIELD • • • • •   297 HEINES GRAVE   170
    OVER HIS BOILING CAULDRON BROODS   • • •   299 GRANDE CHARTR   12
    YOU TRIUMPH OVER TIME AND SPACE   • • •   304 GRANDE CHARTR   166
    EMBLEMS OF HOPE OVER THE GRAVE • • • •   305 GRANDE CHARTR   201
    OVER HIS BOILING CAULDRONS BROODS   • • •   299 GRANDE CHARTR   V 12
    DOWN OVER HILL AND WOOD   • • • • •   314 OBERMANN MORE   58
    HOW OF ALL HUMAN RULES THE OVER-TENSE   • •   339 MEROPE   307
    BUT STILL OVER HIS SPEECH A GLOOM THERE HUNG   •   356 MEROPE   764
    O THAT MY OVER-SPEED AND BURSTING GRIEF   • •   362 MEROPE   939
    DREADING THINE OVER-WROUGHT MOOD   • • •   371 MEROPE   1131
    MY CHILD UNHURT ONLY BY OVER JOY   • • •   377 MEROPE   1220
    MOTHER MY HEART RUNS OVER BUT THE TIME   • •   378 MEROPE   1232
    OVER THY CORPSE TRIUMPH NOT NEITHER MOURN   • •   404 MEROPE   1989
    TAKE THESE MY SON OVER THINE ENEMYS CORPSE   •   404 MEROPE   2010
    OVER THEIR OWN DEAR CHILDREN ROLLD   • • •   427 EMPEDOCLES I 2   446
    BUT OVER ALL THE WORLD   • • • • •   432 EMPEDOCLES II   99
    WITH ONE ARM OVER HIS HEAD • • • • •   434 EMPEDOCLES II   163
    OVER THE GRAVE OF THE SLAIN PYTHO   • • •   435 EMPEDOCLES II   205
    SUNSET OVER THE SEA   • • • • • •   436 EMPEDOCLES II   253
    THAT THE WORLD WIN NO MASTERY OVER HIM   • •   437 EMPEDOCLES II   270
    OH THAT IT BROODED OVER THE WORLD LIKE THE AIR   •   438 EMPEDOCLES II   326
    OVER THE UNALLIED UNOPENING EARTH   • • •   439 EMPEDOCLES II   360
    OVER THE UNRECOGNISING SEA WHILE AIR   • • •   439 EMPEDOCLES II   361
    RUSH OVER IT AGAIN   • • • • • •   441 EMPEDOCLES II   415
    AND DOWN OVER THE THAMES THE DARKNESS DREW   •   444 WESTMIN ABBEY   13
    BY THIS DEAR GUEST OVER THY PRECINCT SHED   • •   449 WESTMIN ABBEY   173
    BY THIS DEAR SOUL OVER THY PRECINCT SHED   • •   449 WESTMIN ABBEY   V 173
    A FIT ALLS OVER   • • • • • • •   460 KAISER DEAD   64
    THAT TROUBLOUS NIGHT IS OVER ON THE BROW   • •   468 ALARIC AT ROME   151

OVERAWE
    RISING ALL ROUND OVERAWE • • • • • • •   291 RUGBY CHAPEL   179

OVERBLOWN
    AND YOUR FLOWERS ARE OVERBLOWN   • • • •   34 NEW SIRENS   254

OVERFEEDING
    A STRAIND LIFE WHILE OVERFEEDING   • • • •   49 SECOND BEST   14

OVERGREW
    GERMS YOUR UNTRIMMD PASSION OVERGREW • • •   30 NEW SIRENS   138

OVERGROWN
    THE GARDEN OVERGROWN YET MILD   • • • • •   301 GRANDE CHARTR   55
    WITH MANY A WILD WEED OVERGROWN   • • • •   479 HAYSWATER BOAT   14

OVERHEAD
    WHILE THE DEEP-BURNISHD FOLIAGE OVERHEAD   • • • •   11 MYCERINUS   98
    AND OVERHEAD THE CLOUDLESS SKY OF MAY   • • • •   133 TRISTRAM 1   96
    TWAS AUGUST AND THE FIERCE SUN OVERHEAD   • • • •   169 EAST LONDON   1
    SOMETIMES A THRUSH FLIT OVERHEAD   • • • • •   248 KENSINGTON GARD   11
    THE BROWN THRUSH CROSSES OVERHEAD   • • • • •   KENSINGTON GARD V 11
    FIERCER THE SUN OVERHEAD   • • • • • • • •   253 FUTURE   65
    WILD BEASTS AND VULTURES SAILING OVERHEAD   • • • •   373 MEROPE   1170

OVERHEAT
    AND AN UNNATURAL OVERHEAT AT BEST   • • • • •   153 TRISTRAM 3   136

OVERLAID
    BEFORE THE SOPHIST-BROOD HATH OVERLAID   • • • •   429 EMPEDOCLES II   29

OVERMUCH
    NOT OVERMUCH I PRIZE   • • • • • • • • •   426 EMPEDOCLES I 2 V 407

OVERPEER
    GREY RAIN-BLEARD STATUES OVERPEER   • • • • • •   191 STRAYED REVEL   179

OVERTURND
    ALTARS UNFED AND TEMPLES OVERTURND   • • • • • •   8 MYCERINUS   3

OVERWEIGHD
    THAT HE SITS OVERWEIGHD   • • • • • • • •   188 STRAYED REVEL   91

OWE
    TO OUR UNHAPPY HOUSE THE DEBT WE OWE   • • • • •   367 MEROPE   1048
    TO ONE UNHAPPY HOUSE THE DEBT WE OWE   • • • • •   367 MEROPE   V1048

OWN
    BREASTS HER OWN GRIEFS AND URGED TOO FIERCELY SAYS   6 GEO CRUIKSHANK   10
    TO PAIN TO DEATH THE BENT OF HIS OWN DAYS   • • • •   6 GEO CRUIKSHANK   13
    EVER IN THEIR OWN EAGER PASTIME BENT   • • • • • •   8 RELIGIOUS ISOL   2
    ON HIS OWN SWARMING THOUGHTS AN INTEREST OWN   • •   8 RELIGIOUS ISOL   4
    ON HIS OWN SWARMING THOUGHTS AN INTEREST OWN   • •   8 RELIGIOUS ISOL   4
    DO THOU WHOM LIGHT IN THINE OWN INMOST SOUL   • •   8 RELIGIOUS ISOL   6
    TO ITS OWN IMPULSE EVERY CREATURE STIRS   • • • •   8 RELIGIOUS ISOL   13
    REVELS MORE DEEP JOY KEENER THAN THEIR OWN   • • • •   10 MYCERINUS   66
    NOR PALLD WITH ITS OWN FULNESS EBBD AND DIED   • •   12 MYCERINUS   116
    AH WE OWN DIVINER FEATURES   • • • • • • •   28 NEW SIRENS   63
    TILL SHE SEARCH AND LEARN HER OWN   • • • • •   28 NEW SIRENS   74
    SOULS AS LITTLE GODLIKE AS THEIR OWN   • • • • •   34 NEW SIRENS   250
    THOU WHO DOST KNOW THINE OWN   • • • • • •   38 STAGIRIUS   2
    OF HER OWN ELOQUENCE   • • • • • • • • •   39 STAGIRIUS   27
    WAFTS NOT FROM THINE OWN THOUGHTS NOR LONGINGS VAIN   42 GIPSY CHILD   10
    FROM THINE OWN MOTHERS BREAST THAT KNOWS NOT THEE   42 GIPSY CHILD   14
    THY SORROW AND THY CALMNESS ARE THINE OWN   • • • •   42 GIPSY CHILD   19
    TO HALVE A LODGING THAT WAS ALL HER OWN   • • •   44 GIPSY CHILD   64
    WAFTS NOT FROM THINE OWN THOUGHTS OF GRAVER STRAIN   41 GIPSY CHILD V 10
    TO HALVE A HOUSE THAT SHOULD BE ALL HER OWN   • •   44 GIPSY CHILD V 64
    CHIEF DREAMER OWN THY DREAM   • • • • • •   46 IN UTRUMQUE PAR   37
    DEAFEND BY HIS OWN STIR   • • • • • • • • •   47 WORLD QUIETIST   20
    HER OWN SWEET ERRANDS ALL FORGONE   • • • •   53 RESIGNATION   36
    NOT HIS OWN COURSE BUT THAT OF MAN   • • • • •   56 RESIGNATION   147
    EACH WITH SOME ERRAND OF ITS OWN   • • • • • •   57 RESIGNATION   168
    WHETHER THAT HIS OWN MIGHTY STRENGTH AT LAST   • •   63 SOHRAB RUSTUM   83
    AND CLASPD HIS HAND WITHIN HIS OWN AND SAID   •   71 SOHRAB RUSTUM   342
    O BY THY FATHERS HEAD BY THINE OWN SOUL   • • •   71 SOHRAB RUSTUM   343
    AND TURND AWAY AND SPAKE TO HIS OWN SOUL   • • •   71 SOHRAB RUSTUM   346
    AND RUSTUM FOLLOWD HIS OWN BLOW AND FELL   • • •   73 SOHRAB RUSTUM   420
    SO RUSTUM KNEW NOT HIS OWN LOSS BUT STOOD   • • •   78 SOHRAB RUSTUM   574
    THINKING OF HER HE LEFT AND HIS OWN DEATH   • • •   79 SOHRAB RUSTUM   603
    FOR HE REMEMBERD HIS OWN EARLY YOUTH   • • •   79 SOHRAB RUSTUM   619
    OF AGE AND LOOKS TO BE HIS OWN DEAR SON   • • •   80 SOHRAB RUSTUM   632
    AND TURND AWAY AND SPOKE TO HIS OWN SOUL   • • •   71 SOHRAB RUSTUM V 346
    THOU TELLER OF SWEET TALES THINE OWN   • • • •   87 SICK KING BOKH   11
    NAY WERE HE THINE OWN MOTHERS SON   • • • • •   92 SICK KING BOKH   137
    BUT OTHER LOADS THAN THIS HIS OWN   • • • • •   92 SICK KING BOKH   153
    BESIDES TO EACH ARE HIS OWN FRIENDS   • • • •   92 SICK KING BOKH   155
    EAT NOT THE FRUIT OF THEIR OWN HANDS   • • • •   93 SICK KING BOKH   170
    THOUGH SIGHTLESS YET HIS OWN MIND LED THE GOD   •   97 BALDER DEAD 1   76
    THROUGH THE FAST-DARKENING STREETS TO HIS OWN HOUSE   101 BALDER DEAD 1   207
    TO KEEP HIS OWN LIFE SAFE AND SEE THE SUN   • • •   101 BALDER DEAD 1   213
    THEY SPAKE AND EACH WENT HOME TO HIS OWN HOUSE   •   101 BALDER DEAD 1   219
    HOME AND LAY DOWN TO SLEEP IN HIS OWN HOUSE   •   102 BALDER DEAD 1   247
    AND ALL THE GODS LAY DOWN IN THEIR OWN HOMES   •   102 BALDER DEAD 1   248
    SLEIPNER AND SLEIPNER WENT TO HIS OWN STALL   •   102 BALDER DEAD 1   266
    AND EVERY GOD WENT HOME TO HIS OWN HOUSE   • • •   106 BALDER DEAD 2   69
    BUT HOME HIS MASTER COMES TO HIS OWN FARM   • • •   114 BALDER DEAD 3   17
    HODER HIS BROTHER WHOM HIS OWN HAND SLEW   • • •   118 BALDER DEAD 3   165
    IN MINE OWN BREAST AND HAVE TO NONE REVEALD   • •   121 BALDER DEAD 3   287
    HODER THE UNHAPPY WHOM HIS OWN HAND SLEW   • • •   124 BALDER DEAD 3   384
    BUT ALL I LEFT OF MY OWN ACT AND FLED   • • • •   125 BALDER DEAD 3   405
    IN THY OWN HOUSE BREIDABLIK NOR ENJOY   • • • •   126 BALDER DEAD 3   449
    IN MY OWN BREAST AND HAVE TO NONE REVEALD   • • •   121 BALDER DEAD 3 V 287
    OF THEIR OWN COUNTRY AND CAN CLEAR DESCRY   • • •   123 BALDER DEAD 3 V 360
    IF ONES OWN HEART BEATS NOT LIGHT   • • • • •   138 TRISTRAM 1   265

578

OWN   (CONTINUED)

Text	Page	Poem		Line
THAN THE SEA-CHILDREN OWN	159	NECKAN		20
HER GENIUS AND HER GLORY ARE HER OWN	168	RACHEL 3		14
WITH HER OWN HUSBAND BY THE LIBYAN SEA	173	MONICAS PRAYER		8
AH WHO KNOWS HIS OWN	177	PARTING		74
WITH THE BLIND GUSTS THAT SHAKE THEIR OWN	178	FAREWELL		28
WITH THE BLIND GUSTS WHICH SHAKE THEIR OWN	178	FAREWELL	V	28
THIS TRUTH TO PROVE AND MAKE THINE OWN	181	ISOLATION MARG		29
OF ALL THAT WAS MY MARGUERITES OWN	185	TERRACE BERNE		40
DECLINES HER MINISTRY AND CARVES HIS OWN	195	FRAG ANTIGONE		6
MAKES HIS OWN WELFARE HIS UNSWERVED-FROM LAW	195	FRAG ANTIGONE		8
AND OUR OWN PLACE ONCE LEFT	195	FRAG ANTIGONE		18
EACH ON HIS OWN STRICT LINE WE MOVE	206	TOO LATE		1
FROM THE TWIN SOUL WHICH HALVES THEIR OWN	206	TOO LATE		4
FROM THE TWIN SOUL THAT HALVES THEIR OWN	206	TOO LATE	V	4
THUS SAITH THE LORD TO HIS OWN	216	LORDS MESSENGER		1
THEN SAITH THE LORD TO HIS OWN	216	LORDS MESSENGER	V	1
YET EACH WILL HAVE ONE ANGUISH HIS OWN SOUL	238	PROGRESS		31
IN THEIR OWN TASKS ALL THEIR POWERS POURING	240	SELF-DEPENDENCE		27
A CRY LIKE THINE IN MINE OWN HEART I HEAR	240	SELF-DEPENDENCE		30
A CRY LIKE THINE IN MY OWN HEART I HEAR	240	SELF-DEPENDENCE	V	30
AND WELL-NIGH CHANGE HIS OWN IDENTITY	246	BURIED LIFE		34
EVEN IN HIS OWN DESPITE HIS BEINGS LAW	246	BURIED LIFE		37
AND MANY A MAN IN HIS OWN BREAST THEN DELVES	246	BURIED LIFE		55
BEEN ON OUR OWN LINE HAVE WE BEEN OURSELVES	246	BURIED LIFE		60
YET A SOLEMN PEACE OF ITS OWN	254	FUTURE		77
AND WE SHOULD WIN THEE FROM THY OWN FAIR LIFE	261	SCHOLAR-GIPSY		224
BUT THYRSIS OF HIS OWN WILL WENT AWAY	264	THYRSIS		40
YET ON HE FARES BY HIS OWN HEART INSPIRED	269	THYRSIS		210
FOR THESE ARE ALL THEIR OWN REWARD	273	EDW QUILLINAN		5
WANDER UNQUIET AND MY OWN	275	SOUTHERN NIGHT		15
ALL PLAINT IN HER OWN CAUSE CONTROLLD	279	SOUTHERN NIGHT		122
TRUST ITS OWN THOUGHTS BEFORE YET	281	HAWORTH CHURCH		42
BLOWS FROM THEIR GRAVES TO THY OWN	284	HAWORTH CHURCH		89
HELPLESSLY GAZING ON THEIR OWN DECLINE	282	HAWORTH CHURCH	V	
TRICKLED IN SILENCE THINE OWN	296	HEINES GRAVE		126
EACH ITS OWN PILGRIM-HOST OF OLD	301	GRANDE CHARTR		62
THINKING OF HIS OWN GODS A GREEK	301	GRANDE CHARTR		81
AND EUROPE MADE HIS WOE HER OWN	303	GRANDE CHARTR		138
ALL SHIPWRECK IN THY OWN WEAK HEART	307	OBERMANN		19
WHO HATH RENOUNCED HIS OWN	309	OBERMANN		104
OF MY OWN DEATH BUT LAIAS WELL I HOPE	331	MEROPE		49
OF A VALIANT CHIEF TO HIS OWN	345	MEROPE		486
BUT ZEUS WHO ACCOUNTETH THY QUARREL HIS OWN	347	MEROPE		526
BUT EVEN OUR OWN HEART THAT NARROW WORLD	352	MEROPE		638
BOUNDED IN OUR OWN BREAST WE HARDLY KNOW	352	MEROPE		639
OF OUR OWN ACTIONS DIMLY TRACE THE CAUSES	352	MEROPE		640
OR OUR OWN WANT OF EFFORT BE THE BAR	352	MEROPE		643
THE STORY OF SPOTS MENTIOND TO HIS OWN	356	MEROPE		767
HE BROUGHT REPORT THAT HIS OWN EYES HAD SEEN	363	MEROPE		958
OUR MISERY MORE AND THINE OWN RUIN SURE	368	MEROPE		1081
DEALT AT MY OWN SOLE RISK BEFORE THEIR EYES	383	MEROPE		1354
OUR OWN RIGHT HAND IN THE DETESTED BLOOD	387	MEROPE		1468
MORE FOR THIS LANDS SAKE GRIEVE I THAN MINE OWN	398	MEROPE		1784
WHAT I HAVE DONE IS DONE BY MY OWN DEED	398	MEROPE		1787
LIVING HIS OWN FUNERAL-PILE	399	MEROPE		1834
LIVING HIS OWN SACRIFICE-BLOCK	400	MEROPE		1859
WHERE MY OWN YOUTH FALLS SHORT BUT LAIAS NOW	405	MEROPE		2016
THE FAITHLESS MURDERERS OWN NO OTHER TONGUE	364	MEROPE	V	
THOU HAST SOME WRONG FROM THINE OWN CITIZENS	411	EMPEDOCLES I 1		142
KNOW THAT AND HELP THYSELF BUT THINE OWN WORDS	413	EMPEDOCLES I 2		29
IN HIS OWN BOSOM DELVES	416	EMPEDOCLES I 2		130
ONCE READ THY OWN BREAST RIGHT	417	EMPEDOCLES I 2		142
FAILS THEIR OWN WILL TO PLEASE	417	EMPEDOCLES I 2		150
WHEN THY OWN LOT WENT HARD	417	EMPEDOCLES I 2		165
BUT WE ARE ALL THE SAME THE FOOLS OF OUR OWN WOES	417	EMPEDOCLES I 2		166
BAFFLERS OF OUR OWN PRAYERS FROM YOUTH TO LIFES LAST SCENES	420	EMPEDOCLES I 2		231
BUT OUR OWN ACTS FOR GOOD OR ILL ARE MIGHTIER POWERS	420	EMPEDOCLES I 2		241
HOW OUR OWN MINDS ARE MADE	423	EMPEDOCLES I 2		328
OVER THEIR OWN DEAR CHILDREN ROLLD	427	EMPEDOCLES I 2		446
KNOW THAT AND HELP THYSELF BUT THY OWN WORDS	413	EMPEDOCLES I 2	V	29
AND THE BEATING OF HIS OWN HEART	435	EMPEDOCLES II		214
OF HIS OWN BREAST FETTERD TO WHAT HE GUARDS	437	EMPEDOCLES II		269
IN ALL THINGS MY OWN DEADNESS	438	EMPEDOCLES II		322
TO OUR OWN ONLY TRUE DEEP-BURIED SELVES	440	EMPEDOCLES II		371
LIVED EVER IN THE LIGHT OF MY OWN SOUL	440	EMPEDOCLES II		393
FAR FROM MY OWN SOUL FAR FROM WARMTH AND LIGHT	440	EMPEDOCLES II		396
IF YOUR OWN HANDS THE GOOD BEGUN UNDO	447	WESTMIN ABBEY		103
EVEN TO A DATE BEYOND OUR OWN	451	GEISTS GRAVE		62
BY THEIR OWN CRIMES A LESSON TO ALL EYES	462	ALARIC AT ROME		11
THAT YOUR OWN HANDS MUST OPEN WIDE THE GATE	466	ALARIC AT ROME		117
AND YOUR OWN VOICE GUIDE HIM TO HIS PREY	466	ALARIC AT ROME		118
AND MINGLE WITH THY RUINS SOMEWHAT OF OUR OWN	470	ALARIC AT ROME		204
SOME LIFELESS SOULLESS PHANTOM OF THEIR OWN	474	CROMWELL		100
THAT FORM WAS HIS THOSE FEATURES WERE HIS OWN	478	CROMWELL		204
AND HE SHOOK HIS HEAD AND THUS ADDRESSD HIS OWN BOSOM		HOMER TRANS		8
NOR WOULD MY OWN HEART LET ME MY HEART WHICH HAS BID ME BE VALIANT		HOMER TRANS		17
BUSY FOR PRIAMS FAME AND MY OWN IN SPITE OF THE FUTURE		HOMER TRANS		19

OWND

FROM FAR AND A MORE DOUBTFUL SERVICE OWND • • • • 64 SOHRAB RUSTUM 127
ALL WHICH HE OWND AND PRAISED WITH GRATEFUL MIND • • 356 MEROPE 763
EXAMIND CLOSE HE OWND THIS STORY FALSE • • • • 365 MEROPE V

OWNER

AS IF THEIR BABY-OWNER CHASED • • • • • • • • 141 TRISTRAM 1 347

OXFORD

THE STORY OF THE OXFORD SCHOLAR POOR • • • • • 256 SCHOLAR-GIPSY 33
BUT CAME TO OXFORD AND HIS FRIENDS NO MORE • • • 256 SCHOLAR-GIPSY 40
THEE AT THE FERRY OXFORD RIDERS BLITHE • • • 257 SCHOLAR-GIPSY 72
SINCE FIRST THY STORY RAN THROUGH OXFORD HALLS • • 259 SCHOLAR-GIPSY 132
THE STORY OF THAT OXFORD SCHOLAR POOR • • • • 256 SCHOLAR-GIPSY V 33
TO-NIGHT FROM OXFORD UP YOUR PATHWAY STRAYS • • 263 THYRSIS 8
A TROOP OF OXFORD HUNTERS GOING HOME • • • • • 267 THYRSIS 153

OXFORDS

AND THE EYE TRAVELS DOWN TO OXFORDS TOWERS • • • • 256 SCHOLAR-GIPSY 30

OXUS

AND THE FOG ROSE OUT OF THE OXUS STREAM • • • • 61 SOHRAB RUSTUM 2
OF OXUS WHERE THE SUMMER-FLOODS OERFLOW • • • • 61 SOHRAB RUSTUM 14
FROM THE BROAD OXUS AND THE GLITTERING SANDS • • 64 SOHRAB RUSTUM 105
THE TARTARS OF THE OXUS THE KINGS GUARD • • • • 64 SOHRAB RUSTUM 117
BESIDE THE OXUS ALL THE PERSIAN LORDS • • • • 72 SOHRAB RUSTUM 358
BLEACH THEM OR OXUS WITH HIS SUMMER-FLOODS • • 72 SOHRAB RUSTUM 377
OXUS IN SUMMER WASH THEM ALL AWAY • • • • • 72 SOHRAB RUSTUM 378
BUT ON THE OXUS-SANDS AND IN THE DANCE • • • 75 SOHRAB RUSTUM 462
AND THE SUN SPARKLED ON THE OXUS STREAM • • • 75 SOHRAB RUSTUM 489
AND OXUS CURDLED AS IT CROSSD HIS STREAM • • • 76 SOHRAB RUSTUM 508
BY THE FAR-DISTANT OXUS HE IS SLAIN • • • 79 SOHRAB RUSTUM 601
THE NORTHERN SIR AND THIS GREAT OXUS STREAM • • 83 SOHRAB RUSTUM 765
THE YELLOW OXUS BY WHOSE BRINK I DIE • • • • 83 SOHRAB RUSTUM 766
LET THEM ALL CROSS THE OXUS BACK IN PEACE • • 84 SOHRAB RUSTUM 782
LET THEM ALL CROSS THE OXUS BACK IN PEACE • • 85 SOHRAB RUSTUM 807
CREPT FROM THE OXUS SOON A HUM AROSE • • • • 86 SOHRAB RUSTUM 868
THE SHORN AND PARCELLD OXUS STRAINS ALONG • • 87 SOHRAB RUSTUM 884
OXUS FORGETTING THE BRIGHT SPEED HE HAD • • • 87 SOHRAB RUSTUM 886
AND OXUS CURDLED AS IT REACHD HIS STREAM • • • 76 SOHRAB RUSTUM V 508
ON THE OXUS STREAM BUT CARE • • • • • • • 193 STRAYED REVEL 245

PACE

AND SHRANK AMAZED BACK HE RECOILD ONE PACE • • • 76 SOHRAB RUSTUM V 517
LONG SINCE WE PACE THIS SHADOWD NAVE • • • • • 305 GRANDE CHARTR 199
FOR BY NO SLOW PACE OR WANT OF SWIFTNESS OF OURS • • HOMER TRANS 50

PACIFY

BENT ABOVE ALL TO PACIFY TO RULE • • • • • • • 388 MEROPE 1490

PACING

LONG THEY STAYD STILL THEN PACING AT THEIR EASE • • 150 TRISTRAM 3 42

PACINGS

BUT THE SAME RESTLESS PACINGS TO AND FRO • • • • 242 SUMMER NIGHT 23

PACK

WITH HIS PACK ROUND HIM AND DELAYS • • • • • • 148 TRISTRAM 2 156

PADDLES

SLOW ROUND HER PADDLES DIES AWAY • • • • • • 276 SOUTHERN NIGHT 31

PAGAN

CHRISTIAN AND PAGAN KING AND SLAVE • • • • • • 311 OBERMANN 149
ON THAT HARD PAGAN WORLD DISGUST • • • • • • 315 OBERMANN MORE 93

PAGE

RAISE ME MY PAGE THIS CANNOT LONG ENDURE • • • • 130 TRISTRAM 1 3
IS MY PAGE HERE COME TURN ME TO THE FIRE • • • 139 TRISTRAM 1 298
I HAVE HAD DREAMS I HAVE HAD DREAMS MY PAGE • • 140 TRISTRAM 1 304
TO-NIGHT MY PAGE SHALL KEEP ME COMPANY • • • • 140 TRISTRAM 1 310
RAISE THE LIGHT MY PAGE THAT I MAY SEE HER • • • 142 TRISTRAM 2 1
PAGE AFTER PAGE OF MUSIC TURN • • • • • • • 224 EPILOG LAOCOON 103
PAGE AFTER PAGE OF MUSIC TURN • • • • • • • 224 EPILOG LAOCOON 103
AND LIVING AS THOU LIVST ON GLANVILS PAGE • • • 259 SCHOLAR-GIPSY 159
O OBERMANN THE SAD STERN PAGE • • • • • • • 304 GRANDE CHARTR 146
YET STAINS THERE ARE TO BLOT THY BRIGHTEST PAGE • • 463 ALARIC AT ROME 37

PAGEANT

THE PAGEANT OF HIS BLEEDING HEART • • • • • • 303 GRANDE CHARTR 136
NO PASSING PAGEANT BORN BUT TO EXPIRE • • • • 463 ALARIC AT ROME 34
TWICE HAD THE PAGEANT OF THAT VAST ARRAY • • • 465 ALARIC AT ROME 77
AND AS THE PAGEANT SWEPT BEFORE THEIR EYES • • • 467 ALARIC AT ROME 122

PAGEANTS

PAGEANTS HAVE PASSD AND TOMBS OF MIGHTY KINGS • • 445 WESTMIN ABBEY 53

PAGES

A FEVER IN THESE PAGES BURNS • • • • • • • • 307 OBERMANN 21
FRESH THROUGH THESE PAGES BLOWS • • • • • • • 307 OBERMANN 26

PAID
ARE ALL DEBTS PAID HAS ALL BEEN SAID • • • • • • 21 YOUTH AND CALM 8
THE DEAD HATH NOW HIS OFFERINGS DULY PAID • • • • 350 MEROPE 596
FOR THAT IN THIS MY WARNING THOU ART PAID • • • • 396 MEROPE 1765
BUT THAT IS PASSD HE WOULD HAVE PAID THY STRAIN • • • 409 EMPEDOCLES I 1 80
HE HATH HIS LESSON TOO AND THAT DEBTS PAID • • • • 429 EMPEDOCLES II 7
HE HAS HIS LESSON TOO AND THAT DEBTS PAID • • • • 429 EMPEDOCLES II V 7

PAILS
FULL-FOAMING MILK-PAILS ALPINE FARE • • • • • • 313 OBERMANN MORE. 17
OR BEAR PAILS TO THE WELL OF MESSEIS OR HYPEREIA • • HOMER TRANS 30

PAIN
TO PAIN TO DEATH THE BENT OF HIS OWN DAYS • • • • 6 GEO CRUIKSHANK 13
MEANS PARTING THAT ONLY IN ABSENCE LIES PAIN • • 19 MODERN SAPPHO V
DUE TO PLEASURE AS TO PAIN • • • • • • • 28 NEW SIRENS 60
FITS OF JOY AND FITS OF PAIN • • • • • • • 33 NEW SIRENS 206
REMAINING IN THY HUNGER AND THY PAIN • • • • • 42 GIPSY CHILD 12
THOU DRUGGING PAIN BY PATIENCE HALF AVERSE • • • 42 GIPSY CHILD 13
O MEEK ANTICIPANT OF THAT SURE PAIN • • • • • 43 GIPSY CHILD 41
A WEIGHT OF MEDITATION MIXD WITH PAIN • • • • • 41 GIPSY CHILD V 12
HOLDS ONLY PAIN • • • • • • • • • • 51 CONSOLATION 40
WHERE THEY STOOD ONCE TO THEM WERE PAIN • • • • 53 RESIGNATION 19
PAIN TO THREAD BACK AND TO RENEW • • • • • • 53 RESIGNATION 20
THIS POMP OF WORLDS THIS PAIN OF BIRTH • • • • 60 RESIGNATION 264
THIS PAIN ALONE WHICH MUST BE BORNE • • • • • 92 SICK KING BOKH 151
IN DIVERS PLACES IF THAT PAIN • • • • • • • 94 SICK KING BOKH 204
THE STORM THE ABYSS THE HOWLING AND THE PAIN • • • 109 BALDER DEAD 2 154
TILL THEN IN PERIL OR IN PAIN WE LIVE • • • • 111 BALDER DEAD 2 225
BUT NEITHER GOD NOR MORTAL HEEDS MY PAIN • • • • 116 BALDER DEAD 3 111
HE IS WEAK WITH FEVER AND PAIN • • • • • • • 133 TRISTRAM 1 85
WITH A WILD DELICIOUS PAIN , • • • • • • • • 135 TRISTRAM 1 151
AND HIS BURNING FEVER-PAIN • • • • • • • 136 TRISTRAM 1 182
TO OUR FORESTS TELL THY PAIN • • • • • • • 139 TRISTRAM 1 275
I WILL WATCH THEE TEND THEE SOOTHE THY PAIN • • • 143 TRISTRAM 2 30
POWER TO BE MOVED AND SOOTHED FOR ALL OUR PAIN • • 153 TRISTRAM 3 117
THAT JOPPAN LEPERS EASE WAS PAIN • • • • • • 158 SAINT BRANDAN 72
CHILDRENS VOICES WILD WITH PAIN • • • • • • 162 FORSAKEN MERM 16
IN THIS HER LIFES LAST DAY OUR POOR OUR PAIN • • • 168 RACHEL 2 10
AND LIFE AND OTHERS JOY AND PAIN • • • • • • 181 ISOLATION MARG 35
O PRINCE WHAT PAIN • • • • • • • • • • 192 STRAYED REVEL 211
SWELL THEIR LARGE VEINS TO BURSTING IN WILD PAIN • • 192 STRAYED REVEL 226
WITHOUT PAIN WITHOUT LABOUR • • • • • • • 194 STRAYED REVEL 274
GIVE HIM EMOTION THOUGH PAIN • • • • • • • 200 EARLY DEATH 16
WHAT TRIUMPH HARK WHAT PAIN • • • • • • • 200 PHILOMELA 4
THAT WILD UNQUENCHD DEEP-SUNKEN OLD-WORLD PAIN • • 200 PHILOMELA 8
ETERNAL PAIN • • • • • • • • • • • 201 PHILOMELA 32
OF THAT OLD PAIN • • • • • • • • • • 200 PHILOMELA V
AH LET ME WEEP AND TELL MY PAIN • • • • • • 206 RIVER 11
NOR CERTITUDE NOR PEACE NOR HELP FOR PAIN • • • • 212 DOVER BEACH 34
TO MONTH WITH WEARY PAIN • • • • • • • 212 GROWING OLD 25
ITS PAIN AND PLEASURE REST AND STRIFE • • • • 225 EPILOG LAOCOON 144
IN PAIN IN TERROR IN DISTRESS • • • • • • • 226 EPILOG LAOCOON 175
THESE SURVIVE YET NOT WITHOUT PAIN • • • • • 229 YOUTH OF NATURE 25
PAIN AND DEJECTION TO-NIGHT • • • • • • • 229 YOUTH OF NATURE 26
DARKEN IN LABOUR AND PAIN • • • • • • • 229 YOUTH OF NATURE 52
WEAK IS THE TREMOR OF PAIN • • • • • • • 230 YOUTH OF NATURE 92
TO GROW OLD IN DARKNESS AND PAIN • • • • • 234 YOUTH OF MAN 58
HATH WITHOUT PAIN SEEN NO RELIGION DIE • • • • 238 PROGRESS V 39
A TINGE IT MAY BE OF THEIR SILENT PAIN • • • • 244 SUMMER NIGHT 84
THE SOUTH WAS PARENT OF HIS PAIN • • • • • 275 STANZAS CARNAC 47
THY MEMORY THY PAIN TO-NIGHT • • • • • • • 276 SOUTHERN NIGHT 18
FILLD EUROPE ONCE WITH HIS LOVE-PAIN • • • • 278 SOUTHERN NIGHT 98
DEADEN THE INFINITE PAIN • • • • • • • • 283 HAWORTH CHURCH V
HALF BLIND PALSIED IN PAIN • • • • • • • 292 HEINES GRAVE 13
AH NOT LITTLE WHEN PAIN • • • • • • • 293 HEINES GRAVE 23
NOT TO HAVE YIELDED TO PAIN • • • • • • • 293 HEINES GRAVE 28
YE SOLEMN SEATS OF HOLY PAIN • • • • • • • 302 GRANDE CHARTR 92
AT LEAST THE RESTLESSNESS THE PAIN • • • • • 302 GRANDE CHARTR 104
THE SUFFERERS DIED THEY LEFT THEIR PAIN • • • • 303 GRANDE CHARTR 131
HERE ON ITS BED OF PAIN • • • • • • • 307 OBERMANN 24
IS FRAUGHT TOO DEEP WITH PAIN • • • • • • • 307 OBERMANN 38
ITS WARFARE WAGED WITH PAIN • • • • • • • 313 OBERMANN MORE 42
OR MAN MUST TOSS IN PAIN • • • • • • • 321 OBERMANN MORE 244
IMMEDICABLE PAIN • • • • • • • • • 323 OBERMANN MORE 316
PAIN AND CARE WITH A DARK STORE • • • • • 431 EMPEDOCLES II 86
PAIN HEROICALLY BORNE • • • • • • • • 454 POOR MATTHIAS 64
EBB OF LIFE AND MORTAL PAIN • • • • • • • 456 POOR MATTHIAS 124
THE SUN THAT ON THY TOSSING PAIN • • • • • • 482 COURAGE 21

PAIND
OF SOME PAIND DESERT-LION WHO ALL DAY • • • • 76 SOHRAB RUSTUM 504
IF HE FOR STRANGERS PAIND HIS HEART • • • • • 92 SICK KING BOKH 147

PAINFUL
SUCH HAPPY ISSUE CROWND HER PAINFUL CARE • • • • 46 IN UTRUMQUE PAR 34
IN WHAT IT HATH OF PAINFUL WHETHER NOW • • • • 359 MEROPE 864
HIS PAINFUL SOLEMN • • • • • • • • • • 399 MEROPE 1817
IN WHAT IT HAS OF PAINFUL WHETHER NOW • • • • 359 MEROPE V 864

PAINFULLY
    SO ANXIOUSLY AND PAINFULLY • • • • • • • • 36 VOICE 25
    WEDGED IN THE SNOW THEN PAINFULLY THE HINDS • • 107 BALDER DEAD 2 95

PAINLESS
    BUT PAINLESS SHALL A STROKE FROM FREA COME • • • • 103 BALDER DEAD 1 302
    PAINLESS AND SWIFT SET FREE HER AIRY SOUL • • • • 104 BALDER DEAD 1 340

PAINS
    ALL PAINS THE IMMORTAL SPIRIT MUST ENDURE • • • • 3 SHAKESPEARE 12
    ALL PAINS BEGUILED • • • • • • • • • • 40 STAGIRIUS 56
    THOUGH HE HATH BORNE IMMORTAL PAINS • • • • • • 56 RESIGNATION 151
    WHEN THE FIERCE PAINS TOOK HER IN THE FOREST • • 145 TRISTRAM 2 83
    THEY YIELD US NOT TO SOOTHE OUR PAINS • • • • 222 EPILOG LAOCOON 32
    BUT WE AN EASIER WAY TO CHEAT OUR PAINS HAVE FOUND 421 EMPEDOCLES I 2 271
    SAW THE CEDARS OF PAINS HILL • • • • • • • • 458 POOR MATTHIAS 199

PAINT
    PAINT THAT LILAC KERCHIEF BOUND • • • • • • 23 MEMORY-PICTURE 25
    PAINT THAT FIGURES PLIANT GRACE • • • • • • 23 MEMORY-PICTURE 33
    PAINT THOSE EYES SO BLUE SO KIND · • • • • • 24 MEMORY-PICTURE 41
    PAINT WITH THEIR IMPETUOUS STRESS • • • • • • 24 MEMORY-PICTURE 43
    TO PAINT ILL AS I HAVE DONE • • • • • • • • 24 MEMORY-PICTURE 51
    CANST THOU PAINT THE INEFFABLE SMILE • • • • • 231 YOUTH OF NATURE 113
    LIVES IN OUR EYES WHICH CAN PAINT • • • • • 233 YOUTH OF MAN 36
    THEY PAINT OF SOULS THE INNER STRIFE • • • • • 301 GRANDE CHARTR 53
    MIGHT PAINT THE CALM SWEET PEACE THE REST OF HOME 475 CROMWELL 113

PAINTED
    FROM THE RICH PAINTED WINDOWS OF THE NAVE • • • • 17 CHURCH BROU 3 5
    PAINTED HE WILLD IT IN THE GALLERY • • • • • 166 PICT NEWSTEAD 7

PAINTER
    BE PAINTER AND MUSICIAN TOO • • • • • • • • 225 EPILOG LAOCOON 130
    BUT NOT AS PAINTER CAN POURTRAY • • • • • • 226 EPILOG LAOCOON 182
    NO PAINTER YET HATH SUCH A WAY • • • • • • • 227 EPILOG LAOCOON 201

PAINTERS
    THE FAMOUS PAINTERS FILLD THEIR WALL • • • • • • 219 BACCHANALIA 2 8
    BEHOLD I SAID THE PAINTERS SPHERE • • • • • • 222 EPILOG LAOCOON 49
    CLEAR AS THE PAINTERS ART CAN DRESS • • • • • • 225 EPILOG LAOCOON 134

PAINTING
    AND THE WISDOM OF MANS PAINTING • • • • • • • 28 NEW SIRENS 75
    WHAT PAINTING IS WHAT POETRY • • • • • • • • 221 EPILOG LAOCOON 6

PAINTS
    AN EMPERORS GIFT AT EARLY MORN HE PAINTS • • • • 81 SOHRAB RUSTUM 674

PAIR
    THE PRINCELY PAIR ARE LEFT ALONE • • • • • 17 CHURCH BROU 2 39
    SO REST FOR EVER REST O PRINCELY PAIR • • • • 17 CHURCH BROU 3 1
    SO SLEEP FOR EVER SLEEP O MARBLE PAIR • • • • 18 CHURCH BROU 3 16
    AND IN A SANDY WHIRLWIND WRAPPD THE PAIR • • • • 75 SOHRAB RUSTUM 485
    THE CLOUD AND THE TWO ARMIES SAW THE PAIR • • • • 77 SOHRAB RUSTUM 524
    AND THE TWO GAZING HOSTS AND THAT SOLE PAIR • • 86 SOHRAB RUSTUM 866
    LATELY BELOW AND JOIND HIM AND THE PAIR • • • • 125 BALDER DEAD 3 434
    UNDER THE FEATHERD HATS OF THE SWEET PAIR • • • • 150 TRISTRAM 3 33
    BEHOLD O NATURE THIS PAIR • • • • • • • 232 YOUTH OF MAN 17
    PLACED SAFELY IN CHANGED FORMS THE PAIR • • • • 427 EMPEDOCLES I 2 457
    THAT PAIR WHOSE HEAD DID PLAN WHOSE HANDS DID FORGE 448 WESTMIN ABBEY 134
    AH UNHAPPY PAIR TO PELEUS WHY DID WE GIVE YOU • • HOMER TRANS 9

PALACE
    FROM YOUR DARKEND PALACE ROOMS • • • • • • 26 NEW SIRENS 4
    SEEKING CEILED CHAMBERS AND A PALACE-HALL • • • • 27 NEW SIRENS 40
    IN SUSAS PALACE PROUD • • • • • • • • • 47 WORLD QUIETIST 26
    TO CORNWALLS PALACE TO THE SIDE • • • • • • 132 TRISTRAM 1 V 61
    THE PALACE TOWERS OF TYNTAGIL • • • • • • 136 TRISTRAM 1 V 177
    IN TYNTAGELS PALACE PROUD • • • • • • • 146 TRISTRAM 2 115
    EVEN IN A PALACE LIFE MAY BE LED WELL • • • 168 WORLDLY PLACE 1
    MATCHD WITH A PALACE IS NOT THIS A HELL • • • 169 WORLDLY PLACE 8
    EVEN IN A PALACE ON HIS TRUTH SINCERE • • • 169 WORLDLY PLACE 9
    THY PALACE GODDESS • • • • • • • • • 187 STRAYED REVEL 44
    FORTH FROM THE PALACE HITHERWARD COMES • • • • 196 FRAG ANTIGONE 44
    THE UNFRIENDLY PALACE IN THE THRACIAN WILD • • • 201 PHILOMELA 18
    TOO MUCH OF PALACE AND DOME • • • • • • 214 NEW ROME 12
    SOME GIRL WHO HERE FROM PALACE-BOWER • • • • • 278 SOUTHERN NIGHT V 101
    A PALACE OF THE KINGS OF FRANCE • • • • • 300 GRANDE CHARTR 24
    LET US CONSULT BEFORE THIS PALACE SENDS • • • • 330 MEROPE 26
    MEANWHILE WITHIN MY FATHERS PALACE I • • • • • 331 MEROPE 47
    SOFTLY STAND BACK SEE TO THESE PALACE GATES • • 331 MEROPE 51
    WAILD FROM THE PALACE WITHIN • • • • • • • 346 MEROPE 496
    A PALACE DEFILED BY A DEATH UNAVENGED • • • 346 MEROPE 508
    A WHISPER THROUGH THE PALACE FLIES OF ONE • • • 361 MEROPE 914
    IN THIS BLOOD-DELUGED PALACE IN WHOSE HALLS • • • 366 MEROPE 1018
    IN THE DETESTED PALACE OF THY FOE • • • 367 MEROPE 1044
    EVEN IN THE DEADLY PALACE OF MY FOE • • • 375 MEROPE 1205
    SOFTLY STAND BACK SEE TOWRD THE PALACE GATES • • 331 MEROPE V 51
    NOR THE UNHAPPY PALACE OF THEIR RACE • • • • • 427 EMPEDOCLES I 2 441

PALACES
    THE COLUMNS OF THE HEAVENLY PALACES • • • • • • 19 CHURCH BROU 3   42
    THE RUIND PALACES OF ODIN SEATS • • • • • • 128 BALDER DEAD 3   533
    SOUTHERN PALACES STEPS • • • • • • • • 296 HEINES GRAVE   132
    SHE FLED HER PALACES • • • • • • • • • 316 OBERMANN MORE   132
    THY DEAD ARE KINGS THY DUST ARE PALACES • • • 464 ALARIC AT ROME   61

PALE
    HEMMD BY TWO BANKS OF CLOUD PEERS PALE AND WEAK • • 10 MYCERINUS   57
    WHO WRESTLES WITH HIS DREAM AS SOME PALE SHAPE • • 11 MYCERINUS   103
    PALE AND BREATHLESS CAME THE HUNTERS • • • • 13 CHURCH BROU 1   25
    LIFELIKE IN THE MARBLE PALE • • • • • • 16 CHURCH BROU 1   106
    ALL HER PALE SWEET-ROUNDED CHEEK • • • • • 23 MEMORY-PICTURE   30
    PLUCK PLUCK CYPRESS O PALE MAIDENS • • • • 30 NEW SIRENS   113
    PLUCK PLUCK CYPRESS O PALE MAIDENS • • • • 35 NEW SIRENS   269
    PLUCK PLUCK CYPRESS O PALE MAIDENS • • • • 35 NEW SIRENS   275
    DOWN THE PALE CHEEK LONG LINES OF SHADOW SLOPE • • 43 GIPSY CHILD   37
    DOWN THY PALE CHEEK THOSE LINES OF SHADOW SLOPE • • 43 GIPSY CHILD   V 37
    PALE DEW-DRENCHD HALF-SHUT ROSES GLEAM • • • 57 RESIGNATION   179
    SO THE PALE PERSIANS HELD THEIR BREATH WITH FEAR • • 66 SOHRAB RUSTUM   169
    OF HIS PALE WIFE WHO WAITS AND WEEPS ON SHORE • • 69 SOHRAB RUSTUM   285
    SO DEAR TO THE PALE PERSIANS RUSTUM CAME • • • 70 SOHRAB RUSTUM   290
    I AM NO GIRL TO BE MADE PALE BY WORDS • • • 72 SOHRAB RUSTUM   381
    OF HIS PALE WIFE WHO WAITS AND WEEPS ASHORE • • 69 SOHRAB RUSTUM V 285
    NOR LOOKST THOU PALE AND WAN LIKE MEN DECEASED • • 108 BALDER DEAD 2   109
    HELAS PALE SWARMS AND THERE WAS BALDER BOUND • • 108 BALDER DEAD 2   133
    WHAT KNIGHT IS THIS SO WEAK AND PALE • • • • 130 TRISTRAM 1   9
    BUT HER CHEEKS ARE SUNK AND PALE • • • • • 131 TRISTRAM 1   32
    LEAVING HER SUNK AND PALE THOUGH FAIR • • • • 132 TRISTRAM 1   48
    WATCHES PALE BY TRISTRAMS BED • • • • • • 132 TRISTRAM 1   75
    THY LOVELY YOUTHFUL WIFE GROWS PALE • • • • 138 TRISTRAM 1   269
    POOR CHILD THOU ART ALMOST AS PALE AS I • • • 140 TRISTRAM 1   312
    AND HER CHEEKS ARE SUNK AND PALE • • • • • 131 TRISTRAM 1 V 32
    THE LOVELY YOUTHFUL WIFE GROWS PALE • • • • 138 TRISTRAM 1 V 269
    WHEN SHE SEES HER HUMBLED PALE AND STILL • • 144 TRISTRAM 2   60
    STAY PALE QUEEN FOR EVER BY MY SIDE • • • • 144 TRISTRAM 2   68
    WHAT LOVE COURAGE CHRIST HE IS SO PALE • • • 145 TRISTRAM 2   80
    AS PALE AND STILL AS WITHERD FLOWERS • • • • 147 TRISTRAM 2   127
    AND ON HIS PILLOWS THAT PALE KNIGHT • • • • 148 TRISTRAM 2   166
    CREEPS THICKLY GROWS NOT HERE BUT THE PALE GRASS • • 150 TRISTRAM 3   15
    THE HEATHER DISAPPEARS AND THE PALE GRASS • • • TRISTRAM 3 V 15
    ITS SHELLS AND ROSES PALE • • • • • • • • 159 NECKAN   10
    AND THE PALE WEAVER THROUGH HIS WINDOWS SEEN • • 169 EAST LONDON   3
    SIT PALE BESIDE THEIR WEALTH • • • • • • 191 STRAYED REVEL   192
    MUST VISIT FIRST THEM TOO AND MAKE THEM PALE • • 193 STRAYED REVEL   246
    ROBS OF A LOVED BRIDE PALE IMPLORING • • • • 196 FRAG ANTIGONE   42
    OF BLOSSOMD CLUSTERS PALE • • • • • • • 200 PHILOMELA   V
    AND PALE DOG-ROSES IN THE HEDGE • • • • • 218 BACCHANALIA 1   12
    AND THE PALE MASTER ON HIS SPAR-STREWN DECK • • 244 SUMMER NIGHT   65
    AS THE PALE WASTE WIDENS AROUND HIM • • • • 254 FUTURE   83
    PALE PINK CONVOLVULUS IN TENDRILS CREEP • • • 255 SCHOLAR-GIPSY   25
    PALE BLUE CONVOLVULUS IN TENDRILS CREEP • • • 255 SCHOLAR-GIPSY V 25
    THE ORANGE AND PALE VIOLET EVENING-SKY • • • 267 THYRSIS   159
    UNDER THE FLOWERY OLEANDERS PALE • • • • • 267 THYRSIS   170
    THESE BRAMBLES PALE WITH MIST ENGARLANDED • • 267 THYRSIS   173
    AND WORDSWORTH AH PALE GHOSTS REJOICE • • • 271 MEMORIAL VERSES   34
    SHOWD ME THE PALE COLD STAR OF TRUTH • • • • 301 GRANDE CHARTR V 69
    WITH THE PALE CROCUS STARRD • • • • • • 310 OBERMANN   118
    THE CONE OF JAMAN PALE AND GREY • • • • • 313 OBERMANN MORE   31
    A PALE UNMEANING GHOST POWERLESS TO FRIGHT • • 366 MEROPE   1021
    WITH PALE-SPIKED LAVENDER • • • • • • • 392 MEROPE   1642
    PALE PHANTOM HOSTS LIKE SHADOWS FAINT AND FAR • • 476 CROMWELL   141
    THAT BROW SO SAD SO PALE SO FULL OF CARE • • • 477 CROMWELL   183
    TILL THE PALE MONARCH AND THE LONG ARRAY • • • 477 CROMWELL   197

PALED
    WHEN THE LAMPS ARE PALED AT MORNING • • • • • 35 NEW SIRENS   263
    THINND AND PALED BEFORE HIS TIME • • • • • • 134 TRISTRAM 1   108

PALENESS
    THE CHEEKS THAT STILL THEIR GENTLE PALENESS WEAR • • 175 PARTING   38

PALER
    THOU ART PALER BUT THY SWEET CHARM ISEULT • • • 143 TRISTRAM 2   25
    SEVERER PALER STATELIER THAN THEY ALL • • • • 331 MEROPE   57

PALES
    EMERGE AND RESTING ON THE MOONLIT PALES • • • • 261 SCHOLAR-GIPSY   217

PALFREY
    ON HER PALFREY WHITE THE DUCHESS • • • • • • 15 CHURCH BROU 1   93
    CLAD IN BLACK ON HER WHITE PALFREY • • • • • 15 CHURCH BROU 1   97
    ON HER WHITE PALFREY HERE HE MET HIS END • • • 154 TRISTRAM 3   162
    NODDED AND TIED HER PALFREY TO A TREE • • • • 155 TRISTRAM 3   212

PALFREYS
    HER PALFREYS FLANKS WERE MIRED AND BATHED IN SWEAT   154 TRISTRAM 3   171

PALL
        MATCH THAT FUNEREAL ASPECT WITH HER PALL . . . . 43 GIPSY CHILD   46

PALLADIUM
        WAS THE PALLADIUM HIGH MID ROCK AND WOOD . . . . 236 PALLADIUM   2

PALLD
        NOR PALLD WITH ITS OWN FULNESS EBBD AND DIED . . 12 MYCERINUS   116

PALM
        FROM PALM-GROVE ON TO PALM-GROVE HAPPY TREES . . 11 MYCERINUS   86
        FROM PALM-GROVE ON TO PALM-GROVE HAPPY TREES . . 11 MYCERINUS   86
        NOR WITHERD WHEN THE PALM-TREE PLUMES THAT ROOFD . . 12 MYCERINUS   118
        AT EVE BY THE PALM-SHADED WELL . . . . 252 FUTURE   37
        THE STRIFE WITH THE PALM . . . . 443 EMPEDOCLES II   466

PALMERS
        SANDALLD PALMERS FARING HOMEWARD . . . . 15 CHURCH BROU 1   77
        AUSTRIAN KNIGHTS AND MARCH-WORN PALMERS . . . . 15 CHURCH BROU 1   85

PALMS
        AND TO-MORROW FOLDED PALMS . . . . 33 NEW SIRENS   198

PALSIED
        IN GRAY AGE WITH PALSIED HANDS . . . . 14 CHURCH BROU 1   66
        PALSIED WITH TERROR BRANDAN SATE . . . . . . 157 SAINT BRANDAN   21
        ITS HEADS OERTAXD ITS PALSIED HEARTS WAS RIFE . . 261 SCHOLAR-GIPSY   205
        HALF BLIND PALSIED IN PAIN . . . . 292 HEINES GRAVE   13
        AND PALSIED ALL OUR WORD WITH DOUBT . . . . . 323 OBERMANN MORE   319
        AND PALSIED ALL OUR DEED WITH DOUBT . . . . . 323 OBERMANN MORE   V 319

PAMERE
        WHEN THE SUN MELTS THE SNOWS IN HIGH PAMERE . . 61 SOHRAB RUSTUM   15
        WHO COME ON SHAGGY PONIES FROM PAMERE . . . . 65 SOHRAB RUSTUM   134
        IN HIS HIGH MOUNTAIN-CRADLE IN PAMERE . . . . 87 SOHRAB RUSTUM   887

PAMISUS
        PAMISUS WATERING THE MESSENIAN PLAIN . . . . . . 330 MEROPE   19

PAN
        OR SOME YOUTH BELOVED OF PAN . . . . 188 STRAYED REVEL   80
        OF PAN AND THE NYMPHS . . . . 188 STRAYED REVEL   81
        WAS BREATHED ON BY THE RURAL PAN . . . . . . 249 KENSINGTON GARD   24
        WAS LOOKED ON BY THE RURAL PAN . . . . KENSINGTON GARD   V 24
        AND SCARCELY WILL THEY BUDGE A YARD O PAN . . . 406 EMPEDOCLES I 1   5
        WHEN JEALOUS PAN WITH MARSYAS DID CONSPIRE . . . 432 EMPEDOCLES II   128
        CAUGHT AS HE JOURNEYED FROM THE LIPS OF PAN . . 473 CROMWELL   40

PANE
        CHRIST WHAT A NIGHT HOW THE SLEET WHIPS THE PANE . . 130 TRISTRAM 1   4
        WE GREET THEE BY THE WINDOW-PANE . . . . . . 451 GEISTS GRAVE   47

PANES
        WHEN THE FROST FLOWERS THE WHITEND WINDOW-PANES . . 70 SOHRAB RUSTUM   306
        UPON THE WINDOW-PANES THE MOON SHINES BRIGHT . . 139 TRISTRAM 1   299
        AND WE GAZED UP THE AISLE THROUGH THE SMALL 163 FORSAKEN MERM   75
            LEADED PANES

PANG
        WHOM I MAY MEET AND STRIKE AND FEEL NO PANG . . 74 SOHRAB RUSTUM   444
        AH LEAVE US NOT THE PANG ALONE . . . . 302 GRANDE CHARTR   V 108
        CURSE UPON CURSE PANG UPON PANG . . . . . . 427 EMPEDOCLES I 2   447
        CURSE UPON CURSE PANG UPON PANG . . . . . . 427 EMPEDOCLES I 2   447

PANGS
        SEEK TO AFFLICT OUR FOES WITH PETTY PANGS . . . 111 BALDER DEAD 2   229
        THE PANGS WHICH TORTURED THEM REMAIN . . . . . 303 GRANDE CHARTR   132
        THESE THESE ARE PANGS WHICH MAKE THE MIND A HELL . . LUCRETIUS 2   16

PANIC
        PANIC DESPAIR FLEE AWAY . . . . 292 RUGBY CHAPEL   197
        AGAINST SURPRISE AND SUDDEN PANIC PROOF . . . . 381 MEROPE   1305

PANS
        THAN PANS FLUTE-MUSIC . . . . 187 STRAYED REVEL   67

PANTHEIA
        THOU HAST HEARD ALL MEN SPEAKING OF PANTHEIA . . 410 EMPEDOCLES I 1   108
        I ASKD HIM OF PANTHEIA YESTERDAY . . . . . . 410 EMPEDOCLES I 1   126
        PANTHEIA FOR I KNOW HER KINSMEN WELL . . . . . 410 EMPEDOCLES I 1   135
        IN TRANCE PANTHEIA LAY . . . . 416 EMPEDOCLES I 2   108

PANTHEIAS
        PANTHEIAS HISTORY HARK WHAT SOUND WAS THAT . . . 412 EMPEDOCLES I 2   8
        INSTRUCT ME OF PANTHEIAS STORY MASTER . . . . 412 EMPEDOCLES I 2   20

PANTING
        AND LATE AT EVENING SPENT AND PANTING FALLS . . 114 BALDER DEAD 3   12

PANTS
        AND TRAVAILS PANTS AND MOANS . . . . 422 EMPEDOCLES I 2   295
        AND STRUGGLES PANTS AND MOANS . . . . 422 EMPEDOCLES I 2   V 295

PARALYSING
    AND PARALYSING CONSCIENCE STOP MY ARM   • • • •   333 MEROPE   98

PARALYTIC
    OF PARALYTIC FACTIONS AND NO SOUL   • • • • •   282 HAWORTH CHURCH   V

PARAMOUNT
    WHERE HE WAS PARAMOUNT SINCE HE IS BANISHD • • • •   410 EMPEDOCLES I 1   123

PARCELLD
    THE SHORN AND PARCELLD OXUS STRAINS ALONG • • • •   87 SOHRAB RUSTUM   884
    HE PARCELLD OUT IN FIVE CONFEDERATE STATES • • • •   337 MEROPE   249

PARCH
    STILL SHARP AS EVER FREEZE AND PARCH • • • • •   56 RESIGNATION   131
    PARCH THEM IN WINTER-TIME ON THE BARE STEPP • •   193 STRAYED REVEL   241

PARCHD
    PARCHD AND ROAD-WORN WE MADE THAT DAY • • • •   54 RESIGNATION   81
    SLAKE THEIR PARCHD THROATS WITH SUGARD MULBERRIES   66 SOHRAB RUSTUM   166

PARDON
    OH YOUR PARDON THE UNCOUTHNESS • • • • • • •   27 NEW SIRENS   49

PARDONING
    THEN AT A PARDONING WORD RE-FURLD   • • • • • •   460 KAISER DEAD   57

PARENT
    GRAVE GAY CHILD PARENT HUSBAND WIFE • • • • • •   226 EPILOG LAOCOON   161
    THE SOUTH WAS PARENT OF HIS PAIN   • • • • •   275 STANZAS CARNAC   47
    WHERE WILL THEY FIND THEIR PARENT ELEMENT • • •   439 EMPEDOCLES II   347
    BOLD ACTIONS PARENT AND A PIERCING KEN • • • •   478 CROMWELL   229

PARENTS
    ORPHAND OF BOTH MY PARENTS BY HIS FOES • • •   385 MEROPE   1411
    FORTH FROM HIS PARENTS STEM • • • • • • •   418 EMPEDOCLES I 2   188

PARIS
    IN PARIS ALL LOOKD HOT AND LIKE TO FADE • • • •   167 RACHEL 1   1
    MURMUR OF PARIS OUTSIDE • • • • • • • •   292 HEINES GRAVE   10
    PARIS DRAWING-ROOMS AND LAMPS • • • • • •   296 HEINES GRAVE   141
    IF PARIS THAT BRIEF FLIGHT ALLOW • • • • • •   321 OBERMANN MORE   269

PARISIAN
    TRICKD OUT WITH A PARISIAN SPEECH AND FACE • • •   168 RACHEL 3   4

PARK
    TO SEE THE PARK-GLADES WHERE YOU PLAY • • • •   141 TRISTRAM 1   355
    OF THE CASTLE-PARK ONE SEES • • • • • • •   141 TRISTRAM 1   363
    ONE MORN AS THROUGH HYDE PARK WE WALKD • • •   221 EPILOG LAOCOON   1

PARLOUR
    THE SOUTHERN WINTER-PARLOUR BY MY FAY • • • •   135 TRISTRAM 1   164

PARMENIDES
    AND YET WHAT DAYS WERE THOSE PARMENIDES • • • •   436 EMPEDOCLES II   235

PARNASSIAN
    THE TEMPLE IN THE PURE PARNASSIAN GORGE • • • •   448 WESTMIN ABBEY   135

PARNASSUS
    OF PARNASSUS SNOWILY CLEAR • • • • • • • •   229 YOUTH OF NATURE   40
    WHEN FROM FAR PARNASSUS SIDE • • • • • • • •   433 EMPEDOCLES II   129
    OF THE ROCKS OF PARNASSUS • • • • • • • •   435 EMPEDOCLES II   201

PARNES
    OF PARNES WHERE THY WAVES • • • • • • •   197 FRAG ANTIGONE   62

PARSONAGE
    THE PARSONAGE-HOUSE AND THE GRAVES • • • • • •   283 HAWORTH CHURCH   65

PART
    WHO HATH A MONARCHS HATH NO BROTHERS PART • • •   46 IN UTRUMQUE PAR   39
    AND YOU WOULD SAY THAT SUN AND STARS TOOK PART • •   75 SOHRAB RUSTUM   480
    RESTORE HIM FOR WHAT PART FULFILS HE HERE • • •   110 BALDER DEAD 2   194
    YE GUIDING POWERS WHO JOIN AND PART • • • • •   174 MEETING   13
    AND PART MY HAIR AND KISS MY BROW • • • • •   209 LONGING   11
    TO CHOOSE IT RIGHTLY IS HIS PART • • • • •   223 EPILOG LAOCOON   87
    FAREWELL UNDER THE SKY WE PART • • • • •   312 OBERMANN   181
    THY PART IT WERE TO ADVISE AND MINE TO OBEY • •   331 MEROPE   34
    YET NOT FOR THIS ELSE MIGHT THY CRIME IN PART • •   339 MEROPE   314
    BUT THOU THE ZEALOUS BEARER HAST NO PART • • •   359 MEROPE   863
    WEAK WOMEN WITH A THOUSANDTH PART MY WRONGS • •   366 MEROPE   1013
    ART THOU THEN COME NEVER TO PART AGAIN • • • •   377 MEROPE   1221
    THAT HE ENJOYD BUT PART BEING HEIR TO ALL • • •   394 MEROPE   1701
    THEN PLAY THY KIND PART WELL FAREWELL TILL NIGHT • •   411 EMPEDOCLES I 1   167
    IF THESE HAVE BEEN THE MASTER PART OF US • • •   439 EMPEDOCLES II   346

PARTED
    IN HEAVEN WAS SELDOM PARTED FROM MY SIDE • • • 126 BALDER DEAD 3   460
    SING THEE TALES OF TRUE LONG-PARTED LOVERS • • • 143 TRISTRAM 2   31
    THE COMBATANTS ARE PARTED NOW   • • • 219 BACCHANALIA 2   10
    BEFORE MAN PARTED FOR THIS EARTHLY STRAND • • • 239 REVOLUTIONS   1
    SCANS THOSE PARTED LIPS THAT PURELY • • • •   META CLOISTER   37
    FREEZES THE SWEET STRAIN ON THE PARTED LIPS • •   FRAGMENT 1   7

PARTIALITY
    SHOWS PARTIALITY • • • • • • • • • • 52 CONSOLATION   73

PARTIES
    STILL TO ENQUIRE HOW PARTIES TEND • • • • • 47 HORATIAN ECHO   2
    THE BREACH BETWEEN OUR PARTIES HELP ME CLOSE • • 335 MEROPE   163

PARTING
    MEANS PARTING THAT ONLY IN ABSENCE LIES PAIN • • 19 MODERN SAPPHO   V
    ERE THE PARTING HOUR GO BY • • • • • • • 22 MEMORY-PICTURE   7
    ERE THE PARTING HOUR GO BY • • • • • • • 23 MEMORY-PICTURE   15
    ERE THE PARTING HOUR GO BY • • • • • • • 23 MEMORY-PICTURE   23
    ERE THE PARTING HOUR GO BY • • • • • • • 23 MEMORY-PICTURE   31
    ERE THE PARTING HOUR GO BY • • • • • • • 23 MEMORY-PICTURE   39
    ERE THE PARTING HOUR GO BY • • • • • • • 24 MEMORY-PICTURE   47
    ERE THE PARTING HOUR GO BY • • • • • • • 24 MEMORY-PICTURE   63
    ERE THE PARTING KISS BE DRY • • • • • • 22 MEMORY-PICTURE   V
    SO HAVE I HEARD THE CUCKOOS PARTING CRY • • • • 264 THYRSIS   57

PARTRIDGE
    AS ON SOME PARTRIDGE IN THE CORN A HAWK • • • • 73 SOHRAB RUSTUM   400

PARTS
    WE SCHOOL OUR MANNERS ACT OUR PARTS • • • • • 179 FAREWELL   45
    PARTS OF A SINGLE CONTINENT • • • • • • • 182 TO MARG CONT   16
    OUTWEARIED WITH THEIR LONELY PARTS • • • • 203 EUPHROSYNE   7
    WHAT THE PARTS AND WHAT THE WHOLE SHOULD BE • 210 SELF-DECEPTION   V 16
    OFTENER PERFORM ARIGHT THEIR PARTS • • • • 221 EPILOG LAOCOON   10
    AND NOT ITS SEPARATE PARTS ALONE • • • • 225 EPILOG LAOCOON   142
    OF PREGNANT PARTS AND QUICK INVENTIVE BRAIN • 256 SCHOLAR-GIPSY   34
    OF SHINING PARTS AND QUICK INVENTIVE BRAIN • • • 256 SCHOLAR-GIPSY   V 34
    KNIT ALL YOUR PARTS AND KEPT YOU ONE • • • • 320 OBERMANN MORE   223
    PARTS FROM THIS CAVE-PIERCED CLIFF THE SHELVING BAY 358 MEROPE   818
    PARTS FROM THE CAVE-PIERCD CLIFF THE SHELVING BAY 358 MEROPE   V 818

PARTY
    WHOM IN OUR PARTY WE BRING • • • • • • 289 RUGBY CHAPEL   115
    HE HAD HIS COUNSEL PARTY FRIENDS I MINE • • • 334 MEROPE   128
    HE ON A HUNTING PARTY TWO DAYS SINCE • • • • 364 MEROPE   973
    HE ON A HUNTING PARTY THREE DAYS SINCE • • • • 364 MEROPE   V 973

PASS
    DIDST PASS ON EARTH UNGUESSD AT BETTER SO • • • 3 SHAKESPEARE   V 11
    FOOL IF THOU CANST NOT PASS HER REST HER SLAVE • • 5 HARMONY NATURE   14
    AND OLD MEN DIE AND YOUNG MEN PASS THEIR PRIME • • 10 MYCERINUS   63
    THE DOOM THEY PASS REVOKE NOT NOR DELAY • • • 10 MYCERINUS   70
    FROM THE WALLD TOWN BEYOND THE PASS • • • • 17 CHURCH BROU 2   26
    PASS COUNTLESS MOODS • • • • • • • 50 CONSOLATION   10
    THEY RAMBLE LEAVING WHERE THEY PASS • • • • 55 RESIGNATION   110
    THEY PASS HE MINGLED WITH THE CROWD • • • • 57 RESIGNATION   162
    CROSSING SO HIGH THAT AS THEY MOUNT THEY PASS • • 66 SOHRAB RUSTUM   163
    WINDING SO HIGH THAT AS THEY MOUNT THEY PASS • • 66 SOHRAB RUSTUM   V 163
    IN SINGLE FILE THEY PASS AND STOP THEIR BREATH • • 66 SOHRAB RUSTUM   V 167
    THEIR KINE ACROSS A SNOWY MOUNTAIN-PASS • • • 107 BALDER DEAD 2   92
    RIDE ON PASS FREE BUT HE BY THIS IS THERE • • • 108 BALDER DEAD 2   134
    AND CANST THOU NOT EVEN HERE PASS PITYING BY • • 125 BALDER DEAD 3   400
    THE GENERATIONS PASS THE AGES GROW • • • • 127 BALDER DEAD 3   473
    FLOCKS OF HIS KIND PASS FLYING OER HIS HEAD • • 129 BALDER DEAD 3   561
    HER MOODS GOOD LACK THEY PASS LIKE SHOWERS • • 146 TRISTRAM 2   125
    THE RICH SHE HAD LET PASS WITH FROZEN STARE • • 170 WEST LONDON   8
    CREEDS PASS RITES CHANGE NO ALTAR STANDETH WHOLE • • 173 MONICAS PRAYER   12
    IN BEATING WHERE WE MUST NOT PASS • • • • 179 FAREWELL   51
    LIKE DRIFTWOOD SPARS WHICH MEET AND PASS • • • 185 TERRACE BERNE   45
    LIKE SHIPS THAT MEET AND SPEAK AND PASS • • • 185 TERRACE BERNE   V 45
    AND WATCH THEE PASS UNCONSCIOUS BY • • • • 205 CALAIS SANDS   28
    AND SEE THEE PASS UNCONSCIOUS BY • • • • 205 CALAIS SANDS   V 28
    RIOTING THEY PASS • • • • • • • 218 BACCHANALIA 1   33
    WHILE THUS MY FRIEND DISCOURSED WE PASS • • • 222 EPILOG LAOCOON   36
    HIS THOUGHT MUST FOLLOW WHERE THEY PASS • • • 225 EPILOG LAOCOON   154
    NO JOT NO TITTLE FROM THE LAW SHALL PASS • • • 237 PROGRESS   11
    HERE AT MY FEET WHAT WONDERS PASS • • • • 248 KENSINGTON GARD   13
    THEN TO THEIR HAPPY REST THEY PASS • • • • 249 KENSINGTON GARD   33
    HERE WHERE I LIE WHAT MARVELS PASS • • • • KENSINGTON GARD   V 13
    WHERE THE SNOWY MOUNTAINOUS PASS • • • • 252 FUTURE   9
    TO BATHE IN THE ABANDOND LASHER PASS • • • • 258 SCHOLAR-GIPSY   95
    STOOD WITH SUSPENDED SCYTHE TO SEE US PASS • • 266 THYRSIS   129
    THEY HUSTLE ONE ANOTHER AND THEY PASS • • • 262 THYRSIS   V
    WHEN FROM THEIR DUSTY LIFE THEY PASS • • • • 277 SOUTHERN NIGHT   59
    KNOCK PASS THE WICKET THOU ART COME • • • • 300 GRANDE CHARTR   29
    PASS BANNERS PASS AND BUGLES CEASE • • • • 306 GRANDE CHARTR   209
    PASS BANNERS PASS AND BUGLES CEASE • • • • 306 GRANDE CHARTR   209
    BEFORE HE CLIMB THE PASS • • • • • • 313 OBERMANN MORE   20
    THE GENTIAN-FLOWERD PASS ITS CROWN • • • • 313 OBERMANN MORE   21

PASS   (CONTINUED)
          IF THESE CONDEMN HIM LET THEM PASS HIS DOOM   • • •   349 MEROPE   557
          FOR ALL WHO PASS PURSUERS AND PURSUED   • • • •   349 MEROPE   582
          YE HAVE NOT LEFT THIS GATE WHICH HE MUST PASS   • •   361 MEROPE   917
          WHERE TRAVELLERS NEVER PASS WHERE ONLY COME   • •   373 MEROPE   1169
          STAND AND LET VENGEANCE PASS HOLD O QUEEN HOLD   • •   374 MEROPE   1198
          AGAIN FROM LIP TO LIP WILL PASS HIS NAME   • • • •   449 WESTMIN ABBEY   180
          THEN SOME WHO THROUGH THIS GARDEN PASS   • • • •   452 GEISTS GRAVE   73
          HOW SHOULD THAT MIGHTIEST CITY PASS AWAY   • • •   467 ALARIC AT ROME   129
          SO PASS WE ON BUT OH TO HARP ARIGHT   • • • • •   471 ALARIC AT ROME   223

PASSAGE
          THE PASSAGE OF THE ANGELS WINGS WILL HEAR   • • • •   19 CHURCH BROU 3   44
          IN THE STRAIT PASSAGE AT THE FARTHER END   • • •   107 BALDER DEAD 2   88
          IN THE STRAIT PASSAGE AT THE FURTHER END   • • •   107 BALDER DEAD 2   V   88
          AND HEAR THE PASSAGE OF A HORSE OF HEAVEN   • • •   125 BALDER DEAD 3   419
          WAITING HER PASSAGE   • • • • • • •   196 FRAG ANTIGONE   43
          PASSAGE FROM THEIR SOULS TO MAN   • • • • •   455 POOR MATTHIAS   98

PASSAGES
          HATH SOWN WITH CLOUDLESS PASSAGES THE TALE   • • • •   43 GIPSY CHILD   51

PASSD
          MAN AFTER MAN THE WORLD SMILED AND PASSD BY   • •   3 EMERSONS ESSAYS   6
          IS PASSD BY OTHERS • • • • • • • • • • •   52 CONSOLATION   69
          BE PASSD ON THE PROUD HEIGHTS OF SWAY   • • • •   56 RESIGNATION   149
          THROUGH THE BLACK TARTAR TENTS HE PASSD WHICH STOOD   61 SOHRAB RUSTUM   12
          THROUGH THE BLACK TENTS HE PASSD OER THAT LOW STRAND   61 SOHRAB RUSTUM   16
          HE PASSD AND TIED HIS SANDALS ON HIS FEET   • • • •   64 SOHRAB RUSTUM   97
          AND THEN A DARK CLOUD PASSD BEFORE HIS EYES   • •   81 SOHRAB RUSTUM   692
          AND TO THE MOSQUE MY LORD PASSD ON   • • • •   89 SICK KING BOKH   45
          THERE HE WENT UP AND PASSD THE OPEN DOORS   • • •   97 BALDER DEAD 1   87
          AND THEY CAME OUT UPON THE PLAIN AND PASSD   • • •   106 BALDER DEAD 2   65
          BUT YESTERMORN FIVE TROOPS OF DEAD PASSD BY   • •   107 BALDER DEAD 2   104
          BUT ALL HE PASSD UNHAILD AND REACHD THE THRONE   • •   109 BALDER DEAD 2   176
          AND THROUGH THE EMPTY STREETS HE RODE AND PASSD   •   113 BALDER DEAD 2   308
          BUT NOW THE SUN HAD PASSD THE HEIGHT OF HEAVEN   •   118 BALDER DEAD 3   154
          PASSD AMONG THESE HEATHS OF OURS   • • • • •   137 TRISTRAM 1   230
          BOTH HAVE PASSD A YOUTH CONSUMED AND SAD   • • •   144 TRISTRAM 2   54
          BOTH HAVE PASSD A YOUTH CONSTRAIND AND SAD   • • •   144 TRISTRAM 2   V   54
          BOTH HAVE PASSD A YOUTH REPRESSD AND SAD   • • •   144 TRISTRAM 2   V   54
          BOTH HAVE PASSD A YOUTH FORLORN AND SAD   • • •   144 TRISTRAM 2   V   54
          HE GAZED UPON ME AS I PASSD   • • • • • • •   158 SAINT BRANDAN   49
          PASSD OPPOSITE SHE TOUCHD HER GIRL WHO HIED   • •   170 WEST LONDON   6
          THE POPLAR AVENUE WAS PASSD   • • • • • • •   177 FAREWELL   5
          PASSD THROUGH THE CRUCIBLE OF TIME   • • • • •   184 TERRACE BERNE   36
          QUICK I PASSD FOLLOWING   • • • • • • • •   187 STRAYED REVEL   40
          FIRED THEIR RINGING SHOT AND PASSD   • • • • •   215 LAST WORD   11
          I ASK IF THOU HAST PASSD THEIR QUIET PLACE   • • •   257 SCHOLAR~GIPSY   65
          HAVE OFTEN PASSD THEE NEAR   • • • • • • •   258 SCHOLAR~GIPSY   96
          HAVE I NOT PASSD THEE ON THE WOODEN BRIDGE   • • •   258 SCHOLAR~GIPSY   123
          ONCE PASSD I BLINDFOLD HERE AT ANY HOUR   • • •   263 THYRSIS   24
          WHEN GOETHE PASSD AWAY WE SAID   • • • • • •   270 MEMORIAL VERSES V   15
          IN THE GLOOM OF NOVEMBER WE PASSD   • • • • •   286 RUGBY CHAPEL   19
          THE STRANGE GUEST SPARKLED NOW TIS PASSD AWAY   •   298 HEINES GRAVE   211
          IS A PASSD MODE AN OUTWORN THEME   • • • • •   302 GRANDE CHARTR   100
          AH IF IT BE PASSD TAKE AWAY   • • • • • • •   302 GRANDE CHARTR   103
          WHO PASSD WITHIN THEIR PUISSANT HAIL   • • • •   303 GRANDE CHARTR   124
          YET IN A TRANQUIL WORLD WAS PASSD   • • • • •   308 OBERMANN   67
          NO EASIER NOR NO QUICKER PASSD   • • • • • •   316 OBERMANN MORE   103
          NO LONELY LIFE HAD PASSD TOO SLOW   • • • • •   317 OBERMANN MORE   153
          DOWN CAME THE STORM OER FRANCE IT PASSD   • • •   319 OBERMANN MORE   201
          IT PASSD THAT ELEMENTAL SWELL   • • • • • • •   319 OBERMANN MORE   207
          I PASSD OBSCURE ALONE   • • • • • • • • •   321 OBERMANN MORE   262
          OF PLACES WE HAD PASSD SPORT WE HAD HAD   • • •   356 MEROPE   756
          AND THEN HE BADE REMEMBER HOW WE PASSD   • • •   356 MEROPE   774
          NOW TOLD BUT IN ONE FLASHING INSTANT PASSD   • • •   358 MEROPE   828
          PASSD YOU A LITTLE SINCE AS MORNING DAWND   • •   408 EMPEDOCLES I 1   46
          CROUCH IN THE WOOD FIRST TILL THE MULES HAVE PASSD   408 EMPEDOCLES I 1   50
          BUT THAT IS PASSD HE WOULD HAVE PAID THY STRAIN   •   409 EMPEDOCLES I 1   80
          CROUCH IN THE BRUSHWOOD TILL THE MULES HAVE PASSD   411 EMPEDOCLES I 1   166
          CHEERD US AND NOW IS PASSD INTO THE NIGHT   • • •   444 WESTMIN ABBEY   3
          PAGEANTS HAVE PASSD AND TOMBS OF MIGHTY KINGS   •   445 WESTMIN ABBEY   53
          SHE SPAKE AND FROM THE PORTAL PASSD AWAY   • • •   447 WESTMIN ABBEY   110
          BY WORCESTERS FIELD THE WARRIOR~VISION PASSD   •   476 CROMWELL   150
          PASSD LIKE A MORNING MIST IN TEARS AWAY   • • •   477 CROMWELL   198
          WHEN MY FLEETING SHADOW PASSD FROM THEE   • • •   482 THEKLAS ANSWER   2
          I PASSD TO-DAY OER WALTON HEATH   • • • • •   483 ROME~SICKNESS   5
          TO THE GREAT MAIN PASSD SEVILLE ON THE RIGHT   •   484 S S LUSITANIA   4
          WITH OMEN OH WERE THAT MOUNT PASSD I SAY   • • •   485 S S LUSITANIA   12

PASSED
          MAN AFTER MAN THEY SMILED AND PASSED ON   • • • •   EMERSONS ESSAYS V   6

PASSENGER
          THE UNKNOWN PASSENGER RETURNING STANDS   • • • •   445 WESTMIN ABBEY   43

PASSERS
          SCANT SPACE THAT WARDER LEFT FOR PASSERS BY   • •   107 BALDER DEAD 2   90
          SOULS BOUND BELOW MY DAILY PASSERS HERE   • • • •   108 BALDER DEAD 2   '110

PASSERS   (CONTINUED)
    AND PITEOUSLY HE EYES THE PASSERS BY   • • • • • 114 BALDER DEAD 3   16
    TOOTHLESS AND OLD SHE GIBES THE PASSERS BY • • • • 123 BALDER DEAD 3   334
    WHO ASKD THE PASSERS—BY FOR AID   • • • • • 157 SAINT BRANDAN   39
    ARE BUT THE CASUAL PASSERS BY WHO COME   • • • LUCRETIUS 5   6

PASSES
    IN THE WALLD CITIES THE WAY PASSES THROUGH   • • • • 193 STRAYED REVEL   250
    RAISED BY THE OBJECTS HE PASSES ARE HIS   • • • • 252 FUTURE   26
    SALUTES AND PASSES BY   • • • • • • • 283 HAWORTH CHURCH   V
    HAIL AS IT PASSES FROM EARTH   • • • • • • 298 HEINES GRAVE   204
    IN THE PASSES OF DELPHI   • • • • • • • • 344 MEROPE   463

PASSEST
    FOR WHOM AS I SUPPOSE THOU PASSEST HERE   • • • • 379 MEROPE   1271

PASSETH
    THERE ARE WHOSE GLORY PASSETH NOT AWAY   • • • • 462 ALARIC AT ROME   7

PASSING
    DOUBTLESS YOU ARE PASSING FAIR   • • • • • 32 NEW SIRENS   188
    OBEDIENCE TO THE PASSING DAY   • • • • • • 53 RESIGNATION   29
    SUDDEN AND SWIFT AND LIKE A PASSING WIND   • • • • 82 SOHRAB RUSTUM   724
    THAT SO THE PASSING HORSEMAN ON THE WASTE   • • • 84 SOHRAB RUSTUM   790
    WHO TELLS THE PASSING TROOPS OF DEAD THEIR WAY   • • 99 BALDER DEAD 1   150
    PASSING ALL HER YOUTHFUL HOUR   • • • • • • 131 TRISTRAM 1   39
    PASSING THE LONG SUMMERS DAY   • • • • • 137 TRISTRAM 1   222
    FOR SHE WAS PASSING WEARY OF HIS LOVE   • • • 156 TRISTRAM 3   224
    I SHIVER FOR THE PASSING DAY   • • • • • • 183 ABSENCE   3
    I SHUDDER FOR THE PASSING DAY   • • • • • • 183 ABSENCE   V   3
    PASSING OUT FROM THE WET TURF   • • • • • • 186 STRAYED REVEL   31
    PASSING THROUGH THE DARK STEMS   • • • • • 194 STRAYED REVEL   278
    THE PASSING GROUP THE SUMMER—MORN   • • • • 222 EPILOG LAOCOON   51
    HE COULD NOT WAIT THEIR PASSING HE IS DEAD   • • • 264 THYRSIS   50
    OF OUR BOAT PASSING HEAVED THE RIVER—GRASS   • • 266 THYRSIS   128
    WHERE THAT FAR SAIL IS PASSING NOW   • • • • 274 STANZAS CARNAC   34
    PASSING THE HOST FROM HAND TO HAND   • • • • 300 GRANDE CHARTR   42
    OF PASSING TROOPS IN THE SUNS BEAM   • • • • 305 GRANDE CHARTR   177
    MELT LIKE A PASSING SMOKE A NIGHTLY DREAM   • • • 402 MEROPE   1945
    THY PASSING BY DOTH VAINLY WAIT   • • • • • 461 KAISER DEAD   74
    NO PASSING PAGEANT BORN BUT TO EXPIRE   • • • 463 ALARIC AT ROME   34

PASSION
    BUSINESS COULD NOT MAKE DULL NOR PASSION WILD   • • 2 TO A FRIEND   11
    THEIR PASSION BURN MORE ERE IT CEASES TO BURN   • • 19 MODERN SAPPHO   14
    THE STRONG BAND WHICH PASSION AROUND HIM HATH FURLD   20 MODERN SAPPHO   22
    THE STRONG SPELL WHICH PASSION UPON HIM HATH HURLD   20 MODERN SAPPHO   V 22
    GERMS YOUR UNTRIMMD PASSION OVERGREW   • • • • 30 NEW SIRENS   138
    ALL FRANK FAITH WHICH PASSION BREEDS   • • • • 34 NEW SIRENS   230
    FROM GRIEF THAT IS BUT PASSION   • • • • • • 39 STAGIRIUS   33
    WIDER THAN ONE MANS PASSION THERES NO MOOD   • • • 50 CONSOLATION   V
    OF PASSION WHICH SUBDUES OUR SOULS TO IT   • • • 153 TRISTRAM 3   128
    HOW THIS FOOL PASSION GULLS MEN POTENTLY   • • 153 TRISTRAM 3   134
    ETERNAL PASSION   • • • • • • • • • 201 PHILOMELA   31
    WHILE WE FOR HOPELESS PASSION DIE   • • • • 202 URANIA   6
    OUR LABOURD PUNY PASSION—FITS   • • • • • 202 URANIA   14
    WHAT POWER OF PASSION WEALTH OF CHANGE   • • • 223 EPILOG LAOCOON   82
    ETERNAL PASSION—FRAUGHT AND FREE   • • • • 224 EPILOG LAOCOON   105
    PERENNIAL PASSION—FRAUGHT AND FREE   • • • 224 EPILOG LAOCOON   V 105
    NEVER BY PASSION QUITE POSSESSD   • • • • • 243 SUMMER NIGHT   32
    OF PASSION WITH ETERNAL LAW   • • • • • 270 MEMORIAL VERSES   11
    PASSION VEHEMENCE GRIEF   • • • • • • 284 HAWORTH CHURCH   95
    COME LIGHTNING PASSION THAT WITH FOOT OF FIRE   • • 367 MEROPE   1060
    THEIR LOYAL PASSION TOWRD MY FATHERS HOUSE   • • 383 MEROPE   1359
    HATE DUTY INTEREST PASSION CALL ONE WAY   • • • 383 MEROPE   1382
    INDEED THY LIFELONG PASSION AND SOLE AIM   • • • 404 MEROPE   1983
    THY FATHERS PASSION WAS THIS PEOPLES EASE   • • • 404 MEROPE   2000

PASSIONATE
    WHO WITH SUCH PASSIONATE WILL   • • • • • • 46 WORLD QUIETIST   7
    BE PASSIONATE HOPES NOT ILL RESIGND   • • • • 59 RESIGNATION   243
    AND A LOOK OF PASSIONATE DESIRE   • • • • • 240 SELF-DEPENDENCE   5
    STORY OF PASSIONATE LIFE   • • • • • • • 280 HAWORTH CHURCH   12
    HISTORY OF PASSIONATE LIFE   • • • • • • 280 HAWORTH CHURCH   V 12
    OF YOUNGER PASSIONATE SOULS   • • • • • 282 HAWORTH CHURCH   V
    PASSIONATE EAGER HIS YOUTH   • • • • • • 298 HEINES GRAVE   194
    HATRED AND PASSIONATE ENVY BLIND THINE EYES   • • 397 MEROPE   1772
    WITH PASSIONATE WARMTH WE CLASP   • • • • 424 EMPEDOCLES I 2   359
    ARE NOT THE PASSIONATE BREATH   • • • • • • 432 EMPEDOCLES II   97
    TO CHANT THY REQUIEM WITH MORE PASSIONATE BREATH   • 471 ALARIC AT ROME   227

PASSIONS
    ILL DEEDS ILL PASSIONS ZEALOUS TO FULFIL   • • • 11 MYCERINUS   76
    OF PASSIONS THAT FOR EVER EBB AND FLOW   • • • 37 YOUTHS AGIT   4
    BUT SO MANY PASSIONS FEEDEST   • • • • • SECOND BEST   V   7
    BUT SUCH FURIOUS PASSIONS FEEDEST   • • • • SECOND BEST   V   7
    HATH FREED FROM PASSIONS AND THE STATE   • • • 53 RESIGNATION   24
    BEYOND HIS PASSIONS WIDEST RANGE   • • • • 58 RESIGNATION   221
    TO HAUNT THE PLACE WHERE PASSIONS REIGN   • • • 181 ISOLATION MARG   17
    OUR PASSIONS FROM OUR BRAIN   • • • • • • • 183 ABSENCE   8

PASSIONS   (CONTINUED)
    PASSIONS FIRST FURIOUS LONGING TO IMBRUE • • •   387 MEROPE   1467
    WHAT ONCE HAD HUMAN PASSIONS HOPES AND FEARS   • •   464 ALARIC AT ROME   52
    THE FEARS AND HOPES AND PASSIONS OF MANKIND   • •   479 CROMWELL   232

PASSIVE
    PASSIVE AT THE NADIR OF DISMAY • • • •   33 NEW SIRENS   202
    PASSIVE AT THE MIDNIGHT OF DESPAIR • • • •   33 NEW SIRENS   V 202
    PASSIVE PERMITTING THEE WHAT COURSE THOU WILT   • •   333 MEROPE   96
    A PASSIVE ENGINE AT THEIR GENERALS WILL   • • •   382 MEROPE   1340

PASSIVELY
    NOR LEFT GOES PASSIVELY BY   • • • • • • •   295 HEINES GRAVE   91

PAST
    EVEN SO DO PAST AND FUTURE INTERTWINE   • • •   10 MYCERINUS   59
    FROM THE CASTLE PAST THE DRAWBRIDGE • • •   13 CHURCH BROU 1   7
    TO THE CASTLE PAST THE DRAWBRIDGE • • •   13 CHURCH BROU 1   31
    SOME EXILES MINDFUL HOW THE PAST WAS GLAD   •   42 GIPSY CHILD   25
    SOME EXILES MINDFUL HOW HIS PAST WAS GLAD •   42 GIPSY CHILD   V 25
    PAST STRAITS AND CURRENTS LONG STEERD THROUGH •   53 RESIGNATION   21
    OF ITS DARK UPLAND FARMS IS PAST   •   54 RESIGNATION   55
    ALL PAST AND THROUGH THE TREES WE GLIDE   •   54 RESIGNATION   58
    FAUSTA TIMES PAST WITH TIMES THAT ARE   •   56 RESIGNATION   137
    IS THIS THEN RUKSH HOW OFTEN IN PAST DAYS   •   83 SOHRAB RUSTUM   742
    RIGHT FOR THE POLAR STAR PAST ORGUNJE   • •   87 SOHRAB RUSTUM   880
    AND PAST THE HAVEN WHERE THE GODS HAVE MOORD   •   97 BALDER DEAD 1   74
    PAST MIDGARD FORTRESS DOWN TO EARTH AND MEN   • •   99 BALDER DEAD 1   142
    PAST MIDGARD FORTRESS DOWN TO EARTH THEY CAME   •   105 BALDER DEAD 2   23
    WITH GOAD AND SHOUTING URGE THEIR CATTLE PAST   •   107 BALDER DEAD 2   96
    IS ALREADY GONE AND PAST • • • •   136 TRISTRAM 1   174
    CHIDE NOT WITH THE PAST BUT FEEL THE PRESENT   •   142 TRISTRAM 2   7
    HE SEES FLOAT PAST AN ICEBERG WHITE • • •   156 SAINT BRANDAN   15
    HARK THE WIND RUSHES PAST US • • • •   176 PARTING   43
    OUR DIFFERENT PAST • • • • •   176 PARTING   66
    YET WE SHALL ONE DAY GAIN LIFE PAST • • •   179 FAREWELL   53
    DEAD BE THE PAST AND ITS PHANTOMS TO ME   • •   206 SEPARATION   12
    AND WEEP AND FEEL THE FULNESS OF THE PAST   • •   212 GROWING OLD   19
    THROUGH CENTURIES PAST IT HAS HUNG SO   • •   214 NEW ROME   19
    ALL THE CENTURIES PAST IT HAS HUNG SO   • •   214 NEW ROME   V 19
    SCATTERING THE PAST ABOUT • • • •   220 BACCHANALIA 2   35
    THE POET FEELS THE PAST AS WELL   • •   221 BACCHANALIA 2   66
    OF HIS RACE IS PAST ON THE EARTH   • •   229 YOUTH OF NATURE   57
    THE PAST RETURNS THEY FEEL • • •   235 YOUTH OF MAN   93
    COLD PLASHING PAST IT CRYSTAL WATERS ROLL   • •   236 PALLADIUM   11
    OF A PAST NIGHT AND A FAR DIFFERENT SCENE   • •   242 SUMMER NIGHT   13
    SO OFTEN HAS HE KNOWN THEE PAST HIM STRAY   •   258 SCHOLAR-GIPSY   118
    PAST THE HIGH WOOD TO WHERE THE ELM-TREE CROWNS   •   263 THYRSIS   12
    UP PAST THE WOOD TO WHERE THE ELM-TREE CROWNS   •   263 THYRSIS   V 12
    PAST THE LOIRES MOUTH AND BY THE FOAM   • •   274 STANZAS CARNAC   35
    CONSCIOUS OR NOT OF THE PAST • • • •   287 RUGBY CHAPEL   45
    OTHERS LIKE THEE IN THE PAST • • • •   290 RUGBY CHAPEL   154
    IN THE LONG-PAST WINTER HE CAME   • •   298 HEINES GRAVE   192
    PAST THE DARK FORGES LONG DISUSED   • •   299 GRANDE CHARTR   3
    PAST LIMESTONE SCARS WITH RAGGED PINES   •   299 GRANDE CHARTR   14
    SHE LET THE LEGIONS THUNDER PAST   • •   316 OBERMANN MORE   111
    BLOCKS OF THE PAST LIKE ICEBERGS HIGH   •   319 OBERMANN MORE   211
    THE PAST ITS MASK OF UNION ON • • •   320 OBERMANN MORE   225
    THE PAST ITS MASK OF UNION GONE   • •   320 OBERMANN MORE   227
    AS WHEN THE PAST WAS NEW • • • •   320 OBERMANN MORE   240
    AH NOT THE EMOTION OF THAT PAST   • •   321 OBERMANN MORE   241
    WAS PAST OF CHEERFUL YOUTH • • •   322 OBERMANN MORE   278
    HE BREAKS THE WINTER OF THE PAST   • •   322 OBERMANN MORE   285
    THOUGH MORE THAN HALF THY YEARS BE PAST   •   323 OBERMANN MORE   305
    PAST SONCHAUDS PINY FLANKS I GAZE   • •   324 OBERMANN MORE   337
    BUT NOW THE PAST IS OUT OF DATE   • •   321 OBERMANN MORE V 245
    HE MELTS THE ICEBERGS OF THE PAST   • •   322 OBERMANN MORE V 285
    PAST ARNE SPRING WHERE RHEA GAVE THE BABE   •   355 MEROPE   736
    PAST EXPECTATION HATH THY MURDERER BUILT   •   386 MEROPE   1435
    THOUGH INJURED PAST FORGIVENESS AS MEN DEEM   •   394 MEROPE   1707
    SON OF CRESPHONTES PAST WHAT PERILS • •   405 MEROPE   2021
    AND THE FEAST PAST ITS PRIME SO WE SLIPPD OUT   •   407 EMPEDOCLES I 1   37
    TILL THE ROUGH COW-HERDS DRIVE THEM PAST   •   413 EMPEDOCLES I 2   40
    OF LONG-PAST HUMAN THINGS • • •   423 EMPEDOCLES I 2   323
    AND WE SHALL FLY FOR REFUGE TO PAST TIMES   •   440 EMPEDOCLES II   383
    CAN EVER QUITE REPEAT THE PAST   • •   450 GEISTS GRAVE   27
    COMRADES OF OUR PAST WERE THEY • • •   453 POOR MATTHIAS   49
    PRESENT AND PAST THE LIVING AND THE DEAD   •   463 ALARIC AT ROME   44
    THOUGHTS OF THE PAST AND OF THE FUTURE TIME   •   467 ALARIC AT ROME   128
    FELL ON THE CHERISHD PAST WITH TEARFUL SMILE   •   474 CROMWELL   70
    OH THAT PAST TIMES COULD GIVE OUR DAY   • •   482 COURAGE   27
    SLOWLY PAST THE OPEN SPACES • • • •   META CLOISTER   5

PASTIME
    EVER IN THEIR OWN EAGER PASTIME BENT • • •   8 RELIGIOUS ISOL   2
    AND PASTIME OF THE GODS THE WISE DISCOURSE   • •   129 BALDER DEAD 3   541
    AND THROUGH THE GLADES THY PASTIME TAKE   • •   149 TRISTRAM 2   189
    NEWS OF MY BUSINESS PASTIME TEMPER FRIENDS   • •   380 MEROPE   1281

PASTORAL
NOTES OF WILD PASTORAL MUSIC OVER ALL	• • •	25	DREAM	12
RARE THE LONE PASTORAL HUTS MARVEL NOT THOU	• •	45	IN UTRUMQUE PAR	17
ON SOME MILD PASTORAL SLOPE	• • • • • • •	261	SCHOLAR-GIPSY	216
NURSED BY HIS PASTORAL FLOW	• • • • • •	313	OBERMANN MORE	28
AND PASTORAL HUTS I HID MY HEAD	• • • • •	321	OBERMANN MORE	251
OF PASTORAL ARCADIA WHERE A BABE	• • • •	330	MEROPE	21
THRICE ISSUED WITH US FROM THEIR PASTORAL VALES	• •	337	MEROPE	226
BUT IN THE PASTORAL ARCADIA REARD	• • • • •	388	MEROPE	1514

PASTURE
THE SHIAH DOGS WHO PASTURE SHEEP	• • • •	93	SICK KING BOKH	167
TO WINTER-PASTURE ON THE SOUTHERN SIDE	• • • •	107	BALDER DEAD 2	93
FEED IN THE OOZE OF THEIR PASTURE-GROUND	• • • •	162	FORSAKEN MERM	40

PASTURED
AS THOSE WHICH PASTURED BY THE SEA	• • • • • •	222	EPILOG LAOCOON	44
AS THOSE THAT PASTURED BY THE SEA	• • • • • •	222	EPILOG LAOCOON	V	44

PASTURES
THE VALLEY-PASTURES ONE BY ONE	• • • • • •	53	RESIGNATION	50
THE PASTURES AND THE QUIET TREES	• • • • • •	57	RESIGNATION	173
VINEYARDS AND CROFTS AND PASTURES BRIGHT WITH SUN	113	BALDER DEAD 3	300
THE SPRINGING PASTURES AND THE FEEDING KINE	•	258	SCHOLAR-GIPSY	108
O PASTURES OF THE MOUNTAIN	• • • • • • •	399	MEROPE	1822
TO THE HIGH MOUNTAIN-PASTURES AND TO STAY	• • •	413	EMPEDOCLES I 2	39

PASTURING
OF THE HIGH-PASTURING KINE	• • • • • • •	307	OBERMANN	32
WAYS FOR THE PASTURING KINE	• • • • • • •	312	OBERMANN MORE	16

PATCH
WHO CAN PATCH UNION HERE WHAT CAN THERE BE	• • •	336	MEROPE	192

PATCHES
WITH SCARLET PATCHES TAGGD AND SHREDS OF GREY	• •	258	SCHOLAR-GIPSY	114

PATE
SAND RAKED HIS SORES FROM HEEL TO PATE	• • • •	157	SAINT BRANDAN	47
LETS FROM HIS SHAGGY HIGHLAND PATE	• • • • •	461	KAISER DEAD	77

PATH
ON EITHER SIDE THE BLACK DEEP-FURROWD PATH	• • •	41	HUMAN LIFE	22
PRICK ME THE FELLOW FROM THE PATH	• • • • •	89	SICK KING BOKH	43
IN THE KINGS PATH BEHOLD THE MAN	• • • • •	90	SICK KING BOKH	94
NAY BUT I SWEAR FROM THIS THY PATH	• • • •	91	SICK KING BOKH	103
AND THROUGH THE SQUARE HIS PATH HE TOOK	• • •	89	SICK KING BOKH	V	49
NOR MUST HE CHOOSE THAT COMMON PATH OF GODS	•	99	BALDER DEAD 1	139
WHICH BORDERS THE SEA-SHORE A COUNTRY PATH	• • •	149	TRISTRAM 3	8
AND BROUGHT HER TALE TO AN END AND FOUND THE PATH	151	TRISTRAM 3	62
OUT OF THE PATH AND TAKE THE GRASS	• • • • •	222	EPILOG LAOCOON	37
EARLY SHE GOES ON THE PATH	• • • • • • •	283	HAWORTH CHURCH	68
WE WE HAVE CHOSEN OUR PATH	• • • • • • •	288	RUGBY CHAPEL	84
PATH TO A CLEAR-PURPOSED GOAL	• • • • • •	288	RUGBY CHAPEL	85
PATH OF ADVANCE BUT IT LEADS	• • • • • •	288	RUGBY CHAPEL	86
WHENCE DROPS THE PATH TO ALLIERE DOWN	• • •	313	OBERMANN MORE	23
DIZZY THE PATH AND PERILOUS THE WAY	• • • •	341	MEROPE	368
INTO THE NARROW PATH OF RIGHT	• • • • • •	353	MEROPE	672
GIRD THEE AND ON UPON THY FATEFUL PATH	• • •	465	ALARIC AT ROME	88
CROSS HIS LONE PATH OR SHARE HIS PILGRIMAGE	•	476	CROMWELL	162
THAT STREWD THE BLOOD-STAIND PATH WHERE EMPIRE LED	478	CROMWELL	226

PATHETIC
FROM WHOSE PATHETIC SOUL-FED SPRINGS	• • • • •	450	GEISTS GRAVE	14
O FOR THE CROON PATHETIC SWEET	• • • • • •	459	KAISER DEAD	11

PATHLESS
FAR OER THE PATHLESS WASTE OF LABOURING FOAM	• •	475	CROMWELL	114

PATHOS
MIGHTY THEIR PATHOS BUT TIS GONE	• • • • •	224	EPILOG LAOCOON	92
IT GIVES THEM PATHOS GIVES THEM POWER	• • •	227	EPILOG LAOCOON	200
ALL THAT HUMAN PATHOS DEAR	• • • • • •	454	POOR MATTHIAS	62

PATHS
AND BY THE DARKLING FOREST-PATHS THE GODS	• • •	106	BALDER DEAD 2	63
FOR IN THE PATHS OF HEAVEN HE IS NOT FOUND	• • •	116	BALDER DEAD 3	102
DIVIDING CLEAR THE PATHS OF NIGHT AND DAY	• • •	121	BALDER DEAD 3	265
UP THE STEEP PINE-PLUMED PATHS OF THE ESTRELLE	•	167	RACHEL 2	4
BUT FLY OUR PATHS OUR FEVERISH CONTACT FLY	• •	261	SCHOLAR-GIPSY	221
IF IN THE PATHS OF THE WORLD	• • • • • •	290	RUGBY CHAPEL	134
THE LEAVES ARE ON THE VALLEY-PATHS	• • • •	306	OBERMANN	7
BUT LEAD HIM THROUGH THE LOVELY MOUNTAIN-PATHS	•	411	EMPEDOCLES I 1	156

PATHWAY
TO-NIGHT FROM OXFORD UP YOUR PATHWAY STRAYS	• •	263	THYRSIS	8

PATIENCE
RATHER TO PATIENCE PROMPTED THAN THAT PROUD	• •	7	REP FRIEND CONT	2
THOU DRUGGING PAIN BY PATIENCE HALF AVERSE	• • • •	42	GIPSY CHILD	13
AND PATIENCE IN ANOTHER LIFE WE SAY	• • • • •	172	IMMORTALITY	3

PATIENCE   (CONTINUED)
  WITH CLOSE—LIPPD PATIENCE FOR OUR ONLY FRIEND • • 260 SCHOLAR—GIPSY 194
  SAD PATIENCE TOO NEAR NEIGHBOUR TO DESPAIR • • • • 261 SCHOLAR—GIPSY 195
  ONE VOICE PREACHD PATIENCE AND THAT VOICE WAS MINE 337 MEROPE 258
  PATIENCE WAS THENCEFORTH SELF DESTRUCTION I • • 338 MEROPE 266
  WITH PATIENCE ON THY FACE DEATH IN THY HEART • 367 MEROPE 1045
  OUR DASTARD PATIENCE BE OUR DARING NOW • • • • 367 MEROPE 1055
  NO PATIENCE TOO PROFOUND • • • • • • • • • • 419 EMPEDOCLES I 2 214

PATIENT
  NOT BY THEIR HANDS WHO VEX THE PATIENT GROUND • • 4 DUKE WELLINGTON 3
  PATIENT OF A LONG REVIEW • • • • • • • • • 30 NEW SIRENS 132
  BEHOLD HER HERE THE PATIENT FLOWER • • • • • • 132 TRISTRAM 1 72
  IN PATIENT DEEP DISDAIN • • • • • • • • • 316 OBERMANN MORE 110
  SAD PATIENT AND RESIGND • • • • • • • • • 321 OBERMANN MORE 254
  WILLING PATIENT TO ZEUS TO HIS CARE • • • • • • 348 MEROPE V
  THAT LOVING HEART THAT PATIENT SOUL • • • • • • 450 GEISTS GRAVE 9

PATIENTLY
  AND PATIENTLY EXACT • • • • • • • • • • 422 EMPEDOCLES I 2 297
  AND PATIENTLY DECLAIMS THE CURSINGS OF HIMSELF • • 422 EMPEDOCLES I 2 V 301

PATRIARCHAL
  THE SIMPLE PATRIARCHAL STATE OF KINGS • • • • 388 MEROPE 1516

PATROCLUS
  AND NOT LEAVE HIM BEHIND A CORPSE ON THE PLAIN HOMER TRANS 42
   LIKE PATROCLUS
  DID THE TROJANS OBTAIN TO STRIP THE ARMS FROM HOMER TRANS 51
   PATROCLUS

PATTER
  THE DROPPING PATTER OF A CHILDS SMALL FEET • • • • FRAGMENT 7 1

PATTERN
  BUT HIS THE PRIOR PATTERN HE DESIGNED • • • • LUCRETIUS 5 2
  HIS IS THE PRIOR PATTERN HE DESIGNED • • • • • • LUCRETIUS 5 V 2

PATTERS
  LOUD HOWLS THE WIND SHARP PATTERS THE RAIN • • • • 133 TRISTRAM 1 83

PAUPERS
  O LEARN OF LONDON WHOSE PAUPERS • • • • • • 214 NEW ROME 13
  BE MADE LIKE LONDON WHERE PAUPERS • • • • • • 214 NEW ROME V 13

PAUSANIAS
  PAUSANIAS ON HIS TRAVELS FOUND • • • • • • • • 221 EPILOG LAOCOON 16
  PAUSANIAS HIS SAGE FRIEND WHO MOUNTS WITH HIM • • 407 EMPEDOCLES I 1 25
  PAUSANIAS AND ON FOOT ALONE AND THOU THEN • • • 407 EMPEDOCLES I 1 30
  BUT OH PAUSANIAS HE IS CHANGED OF LATE • • • • 408 EMPEDOCLES I 1 67
  MORE THAN A DAY AND NIGHT PAUSANIAS • • • • • 409 EMPEDOCLES I 1 100
  SIMPLE PAUSANIAS TWAS NO MIRACLE • • • • • • 410 EMPEDOCLES I 1 134
  IS THIS PAUSANIAS SO • • • • • • • • • 415 EMPEDOCLES I 2 92
  COULDST THOU PAUSANIAS LEARN • • • • • • • 417 EMPEDOCLES I 2 157
  BUT THE DAY WEARS GO NOW PAUSANIAS • • • • • 427 EMPEDOCLES I 2 464
  MEANWHILE STAY ME NOT NOW FAREWELL PAUSANIAS • • 428 EMPEDOCLES I 2 478
  PAUSANIAS IS FAR HENCE AND THAT IS WELL • • • • 429 EMPEDOCLES II 5

PAUSANIUS
  LISTEN PAUSANIUS AY TIS CALLICLES • • • • • • 413 EMPEDOCLES I 2 34

PAUSE
  AND TURNING LEFT THEM THERE AND WITH BRIEF PAUSE • • 11 MYCERINUS 82
  LET ME PAUSE LET ME STRIVE IN MYSELF MAKE SOME ORDER 19 MODERN SAPPHO 7
  LET ME PAUSE LET ME STRIVE IN MYSELF FIND SOME ORDER 19 MODERN SAPPHO V 7
  AT A PAUSE OF SIREN VOICINGS • • • • • • • 27 NEW SIRENS 47
  NO PAUSE ITS ACTION KNEW • • • • • • • • • • 315 OBERMANN MORE 88
  WE PAUSE WE HUSH OUR HEART • • • • • • • • 424 EMPEDOCLES I 2 372

PAUSEFULLY
  LAID PAUSEFULLY UPON LIFES HEADLONG TRAIN • • • • 266 THYRSIS 137

PAUSES
  OF SUDDEN STIRS AND PAUSES FAIR • • • • • • 223 EPILOG LAOCOON 64
  THIS WAY MOVES AND PAUSES GAZES • • • • • • META CLOISTER 11
  THIS WAY MOVES AND PAUSES GAZING • • • • • • META CLOISTER V 11

PAUSING
  TO THE JUST—PAUSING GENIUS WE REMIT • • • • • • 259 SCHOLAR—GIPSY 149

PAVED
  THROUGH THE NARROW PAVED STREETS WHERE ALL WAS STILL 163 FORSAKEN MERM 70

PAVEMENT
  AND ON THE PAVEMENT ROUND THE TOMB THERE GLINTS • • 18 CHURCH BROU 3 22
  BEHOLD THE PAVEMENT OF THE COURTS OF HEAVEN • • 18 CHURCH BROU 3 31
  A PAVEMENT OF PEARL • • • • • • • • • • 165 FORSAKEN MERM 119
  CROUCHD ON THE PAVEMENT CLOSE BY BELGRAVE SQUARE • • 169 WEST LONDON 1

PAVES
  MOUNTAIN GREENSWARD PAVES THE CHANCEL • • • • 15 CHURCH BROU 1 71

PAVILION

    JUST PITCHD THE HIGH PAVILION IN THE MIDST • • • • 67 SOHRAB RUSTUM 193
    NEW PITCHD THE HIGH PAVILION IN THE MIDST • • • • 67 SOHRAB RUSTUM V 193

PAWS

    WE STROKE THY BROAD BROWN PAWS AGAIN • • • • • • 451 GEISTS GRAVE 45

PAY

    THESE MOURN NOT THAT THEIR GOINGS PAY • • • • 53 RESIGNATION 28
    TO-MORROW COME AND YE SHALL PAY • • • • • 87 SICK KING BOKH 7
    AND PAY HER HOMAGE AND ENTREAT WITH PRAYERS • 100 BALDER DEAD 1 179
    FOR THEN THE NIGHT WILL MORE THAN PAY • • • 208 LONGING 3
    FOR THEN THE NIGHT WILL MORE THAN PAY • • • 209 LONGING 15
    FOR SO THE NIGHT WILL MORE THAN PAY • • • • • 208 LONGING V
    FIRST TO THE LIVING WE PAY • • • • • • • 281 HAWORTH CHURCH 34
    NOR PAY HIS BROTHERS DEBT • • • • • • • 318 OBERMANN MORE V
    NOT SO THY HEART WOULD PAY ITS MOMENTS SPEECH • 332 MEROPE 61
    THAT OUR JOINT HANDS MIGHT THEN TOGETHER PAY • 367 MEROPE 1047
    EVERY MORNING DID WE PAY • • • • • • • • • 455 POOR MATTHIAS 111

PAYS

    KNOWING HE DID IT UNKNOWING PAYS FOR IT • • • • 400 MEROPE 1870

PEACE

    BUT FOR PEACE HER SOUL WAS YEARNING • • • • • 21 REQUIESCAT 11
    AND NOW PEACE LAPS HER ROUND • • • • • • • 21 REQUIESCAT 12
    TIS DEATH AND PEACE INDEED IS HERE • • • • • 21 YOUTH AND CALM 1
    BUT AH THOUGH PEACE AND REST FROM FEAR • • • 21 YOUTH AND CALM V 2
    WHO WILL NOT MOUNT IN PEACE BUT LOVE • • • • HORATIAN ECHO V
    WHOSE SECRET IS NOT JOY BUT PEACE • • • • • 58 RESIGNATION 192
    SEEK HIM IN PEACE AND CARRY TO HIS ARMS • • • 63 SOHRAB RUSTUM 76
    TO US FAIN THEREFORE SEND THEE HENCE IN PEACE • 63 SOHRAB RUSTUM 89
    BUT OH LET THERE BE PEACE TWIXT THEE AND ME • 74 SOHRAB RUSTUM 447
    LET THEM ALL CROSS THE OXUS BACK IN PEACE • • • 84 SOHRAB RUSTUM 782
    LET THEM ALL CROSS THE OXUS BACK IN PEACE • • • 85 SOHRAB RUSTUM 807
    BUT THOU SHALT YET HAVE PEACE ONLY NOT NOW • • 85 SOHRAB RUSTUM 829
    PEACE LEST OUR FATHER ODIN HEAR THEE GIBE • • • 114 BALDER DEAD 3 23
    WHO THEN SHALL LIVE IN PEACE AS NOW IN WAR • • • 128 BALDER DEAD 3 531
    THE GENTLENESS THE THIRST FOR PEACE • • • • • 180 FAREWELL 84
    THE THIRST FOR PEACE A RAVING WORLD • • • • • 180 FAREWELL 87
    NOR CERTITUDE NOR PEACE NOR HELP FOR PAIN • • • 212 DOVER BEACH 34
    CARRY MY PEACE UPON EARTH • • • • • • • 216 LORDS MESSENGER 6
    AND THEY ARE SILENT AND AT PEACE • • • • • 226 EPILOG LAOCOON 186
    THAT PEACE HAS LEFT THE UPPER WORLD • • • • 249 KENSINGTON GARD 27
    YET HERE IS PEACE FOR EVER NEW • • • • • • 249 KENSINGTON GARD 29
    THAT THERE ABIDES A PEACE OF THINE • • • • • 249 KENSINGTON GARD 39
    THAT THERE SUBSISTS A PEACE OF THINE • • • • • KENSINGTON GARD V 39
    YET A SOLEMN PEACE OF ITS OWN • • • • • • 254 FUTURE 77
    PEACE TO THE SOUL OF THE MAN ON ITS BREAST • • 254 FUTURE 82
    POISONS THE PEACE OF THY GRAVE • • • • • • 294 HEINES GRAVE 69
    MAYST THOU THE RAPTURE OF PEACE • • • • • 299 HEINES GRAVE 229
    AND LEAVE OUR DESERT TO ITS PEACE • • • • • 306 GRANDE CHARTR 210
    AND LEAVE OUR FOREST TO ITS PEACE • • • • • 306 GRANDE CHARTR V 210
    PEACE PEACE IS WHAT I SEEK AND PUBLIC CALM • • • 333 MEROPE 101
    PEACE PEACE IS WHAT I SEEK AND PUBLIC CALM • • • 333 MEROPE 101
    TOO WIDE AT VARIANCE WITH THE PEACE I SEEK • • • 333 MEROPE 107
    HENCEFORTH BE HONOURD AS THE DATE OF PEACE • • • 333 MEROPE 116
    FOR THAT DESTROYD HIM GIVE THEM PEACE THOU CANST • 335 MEROPE 176
    THOU STANDEST OUT I SEE REPELLEST PEACE • • • 341 MEROPE 354
    OF PEACE AND BEEN REPULSED WITH HATE AND SCORN • 360 MEROPE 881
    A PRIVATE LOSS HERE FOUNDS A NATIONS PEACE • • 360 MEROPE 889
    PEACE WHO TARRIEST TOO LONG • • • • • • • 360 MEROPE 890
    PEACE WITH DELIGHT IN THY TRAIN • • • • • 360 MEROPE 891
    LET HER COME FAIR PEACE LET HER COME • • • • 361 MEROPE 908
    PEACE PEACE ALLS CLEAR THE WICKED WATCH AND WORK • 365 MEROPE 995
    PEACE PEACE ALLS CLEAR THE WICKED WATCH AND WORK • 365 MEROPE 995
    PERMIT NO PEACE TILL YOUR BEHESTS ARE DONE • • • 367 MEROPE 1057
    PEACE WHAT IS IT ALAS • • • • • • • • 368 MEROPE 1086
    APPOINTS THE WAY TO PEACE THROUGH SHEDDING BLOOD • 378 MEROPE 1248
    SORROWFUL PEACE • • • • • • • • • • 378 MEROPE 1249
    AND YET THE ONLY PEACE TO US ALLOWD • • • • 378 MEROPE 1250
    TO WHOM THIS DAY HE CAME TO PROFFER PEACE • • • 387 MEROPE 1482
    AND GRANT HENCEFORTH TO THE MESSENIANS PEACE • • 402 MEROPE 1917
    HIS KINSMAN HIS RIGHT HAND IN PEACE AND WAR • • 403 MEROPE 1974
    WE WOULD HAVE INWARD PEACE • • • • • • • 420 EMPEDOCLES I 2 232
    THE PEACE OF CHILDHOOD AND THE THOUGHTS THAT ROAM • 474 CROMWELL 73
    MIGHT PAINT THE CALM SWEET PEACE THE REST OF HOME • 475 CROMWELL 113
    PEACE THAT RECALLD HIS CHILDISH HOURS ANEW • • • 475 CROMWELL 115
    SHOOK BACK HIS TANGLED LOCKS AND MURMURD PEACE • 477 CROMWELL 174
    YOU SAY TRUE MY DAUGHTER PEACE IS HERE • • • • META CLOISTER 40

PEACEFUL

    AND LET THE PEACEFUL BE • • • • • • • • • 174 MEETING 16
    SUCH PEACEFUL GRAVES • • • • • • • • • 277 SOUTHERN NIGHT 60
    EARTHS OLD HEROIC FORMS IN PEACEFUL SLUMBERS DEEP • 464 ALARIC AT ROME 60
    AND PEACEFUL JOYS AND GENTLER THOUGHTS SWEPT BY • • 474 CROMWELL 71

PEACEFULLY

    THUS PEACEFULLY DO YE LET SINNERS SLEEP • • • • 372 MEROPE 1154

PEAK
THE PEAK OF JAMAN STOOD . . . . 323 OBERMANN MORE 332
SLOPE BEHIND SLOPE UP TO THE PEAK LIES BARE . . 414 EMPEDOCLES I 2 55
THE PEAK ROUND WHICH THE WHITE CLOUDS PLAY . . . . 414 EMPEDOCLES I 2 56
CROWND BY THE AWFUL PEAK ETNAS GREAT MOUTH . . . . 429 EMPEDOCLES II 3

PEAKS
OR CLUSTERD PEAKS WITH PLUNGING GULFS BETWEEN . . 4 BUTLERS SERMONS 11
ALL THE FRORE PEAKS AWFUL CROWN . . . . . . 31 NEW SIRENS 144
THE SOLEMN PEAKS BUT TO THE STARS ARE KNOWN . . 45 IN UTRUMQUE PAR 18
ITS WHITE PEAKS IN AIR . . . . 175 PARTING 14
ITS FIRS AND AFAR ROSE THE PEAKS . . . . . 229 YOUTH OF NATURE 39
FADE FROM THE DISTANT PEAKS OF SNOW . . . . 310 OBERMANN 123
SOUTHWARD AND WEST BEHOLD THOSE SNOWY PEAKS . . 330 MEROPE 16
THENCE TO THE SOUTH BEHOLD THOSE SNOWY PEAKS . . 330 MEROPE V 16
AND THE WHITE OLYMPUS-PEAKS . . . . 431 EMPEDOCLES II 80
OF THE MOONLIT PEAKS AND THE CAVES . . . . . 435 EMPEDOCLES II 203

PEAL
BY NIGHT WITH BOISTEROUS BUGLE-PEAL . . . . . 148 TRISTRAM 2 177
THEN HUSH THOU BOISTEROUS BUGLE-PEAL . . . . . 149 TRISTRAM 2 182
THE CHAPEL WHERE NO ORGANS PEAL . . . . . 300 GRANDE CHARTR 37

PEALD
A VOICE ORACULAR HATH PEALD TO-DAY . . . . . 3 EMERSONS ESSAYS 3
APOLLO PEALD IT FROM HIS DELPHIAN CAVE . . . . 385 MEROPE 1401

PEALING
THROW HIM A PEALING WORD OF SUMMONS DOWN . . . . 349 MEROPE 576

PEALS
AND WHEN THE CLOCK PEALS MIDNIGHT SHE WILL MOVE . . 152 TRISTRAM 3 86

PEARL
A PAVEMENT OF PEARL . . . . 165 FORSAKEN MERM 119

PEARLED
WHEN THE DEW GLISTENS ON THE PEARLED EARS . . . . 65 SOHRAB RUSTUM 155

PEARLS
HAVING MADE UP HIS TALE OF PRECIOUS PEARLS . . . 69 SOHRAB RUSTUM 288
STRUNG LIKE WHITE STARS THE PEARLS STILL ARE . . 146 TRISTRAM 2 109

PEASANT
THE EARLY PEASANT STILL RECALLS . . . . . . 311 OBERMANN 171

PEASANTS
THE ALPINE PEASANTS TWO AND THREE . . . . . 17 CHURCH BROU 2 18
AND WIDEN AND THE PEASANTS HEART IS GLAD . . . 122 BALDER DEAD 3 316

PEBBLES
OF PEBBLES WHICH THE WAVES DRAW BACK AND FLING . . 211 DOVER BEACH 10
OF PEBBLES WHICH THE WAVES SUCK BACK AND FLING . . 211 DOVER BEACH V 10

PEBBLY
AND THROUGH THE BRUSHWOOD TO THE PEBBLY STRAND . . 357 MEROPE 807

PEDLARS
BUT AS A TROOP OF PEDLARS FROM CABOOL . . . . 65 SOHRAB RUSTUM 160

PEEP
OF GRASS PEEP OUT AMID SURROUNDING SNOW . . . 122 BALDER DEAD 3 315
HARDLY LETS PEEP THE GOLDEN HAIR . . . . . 141 TRISTRAM 1 341
THROUGH THE THICK CORN THE SCARLET POPPIES PEEP . . 255 SCHOLAR-GIPSY 23

PEER
WHO RATES US IF WE PEER OUTSIDE OUR PEN . . . . 169 WORLDLY PLACE 7

PEERD
UNDER THE EAVES PEERD ROWS OF INDIAN CORN . . . . 25 DREAM 19
PEERD TWIXT THE STEMS AND THE GROUND BROKE AWAY . . 155 TRISTRAM 3 186

PEERING
PEERING TO SPY A GOAT-TRACK DOWN THE CLIFF . . . . 357 MEROPE 804

PEERLESS
ON THE PEERLESS CHEEK OF QUEENS . . . . . . 33 NEW SIRENS 214
THE PEERLESS HUNTER HARPER KNIGHT . . . . . . 131 TRISTRAM 1 22
PRINCE ALEXANDER PHILIPS PEERLESS SON . . . . 153 TRISTRAM 3 147
PEERLESS IN RADIANCE IN JOY . . . . 294 HEINES GRAVE 66

PEERS
HEMMD BY TWO BANKS OF CLOUD PEERS PALE AND WEAK . . 10 MYCERINUS 57
THOU AND THE OTHER PEERS OF KAI KHOSROO . . 85 SOHRAB RUSTUM 832
OUTLIVED HIS BRETHREN HIS PEERS . . . . . 229 YOUTH OF NATURE 33
THROUGH SILKEN RIFTS SOFT PEERS THE SUN . . 248 KENSINGTON GARD V
THE GENERATIONS OF THY PEERS ARE FLED . . . . 259 SCHOLAR-GIPSY 155

PEEVISH
WITH SUCH A PEEVISH HARDIHOOD OF SCORN . . . . RUDE ORATOR 20

PEISIANAX
```
    I LEFT THEE SUPPING WITH PEISIANAX          • • • • •   407 EMPEDOCLES I 1     31
    PEISIANAX THOU KNOWST DRINKS LATE AND THEN  • • • •     407 EMPEDOCLES I 1     39
    WHEN FIRST HE SOJOURND WITH PEISIANAX         • • • •   408 EMPEDOCLES I 1     73
    WHEN WE WERE GATHERD WITH PEISIANAX         • • • • •   410 EMPEDOCLES I 1    127
    AND BRING PEISIANAX TO HIM FROM THE CITY    • • • • •   428 EMPEDOCLES I 2    481
```

PEKIN
```
    PRICKD AS A CUNNING WORKMAN IN PEKIN  • • • • • •        81 SOHRAB RUSTUM      672
```

PELASGUS
```
    PELASGUS OUR FOREFATHER AND MANKINDS  • • • • •        389 MEROPE            1538
```

PELEUS
```
    TO PELEUS IN LONG DISTANT YEARS         • • • • • •    414 EMPEDOCLES I 2     70
    AH UNHAPPY PAIR TO PELEUS WHY DID WE GIVE YOU    • •       HOMER TRANS          9
```

PELION
```
    OF PELION IN THE STREAMS  • • • • • • • •              190 STRAYED REVEL      145
    ON PELION THEN THEY FEEL  • • • • • • • • • •          192 STRAYED REVEL      224
    ON PELION ON THE GRASSY GROUND  • • • • • • •          414 EMPEDOCLES I 2     58
```

PELL
```
    OF COMMON LIFE WHERE CROWDED UP PELL-MELL  • • • •     168 WORLDLY PLACE        4
```

PELLUCID
```
    AS DEEP AS PELLUCID A SPRING  • • • • • • •            252 FUTURE              39
```

PELOPS
```
    THE HERACLEIDAE BACK TO PELOPS ISLE  • • • • • •       330 MEROPE               7
    TOGETHER TO THIS ISLE OF PELOPS CAME  • • • • •        334 MEROPE             124
    THEIR FATHERS REALM THIS ISLE FROM PELOPS NAMED  • •   336 MEROPE             219
    OF THEIR HERITAGE PELOPS ISLE  • • • • • • •           343 MEROPE             416
```

PEN
```
    HE LEAVES HIS KIND OERLEAPS THEIR PEN    • • • •        58 RESIGNATION        211
    WHO RATES US IF WE PEER OUTSIDE OUR PEN    • • •       169 WORLDLY PLACE        7
    GRAVE IT ON BRASS WITH ADAMANTINE PEN    • • • •       171 DIVINITY             2
    BREATHINGS OF SONG WITH A PEN  • • • • • •             281 HAWORTH CHURCH      24
    WELL PURPOSE TO PEN BACK  • • • • • • • • •            353 MEROPE             671
    IN A LOW DIM-LIGHTED PEN  • • • • • • • •              457 POOR MATTHIAS      186
    OR WITH PEN-BRYNS BOLD BARD PURSUES  • • • • •         458 KAISER DEAD          5
    AND WREST ONE TEAR FROM JOY OH WHO SHALL PEN    • •    468 ALARIC AT ROME     167
```

PENCIL
```
    CAN THY PENCIL O ARTIST RESTORE   • • • • • •          231 YOUTH OF NATURE    110
```

PENITENT
```
    THE PENITENT WITH ANGUISH BOWD  • • • • • • •          225 EPILOG LAOCOON     155
    PENITENT FOR WANT OF RACE      • • • • • • •           454 POOR MATTHIAS       74
```

PENITENTIAL
```
    DEEP IS THEIR PENITENTIAL MOAN  • • • • • • •          224 EPILOG LAOCOON      91
    WITH PENITENTIAL CRIES THEY KNEEL  • • • • •           300 GRANDE CHARTR       39
```

PENMON
```
    ONE CAME FROM PENMON WESTWARD AND A GLOW  • • • •      170 EAST AND WEST        5
```

PENNON
```
    PENNON AND PLUME AND FLASHING LANCE  • • • • •         305 GRANDE CHARTR      178
```

PENSIVE
```
    SHEDDING HER PENSIVE LIGHT AT INTERVALS  • • • •        18 CHURCH BROU 3       35
    WHO ARE THEY O PENSIVE GRACES   • • • • • •             26 NEW SIRENS           9
    SEEN BY RARE GLIMPSES PENSIVE AND TONGUE-TIED  • •     256 SCHOLAR-GIPSY       54
    AND LEANING BACKWARD IN A PENSIVE DREAM  • • •         257 SCHOLAR-GIPSY       77
    AND LEANING BACKWARDS IN A PENSIVE DREAM  • • •        257 SCHOLAR-GIPSY    V  77
    THE PENSIVE STRANGERS FACE   • • • • • • •             311 OBERMANN           172
    THOSE PENSIVE FEATURES WELL I KNEW  • • • • •          314 OBERMANN MORE       61
```

PENT
```
    SO THEY WITH PENT-UP HEARTS AND TEARLESS EYES   • •     97 BALDER DEAD 1       69
    NOT PENT ON SHIP-BOARD THIS DELICIOUS DAY  • • •       133 TRISTRAM 1          98
    MY PENT-UP TEARS OPPRESS MY BRAIN   • • • • •          206 RIVER                9
    IN VAIN OUR PENT WILLS FRET   • • • • • •              418 EMPEDOCLES I 2     182
    OF THE PENT WINDS THAT SCREAM IN AGONY  • • • •        472 CROMWELL            26
    AND OFT THE SPIRIT PENT AT HOME   • • • • •            483 ROME-SICKNESS        2
```

PEOPLE
```
    YET SURELY O MY PEOPLE DID I DEEM   • • • • •            9 MYCERINUS           19
    BROKE FROM HIS SORROWING PEOPLE SO HE SPAKE    • •      11 MYCERINUS           81
    TO TELL HIS WONDERING PEOPLE OF THEIR KING  • •         12 MYCERINUS          125
    AND THE PEOPLE PRAY   • • • • • • • • •                 17 CHURCH BROU 2       30
    THE PEOPLE TO THE NAVE REPAIR   • • • • • •             17 CHURCH BROU 2       34
    A RULER OF THE PEOPLE STAND   • • • • • • •             56 RESIGNATION        155
    JOIND WE ARE HENCEFORTH NOR WILL THY PEOPLE    • •     144 TRISTRAM 2          57
    THE CHIEFS AND PEOPLE    • • • • • • • • •             189 STRAYED REVEL      122
    THE CHIEFS AND THE PEOPLE   • • • • • • • •            189 STRAYED REVEL    V 122
    HER FELLOW-PEOPLE SIT   • • • • • • • • •              282 HAWORTH CHURCH   V
```

PEOPLE   (CONTINUED)
          LAST OF THE PEOPLE WHO BELIEVE . . . . 302 GRANDE CHARTR   112
          WHATEER IN THE MESSENIAN PEOPLE STIRS . . . . . . 331 MEROPE   38
          IN THE MESSENIAN PEOPLE WHAT REMAINS . . . . 334 MEROPE   138
          CONSIDER TOO THIS PEOPLE WHO WERE DEAR . . . . . . 335 MEROPE   174
          WHOSE PEOPLE WHEN THE HERACLEIDAE CAME . . . . . . 338 MEROPE   285
          FROM THE TERRIFIED PEOPLE . . . . 345 MEROPE   488
          HOW USELESS AN ALLY A PEOPLE IS . . . . 381 MEROPE   1312
          MIGHT FROM THE PEOPLE DRAW IF RIGHTLY USED . . . 382 MEROPE   1336
          A PEOPLE IS NO ARMY TRAIND TO FIGHT . . . . . . 382 MEROPE   1339
          A PEOPLE LIKE A COMMON MAN IS DULL . . . . 382 MEROPE   1342
          A PEOPLE THEN IS AN ALLY INDEED . . . . 382 MEROPE   1347
          HE IS AND BY THE PEOPLE HAILD FOR KING . . . . . 401 MEROPE   1890
          AT THY DEAD HUSBANDS NAME THE PEOPLE SHOW . . . . 401 MEROPE   1894
          AS THE CHIEFS RULE MY SON THE PEOPLE ARE . . . . 404 MEROPE   2002
          UNHAPPY PEOPLE WHERE THE CHIEFS THEMSELVES . . . 404 MEROPE   2003
          AS THE CHIEFS RULE INDEED THE PEOPLE ARE . . . . 404 MEROPE   V2002
          AS DREW OF OLD THE PEOPLE AFTER HIM . . . . . . 408 EMPEDOCLES I 1   63
          BUT HE STILL LETS THE PEOPLE WHOM HE SCORNS . . . 410 EMPEDOCLES I 1   138
          AMONG A PEOPLE OF CHILDREN . . . . 432 EMPEDOCLES II   112
          THE SPORTS OF THE COUNTRY-PEOPLE . . . . 436 EMPEDOCLES II   251
          PEOPLE WHO LIVED HERE LONG AGO . . . . 452 GEISTS GRAVE   77
          TROY AND WARLIKE PRIAM TOO AND THE PEOPLE OF PRIAM   HOMER TRANS   22

PEOPLED
          AND PEOPLED CITIES . . . . 189 STRAYED REVEL   126
          IN AN OLDER WORLD PEOPLED BY GODS . . . . 437 EMPEDOCLES II   285
          PEOPLED NIGHTS VOICELESS SHADES WITH FORMS OF LONG AGO 467 ALARIC AT ROME 126
          BREATHE THERE NOT SPIRITS ON THE PEOPLED AIR . . 468 ALARIC AT ROME   163

PEOPLES
          AND FUTURE KING BEFORE THIS PEOPLES EYES . . . . 335 MEROPE   172
          BUT TO MATCH THESE THOU HAST THE PEOPLES LOVE . . 381 MEROPE   1309
          THY FATHER PERISHD IN THIS PEOPLES CAUSE . . . . 381 MEROPE   1314
          THAT KINGS LIVE FOR THEIR PEOPLES NOT THEMSELVES . 394 MEROPE   1715
          THY FATHERS PASSION WAS THIS PEOPLES EASE . . . . 404 MEROPE   2000
          THIS PEOPLES ANARCHY THY FOES PRETENCE . . . . . 404 MEROPE   2001

PEOPLING
          WE PEOPLING THE VOID AIR . . . . 421 EMPEDOCLES I 2   278

PERAN
          THROUGH THE DIM CAMP TO PERAN-WISAS TENT . . . . 61 SOHRAB RUSTUM   11
          THE TARTARS BUILT THERE PERAN-WISAS TENT . . . . 61 SOHRAB RUSTUM   22
          AND PERAN-WISA HEARD HIM THOUGH THE STEP . . . . 62 SOHRAB RUSTUM   28
          THOU KNOWST ME PERAN-WISA IT IS I . . . . 62 SOHRAB RUSTUM   34
          HE SPOKE AND PERAN-WISA TOOK THE HAND . . . . . 63 SOHRAB RUSTUM   63
          HAMAN WHO NEXT TO PERAN-WISA RULED . . . . 64 SOHRAB RUSTUM   108
          BUT PERAN-WISA WITH HIS HERALD CAME . . . . . . 65 SOHRAB RUSTUM   141
          THAT PERAN-WISA KEPT THE TARTARS BACK . . . . . 65 SOHRAB RUSTUM   145
          SO WHEN THEY HEARD WHAT PERAN-WISA SAID . . . . 65 SOHRAB RUSTUM   157
          HE SPAKE AND PERAN-WISA TURND AND STRODE . . . . 66 SOHRAB RUSTUM   187
          THROUGH THE HUSHD CAMP TO PERAN-WISAS TENT . . . 61 SOHRAB RUSTUM   V. 11
          AND PERAN WISA CAME UPON THE SAND . . . . 65 SOHRAB RUSTUM   V 148
          HE SPOKE AND PERAN-WISA TURND AND STRODE . . . . 66 SOHRAB RUSTUM   V 187

PERCEIVE
          PERCEIVE BUT A VOICE AS I COME TO HIS SIDE . . . 20 MODERN SAPPHO   26
          NO I NOTHING CAN PERCEIVE . . . . 215 PIS-ALLER   9
          NOW DO WE SOON PERCEIVE HOW FAST OUR YOUTH IS SPENT 424 EMPEDOCLES I 2 361
          NOR DO WE SOON PERCEIVE HOW FAST OUR YOUTH IS SPENT 424 EMPEDOCLES I 2 V 361

PERCEIVED
          AND HERMOD STRAIGHT PERCEIVED THEM WHO THEY WERE . 126 BALDER DEAD 3   444
          THINGS THAT ARE NOW PERCEIVED . . . . 421 EMPEDOCLES I 2   283

PERCEIVST
          PERCEIVST THOU NOT THE CHANGE OF DAY . . . . . . 315 OBERMANN MORE   81

PERCH
          AND IN VALHALLA FROM HIS GABLE-PERCH . . . . . . 105 BALDER DEAD 2   3
          FALLN BENEATH HIS PERCH AND DYING . . . . 452 POOR MATTHIAS   2
          SATST UPON THY PERCH TO HEAR . . . . 455 POOR MATTHIAS   120
          FALLEN DYING OFF THY PERCH . . . . 456 POOR MATTHIAS   130
          ON HIS PERCH A SPRIGHTLIER BIRD . . . . 458 POOR MATTHIAS   193

PERCHANCE
          PERCHANCE SOME MUTE MEMORIAL AT THEIR HEAD . . . 464 ALARIC AT ROME   58
          PERCHANCE HIS WANDERING HEART WAS FAR AWAY . . . 468 ALARIC AT ROME   169
          CROWNING HIS WILDEST HOPES PERCHANCE HIS EYES . . 468 ALARIC AT ROME   173
          PERCHANCE THAT SOLEMN SIGHT MIGHT QUENCH THE FIRE 469 ALARIC AT ROME   177
          PERCHANCE THAT WONDROUS CITY WAS TO HIM . . . . 469 ALARIC AT ROME   181
          PERCHANCE HAD QUICKEND WITH A LIVING TRUTH . . . 473 CROMWELL   53
          ONE MOMENTS SPACE PERCHANCE MIGHT CHARM HIS EYE . 475 CROMWELL   109

PERCHD
          OER THE VALLEY THE DIZZILY PERCHD . . . . 297 HEINES GRAVE   187
          OF CRAG-PERCHD NONACRIS . . . . 392 MEROPE   1650

PERENNIAL
    PERENNIAL PASSION-FRAUGHT AND FREE   • • • • • •   224 EPILOG LAOCOON   V 105
    AND THEN THY GLAD PERENNIAL YOUTH WOULD FADE   • •   261 SCHOLAR-GIPSY   229

PERFECT
    AND NOBLY PERFECT IN OUR DAY   • • • • • • •   222 EPILOG LAOCOON   26
    AND FEIGN KIND GODS WHO PERFECT WHAT MAN VAINLY TRIES   422 EMPEDOCLES I 2   316
    LIVE HAPPY THEN EXPECT YOUR PERFECT MEED   • • • •   448 WESTMIN ABBEY   138
    STILL TOILS TO PERFECT WHAT THE CHILD BEGAN   • •   473 CROMWELL   46

PERFECTING
    THEIR GLORIOUS TASKS IN SILENCE PERFECTING   • • • •   2 QUIET WORK   12
    THEIR GLORIOUS COURSE IN SILENCE PERFECTING   • •   2 QUIET WORK   V 12

PERFECTLY
    SO PERFECTLY THE LINES EXPRESS   • • • • • • • •   147 TRISTRAM 2   144

PERFIDIOUS
    AND THIS PERFIDIOUS MURDER WHO REVEALD   • • • •   364 MEROPE   V

PERFORM
    OFTENER PERFORM ARIGHT THEIR PARTS   • • • • • •   221 EPILOG LAOCOON   10
    AND WITH JOY THE STARS PERFORM THEIR SHINING   •   240 SELF-DEPENDENCE   21
    WHICH TO PERFORM WE MADE IT MEANS FOR THAT   • • •   330 MEROPE   25

PERFORMD
    LO HOME HAVING PERFORMD YOUR WILL I COME   • • • •   114 BALDER DEAD 3   37
    PERFORMD GOOD SERVICE FOR HIS BLOODY WAGE   • • • •   364 MEROPE   975
    HAS BEEN PERFORMD WHICH CAN BE WHEN THE MAN   • •   LUCRETIUS 2   8

PERFORMEST
    STILL THOU PERFORMEST THE WORD   • • • • • • • •   287 RUGBY CHAPEL   46

PERFORMS
    PERFORMS THIS NOON A SOLEMN SACRIFICE   • • • •   391 MEROPE   1589

PERFUME
    THE PERFUME WHICH THE DAY FORGOES   • • • • • •   218 BACCHANALIA 1   15
    THE BLUE-BELLS PERFUME ALL THE AIR   • • • • •   274 STANZAS CARNAC   20

PERFUMED
    THEIR SCENT AND RUSTLE DOWN THEIR PERFUMED SHOWERS   256 SCHOLAR-GIPSY   27

PERFUMES
    PERFUMES THE EVENING AIR   • • • • • • • • •   234 YOUTH OF MAN   69
    THE FURZE-SCENT PERFUMES ALL THE AIR   • • • • •   274 STANZAS CARNAC   V 20
    OUT-PERFUMES THE THYME   • • • • • • • •   442 EMPEDOCLES II   442

PERHAPS
    OR IN MID-HEAVEN PERHAPS YOUR GOLDEN CARS   • • • •   10 MYCERINUS   43
    TIS ALL PERHAPS WHICH MAN ACQUIRES   • • • • •   22 YOUTH AND CALM   24
    TIS ALL PERHAPS THAT MAN ACQUIRES   • • • • •   22 YOUTH AND CALM   V 24
    OR PERHAPS IF HOPE WERE STRONGER   • • • • • •   29 NEW SIRENS   111
    A BELT OR SWORD PERHAPS AND GO HIS WAY   • • • •   71 SOHRAB RUSTUM   354
    SO WILL HE SPEAK PERHAPS WHILE MEN APPLAUD   • • • •   72 SOHRAB RUSTUM   362
    OR PERHAPS HAS HER YOUNG HEART   • • • • • • •   131 TRISTRAM 1   45
    AND NOW AND THEN PERHAPS THERE SWELLS   • • • •   224 EPILOG LAOCOON   122
    YEARS HENCE PERHAPS MAY DAWN AN AGE   • • • • •   304 GRANDE CHARTR   157
    THERE MAY PERHAPS YET DAWN AN AGE   • • • • •   304 GRANDE CHARTR   V 157
    THERE YET PERHAPS MAY DAWN AN AGE   • • • • •   304 GRANDE CHARTR   V 157
    WITH GRIEVOUS DEEDS PERHAPS WITH MURDER NO   • • •   336 MEROPE   209
    NOT HELP OF MEN ALTHOUGH PERHAPS OF GODS   • • •   341 MEROPE   357
    DISCONTENTED PERHAPS   • • • • • • • •   343 MEROPE   404
    IF PERHAPS UNPIERCED BY THE SWORD   • • • • •   370 MEROPE   1116
    INEVITABLY HAD SURGED UP PERHAPS   • • • • •   394 MEROPE   1698
    ATONED THIS VERY DAY PERHAPS IT IS   • • • • •   397 MEROPE   1769
    THE GODS PERHAPS ALLOWD YOU   • • • • • • •   398 MEROPE   1799
    THOU WILT EARN MY THANKS SURE AND PERHAPS HIS   • •   409 EMPEDOCLES I 1   99
    PRAISED PERHAPS THY COURTEOUS EYE   • • • • •   455 POOR MATTHIAS   117
    THEN PERHAPS THOU SHALT WORK AT THE LOOM OF   HOMER TRANS   29
        ANOTHER IN ARGOS

PERIL
    AND SHUNS TO PERIL IT WITH YOUNGER MEN   • • • •   68 SOHRAB RUSTUM   248
    TILL THEN IN PERIL OR IN PAIN WE LIVE   • • • •   111 BALDER DEAD 2   225
    WILL HAVE MORE PERIL FOR US THAN THE LAST   • • • •   440 EMPEDOCLES II   378

PERILOUS
    OER THE CLOUD-WRAPT PERILOUS PLAIN   • • • • •   217 LORDS MESSENGER   V 21
    PUTTING HIS SICKLE TO THE PERILOUS GRAIN   • • • •   268 THYRSIS   182
    DIZZY THE PATH AND PERILOUS THE WAY   • • • •   341 MEROPE   368
    WAKES ME THUS KINDLY FROM THE PERILOUS SLEEP   • •   375 MEROPE   1203
    THE DARING CLAIMANT OF A PERILOUS THRONE   • • • •   383 MEROPE   1357
    MURDERS UNCERTAIN SECRET PERILOUS GAME   • • • •   388 MEROPE   1501
    BUT THAT WE KNOW HOW EVERY PERILOUS FEAT   • • • •   402 MEROPE   1948

PERILS
    SON OF CRESPHONTES PAST WHAT PERILS   • • • • • •   405 MEROPE   2021

PERISH
    AND PERISH AGAINST FATE BEFORE THY DAY   • • • •   114 BALDER DEAD 3   29
    THOU HAST NOT LIVED WHY SHOULDST THOU PERISH SO   • •   259 SCHOLAR-GIPSY   151

PERISH   (CONTINUED)
      PERISH AND NO ONE ASKS   . . . .   288 RUGBY CHAPEL   67
      THE SON TO PERISH AS YE LEFT THE SIRE   . . . . .   402 MEROPE   1935
      I OF MYSELF KNOW WELL THAT HERE I AM DESTIND TO PERISH   HOMER TRANS   60

PERISHD
      PERISHD IN SIGHT OF THE GOAL   . . . .   345 MEROPE   466
      HE PERISHD IN ARCADIA WHERE HE DWELT . . . . . .   355 MEROPE   717
      THY FATHER PERISHD IN THIS PEOPLES CAUSE   . . . .   381 MEROPE   1314
      PERISHD BEFORE THEIR EYES YET NO MAN STIRRD   . .   381 MEROPE   1315
      PERISHD IN ARGOS BY HIS JEALOUS SONS   . . . .   389 MEROPE   1557
      HE PERISHD IN ARCADIA WHERE HE LIVD . . . . . .   355 MEROPE   V 717

PERISHES
      WHICH PERISHES OF COLD   . . . .   238 PROGRESS   32

PERMANENCE
      FAST PERMANENCE TO AN ILL-GOTTEN THRONE   . . . .   388 MEROPE   1509
      WHAT PERMANENCE WHAT STABILITY LIKE OURS   . . . .   389 MEROPE   1544

PERMISSION
      BY HIGH PERMISSION I AM HERE   . . . .   157 SAINT BRANDAN   24

PERMIT
      PERMIT NO PEACE TILL YOUR BEHESTS ARE DONE . . . .   367 MEROPE   1057

PERMITTING
      PASSIVE PERMITTING THEE WHAT COURSE THOU WILT   . .   333 MEROPE   96

PERPETUAL
      LIFE ONE PERPETUAL FIGHT A BATH OF BLOOD   . . . .   128 BALDER DEAD 3   506
      PERPETUAL PROMPTINGS TO REBELLIOUS HOPE   . . . .   333 MEROPE   91
      THAT REGION IN PERPETUAL CLOUD . . . .   352 MEROPE   642
      HIS FIXD CONDITION AND PERPETUAL WALK   . . . .   404 MEROPE   1993

PERPETUALLY
      HATH TOIL PERPETUALLY   . . . .   422 EMPEDOCLES I 2   294
      HAS TOIL PERPETUALLY   . . . .   422 EMPEDOCLES I 2   V 294

PERSEPOLIS
      BY JEMSHID IN PERSEPOLIS TO BEAR   . . . . . .   86 SOHRAB RUSTUM   861

PERSEVERING
      LABORIOUS PERSEVERING SERIOUS FIRM   . . . . . .   5 DUKE WELLINGTON   10

PERSIA
      THE ROYAL TROOPS OF PERSIA HORSE AND FOOT . . . .   65 SOHRAB RUSTUM   139

PERSIAN
      WILL CHALLENGE FORTH THE BRAVEST PERSIAN LORDS   . .   62 SOHRAB RUSTUM   56
      OR IN SOME QUARREL WITH THE PERSIAN KING   . . . .   63 SOHRAB RUSTUM   85
      FOR THE WARM PERSIAN SEA-BOARD SO THEY STREAMD   . .   64 SOHRAB RUSTUM   116
      BUT CHOOSE A CHAMPION FROM THE PERSIAN LORDS   . .   65 SOHRAB RUSTUM   152
      AND FERABURZ WHO RULED THE PERSIAN HOST   . . .   66 SOHRAB RUSTUM   172
      TO PICK A CHAMPION FROM THE PERSIAN LORDS   . . .   67 SOHRAB RUSTUM   212
      THE CAMP AND TO THE PERSIAN HOST APPEARD   . . .   69 SOHRAB RUSTUM   281
      BY SANDY BAHREIN IN THE PERSIAN GULF . . . .   69 SOHRAB RUSTUM   286
      AND RUSTUM TO THE PERSIAN FRONT ADVANCED   . . .   70 SOHRAB RUSTUM   291
      BESIDE THE OXUS ALL THE PERSIAN LORDS   . . . .   72 SOHRAB RUSTUM   358
      THERE ARE ENOUGH FOES IN THE PERSIAN HOST . . .   74 SOHRAB RUSTUM   443
      A PERSIAN LORD THIS DAY AND STRIP HIS CORPSE   . .   77 SOHRAB RUSTUM   529

PERSIANS
      AND BEAT THE PERSIANS BACK ON EVERY FIELD   . . .   62 SOHRAB RUSTUM   48
      AND ON THE OTHER SIDE THE PERSIANS FORMD   . . .   65 SOHRAB RUSTUM   136
      AND WHEN FEROOD WHO LED THE PERSIANS SAW   . . .   65 SOHRAB RUSTUM   144
      FEROOD AND YE PERSIANS AND TARTARS HEAR   . . .   65 SOHRAB RUSTUM   150
      SO THE PALE PERSIANS HELD THEIR BREATH WITH FEAR   .   66 SOHRAB RUSTUM   169
      BUT THROUGH THE ANXIOUS PERSIANS GUDURZ RAN   . .   66 SOHRAB RUSTUM   189
      AND ALL THE PERSIANS KNEW HIM AND WITH SHOUTS   . .   69 SOHRAB RUSTUM   282
      SO DEAR TO THE PALE PERSIANS RUSTUM CAME   . . .   70 SOHRAB RUSTUM   290
      THE PERSIANS TOOK IT ON THE OPEN SANDS   . . . .   86 SOHRAB RUSTUM   872

PERSISTENCE
      TO THE WORDS HOPE LIGHT PERSISTENCE   . . . . . .   49 SECOND BEST   23
      IS PERSISTENCE ALL-ENDURING   . . . .   SECOND BEST   V 22

PERSONAL
      OF FESTERING THOUGHTS AND PERSONAL FEARS   . . .   271 MEMORIAL VERSES   V
      OR SELFISH LUST OF PERSONAL POWER   . . . . .   353 MEROPE   661
      HIS DEATH A PUBLIC NOT A PERSONAL ACT   . . . .   387 MEROPE   1480
      OF PERSONAL FEELING TO THE PUBLIC WEAL   . . . .   394 MEROPE   1712
      OF PERSONAL VENGEANCE TO THE PUBLIC WEAL   . . .   394 MEROPE   V1712

PERSUADED
      BUT TELL ME HOW HAST THOU PERSUADED HIM   . . . .   409 EMPEDOCLES I 1   105

PERSUASIVE
      THAT TRIUMPH OF THE SWEET PERSUASIVE LYRE   . . . .   432 EMPEDOCLES II   126

PERUSE
    DOST THOU AGAIN PERUSE . . . . 201 PHILOMELA   19
    DOST THOU STILL PERUSE . . . . 201 PHILOMELA   V 19

PERUSED
    ALL THE MOST VALIANT CHIEFS LONG HE PERUSED . . 70 SOHRAB RUSTUM   311

PERVADES
    AND AN UNWONTED CALM PERVADES HIS BREAST . . . . 247 BURIED LIFE   95

PERVERSE
    THOUGH FOUND PERVERSE THE BLOOD OF HERACLES . . 337 MEROPE   256

PESTER
    PESTER HIM NOT IN THIS HIS SOMBRE MOOD . . . . 411 EMPEDOCLES I 1   154

PET
    CALLD US TO PET THEE OR TO PRAISE . . . . . . 450 GEISTS GRAVE   7

PETER
    PETER HIS FRIEND WITH LIGHT DID CONSECRATE . . . . 445 WESTMIN ABBEY   50

PETERS
    HOW HIS ST PETERS CHURCH IN THORNEY ISLE . . . . 445 WESTMIN ABBEY   49

PETRARCHS
    IN DANTES PETRARCHS TASSOS LINE . . . . . . 222 EPILOG LAOCOON   21

PETTY
    SEEK TO AFFLICT OUR FOES WITH PETTY PANGS . . . . 111 BALDER DEAD 2   229
    BUT EACH DAY BRINGS ITS PETTY DUST . . . . . 183 ABSENCE   9
    OUR PETTY SOULS OUR STRUTTING WITS . . . . . 202 URANIA   13

PETULANT
    AND HER PETULANT QUICK REPLIES . . . . 134 TRISTRAM 1   120
    POURS HER PETULANT YOUTH . . . . 297 HEINES GRAVE   185

PHANTOM
    THE PHANTOM OF OURSELVES . . . . 213 GROWING OLD   33
    SOME LIFELESS SOULLESS PHANTOM OF THEIR OWN . . 474 CROMWELL   100
    PALE PHANTOM HOSTS LIKE SHADOWS FAINT AND FAR . . 476 CROMWELL   141

PHANTOMS
    MERE PHANTOMS OF MANS SELF-TORMENTING HEART . . 9 MYCERINUS   25
    DEAD BE THE PAST AND ITS PHANTOMS TO ME . . . . 206 SEPARATION   12
    FIERY PHANTOMS OF DEATH . . . . 346 MEROPE   503
    STILL AS HE GAZD THE PHANTOMS MOURNFUL GLANCE . . 477 CROMWELL   193

PHARISEES
    THE OLD LAW OBSERVED BY SCRIBES AND PHARISEES . . 237 PROGRESS   6

PHENEOS
    TO PHENEOS WITH ITS CRAGGY CITADEL . . . . . 356 MEROPE   745

PHIAL
    REACH ME MY GOLDEN PHIAL STANDS BY THEE . . . . 133 TRISTRAM 1   100
    AND THAT PHIAL RARE HER MOTHER . . . . 134 TRISTRAM 1   V 136

PHIDIAS
    SCULPTORS LIKE PHIDIAS . . . . 221 BACCHANALIA 2   57

PHILIPS
    PRINCE ALEXANDER PHILIPS PEERLESS SON . . . . 153 TRISTRAM 3   147

PHILISTINE
    PURSY PLAYD-OUT PHILISTINE . . . . 457 POOR MATTHIAS   190

PHILOCTETES
    WHERE PHILOCTETES PINED TAKE SHIP AND FLEE . . . 395 MEROPE   1747

PHILOSOPHY
    FOND FANCIES HERE THERE FALSE PHILOSOPHY . . . . 446 WESTMIN ABBEY   66

PHOEBUS
    EVEN IN THAT PHOEBUS-GUARDED GROUND . . . . . 221 EPILOG LAOCOON   15

PHRASE
    SOME DOCTOR FULL OF PHRASE AND FAME . . . . . 250 WISH   18

PHRYGIAN
    LET THIS SOBBING PHRYGIAN STRAIN . . . . . . 32 NEW SIRENS   168
    AND THIS SOBBING PHRYGIAN STRAIN . . . . . . 32 NEW SIRENS   V 168
    LET THIS THROBBING PHRYGIAN STRAIN . . . . . 32 NEW SIRENS   V 168
    OF THAT UNPITYING PHRYGIAN SECT WHICH CRIED . . 172 GOOD SHEPHERD   3
    IN THE HOT CORNFIELD OF THE PHRYGIAN KING . . . . 268 THYRSIS   183
    OF THE PHRYGIAN FLUTES TO TAME . . . . 433 EMPEDOCLES II   131
    TO THE PHRYGIAN HIGHLANDS CAME . . . . 433 EMPEDOCLES II   132
    THERE THE PHRYGIAN BROUGHT HIS FLUTES . . . . 433 EMPEDOCLES II   141
    THE RED-SNOODED PHRYGIAN GIRLS . . . . 434 EMPEDOCLES II   180

PHTHIA
        HE SHOWD HIM PHTHIA FAR AWAY   . . . .   414 EMPEDOCLES I 2   68

PHYSICIAN
        PHYSICIAN OF THE IRON AGE   . . . .   270 MEMORIAL VERSES   17

PICK
        TO PICK A CHAMPION FROM THE PERSIAN LORDS . . . .   67 SOHRAB RUSTUM   212
        AND PICK THE BRAVEST WARRIORS OUT FOR DEATH   . .   105 BALDER DEAD 2   26

PICKING
        THE BLACKBIRD PICKING FOOD   . . . .   258 SCHOLAR-GIPSY   116

PICTURE
        THEY HANG THE PICTURE DOTH THE STORY TELL . . . .   166 PICT NEWSTEAD   8

PIECE
        WHERE BEST THE POET FRAMED HIS PIECE . . . . . .   221 EPILOG LAOCOON   14

PIECEMEAL
        ALL THIS O KING NOT PIECEMEAL AS TO THEE   . . . .   358 MEROPE   827

PIER
        THE SWINGING WATERS AND THE CLUSTERD PIER . . . .   42 GIPSY CHILD   6
        GAY SHINE THE WATERS AND THE CLUSTERD PIER . . . .   41 GIPSY CHILD   V   6
        MIXT WITH THE IDLERS ON THE PIER   . . . . . .   205 CALAIS SANDS   30

PIERCD
        PARTS FROM THE CAVE-PIERCD CLIFF THE SHELVING BAY   358 MEROPE   V 818

PIERCE
        PIERCE FATES IMPENETRABLE EAR . . . .   60 RESIGNATION   274
        AND PIERCE HIM LIKE A STAB AND MAKE HIM LEAP . .   78 SOHRAB RUSTUM   584
        IN ALL HIS LOVELY MIEN LET PIERCE . . . . . .   202 URANIA   23
        EVEN NOW THEIR WHISPERS PIERCE THE GLOOM   . . . .   301 GRANDE CHARTR   71

PIERCED
        AND PIERCED THE MIGHTY RUSTUM WHILE HE LAY . . . .   73 SOHRAB RUSTUM   423
        HIS COVERING SHIELD AND THE SPEAR PIERCED HIS SIDE   76 SOHRAB RUSTUM   520
        AND PIERCED HER WITH AN ARROW AS SHE ROSE . . . .   78 SOHRAB RUSTUM   559
        AT BALDER WHOM NO WEAPON PIERCED OR CLOVE . . . .   95 BALDER DEAD 1   4
        PARTS FROM THIS CAVE-PIERCED CLIFF THE SHELVING BAY   358 MEROPE   818

PIERCING
        PIERCING THE SOLEMN CLOUD   . . . .   45 IN UTRUMQUE PAR   30
        WITH PIERCING UNTOLD ANGUISH   . . . .   235 YOUTH OF MAN   102
        MORE PIERCING THE SECOND CRY RANG . . . . . .   346 MEROPE   495
        AH WHO ARE THESE WHAT SHRILL EAR-PIERCING SCREAM . 375 MEROPE   1202
        BOLD ACTIONS PARENT AND A PIERCING KEN   . . . .   478 CROMWELL   229

PIGEONS
        ON THE CLIFF-SIDE THE PIGEONS . . . .   442 EMPEDOCLES II   431

PIGMY
        THE STRONG BLAST BROUGHT A PIGMY THRONG   . . . .   479 HAYSWATER BOAT   19

PILD
        OR FAR EASTWARD WHERE UP-PILD . . . .   PILLARS UNIVERS   6
        THERE OR EASTWARD WHERE UP-PILD   . . . . . .   PILLARS UNIVERS V   6

PILE
        OF THE NEW PILE THE SUNLIGHT SHINES . . . . . .   16 CHURCH BROU 2   2
        AND ON THE DECK BUILD HIGH A FUNERAL-PILE . . . .   96 BALDER DEAD 1   42
        TO GATHER WOOD AND BUILD A FUNERAL-PILE   . . . .   103 BALDER DEAD 1   296
        AND MAKE A FUNERAL-PILE ON BALDERS SHIP   . . . .   106 BALDER DEAD 2   43
        WHEN YE ENOUGH HAVE WEPT THEN BUILD A PILE . . . .   115 BALDER DEAD 3   53
        THE WOOD TO BALDERS SHIP AND BUILT A PILE . . . .   118 BALDER DEAD 3   161
        AND THE PILE CRACKLED AND BETWEEN THE LOGS . . . .   118 BALDER DEAD 3   187
        THE SUMMIT OF THE PILE THE DEAD THE MAST   . . . .   119 BALDER DEAD 3   190
        AND LONG IN THE FAR DARK BLAZED BALDERS PILE . .   119 BALDER DEAD 3   200
        THE BODIES WERE CONSUMED ASH CHOKED THE PILE . .   119 BALDER DEAD 3   202
        SO WITH A SHOWER OF SPARKS THE PILE FELL IN   . .   119 BALDER DEAD 3   205
        NOR DID THERE NEED LESS THAN THE BURNING PILE . .   198 FRAG ANTIGONE   98
        SOARING FROM HIS DEATH-PILE ON OETA LEFT   . . . .   336 MEROPE   213
        LIVING HIS OWN FUNERAL-PILE   . . . .   399 MEROPE   1834
        PUT THE TORCH TO THE PILE   . . . .   399 MEROPE   1839
        ONE STILL LAGS LAST AND TURNS AND EYES THE PILE . . 444 WESTMIN ABBEY   14
        LO ON A SUDDEN ALL THE PILE IS BRIGHT   . . . .   445 WESTMIN ABBEY   34

PILED
        UPON THE THICK PILED CARPETS IN THE TENT   . . . .   61 SOHRAB RUSTUM   25
        FLING THE PILED SHEAVES ABOUT . . . .   218 BACCHANALIA 1   V 34

PILGRIM
        EACH ITS OWN PILGRIM-HOST OF OLD   . . . . . .   301 GRANDE CHARTR   62

PILGRIMAGE
        GOETHE HAS DONE HIS PILGRIMAGE . . . .   270 MEMORIAL VERSES   18
        CROSS HIS LONE PATH OR SHARE HIS PILGRIMAGE   . .   476 CROMWELL   162

PILGRIMS
    SO PILGRIMS BOUND FOR MECCA PRAYD   • • • • • •   52 RESIGNATION   3

PILLAR
    AND PLANT A FAR-SEEN PILLAR OVER ALL • • • • •   84 SOHRAB RUSTUM   789
    AND PLANT A FAR-SEEN PILLAR OVER ALL • • • • •   84 SOHRAB RUSTUM   804
    SHE SATE BY THE PILLAR WE SAW HER CLEAR • • • •   163 FORSAKEN MERM   76
    THE PILLAR STILL BROODS OER THE FIELDS • • • •   228 YOUTH OF NATURE   15
    FROM THE PILLAR WHERE HE LEANS • • • • • • •   META CLOISTER   34

PILLARS
    THE GAZING UP MID THE DIM PILLARS HIGH   • • • •   18 CHURCH BROU 3   38
    THEN GAZING UP THROUGH THE DIM PILLARS HIGH   • •   18 CHURCH BROU 3 V 38
    AS THOSE BLACK GRANITE PILLARS ONCE HIGH-REARD   • •   86 SOHRAB RUSTUM   860
    BEHOLDING HIM WHERE THE TWO PILLARS STAND • • •   198 FRAG ANTIGONE   91
    MOVES THROUGH THEIR ROWS OF PILLARS OLD • • •   274 STANZAS CARNAC   14
    STREAMS THROUGH THEIR ROWS OF PILLARS OLD • • •   274 STANZAS CARNAC V 14

PILLOW
    TEARS WET THE PILLOW BY THY CHEEK BUT THOU • • •   103 BALDER DEAD 1   290
    AND ON THE SNOWY PILLOW FALLS • • • • • •   141 TRISTRAM 1   336
    I A FADED WATCHER BY THY PILLOW • • • •   144 TRISTRAM 2   61
    HEAVEN HIS HEAD SINKS BACK UPON THE PILLOW • • •   145 TRISTRAM 2   77

PILLOWS
    AND FROM YOUR BROIDERD PILLOWS LIFT YOUR HEADS   • •   18 CHURCH BROU 3   26
    PROP ME UPON THE PILLOWS ONCE AGAIN • • • •   130 TRISTRAM 1   2
    PROPT ON PILLOWS IN HIS BED • • • • • •   130 TRISTRAM 1   11
    AND THE KNIGHT SINKS BACK ON HIS PILLOWS AGAIN • •   133 TRISTRAM 1   84
    AND ON HIS PILLOWS THAT PALE KNIGHT • • • •   148 TRISTRAM 2   166
    AND PILLOWS ON HER FROZEN BREAST AND LOCKS • • •   FRAGMENT 1   3

PINE
    WHEN THE PINE-BOUGHS YIELDED ROUND YOU • • •   29 NEW SIRENS   99
    FOR HE MY HUSBAND LEFT ME HERE TO PINE • • •   116 BALDER DEAD 3   106
    SPLINTERS OF PINE-WOOD SOAKD WITH TURPENTINE   •   118 BALDER DEAD 3   168
    UP THE STEEP PINE-PLUMED PATHS OF THE ESTRELLE   •   167 RACHEL 2   4
    YE PINE-WOODS I COME • • • • • • •   176 PARTING   58
    UPON THE PINE-GROWN LATMIAN STEEP • • •   181 ISOLATION MARG   24
    FROM THE PINE-DOTTED SPURS • • • • •   197 FRAG ANTIGONE   61
    GAILY THEIR PINE-STAFF GREEN • • • • •   218 BACCHANALIA 1   24
    FOR SELF-POISED THEY LIVE NOR PINE WITH NOTING   •   240 SELF-DEPENDENCE   23
    FOR ALONE THEY LIVE NOR PINE WITH NOTING • • •   240 SELF-DEPENDENCE V 23
    WHY SELF-POISED THEY LIVE NOR PINE WITH NOTING   •   240 SELF-DEPENDENCE V 23
    THOSE BLACK-CROWND RED-BOLED PINE-TREES STAND   •   248 KENSINGTON GARD   4
    THOSE BLACK-TOPPD RED-BOLED PINE-TREES STAND   •   248 KENSINGTON GARD V   4
    THIS FOR OUR WISEST AND WE OTHERS PINE • • •   260 SCHOLAR-GIPSY   191
    OF MANY A DARK-BOUGHD PINE • • • • •   307 OBERMANN   30
    THROUGH THE PINE BRANCHES PLAY • • • •   310 OBERMANN   126
    BETWEEN THE PINE-WOODS AND THE CLIFFS • • •   399 MEROPE   1824
    WHENCE THE RIDGED PINE-WOODED ROOTS • • • •   433 EMPEDOCLES II   137
    WHERE THE RIDGD PINE-DARKEND ROOTS • • • •   433 EMPEDOCLES II V 137
    WHENCE THE RIDGD PINE-MUFFLED ROOTS • • • •   433 EMPEDOCLES II V 137
    WHERE THE RIDGD PINE-WOODED ROOTS • • • •   433 EMPEDOCLES II V 137
    AND NEVER PINE • • • • • • •   460 KAISER DEAD   60
    TO GLUE MY FRUITLESS GAZE ON AND TO PINE • • •   FRAGMENT 5   6

PINED
    THEN LEARNT HIS DEATH AND PINED AWAY • • • • •   279 SOUTHERN NIGHT   110
    THEY DO NOT ASK WHO PINED UNSEEN • • • • •   311 OBERMANN   153
    WHERE PHILOCTETES PINED TAKE SHIP AND FLEE • • •   395 MEROPE   1747

PINES
    BY THE STREAM BELOW THE PINES • • • • • •   15 CHURCH BROU 1   92
    THE HILLS ARE CLOTHED WITH PINES SUN-PROOF • • •   16 CHURCH BROU 2   4
    MID BRIGHT GREEN FIELDS BELOW THE PINES • • •   16 CHURCH BROU 2   5
    AND THE WIND WASHES THROUGH THE MOUNTAIN-PINES   •   18 CHURCH BROU 3   37
    AND THE WIND WASHES IN THE MOUNTAIN PINES • • •   18 CHURCH BROU 3 V 37
    AND THE WIND WAILS AMONG THE MOUNTAIN PINES   •   18 CHURCH BROU 3 V 37
    AND THE WIND WASHES MID THE MOUNTAIN PINES • •   18 CHURCH BROU 3 V 37
    BORDERD EACH BANK WITH PINES THE MORNING SUN   •   24 DREAM   3
    DREW A WARM SCENT ABROAD BEHIND THE PINES • • •   25 DREAM   6
    BACKD BY THE PINES A PLANK-BUILT COTTAGE STOOD   •   25 DREAM   15
    SOON THE PLANKD COTTAGE BY THE SUN-WARMD PINES   •   25 DREAM   35
    UNDER OERHANGING PINES THE MORNING SUN • •   24 DREAM V   3
    SOON THE PLANKD COTTAGE MID THE SUN-WARMD PINES   •   25 DREAM V 35
    HANGING GARLANDS ON YOUR ODOROUS PINES • • •   29 NEW SIRENS   96
    IN THE PINES THE THRUSH IS WAKING • • • •   35 NEW SIRENS   259
    HANGING GARLANDS ON THE ODOROUS PINES • • •   29 NEW SIRENS V 96
    SMOTE MID THE ROCKS THE LICHEN-BEARDED PINES   • •   106 BALDER DEAD 2   56
    FRINGED WITH DARK PINES AND SANDS WHERE SEAFOWL SCREAM 123 BALDER DEAD 3   327
    THERE THE PINES SLOPE THE CLOUD-STRIPS • • •   176 PARTING   53
    OF RAVENNA PINES FOR A HIGH • • • • •   294 HEINES GRAVE   61
    PAST LIMESTONE SCARS WITH RAGGED PINES • • •   299 GRANDE CHARTR   14
    THE SCENTED PINES OF SWITZERLAND • • • •   311 OBERMANN   167
    THE TURF THE PINES THE SKY • • • • • •   312 OBERMANN MORE   6
    ITS PINES UNDER THEIR BRANCHES OPE • • • •   312 OBERMANN MORE   15
    ON SOME TALL SCAR FRINGED WITH DARK FEATHERY PINES   357 MEROPE   803
    AND ON THE HIGHEST PINES BUT FARTHER DOWN • • • •   406 EMPEDOCLES I 1   11
    ONES BREATH CURLS IN THE AIR AND ON THESE PINES • • 406 EMPEDOCLES I 1   15

PINES   (CONTINUED)
        UP BY THE TORRENT-SIDE UNDER THE PINES . . . . 411 EMPEDOCLES I 1   164
        AND ON THE HIGHEST PINES BUT FURTHER DOWN . . . . 406 EMPEDOCLES I 1   V 11
        LONGS OFTENER YET AND PINES FOR ROME . . . . . 483 ROME-SICKNESS   4
        CHAFES IN HIS PLACE AND PINES FOR CHANGE . . . . 484 ROME-SICKNESS   24

PINETREES
        THOSE DARK-TOPPD RED-BOLD PINETREES STAND . . . . .   KENSINGTON GARD V 4

PINING
        SICK PINING COMES NOT WHERE THESE ARE . . . . 138 TRISTRAM 1   260
        THEE A PINING EXILE IN THY FOREST . . . . . . 144 TRISTRAM 2   51

PININGS
        ON THE RED PININGS OF THEIR FOREST-FLOOR . . . .   25 DREAM   5

PINION
        HIS PINION AND WITH SHORT UNEASY SWEEPS . . . .   78 SOHRAB RUSTUM   564

PINIOND
        OF SINNERS PINIOND ON THE TORTURING WHEEL . . . . 373 MEROPE   1186

PINK
        OF THE FRAGRANT STOCK AND THE PINK . . . . . . 234 YOUTH OF MAN   68
        PALE PINK CONVOLVULUS IN TENDRILS CREEP . . . . 255 SCHOLAR-GIPSY   25
        AND THE PINK-FLOWERD OLEANDER . . . . 391 MEROPE   1617

PINNACE
        BEACHES THE PINNACE IN A DARKENING COVE . . . .   69 SOHRAB RUSTUM   V 288

PINND
        PINND BY THE THUNDER TO REAR . . . . 293 HEINES GRAVE   31

PINY
        BENEATH THE PINY SWARD . . . . 310 OBERMANN   120
        PAST SONCHAUDS PINY FLANKS I GAZE . . . . . . 324 OBERMANN MORE   337
        AND SONCHAUDS PINY FLANKS I GAZE . . . . . . 324 OBERMANN MORE   V 337

PIONEER
        I HIS CHIEF KINSMAN I HIS PIONEER . . . . . . 338 MEROPE   267

PIOUS
        O SCAN THY NATIVE WORLD WITH PIOUS EYES . . . .   46 IN UTRUMQUE PAR   V 40
        PIOUS BUT IMPIOUS SURELY IF THEIR SCOPE . . . . 342 MEROPE   380
        THE PIOUS WAIL FORSAKE . . . . . . 416 EMPEDOCLES I 2   134
        UNTO THIS PIOUS HOUSEHOLD TO REPAY . . . . . 447 WESTMIN ABBEY   108

PIPE
        MY PIPE IS LOST MY SHEPHERDS HOLIDAY . . . . . 264 THYRSIS   37
        SHE LOVED THE DORIAN PIPE THE DORIAN STRAIN . . 265 THYRSIS   97
        WHICH TASKD THY PIPE TOO SORE AND TIRED THY THROAT   269 THYRSIS   225
        OF THE HARP BE HEARD WITH THE PIPE . . . . . . 360 MEROPE   895

PIPES
        HERE TOO OUR SHEPHERD-PIPES WE FIRST ASSAYD . . 263 THYRSIS   35

PIPING
        HE WENT HIS PIPING TOOK A TROUBLED SOUND . . . . 264 THYRSIS   48
        PIPING A DITTY SAD FOR BIONS FATE . . . . . . 265 THYRSIS   84

PIRATE
        TO MEET HER PIRATE-LOVERS SHIP . . . . 278 SOUTHERN NIGHT   105

PIRATES
        OR ON THE SEA THE FIELD OF PIRATES SAIL . . . . 121 BALDER DEAD 3   270

PIT
        AND FRIENDS ME IN THE PIT OF FIRE . . . . . . 158 SAINT BRANDAN   64

PITCH
        HATH MAN NO SECOND LIFE PITCH THIS ONE HIGH . . 171 BETTER PART   10
        PITCH THEIR SMOKED TENTS AND EVERY BUSH YOU SEE . 258 SCHOLAR-GIPSY   113
        WHEREON MEN PITCH THEIR TENT . . . . 320 OBERMANN MORE   218
        WHEREON WE PITCH OUR TENT . . . . 320 OBERMANN MORE   V 218

PITCHD
        THE DINGY TENTS ARE PITCHD THE FIRES . . . . .   55 RESIGNATION   116
        AND SULLEN AND HAS PITCHD HIS TENTS APART . . . .   66 SOHRAB RUSTUM   179
        JUST PITCHD THE HIGH PAVILION IN THE MIDST . . .   67 SOHRAB RUSTUM   193
        NEW PITCHD THE HIGH PAVILION IN THE MIDST . . . .   67 SOHRAB RUSTUM V 193

PITCHER
        I FILLD MY PITCHER AND STOLE HOME . . . . . .   90 SICK KING BOKH   70
        THE WATER-PITCHER WHERE IT STOOD . . . . . .   90 SICK KING BOKH   78
        MOST SULTRY DRAIND THE PITCHER THERE . . . . .   90 SICK KING BOKH   82

PITCHERS
        WITH PITCHERS IN THEIR HANDS AND FRESH-PULLD FLOWERS 331 MEROPE   54
        SET DOWN YOUR PITCHERS MAIDENS AND FALL BACK . . 332 MEROPE   76

PITEOUS
                PITEOUS AND LOVELY LYING ON THE SAND • • • • • •   80 SOHRAB RUSTUM   633
                BEHIND FLOCKD WRANGLING UP A PITEOUS CREW • • • •   109 BALDER DEAD 2   170
                TURNING WITH PITEOUS • • • • • • • • • •   393 MEROPE   1662
                AT HIS MASTERS PITEOUS CRIES • • • • • • • • •   434 EMPEDOCLES II   186

PITEOUSLY
                AND PITEOUSLY HE EYES THE PASSERS BY • • • • • •   114 BALDER DEAD 3   16

PITIED
                AS WHOLLY TO BE PITIED QUITE FORLORN • • • • • •   126 BALDER DEAD 3   458

PITILESS
                BUT THOU TOO-BOLD HEADSTRONG PITILESS • • • •   196 FRAG ANTIGONE   50
                BY A PITILESS ARROW OF DEATH • • • • • • • •   216 LORDS MESSENGER   18

PITS
                DOUBLE OF ISSUE FULL OF PITS AND SNARES • • • •   349 MEROPE   581

PITT
                STATESMEN LIKE PITT • • • • • • • • • • •   220 BACCHANALIA 2   56

PITY
                AND A DEEP PITY ENTERD RUSTUMS SOUL • • • • •   70 SOHRAB RUSTUM   319
                AND CUNNING ALL THE PITY I HAD IS GONE • • • •   75 SOHRAB RUSTUM   467
                YET HIM I PITY NOT SO MUCH BUT HER • • • • •   78 SOHRAB RUSTUM   589
                HER MOST I PITY WHO NO MORE WILL SEE • • • • •   78 SOHRAB RUSTUM   593
                WILT THOU HAVE PITY ON ALL THESE • • • • • •   93 SICK KING BOKH   179
                THIS MAN MY PITY COULD NOT SAVE • • • • • •   95 SICK KING BOKH   226
                IN PITY AND SILENT AWE • • • • • • • •   283 HAWORTH CHURCH   V
                NOT IN PITY AND NOT • • • • • • • • • •   298 HEINES GRAVE   202
                IN PITY AND MOURNFUL AWE MIGHT STAND • • • • •   301 GRANDE CHARTR   82
                WITH PITY NAY WITH REVERENCE YET BEWARE • • • •   341 MEROPE   361
                WOMANLY PITY NOR MATERNAL FEAR • • • • • •   389 MEROPE   1526
                THE GODS HAD PITY MADE THEM STARS • • • • •   393 MEROPE   1674
                I PITY THEE AND WISH THEE CALMER MIND • • • •   396 MEROPE   1760
                PITY THYSELF NONE NEEDS COMPASSION MORE • • • •   396 MEROPE   1761
                MORE THAN PITY CLAIMST A STAVE • • • • • • •   453 POOR MATTHIAS   22
                AND WITH PITY THE SON OF SATURN SAW THEM BEWAILING   HOMER TRANS   7

PITYING
                AND CANST THOU NOT EVEN HERE PASS PITYING BY • •   125 BALDER DEAD 3   400
                OF PITYING FRIENDS DERISIVE ENEMIES • • • • • •   LUCRETIUS 2   15

PLACD
                AND ON HIS HEAD HE PLACD HIS SHEEP-SKIN CAP •• •   64 SOHRAB RUSTUM   V 100

PLACE
                MAKING THE HEAVEN OF HEAVENS HIS DWELLING-PLACE • •   3 SHAKESPEARE   6
                BOTH ARE LAID IN ONE COLD PLACE • • • • • •   44 QUESTION   6
                AND OFTEN TO SOME KINDLY PLACE • • • • • • •   55 RESIGNATION   112
                ENVIES THE ALL-REGARDED PLACE • • • • • • •   57 RESIGNATION   159
                AND PLACE ME ON A BED AND MOURN FOR ME • • • •   84 SOHRAB RUSTUM   785
                AND PLACE THEE ON A BED AND MOURN FOR THEE • • •   84 SOHRAB RUSTUM   800
                ALONE AND IN A DARKSOME PLACE • • • • • •   90 SICK KING BOKH   66
                HAVE I SEEN REIGNING IN THIS PLACE • • • • •   92 SICK KING BOKH   144
                LOOK THIS IS BUT ONE SINGLE PLACE • • • • •   92 SICK KING BOKH   157
                NOR DID THEY TO THEIR JUDGMENT-PLACE REPAIR • •   105 BALDER DEAD 2   32
                THITHER RESTORE HIM FOR HIS PLACE IS THERE • • •   110 BALDER DEAD 2   200
                HIS PLACE OF STATE REMAINS BY HELAS SIDE • • •   125 BALDER DEAD 3   432
                CHANGES PLACE AND TIME OF YEAR • • • • • •   133 TRISTRAM 1   89
                HAD BEEN THE LIKELIEST TRYSTING-PLACE TO-DAY • •   135 TRISTRAM 1   165
                HIS TRANQUIL LIFE IN THIS LONE PLACE • • • •   137 TRISTRAM 1   212
                WHAT PLACE IS THIS AND WHO ARE THEY • • • • •   148 TRISTRAM 2   164
                NO FAIRER RESTING-PLACE A MAN COULD FIND • • •   155 TRISTRAM 3   210
                WHILE BY HER BEDSIDE HEBREW RITES HAVE PLACE •   168 RACHEL 3   8
                TO HAUNT THE PLACE WHERE PASSIONS REIGN • • •   181 ISOLATION MARG   17
                BUT THOU HAST LONG HAD PLACE TO PROVE • • • •   181 ISOLATION MARG   28
                AND OUR OWN PLACE ONCE LEFT • • • • • • •   195 FRAG ANTIGONE   18
                FAILD TO PLACE THAT MASTER-FEELING CLEAR • • •   210 SELF-DECEPTION   24
                FAILD TO PLACE OUR MASTER-FEELING CLEAR • • • •   210 SELF-DECEPTION   V 24
                WHERE POOR HAVE PLACE LIKE THE SWELLS • • • •   214 NEW ROME   V 14
                GIVES THEN THE FIRST THE FAIREST PLACE • • • •   227 EPILOG LAOCOON   208
                I SAW IT IN SOME OTHER PLACE • • • • • • •   242 MORALITY   34
                I ASK IF THOU HAST PASSD THEIR QUIET PLACE • •   257 SCHOLAR-GIPSY   65
                WITH PLACE WITH HONOUR AND A FLATTERING CREW • •   268 THYRSIS   204
                AND STRUCK HIS FINGER ON THE PLACE • • • • •   270 MEMORIAL VERSES   21
                AH GENTLY PLACE HIM ON THE BENCH • • • • •   276 SOUTHERN NIGHT   34
                THE MOORLAND PLACE BUT THE CHURCH • • • • •   283 HAWORTH CHURCH   V 62
                IN THE PLACE WHERE THE WAYFARER ONCE • • • •   289 RUGBY CHAPEL   96
                AND PLACE WITH THOSE DOST CLAIM • • • • • •   310 OBERMANN   142
                ISSUING ON THAT GREEN PLACE • • • • • • •   311 OBERMANN   170
                MANS WORK-PLACE LAY IN GLOOM • • • • • • •   315 OBERMANN MORE   78
                MID WEEDS AND WRECKS SHE STOOD A PLACE • • • •   317 OBERMANN MORE   139
                REGARD HIS DEATH-PLACE DUMB • • • • • •   318 OBERMANN MORE   178
                GREAT HERACLES AND IN THAT PUBLIC PLACE • • •   330 MEROPE   14
                HAD IN A FATHERS PLACE HE BASELY MURDERD • • •   364 MEROPE   977
                THY FATHERS MURDERER IN THE PUBLIC PLACE • • •   391 MEROPE   1588
                IN HER HIDING-PLACE OF THE THICKETS • • • • •   392 MEROPE   1632
                BEFORE THEY REACH THE ELYSIAN PLACE • • • • •   414 EMPEDOCLES I 2   74

PLACE   (CONTINUED)
          NOR DO THEY SEE THEIR COUNTRY NOR THE PLACE   . . .   427 EMPEDOCLES I 2   439
          FROM THE GRASSY SUN-WARMD PLACE   . . . .   433 EMPEDOCLES II   161
          THIS UNCONGENIAL PLACE THIS HUMAN LIFE   . . .   440 EMPEDOCLES II   366
          AND TO MENS HEARTS THIS ANCIENT PLACE ENDEARD   . .   444 WESTMIN ABBEY   9
          BUT AS ONE VOICELESS BLANK A PLACE OF GRAVES   . .   469 ALARIC AT ROME   182
          TO WESTERN SHORES THE DEATH-PLACE OF THE DAY   . .   475 CROMWELL   112
          YET NOW WHEN BOLDEST WILLS GIVE PLACE   . . . .   481 COURAGE   5
          CHAFES IN HIS PLACE AND PINES FOR CHANGE   . . .   484 ROME-SICKNESS   24

PLACED
          AND BEFORE EACH THE COOKS WHO SERVED THEM PLACED . .   97 BALDER DEAD 1   66
          AND PLACED THEM ON THE PYRE AND ODIN THREW . . . .   118 BALDER DEAD 3   172
          AH AND HE WHO PLACED OUR MASTER-FEELING   . . .   210 SELF-DECEPTION   23
          WHY NOT ON THEM HAVE PLACED THE FORFEIT CROWN   . .   339 MEROPE   320
          PLACED SAFELY IN CHANGED FORMS THE PAIR   . . . .   427 EMPEDOCLES I 2   457

PLACES
          WHO ON SHORES AND SEA-WASHD PLACES   . . . . . .   26 NEW SIRENS   11
          FROM THIS DUSK OF LEAF-STREWN PLACES   . . . . . .   32 NEW SIRENS   193
          IN DIVERS PLACES IF THAT PAIN   . . . .   94 SICK KING BOKH   204
          OF PLACES WE HAD PASSD SPORT WE HAD HAD   . . . .   356 MEROPE   756
          GREEN HAPPY PLACES LIKE A FLOWERY LEA   . . . .   475 CROMWELL   117

PLACID
          A PLACID AND CONTINUOUS WHOLE   . . . .   57 RESIGNATION   190
          A PLACID SETTLED LOVELINESS   . . . .   147 TRISTRAM 2   V 145
          FOR EVER THROUGH THE GLENS PLACID AND DUMB   . . .   427 EMPEDOCLES I 2   460

PLAGUE
          WHERE THIS PLAGUE DRIVES THEM AND HAVE LITTLE EASE   153 TRISTRAM 3   141
          VISIT US AS THEY DO WITH SIGN AND PLAGUE   . . . .   413 EMPEDOCLES I 2   24

PLAGUED
          MID THE SOULS PLAGUED BY HEAVENLY POWER   . . . .   157 SAINT BRANDAN   34

PLAGUES
          WHICH IS THE HEAVIEST OF ALL PLAGUES . . . . . .   93 SICK KING BOKH   171
          THERE ARE WORSE PLAGUES ON EARTH THAN TEARS   . .   250 WISH   8
          SORE THIRST PLAGUES THEM THE ROCKS   . . . . . .   291 RUGBY CHAPEL   178

PLAIN
          OF THE GREAT GODS IS PLAIN AND YE MUST BRING   . .   11 MYCERINUS   75
          THE TOWN THE HIGHWAY AND THE PLAIN   . . . . . .   54 RESIGNATION   79
          INTO THE OPEN PLAIN SO HAMAN BADE   . . . . . .   64 SOHRAB RUSTUM   107
          THESE ALL FILED OUT FROM CAMP INTO THE PLAIN   . .   65 SOHRAB RUSTUM   135
          BUT I WILL FIGHT UNKNOWN AND IN PLAIN ARMS . . . .   68 SOHRAB RUSTUM   257
          WERE PLAIN AND ON HIS SHIELD WAS NO DEVICE . . . .   69 SOHRAB RUSTUM   266
          UNDER THEIR FEET AND MOANING SWEPT THE PLAIN   . .   75 SOHRAB RUSTUM   484
          EDDYING AND MOANING ROUND AND SWEPT THE PLAIN   . .   75 SOHRAB RUSTUM   V 484
          NOR DID HE LOOK ONCE MORE TO IDAS PLAIN   . . . .   97 BALDER DEAD 1   57
          BY THE ASH IGDRASIL IN IDAS PLAIN   . . . . . .   105 BALDER DEAD 2   33
          AND THEY CAME OUT UPON THE PLAIN AND PASSD . . . .   106 BALDER DEAD 2   65
          TO THE ASH IGDRASIL AND IDAS PLAIN   . . . . . .   120 BALDER DEAD 3   217
          OF THEIR DEAR COUNTRY AND CAN PLAIN DESCRY . . . .   123 BALDER DEAD 3   360
          MAKE TOWARD THEM OER THE STRETCHING CLOUDY PLAIN .   126 BALDER DEAD 3   443
          AND WE SHALL TREAD ONCE MORE THE WELL-KNOWN PLAIN   128 BALDER DEAD 3   537
          DEPARTED OER THE CLOUDY PLAIN AND SOON   . . . .   129 BALDER DEAD 3   552
          MAKE TOWARDS THEM OER THE STRETCHING CLOUDY PLAIN   126 BALDER DEAD 3   V 443
          THE WIDE PLAIN RINGS THE DAZED AIR THROBS WITH BLOWS 137 TRISTRAM 1   235
          THE UNQUIET BRIGHT ATLANTIC PLAIN   . . . . . .   148 TRISTRAM 2   174
          NOW ROUND US SPREADS THE WATERY PLAIN   . . . .   182 TO MARG CONT   17
          UPON THE BOUNDLESS OCEAN-PLAIN   . . . .   185 TERRACE BERNE   46
          ACROSS THIS WIDE AERIAL PLAIN   . . . .   204 CALAIS SANDS   6
          OER CALAIS AND ITS FAMOUS PLAIN . . . .   205 CALAIS SANDS   18
          SPREAD WIDE AWAY THE LUMINOUS PLAIN   . . . . . .   204 CALAIS SANDS   V 6
          ON CALAIS AND ITS SHINING PLAIN . . . .   205 CALAIS SANDS   V 18
          AND WE ARE HERE AS ON A DARKLING PLAIN   . . . .   212 DOVER BEACH   35
          GLADLY DESCEND TO THE PLAIN   . . . .   216 LORDS MESSENGER   9
          AT THE CLOSE OF DAY FROM THE PLAIN   . . . . . .   217 LORDS MESSENGER   21
          MADLY BELOW IN THE PLAIN   . . . .   216 LORDS MESSENGER   V
          OER THE CLOUD-WRAPT PERILOUS PLAIN   . . . . . .   217 LORDS MESSENGER   V 21
          DESERTED IS THE HALF-MOWN PLAIN . . . .   217 BACCHANALIA 1   4
          AND OER THE PLAIN WHERE THE DEAD AGE   . . . . . .   219 BACCHANALIA 2   19
          OER THAT WIDE PLAIN NOW WRAPT IN GLOOM   . . . .   220 BACCHANALIA 2   21
          SEE ON THE CUMBERD PLAIN   . . . . . , . . .   220 BACCHANALIA 2   33
          WE SHALL RENEW THE BATTLE IN THE PLAIN   . . . .   236 PALLADIUM   13
          MEN WILL RENEW THE BATTLE IN THE PLAIN   . . . .   236 PALLADIUM   V 13
          THE EYE SINKS INWARD AND THE HEART LIES PLAIN   . . 247 BURIED LIFE   86
          SLUGGISHLY WINDS THROUGH THE PLAIN   . . . . . .   252 FUTURE   15
          NOW FLOWS THROUGH WITH US IS THE PLAIN   . . . .   253 FUTURE   51
          FLATTER THE PLAIN WHERE IT FLOWS   . . . . . .   253 FUTURE   64
          PAMISUS WATERING THE MESSENIAN PLAIN   . . . . . .   330 MEROPE   19
          FAR ON MARATHON PLAIN   . . . .   343 MEROPE   431
          AND THE PLAIN OF TEGEA   . . . .   344 MEROPE   435
          ON TO THE MARSHY ORCHOMENIAN PLAIN   . . . . . .   356 MEROPE   743
          ALL THE STYMPHALIAN PLAIN ARE NOW SUCKD DOWN   . .   358 MEROPE   816
          THAT THOU MAYST READ THINE ENEMYS COUNSEL PLAIN . . 380 MEROPE   1278
          THROUGH WHICH TO SEE LESS PLAIN . . . .   419 EMPEDOCLES I 2   V 205
          PLAIN WE SAW IF THEY WERE SAD   . . . .   455 POOR MATTHIAS   90

PLAIN   (CONTINUED)
    AND THIS PLAIN STAVE • • • • • • • • •   461 KAISER DEAD   84
    SLOPE STATELY DOWN AND MELT INTO THE PLAIN • • •   473 CROMWELL   38
    WHILE OER THE DUSTY PLAIN THE MURMUROUS THRONG • •   473 CROMWELL   43
    LIKE A SWIFT RIVER THRO A SILENT PLAIN • • • •   473 CROMWELL   64
    OER FLOWERING PLAIN AND BLOSSOMD MEADOW FLING • •   474 CROMWELL   91
    THE SUNLESS FOREST AND THE SEALIKE PLAIN • • • •   475 CROMWELL   106
    IN THE PLAIN THERE WERE KINDLED A THOUSAND   HOMER TRANS   3
        FIRES BY EACH ONE
    AND NOT LEAVE HIM BEHIND A CORPSE ON THE PLAIN   HOMER TRANS   42
        LIKE PATROCLUS

PLAINNESS
    PLAINNESS AND CLEARNESS WITHOUT SHADOW OF STAIN • •   244 SUMMER NIGHT   76
    WITH A PLAINNESS AS NEAR • • • • • • • • •   253 FUTURE   44
    OF PLAINNESS OPPRESSD BY CUNNING • • • • • •   432 EMPEDOCLES II   101

PLAINS
    FADED THE MOSS THE ROCKS US BURNING PLAINS • • •   25 DREAM   36
    WENT LURID DOWN OER FLOODED PLAINS • • • • • •   52 RESIGNATION   11
    STILL ROUGH LIKE THOSE WHICH MEN IN TREELESS PLAINS   73 SOHRAB RUSTUM   410
    LIKE THOSE WHICH MEN WHO DWELL IN TREELESS PLAINS   73 SOHRAB RUSTUM V 410
    THE PLAINS OF NIFLHEIM WHERE DWELL THE DEAD • •   100 BALDER DEAD 1   172
    THE PLAINS OF NIFLHEIM WHERE DWELL THE DEAD • •   109 BALDER DEAD 2   150
    THE JOYLESS-PLAINS AND HEARD THE STREAMS OF HELL • •   124 BALDER DEAD 3   380
    AGAINST THE GODS UPON THE PLAINS OF HEAVEN • • •   127 BALDER DEAD 3   481
    THE BOUNDLESS WAVING GRASS-PLAINS STRETCH THICK-STARRD   191 STRAYED REVEL   168
    ON TO THE PLAINS TO THE SEA • • • • • • •   234 YOUTH OF MAN   86
    TO THE INVISIBLE PLAINS TO ROAM WITH THEE • • •   367 MEROPE   1030

PLAINT
    AND WE SHOULD TEASE HER WITH OUR PLAINT IN VAIN • •   265 THYRSIS   100
    ALL PLAINT IN HER OWN CAUSE CONTROLLD • • •   279 SOUTHERN NIGHT 122

PLAINTIVE
    THESE OER THE CORPSE INTONED A PLAINTIVE STRAIN • •   103 BALDER DEAD 1   273
    AND SINGS HIS PLAINTIVE SONG • • • • • • •   159 NECKAN   4
    AND SINGS THIS PLAINTIVE SONG • • • • • • •   161 NECKAN   68

PLAN
    BY SELFISH OCCUPATION PLOT AND PLAN • • • • •   7 REP FRIEND CONT   11
    TO-MORROW ON THE SELF-SAME PLAN • • • • • •   56 RESIGNATION   141
    FINDS HIM WITH MANY AN UNSOLVED PLAN • • • • •   58 RESIGNATION   224
    LIVE WE LIKE BRUTES OUR LIFE WITHOUT A PLAN • •   171 BETTER PART   8
    NOTHING SURE NO MORAL PLAN • • • • • • •   215 PIS-ALLER   7
    HIS EYES ON NATURES PLAN • • • • • • • •   308 OBERMANN   58
    YE LIVE I CRIED YE WORK AND PLAN • • • • • •   320 OBERMANN MORE   215
    THEY COME AND GO THEY WORK AND PLAN • • • • •   320 OBERMANN MORE V 215
    MAN HAS A MIND WITH WHICH TO PLAN HIS SAFETY • •   413 EMPEDOCLES I 2   28
    WHOSE MIND ALLOWS A PLAN • • • • • • • •   415 EMPEDOCLES I 2   99
    WHAT WERE THE WISE MANS PLAN • • • • • • •   421 EMPEDOCLES I 2 267
    THAT PAIR WHOSE HEAD DID PLAN WHOSE HANDS DID FORGE   448 WESTMIN ABBEY   134
    MAKING WANT OF THEIRS AND PLAN • • • • • • •   456 POOR MATTHIAS   151
    IN WHOSE CAPACIOUS SPIRIT LAY HIS PLAN • • • •   LUCRETIUS 5   4
    IN WHOSE PROPHETIC SPIRIT LAY THE PLAN • • • •   LUCRETIUS 5   V 4

PLANE
    A HEADLAND WITH ONE AGED PLANE-TREE CROWND • • • •   358 MEROPE   817

PLANET
    SOME ANGELS IN AN ALIEN PLANET BORN • • • • •   42 GIPSY CHILD   26
    WHAT SERAPHS IN SOME ALIEN PLANET BORN • • • •   42 GIPSY CHILD   V 26

PLANK
    BACKD BY THE PINES A PLANK-BUILT COTTAGE STOOD • •   25 DREAM   15

PLANKD
    SOON THE PLANKD COTTAGE BY THE SUN-WARMD PINES • •   25 DREAM   35
    SOON THE PLANKD COTTAGE MID THE SUN-WARMD PINES • •   25 DREAM   V 35

PLANKS
    TO SAW THEM PLANKS FISH FROM THE FLOODED RIVERS • •   73 SOHRAB RUSTUM V 411
    THROUGH THE ROUGH FIR-PLANKS • • • • • • • •   186 STRAYED REVEL   25

PLANND
    TRISTRAM SWEET LOVE WE ARE BETRAYD OUT-PLANND • •   135 TRISTRAM 1   167
    ALMOST BEFORE TIS PLANND COME GLOWING HATE • • •   367 MEROPE   1062

PLANNING
    TRULY THOU SAYST THE PLANNING GUILTY MIND • • • •   125 BALDER DEAD 3   424

PLANS
    TEEMING WITH PLANS ALERT AND GLAD • • • • • •   460 KAISER DEAD   45

PLANT
    COME PLANT WE HERE IN EARTH OUR ANGRY SPEARS • •   74 SOHRAB RUSTUM   439
    AND PLANT A FAR-SEEN PILLAR OVER ALL • • • • •   84 SOHRAB RUSTUM   789
    AND PLANT A FAR-SEEN PILLAR OVER ALL • • • • •   84 SOHRAB RUSTUM   804
    AND FROM THE MINT-PLANT IN THE SEDGE • • • • •   218 BACCHANALIA 1   13

PLANTED
    HIS GIANT FIGURE PLANTED ON THE SAND • • • • •   71 SOHRAB RUSTUM   336

PLANTED   (CONTINUED)
        THE LAW IS PLANTED TO ABIDE   • • • • • • • •   94 SICK KING BOKH   208
        PLANTED HIS FOOTSTEP THE SPRAY   • • • • • • • •   289 RUGBY CHAPEL   97

PLANTING
        PLANTING HIS STEADFAST FOOTSTEPS IN THE SEA   • •   3 SHAKESPEARE   5

PLANTS
        BRIGHT IN THE SUN THE CLIMBING GOURD-PLANTS LEAVES   25 DREAM   16
        THE LIFE OF PLANTS AND STONES AND RAIN   • • • •   58 RESIGNATION   195
        LET GODS MEN BRUTES BEWEEP HIM PLANTS AND STONES • •   111 BALDER DEAD 2   238
        LET GODS MEN BRUTES BEWEEP HIM PLANTS AND STONES • •   114 BALDER DEAD 3   44
        WITH THE DARK IVY-PLANTS   • • • • • • • •   188 STRAYED REVEL   88
        WITH LARGE-LEAVED LOW-CREEPING MELON-PLANTS   •   190 STRAYED REVEL   155
        OF IVY-PLANTS AND FRAGRANT HANGING BELLS   • • •   414 EMPEDOCLES I 2   49
        IN MEN AND PLANTS AND STONES   • • • • • • •   422 EMPEDOCLES I 2   293
        THE TENDER FOXGLOVE-PLANTS DISPLAY   • • • • •   484 ROME-SICKNESS   15

PLASHING
        LIGHT-PLASHING WAVES AN ANSWER MADE   • • • •   223 EPILOG LAOCOON   68
        COLD PLASHING PAST IT CRYSTAL WATERS ROLL   • • • •   236 PALLADIUM   11

PLATES
        THE IRON PLATES RANG SHARP BUT TURND THE SPEAR   • •   73 SOHRAB RUSTUM   407
        RENT THE TOUGH PLATES BUT FAILD TO REACH THE SKIN   76 SOHRAB RUSTUM   493
        RENT THE TOUGH PLATES BUT MISSD TO REACH THE SKIN   76 SOHRAB RUSTUM   V 493

PLATFORM
        A PROP GAVE WAY CRASH FELL A PLATFORM LO   • • • •   166 AUSTERITY POET   8

PLATFORMS
        ON THY HIGH MOUNTAIN-PLATFORMS   • • • • • • • •   177 PARTING   85

PLATTER
        CORN IN A GOLDEN PLATTER SOAKD WITH WINE   • • • •   83 SOHRAB RUSTUM   754

PLAY
        TOO FEARFUL OR TOO FOND TO PLAY ALONE   • • • •   8 RELIGIOUS ISOL   5
        PLAY THROUGH THIS GRASSY UPLAND GLEN   • • • • •   55 RESIGNATION   99
        OF BATTLE AND WITH ME WHO MAKE NO PLAY   • • •   75 SOHRAB RUSTUM   463
        AH WOULD I WERE IN THOSE GREEN FIELDS AT PLAY   •   133 TRISTRAM 1   97
        IN THE WOODS WHERE THE GLEAMS PLAY   • • • • •   137 TRISTRAM 1   220
        AND ON TWO ANGEL-HEADS DOTH PLAY   • • • • •   141 TRISTRAM 1   337
        TO SEE THE PARK-GLADES WHERE YOU PLAY   • • •   141 TRISTRAM 1   355
        HAD WANDERD FORTH HER CHILDREN WERE AT PLAY   •   149 TRISTRAM 3   6
        WATCHING HER CHILDREN PLAY THEIR LITTLE HANDS   •   150 TRISTRAM 3   24
        HER LAUGHING CHILDREN IN THEIR BEDS AND PLAY   •   151 TRISTRAM 3   77
        IS WITH THEM AND THE WIDE HEATHS WHERE THEY PLAY   •   152 TRISTRAM 3   103
        DREW ISEULT FORTH HER CHILDREN WERE AT PLAY   TRISTRAM 3   V   5
        NOW THE WILD WHITE HORSES PLAY   • • • • • •   161 FORSAKEN MERM   6
        WHY STOPS SHE BY THIS EMPTY PLAY-HOUSE DREAR   •   167 RACHEL 1   11
        TWO SPRINGS WHICH CLOSE BY ONE ANOTHER PLAY   •   170 EAST AND WEST   2
        WE HEARD AFAR FAINT MUSIC PLAY   • • • • • •   224 EPILOG LAOCOON   110
        THEIR CHILDREN PLAY ON THE LAWNS   • • • • •   234 YOUTH OF MAN   70
        THAT IT MIGHT KEEP FROM HIS CAPRICIOUS PLAY   •   246 BURIED LIFE   35
        LIGHT THE GREEN-FOLIAGD CHESTNUTS PLAY   • • •   248 KENSINGTON GARD   V
        LIGHT THE CLEAR FOLIAGED CHESTNUTS PLAY   KENSINGTON GARD   V
        AND MEN WERE SPECKS AND LIFE A PLAY   • • • •   277 SOUTHERN NIGHT   78
        FROM A FEW BOYS LATE AT THEIR PLAY   • • • •   286 RUGBY CHAPEL   7
        THE SPLASHING ICY FOUNTAINS PLAY   • • • •   300 GRANDE CHARTR   33
        THROUGH THE PINE BRANCHES PLAY   • • • • • •   310 OBERMANN   126
        THY BROTHERS PLAY AT MY FEET   • • • • • • •   378 MEROPE   1238
        PLAY WHEN WE HALT AND WHEN THE EVENING COMES   •   409 EMPEDOCLES I 1   90
        THEN PLAY THY KIND PART WELL FAREWELL TILL NIGHT   •   411 EMPEDOCLES I 1   167
        THE PEAK ROUND WHICH THE WHITE CLOUDS PLAY   • •   414 EMPEDOCLES I 2   56
        MEANT MERELY FOR HIS PLAY   • • • • • • •   418 EMPEDOCLES I 2   180
        LOVE TO HAVE SCOPE AND PLAY   • • • • • • •   420 EMPEDOCLES I 2   248
        SEES ALL HER SONS AT PLAY   • • • • • • •   421 EMPEDOCLES I 2   258
        CALLICLES MUST WAIT HERE AND PLAY TO HIM   • •   428 EMPEDOCLES I 2   484
        WILL FRET OUR MINDS TO AN INTENSER PLAY   • •   440 EMPEDOCLES II   380
        WHILE TONGUES OF FIRE ON COIGN AND CARVING PLAY   •   445 WESTMIN ABBEY   36
        GREET UPON THE LAWN AT PLAY   • • • • • •   454 POOR MATTHIAS   68
        IN WORK OR PLAY   • • • • • • • • • •   460 KAISER DEAD   46
        WOULD PLAY THE TRAITOR TO THE STEDFAST WILL   •   475 CROMWELL   108
        LOFTY THOUGHT LIES OFT IN CHILDISH PLAY   • • •   483 THEKLAS ANSWER   24

PLAYD
        WHICH DANCED AND ON THEIR SHOULDERS FLUTTERING PLAYD   25 DREAM   25
        WHICH WAVD AND ON THEIR SHOULDERS FLUTTERING PLAYD   25 DREAM   V   25
        WHICH STIRRD AND ON THEIR SHOULDERS FLUTTERING PLAYD   25 DREAM   V   25
        AND PLAYD WITH IT BUT GUDURZ CAME AND STOOD   •   67 SOHRAB RUSTUM   201
        THE GOLDEN DICE WHEREWITH WE PLAYD OF YORE   • •   128 BALDER DEAD 3   539
        THE GOLDEN DICE WITH WHICH WE PLAYD OF YORE   •   128 BALDER DEAD 3   V 539
        WHICH PLAYD ON HER FLUSHD CHEEK AND HER BLUE EYES   154 TRISTRAM 3   169
        HE SATE AND PLAYD HIS HARP OF GOLD   • • • • •   160 NECKAN   43
        AND ON THE SPARKLING WATERS PLAYD   • • • • •   223 EPILOG LAOCOON   67
        SO HE PLAYD ON THEN ENDED WITH A SMILE   • • •   357 MEROPE   784
        UPON THE HEARTH AND PLAYD WITH THEM AND SMILED   •   446 WESTMIN ABBEY   90
        PURSY PLAYD-OUT PHILISTINE   • • • • • • • •   457 POOR MATTHIAS   190

PLAYER
    THE SWEETEST HARP-PLAYER IN CATANA • • • • • • 412 EMPEDOCLES I 2   13
    THAT WAS MY HARP-PLAYER AGAIN WHERE IS HE • • • • 427 EMPEDOCLES I 2   461

PLAYERS
    THE FAMOUS PLAYERS SCULPTORS WROUGHT • • • • • • 219 BACCHANALIA 2   7

PLAYING
    ON THESE LAWNS I SAW YOU PLAYING • • • • •   29 NEW SIRENS   95
    YET THOU MAYST TRY THY PLAYING IF THOU WILT • • 409 EMPEDOCLES I 1   85
    AND HE TAUGHT HIM FLUTE-PLAYING • • • • • 434 EMPEDOCLES II   170

PLAYS
    PLAYS FONDLY ROUND THEM • • • • • • • •   51 CONSOLATION   44
    GOD TIS HER FACE PLAYS IN THE WATERS BRIGHT • • 139 TRISTRAM 1   284
    WHICH GLISTERING PLAYS ALL ROUND THEM LONE AND MILD 155 TRISTRAM 3   203
    STILL PLAYS ON THE CITY SPIRES • • • • • • 234 YOUTH OF MAN   82
    PLAYS ON THEIR FACES THEY GAZE • • • • • • 235 YOUTH OF MAN   90
    AN AIR OF COOLNESS PLAYS UPON HIS FACE • • • 247 BURIED LIFE   94
    WHICH FOOLISH INNOCENCE PLAYS WITH SUBTLE GUILT • • 366 MEROPE   V
    TO WHERE THE WEST-WIND PLAYS • • • • • • 427 EMPEDOCLES I 2   454

PLAYST
    AND PLAYST THY HARP OF GOLD • • • • • • • 160 NECKAN   50

PLEA
    OUR CRY FOR BLISS OUR PLEA • • • • • • • 419 EMPEDOCLES I 2   209

PLEAD
    AND WE PLEAD AS STAUNCH ADHERENCE • • • •   28 NEW SIRENS   59
    AND WE PLEAD AS FIRM ADHERENCE • • • • • •   28 NEW SIRENS   V 59

PLEADED
    SO WHEN HE PLEADED FOR OUR LEAGUE BUT NOW • • • • 404 MEROPE   1978

PLEADER
    NOR ANY PLEADER ELSE SHALL BE INDULGED • • • • 389 MEROPE   1527

PLEADERS
    O SWEET PLEADERS DOTH MY LOT • • • • • • •   31 NEW SIRENS   164

PLEADING
    WHO TAUGHT THIS PLEADING TO UNPRACTISED EYES • •   41 GIPSY CHILD   1
    PLEADING GAZE THAT FOREHEAD CLEAR • • • • •   META CLOISTER   38

PLEASANT
    TO SPURN MANS COMMON LURE LIFES PLEASANT THINGS • •   9 MYCERINUS   32
    OF ONE SHORT JOY ONE LUST ONE PLEASANT DREAM • •   10 MYCERINUS   50
    THIN THIN THE PLEASANT HUMAN NOISES GROW • • • •   45 IN UTRUMQUE PAR   15
    WITH PLEASANT SMILE LET US TAKE CARE • • • •   48 HORATIAN ECHO   21
    AND WARM AND PLEASANT BUT THE GRAVE IS COLD • •   71 SOHRAB RUSTUM   323
    WITH JOY AND ALL THE PLEASANT LIFE THEY LED • •   79 SOHRAB RUSTUM   627
    WE WANT ALL PLEASANT ENDS BUT WILL USE NO HARSH MEANS 420 EMPEDOCLES I 2   236
    O PLEASANT REST IF ONCE THE RACE WERE RUN • • • • 475 CROMWELL   119

PLEASAUNCE
    CHILL BLOWS THE WIND THE PLEASAUNCE-WALKS ARE DREAR   135 TRISTRAM 1   161
    THE PLEASAUNCE-WALKS THE WEEPING QUEEN • • • • 136 TRISTRAM 1   178

PLEASE
    ARE FURIOUS WITH THEMSELVES AND HARD TO PLEASE • • 153 TRISTRAM 3   142
    CAN NEVER END THEIR TASKS ARE HARD TO PLEASE • • 153 TRISTRAM 3   V 142
    ARE FRETFUL WITH THEMSELVES AND HARD TO PLEASE • • 153 TRISTRAM 3   V 142
    HER ARTISTS COULD NOT PLEASE • • • • • • • 316 OBERMANN MORE   130
    FAILS THEIR OWN WILL TO PLEASE • • • • • • 417 EMPEDOCLES I 2   150
    AND HE TAUGHT HIM HOW TO PLEASE • • • • • 434 EMPEDOCLES II   179

PLEASED
    TIMES GAY MINIONS PLEASED YOU SEE • • • • •   24 MEMORY-PICTURE   53
    PLEASED YOU MOCK THE FRUITLESS CRY • • • • •   24 MEMORY-PICTURE   55
    WELL PLEASED SEE END • • • • • • • • •   52 CONSOLATION   65
    BY WHAT OF OLD PLEASED US AND WILL AGAIN • • • 153 TRISTRAM 3   118
    HE HATH PLEASED OUR EYES AND EARS • • • • • 458 POOR MATTHIAS   203

PLEASURE
    THE FEEBLE SONS OF PLEASURE SET THEIR HAND • • • •   5 DUKE WELLINGTON   7
    AND LANGUID PLEASURE FADE AND FLOWER AGAIN • • • •   10 MYCERINUS   64
    THEIR PLEASURE TO THEIR FEET AND REAP THEIR PRAISE   11 MYCERINUS   77
    HAST THOU WITH MYRTLE-LEAF CROWND HIM O PLEASURE • •   20 MODERN SAPPHO   35
    DUE TO PLEASURE AS TO PAIN • • • • • • •   28 NEW SIRENS   60
    IS THE PLEASURE THAT IS TASTED • • • • • •   30 NEW SIRENS   191
    JOYOUS AT THE HEIGHT OF PLEASURE • • • • •   33 NEW SIRENS   201
    HAPPY AT THE NOON OF PLEASURE • • • • • •   33 NEW SIRENS   V 201
    BOTH IN SUFFERING AND IN PLEASURE • • • • •   49 SECOND BEST   3
    OF STARTLED PLEASURE FLOODS THY BROW • • • • 184 TERRACE BERNE   14
    ITS PAIN AND PLEASURE REST AND STRIFE • • • • 225 EPILOG LAOCOON   144
    A PLEASURE IN CREATING • • • • • • • • 228 CAUTION POETS   2
    PLEASURE IN CONTEMPLATING • • • • • • • 228 CAUTION POETS   4

PLEASURE   (CONTINUED)
        ACTION AND PLEASURE WILL YE ROAM   • • • • • • •   305 GRANDE CHARTR   194
        THE CAPITAL OF PLEASURE SEES   • • • • • • •   312 OBERMANN   179
        AND I MUST LEAVE HIM FOR HIS PLEASURE IS   • • • •   409 EMPEDOCLES I 1   91
        THY PLEASURE RIGHT OR WRONG   • • • • • • • •   416 EMPEDOCLES I 2   133
        PLEASURE TO OUR HOT GRASP   • • • • • • • • •   424 EMPEDOCLES I 2   357
        BUT AN AWFUL PLEASURE BLAND   • • • • • • • •   431 EMPEDOCLES II   67
        THE SMALLEST THING COULD GIVE US PLEASURE THEN   • •   436 EMPEDOCLES II   250

PLEASURES
        VAIN DREAMS WHICH QUENCH OUR PLEASURES THEN DEPART   9 MYCERINUS   27
        VAIN DREAMS THAT QUENCH OUR PLEASURES THEN DEPART   9 MYCERINUS   V 27
        TO MAKE OUR FORMER PLEASURES ALL SEEM STALE   • •   153 TRISTRAM 3   126
        AND THOU HAST PLEASURES TOO TO SHARE • • • • • •   309 OBERMANN   109
        WHAT PLEASURES MAY BE HAD   • • • • • • • • •   426 EMPEDOCLES I 2   408

PLEASURING
        THAT YE COME PLEASURING TO THOKS IRON WOOD • • • •   123 BALDER DEAD 3   338

PLEDGE
        AND PLEDGE EACH OTHER IN RED WINE LIKE FRIENDS   • •   74 SOHRAB RUSTUM   441
        SPEAK NOT TO ME OF TRUCE AND PLEDGE AND WINE   • •   75 SOHRAB RUSTUM   465
        BUT PLEDGE ME IN IT FIRST FOR COURTESY   • • • •   133 TRISTRAM 1   101
        PLEDGE ME IN MY GOLDEN CUP   • • • • • • • •   135 TRISTRAM 1   146
        AND PLEDGE ME IN IT FIRST FOR COURTESY   • • • •   133 TRISTRAM 1   V 101

PLIANT
        PAINT THAT FIGURES PLIANT GRACE   • • • • • •   23 MEMORY-PICTURE   33

PLIES
        PLIES SOME LIGHT FEMALE TASK NOR DREAMS OF US   • •   80 SOHRAB RUSTUM   647
        UPON THEM PLIES THE RACE OF MAN   • • • • • •   320 OBERMANN MORE   213
        THIS COMMERCE FOR MY BEST BEHOOF HE PLIES   • • • •   380 MEROPE   1277

PLIGHT
        THESE ASK NO LOVE THESE PLIGHT NO FAITH   • • • •   203 EUPHROSYNE   15

PLODS
        ERE HE PLODS ON AGAIN   • • • • • • • • • •   311 OBERMANN   174

PLOT
        BY SELFISH OCCUPATION PLOT AND PLAN   • • • • •   7 REP FRIEND CONT   11
        AND MADE A LITTLE PLOT OF MAGIC GROUND   • • • •   156 TRISTRAM 3   220
        ROUND HIS GREEN HARVEST-PLOT   • • • • • • • •   190 STRAYED REVEL   159
        AND CANST TEACH SIMPLE ONES TO PLOT AND FEIGN   • •   367 MEROPE   1059
        SWORN TO OUR PLOT HE IS IF FALSE SURMISE   • • • •   379 MEROPE   1272
        SWORN TO OUR PLOT HE IS BUT THAT SURMISE   • • • •   379 MEROPE   V1272

PLOTS
        MOWING THE GARDEN GRASS-PLOTS NEAR ITS BED • • •   80 SOHRAB RUSTUM   636
        AND IN FIELDS SLOPING TO THE SOUTH DARK PLOTS   • •   122 BALDER DEAD 3   314
        FOR THAT HE PLOTS THY DEATH ACCOUNT IT FALSE   • •   387 MEROPE   1485
        FIGMENTS OF PLOTS WHEREWITH INTRIGUERS FILL   • •   387 MEROPE   1487

PLOTTED
        TREACHEROUSLY PLOTTED TWIXT MY SON AND ME   • • • •   387 MEROPE   1481

PLOTTING
        IF CLEAR FROM PLOTTING BALDERS DEATH TO SWIM   • •   114 BALDER DEAD 3   27

PLOUGH
        IN THE SUNSHINE UNWORN BY THE PLOUGH • • • • • •   252 FUTURE   30

PLOUGHBOYS
        DOWN EACH GREEN BANK HATH GONE THE PLOUGHBOYS TEAM   266 THYRSIS   118

PLOUGHD
        FROM THE DEEP TRENCH SHE PLOUGHD SO STRONG A GOD • •   118 BALDER DEAD 3   178

PLOVER
        AND THE PLOVER IS HEARD ON THE MOORS • • • • • •   285 HAWORTH CHURCH   116

PLUCK
        PLUCK PLUCK CYPRESS O PALE MAIDENS   • • • • •   30 NEW SIRENS   113
        PLUCK PLUCK CYPRESS O PALE MAIDENS   • • • • •   30 NEW SIRENS   113
        PLUCK NO MORE RED ROSES MAIDENS   • • • • • •   35 NEW SIRENS   267
        PLUCK PLUCK CYPRESS O PALE MAIDENS   • • • • •   35 NEW SIRENS   269
        PLUCK PLUCK CYPRESS O PALE MAIDENS   • • • • •   35 NEW SIRENS   269
        PLUCK PLUCK CYPRESS O PALE MAIDENS   • • • • •   35 NEW SIRENS   275
        PLUCK PLUCK CYPRESS O PALE MAIDENS   • • • • •   35 NEW SIRENS   275
        WHEN IT SHOULD PLUCK THEE FROM THY HOSTILE WAY   • •   333 MEROPE   99
        AND THE REALITY WILL PLUCK US BACK   • • • • •   440 EMPEDOCLES II   385

PLUCKD
        AND RUSTUM PLUCKD IT BACK WITH ANGRY GROAN • • • •   76 SOHRAB RUSTUM   494
        PLUCKD IN SHY FIELDS AND DISTANT WYCHWOOD BOWERS • •   257 SCHOLAR-GIPSY   79
        PLUCKD IN SHY FIELDS AND DISTANT WOODLAND BOWERS • •   257 SCHOLAR-GIPSY   V 79
        PLUCKD FROM THE FIRE THE CHILD AND LAID HIM DOWN • •   447 WESTMIN ABBEY   95

PLUCKING
AND PLUCKING UP THE MARBLE FLAGS . . . . . . 95 SICK KING BOKH 227
OR THE CHILDREN PLUCKING . . . . 392 MEROPE 1637

PLUMAGE
SMOOTH HIS RUFFLED PLUMAGE FINE . . . . . . 452 POOR MATTHIAS 11
LAUD THEIR PLUMAGE GREET THEIR LAYS . . . . . 455 POOR MATTHIAS 100

PLUMB
CONCEALS FROM MAN WHO CANNOT PLUMB ITS DEPTHS . . 351 MEROPE 623

PLUME
AND FROM THE FLUTED SPINE ATOP A PLUME . . . . 69 SOHRAB RUSTUM 268
OF HORSEHAIR WAVED A SCARLET HORSEHAIR PLUME . . 69 SOHRAB RUSTUM 269
HE SHORE AWAY AND THAT PROUD HORSEHAIR PLUME . . 76 SOHRAB RUSTUM 497
PENNON AND PLUME AND FLASHING LANCE . . . . . 305 GRANDE CHARTR 178

PLUMED
UP THE STEEP PINE-PLUMED PATHS OF THE ESTRELLE . . 167 RACHEL 2 4

PLUMES
NOR WITHERD WHEN THE PALM-TREE PLUMES THAT ROOFD . . 12 MYCERINUS 118
WITH LONG PLUMES AND SOFT BROWN SEEDS . . . . 434 EMPEDOCLES II 175

PLUMMET
DROPS LIKE A PLUMMET SOHRAB SAW IT COME . . . . 73 SOHRAB RUSTUM 402

PLUNGD
PLUNGD IN THEMSELVES WHO DEMAND . . . . . . 282 HAWORTH CHURCH V

PLUNGE
WHY TARRIEST THOU TO PLUNGE THEE IN THE GULPH . . 124 BALDER DEAD 3 388
STILL FLY PLUNGE DEEPER IN THE BOWERING WOOD . . 261 SCHOLAR-GIPSY 207

PLUNGED
WAS HUSHD AND STILL THE MEN WERE PLUNGED IN SLEEP 61 SOHRAB RUSTUM 4
HE SPOKE BUT RUSTUM LISTEND PLUNGED IN THOUGHT . . 79 SOHRAB RUSTUM 604
SO DEEMD HE YET HE LISTEND PLUNGED IN THOUGHT . . 79 SOHRAB RUSTUM 615
HIS EYE PLUNGED DOWN THE WELTERING STRIFE . . . 270 MEMORIAL VERSES 25
HIS EYE PLUNGED DOWN THE SEETHING STRIFE . . . 270 MEMORIAL VERSES V 25
AND PLUNGED IN THOUGHT AGAIN . . . . 316 OBERMANN MORE 112
AND LOOK TO MEET THEM THAT ONE GRIEF-PLUNGED FORM 331 MEROPE 56
WE BOUNDED DOWN THE SWARDED SLOPE WE PLUNGED . . 357 MEROPE 790
THEN CAME THE PRINCE HE SHOUTED AND PLUNGED IN . 358 MEROPE 810
WHERE FIRST THE CHASE PLUNGED IN THE BAY IS SMOOTH 358 MEROPE 819
AND SEE TO MEET THEM THAT ONE GRIEF-PLUNGED FORM . . 331 MEROPE V 56

PLUNGING
OR CLUSTERD PEAKS WITH PLUNGING GULFS BETWEEN . . 4 BUTLERS SERMONS 11
PLUNGING ALL DAY IN THE BLUE WAVES AT NIGHT . . 69 SOHRAB RUSTUM 287
PLUNGING THROUGH DEEP UNTRODDEN BANKS OF SNOW . . 107 BALDER DEAD 2 97
FRESHEND BY PLUNGING TIDES BY SHOWERS . . . . 275 STANZAS CARNAC 42

PLUTOS
AND RELAX PLUTOS BROW . . . . 265 THYRSIS 86
AND UNBEND PLUTOS BROW . . . . 265 THYRSIS V 86

PLY
MAY THEN MORE NEIGHBOURING COURSES PLY . . . . 180 FAREWELL 74
PLY HIS BOW SUCH A PRICE . . . . 193 STRAYED REVEL 232
UPON THEM PLY THE RACE OF MAN . . . . 320 OBERMANN MORE V 213
TO PLY TWIXT THE MESSENIAN KING AND HIM . . . . 364 MEROPE 981

POACH
POACH THE DEEP WAYS COMING DOWN . . . . . . 282 HAWORTH CHURCH 59

PODARGA
XANTHUS AND BALIUS BOTH YE FAR-FAMD SEED OF PODARGA HOMER TRANS 39

POEMS
BARDS MAKE NEW POEMS . . . . 220 BACCHANALIA 2 37
GOOD POEMS IF HE LOOKD MORE RARE . . . . . . 221 EPILOG LAOCOON 17

POET
THE POET TO WHOSE MIGHTY HEART . . . . 56 RESIGNATION 144
ARE LESS THE POET MORE THAN MAN . . . . . . 58 RESIGNATION 204
DEEPER THE POET FEELS BUT HE . . . . 58 RESIGNATION 206
NOT DEEP THE POET SEES BUT WIDE . . . . . . 58 RESIGNATION 214
DEEPLY THE POET FEELS BUT HE . . . . 58 RESIGNATION V 206
POET WHAT AILS THEE THEN . . . . 220 BACCHANALIA 2 45
THE POET FEELS THE PAST AS WELL . . . . . . 221 BACCHANALIA 2 66
WHERE BEST THE POET FRAMED HIS PIECE . . . . . 221 EPILOG LAOCOON 14
CAN I FEEL THAT THEIR POET IS GONE . . . . . 229 YOUTH OF NATURE 27
OF A SACRED POET LIES LOW . . . . 229 YOUTH OF NATURE 49
OR THE POET WHO SINGS YOU SO WELL . . . . . . 230 YOUTH OF NATURE 62
THE POET WHO SINGS THEM MAY DIE . . . . . . 230 YOUTH OF NATURE 84
WHEN YE MOURN THAT A POET IS DEAD . . . . . . 230 YOUTH OF NATURE 88
POET AND STEEP HIM IN CALM . . . . 294 HEINES GRAVE 51
SONG OF THE POET DIVINE . . . . 295 HEINES GRAVE 104
POET THE WORLD TO THY WAY . . . . 295 HEINES GRAVE 107
GOD GAVE THE POET HIS SONG . . . . 296 HEINES GRAVE 120

POET   (CONTINUED)
        SOME SECRETS MAY THE POET TELL • • • • • • • • •   307 OBERMANN   41

POETIC
        THE LAST POETIC VOICE IS DUMB • • • • • • • • •   270 MEMORIAL VERSES   4

POETRY
        WHAT PAINTING IS WHAT POETRY • • • • • • • • •   221 EPILOG LAOCOON   6
        THAN POETRY WHY SHE THAN THEY • • • • • • • • •   221 EPILOG LAOCOON   11

POETS
        THE POETS RAPT SECURITY • • • • • • • • • • •   59 RESIGNATION   246
        SUCH POETS IS YOUR BRIDE THE MUSE YOUNG GAY • •   166 AUSTERITY POET   12
        THE FAMOUS POETS SUNG AND GONE • • • • • • • • •   219 BACCHANALIA 2   4
        POETS LIKE SHAKESPEARE • • • • • • • • • • •   221 BACCHANALIA 2   59
        BEHOLD AT LAST THE POETS SPHERE • • • • • • • •   225 EPILOG LAOCOON   127
        WHAT POETS FEEL NOT WHEN THEY MAKE • • • • • •   228 CAUTION POETS   1
        CHARM IS THE POETS ALONE • • • • • • • • • •   295 HEINES GRAVE   112
        THE POETS FEVERISH BLOOD • • • • • • • • • •   309 OBERMANN   94
        POETS FIRE GETS FAINT AND LOW • • • • • • • • •   454 POOR MATTHIAS   78

POINT
        WHOSE FIERY POINT NOW IN HIS MAILD RIGHT-HAND • • 74 SOHRAB RUSTUM   451
        THEN AT THE POINT OF DEATH SOHRAB REPLIED • • • •   85 SOHRAB RUSTUM   827
        THERE ON A HIGH GREEN SPUR WHICH BATHES ITS POINT 356 MEROPE   751
        BUT ROUND THE HEADLANDS POINT A CURRENT SETS • • 358 MEROPE   820
        BUT WHEN THEY CAME ABREAST THE POINT THE RACE • • 358 MEROPE   823
        HIS MESSAGES THEN POINT NOT TO THY MURDER • • • • 380 MEROPE   1282

POINTED
        WHAT POINTED ROOFS ARE THESE ADVANCE • • • • • •   300 GRANDE CHARTR   23
        THAT RIGHT THAT CONSCIENCE POINTED TO A DEED • • 341 MEROPE   363
        FULL ON THE SHARP-POINTED   • • • • • • • • •   400 MEROPE   1880

POINTING
        POINTING TO EARTHS CAREWORN CREATURES   • • • •   28 NEW SIRENS   61
        POINTING TO SOME WORLD-WORN CREATURES   • • • •   28 NEW SIRENS   V 61
        THAT LONE SKY-POINTING TREE ARE NOT FOR HIM • •   267 THYRSIS   174

POINTS
        AND SHOWD A SIGN IN FAINT VERMILION POINTS • • • • 81 SOHRAB RUSTUM   671
        AND POINTS US TO A BETTER TIME THAN OURS • • • •   170 WEST LONDON   14

POISE
        BRING HIM TO POISE THERE IS NO OTHER WAY • • • • 436 EMPEDOCLES II   234
        TO SEE IF WE WILL POISE OUR LIFE AT LAST • • • • 440 EMPEDOCLES II   369

POISED
        HUNG POISED AND THEN THE DARTING RIVER OF LIFE • • 25 DREAM   31
        POISED ON THE TOP OF A HUGE WAVE OF FATE • • • •   72 SOHRAB RUSTUM   391
        FOR SELF-POISED THEY LIVE NOR PINE WITH NOTING • • 240 SELF-DEPENDENCE   23
        WHY SELF-POISED THEY LIVE NOR PINE WITH NOTING • • 240 SELF-DEPENDENCE   V 23
        ALONE SELF-POISED HENCEFORWARD MAN • • • • • •   319 OBERMANN MORE   V 185
        SELF-POISED CLEAR-MINDED HENCEFORTH MAN • • • •   319 OBERMANN MORE   V 185

POISON
        HAST THOU SO RARE A POISON LET ME BE • • • • • •   38 WORLDS TRIUMPHS   13
        KEENER TO SLAY THEE LEST THOU POISON ME • • • •   38 WORLDS TRIUMPHS   14
        WHEN THE SHIRT-WRAPT POISON-BLISTERD HERO • • • • 399 MEROPE   1832

POISOND
        CHILD TIS NO TRUE DRAUGHT THIS TIS POISOND WINE • • 133 TRISTRAM 1   103
        CHILD TIS NO WATER THIS TIS POISOND WINE • • • •   133 TRISTRAM 1   V 103

POISONOUS
        CLEANSE TO SWEET AIRS THE BREATH OF POISONOUS STREAMS 410 EMPEDOCLES I 1   117

POISONS
        POISONS THE PEACE OF THY GRAVE • • • • • • • • •   294 HEINES GRAVE   69

POLAR
        RIGHT FOR THE POLAR STAR PAST ORGUNJE   • • • •   87 SOHRAB RUSTUM   880
        THE HURTLING POLAR LIGHTS ARE NEARD • • • • • •   156 SAINT BRANDAN   11

POLE
        NEAREST THE POLE AND WANDERING KIRGHIZZES • • • •   65 SOHRAB RUSTUM   133
        AND SEE ALL SIGHTS FROM POLE TO POLE • • • • • •   277 SOUTHERN NIGHT   69
        AND SEE ALL SIGHTS FROM POLE TO POLE • • • • • •   277 SOUTHERN NIGHT   69
        THAT RUNNST FROM POLE TO POLE • • • • • • • •   316 OBERMANN MORE   118
        THAT RUNNST FROM POLE TO POLE • • • • • • • •   316 OBERMANN MORE   118

POLES
        THE SEA THE STARRY POLES • • • • • • • • • • •   161 NECKAN   62

POLICY
        OF COMMERCE LAWS AND POLICY • • • • • • • • •   48 HORATIAN ECHO   15
        O POLICY TOO SUBTLE FAR FOR SENSE • • • • • •   339 MEROPE   311
        PRACTISE THE INDULGENT BLOODLESS POLICY • • • •   390 MEROPE   1561
        SINCE POLICY BIDS THUS WHAT FOULER DEATH • • • • 390 MEROPE   1568
        WAS POLICY OF STATE THE ASCENDENCY • • • • • •   404 MEROPE   1981

POLISHD
    OER THEIR POLISHD BOSOMS BLOWING   • • • • • •   433 EMPEDOCLES II   154

POLITIC
    THIS POLITIC SOVEREIGN LYING AT OUR FEET   • • • •   403 MEROPE   1965

POLITICS
    HISTORY POLITICS MIND   • • • • • • • • • • •   280 HAWORTH CHURCH   17

POLLUTED
    OF WIDOWHOOD IN THESE POLLUTED HALLS   • • • • •   383 MEROPE   1370

POLYMNIA
    POLYMNIA FULL ON HER DEATH-BED TWAS WELL   • • • •   168 RACHEL 2   8

POLYNICES
    AGAINST CREONS LAW POLYNICES   • • • • • • •   196 FRAG ANTIGONE   41

POLYPHONTES
    AND THOU ART POLYPHONTES FIRST HIS FRIEND   • • • •   335 MEROPE   185
    HERE THEN IT IS WHERE POLYPHONTES DWELLS   • • • •   354 MEROPE   706
    BY POLYPHONTES NEVER FAILD-IN ONCE   • • • • •   387 MEROPE   1476
    SHALL WE SELECT THAN POLYPHONTES WHAT   • • • •   390 MEROPE   1570
    NOT MEROPE AND POLYPHONTES FOES   • • • • •   394 MEROPE   1719
    OH HADST THOU POLYPHONTES STILL BUT KEPT   • • • •   395 MEROPE   1725
    ACCEPT IT POLYPHONTES IS NO MORE   • • • •   401 MEROPE   1888
    WHAT MEANTEST THOU O POLYPHONTES WHAT   • • • •   404 MEROPE   1979

POMP
    ENNOBLING THIS DULL POMP THE LIFE OF KINGS   • • • •   9 MYCERINUS   11
    THIS POMP OF WORLDS THIS PAIN OF BIRTH   • • • •   60 RESIGNATION   264
    SITS BALDER STILL IN POMP BY HELAS SIDE   • • • •   125 BALDER DEAD 3   429
    AH AS OF OLD FROM THE POMP   • • • • • •   296 HEINES GRAVE   129
    COUNCILS AND ARMIES AND THE POMP OF WAR   • • • •   476 CROMWELL   142

POMPOUS
    DOOMD POMPOUS AND ABSURD   • • • • • • • • •   48 HORATIAN ECHO   12

POMPS
    SOON WILL THE HIGH MIDSUMMER POMPS COME ON   • • • •   264 THYRSIS   62

PONDER
    TELL ME THAT I MAY PONDER IT WHEN GONE   • • • •   128 BALDER DEAD 3   516

PONDERED
    WHO WHILE I PONDERED ON THE LOT OF SOULS   • • • •   RUDE ORATOR   2

PONDERING
    PONDERING ON THAT WHICH FREA SAID SHOULD BE   • •   101 BALDER DEAD 1   201
    PONDERING GODS MYSTERIES UNTOLD   • • • • • •   278 SOUTHERN NIGHT   89

PONDERS
    ACHILLES PONDERS IN HIS TENT   • • • • • • • •   303 GRANDE CHARTR   115

PONIES
    WHO COME ON SHAGGY PONIES FROM PAMERE   • • •   65 SOHRAB RUSTUM   134

POOL
    THE SAILING FOAM THE SHINING POOL   • • • • •   55 RESIGNATION   105
    A LITTLE POOL AND IN SHORT SPACE   • • • • • •   90 SICK KING BOKH   68
    A LITTLE POOL AND IN BRIEF SPACE   • • • • • •   90 SICK KING BOKH   V 68
    BESIDE THE RIVER-POOL   • • • • •   160 NECKAN   44
    BESIDE THE POOL SATE NECKAN   • • • • • • •   160 NECKAN   45
    WEPT BY THE RIVER-POOL   • • • • • • • •   161 NECKAN   60

POOLS
    THE CLEAR-BROWN SHALLOW POOLS   • • • • • • •   190 STRAYED REVEL   147

POOR
    WILL BE BROUGHT THOU POOR HEART HOW MUCH NEARER   20 MODERN SAPPHO   20
         TO THEE
    FROM THIS POOR PRESENT SELF WHICH I AM NOW   • • •   37 YOUTHS AGIT   2
    POOR CHILD WHOM THE LIGHT AIR OF CHILDISH JOY   • •   41 GIPSY CHILD   V   9
    THAN THE POOR FACE SHE SLIGHTS IN THEE   • • •   48 HORATIAN ECHO   35
    THAT THY POOR HEAD ALMOST TURNS   • • • • •   49 SECOND BEST   8
    EYES THROUGH HER SILKEN CURTAINS THE POOR DRUDGE   • •   70 SOHRAB RUSTUM   303
    OF THAT POOR DRUDGE MAY BE SO RUSTUM EYED   • • •   70 SOHRAB RUSTUM   308
    AS THAT POOR BIRD FLIES HOME NOR KNOWS HIS LOSS   •   78 SOHRAB RUSTUM   573
    A POOR MEAN SOLDIER AND WITHOUT RENOWN   • • •   85 SOHRAB RUSTUM   814
    THERE ARE THE POOR WHO FAINT ALWAY   • • • •   93 SICK KING BOKH   176
    GAZING UP HITHER THE POOR MAN   • • • • • •   93 SICK KING BOKH   190
    THOU WAST A SINNER THOU POOR MAN   • • • • •   94 SICK KING BOKH   209
    THOU WERT A SINNER THOU POOR MAN   • • • • •   94 SICK KING BOKH   V 209
    POOR LAMB THOU SLEEPEST AND FORGETTST THY WOE   •   103 BALDER DEAD 1   288
    THROUGH MANY STREETS THE POOR BEAST RUNS IN VAIN   •   114 BALDER DEAD 3   10
    AH POOR SOUL IF THIS BE SO   • • • • • • •   139 TRISTRAM 1   288
    POOR CHILD THOU ART ALMOST AS PALE AS I   • • •   140 TRISTRAM 1   312
    BLAME ME NOT POOR SUFFERER THAT I TARRIED   • •   142 TRISTRAM 2   5
    TO THE POOR WRETCH MY CLOAK I CAST   • • • •   158 SAINT BRANDAN   51
    AND I LOSE MY POOR SOUL MERMAN HERE WITH THEE   • •   163 FORSAKEN MERM   59

POOR   (CONTINUED)
     IN THIS HER LIFES LAST DAY OUR POOR OUR PAIN   •   •   168 RACHEL 2   10
     THE WORLDS POOR ROUTED LEAVINGS OR WILL THEY   •   •   172 IMMORTALITY   6
     POOR FUGITIVE THE FEATHERY CHANGE   •   •   •   •   •   201 PHILOMELA   24
     HAST THOU NOT YET POOR BIRD   •   •   •   •   •   •   200 PHILOMELA   V
     WHERE POOR HAVE PLACE LIKE THE SWELLS   •   •   •   •   214 NEW ROME   V   14
     MOCKD HER POOR LOVELORN GIANTS LAY   •   •   •   •   •   222 EPILOG LAOCOON   48
     POOR BOUNDED WORDS AND MAKES THEM NEW   •   •   •   •   224 EPILOG LAOCOON   96
     OF THE POOR SINNER BOUND FOR DEATH   •   •   •   •   •   250 WISH   22
     THE STORY OF THE OXFORD SCHOLAR POOR   •   •   •   •   256 SCHOLAR-GIPSY   33
     THE STORY OF THAT OXFORD SCHOLAR POOR   •   •   •   •   256 SCHOLAR-GIPSY   V   33
     BUT AH OF OUR POOR THAMES SHE NEVER HEARD   •   •   •   265 THYRSIS   98
     POOR GALLANT BOY FOR SUCH THOU WAST   •   •   •   •   •   276 SOUTHERN NIGHT   39
     POOR GALLANT BOY FOR SUCH THOU WERT   •   •   •   •   •   276 SOUTHERN NIGHT   V   39
     SUCH SO SOULLESS SO POOR   •   •   •   •   •   •   •   •   290 RUGBY CHAPEL   149
     OF PRAISE HOT HEADY FUMES TO THE POOR BRAIN   •   •   296 HEINES GRAVE   146
     FLY HENCE POOR WRETCH WHOEER THOU ART   •   •   •   •   307 OBERMANN   17
     POOR WORLD SHE CRIED SO DEEP ACCURST   •   •   •   •   316 OBERMANN MORE   117
     POOR FRAGMENTS OF A BROKEN WORLD   •   •   •   •   •   320 OBERMANN MORE   217
     NO BUT TO THY AMBITION THEIR POOR LIVES   •   •   •   339 MEROPE   325
     THESE POOR EARS STILL AND THESE EYES   •   •   •   •   •   346 MEROPE   501
     OF THIS POOR SOUL WHO BARE HIM AND HIS SIRE   •   •   349 MEROPE   578
     POOR CHANGELING TREMBLED   •   •   •   •   •   •   •   •   392 MEROPE   1636
     OF THIS POOR SOUL WHO BORE HIM AND HIS SIRE   •   •   349 MEROPE   V 578
     IS FATE INDEED SO STRONG MANS STRENGTH INDEED SO POOR   415 EMPEDOCLES I 2   96
     AH POOR FAUN POOR FAUN AH POOR FAUN   •   •   •   •   434 EMPEDOCLES II   190
     AH POOR FAUN POOR FAUN AH POOR FAUN   •   •   •   •   434 EMPEDOCLES II   190
     AH POOR FAUN POOR FAUN AH POOR FAUN   •   •   •   •   434 EMPEDOCLES II   190
     POOR MATTHIAS FOUND HIM LYING   •   •   •   •   •   •   452 POOR MATTHIAS   1
     POOR CANARY MANY A YEAR   •   •   •   •   •   •   •   •   452 POOR MATTHIAS   5
     POOR MATTHIAS WOULDST THOU HAVE   •   •   •   •   •   •   453 POOR MATTHIAS   21
     POOR MATTHIAS WERE THEY THINE   •   •   •   •   •   •   454 POOR MATTHIAS   66
     YET POOR BIRD THY TINY CORSE   •   •   •   •   •   •   454 POOR MATTHIAS   83
     POOR MATTHIAS COULDST THOU SPEAK   •   •   •   •   •   455 POOR MATTHIAS   109
     GRAVELY THOU THE WHILE POOR DEAR   •   •   •   •   •   455 POOR MATTHIAS   119
     POOR MATTHIAS SEE THY END   •   •   •   •   •   •   •   457 POOR MATTHIAS   173
     WHAT POOR KAI DEAD SAY ALL I MEET   •   •   •   •   •   459 KAISER DEAD   9
     POOR MAX WITH DOWNCAST REVERENT HEAD   •   •   •   •   •   460 KAISER DEAD   67

POPLAR
     THE POPLAR AVENUE WAS PASSD   •   •   •   •   •   •   •   177 FAREWELL   5

POPLARS
     UNDER THE RUSTLING POPLARS SHADE   •   •   •   •   •   206 RIVER   2

POPPIES
     THROUGH THE THICK CORN THE SCARLET POPPIES PEEP   •   •   255 SCHOLAR-GIPSY   23

POPPY
     AH NOT THE NECTAROUS POPPY LOVERS USE   •   •   •   •   43 GIPSY CHILD   53

POPULACE
     OF THE INVADING POPULACE   •   •   •   •   •   •   •   •   •   48 HORATIAN ECHO   8

POPULAR
     POPULAR REVERENCE TO THESE RECENT LINES   •   •   •   •   390 MEROPE   1564

POPULOUS
     AT SUNSET ON A POPULOUS TOWN   •   •   •   •   •   •   •   •   57 RESIGNATION   165

PORCELAIN
     PRICKS WITH VERMILION SOME CLEAR PORCELAIN VASE   •   •   81 SOHRAB RUSTUM   673

PORT
     THE PORT LIES BRIGHT UNDER THE AUGUST SUN   •   •   •   •   41 GIPSY CHILD   V   5
     OF PORT THEY HAD MAKES BITTERER FAR THEIR TOIL   •   •   124 BALDER DEAD 3   367
     STILL BENT TO MAKE SOME PORT HE KNOWS NOT WHERE   •   •   244 SUMMER NIGHT   68
     PROUD OF PORT THOUGH SOMETHING SQUAT   •   •   •   •   •   457 POOR MATTHIAS   189

PORTAL
     SHRILLS ROUND THEIR PORTAL   •   •   •   •   •   •   •   50 CONSOLATION   22
     SHE SPAKE AND FROM THE PORTAL PASSD AWAY   •   •   •   •   447 WESTMIN ABBEY   110

PORTEND
     MAY IT TURN HAPPIER THAN MY DOUBTS PORTEND   •   •   •   •   390 MEROPE   1583

PORTICO
     BLOWS THROUGH THE PORTICO   •   •   •   •   •   •   •   186 STRAYED REVEL   20
     ON THE STEPS OF THY PORTICO   •   •   •   •   •   •   •   187 STRAYED REVEL   52
     SO LATE IN THY PORTICO   •   •   •   •   •   •   •   •   •   188 STRAYED REVEL   93
     SOME OF US TO THE PORTICO TO BREATHE   •   •   •   •   •   407 EMPEDOCLES I 1   38

PORTION
     WHY SHOULD WE MEET ANOTHERS PORTION SO   •   •   •   •   96 BALDER DEAD 1   33
     ARE GODS WORST PORTION TO MANKIND   •   •   •   •   •   •   217 NAMELESS EPIT   V

PORTIOND
     THAT ONE LONG PORTIOND WITH HIS DOOM OF DEATH   •   •   98 BALDER DEAD 1   114

PORTSMOUTH
    TO TRAVELLERS ON THE PORTSMOUTH ROAD • • • • • • 452 GEISTS GRAVE 70

POSEIDON
    POSEIDON TO THE SHEPHERD-BOYS TO HIDE • • • • • 355 MEROPE 737

POSSESS
    NOT HAVING IT WHICH WHEN THEY DO POSSESS • • • • 153 TRISTRAM 3 138
    POSSESS ME QUITE • • • • • • • • • • • 276 SOUTHERN NIGHT 20
    AND NEVER ONCE POSSESS OUR SOUL • • • • • • 277 SOUTHERN NIGHT 71
    TILL I POSSESS MY SOUL AGAIN • • • • • • • • 302 GRANDE CHARTR 94

POSSESSD
    BUT ONE POSSESSD HIS WANING TIME • • • • • • 132 TRISTRAM 1 70
    WHO POSSESSD HIS DARKER HOUR • • • • • • • 132 TRISTRAM 1 73
    NEVER BY PASSION QUITE POSSESSD • • • • • • 243 SUMMER NIGHT 32
    BY WHAT DISTRACTIONS HE WOULD BE POSSESSD • • • • 246 BURIED LIFE 32
    POSSESSD IN HATRED LOST IN BLOOD • • • • • • 399 MEROPE 1849

POSSESSES
    WIT IT POSSESSES AND SCORN • • • • • • • • 295 HEINES GRAVE 111

POSSESSEST
    BUT THOU POSSESSEST AN IMMORTAL LOT • • • • • • 259 SCHOLAR-GIPSY 157

POSSESSING
    OF POSSESSING POWERS NOT OUR SHARE • • • • • • 209 SELF-DECEPTION 2

POSSESSION
    BUT INDEED THIS PROUD POSSESSION • • • • • • 33 NEW SIRENS 203

POSSIBLE
    ROSE FROM BELOW IF IT WERE POSSIBLE • • • • • • 412 EMPEDOCLES I 2 9

POST
    ACROSS THE BRIDGE THEN SHE TOOK POST AGAIN • • • 108 BALDER DEAD 2 137
    AH ME WITH WHAT A FOOT DOTH TREASON POST • • • • 363 MEROPE 962
    EACH TO HIS POST WHERE THE OCCASION CALLS • • • 386 MEROPE 1441
    POST-HASTE TO COBHAM CALLS THE MUSE • • • • • 458 KAISER DEAD 2
    THAT PREFACE AND POST-SCRIBE THEE • • • • • • FRAGMENT 5 10

POSTED
    THEY POSTED THROUGH TO REACH IT • • • • • • • LUCRETIUS 6 5

POSTING
    AND SPEND THEIR LIVES IN POSTING HERE AND THERE • • 153 TRISTRAM 3 140
    YEAR POSTING AFTER YEAR • • • • • • • • • 424 EMPEDOCLES I 2 364

POSTPONING
    TO HIM POSTPONING AN ETERNAL LAW • • • • • • 197 FRAG ANTIGONE 75

POSTURE
    POSTURE AND OPIUM NO MORE • • • • • • • • 293 HEINES GRAVE 20

POSTURES
    POSTURES OF RUNES AND HEALING HERBS HE KNEW • • 101 BALDER DEAD 1 211

POTENT
    IS POTENT STILL ON ME IN HIS DECLINE • • • • • 408 EMPEDOCLES I 1 66

POTENTLY
    HOW THIS FOOL PASSION GULLS MEN POTENTLY • • • • 153 TRISTRAM 3 134

POTION
    AND THAT POTION RARE HER MOTHER • • • • • • 134 TRISTRAM 1 136

POTIONS
    HATH IT DRUNK OF OUR LOVE-POTIONS • • • • • • 29 NEW SIRENS 87

POTSDAM
    OF BLOOD-UNMIXD FROM POTSDAM CAME • • • • • • 459 KAISER DEAD 20

POUCH
    CATES FROM OUR HUNTERS POUCH ARCADIAN FARE • • • • 356 MEROPE 753

POUR
    AND BUCKLERS CLASH AND SPEARS BEGIN TO POUR • • 127 BALDER DEAD 3 498
    ACROSS THE SOUNDS AND CHANNELS POUR • • • • • 182 TO MARG CONT 12
    POUR ALL THE SOUL OF THEIR COMPLAINT • • • • • 224 EPILOG LAOCOON 100
    HOW HE WOULD POUR HIMSELF IN EVERY STRIFE • • • 246 BURIED LIFE 33
    POUR THE LIBATION OF MILK • • • • • • • 342 MEROPE 387
    I SEND AND THESE LIBATIONS POUR THE WHILE • • • 350 MEROPE 595
    POUR FORTH THE FOAMING VIALS OF THY WRATH • • • 465 ALARIC AT ROME 86
    POUR FROM A THOUSAND HILLS THY WARRIORS OF THE NORTH 465 ALARIC AT ROME 96
    NOT IN RICH ENGLAND BENT BUT TO MAKE POUR • • • 480 HUNGARIAN NAT 2

POURD
    THE CRIMSON TORRENT POURD DIM NOW AND SOILD • • 86 SOHRAB RUSTUM V 843
    POURD IN PRAYER BEFORE THE VIRGIN-MOTHER • • • • 144 TRISTRAM 2 63
    POURD IN GRIEF BEFORE THE VIRGIN-MOTHER • • • • 144 TRISTRAM 2 V 63
    POURD FLUSHING TO THY LANGUID CHEEK • • • • • 178 FAREWELL 10

POURD   (CONTINUED)
        HERE HE POURD HIS LITTLE SOUL • • • • • • • •   458 POOR MATTHIAS   200

POURING
        IN THEIR OWN TASKS ALL THEIR POWERS POURING   • •   240 SELF-DEPENDENCE   27
        THROUGH POURING TIDE HE PULLS AND DRIZZLING HAZE • •   445 WESTMIN ABBEY   29

POURS
        WHILE THE HEART STILL POURS   • • • • • • •   235 YOUTH OF MAN   114
        POURS HER PETULANT YOUTH • • • • • • • • • •   297 HEINES GRAVE   185

POURST
        PRAY AS THOU POURST LIBATIONS ON THIS TOMB • • • •   342 MEROPE   382

POURTRAY
        BUT NOT AS PAINTER CAN POURTRAY   • • • • • •   226 EPILOG LAOCOON   182

POWDERY
        ITS POWDERY FALL • • • • • • • • • • • •   176 PARTING   50

POWER
        THE SEEDS OF GODLIKE POWER ARE IN US STILL • • • •   4 EMERSONS ESSAYS   12
        OR IS IT THAT SOME POWER TOO WISE TOO STRONG   • •   9 MYCERINUS   V   37
        YE IMBECILES IN PRESENT POWER • • • • • • •   48 HORATIAN ECHO   11
        MOUNTING TO POWER LONG DENIED • • • • • • •   HORATIAN ECHO   V
        FOR HANDMAID TO THEIR STRIDING POWER • • • •   53 RESIGNATION   31
        WHO NEEDS NOT LOVE AND POWER TO KNOW • • • •   59 RESIGNATION   235
        LOVE TRANSIENT POWER AN UNREAL SHOW • • • •   59 RESIGNATION   236
        IN VAIN HATH A KING POWER TO BUILD • • • •   94 SICK KING BOKH   198
        CAN I WITH HELAS POWER A COMPACT STRIKE • •   98 BALDER DEAD 1   109
        AND THEY SHALL BE THY GUIDES WHO HAVE THE POWER • •   102 BALDER DEAD 1   238
        THEN BUT A POWER HE COULD NOT BREAK WITHHELD   • •   129 BALDER DEAD 3   558
        POWER TO BE MOVED AND SOOTHED FOR ALL OUR PAIN • •   153 TRISTRAM 3   117
        BUT TAKES AWAY THE POWER THIS CAN AVAIL   • • •   153 TRISTRAM 3   124
        MID THE SOULS PLAGUED BY HEAVENLY POWER   • •   157 SAINT BRANDAN   34
        HATH SUCH INESTIMABLE POWER   • • • • •   158 SAINT BRANDAN   56
        HATH SUCH INALIENABLE POWER   • • • • •   158 SAINT BRANDAN   V   56
        SHE HAD ONE POWER WHICH MADE HER BREAST ITS HOME • •   168 RACHEL 3   10
        THEN AS NOW A POWER BEYOND OUR SEEING   • • •   210 SELF-DECEPTION   11
        AH SOME POWER EXISTS THERE WHICH IS OURS   • •   210 SELF-DECEPTION   27
        WITH POWER DIVINE ITS STORY TELL   • • • •   223 EPILOG LAOCOON   60
        WHAT POWER OF PASSION WEALTH OF CHANGE   • •   223 EPILOG LAOCOON   82
        IT GIVES THEM PATHOS GIVES THEM POWER   • • •   227 EPILOG LAOCOON   200
        WELL FOR US THAT THE POWER   • • • • • •   232 YOUTH OF MAN   12
        NOR LIFE NOR EMOTION NOR POWER • • • • •   233 YOUTH OF MAN   31
        CHILDREN OF MEN THE UNSEEN POWER WHOSE EYE • •   238 PROGRESS   37
        AND WE HAVE SHOWN ON EACH SPIRIT AND POWER • •   246 BURIED LIFE   58
        THEIR STUPEFYING POWER   • • • • • •   247 BURIED LIFE   70
        AND WE HAVE SHOWN ON EACH TALENT AND POWER • •   246 BURIED LIFE   V   58
        THEIR STUPIFYING POWER   • • • • • •   247 BURIED LIFE   V   70
        THE POWER TO FEEL WITH OTHERS GIVE • • •   249 KENSINGTON GARD   42
        ONLY METHINKS SOME LOSS OF HABITS POWER   • •   263 THYRSIS   22
        WHO IF NOT I FOR QUESTING HERE HATH POWER   • •   265 THYRSIS   104
        IF MEN ESTEEMD THEE FEEBLE GAVE THEE POWER • •   269 THYRSIS   214
        OF FITFUL DREAM AND FEVERISH POWER • • • •   270 MEMORIAL VERSES   24
        AGAIN FIND WORDSWORTHS HEALING POWER • • •   272 MEMORIAL VERSES   63
        HEIGHTEND AND MULTIPLIED POWER • • • • •   281 HAWORTH CHURCH   29
        POWER DROPPING FROM THE HAND   • • • • •   282 HAWORTH CHURCH   V
        WHERE TARRIES HE THE POWER WHO SAID • • • •   320 OBERMANN MORE   231
        SHORN OF THE JOY THE BLOOM THE POWER • • •   322 OBERMANN MORE   303
        TO AVENGE THAT FALL AND BRING THEM BACK TO POWER • •   334 MEROPE   146
        BUT PRINCE ADOPTED BY THE WILL OF POWER   • •   335 MEROPE   171
        AGAINST A POWER EXEMPT FROM COMMON CHECKS • •   336 MEROPE   206
        POWER FAILS US TO TRY CLEARLY IF THAT CAUSE • •   352 MEROPE   647
        POWER FAILS THE MAN HIMSELF TO FIX DISTINCTLY • •   352 MEROPE   649
        OR SELFISH LUST OF PERSONAL POWER   • • • •   353 MEROPE   661
        THAT HE TO POWER MAKES WAY BY ARMS   • • •   353 MEROPE   681
        ATTEMPTING DEEDS BEYOND THY POWER TO DO   • •   368 MEROPE   1079
        TO KEEP THEIR MASTERS POWER THOU WILT FIND • •   381 MEROPE   1307
        AGAINST THE ONE AND CERTAIN ARM OF POWER • •   381 MEROPE   1313
        TO WITNESS OFFERING HIM RETURN AND POWER • •   394 MEROPE   1696
        ALONE I MASTERD POWER AND ALONE   • • • •   398 MEROPE   1792
        THE POWER OF THIS TYRANT AND HIS LORDS   • •   402 MEROPE   1944
        ASSUME THE ENSIGNS OF MY FATHERS POWER   • •   405 MEROPE   2020
        THOU ART TOO YOUNG TO NOTE IT BUT HIS POWER • •   410 EMPEDOCLES I 1   112
        ONE WITH THE OERLABOURD POWER THAT THROUGH   422 EMPEDOCLES I 2   291
            THE BREADTH AND L
        WE HAVE THE POWER TO FEEL THE PRESSURE EASED • •   436 EMPEDOCLES II   245
        FULNESS OF LIFE AND POWER OF FEELING YE   • •   436 EMPEDOCLES II   258
        FORGED BY THE IMPERIOUS LONELY THINKING-POWER • •   440 EMPEDOCLES II   376
        AND JOY IN LIGHT AND POWER TO SPREAD THE JOY • •   446 WESTMIN ABBEY   80
        AND I HAVE NOW NO POWER   • • • • • •   447 WESTMIN ABBEY   107
        OF CHILDHOOD ARTHUR DID SOME CHECK HAVE POWER • •   447 WESTMIN ABBEY   118
        THAT BINDS THE HEART OF MAN WITH MIGHTIEST POWER • •   467 ALARIC AT ROME   146
        THE CHANGE OF LIFE THE NOTHINGNESS OF POWER   469 ALARIC AT ROME   188
        NO BUT THE WILL OF HEAVEN AND FATES INVINCIBLE POWER   HOMER TRANS   49
        A GIFTED MAN THE POWER TO SHEW HIS GIFT   • • • •   LUCRETIUS 2   2
        TO THE BLIND SLAVES OF POWER TO MAKE IT KNOWN • •   FRAGMENT 2   3

POWERLESS
        ARE EVEN LOVERS POWERLESS TO REVEAL   • • • • •   245 BURIED LIFE   14

POWERLESS   (CONTINUED)
        THE OTHER POWERLESS TO BE BORN • • • • • • • •   302 GRANDE CHARTR   86
        A PALE UNMEANING GHOST POWERLESS TO FRIGHT • • • • 366 MEROPE   1021

POWERS
        AFFECTIONS INSTINCTS PRINCIPLES AND POWERS • • • •   4 BUTLERS SERMONS   1
        AND RAYS HER POWERS LIKE SISTER-ISLANDS SEEN   • •   4 BUTLERS SERMONS   9
        STERN SENTENCE OF THE POWERS OF DESTINY • • • • •   8 MYCERINUS   6
        SEEMS IT SO LIGHT A THING THEN AUSTERE POWERS • •   9 MYCERINUS   31
        AND THE GREAT POWERS WE SERVE THEMSELVES MAY BE • • 10 MYCERINUS   41
        STRINGING VAIN WORDS OF POWERS WE CANNOT SEE   • •   10 MYCERINUS   51
        AS CHARTERD BY SOME UNKNOWN POWERS • • • • •   41 HUMAN LIFE   26
        OR WHAT WE FIX WITH FOREIGN POWERS   • • • • •   47 HORATIAN ECHO   3
        FOR OF ALL POWERS THE MIGHTIEST FAR ART THOU   • • 120 BALDER DEAD 3   250
        IN HER LIKE US THERE CLASHD CONTENDING POWERS • • 168 RACHEL 3   11
        YE GUIDING POWERS WHO JOIN AND PART • • • • • •   174 MEETING   13
        YET SHOW HER ONCE YE HEAVENLY POWERS • • • • •   202 URANIA   17
        OF POSSESSING POWERS NOT OUR SHARE   • • • • •   209 SELF-DECEPTION   2
        SAW THE GIFTS THE POWERS IT MIGHT INHERIT • • •   209 SELF-DECEPTION   7
        POWERS STIR IN US STIR AND DISAPPEAR • • • • •   210 SELF-DECEPTION   22
        WE BUT DREAM WE HAVE OUR WISHD-FOR POWERS • • •   210 SELF-DECEPTION   25
        IN THEIR OWN TASKS ALL THEIR POWERS POURING   •   240 SELF-DEPENDENCE   27
        AND NUMB THE ELASTIC POWERS   • • • • • • • •   259 SCHOLAR-GIPSY   146
        FOR EARLY DIDST THOU LEAVE THE WORLD WITH POWERS • 260 SCHOLAR-GIPSY   161
        THY HOPES GROW TIMOROUS AND UNFIXD THY POWERS •   261 SCHOLAR-GIPSY   227
        YOUR PRIDE OF LIFE YOUR TIRELESS POWERS • • • •   304 GRANDE CHARTR   167
        WE IN SOME UNKNOWN POWERS EMPLOY   • • • • • •   310 OBERMANN   133
        A FALSE COURSE FOR THE WORLD AND FOR OURSELVES   419 EMPEDOCLES I 2   226
            FALSE POWERS
        BUT OUR OWN ACTS FOR GOOD OR ILL ARE MIGHTIER POWERS 420 EMPEDOCLES I 2 241
        THOUGH THE NON-HUMAN POWERS • • • • • • • •   421 EMPEDOCLES I 2   264
        STERN POWERS WHO MAKE THEIR CARE • • • • • •   422 EMPEDOCLES I 2   311
        FALSE WEAKNESS IN THE WORLD AND IN OURSELVES   419 EMPEDOCLES I 2 V 226
            FALSE POWERS
        AND WE SHALL FEEL OUR POWERS OF EFFORT FLAG   •   440 EMPEDOCLES II   387
        NEARER HUMAN WERE THEIR POWERS • • • • • • •   453 POOR MATTHIAS   45
        PROOF THEY GIVE TOO PRIMAL POWERS • • • • •   456 POOR MATTHIAS   137
        WHO ASSURE US SUNDERING POWERS • • • • • • •   457 POOR MATTHIAS   171
        ASK OF THE POWERS THAT SPORT WITH MAN • • • •   481 DESTINY   4
        BETWIXT SUCH UNLIKE POWERS • • • • • • • •   LUCRETIUS 5   10

PRACTISE
        PRACTISE THE INDULGENT BLOODLESS POLICY   • • • •   390 MEROPE   1561

PRACTISED
        THOSE VIRTUES PRIZED AND PRACTISED BY TOO FEW   • • 6 REP FRIEND   2
        TO THE LESS PRACTISED EYE OF SANGUINE YOUTH   • • 267 THYRSIS   142
        OF BEING IS PRACTISED THAT STRENGTH • • • • •   287 RUGBY CHAPEL   42
        THEIR DAILY-PRACTISED CHAFINGS KEEP ALIVE • • •   331 MEROPE   44

PRAISD
        A SON SO PRAISD SO BRAVE TO SEND TO WAR   • • •   68 SOHRAB RUSTUM   V 231
        YES BE THE SECOND CATO PRAISD • • • • • • •   481 COURAGE   13

PRAISE
        THEIR PLEASURE TO THEIR FEET AND REAP THEIR PRAISE   11 MYCERINUS   77
        THE PRAISE OF GODS RICH BOON AND LENGTH OF DAYS • • 11 MYCERINUS   78
        AND PRAISE THE CHISELLD BROIDERIES RARE   • • •   17 CHURCH BROU 2   37
        THEN I SHALL PRAISE THE HEAT WHICH THEN I LACK •   37 YOUTHS AGIT   11
        HIM BLAME NOT FAUSTA RATHER PRAISE   • • • • •   59 RESIGNATION   238
        AND PRAISE MY FAME AND PROFFER COURTEOUS GIFTS •   71 SOHRAB RUSTUM   353
        AND THEN THAT ALL THE TARTAR HOST WOULD PRAISE •   77 SOHRAB RUSTUM   534
        WHAT IRKS IT ME THAT MEN SPEAK SOHRABS PRAISE • •   68 SOHRAB RUSTUM   V 228
        I AM NOT WRONGD WHEN MEN SPEAK SOHRABS PRAISE •   68 SOHRAB RUSTUM   V 228
        O KING IN THIS I PRAISE THEE NOT   • • • • • •   92 SICK KING BOKH   133
        HIM THEN I PRAISE WHO DARES   • • • • • •   196 FRAG ANTIGONE   28
        NO END BUT THIS YOU PRAISE • • • • • • • •   199 FRAG DEJANEIRA   24
        I PRAISE THE LIFE WHICH SLIPS AWAY   • • • • •   199 EARLY DEATH   2
        EARNING SHE TOO HER PRAISE • • • • • • • •   280 HAWORTH CHURCH   14
        STOPS IT FOR EVER TO PRAISE   • • • • • • •   282 HAWORTH CHURCH   54
        YOURS IS THE PRAISE IF MANKIND • • • • • • •   291 RUGBY CHAPEL   168
        PRAISE RE-INSPIRE THE BRAVE   • • • • • • •   292 RUGBY CHAPEL   200
        THRILLS AT EACH SMART IS THE PRAISE • • • • •   293 HEINES GRAVE   27
        OF PRAISE HOT HEADY FUMES TO THE POOR BRAIN   •   296 HEINES GRAVE   146
        QUICKEST TO ILL IS THE PRAISE • • • • • • • •   293 HEINES GRAVE   V 27
        WE PRAISE THEM BUT THEY ARE NOT OURS   • • • •   304 GRANDE CHARTR   V 168
        CLAMOURS TO FIND FULFILLD WHICH GOOD MEN PRAISE •   386 MEROPE   1428
        WHOSE PRAISE DO THEY MENTION   • • • • • • •   443 EMPEDOCLES II   457
        CALLD US TO PET THEE OR TO PRAISE • • • • •   450 GEISTS GRAVE   7
        KINDNESS WE BESTOW AND PRAISE • • • • • • •   455 POOR MATTHIAS   99

PRAISED
        BUT HE PRAISED ALLAH WITH LOUD VOICE • • • • •   91 SICK KING BOKH   123
        HAVE PRAISED THE KEEN UNSCRUPULOUS COURSE • • •   178 FAREWELL   35
        ALL WHICH HE OWND AND PRAISED WITH GRATEFUL MIND • 356 MEROPE   763
        AND PRAISED AND SPOILD BY MASTER AND BY GUESTS •   407 EMPEDOCLES I 1   34
        PRAISED PERHAPS THY COURTEOUS EYE • • • • •   455 POOR MATTHIAS   117
        PRAISED THY GOLDEN LIVERY • • • • • • • •   455 POOR MATTHIAS   118

PRAISES
        INSINCERE PRAISES WHICH DESCENDS   • • • • • •   199 EARLY DEATH   6
        TELLS THE PRAISES OF THEIR PRIME   • • • • • •   453 POOR MATTHIAS   28

PRAISING
    AND THOSE WARM LOCKS MEN WERE PRAISING · · · · 30 NEW SIRENS 121
    FORTH WITH THY PRAISING VOICE · · · · · · · 220 BACCHANALIA 2 47

PRANK
    WHITE HOUSES PRANK WHERE ONCE WERE HUTS · · · · 312 OBERMANN MORE 3

PRATE
    WHAT PRATE IS THIS OF FATHERS AND REVENGE · · · · 78 SOHRAB RUSTUM 577
    WHO PRATE OF NATURE FOR SHE · · · · · · · · 233 YOUTH OF MAN 29
    WHO PRATE OF NATURE BUT SHE · · · · · · · · 233 YOUTH OF MAN V 29

PRATING
    THE KING RETURN AND FIND YOU PRATING HERE · · · · 386 MEROPE 1443

PRAY
    CLIMB UP HERE TO PRAY · · · · · · · · · · 17 CHURCH BROU 2 19
    AND THE PEOPLE PRAY · · · · · · · · · · · 17 CHURCH BROU 2 30
    AND THOUGH THE JUST SUN GILD AS MORTALS PRAY · · 43 GIPSY CHILD 59
    AND THOUGH THE JUST SUN GILD AS ALL MEN PRAY · · 43 GIPSY CHILD V 59
    TO THE DREAR EUXINE SO PRAY ALL · · · · · 52 RESIGNATION 13
    SO PRAY THEY AND TO STAND AGAIN · · · · · 53 RESIGNATION 18
    RATHER THYSELF FOR SOME AIM PRAY · · · · · 59 RESIGNATION 239
    WHICH FOLLOW ME I PRAY THEE SLAY NOT THESE · · 84 SOHRAB RUSTUM 779
    MY LORD O KING DO RIGHT I PRAY · · · · · 89 SICK KING BOKH 53
    WHAT WILT THOU PRAY AND GET THEE GRACE · · 91 SICK KING BOKH 101
    GO QUICKLY FORTH THROUGH ALL THE WORLD AND PRAY · 122 BALDER DEAD 3 299
    O HERMOD PRAY THAT THOU MAYST JOIN US THEN · · 129 BALDER DEAD 3 543
    TRISTRAM I PRAY THEE OF THY COURTESY · · · 133 TRISTRAM 1 99
    SHE SAID I MUST GO FOR MY KINSFOLK PRAY · · 163 FORSAKEN MERM 56
    AND I I KNOW NOT IF TO PRAY · · · · · · 243 SUMMER NIGHT 34
    PRAY AS THOU POURST LIBATIONS ON THIS TOMB · · 342 MEROPE 382
    I PRAY THE FURIES EVER-RESTLESS BAND · · · 349 MEROPE 569
    AND PRAY THE GODS AND PRAY THE ALL-SEEING SUN · 349 MEROPE 570
    AND PRAY THE GODS AND PRAY THE ALL-SEEING SUN · 349 MEROPE 570
    THIS FOR OUR SON AND FOR MYSELF I PRAY · · 350 MEROPE 591
    WHY SHOULD HE PRAY TO RANGE · · · · · · 448 WESTMIN ABBEY 147

PRAYD
    SO PILGRIMS BOUND FOR MECCA PRAYD · · · · 52 RESIGNATION 3
    YET WE HER MEMORY AS SHE PRAYD WILL KEEP · · · 173 MONICAS PRAYER 13
    THINKING THAT SO I PRAYD ARIGHT I PRAYD · · · 348 MEROPE 546
    THINKING THAT SO I PRAYD ARIGHT I PRAYD · · · 348 MEROPE 546
    IF I PRAYD WRONGLY I REVOKE THE PRAYER · · · 348 MEROPE 547
    THAT MOMENT WHILE WITH UPTURND EYES HE PRAYD · · 402 MEROPE 1918
    AS I HAVE PRAYD THEE THAT AND TO WHAT END · · · 412 EMPEDOCLES I 2 21

PRAYER
    AND EVEN COULD THE INTEMPERATE PRAYER · · · 60 RESIGNATION 271
    EVER SINCE PRAYER-TIME HE DOTH WAIT · · · · 88 SICK KING BOKH 14
    THREE DAYS SINCE AT THE TIME OF PRAYER · · · 88 SICK KING BOKH 30
    AND TO YOUR PRAYER SHE SENDS YOU THIS REPLY · · 114 BALDER DEAD 3 41
    POURD IN PRAYER BEFORE THE VIRGIN-MOTHER · · · 144 TRISTRAM 2 63
    THAT KNIGHTS ASLEEP AND AT HER PRAYER · · · 149 TRISTRAM 2 180
    HE BOWD HIS HEAD HE BREATHED A PRAYER · · · 158 SAINT BRANDAN 74
    SAY THY PRAYER AND COME BACK TO THE KIND SEA-CAVES · 163 FORSAKEN MERM 61
    BUT IF THE PRAYER BE IN VAIN · · · · · · 282 HAWORTH CHURCH V
    INVESTS THE STERN AND NAKED PRAYER · · · · 300 GRANDE CHARTR 38
    OF REVERIE OF SHADE OF PRAYER · · · · · · 306 GRANDE CHARTR 206
    AND FILL THY LEISURE WITH AN EARNEST PRAYER · · 332 MEROPE 72
    THE PRAYER I CAME TO URGE I WILL DEFER · · · 333 MEROPE 109
    HIS MOST JUST PRAYER YET HIS HOUSE · · · · 343 MEROPE 409
    IF I PRAYD WRONGLY I REVOKE THE PRAYER · · · 348 MEROPE 547
    IF THIS WILL BRING HIM BACK BE THIS MY PRAYER · · 349 MEROPE 579
    THAT WAY IS DUBIOUS FOR A MOTHERS PRAYER · · 349 MEROPE 583
    COME COME BACK TO OUR PRAYER · · · · · · 360 MEROPE 892
    THY MOTHERS PRAYERS AND THIS PRAYER LAST OF ALL · · 405 MEROPE 2011
    HIS MOST JUST PRAYER YET HIS RACE · · · · · 343 MEROPE V 409
    HAPPINESS MOCKD OUR PRAYER · · · · · · · 425 EMPEDOCLES I 2 383
    AND WITH ITS CLEAR CALM TONES THAT DYING PRAYER · · 478 CROMWELL 217

PRAYERS
    AND PRAYERS AND GIFTS AND TEARS ARE FRUITLESS ALL · 10 MYCERINUS 71
    PRAYERS THAT TO-MORROW · · · · · · · · · 36 VOICE 11
    AND PAY HER HOMAGE AND ENTREAT WITH PRAYERS · · 100 BALDER DEAD 1 179
    THY WAY AND THIS AT LEAST MY PRAYERS AVAIL · · · 104 BALDER DEAD 1 309
    LONG PRAYERS I SAID IN THE WORLD THEY SAY · · · · 163 FORSAKEN MERM 66
    FROM THE CHURCH CAME A MURMUR OF FOLK AT THEIR PRAYERS · 163 FORSAKEN MERM 72
    EYES REKINDLING AND PRAYERS · · · · · · · 292 RUGBY CHAPEL 202
    HOW SAY YE MAIDENS DO YE KNOW THESE PRAYERS · · 368 MEROPE 1067
    THY MOTHERS PRAYERS AND THIS PRAYER LAST OF ALL · · 405 MEROPE 2011
    BAFFLERS OF OUR OWN PRAYERS FROM YOUTH TO LIFES · 420 EMPEDOCLES I 2 231
       LAST SCENES
    REPENTANT PRAYERS THAT HAD BEEN STRONG TO SAVE · · 474 CROMWELL 81

PRAYS
    LOUD PRAYS THE PRIEST SHUT STANDS THE DOOR · · · · 163 FORSAKEN MERM 82

PRE
    SEE THE WIFE OF HECTOR THAT GREAT PRE-EMINENT CAPTAIN · · HOMER TRANS 33

PREACH
    WHO WITH SUCH HEAT DOST PREACH WHAT WERE TO THEE • •   5 HARMONY NATURE   2
    TO PREACH THEE TO THEIR SCHOOL • • • • • • • 417 EMPEDOCLES I 2   138
    NOR TONGUE OF MAN NOR FEAR NOR SHAME CAN PREACH • • 467 ALARIC AT ROME   141

PREACHD
    ONE VOICE PREACHD PATIENCE AND THAT VOICE WAS MINE   337 MEROPE   258

PREACHER
    I MET A PREACHER THERE I KNEW AND SAID • • • • 169 EAST LONDON   5

PREACHES
    THIS NO SAINT PREACHES AND THIS NO CHURCH RULES • • 171 DIVINITY   13

PRECARIOUSLY
    PRECARIOUSLY RULED BY FOREIGN LORDS • • • • • • 337 MEROPE   235

PRECEDED
    HAVE PRECEDED THEE YOUNG • • • • • • • • • 284 HAWORTH CHURCH   80

PRECEDENTS
    THY PROOFS THY WITNESS AND THY PRECEDENTS • • • •   RUDE ORATOR   9

PRECINCT
    BY THIS DEAR GUEST OVER THY PRECINCT SHED • • • • 449 WESTMIN ABBEY   173
    BY THIS DEAR SOUL OVER THY PRECINCT SHED • • • • 449 WESTMIN ABBEY V 173

PRECINCTS
    THE WHILE THERE SLEEPS WITHIN THY PRECINCTS DREAD   464 ALARIC AT ROME   51

PRECIOUS
    HAVING MADE UP HIS TALE OF PRECIOUS PEARLS • • • • 69 SOHRAB RUSTUM   288
    HOW MANY PRECIOUS FEELINGS OF MANS HEART • • • • 335 MEROPE   178

PRECIPICE
    OF THAT UNFOOTED PRECIPICE WHOSE ROCK • • • • 358 MEROPE   812

PRECIPICES
    NEVER THE BLACK AND DRIPPING PRECIPICES • • • • 78 SOHRAB RUSTUM   571
    BY THE PRECIPICES OF KHELMOS • • • • • • • • 393 MEROPE   1655
    UP THE PRECIPICES OF TRACHIS • • • • • • • • 399 MEROPE   1828

PRECISE
    WHAT ORDER MORE PRECISE HAD HE THAN I • • • • 384 MEROPE   1400

PREDESTINED
    SWAYING THE SCEPTRE WITH PREDESTINED HAND • • • • 345 MEROPE   473
    PREDESTINED TO THE RAY • • • • • • • • • • 449 WESTMIN ABBEY   172

PREEMINENCE
    MOURNFUL PREEMINENCE NOT • • • • • • • • • 370 MEROPE   1110
    OF MY UNLOVED PREEMINENCE • • • • • • • • 432 EMPEDOCLES II   110

PREFACE
    THAT PREFACE AND POST-SCRIBE THEE • • • • • •   FRAGMENT 5   10

PREFER
    PREFER OBEDIENCE TO THE PRIMAL LAW • • • • • • 196 FRAG ANTIGONE   30

PREFERMENTS
    WHO TIRED OF KNOCKING AT PREFERMENTS DOOR • • • • 256 SCHOLAR-GIPSY   35

PREFERRD
    BUT HE PREFERRD FATE TO HIS STRONG DESIRE • • • • 198 FRAG ANTIGONE   97
    OF MEN THE LINE OF HERACLES PREFERRD • • • • • • 338 MEROPE   269
    PREFERRD MESSENIAN SERFS TO DORIAN LORDS • • • • 339 MEROPE   324

PREGNANT
    SUCH PREGNANT AND INFECTIOUS QUALITY • • • • • • 50 CONSOLATION   V
    OF PREGNANT PARTS AND QUICK INVENTIVE BRAIN • • 256 SCHOLAR-GIPSY   34

PREOCCUPIED
    BUT KEEP HIM SELF-IMMERSED PREOCCUPIED • • • • 237 PROGRESS   19

PREPARE
    FOR WITH TO-MORROWS DAWN THE GODS PREPARE • • • • 103 BALDER DEAD 1   295

PREPARED
    FOR ILL PREPARED FOR SUCH A WAY • • • • • • 226 EPILOG LAOCOON V 171

PREPARES
    AND THE SLOW-RIPENING TIME AT LAST PREPARES • • 379 MEROPE   1264

PRESCIENCE
    OF A PRESCIENCE MORE THAN OURS • • • • • • • • 456 POOR MATTHIAS   138

PRESCRIBED
    CLEAR PRESCRIBED WITHOUT YOUR CREED • • • • • • 215 PIS-ALLER   8

PRESENCE
    NOR WITH A HATEFUL PRESENCE CUMBER HEAVEN   125 BALDER DEAD 3   399
    TO FEEL THE PRESENCE OF A BROTHER GOD   125 BALDER DEAD 3   418
    THY LOVELY PRESENCE AT MY SIDE   204 CALAIS SANDS   11
    IN THE MASTERS PRESENCE AGAIN   216 LORDS MESSENGER   12
    IN THEIR MASTERS PRESENCE AGAIN   216 LORDS MESSENGER   V   12
    OF A DREADFUL PRESENCE OF FEAR   346 MEROPE   494
    A PRESENCE SAD FOR SOME ONE THROUGH THOSE DOORS   359 MEROPE   874
    HIS PRESENCE WITH THE KING THOU MEANST IMPLIES   365 MEROPE   V
    AND RID HIM OF THE PRESENCE OF HIMSELF   435 EMPEDOCLES II   223
    WHAT SWEET-BREATHING PRESENCE   442 EMPEDOCLES II   441
    THE PRESENCE OF THAT GRACIOUS INMATE LIGHT   444 WESTMIN ABBEY   6
    WHICH MAKE ME FOR THY PRESENCE YEARN   450 GEISTS GRAVE   6
    ALWAY FROM THEIR PRESENCE BROKE   454 POOR MATTHIAS   53

PRESENT
    FROM THIS POOR PRESENT SELF WHICH I AM NOW   37 YOUTHS AGIT   2
    YE IMBECILES IN PRESENT POWER   48 HORATIAN ECHO   11
    FOR HIM THE PRESENT   51 CONSOLATION   39
    PROLONG THE PRESENT   51 CONSOLATION   49
    THITHER WHEN OER THIS PRESENT EARTH AND HEAVENS   128 BALDER DEAD 3   522
    CHIDE NOT WITH THE PAST BUT FEEL THE PRESENT   142 TRISTRAM 2   7
    IN THE HOT PRISON OF THE PRESENT MONTH   212 GROWING OLD   24
    I MARKD THE PRESENT DIE   322 OBERMANN MORE   298
    OR HATRED TO THEIR PRESENT IN THIS LAST   331 MEROPE   40
    BROTHER IT SEEMS THY SISTER MUST PRESENT   386 MEROPE   1451
    IN THIS HIS PRESENT FIERCE MAN-HATING MOOD   409 EMPEDOCLES I 1   106
    LOSE ALL OUR PRESENT STATE   425 EMPEDOCLES I 2   405
    OUR ARTHUR WILL AGAIN BE PRESENT HERE   449 WESTMIN ABBEY   179
    PRESENT AND PAST THE LIVING AND THE DEAD   463 ALARIC AT ROME   44
    WE PRIZE NOT WHEN TIS PRESENT BUT WHEN LOST   LUCRETIUS 7   2

PRESENTLY
    LEST FROM THE COUNCIL-CHAMBER PRESENTLY   386 MEROPE   1442
    TILL PRESENTLY THE KING CAME FORTH IN ROBE   401 MEROPE   1903

PRESENTS
    FORTUNE PRESENTS UNPRAYD   195 FRAG ANTIGONE   5
    THE WORLD BUT FEELS THE PRESENTS SPELL   221 BACCHANALIA 2   65

PRESERVED
    SELF-SPRINGING AND A SEED OF MAN PRESERVED   128 BALDER DEAD 3   530

PRESERVER
    TO THE PRESERVER ZEUS LET ME RETURN   395 MEROPE   1723

PRESIDES
    WHOM HELA WITH AUSTERE CONTROL PRESIDES   104 BALDER DEAD 1   317

PRESS
    WHO LOVE THEE BUT MUST PRESS FOR EVER FIRST   63 SOHRAB RUSTUM   68
    LEAVES NO LEISURE TO PRESS   199 EARLY DEATH   12
    IN THE HOT PRESS OF THE NOON-DAY   219 BACCHANALIA 2   18
    AND PRESS INTO ITS INMOST HEART   224 EPILOG LAOCOON   88
    THAT MAN MUST STILL TO SOME NEW WORSHIP PRESS   238 PROGRESS   V

PRESSD
    AND TO HIS HEART HE PRESSD THE OTHER HAND   80 SOHRAB RUSTUM   665
    THE PRESSD FUGITIVE DEAD   136 TRISTRAM 1   185
    HE LONGD FOR IT PRESSD ON IN VAIN   275 STANZAS CARNAC   45
    HE LONGD IT HE PRESSD ON IN VAIN   275 STANZAS CARNAC   V   45

PRESSES
    PRESSES ME CHIDES ME WILL NOT LET ME WEEP   378 MEROPE   1233
    TIME PRESSES SO THAT THEME FORBEAR I NOW   389 MEROPE   1530

PRESSING
    AND THE PRINCE SINGLE PRESSING ON THE REAR   357 MEROPE   799
    PRESSING FAST WITH BOTH HIS HANDS   434 EMPEDOCLES II   187

PRESSURE
    WE HAD THE POWER TO FEEL THE PRESSURE EASED   436 EMPEDOCLES II   245

PREST
    THOSE LIPS HAVE BEEN PREST   176 PARTING   68
    THE WAVES OF MOURNFUL THOUGHT BY WHICH THEY ARE PREST   243 SUMMER NIGHT   48
    THAT THY GROANS LIKE THUNDER PREST   430 EMPEDOCLES II   62
    OR PREST TOGETHER   460 KAISER DEAD   52

PRETENCE
    BE ERROR DEEMD BUT THAT PRETENCE IS VAIN   339 MEROPE   315
    THIS PEOPLES ANARCHY THY FOES PRETENCE   404 MEROPE   2001

PRETENDED
    THROUGH THAT PRETENDED DEATH TO LIVE AND REIGN   331 MEROPE   50

PRETENTIOUS
    FROM PRETENTIOUS TEASD RELATIONS   SECOND BEST   V   18

PRETEXT
    BUT HE WILL FIND SOME PRETEXT NOT TO FIGHT • • • •   71 SOHRAB RUSTUM   352
    THEN WILL HE FIND SOME PRETEXT NOT TO FIGHT • •   71 SOHRAB RUSTUM V 352

PREVAIL
    TO MEET ME MAN TO MAN IF I PREVAIL • • • • • •   62 SOHRAB RUSTUM   57
    NOR DOTH HE KNOW HOW THERE PREVAIL • • • • • • 243 SUMMER NIGHT   56
    NOR DOES HE KNOW HOW THERE PREVAIL • • • • • • 243 SUMMER NIGHT V 56
    ONE AND A WOMAN HOW CAN I PREVAIL • • • • • • 390 MEROPE   1580
    BUT THOU MY SON STUDY TO MAKE PREVAIL • • • • 404 MEROPE   1995

PREVAILD
    ME TOO HAD HE PREVAILD HE HAD NOT SCORND • • • • 334 MEROPE   133

PREY
    SPIED PREY AFAR • • • • • • •   51 CONSOLATION   35
    TOGETHER AS TWO EAGLES ON ONE PREY • • • • •   75 SOHRAB RUSTUM   472
    SEEKING A PREY UNTO HIS HAND • • • • •   93 SICK KING BOKH   164
    COME THEN SINCE HELA HOLDS BY RIGHT HER PREY • 121 BALDER DEAD 3   288
    BALDER IS DEAD AND HELA HOLDS HER PREY • • • 123 BALDER DEAD 3   347
    I WEEP HIM NOT LET HELA KEEP HER PREY • • • 123 BALDER DEAD 3   354
    LOK TRIUMPHS STILL AND HELA KEEPS HER PREY • • • 126 BALDER DEAD 3   447
    BE MAN HENCEFORTH NO MORE A PREY • • • • 302 GRANDE CHARTR   105
    READY TO SLIP ON HIS UNCONSCIOUS PREY • • • 364 MEROPE   972
    WHEN THE GOTH STOOPED UPON HIS STRICKEN PREY • 464 ALARIC AT ROME   68
    AND YOUR OWN VOICE GUIDE HIM TO HIS PREY • • • 466 ALARIC AT ROME   118

PREYING
    AND KEEP HIS MIND FROM PREYING ON ITSELF • • • • 411 EMPEDOCLES I 1   157

PRIAM
    TROY AND WARLIKE PRIAM TOO AND THE PEOPLE OF PRIAM   HOMER TRANS   22
    TROY AND WARLIKE PRIAM TOO AND THE PEOPLE OF PRIAM   HOMER TRANS   22
    MOVES ME SO MUCH NOT HECUBAS GRIEF NOR PRIAM   HOMER TRANS   24
        MY FATHERS

PRIAMS
    BUSY FOR PRIAMS FAME AND MY OWN IN SPITE OF THE FUTURE   HOMER TRANS   19

PRICE
    NOR DOTH SHE COUNT THIS LIFE A PRICE FOR THAT • •   98 BALDER DEAD 1   118
    PLY HIS BOW SUCH A PRICE • • • • • • • 193 STRAYED REVEL   232
    HAD FINISHD AND A MEED OF PRICE REQUIRED • • • • 448 WESTMIN ABBEY V 136

PRICK
    THAT SHE MIGHT PRICK IT ON THE BABE SHE BORE • •   80 SOHRAB RUSTUM   660
    MY GUARDS WHAT PRICK HIM WITH YOUR SPEARS • • • 89 SICK KING BOKH   42
    PRICK ME THE FELLOW FROM THE PATH • • • • 89 SICK KING BOKH   43

PRICKD
    I TELL THEE PRICKD UPON THIS ARM I BEAR • • • 80 SOHRAB RUSTUM   658
    PRICKD AS A CUNNING WORKMAN IN PEKIN • • • • 81 SOHRAB RUSTUM   672
    SO DELICATELY PRICKD THE SIGN APPEARD • • • 81 SOHRAB RUSTUM   677

PRICKERS
    HOUNDS ARE PULLING PRICKERS SWEARING • • • •   13 CHURCH BROU 1   17
    THE PRICKERS SHOUTED THAT THE STAG WAS GONE • • 357 MEROPE   788

PRICKS
    PRICKS WITH VERMILION SOME CLEAR PORCELAIN VASE • •   81 SOHRAB RUSTUM   673

PRIDE
    BUT THE ARCH-FIEND PRIDE • • • • • •   38 STAGIRIUS   18
    OF PRIDE AND HOPE FOR SOHRAB WHOM THEY LOVED • •   65 SOHRAB RUSTUM   159
    MY FATHER AND HIS PRIDE THE WARRIOR THOR • • • 127 BALDER DEAD 3   491
    NOT WITH A LOOK OF WOUNDED PRIDE • • • • 140 TRISTRAM 1   320
    TO SEEM AS FREE FROM PRIDE AND GUILE • • • • 179 FAREWELL   63
    IN PRIDE OF LIFE THE AGES OF YOUR SIRES • • • 238 PROGRESS   46
    NOT TO FEED PRIESTLY PRIDE ARE THERE • • • • 300 GRANDE CHARTR   50
    YOUR PRIDE OF LIFE YOUR TIRELESS POWERS • • • 304 GRANDE CHARTR   167
    LUST OF THE EYE AND PRIDE OF LIFE • • • • 317 OBERMANN MORE   133
    TYRANNY PRIDE AND LUST FILL SICILYS ABODES • • 416 EMPEDOCLES I 2   121
    STREAMS WILL NOT CURB THEIR PRIDE • • • • 420 EMPEDOCLES I 2   252
    YOUNG APOLLO ALL THE PRIDE • • • • 433 EMPEDOCLES II   130
    OER HUMBLED PRIDE AND SELF-REPROACHING WOE • • 462 ALARIC AT ROME   4
    BUT OER HER VANISHT MIGHT AND HUMBLED PRIDE • • 468 ALARIC AT ROME   161
    WHEREON THOU BUILDEST SUCH A GOODLY PRIDE • • • RUDE ORATOR   8
    NEITHER HATE HAVE THEY NOR FEAR NOR PRIDE • • • META CLOISTER   8

PRIE
    AND AT HER PRIE-DIEU KNEEL UNTIL SHE HAVE TOLD • • 152 TRISTRAM 3   92

PRIEST
    ON SUNDAYS TOO A PRIEST DOTH COME • • • •   17 CHURCH BROU 2   25
    YOU HEAR THE WHITE-ROBED PRIEST SAY MASS • • • •   17 CHURCH BROU 2   29
    PRIEST KNIGHTS AND LADIES GAY • • • • • • 159 NECKAN   22
    AND WHO ART THOU THE PRIEST BEGAN • • • • 159 NECKAN   23
    THE SURPLICED PRIEST STOOD DUMB • • • • • 159 NECKAN   28
    AND SOUGHT A PRIEST TO SIGN THE CROSS • • • 160 NECKAN   39
    A CASSOCKD PRIEST RODE BY • • • • • • 160 NECKAN   48
    O RUTH OF GOD THE PRIEST CRIED OUT • • • • 160 NECKAN   55
    THE CASSOCKD PRIEST RODE ONWARDS • • • • 161 NECKAN   57

PRIEST   (CONTINUED)
        LOUD PRAYS THE PRIEST SHUT STANDS THE DOOR • • • •   163 FORSAKEN MERM   82
        FOR THE PRIEST AND THE BELL AND THE HOLY WELL   • • •   164 FORSAKEN MERM   91
        BUT HE WAS A PRIEST TO US ALL • • • • • •   229 YOUTH OF NATURE   53

PRIESTLY
        NO PRIESTLY STERN PROCESSION NOW • • • • •   274 STANZAS CARNAC   13
        NOT TO FEED PRIESTLY PRIDE ARE THERE • • • • •   300 GRANDE CHARTR   50
        IN PRIESTLY GARB A FRAIL OLD MAN WENT BY • • • •   476 CROMWELL   166

PRIESTS
        BEFORE THE PRIESTS THOU SHALT BE HEARD • • • •   91 SICK KING BOKH   108
        FOR THE PRIESTS HAVE GOT HIM IN PRISON • • • •   214 NEW ROME   3

PRIMAL
        OF THAT PRIMAL AGE IS GONE • • • • • •   27 NEW SIRENS   50
        PREFER OBEDIENCE TO THE PRIMAL LAW • • • • •   196 FRAG ANTIGONE   30
        ATTEND IT FROM ITS PRIMAL SOURCE • • • • • •   225 EPILOG LAOCOON   148
        WHEN THE YEARS PRIMAL BURST OF BLOOM IS OER • • •   264 THYRSIS   52
        ONLY THAT PRIMAL GUEST THE FISHER SAW • • •   445 WESTMIN ABBEY   59
        PROOF THEY GIVE TOO PRIMAL POWERS • • • • •   456 POOR MATTHIAS   137

PRIME
        I SATE OBEDIENT IN THE FIERY PRIME • • • • •   9 MYCERINUS   9
        AND OLD MEN DIE AND YOUNG MEN PASS THEIR PRIME • •   10 MYCERINUS   63
        BURGHERS AND DAMES AT SUMMERS PRIME • • • •   17 CHURCH BROU 2   20
        THE HOST AND STILL WAS IN HIS LUSTY PRIME • • •   64 SOHRAB RUSTUM   109
        THE OTHER HIS RESPLENDENT PRIME • • • • • •   132 TRISTRAM 1   71
        IN THE GLORY OF HIS PRIME • • • • • • •   134 TRISTRAM 1   110
        A FRESHNESS BACK AS OF HER PRIME • • • • •   147 TRISTRAM 2   142
        BUT NOT THE MARGUERITE OF THY PRIME • • • •   184 TERRACE BERNE   34
        BUT HIM IN HIS SWEET PRIME • • • • • •   197 FRAG ANTIGONE   65
        BUT HIM ON WHOM IN THE PRIME • • • • • •   199 FRAG DEJANEIRA   25
        SO BUT THY IMAGE ENDURE IN ITS PRIME • • • •   206 SEPARATION   4
        WHICH IN OUR MORNING-PRIME • • • • • • •   232 YOUTH OF MAN   13
        PRIMROSES ORPHANS OF THE FLOWERY PRIME • • • •   266 THYRSIS   120
        HERE WAS THINE HEIGHT OF STRENGTH THY GOLDEN PRIME •   269 THYRSIS   219
        HIS TENDERER YOUTHFUL PRIME • • • • • • •   308 OBERMANN   68
        AND STILL WAS AT ITS PRIME • • • • • •   318 OBERMANN MORE   164
        AND SPENT THY YOUTHFUL PRIME • • • • • •   323 OBERMANN MORE   306
        AND THE FEAST PAST ITS PRIME SO WE SLIPPD OUT •   407 EMPEDOCLES I 1   37
        THE NIGHTS BALMY PRIME • • • • • • • •   442 EMPEDOCLES II   444
        THE PROMISE OF THE PRIME • • • • • • • •   446 WESTMIN ABBEY   72
        THAT PROMISE OF THE PRIME • • • • • • •   446 WESTMIN ABBEY   V   72
        TELLS THE PRAISES OF THEIR PRIME • • • • •   453 POOR MATTHIAS   28
        AND NOT BETHINK HER OF HER GLORIOUS PRIME • • •   467 ALARIC AT ROME   130

PRIMEVAL
        IN THE PRIMEVAL MOUNTAIN-FORESTS BORE • • • •   389 MEROPE   1537

PRIMITIVE
        HER VIGOROUS PRIMITIVE SONS • • • • • • •   252 FUTURE   33

PRIMROSES
        STARRD THE COOL TURF AND CLUMPS OF PRIMROSES • •   155 TRISTRAM 3   208
        PRIMROSES ORPHANS OF THE FLOWERY PRIME • • • •   266 THYRSIS   120

PRINCE
        WHERE THOU YOUNG PRINCE SHALT NEVER MORE ARISE • •   18 CHURCH BROU 3   7
        WHERE THE PRINCE WHOM SHE MUST WED • • • • •   134 TRISTRAM 1   133
        PRINCE ALEXANDER PHILIPS PEERLESS SON • • • •   153 TRISTRAM 3   147
        O PRINCE WHAT PAIN • • • • • • • • •   192 STRAYED REVEL   211
        BUT PRINCE ADOPTED BY THE WILL OF POWER • • • •   335 MEROPE   171
        AEPYTUS THE MESSENIAN PRINCE IS DEAD • • • • •   355 MEROPE   714
        THE PRINCE AT START SEEMD SAD BUT HIS REGARD • •   355 MEROPE   733
        SAD REVERENTIAL HOMAGE HAD OUR PRINCE • • • •   356 MEROPE   761
        AND THE PRINCE SINGLE PRESSING ON THE REAR • • •   357 MEROPE   799
        THEN CAME THE PRINCE HE SHOUTED AND PLUNGED IN • •   358 MEROPE   810
        A MOMENT MORE I SAW THE PRINCE TURN ROUND • • •   358 MEROPE   831
        BUT OF THE PRINCE NOTHING REMAIND SAVE THIS • •   358 MEROPE   839
        THE PRINCE IN CHASE AFTER A SWIMMING STAG • • •   363 MEROPE   959
        IN ONE THING ONLY THAT THE PRINCE IS DEAD • • •   364 MEROPE   966
        OUR PRINCE AND THE GOOD LAIAS WHOM HIS WARD • •   364 MEROPE   976
        FOR THE MESSENIAN HEARTS WHO LOVED THE PRINCE • •   365 MEROPE   993
        I HAVE HEARD O QUEEN HOW A PRINCE • • • • •   368 MEROPE   1082
        ANNOUNCES ME THEIR RIGHTFUL PRINCE RETURND • • •   383 MEROPE   1955
        MESSENIA SPEAKS THE PRINCE THY SON IS DEAD • • •   393 MEROPE   1686
        I TREMBLED FOR OUR PRINCE AND HIS ATTEMPT • • •   401 MEROPE   1901
        BEFORE HIM AT HIS SIDE THE PRINCE THY SON • • •   401 MEROPE   1905
        THE PRINCE SNATCHD FROM THE SACRIFICERS HAND • •   402 MEROPE   1915
        TO CIRCLE THE PRINCE ROUND WHEN SUDDENLY • • •   402 MEROPE   1932
        THE PRINCE HIS UNCLE LAIAS WHOM HIS WARD • • •   364 MEROPE   V   976
        THIS STRANGE UNLIKELY TALE THE PRINCE WAS DROWND • •   364 MEROPE   V
        WHO SAW THE PRINCE AND LAIAS LAST WITH HIM • • •   365 MEROPE   V
        BUT THAT PRINCE AMONG GODS THE SON OF THE LOVELY-HAIRD   HOMER TRANS   52
           LETO

PRINCELY
        DEAD HER PRINCELY YOUTHFUL HUSBAND • • • • • •   14 CHURCH BROU 1   49
        THE PRINCELY PAIR ARE LEFT ALONE • • • • • •   17 CHURCH BROU 2   39
        SO REST FOR EVER REST O PRINCELY PAIR • • • •   17 CHURCH BROU 3   1

PRINCELY   (CONTINUED)
      WHEN THE PRINCELY HEART IS DEAD   . . . . . .   28 NEW SIRENS   V. 78
      WHILE THE PRINCELY HEART IS DEAD   . . . . . .   28 NEW SIRENS   V 78
      O PRINCELY LAIAS TO WHAT PURPOSE CALLS   . . . .   386 MEROPE   1446
      HE TOO WAS THERE IT WAS THE PRINCELY BOY . . . . 477 CROMWELL   179

PRINCES
      OF AN ARCADIAN LORD OUR PRINCES FRIEND   . . . . 363 MEROPE   956
      AND HAD HIM AT THE PRINCES SIDE IN LEASH . . . . 364 MEROPE   971
      FOR THEIR HERACLES-ISSUED PRINCES   . . . . . .   400 MEROPE   1853

PRINCESS
      AND THOU O PRINCESS SHALT NO MORE RECEIVE . . . . 18 CHURCH BROU 3   12
      AND SHE TOO THAT PRINCESS FAIR   . . . .   134 TRISTRAM 1   115
      THAT FIRST ISEULT PRINCESS BRIGHT   . . . . . .   134 TRISTRAM 1   126
      MY PRINCESS ART THOU THERE SWEET DO NOT WAIT . . 140 TRISTRAM 1   308
      MY PRINCESS ART THOU THERE SWEET TIS TOO LATE . . 140 TRISTRAM 1   V 308
      CLOSE MINE EYES THEN SEEK THE PRINCESS ISEULT . . 145 TRISTRAM 2   93
      RISE GO HENCE AND SEEK THE PRINCESS ISEULT . . . 145 TRISTRAM 2   V 93
      BUT AN ARCADIAN PRINCESS MORE AKIN   . . . . . .   337 MEROPE   241

PRINCIPLES
      AFFECTIONS INSTINCTS PRINCIPLES AND POWERS . . . .   4 BUTLERS SERMONS   1

PRINKING
      PRINKING EARS AND DEWLAP THROAT   . . . . . .   454 POOR MATTHIAS   72

PRIOR
      BUT HIS THE PRIOR PATTERN HE DESIGNED   . . . .   LUCRETIUS 5   2
      HIS IS THE PRIOR PATTERN HE DESIGNED . . . . . .   LUCRETIUS 5   V 2

PRISON
      IN THE HOT PRISON OF THE PRESENT MONTH   . . . . 212 GROWING OLD   24
      FOR THE PRIESTS HAVE GOT HIM IN PRISON   . . . . 214 NEW ROME   3
      FOR MOST MEN IN A BRAZEN PRISON LIVE . . . . . . 243 SUMMER NIGHT   37
      DREAMING OF NOUGHT BEYOND THEIR PRISON-WALL . .   243 SUMMER NIGHT   41
      DEATH IN THEIR PRISON REACHES THEM   . . . . . .   243 SUMMER NIGHT   49
      ESCAPE THEIR PRISON AND DEPART   . . . .   243 SUMMER NIGHT   52
      HE TORE US FROM THE PRISON-CELL   . . . . . .   271 MEMORIAL VERSES V
      NOR BE COLD GLOOM THY PRISON   . . . .   322 OBERMANN MORE   282
      SUNLESS PRISON OF ROCK   . . . .   370 MEROPE   1118
      THY PRISON-HOUSE RAISED ONE IMPLORING CRY . . .   383 MEROPE   1371
      CHOSEN A PRISON FOR PROMETHEUS CLIMB . . . . .   395 MEROPE   1750
      SUNLESS PRISON OF ROCKS   . . . .   370 MEROPE   V1118
      WITHIN THE MARBLE PRISON OF HER ARMS . . . . . .   FRAGMENT 1   4

PRISONER
      TIMES CHAFING PRISONER ASK IT NOW   . . . . . .   53 RESIGNATION   39
      AN UNRECOVERD PRISONER SHADE WITH SHADES . . . . 120 BALDER DEAD 3   229
      IS MERLIN PRISONER TILL THE JUDGMENT-DAY . . . . 156 TRISTRAM 3   222
      THERE THE FREED PRISONER WHEREER HIS HEART . . . 243 SUMMER NIGHT   54

PRISONERS
      SOME AS PRISONERS DRAW BREATH   . . . .   216 LORDS MESSENGER   15
      MERE PRISONERS MEANT OR NOT AMONG OUR FOES . . . 337 MEROPE   251
      PRISONERS OF DEATH FROM THE GRAVE   . . . . .   347 MEROPE   525
      AND KEEP US PRISONERS OF OUR CONSCIOUSNESS . . . 439 EMPEDOCLES II   352

PRISONING
      PRISONING IN HIS CREVICD STONES   . . . . . .   PILLARS UNIVERS   11
      PRISONING IN HIS RIFTED STONES   . . . .   PILLARS UNIVERS V 11

PRIVATE
      WITH PUBLIC TOIL AND PRIVATE TEEN   . . . . . .   276 SOUTHERN NIGHT   27
      PRIVATE AFFECTIONS FOR THESE   . . . .   282 HAWORTH CHURCH   V
      FOR PRIVATE GAIN OR HATRED TAKES A LIFE   . . . . 336 MEROPE   202
      A PRIVATE LOSS HERE FOUNDS A NATIONS PEACE . . . 360 MEROPE   889
      FOR THE KINGS PRIVATE EAR RESERVES LIKE THIS . . 364 MEROPE   965
      AND HOW THEN RUNS THIS TRUE AND PRIVATE TALE . . 364 MEROPE   967

PRIVILEGED
      ITS PRIVILEGED IMMUNITY FROM BLOOD   . . . . . .   389 MEROPE   1535

PRIZE
      GOD KNOWS IT I AM WITH YOU IF TO PRIZE   . . . .   6 REP FRIEND   1
      AH THE DIM REMEMBRANCE PRIZE   . . . .   24 MEMORY-PICTURE   62
      NOW AND I KNOW NOT HOW THEY PRIZE THEE THERE . . 115 BALDER DEAD 3   77
      FIXD FULL ON MERLINS FACE HER STATELY PRIZE . .   154 TRISTRAM 3   178
      GARLANDS THEIR PRIZE   . . . .   218 BACCHANALIA 1   37
      LIFE IS THEIR PRIZE   . . . .   220 BACCHANALIA 2   42
      BUT OF THAT INWARD PRIZE   . . . .   315 OBERMANN MORE   V
      FELL TO THY FATHERS LOT THE SECOND PRIZE . . .   330 MEROPE   8
      THOU CONFESSEST THE PRIZE   . . . .   370 MEROPE   1104
      NOT MUCH I KNOW YOU PRIZE   . . . .   426 EMPEDOCLES I 2   407
      NOT MUCH THOU KNOWST I PRIZE   . . . .   426 EMPEDOCLES I 2   V 407
      NOT OVERMUCH I PRIZE   . . . .   426 EMPEDOCLES I 2   V 407
      THOSE STERNER SPIRITS LET ME PRIZE   . . . . . .   481 COURAGE   9
      WE PRIZE NOT WHEN TIS PRESENT BUT WHEN LOST . .   LUCRETIUS 7   2

PRIZED
　　THOSE VIRTUES PRIZED AND PRACTISED BY TOO FEW　•　•　　6 REP FRIEND　　　2
　　BUT PRIZED BUT LOVED BUT EMINENT IN YOU　•　•　•　•　　6 REP FRIEND　　　3
　　WE PRIZED IT DEARLY WHILE IT STOOD WE SAID　•　•　•　•　263 THYRSIS　　　28

PROBATION
　　GO THROUGH THE SAD PROBATION ALL AGAIN　　•　•　•　•　440 EMPEDOCLES II　　368

PROCEED
　　BUT STILL AS WE PROCEED　•　•　•　•　•　•　•　•　•　•　423 EMPEDOCLES I 2　　332

PROCEEDS
　　IF BIRTH PROCEEDS IF THINGS SUBSIST　•　•　•　•　•　•　　58 RESIGNATION　　194
　　PROCEEDS AT ANY NOD　•　•　•　•　•　•　•　•　•　•　422 EMPEDOCLES I 2　　300

PROCEEDST
　　FORESEEN THY HARVEST YET PROCEEDST TO LIVE　•　•　•　•　43 GIPSY CHILD　　40

PROCESSION
　　THE SACRED WORLD AND BY PROCESSION SURE　•　•　•　•　45 IN UTRUMQUE PAR　　3
　　AND IN PROCESSION ALL COME NEAR AND WEEP　•　•　•　•　115 BALDER DEAD 3　　51
　　THE BRIGHT PROCESSION　•　•　•　•　•　•　•　•　•　185 STRAYED REVEL　　4
　　THE BRIGHT PROCESSION　•　•　•　•　•　•　•　•　•　194 STRAYED REVEL　　295
　　NO PRIESTLY STERN PROCESSION NOW　•　•　•　•　•　274 STANZAS CARNAC　　13
　　WHAT BLACK PROCESSION SLOWLY MAKES APPROACH　•　•　331 MEROPE　　52

PROCLAIM
　　THOUGH THE LOUD WORLD PROCLAIM THEIR ENMITY　•　•　1 QUIET WORK　　4

PROCLAIMD
　　AND PROCLAIMD YOUR VAIN OVATION　•　•　•　•　•　•　31 NEW SIRENS　　153

PROCLAIMS
　　PROSPECT OF HOPE WHICH FRANCE PROCLAIMS SO LOUD　•　•　7 REP FRIEND CONT　　3
　　AT DIVORCE WHICH IT PROCLAIMS　•　•　•　•　•　•　•　35 NEW SIRENS　　262
　　PROCLAIMS SALVATION AT HAND　•　•　•　•　•　•　•　214 NEW ROME　　8
　　THE WORLD PROCLAIMS THE TERMS　•　•　•　•　•　•　•　419 EMPEDOCLES I 2　V 222

PROCLES
　　THY SPARTAN COUSINS PROCLES AND HIS BROTHER　•　•　384 MEROPE　　1393

PROCURED
　　IF MEN PROCURED THEE TROUBLE GAVE THEE REST　•　•　269 THYRSIS　　215

PRODIGALITY
　　BUT SHE WITH PRODIGALITY BRINGS FORTH　•　•　•　•　EVERLASTING SUB　　4

PRODIGY
　　THE PRODIGY OF FULL-BLOWN CRIME AMONG　•　•　•　•　6 GEO CRUIKSHANK　　3

PRODUCTS
　　FRESH PRODUCTS OF THEIR BARREN LABOUR FALL　•　•　•　•　243 SUMMER NIGHT　　43

PROFANE
　　AND ARTISTS ENVIOUS AND THE MOB PROFANE　•　•　•　295 HEINES GRAVE　　114
　　THOU KEEPEST ALOOF THE PROFANE　•　•　•　•　•　•　435 EMPEDOCLES II　　207

PROFESSD
　　THE MANNERS THERE PROFESSD　•　•　•　•　•　•　•　419 EMPEDOCLES I 2　　219

PROFFER
　　AND PRAISE MY FAME AND PROFFER COURTEOUS GIFTS　•　•　71 SOHRAB RUSTUM　　353
　　TO WHOM THIS DAY HE CAME TO PROFFER PEACE　•　•　•　387 MEROPE　　1482

PROFIT
　　NO SMALL PROFIT THAT MAN EARNS　•　•　•　•　•　•　•　49 SECOND BEST　　16
　　WHY DOST THOU ONLY PROFIT BY HIS DEATH　•　•　•　•　340 MEROPE　　331
　　YOUR KING DESIRED THE PROFIT OF HIS DEATH　•　•　•　365 MEROPE　　990
　　WHO CHIEFLY PROFIT RUN NO MORE THAN THEY　•　•　•　382 MEROPE　　1351
　　WHO STILL WAS FAITHFUL WHAT MIGHT PROFIT ME　•　•　410 EMPEDOCLES I 1　　131

PROFITEST
　　THOU NOTHING PROFITEST THY FRIENDS BUT MAKST　•　•　368 MEROPE　　1080

PROFOUND
　　IN PROFOUND SILENCE STERN　•　•　•　•　•　•　•　198 FRAG DEJANEIRA　　8
　　PROFOUND YET TOUCHING SWEET YET STRONG　•　•　•　•　222 EPILOG LAOCOON　　28
　　LARGE AND PROFOUND HATH GENIUS HERE　•　•　•　•　223 EPILOG LAOCOON　　80
　　OH HIDE ME IN YOUR GLOOM PROFOUND　•　•　•　•　•　302 GRANDE CHARTR　　91
　　SEE IN THE BLUE PROFOUND　•　•　•　•　•　•　•　313 OBERMANN MORE　　32
　　HIGH IN THE VALAIS-DEPTH PROFOUND　•　•　•　•　•　324 OBERMANN MORE　　347
　　NO PATIENCE TOO PROFOUND　•　•　•　•　•　•　•　419 EMPEDOCLES I 2　　214

PROFOUNDEST
　　THESE MENS PROFOUNDEST MIND　•　•　•　•　•　•　•　238 PROGRESS　　36

PROFOUNDLY
　　AND HEART PROFOUNDLY STIRRD　•　•　•　•　•　•　•　212 GROWING OLD　　18

PROJECT
　　NURSING THY PROJECT IN UNCLOUDED JOY　•　•　•　•　•　261 SCHOLAR-GIPSY　　199

PROJECT   (CONTINUED)
     A LAST LONG-CHERISHD PROJECT IN MY AIM   . . . . 360 MEROPE   880

PROLONG
     PROLONG THE PRESENT   . . . .   51 CONSOLATION   49
     PROLONG THY LIFE THOUGH NOT BY THEE DESIRED   . . 104 BALDER DEAD 1   312

PROLONGD
     PROLONGD NOR KNEW ALTHOUGH NOT LESS   . . . . . 181 ISOLATION MARG   41
     ITS GREATNESS NOR THE REIGN OF FOOLS PROLONGD   . . 282 HAWORTH CHURCH   V
     NOT IN SUNK SPAINS PROLONGD DEATH AGONY   . . . . 480 HUNGARIAN NAT   1

PROMETHEUS
     CHOSEN A PRISON FOR PROMETHEUS CLIMB . . . . . . 395 MEROPE   1750

PROMISE
     A WIND OF PROMISE AND REPOSE   . . . .   21 YOUTH AND CALM   12
     MANY A BROKEN PROMISE THEN   . . . .   23 MEMORY-PICTURE   37
     STERN STRENGTH AND PROMISE OF CONTROL   . . . . 178 FAREWELL   24
     I PROMISE BUT I FEAR   . . . . 371 MEROPE   1136
     PROMISE NOT FAIR LET HIM A LITTLE WHILE   . . . . 388 MEROPE   1506
     THE PROMISE OF THE PRIME . . . . 446 WESTMIN ABBEY   72
     THAT PROMISE OF THE PRIME   . . . . 446 WESTMIN ABBEY   V 72
     THAT DAY OF BOUNDLESS HOPE AND PROMISE HIGH   . . 478 CROMWELL   211

PROMISED
     NOR PROMISED LOVE IT COULD NOT GIVE   . . . . . 251 WISH   38

PROMONTORIES
     HALLOW THE SALAMINIAN PROMONTORIES   . . . . . 481 HUNGARIAN NAT   13

PROMONTORY
     AND THE PROMONTORY OF CENAEUM   . . . . 399 MEROPE   1816

PROMOTION
     WERE AIMD AT THEIR PROMOTION OUR DECLINE   . . . . 337 MEROPE   244

PROMPT
     THE PROMPT STERN GODDESS . . . .   51 CONSOLATION   51
     THE FOOT LESS PROMPT TO MEET THE MORNING DEW   . . 266 THYRSIS   138
     PROMPT UNWEARIED AS HERE . . . . 287 RUGBY CHAPEL   48
     NOT SO LET HIM AND NONE SHALL BE MORE PROMPT   . . 388 MEROPE   1496

PROMPTED
     RATHER TO PATIENCE PROMPTED THAN THAT PROUD   . .   7 REP FRIEND CONT   2

PROMPTER
     HE COMES TO TELL HIS PROMPTER HE HATH SPED . . . . 365 MEROPE   986

PROMPTINGS
     I KNOW IT BUT FATE TROD THOSE PROMPTINGS DOWN   . .   82 SOHRAB RUSTUM   713
     PERPETUAL PROMPTINGS TO REBELLIOUS HOPE   . . . . 333 MEROPE   91

PROMPTS
     BUT SOMETHING PROMPTS ME NOT THUS   . . . . . . 298 HEINES GRAVE   199

PRONE
     LIE PRONE ENORMOUS DOWN THE MOUNTAIN SIDE   . . .   86 SOHRAB RUSTUM   863
     NOT PRONE ALL SAY AVERSE TO BLOODSHED NOW   . . . 388 MEROPE   1492
     NOT PRONE ALL SAY TO USELESS BLOODSHED NOW   . . . 388 MEROPE   V1492

PRONOUNCE
     AND DARED PRONOUNCE IT HAPPY WHAT ARE THESE   . .   RUDE ORATOR   7
     AND DARED PRONOUNCE THEM HAPPY WHAT ARE THESE   . .   RUDE ORATOR   V   7

PRONOUNCED
     THE DOOM PRONOUNCED THE BATTLE-FLAG UNFURLED   . . 465 ALARIC AT ROME   93

PROOF
     THE HILLS ARE CLOTHED WITH PINES SUN-PROOF . . . .   16 CHURCH BROU 2   4
     THROUGH SUN-PROOF ALLEYS . . . .   51 CONSOLATION   26
     SOHRAB THAT WERE A PROOF WHICH COULD NOT LIE   . .   81 SOHRAB RUSTUM   667
     DOST THOU ASK PROOF OUR TREE YET CROWNS THE HILL . . 269 THYRSIS   239
     IF IN THE EVENT BE ANY PROOF   . . . . 354 MEROPE   701
     TIS SO TIS SO ALAS FOR SEE THE PROOF   . . . . 364 MEROPE   978
     SUSPICION GRAVE I SEE BUT NO FIRM PROOF   . . . 365 MEROPE   994
     PROOF NOT SURMISE SHOWS HIM IN COMMERCE CLOSE   . . 380 MEROPE   1274
     AGAINST SURPRISE AND SUDDEN PANIC PROOF   . . . 381 MEROPE   1305
     AUTHENTIC PROOF OF WHAT THOU TELLST OUR EARS   . . 403 MEROPE   1952
     SUSPICION GRAVE I SEE BUT NO CLEAR PROOF   . . . 365 MEROPE   V 994
     REASON THE PROOF CONFIRMS   . . . . 419 EMPEDOCLES I 2   224
     PROOF THEY GIVE TOO PRIMAL POWERS   . . . . . . 456 POOR MATTHIAS   137
     THOU DOST ALLEDGE FOR PROOF SUCH INSTANCES   . . .   RUDE ORATOR   15

PROOFS
     THY PROOFS THY WITNESS AND THY PRECEDENTS   . . .   RUDE ORATOR   9

PROP
     WHO PROP THOU ASKST IN THESE BAD DAYS MY MIND   . .   2 TO A FRIEND   1
     PROP ME UPON THE PILLOWS ONCE AGAIN   . . . . . 130 TRISTRAM 1   2

PROP   (CONTINUED)
        A PROP GAVE WAY CRASH FELL A PLATFORM LO   . . . .   166 AUSTERITY POET   8

PROPER
        HOW SAYST THOU IS THAT SIGN THE PROPER SIGN   . .   81 SOHRAB RUSTUM   687

PROPHESY
        WHY DOST THOU PROPHESY SO MY DEATH TO ME XANTHUS   HOMER TRANS   59
            IT NEEDS NOT

PROPHET
        SEE SUCH A PROPHET AGAIN . . . .   229 YOUTH OF NATURE   47

PROPHETESSES
        THE PROPHETESSES WHO BY RITE ETERNE   . . . . . .   97 BALDER DEAD 1   89

PROPHETIC
        AS FROM A HEIGHT WITH RAPT PROPHETIC EYES   . . .   212 GROWING OLD   17
        UPON ITS HEADLONG COURSE WITH SAD PROPHETIC EYE . .   463 ALARIC AT ROME   24
        IN WHOSE PROPHETIC SPIRIT LAY THE PLAN   . . . .   LUCRETIUS 5   V   4

PROPHETS
        PROPHETS TRANSFIGURED SAINTS AND MARTYRS BRAVE . .   18 CHURCH BROU 3   20

PROPOSAL
        BUT FAIR PROPOSAL MERITS FAIR REPLY   . . . . . .   395 MEROPE   1728

PROPOSE
        BECAUSE THEY TO THEMSELVES PROPOSE   . . . . . .   53 RESIGNATION   15

PROPPING
        THE HANDS PROPPING THE SUNK HEAD   . . . . . .   30 NEW SIRENS   128

PROPS
        PROPS THY SOFT CHEEK   . . . .   186 STRAYED REVEL   10

PROPT
        PROPT ON PILLOWS IN HIS BED   . . . .   130 TRISTRAM 1   11

PRORE
        CUT BY AN ONWARD-LABOURING VESSELS PRORE   . . . .   41 HUMAN LIFE   23

PROSE
        DEAD AND NEITHER PROSE NOR RHYME   . . . . . .   453 POOR MATTHIAS   27

PROSERPINE
        OF PROSERPINE AMONG WHOSE CROWNED HAIR   . . . .   265 THYRSIS   88
        WHEN DORIAN SHEPHERDS SANG TO PROSERPINE   . . . .   265 THYRSIS   92

PROSPECT
        SAW THE WIDE PROSPECT AND THE ASIAN FEN   . . . .   2 TO A FRIEND   3
        PROSPECT OF HOPE WHICH FRANCE PROCLAIMS SO LOUD . .   7 REP FRIEND CONT   3
        CLEAR PROSPECT OER OUR BEINGS WHOLE   . . . . . .   179 FAREWELL   54

PROSPECTS
        PROSPECTS UNROLL THEMSELVES   . . . .   50 CONSOLATION   8

PROSPERITY
        LITTLE IN YOUR PROSPERITY   . . . .   198 FRAG DEJANEIRA   5

PROSPEROUS
        TO GUIDE OUR VENGEANCE TO A PROSPEROUS CLOSE   . .   332 MEROPE   75
        AND I AM SEATED ON A PROSPEROUS THRONE   . . . .   334 MEROPE   136
        PROSPEROUS MIGHTY CAME BACK   . . . .   343 MEROPE   411
        TO GUIDE OUR EFFORT TO A PROSPEROUS CLOSE   . . .   332 MEROPE   V   75
        TIS AS AN ORPHAN AMONG PROSPEROUS BOYS   . . . .   408 EMPEDOCLES I 1   71
        BUT HE WHO HAS OUTLIVED HIS PROSPEROUS DAYS   . .   436 EMPEDOCLES II   261

PROTECTED
        OF A PROTECTED EXILE ANY MORE   . . . .   383 MEROPE   1381

PROTECTORS
        INFIRM PROTECTORS DUBIOUS ORACLES   . . . . . .   336 MEROPE   215

PROUD
        RATHER TO PATIENCE PROMPTED THAN THAT PROUD   . .   7 REP FRIEND CONT   2
        OF DARK ELMS SHOOT ROUND DROPPING DOWN THE   19 MODERN SAPPHO   6
            PROUD STREAM
        OF DARK ELMS COME ROUND DROPPING DOWN THE PROUD STREAM   19 MODERN SAPPHO   V   6
        AND YOUR PROUD HEADS BACKWARD THROWN . . . . .   32 NEW SIRENS   192
        BUT INDEED THIS PROUD POSSESSION   . . . . . .   33 NEW SIRENS   203
        THOUGH EASE DULLS GRACE AND WISDOM BE TOO PROUD . .   44 GIPSY CHILD   63
        THOUGH EASE DULLS GRACE AND WISDOM IS TOO PROUD . .   44 GIPSY CHILD   V 63
        BE NOT TOO PROUD . . . .   46 IN UTRUMQUE PAR   35
        AND PROUD SELF-SEVERANCE FROM THEM WERE DISEASE . .   46 IN UTRUMQUE PAR V 39
        IN SUSAS PALACE PROUD   . . . .   47 WORLD QUIETIST   26
        BE PASSD ON THE PROUD HEIGHTS OF SWAY   . . . .   56 RESIGNATION   149
        IS IN THEIR FAR-OFF TRIUMPHS PROUD   . . . . .   57 RESIGNATION   163
        HE SHORE AWAY AND THAT PROUD HORSEHAIR PLUME   . .   76 SOHRAB RUSTUM   497
        THOU DOST NOT SLAY ME PROUD AND BOASTFUL MAN   . .   77 SOHRAB RUSTUM   542
        THAT PROUD FIRST ISEULT CORNWALLS QUEEN   . . .   132 TRISTRAM 1   58
        LET HER HAVE HER PROUD DARK EYES   . . . . . .   134 TRISTRAM 1   119

PROUD   (CONTINUED)
    DWELLS ON PROUD TYNTAGELS HILL • • • • • • • • • 134 TRISTRAM 1   V 134
    SITS ON PROUD TYNTAGELS HILL   • • • • • • • • 134 TRISTRAM 1   V 134
    BUT THY DARK EYES ARE NOT DIMMD PROUD ISEULT • • 142 TRISTRAM 2   19
    IN TYNTAGELS PALACE PROUD   • • • • • • • • 146 TRISTRAM 2   115
    PROUD IGNORANT SELF-ADORED YOU LIVE ALONE • • • • 198 FRAG DEJANEIRA   7
    THE PROUD BOASTING OF THEIR YOUTH   • • • • • 235 YOUTH OF MAN   103
    THE SHORT PROUD LIP SHOWING THY RACE THY CHEEKS • • 373 MEROPE   1163
    FORSAKE THIS AMPLE PROUD MESSENIAN REALM • • • • 395 MEROPE   1744
    AND I COULD WATCH HIM WITH HIS PROUD SAD FACE • • 408 EMPEDOCLES I 1   59
    IS THY TORTURED HEART STILL PROUD   • • • • • 430 EMPEDOCLES II   49
    WHERE IN PROUD REPOSE HE LAY • • • • • • • 433 EMPEDOCLES II   162
    WHICH MAN PROUD MAN FINDS HARD TO BEAR   • • • 450 GEISTS GRAVE   30
    PROUD OF PORT THOUGH SOMETHING SQUAT • • • • • 457 POOR MATTHIAS   189

PROUDER
    LOFTIER BEARING AND A PROUDER EYE   • • • • • • 28 NEW SIRENS   64

PROUDEST
    AND THE PROUDEST NO MORE SMILE • • • • • • • • 33 NEW SIRENS   216

PROUDLY
    PROUDLY LIKE A KING BEWAILING   • • • • • • • • 34 NEW SIRENS   225
    REARD PROUDLY SNUFFING   • • • • • • • • • • 190 STRAYED REVEL   149
    ALLOWS THE PROUDLY-RIDING AND THE FOUNDERING BARK • 421 EMPEDOCLES I 2   261
    ALLOWS THE PROUDLY-RIDING AND THE FOUNDERD BARK • • 421 EMPEDOCLES I 2 V 261
    WHERE THE DARK SHIPS RODE PROUDLY WOOD THE GALE • • 479 CROMWELL   238

PROVE
    AT SUCH DESPOTIC LENGTH TO PROVE   • • • • • •   HORATIAN ECHO   V
    THOU TOO WILT SURELY ONE DAY PROVE • • • • • • 178 FAREWELL   38
    BUT THOU HAST LONG HAD PLACE TO PROVE   • • • • 181 ISOLATION MARG   28
    THIS TRUTH TO PROVE AND MAKE THINE OWN   • • • • 181 ISOLATION MARG   29
    ONE FOR WHOSE SAKE SHE ONCE MIGHT PROVE • • • • 202 URANIA   19
    NEPHEW THY FRIENDS ARE SOUNDED AND PROVE TRUE • • 390 MEROPE   1587
    NOR DOES BEING WEARY PROVE THAT HE HAS WHERE TO REST 424 EMPEDOCLES I 2 351
    PROVE US SO REMOTE IN KIND • • • • • • • • 457 POOR MATTHIAS   156

PROVED
    AND THOU ART PROVED I KNOW AND I AM YOUNG • • • • 72 SOHRAB RUSTUM   386
    YET SHE CHASTE QUEEN HAD NEVER PROVED   • • • • 181 ISOLATION MARG   25
    AND THOU PROVED MUCH ENDURING   • • • • • • • 194 STRAYED REVEL   287
    WHAT FOR SO FAR FATE HATH NOT PROVED MY FOE • • 397 MEROPE   1778
    WHAT FOR SO FAR SHE HATH NOT PROVED MY FOE • • • 397 MEROPE   V1778

PROVENCAL
    ABOVE THE FRAGRANT WARM PROVENCAL SHORE • • • • 167 RACHEL 2   2

PROVES
    PROVES FORGETFULNESS BEGUN • • • • • • • • • 24 MEMORY-PICTURE   52
    STILL THE ATTEMPT TO USE THEM PROVES THEM NULL • • 210 SELF-DECEPTION   20
    AND IF SO USED PROVES AS THOU SAYST UNSURE • • • 382 MEROPE   1341
    MY FINAL VICTORY PROVES THE GODS APPEASED • • • 397 MEROPE   1770
    THE WORLDS COURSE PROVES THE TERMS • • • • • 419 EMPEDOCLES I 2   222

PROVIDE
    AND BID THE CHIEF TORMENTORS THERE PROVIDE • • • 373 MEROPE   1188

PROW
    STANDS AT THE PROW AND GUIDES THEM BUT ASTERN • • 191 STRAYED REVEL   190
    AT THIS VESSELS PROW I STAND WHICH BEARS ME • • 239 SELF-DEPENDENCE   3
    AT THE VESSELS PROW I STAND WHICH BEARS ME • • • • 239 SELF-DEPENDENCE V 3
    DESCRIED AT SUNRISE AN EMERGING PROW • • • • • 262 SCHOLAR-GIPSY   233

PROWESS
    FOES DAZZLED WITH YOUR PROWESS WELL INCLINED • • 339 MEROPE   302

PRUDENCE
    MANS PRUDENCE AND MANS FIERY MIGHT • • • • • • 272 MEMORIAL VERSES   59
    PRUDENCE IS ON THE OTHER SIDE BUT DEEDS • • • • 383 MEROPE   1384
    CONDEMND BY PRUDENCE HAVE SOMETIMES GONE WELL • • 383 MEROPE   1385
    NOT TILL THE WAYS OF PRUDENCE ALL ARE TRIED • • 384 MEROPE   1386
    IF PRUDENCE COUNSELS THEE TO GO UNARMD • • • • 391 MEROPE   1591

PRUND
    AND PRUND ITS FAITH AND QUENCHD ITS FIRE • • • • 301 GRANDE CHARTR   V 68

PSYCHE
    AND PSYCHE LONG HAS BEEN DEAD • • • • • • • • 214 NEW ROME   4

PUBLIC
    IN JOPPA THROUGH THE PUBLIC STREET • • • • • 157 SAINT BRANDAN   42
    SATE WITH HIS BRIDE TO SEE A PUBLIC SHOW • • • 166 AUSTERITY POET   4
    OR CROSS A STILE INTO THE PUBLIC WAY • • • • • 257 SCHOLAR-GIPSY   85
    WITH PUBLIC TOIL AND PRIVATE TEEN • • • • • • 276 SOUTHERN NIGHT   27
    COUNTRY AND PUBLIC CARES • • • • • • • • • 282 HAWORTH CHURCH   V
    PUBLIC CARES WHICH MOVE • • • • • • • • • 282 HAWORTH CHURCH   V
    GREAT HERACLES AND IN THAT PUBLIC PLACE • • • 330 MEROPE   14
    BY SAD OBSERVANCES AND PUBLIC GRIEF • • • • 332 MEROPE   81
    PEACE PEACE IS WHAT I SEEK AND PUBLIC CALM • • • 333 MEROPE   101

PUBLIC   (CONTINUED)
          BUT WHEN FOR SOME GREAT PUBLIC CAUSE AN ARM   •   •   336 MEROPE   204
          HIS DEATH A PUBLIC NOT A PERSONAL ACT   •   •   •   •   387 MEROPE   1480
          THY FATHERS MURDERER IN THE PUBLIC PLACE   •   •   •   •   391 MEROPE   1588
          OF PERSONAL FEELING TO THE PUBLIC WEAL   •   •   •   •   394 MEROPE   1712
          BASED ON PURE PUBLIC WELFARE LET US BE   •   •   •   •   394 MEROPE   1718
          FOR WHEN THIS MORNING IN THE PUBLIC SQUARE •   •   •   •   401 MEROPE   1895
          OF PERSONAL VENGEANCE TO THE PUBLIC WEAL   •   •   •   •   394 MEROPE   V1712

PUDDLE
          IS TO A PUTRID PUDDLE TURND   •   •   •   •   •   •   •   89 SICK KING BOKH   61

PUFF
          HE SPAKE AND AS HE CEASED A PUFF OF WIND   •   •   •   •   126 BALDER DEAD 3   440

PUFFS
          IN PUFFS OF BALM THE NIGHT-AIR BLOWS   •   •   •   •   •   218 BACCHANALIA 1   14

PUISSANT
          THE PUISSANT CROWND THE WEAK LAID LOW   •   •   •   •   219 BACCHANALIA 2   12
          PUISSANT LIKE THINE WAS YET   •   •   •   •   •   •   •   284 HAWORTH CHURCH   91
          WHO PASSD WITHIN THEIR PUISSANT HAIL   •   •   •   •   •   303 GRANDE CHARTR   124
          SEEMD PUISSANT AND ALIVE   •   •   •   •   •   •   •   •   315 OBERMANN MORE   90
          INTO ONE PUISSANT FOLK AS HE DESIGND   •   •   •   •   •   338 MEROPE   290

PULL
          WHOM ANTLERD REINDEER PULL OVER THE SNOW   •   •   •   •   96 BALDER DEAD 1   54
          FIELDS WHERE SOFT SHEEP FROM CAGES PULL THE HAY   •   •   268 THYRSIS   198
          FIELDS WHERE THE SHEEP FROM CAGES PULL THE HAY   •   •   268 THYRSIS   V 198

PULLD
          WITH PITCHERS IN THEIR HANDS AND FRESH-PULLD FLOWERS   331 MEROPE   54
          OF FRESH-PULLD VIOLETS WREATHED AND NODDING OER   •   •   431 EMPEDOCLES II   87

PULLING
          HOUNDS ARE PULLING PRICKERS SWEARING   •   •   •   •   •   13 CHURCH BROU 1   17

PULLS
          THROUGH POURING TIDE HE PULLS AND DRIZZLING HAZE   •   •   445 WESTMIN ABBEY   29

PULLULATING
          AND PULLULATING RITES EXTERNE AND VAIN   •   •   •   •   449 WESTMIN ABBEY   160

PULSE
          HEAVEN DOTH A QUICKER PULSE IMPART   •   •   •   •   •   56 RESIGNATION   145
          SOME PULSE OF FEELING HE MUST CHOOSE   •   •   •   •   •   223 EPILOG LAOCOON   V 83
          AND A LOST PULSE OF FEELING STIRS AGAIN   •   •   •   •   247 BURIED LIFE   85
          AND PULSE BY PULSE EXPIRED   •   •   •   •   •   •   •   •   319 OBERMANN MORE   192
          AND PULSE BY PULSE EXPIRED   •   •   •   •   •   •   •   •   319 OBERMANN MORE   192
          STOUT WAS ITS ARM EACH PULSE AND BONE   •   •   •   •   315 OBERMANN MORE   V 89

PULSES
          ALL OUR UNQUIET PULSES CEASE   •   •   •   •   •   •   •   180 FAREWELL   82
          TRIPLE HIS PULSES WITH FAME   •   •   •   •   •   •   •   200 EARLY DEATH   19
          QUICKEN HIS PULSES WITH FAME   •   •   •   •   •   •   •   200 EARLY DEATH   V 19
          QUICKEND ITS PULSES NO MORE   •   •   •   •   •   •   •   233 YOUTH OF MAN   45

PULSING
          SEE PULSING WITH THE FIRST-BORN STAR   •   •   •   •   •   218 BACCHANALIA 1   17

PUNCTUAL
          THESE PUNCTUAL FUNERAL HONOURS YEAR BY YEAR   •   •   332 MEROPE   86

PUNCTUALLY
          AND PUNCTUALLY EXACT   •   •   •   •   •   •   •   •   •   422 EMPEDOCLES I 2   V 297

PUNISH
          HE SHALL AVENGE MY DEATH AND PUNISH THEE   •   •   •   •   77 SOHRAB RUSTUM   555
          NO THE AVENGING GODS WHO PUNISH CRIME •   •   •   •   341 MEROPE   359

PUNISHMENT
          PUNISHMENT WITNESSD   •   •   •   •   •   •   •   •   •   399 MEROPE   1818

PUNT
          AS THE SLOW PUNT SWINGS ROUND   •   •   •   •   •   •   •   257 SCHOLAR-GIPSY   V 76

PUNTS
          AS THE PUNTS ROPE CHOPS ROUND   •   •   •   •   •   •   •   257 SCHOLAR-GIPSY   76

PUNY
          HAD BEEN A PUNY GIRL NO BOY AT ALL   •   •   •   •   •   79 SOHRAB RUSTUM   609
          OUR LABOURD PUNY PASSION-FITS   •   •   •   •   •   •   202 URANIA   14
          HIS PUNY CALLOW EAGLETS AND WHAT TRIALS   •   •   •   •   336 MEROPE   214

PURCHASE
          WOULD FREELY DIE TO PURCHASE BALDER BACK   •   •   •   •   98 BALDER DEAD 1   120

PURE
          CHANGING THE PURE EMOTION   •   •   •   •   •   •   •   •   39 STAGIRIUS   24
          FREEZING THE PURE EMOTION   •   •   •   •   •   •   •   •   39 STAGIRIUS   V 24

PURE   (CONTINUED)
         IF IN THE SILENT MIND OF ONE ALL-PURE   • • • •   45 IN UTRUMQUE PAR   1
         BY LONELY PURENESS TO THE ALL-PURE FOUNT   • • • •   45 IN UTRUMQUE PAR   12
         HOLD THE PURE MUSES   • • • • • • •   50 CONSOLATION   17
         STOOD IN BROAD DAYLIGHT AND THE SKY WAS PURE • •   75 SOHRAB RUSTUM   488
         STOOD IN BRIGHT DAYLIGHT AND THE SKY WAS PURE • •   75 SOHRAB RUSTUM   V 488
         HAD BEEN BUT AT THE END TO HER PURE SOUL   • • •   173 MONICAS PRAYER   9
         A SYMPATHY AUGUST AND PURE   • • • • • •   179 FAREWELL   70
         FLASH THROUGH HER PURE IMMORTAL FRAME   • • • •   181 ISOLATION MARG   21
         THEIR PURE UNWAVERING DEEP DISDAIN   • • • • •   202 URANIA   32
         AND ON THE PURE HORIZON FAR   • • • • • • •   218 BACCHANALIA 1   16
         ASCENDING PURE THE BELL-LIKE FAME   • • • • •   219 BACCHANALIA 2   15
         CLEAR IN THE PURE JUNE-NIGHT   • • • • • • •   228 YOUTH OF NATURE   6
         ON THE PURE COLUMNS OF ITS GLEN-BUILT HALL   • • •   236 PALLADIUM   6
         YE HEAVENS WHOSE PURE DARK REGIONS HAVE NO SIGN • •   244 SUMMER NIGHT   78
         THE PURE ETERNAL COURSE OF LIFE   • • • • •   251 WISH   47
         LESS MODEST PURE AND KIND   • • • • • •   273 EDW QUILLINAN   8
         AND THE PURE GOAL OF BEING REACH   • • • • •   278 SOUTHERN NIGHT   85
         ACTIVE BENEFICENT PURE   • • • • • • •   281 HAWORTH CHURCH   V
         PURE SOULS HONOURD AND BLEST   • • • • • •   290 RUGBY CHAPEL   147
         PURE LIBATIONS AND FRESH   • • • • • • •   342 MEROPE   402
         THIS PURE THAT GUILTY MAY HAVE EACH IMPELLD • •   352 MEROPE   646
         ZEUS AND PURE-THOUGHTED JUSTICE BRAND   • • •   353 MEROPE   688
         OUR FATHERS KINGDOM BECAUSE PURE IS SAFE   • •   389 MEROPE   1533
         BASED ON PURE PUBLIC WELFARE LET US BE   • • •   394 MEROPE   1718 •
         IN YOUTHS PURE MORNING NOR THINKS   • • • •   347 MEROPE   V
         ALL SIN IS JUST IS PURE   • • • • • • •   420 EMPEDOCLES I 2   243
         ON SIMPLE MINDS WITH A PURE NATURAL JOY   • •   436 EMPEDOCLES II   243
         YE AND THE PURE DARK ETHER WHERE YE RIDE   • •   438 EMPEDOCLES II   304
         AND TEMPER SWEET AND LOVE OF ALL THINGS PURE • •   446 WESTMIN ABBEY   79
         THE TEMPLE IN THE PURE PARNASSIAN GORGE   • • •   448 WESTMIN ABBEY   135

PURELY
         SCANS THOSE PARTED LIPS THAT PURELY   • • • • •   META CLOISTER   37

PURENESS
         BY LONELY PURENESS TO THE ALL-PURE FOUNT   • • • •   45 IN UTRUMQUE PAR   12

PURER
         WATCHERS FOR A PURER FIRE   • • • • • •   31 NEW SIRENS   140
         AND PURER OR MORE SUBTLE SOUL THAN THEE   • • •   268 THYRSIS   178

PUREST
         HER YOUNGER RIVALS PUREST GRACE   • • • •   147 TRISTRAM 2   146
         SO SPAKE THE IMPERIAL SAGE PUREST OF MEN   • • •   168 WORLDLY PLACE   2
         SO SPOKE THE IMPERIAL SAGE PUREST OF MEN   • • •   168 WORLDLY PLACE   V   2

PURGE
         AH AN HOUR OF HEALTH WOULD PURGE HIS EYESIGHT   • •   144 TRISTRAM 2   67

PURGED
         AND PURGED CONSIDERATE MINDS   • • • • • • •   198 FRAG DEJANEIRA   17
         AND PURGED ITS FAITH AND TRIMMD ITS FIRE   • • •   301 GRANDE CHARTR   68

PURIFIES
         WHEN MORNING PURIFIES THE EARTH   • • • • • •   57 RESIGNATION   171

PURPLE
         AND LIES A FRAGRANT TOWER OF PURPLE BLOOM   • • •   80 SOHRAB RUSTUM   637
         AND THAT FAR PURPLE MOUNTAIN-LINE   • • • •   208 ON THE RHINE   13
         AND PURPLE ORCHISES WITH SPOTTED LEAVES   • • •   257 SCHOLAR-GIPSY   89
         THE TENDER PURPLE SPRAY ON COPSE AND BRIERS • •   263 THYRSIS   18
         I KNOW WHAT WHITE WHAT PURPLE FRITILLARIES   • •   266 THYRSIS   107
         HIGH TOWERD THE SPIKES OF PURPLE ORCHISES   • • •   266 THYRSIS   115
         HER STATELY PURPLE SHE ABHORRD   • • • • • •   316 OBERMANN MORE   127
         MY PURPLE ROBE   • • • • • • • • •   432 EMPEDOCLES II   120

PURPOSE
         HAST LABOURD BUT WITH PURPOSE HAST BECOME   • • •   5 DUKE WELLINGTON   9
         BUT LET US KEEP THAT PURPOSE WHICH AT HOME   • • •   331 MEROPE   35
         WELL PURPOSE TO PEN BACK   • • • • • •   353 MEROPE   671
         GIVE THEM COHESION PURPOSE AND RESOLVE   • • •   382 MEROPE   1323
         O PRINCELY LAIAS TO WHAT PURPOSE CALLS   • • •   386 MEROPE   1446
         A LIFE THAT WROTE ITS PURPOSE WITH A SWORD   • • •   478 CROMWELL   221

PURPOSED
         PATH TO A CLEAR-PURPOSED GOAL   • • • • • • •   288 RUGBY CHAPEL   85

PURPOSELESS
         IN AN EDDY OF PURPOSELESS DUST   • • • • • _ • •   288 RUGBY CHAPEL   77

PURPOSES
         PURPOSES THY DESPAIR   • • • • • • • • •   371 MEROPE   1135

PURPOSEST
         THE STROKE THOU PURPOSEST IS DESPERATE RASH   • •   381 MEROPE   1295

PURSUE
         YOUR EYES PURSUE THE BELLS OF FOAM   • • • • •   58 RESIGNATION   201
         HERMOD THE NIMBLE DOST THOU STILL PURSUE   • • • •   124 BALDER DEAD 3   395

PURSUE   (CONTINUED)
    PURSUE WITH INDISCERNIBLE FLOW ITS WAY • • • 246 BURIED LIFE 40
    FAR ON THE FOREST-SKIRTS WHERE NONE PURSUE • • • 261 SCHOLAR-GIPSY 215
    WE WHO PURSUE • • • • • • • • • • 277 SOUTHERN NIGHT 64
    UNQUIET DROVE HIM EVER TO PURSUE • • • • • 355 MEROPE 726

PURSUED
    BUT STILL AS THEY PURSUED THEIR WARM DRY ROAD • • 150 TRISTRAM 3 44
    FOR HE PURSUED A LONELY ROAD • • • • • • • 308 OBERMANN 57
    WITH HAPPIER ZEAL PURSUED • • • • • • 322 OBERMANN MORE 296
    FOR ALL WHO PASS PURSUERS AND PURSUED • • • 349 MEROPE 582
    AND TOOK THE LAKE TWO HOUNDS ALONE PURSUED • • 357 MEROPE 809
    THE SCHEMES PURSUED IN VAIN FOR TWENTY YEARS • • 360 MEROPE 876

PURSUERS
    FOR ALL WHO PASS PURSUERS AND PURSUED • • • • 349 MEROPE 582

PURSUES
    OR WITH PEN-BRYNS BOLD BARD PURSUES • • • • • • 458 KAISER DEAD 5

PURSY
    PURSY PLAYD-OUT PHILISTINE • • • • • • • • 457 POOR MATTHIAS 190

PUSH
    TO PUSH THE SHIP THROUGH THE THICK SAND SPARKS FLEW 118 BALDER DEAD 3 177

PUSHD
    WATCHD MY LORDS COMING FORTH AND PUSHD • • • • 88 SICK KING BOKH 33
    DELICATE SPIRITS PUSHD AWAY • • • • • • • 219 BACCHANALIA 2 17
    ONE ROOD FROM LAND THEY PUSHD NO MORE • • • • 480 HAYSWATER BOAT 27

PUSHED
    ARE NOT PUSHED OUT BY THE SWELLS • • • • • • 214 NEW ROME 14

PUT
    WAS AT EASTER-TIDE PUT ON • • • • • • 16 CHURCH BROU 1 110
    AND ON THE TOP LAY BALDERS CORPSE AND PUT • • • • 96 BALDER DEAD 1 43
    AND IN HIS FATHERS HAND PUT SLEIPNERS REIN • • • 114 BALDER DEAD 3 34
    BUT NOW PUT ON YOUR ARMS AND MOUNT YOUR STEEDS • • 115 BALDER DEAD 3 50
    THEN THEY PUT FIRE TO THE WOOD AND THOR • • • 118 BALDER DEAD 3 175
    FOR YOU WILL NOT PUT ON • • • • • • 198 FRAG DEJANEIRA 15
    AND FANCY THAT WE PUT FORTH ALL OUR LIFE • • • 236 PALLADIUM 19
    GOD PUT A HEAP OF LETTERS IN HIS HAND • • • • 239 REVOLUTIONS 3
    AND PUT THE SHEPHERDS WANDERER ON THY TRACE • • 257 SCHOLAR-GIPSY 63
    HATH SINCE OUR DAY PUT BY • • • • • • 266 THYRSIS 116
    BUT WHO LIKE HIM WILL PUT IT BY • • • • • 272 MEMORIAL VERSES 70
    CHIDE AND PUT BACK AND DELAY • • • • 283 HAWORTH CHURCH V
    PUT TIGHTNESS IN THY GOLD-EMBOSSED REIN • • • 349 MEROPE 574
    PUT THE TORCH TO THE PILE • • • • • • • 399 MEROPE 1839
    EVER AGAIN PUT EARTHLY LIKENESS ON • • • • 470 ALARIC AT ROME 206
    AND WIN DELIBERATE REASON TO PUT ON FEAR • • • RUDE ORATOR 11

PUTRID
    IS TO A PUTRID PUDDLE TURND • • • • • • • 89 SICK KING BOKH 61

PUTS
    WHERE SORROW PUTS OUT JOY • • • • • • • • 39 STAGIRIUS V 43

PUTTING
    PUTTING HIS SICKLE TO THE PERILOUS GRAIN • • • • 268 THYRSIS 182

PYLADES
    AH PYLADES AND ELECTRA • • • • • • • • • 344 MEROPE 459

PYLOS
    DEGRADING PYLOS FROM ITS ANCIENT RULE • • • • 330 MEROPE 12

PYMS
    PYMS LOOK OF HATE AND STRAFFORDS GLANCE OF FLAME • • 476 CROMWELL 164

PYRE
    AND CEASE TO MOURN AND THINK OF BALDERS PYRE • • 97 BALDER DEAD 1 60
    HEAP ON THE DECK THE LOGS AND BUILD THE PYRE • • 118 BALDER DEAD 3 159
    AND PLACED THEM ON THE PYRE AND ODIN THREW • • • 118 BALDER DEAD 3 172
    THOK WITH DRY EYES WILL WEEP OER BALDERS PYRE • • 123 BALDER DEAD 3 352
    AND THREW THEM ON THE PYRE AND ODIN THREW • • • 118 BALDER DEAD 3 V 172
    SO FLARD IN THE FAR DARKNESS BALDERS PYRE • • • 119 BALDER DEAD 3 V 200
    SO SHOWED IN THE FAR DARKNESS BALDERS PYRE • • • 119 BALDER DEAD 3 V 200
    FROM THE OAK-BUILT FIERCELY-BURNING PYRE • • • 399 MEROPE 1827

PYTHO
    OVER THE GRAVE OF THE SLAIN PYTHO • • • • • 435 EMPEDOCLES II 205

QUAFFD
    SHE WHO AS THEY VOYAGED QUAFFD • • • • • • • 132 TRISTRAM 1 63

QUAILD
    AND HIS MIRTH QUAILD NOT AT THE MILD REPROOF • • 12 MYCERINUS 114
    BUT SOHRAB HEARD AND QUAILD NOT BUT RUSHD ON • • 76 SOHRAB RUSTUM 509
    BUT SOHRAB HEARD AND QUAILD NOT BUT SPRANG ON • • 76 SOHRAB RUSTUM V 509

QUAILD   (CONTINUED)
      THE STATESMAN QUAILD BEFORE HIS GLANCE OF IRE   • •   476 CROMWELL   154

QUAINT
      IN HIS WHITE QUAINT-EMBROIDERD FROCK • • • • • • •   57 RESIGNATION   182

QUAKE
      BEGIN TO QUAKE AND DISBAND   • • • • • • • •   214 NEW ROME   6

QUAKED
      THE TWO HOSTS HEARD THAT CRY AND QUAKED FOR FEAR   • •   76 SOHRAB RUSTUM   507

QUAKING
      UPON WHOSE CHARRD AND QUAKING CRUST I STAND   • •   438 EMPEDOCLES II   307

QUALITIES
      GREAT QUALITIES ARE TRODDEN DOWN   • • • • • •   431 EMPEDOCLES II   92

QUALITY
      SUCH PREGNANT AND INFECTIOUS QUALITY • • • • • •   50 CONSOLATION   V

QUANTOCK
      STILL BLOWS IN THE QUANTOCK COOMBS   • • • • • •   229 YOUTH OF NATURE   23

QUARREL
      OR IN SOME QUARREL WITH THE PERSIAN KING   • • • •   63 SOHRAB RUSTUM   85
      BUT ZEUS WHO ACCOUNTETH THY QUARREL HIS OWN   • •   347 MEROPE   526

QUARRY
      OF THAT UNFLAGGING QUARRY AND THE HOUNDS   • • • •   357 MEROPE   800
      AND TOOK THREE STRIDES QUARRY AND DOGS WERE GONE   • •   358 MEROPE   830

QUARTERS
      LAST OF OUR QUARTERS WITH THE ARCADIAN CHIEFS   • •   356 MEROPE   759

QUARTZ
      OF VEIND WHITE-GLEAMING QUARTZ AND HERE AND THERE   150 TRISTRAM 3   17
      ARE BUSY GATHERING SPARS OF QUARTZ AND STREAMS   • •   150 TRISTRAM 3   25

QUEEN
      WHERE MANS ONE NATURE QUEEN-LIKE SITS ALONE   • •   4 BUTLERS SERMONS   7
      QUEEN-LIKE AND CLEAR   • •   35 VOICE   2
      BUT HE MUST STRAIGHT ACCOST THEIR SOLEMN QUEEN   • •   100 BALDER DEAD 1   178
      SAVE ME ALONE AND HELA SOLEMN QUEEN   • • • • •   104 BALDER DEAD 1   319
      AND THUS BESPAKE HIM FIRST THE SOLEMN QUEEN   • •   110 BALDER DEAD 2   179
      NOT FOR SUCH END O QUEEN THOU HOLDST THY REALM   • •   110 BALDER DEAD 2   197
      HE SPOKE AND GRAVE REPLIED THE SOLEMN QUEEN   • •   110 BALDER DEAD 2   201
      AND WITH INSCRUTABLE REGARD THE QUEEN   • • • •   112 BALDER DEAD 2   280
      KNEELD AND DID HOMAGE TO THE SOLEMN QUEEN   • •   112 BALDER DEAD 2   283
      OF GHOSTS AND COMMUNED WITH THEIR SOLEMN QUEEN   • •   114 BALDER DEAD 3   40
      A QUEEN AND EMPIRE OVER ALL THE DEAD • • • •   121 BALDER DEAD 3   278
      THAT PROUD FIRST ISEULT CORNWALLS QUEEN   • • •   132 TRISTRAM 1   58
      THE PLEASAUNCE-WALKS THE WEEPING QUEEN   • • •   136 TRISTRAM 1   178
      THOU ART COME AT LAST THEN HAUGHTY QUEEN • • •   142 TRISTRAM 2   2
      ME A SMILING QUEEN UPON MY THRONE   • • • •   144 TRISTRAM 2   52
      STAY PALE QUEEN FOR EVER BY MY SIDE   • • • •   144 TRISTRAM 2   68
      IN CORNWALL TRISTRAM AND QUEEN ISEULT LAY   • •   149 TRISTRAM 3   2
      LAY TRISTRAM AND QUEEN ISEULT DEAD AND COLD   • •   149 TRISTRAM 3   V 2
      THE ROSE-CROWND QUEEN OF LEGENDARY LORE   • • •   168 RACHEL 2   7
      YET SHE CHASTE QUEEN HAD NEVER PROVED   • • •   181 ISOLATION MARG   25
      BENEATH ONE ROOF MY QUEEN WITH MINE   • • • •   205 CALAIS SANDS   36
      FOLLOWS THE APPROACHING QUEEN WHO STOPS AS CALLD • •   332 MEROPE   64
      SHORTLY YE SHALL RESUME THEM WITH YOUR QUEEN   • •   332 MEROPE   78
      WAKENS O QUEEN REMEMBRANCE IN THY HEART   • • •   333 MEROPE   106
      BUT WHILE I SMOTE HIM QUEEN I HONOURD HIM   • •   334 MEROPE   132
      LET US IN MARRIAGE KING AND QUEEN UNITE   • • •   335 MEROPE   167
      VENGEANCE O QUEEN IS HIS DUE   • • • • • •   343 MEROPE   408
      SORROW O QUEEN OF MANKIND   • • • • • •   346 MEROPE   506
      O QUEEN FOR AN AVENGER TO APPEAR   • • • •   348 MEROPE   545
      BUT WHITHER GOST THOU HENCE O QUEEN AWAY • • •   350 MEROPE   597
      LEARN THAT FROM OTHER LIPS O QUEEN THAN MINE   • •   362 MEROPE   927
      O HONOURD QUEEN THY SON MY CHARGE IS GONE   • •   362 MEROPE   944
      LOOK UP O QUEEN LOOK UP O MISTRESS DEAR   • • •   363 MEROPE   946
      AND YET NO ENEMY DID THIS O QUEEN   • • • •   363 MEROPE   951
      I HAVE HEARD O QUEEN HOW A PRINCE   • • • •   368 MEROPE   1082
      YOUR QUEEN WHAT IS THIS YE KNEW   • • • •   371 MEROPE   1126
      STAND AND LET VENGEANCE PASS HOLD O QUEEN HOLD   • •   374 MEROPE   1198
      BLOOD-SEVERD BUT MESSENIAS KING AND QUEEN   • • •   394 MEROPE   1720
      O HONOURD QUEEN O FAITHFUL FOLLOWERS • • • • •   400 MEROPE   1882
      FOLLOWS THE ISSUING QUEEN WHO STOPS AS CALLD   • •   332 MEROPE   V 64
      I GO I GO YET QUEEN TAKE THIS ONE WORD   • • •   368 MEROPE   V1077

QUEENLY
      A GOLDEN CIRCLET ON HER QUEENLY BROW • • • • • •   331 MEROPE   58

QUEENS
      ON THE PEERLESS CHEEK OF QUEENS   • • • • •   33 NEW SIRENS   214
      WHICH IN A QUEENS SECLUDED GARDEN THROWS • • • •   70 SOHRAB RUSTUM   315
      FAMOUS OF WOMEN THE QUEENS   • • • • • • •   296 HEINES GRAVE   144

QUELL
     BEGET A CRUEL TEMPER HELP ME QUELL   • • • • • •   335 MEROPE   162

QUELLD
     EASILY QUELLD AND THE FINE   • • • • • • • •   293 HEINES GRAVE   25

QUELLING
     IS MOST QUELLING AND MAN • • • • • • • • • • •   293 HEINES GRAVE   24

QUENCH
     VAIN DREAMS WHICH QUENCH OUR PLEASURES THEN DEPART   9 MYCERINUS   27
     VAIN DREAMS THAT QUENCH OUR PLEASURES THEN DEPART   9 MYCERINUS   V 27
     FOR WHAT CARE I THAT SOHRABS FAME QUENCH THEIRS   • •   68 SOHRAB RUSTUM   V 228
     QUENCH THEN THE ALTAR FIRES OF YOUR OLD GODS   • •   237 PROGRESS   V 27
     QUENCH NOT THE FIRE WITHIN   • • • • • • •   237 PROGRESS   V 28
     A BREATH MIGHT QUENCH   • • • • • • • •   276 SOUTHERN NIGHT   36
     RECEIVE ME HIDE ME QUENCH ME TAKE ME HOME   • • • •   429 EMPEDOCLES II   36
     PERCHANCE THAT SOLEMN SIGHT MIGHT QUENCH THE FIRE   469 ALARIC AT ROME   177

QUENCHD
     AND PRUND ITS FAITH AND QUENCHD ITS FIRE   • • • •   301 GRANDE CHARTR   V 68
     HE FAILS NOT TO JUDGE CLEAR IF THIS BE QUENCHD OR NO   418 EMPEDOCLES I 2   171
     HE FAILS NOT TO JUDGE CLEAR IF THIS IS QUENCHD OR NO   418 EMPEDOCLES I 2   V 171

QUEST
     COME SHEPHERD AND AGAIN BEGIN THE QUEST   • • • •   255 SCHOLAR-GIPSY   10
     COME SHEPHERD AND AGAIN RENEW THE QUEST   • • • •   255 SCHOLAR-GIPSY   V 10
     THOU TOO O THYRSIS ON LIKE QUEST WAST BOUND   • •   269 THYRSIS   211
     MEN GAVE THEE NOTHING BUT THIS HAPPY QUEST   • • •   269 THYRSIS   213
     THOU TOO O THYRSIS ON LIKE QUEST WERT BOUND   • •   269 THYRSIS   V 211

QUESTING
     WHO IF NOT I FOR QUESTING HERE HATH POWER   • • • •   265 THYRSIS   104

QUESTION
     OTHERS ABIDE OUR QUESTION THOU ART FREE   • • • •   2 SHAKESPEARE   1
     RISE WHEREFORE DOST THOU VAINLY QUESTION THUS   • •   72 SOHRAB RUSTUM   365
     IS MY SON SAFE THAT QUESTION BOUNDS MY CARE   • •   401 MEROPE   1889
     SPARE ME META QUESTION RATHER   • • • • • • •   META CLOISTER   25

QUESTIOND
     AND QUESTIOND HERMOD AS HE CAME AND SAID   • • • •   107 BALDER DEAD 2   100

QUESTIONINGS
     WITH QUESTIONINGS ABOUT AN IDLE TALE   • • • • • •   411 EMPEDOCLES I 1   155

QUESTIONS
     OR WITH WHAT VOICE SHALL I THE QUESTIONS MEET   • •   367 MEROPE   1037

QUIBERON
     THE SICKLE-SWEEP OF QUIBERON BAY   • • • • • •   274 STANZAS CARNAC   27

QUICK
     TRAMP OF MEN AND QUICK COMMANDS   • • • • • •   14 CHURCH BROU 1   38
     NOTHING STIRS ON THE LAWN BUT THE QUICK LILAC-SHADE   19 MODERN SAPPHO   2
     NOTHING MOVES ON THE LAWN BUT THE QUICK LILAC-SHADE   19 MODERN SAPPHO   V   2
     QUICK THY TABLETS MEMORY • • • • • • • • • •   22 MEMORY-PICTURE   8
     QUICK THY TABLETS MEMORY • • • • • • • • • •   23 MEMORY-PICTURE   16
     QUICK THY TABLETS MEMORY • • • • • • • • • •   23 MEMORY-PICTURE   24
     QUICK THY TABLETS MEMORY • • • • • • • • • •   23 MEMORY-PICTURE   32
     QUICK THY TABLETS MEMORY • • • • • • • • • •   23 MEMORY-PICTURE   40
     QUICK THY TABLETS MEMORY • • • • • • • • • •   24 MEMORY-PICTURE   48
     QUICK THY TABLETS MEMORY • • • • • • • • • •   24 MEMORY-PICTURE   56
     QUICK THY TABLETS MEMORY • • • • • • • • • •   24 MEMORY-PICTURE   64
     AND SPRANG ASIDE QUICK AS A FLASH THE SPEAR   • •   73 SOHRAB RUSTUM   403
     QUICK QUICK FOR NUMBERD ARE MY SANDS OF LIFE   • •   82 SOHRAB RUSTUM   721
     QUICK QUICK FOR NUMBERD ARE MY SANDS OF LIFE   • •   82 SOHRAB RUSTUM   721
     AND THEIR QUICK TWITTERING FILLS THE BANKS AND SHORES   109 BALDER DEAD 2   162
     AND HER PETULANT QUICK REPLIES   • • • • • •   134 TRISTRAM 1   120
     MARGARET HIST COME QUICK WE ARE HERE   • • • • •   163 FORSAKEN MERM   77
     QUICK THROUGH THE OLEANDERS BRUSH   • • • • •   184 TERRACE BERNE   15
     QUICK I PASSD FOLLOWING   • • • • • • •   187 STRAYED REVEL   40
     QUICK-EYED STRANGER   • • • • • • • •   189 STRAYED REVEL   103
     IN THE QUICK WORLD THAT RUMBLES NIGH   • • • • •   KENSINGTON GARD V 21
     OF PREGNANT PARTS AND QUICK INVENTIVE BRAIN   • •   256 SCHOLAR-GIPSY   34
     OF SHINING PARTS AND QUICK INVENTIVE BRAIN   • •   256 SCHOLAR-GIPSY   V 34
     TOO QUICK DESPAIRER WHEREFORE WILT THOU GO   • • •   264 THYRSIS   61
     AND HOPE ONCE CRUSHD LESS QUICK TO SPRING AGAIN   • •   266 THYRSIS   140
     QUICK LET ME FLY AND CROSS   • • • • • • •   267 THYRSIS   156
     QUICK FROM DISTRESSFUL THOUGHT AND FLOATS IN JOY   • •   351 MEROPE   615
     QUICK BREAKS THE RED FLAME   • • • • • • •   441 EMPEDOCLES II   V 418
     QUICK RAISED TO ASK WHICH WAY WE GO   • • • • •   451 GEISTS GRAVE   50

QUICKEN
     QUICKEN HIS PULSES WITH FAME   • • • • • • •   200 EARLY DEATH   V 19

QUICKEND
     QUICKEND ITS PULSES NO MORE   • • • • • • •   233 YOUTH OF MAN   45
     PERCHANCE HAD QUICKEND WITH A LIVING TRUTH   • • • •   473 CROMWELL   53

QUICKENED
    QUICKENED AND MOVED A HAPPY BREATH • • • • • • •   483 ROME-SICKNESS   7

QUICKENING
    US NOT THE DAILY QUICKENING RACE • • • • • •   48 HORATIAN ECHO   7

QUICKER
    HEAVEN DOTH A QUICKER PULSE IMPART • • • • • •   56 RESIGNATION   145
    NO EASIER NOR NO QUICKER PASSD • • • • • • • •   316 OBERMANN MORE   103

QUICKEST
    QUICKEST TO ILL IS THE PRAISE • • • • • • • •   293 HEINES GRAVE   V 27

QUICKLY
    CROWN CROWN HIM QUICKLY AND LEAVE HIM FOR ME • •   20 MODERN SAPPHO   36
    AND HE ROSE QUICKLY ON ONE ARM AND SAID • • • •   62 SOHRAB RUSTUM   30
    BACK QUICKLY THROUGH THE CAMP IN FEAR AND JOY • •   69 SOHRAB RUSTUM   261
    TURNING HIM QUICKLY TO GO IN • • • • • • • • •   91 SICK KING BOKH   127
    SO QUICKLY AND WILL WAIT FOR NO REPLY • • • •   102 BALDER DEAD 1   242
    GO QUICKLY GODS BRING WOOD TO THE SEASHORE • •   106 BALDER DEAD 2   41
    GO QUICKLY FORTH THROUGH ALL THE WORLD AND PRAY • •   122 BALDER DEAD 3   299
    THE EVENT WILL QUICKLY SHOW • • • • • • • • •   354 MEROPE   702

QUIET
    STILL DO THY QUIET MINISTERS MOVE ON • • • • •   1 QUIET WORK   V 11
    IN QUIET SHE REPOSES • • • • • • • • • •   20 REQUIESCAT   3
    QUIET LIVING STRICT-KEPT MEASURE • • • • • •   49 SECOND BEST   2
    ARE THREADED QUIET IN THE SUN • • • • • • • •   54 RESIGNATION   51
    THE PASTURES AND THE QUIET TREES • • • • • •   57 RESIGNATION   173
    FOR QUIET AND A FEARLESS MIND • • • • • • • •   59 RESIGNATION   244
    IS BUT A QUIET WATERSHED • • • • • • • • •   59 RESIGNATION   259
    HITHER TO THE QUIET HOURS • • • • • • • • •   137 TRISTRAM 1   229
    SO HEALING IS HER QUIET NOW • • • • • • •   147 TRISTRAM 2   143
    AS IF TO ITSELF THE QUIET FOREST SMILED • •   155 TRISTRAM 3   204
    THE QUIET MOSSY TRACK TO AGE • • • • • • •   199 EARLY DEATH   7
    THE MOSSY QUIET TRACK TO AGE • • • • • • •   199 EARLY DEATH   V 7
    MY DARLING ON THIS QUIET AIR • • • • • • •   205 CALAIS SANDS   V 14
    AH QUIET ALL THINGS FEEL THY BALM • • • • •   208 ON THE RHINE   21
    SEE THROUGH THE QUIET LAND • • • • • • • •   218 BACCHANALIA 1   32
    AH SO THE QUIET WAS • • • • • • • • • •   219 BACCHANALIA 1   50
    SEE THROUGH THE QUIET CORN • • • • • • • •   218 BACCHANALIA 1   V 32
    THE CHANGES OF THEIR QUIET DAY • • • • • •   249 KENSINGTON GARD   32
    THE STAGES OF THEIR QUIET DAY • • • • • •   KENSINGTON GARD   V 32
    DRINK OF THE FEELING OF QUIET AGAIN • • • •   253 FUTURE   68
    I ASK IF THOU HAST PASSD THEIR QUIET PLACE • •   257 SCHOLAR-GIPSY   65
    LONG SINCE AND IN SOME QUIET CHURCHYARD LAID • •   259 SCHOLAR-GIPSY   137
    OF QUIET LOOK ADOWN THE DUSK HILL-SIDE • • •   267 THYRSIS   152
    ITS FIR-TOPPED HURST ITS FARMS ITS QUIET FIELDS • •   269 THYRSIS   217
    ENOUGH THE BOAT WITH QUIET SHOCK • • • • •   276 SOUTHERN NIGHT   45
    QUIET TO ASK FOR CLOSED • • • • • • • • •   293 HEINES GRAVE   17
    HERE IN THE QUIET TO SNATCH • • • • • • •   294 HEINES GRAVE   49
    HIS QUIET HOME ONE KEEPS • • • • • • • •   308 OBERMANN   50
    INTO THE QUIET GLOOM WHERE THOU ART NOW • •   350 MEROPE   593
    IN BREATHLESS QUIET AFTER ALL THEIR ILLS • •   427 EMPEDOCLES I 2   438
    AND THE GOOD LEARNED FRIENDLY QUIET MAN • •   429 EMPEDOCLES II   8
    QUIET IN SLEEP THE SEVENTH NIGHT THEY DIED • • •   448 WESTMIN ABBEY   139
    TELL ME IS IT QUIET HERE • • • • • • • • •   META CLOISTER   28

QUIETLY
    AND QUIETLY DECLAIMS THE CURSINGS OF HIMSELF • •   422 EMPEDOCLES I 2   301

QUIT
    LIGHTLY QUIT WHAT LIGHTLY CAME • • • • • •   22 MEMORY-PICTURE   2
    BE GOVERND QUIT THE TARTAR HOST AND COME • • •   71 SOHRAB RUSTUM   330
    HE WILL NOT YIELD INDEED NOR QUIT OUR FOES • • •   71 SOHRAB RUSTUM   351
    AND QUIT THE HOST AND BEAR THEE HENCE WITH ME • •   84 SOHRAB RUSTUM   798
    THE BAND WILL QUIT MANS HEART HE WILL BREATHE FREE   239 REVOLUTIONS   20
    THEN THEN AT LAST TO QUIT MY SIDE • • • • •   250 WISH   12

QUITE
    SO MANY FIERY SPIRITS QUITE COOLD DOWN • • •   37 WORLDS TRIUMPHS   6
    NOR WHOLLY ITS STEEL QUITE THROUGH BUT ALL THE CREST   76 SOHRAB RUSTUM   496
    AS WHOLLY TO BE PITIED QUITE FORLORN • • •   126 BALDER DEAD 3   458
    SWOOPING TO LANDWARD NOR TO WHERE QUITE CLEAR • •   151 TRISTRAM 3   54
    OR IF NOT QUITE ALONE YET THEY • • • • • •   181 ISOLATION MARG   31
    WHEN WE ARE FROZEN UP WITHIN AND QUITE • •   213 GROWING OLD   32
    NOR THE DULLEST BEEN DEAD TO THEM QUITE • •   230 YOUTH OF NATURE   83
    NEVER BY PASSION QUITE POSSESSD • • • • •   243 SUMMER NIGHT   32
    AND NEVER QUITE BENUMBD BY THE WORLDS SWAY • •   243 SUMMER NIGHT   33
    POSSESS ME QUITE • • • • • • • • • • •   276 SOUTHERN NIGHT   20
    NOW CRUSHD BUT NOT QUITE LIFELESS BY HIS FALL • •   334 MEROPE   140
    OF YOUTH TIS LIKE HAD NEVER QUITE FORGONE • •   394 MEROPE   1703
    THE THOUGHT OF VENGEANCE ON ME NEVER QUITE • •   394 MEROPE   1704
    ERE THE BEING OF MAN ERE QUITE THE WORLD • •   429 EMPEDOCLES II   31
    ERE QUITE THE BEING OF MAN ERE QUITE THE WORLD • •   429 EMPEDOCLES II   31
    CAN EVER QUITE REPEAT THE PAST • • • • • •   450 GEISTS GRAVE   27

QUITS
    HEART QUITS HEART AND HAND QUITS HAND • • • •   35 NEW SIRENS   264
    HEART QUITS HEART AND HAND QUITS HAND • • • •   35 NEW SIRENS   264

QUITS   (CONTINUED)
    MAN MEETS MAN AND QUITS AGAIN   • • • • • •   185 TERRACE BERNE   48
    SEE ONE FIGURE QUITS THE MAZES • • • • • • •   META CLOISTER   9

QUITTING
    QUITTING AT HER FATHERS WILL·   • • • • • • •   134 TRISTRAM 1   129

QUIVER
    THEY ARE GONE ALL IS STILL FOOLISH HEART DOST   19 MODERN SAPPHO   1
        THOU QUIVER
    WHERE THE SPENT LIGHTS QUIVER AND GLEAM   • • • •   162 FORSAKEN MERM   37

QUIVERING
    HISSD AND WENT QUIVERING DOWN INTO THE SAND   • •   73 SOHRAB RUSTUM   404
    DEEP HEAVY GASPS QUIVERING THROUGH ALL HIS FRAME • •   86 SOHRAB RUSTUM   850
    QUIVERING AND OTHERS SKIM THE RIVER=STREAMS   • •   109 BALDER DEAD 2   161
    HANGS QUIVERING OUT BETWEEN HIS DUST=SMEARD JAWS •   114 BALDER DEAD 3   15
    SHARP QUIVERING TONGUES OF FLAME SHOT OUT AND LEAPT   119 BALDER DEAD 3   188
    AND QUIVERING LIPS ON WHICH THE TIDE • • • • •   146 TRISTRAM 2   118
    BECKOND HIM ON WITH QUIVERING LIP   • • • • • •   278 SOUTHERN NIGHT   107

RACE
    US NOT THE DAILY QUICKENING RACE   • • • • • •   48 HORATIAN ECHO   7
    HIM NOT THE NOISY SWARMING RACE   • • • • • •   HORATIAN ECHO   V   7
    THROUGH THE COLD GLOOM WITH MEASURED RACE   • • • •   53 RESIGNATION   34
    CHANCE GUIDES THE MIGRATORY RACE   • • • • • •   55 RESIGNATION   113
    TO WHOM EACH MOMENT IN ITS RACE   • • • • • •   59 RESIGNATION   257
    FOR OF THE RACE OF GODS IS NO ONE THERE   • • •   104 BALDER DEAD 1   318
    RUMBLES AND SHAKES TELL ME THY RACE AND HOME   • •   107 BALDER DEAD 2   103
    SMALL BLISS MY RACE HATH OF THE GODS OBTAINED   • •   110 BALDER DEAD 2   205
    AND ALL THE RACE OF YMIR THOU DIDST DROWN   • • • •   121 BALDER DEAD 3   271
    SPRUNG FROM THE BLOOD OF ISRAELS SCATTERD RACE • •   168 RACHEL 3   1
    LONG FED ON BOUNDLESS HOPES O RACE OF MAN   • • • •   170 BETTER PART   1
    ONE OF SOME WORTHIER RACE THAN OURS   • • • • • •   202 URANIA   18
    ONE OF SOME BETTER RACE THAN WE   • • • • • •   202 URANIA   V   18
    ONE OF SOME WORTHIER RACE THAN WE   • • • • • •   202 URANIA   V   18
    TO THESE TO THESE THEIR THANKFUL RACE   • • • •   227 EPILOG LAOCOON   207
    OF HIS RACE IS PAST ON THE EARTH   • • • • • •   229 YOUTH OF NATURE   57
    RACE AFTER RACE MAN AFTER MAN   • • • • • •   232 YOUTH OF NATURE 129
    RACE AFTER RACE MAN AFTER MAN   • • • • • •   232 YOUTH OF NATURE 129
    AND THERE ARRIVES A LULL IN THE HOT RACE   • • •   247 BURIED LIFE   91
    HE TOOK THE SUFFERING HUMAN RACE   • • • • • •   270 MEMORIAL VERSES   19
    AND A ROUGH GRIMED RACE HAVE THEIR HOMES   • • •   283 HAWORTH CHURCH   60
    OF ALL THAT GIFTED RACE   • • • • • • • •   285 HAWORTH CHURCH   103
    OF ALL HIS GIFTED RACE   • • • • • • •   285 HAWORTH CHURCH   103
    IS THE RACE OF MEN WHOM I SEE   • • • • • •   285 HAWORTH CHURCH V 103
    OF YOUR FAINTING DISPIRITED RACE   • • • • • •   290 RUGBY CHAPEL   150
    LAST OF THE RACE OF THEM WHO GRIEVE   • • • • •   291 RUGBY CHAPEL   189
    THE EXULTING THUNDER OF YOUR RACE   • • • • • •   302 GRANDE CHARTR   110
    UPON THEM PLIES THE RACE OF MAN   • • • • • •   304 GRANDE CHARTR   164
    UPON THEM PLY THE RACE OF MAN   • • • •   320 OBERMANN MORE   213
    THE FEARD AND BLACKEND RULER OF THEIR RACE   • • •   320 OBERMANN MORE V 213
    A CLOUD OF VULTURES ON THIS VIGOROUS RACE   • • •   336 MEROPE   198
    VICTORY SURE TO HER RACE • • • • • • • •   339 MEROPE   296
    YET SHALL RESTORER APPEAR TO THE RACE   • • • •   343 MEROPE   428
    THE BONES OF ARCAS WHENCE OUR RACE IS NAMED   • •   344 MEROPE   453
    THIS REGION IS NOT HAPPY FOR MY RACE   • • • •   356 MEROPE   742
    BUT WHEN THEY CAME ABREAST THE POINT THE RACE   •   357 MEROPE   785
    ONCE IN THE BLACK AND ARROWY RACE AND CAST   • • •   358 MEROPE   823
    TRIUMPHANT AND CONDEMNEST ALL OUR RACE   • • • •   358 MEROPE   832
    RACE OF CALAMITY MINE   • • • • • • • •   367 MEROPE   1051
    THE SHORT PROUD LIP SHOWING THY RACE THY CHEEKS • •   370 MEROPE   1108
    FATAL TO ALL THE RACE OF HERACLES   • • • • •   373 MEROPE   1163
    THE ROYAL RACE OF TEMENUS IN ARGOS • • • • •   382 MEROPE   1330
    THAT NEITHER GRATITUDE NOR TIE OF RACE   • • • •   384 MEROPE   1391
    LIGHT TO SPRING UP TO THY RACE   • • • • • •   389 MEROPE   1525
    HIS MOST JUST PRAYER YET HIS RACE   • • • • •   343 MEROPE   V 407
    YET SHALL RESTORERS APPEAR TO THE RACE   • • • •   343 MEROPE   V 409
    AND ALL THE WISDOM OF HIS RACE   • • • • • •   344 MEROPE   V 453
    NOR THE UNHAPPY PALACE OF THEIR RACE   • • • •   414 EMPEDOCLES I 2   76
    GODS AND THE RACE OF MORTALS LOVE SO WELL   • • •   427 EMPEDOCLES I 2   441
    ABOVE A RACE YOU KNOW NOT   • • • • • •   431 EMPEDOCLES II   65
    O IGNORANT RACE OF MAN   • • • • • • •   437 EMPEDOCLES II   296
    PENITENT FOR WANT OF RACE   • • • • • • •   447 WESTMIN ABBEY   101
    AND KAISERS RACE WE DEEMD THE SAME   • • • • •   454 POOR MATTHIAS   74
    O PLEASANT REST IF ONCE THE RACE WERE RUN   • • •   459 KAISER DEAD   21
    AND IN THEIR RUSH THE HUMAN RACE   • • • • •   475 CROMWELL   119
                                                     481 COURAGE   7

RACED
    BLACK UNDER CLIFFS IT RACED ROUND HEADLANDS SHONE   25 DREAM   34

RACES
    YOUR RACES FOUNDERS   • • • • • • • • • • •   391 MEROPE   1601

RACHEL
    RACHEL WITH EYES NO GAZING CAN APPEASE   • • • •   167 RACHEL 1   7
    THE DYING RACHEL IN A CHAIR THEY BORE   • • • •   167 RACHEL 2   3

RACHELS
    AND RACHELS SWITZERLAND HER RHINE IS HERE   • • • •   167 RACHEL 1   14

RACING
        RACING FULL SPEED AND STARTLING IN THEIR RUSH   • • 150 TRISTRAM 3   29

RACK
        NOR LET THY BAWLING FELLOWS RACK THEIR THROATS   • • 255 SCHOLAR-GIPSY   4
        THE AUTUMN STORM-WINDS DRIVE THE RACK   • • • • 306 OBERMANN   3

RACKD
        TO THY RACKD HEART AND BRAIN   • • • • • • • • 200 PHILOMELA   14
        AND THEN WE WILL NO MORE BE RACKD   • • • • • • • 247 BURIED LIFE   67
        THE WANT WHICH RACKD OUR BRAIN • • • • • • • • 323 OBERMANN MORE   314

RADIANCE
        PEERLESS IN RADIANCE IN JOY   • • • • • • • • 294 HEINES GRAVE   66

RADIANT
        SHALL YOU FIND THE RADIANT LOVER   • • • • • • • 33 NEW SIRENS   221
        NOT WITHOUT JOY SO RADIANT SO ENDOWD • • • • • • • 46 IN UTRUMQUE PAR   33
        IF I IF ODIN CLAD IN RADIANT ARMS   • • • • • • 120 BALDER DEAD 3   238
        RADIANT ADORND OUTSIDE A HIDDEN GROUND   • • • • • 166 AUSTERITY POET   13
        DO FOR THIS RADIANT GREEK-SOULD ARTIST CEASE   • • 168 RACHEL 2   12
        AH NOT THE RADIANT SPIRIT OF GREECE ALONE • • • • 168 RACHEL 3   9
        A MESSENGER FROM RADIANT CLIMES   • • • • • • • 208 LONGING   6
        OF THY RADIANT VIGOUR AGAIN   • • • • • • • • 286 RUGBY CHAPEL   18
        RADIANT WITH ARDOUR DIVINE   • • • • • • • • 291 RUGBY CHAPEL   191
        RADIANT WITH FORTUNE AND JOY   • • • • • • • • 393 MEROPE   1683
        THE RADIANT REJOICING INTELLIGENT SONS OF HEAVEN • • 437 EMPEDOCLES II   287
        OR WITH THE NIMBLE RADIANT LIFE OF FIRE   • • • • 439 EMPEDOCLES II   344
        OR WITH THE ACTIVE RADIANT LIFE OF FIRE   • • • • 439 EMPEDOCLES II   V 344
        THAT RADIANT THOUGH THOU WERT THOU COULDST BUT STAY 447 WESTMIN ABBEY   119

RAGE
        AND STOOD ERECT TREMBLING WITH RAGE HIS CLUB   • • 74 SOHRAB RUSTUM   449
        WAS CHOKED WITH RAGE AT LAST THESE WORDS BROKE WAY   74 SOHRAB RUSTUM   456
        OF STORMS THAT RAGE OUTSIDE OUR HAPPY GROUND   • • 264 THYRSIS   49
        IF WITH NO RAGE NO FIRE OF RIGHTEOUS HATE • • • • 366 MEROPE   1011
        WHEREON TO VENT THEIR RAGE   • • • • • • • • 421 EMPEDOCLES I 2   275

RAGES
        BEHOLD SHE CRIES SO MANY RAGES LULLD • • • • • • • 37 WORLDS TRIUMPHS   5

RAGGED
        PAST LIMESTONE SCARS WITH RAGGED PINES   • • • • • 299 GRANDE CHARTR   14

RAGS
        A GIRL THEIR CLOTHES WERE RAGS THEIR FEET WERE BARE 169 WEST LONDON   4

RAIL
        WITH GOD AND FATE TO RAIL AT SUFFERING EASILY   • • 421 EMPEDOCLES I 2   281
        THAT WE WHO RAIL ARE STILL   • • • • • • • • • 422 EMPEDOCLES I 2   289
        WITH WHAT WE RAIL AT ONE • • • • • • • • • • 422 EMPEDOCLES I 2   290

RAILD
        RAILD AND HUNTED FROM THE WORLD   • • • • • • 432 EMPEDOCLES II   105

RAILS
        SOME HANG UPON THE RAILS AND SOME   • • • • • • 224 EPILOG LAOCOON   113

RAIMENT
        WITH SILKEN RAIMENT STORE OF RICE   • • • • • • 94 SICK KING BOKH   194
        GAY RAIMENT SPARKLING GAUDS ELATION STRONG • • • • 166 AUSTERITY POET   7
        BUT RAIMENT OF CELESTIAL SHEEN SHE WORE   • • • • 447 WESTMIN ABBEY   99

RAIN
        OR LET IT BE ON AUTUMN NIGHTS WHEN RAIN   • • • • 18 CHURCH BROU 3   32
        THE RUSTLE OF THE ETERNAL RAIN OF LOVE   • • • • 19 CHURCH BROU 3   46
        THE LIFE OF PLANTS AND STONES AND RAIN   • • • • 58 RESIGNATION   195
        WITH CISTERNS FOR THE WINTER-RAIN   • • • • • • 94 SICK KING BOKH   202
        LOUD HOWLS THE WIND SHARP PATTERS THE RAIN • • • • 133 TRISTRAM 1   83
        ARE JEWELLD WITH BRIGHT DROPS OF RAIN   • • • • 141 TRISTRAM 1   360
        THE CASTLE-COURT ALL WET WITH RAIN   • • • • • 148 TRISTRAM 2   170
        GREY RAIN-BLEARD STATUES OVERPEER   • • • • • 191 STRAYED REVEL   179
        THE THOUGHTS THAT RAIN THEIR STEADY GLOW • • • • 209 DESPONDENCY   1
        WHICH HAS NOT FALLN ON THE DRY HEART LIKE RAIN • • 238 PROGRESS   42
        COME WITH THE VOLLEYING RAIN AND TOSSING BREEZE • • 264 THYRSIS   59
        OUR FOREHEADS FELT THE WIND AND RAIN • • • • • • 271 MEMORIAL VERSES   53
        ITS GOLDEN RAIN ON EARTH CONFERS   • • • • • 277 SOUTHERN NIGHT   54
        LOOM THE BLURRD HILLS THE RAIN   • • • • • • • 286 HAWORTH CHURCH   132
        SUNSHINE AND RAIN AS WE MIGHT   • • • • • • • 287 RUGBY CHAPEL   34
        WITH RAIN WHERE THICK THE CROCUS BLOWS   • • • • 299 GRANDE CHARTR   2
        THE WIND IS UP AND DRIVES THE RAIN   • • • • • 299 GRANDE CHARTR   8
        NOT RAIN NOT THUNDER   • • • • • • • • • 398 MEROPE   1803
        DID FALL LIKE RAIN IN THE FORSAKEN STREET   • • • •   FRAGMENT 7   2

RAIND
        DOWN ON HIS WASTED FINGERS RAIND   • • • • • • 140 TRISTRAM 1   318
        DOWN ON HER SLENDER FINGERS RAIND   • • • • • • 140 TRISTRAM 1   V 318
        IT STOOD AND SUN AND MOONSHINE RAIND THEIR LIGHT • • 236 PALLADIUM   5

RAINS

    WE CLIMBD ON THE GRAVES ON THE STONES WORN WITH RAINS   163 FORSAKEN MERM   74
    THE LOUD RAINS LASHD THE MOUNTAINS CROWN • • • 480 HAYSWATER BOAT   29

RAISD

    TO HAVE RAISD FAITHFUL FRIENDS AND CUT DOWN   425 EMPEDOCLES I 2   V 401
        SPITEFUL FOES
    BUT THAT WHEN GAINST HIMSELF HE RAISD • • • • 481 COURAGE   15
    HIS ARM HE RAISD IT DAUNTLESSLY • • • • • 481 COURAGE   16

RAISE

    AND RAISE YOU ON YOUR COLD WHITE MARBLE BEDS • • 18 CHURCH BROU 3   V 27
    6IGNS ARE NOT WANTING WHICH MIGHT RAISE • • • 56 RESIGNATION   122
    RAISE ME MY PAGE THIS CANNOT LONG ENDURE • • • 130 TRISTRAM 1   3
    RAISE THE LIGHT MY PAGE THAT I MAY SEE HER • • • 142 TRISTRAM 2   1
    THAN I TO HELP RAISE HIS MESSENIAN FRIENDS • • • 388 MEROPE   1497
    VAINLY RAISE HIS RIGID FRAME • • • • • • 452 POOR MATTHIAS   8

RAISED

    AND RAISED THE CURTAIN OF HIS TENT AND CALLD • • 64 SOHRAB RUSTUM   102
    THEN RUSTUM RAISED HIS HEAD HIS DREADFUL EYES • • 76 SOHRAB RUSTUM   514
    HE SPAKE AND RAISED HIS HAND AND GAVE THE RING • • 112 BALDER DEAD 2   279
    SHE RAISED HER EYES UPON HIS FACE • • • • 140 TRISTRAM 1   319
    RAISED ARE THE DRIPPING OARS • • • • • 228 YOUTH OF NATURE   1
    RAISED BY THE OBJECTS HE PASSES ARE HIS • • • 252 FUTURE   26
    GATHER AND SQUANDER ARE RAISED • • • • 288 RUGBY CHAPEL   63
    IS WITHOUT LOVE OR HATE AUSTERELY RAISED • • • 336 MEROPE   205
    THY PRISON-HOUSE RAISED ONE IMPLORING CRY • • 383 MEROPE   1371
    HE TO FULFIL AN ORDER RAISED HIS HAND • • • 384 MEROPE   1399
    AND RAISED HIS SPEAR • • • • • • • 393 MEROPE   1661
    AND SEEMD TO MUSE AWHILE THEN RAISED HIS EYES • • 402 MEROPE   1913
    THEN RAISED HER FACE AND GLORY ROUND HER STREAMD • • 447 WESTMIN ABBEY   96
    THEN RAISED HER FACE AND GLORY ROUND HER BEAMD • • 447 WESTMIN ABBEY   V 96
    QUICK RAISED TO ASK WHICH WAY WE GO • • • • 451 GEISTS GRAVE   50

RAISES

    FLIES VICTORY WINGD AND JUSTICE RAISES THEN • • 388 MEROPE   1503

RAISING

    THEN YOU WEPT AND SLOWLY RAISING • • • • • • 31 NEW SIRENS   147

RAKED

    SAND RAKED HIS SORES FROM HEEL TO PATE • • • 157 SAINT BRANDAN   47
    RAKED FROM THE SWARMING GULF OF SORROWS HELL • • RUDE ORATOR   16
    RAKED FROM THE SWARMING GULFS OF SORROWS HELL • • RUDE ORATOR   V 16

RAKES

    AND FEEBLY RAKES AMONG THE STONES • • • • • 213 PROGRESS POESY   10

RALLY

    RALLY THE GOOD IN THE DEPTHS OF THYSELF • • • 235 YOUTH OF MAN   118
    FIRST RALLY THE MESSENIANS TO THY CAUSE • • • 382 MEROPE   1322
    TO RALLY THEM AND LEAD THEM TO REVENGE • • • 383 MEROPE   1365
    AND RALLY THEM FOR ONE LAST FIGHT AND FAIL • • • 440 EMPEDOCLES II   388

RAMBLE

    THEY RAMBLE LEAVING WHERE THEY PASS • • • • • 55 RESIGNATION   110

RAMBLES

    HIS LONG RAMBLES BY THE SHORE • • • • • • 137 TRISTRAM 1   215
    YOUTH RAMBLES ON LIFES ARID MOUNT • • • • 213 PROGRESS POESY   1
    AND ON THE HUNTING-RAMBLES WHICH HIS HEART • • • 355 MEROPE   725

RAN

    A THRILL THROUGH ALL THE TARTAR SQUADRONS RAN • • 65 SOHRAB RUSTUM   158
    BUT THROUGH THE ANXIOUS PERSIANS GUDURZ RAN • • 66 SOHRAB RUSTUM   189
    HE SPOKE AND FROWND AND GUDURZ TURND AND RAN • • 69 SOHRAB RUSTUM   260
    AND HE RAN FORWARD AND EMBRACED HIS KNEES • • • 71 SOHRAB RUSTUM   341
    THE CRIMSON TORRENT RAN DIM NOW AND SOILD • • • 86 SOHRAB RUSTUM   843
    AND HE RAN FORWARDS AND EMBRACED HIS KNEES • • • 71 SOHRAB RUSTUM   V 341
    KNEELD DOWN AND CRIED NOT NEITHER RAN • • • 91 SICK KING BOKH   120
    RAN BLACK OER THE SEAS FACE THEN STEADY RUSHD • • 118 BALDER DEAD 3   183
    RAN OUT FROM THE DARK UNDERWOOD BEHIND • • • 155 TRISTRAM 3   209
    DEAD AND NO WARNING SHIVER RAN • • • • 184 TERRACE BERNE   26
    RAN OFF AND VANISHD OUT OF HAND • • • • 213 PROGRESS POESY   8
    TO THAT WHICH ONCE RAN THROUGH HIS SOUL • • • 231 YOUTH OF NATURE   94
    SINCE FIRST THY STORY RAN THROUGH OXFORD HALLS • • 259 SCHOLAR-GIPSY   132
    AND LIFE RAN GAILY AS THE SPARKLING THAMES • • • 261 SCHOLAR-GIPSY   202
    WHOSE BEACH ONCE RAN WITH LOYAL BLOOD • • • 274 STANZAS CARNAC   28
    WHILE THUS I MUSED NIGHT GENTLY RAN • • • • 314 OBERMANN MORE   57
    AND CENTURIES CAME AND RAN THEIR COURSE • • • 318 OBERMANN MORE   161
    AND COLD BESIDES HIS BLUE BLOOD RAN • • • • 460 KAISER DEAD   39

RANDOM

    AT RANDOM AND NOT STEER BY RULE • • • • 40 HUMAN LIFE   14
    AT RANDOM ON THE COUNTERPANE • • • • • • 141 TRISTRAM 1   345

RANG

    IN TURN AND FULL STRUCK RUSTUMS SHIELD SHARP RANG   73 SOHRAB RUSTUM   406
    THE IRON PLATES RANG SHARP BUT TURND THE SPEAR • • 73 SOHRAB RUSTUM   407
    WEEPING AND WAILING AND VALHALLA RANG • • • 95 BALDER DEAD 1   11
    FOR THERE RANG NOTE DIVINE IN THAT COMMAND • • • 102 BALDER DEAD 1   245

RANG   (CONTINUED)
        AND TERRIBLY THE HOOFS OF SLEIPNER RANG   • • •   102 BALDER DEAD 1   260
        RANG LONELILY AND SHARP THE SKY WAS FAIR   • • • •   155 TRISTRAM 3   199
        SO RANG TERTULLIANS SENTENCE ON THE SIDE   • • • •   172 GOOD SHEPHERD   2
        AND HOW A CALL CELESTIAL ROUND HIM RANG   • • • •   268 THYRSIS   188
        MORE PIERCING THE SECOND CRY RANG   • • • • • •   346 MEROPE   495
        FAR IN THE WOODS AHEAD THEIR MUSIC RANG   • • • •   357 MEROPE   792
        RANG AS HE TRODE THEM WITH THE VOICE OF WAR   • •   476 CROMWELL   152

RANGE
        LOVE FREE TO RANGE AND REGAL BANQUETINGS   • • • •   9 MYCERINUS   34
        BEYOND HIS PASSIONS WIDEST RANGE   • • • • • •   58 RESIGNATION   221
        THE VAST RANGE OF SNOW   • • • • • • •   175 PARTING   12
        WHILE WE RANGE THE WOODLAND   • • • • • •   188 STRAYED REVEL   73
        THE INSPIRED MUSICIAN WHAT A RANGE   • • • • •   223 EPILOG LAOCOON   81
        CHILDREN WHO EARLY RANGE THESE SLOPES AND LATE • •   258 SCHOLAR-GIPSY   105
        AND GAIND THE WHITE BROW OF THE CUMNER RANGE   • •   259 SCHOLAR-GIPSY   127
        WHY SHOULD HE PRAY TO RANGE   • • • • • • •   448 WESTMIN ABBEY   147
        CRYING COME ON AND RANGE THE WORLD   • • •   460 KAISER DEAD   59
        TO COME AND GO TO SHIFT AND RANGE   • • • • •   484 ROME-SICKNESS   22

RANGED
        RANGED DIAMOND-BRIGHT THE ETERNAL WALL OF SNOW • •   25 DREAM   13
        WERE RANGED AND THEN THE DAILY FRAY BEGAN   • • •   105 BALDER DEAD 2   14
        WHERE ARE IN CIRCLE RANGED TWELVE GOLDEN CHAIRS • •   106 BALDER DEAD 2   37
        AND RANGED THE WOOD IN STACKS BY BALDERS SHIP • •   106 BALDER DEAD 2   68
        WHERE THE SEA-BEASTS RANGED ALL ROUND   • • •   162 FORSAKEN MERM   39
        THE HILLS IN THEIR OLD ORDER RANGED   • • • •   312 OBERMANN MORE   7

RANGES
        THEN WATCH HIM FOR HE RANGES SWIFT AND FAR   • • • •   409 EMPEDOCLES I 1   94

RANGING
        BY FAINT MUSIC GUIDED RANGING   • • • • • • • •   27 NEW SIRENS   29

RANK
        FROM THE RANK LIFE OF TOWNS THIS LEAF AND FLUNG • •   6 GEO CRUIKSHANK   2

RANKS
        REVIEWS AND RANKS HIS MOTLEY BANDS   • • • • •   53 RESIGNATION   45
        AND WITH HIS STAFF KEPT BACK THE FOREMOST RANKS • •   65 SOHRAB RUSTUM   143
        AND CHECKD HIS RANKS AND FIXD THEM WHERE THEY STOOD   65 SOHRAB RUSTUM   147
        YE MOVE THROUGH THE RANKS RECALL   • • • • •   292 RUGBY CHAPEL   198
        RANKS ANY MAN WITH MURDER SUCH AN ACT   • • •   336 MEROPE   208

RAPHAEL
        OF RAPHAEL AND HIS BROTHERHOOD   • • • • • • •   222 EPILOG LAOCOON   25
        BEETHOVEN RAPHAEL CANNOT REACH   • • • • • • •   227 EPILOG LAOCOON   205

RAPHAELS
        RAPHAELS IN SHOALS   • • • • • • • • • • • •   221 BACCHANALIA 2   58

RAPIDS
        ONE MOMENT ON THE RAPIDS TOP OUR BOAT   • • • •   25 DREAM   30

RAPT
        MY CRIME THAT RAPT IN REVERENTIAL AWE   • • • •   9 MYCERINUS   8
        OUR RAPT SOULS ON YOUR REPLIES   • • • • • •   34 NEW SIRENS   236
        SITS RAPT AND HEARS THE BATTLE BREAK BELOW   • • • •   42 GIPSY CHILD   23
        THE POETS RAPT SECURITY   • • • • • • •   59 RESIGNATION   246
        AS FROM A HEIGHT WITH RAPT PROPHETIC EYES   • • •   212 GROWING OLD   17
        RAPT TWIRLING IN THY HAND A WITHERD SPRAY   • • •   258 SCHOLAR-GIPSY   119
        IN SIGHT OF BLOOD BUT WERE RAPT FAR AWAY   • • •   427 EMPEDOCLES I 2   453

RAPTURE
        AND ALL ITS BOUNDING RAPTURE AS AT DAWN   • • • •   79 SOHRAB RUSTUM   620
        NOT WITH THE RAPTURE OF SPRING   • • • • • •   233 YOUTH OF MAN   22
        MAYST THOU THE RAPTURE OF PEACE   • • • • • •   299 HEINES GRAVE   229
        CLAIMS RAPTURE AS ITS RIGHT   • • • • • •   424 EMPEDOCLES I 2   353
        LIT WITH NO RAPTURE AS THE STORM SWEPT BY   • • • •   472 CROMWELL   22
        TO BEND IN RAPTURE AT SOME IDOL THRONE   • • • •   474 CROMWELL   99

RAPTURES
        AND ON RAPTURES FOLLOW CALMS   • • • • • • •   30 NEW SIRENS   120
        FOR THOSE MIMIC RAPTURES YOU HAD WON   • • • •   31 NEW SIRENS   154
        FOR THE MIMIC RAPTURES YOU HAD WON   • • • • •   31 NEW SIRENS   V 154
        AND DASH OUR HOLIEST RAPTURES WHILE WE GAZE   • •   470 ALARIC AT ROME   200

RARE
        AND PRAISE THE CHISELLD BROIDERIES RARE   • • •   17 CHURCH BROU 2   37
        ARE RARE AH MOST LOVES BUT FLOW ONCE AND RETURN • •   19 MODERN SAPPHO   16
        AH I HUSBAND WHATS GROWN RARE   • • • • • • •   22 MEMORY-PICTURE V
        HAST THOU SO RARE A POISON LET ME BE   • • • •   38 WORLDS TRIUMPHS   13
        RARE THE LONE PASTORAL HUTS MARVEL NOT THOU   • •   45 IN UTRUMQUE PAR   17
        I KNOW HER BY HER MILDNESS RARE   • • • • • •   132 TRISTRAM 1   50
        IF HER BLOOM BE NOW LESS RARE   • • • • • •   134 TRISTRAM 1   116
        AND THAT POTION RARE HER MOTHER   • • • • •   134 TRISTRAM 1   136
        AND THAT PHIAL RARE HER MOTHER   • • • • • •   134 TRISTRAM 1   V 136
        AND THE GOLDEN BRACELETS HEAVY AND RARE   • • •   146 TRISTRAM 2   110
        FRINGD WITH DEAD LEAVES AND MOSSES RARE   • • •   148 TRISTRAM 2   V

RARE   (CONTINUED)
        THY CHEEK WAS GRAVE THY SPEECH GREW RARE   .   .   .   .   178 FAREWELL   16
        THAT WILL THAT ENERGY THOUGH RARE   .   .   .   .   .   178 FAREWELL   39
        ARE YET FAR FAR LESS RARE THAN LOVE   .   .   .   .   .   178 FAREWELL   40
        GOOD POEMS IF HE LOOKD MORE RARE   .   .   .   .   .   221 EPILOG LAOCOON   17
        WE VISIT IT BY MOMENTS AH TOO RARE   .   .   .   .   .   236 PALLADIUM   12
        ONLY BUT THIS IS RARE   .   .   .   .   247 BURIED LIFE   77
        SEEN BY RARE GLIMPSES PENSIVE AND TONGUE-TIED   .   .   256 SCHOLAR-GIPSY   54
        TOO RARE TOO RARE GROW NOW MY VISITS HERE   .   .   .   263 THYRSIS   31
        TOO RARE TOO RARE GROW NOW MY VISITS HERE   .   .   .   263 THYRSIS   31
        TOO RARE TOO RARE GROW NOW MY VISITS HERE   .   .   .   269 THYRSIS   231
        TOO RARE TOO RARE GROW NOW MY VISITS HERE   .   .   .   269 THYRSIS   231
        RARE STRAGGLING HUNTERS FOILD BY BRAKE AND CRAG .   .   357 MEROPE   798
        THOU HAST INDEED A RARE TOUCH ON THY HARP   .   .   .   409 EMPEDOCLES I 1   78
        STILL HUNGRIER FOR DELIGHT AS DELIGHTS GROW MORE RARE   424 EMPEDOCLES I 2   371

RARELY
        O HERMOD RARELY DO THE FEET OF GODS   .   .   .   .   .   108 BALDER DEAD 2   119
        SO SUNK SO RARELY LIFTED SAVE TO MEET   .   .   .   .   151 TRISTRAM 3   71
        SHAME RARELY CHECKS THE GENUINE TYRANTS WILL   .   .   340 MEROPE   352
        ON LIPS THAT RARELY FORM THEM NOW   .   .   .   .   .   451 GEISTS GRAVE   42

RARER
        RARER SECRETS THAN THE TOILING HEAD   .   .   .   .   .   .   28 NEW SIRENS   80

RASH
        RASH BOY MEN LOOK ON RUSTUMS FACE AND FLEE   .   .   .   72 SOHRAB RUSTUM   369
        O MISTRESS BY THE GODS DO NOTHING RASH   .   .   .   .   368 MEROPE   1075
        THE STROKE THOU PURPOSEST IS DESPERATE RASH   .   .   381 MEROPE   1295
        IS THY FIRE-SCATHED ARM STILL RASH   .   .   .   .   .   430 EMPEDOCLES II   50
        THE USHERS RASH AND FEVERISH MELANCHOLY   .   .   .   FRAGMENT 1   5

RASHNESS
        AND TRIED IN VAIN THE TURN OF RASHNESS COMES   .   .   384 MEROPE   1387

RATE
        AND BEND THEIR LITTLE FISTS AND RATE THE SENSELESS   421 EMPEDOCLES I 2   276
            GROUND

RATES
        WHO RATES US IF WE PEER OUTSIDE OUR PEN   .   .   .   .   169 WORLDLY PLACE   7

RATHER
        RATHER TO PATIENCE PROMPTED THAN THAT PROUD   .   .   7 REP FRIEND CONT   2
        HIM BLAME NOT FAUSTA RATHER PRAISE   .   .   .   .   .   59 RESIGNATION   238
        RATHER THYSELF FOR SOME AIM PRAY   .   .   .   .   .   59 RESIGNATION   239
        RATHER THAT HEART WHICH BURNS IN THEE   .   .   .   .   59 RESIGNATION   241
        SEEM TO BEAR RATHER THAN REJOICE   .   .   .   .   .   .   60 RESIGNATION   270
        OR RATHER WOULD THAT I EVEN I MYSELF   .   .   .   .   .   85 SOHRAB RUSTUM   816
        RATHER IT FITS YOU HAVING WEPT YOUR HOUR   .   .   .   96 BALDER DEAD 1   34
        SO ANSWEREST THOU BUT WHY NOT RATHER SAY   .   .   .   171 BETTER PART   9
        BUT I WILL RATHER SAY THAT YOU REMAIN   .   .   .   .   244 SUMMER NIGHT   86
        RATHER ON THEE I CALL HUSBAND BELOVED   .   .   .   .   349 MEROPE   584
        SPARE ME META QUESTION RATHER   .   .   .   .   META CLOISTER   25

RAVAGES
        ERASED THE RAVAGES OF TIME   .   .   .   .   147 TRISTRAM 2   140

RAVE
        THINK OFTEN AS I HEAR THEM RAVE   .   .   .   .   .   .   249 KENSINGTON GARD   26
        THINK SOMETIMES AS I HEAR THEM RAVE   .   .   .   .   .   249 KENSINGTON GARD   V 26
        THINK SADLY AS I HEAR THEM RAVE   .   .   .   .   .   .   KENSINGTON GARD   V 26
        WHAT MAKES THEE STRUGGLE AND RAVE   .   .   .   .   .   417 EMPEDOCLES I 2   147

RAVEN
        AND SHAKE BACK HER RAVEN HAIR   .   .   .   .   134 TRISTRAM 1   123
        OER THE BLANCHD SHEET HER RAVEN HAIR   .   .   .   .   .   146 TRISTRAM 2   107

RAVENING
        FROM RAVENING AND WHO GOVERN RUSTUMS SON   .   .   .   63 SOHRAB RUSTUM   92

RAVENNA
        ON RAVENNA SANDS IN THE SHADE   .   .   .   .   294 HEINES GRAVE   60
        OF RAVENNA PINES FOR A HIGH   .   .   .   .   294 HEINES GRAVE   61

RAVES
        TO WHERE THE ATLANTIC RAVES   .   .   .   .   262 SCHOLAR-GIPSY   246
        STILL THE SAME OCEAN ROUND US RAVES   .   .   .   .   .   303 GRANDE CHARTR   125

RAVIN
        RAVIN A LITTLE WHILE IN SPOIL AND BLOOD   .   .   .   .   339 MEROPE   297

RAVING
        THE THIRST FOR PEACE A RAVING WORLD   .   .   .   .   .   .   180 FAREWELL   87

RAVISHD
        MY RAVISHD SPIRIT TOO   .   .   .   .   317 OBERMANN MORE   144

RAY
        MY SAND RUNS SHORT AND AS YON STAR-SHOT RAY   .   .   10 MYCERINUS   56
        AND THE RAY-CROWNED BALDER ANSWERD HIM   .   .   .   .   128 BALDER DEAD 3   517

RAY   (CONTINUED)

FULL ON THEIR WINDOW THE MOONS RAY	• • • • • •	140 TRISTRAM 1	333
WHITEND HIS FACE FROM THE SUNS FRONTING RAY	• •	170 EAST AND WEST	6
SEASONS IMPAIRD NOT THE RAY	• • • • • • •	287 RUGBY CHAPEL	21
MADE IT A RAY OF THY THOUGHT	• • • • • • • •	299 HEINES GRAVE	231
PREDESTINED TO THE RAY	• • • • • • • •	449 WESTMIN ABBEY	172
AN INWARD LIGHT THAT WITH ITS STREAMING RAY	• •	473 CROMWELL	61
NO SOFTENING RAY NO VISIONS FALSE AND WILD	• • • •	475 CROMWELL	125

RAYLESS

LOVELESS RAYLESS JOYLESS YOU SHALL STAND	• • • •	35 NEW SIRENS	266

RAYS

AND RAYS HER POWERS LIKE SISTER-ISLANDS SEEN	• •	4 BUTLERS SERMONS	9
SEE THE WHITE EAST AND THE MORNING RAYS	• • • •	34 NEW SIRENS	242
AND THE FIRST RAYS OF MORNING STREAKD THE EAST	• •	61 SOHRAB RUSTUM	V 1
ALIVE AND STILL THE RAYS WERE ROUND HIS HEAD	• •	103 BALDER DEAD 1	284
WHERE THE SUNS RAYS STRUCK FULL AND FLASHD BACK KEEN		TRISTRAM 3	V 21

RE

THERE RE-ASSEMBLING WE SHALL SEE EMERGE	• • • •	128 BALDER DEAD 3	527
RE-ENTER THEM WITH WONDER NEVER FILL	• • • • • •	128 BALDER DEAD 3	535
WITH ALL THY BEING RE-ARRANGED	• • • • • • •	184 TERRACE BERNE	35
WHICH NOW IS MINE MUST RE-ATTAIN	• • • • • •	206 RIVER	14
WHAT CHARMD YOU IN OTHERS RE-LIVE	• • • • • •	231 YOUTH OF NATURE	109
PRAISE RE-INSPIRE THE BRAVE	• • • • • • • •	292 RUGBY CHAPEL	200
HOPE TO A WORLD RE-MADE	• • • • • • • • •	323 OBERMANN MORE	V 312
FOLLY REVIVED RE-FURBISHD SOPHISTRIES	• • •	449 WESTMIN ABBEY	159
THEN AT A PARDONING WORD RE-FURLD	• • • • •	460 KAISER DEAD	57

REACH

REACH THE VALLEY WHERE THE FABRIC	• • • • •	15 CHURCH BROU 1	87
RENT THE TOUGH PLATES BUT FAILD TO REACH THE SKIN	•	76 SOHRAB RUSTUM	493
SURELY THE NEWS WILL ONE DAY REACH HIS EAR	• • •	78 SOHRAB RUSTUM	581
REACH RUSTUM WHERE HE SITS AND TARRIES LONG	• •	78 SOHRAB RUSTUM	582
FROM TRIBE TO TRIBE UNTIL IT REACH HER EAR	• • •	79 SOHRAB RUSTUM	597
RENT THE TOUGH PLATES BUT MISSD TO REACH THE SKIN		76 SOHRAB RUSTUM	V 493
AND HE WILL REACH ON THE TENTH MORN A BRIDGE	• •	99 BALDER DEAD 1	147
BUT HE WILL REACH ITS UNKNOWN NORTHERN SHORE	• •	99 BALDER DEAD 1	162
REACH ME MY GOLDEN PHIAL STANDS BY THEE	• • •	133 TRISTRAM 1	100
REACH ME MY GOLDEN CUP THAT STANDS BY THEE	• • •	133 TRISTRAM 1	V 100
COURTLY LIFE IS LIGHT AND CANNOT REACH IT	• • •	143 TRISTRAM 2	39
WOULD THESE ARMS REACH TO CLASP THEE	• • • • •	176 PARTING	61
DOST THOU STILL REACH	• • • • • • • •	201 PHILOMELA	V
AND SHE TO HIM WILL REACH HER HAND	• • • • •	202 URANIA	25
BEETHOVEN RAPHAEL CANNOT REACH	• • • • • •	227 EPILOG LAOCOON	205
OR SHALL REACH WHEN HIS EYES HAVE BEEN CLOSED	•	252 FUTURE	23
I CANNOT REACH THE SIGNAL-TREE TO-NIGHT	• • •	267 THYRSIS	165
THYRSIS IN REACH OF SHEEP-BELLS IS MY HOME	• • •	269 THYRSIS	233
AND THE PURE GOAL OF BEING REACH	• • • • •	278 SOUTHERN NIGHT	85
THEN CROSS THE SWARD AND REACH THAT GATE	• • •	300 GRANDE CHARTR	28
AND REACH THAT GLIMMERING SHEET OF GLASS	• • •	310 OBERMANN	119
HELP IT TO REACH OUR DEEP DESIRE	• • • • •	323 OBERMANN MORE	V 313
O ARTS ABOVE THE VULGAR TYRANTS REACH	• • • •	339 MEROPE	310
BEFORE THEY REACH THE ELYSIAN PLACE	• • • •	414 EMPEDOCLES I 2	74
WHOSE WEARINESS NO ENERGY CAN REACH	• • • •	429 EMPEDOCLES II	13
THE JARS OF MEN REACH HIM NOT IN THY VALLEY	• •	435 EMPEDOCLES II	209
BUT CAN LIFE REACH HIM	• • • • • • • •	435 EMPEDOCLES II	210
TO RUN THEIR COURSE AND REACH THEIR GOAL	• • •	450 GEISTS GRAVE	11
WE LAY THEE CLOSE WITHIN OUR REACH	• • • • •	451 GEISTS GRAVE	65
TO HOLD THE LIGHT AND REACH THE HAND	• • • • •	484 ROME-SICKNESS	31
THEY POSTED THROUGH TO REACH IT	• • • • •	LUCRETIUS 6	5

REACHD

AND CROSSD THE CAMP WHICH LAY BEHIND AND REACHD	• •	66 SOHRAB RUSTUM	190
AND OXUS CURDLED AS IT REACHD HIS STREAM	• • •	76 SOHRAB RUSTUM	V 508
BUT ALL HE PASSD UNHAILD AND REACHD THE THRONE	•	109 BALDER DEAD 2	176
HATH REACHD IT THERE HEREAFTER SHALL ARISE	• • •	128 BALDER DEAD 3	520
ONWARD WE MOVED AND REACHD THE RIDE	• • • •	224 EPILOG LAOCOON	107
OH COULD HE ONCE HAVE REACHD THIS AIR	• • • •	275 STANZAS CARNAC	41
SON OF CRESPHONTES WE HAVE REACHD THE GOAL	• •	330 MEROPE	1
AT LAST IT REACHD US THAT HE STILL MISTRUSTFUL	•	338 MEROPE	259
WITH HIM CONFERRING THE KING SLOWLY REACHD	• • •	401 MEROPE	1907
REACHD CAPE VERDE ISLANDS LUSITANIA	• • • •	485 S S LUSITANIA	14
HAS REACHD THE LIMIT OF HIS UTMOST GROWTH	• • •	LUCRETIUS 2	9
TO WHOM THEIR DESTINATION WHEN TIS REACHD	• • •	LUCRETIUS 6	3

REACHES

SOME REACHES OF THY STORM-VEXT STREAM OF LIFE	• •	43 GIPSY CHILD	60
DEATH IN THEIR PRISON REACHES THEM	• • • • •	243 SUMMER NIGHT	49
SOONER THAN THOSE TWIN REACHES OF GREAT TIME	• •	FRAGMENT 5	7

REACHING

THIS FAR-REACHING MAGIC CHAIN	• • • • • • • •	33 NEW SIRENS	204

READ

THE CLEAREST THE BEST WHO HAVE READ	• • • • •	231 YOUTH OF NATURE	104
WILL YE SCAN ME AND READ ME AND TELL	• • • • •	231 YOUTH OF NATURE	119
AND LET ME READ THERE LOVE THY INMOST SOUL	• • •	245 BURIED LIFE	11
OUR EYES CAN IN ANOTHERS EYES READ CLEAR	• • • •	247 BURIED LIFE	81

READ   (CONTINUED)
    MUST NEEDS READ CLEARER SURE THAN HE   • • • • • •   250 WISH   28
    AS REBEKAH READ WHEN SHE SATE   • • • • • •   252 FUTURE   36
    COME LET ME READ THE OFT-READ TALE AGAIN   • • • •   256 SCHOLAR-GIPSY   32
    COME LET ME READ THE OFT-READ TALE AGAIN   • • • •   256 SCHOLAR-GIPSY   32
    HE READ EACH WOUND EACH WEAKNESS CLEAR   • • • •   270 MEMORIAL VERSES   20
    OR ARE WE EASIER TO HAVE READ   • • • • • •   304 GRANDE CHARTR   145
    THOUGH AS YOU READ YOU HEAR THE BELLS   • • • •   307 OBERMANN   31
    AH ME WE ANCHORITES READ THINGS BEST • • • • • •   314 OBERMANN MORE   75
    READ IN THESE ACTIONS INNOCENT IN THEE   • • • •   333 MEROPE   90
    THAT THOU MAYST READ THINE ENEMYS COUNSEL PLAIN • •   380 MEROPE   1278
    ONCE READ THY OWN BREAST RIGHT • • • • • • • •   417 EMPEDOCLES I 2   142
    OF VOLUMES YET TO READ   • • • • • • • •   423 EMPEDOCLES I 2   334
    AM DEAD TO LIFE AND JOY THEREFORE I READ   • • • •   438 EMPEDOCLES II   321
    AND READ THEIR HOMILY TO MAN   • • • • • •   450 GEISTS GRAVE   12
    IN COMMON SIGHTS READ SECRET SYMPATHY   • • •   472 CROMWELL   32
    TO READ EACH THOUGHT AND TEACH THAT MASTER MIND • •   478 CROMWELL   231
    I READ IN DANTE HOW THAT HORNED LIGHT   • • •   484 S S LUSITANIA   1

READEST
    BUT SO MANY BOOKS THOU READEST • • • • • • •   49 SECOND BEST   5

READIER
    WITH READIER TONGUE THAN WE   • • • • • • • •   48 HORATIAN ECHO   18

READING
    IN A WISTFUL SILENCE READING   • • • • • • •   34 NEW SIRENS   237
    LIKE THE REST HIS WIT WITH READING   • • • • • •   49 SECOND BEST   15
    WHO WEPT AT READING OF A GRECIAN KNIGHT   • • • •   153 TRISTRAM 3   144

READS
    NOW READS IN HER BOSOM AS CLEAR   • • • • • •   252 FUTURE   35
    MAIDENS AND READS EXPERIENCE MUCH AMISS   • • • •   382 MEROPE   1334

READY
    READY TO SLIP ON HIS UNCONSCIOUS PREY   • • • •   364 MEROPE   972
    HE HAD HIS MURDERER READY AND THE SWORD   • • • •   366 MEROPE   1000
    SIT AND MAKE READY THE SERPENT THE SCOURGE   • • • •   347 MEROPE   V 531

REAL
    FEWER REAL SUCCESSES CAN DISPLAY   • • • • •   221 EPILOG LAOCOON   V 12
    AND NEAR AND REAL THE CHARM OF THY REPOSE   • • • •   267 THYRSIS   149

REALITY
    AND THE REALITY WILL PLUCK US BACK   • • • • • •   440 EMPEDOCLES II   385
    A MOMENT DISPOSSESSD REALITY   • • • • • • •   474 CROMWELL   94

REALLY
    IF FRANCE AND WE ARE REALLY FRIENDS   • • • • •   47 HORATIAN ECHO   4
    HATH REALLY NEITHER JOY NOR LOVE NOR LIGHT   • • • •   211 DOVER BEACH   33

REALM
    AND WEND THEMSELVES TO HELAS GLOOMY REALM   • • •   98 BALDER DEAD 1   121
    THERE IS A ROAD WHICH LEADS TO HELAS REALM   • • • •   99 BALDER DEAD 1   135
    TO THE LOW SHORE OF GHOSTS AND HELAS REALM   • • • •   99 BALDER DEAD 1   151
    AND HE WILL SEE STRETCH ROUND HIM HELAS REALM   • • •   100 BALDER DEAD 1   171
    IN THAT DIM WORLD IN HELAS MOULDERING REALM   • • •   104 BALDER DEAD 1   315
    THERE IS A WAY WHICH LEADS TO HELAS REALM   • • • •   99 BALDER DEAD 1   V 135
    BOUND ON THEIR WAY BELOW TO HELAS REALM   • • • •   107 BALDER DEAD 2   105
    BELOW THERE TO THE NORTH TOWRD HELAS REALM   • • • •   108 BALDER DEAD 2   123
    AND HE BEHELD SPREAD ROUND HIM HELAS REALM   • • • •   109 BALDER DEAD 2   149
    AND NOW HAVE CHIEF REGARD IN HELAS REALM   • • • •   109 BALDER DEAD 2   169
    NOT FOR SUCH END O QUEEN THOU HOLDST THY REALM   • •   110 BALDER DEAD 2   197
    EVEN HERE THEY SEEK THEE OUT IN HELAS REALM   • • •   112 BALDER DEAD 2   256
    SHOULD MAKE IRRUPTION INTO HELAS REALM   • • •   120 BALDER DEAD 3   242
    I MUST AGAIN BELOW TO HELAS REALM   • • • •   124 BALDER DEAD 3   372
    FREQUENT THE STILL RECESSES OF THE REALM   • • •   126 BALDER DEAD 3   435
    WHOM THIS REALM OF FRANCE CAN BOAST   • • • •   136 TRISTRAM 1   195
    THAT THIS REALM OF FRANCE CAN BOAST   • • • •   136 TRISTRAM 1   V 195
    INTO THE SOUDANS REALM AND THUNDERED ON   • • •   154 TRISTRAM 3   149
    THY REALM OF THOUGHT IS DREAR AND COLD   • • •   309 OBERMANN   107
    BEHOLD THY HERITAGE THY FATHERS REALM • • • •   330 MEROPE   3
    OF HIS FRESH-CONQUERD REALM THE ROYAL SEAT   • • •   330 MEROPE   11
    THEIR FATHERS REALM THIS ISLE FROM PELOPS NAMED • •   336 MEROPE   219
    A GENERAL ASSEMBLAGE OF THE REALM   • • • •   338 MEROPE   263
    STRUCK ONCE AND AWED HIS MOB AND SAVED THIS REALM   338 MEROPE   275
    A WOLFISH BAND IN A DISPEOPLED REALM   • • • •   338 MEROPE   288
    RIGIDLY YET IN SETTLED CALM THIS REALM   • • •   388 MEROPE   1491
    FORSAKE THIS AMPLE PROUD MESSENIAN REALM   • • •   395 MEROPE   1744
    THE INHERITOR OF THE REALM   • • • • • •   400 MEROPE   1862

REALMS
    AND GAVE ME NINE UNLIGHTED REALMS TO RULE   • • • •   110 BALDER DEAD 2   213

REAP
    THEIR PLEASURE TO THEIR FEET AND REAP THEIR PRAISE   11 MYCERINUS   77
    AND REAP A SECOND GLORY IN THINE AGE   • • • • •   84 SOHRAB RUSTUM   776

REAPD
    DESERTED IS THE NEW-REAPD GRAIN   • • • • • •   217 BACCHANALIA 1   V   4

REAPD   (CONTINUED)
        SCREEND IS THIS NOOK OER THE HIGH HALF-REAPD FIELD   255 SCHOLAR-GIPSY   21
        SCREEND IN THIS NOOK OER THE HIGH HALF-REAPD FIELD   255 SCHOLAR-GIPSY   V 21

REAPER
        HERE WHERE THE REAPER WAS AT WORK OF LATE . . . .   255 SCHOLAR-GIPSY   11

REAPERS
        AND AS AFIELD THE REAPERS CUT A SWATH   . . . .   70 SOHRAB RUSTUM   293
        AND AS AFIELD THE REAPERS CUT A SWATHE   . . . .   70 SOHRAB RUSTUM   V 293
        THE REAPERS CRY THE DOGS ALARMS   . . . . .   218 BACCHANALIA 1   V   6
        WITH DISTANT CRIES OF REAPERS IN THE CORN   . . . .   255 SCHOLAR-GIPSY   19
        THE REAPERS IN THE CORN . . . .   436 EMPEDOCLES II   255

REAPPEAR
        LIGHT ONLY LIGHT WAS SLOW TO REAPPEAR   . . . .   445 WESTMIN ABBEY   60

REAPS
        HE REAPS AND STOWS THEM . . . .   190 STRAYED REVEL   157

REAR
        IN AN AGE WHICH CAN REAR THEM NO MORE   . . . .   229 YOUTH OF NATURE   50
        PINND BY THE THUNDER TO REAR . . . .   293 HEINES GRAVE   31
        AND THE PRINCE SINGLE PRESSING ON THE REAR . . . .   357 MEROPE   799

REARD
        LAST OF ALL THE BUILDERS REARD HER   . . . . . .   16 CHURCH BROU 1   103
        AND REARD HIM A BRIGHT BAY WITH LOFTY CREST . .   69 SOHRAB RUSTUM   276
        FOR VERY YOUNG HE SEEMD TENDERLY REARD   . . .   70 SOHRAB RUSTUM   313
        SO SLENDER SOHRAB SEEMD SO SOFTLY REARD   . . .   70 SOHRAB RUSTUM   318
        IT WAS THAT GRIFFIN WHICH OF OLD REARD ZAL . . . .   81 SOHRAB RUSTUM   679
        HIM THAT KIND CREATURE FOUND AND REARD AND LOVED . .   81 SOHRAB RUSTUM   682
        AS THOSE BLACK GRANITE PILLARS ONCE HIGH-REARD . .   86 SOHRAB RUSTUM   860
        NOT BORN IN HEAVEN HE WAS IN VANHEIM REARD . . . .   122 BALDER DEAD 3   324
        REARD PROUDLY SNUFFING   . . . .   190 STRAYED REVEL   149
        WE ARE LIKE CHILDREN REARD IN SHADE   . . . . .   304 GRANDE CHARTR   169
        BUT WE BROUGHT FORTH AND REARD IN HOURS   . . . .   308 OBERMANN   69
        THY MOTHERS KIN RECEIVED THEE AND REARD UP . . . .   330 MEROPE   23
        BUT IN THE PASTORAL ARCADIA REARD   . . . . . .   388 MEROPE   1514
        AND MAIA REARD HIM . . . .   392 MEROPE   1621

REAREST
        THOU TOO REAREST IN HOPE . . . .   346 MEROPE   511
        THOU TOO REAREST IN JOY . . . .   346 MEROPE   V 511

REASON
        IMPULSE AND REASON FREEDOM AND CONTROL   . . . .   4 BUTLERS SERMONS   2
        SO MIGHT THEY REASON SO COMPARE   . . . . .   56 RESIGNATION   136
        AND HIS CHILDS REASON FLICKERD AND DID DIE . . . .   166 PICT NEWSTEAD   6
        AND THE CHILDS REASON FLICKERD AND DID DIE . . . .   166 PICT NEWSTEAD   V 6
        UNCLOUDED REASON I WOULD NOT DECLINE . . . . .   335 MEROPE   158
        IN REASON GOOD WHICH JUSTIFIED MY DEED   . . . .   340 MEROPE   340
        YET OH COULDST THOU BUT ACT AS REASON BIDS . . . .   396 MEROPE   1762
        REASON THE PROOF CONFIRMS   . . . . . .   419 EMPEDOCLES I 2   224
        REASON ITS VOICE CONFIRMS   . . . . . .   419 EMPEDOCLES I 2 V 224
        BUT THY DAY OF DEATH IS AT HAND NOR SHALL WE   HOMER TRANS   48
            BE THE REASON
        AND WIN DELIBERATE REASON TO PUT ON FEAR   . . . .   RUDE ORATOR   11
        INVITEST REASON TO FORSWEAR HER STATE   . . . .   RUDE ORATOR   18

REASONS
        MANS GRAVE REASONS DISAPPEAR . . . .   29 NEW SIRENS   90
        BORN REASONS HEIRS AND OF THAT HERITAGE   . . . .   RUDE ORATOR   3

REBEKAH
        AS REBEKAH READ WHEN SHE SATE   . . . .   252 FUTURE   36

REBEL
        TO TYPHO ONLY THE REBEL OERTHROWN   . . . .   430 EMPEDOCLES II   42
        AND WE SHALL STRUGGLE AWHILE GASP AND REBEL . .   440 EMPEDOCLES II   382
        ONLY TO TYPHO THE REBEL OERTHROWN   . . . . .   430 EMPEDOCLES II   V 42
        TRUE WE MUST TAME OUR REBEL WILL   . . . . .   481 COURAGE   1

REBELLIOUS
        PERPETUAL PROMPTINGS TO REBELLIOUS HOPE   . . . .   333 MEROPE   91
        RUTHLESSLY THEIR REBELLIOUS SUBJECTS CRUSHD . .   390 MEROPE   1567

REBUILD
        OUR EYES WITH GAZING AND REBUILD WITH TEARS . .   128 BALDER DEAD 3   536

REBUKE
        SO FAR AS I CONCEIVE THE WORLDS REBUKE   . . . .   37 WORLDS TRIUMPHS   1

REBUKES
        BECAUSE ITS SIMPLICITY REBUKES . . . .   432 EMPEDOCLES II   106

RECALL
        THE ENCHANTMENTS THAT RECALL THE DEAD TO LIFE . .   101 BALDER DEAD 1   209
        ABBEY RECALL IT WHAT A SPHERE   . . . . . .   223 EPILOG LAOCOON   79
        THE SPOTS WHICH RECALL HIM SURVIVE . . . . .   228 YOUTH OF NATURE   13
        YE MOVE THROUGH THE RANKS RECALL   . . . . .   292 RUGBY CHAPEL   198

RECALL   (CONTINUED)
    WHAT THOUGHTS TO ME HIS ROCKS RECALL   . . . . . .   313 OBERMANN MORE   35

RECALLD
    THERE GLEAMD SOMETHING WHICH RECALLD   . . . . . .   136 TRISTRAM 1   201
    THERE GLEAMD SOMETHING THAT RECALLD   . . . . . .   136 TRISTRAM 1   V 201
    FAIN WOULD HE HAVE RECALLD   . . . . .   198 FRAG ANTIGONE   94
    PEACE THAT RECALLD HIS CHILDISH HOURS ANEW . . . .   475 CROMWELL   115

RECALLS
    THICKENS AND TO ITS INNER GULPH RECALLS   . . . .   129 BALDER DEAD 3   547
    RECALLS THE OBSCURE OPPOSER HE OUTWEIGHD   . . . .   171 DIVINITY   8
    THE EARLY PEASANT STILL RECALLS   . . . . . .   311 OBERMANN   171

RECAST
    TO HIM ADDRESSD WHO WOULD RECAST HER NEW   . . . .   37 WORLDS TRIUMPHS   2
    TO HIM ADDRESSD WHO WOULD RECAST IT NEW   . . . .   37 WORLDS TRIUMPHS V   2

RECEDING
    FAIN HAD HE FOLLOWD THEIR RECEDING STEPS   . . . .   129 BALDER DEAD 3   556

RECEIVD
    AND MANY A GUEST HATH SHE THEREIN RECEIVD   . . . .   251 FUTURE   V

RECEIVE
    AND THOU O PRINCESS SHALT NO MORE RECEIVE   . . . .   18 CHURCH BROU 3   12
    TRISTRAM TRISTRAM STAY RECEIVE ME WITH THEE   . .   146 TRISTRAM 2   99
    BUT THEY BRING MORE THAN THEY RECEIVE   . . . .   203 EUPHROSYNE   20
    THEY LIKE FRIENDS SHALL RECEIVE   . . . . .   284 HAWORTH CHURCH   84
    BEWARE FROM THEE UPBRAIDINGS I RECEIVE   . . . .   341 MEROPE   360
    TO RECEIVE ARCAS WHO TO-DAY SHOULD COME   . .   350 MEROPE   598
    RECEIVE ME HIDE ME QUENCH ME TAKE ME HOME . . . .   429 EMPEDOCLES II   36
    WHAT WILL RECEIVE THEM WHO WILL CALL THEM HOME   . . 439 EMPEDOCLES II   348
    RECEIVE ME SAVE ME . . . .   441 EMPEDOCLES II   416

RECEIVED
    BRISTLED WITH CITIES US THE SEA RECEIVED   . . . .   25 DREAM   37
    OF LIFE TIS TRUE RECEIVED   . . . .   318 OBERMANN MORE   166
    THY MOTHERS KIN RECEIVED THEE AND REARD UP . . .   330 MEROPE   23
    HERACLEIDAE RECEIVED   . . . .   343 MEROPE   421
    OF IMPORT AND IN SILENCE BEST RECEIVED   . . . .   359 MEROPE   861
    BUT WE RECEIVED THE SHOCK OF MIGHTY THOUGHTS   . .   436 EMPEDOCLES II   242

RECEIVES
    RECEIVES THE RIVER . . . .   391 MEROPE   1610

RECENT
    STREAM ON HER FROM HER LORDS YET RECENT GRAVE   . .   172 GOOD SHEPHERD   8
    BRILLIANT WITH RECENT RENOWN   . . . . . .   280 HAWORTH CHURCH   9
    BEFORE THY FEET THIS RECENT CITY SPREADS   . . .   330 MEROPE   9
    POPULAR REVERENCE TO THESE RECENT LINES   . . .   390 MEROPE   1564

RECESSES
    FREQUENT THE STILL RECESSES OF THE REALM   . . . .   126 BALDER DEAD 3   435
    BADE THROUGH THE DEEP RECESSES OF OUR BREAST   . .   246 BURIED LIFE   38

RECKD
    A HEART THAT RECKD NOT OF THE COUNTLESS DEAD   . .   478 CROMWELL   225

RECKLESSLY
    O SELF-WILL RECKLESSLY INDULGED   . . . . . .   398 MEROPE   1801

RECKONEST
    DOUBTLESS THOU RECKONEST ON THE HELP OF FRIENDS   . . 341 MEROPE   356
    DOUBTLESS THOU RECKONEST ON THE HOPE OF FRIENDS   . . 341 MEROPE   V 356

RECKS
    OF ME SHE RECKS NOT NOR MY VAIN DESIRE   . . . .   140 TRISTRAM 1   303
    OF ME SHE RECKS NOT NOR OF MY DESIRE   . . . . .   140 TRISTRAM 1   V 303

RECLUSES
    YE SHY RECLUSES FOLLOW TOO   . . . .   305 GRANDE CHARTR   192

RECOGNISE
    THEY RECOGNISE A FORMER SCENE   . . . .   55 RESIGNATION   115

RECOGNIZE
    THEY LESS THAN US MIGHT RECOGNIZE   . . . . . .   481 COURAGE   11

RECOILD
    AND SHRANK AMAZED BACK HE RECOILD ONE STEP   . . . . 76 SOHRAB RUSTUM   517
    AND SHRANK AMAZED BACK HE RECOILD ONE PACE   . . . . 76 SOHRAB RUSTUM   V 517

RECOLLECT
    THE LEPER RECOLLECT SAID HE   . . . .   157 SAINT BRANDAN   38

RECOLLECTIONS
    AND RECOLLECTIONS INDISTINCT AND DIM   . . . . . .   469 ALARIC AT ROME   183

RECOMMENCE
    THAT HE HAS STILL THOUGH OLD TO RECOMMENCE • • • • 239 REVOLUTIONS   11
    LET HIM DO THIS DO AUGHT BUT RECOMMENCE • • • • 388 MEROPE   1500

RECOMPENCE
    THE GODS DECLARE MY RECOMPENCE TO-DAY • • • •   9 MYCERINUS   16

RECONCILED
    ALL STRIFES BE RECONCILED • • • • • • • • 40 STAGIRIUS   55

RECONCILEMENT
    FAIR TERMS OF RECONCILEMENT EQUAL RULE • • • • 360 MEROPE   882

RECORD
    DO THOU RECORD IT IN THINE INMOST SOUL • • • •   72 SOHRAB RUSTUM   374

RECORDED
    EVEN AS THAT LOVED THAT WELL-RECORDED FRIEND • • 449 WESTMIN ABBEY   168

RECORDS
    FROM SIN WHICH HEAVEN RECORDS NOT WHY FORBEAR • • 171 BETTER PART   7

RECOVERD
    IN NEW-RECOVERD SEATS THE HAPPIER DAY • • • • 128 BALDER DEAD 3   513

RECROSS
    CROSS AND RECROSS THE STRIPS OF MOON-BLANCHD GREEN   255 SCHOLAR-GIPSY   9

RED
    ON THE RED PININGS OF THEIR FOREST-FLOOR • • • •   25 DREAM   5
    PLUCK NO MORE RED ROSES MAIDENS • • • • • •   35 NEW SIRENS   267
    STREW NO MORE RED ROSES MAIDENS • • • • • •   35 NEW SIRENS   V 267
    THE RED-GROUSE SPRINGING AT OUR SOUND • • • •   54 RESIGNATION   70
    AND PLEDGE EACH OTHER IN RED WINE LIKE FRIENDS • •   74 SOHRAB RUSTUM   441
    DEARER TO THE RED JACKALS SHALT THOU BE • • • •   77 SOHRAB RUSTUM   538
    ALL RED WITH BLOOD THE WHIRLING RIVER FLOWS • • 137 TRISTRAM 1   234
    OF THOSE OLD OAKS WHOSE WET RED LEAVES • • • • 141 TRISTRAM 1   359
    BUT WHEN THE RED GLOW ON THE SEA GREW COLD • • 151 TRISTRAM 3   58
    OF HAIR THAT RED AND TUFTED FELL • • • • • • 157 SAINT BRANDAN   18
    ON A RED GOLD THRONE IN THE HEART OF THE SEA • • 163 FORSAKEN MERM   51
    THE RED CREAMING LIQUOR • • • • • • • • 187 STRAYED REVEL   57
    SMEARD WITH RED WINE-STAINS WHO IS HE • • • • 188 STRAYED REVEL   90
    WHERE RED-BERRIED ASHES FRINGE • • • • • • 190 STRAYED REVEL   146
    HIGH ON A JUTTING ROCK IN THE RED STREAM • • • 192 STRAYED REVEL   230
    TO-MORROW RED WITH BLOOD WILL XANTHUS BE • • • 236 PALLADIUM   14
    THOSE BLACK-CROWND RED-BOLED PINE-TREES STAND • • 248 KENSINGTON GARD   4
    THOSE BLACK-TOPPD RED-BOLED PINE-TREES STAND • • 248 KENSINGTON GARD V 4
    THOSE DARK-TOPPD RED-BOLD PINETREES STAND • • •   KENSINGTON GARD V 4
    UNDER A DARK RED-FRUITED YEW-TREES SHADE • • • 259 SCHOLAR-GIPSY   140
    WITH BLOSSOMS RED AND WHITE OF FALLEN MAY • • • 264 THYRSIS   55
    RED LOOSESTRIFE AND BLOND MEADOW-SWEET AMONG • • 266 THYRSIS   124
    THE ORCHIS RED GLEAMS EVERYWHERE • • • • • • 274 STANZAS CARNAC   18
    THE BROAD RED SUN OVER FIELD • • • • • • • 297 HEINES GRAVE   170
    TYPHO SUCH RED JETS OF FLAME • • • • • • • 430 EMPEDOCLES II   48
    THE RED-SNOODED PHRYGIAN GIRLS • • • • • • 434 EMPEDOCLES II   180
    THICK BREAKS THE RED FLAME • • • • • • • 441 EMPEDOCLES II   418
    QUICK BREAKS THE RED FLAME • • • • • • • 441 EMPEDOCLES II V 418

REDDEND
    OER THE SUN-REDDEND WESTERN STRAITS • • • • • • 198 FRAG ANTIGONE   92

REDDENING
    REDDENING THE SEA AROUND AND ALL WAS DARK • • • • 119 BALDER DEAD 3   206

REDOUBLE
    SO SOME MAN WILL SAY AND THEN THY GRIEF WILL REDOUBLE   HOMER TRANS   35

REDOUBLED
    SHORT BUT REDOUBLED BY FAME • • • • • • • • 283 HAWORTH CHURCH   73
    SHORT YET REDOUBLED BY FAME • • • • • • • • 283 HAWORTH CHURCH   V 73

REED
    OR SOME FRORE CASPIAN REED-BED SOUTHWARD BOUND • •   64 SOHRAB RUSTUM   115
    SEE HIM COME BACK AND CUT A SMOOTHER REED • • • 265 THYRSIS   78
    ON WHAT A REED MY CHILD THOU LEANEST THERE • • • 381 MEROPE   1310
    WHERE THE LONG GREEN REED-BEDS SWAY • • • • • 433 EMPEDOCLES II   133
    OF ROBINS REED • • • • • • • • • • • 459 KAISER DEAD   12

REEDS
    THE TALL CRESTED WATER-REEDS • • • • • • • • 434 EMPEDOCLES II   174

REEFS
    TO ALL REEFS AND NARROWS WENDING • • • • • •   26 NEW SIRENS   15
    THE SUNKEN REEFS AND FAR AWAY • • • • • • • 148 TRISTRAM 2   173
    UPON THE REEFS AND SANDBANKS OF THE WORLD • • • •   LUCRETIUS 2   5

REEL
    MAKE THEIR SKIFF REEL AND WORMS • • • • • • 193 STRAYED REVEL   237

REELD
    HE REELD AND STAGGERING BACK SANK TO THE GROUND • •   76 SOHRAB RUSTUM   521

REELD   (CONTINUED)
        HE REELD AND STAGGERING BACK SUNK TO THE GROUND   • •   76 SOHRAB RUSTUM   V 521

REELING
        AND ON EARTH WE WANDER GROPING REELING   • • • •   210 SELF-DECEPTION   21
        TO MARK WITH SHIVERD CREST THE REELING WAVE   • •   472 CROMWELL   23

REELS
        REELS AND SHIVERS ON THE RUFFLED GLOOM   • • • •   32 NEW SIRENS   186

REFLECTED
        THAT HAST SO MUCH REFLECTED BUT ALAS   • • • • • •   LUCRETIUS 1   3

REFLEX
        OURS IS THE REFLEX IMAGE OF THE WORLD   • • • •   LUCRETIUS 5   1

REFRAIND
        LONG WE REFRAIND OURSELVES SUBMITTED LONG   • • • • 337 MEROPE   254

REFRESH
        THE STRAGGLERS REFRESH THE OUTWORN   • • • • • •   292 RUGBY CHAPEL   199

REFRESHD
        COMPOSED REFRESHD ENNOBLED CLEAR   • • • • • •   251 WISH   50
        REFRESHD AND CLAIM THY MASTERS THANKS AND GOLD   • • 373 MEROPE   1182

REFRESHMENT
        REFRESHMENT NEEDED BY THEE AS I JUDGE   • • • •   359 MEROPE   867

REFUGE
        ART STILL HAS TRUTH TAKE REFUGE THERE   • • • •   271 MEMORIAL VERSES   28
        MY REFUGE AND NO MORE   • • • • • •   321 OBERMANN MORE   272
        AND WE SHALL FLY FOR REFUGE TO PAST TIMES   • • • • 440 EMPEDOCLES II   383

REFUSE
        THE LIMBS THEIR WONTED TASKS REFUSE   • • • • • •   276 SOUTHERN NIGHT   41

REFUSED
        HALF REFUSED AND HALF RESIGND   • • • • • •   23 MEMORY-PICTURE   35
        SHREDS OF GIFTS WHICH HE REFUSED IN FULL   • • • •   210 SELF-DECEPTION   18
        I OFFERD TO MY FOES AND THEY REFUSED   • • • • •   360 MEROPE   883
        WHAT SPEECH REFUSED HER   • • • • • • • •   393 MEROPE   1668

REGAIND
        HE LEFT TO LIE BUT HAD REGAIND HIS SPEAR   • • •   74 SOHRAB RUSTUM   450
        HARDLY THE FOURTH WITH GRIEVOUS LOSS REGAIND   • •   336 MEROPE   218
        HARDLY THE THIRD WITH GRIEVOUS LOSS REGAIND   • •   336 MEROPE   V 218

REGAL
        LOVE FREE TO RANGE AND REGAL BANQUETINGS   • • • •   9 MYCERINUS   34

REGARD
        THEN MUST HE NOT REGARD THE WAILFUL GHOSTS   • • •   100 BALDER DEAD 1   176
        THEN HE MUST NOT REGARD THE WAILFUL GHOSTS   • • •   100 BALDER DEAD 1 V 176
        AND NOW HAVE CHIEF REGARD IN HELAS REALM   • • •   109 BALDER DEAD 2   169
        AND WITH INSCRUTABLE REGARD THE QUEEN   • • •   112 BALDER DEAD 2   280
        REGARD HIS DEATH-PLACE DUMB   • • • • • •   318 OBERMANN MORE   178
        THE PRINCE AT START SEEMD SAD BUT HIS REGARD   • •   355 MEROPE   733
        FIXING WITH A MUTE REGARD   • • • • • • •   456 POOR MATTHIAS   121

REGARDED
        ENVIES THE ALL-REGARDED PLACE   • • • • • • • •   57 RESIGNATION   159
        ALL-REGARDED AFAR   • • • • • • • • • •   345 MEROPE   484
        MUTELY SHE REGARDED   • • • • • • • •   393 MEROPE   1665

REGARDING
        REGARDING NEITHER TO RIGHT   • • • • • • • •   295 HEINES GRAVE   90

REGARDS
        WHO LET ME SAY IS THIS STRANGER REGARDS ME   • • •   206 SEPARATION   15
        REGARDS HIS BROTHERS FORM OUTSPREAD   • • • • •   460 KAISER DEAD   68

REGION
        TO THE COOL REGION OF THE GROVES HE LOVED   • • •   11 MYCERINUS   84
        AND IN THAT GRACIOUS REGION BLAND   • • • • •   311 OBERMANN   165
        THAT REGION IN PERPETUAL CLOUD   • • • • • •   352 MEROPE   642
        THIS REGION IS NOT HAPPY FOR MY RACE   • • • •   357 MEROPE   785
        A REGION DESOLATE AND WILD   • • • • • • •   479 HAYSWATER BOAT   1

REGIONS
        THOSE UPPER REGIONS WE MUST TREAD   • • • • •   54 RESIGNATION   65
        FAR REGIONS OF ETERNAL CHANGE   • • • • • • •   58 RESIGNATION   222
        YE HEAVENS WHOSE PURE DARK REGIONS HAVE NO SIGN   • • 244 SUMMER NIGHT   78

REGISTAN
        LOOKING INTO THE REGISTAN   • • • • • • •   88 SICK KING BOKH   17
        BELOW THERE IN THE REGISTAN   • • • • • • •   93 SICK KING BOKH   192

REGISTERED
        YES THERE ARE STORIES REGISTERED ON HIGH   • • • •   462 ALARIC AT ROME   13

REGNER
    REGNER WHO SWEPT THE NORTHERN SEA WITH FLEETS   • •   117 BALDER DEAD 3   126
    SO REGNER SPAKE AND ALL THE HEROES GROAND • • • • 117 BALDER DEAD 3   153

REGRET
    ENNOBLED BY A VAST REGRET • • • • • • • • 179 FAREWELL   71
    TILL FANCIFUL REGRET AND DREAMY WOE • • • • • • 467 ALARIC AT ROME   125

REGRETTING
    REGRETTING THE WARM MANSION WHICH IT LEFT • • • • 86 SOHRAB RUSTUM   855

REGULAR
    WITH REGULAR CADENCE SLOW AND BRING • • • • • 211 DOVER BEACH   V 13

REHEARSE
    WHILE TO EACH OTHER WE REHEARSE • • • • • • 451 GEISTS GRAVE   43
    SAYS IT FITS THAT I REHEARSE • • • • • • • 453 POOR MATTHIAS   17

REIGN
    TO HAUNT THE PLACE WHERE PASSIONS REIGN • • • 181 ISOLATION MARG   17
    ITS GREATNESS NOR THE REIGN OF FOOLS PROLONGD • • 282 HAWORTH CHURCH   V
    THROUGH THAT PRETENDED DEATH TO LIVE AND REIGN • • 331 MEROPE   50
    CLOSING IN BLOOD AND GLOOM HIS SULLEN REIGN • • 335 MEROPE   160
    THAT THOU MIGHTST REIGN HE DIED NOT FOR HIS FAULT • • 339 MEROPE   327
    GRANT HIM TO REIGN THERE WISE AND JUST LIKE THEE • • 350 MEROPE   589
    THE REIGN OF FOLLY USURPATION EVER • • • • 353 MEROPE   668
    TO-DAY I REIGN THE REST I LEAVE TO FATE • • • 397 MEROPE   1776
    AS IF THE REIGN OF JOY DID NOW BEGIN • • • • 445 WESTMIN ABBEY   40
    ALTERNATING WITH WISDOMS TOO SHORT REIGN • • • 449 WESTMIN ABBEY   158

REIGND
    YET OF THE SPIRITS WHO HAVE REIGND • • • • • 307 OBERMANN   45
    NOT NOW OF SPARTA WHERE HIS NEPHEWS REIGND • • • 337 MEROPE   232
    WHEN HIS STAR REIGND BEFORE HIS BANISHMENT • • • • 408 EMPEDOCLES I 1   65

REIGNING
    HAVE I SEEN REIGNING IN THIS PLACE • • • • • 92 SICK KING BOKH   144

REIGNS
    AND FROM THE FLAMING WORLD WHERE MUSPEL REIGNS • • 121 BALDER DEAD 3   262
    NONE SINCE A TWOFOLD COLOUR REIGNS IN ALL • • • 404 MEROPE   1994

REIN
    AND IN HIS FATHERS HAND PUT SLEIPNERS REIN • • • 114 BALDER DEAD 3   34
    SWAYING THE LONG-HAIRD GOATS WITH SILVERD REIN • • 115 BALDER DEAD 3   73
    PUT TIGHTNESS IN THY GOLD-EMBOSSED REIN • • • 349 MEROPE   574

REIND
    A THOUSAND KNIGHTS HAVE REIND THEIR STEEDS • • • 204 CALAIS SANDS   1

REINDEER
    WHOM ANTLERD REINDEER PULL OVER THE SNOW • • • • 96 BALDER DEAD 1   54

REINS
    HE GRASPS THE VERY REINS OF LIFE AND DEATH • • • 410 EMPEDOCLES I 1   125

REJECT
    CAN REJECT WHAT CANNOT CLEAR HIM • • • • • 49 SECOND BEST   18
    ACCEPT THEM OR REJECT THEM BOTH HAVE GROUNDS • • 120 BALDER DEAD 3   226

REJECTEST
    ONCE MORE MY FRIENDSHIP THOU REJECTEST WELL • • 398 MEROPE   1783

REJOICE
    SEEM TO BEAR RATHER THAN REJOICE • • • • • 60 RESIGNATION   270
    THAT SOHRAB WILL REJOICE HER SIGHT NO MORE • • • • 79 SOHRAB RUSTUM   599
    FOR EVER MAKES THEIR EAR REJOICE • • • • 227 EPILOG LAOCOON   196
    AND WORDSWORTH AH PALE GHOSTS REJOICE • • • • 271 MEMORIAL VERSES   34
    REJOICE WITH US AND TRUST ME HE WHO WISHD • • • 403 MEROPE   1958
    O SPEED AND REJOICE • • • • • • • • 442 EMPEDOCLES II   428

REJOICED
    SHARED AND REJOICED IN BY ALL • • • • • • • • 230 YOUTH OF NATURE   67

REJOICING
    REJOICING THROUGH THE HUSHD CHORASMIAN WASTE • • 87 SOHRAB RUSTUM   878
    THE RADIANT REJOICING INTELLIGENT SONS OF HEAVEN • • 437 EMPEDOCLES II   287

REJOICINGS
    THAT WE SOUGHT YOU WITH REJOICINGS • • • • • 27 NEW SIRENS   45

REJOIN
    I MUST REJOIN EMPEDOCLES DO THOU • • • • • 411 EMPEDOCLES I 1   165

REJOIND
    FOR NANNA HATH REJOIND ME WHO OF OLD • • • • • 126 BALDER DEAD 3   459
    THOU ART COME INDEED THOU HAST REJOIND ME • • • • 142 TRISTRAM 2   9

REJOINS
    REJOINS HER IN THEIR HUT UPON THE SANDS   • • • •   70 SOHRAB RUSTUM   289

REKINDLING
    EYES REKINDLING AND PRAYERS   • • • • • • •   292 RUGBY CHAPEL   202

RELATE
    FLUENT OF HORRORS FALTERS TO RELATE IT   • • • •   385 MEROPE   1419
    MUST FROM SOME MOUTH BE HEARD RELATE IT THOU   • •   401 MEROPE   1892
    AT DAWN THOU TO KING SEBERT SHALT RELATE   • • • •   445 WESTMIN ABBEY   48

RELATIONS
    FROM PRETENTIOUS TEASD RELATIONS   • • • • • •   SECOND BEST   V   18

RELAX
    AND RELAX PLUTOS BROW   • • • • • • • • •   265 THYRSIS   86
    AND ALL WHICH MIGHT RELAX HIS SETTLED GLOOM   • •   409 EMPEDOCLES I 1   84

RELAXD
    THE IRON FROWN OF HELA IS RELAXD   • • • • • •   126 BALDER DEAD 3   463

RELEASE
    BUT OFFERS TERMS FOR HIS RELEASE TO HEAVEN   • • • •   122 BALDER DEAD 3   289
    BUT OFFER TERMS FOR HIS RELEASE TO HEAVEN   • • • •   122 BALDER DEAD 3   V 289

RELEASED
    SO SAID HE AND HIS VOICE RELEASED THE HEART   • •   82 SOHRAB RUSTUM   726
    IN ONE AND WERE THROUGH FAITH RELEASED   • • • •   181 ISOLATION MARG   39
    THE LABOUR-RELEASED HERO   • • • • • • • •   399 MEROPE   1844

RELEASEMENT
    THE TERMS OF THY RELEASEMENT HENCE TO HEAVEN   • •   112 BALDER DEAD 2   252

RELEGATE
    AND RELEGATE TO WORLDS YET DISTANT OUR REPOSE   • •   425 EMPEDOCLES I 2   406

RELENTING
    THE LATE-RELENTING GODS WITH VICTORY BROUGHT   • •   330 MEROPE   6

RELICS
    RELICS OF NATIONS THY MEMORIAL-STONES   • • • •   464 ALARIC AT ROME   62

RELIEF
    BUT IS DESPAIR RELIEF   • • • • • • • • •   208 ON THE RHINE   10

RELIGION
    HATH LOOKD ON NO RELIGION SCORNFULLY   • • • •   238 PROGRESS   39
    HATH WITHOUT PAIN SEEN NO RELIGION DIE   • • • •   238 PROGRESS   V   39

RELIGIOUS
    RELIGIOUS FERVOURS ARDOUR MISAPPLIED   • • • • •   237 PROGRESS   17

RELUCTANT
    AND SLOW RELUCTANT STEPS ARE GATHERING ROUND   • •   476 CROMWELL   160

RELUCTANTLY
    RELUCTANTLY THE REST BUT AGAINST ALL   • • • • •   337 MEROPE   257

RELYING
    ON WHAT RELYING TO CRUSH SUCH A FOE   • • • • •   380 MEROPE   1286

REMAIN
    WE RUSH BY COASTS WHERE WE HAD LIEF REMAIN   • • •   40 HUMAN LIFE   17
    SOLE OBJECT OF HER DYING EYES REMAIN   • • • • •   168 RACHEL 2   13
    UNVISITED REMAIN   • • • • • • • • • •   198 FRAG DEJANEIRA   10
    BUT THEY WILL NOT REMAIN   • • • • • • • •   209 DESPONDENCY   6
    I REMAIN   • • • • • • • • • • • •   232 YOUTH OF NATURE   134
    BUT I WILL RATHER SAY THAT YOU REMAIN   • • •   244 SUMMER NIGHT   86
    THE PANGS WHICH TORTURED THEM REMAIN   • • • • •   303 GRANDE CHARTR   132
    YET REMAIN SPENDTHRIFTS STILL   • • • • • •   420 EMPEDOCLES I 2   228

REMAIND
    AND IN THE HAND THE HILT REMAIND ALONE   • • • •   76 SOHRAB RUSTUM   513
    AND IN HIS HAND THE HILT REMAIND ALONE   • • • •   76 SOHRAB RUSTUM   V 513
    AND REMAIND KNEELING AS BEFORE   • • • • • •   91 SICK KING BOKH   124
    BUT ONE SUCH DEATH REMAIND TO COME   • • • • •   270 MEMORIAL VERSES   3
    OF EITHER GULF AND REMAIND   • • • • • • •   345 MEROPE   483
    BUT OF THE PRINCE NOTHING REMAIND SAVE THIS   • •   358 MEROPE   839

REMAINING
    REMAINING IN THY HUNGER AND THY PAIN   • • • • •   42 GIPSY CHILD   12

REMAINS
    CONVERSE HIS SPEECH REMAINS THOUGH HE BE DEAD   • •   111 BALDER DEAD 2   248
    HIS PLACE OF STATE REMAINS BY HELAS SIDE   • • • •   125 BALDER DEAD 3   432
    UNGUIDED HE REMAINS   • • • • • • • •   195 FRAG ANTIGONE   15
    OUR JOURNEY IS WELL MADE THE WORK REMAINS   • • •   330 MEROPE   24
    IN THE MESSENIAN PEOPLE WHAT REMAINS   • • • •   334 MEROPE   138
    IS LIFELESS WHILE ITS HEART REMAINS UNTOUCHD   • •   382 MEROPE   1343

REMEMBER
    BUT FAUSTA I REMEMBER WELL . . . .   54 RESIGNATION   82
    REMEMBER ALL THY VALOUR TRY THY FEINTS . . . .   75 SOHRAB RUSTUM   466
    BUT AT GODS ALTAR OH REMEMBER ME . . . . . .   173 MONICAS PRAYER   4
    REMEMBER EACH UNTO THE END . . . .   217 NAMELESS EPIT   4
    AND THEY REMEMBER . . . .   235 YOUTH OF MAN   101
    AND THEN HE BADE REMEMBER HOW WE PASSD . . . . 356 MEROPE   774
    REMEMBER TO REVENGE HIS DEATH I COME . . . . . 378 MEROPE   1241

REMEMBERD
    FOR HE REMEMBERD HIS OWN EARLY YOUTH . . . . .   79 SOHRAB RUSTUM   619
    YES AND I TOO REMEMBERD THEN NO MORE . . . . . 117 BALDER DEAD 3   145
    THEN I REMEMBERD HOW I WENT . . . .   157 SAINT BRANDAN   41

REMEMBERED
    TO BE REMEMBERED THUS AND YET THEY CANNOT LIVE . . 462 ALARIC AT ROME   18

REMEMBERS
    EXILED REMEMBERS HIS HOME . . . .   347 MEROPE   533

REMEMBRANCE
    AH THE DIM REMEMBRANCE PRIZE . . . .   24 MEMORY-PICTURE   62
    REMEMBRANCE IN OUR SOUL OF WARS ALONE . . . .   117 BALDER DEAD 3   138
    WILLS THAT REMEMBRANCE SHOULD ALWAYS DECAY . . . 206 SEPARATION   6
    FESTERS THE DULL REMEMBRANCE OF A CHANGE . . . . 213 GROWING OLD   29
    WAKENS O QUEEN REMEMBRANCE IN THY HEART . . . . 333 MEROPE   106
    SOMEWHAT WHICH REMEMBRANCE WOKE . . . . . .   454 POOR MATTHIAS   54
    ALL SHAPES THAT HAUNT REMEMBRANCE SOFT AND FAIR . . 474 CROMWELL   83

REMINDS
    BUT MY YOUTH REMINDS ME THOU . . . .   22 MEMORY-PICTURE   V

REMISSLY
    THE SCEPTRE NOT REMISSLY LET IT FALL . . . . . 334 MEROPE   135

REMISSNESS
    OF TYRANNOUS HARSHNESS OR REMISSNESS WEAK . . . 404 MEROPE   2007

REMIT
    TO THE JUST-PAUSING GENIUS WE REMIT . . . . .   259 SCHOLAR-GIPSY   149

REMNANT
    SHALL A SMALL REMNANT OF THE GODS REPAIR . . . . 128 BALDER DEAD 3   525

REMORSE
    REMORSE GRIEF JOY AND WERE THE SCOPE . . . . .   58 RESIGNATION   218
    CALL IT AMBITION OR REMORSE OR LOVE . . . . .   153 TRISTRAM 3   130
    BARING HIS DUMB REMORSE TO FUTURE DAYS . . . . 167 PICT NEWSTEAD   13
    WHICH NEVER YET WITHOUT REMORSE . . . . . .   181 ISOLATION MARG   14
    THERE NURSE A LATE REMORSE AND THANK THE GODS . . 396 MEROPE   1755
    MOVES ME SOMEHOW TO REMORSE . . . .   454 POOR MATTHIAS   84

REMORSEFUL
    YES THE CROWD MUTTERS THAT REMORSEFUL FEAR . . . 333 MEROPE   97
    REMORSEFUL TOWRD MY HOSTILE SOLITUDE . . . . . 387 MEROPE   1475

REMOTE
    FROM THY REMOTE AND SPHERED COURSE . . . . .   181 ISOLATION MARG   16
    REMOTE FROM THINE . . . .   277 SOUTHERN NIGHT   52
    PROVE US SO REMOTE IN KIND . . . .   457 POOR MATTHIAS   156

REMOUNT
    OF LIFE REMOUNT . . . .   45 IN UTRUMQUE PAR   14

REMOVE
    I BEAR THAT YE REMOVE . . . .   183 ABSENCE   16
    REMOVE YET FURTHER OFF IF AUGHT COMES NEAR . . . 332 MEROPE   69

REMOVED
    BUT ALL THAT BROOD THOU HAST REMOVED FAR OFF . . 121 BALDER DEAD 3   274
    WANDERING IN HEAVEN FAR REMOVED . . . . . .   181 ISOLATION MARG   27

REND
    REND IN A THOUSAND SHREDS THIS LIFE OF OURS . .   4 BUTLERS SERMONS   4
    AND REND HIS HEART WHO SEES THEM . . . . .   LUCRETIUS 2   17

RENDER
    TO RENDER TO MY TRUE MESSENIANS THANKS . . . . 405 MEROPE   2018

RENDERD
    TO HAVE RENDERD THE GLEAM OF MY SKIES . . . . . 231 YOUTH OF NATURE 123

RENDERS
    WHO RENDERS VAIN THEIR DEEP DESIRE . . . . . . 182 TO MARG CONT   21

RENEW
    PAIN TO THREAD BACK AND TO-RENEW . . . . .   53 RESIGNATION   20
    WE SHALL RENEW THE BATTLE IN THE PLAIN . . . . 236 PALLADIUM   13
    MEN WILL RENEW THE BATTLE IN THE PLAIN . . . . 236 PALLADIUM   V 13
    ON MY HEART YOUR MIGHTY CHARM RENEW . . . . .   240 SELF-DEPENDENCE 10
    COME SHEPHERD AND AGAIN RENEW THE QUEST . . . . 255 SCHOLAR-GIPSY V 10

RENEW   (CONTINUED)
          AND RENEW BY NECESSITY • • • • • • • • • • 437 EMPEDOCLES II   293
          HUNGARIANS SAVE THE WORLD RENEW THE STORIES   • • 480 HUNGARIAN NAT   9
          ON LAND RENEW THAT GREEK EXPLOIT WHOSE GLORIES • • 481 HUNGARIAN NAT   12

RENEWD
          IMPARTING LIFE RENEWD OLD CLASSIC GRACE   • • • • 168 RACHEL 3   5
          FRESH BE THE WOUND STILL-RENEWD BE ITS SMARTING • • 206 SEPARATION   3
          WAR-CRIES TO FACTION YEAR BY YEAR RENEWD • • • • 333 MEROPE   92

RENOUNCE
          EITHER THOU SHALT RENOUNCE THY VAUNT AND YIELD • •   72 SOHRAB RUSTUM   375
          MUST LEARN TO WAIT RENOUNCE WITHDRAW • • • • • • 481 COURAGE   4

RENOUNCED
          WHO HATH RENOUNCED HIS OWN   • • • • • • • • • 309 OBERMANN   104

RENOWN
          RUKSH WHOSE RENOWN WAS NOISED THROUGH ALL THE EARTH   69 SOHRAB RUSTUM   272
          A POOR MEAN SOLDIER AND WITHOUT RENOWN • • • •   85 SOHRAB RUSTUM   814
          BRILLIANT WITH RECENT RENOWN • • • • • • • • 280 HAWORTH CHURCH   9
          UNDER THE WINGS OF RENOWN   • • • • • • • • 293 HEINES GRAVE   22
          AND VOUCHD BY GLORIOUS RENOWN • • • • • • • • 459 KAISER DEAD   17

RENOWND
          OR THAT RENOWND MIRROR OF CHIVALRY • • • • • • 153 TRISTRAM 3   146

RENT
          RENT THE TOUGH PLATES BUT FAILD TO REACH THE SKIN   76 SOHRAB RUSTUM   493
          AND LIGHTNINGS RENT THE CLOUD AND RUKSH THE HORSE   76 SOHRAB RUSTUM   501
          RENT THE TOUGH PLATES BUT MISSD TO REACH THE SKIN   76 SOHRAB RUSTUM V 493
          ALL RENT AND DUST UPON HIS HAIR • • • • • •   88 SICK KING BOKH   32
          RENT WITH TUMULTUOUS THOUGHTS WHOSE CONFLICT RUNG   478 CROMWELL   223

REPAIR
          THE PEOPLE TO THE NAVE REPAIR • • • • • • • •   17 CHURCH BROU 2   34
          THOSE THAT DO THEMSELVES REPAIR • • • • • •   23 MEMORY-PICTURE   12
          NOR DID THEY TO THEIR JUDGMENT-PLACE REPAIR • • 105 BALDER DEAD 2   32
          SHALL A SMALL REMNANT OF THE GODS REPAIR • • • 128 BALDER DEAD 3   525

REPAY
          UNTO THIS PIOUS HOUSEHOLD TO REPAY • • • • • • 447 WESTMIN ABBEY   108

REPEAT
          CAN EVER QUITE REPEAT THE PAST • • • • • • • • 450 GEISTS GRAVE   27
          BIRDS WE BUT REPEAT ON YOU   • • • • • • • • 457 POOR MATTHIAS   157

REPEATED
          TO-DAYS EXACT REPEATED EFFIGY • • • • • • • 152 TRISTRAM 3   95
          TIS THAT REPEATED SHOCKS AGAIN AGAIN • • • • • 259 SCHOLAR-GIPSY   144
          REPEATED ARE IN THEE I WELL BELIEVE • • • • • 333 MEROPE   87

REPEATS
          STILL HE REPEATS THE DROWNING STORY HERE • • • • 365 MEROPE   987

REPEL
          AND FIRE REPEL US FROM ITS LIVING WAVES   • • • • 439 EMPEDOCLES II   363

REPELLD
          THY SWORD REPELLD IT LONG AGO NOT I • • • • • 341 MEROPE   355
          HIS OFFERS I REPELLD BUT WHAT OF THAT • • • • 366 MEROPE   1010
          HIS OFFERS COLDLY HEARD THEM COLD REPELLD • • • 366 MEROPE   1015
          OF MEN WHO AGAINST HOPE REPELLD THE CHAIN • • • 480 HUNGARIAN NAT   10

REPELLENT
          REPELLENT AS THE WORLD BUT SEE • • • • • • • • 242 SUMMER NIGHT   5

REPELLEST
          THOU STANDEST OUT I SEE REPELLEST PEACE   • • • • 341 MEROPE   354

REPENTANT
          REPENTANT PRAYERS THAT HAD BEEN STRONG TO SAVE • • 474 CROMWELL   81

REPLACE
          DOTH RIOTOUS LAUGHTER NOW REPLACE • • • • • • 184 TERRACE BERNE   21

REPLIED
          AND WITH A FEARLESS MIEN SOHRAB REPLIED   • • • •   77 SOHRAB RUSTUM   540
          AND WITH A FAILING VOICE SOHRAB REPLIED   • • • •   78 SOHRAB RUSTUM   579
          BUT WITH A GRAVE MILD VOICE SOHRAB REPLIED • • • •   84 SOHRAB RUSTUM   771
          AND WITH A MOURNFUL VOICE RUSTUM REPLIED • • • •   84 SOHRAB RUSTUM   795
          THEN AT THE POINT OF DEATH SOHRAB REPLIED • • • •   85 SOHRAB RUSTUM   827
          AND WITH A HEAVY GROAN RUSTUM REPLIED • • • •   83 SOHRAB RUSTUM V 767
          AND WITH A GRAVE MILD VOICE SOHRAB REPLIED • • •   84 SOHRAB RUSTUM V 771
          HE SPOKE THE MOTHER OF THE GODS REPLIED   • • • •   98 BALDER DEAD 1   111
          AND STRAIGHT THE MOTHER OF THE GODS REPLIED • •   99 BALDER DEAD 1   134
          AND STRAIGHT THE MOTHER OF THE GODS REPLIED • • 100 BALDER DEAD 1   187
          A DIRGE AND NANNA AND HER TRAIN REPLIED   • • • 103 BALDER DEAD 1   274
          HE SPAKE THE WARDER OF THE BRIDGE REPLIED • • • 108 BALDER DEAD 2   118
          HE SPOKE AND GRAVE REPLIED THE SOLEMN QUEEN • • 110 BALDER DEAD 2   201

REPLIED   (CONTINUED)
```
        AND STRAIGHT HIS NEIGHBOUR MOVED WITH WRATH REPLIED      114 BALDER DEAD 3        20
        THEN WITH A LOUDER LAUGH THE HAG REPLIED      .    .    .   123 BALDER DEAD 3       350
        HE SPAKE AND THE FLEET HERMOD THUS REPLIED    .    .    .   128 BALDER DEAD 3       514
        BUT WITH A LOUDER LAUGH THE HAG REPLIED       .    .    .   123 BALDER DEAD 3     V 350
        WHEN MY GREAT FATHER FELL THEY HAD REPLIED    .    .    .   383 MEROPE            1366
        SEVEN DAYS THE GOD REPLIED      .    .    .    .    .    .   448 WESTMIN ABBEY      137
```

REPLIES
```
        OUR RAPT SOULS ON YOUR REPLIES    .    .    .    .    .    .    34 NEW SIRENS        236
        OUR SAD SOULS ON YOUR REPLIES     .    .    .    .    .    .    34 NEW SIRENS      V 236
        AND HER PETULANT QUICK REPLIES    .    .    .    .    .    .   134 TRISTRAM 1        120
```

REPLY
```
        THE WORLD SPEAKS WELL YET MIGHT HER FOE REPLY      .    .    38 WORLDS TRIUMPHS     11
        WEAK YET NOT WEAK I MIGHT REPLY       .    .    .    .    .    59 RESIGNATION       255
        HE SPOKE AND SMILED AND GUDURZ MADE REPLY    .    .    .     68 SOHRAB RUSTUM       242
        AND GREATLY MOVED THEN RUSTUM MADE REPLY     .    .    .     68 SOHRAB RUSTUM       249
        SO QUICKLY AND WILL WAIT FOR NO REPLY        .    .    .    102 BALDER DEAD 1       242
        HE SPAKE AND BALDER UTTERD HIM REPLY    .    .    .    .    112 BALDER DEAD 2       262
        AND TO YOUR PRAYER SHE SENDS YOU THIS REPLY       .    .    114 BALDER DEAD 3        41
        AND THE FLEET-FOOTED HERMOD MADE REPLY       .    .    .    126 BALDER DEAD 3       468
        AND HIS BLACK BROTHER-BIRD FROM HENCE REPLY       .    .    127 BALDER DEAD 3       497
        THE MURMUR OF NATURE REPLY     .    .    .    .    .    .    230 YOUTH OF NATURE      78
        TO ROCK THE CATARACTS REPLY    .    .    .    .    .    .    289 RUGBY CHAPEL        92
        O CHILDREN WHAT DO YE REPLY    .    .    .    .    .    .    305 GRANDE CHARTR      193
        WHY DOST THOU FALTER AND MAKE HALF REPLY     .    .    .    362 MEROPE             930
        OR HOW REPLY TO THEE MY CHILD LAST-BORN      .    .    .    367 MEROPE            1041
        DIRECT TO THY DISSUASIONS I REPLY       .    .    .    .    389 MEROPE            1531
        BUT FAIR PROPOSAL MERITS FAIR REPLY     .    .    .    .    395 MEROPE            1728
        THAT SCANTY GRACE SHALL EARN THEE THIS REPLY      .    .    395 MEROPE            1732
```

REPORT
```
        HOWBEIT REPORT THY MESSAGE AND THEREWITH     .    .    .    112 BALDER DEAD 2       273
        BUT NONE HATH WORDS SHE CAN REPORT OF THEE   .    .    .    257 SCHOLAR-GIPSY        90
        BUT NONE HAS WORDS SHE CAN REPORT OF THEE    .    .    .    257 SCHOLAR-GIPSY      V 90
        HE BROUGHT REPORT THAT HIS OWN EYES HAD SEEN      .    .    363 MEROPE             958
        BY THE CONSTRUCTION AND REPORT OF MEN        .    .    .    398 MEROPE            1790
```

REPOSE
```
        FAR NOISIER SCHEMES ACCOMPLISHD IN REPOSE    .    .    .      1 QUIET WORK           7
        MANS NOISY SCHEMES ACCOMPLISHD IN REPOSE     .    .    .      1 QUIET WORK         V 7
        MANS NOISY FEATS ACCOMPLISHD IN REPOSE       .    .    .      1 QUIET WORK         V 7
        MANS NOISY WORK ACCOMPLISHD IN REPOSE        .    .    .      1 QUIET WORK         V 7
        MUCH NOISIER WORK ACCOMPLISHD IN REPOSE      .    .    .      1 QUIET WORK         V 7
        YOUR EYELIDS ON THE STONE WHERE YE REPOSE    .    .    .     18 CHURCH BROU 3       25
        A WIND OF PROMISE AND REPOSE     .    .    .    .    .    .    21 YOUTH AND CALM      12
        A GOAL WHICH GAIND MAY GIVE REPOSE      .    .    .    .     53 RESIGNATION         17
        ON EARTH THE CHRISTMAS-NIGHTS REPOSE    .    .    .    .    158 SAINT BRANDAN       66
        THE GODS HAVE SAID THAT REPOSE    .    .    .    .    .    199 FRAG DEJANEIRA      20
        ATTEND IT TO THE LAST REPOSE      .    .    .    .    .    .   225 EPILOG LAOCOON     151
        AND WE SAY THAT REPOSE HAS FLED       .    .    .    .    .   253 FUTURE             58
        AND NEAR AND REAL THE CHARM OF THY REPOSE    .    .    .    267 THYRSIS            149
        MIGHT WELL REPOSE    .    .    .    .    .    .    .    .    278 SOUTHERN NIGHT      92
        BREAK YOUR UNITED REPOSE    .    .    .    .    .    .    .   285 HAWORTH CHURCH     124
        MARS THE BENIGNANT REPOSE      .    .    .    .    .    .    293 HEINES GRAVE        44
        AND SOUGHT AND FOUND REPOSE    .    .    .    .    .    .    321 OBERMANN MORE      252
        NO TITLE FROM THE GODS TO WELFARE AND REPOSE      .    .    417 EMPEDOCLES I 2     161
        AND RELEGATE TO WORLDS YET DISTANT OUR REPOSE     .    .    425 EMPEDOCLES I 2     406
        WHERE IN PROUD REPOSE HE LAY    .    .    .    .    .    .   433 EMPEDOCLES II      162
        WITH NIGHT COMES SILENCE AND WITH THAT REPOSE     .    .        FRAGMENT 1           2
```

REPOSED
```
        THE LASHES ON THE CHEEKS REPOSED      .    .    .    .    .   141 TRISTRAM 1        339
        TO THE DIM HORIZON REPOSED     .    .    .    .    .    .    234 YOUTH OF MAN        77
```

REPOSES
```
        IN QUIET SHE REPOSES      .    .    .    .    .    .    .    .    20 REQUIESCAT         3
```

REPRESSD
```
        BOTH HAVE PASSD A YOUTH REPRESSD AND SAD     .    .    .    144 TRISTRAM 2         V 54
```

REPRESSEST
```
        STERNLY REPRESSEST THE BAD     .    .    .    .    .    .    .   287 RUGBY CHAPEL      51
```

REPRESSIVE
```
        THE LONG REPRESSIVE ATTITUDE OF RULE    .    .    .    .    334 MEROPE             154
```

REPROACH
```
        THE UNHAPPY WITH REPROACH EVEN IN THE GRAVE       .    .    124 BALDER DEAD 3       396
        THINE ATTITUDE OF COLD ESTRANGED REPROACH    .    .    .    332 MEROPE              85
```

REPROACHFULLY
```
        LAST-MURDERD WHO REPROACHFULLY WILT SAY      .    .    .    367 MEROPE            1042
```

REPROACHING
```
        OER HUMBLED PRIDE AND SELF-REPROACHING WOE   .    .    .    462 ALARIC AT ROME       4
```

REPROOF
```
        AND HIS MIRTH QUAILD NOT AT THE MILD REPROOF      .    .     12 MYCERINUS          114
```

REPROVED
    WITH BLANK INDIFFERENCE OR WITH BLAME REPROVED   • • 245 BURIED LIFE   19

REPULSED
    OF PEACE AND BEEN REPULSED WITH HATE AND SCORN   • • 360 MEROPE   881

REQUIEM
    TO CHANT THY REQUIEM WITH MORE PASSIONATE BREATH • • 471 ALARIC AT ROME   227

REQUIRE
    AND FOR SUCH DOING THEY REQUIRE NOT EYES • • • •   7 REP FRIEND   8
    AND FOR SUCH DOING THEY REQUIRE NO EYES • • •   7 REP FRIEND   V   8
    TO FIND WITH YOU THE JOY WE IN VAIN HERE REQUIRE • • 425 EMPEDOCLES I 2   381

REQUIRED
    HER MIRTH THE WORLD REQUIRED • • • • • • •   21 REQUIESCAT   5
    THE FIERCELY-REQUIRED VICTIM • • • • • • • 400 MEROPE   1869
    FINISHD THEIR WORK AND THEN A MEED REQUIRED   • • 448 WESTMIN ABBEY   136
    HAD FINISHD AND A MEED OF PRICE REQUIRED • • • 448 WESTMIN ABBEY V 136

REQUIRES
    WHICH LAID THEE LOW FOR BLOOD REQUIRES BLOOD   • • 404 MEROPE   1987

REQUIREST
    STERNLY REQUIREST A MAN • • • • • • • 343 MEROPE   406

REQUITE
    REQUITE HIM WORDS SEVERE FOR SEEMING KIND • • • • 349 MEROPE   551

RESERVES
    FOR THE KINGS PRIVATE EAR RESERVES LIKE THIS   • • 364 MEROPE   965

RESIDES
    THE FIRE WHICH IN THE HEART RESIDES • • • • 241 MORALITY   2
    THE FIRE THAT IN THE HEART RESIDES • • • • • 241 MORALITY   V   2

RESIGN
    NOR WHEN WE WILL RESIGN • • • • • • • 310 OBERMANN   136
    MUST LABOUR MUST RESIGN • • • • • • • 319 OBERMANN MORE   186
    WHICH HENCEFORTH WE RESIGN • • • • • • 423 EMPEDOCLES I 2   345

RESIGND
    HALF REFUSED AND HALF RESIGND • • • • •   23 MEMORY-PICTURE   35
    HATH MADE OR BIRTH HATH FOUND RESIGND   • • •   53 RESIGNATION   27
    BE PASSIONATE HOPES NOT ILL RESIGND • • • •   59 RESIGNATION   243
    SO MUCH UNLEARNT SO MUCH RESIGND • • • 301 GRANDE CHARTR   75
    SAD PATIENT AND RESIGND • • • • • • • 321 OBERMANN MORE   254
    EYED THEE WITH A SOUL RESIGND • • • • • 453 POOR MATTHIAS   37

RESOLVE
    RESOLVE TO BE THYSELF AND KNOW THAT HE   • • • 240 SELF-DEPENDENCE   31
    I AUGUR THOU WILT HEAR SOME BOLD RESOLVE • • • 351 MEROPE   610
    GIVE THEM COHESION PURPOSE AND RESOLVE   • • 382 MEROPE   1323
    OF SOLITARY THOUGHT UNSHARED RESOLVE • • • • 403 MEROPE   1969
    WITH HEART NEW STRUNG AND STERN RESOLVE HE STOOD • • 473 CROMWELL   66

RESOLVES
    WHOSE VAGUE RESOLVES NEVER HAVE BEEN FULFILLD   • • 260 SCHOLAR-GIPSY   175
    WHOSE WEAK RESOLVES NEVER HAVE BEEN FULFILLD   • • 260 SCHOLAR-GIPSY V 175

RESOUND
    OR OF THE HORSES OF THE GODS RESOUND • • • • • 108 BALDER DEAD 2   120
    ONCE MORE AND ONCE MORE SEEM TO MAKE RESOUND   • • 201 PHILOMELA   25

RESOUNDS
    HARK THROUGH THE ALLEY RESOUNDS • • • • • 293 HEINES GRAVE   37

RESOURCE
    AND NOT THE INFINITE RESOURCE • • • • • • 450 GEISTS GRAVE   23

RESPECT
    NOTHING BUT THAT WE SEE IT WHAT RESPECT   • • • •   LUCRETIUS 5   8

RESPITE
    AH TELL THEM OF MY RESPITE TOO • • • • • • 157 SAINT BRANDAN   28

RESPLENDENT
    THE OTHER HIS RESPLENDENT PRIME   • • • • • 132 TRISTRAM 1   71

REST
    NATURE IS FICKLE MAN HATH NEED OF REST   • • •   5 HARMONY NATURE   9
    FOOL IF THOU CANST NOT PASS HER REST HER SLAVE • •   5 HARMONY NATURE   14
    THE REST I GIVE TO JOY EVEN WHILE I SPEAK   • •   10 MYCERINUS   55
    SO REST FOR EVER REST O PRINCELY PAIR   • • •   17 CHURCH BROU 3   1
    SO REST FOR EVER REST O PRINCELY PAIR   • • •   17 CHURCH BROU 3   1
    AND EASE FROM SHAME AND REST FROM FEAR   • • •   21 YOUTH AND CALM   2
    IT DREAMS A REST IF NOT MORE DEEP • • • •   22 YOUTH AND CALM   20
    BUT AH THOUGH PEACE AND REST FROM FEAR   • • •   21 YOUTH AND CALM V   2
    IT ASKS A REST IF NOT MORE DEEP   • • • • •   22 YOUTH AND CALM V 20

REST   (CONTINUED)

BRINGING NO REST	36	VOICE	16
LIKE THE REST HIS WIT WITH READING	49	SECOND BEST	15
LET THE TWO ARMIES REST TO-DAY BUT I	62	SOHRAB RUSTUM	55
CANST THOU NOT REST AMONG THE TARTAR CHIEFS	63	SOHRAB RUSTUM	66
AND REST MY AGE AND HEAR OF SOHRABS FAME	68	SOHRAB RUSTUM	239
BUT THEY WENT ODIN FIRST THE REST BEHIND	105	BALDER DEAD 2	35
AND LED THE WAY ON SLEIPNER AND THE REST	115	BALDER DEAD 3	59
THOR CAME ON FOOT THE REST ON HORSEBACK RODE	120	BALDER DEAD 3	218
I REST THE THRALL OF HELA AND ENDURE	129	BALDER DEAD 3	545
WHICH WILL NEVER LET HIM REST	138	TRISTRAM 1	246
BUT THEY SLEEP IN SHELTERD REST	140	TRISTRAM 1	327
THAT WILL NEVER LET HIM REST	138	TRISTRAM 1	V 246
TO REST UNGLOVED ON HER GREEN RIDING-DRESS	154	TRISTRAM 3	175
O BRANDAN TO THIS HOUR OF REST	158	SAINT BRANDAN	71
AH MIGHT I ALWAYS REST UNSEEN	205	CALAIS SANDS	31
OH MIGHT I ALWAYS REST UNSEEN	205	CALAIS SANDS	V 31
AH LET THEM REST THOSE EYES ON MINE	206	RIVER	7
ON MINE LET REST THAT LOVELY HAND	206	RIVER	8
AND ON THY SHOULDER REST MY HEAD	206	RIVER	12
AS KIND TO ALL THE REST AS ME	208	LONGING	V 8
TOO KEEN TO REST TOO WEAK TO FIND	217	NAMELESS EPIT	V
AFAR IN REST THE CATTLE LAY	224	EPILOG LAOCOON	109
ITS PAIN AND PLEASURE REST AND STRIFE	225	EPILOG LAOCOON	144
WHICH NEITHER DEADENS INTO REST	243	SUMMER NIGHT	28
FROM THEIR TIRED HANDS AND REST	243	SUMMER NIGHT	44
AND THE REST A FEW	243	SUMMER NIGHT	51
THAT NEITHER DEADENS INTO REST	243	SUMMER NIGHT	V 28
WHICH NEVER DEADENS INTO REST	243	SUMMER NIGHT	V 28
TO WHICH THY LIGHT WORDS BRING NO REST	245	BURIED LIFE	7
TRICKD IN DISGUISES ALIEN TO THE REST	245	BURIED LIFE	21
THAT FLYING AND ELUSIVE SHADOW REST	247	BURIED LIFE	93
THEN TO THEIR HAPPY REST THEY PASS	249	KENSINGTON GARD	33
AND THE TIRED MEN AND DOGS ALL GONE TO REST	255	SCHOLAR-GIPSY	7
WHICH THOUGH IT GIVES NO BLISS YET SPOILS FOR REST	261	SCHOLAR-GIPSY	223
IT IRKD HIM TO BE HERE HE COULD NOT REST	264	THYRSIS	41
IF MEN PROCURED THEE TROUBLE GAVE THEE REST	269	THYRSIS	215
SIGHT OF THE REST IN THE STORM	289	RUGBY CHAPEL	119
LEAVING THE REST IN THE WILD	290	RUGBY CHAPEL	127
FOR REST IN THIS OUTBUILDING NEAR	300	GRANDE CHARTR	27
WITH NOWHERE YET TO REST MY HEAD	302	GRANDE CHARTR	87
NO MORE SO HE BUT REST LIKE THEE	311	OBERMANN	159
INVITE TO REST THE TRAVELLER THERE	313	OBERMANN MORE	19
MY SOUL HIS EYES DID REST	314	OBERMANN MORE	68
RELUCTANTLY THE REST BUT AGAINST ALL	337	MEROPE	257
BRING TO ME SAFE LET THE REST	348	MEROPE	535
NO CERTAIN NEWS IF LIKE THE REST IT RUN	350	MEROPE	600
TO ME AND THE MESSENIANS LEAVE THE REST	391	MEROPE	1593
TO-DAY I REIGN THE REST I LEAVE TO FATE	397	MEROPE	1776
THE REST TO ME IS LITTLE YET SINCE THAT	401	MEROPE	1891
BRING TO HIS MOTHER THE REST I COMMIT	348	MEROPE	V
LET US REST HERE AND NOW EMPEDOCLES	412	EMPEDOCLES I 2	7
AND THE TIRED CENTAURS COME TO REST	414	EMPEDOCLES I 2	63
AND REST IN THE IMMORTAL MEAD	414	EMPEDOCLES I 2	75
WE REST OUR FACULTIES	423	EMPEDOCLES I 2	337
NOR DOES BEING WEARY PROVE THAT HE HAS WHERE TO REST	424	EMPEDOCLES I 2	351
TAKE DOWN WITH THEE THE REST TO CATANA	428	EMPEDOCLES I 2	466
NEVER TO CEASE TO WRITHE AND TRY TO REST	430	EMPEDOCLES II	60
THE REST OF IMMORTALS	443	EMPEDOCLES II	463
I WOULD NOT BREAK THY REST NOR CHANGE THY DOOM	449	WESTMIN ABBEY	166
ONE LITTLE YEAR THAT RESTLESS SOUL SHALL REST	469	ALARIC AT ROME	193
AND REST HIS WEARY EYES ON THE GREEN LAND AND THEE	470	ALARIC AT ROME	222
WHO SCALE THE CLOUD-CAPT HEIGHT OR SINK TO REST	472	CROMWELL	11
MIGHT PAINT THE CALM SWEET PEACE THE REST OF HOME	475	CROMWELL	113
O PLEASANT REST IF ONCE THE RACE WERE RUN	475	CROMWELL	119
HIS HANDS WERE FOLDED LIKE A SAINT AT REST	476	CROMWELL	168
LEAVES HIM NO REST AND CHANGE HE WILL	484	ROME-SICKNESS	26

RESTED

OF HER EYES AS THEY RESTED ON THINE	231	YOUTH OF NATURE	114
RESTED AS UNDER THE BOUGHS	287	RUGBY CHAPEL	32
RESTED BY SLUMBER AND HEART	297	HEINES GRAVE	177
AND AS WE ATE AND RESTED THERE WE TALKD	356	MEROPE	755
THEN RESTED LISTENING SILENTLY	480	HAYSWATER BOAT	28

RESTING

ON SOME GREAT ROAD OR RESTING IN AN INN	116	BALDER DEAD 3	117
NO FAIRER RESTING-PLACE A MAN COULD FIND	155	TRISTRAM 3	210
THE KINE WERE RESTING IN THE SHADE	222	EPILOG LAOCOON	40
AND THINE EYES RESTING ON THE MOONLIT STREAM	257	SCHOLAR-GIPSY	80
EMERGE AND RESTING ON THE MOONLIT PALES	261	SCHOLAR-GIPSY	217
AND RESTING THERE TO BREATHE I WATCHD THE CHASE	357	MEROPE	797
AND RESTING THERE TO BREATHE I SAW BELOW	357	MEROPE	V 797

RESTLESS

IN HARMONY WITH NATURE RESTLESS FOOL	5	HARMONY NATURE	1
BUT THEN THEY DECKD A RESTLESS GHOST	146	TRISTRAM 2	116
TOO STRANGE TOO RESTLESS TOO UNTAMED	178	FAREWELL	20
WERE RESTLESS ONCE BUT LONG AGO	208	ON THE RHINE	23
BUT THE SAME RESTLESS PACINGS TO AND FRO	242	SUMMER NIGHT	23

RESTLESS   (CONTINUED)
        A THIRST TO SPEND OUR FIRE AND RESTLESS FORCE   • •   246 BURIED LIFE   49
        HAVE RESTLESS HEARTS ONE THROB THE LESS   • • •   303 GRANDE CHARTR   144
        I PRAY THE FURIES EVER-RESTLESS BAND   • • • • •   349 MEROPE   569
        BUT A NAKED ETERNALLY RESTLESS MIND   • • • •   438 EMPEDOCLES II   330
        ONE LITTLE YEAR THAT RESTLESS SOUL SHALL REST   • •   469 ALARIC AT ROME   193
        WHEN RESTLESSNESS IS RESTLESS GOOD   • • • • •   484 ROME-SICKNESS   27
        RESTLESS HEART IN THIS RETREAT • • • • • • • •   META CLOISTER   30

RESTLESSNESS
        THE DEPTH OF THAT CONSUMING RESTLESSNESS   • • • •   238 PROGRESS   V
        AT LEAST THE RESTLESSNESS THE PAIN   • • • • •   302 GRANDE CHARTR   104
        WHEN RESTLESSNESS IS RESTLESS GOOD   • • • • •   484 ROME-SICKNESS   27

RESTORE
        RESTORE HIM FOR WHAT PART FULFILS HE HERE   • • • •   110 BALDER DEAD 2   194
        THITHER RESTORE HIM FOR HIS PLACE IS THERE   • • •   110 BALDER DEAD 2   200
        BUT WILL RESTORE IF ALL THINGS GIVE HIM TEARS   • •   123 BALDER DEAD 3   348
        MIGHT THY DYING KNIGHT RESTORE • • • • • • •   132 TRISTRAM 1   79
        LET A DREAM LIKE THIS RESTORE • • • • • • • •   135 TRISTRAM 1   159
        AH CALM ME RESTORE ME   • • • • • • • • •   177 PARTING   83
        CAN THY PENCIL O ARTIST RESTORE   • • • • •   231 YOUTH OF NATURE   110
        TIME MAY RESTORE US IN HIS COURSE   • • • • •   272 MEMORIAL VERSES   60
        TIME MAY RESTORE US IN ITS COURSE   • • • • •   272 MEMORIAL VERSES   V 60
        OR JUST THY LITTLE SELF RESTORE   • • • • •   450 GEISTS GRAVE   28

RESTORED
        SO IT RESTORED THEE NANNA TO MY SIDE   • • • • •   103 BALDER DEAD 1   307
        HEAR HOW TO HEAVEN MAY BALDER BE RESTORED   • • •   111 BALDER DEAD 2   233
        RISK FROM MY NEW-RESTORED MY ONLY SON   • • • •   387 MEROPE   1456

RESTORER
        YET SHALL RESTORER APPEAR TO THE RACE   • • • •   344 MEROPE   453

RESTORERS
        YET SHALL RESTORERS APPEAR TO THE RACE   • • • •   344 MEROPE   V 453

RESTORES
        HE WHO RESTORES THEE SHALL BE • • • • • • • •   360 MEROPE   903

RESTS
        AND THY DARK MOURNFUL VISION RESTS ON ME   • • • •   41 GIPSY CHILD   V 16
        FEEBLE HE RESTS IF FEEBLE HE WAS BORN   • • • •   LUCRETIUS 3   7

RESULTS
        WITH LARGE RESULTS SO LITTLE RIFE   • • • • • •   60 RESIGNATION   262

RESUME
        SHORTLY YE SHALL RESUME THEM WITH YOUR QUEEN   • •   332 MEROPE   78

RESUMED
        AND SOON THY FOOT RESUMED ITS WANDERING WAY   • •   269 THYRSIS   229

RETAIN
        AH RETAIN WE ALL WE CAN • • • • • • • •   24 MEMORY-PICTURE   60
        NO WE MAY SUFFER DEEPLY YET RETAIN   • • • • •   153 TRISTRAM 3   116
        HIS BELOVED ARGIVE SEER WOULD ZEUS RETAIN   • • •   197 FRAG ANTIGONE   82
        I WILL NOT SAY THAT YOUR MILD DEEPS RETAIN   • • •   244 SUMMER NIGHT   83
        NO MORE AND WE RETAIN   • • • • • • • • •   273 EDW QUILLINAN   14
        UNALTERD TO RETAIN • • • • • • • • • • •   419 EMPEDOCLES I 2   199

RETAIND
        A GESTURE ANYTHING RETAIND   • • • • • • •   185 TERRACE BERNE   39
        RETAIND SO LITTLE IN THY CARELESS DEPTHS   • • • •   LUCRETIUS 1   4

RETAINING
        FOR ALAS HE LEFT US EACH RETAINING   • • • • • •   210 SELF-DECEPTION   17

RETIRE
        BE COUNSELLD AND RETIRE   • • • • • • • • •   174 MEETING   12
        AT LAST THE ENCIRCLING TREES RETIRE   • • • • •   300 GRANDE CHARTR   21

RETIRED
        FOR MOST I KNOW THOU LOVST RETIRED GROUND   • • • •   257 SCHOLAR-GIPSY   71
        WHICH BATHED OUR LIFE RETIRED • • • • • • • •   319 OBERMANN MORE   190

RETORT
        AND UNDAUNTED RETORT   • • • • • • • • • •   293 HEINES GRAVE   33

RETRACE
        AH TIS WELL HE SHOULD RETRACE • • • • • • • •   137 TRISTRAM 1   211

RETREAT
        EXPECT NO WAVERING NO RETREAT NO CHANGE   • • • •   342 MEROPE   378
        RESTLESS HEART IN THIS RETREAT • • • • • • • •   META CLOISTER   30

RETREATING
        RETREATING TO THE BREATH • • • • • • • • • • •   211 DOVER BEACH   26

RETREATS
    AND WONDER IF THOU HAUNTST THEIR SHY RETREATS   257 SCHOLAR-GIPSY   70

RETURN
    I GO AND I RETURN NOT BUT THE WILL   11 MYCERINUS   74
    ARE RARE AH MOST LOVES BUT FLOW ONCE AND RETURN   19 MODERN SAPPHO   16
    ERE THE LONG EVENING CLOSE THOU SHALT RETURN   44 GIPSY CHILD   67
    BUT ALL AT NIGHT RETURN TO ODINS HALL   105 BALDER DEAD 2   17
    TO BE FULFILLD NOR MY RETURN AS SURE   112 BALDER DEAD 2   269
    WORSE WAS THAT WAY TO GO THAN TO RETURN   113 BALDER DEAD 2   291
    FOR HIM FOR OTHERS ALL RETURN IS BARRD   113 BALDER DEAD 2   292
    NINE DAYS HE TOOK TO GO TWO TO RETURN   113 BALDER DEAD 2   293
    ONE DAY THE WANDERING ODER WILL RETURN   116 BALDER DEAD 3   115
    STILL LIFTED WELL WAS HIS RETURN FOREKNOWN   124 BALDER DEAD 3   378
    FROM THE DEEP GLOOM WHERE I WILL NOW RETURN   125 BALDER DEAD 3   415
    OF AGES AND MY LATE RETURN TO LIGHT   128 BALDER DEAD 3   511
    AT THEIR RETURN UP THE HIGH STRAND   211 DOVER BEACH   11
    AT THEIR RETURN UP THE STEEP STRAND   211 DOVER BEACH   V   11
    AT THEIR RETURN UP THE BARRD STRAND   211 DOVER BEACH   V   11
    NOT TILL THE HOURS OF LIGHT RETURN   241 MORALITY   11
    WHAT MATTERS IT NEXT YEAR HE WILL RETURN   265 THYRSIS   72
    ORDER COURAGE RETURN   292 RUGBY CHAPEL   201
    THAT DELPHIC HEST TO RETURN   343 MEROPE   422
    A RETURN O FATHER GIVE TO THY BOY   348 MEROPE   542
    WHAT KEEPS HIM IN ARCADIA FROM RETURN   350 MEROPE   602
    THE KING RETURN AND FIND YOU PRATING HERE   386 MEROPE   1443
    TO WITNESS OFFERING HIM RETURN AND POWER   394 MEROPE   1696
    TO THE PRESERVER ZEUS LET ME RETURN   395 MEROPE   1723
    THE DEAD RETURN TO LIFE   416 EMPEDOCLES I 2   124
    THOU WILT RETURN TO-MORROW TO THE CITY   428 EMPEDOCLES I 2   470
    EVERYTHING WILL RETURN   439 EMPEDOCLES II   332
    AND THEN WE SHALL UNWILLINGLY RETURN   440 EMPEDOCLES II   364
    ONCE MORE THINE IMMEMORIAL GLEAM RETURN   449 WESTMIN ABBEY   175
    ONE DAY THINE IMMEMORIAL GLEAM RETURN   449 WESTMIN ABBEY   V 175

RETURND
    THIS SAID HE LEFT THEM AND RETURND NO MORE   256 SCHOLAR-GIPSY   51
    OUR YOUTH RETURND FOR THERE WAS SHED   271 MEMORIAL VERSES   54
    ANNOUNCES ME THEIR RIGHTFUL PRINCE RETURND   383 MEROPE   1355
    THEN HOME RETURND ONCE MORE DEPART   460 KAISER DEAD   51

RETURNING
    OR ARE THOSE OLD THOUGHTS RETURNING   30 NEW SIRENS   135
    SOHRAB RETURNING FROM THE TARTAR CAMP   79 SOHRAB RUSTUM   594
    RETURNING HOME OVER THE SALT BLUE SEA   85 SOHRAB RUSTUM   833
    RETURNING HOME ON SUMMER-NIGHTS HAVE MET   257 SCHOLAR-GIPSY   73
    THAT I TO-DAY RETURNING FIND MYSELF   385 MEROPE   1410
    THE UNKNOWN PASSENGER RETURNING STANDS   445 WESTMIN ABBEY   43

RETURNS
    AND DARKNESS RETURNS TO OUR EYES   229 YOUTH OF NATURE   58
    THE PAST RETURNS THEY FEEL   235 YOUTH OF MAN   93
    BROUGHT BY THE WEST-WIND RETURNS   285 HAWORTH CHURCH   114

RETURNST
    RETURNST THOU IN HER HOUR OF BIRTH   315 OBERMANN MORE   79

REVEAL
    ARE EVEN LOVERS POWERLESS TO REVEAL   245 BURIED LIFE   14

REVEALD
    BEFORE THY FACE THIS DAY AND WERE REVEALD   72 SOHRAB RUSTUM   371
    IN MINE OWN BREAST AND HAVE TO NONE REVEALD   121 BALDER DEAD 3   287
    IN MY OWN BREAST AND HAVE TO NONE REVEALD   121 BALDER DEAD 3   V 287
    THEIR THOUGHTS FOR FEAR THAT IF REVEALD   245 BURIED LIFE   17
    AND THIS PERFIDIOUS MURDER WHO REVEALD   364 MEROPE   V
    SPOKE AND REVEALD THAT TRAFFIC AND THE TRAITOR   365 MEROPE   V

REVEALING
    REVEALING ALL THE TUMULT OF THE FEAST   11 MYCERINUS   96
    THINE OLD STRENGTH REVEALING   39 STAGIRIUS   37
    THY TRUE STRENGTH REVEALING   39 STAGIRIUS   V   37
    BUT CLEAR AS WORDS CAN MAKE REVEALING   225 EPILOG LAOCOON   137

REVEALS
    OR THE VOICE WHICH REVEALS WHAT YOU ARE   230 YOUTH OF NATURE   65

REVEL
    KINGS HOLD REVEL GALLANTS MEET   14 CHURCH BROU 1   54
    TEMPTS NOT THE REVEL BLITHE   219 BACCHANALIA 1   44
    THEN SHALL THE REVEL AGAIN   360 MEROPE   893

REVELATION
    REVELATION MAKES HIM SURE   215 PIS-ALLER   2

REVELLD
    SO SIX LONG YEARS HE REVELLD NIGHT AND DAY   12 MYCERINUS   122

REVELLERS
    GIRT WITH A THRONG OF REVELLERS BENT HIS WAY   11 MYCERINUS   83
    OR WITH THE REVELLERS FROM THE MOUNTAIN-TOWNS   406 EMPEDOCLES I 1   8

REVELLING
    WITH A GAY REVELLING BAND HE BREAKS FROM THEM   • •   412 EMPEDOCLES I 2   16

REVELS
    REVELS MORE DEEP JOY KEENER THAN THEIR OWN • • • •   10 MYCERINUS   66
    AND YOUR TRAGIC-VAUNTED REVELS • • • • • •   26 NEW SIRENS   19

REVENGE
    WHAT PRATE IS THIS OF FATHERS AND REVENGE • • • •   78 SOHRAB RUSTUM   577
    WHO SADLY ASK ME WHAT IF NOT REVENGE • • • •   367 MEROPE   1039
    AND EYEBALLS STARING FOR REVENGE IN VAIN • • •   373 MEROPE   1175
    MY FIRST STROKE OF REVENGE HAD NEARLY FALLEN • •   377 MEROPE   1224
    REMEMBER TO REVENGE HIS DEATH I COME • • • •   378 MEROPE   1241
    AH REVENGE • • • • • • • •   378 MEROPE   1242
    A NEVER-CHANGING INDEX TO REVENGE • • • •   381 MEROPE   1317
    TO RALLY THEM AND LEAD THEM TO REVENGE • •   383 MEROPE   1365
    HIS JUST REVENGE TO AN UNNATURAL DEED • •   385 MEROPE   1417
    SINCE FROM THY FAITHFUL SUBJECTS WHAT REVENGE •   386 MEROPE   1432
    TO BREATHE A SYLLABLE TO BAR REVENGE • • • •   389 MEROPE   1528

REVENGEFUL
    IN ME THE FEVER OF REVENGEFUL HATE • • • • •   387 MEROPE   1466

REVERE
    BY THOSE WHOM I REVERE • • • • • • • •   354 MEROPE   697

REVERED
    CONSTRUED HIS ACTS INDULGENTLY REVERED • • •   337 MEROPE   255

REVERENCE
    TO REVERENCE YOUR LINEAGE MORE TO OBEY • • •   339 MEROPE   303
    WITH PITY NAY WITH REVERENCE YET BEWARE • • •   341 MEROPE   361
    I HIDE NOT EVEN THIS THE REVERENCE DEEP • • •   387 MEROPE   1474
    POPULAR REVERENCE TO THESE RECENT LINES • • •   390 MEROPE   1564

REVERENT
    POOR MAX WITH DOWNCAST REVERENT HEAD • • • • •   460 KAISER DEAD   67

REVERENTIAL
    MY CRIME THAT RAPT IN REVERENTIAL AWE • • •   9 MYCERINUS   8
    AND YET WITH REVERENTIAL AWE • • • • •   270 MEMORIAL VERSES   12
    SAD REVERENTIAL HOMAGE HAD OUR PRINCE • • •   356 MEROPE   761

REVERIE
    OF REVERIE OF SHADE OF PRAYER • • • • • •   306 GRANDE CHARTR   206

REVERIES
    OR HIS ENDLESS REVERIES • • • • • • • •   137 TRISTRAM 1   219

REVERING
    REVERING WHAT SHE CANNOT SOOTHE • • • • •   283 HAWORTH CHURCH   V

REVERSAL
    ITS DUE REVERSAL • • • • • • • • •   51 CONSOLATION   54

REVERSE
    BUT NEXT WE WOULD REVERSE • • • • • •   422 EMPEDOCLES I 2   312

REVERSION
    AND TO MY SON REVERSION TO THY THRONE • • •   340 MEROPE   334

REVIEW
    PATIENT OF A LONG REVIEW • • • • • • •   30 NEW SIRENS   132

REVIEWS
    REVIEWS AND RANKS HIS MOTLEY BANDS • • • •   53 RESIGNATION   45

REVISIT
    GOOD FRIEND I SHALL REVISIT CATANA • • • •   428 EMPEDOCLES I 2   473

REVIVE
    SEEK THIS REVIVE UNITE IT GIVE IT HOPE • • •   331 MEROPE   45
    HOW MIGHT NOT SUCH A SIGHT AS THIS REVIVE • • •   383 MEROPE   1358

REVIVED
    FOLLY REVIVED RE-FURBISHD SOPHISTRIES • • •   449 WESTMIN ABBEY   159

REVIVING
    NOR DID REVIVING THEBES • • • • • • •   229 YOUTH OF NATURE   46

REVIVST
    TWIXT VICE AND VIRTUE REVIVST • • • • • •   288 RUGBY CHAPEL   55

REVOKE
    THE DOOM THEY PASS REVOKE NOT NOR DELAY • • •   10 MYCERINUS   70
    IF I PRAYD WRONGLY I REVOKE THE PRAYER • • •   348 MEROPE   547
    REVOKE ASSUAGE HER SENTENCE • • • • • •   398 MEROPE   1807

REVOLUTIONS
          IN THE SURE REVOLUTIONS OF THE WORLD • • • • • •   428 EMPEDOCLES I 2   472

REVOLVING
          WITH FOLDED HANDS REVOLVING THINGS TO COME • • • •   98 BALDER DEAD 1   93
          REVOLVING INLY   • • • • • • • • • • •   190 STRAYED REVEL   141

REWARD
          FOR THESE ARE ALL THEIR OWN REWARD   • • • • • •   273 EDW QUILLINAN   5

REWARDS
          AND WHEN THIS BOON REWARDS THE DEAD   • • • • • •   21 YOUTH AND CALM   7

RHEA
          PAST ARNE SPRING WHERE RHEA GAVE THE BABE • • • •   355 MEROPE   736

RHINE
          THE HEATHEN SAXONS ON THE RHINE   • • • • • •   138 TRISTRAM 1   253
          TO SWITZERLAND TO BADEN TO THE RHINE • • • • • •   167 RACHEL 1   10
          AND RACHELS SWITZERLAND HER RHINE IS HERE • • • •   167 RACHEL 1   14
          OF FLANDERS TO THE STORIED RHINE   • • • • • •   205 CALAIS SANDS   34
          OF FLANDERS TO THE ANCIENT RHINE   • • • • • •   205 CALAIS SANDS   V 34
          AND AS THIS BRIMMD UNWRINKLED RHINE • • • • • •   208 ON THE RHINE   12

RHONE
          THE MISTS ARE ON THE RHONE   • • • • • • • •   306 OBERMANN   8

RHONES
          WHICH THE RHONES MURMUR FILLS • • • • • • • • •   324 OBERMANN MORE   344

RHYME
          DEAD AND NEITHER PROSE NOR RHYME   • • • • • •   453 POOR MATTHIAS   27
          A RIVAL RHYME   • • • • • • • • • • • • •   458 KAISER DEAD   6

RHYMES
          WHY WITH THESE MOURNFUL RHYMES • • • • • • • •   46 WORLD QUIETIST   4

RIBBON
          A RIBBON BLUE   • • • • • • • • • • • •   459 KAISER DEAD   16

RIBBOND
          EACH HER RIBBOND TAMBOURINE   • • • • • • •   433 EMPEDOCLES II   155

RIBBONS
          STRAW HATS BEDECKD THEIR HEADS WITH RIBBONS BLUE • •   25 DREAM   24

RICE
          WITH SILKEN RAIMENT STORE OF RICE   • • • • • •   94 SICK KING BOKH   194

RICH
          THE PRAISE OF GODS RICH BOON AND LENGTH OF DAYS • •   11 MYCERINUS   78
          IN THE RICH LANGUOR OF LONG SUMMER-DAYS   • • •   12 MYCERINUS   117
          FROM THE RICH PAINTED WINDOWS OF THE NAVE • • •   17 CHURCH BROU 3   5
          RICH TO-MORROW AS TO-DAY • • • • • • • •   22 MEMORY-PICTURE   3
          ONLY HIS HELM WAS RICH INLAID WITH GOLD   • • •   69 SOHRAB RUSTUM   267
          DOWN THROUGH THE MIDDLE OF A RICH MANS CORN • •   70 SOHRAB RUSTUM   294
          AS SOME RICH WOMAN ON A WINTERS MORN • • • •   70 SOHRAB RUSTUM   302
          LIKE SOME RICH HYACINTH WHICH BY THE SCYTHE • •   80 SOHRAB RUSTUM   634
          AS SOME RICH LADY ON A WINTERS MORN • • • •   70 SOHRAB RUSTUM   V 302
          GLEAMS SO RICH IN THE LIGHT OF THE FIRE   • • •   131 TRISTRAM 1   25
          I KNOW HER BY HER RICH SILK DRESS   • • • •   132 TRISTRAM 1   52
          SO SLIGHT A FORM IN SO RICH A DRESS • • • •   131 TRISTRAM 1   V
          MANTLES WITH THOSE RICH FURS DEEP GLISTERING • •   150 TRISTRAM 3   40
          THE RICH SHE HAD LET PASS WITH FROZEN STARE • •   170 WEST LONDON   8
          FURROWS THE RICH SOIL HERE AND THERE • • • •   191 STRAYED REVEL   176
          SUMPTUOUS ITS CLOTHING RICH ITS FARE • • • •   315 OBERMANN MORE   87
          IN A RICH CHAMBER ON A HAPPY BED   • • • •   373 MEROPE   1178
          OF RICH SOIL CHOSEN BY CRAFT   • • • • • •   399 MEROPE   1848
          NOT IN RICH ENGLAND BENT BUT TO MAKE POUR • • •   480 HUNGARIAN NAT   2

RICHES
          RICHES WE WISH TO GET   • • • • • • • • •   420 EMPEDOCLES I 2   227

RICK
          BY BARN IN THRESHING-TIME BY NEW-BUILT RICK   • •   263 THYRSIS   34

RID
          AND RID HIM OF THE PRESENCE OF HIMSELF   • • • •   435 EMPEDOCLES II   223

RIDDLE
          LEAVES HER RIDDLE HALF UNKNOWN • • • • • • •   28 NEW SIRENS   76

RIDE
          RIDE OUT TO CHURCH FROM CHAMBERY   • • • • •   17 CHURCH BROU 2   21
          AND RIDE ACROSS THE DRAWBRIDGE WITH THY HOUNDS • •   18 CHURCH BROU 3   10
          TO RIDE BUT SLEIPNER ODINS HORSE ALONE   • • •   99 BALDER DEAD 1   138
          WHICH BRANCHES FROM THE NORTH OF HEAVEN AND RIDE • •   99 BALDER DEAD 1   144
          THEIR HORSES FETLOCK-DEEP IN BLOOD THEY RIDE • •   105 BALDER DEAD 2   25
          BUT HERMOD THOU TAKE SLEIPNER AND RIDE DOWN • •   106 BALDER DEAD 2   45
          AND SLEIPNER ODINS HORSE IS THIS I RIDE   • • •   108 BALDER DEAD 2   115
          RIDE ON PASS FREE BUT HE BY THIS IS THERE • • •   108 BALDER DEAD 2   134

RIDE   (CONTINUED)
        THEN MOUNTED SLEIPNER AND SET FORTH TO RIDE   • •   112 BALDER DEAD 2   284
        AND TOOK THEIR HORSES AND SET FORTH TO RIDE   • •   119 BALDER DEAD 3   215
        RIDE BACK AND TELL IN HEAVEN THIS HEAVY NEWS   • •   124 BALDER DEAD 3   371
        RIDE DOWN AND BATHE MY HOT BROW IN THE FLOOD   • •   139 TRISTRAM 1   282
        ONWARD WE MOVED AND REACHD THE RIDE   • • • •   224 EPILOG LAOCOON   107
        THIS THROUGH THE RIDE UPON HIS STEED   • • • • •   224 EPILOG LAOCOON   115
        AS IN OLD DAYS JOVIAL AND TALKING RIDE   • • •   267 THYRSIS   154
        THE BRIDGE IS CROSSD AND SLOW WE RIDE   • • •   299 GRANDE CHARTR   5
        YE AND THE PURE DARK ETHER WHERE YE RIDE   • • •   438 EMPEDOCLES II   304
        SINCE THAT STRANGE CREW DID RIDE AFLOAT   • • •   480 HAYSWATER BOAT   36

RIDER
        ON HIS BROAD BACK NO LESSER RIDER BORE   • • • •   107 BALDER DEAD 2   74

RIDERS
        THEE AT THE FERRY OXFORD RIDERS BLITHE   • • • •   257 SCHOLAR-GIPSY   72

RIDES
        WHAT FOUL FIEND RIDES THEE ON INTO THE FIGHT   • •   137 TRISTRAM 1   239

RIDGD
        WHERE THE RIDGD PINE-DARKEND ROOTS   • • • • •   433 EMPEDOCLES II   V 137
        WHENCE THE RIDGD PINE-MUFFLED ROOTS   • • • •   433 EMPEDOCLES II   V 137
        WHERE THE RIDGD PINE-WOODED ROOTS   • • • • •   433 EMPEDOCLES II   V 137

RIDGE
        SLOPES GRACIOUS UP THE WESTERN RIDGE • • • •   54 RESIGNATION   53
        AND ON THE RIDGE A WAGGON CHOKES THE WAY   • • •   107 BALDER DEAD 2   94
        THY FACE TOWRD HINKSEY AND ITS WINTRY RIDGE   • •   258 SCHOLAR-GIPSY   125
        THY FACE TOWARDS HINKSEY AND ITS WINTRY RIDGE   • •   258 SCHOLAR-GIPSY   V 125
        THE HILL BEHIND WHOSE RIDGE THE SUNSET FLAMES   • •   263 THYRSIS   13
        BARE ON ITS LONELY RIDGE THE TREE THE TREE • • • •   267 THYRSIS   160

RIDGED
        WHENCE THE RIDGED PINE-WOODED ROOTS   • • • • •   433 EMPEDOCLES II   137

RIDGES
        OVER THE GREY SEA-RIDGES AND THE GLIMPSE   • • • •   124 BALDER DEAD 3   366

RIDGING
        FREEZING AND RIDGING IN THEIR ONWARD FLOW   • • • •   108 BALDER DEAD 2   129

RIDING
        TO REST UNGLOVED ON HER GREEN RIDING-DRESS • • •   154 TRISTRAM 3   175
        ALLOWS THE PROUDLY-RIDING AND THE FOUNDERING BARK   421 EMPEDOCLES I 2   261
        ALLOWS THE PROUDLY-RIDING AND THE FOUNDERD BARK • •   421 EMPEDOCLES I 2   V 261

RIDINGS
        DOWN THE FOREST-RIDINGS LONE   • • • • • • •   13 CHURCH BROU 1   22

RIFE
        WITH LARGE RESULTS SO LITTLE RIFE   • • • • • •   60 RESIGNATION   262
        FOR HAUGHTY SPIRITS AND HIGH WRATHS ARE RIFE   • •   115 BALDER DEAD 3   79
        ITS HEADS OERTAXD ITS PALSIED HEARTS WAS RIFE   • •   261 SCHOLAR-GIPSY   205

RIFLED
        TEAR FROM THE RIFLED HEDGE   • • • • • • • •   218 BACCHANALIA 1   36

RIFTED
        THERE IS A CHASM RIFTED IN THE BASE   • • • • •   358 MEROPE   811
        SWEPT DOWN A CHASM RIFTED IN THE CLIFF   • • • •   363 MEROPE   960
        PRISONING IN HIS RIFTED STONES • • • • • • • •   PILLARS UNIVERS V 11

RIFTS
        THROUGH SILKEN RIFTS SOFT PEERS THE SUN   • • • •   248 KENSINGTON GARD V
        THROUGH SILKEN RIFTS SOFT WINKS THE SUN   • • • •   KENSINGTON GARD V

RIGHT
        THE FRIENDS TO WHOM WE HAD NO NATURAL RIGHT   • •   41 HUMAN LIFE   29
        THAT RIGHT IS ON THEIR SIDE   • • • • • • • •   HORATIAN ECHO   V
        IN HIS RIGHT HAND A RULERS STAFF NO SWORD   • • •   64 SOHRAB RUSTUM   99
        WHOSE FIERY POINT NOW IN HIS MAILD RIGHT-HAND   •   74 SOHRAB RUSTUM   451
        RIGHT FOR THE POLAR STAR PAST ORGUNJE   • • •   87 SOHRAB RUSTUM   880
        CARRIED BEFORE HIM AS IS RIGHT • • • • • • •   89 SICK KING BOKH   48
        MY LORD O KING DO RIGHT I PRAY   • • • • • •   89 SICK KING BOKH   53
        ONE WAS MY MOTHER NOW DO RIGHT   • • • • •   90 SICK KING BOKH   88
        RIGHT OPPOSITE AND THUS BEGAN   • • • • • •   90 SICK KING BOKH   96
        UPON A HILL ON THE RIGHT HAND   • • • • •   94 SICK KING BOKH   222
        FOR BALDER WHOM SHE HOLDS BY RIGHT BELOW   • •   100 BALDER DEAD 1   181
        BUT RIGHT BARS THIS NOT ONLY THY DESIRE   • • •   104 BALDER DEAD 1   313
        TO RIGHT AND LEFT AND WARM STEAM FILLS THE AIR   • •   107 BALDER DEAD 2   98
        FOR BALDER WHOM THOU HOLDST BY RIGHT BELOW   • • •   110 BALDER DEAD 2   193
        WITH NANNA ON HIS RIGHT AND ON HIS LEFT   • •   118 BALDER DEAD 3   164
        COME THEN SINCE HELA HOLDS BY RIGHT HER PREY   • •   121 BALDER DEAD 3   288
        HAD SCORED HER WHITE RIGHT HAND WHICH SHE ALLOWS • •   154 TRISTRAM 3   174
        TO CHEER THEE AND TO RIGHT THEE IF THOU ROAM   •   169 EAST LONDON   12
        DOWN ON ME THY RIGHT ARM • • • • • • • • • •   186 STRAYED REVEL   8
        HAVE FELT THEIR HUGE FRAMES NOT CONSTRUCTED RIGHT   239 REVOLUTIONS   15
        HEARS THY VOICE RIGHT NOW HE IS GONE • • • • •   272 MEMORIAL VERSES   74

RIGHT   (CONTINUED)
        REGARDING NEITHER TO RIGHT   •   •   •   •   •   295 HEINES GRAVE   90
        THAT RIGHT THAT CONSCIENCE POINTED TO A DEED   341 MEROPE   363
        THE BEST THEN TO DOMINION HATH THE RIGHT   •   •   •   352 MEROPE   654
        INTO THE NARROW PATH OF RIGHT   •   •   •   •   353 MEROPE   672
        ARMD FOR RIGHT ONLY AND THE GENERAL GOOD   •   •   •   353 MEROPE   685
        HE DOTH THOU HAST BOTH HOUSE AND MASTER RIGHT   •   354 MEROPE   707
        OUR OWN RIGHT HAND IN THE DETESTED BLOOD   •   •   •   387 MEROPE   1468
        RIGHT AT THE HARBOUR-MOUTH   •   •   •   •   •   400 MEROPE   1878
        IS EASY AT NO MOMENT BUT THE RIGHT   •   •   •   •   403 MEROPE   1950
        HIS KINSMAN HIS RIGHT HAND IN PEACE AND WAR   •   403 MEROPE   1974
        THE BEST THEN TO DOMINION HAVE THE RIGHT   •   •   •   352 MEROPE   V 654
        THY PLEASURE RIGHT OR WRONG   •   •   •   •   •   •   416 EMPEDOCLES I 2   133
        ONCE READ THY OWN BREAST RIGHT   •   •   •   •   •   417 EMPEDOCLES I 2   142
        THOU HAST NO RIGHT TO BLISS   •   •   •   •   •   •   417 EMPEDOCLES I 2   160
        CLAIMS RAPTURE AS ITS RIGHT   •   •   •   •   •   •   424 EMPEDOCLES I 2   353
        AS HE LETS HIS LAX RIGHT HAND   •   •   •   •   •   431 EMPEDOCLES II   71
        AND BORNE TO LIGHT AND RIGHT HIS WITNESS HIGH   •   448 WESTMIN ABBEY   144
        TO THE GREAT MAIN PASSD SEVILLE ON THE RIGHT   •   484 S S LUSITANIA   4

RIGHTEND
        HOW RIGHTEND HOW BETRAYD •   •   •   •   •   •   •   •   423 EMPEDOCLES I 2   330

RIGHTEOUS
        I SELF-DEFENCE AND RIGHTEOUS EXECUTION   •   •   •   338 MEROPE   277
        AND RIGHTEOUS IF HE FALLS I COUNT HIS FALL   •   •   349 MEROPE   552
        I THE ONE RIGHTEOUS THEY THE MANY BAD   •   •   •   353 MEROPE   679
        IF WITH NO RAGE NO FIRE OF RIGHTEOUS HATE   •   •   366 MEROPE   1011
        AND I WHEN TO HIS RIGHTEOUS STANDARD DOWN   •, •   •   388 MEROPE   1502

RIGHTFUL
        ANNOUNCES ME THEIR RIGHTFUL PRINCE RETURND •   •   •   383 MEROPE   1355

RIGHTLY
        TO CHOOSE IT RIGHTLY IS HIS PART   •   •   •   •   •   223 EPILOG LAOCOON   87
        RIGHTLY THEY TOLD THEE AND THOU ART ARRIVED   •   •   354 MEROPE   705
        MIGHT FROM THE PEOPLE DRAW IF RIGHTLY USED •   •   •   382 MEROPE   1336

RIGHTS
        AND WHAT THE RIGHTS OF MAN MAY MEAN   •   •   •   •   48 HORATIAN ECHO   17
        RIGHTS UNCONCEDED AND DENIED   •   •   •   •   •   •   352 MEROPE   655
        SURELY IF RIGHTS MAY BE BY FORCE ASSERTED   •   •   •   352 MEROPE   656
        AND FROM HIS NATURAL RIGHTS MY SON DEBAR   •   •   •   388 MEROPE   1495
        THE MEASURE OF HIS RIGHTS   •   •   •   •   •   •   •   417 EMPEDOCLES I 2   155

RIGID
        VAINLY RAISE HIS RIGID FRAME   •   •   •   •   •   •   •   452 POOR MATTHIAS   8

RIGIDLY
        RIGIDLY YET IN SETTLED CALM THIS REALM   •   •   •   •   388 MEROPE   1491

RIGOROUS
        FOR RIGOROUS TEACHERS SEIZED MY YOUTH   •   •   •   •   301 GRANDE CHARTR   67
        MOVE ON A RIGOROUS LINE •   •   •   •   •   •   •   •   •   310 OBERMANN   134

RILL
        THE TINKLE OF THE THIRSTY RILL •   •   •   •   •   •   •   217 BACCHANALIA 1   2

RILLS
        FOR CRESSES FROM THE RILLS   •   •   •   •   •   •   •   258 SCHOLAR-GIPSY   106
        SOFT LULLD BY THE RILLS •   •   •   •   •   •   •   •   •   442 EMPEDOCLES II   434

RIM
        DOWN AT THE FAR HORIZONS RIM •   •   •   •   •   •   •   242 SUMMER NIGHT   9

RIMMD
        AND IN THE HORNS AND GOLD-RIMMD SKULLS THE WINE   •   95 BALDER DEAD 1   14
        AND IN THE HORNS AND GOLD-RIMMD SCULLS THE WINE   •   95 BALDER DEAD 1   V 14
        AND FROM THEIR HORNS WITH SILVER RIMMD DRANK MEAD   119 BALDER DEAD 3   211

RING
        YES WHILE ON EARTH A THOUSAND DISCORDS RING   •   •   1 QUIET WORK   9
        HUNTERS GATHER BUGLES RING •   •   •   •   •   •   •   •   13 CHURCH BROU 1   16
        SIX YARDS ROUND SHALL NOT RING IT •   •   •   •   •   •   50 CONSOLATION   V
        OCEAN WHOSE WATERY RING ENFOLDS THE WORLD •   •   •   99 BALDER DEAD 1   160
        AND NOW WITH GLEAMING RING ENFOLDS THE WORLD •   •   110 BALDER DEAD 2   211
        TO ODIN TO MY FATHER TAKE THIS RING   •   •   •   •   112 BALDER DEAD 2   274
        HE SPAKE AND RAISED HIS HAND AND GAVE THE RING   •   112 BALDER DEAD 2   279
        BUT HERMOD TOOK THE RING AND YET ONCE MORE •   •   •   112 BALDER DEAD 2   282
        A LAST CHOICE GIFT THEREON HIS GOLDEN RING •   •   •   118 BALDER DEAD 3   173
        OVER THE WASTE THIS RING OF OPEN GROUND •   •   •   •   150 TRISTRAM 3   V 13
        THE MOUNTAINS RING THEM •   •   •   •   •   •   •   •   •   190 STRAYED REVEL   161
        IN THESE EARS THEY THUNDER THEY RING •   •   •   •   •   346 MEROPE   500
        AND MANY TIMES THAT MORN WE COURSED IN RING •   •   357 MEROPE   793
        SERRIED AND GRIM THE RING OF DORIAN LORDS •   •   •   401 MEROPE   1900
        LAY ON THE HEARTH AMID A FIERY RING •   •   •   •   •   446 WESTMIN ABBEY   84
        THE TAILS INDOMITABLE RING •   •   •   •   •   •   •   •   459 KAISER DEAD   27

RINGING
        AND HIS CLEAR LAUGH FLED RINGING THROUGH THE GLOOM   12 MYCERINUS   113

RINGING   (CONTINUED)
    STONES ARE SAWING HAMMERS RINGING   • • • • •   15 CHURCH BROU 1   89
    AND BLOOD AND RINGING BLOWS AND VIOLENT DEATH • •   117 BALDER DEAD 3   140
    THE NEIGHING STEEDS THE RINGING BLOWS   • • • •   138 TRISTRAM 1   259
    FIRED THEIR RINGING SHOT AND PASSD   • • • • •   215 LAST WORD   11
    SILENT THE SWATHS THE RINGING WAIN   • • • • • •   21/ BACCHANALIA 1   5
    SILENT THE SHEAVES THE RINGING WAIN   • • • • • •   217 BACCHANALIA 1   V   5
    SET THINE EARS WITH SOUL-FRAUGHT MUSIC RINGING • •   482 THEKLAS ANSWER   7

RINGLET
    COME BIND UP THOSE RINGLET SHOWERS   • • • • • •   32 NEW SIRENS   173

RINGLETS
    THE RINGLETS ON HER SHOULDERS LYING   • • • • • •   131 TRISTRAM 1   26

RINGS
    THE WIDE PLAIN RINGS THE DAZED AIR THROBS WITH BLOWS   137 TRISTRAM 1   235
    HOW LONELY RINGS THE ECHO OF MY FEET • • • • • •   242 SUMMER NIGHT   2
    WHERE THE RIVER IN GLEAMING RINGS   • • • • • •   252 FUTURE   14
    WHEREWITH FROM END TO END ARCADIA RINGS   • • • •   362 MEROPE   943

RIOTING
    RIOTING THEY PASS   • • • • • • • • • • • •   218 BACCHANALIA 1   33

RIOTOUS
    DOTH RIOTOUS LAUGHTER NOW REPLACE   • • • • • •   184 TERRACE BERNE   21

RIPE
    MUSINGS THAT ERE THEY COULD GROW RIPE WERE FLOWN • •   41 GIPSY CHILD   V 19
    WHAT SHELTER TO GROW RIPE IS OURS   • • • • • •   308 OBERMANN   71
    TILL THE SINNER THE VENGEANCE BE RIPE • • • •   347 MEROPE   528

RIPENING
    AND THE SLOW-RIPENING TIME AT LAST PREPARES   • •   379 MEROPE   1264

RIPENS
    DOWN THE LONG AGE OF TRUTH THAT RIPENS SLOW   • •   448 WESTMIN ABBEY   148

RIPPLE
    WHERE THE SHOREWARD RIPPLE BREAKS   • • • • • •   434 EMPEDOCLES II   178

RIPPLED
    IN THE RIPPLED WATERS GREY   • • • • • • • •   433 EMPEDOCLES II   134

RIPPLES
    THE RIPPLES OF WHOSE BLUE WAVES CHEER   • • • •   311 OBERMANN   163
    AND GENTLY SHALL THE MURMURING RIPPLES FLOW   • •   469 ALARIC AT ROME   197

RISE
    YET SUNS SHALL RISE AND MANY MOONS SHALL WANE   • •   10 MYCERINUS   62
    AND RISE UPON YOUR COLD WHITE MARBLE BEDS • • • •   18 CHURCH BROU 1   27
    AND THESE TOO RISE • • • • • • • • • • •   46 IN UTRUMQUE PAR   V 42
    THE YOUNG MAY RISE AT SOHRABS VAUNTS NOT I • • •   68 SOHRAB RUSTUM   227
    RISE WHEREFORE DOST THOU VAINLY QUESTION THUS   •   72 SOHRAB RUSTUM   365
    BUT RISE AND BE NOT WROTH NOT WROTH AM I • • •   74 SOHRAB RUSTUM   429
    YET HE SHALL ONE DAY RISE AND BURST HIS BONDS •   111 BALDER DEAD 2   222
    AND HERMOD SAW THE TOWERS OF ASGARD RISE   • • •   113 BALDER DEAD 2   304
    AND TOWARDS EVENING SEE THE HEADLANDS RISE • • •   123 BALDER DEAD 3   359
    RISE GO HENCE AND SEEK THE PRINCESS ISEULT • • •   145 TRISTRAM 2   V 93
    FIXT HER SLIGHT HANDS CLASPD ON HER LAP THEN RISE   152 TRISTRAM 3   91
    I CAME I SAW THEE RISE THE BLOOD   • • • • • •   178 FAREWELL   9
    GLADLY THEY RISE AT HIS CALL   • • • • • • • •   216 LORDS MESSENGER   7
    RISE SLOWLY UP INTO THE SKY   • • • • • • • •   220 BACCHANALIA 1   25
    THOSE CATTLE COUCHD OR AS THEY RISE   • • • • •   222 EPILOG LAOCOON   53
    BEHOLD THE NEW WORLD RISE   • • • • • • • •   237 PROGRESS   4
    CAN RISE AND OBEY   • • • • • • • • • • •   253 FUTURE   48
    RISE UP ALL ROUND THE CHRISTIAN SPIRES   • • •   274 STANZAS CARNAC   22
    BUT TILL THEY RISE ALLOW OUR TEARS   • • • • •   304 GRANDE CHARTR   V 162
    BID IT RISE BOLDLY AT THE SIGNAL GIVEN   • • •   331 MEROPE   46
    AND COUNT ON LIKE IMPUNITY AND RISE   • • • • •   342 MEROPE   374
    AND THE OLD MEN RISE FROM THEIR BENCH   • • •   360 MEROPE   900
    RISE FAINTLY TO ME NOW IT STOPS WHOS HERE • •   407 EMPEDOCLES I 1   29
    IN THIS CLEAR MOUNTAIN-AIR A VOICE WILL RISE   •   409 EMPEDOCLES I 1   88
    AND HOLDS MEN MUTE TO SEE WHERE IT WILL RISE   •   410 EMPEDOCLES I 1   114
    AND SO THERE RISE THESE LINES OF VERSE   • • • •   451 GEISTS GRAVE   41
    NO SHAME THAT SUNS SHOULD RISE TO LIGHT A CONQUERD   468 ALARIC AT ROME   150
        ROME
    AND LO THE ETERNAL CITY AS THEY RISE • • • • •   468 ALARIC AT ROME   155
    AND WHILE THEY RISE HERE MIGHT WE STAND ALONE   •   470 ALARIC AT ROME   203

RISEN
    HIGH AS THY LIFE BE RISEN TIS FROM THESE   • • •   46 IN UTRUMQUE PAR   V 41
    THE SUN IS NOT YET RISEN AND THE FOE • • • • •   62 SOHRAB RUSTUM   35
    THE SUN BY THIS HAD RISEN AND CLEARD THE FOG   •   64 SOHRAB RUSTUM   104
    HE CEASED BUT WHILE HE SPAKE RUSTUM HAD RISEN •   74 SOHRAB RUSTUM   448
    BY THIS THE SUN HAD RISEN AND CLEARD THE FOG   •   64 SOHRAB RUSTUM   V 104
    HATH RISEN GOETHES WORDSWORTHS SONG   • • • • •   222 EPILOG LAOCOON   29
    AND SEE THE SUN IS RISEN • • • • • • • • •   322 OBERMANN MORE   284
    THEN HAD HIS SEPULCHRE RISEN   • • • • • • • •   345 MEROPE   481
    FAIN WOULD WE DEEM THAT THOU HAST RISEN SO HIGH •   463 ALARIC AT ROME   31

RISES

RISES HIGHER DAY BY DAY   15 CHURCH BROU 1   88
THERE RISES AN UNSPEAKABLE DESIRE   246 BURIED LIFE   47
IN FRONT THE DUMB ROCK RISES STEEP   479 HAYSWATER BOAT   11
SINKS AND RISES THROUGH THIS COOL ARCADE   META CLOISTER   16
AT YOUR VOICE HE RISES SLOWLY   META CLOISTER   33
SINKS AND RISES THROUGH THIS CHARMD ARCADE   META CLOISTER   V 16

RISING

WHEN THE SOUL RISING HIGHER TO GOD COMES NO NIGHER   38 STAGIRIUS   V 14
AND RISING STERNLY ON ONE ARM HE SAID   80 SOHRAB RUSTUM   654
THE CATTLE RISING FROM THE GRASS   225 EPILOG LAOCOON   153
WHERE CRIES ARE RISING EVER NEW   277 SOUTHERN NIGHT   62
RISING ALL ROUND OVERAWE   291 RUGBY CHAPEL   179
AND WRESTLE RISING THEN WITH BARE   300 GRANDE CHARTR   40

RISK

IN SINGLE FIGHT INCURRING SINGLE RISK   63 SOHRAB RUSTUM   69
HIS GRANDSIRE AND HIS UNCLES FEAR THE RISK   350 MEROPE   603
OF WHAT IT LIES WITH THEM TO MAKE RISK NONE   350 MEROPE   604
NOW I IF I INVITE THEM TO RUN RISK   382 MEROPE   1349
DEALT AT MY OWN SOLE RISK BEFORE THEIR EYES   383 MEROPE   1354
RISK FROM MY NEW-RESTORED MY ONLY SON   387 MEROPE   1456
RISK WHAT HE MIGHT NOW THAT I HAVE HIM HERE   387 MEROPE   1458

RITE

THE PROPHETESSES WHO BY RITE ETERNE   97 BALDER DEAD 1   89
WITH ME FOR THUS ORDAINS THE COMMON RITE   103 BALDER DEAD 1   300

RITES

WHILE BY HER BEDSIDE HEBREW RITES HAVE PLACE   168 RACHEL 3   8
CREEDS PASS RITES CHANGE NO ALTAR STANDETH WHOLE   173 MONICAS PRAYER   12
YOUR CREEDS ARE DEAD YOUR RITES ARE DEAD   320 OBERMANN MORE   229
SUSPEND YOUR MELANCHOLY RITES AWHILE   332 MEROPE   77
THIS DAY AMID THESE RITES THIS BLACK-ROBED TRAIN   333 MEROPE   105
THESE OFFERINGS HOME OUR RITES ARE SPOILD TO-DAY   336 MEROPE   196
AND NOW I LEAVE THEE TO THESE RITES ESTEEMD   342 MEROPE   379
AND PULLULATING RITES EXTERNE AND VAIN   449 WESTMIN ABBEY   160

RIVAL

THAT A FORMER RIVAL SHARES HER OFFICE   144 TRISTRAM 2   59
THAT AN ANCIENT RIVAL SHARES HER OFFICE   144 TRISTRAM 2   V 59
ALACK FOR CORYDON NO RIVAL NOW   265 THYRSIS   81
AND ME HENCEFORTH SOLE RIVAL WITH HIMSELF   366 MEROPE   1003
A RIVAL RHYME   458 KAISER DEAD   6

RIVALRY

TOO GREAT FOR HASTE TOO HIGH FOR RIVALRY   1 QUIET WORK   8

RIVALS

ROUSE NO ANGER MAKE NO RIVALS MORE   144 TRISTRAM 2   64
HER YOUNGER RIVALS PUREST GRACE   147 TRISTRAM 2   146
HER YOUNGEST RIVALS FRESHEST GRACE   147 TRISTRAM 2   V 146
HER YOUNGER RIVALS CALMEST GRACE   147 TRISTRAM 2   V 146

RIVE

WINDS FROM OUR SIDE THE UNSUITING CONSORT RIVE   40 HUMAN LIFE   16
OF THOSE THAT IN SECRET THE HEART-STRINGS RIVE   132 TRISTRAM 1   47
RIVE ITS DRY BONES AND WITH NEW FORCE   319 OBERMANN MORE   199

RIVER

THERE BY THE RIVER-BANKS HE WANDERD ON   11 MYCERINUS   85
FAR UP SHINES THE HOUSE AND BENEATH FLOWS THE RIVER   19 MODERN SAPPHO   3
FAR UP GLEAMS THE HOUSE AND BENEATH FLOWS THE RIVER   19 MODERN SAPPHO   V 3
HUNG POISED AND THEN THE DARTING RIVER OF LIFE   25 DREAM   31
SUCH NOW METHOUGHT IT WAS THE RIVER OF LIFE   25 DREAM   32
IN THE MIDST OF RIVER-MEADOWS   32 NEW SIRENS   181
IN THE MIST OF RIVER MEADOWS   32 NEW SIRENS   V 181
DID IN BOKHARA BY THE RIVER FIND   69 SOHRAB RUSTUM   274
AND SEEN THE RIVER OF HELMUND AND THE LAKE   83 SOHRAB RUSTUM   751
SOUTHWARD THE TARTARS BY THE RIVER MARGE   86 SOHRAB RUSTUM   873
BUT THE MAJESTIC RIVER FLOATED ON   86 SOHRAB RUSTUM   875
FOR NEAR THE WALL THE RIVER OF ROARING FLOWS   109 BALDER DEAD 2   152
OF SOME CLEAR RIVER ISSUING FROM A LAKE   109 BALDER DEAD 2   158
QUIVERING AND OTHERS SKIM THE RIVER-STREAMS   109 BALDER DEAD 2   161
THROUGH WHICH A RIVER FLOWS AND SEES BENEATH   113 BALDER DEAD 2   297
SWINGING AND OTHERS SKIM THE RIVER-STREAMS   109 BALDER DEAD 2   V 161
ALL RED WITH BLOOD THE WHIRLING RIVER FLOWS   137 TRISTRAM 1   234
BESIDE THE RIVER-POOL   160 NECKAN   44
WEPT BY THE RIVER-POOL   161 NECKAN   60
THE UNREGARDED RIVER OF OUR LIFE   246 BURIED LIFE   39
ON THE BREAST OF THE RIVER OF TIME   251 FUTURE   3
WHERE THE RIVER IN GLEAMING RINGS   252 FUTURE   14
OF THE LANDS WHICH THE RIVER OF TIME   252 FUTURE   21
THIS TRACT WHICH THE RIVER OF TIME   253 FUTURE   50
FOR EVER THE COURSE OF THE RIVER OF TIME   253 FUTURE   59
HAPLY THE RIVER OF TIME   253 FUTURE   71
SITTING UPON THE RIVER BANK OERGROWN   258 SCHOLAR-GIPSY   97
THE GRASSY HARVEST OF THE RIVER-FIELDS   266 THYRSIS   108

RIVER (CONTINUED)
```
        OF OUR BOAT PASSING HEAVED THE RIVER-GRASS  • • • •    266 THYRSIS            128
        BY THEIR GREEN RIVER WHO DOTH CHANGE  • • • • • •      313 OBERMANN MORE        25
        RECEIVES THE RIVER  • • • • • • • • • • •             391 MEROPE              1610
        LIKE A SWIFT RIVER THRO A SILENT PLAIN  • • • •        473 CROMWELL             64
        THEN LIKE A KINGLY RIVER SWIFT AND STRONG  • • • •     475 CROMWELL            133
```

RIVERS
```
        TO BUILD THEM BOATS FISH FROM THE FLOODED RIVERS  • •   73 SOHRAB RUSTUM       411
        THE DESERT RIVERS MOORGHAB AND TEJEND  • • • •         83 SOHRAB RUSTUM       763
        TO SAW THEM PLANKS FISH FROM THE FLOODED RIVERS  • •   73 SOHRAB RUSTUM     V 411
        ON SOME GREAT RIVERS MARGE  • • • • • • •             193 STRAYED REVEL       252
        THOSE BLUE HILLS TOO THIS RIVERS FLOW  • • •          208 ON THE RHINE         22
        RIVERS AND HIGH-ROOFD TOWNS  • • • • • • •            296 HEINES GRAVE        138
        RIVERS ARE DRIED WINDS STAYD  • • • • • • •           416 EMPEDOCLES I 2      125
```

RIVETS
```
        RIVETS HIS GAZE ON THE BANKS OF THE STREAM  • • •     251 FUTURE                6
```

ROAD
```
        DOWN THE LEAF-STREWN FOREST-ROAD  • • • • •            13 CHURCH BROU 1        30
        ALREADY FROM THE SILENT ROAD  • • • • • •             53 RESIGNATION          49
        PARCHD AND ROAD-WORN WE MADE THAT DAY  • • •          54 RESIGNATION          81
        ONCE MORE WE TREAD THIS SELF-SAME ROAD  • • •         55 RESIGNATION          86
        UPON THE ROAD OF SAMARCAND  • • • • •                 94 SICK KING BOKH      224
        THERE IS A ROAD WHICH LEADS TO HELAS REALM  • •       99 BALDER DEAD 1        135
        BUT HE MUST TREAD A DARK UNTRAVELLD ROAD  • • •       99 BALDER DEAD 1        143
        IN SILENCE UP THE DARK UNTRAVELLD ROAD  • • •        107 BALDER DEAD 2         79
        WHERE THE ROAD ISSUES BETWEEN WALLING ROCKS  •       107 BALDER DEAD 2         89
        AND I COME SENT THIS ROAD ON BALDERS TRACK  • •      108 BALDER DEAD 2        116
        BALDER HATH GONE THIS WAY AND TAEN THE ROAD  •       108 BALDER DEAD 2        122
        WHICH HANGS OVER THE ICE WHERE LIES THE ROAD  •      108 BALDER DEAD 2        127
        AND UP FROM THENCE A WET AND MISTY ROAD  • • •       113 BALDER DEAD 2        289
        BALDER MY BROTHER THOU ART GONE A ROAD  • • •        116 BALDER DEAD 3         99
        ON SOME GREAT ROAD OR RESTING IN AN INN  • • •       116 BALDER DEAD 3        117
        BUT STILL AS THEY PURSUED THEIR WARM DRY ROAD  •     150 TRISTRAM 3           44
        ASKD AN OUTFIT FOR ITS EARTHLY ROAD  • • • •         209 SELF-DECEPTION        8
        WHERE BEHIND KEIGHLEY THE ROAD  • • • • •            282 HAWORTH CHURCH       55
        IN THE SUMMER-MORNING THE ROAD  • • • • •            287 RUGBY CHAPEL         28
        BUT WHERE THE ROAD RUNS NEAR THE STREAM  • •         305 GRANDE CHARTR       175
        FOR HE PURSUED A LONELY ROAD  • • • •                308 OBERMANN             57
        YE SUN-BORN VIRGINS ON THE ROAD OF TRUTH  • •        436 EMPEDOCLES II       239
        OER WHOSE LIT FLOOR A ROAD OF MOONBEAMS LEADS  •     438 EMPEDOCLES II       312
        IN THE SPRING BY THEIR ROAD  • • • • •               442 EMPEDOCLES II       454
        TO TRAVELLERS ON THE PORTSMOUTH ROAD  • • • •        452 GEISTS GRAVE         70
        AS TOWERED ON HIGH ABOVE THEIR MOONLIT ROAD  •       466 ALARIC AT ROME      113
```

ROADS
```
        SAY YE THE SPIRIT OF MAN HAS FOUND NEW ROADS  • •    237 PROGRESS             25
```

ROAM
```
        WHO ROAM OER KIPCHAK AND THE NORTHERN WASTE  •        65 SOHRAB RUSTUM       131
        TO MATE BUT LEFT HER TO ROAM DISTANT LANDS  • • •    116 BALDER DEAD 3        94
        TO CHEER THEE AND TO RIGHT THEE IF THOU ROAM  • •    169 EAST LONDON          12
        OFT THROUGH THE DARKENING FIELDS HAVE SEEN THEE ROAM 257 SCHOLAR-GIPSY        84
        ROAM ON THE LIGHT WE SOUGHT IS SHINING STILL  • •    269 THYRSIS             238
        ACTION AND PLEASURE WILL YE ROAM  • • • • •          305 GRANDE CHARTR       194
        TO THE INVISIBLE PLAINS TO ROAM WITH THEE  • • •     367 MEROPE             1030
        WOULD CHANGE WHEREER HE ROAM  • • • • •              419 EMPEDOCLES I 2      218
        LIKE US THE LIBYAN WIND DELIGHTS TO ROAM AT LARGE    420 EMPEDOCLES I 2      251
        THE PEACE OF CHILDHOOD AND THE THOUGHTS THAT ROAM    474 CROMWELL             73
```

ROAMD
```
        THEY TOO HAVE LONG ROAMD TO AND FRO  • • • • •        55 RESIGNATION         109
        AND UP AND DOWN AND SIDE AND SLANT THEY ROAMD  • •   106 BALDER DEAD 2        53
        NORTH SOUTH EAST WEST THEY STRUCK AND ROAMD THE WORLD 122 BALDER DEAD 3      304
        ROAMD ERE BIRTH THE TREASURIES OF GOD  • • • •       209 SELF-DECEPTION        6
        THE TRIBES WHO THEN ROAMD ON HER BREAST  • • • •     252 FUTURE               32
        AND ROAMD THE WORLD WITH THAT WILD BROTHERHOOD  • •   256 SCHOLAR-GIPSY       38
```

ROAMING
```
        ROAMING THE COUNTRY-SIDE A TRUANT BOY  • • • •        261 SCHOLAR-GIPSY       198
```

ROAR
```
        FALLS HEAVILY AWAY WITH LONG-DRAWN ROAR  • • • •      40 HUMAN LIFE           21
        AND HEARD THEIR HOLLOW ROAR OF DYING MEN  • • •      74 SOHRAB RUSTUM       435
        NO HORSES CRY WAS THAT MOST LIKE THE ROAR  • • •     76 SOHRAB RUSTUM       503
        ON WINTER-EVENINGS WHEN THE ROAR  • • • • •         137 TRISTRAM 1          216
        WHERE FEEBLY COMES THE MOURNFUL ROAR  • • • • •     140 TRISTRAM 1          330
        WILL HEAR THE WAVES ROAR  • • • • • • • •           164 FORSAKEN MERM       115
        THE WAVES ROAR AND WHIRL  • • • • • • • •           165 FORSAKEN MERM       117
        LISTEN YOU HEAR THE GRATING ROAR  • • • •           211 DOVER BEACH           9
        ITS MELANCHOLY LONG WITHDRAWING ROAR  • • • • •     211 DOVER BEACH          25
        AND STERNER COMES THE ROAR  • • • • • • •           244 SUMMER NIGHT         70
        THEN THROUGH THE GREAT TOWNS HARSH HEART-WEARYING ROAR 269 THYRSIS           234
        I HEAR THE TORRENTS ROAR  • • • • • • •             306 OBERMANN             10
        LEAP AND ROAR THOU SEA OF FIRE  • • • • • • •       441 EMPEDOCLES II       411
        ALL FREEDOMS MYSTIC LANGUAGE STORMS THAT ROAR  • •   472 CROMWELL             29
        AFFLICTS GRAVE HEAVEN WITH ITS LONG SENSELESS ROAR   480 HUNGARIAN NAT         5
```

ROARING
    DOWN TO THE MARGIN OF THE ROARING SEA   • • • •   97 BALDER DEAD 1   77
    THROUGH VALLEYS DEEP-ENGULPHD WITH ROARING STREAMS   99 BALDER DEAD 1   146
    AND HEAR THE ROARING OF THE STREAMS OF HELL   • •   100 BALDER DEAD 1   173
    AND CAME AGAIN DOWN TO THE ROARING WAVES   • •   101 BALDER DEAD 1   199
    THROUGH VALLEYS DEEP-ENGULPHD BY ROARING STREAMS • •   107 BALDER DEAD 2   84
    FOR NEAR THE WALL THE RIVER OF ROARING FLOWS   • •   109 BALDER DEAD 2   152
    SOON WITH A ROARING ROSE THE MIGHTY FIRE   • •   118 BALDER DEAD 3   186
    ROARING TORRENTS HAVE BREACHD   • • • • • • •   289 RUGBY CHAPEL   94

ROARS
    IN THE HUGE WORLD WHICH ROARS HARD BY   • • • • 249 KENSINGTON GARD   21

ROASTED
    A SIDE OF ROASTED SHEEP AND CAKES OF BREAD • • • •   67 SOHRAB RUSTUM   198
    A SIDE OF ROASTED SHEEP AND LOAVES OF BREAD   • •   67 SOHRAB RUSTUM   V 198

ROBBER
    NO BOLDER ROBBER   • • • • • • • • •   51 CONSOLATION   31
    MY FATHER WHOM THE ROBBER AFGHANS VEX   • • • •   68 SOHRAB RUSTUM   233
    A CLOUD OF DESERT ROBBER-HORSE HAVE BURST   • • • •   193 STRAYED REVEL   248
    A CLOUD OF DESERT ROBBER-HORSE HAS BURST   • • • •   193 STRAYED REVEL   V 248

ROBBERS
    AGAINST THE ROBBERS AND HE SAW THAT HEAD   • • • •   71 SOHRAB RUSTUM   339

ROBBING
    ROBBING HERSELF OF LIFE IN BURYING   • • • • • •   196 FRAG ANTIGONE   40

ROBE
    A CERTAIN MOOLLAH WITH HIS ROBE   • • • • • •   88 SICK KING BOKH   31
    WHICH HER HEAVY ROBE DOTH HOLD   • • • • • • •   131 TRISTRAM 1   29
    A ROBE OF SACKCLOTH NEXT THE SMOOTH WHITE SKIN • •   166 AUSTERITY POET   11
    WAVES THY WHITE ROBE   • • • • • • • •   186 STRAYED REVEL   22
    HIS ROBE DRAWN OVER   • • • • • • • •   190 STRAYED REVEL   139
    NEW HEARTS WITH THE ENQUIRERS HOLY ROBE   • • • •   198 FRAG DEJANEIRA   16
    TILL PRESENTLY THE KING CAME FORTH IN ROBE • • • •   401 MEROPE   1903
    MY PURPLE ROBE   • • • • • • • • • •   432 EMPEDOCLES II   120
    TOUCH HIS ROBE AND SAY MY FATHER   • • • • •   META CLOISTER   27

ROBED
    YOU HEAR THE WHITE-ROBED PRIEST SAY MASS   • • • •   17 CHURCH BROU 2   29
    A WHITE-ROBED SLAVE STOLE TO THE GREAT KINGS SIDE   47 WORLD QUIETIST   27
    A WHITE-ROBED SLAVE STOLE TO THE MONARCHS SIDE • •   47 WORLD QUIETIST   V 27
    FLOWING-ROBED THE BELOVED   • • • • • •   194 STRAYED REVEL   279
    THIS DAY AMID THESE RITES THIS BLACK-ROBED TRAIN • •   333 MEROPE   105
    THAT BLACK-ROBED SWOONING FIGURE MEROPE   • • •   376 MEROPE   1212
    WHEN THE WHITE-ROBED GARLAND-CROWNED MONARCH • •   400 MEROPE   1857

ROBES
    THE COWERING MERCHANTS IN LONG ROBES   • • • • •   191 STRAYED REVEL   191
    SAD-CHANTING MAIDENS CLAD IN MOURNING ROBES   • •   331 MEROPE   53
    WITH BLOOD-BESPATTERD ROBES AND CHAPLET SHORN • •   403 MEROPE   1966
    LEFT THEIR FRIEND AND WITH ROBES FLOWING   • • • •   433 EMPEDOCLES II   152

ROBINS
    OF ROBINS REED   • • • • • • • • • • •   459 KAISER DEAD   12

ROBS
    ROBS OF A LOVED BRIDE PALE IMPLORING   • • • • •   196 FRAG ANTIGONE   42

ROCK
    YES WRITE IT IN THE ROCK SAINT BERNARD SAID   • •   171 DIVINITY   1
    THEIR ROCK-STRANGLED HUM   • • • • • • • • • •   175 PARTING   30
    HIGH ON A JUTTING ROCK IN THE RED STREAM   • • •   192 STRAYED REVEL   230
    ASOPUS GLEAM ROCK-HEMMD   • • • • • • •   197 FRAG ANTIGONE   63
    AND STRIKES THE ROCK AND FINDS THE VEIN   • • •   213 PROGRESS POESY   2
    WAS THE PALLADIUM HIGH MID ROCK AND WOOD   • • •   236 PALLADIUM   2
    HE TARRIES WHERE THE ROCK OF SPAIN   • • • •   275 STANZAS CARNAC   38
    HE LINGERS WHERE THE ROCK OF SPAIN   • • • •   275 STANZAS CARNAC   V 38
    TOUCHES AND ON GIBRALTARS ROCK   • • • • •   276 SOUTHERN NIGHT   47
    THUNDER CRASHES FROM ROCK   • • • • • • •   289 RUGBY CHAPEL   91
    TO ROCK THE CATARACTS REPLY   • • • • • • •   289 RUGBY CHAPEL   92
    IN THE LAURELLD ROCK OER THE BLUE   • • • • •   294 HEINES GRAVE   57
    UP OER THE ROCK-STREWN SLOPE   • • • • • •   297 HEINES GRAVE   162
    CLIMBING THE ROCK WHICH JUTS   • • • • • •   297 HEINES GRAVE   186
    ROCK TO ITS IRON CROSS   • • • • • • • •   298 HEINES GRAVE   188
    OF THAT UNFOOTED PRECIPICE WHOSE ROCK   • •   358 MEROPE   812
    SUNLESS PRISON OF ROCK   • • • • • • • • •   370 MEROPE   1118
    SOME ROCK MORE LONELY THAN THAT LEMNIAN ISLE •   395 MEROPE   1746
    AND IN THE LONELY ROCK-STREWN MOUNTAIN-GLEN   •   430 EMPEDOCLES II   39
    IN FRONT THE DUMB ROCK RISES STEEP   • • • • •   479 HAYSWATER BOAT   11

ROCKD
    AND THE SHIP FLOATED ON THE WAVES AND ROCKD   • •   118 BALDER DEAD 3   180

ROCKING
    ROCKING HER OBSCURE BODY TO AND FRO   • • • • •   45 IN UTRUMQUE PAR   25
    OF THE BRIGHT ROCKING OCEAN SETS TO SHORE   • • • •   79 SOHRAB RUSTUM   617
    AND LEFT IT ROCKING IN THE BAY • • • • • • • •   480 HAYSWATER BOAT   32

ROCKS

UPON THE MOSSY ROCKS AT THE STREAMS EDGE		25 DREAM	14
FADED THE MOSS THE ROCKS US BURNING PLAINS		25 DREAM	36
THE STRANGE-SCRAWLD ROCKS THE LONELY SKY		60 RESIGNATION	268
A HELPLESS BABE AMONG THE MOUNTAIN-ROCKS		81 SOHRAB RUSTUM	681
SMOTE MID THE ROCKS THE LICHEN-BEARDED PINES		106 BALDER DEAD 2	56
WHERE THE ROAD ISSUES BETWEEN WALLING ROCKS		107 BALDER DEAD 2	89
AND IN A CAVE A BED OF NEEDLE-ROCKS		111 BALDER DEAD 2	220
IS STREWN WITH ROCKS AND MANY A SHIVERD MASS		150 TRISTRAM 3	16
AND HIGH ROCKS THROW MILDLY		165 FORSAKEN MERM	130
TO THE LONELY INN MID THE ROCKS		289 RUGBY CHAPEL	109
SEE IN THE ROCKS OF THE WORLD		291 RUGBY CHAPEL	171
SORE THIRST PLAGUES THEM THE ROCKS		291 RUGBY CHAPEL	178
SOLE THEY SHALL STRAY IN THE ROCKS		291 RUGBY CHAPEL	185
SOLE THEY SHALL STRAY ON THE ROCKS		291 RUGBY CHAPEL	V 185
WHAT THOUGHTS TO ME HIS ROCKS RECALL		313 OBERMANN MORE	35
ALONG THE ROCKS OF NAYE		324 OBERMANN MORE	336
AS FROM A FASTNESS IN THE ROCKS OUR SCANT		337 MEROPE	247
IN SOME DARK FIR-TREES SHADOW AMID ROCKS		373 MEROPE	1167
SUNLESS PRISON OF ROCKS		370 MEROPE	V1118
BUT HIDE THEE IN THE ROCKS A GREAT WAY DOWN		409 EMPEDOCLES I 1	96
OF THE ROCKS OF PARNASSUS		435 EMPEDOCLES II	201
ROOST DEEP IN THE ROCKS		442 EMPEDOCLES II	432
INLAND FROM THE ROCKS AND SEA		457 POOR MATTHIAS	180

ROCKY

HE KNOWS EACH FRITH AND EVERY ROCKY CREEK		123 BALDER DEAD 3	326
THE ROCKY BANKS THE TERRACE HIGH		183 TERRACE BERNE	3
SAW IN THE ROCKY ISLE OF DELOS DIE		197 FRAG ANTIGONE	69
FAR ON ITS ROCKY KNOLL DESCRIED		273 STANZAS CARNAC	1
CRAWLS UP ITS ROCKY STAIR		306 OBERMANN	2

ROD

AND EASED OF BASKET AND OF ROD		248 KENSINGTON GARD	19

RODE

AND MOUNTED HIS HORSE SLEIPNER WHOM HE RODE		96 BALDER DEAD 1	47
AND FROM THE HALL OF HEAVEN HE RODE AWAY		96 BALDER DEAD 1	48
AND MOUNTED SLEIPNER AND IN DARKNESS RODE		102 BALDER DEAD 1	255
AND TO VALHALLAS GATE HE RODE AND LEFT		102 BALDER DEAD 1	265
SKULDA THE YOUNGEST OF THE NORNIES RODE		105 BALDER DEAD 2	21
AND ALL THAT NIGHT HE RODE AND JOURNEYD SO		107 BALDER DEAD 2	82
BUT NORTHWARD HERMOD RODE THE WAY BELOW		108 BALDER DEAD 2	138
AND THROUGH THE EMPTY STREETS HE RODE AND PASSD		113 BALDER DEAD 2	308
AND THRICE IN ARMS AROUND THE DEAD THEY RODE		115 BALDER DEAD 3	61
THOR CAME ON FOOT THE REST ON HORSEBACK RODE		120 BALDER DEAD 3	218
THEIR HORSES AND RODE FORTH THROUGH ALL THE WORLD		122 BALDER DEAD 3	303
BUT HERMOD RODE WITH NIORD WHOM HE TOOK		122 BALDER DEAD 3	320
AND THEY RODE HOME TOGETHER THROUGH THE WOOD		123 BALDER DEAD 3	329
BUT NORTHWARD HERMOD RODE THE WAY BELOW		124 BALDER DEAD 3	374
A CASSOCKD PRIEST RODE BY		160 NECKAN	48
THE CASSOCKD PRIEST RODE ONWARDS		161 NECKAN	57
WE RODE FROM TEGEA THROUGH THE WOODS OF OAKS		355 MEROPE	735
WHERE RODE THE TALL DARK SHIPS WHOSE LOOSEND SAIL		473 CROMWELL	67
WHERE THE DARK SHIPS RODE PROUDLY WOOD THE GALE		479 CROMWELL	238

ROE

WILD HOG AND BEAR AND MOUNTAIN-DEER AND ROE		356 MEROPE	758

ROLL

ROLL THROUGH THE HEAVING MULTITUDE		57 RESIGNATION	157
OR WHETHER IT WILL ROLL US OUT TO SEA		73 SOHRAB RUSTUM	394
ROLL TUMBLING IN THE CURRENT OER MY HEAD		83 SOHRAB RUSTUM	770
RUSTING FOR EVER AND THE YEARS ROLL ON		127 BALDER DEAD 3	472
AND ROLL ADOWN A CHANNEL LARGE		224 EPILOG LAOCOON	101
COLD PLASHING PAST IT CRYSTAL WATERS ROLL		236 PALLADIUM	11
BRIGHT ELSE AND FAST THE STREAM OF LIFE MAY ROLL		238 PROGRESS	29
AND THE SEA ITS LONG MOON-SILVERD ROLL		240 SELF-DEPENDENCE	22
I FEEL A NAMELESS SADNESS OER ME ROLL		245 BURIED LIFE	3
HAD FELT HIM LIKE THE THUNDERS ROLL		270 MEMORIAL VERSES	9
TILL FREE MY THOUGHTS BEFORE ME ROLL		302 GRANDE CHARTR	95
ONCE MORE UPON ME ROLL		306 OBERMANN	14
FROM DAVIDS LIPS THIS WORD DID ROLL		318 OBERMANN MORE	V
FROM DAVIDS LIPS THAT WORD DID ROLL		318 OBERMANN MORE	V
ONCE MORE ROLL BACK ON MY HOUSE		378 MEROPE	1244
BEGIN TO ROLL AND ALMOST DROWN		431 EMPEDOCLES II	63
AND MAKES THE MASSD CLOUDS ROLL		432 EMPEDOCLES II	122
WHILE FULL AND CEASELESS AS THE OCEAN ROLL		464 ALARIC AT ROME	71
THE MORNING MISTS FROM TOWER AND TEMPLE ROLL		468 ALARIC AT ROME	154
SPRANG FROM ITS SLEEP AND LO THE WATERS ROLL		479 CROMWELL	236

ROLLD

WHEREOER THE CHARIOT WHEELS OF LIFE ARE ROLLD		4 BUTLERS SERMONS	13
THE BIG WARM TEARS ROLLD DOWN AND CAKED THE SAND		82 SOHRAB RUSTUM	736
ROLLD HEAVILY THE LEADEN MIST ASIDE		126 BALDER DEAD 3	441
TWAS DAWN A BROUGHAM ROLLD THROUGH THE STREETS AND MADE		167 RACHEL 1	4
BACKWARD AND FORWARD ROLLD THE WAVES OF FIGHT		236 PALLADIUM	7
TO THEE WE COME THEN CLOUDS ARE ROLLD		309 OBERMANN	105

ROLLD   (CONTINUED)
        OVER THEIR OWN DEAR CHILDREN ROLLD   • • • • •   427 EMPEDOCLES I 2   446
        WITH WHAT ROLLD OF US IN THE STORMY MAIN   • • • •   439 EMPEDOCLES II   342
        WITH WHAT ROLLD OF US IN THE STORMY DEEP   • • • •   439 EMPEDOCLES II   V 342
        THE FUTURE ROLLD ITS GATHERING TIDES ALONG   • • • •   475 CROMWELL   134

ROLLING
        FELT THE SLOW-ROLLING WORD   • • • • • • •   47 WORLD QUIETIST   29
        THROUGH MANY ROLLING CLOUDS SO RUSTUM SAW   • • • •   79 SOHRAB RUSTUM   623
        CLOUDS OF WHITE ROLLING VAPOURS FILL THE VALE   • • •   113 BALDER DEAD 2   298
        HANGS DARK UPON THE ROLLING SEA   • • • • • •   205 CALAIS SANDS   22
        THE WHITE MISTS ROLLING LIKE A SEA   • • • • • •   306 OBERMANN   9
        FLOAT ON A ROLLING SEA   • • • • • • • • •   319 OBERMANN MORE   212
        FLOAT IN A ROLLING SEA   • • • • • • • • •   319 OBERMANN MORE   V 212
        THE WORLD A ROLLING FLOOD   • • • • • • • •   424 EMPEDOCLES I 2   354

ROLLS
        BRING WATER NARD AND LINEN ROLLS   • • • • •   95 SICK KING BOKH   229
        WHICH SINCE THEN FOR EVER ROLLS   • • • • • •   132 TRISTRAM 1   65
        GREEN ROLLS BENEATH THE HEADLANDS   • • • • • •   159 NECKAN   5
        GREEN ROLLS THE BALTIC SEA   • • • • • • •   159 NECKAN   6
        THE SALT TIDE ROLLS SEAWARD   • • • • • • •   164 FORSAKEN MERM   V 110
        BUT A SEA ROLLS BETWEEN US   • • • • • •   176 PARTING   65
        TIS THAT FROM CHANGE TO CHANGE THEIR BEING ROLLS   • • 259 SCHOLAR-GIPSY   143
        THE BLUE SEINE ROLLS HER WAVE   • • • • • • •   312 OBERMANN   178
        ROUND WHICH THE SULLEN VAPOUR ROLLS ALONE   • • • •   429 EMPEDOCLES II   4

ROMAN
        WITH THE ROMAN EMPEROR   • • • • • • • •   138 TRISTRAM 1   255
        LIKE THAT BALD CAESAR THE FAMED ROMAN WIGHT   • • •   153 TRISTRAM 3   143
        LIKE THAT BOLD CAESAR THE FAMED ROMAN WIGHT   • • •   153 TRISTRAM 3   V 143
        THE ROMAN NOBLE LAY   • • • • • • • • •   315 OBERMANN MORE   98
        THE ROMAN TEMPEST SWELLD AND SWELLD   • • • • • •   316 OBERMANN MORE   107

ROMANCE
        O CHARM O ROMANCE THAT WE FEEL • • • • • • • • •   230 YOUTH OF NATURE   64
        SUCH BY THESE WATERS OF ROMANCE   • • • • • •   279 SOUTHERN NIGHT   111

ROMANTIC
        ROMANTIC SOLITARY STILL   • • • • • • • • • • •   279 SOUTHERN NIGHT   114

ROME
        CLEARD ROME OF WHAT MOST SHAMED HIM BUT BE HIS   • •   2 TO A FRIEND   8
        THE GOTH BOUND ROME-WARDS SO THE HUN   • • • • •   52 RESIGNATION   9
        UPON US ARE THE CHIVALRY OF ROME   • • • • • •   137 TRISTRAM 1   236
        TO FORMS FROM ANTIQUE GREECE AND ROME UPTORN   • •   168 RACHEL 3   3
        GERMANY FRANCE CHRIST MOSES ATHENS ROME   • • • •   168 RACHEL 3   12
        SAYS APOLLO MODERNISE ROME   • • • • • • •   214 NEW ROME   10
        SAYS APOLLO MODERNISED ROME   • • • • • • •   214 NEW ROME   V 10
        ROME ENGLAND FRANCE YES NOR IN VAIN ESSAYD   • • •   239 REVOLUTIONS   6
        TO HYMN THE CONQUERING MARCH OF ROME   • • • •   300 GRANDE CHARTR   51
        SWEPT FROM THY WALLS O ROME ON ITS TRIUMPHANT WAY   465 ALARIC AT ROME   78
        THE WORLD HATH BOWED TO ROME OH COLD WERE HE   • •   465 ALARIC AT ROME   89
        NO SHAME THAT SUNS SHOULD RISE TO LIGHT A CONQUERD   468 ALARIC AT ROME   150
            ROME
        BEHELD HIM MASTER OF IMPERIAL ROME   • • • • • •   468 ALARIC AT ROME   172
        STILL SHOULD THE SPIRIT HOLD COMMUNION ROME WITH THEE 470 ALARIC AT ROME   210
        LONGS OFTENER YET AND PINES FOR ROME   • • • • • •   483 ROME-SICKNESS   4

ROMPING
        BY ROMPING CHILDREN WHOM THEIR NURSES CALL   • • • •   86 SOHRAB RUSTUM   V 846

ROOD
        ONE ROOD FROM SHORE THAT SINGLE BOAT   • • • • • •   479 HAYSWATER BOAT   16
        ONE ROOD FROM LAND THEY PUSHD NO MORE   • • • •   480 HAYSWATER BOAT   27

ROOF
        UPON THE GLISTENING LEADEN ROOF   • • • • • •   16 CHURCH BROU 2   1
        ON THE SMOOTH LEADEN ROOF AND ON THE WALLS   • • • •   18 CHURCH BROU 3   34
        MUFFLED ITS WALLS AND ON THE STONE-STREWN ROOF   • •   25 DREAM   17
        AND WENT UP ON THE ROOF TO SLEEP   • • • • • •   90 SICK KING BOKH   73
        UP TO ITS GOLDEN ROOF WITH SOBS AND CRIES   • • • •   95 BALDER DEAD 1   12
        BENEATH ONE ROOF MY QUEEN WITH MINE   • • • • •   205 CALAIS SANDS   36
        ON THE ROOF OF THE BROCKEN-TOWER   • • • • • •   297 HEINES GRAVE   168

ROOFD
        NOR WITHERD WHEN THE PALM-TREE PLUMES THAT ROOFD   • •   12 MYCERINUS   118
        TILL THE CHURCH WAS ROOFD AND DONE   • • • • • •   16 CHURCH BROU 1   102
        OF ODIN AND MY HIGH-ROOFD HOUSE IS BUILT   • • • •   108 BALDER DEAD 2   113
        AND THE ROOFD BRIDGE THAT SPANS THE STREAM   • • • •   177 FAREWELL   6
        RIVERS AND HIGH-ROOFD TOWNS   • • • • • • •   296 HEINES GRAVE   138
        TO THE STONE-ROOFD HUT AT THE TOP   • • • • • •   297 HEINES GRAVE   166

ROOFS
        ON THE SMOOTH CONVENT-ROOFS   • • • • • • • •   50 CONSOLATION   12
        ONCE MORE THE ROOFS OF BERNE APPEAR   • • • • • •   183 TERRACE BERNE   2
        AND FROM THE ROOFS THE TWISTED CHIMNEY-STACKS   • • •   263 THYRSIS   5
        WHAT POINTED ROOFS ARE THESE ADVANCE   • • • • •   300 GRANDE CHARTR   23

ROOKS
        AND BOYS WHO IN LONE WHEATFIELDS SCARE THE ROOKS   • • 257 SCHOLAR-GIPSY   64

ROOM

    FROM YOUR HUMMING FESTAL ROOM • • • • • • • •   32 NEW SIRENS   184
    FROM THE HUMMING FESTAL ROOM • • • • • • • •   32 NEW SIRENS   V 184
    THEY WINNING ROOM TO SEE AND HEAR • • • • • •   59 RESIGNATION   249
    CROWD AS WE WILL ITS NEUTRAL ROOM • • • • •   59 RESIGNATION   V 258
    SHE SPAKE AND STEPPD ASIDE AND LEFT HIM ROOM • •   108 BALDER DEAD 2   135
    THROUGH MANY A ROOM AND CORRIDOR • • • • • •   140 TRISTRAM 1   332
    HE GAZES DOWN INTO THE ROOM • • • • • • •   148 TRISTRAM 2   161
    AND LAID HER IN A STATELY ROOM WHERE FELL • • •   168 RACHEL 2   5
    SPARE ME THE WHISPERING CROWDED ROOM • • • • •   250 WISH   13
    OF THE SICK-ROOM THE MORTAL STRIFE • • • • •   251 WISH   45
    OF A SICK ROOM A MORTAL STRIFE • • • • • •   251 WISH   V 45
    IN THE SCHOOL-ROOM WINDOWS BUT COLD • • • •   286 RUGBY CHAPEL   9
    SHUTTERS AND DARKEND ROOM • • • • • • •   293 HEINES GRAVE   18
    TO GIVE HIS VIRTUES ROOM • • • • • • • • •   420 EMPEDOCLES I 2   255
    TO LEAVE HIS VIRTUES ROOM • • • • • • • •   420 EMPEDOCLES'I 2   V 255

ROOMS

    FROM YOUR DARKEND PALACE ROOMS • • • • • • •   26 NEW SIRENS   4
    AND ROOMS OF TREASURES NOT A FEW • • • • • •   94 SICK KING BOKH   214
    PARIS DRAWING-ROOMS AND LAMPS • • • • • • •   296 HEINES GRAVE   141

ROOST

    ROOST DEEP IN THE ROCKS • • • • • • • • •   442 EMPEDOCLES II   432

ROOT

    THERE ON A GRASSY SPUR WHICH BATHES ITS ROOT • • • 356 MEROPE   V 751
    THERE IS SOME ROOT OF SUFFERING IN HIMSELF • • • • 411 EMPEDOCLES I 1   151
    SO EACH NEW MAN STRIKES ROOT INTO A FAR FORE-TIME   418 EMPEDOCLES I 2   191

ROOTED

    BUT LORD AND HOUNDS KEEP ROOTED THERE • • • •   149 TRISTRAM 2   185
    AS ROOTED TO THE EARTH NOR SOUNDS • • • • •   148 TRISTRAM 2   V

ROOTS

    AND BURST THEIR ROOTS WHILE TO THEIR TOPS THE GODS 106 BALDER DEAD 2   57
    AND SAW THE NORNIES WATERING THE ROOTS • • •   120 BALDER DEAD 3   221
    AND ROUND GREEN ROOTS AND YELLOWING STALKS I SEE • 255 SCHOLAR-GIPSY   24
    WHO MADE THE ROOTS OF TREES HIS BED • • • •   277 SOUTHERN NIGHT   79
    ETERNAL SHOWERS OF SPRAY ON THE MOSSD ROOTS •   414 EMPEDOCLES I 2   47
    THROUGH WHOSE HEART ETNA DRIVES HER ROOTS OF STONE 430 EMPEDOCLES II   43
    WHENCE THE RIDGED PINE-WOODED ROOTS • • • • •   433 EMPEDOCLES II   137
    AND HAD TORN UP BY THE ROOTS • • • • • • •   434 EMPEDOCLES II   173
    WHERE THE RIDGD PINE-DARKEND ROOTS • • • • •   433 EMPEDOCLES II   V 137
    WHENCE THE RIDGD PINE-MUFFLED ROOTS • • • • •   433 EMPEDOCLES II   V 137
    WHERE THE RIDGD PINE-WOODED ROOTS • • • • • •   433 EMPEDOCLES II   V 137

ROPE

    AS THE PUNTS ROPE CHOPS ROUND • • • • • • •   257 SCHOLAR-GIPSY   76

ROPES

    AXES AND ROPES AND AT THEIR HEAD CAME THOR • • •   106 BALDER DEAD 2   48
    MADE FAST THE WOVEN ROPES AND HALED THEM DOWN • •   106 BALDER DEAD 2   58
    THE FERRY-BOAT WITH WOVEN ROPES • • • • • •   191 STRAYED REVEL   186

ROSARY

    HER ROSARY-BEADS OF EBONY TIPPD WITH GOLD • • • •   152 TRISTRAM 3   93

ROSE

    ROSE-CROWND AND EVER WHEN THE SUN WENT DOWN • •   11 MYCERINUS   93
    FLASHD ONCE LIKE FALLING STREAMS WE ROSE WE GAZED   25 DREAM   29
    WHEN THE FIRST ROSE FLUSH WAS STEEPING • • • •   31 NEW SIRENS   143
    A WILD ROSE CLIMBING UP A MOULDERING WALL • •   36 VOICE   20
    FRESH GARLANDS OF THIS DEWY ROSE • • • • •   48 HORATIAN ECHO   23
    ROUND ALPINE SUMMITS EDDYING ROSE • • • • •   52 RESIGNATION   8
    AND THE FOG ROSE OUT OF THE OXUS STREAM • • •   61 SOHRAB RUSTUM   2
    HE ROSE AND CLAD HIMSELF AND GIRT HIS SWORD •   61 SOHRAB RUSTUM   8
    AND HE ROSE QUICKLY ON ONE ARM AND SAID • • •   62 SOHRAB RUSTUM   30
    ROSE SUCH AS THAT THE SINEWY WOODCUTTERS •   75 SOHRAB RUSTUM   476
    OVER THE FIGHTERS HEADS AND A WIND ROSE •   75 SOHRAB RUSTUM   483
    AND PIERCED HER WITH AN ARROW AS SHE ROSE • •   78 SOHRAB RUSTUM   559
    SO SPAKE THE KING OF GODS AND STRAIGHTWAY ROSE •   96 BALDER DEAD 1   46
    BUT FROM THE HILL OF LIDSKIALF ODIN ROSE • •   102 BALDER DEAD 1   253
    AND FROM THEIR BEDS THE HEROES ROSE AND DONND •   105 BALDER DEAD 2   11
    SOON WITH A ROARING ROSE THE MIGHTY FIRE • •   118 BALDER DEAD 3   186
    BUT FAINTER AS THE STARS ROSE HIGH IT FLARED •   119 BALDER DEAD 3   201
    BUT FAINTER AS THE STARS ROSE HIGH IT BURND •   119 BALDER DEAD 3   V 201
    HER FINGER ON HER LIPS THEN VIVIAN ROSE • • •   156 TRISTRAM 3   215
    HE ROSE TO EARTH AGAIN • • • • • • • • •   160 NECKAN   38
    COME I SAID AND WE ROSE THROUGH THE SURF IN THE BAY 163 FORSAKEN MERM   67
    THE ROSE-CROWND QUEEN OF LEGENDARY LORE • • • •   168 RACHEL 2   7
    ITS FIRS AND AFAR ROSE THE PEAKS • • • • • •   229 YOUTH OF NATURE   39
    THE HILLS WHERE HIS LIFE ROSE ʃ • • • • • •   247 BURIED LIFE   97
    EACH ROSE WITH BLUSHING FACE • • • • • • •   265 THYRSIS   96
    MYRTLE AND ROSE FIT THE YOUNG • • • • • • •   282 HAWORTH CHURCH   V
    ROSE AND WITH FIRE AND SWORD ASSAILED MY HOUSE • • 340 MEROPE   344
    THERE ROSE UP A CRY IN THE STREETS • • • • •   345 MEROPE   487
    WITH HEDGES OF THE WILD ROSE • • • • • • •   399 MEROPE   1821
    ROSE FROM BELOW IF IT WERE POSSIBLE • • • • •   412 EMPEDOCLES I 2   9

ROSE   (CONTINUED)
        HOW HIS BROW LIGHTEND AS THE MUSIC ROSE   •   •   •   428 EMPEDOCLES I 2   483
        ROSE DIM FROM THE MORASS   •   •   •   •   •   •   •   •   445 WESTMIN ABBEY   32
        CRUSHD AS THEY ROSE BY MANHOODS STERNER WILL   •   •   474 CROMWELL   80
        UNTIL ANOTHER ROSE AND SMOTE HIM DOWN   •   •   •   •   476 CROMWELL   144
        AT LAST IN AIR FAR OFF DIM ROSE A HEIGHT   •   •   •   •   484 S S LUSITANIA   6
        OER THOSE SAME SEAS DARK TENERIFFE ROSE FRAUGHT   •   •   485 S S LUSITANIA   11

ROSEATE
        IN HIS ROSEATE LIGHT AUSTERE   •   •   •   •   •   •   •   PILLARS UNIVERS   V   9

ROSES
        STREW ON HER ROSES ROSES   •   •   •   •   •   •   •   •   20 REQUIESCAT   1
        STREW ON HER ROSES ROSES   •   •   •   •   •   •   •   •   20 REQUIESCAT   1
        ROSES FOR THAT DREAMING BROW   •   •   •   •   •   •   •   32 NEW SIRENS   174
        PLUCK NO MORE RED ROSES MAIDENS   •   •   •   •   •   •   35 NEW SIRENS   267
        STREW NO MORE RED ROSES MAIDENS   •   •   •   •   •   •   35 NEW SIRENS   V 267
        PALE DEW-DRENCHD HALF-SHUT ROSES GLEAM   •   •   •   •   57 RESIGNATION   179
        ITS SHELLS AND ROSES PALE   •   •   •   •   •   •   •   •   159 NECKAN   10
        AND PALE DOG-ROSES IN THE HEDGE   •   •   •   •   •   •   218 BACCHANALIA 1   12
        BEFORE THE ROSES AND THE LONGEST DAY   •   •   •   •   •   264 THYRSIS   53
        ROSES THAT DOWN THE ALLEYS SHINE AFAR   •   •   •   •   264 THYRSIS   67
        STREW WITH ROSES THE GRAVE   •   •   •   •   •   •   •   283 HAWORTH CHURCH   V 66

ROSILY
        ROSILY BRIGHTEN AND THE SOOTHED GODS SMILE   •   •   •   •   431 EMPEDOCLES II   81

ROSY
        AND LOOKING DOWN ON THE WARM ROSY TINTS   •   •   •   •   18 CHURCH BROU 3   28
        AND WATCHD THE ROSY LIGHT   •   •   •   •   •   •   •   •   310 OBERMANN   122

ROTHA
        O ROTHA WITH THY LIVING WAVE   •   •   •   •   •   •   •   272 MEMORIAL VERSES   72
        OF ROTHA SPARKLES THROUGH FIELDS   •   •   •   •   •   •   280 HAWORTH CHURCH   2
        OF ROTHA SPARKLES THE FIELDS   •   •   •   •   •   •   •   280 HAWORTH CHURCH   V 2

ROTTED
        SHOULD FIRST HAVE ROTTED ON THEIR NIMBLE JOINTS   •   •   83 SOHRAB RUSTUM   739
        SHOULD THEN HAVE ROTTED ON THY NIMBLE JOINTS   •   •   83 SOHRAB RUSTUM   V 739
        SHOULD THEN HAVE ROTTED ON THEIR NIMBLE JOINTS   •   •   83 SOHRAB RUSTUM   V 739

ROUGE
        THY SMILE AND ROUGE WITH STONY GLARE   •   •   •   •   •   184 TERRACE BERNE   22

ROUGH
        STILL ROUGH LIKE THOSE WHICH MEN IN TREELESS PLAINS   73 SOHRAB RUSTUM   410
        COULD WIELD AN UNLOPPD TRUNK IT WAS STILL ROUGH   •   •   73 SOHRAB RUSTUM   V 409
        AND STREWN THE CHANNELS WITH TORN BOUGHS SO ROUGH   73 SOHRAB RUSTUM   V 415
        AND THIS ROUGH DECEMBER-NIGHT   •   •   •   •   •   •   •   136 TRISTRAM 1   181
        DRAGGING THEIR NETS THROUGH THE ROUGH WAVES AFAR   •   •   151 TRISTRAM 3   80
        THROUGH THE ROUGH FIR-PLANKS   •   •   •   •   •   •   •   186 STRAYED REVEL   25
        TOPPD WITH ROUGH-HEWN   •   •   •   •   •   •   •   •   •   191 STRAYED REVEL   178
        AND A ROUGH GRIMED RACE HAVE THEIR HOMES   •   •   •   •   283 HAWORTH CHURCH   60
        IN HER ROUGH FORM FEARING   •   •   •   •   •   •   •   •   392 MEROPE   1634
        TILL THE ROUGH COW-HERDS DRIVE THEM PAST   •   •   •   •   413 EMPEDOCLES I 2   40
        NOR IS THAT WIND LESS ROUGH WHICH BLOWS A GOOD   420 EMPEDOCLES I 2   256
              MANS BARGE
        NOR IS THE WIND LESS ROUGH THAT BLOWS A GOOD   420 EMPEDOCLES I 2   V 256
              MANS BARGE
        ROUGH WAS THE WINTER EVE   •   •   •   •   •   •   •   •   444 WESTMIN ABBEY   11
        AND THE ROUGH WAVES OF LIFE FOR EVER LAID   •   •   •   •   449 WESTMIN ABBEY   165
        MADE ROUGH WITH CARE BECOME THE CHANGEFUL SEA   •   •   473 CROMWELL   49

ROUND
        STAND NEVER IDLE BUT GO ALWAYS ROUND   •   •   •   •   •   4 DUKE WELLINGTON   2
        ECHOING ROUND THIS CASTLE OLD   •   •   •   •   •   •   •   12 CHURCH BROU 1   2
        LADIES WAITING ROUND HER SEAT   •   •   •   •   •   •   •   13 CHURCH BROU 1   34
        ROUND THE TOMB THE CARVED STONE FRETWORK   •   •   •   •   16 CHURCH BROU 1   109
        ROUND THE WALL TO STRAY   •   •   •   •   •   •   •   •   16 CHURCH BROU 2   11
        ROUND THE CHURCH OF BROU   •   •   •   •   •   •   •   •   16 CHURCH BROU 2   16
        ROUND THE CHURCH OF BROU   •   •   •   •   •   •   •   •   17 CHURCH BROU 2   24
        ROUND THE CHURCH OF BROU   •   •   •   •   •   •   •   •   17 CHURCH BROU 2   32
        ROUND THE TOMB TO STRAY   •   •   •   •   •   •   •   •   17 CHURCH BROU 2   35
        AND ON THE PAVEMENT ROUND THE TOMB THERE GLINTS   •   •   18 CHURCH BROU 3   22
        OF DARK ELMS SHOOT ROUND DROPPING DOWN THE   19 MODERN SAPPHO   6
              PROUD STREAM
        LOOKS LANGUIDLY ROUND ON A GLOOM-BURIED WORLD   •   •   20 MODERN SAPPHO   24
        TIS HE TIS THEIR FLAG SHOOTING ROUND BY THE TREES   20 MODERN SAPPHO   30
        OF DARK ELMS COME ROUND DROPPING DOWN THE PROUD STREAM   19 MODERN SAPPHO   V   6
        TIS HE TIS THE BOAT SHOOTING ROUND BY THE TREES   •   •   20 MODERN SAPPHO   V 30
        AND NOW PEACE LAPS HER ROUND   •   •   •   •   •   •   •   21 REQUIESCAT   12
        BLACK UNDER CLIFFS IT RACED ROUND HEADLANDS SHONE   25 DREAM   34
        ROUND OUR HEARTS WITH LONG CARESSES   •   •   •   •   •   28 NEW SIRENS   69
        WHEN THE PINE-BOUGHS YIELDED ROUND YOU   •   •   •   •   29 NEW SIRENS   99
        WHO MASSD ROUND THAT SLIGHT BROW THESE CLOUDS OF DOOM   41 GIPSY CHILD   4
        ROUND THY STILL DREAMING BROTHER-WORLD OUTSPREAD   •   •   45 IN UTRUMQUE PAR   31
        YET AS THE WHEEL FLIES ROUND   •   •   •   •   •   •   •   47 WORLD QUIETIST   17
        HEM ME ROUND EVERYWHERE   •   •   •   •   •   •   •   •   50 CONSOLATION   3
        SHRILLS ROUND THEIR PORTAL   •   •   •   •   •   •   •   50 CONSOLATION   22
        PLAYS FONDLY ROUND THEM   •   •   •   •   •   •   •   •   51 CONSOLATION   44
        BRINGS ROUND TO ALL MEN   •   •   •   •   •   •   •   •   52 CONSOLATION   74
        SIX YARDS ROUND SHALL NOT RING IT   •   •   •   •   •   •   50 CONSOLATION   V
        ROUND ALPINE SUMMITS EDDYING ROSE   •   •   •   •   •   52 RESIGNATION   ·8

ROUND   (CONTINUED)

IN DARK KNOTS CROUCH ROUND THE WILD FLAME	• • • •	55 RESIGNATION	118
RUNS HIS OLD ROUND OF DUBIOUS CHEER	• • • • •	56 RESIGNATION	129
FOLDS THE STILL VALLEY ALMOST ROUND	• • • • •	57 RESIGNATION	175
IN THE DAYS LIFE WHOSE IRON ROUND	• • • • •	58 RESIGNATION	209
AND THREW A WHITE CLOAK ROUND HIM AND HE TOOK	• •	64 SOHRAB RUSTUM	98
HIS ARMS ROUND HIS SONS NECK AND WEPT ALOUD	• •	82 SOHRAB RUSTUM	728
AND CLIP HIS BORDERS ROUND AND DRIVE HIS HERDS	• •	68 SOHRAB RUSTUM	V 234
EDDYING AND MOANING ROUND AND SWEPT THE PLAIN	• •	75 SOHRAB RUSTUM	V 484
THOUGH IT BE GREAT ALL THE EARTH ROUND	• • •	92 SICK KING BOKH	158
SO ON THE FLOOR LAY BALDER DEAD AND ROUND	• • •	95 BALDER DEAD 1	1
AND STOOD ROUND BALDER ON THE BLOODY FLOOR	• • •	95 BALDER DEAD 1	10
AND HE WILL SEE STRETCH ROUND HIM HELAS REALM	• •	100 BALDER DEAD 1	171
ALIVE AND STILL THE RAYS WERE ROUND HIS HEAD	• •	103 BALDER DEAD 1	284
AND STOOD ROUND BALDER LYING ON HIS BIER	• • •	102 BALDER DEAD 1	V 270
AND HE BEHELD SPREAD ROUND HIM HELAS REALM	• • •	109 BALDER DEAD 2	149
AND ROUND THEM STILL THE WATTLED HURDLES HUNG	• •	109 BALDER DEAD 2	173
ROUND BALDERS CORPSE WHICH THEY HAD THITHER BORNE		113 BALDER DEAD 3	2
ROUND WHERE THEY STOOD AND THEY BEHELD TWO FORMS	• •	126 BALDER DEAD 3	442
DEATH AND THE GLOOM WHICH ROUND ME EVEN NOW	• •	129 BALDER DEAD 3	546
ONCE MORE ROUND THEM AND THE SEA	• • • • •	135 TRISTRAM 1	154
ALL ROUND THE FOREST SWEEPS OFF BLACK IN SHADE	• •	139 TRISTRAM 1	276
ROUND EACH SWEET BROW THE CAP CLOSE-SET	• • •	141 TRISTRAM 1	340
AND ROUND HIM A FRESH FOREST-SCENE	• • • •	147 TRISTRAM 2	154
WITH HIS PACK ROUND HIM AND DELAYS	• • • •	148 TRISTRAM 2	156
IS LIGHT AND GREEN THE HEATHER WHICH ALL ROUND	• •	150 TRISTRAM 3	14
NOR TO THE BROWN HEATHS ROUND THEM BRIGHT AND WIDE	•	151 TRISTRAM 3	49
WHICH GLISTERING PLAYS ALL ROUND THEM LONE AND MILD		155 TRISTRAM 3	203
NINE TIMES SHE WAVED THE FLUTTERING WIMPLE ROUND	• •	156 TRISTRAM 3	219
THE YEAR HAD TRAVELLD ROUND AND ONE BRIGHT DAY	• •	TRISTRAM 3	V 1
FIRST MEETS THE FRINGING HEATH AT ONCE ALL ROUND		TRISTRAM 3	V 14
FIRST LEAVES THE FRINGING HEATH AT ONCE ALL ROUND		TRISTRAM 3	V 14
FIRST MEETS THE ENCIRCLING HEATH AT ONCE ALL ROUND		TRISTRAM 3	V 14
FIRST LEAVES THE ENCIRCLING HEATH AT ONCE ALL ROUND		TRISTRAM 3	V 14
IS GREEN AND CLEAR THE HEATHER WHICH ALL ROUND	• •	TRISTRAM 3	V 14
IS LIGHT AND GREEN THE HEATHER WHICH ALL ROUND		TRISTRAM 3	V 14
NOR TO THE BROWN HEATHS ROUND THEM WARM AND WIDE	•	TRISTRAM 3	V 49
WHICH GLISTERING LAY ALL ROUND THEM LONE AND MILD		155 TRISTRAM 3	V 203
MID SHELLS THAT ROUND HER LIE	• • • • • •	160 NECKAN	34
WHERE THE SEA-BEASTS RANGED ALL ROUND	• • • •	162 FORSAKEN MERM	39
ROUND THE WORLD FOR EVER AND AYE	• • • • •	162 FORSAKEN MERM	45
THINE ARMS ROUND THY CHILD	• • • • • •	177 PARTING	78
NOW ROUND US SPREADS THE WATERY PLAIN	• • •	182 TO MARG CONT	17
I SPRANG UP I THREW ROUND ME	• • • • •	186 STRAYED REVEL	29
IN THE TOWN ROUND THE TEMPLE	• • • • •	186 STRAYED REVEL	37
DRIFTING DRIFTING ROUND HIM	• • • • • •	190 STRAYED REVEL	158
ROUND HIS GREEN HARVEST-PLOT	• • • • •	190 STRAYED REVEL	159
AND WANDER ROUND THE WORLD AGAIN	• • • • •	206 RIVER	16
WAS ONCE TOO AT THE FULL AND ROUND EARTHS SHORE	• •	211 DOVER BEACH	22
THEY SEE ALL ROUND A WILDERNESS	• • • •	226 EPILOG LAOCOON	176
ITS SPELL IS ROUND THEM LIKE A SHOWER	• • •	227 EPILOG LAOCOON	199
ROUND TROY BUT WHILE THIS STOOD TROY COULD NOT FALL		236 PALLADIUM	8
UNAFFRIGHTED BY THE SILENCE ROUND THEM	• • •	240 SELF-DEPENDENCE	17
AND ROUND GREEN ROOTS AND YELLOWING STALKS I SEE	• •	255 SCHOLAR-GIPSY	24
AS THE PUNTS ROPE CHOPS ROUND	• • • • •	257 SCHOLAR-GIPSY	76
AS THE SLOW PUNT SWINGS ROUND	• • • • •	257 SCHOLAR-GIPSY	V 76
YES THOU ART GONE AND ROUND ME TOO THE NIGHT	• •	266 THYRSIS	131
AND HOW A CALL CELESTIAL ROUND HIM RANG	• • •	268 THYRSIS	188
OUR SOULS IN ITS BENUMBING ROUND	• • • •	271 MEMORIAL VERSES	46
THE HILLS WERE ROUND US AND THE BREEZE	• • •	271 MEMORIAL VERSES	51
OUR SPIRITS IN A BRAZEN ROUND	• • • • •	271 MEMORIAL VERSES	V 46
RISE UP ALL ROUND THE CHRISTIAN SPIRES	• • •	274 STANZAS CARNAC	22
ALL ROUND NO SOUL NO BOAT NO HAIL	• • • •	274 STANZAS CARNAC	30
HOME ROUND INTO THE ENGLISH WAVE	• • • •	275 STANZAS CARNAC	37
SLOW ROUND HER PADDLES DIES AWAY	• • • •	276 SOUTHERN NIGHT	31
ROUND THEE THEY LIE THE GRASS	• • • • •	284 HAWORTH CHURCH	88
FIFTEEN YEARS HAVE GONE ROUND	• • • • •	287 RUGBY CHAPEL	26
NOT WITHOUT AIM TO GO ROUND	• • • • •	288 RUGBY CHAPEL	76
WHO ALL ROUND ME TO-DAY	• • • • • •	290 RUGBY CHAPEL	156
RISING ALL ROUND OVERAWE	• • • • • •	291 RUGBY CHAPEL	179
STUPIDLY TRAVELS HER ROUND	• • • • •	294 HEINES GRAVE	81
THE AUTUMNAL EVENING DARKENS ROUND	• • • •	299 GRANDE CHARTR	7
TAKE ME COWLD FORMS AND FENCE ME ROUND	• • •	302 GRANDE CHARTR	93
STILL THE SAME OCEAN ROUND US RAVES	• • • •	303 GRANDE CHARTR	125
DEEP DEEP THE GREENWOOD ROUND THEM WAVES	• •	305 GRANDE CHARTR	173
ROUND SOME FAIR FOREST-LODGE AT MORN	• • •	305 GRANDE CHARTR	184
FENCED EARLY IN THIS CLOISTRAL ROUND	• • •	306 GRANDE CHARTR	205
INVEST ME STEEP ME FOLD ME ROUND	• • • •	302 GRANDE CHARTR	V 93
ROUND SOME OLD FOREST-LODGE AT MORN	• • •	305 GRANDE CHARTR	V 184
STAND DARK ROUND THY GREEN GRAVE	• • • •	311 OBERMANN	168
THOUGH ROUND THY FIRMER MANHOOD CAST	• • • •	323 OBERMANN MORE	307
THE FORESTS ROUND THAT BELT CYLLENES SIDE	• •	357 MEROPE	794
BUT ROUND THE HEADLANDS POINT A CURRENT SETS	• •	358 MEROPE	820
CAUGHT THEM AS WIND TAKES FEATHERS WHIRLD THEM ROUND		358 MEROPE	824
A MOMENT MORE I SAW THE PRINCE TURN ROUND	• •	358 MEROPE	831
RUSTLED ROUND HIS CRADLE	• • • • • •	392 MEROPE	1620
TO CIRCLE THE PRINCE ROUND WHEN SUDDENLY	• •	402 MEROPE	1932
THE FORESTS ROUND WHICH BELT CYLLENES SIDE	• •	357 MEROPE	V 794
THE PEAK ROUND WHICH THE WHITE CLOUDS PLAY	• • •	414 EMPEDOCLES I 2	56
ROUND WHICH THE SULLEN VAPOUR ROLLS ALONE	• • •	429 EMPEDOCLES II	4

ROUND   (CONTINUED)
        AND NO ONE ROUND THE CHARMED CIRCLE SPEAKS • • •   431 EMPEDOCLES II   83
        THEN RAISED HER FACE AND GLORY ROUND HER STREAMD • • 447 WESTMIN ABBEY   96
        THEN RAISED HER FACE AND GLORY ROUND HER BEAMD • •   447 WESTMIN ABBEY   V 96
        ROUND HIS SMALL THROAT OF BLACK AND BROWN • • •   459 KAISER DEAD   15
        AND LEAVE IT ROUND THY NECK TO TWINE • • • •   461 KAISER DEAD   81
        ROUND THE WAN TEMPLES OF THE HALLOWED DEAD • • •   463 ALARIC AT ROME   26
        WITH SOLEMN CADENCE ROUND HER CITADEL • • • •   472 CROMWELL   20
        LIKE LOVING SHADOWS ROUND THAT CHILDHOODS HOME • •   474 CROMWELL   74
        AND SLOW RELUCTANT STEPS ARE GATHERING ROUND • •   476 CROMWELL   160
        AND THE WIND MURMURD ROUND HIM AND HE STOOD • •   479 CROMWELL   239

ROUNDED
        ALL HER PALE SWEET-ROUNDED CHEEK • • • • • • •   23 MEMORY-PICTURE   30

ROUNDS
        IN FILES AND IN ROUNDS • • • • • • • • • •   218 BACCHANALIA 1   23

ROUSE
        ROUSE NO ANGER MAKE NO RIVALS MORE • • • • • •   144 TRISTRAM 2   64
        FOR THOU WILT ROUSE NO SLEEPERS HERE • • • • •   149 TRISTRAM 2   190
        STILL LIKE A TRUMPET DOST ROUSE • • • • • •   287 RUGBY CHAPEL   52
        SOME STRAGGLING HUNTERS TO MY AID TO ROUSE • • •   358 MEROPE   836
        HOW SHALL I ROUSE THEIR LOVE THEIR ARDOUR SO • •   382 MEROPE   1352

ROUSED
        AND THE ROUSED MALIAC GULPH • • • • • • • •   198 FRAG ANTIGONE   101

ROUSES
        MISERY WHICH ROUSES OTHERS BREAKS THE SPRING • •   366 MEROPE   1025

ROUT
        THE ROUT EARLY GATHERD • • • • • • • • • •   186 STRAYED REVEL   36
        THINE ANCIENT ROUT BY THE CILICIAN HILLS • • • •   430 EMPEDOCLES II   53
        THY ANCIENT ROUT BY THE CILICIAN HILLS • • • •   430 EMPEDOCLES II   V 53
        THE ANCIENT ROUT BY THE CILICIAN HILLS • • • •   430 EMPEDOCLES II   V 53

ROUTED
        THE WORLDS POOR ROUTED LEAVINGS OR WILL THEY • •   172 IMMORTALITY   6
        STAY THIS HAND FROM FIGHT TILL THE TROJANS   HOMER TRANS   62
            ARE UTTERLY ROUTED

ROVE
        WHO ROVE OER KIPCHAK AND THE NORTHERN WASTE • •   65 SOHRAB RUSTUM   V 131
        HER WORK AWAY AND LET HER FINGERS ROVE • • • •   152 TRISTRAM 3   87
        BUT SHE HERSELF WHITHER SHE WILL CAN ROVE • • • •   156 TRISTRAM 3   223

ROVED
        YET NOW MY GLANCE BUT ONCE HATH ROVED • • • •   205 CALAIS SANDS   17
        BUT NOW MY GLANCE BUT ONCE HATH ROVED • • • •   205 CALAIS SANDS   V 17

ROVER
        ROVER WITH THE GOOD BROWN HEAD • • • • • • •   453 POOR MATTHIAS   25
        ROVER DIED ATOSSA TOO • • • • • • • • •   453 POOR MATTHIAS   43
        AND TOSS AND ROVER • • • • • • • • • • •   460 KAISER DEAD   66

ROVING
        THEN FANCYS ROVING VISIONS BOLD AND FREE • • • •   474 CROMWELL   93

ROW
        AND ROW HIM STRAIGHTWAY TO THE FURTHER SHORE • •   444 WESTMIN ABBEY   25

ROWS
        UNDER THE EAVES PEERD ROWS OF INDIAN CORN • • •   25 DREAM   19
        MOVES THROUGH THEIR ROWS OF PILLARS OLD • • •   274 STANZAS CARNAC   14
        STREAMS THROUGH THEIR ROWS OF PILLARS OLD • • •   274 STANZAS CARNAC   V 14

ROYAL
        THE ROYAL TROOPS OF PERSIA HORSE AND FOOT • • •   65 SOHRAB RUSTUM   139
        ROYAL STATE WITH MARC MY DEEP-WRONGD HUSBAND • •   144 TRISTRAM 2   45
        THIS HIS IDOL THIS THAT ROYAL BRIDE • • • •   144 TRISTRAM 2   66
        SPEAK HER FAIR SHE IS OF ROYAL BLOOD • • • •   145 TRISTRAM 2   94
        OF HIS FRESH-CONQUERD REALM THE ROYAL SEAT • • •   330 MEROPE   11
        WHO BUT THE KINSMEN OF THE ROYAL BROOD • • • •   336 MEROPE   221
        WHO TOLD ME THAT THE ROYAL HOUSE WAS HERE • • •   354 MEROPE   704
        SET FORTH FROM TEGEA THE ROYAL TOWN • • • •   355 MEROPE   732
        SO DIES THE LAST SHOOT OF OUR ROYAL TREE • • •   359 MEROPE   857
        AND SUCH AS FITS A ROYAL HOUSE TO SHOW • • •   359 MEROPE   871
        THE ROYAL RACE OF TEMENUS IN ARGOS • • •   384 MEROPE   1391
        MY ROYAL SISTER BUT WITHOUT SOME CAUSE • • •   386 MEROPE   1449

RUB
        AND THEY WILL RUB THROUGH IF THEY CAN • • • •   56 RESIGNATION   140
        AND RUB THE STEEL AND MAKE IT SHINE • • • • •   461 KAISER DEAD   80

RUBBD
        BUT NO THEY RUBBD THROUGH YESTERDAY • • • • •   56 RESIGNATION   138

RUBY
        AND AMETHYST AND RUBY THEN UNCLOSE • • • • • •   18 CHURCH BROU 3   24

RUDDER
    GRASPING THE RUDDER HARD . . . .   244 SUMMER NIGHT   67
    AND SNATCHD HIS RUDDER AND SHOOK OUT MORE SAIL . . .   262 SCHOLAR-GIPSY   242
    THE RUDDER SWINGS YET NONE DOTH STEER   . . . .   480 HAYSWATER BOAT   39

RUDDY
    RUDDY IN THE FIRES LIGHT . . . .   131 TRISTRAM 1   18
    THERE SATE FIFTY MEN IN THE RUDDY LIGHT OF THE FIRE   HOMER TRANS   4

RUDE
    ON THE BROWN RUDE-CARVED BALCONY TWO FORMS . . . .   25 DREAM   21
    AND NOW BEYOND THE RUDE STONE BRIDGE . . . . . .   54 RESIGNATION   52
    AND THIS RUDE CUMNER GROUND   . . . .   269 THYRSIS   216
    AND THIS RUDE CUMNOR GROUND   . . . .   269 THYRSIS   V 216
    AFTER LONG DARKNESS RUDE . . . .   322 OBERMANN MORE   294
    BUT WE AS SOME RUDE GUEST   . . . .   419 EMPEDOCLES I 2   217
    FLASHT ON THE RUDE BARBARIANS WILD ARRAY . . . .   464 ALARIC AT ROME   70
    RUDE ORATOR . . . .   RUDE ORATOR   1

RUDELY
    THE GENTLENESS TOO RUDELY HURLD   . . . .   180 FAREWELL   85
    SHAKEN AND RUDELY HURLD . . . .   416 EMPEDOCLES I 2   V 115

RUE
    BUT FROM THEIR WEAKNESS WHO WOULD WORK HER RUE   . .   37 WORLDS TRIUMPHS   4
    BUT FROM THEIR BASENESS WHO WOULD WORK HER RUE   . .   37 WORLDS TRIUMPHS   V   4
    TO RUE MY GUILT IN ENDLESS FLAME . . . . . .   157 SAINT BRANDAN   32

RUFFLE
    THE WINDOW AND RUFFLE   . . . .   174 PARTING   3

RUFFLED
    REELS AND SHIVERS ON THE RUFFLED GLOOM   . . . .   32 NEW SIRENS   186
    SMOOTH HIS RUFFLED PLUMAGE FINE   . . . . . .   452 POOR MATTHIAS   11

RUFFLES
    RUFFLES THE WARM AFTERNOON   . . . .   293 HEINES GRAVE   40

RUGGED
    THE RUGGED LABOURER   . . . .   47 WORLD QUIETIST   21

RUGS
    OF RUGS AND FELTS AND NEAR HIM LAY HIS ARMS   . .   61 SOHRAB RUSTUM   27
    HIS BED AND THE WARM RUGS WHEREON HE LAY   . . .   63 SOHRAB RUSTUM   95

RUIN
    KNOWLEDGE NO RUIN   . . . .   40 STAGIRIUS   59
    HELPLESS TO BETTER US OR RUIN THEM   . . . . .   111 BALDER DEAD 2   230
    THEIR HANGING RUIN ALAS . . . .   289 RUGBY CHAPEL   100
    OF RUIN BUT SHE SMILED   . . . .   317 OBERMANN MORE   140
    DOWN CAME THE STORM IN RUIN FELL   . . . . .   319 OBERMANN MORE   V 205
    HE SACRIFICED OUR RUIN IN HIS HEART   . . . .   338 MEROPE   273
    HE BEARS THE SEED OF RUIN IN HIMSELF   . . . .   359 MEROPE   856
    OUR MISERY MORE AND THINE OWN RUIN SURE   . . .   368 MEROPE   1081
    TO ANNOUNCE THE RUIN OF MY HUSBANDS HOUSE   . . .   395 MEROPE   1738
    FATE SEALS MY LIPS AND DRAGS TO RUIN THEE   . . .   397 MEROPE   1779
    NEEDLE OF RUIN   . . . .   400 MEROPE   1881
    AND MAKES THY VERY RUIN FRESH AND BEAUTIFUL   . .   464 ALARIC AT ROME   54

RUIND
    A GUSH OF SUNBEAMS THROUGH A RUIND HALL   . . . .   36 VOICE   21
    THE RUIND PALACES OF ODIN SEATS   . . . . . .   128 BALDER DEAD 3   533
    BUT RUIND AND SOLEMN AND GREY . . . .   228 YOUTH OF NATURE   20
    BETWEEN A RUIND CHURCH AND SHATTERD THRONE . . . .   477 CROMWELL   188

RUINS
    DOWN CAME THE STORM IN RUINS FELL   . . . .   319 OBERMANN MORE   205
    THOU SHATTERED MASS WHOSE GLORIOUS RUINS TELL   . .   463 ALARIC AT ROME   45
    AND MINGLE WITH THY RUINS SOMEWHAT OF OUR OWN   . .   470 ALARIC AT ROME   204

RUKSH
    SO ARMD HE ISSUED FORTH AND RUKSH HIS HORSE   . .   69 SOHRAB RUSTUM   270
    RUKSH WHOSE RENOWN WAS NOISED THROUGH ALL THE EARTH   69 SOHRAB RUSTUM   272
    AND LIGHTNINGS RENT THE CLOUD AND RUKSH THE HORSE   76 SOHRAB RUSTUM   501
    WHEN THEY SAW RUSTUMS GRIEF AND RUKSH THE HORSE   . .   82 SOHRAB RUSTUM   730
    RUKSH NOW THOU GRIEVEST BUT O RUKSH THY FEET   . .   83 SOHRAB RUSTUM   738
    RUKSH NOW THOU GRIEVEST BUT O RUKSH THY FEET   . .   83 SOHRAB RUSTUM   738
    IS THIS THEN RUKSH HOW OFTEN IN PAST DAYS . . . .   83 SOHRAB RUSTUM   742
    O RUKSH THOU ART MORE FORTUNATE THAN I   . . . .   83 SOHRAB RUSTUM   747
    AND SAID O RUKSH BEAR RUSTUM WELL BUT I   . . . .   83 SOHRAB RUSTUM   755

RULE
    I LOOKD FOR LIFE MORE LASTING RULE MORE HIGH   . .   9 MYCERINUS   17
    AT RANDOM AND NOT STEER BY RULE   . . . . . .   40 HUMAN LIFE   14
    THEY THAT BEAR RULE AND ARE OBEYD   . . . . .   93 SICK KING BOKH   186
    UNTO A RULE MORE STRONG THAN THEIRS   . . . . .   93 SICK KING BOKH   187
    AND GAVE ME NINE UNLIGHTED REALMS TO RULE   . . .   110 BALDER DEAD 2   213
    THAN BE A CROWND KING HERE AND RULE THE DEAD   . .   112 BALDER DEAD 2   267
    AND GAVST HER NINE UNLIGHTED WORLDS TO RULE   . .   121 BALDER DEAD 3   277
    TILL THEY RULE IT TILL HE SEEM . . . .   136 TRISTRAM 1   184

RULE (CONTINUED)

THOUGH SHE RULE NOT EARTH TO-DAY	227	PERSIST POETRY	V	2
HIS MATES HAD ARTS TO RULE AS THEY DESIRED	256	SCHOLAR-GIPSY		45
MADE HIS LIFES RULE ONCE MORE	314	OBERMANN MORE		54
DEGRADING PYLOS FROM ITS ANCIENT RULE	330	MEROPE		12
HATE TO THEIR RULE WHICH ELSE WOULD DIE AWAY	331	MEROPE		43
ALAS THAT HOW TO RULE IT WAS OUR BROIL	334	MEROPE		127
THE LONG REPRESSIVE ATTITUDE OF RULE	334	MEROPE		154
ASSIST ME TO RULE MILDLY LET US JOIN	335	MEROPE		164
TO RULE THIS KINGDOM I INTEND WITH SWAY	342	MEROPE		376
CLEMENT IF MAY BE BUT TO RULE IT THERE	342	MEROPE		377
HOLDS RULE AH ME AH	345	MEROPE		475
LET THE BEST RULE THEY SAY AGAIN	352	MEROPE		653
THAT BEST WHO OUGHT TO RULE AM I	353	MEROPE		677
FAIR TERMS OF RECONCILEMENT EQUAL RULE	360	MEROPE		882
THE WILLING SHARER OF HIS GUILTY RULE	366	MEROPE		1007
WHEN THEY CORRUPT THE SOULS OF THOSE THEY RULE	386	MEROPE		1437
BENT ABOVE ALL TO PACIFY TO RULE	388	MEROPE		1490
LET US FORGET OURSELVES FOR THOSE WE RULE	394	MEROPE		1721
AS THE CHIEFS RULE MY SON THE PEOPLE ARE	404	MEROPE		2002
SO RULE THAT EVEN THINE ENEMIES MAY FAIL	404	MEROPE		2005
SO RULE THAT AS THY FATHER THOU BE LOVED	404	MEROPE		2008
SO RULE THAT AS HIS FOE THOU BE OBEYD	404	MEROPE		2009
AS THE CHIEFS RULE INDEED THE PEOPLE ARE	404	MEROPE		V2002
SO RULE THAT AS THY FOE THOU BE OBEYD	404	MEROPE		V2009

RULED

HAMAN WHO NEXT TO PERAN-WISA RULED	64	SOHRAB RUSTUM	108
AND FERABURZ WHO RULED THE PERSIAN HOST	66	SOHRAB RUSTUM	172
AND RULED OER DENMARK AND THE HEATHY ISLES	117	BALDER DEAD 3	127
ONE THING TO UNDO WHAT THOU THYSELF HAST RULED	120	BALDER DEAD 3	253
A GOD A GOD THEIR SEVERANCE RULED	182	TO MARG CONT	22
PRECARIOUSLY RULED BY FOREIGN LORDS	337	MEROPE	235
RULED IN THEIR NAME AND TRAIND THEM TO YOUR WILL	339	MEROPE	321
AND TRULY IN THIS ILL-RULED WORLD	353	MEROPE	664
IN ALL BY THY EXPERIENCE TO BE RULED	405	MEROPE	2015

RULER

A RULER OF THE PEOPLE STAND	56	RESIGNATION	155
THE FEARD AND BLACKEND RULER OF THEIR RACE	336	MEROPE	198
WELL THIRST TO DRAG THE WRONGFUL RULER DOWN	353	MEROPE	670

RULERS

IN HIS RIGHT HAND A RULERS STAFF NO SWORD	64	SOHRAB RUSTUM	99
THEIR MURDERD RULERS TERRIBLY AVENGED	390	MEROPE	1566

RULES

BUT IF THIS ONE DESIRE INDEED RULES ALL	63	SOHRAB RUSTUM	74
WITH AGE AND RULES OVER THE VALIANT KOORDS	78	SOHRAB RUSTUM	592
OR IF INDEED THIS ONE DESIRE RULES ALL	63	SOHRAB RUSTUM	V 74
THIS NO SAINT PREACHES AND THIS NO CHURCH RULES	171	DIVINITY	13
CRITICS NEW RULES	220	BACCHANALIA 2	40
HOW OF ALL HUMAN RULES THE OVER-TENSE	339	MEROPE	307
STILL RULES STILL WATCHES AND NUMBRETH THE HOURS	347	MEROPE	527
STILL RULES STILL WATCHES AND NUMBERS THE HOURS	347	MEROPE	V 527
BY OTHER RULES THAN ARE IN VOGUE TO-DAY	436	EMPEDOCLES II	265

RULING

NOR DID THE ALL-RULING ODIN SLIGHT HER WORD	122	BALDER DEAD 3	297
UPON OUR LIFE A RULING EFFLUENCE SEND	236	PALLADIUM	22
HIM IF HIGH-RULING ZEUS	347	MEROPE	534

RUMBLED

GREW BLACKER THUNDER RUMBLED IN THE AIR	76	SOHRAB RUSTUM	500

RUMBLES

RUMBLES AND SHAKES TELL ME THY RACE AND HOME	107	BALDER DEAD 2	103
IN THE QUICK WORLD THAT RUMBLES NIGH		KENSINGTON GARD	V 21
IN THE HUGE WORLD THAT RUMBLES NIGH		KENSINGTON GARD	V 21

RUMBLING

CAST BY THE RUMBLING SUBTERRANEAN STREAM	358	MEROPE	841

RUMBLINGS

THESE RUMBLINGS ARE NOT TYPHOS GROANS I KNOW	431	EMPEDOCLES II	95

RUMOUR

DIM IS THE RUMOUR OF A COMMON FIGHT	62	SOHRAB RUSTUM	60
BUT A DARK RUMOUR WILL BE BRUITED UP	79	SOHRAB RUSTUM	596

RUMOURS

THIS LONG TIME RUMOURS	189	STRAYED REVEL	109
BUT RUMOURS HUNG ABOUT THE COUNTRY-SIDE	256	SCHOLAR-GIPSY	52
NUMBER IT WITH THE THOUSAND RUMOURS VAIN	387	MEROPE	1486

RUN

COULD LIFE RUN NO HAPPIER WAY	33	NEW SIRENS	200
COULD LIFE RUN NO EASIER WAY	33	NEW SIRENS	V 200
WHICH FROM THE FOUNTAIN OF VERGELMER RUN	108	BALDER DEAD 2	130
OUTMOST THE OTHERS NEAR THE CENTRE RUN	109	BALDER DEAD 2	153

RUN (CONTINUED)

HOW WOULD YOUR VOICES RUN AGAIN		141 TRISTRAM 1	361
TO WATCH THIS LINE OF SAND-HILLS RUN		204 CALAIS SANDS	2
TO SEE THIS LINE OF SAND-HILLS RUN		204 CALAIS SANDS	V 2
HAVE RUN THEIR CIRCLE AND LEFT		282 HAWORTH CHURCH	V
NO CERTAIN NEWS IF LIKE THE REST IT RUN		350 MEROPE	600
NOW I IF I INVITE THEM TO RUN RISK		382 MEROPE	1349
WHO CHIEFLY PROFIT RUN NO MORE THAN THEY		382 MEROPE	1351
HATH RUN HIS BRIGHT CAREER		448 WESTMIN ABBEY	142
TO RUN THEIR COURSE AND REACH THEIR GOAL		450 GEISTS GRAVE	11
O PLEASANT REST IF ONCE THE RACE WERE RUN		475 CROMWELL	119
THERE WHERE TEARS ARE NEVER MORE TO RUN		482 THEKLAS ANSWER	12

RUNES

POSTURES OF RUNES AND HEALING HERBS HE KNEW		101 BALDER DEAD 1	211

RUNG

RENT WITH TUMULTUOUS THOUGHTS WHOSE CONFLICT RUNG		478 CROMWELL	223

RUNIC

BEFORE SOME FALLEN RUNIC STONE		301 GRANDE CHARTR	83

RUNNING

RUNNING FAST HOMEWARD WITH THE TURN OF TIDE		69 SOHRAB RUSTUM	V 287
MY MAN COMES RUNNING FLECKD WITH BLOOD		89 SICK KING BOKH	50

RUNNST

THAT RUNNST FROM POLE TO POLE		316 OBERMANN MORE	118

RUNS

MY SAND RUNS SHORT AND AS YON STAR-SHOT RAY		10 MYCERINUS	56
RUNS HIS OLD ROUND OF DUBIOUS CHEER		56 RESIGNATION	129
A SHIVER RUNS THROUGH THE DEEP CORN FOR JOY		65 SOHRAB RUSTUM	156
WASTES AND RUNS THINNER EVERY DAY		89 SICK KING BOKH	64
THROUGH THE CLIFF-WALL AND A FRESH STREAM RUNS DOWN		97 BALDER DEAD 1	82
THROUGH MANY STREETS THE POOR BEAST RUNS IN VAIN		114 BALDER DEAD 3	10
THEY FEEL RUNS OER IN EVERY LINE		227 EPILOG LAOCOON	198
RUNS IT NOT HERE THE TRACK BY CHILDSWORTH FARM		263 THYRSIS	11
RUNS AND COLLIERS CARTS		282 HAWORTH CHURCH	58
BUT WHERE THE ROAD RUNS NEAR THE STREAM		305 GRANDE CHARTR	175
AND HOW THEN RUNS THIS TRUE AND PRIVATE TALE		364 MEROPE	967
MOTHER MY HEART RUNS OVER BUT THE TIME		378 MEROPE	1232

RURAL

WAS BREATHED ON BY THE RURAL PAN		249 KENSINGTON GARD	24
WAS LOOKED ON BY THE RURAL PAN		KENSINGTON GARD	V 24

RUSH

WE RUSH BY COASTS WHERE WE HAD LIEF REMAIN		40 HUMAN LIFE	17
O SOHRAB WHEREFORE WILT THOU RUSH ON DEATH		71 SOHRAB RUSTUM	329
RACING FULL SPEED AND STARTLING IN THEIR RUSH		150 TRISTRAM 3	29
WHO RUSH BY WHO SHAKE		174 PARTING	2
I RUSH WITH THE SWIFT SPHERES AND GLOW		241 MORALITY	27
WHEN JADED WITH THE RUSH AND GLARE		247 BURIED LIFE	79
RUSH OER THE YORKSHIRE MOORS		286 HAWORTH CHURCH	130
SWIFT RUSH THE SPECTRAL VAPOURS WHITE		299 GRANDE CHARTR	13
FAST RUSH THE SPECTRAL VAPOURS WHITE		299 GRANDE CHARTR	V 13
RUSH OVER IT AGAIN		441 EMPEDOCLES II	415
OR LOUDER RUSH OF WHIRLWINDS SWEEPING BY		466 ALARIC AT ROME	111
SMOTE LIKE THE RUSH OF WATERS ON HIS EAR		475 CROMWELL	136
AND IN THEIR RUSH THE HUMAN RACE		481 COURAGE	7

RUSHD

AND HE TOO DREW HIS SWORD AT ONCE THEY RUSHD		75 SOHRAB RUSTUM	471
BUT SOHRAB HEARD AND QUAILD NOT BUT RUSHD ON		76 SOHRAB RUSTUM	509
RAN BLACK OER THE SEAS FACE THEN STEADY RUSHD		118 BALDER DEAD 3	183
AND SHOOK AS IT RUSHD BY HER		319 OBERMANN MORE	204
BROKE FROM THE DORIAN LORDS FORWARD THEY RUSHD		402 MEROPE	1931
WE CHEERD BUT FROM IT RUSHD A BLAST OF MIGHT		484 S S LUSITANIA	7

RUSHES

STILL THIS WILD BROOK THE RUSHES COOL		55 RESIGNATION	104
WHO SCATTERS RUSHES IN A MASTERS HALL		112 BALDER DEAD 2	266
AND THOSE BLOWN RUSHES ON THE FLOOR		148 TRISTRAM 2	160
AND THE BLOWN RUSHES ON THE FLOOR		148 TRISTRAM 2	V 160
HARK THE WIND RUSHES PAST US		176 PARTING	43
THAT THE BLOOD RUSHES IN STREAMS TO THE DUST		400 MEROPE	1865
THE GLOSSY RUSHES NODDED BY		480 HAYSWATER BOAT	26

RUSHING

LIKE THE BROAD RUSHING OF THE INSURGENT NILE		10 MYCERINUS	V 40
LIKE THE BROAD RUSHING OF THE COLUMND NILE		10 MYCERINUS	V 40
LIKE THE BROAD RUSHING OF THE INSURGED NILE		10 MYCERINUS	V 40
COME RUSHING DOWN TOGETHER FROM THE CLOUDS		75 SOHRAB RUSTUM	473
THE RUSHING BATTLE CLEARD THY BLOOD		139 TRISTRAM 1	292
THE RUSHING WINDS GO		175 PARTING	26
BY THE SWIFT-RUSHING MISSILE OF DEATH		216 LORDS MESSENGER	V 18
HE LOOKD ON THE RUSHING DECAY		229 YOUTH OF NATURE	29
IN THE RUSHING THUNDERING MAD		370 MEROPE	1105
THEN TRY THE ISSUE AND NOT RUSHING ON		382 MEROPE	1325

RUSHING   (CONTINUED)
        THROUGH THE BLACK RUSHING SMOKE-BURSTS   • • • •   441 EMPEDOCLES II   417

RUSHY
        THROUGH BEDS OF SAND AND MATTED RUSHY ISLES   • •   87 SOHRAB RUSTUM   885

RUSSIAN
        AND WHAT THE RUSSIAN CZAR INTENDS   • • • • • •   47 HORATIAN ECHO   5
        UPON THE RUSSIAN FRONTIER WHERE   • • • • • • •   93 SICK KING BOKH   161

RUST
        THEN WE SHALL RUST IN SHADE OR SHINE IN STRIFE   • •   236 PALLADIUM   17

RUSTIC
        COOL SHADE IS THERE AND RUSTIC CHEER   • • • • • •   54 RESIGNATION   75
        WHAT THOUGH THE MUSIC OF THY RUSTIC FLUTE   • • • •   269 THYRSIS   221

RUSTING
        RUSTING FOR EVER AND THE YEARS ROLL ON   • • • •   127 BALDER DEAD 3   472

RUSTLE
        THE RUSTLE OF THE ETERNAL RAIN OF LOVE   • • • •   19 CHURCH BROU 3   46
        THEIR SCENT AND RUSTLE DOWN THEIR PERFUMED SHOWERS   256 SCHOLAR-GIPSY   27

RUSTLED
        RUSTLED ROUND HIS CRADLE   • • • • • • • • •   392 MEROPE   1620

RUSTLES
        THE WILD BOAR RUSTLES IN HIS LAIR   • • • • • •   149 TRISTRAM 2   183
        THIS BREEZE THAT RUSTLES BY THAT FAMED   • • • •   223 EPILOG LAOCOON   78

RUSTLING
        UNDER THE RUSTLING POPLARS SHADE   • • • • • •   206 RIVER   2
        CAME RUSTLING FROM THE GARDEN-TREES   • • • • •   223 EPILOG LAOCOON   66
        IN THE RUSTLING NIGHT-AIR CAME THE ANSWER   • • •   240 SELF-DEPENDENCE   15
        WHERE WITH CLEAR-RUSTLING WAVE   • • • • • • •   311 OBERMANN   166

RUSTLINGLY
        DOTH RUSTLINGLY ABOVE YOUR HEADS COMPLAIN   • • • •   18 CHURCH BROU 3   33

RUSTUM
        RUSTUM MY FATHER WHO I HOPED SHOULD GREET   • • • •   62 SOHRAB RUSTUM   50
        RUSTUM WILL SURELY HEAR IT IF I FALL   • •   • • •   62 SOHRAB RUSTUM   58
        TO SEEK OUT RUSTUM SEEK HIM NOT THROUGH FIGHT   • •   63 SOHRAB RUSTUM   75
        WHEN RUSTUM WAS IN FRONT OF EVERY FRAY   • • • •   63 SOHRAB RUSTUM   80
        BUT RUSTUM CAME LAST NIGHT ALOOF HE SITS   • • •   66 SOHRAB RUSTUM   178
        RUSTUM HIS MORNING MEAL WAS DONE BUT STILL   • • •   67 SOHRAB RUSTUM   196
        AND DARK GREEN MELONS AND THERE RUSTUM SATE   • •   67 SOHRAB RUSTUM   199
        O RUSTUM LIKE THY MIGHT IS THIS YOUNG MANS   • •   67 SOHRAB RUSTUM   215
        COME DOWN AND HELP US RUSTUM OR WE LOSE   • • •   67 SOHRAB RUSTUM   219
        HE SPOKE BUT RUSTUM ANSWERD WITH A SMILE   • •   67 SOHRAB RUSTUM   220
        RUSTUM HE LOVES NO MORE BUT LOVES THE YOUNG   • •   67 SOHRAB RUSTUM   226
        WHAT THEN O RUSTUM WILL MEN SAY TO THIS   • • •   68 SOHRAB RUSTUM   243
        LIKE SOME OLD MISER RUSTUM HOARDS HIS FAME   • •   68 SOHRAB RUSTUM   247
        AND GREATLY MOVED THEN RUSTUM MADE REPLY   • •   68 SOHRAB RUSTUM   249
        COME THOU SHALT SEE HOW RUSTUM HOARDS HIS FAME   •   68 SOHRAB RUSTUM   256
        LET NOT MEN SAY OF RUSTUM HE WAS MATCHD   • • •   69 SOHRAB RUSTUM   258
        FEAR AT HIS WRATH BUT JOY THAT RUSTUM CAME   • •   69 SOHRAB RUSTUM   262
        BUT RUSTUM STRODE TO HIS TENT-DOOR AND CALLD   •   69 SOHRAB RUSTUM   263
        THE HORSE WHOM RUSTUM ON A FORAY ONCE   • • • •   69 SOHRAB RUSTUM   273
        SO FOLLOWD RUSTUM LEFT HIS TENTS AND CROSSD   •   69 SOHRAB RUSTUM   280
        SO DEAR TO THE PALE PERSIANS RUSTUM CAME   • • •   70 SOHRAB RUSTUM   290
        AND RUSTUM TO THE PERSIAN FRONT ADVANCED   • •   70 SOHRAB RUSTUM   291
        AND RUSTUM CAME UPON THE SAND AND CAST   • • •   70 SOHRAB RUSTUM   299
        OF THAT POOR DRUDGE MAY BE SO RUSTUM EYED   • •   70 SOHRAB RUSTUM   308
        CAME SEEKING RUSTUM AND DEFYING FORTH   • • • •   70 SOHRAB RUSTUM   310
        THE MIGHTY VOICE OF RUSTUM AND HE SAW   • • • •   71 SOHRAB RUSTUM   335
        ART THOU NOT RUSTUM SPEAK ART THOU NOT HE   • •   71 SOHRAB RUSTUM   344
        BUT RUSTUM EYED ASKANCE THE KNEELING YOUTH   • •   71 SOHRAB RUSTUM   345
        AND HIDE IT NOT BUT SAY RUSTUM IS HERE   • • •   71 SOHRAB RUSTUM   350
        SHRANK ONLY RUSTUM DARED THEN HE AND I   • • •   72 SOHRAB RUSTUM   360
        OF RUSTUM I AM HERE WHOM THOU HAST CALLD   • •   72 SOHRAB RUSTUM   366
        IS IT WITH RUSTUM ONLY THOU WOULDST FIGHT   • •   72 SOHRAB RUSTUM   368
        FOR WELL I KNOW THAT DID GREAT RUSTUM STAND   •   72 SOHRAB RUSTUM   370
        YET THIS THOU HAST SAID WELL DID RUSTUM STAND   •   72 SOHRAB RUSTUM   382
        BUT RUSTUM IS FAR HENCE AND WE STAND HERE   • •   72 SOHRAB RUSTUM   384
        HE SPOKE AND RUSTUM ANSWERD NOT BUT HURLD   • •   73 SOHRAB RUSTUM   398
        AND RUSTUM SEIZED HIS CLUB WHICH NONE BUT HE   •   73 SOHRAB RUSTUM   408
        THE CLUB WHICH RUSTUM LIFTED NOW AND STRUCK   •   73 SOHRAB RUSTUM   416
        AND RUSTUM FOLLOWD HIS OWN BLOW AND FELL   • • •   73 SOHRAB RUSTUM   420
        AND PIERCED THE MIGHTY RUSTUM WHILE HE LAY   • •   73 SOHRAB RUSTUM   423
        THOU SAYST THOU ART NOT RUSTUM BE IT SO   • • •   74 SOHRAB RUSTUM   431
        HE CEASED BUT WHILE HE SPAKE RUSTUM HAD RISEN   •   74 SOHRAB RUSTUM   448
        RUSTUM AND SOHRAB ON EACH OTHER HAILD   • • • •   75 SOHRAB RUSTUM   479
        AND LABOURING BREATH FIRST RUSTUM STRUCK THE SHIELD   75 SOHRAB RUSTUM   491
        AND RUSTUM PLUCKD IT BACK WITH ANGRY GROAN   • • •   76 SOHRAB RUSTUM   494
        AND RUSTUM BOWD HIS HEAD BUT THEN THE GLOOM   • •   76 SOHRAB RUSTUM   499
        AND STRUCK AGAIN AND AGAIN RUSTUM BOWD   • • •   76 SOHRAB RUSTUM   510
        THEN RUSTUM RAISED HIS HEAD HIS DREADFUL EYES   •   76 SOHRAB RUSTUM   514
        AND SHOUTED RUSTUM SOHRAB HEARD THAT SHOUT   • • •   76 SOHRAB RUSTUM   516

RUSTUM   (CONTINUED)
SAW RUSTUM STANDING SAFE UPON HIS FEET   •   •   •   •   77 SOHRAB RUSTUM   525
THEN WITH A BITTER SMILE RUSTUM BEGAN   •   •   •   •   77 SOHRAB RUSTUM   527
OR ELSE THAT THE GREAT RUSTUM WOULD COME DOWN   •   •   77 SOHRAB RUSTUM   531
NO RUSTUM SLAYS ME AND THIS FILIAL HEART   •   •   •   •   77 SOHRAB RUSTUM   543
THE MIGHTY RUSTUM SHALL AVENGE MY DEATH   •   •   •   •   77 SOHRAB RUSTUM   553
SO RUSTUM KNEW NOT HIS OWN LOSS BUT STOOD   •   •   •   •   78 SOHRAB RUSTUM   574
THE MIGHTY RUSTUM NEVER HAD A SON   •   •   •   •   78 SOHRAB RUSTUM   578
REACH RUSTUM WHERE HE SITS AND TARRIES LONG   •   •   78 SOHRAB RUSTUM   582
HE SPOKE BUT RUSTUM LISTEND PLUNGED IN THOUGHT   •   •   79 SOHRAB RUSTUM   604
RUSTUM SHOULD SEEK THE BOY TO TRAIN IN ARMS   •   •   79 SOHRAB RUSTUM   611
THROUGH MANY ROLLING CLOUDS SO RUSTUM SAW   •   •   •   79 SOHRAB RUSTUM   623
AND RUSTUM GAZED ON HIM WITH GRIEF AND SAID   •   •   80 SOHRAB RUSTUM   640
WHOM RUSTUM WERT THOU HIS MIGHT WELL HAVE LOVED   •   •   80 SOHRAB RUSTUM   642
FOR RUSTUM HAD NO SON ONE CHILD HE HAD   •   •   •   80 SOHRAB RUSTUM   645
THAT SEAL WHICH RUSTUM TO MY MOTHER GAVE   •   •   •   80 SOHRAB RUSTUM   659
THEN RUSTUM TOOK IT FOR HIS GLORIOUS SIGN   •   •   •   81 SOHRAB RUSTUM   683
HE SPOKE BUT RUSTUM GAZED AND GAZED AND STOOD   •   •   81 SOHRAB RUSTUM   689
CAME BACK TO RUSTUM AND HE OPED HIS EYES   •   •   •   81 SOHRAB RUSTUM   698
OF RUSTUM AND HIS TEARS BROKE FORTH HE CAST   •   •   82 SOHRAB RUSTUM   727
BUT RUSTUM CHID HIM WITH STERN VOICE AND SAID   •   •   82 SOHRAB RUSTUM   737
AND SAID O RUKSH BEAR RUSTUM WELL BUT I   •   •   •   83 SOHRAB RUSTUM   755
THEN WITH A HEAVY GROAN RUSTUM BEWAILD   •   •   •   83 SOHRAB RUSTUM   767
AND WITH A MOURNFUL VOICE RUSTUM REPLIED   •   •   •   84 SOHRAB RUSTUM   795
AND RUSTUM GAZED IN SOHRABS FACE AND SAID   •   •   •   85 SOHRAB RUSTUM   835
AND THE GREAT RUSTUM DREW HIS HORSEMANS CLOAK   •   •   86 SOHRAB RUSTUM   858
SO IN THE SAND LAY RUSTUM BY HIS SON   •   •   •   86 SOHRAB RUSTUM   864
AND RUSTUM AND HIS SON WERE LEFT ALONE   •   •   •   86 SOHRAB RUSTUM   874
FEAR AT HIS WRATH AND JOY THAT RUSTUM CAME   •   •   •   69 SOHRAB RUSTUM   V 262
SO FOLLOWD RUSTUM ISSUED FORTH AND CROSSD   •   •   •   69 SOHRAB RUSTUM   V 280
WENT SEEKING RUSTUM AND DEFYING FORTH   •   •   •   70 SOHRAB RUSTUM   V 310
THEN RUSTUM SEIZED HIS CLUB WHICH NONE BUT HE   •   •   73 SOHRAB RUSTUM   V 408
RUSTUM SHOULD TAKE THE BOY TO TRAIN IN ARMS   •   •   79 SOHRAB RUSTUM   V 611
AND WITH A HEAVY GROAN RUSTUM REPLIED   •   •   •   •   83 SOHRAB RUSTUM   V 767
AND RUSTUM GAZED ON SOHRABS FACE AND SAID   •   •   85 SOHRAB RUSTUM   V 835

RUSTUMS
FROM RAVENING AND WHO GOVERN RUSTUMS SON   •   •   •   •   63 SOHRAB RUSTUM   92
OUT ON THE SANDS BEYOND IT RUSTUMS TENTS   •   •   •   •   66 SOHRAB RUSTUM   191
WAS RUSTUMS AND HIS MEN LAY CAMPD AROUND   •   •   •   •   67 SOHRAB RUSTUM   194
AND GUDURZ ENTERD RUSTUMS TENT AND FOUND   •   •   •   •   67 SOHRAB RUSTUM   195
AND A DEEP PITY ENTERD RUSTUMS SOUL   •   •   •   •   70 SOHRAB RUSTUM   319
RASH BOY MEN LOOK ON RUSTUMS FACE AND FLEE   •   •   •   72 SOHRAB RUSTUM   369
IN TURN AND FULL STRUCK RUSTUMS SHIELD SHARP RANG   •   73 SOHRAB RUSTUM   406
THUNDERING TO EARTH AND LEAPT FROM RUSTUMS HAND   •   •   73 SOHRAB RUSTUM   419
AND THOU SHALT TALK TO ME OF RUSTUMS DEEDS   •   •   •   74 SOHRAB RUSTUM   442
THEN SOHRAB WITH HIS SWORD SMOTE RUSTUMS HELM   •   •   76 SOHRAB RUSTUM   495
BY A FALSE BOAST THE STYLE OF RUSTUMS SON   •   •   •   79 SOHRAB RUSTUM   613
HAVE TOLD THEE FALSE THOU ART NOT RUSTUMS SON   •   •   80 SOHRAB RUSTUM   644
HE SPOKE AND ALL THE BLOOD LEFT RUSTUMS CHEEKS   •   •   80 SOHRAB RUSTUM   661
IF THOU SHOW THIS THEN ART THOU RUSTUMS SON   •   •   81 SOHRAB RUSTUM   668
ON SOHRABS ARM THE SIGN OF RUSTUMS SEAL   •   •   •   81 SOHRAB RUSTUM   678
RUSTUMS GREAT FATHER WHOM THEY LEFT TO DIE   •   •   •   81 SOHRAB RUSTUM   680
OF RUSTUMS SON OR OF SOME OTHER MANS   •   •   •   •   81 SOHRAB RUSTUM   688
WHEN THEY SAW RUSTUMS GRIEF AND RUKSH THE HORSE   •   •   82 SOHRAB RUSTUM   730
SOHRAB THE MIGHTY RUSTUMS SON LIES THERE   •   •   •   84 SOHRAB RUSTUM   792

RUTH
O RUTH OF GOD THE PRIEST CRIED OUT   •   •   •   •   •   160 NECKAN   55
BY THE FAVOURITE WATERS OF RUTH   •   •   •   •   •   229 YOUTH OF NATURE   24
I SEEK THESE ANCHORITES NOT IN RUTH   •   •   •   •   •   301 GRANDE CHARTR   77

RUTHLESS
MERE RUTHLESS AND UNCOUNSELLD WOLVES OF WAR   •   •   381 MEROPE   1301
MERE RUTHLESS AND UNCOUNSELLD TOOLS OF WAR   •   •   •   •   381 MEROPE   V1301

RUTHLESSLY
RUTHLESSLY THEIR REBELLIOUS SUBJECTS CRUSHD   •   •   390 MEROPE   1567

RYDAL
RYDAL AND FAIRFIELD ARE THERE   •   •   •   •   •   •   •   228 YOUTH OF NATURE   8

RYMER
WHILE FROM THE EAST THE GIANT RYMER STEERS   •   •   •   127 BALDER DEAD 3   478

SACKCLOTH
A ROBE OF SACKCLOTH NEXT THE SMOOTH WHITE SKIN   •   •   166 AUSTERITY POET   11
IN GREATNESS ONCE IN SACKCLOTH NOW AND TEARS   •   •   463 ALARIC AT ROME   20

SACRED
THE SACRED WORLD AND BY PROCESSION SURE   •   •   •   45 IN UTRUMQUE PAR   3
WHILE TWILIGHT FELL AND SACRED NIGHT CAME ON   •   •   97 BALDER DEAD 1   71
ON FREAS HEARTH FEED HIGH THE SACRED FIRE   •   •   •   97 BALDER DEAD 1   90
BEGAN AGAIN TO HEAP THE SACRED FIRE   •   •   •   •   100 BALDER DEAD 1   196
AND INSTANTLY THE SACRED MORN APPEARD   •   •   •   104 BALDER DEAD 1   342
SILENT AND WAITED FOR THE SACRED MORN   •   •   •   119 BALDER DEAD 3   212
ERE DANTE CAME THE TRUMP OF SACRED SONG   •   •   •   166 AUSTERITY POET   2
AND SEES NOT THAT THE SACRED DROPS   •   •   •   •   •   213 PROGRESS POESY   7
OF A SACRED POET LIES LOW   •   •   •   •   •   •   229 YOUTH OF NATURE   49
BATHED IN THE SACRED DEWS OF MORN   •   •   •   •   •   250 WISH   33

SACRED   (CONTINUED)
          FOR THERE WHERE MORNINGS SACRED FOUNT   • • •   277 SOUTHERN NIGHT   53
          AH OER THAT SILENT SACRED LAND   • • • • • •   318 OBERMANN MORE   181
          AH FROM THAT SILENT SACRED LAND   • • • • •   318 OBERMANN MORE   V 181
          AND IF THE SACRED LOAD OPPRESSD OUR BRAIN   • • • • 436 EMPEDOCLES II   244
          AND MAJESTY AND SACRED FORM AND FEAR • • • • • •   445 WESTMIN ABBEY   58
          IT WILL COME WHEN SACRED TROY SHALL GO TO DESTRUCTION   HOMER TRANS   21

SACRIFICE
          FETCH ME THE SACRIFICE-AXE   • • • •   371 MEROPE   1138
          PERFORMS THIS NOON A SOLEMN SACRIFICE   • • • •   391 MEROPE   1589
          HAVE LEARND THAT WE MUST SACRIFICE THE BENT   • •   394 MEROPE   1711
          SPEAK I GO HENCE TO OFFER SACRIFICE   • • • • •   394 MEROPE   1722
          A WILLING A WILLING SACRIFICE ON THAT DAY   • • •   399 MEROPE   1830
          ANOTHER ANOTHER SACRIFICE ON THIS DAY   • • • •   400 MEROPE   1855
          LIVING HIS OWN SACRIFICE-BLOCK   • • • • •   400 MEROPE   1859
          OF SACRIFICE HIS GUARDS CLEARING THE WAY   • • •   401 MEROPE   1904
          TO THE GODS GRATEFUL SACRIFICE AND THEN   • • • •   405 MEROPE   2019
          HAVE LEARND THAT WE MUST SACRIFICE THE THIRST • •   394 MEROPE   V1711

SACRIFICED
          HE SACRIFICED OUR RUIN IN HIS HEART   • • • • •   338 MEROPE   273

SACRIFICERS
          THE SACRIFICERS AXE WILL SERVE THY TURN   • • •   391 MEROPE   1592
          THE PRINCE SNATCHD FROM THE SACRIFICERS HAND   • •   402 MEROPE   1919

SACRIFICING
          WHERE BY THE SACRIFICING MINISTER   • • • • • •   401 MEROPE   1909

SAD
          SIGHD OUT BY WINTERS SAD TRANQUILLITY   • • • •   12 MYCERINUS   115
          WITH A SAD MAJESTIC MOTION   • • • • • •   31 NEW SIRENS   155
          OUR SAD SOULS ON YOUR REPLIES • • • • • •   34 NEW SIRENS   V 236
          SO SAD AND WITH SO WILD A START   • • • • •   36 VOICE   23
          NO EXILES DREAM WAS EVER HALF SO SAD   • • • •   42 GIPSY CHILD   27
          NEVER WAS EXILES MEMORY HALF SO SAD   • • • • •   42 GIPSY CHILD   V 27
          A FEW SAD SMILES AND THEN   • • • • • •   44 QUESTION   5
          HIS SAD LUCIDITY OF SOUL   • • • • • •   58 RESIGNATION   198
          SO THAT SAD MOTHER SENT HIM WORD FOR FEAR   • • •   79 SOHRAB RUSTUM   610
          WHY FOR NO CAUSE MAKE SAD THY FACE   • • •   92 SICK KING BOKH   142
          THAT SAD SOLE HONOUR OF THE DEAD AND THEE   • • •   103 BALDER DEAD 1   298
          THEN SAD AT HEART TO NIORD HERMOD SPAKE   • • •   124 BALDER DEAD 3   369
          HER LOOK WAS LIKE A SAD EMBRACE   • • • •   140 TRISTRAM 1   322
          BOTH HAVE PASSD A YOUTH CONSUMED AND SAD   • • •   144 TRISTRAM 2   54
          BOTH HAVE PASSD A YOUTH CONSTRAIND AND SAD • • •   144 TRISTRAM 2   V 54
          BOTH HAVE PASSD A YOUTH REPRESSD AND SAD   • • •   144 TRISTRAM 2   V 54
          BOTH HAVE PASSD A YOUTH FORLORN AND SAD   • •   144 TRISTRAM 2   V 54
          THE OLD THE SAD THE WORN WERE THERE   • • •   224 EPILOG LAOCOON   118
          AND ALL HIS STORE OF SAD EXPERIENCE HE   • • •   260 SCHOLAR-GIPSY   185
          SAD PATIENCE TOO NEAR NEIGHBOUR TO DESPAIR • • •   261 SCHOLAR-GIPSY   195
          PIPING A DITTY SAD FOR BIONS FATE   • • • •   265 THYRSIS   84
          HEAVY AND SAD FOR HER SONS   • • • • • •   294 HEINES GRAVE   73
          FEARFUL AND SAD FOR HER SONS   • • • •   294 HEINES GRAVE   V 73
          TROUBLOUS AND SAD FOR HER SONS   • • • • •   294 HEINES GRAVE   V 73
          A FAITH OR SCIOLISTS BEEN SAD   • • • • •   302 GRANDE CHARTR   102
          O OBERMANN THE SAD STERN PAGE   • • • • •   304 GRANDE CHARTR   146
          AND THOU SAD GUIDE ADIEU   • • • • • •   310 OBERMANN   130
          AND THY SAD TRANQUIL LORE   • • • • • •   313 OBERMANN MORE   48
          SAD PATIENT AND RESIGND   • • • • • •   321 OBERMANN MORE   254
          HANG WEEDS OF OUR SAD TIME   • • • • •   323 OBERMANN MORE   308
          SAD-CHANTING MAIDENS CLAD IN MOURNING ROBES   331 MEROPE   53
          BY SAD OBSERVANCES AND PUBLIC GRIEF   • • • •   332 MEROPE   81
          THE PRINCE AT START SEEMD SAD BUT HIS REGARD   • •   355 MEROPE   733
          SAD REVERENTIAL HOMAGE HAD OUR PRINCE   • •   356 MEROPE   761
          A PRESENCE SAD FOR SOME ONE THROUGH THOSE DOORS •   359 MEROPE   874
          BEARS SAD WITNESS IS LOST   • • • • •   369 MEROPE   1092
          SAD EAGER EYES   • • • • • •   393 MEROPE   1664
          EVEN AFTER NEWS OF THIS SAD DEATH OUR LEAGUE   • •   394 MEROPE   1689
          COMING SWIFTLY THROUGH THE SAD TRACHINIANS   • •   399 MEROPE   1838
          AND I COULD WATCH HIM WITH HIS PROUD SAD FACE   •   408 EMPEDOCLES I 1   59
          WHICH MAKES THE TIME LOOK BLACK AND SAD TO HIM   •   411 EMPEDOCLES I 1   153
          WHICH MAKES THE TIMES LOOK BLACK AND SAD TO HIM •   411 EMPEDOCLES I 1   V 153
          ESTRANGED LIKE MINE AND SAD   • • • • •   426 EMPEDOCLES I 2   410
          WHOLLY FORGET THEIR FIRST SAD LIFE AND HOME   •   427 EMPEDOCLES I 2   458
          NOT EAGER NOR NOT SAD   • • • • •   426 EMPEDOCLES I 2   V 410
          HAST THOU SWORN IN THY SAD LAIR   • • • •   430 EMPEDOCLES II   58
          GO THROUGH THE SAD PROBATION ALL AGAIN   • •   440 EMPEDOCLES II   368
          KNOW THEM IN THEIR SAD DECAY   • • • • •   453 POOR MATTHIAS   30
          SAD COMPUNCTIOUS VISITINGS   • • • • •   455 POOR MATTHIAS   86
          PLAIN WE SAW IF THEY WERE SAD   • • • •   455 POOR MATTHIAS   90
          YES MAX AND WE GREW SLOW AND SAD   • •   460 KAISER DEAD   43
          UPON ITS HEADLONG COURSE WITH SAD PROPHETIC EYE •   463 ALARIC AT ROME   24
          HOW CALMLY SAD HOW SADLY BEAUTIFUL   • • • •   466 ALARIC AT ROME   100
          WAS COLD AND SAD BENEATH THAT BREATHLESS VOICELESS   466 ALARIC AT ROME   108
            NIGHT
          YEARS THAT WERE SWEET OR SAD BECALMD OR TOSSD   • • 474 CROMWELL   77
          THAT BROW SO SAD SO PALE SO FULL OF CARE   • •   477 CROMWELL   183
          SAD FACES WATCHD AROUND HIM AND HIS BREATH   • •   478 CROMWELL   207
          IT IS A SAD SIGHT WHEN THE WORLD DENIES   • • •   LUCRETIUS 2   1

SADDENING
    THE SADDENING TALE THAT TELLS OF SORROW AND DECAY   462 ALARIC AT ROME   6
    THE SADDENING VISIONS OF DEPARTED DAYS • • • 470 ALARIC AT ROME   202
    THERE IS A SIGHT MORE SADDENING YET WHEN ALL • •   LUCRETIUS 2   7

SADDENS
    SADDENS MY SOUL WITH ITS CHILL • • • • • • • • 293 HEINES GRAVE   41

SADDER
    AND THEN WE TURN THOU SADDER SAGE • • • • · • 309 OBERMANN   81

SADDLE
    CROUCHD ON HIS SADDLE WHILE THE SUN • • • • • 52 RESIGNATION   10
    CROUCHD ON HIS SADDLE WHEN THE SUN • • • • • 52 RESIGNATION V 10
    DIGHT WITH A SADDLE-CLOTH OF BROIDERD GREEN • • 69 SOHRAB RUSTUM   277
    THERE HAMPDEN BENT HIM OER HIS SADDLE BOW • • • • 476 CROMWELL   169

SADDLED
    AND SADDLED HIM BEFORE THAT SLEIPNER BROOKD • • 107 BALDER DEAD 2   72
    I SADDLED MY WHITE MULE AND ALL NIGHT LONG • • • • 407 EMPEDOCLES I 1   44

SADLY
    SADLY BACK THE SEATS OF MEN • • • • • • 31 NEW SIRENS   150
    HE CAME AND SADLY WENT ALONG THE SAND • • • • 97 BALDER DEAD 1   78
    BUT HERMOD MOUNTED HIM AND SADLY FARED • • • • 107 BALDER DEAD 2   78
    OF THE NEAR WAVES CAME SADLY GRAND • • • • • 137 TRISTRAM 1   217
    WHERE THE HIGH WOODS STRIP SADLY • • • • • • 175 PARTING   7
    THINK SADLY AS I HEAR THEM RAVE • • • • •   KENSINGTON GARD V 26
    COLDLY SADLY DESCENDS • • • • • • • • 286 RUGBY CHAPEL   1
    SADLY WE ANSWER WE BRING • • • • • • • • 289 RUGBY CHAPEL   117
    WHO SADLY ASK ME WHAT IF NOT REVENGE • • • • • 367 MEROPE   1039
    HOW CALMLY SAD HOW SADLY BEAUTIFUL • • • • • 466 ALARIC AT ROME   100
    GAZD SADLY DOWN ON HIS UNRESTFUL LOT • • • • • 474 CROMWELL   86
    SO SADLY CALM SO KINGLY SO SERENE • • • • • • 477 CROMWELL   186

SADNESS
    IF SADNESS AT THE LONG HEART-WASTING SHOW • • • • 7 REP FRIEND   9
    O SPEAK ONCE AND SHAME MY SADNESS • • • • • 32 NEW SIRENS   167
    O SPEAK ONCE AND LET MY SADNESS • • • • • • 32 NEW SIRENS V 167
    MOODS OF FANTASTIC SADNESS NOTHING WORTH • • • • 42 GIPSY CHILD   18
    THE ETERNAL NOTE OF SADNESS IN • • • • • • • 211 DOVER BEACH   14
    MY LONGING MY SADNESS MY JOY • • • • • • • 231 YOUTH OF NATURE   121
    I FEEL A NAMELESS SADNESS OER ME ROLL • • • • 245 BURIED LIFE   3
    GRACE TO YOUR MOOD OF SADNESS GAVE • • • • • 304 GRANDE CHARTR   153
    GRACE TO THEIR MOOD OF SADNESS GAVE • • • • • 304 GRANDE CHARTR V 153
    BY SADNESS AND SELF-WILL • • • • • • • • 425 EMPEDOCLES I 2   395
    OH SOUND THERE NOT SOME STRAINS OF SADNESS THERE • • 468 ALARIC AT ROME   165

SAFE
    MAN WOULD BE MILD AND WITH SAFE CONSCIENCE BLEST • • 5 HARMONY NATURE   11
    FAIN WOULD I KNOW THEE SAFE AND WELL THOUGH LOST • • 63 SOHRAB RUSTUM   88
    SAW RUSTUM STANDING SAFE UPON HIS FEET • • • • 77 SOHRAB RUSTUM   525
    TO KEEP HIS OWN LIFE SAFE AND SEE THE SUN • • • 101 BALDER DEAD 1   213
    AND NOW I COUNT NOT OF THESE TERMS AS SAFE • • • 112 BALDER DEAD 2   268
    SAFE THROUGH THE SMOKE OF THE FIGHT • • • • • 217 LORDS MESSENGER   23
    WITH SAFE UNWANDERING FEET EXPLORE • • • • • 226 EPILOG LAOCOON   190
    A JUST THEREFORE A SAFE SUPREMACY • • • • • 339 MEROPE   305
    EXILE ABROAD MORE SAFE THAN HEIRSHIP HERE • • • • 340 MEROPE   337
    BRING TO ME SAFE LET THE REST • • • • • • 348 MEROPE   535
    OUR FATHERS KINGDOM BECAUSE PURE IS SAFE • • • • 389 MEROPE   1533
    IS MY SON SAFE THAT QUESTION BOUNDS MY CARE • • 401 MEROPE   1889
    COMST THOU GUIDED SAFE TO THY HOME • • • • • 405 MEROPE   2022

SAFELY
    PLACED SAFELY IN CHANGED FORMS THE PAIR • • •• • 427 EMPEDOCLES I 2   457

SAFETY
    SOMEWHERE IN SAFETY A NURSLING A LIGHT • • • • 346 MEROPE V 513
    MAN HAS A MIND WITH WHICH TO PLAN HIS SAFETY • • 413 EMPEDOCLES I 2   28

SAFFRON
    WITH SAFFRON AND THE YELLOW HOLLYHOCK • • • • 191 STRAYED REVEL   169
    WITH SAFFRON AND THE YELLOW HOLYHOCK • • • • • 191 STRAYED REVEL V 169

SAGACIOUS
    SAGACIOUS MEN OF IRON WATCHFUL FIRM • • • • • 381 MEROPE   1304

SAGE
    SO SPAKE THE IMPERIAL SAGE PUREST OF MEN • • • 168 WORLDLY PLACE   2
    SO SPOKE THE IMPERIAL SAGE PUREST OF MEN • • • 168 WORLDLY PLACE V 2
    WHICH ARISE ON THE GLASS OF THE SAGE • • • • 230 YOUTH OF NATURE   73
    GOETHES SAGE MIND AND BYRONS FORCE • • • • 272 MEMORIAL VERSES   61
    SOME SAGE TO WHOM THE WORLD WAS DEAD • • • • 277 SOUTHERN NIGHT   77
    BUT YOU A GRAVE FOR KNIGHT OR SAGE • • • • • 279 SOUTHERN NIGHT .113
    BUT YOU A GRAVE FOR GIRL OR SAGE • • • • • • 279 SOUTHERN NIGHT V .113
    WHICH WITHOUT HARDNESS WILL BE SAGE • • • • 304 GRANDE CHARTR   159
    AND ONE THE STRONG MUCH-TOILING SAGE • • • • 308 OBERMANN   51
    AND THEN WE TURN THOU SADDER SAGE • • • • • 309 OBERMANN   81
    WITH SAGE EXPERIENCE SHE SPEAKS AND THOU • • • 382 MEROPE   1331
    THAT JUSTICE THAT SAGE ORDER NOT ALONE • • • • 404 MEROPE   1997

SAGE   (CONTINUED)
    PAUSANIAS HIS SAGE FRIEND WHO MOUNTS WITH HIM   • • 407 EMPEDOCLES I 1   25
    O SAGE O SAGE TAKE THEN THE ONE WAY LEFT   • • • • 429 EMPEDOCLES II   24
    O SAGE O SAGE TAKE THEN THE ONE WAY LEFT   • • • • 429 EMPEDOCLES II   24
    THOU HAST SEEN ATOSSA SAGE • • • • • • • 453 POOR MATTHIAS   31
    BUT WITH ALL THIS TRAVAIL SAGE • • • • • • 456 POOR MATTHIAS   147

SAGEST
    SUNK THEN IS EUROPES SAGEST HEAD • • • • • 270 MEMORIAL VERSES   16

SAHARAN
    SAHARAN SAND-WINDS • • • • • • • • 51 CONSOLATION   36

SAID
    HAST THOU NO LIP FOR WELCOME SO I SAID • • • 3 EMERSONS ESSAYS   5
    SAID THE DUCHESS MARGUERITE THEN • • • 15 CHURCH BROU 1   74
    ARE ALL DEBTS PAID HAS ALL BEEN SAID • • • 21 YOUTH AND CALM   8
    ONCE I SAID A FACE IS GONE • • • • 23 MEMORY-PICTURE   9
    YOUNG I SAID A FACE IS GONE • • • • 23 MEMORY-PICTURE V 9
    LONG I SAID A FACE IS GONE • • • • • 23 MEMORY-PICTURE V 9
    AT BURNING NOON SO WARRIORS SAID • • • • 52 RESIGNATION   4
    AND HE ROSE QUICKLY ON ONE ARM AND SAID • • 62 SOHRAB RUSTUM   30
    BUT SOHRAB CAME TO THE BEDSIDE AND SAID • • 62 SOHRAB RUSTUM   33
    OF THE YOUNG MAN IN HIS AND SIGHD AND SAID • • 63 SOHRAB RUSTUM   64
    SO SAID HE AND DROPPD SOHRABS HAND AND LEFT • 63 SOHRAB RUSTUM   94
    BETWIXT THE SILENT HOSTS AND SPAKE AND SAID • 65 SOHRAB RUSTUM   149
    SO WHEN THEY HEARD WHAT PERAN-WISA SAID • • 65 SOHRAB RUSTUM   157
    THESE CAME AND COUNSELLD AND THEN GUDURZ SAID   66 SOHRAB RUSTUM   174
    OLD MAN BE IT AGREED AS THOU HAST SAID • • 66 SOHRAB RUSTUM   185
    AND GREETED GUDURZ WITH BOTH HANDS AND SAID • 67 SOHRAB RUSTUM   204
    BUT GUDURZ STOOD IN THE TENT-DOOR AND SAID • 67 SOHRAB RUSTUM   207
    AND BECKOND TO HIM WITH HIS HAND AND SAID • • 70 SOHRAB RUSTUM   321
    AND CLASPD HIS HAND WITHIN HIS OWN AND SAID • 71 SOHRAB RUSTUM   342
    YET THIS THOU HAST SAID WELL DID RUSTUM STAND • 72 SOHRAB RUSTUM   382
    BUT COURTEOUSLY DREW BACK AND SPOKE AND SAID • 74 SOHRAB RUSTUM   426
    BUT WITH A COLD INCREDULOUS VOICE HE SAID • • • 78 SOHRAB RUSTUM   576
    AND RUSTUM GAZED ON HIM WITH GRIEF AND SAID • 80 SOHRAB RUSTUM   640
    AND RISING STERNLY ON ONE ARM HE SAID • • • 80 SOHRAB RUSTUM   654
    AND IN A HOLLOW VOICE HE SPAKE AND SAID • • 80 SOHRAB RUSTUM   666
    AND THEN HE TOUCHD IT WITH HIS HAND AND SAID • 81 SOHRAB RUSTUM   686
    AND WITH A SOOTHING VOICE HE SPAKE AND SAID • 82 SOHRAB RUSTUM   707
    SO SAID HE AND HIS VOICE RELEASED THE HEART • 82 SOHRAB RUSTUM   726
    BUT RUSTUM CHID HIM WITH STERN VOICE AND SAID • 82 SOHRAB RUSTUM   737
    BUT SOHRAB LOOKD UPON THE HORSE AND SAID • • 83 SOHRAB RUSTUM   741
    MY TERRIBLE FATHERS TERRIBLE HORSE AND SAID • 83 SOHRAB RUSTUM   744
    AND SAID O RUKSH BEAR RUSTUM WELL BUT I • • • 83 SOHRAB RUSTUM   755
    FEAR NOT AS THOU HAST SAID SOHRAB MY SON • • 84 SOHRAB RUSTUM   796
    AND RUSTUM GAZED IN SOHRABS FACE AND SAID • • 85 SOHRAB RUSTUM   835
    BETWIXT THE SILENT HOSTS AND SPOKE AND SAID • 65 SOHRAB RUSTUM V 149
    SO SPAKE HE AND FEROOD STOOD FORTH AND SAID • 66 SOHRAB RUSTUM V 184
    AND WITH A COLD INCREDULOUS VOICE HE SAID • 78 SOHRAB RUSTUM V 576
    AND WITH A SOOTHING VOICE HE SPOKE AND SAID • 82 SOHRAB RUSTUM V 707
    AND RUSTUM GAZED ON SOHRABS FACE AND SAID • • 85 SOHRAB RUSTUM V 835
    AS THE KING SAID SO IT WAS DONE • • • 89 SICK KING BOKH   44
    BUT MY LORD MUSED A SPACE AND SAID • • • 90 SICK KING BOKH   89
    IT IS SOME MADMAN THE KING SAID • • • 90 SICK KING BOKH   91
    TILL THAT THE KING STOOD FORTH AND SAID • • 91 SICK KING BOKH   107
    BRING THOU TO ME HIS CORPSE HE SAID • • • 91 SICK KING BOKH   128
    AS THE KING SAID SO WAS IT DONE • • • 89 SICK KING BOKH V 44
    AS THE KING SAID SO WAS IT DONE • • • 90 SICK KING BOKH V 92
    TO HER DREW HODER NEAR AND SPAKE AND SAID • 98 BALDER DEAD 1   94
    AND THE BLIND HODER ANSWERD HER AND SAID • 99 BALDER DEAD 1   131
    SHE SPOKE BUT HODER ANSWERD HER AND SAID • 100 BALDER DEAD 1   184
    PONDERING ON THAT WHICH FREA SAID SHOULD BE   101 BALDER DEAD 1   201
    SO HODER BRUSHD BY HERMODS SIDE AND SAID • 101 BALDER DEAD 1   235
    AND HERMOD GAZED INTO THE NIGHT AND SAID • 102 BALDER DEAD 1   240
    SO SAID HE AND THE GODS AROSE AND TOOK • • 106 BALDER DEAD 2   47
    AND QUESTIOND HERMOD AS HE CAME AND SAID • 107 BALDER DEAD 2   100
    AND SPAKE AND MILD ENTREATED HER AND SAID • 110 BALDER DEAD 2   188
    SHE SPAKE AND HERMOD ANSWERD HER AND SAID • 111 BALDER DEAD 2   241
    BUT FEEBLY AS A VOICE FAR OFF HE SAID • • 112 BALDER DEAD 2   263
    AND GREETED ODIN AND THE GODS AND SAID • • 114 BALDER DEAD 3   35
    AND STRAIGHT THE FATHER OF THE AGES SAID • 115 BALDER DEAD 3   48
    SO BALDER SAID BUT ODER WELL I KNOW • • • 117 BALDER DEAD 3   119
    HE LAST APPROACHD THE CORPSE AND SPAKE AND SAID 117 BALDER DEAD 3   131
    BUT THEN THE FATHER OF THE AGES SAID • • 118 BALDER DEAD 3   156
    AND THUS THE FATHER OF THE AGES SAID • • 120 BALDER DEAD 3   224
    DAUGHTER AND WIFE OF ODIN THUS SHE SAID • 120 BALDER DEAD 3   247
    SHE GREETED THEM THE FIRST AND LAUGHD AND SAID 123 BALDER DEAD 3   336
    SHE SPAKE BUT HERMOD ANSWERD HER AND SAID • 123 BALDER DEAD 3   345
    AND CALLD HIM BY HIS NAME AND STERNLY SAID • 124 BALDER DEAD 3   386
    HE SPOKE BUT HODER ANSWERD HIM AND SAID • 124 BALDER DEAD 3   394
    WELCOME HE SAID IF THERE BE WELCOME HERE • 125 BALDER DEAD 3   411
    BUT HERMOD STAYD HIM WITH MILD WORDS AND SAID • 125 BALDER DEAD 3   422
    BALDER AND NANNA AND TO BALDER SAID • • 126 BALDER DEAD 3   445
    HE SPAKE AND BALDER ANSWERD HIM AND SAID • 126 BALDER DEAD 3   454
    HE SPAKE BUT BALDER ANSWERD HIM AND SAID • 127 BALDER DEAD 3   483
    THIS IS WHAT MY MOTHER SAID SHOULD BE • • 145 TRISTRAM 2   82
    SON SHE SAID THY NAME SHALL BE OF SORROW • 145 TRISTRAM 2   85
    SO SHE SAID AND DIED IN THE DREAR FOREST • • 145 TRISTRAM 2   87

SAID   (CONTINUED)
    HERE LET US HALT SAID MERLIN THEN AND SHE   •   •   •   •   155 TRISTRAM 3   211
    AH WHENCE THIS MERCY LORD I SAID   •   •   •   •   •   157 SAINT BRANDAN   37
    THE LEPER RECOLLECT SAID HE   •   •   •   •   •   •   157 SAINT BRANDAN   38
    HE SAID THE EARTH HATH KINDNESS   •   •   •   •   161 NECKAN   V   61
    SHE SAID I MUST GO FOR MY KINSFOLK PRAY   •   •   163 FORSAKEN MERM   56
    I SAID GO UP DEAR HEART THROUGH THE WAVES   •   •   163 FORSAKEN MERM   60
    LONG PRAYERS I SAID IN THE WORLD THEY SAY   •   •   163 FORSAKEN MERM   66
    COME I SAID AND WE ROSE THROUGH THE SURF IN THE BAY   •   163 FORSAKEN MERM   67
    DEAR HEART I SAID WE ARE LONG ALONE   •   •   •   163 FORSAKEN MERM   78
    I MET A PREACHER THERE I KNEW AND SAID   •   •   •   169 EAST LONDON   5
    BRAVELY SAID HE FOR I OF LATE HAVE BEEN   •   •   •   169 EAST LONDON   7
    SEIRIOL THE BRIGHT KYBI THE DARK MEN SAID   •   •   170 EAST AND WEST   9
    YES WRITE IT IN THE ROCK SAINT BERNARD SAID   •   171 DIVINITY   1
    THE GODS HAVE SAID THAT REPOSE   •   •   •   •   •   199 FRAG DEJANEIRA   20
    CREEP AND LET NO MORE BE SAID   •   •   •   •   •   215 LAST WORD   2
    BEHOLD I SAID THE PAINTERS SPHERE   •   •   •   •   222 EPILOG LAOCOON   49
    BUT WHO I SAID SUFFICES HERE   •   •   •   •   •   225 EPILOG LAOCOON   128
    IN THIS SELF-SAME GARDEN AND SAID   •   •   •   •   233 YOUTH OF MAN   25
    WAS IT THE LORD THEN SAID WITH SCORN YE SAW   •   237 PROGRESS   5
    SO CHRIST SAID EIGHTEEN HUNDRED YEARS AGO   •   •   237 PROGRESS   13
    AND WHAT THEN SHALL BE SAID TO THOSE TO-DAY   •   237 PROGRESS   14
    THE OLD LAW THEY SAID IS WHOLLY COME TO NOUGHT   •   237 PROGRESS   V   3
    AND I HE SAID THE SECRET OF THEIR ART   •   •   •   256 SCHOLAR-GIPSY   48
    THIS SAID HE LEFT THEM AND RETURND NO MORE   •   •   256 SCHOLAR-GIPSY   51
    WE PRIZED IT DEARLY WHILE IT STOOD WE SAID   •   •   263 THYRSIS   28
    WHEN GOETHES DEATH WAS TOLD WE SAID   •   •   •   270 MEMORIAL VERSES   15
    AND SAID THOU AILEST HERE AND HERE   •   •   •   •   270 MEMORIAL VERSES   22
    HE SAID THE END IS EVERYWHERE   •   •   •   •   271 MEMORIAL VERSES   27
    WHAT SHALL BE SAID OER WORDSWORTHS TOMB   •   •   270 MEMORIAL VERSES   V   5
    WHEN GOETHE PASSD AWAY WE SAID   •   •   •   •   270 MEMORIAL VERSES   V   15
    UNNAMED WHO GOETHE SAID   •   •   •   •   •   •   295 HEINES GRAVE   99
    YES AS THE SON OF THETIS SAID   •   •   •   •   •   309 OBERMANN   89
    WHERE TARRIES HE THE POWER WHO SAID   •   •   •   320 OBERMANN MORE   231
    WILL LIE MY GRANDSIRE SAID OUR FAIREST CHANCE   •   331 MEROPE   41
    THE MOST ARE BAD WISE MEN HAVE SAID   •   •   •   352 MEROPE   652
    DIED OF A SNAKE-BITE SAID HE ON THAT BROW   •   •   357 MEROPE   781
    A YOUTH ARRIVED BUT NOW THE SON HE SAID   •   •   363 MEROPE   955
    THY SON IS HERE ONE SAID SO SURE BUT NOW   •   •   376 MEROPE   1216
    I SHOULD HAVE SAID THAT SOME ONE TOUCHD A HARP   •   412 EMPEDOCLES I 2   11
    AND SAID O BOY I TAUGHT THIS LORE   •   •   •   •   414 EMPEDOCLES I 2   69
    THY CITIZENS TIS SAID   •   •   •   •   •   •   416 EMPEDOCLES I 2   117
    AND THE ATTENTIVE MUSES SAID   •   •   •   •   •   433 EMPEDOCLES II   145
    AND JOKES IN DOGGISH LANGUAGE SAID   •   •   •   460 KAISER DEAD   71
    WHICH HID ULYSSES WAVED ITSELF AND SAID   •   •   484 S S LUSITANIA   2

SAIDST
    OF THE HERACLEIDAN CONQUERORS AS THOU SAIDST   •   •   404 MEROPE   1982

SAIL
    WHEN THOU SHALT SAIL IN A HIGH-MASTED SHIP   •   •   85 SOHRAB RUSTUM   831
    OR ON THE SEA THE FIELD OF PIRATES SAIL   •   •   121 BALDER DEAD 3   270
    FOR THE GLEAM OF THEIR WHITE SAIL   •   •   •   •   138 TRISTRAM 1   272
    NOW TO SAIL THE SEAS OF DEATH I LEAVE THEE   •   •   145 TRISTRAM 2   97
    SAIL AND SAIL WITH UNSHUT EYE   •   •   •   •   •   162 FORSAKEN MERM   44
    SAIL AND SAIL WITH UNSHUT EYE   •   •   •   •   •   162 FORSAKEN MERM   44
    LISTETH WILL SAIL   •   •   •   •   •   •   •   243 SUMMER NIGHT   55
    AND SNATCHD HIS RUDDER AND SHOOK OUT MORE SAIL   •   262 SCHOLAR-GIPSY   242
    HANGS TOUCHD WITH LIGHT ONE SNOWY SAIL   •   •   274 STANZAS CARNAC   32
    WHERE THAT FAR SAIL IS PASSING NOW   •   •   •   274 STANZAS CARNAC   34
    HANGS TOUCHD WITH LIGHT ONE DISTANT SAIL   •   •   274 STANZAS CARNAC   V   32
    THIS SEA OF TIME WHEREON WE SAIL   •   •   •   •   303 GRANDE CHARTR   122
    STRIKES WITH ALL SAIL SET   •   •   •   •   •   400 MEROPE   1879
    WHEN TO SAIL AND WHEN TO SOW   •   •   •   •   •   456 POOR MATTHIAS   140
    WHERE RODE THE TALL DARK SHIPS WHOSE LOOSEND SAIL   •   473 CROMWELL   67
    ONCE MORE BENEATH HIM AND THE FLUTTERING SAIL   •   •   479 CROMWELL   237

SAILD
    WAS IT A DREAM WE SAILD I THOUGHT WE SAILD   •   •   24 DREAM   1
    WAS IT A DREAM WE SAILD I THOUGHT WE SAILD   •   •   24 DREAM   1
    SAILD BY THE FATE-MEANT GULF TO THEIR CONQUEST   •   344 MEROPE   450

SAILING
    THE SAILING FOAM THE SHINING POOL   •   •   •   •   55 RESIGNATION   105
    WHERE GREAT WHALES COME SAILING BY   •   •   •   •   162 FORSAKEN MERM   43
    WILD BEASTS AND VULTURES SAILING OVERHEAD   •   •   373 MEROPE   1170

SAILORS
    HIS SAILORS BONNET   •   •   •   •   •   •   •   •   189 STRAYED REVEL   105

SAILS
    LO SAILS THAT GLEAM A MOMENT AND ARE GONE   •   •   42 GIPSY CHILD   5
    ECHO HER STORMY SCREAM AS SHE SAILS BY   •   •   78 SOHRAB RUSTUM   572
    THE MAST THEY FIXT AND HOISTED UP THE SAILS   •   118 BALDER DEAD 3   174
    THE BREEZE AND FILLD THE SAILS AND BLEW THE FIRE   •   118 BALDER DEAD 3   184
    AND ATE THE SHRIVELLING SAILS BUT STILL THE SHIP   •   119 BALDER DEAD 3   191
    THEY FIXT THE MAST AND HOISTED UP THE SAILS   •   118 BALDER DEAD 3   V 174
    THE CALM SEA SHINES LOOSE HANG THE VESSELS SAILS   •   133 TRISTRAM 1   94
    WANDERING THROUGH THEIR DROOPING SAILS   •   •   •   135 TRISTRAM 1   157
    THE SAND THE SEA-BIRDS AND THE DISTANT SAILS   •   •   152 TRISTRAM 3   105

```
SAILS          ( CONTINUED )
       SAINT BRANDAN SAILS THE NORTHERN MAIN      • • • •        156 SAINT BRANDAN       1
       HE GREETS THEM ONCE HE SAILS AGAIN  • • • • • •          156 SAINT BRANDAN       3
       ONLY THE TRACT WHERE HE SAILS   • • • • • •             252 FUTURE              24
       OUTSIDE THE WESTERN STRAITS AND UNBENT SAILS    • •     262 SCHOLAR-GIPSY      247
       NO MAST NO SAILS ARE SET THEREON    • • • • •           479 HAYSWATER BOAT       5

SAINT
       SAINT BRANDAN SAILS THE NORTHERN MAIN      • • • •      156 SAINT BRANDAN       1
       SO LATE SUCH STORMS THE SAINT IS MAD  • • • • •        156 SAINT BRANDAN       4
       BUT NORTH STILL NORTH SAINT BRANDAN STEERD  • • • •    156 SAINT BRANDAN       9
       TEARS STARTED TO SAINT BRANDANS EYES  • • • • •        158 SAINT BRANDAN      73
       YES WRITE IT IN THE ROCK SAINT BERNARD SAID    • •     171 DIVINITY            1
       WELL SPAKE THE IMPETUOUS SAINT AND BORE OF MEN    •    171 DIVINITY            6
       THIS NO SAINT PREACHES AND THIS NO CHURCH RULES   •    171 DIVINITY           13
       SAINT MICHAELS CHAPEL CUTS THE SKY   • • • • •         273 STANZAS CARNAC      2
       WHO BORE SAINT LOUIS COMPANY   • • • • • • •           278 SOUTHERN NIGHT     94
       THE MULE-TRACK FROM SAINT LAURENT GOES   • • • •       299 GRANDE CHARTR       4
       BE NEITHER SAINT NOR SOPHIST-LED BUT BE A MAN   •      416 EMPEDOCLES I 2    136
       HIS HANDS WERE FOLDED LIKE A SAINT AT REST   • • •     476 CROMWELL          168

SAINTS
       GODS ARE WE BARDS SAINTS HEROES IF WE WILL  • • •        4 EMERSONS ESSAYS   13
       ONLY THE BLESSED SAINTS ARE SMILING DUMB   • • • •      17 CHURCH BROU 3      4
       PROPHETS TRANSFIGURED SAINTS AND MARTYRS BRAVE  • • •   18 CHURCH BROU 3     20
       AH SWEET SAINTS UNWITTINGLY   • • • • • • •            135 TRISTRAM 1       142
       AH SWEET SAINTS HIS DREAM DOTH MOVE   • • • • •        135 TRISTRAM 1       170
       DEAR SAINTS IT IS NOT SORROW AS I HEAR   • • • •       152 TRISTRAM 3       112
       THE BROTHERHOODS OF SAINTS ARE GLAD   • • • • •        156 SAINT BRANDAN      2
       TWO SAINTS MET OFTEN WHERE THOSE WATERS FLOW   • •     170 EAST AND WEST      4

SAITH
       THUS SAITH THE LORD TO HIS OWN  • • • • • • •          216 LORDS MESSENGER    1
       THEN SAITH THE LORD TO HIS OWN  • • • • • • •          216 LORDS MESSENGER  V  1
       SO SAITH HE BLESSING HIM WITH OUTSPREAD HANDS   • •    445 WESTMIN ABBEY     46

SAKE
       THAT ONE SHOULD GRUDGE ITS LOSS FOR BALDERS SAKE • •    98 BALDER DEAD 1    125
       TRISTRAM ART THOU CALLD FOR MY DEATHS SAKE  • • • •    145 TRISTRAM 2        86
       TILL FOR ITS SAKE ALONE WE LIVE AND MOVE   • • • •     153 TRISTRAM 3       129
       ONE FOR WHOSE SAKE SHE ONCE MIGHT PROVE   • • • •      202 URANIA            19
       FOR GODS SAKE BELIEVE IT THEN   • • • • • • •          215 PIS-ALLER         12
       MORE FOR THIS LANDS SAKE GRIEVE I THAN MINE OWN • •    398 MEROPE          1784

SALAMINIAN
       HALLOW THE SALAMINIAN PROMONTORIES    • • • • • •      481 HUNGARIAN NAT     13

SALLIES
       LEANS HER EAR TO YOUR MAD SALLIES    • • • • • •        27 NEW SIRENS        27

SALORE
       THE TUKAS AND THE LANCES OF SALORE   • • • • • •        64 SOHRAB RUSTUM    122

SALT
       RETURNING HOME OVER THE SALT BLUE SEA     • • •         85 SOHRAB RUSTUM    833
       WATCHING BY THE SALT SEA-TIDE   • • • • • • •          138 TRISTRAM 1       270
       BENEATH THE SALT SEA-TIDE   • • • • • •                160 NECKAN            32
       NOW THE SALT TIDES SEAWARD FLOW   • • • • •            161 FORSAKEN MERM      5
       WHERE THE SALT WEED SWAYS IN THE STREAM   • • •        162 FORSAKEN MERM     38
       NOW THE SALT TIDES SEAWARDS FLOW    • • • •            161 FORSAKEN MERM    V  5
       THE SALT TIDE ROLLS SEAWARD   • • • • • •              164 FORSAKEN MERM    V 110
       THE UNPLUMBD SALT ESTRANGING SEA   • • • • •           182 TO MARG CONT      24
       LEAVING THE SALT SEA-BEDS   • • • • • • •              196 FRAG ANTIGONE     57

SALUTATIONS
       STUPID SALUTATIONS GAY   • • • • • • • •               455 POOR MATTHIAS    112

SALUTES
       SALUTES AND PASSES BY   • • • • • • • • •              283 HAWORTH CHURCH   V

SALVATION
       PROCLAIMS SALVATION AT HAND   • • • • • • •            214 NEW ROME           8
       INSTILLS SALVATION AT HAND   • • • • • • •             214 NEW ROME         V  8

SAMARCAND
       IN SAMARCAND BEFORE THE ARMY MARCHD   • • • • •         62 SOHRAB RUSTUM     40
       IN SAMARCAND HE WILL ARISE AND CRY   • • • • •          72 SOHRAB RUSTUM    356
       AFRASIABS CITIES ONLY SAMARCAND   • • • • •             83 SOHRAB RUSTUM    760
       OF SAMARCAND IS BROUGHT THIS WAY   • • • • •            89 SICK KING BOKH    63
       UPON THE ROAD OF SAMARCAND   • • • • • • •              94 SICK KING BOKH   224

SAME
       ONCE MORE WE TREAD THIS SELF-SAME ROAD   • • • •        55 RESIGNATION       86
       THE SELF-SAME SHADOWS NOW AS THEN   • • • • •           55 RESIGNATION       98
       TO-MORROW ON THE SELF-SAME PLAN   • • • • •             56 RESIGNATION      141
       THE MORROW AT THE SELF-SAME HOUR   • • • • •            90 SICK KING BOKH    93
       THE VERY SAME WHICH YESTERNIGHT   • • • • •            146 TRISTRAM 2       112
       IN THIS SELF-SAME GARDEN AND SAID   • • • •            233 YOUTH OF MAN      25
       BUT THE SAME RESTLESS PACINGS TO AND FRO   • • •       242 SUMMER NIGHT      23
       AND THE SAME VAINLY THROBBING HEART WAS THERE   • •    242 SUMMER NIGHT      24
```

SAME   (CONTINUED)
        AND THE SAME BRIGHT CALM MOON   242 SUMMER NIGHT   25
        AND THE SAME AGITATED HEART WAS THERE   242 SUMMER NIGHT   V   24
        THE SAME HEART BEATS IN EVERY HUMAN BREAST   245 BURIED LIFE   23
        THE SAME THE GIPSIES WORE   256 SCHOLAR-GIPSY   56
        IN THE TWO HINKSEYS NOTHING KEEPS THE SAME   262 THYRSIS   2
        STILL THE SAME OCEAN ROUND US RAVES   303 GRANDE CHARTR   125
        GLION BUT NOT THE SAME   312 OBERMANN MORE   4
        BUT YE YE ARE THE SAME   320 OBERMANN MORE   224
        HE STOOD BY WHAT HE WISHD FOR I THE SAME   334 MEROPE   129
        ON THAT SAME SPUR WHERE WE HAD SATE AT MORN   357 MEROPE   796
        AND IN MY TURN I WISH THE SAME FOR THEE   396 MEROPE   1763
        ON THE SAME SPUR WHERE WE HAD SATE AT MORN   357 MEROPE   V   796
        TRUMPET IT AS THEY WILL IS BUT THE SAME AS THINE   417 EMPEDOCLES I 2   141
        BUT WE ARE ALL THE SAME THE FOOLS OF OUR OWN WOES   417 EMPEDOCLES I 2   166
        TIS THE SAME UNSKILFULNESS   457 POOR MATTHIAS   160
        AND KAISERS RACE WE DEEMD THE SAME   459 KAISER DEAD   21
        AND THE SAME WORLD HAS TONGUE AND EAR AND EYE   470 ALARIC AT ROME   218
        WITH STERN SLOW STEPS UNSEEN YET STILL THE SAME   476 CROMWELL   147
        OER THOSE SAME SEAS DARK TENERIFFE ROSE FRAUGHT   485 S S LUSITANIA   11
        TOUCH THE SAME SURFACE WHICH OUR FATHERS TROD   EVERLASTING SUB   3
        HAVE THE SAME SURFACE WHICH OUR FATHERS TROD   EVERLASTING SUB   V   3
        HAVE THE SAME SURFACE WHICH OUR FATHERS FELT   EVERLASTING SUB   V   3
        HAVE THE SAME SURFACE WHICH OUR FATHERS TOUCHD   EVERLASTING SUB   V   3
        TOUCH THE SAME SURFACE WHICH OUR FATHERS FELT   EVERLASTING SUB   V   3
        TOUCH THE SAME SURFACE WHICH OUR FATHERS TOUCHD   EVERLASTING SUB   V   3

SANCTIFY
        THEY SHALL NOT DECK YOUR LIFE BUT SANCTIFY YOUR GRAVE   467 ALARIC AT ROME   138

SANCTION
        THOUGH FENCED BY SANCTION OF A THOUSAND YEARS   353 MEROPE   669

SANCTIONS
        WHICH NATURE SANCTIONS WHICH THE INNOCENT BLOOD   386 MEROPE   1427

SANCTUARY
        THENCE BY THE SEA-GODS SANCTUARY AND THE TOMB   356 MEROPE   740
        THE MANTINEAN SANCTUARY FORBID   357 MEROPE   775

SAND
        URGED AND TO FEED WHOSE MOVEMENT SPINNING SAND   5 DUKE WELLINGTON   6
        MY SAND RUNS SHORT AND AS YON STAR-SHOT RAY   10 MYCERINUS   56
        IN A LONE SAND-HEMMD   51 CONSOLATION   27
        SAHARAN SAND-WINDS   51 CONSOLATION   36
        AND THE OLD TARTAR CAME UPON THE SAND   65 SOHRAB RUSTUM   148
        BRISTLING AND IN THE MIDST THE OPEN SAND   70 SOHRAB RUSTUM   298
        AND RUSTUM CAME UPON THE SAND AND CAST   70 SOHRAB RUSTUM   299
        HIS GIANT FIGURE PLANTED ON THE SAND   71 SOHRAB RUSTUM   336
        OR ELSE THY BONES SHALL STREW THIS SAND TILL WINDS   72 SOHRAB RUSTUM   376
        HISSD AND WENT QUIVERING DOWN INTO THE SAND   73 SOHRAB RUSTUM   404
        TO HIS KNEES AND WITH HIS FINGERS CLUTCHD THE SAND   73 SOHRAB RUSTUM   421
        DIZZY AND ON HIS KNEES AND CHOKED WITH SAND   74 SOHRAB RUSTUM   424
        AND MAKE A TRUCE AND SIT UPON THIS SAND   74 SOHRAB RUSTUM   440
        AND COMES AT NIGHT TO DIE UPON THE SAND   76 SOHRAB RUSTUM   506
        AND SOHRAB WOUNDED ON THE BLOODY SAND   77 SOHRAB RUSTUM   526
        PITEOUS AND LOVELY LYING ON THE SAND   80 SOHRAB RUSTUM   633
        LOVELY IN DEATH UPON THE COMMON SAND   80 SOHRAB RUSTUM   639
        COME SIT BESIDE ME ON THIS SAND AND TAKE   82 SOHRAB RUSTUM   718
        THE BIG WARM TEARS ROLLD DOWN AND CAKED THE SAND   82 SOHRAB RUSTUM   736
        MIGHT NOW BE LYING ON THIS BLOODY SAND   85 SOHRAB RUSTUM   817
        SO ON THE BLOODY SAND SOHRAB LAY DEAD   86 SOHRAB RUSTUM   857
        SO IN THE SAND LAY RUSTUM BY HIS SON   86 SOHRAB RUSTUM   864
        THROUGH BEDS OF SAND AND MATTED RUSHY ISLES   87 SOHRAB RUSTUM   885
        AND PERAN WISA CAME UPON THE SAND   65 SOHRAB RUSTUM   V   148
        TO HIS KNEES AND WITH HIS FINGERS GRASPD THE SAND   73 SOHRAB RUSTUM   V   421
        HE CAME AND SADLY WENT ALONG THE SAND   97 BALDER DEAD 1   78
        TO PUSH THE SHIP THROUGH THE THICK SAND SPARKS FLEW   118 BALDER DEAD 3   177
        THROUGH THE DARK UP THE DROWND SAND   137 TRISTRAM 1   218
        AND MANY A STRETCH OF WATERY SAND   141 TRISTRAM 1   369
        THE SAND THE SEA-BIRDS AND THE DISTANT SAILS   152 TRISTRAM 3   105
        SAND RAKED HIS SORES FROM HEEL TO PATE   157 SAINT BRANDAN   47
        SAND-STREWN CAVERNS COOL AND DEEP   162 FORSAKEN MERM   35
        SHE STEALS TO THE WINDOW AND LOOKS AT THE SAND   164 FORSAKEN MERM   98
        AND OVER THE SAND AT THE SEA   164 FORSAKEN MERM   99
        WE WILL GAZE FROM THE SAND-HILLS   165 FORSAKEN MERM   136
        WHETHER THROUGH WHIRLING SAND   193 STRAYED REVEL   247
        TO WATCH THIS LINE OF SAND-HILLS RUN   204 CALAIS SANDS   2
        I SAW UPON THE OPEN SAND   204 CALAIS SANDS   10
        TO SEE THIS LINE OF SAND-HILLS RUN   204 CALAIS SANDS   V   2
        AND SEE UPON THE LOVELY SAND   204 CALAIS SANDS   V   10
        WHERE THE EBB MEETS THE MOON-BLANCHD SAND   211 DOVER BEACH   V   8
        WHERE THE SEA MEETS THE MOON-BLANCHD SAND   211 DOVER BEACH   V   8
        AND CRUMBLING WALL AND SULTRY SAND   318 OBERMANN MORE   183
        TILL THE SAND THY FEATHERS SMIRCH   456 POOR MATTHIAS   129
        SO FEATLY STREWN WITH DRIFTED SAND   480 HAYSWATER BOAT   22

SANDALLD
        SANDALLD PALMERS FARING HOMEWARD   15 CHURCH BROU 1   77

SANDALS
    HE PASSD AND TIED HIS SANDALS ON HIS FEET • • • •   64 SOHRAB RUSTUM   97
    WITH THY SOILD HUNTING-COAT AND SANDALS TORN • • 372 MEROPE   1159

SANDBANKS
    UPON THE REEFS AND SANDBANKS OF THE WORLD • • • •   LUCRETIUS 2   5

SANDFORD
    ABOVE BY ENSHAM DOWN BY SANDFORD YIELDS • • • 266 THYRSIS   109

SANDS
    TROOP ACROSS THE FLUSHING SANDS • • •   26 NEW SIRENS   14
    FROM THE BROAD OXUS AND THE GLITTERING SANDS • • 64 SOHRAB RUSTUM   105
    AND THOSE FROM ATTRUCK AND THE CASPIAN SANDS • • 64 SOHRAB RUSTUM   123
    OUT ON THE SANDS BEYOND IT RUSTUMS TENTS • • • 66 SOHRAB RUSTUM   191
    REJOINS HER IN THEIR HUT UPON THE SANDS • • • 70 SOHRAB RUSTUM   289
    BUT ON THE OXUS-SANDS AND IN THE DANCE • • • 75 SOHRAB RUSTUM   462
    QUICK QUICK FOR NUMBERD ARE MY SANDS OF LIFE • 82 SOHRAB RUSTUM   721
    AND THOU HAST TROD THE SANDS OF SEISTAN • • • 83 SOHRAB RUSTUM   750
    THE PERSIANS TOOK IT ON THE OPEN SANDS • • • 86 SOHRAB RUSTUM   872
    BRIMMING AND BRIGHT AND LARGE THEN SANDS BEGIN   87 SOHRAB RUSTUM   881
    UNDER THE GATE-HOUSE TO THE SANDS AND FOUND • • 113 BALDER DEAD 2   309
    WEEPING THE SANDS WERE WETTED AND THEIR ARMS • • 115 BALDER DEAD 3   62
    FRINGED WITH DARK PINES AND SANDS WHERE SEAFOWL SCREAM 123 BALDER DEAD 3   327
    ON THE BLANCHD SANDS A GLOOM • • • • • • • 165 FORSAKEN MERM   131
    ON RAVENNA SANDS IN THE SHADE • • • • • • 294 HEINES GRAVE   60
    WE MEASURE THE SEA-TIDES WE NUMBER THE SEA-SANDS • 423 EMPEDOCLES I 2 321

SANDY
    DEEP IN THE SANDY WASTE • • • • • • • 51 CONSOLATION   33
    BY SANDY BAHREIN IN THE PERSIAN GULF • • • • 69 SOHRAB RUSTUM   286
    AND IN A SANDY WHIRLWIND WRAPPD THE PAIR • • 75 SOHRAB RUSTUM   485
    WE WENT UP THE BEACH BY THE SANDY DOWN • • • 163 FORSAKEN MERM   68
    THE SANDY SPITS THE SHORE-LOCKD LAKES • • • 275 SOUTHERN NIGHT   1

SANE
    FROM MISTS AND SANE AND CLEAR • • • • 308 OBERMANN   62
    THOU ART BEWILDERD THE SANE HEAD IS MINE • • • 396 MEROPE   1759

SANG
    STROLLD AND SANG WITH JOYFUL MIND • • •   26 NEW SIRENS   6
    AND THROUGH THE VOID AIR SANG • • • • 197 FRAG ANTIGONE   88
    WHEN DORIAN SHEPHERDS SANG TO PROSERPINE • • 265 THYRSIS   92
    SO SANG I BUT THE MIDNIGHT BREEZE • • • 279 SOUTHERN NIGHT 117
    SO I SANG BUT THE MUSE • • • • 285 HAWORTH CHURCH 125
    AND AT THE BANQUET ALL THE MUSES SANG • • • 427 EMPEDOCLES I 2 451
    HERE MATTHIAS SANG HIS FILL • • • • • 458 POOR MATTHIAS 198

SANGEST
    BUT WHEN THOU SANGEST BALDER THOU DIDST STRIKE • 117 BALDER DEAD 3   141

SANGUINE
    TO THE LESS PRACTISED EYE OF SANGUINE YOUTH • • 267 THYRSIS   142
    TO THE UNPRACTISED EYE OF SANGUINE YOUTH • • • 267 THYRSIS   V 142

SANK
    WHEN SHE SANK INTO HER GRAVE • • • • • 15 CHURCH BROU 1   70
    NEVER TILL NOW DEFILED SANK TO THE DUST • • 76 SOHRAB RUSTUM   498
    HE REELD AND STAGGERING BACK SANK TO THE GROUND • 76 SOHRAB RUSTUM   521
    AND HIS HEAD SWAM AND HE SANK DOWN TO EARTH • 81 SOHRAB RUSTUM   693
    AND NANNA ON HER BED SANK BACK BUT THEN • • 104 BALDER DEAD 1   338
    AND SANK DOWN HERE SLEEPING • • • • • 187 STRAYED REVEL   51
    HOTLY CHARGED AND SANK AT LAST • • • • 215 LAST WORD   12
    THAT WORLD-FAMED SON OF FIRE SHE WHO SANK • • 285 HAWORTH CHURCH   97
    DOWN SHE SANK AMID HER FUR • • • • • 453 POOR MATTHIAS   36

SANKST
    THOU SANKST ALONE • • • • • • • • • 276 SOUTHERN NIGHT   28

SAPIENT
    TO SHAKE HIS SAPIENT HEAD AND GIVE • • • • 250 WISH   19

SAPPD
    HEALTH SAPPD BY LIVING ILL • • • • • 425 EMPEDOCLES I 2 393

SAPPHIRE
    A CHEQUER-WORK OF GLOWING SAPPHIRE-TINTS • • • 18 CHURCH BROU 3   23

SAPPST
    THAT SAPPST THE VITALS OF THIS TERRIBLE MOUNT • • 438 EMPEDOCLES II 306

SARDONIC
    THEIR VAUNTS THEIR FEATS LET A SARDONIC SMILE • • 298 HEINES GRAVE 208

SAT
    AND HELA SAT THEREON WITH COUNTENANCE STERN • • 110 BALDER DEAD 2 V 178
    SO TIBERIUS MIGHT HAVE SAT • • • • • • 453 POOR MATTHIAS   41

SATE
    I SATE OBEDIENT IN THE FIERY PRIME • • • • • 9 MYCERINUS   9

SATE   (CONTINUED)
        SATE THE DUCHESS MARGUERITE   • • • • • • •   13 CHURCH BROU 1   36
        SATE AND WATCHD HER WORKING TRAIN   • • • • • •   15 CHURCH BROU 1   94
        THERE SHE SATE AND WATCHD THE BUILDERS   • • • •   16 CHURCH BROU 1   101
        AND DARK GREEN MELONS AND THERE RUSTUM SATE   • •   67 SOHRAB RUSTUM   199
        DOWN OER HIS FACE AND SATE BY HIS DEAD SON • • • • •   86 SOHRAB RUSTUM   859
        THAT THEY SATE WITH IT IN MY SIGHT   • • • • •   90 SICK KING BOKH   83
        TO LIDSKIALF AND SATE UPON HIS THRONE   • • • •   96 BALDER DEAD 1   49
        AND ON THEIR GOLDEN CHAIRS THEY SATE AGAIN   • • •   97 BALDER DEAD 1   64
        UPON HER GOLDEN CHAIR THE MOTHER SATE   • • • •   98 BALDER DEAD 1   92
        AND BOWD HER HEAD AND SATE WITH FOLDED HANDS   • •   100 BALDER DEAD 1   193
        THERE ALL THE GODS IN SILENCE SATE THEM DOWN   • •   106 BALDER DEAD 2   39
        TO ASGARD AND SATE DOWN IN ODINS HALL   • •   119 BALDER DEAD 3   208
        THERE CAME THE GODS AND SATE THEM DOWN ON STONES   •   120 BALDER DEAD 3   223
        AND BOWD HER HEAD AND SATE WITH FOLDED HANDS   • •   122 BALDER DEAD 3   296
        WHERE SATE IN THE CAVES MOUTH A SKINNY HAG   • • •   123 BALDER DEAD 3   333
        THEY SATE THEM DOWN TOGETHER AND A SLEEP   • • •   155 TRISTRAM 3   213
        PALSIED WITH TERROR BRANDAN SATE   • • • • •   157 SAINT BRANDAN   21
        AND IN THE STREET A LEPER SATE   • • • • • • •   157 SAINT BRANDAN   45
        HE SATE AND PLAYD HIS HARP OF GOLD   • • • • •   160 NECKAN   43
        BESIDE THE POOL SATE NECKAN   • • • • • • •   160 NECKAN   45
        ONCE SHE SATE WITH YOU AND ME   • • • • • • •   163 FORSAKEN MERM   50
        AND THE YOUNGEST SATE ON HER KNEE   • • • • •   163 FORSAKEN MERM   52
        SHE SATE BY THE PILLAR WE SAW HER CLEAR   • • •   163 FORSAKEN MERM   76
        SATE WITH HIS BRIDE TO SEE A PUBLIC SHOW   • • •   166 AUSTERITY POET   4
        SATE IN THE BROUGHAM AND THOSE BLANK WALLS SURVEYD   167 RACHEL 1   8
        AS REBEKAH READ WHEN SHE SATE   • • • • • • •   252 FUTURE   36
        ON JAMAN HAST THOU SATE   • • • • • •   310 OBERMANN   114
        FAR IN THE LIQUID LAKE WE SATE AND DREW   • •   356 MEROPE   752
        ON THAT SAME SPUR WHERE WE HAD SATE AT MORN   • •   357 MEROPE   796
        ON THE SAME SPUR WHERE WE HAD SATE AT MORN   • • •   357 MEROPE   V 796
        AND IN THE LITTER SATE EMPEDOCLES   • • • • •   407 EMPEDOCLES I 1   42
        AND HAVE THIS HOUR SATE BY THE TORRENT HERE   • •   408 EMPEDOCLES I 1   47
        ALL NIGHT THEY SATE THEN STOLE AWAY   • • • • •   480 HAYSWATER BOAT   31
        THERE SATE FIFTY MEN IN THE RUDDY LIGHT OF THE FIRE   HOMER TRANS   4
        WHILE THEIR MASTERS SATE BY THE FIRE AND WAITED   HOMER TRANS   6
                FOR MORNING

SATED
        DEEP WEARINESS AND SATED LUST   • • • • • • • •   315 OBERMANN MORE   95
        SATED AND MORE THAN ENOUGH   • • • • • • • •   348 MEROPE   V

SATIATE
        WOULD NEVER LET US SATIATE HERE   • • • • • •   180 FAREWELL   88

SATISFIED
        IF HIS WILL BE NOT SATISFIED   • • • • • • •   • •   94 SICK KING BOKH   206
        BUT WHEN THEIR SOULS WERE SATISFIED WITH WAIL   • •   103 BALDER DEAD 1   276
        ACROSS AND BEGGD AND CAME BACK SATISFIED   • • • •   170 WEST LONDON   7

SATST
        BUT MUTE THOU SATST AND EACH MESSENIAN HEART   • •   383 MEROPE   1373
        SATST UPON THY PERCH TO HEAR   • • • • • • • •   455 POOR MATTHIAS   120

SATURN
        AND WITH PITY THE SON OF SATURN SAW THEM BEWAILING   HOMER TRANS   7

SATURNS
        FROM SATURNS SEARCH AMONG THE NEW-YEAND LAMBS   • •   355 MEROPE   738

SAUNTER
        WITH SAUNTER WITH BOUNDS • • • • • • • • • • •   218 BACCHANALIA 1   21

SAVAGE
        AMONG THEIR SAVAGE GORGES AND COLD SPRINGS   • • • •   198 FRAG DEJANEIRA   9
        HE WOULD NOT LET HIS SAVAGE CHIEFS ALIGHT   • • •   339 MEROPE   295
        THESE ARE NOT NOW THE SAVAGE BAND WHO ERST   • • •   381 MEROPE   1299

SAVE
        SAVE OH SAVE   • • • • • • • • • • • • • • •   38 STAGIRIUS   5
        SAVE OH SAVE   • • • • • • • • • • • • • • •   38 STAGIRIUS   5
        SAVE OH SAVE   • • • • • • • • • • • • • • •   38 STAGIRIUS   13
        SAVE OH SAVE   • • • • • • • • • • • • • • •   38 STAGIRIUS   13
        SAVE OH SAVE   • • • • • • • • • • • • • • •   39 STAGIRIUS   29
        SAVE OH SAVE   • • • • • • • • • • • • • • •   39 STAGIRIUS   29
        SAVE OH SAVE   • • • • • • • • • • • • • • •   39 STAGIRIUS   38
        SAVE OH SAVE   • • • • • • • • • • • • • • •   39 STAGIRIUS   38
        SAVE OH SAVE   • • • • • • • • • • • • • • •   40 STAGIRIUS   62
        SAVE OH SAVE   • • • • • • • • • • • • • • •   40 STAGIRIUS   62
        NO LIFE SAVE HIS AND OURS INTRUDES   • • • • • •   54 RESIGNATION   72
        THIS MAN MY PITY COULD NOT SAVE   • • • • •   95 SICK KING BOKH   226
        SAVE ME ALONE AND HELA SOLEMN QUEEN   • • • • •   104 BALDER DEAD 1   319
        SAVE ONE BERGELMER HE ON SHIPBOARD FLED   • • •   121 BALDER DEAD 3   272
        BUT WHAT WERE I TO SAVE THEM IN THAT HOUR   • • •   127 BALDER DEAD 3   489
        IF STRENGTH MIGHT SAVE THEM COULD NOT ODIN SAVE • •   127 BALDER DEAD 3   490
        IF STRENGTH MIGHT SAVE THEM COULD NOT ODIN SAVE • •   127 BALDER DEAD 3   490
        IF STRENGTH COULD SAVE THEM COULD NOT ODIN SAVE • •   127 BALDER DEAD 3   V 490
        IF STRENGTH COULD SAVE THEM COULD NOT ODIN SAVE • •   127 BALDER DEAD 3   V 490
        FLY SAVE THYSELF SAVE ME I DARE NOT STAY   • • •   135 TRISTRAM 1   168
        FLY SAVE THYSELF SAVE ME I DARE NOT STAY   • • •   135 TRISTRAM 1   168
        THOU HAST DARED IT BUT TOO LATE TO SAVE   • • •   142 TRISTRAM 2   10

SAVE   (CONTINUED)
        ME THY LIVING FRIEND THOU CANST NOT SAVE   • • • •   145 TRISTRAM 2   90
        SO SUNK SO RARELY LIFTED SAVE TO MEET   • • • •   151 TRISTRAM 3   71
        HE SAVES THE SHEEP THE GOATS HE DOTH NOT SAVE   • • •   172 GOOD SHEPHERD   1
        AND WHAT CRIES CUPID WILL SAVE US   • • • • • •   214 NEW ROME   9
        AND WHAT ASKS CUPID WILL SAVE US   • • • • • •   214 NEW ROME   V 9
        IT DRAWS THEM ON THEY CANNOT SAVE   • • • • •   226 EPILOG LAOCOON   165
        HER WHOM WE CANNOT SAVE   • • • • • • • •   282 HAWORTH CHURCH   V
        MANY TO SAVE WITH THYSELF   • • • • • • •   290 RUGBY CHAPEL   141
        SAVE THEE TO SEE THEIR WAY   • • • • • • •   307 OBERMANN   48
        AND CHRIST WAS BY TO SAVE   • • • • • •   318 OBERMANN MORE   172
        NO MAN CAN SAVE HIS BROTHERS SOUL   • • • •   318 OBERMANN MORE   V
        SAVE FOR THIS ANNUAL CHARGE I HOPE TO HEAR • • • •   351 MEROPE   619
        BUT OF THE PRINCE NOTHING REMAIND SAVE THIS   • •   358 MEROPE   839
        SAVE MINE HE MUST NOT MEET A HUMAN EYE   • • • •   408 EMPEDOCLES I 1   53
        RECEIVE ME SAVE ME   • • • • • • • • • •   441 EMPEDOCLES II   416
        REPENTANT PRAYERS THAT HAD BEEN STRONG TO SAVE   • •   474 CROMWELL   81
        HUNGARIANS SAVE THE WORLD RENEW THE STORIES   480 HUNGARIAN NAT   9
        AT THY WANT OF A MAN LIKE ME TO SAVE THEE FROM BONDAGE   HOMER TRANS   36
        TRULY YET THIS TIME WILL WE SAVE THEE MIGHTY ACHILLES   HOMER TRANS   47

SAVED
        NEVER WAS THAT FIELD LOST OR THAT FOE SAVED   • •   71 SOHRAB RUSTUM   328
        MEMORIAL OF ME WHETHER SAVED OR NO   • • • • •   112 BALDER DEAD 2   275
        THIS LOST SEA-CREATURE SAVED   • • • • • • •   160 NECKAN   56
        AND FAIN WOULD ZEUS HAVE SAVED HIS TIRED SON   • •   198 FRAG ANTIGONE   90
        BE SAVED MY FATHER ALONE   • • • • • • • • •   290 RUGBY CHAPEL   125
        STRUCK ONCE AND AWED HIS MOB AND SAVED THIS REALM   338 MEROPE   275
        HE WOULD HAVE SAVED YOU FROM YOUR FURIOUS SELVES •   339 MEROPE   299
        I SAVED THEM MEANT THEIR HONOUR BUT THY FRIENDS   •   340 MEROPE   343
        WHO SAVED HIM FROM THESE MURDEROUS HALLS A BABE •   351 MEROPE   617
        WAS SAVED A BABE BUT TO A LIFE OBSCURE   • • •   356 MEROPE   769
        AND THIS AT LANDING SPIED BY US AND SAVED   • • • •   358 MEROPE   842
        ONE LAST MURDER-SAVED CHILD   • • • • • • •   369 MEROPE   1102

SAVES
        HE SAVES THE SHEEP THE GOATS HE DOTH NOT SAVE   • •   172 GOOD SHEPHERD   1
        WHICH FOR TWO JADED ENGLISH SAVES   • • • • • •   277 SOUTHERN NIGHT   58

SAVIOURS
        THE SAVIOURS HAPPY LIGHT • • • • • • • • • • •   446 WESTMIN ABBEY   61

SAVOY
        DOWN THE SAVOY VALLEYS SOUNDING   • • • • • •   12 CHURCH BROU 1   1
        MID THE SAVOY MOUNTAIN VALLEYS • • • • • • • • •   14 CHURCH BROU 1   61
        IN THE SAVOY MOUNTAIN-MEADOWS   • • • • • • • •   15 CHURCH BROU 1   91

SAVOYS
        SAVOYS DUKE HAD LEFT HIS BRIDE • • • • • • • •   13 CHURCH BROU 1   6

SAW
        SAW THE WIDE PROSPECT AND THE ASIAN FEN   • • •   2 TO A FRIEND   3
        WHO SAW LIFE STEADILY AND SAW IT WHOLE   • • • •   2 TO A FRIEND   12
        WHO SAW LIFE STEADILY AND SAW IT WHOLE   • • • •   2 TO A FRIEND   12
        WHICH SAW ONE CLUE TO LIFE AND FOLLOWD IT   • • • •   5 DUKE WELLINGTON   14
        IT WAS WELL WITH ME ONCE IF I SAW HIM TO-MORROW • •   19 MODERN SAPPHO   V
        THEY SAW US THEY CONFERRD THEIR BOSOMS HEAVED   • •   25 DREAM   26
        ON THESE LAWNS I SAW YOU PLAYING   • • • • • •   29 NEW SIRENS   95
        SAW THE HOARSE BOUGHS LABOUR IN THE WIND   • • • •   26 NEW SIRENS   V 8
        WHAT MORTAL WHEN HE SAW   • • • • • • • •   40 HUMAN LIFE   1
        AND WHEN FEROOD WHO LED THE PERSIANS SAW   • • • •   65 SOHRAB RUSTUM   144
        BEFORE HIM AND HE LOOKD AND SAW HIM STAND   • • • •   67 SOHRAB RUSTUM   202
        HIS EYES TOWARD THE TARTAR TENTS AND SAW   • • • •   70 SOHRAB RUSTUM   300
        THE MIGHTY VOICE OF RUSTUM AND HE SAW   • • • •   71 SOHRAB RUSTUM   335
        AGAINST THE ROBBERS AND HE SAW THAT HEAD   • • • •   71 SOHRAB RUSTUM   339
        DROPS LIKE A PLUMMET SOHRAB SAW IT COME   • • • •   73 SOHRAB RUSTUM   402
        THE CLOUD AND THE TWO ARMIES SAW THE PAIR   • • • •   77 SOHRAB RUSTUM   524
        SAW RUSTUM STANDING SAFE UPON HIS FEET   • • • •   77 SOHRAB RUSTUM   525
        THROUGH MANY ROLLING CLOUDS SO RUSTUM SAW   • • • •   79 SOHRAB RUSTUM   623
        HIS YOUTH SAW SOHRABS MOTHER IN HER BLOOM   • • • •   79 SOHRAB RUSTUM   624
        IN ADER-BAIJAN AND HE SAW THAT YOUTH   • • • •   80 SOHRAB RUSTUM   631
        BUT SOHRAB SAW HIS THOUGHT AND HELD HIS HANDS   • •   82 SOHRAB RUSTUM   706
        WHEN FIRST I SAW THEE AND THY HEART SPOKE TOO   • •   82 SOHRAB RUSTUM   712
        WHEN THEY SAW RUSTUMS GRIEF AND RUKSH THE HORSE • •   82 SOHRAB RUSTUM   730
        OH THAT I SAW ITS GRAINS OF YELLOW SILT   • • • •   83 SOHRAB RUSTUM   769
        HIS EYES TOWARDS THE TARTAR TENTS AND SAW   • • • •   70 SOHRAB RUSTUM   V 300
        TO SAW THEM PLANKS FISH FROM THE FLOODED RIVERS • •   73 SOHRAB RUSTUM   V 411
        OF HELA AND SAW NEAR IT BALDER CROWND   • • • •   109 BALDER DEAD 2   177
        AND ON THE TWELFTH MORN SAW THE LIGHT OF HEAVEN • •   113 BALDER DEAD 2   294
        SO HERMOD OER THE FOG BETWEEN SAW HEAVEN   • • • •   113 BALDER DEAD 2   301
        AND HERMOD SAW THE TOWERS OF ASGARD RISE   • • • •   113 BALDER DEAD 2   304
        BUT ODIN LOOKD TOWARD THE LAND AND SAW   • • • •   114 BALDER DEAD 3   31
        AND SAW MY SHEPHERDESS ASLAUGA TEND   • • • • •   117 BALDER DEAD 3   149
        AND SAW THE NORNIES WATERING THE ROOTS   • • • •   120 BALDER DEAD 3   221
        AND ONCE MORE HERMOD SAW AROUND HIM SPREAD   • • • •   124 BALDER DEAD 3   379
        OF NIFLHEIM HE SAW ONE GHOST COME NEAR   • • • •   124 BALDER DEAD 3   382
        THEN WHITE WITH BLOSSOM AND YOU SAW THE HORNS   • •   155 TRISTRAM 3   192
        YOU SAW THE BRIGHT-EYED SQUIRRELS DART ALONG   • •   155 TRISTRAM 3   195
        THE GRASS WAS DRY AND MOSSD AND YOU SAW CLEAR   • •   155 TRISTRAM 3   206
        HE SAW ON SPRAY-SWEPT HEBRIDES • • • • • • • •   156 SAINT BRANDAN   7

SAW   (CONTINUED)

```
SAW HIM LOOK EASED AND HURRIED BY               158 SAINT BRANDAN      52
OF ALL HE SAW AND FELT ON EARTH                 159 NECKAN             15
SHE SATE BY THE PILLAR WE SAW HER CLEAR         163 FORSAKEN MERM      76
A TRAMP I SAW ILL MOODY AND TONGUE-TIED         169 WEST LONDON         2
I CAME I SAW THEE RISE THE BLOOD                178 FAREWELL            9
DOWN THE DARK VALLEY I SAW                      187 STRAYED REVEL      42
OF LOUD EURIPUS SAW                             196 FRAG ANTIGONE      59
SAW AND SNATCHD WILD WITH LOVE                  196 FRAG ANTIGONE      60
SAW IN THE ROCKY ISLE OF DELOS DIE              197 FRAG ANTIGONE      69
SHE LOOKD AND SMILED AND SAW THEM THROUGH       202 URANIA             12
I SAW UPON THE OPEN SAND                        204 CALAIS SANDS       10
SAW THE GIFTS THE POWERS IT MIGHT INHERIT       209 SELF-DECEPTION      7
STRAIND AND LONGD AND GRASPD EACH GIFT IT SAW   210 SELF-DECEPTION     10
WHICH WE SAW WITH HIS EYES AND WERE GLAD        229 YOUTH OF NATURE    55
SAW THE MISTAKES OF OUR YOUTH                   232 YOUTH OF MAN       14
NATURE THEY SAW NO MORE                         233 YOUTH OF MAN       50
AND FOUGHT AND SAW IT NOT BUT THERE IT STOOD    236 PALLADIUM           4
HE SAW A FIRE IN HIS DISCIPLES EYES             237 PROGRESS            2
WAS IT THE LORD THEN SAID WITH SCORN YE SAW     237 PROGRESS            5
I SAW I FELT IT ONCE BUT WHERE                  241 MORALITY           30
I SAW IT IN SOME OTHER PLACE                    242 MORALITY           34
AND SAW THE MERRY GRECIAN COASTER COME          262 SCHOLAR-GIPSY     237
LONG SINCE SAW BYRONS STRUGGLE CEASE            270 MEMORIAL VERSES     2
WITH SHIVERING HEART THE STRIFE WE SAW          270 MEMORIAL VERSES    10
I SAW HIM SENSITIVE IN FRAME                    272 EDW QUILLINAN       1
SO MOONLIT SAW ME ONCE OF YORE                  275 SOUTHERN NIGHT     14
I SAW THE MEETING OF TWO                        280 HAWORTH CHURCH      7
EVENING A MEETING I SAW                         280 HAWORTH CHURCH    V
SAW THE FAMOUS ALAS                             281 HAWORTH CHURCH    V
THY SPIRIT OF THAT WE SAW                       290 RUGBY CHAPEL      137
AH I KNEW THAT I SAW                            294 HEINES GRAVE       55
AND WHAT FROM HEAVEN SAW HE                     319 OBERMANN MORE     210
IN DREAMS I SAW THE FUTURE SHINE                321 OBERMANN MORE     259
I SAW THE MORNING BREAK                         324 OBERMANN MORE     348
NOW IN THE WOODS FAR DOWN I SAW THEM CROSS      357 MEROPE            801
A MOMENT MORE I SAW THE PRINCE TURN ROUND       358 MEROPE            831
THE YOUTH THOU SAYST WE SAW AND HEARD BUT NOW   365 MEROPE            985
TO MURDERS DREAD ARENA WHERE I SAW              387 MEROPE           1462
WITH CYPSELUS OUR FATHER WHERE WE SAW           388 MEROPE           1515
I TOOK MY STAND AND SAW THE UNARMD CROWDS       401 MEROPE           1896
AND FROM THAT MOMENT I SAW NOTHING CLEAR        402 MEROPE           1936
I HEARD THE CLASH OF WEAPONS THEN I SAW         402 MEROPE           1941
AND RESTING THERE TO BREATHE I SAW BELOW        357 MEROPE          V 797
WHO SAW THE PRINCE AND LAIAS LAST WITH HIM      365 MEROPE          V
I SAW THE MULES AND LITTER IN THE COURT         407 EMPEDOCLES I 1     41
I SAW HIM THROUGH THE CHESTNUTS FAR BELOW       428 EMPEDOCLES I 2    485
ONLY THAT PRIMAL GUEST THE FISHER SAW           445 WESTMIN ABBEY      59
AND SAW HER BABE AMIDST THE FIRE AND SCREAMD    446 WESTMIN ABBEY      93
PLAIN WE SAW IF THEY WERE SAD                   455 POOR MATTHIAS      90
SAW THE CEDARS OF PAINS HILL                    458 POOR MATTHIAS     199
SAW BUT ANOTHER STEP TO CLIMB TO VICTORY        469 ALARIC AT ROME    186
THAT DAY THAT HAILD HIS TRIUMPHS SAW HIM DIE    478 CROMWELL          212
AND WITH PITY THE SON OF SATURN SAW THEM BEWAILING  HOMER TRANS        7
```

SAWING
```
STONES ARE SAWING HAMMERS RINGING                15 CHURCH BROU 1      89
```

SAWST
```
NOT LITTLE IF THOU SAWST WHAT LOVE WHAT ZEAL    401 MEROPE           1893
```

SAXIFRAGE
```
ON EVERY BANK THE VIRGIN SAXIFRAGE                  EVERLASTING SUB     5
```

SAXON
```
O SAXON FISHER THOU HAST HAD WITH THEE          445 WESTMIN ABBEY      44
```

SAXONS
```
THE HEATHEN SAXONS ON THE RHINE                 138 TRISTRAM 1        253
```

SAY
```
SAY WHAT SHALL CALM US WHEN SUCH GUESTS INTRUDE   6 GEO CRUIKSHANK     6
I WILL GO FORTH THOUGH SOMETHING WOULD I SAY     10 MYCERINUS         68
I WILL GO FORTH BUT SOMETHING WOULD I SAY        10 MYCERINUS       V 68
YOU HEAR THE WHITE-ROBED PRIEST SAY MASS         17 CHURCH BROU 2     29
SAY WHAT IS THIS WE ARE IN BLISS FORGIVEN        18 CHURCH BROU 3     30
HUSH YE WILL SAY IT IS ETERNITY                  19 CHURCH BROU 3     40
WHAT MAY CHAIN US WHO CAN SAY                    23 MEMORY-PICTURE    22
SHOW YOU SAY MY LOVE DECLINES                    24 MEMORY-PICTURE    50
AH YOU SAY THE LARGE APPEARANCE                  28 NEW SIRENS        57
COME YOU SAY THE HOURS WERE DREARY               28 NEW SIRENS        65
COME YOU SAY THE SOUL IS FAINTING                28 NEW SIRENS        73
COME YOU SAY THE BRAIN IS SEEKING                28 NEW SIRENS        77
COME YOU SAY OPINION TREMBLES                    29 NEW SIRENS        81
SHEPHERDS SAY THEY FOUND YOU SLEEPING            31 NEW SIRENS       145
HALF IN DOUBT THEY SAY AND GAZING                31 NEW SIRENS       149
COME YOU SAY THE LARGE APPEARANCE                28 NEW SIRENS      V 57
COME YOU SAY THE HOURS ARE DREARY                28 NEW SIRENS      V 65
WHY YOU SAY CRITIAS BE DEBATING STILL            46 WORLD QUIETIST     3
WE LEFT JUST TEN YEARS SINCE YOU SAY             53 RESIGNATION       40
```

SAY (CONTINUED)

THESE ARE NOT CHANGED AND WE YOU SAY	55	RESIGNATION	106
AND DOES NOT SAY I AM ALONE	57	RESIGNATION	169
WHAT THEN O RUSTUM WILL MEN SAY TO THIS	68	SOHRAB RUSTUM	243
HIDEST THY FACE TAKE HEED LEST MEN SHOULD SAY	68	SOHRAB RUSTUM	246
O GUDURZ WHEREFORE DOST THOU SAY SUCH WORDS	68	SOHRAB RUSTUM	250
THOU KNOWEST BETTER WORDS THAN THIS TO SAY	68	SOHRAB RUSTUM	251
LET NOT MEN SAY OF RUSTUM HE WAS MATCHD	69	SOHRAB RUSTUM	258
AND HIDE IT NOT BUT SAY RUSTUM IS HERE	71	SOHRAB RUSTUM	350
AND YOU WOULD SAY THAT SUN AND STARS TOOK PART	75	SOHRAB RUSTUM	480
AND WASH THEM WITH THY TEARS AND SAY MY SON	82	SOHRAB RUSTUM	720
AND SAY O SON I WEEP THEE NOT TOO SORE	85	SOHRAB RUSTUM	822
MAY SEE MY TOMB A GREAT WAY OFF AND SAY	84	SOHRAB RUSTUM	V 791
THEN SAY HE WAS NOT WHOLLY VILE	95	SICK KING BOKH	231
SAY THEN IF HE HATH CROSSD THY BRIDGE OR NO	108	BALDER DEAD 2	117
AND OVER BALDERS CORPSE THESE WORDS DIDST SAY	115	BALDER DEAD 3	74
TO TAKE MY HAND AND WIPE MY TEARS AND SAY	116	BALDER DEAD 3	113
BUT HOW YE SAY SHOULD THE FULFILMENT FAIL	120	BALDER DEAD 3	230
AND TO TRISTRAM LAUGHING SAY	135	TRISTRAM 1	144
BEND BEND DOWN I YET HAVE MUCH TO SAY	145	TRISTRAM 2	76
SAY I WILLD SO THAT THOU STAY BESIDE ME	145	TRISTRAM 2	95
AND TO HIMSELF HE SEEMS TO SAY	148	TRISTRAM 2	163
SHE WILL SAY IS THIS THE FORM I DREADED	144	TRISTRAM 2	V 65
SAY I CHARGD HER THAT YE LIVE TOGETHER	145	TRISTRAM 2	V 95
SAY I CHARGD HER THAT THOU STAY BESIDE ME	145	TRISTRAM 2	V 95
SAY I CHARGD THEE THAT THOU STAY BESIDE HER	145	TRISTRAM 2	V 95
WHAT TALE DID ISEULT TO THE CHILDREN SAY	154	TRISTRAM 3	151
AND IN THAT DAISIED CIRCLE AS MEN SAY	156	TRISTRAM 3	221
AN ANGEL TOUCH MINE ARM AND SAY	157	SAINT BRANDAN	35
SAY THY PRAYER AND COME BACK TO THE KIND SEA-CAVES	163	FORSAKEN MERM	61
LONG PRAYERS I SAID IN THE WORLD THEY SAY	163	FORSAKEN MERM	66
ILL STOP AND SAY THERE WERE NO SUCCOUR HERE	169	WORLDLY PLACE	13
AND THIRTEEN HUNDRED YEARS AGONE THEY SAY	170	EAST AND WEST	3
SO ANSWEREST THOU BUT WHY NOT RATHER SAY	171	BETTER PART	9
AND PATIENCE IN ANOTHER LIFE WE SAY	172	IMMORTALITY	3
SAY HAS SOME WET BIRD-HAUNTED ENGLISH LAWN	175	PARTING	19
ACROSS MY HEART TO SAY THY THREAD	184	TERRACE BERNE	27
SAY WILL IT NEVER HEAL	200	PHILOMELA	9
I MUST NOT SAY THAT THOU WAST TRUE	203	EUPHROSYNE	1
YET LET ME SAY THAT THOU WAST FAIR	203	EUPHROSYNE	2
ADIEU AND SAY THAT ONE AT LEAST	204	EUPHROSYNE	27
I MUST NOT SAY THAT THOU WERT TRUE	203	EUPHROSYNE	V 1
I WILL NOT SAY THAT THOU WAST TRUE	203	EUPHROSYNE	V 1
I MUST NOT SAY THAT SHE WAS TRUE	203	EUPHROSYNE	V 1
YET LET ME SAY THAT THOU WERT FAIR	203	EUPHROSYNE	V 2
YET LET ME SAY THAT SHE WAS FAIR	203	EUPHROSYNE	V 2
WHO LET ME SAY IS THIS STRANGER REGARDS ME	206	SEPARATION	15
AND SAY MY LOVE WHY SUFFEREST THOU	209	LONGING	12
AND SAY MY FRIEND WHY SUFFEREST THOU	209	LONGING	V 12
WHICH OTHERS KNOW OR SAY THEY KNOW	209	DESPONDENCY	3
SAY WHAT BLINDS US THAT WE CLAIM THE GLORY	209	SELF-DECEPTION	1
SAY WHY SO MUTE	220	BACCHANALIA 2	46
THAT TRANSIENT GLIMPSE IN SONG THEY SAY	226	EPILOG LAOCOON	181
WHEN YOUR GREAT ONES DEPART WILL YE SAY	231	YOUTH OF NATURE	126
I SAY UNTO YOU SEE YE KEEP THAT LAW	237	PROGRESS	7
I SAY UNTO YOU SEE THAT YOUR SOULS LIVE	237	PROGRESS	23
SAY YE THE SPIRIT OF MAN HAS FOUND NEW ROADS	237	PROGRESS	25
AND THE CALM MOONLIGHT SEEMS TO SAY	243	SUMMER NIGHT	26
I WILL NOT SAY THAT YOUR MILD DEEPS RETAIN	244	SUMMER NIGHT	83
BUT I WILL RATHER SAY THAT YOU REMAIN	244	SUMMER NIGHT	86
OUR HIDDEN SELF AND WHAT WE SAY AND DO	247	BURIED LIFE	65
AND WHAT WE MEAN WE SAY AND WHAT WE WOULD WE KNOW	247	BURIED LIFE	87
AND WE SAY THAT REPOSE HAS FLED	253	FUTURE	58
WHAT MIGHT WE SAY TO CONSOLE	282	HAWORTH CHURCH	V
WE TOO SAY THAT SHE NOW	294	HEINES GRAVE	77
MY MELANCHOLY SCIOLISTS SAY	302	GRANDE CHARTR	99
SAY HAVE THEIR SONS ACHIEVED MORE JOYS	303	GRANDE CHARTR	129
SAY IS LIFE LIGHTER NOW THAN THEN	303	GRANDE CHARTR	130
SAY HAVE THEIR SONS OBTAIND MORE JOYS	303	GRANDE CHARTR	V 129
AND SAY THE STONE IS NOT YET TO	318	OBERMANN MORE	179
SAY IS IT MORE ALIVE	320	OBERMANN MORE	228
INFER THEE THEIR ACCOMPLICE AND THEY SAY	334	MEROPE	143
LET THE BEST RULE THEY SAY AGAIN	352	MEROPE	653
BUT WHO CAN SAY WITHOUT A FEAR	353	MEROPE	676
I SPEAK NO WORD OF BOAST BUT THIS I SAY	360	MEROPE	888
AH AH AH ME AND I TOO SAY AH ME	363	MEROPE	948
LAST-MURDERD WHO REPROACHFULLY WILT SAY	367	MEROPE	1042
HOW SAY YE MAIDENS DO YE KNOW THESE PRAYERS	368	MEROPE	1067
WE SEE DEAR MISTRESS AND WE SAY THE GODS	377	MEROPE	1225
AND HARDLY YET SOME SAY HATH FOUND A GRAVE	385	MEROPE	1425
NOT PRONE ALL SAY AVERSE TO BLOODSHED NOW	388	MEROPE	1492
NOT PRONE ALL SAY TO USELESS BLOODSHED NOW	388	MEROPE	V1492
BUT IF AS MOST MEN SAY HE IS HALF MAD	407	EMPEDOCLES I 1	23
EMPEDOCLES WOULD SAY SO DID HE DEIGN	410	EMPEDOCLES I 1	137
BUT I WILL ALSO SAY THAT WHEN THE GODS	413	EMPEDOCLES I 2	23
WHY SHOULD I SAY THAT LIFE NEED YIELD BUT MODERATE BLISS	425	EMPEDOCLES I 2	391
I SAY FEAR NOT LIFE STILL	426	EMPEDOCLES I 2	422
AND THERE THEY SAY TWO BRIGHT AND AGED SNAKES	427	EMPEDOCLES I 2	435
AND SAY YE HELPERS HEAR EMPEDOCLES	429	EMPEDOCLES II	27
AND WHO CAN SAY I HAVE BEEN ALWAYS FREE	440	EMPEDOCLES II	392

SAY   (CONTINUED)
    AND SAY YE SERVANTS HEAR EMPEDOCLES   • • • • • •   429 EMPEDOCLES II   V 27
    AND STOP BEFORE THE STONE AND SAY   • • • • • •   452 GEISTS GRAVE   76
    FOUND HIM STIFF YOU SAY THOUGH WARM   • • • • • •   452 POOR MATTHIAS   3
    WHAT POOR KAI DEAD SAY ALL I MEET   • • • • • •   459 KAISER DEAD   9
    WHERE ALL WE SEE OR DO OR HEAR OR SAY   • • • • • •   464 ALARIC AT ROME   47
    SAY NOT SUCH DREAMS ARE IDLE FOR THE MAN • • • • •   473 CROMWELL   45
    OF WHAT WE SAY WE FEEL BELOW THE STREAM   • • • •   483 BELOW SURFACE   2
    WITH OMEN OH WERE THAT MOUNT PASSD I SAY • • • •   485 S S LUSITANIA   12
    AND SOME MAN MAY SAY AS HE LOOKS AND SEES THY   HOMER TRANS   32
         TEARS FALLING
    SO SOME MAN WILL SAY AND THEN THY GRIEF WILL REDOUBLE   HOMER TRANS   35
    WHICH MEN SAY IS THE FLEETEST OF WINDS TIS   HOMER TRANS   55
         THOU WHO ART FATED
    TOUCH HIS ROBE AND SAY MY FATHER   • • • • • •   META CLOISTER   27
    SAY MY FATHER DOES THE TIRED   • • • • •   META CLOISTER   29
    YOU SAY TRUE MY DAUGHTER PEACE IS HERE   • • • •   META CLOISTER   40
    SAY THIS OF HER   • • • • • • • • •   FRAGMENT 5   1

SAYING
    SO SAYING THE KING TOOK A STONE   • • • • • •   91 SICK KING BOKH   117
    I HEAR THEE SAYING NOW • • • • • • • • • •   309 OBERMANN   90
    ONE HEARS THEE SAYING NOW   • • • • • • • •   309 OBERMANN   V 90

SAYS
    BREASTS HER OWN GRIEFS AND URGED TOO FIERCELY SAYS   6 GEO CRUIKSHANK   10
    MARGUERITE SAYS AS LAST YEAR WENT   • • • • • •   23 MEMORY-PICTURE   17
    SAYS HAPPY HE WHO LODGES THERE • • • • • • •   94 SICK KING BOKH   193
    FAIR LOVE SHE SAYS CANST THOU FORGET SO SOON   •   139 TRISTRAM 1   285
    CHRIST SOME ONE SAYS WAS HUMAN AS WE ARE   • • •   170 BETTER PART   3
    SAYS APOLLO MODERNISE ROME   • • • • • • •   214 NEW ROME   10
    SAYS APOLLO MODERNISED ROME   • • • • • • (214 NEW ROME   V 10
    IT KNOWS NOT WHAT HE SAYS   • • • • • • • •   307 OBERMANN   44
    SAYS IT FITS THAT I REHEARSE   • • • • • • •   453 POOR MATTHIAS   17

SAYST
    THOU SAYST THOU ART NOT RUSTUM BE IT SO   • • • •   74 SOHRAB RUSTUM   431
    HOW SAYST THOU IS THAT SIGN THE PROPER SIGN • •   81 SOHRAB RUSTUM   687
    O VIZIER BE IT AS THOU SAYST   • • • • • •   88 SICK KING BOKH   29
    HELA SUCH AS THOU SAYST THE TERMS SHALL BE • •   111 BALDER DEAD 2   242
    TRULY THOU SAYST THE PLANNING GUILTY MIND   • •   125 BALDER DEAD 3   424
    ONE DAY THOU SAYST THERE WILL AT LAST APPEAR   •   239 REVOLUTIONS   17
    THE YOUTH THOU SAYST WE SAW AND HEARD BUT NOW •   365 MEROPE   985
    IF HOW SAYST THOU WITHIN • • • • • • •   370 MEROPE   1122
    AND IF SO USED PROVES AS THOU SAYST UNSURE • • •   382 MEROPE   1341
    BLOOD-FOUNDED THRONES THOU SAYST ARE INSECURE •   389 MEROPE   1532

SCALD
    STILL LEFT AND THAT CHIEF SCALD THY BROTHER BRAGE 117 BALDER DEAD 3   133

SCALDS
    AND AT HIS HEAD AND FEET SHE STATIOND SCALDS • • 102 BALDER DEAD 1   271
    BALDER THERE YET ARE MANY SCALDS IN HEAVEN • • • • 117 BALDER DEAD 3   132

SCALE
    WHO SCALE THE CLOUD-CAPT HEIGHT OR SINK TO REST • • 472 CROMWELL   11
    DIDST FORCE AN AUDIENCE ERE I STRUCK THE SCALE   • •   RUDE ORATOR   6

SCALES
    AND THE SCALES OF HABIT   • • • • • • • • • •   235 YOUTH OF MAN   106

SCAN
    O SCAN THY NATIVE WORLD WITH PIOUS EYES   • • •   46 IN UTRUMQUE PAR V 40
    SUBDUES THAT ENERGY TO SCAN   • • • • • • •   56 RESIGNATION   146
    THOSE GIPSIES SO YOUR THOUGHTS I SCAN   • • •   58 RESIGNATION   203
    NO JUDGE EYES US FROM HEAVEN OUR SIN TO SCAN   •   170 BETTER PART   4
    WILL YE SCAN ME AND READ ME AND TELL   • • • •   231 YOUTH OF NATURE 119
    HOLDS HIS LANTERN TO SCAN   • • • • • • •   289 RUGBY CHAPEL   113
    WHEN I COULD HOURLY SCAN • • • • • • • •   317 OBERMANN MORE   154
    HIS ALL TOO HUMAN CREEDS AND SCAN   • • • • •   319 OBERMANN MORE   187
    WORN WAS HIS BROW WITH CARES NO THOUGHT COULD SCAN 476 CROMWELL   155
    A LIFE WHOSE WAYS NO HUMAN THOUGHT COULD SCAN • • 478 CROMWELL   219

SCANND
    SELF-SCHOOLD SELF-SCANND SELF-HONOURD SELF-SECURE   3 SHAKESPEARE   10
    AND SCANND WITH BLINKING EYES THE ADVANCING FORM • 76 SOHRAB RUSTUM   518
    AND HIMSELF SCANND IT LONG WITH MOURNFUL EYES •   81 SOHRAB RUSTUM   685
    HE SCANND EACH WOUND EACH WEAKNESS NEAR   • • •   270 MEMORIAL VERSES V 20
    THOU TOO HAST SCANND IT WELL   • • • • • •   309 OBERMANN   84
    BENT ON MY FACE WITH GAZE WHICH SCANND   • • •   314 OBERMANN MORE   67
    BENT ON MY FACE WITH GAZE THAT SCANND   • • •   314 OBERMANN MORE V 67
    SCANND OF TRAMPS AND FISHERMEN • • • • • • •   457 POOR MATTHIAS   187

SCANNING
    SCANNING MY FACE AND THE CHANGES WROUGHT THERE   • • 206 SEPARATION   14

SCANS
    SCANS THOSE PARTED LIPS THAT PURELY • • • • • •   META CLOISTER   37

SCANT
    SCANT SPACE THAT WARDER LEFT FOR PASSERS BY   • •   107 BALDER DEAD 2   90
    SCANT LEISURE FOR A SECOND MESSENGER • • • • • •   140 TRISTRAM 1   307

SCANT   (CONTINUED)
        AS FROM A FASTNESS IN THE ROCKS OUR SCANT   • • • •   337 MEROPE   247
        WHAT FOR A TERM SO SCANT • • • • • • • • • •   444 WESTMIN ABBEY   1

SCANTY
        OF THE JAXARTES MEN WITH SCANTY BEARDS   • • • •   64 SOHRAB RUSTUM   129
        THAT SCANTY GRACE SHALL EARN THEE THIS REPLY   • •   395 MEROPE   1732

SCAR
        ON SOME TALL SCAR FRINGED WITH DARK FEATHERY PINES   357 MEROPE   803

SCARCE
        ARE SCARCE MORE CHANGED IN TRUTH THAN THEY • • • •   55 RESIGNATION   107
        CHOKED BY THE AIR AND SCARCE CAN THEY THEMSELVES • •   66 SOHRAB RUSTUM   165
        SCARCE FRESHER IS THE MOUNTAIN-SOD   • • • • • •   248 KENSINGTON GARD   17
        SCARCE COMPREHENDING THE VOICE • • • • • • • •   294 HEINES GRAVE   78
        OF HERACLES SCARCE HERACLEIDAE LESS • • • • • •   337 MEROPE   222
        SCARCE DANGEROUS LESS THAN HIM THE DORIAN LORDS • •   381 MEROPE   1298
        COULD SCARCE HAVE LIGHTED ON A LOVELIER CURE • • •   407 EMPEDOCLES I 1   26
        SCARCE CAN ONE THINK IN CALM SO THREATENING   416 EMPEDOCLES I 2   126
                   ARE THE GODS
        AND SCARCE THE BOON OF LIFE COULD STRUGGLE THROUGH   446 WESTMIN ABBEY   69

SCARCELY
        SCARCELY MOVES THE COVERLET   • • • • • • • •   141 TRISTRAM 1   343
        AND SCARCELY WILL THEY BUDGE A YARD O PAN • • • •   406 EMPEDOCLES I 1   5
        FOR MIST CAN SCARCELY SEE   • • • • • • • • •   444 WESTMIN ABBEY   22

SCARE
        AND BOYS WHO IN LONE WHEATFIELDS SCARE THE ROOKS • •   257 SCHOLAR-GIPSY   64
        A FOOL CAN DRIVE IT AND A FLY MAY SCARE   • • • •   382 MEROPE   1344

SCARED
        THE SCARED GLENS WE WANDERD ON • • • • • • • •   27 NEW SIRENS   30
        AND SCARED OETAEAN SNOWS • • • • • • • • • •   198 FRAG ANTIGONE   102
        WILD GOOSEBERRIES SCARED HER   • • • • • • • •   392 MEROPE   1639

SCARFD
        SCARFD WITH THE CROSS WHO WATCHD THE MILES • • • •   52 RESIGNATION   5

SCARLET
        AND THE FRAIL SCARLET-BERRIED ASH BEGAN   • • • •   25 DREAM   9
        OF SCARLET CLOTH THEY WERE AND GLITTERING GAY   • •   66 SOHRAB RUSTUM   192
        OF HORSEHAIR WAVED A SCARLET HORSEHAIR PLUME   • •   69 SOHRAB RUSTUM   269
        WITH SCARLET BERRIES GEMMD THE FELL-FARES FOOD   • •   150 TRISTRAM 3   22
        WITH SCARLET BERRIES BRIGHT THE FELLFARES FOOD   • •   TRISTRAM 3   V 22
        THROUGH THE THICK CORN THE SCARLET POPPIES PEEP   • •   255 SCHOLAR-GIPSY   23
        WITH SCARLET PATCHES TAGGD AND SHREDS OF GREY   • •   258 SCHOLAR-GIPSY   114

SCARS
        PAST LIMESTONE SCARS WITH RAGGED PINES   • • • •   299 GRANDE CHARTR   14

SCATHED
        HIS BOLT-SCATHED FRONT TO THE STARS   • • • • • •   293 HEINES GRAVE   32
        IS THY FIRE-SCATHED ARM STILL RASH   • • • • • •   430 EMPEDOCLES II   50

SCATHING
        IN SHEETS OF SCATHING FIRE   • • • • • • • •   319 OBERMANN MORE   202

SCATTER
        HARK THE GAMES ON FOOT THEY SCATTER   • • • • • •   13 CHURCH BROU 1   21

SCATTERD
        SPRUNG FROM THE BLOOD OF ISRAELS SCATTERD RACE   • •   168 RACHEL 3   1
        AND IN THE SCATTERD FARMS THE LIGHTS COME OUT   • •   267 THYRSIS   164

SCATTERING
        SCATTERING THE PAST ABOUT   • • • • • • • • •   220 BACCHANALIA 2   35
        SCATTERING LIGHTNINGS THAT SOUL   • • • • • • •   298 HEINES GRAVE   205

SCATTERS
        WHO SCATTERS RUSHES IN A MASTERS HALL   • • • • •   112 BALDER DEAD 2   266

SCENE
        THEY RECOGNISE A FORMER SCENE • • • • • • • •   55 RESIGNATION   115
        AND ROUND HIM A FRESH FOREST-SCENE • • • • • •   147 TRISTRAM 2   154
        ILL AND OERWORKD HOW FARE YOU IN THIS SCENE • • •   169 EAST LONDON   6
        CAN CHANGE OF SCENE AND NIGHT • • • • • • • •   200 PHILOMELA   V
        OH THAT TO SHARE THIS FAMOUS SCENE   • • • • • •   204 CALAIS SANDS   9
        OF A PAST NIGHT AND A FAR DIFFERENT SCENE   • • • •   242 SUMMER NIGHT   13
        WOULD FIX OUR FAVOURITE ON THE SCENE • • • • • •   451 GEISTS GRAVE   38
        THAT SPOT THE SOLITARY SCENE   • • • • • • • •   480 HAYSWATER BOAT   24

SCENES
        BAFFLERS OF OUR OWN PRAYERS FROM YOUTH TO LIFES   420 EMPEDOCLES I 2   231
                  LAST SCENES
        SCENES WHERE A CAESAR TRIUMPHT OR A SCIPIO TROD   • •   466 ALARIC AT ROME   114

SCENT
        DREW A WARM SCENT ABROAD BEHIND THE PINES   • • • •   25 DREAM   6
        SCENT AND SONG AND LIGHT AND FLOWERS • • • • • •   32 NEW SIRENS   171
        ON ITS IVIED WINDOWS A SCENT   • • • • • • • •   234 YOUTH OF MAN   66

SCENT   (CONTINUED)
  THEIR SCENT AND RUSTLE DOWN THEIR PERFUMED SHOWERS 256 SCHOLAR-GIPSY 27
  AND SCENT OF HAY NEW-MOWN • • • • • • • 265 THYRSIS 76
  THE FURZE-SCENT PERFUMES ALL THE AIR • • • • • • 274 STANZAS CARNAC V 20

SCENTED
  THE SCENTED PINES OF SWITZERLAND • • • • • • 311 OBERMANN 167

SCENTS
  AND YOUR SCENTS HAVE SHED THEIR SWEETNESS • • • • 34 NEW SIRENS 253
  MURMURS AND SCENTS OF THE INFINITE SEA • • • • 254 FUTURE 87

SCEPTIC
  AND SCEPTIC AS HE IS • • • • • • • 418 EMPEDOCLES I 2 170

SCEPTRE
  AND LAID HER SCEPTRE DOWN • • • • • • • 316 OBERMANN MORE 126
  THE SCEPTRE NOT REMISSLY LET IT FALL • • • • 334 MEROPE 135
  SWAYING THE SCEPTRE WITH PREDESTINED HAND • • • 345 MEROPE 473
  MAKE CESSION OF HER SCEPTRE DOOM HERSELF • • • • RUDE ORATOR 19

SCEPTRES
  THAT SPOTLESS HANDS UNSHAKEN SCEPTRES HOLD • • • • 388 MEROPE 1519

SCHEME
  THE SCHEME OURSELVES HAVE SPUN • • • • • • • 422 EMPEDOCLES I 2 313

SCHEMERS
  OR DIDST THOU BUT AS CAUTIOUS SCHEMERS USE • • • • 404 MEROPE 1984

SCHEMES
  FAR NOISIER SCHEMES ACCOMPLISHD IN REPOSE • • • • 1 QUIET WORK 7
  MANS NOISY SCHEMES ACCOMPLISHD IN REPOSE • • • • 1 QUIET WORK V 7
  BUT SO MANY SCHEMES THOU BREEDEST • • • • 49 SECOND BEST 6
  BUT SUCH ANXIOUS SCHEMES THOU BREEDEST SECOND BEST V 6
  AND TIRED UPON A THOUSAND SCHEMES OUR WIT • • • • 259 SCHOLAR-GIPSY 148
  THE SCHEMES PURSUED IN VAIN FOR TWENTY YEARS • • 360 MEROPE 876

SCHEMING
  OF THIS FAR-SCHEMING TYRANT AND HIS BOON • • • • 366 MEROPE 998

SCHOLAR
  THE STORY OF THE OXFORD SCHOLAR POOR • • • • • 256 SCHOLAR-GIPSY 33
  THAT THE LOST SCHOLAR LONG WAS SEEN TO STRAY • • 256 SCHOLAR-GIPSY 53
  THE STORY OF THAT OXFORD SCHOLAR POOR • • • • 256 SCHOLAR-GIPSY V 33
  OUR FRIEND THE GIPSY-SCHOLAR WAS NOT DEAD • • • 263 THYRSIS 29
  OUR GIPSY-SCHOLAR HAUNTS OUTLIVING THEE • • • 268 THYRSIS 197
  OUR SCHOLAR TRAVELS YET THE LOVED HILL-SIDE • • 269 THYRSIS 240
  OUR FRIEND THE SCHOLAR-GIPSY WAS NOT DEAD • • • 263 THYRSIS V 29

SCHOLARS
  WHOSE SURENESS GRAY-HAIRD SCHOLARS HARDLY LEARN • • 43 GIPSY CHILD 42
  TWO SCHOLARS WHOM AT COLLEGE ERST HE KNEW • • • • 256 SCHOLAR-GIPSY 42

SCHOOL
  WE SCHOOL OUR MANNERS ACT OUR PARTS • • • • • 179 FAREWELL 45
  IN THE SCHOOL-ROOM WINDOWS BUT COLD • • • • • 286 RUGBY CHAPEL 9
  YET HAST BEEN LONG AT SCHOOL WITH THOUGHTFUL TIME 394 MEROPE 1708
  TO PREACH THEE TO THEIR SCHOOL • • • • • • • • 417 EMPEDOCLES I 2 138

SCHOOLD
  SELF-SCHOOLD SELF-SCANND SELF-HONOURD SELF-SECURE 3 SHAKESPEARE 10
  AND WHEN MY ILL-SCHOOLD SPIRIT IS AFLAME • • • • 169 WORLDLY PLACE 11
  THUS THOUGH A WOMAN I WAS SCHOOLD • • • • • 354 MEROPE 696

SCHOOLING
  WHOM SCHOOLING OF THE STUBBORN MIND • • • • • • 53 RESIGNATION 26

SCHOOLS
  WISDOM AND GOODNESS THEY ARE GOD WHAT SCHOOLS • • 171 DIVINITY 11
  THINKERS NEW SCHOOLS • • • • • • • • 220 BACCHANALIA 2 38
  OF SOPHISTS HAS GOT EMPIRE IN OUR SCHOOLS • • • • 410 EMPEDOCLES I 1 122

SCIENCE
  ART SCIENCE WIT • • • • • • • • • • 220 BACCHANALIA 2 54
  TRUE SCIENCE IF THERE IS • • • • • • • • • 423 EMPEDOCLES I 2 339

SCIOLISTS
  MY MELANCHOLY SCIOLISTS SAY • • • • • • 302 GRANDE CHARTR 99
  A FAITH OR SCIOLISTS BEEN SAD • • • • • • • 302 GRANDE CHARTR 102

SCIPIO
  SCENES WHERE A CAESAR TRIUMPHT OR A SCIPIO TROD • • 466 ALARIC AT ROME 114

SCOFF
  MEN SCOFF AT HEAVEN AND FATE • • • • • • • • 426 EMPEDOCLES I 2 418

SCOFFINGLY
  AND THE DAMES WHISPERED SCOFFINGLY • • • • • • 146 TRISTRAM 2 124

SCONCES

IN THE HALL WITH SCONCES BLAZING	13 CHURCH BROU 1	33
BLOODY NEATH THE FLARING SCONCES	14 CHURCH BROU 1	51
FLASHD IN THE SILVER SCONCES LIGHT	146 TRISTRAM 2	113

SCOOP

SCOOP THE SHELVES AND FRET THE STORMS	26 NEW SIRENS	12

SCOPE

OF VEHEMENT ACTIONS WITHOUT SCOPE OR TERM	5 DUKE WELLINGTON	12
REMORSE GRIEF JOY AND WERE THE SCOPE	58 RESIGNATION	218
WHO FLUCTUATE IDLY WITHOUT TERM OR SCOPE	260 SCHOLAR-GIPSY	167
PIOUS BUT IMPIOUS SURELY IF THEIR SCOPE	342 MEROPE	380
LOVE TO HAVE SCOPE AND PLAY	420 EMPEDOCLES I 2	248
LEAVES HUMAN EFFORT SCOPE	426 EMPEDOCLES I 2	423

SCORE

WOULD TAKE A SCORE YEARS FROM A STRONG MANS AGE	140 TRISTRAM 1	305

SCORED

HAD SCORED HER WHITE RIGHT HAND WHICH SHE ALLOWS	154 TRISTRAM 3	174

SCORES

SCORES OF TRUE LOVE KNOTS ARE BREAKING	35 NEW SIRENS	261

SCORN

SO SPAKE HE HALF IN ANGER HALF IN SCORN	11 MYCERINUS	79
SHALL I SEEK THAT I MAY SCORN HER	35 NEW SIRENS	271
AND SCORN US AS OUR MISTRESS MAY	48 HORATIAN ECHO	33
AND WILL NOT THEN THE IMMORTAL ARMIES SCORN	172 IMMORTALITY	5
AH MAY SHE SCORN THEM STILL TILL WE	202 URANIA	15
SCORN THEM AS BITTERLY AS SHE	202 URANIA	16
WAS IT THE LORD THEN SAID WITH SCORN YE SAW	237 PROGRESS	5
SCORN YE THIS WORLD THEIR TEARS THEIR INWARD CARES	237 PROGRESS	22
GIBING OF SPIRITS IN SCORN	293 HEINES GRAVE	42
NOT BY THE THUNDER OF SCORN	295 HEINES GRAVE	109
WIT IT POSSESSES AND SCORN	295 HEINES GRAVE	111
WITH HAUGHTY SCORN WHICH MOCKD THE SMART	303 GRANDE CHARTR	134
OF PEACE AND BEEN REPULSED WITH HATE AND SCORN	360 MEROPE	881
NOT TO SEE APOLLOS SCORN	434 EMPEDOCLES II	189
WITH SUCH A PEEVISH HARDIHOOD OF SCORN	RUDE ORATOR	20

SCORND

I LOVED THE GOOD HE SCORND AND HATED WRONG	9 MYCERINUS	15
HIS SCORND WHITE HAIRS	192 STRAYED REVEL	219
ME TOO HAD HE PREVAILD HE HAD NOT SCORND	334 MEROPE	133

SCORNFUL

SCORNFUL AND STRANGE AND SORROWFUL AND FULL	4 EMERSONS ESSAYS	9
SO SCORNFUL SEEMED THAT SMILE SO STRANGE SO FULL	EMERSONS ESSAYS V	9
HE IS TOO SCORNFUL TOO HIGH-WROUGHT TOO BITTER	411 EMPEDOCLES I 1	149
SCORNFUL APOLLOS ENSIGN LIE THOU THERE	434 EMPEDOCLES II	193

SCORNFULLY

HATH LOOKD ON NO RELIGION SCORNFULLY	238 PROGRESS	39

SCORNS

HOW DEEPLY SHE WHO SCORNS CAN LOVE	202 URANIA	20
BUT HE STILL LETS THE PEOPLE WHOM HE SCORNS	410 EMPEDOCLES I 1	138

SCOTT

SCOTT HAD BESTOWD THERE HIS LAST	281 HAWORTH CHURCH	23
SCOTT HAD CONSIGND THERE HIS LAST	281 HAWORTH CHURCH V	23

SCOURD

THEY TWO SCOURD EVERY COAST AND ALL THINGS WEPT	123 BALDER DEAD 3	328

SCOURGE

BUT DOWN THOU FLEEST HERE AND LEAVST OUR SCOURGE	367 MEROPE	1050
AND THE STANCH FURIES NEVER-SILENT SCOURGE	373 MEROPE	1187
SIT AND MAKE READY THE SERPENT THE SCOURGE	347 MEROPE V	531
SCOURGE OF THE NATIONS WOULDEST THOU LINGER YET	465 ALARIC AT ROME	94

SCOURGED

INTO A JEALOUS TYRANT SCOURGED WITH FEARS	335 MEROPE	159

SCOWLING

THAT FURTIVE MIEN THAT SCOWLING EYE	157 SAINT BRANDAN	17

SCRAPES

CROSSING THE STREAM IN SUMMER SCRAPES THE LAND	61 SOHRAB RUSTUM	19

SCRATCHD

SCRATCHD BY A FALL WITH MOANS	421 EMPEDOCLES I 2	272

SCRAWLD

THE STRANGE-SCRAWLD ROCKS THE LONELY SKY	60 RESIGNATION	268
BEARDED WITH LICHEN SCRAWLD AND GREY	274 STANZAS CARNAC	10

SCREAM
    ECHO HER STORMY SCREAM AS SHE SAILS BY   • • •   78 SOHRAB RUSTUM   572
    FRINGED WITH DARK PINES AND SANDS WHERE SEAFOWL SCREAM 123 BALDER DEAD 3   327
    AH WHO ARE THESE WHAT SHRILL EAR-PIERCING SCREAM • •   375 MEROPE   1202
    OF THE PENT WINDS THAT SCREAM IN AGONY   • • •   472 CROMWELL   26

SCREAMD
    THE KNIGHTS DREW SWORD THE LADIES SCREAMD   • • •   159 NECKAN   27
    AND SAW HER BABE AMIDST THE FIRE AND SCREAMD   • •   446 WESTMIN ABBEY   93

SCREAMING
    WHERE IN AND OUT THE SCREAMING SEAFOWL FLY • • •   97 BALDER DEAD 1   80
    DROVE THEM SCREAMING FROM THEIR EYRIES   • • •   399 MEROPE   1829

SCREAMS
    CIRCLES ABOVE HIS EYRY WITH LOUD SCREAMS   • • •   78 SOHRAB RUSTUM   565
    OF STAGSHORN FOR THEIR HATS ANON WITH SCREAMS   • •   150 TRISTRAM 3   26
    NOR TO THE SHINING SEA-FOWL THAT WITH SCREAMS   • •   151 TRISTRAM 3   52
    ECHOING THE SCREAMS OF THE EAGLES   • • • •   252 FUTURE   10

SCREEN
    THREE HOLLIES SIDE BY SIDE AND MADE A SCREEN   • •   150 TRISTRAM 3   20
    CLUSTERD UNDER THE HOLLY-SCREEN AND SHE   • • •   150 TRISTRAM 3   36

SCREEND
    SCREEND BY DEEP BOUGHS ON EITHER HAND   • • •   248 KENSINGTON GARD   2
    SCREEND BY DARK TREES ON EITHER HAND • • • •   248 KENSINGTON GARD V   2
    SCREEND IS THIS NOOK OER THE HIGH HALF-REAPD FIELD   255 SCHOLAR-GIPSY   21
    SCREEND IN THIS NOOK OER THE HIGH HALF-REAPD FIELD   255 SCHOLAR-GIPSY V 21

SCREENS
    SCREENS NOT NOW A HEART OF STONE   • • • • •   27 NEW SIRENS   52

SCRIBE
    THAT PREFACE AND POST-SCRIBE THEE   • • • •   FRAGMENT 5   10

SCRIBES
    THE OLD LAW OBSERVED BY SCRIBES AND PHARISEES   • •   237 PROGRESS   6

SCRUTINISE
    WE SCRUTINISE THE DATES   • • • • • • •   423 EMPEDOCLES I 2   322

SCUFFLE
    WE HEAR THY SCUFFLE ON THE STAIR   • • • • •   451 GEISTS GRAVE   48

SCULLS
    AND IN THE HORNS AND GOLD-RIMMD SCULLS THE WINE   • •   95 BALDER DEAD 1 V 14

SCULPTORS
    THE FAMOUS PLAYERS SCULPTORS WROUGHT • • • •   219 BACCHANALIA 2   7
    SCULPTORS LIKE PHIDIAS   • • • • • •   221 BACCHANALIA 2   57

SCULPTURED
    ON THE TOMB TWO FORMS THEY SCULPTURED   • • •   16 CHURCH BROU 1   105
    LIKE STONE-SCULPTURED ANTIQUE KINGS   • • • •   META CLOISTER   4

SCYTHE
    LIKE SOME RICH HYACINTH WHICH BY THE SCYTHE   • •   80 SOHRAB RUSTUM   634
    IN JUNE AND MANY A SCYTHE IN SUNSHINE FLAMES   • •   257 SCHOLAR-GIPSY   92
    STOOD WITH SUSPENDED SCYTHE TO SEE US PASS • • •   266 THYRSIS   129

SCYTHIAN
    THEY SEE THE SCYTHIAN   • • • • • • •   191 STRAYED REVEL   162
    THE SCYTHIAN BUT LONG FROSTS   • • • • • •   193 STRAYED REVEL   240

SEA
    PLANTING HIS STEADFAST FOOTSTEPS IN THE SEA   • •   3 SHAKESPEARE   5
    LINKING THEIR CORAL ARMS UNDER THE SEA   • • •   4 BUTLERS SERMONS   10
    HAVE WHISPERD IT TO THE COMPLAINING SEA   • • •   8 RELIGIOUS ISOL   11
    BRISTLED WITH CITIES US THE SEA RECEIVED   • • •   25 DREAM   37
    WHO ON SHORES AND SEA-WASHD PLACES   • • • •   26 NEW SIRENS   11
    HUNGRY AND BARREN AND SHARP AS THE SEA   • • •   39 STAGIRIUS   47
    ON LIFES INCOGNISABLE SEA   • • • • • •   40 HUMAN LIFE   8
    WE STEM ACROSS THE SEA OF LIFE BY NIGHT   • • •   41 HUMAN LIFE   27
    WE STEM ACROSS THE SEA BY NIGHT   • • • •   41 HUMAN LIFE V 27
    NOR IDLY DO THESE SEA-BIRDS HOVER NEAR   • • •   42 GIPSY CHILD   8
    AND BLITHELY DO THESE SEA-BIRDS HOVER NEAR • • •   41 GIPSY CHILD V   8
    THAT NIGHT IN THE WIDE-GLIMMERING SEA   • • •   54 RESIGNATION   85
    FOR THE WARM PERSIAN SEA-BOARD SO THEY STREAMD   •   64 SOHRAB RUSTUM   116
    FOR WE ARE ALL LIKE SWIMMERS IN THE SEA   • • •   72 SOHRAB RUSTUM   390
    OR WHETHER IT WILL ROLL US OUT TO SEA   • • •   73 SOHRAB RUSTUM   394
    BACK OUT TO SEA TO THE DEEP WAVES OF DEATH • • •   73 SOHRAB RUSTUM   395
    RETURNING HOME OVER THE SALT BLUE SEA   • • •   85 SOHRAB RUSTUM   833
    SOON BE THAT DAY MY SON AND DEEP THAT SEA   • • •   85 SOHRAB RUSTUM   836
    EMERGE AND SHINE UPON THE ARAL SEA   • • • •   87 SOHRAB RUSTUM   892
    FIRE TO THE WOOD AND SEND HIM OUT TO SEA   • • •   96 BALDER DEAD 1   44
    DOWN TO THE MARGIN OF THE ROARING SEA   • • •   97 BALDER DEAD 1   77
    FROM THE HIGH MOORS BEHIND AND MEETS THE SEA   • •   97 BALDER DEAD 1   83
    FENSALER WHOSE LIT WINDOWS LOOK TO SEA   • • •   100 BALDER DEAD 1   198
    FROM THE SEA CITYWARD AND KNEW HIS STEP   • • •   101 BALDER DEAD 1   227
    ON AUTUMN-DAYS BEFORE THEY CROSS THE SEA   • • •   109 BALDER DEAD 2   159

SEU   (CONTINUED)

OF THESE THE SERPENT IN THE SEA YE CAST	110	BALDER DEAD 2	209
THE GODS ON THE SEA-SHORE BY BALDERS SHIP	113	BALDER DEAD 2	310
REGNER WHO SWEPT THE NORTHERN SEA WITH FLEETS	117	BALDER DEAD 3	126
AND CAME DOWN MOANING TO THE SEA FIRST SQUALLS	118	BALDER DEAD 3	182
AND WREATHED IN SMOKE THE SHIP STOOD OUT TO SEA	118	BALDER DEAD 3	185
INTO THE SMOKE-WRAPT SEA AND NIGHT CAME ON	119	BALDER DEAD 3	195
REDDENING THE SEA AROUND AND ALL WAS DARK	119	BALDER DEAD 3	206
LAST WALKING BY THE SEA THOU FOUNDEST SPARS	121	BALDER DEAD 3	268
OR ON THE SEA THE FIELD OF PIRATES SAIL	121	BALDER DEAD 3	270
TO SHOW HIM SPITS AND BEACHES OF THE SEA	122	BALDER DEAD 3	321
CATCHES THEM AND DRIVES OUT AGAIN TO SEA	124	BALDER DEAD 3	364
OVER THE GREY SEA-RIDGES AND THE GLIMPSE	124	BALDER DEAD 3	366
THEN WALKING BY THE SEA THOU FOUNDEST SPARS	121	BALDER DEAD 3	V 268
THE LANTERNS OF THE FISHING-BOATS AT SEA	130	TRISTRAM 1	6
IS IT THAT THE BLEAK SEA-GALE	131	TRISTRAM 1	33
BEATING FROM THE ATLANTIC SEA	131	TRISTRAM 1	34
WHO IS THIS SNOWDROP BY THE SEA	132	TRISTRAM 1	49
OER SOME FAIR UNWINTRY SEA	133	TRISTRAM 1	91
THE CALM SEA SHINES LOOSE HANG THE VESSELS SAILS	133	TRISTRAM 1	94
AS HE STEERS HER OER THE SEA	134	TRISTRAM 1	128
HIGH ABOVE THE SOUNDING SEA	134	TRISTRAM 1	135
ONCE MORE ROUND THEM AND THE SEA	135	TRISTRAM 1	154
OUR SNOWDROP BY THE ATLANTIC SEA	136	TRISTRAM 1	196
BY THE GREY ATLANTIC SEA	137	TRISTRAM 1	231
WATCHING BY THE SALT SEA-TIDE	138	TRISTRAM 1	270
TO OUR LONELY SEA COMPLAIN	139	TRISTRAM 1	274
LONG INLETS OF SMOOTH GLITTERING SEA	141	TRISTRAM 1	368
IS IT THAT THE BLACK SEA-GALE	131	TRISTRAM 1	V 33
FAST BESIDE THE SOUNDING SEA	134	TRISTRAM 1	V 135
THROUGH SOME OLD SEA-SIDE KNIGHTLY HALL	148	TRISTRAM 2	178
A YEAR HAD FLOWN AND OER THE SEA AWAY	149	TRISTRAM 3	1
WHICH BORDERS THE SEA-SHORE A COUNTRY PATH	149	TRISTRAM 3	8
NOR DID THEIR LOOKS STRAY ONCE TO THE SEA-SIDE	151	TRISTRAM 3	48
NOR TO THE SHINING SEA-FOWL THAT WITH SCREAMS	151	TRISTRAM 3	52
BUT WHEN THE RED GLOW ON THE SEA GREW COLD	151	TRISTRAM 3	58
THE HOLLIES AND THE CLIFF AND THE SEA-SHORE	152	TRISTRAM 3	104
THE SAND THE SEA-BIRDS AND THE DISTANT SAILS	152	TRISTRAM 3	105
IN EVERY HUT ALONG THIS SEA-COAST WILD	152	TRISTRAM 3	109
BEYOND THE HEATHS EDGED BY THE LONELY SEA	154	TRISTRAM 3	155
TO GAZE ON THE LIGHT SEA OF LEAF AND BOUGH	155	TRISTRAM 3	202
TO GAZE ON THE GREEN SEA OF LEAF AND BOUGH	155	TRISTRAM 3	V 202
THE SEA WITHOUT A HUMAN SHORE	156	SAINT BRANDAN	12
THE BALTIC SEA ALONG	159	NECKAN	2
GREEN ROLLS THE BALTIC SEA	159	NECKAN	6
FAR FROM THE KIND SEA-WAVE	159	NECKAN	16
THAN THE SEA-CHILDREN OWN	159	NECKAN	20
FROM THE SEA-WAVES I COME	159	NECKAN	26
AND BORE HER DOWN TO THE SEA-HALLS	160	NECKAN	31
BENEATH THE SALT SEA-TIDE	160	NECKAN	32
THIS LOST SEA-CREATURE SAVED	160	NECKAN	56
THE SEA THE STARRY POLES	161	NECKAN	62
EARTH SEA AND SKY AND GOD ABOVE	161	NECKAN	63
THE BALTIC SEA ALONG	161	NECKAN	66
FAR FROM THE GREEN SEA WAVE	159	NECKAN	V 16
BENEATH THE COLD SEA TIDE	160	NECKAN	V 32
WHERE THE SEA-BEASTS RANGED ALL ROUND	162	FORSAKEN MERM	39
WHERE THE SEA-SNAKES COIL AND TWINE	162	FORSAKEN MERM	41
ON A RED GOLD THRONE IN THE HEART OF THE SEA	163	FORSAKEN MERM	51
SHE SIGHD SHE LOOKD UP THROUGH THE CLEAR GREEN SEA	163	FORSAKEN MERM	55
SAY THY PRAYER AND COME BACK TO THE KIND SEA-CAVES	163	FORSAKEN MERM	61
THE SEA GROWS STORMY THE LITTLE ONES MOAN	163	FORSAKEN MERM	65
WHERE THE SEA-STOCKS BLOOM TO THE WHITE-WALLD TOWN	163	FORSAKEN MERM	69
THE SEA GROWS STORMY THE LITTLE ONES MOAN	163	FORSAKEN MERM	79
DOWN TO THE DEPTHS OF THE SEA	164	FORSAKEN MERM	86
AND OVER THE SAND AT THE SEA	164	FORSAKEN MERM	99
THE KINGS OF THE SEA	165	FORSAKEN MERM	123
THE KINGS OF THE SEA	165	FORSAKEN MERM	143
WITH HER OWN HUSBAND BY THE LIBYAN SEA	173	MONICAS PRAYER	8
BUT AS ROLLS BETWEEN US	176	PARTING	65
THE CALM UPON THE MOONLIT SEA	180	FAREWELL	80
YES IN THE SEA OF LIFE ENISLED	182	TO MARG CONT	1
THE UNPLUMBD SALT ESTRANGING SEA	182	TO MARG CONT	24
SO ON THE SEA OF LIFE ALAS	185	TERRACE BERNE	47
BY THE GREY SEA IF SO THEN HAIL	189	STRAYED REVEL	128
VIOLET SEA	192	STRAYED REVEL	204
STARTLED THE UNKNOWN SEA	193	STRAYED REVEL	260
LEAVING THE SALT SEA-BEDS	196	FRAG ANTIGONE	57
HOW SWEETLY WOULD THE FRESH SEA-BREEZE	205	CALAIS SANDS	15
HANGS DARK UPON THE ROLLING SEA	205	CALAIS SANDS	22
OH THAT YON SEA-BIRDS WINGS WERE MINE	205	CALAIS SANDS	23
HOW SWEETLY WOULD THE FRESH SEA-WIND	205	CALAIS SANDS	V 15
ON THE BLUE SEA MY GAZE I STRAIN	205	CALAIS SANDS	V 20
OH THAT THAT SEA-BIRDS WINGS WERE MINE	205	CALAIS SANDS	V 23
LIKE STARS ON LIFES COLD SEA	209	DESPONDENCY	2
THE SEA IS CALM TO-NIGHT	210	DOVER BEACH	1
WHERE THE SEA MEETS THE MOON-BLANCHD LAND	211	DOVER BEACH	8
HEARING IT BY THIS DISTANT NORTHERN SEA	211	DOVER BEACH	20
THE SEA OF FAITH	211	DOVER BEACH	21
WHERE THE SEA MEETS THE MOON-BLANCHD SAND	211	DOVER BEACH	V 8

SEA   (CONTINUED)
    AS THOSE WHICH PASTURED BY THE SEA . . . . . . 222 EPILOG LAOCOON   44
    AS THOSE THAT PASTURED BY THE SEA . . . . . . 222 EPILOG LAOCOON V 44
    AND EGREMONT SLEEPS BY THE SEA . . . . . . 228 YOUTH OF NATURE   17
    ON TO THE PLAINS TO THE SEA . . . . . . 234 YOUTH OF MAN   86
    FORWARDS FORWARDS OER THE STARLIT SEA . . . . 239 SELF-DEPENDENCE   4
    OER THE SEA AND TO THE STARS I SEND . . . . . 240 SELF-DEPENDENCE   6
    AND THE SEA ITS LONG MOON-SILVERD ROLL . . . . 240 SELF-DEPENDENCE   22
    DESPOTIC ON THAT SEA . . . . 243 SUMMER NIGHT   57
    OF SEA AND WIND AND THROUGH THE DEEPENING GLOOM . . 244 SUMMER NIGHT   71
    DESPOTIC ON LIFES SEA . . . . 243 SUMMER NIGHT V 57
    AND THE SEA WHERE IT GOES . . . . 247 BURIED LIFE   98
    WHETHER IN SOUND OF THE SWALLOWING SEA . . . . 252 FUTURE   16
    MURMURS AND SCENTS OF THE INFINITE SEA . . . . 254 FUTURE   87
    AS SOME GRAVE TYRIAN TRADER FROM THE SEA . . . . 262 SCHOLAR-GIPSY 232
    MELT INTO OPEN MOONLIT SEA . . . . 275 SOUTHERN NIGHT   2
    NOT BY THIS GRACIOUS MIDLAND SEA . . . . . 277 SOUTHERN NIGHT   74
    THIS SEA OF TIME WHEREON WE SAIL . . . . . 303 GRANDE CHARTR 122
    THE WHITE MISTS ROLLING LIKE A SEA . . . . . 306 OBERMANN   9
    THAT MUCH-LOVED INLAND SEA . . . . . . 311 OBERMANN 162
    FLOAT ON A ROLLING SEA . . . . 319 OBERMANN MORE 212
    FLOAT IN A ROLLING SEA . . . . 319 OBERMANN MORE V 212
    ON THE HIGH SEA-BANK IN THE SIGHT . . . . . 345 MEROPE 482
    MUCH IS THERE WHICH THE SEA . . . . . . 351 MEROPE 622
    THENCE BY THE SEA-GODS SANCTUARY AND THE TOMB . . 356 MEROPE 740
    OF THE THRACIAN SEA LET HER LEAVE . . . . . 361 MEROPE 912
    AND THE SEA-EAGLES BUILD THEIR NEST . . . . 414 EMPEDOCLES I 2 67
    EXPERIENCE LIKE A SEA SOAKS ALL-EFFACING IN . . 419 EMPEDOCLES I 2 201
    OF EARTH AND AIR AND SEA . . . . 422 EMPEDOCLES I 2 292
    WE MEASURE THE SEA-TIDES WE NUMBER THE SEA-SANDS . 423 EMPEDOCLES I 2 321
    WE MEASURE THE SEA-TIDES WE NUMBER THE SEA-SANDS . 423 EMPEDOCLES I 2 321
    AND BY THE SEA AND IN THE BRAKES . . . . . 426 EMPEDOCLES I 2 431
    THE GRASS IS COOL THE SEA-SIDE AIR . . . . . 426 EMPEDOCLES I 2 432
    BASK IN THE GLENS OR ON THE WARM SEA-SHORE . . . 427 EMPEDOCLES I 2 437
    TO IMBED THEM IN THE SEA . . . . 430 EMPEDOCLES II 4(
    WHERE ERST THE STRONG SEA-CURRENTS SUCKD THEE DOWN 430 EMPEDOCLES II 59
    LETTING THE SEA-STREAM WANDER THROUGH THY HAIR . 430 EMPEDOCLES II 61
    LIKE A SEA-WAVE BETWIXT THE WORLD AND THEE . . . 436 EMPEDOCLES II 231
    SUNSET OVER THE SEA . . . . 436 EMPEDOCLES II 253
    THOU TOO BRIMMEST WITH LIFE THE SEA OF CLOUD . . 438 EMPEDOCLES II 308
    LIVES AND THAT OTHER FAINTER SEA FAR DOWN . . 438 EMPEDOCLES II 311
    OH THAT MY HEART BOUNDED WITH THE SWELL OF THE SEA 438 EMPEDOCLES II 324
    OVER THE UNRECOGNISING SEA WHILE AIR . . . . 439 EMPEDOCLES II 361
    WILL BLOW US FIERCELY BACK TO SEA AND EARTH . . 439 EMPEDOCLES II 362
    LEAP AND ROAR THOU SEA OF FIRE . . . . . 441 EMPEDOCLES II 411
    IN CLIFF TO THE SEA . . . . 441 EMPEDOCLES II 424
    THY LAST DEFEAT IN THIS SICILIAN SEA . . . . 430 EMPEDOCLES II V 57
    OR OERPASS THE SEVERING SEA . . . . . . 456 POOR MATTHIAS 127
    INLAND FROM THE ROCKS AND SEA . . . . . 457 POOR MATTHIAS 180
    WHO WOULD NOT TURN HIM FROM THE BARREN SEA . . . 470 ALARIC AT ROME 221
    AND GLADSOME GREETINGS OF THE BUOYANT SEA . . 472 CROMWELL 8
    MADE ROUGH WITH CARE BECOME THE CHANGEFUL SEA . 473 CROMWELL 49
    BETWEEN THE BARREN MOUNTAINS AND THE STORMY SEA . 475 CROMWELL 118
    AND STRUCK AND OER US THE SEA-WATERS SPREAD . 484 S S LUSITANIA 8
    FROM THE ENCROACHING EUXINE SEA . . . . .   PILLARS UNIVERS 8
    FROM THE TYRANNOUS EUXINE SEA . . . . .   PILLARS UNIVERS V 8
    FROM THE FIERCER EUXINE SEA . . . . . .   PILLARS UNIVERS V 8

SEAFARING
    AND AS SEAFARING MEN WHO LONG HAVE WROUGHT . . . . 123 BALDER DEAD 3   357

SEAFOWL
    WHERE IN AND OUT THE SCREAMING SEAFOWL FLY . . . . 97 BALDER DEAD 1   80
    FRINGED WITH DARK PINES AND SANDS WHERE SEAFOWL SCREAM 123 BALDER DEAD 3   327

SEAL
    THAT SEAL WHICH RUSTUM TO MY MOTHER GAVE . . . . 80 SOHRAB RUSTUM   659
    ON SOHRABS ARM THE SIGN OF RUSTUMS SEAL . . . . 81 SOHRAB RUSTUM   678
    AND FATE SET SEAL THAT SO HIS END MUST BE . . . . 96 BALDER DEAD 1   25
    LOOKS ON IN FEAR AND WHEN THE SEAL IS SET . . . . 465 ALARIC AT ROME   92

SEALD
    AND FREA SEALD HER TIRED LIDS WITH SLEEP . . . . 103 BALDER DEAD 1   279
    FOR HER EYES WERE SEALD TO THE HOLY BOOK . . . . 163 FORSAKEN MERM   81
    AND BY CONTRITION SEALD THRICE SURE . . . . . 179 FAREWELL   72

SEALIKE
    THE SUNLESS FOREST AND THE SEALIKE PLAIN . . . . 475 CROMWELL   106

SEALING
    SEALING HER EAGLE EYES . . . . 38 STAGIRIUS   21

SEALS
    THEIR HOT SEALS AND LET HIM WAKE . . . . . . 139 TRISTRAM 1   295
    FOR THAT WHICH SEALS THEM HATH BEEN DEEP-ORDAIND . . 245 BURIED LIFE   29
    FATE SEALS MY LIPS AND DRAGS TO RUIN THEE . . . . 397 MEROPE   1779

SEARCH
    TILL SHE SEARCH AND LEARN HER OWN . . . . . . 28 NEW SIRENS   74
    WE KNOW NOT AND NO SEARCH WILL MAKE US KNOW . . 73 SOHRAB RUSTUM   396

SEARCH   (CONTINUED)
    OR THOU WILT FIND HIM IN THY FAITHFUL SEARCH   • • 116 BALDER DEAD 3   116
    FROM SATURNS SEARCH AMONG THE NEW-YEAND LAMBS • • 355 MEROPE   738
    SEARCH HE A THOUSAND YEARS • • • • • • • 417 EMPEDOCLES I 2   145
    WE SEARCH OUT DEAD MENS WORDS AND WORKS OF   423 EMPEDOCLES I 2   326
        DEAD MENS HANDS
    OUR DESPERATE SEARCH WAS SIN • • • • • • • 423 EMPEDOCLES I 2   344

SEARCHING
    TO THE FOILD SEARCHING OF MORTALITY • • • • • 3 SHAKESPEARE   8
    AND THAT SOUL-SEARCHING VISION FELL ON ME • • • • 42 GIPSY CHILD   16

SEARD
    SEARD HIS KEEN EYEBALLS • • • • • • • • • 51 CONSOLATION   37
    WITH HOT CHEEKS AND SEARD EYES • • • • • • • 201 PHILOMELA   20

SEAS
    WHENCE EQUALLY THE SEAS OF LIFE AND DEATH ARE FED   60 RESIGNATION   260
    RAN BLACK OER THE SEAS FACE THEN STEADY RUSHD • 118 BALDER DEAD 3   183
    NOW TO SAIL THE SEAS OF DEATH I LEAVE THEE • • • 145 TRISTRAM 2   97
    HE HEARD ACROSS THE HOWLING SEAS • • • • • 156 SAINT BRANDAN   5
    THE VAST SEAS OF SNOW • • • • • • • • 175 PARTING   28
    TO HAVE ECHOED THE MOAN OF MY SEAS • • • • 231 YOUTH OF NATURE   124
    OVER THE LIT SEAS UNQUIET WAY • • • • • 240 SELF-DEPENDENCE   14
    OER THOSE SAME SEAS DARK TENERIFFE ROSE FRAUGHT • 485 S S LUSITANIA   11

SEASHORE
    BRING WOOD TO THE SEASHORE TO BALDERS SHIP • 96 BALDER DEAD 1   41
    GO QUICKLY GODS BRING WOOD TO THE SEASHORE • • • 106 BALDER DEAD 2   41
    AND LOOSED THEM OF THEIR LOADS ON THE SEASHORE • • 106 BALDER DEAD 2   67

SEASONS
    SEASONS ALTERNATING AND NIGHT AND DAY • • • 45 IN UTRUMQUE PAR   5
    SEASONS IMPAIRD NOT THE RAY • • • • • • 287 RUGBY CHAPEL   21
    MARK THE SEASONS MAP OUR YEAR • • • • • • 456 POOR MATTHIAS   145

SEAT
    SOME BETTER ARCHETYPE WHOSE SEAT WAS HEAVEN • • 9 MYCERINUS   22
    LADIES WAITING ROUND HER SEAT • • • • • • 13 CHURCH BROU 1   34
    HIS SEAT UPON THE INTELLECTUAL THRONE • • • 260 SCHOLAR-GIPSY   184
    OF HIS FRESH-CONQUERD REALM THE ROYAL SEAT • • 330 MEROPE   11
    IF STILL INDEED HE LIVES WHOM THOU WOULDST SEAT • 336 MEROPE   189
    WHICH FROM ONE CENTRAL CITYS GUARDED SEAT • • • 337 MEROPE   246
    WHEN THE SOUND CLIMBS NEAR HIS SEAT • • • • 431 EMPEDOCLES II   69

SEATED
    HAD FOUND HIM SEATED AT THEIR ENTERING • • • 256 SCHOLAR-GIPSY   60
    AND I AM SEATED ON A PROSPEROUS THRONE • • • 334 MEROPE   136
    CAN HOUSES THUS ILL-SEATED THUS EMBROILD • • • 390 MEROPE   1559

SEATS
    SADLY BACK THE SEATS OF MEN • • • • • • 31 NEW SIRENS   150
    IN DIVINE SEATS HATH KNOWN • • • • • • 45 IN UTRUMQUE PAR   23
    THERE ARE THE JOYLESS SEATS THE HAUNT OF GHOSTS • 108 BALDER DEAD 2   132
    SHALL HE SHED CHEER OVER THE CHEERLESS SEATS • 110 BALDER DEAD 2   195
    IN NEW-RECOVERD SEATS THE HAPPIER DAY • • • 128 BALDER DEAD 3   513
    BROTHER WHAT SEATS ARE THESE WHAT HAPPIER DAY • 128 BALDER DEAD 3   515
    THE RUIND PALACES OF ODIN SEATS • • • • 128 BALDER DEAD 3   533
    YE SOLEMN SEATS OF HOLY PAIN • • • • • • 302 GRANDE CHARTR   92

SEAWARD
    GAZING SEAWARD FOR THE LIGHT • • • • • • 130 TRISTRAM 1   12
    NOW THE SALT TIDES SEAWARD FLOW • • • • 161 FORSAKEN MERM   5
    WHEN SWEET AIRS COME SEAWARD • • • • • 165 FORSAKEN MERM   128
    THE SALT TIDE ROLLS SEAWARD • • • • • • 164 FORSAKEN MERM   V 110

SEAWARDS
    GAZING SEAWARDS MANY A LEAGUE • • • • • 131 TRISTRAM 1   42
    GAZING SEAWARDS FOR THE LIGHT • • • • • 130 TRISTRAM 1   V 12
    NOW THE SALT TIDES SEAWARDS FLOW • • • • 161 FORSAKEN MERM   V 5

SEAWEED
    OVER BANKS OF BRIGHT SEAWEED • • • • • • 165 FORSAKEN MERM   134

SEBERT
    AT DAWN THOU TO KING SEBERT SHALT RELATE • • • 445 WESTMIN ABBEY   48

SEBERTS
    KING SEBERTS WORK THE WONDROUS MINSTER NEW • • • 444 WESTMIN ABBEY   16
    EFFACE THE HUMBLER GRAVES OF SEBERTS LINE • • • 445 WESTMIN ABBEY   54

SECLUDED
    WHICH IN A QUEENS SECLUDED GARDEN THROWS • • • 70 SOHRAB RUSTUM   315
    THROUGH THESE SECLUDED DELLS TO CRY • • • • 305 GRANDE CHARTR   195

SECLUSION
    THY DEEP SECLUSION THINE UNYIELDING GLOOM • • • 332 MEROPE   84
    WHERE IN SECRET SECLUSION • • • • • • 344 MEROPE   437

SECOND
    SECOND AND WAS THE UNCLE OF THE KING • • • • • 66 SOHRAB RUSTUM   173

SECOND   (CONTINUED)
        AND REAP A SECOND GLORY IN THINE AGE • • • • • •   84 SOHRAB RUSTUM   776
        THE SECOND ASGARD WITH ANOTHER NAME • • • • • •   128 BALDER DEAD 3   521
        SCANT LEISURE FOR A SECOND MESSENGER • • • • • •   140 TRISTRAM 1   307
        HATH MAN NO SECOND LIFE PITCH THIS ONE HIGH • •   171 BETTER PART   10
        THE SECOND WAVE SUCCEEDS BEFORE   • • • • • •   308 OBERMANN   75
        THE CHILDREN OF THE SECOND BIRTH   • • • • • •   310 OBERMANN   143
        MAN GETS NO SECOND DAY • • • • • • • • •   321 OBERMANN MORE   258
        FELL TO THY FATHERS LOT THE SECOND PRIZE • • • •   330 MEROPE   8
        AND SECOND FATHER FROM THAT HOUR WHEN FIRST • •   331 MEROPE   30
        MORE PIERCING THE SECOND CRY RANG   • • • • • •   346 MEROPE   495
        THE STRICKEN KING A SECOND ENEMY   • • • • • •   381 MEROPE   1297
        OF SECOND LIFE I KNOW NOT WHERE   • • • • • •   450 GEISTS GRAVE   32
        YES BE THE SECOND CATO PRAISD • • • • • • • •   481 COURAGE   13

SECONDS
        SOMETIMES A SECONDS SPACE THEIR EAR • • • • • •   226 EPILOG LAOCOON   179

SECRET
        WHAT THOUGH THE HOLY SECRET WHICH MOULDS THEE • •   8 RELIGIOUS ISOL   9
        YET THERE THY SECRET LIES • • • • • • • •   46 IN UTRUMQUE PAR V 37
        WHOSE SECRET IS NOT JOY BUT PEACE   • • • • • •   58 RESIGNATION   192
        YET IN MY SECRET MIND ONE WAY I KNOW • • • • • •   99 BALDER DEAD 1   128
        OF THOSE THAT IN SECRET THE HEART-STRINGS RIVE • •   132 TRISTRAM 1   47
        THERES A SECRET IN HIS BREAST   • • • • • •   138 TRISTRAM 1   245
        HAVE THOUGHT THAT MY SECRET WAS THEIRS • • • •   232 YOUTH OF NATURE   130
        HAVE DREAMD THAT MY SECRET WAS THEIRS • • • •   232 YOUTH OF NATURE V 130
        AND I HE SAID THE SECRET OF THEIR ART • • • •   256 SCHOLAR-GIPSY   48
        THEREFORE A SECRET UNREST • • • • • • •   296 HEINES GRAVE   121
        AND SECRET FROM THE EYES OF ALL   • • • • • •   305 GRANDE CHARTR   172
        AND SECRET LOATHING FELL • • • • • • • •   315 OBERMANN MORE   94
        THAT THOU IN SECRET NURTUREST UP THY SON • • •   334 MEROPE   144
        WHERE IN SECRET SECLUSION • • • • • • • •   344 MEROPE   437
        HIM IN SECRET IN TEARS   • • • • • • • •   347 MEROPE   516
        TOO DEAR HIS SECRET WILES HAVE COST OUR HOUSE • •   380 MEROPE   1279
        MURDERS UNCERTAIN SECRET PERILOUS GAME • • • •   388 MEROPE   1501
        THAT IS THE SECRET OF THIS MIRACLE • • • • • •   410 EMPEDOCLES I 1   132
        SOME SECRET AND UNFOLLOWD VEIN OF WOE • • • •   411 EMPEDOCLES I 1   152
        OUR SHIVERING HEART IS MINED BY SECRET DISCONTENT   424 EMPEDOCLES I 2   366
        IN COMMON SIGHTS READ SECRET SYMPATHY • • • •   472 CROMWELL   32

SECRETLY
        NOW THE KING CHARGED US SECRETLY   • • • • • •   91 SICK KING BOKH   113

SECRETS
        RARER SECRETS THAN THE TOILING HEAD • • • • • •   28 NEW SIRENS   80
        THE SECRETS OF THE WORLDS MACHINE   • • • • • •   48 HORATIAN ECHO   16
        SOME SECRETS MAY THE POET TELL • • • • • • •   307 OBERMANN   41
        MORE THAN ALL SECRETS HID THE WAY IT KEEPS • • • •   352 MEROPE   631
        OF SECRETS YET TO EXPLORE • • • • • • • •   423 EMPEDOCLES I 2   335

SECT
        OF THAT UNPITYING PHRYGIAN SECT WHICH CRIED • •   172 GOOD SHEPHERD   3

SECURE
        SELF-SCHOOLD SELF-SCANND SELF-HONOURD SELF-SECURE   3 SHAKESPEARE   10
        WHO MADE THAT TRIUMPH THOUGH DEFERRD SECURE • •   336 MEROPE   220
        AND NOW GLORIOUS SECURE • • • • • • • •   343 MEROPE   414
        TO SEE SECURE TO LIVE WITH THOSE SHE LOVES • • •   349 MEROPE   566
        FLING OFF THY CROWN SUPPOSED AT LAST SECURE • •   395 MEROPE   1743
        TO AFFRIGHT A FORTUNE WHICH THE GODS SECURE • •   398 MEROPE   1782

SECURES
        THY SHAME SECURES MY FREEDOM NOT THY WILL • • • •   340 MEROPE   351

SECURITY
        THE POETS RAPT SECURITY • • • • • • • • • •   59 RESIGNATION   246

SEDGE
        AND FROM THE MINT-PLANT IN THE SEDGE • • • • • •   218 BACCHANALIA 1   13
        SWALLOWS TROOPING IN THE SEDGE • • • • • • •   456 POOR MATTHIAS   143

SEDGED
        AND WHAT SEDGED BROOKS ARE THAMESS TRIBUTARIES • •   266 THYRSIS   110

SEDGY
        YET IN THE SEDGY BOTTOM THERE • • • • • • •   148 TRISTRAM 2   V

SEDUCED
        TO AEPYTUS THE KING SEDUCED WITH GOLD • • • •   364 MEROPE   970

SEE
        VAIN LABOUR DEEP AND BROAD WHERE NONE MAY SEE • •   4 BUTLERS SERMONS   5
        STRINGING VAIN WORDS OF POWERS WE CANNOT SEE • •   10 MYCERINUS   51
        THROUGH THAT GLOOM HE WILL SEE BUT A SHADOW APPEARING 20 MODERN SAPPHO   25
        THOSE FRANK EYES WHERE DEEP I SEE   • • • • • •   24 MEMORY-PICTURE   45
        TIMES GAY MINIONS PLEASED YOU SEE   • • • • • •   24 MEMORY-PICTURE   53
        YET I SEE THE HOWLING LEVELS • • • • • • •   26 NEW SIRENS   17
        SEE THE WHITE EAST AND THE MORNING RAYS • • • •   34 NEW SIRENS   242
        WELL PLEASED SEE END   • • • • • • • • •   52 CONSOLATION   65

SEE   (CONTINUED)

THEY SEE THEIR SHACKLED BEASTS AGAIN   • • • • • •   55 RESIGNATION   120
THEY FEEL NOT THOUGH THEY MOVE AND SEE • • • •   58 RESIGNATION   205
MAN STILL WOULD SEE AND SEE DISMAYD   • • • • • •   58 RESIGNATION   220
MAN STILL WOULD SEE AND SEE DISMAYD   • • • • • •   58 RESIGNATION   220
THEY WINNING ROOM TO SEE AND HEAR   • • • • • •   59 RESIGNATION   249
WELCOME THESE EYES COULD SEE NO BETTER SIGHT   • •   67 SOHRAB RUSTUM   205
COME THOU SHALT SEE HOW RUSTUM HOARDS HIS FAME • •   68 SOHRAB RUSTUM   256
NO WHEN I SEE THEE WRATH FORSAKES MY SOUL • • • •   74 SOHRAB RUSTUM   430
HER MOST I PITY WHO NO MORE WILL SEE   • • • • •   78 SOHRAB RUSTUM   593
MAY SEE MY TOMB A GREAT WAY OFF AND CRY • • • •   84 SOHRAB RUSTUM   791
MAY SEE MY TOMB A GREAT WAY OFF AND SAY • • • •   84 SOHRAB RUSTUM   V 791
CLEAR IN THESE THINGS I CANNOT SEE   • • • •   93 SICK KING BOKH   182
THOU WAST ATHIRST AND DIDST NOT SEE   • • • • •   94 SICK KING BOKH   210
THOU WERT ATHIRST AND DIDST NOT SEE   • • • • •   94 SICK KING BOKH   V 210
NOR SEE THE SUN ARISE NOR SEE IT SET   • • • • •   99 BALDER DEAD 1   154
NOR SEE THE SUN ARISE NOR SEE IT SET   • • • • •   99 BALDER DEAD 1   154
AND HE WILL SEE STRETCH ROUND HIM HELAS REALM   •   100 BALDER DEAD 1   171
AND HE WILL SEE THE FEEBLE SHADOWY TRIBES   • • •   100 BALDER DEAD 1   174
TO KEEP HIS OWN LIFE SAFE AND SEE THE SUN   • • •   101 BALDER DEAD 1   213
NOR YET COULD HERMOD SEE HIS BROTHERS FACE • • •   101 BALDER DEAD 1   228
HOWBEIT I WILL SEE AND DO HIS HEST   • • • •   102 BALDER DEAD 1   244
WHO SEE THE LIGHT AND BLEST IN ASGARD DWELL   •   112 BALDER DEAD 2   255
SEE HERE IS HERMOD WHO COMES SINGLE BACK   • • •   113 BALDER DEAD 3   6
WOULD I MIGHT SEE HIM SNATCH THEE IN HIS HAND   •   114 BALDER DEAD 3   24
MY TRUANT ODER I SHALL SEE NO MORE   • • • •   117 BALDER DEAD 3   120
AND TOWARDS EVENING SEE THE HEADLANDS RISE • • •   123 BALDER DEAD 3   359
WHO LIVE AND WITH THEIR EYES SHALL SEE THAT DAY •   127 BALDER DEAD 3   486
THERE RE-ASSEMBLING WE SHALL SEE EMERGE • • • •   128 BALDER DEAD 3   527
SEE IT SHINE AND TAKE IT UP   • • • • • • •   135 TRISTRAM 1   143
WHAT HIS EYE MUST SEE NO MORE   • • • • • • •   135 TRISTRAM 1   160
I SEE HER FORM GLIDE THROUGH THE CROSSING SPEARS •   138 TRISTRAM 1   241
BEYOND THE MOUNTAINS WILL HE SEE   • • • • •   138 TRISTRAM 1   250
WHAT NEW CHANGE SHALL WE NOW SEE   • • • •   139 TRISTRAM 1   296
TO SEE THE PARK-GLADES WHERE YOU PLAY   • • • •   141 TRISTRAM 1   355
TO SEE THE SPARKLE ON THE EAVES • • • • •   141 TRISTRAM 1   357
BUT YOU SEE FAIRER IN YOUR DREAMS   • • • •   141 TRISTRAM 1   371
RAISE THE LIGHT MY PAGE THAT I MAY SEE HER • • •   142 TRISTRAM 2   1
SEE MY CHEEK AND LIPS HOW WHITE THEY ARE   • • •   143 TRISTRAM 2   24
HUSH NO WORDS THAT SMILE I SEE FORGIVES ME • • •   144 TRISTRAM 2   69
THROUGH A MIST I SEE THEE NEAR COME NEARER • • •   145 TRISTRAM 2   75
YOU SEE THEM CLEAR THE MOON SHINES BRIGHT   • • •   146 TRISTRAM 2   101
AND ON THE ARRAS WROUGHT YOU SEE   • • • •   147 TRISTRAM 2   152
AND THERE UPON THE WALL YOU SEE • • • • •   147 TRISTRAM 2   V 152
AND IS SHE HAPPY DOES SHE SEE UNMOVED   • • • •   151 TRISTRAM 3   64
AND YET I SWEAR IT ANGERS ME TO SEE   • • • •   153 TRISTRAM 3   133
WE SHALL SEE WHILE ABOVE US   • • • • •   165 FORSAKEN MERM   116
SATE WITH HIS BRIDE TO SEE A PUBLIC SHOW   • • •   166 AUSTERITY POET   4
SITS THERE NO JUDGE IN HEAVEN OUR SIN TO SEE   •   171 BETTER PART   11
AGAIN I SEE MY BLISS AT HAND   • • • • •   174 MEETING   1
BUT SEE TIS IN VAIN   • • • • • • •   176 PARTING   62
SHALL SEE OURSELVES AND LEARN AT LAST   • • • •   179 FAREWELL   55
THINE EYES MY LOVE I SEE   • • • • • • •   183 ABSENCE   2
AH SHALL I SEE THEE WHILE A FLUSH   • • • •   184 TERRACE BERNE   13
AND MARGUERITE I SHALL SEE NO MORE   • • • •   185 TERRACE BERNE   52
SO SOON I SEE THE NIGHT-DEWS   • • • • • •   186 STRAYED REVEL   15
WOULDST MORE OF IT SEE HOW GLOWS   • • • •   187 STRAYED REVEL   55
SEE WHAT THE DAY BRINGS • • • • • • •   188 STRAYED REVEL   74
AH AND I SEE TOO   • • • • •   189 STRAYED REVEL   104
AND SEE BELOW THEM   • • • • • • •   190 STRAYED REVEL   133
THEY SEE TIRESIAS   • • • • • • •   190 STRAYED REVEL   135
THEY SEE THE CENTAURS   • • • • • • •   190 STRAYED REVEL   143
THEY SEE THE INDIAN   • • • • • • •   190 STRAYED REVEL   151
THEY SEE THE SCYTHIAN   • • • • • • •   191 STRAYED REVEL   162
THEY SEE THE FERRY   • • • • • • • •   191 STRAYED REVEL   181
THEY SEE THE HEROES   • • • • • • •   192 STRAYED REVEL   201
THEY TOO CAN SEE   • • • • • • •   192 STRAYED REVEL   212
THEY SEE THE CENTAURS   • • • • • • •   192 STRAYED REVEL   223
THEY SEE THE INDIAN   • • • • • • •   193 STRAYED REVEL   235
THEIR MELON-HARVEST TO THE HEART THEY SEE   • • •   193 STRAYED REVEL   239
THEY SEE THE MERCHANTS • • • • • • •   193 STRAYED REVEL   244
THEY SEE THE HEROES   • • • • • • •   193 STRAYED REVEL   254
FOR HIM WHO MUST SEE MANY YEARS • • • •   199 EARLY DEATH   1
YET OH THAT FATE WOULD LET HER SEE   • • • •   202 URANIA   V 17
TO SEE THIS LINE OF SAND-HILLS RUN   • • • •   204 CALAIS SANDS   V   2
TO SEE TOWRD ARDRES GOLDEN FIELD   • • • •   204 CALAIS SANDS   V   5
AND SEE UPON THE LOVELY SAND   • • • • •   204 CALAIS SANDS   V 10
AND SEE THEE PASS UNCONSCIOUS BY   • • • •   205 CALAIS SANDS   V 28
TIS NOT TO SEE THE WORLD   • • • • •   212 GROWING OLD   16
BUT SEE HIS SHAVEN OPPRESSORS   • • • • •   214 NEW ROME   5
BUT SEE HIS BLACK-COATED GAOLERS   • • • •   214 NEW ROME   V   5
SEE YE THE TROUBLE BELOW   • • • • •   216 LORDS MESSENGER   2
SEE YE THE BATTLE BELOW • • • • •   216 LORDS MESSENGER   V   2
SEE PULSING WITH THE FIRST-BORN STAR   • • • •   218 BACCHANALIA 1   17
SEE THE WILD MAENADS   • • • • • •   218 BACCHANALIA 1   28
SEE THROUGH THE QUIET LAND   • • • • •   218 BACCHANALIA 1   32
SEE THROUGH THE QUIET CORN   • • • • •   218 BACCHANALIA 1   V 32
SEE ON THE CUMBERD PLAIN   • • • • •   220 BACCHANALIA 2   33
SEE ON THEIR GLOWING CHEEKS   • • • • •   221 BACCHANALIA 2   61
IN LESSINGS TRACK AND TRIED TO SEE   • • • • •   221 EPILOG LAOCOON   5

SEE   (CONTINUED)

THEY SEE ALL ROUND A WILDERNESS	226 EPILOG LAOCOON	176
SEE SUCH A PROPHET AGAIN	229 YOUTH OF NATURE	47
SEE THEM TO-NIGHT WHERE THEY STAND	232 YOUTH OF MAN	18
AND THEY SEE FOR A MOMENT	235 YOUTH OF MAN	108
HELEN WILL COME UPON THE WALL TO SEE	236 PALLADIUM	16
I SAY UNTO YOU SEE YE KEEP THAT LAW	237 PROGRESS	7
I SAY UNTO YOU SEE THAT YOUR SOULS LIVE	237 PROGRESS	23
UNDISTRACTED BY THE SIGHTS THEY SEE	240 SELF-DEPENDENCE	18
THESE ATTAIN THE MIGHTY LIFE YOU SEE	240 SELF-DEPENDENCE	28
SEE ON HER FACE A GLOW IS SPREAD	241 MORALITY	21
REPELLENT AS THE WORLD BUT SEE	242 SUMMER NIGHT	5
LIKE ALL THE OTHER MEN I SEE	243 SUMMER NIGHT	36
A WORLD ABOVE MANS HEAD TO LET HIM SEE	244 SUMMER NIGHT	87
AND THAT WE SHOULD NOT SEE	246 BURIED LIFE	41
NOR BRING TO SEE ME CEASE TO LIVE	250 WISH	17
MOVED TO THE WINDOW NEAR AND SEE	250 WISH	31
WHO CAN SEE THE GREEN EARTH ANY MORE	252 FUTURE	27
CHANGING AND SHOT AS THE SIGHTS WHICH WE SEE	253 FUTURE	57
SEE AN ENNOBLING SIGHT	253 FUTURE	67
AND ROUND GREEN ROOTS AND YELLOWING STALKS I SEE	255 SCHOLAR-GIPSY	24
PITCH THEIR SMOKED TENTS AND EVERY BUSH YOU SEE	258 SCHOLAR-GIPSY	113
FOR WHOM EACH YEAR WE SEE	260 SCHOLAR-GIPSY	176
SEE TIS NO FOOT OF UNFAMILIAR MEN	263 THYRSIS	7
BUT THYRSIS NEVER MORE WE SWAINS SHALL SEE	265 THYRSIS	77
SEE HIM COME BACK AND CUT A SMOOTHER REED	265 THYRSIS	78
STOOD WITH SUSPENDED SCYTHE TO SEE US PASS	266 THYRSIS	129
I SEE HER VEIL DRAW SOFT ACROSS THE DAY	266 THYRSIS	133
INTO YON FARTHER FIELD TIS DONE AND SEE	267 THYRSIS	157
I TROW THE MIGHTY MOTHER DOTH NOT SEE	268 THYRSIS	179
INTO YON FURTHER FIELD TIS DONE AND SEE	267 THYRSIS	V 157
HIS FEET TO SEE THE LURID FLOW	271 MEMORIAL VERSES	31
SEE LOW ABOVE THE TIDE AT FLOOD	274 STANZAS CARNAC	26
I SEE THE SMOKE-CROWND VESSEL COME	276 SOUTHERN NIGHT	30
THE MIEN OF YOUTH WE USED TO SEE	276 SOUTHERN NIGHT	38
AND SEE ALL SIGHTS FROM POLE TO POLE	277 SOUTHERN NIGHT	69
I SEE THEM STILL I SEE THEM NOW	279 SOUTHERN NIGHT	127
I SEE THEM STILL I SEE THEM NOW	279 SOUTHERN NIGHT	127
SHALL ALWAYS SEE	279 SOUTHERN NIGHT	128
SHE WILL NOT SEE HER COUNTRY LOSE	282 HAWORTH CHURCH	V
TO SNATCH AND WIELD IT WILL NOT SEE	282 HAWORTH CHURCH	V
SEE IN THE DESOLATE HOUSE	283 HAWORTH CHURCH	V
ANOTHER GRIEF I SEE	283 HAWORTH CHURCH	V
IS THE RACE OF MEN WHOM I SEE	290 RUGBY CHAPEL	150
SEE IN THE ROCKS OF THE WORLD	291 RUGBY CHAPEL	171
SEE IN THE MAY-AFTERNOON	297 HEINES GRAVE	152
THOU STANDEST GAZING TO SEE	297 HEINES GRAVE	169
SEE FRAGRANT HERBS ARE FLOWERING THERE	301 GRANDE CHARTR	56
AND WAIT TO SEE THE FUTURE COME	303 GRANDE CHARTR	118
SAVE THEE TO SEE THEIR WAY	307 OBERMANN	48
AND HEALING SIGHTS TO SEE	309 OBERMANN	112
WILT NOT IF THOU CANST SEE ME NOW	310 OBERMANN	139
THERE WITHOUT ANGER THOU WILT SEE	311 OBERMANN	157
SEE IN THE BLUE PROFOUND	313 OBERMANN	32
COULD SEE THE MOTHER WITH HER CHILD	317 OBERMANN MORE	157
SEE I MAKE ALL THINGS NEW	320 OBERMANN MORE	232
AND SEE THE SUN IS RISEN	322 OBERMANN MORE	284
WHEN I COULD HOURLY SEE	315 OBERMANN MORE	V 154
COULD SEE THE MOTHER WITH THE CHILD	317 OBERMANN MORE	V 157
SOFTLY STAND BACK SEE TO THESE PALACE GATES	331 MEROPE	51
IT LIVES AND WHILE I SEE THE LIGHT WILL LIVE	334 MEROPE	121
DO TWENTY YEARS WEAR OUT AND SEE EXPIRE	335 MEROPE	180
THOU STANDEST OUT I SEE REPELLEST PEACE	341 MEROPE	354
NIGHT AND DAY SEE THEM FALL	346 MEROPE	502
TO SEE ANOTHER MIGHTY VICTIM BLEED	349 MEROPE	563
TO SEE SECURE TO LIVE WITH THOSE SHE LOVES	349 MEROPE	566
LOOK UP AND SEE THY FRIENDS WHO COMFORT THEE	363 MEROPE	947
TIS SO TIS SO ALAS FOR SEE THE PROOF	364 MEROPE	978
SUSPICION GRAVE I SEE BUT NO FIRM PROOF	365 MEROPE	994
WHAT DO I SEE A MURDERER AT DEATHS DOOR	374 MEROPE	1195
BEAR WITNESS SEE MARK WELL ON WHAT A HEAD	377 MEROPE	1223
WE SEE DEAR MISTRESS AND WE SAY THE GODS	377 MEROPE	1225
THAT WORD IT KILLS ME I SEE	378 MEROPE	1243
THOU WILT DESTROY I SEE THYSELF AND US	385 MEROPE	1405
AND ONLY BAD MEN JOY TO SEE UNDONE	386 MEROPE	1429
INSCRUTABLE AS EVER SEE IT KEEPS	403 MEROPE	1967
SOFTLY STAND BACK SEE TOWRD THE PALACE GATES	331 MEROPE	V 51
AND SEE TO MEET THEM THAT ONE GRIEF-PLUNGED FORM	331 MEROPE	V 56
SUSPICION GRAVE I SEE BUT NO CLEAR PROOF	365 MEROPE	V 994
HE LOVES THEE BUT HE MUST NOT SEE THEE NOW	409 EMPEDOCLES I 1	77
AND HOLDS MEN MUTE TO SEE WHERE IT WILL RISE	410 EMPEDOCLES I 1	114
ENOUGH OF THIS I SEE THE LITTER WIND	411 EMPEDOCLES I 1	163
SEE HOW THE GIANT SPIRES OF YELLOW BLOOM	412 EMPEDOCLES I 2	4
AND HE TREATS DOUBT THE BEST WHO TRIES TO SEE LEAST ILL	415 EMPEDOCLES I 2	101
MAYST SEE WITHOUT DISMAY	416 EMPEDOCLES I 2	110
FILL THEE TO SEE OUR TIME	416 EMPEDOCLES I 2	113
THROUGH WHICH TO SEE LESS CLEAR	419 EMPEDOCLES I 2	205
GRANT THAT THE WORLD WERE FULL OF GODS WE CANNOT SEE	421 EMPEDOCLES I 2	286
WE SEE IN BLANK DISMAY	424 EMPEDOCLES I 2	363
NOR DO THEY SEE THEIR COUNTRY NOR THE PLACE	427 EMPEDOCLES I 2	439

SEE   (CONTINUED)

THEY HAD STAYD LONG ENOUGH TO SEE	427	EMPEDOCLES I 2	444
AND I SHALL DOUBTLESS SEE THEM ALL AGAIN	428	EMPEDOCLES I 2	476
FILL THEE TO SEE OUR DAY	416	EMPEDOCLES I 2	V 113
FILL THEE TO SEE OUR WORLD	416	EMPEDOCLES I 2	V 113
THROUGH WHICH TO SEE LESS PLAIN	419	EMPEDOCLES I 2	V 205
WHO STRIVE TO SEE WITH EYES	426	EMPEDOCLES I 2	V 409
OH THAT FATE HAD LET ME SEE	432	EMPEDOCLES II	125
NOT TO SEE APOLLOS SCORN	434	EMPEDOCLES II	189
TO SEE IF WE WILL POISE OUR LIFE AT LAST	440	EMPEDOCLES II	369
TO SEE IF WE WILL NOW AT LAST BE TRUE	440	EMPEDOCLES II	370
DO THY BLOODSHOT EYES STILL SEE	430	EMPEDOCLES II	V 55
FOR MIST CAN SCARCELY SEE	444	WESTMIN ABBEY	22
WHAT HAD OUR ARTHUR GAIND TO STOP AND SEE	448	WESTMIN ABBEY	154
TO LIVE AND SEE ARISE	449	WESTMIN ABBEY	157
FOR MIST CAN HARDLY SEE	444	WESTMIN ABBEY	V 22
WE SEE THE FLAPS OF THY LARGE EARS	451	GEISTS GRAVE	49
SHALL SEE THY GRAVE UPON THE GRASS	452	GEISTS GRAVE	75
POOR MATTHIAS SEE THY END	457	POOR MATTHIAS	173
STILL STILL I SEE THE FIGURE SMART	460	KAISER DEAD	49
I SEE THE TAIL LIKE BRACELET TWIRLD	460	KAISER DEAD	55
WHERE ALL WE SEE OR DO OR HEAR OR SAY	464	ALARIC AT ROME	47
YEA THOUGH HAND TOUCH THEE NOT NOR EYE SHOULD SEE	470	ALARIC AT ROME	209
ALL WONDROUS DEEDS THE COMING DAYS SHOULD SEE	475	CROMWELL	139
SEE THE WIFE OF HECTOR THAT GREAT PRE-EMINENT CAPTAIN		HOMER TRANS	33
SEE THAT YE BRING YOUR MASTER HOME TO THE HOST		HOMER TRANS	40
OF THE ARGIVES			
OF THEIR CLOISTER SEE THEY GLIDE		META CLOISTER	6
SEE ONE FIGURE QUITS THE MAZES		META CLOISTER	9
NOTHING BUT THAT WE SEE IT WHAT RESPECT		LUCRETIUS 5	8

SEED

FOR DOUBLE-MINDED EVER WAS THE SEED	112	BALDER DEAD 2	271
BUT FROM THE TRAITOROUS SEED OF LOK THEY COME	120	BALDER DEAD 3	234
AND ODIN AND HIS SONS THE SEED OF HEAVEN	127	BALDER DEAD 3	488
SELF-SPRINGING AND A SEED OF MAN PRESERVED	128	BALDER DEAD 3	530
YES BUT HIS SEED STILL WISER-COUNSELLD	344	MEROPE	449
WHICH HE THE SEED OF HERACLES DRAGGD ON	356	MEROPE	770
HE BEARS THE SEED OF RUIN IN HIMSELF	359	MEROPE	856
WHEN THE SEED OF LYCAON	391	MEROPE	1603
YES BUT HIS SONS SEED WISER-COUNSELLD	344	MEROPE	V 449
SEED-TIME AND HARVEST	436	EMPEDOCLES II	254
CAKE WE OFFERD SUGAR SEED	455	POOR MATTHIAS	115
XANTHUS AND BALIUS BOTH YE FAR-FAMD SEED OF PODARGA		HOMER TRANS	39

SEEDS

THE SEEDS OF GODLIKE POWER ARE IN US STILL	4	EMERSONS ESSAYS	12
STROWN WITH DARK SEEDS	187	STRAYED REVEL	58
WITH LONG PLUMES AND SOFT BROWN SEEDS	434	EMPEDOCLES II	175

SEEING

SEEING THIS VALE THIS EARTH WHEREON WE DREAM	7	REP FRIEND CONT	5
THEN AS NOW A POWER BEYOND OUR SEEING	210	SELF-DECEPTION	11
AND PRAY THE GODS AND PRAY THE ALL-SEEING SUN	349	MEROPE	570
HE SLEEPS SLEEPS CALM O YE ALL-SEEING GODS	372	MEROPE	1153

SEEK

SEEK HER AT THE CHURCH OF BROU	15	CHURCH BROU 1	84
SHALL I SEEK THAT I MAY SCORN HER	35	NEW SIRENS	271
WITH EYES WHICH SEEK THINE EYES THOU DOST CONVERSE	41	GIPSY CHILD	V 15
FOR SO DID KING AFRASIAB BID ME SEEK	62	SOHRAB RUSTUM	38
I SEEK ONE MAN ONE MAN AND ONE ALONE	62	SOHRAB RUSTUM	49
TO SEEK OUT RUSTUM SEEK HIM NOT THROUGH FIGHT	63	SOHRAB RUSTUM	75
TO SEEK OUT RUSTUM SEEK HIM NOT THROUGH FIGHT	63	SOHRAB RUSTUM	75
SEEK HIM IN PEACE AND CARRY TO HIS ARMS	63	SOHRAB RUSTUM	76
BUT FAR HENCE SEEK HIM FOR HE IS NOT HERE	63	SOHRAB RUSTUM	78
TO SEEK THY FATHER NOT SEEK SINGLE FIGHTS	63	SOHRAB RUSTUM	90
TO SEEK THY FATHER NOT SEEK SINGLE FIGHTS	63	SOHRAB RUSTUM	90
HIM WILL I SEEK AND CARRY TO HIS EAR	66	SOHRAB RUSTUM	180
MY FATHER WHOM I SEEK THROUGH ALL THE WORLD	77	SOHRAB RUSTUM	554
RUSTUM SHOULD SEEK THE BOY TO TRAIN IN ARMS	79	SOHRAB RUSTUM	611
YET IF HE SEEK TO FLY GIVE WAY	91	SICK KING BOKH	115
KNOWING THE GOD THEY WENT TO SEEK HOW DEAR	107	BALDER DEAD 2	77
SEEK TO AFFLICT OUR FOES WITH PETTY PANGS	111	BALDER DEAD 2	229
EVEN HERE THEY SEEK THEE OUT IN HELAS REALM	112	BALDER DEAD 2	256
SINCE THEN I VAINLY SEEK HIM THROUGH THE WORLD	116	BALDER DEAD 3	109
CLOSE MINE EYES THEN SEEK THE PRINCESS ISEULT	145	TRISTRAM 2	93
RISE GO HENCE AND SEEK THE PRINCESS ISEULT	145	TRISTRAM 2	V 93
THEY SEEK TO FIND IN THOSE THEY LOVE	178	FAREWELL	23
DO YOU SEEK COUNSEL OF THE GODS	198	FRAG DEJANEIRA	6
TO WOO THY SMILE TO SEEK THINE EYE	205	CALAIS SANDS	26
TO CATCH THY SMILE TO SEEK THINE EYE	205	CALAIS SANDS	V 26
ENDS WE SEEK WE NEVER SHALL ATTAIN	210	SELF-DECEPTION	26
WHOSE EYE THOU WAST AFRAID TO SEEK	241	MORALITY	20
WHOSE EYE THOU WERT AFRAID TO SEEK	241	MORALITY	V 20
SHY TO ILLUMINE AND I SEEK IT TOO	268	THYRSIS	202
APPROACH FOR WHAT WE SEEK IS HERE	300	GRANDE CHARTR	25
I SEEK THESE ANCHORITES NOT IN RUTH	301	GRANDE CHARTR	77
TO SEEK A DRAUGHT TO SLAKE THY THIRST	316	OBERMANN MORE	119
GO SEEK IT IN THY SOUL	316	OBERMANN MORE	120
DIDST SEEK THE SOLITARY MAN	322	OBERMANN MORE	V 279

SEEK   (CONTINUED)
        GO THOU INTO THE CITY AND SEEK OUT   • •   • •   331 MEROPE   37
        SEEK THIS REVIVE UNITE IT GIVE IT HOPE • •   • •   331 MEROPE   45
        ALL THIS I BEAR FOR WHAT I SEEK I KNOW • •   • •   333 MEROPE   100
        PEACE PEACE IS WHAT I SEEK AND PUBLIC CALM • • • •   333 MEROPE   101
        TOO WIDE AT VARIANCE WITH THE PEACE I SEEK • • • •   333 MEROPE   107
        WILL I SEEK TIDINGS TAKE THE WHILE THIS WORD • •   368 MEROPE   1078
        ARCAS SEEK OUT MY UNCLE LAIAS NOW   • •   • •   379 MEROPE   1260
        YET EXCULPATION NEEDS IT IF I SEEK   • • • • •   387 MEROPE   1454

SEEKER
        DROP BY AND LEAVE ITS SEEKER STILL UNTIRED • • • • 268 THYRSIS   207

SEEKING
        SEEKING CEILED CHAMBERS AND A PALACE-HALL • • • •   27 NEW SIRENS   40
        COME YOU SAY THE BRAIN IS SEEKING   • • • • •   28 NEW SIRENS   77
        CAME SEEKING RUSTUM AND DEFYING FORTH   • • • •   70 SOHRAB RUSTUM   310
        WENT SEEKING RUSTUM AND DEFYING FORTH   • • • •   70 SOHRAB RUSTUM   V 310
        SEEKING A PREY UNTO HIS HAND   • • • • •   93 SICK KING BOKH   164
        IN SEEKING WHAT WE SHALL NOT FIND   • • • • •   179 FAREWELL   52

SEEKS
        WHEN SOHRAB DARES OUR BRAVEST FORTH AND SEEKS   • •   68 SOHRAB RUSTUM   244
        THEE MOST OF ALL AND THOU WHOM MOST HE SEEKS   • •   68 SOHRAB RUSTUM   245
        SINCE THEN SHE SEEKS HIM AND WEEPS TEARS OF GOLD • • 116 BALDER DEAD 3   95
        A FUGITIVE AND GRACIOUS LIGHT HE SEEKS   • • • •   268 THYRSIS   201
        WHAT SEEKS ON THIS MOUNTAIN   • • • • • • •   442 EMPEDOCLES II   451

SEEM
        YET WHEN I MUSE ON WHAT LIFE IS I SEEM   • • • •   7 REP FRIEND CONT   1
        I TOO BUT SEEM   • • • • • • • • • • • • •   46 IN UTRUMQUE PAR   42
        THOUGH BEARABLE SEEM HARDLY WORTH   • • • • •   60 RESIGNATION   263
        SEEM TO BEAR RATHER THAN REJOICE   • • • • •   60 RESIGNATION   270
        KEEP HIS EYELIDS LET HIM SEEM   • • • • •   133 TRISTRAM 1   106
        TILL THEY RULE IT TILL HE SEEM • • • • • • •   136 TRISTRAM 1   184
        TO MAKE OUR FORMER PLEASURES ALL SEEM STALE   • •   153 TRISTRAM 3   126
        THIS TOO CAN CHANGE US WHOLLY AND MAKE SEEM   • •   153 TRISTRAM 3   131
        TO SEEM AS FREE FROM PRIDE AND GUILE   • • • • •   179 FAREWELL   63
        ONCE MORE AND ONCE MORE SEEM TO MAKE RESOUND • •   201 PHILOMELA   25
        THE BURIED STREAM AND SEEM TO BE   • • • • •   246 BURIED LIFE   42
        AND I MYSELF SEEM HALF TO KNOW THY LOOKS   • • • •   257 SCHOLAR-GIPSY   62
        FORGIVE ME MAIDENS IF I SEEM TOO SLACK   • • • •   348 MEROPE   548
        THAT WILDEST VISIONS STILL SHOULD LOVELIEST SEEM • • 470 ALARIC AT ROME   213

SEEMD
        FIRST A LIGHT CLOUD OF HORSE TARTARS THEY SEEMD • •   65 SOHRAB RUSTUM   137
        FOR VERY YOUNG HE SEEMD TENDERLY REARD   • • • •   70 SOHRAB RUSTUM   313
        SO SLENDER SOHRAB SEEMD SO SOFTLY REARD   • • • •   70 SOHRAB RUSTUM   318
        ALL TIE WITH ALL BESIDE SEEMD VAIN AND CHEAP   • •   173 MONICAS PRAYER   10
        AND LONG THE WAY APPEARS WHICH SEEMD SO SHORT   • •   267 THYRSIS   141
        YEARS IN NUMBER IT SEEMD   • • • • • • •   281 HAWORTH CHURCH   27
        SEEMD BUT A DREAM OF THE HEART • • • • • • •   290 RUGBY CHAPEL   151
        SEEMD BUT A CRY OF DESIRE   • • • • • • •   290 RUGBY CHAPEL   152
        SEEMD PUISSANT AND ALIVE   • • • • • • • •   315 OBERMANN MORE   90
        THE PRINCE AT START SEEMD SAD BUT HIS REGARD   • •   355 MEROPE   733
        AND SEEMD TO MUSE AWHILE THEN RAISED HIS EYES   • •   402 MEROPE   1913
        TILL THEN WE ALL SEEMD STONE BUT THEN A CRY   • •   402 MEROPE   1930
        FOR FROM ALL SIDES A DELUGE AS IT SEEMD   • • • •   402 MEROPE   1937
        AND TRULY ONE WHO SEES WHAT SEEMD SO STRONG   • •   402 MEROPE   1943
        SEEMD TO COME TRUE AT LAST O ABBEY OLD   • • • •   446 WESTMIN ABBEY   73
        IT SEEMD A CHILD OF LIGHT DID BRING THE DOWER   • •   446 WESTMIN ABBEY   74
        SEEMD SURGING THE VIRGILIAN CRY   • • • • • •   450 GEISTS GRAVE   15
        DWELT IT SEEMD IN SYMPATHY   • • • • • • •   454 POOR MATTHIAS   52

SEEMED
        SO SCORNFUL SEEMED THAT SMILE SO STRANGE SO FULL • •   EMERSONS ESSAYS V 9

SEEMING
        DWELT WITH MERE OUTWARD SEEMING HE WITHIN • • • •   12 MYCERINUS   108
        O SEEMING SOLE TO AWAKE THY SUN-BATHED HEAD   • •   45 IN UTRUMQUE PAR   29
        REQUITE HIM WORDS SEVERE FOR SEEMING KIND • • • •   349 MEROPE   551
        CUT SHORT THY TRIUMPH SEEMING AT ITS HEIGHT   • •   395 MEROPE   1742
        MISLED BY SEEMING   • • • • • • • • • • •   398 MEROPE   1796
        ALL THOU AUGUREST HERE OF LOVELY SEEMING   • • • •   483 THEKLAS ANSWER   21

SEEMS
        SEEMS IT SO LIGHT A THING THEN AUSTERE POWERS   • •   9 MYCERINUS   31
        SEEMS THERE NO JOY IN DANCES CROWND WITH FLOWERS • •   9 MYCERINUS   33
        LIE STREWN IT SEEMS WHERE THEN THEY LAY   • • • •   55 RESIGNATION   101
        IT SEEMS AS IF IN THEIR DECAY   • • • • • • •   56 RESIGNATION   134
        FROM HELL AND SHALL I TELL THEE HOW HE SEEMS   • •   113 BALDER DEAD 3   7
        HAPLY HE SEEMS AGAIN TO MOVE   • • • • • • •   136 TRISTRAM 1   206
        AND TO HIMSELF HE SEEMS TO SAY • • • • • • •   148 TRISTRAM 2   163
        WHO SEEMS OF MARBLE ON A TOMB   • • • • • • •   148 TRISTRAM 2   167
        SHE SEEMS ONE DYING IN A MASK OF YOUTH   • • • •   151 TRISTRAM 3   75
        SHE IS NOT COLD THOUGH SHE SEEMS SO   • • • • •   201 URANIA   2
        TO ONE ANOTHER FOR THE WORLD WHICH SEEMS   • • • •   211 DOVER BEACH   30
        AND THE CALM MOONLIGHT SEEMS TO SAY   • • • • •   243 SUMMER NIGHT   26
        WHERE INTEREST SEEMS TO HAVE ENJOIND IT TOO   • •   341 MEROPE   364
        INTERPRET THEN FOR WE IT SEEMS ARE DULL   • • • •   365 MEROPE   989

SEEMS   (CONTINUED)
     SEEMS IT LIGHTER MY LOSS • • • • • • • • • •   370 MEROPE   1115
     BROTHER IT SEEMS THY SISTER MUST PRESENT   • • • •   386 MEROPE   1451
     OF DARING EASY AS IT SEEMS WHEN DONE • • • • • •   403 MEROPE   1949
     DID BY THIS STONE IT SEEMS INTEND   • • • • • •   452 GEISTS GRAVE   78
     SEEMS STRANGELY ECHOED BACK BY TONES OF YESTERDAY   464 ALARIC AT ROME   48
     IN SOOTH IT SEEMS A HUNDRED YEAR   • • • • • •   480 HAYSWATER BOAT   35
     TO ME IT SEEMS AS VAIN LUCRETIUS   • • • • • •   LUCRETIUS 3   1
     SOON SEEMS AS TEDIOUS AS EACH TEDIOUS STAGE   • •   LUCRETIUS 6   4
     IT SEEMS AN IDLE THING WHICH COULD NOT LIVE   • •   FRAGMENT 9   1

SEEMST
     FLY BACK MY CHILD AND THOU SEEMST   • • • • • •   377 MEROPE   1229

SEEN
     AND RAYS HER POWERS LIKE SISTER-ISLANDS SEEN   • •   4 BUTLERS SERMONS   9
     CROSSING THE STREAM THE KINE ARE SEEN   • • • •   16 CHURCH BROU 2   10
     HAVE YOU SEEN IT AT THE CLOSING   • • • • • •   33 NEW SIRENS   207
     TOOK THEN ITS ALL-SEEN WAY   • • • • • • • •   45 IN UTRUMQUE PAR   7
     THERE CLIMBING HANGS A FAR-SEEN SIGN • • • • • •   54 RESIGNATION   60
     TO FIND A FATHER THOU HAST NEVER SEEN   • • • •   63 SOHRAB RUSTUM   70
     BOY AS I AM I HAVE SEEN BATTLES TOO • • • •   74 SOHRAB RUSTUM   433
     OH COULD I LIVE TILL I THAT GRIEF HAD SEEN • • •   78 SOHRAB RUSTUM   588
     AND SEEN THE RIVER OF HELMUND AND THE LAKE • • •   83 SOHRAB RUSTUM   751
     NOR SEEN HIS LOFTY HOUSE IN SEISTAN • • • • •   83 SOHRAB RUSTUM   757
     BUT LODGED AMONG MY FATHERS FOES AND SEEN • • •   83 SOHRAB RUSTUM   759
     AND PLANT A FAR-SEEN PILLAR OVER ALL • • • • •   84 SOHRAB RUSTUM   789
     AND PLANT A FAR-SEEN PILLAR OVER ALL • • • • •   84 SOHRAB RUSTUM   804
     HAVE I SEEN REIGNING IN THIS PLACE   • • • • • •   92 SICK KING BOKH   144
     AND TELL THE HEAVEN-BORN GODS HOW THOU HAST SEEN • •   112 BALDER DEAD 2   276
     AND INSTEAD THEREOF IS SEEN   • • • • • • • •   136 TRISTRAM 1   175
     NEVER SURELY HAS BEEN SEEN   • • • • • • • •   131 TRISTRAM 1   V
     AND THE PALE WEAVER THROUGH HIS WINDOWS SEEN   • •   169 EAST LONDON   3
     ALL DAY LONG HAVE SEEN   • • • • • • • • • •   194 STRAYED REVEL   273
     HATH WITHOUT PAIN SEEN NO RELIGION DIE   • • • •   238 PROGRESS   V 39
     UNFREED HAVING SEEN NOTHING STILL UNBLEST   • • •   243 SUMMER NIGHT   50
     THE LIGHTNING-BURSTS IS SEEN   • • • • • • • •   244 SUMMER NIGHT   63
     AND ONLY THE WHITE SHEEP ARE SOMETIMES SEEN   • •   255 SCHOLAR-GIPSY   8
     THAT THE LOST SCHOLAR LONG WAS SEEN TO STRAY   • •   256 SCHOLAR-GIPSY   53
     SEEN BY RARE GLIMPSES PENSIVE AND TONGUE-TIED   •   256 SCHOLAR-GIPSY   54
     AND THEN THEY LAND AND THOU ART SEEN NO MORE   • •   257 SCHOLAR-GIPSY   81
     OFT THROUGH THE DARKENING FIELDS HAVE SEEN THEE ROAM   257 SCHOLAR-GIPSY   84
     THOU HAST BEEN SEEN OR HANGING ON A GATE   • • • •   258 SCHOLAR-GIPSY   103
     BY SOME HIGH CHALET-DOOR AND SEEN   • • • • • •   310 OBERMANN   115
     DIVINELIER IMAGED CLEARER SEEN • • • • • • • •   322 OBERMANN MORE   295
     HE BROUGHT REPORT THAT HIS OWN EYES HAD SEEN   • •   363 MEROPE   958
     O THOU LONG-LOST LONG SEEN IN DREAMS ALONE   • • •   381 MEROPE   1288
     BUT NOW SEEN FACE TO FACE MY ONLY CHILD • • • •   381 MEROPE   1289
     WHAT ONCE-FAMED WRETCH HE HATH SEEN LURKING THERE   396 MEROPE   V1754
     I HAVE SEEN MANY CITIES IN MY TIME   • • • • • •   428 EMPEDOCLES I 2   474
     WHAT SUFFERING IS THERE NOT SEEN   • • • • • •   432 EMPEDOCLES II   100
     THOU HAST SEEN ATOSSA SAGE   • • • • • • • •   453 POOR MATTHIAS   31
     NO METEOR BRIGHTNESS TO BE SEEN AND DIE • • • •   463 ALARIC AT ROME   33

SEER
     THE SEER FROM THE EAST WAS THEN IN LIGHT   • • • •   170 EAST AND WEST   10
     THE SEER FROM THE WEST WAS THEN IN SHADE   • • • •   170 EAST AND WEST   11
     HIS BELOVED ARGIVE SEER WOULD ZEUS RETAIN   • • •   197 FRAG ANTIGONE   82
     AND LIKE THE THEBAN SEER • • • • • • • • • •   229 YOUTH OF NATURE   34
     THE THEBAN SEER TO THE SPRING • • • • • • • •   229 YOUTH OF NATURE   44
     WHERE THOU O SEER ART SET • • • • • • • • •   309 OBERMANN   106

SEES
     SEES GOD NO NEARER • • • • • • • • • • • •   38 STAGIRIUS   15
     WHEN THE MIND WAXING CLEARER SEES GOD NO NEARER • •   38 STAGIRIUS   V 16
     HERE WHENCE THE EYE FIRST SEES FAR DOWN   • • • •   55 RESIGNATION   92
     HE SEES IN SOME GREAT-HISTORIED LAND • • • • • •   56 RESIGNATION   154
     SEES HIS STRONG THOUGHT IN FIERY FLOOD   • • • •   56 RESIGNATION   156
     HE SEES THE GENTLE STIR OF BIRTH   • • • • • •   57 RESIGNATION   170
     HE LEANS UPON A GATE AND SEES • • • • • • • •   57 RESIGNATION   172
     HE SEES THE DROWSY NEW-WAKED CLOWN   • • • • • •   57 RESIGNATION   181
     BEFORE HIM HE SEES LIFE UNROLL • ′ • • • • • •   57 RESIGNATION   189
     NOT DEEP THE POET SEES BUT WIDE • • • • • • •   58 RESIGNATION   214
     AND AS THE WOODMAN SEES A LITTLE SMOKE   • • • •   104 BALDER DEAD 1   335
     THROUGH WHICH A RIVER FLOWS AND SEES BENEATH   • •   113 BALDER DEAD 2   297
     AND TIED HIM IN A YARD AT AUTUMN SEES   • • • •   129 BALDER DEAD 3   560
     SEES SUDDENLY A SPIRE OF FLAME SHOOT UP • • • •   119 BALDER DEAD 3 V
     OF THE CASTLE-PARK ONE SEES   • • • • • • • •   141 TRISTRAM 1   363
     WHEN SHE SEES HER HUMBLED PALE AND STILL   • • • •   144 TRISTRAM 2   60
     HE SEES FLOAT PAST AN ICEBERG WHITE • • • • • •   156 SAINT BRANDAN   15
     HE SEES FLOAT NEAR AN ICEBERG WHITE • • • • •   156 SAINT BRANDAN   V 15
     BUT HE WHO SEES US THROUGH AND THROUGH   • • • •   179 FAREWELL   46
     AND SEES NOT THAT THE SACRED DROPS   • • • • • •   213 PROGRESS POESY   7
     SEES THE CONTRITION OF AGE   • • • • • • • •   232 YOUTH OF MAN   16
     AND HEARS ITS WINDING MURMUR AND HE SEES   • • • •   247 BURIED LIFE   89
     AS WHAT HE SEES IS SO HAVE HIS THOUGHTS BEEN   • •   252 FUTURE   7
     WHETHER HE FIRST SEES LIGHT   • • • • • • • •   252 FUTURE   13
     SEES THEE NOR STOPS HIS MEAL NOR FEARS AT ALL   •   258 SCHOLAR-GIPSY   117
     HIS WHO UNWILLINGLY SEES • • • • • • • • • •   291 RUGBY CHAPEL   166
     THE CAPITAL OF PLEASURE SEES   • • • • • • • •   312 OBERMANN   179

SEES   (CONTINUED)
            AND TRULY ONE WHO SEES WHAT SEEMD SO STRONG   •   •   402 MEROPE   1943
            ONE SEES ONES FOOTPRINTS CRUSHD IN THE WET GRASS •   •   406 EMPEDOCLES I 1   14
            AND NEVER SEES A WHOLE •   •   •   •   •   •   •   • 415 EMPEDOCLES I 2   85
            SINCE HE SEES NOTHING CLEAR •   •   •   •   •   •   • 415 EMPEDOCLES I 2   90
            SEES ALL HER SONS AT PLAY •   •   •   •   •   •   •   • 421 EMPEDOCLES I 2   258
            SEES MAN CONTROL THE WIND •   •   •   •   •   •   •   • 421 EMPEDOCLES I 2   259
            SURE ONLY THAT YOUR MIND SEES ALL THINGS WHICH BEFAL • 423 EMPEDOCLES I 2   346
            WHERE HE SEES NOTHING CLEAR •   •   •   •   •   •   • 415 EMPEDOCLES I 2   V   90
            THE OLYMPIAN COUNCIL SEES •   •   •   •   •   •   •   • 431 EMPEDOCLES II   70
            WHOM THE SUMMER EVENING SEES •   •   •   •   •   •   • 434 EMPEDOCLES II   181
            AND SOME MAN MAY SAY AS HE LOOKS AND SEES THY   HOMER TRANS   32
                TEARS FALLING
            AND REND HIS HEART WHO SEES THEM •   •   •   •   •   • LUCRETIUS 2   17

SEEST
            BUT COME THOU SEEST THIS GREAT HOST OF MEN •   •   •   •   84 SOHRAB RUSTUM   778
            FOR THESE THOU SEEST ARE UNMOVED •   •   •   •   •   • 149 TRISTRAM 2   191
            THOU WHO SEEST US DIE •   •   •   •   •   •   •   •   • 232 YOUTH OF MAN   5
            SEEST US CHANGE WHILE WE LIVE •   •   •   •   •   •   • 232 YOUTH OF MAN   6
            SEEST OUR DREAMS ONE BY ONE •   •   •   •   •   •   • 232 YOUTH OF MAN   7
            SEEST OUR ERRORS DEPART •   •   •   •   •   •   •   • 232 YOUTH OF MAN   8
            OF OUR NIGHT-JOURNEY AND THOU SEEST THY HOME •   •   • 330 MEROPE   2
            AND SEEST MY STRIPLING HUNTER THERE AFIELD •   •   •   • 349 MEROPE   573
            AND WISDOM NOW THOU SEEST DEMANDS IT TOO •   •   •   • 390 MEROPE   1573

SEETHING
            HIS EYE PLUNGED DOWN THE SEETHING STRIFE •   •   •   • 270 MEMORIAL VERSES   V 25
            THE SEETHING FOAM •   •   •   •   •   •   •   •   •   • 276 SOUTHERN NIGHT   32

SEINE
            THE BLUE SEINE ROLLS HER WAVE •   •   •   •   •   •   • 312 OBERMANN   178
            THE SEINE CONDUCTS HER WAVE •   •   •   •   •   •   • 312 OBERMANN   V 178
            AT SEVRES BY THE SEINE •   •   •   •   •   •   •   •   • 321 OBERMANN MORE   268

SEIRIOL
            SEIRIOL THE BRIGHT KYBI THE DARK MEN SAID •   •   •   • 170 EAST AND WEST   9

SEISTAN
            IN SEISTAN WITH ZAL HIS FATHER OLD •   •   •   •   •   •   63 SOHRAB RUSTUM   82
            AND THOU HAST TROD THE SANDS OF SEISTAN •   •   •   •   83 SOHRAB RUSTUM   750
            NOR SEEN HIS LOFTY HOUSE IN SEISTAN •   •   •   •   •   83 SOHRAB RUSTUM   757
            BUT CARRY ME WITH THEE TO SEISTAN •   •   •   •   •   •   84 SOHRAB RUSTUM   784
            AND CARRY THEE AWAY TO SEISTAN •   •   •   •   •   •   •   84 SOHRAB RUSTUM   799
            AND I NOT THOU BE BORNE TO SEISTAN •   •   •   •   •   •   85 SOHRAB RUSTUM   820

SEIZED
            AND RUSTUM SEIZED HIS CLUB WHICH NONE BUT HE   •   •   73 SOHRAB RUSTUM   408
            AND THEY STOOD WIDE WITH HORROR AND HE SEIZED   •   •   81 SOHRAB RUSTUM   699
            THEN RUSTUM SEIZED HIS CLUB WHICH NONE BUT HE   •   •   73 SOHRAB RUSTUM   V 408
            WELL HE HATH DONE WHO HATH SEIZED HAPPINESS   •   • 195 FRAG ANTIGONE   1
            FOR RIGOROUS TEACHERS SEIZED MY YOUTH •   •   •   •   • 301 GRANDE CHARTR   67
            SEIZED HE ESCAPES AND NEXT I FIND HIM HERE •   •   •   • 364 MEROPE   983

SELDOM
            IN HEAVEN WAS SELDOM PARTED FROM MY SIDE •   •   •   • 126 BALDER DEAD 3   460
            NOW SELDOM COME I SINCE I CAME WITH HIM •   •   •   • 263 THYRSIS   25
            SELDOM AND FAINTLY THE DEPTH •   •   •   •   •   •   • 282 HAWORTH CHURCH   V

SELECT
            SHALL WE SELECT THAN POLYPHONTES WHAT   •   •   •   • 390 MEROPE   1570

SELECTED
            TO SELF-SELECTED GOOD •   •   •   •   •   •   •   •   • 196 FRAG ANTIGONE   29

SELF
            SELF-SCHOOLD SELF-SCANND SELF-HONOURD SELF-SECURE   3 SHAKESPEARE   10
            SELF-SCHOOLD SELF-SCANND SELF-HONOURD SELF-SECURE   3 SHAKESPEARE   10
            SELF-SCHOOLD SELF-SCANND SELF-HONOURD SELF-SECURE   3 SHAKESPEARE   10
            SELF-SCHOOLD SELF-SCANND SELF-HONOURD SELF-SECURE   3 SHAKESPEARE   10
            OF YOUTH SELF-GOVERND AT THE FEET OF LAW •   •   •   •   9 MYCERINUS   10
            MERE PHANTOMS OF MANS SELF-TORMENTING HEART •   •   •   9 MYCERINUS   25
            WHEN THE DUPED SOUL SELF-MASTERD CLAIMS ITS MEED •   •   9 MYCERINUS   28
            FROM THIS POOR PRESENT SELF WHICH I AM NOW •   •   •   • 37 YOUTHS AGIT   2
            STAND MUTE SELF-CENTRED STERN AND DREAM NO MORE •   •   42 GIPSY CHILD   32
            OH WHEN MOST SELF-EXALTED MOST ALONE •   •   •   •   •   46 IN UTRUMQUE PAR   36
            AND PROUD SELF-SEVERANCE FROM THEM WERE DISEASE •   •   46 IN UTRUMQUE PAR   V 39
            WHOM LABOURS SELF-ORDAIND ENTHRALL •   •   •   •   •   •   52 RESIGNATION   14
            ONCE MORE WE TREAD THIS SELF-SAME ROAD •   •   •   •   •   55 RESIGNATION   86
            THE SELF-SAME SHADOWS NOW AS THEN •   •   •   •   •   •   55 RESIGNATION   98
            TO-MORROW ON THE SELF-SAME PLAN •   •   •   •   •   •   •   56 RESIGNATION   141
            THE MORROW AT THE SELF-SAME HOUR •   •   •   •   •   •   90 SICK KING BOKH   93
            SELF-SPRINGING AND A SEED OF MAN PRESERVED •   •   •   • 128 BALDER DEAD 3   530
            BREATHING SELF-MURDER FRENZY SPITE •   •   •   •   •   • 157 SAINT BRANDAN   31
            SELF-SWAYD OUR FEELINGS EBB AND SWELL •   •   •   •   • 180 ISOLATION MARG   11
            TO SELF-SELECTED GOOD •   •   •   •   •   •   •   •   • 196 FRAG ANTIGONE   29
            PROUD IGNORANT SELF-ADORED YOU LIVE ALONE •   •   •   • 198 FRAG DEJANEIRA   7
            IN THIS SELF-SAME GARDEN AND SAID •   •   •   •   •   • 233 YOUTH OF MAN   25
            BUT KEEP HIM SELF-IMMERSED PREOCCUPIED •   •   •   •   • 237 PROGRESS   19
            WHICH HAS NOT CRIED TO SUNK SELF-WEARY MAN •   •   •   • 238 PROGRESS   43
            FOR SELF-POISED THEY LIVE NOR PINE WITH NOTING •   • 240 SELF-DEPENDENCE   23

SELF   (CONTINUED)
      WHY SELF-POISED THEY LIVE NOR PINE WITH NOTING   • •   240 SELF-DEPENDENCE V 23
      ASK HOW SHE VIEWD THY SELF-CONTROL   • • • •   241 MORALITY   15
      HIS GENUINE SELF AND FORCE HIM TO OBEY   • • • •   246 BURIED LIFE   36
      OUR HIDDEN SELF AND WHAT WE SAY AND DO   • • • •   247 BURIED LIFE   65
      BAFFLED UNKNOWN SELF-CONSUMED   • • • •   285 HAWORTH CHURCH   98
      ALONE SELF-POISED HENCEFORWARD MAN   • • • •   319 OBERMANN MORE   V 185
      SELF-POISED CLEAR-MINDED HENCEFORTH MAN • • •   319 OBERMANN MORE   V 185
      ALBEIT WITH LIPS UNAPT TO SELF-EXCUSE   • • • •   336 MEROPE   199
      PATIENCE WAS THENCEFORTH SELF DESTRUCTION I •   338 MEROPE   266
      I SELF-DEFENCE AND RIGHTEOUS EXECUTION   • • •   338 MEROPE   277
      WHO SELF-EXCULPATES LEND TO FOULEST DEEDS • •   338 MEROPE   279
      IMPERIOUS SELF-ASSERTING VIOLENCE   • • • •   353 MEROPE   689
      O SELF-WILL RECKLESSLY INDULGED   • • • •   398 MEROPE   1801
      BY SADNESS AND SELF-WILL   • • • • • •   425 EMPEDOCLES I 2   395
      AND DRIED ITS SELF-SUFFICING FOUNT OF JOY •   429 EMPEDOCLES II   22
      THAT SELF-HELPING SON OF EARTH   • • • •   432 EMPEDOCLES II   103
      THE SELF-HELPING SON OF EARTH   • • • • •   432 EMPEDOCLES II   V 103
      OR JUST THY LITTLE SELF RESTORE   • • • •   450 GEISTS GRAVE   28
      OER HUMBLED PRIDE AND SELF-REPROACHING WOE • • •   462 ALARIC AT ROME   4
      SHARP SENSE OF DEEP SELF-IGNORANCE FEAR OF LOOKS • •   LUCRETIUS 2   14

SELFISH
      BY SELFISH OCCUPATION PLOT AND PLAN   • • • • • •   7 REP FRIEND CONT   11
      OR SELFISH LUST OF PERSONAL POWER   • • • • •   353 MEROPE   661

SELL
      OUR FREEDOM FOR A LITTLE BREAD WE SELL   • • • •   169 WORLDLY PLACE   5

SELLERS
      WHERE THROUGH THE SELLERS BOOTHS THE SLAVES   • •   88 SICK KING BOKH   18

SELVES
      HE WOULD HAVE SAVED YOU FROM YOUR FURIOUS SELVES • •   339 MEROPE   299
      TO OUR OWN ONLY TRUE DEEP-BURIED SELVES   • • • •   440 EMPEDOCLES II   371

SEMBLANCE
      WHEN SEMBLANCE OF IT FAINT LIKE MINE   • • • • •   158 SAINT BRANDAN   V 55
      IF SEMBLANCE OF IT FAINT LIKE MINE   • • • • •   158 SAINT BRANDAN   V 55
      IN OUTWARD SEMBLANCE HE MUST GIVE   • • • • •   223 EPILOG LAOCOON   57

SEND
      STILL DOTH FOR LABOURERS SEND   • • • • • •   47 WORLD QUIETIST   14
      TO US FAIN THEREFORE SEND THEE HENCE IN PEACE • •   63 SOHRAB RUSTUM   89
      A SON SO FAMED SO BRAVE TO SEND TO WAR   • • • •   68 SOHRAB RUSTUM   231
      BUT ME THOU MUST BEAR HENCE NOT SEND WITH THEM • • 84 SOHRAB RUSTUM   783
      A SON SO PRAISD SO BRAVE TO SEND TO WAR   • • • •   68 SOHRAB RUSTUM   V 231
      O MOST JUST VIZIER SEND AWAY   • • • • • •   87 SICK KING BOKH   1
      SEND HIM AWAY SIRS AND MAKE ON   • • • • •   90 SICK KING BOKH   90
      FIRE TO THE WOOD AND SEND HIM OUT TO SEA   • • • •   96 BALDER DEAD 1   44
      DO THE GODS SEND TO ME TO MAKE THEM BLEST • •   110 BALDER DEAD 2   204
      SEND THROUGH THE WORLD THY MESSENGERS ENTREAT •   122 BALDER DEAD 3   291
      UPON OUR LIFE A RULING EFFLUENCE SEND   • • •   236 PALLADIUM   22
      OER THE SEA AND TO THE STARS I SEND   • • • • •   240 SELF-DEPENDENCE   6
      SEND US THE YOUTH WHOM YE HIDE   • • • •   342 MEROPE   393
      SEND AN AVENGER GODS OF THE DEAD   • • • •   348 MEROPE   543
      AN AVENGER I ASK NOT SEND ME MY SON   • • • •   348 MEROPE   544
      I SEND AND THESE LIBATIONS POUR THE WHILE • • •   350 MEROPE   595
      WITH ARMS THEN THEY SHOULD SEND HIM NOT BY STEALTH 351 MEROPE   606
      SEND FAR THEIR LIGHT VOICE   • • • • • •   442 EMPEDOCLES II   426

SENDER
      TO CHUCKLE WITH HIS SENDER OER THE GAME   • • • •   366 MEROPE   V

SENDS
      AND TO YOUR PRAYER SHE SENDS YOU THIS REPLY   • •   114 BALDER DEAD 3   41
      LET US CONSULT BEFORE THIS PALACE SENDS   • • • •   330 MEROPE   26
      HE TO THEE SENDS ME ON IN ONE THING GLAD   • • • • 359 MEROPE   850

SENESCHAL
      THE CHILDREN AND THE GREY-HAIRD SENESCHAL   • • • • 152 TRISTRAM 3   97

SENSE
      GUESTS THE DULL SENSE NEVER KNEW   • • • • •   30 NEW SIRENS   136
      TO A SKIN-DEEP SENSE   • • • • •   39 STAGIRIUS   26
      CAUGHT NOT TILL THEN A SENSE   • • • • •   47 WORLD QUIETIST   22
      IN SOME SENSE FAUSTA OUTLASTS DEATH   • •   59 RESIGNATION   230
      WHERE NO MORE LIGHTS OF SENSE OR KNOWLEDGE ARE •   167 PICT NEWSTEAD   11
      GIVES US A SENSE OF THE AWE   • • • • •   231 YOUTH OF NATURE   100
      BUT AH AN INEXTINGUISHABLE SENSE   • • •   239 REVOLUTIONS   9
      OF SWAY HAVE FELT THIS BODING SENSE COME ON • •   239 REVOLUTIONS   14
      WEAKEN THE SENSE OF HIS LOSS   • • • • •   283 HAWORTH CHURCH   V
      O POLICY TOO SUBTLE FAR FOR SENSE   • • •   339 MEROPE   311
      NOT ONLY WOUND THE SENSE BUT KILL THE SOUL • •   385 MEROPE   1408
      YET GRANT AS SENSE LONG MISSD   • • • •   421 EMPEDOCLES I 2   282
      SENSE AFTER SENSE DECAY   • • • • • •   424 EMPEDOCLES I 2   365
      SENSE AFTER SENSE DECAY   • • • • • •   424 EMPEDOCLES I 2   365
      SOME SLOUGH OF SENSE OR SOME FANTASTIC MAZE •   440 EMPEDOCLES II   375
      AND BE ASTRAY FOR EVER SLAVE OF SENSE   • • •   440 EMPEDOCLES II   390
      THE SENSE OF TEARS IN MORTAL THINGS   • • • • •   450 GEISTS GRAVE   16

SENSE   (CONTINUED)
        WHAT SENSE WHAT CHEER . . . .   459 KAISER DEAD   34
        WHOSE SPELL-BOUND SENSE FROM CHILDHOODS HOUR   471 CROMWELL   3
            HATH KNOWN
        SHARP SENSE OF DEEP SELF-IGNORANCE FEAR OF LOOKS . .   LUCRETIUS 2   14

SENSELESS
        MANS SENSELESS UPROAR MINGLING WITH HIS TOIL   . .   1 QUIET WORK   V 10
        OUR SENSELESS UPROAR MINGLING WITH OUR TOIL   . .   1 QUIET WORK   V 10
        SENSELESS WELTERING IN HIS GORE   . . . . . . 13 CHURCH BROU 1   28
        THE SENSELESS WORLD WITH THEM ALL   . . . . . 233 YOUTH OF MAN   34
        AND BEND THEIR LITTLE FISTS AND RATE THE SENSELESS 421 EMPEDOCLES I 2   276
            GROUND
        AFFLICTS GRAVE HEAVEN WITH ITS LONG SENSELESS ROAR 480 HUNGARIAN NAT   5

SENSES
        BETWIXT OUR SENSES AND OUR SORROW KEEPS   . . . . 43 GIPSY CHILD   50
        ABOVE THE HOWLING SENSES EBB AND FLOW   . . . . 169 EAST LONDON   11
        WILL GOAD OUR SENSES WITH A SHARPER SPUR   . . . . 440 EMPEDOCLES II   379

SENSITIVE
        I SAW HIM SENSITIVE IN FRAME   . . . . 272 EDW QUILLINAN   1

SENT
        WHICH IT SENT FLYING WIDE THEN SOHRAB THREW   . . 73 SOHRAB RUSTUM   405
        SO THAT SAD MOTHER SENT HIM WORD FOR FEAR   . . . 79 SOHRAB RUSTUM   610
        AND I COME SENT THIS ROAD ON BALDERS TRACK   . . . 108 BALDER DEAD 2   116
        AND SENT ME WITH MY DOGS TO SWEEP   . . . . . . 148 TRISTRAM 2   176
        AND SENT HIM WITH HIS DOGS TO SWEEP   . . . . . . 148 TRISTRAM 2   V 176
        SENT ECHOES THROUGH THE NIGHT TO WAKE   . . . . 177 FAREWELL   3
        IS TO THEIR FARTHEST CAVERNS SENT   . . . . . . 182 TO MARG CONT   14
        BUT IT NEEDS HEAVEN-SENT MOMENTS FOR THIS SKILL . 256 SCHOLAR-GIPSY   50
        SUFFERING SENT THEM DEATH   . . . . 343 MEROPE   417
        SENT FORTH ECHEMUS THE VICTOR THE KING   . . . 344 MEROPE   442
        A MESSENGER SENT FROM ARCADIA HERE   . . . . . 361 MEROPE   920
        HE WHO WAS SENT HATH SPED AND NOW COMES BACK   . . 366 MEROPE   V

SENTENCE
        STERN SENTENCE OF THE POWERS OF DESTINY   . . . .   8 MYCERINUS   6
        I WILL UNFOLD MY SENTENCE AND MY CRIME   . . . .   9 MYCERINUS   7
        SO RANG TERTULLIANS SENTENCE ON THE SIDE   . . . . 172 GOOD SHEPHERD   2
        THIS SENTENCE HAVE I LEFT BEHIND   . . . . . . 217 NAMELESS EPIT   V
        BY THE ORACULAR SENTENCE OF THE GODS . . . . . . 385 MEROPE   1422
        REVOKE ASSUAGE HER SENTENCE   . . . . 398 MEROPE   1807

SENTENCED
        BUT SENTENCED HIM AS THE LAW IS   . . . . . . 91 SICK KING BOKH   111

SENTST
        THOU SENTST AND FETCHEDST FIRE AND MADEST LIGHTS . . 121 BALDER DEAD 3   263

SEPARATE
        AND NOT ITS SEPARATE PARTS ALONE   . . . . . . 225 EPILOG LAOCOON   142

SEPTEMBER
        SERE WITH SEPTEMBER DROOPD THE CHESTNUT-TREES . . 167 RACHEL 1   3
        BROWN WITH SEPTEMBER DROOPD THE CHESTNUT-TREES . . 167 RACHEL 1   V 3

SEPTEMBERS
        IN SEPTEMBERS BRIGHT AFTERNOON . . . . 292 HEINES GRAVE   7

SEPULCHRE
        HERE NO SEPULCHRE BUILT   . . . . 294 HEINES GRAVE   56
        THEN HAD HIS SEPULCHRE RISEN   . . . . 345 MEROPE   481
        ALAS NO COMMON SEPULCHRE ART THOU   . . . . . . 464 ALARIC AT ROME   55

SEQUESTERD
        THEN SOUGHT THY STRAW IN SOME SEQUESTERD GRANGE . . 259 SCHOLAR-GIPSY   130

SERAPHS
        WHAT SERAPHS IN SOME ALIEN PLANET BORN   . . . . 42 GIPSY CHILD   V 26

SERE
        SERE IN THE GARDEN OF THE TUILERIES . . . . . . 167 RACHEL 1   2
        SERE WITH SEPTEMBER DROOPD THE CHESTNUT-TREES . . 167 RACHEL 1   3
        WERE MINGLING WITH THE SERE AND WITHERED HUES OF DEATH 466 ALARIC AT ROME 102

SERENE
        DRINKING DEEP DRAUGHTS OF JOY YE DWELL SERENE . . 10 MYCERINUS   48
        WHAT ELSE SERENE . . . . 279 SOUTHERN NIGHT   136
        MAYST THOU A MOOD MORE SERENE   . . . . 299 HEINES GRAVE   227
        THEIR MOURNFUL CALM SERENE   . . . . 314 OBERMANN MORE   50
        SO SADLY CALM SO KINGLY SO SERENE   . . . . . . 477 CROMWELL   186

SERENELY
        KNOWING CLASP IT AND SERENELY BEAT   . . . . . .   META CLOISTER   32

SERENITY
        WHOM AN UNBLAMED SERENITY   . . . . 53 RESIGNATION   23

SERF
        BETTER TO LIVE A SERF A CAPTURED MAN . . . . . . 112 BALDER DEAD 2   265

SERFS
    PREFERRD MESSENIAN SERFS TO DORIAN LORDS • • • • 339 MEROPE   324

SERIMNERS
    NEW MESSES OF THE BOAR SERIMNERS FLESH • • • • 97 BALDER DEAD 1   67
    ALL NIGHT THEY ATE THE BOAR SERIMNERS FLESH • • 119 BALDER DEAD 3   210

SERIOUS
    LABORIOUS PERSEVERING SERIOUS FIRM • • • • • 5 DUKE WELLINGTON   10
    SOME TWO HOURS MARCH WITH SERIOUS AIR • • • • 54 RESIGNATION   68
    BUT LIGHT THE SERIOUS VISAGE GREW • • • • • 202 URANIA   11
    IMMERSED IN SERIOUS STATE-CRAFT IS THE KING • • 387 MEROPE   1489

SERPENT
    FENRIS THE WOLF THE SERPENT HUGE AND ME • • • 110 BALDER DEAD 2   208
    OF THESE THE SERPENT IN THE SEA YE CAST • • • 110 BALDER DEAD 2   209
    AND LOK THE FATHER OF THE SERPENT FIRST • • • 113 BALDER DEAD 3   4
    HIS SHIP AND THE GREAT SERPENT MAKES TO LAND • 127 BALDER DEAD 3   479
    AND THOU THOU FAIR-SKINND SERPENT THOU ART LAID • 373 MEROPE   1177
    SIT AND MAKE READY THE SERPENT THE SCOURGE • • 347 MEROPE   V 531

SERPENTS
    AND OER HIS VISAGE SERPENTS DROPPING GALL • • • 111 BALDER DEAD 2   221
    MY DUNGEON WHERE THE SERPENTS STUNG ME DEAD • 117 BALDER DEAD 3   146

SERRIED
    THROUGH BLACK DEPTHS OF SERRIED SHADOWS • • • 32 NEW SIRENS   179
    BEHIND HIS CORPSE THEIR HEDGE OF SERRIED SPEARS • 381 MEROPE   1308
    SERRIED AND GRIM THE RING OF DORIAN LORDS • • • 401 MEROPE   1900

SERVANT
    MASTER AND SERVANT YOUNG AND OLD • • • • • 226 EPILOG LAOCOON   160
    MY MOTHERS FAITHFUL SERVANT LAID ME DOWN • • 331 MEROPE   31
    THY TRUSTING LORD DIDST THOU HIS SERVANT SLAY • 338 MEROPE   280
    THUS MUCH FROM ARCAS MY OLD SERVANT TRUE • • • 351 MEROPE   616
    UNFAITHFUL SERVANT DOST THOU TOO DESERT ME • • 368 MEROPE   1076
    BUT THE FAITHFUL SERVANT AND NURSE • • • • 369 MEROPE   1090
    BUT THE FAITHFUL SERVANT AND GUARD • • • • 369 MEROPE   V1090

SERVANTS
    THOSE WILLING SERVANTS SHALL STAND • • • • • 216 LORDS MESSENGER   11
    SERVANTS OF GOD OR SONS • • • • • • • 291 RUGBY CHAPEL   162
    NOT AS SERVANTS YE KNEW • • • • • • 291 RUGBY CHAPEL   164
    AND SAY YE SERVANTS HEAR EMPEDOCLES • • • • 429 EMPEDOCLES II   V 27

SERVD
    ONE LESSON OF TWO DUTIES SERVD IN ONE • • • 1 QUIET WORK   V   3
    WITH CHERRIES SERVD IN DRIFTS OF SNOW • • • 94 SICK KING BOKH   197
    HATH IN HIS EYE EVER BUT SERVD TO SHOW • • • 238 PROGRESS   V

SERVE
    AND THE GREAT POWERS WE SERVE THEMSELVES MAY BE • 10 MYCERINUS   41
    BENT ONLY TO SERVE VIRTUE • • • • • • 353 MEROPE   662
    THE SACRIFICERS AXE WILL SERVE THY TURN • • • 391 MEROPE   1592
    BUT I WOULD SERVE HIM SOOTHE HIM IF I COULD • 408 EMPEDOCLES I 1   75
    THE HUMBLER SORT WHO SERVE AND TEND • • • • 459 KAISER DEAD   32

SERVED
    I HAVE STILL SERVED AFRASIAB WELL AND SHOWN • • 62 SOHRAB RUSTUM   44
    AND BEFORE EACH THE COOKS WHO SERVED THEM PLACED • • 97 BALDER DEAD 1   66
    WHICH SERVED FOR THAT TITANIC STRIFE • • • • 270 MEMORIAL VERSES   14
    THE UNIVERSAL ORDER SERVED • • • • • • 314 OBERMANN MORE   55
    AND SERVED MEN NOBLY AND ACCEPTANCE FOUND • • • 448 WESTMIN ABBEY   143

SERVICE
    FROM FAR AND A MORE DOUBTFUL SERVICE OWND • • • 64 SOHRAB RUSTUM   127
    PERFORMD GOOD SERVICE FOR HIS BLOODY WAGE • • • 364 MEROPE   975
    THE TOILS OF THY FOUL SERVICE TILL THOU WAKE • 373 MEROPE   1181
    UNSPARING IN HIS SERVICE OF HIS TOIL • • • • 404 MEROPE   1975
    WHO ASKS THIS FINAL SERVICE AT YOUR HANDS • • • 429 EMPEDOCLES II   28

SET
    THE FEEBLE SONS OF PLEASURE SET THEIR HAND • • • 5 DUKE WELLINGTON   7
    FOR A BOUND WAS SET TO MEETINGS • • • • • 30 NEW SIRENS   115
    STARS SET DEEP YET INLY BURNING • • • • • 30 NEW SIRENS   137
    O LET FALL ONE TEAR AND SET US FREE • • • • 34 NEW SIRENS   226
    BUT A BOUND WAS SET TO MEETINGS • • • • • 30 NEW SIRENS   V 115
    OH SET US FREE • 39 STAGIRIUS   48
    LONG SINCE THE WORLD HATH SET ITS HEART TO LIVE • 46 WORLD QUIETIST   11
    ASK NOT TO AMUSE BUT TO SET FREE • • • • 59 RESIGNATION   242
    AND ON HIS HEAD HE SET HIS SHEEP-SKIN CAP • • • 64 SOHRAB RUSTUM   100
    AND CLOSE-SET SKULL-CAPS AND THOSE WILDER HORDES • 64 SOHRAB RUSTUM   130
    AND HIS SOUL SET TO GRIEF AS THE VAST TIDE • • 79 SOHRAB RUSTUM   616
    WASH OFF ALL BLOOD SET SMOOTH EACH LIMB • • • 95 SICK KING BOKH   230
    AND FATE SET SEAL THAT SO HIS END MUST BE • • 96 BALDER DEAD 1   25
    NOR SEE THE SUN ARISE NOR SEE IT SET • • • 99 BALDER DEAD 1   154
    TAKE SLEIPNER HERMOD AND SET FORTH WITH DAWN • 102 BALDER DEAD 1   236
    PAINLESS AND SWIFT SET FREE HER AIRY SOUL • • 104 BALDER DEAD 1   340
    AND HELA SET THEREON WITH COUNTENANCE STERN • 110 BALDER DEAD 2   178

SET   (CONTINUED)
     AND WITH HIMSELF SET US HIS OFFSPRING FREE •   •   •   111 BALDER DEAD 2   223
     THEN MOUNTED SLEIPNER AND SET FORTH TO RIDE   •   •   112 BALDER DEAD 2   284
     AND THEY SET JARS OF WINE AND OIL TO LEAN   •   •   •   118 BALDER DEAD 3   166
     SET HIS STOUT SHOULDER HARD AGAINST THE STERN   •   •   118 BALDER DEAD 3   176
     AND TOOK THEIR HORSES AND SET FORTH TO RIDE   •   •   119 BALDER DEAD 3   215
     AND SET THE FIELDS OF GLOOM ABLAZE WITH LIGHT   •   •   120 BALDER DEAD 3   243
     AND SET BY OCEANS UTMOST MARGE TO DWELL   •   )   •   121 BALDER DEAD 3   275
     HE SPOKE AND NIORD SET FORTH BACK TO HEAVEN   •   •   124 BALDER DEAD 3   373
     AT LAST HE SIGHD AND SET FORTH BACK TO HEAVEN   •   •   129 BALDER DEAD 3   566
     ROUND EACH SWEET BROW THE CAP CLOSE-SET   •   •   •   141 TRISTRAM 1   340
     AND HER EYES ARE SET IN A STARE   •   •   •   •   •   164 FORSAKEN MERM   100
     SET UP A MARK OF EVERLASTING LIGHT •   •   •   •   •   169 EAST LONDON   10
     THEY ARE HERE THEY ARE SET IN THE WORLD   •   •   •   230 YOUTH OF NATURE   80
     SET WHERE THE UPPER STREAMS OF SIMOIS FLOW •   •   •   236 PALLADIUM   1
     CHEERFUL WITH FRIENDS WE SET FORTH •   •   •   •   •   289 RUGBY CHAPEL   89
     FRIENDS WHO SET FORTH AT OUR SIDE   •   •   •   •   •   289 RUGBY CHAPEL   102
     WHERE THOU O SEER ART SET   •   •   •   •   •   •   •   309 OBERMANN   106
     OF LOVE WHICH SET SO DEEP AND STRONG   •   •   •   •   317 OBERMANN MORE   147
     SET DOWN YOUR PITCHERS MAIDENS AND FALL BACK   •   •   332 MEROPE   76
     CLAIMS EVER HOSTILE ELSE AND SET THY SON   •   •   •   335 MEROPE   168
     SET FORTH FROM TEGEA THE ROYAL TOWN •   •   •   •   •   355 MEROPE   732
     WHY SHOULD THIS HEART OF MINE SET MIGHTY STORE •   •   398 MEROPE   1789
     STRIKES WITH ALL SAIL SET   •   •   •   •   •   •   •   400 MEROPE   1879
     LIMITS WE DID NOT SET   •   •   •   •   •   •   •   •   418 EMPEDOCLES I 2   184
     THROUGH THIS SHARP TOIL-SET LIFE   •   •   •   •   •   421 EMPEDOCLES I 2   268
     TAKE THY BOUGH SET ME FREE FROM MY SOLITUDE   •   •   435 EMPEDOCLES II   218
     THOUGH MOVING INLY TO ONE FAR-SET GOAL •   •   •   •   448 WESTMIN ABBEY   153
     SET BETWIXT OURSELVES AND THEE •   •   •   •   •   •   456 POOR MATTHIAS   128
     LOOKS ON IN FEAR AND WHEN THE SEAL IS SET   •   •   •   465 ALARIC AT ROME   92
     NO MAST NO SAILS ARE SET THEREON   •   •   •   •   •   479 HAYSWATER BOAT   5
     SET THINE EARS WITH SOUL-FRAUGHT MUSIC RINGING •   •   482 THEKLAS ANSWER   7
     TO DAILY TASKS WE SET OUR HAND •   •   •   •   •   •   483 ROME-SICKNESS   1
     FOLLOWING THE SUN WE SET OUR VESSELS HEAD   •   •   •   484 S S LUSITANIA   3

SETS
     WHEN THE SLOW TIDE SETS ONE WAY   •   •   •   •   •   33 NEW SIRENS   220
     STRONGLY SETS AND TRULY BURNS   •   •   •   •   •   •   49 SECOND BEST   24
     OF THE BRIGHT ROCKING OCEAN SETS TO SHORE   •   •   •   79 SOHRAB RUSTUM   617
     AND A WARM WEST-WIND BLOWS AND THAW SETS IN •   •   •   122 BALDER DEAD 3   309
     BUT ROUND THE HEADLANDS POINT A CURRENT SETS   •   •   358 MEROPE   820
     AND SETS HIS FREIGHT ASHORE ON THORNEY STRAND   •   •   445 WESTMIN ABBEY   30

SETTER
     THE MURDERER AND HIS IMPIOUS SETTER-ON •   •   •   •   368 MEROPE   1072

SETTING
     STREAMS FROM THE SETTING SUN AND COLOURS BRIGHT •   •   18 CHURCH BROU 3   19

SETTLED
     A TRANQUIL SETTLED LOVELINESS   •   •   •   •   •   •   147 TRISTRAM 2   145
     A PLACID SETTLED LOVELINESS   •   •   •   •   •   •   147 TRISTRAM 2   V 145
     THE FELL-FARES SETTLED ON THE THICKETS NEAR •   •   •   151 TRISTRAM 3   55
     RIGIDLY YET IN SETTLED CALM THIS REALM •   •   •   •   388 MEROPE   1491
     THERE IS A SETTLED TROUBLE IN HIS AIR   •   •   •   •   408 EMPEDOCLES I 1   68
     AND ALL WHICH MIGHT RELAX HIS SETTLED GLOOM •   •   •   409 EMPEDOCLES I 1   84

SETTLES
     GLOOM SETTLES SLOWLY DOWN OVER THEIR BREAST •   •   243 SUMMER NIGHT   46

SEVEN
     TO SEVEN AGES   •   •   •   •   •   •   •   •   •   •   192 STRAYED REVEL   222
     SEVEN-GATED THEBES OR TROY •   •   •   •   •   •   •   193 STRAYED REVEL   257
     SEVEN-CUBIT-STATURED SON   •   •   •   •   •   •   •   344 MEROPE   441
     SEVEN DAYS THE GOD REPLIED   •   •   •   •   •   •   •   448 WESTMIN ABBEY   137

SEVENTH
     QUIET IN SLEEP THE SEVENTH NIGHT THEY DIED •   •   •   448 WESTMIN ABBEY   139

SEVER
     FIND I HIM FROM WHOM I HAD TO SEVER •   •   •   •   •   482 THEKLAS ANSWER   9

SEVERANCE
     AND PROUD SELF-SEVERANCE FROM THEM WERE DISEASE •   •   46 IN UTRUMQUE PAR V 39
     A GOD A GOD THEIR SEVERANCE RULED   •   •   •   •   •   182 TO MARG CONT   22
     BY SEVERANCE IMMATURE   •   •   •   •   •   •   •   •   197 FRAG ANTIGONE   66

SEVERD
     THAT SEVERD THE WORLDS MARCH AND THINE BE GONE •   •   44 GIPSY CHILD   62
     THAT SEVERD THE WORLDS MARCH AND THINE IS GONE •   •   44 GIPSY CHILD   V 62
     AND KNOW NOT YE ARE SEVERD •   •   •   •   •   •   •   320 OBERMANN MORE   216
     AND KNOW NOT THEY ARE SEVERD   •   •   •   •   •   •   320 OBERMANN MORE   V 216
     BLOOD-SEVERD BUT MESSENIAS KING AND QUEEN   •   •   •   394 MEROPE   1720

SEVERE
     WHOSE SEVERE MOMENTS   •   •   •   •   •   •   •   •   52 CONSOLATION   67
     YET THAT SEVERE THAT EARNEST AIR   •   •   •   •   •   241 MORALITY   29
     REQUITE HIM WORDS SEVERE FOR SEEMING KIND   •   •   •   349 MEROPE   551
     IN HIS SEVERE LOOKS SUCH A MAJESTY •   •   •   •   •   408 EMPEDOCLES I 1   62
     THOUGH YOUNG INTOLERABLY SEVERE •   •   •   •   •   •   435 EMPEDOCLES II   206

SEVERELY
    O AIR-BORN VOICE LONG SINCE SEVERELY CLEAR • • • • 240 SELF-DEPENDENCE 29

SEVERER
    SEVERER PALER STATELIER THAN THEY ALL • • • • 331 MEROPE 57

SEVERING
    OR OERPASS THE SEVERING SEA • • • • • • • 456 POOR MATTHIAS 127

SEVERITY
    NO VIGOUR AND SEVERITY MUST CHAIN • • • • • 390 MEROPE 1563

SEVILLE
    TO THE GREAT MAIN PASSD SEVILLE ON THE RIGHT • • 484 S S LUSITANIA 4

SEVRES
    AT SEVRES BY THE SEINE • • • • • • • • • • 321 OBERMANN MORE 268

SHACKLED
    THEY SEE THEIR SHACKLED BEASTS AGAIN • • • • • • 55 RESIGNATION 120

SHADE
    NOTHING STIRS ON THE LAWN BUT THE QUICK LILAC-SHADE 19 MODERN SAPPHO 2
    NOTHING MOVES ON THE LAWN BUT THE QUICK LILAC-SHADE 19 MODERN SAPPHO V 2
    IN THE SLUMBROUS CEDARN SHADE • • • • • • • • 28 NEW SIRENS 68
    SYLVAN GODS OF THIS FAIR SHADE • • • • • • • • 34 NEW SIRENS 244
    IN THIS SLUMBROUS CEDARN SHADE • • • • • • • • 28 NEW SIRENS V 68
    COOL SHADE IS THERE AND RUSTIC CHEER • • • • • • 54 RESIGNATION 75
    AN UNRECOVERD PRISONER SHADE WITH SHADES • • • • 120 BALDER DEAD 3 229
    ALL ROUND THE FOREST SWEEPS OFF BLACK IN SHADE • • 139 TRISTRAM 1 276
    THE SEER FROM THE WEST WAS THEN IN SHADE • • • • 170 EAST AND WEST 11
    OF A TRANQUIL LIFE IN THE SHADE • • • • • • 199 EARLY DEATH 14
    UNDER THE RUSTLING POPLARS SHADE • • • • • • 206 RIVER 2
    THE KINE WERE RESTING IN THE SHADE • • • • • • 222 EPILOG LAOCOON 40
    THEN WE SHALL RUST IN SHADE OR SHINE IN STRIFE • • 236 PALLADIUM 17
    AND BOWER ME FROM THE AUGUST SUN WITH SHADE • • 256 SCHOLAR-GIPSY 29
    UNDER A DARK RED-FRUITED YEW-TREES SHADE • • • • 259 SCHOLAR-GIPSY 140
    STILL CLUTCHING THE INVIOLABLE SHADE • • • • • • 261 SCHOLAR-GIPSY 212
    IN EVER-NEARING CIRCLE WEAVES HER SHADE • • • • 266 THYRSIS 132
    SINCE ERST AT MORN SOME WANDERING SHADE • • • • 271 MEMORIAL VERSES 37
    WE WHO TILL THEN IN THY SHADE • • • • • • 287 RUGBY CHAPEL 31
    ON RAVENNA SANDS IN THE SHADE • • • • • • 294 HEINES GRAVE 60
    CHEQUERING THE GRASS WITH THEIR SHADE • • • • 297 HEINES GRAVE 158
    WE ARE LIKE CHILDREN REARD IN SHADE • • • • • 304 GRANDE CHARTR 169
    OF REVERIE OF SHADE OF PRAYER • • • • • • 306 GRANDE CHARTR 206
    THOU MELANCHOLY SHADE • • • • • • • • 310 OBERMANN 138
    AND TRAVERSED ALL THE SHADE • • • • • • 323 OBERMANN MORE 310
    TO HIS AVENGING SHADE AND TO THE GODS • • • • 332 MEROPE 73
    HEAR US AND HELP US SHADE OF OUR KING • • • • 348 MEROPE 541
    HERE IN THE VALLEY IS IN SHADE THE SWARD • • • • 406 EMPEDOCLES I 1 12
    OF THE HOT NOON WITHOUT A SHADE • • • • • • 414 EMPEDOCLES I 2 54
    THOUGH THOU HAST BEEN MY SHADE IN THE WORLDS HEAT 434 EMPEDOCLES II 194
    THUS SLEEPING IN THINE ABBEYS FRIENDLY SHADE • • 449 WESTMIN ABBEY 164
    HERE SLEEPING IN THINE ABBEYS FRIENDLY SHADE • • 449 WESTMIN ABBEY V 164
    DARK THE VALLEY SLEEPS IN SHADE • • • • • • META CLOISTER 14

SHADED
    AT EVE BY THE PALM-SHADED WELL • • • • • • • • 252 FUTURE 37

SHADES
    WHERE IDLY FLIT ABOUT THE FEEBLE SHADES • • • • 110 BALDER DEAD 2 182
    AN UNRECOVERD PRISONER SHADE WITH SHADES • • • • 120 BALDER DEAD 3 229
    PEOPLED NIGHTS VOICELESS SHADES WITH FORMS OF LONG AGO 467 ALARIC AT ROME 126

SHADOW
    DID SHADOW SOMEWHAT OF THE LIFE OF GODS • • • • 9 MYCERINUS 24
    THROUGH THAT GLOOM HE WILL SEE BUT A SHADOW APPEARING 20 MODERN SAPPHO 25
    IN THE CEDARN SHADOW SLEEPING • • • • • • • • 26 NEW SIRENS 1
    IN THE CEDAR SHADOW SLEEPING • • • • • • • • 26 NEW SIRENS V 1
    DOWN THE PALE CHEEK LONG LINES OF SHADOW SLOPE • • 43 GIPSY CHILD 37
    DOWN THY PALE CHEEK THOSE LINES OF SHADOW SLOPE • • 43 GIPSY CHILD V 37
    ITS SLIGHT DARK SHADOW ON THE MOONLIT TURF • • • 70 SOHRAB RUSTUM 316
    COME LET ME LEAVE THE SHADOW OF THIS WOOD • • • 139 TRISTRAM 1 281
    ALL WHICH WE DID BEFORE SHADOW AND DREAM • • • 153 TRISTRAM 3 132
    ALL THAT WE DID BEFORE SHADOW AND DREAM • • • 153 TRISTRAM 3 V 132
    THE SHADOW OF A MARBLE MUSE OF YORE • • • • 168 RACHEL 2 6
    WHO SPOKE THESE WORDS NO SHADOW EVER CAME • • • 169 WORLDLY PLACE 10
    WHOSE FIGURE CASTS A SHADOW ON THE FLOOR • • • • 175 PARTING 36
    IN THE SHADOW WORDSWORTH LIES DEAD • • • • • 228 YOUTH OF NATURE 9
    MOONLIGHT AND SHADOW AND LAKE • • • • • • • 230 YOUTH OF NATURE 60
    PLAINNESS AND CLEARNESS WITHOUT SHADOW OF STAIN • • 244 SUMMER NIGHT 76
    THAT FLYING AND ELUSIVE SHADOW REST • • • • •) 247 BURIED LIFE 93
    FOR THAT A SHADOW LOURD ON THE FIELDS • • • • 264 THYRSIS 44
    FOR THAT A SHADOW LOWERD ON THE FIELDS • • • • 264 THYRSIS V 44
    BUT SOME DARK SHADOW CAME • • • • • • • 285 HAWORTH CHURCH 110
    SHADOW AND VERDURE AND COOL • • • • • • 292 HEINES GRAVE 8
    IN SOME DARK FIR-TREES SHADOW AMID ROCKS • • • • 373 MEROPE 1167
    THE COLD DULL SHADOW OF THEIR ICY WING • • • • 474 CROMWELL 92
    WHEN MY FLEETING SHADOW PASSD FROM THEE • • • • 482 THEKLAS ANSWER 2

SHADOWD
LONG SINCE WE PACE THIS SHADOWD NAVE • • • • • • 305 GRANDE CHARTR 199
AS OF ONE SHADOWD BY IMPENDING DEATH • • • • • • 356 MEROPE 765
AS ERST THEY SHADOWD • • • • • • • • • • 391 MEROPE 1600
FROM THE FOUR-TOWND MOUNTAIN-SHADOWD DORIS • • • • 400 MEROPE 1852

SHADOWING
OF THAT WORLD-SHADOWING TREE WITH HONEY-DEW • • 120 BALDER DEAD 3 222

SHADOWS
AND THE NIGHT WAXES AND THE SHADOWS FALL • • • • 10 MYCERINUS 72
THROUGH BLACK DEPTHS OF SERRIED SHADOWS • • • • 32 NEW SIRENS 179
THE SELF-SAME SHADOWS NOW AS THEN • • • • • 55 RESIGNATION 98
SHADOWS OF HATES BUT THEY DISTRESS THEM STILL • • 126 BALDER DEAD 3 467
LIKE SHADOWS FORTH IN SPRING • • • • • • • 193 STRAYED REVEL 243
CHILL AND THE SHADOWS NOW • • • • • • • • 297 HEINES GRAVE 164
THE ETERNAL HILLS THEIR GIANT SHADOWS FLUNG • • 472 CROMWELL 14
ITS SHADOWS OER THE FUTURE FLOWERD AND GREW • • 473 CROMWELL 56
LIKE LOVING SHADOWS ROUND THAT CHILDHOODS HOME • 474 CROMWELL 74
PALE PHANTOM HOSTS LIKE SHADOWS FAINT AND FAR • • 476 CROMWELL 141

SHADOWY
SPRING THE FOUNDATIONS OF THAT SHADOWY THRONE • • 4 BUTLERS SERMONS 6
SPRING THE FOUNDATIONS OF THE SHADOWY THRONE • • 4 BUTLERS SERMONS V 6
AND HE WILL SEE THE FEEBLE SHADOWY TRIBES • • • 100 BALDER DEAD 1 174
AND FROM THE DARK FLOCKD UP THE SHADOWY TRIBES • 109 BALDER DEAD 2 156
BELOW AND LOOKD UPON THE SHADOWY TRIBES • • • 114 BALDER DEAD 3 39
A SHADOWY DURABILITY • • • • • • • • • 185 TERRACE BERNE 43
BEEN TO YOUR SHADOWY WORLD CONVEYD • • • • • 271 MEMORIAL VERSES 36
SOME SHADOWY VISION OF A TRANQUIL LIFE • • • • 474 CROMWELL 101

SHAFT
HIS BOAR-SPEARS BROKEN SHAFT BACK ON THE LAKE • • 358 MEROPE 840

SHAFTS
BY ARTEMIS SOFT SHAFTS • • • • • • • • • • 197 FRAG ANTIGONE 67

SHAGGY
WHO COME ON SHAGGY PONIES FROM PAMERE • • • • 65 SOHRAB RUSTUM 134
ACROSS THE SHAGGY BROWS OF TRISTRAMS HOUND • • • 152 TRISTRAM 3 88
LETS FROM HIS SHAGGY HIGHLAND PATE • • • • • • 461 KAISER DEAD 77

SHAKE
YET COULD NOT SHAKE IT • • • • • • • • • 36 VOICE 38
AND SHAKE BACK HER RAVEN HAIR • • • • • • • 134 TRISTRAM 1 123
WHEN GUSTS SHAKE THE DOOR • • • • • • • • 164 FORSAKEN MERM 113
WHO RUSH BY WHO SHAKE • • • • • • • • • 174 PARTING 2
WITH THE BLIND GUSTS THAT SHAKE THEIR OWN • • • 178 FAREWELL 28
WITH THE BLIND GUSTS WHICH SHAKE THEIR OWN • • • 178 FAREWELL V 28
SHAKE LOOSE SOME BAND OF SOFT BROWN HAIR • • • 205 CALAIS SANDS 16
SHAKE BACK THY BANDS OF SOFT BROWN HAIR • • • 205 CALAIS SANDS V 16
SHAKE LOOSE SOME LOCK OF SOFT BROWN HAIR • • • 205 CALAIS SANDS V 16
TO SHAKE HIS SAPIENT HEAD AND GIVE • • • • • 250 WISH 19

SHAKEN
WITH SHOUT AND SHAKEN SPEAR • • • • • • • 191 STRAYED REVEL 189
AND THE SPERCHEIOS VALE SHAKEN WITH GROANS • • • 198 FRAG ANTIGONE 100
SHAKEN AND OUT OF CHIME • • • • • • • • • 416 EMPEDOCLES I 2 115
SHAKEN AND IN DISMAY • • • • • • • • • • 416 EMPEDOCLES I 2 V 115
SHAKEN AND RUDELY HURLD • • • • • • • • • 416 EMPEDOCLES I 2 V 115

SHAKES
OH WHAT A SPASM SHAKES THE DREAMERS HEART • • • 46 IN UTRUMQUE PAR 41
SHAKES HER HEAD FROWNING • • • • • • • • • 51 CONSOLATION 52
RUMBLES AND SHAKES TELL ME THY RACE AND HOME • • 107 BALDER DEAD 2 103
SHAKES EVERY LEAF OF THE GROVE • • • • • • • 293 HEINES GRAVE 43
APPALS ME SHAKES ME WITH AWE • • • • • • • 372 MEROPE 1146

SHAKESPEARE
POETS LIKE SHAKESPEARE • • • • • • • • • • 221 BACCHANALIA 2 59
THE CHARM WHICH HOMER SHAKESPEARE TEACH • • • • 227 EPILOG LAOCOON 206
SHAKESPEARE LOVELIEST OF SOULS • • • • • • • 294 HEINES GRAVE 65

SHAKING
SHAKING HER HEAD TOOK THE HARP • • • • • • • 285 HAWORTH CHURCH 126
SHAKING HIS THIN WHITE HAIRS • • • • • • • • 289 RUGBY CHAPEL 112

SHALLOW
IN ITS CLEAR SHALLOW TURF-FRINGED BED • • • • 55 RESIGNATION 91
THE CLEAR-BROWN SHALLOW POOLS • • • • • • • 190 STRAYED REVEL 147
BELOW THE SURFACE-STREAM SHALLOW AND LIGHT • • • 483 BELOW SURFACE 1

SHALLOWS
TO CROSS THE SPARKLING SHALLOWS THERE • • • • 413 EMPEDOCLES I 2 37

SHAMD
SHAMD AND BAFFLED BY YOUR GLADNESS • • • • • 32 NEW SIRENS V 169
NEVER DEFACD TILL NOW SHAMD TO THE DUST • • • • 76 SOHRAB RUSTUM V 498

SHAME
    AND EASE FROM SHAME AND REST FROM FEAR   • • •   21 YOUTH AND CALM   2
    O SPEAK ONCE AND SHAME MY SADNESS   • • • •   32 NEW SIRENS   167
    FEROOD SHAME BIDS US TAKE THEIR CHALLENGE UP   •   66 SOHRAB RUSTUM   175
    AND WRING HIS HEART WITH SHAME TO HEAR THY WORD   •   116 BALDER DEAD 3   105
    WHICH DOGGD BY FEAR AND FOUGHT BY SHAME   • •   147 TRISTRAM 2   132
    BACK WITH THE CONSCIOUS THRILL OF SHAME   • •   181 ISOLATION MARG   19
    THE TOO CLEAR WEB AND THY DUMB SISTERS SHAME   •   201 PHILOMELA   21
    THY SHAME SECURES MY FREEDOM NOT THY WILL   • •   340 MEROPE   351
    SHAME RARELY CHECKS THE GENUINE TYRANTS WILL   •   340 MEROPE   352
    AS MUCH TO THE KINGS WISH MORE TO HIS SHAME   •   364 MEROPE   968
    WHAT HATE AND AWE AND SHAME   • • • •   416 EMPEDOCLES I 2   112
    TWICE ERE THAT DAY OF SHAME THE EMBATTLED FOE   •   465 ALARIC AT ROME   73
    NOR TONGUE OF MAN NOR FEAR NOR SHAME CAN PREACH   •   467 ALARIC AT ROME   141
    NO SHAME THAT SUNS SHOULD RISE TO LIGHT A CONQUERD   468 ALARIC AT ROME   150
        ROME
    THE TRUE HEART-BREAKING BAFFLED HOPE AND SHAME   •   LUCRETIUS 2   13

SHAMED
    CLEARD ROME OF WHAT MOST SHAMED HIM BUT BE HIS   •   2 TO A FRIEND   8
    THEN WERE THE CHIEFS OF IRAN SHAMED THROUGH ME   •   72 SOHRAB RUSTUM   363
    BECAUSE THOU HAST SHAMED ME BEFORE BOTH THE HOSTS   •   75 SOHRAB RUSTUM   468
    IF THIS WAS FEAR OF THEM IT SHAMED THE KING   •   337 MEROPE   252
    IF JEALOUSY OF US IT SHAMED THE MAN   • • • •   337 MEROPE   253

SHAMEFUL
    TO HIDE THEIR SHAMEFUL MEMORY FROM MEN   • • •   109 BALDER DEAD 2   175

SHAPE
    WHO WRESTLES WITH HIS DREAM AS SOME PALE SHAPE   •   11 MYCERINUS   103
    THOK IS SHE CALLD BUT NOW LOK WORE HER SHAPE   •   123 BALDER DEAD 3   335
    IN HAT OF ANTIQUE SHAPE AND CLOAK OF GREY   • •   256 SCHOLAR-GIPSY   55

SHAPES
    ALL SHAPES THAT HAUNT REMEMBRANCE SOFT AND FAIR   •   474 CROMWELL   83

SHARE
    THEN AM I YOURS AND WHAT YOU FEEL I SHARE   • •   7 REP FRIEND   14
    AND SHARE THE BATTLES COMMON CHANCE WITH US   •   63 SOHRAB RUSTUM   67
    NEAR HARBOUR BUT THEY SHARE   • • •   193 STRAYED REVEL   255
    OH THAT TO SHARE THIS FAMOUS SCENE   • • •   204 CALAIS SANDS   9
    OF POSSESSING POWERS NOT OUR SHARE   •   209 SELF-DECEPTION   2
    WHO THOUGH SO NOBLE SHARE IN THE WORLDS TOIL   •   244 SUMMER NIGHT   81
    AND THOU HAST PLEASURES TOO TO SHARE   • •   309 OBERMANN   109
    YES AND ALONE IS WITH ME HERE TO SHARE   •   379 MEROPE   1268
    TO BID HER SHARE THINE UNENDANGERD THRONE   •   395 MEROPE   1740
    AND WE MIGHT GLADLY SHARE THE FRUITFUL STIR   •   439 EMPEDOCLES II   339
    CROSS HIS LONE PATH OR SHARE HIS PILGRIMAGE   •   476 CROMWELL   162

SHARED
    SHARED AND REJOICED IN BY ALL   • • • • •   230 YOUTH OF NATURE   67
    HE WHO HATH WATCHD NOT SHARED THE STRIFE   • • •   309 OBERMANN   101

SHAREDST
    NOT OF HIM OF CRESPHONTES THOU SHAREDST THE LOT   •   345 MEROPE   471

SHARER
    THE WILLING SHARER OF HIS GUILTY RULE   • • •   366 MEROPE   1007

SHARERS
    OF SHARERS IN A COMMON HUMAN FATE   • • • • •   170 WEST LONDON   11

SHARES
    THAT A FORMER RIVAL SHARES HER OFFICE   • • •   144 TRISTRAM 2   59
    THAT AN ANCIENT RIVAL SHARES HER OFFICE   • • •   144 TRISTRAM 2   V 59
    FALSE NECKAN SHARES MY BED SHE WEEPS   • • • •   160 NECKAN   35

SHARP
    HUNGRY AND BARREN AND SHARP AS THE SEA   • •   39 STAGIRIUS   47
    STILL SHARP AS EVER FREEZE AND PARCH   • • •   56 RESIGNATION   131
    IN TURN AND FULL STRUCK RUSTUMS SHIELD SHARP RANG   73 SOHRAB RUSTUM   406
    THE IRON PLATES RANG SHARP BUT TURND THE SPEAR   •   73 SOHRAB RUSTUM   407
    SPEECHLESS AND THEN HE UTTERD ONE SHARP CRY   •   81 SOHRAB RUSTUM   690
    SHARP QUIVERING TONGUES OF FLAME SHOT OUT AND LEAPT   •   119 BALDER DEAD 3   188
    LOUD HOWLS THE WIND SHARP PATTERS THE RAIN   •   133 TRISTRAM 1   83
    HIS SWORD IS SHARP HIS HORSE IS GOOD   • • •   138 TRISTRAM 1   249
    RANG LONELILY AND SHARP THE SKY WAS FAIR   • •   155 TRISTRAM 3   199
    I CHIDE WITH THEE NOT THAT THY SHARP   • • •   294 HEINES GRAVE   70
    BY THE LAKE-EDGE BROKE THE SHARP CRY OF HOUNDS   •   357 MEROPE   787
    FULL ON THE SHARP-POINTED   • • • •   400 MEROPE   1880
    THROUGH THIS SHARP TOIL-SET LIFE   • • • •   421 EMPEDOCLES I 2   268
    SHARP SENSE OF DEEP SELF-IGNORANCE FEAR OF LOOKS   •   LUCRETIUS 2   14

SHARPER
    WILL GOAD OUR SENSES WITH A SHARPER SPUR   • •   440 EMPEDOCLES II   379

SHATTERD
    BETWEEN A RUIND CHURCH AND SHATTERD THRONE   • • •   477 CROMWELL   188

SHATTERED
    THOU SHATTERED MASS WHOSE GLORIOUS RUINS TELL   •   463 ALARIC AT ROME   45

SHAVEN
    OF SHAVEN HILL-SWARD TRIM AND GREEN   • • • • • •   16 CHURCH BROU 2   V 13
    BUT SEE HIS SHAVEN OPPRESSORS • • • • • •   214 NEW ROME   5

SHAWL
    THY SHAWL THY LOOK THY SMILE THY HAND • • • •   204 CALAIS SANDS   12
    THAT SHAWL THAT STEP THAT LOOK THAT HAND • • • •   204 CALAIS SANDS   V 12

SHEAVES
    SILENT THE SHEAVES THE RINGING WAIN • • • • •   217 BACCHANALIA 1   V 5
    FLING THE PILED SHEAVES ABOUT • • • • • •   218 BACCHANALIA 1   V 34
    AND IN THE SUN ALL MORNING BINDS THE SHEAVES • •   255 SCHOLAR-GIPSY   14

SHED
    AND YOUR SCENTS HAVE SHED THEIR SWEETNESS • • •   34 NEW SIRENS   253
    MOTHERS HAVE SHED • • • • • • • • • • •   36 VOICE   10
    SHALL HE SHED CHEER OVER THE CHEERLESS SEATS •   110 BALDER DEAD 2   195
    HE STRAINS TO JOIN THEIR FLIGHT AND FROM HIS SHED   129 BALDER DEAD 3   563
    OUR YOUTH RETURND FOR THERE WAS SHED • • •   271 MEMORIAL VERSES   54
    OUR YOUTH CAME BACK FOR THERE WAS SHED • •   271 MEMORIAL VERSES V 54
    I COME TO SHED THEM AT THEIR SIDE • • • •   302 GRANDE CHARTR   90
    AND SHED THEIR BLOOD LIKE WATER IN OUR CAUSE •   337 MEROPE   227
    BY THIS DEAR GUEST OVER THY PRECINCT SHED • •   449 WESTMIN ABBEY   173
    BY THIS DEAR SOUL OVER THY PRECINCT SHED • •   449 WESTMIN ABBEY V 173
    WHY SPEEDST THOU NOT THY DEATHLIKE WAVE TO SHED • • 462 ALARIC AT ROME   3

SHEDDING
    SHEDDING HER PENSIVE LIGHT AT INTERVALS • • •   18 CHURCH BROU 3   35
    APPOINTS THE WAY TO PEACE THROUGH SHEDDING BLOOD •   378 MEROPE   1248

SHEDS
    SHEDS BLOOD IMPRISONS BANISHES ATTAINTS • • •   353 MEROPE   682

SHEEN
    OR IN DEAF EASE ON THRONES OF DAZZLING SHEEN • •   10 MYCERINUS   47
    AND BRIGHTEST IS THEIR GLORYS SHEEN • • • •   227 EPILOG LAOCOON   209
    SWIMS IN THE SHEEN OF THE MOON • • • •   228 YOUTH OF NATURE   4
    WHAT ELSE IS STEEPD IN LUCID SHEEN • • •   279 SOUTHERN NIGHT   134
    THE WORLDS GREAT ORDER DAWNS IN SHEEN • • •   322 OBERMANN MORE   293
    BUT RAIMENT OF CELESTIAL SHEEN SHE WORE • • •   447 WESTMIN ABBEY   99

SHEENY
    DROOPS ALL HIS SHEENY BROWN DEEP-FEATHERD NECK • • 431 EMPEDOCLES II   76

SHEEP
    AND ON HIS HEAD HE SET HIS SHEEP-SKIN CAP • • •   64 SOHRAB RUSTUM   100
    FIRST WITH BLACK SHEEP-SKIN CAPS AND WITH LONG SPEARS   64 SOHRAB RUSTUM   118
    A SIDE OF ROASTED SHEEP AND CAKES OF BREAD • •   67 SOHRAB RUSTUM   198
    KOHIK AND WHERE THE KALMUKS FEED THEIR SHEEP •   83 SOHRAB RUSTUM   764
    AND ON HIS HEAD HE PLACD HIS SHEEP-SKIN CAP • •   64 SOHRAB RUSTUM V 100
    A SIDE OF ROASTED SHEEP AND LOAVES OF BREAD • •   67 SOHRAB RUSTUM V 198
    THE SHIAH DOGS WHO PASTURE SHEEP • • • •   93 SICK KING BOKH   167
    HE SAVES THE SHEEP THE GOATS HE DOTH NOT SAVE •   172 GOOD SHEPHERD   1
    HOW THICK THE TREMULOUS SHEEP-CRIES COME • • •   248 KENSINGTON GARD   8
    HOW STRANGE THE TREMULOUS SHEEP-CRIES COME • • •   KENSINGTON GARD V 8
    AND ONLY THE WHITE SHEEP ARE SOMETIMES SEEN •   255 SCHOLAR-GIPSY   8
    HERE WITH THE SHEPHERDS AND THE SILLY SHEEP •   264 THYRSIS   45
    HIS SHEEP HIS HAPLESS LOVE HIS BLINDED EYES •   268 THYRSIS   187
    FIELDS WHERE SOFT SHEEP FROM CAGES PULL THE HAY •   268 THYRSIS   198
    THYRSIS IN REACH OF SHEEP-BELLS IS MY HOME • •   269 THYRSIS   233
    FIELDS WHERE THE SHEEP FROM CAGES PULL THE HAY •   268 THYRSIS V 198
    SHEEP MAKE THE DAISIED AISLES THEIR FOLD • •   274 STANZAS CARNAC   16
    SHEEP MAKE THE FURZE-GROWN AISLES THEIR FOLD •   274 STANZAS CARNAC V 16
    SHEEP MAKE THE FURZE-GROWN NAVE THEIR FOLD • •   STANZAS CARNAC V 16
    BRINGING THY SHEEP IN THY HAND • • • •   290 RUGBY CHAPEL   144
    ARE SWEPT LIKE HUDDLING SHEEP ALONG • • • •   481 COURAGE   8

SHEEPFOLD
    THE SHEEPFOLD OF MICHAEL SURVIVES • • • • •   228 YOUTH OF NATURE   21

SHEET
    OER THE BLANCHD SHEET HER RAVEN HAIR • • • •   146 TRISTRAM 2   107
    AND REACH THAT GLIMMERING SHEET OF GLASS • • •   310 OBERMANN   119

SHEETS
    THERE WHERE DOWN CLOUDY CLIFFS THROUGH SHEETS OF FOAM   262 SCHOLAR-GIPSY   248
    IN SHEETS OF SCATHING FIRE • • • • • • •   319 OBERMANN MORE   202
    FAR OER THE GLISTENING SHEETS OF WINDY CORN • • 473 CROMWELL   36

SHELF
    AND FROM SOME SWARDED SHELF HIGH UP THERE CAME • •   25 DREAM   11

SHELL
    THE WIND IS DOWN BUT SHELL NOT COME TO-NIGHT •   139 TRISTRAM 1   300
    SHELL LIGHT HER SILVER LAMP WHICH FISHERMEN •   151 TRISTRAM 3   79
    AND TAKE HER BROIDERY-FRAME AND THERE SHELL SIT •   152 TRISTRAM 3   82
    WHOSE STRIPED SHELL FOUNDED • • • • • • •   392 MEROPE   1628

SHELLEY
WHAT BOOTS IT SHELLEY THAT THE BREEZE   • • • •   303 GRANDE CHARTR   139

SHELLS
ITS SHELLS AND ROSES PALE   • • • • • • • •   159 NECKAN   10
MID SHELLS THAT ROUND HER LIE   • • • • • • • •   160 NECKAN   34

SHELTER
AH THINE WAS NOT THE SHELTER BUT THE FRAY   • • • •   42 GIPSY CHILD   24
LACKING THE SHELTER OF THEE   • • • • • • • •   287 RUGBY CHAPEL   36
WHAT SHELTER TO GROW RIPE IS OURS   • • • • • •   308 OBERMANN   71
BEHIND THE SHELTER OF THY FATHERS TOMB   • • • •   332 MEROPE   68

SHELTERD
BUT THEY SLEEP IN SHELTERD REST   • • • • • • • •   140 TRISTRAM 1   327
OF THE TIMES WHICH HAD SHELTERD HIS YOUTH   • • • •   229 YOUTH OF NATURE   30
WHICH SHELTERD THEIR CHILDHOOD THE SUN   • • • •   234 YOUTH OF MAN   65

SHELTRING
IN THE DEEP STILLNESS OF ITS SHELTRING BREAST   • •   472 CROMWELL   12

SHELVES
SCOOP THE SHELVES AND FRET THE STORMS   • • • •   26 NEW SIRENS   12

SHELVING
PARTS FROM THIS CAVE-PIERCED CLIFF THE SHELVING BAY   358 MEROPE   818
PARTS FROM THE CAVE-PIERCD CLIFF THE SHELVING BAY   358 MEROPE   V 818

SHEPHERD
THE SHEPHERD FROM HIS MOUNTAIN-LODGE DESCRIES   • •   79 SOHRAB RUSTUM   621
SHEPHERD WHAT AILS THEE THEN   • • • • • • • •   219 BACCHANALIA 1   40
SHEPHERD WHY MUTE   • • • • • • • • • •   219 BACCHANALIA 1   41
GO FOR THEY CALL YOU SHEPHERD FROM THE HILL   • •   255 SCHOLAR-GIPSY   1
GO SHEPHERD AND UNTIE THE WATTLED COTES   • • • •   255 SCHOLAR-GIPSY   2
COME SHEPHERD AND AGAIN BEGIN THE QUEST   • • • •   255 SCHOLAR-GIPSY   10
AND HERE TILL SUN-DOWN SHEPHERD WILL I BE   • • • •   255 SCHOLAR-GIPSY   22
COME SHEPHERD AND AGAIN RENEW THE QUEST   • • • •   255 SCHOLAR-GIPSY   V 10
HERE TOO OUR SHEPHERD-PIPES WE FIRST ASSAYD   • •   263 THYRSIS   35
O FAITHFUL SHEPHERD TO COME   • • • • • • • •   290 RUGBY CHAPEL   143
POSEIDON TO THE SHEPHERD-BOYS TO HIDE   • • • •   355 MEROPE   737
BEQUEATHS THE ALLEGIANCE OF OUR SHEPHERD-TRIBES   • •   389 MEROPE   1540
BUT KAI A TIRELESS SHEPHERD-LAD   • • • • •   460 KAISER DEAD   44

SHEPHERDESS
AND SAW MY SHEPHERDESS ASLAUGA TEND   • • • • •   117 BALDER DEAD 3   149

SHEPHERDING
SHEPHERDING HIS FLOCK OF GOLD   • • • • • • • •   457 POOR MATTHIAS   185

SHEPHERDS
SHEPHERDS SAY THEY FOUND YOU SLEEPING   • • • •   31 NEW SIRENS   145
SHE HER GOOD SHEPHERDS HASTY IMAGE DREW   • • • •   172 GOOD SHEPHERD   13
SHEPHERDS HAD MET HIM ON THE HURST IN SPRING   • •   256 SCHOLAR-GIPSY   57
AND PUT THE SHEPHERDS WANDERER ON THY TRACE   • •   257 SCHOLAR-GIPSY   63
MY PIPE IS LOST MY SHEPHERDS HOLIDAY   • • • •   264 THYRSIS   37
HERE WITH THE SHEPHERDS AND THE SILLY SHEEP   • •   264 THYRSIS   45
BUT WHEN SICILIAN SHEPHERDS LOST A MATE   • • • •   265 THYRSIS   82
WHEN DORIAN SHEPHERDS SANG TO PROSERPINE   • • • •   265 THYRSIS   92
A SHEPHERDS GARB HE WORE   • • • • • • • •   314 OBERMANN MORE   64
OR THE SHEPHERDS ON SLOPES   • • • • • • • •   392 MEROPE   1641
IN THE MOONLIGHT THE SHEPHERDS   • • • • • • • •   442 EMPEDOCLES II   433

SHEW
A GIFTED MAN THE POWER TO SHEW HIS GIFT   • • • •   LUCRETIUS 2   2

SHIAH
THE SHIAH DOGS WHO PASTURE SHEEP   • • • • • •   93 SICK KING BOKH   167

SHIELD
WERE PLAIN AND ON HIS SHIELD WAS NO DEVICE   • • • •   69 SOHRAB RUSTUM   266
IN TURN AND FULL STRUCK RUSTUMS SHIELD SHARP RANG   73 SOHRAB RUSTUM   406
AND LABOURING BREATH FIRST RUSTUM STRUCK THE SHIELD   75 SOHRAB RUSTUM   491
HIS COVERING SHIELD AND THE SPEAR PIERCED HIS SIDE   76 SOHRAB RUSTUM   520
WHICH TROUBLES ALL MY HEART AND MADE MY SHIELD   • •   77 SOHRAB RUSTUM   549

SHIELDS
ONE FROM THE EAST ONE FROM THE WEST THEIR SHIELDS   75 SOHRAB RUSTUM   474
TOO SOON FOR FAME WITH WHITE UNGRAVEN SHIELDS   • •   109 BALDER DEAD 2   165

SHIFT
TO COME AND GO TO SHIFT AND RANGE   • • • • • •   484 ROME-SICKNESS   22

SHIFTING
AND THY CLEAR AIMS BE CROSS AND SHIFTING MADE   • •   261 SCHOLAR-GIPSY   228

SHIFTS
JUDGMENT SHIFTS CONVICTIONS GO   • • • • • • • •   29 NEW SIRENS   82

SHINE
GAY SHINE THE WATERS AND THE CLUSTERD PIER   • • • •   41 GIPSY CHILD   V 6
EMERGE AND SHINE UPON THE ARAL SEA   • • • • • •   87 SOHRAB RUSTUM   892

SHINE   (CONTINUED)
        SEE IT SHINE AND TAKE IT UP . . . .   135 TRISTRAM 1   143
        AND IN THE BOTTOM OF THE GLADE SHINE CLEAR . . . .   139 TRISTRAM 1   278
        LIGHTS SHINE IN THE TOWN . . . .   164 FORSAKEN MERM   111
        THEY SHINE UPON THE WORLD THEIR EARS . . . . .   203 EUPHROSYNE   21
        LET THOSE ARCH EYES NOW SOFTLY SHINE . . . . .   206 RIVER   5
        TO SHINE THERE EVERLASTINGLY . . . .   220 BACCHANALIA 2   26
        THEN WE SHALL RUST IN SHADE OR SHINE IN STRIFE . .   236 PALLADIUM   17
        AND MARKD THEE WHEN THE STARS COME OUT AND SHINE .   258 SCHOLAR-GIPSY   109
        ROSES THAT DOWN THE ALLEYS SHINE AFAR . . . .   264 THYRSIS   67
        MILD OER HER GRAVE YE MOUNTAINS SHINE . . . .   279 SOUTHERN NIGHT   137
        WE WATCH THOSE YELLOW TAPERS SHINE . . . . . .   305 GRANDE CHARTR   200
        THE HUTS OF AVANT SHINE . . . .   312 OBERMANN MORE   14
        IN DREAMS I SAW THE FUTURE SHINE . . . . . .   321 OBERMANN MORE   259
        AND RUB THE STEEL AND MAKE IT SHINE . . . . .   461 KAISER DEAD   80
        DID WITH SUCH COLD DERISION SHINE . . . . . .   482 COURAGE   22

SHINES
        ON THE WORK THE BRIGHT SUN SHINES . . . . .   15 CHURCH BROU 1   90
        OF THE NEW PILE THE SUNLIGHT SHINES . . . . .   16 CHURCH BROU 2   2
        THE MOON THROUGH THE CLERE-STORY WINDOWS SHINES . .   18 CHURCH BROU 3   36
        FAR UP SHINES THE HOUSE AND BENEATH FLOWS THE RIVER   19 MODERN SAPPHO   3
        BRIGHT SHINES THE SUN . . . .   50 CONSOLATION   15
        HERE WHERE THE BROOK SHINES NEAR ITS HEAD . . . .   55 RESIGNATION   90
        THE CALM SEA SHINES LOOSE HANG THE VESSELS SAILS . .   133 TRISTRAM 1   94
        MILD SHINES THE COLD SPRING IN THE MOONS CLEAR LIGHT   139 TRISTRAM 1   283
        UPON THE WINDOW-PANES THE MOON SHINES BRIGHT . .   139 TRISTRAM 1   299
        IT SHINES UPON THE BLANK WHITE WALLS . . . . .   141 TRISTRAM 1   335
        YOU SEE THEM CLEAR THE MOON SHINES BRIGHT . . .   146 TRISTRAM 2   101
        SHINES THE GHOSTLIKE TAPESTRY . . . .   147 TRISTRAM 2   V 151
        SHINES AND IS GONE THE CLIFFS OF ENGLAND . . . .   210 DOVER BEACH   V 4
        SHINES NOT ITS STREAM . . . .   220 BACCHANALIA 2   52
        HALT THROUGH THE CLOUD-DRIFT SOMETHING SHINES . .   299 GRANDE CHARTR   16

SHINGLE
        THE GRATING SHINGLE STRAGGLED DOWN . . . . . .   480 HAYSWATER BOAT   30

SHINGLES
        AND NAKED SHINGLES OF THE WORLD . . . . . .   211 DOVER BEACH   28

SHINING
        A LIGHT THAT SHINING FROM THE BLEST ABODES . . .   9 MYCERINUS   23
        THEIR SMOOTH TOPS SHINING SUNWARD AND BENEATH . .   11 MYCERINUS   87
        THEIR SMOOTH TOPS SHINING SUNWARDS AND BENEATH . .   11 MYCERINUS   V 87
        ERE HE COME ERE THE BOAT BY THE SHINING-BRANCHD BORDER   19 MODERN SAPPHO   5
        SKIMS NOW AND THEN THE SHINING GROUND . . . .   54 RESIGNATION   71
        THE SAILING FOAM THE SHINING POOL . . . . . .   55 RESIGNATION   105
        TOIL ENDED THROUGH THE SHINING STREETS . . . .   57 RESIGNATION   167
        AND FAR FROM HEAVEN HE TURND HIS SHINING ORBS . .   96 BALDER DEAD 1   51
        DAY DROVE HIS COURSER WITH THE SHINING MANE . .   105 BALDER DEAD 2   2
        ALL SHINING IN THE WHITE MOON-BEAMS . . . . .   141 TRISTRAM 1   370
        NOR TO THE SHINING SEA-FOWL THAT WITH SCREAMS . .   151 TRISTRAM 3   52
        THE HUSH AMONG THE SHINING STARS . . . . . .   180 FAREWELL   79
        THEIR SHINING EYES . . . .   190 STRAYED REVEL   132
        ON CALAIS AND ITS SHINING PLAIN . . . . . .   205 CALAIS SANDS   V 18
        GIRT BY HIS FAR-SHINING TRAIN . . . .   216 LORDS MESSENGER   V
        THEIR SHINING FLANKS THEIR LIQUID EYES . . . .   223 EPILOG LAOCOON   54
        AND WITH JOY THE STARS PERFORM THEIR SHINING . .   240 SELF-DEPENDENCE   21
        OF SHINING PARTS AND QUICK INVENTIVE BRAIN . . . .   256 SCHOLAR-GIPSY   V 34
        ROAM ON THE LIGHT WE SOUGHT IS SHINING STILL . .   269 THYRSIS   238
        THE SHINING MOORLAND TO HEAR . . . .   285 HAWORTH CHURCH   119
        YES IN SOME FAR-SHINING SPHERE . . . .   287 RUGBY CHAPEL   44
        AND ON HIS GRAVE WITH SHINING EYES . . . . .   318 OBERMANN MORE   175
        IS SHINING ON THE BRILLIANT MOUNTAIN-CRESTS . .   406 EMPEDOCLES I 1   10
        ARE SHINING ON THOSE NAKED SLOPES LIKE FLAME . .   412 EMPEDOCLES I 2   6
        DRAWS IN THE ENAMOURD GAZER TO ITS SHINING BREAST   424 EMPEDOCLES I 2   356
        YOUR LONELY COLD-SHINING LIGHTS . . . . . .   437 EMPEDOCLES II   289
        OUR SHINING VISITANT . . . .   444 WESTMIN ABBEY   2
        AND IN THY COURTS HIS SHINING FREIGHT UNROLLD . .   446 WESTMIN ABBEY   76
        MAX WITH SHINING YELLOW COAT . . . .   454 POOR MATTHIAS   71
        IN MOSS AND GORSE AND SHINING FIR . . . . . .   483 ROME-SICKNESS   8

SHIP
        AND NEVER TOUCHES THE SHIP-SIDE AGAIN . . . .   41 HUMAN LIFE   24
        WHEN THOU SHALT SAIL IN A HIGH-MASTED SHIP . . .   85 SOHRAB RUSTUM   831
        BRING WOOD TO THE SEASHORE TO BALDERS SHIP . .   96 BALDER DEAD 1   41
        UPON MY SHIP AND BURN MY CORPSE WITH FIRE . . .   103 BALDER DEAD 1   297
        AND MAKE A FUNERAL-PILE ON BALDERS SHIP . . .   106 BALDER DEAD 2   43
        AND RANGED THE WOOD IN STACKS BY BALDERS SHIP . .   106 BALDER DEAD 2   68
        THE GODS ON THE SEA-SHORE BY BALDERS SHIP . . .   113 BALDER DEAD 2   310
        BRING NOW THE GATHERD WOOD TO BALDERS SHIP . .   118 BALDER DEAD 3   158
        THE WOOD TO BALDERS SHIP AND BUILT A PILE . . .   118 BALDER DEAD 3   161
        TO PUSH THE SHIP THROUGH THE THICK SAND SPARKS FLEW   118 BALDER DEAD 3   177
        AND THE SHIP FLOATED ON THE WAVES AND ROCKD . .   118 BALDER DEAD 3   180
        AND WREATHED IN SMOKE THE SHIP STOOD OUT TO SEA . .   118 BALDER DEAD 3   185
        AND ATE THE SHRIVELLING SAILS BUT STILL THE SHIP .   119 BALDER DEAD 3   191
        BUT THROUGH THE DARK THEY WATCHD THE BURNING SHIP   119 BALDER DEAD 3   197
        HIS SHIP AND THE GREAT SERPENT MAKES TO LAND . .   127 BALDER DEAD 3   479
        OF SOME SHIP THAT FIGHTS THE GALE . . . . . .   130 TRISTRAM 1   13
        SHE WHOM TRISTRAMS SHIP OF YORE . . . . . .   132 TRISTRAM 1   59

SHIP   (CONTINUED)
        NOT PENT ON SHIP-BOARD THIS DELICIOUS DAY   • • •   133 TRISTRAM 1   98
        THERE IN A SHIP THEY BORE THOSE LOVERS COLD   • •   149 TRISTRAM 3   4
        SITTING IN THE DARK SHIP   • • • • • • • • •   192 STRAYED REVEL   202
        HE WAS BORN IN A SHIP   • • • • • • • • • •   251 FUTURE   2
        TO MEET HER PIRATE-LOVERS SHIP   • • • • • •   278 SOUTHERN NIGHT   105
        WHERE PHILOCTETES PINED TAKE SHIP AND FLEE   • • • •   395 MEROPE   1747
        IN HIS LONG BLACK SHIP SPEEDING NIGHT AND DAY   • •   485 S S LUSITANIA   10

SHIPBOARD
        SAVE ONE BERGELMER HE ON SHIPBOARD FLED   • • • •   121 BALDER DEAD 3   272

SHIPS
        WHO WHEN SHIPS ARE THAT WAY TENDING   • • • • •   26 NEW SIRENS   13
        THEIR SHIPS AND THROUGH THE GATE BEYOND THE WALL   • •   97 BALDER DEAD 1   75
        WHICH VENICE SHIPS DO FROM SWART EGYPT BRING   • •   150 TRISTRAM 3   41
        LIKE SHIPS THAT MEET AND SPEAK AND PASS   • • • •   185 TERRACE BERNE   V 45
        WHERE RODE THE TALL DARK SHIPS WHOSE LOOSEND SAIL   •   473 CROMWELL   67
        WHERE THE DARK SHIPS RODE PROUDLY WOOD THE GALE   • • •   479 CROMWELL   238
        BETWEEN THAT AND THE SHIPS THE TROJANS NUMEROUS FIRES   HOMER TRANS   2

SHIPWRECK
        ALL SHIPWRECK IN THY OWN WEAK HEART   • • • • • • •   307 OBERMANN   19

SHIRT
        OOZING THROUGH THY SOAKD HUNTING-SHIRT WITH LIMBS   373 MEROPE   1173
        WHEN THE SHIRT-WRAPT POISON-BLISTERD HERO   • • • •   399 MEROPE   1832

SHIVER
        SHIVER AND DIE   • • • • • • • • • • •   35 VOICE   8
        A SHIVER RUNS THROUGH THE DEEP CORN FOR JOY   • •   65 SOHRAB RUSTUM   156
        I SHIVER FOR THE PASSING DAY   • • • • • • • •   183 ABSENCE   3
        DEAD AND NO WARNING SHIVER RAN   • • • • • • • •   184 TERRACE BERNE   26

SHIVERD
        IS STREWN WITH ROCKS AND MANY A SHIVERD MASS   • •   150 TRISTRAM 3   16
        SHE SHIVERD AND OBEYD   • • • • • • • • • •   316 OBERMANN MORE   124
        TO MARK WITH SHIVERD CREST THE REELING WAVE   • •   472 CROMWELL   23

SHIVERING
        SHIVERING WITH FEVER NAKED OLD   • • • • • • •   157 SAINT BRANDAN   46
        WITH SHIVERING HEART THE STRIFE WE SAW   • • • •   270 MEMORIAL VERSES   10
        OUR SHIVERING HEART IS MINED BY SECRET DISCONTENT   424 EMPEDOCLES I 2   366

SHIVERS
        REELS AND SHIVERS ON THE RUFFLED GLOOM   • • • •   32 NEW SIRENS   186
        SPRANG IN A THOUSAND SHIVERS ON THE HELM   • • • •   76 SOHRAB RUSTUM   512

SHOALS
        RAPHAELS IN SHOALS   • • • • • • • • • • • •   221 BACCHANALIA 2   58

SHOCK
        ENOUGH THE BOAT WITH QUIET SHOCK   • • • • • •   276 SOUTHERN NIGHT   45
        BUT WE RECEIVED THE SHOCK OF MIGHTY THOUGHTS   • •   436 EMPEDOCLES II   242

SHOCKS
        BY CITY AND HOUSEHOLD GROUPD WE LIVE AND MANY SHOCKS   195 FRAG ANTIGONE   20
        TIS THAT REPEATED SHOCKS AGAIN AGAIN   • • • • • •   259 SCHOLAR-GIPSY   144

SHONE
        BLACK UNDER CLIFFS IT RACED ROUND HEADLANDS SHONE   25 DREAM   34
        AND YOUR HEAVENLY EYES SHONE THROUGH   • • • • • •   29 NEW SIRENS   98
        STARS SHONE AFTER A DAY OF STORM   • • • • • •   156 SAINT BRANDAN   14
        THEY NEVER SHONE FOR ME   • • • • • • • • •   209 DESPONDENCY   4
        THE FAMOUS ORATORS HAVE SHONE   • • • • • • •   219 BACCHANALIA 2   3
        THE SUN SHONE IN THE NEW-WASHD SKY   • • • • • •   319 OBERMANN MORE   209
        SHONE OFT SO HIGH A LIGHT   • • • • • • • • •   446 WESTMIN ABBEY   82
        THINE EYE WAS BRIGHT THY COAT IT SHONE   • • • •   460 KAISER DEAD   61
        IN BROAD CLEAR LIGHT THE GHASTLY VISION SHONE   • •   477 CROMWELL   203
        SO SHONE FORTH IN FRONT OF TROY BY THE BED OF XANTHUS   HOMER TRANS   1

SHOOK
        ON THE DRY NOON SHOOK THEIR DEW   • • • • • •   29 NEW SIRENS   108
        GLARED AND HE SHOOK ON HIGH HIS MENACING SPEAR   • •   76 SOHRAB RUSTUM   515
        AND STRONG CONVULSIVE GROANINGS SHOOK HIS BREAST   • •   82 SOHRAB RUSTUM   703
        MOURNFULLY SHOOK HIS HEAD AND DISAPPEARD   • • •   104 BALDER DEAD 1   334
        NOR SHOOK THE BRIDGE SO MUCH AS THOU ALONE   • • •   107 BALDER DEAD 2   106
        SHOOK HER WEAK BOSOM DAY AND NIGHT   • • • • •   147 TRISTRAM 2   133
        AND SNATCHD HIS RUDDER AND SHOOK OUT MORE SAIL   • •   262 SCHOLAR-GIPSY   242
        SHOOK LIKE A CLARION-BLAST MY SOUL   • • • • •   284 HAWORTH CHURCH V 100
        AND SHOOK AS IT RUSHD BY HER   • • • • • • •   319 OBERMANN MORE   204
        WHO SHOOK THE FIERCE NELEIDAE ON THEIR THRONE   • •   338 MEROPE   292
        SHOOK BACK HIS TANGLED LOCKS AND MURMURD PEACE   • •   477 CROMWELL   174
        SHOOK THE DEEP SLUMBER OF HIS DEATHLIKE TRANCE   • •   477 CROMWELL   194
        AND HE SHOOK HIS HEAD AND THUS ADDRESSD HIS OWN BOSOM   HOMER TRANS   8

SHOOT
        OF DARK ELMS SHOOT ROUND DROPPING DOWN THE   19 MODERN SAPPHO   6
            PROUD STREAM
        SEES SUDDENLY A SPIRE OF FLAME SHOOT UP   • • • •   119 BALDER DEAD 3   V
        NOR THE CROPPD HERBAGE SHOOT ANOTHER HEAD   • • • •   255 SCHOLAR-GIPSY   5

SHOOT   (CONTINUED)
        NOR THE CROPPD GRASSES SHOOT ANOTHER HEAD   • • • •   255 SCHOLAR-GIPSY   V   5
        SO DIES THE LAST SHOOT OF OUR ROYAL TREE   • • • •   359 MEROPE   857

SHOOTING
        TIS HE TIS THEIR FLAG SHOOTING ROUND BY THE TREES   20 MODERN SAPPHO   30
        TIS HE TIS THE BOAT SHOOTING ROUND BY THE TREES   • •   20 MODERN SAPPHO   V 30
        OF SHOOTING CLIFF AND CRUMBLED STONE   • • • • •   •   479 HAYSWATER BOAT   13

SHOOTS
        OF TREES AND VEINS OF TURF AND LONG DARK SHOOTS   • •   414 EMPEDOCLES I 2   48

SHORE
        OF HIS PALE WIFE WHO WAITS AND WEEPS ON SHORE   • •   69 SOHRAB RUSTUM   285
        HE SHORE AWAY AND THAT PROUD HORSEHAIR PLUME   • •   76 SOHRAB RUSTUM   497
        OF THE BRIGHT ROCKING OCEAN SETS TO SHORE   • • • •   79 SOHRAB RUSTUM   617
        TO THE LOW SHORE OF GHOSTS AND HELAS REALM   • • • •   99 BALDER DEAD 1   151
        BUT HE WILL REACH ITS UNKNOWN NORTHERN SHORE   • •   99 BALDER DEAD 1   162
        BEING ALIVE AND COME TO OCEANS SHORE   • • • • •   •   110 BALDER DEAD 2   184
        THE GODS ON THE SEA-SHORE BY BALDERS SHIP   • • • •   113 BALDER DEAD 2   310
        AND WEEP FROM SHORE TO SHORE MY GOLDEN TEARS   • •   116 BALDER DEAD 3   110
        AND WEEP FROM SHORE TO SHORE MY GOLDEN TEARS   • •   116 BALDER DEAD 3   110
        BUT THE GODS WENT BY STARLIGHT UP THE SHORE   • •   119 BALDER DEAD 3   207
        FROM HER LONELY SHORE-BUILT TOWER • • • • • •   •   131 TRISTRAM 1   43
        HIS LONG RAMBLES BY THE SHORE • • • • • • •   •   137 TRISTRAM 1   215
        ONE LAST KISS UPON THE LIVING SHORE   • • • • •   •   145 TRISTRAM 2   98
        WHICH BORDERS THE SEA-SHORE A COUNTRY PATH   • • • •   149 TRISTRAM 3   8
        THE HOLLIES AND THE CLIFF AND THE SEA-SHORE   • •   152 TRISTRAM 3   104
        THE SEA WITHOUT A HUMAN SHORE • • • • • • •   •   156 SAINT BRANDAN   12
        AND THE LITTLE GREY CHURCH ON THE WINDY SHORE   • •   162 FORSAKEN MERM   26
        IN THE LITTLE GREY CHURCH ON THE SHORE TO-DAY   • •   163 FORSAKEN MERM   57
        ABOVE THE FRAGRANT WARM PROVENCAL SHORE   • • • •   167 RACHEL 2   2
        AND LOVELY NOTES FROM SHORE TO SHORE   • • • • •   •   182 TO MARG CONT   11
        AND LOVELY NOTES FROM SHORE TO SHORE   • • • • •   •   182 TO MARG CONT   11
        O WANDERER FROM A GRECIAN SHORE   • • • • • •   •   200 PHILOMELA   5
        WAS ONCE TOO AT THE FULL AND ROUND EARTHS SHORE   • •   211 DOVER BEACH   22
        ONLY A FEW THE LIFE-STREAMS SHORE • • • • • •   •   226 EPILOG LAOCOON   189
        STILL STANDING FOR SOME FALSE IMPOSSIBLE SHORE   • •   244 SUMMER NIGHT   69
        GONE IS THE CALM OF ITS EARLIER SHORE • • • • •   •   253 FUTURE   52
        OF ITS EARLY MOUNTAINOUS SHORE   • • • • • •   •   254 FUTURE   76
        WE TRACKD THE SHY THAMES SHORE   • • • • • •   •   266 THYRSIS   126
        THE SANDY SPITS THE SHORE-LOCKD LAKES • • • •   •   275 SOUTHERN NIGHT   1
        TOUCHD SHORE TO DIE   • • • • • • • •   •   278 SOUTHERN NIGHT   V 96
        O STRONG SOUL BY WHAT SHORE   • • • • • • •   •   287 RUGBY CHAPEL   37
        THROUGH EUROPE TO THE AETOLIAN SHORE   • • • • •   •   303 GRANDE CHARTR   135
        LIKE CHILDREN BATHING ON THE SHORE   • • • • •   •   308 OBERMANN   73
        BASK IN THE GLENS OR ON THE WARM SEA-SHORE   • • • •   427 EMPEDOCLES I 2   437
        AND ROW HIM STRAIGHTWAY TO THE FURTHER SHORE   • •   444 WESTMIN ABBEY   25
        BY HILL OR WAVE THE MOUNTAIN OR THE SHORE   • • • •   472 CROMWELL   30
        ONE ROOD FROM SHORE THAT SINGLE BOAT   • • • •   •   479 HAYSWATER BOAT   16
        THIS BOAT THEY FOUND AGAINST THE SHORE   • • • •   •   480 HAYSWATER BOAT   25
        THE FLOOD OF THE WORLDS COMMERCE ON HER SHORE   • •   480 HUNGARIAN NAT   3

SHORELESS
        DOTTING THE SHORELESS WATERY WILD   • • • • • •   •   182 TO MARG CONT   3

SHORES
        WHO ON SHORES AND SEA-WASHD PLACES   • • • • • • •   26 NEW SIRENS   11
        AND THEIR QUICK TWITTERING FILLS THE BANKS AND SHORES   109 BALDER DEAD 2   162
        AND BADE BETWIXT THEIR SHORES TO BE • • • • •   •   182 TO MARG CONT   23
        TO WESTERN SHORES THE DEATH-PLACE OF THE DAY   • •   475 CROMWELL   112

SHOREWARD
        NOW THE GREAT WINDS SHOREWARD BLOW   • • • • • •   •   161 FORSAKEN MERM   4
        WHERE THE SHOREWARD RIPPLE BREAKS   • • • • • •   •   434 EMPEDOCLES II   178

SHOREWARDS
        NOW THE GREAT WINDS SHOREWARDS BLOW   • • • • • •   •   161 FORSAKEN MERM   V   4

SHORN
        THE SHORN AND PARCELLD OXUS STRAINS ALONG   • • • •   87 SOHRAB RUSTUM   884
        SHORN OF THE JOY THE BLOOM THE POWER   • • • •   •   322 OBERMANN MORE   303
        WITH BLOOD-BESPATTERD ROBES AND CHAPLET SHORN   • •   403 MEROPE   1966

SHORT
        OF LABOUR THAT IN ONE SHORT HOUR OUTGROWS   • • • •   1 QUIET WORK   V   6
        OF ONE SHORT JOY ONE LUST ONE PLEASANT DREAM   • •   10 MYCERINUS   50
        MY SAND RUNS SHORT AND AS YON STAR-SHOT RAY   • •   10 MYCERINUS   56
        AFTER SHORT COMMERCE WITH ME FEAR MY FROWN   • • • •   37 WORLDS TRIUMPHS   8
        AND CLIP HIS BORDERS SHORT AND DRIVE HIS HERDS   • •   68 SOHRAB RUSTUM   234
        AND IN THE MIDST A STUBBLE SHORT AND BARE   • • • •   70 SOHRAB RUSTUM   296
        HIS PINION AND WITH SHORT UNEASY SWEEPS   • • • • •   78 SOHRAB RUSTUM   564
        A LITTLE POOL AND IN SHORT SPACE   • • • • •   •   90 SICK KING BOKH   68
        AND HAVE NOW SHORT SPACE FOR BEING GLAD   • • • •   144 TRISTRAM 2   56
        HIS SHORT COAT TRAVEL-TARNISHD   • • • • • •   •   189 STRAYED REVEL   106
        AND LONG THE WAY APPEARS WHICH SEEMD SO SHORT   • •   267 THYRSIS   141
        SHORT BUT REDOUBLED BY FAME   • • • • • • •   •   283 HAWORTH CHURCH   73
        SHORT YET REDOUBLED BY FAME   • • • • • •   •   283 HAWORTH CHURCH   V 73
        OER THE FRESH SHORT TURF OF THE HARTZ • • • •   •   297 HEINES GRAVE   153
        FOR ONE SHORT MOMENT WANDER OER HIS LIPS   • • • •   298 HEINES GRAVE   209

SHORT   (CONTINUED)
       SO WOULD HAVE BUILT YOU IN A FEW SHORT YEARS   • • 339 MEROPE   304
       SHORT ANSWER IS SUFFICIENT LEAGUE WITH THEE   • • 340 MEROPE   335
       ADMIRE THEN MAIDENS HOW IN ONE SHORT HOUR   • • 360 MEROPE   875
       THE SHORT PROUD LIP SHOWING THY RACE THY CHEEKS   • • 373 MEROPE   1163
       CUT SHORT THY TRIUMPH SEEMING AT ITS HEIGHT   • • 395 MEROPE   1742
       OF SHORT GRASS BEADED WITH DEW • • • • •   • • 399 MEROPE   1823
       WITH SHORT IMPATIENT LOWINGS THERE HE STOPPD   • • 402 MEROPE   1912
       WHERE MY OWN YOUTH FALLS SHORT BUT LAIAS NOW   • • 405 MEROPE   2016
       CAN CUT HIS OSCILLATIONS SHORT AND SO   • • • • 436 EMPEDOCLES II   233
       SHALL CUT HIS OSCILLATIONS SHORT AND SO   • • • • 436 EMPEDOCLES II   V 233
       ALTERNATING WITH WISDOMS TOO SHORT REIGN   • • 449 WESTMIN ABBEY   158
       WHAT WAS FOUR YEARS THEIR WHOLE SHORT DAY   • • • • 450 GEISTS GRAVE   20
       WHAT WAS FOUR YEARS THEIR WHOLE SHORT STAY   • • • • 450 GEISTS GRAVE   V 20
       CUTS SHORT THE FEIGNINGS OF FANTASTIC GRIEF   • •   FRAGMENT 1   6

SHORTLY
       SHORTLY YE SHALL RESUME THEM WITH YOUR QUEEN   • • • 332 MEROPE   78
       FOR A GRAND CULPRIT SHORTLY COMING DOWN   • • • • 373 MEROPE   1189

SHOT
       MY SAND RUNS SHORT AND AS YON STAR-SHOT RAY   • •   10 MYCERINUS   56
       WE SHOT BENEATH THE COTTAGE WITH THE STREAM   • •   25 DREAM   20
       SHARP QUIVERING TONGUES OF FLAME SHOT OUT AND LEAPT   119 BALDER DEAD 3   188
       FIRED THEIR RINGING SHOT AND PASSD   • • • • • • 215 LAST WORD   11
       A BOLT IS SHOT BACK SOMEWHERE IN OUR BREAST   • • 247 BURIED LIFE   84
       CHANGING AND SHOT AS THE SIGHTS WHICH WE SEE   • • 253 FUTURE   57

SHOULDER
       HIS SPEAR DOWN FROM THE SHOULDER DOWN IT CAME   • •   73 SOHRAB RUSTUM   399
       HIS BELT AND NEAR THE SHOULDER BARED HIS ARM   • •   81 SOHRAB RUSTUM   670
       SET HIS STOUT SHOULDER HARD AGAINST THE STERN   • • 118 BALDER DEAD 3   176
       ON THY WHITE SHOULDER • • • • • • • • • • • 186 STRAYED REVEL   18
       AND ON THY SHOULDER REST MY HEAD   • • • • • • 206 RIVER   12
       UPON THE OPEN SHOULDER OF THE HILL   • • • • • • 412 EMPEDOCLES I 2   3

SHOULDERING
       SHALL DRAW TO SWELL THAT SHOULDERING HERD   • • • •   48 HORATIAN ECHO   9
       SHOULDERING HIS HAMMER WHICH THE GIANTS KNOW   • • 106 BALDER DEAD 2   49
       SHOULDERING THY HAMMER IN THY CHARIOT DRAWN   • • 115 BALDER DEAD 3   72

SHOULDERS
       WHICH DANCED AND ON THEIR SHOULDERS FLUTTERING PLAYD   25 DREAM   25
       WHICH WAVD AND ON THEIR SHOULDERS FLUTTERING PLAYD   25 DREAM   V 25
       WHICH STIRRD AND ON THEIR SHOULDERS FLUTTERING PLAYD   25 DREAM   V 25
       FOLLOWD AND ON THEIR SHOULDERS CARRIED BOUGHS   • • 106 BALDER DEAD 2   64
       THE RINGLETS ON HER SHOULDERS LYING   • • • • • • 131 TRISTRAM 1   26
       AND ON HIS SHOULDERS NOT A LAMB A KID   • • • • 172 GOOD SHEPHERD   14
       LOOSE OER THEIR SHOULDERS WHITE   • • • • • • 218 BACCHANALIA 1   26
       GLOW NOT THEIR SHOULDERS SMOOTH   • • • • • • 219 BACCHANALIA 1   46
       BEARING ON SHOULDERS IMMENSE   • • • • • • • • 295 HEINES GRAVE   93
       BEARING ON HIS SHOULDERS BROAD   • • • • • • • •   PILLARS UNIVERS   3

SHOUT
       HARK A SHOUT A CRASH A GROAN   • • • • • • • • •   13 CHURCH BROU 1   24
       AND SHOUTED RUSTUM SOHRAB HEARD THAT SHOUT   • • • •   76 SOHRAB RUSTUM   516
       WITH SHOUT AND SHAKEN SPEAR   • • • • • • • • • 191 STRAYED REVEL   189
       SILENT HARDLY A SHOUT   • • • • • • • • • • 286 RUGBY CHAPEL   6
       WAS THE WILD SHOUT THOSE GOTHIC MYRIADS GAVE   • • 466 ALARIC AT ROME   112
       JARRD WITH THE BURSTING SHOUT THEY COME THE   • • 467 ALARIC AT ROME   132
           GOTH THEY COME
       THE SHOUT OF ONSET AND THE SHRIEK OF FEAR   • • • • 475 CROMWELL   135

SHOUTED
       AND SHOUTED RUSTUM SOHRAB HEARD THAT SHOUT   • • • •   76 SOHRAB RUSTUM   516
       THE PRICKERS SHOUTED THAT THE STAG WAS GONE   • • 357 MEROPE   788
       THEN CAME THE PRINCE HE SHOUTED AND PLUNGED IN   • • 358 MEROPE   810
       AND SHOUTED SINCE BY THEE DEFILEMENT CAME   • • • • 402 MEROPE   1923

SHOUTING
       WITH GOAD AND SHOUTING URGE THEIR CATTLE PAST   • • 107 BALDER DEAD 2   96
       CAROLLING AND SHOUTING   • • • • • • • • • • 220 BACCHANALIA 2   31
       I AT THAT ALTAR WHERE MID SHOUTING CROWDS   • • • • 338 MEROPE   272
       AND STOOD SHOUTING FOR A FIERY TORCH   • • • • • • 399 MEROPE   1835
       AND STANDS SHOUTING FOR A SLAUGHTEROUS AXE   • • • • 400 MEROPE   1860
       HARK HOW THE SHOUTING CROWDS TRAMP HITHERWARD   • • 401 MEROPE   1886

SHOUTS
       SHOUTS GREETING FROM HIS EASY CHAIR   • • • • • •   53 RESIGNATION   43
       AND ALL THE PERSIANS KNEW HIM AND WITH SHOUTS   • •   69 SOHRAB RUSTUM   282
       THE CHILDRENS SHOUTS AND AT TIMES   • • • • • • 234 YOUTH OF MAN   72

SHOW
       IF SADNESS AT THE LONG HEART-WASTING SHOW   • • • •   7 REP FRIEND   9
       SHOW YOU SAY MY LOVE DECLINES   • • • • • • • • •   24 MEMORY-PICTURE   50
       LOVE TRANSIENT POWER AN UNREAL SHOW   • • • • • •   59 RESIGNATION   236
       IF THOU SHOW THIS THEN ART THOU RUSTUMS SON   • •   81 SOHRAB RUSTUM   668
       TO MOURN WITH HIM AND SHOW HIM CARE   • • • • • •   92 SICK KING BOKH   156
       SHOW ME THROUGH ALL THE WORLD THE SIGNS OF GRIEF • • 111 BALDER DEAD 2   234
       SHOW HER THROUGH ALL THE WORLD THE SIGNS OF GRIEF   114 BALDER DEAD 3   42

SHOW   (CONTINUED)
```
        TO SHOW HIM SPITS AND BEACHES OF THE SEA    . . .    122 BALDER DEAD 3        321
        SATE WITH HIS BRIDE TO SEE A PUBLIC SHOW     . . .    166 AUSTERITY POET         4
        IN THE BARE MIDST OF ANGLESEY THEY SHOW      . . .    170 EAST AND WEST          1
        YET SHOW HER ONCE YE HEAVENLY POWERS   . . . . .      202 URANIA                17
        THE ASPECT OF THE MOMENT SHOW    . . . . .           225 EPILOG LAOCOON        131
        HATH IN HIS EYE EVER BUT SERVD TO SHOW    . . .      238 PROGRESS              V
        ALL WHICH MAKES DEATH A HIDEOUS SHOW   . . . .       250 WISH                  16
        ALL THAT MAKES DEATH A HIDEOUS SHOW    . . . .       250 WISH                V 16
        THE EVENT WILL QUICKLY SHOW    . . . . .             354 MEROPE               702
        WASHD AS THE MARKS UPON THE HILLS STILL SHOW  .      358 MEROPE               815
        AND SUCH AS FITS A ROYAL HOUSE TO SHOW    . . .      359 MEROPE               871
        AT THY DEAD HUSBANDS NAME THE PEOPLE SHOW   . .      401 MEROPE              1894
        THAT EVEN IN THY VICTORY THOU SHOW   . . . . .       405 MEROPE              2012
        SYMPATHY COULD FEEL AND SHOW    . . . . .           455 POOR MATTHIAS         93
        AS THEY SHOW AND DISAPPEAR    . . . . . .            456 POOR MATTHIAS        146

SHOWD
        AND SHOWD A SIGN IN FAINT VERMILION POINTS   . . .   81 SOHRAB RUSTUM        671
        THE LAND OF ARIOSTO SHOWD    . . . . . .            222 EPILOG LAOCOON        22
        SHOWD ME THE HIGH WHITE STAR OF TRUTH    . . .      301 GRANDE CHARTR         69
        SHOWD ME THE PALE COLD STAR OF TRUTH   . . . .      301 GRANDE CHARTR       V 69
        HE SHOWD HIM PHTHIA FAR AWAY   . . . . .            414 EMPEDOCLES I 2        68

SHOWED
        SO SHOWED IN THE FAR DARKNESS BALDERS PYRE   . . .  119 BALDER DEAD 3      V 200

SHOWER
        A CHARRD LOG FALLING MAKES A SHOWER OF SPARKS   . . 119 BALDER DEAD 3        204
        SO WITH A SHOWER OF SPARKS THE PILE FELL IN     . . 119 BALDER DEAD 3        205
        WHAT BLESSING MUST FULL GOODNESS SHOWER    . . .   158 SAINT BRANDAN         54
        WHAT BLESSING MUST TRUE GOODNESS SHOWER    . . .   158 SAINT BRANDAN       V 54
        ITS SPELL IS ROUND THEM LIKE A SHOWER    . . .     227 EPILOG LAOCOON       199

SHOWERD
        IN BLINDING MASSES SHOWERD THE GOLDEN HAIR   . . .  150 TRISTRAM 3           34

SHOWERING
        WHEN YOUR SHOWERING LOCKS ENWOUND YOU    . . . .    29 NEW SIRENS           97
        SHOWERING THEIR HAIR    . . . . . . . .            218 BACCHANALIA 1        27

SHOWERLESS
        BENT TO THE COLD WINDS OF THE SHOWERLESS SPRING  . . 12 MYCERINUS          120

SHOWERS
        COME BIND UP THOSE RINGLET SHOWERS    . . . . .    32 NEW SIRENS          173
        HER MOODS GOOD LACK THEY PASS LIKE SHOWERS   . . . 146 TRISTRAM 2          125
        THROUGH WHOSE FRAIL LEAVES AND SHOWERS   . . . .   200 PHILOMELA          V
        THROUGH WHOSE LIGHT LEAVES AND SHOWERS   . . . .   200 PHILOMELA          V
        THEIR SCENT AND RUSTLE DOWN THEIR PERFUMED SHOWERS  256 SCHOLAR-GIPSY       27
        FRESHEND BY PLUNGING TIDES BY SHOWERS    . . . .   275 STANZAS CARNAC      42
        APRIL SHOWERS    . . . . . . . . . .              286 HAWORTH CHURCH     129
        ETERNAL SHOWERS OF SPRAY ON THE MOSSD ROOTS    .   414 EMPEDOCLES I 2      47
        STRESS OF GALE AND SHOWERS OF SPRAY   . . . . .   457 POOR MATTHIAS       178

SHOWERY
        BETWEEN HEATH-CLAD SHOWERY HILLS    . . . . .     282 HAWORTH CHURCH      57
        LOOK THROUGH THE SHOWERY TWILIGHT GREY   . . . .  300 GRANDE CHARTR       22

SHOWING
        SHOWING THEN BLOTTING FROM OUR SIGHT   . . . . .  299 GRANDE CHARTR       15
        THE SHORT PROUD LIP SHOWING THY RACE THY CHEEKS  . . 373 MEROPE          1163

SHOWN
        I HAVE STILL SERVED AFRASIAB WELL AND SHOWN    .   62 SOHRAB RUSTUM       44
        AND WE HAVE SHOWN ON EACH SPIRIT AND POWER   . . . 246 BURIED LIFE        58
        AND WE HAVE SHOWN ON EACH TALENT AND POWER   . . . 246 BURIED LIFE      V 58
        WHEREVER SHOWN HOWEER INSPIRED    . . . . . .    279 SOUTHERN NIGHT     131
        WHATEVER SHOWN HOWEER ATTIRD    . . . . . .      279 SOUTHERN NIGHT   V 131
        SOMETHING TOO STUDIOUSLY FORGIVE ME SHOWN    . .  334 MEROPE             142
        BY HIM SHOWN FAIR BUT I BELIEVE MOST FOUL    . .  349 MEROPE             556
        HIS GROUNDS HOWEVER SPECIOUS SHOWN    . . . .     354 MEROPE             694
        FIRST HEARD OR IN ITS FUTURE ISSUE SHOWN   . . .  359 MEROPE             865
        WHEN ALL TURND TOWRDS ME ME HE WOULD HAVE SHOWN  .  366 MEROPE          1005
        THEIR KINDNESS SHOWN ME IN MY WANDERING HOUR   .  447 WESTMIN ABBEY      109

SHOWS
        SHOWS PARTIALITY    . . . . . . . . . .           52 CONSOLATION        73
        AND SHOWS ITS LIGHTED WINDOWS TO THE MAIN    . .   97 BALDER DEAD 1      86
        A BREAK BETWEEN THE HOUSETOPS SHOWS    . . . .    242 SUMMER NIGHT        6
        PROOF NOT SURMISE SHOWS HIM IN COMMERCE CLOSE   .  380 MEROPE           1274

SHOWST
        WHAT WAY IS THIS O MOTHER THAT THOU SHOWST   . . .  99 BALDER DEAD 1     132
        MOTHER A DREADFUL WAY IS THIS THOU SHOWST    . . . 100 BALDER DEAD 1     185

SHRANK
        SHRANK ONLY RUSTUM DARED THEN HE AND I   . . . .   72 SOHRAB RUSTUM     360
        AND SHRANK AMAZED BACK HE RECOILD ONE STEP   . . . 76 SOHRAB RUSTUM     517
        AND SHRANK AMAZED BACK HE RECOILD ONE PACE   . . . 76 SOHRAB RUSTUM   V 517
```

SHREDS
    REND IN A THOUSAND SHREDS THIS LIFE OF OURS   4 BUTLERS SERMONS   4
    SHREDS OF GIFTS WHICH HE REFUSED IN FULL   210 SELF-DECEPTION   18
    WITH SCARLET PATCHES TAGGD AND SHREDS OF GREY   258 SCHOLAR-GIPSY   114

SHRIEK
    THE SHOUT OF ONSET AND THE SHRIEK OF FEAR   475 CROMWELL   135

SHRILL
    WITH SHRILL AND DISMAL CRIES THAT BIRD SHALL CROW   105 BALDER DEAD 2   6
    WHEN THE FEAST WAS LOUD AND THE LAUGHTER SHRILL   146 TRISTRAM 2   V 114
    AH WHO ARE THESE WHAT SHRILL EAR-PIERCING SCREAM   375 MEROPE   1202

SHRILLS
    SHRILLS ROUND THEIR PORTAL   50 CONSOLATION   22

SHRINE
    SINK IN THYSELF THERE ASK WHAT AILS THEE AT   417 EMPEDOCLES I 2   146
      THAT SHRINE

SHRINES
    THE GREAT ORACULAR SHRINES   198 FRAG DEJANEIRA   11

SHRINK
    MIGHT SHRINK HALF STARTLED LIKE A GUILTY MAN   11 MYCERINUS   102

SHRIVELLING
    AND ATE THE SHRIVELLING SAILS BUT STILL THE SHIP   119 BALDER DEAD 3   191

SHROUD
    UNWELCOME SHROUD OF THE FORGOTTEN DEAD   462 ALARIC AT ROME   1
    FOLD LIKE A SHROUD AROUND THY WITHERED BONES   464 ALARIC AT ROME   64

SHROUDED
    HAUNTING THE SHROUDED CHAMBERS OF HIS HEART   473 CROMWELL   58
    A FORM HE KNEW BUT IT WAS SHROUDED THEN   476 CROMWELL   146

SHRUNK
    A DARING HAND THAT SHRUNK NOT TO FULFIL   478 CROMWELL   227

SHUDDER
    I SHUDDER FOR THE PASSING DAY   183 ABSENCE   V 3
    I SHUDDER LAIAS TO COMMIT MY CHILD   387 MEROPE   1461

SHUDDERING
    SHUDDERING THEY DREW HER GARMENTS OFF AND FOUND   166 AUSTERITY POET   10

SHUFFLE
    AND FROM THE BOUGHS THE SNOWLOADS SHUFFLE DOWN   122 BALDER DEAD 3   313

SHUFFLES
    WHO SHUFFLES THROUGH THE DEEP DEW-MOISTEND DUST   101 BALDER DEAD 1   232

SHUNS
    AND SHUNS TO PERIL IT WITH YOUNGER MEN   68 SOHRAB RUSTUM   248

SHUT
    PALE DEW-DRENCHD HALF-SHUT ROSES GLEAM   57 RESIGNATION   179
    FOR ALLAH SHUT MY EARS AND MIND   88 SICK KING BOKH   24
    AND HE WENT IN AND SHUT THE DOOR AND FIXT   102 BALDER DEAD 1   251
    LOUD PRAYS THE PRIEST SHUT STANDS THE DOOR   163 FORSAKEN MERM   82
    WHEN BYRONS EYES WERE SHUT IN DEATH   270 MEMORIAL VERSES   6
    SHUT OUT THE GRIEF THE DESPAIR   283 HAWORTH CHURCH   V
    SHE TORE HER BOOKS SHE SHUT HER COURTS   316 OBERMANN MORE   131
    WE SHUT OUR EYES AND MUSE   423 EMPEDOCLES I 2   327

SHUTS
    NOT SUFFERING WHICH SHUTS UP EYE AND EAR   152 TRISTRAM 3   113
    NOT SUFFERING THAT SHUTS UP EYE AND EAR   152 TRISTRAM 3   V 113

SHUTTERS
    SHUTTERS AND DARKEND ROOM   293 HEINES GRAVE   18

SHUTTLE
    TILL THE SHUTTLE FALLS FROM HER HAND   164 FORSAKEN MERM   V 96

SHY
    SHALL BREATHLESS GLADES CHEERD BY SHY DIANS HORN   6 GEO CRUIKSHANK   8
    THROUGH LAST YEARS FERN OF THE SHY FALLOW-DEER   155 TRISTRAM 3   193
    THROUGH THE GREEN FERN OF THE SHY FALLOW-DEER   155 TRISTRAM 3   V 193
    AND WONDER IF THOU HAUNTST THEIR SHY RETREATS   257 SCHOLAR-GIPSY   70
    PLUCKD IN SHY FIELDS AND DISTANT WYCHWOOD BOWERS   257 SCHOLAR-GIPSY   79
    SHY TRAFFICKERS THE DARK IBERIANS COME   262 SCHOLAR-GIPSY   249
    PLUCKD IN SHY FIELDS AND DISTANT WOODLAND BOWERS   257 SCHOLAR-GIPSY   V 79
    WE TRACKD THE SHY THAMES SHORE   266 THYRSIS   126
    SHY TO ILLUMINE AND I SEEK IT TOO   268 THYRSIS   202
    YE SHY RECLUSES FOLLOW TOO   305 GRANDE CHARTR   192
    THE SHY MOUNTAIN-BEAR   392 MEROPE   1640

SIBYLLAS
    AND FROM THE SIGN IS GONE SIBYLLAS NAME • • • • 262 THYRSIS   4

SICILIAN
    BUT WHEN SICILIAN SHEPHERDS LOST A MATE • • • • 265 THYRSIS   82
    ARE FLOWERS FIRST OPEND ON SICILIAN AIR • • • • 265 THYRSIS   89
    FOR SHE HERSELF HAD TROD SICILIAN FIELDS • • • • 265 THYRSIS   93
    SINGS HIS SICILIAN FOLD • • • • • • • 268 THYRSIS   186
    THY LAST MISCHANCE ON THIS SICILIAN DEEP • • • • 430 EMPEDOCLES II   57
    THY LAST DEFEAT IN THIS SICILIAN SEA • • • • • 430 EMPEDOCLES II V 57

SICILY
    THAT OLD-WORLD MORN IN SICILY • • • • • 222 EPILOG LAOCOON   45
    ᴮETWIXT THE SYRTES AND SOFT SICILY • • • • • 262 SCHOLAR-GIPSY   245
    CLOUDS AND GROWS DAILY WORSE IN SICILY • • • • 410 EMPEDOCLES I 1   120

SICILYS
    TYRANNY PRIDE AND LUST FILL SICILYS ABODES • • • 416 EMPEDOCLES I 2   121

SICK
    NATURE IS CRUEL MAN IS SICK OF BLOOD • • • • • 5 HARMONY NATURE   7
    WHERE OUR SICK SOULS DO LIE • • • • • • 39 STAGIRIUS   50
    MAZED WITH DOUBTS AND SICK WITH FEARS • • • • 44 QUESTION   13
    TURNING SICK AND BAFFLED LEARNS • • • • • SECOND BEST V 20
    O KING THOU KNOWST I HAVE BEEN SICK • • • • 88 SICK KING BOKH   22
    NOW MARK I BEING FEVERD SICK • • • • • 90 SICK KING BOKH   85
    THERE ARE THE LEPERS AND ALL SICK • • • • • 93 SICK KING BOKH   175
    BUT I AM SICK NOR HEED I THESE • • • • • 94 SICK KING BOKH   215
    MINE EARS ARE STUNND WITH BLOWS AND SICK FOR CALM   128 BALDER DEAD 3   508
    OVER THE SICK MANS FEET IS SPREAD • • • • • 131 TRISTRAM 1   15
    SICK PINING COMES NOT WHERE THESE ARE • • • 138 TRISTRAM 1   260
    SICK WITH GRIEF I AM AND FAINT WITH TRAVEL • • 142 TRISTRAM 2   15
    WEARY OF MYSELF AND SICK OF ASKING • • • • 239 SELF-DEPENDENCE   1
    OF THE SICK ROOM THE MORTAL STRIFE • • • • 251 WISH   45
    OF A SICK ROOM A MORTAL STRIFE • • • • • 251 WISH V 45
    FREE FROM THE SICK FATIGUE THE LANGUID DOUBT • 260 SCHOLAR-GIPSY   164
    WITH ITS SICK HURRY ITS DIVIDED AIMS • • • 261 SCHOLAR-GIPSY   204
    WHAT MORTAL COULD BE SICK OR SORRY HERE • • • 407 EMPEDOCLES I 1   20

SICKLE
    PUTTING HIS SICKLE TO THE PERILOUS GRAIN • • • 268 THYRSIS   182
    THE SICKLE-SWEEP OF QUIBERON BAY • • • • • 274 STANZAS CARNAC   27

SICKNESS
    MEN SPENT BY SICKNESS OR OBSCURE DECAY • • • 104 BALDER DEAD 1   325
    ANGER AND STRIFE AND SICKNESS ARE WITHIN • • 465 ALARIC AT ROME   81
    AGAINST A SICKNESS OR DEFORMITY • • • • • LUCRETIUS 3   4
    THE CLOUDS OF SICKNESS CAST NO STAIN UPON • • • FRAGMENT 8   1

SIDE
    WESTWARD ON THE SIDE OF FRANCE • • • • • • 13 CHURCH BROU 1   20
    PERCEIVE BUT A VOICE AS I COME TO HIS SIDE • • • 20 MODERN SAPPHO   26
    YOUTH DREAMS A BLISS ON THIS SIDE DEATH • • • 22 YOUTH AND CALM   19
    YOUTH DREAMS A JOY ON THIS SIDE DEATH • • • 22 YOUTH AND CALN V 19
    STANDS AT DAYBREAK WEEPING BY MY SIDE • • • 35 NEW SIRENS   274
    MOUNTS AT HER SIDE • • • • • • • • 38 STAGIRIUS   19
    WINDS FROM OUR SIDE THE UNSUITING CONSORT RIVE • 40 HUMAN LIFE   16
    ON EITHER SIDE THE BLACK DEEP-FURROWD PATH • • • 41 HUMAN LIFE   22
    AND NEVER TOUCHES THE SHIP-SIDE AGAIN • • • 41 HUMAN LIFE   24
    A WHITE-ROBED SLAVE STOLE TO THE GREAT KINGS SIDE   47 WORLD QUIETIST   27
    A WHITE-ROBED SLAVE STOLE TO THE MONARCHS SIDE • • 47 WORLD QUIETIST V 27
    THAT RIGHT IS ON THEIR SIDE • • • • • • HORATIAN ECHO V
    ON THIS SIDE THE ALL-COMMON CLOSE • • • • 53 RESIGNATION   16
    EMERGING ON THE GREEN HILL-SIDE • • • • 54 RESIGNATION   59
    BUT WHERE THE FARTHER SIDE SLOPES DOWN • • • 57 RESIGNATION   180
    BUT WHERE THE FURTHER SIDE SLOPES DOWN • • • 57 RESIGNATION V 180
    HIS HERALD TO HIS SIDE AND WENT ABROAD • • • 64 SOHRAB RUSTUM   103
    AND ON THE OTHER SIDE THE PERSIANS FORMD • • 65 SOHRAB RUSTUM   136
    A SIDE OF ROASTED SHEEP AND CAKES OF BREAD • • 67 SOHRAB RUSTUM   198
    AND ON EACH SIDE ARE SQUARES OF STANDING CORN • • 70 SOHRAB RUSTUM   295
    SO ON EACH SIDE WERE SQUARES OF MEN WITH SPEARS • • 70 SOHRAB RUSTUM   297
    WHICH HANGS UNCERTAIN TO WHICH SIDE TO FALL • • 72 SOHRAB RUSTUM   392
    HATH TRAILD THE HUNTERS JAVELIN IN HIS SIDE • • 76 SOHRAB RUSTUM   505
    HIS COVERING SHIELD AND THE SPEAR PIERCED HIS SIDE   76 SOHRAB RUSTUM   520
    LIES DYING WITH THE ARROW IN HER SIDE • • • 78 SOHRAB RUSTUM   567
    THE SPEAR AND DREW IT FROM HIS SIDE AND EASED • • 85 SOHRAB RUSTUM   839
    FLOWD WITH THE STREAM ALL DOWN HIS COLD WHITE SIDE   86 SOHRAB RUSTUM   842
    LIE PRONE ENORMOUS DOWN THE MOUNTAIN SIDE • • • 86 SOHRAB RUSTUM   863
    A SIDE OF ROASTED SHEEP AND LOAVES OF BREAD • • 67 SOHRAB RUSTUM V 198
    HAS TRAILD THE HUNTERS JAVELIN IN HIS SIDE • • 76 SOHRAB RUSTUM V 505
    SO HODER BRUSHD BY HERMODS SIDE AND SAID • • • 101 BALDER DEAD 1   235
    SO IT RESTORED THEE NANNA TO MY SIDE • • • 103 BALDER DEAD 1   307
    TOWRD EARTH AND FIGHTS OF MEN AND AT THEIR SIDE • • 105 BALDER DEAD 2   20
    AND UP AND DOWN AND SIDE AND SLANT THEY ROAMD • • 106 BALDER DEAD 2   53
    YET DOCILE NOW HE STOOD AT HERMODS SIDE • • 107 BALDER DEAD 2   75
    TO WINTER-PASTURE ON THE SOUTHERN SIDE • • • 107 BALDER DEAD 2   93
    AND NOW THOU SITTEST CROWND BY HELAS SIDE • • 112 BALDER DEAD 2   260
    ME SITTING HERE BELOW BY HELAS SIDE • • • • 112 BALDER DEAD 2   277
    SITS BALDER STILL IN POMP BY HELAS SIDE • • 125 BALDER DEAD 3   429
    HIS PLACE OF STATE REMAINS BY HELAS SIDE • • 125 BALDER DEAD 3   432
    IN HEAVEN WAS SELDOM PARTED FROM MY SIDE • • 126 BALDER DEAD 3   460

SIDE   (CONTINUED)
          TO TYNTAGEL TO THE SIDE . . . .   132 TRISTRAM 1   61
          AT THY SIDE THOU LOVELY CHARGE . . . . . .   134 TRISTRAM 1   112
          HIS GENTLE BEARING AT THE SIDE . . . . . .   137 TRISTRAM 1   213
          AT ARTHURS SIDE HE FIGHTS ONCE MORE . . .   138 TRISTRAM 1   254
          WITH HER CHILDREN AT HER SIDE . . . . . .   138 TRISTRAM 1   271
          SHE CAME TO THE BED-SIDE . . . .   140 TRISTRAM 1   316
          ON THE CASTLES SOUTHERN SIDE . . . . . .   140 TRISTRAM 1   329
          TO CORNWALLS PALACE TO THE SIDE . . . . .   132 TRISTRAM 1   V 61
          STAY PALE QUEEN FOR EVER BY MY SIDE . . .   144 TRISTRAM 2   68
          THROUGH SOME OLD SEA-SIDE KNIGHTLY HALL .   148 TRISTRAM 2   178
          THREE HOLLIES SIDE BY SIDE AND MADE A SCREEN   150 TRISTRAM 3   20
          THREE HOLLIES SIDE BY SIDE AND MADE A SCREEN   150 TRISTRAM 3   20
          NOR DID THEIR LOOKS STRAY ONCE TO THE SEA-SIDE 151 TRISTRAM 3   48
          AWAY THE OTHER SIDE OF BRITTANY . . . . .   154 TRISTRAM 3   154
          ON THE BROOKS FARTHER SIDE WAS CLEAR BUT THEN 155 TRISTRAM 3   189
          ON THE BROOKS FURTHER SIDE WAS CLEAR BUT THEN 155 TRISTRAM 3   V 189
          AT THE CHURCH ON THE HILL-SIDE . . . . . .   165 FORSAKEN MERM   138
          A BABE WAS IN HER ARMS AND AT HER SIDE . .   169 WEST LONDON   3
          SO RANG TERTULLIANS SENTENCE ON THE SIDE .   172 GOOD SHEPHERD   2
          WHO CROSS TO THE HILL-SIDE . . . .   175 PARTING   5
          TO THE CLEAR WANING HILL-SIDE . . . . . .   176 PARTING   45
          TO THY SIDE GODDESS FROM WITHIN . . . . .   189 STRAYED REVEL   100
          DOWN AT THE WATER-SIDE . . . .   194 STRAYED REVEL   266
          VOW TO BEAT HENCEFORTH SIDE BY SIDE . . .   203 EUPHROSYNE   8
          VOW TO BEAT HENCEFORTH SIDE BY SIDE . . .   203 EUPHROSYNE   8
          THY LOVELY PRESENCE AT MY SIDE . . . . .   204 CALAIS SANDS   11
          THAT SLIGHT SWEET FIGURE AT MY SIDE . . .   204 CALAIS SANDS   V 11
          YEARS AGO AT MY SIDE . . . .   233 YOUTH OF MAN   24
          THEN THEN AT LAST TO QUIT MY SIDE . . . .   250 WISH   12
          BUT RUMOURS HUNG ABOUT THE COUNTRY-SIDE .   256 SCHOLAR-GIPSY   52
          ROAMING THE COUNTRY-SIDE A TRUANT BOY . .   261 SCHOLAR-GIPSY   198
          BUT MANY A DINGLE ON THE LOVED HILL-SIDE .   266 THYRSIS   112
          OF QUIET LOOK ADOWN THE DUSK HILL-SIDE . .   267 THYRSIS   152
          OUR SCHOLAR TRAVELS YET THE LOVED HILL-SIDE   269 THYRSIS   240
          A BOAT IS LOWERD FROM HER SIDE . . . . . .   276 SOUTHERN NIGHT   33
          THE SOFT MEDITERRANEAN SIDE . . . .   277 SOUTHERN NIGHT   67
          LONELY AND BLEAK AT ITS SIDE . . . . . .   283 HAWORTH CHURCH   64
          DAYS NOT DARK AT THY SIDE . . . .   287 RUGBY CHAPEL   20
          FRIENDS WHO SET FORTH AT OUR SIDE . . . .   289 RUGBY CHAPEL   102
          THE AVALANCHE SWEPT FROM OUR SIDE . . . .   289 RUGBY CHAPEL   123
          DAYS NOT OF GLOOM AT THY SIDE . . . . . .   287 RUGBY CHAPEL   V 20
          BY THE AVON SIDE IN THE BRIGHT . . . . . .   294 HEINES GRAVE   63
          LONG ON THE GREY HILL-SIDE . . . .   297 HEINES GRAVE   165
          THROUGH FOREST UP THE MOUNTAIN-SIDE . . .   299 GRANDE CHARTR   6
          I COME TO SHED THEM AT THEIR SIDE . . . .   302 GRANDE CHARTR   90
          AND ON THIS SIDE THOSE CONFLUENT STREAMS WHICH MAKE 330 MEROPE   18
          FROM CHIEF TO CHIEF I WANDERD AT HIS SIDE .   355 MEROPE   728
          TO DRAW THE COVERTS ON CYLLENES SIDE . . .   356 MEROPE   750
          THE FORESTS ROUND THAT BELT CYLLENES SIDE .   357 MEROPE   794
          WALLS ON ONE SIDE THE DEEP STYMPHALIAN LAKE   358 MEROPE   813
          FISHERS WHO LIVE ON THE LAKE-SIDE TO LAUNCH   358 MEROPE   837
          AND HAD HIM AT THE PRINCES SIDE IN LEASH .   364 MEROPE   971
          AMONG THE FORESTS ON CYLLENES SIDE . . . .   364 MEROPE   974
          KEPT ME THEIR MOTHER FROM THEIR SIDE SO LONG   367 MEROPE   1040
          UNTRODDEN ON CYLLENES DESOLATE SIDE . . .   373 MEROPE   1168
          PRUDENCE IS ON THE OTHER SIDE BUT DEEDS .   383 MEROPE   1384
          TO THE SIDE OF HEBE . . . .   399 MEROPE   1842
          BEFORE HIM AT HIS SIDE THE PRINCE THY SON .   401 MEROPE   1905
          SWAYING FROM SIDE TO SIDE HIS MASSY HEAD .   401 MEROPE   1911
          SWAYING FROM SIDE TO SIDE HIS MASSY HEAD .   401 MEROPE   1911
          LAIAS IN ARMS SPRANG TO HIS NEPHEWS SIDE .   402 MEROPE   1933
          AND FOUND HIM AT MY HUSBANDS SIDE HIS FRIEND   403 MEROPE   1973
          THE FORESTS ROUND WHICH BELT CYLLENES SIDE .   357 MEROPE   V 794
          BY THE STREAM-SIDE AFTER THE DUSTY LANES .   406 EMPEDOCLES I 1   3
          UP BY THE TORRENT-SIDE UNDER THE PINES . .   411 EMPEDOCLES I 1   164
          THE GRASS IS COOL THE SEA-SIDE AIR . . . .   426 EMPEDOCLES I 2   432
          WHEN FROM FAR PARNASSUS SIDE . . . .   433 EMPEDOCLES II   129
          ON THE CLIFF-SIDE THE PIGEONS . . . . . .   442 EMPEDOCLES II   431
          A STRANGE WAYFARER COMING TO HIS SIDE . .   444 WESTMIN ABBEY   23
          IN SOME CHANCE BATTLE ON CITHAERON-SIDE .   447 WESTMIN ABBEY   114
          HUMAN SUFFERING AT OUR SIDE . . . .   457 POOR MATTHIAS   163

SIDES
          IS ON ALL SIDES OERSHADOWD BY THE HIGH . .   7 REP FRIEND CONT   6
          THEY TURN ON ALL SIDES . . . .   190 STRAYED REVEL   131
          FOR INSTANT COMMENT HAVING MANY SIDES . .   359 MEROPE   860
          FOR FROM ALL SIDES A DELUGE AS IT SEEMD .   402 MEROPE   1937
          DOWN ITS STEEP VERDANT SIDES THE AIR . . .   414 EMPEDOCLES I 2   45

SIGH
          COME YOU MURMUR WITH A SIGH . . . .   28 NEW SIRENS   62
          AND SIGH THAT ONE THING ONLY HAS BEEN LENT   37 YOUTHS AGIT   13
          HE HEARS A VOICE SIGH HUMBLY WAIT . . . .   157 SAINT BRANDAN   23
          AND ANON THERE BREAKS A SIGH . . . .   164 FORSAKEN MERM   101
          A LONG LONG SIGH . . . .   164 FORSAKEN MERM   105
          SHE SMILES AND SMILES AND WILL NOT SIGH .   202 URANIA   5
          A SIGH A TEAR BUT IN THE THRONG . . . . .   225 EPILOG LAOCOON   123
          WE TOO SIGH THAT SHE FLAGS . . . .   294 HEINES GRAVE   76
          CLINGEST WITH SMILES WITH A SIGH . . . . .   298 HEINES GRAVE   190

SIGH   (CONTINUED)
```
    A SIGH THE GODDESS GAVE AND WITH A FROWN    •   •   •   447 WESTMIN ABBEY      94
    AND OER THY TOWERS THE WINDS HALF UTTERED SIGH  •   •  464 ALARIC AT ROME      65
    MIGHT WELL BE MINGLING AT THAT MURMURED SIGH    •   •  469 ALARIC AT ROME     179
```

SIGHD
```
    SIGHD OUT BY WINTERS SAD TRANQUILLITY       •   •   •    12 MYCERINUS         115
    OF THE YOUNG MAN IN HIS AND SIGHD AND SAID  •   •   •    63 SOHRAB RUSTUM      64
    AT LAST HE SIGHD AND SET FORTH BACK TO HEAVEN   •   •   129 BALDER DEAD 3     566
    SHE SIGHD SHE LOOKD UP THROUGH THE CLEAR GREEN SEA  163 FORSAKEN MERM       55
    SO SPAKE THE FIERCE TERTULLIAN BUT SHE SIGHD    •   •   172 GOOD SHEPHERD       6
```

SIGHINGS
```
    WITH LOW SIGHINGS SILENCE STOLE     •   •   •   •   •   •    28 NEW SIRENS       70
```

SIGHS
```
    WITH LOW SIGHS HATH SILENCE STOLE   •   •   •   •   •   •    28 NEW SIRENS     V 70
```

SIGHT
```
    AND THE SIGHT FROZE ALL HER LIFE    •   •   •   •   •   •    14 CHURCH BROU 1    52
    WELCOME THESE EYES COULD SEE NO BETTER SIGHT    •   •    67 SOHRAB RUSTUM     205
    THAT SOHRAB WILL REJOICE HER SIGHT NO MORE  •   •   •    79 SOHRAB RUSTUM     599
    THAT THEY SATE WITH IT IN MY SIGHT  •   •   •   •   •    90 SICK KING BOKH     83
    MOST UNBLEST ALSO AT THAT SIGHT     •   •   •   •   •    90 SICK KING BOKH     86
    FOR WHO WILL BEAR MY HATEFUL SIGHT IN HEAVEN    •   •    98 BALDER DEAD 1     106
    OUT OF OUR SIGHT THAT WE MAY TURN FROM GRIEF    •   •   115 BALDER DEAD 3      55
    AND THEY FROM SIGHT HAVE DISAPPEARD AND SUNK    •   •   128 BALDER DEAD 3     524
    FADED FROM SIGHT INTO THE INTERIOR GLOOM    •   •   •   129 BALDER DEAD 3     553
    TO LOOK FORTH ON THE FAIRY SIGHT    •   •   •   •   •   141 TRISTRAM 1        353
    IT WAS THE SIGHT OF THAT LORD ARUNDEL   •   •   •   •   166 PICT NEWSTEAD       4
    SEE AN ENNOBLING SIGHT  •   •   •   •   •   •   •   •   253 FUTURE             67
    SIGHT OF THE REST IN THE STORM  •   •   •   •   •   •   289 RUGBY CHAPEL      119
    SHOWING THEN BLOTTING FROM OUR SIGHT    •   •   •   •   299 GRANDE CHARTR      15
    ARE NOTHING IN THEIR SIGHT  •   •   •   •   •   •   •   311 OBERMANN          152
    PERISHD IN SIGHT OF THE GOAL    •   •   •   •   •   •   345 MEROPE            466
    ON THE HIGH SEA-BANK IN THE SIGHT   •   •   •   •   •   345 MEROPE            482
    FOR YEARS HIS WIDOW IN THEIR SIGHT I STAND  •   •   •   381 MEROPE           1316
    HOW MIGHT NOT SUCH A SIGHT AS THIS REVIVE   •   •   •   383 MEROPE           1358
    O ERYMANTHUS FROM SIGHT •   •   •   •   •   •   •   •   347 MEROPE            V
    TILL THE SLOW MULES SHOULD CLIMB IN SIGHT AGAIN •   •   408 EMPEDOCLES I 1     48
    IN SIGHT OF BLOOD BUT WERE RAPT FAR AWAY    •   •   •   427 EMPEDOCLES I 2    453
    HAD GAZED IN WONDER ON THAT GLORIOUS SIGHT  •   •   •   465 ALARIC AT ROME     74
    PERCHANCE THAT SOLEMN SIGHT MIGHT QUENCH THE FIRE   469 ALARIC AT ROME     177
    IT MAY BE IN THAT DESOLATE SIGHT HIS EYE    •   •   •   469 ALARIC AT ROME     185
    IT IS A SAD SIGHT WHEN THE WORLD DENIES •   •   •   •       LUCRETIUS 2         1
    THERE IS A SIGHT MORE SADDENING YET WHEN ALL    •   •       LUCRETIUS 2         7
```

SIGHTLESS
```
    THOUGH SIGHTLESS YET HIS OWN MIND LED THE GOD   •   •    97 BALDER DEAD 1      76
    SIGHTLESS AND HELPLESS WANDERING WEAK IN HEAVEN •   •    98 BALDER DEAD 1      97
    SIGHTLESS IN SOUL AND EYE WHAT WORDS ARE THESE  •   •    98 BALDER DEAD 1     113
    NO JOURNEY FOR A SIGHTLESS GOD TO GO    •   •   •   •   100 BALDER DEAD 1     186
    HIS OLD SIGHTLESS HEAD  •   •   •   •   •   •   •   •   190 STRAYED REVEL     140
```

SIGHTS
```
    UNDISTRACTED BY THE SIGHTS THEY SEE •   •   •   •   •   240 SELF-DEPENDENCE    18
    CHANGING AND SHOT AS THE SIGHTS WHICH WE SEE    •   •   253 FUTURE             57
    AND SEE ALL SIGHTS FROM POLE TO POLE    •   •   •   •   277 SOUTHERN NIGHT     69
    AND HEALING SIGHTS TO SEE   •   •   •   •   •   •   •   309 OBERMANN          112
    BUT ASK HOW THOU SUCH SIGHTS    •   •   •   •   •   •   416 EMPEDOCLES I 2    109
    IN COMMON SIGHTS READ SECRET SYMPATHY   •   •   •   •   472 CROMWELL           32
```

SIGN
```
    THERE CLIMBING HANGS A FAR-SEEN SIGN    •   •   •   •    54 RESIGNATION        60
    THE BALEFUL SIGN OF FEVERS DUST HAD SOILD   •   •   •    74 SOHRAB RUSTUM     453
    AND SHOWD A SIGN IN FAINT VERMILION POINTS  •   •   •    81 SOHRAB RUSTUM     671
    SO DELICATELY PRICKD THE SIGN APPEARD   •   •   •   •    81 SOHRAB RUSTUM     677
    ON SOHRABS ARM THE SIGN OF RUSTUMS SEAL •   •   •   •    81 SOHRAB RUSTUM     678
    THEN RUSTUM TOOK IT FOR HIS GLORIOUS SIGN   •   •   •    81 SOHRAB RUSTUM     683
    HOW SAYST THOU IS THAT SIGN THE PROPER SIGN •   •   •    81 SOHRAB RUSTUM     687
    HOW SAYST THOU IS THAT SIGN THE PROPER SIGN •   •   •    81 SOHRAB RUSTUM     687
    AND LABEL WITH THE BLESSED SIGN •   •   •   •   •   •   138 TRISTRAM 1        252
    AND SOUGHT A PRIEST TO SIGN THE CROSS   •   •   •   •   160 NECKAN             39
    YE HEAVENS WHOSE PURE DARK REGIONS HAVE NO SIGN •   •   244 SUMMER NIGHT       78
    AND FROM THE SIGN IS GONE SIBYLLAS NAME •   •   •   •   262 THYRSIS             4
    AND THOU MY MOTHER HADST THOU MADE A SIGN   •   •   •   383 MEROPE           1368
    VISIT US AS THEY DO WITH SIGN AND PLAGUE    •   •   •   413 EMPEDOCLES I 2     24
    THE BOON THY DEDICATION-SIGN FORETOLD   •   •   •   •   444 WESTMIN ABBEY       5
    OUR COMPANIONS DYING SIGN   •   •   •   •   •   •   •   456 POOR MATTHIAS     126
    BROTHER MANS DESPAIRING SIGN    •   •   •   •   •   •   457 POOR MATTHIAS     169
    A CONQUERING SIGN   •   •   •   •   •   •   •   •   •   460 KAISER DEAD        58
    THERE OF THY MASTER KEEP THAT SIGN  •   •   •   •   •   461 KAISER DEAD        83
```

SIGNAL
```
    THE SIGNAL-ELM THAT LOOKS ON ILSLEY DOWNS   •   •   •   263 THYRSIS            14
    I CANNOT REACH THE SIGNAL-TREE TO-NIGHT •   •   •   •   267 THYRSIS           165
    BID IT RISE BOLDLY AT THE SIGNAL GIVEN  •   •   •   •   331 MEROPE             46
    BUT IF SOME SIGNAL UNASSISTED STROKE    •   •   •   •   383 MEROPE           1353
    BUT THE SIGNAL EXAMPLE  •   •   •   •   •   •   •   •   398 MEROPE           1810
```

SIGND

WARRIOR STATESMAN HAD SIGND · · · · · · · · 281 HAWORTH CHURCH 21

SIGNIFIED

WHERE TIME ELSE DUMB HATH SIGNIFIED HIS SWAY · · FRAGMENT 2 2

SIGNS

SIGNS ARE NOT WANTING WHICH MIGHT RAISE · · · · 56 RESIGNATION 122
SIGNS ARE NOT WANTING IF THEY WOULD · · · · · · 56 RESIGNATION 124
SHOW ME THROUGH ALL THE WORLD THE SIGNS OF GRIEF · 111 BALDER DEAD 2 234
SHOW HER THROUGH ALL THE WORLD THE SIGNS OF GRIEF · 114 BALDER DEAD 3 42
BY THWARTING SIGNS AND BRAVES · · · · · · · · 244 SUMMER NIGHT 60
TELLS US HIS MISERYS BIRTH AND GROWTH AND SIGNS · 260 SCHOLAR-GIPSY 187
SIGNS MAKE THY SOUL AFRAID · · · · · · · · 416 EMPEDOCLES I 2 123
SIGNS THE CROSS AND ANSWERS SURELY · · · · · · META CLOISTER 39

SILENCE

THEIR GLORIOUS TASKS IN SILENCE PERFECTING · · · · 2 QUIET WORK 12
THEIR GLORIOUS COURSE IN SILENCE PERFECTING · · 2 QUIET WORK V 12
INTO THE SILENCE OF THE GROVES AND WOODS · · · 10 MYCERINUS 67
WITH LOW SIGHINGS SILENCE STOLE · · · · · · 28 NEW SIRENS 70
IN A WISTFUL SILENCE READING · · · · · · 34 NEW SIRENS 237
WITH LOW SIGHS HATH SILENCE STOLE · · · · · 28 NEW SIRENS V 70
BUT IN DISDAINFUL SILENCE TURN AWAY · · · · · 42 GIPSY CHILD 31
THE CHEERFUL SILENCE OF THE FELLS · · · · · 54 RESIGNATION 67
WAILING NO MORE IN SILENCE ATE AND DRANK · · 97 BALDER DEAD 1 70
THERE ALL THE GODS IN SILENCE SATE THEM DOWN · 106 BALDER DEAD 2 39
IN SILENCE UP THE DARK UNTRAVELLD ROAD · · · 107 BALDER DEAD 2 79
WITH SILENCE BALM MY WHIRLING BRAIN · · · · 158 SAINT BRANDAN 70
IN PROFOUND SILENCE STERN · · · · · · 198 FRAG DEJANEIRA 8
AND IN THE AFTER-SILENCE SWEET · · · · · · 219 BACCHANALIA 2 13
AH SO THE SILENCE WAS · · · · · · 221 BACCHANALIA 2 63
AND SOLEMN SILENCE OF ITS CLOSE · · · · · 225 EPILOG LAOCOON 152
UNAFFRIGHTED BY THE SILENCE ROUND THEM · · 240 SELF-DEPENDENCE 17
WHILE ALL AROUND IN SILENCE LIES · · · · · 250 WISH 30
TRICKLED IN SILENCE THINE OWN · · · · · · 296 HEINES GRAVE 126
THE SILENCE FAR BELOW · · · · · · 323 OBERMANN MORE 328
BY SILENCE EVER AFTER FOR BEHOLD · · · · · 332 MEROPE 62
TOWRD THEE TOWARD THY SILENCE AS THY SPEECH · 333 MEROPE 112
SPEAK THEREFORE OR KEEP SILENCE WHICH THOU WILT · 333 MEROPE 113
DEEMING AS TYRANTS DEEM OUR SILENCE HATE · · 338 MEROPE 260
FOR YEARS IN SILENCE DEVOURING HER HEART · · 346 MEROPE 509
OF IMPORT AND IN SILENCE BEST RECEIVED · · 359 MEROPE 861
AND YE KEEP FAITHFUL SILENCE FRIENDS AND MARK · 368 MEROPE 1073
YE KEPT SILENCE IN FEAR · · · · · · 371 MEROPE 1129
MEANTIME ON THEE THE TASK OF SILENCE ONLY · · 390 MEROPE 1584
THE SILENCE THOU HAST KEPT FOR TWENTY YEARS · 395 MEROPE 1726
SILENCE AND EXPECTATION HELD US ALL · · · · 401 MEROPE 1902
TOWRDS THEE TOWARDS THY SILENCE AS THY SPEECH · 333 MEROPE V 112
IN ECHOING UNNEARD SILENCE · · · · · · 437 EMPEDOCLES II 295
THE NIGHT IN HER SILENCE · · · · · · 443 EMPEDOCLES II 467
THE NIGHT IN ITS SILENCE · · · · · · 443 EMPEDOCLES II V 467
YES IN SUCH ELOQUENT SILENCE DIDST THOU LIE · 464 ALARIC AT ROME 67
MUST BEAR IN SILENCE MANY AN ILL · · · · 481 COURAGE 3
NIGHT COMES WITH NIGHT COMES SILENCE HAND IN HAND FRAGMENT 1 1
WITH NIGHT COMES SILENCE AND WITH THAT REPOSE · · FRAGMENT 1 2

SILENT

AND BY THAT SILENT KNOWLEDGE DAY BY DAY · · · 12 MYCERINUS 110
IF IN THE SILENT MIND OF ONE ALL-PURE · · · 45 IN UTRUMQUE PAR 1
ALREADY FROM THE SILENT ROAD · · · · · · 53 RESIGNATION 49
BETWIXT THE SILENT HOSTS AND SPAKE AND SAID · 65 SOHRAB RUSTUM 149
BETWIXT THE SILENT HOSTS AND SPOKE AND SAID · 65 SOHRAB RUSTUM V 149
SILENT AND WAITED FOR THE SACRED MORN · · · 119 BALDER DEAD 3 212
VIDAR THE SILENT THE IMPETUOUS TYR · · · 127 BALDER DEAD 3 492
HALT AT THE WHITE AND SILENT COLONNADE · · 167 RACHEL 1 5
THE COURT ALL SILENT · · · · · · 187 STRAYED REVEL 47
ALONG THE NEVER-SILENT STRAIT · · · · · 204 CALAIS SANDS 3
ALONG THE NEVER-SILENT BEACH · · · · · 204 CALAIS SANDS V 3
SILENT THE SWANS BESIDE US FLOAT · · · · 206 RIVER 3
SILENT THE LORD OF THE WORLD · · · · · 216 LORDS MESSENGER V
SILENT THE SWATHS THE RINGING WAIN · · · 217 BACCHANALIA 1 5
SILENT THE SHEAVES THE RINGING WAIN · · · 217 BACCHANALIA 1 V 5
DID ITS NOW SILENT WARFARE WAGE · · · · 219 BACCHANALIA 2 20
AND THEY ARE SILENT AND AT PEACE · · · 226 EPILOG LAOCOON 186
SILENT THE BOAT THE LAKE · · · · · 228 YOUTH OF NATURE 2
THROUGH THE SILENT FLOWERY LAND · · · 234 YOUTH OF MAN 85
SILENT AND WHITE UNOPENING DOWN · · · · 242 SUMMER NIGHT 4
A TINGE IT MAY BE OF THEIR SILENT PAIN · · 244 SUMMER NIGHT 84
TO THE SILENT COUNTRY AND LEAVES · · · · 283 HAWORTH CHURCH 69
IN PITY AND SILENT AWE · · · · · · 283 HAWORTH CHURCH V
SILENT HARDLY A SHOUT · · · · · · 286 RUGBY CHAPEL 6
THE SILENT COURTS WHERE NIGHT AND DAY · · 300 GRANDE CHARTR 31
SILENT WHILE YEARS ENGRAVE THE BROW · · · 302 GRANDE CHARTR 113
SILENT THE BEST ARE SILENT NOW · · · · · 302 GRANDE CHARTR 114
SILENT THE BEST ARE SILENT NOW · · · · 302 GRANDE CHARTR 114
SILENT THEY ARE THOUGH NOT CONTENT · · · 303 GRANDE CHARTR 117
YE SLUMBER IN YOUR SILENT GRAVE · · · · 304 GRANDE CHARTR 151
THEY SLUMBER IN THEIR SILENT GRAVE · · · · 304 GRANDE CHARTR V 151
AH OER THAT SILENT SACRED LAND · · · · · 318 OBERMANN MORE 181

SILENT   (CONTINUED)
            AH FROM THAT SILENT SACRED LAND   . . . . .   318 OBERMANN MORE   V 181
            AND THE STANCH FURIES NEVER=SILENT SCOURGE . . . .   373 MEROPE   1187
            SILENT NOW FOR EVERMORE . . . .   453 POOR MATTHIAS   20
            WHISPERS IN MOURNFUL TONES THY SILENT ELEGY . . .   464 ALARIC AT ROME   66
            YES THERE HE STOOD UPON THAT SILENT HILL . . . .   468 ALARIC AT ROME   157
            HIGH FATE IS THEIRS WHO WHERE THE SILENT SKY . .   472 CROMWELL   9
            LIKE A SWIFT RIVER THRO A SILENT PLAIN . . . .   473 CROMWELL   64

SILENTLY
            ONE FORM STANDS GAZING SILENTLY BELOW   . . . .   468 ALARIC AT ROME   153
            THEN RESTED LISTENING SILENTLY . . . .   480 HAYSWATER BOAT   28

SILENUS
            THE OLD SILENUS   . . . .   193 STRAYED REVEL   261

SILK
            WHAT LADY IS THIS WHOSE SILK ATTIRE   . . . . .   131 TRISTRAM 1   24
            I KNOW HER BY HER RICH SILK DRESS   . . . . .   132 TRISTRAM 1   52
            OF SILK=BALES AND OF BALSAM=DROPS   . . . . .   191 STRAYED REVEL   193

SILKEN
            EYES THROUGH HER SILKEN CURTAINS THE POOR DRUDGE . .   70 SOHRAB RUSTUM   303
            WITH SILKEN RAIMENT STORE OF RICE   . . . . .   94 SICK KING BOKH   194
            SILKEN COURTIERS WHISPERING HONIED NOTHINGS . .   144 TRISTRAM 2   47
            THROUGH SILKEN RIFTS SOFT PEERS THE SUN   . . .   248 KENSINGTON GARD   V
            THROUGH SILKEN RIFTS SOFT WINKS THE SUN   . . .   KENSINGTON GARD   V

SILLY
            HERE WITH THE SHEPHERDS AND THE SILLY SHEEP   . .   264 THYRSIS   45

SILT
            OH THAT I SAW ITS GRAINS OF YELLOW SILT   . . . .   83 SOHRAB RUSTUM   769

SILVER
            SPLINTERD THE SILVER ARROWS OF THE MOON   . . . .   11 MYCERINUS   99
            AND FROM THEIR HORNS WITH SILVER RIMMD DRANK MEAD .   119 BALDER DEAD 3   211
            FLASHD IN THE SILVER SCONCES LIGHT   . . . . .   146 TRISTRAM 2   113
            HATH YET AN INFANTINE AND SILVER TONE   . . . .   151 TRISTRAM 3   73
            SHELL LIGHT HER SILVER LAMP WHICH FISHERMEN   . .   151 TRISTRAM 3   79
            HAS YET AN INFANTINE AND SILVER TONE . . . . .   151 TRISTRAM 3   V   73
            THE FAR-OFF SOUND OF A SILVER BELL   . . . . .   162 FORSAKEN MERM   34
            YOUNG DAPHNIS WITH HIS SILVER VOICE DOTH SING . .   268 THYRSIS   185
            BOUND ALL HIS BEING WITH A SILVER CHAIN   . . . .   473 CROMWELL   63
            OF MANY A LAWNY HILL AND STREAMS WITH SILVER FLOW   474 CROMWELL   104

SILVERD
            SWAYING THE LONG-HAIRD GOATS WITH SILVERD REIN   . . 115 BALDER DEAD 3   73
            AND THE SEA ITS LONG MOON=SILVERD ROLL   . . .   240 SELF=DEPENDENCE   22
            BY NIGHT THE SILVERD BRANCHES OF THE GLADE . . .   261 SCHOLAR=GIPSY   214
            WHERE THE MOON=SILVERD INLETS . . . .   442 EMPEDOCLES II   425

SIMOIS
            SET WHERE THE UPPER STREAMS OF SIMOIS FLOW . . .   236 PALLADIUM   1

SIMPLE
            OMIT OMIT MY SIMPLE FRIEND . . . .   47 HORATIAN ECHO   1
            HE LOVED EACH SIMPLE JOY THE COUNTRY YIELDS . .   264 THYRSIS   42
            AND CANST TEACH SIMPLE ONES TO PLOT AND FEIGN . .   367 MEROPE   1059
            THE SIMPLE PATRIARCHAL STATE OF KINGS   . . . .   388 MEROPE   1516
            SIMPLE PAUSANIAS TWAS NO MIRACLE   . . . . . .   410 EMPEDOCLES I 1   134
            ON SIMPLE MINDS WITH A PURE NATURAL JOY   . . .   436 EMPEDOCLES II   243

SIMPLER
            HOW ANGRILY THOU SPURNST ALL SIMPLER FARE   . . .   170 BETTER PART   2
            HAVE YET SO MUCH AS HEARD THIS SIMPLER LORE   . .   171 DIVINITY   12

SIMPLICITY
            BECAUSE ITS SIMPLICITY REBUKES . . . .   432 EMPEDOCLES II   106

SIMPLY
            SIMPLY THE WAY DIVINE   . . . .   319 OBERMANN MORE   188

SIN
            NO JUDGE EYES US FROM HEAVEN OUR SIN TO SCAN   . .   170 BETTER PART   4
            FROM SIN WHICH HEAVEN RECORDS NOT WHY FORBEAR . .   171 BETTER PART   7
            SITS THERE NO JUDGE IN HEAVEN OUR SIN TO SEE   . .   171 BETTER PART   11
            MAN IS BLIND BECAUSE OF SIN   . . . .   215 PIS=ALLER   1
            WHO ARE NOT EXPIATE THE GENERAL SIN   . . . . .   341 MEROPE   366
            VENGEANCE ON SINNER AND SIN   . . . .   348 MEROPE   539
            YET WILL NOT CEASE FROM SIN   . . . .   420 EMPEDOCLES I 2   235
            ALL SIN IS JUST IS PURE   . . . .   420 EMPEDOCLES I 2   243
            OUR DESPERATE SEARCH WAS SIN . . . .   423 EMPEDOCLES I 2   344
            DREAMS THAT WERE SWEET AT EVE AT MORN WERE SIN . .   475 CROMWELL   121
            THERE FROM SIN DELIVERD DWELLS MY FATHER   . . .   482 THEKLAS ANSWER   15

SINCE
            MUCH HE WHOSE FRIENDSHIP I NOT LONG SINCE WON . .   2 TO A FRIEND   5
            CRITIAS LONG SINCE I KNOW   . . . .   46 WORLD QUIETIST   9
            LONG SINCE THE WORLD HATH SET ITS HEART TO LIVE . . 46 WORLD QUIETIST   11

SINCE   (CONTINUED)

LONG SINCE WITH CREDULOUS ZEAL	46	WORLD QUIETIST	12
WE LEFT JUST TEN YEARS SINCE YOU SAY	53	RESIGNATION	40
FAUSTA WHICH TEN YEARS SINCE WE TROD	55	RESIGNATION	87
NAY AND SINCE DEATH WHICH WIPES OUT MAN	58	RESIGNATION	223
THOU KNOWST IF SINCE FROM ADER-BAIJAN FIRST	62	SOHRAB RUSTUM	42
THOU KNOWEST IF SINCE FROM ADER-BAIJAN FIRST	62	SOHRAB RUSTUM V	42
EVER SINCE PRAYER-TIME HE DOTH WAIT	88	SICK KING BOKH	14
THREE DAYS SINCE AT THE TIME OF PRAYER	88	SICK KING BOKH	30
WHO SINCE IN YOUR DESPITE HATH WAXD AMAIN	110	BALDER DEAD 2	210
SINCE THEN SHE SEEKS HIM AND WEEPS TEARS OF GOLD	116	BALDER DEAD 3	95
SINCE THEN I VAINLY SEEK HIM THROUGH THE WORLD	116	BALDER DEAD 3	109
COME THEN SINCE HELA HOLDS BY RIGHT HER PREY	121	BALDER DEAD 3	288
FOR I AM LONG SINCE WEARY OF YOUR STORM	127	BALDER DEAD 3	503
WHICH SINCE THEN FOR EVER ROLLS	132	TRISTRAM 1	65
GRIEF SINCE THEN HIS HOME WITH ME DOTH MAKE	145	TRISTRAM 2	88
BUT SINCE LIVING WE WERE UNUNITED	145	TRISTRAM 2	91
OR HAST THOU LONG SINCE WANDERD BACK	184	TERRACE BERNE	17
SINCE MAN WOKE ON EARTH HE KNOWS HIS STORY	209	SELF-DECEPTION	3
LONG LONG SINCE UNDOWERD YET OUR SPIRIT	209	SELF-DECEPTION	5
MANS NEW SPIRIT SINCE IT WAS NOT WE	210	SELF-DECEPTION	14
MANS BLANK SPIRIT SINCE IT WAS NOT WE	210	SELF-DECEPTION V	14
SINCE FIRST THE WORLD BEGAN	238	PROGRESS V	40
SINCE HE HAS NOT YET FOUND THE WORD GOD WOULD	239	REVOLUTIONS	12
O AIR-BORN VOICE LONG SINCE SEVERELY CLEAR	240	SELF-DEPENDENCE	29
SINCE FIRST THY STORY RAN THROUGH OXFORD HALLS	259	SCHOLAR-GIPSY	132
LONG SINCE AND IN SOME QUIET CHURCHYARD LAID	259	SCHOLAR-GIPSY	137
ELSE WERT THOU LONG SINCE NUMBERD WITH THE DEAD	259	SCHOLAR-GIPSY	153
NOW SELDOM COME I SINCE I CAME WITH HIM	263	THYRSIS	25
HATH SINCE OUR DAY PUT BY	266	THYRSIS	116
LONG SINCE SAW BYRONS STRUGGLE CEASE	270	MEMORIAL VERSES	2
SINCE ERST AT MORN SOME WANDERING SHADE	271	MEMORIAL VERSES	37
AH SINCE DARK DAYS STILL BRING TO LIGHT	272	MEMORIAL VERSES	58
FOUR YEARS SINCE IN THE HOUSE	280	HAWORTH CHURCH	4
FIRST IN FICTION HAD SINCE	280	HAWORTH CHURCH	15
DARING SINCE BYRON DIED	284	HAWORTH CHURCH	96
FOUR YEARS SINCE ON A MARKD	280	HAWORTH CHURCH V	
SINCE THOU AROSEST TO TREAD	287	RUGBY CHAPEL	27
LONG SINCE DEEP IN OUR HEARTS	294	HEINES GRAVE	74
LONG SINCE HATH FLUNG HER WEEDS AWAY	304	GRANDE CHARTR	154
LONG SINCE WE PACE THIS SHADOWD NAVE	305	GRANDE CHARTR	199
LONG SINCE HATH THROWN HER WEEDS AWAY	304	GRANDE CHARTR V	154
SINCE LAST ON EARTH THERE LIVED AND WROUGHT	315	OBERMANN MORE V	83
ENOUGH OF THIS SINCE THAT I HAVE MAINTAIND	334	MEROPE	134
AND SINCE HAS FONDLY WATCHD HIM NIGHT AND DAY	351	MEROPE	618
WITH CYPSELUS AND TWO DAYS SINCE HE DIED	355	MEROPE	718
ON SUCH A HUNTING-JOURNEY THREE MORNS SINCE	355	MEROPE	730
HE ON A HUNTING PARTY TWO DAYS SINCE	364	MEROPE	973
SINCE FROM THY FAITHFUL SUBJECTS WHAT REVENGE	386	MEROPE	1432
BUT THAT SINCE FIRST THE BLACK AND FRUITFUL EARTH	389	MEROPE	1536
FIXD YESTERDAY AND TEN TIMES CHANGED SINCE THEN	389	MEROPE	1547
SINCE POLICY BIDS THUS WHAT FOULER DEATH	390	MEROPE	1568
FOR FATE THOU WAITST NOT LONG SINCE IN THIS HOUR	397	MEROPE	1777
SINCE SO THOU WILT I DARE MAINTAIN IT STILL	398	MEROPE	1793
THE REST TO ME IS LITTLE YET SINCE THAT	401	MEROPE	1891
AND SHOUTED SINCE BY THEE DEFILEMENT CAME	402	MEROPE	1923
NONE SINCE A TWOFOLD COLOUR REIGNS IN-ALL	404	MEROPE	1994
ENOUGH OF THIS SINCE THEN I HAVE MAINTAIND	334	MEROPE V	134
HE ON A HUNTING PARTY THREE DAYS SINCE	364	MEROPE V	973
SINCE SO THOU WILT I WILL MAINTAIN IT STILL	398	MEROPE	V1793
PASSD YOU A LITTLE SINCE AS MORNING DAWND	408	EMPEDOCLES I 1	46
THIS HE COULD DO.OF OLD BUT NOW SINCE ALL	410	EMPEDOCLES I 1	119
SINCE BROILS TEAR US IN TWAIN SINCE THIS NEW SWARM	410	EMPEDOCLES I 1	121
SINCE BROILS TEAR US IN TWAIN SINCE THIS NEW SWARM	410	EMPEDOCLES I 1	121
WHERE HE WAS PARAMOUNT SINCE HE IS BANISHD	410	EMPEDOCLES I 1	123
SINCE HE SEES NOTHING CLEAR	415	EMPEDOCLES I 2	90
BUT SINCE LIFE TEEMS WITH ILL	426	EMPEDOCLES I 2	424
JUST SINCE DOWN AT THE STREAM HO CALLICLES	428	EMPEDOCLES I 2	486
LONG SINCE HIS NAME IS HEARD ON EARTH NO MORE	447	WESTMIN ABBEY	113
SINCE GAINST THE CLASSES	460	KAISER DEAD	40
SINCE THAT STRANGE CREW DID RIDE AFLOAT	480	HAYSWATER BOAT	36
YET HAPPY SINCE HIS FEVERISH BLOOD	484	ROME-SICKNESS	25

SINCERE

EVEN IN A PALACE ON HIS TRUTH SINCERE	169	WORLDLY PLACE	9
AH LET THEM KEEP THEIR FAITH SINCERE	203	EUPHROSYNE	11

SINEWY

ROSE SUCH AS THAT THE SINEWY WOODCUTTERS	75	SOHRAB RUSTUM	476

SING

WHILST OTHER MEN MAKE CHEER AND SING	93	SICK KING BOKH	178
WHOM WE MAY BID TO SING THOUGH THOU ART GONE	117	BALDER DEAD 3	134
SING THEE TALES OF TRUE LONG-PARTED LOVERS	143	TRISTRAM 2	31
THE NIGHTINGALES DIVINELY SING	182	TO MARG CONT	10
BEHOLD AND SING	192	STRAYED REVEL	209
TO BECOME WHAT WE SING	193	STRAYED REVEL	234
THE BIRDS SING SWEETLY IN THESE TREES	248	KENSINGTON GARD V	5
THE BIRDS SING SWEETLY IN THEIR TREES		KENSINGTON GARD V	5
YOUNG DAPHNIS WITH HIS SILVER VOICE DOTH SING	268	THYRSIS	185

SING   (CONTINUED)
       SING HIM THY BEST FOR FEW OR NONE . . . . . . 272 MEMORIAL VERSES   73
       HOW SHALL I SING HER WHOSE SOUL . . . . 284 HAWORTH CHURCH   93
       FOR HE TAUGHT HIM HOW TO SING . . . . 434 EMPEDOCLES II   169

SINGER
       SINGER OF SWEET COLONUS AND ITS CHILD . . . .   2 TO A FRIEND   14
       THAT THE SINGER WAS LESS THAN HIS THEMES . . . 230 YOUTH OF NATURE   89
       MORE THAN THE SINGER ARE THESE . . . . 230 YOUTH OF NATURE   91

SINGING
       SINGING MOST JOYFULLY . . . . 164 FORSAKEN MERM   88
       SINGING MOST JOYFULLY . . . . 164 FORSAKEN MERM   95
       SINGING HERE CAME A MORTAL . . . . 165 FORSAKEN MERM   120
       SINGING THERE DWELLS A LOVED ONE . . . . . . 165 FORSAKEN MERM   140
       ASK WHERE NOW THOSE NIGHTINGALES ARE SINGING . . 482 THEKLAS ANSWER   5

SINGLE
       FURIOUS SINGLE HORSEMEN GALLOP . . . .   13 CHURCH BROU 1   23
       BUT OF A SINGLE COMBAT FAME SPEAKS CLEAR . . .   62 SOHRAB RUSTUM   62
       IN SINGLE FIGHT INCURRING SINGLE RISK . . .   63 SOHRAB RUSTUM   69
       IN SINGLE FIGHT INCURRING SINGLE RISK . . .   63 SOHRAB RUSTUM   69
       TO SEEK THY FATHER NOT SEEK SINGLE FIGHTS . .   63 SOHRAB RUSTUM   90
       IN SINGLE FILE THEY MOVE AND STOP THEIR BREATH .   66 SOHRAB RUSTUM   167
       IN SINGLE FIGHT WITH ANY MORTAL MAN . . . . .   69 SOHRAB RUSTUM   259
       SOLE LIKE SOME SINGLE TOWER WHICH A CHIEF . .   71 SOHRAB RUSTUM   337
       TO COPE WITH ME IN SINGLE FIGHT BUT THEY . . .   72 SOHRAB RUSTUM   359
       IN SINGLE FILE THEY PASS AND STOP THEIR BREATH .   66 SOHRAB RUSTUM V 167
       IN SINGLE FILE THEY WIND AND STOP THEIR BREATH .   66 SOHRAB RUSTUM V 167
       LOOK THIS IS BUT ONE SINGLE PLACE . . . . . .   92 SICK KING BOKH   157
       SEE HERE IS HERMOD WHO COMES SINGLE BACK . . . 113 BALDER DEAD 3   6
       THIS OR SOME TYRANNOUS SINGLE THOUGHT SOME FIT . 153 TRISTRAM 3   127
       PARTS OF A SINGLE CONTINENT . . . . 182 TO MARG CONT   16
       THAT SINGLE ELM-TREE BRIGHT . . . . 263 THYRSIS   26
       A SINGLE MOOD OF THE LIFE . . . . 298 HEINES GRAVE   215
       WITHOUT A SINGLE GUILTY THOUGHT . . . . 353 MEROPE   684
       AND THE PRINCE SINGLE PRESSING ON THE REAR . . 357 MEROPE   799
       SINGLE AND FRIENDLESS GIVE TO CERTAIN DEATH . . 382 MEROPE   1326
       SINGLE AND FRIENDLESS THROW TO CERTAIN DEATH . . 382 MEROPE   V1326
       SINGLE NOT FOR DISTRESS . . . .   EMPEDOCLES I 2   V
       IN A WASTE WOOD A SINGLE BOAT . . . . 479 HAYSWATER BOAT   4
       ONE ROOD FROM SHORE THAT SINGLE BOAT . . . . . 479 HAYSWATER BOAT   16

SINGS
       AND SINGS HIS PLAINTIVE SONG . . . . 159 NECKAN   4
       HE SINGS NOT OF THE OCEAN . . . . 159 NECKAN   9
       OF EARTH OF EARTH THE NECKAN SINGS . . . . . . 159 NECKAN   11
       AND SINGS A MOURNFUL STAVE . . . . 159 NECKAN   14
       SINGS HOW A KNIGHT HE WANDERD . . . . 159 NECKAN   17
       SINGS OF HIS EARTHLY BRIDAL . . . . 159 NECKAN   21
       HE SINGS HOW FROM THE CHAPEL . . . . 160 NECKAN   29
       HE SINGS HOW SHE SITS WEEPING . . . . 160 NECKAN   33
       HE SINGS HOW THROUGH THE BILLOWS . . . . 160 NECKAN   37
       HE SINGS HOW ON AN EVENING . . . . 160 NECKAN   41
       AND SINGS THIS PLAINTIVE SONG . . . . 161 NECKAN   68
       HARK WHAT SHE SINGS O JOY O JOY . . . . 164 FORSAKEN MERM   89
       AND SO SHE SINGS HER FILL . . . . 164 FORSAKEN MERM   94
       OR THE POET WHO SINGS YOU SO WELL . . . . . . 230 YOUTH OF NATURE   62
       THE POET WHO SINGS THEM MAY DIE . . . . 230 YOUTH OF NATURE   84
       SINGS HIS SICILIAN FOLD . . . . 268 THYRSIS   186
       WAS IT AS THE GRECIAN SINGS . . . . 456 POOR MATTHIAS   131

SINK
       AND HURL THEE IN A LAKE TO SINK OR SWIM . . . 114 BALDER DEAD 3   26
       SINK O YOUTH IN THY SOUL . . . . 235 YOUTH OF MAN   116
       HOW IT WERE GOOD TO SINK THERE AND BREATHE FREE . 244 SUMMER NIGHT   V 90
       THERE IN UNVOICED OBLIVION SINK THY NAME . . . 395 MEROPE   1751
       SINK IN THYSELF THERE ASK WHAT AILS THEE AT
           THAT SHRINE   417 EMPEDOCLES I 2   146
       SINK UPON HIS MIGHTY KNEES . . . . 431 EMPEDOCLES II   73
       AND WE SHALL SINK IN THE IMPOSSIBLE STRIFE . . 440 EMPEDOCLES II   389
       WHO SCALE THE CLOUD-CAPT HEIGHT OR SINK TO REST . 472 CROMWELL   11
       TO ALL WHO SINK TO ALL WHO STRAY . . . . . . 484 ROME-SICKNESS   32

SINKING
       OF THE SLOW-SINKING SUN . . . . 208 ON THE RHINE   15
       WITH THE SINKING SUN AND THE AIR . . . . . . 297 HEINES GRAVE   163

SINKS
       AND THE KNIGHT SINKS BACK ON HIS PILLOWS AGAIN . . 133 TRISTRAM 1   84
       HEAVEN HIS HEAD SINKS BACK UPON THE PILLOW . . 145 TRISTRAM 2   77
       SHE SINKS UPON THE GROUND HER HOOD . . . . . 146 TRISTRAM 2   103
       THE EYE SINKS INWARD AND THE HEART LIES PLAIN . . 247 BURIED LIFE   86
       SINKS AND RISES THROUGH THIS COOL ARCADE . . .   META CLOISTER   16
       SINKS AND RISES THROUGH THIS CHARMD ARCADE . . .   META CLOISTER V 16

SINND
       SON LOVED OF ZEUS HIS FATHER FOR HE SINND . . . 398 MEROPE   1814

SINNER
       ON THIS GREAT SINNER WHO DID BREAK . . . . .   89 SICK KING BOKH   37

SINNER   (CONTINUED)
      THOU WAST A SINNER THOU POOR MAN   . . . . . .   94 SICK KING BOKH   209
      ON THIS GREAT SINNER WHO HATH BROKE   . . . . . .   89 SICK KING BOKH V   37
      THOU WERT A SINNER THOU POOR MAN   . . . . . .   94 SICK KING BOKH V 209
      OF THE POOR SINNER BOUND FOR DEATH   . . . . . . 250 WISH   22
      TILL THE SINNER THE VENGEANCE BE RIPE . . . .   347 MEROPE   528
      VENGEANCE ON SINNER AND SIN   . . . .   348 MEROPE   539
      SURELY NO SINNER THE MAN . . . .   361 MEROPE   905

SINNERS
      ARISING FROM THE SINNERS LAKE   . . . .   158 SAINT BRANDAN   67
      THUS PEACEFULLY DO YE LET SINNERS SLEEP . . . .   372 MEROPE   1154
      OF SINNERS PINIOND ON THE TORTURING WHEEL . . .   373 MEROPE   1186

SINS
      WHO SINS ONCE WASHD BY THE BAPTISMAL WAVE . . . . 172 GOOD SHEPHERD   5

SIR
      THE NORTHERN SIR AND THIS GREAT OXUS STREAM . .   83 SOHRAB RUSTUM   765
      SIR TRISTRAM OF THY COURTESY   . . . .   135 TRISTRAM 1   145
      HER WOMEN AND SIR TRISTRAMS AGED HOUND   . . . .   152 TRISTRAM 3   98
      SIR KNIGHT WHO WEDDST TO-DAY   . . . .   159 NECKAN   24

SIRE
      THRICE SON FOLLOWD SIRE   . . . .   345 MEROPE   467
      OF THIS POOR SOUL WHO BARE HIM AND HIS SIRE . .   349 MEROPE   578
      WHERE SIRE TO SON TRANSMITS THE UNQUESTIOND CROWN 388 MEROPE   1517
      LEGITIMATELY SIRE TO SON WITH US   . . . . . .   389 MEROPE   1539
      THE SON TO PERISH AS YE LEFT THE SIRE   . . . . 402 MEROPE   1935
      GRANDSON FOLLOWD SIRE   . . . .   345 MEROPE   V 467
      OF THIS POOR SOUL WHO BORE HIM AND HIS SIRE . .   349 MEROPE   V 578
      BUT AH HIS SIRE   . . . .   459 KAISER DEAD   24

SIREN
      AT A PAUSE OF SIREN VOICINGS   . . . .   27 NEW SIRENS   47

SIRES
      IN PRIDE OF LIFE THE AGES OF YOUR SIRES   . . . . 238 PROGRESS   46

SIROCCO
      ONE MORN WHEN THE SIROCCO SPENT   . . . . . . 157 SAINT BRANDAN   43

SIRS
      SEND HIM AWAY SIRS AND MAKE ON . . . .   90 SICK KING BOKH   90

SISTER
      AND RAYS HER POWERS LIKE SISTER-ISLANDS SEEN . .   4 BUTLERS SERMONS   9
      MY SISTER TO MAINTAIN WITH THEE   . . . . . . 180 FAREWELL   78
      MY SISTER TO BEHOLD WITH THEE   . . . .   180 FAREWELL   V 78
      WELCOME THE SISTER THE FRIEND   . . . .   284 HAWORTH CHURCH   86
      BROTHER FOLLOWD SISTER   . . . .   344 MEROPE   447
      MY ROYAL SISTER BUT WITHOUT SOME CAUSE   . . . . 386 MEROPE   1449
      BROTHER IT SEEMS THY SISTER MUST PRESENT   . . . 386 MEROPE   1451
      JUSTICE MY SISTER LONG DEMANDS THIS BLOW   . . . 390 MEROPE   1572
      SISTER FROM THIS DAY FORTH THOU ART NO MORE . . 403 MEROPE   1954
      TO ETNAS LIPAREAN SISTER-FIRES   . . . .   438 EMPEDOCLES II   313

SISTERLY
      LOVING A SISTERLY BAND   . . . .   284 HAWORTH CHURCH   81

SISTERS
      THE TOO CLEAR WEB AND THY DUMB SISTERS SHAME . . 201 PHILOMELA   21

SIT
      HERE SIT WE AND AGAIN UNROLL   . . . .   55 RESIGNATION   94
      WHAT NEWS BUT SIT DOWN FIRST AND EAT AND DRINK . . 67 SOHRAB RUSTUM   206
      AND MAKE A TRUCE AND SIT UPON THIS SAND   . . .   74 SOHRAB RUSTUM   440
      COME SIT BESIDE ME ON THIS SAND AND TAKE   . . .   82 SOHRAB RUSTUM   718
      SIT SIT BY ME I WILL THINK WEVE LIVED SO   . . . 143 TRISTRAM 2   35
      SIT SIT BY ME I WILL THINK WEVE LIVED SO   . . . 143 TRISTRAM 2   35
      AND TAKE HER BROIDERY-FRAME AND THERE SHELL SIT . 152 TRISTRAM 3   82
      SIT PALE BESIDE THEIR WEALTH   . . . .   191 STRAYED REVEL   192
      HERE WILL I SIT AND WAIT   . . . .   255 SCHOLAR-GIPSY   16
      HER FELLOW-PEOPLE SIT   . . . .   282 HAWORTH CHURCH   V
      SIT AND EYE GRIMLY THE VICTIM UNSCOURGED   . . . 347 MEROPE   531
      WHO IN MANS INMOST BOSOM SIT AND JUDGE   . . . 349 MEROPE   554
      SIT AND MAKE READY THE SERPENT THE SCOURGE . . . 347 MEROPE   V 531
      SIT FOR HOURS BESIDE THY CAGE   . . . .   453 POOR MATTHIAS   32

SITS
      WHERE MANS ONE NATURE QUEEN-LIKE SITS ALONE . .   4 BUTLERS SERMONS   7
      SITS RAPT AND HEARS THE BATTLE BREAK BELOW . . . 42 GIPSY CHILD   23
      BUT NOW HE KEEPS APART AND SITS AT HOME   . . .   63 SOHRAB RUSTUM   81
      BUT RUSTUM CAME LAST NIGHT ALOOF HE SITS   . . .   66 SOHRAB RUSTUM   178
      REACH RUSTUM WHERE HE SITS AND TARRIES LONG . .   78 SOHRAB RUSTUM   582
      TRUTH SITS UPON THE LIPS OF DYING MEN   . . .   80 SOHRAB RUSTUM   656
      SITS BALDER STILL IN POMP BY HELAS SIDE   . . . 125 BALDER DEAD 3   429
      LET HER AS SHE SITS ON BOARD   . . . .   135 TRISTRAM 1   141
      SITS ON PROUD TYNTAGELS HILL   . . . .   134 TRISTRAM 1   V 134
      SITS NECKAN WITH HIS HARP OF GOLD   . . . . . . 159 NECKAN   3

SITS   (CONTINUED)
       HE SITS UPON THE HEADLANDS   • • • • • • • •   159 NECKAN   13
       HE SINGS HOW SHE SITS WEEPING   • • • • • • •   160 NECKAN   33
       SITS NECKAN WITH HIS HARP OF GOLD   • • • • • •   161 NECKAN   67
       SHE SITS AT HER WHEEL IN THE HUMMING TOWN • • • •   164 FORSAKEN MERM   87
       SITS THERE NO JUDGE IN HEAVEN OUR SIN TO SEE   • •   171 BETTER PART   11
       THAT HE SITS BENDING DOWNWARD   • • • • • • • •   188 STRAYED REVEL   82
       THAT HE SITS OVERWEIGHD   • • • • • • • •   188 STRAYED REVEL   91

SITTEST
       AND NOW THOU SITTEST CROWND BY HELAS SIDE   • • • •   112 BALDER DEAD 2   260
       LOITERER WHY SITTEST THOU   • • • • • • • •   220 BACCHANALIA 2   49
       IMMOVEABLE THOU SITTEST STILL   • • • • • • • •   309 OBERMANN   85

SITTING
       SITTING CHEERLESS IN YOUR BOWERS   • • • • • • •   30 NEW SIRENS   127
       BY MOSS-BORDERD STATUES SITTING   • • • • • • •   34 NEW SIRENS   239
       A BREEDING EAGLE SITTING ON HER NEST • • • • • •   77 SOHRAB RUSTUM   557
       AND BALDER SITTING CROWND AND HELAS THRONE • • • •   100 BALDER DEAD 1   175
       ME SITTING HERE BELOW BY HELAS SIDE • • • • • •   112 BALDER DEAD 2   277
       AND THEY FOUND MIMIR SITTING BY HIS FOUNT   • • • •   120 BALDER DEAD 3   219
       SITTING IN THE GILDED BARGE   • • • • • •   134 TRISTRAM 1   111
       SITTING STAFF IN HAND   • • • • • • •   190 STRAYED REVEL   136
       SITTING IN HIS CART   • • • • • • • •   191 STRAYED REVEL   171
       SITTING IN THE DARK SHIP   • • • • • • •   192 STRAYED REVEL   202
       SITTING BY ME WHILE HIS FAUNS   • • • • • • •   194 STRAYED REVEL   265
       SITTING ON THE WARM STEPS   • • • • • • •   194 STRAYED REVEL   271
       SITTING UPON THE RIVER BANK OERGROWN • • • • •   258 SCHOLAR-GIPSY   97
       FOR YEARS THEY SITTING HELPLESS IN THEIR HOME • •   427 EMPEDOCLES I 2   448
       SITTING ON A TABLED STONE   • • • • • •   434 EMPEDOCLES II   177

SITTST
       YET MOURN NOT FOR ME HERMOD WHEN THOU SITTST   • •   126 BALDER DEAD 3   456
       WHY SITTST THOU THERE O NECKAN   • • • • • • • •   160 NECKAN   49

SIX
       AND WHEN SIX YEARS ARE MEASURED LO I DIE   • • • •   9 MYCERINUS   18
       BLOTTING THIS SIX YEARS SPACE WHICH YET IS MINE • •   10 MYCERINUS   60
       SIX YEARS SIX LITTLE YEARS SIX DROPS OF TIME   • •   10 MYCERINUS   61
       SIX YEARS SIX LITTLE YEARS SIX DROPS OF TIME   • •   10 MYCERINUS   61
       SIX YEARS SIX LITTLE YEARS SIX DROPS OF TIME   • •   10 MYCERINUS   61
       SO SIX LONG YEARS HE REVELLD NIGHT AND DAY • • •   12 MYCERINUS   122
       SIX YARDS ROUND SHALL NOT RING IT   • • • • •   50 CONSOLATION   V
       SIX YEARS AGO I BROUGHT HIM DOWN   • • • • • •   459 KAISER DEAD   13

SIXTH
       ISTER TETHYS AND OCEANS SIXTH-BORN SON   • • • •   FRAGMENT 4   2

SKIES
       THEN LOOKD AND LO THE FROSTY SKIES • • • • • •   158 SAINT BRANDAN   75
       TO HAVE RENDERD THE GLEAM OF MY SKIES • • • • •   231 YOUTH OF NATURE   123
       AND ALL THE MARVEL OF THE GOLDEN SKIES • • • •   268 THYRSIS   190
       OR WONDROUS SOUNDS FROM TRANQUIL SKIES WERE BORNE   472 CROMWELL   35
       SKIES THAT UNBOUND BY CLASP OF MOUNTAIN CHAIN • •   473 CROMWELL   37

SKIFF
       MAKE THEIR SKIFF REEL AND WORMS   • • • • • •   193 STRAYED REVEL   237
       UNMOORD OUR SKIFF WHEN THROUGH THE WYTHAM FLATS • •   266 THYRSIS   123

SKILL
       HARDLY HAD SKILL TO UTTER ONE OF ALL • • • • •   246 BURIED LIFE   61
       BUT IT NEEDS HEAVEN-SENT MOMENTS FOR THIS SKILL   • •   256 SCHOLAR-GIPSY   50
       BUT IT NEEDS HAPPY MOMENTS FOR THIS SKILL   • • •   256 SCHOLAR-GIPSY   V 50
       ALL SKILL I WIELD ARE FREE   • • • • • • •   415 EMPEDOCLES I 2   105

SKIM
       QUIVERING AND OTHERS SKIM THE RIVER-STREAMS   • • •   109 BALDER DEAD 2   161
       SWINGING AND OTHERS SKIM THE RIVER-STREAMS • • •   109 BALDER DEAD 2   V 161

SKIMMING
       SWALLOW SKIMMING BY THE MILL   • • • • • • •   456 POOR MATTHIAS   142

SKIMS
       SKIMS NOW AND THEN THE SHINING GROUND   • • • •   54 RESIGNATION   71

SKIN
       AND THE SKIN OF DAZZLING SMOOTHNESS • • • • • •   27 NEW SIRENS   51
       TO A SKIN-DEEP SENSE   • • • • • • • • •   39 STAGIRIUS   26
       AND ON HIS HEAD HE SET HIS SHEEP-SKIN CAP   • • • • •   64 SOHRAB RUSTUM   100
       FIRST WITH BLACK SHEEP-SKIN CAPS AND WITH LONG SPEARS   64 SOHRAB RUSTUM   118
       RENT THE TOUGH PLATES BUT FAILD TO REACH THE SKIN   76 SOHRAB RUSTUM   493
       AND ON HIS HEAD HE PLACD HIS SHEEP-SKIN CAP   • •   64 SOHRAB RUSTUM   V 100
       RENT THE TOUGH PLATES BUT MISSD TO REACH THE SKIN   76 SOHRAB RUSTUM   V 493
       IS IN MY SKIN WHICH ANGERS ME   • • • • • • •   93 SICK KING BOKH   184
       A ROBE OF SACKCLOTH NEXT THE SMOOTH WHITE SKIN   • •   166 AUSTERITY POET   11
       MY DAPPLED FAWN-SKIN   • • • • • • • •   186 STRAYED REVEL   30
       HIS FAWN-SKIN HALF UNTIED   • • • • • • • •   188 STRAYED REVEL   89

SKINND
       AND THOU THOU FAIR-SKINND SERPENT THOU ART LAID • •   373 MEROPE   1177

SKINNY
        WHERE SATE IN THE CAVES MOUTH A SKINNY HAG • • • •   123 BALDER DEAD 3   333

SKIPPING
        WITH THY LIGHT SKIPPING TRICKS AND THY GIRLS WILES   75 SOHRAB RUSTUM   469

SKIRTS
        THE MOUNTAIN-SKIRTS WITH ALL THEIR SYLVAN CHANGE • •   25 DREAM   7
        IN AUTUMN ON THE SKIRTS OF BAGLEY WOOD   • • • • 258 SCHOLAR-GIPSY   111
        FAR ON THE FOREST-SKIRTS WHERE NONE PURSUE • • • • 261 SCHOLAR-GIPSY   215

SKULDA
        SKULDA THE YOUNGEST OF THE NORNIES RODE   • • • • 105 BALDER DEAD 2   21

SKULKD
        IF LIKE A COWARD I SKULKD BEHIND APART FROM THE BATTLE   HOMER TRANS   16

SKULL
        AND CLOSE-SET SKULL-CAPS AND THOSE WILDER HORDES • •   64 SOHRAB RUSTUM   130

SKULLS
        AND IN THE HORNS AND GOLD-RIMMD SKULLS THE WINE • •   95 BALDER DEAD 1   14

SKY
        THESE VEXT BRANCHES AND THIS HOWLING SKY • • • •   27 NEW SIRENS   48
        THE STRANGE-SCRAWLD ROCKS THE LONELY SKY • • • •   60 RESIGNATION   268
        THAT VAST SKY-NEIGHBOURING MOUNTAIN OF MILK SNOW • •   66 SOHRAB RUSTUM   162
        STOOD IN BROAD DAYLIGHT AND THE SKY WAS PURE   • •   75 SOHRAB RUSTUM   488
        STOOD IN BRIGHT DAYLIGHT AND THE SKY WAS PURE   • •   75 SOHRAB RUSTUM   V 488
        GREW DEEPER THUNDER CRASHD ALONG THE SKY • • • •   76 SOHRAB RUSTUM   V 500
        AND OVERHEAD THE CLOUDLESS SKY OF MAY   • • • • 133 TRISTRAM 1   96
        RANG LONELILY AND SHARP THE SKY WAS FAIR • • • • 155 TRISTRAM 3   199
        EARTH SEA AND SKY AND GOD ABOVE   • • • • • • 161 NECKAN   63
        THOUGHTS LIGHT LIKE GLEAMS MY SPIRITS SKY • • • • 209 DESPONDENCY   5
        THE LIQUID SKY ABOVE THE HILL   • • • • • • • 218 BACCHANALIA 1   18
        RISE SLOWLY UP INTO THE SKY   • • • • • • • • 220 BACCHANALIA 2   25
        LIKE STARS IN THE DEEP OF THE SKY   • • • • • • 230 YOUTH OF NATURE   72
        THE CLOUDED SKY IS STILL AND GREY   • • • • • • 248 KENSINGTON GARD   V
        THE ORANGE AND PALE VIOLET EVENING-SKY   • • • • 267 THYRSIS   159
        THAT LONE SKY-POINTING TREE ARE NOT FOR HIM   • • 267 THYRSIS   174
        THAT LONELY TREE AGAINST THE WESTERN SKY • • • • 268 THYRSIS   195
        SAINT MICHAELS CHAPEL CUTS THE SKY   • • • • • • 273 STANZAS CARNAC   2
        THE OPENING SUMMER THE SKY   • • • • • • • • • 285 HAWORTH CHURCH   118
        FAREWELL UNDER THE SKY WE PART • • • • • • • • 312 OBERMANN   181
        THE TURF THE PINES THE SKY   • • • • • • • • 312 OBERMANN MORE   6
        THE SUN SHONE IN THE NEW-WASHD SKY   • • • • • • 319 OBERMANN MORE   209
        IN THE YET STAR-SOWN NIGHTLY SKY   • • • • • • 323 OBERMANN MORE   331
        AS IF THE SKY WAS IMPIOUS NOT TO FALL   • • • • 411 EMPEDOCLES I 1   145
        WE MAP THE STARRY SKY   • • • • • • • • • • 423 EMPEDOCLES I 2   319
        AS THE SKY-BRIGHTENING SOUTH-WIND CLEARS THE DAY • • 432 EMPEDOCLES II   121
        AND THE DEEP HUES OF AN ITALIAN SKY • • • • • • 464 ALARIC AT ROME   69
        HIGH FATE IS THEIRS WHO WHERE THE SILENT SKY   • • 472 CROMWELL   9
        LIKE SUMMER LIGHTNINGS OER A DARKEND SKY • • • • 474 CROMWELL   72
        FAR ON THE DIM HORIZON WHEN THE SKY • • • • • • 475 CROMWELL   129
        THAT KNEW NOT EARTH SOARD UPWARDS TO THE SKY   • • 477 CROMWELL   178
        LAST NIGHT I LOOKD THE SKY WAS CLEAR • • • • • • 480 HAYSWATER BOAT   33

SKYE
        THE CHIEL FROM SKYE   • • • • • • • • • • 461 KAISER DEAD   76

SLACK
        HIS LIMBS GREW SLACK MOTIONLESS WHITE HE LAY   • •   86 SOHRAB RUSTUM   848
        FORGIVE ME MAIDENS IF I SEEM TOO SLACK   • • • • 348 MEROPE   548
        IF FOLLOWD MAKE THEIR SUCCOUR SLACK AND NULL   • • 382 MEROPE   1338

SLACKEND
        AND THOSE SLACKEND ARMS FORGO   • • • • • • • •   27 NEW SIRENS   54
        AND YOUR SLACKEND ARMS FOREGO   • • • • • • • •   27 NEW SIRENS   V 54

SLAIN
        FOOL THOU ART SLAIN AND BY AN UNKNOWN MAN • • • •   77 SOHRAB RUSTUM   537
        BY THE FAR-DISTANT OXUS HE IS SLAIN • • • • •   79 SOHRAB RUSTUM   601
        FOR WOULD THAT ALL WHOM I HAVE EVER SLAIN • • • •   85 SOHRAB RUSTUM   809
        FOR WOULD THAT ALL THAT I HAVE EVER SLAIN • • • •   85 SOHRAB RUSTUM   V 809
        THEN GORGED AND HELPLESS BE ASSAILD AND SLAIN   • • 339 MEROPE   298
        BY NIGHT IN THAT BLIND TUMULT THEY WERE SLAIN   • • 340 MEROPE   345
        OF MY TWO ELDER SONS SLAIN LONG AGO • • • • • • 367 MEROPE   1038
        EARLY-SLAIN INNOCENTS NEAR   • • • • • • • • • 378 MEROPE   1239
        MY FATHER BY YOUR STROKES MY MOTHER SLAIN • • • • 385 MEROPE   1412
        THINE ENEMY IS SLAIN THY SON IS KING • • • • • • 403 MEROPE   1957
        OVER THE GRAVE OF THE SLAIN PYTHO   • • • • • • 435 EMPEDOCLES II   205

SLAKE
        SLAKE THEIR PARCHD THROATS WITH SUGARD MULBERRIES   66 SOHRAB RUSTUM   166
        TO SEEK A DRAUGHT TO SLAKE THY THIRST   • • • • 316 OBERMANN MORE   119

SLAKED
        NOR SLAKED MY THIRST AT THE CLEAR HELMUND STREAM • •   83 SOHRAB RUSTUM   758

SLANT
    AND UP AND DOWN AND SIDE AND SLANT THEY ROAMD   • • 106 BALDER DEAD 2   53

SLAUGHTER
    SNATCHD FROM THE SLAUGHTER OF THY FATHERS HOUSE   • • 330 MEROPE   22

SLAUGHTERD
    HERE HERE THOU HAST HIM SLAUGHTERD BY THIS HAND   • • 376 MEROPE   1217

SLAUGHTEROUS
    AND WITH THESE SLAUGHTEROUS HANDS DRAW SWORD NO MORE   68 SOHRAB RUSTUM   241
    AND STANDS SHOUTING FOR A SLAUGHTEROUS AXE • • • • 400 MEROPE   1860

SLAVE
    THAT HALTING SLAVE WHO IN NICOPOLIS • • • • • •   2 TO A FRIEND   6
    OF THAT LAME SLAVE WHO IN NICOPOLIS • • • • •   2 TO A FRIEND   V   6
    FOOL IF THOU CANST NOT PASS HER REST HER SLAVE • •   5 HARMONY NATURE   14
    A WHITE-ROBED SLAVE STOLE TO THE GREAT KINGS SIDE   47 WORLD QUIETIST   27
    A WHITE-ROBED SLAVE STOLE TO THE MONARCHS SIDE • • 47 WORLD QUIETIST   V 27
    WITH FOLLY OR WHAT DRUNKEN SLAVE • • • • • • 89 SICK KING BOKH   41
    HATH SNATCHD A LITTLE FAIR-HAIRD SLAVE • • • • 93 SICK KING BOKH   165
    BETTER TO LIVE A SLAVE A CAPTURED MAN • • • • 112 BALDER DEAD 2   V 265
    MADMAN OR SLAVE MUST MAN BE ONE • • • • • • 244 SUMMER NIGHT   75
    CHRISTIAN AND PAGAN KING AND SLAVE • • • • • 311 OBERMANN   149
    BE NOT THEN FEARS BLIND SLAVE • • • • • • • 415 EMPEDOCLES I 2   102
    AND BE ASTRAY FOR EVER SLAVE OF SENSE • • • • 440 EMPEDOCLES II   390
    I HAVE IN NO WISE BEEN BUT SLAVE OF THOUGHT • • 440 EMPEDOCLES II   391

SLAVES
    SLAVES OF A TYRANNOUS NECESSITY • • • • • • 10 MYCERINUS   42
    WHERE THROUGH THE SELLERS BOOTHS THE SLAVES • • 88 SICK KING BOKH   18
    AND ONLY SLAVES AND TYRANTS LEFT ALIVE • • • • 383 MEROPE   1378
    THOUGHTS SLAVES AND DEAD TO EVERY NATURAL JOY • • 436 EMPEDOCLES II   249
    WHOSE SONS WERE CONQUERORS ONCE AND NOW WERE SLAVES 469 ALARIC AT ROME   184
    TO THE BLIND SLAVES OF POWER TO MAKE IT KNOWN • •   FRAGMENT 2   3

SLAY
    KEENER TO SLAY THEE LEST THOU POISON ME • • • • 38 WORLDS TRIUMPHS   14
    THOU DOST NOT SLAY ME PROUD AND BOASTFUL MAN • • 77 SOHRAB RUSTUM   542
    WHICH FOLLOW ME I PRAY THEE SLAY NOT THESE • • • 84 SOHRAB RUSTUM   779
    BEFORE THE HEAVENS WERE BUILDED THOU DIDST SLAY • • 121 BALDER DEAD 3   256
    THY BROTHER WHOM THROUGH FOLLY THOU DIDST SLAY • • 124 BALDER DEAD 3   393
    THY TRUSTING LORD DIDST THOU HIS SERVANT SLAY • • 338 MEROPE   280
    WHY WITH THE OFFENDING FATHER DID YE SLAY • • • 339 MEROPE   318

SLAYING
    WHAT SHOULD I DO WITH SLAYING ANY MORE • • • • 85 SOHRAB RUSTUM   808
    FOR HE HE AT LEAST BY SLAYING HER • • • • • • 196 FRAG ANTIGONE   48

SLAYS
    NO RUSTUM SLAYS ME AND THIS FILIAL HEART • • • • 77 SOHRAB RUSTUM   543

SLAYST
    NO BY THE GODS THOU SLAYST STAND OFF THY SON • • 375 MEROPE   1201

SLEEP
    SO SLEEP FOR EVER SLEEP O MARBLE PAIR • • • • 18 CHURCH BROU 3   16
    SO SLEEP FOR EVER SLEEP O MARBLE PAIR • • • • 18 CHURCH BROU 3   16
    MORE GRATEFUL THAN THIS MARBLE SLEEP • • • • • 22 YOUTH AND CALM   21
    SLEEP IN THE JULY SUNSHINE STILL • • • • • • 55 RESIGNATION   97
    WAS HUSHD AND STILL THE MEN WERE PLUNGED IN SLEEP 61 SOHRAB RUSTUM   4
    WAS DULLD FOR HE SLEPT LIGHT AN OLD MANS SLEEP • • 62 SOHRAB RUSTUM   29
    SLEEP BUT I SLEEP NOT ALL NIGHT LONG I LIE • • • 62 SOHRAB RUSTUM   36
    SLEEP BUT I SLEEP NOT ALL NIGHT LONG I LIE • • • 62 SOHRAB RUSTUM   36
    AND WENT UP ON THE ROOF TO SLEEP • • • • • • 90 SICK KING BOKH   73
    HOME AND LAY DOWN TO SLEEP IN HIS OWN HOUSE • • 102 BALDER DEAD 1   247
    AND FREA SEALD HER TIRED LIDS WITH SLEEP • • • 103 BALDER DEAD 1   279
    LIKE A YOUNG CHILD HAST CRIED THYSELF TO SLEEP • • 103 BALDER DEAD 1   291
    SLEEP ON I WATCH THEE AND AM HERE TO AID • • • 103 BALDER DEAD 1   292
    TO FADE AND NANNA IN HER SLEEP STRETCHD OUT • • 104 BALDER DEAD 1   332
    HARK HE MUTTERS IN HIS SLEEP • • • • • • • 133 TRISTRAM 1   87
    TO BED AND SLEEP MY FEVER IS GONE BY • • • • 140 TRISTRAM 1   309
    WHERE DO THE CHILDREN SLEEP KISS THEM FOR ME • • 140 TRISTRAM 1   311
    BUT THEY SLEEP IN SHELTERD REST • • • • • • 140 TRISTRAM 1   327
    FAR HENCE HER DREAMS ARE FAIR HER SLEEP IS STILL • 139 TRISTRAM 1   V 302
    I AM NOW THY NURSE I BID THEE SLEEP • • • • • 144 TRISTRAM 2   70
    WHAT HAS SOME GLAMOUR MADE ME SLEEP • • • • • 148 TRISTRAM 2   175
    HAS THEN SOME GLAMOUR MADE HIM SLEEP • • • • • 148 TRISTRAM 2   V 175
    AWHILE WITH THEM BEFORE THEY SLEEP AND THEN • • 151 TRISTRAM 3   78
    THEN TO HER SOFT SLEEP AND TO-MORROWLL BE • • • 152 TRISTRAM 3   94
    THEY SATE THEM DOWN TOGETHER AND A SLEEP • • • 155 TRISTRAM 3   213
    TO HANG OVER ENDYMIONS SLEEP • • • • • • • 181 ISOLATION MARG   23
    AGAIN THE SWEET SLEEP • • • • • • • • • 187 STRAYED REVEL   69
    BY FUMES OF WINE AND SLEEP • • • • • • • 188 STRAYED REVEL   92
    IN JOY AND WHEN I WILL I SLEEP • • • • • • 241 MORALITY   28
    THE MORNINGLESS AND UNAWAKENING SLEEP • • • • 267 THYRSIS   169
    THE GIANT STONES OF CARNAC SLEEP • • • • • • 274 STANZAS CARNAC   11
    O BOY IF HERE THOU SLEEPST SLEEP WELL • • • • 285 HAWORTH CHURCH   107
    SLEEP O CLUSTER OF FRIENDS • • • • • • • • 285 HAWORTH CHURCH   112
    SLEEP OR ONLY WHEN MAY • • • • • • • • • 285 HAWORTH CHURCH   113

SLEEP   (CONTINUED)
          SLEEP OR ONLY FOR THIS   • • • • • • • • •   285 HAWORTH CHURCH   123
          HITHER TO COME AND TO SLEEP   • • • • • • •   293 HEINES GRAVE   21
          AND WHERE THEY SLEEP THAT WOODEN BED • • • • • •   300 GRANDE CHARTR   47
          AS OUT OF SLEEP AND NO   • • • • • • • •   323 OBERMANN MORE   326
          WHILE THE GOOD SLEEP THE WORKERS HAVE THE DAY • •   366 MEROPE   996
          THUS PEACEFULLY DO YE LET SINNERS SLEEP   • • • •   372 MEROPE   1154
          WHAT SWEETER SLEEP THAN THIS COULD I DESIRE   • • •   372 MEROPE   1156
          AND WHERE DOST THOU SLEEP NOW MY INNOCENT BOY • •   373 MEROPE   1166
          AND DRINKST UNTROUBLED SLUMBER TO SLEEP OFF   • • •   373 MEROPE   1180
          WAKE UP IN HELL FROM THINE UNHALLOWD SLEEP   • • •   373 MEROPE   1183
          WAKES ME THUS KINDLY FROM THE PERILOUS SLEEP   • •   375 MEROPE   1203
          NEVER TO CEASE TO WRITHE AND TRY TO SLEEP   • • • • 430 EMPEDOCLES II   V 60
          HIS MOTHER WOKE FROM SLEEP   • • • • • •   446 WESTMIN ABBEY   92
          QUIET IN SLEEP THE SEVENTH NIGHT THEY DIED   • • •   448 WESTMIN ABBEY   139
          BUT ONE VAST FANE WHERE ALL UNCONSCIOUS SLEEP • •   464 ALARIC AT ROME   59
          OF SLEEP UNSHADOWD BY A DREAM OF WOE   • • • • •   474 CROMWELL   103
          HIS WERE NO TRANQUIL YEARS NO LANGUID SLEEP   • • •   475 CROMWELL   123
          SPRANG FROM ITS SLEEP AND LO THE WATERS ROLL • •   479 CROMWELL   236
          BEHIND A BURIED VALE DOTH SLEEP   • • • • •   479 HAYSWATER BOAT   9

SLEEPER
          WHENCE ART THOU SLEEPER   • • • • • • • • •   186 STRAYED REVEL   23
          AND THOU TOO SLEEPER   • • • • • • • • • •   189 STRAYED REVEL   115

SLEEPERS
          FOR THOU WILT ROUSE NO SLEEPERS HERE • • • • • •   149 TRISTRAM 2   190

SLEEPEST
          POOR LAMB THOU SLEEPEST AND FORGETTST THY WOE   • •   103 BALDER DEAD 1   288

SLEEPING
          IN THE CEDARN SHADOW SLEEPING   • • • • •   26 NEW SIRENS   1
          SHEPHERDS SAY THEY FOUND YOU SLEEPING   • • • •   31 NEW SIRENS   145
          IN THE CEDAR SHADOW SLEEPING   • • • • • •   26 NEW SIRENS   V   1
          AND FOUND THE OLD MAN SLEEPING ON HIS BED   • • •   61 SOHRAB RUSTUM   26
          OR AT A FORD OR SLEEPING BY A TREE   • • • • •   117 BALDER DEAD 3   118
          THE BLOSSOMD THORN-TREE AND HER SLEEPING LOVER •   156 TRISTRAM 3   218
          AT THE WHITE SLEEPING TOWN   • • • • • • •   165 FORSAKEN MERM   137
          THE LIONS SLEEPING   • • • • • • • • • •   187 STRAYED REVEL   48
          AND SANK DOWN HERE SLEEPING   • • • • • •   187 STRAYED REVEL   51
          AND SUNK DOWN HERE SLEEPING   • • • • • •   187 STRAYED REVEL   V 51
          ALL HOUSED WITHIN THE SLEEPING FARMS   • • • •   218 BACCHANALIA 1   7
          AND WAIT THE ISSUE SLEEPING UNDERGROUND   • • •   448 WESTMIN ABBEY   146
          THUS SLEEPING IN THINE ABBEYS FRIENDLY SHADE •   449 WESTMIN ABBEY   164
          HERE SLEEPING IN THINE ABBEYS FRIENDLY SHADE •   449 WESTMIN ABBEY   V 164
          OF OCEANS SLEEPING FACE OR HEAVENS UNBROKEN BLUE •   463 ALARIC AT ROME   36

SLEEPLESS
          STILL DO THY SLEEPLESS MINISTERS MOVE ON   • • • •   1 QUIET WORK   11
          AT THE SLEEPLESS WATERS   • • • • • • •   35 VOICE   5
          HIGH FATE IS THEIRS YE SLEEPLESS WAVES WHOSE EAR •   471 CROMWELL   1

SLEEPS
          OF GRIEF AND EASED US WITH A THOUSAND SLEEPS   • •   43 GIPSY CHILD   52
          WHERE MERLIN BY THE ENCHANTED THORN-TREE SLEEPS •   154 TRISTRAM 3   158
          AND EGREMONT SLEEPS BY THE SEA   • • • • • •   228 YOUTH OF NATURE   17
          THE CHILD SLEEPS WARMLY IN HIS BED   • • • • •   249 KENSINGTON GARD   36
          THE CHILD SLEEPS SWEETLY IN HIS BED   • • • • •   KENSINGTON GARD V 36
          GOETHE IN WEIMAR SLEEPS AND GREECE   • • • • •   270 MEMORIAL VERSES   1
          A BROTHER SLEEPS HE HERE   • • • • • • • •   285 HAWORTH CHURCH   102
          IN GERMAN WEIMAR SLEEPS   • • • • • • • •   308 OBERMANN   52
          SLEEPS AGAMEMNONS UNHAPPY   • • • • • •   344 MEROPE   439
          HE SLEEPS SLEEPS CALM O YE ALL-SEEING GODS   • • •   372 MEROPE   1153
          HE SLEEPS SLEEPS CALM O YE ALL-SEEING GODS   • • •   372 MEROPE   1153
          THE WHILE THERE SLEEPS WITHIN THY PRECINCTS DREAD   464 ALARIC AT ROME   51
          DARK THE VALLEY SLEEPS IN SHADE   • • • • •   META CLOISTER   14

SLEEPST
          O BOY IF HERE THOU SLEEPST SLEEP WELL   • • • •   285 HAWORTH CHURCH   107

SLEET
          CHRIST WHAT A NIGHT HOW THE SLEET WHIPS THE PANE • 130 TRISTRAM 1   4

SLEEVE
          THE GODS LAUGH IN THEIR SLEEVE   • • • • • • •   415 EMPEDOCLES I 2   87

SLEIPNER
          AND MOUNTED HIS HORSE SLEIPNER WHOM HE RODE   • •   96 BALDER DEAD 1   47
          TO RIDE BUT SLEIPNER ODINS HORSE ALONE   • • •   99 BALDER DEAD 1   138
          TIGHTEN THE GIRTHS OF SLEIPNER ODINS HORSE   • • • 100 BALDER DEAD 1   169
          TAKE SLEIPNER HERMOD AND SET FORTH WITH DAWN • •   102 BALDER DEAD 1   236
          AND MOUNTED SLEIPNER AND IN DARKNESS RODE   • • •   102 BALDER DEAD 1   255
          AND TERRIBLY THE HOOFS OF SLEIPNER RANG   • • •   102 BALDER DEAD 1   260
          SLEIPNER AND SLEIPNER WENT TO HIS OWN STALL • • • 102 BALDER DEAD 1   266
          SLEIPNER AND SLEIPNER WENT TO HIS OWN STALL • • • 102 BALDER DEAD 1   266
          BUT HERMOD THOU TAKE SLEIPNER AND RIDE DOWN   • •   106 BALDER DEAD 2   45
          HERMOD LED SLEIPNER FROM VALHALLA FORTH   • • •   106 BALDER DEAD 2   71
          AND SADDLED HIM BEFORE THAT SLEIPNER BROOKD   • •   107 BALDER DEAD 2   72
          AND SLEIPNER ODINS HORSE IS THIS I RIDE   • • • • 108 BALDER DEAD 2   115

SLEIPNER   (CONTINUED)
    ON THE SMOOTH ICE OF SLEIPNER ODINS HORSE   • • •   109 BALDER DEAD 2   147
    SHE SPAKE BUT DOWN OFF SLEIPNER HERMOD SPRANG   • •   110 BALDER DEAD 2   186
    THEN MOUNTED SLEIPNER AND SET FORTH TO RIDE   • •   112 BALDER DEAD 2   284
    AND SLEIPNER SNORTED FOR HE SMELT THE AIR   • • • •   113 BALDER DEAD 2   302
    AND HERMOD CAME AND LEAPT FROM SLEIPNER DOWN   • •   114 BALDER DEAD 3   33
    AND LED THE WAY ON SLEIPNER AND THE REST   • • • •   115 BALDER DEAD 3   59
    MOUNTED ON SLEIPNER WITH THE WARRIOR THOR   • • • •   120 BALDER DEAD 3   239

SLEIPNERS
    AND IN HIS FATHERS HAND PUT SLEIPNERS REIN   • • • •   114 BALDER DEAD 3   34

SLENDER
    SO SLENDER SOHRAB SEEMD SO SOFTLY REARD   • • •   70 SOHRAB RUSTUM   318
    WITH FLANKS A-TREMBLE AND HIS SLENDER TONGUE   • •   114 BALDER DEAD 3   14
    DOWN ON HER SLENDER FINGERS RAIND   • • • • •   140 TRISTRAM 1   V 318
    THE SLENDER TORRENT   • • • • • • • • •   392 MEROPE   1652

SLEPT
    SOHRAB ALONE HE SLEPT NOT ALL NIGHT LONG   • • • •   61 SOHRAB RUSTUM   5
    WAS DULLD FOR HE SLEPT LIGHT AN OLD MANS SLEEP   • •   62 SOHRAB RUSTUM   29
    AND GAZED ON NANNA AS SHE SLEPT AND SPAKE   • • • •   103 BALDER DEAD 1   287

SLEW
    NOT FOR THE THOUSANDS WHOM MY FATHER SLEW   • • • •   8 MYCERINUS   2
    LIVING BUT ELLA CAPTURED HIM AND SLEW   • • • •   117 BALDER DEAD 3   128
    HODER HIS BROTHER WHOM HIS OWN HAND SLEW   • • • •   118 BALDER DEAD 3   165
    AND SLEW THE DOGS WHO AT HIS TABLE FED   • • • •   118 BALDER DEAD 3   170
    HODER THE UNHAPPY WHOM HIS OWN HAND SLEW   • • • •   124 BALDER DEAD 3   384
    AND SLEW THE DOGS WHICH AT HIS TABLE FED   • • • •   118 BALDER DEAD 3   V 170
    FOR IF YE SLEW HIM FOR SUPPOSED MISRULE   • • • •   339 MEROPE   316
    SLEW THEIR ENEMIES KING TISAMENUS   • • • • •   344 MEROPE   451
    WHAT FOLLOWD HIS MOST TRUSTED KINSMAN SLEW   • • •   389 MEROPE   1555
    SLEW HIM FIGHTING IN FRONT OF THE FRAY AND   HOMER TRANS   53
        GLORIFIED HECTOR

SLEWST
    BECAUSE THOU SLEWST HIS BROTHERS WITH THEIR FATHER   336 MEROPE   191
    KINSMAN THOU SLEWST THY KINSMAN FRIEND THY FRIEND   338 MEROPE   281

SLIDDEN
    HATH FRAYD AND SLIDDEN DOWN AND WE NO MORE   • • • •   EVERLASTING SUB   2
    HATH FRAYD AND SLIDDEN DOWN AND THEY NO MORE   • •   EVERLASTING SUB   V   2

SLIGHT
    WHO MASSD ROUND THAT SLIGHT BROW THESE CLOUDS OF DOOM   41 GIPSY CHILD   4
    AND NOT THAT ONE SLIGHT HELPLESS GIRL I HAVE   • •   68 SOHRAB RUSTUM   230
    ITS SLIGHT DARK SHADOW ON THE MOONLIT TURF   • • •   70 SOHRAB RUSTUM   316
    NOR DO I MERIT ODIN THOU SHOULDST SLIGHT   • • • •   121 BALDER DEAD 3   282
    NOR DID THE ALL-RULING ODIN SLIGHT HER WORD   • •   122 BALDER DEAD 3   297
    HER LOOKS ARE MILD HER FINGERS SLIGHT   • • • •   131 TRISTRAM 1   30
    SO SLIGHT A FORM IN SO RICH A DRESS   • • • • •   131 TRISTRAM 1   V
    FIXT HER SLIGHT HANDS CLASPD ON HER LAP THEN RISE   152 TRISTRAM 3   91
    COULD FROM EARTHS WAYS THAT FIGURE SLIGHT   • • •   184 TERRACE BERNE   29
    THAT SLIGHT SWEET FIGURE AT MY SIDE   • • • •   204 CALAIS SANDS   V 11
    WITH SUCH SLIGHT MEANS TO COPE WITH SUCH A FOE   • •   381 MEROPE   1293

SLIGHTS
    THAN THE POOR FACE SHE SLIGHTS IN THEE   • • • •   48 HORATIAN ECHO   35

SLIM
    COURTEOUS-EYED ERECT AND SLIM   • • • • • • •   458 POOR MATTHIAS   194

SLIP
    SLIP WITHOUT BRINGING BLISS SLOWLY AWAY   • • • •   151 TRISTRAM 3   66
    ONCE MORE I SLIP MY CHAIN   • • • • • • •   313 OBERMANN MORE   44
    READY TO SLIP ON HIS UNCONSCIOUS PREY   • • • •   364 MEROPE   972

SLIPPD
    AND THE FEAST PAST ITS PRIME SO WE SLIPPD OUT   • •   407 EMPEDOCLES I 1   37

SLIPPERY
    I LOATHE FOR HIM THE SLIPPERY WAY OF BLOOD   • • • •   387 MEROPE   1464

SLIPPING
    BEEN HELPD BY SLIPPING YEARS   • • • • • • •   200 PHILOMELA   V
    BUT THE SMOOTH-SLIPPING WEEKS   • • • • • • •   268 THYRSIS   206

SLIPS
    I PRAISE THE LIFE WHICH SLIPS AWAY   • • • • • •   199 EARLY DEATH   2
    THAT LIFE IS BEST WHICH SLIPS AWAY   • • • • • •   199 EARLY DEATH   V   2

SLOPE
    DOWN THE PALE CHEEK LONG LINES OF SHADOW SLOPE   • •   43 GIPSY CHILD   37
    DOWN THY PALE CHEEK THOSE LINES OF SHADOW SLOPE   • •   43 GIPSY CHILD   V 37
    BUT OER THEM ON THE FARTHER SLOPE DESCRIES   • • •   113 BALDER DEAD 2   299
    BUT THEIR SLOPE WAS NOT DEEP AND FAR AND NEAR   • •   TRISTRAM 3   V 11
    THERE THE PINES SLOPE THE CLOUD-STRIPS   • • • •   176 PARTING   53
    ON SOME MILD PASTORAL SLOPE   • • • • • •   261 SCHOLAR-GIPSY   216
    THERE ON ITS SLOPE IS BUILT   • • • • • • •   283 HAWORTH CHURCH   61
    UP OER THE ROCK-STREWN SLOPE   • • • • • • •   297 HEINES GRAVE   162

SLOPE   (CONTINUED)
       ACROSS THE VALLEY ON THAT SLOPE • • • • • •   312 OBERMANN MORE   13
       WE BOUNDED DOWN THE SWARDED SLOPE WE PLUNGED • • 357 MEROPE   790
       SLOPE BEHIND SLOPE UP TO THE PEAK LIES BARE • •   414 EMPEDOCLES I 2   55
       SLOPE BEHIND SLOPE UP TO THE PEAK LIES BARE • •   414 EMPEDOCLES I 2   55
       SLOPE STATELY DOWN AND MELT INTO THE PLAIN • • • • 473 CROMWELL   38

SLOPED
       IN A SLOPED SWARD DOWN TO A BRAWLING BROOK • • • • 155 TRISTRAM 3   187

SLOPES
       SWISS CHALETS GLITTERD ON THE DEWY SLOPES • • • •   25 DREAM   10
       SLOPES GRACIOUS UP THE WESTERN RIDGE • • • • • •   54 RESIGNATION   53
       BUT WHERE THE FARTHER SIDE SLOPES DOWN • • • •   57 RESIGNATION   180
       BUT WHERE THE FURTHER SIDE SLOPES DOWN • • • •   57 RESIGNATION   V 180
       STREAM OVER CASBIN AND THE SOUTHERN SLOPES • • • •   64 SOHRAB RUSTUM   113
       MERLIN AND VIVIAN STOPPD ON THE SLOPES BROW • •   155 TRISTRAM 3   201
       CHILDREN WHO EARLY RANGE THESE SLOPES AND LATE • • 258 SCHOLAR-GIPSY   105
       I KNOW THESE SLOPES WHO KNOWS THEM IF NOT I • •   266 THYRSIS   111
       STILL STILL THESE SLOPES TIS CLEAR • • • • • •   268 THYRSIS   196
       HOW OFTEN WHERE THE SLOPES ARE GREEN • • • • •   310 OBERMANN   113
       OR THE SHEPHERDS ON SLOPES • • • • • • • •   392 MEROPE   1641
       ARE SHINING ON THOSE NAKED SLOPES LIKE FLAME • •   412 EMPEDOCLES I 2   6
       OR DOT THE SLOPES TO VEVEY DOWN • • • • • •   483 ROME-SICKNESS   12

SLOPING
       AND IN FIELDS SLOPING TO THE SOUTH DARK PLOTS • • 122 BALDER DEAD 3   314

SLOUGH
       SOME SLOUGH OF SENSE OR SOME FANTASTIC MAZE • •   440 EMPEDOCLES II   375

SLOUGHS
       COWARDS WHO WERE IN SLOUGHS INTERRD ALIVE • • • • 109 BALDER DEAD 2   172

SLOW
       SLOW AND TIRED CAME THE HUNTERS • • • • • •   14 CHURCH BROU 1   41
       SLOW THEY ENTERD WITH THEIR MASTER • • • • • •   14 CHURCH BROU 1   45
       WITH A STATELY SLOW SURPRISE • • • • • • •   31 NEW SIRENS   156
       WHEN THE SLOW TIDE SETS ONE WAY • • • • • •   33 NEW SIRENS   220
       FELT THE SLOW-ROLLING WORD • • • • • • •   47 WORLD QUIETIST   29
       SLOW THROUGH THE TARTAR SQUADRONS TO THE FRONT • •   65 SOHRAB RUSTUM V 142
       SLOW SLOW AND SOFTLY WHERE SHE STOOD • • • • •   146 TRISTRAM 2   102
       SLOW SLOW AND SOFTLY WHERE SHE STOOD • • • • •   146 TRISTRAM 2   102
       WHERE THE DEEP FOREST STREAM CREEPS SLOW • •   148 TRISTRAM 2   V
       HER CHILDRENS SHE MOVES SLOW HER VOICE ALONE • •   151 TRISTRAM 3   72
       SLOW AND SURELY THE SWEETS • • • • • • •   199 EARLY DEATH   13
       SLOW AND SURELY THE SWEET • • • • • • •   199 EARLY DEATH   V 13
       STILL GLIDES THE STREAM SLOW DROPS THE BOAT • •   206 RIVER   1
       OF THE SLOW-SINKING SUN • • • • • • • •   208 ON THE RHINE   15
       WITH TREMULOUS CADENCE SLOW AND BRING • •   211 DOVER BEACH   13
       WITH REGULAR CADENCE SLOW AND BRING • • • •   211 DOVER BEACH   V 13
       WITH MOURNFUL CADENCE SLOW AND BRING • • •   211 DOVER BEACH   V 13
       THROUGH THE LONG DEWY GRASS MOVE SLOW AWAY • •   258 SCHOLAR-GIPSY   110
       AS THE SLOW PUNT SWINGS ROUND • • • • • •   257 SCHOLAR-GIPSY V 76
       SLOW TO A STOP AT MORNING GREY • • • • • •   276 SOUTHERN NIGHT   29
       SLOW ROUND HER PADDLES DIES AWAY • • • • •   276 SOUTHERN NIGHT   31
       SLOW DIE OUT OF HER LIFE • • • • • • •   295 HEINES GRAVE   83
       THE BRIDGE IS CROSSD AND SLOW WE RIDE • • • •   299 GRANDE CHARTR   5
       NO LONELY LIFE HAD PASSD TOO SLOW • • • •   317 OBERMANN MORE   153
       BUT SLOW THAT TIDE OF COMMON THOUGHT • • • •   319 OBERMANN MORE   189
       SLOW SLOW THE OLD WORLD WORE TO NOUGHT • • •   319 OBERMANN MORE   191
       SLOW SLOW THE OLD WORLD WORE TO NOUGHT • • •   319 OBERMANN MORE   191
       SO FEEBLE IS HIS MARCH SO SLOW • • • • • •   352 MEROPE   627
       WHILE LOYALTY WITH ALL HER SPEED IS SLOW • •   363 MEROPE   963
       STRETCHD AMONG BRIARS AND STONES THE SLOW BLACK GORE • • 373 MEROPE 1172
       AND THE SLOW-RIPENING TIME AT LAST PREPARES • •   379 MEROPE   1264
       MONTH AFTER MONTH THROUGH THE SLOW-DRAGGING YEAR • • 347 MEROPE   V
       HERE WILL I STAY TILL THE SLOW LITTER COMES • •   407 EMPEDOCLES I 1   18
       TILL THE SLOW MULES SHOULD CLIMB IN SIGHT AGAIN • • 408 EMPEDOCLES I 1 48
       LIGHT ONLY LIGHT WAS SLOW TO REAPPEAR • • •   445 WESTMIN ABBEY   60
       DOWN THE LONG AGE OF TRUTH THAT RIPENS SLOW • •   448 WESTMIN ABBEY   148
       YES MAX AND WE GREW SLOW AND SAD • • • • •   460 KAISER DEAD   43
       THINK YE IT STRIKES TOO SLOW THE SWORD OF FATE • • 466 ALARIC AT ROME 115
       FATES THREATNINGS ARE NOT VAIN THE SPOILER   466 ALARIC AT ROME 120
           COMES NOT SLOW
       WITH STERN SLOW STEPS UNSEEN YET STILL THE SAME • • 476 CROMWELL   147
       AND SLOW RELUCTANT STEPS ARE GATHERING ROUND • •   476 CROMWELL   160
       FOR BY NO SLOW PACE OR WANT OF SWIFTNESS OF OURS • •   HOMER TRANS   50
       WITHIN THE BALANCE OF A SLOW SUSPENSE • • • •   RUDE ORATOR   5
       OF THAT DUSK SLOW-MOVING BAND • • • • • •   META CLOISTER   10

SLOWLY
       THEN YOU WEPT AND SLOWLY RAISING • • • • •   31 NEW SIRENS   147
       WIDENS SLOWLY WESTWARD ALL THAT WHILE • •   33 NEW SIRENS   V 218
       THERE WINDS UPSTREAMING SLOWLY STILL • • • •   54 RESIGNATION   62
       THOUGH SLOWLY THE FAMILIAR WHOLE • • • • •   55 RESIGNATION   95
       SLOWLY BEHIND HIS HEAVY TREAD • • • • •   57 RESIGNATION   184
       SLOWLY BEHIND THE HEAVY TREAD • • • • •   57 RESIGNATION   V 184
       AH HIS EYELIDS SLOWLY BREAK • • • • • • •   139 TRISTRAM 1   294
       SLIP WITHOUT BRINGING BLISS SLOWLY AWAY • • •   151 TRISTRAM 3   66
       RISE SLOWLY UP INTO THE SKY • • • • • • •   220 BACCHANALIA 2   25

SLOWLY   (CONTINUED)
         GOES SLOWLY BY AND THIS AT SPEED   . . . .   224 EPILOG LAOCOON   116
         SLOWLY WITHIN THE WALLS . . . .   233 YOUTH OF MAN   46
         AND DROOPD AND SLOWLY DIED UPON THEIR THRONE   . .   239 REVOLUTIONS   16
         GLOOM SETTLES SLOWLY DOWN OVER THEIR BREAST   . .   243 SUMMER NIGHT   46
         I FEEL HER SLOWLY CHILLING BREATH INVADE   . . . .   266 THYRSIS   134
         WHAT BLACK PROCESSION SLOWLY MAKES APPROACH   . . .   331 MEROPE   52
         WITH HIM CONFERRING THE KING SLOWLY REACHD   . . . .   401 MEROPE   1907
         THE CURTAINS OF THE BLUE FILMS SLOWLY MEET   . . . .   431 EMPEDOCLES II   79
         WHO SLOWLY BEGIN TO MARSHAL   . . . . . .   437 EMPEDOCLES II   277
         SLOWLY THREAD THEM WHEN BEHOLD   . . . .   457 POOR MATTHIAS   183
         THEN SLOWLY BRIGHTEN AS THE DAYS HAD FLOWN   . .   474 CROMWELL   76
         SLOWLY PAST THE OPEN SPACES   . . . .   META CLOISTER   5
         AT YOUR VOICE HE RISES SLOWLY   . . . .   META CLOISTER   33

SLUGGISHLY
         SLUGGISHLY WINDS THROUGH THE PLAIN   . . . . . .   252 FUTURE   15

SLUMBER
         MIGHT FADE IN SLUMBER AND THE FEET OF JOY   . . . .   11 MYCERINUS   90
         HEARD IN SLUMBER SOUNDS OF WARNING   . . . . . .   26 NEW SIRENS   7
         SHE WILL START FROM HER SLUMBER   . . . .   164 FORSAKEN MERM   112
         DEEP BE THE DARKNESS AND STILL BE THE SLUMBER   . .   206 SEPARATION   11
         RESTED BY SLUMBER AND HEART   . . . .   297 HEINES GRAVE   177
         YE SLUMBER IN YOUR SILENT GRAVE   . . . . . .   304 GRANDE CHARTR   151
         THEY SLUMBER IN THEIR SILENT GRAVE   . . . . .   304 GRANDE CHARTR   V 151
         AND DRINKST UNTROUBLED SLUMBER TO SLEEP OFF   . .   373 MEROPE   1180
         O HAPPY SLUMBER IF THE DAY WERE DONE   . . . . .   475 CROMWELL   120
         SHOOK THE DEEP SLUMBER OF HIS DEATHLIKE TRANCE   .   477 CROMWELL   194
         THRILLD WITH A DREAD NO SLUMBER COULD CONTROL   . .   477 CROMWELL   200

SLUMBERD
         HE SLUMBERD AND AMBROSIA BALMD THE CHILD   . . . .   446 WESTMIN ABBEY   88
         THEN HIS EYE SLUMBERD AND THE CHAIN WAS BROKE   . .   475 CROMWELL   131

SLUMBERETH
         WHEN THE WIND SLUMBERETH IN A SUDDEN LULL   . . . .   466 ALARIC AT ROME   98

SLUMBERING
         TREADS ON THE SLUMBERING DUST OF OTHER YEARS   . .   464 ALARIC AT ROME   50

SLUMBERS
         EARTHS OLD HEROIC FORMS IN PEACEFUL SLUMBERS DEEP   464 ALARIC AT ROME   60
         NOR WAKE THE WEARY SOUL THAT SLUMBERS ON BELOW   . . 469 ALARIC AT ROME   198

SLUMBROUS
         IN THE SLUMBROUS CEDARN SHADE   . . . .   28 NEW SIRENS   68
         IN THIS SLUMBROUS CEDARN SHADE   . . . .   28 NEW SIRENS   V 68

SLUNG
         A CORD THE GODS FIRST SLUNG   . . . .   415 EMPEDOCLES I 2   78

SMALL
         NO SMALL PROFIT THAT MAN EARNS   . . . .   49 SECOND BEST   16
         WHETHER A THING BE GREAT OR SMALL   . . . .   89 SICK KING BOKH   56
         SMALL BLISS MY RACE HATH OF THE GODS OBTAINED   . .   110 BALDER DEAD 2   205
         SHALL A SMALL REMNANT OF THE GODS REPAIR   . . . .   128 BALDER DEAD 3   525
         WHEN FRAGMENT OF IT SMALL LIKE MINE   . . . . . .   158 SAINT BRANDAN   55
         IF FRAGMENT OF IT SMALL LIKE MINE   . . . . . .   158 SAINT BRANDAN   V 55
         AND WE GAZED UP THE AISLE THROUGH THE SMALL   163 FORSAKEN MERM   75
              LEADED PANES
         NO SMALL BOAST FOR A WEAK   . . . .   293 HEINES GRAVE   29
         AND WITH THAT SMALL TRANSFIGURED BAND   . . . .   311 OBERMANN   145
         SMALL COMFORT OFFERS FOR A WOMAN THERE   . . . .   349 MEROPE   564
         TO SOME SMALL HUMBLE AND UNNOTED STRAND   . . .   395 MEROPE   1745
         THERE IS SMALL COMFORT FOR A WOMAN HERE   . . . .   349 MEROPE   V 564
         IS IT SO SMALL A THING   . . . .   425 EMPEDOCLES I 2   397
         THY SMALL BLACK FIGURE ON THE SNOW   . . . . .   451 GEISTS GRAVE   52
         DROVE MY DAUGHTER SMALL AND ME   . . . .   457 POOR MATTHIAS   179
         ROUND HIS SMALL THROAT OF BLACK AND BROWN   . . .   459 KAISER DEAD   15
         THE DROPPING PATTER OF A CHILDS SMALL FEET   . . . .   FRAGMENT 7   1

SMALLEST
         THE SMALLEST THING COULD GIVE US PLEASURE THEN   . . 436 EMPEDOCLES II   250

SMART
         FELT ALREADY SOME DEEPER SMART   . . . .   131 TRISTRAM 1   46
         DEAD TO ITS DEEP HABITUAL SMART   . . . . . .   206 RIVER   19
         THRILLS AT EACH SMART IS THE PRAISE   . . . . .   293 HEINES GRAVE   27
         WITH HAUGHTY SCORN WHICH MOCKD THE SMART   . . . .   303 GRANDE CHARTR   134
         STILL STILL I SEE THE FIGURE SMART   . . . . . .   460 KAISER DEAD   49

SMARTING
         FRESH BE THE WOUND STILL-RENEWD BE ITS SMARTING   . . 206 SEPARATION   3

SMEARD
         HANGS QUIVERING OUT BETWEEN HIS DUST-SMEARD JAWS   . . 114 BALDER DEAD 3   15
         SMEARD WITH RED WINE-STAINS WHO IS HE   . . . .   188 STRAYED REVEL   90

SMELL
         SWEET-WILLIAM WITH HIS HOMELY COTTAGE-SMELL   . .   264 THYRSIS   65

SMELLING
　　　BUT THE SWEET-SMELLING MYRTLE　•　•　•　•　•　•　•　•　391 MEROPE　　　　　　　1616

SMELT
　　　AND SLEIPNER SNORTED FOR HE SMELT THE AIR　•　•　•　•　113 BALDER DEAD 2　　　302

SMILE
　　　A SMILE OF WISTFUL INCREDULITY　•　•　•　•　•　•　•　•　　3 EMERSONS ESSAYS　　　7
　　　A SMILE OF MOURNFUL INCREDULITY　•　•　•　•　•　•　　　　EMERSONS ESSAYS　V　7
　　　SO SCORNFUL SEEMED THAT SMILE SO STRANGE SO FULL　•　•　　EMERSONS ESSAYS　V　9
　　　AND THE PROUDEST NO MORE SMILE　•　•　•　•　•　•　•　•　33 NEW SIRENS　　　　216
　　　AND GRIEF THAT HEALD AT EVERY SMILE OF EARTH　•　•　41 GIPSY CHILD　　　V　20
　　　DREAMS DAWN AND FLY FRIENDS SMILE AND DIE　•　•　•　•　44 QUESTION　　　　　　8
　　　WITH PLEASANT SMILE LET US TAKE CARE　•　•　•　•　•　•　48 HORATIAN ECHO　　21
　　　YOU LISTEN BUT THAT WANDERING SMILE　•　•　•　•　•　•　58 RESIGNATION　　　199
　　　HE SPOKE BUT RUSTUM ANSWERD WITH A SMILE　•　•　•　•　67 SOHRAB RUSTUM　　220
　　　THEN WITH A BITTER SMILE RUSTUM BEGAN　•　•　•　•　•　77 SOHRAB RUSTUM　　527
　　　HUSH NO WORDS THAT SMILE I SEE FORGIVES ME　•　•　•　144 TRISTRAM 2　　　　69
　　　THE LOVELY LIPS WITH THEIR ARCH SMILE THAT TELLS　•　•　176 PARTING　　　　　39
　　　THEN IN THE ETERNAL FATHERS SMILE　•　•　•　•　•　•　179 FAREWELL　　　　　61
　　　THY SMILE AND ROUGE WITH STONY GLARE　•　•　•　•　•　184 TERRACE BERNE　　22
　　　THEY SMILE UPON THE WORLD THEIR EARS　•　•　•　•　•　•　203 EUPHROSYNE　　　V　21
　　　THY SHAWL THY LOOK THY SMILE THY HAND　•　•　•　•　•　204 CALAIS SANDS　　12
　　　TO WOO THY SMILE TO SEEK THINE EYE　•　•　•　•　•　•　205 CALAIS SANDS　　26
　　　TO CATCH THY SMILE TO SEEK THINE EYE　•　•　•　•　•　205 CALAIS SANDS　V　26
　　　AND SMILE ON THY NEW WORLD AND BE　•　•　•　•　•　•　208 LONGING　　　　　　7
　　　CANST THOU PAINT THE INEFFABLE SMILE　•　•　•　•　•　231 YOUTH OF NATURE　113
　　　WE KNOW WE KNOW THAT WE CAN SMILE　•　•　•　•　•　•　245 BURIED LIFE　　　　5
　　　BRIGHT IN THY CRADLE SMILE　•　•　•　•　•　•　•　285 HAWORTH CHURCH　109
　　　THEIR VAUNTS THEIR FEATS LET A SARDONIC SMILE　•　•　298 HEINES GRAVE　　208
　　　THAT SMILE WAS HEINE FOR ITS EARTHLY HOUR　•　•　•　298 HEINES GRAVE　　210
　　　SO HE PLAYD ON THEN ENDED WITH A SMILE　•　•　•　•　357 MEROPE　　　　　　784
　　　ROSILY BRIGHTEN AND THE SOOTHED GODS SMILE　•　•　•　431 EMPEDOCLES II　　81
　　　THE CARELESS GLANCE THE COLD UNMEANING SMILE　•　•　470 ALARIC AT ROME　219
　　　AGE OF ITS TEARS AND CHILDHOOD OF ITS SMILE　•　•　472 CROMWELL　　　　　6
　　　FELL ON THE CHERISHD PAST WITH TEARFUL SMILE　•　•　474 CROMWELL　　　　70
　　　CHILDHOODS BRIGHT GLANCE AND SUNNY SMILE NO MORE　•　•　477 CROMWELL　　　182

SMILED
　　　MAN AFTER MAN THE WORLD SMILED AND PASSD BY　•　•　　3 EMERSONS ESSAYS　　6
　　　MAN AFTER MAN THEY SMILED AND PASSED ON　•　•　•　•　　EMERSONS ESSAYS　V　6
　　　BUT FROM THEN SHE NEVER SMILED　•　•　•　•　•　•　•　14 CHURCH BROU 1　　60
　　　FACES THAT SMILED AND FLED　•　•　•　•　•　•　•　•　44 QUESTION　　　　　19
　　　HE SPOKE AND SMILED AND GUDURZ MADE REPLY　•　•　•　68 SOHRAB RUSTUM　　242
　　　BUT HE LOOKD ON AND SMILED NOR BARED HIS SWORD　•　•　74 SOHRAB RUSTUM　　425
　　　HE SPOKE AND SOHRAB SMILED ON HIM AND TOOK　•　•　•　85 SOHRAB RUSTUM　　838
　　　BUT HE LOOKD ON AND SMILED NOR DREW HIS SWORD　•　•　74 SOHRAB RUSTUM　V 425
　　　AS IF TO ITSELF THE QUIET FOREST SMILED　•　•　•　•　155 TRISTRAM 3　　　204
　　　SHE SMILED SHE WENT UP THROUGH THE SURF IN THE BAY　•　163 FORSAKEN MERM　　62
　　　AND THEN SHE SMILED AND IN THE CATACOMBS　•　•　•　•　172 GOOD SHEPHERD　　9
　　　SHE LOOKD AND SMILED AND SAW THEM THROUGH　•　•　•　202 URANIA　　　　　12
　　　ON ONE SHE SMILED AND HE WAS BLEST　•　•　•　•　•　•　204 EUPHROSYNE　　　V
　　　HOPE AT THAT MEETING SMILED FAIR　•　•　•　•　•　•　281 HAWORTH CHURCH　26
　　　OF RUIN BUT SHE SMILED　•　•　•　•　•　•　•　•　317 OBERMANN MORE　140
　　　UPON THE HEARTH AND PLAYD WITH THEM AND SMILED　•　•　446 WESTMIN ABBEY　　90
　　　NO GLITTERING HOPES ON LIFES GREY DISTANCE SMILED　•　475 CROMWELL　　　　126

SMILES
　　　SMILES THE DUCHESS MARGUERITE　•　•　•　•　•　•　•　13 CHURCH BROU 1　　12
　　　CLOTHED IN SMILES BENEATH THE DAIS　•　•　•　•　•　•　13 CHURCH BROU 1　　35
　　　SHE BATHED IT IN SMILES OF GLEE　•　•　•　•　•　•　21 REQUIESCAT　　　　6
　　　A FEW SAD SMILES AND THEN　•　•　•　•　•　•　•　44 QUESTION　　　　　　5
　　　MY MARGUERITE SMILES UPON THE STRAND　•　•　•　•　•　174 MEETING　　　　　　3
　　　SHE SMILES AND SMILES AND WILL NOT SIGH　•　•　•　•　202 URANIA　　　　　　5
　　　SHE SMILES AND SMILES AND WILL NOT SIGH　•　•　•　•　202 URANIA　　　　　　5
　　　THEN WILL SHE WEEP WITH SMILES TILL THEN　•　•　•　•　202 URANIA　　　　　29
　　　SHE SMILES ELSEWHERE WE MAKE A DIN　•　•　•　•　•　•　204 EUPHROSYNE　　　V
　　　NODS SMILES AND GREETINGS AND FAREWELLS　•　•　•　•　224 EPILOG LAOCOON　121
　　　AND THY GAY SMILES NO ANODYNE　•　•　•　•　•　•　•　245 BURIED LIFE　　　　8
　　　THEN FLY OUR GREETINGS FLY OUR SPEECH AND SMILES　•　•　262 SCHOLAR-GIPSY　　231
　　　SMILES BROKE FROM US AND WE HAD EASE　•　•　•　•　•　271 MEMORIAL VERSES　50
　　　CLINGEST WITH SMILES WITH A SIGH　•　•　•　•　•　•　298 HEINES GRAVE　　190
　　　HAVE THOUGHTS AND SMILES AND TEARS　•　•　•　•　•　•　322 OBERMANN MORE　288

SMILEST
　　　WE ASK AND ASK THOU SMILEST AND ART STILL　•　•　•　•　　2 SHAKESPEARE　　　　2
　　　A BABE THOU SMILEST AGAIN　•　•　•　•　•　•　•　•　378 MEROPE　　　　　　1237

SMILING
　　　GAY HER SMILING LORD TO GREET　•　•　•　•　•　•　•　13 CHURCH BROU 1　　10
　　　ONLY THE BLESSED SAINTS ARE SMILING DUMB　•　•　•　•　17 CHURCH BROU 3　　4
　　　DUMBLY SMILING AS YOU GO　•　•　•　•　•　•　•　•　31 NEW SIRENS　　　160
　　　ME A SMILING QUEEN UPON MY THRONE　•　•　•　•　•　•　144 TRISTRAM 2　　　　52
　　　THOU STANDEST SMILING　•　•　•　•　•　•　•　•　186 STRAYED REVEL　　7
　　　AH GOLDEN-HAIRD STRANGELY SMILING GODDESS　•　•　•　194 STRAYED REVEL　286
　　　THOU SMILING FIEND AND CLAIM THY GUERDON THERE　•　•　373 MEROPE　　　　　1184

SMILINGLY
　　　SMILINGLY FORTH UPON HER SUNNY BAY　•　•　•　•　•　•　468 ALARIC AT ROME　160

SMIRCH
        TILL THE SAND THY FEATHERS SMIRCH   • • • • • •   456 POOR MATTHIAS   129

SMIRCHD
        AND THREW IT ON HIS HEAD AND SMIRCHD HIS HAIR   • •   81 SOHRAB RUSTUM   701

SMIT
        HE HAD SMIT ME HAD HE BEEN SWIFT AS I   • • • •   334 MEROPE   131.

SMITHS
        GERMAN MASONS SMITHS FROM SPAIN   • • • • • •   15 CHURCH BROU 1   96

SMITTEN
        A FAR BRIGHT CITY SMITTEN BY THE SUN • • • • • •   79 SOHRAB RUSTUM   622

SMOCK
        ON THE WARM INGLE-BENCH THE SMOCK-FROCKD BOORS   • •   256 SCHOLAR-GIPSY   59

SMOKE
        CAPPD WITH FAINT SMOKE THE NOISY TOWN   • • • •   55 RESIGNATION   93
        AND AS THE WOODMAN SEES A LITTLE SMOKE   • • • •   104 BALDER DEAD 1   335
        AND WREATHED IN SMOKE THE SHIP STOOD OUT TO SEA   • •   118 BALDER DEAD 3   185
        INTO THE SMOKE-WRAPT SEA AND NIGHT CAME ON   • • • •   119 BALDER DEAD 3   195
        UPON THE CLIFFS OR SMOKE OF BURNING WEEDS   • • • •   124 BALDER DEAD 3   362
        SAFE THROUGH THE SMOKE OF THE FIGHT   • • •   217 LORDS MESSENGER   23
        I SEE THE SMOKE-CROWND VESSEL COME   • • • •   276 SOUTHERN NIGHT   30
        WHERE THAT WET SMOKE AMONG THE WOODS   • • • •   299 GRANDE CHARTR   11
        ON THAT MORN WHEN THE SMOKE-CLOUD   • • • • •   399 MEROPE   1826
        MELT LIKE A PASSING SMOKE A NIGHTLY DREAM   • • • •   402 MEROPE   1945
        THESE ANGRY SMOKE-BURSTS • • • • • •   • • • •   432 EMPEDOCLES II   96
        THROUGH THE BLACK RUSHING SMOKE-BURSTS   • • • •   441 EMPEDOCLES II   417

SMOKED
        PITCH THEIR SMOKED TENTS AND EVERY BUSH YOU SEE   • •   258 SCHOLAR-GIPSY   113

SMOKELESS
        SMOKELESS EMPTY   • • • • • • • • • • •   187 STRAYED REVEL   45

SMOKY
        SMOKY DWARF HOUSES   • • • • • • • • • • •   50 CONSOLATION   2

SMOOTH
        THEIR SMOOTH TOPS SHINING SUNWARD AND BENEATH   • •   11 MYCERINUS   87
        IT MAY BE BUT NOT LESS HIS BROW WAS SMOOTH   • • •   12 MYCERINUS   112
        THEIR SMOOTH TOPS SHINING SUNWARDS AND BENEATH   • •   11 MYCERINUS   V 87
        ON THE SMOOTH LEADEN ROOF AND ON THE WALLS   • • •   18 CHURCH BROU 3   34
        ON THE SMOOTH CONVENT-ROOFS   • • • • •   50 CONSOLATION   12
        WASH OFF ALL BLOOD SET SMOOTH EACH LIMB   • • •   95 SICK KING BOKH   230
        WHOM THOU SO WELL HAST LOVED BUT I CAN SMOOTH   • •   103 BALDER DEAD 1   308
        ON THE SMOOTH ICE OF SLEIPNER ODINS HORSE   • • •   109 BALDER DEAD 2   147
        SMOOTH SOUND THE TERMS AND LIGHT TO BE FULFILLD   • •   120 BALDER DEAD 3   231
        FAR HENCE HER DREAMS ARE FAIR SMOOTH IS HER BROW   •   139 TRISTRAM 1   302
        LONG INLETS OF SMOOTH GLITTERING SEA   • • • •   141 TRISTRAM 1   368
        IN THE SMOOTH CENTRE OF THE OPENING STOOD   • • •   150 TRISTRAM 3   19
        IN THE SMOOTH CENTRE OF THE HOLLOW STOOD   • • •   TRISTRAM 3   V 19
        A ROBE OF SACKCLOTH NEXT THE SMOOTH WHITE SKIN   • •   166 AUSTERITY POET   11
        GLOW NOT THEIR SHOULDERS SMOOTH   • • • • • •   219 BACCHANALIA 1   46
        BUT THE SMOOTH-SLIPPING WEEKS   • • • • • • •   268 THYRSIS   206
        THE SMOOTH TO-DAY OF GOD   • • • • • • •   262 THYRSIS   V
        CARVED THERE NO MORE AND THE SMOOTH   • • • • •   292 HEINES GRAVE   3
        WHERE FIRST THE CHASE PLUNGED IN THE BAY IS SMOOTH   358 MEROPE   819
        HERE WHERE THE GRASS IS SMOOTH AND WARM   • • •   451 GEISTS GRAVE   66
        SMOOTH HIS RUFFLED PLUMAGE FINE   • • • • •   452 POOR MATTHIAS   11

SMOOTHED
        FOR WE LOSE HIM WHO SMOOTHED ALL STRIFE IN HEAVEN   116 BALDER DEAD 3   88
        SPRINKLED AND SMOOTHED   • • • • • • • • •   194 STRAYED REVEL   267

SMOOTHER
        SEE HIM COME BACK AND CUT A SMOOTHER REED   • • • •   265 THYRSIS   78

SMOOTHNESS
        THE SMOOTHNESS OF THAT LIMPID BROW   • • • • • •   21 YOUTH AND CALM   4
        AND THE SKIN OF DAZZLING SMOOTHNESS   • • • • •   27 NEW SIRENS   51

SMOTE
        THEN SOHRAB WITH HIS SWORD SMOTE RUSTUMS HELM   • •   76 SOHRAB RUSTUM   495
        AND HIS KNEES TOTTERD AND HE SMOTE HIS HAND   • •   80 SOHRAB RUSTUM   662
        SMOTE MID THE ROCKS THE LICHEN-BEARDED PINES   • •   106 BALDER DEAD 2   56
        SMOTE ON THE SQUALID STREETS OF BETHNAL GREEN   • •   169 EAST LONDON   2
        ANGRILY SMOTE ON THE CHORDS   • • • • •   285 HAWORTH CHURCH   128
        I SMOTE HIM WHEN OUR WISHES CLASHD IN ARMS   • • •   334 MEROPE   130
        BUT WHILE I SMOTE HIM QUEEN I HONOURD HIM   • • •   334 MEROPE   132
        OF GOTHIC CLARION SMOTE THY STARTLED EAR   • • •   465 ALARIC AT ROME   80
        OR THAT MYSTERIOUS CRY THAT SMOTE WITH FEAR   • •   473 CROMWELL   41
        SMOTE LIKE THE RUSH OF WATERS ON HIS EAR   • • •   475 CROMWELL   136
        UNTIL ANOTHER ROSE AND SMOTE HIM DOWN   • • •   476 CROMWELL   144
        HIS LATEST LOFTIEST MUSIC SMOTE HIS EAR   • • • •   478 CROMWELL   210

SMYRNA
    AND TMOLUS HILL AND SMYRNA BAY THOUGH BLIND   • •   2 TO A FRIEND   4

SMYRNAS
    AND TMOLUS HILL AND SMYRNAS BAY THOUGH BLIND   • •   2 TO A FRIEND   V 4

SNAKE
    LITHE AS THE GLANCING SNAKE AND THE CLUB CAME   • •   73 SOHRAB RUSTUM   418
    DIED OF A SNAKE-BITE SAID HE ON THAT BROW   • • • • 357 MEROPE   781

SNAKES
    WHERE THE SEA-SNAKES COIL AND TWINE • • • • • • 162 FORSAKEN MERM   41
    AND THERE THEY SAY TWO BRIGHT AND AGED SNAKES   • •   427 EMPEDOCLES I 2   435

SNAP
    ARE APT TO SNAP THE EASY-STRETCHD ENDURE   • • • • 339 MEROPE   308

SNAPDRAGON
    SOON SHALL WE HAVE GOLD-DUSTED SNAPDRAGON   • • • • 264 THYRSIS   64

SNAPPD
    SHE VEILD HER EAGLES SNAPPD HER SWORD   • • • • 316 OBERMANN MORE   125

SNAPT
    AND WERE IT SNAPT THOU LOVST ME NOT • • • • • 208 ON THE RHINE   9

SNARE
    BALDER TOO TRULY THOU FORESAWST A SNARE   • • • • 126 BALDER DEAD 3   446

SNARES
    BUT HIM TOO FOES AWAIT AND NETTED SNARES   • • • • 111 BALDER DEAD 2   219
    DOUBLE OF ISSUE FULL OF PITS AND SNARES   • • • 349 MEROPE   581

SNATCH
    THEY SNATCH ALSO TOWARDS MERVE • • • 93 SICK KING BOKH   166
    WE MUST NOT SNATCH IT EAGERLY • • • • • 94 SICK KING BOKH   212
    THAT THOUGH WE SNATCH WHAT WE DESIRE • • • • 94 SICK KING BOKH   V 211
    WOULD I MIGHT SEE HIM SNATCH THEE IN HIS HAND   • • 114 BALDER DEAD 3   24
    TO SNATCH AND WIELD IT WILL NOT SEE • • • • 282 HAWORTH CHURCH   V
    FRUITLESS BUT SOMETHING TO SNATCH • • • • 288 RUGBY CHAPEL   81
    HERE IN THE QUIET TO SNATCH • • • • • 294 HEINES GRAVE   49

SNATCHD
    SNATCHD A TURBID INSPIRATION • • • • 31 NEW SIRENS   151
    SNATCHD AN EARTHLY INSPIRATION • • • • • 31 NEW SIRENS   V 151
    HATH SNATCHD A LITTLE FAIR-HAIRD SLAVE   • • • 93 SICK KING BOKH   165
    I SNATCHD UP MY VINE-CROWN MY FIR-STAFF   • • • 186 STRAYED REVEL   33
    SAW AND SNATCHD WILD WITH LOVE • • • • 196 FRAG ANTIGONE   60
    AND SNATCHD HIS RUDDER AND SHOOK OUT MORE SAIL   • 262 SCHOLAR-GIPSY   242
    SNATCHD FROM THE SLAUGHTER OF THY FATHERS HOUSE   • 330 MEROPE   22
    WE SPRANG UPON OUR FEET WE SNATCHD OUR SPEARS   • • 357 MEROPE   789
    THE PRINCE SNATCHD FROM THE SACRIFICERS HAND   • • 402 MEROPE   1919

SNATCHES
    AND WHEN AT LAST THEIR SNATCHES CEASE   • • • • 226 EPILOG LAOCOON   185
    AND WHEN AT LAST THESE SNATCHES CEASE   • • • • 226 EPILOG LAOCOON   V 185

SNEERS
    THE SOPHIST SNEERS FOOL TAKE • • • • • 416 EMPEDOCLES I 2   132

SNIFF
    SO YE GROW SQUEAMISH GODS AND SNIFF AT HEAVEN   • • 123 BALDER DEAD 3   344

SNOODED
    THE RED-SNOODED PHRYGIAN GIRLS • • • • • • 434 EMPEDOCLES II   180

SNORT
    WITH SNORT AND STRAIN • • • • • • • 191 STRAYED REVEL   184

SNORTED
    AND SLEIPNER SNORTED FOR HE SMELT THE AIR   • • • 113 BALDER DEAD 2   302

SNORTING
    AND DRAVE THEM HOMEWARD AND THE SNORTING STEEDS   • • 106 BALDER DEAD 2   61
    AND DROVE THEM HOMEWARD AND THE SNORTING STEEDS   • • 106 BALDER DEAD 2   V 61

SNOW
    RANGED DIAMOND-BRIGHT THE ETERNAL WALL OF SNOW   • • 25 DREAM   13
    THAT VAST SKY-NEIGHBOURING MOUNTAIN OF MILK SNOW   • • 66 SOHRAB RUSTUM   162
    LONG FLOCKS OF TRAVELLING BIRDS DEAD ON THE SNOW   • • 66 SOHRAB RUSTUM   164
    AND I TO TARRY WITH THE SNOW-HAIRD ZAL   • • 68 SOHRAB RUSTUM   232
    THOU AND THE SNOW-HAIRD ZAL AND ALL THY FRIENDS   • • 84 SOHRAB RUSTUM   786
    WITH THE SNOW-HEADED ZAL AND ALL MY FRIENDS   • • 84 SOHRAB RUSTUM   801
    WITH CHERRIES SERVD IN DRIFTS OF SNOW   • • 94 SICK KING BOKH   197
    WHOM ANTLERD REINDEER PULL OVER THE SNOW   • • • 96 BALDER DEAD 1   54
    AT THE CHINKD FIELDS OF ICE THE WASTE OF SNOW   • • 100 BALDER DEAD 1   164
    WEDGED IN THE SNOW THEN PAINFULLY THE HINDS   • • 107 BALDER DEAD 2   95
    PLUNGING THROUGH DEEP UNTRODDEN BANKS OF SNOW   • • 107 BALDER DEAD 2   97
    IN ALL THE FORESTS AND THE SOFT-STREWN SNOW   • • 122 BALDER DEAD 3   311
    OF GRASS PEEP OUT AMID SURROUNDING SNOW   • • • 122 BALDER DEAD 3   315

SNOW   (CONTINUED)
          AS THE DRIVEN SNOW ARE WHITE . . . .   131 TRISTRAM 1   31
          HER SNOW-WHITE HANDS HER GOLDEN HAIR . . . . . .   132 TRISTRAM 1   51
          ISEULT OF THE SNOW-WHITE HAND . . . .   132 TRISTRAM 1   74
          NOR TO THE SNOW WHICH THOUGH TWAS ALL AWAY . . . .   151 TRISTRAM 3   50
          THE VAST RANGE OF SNOW . . . .   175 PARTING   12
          THE VAST SEAS OF SNOW . . . .   175 PARTING   28
          UNSPOTTED BY SNOW . . . .   176 PARTING   46
          WHERE THE NICHED SNOW-BED SPRAYS DOWN . . . .   176 PARTING   49
          THE VAST FIELDS OF SNOW . . . .   PARTING   V 28
          AS IS THE ETERNAL MOONLIT SNOW . . . .   207 ON THE RHINE   3
          WRAPT IN THY CLOAK AND BATTLING WITH THE SNOW . .   258 SCHOLAR-GIPSY   124
          GORGES OER MOUNTAINS IN SNOW . . . .   289 RUGBY CHAPEL   88
          THE UNSEEN SNOW-BEDS DISLODGE . . . .   289 RUGBY CHAPEL   99
          WHOM WE HAVE LEFT IN THE SNOW . . . .   289 RUGBY CHAPEL   116
          OR CHALETS NEAR THE ALPINE SNOW . . . . . .   304 GRANDE CHARTR   150
          FADE FROM THE DISTANT PEAKS OF SNOW . . . . .   310 OBERMANN   123
          OUR LIFE TO ALPINE SNOW . . . .   323 OBERMANN MORE   318
          IN THE SNOW-FILLD HOLLOWS . . . .   392 MEROPE   1623
          THY SMALL BLACK FIGURE ON THE SNOW . . . . .   451 GEISTS GRAVE   52
          FROM A FAR LAND THE CHILDREN OF THE SNOW . . . .   474 CROMWELL   90

SNOWDROP
          WHO IS THIS SNOWDROP BY THE SEA . . . . . .   132 TRISTRAM 1   49
          OUR SNOWDROP BY THE ATLANTIC SEA . . . . . .   136 TRISTRAM 1   196

SNOWFLAKES
          TURND ONCE TO WATCH WHILE THICK THE SNOWFLAKES FALL   259 SCHOLAR-GIPSY   128

SNOWILY
          OF PARNASSUS SNOWILY CLEAR . . . .   229 YOUTH OF NATURE   40

SNOWLOADS
          AND FROM THE BOUGHS THE SNOWLOADS SHUFFLE DOWN . .   122 BALDER DEAD 3   313

SNOWS
          DOWN LYDIAN MOUNTAINS SO WHEN SNOWS . . . . .   52 RESIGNATION   7
          WHEN THE SUN MELTS THE SNOWS IN HIGH PAMERE . .   61 SOHRAB RUSTUM   15
          FOR FEAR THEY SHOULD DISLODGE THE OERHANGING SNOWS   66 SOHRAB RUSTUM   168
          I JOURNEY TO THESE HEALING SNOWS . . . . . .   158 SAINT BRANDAN   68
          THE JUNGFRAU SNOWS LOOK FAINT AND FAR . . . .   184 TERRACE BERNE   6
          AND SCARED OETAEAN SNOWS . . . .   198 FRAG ANTIGONE   102
          AND TRANQUIL AS THE GLACIER-SNOWS . . . . . .   278 SOUTHERN NIGHT   90
          THE SOUL OF THEIR WHITE SNOWS . . . .   307 OBERMANN   28
          THE SOUL OF THEIR MUTE SNOWS . . . .   307 OBERMANN   V 28
          THERE AMONG ALPINE SNOWS . . . .   321 OBERMANN MORE   250
          AND THE DOMED VELAN WITH HIS SNOWS . . . . .   324 OBERMANN MORE   341

SNOWY
          THEIR KINE ACROSS A SNOWY MOUNTAIN-PASS . . . .   107 BALDER DEAD 2   92
          AND ON THE SNOWY PILLOW FALLS . . . .   141 TRISTRAM 1   336
          WHERE THE SNOWY MOUNTAINOUS PASS . . . . . .   252 FUTURE   9
          HANGS TOUCHD WITH LIGHT ONE SNOWY SAIL . . . .   274 STANZAS CARNAC   32
          THE SNOWY HIMALAYAN MOUNT . . . .   277 SOUTHERN NIGHT   55
          SOUTHWARD AND WEST BEHOLD THOSE SNOWY PEAKS . .   330 MEROPE   16
          THENCE TO THE SOUTH BEHOLD THOSE SNOWY PEAKS . .   330 MEROPE   V 16
          IN HIS SNOWY LIGHT AUSTERE . . . .   PILLARS UNIVERS   9

SNUFF
          THE FIERCE HOUNDS SNUFF THE TAINTED AIR . . . .   149 TRISTRAM 2   184

SNUFFD
          AND SNUFFD THE BREEZES OF MY FATHERS HOME . . .   83 SOHRAB RUSTUM   749

SNUFFING
          REARD PROUDLY SNUFFING . . . .   190 STRAYED REVEL   149

SNUFFS
          SNUFFS AT IT DAINTILY AND STOOPS HER HEAD . . .   123 BALDER DEAD 3   342

SOAKD
          CORN IN A GOLDEN PLATTER SOAKD WITH WINE . . .   83 SOHRAB RUSTUM   . 754
          SPLINTERS OF PINE-WOOD SOAKD WITH TURPENTINE . .   118 BALDER DEAD 3   168
          OOZING THROUGH THY SOAKD HUNTING-SHIRT WITH LIMBS   373 MEROPE   1173

SOAKING
          AND WHERE THE SOAKING SPRINGS ABOUND . . . . .   414 EMPEDOCLES I 2   64

SOAKS
          EXPERIENCE LIKE A SEA SOAKS ALL-EFFACING IN . .   419 EMPEDOCLES I 2   201

SOAR
          AND WHEN SHE FAIN WOULD SOAR . . . .   39 STAGIRIUS   22

SOARD
          THAT KNEW NOT EARTH SOARD UPWARDS TO THE SKY . .   477 CROMWELL   178

SOARING
          SOARING FROM HIS DEATH-PILE ON OETA LEFT . . .   336 MEROPE   213
          STOOPS TO THE SOARING MOUNTAINS LIVE AND DIE . .   472 CROMWELL   10

SOBBING
    LET THIS SOBBING PHRYGIAN STRAIN   • • • • • •   32 NEW SIRENS   168
    AND THIS SOBBING PHRYGIAN STRAIN   • • • • • •   32 NEW SIRENS   V 168

SOBER
    AMBITIONS BOLDEST DREAM MIGHT SOBER AND APPAL   • •   463 ALARIC AT ROME   42

SOBERD
    TO THIS DEEP-SOBERD HEART   • • • • • •   36 VOICE   24
    TO THIS LONG SOBERD HEART   • • • • • •   36 VOICE   V 24

SOBS
    AND HIS SOBS CHOKED HIM AND HE CLUTCHD HIS SWORD • •   82 SOHRAB RUSTUM   704
    UP TO ITS GOLDEN ROOF WITH SOBS AND CRIES • • •   95 BALDER DEAD 1   12
    THERE SOBS I KNOW NOT WHAT GROUND-TONE • • •   307 OBERMANN   35

SOCIAL
    OF A SOCIAL ORDER HE LOVED • • • • • • • •   229 YOUTH OF NATURE   32
    YOUR SOCIAL ORDER TOO • • • • • • • •   320 OBERMANN MORE   230

SOD
    SCARCE FRESHER IS THE MOUNTAIN-SOD • • • • •   248 KENSINGTON GARD   17
    NOT FRESHER IS THE MOUNTAIN SOD • • • • •   KENSINGTON GARD V 17
    FLINGING ON THE MOUNTAIN-SOD • • • • • •   433 EMPEDOCLES II   156

SOFT
    HER SOFT FACE HER HAIR AROUND • • • •   23 MEMORY-PICTURE   26
    O THOU YOUNG MAN THE AIR OF HEAVEN IS SOFT • • •   70 SOHRAB RUSTUM   322
    HE SPAKE AND BRUSHD SOFT BY AND DISAPPEARD • • •   102 BALDER DEAD 1   239
    SO THEY TWO SOFT TO ONE ANOTHER SPAKE • • •   114 BALDER DEAD 3   30
    IN ALL THE FORESTS AND THE SOFT-STREWN SNOW • •   122 BALDER DEAD 3   311
    SOFT WHO IS THAT STANDS BY THE DYING FIRE • • •   130 TRISTRAM 1   7
    AT THIS SOFT HOUR UNDER THIS SWEET MOON • • •   139 TRISTRAM 1   286
    THROUGH THE SOFT-OPEND LIPS THE AIR • • • •   141 TRISTRAM 1   342
    THE HOLLOWS GRASSY BANKS ARE SOFT-INCLINED • •   149 TRISTRAM 3   10
    LIFTING HER SOFT-BENT HEAD ONLY TO MIND • • •   152 TRISTRAM 3   84
    THEN TO HER SOFT SLEEP AND TO-MORROWLL BE • • •   152 TRISTRAM 3   94
    THE OPENINGS GRASSY BANKS ARE SOFT INCLINED   TRISTRAM 3 V 10
    THE OPENINGS GRASSY BANKS WERE SOFT INCLINED   TRISTRAM 3 V 10
    WHEN SOFT THE WINDS BLOW • • • • • • • •   165 FORSAKEN MERM   125
    I KNOW THAT SOFT ENKERCHIEFD HAIR • • •   174 MEETING   7
    THE SWEET BLUE EYES THE SOFT ASH-COLOURED HAIR • •   175 PARTING   37
    HUNG SOFT IN THEIR HEADS • • • • • •   176 PARTING   54
    THY CHEEKS SOFT HUE AND FLUTTERING LACE • • •   184 TERRACE BERNE   23
    PROPS THY SOFT CHEEK • • • • • • • •   186 STRAYED REVEL   10
    MORE SOFT AH ME • • • • • • • •   187 STRAYED REVEL   65
    BY ARTEMIS SOFT SHAFTS • • • • • • • •   197 FRAG ANTIGONE   67
    SHAKE LOOSE SOME BAND OF SOFT BROWN HAIR • • •   205 CALAIS SANDS   16
    TO-NIGHT THOSE SOFT-FRINGED EYES SHALL CLOSE • •   205 CALAIS SANDS   35
    SHAKE BACK THY BANDS OF SOFT BROWN HAIR • • •   205 CALAIS SANDS V 16
    SHAKE LOOSE SOME LOCK OF SOFT BROWN HAIR • • •   205 CALAIS SANDS V 16
    TO-NIGHT THOSE SOFT-VEILED EYES SHALL CLOSE • •   205 CALAIS SANDS V 35
    THOSE EYES OF DEEP SOFT LUCENT HUE • • • •   208 ON THE RHINE   18
    THE SOFT-COUCHD CATTLE WERE AS FAIR • • • •   222 EPILOG LAOCOON   43
    LOVELY AND SOFT AS A DREAM • • • • • •   228 YOUTH OF NATURE   3
    BEHIND THROUGH THE SOFT AIR • • • • •   242 SUMMER NIGHT   20
    THROUGH SILKEN RIFTS SOFT PEERS THE SUN • • •   248 KENSINGTON GARD V
    THROUGH SILKEN RIFTS SOFT WINKS THE SUN • • •   KENSINGTON GARD V
    THY DARK VAGUE EYES AND SOFT ABSTRACTED AIR • •   258 SCHOLAR-GIPSY   99
    BETWIXT THE SYRTES AND SOFT SICILY • • •   262 SCHOLAR-GIPSY   245
    HUMID THE AIR LEAFLESS YET SOFT AS SPRING • • •   263 THYRSIS   17
    I SEE HER VEIL DRAW SOFT ACROSS THE DAY • • •   266 THYRSIS   133
    FIELDS WHERE SOFT SHEEP FROM CAGES PULL THE HAY • •   268 THYRSIS   198
    NEATH THE SOFT CANOPY OF ENGLISH AIR • • • •   268 THYRSIS V 194
    THE SOFT MEDITERRANEAN BREAKS • • • • •   275 SOUTHERN NIGHT   3
    AH SUCH A NIGHT SO SOFT SO LONE • • • • •   275 SOUTHERN NIGHT   13
    THE SOFT MEDITERRANEAN SIDE • • • • •   277 SOUTHERN NIGHT   67
    THROUGH ALPINE MEADOWS SOFT-SUFFUSED • • •   299 GRANDE CHARTR   1
    WHICH FRINGE THY SOFT BLUE SPEZZIAN BAY • • •   303 GRANDE CHARTR   142
    THAT FRINGE THY SOFT BLUE SPEZZIAN BAY • • •   303 GRANDE CHARTR V 142
    SOFT DARKNESS ON THE TURF DID LIE • • • •   323 OBERMANN MORE   329
    TO BE LEFT MUSING THESE SOFT NIGHTS ALONE • • •   409 EMPEDOCLES I 1   92
    WITH LONG PLUMES AND SOFT BROWN SEEDS • • •   434 EMPEDOCLES II   175
    SOFT LULLD BY THE RILLS • • • • • • •   442 EMPEDOCLES II   434
    ALL SHAPES THAT HAUNT REMEMBRANCE SOFT AND FAIR • •   474 CROMWELL   83
    WHO OF LATE ON THE SOFT NIGHTS OF MAY • • • •   482 THEKLAS ANSWER   6

SOFTEND
    MELLOWD AND SOFTEND AS WITH SUNSET-GLOW • • • •   212 GROWING OLD   14

SOFTENING
    NO SOFTENING RAY NO VISIONS FALSE AND WILD • • • •   475 CROMWELL   125

SOFTENINGS
    ARE THEY FROM HEAVEN THESE SOFTENINGS OF THE HEART   74 SOHRAB RUSTUM   437

SOFTLY
    SO SLENDER SOHRAB SEEMD SO SOFTLY REARD • • • •   70 SOHRAB RUSTUM   318
    AND CAST IT SOFTLY BUT THE MAN • • • • • • • •   91 SICK KING BOKH   118

SOFTLY   (CONTINUED)
    SLOW SLOW AND SOFTLY WHERE SHE STOOD • • • • • • 146 TRISTRAM 2   102
    AND NOW SHE WILL GO HOME AND SOFTLY LAY • • • • • 151 TRISTRAM 3   76
    LET THOSE ARCH EYES NOW SOFTLY SHINE • • • • • • 206 RIVER   5
    COMES SOFTLY THROUGH THE OLIVE-TREES • • • • • • 279 SOUTHERN NIGHT   119
    SOFTLY STAND BACK SEE TO THESE PALACE GATES • • 331 MEROPE   51
    THY HEAD DROOPD SOFTLY AND THE GOLDEN CURLS • • 373 MEROPE   1161
    SOFTLY STAND BACK SEE TOWRD THE PALACE GATES • • 331 MEROPE   V 51
    SOFTLY GLEAM THE FAR BLUE MOUNTAINS • • • • • • META CLOISTER   13
    OF A SPIRIT SOFTLY CLEAR • • • • • • • • • • META CLOISTER   22

SOHRAB
    SOHRAB ALONE HE SLEPT NOT ALL NIGHT LONG • • • • 61 SOHRAB RUSTUM   5
    AND SOHRAB CAME THERE AND WENT IN AND STOOD • • • 61 SOHRAB RUSTUM   24
    BUT SOHRAB CAME TO THE BEDSIDE AND SAID • • • • 62 SOHRAB RUSTUM   33
    O SOHRAB AN UNQUIET HEART IS THINE • • • • • • 63 SOHRAB RUSTUM   65
    O SOHRAB CARRY AN UNWOUNDED SON • • • • • • • 63 SOHRAB RUSTUM   77
    TO FIGHT OUR CHAMPION SOHRAB MAN TO MAN • • • • 65 SOHRAB RUSTUM   153
    OF PRIDE AND HOPE FOR SOHRAB WHOM THEY LOVED • • 65 SOHRAB RUSTUM   159
    LET SOHRAB ARM AND WE WILL FIND A MAN • • • • 66 SOHRAB RUSTUM   186
    SOHRAB MEN CALL HIM BUT HIS BIRTH IS HID • • • 67 SOHRAB RUSTUM   214
    WHEN SOHRAB DARES OUR BRAVEST FORTH AND SEEKS • 68 SOHRAB RUSTUM   244
    AND SOHRAB ARMD IN HAMANS TENT AND CAME • • • • 70 SOHRAB RUSTUM   292
    SOHRAB COME FORTH AND EYED HIM AS HE CAME • • • 70 SOHRAB RUSTUM   301
    SO SLENDER SOHRAB SEEMD SO SOFTLY REARD • • • • 70 SOHRAB RUSTUM   318
    O SOHRAB WHEREFORE WILT THOU RUSH ON DEATH • • 71 SOHRAB RUSTUM   329
    SO HE SPAKE MILDLY SOHRAB HEARD HIS VOICE • • • 71 SOHRAB RUSTUM   334
    HE SPOKE AND SOHRAB ANSWERD ON HIS FEET • • • • 72 SOHRAB RUSTUM   379
    DROPS LIKE A PLUMMET SOHRAB SAW IT COME • • • • 73 SOHRAB RUSTUM   402
    WHICH IT SENT FLYING WIDE THEN SOHRAB THREW • • 73 SOHRAB RUSTUM   405
    ONE STROKE BUT AGAIN SOHRAB SPRANG ASIDE • • • 73 SOHRAB RUSTUM   417
    AND NOW MIGHT SOHRAB HAVE UNSHEATHED HIS SWORD • 73 SOHRAB RUSTUM   422
    HE SPOKE AND SOHRAB KINDLED AT HIS TAUNTS • • • 75 SOHRAB RUSTUM   470
    RUSTUM AND SOHRAB ON EACH OTHER HAILD • • • • 75 SOHRAB RUSTUM   479
    WHICH SOHRAB HELD STIFF OUT THE STEEL-SPIKED SPEAR 75 SOHRAB RUSTUM   492
    THEN SOHRAB WITH HIS SWORD SMOTE RUSTUMS HELM • 76 SOHRAB RUSTUM   495
    BUT SOHRAB HEARD AND QUAILD NOT BUT RUSHD ON • 76 SOHRAB RUSTUM   509
    AND SHOUTED RUSTUM SOHRAB HEARD THAT SHOUT • • 76 SOHRAB RUSTUM   516
    AND SOHRAB WOUNDED ON THE BLOODY SAND • • • • 77 SOHRAB RUSTUM   526
    SOHRAB THOU THOUGHTTEST IN THY MIND TO KILL • • 77 SOHRAB RUSTUM   528
    AND WITH A FEARLESS MIEN SOHRAB REPLIED • • • • 77 SOHRAB RUSTUM   540
    AND WITH A FAILING VOICE SOHRAB REPLIED • • • 78 SOHRAB RUSTUM   579
    SOHRAB RETURNING FROM THE TARTAR CAMP • • • • 79 SOHRAB RUSTUM   594
    THAT SOHRAB WILL REJOICE HER SIGHT NO MORE • • 79 SOHRAB RUSTUM   599
    AND SO HE DEEMD THAT EITHER SOHRAB TOOK • • • 79 SOHRAB RUSTUM   612
    ON THE MOWN DYING GRASS SO SOHRAB LAY • • • • 80 SOHRAB RUSTUM   638
    O SOHRAB THOU INDEED ART SUCH A SON • • • • 80 SOHRAB RUSTUM   641
    YET HERE THOU ERREST SOHRAB OR ELSE MEN • • • 80 SOHRAB RUSTUM   643
    BUT SOHRAB ANSWERD HIM IN WRATH FOR NOW • • • 80 SOHRAB RUSTUM   649
    SOHRAB THAT WERE A PROOF WHICH COULD NOT LIE • 81 SOHRAB RUSTUM   667
    THEN WITH WEAK HASTY FINGERS SOHRAB LOOSED • • 81 SOHRAB RUSTUM   669
    AND SOHRAB BARED THAT IMAGE ON HIS ARM • • • • 81 SOHRAB RUSTUM   684
    BUT SOHRAB CRAWLD TO WHERE HE LAY AND CAST • • 81 SOHRAB RUSTUM   694
    BUT SOHRAB SAW HIS THOUGHT AND HELD HIS HANDS • 82 SOHRAB RUSTUM   706
    BUT SOHRAB LOOKD UPON THE HORSE AND SAID • • • 83 SOHRAB RUSTUM   741
    BUT WITH A GRAVE MILD VOICE SOHRAB REPLIED • • 84 SOHRAB RUSTUM   771
    SOHRAB THE MIGHTY RUSTUMS SON LIES THERE • • • 84 SOHRAB RUSTUM   792
    FEAR NOT AS THOU HAST SAID SOHRAB MY SON • • • 84 SOHRAB RUSTUM   796
    THEN AT THE POINT OF DEATH SOHRAB REPLIED • • • 85 SOHRAB RUSTUM   827
    HE SPOKE AND SOHRAB SMILED ON HIM AND TOOK • • 85 SOHRAB RUSTUM   838
    SO ON THE BLOODY SAND SOHRAB LAY DEAD • • • • 86 SOHRAB RUSTUM   857
    WHICH SOHRAB HELD ADVANCD THE STEEL-SPIKED SPEAR 75 SOHRAB RUSTUM V 492
    BUT SOHRAB HEARD AND QUAILD NOT BUT SPRANG ON • 76 SOHRAB RUSTUM V 509
    AND SOHRAB BARED THAT FIGURE ON HIS ARM • • • • 81 SOHRAB RUSTUM V 684
    AND WITH A GRAVE MILD VOICE SOHRAB REPLIED • • • 84 SOHRAB RUSTUM V 771

SOHRABS
    SO SAID HE AND DROPPD SOHRABS HAND AND LEFT • • 63 SOHRAB RUSTUM   94
    THE YOUNG MAY RISE AT SOHRABS VAUNTS NOT I • • 68 SOHRAB RUSTUM   227
    FOR WHAT CARE I THOUGH ALL SPEAK SOHRABS FAME • 68 SOHRAB RUSTUM   228
    AND REST MY AGE AND HEAR OF SOHRABS FAME • • • 68 SOHRAB RUSTUM   239
    HIS YOUTH SAW SOHRABS MOTHER IN HER BLOOM • • • 79 SOHRAB RUSTUM   624
    ON SOHRABS ARM THE SIGN OF RUSTUMS SEAL • • • 81 SOHRAB RUSTUM   678
    AND RUSTUM GAZED IN SOHRABS FACE AND SAID • • 85 SOHRAB RUSTUM   835
    WHAT IRKS IT ME THAT MEN SPEAK SOHRABS PRAISE • 68 SOHRAB RUSTUM V 228
    I AM NOT WRONGD WHEN MEN SPEAK SOHRABS PRAISE • 68 SOHRAB RUSTUM V 228
    FOR WHAT CARE I THAT SOHRABS FAME QUENCH THEIRS • 68 SOHRAB RUSTUM V 228
    AND RUSTUM GAZED ON SOHRABS FACE AND SAID • • 85 SOHRAB RUSTUM V 835

SOIL
    FURROWS THE RICH SOIL HERE AND THERE • • • • • 191 STRAYED REVEL   176
    AND THOUGH SO TASKD KEEP FREE FROM DUST AND SOIL • 244 SUMMER NIGHT   82
    AND HALF-BESTOWD HALF YIELDED UP THEIR SOIL • • 339 MEROPE   294
    OF RICH SOIL CHOSEN BY CRAFT • • • • • • • 399 MEROPE   1848
    THE COLD DULL SOIL OF HIS UNFRUITFUL YOUTH • • • 473 CROMWELL   54

SOILD
    OF THE SOILD GLORY AND THE TRAILING WING • • • 43 GIPSY CHILD   56
    THE BALEFUL SIGN OF FEVERS DUST HAD SOILD • • • 74 SOHRAB RUSTUM   453
    THE CRIMSON TORRENT RAN DIM NOW AND SOILD • • • 86 SOHRAB RUSTUM   843

SOILD   (CONTINUED)
        LIKE THE SOILD TISSUE OF WHITE VIOLETS   • • •   86 SOHRAB RUSTUM   844
        THE CRIMSON TORRENT POURD DIM NOW AND SOILD   • •   86 SOHRAB RUSTUM   V 843
        WITH THY SOILD HUNTING-COAT AND SANDALS TORN   372 MEROPE   1159
        UNARMD AND TRAVEL-SOILD JUST AS HE WAS   • • • •   401 MEROPE   1906
        AS I WAS LIFTING MY SOILD GARLAND OFF   • • • •   407 EMPEDOCLES I 1   40

SOJOURND
        WHEN FIRST HE SOJOURND WITH PEISIANAX   • • • •   408 EMPEDOCLES I 1   73

SOLACE
        SOME SOLACE IN EACH OTHERS LOOK AND SPEECH • • • •   104 BALDER DEAD 1   327
        THOU HAST THEN ALL THE SOLACE DEATH ALLOWS • • • •   126 BALDER DEAD 3   469
        SO BE IT YET WILL THAT MORE SOLACE BRING   • • • •   349 MEROPE   559

SOLD
        TIS NOT IN THE WORLDS MARKET BOUGHT AND SOLD   • •   268 THYRSIS   205

SOLDIER
        A POOR MEAN SOLDIER AND WITHOUT RENOWN   • • • •   85 SOHRAB RUSTUM   814
        GIRL STATESMAN MERCHANT SOLDIER BOLD • • • • •   226 EPILOG LAOCOON   159
        SOLDIER AND ANCHORITE   • • • • • • • •   311 OBERMANN   150
        THE SOLDIER KINDLED, AT HIS WORDS OF FIRE   • • • •   476 CROMWELL   153

SOLDIERS
        SOLDIERS LIKE CAESAR   • • • • • • • • •   220 BACCHANALIA 2   55
        FORTH TO THE WORLD THOSE SOLDIERS FARE   • • • •   305 GRANDE CHARTR   179

SOLE
        FIND THEIR SOLE SPEECH IN THAT VICTORIOUS BROW   • •   3 SHAKESPEARE   14
        FIND THEIR SOLE VOICE IN THAT VICTORIOUS BROW   • •   3 SHAKESPEARE   V 14
        O SEEMING SOLE TO AWAKE THY SUN-BATHED HEAD   • •   45 IN UTRUMQUE PAR   29
        SOLE LIKE SOME SINGLE TOWER WHICH A CHIEF   • • •   71 SOHRAB RUSTUM   337
        HIS HUDDLING YOUNG LEFT SOLE AT THAT HE CHECKS   • •   78 SOHRAB RUSTUM   563
        AND THE TWO GAZING HOSTS AND THAT SOLE PAIR   • •   86 SOHRAB RUSTUM   866
        THAT SAD SOLE HONOUR OF THE DEAD AND THEE   • • •   103 BALDER DEAD 1   298
        ARE THERE THE SOLE COMPANIONS TO BE FOUND   • • •   152 TRISTRAM 3   99
        SOLE OBJECT OF HER DYING EYES REMAIN • • • •   168 RACHEL 2   13
        SOLE IN THESE FIELDS YET WILL I NOT DESPAIR   • • 268 THYRSIS   192
        SOLE THEY SHALL STRAY IN THE ROCKS   • • • • •   291 RUGBY CHAPEL   185
        SOLE THEY SHALL STRAY ON THE ROCKS   • • • • •   291 RUGBY CHAPEL   V 185
        SOLE OFFERING THAT THOU HAST LOCKS FROM THY HEAD   • • 332 MEROPE   71
        AND ME HENCEFORTH SOLE RIVAL WITH HIMSELF   • • •   366 MEROPE   1003
        DEALT AT MY OWN SOLE RISK BEFORE THEIR EYES • • •   383 MEROPE   1354
        ARE THE SOLE CLAIMANTS LEFT WHAT CAUSE OF STRIFE • •   394 MEROPE   1693
        INDEED THY LIFELONG PASSION AND SOLE AIM   • • • •   404 MEROPE   1983

SOLEMN
        THE SOLEMN PEAKS BUT TO THE STARS ARE KNOWN   • •   45 IN UTRUMQUE PAR   18
        PIERCING THE SOLEMN CLOUD   • • • • • •   45 IN UTRUMQUE PAR   30
        THE SOLEMN WASTES OF HEATHY HILL   • • • • •   55 RESIGNATION   96
        THE SOLEMN HILLS AROUND US SPREAD   • • • • •   60 RESIGNATION   266
        AND NIGHT CAME DOWN OVER THE SOLEMN WASTE • • •   86 SOHRAB RUSTUM   865
        BUT HE MUST STRAIGHT ACCOST THEIR SOLEMN QUEEN   • •   100 BALDER DEAD 1   178
        SAVE ME ALONE AND HELA SOLEMN QUEEN   • • • •   104 BALDER DEAD 1   319
        AND THUS BESPAKE HIM FIRST THE SOLEMN QUEEN   • • 110 BALDER DEAD 2   179
        HE SPOKE AND GRAVE REPLIED THE SOLEMN QUEEN   • • 110 BALDER DEAD 2   201
        KNEELD AND DID HOMAGE TO THE SOLEMN QUEEN   • • •   112 BALDER DEAD 2   283
        OF GHOSTS AND COMMUNED WITH THEIR SOLEMN QUEEN   • •   114 BALDER DEAD 3   40
        AND SOLEMN SILENCE OF ITS CLOSE   • • • •   225 EPILOG LAOCOON   152
        BUT RUIND AND SOLEMN AND GREY   • • • • • •   228 YOUTH OF NATURE   20
        YET A SOLEMN PEACE OF ITS OWN   • • • • • •   254 FUTURE   77
        SOLEMN UNLIGHTED AUSTERE   • • • • • • •   286 RUGBY CHAPEL   10
        YE SOLEMN SEATS OF HOLY PAIN   • • • • • •   302 GRANDE CHARTR   92
        SOLEMN OER HUT AND WOOD   • • • • • • • •   323 OBERMANN MORE   330
        OUR HANDS IN SOLEMN UNION MAKING FRIENDS   • • •   335 MEROPE   165
        PERFORMS THIS NOON A SOLEMN SACRIFICE   • • •   391 MEROPE   1589
        HIS PAINFUL SOLEMN   • • • • • • • • •   399 MEROPE   1817
        BEFORE THE SOUL LOSE ALL HER SOLEMN JOYS   • • •   429 EMPEDOCLES II   33
        THOU SOLEMN GRAVE WHERE EVERY STEP WE TREAD   • • 464 ALARIC AT ROME   49
        PERCHANCE THAT SOLEMN SIGHT MIGHT QUENCH THE FIRE   469 ALARIC AT ROME   177
        WITH SOLEMN CADENCE ROUND HER CITADEL   • • • •   472 CROMWELL   20

SOLID
        MOULD NOT THE SOLID EARTH THOUGH NEVER WINDS   • •   8 RELIGIOUS ISOL   10
        MOULDS NOT THE SOLID EARTH THOUGH NEVER WINDS   • •   8 RELIGIOUS ISOL V 10

SOLITARY
        UNDER THE SOLITARY MOON HE FLOWD   • • • • • •   87 SOHRAB RUSTUM   879
        ROMANTIC SOLITARY STILL   • • • • • • • • •   279 SOUTHERN NIGHT   114
        DIDST FIND THE SOLITARY MAN   • • • • • •   322 OBERMANN MORE   279
        DIDST SEEK THE SOLITARY MAN   • • • • • •   322 OBERMANN MORE   V 279
        OF SOLITARY THOUGHT UNSHARED RESOLVE • • • •   403 MEROPE   1969
        OF THAT SOLITARY LAKE   • • • • • • • •   433 EMPEDOCLES II   135
        THAT SPOT THE SOLITARY SCENE   • • • • • •   480 HAYSWATER BOAT   24

SOLITUDE
        LIKE COMETS ON THE HEAVENLY SOLITUDE • • • • • •   6 GEO CRUIKSHANK   7
        IN THE BLANK ECHOING SOLITUDE IF EARTH   • • • •   45 IN UTRUMQUE PAR   24
        AS LITTLE AS DID SOLITUDE   • • • • • • • •   139 TRISTRAM 1   293

SOLITUDE   (CONTINUED)
    BACK TO THY SOLITUDE AGAIN   • • • • • • • 181 ISOLATION MARG   18
    WAVE US AWAY AND KEEP THY SOLITUDE   • • • • • 261 SCHOLAR-GIPSY   210
    AND ONE TO SOLITUDE   • • • • (• • • • • 309 OBERMANN   96
    COME TO MY MOUNTAIN-SOLITUDE   • • • • • • 322 OBERMANN MORE   275
    REMORSEFUL TOWRD MY HOSTILE SOLITUDE   • • • • 387 MEROPE   1475
    THE SOLITUDE OF HER WHOM THOU HAST WRONGD   • • • 395 MEROPE   1731
    SOME SOLITUDE MORE INACCESSIBLE   • • • • • 395 MEROPE   1748
    I AM WEARY OF THE SOLITUDE   • • • • • • 435 EMPEDOCLES II   199
    BUT THE SOLITUDE OPPRESSES THY VOTARY   • • • 435 EMPEDOCLES II   208
    TAKE THY BOUGH SET ME FREE FROM MY SOLITUDE   • 435 EMPEDOCLES II   218
    AND HE WILL FLY TO SOLITUDE AGAIN   • • • • 435 EMPEDOCLES II   227
    I WHO HAVE NOT LIKE THESE IN SOLITUDE   • • • 438 EMPEDOCLES II   318
    THAT IN THE SOLITUDE BEYOND THE STARS   • • • FRAGMENT 6   2

SOLITUDES
    UPON THESE BREATHLESS SOLITUDES   • • • • • 54 RESIGNATION   73
    THE SOLITUDES OF THE GREEN WOOD   • • • • • 139 TRISTRAM 1   290
    IN THE MOONLIT SOLITUDES MILD   • • • • • 288 RUGBY CHAPEL   70
    AND KEEPS ITS LIQUID SOLITUDES UNSCALED   • • 351 MEROPE   625
    BUT AT A DISTANCE IN THESE SOLITUDES   • • • • 409 EMPEDOCLES I 1   87

SOLUTION
    WISHD TRULY WISHD SOLUTION TO OUR BROIL   • • • • 360 MEROPE   886

SOMBRE
    AND THE SOMBRE DAY DRAGGD ON   • • • • • • • 30 NEW SIRENS   116
    ITS SOMBRE ASPECT OF MAJESTIC CARE   • • • • 403 MEROPE   1968
    PESTER HIM NOT IN THIS HIS SOMBRE MOOD   • • • • 411 EMPEDOCLES I 1   154

SOME
    OUT-TOPPING KNOWLEDGE SO SOME SOVRAN HILL   • • • 2 SHAKESPEARE   V 3
    A LIGHT THAT FROM SOME UPPER FOUNT DID BEAM   • • 9 MYCERINUS   21
    SOME BETTER ARCHETYPE WHOSE SEAT WAS HEAVEN   • • 9 MYCERINUS   22
    OR IS IT THAT SOME FORCE TOO WISE TOO STRONG   • • 9 MYCERINUS   37
    WHO WRESTLES WITH HIS DREAM AS SOME PALE SHAPE   • • 11 MYCERINUS   103
    OR IS IT THAT SOME POWER TOO WISE TOO STRONG   • • 9 MYCERINUS   V 37
    OR IS IT THAT SOME FORCE TOO STERN TOO STRONG   • • 9 MYCERINUS   V 37
    GUIDE ME SOME ONE TO THE MOUNTAIN   • • • • • 15 CHURCH BROU 1   75
    LET ME PAUSE LET ME STRIVE IN MYSELF MAKE SOME ORDER   19 MODERN SAPPHO   7
    LET ME PAUSE LET ME STRIVE IN MYSELF FIND SOME ORDER   19 MODERN SAPPHO   V 7
    SOME DAY NEXT YEAR I SHALL BE   • • • • • • 23 MEMORY-PICTURE   19
    AND FROM SOME SWARDED SHELF HIGH UP THERE CAME   • • 25 DREAM   11
    WHERE SOME MUSE WITH HALF-CURVED FROWN   • • • 27 NEW SIRENS   26
    SOME LARGE ANSWER YOU SHALL HEAR   • • • • • 29 NEW SIRENS   92
    IN SOME WINDLESS VALLEY FARTHER DOWN   • • • • 31 NEW SIRENS   146
    FROM SOME TRANSIENT EARTHLY SUN   • • • • • 31 NEW SIRENS   152
    POINTING TO SOME WORLD-WORN CREATURES   • • • 28 NEW SIRENS   V 61
    FROM SOME TRANSIENT HUMAN SUN   • • • • • • 31 NEW SIRENS   V 152
    WHEN I SHALL BE DIVORCED SOME TEN YEARS HENCE   ) • 37 YOUTHS AGIT   1
    IF SOME FAIR COAST HAVE LURED US TO MAKE STAY   • • 40 HUMAN LIFE   11
    OR SOME FRIEND HAILD US TO KEEP COMPANY   • • 40 HUMAN LIFE   12
    AS CHARTERD BY SOME UNKNOWN POWERS   • • (• • 41 HUMAN LIFE   26
    IF SOME FAIR COAST HAS LURED US TO MAKE STAY   • 40 HUMAN LIFE   V 11
    SOME EXILES MINDFUL HOW THE PAST WAS GLAD   • • • 42 GIPSY CHILD   25
    SOME ANGELS IN AN ALIEN PLANET BORN   • • • • 42 GIPSY CHILD   26
    OR DO I WAIT TO HEAR SOME GRAY-HAIRD KING   • • 43 GIPSY CHILD   33
    SOME REACHES OF THY STORM-VEXT STREAM OF LIFE   • • 43 GIPSY CHILD   60
    SOME DREAMERS WHO FAR OFF A SUMMERS DAY   • • 42 GIPSY CHILD   V 22
    SOME EXILES MINDFUL HOW HIS PAST WAS GLAD   • • • 42 GIPSY CHILD   V 25
    WHAT SERAPHS IN SOME ALIEN PLANET BORN   • • • 42 GIPSY CHILD   V 26
    SOME UNDIMMD HOURS   • • • • • • • • • 52 CONSOLATION   75
    SOME TWO HOURS MARCH WITH SERIOUS AIR   • • • 54 RESIGNATION   68
    AND OFTEN TO SOME KINDLY PLACE   • • • • • 55 RESIGNATION   112
    HE SEES IN SOME GREAT-HISTORIED LAND   • • • • 56 RESIGNATION   154
    FROM SOME HIGH STATION HE LOOKS DOWN   • • • • 57 RESIGNATION   164
    EACH WITH SOME ERRAND OF ITS OWN   • • • • • 57 RESIGNATION   168
    THE CUCKOO LOUD ON SOME HIGH LAWN   • • • • • 57 RESIGNATION   176
    IN SOME SENSE FAUSTA OUTLASTS DEATH   • • • • 59 RESIGNATION   230
    RATHER THYSELF FOR SOME AIM PRAY   • • • • • 59 RESIGNATION   239
    SHOULD ONE DAY GREET UPON SOME WELL-FOUGHT FIELD   • 62 SOHRAB RUSTUM   51
    OR IN SOME QUARREL WITH THE PERSIAN KING   • • 63 SOHRAB RUSTUM   85
    AS WHEN SOME GREY NOVEMBER MORN THE FILES   • • 64 SOHRAB RUSTUM   111
    OR SOME FRORE CASPIAN REED-BED SOUTHWARD BOUND   • 64 SOHRAB RUSTUM   115
    LIKE SOME OLD MISER RUSTUM HOARDS HIS FAME   • • 68 SOHRAB RUSTUM   247
    AS SOME RICH WOMAN ON A WINTERS MORN   • • • 70 SOHRAB RUSTUM   302
    LIKE SOME YOUNG CYPRESS TALL AND DARK AND STRAIGHT   70 SOHRAB RUSTUM   314
    SOLE LIKE SOME SINGLE TOWER WHICH A CHIEF   • • • 71 SOHRAB RUSTUM   337
    BUT HE WILL FIND SOME PRETEXT NOT TO FIGHT   • • • 71 SOHRAB RUSTUM   352
    AS ON SOME PARTRIDGE IN THE CORN A HAWK   • • • 73 SOHRAB RUSTUM   400
    OF SOME PAIND DESERT-LION WHO ALL DAY   • • • 76 SOHRAB RUSTUM   504
    AS WHEN SOME HUNTER IN THE SPRING HATH FOUND   • • 77 SOHRAB RUSTUM   556
    IN SOME FAR STONY GORGE OUT OF HIS KEN   • • • 78 SOHRAB RUSTUM   568
    LIKE SOME RICH HYACINTH WHICH BY THE SCYTHE   • • 80 SOHRAB RUSTUM   634
    PLIES SOME LIGHT FEMALE TASK NOR DREAMS OF US   • • 80 SOHRAB RUSTUM   647
    PRICKS WITH VERMILION SOME CLEAR PORCELAIN VASE   • 81 SOHRAB RUSTUM   673
    OF RUSTUMS SON OR OF SOME OTHER MANS   • • • • 81 SOHRAB RUSTUM   688
    FOR SOME ARE BORN TO DO GREAT DEEDS AND LIVE   • • 84 SOHRAB RUSTUM   773
    AS SOME ARE BORN TO BE OBSCURED AND DIE   • • • 84 SOHRAB RUSTUM   774
    AS SOME RICH LADY ON A WINTERS MORN   • • • • 70 SOHRAB RUSTUM   V 302

SOME   (CONTINUED)

THEN WILL HE FIND SOME PRETEXT NOT TO FIGHT	71	SOHRAB RUSTUM	V 352
UNDER SOME MULBERRY-TREES I FOUND	90	SICK KING BOKH	67
IT IS SOME MADMAN THE KING SAID	90	SICK KING BOKH	91
SOME SOLACE IN EACH OTHERS LOOK AND SPEECH	104	BALDER DEAD 1	327
THERE THROUGH SOME BATTLE-FIELD WHERE MEN FALL FAST	105	BALDER DEAD 2	24
OF SOME CLEAR RIVER ISSUING FROM A LAKE	109	BALDER DEAD 2	158
WE DO NOT AS SOME FEEBLER HATERS DO	111	BALDER DEAD 2	228
TO THE STEEP EDGE OF SOME GREAT VALLEY COMES	113	BALDER DEAD 2	296
SOME MORN AT MARKET IN A CROWDED TOWN	114	BALDER DEAD 3	9
ON SOME GREAT ROAD OR RESTING IN AN INN	116	BALDER DEAD 3	117
THESE TERMS AND I SUSPECT SOME HIDDEN FRAUD	120	BALDER DEAD 3	235
FAR OFF WHERE SOME UNWARND MIGHT FAIL TO WEEP	122	BALDER DEAD 3	322
LOOK AS IN SOME BOORS YARD A SWEET-BREATHD COW	123	BALDER DEAD 3	340
OF SOME SHIP THAT FIGHTS THE GALE	130	TRISTRAM 1	13
FELT ALREADY SOME DEEPER SMART	131	TRISTRAM 1	46
OER SOME FAIR UNWINTRY SEA	133	TRISTRAM 1	91
WHAT HAS SOME GLAMOUR MADE ME SLEEP	148	TRISTRAM 2	175
THROUGH SOME OLD SEA-SIDE KNIGHTLY HALL	148	TRISTRAM 2	178
HAS THEN SOME GLAMOUR MADE HIM SLEEP	148	TRISTRAM 2	V 175
THIS OR SOME TYRANNOUS SINGLE THOUGHT SOME FIT	153	TRISTRAM 3	127
THIS OR SOME TYRANNOUS SINGLE THOUGHT SOME FIT	153	TRISTRAM 3	127
AND DRUDGE UNDER SOME FOOLISH MASTERS KEN	169	WORLDLY PLACE	6
SOME NOBLER AMPLER STAGE OF LIFE TO WIN	169	WORLDLY PLACE	12
SOME LABOURING MEN WHOSE WORK LAY SOMEWHERE THERE	170	WEST LONDON	5
CHRIST SOME ONE SAYS WAS HUMAN AS WE ARE	170	BETTER PART	3
AH WARN SOME MORE AMBITIOUS HEART	174	MEETING	15
SAY HAS SOME WET BIRD-HAUNTED ENGLISH LAWN	175	PARTING	19
OR WAS IT FROM SOME SUN-FLECKD MOUNTAIN-BROOK	175	PARTING	21
OR SOME YOUTH BELOVED OF PAN	188	STRAYED REVEL	80
THROUGH THE ISLANDS SOME DIVINE BARD	189	STRAYED REVEL	118
ON SOME GREAT RIVERS MARGE	193	STRAYED REVEL	252
ONE OF SOME WORTHIER RACE THAN OURS	202	URANIA	18
ONE OF SOME BETTER RACE THAN WE	202	URANIA	V 18
ONE OF SOME WORTHIER RACE THAN WE	202	URANIA	V 18
BUT SOULS WHOM SOME BENIGNANT BREATH	203	EUPHROSYNE	13
SHAKE LOOSE SOME BAND OF SOFT BROWN HAIR	205	CALAIS SANDS	16
SHAKE LOOSE SOME LOCK OF SOFT BROWN HAIR	205	CALAIS SANDS	V 16
AND SOME FIND DEATH ERE THEY FIND LOVE	206	TOO LATE	2
SOME DAY I SHALL BE COLD I KNOW	207	ON THE RHINE	2
AH SOME POWER EXISTS THERE WHICH IS OURS	210	SELF-DECEPTION	27
SOME END IS THERE WE INDEED MAY GAIN	210	SELF-DECEPTION	28
SOME IN THE TUMULT ARE LOST	216	LORDS MESSENGER	13
SOME AS PRISONERS DRAW BREATH	216	LORDS MESSENGER	15
SOME UNCONQUERD ARE CROSSD	216	LORDS MESSENGER	16
SOME SOURCE OF FEELING HE MUST CHOOSE	223	EPILOG LAOCOON	83
SOME HANG UPON THE RAILS AND SOME	224	EPILOG LAOCOON	113
SOME HANG UPON THE RAILS AND SOME	224	EPILOG LAOCOON	113
SOME VACANT AND SOME MUSING WENT	224	EPILOG LAOCOON	119
SOME VACANT AND SOME MUSING WENT	224	EPILOG LAOCOON	119
AND SOME IN TALK AND MERRIMENT	224	EPILOG LAOCOON	120
SOME PULSE OF FEELING HE MUST CHOOSE	223	EPILOG LAOCOON	V 83
AH FROM THE OLD WORLD LET SOME ONE ANSWER GIVE	237	PROGRESS	21
THAT MAN MUST STILL TO SOME NEW WORSHIP PRESS	238	PROGRESS	V
ALL THE FEVER OF SOME DIFFERING SOUL	240	SELF-DEPENDENCE	24
I FELT IT IN SOME OTHER CLIME	242	MORALITY	33
I SAW IT IN SOME OTHER PLACE	242	MORALITY	34
THEIR LIVES TO SOME UNMEANING TASKWORK GIVE	243	SUMMER NIGHT	40
AWHILE HE HOLDS SOME FALSE WAY UNDEBARRD	244	SUMMER NIGHT	59
STILL BENT TO MAKE SOME PORT HE KNOWS NOT WHERE	244	SUMMER NIGHT	68
STILL STANDING FOR SOME FALSE IMPOSSIBLE SHORE	244	SUMMER NIGHT	69
SOME DOCTOR FULL OF PHRASE AND FAME	250	WISH	18
AT SOME LONE ALEHOUSE IN THE BERKSHIRE MOORS	256	SCHOLAR-GIPSY	58
AT SOME LONE HOMESTEAD IN THE CUMNER HILLS	258	SCHOLAR-GIPSY	101
THEN SOUGHT THY STRAW IN SOME SEQUESTERD GRANGE	259	SCHOLAR-GIPSY	130
LONG SINCE AND IN SOME QUIET CHURCHYARD LAID	259	SCHOLAR-GIPSY	137
SOME COUNTRY-NOOK WHERE OER THY UNKNOWN GRAVE	259	SCHOLAR-GIPSY	138
ON SOME MILD PASTORAL SLOPE	261	SCHOLAR-GIPSY	216
AS SOME GRAVE TYRIAN TRADER FROM THE SEA	262	SCHOLAR-GIPSY	232
ONLY METHINKS SOME LOSS OF HABITS POWER	263	THYRSIS	22
SOME LIFE OF MEN UNBLEST	264	THYRSIS	46
SO SOME TEMPESTUOUS MORN IN EARLY JUNE	264	THYRSIS	51
SOME GOOD SURVIVOR WITH HIS FLUTE WOULD GO	265	THYRSIS	83
SINCE ERST AT MORN SOME WANDERING SHADE	271	MEMORIAL VERSES	37
SOME SAGE TO WHOM THE WORLD WAS DEAD	277	SOUTHERN NIGHT	77
SOME GREY CRUSADING KNIGHT AUSTERE	278	SOUTHERN NIGHT	93
SOME YOUTHFUL TROUBADOUR WHOSE TONGUE	278	SOUTHERN NIGHT	97
SOME GIRL WHO HERE FROM CASTLE-BOWER	278	SOUTHERN NIGHT	101
AND LIVED SOME MOONS IN HAPPY TRANCE	279	SOUTHERN NIGHT	109
SOME GIRL WHO HERE FROM PALACE-BOWER	278	SOUTHERN NIGHT	V 101
SOME IN ART SOME IN GIFT	284	HAWORTH CHURCH	82
SOME IN ART SOME IN GIFT	284	HAWORTH CHURCH	82
BUT SOME DARK SHADOW CAME	285	HAWORTH CHURCH	110
SOME IN GIFT SOME IN ART	284	HAWORTH CHURCH	V 82
SOME IN GIFT SOME IN ART	284	HAWORTH CHURCH	V 82
YES IN SOME FAR-SHINING SPHERE	287	RUGBY CHAPEL	44
AND THERE ARE SOME WHOM A THIRST	288	RUGBY CHAPEL	73
AH YES SOME OF US STRIVE	288	RUGBY CHAPEL	79
BUT AS ON SOME FAR NORTHERN STRAND	301	GRANDE CHARTR	80
BEFORE SOME FALLEN RUNIC STONE	301	GRANDE CHARTR	83

SOME   (CONTINUED)
        BENEATH SOME OLD-WORLD ABBEY WALL   • • • • • •   304 GRANDE CHARTR   170
        ROUND SOME FAIR FOREST-LODGE AT MORN • • • • • •   305 GRANDE CHARTR   184
        ROUND SOME OLD FOREST-LODGE AT MORN   • • • • • •   305 GRANDE CHARTR   V 184
        SOME SECRETS MAY THE POET TELL   • • • • • • •   307 OBERMANN   41
        BY SOME HIGH CHALET-DOOR AND SEEN   • • • • • •   310 OBERMANN   115
        WE IN SOME UNKNOWN POWERS EMPLOY   • • • • • •   310 OBERMANN   133
        WHAT SOME TWO THOUSAND YEARS SURVEY   • • • •   315 OBERMANN MORE   83
        SOME NEW SUCH HOPE MUST DAWN AT LAST • • • •   321 OBERMANN MORE   243
        I TURNED BY SOME VAGUE IMPULSE STIRRD • • • •   324 OBERMANN MORE   335
        BUT WHEN FOR SOME GREAT PUBLIC CAUSE AN ARM   • • 336 MEROPE   204
        SOME FORM AH ME AH   • • • • • • • •   346 MEROPE   493
        I AUGUR THOU WILT HEAR SOME BOLD RESOLVE   • •   351 MEROPE   610
        MIGHT SOME ONE STRAIGHT INFORM HIM HE IS SOUGHT •   354 MEROPE   708
        ON SOME TALL SCAR FRINGED WITH DARK FEATHERY PINES 357 MEROPE   803
        SOME STRAGGLING HUNTERS TO MY AID TO ROUSE • • •   358 MEROPE   836
        TO THE GUEST-CHAMBER LEAD HIM SOME ONE GIVE   • • 359 MEROPE   869
        A PRESENCE SAD FOR SOME ONE THROUGH THOSE DOORS •   359 MEROPE   874
        HAVE TEMPERD ME EEN THUS AND IN SOME SOULS • • •   366 MEROPE   1024
        IN SOME DARK FIR-TREES SHADOW AMID ROCKS   • •   373 MEROPE   1167
        BUT IF SOME SIGNAL UNASSISTED STROKE • • • •   383 MEROPE   1353
        AND HARDLY YET SOME SAY HATH FOUND A GRAVE • • •   385 MEROPE   1425
        MY ROYAL SISTER BUT WITHOUT SOME CAUSE   • •   386 MEROPE   1449
        AGREES TO DEEM SOME DEEDS SO DARK IN GUILT • •   389 MEROPE   1524
        SOME GOD MEROPE NOW   • • • • • • •   393 MEROPE   1680
        SOME ILL DESIGN AGAINST HIM JEALOUSY • • • •   394 MEROPE   1700
        TO SOME SMALL HUMBLE AND UNNOTED STRAND   • •   395 MEROPE   1745
        SOME ROCK MORE LONELY THAN THAT LEMNIAN ISLE   •   395 MEROPE   1746
        SOME SOLITUDE MORE INACCESSIBLE   • • • • •   395 MEROPE   1748
        MUST FROM SOME MOUTH BE HEARD RELATE IT THOU   •   401 MEROPE   1892
        AGREES TO DEEM SOME DEEDS SO HORRIBLE • • •   389 MEROPE   V1524
        SOME OF US TO THE PORTICO TO BREATHE • • • •   407 EMPEDOCLES I 1   38
        THOU HAST SOME WRONG FROM THINE OWN CITIZENS   •   411 EMPEDOCLES I 1   142
        THERE IS SOME ROOT OF SUFFERING IN HIMSELF • • •   411 EMPEDOCLES I 1   151
        SOME SECRET AND UNFOLLOWD VEIN OF WOE • • • •   411 EMPEDOCLES I 1   152
        I SHOULD HAVE SAID THAT SOME ONE TOUCHD A HARP •   412 EMPEDOCLES I 2   11
        BUT WE AS SOME RUDE GUEST   • • • • • •   419 EMPEDOCLES I 2   217
        EITHER TO-MORROW OR SOME OTHER DAY   • • • •   428 EMPEDOCLES I 2   471
        THAT WE MUST CLAIM SOME BLISS   • • • • •   425 EMPEDOCLES I 2 V 402
        INTO SOME BONDAGE OF THE FLESH OR MIND   • •   440 EMPEDOCLES II   374
        SOME SLOUGH OF SENSE OR SOME FANTASTIC MAZE   •   440 EMPEDOCLES II   375
        SOME SLOUGH OF SENSE OR SOME FANTASTIC MAZE   •   440 EMPEDOCLES II   375
        IN SOME CHANCE BATTLE ON CITHAERON-SIDE   • • •   447 WESTMIN ABBEY   114
        OF CHILDHOOD ARTHUR DID SOME CHECK HAVE POWER •   447 WESTMIN ABBEY   118
        THEN SOME WHO THROUGH THIS GARDEN PASS   • • •   452 GEISTS GRAVE   73
        YET SOME THERE ARE THEIR VERY LIVES WOULD GIVE •   462 ALARIC AT ROME   17
        PERCHANCE SOME MUTE MEMORIAL AT THEIR HEAD • •   464 ALARIC AT ROME   58
        OH SOUND THERE NOT SOME STRAINS OF SADNESS THERE • 468 ALARIC AT ROME   165
        TO BEND IN RAPTURE AT SOME IDOL THRONE   • •   474 CROMWELL   99
        SOME LIFELESS SOULLESS PHANTOM OF THEIR OWN   •   474 CROMWELL   100
        SOME SHADOWY VISION OF A TRANQUIL LIFE   • •   474 CROMWELL   101
        ON SOME BARE HEADLAND STRAINING MOURNFULLY • • •   477 CROMWELL   190
        LIKE SOME FORGOTTEN STRAIN THAT HAUNTS US STILL •   477 CROMWELL   195
        AS THY GRIEF WHEN IN TEARS SOME BRAZEN-COATED ACHAIAN   HOMER TRANS   27
        AND SOME MAN MAY SAY AS HE LOOKS AND SEES THY   HOMER TRANS   32
             TEARS FALLING
        SO SOME MAN WILL SAY AND THEN THY GRIEF WILL REDOUBLE   HOMER TRANS   35
        IN SOME OTHER SORT THAN YOUR LAST WHEN THE   HOMER TRANS   41
             BATTLE IS ENDED
        IN FRONT OF SOME GREAT FANE WHEREOF WE KNOW   • •   LUCRETIUS 5   7

SOMEHOW
        MOVES ME SOMEHOW TO REMORSE   • • • • • • • •   454 POOR MATTHIAS   84

SOMETHING
        I WILL GO FORTH THOUGH SOMETHING WOULD I SAY   • •   10 MYCERINUS   68
        SOMETHING YET WHAT I KNOW NOT FOR THE GODS • • •   10 MYCERINUS   69
        I WILL GO FORTH BUT SOMETHING WOULD I SAY • • •   10 MYCERINUS   V 68
        THE SOMETHING THAT INFECTS THE WORLD • • • •   60 RESIGNATION   278
        THAT NAME AND SOMETHING I CONFESS IN THEE • • •   77 SOHRAB RUSTUM   548
        SOMETHING TOO MUCH OF WAR AND BROILS WHICH MAKE   128 BALDER DEAD 3   505
        THERE GLEAMD SOMETHING WHICH RECALLD • • • •   136 TRISTRAM 1   201
        THERE GLEAMD SOMETHING THAT RECALLD   • • • •   136 TRISTRAM 1   V 201
        SOMETHING ALTERD IN THY COURTLY TONE • • • •   143 TRISTRAM 2   34
        I AM HAPPY YET I FEEL THERES SOMETHING   • •   145 TRISTRAM 2   73
        FOR SOMETHING IN ITS DEPTHS DOTH GLOW • • • •   178 FAREWELL   19
        THE LETTERS HAVE COMBINED SOMETHING WAS MADE   •   239 REVOLUTIONS   8
        BUT THERES A SOMETHING IN THIS BREAST • • • •   245 BURIED LIFE   6
        FRUITLESS BUT SOMETHING TO SNATCH   • • • •   288 RUGBY CHAPEL   81
        BUT SOMETHING PROMPTS ME NOT THUS   • • • •   298 HEINES GRAVE   199
        HALT THROUGH THE CLOUD-DRIFT SOMETHING SHINES •   299 GRANDE CHARTR   16
        SOMETHING TOO STUDIOUSLY FORGIVE ME SHOWN • • •   334 MEROPE   142
        NO SOMETHING MUST BE DARED AND GREAT AS ERST   •   367 MEROPE   1054
        LOOKD ON TO SOMETHING NEW   • • • • • •   425 EMPEDOCLES I 2   378
        FOR SOMETHING HAS IMPAIRD THY SPIRITS STRENGTH •   429 EMPEDOCLES II   21
        SOMETHING HAUNTS MY CONSCIENCE BRINGS • • • •   455 POOR MATTHIAS   85
        PROUD OF PORT THOUGH SOMETHING SQUAT • • • •   457 POOR MATTHIAS   189

SOMETIMES
        IT MAY BE THAT SOMETIMES HIS WONDERING SOUL   • •   11 MYCERINUS   100
        SOMETIMES FROM THE GROVES CENTRE ECHOES CAME   • •   12 MYCERINUS   124
        SOMETIMES A WILD-HAIRD MAENAD   • • • • • • •   194 STRAYED REVEL   275

SOMETIMES   (CONTINUED)

SOMETIMES A FAUN WITH TORCHES	194	STRAYED REVEL	276
AND SOMETIMES FOR A MOMENT	194	STRAYED REVEL	277
AND SOMETIMES BY STILL HARDER FATE	207	TOO LATE	5
SOMETIMES A MOMENTARY GLEAM	226	EPILOG LAOCOON	177
SOMETIMES A SECONDS SPACE THEIR EAR	226	EPILOG LAOCOON	179
SOMETIMES A CHILD WILL CROSS THE GLADE	248	KENSINGTON GARD	9
SOMETIMES A THRUSH FLIT OVERHEAD	248	KENSINGTON GARD	11
THINK SOMETIMES AS I HEAR THEM RAVE	249	KENSINGTON GARD	V 26
AND ONLY THE WHITE SHEEP ARE SOMETIMES SEEN	255	SCHOLAR-GIPSY	8
BUT IT IS SOMETIMES TRODDEN OH BELIEVE IT	341	MEROPE	370
WELL SOMETIMES MAY THE GOOD DESIRE	353	MEROPE	665
MOTHER SOMETIMES THE JUSTICE OF THE GODS	378	MEROPE	1247
CONDEMND BY PRUDENCE HAVE SOMETIMES GONE WELL	383	MEROPE	1385
SOMETIMES WHEN HE WAS GONE I WISHD HIM BACK	387	MEROPE	1457
ARE NEVER FREE FROM DOUBT THOUGH SOMETIMES DUE	388	MEROPE	1522
AND ASK IF SOMETIMES	398	MEROPE	1798
SOMETIMES TO ETNAS TOP AND TO THE CONE	409	EMPEDOCLES I 1	95
SOMETIMES AND WANDERS FAR AMONG THE GLENS	412	EMPEDOCLES I 2	17
FAIN WOULD DO ALL THINGS WELL BUT SOMETIMES FAILS IN STRENGTH	422	EMPEDOCLES I 2	296

SOMEWHAT

DID SHADOW SOMEWHAT OF THE LIFE OF GODS	9	MYCERINUS	24
SOMEWHAT WHICH REMEMBRANCE WOKE	454	POOR MATTHIAS	54
SOMEWHAT MORE OR SOMEWHAT LESS	457	POOR MATTHIAS	159
SOMEWHAT MORE OR SOMEWHAT LESS	457	POOR MATTHIAS	159
AND MINGLE WITH THY RUINS SOMEWHAT OF OUR OWN	470	ALARIC AT ROME	204
OR SOMEWHAT BUT THAT MOST UNLOVEABLE		FRAGMENT 5	9

SOMEWHERE

SOMEWHERE I KNOW NOT WHERE BUT FAR FROM HERE	78	SOHRAB RUSTUM	583
SOME LABOURING MEN WHOSE WORK LAY SOMEWHERE THERE	170	WEST LONDON	5
A BOLT IS SHOT BACK SOMEWHERE IN OUR BREAST	247	BURIED LIFE	84
SOMEWHERE SURELY AFAR	287	RUGBY CHAPEL	40
SOMEWHERE FOR VENGEANCE A CHAMPION A LIGHT	346	MEROPE	513
SOMEWHERE IN SAFETY A NURSLING A LIGHT	346	MEROPE	V 513

SON

TAUGHT ARRIAN WHEN VESPASIANS BRUTAL SON	2	TO A FRIEND	7
THY COUNSEL AND TO HEED THEE AS THY SON	62	SOHRAB RUSTUM	39
HIS NOT UNWORTHY NOT INGLORIOUS SON	62	SOHRAB RUSTUM	52
THAT WERE FAR BEST MY SON TO STAY WITH US	63	SOHRAB RUSTUM	71
O SOHRAB CARRY AN UNWOUNDED SON	63	SOHRAB RUSTUM	77
FROM RAVENING AND WHO GOVERN RUSTUMS SON	63	SOHRAB RUSTUM	92
FOR WOULD THAT I MYSELF HAD SUCH A SON	68	SOHRAB RUSTUM	229
A SON SO FAMED SO BRAVE TO SEND TO WAR	68	SOHRAB RUSTUM	231
TO IRAN AND BE AS MY SON TO ME	71	SOHRAB RUSTUM	331
OVER HIS DYING SON AND KNEW HIM NOT	78	SOHRAB RUSTUM	575
THE MIGHTY RUSTUM NEVER HAD A SON	78	SOHRAB RUSTUM	578
AH YES HE HAD AND THAT LOST SON AM I	78	SOHRAB RUSTUM	580
FIERCE MAN BETHINK THEE FOR AN ONLY SON	78	SOHRAB RUSTUM	586
NOR DID HE YET BELIEVE IT WAS HIS SON	79	SOHRAB RUSTUM	605
BY A FALSE BOAST THE STYLE OF RUSTUMS SON	79	SOHRAB RUSTUM	613
OF AGE AND LOOKS TO BE HIS OWN DEAR SON	80	SOHRAB RUSTUM	632
O SOHRAB THOU INDEED ART SUCH A SON	80	SOHRAB RUSTUM	641
HAVE TOLD THEE FALSE THOU ART NOT RUSTUMS SON	80	SOHRAB RUSTUM	644
FOR RUSTUM HAD NO SON ONE CHILD HE HAD	80	SOHRAB RUSTUM	645
IF THOU SHOW THIS THEN ART THOU RUSTUMS SON	81	SOHRAB RUSTUM	668
OF RUSTUMS SON OR OF SOME OTHER MANS	81	SOHRAB RUSTUM	688
AND WASH THEM WITH THY TEARS AND SAY MY SON	82	SOHRAB RUSTUM	720
SOHRAB THE MIGHTY RUSTUMS SON LIES THERE	84	SOHRAB RUSTUM	792
FEAR NOT AS THOU HAST SAID SOHRAB MY SON	84	SOHRAB RUSTUM	796
SO THOU MIGHTEST LIVE TOO MY SON MY SON	85	SOHRAB RUSTUM	815
SO THOU MIGHTEST LIVE TOO MY SON MY SON	85	SOHRAB RUSTUM	815
AND SAY O SON I WEEP THEE NOT TOO SORE	85	SOHRAB RUSTUM	822
SOON BE THAT DAY MY SON AND DEEP THAT SEA	85	SOHRAB RUSTUM	836
DOWN OER HIS FACE AND SATE BY HIS DEAD SON	86	SOHRAB RUSTUM	859
SO IN THE SAND LAY RUSTUM BY HIS SON	86	SOHRAB RUSTUM	864
AND RUSTUM AND HIS SON WERE LEFT ALONE	86	SOHRAB RUSTUM	874
A SON SO PRAISD SO BRAVE TO SEND TO WAR	68	SOHRAB RUSTUM	V 231
NAY WERE HE THINE OWN MOTHERS SON	92	SICK KING BOKH	137
I MOST MIGHT WEEP HIS FATHER SUCH A SON	96	BALDER DEAD 1	21
HODER ILL-FATED CHILD OF BALE MY SON	98	BALDER DEAD 1	112
THEREFORE THYSELF THOU SHALT NOT GO MY SON	100	BALDER DEAD 1	188
O DAMSEL HERMOD AM I CALLD THE SON	108	BALDER DEAD 2	112
HERMOD FOR HE THOU ART THOU SON OF HEAVEN	110	BALDER DEAD 2	202
FAREWELL O BALDER BRIGHT AND LOVED MY SON	115	BALDER DEAD 3	67
FORSET THY SON TO BE BELOVED LIKE THEE	126	BALDER DEAD 3	451
SON SHE SAID THY NAME SHALL BE OF SORROW	145	TRISTRAM 2	85
PRINCE ALEXANDER PHILIPS PEERLESS SON	153	TRISTRAM 3	147
THAT SON OF ITALY WHO TRIED TO BLOW	166	AUSTERITY POET	1
THE LITTLE FAIR-HAIRD SON WITH VACANT GAZE	167	PICT NEWSTEAD	10
LAERTES SON	189	STRAYED REVEL	113
ALCMENAS DREADFUL SON	192	STRAYED REVEL	231
AND FAIN WOULD ZEUS HAVE SAVED HIS TIRED SON	198	FRAG ANTIGONE	90
WORDSWORTHS SON-IN-LAW FRIEND	280	HAWORTH CHURCH	6
THAT WORLD-FAMED SON OF FIRE SHE WHO SANK	285	HAWORTH CHURCH	97
SON OF MANKIND TO THE EARTH	293	HEINES GRAVE	30
NEW-COMING SON OF MANKIND	298	HEINES GRAVE	220
THE CELLS THE SUFFERING SON OF MAN	300	GRANDE CHARTR	45

SON (CONTINUED)
YES AS THE SON OF THETIS SAID • • • • • • • 309 OBERMANN 89
SON OF CRESPHONTES WE HAVE REACHD THE GOAL • • • • 330 MEROPE 1
THAT THOU IN SECRET NURTUREST UP THY SON • • • • 334 MEROPE 144
CLAIMS EVER HOSTILE ELSE AND SET THY SON • • • • 335 MEROPE 168
AND TO MY SON REVERSION TO THY THRONE • • • • 340 MEROPE 334
ONE SON AT LEAST I SPARED FOR STILL HE LIVES • • • 340 MEROPE 348
SEVEN-CUBIT-STATURED SON • • • • • • • 344 MEROPE 441
THRICE SON FOLLOWD SIRE • • • • • • • 345 MEROPE 467
AN AVENGER I ASK NOT SEND ME MY SON • • • 348 MEROPE 544
BRING BACK OUR SON IF MAY BE WITHOUT BLOOD • • • 350 MEROPE 587
THIS FOR OUR SON AND FOR MYSELF I PRAY • • • 350 MEROPE 591
THAT MY SON STILL SURVIVES IN HEALTH IN BLOOM • • 351 MEROPE 612
THE SON OF AN ARCADIAN NOBLE I • • • • • • 355 MEROPE 723
O HONOURD QUEEN THY SON MY CHARGE IS GONE • • • 362 MEROPE 944
A YOUTH ARRIVED BUT NOW THE SON HE SAID • • • 363 MEROPE 955
OF HEIRSHIP TO HIS KINGDOM FOR MY SON • • • 366 MEROPE 999
OR HARM AND NURSE MY LONGING FOR MY SON • • • 366 MEROPE 1022
AND EVEN NOW MY SON AH ME MY SON • • • • 366 MEROPE 1026
AND EVEN NOW MY SON AH ME MY SON • • • • 366 MEROPE 1026
AGAMEMNONS SON IN MYCENAE • • • • • • 368 MEROPE 1083
A MORE JUST STROKE THAN THAT THOU GAVST MY SON • • 373 MEROPE 1191
NO BY THE GODS THOU SLAYST STAND OFF THY SON • • 375 MEROPE 1201
THY SON IS HERE ONE SAID SO SURE BUT NOW • • 376 MEROPE 1216
O MY SON • • • • • • • • • • 377 MEROPE 1227
BE GUIDED O MY SON SPURN COUNSEL NOT • • • • 382 MEROPE 1328
HIS SON FROM VENGEANCE ON HIS MURDERER • • • 385 MEROPE 1415
RISK FROM MY NEW-RESTORED MY ONLY SON • • • 387 MEROPE 1456
BESIDES FOR FROM MY BROTHER AND MY SON • • • 387 MEROPE 1473
TREACHEROUSLY PLOTTED TWIXT MY SON AND ME • • • 387 MEROPE 1481
TREATY AND TO THIS KINGDOM FOR MY SON • • • 387 MEROPE 1483
AND FROM HIS NATURAL RIGHTS MY SON DEBAR • • • 388 MEROPE 1495
WHERE SIRE TO SON TRANSMITS THE UNQUESTIOND CROWN • 388 MEROPE 1517
LEGITIMATELY SIRE TO SON WITH US • • • • 389 MEROPE 1539
TO STRIKE IT THEN DISSUADE THY SON NO MORE • • • 390 MEROPE 1574
ALAS AGAINST MY BROTHER SON AND FRIENDS • • • 390 MEROPE 1579
SON WITH A DOUBTING HEART THY MOTHER YIELDS • • 390 MEROPE 1582
O SON AND MOTHER • • • • • • • 391 MEROPE 1596
HER SON HEART-STRICKEN EYED HER • • • • 393 MEROPE 1673
SO LIKE A STAR DAWNS THY SON • • • • • 393 MEROPE 1682
MESSENIA SPEAKS THE PRINCE THY SON IS DEAD • • 393 MEROPE 1686
LAY IN THY SON IS BURIED IN HIS GRAVE • • • 394 MEROPE 1694
SON LOVED OF ZEUS HIS FATHER FOR HE SINND • • 398 MEROPE 1814
IS MY SON SAFE THAT QUESTION BOUNDS MY CARE • • 401 MEROPE 1889
BEFORE HIM AT HIS SIDE THE PRINCE THY SON • • • 401 MEROPE 1905
OF AEPYTUS THY MURDERD MASTERS SON • • • • 402 MEROPE 1926
THE SON TO PERISH AS YE LEFT THE SIRE • • • 402 MEROPE 1935
THE DORIANS LYING DEAD THY SON HAILD KING • • 402 MEROPE 1942
THE ANXIOUS MOTHER OF AN EXILED SON • • • 403 MEROPE 1956
THINE ENEMY IS SLAIN THY SON IS KING • • • 403 MEROPE 1957
O AEPYTUS MY SON BEHOLD BEHOLD • • • • 403 MEROPE 1963
BUT THOU MY SON STUDY TO MAKE PREVAIL • • • 404 MEROPE 1995
AS THE CHIEFS RULE MY SON THE PEOPLE ARE • • • 404 MEROPE 2002
TAKE THESE MY SON OVER THINE ENEMYS CORPSE • • 404 MEROPE 2010
SON OF CRESPHONTES PAST WHAT PERILS • • • 405 MEROPE 2021
WHAT THEY WILL BUT TO ME GIVE MY SON • • • • 348 MEROPE V
SON LOVED OF ZEUS HIS FATHER FOR HE ERRD • • • • 398 MEROPE V1814
ASK WHAT MOST HELPS WHEN KNOWN THOU SON OF ANCHITUS • 416 EMPEDOCLES I 2 111
THAT SELF-HELPING SON OF EARTH • • • • • • 432 EMPEDOCLES II 103
THE SELF-HELPING SON OF EARTH • • • • • • 432 EMPEDOCLES II V 103
AND WITH PITY THE SON OF SATURN SAW THEM BEWAILING HOMER TRANS 7
BUT THAT PRINCE AMONG GODS THE SON OF THE LOVELY-HAIRD HOMER TRANS 52
LETO
ISTER TETHYS AND OCEANS SIXTH-BORN SON • • • • FRAGMENT 4 2

SONCHAUDS
PAST SONCHAUDS PINY FLANKS I GAZE • • • • • • 324 OBERMANN MORE 337
AND SONCHAUDS PINY FLANKS I GAZE • • • • • • 324 OBERMANN MORE V 337

SONG
SCENT AND SONG AND LIGHT AND FLOWERS • • • • • 32 NEW SIRENS 171
WHO IN THEIR LIVES WERE FAMOUS FOR THEIR SONG • • 103 BALDER DEAD 1 272
AND SINGS HIS PLAINTIVE SONG • • • • • • 159 NECKAN 4
AND SINGS THIS PLAINTIVE SONG • • • • • • 161 NECKAN 68
ERE DANTE CAME THE TRUMP OF SACRED SONG • • • 166 AUSTERITY POET 2
THE GODS EXACT FOR SONG • • • • • • • 193 STRAYED REVEL 233
AND THESE BLANCHD SONG-STIRRD BOUGHS • • • • 200 PHILOMELA V
FORTH WITH THY JOYOUS SONG • • • • • 219 BACCHANALIA 1 42
HATH RISEN GOETHES WORDSWORTHS SONG • • • • 222 EPILOG LAOCOON 29
THAT TRANSIENT GLIMPSE IN SONG THEY SAY • • • 226 EPILOG LAOCOON 181
THAT TRANSIENT SOUND IN SONG THEY TELL • • • 226 EPILOG LAOCOON 183
IN HIS GLADDEST AIRIEST SONG • • • • 231 YOUTH OF NATURE 96
BIRDS HERE MAKE SONG EACH BIRD HAS HIS • • • 248 KENSINGTON GARD 5
FOR THEE THE LITYERSES-SONG AGAIN • • • • 268 THYRSIS 184
HEARD THE CLEAR SONG OF ORPHEUS COME • • • • 271 MEMORIAL VERSES 38
BREATHINGS OF SONG WITH A PEN • • • • • • 281 HAWORTH CHURCH 24
WHOSE TOO BOLD DYING SONG • • • • • • 285 HAWORTH CHURCH 99
SONG OF THE POET DIVINE • • • • • • • 295 HEINES GRAVE 104
GOD GAVE THE POET HIS SONG • • • • • • 296 HEINES GRAVE 120
THEIR TINKLING BELLS MIXD WITH THE SONG OF BIRDS • • 407 EMPEDOCLES I 1 28
MEED FOR DAILY SONG OF YORE • • • • • • • 453 POOR MATTHIAS 19

SONG   (CONTINUED)

WHICH COMPELLD FOR GEIST A SONG	• • • • • • •	454 POOR MATTHIAS	60
WITNESS THEIR UNWORLDLY SONG	• • • • • • •	456 POOR MATTHIAS	136
DID THE WAVES CHAUNT THEIR SONG OF LIBERTY	• • • •	472 CROMWELL	16
IF NOT THY FIERCE AND TURBID SONG	• • • • • •	482 COURAGE	18

SONGS

IN THE BANQUET AND LEARND HIS SONGS	• • • • • • •	189 STRAYED REVEL	123
SONGS TO TRILL IN SURREY AIR	• • • • • • •	458 POOR MATTHIAS	197

SONGSTER

SONGSTER THOU OF MANY A YEAR	• • • • • • • •	452 POOR MATTHIAS	15

SONOROUS

SONOROUS WITNESS TO HIS EMPIRE GAVE	• • • • • •	476 CROMWELL	158

SONS

THE FEEBLE SONS OF PLEASURE SET THEIR HAND	• • •	5 DUKE WELLINGTON	7
HIS ARMS ROUND HIS SONS NECK AND WEPT ALOUD	• •	82 SOHRAB RUSTUM	728
BUT HEAR YE THIS YE SONS OF MEN	• • • •	93 SICK KING BOKH	185
DRAWN IN HIS CAR BESIDE ME AND MY SONS	• • •	120 BALDER DEAD 3	240
HE SPAKE AND HIS FIERCE SONS APPLAUDED LOUD	• •	120 BALDER DEAD 3	245
THOU AND THY BRETHREN FIERCE THE SONS OF BOR	•	121 BALDER DEAD 3	258
BUT GODS ARE LIKE THE SONS OF MEN IN THIS	• •	125 BALDER DEAD 3	426
AND ODIN AND HIS SONS THE SEED OF HEAVEN	• • •	127 BALDER DEAD 3	488
TO ACHIEVE HIS SONS DELIVERANCE O MY CHILD	• • •	198 FRAG ANTIGONE	103
WAS TURND UPON THE SONS OF MEN	• • • • •	202 URANIA	10
COLDLY SHE MOCKS THE SONS OF MEN	• • • •	202 URANIA	30
OF FORTUNES FAVOUR SONS NOT ME	• • • •	249 WISH	4
HER VIGOROUS PRIMITIVE SONS	• • • • •	252 FUTURE	33
SERVANTS OF GOD OR SONS	• • • • • •	291 RUGBY CHAPEL	162
HEAVY AND SAD FOR HER SONS	• • • • •	294 HEINES GRAVE	73
OF HER GREATEST GOLDEN-MOUTHD SONS	• • •	294 HEINES GRAVE	79
SO WE ARRAIGN HER HER SONS	• • • • •	295 HEINES GRAVE	86
FEARFUL AND SAD FOR HER SONS	• • • • •	294 HEINES GRAVE	V 73
TROUBLOUS AND SAD FOR HER SONS	• • • •	294 HEINES GRAVE	V 73
SAY HAVE THEIR SONS ACHIEVED MORE JOYS	• •	303 GRANDE CHARTR	129
SONS OF THE WORLD OH SPEED THOSE YEARS	• • •	304 GRANDE CHARTR	161
SAY HAVE THEIR SONS OBTAIND MORE JOYS	• • •	303 GRANDE CHARTR	V 129
SONS OF THE WORLD OH HASTE THOSE YEARS	• • •	304 GRANDE CHARTR	V 161
AND GOETHES COURSE FEW SONS OF MEN	• • • •	308 OBERMANN	55
A HOUSE ONCE GREAT NOW DWINDLING IN ITS SONS	•	337 MEROPE	237
TWO UNOFFENDING BABES HIS INNOCENT SONS	• • •	339 MEROPE	319
SUCH CHANCE AS KILLD THE FATHER KILLD THE SONS		340 MEROPE	347
FELL THE ELDEST OF THE SONS OF HERACLES	• • •	344 MEROPE	445
YOUR SONS LEAP UPON THE FOE OF YOUR KIN	• •	344 MEROPE	462
ON THE FAIR CURLD HEADS OF MY SONS	• • •	346 MEROPE	504
IN THEIR ALLEGIANCE ME IN MY SONS DEATH-HOUR	•	366 MEROPE	1004
OF MY TWO ELDER SONS SLAIN LONG AGO	• • • •	367 MEROPE	1038
MOTHERS LAMENTING THEIR SONS	• • • • •	369 MEROPE	1096
FATHERS SONS GRANDSONS ARE ALL	• • • •	379 MEROPE	1254
PERISHD IN ARGOS BY HIS JEALOUS SONS	• • •	389 MEROPE	1557
YES BUT HIS SONS SEED WISER-COUNSELLD	• • •	344 MEROPE	V 449
SEES ALL HER SONS AT PLAY	• • • • • •	421 EMPEDOCLES I 2	258
THE RADIANT REJOICING INTELLIGENT SONS OF HEAVEN	• •	437 EMPEDOCLES II	287
WHOSE SONS WERE CONQUERORS ONCE AND NOW WERE SLAVES		469 ALARIC AT ROME	184

SOON

SOON THE PLANKD COTTAGE BY THE SUN-WARMD PINES	• •	25 DREAM	35
SOON THE PLANKD COTTAGE MID THE SUN-WARMD PINES	• •	25 DREAM	V 35
I AM DUMB ALAS TOO SOON ALL	• • • • •	29 NEW SIRENS	89
SOON BE THAT DAY MY SON AND DEEP THAT SEA	• • •	85 SOHRAB RUSTUM	836
CREPT FROM THE OXUS SOON A HUM AROSE	• • • •	86 SOHRAB RUSTUM	868
WHEN I AM DEAD WILL SOON GROW STILL	• • • •	94 SICK KING BOKH	218
TOO SOON FOR FAME WITH WHITE UNGRAVEN SHIELDS	•	109 BALDER DEAD 2	165
AND SOON HAD ALL THAT DAY BEEN SPENT IN WAIL	•	118 BALDER DEAD 3	155
SOON WITH A ROARING ROSE THE MIGHTY FIRE	• • •	118 BALDER DEAD 3	186
DEPARTED OER THE CLOUDY PLAIN AND SOON	• • •	129 BALDER DEAD 3	552
FAIR LOVE SHE SAYS CANST THOU FORGET SO SOON	•	139 TRISTRAM 1	285
FORGOT MY GOOD AS SOON AS DONE	• • • •	158 SAINT BRANDAN	60
FORGOT MY DEED AS SOON AS DONE	• • • •	158 SAINT BRANDAN	V 60
DAYS FLEW AH SOON I COULD DISCERN	• • • •	178 FAREWELL	13
WHAT FAR TOO SOON ALAS I LEARND	• • • •	180 ISOLATION MARG	8
SHOULD BE AS SOON AS KINDLED COOLD	• • • •	182 TO MARG CONT	20
OUR SOON-CHOKED SOULS TO FILL	• • • • •	183 ABSENCE	10
SO SOON I SEE THE NIGHT-DEWS	• • • • •	186 STRAYED REVEL	15
SOON SOON THY CHEER WOULD DIE	• • • • •	261 SCHOLAR-GIPSY	226
SOON SOON THY CHEER WOULD DIE	• • • • •	261 SCHOLAR-GIPSY	226
SOON WILL THE HIGH MIDSUMMER POMPS COME ON	• •	264 THYRSIS	62
SOON WILL THE MUSK CARNATIONS BREAK AND SWELL	•	264 THYRSIS	63
SOON SHALL WE HAVE GOLD-DUSTED SNAPDRAGON	• • •	264 THYRSIS	64
LOST IT TOO SOON AND LEARNT A STORMY NOTE	• • •	269 THYRSIS	223
AND SOON THY FOOT RESUMED ITS WANDERING WAY	• •	269 THYRSIS	229
DYING TOO SOON YET GREEN	• • • • • •	283 HAWORTH CHURCH	71
TEMPER OF GENIUS SO SOON	• • • • • •	293 HEINES GRAVE	26
SOON SOON SHALL ZEUS BRING HIM HOME	• • • •	347 MEROPE	514
SOON SOON SHALL ZEUS BRING HIM HOME	• • • •	347 MEROPE	514
SOON SHALL HE DAWN ON THIS LAND	• • • • •	347 MEROPE	515
SOON HAVING ONCE BEHELD HIM TO DESCEND	• • • •	350 MEROPE	592
WHY WILT THOU FLY TO LOSE AS SOON AS FOUND	• •	381 MEROPE	1290

SOON   (CONTINUED)

```
      NOW DO WE SOON PERCEIVE HOW FAST OUR YOUTH IS SPENT      424 EMPEDOCLES I 2      361
      NOR DO WE SOON PERCEIVE HOW FAST OUR YOUTH IS SPENT      424 EMPEDOCLES I 2    V 361
      WHAT IS THE HAPPY GLOW SO SOON EXPIRED     .  .  .  .    444 WESTMIN ABBEY       10
      SOON SOON THE DAYS CONVICTION BRING    .  .  .  .  .  .  459 KAISER DEAD         25
      SOON SOON THE DAYS CONVICTION BRING    .  .  .  .  .  .  459 KAISER DEAD         25
      SOON WAS THAT STILLNESS BROKEN LIKE THE CRY      .  .   466 ALARIC AT ROME      109
      SOON SEEMS AS TEDIOUS AS EACH TEDIOUS STAGE      .  .       LUCRETIUS 6           4
```

SOONER

```
      OR THE DAY WERE SOONER DONE     .  .  .  .  .  .  .  .   29 NEW SIRENS         110
      SOONER SHALL THIS MY STAFF BEAR LEAVES     .  .  .  .   160 NECKAN              51
      SOONER THAN THOSE TWIN REACHES OF GREAT TIME     .  .       FRAGMENT 5           7
```

SOONEST

```
      WHERE SWEET THINGS SOONEST CLOY     .  .  .  .  .  .  .  39 STAGIRIUS           44
      AND SOONEST FADE IN THE BROAD GLARE OF DAY  .  .  .  .  470 ALARIC AT ROME      214
```

SOOTH

```
      OR AS THOU NEVER CAMST IN SOOTH     .  .  .  .  .  .    209 LONGING              9
      IN SOOTH IT SEEMS A HUNDRED YEAR    .  .  .  .  .  .    480 HAYSWATER BOAT      35
```

SOOTHE

```
      I WILL WATCH THEE TEND THEE SOOTHE THY PAIN      .  .   143 TRISTRAM 2          30
      THEY YIELD US NOT TO SOOTHE OUR PAINS      .  .  .  .   222 EPILOG LAOCOON      32
      REVERING WHAT SHE CANNOT SOOTHE     .  .  .  .  .  .    283 HAWORTH CHURCH    V
      IF THAT MIGHT SOOTHE HIM BELOW  .  .  .  .  .  .  .  .  343 MEROPE             410
      ALL I COULD DO TO SOOTHE THEE HAS BEEN TRIED     .  .   396 MEROPE            1764
      BUT I WOULD SERVE HIM SOOTHE HIM IF I COULD      .  .   408 EMPEDOCLES I 1      75
      THOUGH FROM AFAR DISTINCTLY IT MAY SOOTHE HIM    .  .   409 EMPEDOCLES I 1      89
      HIS COUNSEL COULD ONCE SOOTHE HIM BUT APOLLO     .  .   428 EMPEDOCLES I 2     482
```

SOOTHED

```
      POWER TO BE MOVED AND SOOTHED FOR ALL OUR PAIN   .  .   153 TRISTRAM 3         117
      OUR SOOTHED ENCOURAGED SOULS WILL DARE     .  .  .  .   179 FAREWELL            62
      AND HOW THE BREAST WAS SOOTHED AND HOW THE HEAD  .  .   260 SCHOLAR-GIPSY      189
      ROSILY BRIGHTEN AND THE SOOTHED GODS SMILE  .  .  .  .  431 EMPEDOCLES II       81
      SOOTHED THEM IN THEIR LAST DECAY    .  .  .  .  .  .    455 POOR MATTHIAS       92
```

SOOTHING

```
      AND WITH A SOOTHING VOICE HE SPAKE AND SAID      .  .    82 SOHRAB RUSTUM      707
      AND WITH A SOOTHING VOICE HE SPOKE AND SAID      .  .    82 SOHRAB RUSTUM    V 707
      THEN SOOTHING WITH THY CHRISTIAN STRAIN FORLORN  .  .   168 RACHEL 3             6
      FOR NEVER HAS SUCH SOOTHING VOICE   .  .  .  .  .  .    271 MEMORIAL VERSES     35
```

SOPHIST

```
      THE SOPHIST SNEERS FOOL TAKE    .  .  .  .  .  .  .  .  416 EMPEDOCLES I 2     132
      BE NEITHER SAINT NOR SOPHIST-LED BUT BE A MAN    .  .   416 EMPEDOCLES I 2     136
      BEFORE THE SOPHIST-BROOD HATH OVERLAID     .  .  .  .   429 EMPEDOCLES II       29
```

SOPHISTICATED

```
      SOPHISTICATED NO TRUTH     .  .  .  .  .  .  .  .  .  .  441 EMPEDOCLES II      401
```

SOPHISTRIES

```
      THE BARREN OPTIMISTIC SOPHISTRIES     .  .  .  .  .  .    7 REP FRIEND           5
      FOLLY REVIVED RE-FURBISHD SOPHISTRIES      .  .  .  .   449 WESTMIN ABBEY      159
```

SOPHISTS

```
      OF SOPHISTS HAS GOT EMPIRE IN OUR SCHOOLS  .  .  .  .   410 EMPEDOCLES I 1     122
      THE SOPHISTS ARE NO ENEMIES OF HIS    .  .  .  .  .  .  411 EMPEDOCLES I 1     146
      TIS NOT THE TIMES TIS NOT THE SOPHISTS VEX HIM   .  .   411 EMPEDOCLES I 1     150
      A WORLD THESE SOPHISTS THRONG   .  .  .  .  .  .  .  .  416 EMPEDOCLES I 2     135
```

SOPHOCLES

```
      SOPHOCLES LONG AGO  .  .  .  .  .  .  .  .  .  .  .  .   211 DOVER BEACH         15
```

SORE

```
      AND SAY O SON I WEEP THEE NOT TOO SORE     .  .  .  .    85 SOHRAB RUSTUM      822
      THAT THEY FLEW THICK AND BRUISED HIM SORE  .  .  .  .    91 SICK KING BOKH     122
      THAT TRAVAILS SORE AND BRINGS FORTH WIND   .  .  .  .   217 NAMELESS EPIT     V
      THEY HAVE DECLARED THE SPIRITS SORE   .  .  .  .  .  .  224 EPILOG LAOCOON      93
      SORE LOAD AND WORDS CAN DO NO MORE    .  .  .  .  .  .  224 EPILOG LAOCOON      94
      WHICH TASKD THY PIPE TOO SORE AND TIRED THY THROAT     269 THYRSIS            225
      SORE THIRST PLAGUES THEM THE ROCKS    .  .  .  .  .  .  291 RUGBY CHAPEL       178
```

SORELY

```
      SORELY AGAINST THY WILL BY STRONG NECESSITYS ORDER         HOMER TRANS         31
```

SORES

```
      SAND RAKED HIS SORES FROM HEEL TO PATE     .  .  .  .   157 SAINT BRANDAN       47
```

SOREST

```
      BUT AH THEN COMES HIS SOREST SPELL    .  .  .  .  .  .  225 EPILOG LAOCOON     139
```

SORROW

```
      IN MY CASTLE ALL IS SORROW      .  .  .  .  .  .  .  .   15 CHURCH BROU 1       73
      IS IT HOPE MAKES ME LINGER THE DIM THOUGHT THAT SORROW  19 MODERN SAPPHO     V
      DO I BRIGHTEN AT YOUR SORROW    .  .  .  .  .  .  .  .   31 NEW SIRENS         163
      WHICH THE SORROW-STRICKEN DAY DENIES  .  .  .  .  .  .   32 NEW SIRENS         178
      WHEN THE MEAN SHALL NO MORE SORROW    .  .  .  .  .  .   33 NEW SIRENS         218
```

SORROW   (CONTINUED)

AS THE TEARS OF SORROW . . . .   36 VOICE   9
WHERE SORROW TREADS ON JOY   . . . .   39 STAGIRIUS   43
WHERE SORROW PUTS OUT JOY   . . . .   39 STAGIRIUS   V 43
THY SORROW AND THY CALMNESS ARE THINE OWN   .   42 GIPSY CHILD   19
NOR ANY ANGELS SORROW SO FORLORN   . . . . .   42 GIPSY CHILD   28
BETWIXT OUR SENSES AND OUR SORROW KEEPS   . .   43 GIPSY CHILD   50
AND NEVER ANGELS SORROW SO FORLORN   . . . .   42 GIPSY CHILD   V 28
NO MEDITATION NO DELIGHT NO SORROW   . . . .   50 CONSOLATION   V
ALL THESE HAVE SORROW AND KEEP STILL   . . .   93 SICK KING BOKH   177
SON SHE SAID THY NAME SHALL BE OF SORROW   . .   145 TRISTRAM 2   85
TRISTRAM TRISTRAM STAY I COME AH SORROW   . .   146 TRISTRAM 2   V 99
DEAR SAINTS IT IS NOT SORROW AS I HEAR   . .   152 TRISTRAM 3   112
FROM A SORROW-CLOUDED EYE   . . . .   164 FORSAKEN MERM   103
AND A HEART SORROW-LADEN . . . . . (. . .   164 FORSAKEN MERM   104
GROWS FROM SUCH SORROW AS THEIRS   . . . . .   235 YOUTH OF MAN   100
SORROW O QUEEN OF MANKIND   . . . .   346 MEROPE   506
THE SADDENING TALE THAT TELLS OF SORROW AND DECAY   462 ALARIC AT ROME   6
FAMINE AND SORROW ARE NO STRANGERS HERE   . .   465 ALARIC AT ROME   82
TO TOUCH WITH SORROW EVEN A VICTORS MIND   . .   468 ALARIC AT ROME   166
AND THE FIRST SORROW WHICH IS CHILDHOODS GRAVE .   474 CROMWELL   82
MADE VOID AND HELD THE SORROW AND THE JOY   . .   RUDE ORATOR   4

SORROWD
TILL THAT HOUR SHE NEVER SORROWD   . . . . .   14 CHURCH BROU 1   59
CHEERD ALL THE FAILING HEARTS THAT SORROWD THERE .   478 CROMWELL   218

SORROWFUL
SCORNFUL AND STRANGE AND SORROWFUL AND FULL   . .   4 EMERSONS ESSAYS   9
SORROWFUL PEACE   . . . .   378 MEROPE   1249

SORROWING
BROKE FROM HIS SORROWING PEOPLE SO HE SPAKE . . . .   11 MYCERINUS   81
NOR TOWRD VALHALLA AND THE SORROWING GODS   . . . .   97 BALDER DEAD 1   58
NOR TOWARDS VALHALLA AND THE SORROWING GODS   . .   97 BALDER DEAD 1 V 58

SORROWS
THAT WAS BLISS TO MAKE MY SORROWS FLEE   . . .   144 TRISTRAM 2   46
LIKE DREAMS BETWEEN TWO SORROWS WENT AND CAME   .   474 CROMWELL   96
WAS IT THAT YE WITH MAN MIGHT HAVE YOUR THOUSANDS   HOMER TRANS   11
   OF SORROWS
RAKED FROM THE SWARMING GULF OF SORROWS HELL   . .   RUDE ORATOR   16
RAKED FROM THE SWARMING GULFS OF SORROWS HELL   . .   RUDE ORATOR   V 16

SORRY
WHAT MORTAL COULD BE SICK OR SORRY HERE   . . . .   407 EMPEDOCLES I 1   20

SORT
ONLY THE INGLORIOUS SORT ARE THERE BELOW   . . . .   104 BALDER DEAD 1   323
TO SORT WHATS HERE AMASSD   . . . .   419 EMPEDOCLES I 2   215
THE HUMBLER SORT WHO SERVE AND TEND   . . . . . .   459 KAISER DEAD   32
IN SOME OTHER SORT THAN YOUR LAST WHEN THE   HOMER TRANS   41
   BATTLE IS ENDED

SOUDANS
INTO THE SOUDANS REALM AND THUNDERED ON   . . . .   154 TRISTRAM 3   149

SOUGHT
THAT WE SOUGHT YOU WITH REJOICINGS   . . . . . .   27 NEW SIRENS   45
YOU DOZED EYELIDS SOUGHT AGAIN . . . .   31 NEW SIRENS   148
WITH EYES WHICH SOUGHT THINE EYES THOU DIDST CONVERSE   42 GIPSY CHILD   15
WITH EYES THAT SOUGHT THINE EYES THOU DIDST CONVERSE   42 GIPSY CHILD   V 15
AND SOUGHT A PRIEST TO SIGN THE CROSS   . . . .   160 NECKAN   39
THEN SOUGHT THY STRAW IN SOME SEQUESTERD GRANGE   . .   259 SCHOLAR-GIPSY   130
ROAM ON THE LIGHT WE SOUGHT IS SHINING STILL   . .   269 THYRSIS   238
AND SOUGHT AND FOUND REPOSE   . . . .   321 OBERMANN MORE   252
I SOUGHT THEE MEROPE I FIND THEE THUS   . . . .   332 MEROPE   79
MIGHT SOME ONE STRAIGHT INFORM HIM HE IS SOUGHT   . .   354 MEROPE   708

SOUGHTEST
THOU SOUGHTEST LAY IN GLOOM   . . . .   315 OBERMANN MORE V 78

SOUL
MY SPECIAL THANKS WHOSE EVEN-BALANCED SOUL   . . . .   2 TO A FRIEND   9
STRONG IS THE SOUL AND WISE AND BEAUTIFUL . . . .   4 EMERSONS ESSAYS   11
STRONG IS THE SOUL AND FRESH AND BEAUTIFUL . . . .   EMERSONS ESSAYS V 11
COLD-BUBBLING SPRINGS OR CAVES NOT SO THE SOUL   . .   6 GEO CRUIKSHANK   9
DO THOU WHOM LIGHT IN THINE OWN INMOST SOUL   . .   8 RELIGIOUS ISOL   6
WHEN THE DUPED SOUL SELF-MASTERD CLAIMS ITS MEED   . .   9 MYCERINUS   28
IT MAY BE THAT SOMETIMES HIS WONDERING SOUL   . .   11 MYCERINUS   100
TOOK MEASURE OF HIS SOUL AND KNEW ITS STRENGTH   . .   12 MYCERINUS   109
BUT FOR PEACE HER SOUL WAS YEARNING   . . . . .   21 REQUIESCAT   11
FELL LIKE OSSA ON THE CLIMBING SOUL   . . . . .   28 NEW SIRENS   72
COME YOU SAY THE SOUL IS FAINTING   . . . . .   28 NEW SIRENS   73
WHICH THE JEALOUS SOUL CONCEDES   . . . . . .   34 NEW SIRENS   228
WEIGHS LIKE OSSA ON THE AERY SOUL   . . . . .   28 NEW SIRENS   V 72
WEIGHD LIKE OSSA ON THE AERY SOUL   . . . . .   28 NEW SIRENS   V 72
WHEN THE SOUL GROWING CLEARER   . . . . . .   38 STAGIRIUS   14
WHEN THE SOUL MOUNTING HIGHER   . . . . . .   38 STAGIRIUS   16
WHEN THE SOUL RISING HIGHER TO GOD COMES NO NIGHER   38 STAGIRIUS   V 14
AND THAT SOUL-SEARCHING VISION FELL ON ME   . . . .   42 GIPSY CHILD   16
YET DOTH THINE INMOST SOUL WITH YEARNING TEEM   . .   46 IN UTRUMQUE PAR   40

SOUL   (CONTINUED)
SWELL HIS ATTENTIVE SOUL . . . .   47 WORLD QUIETIST   30
WEIGHS DOWN MY SOUL . . . .   50 CONSOLATION   5
HIS SAD LUCIDITY OF SOUL . . . .   58 RESIGNATION   198
AND A DEEP PITY ENTERD RUSTUMS SOUL . . . . . .   70 SOHRAB RUSTUM   319
STREAKD WITH ITS FIRST GREY HAIRS HOPE FILLED HIS SOUL   71 SOHRAB RUSTUM   340
O BY THY FATHERS HEAD BY THINE OWN SOUL . . . .   71 SOHRAB RUSTUM   343
AND TURND AWAY AND SPAKE TO HIS OWN SOUL . . . .   71 SOHRAB RUSTUM   346
DO THOU RECORD IT IN THINE INMOST SOUL . . . .   72 SOHRAB RUSTUM   374
NO WHEN I SEE THEE WRATH FORSAKES MY SOUL . . .   74 SOHRAB RUSTUM   430
WHO ART THOU THEN THAT CANST SO TOUCH MY SOUL .   74 SOHRAB RUSTUM   432
AND HIS SOUL SET TO GRIEF AS THE VAST TIDE . . .   79 SOHRAB RUSTUM   616
AND TURND AWAY AND SPOKE TO HIS OWN SOUL . . .   71 SOHRAB RUSTUM   V 346
THOU BAREST ME AND UNFORESEEING SOUL . . . .   98 BALDER DEAD 1   99
SIGHTLESS IN SOUL AND EYE WHAT WORDS ARE THESE   98 BALDER DEAD 1   113
ALIVE I KEPT NOT FAR FROM THEE DEAR SOUL . . .   103 BALDER DEAD 1   293
TO CUT THY THREAD OF LIFE AND FREE THY SOUL . .   103 BALDER DEAD 1   303
PAINLESS AND SWIFT SET FREE HER.AIRY SOUL . . .   104 BALDER DEAD 1   340
REMEMBRANCE IN OUR SOUL OF WARS ALONE . . . .   117 BALDER DEAD 3   138
THE SWEETEST CHRISTIAN SOUL ALIVE . . . . .   132 TRISTRAM 1   54
AH POOR SOUL IF THIS BE SO . . . .   139 TRISTRAM 1   288
AND I LOSE MY POOR SOUL MERMAN HERE WITH THEE   163 FORSAKEN MERM   59
A-KEMPIS HER DEPARTING SOUL OUTWORN . . . .   168 RACHEL 3   7
THE STRIFE THE MIXTURE IN HER SOUL ARE OURS   168 RACHEL 3   13
O HUMAN SOUL AS LONG AS THOU CANST SO . . . .   169 EAST LONDON   9
HIS SOUL WELL-KNIT AND ALL HIS BATTLES WON . .   172 IMMORTALITY   13
HAD BEEN BUT AT THE END TO HER PURE SOUL . . .   173 MONICAS PRAYER   9
MINED BY THE FEVER OF THE SOUL . . . . . .   178 FAREWELL   22
THEY ASK A SOUL WHICH NEVER SWAYS . . . . .   178 FAREWELL   27
OUR TRUE AFFINITIES OF SOUL . . . .   179 FAREWELL   56
THEY ASK A SOUL THAT NEVER SWAYS . . . . .   178 FAREWELL   V 27
SWEEP THROUGH MY SOUL . . . .   185 STRAYED REVEL   6
SWEEP THROUGH MY SOUL . . . .   194 STRAYED REVEL   297
WITH UNSPENT MIND AND A SOUL . . . .   199 FRAG DEJANEIRA   27
BEFORE I DIE BEFORE THE SOUL . . . .   206 RIVER   13
FROM THE TWIN SOUL WHICH HALVES THEIR OWN . .   206 TOO LATE   4
FROM THE TWIN SOUL THAT HALVES THEIR OWN . .   206 TOO LATE   V   4
MUST WHEN UNSEEN FROM THE SOUL FADE AWAY . .   206 SEPARATION   8
POUR ALL THE SOUL OF THEIR COMPLAINT . . . .   224 EPILOG LAOCOON   100
HATH NEER BEEN MIRRORD ON THEIR SOUL . . . .   226 EPILOG LAOCOON   188
TO THAT WHICH ONCE RAN THROUGH HIS SOUL . . .   231 YOUTH OF NATURE   94
BRUSHD OFF THE BLOOM FROM THEIR SOUL . . . .   233 YOUTH OF MAN   42
SOUL OF THE WORLD . . . .   233 YOUTH OF MAN   53
LEAVE NOT A HUMAN SOUL . . . .   234 YOUTH OF MAN   57
AWAKE AND STIR IN THEIR SOUL . . . . . .   235 YOUTH OF MAN   92
WHILE THE SOUL STILL LOOKS THROUGH THINE EYES   235 YOUTH OF MAN   113
SINK O YOUTH IN THY SOUL . . . .   235 YOUTH OF MAN   116
SO IN ITS LOVELY MOONLIGHT LIVES THE SOUL . .   236 PALLADIUM   9
AND NEVER KNOW HOW WITH THE SOUL IT FARES . .   236 PALLADIUM   20
STILL DOTH THE SOUL FROM ITS LONE FASTNESS HIGH   236 PALLADIUM   21
YET EACH WILL HAVE ONE ANGUISH HIS OWN SOUL   238 PROGRESS   31
FEEL MY SOUL BECOMING VAST LIKE YOU . . . .   240 SELF-DEPENDENCE   12
ALL THE FEVER OF SOME DIFFERING SOUL . . . .   240 SELF-DEPENDENCE   24
IN MYSTERY OUR SOUL ABIDES . . . . . .   241 MORALITY   4
THEN WHEN THE CLOUDS ARE OFF THE SOUL . . .   241 MORALITY   13
AND LET ME READ THERE LOVE THY INMOST SOUL . .   245 BURIED LIFE   11
CALM SOUL OF ALL THINGS MAKE IT MINE . . . .   249 KENSINGTON GARD   37
I ASK NOT EACH KIND SOUL TO KEEP . . . . .   250 WISH   5
HIS BROTHER-DOCTOR OF THE SOUL . . . . .   250 WISH   23
IN SOUL WITH WHAT I GAZE ON WED . . . . .   251 WISH   42
OF GOD OF THE WORLD OF THE SOUL . . . . .   253 FUTURE   43
PEACE TO THE SOUL OF THE MAN ON ITS BREAST . .   254 FUTURE   82
AND PURER OR MORE SUBTLE SOUL THAN THEE . . .   268 THYRSIS   178
HE TAUGHT US LITTLE BUT OUR SOUL . . . . .   270 MEMORIAL VERSES   8
ALL ROUND NO SOUL NO BOAT NO HAIL . . . .   274 STANZAS CARNAC   30
AND NEVER ONCE POSSESS OUR SOUL . . . . .   277 SOUTHERN NIGHT   71
HAIL TO THE STEADFAST SOUL . . . .   281 HAWORTH CHURCH   37
HOW SHALL I SING HER WHOSE SOUL . . . . .   284 HAWORTH CHURCH   93
STIRRD LIKE A CLARION-BLAST MY SOUL . . . .   285 HAWORTH CHURCH   100
OF PARALYTIC FACTIONS AND NO SOUL . . . . .   282 HAWORTH CHURCH   V
SHOOK LIKE A CLARION-BLAST MY SOUL . . . .   284 HAWORTH CHURCH   V 100
O STRONG SOUL BY WHAT SHORE . . . . .   287 RUGBY CHAPEL   37
ARROWY LIGHTNINGS OF SOUL . . . . .   293 HEINES GRAVE   36
SADDENS MY SOUL WITH ITS CHILL . . . . .   293 HEINES GRAVE   41
TASTED AMISS TO THY SOUL . . . . .   296 HEINES GRAVE   124
TO THE FROZEN HARTZ WITH HIS SOUL . . . .   298 HEINES GRAVE   193
SCATTERING LIGHTNINGS THAT SOUL . . . .   298 HEINES GRAVE   205
TILL I POSSESS MY SOUL AGAIN . . . .   302 GRANDE CHARTR   94
WHICH BROODED OER THY SOUL . . . . .   306 OBERMANN   16
THE SOUL OF THEIR WHITE SNOWS . . . . .   307 OBERMANN   28
THE SOUL OF THEIR MUTE SNOWS . . . . .   307 OBERMANN   V 28
MY SOUL HIS EYES DID REST . . . . .   314 OBERMANN MORE   68
GO SEEK IT IN THY SOUL . . . . .   316 OBERMANN MORE   120
STILL IN MY SOUL THE VOICE I HEARD . . . . . .   324 OBERMANN MORE   333
SOUL THAT THAN THEY WE TAKE MORE CARE . . .   315 OBERMANN MORE   V
SOUL THAT WE TAKE MORE COUNT AND CARE . . .   315 OBERMANN MORE   V
NO MAN CAN SAVE HIS BROTHERS SOUL . . . .   318 OBERMANN MORE   V
FIXED IN OUR SOUL A THIRST LIKE FIRE . . . .   323 OBERMANN MORE   V 315
CONSUMD OUR SOUL WITH THIRST LIKE FIRE . . .   323 OBERMANN MORE   V 315
OF THIS POOR SOUL WHO BARE HIM AND HIS SIRE . .   349 MEROPE   578

SOUL   (CONTINUED)
        HAPLY HAD BUT ONE DARING SOUL STOOD FORTH • • • •   383 MEROPE   1364
        NOT ONLY WOUND THE SENSE BUT KILL THE SOUL • • • •   385 MEROPE   1408
        OF THIS POOR SOUL WHO BORE HIM AND HIS SIRE • • •   349 MEROPE   V 578
        AND THEN THE SOUL OF MAN • • • • • • • •   415 EMPEDOCLES I 2   79
        THE WIND-BORNE MIRRORING SOUL • • • • • • •   415 EMPEDOCLES I 2   83
        SIGNS MAKE THY SOUL AFRAID • • • • • • • •   416 EMPEDOCLES I 2   123
        BEFORE THE SOUL LOSE ALL HER SOLEMN JOYS • • • •   429 EMPEDOCLES II   33
        DOTH THY FIERCE SOUL STILL DEPLORE • • • • • •   430 EMPEDOCLES II   52
        THE CLOUDS WHICH WRAP THE SOUL • • • • • • •   432 EMPEDOCLES II   124
        OH THAT MY SOUL WERE FULL OF LIGHT AS THE STARS • • 438 EMPEDOCLES II   325
        THEIR SOUL OF UNWORN YOUTH THEIR BREATH OF GREATNESS 440 EMPEDOCLES II   384
        LIVED EVER IN THE LIGHT OF MY OWN SOUL • • • • •   440 EMPEDOCLES II   393
        FAR FROM MY OWN SOUL FAR FROM WARMTH AND LIGHT • •   440 EMPEDOCLES II   396
        MOUNTS OFF MY SOUL I FEEL IT I BREATHE FREE • •   441 EMPEDOCLES II   408
        MY SOUL GLOWS TO MEET YOU • • • • • • •   441 EMPEDOCLES II   412
        THE CLOUDS THAT WRAP THE SOUL • • • • • •   432 EMPEDOCLES II   V 124
        A CHURCH ONCE LARGE AND THEN GROWN STRAIT IN SOUL   449 WESTMIN ABBEY   156
        BY THIS DEAR SOUL OVER THY PRECINCT SHED • • • •   449 WESTMIN ABBEY   V 173
        THAT LOVING HEART THAT PATIENT SOUL • • • • •   450 GEISTS GRAVE   9
        FROM WHOSE PATHETIC SOUL-FED SPRINGS • • • • •   450 GEISTS GRAVE   14
        EYED THEE WITH A SOUL RESIGND • • • • • • •   453 POOR MATTHIAS   37
        SOUL-FED EYES WITH SUFFERING WORN • • • • • •   454 POOR MATTHIAS   63
        STAND NOT TWIXT HIS SOUL AND OURS • • • • • •   457 POOR MATTHIAS   172
        HERE HE POURD HIS LITTLE SOUL • • • • • • •   458 POOR MATTHIAS   200
        ONE LITTLE YEAR' THAT RESTLESS SOUL SHALL REST • •   469 ALARIC AT ROME   193
        NOR WAKE THE WEARY SOUL THAT SLUMBERS ON BELOW • •   469 ALARIC AT ROME   198
        FLASHD FROM THY SOUL UPON THINE INWARD EAR • • •   472 CROMWELL   28
        THEN ALL HIS DREAM WAS TROUBLED AND HIS SOUL • •   477 CROMWELL   199
        DEEP THRO HIS SOUL AND CHOKD HIS FALTERING TONGUE   478 CROMWELL   224
        THEN ALL HIS VISION FADED AND HIS SOUL • • • •   479 CROMWELL   235
        A HEART OF ICE A SOUL OF FIRE • • • • • • •   481 DESTINY   6
        KEPT MORE THAN US THEIR STRENGTH OF SOUL • • • •   481 COURAGE   12
        SET THINE EARS WITH SOUL-FRAUGHT MUSIC RINGING • •   482 THEKLAS ANSWER   7
        FOR THAT DAY WILL COME MY SOUL IS ASSURD OF ITS COMING HOMER TRANS   20

SOULD
        HE MUCH THE OLD MAN WHO CLEAREST-SOULD OF MEN • •   2 TO A FRIEND   2
        DO FOR THIS RADIANT GREEK-SOULD ARTIST CEASE • •   168 RACHEL 2   12
        IN HEART HIGH-SOULD • • • • • • • • •   279 SOUTHERN NIGHT   124
        THE GODS O MISTRESS DEAR THE HARD-SOULD MAN • •   390 MEROPE   1577

SOULLESS
        SUCH SO SOULLESS SO POOR • • • • • • • • •   290 RUGBY CHAPEL   149
        SOME LIFELESS SOULLESS PHANTOM OF THEIR OWN • •   474 CROMWELL   100

SOULS
        OUR RAPT SOULS ON YOUR REPLIES • • • • • • •   34 NEW SIRENS   236
        SOULS AS LITTLE GODLIKE AS THEIR OWN • • • • •   34 NEW SIRENS   250
        OUR SAD SOULS ON YOUR REPLIES • • • • • • •   34 NEW SIRENS   V 236
        WHERE OUR SICK SOULS DO LIE • • • • • • •   39 STAGIRIUS   50
        NOR WEARINESS THE FULL-FED SOULS ANNOY • • • •   42 GIPSY CHILD   11
        IS THE CALM THINE OF STOIC SOULS WHO WEIGH • • •   42 GIPSY CHILD   29
        BUT WHEN THEIR SOULS WERE SATISFIED WITH WAIL • •   103 BALDER DEAD 1   276
        AND ALL THE NOBLER SOULS OF MORTAL MEN • • •   104 BALDER DEAD 1   320
        FOR ALL THE NOBLER SOULS OF MORTAL MEN • • •   104 BALDER DEAD 1   V 320
        SOULS BOUND BELOW MY DAILY PASSERS HERE • • •   108 BALDER DEAD 2   110
        THROUGH THEIR BLOOD AND BINDS THEIR SOULS • •   132 TRISTRAM 1   66
        OF PASSION WHICH SUBDUES OUR SOULS TO IT • • •   153 TRISTRAM 3   128
        MID THE SOULS PLAGUED BY HEAVENLY POWER • • •   157 SAINT BRANDAN   34
        BUT AH NOT HUMAN SOULS • • • • • • • •   161 NECKAN   64
        OUR SOOTHED ENCOURAGED SOULS WILL DARE • • •   179 FAREWELL   62
        OUR SOON-CHOKED SOULS TO FILL • • • • • • •   183 ABSENCE   10
        BUT OUR IGNOBLE SOULS LACK MIGHT • • • • • •   201 URANIA   4
        OUR PETTY SOULS OUR STRUTTING WITS • • • • •   202 URANIA   13
        BUT SOULS WHOM SOME BENIGNANT BREATH • • • •   203 EUPHROSYNE   13
        BEAUTIFUL SOULS • • • • • • • •   221 BACCHANALIA 2   60
        AND MANY MANY ARE THE SOULS • • • • • •   226 EPILOG LAOCOON   163
        SUCH LOVELY FLOWERS FOR CHEERING SOULS • • •   227 EPILOG LAOCOON   204
        SOULS EREWHILE WHO CAUGHT HER WORD • • • •   227 PERSIST POETRY   3
        THEY ABIDE AND THE FINEST OF SOULS • • • •   230 YOUTH OF NATURE   81
        I SAY UNTO YOU SEE THAT YOUR SOULS LIVE • •   237 PROGRESS   23
        HOW BOUNDLESS MIGHT HIS SOULS HORIZONS BE • •   244 SUMMER NIGHT   88
        FROM THE SOULS SUBTERRANEAN DEPTH UPBORNE • • •   247 BURIED LIFE   73
        EXHAUST THE ENERGY OF STRONGEST SOULS • • •   259 SCHOLAR-GIPSY   145
        OUR SOULS IN ITS BENUMBING ROUND • • • •   271 MEMORIAL VERSES   46
        IN A BOOK WHICH OF WORLD-FAMOUS SOULS • • •   280 HAWORTH CHURCH   19
        UNQUIET SOULS • • • • • • • •   286 HAWORTH CHURCH   134
        IN A BOOK WHICH OF GLORIOUS SOULS • • • •   280 HAWORTH CHURCH V 19
        OF YOUNGER PASSIONATE SOULS • • • • • •   282 HAWORTH CHURCH V
        PURE SOULS HONOURD AND BLEST • • • • • •   290 RUGBY CHAPEL   147
        BUT SOULS TEMPERD WITH FIRE • • • • • • •   291 RUGBY CHAPEL   159
        SHAKESPEARE LOVELIEST OF SOULS • • • • • •   294 HEINES GRAVE   65
        THEY PAINT OF SOULS THE INNER STRIFE • • • •   301 GRANDE CHARTR   53
        HAVE TEMPERD ME EEN THUS AND IN SOME SOULS • •   366 MEROPE   1024
        WHEN THEY CORRUPT THE SOULS OF THOSE THEY RULE • • 386 MEROPE   1437
        AND CAN OUR SOULS NOT STRIVE • • • • • •   415 EMPEDOCLES I 2   93
        THOU FEELEST THY SOULS FRAME • • • • • •   416 EMPEDOCLES I 2   114
        AND THE SOULS DEEP ETERNAL NIGHT COME ON • • •   429 EMPEDOCLES II   35
        ARE FOR THE HAPPY FOR THE SOULS AT EASE • • •   436 EMPEDOCLES II   259

SOULS   (CONTINUED)

PASSAGE FROM THEIR SOULS TO MAN	• • • • • •	455	POOR MATTHIAS	98
WHO WHILE I PONDERED ON THE LOT OF SOULS	• • • •		RUDE ORATOR	2

SOUND

AND WHEN THE MIRTH WAXD LOUDEST WITH DULL SOUND	• •	12	MYCERINUS	123
ERE THEIR BOAT-MUSIC SOUND ERE THEIR BROIDERD FLAGS GLEAM		19	MODERN SAPPHO	8
IN MAZES OF HEAT AND SOUND	• • • • • • • •	21	REQUIESCAT	10
WITH NO UNGRATEFUL SOUND	• • • • • • • • •	47	WORLD QUIETIST	18
THE RED-GROUSE SPRINGING AT OUR SOUND	• • • •	54	RESIGNATION	70
BY MIDNIGHT TO A BUBBLING FOUNTAINS SOUND	• • • •	70	SOHRAB RUSTUM	317
SMOOTH SOUND THE TERMS AND LIGHT TO BE FULFILLD	• •	120	BALDER DEAD 3	231
AFTER AN HOUR A DRIPPING SOUND IS HEARD	• • • •	122	BALDER DEAD 3	310
THE GOLDEN-CRESTED COCK SHALL SOUND ALARM	• • • •	127	BALDER DEAD 3	496
THE FAR-OFF SOUND OF A SILVER BELL	• • • •	162	FORSAKEN MERM	34
WHEN DOWN SWUNG THE SOUND OF A FAR-OFF BELL	• •	163	FORSAKEN MERM	54
WHEN DOWN SWUNG THE SOUND OF THE FAR-OFF BELL	• •	163	FORSAKEN MERM	V 54
FIND ALSO IN THE SOUND A THOUGHT	• • • •	211	DOVER BEACH	19
AS FROM THE KINGS OF SOUND ARE BLOWN	• • • • •	222	EPILOG LAOCOON	34
SOUND AS OF WANDERING BREEZE BUT SOUND	• • • •	223	EPILOG LAOCOON	75
SOUND AS OF WANDERING BREEZE BUT SOUND	• • • •	223	EPILOG LAOCOON	75
THAT TRANSIENT SOUND IN SONG THEY TELL	• • • •	226	EPILOG LAOCOON	183
WHETHER IN SOUND OF THE SWALLOWING SEA	• • • •	252	FUTURE	16
HE WENT HIS PIPING TOOK A TROUBLED SOUND	• • • •	264	THYRSIS	48
WHILE HARK FAR DOWN WITH STRANGLED SOUND	• • • •	299	GRANDE CHARTR	9
IS IT FOR THIS BECAUSE THE SOUND	• • • • •	307	OBERMANN	37
AND GLORIOUS THERE WITHOUT A SOUND	• • • •	324	OBERMANN MORE	345
VISIT OUR STREETS AND THE SOUND	• • • •	360	MEROPE	894
THAT STERN WORD MURDER HAD TOO DREAD A SOUND	• •	365	MEROPE	992
TO SOUND THY TRIUMPH IN HIS WIDOWS EARS	• • •	395	MEROPE	1739
PANTHEIAS HISTORY HARK WHAT SOUND WAS THAT	• • •	412	EMPEDOCLES I 2	8
NO EYE COULD BE TOO SOUND	• • • • •	419	EMPEDOCLES I 2	212
WHEN THE SOUND CLIMBS NEAR HIS SEAT	• • • •	431	EMPEDOCLES II	69
THE SOUND BELOVED OF HIS VICTORIOUS BREATH	• • •	448	WESTMIN ABBEY	128
HERE IS NO ECHO TO THE SOUND OF HOME	• • • •	468	ALARIC AT ROME	149
OH SOUND THERE NOT SOME STRAINS OF SADNESS THERE	• •	468	ALARIC AT ROME	165
THESE HAD NO SOUND FOR THEE THAT COLD CALM EYE	• •	472	CROMWELL	21
WHAT FORMS ARE THESE THAT WITH COMPLAINING SOUND	• •	476	CROMWELL	159

SOUNDED

NEPHEW THY FRIENDS ARE SOUNDED AND PROVE TRUE	• •	390	MEROPE	1587

SOUNDING

SWEEP IN THE SOUNDING STILLNESS OF THE NIGHT	• •	10	MYCERINUS	46
DOWN THE SAVOY VALLEYS SOUNDING	• • • • • •	12	CHURCH BROU 1	1
HIGH ABOVE THE SOUNDING SEA	• • • • • • •	134	TRISTRAM 1	135
FAST BESIDE THE SOUNDING SEA	• • • • • • •	134	TRISTRAM 1	V 135
IN THE SOUNDING LABOUR-HOUSE VAST	• • • • •	287	RUGBY CHAPEL	41

SOUNDS

ON AUTUMN-MORNINGS WHEN THE BUGLE SOUNDS	• • • •	18	CHURCH BROU 3	9
HEARD IN SLUMBER SOUNDS OF WARNING	• • • • • •	26	NEW SIRENS	7
HEARD AT EVENING SOUNDS OF WARNING	• • • • • •	26	NEW SIRENS	V 7
AS ROOTED TO THE EARTH NOR SOUNDS	• • • • • •	148	TRISTRAM 2	V
ACROSS THE SOUNDS AND CHANNELS POUR	• • • • •	182	TO MARG CONT	12
HIS VOICE LIKE SOUNDS OF SUMMER NIGHTS	• • • •	202	URANIA	22
EVEN OF ANGELS SOUNDS AMISS	• • • • • • •	295	HEINES GRAVE	102
SOUNDS NOW ONE WORD ALONE	• • • • • •	318	OBERMANN MORE	184
THE ILL-BODING NOTE WHICH FRANTIC HATRED SOUNDS	• •	397	MEROPE	1781
THE ILL-BODING NOTE WHICH FRANTIC ENVY SOUNDS	• •	397	MEROPE	V1781
ONLY TO TYPHO IT SOUNDS HATEFULLY	• • • • •	430	EMPEDOCLES II	41
SOUNDS OF DEEP IMPORT VOICES THAT BEGUILE	• • •	472	CROMWELL	5
YET ALL HIGH SOUNDS THAT MOUNTAIN CHILDREN HEAR	• •	472	CROMWELL	27
OR WONDROUS SOUNDS FROM TRANQUIL SKIES WERE BORNE	•	472	CROMWELL	35
SOUNDS SUCH AS ERST THE LONE WAYFARING MAN	• • •	473	CROMWELL	39
LIKE SOUNDS FROM OTHER WORLDS THE SPARTANS EAR	• •	473	CROMWELL	42

SOUNDST

KNOWST THOU THEN AUGHT THAT THUS THOU SOUNDST THE ALARM		396	MEROPE	1766

SOURCE

SOME SOURCE OF FEELING HE MUST CHOOSE	• • • •	223	EPILOG LAOCOON	83
ATTEND IT FROM ITS PRIMAL SOURCE	• • • • • •	225	EPILOG LAOCOON	148

SOURCES

AS SHE WAS BY THE SOURCES OF TIME	• • • • • •	252	FUTURE	28

SOURD

THOU ART AS CROSS AS SOURD AS HIMSELF	• • • •	411	EMPEDOCLES I 1	141

SOUTH

THE LONG-MUSED THOUGHT TO NORTH SOUTH EAST AND WEST		45	IN UTRUMQUE PAR	6
NEXT THE MORE TEMPERATE TOORKMUNS OF THE SOUTH	• •	64	SOHRAB RUSTUM	121
CONFRONTS THE DOG AND HUNTER IN THE SOUTH	• • • •	99	BALDER DEAD 1	157
NORTH SOUTH EAST WEST THEY STRUCK AND ROAMD THE WORLD		122	BALDER DEAD 3	304
AND IN FIELDS SLOPING TO THE SOUTH DARK PLOTS	• •	122	BALDER DEAD 3	314
WHEN FROM THE SOUTH SHALL MARCH THE FIERY BAND	• •	127	BALDER DEAD 3	475
FAR TO THE SOUTH BEYOND THE BLUE THERE SPREADS	• •	128	BALDER DEAD 3	518
BRIGHT WAS THE MORN AND SOUTH THE AIR	• • • •	222	EPILOG LAOCOON	42
AND FAR TO THE SOUTH THE HEATH	• • • • • • • •	228	YOUTH OF NATURE	22

SOUTH   (CONTINUED)
                THE SOUTH WAS PARENT OF HIS PAIN . . . . 275 STANZAS CARNAC   47
                THE SOUTH IS MISTRESS OF HIS GRAVE . . . . . . 275 STANZAS CARNAC   48
                THENCE TO THE SOUTH BEHOLD THOSE SNOWY PEAKS . . 330 MEROPE   V 16
                AS THE SKY-BRIGHTENING SOUTH-WIND CLEARS THE DAY . . 432 EMPEDOCLES II   121

SOUTHERN
                STREAM OVER CASBIN AND THE SOUTHERN SLOPES . . . . 64 SOHRAB RUSTUM   113
                TO WINTER-PASTURE ON THE SOUTHERN SIDE . . . . . 107 BALDER DEAD 2   93
                THE SOUTHERN WINTER-PARLOUR BY MY FAY . . . . . 135 TRISTRAM 1   164
                ON THE CASTLES SOUTHERN SIDE . . . . 140 TRISTRAM 1   329
                TO A BOON SOUTHERN COUNTRY HE IS FLED . . . . . 268 THYRSIS   175
                SOUTHERN PALACES STEPS . . . . 296 HEINES GRAVE   132
                LIKE FROZEN WINDS ON SOUTHERN VALES THAT BLOW . . 474 CROMWELL   89

SOUTHWARD
                OR SOME FRORE CASPIAN REED-BED SOUTHWARD BOUND . . 64 SOHRAB RUSTUM   115
                SOUTHWARD THE TARTARS BY THE RIVER MARGE . . . . 86 SOHRAB RUSTUM   873
                THE FRINGES OF A SOUTHWARD-FACING BROW . . . . 262 SCHOLAR-GIPSY   235
                SOUTHWARD AND WEST BEHOLD THOSE SNOWY PEAKS . . . 330 MEROPE   16
                AND CEUTA ON THE LEFT THEN SOUTHWARD SPED . . . 484 S S LUSITANIA   5

SOVEREIGN
                EACH SOVEREIGN FOR HIS DEAR-BOUGHT HOUR BORN . . 388 MEROPE   1513
                THIS POLITIC SOVEREIGN LYING AT OUR FEET . . . . 403 MEROPE   1965
                WHILE OER HIS SOVEREIGN EYE . . . . 431 EMPEDOCLES II   V 78

SOVRAN
                OUT-TOPPING KNOWLEDGE SO SOME SOVRAN HILL . . . .   2 SHAKESPEARE   V 3
                WHILE THE SOVRAN HEART IS DEAD . . . . 28 NEW SIRENS   78
                WHILE OER HIS SOVRAN EYE . . . . 431 EMPEDOCLES II   78

SOW
                WHEN TO SAIL AND WHEN TO SOW . . . . 456 POOR MATTHIAS   140

SOWING
                SOWING HIS VICTORS THINLY THROUGH THEM ALL . . . 337 MEROPE   250

SOWN
                HATH SOWN WITH CLOUDLESS PASSAGES THE TALE . . . 43 GIPSY CHILD   51
                FROM THE INTENSE CLEAR STAR-SOWN VAULT OF HEAVEN . . 240 SELF-DEPENDENCE   13
                IN THE YET STAR-SOWN NIGHTLY SKY . . . . . . 323 OBERMANN MORE   331

SPACE
                BLOTTING THIS SIX YEARS SPACE WHICH YET IS MINE . . 10 MYCERINUS   60
                WHISPERING A LITTLE SPACE AND THOU ART MINE . . 11 MYCERINUS   106
                TO USHER FOR A DESTINED SPACE . . . . 53 RESIGNATION   35
                EXULTS YET FOR NO MOMENTS SPACE . . . . 57 RESIGNATION   158
                CROWD AS WE WILL ITS NEUTRAL SPACE . . . . . . 59 RESIGNATION   258
                A LITTLE POOL AND IN SHORT SPACE . . . . 90 SICK KING BOKH   68
                BUT MY LORD MUSED A SPACE AND SAID . . . . . . 90 SICK KING BOKH   89
                A LITTLE POOL AND IN BRIEF SPACE . . . . 90 SICK KING BOKH   V 68
                SCANT SPACE THAT WARDER LEFT FOR PASSERS BY . . 107 BALDER DEAD 2   90
                AND HAVE NOW SHORT SPACE FOR BEING GLAD . . . . 144 TRISTRAM 2   56
                SOMETIMES A SECONDS SPACE THEIR EAR . . . . . 226 EPILOG LAOCOON   179
                NOR WORE THE MANACLES OF SPACE . . . . 242 MORALITY   32
                SPACE FOR THINGS FAR FROM THEMSELVES . . . . . 282 HAWORTH CHURCH   V
                YOU TRIUMPH OVER TIME AND SPACE . . . . 304 GRANDE CHARTR   166
                AND BADE THE WINDS THROUGH SPACE IMPEL THE GUSTY TOY 415 EMPEDOCLES I 2   81
                WHO HAS NO MINUTES BREATHING SPACE ALLOWD . . . 437 EMPEDOCLES II   272
                AND WAIT WHILE HE DID THERE A SPACE ABIDE . . . 445 WESTMIN ABBEY   26
                ONE MOMENTS SPACE PERCHANCE MIGHT CHARM HIS EYE . 475 CROMWELL   109
                ONE MOMENTS SPACE MIGHT WAFT HIM FAR AWAY . . . 475 CROMWELL   111

SPACES
                SLOWLY PAST THE OPEN SPACES . . . .   META CLOISTER   5

SPACIOUS
                AND IN THE DESERT SPACIOUS INNS . . . . 94 SICK KING BOKH   203

SPAIN
                GERMAN MASONS SMITHS FROM SPAIN . . . . 15 CHURCH BROU 1   96
                HE TARRIES WHERE THE ROCK OF SPAIN . . . . . . 275 STANZAS CARNAC   38
                HE LINGERS WHERE THE ROCK OF SPAIN . . . . . . 275 STANZAS CARNAC   V 38
                FROM ENGLAND GERMANY OR SPAIN . . . . 301 GRANDE CHARTR   63

SPAINS
                NOT IN SUNK SPAINS PROLONGD DEATH AGONY . . . . 480 HUNGARIAN NAT   1

SPAKE
                AS THOUGH ONE SPAKE OF LIFE UNTO THE DEAD . . . .   3 EMERSONS ESSAYS   8
                AS THOUGH ONE SPAKE OF NOISE UNTO THE DEAD . . .   3 EMERSONS ESSAYS V 8
                AS THOUGH MEN SPAKE OF LIFE A JOY WAS FLED . . .   EMERSONS ESSAYS V 8
                SO SPAKE HE HALF IN ANGER HALF IN SCORN . . . . 11 MYCERINUS   79
                BROKE FROM HIS SORROWING PEOPLE SO HE SPAKE . . 11 MYCERINUS   81
                HE SPAKE THE GREAT KING HEARD . . . . 47 WORLD QUIETIST   28
                BETWIXT THE SILENT HOSTS AND SPAKE AND SAID . . 65 SOHRAB RUSTUM   149
                SO SPAKE HE AND FEROOD STOOD FORTH AND CRIED . . 66 SOHRAB RUSTUM   184
                HE SPAKE AND PERAN-WISA TURND AND STRODE . . . . 66 SOHRAB RUSTUM   187
                SO HE SPAKE MILDLY SOHRAB HEARD HIS VOICE . . . 71 SOHRAB RUSTUM   334

SPAKE   (CONTINUED)

AND TURND AWAY AND SPAKE TO HIS OWN SOUL	71	SOHRAB RUSTUM	346
AND THEN HE TURND AND STERNLY SPAKE ALOUD	72	SOHRAB RUSTUM	364
HE CEASED BUT WHILE HE SPAKE RUSTUM HAD RISEN	74	SOHRAB RUSTUM	448
AND IN A HOLLOW VOICE HE SPAKE AND SAID	80	SOHRAB RUSTUM	666
AND WITH A SOOTHING VOICE HE SPAKE AND SAID	82	SOHRAB RUSTUM	707
SO SPAKE HE AND FEROOD STOOD FORTH AND SAID	66	SOHRAB RUSTUM	V 184
VENGEANCE O KING BUT THE KING SPAKE	89	SICK KING BOKH	39
AND THUS THE FATHER OF THE AGES SPAKE	95	BALDER DEAD 1	17
SO SPAKE THE KING OF GODS AND STRAIGHTWAY ROSE	96	BALDER DEAD 1	46
TO HER DREW HODER NEAR AND SPAKE AND SAID	98	BALDER DEAD 1	94
WHO WHILE THE MOTHER SPAKE HAD CEASED THEIR TOIL	100	BALDER DEAD 1	195
THEY SPAKE AND EACH WENT HOME TO HIS OWN HOUSE	101	BALDER DEAD 1	219
HE SPAKE AND BRUSHD SOFT BY AND DISAPPEARD	102	BALDER DEAD 1	239
AND GAZED ON NANNA AS SHE SLEPT AND SPAKE	103	BALDER DEAD 1	287
HE SPAKE AND STRAIGHT HIS LINEAMENTS BEGAN	104	BALDER DEAD 1	331
AND THUS THE FATHER OF THE AGES SPAKE	106	BALDER DEAD 2	40
HE SPAKE THE WARDER OF THE BRIDGE REPLIED	108	BALDER DEAD 2	118
SHE SPAKE AND STEPPD ASIDE AND LEFT HIM ROOM	108	BALDER DEAD 2	135
SHE SPAKE BUT DOWN OFF SLEIPNER HERMOD SPRANG	110	BALDER DEAD 2	186
AND SPAKE AND MILD ENTREATED HER AND SAID	110	BALDER DEAD 2	188
SHE SPAKE AND HERMOD ANSWERD HER AND SAID	111	BALDER DEAD 2	241
HE SPAKE AND STRAIGHTWAY HELA ANSWERED HIM	111	BALDER DEAD 2	246
AND STRAIGHT TO BALDER HERMOD TURND AND SPAKE	111	BALDER DEAD 2	249
HE SPAKE AND BALDER UTTERD HIM REPLY	112	BALDER DEAD 2	262
HE SPAKE AND RAISED HIS HAND AND GAVE THE RING	112	BALDER DEAD 2	279
BEHELD HIM COME AND TO HIS NEIGHBOUR SPAKE	113	BALDER DEAD 3	5
SO THEY TWO SOFT TO ONE ANOTHER SPAKE	114	BALDER DEAD 3	30
HE SPAKE AND ALL THE GODS ASSENTING WAILD	116	BALDER DEAD 3	89
SHE IN HER HANDS TOOK BALDERS HEAD AND SPAKE	116	BALDER DEAD 3	98
SHE SPAKE AND ALL THE GODDESSES BEWAILD	117	BALDER DEAD 3	123
HE LAST APPROACHD THE CORPSE AND SPAKE AND SAID	117	BALDER DEAD 3	131
SO REGNER SPAKE AND ALL THE HEROES GROAND	117	BALDER DEAD 3	153
HE SPAKE AND HIS FIERCE SONS APPLAUDED LOUD	120	BALDER DEAD 3	245
SHE SPAKE AND ON HER FACE LET FALL HER VEIL	122	BALDER DEAD 3	295
STRAIGHTWAY HE SPAKE AND THUS ADDRESSD THE GODS	122	BALDER DEAD 3	298
SHE SPAKE BUT HERMOD ANSWERD HER AND SAID	123	BALDER DEAD 3	345
SHE SPAKE AND TO THE CAVERNS DEPTH SHE FLED	123	BALDER DEAD 3	355
THEN SAD AT HEART TO NIORD HERMOD SPAKE	124	BALDER DEAD 3	369
HE SPAKE AND TURND TO GO TO THE INNER GLOOM	125	BALDER DEAD 3	421
AND THE BLIND HODER ANSWERD HIM AND SPAKE	125	BALDER DEAD 3	431
HE SPAKE AND AS HE CEASED A PUFF OF WIND	126	BALDER DEAD 3	440
HE SPAKE AND BALDER ANSWERD HIM AND SAID	126	BALDER DEAD 3	454
HE SPAKE BUT BALDER ANSWERD HIM AND SAID	127	BALDER DEAD 3	483
HE SPAKE AND THE FLEET HERMOD THUS REPLIED	128	BALDER DEAD 3	514
SO SPAKE THE IMPERIAL SAGE PUREST OF MEN	168	WORLDLY PLACE	2
WELL SPAKE THE IMPETUOUS SAINT AND BORE OF MEN	171	DIVINITY	6
SO SPAKE THE FIERCE TERTULLIAN BUT SHE SIGHD	172	GOOD SHEPHERD	6
AND STILL IT SPAKE ITS WONTED SPEECH	319	OBERMANN MORE	195
AND BEAUTY FILLD HER AND SHE SPAKE ALOUD	447	WESTMIN ABBEY	100
SHE SPAKE AND FROM THE PORTAL PASSD AWAY	447	WESTMIN ABBEY	110
SO HE SPAKE AND DROVE WITH A CRY HIS STEEDS		HOMER TRANS	63
INTO BATTLE			

SPAN

WE LIVE NO MORE WHEN WE HAVE DONE OUR SPAN	171	BETTER PART	5
OF LIFE WAS CUT AND CLOSED THY SPAN	184	TERRACE BERNE	28
HIS MORTAL SPAN	278	SOUTHERN NIGHT	84
AY AGES LONG ENDURED HIS SPAN	318	OBERMANN MORE	165
O THOU WHO ERE THY FLYING SPAN	322	OBERMANN MORE	277
THE OUT-SPREAD WORLD TO SPAN	415	EMPEDOCLES I 2	77
THE HOWLING VOID TO SPAN	415	EMPEDOCLES I 2	V 77
MANS MEASURES CANNOT SPAN THE ILLIMITABLE ALL	423	EMPEDOCLES I 2	V 341
HAD THEY INDEED NO LONGER SPAN	450	GEISTS GRAVE	10
TO FLAG AND FEEL HIS NARROWING SPAN	459	KAISER DEAD	38

SPANGLED

EARTH AND HEAVENS STAR-SPANGLED LOAD		PILLARS UNIVERS	4

SPANND

SPANND BY AERIAL ARCHES ALL OF GOLD	4	BUTLERS SERMONS	12

SPANS

WHICH SPANS WITH GOLDEN ARCHES GIALLS STREAM	99	BALDER DEAD 1	148
WHICH SPANS WITH GOLDEN ARCHES GIALLS STREAM	107	BALDER DEAD 2	86
AND THE ROOFD BRIDGE THAT SPANS THE STREAM	177	FAREWELL	6

SPAR

AND THE PALE MASTER ON HIS SPAR-STREWN DECK	244	SUMMER NIGHT	65

SPARE

AND I WILL SPARE THY HOST YEA LET THEM GO	84	SOHRAB RUSTUM	806
UNSEEN AND HAVING DRINK TO SPARE	90	SICK KING BOKH	71
THIS SPARE DARK-FEATURED	189	STRAYED REVEL	102
SPARE ME THE WHISPERING CROWDED ROOM	250	WISH	13
MARKD THINE OUTLANDISH GARB THY FIGURE SPARE	258	SCHOLAR-GIPSY	98
MARKD THY OUTLANDISH GARB THY FIGURE SPARE	258	SCHOLAR-GIPSY	V 98
THOUGH TO THESE LEAVES THE GLACIERS SPARE	307	OBERMANN	27
TYRANTS THINK HIM THEY MURDER NOT THEY SPARE	340	MEROPE	349
SPARES NOT HIMSELF THEMSELVES THEY WILL NOT SPARE	383	MEROPE	1363
WHO SPARED NOT OTHERS BID NOT US TO SPARE	390	MEROPE	1578

SPARE   (CONTINUED)
        SPARE ME META QUESTION RATHER . . . .   META CLOISTER   25

SPARED
        ONE SON AT LEAST I SPARED FOR STILL HE LIVES . . . . 340 MEROPE   348
        WHO SPARED NOT OTHERS BID NOT US TO SPARE . . . .   390 MEROPE   1578

SPARELY
        ALIGHT AND SPARELY SUP AND WAIT   . . . .   300 GRANDE CHARTR   26

SPARES
        SPARES BUT THE CLOUDY BORDER OF HIS BASE . . . .   3 SHAKESPEARE   7
        SPARES OFTEN BUT THE BORDER OF HIS BASE . . . . .   3 SHAKESPEARE   V   7
        SPARES BUT THE BORDER OFTEN OF HIS BASE . . . . .   3 SHAKESPEARE   V   7
        SPARES NOT A THOUGHT TO HIS HOME   . . . .   347 MEROPE   522
        SPARES NOT HIMSELF THEMSELVES THEY WILL NOT SPARE   383 MEROPE   1363

SPARING
        SPARING US NARROWER MARGIN THAN WE DEEM . . . . .   7 REP FRIEND CONT   8

SPARK
        AND WAITING FOR THE SPARK FROM HEAVEN TO FALL . . .   258 SCHOLAR-GIPSY   120
        ,THOU WAITEST FOR THE SPARK FROM HEAVEN AND WE . .   260 SCHOLAR-GIPSY   171
        AND HOW THE DYING SPARK OF HOPE WAS FED . . . .   260 SCHOLAR-GIPSY   188
        THE LAST SPARK OF MANS CONSCIOUSNESS WITH WORDS . .   429 EMPEDOCLES II   30

SPARKLE
        TO SEE THE SPARKLE ON THE EAVES   . . . .   141 TRISTRAM 1   357
        STARS NOW THEY SPARKLE . . . .   393 MEROPE   1675

SPARKLED
        AND THE SUN SPARKLED ON THE OXUS STREAM . . . . .   75 SOHRAB RUSTUM   489
        SPARKLED WITH MOCKING GLEE AND EXERCISE . . . .   154 TRISTRAM 3   170
        THE STRANGE GUEST SPARKLED NOW TIS PASSD AWAY . .   298 HEINES GRAVE   211

SPARKLES
        THAT SPARKLES IN THE SUN ALONG . . . .   226 EPILOG LAOCOON   158
        OF ROTHA SPARKLES THROUGH FIELDS . . . .   280 HAWORTH CHURCH   2
        OF ROTHA SPARKLES THE FIELDS . . . .   280 HAWORTH CHURCH   V   2

SPARKLING
        ON THE LIFELESS MARGIN OF THE SPARKLING OCEAN . .   36 VOICE   19
        AND FAR BEYOND THE SPARKLING TREES . . . . . .   141 TRISTRAM 1   362
        GAY RAIMENT SPARKLING GAUDS ELATION STRONG . . . .   166 AUSTERITY POET   7
        TO CALAIS SPARKLING IN THE SUN . . . .   204 CALAIS SANDS   V   4
        AND ON THE SPARKLING WATERS PLAYD . . . . . .   223 EPILOG LAOCOON   67
        AND LIFE RAN GAILY AS THE SPARKLING THAMES . . . .   261 SCHOLAR-GIPSY   202
        TO CROSS THE SPARKLING SHALLOWS THERE   . . . .   413 EMPEDOCLES I 2   37

SPARKS
        TO PUSH THE SHIP THROUGH THE THICK SAND SPARKS FLEW   118 BALDER DEAD 3   177
        A CHARRD LOG FALLING MAKES A SHOWER OF SPARKS . .   119 BALDER DEAD 3   204
        SO WITH A SHOWER OF SPARKS THE PILE FELL IN . .   119 BALDER DEAD 3   205

SPARS
        LAST WALKING BY THE SEA THOU FOUNDEST SPARS . .   121 BALDER DEAD 3   268
        THEN WALKING BY THE SEA THOU FOUNDEST SPARS . .   121 BALDER DEAD 3   V 268
        ARE BUSY GATHERING SPARS OF QUARTZ AND STREAMS . .   150 TRISTRAM 3   25
        LIKE DRIFTWOOD SPARS WHICH MEET AND PASS . . . .   185 TERRACE BERNE   45

SPARTA
        NOT NOW OF SPARTA WHERE HIS NEPHEWS REIGND . . . .   337 MEROPE   232
        WORST OF THE THREE THE STONY SPARTA FELL . . . .   389 MEROPE   1553

SPARTAN
        THY SPARTAN COUSINS PROCLES AND HIS BROTHER . . .   384 MEROPE   1393
        HIS ARGIVE OR HIS SPARTAN COUSINS AID . . . .   388 MEROPE   1499
        THE SPARTAN BROTHERS WITH THEIR GUARDIAN STRIVE . . 390 MEROPE   1558

SPARTANS
        LIKE SOUNDS FROM OTHER WORLDS THE SPARTANS EAR . .   473 CROMWELL   42

SPASM
        OH WHAT A SPASM SHAKES THE DREAMERS HEART . . . .   46 IN UTRUMQUE PAR   41

SPEAK
        THE REST I GIVE TO JOY EVEN WHILE I SPEAK . . . .   10 MYCERINUS   55
        O SPEAK ONCE AND SHAME MY SADNESS   . . . . . .   32 NEW SIRENS   167
        O SPEAK ONCE AND LET MY SADNESS   . . . .   32 NEW SIRENS   V 167
        SPEAK IS THERE NEWS OR ANY NIGHT ALARM . . . .   62 SOHRAB RUSTUM   32
        FOR WHAT CARE I THOUGH ALL SPEAK SOHRABS FAME . .   68 SOHRAB RUSTUM   228
        ART THOU NOT RUSTUM SPEAK ART THOU NOT HE . . .   71 SOHRAB RUSTUM   344
        SO WILL HE SPEAK PERHAPS WHILE MEN APPLAUD . . .   72 SOHRAB RUSTUM   362
        SPEAK NOT TO ME OF TRUCE AND PLEDGE AND WINE . .   75 SOHRAB RUSTUM   465
        BUT LET US SPEAK NO MORE OF THIS I FIND . . . .   82 SOHRAB RUSTUM   716
        WHAT IRKS IT ME THAT MEN SPEAK SOHRABS PRAISE . .   68 SOHRAB RUSTUM   V 228
        I AM NOT WRONGD WHEN MEN SPEAK SOHRABS PRAISE . .   68 SOHRAB RUSTUM   V 228
        TO SPEAK IN ORDER WHAT HATH CHANCED . . . . . .   88 SICK KING BOKH   28
        IF I SPEAK FOLLY BUT A KING   . . . .   89 SICK KING BOKH   55
        AND TRULY WHILE I SPEAK O KING . . . .   92 SICK KING BOKH   129

SPEAK   (CONTINUED)
SPEAK WERE NOT THIS A WAY THE WAY FOR GODS	120 BALDER DEAD 3	237
TRISTRAM AH FOR LOVE OF HEAVEN SPEAK KINDLY	142 TRISTRAM 2	13
NO THOU SHALT NOT SPEAK I SHOULD BE FINDING	143 TRISTRAM 2	33
WHAT THOU THINKST MEN SPEAK IN COURTLY CHAMBERS	143 TRISTRAM 2	41
SPEAK HER FAIR SHE IS OF ROYAL BLOOD	145 TRISTRAM 2	94
TRISTRAM FOR THE LOVE OF HEAVEN SPEAK KINDLY	142 TRISTRAM 2 V	13
IN TEARS WITH HEARTS TOO FULL TO SPEAK	178 FAREWELL	12
LIKE SHIPS THAT MEET AND SPEAK AND PASS	185 TERRACE BERNE V	45
SPEAK OF THE SURE CONSOLATIONS OF TIME	206 SEPARATION	2
THEY SPEAK THE HAPPINESS DIVINE	227 EPILOG LAOCOON	197
TO UNLOCK THE HEART AND LET IT SPEAK	245 BURIED LIFE	13
AND LONG WE TRY IN VAIN TO SPEAK AND ACT	247 BURIED LIFE	64
THE EYES ARE GLAZED THOU CANST NOT SPEAK	276 SOUTHERN NIGHT	42
SPEAK THE LAST WORD AT HIS GRAVE	298 HEINES GRAVE	201
NOT AS THEIR FRIEND OR CHILD I SPEAK	301 GRANDE CHARTR	79
O LAIAS LAIAS LET THE HEART SPEAK HERE	331 MEROPE	59
SPEAK THEREFORE OR KEEP SILENCE WHICH THOU WILT	333 MEROPE	113
HEAR ME THEN SPEAK AND LET THIS MOURNFUL DAY	333 MEROPE	114
WERE THEY WE DISPOSSESSED OF US I SPEAK	337 MEROPE	229
I SPEAK NOT NOW OF ARGOS WHERE HIS BROTHER	337 MEROPE	231
SPEAK THEM THAT I MAY JUDGE THEIR KIND MYSELF	354 MEROPE	712
I SPEAK NO WORD OF BOAST BUT THIS I SAY	360 MEROPE	888
SPEAK I GO HENCE TO OFFER SACRIFICE	394 MEROPE	1722
IT IS ENOUGH THAT ALL MEN SPEAK OF IT	413 EMPEDOCLES I 2	22
FOR I MUST HENCEFORTH SPEAK NO MORE WITH MAN	429 EMPEDOCLES II	6
POOR MATTHIAS COULDST THOU SPEAK	455 POOR MATTHIAS	109

SPEAKEST
| AND WHO THOU ART WHO SPEAKEST TO ME I | 335 MEROPE | 183 |
| THOU SPEAKEST WELL BUT HERE TO GIVE OUR EYES | 403 MEROPE | 1951 |

SPEAKING
YET THIS GLEAND WHEN GODS WERE SPEAKING	28 NEW SIRENS	79
SO SPEAKING THE FLEET-FOOTED HERMOD CAME	102 BALDER DEAD 1	246
THY KIND-SPEAKING FATHER STANDS	378 MEROPE	1240
THOU HAST HEARD ALL MEN SPEAKING OF PANTHEIA	410 EMPEDOCLES I 1	108

SPEAKS
THE WORLD SPEAKS WELL YET MIGHT HER FOE REPLY	38 WORLDS TRIUMPHS	11
BUT OF A SINGLE COMBAT FAME SPEAKS CLEAR	62 SOHRAB RUSTUM	62
AND NOW TO-NIGHT SHE LAUGHS AND SPEAKS	147 TRISTRAM 2	128
WHO SPEAKS AH WHO COMES FORTH	189 STRAYED REVEL	99
NONE SPEAKS NONE HEEDS AH TURN THY HEAD	206 RIVER	4
YES OBERMANN ALL SPEAKS OF THEE	306 OBERMANN	11
WITH SAGE EXPERIENCE SHE SPEAKS AND THOU	382 MEROPE	1331
THE GODS COMMAND NOT WHERE THE HEART SPEAKS CLEAR	385 MEROPE	1404
MESSENIA SPEAKS THE PRINCE THY SON IS DEAD	393 MEROPE	1686
I HEAR GORGIAS THEIR CHIEF SPEAKS NOBLY OF HIM	411 EMPEDOCLES I 1	147
AND NO ONE ROUND THE CHARMED CIRCLE SPEAKS	431 EMPEDOCLES II	83
HE FABLES YET SPEAKS TRUTH	431 EMPEDOCLES II	89
THEN FADES BUT SPEAKS THE WHILE	445 WESTMIN ABBEY	47
YET HERE IT SPEAKS NOT YEA THOUGH ALL AROUND	467 ALARIC AT ROME	143

SPEAR
HE TOOK HIS SPEAR AND TO THE FRONT HE CAME	65 SOHRAB RUSTUM	146
HIS SPEAR DOWN FROM THE SHOULDER DOWN IT CAME	73 SOHRAB RUSTUM	399
AND SPRANG ASIDE QUICK AS A FLASH THE SPEAR	73 SOHRAB RUSTUM	403
THE IRON PLATES RANG SHARP BUT TURND THE SPEAR	73 SOHRAB RUSTUM	407
MAYST FIGHT FIGHT THEN WHEN THEY CONFRONT THY SPEAR	74 SOHRAB RUSTUM	446
HE LEFT TO LIE BUT HAD REGAIND HIS SPEAR	74 SOHRAB RUSTUM	450
WHICH SOHRAB HELD STIFF OUT THE STEEL-SPIKED SPEAR	75 SOHRAB RUSTUM	492
GLARED AND HE SHOOK ON HIGH HIS MENACING SPEAR	76 SOHRAB RUSTUM	515
HIS COVERING SHIELD AND THE SPEAR PIERCED HIS SIDE	76 SOHRAB RUSTUM	520
FALL AND THY SPEAR TRANSFIXD AN UNARMD FOE	77 SOHRAB RUSTUM	550
THE ANGUISH OF THE DEEP-FIXD SPEAR GREW FIERCE	80 SOHRAB RUSTUM	650
THE STRIFE AND HURLD ME ON MY FATHERS SPEAR	82 SOHRAB RUSTUM	715
THE SPEAR AND DREW IT FROM HIS SIDE AND EASED	85 SOHRAB RUSTUM	839
WHICH SOHRAB HELD ADVANCD THE STEEL-SPIKED SPEAR	75 SOHRAB RUSTUM V	492
AND WILL LIKE A DIVIDING SPEAR	178 FAREWELL	34
WITH SHOUT AND SHAKEN SPEAR	191 STRAYED REVEL	189
AT LARGE HIS ENEMYS SPEAR	197 FRAG ANTIGONE	89
UPHUNG THE SPEAR UNBENT THE BOW	219 BACCHANALIA 2	11
BY ACHAIAN ARCADIAN SPEAR	345 MEROPE	480
AND RAISED HIS SPEAR	393 MEROPE	1661

SPEARS
HORSES FRET AND BOAR-SPEARS GLANCE	13 CHURCH BROU 1	18
FIRST WITH BLACK SHEEP-SKIN CAPS AND WITH LONG SPEARS	64 SOHRAB RUSTUM	118
SO ON EACH SIDE WERE SQUARES OF MEN WITH SPEARS	70 SOHRAB RUSTUM	297
COME PLANT WE HERE IN EARTH OUR ANGRY SPEARS	74 SOHRAB RUSTUM	439
MY GUARDS WHAT PRICK HIM WITH YOUR SPEARS	89 SICK KING BOKH	42
LAY THICKLY STREWN SWORDS AXES DARTS AND SPEARS	95 BALDER DEAD 1	2
AND BUCKLERS CLASH AND SPEARS BEGIN TO POUR	127 BALDER DEAD 3	498
THEIR SPEARS ARE DOWN THEIR STEEDS ARE BATHED IN FOAM	137 TRISTRAM 1	237
I SEE HER FORM GLIDE THROUGH THE CROSSING SPEARS	138 TRISTRAM 1	241
THEY FEEL THE BITING SPEARS	192 STRAYED REVEL	227
WE SPRANG UPON OUR FEET WE SNATCHD OUR SPEARS	357 MEROPE	789
HIS BOAR-SPEARS BROKEN SHAFT BACK ON THE LAKE	358 MEROPE	840
BEHIND HIS CORPSE THEIR HEDGE OF SERRIED SPEARS	381 MEROPE	1308

SPEARS   (CONTINUED)
        AND THE STRAIGHT ASHES GROW FOR SPEARS   • • • •   414 EMPEDOCLES I 2   65

SPECIAL
        MY SPECIAL THANKS WHOSE EVEN-BALANCED SOUL   • • • •   2 TO A FRIEND   9

SPECIOUS
        HIS GROUNDS HOWEVER SPECIOUS SHOWN   • • • • • •   354 MEROPE   694
        CLOAK THINE AMBITION WITH THESE SPECIOUS WORDS   • •   404 MEROPE   1985

SPECKLED
        THE FELL-FARES AND THE SPECKLED MISSEL-THRUSH   • •   150 TRISTRAM 3   30

SPECKS
        AND MEN WERE SPECKS AND LIFE A PLAY   • • • • • •   277 SOUTHERN NIGHT   78

SPECTACLE
        ETERNAL MUNDANE SPECTACLE   • • • • • • • •   59 RESIGNATION   228
        THE LONG UNPAUSING SPECTACLE   • • • • • • • •   225 EPILOG LAOCOON   146
        THIS IGNOMINIOUS SPECTACLE   • • • • • • •   282 HAWORTH CHURCH   V
        TILL MINE EYES ACHE WITH THE LONG SPECTACLE   • •   428 EMPEDOCLES I 2   475
        TILL MY EYES ACHE WITH THE LONG SPECTACLE   • • • •   428 EMPEDOCLES I 2   V 475

SPECTRAL
        SWIFT RUSH THE SPECTRAL VAPOURS WHITE   • • • • •   299 GRANDE CHARTR   13
        FAST RUSH THE SPECTRAL VAPOURS WHITE • • • • • •   299 GRANDE CHARTR   V 13

SPECULATORS
        THE FAMOUS SPECULATORS THOUGHT   • • • • • • • •   219 BACCHANALIA 2   6

SPED
        SHALL IN VAIN BE SPED   • • • • • • • • •   36 VOICE   12
        HE COMES TO TELL HIS PROMPTER HE HATH SPED   • • •   365 MEROPE   986
        HE WHO WAS SENT HATH SPED AND NOW COMES BACK   • •   366 MEROPE   V
        THOU TOO WAST WITH HIM STRAIGHTWAY I SPED HOME   • •   407 EMPEDOCLES I 1   43
        THOU TOO WERT WITH HIM STRAIGHTWAY I SPED HOME   • •   407 EMPEDOCLES I 1   V 43
        WATCHING HOW THE WHETTING SPED   • • • • • • •   434 EMPEDOCLES II   164
        AND AS YEARS SPED THE MINSTER-AISLES DIVINE   • •   445 WESTMIN ABBEY   55
        AND CEUTA ON THE LEFT THEN SOUTHWARD SPED   • • •   484 S S LUSITANIA   5

SPEECH
        FIND THEIR SOLE SPEECH IN THAT VICTORIOUS BROW   • •   3 SHAKESPEARE   14
        ALL TRUE SPEECH AND LARGE AVOWAL   • • • • •   34 NEW SIRENS   227
        SOME SOLACE IN EACH OTHERS LOOK AND SPEECH   • • •   104 BALDER DEAD 1   327
        CONVERSE HIS SPEECH REMAINS THOUGH HE BE DEAD   • •   111 BALDER DEAD 2   248
        THOU HEARST IF HEARING LIKE AS SPEECH IS THINE   • •   112 BALDER DEAD 2   251
        FAREWELL FOR LONGER SPEECH IS NOT ALLOWD   • •   129 BALDER DEAD 3   548
        OF COURTLY SPEECH ABRUPTLY DIED   • • • •   146 TRISTRAM 2   119
        TRICKD OUT WITH A PARISIAN SPEECH AND FACE   • • •   168 RACHEL 3   4
        THY CHEEK WAS GRAVE THY SPEECH GREW RARE   • •   178 FAREWELL   16
        THEN FLY OUR GREETINGS FLY OUR SPEECH AND SMILES • •   262 SCHOLAR-GIPSY   231
        WITHOUT COMPANION WITHOUT SPEECH   • • • •   278 SOUTHERN NIGHT   87
        AND STILL IT SPAKE ITS WONTED SPEECH   • • • •   319 OBERMANN MORE   195
        NOT SO THY HEART WOULD PAY ITS MOMENTS SPEECH   • •   332 MEROPE   61
        TOWRD THEE TOWARD THY SILENCE AS THY SPEECH • •   333 MEROPE   112
        NOT MUCH A TYRANT THY FREE SPEECH DISPLAYS ME   • •   340 MEROPE   350
        BUT STILL OVER HIS SPEECH A GLOOM THERE HUNG   • •   356 MEROPE   764
        ARRIVED AND OF THE KING HAD SPEECH BUT NOW   • • •   361 MEROPE   921
        AND LOCKD MY SPEECH FOR EVER IN MY BREAST   • • •   362 MEROPE   941
        WHAT SPEECH REFUSED HER   • • • • • • • •   393 MEROPE   1668
        TOWRDS THEE TOWARDS THY SILENCE AS THY SPEECH   • •   333 MEROPE   V 112

SPEECHLESS
        WE BATHED OUR HANDS WITH SPEECHLESS GLEE   • • •   54 RESIGNATION   84
        SPEECHLESS AND THEN HE UTTERD ONE SHARP CRY   • •   81 SOHRAB RUSTUM   690
        TO YEARN WITH SPEECHLESS IMPULSE TO THE FREE   • •   472 CROMWELL   7

SPEED
        OXUS FORGETTING THE BRIGHT SPEED HE HAD   • • •   87 SOHRAB RUSTUM   886
        FOR SPEED AND HERMOD WAS HIS NAME IN HEAVEN   • •   101 BALDER DEAD 1   221
        RACING FULL SPEED AND STARTLING IN THEIR RUSH   • •   150 TRISTRAM 3   29
        GOES SLOWLY BY AND THIS AT SPEED   • • • •   224 EPILOG LAOCOON   116
        SONS OF THE WORLD OH SPEED THOSE YEARS   • • •   304 GRANDE CHARTR   161
        O THAT MY OVER-SPEED AND BURSTING GRIEF   • •   362 MEROPE   939
        WHILE LOYALTY WITH ALL HER SPEED IS SLOW   • • •   363 MEROPE   963
        AND NOW AND NOW BACK TO THE TOWN WITH SPEED   • •   408 EMPEDOCLES I 1   49
        BUT HE IS STRANGELY WROUGHT I WILL SPEED BACK   • •   428 EMPEDOCLES I 2   480
        O SPEED AND REJOICE   • • • • • • • • •   442 EMPEDOCLES II   428
        BUT FOR US WE VIE IN SPEED WITH THE BREATH   HOMER TRANS   54
              OF THE WEST-WIND

SPEEDING
        IN HIS LONG BLACK SHIP SPEEDING NIGHT AND DAY   • •   485 S S LUSITANIA   10

SPEEDS
        IF SO ALLS WELL FOR LOOK THE OLD MAN SPEEDS   • •   362 MEROPE   934

SPEEDST
        WHY SPEEDST THOU NOT THY DEATHLIKE WAVE TO SHED   • • 462 ALARIC AT ROME   3

SPELL
        THE STRONG SPELL WHICH PASSION UPON HIM HATH HURLD   20 MODERN SAPPHO   V 22
        AND SPELL THY LOOKS AND GUESS THY THOUGHTS . . . .   205 CALAIS SANDS   29
        THE WORLD BUT FEELS THE PRESENTS SPELL . . . . .   221 BACCHANALIA 2   65
        ITS ELSE UNUTTERABLE SPELL . . . .   223 EPILOG LAOCOON   86
        BUT AH THEN COMES HIS SOREST SPELL . . . . .   225 EPILOG LAOCOON   139
        ITS SPELL IS ROUND THEM LIKE A SHOWER . . . . .   227 EPILOG LAOCOON   199
        BUT WE MY LOVE DOTH A LIKE SPELL BENUMB . . . .   245 BURIED LIFE   24
        BUT WE MY LOVE DOES A LIKE SPELL BENUMB . . . .   245 BURIED LIFE   V 24
        THE ETERNAL TRIFLER BREAKS YOUR SPELL . . . .   304 GRANDE CHARTR   155
        THE ETERNAL TRIFLER BREAKS THEIR SPELL . . . .   304 GRANDE CHARTR   V 155
        TO THEE WE FEEL THY SPELL . . . .   309 OBERMANN   82
        HIM WHO OBEYS THY SPELL . . . . . .   311 OBERMANN   158
        WHEREOF THY YOUTH FELT ALL THE SPELL . . . .   323 OBERMANN MORE   309
        AND KINGLY GAIT FOR EVER SUCH A SPELL . . . .   408 EMPEDOCLES I 1   61
        MIND IS THE SPELL WHICH GOVERNS EARTH AND HEAVEN . .   413 EMPEDOCLES I 2   27
        THE SWEET NOTES WHOSE LULLING SPELL . . . . .   431 EMPEDOCLES II   64
        WHOSE SPELL-BOUND SENSE FROM CHILDHOODS HOUR   471 CROMWELL   3
            HATH KNOWN

SPELLS
        TO KNOW THOSE SPELLS OF THINE WHICH STAY THEIR HAND   413 EMPEDOCLES I 2   25
        WERE TO LIVE FREE FROM TERROR SPELLS MISTRUST THEM   413 EMPEDOCLES I 2   26
        TO KNOW THOSE SPELLS OF TIME THAT STAY THEIR HAND   413 EMPEDOCLES I 2   V 25
        TO KNOW THOSE SPELLS OF THINE THAT STAY THEIR HAND   413 EMPEDOCLES I 2   V 25
        WERE TO LIVE FREED FROM TERROR SPELLS MISTRUST THEM   413 EMPEDOCLES I 2   V 26
        BUT SPELLS TO MUTTER . . . .   432 EMPEDOCLES II   117

SPEND
        SPEND AS MADLY AS YOU MAY . . . .   22 MEMORY-PICTURE   4
        AND SPEND THE GOODLY TREASUURES I HAVE GOT . . . .   68 SOHRAB RUSTUM   238
        AND SPEND THEIR LIVES IN POSTING HERE AND THERE . .   153 TRISTRAM 3   140
        IT IS TO SPEND LONG DAYS . . . .   212 GROWING OLD   21
        A THIRST TO SPEND OUR FIRE AND RESTLESS FORCE . .   246 BURIED LIFE   49
        AND SPEND OUR WIT TO NAME WHAT MOST EMPLOY UNNAMED   423 EMPEDOCLES I 2   331
        MANY YEARS HAVE NOT TO SPEND . . . .   458 POOR MATTHIAS   211

SPENDTHRIFTS
        YET REMAIN SPENDTHRIFTS STILL . . . .   420 EMPEDOCLES I 2   228

SPENT
        SO THE COMING YEARLL BE SPENT . . . .   23 MEMORY-PICTURE   18
        SPENT IS THE SPOIL HE WON . . . .   51 CONSOLATION   38
        MEN SPENT BY SICKNESS OR OBSCURE DECAY . . . .   104 BALDER DEAD 1   325
        AND LATE AT EVENING SPENT AND PANTING FALLS . .   114 BALDER DEAD 3   12
        AND SOON HAD ALL THAT DAY BEEN SPENT IN WAIL . .   118 BALDER DEAD 3   155
        ONE MORN WHEN THE SIROCCO SPENT . . . .   157 SAINT BRANDAN   43
        WHERE THE SPENT LIGHTS QUIVER AND GLEAM . . . .   162 FORSAKEN MERM   37
        MANY SPENT FAMES AND FALLEN MIGHTS . . . . .   220 BACCHANALIA 2   23
        ELSE HADST THOU SPENT LIKE OTHER MEN THY FIRE . .   259 SCHOLAR-GIPSY   154
        FIRM TO THEIR MARK NOT SPENT ON OTHER THINGS . .   260 SCHOLAR-GIPSY   163
        O SPENT ONES OF A WORK-DAY AGE . . . . . .   279 SOUTHERN NIGHT   115
        NOT WITH THE CROWD TO BE SPENT . . . . .   288 RUGBY CHAPEL   75
        WHEN YOUR WORLDS DAY WAS SPENT . . . . . .   320 OBERMANN MORE   220
        AND SPENT THY YOUTHFUL PRIME . . . . . .   323 OBERMANN MORE   306
        WITH MOUNTAIN-TRAVEL AND NIGHT-WATCHING SPENT . .   359 MEROPE   868
        NOW DO WE SOON PERCEIVE HOW FAST OUR YOUTH IS SPENT   424 EMPEDOCLES I 2   361
        NOR DO WE SOON PERCEIVE HOW FAST OUR YOUTH IS SPENT   424 EMPEDOCLES I 2   V 361
        IN DESERT ICE OF SUBTLETIES WAS SPENT . . . .   446 WESTMIN ABBEY   64
        BETTER THAN WE SPENT WITH THEE . . . . . .   458 POOR MATTHIAS   213

SPERCHEIOS
        AND THE SPERCHEIOS VALE SHAKEN WITH GROANS . . . .   198 FRAG ANTIGONE   100

SPEZZIAN
        WHICH FRINGE THY SOFT BLUE SPEZZIAN BAY . . .   303 GRANDE CHARTR   142
        THAT FRINGE THY SOFT BLUE SPEZZIAN BAY . . .   303 GRANDE CHARTR   V 142
        THAT FRINGE THY DARK BLUE SPEZZIAN BAY . . .   303 GRANDE CHARTR   V 142

SPHERE
        FROM HER TRANQUIL SPHERE . . . .   35 VOICE   4
        FOR MOVEMENT FOR AN AMPLER SPHERE . . . .   60 RESIGNATION   273
        BEHOLD I SAID THE PAINTERS SPHERE . . . .   222 EPILOG LAOCOON   49
        ABBEY RECALL IT WHAT A SPHERE . . . .   223 EPILOG LAOCOON   79
        BEHOLD AT LAST THE POETS SPHERE . . . .   225 EPILOG LAOCOON   127
        YES IN SOME FAR-SHINING SPHERE . . . . .   287 RUGBY CHAPEL   44
        ITS ACCENTS OF ANOTHER SPHERE . . . . .   306 GRANDE CHARTR   204

SPHERED
        FROM THY REMOTE AND SPHERED COURSE . . . . .   181 ISOLATION MARG   16

SPHERES
        I RUSH WITH THE SWIFT SPHERES AND GLOW . . . .   241 MORALITY   27

SPHINX
        WHERE THE SPHINX LIVED AMONG THE FROWNING HILLS . .   427 EMPEDOCLES I 2   440

SPICED
        WITH TRISTRAM THAT SPICED MAGIC DRAUGHT . . . .   132 TRISTRAM 1   64

SPIED
        SPIED PREY AFAR . . . .   51 CONSOLATION   35

SPIED   (CONTINUED)
            AND THIS AT LANDING SPIED BY US AND SAVED . . . . 358 MEROPE   842

SPIKED
            WHICH SOHRAB HELD STIFF OUT THE STEEL-SPIKED SPEAR   75 SOHRAB RUSTUM   492
            WHICH SOHRAB HELD ADVANCD THE STEEL-SPIKED SPEAR . .   75 SOHRAB RUSTUM   V 492
            WITH PALE-SPIKED LAVENDER   . . . . 392 MEROPE   1642

SPIKES
            HIGH TOWERD THE SPIKES OF PURPLE ORCHISES . . . . 266 THYRSIS   115

SPILL
            MADE MY TOST HEART ITS VERY LIFE-BLOOD SPILL   . .   36 VOICE   39
            DRAIND ALL THE LIFE MY FULL HEART HAD TO SPILL . .   36 VOICE   V 39

SPINDLE
            TILL THE SPINDLE DROPS FROM HER HAND . . . . . . 164 FORSAKEN MERM   96

SPINE
            AND FROM THE FLUTED SPINE ATOP A PLUME   . . . .   69 SOHRAB RUSTUM   268

SPINNING
            URGED AND TO FEED WHOSE MOVEMENT SPINNING SAND . .   5 DUKE WELLINGTON   6
            SPINNING WITH HER MAIDENS HERE . . . . 131 TRISTRAM 1   40

SPINS
            AND HE SPINS ILL WHO MISSES ONE   . . . .   48 HORATIAN ECHO   26
            HITHER AND THITHER SPINS . . . . 415 EMPEDOCLES I 2   82

SPIRE
            SEES SUDDENLY A SPIRE OF FLAME SHOOT UP   . . . . 119 BALDER DEAD 3   V
            FOREST AND CITY AND SPIRE   . . . . 297 HEINES GRAVE   171

SPIRES
            GIVE TO THE WIND THEIR WAVERING SPIRES   . . . .   55 RESIGNATION   117
            STILL PLAYS ON THE CITY SPIRES . . . . 234 YOUTH OF MAN   82
            AND THAT SWEET CITY WITH HER DREAMING SPIRES   . . 263 THYRSIS   19
            RISE UP ALL ROUND THE CHRISTIAN SPIRES   . . . . 274 STANZAS CARNAC   22
            WITH YELLOW SPIRES AFLAME   . . . . 313 OBERMANN MORE   22
            SEE HOW THE GIANT SPIRES OF YELLOW BLOOM   . . . . 412 EMPEDOCLES I 2   4

SPIRIT
            ALL PAINS THE IMMORTAL SPIRIT MUST ENDURE . . . .   3 SHAKESPEARE   12
            HER CABIND AMPLE SPIRIT . . . .   21 REQUIESCAT   13
            THAT MANS SPIRIT AT ITS LURING . . . .   SECOND BEST   V 23
            UNWILLINGLY THE SPIRIT FLED AWAY   . . . .   86 SOHRAB RUSTUM   854
            THEN BALDERS SPIRIT THROUGH THE GLOOM DREW NEAR . . 103 BALDER DEAD 1   282
            IN TIMES LESS ALIEN TO A SPIRIT MILD   . . . . . 128 BALDER DEAD 3   512
            AND HIS SPIRIT IS NOT CLEAR   . . . . 133 TRISTRAM 1   86
            THE SPIRIT OF THE WOODS WAS IN HER FACE   . . . . 154 TRISTRAM 3   180
            AH WHERE THE SPIRIT ITS HIGHEST LIFE HATH LED   . . 167 RACHEL 1   12
            AH NOT THE RADIANT SPIRIT OF GREECE ALONE . . . . 168 RACHEL 3   9
            AND WHEN MY ILL-SCHOOLD SPIRIT IS AFLAME   . . . . 169 WORLDLY PLACE   11
            THOUGHT I ABOVE HER STATE THIS SPIRIT TOWERS   . . 170 WEST LONDON   9
            THE UNCONQUERD JOY IN WHICH HER SPIRIT DWELLS   . . 176 PARTING   40
            WITH SPIRIT VANISHD BEAUTY WANED   . . . . 185 TERRACE BERNE   37
            LONG LONG SINCE UNDOWERD YET OUR SPIRIT   . . . . 209 SELF-DECEPTION   5
            MANS NEW SPIRIT SINCE IT WAS NOT WE . . . . 210 SELF-DECEPTION   14
            MANS BLANK SPIRIT SINCE IT WAS NOT WE   . . . . . 210 SELF-DECEPTION   V 14
            TO THE DYING SPIRIT OF YOUTH   . . . . 234 YOUTH OF MAN   55
            SAY YE THE SPIRIT OF MAN HAS FOUND NEW ROADS   . . 237 PROGRESS   25
            THE SPIRIT BLOWETH AND IS STILL   . . . . 241 MORALITY   3
            THAT WHIRLS THE SPIRIT FROM ITSELF AWAY   . . . . 243 SUMMER NIGHT   30
            AND WE HAVE SHOWN ON EACH SPIRIT AND POWER . . . . 246 BURIED LIFE   58
            THEN WILLING LET MY SPIRIT GO   . . . . 251 WISH   51
            THE BECK OF THE SPIRIT LIKE HIM   . . . . 253 FUTURE   49
            AT THE STRAITS FAILD THAT SPIRIT BRAVE   . . . . 275 STANZAS CARNAC   46
            THAT SPIRIT IF ALL HAVE NOT YET DIED   . . . . . 276 SOUTHERN NIGHT   35
            OF A GENTLE SPIRIT NOW DEAD   . . . . 280 HAWORTH CHURCH   5
            HAIL TO THE SPIRIT WHICH DARED . . . . 281 HAWORTH CHURCH   41
            OF THE SPIRIT IN WHOM THOU DOST LIVE   . . . . . 287 RUGBY CHAPEL   47
            THY SPIRIT OF THAT WE SAW   . . . . 290 RUGBY CHAPEL   137
            HEINES SPIRIT OUTWORN   . . . . 296 HEINES GRAVE   148
            THE SPIRIT OF THE WORLD . . . . 298 HEINES GRAVE   206
            OF THE SPIRIT IN WHOM WE EXIST . . . . 298 HEINES GRAVE   216
            SPIRIT WHO FILLEST US ALL   . . . . 298 HEINES GRAVE   218
            SPIRIT WHO UTTEREST IN EACH   . . . . 298 HEINES GRAVE   219
            A WOUNDED HUMAN SPIRIT TURNS   . . . . 307 OBERMANN   23
            STRONG WAS HE WITH A SPIRIT FREE   . . . . 308 OBERMANN   61
            ACROSS HER SPIRIT GREY   . . . . 316 OBERMANN MORE   114
            MY RAVISHD SPIRIT TOO   . . . . 317 OBERMANN MORE   144
            YET WITH A LIGHT UNCAREWORN SPIRIT TURNS   . . . . 351 MEROPE   614
            WHAT MOOD OF SPIRIT THEREFORE SHALL WE CALL . . . 404 MEROPE   1991
            WHOSE SPRING OF HOPE IS DRIED WHOSE SPIRIT HAS FAILD   438 EMPEDOCLES II   317
            EVEN OF THAT ARDENT SPIRIT HOPES AND FEARS . . . . 469 ALARIC AT ROME   178
            ALAS THAT FIERY SPIRIT LITTLE KNEW . . . . 469 ALARIC AT ROME   187
            STILL SHOULD THE SPIRIT HOLD COMMUNION ROME WITH THEE 470 ALARIC AT ROME   210
            ALL THESE HAD STIRRD THY SPIRIT AND THINE EYE   . . 472 CROMWELL   31
            THAT BOUND HIS SPIRIT AND HIS HEART AWOKE . . . . 475 CROMWELL   132
            AND MAKE THE WORLDS DEAD SPIRIT LEAP AGAIN . . . . 481 HUNGARIAN NAT   11

SPIRIT   (CONTINUED)
        AND OFT THE SPIRIT PENT AT HOME • • • • • •   483 ROME-SICKNESS   2
        OF A SPIRIT SOFTLY CLEAR • • • • • • • •   META CLOISTER   22
        IN WHOSE CAPACIOUS SPIRIT LAY HIS PLAN • • • •   LUCRETIUS 5   4
        IN WHOSE PROPHETIC SPIRIT LAY THE PLAN • • • •   LUCRETIUS 5   V 4

SPIRITED
        HIS SPIRITED AIR AND WONDERD WHO HE WAS • • • •   70 SOHRAB RUSTUM   312

SPIRITS
        SO MANY FIERY SPIRITS QUITE COOLD DOWN • • • •   37 WORLDS TRIUMPHS   6
        BECAUSE OUR SPIRITS HAVE FORGOT • • • • • •   60 RESIGNATION   276
        FOR HAUGHTY SPIRITS AND HIGH WRATHS ARE RIFE • •   115 BALDER DEAD 3   79
        IN WHOSE HOT AIR OUR SPIRITS ARE UPCURLD • • •   153 TRISTRAM 3   120
        OUR SPIRITS HAVE GROWN • • • • • • • •   177 PARTING   72
        THOUGHTS LIGHT LIKE GLEAMS MY SPIRITS SKY • • •   209 DESPONDENCY   5
        DELICATE SPIRITS PUSHD AWAY • • • • • • •   219 BACCHANALIA 2   17
        THEY HAVE DECLARED THE SPIRITS SORE • • • • •   224 EPILOG LAOCOON   93
        ON SPIRITS THAT HAD LONG BEEN DEAD • • • • •   272 MEMORIAL VERSES   55
        SPIRITS DRIED UP AND CLOSELY FURLD • • • • •   272 MEMORIAL VERSES   56
        OUR SPIRITS IN A BRAZEN ROUND • • • • • •   271 MEMORIAL VERSES V 46
        SPIRITS DEEP-CRUSHED AND CLOSELY FURLD • • • •   272 MEMORIAL VERSES V 56
        I KNEW HIS SPIRITS LOW • • • • • • • •   272 EDW QUILLINAN   2
        GIBING OF SPIRITS IN SCORN • • • • • • •   293 HEINES GRAVE   42
        BITTER SPIRITS YE CLAIM • • • • • • • •   293 HEINES GRAVE   46
        YET OF THE SPIRITS WHO HAVE REIGND • • • • •   307 OBERMANN   45
        THOUGH ALL FREE SPIRITS IN THIS LAND WERE DEAD • • 383 MEROPE   1377
        THOUGH ALL FREE SPIRITS IN THIS LAND BE DEAD • •   383 MEROPE   V1377
        FOR SOMETHING HAS IMPAIRD THY SPIRITS STRENGTH • • 429 EMPEDOCLES II   21
        BY SPIRITS GLORIOUSLY GAY • • • • • • •   450 GEISTS GRAVE   18
        BREATHE THERE NOT SPIRITS ON THE PEOPLED AIR • •   468 ALARIC AT ROME   163
        THOSE STERNER SPIRITS LET ME PRIZE • • • • •   481 COURAGE   9
        ALL YOUR SPIRITS HISTORY GLEANS • • • • • •   META CLOISTER   36

SPITALFIELDS
        IN SPITALFIELDS LOOKD THRICE DISPIRITED • • • •   169 EAST LONDON   4

SPITE
        BREATHING SELF-MURDER FRENZY SPITE • • • • • • 157 SAINT BRANDAN   31
        YET STILL IN SPITE OF TRUTH • • • • • • • •   424 EMPEDOCLES I 2   367
        IN SPITE OF HOPES ENTOMBD • • • • • • • •   424 EMPEDOCLES I 2   368
        BUSY FOR PRIAMS FAME AND MY OWN IN SPITE OF THE FUTURE   HOMER TRANS   19

SPITEFUL
        TO HAVE RAISD FAITHFUL FRIENDS AND CUT DOWN   425 EMPEDOCLES I 2 V 401
                SPITEFUL FOES

SPITS
        TO SHOW HIM SPITS AND BEACHES OF THE SEA • • • • 122 BALDER DEAD 3   321
        THE SANDY SPITS THE SHORE-LOCKD LAKES • • • •   275 SOUTHERN NIGHT   1

SPLASHING
        THE SPLASHING ICY FOUNTAINS PLAY • • • • • •   300 GRANDE CHARTR   33

SPLENDOUR
        CALLD HISTORY KEEPS A SPLENDOUR DUE TO WIT • • • •   5 DUKE WELLINGTON   13
        FREELY DID THEY FLASH THEIR SPLENDOUR • • • •   35 NEW SIRENS   257
        WHERE MANY A SPLENDOUR FINDS ITS TOMB • • • •   220 BACCHANALIA 2   22
        OR THE BRIEF SPLENDOUR OF THAT METEOR LIGHT • •   463 ALARIC AT ROME   29

SPLINTERD
        SPLINTERD THE SILVER ARROWS OF THE MOON • • • •   11 MYCERINUS   99

SPLINTERS
        SPLINTERS OF PINE-WOOD SOAKD WITH TURPENTINE • • 118 BALDER DEAD 3   168

SPLIT
        AND SPLIT HIS CURRENTS THAT FOR MANY A LEAGUE • • 87 SOHRAB RUSTUM   883

SPOIL
        SPENT IS THE SPOIL HE WON • • • • • • • •   51 CONSOLATION   38
        COUNTS HIS DAYS SPOIL THE SPOTTED TROUT • • • • 248 KENSINGTON GARD   20
        RAVIN A LITTLE WHILE IN SPOIL AND BLOOD • • • • 339 MEROPE   297
        NO WEAKNESS SPOIL OUR LOT • • • • • • • •   421 EMPEDOCLES I 2   263

SPOILD
        THESE OFFERINGS HOME OUR RITES ARE SPOILD TO-DAY • • 336 MEROPE   196
        AND PRAISED AND SPOILD BY MASTER AND BY GUESTS • • 407 EMPEDOCLES I 1   34
        SHALL WE WITH TEMPER SPOILD • • • • • • • •   425 EMPEDOCLES I 2   392
        SHALL WE WITH TEMPERS SPOILD • • • • • • • •   425 EMPEDOCLES I 2 V 392

SPOILER
        FATES THREATNINGS ARE NOT VAIN THE SPOILER   466 ALARIC AT ROME   120
                COMES NOT SLOW

SPOILS
        WITH SPOILS AND HONOUR WHEN THE WAR IS DONE • •   79 SOHRAB RUSTUM   595
        OF MAD DELIGHT THEY DROP THEIR SPOILS AND BOUND • • 150 TRISTRAM 3   27
        WHICH THOUGH IT GIVES NO BLISS YET SPOILS FOR REST   261 SCHOLAR-GIPSY   223

SPOILST
        O GODS FOOLISH OLD MAN THOU SPOILST MY BLOW • •   374 MEROPE   1194

SPOKE

HE SPOKE THE MONARCH HEARD	47	WORLD QUIETIST	V 28
HE SPOKE THE GREAT KING HEARD	47	WORLD QUIETIST	V 28
HE SPOKE AND PERAN-WISA TOOK THE HAND	63	SOHRAB RUSTUM	63
HE SPOKE BUT RUSTUM ANSWERD WITH A SMILE	67	SOHRAB RUSTUM	220
HE SPOKE AND SMILED AND GUDURZ MADE REPLY	68	SOHRAB RUSTUM	242
HE SPOKE AND FROWND AND GUDURZ TURND AND RAN	69	SOHRAB RUSTUM	260
HE SPOKE AND SOHRAB ANSWERD ON HIS FEET	72	SOHRAB RUSTUM	379
HE SPOKE AND RUSTUM ANSWERD NOT BUT HURLD	73	SOHRAB RUSTUM	398
BUT COURTEOUSLY DREW BACK AND SPOKE AND SAID	74	SOHRAB RUSTUM	426
HE SPOKE AND SOHRAB KINDLED AT HIS TAUNTS	75	SOHRAB RUSTUM	470
HE SPOKE AND AS HE CEASED HE WEPT ALOUD	79	SOHRAB RUSTUM	602
HE SPOKE BUT RUSTUM LISTEND PLUNGED IN THOUGHT	79	SOHRAB RUSTUM	604
WHO SPOKE ALTHOUGH HE CALLD BACK NAMES HE KNEW	79	SOHRAB RUSTUM	606
HE SPOKE AND ALL THE BLOOD LEFT RUSTUMS CHEEKS	80	SOHRAB RUSTUM	661
HE SPOKE BUT RUSTUM GAZED AND GAZED AND STOOD	81	SOHRAB RUSTUM	689
WHEN FIRST I SAW THEE AND THY HEART SPOKE TOO	82	SOHRAB RUSTUM	712
HE SPOKE AND SOHRAB SMILED ON HIM AND TOOK	85	SOHRAB RUSTUM	838
BETWIXT THE SILENT HOSTS AND SPOKE AND SAID	65	SOHRAB RUSTUM	V 149
HE SPOKE AND PERAN-WISA TURND AND STRODE	66	SOHRAB RUSTUM	V 187
AND TURND AWAY AND SPOKE TO HIS OWN SOUL	71	SOHRAB RUSTUM	V 346
AND WITH A SOOTHING VOICE HE SPOKE AND SAID	82	SOHRAB RUSTUM	V 707
VENGEANCE O KING BUT THE KING SPOKE	89	SICK KING BOKH	V 39
HE SPOKE THE MOTHER OF THE GODS REPLIED	98	BALDER DEAD 1	111
SHE SPOKE BUT HODER ANSWERD HER AND SAID	100	BALDER DEAD 1	184
SHE SPOKE AND ON HER FACE LET FALL HER VEIL	100	BALDER DEAD 1	192
SO HAVING SPOKE THE KING OF GODS AROSE	96	BALDER DEAD 1	V 46
HE SPOKE AND GRAVE REPLIED THE SOLEMN QUEEN	110	BALDER DEAD 2	201
HE SPOKE AND ALL THE GODS TO ODIN LOOKD	115	BALDER DEAD 3	47
HE SPOKE AND THE GODS ARMD AND ODIN DONND	115	BALDER DEAD 3	57
HE SPOKE AND NIORD SET FORTH BACK TO HEAVEN	124	BALDER DEAD 3	373
HE SPOKE BUT HODER ANSWERD HIM AND SAID	124	BALDER DEAD 3	394
HE SPOKE AND WAVED FAREWELL AND GAVE HIS HAND	129	BALDER DEAD 3	549
WHO SPOKE THESE WORDS NO SHADOW EVER CAME	169	WORLDLY PLACE	10
SO SPOKE THE IMPERIAL SAGE PUREST OF MEN	168	WORLDLY PLACE	V 2
HE SPOKE AND LOOSED OUR HEART IN TEARS	271	MEMORIAL VERSES	47
SPOKE AND REVEALD THAT TRAFFIC AND THE TRAITOR	365	MEROPE	V
I SPOKE WITH HIM THIS MORNING ONCE MORE THEREFORE	412	EMPEDOCLES I 2	19

SPORT

TO THE HALL WHAT SPORT WHAT SPORT	14	CHURCH BROU 1	44
TO THE HALL WHAT SPORT WHAT SPORT	14	CHURCH BROU 1	44
WHICH ALL THE GODS IN SPORT HAD IDLY THROWN	95	BALDER DEAD 1	3
AT WHOM THE GODS IN SPORT THEIR WEAPONS THREW	98	BALDER DEAD 1	103
BROTHER AND FELLOW-SPORT OF LOK WITH ME	125	BALDER DEAD 3	412
OF PLACES WE HAD PASSD SPORT WE HAD HAD	356	MEROPE	756
ASK OF THE POWERS THAT SPORT WITH MAN	481	DESTINY	4

SPORTS

FILL WITH THEIR SPORTS THE FIELD	218	BACCHANALIA 1	38
SHE BROKE HER FLUTES SHE STOPPD HER SPORTS	316	OBERMANN MORE	129
THE SPORTS OF THE COUNTRY-PEOPLE	436	EMPEDOCLES II	251

SPOT

FROM THE STREAMS BRINK THE SPOT WHERE FIRST A BOAT	61	SOHRAB RUSTUM	18
TO DIE BY STONING ON THE SPOT	91	SICK KING BOKH	112
ALL SPOTS MATCHD WITH THAT SPOT ARE LESS DIVINE	167	RACHEL 1	13
HOW CHANGED IS HERE EACH SPOT MAN MAKES OR FILLS	262	THYRSIS	1
BLOW OFF THE SPOT OF MURDER FROM HIS NAME	336	MEROPE	200
THAT SPOT THE SOLITARY SCENE	480	HAYSWATER BOAT	24

SPOTLESS

THAT SPOTLESS HANDS UNSHAKEN SCEPTRES HOLD	388	MEROPE	1519

SPOTS

ALL SPOTS MATCHD WITH THAT SPOT ARE LESS DIVINE	167	RACHEL 1	13
THE SPOTS WHICH RECALL HIM SURVIVE	228	YOUTH OF NATURE	13
THE STORY OF SPOTS MENTIOND TO HIS OWN	356	MEROPE	767
IN THE HIGH UNFREQUENTED MOUNTAIN-SPOTS	409	EMPEDOCLES I 1	93
THE BOORS WITH WHOM HE TALKD THE COUNTRY-SPOTS HE KNEW	426	EMPEDOCLES I 2	416

SPOTTED

COUNTS HIS DAYS SPOIL THE SPOTTED TROUT	248	KENSINGTON GARD	20
FRESHENING ITS CURRENT AND SPOTTED WITH FOAM	254	FUTURE	80
AND PURPLE ORCHISES WITH SPOTTED LEAVES	257	SCHOLAR-GIPSY	89

SPRANG

AND WITH A CRY SPRANG UP AND DROPPD THE BIRD	67	SOHRAB RUSTUM	203
AND SPRANG ASIDE QUICK AS A FLASH THE SPEAR	73	SOHRAB RUSTUM	403
ONE STROKE BUT AGAIN SOHRAB SPRANG ASIDE	73	SOHRAB RUSTUM	417
SPRANG IN A THOUSAND SHIVERS ON THE HELM	76	SOHRAB RUSTUM	512
BUT SOHRAB HEARD AND QUAILD NOT BUT SPRANG ON	76	SOHRAB RUSTUM	V 509
SHE SPAKE BUT DOWN OFF SLEIPNER HERMOD SPRANG	110	BALDER DEAD 2	186
THY DELUGE AND FROM HIM THE GIANTS SPRANG	121	BALDER DEAD 3	273
I SPRANG UP I THREW ROUND ME	186	STRAYED REVEL	29
AND HEAVENWARD FROM THE FOUNTAIN-BRINK HE SPRANG	268	THYRSIS	189
WE SPRANG UPON OUR FEET WE SNATCHD OUR SPEARS	357	MEROPE	789
WHILE FROM THE TURF WHEREON I LAY I SPRANG	358	MEROPE	829
LAIAS IN ARMS SPRANG TO HIS NEPHEWS SIDE	402	MEROPE	1933

SPRANG   (CONTINUED)
        SPRANG FROM ITS SLEEP AND LO THE WATERS ROLL   • • 479 CROMWELL   236

SPRAY
        AND NEVER A SPRAY OF YEW • • • • • • • • • •   20 REQUIESCAT   2
        AND AS A SPRAY OF HONEYSUCKLE FLOWERS   • • • • 101 BALDER DEAD 1   230
        YES THE SPRAY IS ON THY CLOAK AND HAIR   • • • • 142 TRISTRAM 2   18
        AND THEN THE BEACH AND MARKD WITH SPRAY   • • • • 148 TRISTRAM 2   172
        HE SAW ON SPRAY–SWEPT HEBRIDES • • • • • • • •   156 SAINT BRANDAN   7
        CHAMP AND CHAFE AND TOSS IN THE SPRAY   • • • • 161 FORSAKEN MERM   7
        ONLY FROM THE LONG LINE OF SPRAY   • • • • • •   211 DOVER BEACH   7
        RAPT TWIRLING IN THY HAND A WITHERD SPRAY • • • • 258 SCHOLAR–GIPSY   119
        THE TENDER PURPLE SPRAY ON COPSE AND BRIERS • •   263 THYRSIS   18
        PLANTED HIS FOOTSTEP THE SPRAY • • • • • • • •   289 RUGBY CHAPEL   97
        SPRAY–DRIZZLED LONELY   • • • • • • • • • •   392 MEROPE   1647
        ETERNAL SHOWERS OF SPRAY ON THE MOSSD ROOTS • •   414 EMPEDOCLES I 2   47
        STRESS OF GALE AND SHOWERS OF SPRAY • • • • • •   457 POOR MATTHIAS   178

SPRAYS
        WHERE THE NICHED SNOW–BED SPRAYS DOWN   • • • • 176 PARTING   49

SPREAD
        THE SOLEMN HILLS AROUND US SPREAD • • • • •   60 RESIGNATION   266
        A DOME OF LATHS AND OER IT FELTS WERE SPREAD • • 61 SOHRAB RUSTUM   23
        IN MARCHING ORDER SPREAD OF LONG–NECKD CRANES • • 64 SOHRAB RUSTUM   112
        THY COURAGE OR THY CRAFT AND SPREAD THY FAME • • 77 SOHRAB RUSTUM   535
        AND HE BEHELD SPREAD ROUND HIM HELAS REALM • • • 109 BALDER DEAD 2   149
        AND MORNING OVER ALL THE WORLD WAS SPREAD • • •   119 BALDER DEAD 3   213
        AND ONCE MORE HERMOD SAW AROUND HIM SPREAD • • • 124 BALDER DEAD 3   379
        OVER THE SICK MANS FEET IS SPREAD • • • • •   131 TRISTRAM 1   15
        ARE SPREAD AND UPFURLD   • • • • • • • • •   177 PARTING   88
        SPREAD WIDE AWAY THE LUMINOUS PLAIN • • • • •   204 CALAIS SANDS   V   6
        SEE ON HER FACE A GLOW IS SPREAD   • • • • • •   241 MORALITY   21
        THE BLUE HAZE–CRADLED MOUNTAINS SPREAD AWAY • •   242 SUMMER NIGHT   21
        THE WIDE AERIAL LANDSCAPE SPREAD   • • • • •   250 WISH   34
        THE OUT–SPREAD WORLD TO SPAN • • • • • •   415 EMPEDOCLES I 2   77
        AND JOY IN LIGHT AND POWER TO SPREAD THE JOY • • 446 WESTMIN ABBEY   80
        ARISE AND ARM THEE SPREAD THY BANNERS FORTH • •   465 ALARIC AT ROME   95
        AND STRUCK AND OER US THE SEA–WATERS SPREAD • •   484 S S LUSITANIA   8

SPREADING
        THE BARE HEATHS SPREADING CLEAR AS DAY   • • • • 141 TRISTRAM 1   364
        THE LONE UNBROKEN VIEW GOES SPREADING CLEAR • • •   TRISTRAM 3   V 12
        SPREADING OER THE THUNDERERS FACE • • • • • •   431 EMPEDOCLES II   68

SPREADS
        SPREADS ITS COLD LIGHT WIDER ALL THAT WHILE • •   33 NEW SIRENS   218
        FAR TO THE SOUTH BEYOND THE BLUE THERE SPREADS • • 128 BALDER DEAD 3   518
        THE LONE UNBROKEN VIEW SPREADS BRIGHT AND CLEAR • 150 TRISTRAM 3   12
        THE ACONITE SPREADS • • • • • • • • • • •   176 PARTING   52
        NOW ROUND US SPREADS THE WATERY PLAIN • • • •   182 TO MARG CONT   17
        HE SPREADS OUT HIS ARMS TO THE LIGHT • • • • •   251 FUTURE   5
        BEFORE THY FEET THIS RECENT CITY SPREADS • • • • 330 MEROPE   9

SPRENT
        THE CHEEK GROWN THIN THE BROWN HAIR SPRENT WITH GREY 266 THYRSIS   135

SPRIGHTLIER
        ON HIS PERCH A SPRIGHTLIER BIRD   • • • • • •   458 POOR MATTHIAS   193

SPRING
        SPRING THE FOUNDATIONS OF THAT SHADOWY THRONE • • 4 BUTLERS SERMONS   6
        SPRING THE FOUNDATIONS OF THE SHADOWY THRONE • •   4 BUTLERS SERMONS V 6
        BENT TO THE COLD WINDS OF THE SHOWERLESS SPRING • • 12 MYCERINUS   120
        HERE SHE CAME A BRIDE IN SPRING • • • • • •   13 CHURCH BROU 1   14
        NOT DAILY LABOURS DULL LETHAEAN SPRING   • • • • 43 GIPSY CHILD   54
        LIKE SPRING FLOWERS • • • • • • • • • • •   44 QUESTION   9
        SPRING THE GREAT STREAMS • • • • • • • •   45 IN UTRUMQUE PAR   21
        AS WHEN SOME HUNTER IN THE SPRING HATH FOUND • •   77 SOHRAB RUSTUM   556
        THE SPRING THAT BUBBLES UP BY HELAS THRONE • • •   108 BALDER DEAD 2   131
        THESE FLOW BY HELAS THRONE AND NEAR THEIR SPRING • • 109 BALDER DEAD 2 155
        ANOTHER NOTE AND LIKE A BIRD IN SPRING   • • • • 117 BALDER DEAD 3   142
        AT WINTERS END BEFORE THE SPRING BEGINS   • • • • 122 BALDER DEAD 3   308
        ALL THE SPRING–TIME OF HIS LOVE • • • • • •   136 TRISTRAM 1   173
        MILD SHINES THE COLD SPRING IN THE MOONS CLEAR LIGHT 139 TRISTRAM 1   283
        WHICH KILLS IN US THE BLOOM THE YOUTH THE SPRING • • 153 TRISTRAM 3   122
        AND A FRESH BREATH OF SPRING STIRRD EVERYWHERE • • 155 TRISTRAM 3   200
        WHEN SPRING–TIDES ARE LOW • • • • • • • • •   165 FORSAKEN MERM   127
        AGAIN I SPRING TO MAKE MY CHOICE   • • • • • •   174 MEETING   9
        AND THEY ARE SWEPT BY BALMS OF SPRING   • • • • 182 TO MARG CONT   8
        IN THE UNKIND SPRING HAVE GNAWN   • • • • • •   193 STRAYED REVEL   238
        LIKE SHADOWS FORTH IN SPRING • • • • • • • •   193 STRAYED REVEL   243
        IN THE UNKIND SPRING HAVE GNAWD   • • • • • •   193 STRAYED REVEL   V 238
        I MUST NOT SPRING TO GRASP THY HAND • • • • •   205 CALAIS SANDS   25
        I MUST NOT SPRING TO TOUCH THY HAND • • • • •   205 CALAIS SANDS   V 25
        COLD BUBBLED THE SPRING OF TILPHUSA • • • • •   229 YOUTH OF NATURE   36
        THE THEBAN SEER TO THE SPRING • • • • • • • •   229 YOUTH OF NATURE   44
        AS SHE WAS IN HER MORNING OF SPRING • • • • •   231 YOUTH OF NATURE   112
        NOT WITH THE RAPTURE OF SPRING • • • • • • •   233 YOUTH OF MAN   22
        COME LIKE THE BREATH OF THE SPRING • • • • • •   234 YOUTH OF MAN   56

SPRING   (CONTINUED)
        THE SPRING-TIDES BRIMMING FLOW • • • • • • • • 242 SUMMER NIGHT   16
        AS DEEP AS PELLUCID A SPRING • • • • • • • • • 252 FUTURE   39
        SHEPHERDS HAD MET HIM ON THE HURST IN SPRING • • 256 SCHOLAR-GIPSY   57
        HUMID THE AIR LEAFLESS YET SOFT AS SPRING • • • • 263 THYRSIS   17
        AND WE SHALL HAVE HIM IN THE SWEET SPRING-DAYS • • 265 THYRSIS   73
        AND HOPE ONCE CRUSHD LESS QUICK TO SPRING AGAIN • • 266 THYRSIS   140
        LIGHT TO SPRING UP TO THY HOUSE • • • • • • • 343 MEROPE   407
        GIVES HER NAME TO THE SPRING • • • • • • • • 343 MEROPE   432
        PAST ARNE SPRING WHERE RHEA GAVE THE BABE • • • • 355 MEROPE   736
        MISERY WHICH ROUSES OTHERS BREAKS THE SPRING • • 366 MEROPE   1025
        LIGHT TO SPRING UP TO THY RACE • • • • • • • 343 MEROPE   V 407
        TO HAVE LIVED LIGHT IN THE SPRING • • • • • • 425 EMPEDOCLES I 2   399
        WHOSE SPRING OF HOPE IS DRIED WHOSE SPIRIT HAS FAILD 438 EMPEDOCLES II   317
        IN THE SPRING BY THEIR ROAD • • • • • • • • 442 EMPEDOCLES II   454
        WHAT SPRING OF YOUTH IN THAT MAJESTIC MIEN • • • • 477 CROMWELL   185
        THE COMING SPRING-TIMES EARLIEST STIR • • • • 483 ROME-SICKNESS   6

SPRINGING
        THE RED-GROUSE SPRINGING AT OUR SOUND • • • •   54 RESIGNATION   70
        SELF-SPRINGING AND A SEED OF MAN PRESERVED • • • 128 BALDER DEAD 3   530
        AND THE SPRINGING BUSTARD-FOWL • • • • • • • 191 STRAYED REVEL   174
        THE SPRINGING PASTURES AND THE FEEDING KINE • • 258 SCHOLAR-GIPSY   108

SPRINGS
        COLD-BUBBLING SPRINGS OR CAVES NOT SO THE SOUL • •   6 GEO CRUIKSHANK   9
        WHERE THE SPRINGS OF KNOWLEDGE ARE • • • • • •   27 NEW SIRENS   34
        FROM THE GOLDEN SPRINGS OF DAWN • • • • • • •   26 NEW SIRENS   V 22
        O WAKING ON A WORLD WHICH THUS-WISE SPRINGS • •   45 IN UTRUMQUE PAR   8
        THERE SPRINGS THE BROOK WILL GUIDE US DOWN • • •   54 RESIGNATION   76
        BY THEIR DARK SPRINGS THE WIND IN WINTER-TIME • •   73 SOHRAB RUSTUM   413
        OF WISDOM WHICH BENEATH THE ASHTREE SPRINGS • • 120 BALDER DEAD 3   220
        TWO SPRINGS WHICH CLOSE BY ONE ANOTHER PLAY • • 170 EAST AND WEST   2
        LORN AUTUMNS AND TRIUMPHANT SPRINGS • • • • • 181 ISOLATION MARG   34
        AMONG THEIR SAVAGE GORGES AND COLD SPRINGS • • • 198 FRAG DEJANEIRA   9
        WAS BLINDED BY THE OUTGUSHING SPRINGS OF BRINE • • 357 MEROPE   778
        AND WHERE THE SOAKING SPRINGS ABOUND • • • • • 414 EMPEDOCLES I 2   64
        A NEW-MADE WORLD UP-SPRINGS • • • • • • • • 418 EMPEDOCLES I 2   179
        WHAT SPRINGS OF THOUGHT THEY USE • • • • • • 423 EMPEDOCLES I 2   329
        WHERE MAEANDERS SPRINGS ARE BORN • • • • • • 433 EMPEDOCLES II   136
        FROM WHOSE PATHETIC SOUL-FED SPRINGS • • • • • 450 GEISTS GRAVE   14

SPRINKLED
        SPRINKLED WITH HOLLY TREES AND JUNIPER • • • •   TRISTRAM 3   V 18
        THIN-SPRINKLED WITH FARMS • • • • • • • • 175 PARTING   6
        SPRINKLED AND SMOOTHED • • • • • • • • • • 194 STRAYED REVEL   267

SPRITES
        LOVERS OF CHANGE YE ARE FASTIDIOUS SPRITES • • • • 123 BALDER DEAD 3   339

SPRUNG
        THINE ELDEST AND OF ME THE GODS ARE SPRUNG • • • 121 BALDER DEAD 3   285
        SPRUNG FROM THE BLOOD OF ISRAELS SCATTERD RACE • • 168 RACHEL 3   1
        A NEW-SPRUNG WORLD INFORM • • • • • • • • 319 OBERMANN MORE   200
        FROM THE AEOLIAN STOCK OF NELEUS SPRUNG • • • • 337 MEROPE   236
        THIS AWE WHICH GUARDS OUR EARTH-SPRUNG LINEAL KINGS 389 MEROPE   1543
        TOGETHER WE HAD SPRUNG TOGETHER LIVED • • • • 334 MEROPE   V 123

SPUN
        OF LITTLE THREADS OUR LIFE IS SPUN • • • • •   48 HORATIAN ECHO   25
        THE NORNIES WHEN HIS MOTHER BARE HIM SPUN • • •   96 BALDER DEAD 1   24
        FOR THE WHEEL WHERE I SPUN • • • • • • • • 164 FORSAKEN MERM   92
        OF BUT ONE STUFF ARE SPUN • • • • • • • • 422 EMPEDOCLES I 2   288
        THE SCHEME OURSELVES HAVE SPUN • • • • • • • 422 EMPEDOCLES I 2   313

SPUR
        THERE ON A HIGH GREEN SPUR WHICH BATHES ITS POINT   356 MEROPE   751
        ON THAT SAME SPUR WHERE WE HAD SATE AT MORN • • 357 MEROPE   796
        THERE ON A GRASSY SPUR WHICH BATHES ITS ROOT • • 356 MEROPE   V 751
        ON THE SAME SPUR WHERE WE HAD SATE AT MORN • • • 357 MEROPE   V 796
        WILL GOAD OUR SENSES WITH A SHARPER SPUR • • • 440 EMPEDOCLES II   379

SPURN
        TO SPURN MANS COMMON LURE LIFES PLEASANT THINGS • •   9 MYCERINUS   32
        BE GUIDED O MY SON SPURN COUNSEL NOT • • • • • 382 MEROPE   1328
        WE SPURN IT AND INVENT • • • • • • • • • 419 EMPEDOCLES I 2   225
        WE SPURN THEM AND INVENT • • • • • • • • • 419 EMPEDOCLES I 2 V 225

SPURND
        NOT BY THE JUSTICE THAT MY FATHER SPURND • • •   8 MYCERINUS   1
        WITH FEET THAT SPURND THE GROUND LO MILTON THERE • • 477 CROMWELL   175

SPURNST
        HOW ANGRILY THOU SPURNST ALL SIMPLER FARE • • • • 170 BETTER PART   2

SPURRD
        SUCH AS ERE NOW HATH SPURRD TO FEARFUL DEEDS • • 366 MEROPE   1012
        DESIREDST THOU WHAT TRULY SPURRD THEE ON • • • • 404 MEROPE   1980
        THE THOUGHT THAT SPURRD IT AND A DAUNTLESS WILL • • 478 CROMWELL   228

SPURS
    FROM THE PINE-DOTTED SPURS   • • • • • • • • • 197 FRAG ANTIGONE   61
    OER THE GRACIOUS SPURS COMING DOWN • • • • • • 297 HEINES GRAVE   179

SPY
    PEERING TO SPY A GOAT-TRACK DOWN THE CLIFF • • • • 357 MEROPE   804

SQUADRONS
    THREADING THE TARTAR SQUADRONS TO THE FRONT   • • 65 SOHRAB RUSTUM   142
    A THRILL THROUGH ALL THE TARTAR SQUADRONS RAN   • • 65 SOHRAB RUSTUM   158
    BACK THROUGH THE OPENING SQUADRONS TO HIS TENT   • • 66 SOHRAB RUSTUM   188
    SWIFT THROUGH THE TARTAR SQUADRONS TO THE FRONT   • • 65 SOHRAB RUSTUM   V 142
    SLOW THROUGH THE TARTAR SQUADRONS TO THE FRONT   • • 65 SOHRAB RUSTUM   V 142

SQUALID
    SMOTE ON THE SQUALID STREETS OF BETHNAL GREEN   • • 169 EAST LONDON   2

SQUALLS
    AND CAME DOWN MOANING TO THE SEA FIRST SQUALLS   • • 118 BALDER DEAD 3   182
    ON HIS MOUNTAIN LAKE BUT SQUALLS   • • • • • 193 STRAYED REVEL   236

SQUANDER
    GATHER AND SQUANDER ARE RAISED • • • • • • • 288 RUGBY CHAPEL   63

SQUANDERD
    MUCH HAST HAD HAST SQUANDERD MUCH   • • • • • • 22 MEMORY-PICTURE   V

SQUARE
    THE CHURCHYARD WALL THAT CLIPS THE SQUARE • • • • 16 CHURCH BROU 2   12
    AND THROUGH THE SQUARE HIS WAY HE TOOK   • • • 89 SICK KING BOKH   49
    AND THROUGH THE SQUARE HIS PATH HE TOOK   • • • 89 SICK KING BOKH   V 49
    AND ALL ARE MARSHALLD IN ONE FLAMING SQUARE   • • 127 BALDER DEAD 3   480
    CROUCHD ON THE PAVEMENT CLOSE BY BELGRAVE SQUARE • 169 WEST LONDON   1
    FOR WHEN THIS MORNING IN THE PUBLIC SQUARE • • • 401 MEROPE   1895
    THE ALTAR IN THE MIDDLE OF THE SQUARE   • • • 401 MEROPE   1908

SQUARES
    AND ON EACH SIDE ARE SQUARES OF STANDING CORN   • • 70 SOHRAB RUSTUM   295
    SO ON EACH SIDE WERE SQUARES OF MEN WITH SPEARS   • • 70 SOHRAB RUSTUM   297
    GRAPE-SYRUP SQUARES OF COLOURD ICE • • • • • 94 SICK KING BOKH   196

SQUAT
    PROUD OF PORT THOUGH SOMETHING SQUAT • • • • • • 457 POOR MATTHIAS   189

SQUEAMISH
    SO YE GROW SQUEAMISH GODS AND SNIFF AT HEAVEN   • • 123 BALDER DEAD 3   344

SQUIRES
    THE CAPTAIN OF HIS SQUIRES AND HIS GUARD   • • • • 355 MEROPE   729

SQUIRRELS
    YOU SAW THE BRIGHT-EYED SQUIRRELS DART ALONG   • • 155 TRISTRAM 3   195

ST
    AND SHE DIED AT THE ST JOHN   • • • • • • • • 16 CHURCH BROU 1   112
    HOW HIS ST PETERS CHURCH IN THORNEY ISLE   • • • 445 WESTMIN ABBEY   49
    I CROSSD ST GEORGES HILL TO-DAY   • • • • • 484 ROME-SICKNESS   13

STAB
    AND PIERCE HIM LIKE A STAB AND MAKE HIM LEAP   • • 78 SOHRAB RUSTUM   584

STABILITY
    WHAT PERMANENCE WHAT STABILITY LIKE OURS   • • • • 389 MEROPE   1544

STABLISH
    STABLISH CONTINUE OUR MARCH   • • • • • • • 292 RUGBY CHAPEL   206

STACKS
    AND RANGED THE WOOD IN STACKS BY BALDERS SHIP   • • 106 BALDER DEAD 2   68
    AND FROM THE ROOFS THE TWISTED CHIMNEY-STACKS   • • 263 THYRSIS   5

STAFF
    IN HIS RIGHT HAND A RULERS STAFF NO SWORD • • • 64 SOHRAB RUSTUM   99
    AND WITH HIS STAFF KEPT BACK THE FOREMOST RANKS • • 65 SOHRAB RUSTUM   143
    SOONER SHALL THIS MY STAFF BEAR LEAVES   • • • 160 NECKAN   51
    BUT LO THE STAFF IT BUDDED • • • • • • • 160 NECKAN   53
    BEHOLD THE STERN MAILD FATHER STAFF IN HAND   • • 167 PICT NEWSTEAD   9
    I SNATCHD UP MY VINE-CROWN MY FIR-STAFF   • • • 186 STRAYED REVEL   33
    SITTING STAFF IN HAND • • • • • • • • • 190 STRAYED REVEL   136
    GAILY THEIR PINE-STAFF GREEN • • • • • • • 218 BACCHANALIA 1   24
    WITH STAFF AND GOURD HIS WAY DID BEND • • • • 278 SOUTHERN NIGHT   81

STAG
    THE PRICKERS SHOUTED THAT THE STAG WAS GONE   • • 357 MEROPE   788
    BROKE BLACK WITH SWEAT THE ANTLERD MOUNTAIN-STAG • • 357 MEROPE   808
    STAG DOGS AND HUNTER TO THE YAWNING GULPH   • • 358 MEROPE   826
    WHERE FIRST THE STAG TOOK WATER FLOATED STILL   • • 358 MEROPE   844
    THE PRINCE IN CHASE AFTER A SWIMMING STAG • • • 363 MEROPE   959

STAGE
```
THE MELLOW GLORY OF THE ATTIC STAGE    • • • • • •      2 TO A FRIEND           13
SOME NOBLER AMPLER STAGE OF LIFE TO WIN    • • • •    169 WORLDLY PLACE         12
IT IS LAST STAGE OF ALL   • • • • • • • • • • •       213 GROWING OLD           31
CLEARING A STAGE   • • • • • • • • • • • • • •        220 BACCHANALIA 2         34
FORMS THAT WITH HIM SHALL TREAD LIFES CHANGING STAGE  476 CROMWELL            161
SOON SEEMS AS TEDIOUS AS EACH TEDIOUS STAGE    • •        LUCRETIUS 6           4
```

STAGES
```
THE STAGES OF THEIR QUIET DAY   • • • • • • • •          KENSINGTON GARD    V 32
```

STAGGER
```
THEY FAINT THEY STAGGER TO AND FRO   • • • • • •      226 EPILOG LAOCOON       173
STAGGER FOR EVER IN VAIN • • • • • • • • • • •        291 RUGBY CHAPEL         186
```

STAGGERING
```
HE REELD AND STAGGERING BACK SANK TO THE GROUND   • •  76 SOHRAB RUSTUM        521
HE REELD AND STAGGERING BACK SUNK TO THE GROUND   • •  76 SOHRAB RUSTUM      V 521
STAGGERING ON TO HER GOAL   • • • • • • • •          295 HEINES GRAVE          92
```

STAGHOUNDS
```
WHERE HUNTERS GATHER STAGHOUNDS BAY   • • • • • •     305 GRANDE CHARTR        183
```

STAGS
```
HE HAS THE WILD STAGS FOOT THE LIONS HEART   • • • •   66 SOHRAB RUSTUM        177
HE HAS THE WILD STAGS FOOT THE LIONS HEART   • • • •   67 SOHRAB RUSTUM        216
HE HATH THE WILD STAGS FOOT THE LIONS HEART   • •     67 SOHRAB RUSTUM      V 216
```

STAGSHORN
```
OF STAGSHORN FOR THEIR HATS ANON WITH SCREAMS   • •  150 TRISTRAM 3            26
```

STAIN
```
PLAINNESS AND CLEARNESS WITHOUT SHADOW OF STAIN   • • 244 SUMMER NIGHT         76
THE CLOUDS OF SICKNESS CAST NO STAIN UPON   • • • •      FRAGMENT 8            1
```

STAIND
```
THE STAIND ARMS THE MATTED HAIR   • • • • • • •      136 TRISTRAM 1           199
ON THE BLOOD-STAIND HOME OF HIS BIRTH   • • • •      347 MEROPE              V
YOUTH STAIND WITH FOLLIES AND THE THOUGHTS OF ILL    474 CROMWELL             79
THAT STREWD THE BLOOD-STAIND PATH WHERE EMPIRE LED   478 CROMWELL            226
```

STAINS
```
ON HIS COAT WERE LEAVES AND BLOOD-STAINS   • • • •    14 CHURCH BROU 1        47
SMEARD WITH RED WINE-STAINS WHO IS HE   • • • •      188 STRAYED REVEL        90
YET STAINS OUR LAND BE BY THIS BLOOD WASHD OUT   • • 402 MEROPE             1916
YES THERE ARE STAINS TIMES FINGERS CANNOT BLOT   • • 462 ALARIC AT ROME       14
YET STAINS THERE ARE TO BLOT THY BRIGHTEST PAGE   • • 463 ALARIC AT ROME       37
```

STAIR
```
I HEAR THE BEARERS ON THE STAIR   • • • • • •        92 SICK KING BOKH       130
WHAT LIGHTS IN THE COURT WHAT STEPS ON THE STAIR  • • 142 TRISTRAM 1          373
AND FROM THE WAVE-KISSD MARBLE STAIR   • • • • • •   278 SOUTHERN NIGHT       106
CRAWLS UP ITS ROCKY STAIR   • • • • • • • • •        306 OBERMANN              2
WE HEAR THY SCUFFLE ON THE STAIR   • • • • • •       451 GEISTS GRAVE         48
```

STAIRS
```
BUT ON THE STAIRS WHAT VOICE IS THIS I HEAR   • •    175 PARTING              17
```

STALE
```
TO MAKE OUR FORMER PLEASURES ALL SEEM STALE   • •    153 TRISTRAM 3          126
```

STALK
```
EITHER A VENGEFUL FURY I SHOULD STALK   • • • •      366 MEROPE             1019
```

STALKS
```
AND ROUND GREEN ROOTS AND YELLOWING STALKS I SEE  • • 255 SCHOLAR-GIPSY        24
THE BRAZEN-FOOTED FURY EVER STALKS   • • • • • •     395 MEROPE             1734
```

STALL
```
SLEIPNER AND SLEIPNER WENT TO HIS OWN STALL   • •    102 BALDER DEAD 1        266
THEIR ARMS AND LED THEIR HORSES FROM THE STALL   • • 105 BALDER DEAD 2        12
```

STAMP
```
SUCH WERE THE DISPOSSESSORS OF WHAT STAMP   • • • •  337 MEROPE              228
AND STAMP HIMSELF THEREAFTER BAD OR GOOD   • • • •   352 MEROPE              651
AND DARES STAMP NOTHING FALSE WHERE HE FINDS         415 EMPEDOCLES I 2       91
    NOTHING SURE
```

STAMPD
```
WHEREWITH THEY STAMPD THEM DOWN AND TROD THEM DEEP   109 BALDER DEAD 2       174
```

STANCH
```
I STANCH WITH ICE MY BURNING BREAST   • • • • • •    158 SAINT BRANDAN        69
AND THE STANCH FURIES NEVER-SILENT SCOURGE   • • • • 373 MEROPE             1187
```

STAND
```
DIDST STAND ON EARTH UNGUESSD AT BETTER SO   • • • •   3 SHAKESPEARE        V 11
STAND NEVER IDLE BUT GO ALWAYS ROUND   • • • • • •     4 DUKE WELLINGTON      2
WHERE I STAND THE GRASS IS GLOWING   • • • • • •      32 NEW SIRENS          187
LOVELESS RAYLESS JOYLESS YOU SHALL STAND   • • • •    35 NEW SIRENS          266
STAND MUTE SELF-CENTRED STERN AND DREAM NO MORE   • • 42 GIPSY CHILD          32
STAND TRANCED IN JOY   • • • • • • • • • • • •        51 CONSOLATION          45
```

STAND (CONTINUED)

TIME STAND STILL HERE • • • • • • • • • •   51 CONSOLATION   50
SO PRAY THEY AND TO STAND AGAIN   • • • • • • •   53 RESIGNATION   18
A RULER OF THE PEOPLE STAND • • • • • • • • •   56 RESIGNATION   155
STAND FORTH THE WHILE AND TAKE THEIR CHALLENGE UP   66 SOHRAB RUSTUM   183
BEFORE HIM AND HE LOOKD AND SAW HIM STAND • • • •   67 SOHRAB RUSTUM   202
THE ARMIES ARE DRAWN OUT AND STAND AT GAZE • • •   67 SOHRAB RUSTUM   210
FOR WELL I KNOW THAT DID GREAT RUSTUM STAND • • •   72 SOHRAB RUSTUM   370
YET THIS THOU HAST SAID WELL DID RUSTUM STAND • •   72 SOHRAB RUSTUM   382
BUT RUSTUM IS FAR HENCE AND WE STAND HERE • • • •   72 SOHRAB RUSTUM   384
THE WATCHERS OF TWO ARMIES STAND • • • • • • •   93 SICK KING BOKH   162
TEARS STAND UPON THE LASHES OF THINE EYES • • • 103 BALDER DEAD 1   289
NOW STAND CLEAR BEFORE ME IN THE MOONLIGHT • • • 145 TRISTRAM 2   V 97
METHINKS THE WOE WHICH MADE THAT FATHER STAND • • 167 PICT NEWSTEAD   12
WHO CAN STAND STILL • • • • • • • • • • • 194 STRAYED REVEL   289
IGNORANT WHERE TO STAND OR WHOM TO AVOID • • • • 195 FRAG ANTIGONE   19
BEHOLDING HIM WHERE THE TWO PILLARS STAND • • • 198 FRAG ANTIGONE   91
AND GAZING IN HIS EYES WILL STAND • • • • • • 202 URANIA   26
BUT I MAY STAND FAR OFF AND GAZE • • • • • • 205 CALAIS SANDS   27
GLEAMS AND IS GONE THE CLIFFS OF ENGLAND STAND • • 210 DOVER BEACH   4
THOSE WILLING SERVANTS SHALL STAND • • • • • • 216 LORDS MESSENGER   11
THE MOUNTAINS STAND AT ITS HEAD • • • • • • 228 YOUTH OF NATURE   5
SEE THEM TO-NIGHT WHERE THEY STAND • • • • • • 232 YOUTH OF MAN   18
HERE THEY STAND TO-NIGHT • • • • • • • • • 234 YOUTH OF MAN   61
THEY STAND AND LISTEN THEY HEAR • • • • • • 234 YOUTH OF MAN   71
AT THIS VESSELS PROW I STAND WHICH BEARS ME • • 239 SELF-DEPENDENCE   3
AT THE VESSELS PROW I STAND WHICH BEARS ME • • • 239 SELF-DEPENDENCE V 3
THOSE BLACK-CROWND RED-BOLED PINE-TREES STAND • • 248 KENSINGTON GARD   4
THOSE BLACK-TOPPD RED-BOLED PINE-TREES STAND • • 248 KENSINGTON GARD V 4
THOSE DARK-TOPPD RED-BOLD PINETREES STAND • • •   KENSINGTON GARD V 4
THE DARKER ELMS STAND GRAVE AND DUN • • • • • 248 KENSINGTON GARD V
THE MASSIER ELMS STAND GRAVE AND DUN • • • • •   KENSINGTON GARD V
WE STAND TO-DAY BY WORDSWORTHS TOMB • • • • • 270 MEMORIAL VERSES   5
WE STAND TO-DAY AT WORDSWORTHS TOMB • • • • • 270 MEMORIAL VERSES V 5
LIKE GHOSTS THE HUGE GNARLD OLIVES STAND • • • • 275 SOUTHERN NIGHT   6
SUCH THOU WAST AND I STAND • • • • • • • • 287 RUGBY CHAPEL   23
AND WHITE UPLIFTED FACES STAND • • • • • • • 300 GRANDE CHARTR   41
IN PITY AND MOURNFUL AWE MIGHT STAND • • • • • 301 GRANDE CHARTR   82
BUT WE STAND MUTE AND WATCH THE WAVES • • • • 303 GRANDE CHARTR   126
BUT THEY STAND MUTE AND WATCH THE WAVES • • • • 303 GRANDE CHARTR V 126
STAND DARK ROUND THY GREEN GRAVE • • • • • • 311 OBERMANN   168
SOFTLY STAND BACK SEE TO THESE PALACE GATES • • 331 MEROPE   51
AND IGNORANT MEN DESPISE ME THAT I STAND • • • 333 MEROPE   95
BUT MEROPE THE YEARS ADVANCE I STAND • • • • • 334 MEROPE   151
NOT IN ABHORRD ESTRANGEMENT LET YOU STAND • • • 339 MEROPE   300
BUT FOR THY CHILDRENS DEATH I STAND ASSOILD • • 340 MEROPE   342
STAND AND LET VENGEANCE PASS HOLD O QUEEN HOLD • 374 MEROPE   1198
NO BY THE GODS THOU SLAYST STAND OFF THY SON • • 375 MEROPE   1201
FOR YEARS HIS WIDOW IN THEIR SIGHT I STAND • • 381 MEROPE   1316
HERE STAND I NOW AND THE ATTEMPT SHALL BE • • • 383 MEROPE   1383
NEITHER EXULTING NOR ASHAMED I STAND • • • • • 398 MEROPE   1788
I TOOK MY STAND AND SAW THE UNARMD CROWDS • • • 401 MEROPE   1896
AND MAKE IT STAND INDEED THE WILL OF HEAVEN • • 404 MEROPE   1999
SOFTLY STAND BACK SEE TOWRD THE PALACE GATES • 331 MEROPE   V 51
DID THE YOUNG OLYMPUS STAND • • • • • • • • 434 EMPEDOCLES II   166
UPON WHOSE CHARRD AND QUAKING CRUST I STAND • • 438 EMPEDOCLES II   307
STAND NOT TWIXT HIS SOUL AND OURS • • • • • 457 POOR MATTHIAS   172
AND WERE THERE NONE TO STAND AND WEEP ALONE • • 467 ALARIC AT ROME   121
AND WHILE THEY RISE HERE MIGHT WE STAND ALONE • 470 ALARIC AT ROME   203
NEAR WHERE ATLAS HATH HIS STAND • • • • • •   PILLARS UNIVERS   2
YE TOO WHO STAND BESIDE THE HOARY THRONE • • •   FRAGMENT 2   1

STANDARD
AND I WHEN TO HIS RIGHTEOUS STANDARD DOWN • • • • 388 MEROPE   1502

STANDEST
AH HOW FAIR THOU STANDEST IN THE MOONLIGHT • • • 143 TRISTRAM 2   27
THOU STANDEST SMILING • • • • • • • • • • 186 STRAYED REVEL   7
THOU STANDEST GAZING TO SEE • • • • • • • • 297 HEINES GRAVE   169
STANDEST AT NIGHTFALL ALONE • • • • • • • • 297 HEINES GRAVE   175
THOU STANDEST OUT I SEE REPELLEST PEACE • • • • 341 MEROPE   354

STANDETH
CREEDS PASS RITES CHANGE NO ALTAR STANDETH WHOLE • • 173 MONICAS PRAYER   12

STANDING
SHALL BE LEFT STANDING FACE TO FACE WITH GOD • •   7 REP FRIEND CONT   14
AND ON EACH SIDE ARE SQUARES OF STANDING CORN • •   70 SOHRAB RUSTUM   295
SAW RUSTUM STANDING SAFE UPON HIS FEET • • • •   77 SOHRAB RUSTUM   525
THEY SHOULD BE LYING HERE I STANDING THERE • • •   77 SOHRAB RUSTUM   546
AND TO ONE STANDING ON THEM FAR AND NEAR • • • 149 TRISTRAM 3   11
YET LOW AND FROM THE BOTTOM YET TO ONE STANDING IN IT   TRISTRAM 3   V 11
STILL STANDING FOR SOME FALSE IMPOSSIBLE SHORE • • 244 SUMMER NIGHT   69
STANDING FOR HARBOUR • • • • • • • • • • 400 MEROPE   1877
THE YOUNG ACHILLES STANDING BY • • • • • • • 414 EMPEDOCLES I 2   60

STANDS
STANDS A LONELY CHURCH UNFINISHD • • • • • • •   14 CHURCH BROU 1   63
AND THE CHURCH UNFINISHD STANDS • • • • • • •   14 CHURCH BROU 1   68
STANDS AS ERST THE BUILDERS LEFT IT • • • • • •   15 CHURCH BROU 1   69

STANDS   (CONTINUED)

STANDS THE CHURCH ON HIGH	• • • • • • • •	16 CHURCH BROU 2	6
STANDS AT DAYBREAK WEEPING BY MY SIDE	• • • • •	35 NEW SIRENS	274
HIGH ON A BANK OUR LEADER STANDS	• • • • • •	53 RESIGNATION	44
STONED MUST HE BE THE LAW STANDS SO	• • • • • •	91 SICK KING BOKH	114
STILL THOU ART KING AND THE LAW STANDS	• • • • •	92 SICK KING BOKH	138
THERE IN THE GLEN FENSALER STANDS THE HOUSE	• •	97 BALDER DEAD 1	84
SOFT WHO IS THAT STANDS BY THE DYING FIRE	• • • •	130 TRISTRAM 1	7
REACH ME MY GOLDEN PHIAL STANDS BY THEE	• • • •	133 TRISTRAM 1	100
REACH ME MY GOLDEN CUP THAT STANDS BY THEE	• • •	133 TRISTRAM 1	V 100
UNDER THE GLITTERING HOLLIES ISEULT STANDS	• • • •	150 TRISTRAM 3	23
UNDER THE BURNISHD HOLLIES ISEULT STANDS	• • • •	TRISTRAM 3	V 23
LOUD PRAYS THE PRIEST SHUT STANDS THE DOOR	• • • •	163 FORSAKEN MERM	82
AND THE WHIZZING WHEEL STANDS STILL	• • • • •	164 FORSAKEN MERM	97
STANDS AT THE PROW AND GUIDES THEM BUT ASTERN	• •	191 STRAYED REVEL	190
VAIN THY ONSET ALL STANDS FAST	• • • • • • • •	215 LAST WORD	3
STANDS ON THE CREST OF THE HILL	• • • • • • •	283 HAWORTH CHURCH	63
STANDS ON THE THRESHOLD THE WIND	• • • • • •	289 RUGBY CHAPEL	111
THERE STANDS THE TEMPLE OF THINE ANCESTOR	• • • •	330 MEROPE	13
THY KIND-SPEAKING FATHER STANDS	• • • • • •	378 MEROPE	1240
MY MOTHER STANDS ALOOF AND BLAMES OUR DEED	• • • •	386 MEROPE	1448
AND STANDS SHOUTING FOR A SLAUGHTEROUS AXE	• • • •	400 MEROPE	1860
THEREFORE NOW OLYMPUS STANDS	• • • • • •	434 EMPEDOCLES II	185
THE UNKNOWN PASSENGER RETURNING STANDS	• • • •	445 WESTMIN ABBEY	43
ONE FORM STANDS GAZING SILENTLY BELOW	• • • •	468 ALARIC AT ROME	153
UNTHWARTED UNDIVERTED WHEN HE STANDS	• • •	LUCRETIUS 2	10
AND STANDS A FAILURE THEN THEN HAPPENS OPPIUS	• •	LUCRETIUS 2	12

STAR

MY SAND RUNS SHORT AND AS YON STAR-SHOT RAY	• •	10 MYCERINUS	56
AND THE BRIGHT AND MORNING STAR	• • • • • •	27 NEW SIRENS	36
ERE THE LONG NIGHT WHOSE STILLNESS BROOKS NO STAR		43 GIPSY CHILD	45
BLAZED BRIGHT AND BALEFUL LIKE THAT AUTUMN-STAR	• •	74 SOHRAB RUSTUM	452
THEY FOLLOWD ME MY HOPE MY FAME MY STAR	• • •	84 SOHRAB RUSTUM	781
RIGHT FOR THE POLAR STAR PAST ORGUNJE	• • •	87 SOHRAB RUSTUM	880
AND OLD MEN KNOWN TO GLORY BUT THEIR STAR	• • • •	109 BALDER DEAD 2	166
ALONG THIS IRON COAST KNOW LIKE A STAR	• • •	151 TRISTRAM 3	81
YOUTH LIKE A STAR AND WHAT TO YOUTH BELONG	• • •	166 AUSTERITY POET	6
SEE PULSING WITH THE FIRST-BORN STAR	• • • •	218 BACCHANALIA 1	17
THE GLEAM OF THE EVENING STAR	• • • • • •	228 YOUTH OF NATURE	18
FROM THE INTENSE CLEAR STAR-SOWN VAULT OF HEAVEN	• •	240 SELF-DEPENDENCE	13
AND THE FULL MOON AND THE WHITE EVENING-STAR	• •	264 THYRSIS	70
SHOWD ME THE HIGH WHITE STAR OF TRUTH	• • •	301 GRANDE CHARTR	69
SHOWD ME THE PALE COLD STAR OF TRUTH	• • • •	301 GRANDE CHARTR	V 69
IN THE YET STAR-SOWN NIGHTLY SKY	• • • • •	323 OBERMANN MORE	331
SO LIKE A STAR DAWNS THY SON	• • • • • •	393 MEROPE	1682
WHEN HIS STAR REIGND BEFORE HIS BANISHMENT	• • • •	408 EMPEDOCLES I 1	65
EARTH AND HEAVENS STAR-SPANGLED LOAD	• • • • •	PILLARS UNIVERS	4

STARE

AND HER EYES ARE SET IN A STARE	• • • • •	164 FORSAKEN MERM	100
THE RICH SHE HAD LET PASS WITH FROZEN STARE	• •	170 WEST LONDON	8

STARES

HE STARES AND STARES WITH TROUBLED FACE	• • • •	148 TRISTRAM 2	157
HE STARES AND STARES WITH TROUBLED FACE	• • • •	148 TRISTRAM 2	157

STARING

AND EYEBALLS STARING FOR REVENGE IN VAIN	• • • •	373 MEROPE	1175

STARK

YET STARK FROM THE DEATH-STRUGGLE TIGHT-CLENCHD HANDS	373 MEROPE	1174

STARLIGHT

INTO THE FROSTY STARLIGHT AND THERE MOVED	• • • •	87 SOHRAB RUSTUM	877
BUT THE GODS WENT BY STARLIGHT UP THE SHORE	• •	119 BALDER DEAD 3	207

STARLIKE

LED BY THY TAPERS STARLIKE BEAM	• • • • • •	177 FAREWELL	8
LIT BY THY TAPERS STARLIKE BEAM	• • • • • •	177 FAREWELL	V 8

STARLINGS

STARLINGS SWIRLING FROM THE HEDGE	• • • • • •	456 POOR MATTHIAS	144

STARLIT

AT COCK-CROW ON A STARLIT WINTERS MORN	• • • •	70 SOHRAB RUSTUM	305
FORWARDS FORWARDS OER THE STARLIT SEA	• • • •	239 SELF-DEPENDENCE	4
ON THE STARLIT ARABIAN WASTE	• • • • • •	253 FUTURE	47
UNDERNEATH THE STARLIT TREES	• • • • • •	434 EMPEDOCLES II	183

STARRD

AND YOUR BROWS WERE STARRD WITH DEW	• • • • •	29 NEW SIRENS	100
OF THAT STRANGER-KNIGHT ILL-STARRD	• • • • •	136 TRISTRAM 1	200
STARRD THE COOL TURF AND CLUMPS OF PRIMROSES	• •	155 TRISTRAM 3	208
FROM HEATHS STARRD WITH BROOM	• • • • • • •	165 FORSAKEN MERM	129
THE BOUNDLESS WAVING GRASS-PLAINS STRETCH THICK-STARRD	191 STRAYED REVEL	168
HIM I COUNT HIM WELL-STARRD	• • • • • • •	199 FRAG DEJANEIRA	31
STARRD AND JEWELLD OF MEN	• • • • • • •	296 HEINES GRAVE	143
WITH THE PALE CROCUS STARRD	• • • • • • •	310 OBERMANN	118
HIS FATHER AND HIS ILL-STARRD BRETHREN FALL	• •	387 MEROPE	1463

STARRY
THE SEA THE STARRY POLES . . . . 161 NECKAN 62
WHEN SHE FORSOOK THE STARRY HEIGHT . . . . . . 181 ISOLATION MARG 22
AND IN THEIR GLENS ON STARRY NIGHTS . . . . . . 182 TO MARG CONT 9
HIS EYES BE LIKE THE STARRY LIGHTS . . . . . . 202 URANIA 21
WE MAP THE STARRY SKY . . . . 423 EMPEDOCLES I 2 319
AH THEY WALK IN STARRY MUSINGS . . . . META CLOISTER 3

STARS
WHO TO THE STARS UNCROWNS HIS MAJESTY . . . . 2 SHAKESPEARE 4
AND THOU WHO DIDST THE STARS AND SUNBEAMS KNOW . . 3 SHAKESPEARE 9
THAT TO THE STARS UNCROWNS HIS MAJESTY . . . . 2 SHAKESPEARE V 4
AND THOU WHOSE HEAD DID STARS AND SUNBEAMS KNOW . . 3 SHAKESPEARE V 9
AND IN WILD HUNT THROUGH MAZY TRACTS OF STARS . . 10 MYCERINUS 45
STARS SET DEEP YET INLY BURNING . . . . . . 30 NEW SIRENS 137
THE SOLEMN PEAKS BUT TO THE STARS ARE KNOWN . . 45 IN UTRUMQUE PAR 18
BUT TO THE STARS AND THE COLD LUNAR BEAMS . . . 45 IN UTRUMQUE PAR 19
AND YOU WOULD SAY THAT SUN AND STARS TOOK PART . . 75 SOHRAB RUSTUM 480
AND TRANQUIL FROM WHOSE FLOOR THE NEW-BATHED STARS . 87 SOHRAB RUSTUM 891
TO ASGARD AND THE STARS CAME OUT IN HEAVEN . . 102 BALDER DEAD 1 256
WHEN AIR IS CHILLIEST AND THE STARS SUNK LOW . . 103 BALDER DEAD 1 281
BY THE DIM VAPOUR-BLOTTED LIGHT OF STARS . . . 108 BALDER DEAD 2 126
BUT BY THE BLOTTED LIGHT OF STARS HE FARED . . . 108 BALDER DEAD 2 140
BUT FAINTER AS THE STARS ROSE HIGH IT FLARED . . 119 BALDER DEAD 3 201
SUN MOON AND STARS WHICH THOU HAST HUNG IN HEAVEN . 121 BALDER DEAD 3 264
BUT FAINTER AS THE STARS ROSE HIGH IT BURND . . 119 BALDER DEAD 3 V 201
STRUNG LIKE WHITE STARS THE PEARLS STILL ARE . . 146 TRISTRAM 2 109
STARS SHONE AFTER A DAY OF STORM . . . . . 156 SAINT BRANDAN 14
THE HUSH AMONG THE SHINING STARS . . . . . 180 FAREWELL 79
AH COOL NIGHT-WIND TREMULOUS STARS . . . . . 194 STRAYED REVEL 282
LIKE STARS ON LIFES COLD SEA . . . . 209 DESPONDENCY 2
LIKE STARS OVER THE BOUNDING HILL . . . . . 220 BACCHANALIA 2 27
LIKE STARS IN THE DEEP OF THE SKY . . . . . 230 YOUTH OF NATURE 72
OER THE SEA AND TO THE STARS I SEND . . . . . 240 SELF-DEPENDENCE 6
AH ONCE MORE I CRIED YE STARS YE WATERS . . . . 240 SELF-DEPENDENCE 9
AND WITH JOY THE STARS PERFORM THEIR SHINING . . 240 SELF-DEPENDENCE 21
AS THE STARS COME OUT AND THE NIGHT-WIND . . . 254 FUTURE 85
AND MARKD THEE WHEN THE STARS COME OUT AND SHINE . 258 SCHOLAR-GIPSY 109
THE WEST UNFLUSHES THE HIGH STARS GROW BRIGHT . . 267 THYRSIS 163
HIS BOLT-SCATHED FRONT TO THE STARS . . . . . 293 HEINES GRAVE 32
THE SYRIAN STARS LOOK DOWN . . . . 318 OBERMANN MORE 176
THE GODS HAD PITY MADE THEM STARS . . . . . 393 MEROPE 1674
STARS NOW THEY SPARKLE . . . . 393 MEROPE 1675
WITH MUSIC TO HAVE DRAWN THE STARS FROM HEAVEN . 409 EMPEDOCLES I 1 81
HE TOLD HIM OF THE GODS THE STARS . . . . . 414 EMPEDOCLES I 2 71
AND YOU YE STARS . . . . 437 EMPEDOCLES II 276
NO NO YE STARS THERE IS NO DEATH WITH YOU . . . 438 EMPEDOCLES II 301
OH THAT MY SOUL WERE FULL OF LIGHT AS THE STARS . 438 EMPEDOCLES II 325
THE STARS IN THEIR CALM . . . . 443 EMPEDOCLES II 468
THAT IN THE SOLITUDE BEYOND THE STARS . . . . FRAGMENT 6 2

START
SO SAD AND WITH SO WILD A START . . . . . . 36 VOICE 23
HA DOST THOU START ARE THY LIPS BLANCHD LIKE MINE . 133 TRISTRAM 1 102
I AM DYING START NOT NOR LOOK WILDLY . . . . . 145 TRISTRAM 2 89
SHE WILL START FROM HER SLUMBER . . . . . . 164 FORSAKEN MERM 112
THE PRINCE AT START SEEMD SAD BUT HIS REGARD . . 355 MEROPE 733
TROPHY IN MOUTH AGOG TO START . . . . 460 KAISER DEAD 50

STARTED
TEARS STARTED TO MINE EYES WITH YEARNING JOY . . 117 BALDER DEAD 3 151
TEARS STARTED TO SAINT BRANDANS EYES . . . . . 158 SAINT BRANDAN 73

STARTING
THIS STARTING FEVERISH HEART AWAY . . . . . . 178 FAREWELL 32

STARTLED
MIGHT SHRINK HALF STARTLED LIKE A GUILTY MAN . . 11 MYCERINUS 102
OF STARTLED PLEASURE FLOODS THY BROW . . . . . 184 TERRACE BERNE 14
STARTLED THE UNKNOWN SEA . . . . 193 STRAYED REVEL 260
THEN A BOY HE STARTLED . . . . 392 MEROPE 1622
OF GOTHIC CLARION SMOTE THY STARTLED EAR . . . 465 ALARIC AT ROME 80

STARTLING
RACING FULL SPEED AND STARTLING IN THEIR RUSH . . 150 TRISTRAM 3 29

STARTS
AND STARTS HIM THAT HE THINKS A GHOST WENT BY . . 101 BALDER DEAD 1 234

STARWARDS
LURD HIM STARWARDS TO UPLIFT HIS EYE . . . . . 483 THEKLAS ANSWER 18

STATE
THOU AND THY LADIES IN THE HALL OF STATE . . . 18 CHURCH BROU 3 13
OF ALL THE ENGINE-WORK OF STATE . . . . . . 48 HORATIAN ECHO 14
HATH FREED FROM PASSIONS AND THE STATE . . . . 53 RESIGNATION 24
HIS PLACE OF STATE REMAINS BY HELAS SIDE . . . 125 BALDER DEAD 3 432
ROYAL STATE WITH MARC MY DEEP-WRONGD HUSBAND . . 144 TRISTRAM 2 45
THOUGHT I ABOVE HER STATE THIS SPIRIT TOWERS . . 170 WEST LONDON 9

STATE   (CONTINUED)
         IN WHAT STATE GODS OTHER WORKS MAY BE   • • • •   240 SELF-DEPENDENCE   26
         IN THIS HIS MORTAL STATE • • • • • • • • • 273 EDW QUILLINAN   10
         IN THIS HIS LIVING STATE • • • • • • • • • 273 EDW QUILLINAN   V 10
         HADST THOU FROM THY FORLORN AND CAPTIVE STATE   • •   383 MEROPE   1369
         IMMERSED IN SERIOUS STATE-CRAFT IS THE KING   • •   387 MEROPE   1489
         THE SIMPLE PATRIARCHAL STATE OF KINGS   • • • •   388 MEROPE   1516
         WELFARE TO THE MESSENIAN STATE AND CALM   • • • •   403 MEROPE   1959
         WAS POLICY OF STATE THE ASCENDENCY   • • • • •   404 MEROPE   1981
         LOSE ALL OUR PRESENT STATE • • • • • • • • 425 EMPEDOCLES I 2   405
         FAIL TO MAKE BLEST THY STATE • • • • • • 426 EMPEDOCLES I 2   420
         LEARN THAT MEN WILL NOT AND GODS CANNOT HELP THY STATE
                                               EMPEDOCLES I 2   V
         AND IN OUR INDIVIDUAL HUMAN STATE   • • • • •   440 EMPEDOCLES II   367
         INVITEST REASON TO FORSWEAR HER STATE   • • • •   RUDE ORATOR   18
         THAT WE WERE DESTIND TO A HAPPIER STATE   • • • •   LUCRETIUS 3   11

STATELIER
         ON A WIDER STATELIER STREAM   • • • • • • • 253 FUTURE   74
         SEVERER PALER STATELIER THAN THEY ALL   • • • •   331 MEROPE   57

STATELY
         WITH A STATELY SLOW SURPRISE • • • • • • • 31 NEW SIRENS   156
         HIS STATELY CREST AND DIMMD HIS GLITTERING ARMS   • •   74 SOHRAB RUSTUM   454
         AND HEAP A STATELY MOUND ABOVE MY BONES   • • • •   84 SOHRAB RUSTUM   788
         AND HEAP A STATELY MOUND ABOVE THY BONES   • • • •   84 SOHRAB RUSTUM   803
         IN HIS STATELY DEEP DISTRESS • • • • • • • 137 TRISTRAM 1   209
         A STATELY HUNTSMAN CLAD IN GREEN   • • • • •   147 TRISTRAM 2   153
         FIXD FULL ON MERLINS FACE HER STATELY PRIZE   • •   154 TRISTRAM 3   178
         AND LAID HER IN A STATELY ROOM WHERE FELL • • • •   168 RACHEL 2   5
         DOWN OER THE STATELY BRIDGE THE BREEZE   • • • •   223 EPILOG LAOCOON   65
         HER STATELY PURPLE SHE ABHORRD   • • • • •   316 OBERMANN MORE   127
         SLOPE STATELY DOWN AND MELT INTO THE PLAIN • • • •   473 CROMWELL   38

STATES
         HE PARCELLD OUT IN FIVE CONFEDERATE STATES • • • •   337 MEROPE   249
         THE BOUNDS OF EFFACED STATES • • • • • • • 423 EMPEDOCLES I 2   324

STATESMAN
         GIRL STATESMAN MERCHANT SOLDIER BOLD • • • • •   226 EPILOG LAOCOON   159
         WARRIOR STATESMAN HAD SIGND   • • • • • • • 281 HAWORTH CHURCH   21
         WARRIOR STATESMAN HAD LEFT   • • • • • • • 281 HAWORTH CHURCH V 21
         THE STATESMAN QUAILD BEFORE HIS GLANCE OF IRE   • •   476 CROMWELL   154

STATESMEN
         STATESMEN NEW SYSTEMS   • • • • • • • • • 220 BACCHANALIA 2   39
         STATESMEN LIKE PITT   • • • • • • • • • • 220 BACCHANALIA 2   56

STATION
         ONCE LIKE US YOU TOOK YOUR STATION   • • • • •   31 NEW SIRENS   139
         ONCE LIKE ME YOU TOOK YOUR STATION   • • • • •   31 NEW SIRENS   V 139
         FROM SOME HIGH STATION HE LOOKS DOWN • • • • •   57 RESIGNATION   164

STATIOND
         AND AT HIS HEAD AND FEET SHE STATIOND SCALDS   • •   102 BALDER DEAD 1   271

STATUE
         I A STATUE ON THY CHAPEL-FLOOR   • • • • • • 144 TRISTRAM 2   62
         STOOD LIKE A STATUE AND HIS FACE WAS FAIR • • • •   477 CROMWELL   176

STATUED
         DOWN THE STATUED ALLEYS CAME • • • • • • • 29 NEW SIRENS   102

STATUES
         BY MOSS-BORDERD STATUES SITTING   • • • • • • 34 NEW SIRENS   239
         GREY RAIN-BLEARD STATUES OVERPEER   • • • • • 191 STRAYED REVEL   179
         THOUGH MANY THAN GOOD STATUES WERE   • • • • • 221 EPILOG LAOCOON   18
         BORDERD BY STATUES AND WALKS • • • • • • • 296 HEINES GRAVE   133

STATURED
         SEVEN-CUBIT-STATURED SON • • • • • • • • • 344 MEROPE   441

STAUNCH
         AND WE PLEAD AS STAUNCH ADHERENCE   • • • • • 28 NEW SIRENS   59

STAVE
         AND SINGS A MOURNFUL STAVE   • • • • • • • 159 NECKAN   14
         MORE THAN PITY CLAIMST A STAVE   • • • • • • 453 POOR MATTHIAS   22
         DEAD CANARY BIRD A STAVE • • • • • • • • • 457 POOR MATTHIAS   176
         AND THIS PLAIN STAVE • • • • • • • • • • 461 KAISER DEAD   84

STAVED
         STAVED US BACK AND GAVE OUR CHOICE THE LAW • • • •   210 SELF-DECEPTION   12

STAY
         IF SOME FAIR COAST HAVE LURED US TO MAKE STAY   • •   40 HUMAN LIFE   11
         IF SOME FAIR COAST HAS LURED US TO MAKE STAY   • •   40 HUMAN LIFE   V 11
         THAT WERE FAR BEST MY SON TO STAY WITH US • • • •   63 SOHRAB RUSTUM   71
         THERE WOULD I STAY AND HANG MY ARMOUR UP   • • • •   68 SOHRAB RUSTUM   V 296
         HOWBEIT STAY AND BE APPEASED AND TELL   • • • •   129 BALDER DEAD 3   428
         FLY SAVE THYSELF SAVE ME I DARE NOT STAY   • • • •   135 TRISTRAM 1   168

STAY   (CONTINUED)
        I FORGIVE THEE I SEULT THOU WILT STAY . . . . .   143 TRISTRAM 2   28
        STAY PALE QUEEN FOR EVER BY MY SIDE . . . . .   144 TRISTRAM 2   68
        SAY I WILLD SO THAT THOU STAY BESIDE ME . . . .   145 TRISTRAM 2   95
        TRISTRAM TRISTRAM STAY RECEIVE ME WITH THEE . .   146 TRISTRAM 2   99
        SAY I CHARGD HER THAT THOU STAY BESIDE ME . . .   145 TRISTRAM 2   V   95
        SAY I CHARGD THEE THAT THOU STAY BESIDE HER . .   145 TRISTRAM 2   V   95
        TRISTRAM TRISTRAM STAY I COME AH SORROW . . . .   146 TRISTRAM 2   V   99
        MOTHER DEAR WE CANNOT STAY . . . . . .   162 FORSAKEN MERM   20
        STAY WITH ME MARGUERITE STILL . . . . . .   183 ABSENCE   20
        AND AT ITS END TO STAY THE EYE . . . .   248 KENSINGTON GARD   3
        AND AT ITS HEAD TO STAY THE EYE . . . .   248 KENSINGTON GARD V   3
        WHERE ENDS THE GLADE TO STAY THE EYE . . . . .   248 KENSINGTON GARD V   3
        AND LONG WITH MEN OF CARE THOU COULDST NOT STAY . 269 THYRSIS   228
        BUT AH I COULD NOT STAY . . . .   321 OBERMANN MORE   260
        HERE WILL I STAY TILL THE SLOW LITTER COMES . .   407 EMPEDOCLES I 1   18
        I WOULD FAIN STAY AND HELP THEE TEND HIM ONCE .   408 EMPEDOCLES I 1   56
        HE COULD STAY SWIFT DISEASES IN OLD DAYS . . .   410 EMPEDOCLES I 1   115
        TO KNOW THOSE SPELLS OF THINE WHICH STAY THEIR HAND 413 EMPEDOCLES I 2   25
        TO THE HIGH MOUNTAIN-PASTURES AND TO STAY . . .   413 EMPEDOCLES I 2   39
        MEANWHILE STAY ME NOT NOW FAREWELL PAUSANIAS . . 428 EMPEDOCLES I 2   478
        TO KNOW THOSE SPELLS OF TIME THAT STAY THEIR HAND 413 EMPEDOCLES I 2 V   25
        TO KNOW THOSE SPELLS OF THINE THAT STAY THEIR HAND 413 EMPEDOCLES I 2 V   25
        THAT RADIANT THOUGH THOU WERT THOU COULDST BUT STAY 447 WESTMIN ABBEY   119
        FOUR YEARS AND DIDST THOU STAY ABOVE . . . . .   449 GEISTS GRAVE   1
        WHAT WAS FOUR YEARS THEIR WHOLE SHORT STAY . . . 450 GEISTS GRAVE   V   20
        STAY THIS HAND FROM FIGHT TILL THE TROJANS   HOMER TRANS   62
                ARE UTTERLY ROUTED

STAYD
        BUT HERMOD STAYD HIM WITH MILD WORDS AND SAID . . 125 BALDER DEAD 3   422
        LONG THEY STAYD STILL THEN PACING AT THEIR EASE . 150 TRISTRAM 3   42
        WARM IN THEIR MANTLES WRAPT THE THREE STAYD THERE   TRISTRAM 3   V   38
        NOT ONCE TO DAY THESE EYES HAVE STAYD . . . .   205 CALAIS SANDS V   17
        RIVERS ARE DRIED WINDS STAYD . . . .   416 EMPEDOCLES I 2   125
        THEY HAD STAYD LONG ENOUGH TO SEE . . . . . .   427 EMPEDOCLES I 2   444

STAYED
        TWICE HATH THE CLOUD HUNG OER THEE TWICE BEEN STAYED 465 ALARIC AT ROME   83

STAYS
        YET IF LITTLE STAYS WITH MAN . . . .   24 MEMORY-PICTURE   59
        ON THAT CLEAR FOREST-KNOLL HE STAYS . . . . .   148 TRISTRAM 2   155
        TIS NOON WITH HIM AND YET HE STAYS . . . . .   148 TRISTRAM 2   V   155
        IT STAYS IN YOUR ABODES . . . .   423 EMPEDOCLES I 2   340

STEADFAST
        PLANTING HIS STEADFAST FOOTSTEPS IN THE SEA . .   3 SHAKESPEARE   5
        HAIL TO THE STEADFAST SOUL . . . .   281 HAWORTH CHURCH   37
        THAT STEADFAST MOURNFUL STRAIN CONSOLED . . . .   450 GEISTS GRAVE   17

STEADILY
        WHO SAW LIFE STEADILY AND SAW IT WHOLE . . . .   2 TO A FRIEND   12

STEADY
        RAN BLACK OER THE SEAS FACE THEN STEADY RUSHD . . 118 BALDER DEAD 3   183
        THE THOUGHTS THAT RAIN THEIR STEADY GLOW . . . . 209 DESPONDENCY   1

STEAL
        DID STEAL INTO MINE EAR . . . .   36 VOICE   36
        DID STEAL INTO MINE EARS . . . .   36 VOICE   V   36
        BEGIN TO STEAL TO THEIR EYES . . . .   235 YOUTH OF MAN   98
        AND DARKNESS STEAL OER THE WET GRASS . . . . .   310 OBERMANN   117

STEALING
        CAME UPON HER STEALING . . . .   392 MEROPE   1644

STEALS
        STEALS COLDLY AROUND THE CHAMBER BRIGHT . . . .   147 TRISTRAM 2   148
        STEALS OVER IT FROM THE TILLD LAND BEHIND . . .   TRISTRAM 3   V   9
        STEALS OVER IT FROM THE TILLD FIELDS BEHIND . .   TRISTRAM 3   V   9
        SHE STEALS TO THE WINDOW AND LOOKS AT THE SAND . 164 FORSAKEN MERM   98
        AND STEALS THE HONIED MUSIC OF HIS TONGUE . . .   FRAGMENT 1   8

STEALTH
        DISCOVERY OF A VISIT MADE BY STEALTH . . . . .   351 MEROPE   605
        WITH ARMS THEN THEY SHOULD SEND HIM NOT BY STEALTH 351 MEROPE   606
        WITH ARMS THEY DARE NOT AND BY STEALTH THEY FEAR . 351 MEROPE   607

STEALTHILY
        LIFTING THE COOL-HAIRD CREEPERS STEALTHILY . . . 262 SCHOLAR-GIPSY   234

STEAM
        TO RIGHT AND LEFT AND WARM STEAM FILLS THE AIR . . 107 BALDER DEAD 2   98

STEAMING
        IN THE STILL NIGHT ACROSS THE STEAMING FLATS . .   12 MYCERINUS   126
        AND HER LOAD OF STEAMING TRESSES . . . . . .   28 NEW SIRENS   71

STEDFAST
        BUT IF THE STEDFAST COMMANDMENT OF NATURE . . .   206 SEPARATION   5

STEDFAST   (CONTINUED)
     WOULD PLAY THE TRAITOR TO THE STEDFAST WILL   • •   475 CROMWELL   108

STEED
     MY MOTHER TOLD ME OF THEE THOU BRAVE STEED • • • •   83 SOHRAB RUSTUM   743
     THIS THROUGH THE RIDE UPON HIS STEED • • • • • •   224 EPILOG LAOCOON   115

STEEDS
     STEEDS ARE NEIGHING GALLANTS GLITTERING   • • • •   13 CHURCH BROU 1   9
     LARGE MEN LARGE STEEDS WHO FROM BOKHARA COME   • •   64 SOHRAB RUSTUM   119
     LIGHT MEN AND ON LIGHT STEEDS WHO ONLY DRINK   • •   64 SOHRAB RUSTUM   124
     AND THE VALKYRIES ON THEIR STEEDS WENT FORTH   • •   105 BALDER DEAD 2   19
     FORTH WENDED THEY AND DRAVE THEIR STEEDS BEFORE • •   106 BALDER DEAD 2   50
     AND BOUND THE LOGS BEHIND THEIR STEEDS TO DRAW   • •   106 BALDER DEAD 2   60
     AND DRAVE THEM HOMEWARD AND THE SNORTING STEEDS • •   106 BALDER DEAD 2   61
     FORTH WENDED THEY AND DROVE THEIR STEEDS BEFORE • •   106 BALDER DEAD 2   V 50
     AND DROVE THEM HOMEWARD AND THE SNORTING STEEDS • •   106 BALDER DEAD 2   V 61
     BUT NOW PUT ON YOUR ARMS AND MOUNT YOUR STEEDS   • •   115 BALDER DEAD 3   50
     THEIR SPEARS ARE DOWN THEIR STEEDS ARE BATHED IN FOAM 137 TRISTRAM 1   237
     THE NEIGHING STEEDS THE RINGING BLOWS   • • • •   138 TRISTRAM 1   259
     HIS FLYING STEEDS CAME NEAR   • • • • • • •   197 FRAG ANTIGONE   85
     A THOUSAND KNIGHTS HAVE REIND THEIR STEEDS • • • •   204 CALAIS SANDS   1
     AND CHECK THY FIERY STEEDS AND LEANING BACK   • •   349 MEROPE   575
     BY THEIR CHARIOTS STOOD THE STEEDS AND CHAMPD   HOMER TRANS   5
          THE WHITE BARLEY
     SO HE SPAKE AND DROVE WITH A CRY HIS STEEDS   HOMER TRANS   63
          INTO BATTLE

STEEL
     MARSHALLD BATTALIONS BRIGHT IN BURNISHD STEEL   • •   65 SOHRAB RUSTUM   140
     AND CLAD HIMSELF IN STEEL THE ARMS HE CHOSE   • •   69 SOHRAB RUSTUM   265
     WHICH SOHRAB HELD STIFF OUT THE STEEL-SPIKED SPEAR   75 SOHRAB RUSTUM   492
     NOR CLOVE ITS STEEL QUITE THROUGH BUT ALL THE CREST   76 SOHRAB RUSTUM   496
     AND HE DESIRED TO DRAW FORTH THE STEEL   • • • •   80 SOHRAB RUSTUM   651
     WHICH SOHRAB HELD ADVANCD THE STEEL-SPIKED SPEAR • •   75 SOHRAB RUSTUM   V 492
     UNTIL THEY CRUMBLE OR ELSE GROW LIKE STEEL   • •   153 TRISTRAM 3   121
     AND AGAINST FEAR OUR BREAST TO STEEL   • • • • •   272 MEMORIAL VERSES   65
     AND RUB THE STEEL AND MAKE IT SHINE   • • • • •   461 KAISER DEAD   80

STEEP
     TO THE STEEP EDGE OF SOME GREAT VALLEY COMES   • •   113 BALDER DEAD 2   296
     UP THE STEEP PINE-PLUMED PATHS OF THE ESTRELLE   • •   167 RACHEL 2   4
     UP THE STEEP STREET I HURRIED FAST   • • • • •   177 FAREWELL   7
     UPON THE PINE-GROWN LATMIAN STEEP   • • • • • •   181 ISOLATION MARG   24
     TO CROSS THE STEEP ISMENIAN GLEN   • • • • • •   197 FRAG ANTIGONE   86
     AT THEIR RETURN UP THE STEEP STRAND   • • • • •   211 DOVER BEACH   V 11
     THERE WHERE GIBRALTARS CANNOND STEEP   • • • • •   276 SOUTHERN NIGHT   23
     A LONG STEEP JOURNEY THROUGH SUNK   • • • • • •   288 RUGBY CHAPEL   87
     POET AND STEEP HIM IN CALM   • • • • • • •   294 HEINES GRAVE   51
     INVEST ME STEEP ME FOLD ME ROUND   • • • • • •   302 GRANDE CHARTR   V 93
     DOWN ITS STEEP VERDANT SIDES THE AIR   • • • • •   414 EMPEDOCLES I 2   45
     IN FRONT THE DUMB ROCK RISES STEEP   • • • • • •   479 HAYSWATER BOAT   11

STEEPD
     GREEN BURSTING FIGS AND TUNNIES STEEPD IN BRINE • •   262 SCHOLAR-GIPSY   239
     WHAT ELSE IS STEEPD IN LUCID SHEEN   • • • • • •   279 SOUTHERN NIGHT   134

STEEPING
     WHEN THE FIRST ROSE FLUSH WAS STEEPING   • • • •   31 NEW SIRENS   143

STEER
     AT RANDOM AND NOT STEER BY RULE   • • • • • •   40 HUMAN LIFE   14
     WHO THROUGH ALL HE MEETS CAN STEER HIM   • • • •   49 SECOND BEST   17
     AND SHE WILL BID HIM NORTHWARD STEER HIS COURSE • •   99 BALDER DEAD 1   152
     HAVE A WORSE COURSE TO STEER   • • • • • • •   308 OBERMANN   64
     TO HEAVEN AND LAID HIS HAND UPON THE STEER • • • •   402 MEROPE   1914
     THE RUDDER SWINGS YET NONE DOTH STEER   • • • •   480 HAYSWATER BOAT   39

STEERD
     TO GUIDE ME I HAVE STEERD BY TO THE END   • • • •   40 HUMAN LIFE   6
     PAST STRAITS AND CURRENTS LONG STEERD THROUGH   • •   53 RESIGNATION   21
     BUT NORTH STILL NORTH SAINT BRANDAN STEERD • • • •   156 SAINT BRANDAN   9

STEERING
     LIKE THOSE KINGS WITH TREASURE STEERING   • • •   26 NEW SIRENS   21
     IN A TYRIAN GALLEY STEERING   • • • • • • •   26 NEW SIRENS   V 21
     TO TOO EXACT A STEERING OF OUR WAY   • • • • •   40 HUMAN LIFE   9

STEERS
     WHILE FROM THE EAST THE GIANT RYMER STEERS • • • •   127 BALDER DEAD 3   478
     AS HE STEERS HER OER THE SEA   • • • • • • • •   134 TRISTRAM 1   128

STEM
     WE STEM ACROSS THE SEA OF LIFE BY NIGHT   • • • •   41 HUMAN LIFE   27
     WE STEM ACROSS THE SEA BY NIGHT   • • • • • •   41 HUMAN LIFE   V 27
     AND WHILE THEY TRY TO STEM   • • • • • • • •   243 SUMMER NIGHT   47
     FORTH FROM HIS PARENTS STEM   • • • • • • • •   418 EMPEDOCLES I 2   188

STEMMD
     STEMMD BY THE STRENGTH OF MANHOOD FEARLESSLY   • •   473 CROMWELL   50

STEMS

    BURYING THEIR UNSUNND STEMS IN GRASS AND FLOWERS   • •   11 MYCERINUS   88
    GLIDING HALF HIDDEN THROUGH THE DUSKY STEMS   • •   11 MYCERINUS   104
    BLOWING BETWEEN THE STEMS THE FOREST-AIR   • • •   154 TRISTRAM 3   167
    PEERD TWIXT THE STEMS AND THE GROUND BROKE AWAY   • •   155 TRISTRAM 3   186
    PASSING THROUGH THE DARK STEMS • • • • •   • •   194 STRAYED REVEL   278
    HOW GREEN BETWEEN THE STEMS IT IS   • • • • • •   KENSINGTON GARD V   7
    THEY MOORD THEIR BOATS AMONG THE BULRUSH STEMS   • •   444 WESTMIN ABBEY   18

STENYCLAROS

    O STENYCLAROS WHICH HE BUILT AND MADE   • • • • • 330 MEROPE   10
    HAD TO THIS CITY STENYCLAROS CALLD   • • • • •   338 MEROPE   262
    O TOWN HIGH STENYCLAROS   • • • • • • •   • •   399 MEROPE   1850
    SO LOOKD HE WHEN TO STENYCLAROS FIRST   • • • •   403 MEROPE   1971

STEP

    ITS STEP SO FIRM ITS EYE SO BRIGHT   • • • • •   21 YOUTH AND CALM   10
    ITS STEP SO FIRM ITS EYES SO BRIGHT   • • • • •   21 YOUTH AND CALM   V   10
    ITS STEP SO GAY ITS EYE SO BRIGHT   • • • • •   21 YOUTH AND CALM   V   10
    AND PERAN-WISA HEARD HIM THOUGH THE STEP   • • •   62 SOHRAB RUSTUM   28
    AND SHRANK AMAZED BACK HE RECOILD ONE STEP   • • •   76 SOHRAB RUSTUM   517
    FROM THE SEA CITYWARD AND KNEW HIS STEP   • • •   101 BALDER DEAD 1   227
    THAT SHAWL THAT STEP THAT LOOK THAT HAND   • •   204 CALAIS SANDS   V   12
    WITH FURTIVE STEP AND CHEEK OF FLAME   • • • •   278 SOUTHERN NIGHT   102
    THOU SOLEMN GRAVE WHERE EVERY STEP WE TREAD   • •   464 ALARIC AT ROME   49
    SAW BUT ANOTHER STEP TO CLIMB TO VICTORY   • • •   469 ALARIC AT ROME   186
    HIS STEP WAS LOFTIER THAN THE STEPS OF MAN • • •   476 CROMWELL   156

STEPP

    ON THE WIDE STEPP UNHARNESSING • • • • • • •   • •   191 STRAYED REVEL   163
    PARCH THEM IN WINTER-TIME ON THE BARE STEPP   • •   193 STRAYED REVEL   241

STEPPD

    SHE SPAKE AND STEPPD ASIDE AND LEFT HIM ROOM   • •   108 BALDER DEAD 2   135

STEPS

    THE GUIDE OF OUR DARK STEPS A TRIPLE VEIL   • • •   43 GIPSY CHILD   49
    HIS HOUSE NOW MID THEIR BROKEN FLIGHTS OF STEPS   • •   86 SOHRAB RUSTUM   862
    FAIN HAD HE FOLLOWD THEIR RECEDING STEPS   • • •   129 BALDER DEAD 3   556
    WHAT LIGHTS IN THE COURT WHAT STEPS ON THE STAIR • • 142 TRISTRAM 3   373
    ON THE STEPS OF THY PORTICO   • • • • • • •   • •   187 STRAYED REVEL   52
    SITTING ON THE WARM STEPS   • • • • • • •   • •   194 STRAYED REVEL   271
    FOLLOW YOUR STEPS AS YE GO   • • • • • • • • • •   292 RUGBY CHAPEL   203
    SOUTHERN PALACES STEPS   • • • • • • • •   • •   296 HEINES GRAVE   132
    WITH STERN SLOW STEPS UNSEEN YET STILL THE SAME   • • 476 CROMWELL   147
    HIS STEP WAS LOFTIER THAN THE STEPS OF MAN • • •   476 CROMWELL   156
    AND SLOW RELUCTANT STEPS ARE GATHERING ROUND   • •   476 CROMWELL   160
    THERE LAUD WITH NOISELESS STEPS AND GLITTERING EYE   476 CROMWELL   165

STERN

    STERN SENTENCE OF THE POWERS OF DESTINY   • • •   8 MYCERINUS   6
    OR IS IT THAT SOME FORCE TOO STERN TOO STRONG   • •   9 MYCERINUS   V   37
    OLD THAT DUCHESS STERN BEGAN IT   • • • • •   • •   14 CHURCH BROU 1   65
    STAND MUTE SELF-CENTRED STERN AND DREAM NO MORE • •   42 GIPSY CHILD   32
    THE PROMPT STERN GODDESS • • • • • • • • •   • •   51 CONSOLATION   51
    THE BLEAK STERN HOUR   • • • • • • • • •   • •   52 CONSOLATION   66
    BUT RUSTUM CHID HIM WITH STERN VOICE AND SAID   • •   82 SOHRAB RUSTUM   737
    WITH COLD DRY EYES AND HEARTS COMPOSED AND STERN • •   96 BALDER DEAD 1   35
    AND HELA SET THEREON WITH COUNTENANCE STERN   • • 110 BALDER DEAD 2   178
    AND HELA SAT THEREON WITH COUNTENANCE STERN   • • 110 BALDER DEAD 2   V 178
    SET HIS STOUT SHOULDER HARD AGAINST THE STERN   • • 118 BALDER DEAD 3   176
    BEHOLD THE STERN MAILD FATHER STAFF IN HAND   • • 167 PICT NEWSTEAD   9
    STERN STRENGTH AND PROMISE OF CONTROL   • • •   178 FAREWELL   24
    IN PROFOUND SILENCE STERN   • • • • • • •   • •   198 FRAG DEJANEIRA   8
    THE WORLD TO THEM WAS STERN AND DREAR   • • •   203 EUPHROSYNE   9
    AVERSE AS DIDO DID WITH GESTURE STERN   • • •   261 SCHOLAR-GIPSY   208
    NO PRIESTLY STERN PROCESSION NOW   • • • • •   • •   274 STANZAS CARNAC   13
    STERN INTERRUPTED MY STRAIN   • • • • • • •   • •   285 HAWORTH CHURCH   127
    INVESTS THE STERN AND NAKED PRAYER   • • • •   300 GRANDE CHARTR   38
    O OBERMANN THE SAD STERN PAGE • • • • • •   • •   304 GRANDE CHARTR   146
    IN THIS STERN ALPINE DELL   • • • • • • •   • •   312 OBERMANN   182
    THAT STERN WORD MURDER HAD TOO DREAD A SOUND   • • 365 MEROPE   992
    MY HUSBAND WANDERING WITH HIS STERN COMPEERS   • • 367 MEROPE   1033
    AND THE STERN DESTINY-BROUGHT STRANGER • • •   400 MEROPE   1861
    STERN POWERS WHO MAKE THEIR CARE   • • • • •   • •   422 EMPEDOCLES I 2   310
    STERN LAW OF EVERY MORTAL LOT • • • • • • •   • •   450 GEISTS GRAVE   29
    OR TIMES STERN HAND WHY BLOTS IT NOT AWAY   • • •   462 ALARIC AT ROME   5
    YET ONCE AGAIN STERN CHIEF YET ONCE AGAIN   • • •   465 ALARIC AT ROME   85
    SO STERN A LESSON AS NECESSITY   • • • • •   • •   467 ALARIC AT ROME   142
    OF THY STERN HILL THOU MIGHTY CAPITOL   • • •   468 ALARIC AT ROME   152
    WITH HEART NEW STRUNG AND STERN RESOLVE HE STOOD • • 473 CROMWELL   66
    FROM THE STERN FUTURE AND THE YEARS GONE BY   • • 475 CROMWELL   110
    WITH STERN SLOW STEPS UNSEEN YET STILL THE SAME • • 476 CROMWELL   147

STERNER

    AND STERNER COMES THE ROAR   • • • • • • •   • •   244 SUMMER NIGHT   70
    LEAVES ME AUSTERER STERNER THAN I WOULD   • • •   335 MEROPE   155
    CRUSHD AS THEY ROSE BY MANHOODS STERNER WILL   • • 474 CROMWELL   80
    THOSE STERNER SPIRITS LET ME PRIZE   • • • • •   481 COURAGE   9

STERNLY
         AND THEN HE TURND AND STERNLY SPAKE ALOUD   • • •   72 SOHRAB RUSTUM   364
         AND RISING STERNLY ON ONE ARM HE SAID   • • •   80 SOHRAB RUSTUM   654
         NOT KNEELING STERNLY FIXD HE STOOD   • • • • •   90 SICK KING BOKH   95
         AND CALLD HIM BY HIS NAME AND STERNLY SAID • • • •   124 BALDER DEAD 3   386
         LOOKD STERNLY THROUGH THE FROSTY EVENING-AIR • •   151 TRISTRAM 3   60
         STERNLY REPRESSEST THE BAD   • • • • • • •   287 RUGBY CHAPEL   51
         STERNLY COMPRESSD WE STRAIN ON • • • • • • •   289 RUGBY CHAPEL   106
         STERNLY REQUIREST A MAN   • • • • • • • • •   343 MEROPE   406
         STERNLY CONDEMN THE TOO BOLD MAN WHO DARES • • • •   353 MEROPE   690
         AS THEY LOOKED STERNLY ON BEHELD NEW VICTORIES • •   468 ALARIC AT ROME   174

STICK
         BUT ONCE I KNEW EACH FIELD EACH FLOWER EACH STICK   263 THYRSIS   32

STIFF
         WHICH SOHRAB HELD STIFF OUT THE STEEL-SPIKED SPEAR   75 SOHRAB RUSTUM   492
         AND NEATH THOSE CHESTNUT-TREES WHERE STIFF • • • • • 312 OBERMANN MORE   9
         FOUND HIM STIFF YOU SAY THOUGH WARM • • • • • •   452 POOR MATTHIAS   3

STIFFER
         THEIR JOINTS GROW STIFFER BUT THE YEAR • • • •   56 RESIGNATION   128
         GROW STIFFER EVERY FUNCTION LESS EXACT • • • •   212 GROWING OLD   9

STIFLING
         MARCUS AURELIUS BUT THE STIFLING DEN • • • • • • •   168 WORLDLY PLACE   3
         BUT THROUGH THEIR FORMS AND MODES AND STIFLING VEILS 439 EMPEDOCLES II   354

STILE
         OR CROSS A STILE INTO THE PUBLIC WAY • • • • • •   257 SCHOLAR-GIPSY   85

STILL
         STILL DO THY SLEEPLESS MINISTERS MOVE ON • • • •   1 QUIET WORK   11
         STILL WORKING BLAMING STILL OUR VAIN TURMOIL   • •   2 QUIET WORK   13
         STILL WORKING BLAMING STILL OUR VAIN TURMOIL   • •   2 QUIET WORK   13
         OF LABOUR THAT IN STILL ADVANCE OUTGROWS   • • • •   1 QUIET WORK   V 6
         STILL DO THY QUIET MINISTERS MOVE ON • • • • •   1 QUIET WORK   V 11
         STILL WORKING CHIDING STILL OUR VAIN TURMOIL   • •   2 QUIET WORK   V 13
         STILL WORKING CHIDING STILL OUR VAIN TURMOIL   • •   2 QUIET WORK   V 13
         WE ASK AND ASK THOU SMILEST AND ART STILL   • • • •   2 SHAKESPEARE   2
         THE SEEDS OF GODLIKE POWER ARE IN US STILL • • • •   4 EMERSONS ESSAYS   12
         IN THE STILL NIGHT ACROSS THE STEAMING FLATS   • •   12 MYCERINUS   126
         IN YOUR HIGH CHURCH MID THE STILL MOUNTAIN-AIR • •   17 CHURCH BROU 3   2
         THEY ARE GONE ALL IS STILL FOOLISH HEART DOST • •   19 MODERN SAPPHO   1
             THOU QUIVER
         MURMURING ART THOU STILL UNKIND   • • • • • •   23 MEMORY-PICTURE   36
         STILL THEY GALL YOU THE LONG HOURS • • • • • •   30 NEW SIRENS   129
         THOSE MELANCHOLY TONES SO SWEET AND STILL   • • •   36 VOICE   34
         FROM THOSE STILL DEEPS IN FORM AND COLOUR DREST • • 45 IN UTRUMQUE PAR   4
         ROUND THY STILL DREAMING BROTHER-WORLD OUTSPREAD • • 45 IN UTRUMQUE PAR   31
         WHY YOU SAY CRITIAS BE DEBATING STILL   • • • •   46 WORLD QUIETIST   3
         STILL DOTH FOR LABOURERS SEND   • • • • • • •   47 WORLD QUIETIST   14
         WHO STILL THEIR LABOUR GIVE   • • • • • • • •   47 WORLD QUIETIST   15
         AND STILL EXPECTS AN END • • • • • • • • •   47 WORLD QUIETIST   16
         STILL TO ENQUIRE HOW PARTIES TEND   • • • • • •   47 HORATIAN ECHO   2
         THEY STILL LOOK FAIR   • • • • • • • • •   50 CONSOLATION   20
         TIME STAND STILL HERE   • • • • • • • • •   51 CONSOLATION   50
         THE WIDE EARTH IS STILL   • • • • • • • •   50 CONSOLATION   V
         THERE WINDS UPSTREAMING SLOWLY STILL   • • • • •   54 RESIGNATION   62
         SLEEP IN THE JULY SUNSHINE STILL   • • • • • •   55 RESIGNATION   97
         STILL THIS WILD BROOK THE RUSHES COOL   • • • •   55 RESIGNATION   104
         STILL SHARP AS EVER FREEZE AND PARCH • • • • •   56 RESIGNATION   131
         THEY MUST LIVE STILL AND YET GOD KNOWS • • • •   56 RESIGNATION   132
         FOLDS THE STILL VALLEY ALMOST ROUND • • • • •   57 RESIGNATION   175
         MAN STILL WOULD SEE AND SEE DISMAYD • • • • •   58 RESIGNATION   220
         STILL GAZING ON THE EVER FULL   • • • • • • •   59 RESIGNATION   227
         WAS HUSHD AND STILL THE MEN WERE PLUNGED IN SLEEP   61 SOHRAB RUSTUM   4
         I HAVE STILL SERVED AFRASIAB WELL AND SHOWN   • •   62 SOHRAB RUSTUM   44
         THIS TOO THOU KNOWST THAT WHILE I STILL BEAR ON • • 62 SOHRAB RUSTUM   46
         THE HOST AND STILL WAS IN HIS LUSTY PRIME   • • •   64 SOHRAB RUSTUM   109
         RUSTUM HIS MORNING MEAL WAS DONE BUT STILL • •   67 SOHRAB RUSTUM   196
         STILL ROUGH LIKE THOSE WHICH MEN IN TREELESS PLAINS   73 SOHRAB RUSTUM   410
         COULD WIELD AN UNLOPPD TRUNK IT WAS STILL ROUGH • • 73 SOHRAB RUSTUM   V 409
         THEIR LIPS STILL WET WHEN I CAME DOWN   • • •   90 SICK KING BOKH   84
         STILL THOU ART KING AND THE LAW STANDS • • • •   92 SICK KING BOKH   138
         ALL THESE HAVE SORROW AND KEEP STILL • • • • •   93 SICK KING BOKH   177
         WHEN I AM DEAD WILL SOON GROW STILL • • • • •   94 SICK KING BOKH   218
         BUT MUCH MUST STILL BE TRIED WHICH SHALL BUT FAIL   99 BALDER DEAD 1   130
         SO THOU MIGHTST LIVE AND STILL DELIGHT THE GODS • • 101 BALDER DEAD 1   218
         ALIVE AND STILL THE RAYS WERE ROUND HIS HEAD   • • 103 BALDER DEAD 1   284
         STILL NORTH UNTIL HE MET A STRETCHING WALL • • •   109 BALDER DEAD 2   144
         AND ROUND THEM STILL THE WATTLED HURDLES HUNG   • • 109 BALDER DEAD 2   173
         LOK STILL SUBSISTS IN HEAVEN OUR FATHER WISE   • • 111 BALDER DEAD 2   217
         STILL LEFT AND THAT CHIEF SCALD THY BROTHER BRAGE   117 BALDER DEAD 3   133
         AND ATE THE SHRIVELLING SAILS BUT STILL THE SHIP • • 119 BALDER DEAD 3   191
         STILL CARRIED OER THE DISTANT WATERS ON   • •   119 BALDER DEAD 3   198
         STILL LIFTED WELL WAS HIS RETURN FOREKNOWN • • •   124 BALDER DEAD 3   378
         HERMOD THE NIMBLE DOST THOU STILL PURSUE   • •   124 BALDER DEAD 3   395
         SITS BALDER STILL IN POMP BY HELAS SIDE   • •   125 BALDER DEAD 3   429
         FREQUENT THE STILL RECESSES OF THE REALM   • •   126 BALDER DEAD 3   435
         LOK TRIUMPHS STILL AND HELA KEEPS HER PREY • • • •   126 BALDER DEAD 3   447
         AND STILL THE ACCEPTANCE FOLLOWS ME WHICH CROWND • • 126 BALDER DEAD 3   461

STILL   (CONTINUED)

SHADOWS OF HATES BUT THEY DISTRESS THEM STILL • • 126 BALDER DEAD 3   467
ITS WINTER WHICH ENDURETH STILL • • • • • 136 TRISTRAM 1   176
BUT ELSE THEY ARE SO STILL • • • • • • • 141 TRISTRAM 1   350
AH TIRED MADCAPS YOU LIE STILL • • • • • • 141 TRISTRAM 1   351
FAR HENCE HER DREAMS ARE FAIR HER SLEEP IS STILL • • 139 TRISTRAM 1   V 302
WHEN SHE SEES HER HUMBLED PALE AND STILL • • • • 144 TRISTRAM 2   60
STILL HOLD HER LOVERS HAND HER HEAD • • • • • 146 TRISTRAM 2   105
STRUNG LIKE WHITE STARS THE PEARLS STILL ARE • • 146 TRISTRAM 2   109
FLASH ON HER WHITE ARMS STILL • • • • • • 146 TRISTRAM 2   111
AS PALE AND STILL AS WITHERD FLOWERS • • • • 147 TRISTRAM 2   127
STILL HOLD HER LOVERS HANDS HER HEAD • • • • • 146 TRISTRAM 2   V 105
STILL HOLDS HER LOVERS HANDS HER HEAD • • • • 146 TRISTRAM 2   V 105
UNDER THE HOLLIES IN THE CLEAR STILL AIR • • • 150 TRISTRAM 3   39
LONG THEY STAYD STILL THEN PACING AT THEIR EASE • • 150 TRISTRAM 3   42
BUT STILL AS THEY PURSUED THEIR WARM DRY ROAD • • 150 TRISTRAM 3   44
AND STILL THE CHILDREN LISTEND THEIR BLUE EYES • • 150 TRISTRAM 3   46
FROM THE OPEN HEATH STILL BY THE HEDGEROWS LAY • • 151 TRISTRAM 3   51
AND THEY WOULD STILL HAVE LISTEND TILL DARK NIGHT • • 151 TRISTRAM 3   56
IS IT THIS THOUGHT WHICH MAKES HER MIEN SO STILL • • 151 TRISTRAM 3   69
SHE HERSELF LOVES THEM STILL AND WHEN THEY ARE TOLD • 152 TRISTRAM 3   110
BUT STILL SHE CHATTED ON WITH HER BLUE EYES • • 154 TRISTRAM 3   177
IS IT THIS THOUGHT THAT MAKES HER MIEN SO STILL • • 151 TRISTRAM 3   V 69
BUT NORTH STILL NORTH SAINT BRANDAN STEERD • • • • 156 SAINT BRANDAN   9
THROUGH THE NARROW PAVED STREETS WHERE ALL WAS STILL • 163 FORSAKEN MERM   70
AND THE WHIZZING WHEEL STANDS STILL • • • • • 164 FORSAKEN MERM   97
UP THE STILL GLISTENING BEACHES • • • • • • 165 FORSAKEN MERM   132
THE CHEEKS THAT STILL THEIR GENTLE PALENESS WEAR • • 175 PARTING   38
THE THOUSAND SWEET STILL JOYS OF SUCH • • • • 179 FAREWELL   67
STAY WITH ME MARGUERITE STILL • • • • • • 183 ABSENCE   20
OR SHALL I FIND THEE STILL BUT CHANGED • • • • 184 TERRACE BERNE   33
I FEEL IT STILL NOW YOUTH IS OER • • • • • 185 TERRACE BERNE   50
WHO CAN STAND STILL • • • • • • • • • 194 STRAYED REVEL   289
STILL AFTER MANY YEARS IN DISTANT LANDS • • • • 200 PHILOMELA   6
STILL NOURISHING IN THY BEWILDERD BRAIN • • • • 200 PHILOMELA   7
DOST THOU STILL BEHOLD • • • • • • • • 201 PHILOMELA   V 16
DOST THOU STILL PERUSE • • • • • • • • 201 PHILOMELA   V 19
DOST THOU STILL REACH • • • • • • • • 201 PHILOMELA   V
AH MAY SHE SCORN THEM STILL TILL WE • • • • 202 URANIA   15
STILL GLIDES THE STREAM SLOW DROPS THE BOAT • • • 206 RIVER   1
AND SOMETIMES BY STILL HARDER FATE • • • • • 207 TOO LATE   5
FRESH BE THE WOUND STILL-RENEWD BE ITS SMARTING • • 206 SEPARATION   3
DEEP BE THE DARKNESS AND STILL BE THE SLUMBER • • 206 SEPARATION   11
STILL THESE WASTE US WITH THEIR HOPELESS STRAINING • • 210 SELF-DECEPTION   19
STILL THE ATTEMPT TO USE THEM PROVES THEM NULL • • 210 SELF-DECEPTION   20
THOU ART TIRED BEST BE STILL • • • • • • 215 LAST WORD   8
THE EVENING COMES THE FIELDS ARE STILL • • • • 217 BACCHANALIA 1   1
THE EVENING COMES THE FIELDS ARE STILL • • • • 218 BACCHANALIA 1   19
THE EVENING COMES THE FIELD IS STILL • • • • 217 BACCHANALIA 1   V 1
THE EVENING COMES THE FIELD IS STILL • • • • 218 BACCHANALIA 1   V 19
THE EPOCH ENDS THE WORLD IS STILL • • • • • 219 BACCHANALIA 2   1
THE EPOCH ENDS THE WORLD IS STILL • • • • • 220 BACCHANALIA 2   28
THE GRASS HAD STILL THE GREEN OF MAY • • • • 222 EPILOG LAOCOON   38
AND STILL THE UNBLACKEND ELMS WERE GAY • • • • 222 EPILOG LAOCOON   39
STILL WE WALKD ON IN THOUGHTFUL MOOD • • • • 223 EPILOG LAOCOON   61
AND STILL THEY LIVE AND STILL THEY BURN • • • 224 EPILOG LAOCOON   104
AND STILL THEY LIVE AND STILL THEY BURN • • • 224 EPILOG LAOCOON   104
AH STILL HARP ON WHAT THEY HEARD • • • • • 227 PERSIST POETRY   4
THE PILLAR STILL BROODS OER THE FIELDS • • • • 228 YOUTH OF NATURE   15
STILL BLOWS IN THE QUANTOCK COOMBS • • • • • 229 YOUTH OF NATURE   23
CROWNS THE STILL VALLEY BEHIND • • • • • • 234 YOUTH OF MAN   63
STILL PLAYS ON THE CITY SPIRES • • • • • • 234 YOUTH OF MAN   82
WHILE THE SOUL STILL LOOKS THROUGH THINE EYES • • 235 YOUTH OF MAN   113
WHILE THE HEART STILL POURS • • • • • • • 235 YOUTH OF MAN   114
STILL DOTH THE SOUL FROM ITS LONE FASTNESS HIGH • • 236 PALLADIUM   21
THAT MAN MUST STILL TO SOME NEW WORSHIP PRESS • • 238 PROGRESS   V
THAT HE HAS STILL THOUGH OLD TO RECOMMENCE • • • 239 REVOLUTIONS   11
STILL STILL LET ME AS I GAZE UPON YOU • • • • 240 SELF-DEPENDENCE   11
STILL STILL LET ME AS I GAZE UPON YOU • • • • 240 SELF-DEPENDENCE   11
THE SPIRIT BLOWETH AND IS STILL • • • • • 241 MORALITY   3
HAST THOU THEN STILL THE OLD UNQUIET BREAST • • • 243 SUMMER NIGHT   27
STILL TO BE WHAT I AM OR YIELD AND BE • • • 243 SUMMER NIGHT   35
UNFREED HAVING SEEN NOTHING STILL UNBLEST • • • 243 SUMMER NIGHT   50
STILL BENT TO MAKE SOME PORT HE KNOWS NOT WHERE • • 244 SUMMER NIGHT   68
STILL STANDING FOR SOME FALSE IMPOSSIBLE SHORE • • 244 SUMMER NIGHT   69
IS LEFT TO EACH MAN STILL • • • • • • • 244 SUMMER NIGHT   92
YET STILL FROM TIME TO TIME VAGUE AND FORLORN • • 247 BURIED LIFE   72
STILL ALL THINGS IN THIS GLADE GO THROUGH • • • 249 KENSINGTON GARD   31
THE CLOUDED SKY IS STILL AND GREY • • • • • 248 KENSINGTON GARD   V
BUT WHEN THE FIELDS ARE STILL • • • • • • 255 SCHOLAR-GIPSY   6
YES WE AWAIT IT BUT IT STILL DELAYS • • • • 260 SCHOLAR-GIPSY   181
STILL FLY PLUNGE DEEPER IN THE BOWERING WOOD • • 261 SCHOLAR-GIPSY   207
STILL NURSING THE UNCONQUERABLE HOPE • • • • 261 SCHOLAR-GIPSY   211
STILL CLUTCHING THE INVIOLABLE SHADE • • • • 261 SCHOLAR-GIPSY   212
THYRSIS AND I WE STILL HAD THYRSIS THEN • • • 263 THYRSIS   10
HEAR IT O THYRSIS STILL OUR TREE IS THERE • • 267 THYRSIS   171
STILL STILL THESE SLOPES TIS CLEAR • • • • 268 THYRSIS   196
STILL STILL THESE SLOPES TIS CLEAR • • • • 268 THYRSIS   196
KNOW HIM A WANDERER STILL THEN WHY NOT ME • • 268 THYRSIS   200
DROP BY AND LEAVE ITS SEEKER STILL UNTIRED • • • 268 THYRSIS   207

STILL   (CONTINUED)

AND STILL THE HAUNT BELOVED A VIRTUE YIELDS	269	THYRSIS	220
ROAM ON THE LIGHT WE SOUGHT IS SHINING STILL	269	THYRSIS	238
ART STILL HAS TRUTH TAKE REFUGE THERE	271	MEMORIAL VERSES	28
AH SINCE DARK DAYS STILL BRING TO LIGHT	272	MEMORIAL VERSES	58
BRIGHT IN THE SUNSET WEIRD AND STILL	273	STANZAS CARNAC	5
STILL ART TO ME	276	SOUTHERN NIGHT	40
ROMANTIC SOLITARY STILL	279	SOUTHERN NIGHT	114
I SEE THEM STILL I SEE THEM NOW	279	SOUTHERN NIGHT	127
STILL THOU PERFORMEST THE WORD	287	RUGBY CHAPEL	46
STILL THOU UPRAISEST WITH ZEAL	287	RUGBY CHAPEL	49
STILL LIKE A TRUMPET DOST ROUSE	287	RUGBY CHAPEL	52
STILL THOU TURNEDST AND STILL	290	RUGBY CHAPEL	131
STILL THOU TURNEDST AND STILL	290	RUGBY CHAPEL	131
BECKONEDST THE TREMBLER AND STILL	290	RUGBY CHAPEL	132
NOTHING TO US THOU WAST STILL	290	RUGBY CHAPEL	138
NOTHING TO US THOU WERT STILL	290	RUGBY CHAPEL	V 138
SUMMER BUT UNDER THEM STILL	292	HEINES GRAVE	6
STILL THE SAME OCEAN ROUND US RAVES	303	GRANDE CHARTR	125
IMMOVEABLE THOU SITTEST STILL	309	OBERMANN	85
THE EARLY PEASANT STILL RECALLS	311	OBERMANN	171
THEN STILL AND SUDDEN OBERMANN	314	OBERMANN MORE	59
STILL STILL WENT FORTH THAT CHILDS DEAR FORCE	318	OBERMANN MORE	163
STILL STILL WENT FORTH THAT CHILDS DEAR FORCE	318	OBERMANN MORE	163
AND STILL WAS AT ITS PRIME	318	OBERMANN MORE	164
IN VAIN MEN STILL WITH HOPING NEW	318	OBERMANN MORE	177
AND STILL IT SPAKE ITS WONTED SPEECH	319	OBERMANN MORE	195
THE MILLIONS SUFFER STILL AND GRIEVE	320	OBERMANN MORE	233
WHAT THOUGH THERE STILL NEED EFFORT STRIFE	322	OBERMANN MORE	289
THOUGH MUCH BE STILL UNWON	322	OBERMANN MORE	290
WHAT STILL OF STRENGTH IS LEFT EMPLOY	323	OBERMANN MORE	321
STILL IN MY SOUL THE VOICE I HEARD	324	OBERMANN MORE	333
YET STILL FOR I CONCEAL IT NOT FERMENTS	334	MEROPE	137
TILL NOW AND I HAVE STRENGTH TO CHAIN IT STILL	334	MEROPE	150
IF STILL INDEED HE LIVES WHOM THOU WOULDST SEAT	336	MEROPE	189
AT LAST IT REACHD US THAT HE STILL MISTRUSTFUL	338	MEROPE	259
ONE SON AT LEAST I SPARED FOR STILL HE LIVES	340	MEROPE	348
YES BUT HIS SEED STILL WISER-COUNSELLD	344	MEROPE	449
THESE POOR EARS STILL AND THESE EYES	346	MEROPE	501
STILL RULES STILL WATCHES AND NUMBRETH THE HOURS	347	MEROPE	527
STILL RULES STILL WATCHES AND NUMBRETH THE HOURS	347	MEROPE	527
STILL BY ACHERON STREAM	347	MEROPE	529
STILL STILL THE DORIAN BOY	347	MEROPE	532
STILL STILL THE DORIAN BOY	347	MEROPE	532
INSTALL HIM IN THY THRONE STILL WITHOUT BLOOD	350	MEROPE	588
CERTAIN IN THIS THAT TIS UNCERTAIN STILL	350	MEROPE	601
THAT MY SON STILL SURVIVES IN HEALTH IN BLOOM	351	MEROPE	612
TO HEAR THAT STILL HE LOVES STILL LONGS FOR ME	351	MEROPE	613
TO HEAR THAT STILL HE LOVES STILL LONGS FOR ME	351	MEROPE	613
BUT STILL OVER HIS SPEECH A GLOOM THERE HUNG	356	MEROPE	764
STILL AT HIS MOUNTAIN-TOMB MEN MARVEL BUILT	357	MEROPE	782
WASHD AS THE MARKS UPON THE HILLS STILL SHOW	358	MEROPE	815
WHERE FIRST THE STAG TOOK WATER FLOATED STILL	358	MEROPE	844
TO FRIENDS STILL MORE AND LABOURERS IN OUR CAUSE	359	MEROPE	872
STILL HE REPEATS THE DROWNING STORY HERE	365	MEROPE	987
MEAN STILL TO KEEP ALOOF FROM DORIAN BROIL	384	MEROPE	1396
OH HADST THOU POLYPHONTES STILL BUT KEPT	395	MEROPE	1725
SINCE SO THOU WILT I DARE MAINTAIN IT STILL	398	MEROPE	1793
STILL RULES STILL WATCHES AND NUMBERS THE HOURS	347	MEROPE	V 527
STILL RULES STILL WATCHES AND NUMBERS THE HOURS	347	MEROPE	V 527
SINCE SO THOU WILT I WILL MAINTAIN IT STILL	398	MEROPE	V1793
IS DARK AND ON THE STREAM THE MIST STILL HANGS	406	EMPEDOCLES I 1	13
AND STILL I KNOW NOT HOW HE DRAWS ME TO HIM	408	EMPEDOCLES I 1	58
IS POTENT STILL ON ME IN HIS DECLINE	408	EMPEDOCLES I 1	66
HE HATH HIS HARP AND LAUREL WITH HIM STILL	409	EMPEDOCLES I 1	82
WHO STILL WAS FAITHFUL WHAT MIGHT PROFIT ME	410	EMPEDOCLES I 1	131
BUT HE STILL LETS THE PEOPLE WHOM HE SCORNS	410	EMPEDOCLES I 1	138
HE HAS HIS HARP AND LAUREL WITH HIM STILL	409	EMPEDOCLES I 1	V 82
AND WHY IS IT THAT STILL	417	EMPEDOCLES I 2	152
YET REMAIN SPENDTHRIFTS STILL	420	EMPEDOCLES I 2	228
STILL USE OUR BODIES ILL	420	EMPEDOCLES I 2	230
AND MUCH MAY STILL EXIST	421	EMPEDOCLES I 2	284
THAT WE WHO RAIL ARE STILL	422	EMPEDOCLES I 2	289
BUT STILL AS WE PROCEED	423	EMPEDOCLES I 2	332
YET STILL IN SPITE OF TRUTH	424	EMPEDOCLES I 2	367
STILL HUNGRIER FOR DELIGHT AS DELIGHTS GROW MORE RARE	424	EMPEDOCLES I 2	371
CHANGEFUL TILL NOW WE STILL	425	EMPEDOCLES I 2	377
I SAY FEAR NOT LIFE STILL	426	EMPEDOCLES I 2	422
IN THE STILL MOUNTAIN AIR	430	EMPEDOCLES II	40
IS THY TORTURED HEART STILL PROUD	430	EMPEDOCLES II	49
IS THY FIRE-SCATHED ARM STILL RASH	430	EMPEDOCLES II	50
STILL ALERT THY STONE-CRUSHD FRAME	430	EMPEDOCLES II	51
DOTH THY FIERCE SOUL STILL DEPLORE	430	EMPEDOCLES II	52
DO THY BLOODSHOT EYES STILL WEEP	430	EMPEDOCLES II	55
THEN WE COULD STILL ENJOY THEN NEITHER THOUGHT	436	EMPEDOCLES II	240
BUT WE SHALL STILL BE IN THEM AND THEY IN US	439	EMPEDOCLES II	349
BAFFLED FOR EVER AND STILL THOUGHT AND MIND	439	EMPEDOCLES II	358
UP THE STILL VALE OF THISBE	442	EMPEDOCLES II	427
DO THY BLOODSHOT EYES STILL SEE	430	EMPEDOCLES II	V 55
DO THY BLOODSHOT EYES STILL FLEE	430	EMPEDOCLES II	V 55

STILL   (CONTINUED)
     ONE STILL LAGS LAST AND TURNS AND EYES THE PILE   •   •   444 WESTMIN ABBEY   14
     STILL BENEATH THEIR FEATHERD BREAST   •   •   •   •   •   455 POOR MATTHIAS   101
     STILL STILL I SEE THE FIGURE SMART   •   •   •   •   •   460 KAISER DEAD   49
     STILL STILL I SEE THE FIGURE SMART   •   •   •   •   •   460 KAISER DEAD   49
     UNLIKE THAT OCEAN-CITY GAZING STILL   •   •   •   •   •   468 ALARIC AT ROME   159
     STILL SHOULD THE SPIRIT HOLD COMMUNION ROME WITH THEE •   470 ALARIC AT ROME   210
     THAT WILDEST VISIONS STILL SHOULD LOVELIEST SEEM   •   •   470 ALARIC AT ROME   213
     STILL TOILS TO PERFECT WHAT THE CHILD BEGAN   •   •   •   473 CROMWELL   46
     THOSE LINGERING HOPES OF COWARD HEARTS THAT STILL •   •   475 CROMWELL   107
     WITH STERN SLOW STEPS UNSEEN YET STILL THE SAME   •   •   476 CROMWELL   147
     STILL TURND TO WATCH THE BATTLE STILL FORGOT   •   •   •   476 CROMWELL   171
     STILL TURND TO WATCH THE BATTLE STILL FORGOT   •   •   •   476 CROMWELL   171
     STILL AS HE GAZD THE PHANTOMS MOURNFUL GLANCE •   •   •   477 CROMWELL   193
     LIKE SOME FORGOTTEN STRAIN THAT HAUNTS US STILL   •   •   477 CROMWELL   195
     THE GREY-STREAKD WATERS LABOUR STILL •   •   •   •   •   479 HAYSWATER BOAT   18
     STILL WOULD BE TRUE YET STILL GROWS COLD   •   •   •   •   481 DESTINY   3
     STILL WOULD BE TRUE YET STILL GROWS COLD   •   •   •   •   481 DESTINY   3
     THY FIERY COURAGE STILL WAS STRONG   •   •   •   •   •   482 COURAGE   20
     STILL MENDING LESSENING HUMAN ILL   •   •   •   •   •   484 ROME-SICKNESS   28

STILLNESS
     SWEEP IN THE SOUNDING STILLNESS OF THE NIGHT •   •   10 MYCERINUS   46
     ERE THE LONG NIGHT WHOSE STILLNESS BROOKS NO STAR   43 GIPSY CHILD   45
     HOW DEEP IS THEIR STILLNESS   •   •   •   •   •   •   •   175 PARTING   15
     WHAT DEATHLIKE STILLNESS OER THE LANDSCAPE LAY   •   466 ALARIC AT ROME   99
     SOON WAS THAT STILLNESS BROKEN LIKE THE CRY   •   •   466 ALARIC AT ROME   109
     IN THE DEEP STILLNESS OF ITS SHELTRING BREAST   •   472 CROMWELL   12

STINGS
     TO THESE OUT-DATED STINGS AGAIN   •   •   •   •   •   •   302 GRANDE CHARTR   106

STIR
     I WITH LITTLE LAND TO STIR   •   •   •   •   •   •   •   22 MEMORY-PICTURE   5
     DEAFEND BY HIS OWN STIR   •   •   •   •   •   •   •   •   47 WORLD QUIETIST   20
     HE SEES THE GENTLE STIR OF BIRTH •   •   •   •   •   •   57 RESIGNATION   170
     I WILL NOT STIR TILL I BE JUDGED •   •   •   •   •   •   91 SICK KING BOKH   104
     LONGING WILL STIR WITHIN MY BREAST THOUGH VAIN   •   •   127 BALDER DEAD 3   499
     THIS STIR THEY HAVE AND THIS ALONE   •   •   •   •   •   141 TRISTRAM 1   349
     IN THE STIR OF THE FORCES   •   •   •   •   •   •   •   177 PARTING   89
     POWERS STIR IN US STIR AND DISAPPEAR •   •   •   •   •   210 SELF-DECEPTION   22
     POWERS STIR IN US STIR AND DISAPPEAR •   •   •   •   •   210 SELF-DECEPTION   22
     STIR OF EXISTENCE   •   •   •   •   •   •   •   •   •   •   233 YOUTH OF MAN   52
     AWAKE AND STIR IN THEIR SOUL •   •   •   •   •   •   •   235 YOUTH OF MAN   92
     ENOUGH OF THIS THOUGH NOT A FINGER STIR   •   •   •   •   383 MEROPE   1375
     AND WE MIGHT GLADLY SHARE THE FRUITFUL STIR   •   •   •   439 EMPEDOCLES II   339
     THE COMING SPRING-TIMES EARLIEST STIR   •   •   •   •   483 ROME-SICKNESS   6

STIRRD
     WHICH STIRRD AND ON THEIR SHOULDERS FLUTTERING PLAYD   25 DREAM   V 25
     AND A FRESH BREATH OF SPRING STIRRD EVERYWHERE   •   •   155 TRISTRAM 3   200
     AND THESE BLANCHD SONG-STIRRD BOUGHS •   •   •   •   •   200 PHILOMELA   V
     AND HEART PROFOUNDLY STIRRD   •   •   •   •   •   •   •   212 GROWING OLD   18
     AN AIR-STIRRD FOREST FRESH AND CLEAR •   •   •   •   •   248 KENSINGTON GARD   16
     HER FOOT THE CUMNER COWSLIPS NEVER STIRRD   •   •   •   265 THYRSIS   99
     HER FOOT THE CUMNER COWSLIPS NEVER STIRRD   •   •   •   265 THYRSIS   V 99
     STIRRD LIKE A CLARION-BLAST MY SOUL   •   •   •   •   •   285 HAWORTH CHURCH   100
     I TURNED BY SOME VAGUE IMPULSE STIRRD   •   •   •   •   324 OBERMANN MORE   335
     PERISHD BEFORE THEIR EYES YET NO MAN STIRRD   •   •   •   381 MEROPE   1315
     FLUTTER CHIRP SHE NEVER STIRRD   •   •   •   •   •   •   453 POOR MATTHIAS   34
     BUT FAR IN OBSCURE THERE STIRRD   •   •   •   •   •   •   458 POOR MATTHIAS   192
     ALL THESE HAD STIRRD THY SPIRIT AND THINE EYE   •   •   472 CROMWELL   31

STIRREST
     BLITHE ALL ELSE STIRS THOU STIRREST NOT AVERSE   •   •   41 GIPSY CHILD   V 13

STIRS
     TO ITS OWN IMPULSE EVERY CREATURE STIRS   •   •   •   •   8 RELIGIOUS ISOL   13
     NOTHING STIRS ON THE LAWN BUT THE QUICK LILAC-SHADE   19 MODERN SAPPHO   2
     BLITHE ALL ELSE STIRS THOU STIRREST NOT AVERSE   41 GIPSY CHILD   V 13
     THY BROTHER-WORLD STIRS AT THY FEET UNKNOWN   •   •   •   46 IN UTRUMQUE PAR   38
     THY NATIVE WORLD STIRS AT THY FEET UNKNOWN   •   •   •   46 IN UTRUMQUE PAR V 36
     STRONGLY STIRS AND TRULY BURNS   •   •   •   •   •   •   49 SECOND BEST   V 24
     DEEPLY STIRS AND TRULY BURNS •   •   •   •   •   •   •   SECOND BEST   V 24
     STIRS THY HAIR GODDESS   •   •   •   •   •   •   •   •   186 STRAYED REVEL   21
     OF SUDDEN STIRS AND PAUSES FAIR   •   •   •   •   •   •   223 EPILOG LAOCOON   64
     AND A LOST PULSE OF FEELING STIRS AGAIN   •   •   •   •   247 BURIED LIFE   85
     WHAT MEMORIES HE STIRS   •   •   •   •   •   •   •   •   313 OBERMANN MORE   36
     WHATEER IN THE MESSENIAN PEOPLE STIRS   •   •   •   •   331 MEROPE   38
     WHATEER IN THE MESSENIAN CITY STIRS   •   •   •   •   •   331 MEROPE   V 38
     STIRS A HISTORY UNEXPRESSD   •   •   •   •   •   •   •   455 POOR MATTHIAS   102

STOCK
     OF THE FRAGRANT STOCK AND THE PINK   •   •   •   •   •   234 YOUTH OF MAN   68
     FROM THE AEOLIAN STOCK OF NELEUS SPRUNG   •   •   •   •   337 MEROPE   236
     OF THAT STOCK BORN WHO BESTOWD   •   •   •   •   •   •   343 MEROPE   426

STOCKS
     WHERE THE SEA-STOCKS BLOOM TO THE WHITE-WALLD TOWN   163 FORSAKEN MERM   69
     AND STOCKS IN FRAGRANT BLOW   •   •   •   •   •   •   •   264 THYRSIS   66

STOIC
    IS THE CALM THINE OF STOIC SOULS WHO WEIGH • • • •   42 GIPSY CHILD   29

STOLE
    WITH LOW SIGHINGS SILENCE STOLE • • • • • •   28 NEW SIRENS   70
    WITH LOW SIGHS HATH SILENCE STOLE • • • • • •   28 NEW SIRENS   V 70
    A WHITE-ROBED SLAVE STOLE TO THE GREAT KINGS SIDE   47 WORLD QUIETIST   27
    A WHITE-ROBED SLAVE STOLE TO THE MONARCHS SIDE • •   47 WORLD QUIETIST V 27
    BUT WHEN THE GREY DAWN STOLE INTO HIS TENT • • • •   61 SOHRAB RUSTUM   7
    I FILLD MY PITCHER AND STOLE HOME • • • • • •   90 SICK KING BOKH   70
    THE MOURNING-STOLE NO MORE • • • • • •   447 WESTMIN ABBEY   97
    ALL NIGHT THEY SATE THEN STOLE AWAY • • • • • •   480 HAYSWATER BOAT   31

STOLN
    STOLN FROM ARISTOPHANES • • • • • • • • • •   456 POOR MATTHIAS   154

STONE
    IN THE NAVE A TOMB OF STONE • • • • • • • • •   16 CHURCH BROU 1   104
    ROUND THE TOMB THE CARVED STONE FRETWORK • • • •   16 CHURCH BROU 1   109
    AND MARVEL AT THE FORMS OF STONE • • • • •   17 CHURCH BROU 2   36
    YOUR EYELIDS ON THE STONE WHERE YE REPOSE • • •   18 CHURCH BROU 3   25
    MUFFLED ITS WALLS AND ON THE STONE-STREWN ROOF • •   25 DREAM   17
    SCREENS NOT NOW A HEART OF STONE • • • • • •   27 NEW SIRENS   52
    AND NOW BEYOND THE RUDE STONE BRIDGE • • • • •   54 RESIGNATION   52
    SO SAYING THE KING TOOK A STONE • • • • • •   91 SICK KING BOKH   117
    IDLE AS A MOSSY STONE • • • • • • • •   137 TRISTRAM 1   223
    WE DIG AND HEAP LAY STONE ON STONE • • • • •   241 MORALITY   8
    WE DIG AND HEAP LAY STONE ON STONE • • • • •   241 MORALITY   8
    TO THE STONE-ROOFD HUT AT THE TOP • • • • •   297 HEINES GRAVE   166
    INTO THEIR STONE-CARVED BASINS COLD • • • • •   300 GRANDE CHARTR   32
    BEFORE SOME FALLEN RUNIC STONE • • • • • •   301 GRANDE CHARTR   83
    BUT AH ITS HEART ITS HEART WAS STONE • • • •   315 OBERMANN MORE   91
    NO CLOISTER-FLOOR OF HUMID STONE • • • • • •   317 OBERMANN MORE   149
    AND SAY THE STONE IS NOT YET TO • • • • • •   318 OBERMANN MORE   179
    OF SUN AND ARID STONE • • • • • • • •   318 OBERMANN MORE   182
    AND THE STONE COFFINS THEN BY CAPHYAE CLIFFS • •   356 MEROPE   744
    IN THE STONE COFFINS AT ORCHOMENUS • • • • •   356 MEROPE   773
    TILL THEN WE ALL SEEMD STONE BUT THEN A CRY •   402 MEROPE   1930
    THROUGH WHOSE HEART ETNA DRIVES HER ROOTS OF STONE   430 EMPEDOCLES II   43
    STILL ALERT THY STONE-CRUSHD FRAME • • • • •   430 EMPEDOCLES II   51
    SITTING ON A TABLED STONE • • • • • • •   434 EMPEDOCLES II   177
    BY MOUNDED TURF AND GRAVEN STONE • • • • •   451 GEISTS GRAVE   64
    MARKD WITH A STONE THY LAST ABODE • • • • •   452 GEISTS GRAVE   72
    AND STOP BEFORE THE STONE AND SAY • • • • •   452 GEISTS GRAVE   76
    DID BY THIS STONE IT SEEMS INTEND • • • • •   452 GEISTS GRAVE   78
    OF SHOOTING CLIFF AND CRUMBLED STONE • • • •   479 HAYSWATER BOAT   13
    LIKE STONE-SCULPTURED ANTIQUE KINGS • • • • •   META CLOISTER   4
    BEFORE A STONE WAS LIFTED AND WE MEMMIUS • • • •   LUCRETIUS 5   5

STONED
    STONED MUST HE BE THE LAW STANDS SO • • • • • •   91 SICK KING BOKH   114

STONES
    STONES ARE SAWING HAMMERS RINGING • • • • •   15 CHURCH BROU 1   89
    THE LOOSE DARK STONES ON THE GREEN WAY • • • •   55 RESIGNATION   100
    THE LIFE OF PLANTS AND STONES AND RAIN • • • •   58 RESIGNATION   195
    SO THEY WHOSE LOT IT WAS CAST STONES • • • • •   91 SICK KING BOKH   121
    LET GODS MEN BRUTES BEWEEP HIM PLANTS AND STONES •   111 BALDER DEAD 2   238
    LET GODS MEN BRUTES BEWEEP HIM PLANTS AND STONES •   114 BALDER DEAD 3   44
    THERE CAME THE GODS AND SATE THEM DOWN ON STONES •   120 BALDER DEAD 3   223
    WE CLIMBD ON THE GRAVES ON THE STONES WORN WITH RAINS   163 FORSAKEN MERM   74
    THE AGATE BROOCH-STONES • • • • • • • •   186 STRAYED REVEL   17
    AND MILK-BARRD ONYX-STONES • • • • • • • •   192 STRAYED REVEL   197
    AND FEEBLY RAKES AMONG THE STONES • • • • •   213 PROGRESS POESY   10
    THE GIANT STONES OF CARNAC SLEEP • • • • • •   274 STANZAS CARNAC   11
    STONES MIGHT HAVE WOUNDED THY FEET • • • • • •   290 RUGBY CHAPEL   135
    STRETCHD AMONG BRIARS AND STONES THE SLOW BLACK GORE   373 MEROPE   1172
    LEND LIFE TO THE DUMB STONES • • • • • • •   421 EMPEDOCLES I 2   274
    IN MEN AND PLANTS AND STONES • • • • • • •   422 EMPEDOCLES I 2   293
    RELICS OF NATIONS THY MEMORIAL-STONES • • • •   464 ALARIC AT ROME   62
    PRISONING IN HIS CREVICD STONES • • • • • •   PILLARS UNIVERS   11
    PRISONING IN HIS RIFTED STONES • • • • • • •   PILLARS UNIVERS V 11

STONING
    TO DIE BY STONING ON THE SPOT • • • • • • •   91 SICK KING BOKH   112

STONY
    IN SOME FAR STONY GORGE OUT OF HIS KEN • • • •   78 SOHRAB RUSTUM   568
    THY SMILE AND ROUGE WITH STONY GLARE • • • • • •   184 TERRACE BERNE   22
    MOUNTS UP THE STONY FOREST-WAY • • • • • • •   300 GRANDE CHARTR   20
    AND STONY MOUNTS THE WAY • • • • • • • •   312 OBERMANN MORE   10
    WORST OF THE THREE THE STONY SPARTA FELL • • • •   389 MEROPE   1553

STOOD
    LAST NIGHT WE STOOD EARNESTLY TALKING TOGETHER • •   19 MODERN SAPPHO   9
    BACKD BY THE PINES A PLANK-BUILT COTTAGE STOOD • •   25 DREAM   15
    WHERE THEY STOOD ONCE TO THEM WERE PAIN • • •   53 RESIGNATION   19
    THROUGH THE BLACK TARTAR TENTS HE PASSD WHICH STOOD   61 SOHRAB RUSTUM   12
    AND SOHRAB CAME THERE AND WENT IN AND STOOD • •   61 SOHRAB RUSTUM   24

STOOD   (CONTINUED)
        AND CHECKD HIS RANKS AND FIXD THEM WHERE THEY STOOD   65 SOHRAB RUSTUM   147
        SO SPAKE HE AND FEROOD STOOD FORTH AND CRIED   66 SOHRAB RUSTUM   184
        THE TABLE STOOD BEFORE HIM CHARGED WITH FOOD   67 SOHRAB RUSTUM   197
        AND PLAYD WITH IT BUT GUDURZ CAME AND STOOD   67 SOHRAB RUSTUM   201
        BUT GUDURZ STOOD IN THE TENT-DOOR AND SAID   67 SOHRAB RUSTUM   207
        AS HE BEHELD HIM COMING AND HE STOOD   70 SOHRAB RUSTUM   320
        AND TRIED AND I HAVE STOOD ON MANY A FIELD   71 SOHRAB RUSTUM   326
        AND STOOD ERECT TREMBLING WITH RAGE HIS CLUB   74 SOHRAB RUSTUM   449
        STOOD IN BROAD DAYLIGHT AND THE SKY WAS PURE   75 SOHRAB RUSTUM   488
        WHO STOOD AT HAND UTTERD A DREADFUL CRY   76 SOHRAB RUSTUM   502
        AND THEN HE STOOD BEWILDERD AND HE DROPPD   76 SOHRAB RUSTUM   519
        SO RUSTUM KNEW NOT HIS OWN LOSS BUT STOOD   78 SOHRAB RUSTUM   574
        HE SPOKE BUT RUSTUM GAZED AND GAZED AND STOOD   81 SOHRAB RUSTUM   689
        AND THEY STOOD WIDE WITH HORROR AND HE SEIZED   81 SOHRAB RUSTUM   699
        SO SPAKE HE AND FEROOD STOOD FORTH AND SAID   66 SOHRAB RUSTUM   V 184
        THE TABLE STOOD BESIDE HIM CHARGED WITH FOOD   67 SOHRAB RUSTUM   V 197
        THE TABLE STOOD BESIDE HIM CHARGED WITH CATES   67 SOHRAB RUSTUM   V 197
        STOOD IN BRIGHT DAYLIGHT AND THE SKY WAS PURE   75 SOHRAB RUSTUM   V 488
        THE WATER-PITCHER WHERE IT STOOD   90 SICK KING BOKH   78
        NOT KNEELING STERNLY FIXD HE STOOD   90 SICK KING BOKH   95
        THEN THEY WHO STOOD ABOUT THE KING   91 SICK KING BOKH   105
        TILL THAT THE KING STOOD FORTH AND SAID   91 SICK KING BOKH   107
        BUT IN HIS BREAST STOOD FIXT THE FATAL BOUGH   95 BALDER DEAD 1   5
        AND STOOD ROUND BALDER ON THE BLOODY FLOOR   95 BALDER DEAD 1   10
        AND ON THE TABLES STOOD THE UNTASTED MEATS   95 BALDER DEAD 1   13
        AND STOOD BY BALDER LYING ON HIS BIER   102 BALDER DEAD 1   270
        WHICH WERE HIS GLORIOUS MARK IN HEAVEN HE STOOD   103 BALDER DEAD 1   285
        AND STOOD ROUND BALDER LYING ON HIS BIER   102 BALDER DEAD 1   V 270
        YET DOCILE NOW HE STOOD AT HERMODS SIDE   107 BALDER DEAD 2   75
        OF HELL BEHELD THEM AND THE GHOSTS STOOD DUMB   112 BALDER DEAD 2   281
        HIS MESSENGER AND HE STOOD FORTH AND CRIED   114 BALDER DEAD 3   32
        AND WREATHED IN SMOKE THE SHIP STOOD OUT TO SEA   118 BALDER DEAD 3   185
        AND THE GODS STOOD UPON THE BEACH AND GAZED   119 BALDER DEAD 3   193
        ROUND WHERE THEY STOOD AND THEY BEHELD TWO FORMS   126 BALDER DEAD 3   442
        BUT HERMOD STOOD BESIDE HIS DROOPING HORSE   129 BALDER DEAD 3   554
        SLOW SLOW AND SOFTLY WHERE SHE STOOD   146 TRISTRAM 2   102
        IN THE SMOOTH CENTRE OF THE OPENING STOOD   150 TRISTRAM 3   19
        WARM IN THEIR MANTLES WRAPT THE THREE STOOD THERE   150 TRISTRAM 3   38
        AND UP AS HIGH AS WHERE THEY STOOD TO LOOK   155 TRISTRAM 3   188
        DOWN IN THE MIDDLE OF THE HOLLOW STOOD   TRISTRAM 3   V 19
        IN THE SMOOTH CENTRE OF THE HOLLOW STOOD   TRISTRAM 3   V 19
        THE SURPLICED PRIEST STOOD DUMB   159 NECKAN   28
        BUT WE STOOD WITHOUT IN THE COLD BLOWING AIRS   163 FORSAKEN MERM   73
        LOCKD IN EACH OTHERS ARMS WE STOOD   178 FAREWELL   11
        AND NOW UPON THE BRIDGE WE STOOD   223 EPILOG LAOCOON   62
        WHICH THEY HAD OF OLD WHEN THEY STOOD   233 YOUTH OF MAN   23
        AND FOUGHT AND SAW IT NOT BUT THERE IT STOOD   236 PALLADIUM   4
        IT STOOD AND SUN AND MOONSHINE RAIND THEIR LIGHT   236 PALLADIUM   5
        ROUND TROY BUT WHILE THIS STOOD TROY COULD NOT FALL   236 PALLADIUM   8
        THE MASTER STOOD UPON THE MOUNT AND TAUGHT   237 PROGRESS   1
        WHILE YET UPON THE VERGE OF HEAVEN HE STOOD   239 REVOLUTIONS   2
        HEADLANDS STOOD OUT INTO THE MOONLIT DEEP   242 SUMMER NIGHT   14
        WE PRIZED IT DEARLY WHILE IT STOOD WE SAID   263 THYRSIS   28
        STOOD WITH SUSPENDED SCYTHE TO SEE US PASS   266 THYRSIS   129
        ON THE GRASS NEAR ME STOOD   314 OBERMANN MORE   60
        MID WEEDS AND WRECKS SHE STOOD A PLACE   317 OBERMANN MORE   139
        HAD STOOD AGAINST THE WAVE   317 OBERMANN MORE   146
        AND OPEN STOOD HIS GRAVE   318 OBERMANN MORE   170
        ITS FRAME YET STOOD WITHOUT A BREACH   319 OBERMANN MORE   193
        THE PEAK OF JAMAN STOOD   323 OBERMANN MORE   332
        HE STOOD BY WHAT HE WISHD FOR I THE SAME   334 MEROPE   129
        WHILE STOOD OER HIM A FORM   346 MEROPE   492
        HAPLY HAD BUT ONE DARING SOUL STOOD FORTH   383 MEROPE   1364
        ALAS OUR FOE ALONE STOOD FORWARD THEN   383 MEROPE   1367
        AND STOOD SHOUTING FOR A FIERY TORCH   399 MEROPE   1835
        THE FLOWER-DRESSD VICTIM STOOD A MILK-WHITE BULL   401 MEROPE   1910
        WHICH FELLD HIM TO THE EARTH AND OER HIM STOOD   402 MEROPE   1922
        SO CHARGD HE STOOD DUMB-FOUNDERD CYPSELUS   365 MEROPE   V
        ON US WHO STOOD DESPONDENT BY   450 GEISTS GRAVE   34
        KAI STOOD CONFEST   459 KAISER DEAD   30
        BUT THOU IMPERIAL CITY THAT HAST STOOD   463 ALARIC AT ROME   19
        YES THERE HE STOOD UPON THAT SILENT HILL   468 ALARIC AT ROME   157
        WITH HEART NEW STRUNG AND STERN RESOLVE HE STOOD   473 CROMWELL   66
        STOOD LIKE A STATUE AND HIS FACE WAS FAIR   477 CROMWELL   176
        AND THE WIND MURMURD ROUND HIM AND HE STOOD   479 CROMWELL   239
        BY THEIR CHARIOTS STOOD THE STEEDS AND CHAMPD   HOMER TRANS   5
            THE WHITE BARLEY

STOOPED
        WHEN THE GOTH STOOPED UPON HIS STRICKEN PREY   464 ALARIC AT ROME   68

STOOPS
        SNUFFS AT IT DAINTILY AND STOOPS HER HEAD   123 BALDER DEAD 3   342
        AND STOOPS TO CLEAR THY MOSS-GROWN DATE   311 OBERMANN   173
        STOOPS TO THE SOARING MOUNTAINS LIVE AND DIE   472 CROMWELL   10

STOP
        IN SINGLE FILE THEY MOVE AND STOP THEIR BREATH   66 SOHRAB RUSTUM   167
        IN SINGLE FILE THEY PASS AND STOP THEIR BREATH   66 SOHRAB RUSTUM   V 167
        IN SINGLE FILE THEY WIND AND STOP THEIR BREATH   66 SOHRAB RUSTUM   V 167

STOP (CONTINUED)
```
        ILL STOP AND SAY THERE WERE NO SUCCOUR HERE      •   •   169 WORLDLY PLACE    13
        STOP NOT TO ME AT THIS BITTER DEPARTING      •  •  •  •  206 SEPARATION        1
        SLOW TO A STOP AT MORNING GREY   •  •  •  •  •  •  276 SOUTHERN NIGHT    29
        BUT STOP TO FETCH BACK THOUGHTS THAT STRAY  •  •  •  313 OBERMANN MORE     29
        AND PARALYSING CONSCIENCE STOP MY ARM   •  •  •  •  333 MEROPE            98
        WHAT HAD OUR ARTHUR GAIND TO STOP AND SEE  •  •  •  •  448 WESTMIN ABBEY    154
        AND STOP BEFORE THE STONE AND SAY  •  •  •  •  •  452 GEISTS GRAVE      76
```

STOPPD
```
        STOPPD IN DARKNESS IN THE COURT    •  •  •  •   14 CHURCH BROU 1     42
        FOR THEY HAD TRAVELLD FAR AND NOT STOPPD YET    •  •  154 TRISTRAM 3      172
        MERLIN AND VIVIAN STOPPD ON THE SLOPES BROW    •  •  155 TRISTRAM 3      201
        SHE BROKE HER FLUTES SHE STOPPD HER SPORTS   •  •  •  316 OBERMANN MORE    129
        WITH SHORT IMPATIENT LOWINGS THERE HE STOPPD    •  •  402 MEROPE         1912
```

STOPPED
```
        THUS FAR HE AND HERE HIS VOICE WAS STOPPED           HOMER TRANS        57
            BY THE FURIES
```

STOPPING
```
        HOVERING AND STOPPING OFT AS IF AFRAID    •  •  •  •  124 BALDER DEAD 3    383
```

STOPS
```
        FAILS BUT ONE THING TO GRIEVE HERE BALDER STOPS   •  •  111 BALDER DEAD 2    235
        FAILS BUT ONE THING TO GRIEVE THERE BALDER STOPS  •  •  114 BALDER DEAD 3     43
        WHY STOPS SHE BY THIS EMPTY PLAY-HOUSE DREAR   •  •  167 RACHEL 1          11
        SEES THEE NOR STOPS HIS MEAL NOR FEARS AT ALL   •  •  258 SCHOLAR-GIPSY    117
        STOPS IT FOR EVER TO PRAISE   •  •  •  •  •  •  282 HAWORTH CHURCH    54
        FOLLOWS THE APPROACHING QUEEN WHO STOPS AS CALLD  •  •  332 MEROPE            64
        FOLLOWS THE ISSUING QUEEN WHO STOPS AS CALLD    •  •  332 MEROPE          V 64
        RISE FAINTLY TO ME NOW IT STOPS WHOS HERE   •  •  •  •  407 EMPEDOCLES I 1    29
```

STORE
```
        WITH SILKEN RAIMENT STORE OF RICE    •  •  •  •  •  94 SICK KING BOKH   194
        OFT THOU HAST GIVEN THEM STORE   •  •  •  •  •  •  257 SCHOLAR-GIPSY     86
        AND ALL HIS STORE OF SAD EXPERIENCE HE   •  •  •  •  260 SCHOLAR-GIPSY    185
        I THINK ON WHAT THE FUTURE HATH IN STORE   •  •  •  397 MEROPE         1775
        WHY SHOULD THIS HEART OF MINE SET MIGHTY STORE   •  •  398 MEROPE         1789
        PAIN AND CARE WITH A DARK STORE   •  •  •  •  •  431 EMPEDOCLES II     86
        WERE THINE IN STORE THOU FAITHFUL FRIEND   •  •  •  •  459 KAISER DEAD       33
```

STORED
```
        ILL-STORED IN STRENGTH IN WITS ARE THEY   •  •  •  •  226 EPILOG LAOCOON   172
        ORCHARD AND CROFT AND FULL-STORED GRANGE   •  •  •  •  313 OBERMANN MORE     27
```

STORES
```
        COOL FARMS WITH OPEN-LYING STORES   •  •  •  •  •   54 RESIGNATION       56
        LONE FARMS WITH OPEN-LYING STORES   •  •  •  •  •   54 RESIGNATION     V 56
        THEN HERE AT NOON COMES BACK HIS STORES TO USE   •  •  255 SCHOLAR-GIPSY     15
```

STORIED
```
        OF FLANDERS TO THE STORIED RHINE   •  •  •  •  •  •  205 CALAIS SANDS      34
```

STORIES
```
        YES THERE ARE STORIES REGISTERED ON HIGH   •  •  •  •  462 ALARIC AT ROME    13
        HUNGARIANS SAVE THE WORLD RENEW THE STORIES   •  •  480 HUNGARIAN NAT      9
```

STORK
```
        AND AS A STORK WHICH IDLE BOYS HAVE TRAPPD   •  •  •  •  129 BALDER DEAD 3    559
```

STORM
```
        SOME REACHES OF THY STORM-VEXT STREAM OF LIFE   •  •   43 GIPSY CHILD       60
        THE STORM THE ABYSS THE HOWLING AND THE PAIN   •  •  109 BALDER DEAD 2    154
        FOR I AM LONG SINCE WEARY OF YOUR STORM   •  •  •  •  127 BALDER DEAD 3    503
        STARS SHONE AFTER A DAY OF STORM   •  •  •  •  •  156 SAINT BRANDAN     14
        YE STORM-WINDS OF AUTUMN   •  •  •  •  •  •  •  174 PARTING            1
        THEN ON THE HEIGHT COMES THE STORM   •  •  •  •  •  289 RUGBY CHAPEL      90
        FALTER ARE LOST IN THE STORM   •  •  •  •  •  •  289 RUGBY CHAPEL     103
        OUR STORM-BEAT FIGURES AND ASKS   •  •  •  •  •  289 RUGBY CHAPEL     114
        SIGHT OF THE REST IN THE STORM   •  •  •  •  •  •  289 RUGBY CHAPEL     119
        THE AUTUMN STORM-WINDS DRIVE THE RACK   •  •  •  •  306 OBERMANN           3
        MIGHT FALL A FRESHENING STORM   •  •  •  •  •  •  319 OBERMANN MORE    198
        DOWN CAME THE STORM OER FRANCE IT PASSD   •  •  •  •  319 OBERMANN MORE    201
        DOWN CAME THE STORM IN RUINS FELL   •  •  •  •  •  319 OBERMANN MORE    205
        DOWN CAME THE STORM IN RUIN FELL   •  •  •  •  •  319 OBERMANN MORE  V 205
        ABIDES ENTHROND AMID THE MIST AND STORM   •  •  •  •  472 CROMWELL          18
        LIT WITH NO RAPTURE AS THE STORM SWEPT BY   •  •  •  •  472 CROMWELL          22
```

STORMIEST
```
        OF EUROPES STORMIEST TIME   •  •  •  •  •  •  •  308 OBERMANN        V 66
```

STORMILY
```
        STORMILY SWEET HIS TITAN-AGONY   •  •  •  •  •  •  166 PICT NEWSTEAD      3
```

STORMS
```
        SCOOP THE SHELVES AND FRET THE STORMS   •  •  •  •   26 NEW SIRENS        12
        STORMS UNSMOOTHD YOUR FOLDED VALLEYS   •  •  •  •   30 NEW SIRENS       123
        NIORD THE GOD OF STORMS WHOM FISHERS KNOW   •  •  •  •  122 BALDER DEAD 3    323
        SO LATE SUCH STORMS THE SAINT IS MAD   •  •  •  •  •  156 SAINT BRANDAN      4
        ITS STORMS OF DUST WITH BURNING HEAT   •  •  •  •  •  157 SAINT BRANDAN     44
```

STORMS   (CONTINUED)
    ONCE-LONGD-FOR STORMS OF LOVE . . . . 183 ABSENCE   14
    OF STORMS THAT RAGE OUTSIDE OUR HAPPY GROUND   . . 264 THYRSIS   49
    ALL FREEDOMS MYSTIC LANGUAGE STORMS THAT ROAR . . 472 CROMWELL   29

STORMY
    ECHO HER STORMY SCREAM AS SHE SAILS BY   . . . . . 78 SOHRAB RUSTUM   572
    AT TWILIGHT ON A STORMY EVE IN MARCH . . . . 69 SOHRAB RUSTUM   V 286
    FLYING OER THE STORMY MAIN   . . . . 136 TRISTRAM 1   188
    THE SEA GROWS STORMY THE LITTLE ONES MOAN . . . . . 163 FORSAKEN MERM   65
    THE SEA GROWS STORMY THE LITTLE ONES MOAN . . . . . 163 FORSAKEN MERM   79
    UPON TIMES BARREN STORMY FLOW   . . . . 183 ABSENCE   19
    AND COMING FLUSHD OVER THE STORMY FRITH . . . . . 196 FRAG ANTIGONE   58
    LOST IT TOO SOON AND LEARNT A STORMY NOTE . . . . 269 THYRSIS   223
    STORMY THROUGH DRIVING MIST   . . . . 286 HAWORTH CHURCH   131
    IN THE STORMY DESOLATE WAVES . . . . 361 MEROPE   911
    WITH WHAT ROLLD OF US IN THE STORMY MAIN . . . . 439 EMPEDOCLES II   342
    WITH WHAT ROLLD OF US IN THE STORMY DEEP . . . . 439 EMPEDOCLES II   V 342
    TELLING HOW ONE STORMY DAY . . . . 457 POOR MATTHIAS   177
    BETWEEN THE BARREN MOUNTAINS AND THE STORMY SEA . 475 CROMWELL   118

STORY
    THE MOON THROUGH THE CLERE-STORY WINDOWS SHINES . . 18 CHURCH BROU 3   36
    FROM ISEULTS LIPS THE UNBROKEN STORY FLOWD . . . 150 TRISTRAM 1   45
    THEY HANG THE PICTURE DOTH THE STORY TELL . . . . 166 PICT NEWSTEAD   8
    SINCE MAN WOKE ON EARTH HE KNOWS HIS STORY . . . . 209 SELF-DECEPTION   3
    WITH POWER DIVINE ITS STORY TELL . . . . 223 EPILOG LAOCOON   60
    THE STORY OF THE OXFORD SCHOLAR POOR . . . . . . 256 SCHOLAR-GIPSY   33
    SINCE FIRST THY STORY RAN THROUGH OXFORD HALLS . . 259 SCHOLAR-GIPSY   132
    THE STORY OF THAT OXFORD SCHOLAR POOR   . . . . . 256 SCHOLAR-GIPSY   V 33
    STORY OF PASSIONATE LIFE . . . . 280 HAWORTH CHURCH   12
    THE STORY OF SPOTS MENTIOND TO HIS OWN . . . . . 356 MEROPE   767
    STILL HE REPEATS THE DROWNING STORY HERE . . . . 365 MEROPE   987
    EXAMIND CLOSE HE OWND THIS STORY FALSE . . . . . 365 MEROPE   V
    INSTRUCT ME OF PANTHEIAS STORY MASTER   . . . . . 412 EMPEDOCLES I 2   20
    HE EVER LOVED THE THEBAN STORY WELL . . . . . . 427 EMPEDOCLES I 2   463

STOUT
    SET HIS STOUT SHOULDER HARD AGAINST THE STERN . . 118 BALDER DEAD 3   176
    STOUT WAS ITS ARM EACH THEW AND BONE . . . . . 315 OBERMANN MORE   89
    STOUT WAS ITS ARM EACH PULSE AND BONE . . . . 315 OBERMANN MORE   V 89

STOUTLY
    STOUTLY UNDER THE HEADLANDS LEE THEY SWAM . . . . 358 MEROPE   822

STOWS
    HE REAPS AND STOWS THEM . . . . 190 STRAYED REVEL   157

STRAFFORDS
    PYMS LOOK OF HATE AND STRAFFORDS GLANCE OF FLAME . . 476 CROMWELL   164

STRAGGLED
    THE GRATING SHINGLE STRAGGLED DOWN   . . . . . . 480 HAYSWATER BOAT   30

STRAGGLERS
    THE STRAGGLERS REFRESH THE OUTWORN   . . . . . . 292 RUGBY CHAPEL   199

STRAGGLING
    IN THE HEDGE STRAGGLING TO THE STREAM . . . . 57 RESIGNATION   178
    RARE STRAGGLING HUNTERS FOILD BY BRAKE AND CRAG . . 357 MEROPE   798
    SOME STRAGGLING HUNTERS TO MY AID TO ROUSE . . . 358 MEROPE   836

STRAIGHT
    LIKE SOME YOUNG CYPRESS TALL AND DARK AND STRAIGHT   70 SOHRAB RUSTUM   314
    AND STRAIGHT THE MOTHER OF THE GODS REPLIED . . 99 BALDER DEAD 1   134
    AND STRAIGHT HE WILL COME DOWN TO OCEANS STRAND . . 99 BALDER DEAD 1   159
    BUT HE MUST STRAIGHT ACCOST THEIR SOLEMN QUEEN . . 100 BALDER DEAD 1   178
    AND STRAIGHT THE MOTHER OF THE GODS REPLIED . . 100 BALDER DEAD 1   187
    HE SPAKE AND STRAIGHT HIS LINEAMENTS BEGAN . . . . 104 BALDER DEAD 1   331
    AND STRAIGHT TO BALDER HERMOD TURND AND SPAKE . . 111 BALDER DEAD 2   249
    AND STRAIGHT HIS NEIGHBOUR MOVED WITH WRATH REPLIED 114 BALDER DEAD 3   20
    AND STRAIGHT THE FATHER OF THE AGES SAID . . . . 115 BALDER DEAD 3   48
    WHEN THE GODS HEARD THEY STRAIGHT AROSE AND TOOK . . 122 BALDER DEAD 3   302
    AND HERMOD STRAIGHT PERCEIVED THEM WHO THEY WERE . . 126 BALDER DEAD 3   444
    THE TRACK A STRAIGHT BLACK LINE . . . . 191 STRAYED REVEL   175
    NO LINGERING NOW STRAIGHT TO THE CITY I . . . . 332 MEROPE   65
    MIGHT SOME ONE STRAIGHT INFORM HIM HE IS SOUGHT . . 354 MEROPE   708
    AND THE STRAIGHT ASHES GROW FOR SPEARS . . . . 414 EMPEDOCLES I 2   65

STRAIGHTWAY
    WILT THOU THEY STRAIGHTWAY BRING HIM IN . . . . 92 SICK KING BOKH   131
    SO SPAKE THE KING OF GODS AND STRAIGHTWAY ROSE . . 96 BALDER DEAD 1   46
    HE SPAKE AND STRAIGHTWAY HELA ANSWERED HIM . . . . 111 BALDER DEAD 2   246
    STRAIGHTWAY HE SPAKE AND THUS ADDRESSD THE GODS . . 122 BALDER DEAD 3   298
    THEY STRAIGHTWAY ARE BURNT UP WITH FUME AND CARE . . 153 TRISTRAM 3   139
    THOU TOO WAST WITH HIM STRAIGHTWAY I SPED HOME . . 407 EMPEDOCLES I 1   43
    STRAIGHTWAY THOU FALLEST TO ARRAIGN THE TIMES . . 411 EMPEDOCLES I 1   144
    THOU TOO WERT WITH HIM STRAIGHTWAY I SPED HOME . . 407 EMPEDOCLES I 1 V 43
    AND ROW HIM STRAIGHTWAY TO THE FURTHER SHORE . . 444 WESTMIN ABBEY   25

STRAIN
```
LET THIS SOBBING PHRYGIAN STRAIN              32 NEW SIRENS      168
AND THIS SOBBING PHRYGIAN STRAIN              32 NEW SIRENS    V 168
LET THIS THROBBING PHRYGIAN STRAIN            32 NEW SIRENS    V 168
WHAT WONDER SHALL TIME BREED TO SWELL THY STRAIN  43 GIPSY CHILD   43
WAFTS NOT FROM THINE OWN THOUGHTS OF GRAVER STRAIN 41 GIPSY CHILD V 10
THESE OER THE CORPSE INTONED A PLAINTIVE STRAIN  103 BALDER DEAD 1  273
THEN SOOTHING WITH THY CHRISTIAN STRAIN FORLORN  168 RACHEL 3         6
WITH SNORT AND STRAIN                        191 STRAYED REVEL   184
ON THE BLUE STRAIT MINE EYES I STRAIN        205 CALAIS SANDS     20
ON THE BLUE SEA MY GAZE I STRAIN             205 CALAIS SANDS   V 20
OER THE BLUE STRAIT MINE EYES I STRAIN       205 CALAIS SANDS   V 20
HERE LET THAT VOICE MAKE END THEN LET A STRAIN  238 PROGRESS      33
AND BLOW A STRAIN THE WORLD AT LAST SHALL HEED  265 THYRSIS       79
SHE LOVED THE DORIAN PIPE THE DORIAN STRAIN  265 THYRSIS         97
HIS DYING STRAIN                             278 SOUTHERN NIGHT 100
AND CHECKS MY STRAIN                         279 SOUTHERN NIGHT 120
A DYING STRAIN                               278 SOUTHERN NIGHT V 100
STERN INTERRUPTED MY STRAIN                  285 HAWORTH CHURCH 127
STERNLY COMPRESSD WE STRAIN ON               289 RUGBY CHAPEL   106
SO LITTLE LOVES THY STRAIN                   307 OBERMANN        40
BUT THAT IS PASSD HE WOULD HAVE PAID THY STRAIN  409 EMPEDOCLES I 1  80
BUT HUSH THIS MOURNFUL STRAIN                448 WESTMIN ABBEY  131
THAT STEADFAST MOURNFUL STRAIN CONSOLED      450 GEISTS GRAVE    17
LIKE SOME FORGOTTEN STRAIN THAT HAUNTS US STILL  477 CROMWELL    195
FREEZES THE SWEET STRAIN ON THE PARTED LIPS      FRAGMENT 1        7
```
STRAIND
```
A STRAIND LIFE WHILE OVERFEEDING              49 SECOND BEST      14
WERE STRAIND TO THAT BREAST                  176 PARTING          70
MY STRAIND ARMS ARE CAST                     176 PARTING        V 64
STRAIND AND LONGD AND GRASPD EACH GIFT IT SAW  210 SELF-DECEPTION 10
```
STRAINING
```
WENT STRAINING THROUGH THE CRACKLING BRUSHWOOD DOWN  106 BALDER DEAD 2  62
THE FLYING LEAVES THE STRAINING BLAST        136 TRISTRAM 1      179
STILL THESE WASTE US WITH THEIR HOPELESS STRAINING  210 SELF-DECEPTION 19
ON SOME BARE HEADLAND STRAINING MOURNFULLY   477 CROMWELL       190
```
STRAINS
```
STRAINS OF GLAD MUSIC AT A FUNERAL            36 VOICE            22
THROUGH WHICH THE GROANING DANUBE STRAINS     52 RESIGNATION      12
THE SHORN AND PARCELLD OXUS STRAINS ALONG     87 SOHRAB RUSTUM   884
HE STRAINS TO JOIN THEIR FLIGHT AND FROM HIS SHED  129 BALDER DEAD 3  563
SUCH MULTITUDE OF HEAVENLY STRAINS           222 EPILOG LAOCOON   33
THOU HEAREST THE IMMORTAL STRAINS OF OLD     268 THYRSIS        V 181
AND TRY THY NOBLEST STRAINS MY CALLICLES     409 EMPEDOCLES I 1   97
OH SOUND THERE NOT SOME STRAINS OF SADNESS THERE  468 ALARIC AT ROME 165
```
STRAIT
```
IN THE STRAIT PASSAGE AT THE FARTHER END     107 BALDER DEAD 2    88
IN THE STRAIT PASSAGE AT THE FURTHER END     107 BALDER DEAD 2  V 88
ALONG THE NEVER-SILENT STRAIT                204 CALAIS SANDS      3
ON THE BLUE STRAIT MINE EYES I STRAIN        205 CALAIS SANDS     20
OER THE BLUE STRAIT MINE EYES I STRAIN       205 CALAIS SANDS   V 20
UPON THE STRAIT ON THE FRENCH COAST THE LIGHT  DOVER BEACH     V 3
A CHURCH ONCE LARGE AND THEN GROWN STRAIT IN SOUL  449 WESTMIN ABBEY 156
```
STRAITLY
```
TIES STRAITLY UP FROM MINE THY LOT           208 ON THE RHINE      8
```
STRAITS
```
PAST STRAITS AND CURRENTS LONG STEERD THROUGH  53 RESIGNATION     21
WITH ECHOING STRAITS BETWEEN US THROWN       182 TO MARG CONT      2
OER THE SUN-REDDEND WESTERN STRAITS          198 FRAG ANTIGONE    92
UPON THE STRAITS ON THE FRENCH COAST THE LIGHT  210 DOVER BEACH     3
OUTSIDE THE WESTERN STRAITS AND UNBENT SAILS  262 SCHOLAR-GIPSY   247
AT THE STRAITS FAILD THAT SPIRIT BRAVE       275 STANZAS CARNAC   46
AT THE FATE-DENIED STRAITS                   344 MEROPE          444
```
STRAND
```
CLUSTERING LIKE BEE-HIVES ON THE LOW FLAT STRAND  61 SOHRAB RUSTUM  13
THROUGH THE BLACK TENTS HE PASSD OER THAT LOW STRAND  61 SOHRAB RUSTUM  16
AND STRAIGHT HE WILL COME DOWN TO OCEANS STRAND  99 BALDER DEAD 1  159
AND HE CAME DOWN TO OCEANS NORTHERN STRAND   108 BALDER DEAD 2   141
AND OER THE ICE HE FARED TO OCEANS STRAND    113 BALDER DEAD 2   288
FOR THE SURGE-BEAT CORNISH STRAND            134 TRISTRAM 1      132
MY MARGUERITE SMILES UPON THE STRAND         174 MEETING           3
EACH GLISTENING STRAND EACH HEATH-FRINGED BAY  177 FAREWELL        4
AT THEIR RETURN UP THE HIGH STRAND           211 DOVER BEACH      11
AT THEIR RETURN UP THE STEEP STRAND          211 DOVER BEACH    V 11
AT THEIR RETURN UP THE BARRD STRAND          211 DOVER BEACH    V 11
BEFORE MAN PARTED FOR THIS EARTHLY STRAND    239 REVOLUTIONS       1
THE CHURCH OF CARNAC BY THE STRAND           274 STANZAS CARNAC   23
WHILE BY THE STRAND                          275 SOUTHERN NIGHT    8
AH ME GIBRALTARS STRAND IS FAR               277 SOUTHERN NIGHT   49
BUT AS ON SOME FAR NORTHERN STRAND           301 GRANDE CHARTR    80
AND THROUGH THE BRUSHWOOD TO THE PEBBLY STRAND  357 MEROPE        807
TO SOME SMALL HUMBLE AND UNNOTED STRAND      395 MEROPE         1745
AND THE STRAND OF EUBOEA                     399 MEROPE         1815
```

STRAND   (CONTINUED)
        BUT ALOOF ON THE LAKE-STRAND . . . . 434 EMPEDOCLES II   165
        AND SETS HIS FREIGHT ASHORE ON THORNEY STRAND . . 445 WESTMIN ABBEY   30
        FROM THOSE TWIN BROOKS THAT BEACHED STRAND . . . . 480 HAYSWATER BOAT   21
        AND THAT GOLDEN-FRUITED STRAND . . . .   PILLARS UNIVERS   1

STRANGE
        SCORNFUL AND STRANGE AND SORROWFUL AND FULL . .   4 EMERSONS ESSAYS   9
        SO SCORNFUL SEEMED THAT SMILE SO STRANGE SO FULL . .   EMERSONS ESSAYS   V 9
        OF THOUGHT SUCH CONTRAST STRANGE . . . .   36 VOICE   28
        STRANGE UNLOVED UPROAR . . . .   50 CONSOLATION   21
        THE STRANGE-SCRAWLD ROCKS THE LONELY SKY . . . . 60 RESIGNATION   268
        A STRANGE UNLIKELY ERRAND SURE IS THINE . . . . 110 BALDER DEAD 2   203
        VAIN AND STRANGE DEBATE WHERE BOTH HAVE SUFFERD . . 144 TRISTRAM 2   53
        FOR THE COLD STRANGE EYES OF A LITTLE MERMAIDEN . 164 FORSAKEN MERM   106
        TOO STRANGE TOO RESTLESS TOO UNTAMED . . . . .   178 FAREWELL   20
        HOW STRANGE THE TREMULOUS SHEEP-CRIES COME . . .   KENSINGTON GARD V 8
        TO LEARN STRANGE ARTS AND JOIN A GIPSY-TRIBE . . 259 SCHOLAR-GIPSY   135
        BEFORE THIS STRANGE DISEASE OF MODERN LIFE . . . 261 SCHOLAR-GIPSY   203
        AND STRANGE AND VAIN THE EARTHLY TURMOIL GROWS . 267 THYRSIS   148
        STRANGE IRONY OF FATE ALAS . . . .   277 SOUTHERN NIGHT   57
        THE STRANGE GUEST SPARKLED NOW TIS PASSD AWAY . 298 HEINES GRAVE   211
        BITTER AND STRANGE WAS THE LIFE . . . . 299 HEINES GRAVE   223
        OF HEINE HIS STRANGE ALAS . . . .   299 HEINES GRAVE   224
        THIS STRANGE UNLIKELY TALE THE PRINCE WAS DROWND . 364 MEROPE   V
        A STRANGE WAYFARER COMING TO HIS SIDE . . . .   444 WESTMIN ABBEY   23
        WHEREBY STRANGE ARE THEY AND WE . . . . . .   456 POOR MATTHIAS   150
        SINCE THAT STRANGE CREW DID RIDE AFLOAT . . . . 480 HAYSWATER BOAT   36

STRANGELY
        ERRS STRANGELY FOR THE KING FOR KAI KHOSROO . .   67 SOHRAB RUSTUM   223
        AH GOLDEN-HAIRD STRANGELY SMILING GODDESS . . . . 194 STRAYED REVEL   286
        BUT STRANGELY MISINTERPRET ALL YOU HEAR . . . . 198 FRAG DEJANEIRA   14
        AND STRANGELY AS WE TALKD HE WOULD APPLY . . . . 356 MEROPE   766
        BUT HE IS STRANGELY WROUGHT I WILL SPEED BACK . . 428 EMPEDOCLES I 2   480
        SEEMS STRANGELY ECHOED BACK BY TONES OF YESTERDAY   464 ALARIC AT ROME   48

STRANGER
        OF THAT STRANGER-KNIGHT ILL-STARRD . . . . . . 136 TRISTRAM 1   200
        QUICK-EYED STRANGER . . . . 189 STRAYED REVEL   103
        ART THOU HE STRANGER . . . . 189 STRAYED REVEL   111
        WHO LET ME SAY IS THIS STRANGER REGARDS ME . . . . 206 SEPARATION   15
        STRANGER THIS NEWS THOU BRINGEST IS TOO GREAT . 359 MEROPE   859
        WHICH NO STRANGER UNKNOWN . . . .   369 MEROPE   1089
        AND THE STERN DESTINY-BROUGHT STRANGER . . . . 400 MEROPE   1861
        STRANGER THE NEWS THOU BRINGEST IS TOO GREAT . 359 MEROPE   V 859
        AND THITHERWARD THE STRANGER TOOK HIS WAY . . .   445 WESTMIN ABBEY   33

STRANGERS
        IF HE FOR STRANGERS PAIND HIS HEART . . . . . .   92 SICK KING BOKH   147
        BEFORE A STRANGERS THRESHOLD NOT HIS HOME . . . 114 BALDER DEAD 3   13
        IN THIS FAIR STRANGERS EYES OF GREY . . . . . 183 ABSENCE   1
        WITH STRANGERS BUT THE BOND . . . . 196 FRAG ANTIGONE   35
        ONLY WITH STRANGERS TO MEET . . . . 284 HAWORTH CHURCH   75
        THE PENSIVE STRANGERS FACE . . . . 311 OBERMANN   172
        NO WE ARE STRANGERS HERE THE WORLD IS FROM OF OLD   418 EMPEDOCLES I 2   181
        AND WE SHALL BE THE STRANGERS OF THE WORLD . . . 439 EMPEDOCLES II   350
        FAMINE AND SORROW ARE NO STRANGERS HERE . . . . 465 ALARIC AT ROME   82

STRANGLED
        NATURES WISH MUST NOW BE STRANGLED . . . . . .   49 SECOND BEST   11
        THEIR ROCK-STRANGLED HUM . . . .   175 PARTING   30
        WHILE HARK FAR DOWN WITH STRANGLED SOUND . . . . 299 GRANDE CHARTR   9

STRATFORD
        STRATFORD MEADOWS FOR THEE . . . .   294 HEINES GRAVE   64

STRAW
        STRAW HATS BEDECKD THEIR HEADS WITH RIBBONS BLUE . . 25 DREAM   24
        TO CHEW THE STRAW HER LITTER AT HER FEET . . . . 123 BALDER DEAD 3   343
        THEN SOUGHT THY STRAW IN SOME SEQUESTERD GRANGE . 259 SCHOLAR-GIPSY   130

STRAY
        ROUND THE WALL TO STRAY . . . .   16 CHURCH BROU 2   11
        ROUND THE TOMB TO STRAY . . . .   17 CHURCH BROU 2   35
        KALMUCKS AND UNKEMPT KUZZAKS TRIBES WHO STRAY .   65 SOHRAB RUSTUM   132
        KALMUCKS AND UNKEMPD KUZZAKS TRIBES WHO STRAY .   65 SOHRAB RUSTUM   V 132
        NOR DID THEIR LOOKS STRAY ONCE TO THE SEA-SIDE . 151 TRISTRAM 3   48
        BAFFLED BEWILDERD THEY STRAY . . . .   216 LORDS MESSENGER   14
        THAT THE LOST SCHOLAR LONG WAS SEEN TO STRAY . 256 SCHOLAR-GIPSY   53
        SO OFTEN HAS HE KNOWN THEE PAST HIM STRAY . . . 258 SCHOLAR-GIPSY   118
        THOU THROUGH THE FIELDS AND THROUGH THE WOODS   261 SCHOLAR-GIPSY   197
              DOST STRAY
        SOLE THEY SHALL STRAY IN THE ROCKS . . . . . . 291 RUGBY CHAPEL   185
        SOLE THEY SHALL STRAY ON THE ROCKS . . . . . . 291 RUGBY CHAPEL   V 185
        BUT STOP TO FETCH BACK THOUGHTS THAT STRAY . . . 313 OBERMANN MORE   29
        AND ALL THAT THEBAN WOE AND STRAY . . . . . . 427 EMPEDOCLES I 2   459
        TINY THOUGH THOU ART TO STRAY . . . . 458 POOR MATTHIAS   208
        TO ALL WHO SINK TO ALL WHO STRAY . . . . 484 ROME-SICKNESS   32

STRAYING
    BUT FOR ME MY THOUGHTS ARE STRAYING • • • • • •   29 NEW SIRENS   93

STRAYS
    THEN WHEN WE MEET AND THY LOOK STRAYS TOWARD ME • • 206 SEPARATION   13
    THEN WHEN WE MEET AND THY LOOK STRAYS TOWARDS ME • • 206 SEPARATION   V 13
    TO-NIGHT FROM OXFORD UP YOUR PATHWAY STRAYS   • • 263 THYRSIS   8
    O MY COMFORTERS STRAYS • • • • • • • • • • • 348 MEROPE   V

STREAK
    LET THE FLUTTERING FRINGES STREAK   • • • • • • 23 MEMORY-PICTURE   29

STREAKD
    STREAKD WITH ITS FIRST GREY HAIRS HOPE FILLED HIS SOUL 71 SOHRAB RUSTUM   340
    AND THE FIRST RAYS OF MORNING STREAKD THE EAST   • • 61 SOHRAB RUSTUM V   1
    THE GREY-STREAKD WATERS LABOUR STILL • • • • • • 479 HAYSWATER BOAT   18

STREAM
    BY THE STREAM BELOW THE PINES • • • • • • • • 15 CHURCH BROU 1   92
    THE STREAM GOES LEAPING BY • • • • • • • • • • 16 CHURCH BROU 2   3
    CROSSING THE STREAM THE KINE ARE SEEN • • • • • 16 CHURCH BROU 2   10
    OF DARK ELMS SHOOT ROUND DROPPING DOWN THE   19 MODERN SAPPHO   6
        PROUD STREAM
    OF DARK ELMS COME ROUND DROPPING DOWN THE PROUD STREAM 19 MODERN SAPPHO V   6
    MARTIN AND I DOWN A GREEN ALPINE STREAM • • • • 24 DREAM   2
    WE SHOT BENEATH THE COTTAGE WITH THE STREAM • • • 25 DREAM   20
    STREAM ALL DAY THROUGH YOUR ENCHANTED LAWN • • • 26 NEW SIRENS   24
    SOME REACHES OF THY STORM-VEXT STREAM OF LIFE • • 43 GIPSY CHILD   60
    AGES OR HOURS O WAKING ON LIFES STREAM • • • • 45 IN UTRUMQUE PAR 11
    ON THIS MILD BANK ABOVE THE STREAM • • • • • • 55 RESIGNATION   102
    IN THE HEDGE STRAGGLING TO THE STREAM • • • • • 57 RESIGNATION   178
    THIS STREAM WHICH FALLS INCESSANTLY • • • • • • 60 RESIGNATION   267
    THIS STREAM THAT FALLS INCESSANTLY • • • • • • 60 RESIGNATION V 267
    AND THE FOG ROSE OUT OF THE OXUS STREAM • • • • 61 SOHRAB RUSTUM   2
    BUT ALL THE TARTAR CAMP ALONG THE STREAM • • • • 61 SOHRAB RUSTUM   3
    CROSSING THE STREAM IN SUMMER SCRAPES THE LAND • 61 SOHRAB RUSTUM   19
    STREAM OVER CASBIN AND THE SOUTHERN SLOPES • • • 64 SOHRAB RUSTUM   113
    AND THE SUN SPARKLED ON THE OXUS STREAM • • • • 75 SOHRAB RUSTUM   489
    AND OXUS CURDLED AS IT CROSSD HIS STREAM • • • • 76 SOHRAB RUSTUM   508
    NOR SLAKED MY THIRST AT THE CLEAR HELMUND STREAM • 83 SOHRAB RUSTUM   758
    THE NORTHERN SIR AND THIS GREAT OXUS STREAM • • • 83 SOHRAB RUSTUM   765
    FLOWD WITH THE STREAM ALL DOWN HIS COLD WHITE SIDE • 86 SOHRAB RUSTUM   842
    CROSSING THE STREAM IN SUMMER MEETS THE LAND • • 61 SOHRAB RUSTUM V 19
    AND OXUS CURDLED AS IT REACHD HIS STREAM • • • • 76 SOHRAB RUSTUM V 508
    AND THE CANAL WHICH FROM THE STREAM • • • • • • 89 SICK KING BOKH   62
    AND THE CANAL THAT FROM THE STREAM • • • • • • 89 SICK KING BOKH V 62
    THROUGH THE CLIFF-WALL AND A FRESH STREAM RUNS DOWN • 97 BALDER DEAD 1   82
    WHICH SPANS WITH GOLDEN ARCHES GIALLS STREAM • • 99 BALDER DEAD 1 148
    AND IS ALONE NOT DIPT IN OCEANS STREAM • • • • 99 BALDER DEAD 1 158
    WHICH SPANS WITH GOLDEN ARCHES GIALLS STREAM • • 107 BALDER DEAD 2   86
    UNDER WHOSE HOOFS THE BRIDGE OER GIALLS STREAM • 107 BALDER DEAD 2 102
    HOW DIDST THOU CROSS THE BRIDGE OER GIALLS STREAM • 110 BALDER DEAD 2 183
    TO THE ARMD DAMSELS BRIDGE AND GIALLS STREAM • • 113 BALDER DEAD 2 290
    THE WAY HE KNEW AND TRAVERSED GIALLS STREAM • • 124 BALDER DEAD 3 375
    WHERE THE DEEP FOREST STREAM CREEPS SLOW • • • 148 TRISTRAM 2   V
    WHERE THE SALT WEED SWAYS IN THE STREAM • • • • 162 FORSAKEN MERM   38
    STREAM ON HER FROM HER LORDS YET RECENT GRAVE • • 172 GOOD SHEPHERD   8
    AND THE ROOFD BRIDGE THAT SPANS THE STREAM • • • 177 FAREWELL   6
    THE STREAM AND DO I LINGER HERE • • • • • • 183 TERRACE BERNE   4
    LONE CHORASMIAN STREAM THEREON • • • • • • • 191 STRAYED REVEL 183
    HIGH ON A JUTTING ROCK IN THE RED STREAM • • • • 192 STRAYED REVEL 230
    ON THE OXUS STREAM BUT CARE • • • • • • • • 193 STRAYED REVEL 245
    STILL GLIDES THE STREAM SLOW DROPS THE BOAT • • 206 RIVER   1
    FOR THE BRIGHT STREAM A CHANNEL GRAND • • • • 213 PROGRESS POESY   6
    SHINES NOT ITS STREAM • • • • • • • • • • 220 BACCHANALIA 2   52
    AND THROUGH THE STREAM OF MUSIC TELL • • • • • 223 EPILOG LAOCOON   85
    MEN WITH THEIR STREAM OF LIFE WERE HERE • • • • 224 EPILOG LAOCOON 112
    AND WANDERING FROM THE STREAM THEY GO • • • • 226 EPILOG LAOCOON 174
    THEY CATCH OF THE MYSTERIOUS STREAM • • • • • 226 EPILOG LAOCOON 178
    THE STREAM OF LIFES MAJESTIC WHOLE • • • • • 226 EPILOG LAOCOON 187
    FLOATS THE IMPERIAL STREAM • • • • • • • • 234 YOUTH OF MAN   87
    BRIGHT ELSE AND FAST THE STREAM OF LIFE MAY ROLL • 238 PROGRESS   29
    THE BURIED STREAM AND SEEM TO BE • • • • • • 246 BURIED LIFE   42
    RIVETS HIS GAZE ON THE BANKS OF THE STREAM • • • 251 FUTURE   6
    OF THE NEW-BORN CLEAR-FLOWING STREAM • • • • • 252 FUTURE   12
    WITH A THOUSAND CRIES IS ITS STREAM • • • • • 253 FUTURE   54
    DENSER THE TRADE ON ITS STREAM • • • • • • • 253 FUTURE   63
    ON A WIDER STATELIER STREAM • • • • • • • • 253 FUTURE   74
    BRINGS UP THE STREAM • • • • • • • • • • 254 FUTURE   86
    TRAILING IN THE COOL STREAM THY FINGERS WET • • 257 SCHOLAR-GIPSY   75
    AND THINE EYES RESTING ON THE MOONLIT STREAM • • 257 SCHOLAR-GIPSY   80
    AND MENS INCESSANT STREAM GOES BY • • • • • • 277 SOUTHERN NIGHT   63
    WHERE UNDER LOUGHRIGG THE STREAM • • • • • • 280 HAWORTH CHURCH   1
    THE TRACK THE STREAM-BED DESCENDS • • • • • • 289 RUGBY CHAPEL   95
    UP BY THE STREAM WITH ITS HUGE • • • • • • • 297 HEINES GRAVE   159
    AND MIST-TRACKD STREAM OF THE WIDE • • • • • 297 HEINES GRAVE   172
    DOTH THE DEAD GUIERS STREAM COMPLAIN • • • • • 299 GRANDE CHARTR   10
    BUT WHERE THE ROAD RUNS NEAR THE STREAM • • • • 305 GRANDE CHARTR 175
    STILL BY ACHERON STREAM • • • • • • • • • 347 MEROPE   529
    CAST BY THE RUMBLING SUBTERRANEAN STREAM • • • 358 MEROPE   841
    THE AROANIAN STREAM • • • • • • • • • • 391 MEROPE   1612
    BY THE STREAM-SIDE AFTER THE DUSTY LANES • • • • 406 EMPEDOCLES I 1   3

STREAM   (CONTINUED)
    IS DARK AND ON THE STREAM THE MIST STILL HANGS   • • 406 EMPEDOCLES I 1   13
    THE NOON IS HOT WHEN WE HAVE CROSSD THE STREAM   • • 412 EMPEDOCLES I 2   1
    THE TRACK WINDS DOWN TO THE CLEAR STREAM • • • 413 EMPEDOCLES I 2   36
    IS FRESHEND BY THE LEAPING STREAM WHICH THROWS • • 414 EMPEDOCLES I 2   46
    AND STREAM AND SWARD AND CHESTNUT-TREES • • • 414 EMPEDOCLES I 2   52
    THE STREAM LIKE US DESIRES • • • • • 420 EMPEDOCLES I 2   249
    DOWN BY THE STREAM YES MASTER IN THE WOOD • • • 427 EMPEDOCLES I 2   462
    JUST SINCE DOWN AT THE STREAM HO CALLICLES • • • 428 EMPEDOCLES I 2   486
    LETTING THE SEA-STREAM WANDER THROUGH THY HAIR • • 430 EMPEDOCLES II   61
    THEY STREAM UP AGAIN • • • • • • • 442 EMPEDOCLES II   450
    BELOW THE SURFACE-STREAM SHALLOW AND LIGHT • • • 483 BELOW SURFACE   1
    OF WHAT WE SAY WE FEEL BELOW THE STREAM • • • 483 BELOW SURFACE   2
    THE CENTRAL STREAM OF WHAT WE FEEL INDEED • • • 483 BELOW SURFACE   5

STREAMD
    FROM THEIR BLACK TENTS LONG FILES OF HORSE   64 SOHRAB RUSTUM   110
        THEY STREAMD
    FOR THE WARM PERSIAN SEA-BOARD SO THEY STREAMD • • 64 SOHRAB RUSTUM   116
    THEN RAISED HER FACE AND GLORY ROUND HER STREAMD • • 447 WESTMIN ABBEY   96
    STREAMD TO THE GROUND BY THE YOKE ESCAPING   HOMER TRANS   45
        FROM UNDER THE COLLAR

STREAMED
    HORDE AFTER HORDE STREAMED UP THY FROWNING CAPITOL   464 ALARIC AT ROME   72

STREAMING
    FROM YOUR DAZZLED WINDOWS STREAMING • • • • • 32 NEW SIRENS   183
    WITH STREAMING FLANKS AND HEADS • • • • • • 190 STRAYED REVEL   148
    SULLYING HIS GARMENT WITH DARK-STREAMING BLOOD • • 346 MEROPE   491
    COME STREAMING WITH THE FLOODS OF GLORY IN • • • 445 WESTMIN ABBEY   38
    AN INWARD LIGHT THAT WITH ITS STREAMING RAY • • 473 CROMWELL   61

STREAMS
    STREAMS FROM THE SETTING SUN AND COLOURS BRIGHT • • 18 CHURCH BROU 3   19
    UPON THE MOSSY ROCKS AT THE STREAMS EDGE • • • 25 DREAM   14
    FLASHD ONCE LIKE FALLING STREAMS WE ROSE WE GAZED • 25 DREAM   29
    SPRING THE GREAT STREAMS • • • • • • • • 45 IN UTRUMQUE PAR   21
    FROM THE STREAMS BRINK THE SPOT WHERE FIRST A BOAT • 61 SOHRAB RUSTUM   18
    TO HEM HIS WATERY MARCH AND DAM HIS STREAMS • • 87 SOHRAB RUSTUM   882
    THROUGH VALLEYS DEEP-ENGULPHD WITH ROARING STREAMS • 99 BALDER DEAD 1   146
    AND HEAR THE ROARING OF THE STREAMS OF HELL • • 100 BALDER DEAD 1   173
    THROUGH VALLEYS DEEP-ENGULPHD BY ROARING STREAMS • 107 BALDER DEAD 2   84
    FOR IN THAT ICE ARE LOST THOSE NORTHERN STREAMS • • 108 BALDER DEAD 2   128
    AND HEARD THE THUNDER OF THE STREAMS OF HELL • • 109 BALDER DEAD 2   151
    QUIVERING AND OTHERS SKIM THE RIVER-STREAMS • • 109 BALDER DEAD 2   161
    SWINGING AND OTHERS SKIM THE RIVER-STREAMS • • • 109 BALDER DEAD 2 V 161
    THE JOYLESS PLAINS AND HEARD THE STREAMS OF HELL • 124 BALDER DEAD 3   380
    LIES IN DISORDERD STREAMS AND THERE • • • • 146 TRISTRAM 2   108
    ARE BUSY GATHERING SPARS OF QUARTZ AND STREAMS • 150 TRISTRAM 3   25
    OF PELION IN THE STREAMS • • • • • • • 190 STRAYED REVEL   145
    ONLY A FEW THE LIFE-STREAMS SHORE • • • • 226 EPILOG LAOCOON   189
    SET WHERE THE UPPER STREAMS OF SIMOIS FLOW • • 236 PALLADIUM   1
    STREAMS THROUGH THEIR ROWS OF PILLARS OLD • • • 274 STANZAS CARNAC V 14
    AND ON THIS SIDE THOSE CONFLUENT STREAMS WHICH MAKE 330 MEROPE   18
    THAT THE BLOOD RUSHES IN STREAMS TO THE DUST • 400 MEROPE   1865
    THAT CLIMB FROM THE STREAMS EDGE THE LONG GREY TUFTS 406 EMPEDOCLES I 1   16
    CLEANSE TO SWEET AIRS THE BREATH OF POISONOUS STREAMS 410 EMPEDOCLES I 1   117
    STREAMS WILL NOT CURB THEIR PRIDE • • • • • 420 EMPEDOCLES I 2   252
    OF MANY A LAWNY HILL AND STREAMS WITH SILVER FLOW 474 CROMWELL   104

STREET
    IN JOPPA THROUGH THE PUBLIC STREET • • • • • 157 SAINT BRANDAN   42
    AND IN THE STREET A LEPER SATE • • • • • • 157 SAINT BRANDAN   45
    FOR THE HUMMING STREET AND THE CHILD WITH ITS TOY 164 FORSAKEN MERM   90
    UP THE STEEP STREET I HURRIED FAST • • • • 177 FAREWELL   7
    IN THE DESERTED MOON-BLANCHD STREET • • • 242 SUMMER NIGHT   1
    THE VILLAGE STREET ITS HAUNTED MANSION LACKS • 262 THYRSIS   3
    THE LIGHTS COME OUT IN THE STREET • • • • 286 RUGBY CHAPEL   8
    WERE KNOWN TO ALL THE VILLAGE-STREET • • • • 459 KAISER DEAD   8
    DID FALL LIKE RAIN IN THE FORSAKEN STREET • • • FRAGMENT 7   2

STREETS
    TOIL ENDED THROUGH THE SHINING STREETS • • • 57 RESIGNATION   167
    IN ODINS HALL AND WENT THROUGH ASGARD STREETS • 97 BALDER DEAD 1   73
    BUT NIGHT CAME DOWN AND DARKEND ASGARD STREETS • 101 BALDER DEAD 1   202
    THROUGH THE FAST-DARKENING STREETS TO HIS OWN HOUSE 101 BALDER DEAD 1   207
    ALONG THE FLINTY FLOOR OF ASGARD STREETS • • 102 BALDER DEAD 1   261
    AND THROUGH THE EMPTY STREETS HE RODE AND PASSD • 113 BALDER DEAD 2   308
    THROUGH MANY STREETS THE POOR BEAST RUNS IN VAIN • 114 BALDER DEAD 3   10
    THROUGH THE NARROW PAVED STREETS WHERE ALL WAS STILL 163 FORSAKEN MERM   70
    TWAS DAWN A BROUGHAM ROLLD THROUGH THE STREETS 167 RACHEL 1   4
        AND MADE
    SMOTE ON THE SQUALID STREETS OF BETHNAL GREEN • 169 EAST LONDON   2
    WHAT INNS YOUR STREETS TOO HOW NARROW • • • 214 NEW ROME   11
    WIDE STREETS WITH FINE DOUBLE TROTTOIRS • • • 214 NEW ROME   15
    YOUR STREETS ARE ANCIENT AND NARROW • • • • 214 NEW ROME V 11
    YOUR STREETS HOW ANCIENT AND NARROW • • • • 214 NEW ROME V 11
    NEW STREETS WITH FINE DOUBLE TROTTOIRS • • • 214 NEW ROME V 15
    BUT OFTEN IN THE WORLDS MOST CROWDED STREETS • 246 BURIED LIFE   45
    HITHER TO COME FROM THE STREETS • • • • • 292 HEINES GRAVE   14
    THERE ROSE UP A CRY IN THE STREETS • • • • 345 MEROPE   487
    TO HEAR ANOTHER TUMULT IN THESE STREETS • • • 349 MEROPE   561

STREETS   (CONTINUED)
        VISIT OUR STREETS AND THE SOUND   . . . . . .   360 MEROPE   894
        ANCIENT STREETS OF HASTINGS TOWN   . . . . . .   457 POOR MATTHIAS   182

STRENGTH
        TOOK MEASURE OF HIS SOUL AND KNEW ITS STRENGTH   . .   12 MYCERINUS   109
        NOT FROM HERSELF HER FAME OF STRENGTH SHE TOOK   . .   37 WORLDS TRIUMPHS   3
        THINE OLD STRENGTH REVEALING   . . . .   39 STAGIRIUS   37
        THY TRUE STRENGTH REVEALING   . . . .   39 STAGIRIUS   V   37
        CHANGE DOTH UNKNIT THE TRANQUIL STRENGTH OF MEN   . .   44 QUESTION   3
        WHETHER THAT HIS OWN MIGHTY STRENGTH AT LAST   . .   63 SOHRAB RUSTUM   83
        TILL NOW ALL STRENGTH WAS EBBD AND FROM HIS LIMBS   86 SOHRAB RUSTUM   853
        MADE FAST TO THE BORED CRAG BY WILE NOT STRENGTH . . 111 BALDER DEAD 2   215
        IF STRENGTH MIGHT SAVE THEM COULD NOT ODIN SAVE   . . 127 BALDER DEAD 3   490
        IF STRENGTH COULD SAVE THEM COULD NOT ODIN SAVE   . . 127 BALDER DEAD 3   V 490
        FROM STRENGTH TO STRENGTH ADVANCING ONLY HE   . . 172 IMMORTALITY   12
        FROM STRENGTH TO STRENGTH ADVANCING ONLY HE   . . 172 IMMORTALITY   12
        STERN STRENGTH AND PROMISE OF CONTROL   . . . .   178 FAREWELL   24
        IS IT TO FEEL OUR STRENGTH   . . . .   212 GROWING OLD   6
        NOT OUR BLOOM ONLY BUT OUR STRENGTH DECAY   . . .   212 GROWING OLD   7
        ILL-STORED IN STRENGTH IN WITS ARE THEY   . . .   226 EPILOG LAOCOON   172
        ILL FOUND IN STRENGTH IN WITS ARE THEY   . . . .   226 EPILOG LAOCOON   V 172
        HERE WAS THINE HEIGHT OF STRENGTH THY GOLDEN PRIME   269 THYRSIS   219
        OF BEING IS PRACTISED THAT STRENGTH   . . . . .   287 RUGBY CHAPEL   42
        WHAT STILL OF STRENGTH IS LEFT EMPLOY   . . . .   323 OBERMANN MORE   321
        TILL NOW AND I HAVE STRENGTH TO CHAIN IT STILL   . . 334 MEROPE   150
        THINE ENEMY THOU KNOWST NOT NOR HIS STRENGTH   . . 381 MEROPE   1294
        ALAS AN ADAMANTINE STRENGTH INDEED   . . . . .   386 MEROPE   1434
        FOR THIS IS THE TRUE STRENGTH OF GUILTY KINGS   . . 386 MEROPE   1436
        BUILT IN STRENGTH AGAINST THE VANQUISHD   . . . .   400 MEROPE   1854
        IS FATE INDEED SO STRONG MANS STRENGTH INDEED SO POOR 415 EMPEDOCLES I 2   96
        FAIN WOULD DO ALL THINGS WELL BUT SOMETIMES   422 EMPEDOCLES I 2   296
                FAILS IN STRENGTH
        FOR SOMETHING HAS IMPAIRD THY SPIRITS STRENGTH   . . 429 EMPEDOCLES II   21
        AND DEADLY AIRS HIS STRENGTH DID UNDERMINE   . . . . 448 WESTMIN ABBEY   126
        STEMMD BY THE STRENGTH OF MANHOOD FEARLESSLY   . . 473 CROMWELL   50
        KEPT MORE THAN US THEIR STRENGTH OF SOUL   . . . .   481 COURAGE   12

STRENGTHEN
        OTHERS WILL STRENGTHEN US TO BEAR   . . . . . .   272 MEMORIAL VERSES   66
        STRENGTHEN THE WAVERING LINE   . . . .   292 RUGBY CHAPEL   205

STRENUOUS
        WHEN ON THE STRENUOUS JUST MAN HEAVEN BESTOWS   . .   9 MYCERINUS   29
        AND THOUGH THOU GLEAN WHAT STRENUOUS GLEANERS MAY   43 GIPSY CHILD   57

STRESS
        PAINT WITH THEIR IMPETUOUS STRESS   . . . . . .   24 MEMORY-PICTURE   43
        STRESS OF GALE AND SHOWERS OF SPRAY   . . . . . .   457 POOR MATTHIAS   178

STRETCH
        AND HE WILL SEE STRETCH ROUND HIM HELAS REALM   . . 100 BALDER DEAD 1   171
        AND MANY A STRETCH OF WATERY SAND   . . . . . .   141 TRISTRAM 1   369
        COME STRETCH FORTH THY HAND THEN SO   . . . . . .   187 STRAYED REVEL   61
        THE BOUNDLESS WAVING GRASS-PLAINS STRETCH THICK-STARRD 191 STRAYED REVEL   168

STRETCHD
        GOD THE DUKE LIES STRETCHD BESIDE HIM   . . . .   13 CHURCH BROU 1   27
        AND LEFT HIS BODY STRETCHD UPON THE FLOOR   . . .   97 BALDER DEAD 1   63
        TO FADE AND NANNA IN HER SLEEP STRETCHD OUT   . . 104 BALDER DEAD 1   332
        STRETCHD FORTH HIS HAND AND WITH BENIGNANT VOICE . . 125 BALDER DEAD 3   410
        THE LONE UNBROKEN VIEW STRETCHD BRIGHT AND CLEAR . .   TRISTRAM 3   V 12
        MY STRETCHD ARMS ARE CAST   . . . .   176 PARTING   64
        WHERE THE TIRED ANGLER LIES STRETCHD OUT   . . .   248 KENSINGTON GARD   18
        WHERE THE LONE ANGLER LIES STRETCHD OUT   . . . .   KENSINGTON GARD V 18
        WHO TO THE INVADING DORIANS STRETCHD A HAND   . . 338 MEROPE   293
        ARE APT TO SNAP THE EASY-STRETCHD ENDURE   . . . .   339 MEROPE   308
        STRETCHD AMONG BRIARS AND STONES THE SLOW BLACK GORE 373 MEROPE   1172
        AND GLORY STRETCHD AT BURWOOD GATE   . . . . . .   461 KAISER DEAD   73
        STRETCHD ON THAT BED OF DEATH ART NOTHING NOW   . . 479 CROMWELL   234

STRETCHES
        IN DANGEROUS HOUR STRETCHES HIS HAND   . . . . . .   393 MEROPE   1681

STRETCHING
        NORTHWARD UNTIL HE MEETS A STRETCHING WALL   . . . . 100 BALDER DEAD 1   166
        STILL NORTH UNTIL HE MET A STRETCHING WALL   . . . . 109 BALDER DEAD 2   144
        MAKE TOWARD THEM OER THE STRETCHING CLOUDY PLAIN . . 126 BALDER DEAD 3   443
        MAKE TOWARDS THEM OER THE STRETCHING CLOUDY PLAIN   126 BALDER DEAD 3   V 443
        STRETCHING OUT LIKE THE DESERT   . . . .   235 YOUTH OF MAN   109

STREW
        STREW ON HER ROSES ROSES   . . . .   20 REQUIESCAT   1
        STREW NO MORE RED ROSES MAIDENS   . . . .   35 NEW SIRENS   V 267
        OR ELSE THY BONES SHALL STREW THIS SAND TILL WINDS   72 SOHRAB RUSTUM   376
        STREW WITH LAUREL THE GRAVE   . . . .   283 HAWORTH CHURCH   66
        STREW WITH ROSES THE GRAVE   . . . .   283 HAWORTH CHURCH   V 66

STREWD
    THAT STREWD THE BLOOD-STAIND PATH WHERE EMPIRE LED   478 CROMWELL   226

STREWN
    DOWN THE LEAF-STREWN FOREST-ROAD • • • • • • 13 CHURCH BROU 1   30
    MUFFLED ITS WALLS AND ON THE STONE-STREWN ROOF • • 25 DREAM   17
    FROM THIS DUSK OF LEAF-STREWN PLACES • • • • • 32 NEW SIRENS   193
    LIE STREWN IT SEEMS WHERE THEN THEY LAY • • • • 55 RESIGNATION   101
    AND STREWN THE CHANNELS WITH TORN BOUGHS SO HUGE • 73 SOHRAB RUSTUM   415
    AND STREWN THE CHANNELS WITH TORN BOUGHS SO ROUGH 73 SOHRAB RUSTUM   V 415
    LAY THICKLY STREWN SWORDS AXES DARTS AND SPEARS • • 95 BALDER DEAD 1   2
    IN ALL THE FORESTS AND THE SOFT-STREWN SNOW • • 122 BALDER DEAD 3   311
    IS STREWN WITH ROCKS AND MANY A SHIVERD MASS • • 150 TRISTRAM 3   16
    SAND-STREWN CAVERNS COOL AND DEEP • • • • 162 FORSAKEN MERM   35
    AND THE PALE MASTER ON HIS SPAR-STREWN DECK • • 244 SUMMER NIGHT   65
    AND CHESTNUT-FLOWERS ARE STREWN • • • • 264 THYRSIS   56
    STREWN WITH ITS DANK YELLOW DRIFTS • • • 286 RUGBY CHAPEL   3
    UP OER THE ROCK-STREWN SLOPE • • • • • 297 HEINES GRAVE   162
    AND IN THE LONELY ROCK-STREWN MOUNTAIN-GLEN • • 430 EMPEDOCLES II   39
    LIE STREWN THE WHITE FLOCKS • • • • • 442 EMPEDOCLES II   430
    SO FEATLY STREWN WITH DRIFTED SAND • • • • 480 HAYSWATER BOAT   22
    THERE IN THE LEAF-STREWN COPSE I FOUND • • • 484 ROME-SICKNESS   14

STRICKEN
    WHICH THE SORROW-STRICKEN DAY DENIES • • • • 32 NEW SIRENS   178
    TOTTERING A DEATH-STRICKEN HAND • • • • • 281 HAWORTH CHURCH   25
    THE STRICKEN KING A SECOND ENEMY • • • • 381 MEROPE   1297
    HER SON HEART-STRICKEN EYED HER • • • • 393 MEROPE   1673
    WHEN THE GOTH STOOPED UPON HIS STRICKEN PREY • • 464 ALARIC AT ROME   68

STRICT
    QUIET LIVING STRICT-KEPT MEASURE • • • • • 49 SECOND BEST   2
    EACH ON HIS OWN STRICT LINE WE MOVE • • • • 206 TOO LATE   1
    BE THEIR FIRST-FOUNDED ORDER STRICT MAINTAIND • • 390 MEROPE   1565

STRICTLY
    BE STRICTLY CARED FOR IN THE APPOINTED DAY • • • 96 BALDER DEAD 1   39
    MORE STRICTLY THEN THE INWARD JUDGE OBEY • • • 171 BETTER PART   12

STRIDE
    OUR BUSINESS WITH UNSLACKENING STRIDE • • • • 277 SOUTHERN NIGHT   65

STRIDES
    AND TOOK THREE STRIDES QUARRY AND DOGS WERE GONE • • 358 MEROPE   830

STRIDING
    FOR HANDMAID TO THEIR STRIDING POWER • • • • • 53 RESIGNATION   31

STRIFE
    MOVED ONLY BUT BY GENIUS IN THE STRIFE • • • • 4 DUKE WELLINGTON   4
    IN THE THRONGD FIELDS WHERE WINNING COMES BY STRIFE 43 GIPSY CHILD   58
    IN EARTHS THRONGD FIELDS WHERE WINNING COMES BY STRIFE 43 GIPSY CHILD   V 58
    THROUGH CLOUDS OF INDIVIDUAL STRIFE • • • • • 59 RESIGNATION   251
    THE STRIFE AND HURLD ME ON MY FATHERS SPEAR • • 82 SOHRAB RUSTUM   715
    FOR WE LOSE HIM WHO SMOOTHED ALL STRIFE IN HEAVEN 116 BALDER DEAD 3   88
    THE STRIFE THE MIXTURE IN HER SOUL ARE OURS • • 168 RACHEL 3   13
    AND HE WHO FLAGGD NOT IN THE EARTHLY STRIFE • • 172 IMMORTALITY   11
    WILL HAVE BEEN LOST THE HELP IN STRIFE • • • • 179 FAREWELL   66
    FAME AND HER LESS FAIR FOLLOWERS ENVY STRIFE • • 199 EARLY DEATH   4
    NOW STRIFE IS HUSHD OUR EARS DOTH MEET • • • 219 BACCHANALIA 2   V 14
    ITS PAIN AND PLEASURE REST AND STRIFE • • • • 225 EPILOG LAOCOON   144
    THEN WE SHALL RUST IN SHADE OR SHINE IN STRIFE • • 236 PALLADIUM   17
    AH CHILD SHE CRIES THAT STRIFE DIVINE • • • • 241 MORALITY   23
    HOW HE WOULD POUR HIMSELF IN EVERY STRIFE • • 246 BURIED LIFE   33
    BUT OFTEN IN THE DIN OF STRIFE • • • • • 246 BURIED LIFE   46
    OF THE SICK ROOM THE MORTAL STRIFE • • • • 251 WISH   45
    OF A SICK ROOM A MORTAL STRIFE • • • • • 251 WISH   V 45
    FOR STRONG THE INFECTION OF OUR MENTAL STRIFE • • 261 SCHOLAR-GIPSY   222
    WITH SHIVERING HEART THE STRIFE WE SAW • • • 270 MEMORIAL VERSES   10
    WHICH SERVED FOR THAT TITANIC STRIFE • • • • 270 MEMORIAL VERSES   14
    HIS EYE PLUNGED DOWN THE WELTERING STRIFE • • 270 MEMORIAL VERSES   25
    SUFFICD FOR THAT TITANIC STRIFE • • • • • 270 MEMORIAL VERSES   V 14
    WHICH FLOWD FOR THAT TITANIC STRIFE • • • • 270 MEMORIAL VERSES   V 14
    HIS EYE PLUNGED DOWN THE SEETHING STRIFE • • 270 MEMORIAL VERSES   V 25
    THEY PAINT OF SOULS THE INNER STRIFE • • • • 301 GRANDE CHARTR   53
    NOT IN THE WORLD NOT IN THE STRIFE • • • • 309 OBERMANN   99
    HE WHO HATH WATCHD NOT SHARED THE STRIFE • • 309 OBERMANN   101
    AND HURRIED TORN WITH INWARD STRIFE • • • • 317 OBERMANN MORE   135
    DID MAKE FROM HAUNTS OF STRIFE • • • • • 322 OBERMANN MORE   274
    WHAT THOUGH THERE STILL NEED EFFORT STRIFE • • 322 OBERMANN MORE   289
    THE TWENTIETH ANNIVERSARY OF STRIFE • • • • 333 MEROPE   115
    MARCHD WITH THEM HATRED AND STRIFE • • • • 343 MEROPE   418
    ARE THE SOLE CLAIMANTS LEFT WHAT CAUSE OF STRIFE • • 394 MEROPE   1693
    HEAVEN IS WITH EARTH AT STRIFE • • • • • • 416 EMPEDOCLES I 2   122
    AND WIN WHATS WON BY STRIFE • • • • • • 421 EMPEDOCLES I 2   270
    THERE WAS HELD THE FAMOUS STRIFE • • • • • 433 EMPEDOCLES II   140
    TOUCHD THE HILLS THE STRIFE WAS DONE • • • • 433 EMPEDOCLES II   144
    AND WE SHALL SINK IN THE IMPOSSIBLE STRIFE • • 440 EMPEDOCLES II   389
    THE STRIFE WITH THE PALM • • • • • • 443 EMPEDOCLES II   466
    AND MEN IGNOBLE HARASSD HIM WITH STRIFE • • • 447 WESTMIN ABBEY   125
    ANGER AND STRIFE AND SICKNESS ARE WITHIN • • • 465 ALARIC AT ROME   81

STRIFE   (CONTINUED)
        OF JOYS UNCLOUDED YEARS UNSTIRRD BY STRIFE • • •   474 CROMWELL   102
        THERE FALKLAND EYD THE STRIFE THAT WOULD NOT CEASE   477 CROMWELL   173
        THEY YOKD IN HIM FOR ENDLESS STRIFE • • • • • •   481 DESTINY   5

STRIFES
        ALL STRIFES BE RECONCILED   • • • • • • • •   40 STAGIRIUS   55
        AND DAILY STRIFES ARISE AND ANGRY WORDS   • • • •   116 BALDER DEAD 3   82
        NOW STRIFES ARE HUSHD OUR EARS DOTH MEET   • • • •   219 BACCHANALIA 2   14

STRIKE
        WHOM I MAY MEET AND STRIKE AND FEEL NO PANG   • •   74 SOHRAB RUSTUM   444
        CAN I WITH HELAS POWER A COMPACT STRIKE   • • • •   98 BALDER DEAD 1   109
        BUT WHEN THOU SANGEST BALDER THOU DIDST STRIKE • •   117 BALDER DEAD 3   141
        AS IT DRAWS TO THE OCEAN MAY STRIKE • • • • •   254 FUTURE   81
        STRIKE LEFTWARD CRIES OUR GUIDE AND HIGHER • • • •   300 GRANDE CHARTR   19
        AND STRIKE OPPOSERS DOWN   • • • • • • • • •   352 MEROPE   659
        AND I WOULD NOW HAVE JUSTICE STRIKE NOT ME • • • •   387 MEROPE   1472
        TO STRIKE IT THEN DISSUADE THY SON NO MORE • • •   390 MEROPE   1574
        BE WITH HIM CHOOSE THE MOMENT STRIKE THY BLOW • •   391 MEROPE   1590
        WHAT HAND TO STRIKE THEE MEET AS MINE THE HAND • •   402 MEROPE   1925
        GO WITH HIM CHOOSE THE MOMENT STRIKE THY BLOW • •   391 MEROPE   V1590

STRIKES
        AND STRIKES THE ROCK AND FINDS THE VEIN   • • •   213 PROGRESS POESY   2
        AND THEN THE TEMPEST STRIKES HIM AND BETWEEN • •   244 SUMMER NIGHT   62
        STRIKES WITH ALL SAIL SET   • • • • • • • •   400 MEROPE   1879
        SO EACH NEW MAN STRIKES ROOT INTO A FAR FORE-TIME   418 EMPEDOCLES I 2   191
        THINK YE IT STRIKES TOO SLOW THE SWORD OF FATE •   466 ALARIC AT ROME   115

STRIKST
        THOU STRIKST TOO HARD THAT CLUB OF THINE WILL FLOAT   74 SOHRAB RUSTUM   427
        THOU KNOWST NOT WHOM THOU STRIKST I KNOW HIS CRIME   374 MEROPE   1199
        UNHAPPY ONE THOU STRIKST A MOST JUST BLOW • • • •   374 MEROPE   1200

STRING
        BUT THEY HARP EVER ON ONE STRING AND WAKE • • • •   117 BALDER DEAD 3   137

STRINGING
        STRINGING VAIN WORDS OF POWERS WE CANNOT SEE   • •   10 MYCERINUS   51

STRINGS
        OF THOSE THAT IN SECRET THE HEART-STRINGS RIVE • •   132 TRISTRAM 1   47

STRIP
        A PERSIAN LORD THIS DAY AND STRIP HIS CORPSE • • •   77 SOHRAB RUSTUM   529
        WHERE THE HIGH WOODS STRIP SADLY   • • • • • •   175 PARTING   7
        DID THE TROJANS OBTAIN TO STRIP THE ARMS FROM   HOMER TRANS   51
            PATROCLUS

STRIPED
        WHOSE STRIPED SHELL FOUNDED   • • • • • • • • •   392 MEROPE   1628

STRIPLING
        CROSSING THE STRIPLING THAMES AT BAB-LOCK-HITHE • •   257 SCHOLAR-GIPSY   74
        AND SEEST MY STRIPLING HUNTER THERE AFIELD • • • •   349 MEROPE   573
        IS CHARGED AGAINST THIS STRIPLING AGENTS FEED • •   364 MEROPE   980

STRIPPD
        STRIPPD WITHOUT FRIENDS AS WE ARE   • • • • • •   289 RUGBY CHAPEL   121

STRIPS
        THERE THE PINES SLOPE THE CLOUD-STRIPS • • • •   176 PARTING   53
        CROSS AND RECROSS THE STRIPS OF MOON-BLANCHD GREEN   255 SCHOLAR-GIPSY   9

STRIVE
        LET ME PAUSE LET ME STRIVE IN MYSELF MAKE SOME ORDER   19 MODERN SAPPHO   7
        LET ME PAUSE LET ME STRIVE IN MYSELF FIND SOME ORDER   19 MODERN SAPPHO   V 7
        I DO NOT STRIVE I DO NOT WEEP • • • • • • • •   241 MORALITY   26
        THE WILL TO NEITHER STRIVE NOR CRY • • • • • •   249 KENSINGTON GARD   41
        AH YES SOME OF US STRIVE • • • • • • • • • •   288 RUGBY CHAPEL   79
        STRIVE NOT DIE ALSO THOU • • • • • • • • • •   309 OBERMANN   92
        THE SPARTAN BROTHERS WITH THEIR GUARDIAN STRIVE • •   390 MEROPE   1558
        AND CAN OUR SOULS NOT STRIVE   • • • • • • • •   415 EMPEDOCLES I 2   93
        ALL STRIVE TO MAKE IT LESS • • • • • • • • •   416 EMPEDOCLES I 2   120
        WHO STRIVE TO SEE WITH EYES   • • • • • • • •   426 EMPEDOCLES I 2 V 409
        WE STRIVE TO CARRY DOWN THY NAME   • • • • • •   451 GEISTS GRAVE   63

STRIVES
        OF WHOM EACH STRIVES NOR KNOWS FOR WHAT HE STRIVES   260 SCHOLAR-GIPSY   168
        OF WHOM EACH STRIVES NOR KNOWS FOR WHAT HE STRIVES   260 SCHOLAR-GIPSY   168
        AND TRAVAILS STRIVES AND MOANS • • • • • • •   422 EMPEDOCLES I 2 V 295

STRIVING
        WITH INWARD STRIVING AND DEMAND   • • • • • •   247 BURIED LIFE   68
        STRIVING BLINDLY ACHIEVING   • • • • • • • •   288 RUGBY CHAPEL   65
        WHY EACH IS STRIVING FROM OF OLD   • • • • • •   481 DESTINY   1

STRODE
        HE SPAKE AND PERAN-WISA TURND AND STRODE   • • • •   66 SOHRAB RUSTUM   187
        BUT RUSTUM STRODE TO HIS TENT-DOOR AND CALLD   • •   69 SOHRAB RUSTUM   263

```
STRODE            ( CONTINUED )
    HE SPOKE AND PERAN-WISA TURND AND STRODE     • • • •   66 SOHRAB RUSTUM    V 187

STROKE
    ONE STROKE BUT AGAIN SOHRAB SPRANG ASIDE      • • • •   73 SOHRAB RUSTUM      417
    NEAR DEATH AND BY AN IGNORANT STROKE OF THINE   • •     85 SOHRAB RUSTUM      818
    BUT PAINLESS SHALL A STROKE FROM FREA COME    • • • •  103 BALDER DEAD 1      302
    AND WELL I KNOW THAT BY NO STROKE OF DEATH    • • • •  103 BALDER DEAD 1      305
    FREA THE MOTHER OF THE GODS WITH STROKE       • • • •  104 BALDER DEAD 1      339
    OF BARDS FULL MANY A STROKE DIVINE      • • • • •      222 EPILOG LAOCOON      20
    WITH THE CEASELESS STROKE OF HIS WINGS       • • • •   233 YOUTH OF MAN        41
    TURN ON THE FOOLISH THE STROKE    • • • • • •         281 HAWORTH CHURCH    V
    BUT IF THE STROKE MUST FALL     • • • • • •           282 HAWORTH CHURCH    V
    ARE BY A STROKE THOUGH UNDESIRED COMPLETE     • •     360 MEROPE             877
    A MORE JUST STROKE THAN THAT THOU GAVST MY SON  • •   373 MEROPE            1191
    MY FIRST STROKE OF REVENGE HAD NEARLY FALLEN   • •    377 MEROPE            1224
    ONE SUDDEN STROKE AND THE MESSENIANS LOVE     • •     381 MEROPE            1287
    THE STROKE THOU PURPOSEST IS DESPERATE RASH    • •    381 MEROPE            1295
    BUT IF SOME SIGNAL UNASSISTED STROKE   • • • •        383 MEROPE            1353
    I KNOW NOT JUST IN EITHER CASE THE STROKE    • • •    404 MEROPE            1986
    WE STROKE THY BROAD BROWN PAWS AGAIN    • • • • •     451 GEISTS GRAVE        45

STROKED
    AND WITH FOND FALTERING FINGERS STROKED HIS CHEEKS    81 SOHRAB RUSTUM      696
    HAS OFTEN STROKED THY NECK AND GIVEN THEE FOOD  • •    83 SOHRAB RUSTUM      753
    HANDS HAD STROKED THEM WHICH ARE COLD     • • • •     453 POOR MATTHIAS       47

STROKES
    MY FATHER BY YOUR STROKES MY MOTHER SLAIN    • • •    385 MEROPE            1412
    WHICH WAY TO LEAN I KNOW NOT BLOODY STROKES    • •    388 MEROPE            1521

STROLLD
    STROLLD AND SANG WITH JOYFUL MIND      • • • • •       26 NEW SIRENS           6

STRONG
    STRONG IS THE SOUL AND WISE AND BEAUTIFUL     • • •     4 EMERSONS ESSAYS     11
    STRONG IS THE SOUL AND FRESH AND BEAUTIFUL    • • •       EMERSONS ESSAYS   V 11
    TO BE LIKE NATURE STRONG LIKE NATURE COOL     • • •     5 HARMONY NATURE       4
    OR IS IT THAT SOME FORCE TOO WISE TOO STRONG   • •      9 MYCERINUS           37
    OR IS IT THAT SOME POWER TOO WISE TOO STRONG   • •      9 MYCERINUS         V 37
    OR IS IT THAT SOME FORCE TOO STERN TOO STRONG  • •      9 MYCERINUS         V 37
    THEIR LOVE LET ME KNOW MUST GROW STRONG AND           19 MODERN SAPPHO       13
            YET STRONGER
    THE STRONG BAND WHICH PASSION AROUND HIM HATH FURLD   20 MODERN SAPPHO       22
    THE STRONG BAND WHICH BEAUTY AROUND HIM HATH FURLD    20 MODERN SAPPHO     V 22
    THE STRONG SPELL WHICH PASSION UPON HIM HATH HURLD    20 MODERN SAPPHO     V 22
    AH TOO TRUE TIMES CURRENT STRONG     • • • • • •       24 MEMORY-PICTURE      57
    STRONG TO DECEIVE STRONG TO ENSLAVE    • • • • •       39 STAGIRIUS           28
    STRONG TO DECEIVE STRONG TO ENSLAVE    • • • • •       39 STAGIRIUS           28
    WHERE WISE MEN ARE NOT STRONG    • • • • • • •         39 STAGIRIUS           40
    WHERE GOOD MEN ARE NOT STRONG    • • • • • • •         39 STAGIRIUS         V 40
    SEES HIS STRONG THOUGHT IN FIERY FLOOD     • • •       56 RESIGNATION        156
    AND STRONG CONVULSIVE GROANINGS SHOOK HIS BREAST • •   82 SOHRAB RUSTUM      703
    UNTO A RULE MORE STRONG THAN THEIRS  • • • • •         93 SICK KING BOKH     187
    FROM THE DEEP TRENCH SHE PLOUGHD SO STRONG A GOD  • • 118 BALDER DEAD 3      178
    BUT IN THE HILLS A STRONG EAST-WIND AROSE    • • •    118 BALDER DEAD 3      181
    ALL THE STRONG BROOD OF HEAVEN TO SWELL MY TRAIN • • 120 BALDER DEAD 3      241
    WOULD TAKE A SCORE YEARS FROM A STRONG MANS AGE   • • 140 TRISTRAM 1         305
    UNDER THE THORNS ON THE GREEN SWARD AND STRONG   • • 155 TRISTRAM 3         196
    GAY RAIMENT SPARKLING GAUDS ELATION STRONG   • • •   166 AUSTERITY POET       7
    IN A TOO STRONG EMOTIONS SWAY    • • • • • •         178 FAREWELL            30
    BUT HE PREFERRD FATE TO HIS STRONG DESIRE    • • •   198 FRAG ANTIGONE       97
    PROFOUND YET TOUCHING SWEET YET STRONG    • • •      222 EPILOG LAOCOON      28
    A STRONG EMOTION ON HER CHEEK    • • • • • •         241 MORALITY            22
    FOR STRONG THE INFECTION OF OUR MENTAL STRIFE   • •  261 SCHOLAR-GIPSY      222
    O STRONG SOUL BY WHAT SHORE      • • • • • • •       287 RUGBY CHAPEL        37
    STRONG CHILDREN OF THE ALPINE WILD    • • • • •      301 GRANDE CHARTR       57
    AND ONE THE STRONG MUCH-TOILING SAGE    • • • •      308 OBERMANN            51
    STRONG WAS HE WITH A SPIRIT FREE    • • • • •        308 OBERMANN            61
    OF LOVE WHICH SET SO DEEP AND STRONG    • • • •      317 OBERMANN MORE      147
    STRONG BLACK TEMPESTUOUS TO THE CAVERN-MOUTH   • •   358 MEROPE             821
    O LAWLESS DARING OF THE STRONG    • • • • • • •      398 MEROPE            1800
    AND TRULY ONE WHO SEES WHAT SEEMD SO STRONG    • •   402 MEROPE            1943
    IS FATE INDEED SO STRONG MANS STRENGTH INDEED SO POOR 415 EMPEDOCLES I 2     96
    WHERE ERST THE STRONG SEA-CURRENTS SUCKD THEE DOWN   430 EMPEDOCLES II       59
    YES BUT THAT ENFORCEMENT STRONG    • • • • •         454 POOR MATTHIAS       59
    WISHES THERE AND FEELINGS STRONG    • • • • •        455 POOR MATTHIAS      103
    REPENTANT PRAYERS THAT HAD BEEN STRONG TO SAVE      474 CROMWELL            81
    THEN LIKE A KINGLY RIVER SWIFT AND STRONG    • • •   475 CROMWELL           133
    LAST NIGHT THE WIND WAS UP AND STRONG    • • •       479 HAYSWATER BOAT      17
    THE STRONG BLAST BROUGHT A PIGMY THRONG    • • •     479 HAYSWATER BOAT      19
    WHEN FATE AND CIRCUMSTANCE ARE STRONG    • • •       481 COURAGE              6
    THY FIERY COURAGE STILL WAS STRONG    • • • • •      482 COURAGE             20
    WITH NOISELESS CURRENT STRONG OBSCURE AND DEEP   • • 483 BELOW SURFACE        4
    SORELY AGAINST THY WILL BY STRONG NECESSITYS ORDER      HOMER TRANS         31

STRONGER
    THEIR LOVE LET ME KNOW MUST GROW STRONG AND           19 MODERN SAPPHO       13
            YET STRONGER
    OR PERHAPS IF HOPE WERE STRONGER    • • • • • •       29 NEW SIRENS         111
    THE LAW GREW STRONGER EVERY DAY    • • • • • •        56 RESIGNATION        135
```

STRONGEST
        EXHAUST THE ENERGY OF STRONGEST SOULS   • • • • • 259 SCHOLAR-GIPSY   145

STRONGLY
        STRONGLY SETS AND TRULY BURNS   • • • • • • • •   49 SECOND BEST   24
        STRONGLY STIRS AND TRULY BURNS   • • • • • • • •   49 SECOND BEST   V 24
        TWO HORSES STRONGLY SWIMMING TOW   • • • • • •   191 STRAYED REVEL   185

STROVE
        TWO BROTHERS AND THEIR ORPHAN NEPHEWS STROVE   • • 389 MEROPE   1548

STROWN
        STROWN WITH DARK SEEDS   • • • • • • • • •   187 STRAYED REVEL   58

STRUCK
        IN TURN AND FULL STRUCK RUSTUMS SHIELD SHARP RANG   73 SOHRAB RUSTUM   406
        THE CLUB WHICH RUSTUM LIFTED NOW AND STRUCK   •   73 SOHRAB RUSTUM   416
        AND LABOURING BREATH FIRST RUSTUM STRUCK THE SHIELD   75 SOHRAB RUSTUM   491
        AND STRUCK AGAIN AND AGAIN RUSTUM BOWD   76 SOHRAB RUSTUM   510
        NORTH SOUTH EAST WEST THEY STRUCK AND ROAMD THE WORLD 122 BALDER DEAD 3   304
        WHERE THE SUNS RAYS STRUCK FULL AND FLASHD BACK KEEN   TRISTRAM 3   V 21
        WHO STRUCK IN HEAT HIS CHILD HE LOVED SO WELL   • •   166 PICT NEWSTEAD   5
        WHO STRUCK IN HEAT THE CHILD HE LOVED SO WELL   • •   166 PICT NEWSTEAD   V   5
        WHEN HIS AWE-STRUCK CAPTORS LED   • • • • • •   229 YOUTH OF NATURE   43
        AND STRUCK HIS FINGER ON THE PLACE   • • • • •   270 MEMORIAL VERSES   21
        TO ZEUS BEFORE HE STRUCK HIS BLOW STRUCK MINE   338 MEROPE   274
        TO ZEUS BEFORE HE STRUCK HIS BLOW STRUCK MINE   • •   338 MEROPE   274
        STRUCK ONCE AND AWED HIS MOB AND SAVED THIS REALM   338 MEROPE   275
        A BLOW A BLOW WAS STRUCK AND HE FELL   • • • •   346 MEROPE   490
        BUT THOU WHEN STRUCK THINE HOUR TO GO   • • •   450 GEISTS GRAVE   33
        AND STRUCK AND OER US THE SEA-WATERS SPREAD   •   484 S S LUSITANIA   8
        DIDST FORCE AN AUDIENCE ERE I STRUCK THE SCALE   • •   RUDE ORATOR   6
        AWE-STRUCK FAIN WOULD CEASE TO BE   • • • • • •   META CLOISTER   18

STRUGGLE
        OF STRUGGLE THESE NECESSITATE   • • • • • • •   53 RESIGNATION   25
        I STRUGGLE TOWARDS THE LIGHT AND YE   • • • • •   183 ABSENCE   13
        I STRUGGLE TOWARDS THE LIGHT BUT OH   • • • • •   183 ABSENCE   17
        SWEPT WITH CONFUSED ALARMS OF STRUGGLE AND FLIGHT   212 DOVER BEACH   36
        LONG SINCE SAW BYRONS STRUGGLE CEASE   • • • •   270 MEMORIAL VERSES   2
        WITHOUT A CRY A STRUGGLE OR A BLOW   • • • • •   367 MEROPE   1028
        YET STARK FROM THE DEATH-STRUGGLE TIGHT-CLENCHD HANDS 373 MEROPE   1174
        WHAT MAKES THEE STRUGGLE AND RAVE   • • • • •   417 EMPEDOCLES I 2   147
        AND WE SHALL STRUGGLE AWHILE GASP AND REBEL   •   440 EMPEDOCLES II   382
        AND SCARCE THE BOON OF LIFE COULD STRUGGLE THROUGH   446 WESTMIN ABBEY   69

STRUGGLES
        AND STRUGGLES PANTS AND MOANS   • • • • • • • •   422 EMPEDOCLES I 2   V 295

STRUGGLING
        CROWN OF HIS STRUGGLING LIFE AN UNJUST CLOSE   • •   9 MYCERINUS   30
        OF DUST WHICH WREATHED THEIR STRUGGLING FILES   • •   52 RESIGNATION   6
        OF DUST THAT WREATHED THEIR STRUGGLING FILES   • •   52 RESIGNATION   V 6
        MID STRUGGLING SUFFERERS HURT TO DEATH SHE LAY   166 AUSTERITY POET   9
        THY STRUGGLING TASKD MORALITY   • • • • • • •   241 MORALITY   16
        STRUGGLING IN VAIN TO CROSS IT SWEPT THEM ON   • • 358 MEROPE   825

STRUNG
        STRUNG LIKE WHITE STARS THE PEARLS STILL ARE   • • 146 TRISTRAM 2   109
        EACH NERVE MORE LOOSELY STRUNG   • • • • • • • •   212 GROWING OLD   10
        EACH NERVE MORE WEAKLY STRUNG   • • • • • • • •   212 GROWING OLD   V 10
        WITH HEART NEW STRUNG AND STERN RESOLVE HE STOOD • •473 CROMWELL   66

STRUTTING
        OUR PETTY SOULS OUR STRUTTING WITS   • • • • • •   202 URANIA   13

STUBBLE
        AND IN THE MIDST A STUBBLE SHORT AND BARE   • • •   70 SOHRAB RUSTUM   296

STUBBORN
        NATURE IS STUBBORN MAN WOULD FAIN ADORE   • • •   5 HARMONY NATURE   8
        WHOM SCHOOLING OF THE STUBBORN MIND   • • • • •   53 RESIGNATION   26
        BUT FIRST HE WOULD CONVINCE HIS STUBBORN FOE   • •   80 SOHRAB RUSTUM   653

STUCK
        AGAINST THE BODIES AND STUCK TORCHES NEAR   • • • 118 BALDER DEAD 3   167

STUDDED
        THIS OPEN GLEN WAS STUDDED THICK WITH THORNS   • • 155 TRISTRAM 3   191
        WITH THORNS ONCE STUDDED OLD WHITE-BLOSSOMD TREES   266 THYRSIS   113

STUDIOUS
        LIGHTS UP HIS STUDIOUS FOREHEAD AND THIN HANDS   • • 81 SOHRAB RUSTUM   676
        THAT THOU WERT WANDERD FROM THE STUDIOUS WALLS   • • 259 SCHOLAR-GIPSY   134

STUDIOUSLY
        SOMETHING TOO STUDIOUSLY FORGIVE ME SHOWN   • • • • 334 MEROPE   142

STUDY
        BUT THOU MY SON STUDY TO MAKE PREVAIL   • • • • 404 MEROPE   1995

STUFF
          OUT OF THIS STUFF THESE FORCES THOU ART GROWN   • •   46 IN UTRUMQUE PAR   V   38
          AND BROUGHT HIS ARMS AND GOLD AND ALL HIS STUFF   • •   118 BALDER DEAD 3   169
          OF BUT ONE STUFF ARE SPUN   • • • • • • •   • •   422 EMPEDOCLES I 2   288

STUFFD
          WHOSE MANGER IS STUFFD FULL OF GOOD FRESH HAY   • •   123 BALDER DEAD 3   341

STUNG
          MY DUNGEON WHERE THE SERPENTS STUNG ME DEAD   • •   117 BALDER DEAD 3   146

STUNND
          MINE EARS ARE STUNND WITH BLOWS AND SICK FOR CALM   128 BALDER DEAD 3   508

STUPEFYING
          THEIR STUPEFYING POWER   • • • • • • • • • • • •   247 BURIED LIFE   70

STUPID
          STUPID DETRACTION JEALOUSY CABAL   • • • • • • •   199 EARLY DEATH   5
          STUPID SALUTATIONS GAY   • • • • • • • • • • • • •   455 POOR MATTHIAS   112

STUPIDLY
          STUPIDLY TRAVELS HER ROUND   • • • • • • • • • •   294 HEINES GRAVE   81

STUPIFYING
          THEIR STUPIFYING POWER   • • • • • • • • • • • • •   247 BURIED LIFE   V   70

STUPOR
          AND LIGHTS FAIR NURSLING STUPOR FIRST INVADES   • •   448 WESTMIN ABBEY   129

STURDY
          THESE STURDY AND UNWORN MESSENIAN TRIBES   • • • •   338 MEROPE   291

STYLE
          BY A FALSE BOAST THE STYLE OF RUSTUMS SON   • • • •   79 SOHRAB RUSTUM   613

STYMPHALIAN
          TO THE STYMPHALIAN LAKE OUR JOURNEYS END   • • • •   356 MEROPE   749
          WALLS ON ONE SIDE THE DEEP STYMPHALIAN LAKE   • •   358 MEROPE   813
          ALL THE STYMPHALIAN PLAIN ARE NOW SUCKD DOWN   • •   358 MEROPE   816
          WHICH HANGS OER THE STYMPHALIAN LAKE AND DROWND   • •   363 MEROPE   961

STYX
          OF STYX COME DANCING   • • • • • • • • • • • • •   392 MEROPE   1653

STYXS
          WHICH STYXS AWFUL WATERS TRICKLE DOWN   • • • •   368 MEROPE   1065

SUBDUE
          AND WOULD THE WORLD SUBDUE   • • • • • • • • • •   418 EMPEDOCLES I 2   183

SUBDUED
          SUBDUED WITH LIMBER CHAINS LIVES FENRIS BOUND   • •   111 BALDER DEAD 2   216
          AND FINALLY THIS LAND THEN HALF-SUBDUED   • • • •   337 MEROPE   245

SUBDUES
          SUBDUES THAT ENERGY TO SCAN   • • • • • • • • • •   56 RESIGNATION   146
          OF PASSION WHICH SUBDUES OUR SOULS TO IT   • • • •   153 TRISTRAM 3   128

SUBJECT
          HER DARKNESS FROM HER GRASP A SUBJECT TEAR   • • • •   121 BALDER DEAD 3   280
          WAS SUBJECT TO THESE TRANCES FROM A GIRL   • • • •   410 EMPEDOCLES I 1   136

SUBJECTS
          TO HIS NEW SUBJECTS THAN TO US HIS FRIENDS   • • • •   337 MEROPE   242
          A TALE MEANWHILE FORGED FOR HIS SUBJECTS EARS   • •   366 MEROPE   1002
          SINCE FROM THY FAITHFUL SUBJECTS WHAT REVENGE   • •   386 MEROPE   1432
          THUS LITTLE FOUNDED IN THEIR SUBJECTS LOVE   • • • •   390 MEROPE   1560
          RUTHLESSLY THEIR REBELLIOUS SUBJECTS CRUSHD   • •   390 MEROPE   1567

SUBLIME
          THE ODE SUBLIME   • • • • • • • • • • • • • • •   458 KAISER DEAD   4

SUBMITTED
          LONG WE REFRAIND OURSELVES SUBMITTED LONG   • • • •   337 MEROPE   254

SUBSIST
          IF BIRTH PROCEEDS IF THINGS SUBSIST   • • • • • • •   58 RESIGNATION   194
          FOR NEITHER COULD SUBSIST ALONE   • • • • • • • •   203 EUPHROSYNE   12
          BUT IN A WORLD HE LOVES NOT MUST SUBSIST   • • • •   437 EMPEDOCLES II   267

SUBSISTS
          LOK STILL SUBSISTS IN HEAVEN OUR FATHER WISE   • •   111 BALDER DEAD 2   217
          THAT THERE SUBSISTS A PEACE OF THINE   • • • • • • •   KENSINGTON GARD V   39

SUBSTANCE
          AND SUBSTANCE AND A GOLDEN HOUSE IN HEAVEN   • • • •   125 BALDER DEAD 3   404
          THE EVERLASTING SUBSTANCE OF THE HILLS   • • • •   EVERLASTING SUB   1

SUBTERRANEAN
      ON THOSE WALLS SUBTERRANEAN WHERE SHE HID • • • • 172 GOOD SHEPHERD   11
      FROM THE SOULS SUBTERRANEAN DEPTH UPBORNE • • • • 247 BURIED LIFE   73
      CAST BY THE RUMBLING SUBTERRANEAN STREAM • • • • 358 MEROPE   841

SUBTLE
      MORE SUBTLE-WINDING . • • • • • • • • 187 STRAYED REVEL   66
      AND PURER OR MORE SUBTLE SOUL THAN THEE • • • • 268 THYRSIS   178
      O POLICY TOO SUBTLE FAR FOR SENSE • • • • • 339 MEROPE   311
      WHICH FOOLISH INNOCENCE PLAYS WITH SUBTLE GUILT • • 366 MEROPE   V
      TO THE SUBTLE CONTRIVING HEAD • • • • • • • 431 EMPEDOCLES II   91

SUBTLETIES
      IN DESERT ICE OF SUBTLETIES WAS SPENT • • • • 446 WESTMIN ABBEY   64

SUCCEED
      AND WE KNOW NOT WHAT SHALL SUCCEED • • • • • • 253 FUTURE   70

SUCCEEDING
      AND EACH SUCCEEDING AGE IN WHICH WE ARE BORN • • 440 EMPEDOCLES II   377

SUCCEEDS
      THE SECOND WAVE SUCCEEDS BEFORE • • • • • 308 OBERMANN   75
      YET GRANT THAT IT SUCCEEDS THOU HAST BEHIND • • 381 MEROPE   1296

SUCCESS
      OH ONCE ERE NIGHT IN THY SUCCESS THY CHAIN • • • 44 GIPSY CHILD   66
      BUT YET SUCCESS SWAYS WITH THE BREATH OF HEAVEN • • 72 SOHRAB RUSTUM   387
      AND WISHD HIM HEALTH SUCCESS AND FAME • • • 272 EDW QUILLINAN   3
      CROWND WITH SUCCESS NOT IN MY WAY BUT HEAVENS • • 360 MEROPE   878
      SUCCESS OF CRIME • • • • • • • • • • 398 MEROPE   1797

SUCCESSES
      FEWER FINE SUCCESSES CAN DISPLAY • • • • • • 221 EPILOG LAOCOON   12
      FEWER REAL SUCCESSES CAN DISPLAY • • • • • • 221 EPILOG LAOCOON V 12

SUCCESSION
      LINKING IN A MAD SUCCESSION • • • • • • • 33 NEW SIRENS   205
      A LONG SUCCESSION OF CRIMES • • • • • • • 379 MEROPE   1252

SUCCOUR
      ILL STOP AND SAY THERE WERE NO SUCCOUR HERE • • 169 WORLDLY PLACE   13
      SHE TURNS FROM THAT COLD SUCCOUR WHICH ATTENDS • • 170 WEST LONDON   12
      ALL CLAIM TO SUCCOUR FORFEIT TO MYSELF • • • 366 MEROPE   1008
      DISCREDITING THE SUCCOUR WHICH OUR CAUSE • • • 382 MEROPE   1335
      IF FOLLOWD MAKE THEIR SUCCOUR SLACK AND NULL • • 382 MEROPE   1338
      TO SUCCOUR ME IN MY EXTREMEST NEED • • • 383 MEROPE   1376
      DEEP AS THOU CANST FOR HENCE NO SUCCOUR COMES • • 386 MEROPE   1431

SUCCOUREST
      SUCCOUREST THIS WAS THY WORK • • • • • • • 288 RUGBY CHAPEL   56

SUCCOURS
      LET HIM FETCH SUCCOURS FROM ARCADIA GAIN • • • • 388 MEROPE   1498

SUCCUMBD
      SUCCUMBD TO THE ENVY OF UNKIND GODS • • • • • • 197 FRAG ANTIGONE   77

SUCH
      WHO WITH SUCH HEAT DOST PREACH WHAT WERE TO THEE • • 5 HARMONY NATURE   2
      SAY WHAT SHALL CALM US WHEN SUCH GUESTS INTRUDE • • 6 GEO CRUIKSHANK   6
      AND FOR SUCH DOING THEY REQUIRE NOT EYES • • • 7 REP FRIEND   8
      AND FOR SUCH DOING HAVE NO NEED OF EYES • • • 7 REP FRIEND   V 8
      AND FOR SUCH DOING THEY REQUIRE NO EYES • • • 7 REP FRIEND   V 8
      CHILDREN AS SUCH FORGIVE THEM HAVE I KNOWN • • • 8 RELIGIOUS ISOL   1
      AS THESE ARE THOU TOO WERT SUCH • • • • • 22 MEMORY-PICTURE V
      SUCH NOW METHOUGHT IT WAS THE RIVER OF LIFE • • 25 DREAM   32
      BLEW SUCH MUSIC AS A GOD MAY FRAME • • • • 29 NEW SIRENS   104
      AND OH WITH SUCH INTOLERABLE CHANGE • • • • • 36 VOICE   27
      OF THOUGHT SUCH CONTRAST STRANGE • • • • • • 36 VOICE   28
      BLEW SUCH A THRILLING SUMMONS TO MY WILL • • • 36 VOICE   37
      WHO HID SUCH IMPORT IN AN INFANTS GLOOM • • • • 41 GIPSY CHILD   2
      SUCH HAPPY ISSUE CROWND HER PAINFUL CARE • • • 46 IN UTRUMQUE PAR   34
      WHO WITH SUCH PASSIONATE WILL • • • • • • 46 WORLD QUIETIST   7
      AT SUCH DESPOTIC LENGTH TO PROVE • • • • • • HORATIAN ECHO   V
      BUT SUCH ANXIOUS SCHEMES THOU BREEDEST • • • • SECOND BEST   V 6
      BUT SUCH FURIOUS PASSIONS FEEDEST • • • • • • SECOND BEST   V 7
      SUCH PREGNANT AND INFECTIOUS QUALITY • • • • 50 CONSOLATION   V
      FOR WOULD THAT I MYSELF HAD SUCH A SON • • • 68 SOHRAB RUSTUM   229
      O GUDURZ WHEREFORE DOST THOU SAY SUCH WORDS • • 68 SOHRAB RUSTUM   250
      ROSE SUCH AS THAT THE SINEWY WOODCUTTERS • • • 75 SOHRAB RUSTUM   476
      OF HEWING AXES CRASHING TREES SUCH BLOWS • • • 75 SOHRAB RUSTUM   478
      FOR WERE I MATCHD WITH TEN SUCH MEN AS THEE • • 77 SOHRAB RUSTUM   544
      O SOHRAB THOU INDEED ART SUCH A SON • • • • 80 SOHRAB RUSTUM   641
      FOR WERE I MATCHD WITH TEN SUCH MEN AS THOU • • 77 SOHRAB RUSTUM V 544
      TO FIND SUCH FAVOUR IN THINE EYES • • • • • 92 SICK KING BOKH 136
      I MOST MIGHT WEEP HIS FATHER SUCH A SON • • • 96 BALDER DEAD 1   21
      WOUNDLESS AND FRESH SUCH LOT IS THEIRS IN HEAVEN • 105 BALDER DEAD 2 18
      NOT FOR SUCH END O QUEEN THOU HOLDST THY REALM • • 110 BALDER DEAD 2 197
      AND THIS IS TRUE AND SUCH A LOSS IS HEAVENS • • 111 BALDER DEAD 2 232

SUCH   (CONTINUED)
    HELA SUCH AS THOU SAYST THE TERMS SHALL BE • • • •   111 BALDER DEAD 2   242
    SUCH AS ON EARTH WE VALIANTLY HAVE WAGED   • • • •   117 BALDER DEAD 3   139
    SUCH FOR THE FUTURE IS MY HOPE MEANWHILE   • • • •   129 BALDER DEAD 3   544
    ONE SUCH KISS AS THOSE OF YORE • • • • • •   132 TRISTRAM 1   78
    CHRIST KEEP US FROM SUCH FANTASY • • • • • •   147 TRISTRAM 2   130
    HEAVEN KEEP US FROM SUCH FANTASY • • • • • •   147 TRISTRAM 2   V 130
    SO LATE SUCH STORMS THE SAINT IS MAD • • • •   156 SAINT BRANDAN   4
    HATH SUCH INESTIMABLE POWER • • • • • •   158 SAINT BRANDAN   56
    HATH SUCH INALIENABLE POWER • • • • • •   158 SAINT BRANDAN   V 56
    SUCH POETS IS YOUR BRIDE THE MUSE YOUNG GAY • •   166 AUSTERITY POET   12
    IF WE THEN TOO CAN BE SUCH MEN AS HE • • • •   171 BETTER PART   14
    THE THOUSAND SWEET STILL JOYS OF SUCH • • • •   179 FAREWELL   67
    PLY HIS BOW SUCH A PRICE • • • • • •   193 STRAYED REVEL   232
    SUCH END OERTOOK THAT LOVE • • • • • •   197 FRAG ANTIGONE   70
    SUCH MULTITUDE OF HEAVENLY STRAINS • • • • •   222 EPILOG LAOCOON   33
    FOR ILL-ENDOWD FOR SUCH A WAY • • • • •   226 EPILOG LAOCOON   171
    NO PAINTER YET HATH SUCH A WAY • • • • •   227 EPILOG LAOCOON   201
    SUCH LOVELY FLOWERS FOR CHEERING SOULS • • •   227 EPILOG LAOCOON   204
    FOR ILL PREPARED FOR SUCH A WAY • • • • •   226 EPILOG LAOCOON   V 171
    SEE SUCH A PROPHET AGAIN • • • • • •   229 YOUTH OF NATURE   47
    GROWS FROM SUCH SORROW AS THEIRS • • • •   235 YOUTH OF MAN   100
    BUT ONE SUCH DEATH REMAIND TO COME • • • •   270 MEMORIAL VERSES   3
    FOR NEVER HAS SUCH SOOTHING VOICE • • • •   271 MEMORIAL VERSES   35
    AH SUCH A NIGHT SO SOFT SO LONE • • • •   275 SOUTHERN NIGHT   13
    POOR GALLANT BOY FOR SUCH THOU WAST • • •   276 SOUTHERN NIGHT   39
    SUCH PEACEFUL GRAVES • • • • •   277 SOUTHERN NIGHT   60
    SUCH BY THESE WATERS OF ROMANCE • • • •   279 SOUTHERN NIGHT   111
    POOR GALLANT BOY FOR SUCH THOU WERT • • •   276 SOUTHERN NIGHT   V 39
    SUCH THOU WAST AND I STAND • • • • •   287 RUGBY CHAPEL   23
    SUCH SO SOULLESS SO POOR • • • • • •   290 RUGBY CHAPEL   149
    THEN IN SUCH HOUR OF NEED • • • • •   291 RUGBY CHAPEL   188
    FROM SUCH MATES THE OUTWORN • • • •   294 HEINES GRAVE   50
    SUCH BARREN KNOWLEDGE AWHILE • • • •   296 HEINES GRAVE   119
    SUCH OF THY THOUGHTS AS THOU WILT • • •   299 HEINES GRAVE   221
    AND YET MEN HAVE SUCH NEED OF JOY • • •   320 OBERMANN MORE   237
    SOME NEW SUCH HOPE MUST DAWN AT LAST • •   321 OBERMANN MORE   243
    AND YET THEY HAVE SUCH NEED OF JOY • • •   320 OBERMANN MORE   V 237
    A NEW SUCH HOPE MUST DAWN AT LAST • •   321 OBERMANN MORE   V 243
    SUCH ARE THEIR HOPES I ASK NOT IF BY THEE • • •   334 MEROPE   147
    RANKS ANY MAN WITH MURDER SUCH AN ACT • •   336 MEROPE   208
    FIND THEN SUCH CAUSE THE CHARGE OF MURDER FALLS •   336 MEROPE   210
    SUCH WERE THE DISPOSSESSORS OF WHAT STAMP • •   337 MEROPE   228
    SUCH WERE THE CONQUERD SUCH THE CONQUERORS WHO •   337 MEROPE   238
    SUCH WERE THE CONQUERD SUCH THE CONQUERORS WHO •   337 MEROPE   238
    FOR ME I DEEM SUCH IMPIOUS AND FOR HIM • •   340 MEROPE   336
    SUCH CHANCE AS KILLD THE FATHER KILLD THE SONS •   340 MEROPE   347
    AND WHO ART THOU WHO BRINGEST ME SUCH NEWS • •   355 MEROPE   716
    ON SUCH A HUNTING-JOURNEY THREE MORNS SINCE •   355 MEROPE   730
    AND SUCH AS FITS A ROYAL HOUSE TO SHOW • •   359 MEROPE   871
    SUCH A BOON TO BRING HATH BEEN GIVEN • • •   361 MEROPE   907
    TOO SUDDENLY THOU TELLEST SUCH A LOSS • •   363 MEROPE   945
    FORGIVE FORGIVE THE BRINGER OF SUCH NEWS • •   363 MEROPE   949
    SUCH AS ERE NOW HATH SPURRD TO FEARFUL DEEDS •   366 MEROPE   1012
    WHAT SHALL I HAVE TO ANSWER TO SUCH WORDS •   367 MEROPE   1053
    AND ENTERTAINST THOU CHILD SUCH DANGEROUS FRIENDS   380 MEROPE   1276
    NOT YET THOUGH SUCH NO DOUBT HIS FINAL AIM • • •   380 MEROPE   1283
    ON WHAT RELYING TO CRUSH SUCH A FOE • •   380 MEROPE   1286
    WITH SUCH SLIGHT MEANS TO COPE WITH SUCH A FOE •   381 MEROPE   1293
    WITH SUCH SLIGHT MEANS TO COPE WITH SUCH A FOE •   381 MEROPE   1293
    HOW MIGHT NOT SUCH A SIGHT AS THIS REVIVE • •   383 MEROPE   1358
    WITH SUCH A DEED AS THIS THOU MATCHEST MINE •   385 MEROPE   1426
    IF IN THIS FEEBLE BOSOM SUCH A FIRE • • •   387 MEROPE   1470
    IF HAPLY AT THIS MOMENT SUCH ATTEMPT • • •   388 MEROPE   1505
    FIRST WORK AFTER SUCH VICTORY LET US GO • •   405 MEROPE   2017
    AND KINGLY GAIT FOR EVER SUCH A SPELL • •   408 EMPEDOCLES I 1   61
    IN HIS SEVERE LOOKS SUCH A MAJESTY • • •   408 EMPEDOCLES I 1   62
    IN SUCH A GLEN ON SUCH A DAY • • • •   414 EMPEDOCLES I 2   57
    IN SUCH A GLEN ON SUCH A DAY • • • •   414 EMPEDOCLES I 2   57
    BUT ASK HOW THOU SUCH SIGHTS • • • •   416 EMPEDOCLES I 2   109
    TYPHO SUCH RED JETS OF FLAME • • • •   430 EMPEDOCLES II   48
    SUCH WAYS SUCH ARTS SUCH LOOKS HADST THOU • •   451 GEISTS GRAVE   44
    SUCH WAYS SUCH ARTS SUCH LOOKS HADST THOU • •   451 GEISTS GRAVE   44
    SUCH WAYS SUCH ARTS SUCH LOOKS HADST THOU • •   451 GEISTS GRAVE   44
    YES IN SUCH ELOQUENT SILENCE DIDST THOU LIE •   464 ALARIC AT ROME   67
    SOUNDS SUCH AS ERST THE LONE WAYFARING MAN •   473 CROMWELL   39
    SAY NOT SUCH DREAMS ARE IDLE FOR THE MAN • •   473 CROMWELL   45
    DID WITH SUCH COLD DERISION SHINE • • •   482 COURAGE   22
    WHEREON THOU BUILDEST SUCH A GOODLY PRIDE • •   RUDE ORATOR   8
    FOR SUCH A DAMNING CATALOGUE OF ILLS • • •   RUDE ORATOR   14
    THOU DOST ALLEDGE FOR PROOF SUCH INSTANCES •   RUDE ORATOR   15
    WITH SUCH A PEEVISH HARDIHOOD OF SCORN • •   RUDE ORATOR   20
    THOU MIRROR THAT HAST DANCD THROUGH SUCH A WORLD • •   LUCRETIUS 1   1
    BETWIXT SUCH UNLIKE POWERS • • • • • •   LUCRETIUS 5   10

SUCK
    OF PEBBLES WHICH THE WAVES SUCK BACK AND FLING • • 211 DOVER BEACH   V 10

SUCKD
    ALL THE STYMPHALIAN PLAIN ARE NOW SUCKD DOWN • •   358 MEROPE   816

SUCKD   (CONTINUED)
     WHERE ERST THE STRONG SEA-CURRENTS SUCKD THEE DOWN   430 EMPEDOCLES II   59

SUDDEN
     SUDDEN AND SWIFT AND LIKE A PASSING WIND   . . . .   82 SOHRAB RUSTUM   724
     OF SUDDEN STIRS AND PAUSES FAIR   . . . . . .   223 EPILOG LAOCOON   64
     IS ON A SUDDEN BROUGHT   . . . .   242 SUMMER NIGHT   12
     BUT HUSH THE UPLAND HATH A SUDDEN LOSS   . . . .   267 THYRSIS   151
     SUDDEN FOR FIFTEEN YEARS   . . . .   287 RUGBY CHAPEL   30
     THEN STILL AND SUDDEN OBERMANN   . . . . . .   314 OBERMANN MORE   59
     ONE SUDDEN STROKE AND THE MESSENIANS LOVE   . . . .   381 MEROPE   1287
     AGAINST SURPRISE AND SUDDEN PANIC PROOF   . . . .   381 MEROPE   1305
     LO ON A SUDDEN ALL THE PILE IS BRIGHT   . . . .   445 WESTMIN ABBEY   34
     WHEN THE WIND SLUMBERETH IN A SUDDEN LULL   . . . .   466 ALARIC AT ROME   98
     SUDDEN HE BOWD HIS HEAD AND ALL HIS MANE AS HE BOWD IT   HOMER TRANS   44

SUDDENLY
     GREW SUDDENLY IN HEAVEN AND DARKD THE SUN   . . . .   75 SOHRAB RUSTUM   482
     SEES SUDDENLY A SPIRE OF FLAME SHOOT UP   . . . .   119 BALDER DEAD 3   V
     TOO SUDDENLY THOU TELLEST SUCH A LOSS   . . . .   363 MEROPE   945
     TO CIRCLE THE PRINCE ROUND WHEN SUDDENLY   . . . .   402 MEROPE   1932
     THROUGH THE DARK NIGHT SUDDENLY   . . . . . .   430 EMPEDOCLES II   47

SUFFER
     I SHALL SUFFER BUT THEY WILL OUTLIVE THEIR AFFECTION   20 MODERN SAPPHO   17
     WHERE JUST MEN SUFFER WRONG   . . . .   39 STAGIRIUS   42
     NO WE MAY SUFFER DEEPLY YET RETAIN   . . . .   153 TRISTRAM 3   116
     IT IS TO SUFFER THIS   . . . .   213 GROWING OLD   26
     AND THEN WE SUFFER AND AMONGST US ONE   . . . .   260 SCHOLAR-GIPSY   182
     THE MILLIONS SUFFER STILL AND GRIEVE   . . . . .   320 OBERMANN MORE   233
     SO LOATH TO SUFFER MUTE   . . . .   421 EMPEDOCLES I 2   277

SUFFERD
     VAIN AND STRANGE DEBATE WHERE BOTH HAVE SUFFERD   . .   144 TRISTRAM 2   53
     I TOO HAVE SUFFERD YET I KNOW   . . . .   201 URANIA   1
     I TOO HAVE SUFFERD BUT I KNOW   . . . . . .   201 URANIA   V   1
     ALL THINGS HAVE SUFFERD A LOSS   . . . . . .   232 YOUTH OF NATURE   127
     WHO MOST HAS SUFFERD TAKES DEJECTEDLY   . . . .   260 SCHOLAR-GIPSY   183

SUFFERER
     BLAME ME NOT POOR SUFFERER THAT I TARRIED   . . . .   142 TRISTRAM 2   5

SUFFERERS
     MID STRUGGLING SUFFERERS HURT TO DEATH SHE LAY   . .   166 AUSTERITY POET   9
     THE SUFFERERS DIED THEY LEFT THEIR PAIN   . . . .   303 GRANDE CHARTR   131

SUFFEREST
     AND SAY MY LOVE WHY SUFFEREST THOU   . . . . . .   209 LONGING   12
     AND SAY MY FRIEND WHY SUFFEREST THOU   . . . . .   209 LONGING   V   12

SUFFERING
     WHICH YEARS AND CURIOUS THOUGHT AND SUFFERING GIVE   43 GIPSY CHILD   38
     WHICH YEARS TO MOST AND CARE AND SUFFERING GIVE   . .   43 GIPSY CHILD   V   38
     BOTH IN SUFFERING AND IN PLEASURE   . . . . . .   49 SECOND BEST   3
     ACTION AND SUFFERING THOUGH HE KNOW   . . . . .   56 RESIGNATION   152
     NOT SUFFERING WHICH SHUTS UP EYE AND EAR   . . . .   152 TRISTRAM 3   113
     NOT SUFFERING THAT SHUTS UP EYE AND EAR   . . . .   152 TRISTRAM 3   V 113
     HE TOOK THE SUFFERING HUMAN RACE   . . . . . .   270 MEMORIAL VERSES   19
     ALAS YET TO THE SUFFERING MAN   . . . . . .   273 EDW QUILLINAN   9
     THE CELLS THE SUFFERING SON OF MAN   . . . . .   300 GRANDE CHARTR   45
     SUFFERING SENT THEM DEATH   . . . .   343 MEROPE   417
     O SUFFERING O CALAMITY HOW TEN   . . . . . .   385 MEROPE   1406
     THERE IS SOME ROOT OF SUFFERING IN HIMSELF   . . .   411 EMPEDOCLES I 1   151
     WITH GOD AND FATE TO RAIL AT SUFFERING EASILY   . .   421 EMPEDOCLES I 2   281
     WHAT SUFFERING IS THERE NOT SEEN   . . . . . .   432 EMPEDOCLES II   100
     SOUL-FED EYES WITH SUFFERING WORN   . . . . . .   454 POOR MATTHIAS   63
     HUMAN SUFFERING AT OUR SIDE   . . . .   457 POOR MATTHIAS   163

SUFFERINGS
     HIMSELF HIS SUFFERINGS IN HIS COUNTRYS LOT   . . . .   477 CROMWELL   172

SUFFICD
     SUFFICD FOR THAT TITANIC STRIFE   . . . .   270 MEMORIAL VERSES   V 14

SUFFICES
     BUT WHO I SAID SUFFICES HERE   . . . .   225 EPILOG LAOCOON   128

SUFFICIENT
     SHORT ANSWER IS SUFFICIENT LEAGUE WITH THEE   . .   340 MEROPE   335
     WAIT THEN UNTIL SUFFICIENT HELP APPEARS   . . . .   384 MEROPE   1397

SUFFICING
     AND DRIED ITS SELF-SUFFICING FOUNT OF JOY   . . . .   429 EMPEDOCLES II   22

SUFFRAGE
     THE SUFFRAGE CAPTIVE NOW NOT ONE IN TEN   . . . .   171 DIVINITY   7

SUFFUSED
     WITH EYE SUFFUSED BUT HEART INSPIRED TRUE   . . . .   172 GOOD SHEPHERD   10
     THROUGH ALPINE MEADOWS SOFT-SUFFUSED   . . . . .   299 GRANDE CHARTR   1

SUGAR
    CAKE WE OFFERD SUGAR SEED . . . . 455 POOR MATTHIAS 115

SUGARD
    SLAKE THEIR PARCHD THROATS WITH SUGARD MULBERRIES 66 SOHRAB RUSTUM 166

SUGGESTIONS
    SUGGESTIONS TO DISQUIETUDE . . . . 56 RESIGNATION 125

SUITED
    SUITED WELL TO HEALTH BUT HOW . . . . 455 POOR MATTHIAS 113

SUITS
    I DOUBT THEIR CAUTION LITTLE SUITS THEIR WARD . . 351 MEROPE 608

SULLEN
    AND SULLEN AND HAS PITCHD HIS TENTS APART . . . . 66 SOHRAB RUSTUM 179
    CLOSING IN BLOOD AND GLOOM HIS SULLEN REIGN . . 335 MEROPE 160
    ROUND WHICH THE SULLEN VAPOUR ROLLS ALONE . . . 429 EMPEDOCLES II 4
    IN SULLEN HOMAGE TO THE INVADERS MIGHT . . . 465 ALARIC AT ROME 76

SULLYING
    SULLYING HIS GARMENT WITH DARK-STREAMING BLOOD . . 346 MEROPE 491

SULTRY
    MOST SULTRY DRAIND THE PITCHER THERE . . . . . 90 SICK KING BOKH 82
    AND CRUMBLING WALL AND SULTRY SAND . . . . . 318 OBERMANN MORE 183

SUM
    OF NATURE WITH HER COUNTLESS SUM . . . . . . 450 GEISTS GRAVE 24

SUMMER
    IN THE RICH LANGUOR OF LONG SUMMER-DAYS . . . 12 MYCERINUS 117
    BY WELL-HEADS IN SUMMER DAYS . . . . . . 34 NEW SIRENS 240
    FRESH FROM THE SUMMER FIELDS . . . . . . 51 CONSOLATION 43
    OF OXUS WHERE THE SUMMER-FLOODS OERFLOW . . . 61 SOHRAB RUSTUM 14
    CROSSING THE STREAM IN SUMMER SCRAPES THE LAND . 61 SOHRAB RUSTUM 19
    BLEACH THEM OR OXUS WITH HIS SUMMER-FLOODS . . . 72 SOHRAB RUSTUM 377
    OXUS IN SUMMER WASH THEM ALL AWAY . . . . 72 SOHRAB RUSTUM 378
    UPON THE SUMMER-FLOODS AND NOT MY BONES . . . 74 SOHRAB RUSTUM 428
    THEY THREE IN THAT LONG-DISTANT SUMMER-TIME . . 79 SOHRAB RUSTUM 628
    CROSSING THE STREAM IN SUMMER MEETS THE LAND . 61 SOHRAB RUSTUM V 19
    LET THE EARLY SUMMER BE . . . . 135 TRISTRAM 1 153
    IN SUMMER ON THE HEADLANDS . . . . 159 NECKAN 1
    IN SUMMER ON THE HEADLANDS . . . . 161 NECKAN 65
    WHICH LUNA FELT THAT SUMMER-NIGHT . . . . . 181 ISOLATION MARG 20
    HIS VOICE LIKE SOUNDS OF SUMMER NIGHTS . . . 202 URANIA 22
    THE FLIES A SUMMER-MURMUR MADE . . . . . . 222 EPILOG LAOCOON 41
    THE PASSING GROUP THE SUMMER-MORN . . . . . 222 EPILOG LAOCOON 51
    ONE SUMMER-MORN FORSOOK . . . . 256 SCHOLAR-GIPSY 36
    MOORD TO THE COOL BANK IN THE SUMMER-HEATS . . 257 SCHOLAR-GIPSY 67
    RETURNING HOME ON SUMMER-NIGHTS HAVE MET . . 257 SCHOLAR-GIPSY 73
    DARK BLUEBELLS DRENCHD WITH DEWS OF SUMMER EVES . 257 SCHOLAR-GIPSY 88
    THE OPENING SUMMER THE SKY . . . . 285 HAWORTH CHURCH 118
    IN THE SUMMER-MORNING THE ROAD . . . . . . 287 RUGBY CHAPEL 28
    SUMMER BUT UNDER THEM STILL . . . . 292 HEINES GRAVE 6
    THE SUMMER-DAY GROW LATE . . . . 310 OBERMANN 116
    BEHOLD IN SUMMER . . . . 392 MEROPE 1651
    OF THIS FAIR SUMMER-WEATHER ON THESE HILLS . . 409 EMPEDOCLES I 1 101
    IN SUMMER TO ALL COUNTRY-FESTIVALS . . . . 412 EMPEDOCLES I 2 15
    WHOM THE SUMMER EVENING SEES . . . . . . 434 EMPEDOCLES II 181
    LIKE SUMMER LIGHTNINGS OER A DARKEND SKY . . . 474 CROMWELL 72

SUMMERS
    BURGHERS AND DAMES AT SUMMERS PRIME . . . . . 17 CHURCH BROU 2 20
    SOME DREAMERS WHO FAR OFF A SUMMERS DAY . . . 42 GIPSY CHILD V 22
    PASSING THE LONG SUMMERS DAY . . . . . 137 TRISTRAM 1 222
    ALL THE LIVE MURMUR OF A SUMMERS DAY . . . . 255 SCHOLAR-GIPSY 20

SUMMIT
    OVER THE SUMMIT OF THE HILL . . . . . . 54 RESIGNATION 63
    THE SUMMIT OF THE PILE THE DEAD THE MAST . . . 119 BALDER DEAD 3 190
    AND THE BLANCHD SUMMIT BARE . . . . . . 324 OBERMANN MORE 338

SUMMITS
    ROUND ALPINE SUMMITS EDDYING ROSE . . . . . 52 RESIGNATION 8

SUMMONS
    BLEW SUCH A THRILLING SUMMONS TO MY WILL . . . 36 VOICE 37
    SUMMONS THE YOUNGER IS DEAD . . . . . . 281 HAWORTH CHURCH 33
    THROW HIM A PEALING WORD OF SUMMONS DOWN . . . 349 MEROPE 576

SUMPTUOUS
    SUMPTUOUS ITS CLOTHING RICH ITS FARE . . . . . 315 OBERMANN MORE 87

SUN
    ROSE-CROWND AND EVER WHEN THE SUN WENT DOWN . . 11 MYCERINUS 93
    ON THE WORK THE BRIGHT SUN SHINES . . . . . 15 CHURCH BROU 1 90
    THE HILLS ARE CLOTHED WITH PINES SUN-PROOF . . . 16 CHURCH BROU 2 4

SUN   (CONTINUED)

STREAMS FROM THE SETTING SUN AND COLOURS BRIGHT • • 18 CHURCH BROU 3   19
FOR DAYLIGHT FOR THE CHEERFUL SUN • • • • • 22 YOUTH AND CALM   17
BORDERD EACH BANK WITH PINES THE MORNING SUN • • 24 DREAM   3
BRIGHT IN THE SUN THE CLIMBING GOURD-PLANTS LEAVES • 25 DREAM   16
SOON THE PLANKD COTTAGE BY THE SUN-WARMD PINES • • 25 DREAM   35
UNDER OERHANGING PINES THE MORNING SUN • • • 24 DREAM   V 3
SOON THE PLANKD COTTAGE MID THE SUN-WARMD PINES • 25 DREAM   V 35
NO WEAK NURSLING OF AN EARTHLY SUN • • • • 30 NEW SIRENS   112
FROM SOME TRANSIENT EARTHLY SUN • • • • 31 NEW SIRENS   152
FROM SOME TRANSIENT HUMAN SUN • • • • 31 NEW SIRENS   V 152
WHAT HEAVENS WHAT EARTH WHAT SUN SHALT THOU DISCERN 43 GIPSY CHILD   44
AND THOUGH THE JUST SUN GILD AS MORTALS PRAY • • 43 GIPSY CHILD   59
THE PORT LIES BRIGHT UNDER THE AUGUST SUN • • 41 GIPSY CHILD   V 5
AND THOUGH THE JUST SUN GILD AS ALL MEN PRAY • 43 GIPSY CHILD   V 59
ALONE THE SUN ARISES AND ALONE • • • • 45 IN UTRUMQUE PAR   20
O SEEMING SOLE TO AWAKE THY SUN-BATHED HEAD • 45 IN UTRUMQUE PAR   29
BRIGHT SHINES THE SUN • • • • • • • 50 CONSOLATION   15
THROUGH SUN-PROOF ALLEYS • • • • • • 51 CONSOLATION   26
CROUCHD ON HIS SADDLE WHILE THE SUN • • • 52 RESIGNATION   10
ARE THREADED QUIET IN THE SUN • • • • 54 RESIGNATION   51
CROUCHD ON HIS SADDLE WHEN THE SUN • • • 52 RESIGNATION   V 10
WHEN THE SUN MELTS THE SNOWS IN HIGH PAMERE • 61 SOHRAB RUSTUM   15
THE SUN IS NOT YET RISEN AND THE FOE • • • 62 SOHRAB RUSTUM   35
THE SUN BY THIS HAD RISEN AND CLEARD THE FOG • 64 SOHRAB RUSTUM   104
AND YOU WOULD SAY THAT SUN AND STARS TOOK PART • 75 SOHRAB RUSTUM   480
GREW SUDDENLY IN HEAVEN AND DARKD THE SUN • • 75 SOHRAB RUSTUM   482
AND THE SUN SPARKLED ON THE OXUS STREAM • • • 75 SOHRAB RUSTUM   489
AND THE BRIGHT SUN BROKE FORTH AND MELTED ALL • 76 SOHRAB RUSTUM   523
A FAR BRIGHT CITY SMITTEN BY THE SUN • • • 79 SOHRAB RUSTUM   622
BY THIS THE SUN HAD RISEN AND CLEARD THE FOG • 64 SOHRAB RUSTUM   V 104
IN THESE LAST DAYS THE SUN HATH BURND • • • 89 SICK KING BOKH   59
NOR SEE THE SUN ARISE NOR SEE IT SET • • • • 99 BALDER DEAD 1   154
TO KEEP HIS OWN LIFE SAFE AND SEE THE SUN • • 101 BALDER DEAD 1   213
NOR LIT WITH SUN BUT THROUGH THE DARKSOME AIR • 108 BALDER DEAD 2   125
AND OER A DARKSOME TRACT WHICH KNOWS NO SUN • 108 BALDER DEAD 2   139
VINEYARDS AND CROFTS AND PASTURES BRIGHT WITH SUN • 113 BALDER DEAD 2   300
NOT LIT WITH SUN BUT THROUGH THE DARKSOME AIR • 108 BALDER DEAD 2   V 125
BUT NOW THE SUN HAD' PASSD THE HEIGHT OF HEAVEN • 118 BALDER DEAD 3   154
AND WHILE THEY GAZED THE SUN WENT LURID DOWN • 119 BALDER DEAD 3   194
SUN MOON AND STARS WHICH THOU HAST HUNG IN HEAVEN 121 BALDER DEAD 3   264
TO WARMER LANDS AND COASTS THAT KEEP THE SUN • 129 BALDER DEAD 3   562
WARM WITH THE WINTER-SUN OF BURNISHD GREEN • • 150 TRISTRAM 3   21
AND THE BLESSED LIGHT OF THE SUN • • • • 164 FORSAKEN MERM   93
TWAS AUGUST AND THE FIERCE SUN OVERHEAD • • 169 EAST LONDON   1
OR WAS IT FROM SOME SUN-FLECKD MOUNTAIN-BROOK • 175 PARTING   21
OER THE SUN-REDDEND WESTERN STRAITS • • • 198 FRAG ANTIGONE   92
TO CALAIS GLITTERING IN THE SUN • • • • 204 CALAIS SANDS   4
TO CALAIS SPARKLING IN THE SUN • • • • 204 CALAIS SANDS   V 4
OF THE SLOW-SINKING SUN • • • • • • 208 ON THE RHINE   15
THAT SPARKLES IN THE SUN ALONG • • • • 226 EPILOG LAOCOON   158
ARE YE LIKE DAYLIGHT AND SUN • • • • • 230 YOUTH OF NATURE   66
WHICH SHELTERD THEIR CHILDHOOD THE SUN • • 234 YOUTH OF MAN   65
IT STOOD AND SUN AND MOONSHINE RAIND THEIR LIGHT • 236 PALLADIUM   5
THE MEADOWS WHERE IT GLIDES THE SUN THE BREEZE • 247 BURIED LIFE   90
THROUGH SILKEN RIFTS SOFT PEERS THE SUN • • 248 KENSINGTON GARD V
THROUGH SILKEN RIFTS SOFT WINKS THE SUN • •   KENSINGTON GARD V
BUT LIT FOR ALL ITS GENEROUS SUN • • • • 251 WISH   39
FIERCER THE SUN OVERHEAD • • • • • • 253 FUTURE   65
AND IN THE SUN ALL MORNING BINDS THE SHEAVES • 255 SCHOLAR-GIPSY   14
AND HERE TILL SUN-DOWN SHEPHERD WILL I BE • • 255 SCHOLAR-GIPSY   22
AND BOWER ME FROM THE AUGUST SUN WITH SHADE • 256 SCHOLAR-GIPSY   29
TOPS IN LIFES MORNING-SUN SO BRIGHT AND BARE • 267 THYRSIS   145
WENT OER THE SUN-LIT FIELDS AGAIN • • • • 271 MEMORIAL VERSES   52
WARMING THEIR HEADS IN THE SUN • • • • 297 HEINES GRAVE   157
WITH THE SINKING SUN AND THE AIR • • • 297 HEINES GRAVE   163
THE BROAD RED SUN OVER FIELD • • • • 297 HEINES GRAVE   170
AND CHEERFUL WORKS BENEATH THE SUN • • • 301 GRANDE CHARTR   60
ABOVE HIS SUN-WARMD FIRS • • • • • 313 OBERMANN MORE   34
OF SUN AND ARID STONE • • • • • • 318 OBERMANN MORE   182
THE SUN SHONE IN THE NEW-WASHD SKY • • • 319 OBERMANN MORE   209
I FELT THE SUN AND WIND • • • • • 321 OBERMANN MORE   256
AND SEE THE SUN IS RISEN • • • • • 322 OBERMANN MORE   284
AND PRAY THE GODS AND PRAY THE ALL-SEEING SUN • 349 MEROPE   570
SUN WHO CAREEREST THROUGH THE HEIGHT OF HEAVEN • 349 MEROPE   571
AND BID THE SUN THINE ONLY VISITANT • • • 395 MEROPE   1752
BUT NEVER ON SO FAIR A MORN THE SUN • • • 406 EMPEDOCLES I 1   9
OF THE SUN-LOVING GENTIAN IN THE HEAT • • 412 EMPEDOCLES I 2   5
TO HAVE ENJOYD THE SUN • • • • • 425 EMPEDOCLES I 2   398
AND WHEN NOW THE WESTERING SUN • • • • 433 EMPEDOCLES II   143
FROM THE GRASSY SUN-WARMD PLACE • • • 433 EMPEDOCLES II   161
YE SUN-BORN VIRGINS ON THE ROAD OF TRUTH • • 436 EMPEDOCLES II   239
BEFORE THE SUN BEFORE THE WIND • • • • 456 POOR MATTHIAS   133
THE SUN THAT ON THY TOSSING PAIN • • • 482 COURAGE   21
FOLLOWING THE SUN WE SET OUR VESSELS HEAD • • 484 S S LUSITANIA   3

SUNBEAMS

AND THOU WHO DIDST THE STARS AND SUNBEAMS KNOW • • 3 SHAKESPEARE   9
AND THOU WHOSE HEAD DID STARS AND SUNBEAMS KNOW • • 3 SHAKESPEARE   V 9
A GUSH OF SUNBEAMS THROUGH A RUIND HALL • • • 36 VOICE   21

SUNBURNT
    HIS HARD-TASKD SUNBURNT WIFE • • • • • • • • 426 EMPEDOCLES I 2   414

SUNDAYS
    ON SUNDAYS AT THE MATIN-CHIME • • • • • • • 17 CHURCH BROU 2   17
    ON SUNDAYS TOO A PRIEST DOTH COME • • • • • • 17 CHURCH BROU 2   25

SUNDERING
    WHO ASSURE US SUNDERING POWERS • • • • • • • • 457 POOR MATTHIAS   171

SUNG
    THE FAMOUS POETS SUNG AND GONE • • • • • • 219 BACCHANALIA 2   4
    WHO HERE OUTWORN HAD SUNK AND SUNG • • • • • • 278 SOUTHERN NIGHT   99
    WHO HERE OUTWEARIED SUNK AND SUNG • • • • • • 278 SOUTHERN NIGHT V 99
    HONOURD AND SUNG OF BY ALL • • • • • • • 343 MEROPE   430
    AROUND WHOSE FEET THE EXULTING WAVES HAVE SUNG • • 472 CROMWELL   13

SUNK
    WHEN SHE SUNK INTO HER GRAVE • • • • • • 15 CHURCH BROU 1 V 70
    THE HANDS PROPPING THE SUNK HEAD • • • • • • 30 NEW SIRENS   128
    THE SUNK EYES THE WAILING TONE • • • • • • • 34 NEW SIRENS   248
    WHERE HOST MEETS HOST AND MANY NAMES ARE SUNK • • 62 SOHRAB RUSTUM   61
    NEVER TILL NOW DEFILED SUNK TO THE DUST • • • 76 SOHRAB RUSTUM V 498
    HE REELD AND STAGGERING BACK SUNK TO THE GROUND • 76 SOHRAB RUSTUM V 521
    AND HIS HEAD SWAM AND HE SUNK DOWN TO EARTH • • 81 SOHRAB RUSTUM V 693
    WHEN AIR IS CHILLIEST AND THE STARS SUNK LOW • • 103 BALDER DEAD 1   281
    AND NANNA ON HER BED SUNK BACK BUT THEN • • • • 104 BALDER DEAD 1 V 338
    AND THEY FROM SIGHT HAVE DISAPPEARD AND SUNK • • 128 BALDER DEAD 3   524
    BUT HER CHEEKS ARE SUNK AND PALE • • • • • 131 TRISTRAM 1   32
    LEAVING HER SUNK AND PALE THOUGH FAIR • • • • 132 TRISTRAM 1   48
    AND HER CHEEKS ARE SUNK AND PALE • • • • • 131 TRISTRAM 1 V 32
    SO SUNK SO RARELY LIFTED SAVE TO MEET • • • • 151 TRISTRAM 3   71
    THERE TO WATCH OER THE SUNK VALE • • • • • 176 PARTING   47
    AND SUNK DOWN HERE SLEEPING • • • • • • 187 STRAYED REVEL V 51
    SUNK IN THY DREAM • • • • • • • • • • 220 BACCHANALIA 2   50
    OR SUNK AT THE CORE OF THE WORLD • • • • • 230 YOUTH OF NATURE   70
    WHICH HAS NOT CRIED TO SUNK SELF-WEARY MAN • • • 238 PROGRESS   43
    SUNK THEN IS EUROPES SAGEST HEAD • • • • • 270 MEMORIAL VERSES   16
    WHO HERE OUTWORN HAD SUNK AND SUNG • • • • • 278 SOUTHERN NIGHT   99
    WHO HERE OUTWEARIED SUNK AND SUNG • • • • • 278 SOUTHERN NIGHT V 99
    A LONG STEEP JOURNEY THROUGH SUNK • • • • • 288 RUGBY CHAPEL   87
    UPON HIS CROSS WITH HEAD SUNK LOW • • • • • 317 OBERMANN MORE   155
    THOUGH SUNK BE NOW THIS BRIGHT THIS GRACIOUS HEAD • 449 WESTMIN ABBEY   176
    THOUGH SUNK IS NOW THIS BRIGHT THIS GRACIOUS HEAD • 449 WESTMIN ABBEY V 176
    NOT IN SUNK SPAINS PROLONGD DEATH AGONY • • • 480 HUNGARIAN NAT   1

SUNKEN
    THE SUNKEN REEFS AND FAR AWAY • • • • • • 148 TRISTRAM 2   173
    THAT WILD UNQUENCHD DEEP-SUNKEN OLD-WORLD PAIN • • 200 PHILOMELA   8

SUNLESS
    THROUGH THIS WASTE OF SUNLESS GREENS • • • • • 33 NEW SIRENS   212
    SUNLESS PRISON OF ROCK • • • • • • • • 370 MEROPE   1118
    SUNLESS PRISON OF ROCKS • • • • • • • • 370 MEROPE   V1118
    HIDE HIS TORN HEAD BENEATH HIS SUNLESS CAVE • • 472 CROMWELL   24
    THE SUNLESS FOREST AND THE SEALIKE PLAIN • • • 475 CROMWELL   106

SUNLIGHT
    OF THE NEW PILE THE SUNLIGHT SHINES • • • • • 16 CHURCH BROU 2   2
    LIKE ISLES OF SUNLIGHT ON A MOUNTAINS BROW • • • 475 CROMWELL   127

SUNNY
    THE SUNNY WASTE • • • • • • • • • • 191 STRAYED REVEL   180
    SMILINGLY FORTH UPON HER SUNNY BAY • • • • • 468 ALARIC AT ROME   160
    THE SUNNY WATERS HOLD THEIR JOYOUS WAY • • • 469 ALARIC AT ROME   196
    CHILDHOODS BRIGHT GLANCE AND SUNNY SMILE NO MORE • • 477 CROMWELL   182

SUNRISE
    AT SUNRISE FROM THEIR DEWY LAIR • • • • • 16 CHURCH BROU 2   9
    WHERE AT SUNRISE THROUGH YOUR VINES • • • • • 29 NEW SIRENS   94
    WHERE AT SUNRISE THROUGH THE VINES • • • • • 29 NEW SIRENS V 94
    DESCRIED AT SUNRISE AN EMERGING PROW • • • • • 262 SCHOLAR-GIPSY   233

SUNS
    YET SUNS SHALL RISE AND MANY MOONS SHALL WANE • • 10 MYCERINUS   62
    WHAT HEAVENS WHAT EARTH WHAT SUNS SHALT THOU DISCERN 43 GIPSY CHILD V 44
    LIKE LEAVES BY SUNS NOT YET UNCURLD • • • • • 59 RESIGNATION   253
    INDOORS FROM THE SUNS EYE HIS HEAD DROOPD LOW • • 86 SOHRAB RUSTUM   847
    WHERE THE SUNS RAYS STRUCK FULL AND FLASHD BACK KEEN   TRISTRAM 3 V 21
    WHITEND HIS FACE FROM THE SUNS FRONTING RAY • • 170 EAST AND WEST   6
    WHERE IN THE SUNS HOT EYE • • • • • • • 243 SUMMER NIGHT   38
    CATCHES THE WESTERING SUNS LAST FIRES • • • • 274 STANZAS CARNAC   24
    WITH INDIAN SUNS AT LAST FORDONE • • • • • 276 SOUTHERN NIGHT V 26
    OF PASSING TROOPS IN THE SUNS BEAM • • • • • 305 GRANDE CHARTR   177
    NO SHAME THAT SUNS SHOULD RISE TO LIGHT A CONQUERD   468 ALARIC AT ROME   150
        ROME

SUNSET
    AT SUNSET ON A POPULOUS TOWN • • • • • • • 57 RESIGNATION   165
    AT SUNSET NEARING • • • • • • • • • • 192 STRAYED REVEL   205

SUNSET   (CONTINUED)
          MELLOWD AND SOFTEND AS WITH SUNSET-GLOW   • • • •   212 GROWING OLD   14
          THE HILL BEHIND WHOSE RIDGE THE SUNSET FLAMES   • •   263 THYRSIS   13
          BACKD BY THE SUNSET WHICH DOTH GLORIFY   • • • •   267 THYRSIS   158
          BRIGHT IN THE SUNSET WEIRD AND STILL • • • • •   273 STANZAS CARNAC   5
          SUNSET OVER THE SEA   • • • • • • • •   436 EMPEDOCLES II   253
          LIKE A GREEN LAND AT SUNSET ALL WERE THERE   • • • •   474 CROMWELL   84
          BATHD IN A BLAZE OF SUNSET MELT AWAY   • • • • •   478 CROMWELL   216

SUNSHINE
          THOUGH THAT BLANK SUNSHINE BLIND THEE THOUGH THE CLOUD   44 GIPSY CHILD   61
          MIST CLOGS THE SUNSHINE   • • • • • • • • •   50 CONSOLATION   1
          SLEEP IN THE JULY SUNSHINE STILL   • • • • • •   55 RESIGNATION   97
          THROUGH WHOSE GREEN BOUGHS THE GOLDEN SUNSHINE CREEPS   154 TRISTRAM 3   157
          AH NOW TIS CHANGED IN CONQUERING SUNSHINE BRIGHT   • •   170 EAST AND WEST   12
          CAME LOLLING IN THE SUNSHINE   • • • • • • •   193 STRAYED REVEL   262
          NOT WITH THE SUNSHINE OF HOPE   • • • • • • •   233 YOUTH OF MAN   21
          IN THE SUNSHINE UNWORN BY THE PLOUGH   • • • • •   252 FUTURE   30
          MID WIDE GRASS MEADOWS WHICH THE SUNSHINE FILLS   •   257 SCHOLAR-GIPSY   68
          IN JUNE AND MANY A SCYTHE IN SUNSHINE FLAMES   •   257 SCHOLAR-GIPSY   92
          SUNSHINE AND RAIN AS WE MIGHT   • • • • • • •   287 RUGBY CHAPEL   34
          CREEPS OER THE SUNSHINE A BREEZE   • • • • •   293 HEINES GRAVE   39
          THE SUNSHINE IN THE HAPPY GLENS IS FAIR   • • •   426 EMPEDOCLES I 2   430
          LIKE SUNSHINE WENT AND CAME AND BADE   • • • • •   460 KAISER DEAD   47

SUNWARD
          THEIR SMOOTH TOPS SHINING SUNWARD AND BENEATH   • •   11 MYCERINUS   87

SUNWARDS
          THEIR SMOOTH TOPS SHINING SUNWARDS AND BENEATH   • •   11 MYCERINUS   V   87

SUP
     ALIGHT AND SPARELY SUP AND WAIT   • • • • • • •   300 GRANDE CHARTR   26

SUPERFLUITY
     BUT THOU WHOM SUPERFLUITY OF JOY   • • • • • •   42 GIPSY CHILD   9

SUPERPOSED
     WHEN BURSTING THROUGH THE NETWORK SUPERPOSED   • •   7 REP FRIEND CONT   10

SUPERSEDE
          TILL DEATH ARRIVE TO SUPERSEDE • • • • • • • •   56 RESIGNATION   142
          TILL DEATH ARRIVES TO SUPERSEDE   • • • • • • •   56 RESIGNATION   V 142

SUPERSTITIOUS
     BAH THOU A DOCTOR THOU ART SUPERSTITIOUS   • • • •   410 EMPEDOCLES I 1   133

SUPPD
     FAMILIAR HALLS WHERE WE HAVE SUPPD OF OLD   • • • •   128 BALDER DEAD 3   534

SUPPING
     I LEFT THEE SUPPING WITH PEISIANAX   • • • • • •   407 EMPEDOCLES I 1   31

SUPPORT
     SUPPORT THE FERVOURS OF THE HEAVENLY MORN   • • • •   172 IMMORTALITY   8

SUPPOSE
     FOR WHOM AS I SUPPOSE THOU PASSEST HERE   • • • •   379 MEROPE   1271

SUPPOSED
          FOR IF YE SLEW HIM FOR SUPPOSED MISRULE   • • • •   339 MEROPE   316
          FLING OFF THY CROWN SUPPOSED AT LAST SECURE   • •   395 MEROPE   1743

SUPPRESSD
     AH IT LIVES BECAUSE SO DEEP-SUPPRESSD   • • • •   143 TRISTRAM 2   40

SUPREMACY
     A JUST THEREFORE A SAFE SUPREMACY   • • • • • •   339 MEROPE   305

SUPREME
          FRANCE FAMED IN ALL GREAT ARTS IN NONE SUPREME   • •   7 REP FRIEND CONT   4
          BLIND DIVINATIONS OF A WILL SUPREME   • • • • • •   10 MYCERINUS   52
          DEATH DEATH WAS JUDGED THE BOON SUPREME INDEED   • •   448 WESTMIN ABBEY   140

SURE
          O MEEK ANTICIPANT OF THAT SURE PAIN   • • • •   43 GIPSY CHILD   41
          THE SACRED WORLD AND BY PROCESSION SURE   • • • •   45 IN UTRUMQUE PAR   3
          AND THOUGH THOU THINKEST THAT THOU KNOWEST SURE   • •   72 SOHRAB RUSTUM   388
          FOR HE HAD HAD SURE TIDINGS THAT THE BABE   • • •   79 SOHRAB RUSTUM   607
          A STRANGE UNLIKELY ERRAND SURE IS THINE   • • • •   110 BALDER DEAD 2   203
          AND SURE OF ALL THE HAPPIEST FAR ART THOU   • • •   112 BALDER DEAD 2   257
          TO BE FULFILLD NOR MY RETURN AS SURE   • • • •   112 BALDER DEAD 2   269
          IS SHE NOT COME THE MESSENGER WAS SURE   • • • •   130 TRISTRAM 1   1
          AND BY CONTRITION SEALD THRICE SURE   • • • • •   179 FAREWELL   72
          SPEAK OF THE SURE CONSOLATIONS OF TIME   • • • •   206 SEPARATION   2
          REVELATION MAKES HIM SURE   • • • • • • •   215 PIS-ALLER   2
          NOTHING SURE NO MORAL PLAN   • • • • • • •   215 PIS-ALLER   7
          MUST NEEDS READ CLEARER SURE THAN HE   • • • • •   250 WISH   28
          OF FEELING AS TRANQUIL AS SURE   • • • • • • •   252 FUTURE   40
          VICTORY SURE TO HER RACE   • • • • • • • •   343 MEROPE   428

SURE   (CONTINUED)
        MOST LIKELY GRATEFUL BUT IN ALL CASE SURE   · · · ·   354 MEROPE   711
        OUR MISERY MORE AND THINE OWN RUIN SURE   · · · ·   368 MEROPE   1081
        SURE ALL-COMMON TO LOSE   · · · · · · ·   369 MEROPE   1100
        THY SON IS HERE ONE SAID SO SURE BUT NOW   · · · ·   376 MEROPE   1216
        COULD FIND NO WAY TO FOUND THEM SURE AS THIS   · · ·   403 MEROPE   1960
        THOU WILT EARN MY THANKS SURE AND PERHAPS HIS   · ·   409 EMPEDOCLES I 1   99
        AND DARES STAMP NOTHING FALSE WHERE HE FINDS   415 EMPEDOCLES I 2   91
            NOTHING SURE
        SURE ONLY THAT YOUR MIND SEES ALL THINGS WHICH BEFAL   423 EMPEDOCLES I 2   346
        IN THE SURE REVOLUTIONS OF THE WORLD   · · · · · ·   428 EMPEDOCLES I 2   472
        BRIGHT WITS AND INSTINCTS SURE   · · · · · · ·   446 WESTMIN ABBEY   77
        BRIGHT WITS AND INSTINCT SURE   · · · · · · ·   446 WESTMIN ABBEY   V 77

SURELY
        YET SURELY O MY PEOPLE DID I DEEM   · · · · · ·   9 MYCERINUS   19
        SURELY THAN THOSE WHICH SHOULD THINE AGE EMPLOY   · ·   41 GIPSY CHILD   V 11
        WHO EACH DAY MORE SURELY LEARNS   · · · · · ·   49 SECOND BEST   20
        RUSTUM WILL SURELY HEAR IT IF I FALL   · · · · ·   62 SOHRAB RUSTUM   58
        THY VICTORY YET THOU CANST NOT SURELY KNOW   · · ·   72 SOHRAB RUSTUM   389
        SURELY THE NEWS WILL ONE DAY REACH HIS EAR   · · ·   78 SOHRAB RUSTUM   581
        SURELY MY HEART CRIED OUT THAT IT WAS THOU   · · ·   82 SOHRAB RUSTUM   711
        FASTER SURELY THAN IT SHOULD   · · · · · · ·   135 TRISTRAM 1   171
        FROM VIOLENT ANGUISH SURELY FREE   · · · · · ·   137 TRISTRAM 1   233
        NEVER SURELY HAS BEEN SEEN   · · · · · · ·   131 TRISTRAM 1   V
        SURELY SHE WILL COME AGAIN   · · · · · · ·   162 FORSAKEN MERM   17
        THOU TOO WILT SURELY ONE DAY PROVE   · · · · ·   178 FAREWELL   38
        FOR SURELY ONCE THEY FEEL WE WERE   · · · · ·   182 TO MARG CONT   15
        SLOW AND SURELY THE SWEETS   · · · · · ·   199 EARLY DEATH   13
        SLOW AND SURELY THE SWEET   · · · · · ·   199 EARLY DEATH   V 13
        FOR TIS SO SURELY EVEN IN GREECE   · · · · ·   221 EPILOG LAOCOON   13
        SURELY HAS NOT BEEN LEFT VAIN   · · · · · · ·   287 RUGBY CHAPEL   39
        SOMEWHERE SURELY AFAR   · · · · · · ·   287 RUGBY CHAPEL   40
        UPROAR SURELY NOT LOATH   · · · · · · · ·   293 HEINES GRAVE   15
        SURELY IT WAS THAT BARD   · · · · · · ·   295 HEINES GRAVE   98
        PIOUS BUT IMPIOUS SURELY IF THEIR SCOPE   · · · ·   342 MEROPE   380
        SURELY IF RIGHTS MAY BE BY FORCE ASSERTED   · · ·   352 MEROPE   656
        SURELY NO SINNER THE MAN   · · · · · · · ·   361 MEROPE   905
        SIGNS THE CROSS AND ANSWERS SURELY   · · · · ·   META CLOISTER   39

SURENESS
        WHOSE SURENESS GRAY-HAIRD SCHOLARS HARDLY LEARN   · ·   43 GIPSY CHILD   42

SURF
        THROUGH THE SURF AND THROUGH THE SWELL   · · · ·   162 FORSAKEN MERM   33
        SHE SMILED SHE WENT UP THROUGH THE SURF IN THE BAY   163 FORSAKEN MERM   62
        COME I SAID AND WE ROSE THROUGH THE SURF IN THE BAY   163 FORSAKEN MERM   67

SURFACE
        BELOW THE SURFACE-STREAM SHALLOW AND LIGHT   · · ·   483 BELOW SURFACE   1
        TOUCH THE SAME SURFACE WHICH OUR FATHERS TROD   · ·   EVERLASTING SUB   3
        HAVE THE SAME SURFACE WHICH OUR FATHERS TROD   · ·   EVERLASTING SUB   V 3
        HAVE THE SAME SURFACE WHICH OUR FATHERS FELT   · ·   EVERLASTING SUB   V 3
        HAVE THE SAME SURFACE WHICH OUR FATHERS TOUCHD   · ·   EVERLASTING SUB   V 3
        TOUCH THE SAME SURFACE WHICH OUR FATHERS FELT   · ·   EVERLASTING SUB   V 3
        TOUCH THE SAME SURFACE WHICH OUR FATHERS TOUCHD   · ·   EVERLASTING SUB   V 3

SURGE
        FOR THE SURGE-BEAT CORNISH STRAND   · · · · · ·   134 TRISTRAM 1   132
        TYNTAGEL ON ITS SURGE-BEAT HILL   · · · · · ·   136 TRISTRAM 1   177

SURGED
        INEVITABLY HAD SURGED UP PERHAPS   · · · · · ·   394 MEROPE   1698

SURGING
        OF BUFFETING WIND AND SURGING TIDE   · · · · · ·   140 TRISTRAM 1   331
        SEEMD SURGING THE VIRGILIAN CRY   · · · · · ·   450 GEISTS GRAVE   15
        OF THE HOARSE ONSET OF THE SURGING WAVE   · · · ·   466 ALARIC AT ROME   110
        THE SURGING BATTLE AND THE MAILD ARRAY   · · · ·   475 CROMWELL   138

SURMISE
        SWORN TO OUR PLOT HE IS IF FALSE SURMISE   · · · ·   379 MEROPE   1272
        PROOF NOT SURMISE SHOWS HIM IN COMMERCE CLOSE   · ·   380 MEROPE   1274
        SWORN TO OUR PLOT HE IS BUT THAT SURMISE   · · · ·   379 MEROPE   V1272

SURPLICED
        THE SURPLICED PRIEST STOOD DUMB   · · · · · · ·   159 NECKAN   28

SURPRISE
        WITH A STATELY SLOW SURPRISE   · · · · · · ·   31 NEW SIRENS   156
        THAT THE KNIGHTS EYED HER IN SURPRISE   · · · ·   146 TRISTRAM 2   123
        FIXD ON THEIR MOTHERS FACE IN WIDE SURPRISE   · · ·   151 TRISTRAM 3   47
        ARRESTS THEM WITH A CHARMD SURPRISE   · · · · ·   305 GRANDE CHARTR   190
        OF CHANGE ALARM SURPRISE   · · · · · · · · ·   308 OBERMANN   70
        AGAINST SURPRISE AND SUDDEN PANIC PROOF   · · · ·   381 MEROPE   1305

SURPRISED
        OR SURPRISED IN THE GLENS   · · · · · · · ·   392 MEROPE   1626

SURPRIZE
        FIXD ON THEIR MOTHERS FACE IN WIDE SURPRIZE   · ·   TRISTRAM 3   V 47

SURRENDER
     AND YOUR JEWELLD GAUDS SURRENDER   . . . . . .   35 NEW SIRENS   255

SURREY
     SONGS TO TRILL IN SURREY AIR   . . . .   458 POOR MATTHIAS   197

SURROUND
     MOUNTAINS SURROUND IT AND SWEET VIRGIN AIR . . . .   236 PALLADIUM   10

SURROUNDING
     OF GRASS PEEP OUT AMID SURROUNDING SNOW   . . . .   122 BALDER DEAD 3   315

SURVEY
     WHAT SOME TWO THOUSAND YEARS SURVEY   . . . . . .   315 OBERMANN MORE   83
     WE BUT SURVEY HE IS THE ARCHITECT   . . . . . .   LUCRETIUS 5   3

SURVEYD
     SATE IN THE BROUGHAM AND THOSE BLANK WALLS SURVEYD   167 RACHEL 1   8
     WIDEND HER SWEEP AND SURVEYD   . . . .   280 HAWORTH CHURCH   16

SURVEYS
     SURVEYS EACH HAPPY GROUP WHICH FLEETS   . . . .   57 RESIGNATION   166
     SURVEYS EACH HAPPY GROUP THAT FLEETS . . . . . .   57 RESIGNATION   V 166
     THE MOUNT FROM WHENCE HIS EYE SURVEYS THE WORLD . .   96 BALDER DEAD 1   50
     THE THRONE FROM WHICH HIS EYE SURVEYS THE WORLD . .   102 BALDER DEAD 1   254

SURVIVE
     BALDER HAS MET HIS DEATH AND YE SURVIVE   . . . .   96 BALDER DEAD 1   26
     THE SPOTS WHICH RECALL HIM SURVIVE   . . . . . .   228 YOUTH OF NATURE   13
     THESE SURVIVE YET NOT WITHOUT PAIN   . . . . . .   229 YOUTH OF NATURE   25

SURVIVED
     HAVE YOU TOO SURVIVED YOURSELVES   . . . . . .   437 EMPEDOCLES II   280

SURVIVES
     THE SHEEPFOLD OF MICHAEL SURVIVES   . . . . . .   228 YOUTH OF NATURE   21
     THAT MY SON STILL SURVIVES IN HEALTH IN BLOOM   . .   351 MEROPE   612

SURVIVEST
     THOU SURVIVEST US THIS   . . . .   232 YOUTH OF MAN   2

SURVIVING
     THE YOUNG SURVIVING ISEULT ONE BRIGHT DAY   . . . .   149 TRISTRAM 3   5

SURVIVOR
     SOME GOOD SURVIVOR WITH HIS FLUTE WOULD GO . . . .   265 THYRSIS   83

SUSAS
     IN SUSAS PALACE PROUD   . . . .   47 WORLD QUIETIST   26

SUSPECT
     THESE TERMS AND I SUSPECT SOME HIDDEN FRAUD   . .   120 BALDER DEAD 3   235

SUSPEND
     SUSPEND YOUR MELANCHOLY RITES AWHILE . . . . . .   332 MEROPE   77

SUSPENDED
     STOOD WITH SUSPENDED SCYTHE TO SEE US PASS . . . .   266 THYRSIS   129

SUSPENSE
     WITHIN THE BALANCE OF A SLOW SUSPENSE   . . . .   RUDE ORATOR   5

SUSPICION
     INVOLVED IN ONE SUSPICION WITH THE BASE   . . . .   341 MEROPE   367
     UNJUST SUSPICION AND ERRONEOUS FEAR   . . . . . .   342 MEROPE   384
     SUSPICION GRAVE I SEE BUT NO FIRM PROOF   . . . .   365 MEROPE   994
     SUSPICION FROM THY GRANDSIRE OF THY DEATH   . . . .   379 MEROPE   1270
     YET HAD HE LIVED SUSPICION JEALOUSY . .   . . . .   394 MEROPE   1697
     TWIXT THEE AND ME SUSPICION THAT I NURSED   . . . .   394 MEROPE   1699
     ON THIS SUSPICION CAST HIM INTO CHAINS   . . . .   365 MEROPE   V
     SUSPICION GRAVE I SEE BUT NO CLEAR PROOF   . . . .   365 MEROPE   V 994

SUSPICIOUS
     OLD AGE IS MORE SUSPICIOUS THAN THE FREE   . . . .   335 MEROPE   156

SUSTAIND
     WAS CALMD ENNOBLED COMFORTED SUSTAIND   . . . .   12 MYCERINUS   111

SUSTAINS
     IS EVERYWHERE SUSTAINS THE WISE THE FOOLISH ELF . .   422 EMPEDOCLES I 2   306

SWAINS
     BUT THYRSIS NEVER MORE WE SWAINS SHALL SEE . . . .   265 THYRSIS   77

SWALLOW
     AND TO EACH BULRUSH-CREST A SWALLOW HANGS   . . . .   109 BALDER DEAD 2   160
     SWALLOW SKIMMING BY THE MILL   . . . .   456 POOR MATTHIAS   142

SWALLOWING
    WHETHER IN SOUND OF THE SWALLOWING SEA   • • • •   252 FUTURE   16

SWALLOWS
    AND AS THE SWALLOWS CROWD THE BULRUSH-BEDS • • • •   109 BALDER DEAD 2   157
    WHERE BLACK-WINGD SWALLOWS HAUNT THE GLITTERING THAMES   257 SCHOLAR-GIPSY   94
    AND DARTING SWALLOWS AND LIGHT WATER-GNATS • • • •   266 THYRSIS   125
    SWALLOWS TROOPING IN THE SEDGE • • • • • • • 456 POOR MATTHIAS   143

SWAM
    AND HIS HEAD SWAM AND HE SANK DOWN TO EARTH   • •   81 SOHRAB RUSTUM   693
    AND HIS HEAD SWAM AND HE SUNK DOWN TO EARTH   • •   81 SOHRAB RUSTUM   V 693
    STOUTLY UNDER THE HEADLANDS LEE THEY SWAM • • • •   358 MEROPE   822

SWANS
    SILENT THE SWANS BESIDE US FLOAT • • • • • •   206 RIVER   3
    GEESE ARE SWANS AND SWANS ARE GEESE • • • • •   215 LAST WORD   6
    GEESE ARE SWANS AND SWANS ARE GEESE • • • • •   215 LAST WORD   6

SWARD
    OF OPEN HILL-SWARD FRESH AND GREEN • • • • •   16 CHURCH BROU 2   13
    OF SHAVEN HILL-SWARD TRIM AND GREEN • • • • •   16 CHURCH BROU 2   V 13
    AND LOPPD THEIR BOUGHS AND CLOVE THEM ON THE SWARD   106 BALDER DEAD 2   59
    IN A SLOPED SWARD DOWN TO A BRAWLING BROOK • • • •   155 TRISTRAM 3   187
    UNDER THE THORNS ON THE GREEN SWARD AND STRONG • •   155 TRISTRAM 3   196
    THEN CROSS THE SWARD AND REACH THAT GATE • • •   300 GRANDE CHARTR   28
    BENEATH THE PINY SWARD • • • • • • • •   310 OBERMANN   120
    HERE IN THE VALLEY IS IN SHADE THE SWARD • • •   406 EMPEDOCLES I 1   12
    AND STREAM AND SWARD AND CHESTNUT-TREES • • •   414 EMPEDOCLES I 2   52
    ON THE SWARD AT THE CLIFF-TOP • • • • • •   442 EMPEDOCLES II   429

SWARDED
    AND FROM SOME SWARDED SHELF HIGH UP THERE CAME • •   25 DREAM   11
    SWARDED ALLEYS THE LIMES • • • • • • • •   292 HEINES GRAVE   4
    WE BOUNDED DOWN THE SWARDED SLOPE WE PLUNGED • •   357 MEROPE   790

SWARM
    AND THEN A SWARM OF WANDERING HORSE WHO CAME • •   64 SOHRAB RUSTUM   126
    SINCE BROILS TEAR US IN TWAIN SINCE THIS NEW SWARM   410 EMPEDOCLES I 1   121

SWARMD
    SO AROUND HERMOD SWARMD THE TWITTERING GHOSTS • •   109 BALDER DEAD 2   163

SWARMING
    ON HIS OWN SWARMING THOUGHTS AN INTEREST OWN • •   8 RELIGIOUS ISOL   4
    HIM NOT THE NOISY SWARMING RACE • • • • •   HORATIAN ECHO   V 7
    RAKED FROM THE SWARMING GULF OF SORROWS HELL • •   RUDE ORATOR   16
    RAKED FROM THE SWARMING GULFS OF SORROWS HELL • •   RUDE ORATOR   V 16

SWARMS
    HELAS PALE SWARMS AND THERE WAS BALDER BOUND • •   108 BALDER DEAD 2   133
    SHE FOLLOWS THE GAY WORLD WHOSE SWARMS HAVE FLED • •   167 RACHEL 1   9
    AMONG THE SWARMS OF MEN • • • • • • • •   311 OBERMANN   176

SWARMY
    WHAT SWARMY ENDLESS LIFE IS HERE • • • • • •   KENSINGTON GARD   V 14

SWART
    WHICH VENICE SHIPS DO FROM SWART EGYPT BRING • •   150 TRISTRAM 3   41

SWATH
    NO AS THE FOAMING SWATH • • • • • • • •   40 HUMAN LIFE   19
    AND AS AFIELD THE REAPERS CUT A SWATH • • • •   70 SOHRAB RUSTUM   293

SWATHE
    NO AS THE FOAMING SWATHE • • • • • • • •   40 HUMAN LIFE   V 19
    AND AS AFIELD THE REAPERS CUT A SWATHE • • • •   70 SOHRAB RUSTUM   V 293

SWATHS
    SILENT THE SWATHS THE RINGING WAIN • • • • • •   217 BACCHANALIA 1   5

SWAY
    CROWND WITH GRAY HAIRS HE DIED AND FULL OF SWAY • •   9 MYCERINUS   14
    BE PASSD ON THE PROUD HEIGHTS OF SWAY • • • •   56 RESIGNATION   149
    THERE WERE TWO ISEULTS WHO DID SWAY • • • • •   132 TRISTRAM 1   68
    IN A TOO STRONG EMOTIONS SWAY • • • • • •   178 FAREWELL   30
    OF SWAY HAVE FELT THIS BODING SENSE COME ON • •   239 REVOLUTIONS   14
    AND NEVER QUITE BENUMBD BY THE WORLDS SWAY • • • •   243 SUMMER NIGHT   33
    TO RULE THIS KINGDOM I INTEND WITH SWAY • • • •   342 MEROPE   376
    FOR EACH OF WHOM TO SWAY • • • • • • • •   418 EMPEDOCLES I 2   178
    WHERE THE LONG GREEN REED-BEDS SWAY • • • • •   433 EMPEDOCLES II   133
    WHERE TIME ELSE DUMB HATH SIGNIFIED HIS SWAY • •   FRAGMENT 2   2

SWAYD
    SELF-SWAYD OUR FEELINGS EBB AND SWELL • • • •   180 ISOLATION MARG   11
    AH WHO SWAYD OUR CHOICE AND WHO DECIDED • • • •   210 SELF-DECEPTION   15
    AND ONE SWAYD ALL WHO WORE A KINGLY CROWN • • • •   476 CROMWELL   143

SWAYING
    SWAYING THE LONG-HAIRD GOATS WITH SILVERD REIN • •   115 BALDER DEAD 3   73
    SWAYING THE SCEPTRE WITH PREDESTINED HAND • • • •   345 MEROPE   473

SWAYING   (CONTINUED)
        SWAYING FROM SIDE TO SIDE HIS MASSY HEAD   . . . .   401 MEROPE   1911

SWAYS
        BUT YET SUCCESS SWAYS WITH THE BREATH OF HEAVEN . .   72 SOHRAB RUSTUM   387
        WHERE THE SALT WEED SWAYS IN THE STREAM   . . . .   162 FORSAKEN MERM   38
        THEY ASK A SOUL WHICH NEVER SWAYS   . . . . . .   178 FAREWELL   27
        THEY ASK A SOUL THAT NEVER SWAYS   . . . . . .   178 FAREWELL   V 27

SWEAR
        NAY BUT I SWEAR FROM THIS THY PATH   . . . . . .   91 SICK KING BOKH   103
        AND YET I SWEAR IT ANGERS ME TO SEE   . . . . . .   153 TRISTRAM 3   133
        SWEAR BY THE GODS HENCEFORTH TO OBEY ME   . . . .   371 MEROPE   1133

SWEARING
        HOUNDS ARE PULLING PRICKERS SWEARING   . . . . . .   13 CHURCH BROU 1   17

SWEAT
        HER PALFREYS FLANKS WERE MIRED AND BATHED IN SWEAT   154 TRISTRAM 3   171
        BROKE BLACK WITH SWEAT THE ANTLERD MOUNTAIN-STAG . . 357 MEROPE   808

SWEEP
        SWEEP IN THE SOUNDING STILLNESS OF THE NIGHT   . .   10 MYCERINUS   46
        OFF THEY SWEEP THE MARSHY FORESTS   . . . . . .   13 CHURCH BROU 1   19
        AND HIS CLOSED EYE DOTH SWEEP   . . . .   133 TRISTRAM 1   90
        LET HER SWEEP HER DAZZLING HAND   . . . . . .   134 TRISTRAM 1   121
        AND SENT ME WITH MY DOGS TO SWEEP   . . . . . .   148 TRISTRAM 2   176
        AND SENT HIM WITH HIS DOGS TO SWEEP   . . . . . .   148 TRISTRAM 2   V 176
        SWEEP THROUGH MY SOUL   . . . .   185 STRAYED REVEL   6
        SWEEP THROUGH MY SOUL   . . . .   194 STRAYED REVEL   297
        FREE TO THE SWEEP OF LIGHT AND WIND   . . . . . .   223 EPILOG LAOCOON   72
        HOUSES WITH LONG WHITE SWEEP   . . . .   242 SUMMER NIGHT   18
        BEHIND ME ON THEIR GRASSY SWEEP   . . . .   274 STANZAS CARNAC   9
        THE SICKLE-SWEEP OF QUIBERON BAY   . . . . . .   274 STANZAS CARNAC   27
        WIDEND HER SWEEP AND SURVEYD   . . . . . .   280 HAWORTH CHURCH   16
        AN ARM ALOFT FOR HELP THEN SWEEP BENEATH   . . .   358 MEROPE   833
        ONE ARM ALOFT FOR HELP THEN SWEEP BENEATH   . . .   358 MEROPE   V 833
        THE WIND SWEEP MAN AWAY   . . . .   421 EMPEDOCLES I 2   260

SWEEPING
        AND IN THE SWEEPING OF THE WIND YOUR EAR   . . . .   19 CHURCH BROU 3   43
        SWEEPING THE DUST CAME NEAR AND IN MUTE WOE   . .   82 SOHRAB RUSTUM   732
        HOUR AFTER HOUR HER GOLD CURLS SWEEPING IT . . . . 152 TRISTRAM 3   83
        OR LOUDER RUSH OF WHIRLWINDS SWEEPING BY   . . . .   466 ALARIC AT ROME   111

SWEEPS
        SWEEPS EARTH AND HEAVEN AND MEN AND GODS ALONG . .   9 MYCERINUS   39
        HIS PINION AND WITH SHORT UNEASY SWEEPS   . . . .   78 SOHRAB RUSTUM   564
        ALL ROUND THE FOREST SWEEPS OFF BLACK IN SHADE . . 139 TRISTRAM 1   276

SWEET
        SINGER OF SWEET COLONUS AND ITS CHILD   . . . . .   2 TO A FRIEND   14
        ALL HER PALE SWEET-ROUNDED CHEEK   . . . . . .   23 MEMORY-PICTURE   30
        O SWEET PLEADERS DOTH MY LOT   . . . .   31 NEW SIRENS   164
        CAN I LOOK ON YOUR SWEET FACES   . . . . . .   32 NEW SIRENS   191
        THOSE MELANCHOLY TONES SO SWEET AND STILL   . .   36 VOICE   34
        WHERE SWEET THINGS SOONEST CLOY   . . . . . .   39 STAGIRIUS   44
        WITH SWEET JOIND VOICES   . . . .   51 CONSOLATION   46
        HER OWN SWEET ERRANDS ALL FORGONE   . . . . .   53 RESIGNATION   36
        CURLD MINION DANCER COINER OF SWEET WORDS   . .   74 SOHRAB RUSTUM   458
        THOU TELLER OF SWEET TALES THINE OWN   . . . . .   87 SICK KING BOKH   11
        LOOK AS IN SOME BOORS YARD A SWEET-BREATHD COW .   123 BALDER DEAD 3   340
        NIPS TOO KEENLY THE SWEET FLOWER   . . . . .   131 TRISTRAM 1   36
        BEFORE US ARE THE SWEET GREEN FIELDS OF WALES   .   133 TRISTRAM 1   95
        AH SWEET ANGELS LET HIM DREAM   . . . . . .   133 TRISTRAM 1   105
        AH SWEET SAINTS UNWITTINGLY   . . . .   135 TRISTRAM 1   142
        TRISTRAM SWEET LOVE WE ARE BETRAYD OUT-PLANND .   135 TRISTRAM 1   167
        AH SWEET SAINTS HIS DREAM DOTH MOVE   . . . . .   135 TRISTRAM 1   170
        AT THIS SOFT HOUR UNDER THIS SWEET MOON   . . .   139 TRISTRAM 1   286
        MY PRINCESS ART THOU THERE SWEET DO NOT WAIT   .   140 TRISTRAM 1   308
        SWEET FLOWER THY CHILDRENS EYES   . . . . .   140 TRISTRAM 1   325
        ROUND EACH SWEET BROW THE CAP CLOSE-SET   . .   141 TRISTRAM 1   340
        MY PRINCESS ART THOU THERE SWEET TIS TOO LATE .   140 TRISTRAM 1   V 308
        THOU ART PALER BUT THY SWEET CHARM ISEULT   . .   143 TRISTRAM 2   25
        THE SWEET EXPRESSION OF HER BROW   . . . . . .   147 TRISTRAM 2   138
        UNDER THE FEATHERD HATS OF THE SWEET PAIR   . .   150 TRISTRAM 3   33
        HER FEATURES SO FATIGUED HER EYES THOUGH SWEET .   151 TRISTRAM 3   70
        WE HEARD THE SWEET BELLS OVER THE BAY   . . . .   162 FORSAKEN MERM   31
        WHEN SWEET AIRS COME SEAWARD   . . . .   165 FORSAKEN MERM   128
        STORMILY SWEET HIS TITAN-AGONY   . . . . . .   166 PICT NEWSTEAD   3
        AND THOSE SWEET EYES OF BLUE   . . . . . .   174 MEETING   8
        THAT THE SWEET VOICE ITS UPLAND CLEARNESS TOOK .   175 PARTING   22
        SWEET NOTES THIS WAY   . . . .   175 PARTING   24
        THE SWEET BLUE EYES THE SOFT ASH-COLOURD HAIR .   175 PARTING   37
        SWEET LIPS THIS WAY   . . . .   176 PARTING   42
        WHERE SWEET THE UNBROKEN MOONBEAMS LAY   . . . .   177 FAREWELL   2
        THE THOUSAND SWEET STILL JOYS OF SUCH   . . . .   179 FAREWELL   67
        HOW SWEET UNREACHD BY EARTHLY JARS   . . . . .   180 FAREWELL   77
        HOW SWEET TO FEEL ON THE BOON AIR   . . . . .   180 FAREWELL   81
        AH THE SWEET FUMES AGAIN   . . . .   187 STRAYED REVEL   64

```
SWEET            ( CONTINUED )
         AGAIN THE SWEET SLEEP      . . . . . . . . . .    187 STRAYED REVEL         69
         THY VOICE IS SWEET . . . . . . . . . . . .        189 STRAYED REVEL        116
         BUT HIM IN HIS SWEET PRIME      . . . . . . .      197 FRAG ANTIGONE         65
         SLOW AND SURELY THE SWEET       . . . . . . .      199 EARLY DEATH      V    13
         AND THE SWEET TRANQUIL THAMES       . . . . . .    200 PHILOMELA             12
         THAT SLIGHT SWEET FIGURE AT MY SIDE     . . . .    204 CALAIS SANDS     V    11
         COME TO THE WINDOW SWEET IS THE NIGHT-AIR . . . .  210 DOVER BEACH           6
         AND IN THE AFTER-SILENCE SWEET . . . . . . .       219 BACCHANALIA 2         13
         PROFOUND YET TOUCHING SWEET YET STRONG    . . . .  222 EPILOG LAOCOON        28
         FULL OF SWEET BREATHINGS WAS THE AIR    . . . .    223 EPILOG LAOCOON        63
         SWEET AND FORGIVING AND GOOD     . . . . . . .     232 YOUTH OF MAN          15
         MOUNTAINS SURROUND IT AND SWEET VIRGIN AIR . . .   236 PALLADIUM             10
         AND THAT SWEET CITY WITH HER DREAMING SPIRES . .   263 THYRSIS               19
         SWEET-WILLIAM WITH HIS HOMELY COTTAGE-SMELL . .    264 THYRSIS               65
         AND WE SHALL HAVE HIM IN THE SWEET SPRING-DAYS .   265 THYRSIS               73
         RED LOOSESTRIFE AND BLOND MEADOW-SWEET AMONG . .   266 THYRSIS              124
         SWEET GENEROUS AND HUMANE     . . . . . . . .      273 EDW QUILLINAN         16
         WHOSE FLOOR TO-NIGHT SWEET MOONSHINE FILLS . .     277 SOUTHERN NIGHT        75
         SWEET AND GRACEFUL AND SHE      . . . . . . .      284 HAWORTH CHURCH        92
         NAPLES BAY FOR A SWEET       . . . . . . . .       294 HEINES GRAVE          58
         WORDSWORTHS SWEET CALM OR GOETHES WIDE    . . .    308 OBERMANN              79
         SWEET HEAPS OF FRESH-CUT GRASS . . . . . . .       313 OBERMANN MORE         18
         SWEET CHESTNUTS BARLEY-CAKES AND BOARS-FLESH DRIED 356 MEROPE               754
         BUT THE SWEET-SMELLING MYRTLE       . . . . . .    391 MEROPE              1616
         WITH THE SWEET NIGHT TO HELP THY HARMONY    . . .  409 EMPEDOCLES I 1        98
         CLEANSE TO SWEET AIRS THE BREATH OF POISONOUS STREAMS 410 EMPEDOCLES I 1    117
         MORE VIRGINAL AND SWEET THAN OURS    . . . . .     426 EMPEDOCLES I 2       434
         AS VIRGINAL AND SWEET AS OURS      . . . . . .     426 EMPEDOCLES I 2   V 434
         THE SWEET NOTES WHOSE LULLING SPELL    . . . .     431 EMPEDOCLES II         64
         THAT TRIUMPH OF THE SWEET PERSUASIVE LYRE   . . .  432 EMPEDOCLES II        126
         WHAT SWEET-BREATHING PRESENCE       . . . . . .    442 EMPEDOCLES II        441
         THAT VOICE HAD NOTE SO CLEAR OF SWEET COMMAND . .  445 WESTMIN ABBEY         28
         AND TEMPER SWEET AND LOVE OF ALL THINGS PURE . .   446 WESTMIN ABBEY         79
         O FOR THE CROON PATHETIC SWEET      . . . . . .    459 KAISER DEAD           11
         YEARS THAT WERE SWEET OR SAD BECALMD OR TOSSD . .  474 CROMWELL              77
         MIGHT PAINT THE CALM SWEET PEACE THE REST OF HOME  475 CROMWELL             113
         DREAMS THAT WERE SWEET AT EVE AT MORN WERE SIN . . 475 CROMWELL             121
         ON THE SWEET AND MOON-BATHED LAND      . . . . .       META CLOISTER        12
         YOUR SWEET EYES ARE TURNED ON ME      . . . . .       META CLOISTER        20
         FREEZES THE SWEET STRAIN ON THE PARTED LIPS   . .     FRAGMENT 1            7

SWEETER
         WHAT SWEETER SLEEP THAN THIS COULD I DESIRE   . .  372 MEROPE             1156

SWEETEST
         THE SWEETEST CHRISTIAN SOUL ALIVE    . . . . . .   132 TRISTRAM 1            54
         THE SWEETEST HARP-PLAYER IN CATANA    . . . . . .  412 EMPEDOCLES I 2        13

SWEETLY
         HOW SWEETLY WOULD THE FRESH SEA-BREEZE    . . . .  205 CALAIS SANDS          15
         HOW SWEETLY WOULD THE FRESH SEA-WIND    . . . . .  205 CALAIS SANDS     V    15
         THAT MOCKING MOUTH GROW SWEETLY BLAND    . . . .   206 RIVER                 6
         LIE SWEETLY IN THE LOOK DIVINE . . . . . . . .     208 ON THE RHINE          14
         THE BIRDS SING SWEETLY IN THESE TREES    . . . .   248 KENSINGTON GARD  V    5
         THE BIRDS SING SWEETLY IN THEIR TREES    . . . .       KENSINGTON GARD  V    5
         THE CHILD SLEEPS SWEETLY IN HIS BED   . . . . . .     KENSINGTON GARD  V   36

SWEETNESS
         AND YOUR SCENTS HAVE SHED THEIR SWEETNESS   . . .   34 NEW SIRENS          253

SWEETS
         WHICH ON THE SWEETS THAT WOO IT DARES NOT FEED . .   9 MYCERINUS            26
         SLOW AND SURELY THE SWEETS      . . . . . . . .    199 EARLY DEATH          13

SWELL
         WHAT WONDER SHALL TIME BREED TO SWELL THY STRAIN .  43 GIPSY CHILD          43
         SWELL HIS ATTENTIVE SOUL      . . . . . . . . .     47 WORLD QUIETIST       30
         SHALL DRAW TO SWELL THAT SHOULDERING HERD . . . .   48 HORATIAN ECHO         9
         OR THAT MEN GAVE IT HIM TO SWELL HIS FAME . . . .   79 SOHRAB RUSTUM       614
         ALL THE STRONG BROOD OF HEAVEN TO SWELL MY TRAIN . 120 BALDER DEAD 3       241
         THROUGH THE SURF AND THROUGH THE SWELL    . . . .  162 FORSAKEN MERM        33
         WHAT MAY MY HEART AT NEWSTEAD FULLEST SWELL . . .  166 PICT NEWSTEAD         1
         SELF-SWAYD OUR FEELINGS EBB AND SWELL    . . . .   180 ISOLATION MARG       11
         SWELL THEIR LARGE VEINS TO BURSTING IN WILD PAIN . 192 STRAYED REVEL       226
         SOON WILL THE MUSK CARNATIONS BREAK AND SWELL . .  264 THYRSIS              63
         WHERE ARE THE MOWERS WHO AS THE TINY SWELL . . .   266 THYRSIS             127
         IT PASSD THAT ELEMENTAL SWELL . . . . . . . .      319 OBERMANN MORE       207
         WHEN THROUGH THY CAVES THOU HEAREST MUSIC SWELL .  431 EMPEDOCLES II        66
         THE AIR IS THIN THE VEINS SWELL      . . . . . .   435 EMPEDOCLES II       215
         OH THAT MY HEART BOUNDED WITH THE SWELL OF THE SEA 438 EMPEDOCLES II       324
         AND WHISPERS TO THE LISTENING WINDS THAT SWELL . . 472 CROMWELL             19

SWELLD
         OF THE MIDMOST OCEAN HAVE SWELLD    . . . . . . .  288 RUGBY CHAPEL         71
         THE ROMAN TEMPEST SWELLD AND SWELLD   . . . . . .  316 OBERMANN MORE       107
         THE ROMAN TEMPEST SWELLD AND SWELLD   . . . . . .  316 OBERMANN MORE       107

SWELLING
         SWELLS WITH THE SWELLING EVIL OF THIS TIME . . . . 410 EMPEDOCLES I 1      113
```

SWELLING   (CONTINUED)
          WITH HELD-IN JOY SWELLING ITS HEART I ONLY .   .   .   .   438 EMPEDOCLES II   316

SWELLS
          MILD HOLLOWS AND CLEAR HEATHY SWELLS . . . . . .   54 RESIGNATION   66
          SWELLS MY HEART AND TAKES MY BREATH AWAY   . . . .   145 TRISTRAM 2   74
          ARE NOT PUSHED OUT BY THE SWELLS   . . . . . .   214 NEW ROME   14
          WHERE POOR HAVE PLACE LIKE THE SWELLS   . . . .   214 NEW ROME   V 14
          AND NOW AND THEN PERHAPS THERE SWELLS   . . . .   224 EPILOG LAOCOON   122
          THOUGH HERE A MOUNTAIN-MURMUR SWELLS . . . . .   307 OBERMANN   29
          SWELLS WITH THE SWELLING EVIL OF THIS TIME . . . .   410 EMPEDOCLES I 1   113
          THE MASS SWELLS MORE AND MORE   . . . .   423 EMPEDOCLES I 2   333
          AND MEMORYS GUSHING TIDE SWELLS DEEP AND FULL . .   464 ALARIC AT ROME   53
          THE TRUMPET SWELLS YET LOUDER THEY ARE HERE   . .   467 ALARIC AT ROME   133

SWEPT
          UNDER THEIR FEET AND MOANING SWEPT THE PLAIN   . .   75 SOHRAB RUSTUM   484
          EDDYING AND MOANING ROUND AND SWEPT THE PLAIN   . .   75 SOHRAB RUSTUM   V 484
          REGNER WHO SWEPT THE NORTHERN SEA WITH FLEETS   . .   117 BALDER DEAD 3   126
          THE TEMPEST OF THE LATTER DAYS HATH SWEPT   . . .   128 BALDER DEAD 3   523
          HE SAW ON SPRAY-SWEPT HEBRIDES   . . . .   156 SAINT BRANDAN   7
          AND THEY ARE SWEPT BY BALMS OF SPRING   . . . .   182 TO MARG CONT   8
          SWEPT WITH CONFUSED ALARMS OF STRUGGLE AND FLIGHT   212 DOVER BEACH   36
          AND AIR-SWEPT LINDENS YIELD   . . . .   255 SCHOLAR-GIPSY   26
          THE AVALANCHE SWEPT FROM OUR SIDE   . . . . .   289 RUGBY CHAPEL   123
          STRUGGLING IN VAIN TO CROSS IT SWEPT THEM ON   . .   358 MEROPE   825
          SWEPT DOWN A CHASM RIFTED IN THE CLIFF   . . .   363 MEROPE   960
          SWEPT DOWN A CHASM BROKEN IN THE CLIFF   . . . .   363 MEROPE   V 960
          SWEPT FROM THY WALLS O ROME ON ITS TRIUMPHANT WAY   465 ALARIC AT ROME   78
          AND AS THE PAGEANT SWEPT BEFORE THEIR EYES . . . .   467 ALARIC AT ROME   122
          SWEPT OFF THE WITHERED LEAVES THAT HIDE THE NAKED TOMB   469 ALARIC AT ROME   192
          LIT WITH NO RAPTURE AS THE STORM SWEPT BY . . .   472 CROMWELL   22
          OF HEAVENS EMBATTLED MYRIADS SWEPT ALONG   . . . .   473 CROMWELL   44
          SWEPT OER THE FANCY OF THAT HEEDLESS CHILD . . . .   473 CROMWELL   52
          AND PEACEFUL JOYS AND GENTLER THOUGHTS SWEPT BY . .   474 CROMWELL   71
          ARE SWEPT LIKE HUDDLING SHEEP ALONG . . . . .   481 COURAGE   8

SWERVED
          IT WERE NOT MEET THE BALANCE SWERVED . . . . . .   92 SICK KING BOKH   139
          THE HARMONY FROM WHICH MAN SWERVED   . . . . . .   314 OBERMANN MORE   53

SWIFT
          LET MY TURN IF IT WILL COME BE SWIFT IN ARRIVING . .   20 MODERN SAPPHO   31
          LOUD THUNDERING BORE US BY SWIFT SWIFT IT FOAMD   . .   25 DREAM   33
          LOUD THUNDERING BORE US BY SWIFT SWIFT IT FOAMD   . .   25 DREAM   33
          AND SWIFT FOR LIKE THE LIGHTNING TO THIS FIELD   . .   82 SOHRAB RUSTUM   722
          SUDDEN AND SWIFT AND LIKE A PASSING WIND   . . . .   82 SOHRAB RUSTUM   724
          SWIFT THROUGH THE TARTAR SQUADRONS TO THE FRONT . .   65 SOHRAB RUSTUM   V 142
          AND SWIFT TO ASGARD TO THE GATE HE CAME   . . . .   102 BALDER DEAD 1   259
          BUT IT SHALL NOT BE SO BUT MILD BUT SWIFT . . . .   103 BALDER DEAD 1   301
          TARDY OR SWIFT WOULDST THOU BE LOATH TO DIE   . . .   103 BALDER DEAD 1   306
          PAINLESS AND SWIFT SET FREE HER AIRY SOUL . . . .   104 BALDER DEAD 1   340
          CAME SWIFT DOWN TO JOIN   . . . .   186 STRAYED REVEL   35
          BY THE SWIFT-RUSHING MISSILE OF DEATH   . . . . .   216 LORDS MESSENGER   V 18
          I RUSH WITH THE SWIFT SPHERES AND GLOW . . . . .   241 MORALITY   27
          SWIFT RUSH THE SPECTRAL VAPOURS WHITE   . . . . .   299 GRANDE CHARTR   13
          HE HAD SMIT ME HAD HE BEEN SWIFT AS I   . . . . .   334 MEROPE   131
          SWIFT AS I CAME HATH FALSEHOOD BEEN BEFORE . . . .   363 MEROPE   954
          COME YE SWIFT FURIES WHO TO HIM YE HAUNT   . . . .   367 MEROPE   1056
          THEN WATCH HIM FOR HE RANGES SWIFT AND FAR . . . .   409 EMPEDOCLES I 1   94
          HE COULD STAY SWIFT DISEASES IN OLD DAYS   . . . .   410 EMPEDOCLES I 1   115
          LIKE A SWIFT RIVER THRO A SILENT PLAIN . . . . .   473 CROMWELL   64
          THEN LIKE A KINGLY RIVER SWIFT AND STRONG . . . .   475 CROMWELL   133
          THEN WITH A TROUBLED HEART THE SWIFT ACHILLES   HOMER TRANS   58
              ADDRESSD HIM

SWIFTLY
          COMING SWIFTLY THROUGH THE SAD TRACHINIANS . . . .   399 MEROPE   1838
          COMING SWIFTLY THROUGH THE JOCUND DORIANS . . . .   400 MEROPE   1863

SWIFTNESS
          FOR BY NO SLOW PACE OR WANT OF SWIFTNESS OF OURS . .   HOMER TRANS   50

SWIM
          AND HURL THEE IN A LAKE TO SINK OR SWIM   . . . .   114 BALDER DEAD 3   26
          IF CLEAR FROM PLOTTING BALDERS DEATH TO SWIM . . .   114 BALDER DEAD 3   27
          YE FADE YE SWIM YE WAVER BEFORE ME   . . . . . .   194 STRAYED REVEL   290

SWIMMERS
          FOR WE ARE ALL LIKE SWIMMERS IN THE SEA   . . . .   72 SOHRAB RUSTUM   390

SWIMMING
          TWO HORSES STRONGLY SWIMMING TOW   . . . . . .   191 STRAYED REVEL   185
          THE PRINCE IN CHASE AFTER A SWIMMING STAG . . . .   363 MEROPE   959

SWIMS
          SWIMS IN THE SHEEN OF THE MOON . . . .   228 YOUTH OF NATURE   4
          SWIMS ON AN OBSCURE MUCH WE MIGHT HAVE BEEN   . .   FRAGMENT 3   2

SWING
          THE COLLIE HAIR THE COLLIE SWING   . . . . . .   459 KAISER DEAD   26

SWINGING
THE SWINGING WATERS AND THE CLUSTERD PIER • • • • • 42 GIPSY CHILD 6
SWINGING AND OTHERS SKIM THE RIVER-STREAMS • • • • • 109 BALDER DEAD 2 V 161
SWINGING WITH IT IN THE LIGHT • • • • • • • • 147 TRISTRAM 2 150

SWINGS
A GATE SWINGS TO OUR TIDE HATH FLOWD • • • • • • 53 RESIGNATION 48
THE LOADED BOAT SWINGS GROANING • • • • • • 192 STRAYED REVEL 198
AS THE SLOW PUNT SWINGS ROUND • • • • • • 257 SCHOLAR-GIPSY V 76
FOR THIS AND THAT WAY SWINGS • • • • • • • 448 WESTMIN ABBEY 151
THE RUDDER SWINGS YET NONE DOTH STEER • • • • 480 HAYSWATER BOAT 39

SWIRLING
STARLINGS SWIRLING FROM THE HEDGE • • • • • • 456 POOR MATTHIAS 144

SWISS
SWISS CHALETS GLITTERD ON THE DEWY SLOPES • • • • 25 DREAM 10

SWITZERLAND
TO SWITZERLAND TO BADEN TO THE RHINE • • • • • 167 RACHEL 1 10
AND RACHELS SWITZERLAND HER RHINE IS HERE • • • • 167 RACHEL 1 14
THE SCENTED PINES OF SWITZERLAND • • • • • • 311 OBERMANN 167
BREAKS OUT AND LONGS FOR SWITZERLAND • • • • • 483 ROME-SICKNESS 3

SWOLN
MY HEART IS SWOLN WITH LOVE UNSAID • • • • • • 206 RIVER 10

SWOONING
THAT BLACK-ROBED SWOONING FIGURE MEROPE • • • • 376 MEROPE 1212

SWOOPING
SWOOPING TO LANDWARD NOR TO WHERE QUITE CLEAR • • 151 TRISTRAM 3 54

SWORD
HE ROSE AND CLAD HIMSELF AND GIRT HIS SWORD • • 61 SOHRAB RUSTUM 8
IN HIS RIGHT HAND A RULERS STAFF NO SWORD • • • • 64 SOHRAB RUSTUM 99
AND WITH THESE SLAUGHTEROUS HANDS DRAW SWORD NO MORE • 68 SOHRAB RUSTUM 241
A BELT OR SWORD PERHAPS AND GO HIS WAY • • • 71 SOHRAB RUSTUM 354
AND NOW MIGHT SOHRAB HAVE UNSHEATHED HIS SWORD • • 73 SOHRAB RUSTUM 422
BUT HE LOOKD ON AND SMILED NOR BARED HIS SWORD • • 74 SOHRAB RUSTUM 425
AND HE TOO DREW HIS SWORD AT ONCE THEY RUSHD • • 75 SOHRAB RUSTUM 471
THEN SOHRAB WITH HIS SWORD SMOTE RUSTUMS HELM • • 76 SOHRAB RUSTUM 495
AND HIS SOBS CHOKED HIM AND HE CLUTCHD HIS SWORD • • 82 SOHRAB RUSTUM 704
BUT HE LOOKD ON AND SMILED NOR DREW HIS SWORD • • 74 SOHRAB RUSTUM V 425
THE SWORD WERE BROKEN IN THY HANDS • • • • • 92 SICK KING BOKH 140
HIS SWORD UPRIGHT AND FELL ON IT AND DIED • • • • 102 BALDER DEAD 1 252
HIS SWORD IS SHARP HIS HORSE IS GOOD • • • • 138 TRISTRAM 1 249
THE KNIGHTS DREW SWORD THE LADIES SCREAMD • • • • 159 NECKAN 27
IN CROWN AND SWORD ARRAYD • • • • • • • 316 OBERMANN MORE 122
SHE VEILD HER EAGLES SNAPPD HER SWORD • • • • 316 OBERMANN MORE 125
ROSE AND WITH FIRE AND SWORD ASSAILED MY HOUSE • • 340 MEROPE 344
THY SWORD REPELLD IT LONG AGO NOT I • • • • • 341 MEROPE 355
HE HAD HIS MURDERER READY AND THE SWORD • • • 366 MEROPE 1000
IF PERHAPS UNPIERCED BY THE SWORD • • • • • 370 MEROPE 1116
HER SWORD WILL BE THE FIRST TO BID IT FALL • • • 388 MEROPE 1504
UNCLOSED HIS ITCHING FINGERS FROM HIS SWORD • • • 394 MEROPE 1705
THINK YE IT STRIKES TOO SLOW THE SWORD OF FATE • • 466 ALARIC AT ROME 115
A LIFE THAT WROTE ITS PURPOSE WITH A SWORD • • • • 478 CROMWELL 221
TRACKD BY MURDERS BLOODY SWORD NO MORE • • • • 482 THEKLAS ANSWER 16

SWORDS
LAY THICKLY STREWN SWORDS AXES DARTS AND SPEARS • • 95 BALDER DEAD 1 2

SWORN
SWORN TO OUR PLOT HE IS IF FALSE SURMISE • • • • 379 MEROPE 1272
SWORN TO OUR PLOT HE IS BUT THAT SURMISE • • • • 379 MEROPE V1272
HAST THOU SWORN IN THY SAD LAIR • • • • • • 430 EMPEDOCLES II 58

SWUNG
WHEN DOWN SWUNG THE SOUND OF A FAR-OFF BELL • • 163 FORSAKEN MERM 54
WHEN DOWN SWUNG THE SOUND OF THE FAR-OFF BELL • • 163 FORSAKEN MERM V 54

SYCAMORES
UNDER THEIR BURNISHD SYCAMORES • • • • • • • • 54 RESIGNATION 57

SYLLABLE
TO BREATHE A SYLLABLE TO BAR REVENGE • • • • • • 389 MEROPE 1528

SYLVAN
THE MOUNTAIN-SKIRTS WITH ALL THEIR SYLVAN CHANGE • • 25 DREAM 7
SYLVAN GODS OF THIS FAIR SHADE • • • • • • • 34 NEW SIRENS 244
IN THESE LONE SYLVAN GLADES THAT APRIL-DAY • • • • 154 TRISTRAM 3 163
GAY DAMES ARE THERE IN SYLVAN GREEN • • • • • 305 GRANDE CHARTR 185

SYMPATHISE
A GRIEF AND SYMPATHISE • • • • • • • • • • 140 TRISTRAM 1 324

SYMPATHY
A SYMPATHY AUGUST AND PURE • • • • • • • • 179 FAREWELL 70

SYMPATHY   (CONTINUED)
```
     YIELD THEM LOVE AMUSEMENT SYMPATHY    . . . . . .   240 SELF-DEPENDENCE    20
     DWELT IT SEEMD IN SYMPATHY                          454 POOR MATTHIAS      52
     SYMPATHY COULD FEEL AND SHOW          . . . . . .   455 POOR MATTHIAS      93
     ALL NATURAL LOVE ALL HUMAN SYMPATHY   . . . . . .   467 ALARIC AT ROME    147
     THE THOUGHTLESS WORD THE LACK OF SYMPATHY  . . . .  470 ALARIC AT ROME    220
     IN COMMON SIGHTS READ SECRET SYMPATHY     . . . .   472 CROMWELL           32
```

SYRIA
```
     AUSTRIAN KNIGHTS FROM SYRIA CAME      . . . . . . .  15 CHURCH BROU 1      78
```

SYRIAN
```
     IN THE LORN SYRIAN TOWN   . . . . . . . . . . . .   318 OBERMANN MORE     174
     THE SYRIAN STARS LOOK DOWN    . . . . . . . . . .   318 OBERMANN MORE     176
```

SYRTES
```
     BETWIXT THE SYRTES AND SOFT SICILY    . . . . . .   262 SCHOLAR-GIPSY     245
```

SYRUP
```
     GRAPE-SYRUP SQUARES OF COLOURD ICE    . . . . . .    94 SICK KING BOKH    196
```

SYSTEMS
```
     STATESMEN NEW SYSTEMS     . . . . . . . . . . .    220 BACCHANALIA 2      39
```

TABLE
```
     THE TABLE STOOD BEFORE HIM CHARGED WITH FOOD   . .   67 SOHRAB RUSTUM     197
     THE TABLE STOOD BESIDE HIM CHARGED WITH FOOD   . .   67 SOHRAB RUSTUM   V 197
     THE TABLE STOOD BESIDE HIM CHARGED WITH CATES  . .   67 SOHRAB RUSTUM   V 197
     AND SLEW THE DOGS WHO AT HIS TABLE FED     . . . .  118 BALDER DEAD 3     170
     AT TABLE AND THE FUNERAL-FEAST BEGAN   . . . . . .  119 BALDER DEAD 3     209
     AND SLEW THE DOGS WHICH AT HIS TABLE FED   . . . .  118 BALDER DEAD 3   V 170
```

TABLED
```
     SITTING ON A TABLED STONE     . . . . . . . .      434 EMPEDOCLES II     177
```

TABLES
```
     AND ON THE TABLES STOOD THE UNTASTED MEATS  . . . .  95 BALDER DEAD 1      13
     BESIDE THE TABLES IN THE HALL OF HEAVEN     . . . .  97 BALDER DEAD 1      65
```

TABLETS
```
     QUICK THY TABLETS MEMORY  . . . . . . . . . .       22 MEMORY-PICTURE      8
     QUICK THY TABLETS MEMORY  . . . . . . . . . .       23 MEMORY-PICTURE     16
     QUICK THY TABLETS MEMORY  . . . . . . . . . .       23 MEMORY-PICTURE     24
     QUICK THY TABLETS MEMORY  . . . . . . . . . .       23 MEMORY-PICTURE     32
     QUICK THY TABLETS MEMORY  . . . . . . . . . .       23 MEMORY-PICTURE     40
     QUICK THY TABLETS MEMORY  . . . . . . . . . .       24 MEMORY-PICTURE     48
     QUICK THY TABLETS MEMORY  . . . . . . . . . .       24 MEMORY-PICTURE     56
     QUICK THY TABLETS MEMORY  . . . . . . . . . .       24 MEMORY-PICTURE     64
```

TACITURN
```
     WHERE THE GAUNT AND TACITURN HOST     . . . . . .   289 RUGBY CHAPEL      110
```

TAEN
```
     BALDER HATH GONE THIS WAY AND TAEN THE ROAD    . .  108 BALDER DEAD 2     122
```

TAGGD
```
     WITH SCARLET PATCHES TAGGD AND SHREDS OF GREY  . .  258 SCHOLAR-GIPSY     114
```

TAIL
```
     KAIS BRACELET TAIL KAIS BUSY FEET     . . . . . .   459 KAISER DEAD         7
     I SEE THE TAIL LIKE BRACELET TWIRLD   . . . . . .   460 KAISER DEAD        55
```

TAILS
```
     THE TAILS INDOMITABLE RING    . . . . . . . . .     459 KAISER DEAD        27
```

TAINT
```
     IS IT THE BLIGHTING TAINT DISHONOUR BREATHES   . .  463 ALARIC AT ROME     27
```

TAINTED
```
     THE FIERCE HOUNDS SNUFF THE TAINTED AIR    . . . .  149 TRISTRAM 2        184
```

TAKE
```
     WITH PLEASANT SMILE LET US TAKE CARE  . . . . .      48 HORATIAN ECHO      21
     FEROOD SHAME BIDS US TAKE THEIR CHALLENGE UP   . .   66 SOHRAB RUSTUM     175
     STAND FORTH THE WHILE AND TAKE THEIR CHALLENGE UP   66 SOHRAB RUSTUM     183
     HIDEST THY FACE TAKE HEED LEST MEN SHOULD SAY  . .   68 SOHRAB RUSTUM     246
     HIS HEART TO TAKE A GIFT AND LET THEE GO   . . . .   77 SOHRAB RUSTUM     533
     COME SIT BESIDE ME ON THIS SAND AND TAKE   . . . .   82 SOHRAB RUSTUM     718
     RUSTUM SHOULD TAKE THE BOY TO TRAIN IN ARMS    . .   79 SOHRAB RUSTUM   V 611
     THAT THOUGH WE TAKE WHAT WE DESIRE    . . . . .      94 SICK KING BOKH    211
     THAT I ALONE MUST TAKE THE BRANCH FROM LOK  . . .    98 BALDER DEAD 1     100
     WHO GOES THAT WAY MUST TAKE NO OTHER HORSE  . . .    99 BALDER DEAD 1     137
     TAKE SLEIPNER HERMOD AND SET FORTH WITH DAWN   . .  102 BALDER DEAD 1     236
     BUT HERMOD THOU TAKE SLEIPNER AND RIDE DOWN    . .  106 BALDER DEAD 2      45
     TO ODIN TO MY FATHER TAKE THIS RING   . . . . .     112 BALDER DEAD 2     274
     TO TAKE MY HAND AND WIPE MY TEARS AND SAY   . . .   116 BALDER DEAD 3     113
     SEE IT SHINE AND TAKE IT UP   . . . . . . . .       135 TRISTRAM 1        143
     TRISTRAM NAY NAY THOU MUST NOT TAKE MY HAND    . .  135 TRISTRAM 1        166
     WOULD TAKE A SCORE YEARS FROM A STRONG MANS AGE  .  140 TRISTRAM 1        305
     TAKE MY HAND DEAR TRISTRAM LOOK ON ME      . . . .  142 TRISTRAM 2         16
```

TAKE   (CONTINUED)
          TAKE MY HAND AND TOUCH THESE WASTED FINGERS   . . 143 TRISTRAM 2   23
          NOR THY YOUNGER ISEULT TAKE IT ILL   . . . . . . 144 TRISTRAM 2   58
          AND THROUGH THE GLADES THY PASTIME TAKE   . . . . 149 TRISTRAM 2   189
          AND TAKE HER BROIDERY-FRAME AND THERE SHELL SIT . . 152 TRISTRAM 3   82
          WE LEAVE THE BRUTAL WORLD TO TAKE ITS WAY   . . . . 172 IMMORTALITY   2
          AND WHAT THE WORLD CAN GIVE THEY TAKE   . . . . . 203 EUPHROSYNE   19
          GLADLY THEY TAKE HIS COMMAND   . . . . 216 LORDS MESSENGER V   8
          OUT OF THE PATH AND TAKE THE GRASS   . . . . 222 EPILOG LAOCOON   37
          THE WORLD IN ITS TURN WILL NOT TAKE   . . . . . . 228 CAUTION POETS   3
          TO TAKE HIS NURSE HIS BROKEN TOY   . . . . 248 KENSINGTON GARD   10
          NOR FETCH TO TAKE THE ACCUSTOMD TOLL   . . . . . . 250 WISH   21
          I TAKE THE OMEN EVE LETS DOWN HER VEIL   . . . . . 267 THYRSIS   161
          ART STILL HAS TRUTH TAKE REFUGE THERE   . . . . . 271 MEMORIAL VERSES   28
          TAKE LEAVE OF HEINE NOT THUS   . . . . 298 HEINES GRAVE   200
          TAKE ME COWLD FORMS AND FENCE ME ROUND   . . . . 302 GRANDE CHARTR   93
          AH IF IT BE PASSD TAKE AWAY . . . . 302 GRANDE CHARTR   103
          SOUL THAT THAN THEY WE TAKE MORE CARE   . . . . . 315 OBERMANN MORE   V
          SOUL THAT WE TAKE MORE COUNT AND CARE   . . . . . 315 OBERMANN MORE   V
          TO TAKE THE INHERITANCE OF HERACLES   . . . . . . 334 MEROPE   125
          WHO CAN EXTEND THEIR HANDS MAIDENS TAKE BACK   . . 336 MEROPE   195
          TAKE THIS FOR TRUE THE OTHER TALE FOR FEIGND   . . 364 MEROPE   984
          WILL I SEEK TIDINGS TAKE THE WHILE THIS WORD   . . 368 MEROPE   1078
          TAKE NOT WITH HIM TO COUNCIL DID THE KING   . . . 373 MEROPE   1192
          UPBRAIDS THEE NO ONE THOU DOST WELL BUT TAKE   . . 376 MEROPE   1214
          YES ONCE AGAIN I COME I WILL NOT TAKE   . . . . . 394 MEROPE   1690
          TO THIS THOU WOULDST HAVE ANSWER TAKE IT FLY   . . 395 MEROPE   1741
          WHERE PHILOCTETES PINED TAKE SHIP AND FLEE . . . . 395 MEROPE   1747
          TAKE THESE MY SON OVER THINE ENEMYS CORPSE . . . . 404 MEROPE   2010
          I GO I GO YET QUEEN TAKE THIS ONE WORD   . . . . . 368 MEROPE   V1077
          THE SOPHIST SNEERS FOOL TAKE   . . . . 416 EMPEDOCLES I 2   132
          WE MARK NOT THE WORLDS COURSE BUT WOULD HAVE   419 EMPEDOCLES I 2   221
             IT TAKE OURS
          YOU ONLY CAN TAKE IN   . . . . 423 EMPEDOCLES I 2   342
          THEMSELVES WHO WISELY TAKE   . . . . 425 EMPEDOCLES I 2   388
          TAKE DOWN WITH THEE THE REST TO CATANA   . . . . . 428 EMPEDOCLES I 2   466
          O SAGE O SAGE TAKE THEN THE ONE WAY LEFT   . . . . 429 EMPEDOCLES II   24
          RECEIVE ME HIDE ME QUENCH ME TAKE ME HOME   . . . . 429 EMPEDOCLES II   36
          TAKE THY BOUGH SET ME FREE FROM MY SOLITUDE   . . 435 EMPEDOCLES II   218
          YEA I TAKE MYSELF TO WITNESS   . . . . 441 EMPEDOCLES II   399
          WOMAN I TOO TAKE THOUGHT FOR THIS BUT THEN   HOMER TRANS   14
             I BETHINK ME

TAKEN
          WHOSE BENT WAS TAKEN LONG AGO   . . . . 305 GRANDE CHARTR   198

TAKES
          SWELLS MY HEART AND TAKES MY BREATH AWAY   . . . . 145 TRISTRAM 2   74
          BUT TAKES AWAY THE POWER THIS CAN AVAIL   . . . . 153 TRISTRAM 3   124
          AND TAKES IT IN HER HAND AND WAVES IT OVER   . . . 156 TRISTRAM 3   217
          BEETHOVEN TAKES THEM THEN THOSE TWO   . . . . . . 224 EPILOG LAOCOON   95
          WHO MOST HAS SUFFERD TAKES DEJECTEDLY   . . . . . 260 SCHOLAR-GIPSY   183
          EACH TAKES AND THEN HIS VISAGE WAN   . . . . 300 GRANDE CHARTR   43
          FOR PRIVATE GAIN OR HATRED TAKES A LIFE   . . . . 336 MEROPE   202
          CAUGHT THEM AS WIND TAKES FEATHERS WHIRLD THEM ROUND 358 MEROPE   824
          THE INCESSANT WANDERER TAKES HIS WAY   . . . . . . 484 ROME-SICKNESS   30

TALE
          HATH SOWN WITH CLOUDLESS PASSAGES THE TALE . . . . 43 GIPSY CHILD   51
          HAVING MADE UP HIS TALE OF PRECIOUS PEARLS . . . . 69 SOHRAB RUSTUM   288
          AND BROUGHT HER TALE TO AN END AND FOUND THE PATH 151 TRISTRAM 3   62
          WHAT TALE DID ISEULT TO THE CHILDREN SAY   . . . . 154 TRISTRAM 3   151
          THIS TALE OF MERLIN AND THE LOVELY FAY   . . . . . 154 TRISTRAM 3   164
          HE HATH NO OTHER TALE   . . . . 159 NECKAN   12
          COME LET ME READ THE OFT-READ TALE AGAIN   . . . . 256 SCHOLAR-GIPSY   32
          AND THE GRAVE GLANVIL DID THE TALE INSCRIBE   . . 259 SCHOLAR-GIPSY   133
          HE KEPT HIS TALE THEN FOR THE KING ALONE   . . . 362 MEROPE   928
          HIS TALE WAS MEETER FOR THAT EAR THAN THINE   . . 362 MEROPE   929
          FAITHFUL NOT WELCOME WHEN MY TALE IS TOLD   . . . 362 MEROPE   938
          ANOTHER TALE I TROW THY MESSENGER   . . . . 364 MEROPE   964
          AND HOW THEN RUNS THIS TRUE AND PRIVATE TALE   . . 364 MEROPE   967
          TAKE THIS FOR TRUE THE OTHER TALE FOR FEIGND   . . 364 MEROPE   984
          A TALE MEANWHILE FORGED FOR HIS SUBJECTS EARS   . . 366 MEROPE   1002
          THIS STRANGE UNLIKELY TALE THE PRINCE WAS DROWND . 364 MEROPE   V
          WITH QUESTIONINGS ABOUT AN IDLE TALE   . . . . . . 411 EMPEDOCLES I 1   155
          WHAT A TALE OF THY LAST WEEK   . . . . 455 POOR MATTHIAS   110
          THE SADDENING TALE THAT TELLS OF SORROW AND DECAY 462 ALARIC AT ROME   6

TALENT
          AND WE HAVE SHOWN ON EACH TALENT AND POWER . . . . 246 BURIED LIFE   V   58

TALES
          EAGER TELL-TALES OF HER MIND   . . . . 24 MEMORY-PICTURE   42
          THOU TELLER OF SWEET TALES THINE OWN   . . . . . . 87 SICK KING BOKH   11
          SING THEE TALES OF TRUE LONG-PARTED LOVERS . . . . 143 TRISTRAM 2   31
          THESE ARE TO HER DEAR AS TO THEM THE TALES . . . . 152 TRISTRAM 3   106
          NO AWAY WITH TALES LIKE THESE   . . . . 456 POOR MATTHIAS   153

TALK
          THERE WOULD BE THEN NO TALK OF FIGHTING MORE   . . 72 SOHRAB RUSTUM   372
          AND THOU SHALT TALK TO ME OF RUSTUMS DEEDS   . . . 74 SOHRAB RUSTUM   442
          THE GODS HELD TALK TOGETHER GROUPD IN KNOTS   . . 113 BALDER DEAD 3   1

TALK   (CONTINUED)
          AND SOME IN TALK AND MERRIMENT . . . .   224 EPILOG LAOCOON   120
          AND TALK TO HIM OF THINGS AT HAND AND COMMON   . .   411 EMPEDOCLES I 1   158
          WHOSE CORDIAL TALK . . . .   460 KAISER DEAD   70

TALKD
          THEY OUT-TALKD THEE HISSD THEE TORE THEE   . . . .   215 LAST WORD   9
          THE AGE HAS TALKD AND WORKD ITS FILL . . . . . .   219 BACCHANALIA 2   2
          MY FRIEND AND I BY CHANCE WE TALKD . . . .   221 EPILOG LAOCOON   2
          AND AS WE ATE AND RESTED THERE WE TALKD   . . . .   356 MEROPE   755
          AND STRANGELY AS WE TALKD HE WOULD APPLY   . . . .   356 MEROPE   766
          THE BOORS WITH WHOM HE TALKD THE COUNTRY-SPOTS HE KNEW   426 EMPEDOCLES I 2   416

TALKEST
          AND TALKEST WITH THE FEEBLE TRIBES OF GHOSTS   . .   115 BALDER DEAD 3   76

TALKING
          LAST NIGHT WE STOOD EARNESTLY TALKING TOGETHER   . .   19 MODERN SAPPHO   9
          AND TALKING OF THE LIFE WE LED IN HEAVEN   . . . .   104 BALDER DEAD 1   329
          AS IN OLD DAYS JOVIAL AND TALKING RIDE   . . . .   267 THYRSIS   154
          BREAK OFF BREAK OFF YOUR TALKING AND DEPART   . .   386 MEROPE   1440

TALL
          LIKE SOME YOUNG CYPRESS TALL AND DARK AND STRAIGHT   70 SOHRAB RUSTUM   314
          TALL GRASSES AND WHITE FLOWERING NETTLES WAVE   . .   259 SCHOLAR-GIPSY   139
          UP THROUGH THE TALL DARK FIRS . . . .   297 HEINES GRAVE   156
          AH JAMAN DELICATELY TALL . . . .   313 OBERMANN MORE   33
          ON SOME TALL SCAR FRINGED WITH DARK FEATHERY PINES   357 MEROPE   803
          THE TALL CRESTED WATER-REEDS . . . .   434 EMPEDOCLES II   174
          WHERE RODE THE TALL DARK SHIPS WHOSE LOOSEND SAIL   473 CROMWELL   67

TAMBOURINE
          EACH HER RIBBOND TAMBOURINE   . . . .   433 EMPEDOCLES II   155

TAME
          WHOM THE WORLD COULD NOT TAME . . . .   310 OBERMANN   144
          OF THE PHRYGIAN FLUTES TO TAME . . . .   433 EMPEDOCLES II   131
          TRUE WE MUST TAME OUR REBEL WILL   . . . . . .   481 COURAGE   1

TAMED
          TAMED IS THEIR TURBULENT YOUTHFUL GLOW   . . . .   208 ON THE RHINE   24
          OUR HAIR GROWS GREY OUR EYES ARE DIMMD OUR   423 EMPEDOCLES I 2   336
               HEAT IS TAMED

TANAGRAEAN
          THE HUNTER OF THE TANAGRAEAN FIELD   . . . . . .   197 FRAG ANTIGONE   64

TANGLE
          THE HOPELESS TANGLE OF OUR AGE . . . .   309 OBERMANN   83

TANGLED
          INTO THE TANGLED GLEN BELOW   . . . .   148 TRISTRAM 2   V
          A BRIER IN THAT TANGLED WILDERNESS   . . . . . .   154 TRISTRAM 3   173
          A BRIAR IN THAT TANGLED WILDERNESS   . . . . . .   154 TRISTRAM 3   V 173
          SHOOK BACK HIS TANGLED LOCKS AND MURMURD PEACE   . .   477 CROMWELL   174

TANKS
          THAT THE GREEN WATER IN THE TANKS   . . . . . .   89 SICK KING BOKH   60

TANND
          WITH THE LOW BROAD HAT OF THE TANND   . . . . .   342 MEROPE   395

TAPERS
          LED BY THY TAPERS STARLIKE BEAM   . . . .   177 FAREWELL   8
          LIT BY THY TAPERS STARLIKE BEAM   . . . .   177 FAREWELL   V 8
          WE WATCH THOSE YELLOW TAPERS SHINE   . . . . . .   305 GRANDE CHARTR   200

TAPESTRY
          FLAPS THE GHOSTLIKE TAPESTRY . . . .   147 TRISTRAM 2   151
          SHINES THE GHOSTLIKE TAPESTRY   . . . .   147 TRISTRAM 2   V 151

TARDY
          TARDY OR SWIFT WOULDST THOU BE LOATH TO DIE   . .   103 BALDER DEAD 1   306

TARNISHD
          HIS SHORT COAT TRAVEL-TARNISHD . . . .   189 STRAYED REVEL   106

TARRIED
          BLAME ME NOT POOR SUFFERER THAT I TARRIED   . . . .   142 TRISTRAM 2   5

TARRIES
          REACH RUSTUM WHERE HE SITS AND TARRIES LONG   . .   78 SOHRAB RUSTUM   582
          HE TARRIES WHERE THE ROCK OF SPAIN . . . . . .   275 STANZAS CARNAC   38
          WHERE TARRIES HE THE POWER WHO SAID   . . . . .   320 OBERMANN MORE   231

TARRIEST
          WHY TARRIEST THOU TO PLUNGE THEE IN THE GULPH   . .   124 BALDER DEAD 3   388
          TARRIEST THOU NOW FOR THAT FORCE   . . . . . .   287 RUGBY CHAPEL   38
          PEACE WHO TARRIEST TOO LONG   . . . .   360 MEROPE   890

TARRY
AND I TO TARRY WITH THE SNOW-HAIRD ZAL   • • • •   68 SOHRAB RUSTUM   232
AND I TO TARRY WITH THE WHITE-HAIRD ZAL   • • • •   68 SOHRAB RUSTUM   V 232
O MERCHANTS TARRY YET A DAY   • • • • • •   87 SICK KING BOKH   5
HO ENTER YE WHO TARRY THERE   • • • • • • •   92 SICK KING BOKH   132

TARTAR
BUT ALL THE TARTAR CAMP ALONG THE STREAM   • • • •   61 SOHRAB RUSTUM   3
THROUGH THE BLACK TARTAR TENTS HE PASSD WHICH STOOD   61 SOHRAB RUSTUM   12
THE CONQUERING TARTAR ENSIGNS THROUGH THE WORLD   • •   62 SOHRAB RUSTUM   47
CANST THOU NOT REST AMONG THE TARTAR CHIEFS   • • •   63 SOHRAB RUSTUM   66
AND FROM THEIR TENTS THE TARTAR HORSEMEN FILED   • •   64 SOHRAB RUSTUM   106
THREADING THE TARTAR SQUADRONS TO THE FRONT   • • •   65 SOHRAB RUSTUM   142
AND THE OLD TARTAR CAME UPON THE SAND   • • • •   65 SOHRAB RUSTUM   148
A THRILL THROUGH ALL THE TARTAR SQUADRONS RAN   • •   65 SOHRAB RUSTUM   158
THE TARTAR CHALLENGE AND THIS YOUNG MANS NAME   • •   66 SOHRAB RUSTUM   181
HIS EYES TOWARD THE TARTAR TENTS AND SAW   • • • •   70 SOHRAB RUSTUM   300
BE GOVERND QUIT THE TARTAR HOST AND COME   • • •   71 SOHRAB RUSTUM   330
FALSE WILY BOASTFUL ARE THESE TARTAR BOYS   • • •   71 SOHRAB RUSTUM   348
WITH TARTAR GIRLS WITH WHOM THOU ART WONT TO DANCE   75 SOHRAB RUSTUM   461
AND THEN THAT ALL THE TARTAR HOST WOULD PRAISE   • •   77 SOHRAB RUSTUM   534
SOHRAB RETURNING FROM THE TARTAR CAMP   • • •   79 SOHRAB RUSTUM   594
SWIFT THROUGH THE TARTAR SQUADRONS TO THE FRONT   •   65 SOHRAB RUSTUM   V 142
SLOW THROUGH THE TARTAR SQUADRONS TO THE FRONT   •   65 SOHRAB RUSTUM   V 142
HIS EYES TOWARDS THE TARTAR TENTS AND SAW   • • •   70 SOHRAB RUSTUM   V 300

TARTAREAN
UNDER THE DRIPPING BLACK TARTAREAN CLIFF   • • • •   368 MEROPE   1064

TARTARS
THE TARTARS BUILT THERE PERAN-WISAS TENT   • • •   61 SOHRAB RUSTUM   22
I CAME AMONG THE TARTARS AND BORE ARMS   • • •   62 SOHRAB RUSTUM   43
THE TARTARS OF THE OXUS THE KINGS GUARD   • • •   64 SOHRAB RUSTUM   117
THE TARTARS OF FERGHANA FROM THE BANKS   • • •   64 SOHRAB RUSTUM   128
FIRST A LIGHT CLOUD OF HORSE TARTARS THEY SEEMD   •   65 SOHRAB RUSTUM   137
THAT PERAN-WISA KEPT THE TARTARS BACK   • • •   65 SOHRAB RUSTUM   145
FEROOD AND YE PERSIANS AND TARTARS HEAR   • • •   65 SOHRAB RUSTUM   150
FOR FROM THE TARTARS IS A CHALLENGE BROUGHT   • •   67 SOHRAB RUSTUM   211
HAILD BUT THE TARTARS KNEW NOT WHO HE WAS   • • •   69 SOHRAB RUSTUM   283
SOUTHWARD THE TARTARS BY THE RIVER MARGE   • • •   86 SOHRAB RUSTUM   873
THE TARTARS OF BOKHARA THE KINGS GUARD   • • •   64 SOHRAB RUSTUM   V 117

TASK
PLIES SOME LIGHT FEMALE TASK NOR DREAMS OF US   • •   80 SOHRAB RUSTUM   647
MEANTIME ON THEE THE TASK OF SILENCE ONLY   • • •   390 MEROPE   1584

TASKD
THY STRUGGLING TASKD MORALITY   • • • • • •   241 MORALITY   16
AND THOUGH SO TASKD KEEP FREE FROM DUST AND SOIL   •   244 SUMMER NIGHT   82
WHICH TASKD THY PIPE TOO SORE AND TIRED THY THROAT   269 THYRSIS   225
HIS HARD-TASKD SUNBURNT WIFE   • • • • • •   426 EMPEDOCLES I 2   414

TASKS
THEIR GLORIOUS TASKS IN SILENCE PERFECTING   • • •   2 QUIET WORK   12
MODERATE TASKS AND MODERATE LEISURE   • • • •   49 SECOND BEST   1
TO WAKE THE GODS AND HEROES TO THEIR TASKS   • •   105 BALDER DEAD 2   9
CAN NEVER END THEIR TASKS ARE HARD TO PLEASE   •   153 TRISTRAM 3   V 142
IN THEIR OWN TASKS ALL THEIR POWERS POURING   •   240 SELF-DEPENDENCE   27
BUT TASKS IN HOURS OF INSIGHT WILLD   • • • •   241 MORALITY   5
THE LIMBS THEIR WONTED TASKS REFUSE   • • • •   276 SOUTHERN NIGHT   41
OF HUMAN TASKS THEIR ONLY ONE   • • • •   301 GRANDE CHARTR   59
ITS INMATES ON THEIR DAILY TASKS ABROAD   • • •   330 MEROPE   27
TO DAILY TASKS WE SET OUR HAND   • • • • • •   483 ROME-SICKNESS   1

TASKWORK
THEIR LIVES TO SOME UNMEANING TASKWORK GIVE   • •   243 SUMMER NIGHT   40

TASSELLD
THY GOLDEN-TASSELLD BUGLE BLOW   • • • • • • •   149 TRISTRAM 2   188

TASSOS
IN DANTES PETRARCHS TASSOS LINE   • • • • • •   222 EPILOG LAOCOON   21

TASTED
IS THE PLEASURE THAT IS TASTED   • • • • • •   30 NEW SIRENS   131
TASTED AMISS TO THY SOUL   • • • • • • • •   296 HEINES GRAVE   124

TAUGHT
TAUGHT ARRIAN WHEN VESPASIANS BRUTAL SON   • • •   2 TO A FRIEND   7
WHO TAUGHT THIS PLEADING TO UNPRACTISED EYES   •   41 GIPSY CHILD   1
BY AGE TAUGHT MANY THINGS   • • • • • •   189 STRAYED REVEL   119
AH CRIES MY FRIEND BUT WHO HATH TAUGHT   • • •   221 EPILOG LAOCOON   8
THE MASTER STOOD UPON THE MOUNT AND TAUGHT   • •   237 PROGRESS   1
WHICH HAS NOT TAUGHT WEAK WILLS HOW MUCH THEY CAN   238 PROGRESS   41
HE TAUGHT US LITTLE BUT OUR SOUL   • • • •   270 MEMORIAL VERSES   8
IN ALL ELSE WILLING TO BE TAUGHT IN THIS   • • •   379 MEROPE   1258
THE CENTAUR TAUGHT HIM TO EXPLORE   • • • •   414 EMPEDOCLES I 2   61
AND SAID O BOY I TAUGHT THIS LORE   • • • •   414 EMPEDOCLES I 2   69
FOR HE TAUGHT HIM HOW TO SING   • • • • •   434 EMPEDOCLES II   169
AND HE TAUGHT HIM FLUTE-PLAYING   • • • • •   434 EMPEDOCLES II   170
AND HE TAUGHT HIM HOW TO PLEASE   • • • • •   434 EMPEDOCLES II   179

TAUNTS
    HE SPOKE AND SOHRAB KINDLED AT HIS TAUNTS • • • •   75 SOHRAB RUSTUM   470

TAWNY
    THE TAWNY-THROATED • • • • • • • • • • •   200 PHILOMELA   2

TAX
    FEAR NOT NOW THAT MEN SHOULD TAX THINE HONOUR • •   142 TRISTRAM 2   11
    FEAR NOT NOW THAT MEN SHOULD TAX THY HONOUR • •   142 TRISTRAM 2   V 11

TAYGETUS
    TAYGETUS LACONIAS BORDER-WALL • • • • • • •   330 MEROPE   17

TEACH
    ONLY THE EVENT WILL TEACH US IN ITS HOUR • • • •   73 SOHRAB RUSTUM   397
    THE CHARM WHICH HOMER SHAKESPEARE TEACH • • •   227 EPILOG LAOCOON   206
    OTHERS WILL TEACH US HOW TO DARE • • • •   272 MEMORIAL VERSES   64
    AND CANST TEACH SIMPLE ONES TO PLOT AND FEIGN • •   367 MEROPE   1059
    TEACH US WHILE THEY COME AND GO • • • • •   456 POOR MATTHIAS   139
    ALAS NO WREATHS ARE HERE DESPAIR MAY TEACH • • •   467 ALARIC AT ROME   139
    TO READ EACH THOUGHT AND TEACH THAT MASTER MIND • •   478 CROMWELL   231

TEACHER
    AND FROM THAT TEACHER MAYST HAVE LEARND LIKE ME • •   394 MEROPE   1709

TEACHERS
    FOR RIGOROUS TEACHERS SEIZED MY YOUTH • • • •   301 GRANDE CHARTR   67

TEACHES
    TEACHES THE LIMIT OF THE JUST AND TRUE • • • •   7 REP FRIEND   7

TEAM
    DOWN EACH GREEN BANK HATH GONE THE PLOUGHBOYS TEAM   266 THYRSIS   118

TEAR
    O LET FALL ONE TEAR AND SET US FREE • • • • •   34 NEW SIRENS   226
    HER DARKNESS FROM HER GRASP A SUBJECT TEAR • • •   121 BALDER DEAD 3   280
    WITHOUT A WORD WITHOUT A TEAR • • • • • •   137 TRISTRAM 1   210
    AND ANON THERE DROPS A TEAR • • • • • •   164 FORSAKEN MERM   102
    TEAR FROM THE RIFLED HEDGE • • • • • •   218 BACCHANALIA 1   36
    A SIGH A TEAR BUT IN THE THRONG • • • •   225 EPILOG LAOCOON   123
    SINCE BROILS TEAR US IN TWAIN SINCE THIS NEW SWARM   410 EMPEDOCLES I 1   121
    THOU HAST THINE ABSENT MASTERS TEAR • • • •   451 GEISTS GRAVE   55
    AND WREST ONE TEAR FROM JOY OH WHO SHALL PEN • •   468 ALARIC AT ROME   167

TEARFUL
    FELL ON THE CHERISHD PAST WITH TEARFUL SMILE • •   474 CROMWELL   70

TEARING
    AND TEARING UP THE MARBLE FLAGS • • • • •   95 SICK KING BOKH   V 227

TEARLESS
    SO THEY WITH PENT-UP HEARTS AND TEARLESS EYES • •   97 BALDER DEAD 1   69
    TEARLESS WHEN OF MY DEATH HE HEARS • • • • •   250 WISH   6

TEARS
    AND PRAYERS AND GIFTS AND TEARS ARE FRUITLESS ALL   10 MYCERINUS   71
    WILL IT WEEP OUR BURNING TEARS • • • • • • •   29 NEW SIRENS   86
    AS THE TEARS OF SORROW • • • • • • • • •   36 VOICE   9
    FROM TEARS THAT BRING NO HEALING • • • • •   39 STAGIRIUS   35
    MEN DIG GRAVES WITH BITTER TEARS • • • • •   44 QUESTION   11
    LEAND ON HIS GATE HE GAZES TEARS • • • •   57 RESIGNATION   186
    AT THE FULL MOON TEARS GATHERD IN HIS EYES • • •   79 SOHRAB RUSTUM   618
    AND WASH THEM WITH THY TEARS AND SAY MY SON • •   82 SOHRAB RUSTUM   720
    OF RUSTUM AND HIS TEARS BROKE FORTH HE CAST • •   82 SOHRAB RUSTUM   727
    THE BIG WARM TEARS ROLLD DOWN AND CAKED THE SAND • •   82 SOHRAB RUSTUM   736
    NOT LESS THAN THOSE WHO MERIT TEARS • • • •   92 SICK KING BOKH   148
    ENOUGH OF TEARS YE GODS ENOUGH OF WAIL • • •   95 BALDER DEAD 1   18
    WITH WOMENS TEARS AND WEAK COMPLAINING CRIES • •   96 BALDER DEAD 1   32
    TEARS STAND UPON THE LASHES OF THINE EYES • • •   103 BALDER DEAD 1   289
    TEARS WET THE PILLOW BY THY CHEEK BUT THOU • •   103 BALDER DEAD 1   290
    WITH WOMANS TEARS AND WEAK COMPLAINING CRIES • •   96 BALDER DEAD 1   V 32
    FOLLOWD IN TEARS THEIR FATHER AND THEIR KING • •   115 BALDER DEAD 3   60
    WITH THEIR THICK-FALLING TEARS SO GOOD A FRIEND • •   115 BALDER DEAD 3   63
    AND FREYA NEXT CAME NIGH WITH GOLDEN TEARS • • •   116 BALDER DEAD 3   90
    SINCE THEN SHE SEEKS HIM AND WEEPS TEARS OF GOLD • •   116 BALDER DEAD 3   95
    AND WEEP FROM SHORE TO SHORE MY GOLDEN TEARS • •   116 BALDER DEAD 3   110
    TO TAKE MY HAND AND WIPE MY TEARS AND SAY • • •   116 BALDER DEAD 3   113
    WEEP NOT O FREYA WEEP NO GOLDEN TEARS • • •   116 BALDER DEAD 3   114
    TEARS STARTED TO MINE EYES WITH YEARNING JOY • •   117 BALDER DEAD 3   151
    IN HEAVEN AND EARTH AND WHO WOULD GRUDGE HIM TEARS   120 BALDER DEAD 3   233
    THOK NOT FOR GIBES WE COME WE COME FOR TEARS • •   123 BALDER DEAD 3   346
    BUT WILL RESTORE IF ALL THINGS GIVE HIM TEARS • •   123 BALDER DEAD 3   348
    IS BALDER DEAD AND DO YE COME FOR TEARS • • •   123 BALDER DEAD 3   351
    OUR EYES WITH GAZING AND REBUILD WITH TEARS • •   128 BALDER DEAD 3   536
    MUTE GAZING AFTER THEM IN TEARS AND FAIN • • •   129 BALDER DEAD 3   555
    SHE TOOK HIS HANDS IN HERS HER TEARS • • • •   140 TRISTRAM 1   317
    TEARS STARTED TO SAINT BRANDANS EYES • • • •   158 SAINT BRANDAN   73
    TEARS FILLD HIS MILD BLUE EYE • • • • • • •   160 NECKAN   46

TEARS   (CONTINUED)
    TEARS FILLD HIS COLD BLUE EYE • • • • • • • 160 NECKAN   V 46
    TEARS FILLD HIS KIND BLUE EYE • • • • • • • 160 NECKAN   V 46
    AND DRY UP MY TEARS • • • • • • • • • 177 PARTING   84
    IN TEARS WITH HEARTS TOO FULL TO SPEAK • • • 178 FAREWELL   12
    THEY WILL NOT GIVE US LOVE AND TEARS • • • • • 203 EUPHROSYNE   23
    MY PENT-UP TEARS OPPRESS MY BRAIN • • • • • 206 RIVER   9
    HUSH FOR TEARS • • • • • • • • • • • 235 YOUTH OF MAN   97
    SCORN YE THIS WORLD THEIR TEARS THEIR INWARD CARES 237 PROGRESS   22
    BEHOLD WITH TEARS MINE EYES ARE WET • • • • • 245 BURIED LIFE   2
    BEHOLD WITH TEARS MY EYES ARE WET • • • • • 245 BURIED LIFE   V 2
    THERE ARE WORSE PLAGUES ON EARTH THAN TEARS • • 250 WISH   8
    HE SPOKE AND LOOSED OUR HEART IN TEARS • • • • 271 MEMORIAL VERSES   47
    OF MANY HOPES OF MANY TEARS • • • • • • • • 285 HAWORTH CHURCH   106
    THEIR FAITH MY TEARS THE WORLD DERIDE • • • • 302 GRANDE CHARTR   89
    OUR FATHERS WATERD WITH THEIR TEARS • • • • 303 GRANDE CHARTR   121
    BUT WHILE WE WAIT ALLOW OUR TEARS • • • • • 304 GRANDE CHARTR   162
    THEIR FATHERS WATERD WITH THEIR TEARS • • • 303 GRANDE CHARTR   V 121
    BUT TILL THEY RISE ALLOW OUR TEARS • • • • 304 GRANDE CHARTR   V 162
    TEARS WASHD THE TROUBLE FROM HER FACE • • • • 317 OBERMANN MORE   137
    HAVE THOUGHTS AND SMILES AND TEARS • • • • • 322 OBERMANN MORE   288
    AND THEN HIS MURDERER THESE OFFENDING TEARS   335 MEROPE   186
    TEARS FALL THICKLY THE WHILE • • • • • • • 342 MEROPE   389
    HIM IN SECRET IN TEARS • • • • • • • • 347 MEROPE   516
    WHOSE TEARS WARRANT HIS TRUTH • • • • • • • 369 MEROPE   1091
    AH I BESEECH THEE WITH TEARS • • • • • • • 372 MEROPE   1151
    TEARS COURSED TEARS HUMAN • • • • • • • 393 MEROPE   1669
    TEARS COURSED TEARS HUMAN • • • • • • • 393 MEROPE   1669
    THE SENSE OF TEARS IN MORTAL THINGS • • • • 450 GEISTS GRAVE   16
    IN GREATNESS ONCE IN SACKCLOTH NOW AND TEARS • • 463 ALARIC AT ROME   20
    AGE OF ITS TEARS AND CHILDHOOD OF ITS SMILE • • 472 CROMWELL   6
    PASSD LIKE A MORNING MIST IN TEARS AWAY • • • • 477 CROMWELL   198
    THERE WHERE TEARS ARE NEVER MORE TO RUN • • • 482 THEKLAS ANSWER   12
    AS THY GRIEF WHEN IN TEARS SOME BRAZEN-COATED ACHAIAN HOMER TRANS   27
    AND SOME MAN MAY SAY AS HE LOOKS AND SEES THY HOMER TRANS   32
        TEARS FALLING
    TEARS HAVE WASHED THEIR AUSTERE FACES • • • • META CLOISTER   7

TEASD
    FROM PRETENTIOUS TEASD RELATIONS • • • • • • SECOND BEST   V 18

TEASE
    AND WE SHOULD TEASE HER WITH OUR PLAINT IN VAIN • • 265 THYRSIS   100

TEASED
    BEFORE THIS TEASED OERLABOURD HEART • • • • • • 206 RIVER   17

TEDIOUS
    WHEN YOUTH HAS DONE ITS TEDIOUS VAIN EXPENSE • • 37 YOUTHS AGIT   3
    ON NATIVE GROUND THAN DRAG THE TEDIOUS HOURS • • 383 MEROPE   1380
    AND ALL THE TEDIOUS TOSSING TO AND FRO • • • • 448 WESTMIN ABBEY   150
    SOON SEEMS AS TEDIOUS AS EACH TEDIOUS STAGE • • LUCRETIUS 6   4
    SOON SEEMS AS TEDIOUS AS EACH TEDIOUS STAGE • • LUCRETIUS 6   4

TEEM
    YET DOTH THINE INMOST SOUL WITH YEARNING TEEM • • 46 IN UTRUMQUE PAR   40

TEEMING
    TEEMING WITH PLANS ALERT AND GLAD • • • • • • 460 KAISER DEAD   45

TEEMS
    BUT SINCE LIFE TEEMS WITH ILL • • • • • • • 426 EMPEDOCLES I 2   424

TEEN
    WORKING LOVE BUT WORKING TEEN • • • • • • • 132 TRISTRAM 1   67
    TILL HAVING USED OUR NERVES WITH BLISS AND TEEN • • 259 SCHOLAR-GIPSY   147
    WITH PUBLIC TOIL AND PRIVATE TEEN • • • • • 276 SOUTHERN NIGHT   27

TEGEA
    AND THE PLAIN OF TEGEA • • • • • • • • 344 MEROPE   435
    SET FORTH FROM TEGEA THE ROYAL TOWN • • • • • 355 MEROPE   732
    WE RODE FROM TEGEA THROUGH THE WOODS OF OAKS • • 355 MEROPE   735
    ARRIVED FROM TEGEA WITH WEIGHTY NEWS • • • • • 361 MEROPE   915

TEJEND
    THE DESERT RIVERS MOORGHAB AND TEJEND • • • • 83 SOHRAB RUSTUM   763

TELL
    TO TELL HIS WONDERING PEOPLE OF THEIR KING • • • 12 MYCERINUS   125
    IT HEARS A VOICE WITHIN IT TELL • • • • • • 22 YOUTH AND CALM   22
    EAGER TELL-TALES OF HER MIND • • • • • • • 24 MEMORY-PICTURE   42
    COULD EVER YET DARE TELL HIM FEARLESSLY • • • • 40 HUMAN LIFE   3
    AND I WILL TELL THEE WHAT MY HEART DESIRES • • • 62 SOHRAB RUSTUM   41
    BUT BEING WHAT I AM I TELL THEE THIS • • • • 72 SOHRAB RUSTUM   373
    I TELL THEE PRICKD UPON THIS ARM I BEAR • • • 80 SOHRAB RUSTUM   658
    RUMBLES AND SHAKES TELL ME THY RACE AND HOME • • 107 BALDER DEAD 2   103
    BUT COME DECLARE ME THIS AND TRULY TELL • • • 111 BALDER DEAD 2   243
    AND TELL THE HEAVEN-BORN GODS HOW THOU HAST SEEN • • 112 BALDER DEAD 2   276
    FROM HELL AND SHALL I TELL THEE HOW HE SEEMS • • 113 BALDER DEAD 3   7
    OH IF IT BE SO TELL HIM WHAT THOU WAST • • • 116 BALDER DEAD 3   103
    RIDE BACK AND TELL IN HEAVEN THIS HEAVY NEWS • • 124 BALDER DEAD 3   371

TELL   (CONTINUED)
        HOWBEIT STAY AND BE APPEASED AND TELL   . . . .   125 BALDER DEAD 3   428
        TELL ME THAT I MAY PONDER IT WHEN GONE   . . . .   128 BALDER DEAD 3   516
        OH IF IT BE SO TELL HIM WHAT THOU WERT   . . . .   116 BALDER DEAD 3   V 103
        TO OUR FORESTS TELL THY PAIN . . . .   139 TRISTRAM 1   275
        AH TELL THEM OF MY RESPITE TOO . . . .   157 SAINT BRANDAN   28
        TELL THEM ONE BLESSED CHRISTMAS-NIGHT   . . . .   157 SAINT BRANDAN   29
        THEY HANG THE PICTURE DOTH THE STORY TELL . . . .   166 PICT NEWSTEAD   8
        AH LET ME WEEP AND TELL MY PAIN . . . .   206 RIVER   11
        TELL ME CAN YOU FIND INDEED . . . .   215 PIS-ALLER   6
        WITH POWER DIVINE ITS STORY TELL . . . .   223 EPILOG LAOCOON   60
        AND THROUGH THE STREAM OF MUSIC TELL . . . .   223 EPILOG LAOCOON   85
        OF TOIL HE MUST LIFES MOVEMENT TELL . . . .   225 EPILOG LAOCOON   140
        THE MOVEMENT HE MUST TELL OF LIFE . . . .   225 EPILOG LAOCOON   143
        THAT TRANSIENT SOUND IN SONG THEY TELL   . . . .   226 EPILOG LAOCOON   183
        WILL YE SCAN ME AND READ ME AND TELL . . . .   231 YOUTH OF NATURE   119
        SOME SECRETS MAY THE POET SAVE . . . .   307 OBERMANN   41
        TO TELL TOO DEEP ONES IS NOT WELL . . . .   307 OBERMANN   43
        THOUGH LATE THOUGH DIMMD THOUGH WEAK YET TELL . .   323 OBERMANN MORE   311
        THIS WERE ENOUGH BUT LET ME TELL THEE TOO . . . .   338 MEROPE   282
        WHO SHALL TELL MEROPE THIS HEAVY NEWS   . . . . .   359 MEROPE   —   858
        TELL ME HATH ONE NOT COME OR WORSE MISCHANCE   . .   361 MEROPE   918
        AND WHAT ARCADIAN NEWS HAD HE TO TELL   . . . . .   361 MEROPE   926
        HE COMES TO TELL HIS PROMPTER HE HATH SPED . . . .   365 MEROPE   986
        BUT TELL ME HOW HAST THOU PERSUADED HIM . . . . .   409 EMPEDOCLES I 1   105
        AND HE WOULD TELL ME AS HIS OLD TRIED FRIEND   . .   410 EMPEDOCLES I 1   130
        TELL HIM I NEVER FAILD TO LOVE HIS LYRE . . . . .   428 EMPEDOCLES I 2   468
        THOU SHATTERED MASS WHOSE GLORIOUS RUINS TELL . .   463 ALARIC AT ROME   45
        TELL OF OLD TIMES AND HOLIEST MEMORIES   . . . . .   467 ALARIC AT ROME   124
        FLOAT UP TO TELL OF AGES THAT ARE GONE   . . . . .   470 ALARIC AT ROME   208
        TELL ME IS IT QUIET HERE . . . .   META CLOISTER   28

TELLER
        THOU TELLER OF SWEET TALES THINE OWN   . . . . . .   87 SICK KING BOKH   11

TELLEST
        THOU TELLEST THE FATE OF THE LAST   . . . . . .   345 MEROPE   469
        TOO SUDDENLY THOU TELLEST SUCH A LOSS   . . . . .   363 MEROPE   945

TELLING
        TELLING HER ALL THAT GRIEF THEY HAVE IN HEAVEN . .   10C BALDER DEAD 1   180
        TELLING US ARNE MINDED HIM HE TOO   . . . . . .   356 MEROPE   768
        TELLING HOW ONE STORMY DAY   . . . .   457 POOR MATTHIAS   177

TELLS
        WHO TELLS THE PASSING TROOPS OF DEAD THEIR WAY . .   99 BALDER DEAD 1   150
        THE LOVELY LIPS WITH THEIR ARCH SMILE THAT TELLS . . 176 PARTING   39
        TELLS US HIS MISERYS BIRTH AND GROWTH AND SIGNS . . 260 SCHOLAR-GIPSY   187
        WHICH TELLS US HOW THOU HIDDST THY HEAD . . . . .   304 GRANDE CHARTR   147
        TELLS ME ENOUGH THOU KNOWST THE NEWS WHICH ALL . .   393 MEROPE   1685
        TELLS THE PRAISES OF THEIR PRIME   . . . .   453 POOR MATTHIAS   28
        THE SADDENING TALE THAT TELLS OF SORROW AND DECAY   462 ALARIC AT ROME   6

TELLST
        AUTHENTIC PROOF OF WHAT THOU TELLST OUR EARS   . .   403 MEROPE   1952

TEMENUS
        THE ROYAL RACE OF TEMENUS IN ARGOS   . . . . . .   384 MEROPE   1391
        THE ELDEST MIGHTIEST BROTHER TEMENUS TOOK . . . .   389 MEROPE   1550
        CRESPHONTES IN MESSENIA TEMENUS   . . . .   389 MEROPE   1556

TEMPER
        TEMPER OF GENIUS SO SOON . . . .   293 HEINES GRAVE   26
        TEMPER OF GENIUS ALIVE   . . . .   293 HEINES GRAVE   V 26
        BEGET A CRUEL TEMPER HELP ME QUELL   . . . . . .   335 MEROPE   162
        NEWS OF MY BUSINESS PASTIME TEMPER FRIENDS . . . .   380 MEROPE   1281
        SHALL WE WITH TEMPER SPOILD . . . .   425 EMPEDOCLES I 2   392
        AND HARSH THE TEMPER GREW   . . . .   446 WESTMIN ABBEY   67
        AND TEMPER SWEET AND LOVE OF ALL THINGS PURE   . .   446 WESTMIN ABBEY   79
        AND TEMPER OF HEROIC MOULD   . . . .   450 GEISTS GRAVE   19

TEMPERATE
        NEXT THE MORE TEMPERATE TOORKMUNS OF THE SOUTH   . .   64 SOHRAB RUSTUM   121

TEMPERD
        BUT SOULS TEMPERD WITH FIRE . . . .   291 RUGBY CHAPEL   159
        HAVE TEMPERD ME EEN THUS AND IN SOME SOULS . . . .   366 MEROPE   1024

TEMPERS
        SHALL WE WITH TEMPERS SPOILD . . . .   425 EMPEDOCLES I 2   V 392

TEMPEST
        THE TEMPEST OF THE LATTER DAYS HATH SWEPT . . . .   128 BALDER DEAD 3   523
        AND THEN THE TEMPEST STRIKES HIM AND BETWEEN   . .   244 SUMMER NIGHT   62
        FROM THE FIERCE TEMPEST OF THINE AGE . . . . . .   304 GRANDE CHARTR   148
        THE ROMAN TEMPEST SWELLD AND SWELLD . . . . . .   316 OBERMANN MORE   107
        THE GATHERING TEMPEST WITH ITS VOICE OF FEAR   . .   478 CROMWELL   209

TEMPESTS
        TYRANNOUS TEMPESTS OF BALE   . . . .   293 HEINES GRAVE   35

TEMPESTUOUS
    SO SOME TEMPESTUOUS MORN IN EARLY JUNE   • • • • 264 THYRSIS   51
    STRONG BLACK TEMPESTUOUS TO THE CAVERN-MOUTH   • • 358 MEROPE   821

TEMPLE
    IN THE TOWN ROUND THE TEMPLE   • • • • • • 186 STRAYED REVEL   37
    THERE STANDS THE TEMPLE OF THINE ANCESTOR   • • • • 330 MEROPE   13
    IN THE TEMPLE-BUILT GORGE   • • • • • • • 345 MEROPE   464
    THE TEMPLE IN THE PURE PARNASSIAN GORGE   • • • 448 WESTMIN ABBEY 135
    THE MORNING MISTS FROM TOWER AND TEMPLE ROLL   • • 468 ALARIC AT ROME 154

TEMPLES
    ALTARS UNFED AND TEMPLES OVERTURND   • • • • • • 8 MYCERINUS   3
    THE TEMPLES TIGHTEN AND THROB THERE   • • • • • 435 EMPEDOCLES II 216
    ROUND THE WAN TEMPLES OF THE HALLOWED DEAD   • • • 463 ALARIC AT ROME 26

TEMPTATIONS
    FROM THE WORLDS TEMPTATIONS   • • • • • • • 38 STAGIRIUS   6

TEMPTS
    TEMPTS NOT THE REVEL BLITHE   • • • • • • • 219 BACCHANALIA 1 44
    TEMPTS NOT THE BRIGHT NEW AGE   • • • • • • 220 BACCHANALIA 2 51
    LOOK THE WORLD TEMPTS OUR EYE   • • • • • • 423 EMPEDOCLES I 2 317

TEN
    WHEN I SHALL BE DIVORCED SOME TEN YEARS HENCE   • • 37 YOUTHS AGIT   1
    TEN THOUSAND MOURNERS   • • • • • • • • • 52 CONSOLATION 64
    WE LEFT JUST TEN YEARS SINCE YOU SAY   • • • • 53 RESIGNATION 40
    FAUSTA WHICH TEN YEARS SINCE WE TROD   • • • • 55 RESIGNATION 87
    FOR WERE I MATCHD WITH TEN SUCH MEN AS THEE   • • 77 SOHRAB RUSTUM 544
    FOR WERE I MATCHD WITH TEN SUCH MEN AS THOU   • • 77 SOHRAB RUSTUM V 544
    THE SUFFRAGE CAPTIVE NOW NOT ONE IN TEN   • • • 171 DIVINITY   7
    TEN YEARS AND TO MY WAKING EYE   • • • • • • 183 TERRACE BERNE 1
    IT IS TEN THOUSAND FIERY WILLS IN ONE   • • • 382 MEROPE 1348
    O SUFFERING O CALAMITY HOW TEN   • • • • • • 385 MEROPE 1406
    FIXD YESTERDAY AND TEN TIMES CHANGED SINCE THEN   • • 389 MEROPE 1547

TENANT
    THE ICEBERG AND NO TENANT THERE   • • • • • • 158 SAINT BRANDAN V 76

TENANTLESS
    WHEN HE LOOKD UP TENANTLESS LIES   • • • • • • 158 SAINT BRANDAN V 75

TEND
    STILL TO ENQUIRE HOW PARTIES TEND   • • • • 47 HORATIAN ECHO 2
    AND SAW MY SHEPHERDESS ASLAUGA TEND   • • • • 117 BALDER DEAD 3 149
    I WILL WATCH THEE TEND THEE SOOTHE THY PAIN   • • 143 TRISTRAM 2 30
    I WOULD FAIN STAY AND HELP THEE TEND HIM ONCE   • • 408 EMPEDOCLES I 1 56
    THE HUMBLER SORT WHO SERVE AND TEND   • • • • 459 KAISER DEAD 32

TENDED
    TENDED OF HIS FEVER HERE   • • • • • • • 136 TRISTRAM 1 205
    SHE COMBD ITS BRIGHT HAIR AND SHE TENDED IT WELL   • • 163 FORSAKEN MERM 53

TENDENCE
    WHO THOUGH THE TENDENCE OF THE WHOLE   • • • • • 481 COURAGE 10

TENDER
    THE TENDER PURPLE SPRAY ON COPSE AND BRIERS   • • 263 THYRSIS 18
    TENDER VIRGIL NO TOMB   • • • • • • • • 294 HEINES GRAVE 59
    WHOSE TENDER WINNING ARTS   • • • • • • • 317 OBERMANN MORE 158
    THE TENDER FOXGLOVE-PLANTS DISPLAY   • • • • • 484 ROME-SICKNESS 15

TENDERER
    HIS TENDERER YOUTHFUL PRIME   • • • • • • • 308 OBERMANN 68

TENDEREST
    AND NOW TO ME THOU TENDEREST FRIENDLY LEAGUE   • • 340 MEROPE 333

TENDERLY
    FOR VERY YOUNG HE SEEMD TENDERLY REARD   • • • 70 SOHRAB RUSTUM 313

TENDERNESS
    OF INQUIRING TENDERNESS   • • • • • • • • 24 MEMORY-PICTURE 44

TENDING
    WHO WHEN SHIPS ARE THAT WAY TENDING   • • • • 26 NEW SIRENS 13
    WHERE ARE THEY TENDING A GOD   • • • • • • 291 RUGBY CHAPEL 174

TENDRILS
    PALE PINK CONVOLVULUS IN TENDRILS CREEP   • • • 255 SCHOLAR-GIPSY 25
    PALE BLUE CONVOLVULUS IN TENDRILS CREEP   • • • 255 SCHOLAR-GIPSY V 25

TENERIFFE
    OER THOSE SAME SEAS DARK TENERIFFE ROSE FRAUGHT   • • 485 S S LUSITANIA 11

TENSE
    HOW OF ALL HUMAN RULES THE OVER-TENSE   • • • 339 MEROPE 307
    AND HELP HIM TO UNBEND HIS TOO TENSE THOUGHT   • • 435 EMPEDOCLES II 222

TENT

BUT WHEN THE GREY DAWN STOLE INTO HIS TENT	61	SOHRAB RUSTUM	7
AND TOOK HIS HORSEMANS CLOAK AND LEFT HIS TENT	61	SOHRAB RUSTUM	9
THROUGH THE DIM CAMP TO PERAN-WISAS TENT	61	SOHRAB RUSTUM	11
THE TARTARS BUILT THERE PERAN-WISAS TENT	61	SOHRAB RUSTUM	22
UPON THE THICK PILED CARPETS IN THE TENT	61	SOHRAB RUSTUM	25
AND RAISED THE CURTAIN OF HIS TENT AND CALLD	64	SOHRAB RUSTUM	102
BACK THROUGH THE OPENING SQUADRONS TO HIS TENT	66	SOHRAB RUSTUM	188
AND GUDURZ ENTERD RUSTUMS TENT AND FOUND	67	SOHRAB RUSTUM	195
BUT GUDURZ STOOD IN THE TENT-DOOR AND SAID	67	SOHRAB RUSTUM	207
BUT RUSTUM STRODE TO HIS TENT-DOOR AND CALLD	69	SOHRAB RUSTUM	263
AND SOHRAB ARMD IN HAMANS TENT AND CAME	70	SOHRAB RUSTUM	292
AND BEAR THY TROPHIES TO AFRASIABS TENT	77	SOHRAB RUSTUM	530
THROUGH THE HUSHD CAMP TO PERAN-WISAS TENT	61	SOHRAB RUSTUM V	11
ACHILLES PONDERS IN HIS TENT	303	GRANDE CHARTR	115
MEN CALLD FROM CHAMBER CHURCH AND TENT	318	OBERMANN MORE	171
WHEREON MEN PITCH THEIR TENT	320	OBERMANN MORE	218
WHEREON WE PITCH OUR TENT	320	OBERMANN MORE V	218

TENTED

BY LEAGUERD TOWER AND TENTED FIELD IT CAME	476	CROMWELL	148

TENTH

AND HE WILL REACH ON THE TENTH MORN A BRIDGE	99	BALDER DEAD 1	147
AND ON THE TENTH MORN HE BEHELD THE BRIDGE	107	BALDER DEAD 2	85

TENTS

THE DINGY TENTS ARE PITCHD THE FIRES	55	RESIGNATION	116
THROUGH THE BLACK TARTAR TENTS HE PASSD WHICH STOOD	61	SOHRAB RUSTUM	12
THROUGH THE BLACK TENTS HE PASSD OER THAT LOW STRAND	61	SOHRAB RUSTUM	16
UNMURMURING IN OUR TENTS WHILE IT IS WAR	63	SOHRAB RUSTUM	72
AND FROM THEIR TENTS THE TARTAR HORSEMEN FILED	64	SOHRAB RUSTUM	106
FROM THEIR BLACK TENTS LONG FILES OF HORSE THEY STREAMD	64	SOHRAB RUSTUM	110
AND SULLEN AND HAS PITCHD HIS TENTS APART	66	SOHRAB RUSTUM	179
OUT ON THE SANDS BEYOND IT RUSTUMS TENTS	66	SOHRAB RUSTUM	191
SO FOLLOWD RUSTUM LEFT HIS TENTS AND CROSSD	69	SOHRAB RUSTUM	280
HIS EYES TOWARD THE TARTAR TENTS AND SAW	70	SOHRAB RUSTUM	300
AND THE BLACK TOORKMUN TENTS AND ONLY DRUNK	83	SOHRAB RUSTUM	762
SO SHALL IT BE FOR I WILL BURN MY TENTS	84	SOHRAB RUSTUM	797
HIS EYES TOWARDS THE TARTAR TENTS AND SAW	70	SOHRAB RUSTUM V	300
PITCH THEIR SMOKED TENTS AND EVERY BUSH YOU SEE	258	SCHOLAR-GIPSY	113

TERM

OF VEHEMENT ACTIONS WITHOUT SCOPE OR TERM	5	DUKE WELLINGTON	12
WHO FLUCTUATE IDLY WITHOUT TERM OR SCOPE	260	SCHOLAR-GIPSY	167
ITS TERM OF LIFE WAS NEARLY CLOSED	322	OBERMANN MORE	299
FOOLS THAT IN MANS BRIEF TERM	424	EMPEDOCLES I 2	347
WHAT FOR A TERM SO SCANT	444	WESTMIN ABBEY	1
AFTER LIGHTS TERM A TERM OF CECITY	448	WESTMIN ABBEY	155
AFTER LIGHTS TERM A TERM OF CECITY	448	WESTMIN ABBEY	155

TERMS

CHANGED GIFTS AND WENT ON EQUAL TERMS AWAY	72	SOHRAB RUSTUM	361
HELA SUCH AS THOU SAYST THE TERMS SHALL BE	111	BALDER DEAD 2	242
THE TERMS OF THY RELEASEMENT HENCE TO HEAVEN	112	BALDER DEAD 2	252
AND NOW I COUNT NOT OF THESE TERMS AS SAFE	112	BALDER DEAD 2	268
YE GODS THESE TERMS MAY KEEP ANOTHER DAY	115	BALDER DEAD 3	49
YE GODS THE TERMS YE KNOW WHICH HERMOD BROUGHT	120	BALDER DEAD 3	225
SMOOTH SOUND THE TERMS AND LIGHT TO BE FULFILLD	120	BALDER DEAD 3	231
THESE TERMS AND I SUSPECT SOME HIDDEN FRAUD	120	BALDER DEAD 3	235
BUT OFFERS TERMS FOR HIS RELEASE TO HEAVEN	122	BALDER DEAD 3	289
BUT OFFER TERMS FOR HIS RELEASE TO HEAVEN	122	BALDER DEAD 3 V	289
FAIR TERMS OF RECONCILEMENT EQUAL RULE	360	MEROPE	882
WORSE TERMS THAN MINE THEY HAVE OBTAIND FROM HEAVEN	360	MEROPE	884
THE WORLDS COURSE PROVES THE TERMS	419	EMPEDOCLES I 2	222
THE WORLD PROCLAIMS THE TERMS	419	EMPEDOCLES I 2 V	222

TERRACE

THE ROCKY BANKS THE TERRACE HIGH	183	TERRACE BERNE	3

TERRACED

TERRACED AND ORANGE-BOWERS	296	HEINES GRAVE	134

TERRACES

ON THE GILT TERRACES	50	CONSOLATION	13
ON THE GOLD TERRACES	50	CONSOLATION V	13
WHERE BETWEEN GRANITE TERRACES	312	OBERMANN	177

TERRIBLE

MY TERRIBLE FATHERS TERRIBLE HORSE AND SAID	83	SOHRAB RUSTUM	744
MY TERRIBLE FATHERS TERRIBLE HORSE AND SAID	83	SOHRAB RUSTUM	744
TERRIBLE DEITIES THRONED	347	MEROPE	530
THAT SAPPST THE VITALS OF THIS TERRIBLE MOUNT	438	EMPEDOCLES II	306

TERRIBLY

AND TERRIBLY THE HOOFS OF SLEIPNER RANG	102	BALDER DEAD 1	260
THEIR MURDERD RULERS TERRIBLY AVENGED	390	MEROPE	1566

TERRIFIED
         FROM THE TERRIFIED PEOPLE   . . . .   345 MEROPE   488

TERROR
         PALSIED WITH TERROR BRANDAN SATE   . . . . . .   157 SAINT BRANDAN   21
         WITH TERROR FROM THY TREE   . . . .   PHILOMELA   V
         IN PAIN IN TERROR IN DISTRESS   . . . .   226 EPILOG LAOCOON   175
         OF TERROR AND INSANE DISTRESS   . . . .   271 MEMORIAL VERSES   32
         WERE TO LIVE FREE FROM TERROR SPELLS MISTRUST THEM   413 EMPEDOCLES I 2   26
         WERE TO LIVE FREED FROM TERROR SPELLS MISTRUST THEM 413 EMPEDOCLES I 2   V 26

TERRORS
         THE NIGHT OF TERRORS AND THE DAY OF CARE   . . . .   478 CROMWELL   205

TERTULLIAN
         SO SPAKE THE FIERCE TERTULLIAN BUT SHE SIGHD   . .   172 GOOD SHEPHERD   6

TERTULLIANS
         SO RANG TERTULLIANS SENTENCE ON THE SIDE   . . . .   172 GOOD SHEPHERD   2

TEST
         AS THOSE WHEREWITH WE TRY TO TEST   . . . . . .   352 MEROPE   634
         AS THOSE WITH WHICH WE TRY TO TEST   . . . . . .   352 MEROPE   V 634

TESTED
         FROM FIRST YOUTH TESTED UP TO EXTREME OLD AGE   . .   2 TO A FRIEND   10

TETHERS
         HE TETHERS HIS BEAST DOWN AND MAKES HIS MEAL   . .   191 STRAYED REVEL   165

TETHYS
         ISTER TETHYS AND OCEANS SIXTH-BORN SON   . . . .   FRAGMENT 4   2

THAMES
         AND THE SWEET TRANQUIL THAMES   . . . .   200 PHILOMELA   12
         CROSSING THE STRIPLING THAMES AT BAB-LOCK-HITHE . . 257 SCHOLAR-GIPSY   74
         WHERE BLACK-WINGD SWALLOWS HAUNT THE GLITTERING THAMES 257 SCHOLAR-GIPSY   94
         AND LIFE RAN GAILY AS THE SPARKLING THAMES   . . .   261 SCHOLAR-GIPSY   202
         THE VALE THE THREE LONE WEIRS THE YOUTHFUL THAMES   263 THYRSIS   15
         BUT AH OF OUR POOR THAMES SHE NEVER HEARD   . . .   265 THYRSIS   98
         WE TRACKD THE SHY THAMES SHORE   . . . .   266 THYRSIS   126
         AND DOWN OVER THE THAMES THE DARKNESS DREW   . . .   444 WESTMIN ABBEY   13
         THE WORLD-FAMED ABBEY BY THE WESTERING THAMES   . .   444 WESTMIN ABBEY   20

THAMESS
         AND WHAT SEDGED BROOKS ARE THAMESS TRIBUTARIES   . . 266 THYRSIS   110

THAN
         RATHER TO PATIENCE PROMPTED THAN THAT PROUD   . .   7 REP FRIEND CONT   2
         SPARING US NARROWER MARGIN THAN WE DEEM   . . . .   7 REP FRIEND CONT   8
         REVELS MORE DEEP JOY KEENER THAN THEIR OWN   . . .   10 MYCERINUS   66
         MORE GRATEFUL THAN THIS MARBLE SLEEP   . . . . . .   22 YOUTH AND CALM   21
         AND MORE THAN MORTAL IMPULSE FILLD THEIR EYES   . .   25 DREAM   27
         ARE LESS LONELY THAN THEY WERE   . . . .   26 NEW SIRENS   20
         MORE MELODIOUS THAN OF YORE   . . . .   27 NEW SIRENS   42
         THAN THE CHARMS ULYSSES BORE   . . . .   27 NEW SIRENS   44
         RARER SECRETS THAN THE TOILING HEAD   . . . . . .   28 NEW SIRENS   80
         SURELY THAN THOSE WHICH SHOULD THINE AGE EMPLOY . .   41 GIPSY CHILD   V 11
         WITH READIER TONGUE THAN WE   . . . .   48 HORATIAN ECHO   18
         THAN THE POOR FACE SHE SLIGHTS IN THEE   . . . .   48 HORATIAN ECHO   35
         WIDER THAN ONE MANS PASSION THERES NO MOOD   . . .   50 CONSOLATION   V
         ARE SCARCE MORE CHANGED IN TRUTH THAN THEY   . . .   55 RESIGNATION   107
         ARE LESS THE POET MORE THAN MAN   . . . .   58 RESIGNATION   204
         NOBLER THAN THIS TO FILL THE DAY   . . . .   59 RESIGNATION   240
         SEEM TO BEAR RATHER THAN REJOICE   . . . .   60 RESIGNATION   270
         THOU KNOWEST BETTER WORDS THAN THIS TO SAY   . . .   68 SOHRAB RUSTUM   251
         HEAVENS AIR IS BETTER THAN THE COLD DEAD GRAVE . .   71 SOHRAB RUSTUM   324
         BEGIN THOU ART MORE VAST MORE DREAD THAN I   . . .   72 SOHRAB RUSTUM   385
         THAN TO THY FRIENDS AND TO THY FATHER OLD   . . .   77 SOHRAB RUSTUM   539
         O RUKSH THOU ART MORE FORTUNATE THAN I   . . . .   83 SOHRAB RUSTUM   747
         NOT LESS THAN THOSE WHO MERIT TEARS   . . . . . .   92 SICK KING BOKH   148
         BUT OTHER LOADS THAN THIS HIS OWN   . . . .   92 SICK KING BOKH   153
         UNTO A RULE MORE STRONG THAN THEIRS   . . . . . .   93 SICK KING BOKH   187
         NO MEANER HAND THAN ODINS ON HIS MANE   . . . . .   107 BALDER DEAD 2   73
         THAN BE A CROWND KING HERE AND RULE THE DEAD   . .   112 BALDER DEAD 2   267
         WORSE WAS THAT WAY TO GO THAN TO RETURN   . . . .   113 BALDER DEAD 2   291
         NO LESS THAN BALDER HAVE I LOST THE LIGHT   . . .   125 BALDER DEAD 3   401
         MORE FRESH MORE VERDANT THAN THE LAST WITH FRUITS   128 BALDER DEAD 3   529
         FASTER SURELY THAN IT SHOULD   . . . .   135 TRISTRAM 1   171
         ARE NOT MORE INNOCENT THAN THINE   . . . .   140 TRISTRAM 1   326
         FAR LOVELIER THAN THEY ARE BY DAY   . . . .   141 TRISTRAM 1   356
         BUT THESE SHE LOVES AND NOISIER LIFE THAN THIS . .   152 TRISTRAM 3   100
         WHO MADE A NAME AT YOUNGER YEARS THAN HE   . . .   153 TRISTRAM 3   145
         THAN THE SEA-CHILDREN OWN   . . . .   159 NECKAN   20
         THAN THOU SHALT HEAVEN BEHOLD   . . . .   160 NECKAN   52
         WAS WOE THAN BYRONS WOE MORE TRAGIC FAR   . . . .   167 PICT NEWSTEAD   14
         AND POINTS US TO A BETTER TIME THAN OURS   . . . .   170 WEST LONDON   14
         ARE YET FAR FAR LESS RARE THAN LOVE   . . . . . .   178 FAREWELL   40
         THAN I WAST DESTIND TO THIS LORE   . . . .   179 FAREWELL   44
         THAN I WERT DESTIND TO THIS LORE   . . . .   179 FAREWELL   V 44
         ALONE THAN THOU THEIR LONELINESS   . . . .   181 ISOLATION MARG   42
         THAN PANS FLUTE-MUSIC   . . . .   187 STRAYED REVEL   67

805

THAN   (CONTINUED)
        ONE THAN CREON CRUELLER FAR . . . .   196 FRAG ANTIGONE   47
        AH ME HONOUREST MORE THAN THY LOVER . . . . .   196 FRAG ANTIGONE   51
        NOR DID THERE NEED LESS THAN THE BURNING PILE . . 198 FRAG ANTIGONE   98
        WERE BUT MEN NOBLER THAN THEY ARE . . . . . .   202 URANIA   8
        ONE OF SOME WORTHIER RACE THAN OURS . . . . .   202 URANIA   18
        ONE OF SOME BETTER RACE THAN WE . . . .   202 URANIA   V 18
        ONE OF SOME WORTHIER RACE THAN WE . . . . . .   202 URANIA   V 18
        BUT THEY BRING MORE THAN THEY RECEIVE . . . .   203 EUPHROSYNE   20
        FOR THEN THE NIGHT WILL MORE THAN PAY . . . .   208 LONGING   3
        FOR THEN THE NIGHT WILL MORE THAN PAY . . . .   209 LONGING   15
        FOR SO THE NIGHT WILL MORE THAN PAY . . . . .   208 LONGING   V
        THAN POETRY WHY SHE THAN THEY . . . .   221 EPILOG LAOCOON   11
        THAN POETRY WHY SHE THAN THEY . . . .   221 EPILOG LAOCOON   11
        THOUGH MANY THAN GOOD STATUES WERE . . . . .   221 EPILOG LAOCOON   18
        THAT THE SINGER WAS LESS THAN HIS THEMES . . . 230 YOUTH OF NATURE   89
        MORE THAN THE SINGER ARE THESE . . . .   230 YOUTH OF NATURE   91
        LESS THAN THEY LEFT UNREVEALD . . . .   231 YOUTH OF NATURE   106
        YES BUT MORE THAN THIS . . . .   232 YOUTH OF MAN   4
        MORE FAITHFULLY THAN THESE . . . .   237 PROGRESS   8
        A DEEPER LIFE THAN THEIRS . . . .   237 PROGRESS   24
        THERE ARE WORSE PLAGUES ON EARTH THAN TEARS .   250 WISH   8
        MUST NEEDS READ CLEARER SURE THAN HE . . . .   250 WISH   28
        AND PURER OR MORE SUBTLE SOUL THAN THEE . . .   268 THYRSIS   178
        AND WHITER THAN THY WHITE BURNOUS . . . . . .   276 SOUTHERN NIGHT   43
        MORE THAN HE ASKS WHAT WAVES . . . .   288 RUGBY CHAPEL   69
        SAY IS LIFE LIGHTER NOW THAN THEN . . . . . .   303 GRANDE CHARTR   130
        MORE FORTUNATE ALAS THAN WE . . . .   304 GRANDE CHARTR   158
        CLEARER HOW MUCH THAN OURS YET WE . . . . . .   308 OBERMANN   63
        GREATER BY FAR THAN THOU ARE DEAD . . . . . .   309 OBERMANN   91
        EARTH HAPPIER THAN BEFORE . . . .   314 OBERMANN MORE   56
        YET IT HAD MORE THAN I . . . .   322 OBERMANN MORE   300
        THOUGH MORE THAN HALF THY YEARS BE PAST . . .   323 OBERMANN MORE   305
        SOUL THAT THAN THEY WE TAKE MORE CARE . . . .   315 OBERMANN MORE   V
        SEVERER PALER STATELIER THAN THEY ALL . . . .   331 MEROPE   57
        FOR WE WERE KINSMEN MORE THAN KINSMEN FRIENDS . 334 MEROPE   122
        LEAVES ME AUSTERER STERNER THAN I WOULD . . .   335 MEROPE   155
        OLD AGE IS MORE SUSPICIOUS THAN THE FREE . . . 335 MEROPE   156
        THAN THEY THESE AND THE DORIAN LORDS WHOSE KING 337 MEROPE   223
        TO HIS NEW SUBJECTS THAN TO US HIS FRIENDS . . 337 MEROPE   242
        HOTLIER THAN THOU AND WERE BY THEE KEPT BACK . 339 MEROPE   330
        EXILE ABROAD MORE SAFE THAN HEIRSHIP HERE . .   340 MEROPE   337
        TO THE CHAFED HEART OF JUSTICE THAN TO MINE .   349 MEROPE   560
        MORE FORTUNATE THAN THEE MORE FAIRLY JUDGED .   350 MEROPE   590
        BUT MORE THAN ALL UNPLUMBD . . . .   352 MEROPE   629
        MORE THAN ALL SECRETS HID THE WAY IT KEEPS . . 352 MEROPE   631
        WORSE TERMS THAN MINE THEY HAVE OBTAIND FROM HEAVEN 360 MEROPE   884
        OTHER THAN BY THIS DEATH BUT IT HATH COME . .   360 MEROPE   887
        LEARN THAT FROM OTHER LIPS O QUEEN THAN MINE . 362 MEROPE   927
        HIS TALE WAS MEETER FOR THAT EAR THAN THINE .   362 MEROPE   929
        BETTER FROM THINE THAN FROM AN ENEMYS TONGUE . 363 MEROPE   950
        WHAT SWEETER SLEEP THAN THIS COULD I DESIRE .   372 MEROPE   1156
        A MORE JUST STROKE THAN THAT THOU GAVST MY SON 373 MEROPE   1191
        SCARCE DANGEROUS LESS THAN HIM THE DORIAN LORDS 381 MEROPE   1298
        WHO CHIEFLY PROFIT RUN NO MORE THAN THEY . .   382 MEROPE   1351
        ON NATIVE GROUND THAN DRAG THE TEDIOUS HOURS . 383 MEROPE   1380
        WHAT ORDER MORE PRECISE HAD HE THAN I . . . .   384 MEROPE   1400
        THAN I TO HELP RAISE HIS MESSENIAN FRIENDS . . 388 MEROPE   1497
        THAN THINE ILLUSTRIOUS HUSBANDS TO AVENGE . .   390 MEROPE   1569
        SHALL WE SELECT THAN POLYPHONTES WHAT . . . .   390 MEROPE   1570
        MAY IT TURN HAPPIER THAN MY DOUBTS PORTEND . . 390 MEROPE   1583
        SOME ROCK MORE LONELY THAN THAT LEMNIAN ISLE . 395 MEROPE   1746
        THAN THE ICE-BASTIOND CAUCASIAN MOUNT . . . .   395 MEROPE   1749
        MORE FOR THIS LANDS SAKE GRIEVE I THAN MINE OWN 398 MEROPE   1784
        SATED AND MORE THAN ENOUGH . . . .   348 MEROPE   V
        MORE THAN A DAY AND NIGHT PAUSANIAS . . . . .   409 EMPEDOCLES I 1   100
        THAN IN THE BROILING CITY IN THESE HEATS . .   409 EMPEDOCLES I 1   104
        AND YET THE VILLAGE-CHURL FEELS THE TRUTH MORE 426 EMPEDOCLES I 2   411
                THAN YOU
        MORE VIRGINAL AND SWEET THAN OURS . . . . . .   426 EMPEDOCLES I 2   434
        BY OTHER RULES THAN ARE IN VOGUE TO-DAY . . .   436 EMPEDOCLES II   265
        WILL HAVE MORE PERIL FOR US THAN THE LAST . .   440 EMPEDOCLES I 2   378
        WHAT COULD HE BETTER WISH THAN THEN TO DIE . . 448 WESTMIN ABBEY   145
        WHAT CAN HE BETTER CRAVE THAN THEN TO DIE . .   448 WESTMIN ABBEY   V 145
        MORE THAN PITY CLAIMST A STAVE . . . .   453 POOR MATTHIAS   22
        FRIENDS MORE NEAR US THAN A BIRD . . . . . .   453 POOR MATTHIAS   23
        LESS THAN THEY TO US ARE YOU . . . .   453 POOR MATTHIAS   44
        OF A PRESCIENCE MORE THAN OURS . . . .   456 POOR MATTHIAS   138
        BETTER THAN WE SPENT WITH THEE . . . .   458 POOR MATTHIAS   213
        A HOLIER INCENSE THAN THIS FEEBLE LAY . . . .   471 ALARIC AT ROME   226
        MORE CALM MORE DEEP THAN CHILDHOOD EVER KNEW . 475 CROMWELL   116
        HIS STEP WAS LOFTIER THAN THE STEPS OF MAN . . 476 CROMWELL   156
        TO LOVE MORE DEEPLY THAN HE CAN . . . .   481 DESTINY   2
        THEY LESS THAN US MIGHT RECOGNIZE . . . . . .   481 COURAGE   11
        KEPT MORE THAN US THEIR STRENGTH OF SOUL . . . 481 COURAGE   12
        FOR THAN MAN INDEED THERE BREATHES NO WRETCHEDER   HOMER TRANS   12
                CREATURE
        IN SOME OTHER SORT THAN YOUR LAST WHEN THE   HOMER TRANS   41
                BATTLE IS ENDED
        SOONER THAN THOSE TWIN REACHES OF GREAT TIME . .   FRAGMENT 5   7

THANK
        AND HAVE TO THANK THEE FOR A FALL BEWARE . . . . 342 MEROPE   375

THANK (CONTINUED)
    THERE NURSE A LATE REMORSE AND THANK THE GODS   •   •   396 MEROPE   1755
    AND THANK THY BITTEREST FOE THAT HAVING LOST   •   •   396 MEROPE   1756
    AND FOR YOUNG CALLICLES THANK HIM FROM ME   •   •   •   428 EMPEDOCLES I 2   467

THANKFUL
    TO THESE TO THESE THEIR THANKFUL RACE   •   •   •   227 EPILOG LAOCOON   207

THANKLESS
    COLD HEARTS AND THANKLESS TONGUES WHERE THANKS ARE DUE   8 MYCERINUS   4
    COLD HEARTS AND THANKLESS TONGUES WHERE THANKS   8 MYCERINUS   V   4
        WERE DUE
    AND LEAVE TO DEATH THE HOSTS OF THANKLESS KINGS   •   •   68 SOHRAB RUSTUM   240
    A DEAD IGNORANT THANKLESS CORPSE   •   •   •   •   •   196 FRAG ANTIGONE   53

THANKS
    MY SPECIAL THANKS WHOSE EVEN-BALANCED SOUL   •   •   •   2 TO A FRIEND   9
    COLD HEARTS AND THANKLESS TONGUES WHERE THANKS ARE DUE   8 MYCERINUS   4
    COLD HEARTS AND THANKLESS TONGUES WHERE THANKS   8 MYCERINUS   V   4
        WERE DUE
    THANKS GRACIOUS ONE   •   •   •   •   •   •   •   •   •   187 STRAYED REVEL   63
    REFRESHD AND CLAIM THY MASTERS THANKS AND GOLD   •   •   373 MEROPE   1182
    THANKS TO HIM FOR OUR AMITY AS WELL   •   •   •   •   395 MEROPE   1724
    TO RENDER TO MY TRUE MESSENIANS THANKS   •   •   •   405 MEROPE   2018
    THOU WILT EARN MY THANKS SURE AND PERHAPS HIS   •   •   409 EMPEDOCLES I 1   99
    THAT NEEDS NO THANKS ONE IS FAR BETTER HERE   •   •   409 EMPEDOCLES I 1   103

THAW
    OF ALL ITS CHAFING TORRENTS AFTER THAW   •   •   •   5 DUKE WELLINGTON   5
    AND A WARM WEST-WIND BLOWS AND THAW SETS IN   •   •   122 BALDER DEAD 3   309

THEATRE
    OF THE FRENCH THEATRE WORN WITH DISEASE   •   •   •   167 RACHEL 1   6

THEBAN
    AND LIKE THE THEBAN SEER   •   •   •   •   •   •   •   229 YOUTH OF NATURE   34
    THE THEBAN SEER TO THE SPRING   •   •   •   •   •   •   229 YOUTH OF NATURE   44
    AND ALL THAT THEBAN WOE AND STRAY   •   •   •   •   •   427 EMPEDOCLES I 2   459
    HE EVER LOVED THE THEBAN STORY WELL   •   •   •   •   427 EMPEDOCLES I 2   463

THEBANS
    I WEEP THEBANS   •   •   •   •   •   •   •   •   •   •   196 FRAG ANTIGONE   46

THEBES
    THE DOOM OF THEBES   •   •   •   •   •   •   •   •   190 STRAYED REVEL   142
    THEIR LIVES AND FORMER VIOLENT TOIL IN THEBES   •   •   193 STRAYED REVEL   256
    SEVEN-GATED THEBES OR TROY   •   •   •   •   •   193 STRAYED REVEL   257
    IN THIS OUR THEBES BUT WHEN   •   •   •   •   •   197 FRAG ANTIGONE   84
    THEBES WAS BEHIND HIM IN FLAMES   •   •   •   •   229 YOUTH OF NATURE   41
    NOR DID REVIVING THEBES   •   •   •   •   •   •   •   229 YOUTH OF NATURE   46
    WHEN THEBES WHEN ATHENS DARED NOT WHO IN ARMS   •   •   337 MEROPE   225
    NOR THEBES NOR THE ISMENUS ANY MORE   •   •   •   •   427 EMPEDOCLES I 2   442
    IN THEBES THE BILLOW OF CALAMITY   •   •   •   •   427 EMPEDOCLES I 2   445

THEME
    IS A PASSD MODE AN OUTWORN THEME   •   •   •   •   302 GRANDE CHARTR   100
    TIME PRESSES SO THAT THEME FORBEAR I NOW   •   •   •   389 MEROPE   1530

THEMES
    THAT THE SINGER WAS LESS THAN HIS THEMES   •   •   •   230 YOUTH OF NATURE   89

THENCE
    HE ESCAPES THENCE BUT WE ABIDE   •   •   •   •   •   58 RESIGNATION   213
    AND UP FROM THENCE TO ORGUNJE   •   •   •   •   •   93 SICK KING BOKH   168
    AND UP FROM THENCE TO URGHENDJE   •   •   •   93 SICK KING BOKH   V 168
    THENCE ON HE JOURNEYD OER THE FIELDS OF ICE   •   •   109 BALDER DEAD 2   143
    AND UP FROM THENCE A WET AND MISTY ROAD   •   •   •   113 BALDER DEAD 2   289
    THENCE BY THE SEA-GODS SANCTUARY AND THE TOMB   •   •   356 MEROPE   740
    THENCE TO THE SOUTH BEHOLD THOSE SNOWY PEAKS   •   •   330 MEROPE   V   16
    THENCE HE ESCAPD AND NEXT I FIND HIM HERE   •   •   •   365 MEROPE   V

THENCEFORTH
    PATIENCE WAS THENCEFORTH SELF DESTRUCTION I   •   •   338 MEROPE   266

THEREAFTER
    AND STAMP HIMSELF THEREAFTER BAD OR GOOD   •   •   •   352 MEROPE   651

THEREAT
    NOR DOES HEAVEN TOIL THEREAT   •   •   •   •   •   •   EMPEDOCLES I 2   V

THEREIN
    AND WE MUST LEAVE THE OLD FAITHS AND WALK THEREIN   237 PROGRESS   26
    AND MANY A GUEST HATH SHE THEREIN RECEIVD   •   •   •   251 FUTURE   V

THEREOF
    AND INSTEAD THEREOF IS SEEN   •   •   •   •   •   •   136 TRISTRAM 1   175

THEREON
    AND HELA SET THEREON WITH COUNTENANCE STERN   •   •   110 BALDER DEAD 2   178
    AND HELA SAT THEREON WITH COUNTENANCE STERN   •   •   110 BALDER DEAD 2   V 178
    A LAST CHOICE GIFT THEREON HIS GOLDEN RING   •   •   •   118 BALDER DEAD 3   173
    LONE CHORASMIAN STREAM THEREON   •   •   •   •   •   •   191 STRAYED REVEL   183

THEREON   (CONTINUED)
      NO MAST NO SAILS ARE SET THEREON   . . . . . .   479 HAYSWATER BOAT   5

THEREWITH
      HOWBEIT REPORT THY MESSAGE AND THEREWITH   . . . .   112 BALDER DEAD 2   273

THESEUS
      OF THE GRIM LAPITHAE AND THESEUS DRIVE   . . . .   192 STRAYED REVEL   228

THESSALY
      ABOVE THE FOREST-GROUND CALLED THESSALY   . . . .   258 SCHOLAR-GIPSY   115

THETIS
      YES AS THE SON OF THETIS SAID   . . . .   309 OBERMANN   89

THEW
      STOUT WAS ITS ARM EACH THEW AND BONE   . . . . . .   315 OBERMANN MORE   89

THICK
      UPON THE THICK PILED CARPETS IN THE TENT   . . . .   61 SOHRAB RUSTUM   25
      THAT THEY FLEW THICK AND BRUISED HIM SORE   . . . .   91 SICK KING BOKH   122
      WITH THEIR THICK-FALLING TEARS SO GOOD A FRIEND   . .   115 BALDER DEAD 3   63
      TO PUSH THE SHIP THROUGH THE THICK SAND SPARKS FLEW   118 BALDER DEAD 3   177
      UNDER THE TREES IS DIBBLED THICK WITH HOLES   . .   122 BALDER DEAD 3   312
      THIS OPEN GLEN WAS STUDDED THICK WITH THORNS   . .   155 TRISTRAM 3   191
      CLUSTERD IN THICK BEADS DIM   . . . .   186 STRAYED REVEL   16
      A FLOATING ISLE THICK-MATTED   . . . .   190 STRAYED REVEL   154
      THE BOUNDLESS WAVING GRASS-PLAINS STRETCH THICK-STARRD   191 STRAYED REVEL   168
      HOW THICK THE BURSTS COME CROWDING THROUGH THE LEAVES   201 PHILOMELA   29
      HOW THICK THE TREMULOUS SHEEP-CRIES COME   . . . .   248 KENSINGTON GARD   8
      THROUGH THE THICK CORN THE SCARLET POPPIES PEEP   . .   255 SCHOLAR-GIPSY   23
      TURND ONCE TO WATCH WHILE THICK THE SNOWFLAKES FALL   259 SCHOLAR-GIPSY   128
      WHERE THICK THE COWSLIPS GREW AND FAR DESCRIED   . .   266 THYRSIS   114
      GAINST THICK-CRASHING INSANE   . . . .   293 HEINES GRAVE   34
      WITH RAIN WHERE THICK THE CROCUS BLOWS   . . . .   299 GRANDE CHARTR   2
      WHICH THE GOATS LOVE ARE JEWELLD THICK WITH DEW   . .   407 EMPEDOCLES I 1   17
      THICK BREAKS THE RED FLAME   . . . .   441 EMPEDOCLES II   418

THICKENS
      THICKENS AND TO ITS INNER GULPH RECALLS   . . . .   129 BALDER DEAD 3   547

THICKETS
      THE FELL-FARES SETTLED ON THE THICKETS NEAR   . .   151 TRISTRAM 3   55
      THROUGH THE DENSE ILEX-THICKETS TO THE DOGS   . .   357 MEROPE   791
      IN HER HIDING-PLACE OF THE THICKETS   . . . . . .   392 MEROPE   1632

THICKLY
      LAY THICKLY STREWN SWORDS AXES DARTS AND SPEARS   . .   95 BALDER DEAD 1   2
      CREEPS THICKLY GROWS NOT HERE BUT THE PALE GRASS   . .   150 TRISTRAM 3   15
      BLOOMS THICKLY GROWS NOT HERE   . . . .   TRISTRAM 3   V 15
      CREEPS THICKLY GROWS NOT HERE   . . . .   TRISTRAM 3   V 15
      TEARS FALL THICKLY THE WHILE   . . . .   342 MEROPE   389

THIN
      THIN THIN THE PLEASANT HUMAN NOISES GROW   . . . .   45 IN UTRUMQUE PAR   15
      THIN THIN THE PLEASANT HUMAN NOISES GROW   . . . .   45 IN UTRUMQUE PAR   15
      LIGHTS UP HIS STUDIOUS FOREHEAD AND THIN HANDS   . .   81 SOHRAB RUSTUM   676
      THIN-SPRINKLED WITH FARMS   . . . .   175 PARTING   6
      THE CHEEK GROWN THIN THE BROWN HAIR SPRENT WITH GREY   266 THYRSIS   135
      SHAKING HIS THIN WHITE HAIRS   . . . .   289 RUGBY CHAPEL   112
      MOSS-HUNG BOULDERS AND THIN   . . . .   297 HEINES GRAVE   160
      THE AIR IS THIN THE VEINS SWELL   . . . . . .   435 EMPEDOCLES II   215

THING
      SEEMS IT SO LIGHT A THING THEN AUSTERE POWERS   . .   9 MYCERINUS   31
      AND SIGH THAT ONE THING ONLY HAS BEEN LENT   . . . .   37 YOUTHS AGIT   13
      FOR IF I NOW CONFESS THIS THING HE ASKS   . . . .   71 SOHRAB RUSTUM   349
      THESE MANY DAYS AND HEARD NO THING   . . . . . .   88 SICK KING BOKH   23
      WHETHER A THING BE GREAT OR SMALL   . . . . . .   89 SICK KING BOKH   56
      AND THE THING HEARD THEY DOUBTED NOT   . . . . . .   91 SICK KING BOKH   110
      FAILS BUT ONE THING TO GRIEVE HERE BALDER STOPS   . .   111 BALDER DEAD 2   235
      FAILS BUT ONE THING TO GRIEVE THERE BALDER STOPS   . .   114 BALDER DEAD 3   43
      ONE THING TO UNDO WHAT THOU THYSELF HAST RULED   . .   120 BALDER DEAD 3   253
      HOW VAIN A THING IS MORTAL LOVE   . . . . . .   181 ISOLATION MARG   26
      HE TO THEE SENDS ME ON IN ONE THING GLAD   . . . .   359 MEROPE   850
      IN ONE THING ONLY THAT THE PRINCE IS DEAD   . . . .   364 MEROPE   966
      AND WHEN HERE EACH NEW THING   . . . .   418 EMPEDOCLES I 2   194
      IS IT SO SMALL A THING   . . . .   425 EMPEDOCLES I 2   397
      THE SMALLEST THING COULD GIVE US PLEASURE THEN   . .   436 EMPEDOCLES II   250
      THE CASE WAS CLEAR A MONGREL THING   . . . . . .   459 KAISER DEAD   29
      AND WELTERS LIKE A HUMAN THING   . . . .   479 HAYSWATER BOAT   7
      IT SEEMS AN IDLE THING WHICH COULD NOT LIVE   . .   FRAGMENT 9   1

THINGS
      BY CONTEMPLATION OF DIVINER THINGS   . . . . . .   9 MYCERINUS   12
      TO SPURN MANS COMMON LURE LIFES PLEASANT THINGS   . .   9 MYCERINUS   32
      BUT ALL THINGS NOW ARE ORDERD FAIR   . . . . . .   16 CHURCH BROU 2   15
      WHERE SWEET THINGS SOONEST CLOY   . . . . . .   39 STAGIRIUS   44
      BETWIXT THY WAKING AND THE BIRTH OF THINGS   . . . .   45 IN UTRUMQUE PAR   10
      HUMAN THINGS SO FAST ENTANGLED   . . . .   49 SECOND BEST   10

THINGS   (CONTINUED)
        HUMAN THINGS SO DEEP ENTANGLED • • • • • • • •   SECOND BEST   V 10
        IF BIRTH PROCEEDS IF THINGS SUBSIST • • • • • •   58 RESIGNATION   194
        THINGS WHICH MIGHT VEX HIM SHALL BE FOUND • • • •   92 SICK KING BOKH   160
        CLEAR IN THESE THINGS I CANNOT SEE • • • • • • •   93 SICK KING BOKH   182
        WITH FOLDED HANDS REVOLVING THINGS TO COME • • •   98 BALDER DEAD 1   93
        OR FOR THOU KNOWST THE FATES AND THINGS ALLOWD • •   98 BALDER DEAD 1   108
        ALL LIVING AND UNLIVING THINGS TO WEEP • • • • •   122 BALDER DEAD 3   292
        ALL LIVING AND UNLIVING THINGS TO WEEP • • • • •   122 BALDER DEAD 3   300
        ENTREATING ALL THINGS TO WEEP BALDERS DEATH • •   122 BALDER DEAD 3   305
        OF ALL THINGS WEEPING TO BRING BALDER BACK • • •   122 BALDER DEAD 3   318
        THEY TWO SCOURD EVERY COAST AND ALL THINGS WEPT • • 123 BALDER DEAD 3   328
        BUT WILL RESTORE IF ALL THINGS GIVE HIM TEARS • •   123 BALDER DEAD 3   348
        WEEP HIM ALL OTHER THINGS IF WEEP THEY WILL • •   123 BALDER DEAD 3   353
        AND WOMEN THINGS THAT LIVE AND MOVE • • • • •   178 FAREWELL   21
        WHICH TOUCH THEE ARE UNMATING THINGS • • • • •   181 ISOLATION MARG   32
        TO THINGS BY MORTAL COURSE THAT LIVE • • • • •   185 TERRACE BERNE   42
        BY AGE TAUGHT MANY THINGS • • • • • • • • •   189 STRAYED REVEL   119
        THESE THINGS ULYSSES • • • • • • • • • •   192 STRAYED REVEL   207
        HE TOLD ME THESE THINGS • • • • • • • • •   194 STRAYED REVEL   269
        AH QUIET ALL THINGS FEEL THY BALM • • • • •   208 ON THE RHINE   21
        ALL THINGS BEGIN AGAIN • • • • • • • • •   220 BACCHANALIA 2   41
        THESE OR MUCH GREATER THINGS BUT CAUGHT • • •   223 EPILOG LAOCOON   55
        A MOMENTS LIFE OF THINGS THAT LIVE • • • • •   223 EPILOG LAOCOON   58
        ALL THINGS HAVE SUFFERD A LOSS • • • • • •   232 YOUTH OF NATURE   127
        THESE DEMAND NOT THAT THE THINGS WITHOUT THEM • •   240 SELF-DEPENDENCE   19
        STILL ALL THINGS IN THIS GLADE GO THROUGH • • •   249 KENSINGTON GARD   31
        CALM SOUL OF ALL THINGS MAKE IT MINE • • • • •   249 KENSINGTON GARD   37
        THE FUTURE AND ITS VIEWLESS THINGS • • • • •   250 WISH   25
        FIRM TO THEIR MARK NOT SPENT ON OTHER THINGS • •   260 SCHOLAR-GIPSY   163
        CAUSES OF THINGS AND FAR BELOW • • • • • •   271 MEMORIAL VERSES   30
        SPACE FOR THINGS FAR FROM THEMSELVES • • • • •   282 HAWORTH CHURCH   V
        WHO ALONE IS ALL THINGS IN ONE • • • • • •   298 HEINES GRAVE   217
        AH ME WE ANCHORITES READ THINGS BEST • • • • •   314 OBERMANN MORE   75
        SEE I MAKE ALL THINGS NEW • • • • • • • •   320 OBERMANN MORE   232
        ALL THINGS BUT LIFE THOU LOSE NOT LIFE AS WELL • • 396 MEROPE   1757
        WHAT THINGS DARING WHAT ENDURING • • • • •   405 MEROPE   2023
        AND TALK TO HIM OF THINGS AT HAND AND COMMON • •   411 EMPEDOCLES I 1   158
        THINGS THAT ARE NOW PERCEIVED • • • • • • •   421 EMPEDOCLES I 2   283
        ALL THINGS THE WORLD WHICH FILL • • • • • •   422 EMPEDOCLES I 2   287
        FAIN WOULD DO ALL THINGS WELL BUT SOMETIMES • •   422 EMPEDOCLES I 2   296
              FAILS IN STRENGTH
        OF LONG-PAST HUMAN THINGS • • • • • • • •   423 EMPEDOCLES I 2   323
        SURE ONLY THAT YOUR MIND SEES ALL THINGS WHICH BEFAL 423 EMPEDOCLES I 2   346
        HE CANNOT ALL THINGS VIEW • • • • • • • •   424 EMPEDOCLES I 2   348
        ALL THINGS THE WORLD THAT FILL • • • • • • •   422 EMPEDOCLES I 2 V 287
        NOR OUTWARD THINGS WERE CLOSED AND DEAD TO US • •   436 EMPEDOCLES II   241
        IN ALL THINGS MY OWN DEADNESS • • • • • • •   438 EMPEDOCLES II   322
        OF ALL THINGS AND THEN • • • • • • • • •   443 EMPEDOCLES II   462
        AND TEMPER SWEET AND LOVE OF ALL THINGS PURE • •   446 WESTMIN ABBEY   79
        THE FLUX OF MORTAL THINGS • • • • • • • •   448 WESTMIN ABBEY   152
        THE SENSE OF TEARS IN MORTAL THINGS • • • • •   450 GEISTS GRAVE   16
        BIRDS WERE BORN THE FIRST OF THINGS • • • • •   456 POOR MATTHIAS   132
        THINGS THAT MAY CEASE BUT NEVER BE FORGOT • • •   462 ALARIC AT ROME   16
        WHISPERING FROM ALL AROUND ALL EARTHLY THINGS MUST DIE 469 ALARIC AT ROME 180
        BEAUTIFUL CITY IF DEPARTED THINGS • • • • • •   470 ALARIC AT ROME   205
        OF ALL LIVING THINGS THAT ON EARTH ARE BREATHING   HOMER TRANS   13
              AND MOVING
        OF ALL THIRST OF EARTHLY THINGS • • • • • •   META CLOISTER   2
        HERE WHERE LIFE AND ALL THINGS LIVING • • • •   META CLOISTER   17
        THE DOUBT THAT ASSAILS ALL THINGS NEVER WON • •   FRAGMENT 8   3

THINK
        YET I THINK AT GODS TRIBUNAL • • • • • • •   29 NEW SIRENS   91
        I THINK THOU WILT HAVE FATHOMD LIFE TOO FAR • •   43 GIPSY CHILD   47
        AND CEASE TO MOURN AND THINK OF BALDERS PYRE • •   97 BALDER DEAD 1   60
        THEY THINK TO BURN AND ALL MY CHOICEST WEALTH • •   103 BALDER DEAD 1   299
        I THINK I HAVE A FEVER IN MY BLOOD • • • • •   139 TRISTRAM 1   280
        SIT SIT BY ME I WILL THINK WEVE LIVED SO • • • •   143 TRISTRAM 2   35
        OH BRANDAN THINK WHAT GRACE DIVINE • • • • •   158 SAINT BRANDAN   53
        WHATEVER THOUGHT MIGHT THINK IT TOO • • • • •   221 BACCHANALIA 2   68
        THINK NOT THAT I TO ANNUL THE LAW HAVE WILLD • •   237 PROGRESS   10
        BUT THAT YE THINK CLEAR FEEL DEEP BEAR FRUIT WELL   238 PROGRESS   47
        BUT THAT YOU THINK CLEAR FEEL DEEP BEAR FRUIT WELL 238 PROGRESS   V 47
        THINK OFTEN AS I HEAR THEM RAVE • • • • • •   249 KENSINGTON GARD   26
        THINK SOMETIMES AS I HEAR THEM RAVE • • • • •   249 KENSINGTON GARD V 26
        THINK SADLY AS I HEAR THEM RAVE • • • • •   KENSINGTON GARD V 26
        I THINK OF HER WHOSE GENTLE TONGUE • • • • •   279 SOUTHERN NIGHT   121
        OF THEE I THINK MY BROTHER YOUNG • • • • •   279 SOUTHERN NIGHT   123
        IN THE AUTUMN EVENING AND THINK • • • • • •   287 RUGBY CHAPEL   24
        BUT WAS IT THOU I THINK • • • • • • • • •   295 HEINES GRAVE   97
        MAY THINK TO EMULATE • • • • • • • • • •   308 OBERMANN   56
        THOU LEARNST TO THINK AS THEY • • • • • • •   311 OBERMANN   148
        TYRANTS THINK HIM THEY MURDER NOT THEY SPARE • •   340 MEROPE   349
        I KNOW I KNOW HOW HARD IT IS TO THINK • • •   341 MEROPE   362
        EMBOLDEND BY MY LENIENCE THINK IT FEAR • • •   341 MEROPE   373
        HOW MUCH MEN THINK ME ABJECT VOID OF HEART • • •   366 MEROPE   1016
        I FEAR NOT BUT I THINK ON MY DESIGN • • • •   378 MEROPE   1235
        I THINK ON WHAT THE FUTURE HATH IN STORE • • •   397 MEROPE   1775
        THE MULES I THINK WILL NOT BE HERE THIS HOUR • •   406 EMPEDOCLES I 1   1
        I THINK THOU WOULDST NOT VEX HIM NO AND YET • •   408 EMPEDOCLES I 1   55
        SCARCE CAN ONE THINK IN CALM SO THREATENING   416 EMPEDOCLES I 2   126
              ARE THE GODS

THINK   (CONTINUED)
        NOR THINK THE GODS WERE CRAZED . . . . 417 EMPEDOCLES I 2   164
        I THINK MIGHT MAKE US FEAR . . . . 425 EMPEDOCLES I 2   384
        THINK YE IT STRIKES TOO SLOW THE SWORD OF FATE . . 466 ALARIC AT ROME   115
        THINK YE THE AVENGER LOITERS ON HIS WAY . . . . 466 ALARIC AT ROME   116
        AS LIGHT OF WHAT WE THINK WE FEEL THERE FLOWS . . 483 BELOW SURFACE   3
        FORTUNATE FIRS WHO NEVER THINK . . . . 483 ROME-SICKNESS   9

THINKERS
        THINKERS NEW SCHOOLS   . . . . 220 BACCHANALIA 2   38

THINKEST
        AND THOUGH THOU THINKEST THAT THOU KNOWEST SURE . . 72 SOHRAB RUSTUM   388

THINKING
        THINKING OF HER HE LEFT AND HIS OWN DEATH . . . . 79 SOHRAB RUSTUM   603
        THINKING OF HIS OWN GODS A GREEK . . . . 301 GRANDE CHARTR   81
        THINKING THAT SO I PRAYD ARIGHT I PRAYD . . . . 348 MEROPE   546
        AND I CAME THINKING TO FIND ARCAS HERE . . . . . 361 MEROPE   916
        THINKING ATONED-FOR . . . . 400 MEROPE   1872
        THINKING APPEASED . . . . 400 MEROPE   1874
        FORGED BY THE IMPERIOUS LONELY THINKING-POWER . . 440 EMPEDOCLES II   376

THINKS
        AND STARTS HIM THAT HE THINKS A GHOST WENT BY . . 101 BALDER DEAD 1   234
        AND THEN HE THINKS HE KNOWS . . . . 247 BURIED LIFE   96
        WHO THINKS AS THEY THOUGHT . . . . 252 FUTURE   31
        IN YOUTHS PURE MORNING NOR THINKS . . . . . . 347 MEROPE   V

THINKST
        WHAT THOU THINKST MEN SPEAK IN COURTLY CHAMBERS . . 143 TRISTRAM 2   41
        WHAT THOU THINKST THIS ACHING BROW WAS COOLER . . 143 TRISTRAM 2   43

THINLY
        SOWING HIS VICTORS THINLY THROUGH THEM ALL . . . . 337 MEROPE   250

THINND
        THINND AND PALED BEFORE HIS TIME . . . . . . 134 TRISTRAM 1   108

THINNER
        WASTES AND RUNS THINNER EVERY DAY . . . . . . 89 SICK KING BOKH   64

THIRD
        IN THE THIRD GENERATION THE WAY . . . . 343 MEROPE   412
        BUT THE THIRD WHAT DELAYS HIM . . . . 344 MEROPE   457
        HARDLY THE THIRD WITH GRIEVOUS LOSS REGAIND . . 336 MEROPE   V 218

THIRST
        WONDER NOT DEAD AND THIRST NOT DRIED . . . . . . 59 RESIGNATION   226
        NOR SLAKED MY THIRST AT THE CLEAR HELMUND STREAM . . 83 SOHRAB RUSTUM   758
        THE GENTLENESS THE THIRST FOR PEACE . . . . . . 180 FAREWELL   84
        THE THIRST FOR PEACE A RAVING WORLD . . . . . 180 FAREWELL   87
        A THIRST TO SPEND OUR FIRE AND RESTLESS FORCE . . 246 BURIED LIFE   49
        AND THERE ARE SOME WHOM A THIRST . . . . 288 RUGBY CHAPEL   73
        SORE THIRST PLAGUES THEM THE ROCKS . . . . . . 291 RUGBY CHAPEL   178
        TO SEEK A DRAUGHT TO SLAKE THY THIRST . . . . 316 OBERMANN MORE   119
        CONSUMED OUR HEART WITH THIRST LIKE FIRE . . . . 323 OBERMANN MORE   315
        FIXED IN OUR SOUL A THIRST LIKE FIRE . . . . . 323 OBERMANN MORE   V 315
        CONSUMD OUR SOUL WITH THIRST LIKE FIRE . . . . . 323 OBERMANN MORE   V 315
        WELL THIRST TO DRAG THE WRONGFUL RULER DOWN . . 353 MEROPE   670
        HAVE LEARND THAT WE MUST SACRIFICE THE THIRST . . 394 MEROPE   V1711
        OF LIFE THE THIRST FOR BLISS . . . . 418 EMPEDOCLES I 2   168
        NOR IS THE THIRST TO BLAME   . . . . 418 EMPEDOCLES I 2   172
        NOR IS THAT THIRST TO BLAME . . . . 418 EMPEDOCLES I 2   V 172
        AND WE SHALL FEEL THE AGONY OF THIRST . . . . 439 EMPEDOCLES II   356
        OF ALL THIRST OF EARTHLY THINGS . . . . . .   META CLOISTER   2

THIRSTY
        AS THEY WERE THIRSTY AND THE NIGHT . . . . . . 90 SICK KING BOKH   81
        THE TINKLE OF THE THIRSTY RILL . . . . 217 BACCHANALIA 1   2

THIRTEEN
        AND THIRTEEN HUNDRED YEARS AGONE THEY SAY . . . 170 EAST AND WEST   3

THIRTY
        TO DIE AT THIRTY-FIVE IN BABYLON   . . . . . . 154 TRISTRAM 3   150
        THIRTY LONG DAYS IN A COLD TRANCE OF DEATH . . . 410 EMPEDOCLES I 1   110

THISBE
        UP THE STILL VALE OF THISBE . . . . 442 EMPEDOCLES II   427

THITHER
        THITHER O VIZIER WILL I BEAR . . . . 95 SICK KING BOKH   225
        THITHER RESTORE HIM FOR HIS PLACE IS THERE . . . 110 BALDER DEAD 2   200
        ROUND BALDERS CORPSE WHICH THEY HAD THITHER BORNE 113 BALDER DEAD 3   2
        THITHER WHEN OER THIS PRESENT EARTH AND HEAVENS . . 128 BALDER DEAD 3   522
        THITHER IN YOUR ADVERSITY . . . . 198 FRAG DEJANEIRA   12
        HITHER AND THITHER SPINS . . . . 415 EMPEDOCLES I 2   82

THITHERWARD
    AND THITHERWARD THE STRANGER TOOK HIS WAY . . . . 445 WESTMIN ABBEY   33

THOK
    THOK IS SHE CALLD BUT NOW LOK WORE HER SHAPE   . . 123 BALDER DEAD 3   335
    THOK NOT FOR GIBES WE COME WE COME FOR TEARS   . . 123 BALDER DEAD 3   346
    THOK WITH DRY EYES WILL WEEP OER BALDERS PYRE   . . 123 BALDER DEAD 3   352

THOKS
    THAT YE COME PLEASURING TO THOKS IRON WOOD . . . . 123 BALDER DEAD 3   338

THOR
    AXES AND ROPES AND AT THEIR HEAD CAME THOR . . . . 106 BALDER DEAD 2   48
    OF CRASHING FALLS FOR WITH HIS HAMMER THOR . . . . 106 BALDER DEAD 2   55
    THOU CAMEST NEAR THE NEXT O WARRIOR THOR . . . . 115 BALDER DEAD 3   71
    THEN THEY PUT FIRE TO THE WOOD AND THOR . . . . 118 BALDER DEAD 3   175
    THOR CAME ON FOOT THE REST ON HORSEBACK RODE . . . 120 BALDER DEAD 3   218
    MOUNTED ON SLEIPNER WITH THE WARRIOR THOR . . . . 120 BALDER DEAD 3   239
    MY FATHER AND HIS PRIDE THE WARRIOR THOR . . . . 127 BALDER DEAD 3   491

THORA
    BUT I HEARD THORA LAUGH IN GOTHLAND ISLE . . . . 117 BALDER DEAD 3   148

THORN
    WHERE MERLIN BY THE ENCHANTED THORN-TREE SLEEPS . . 154 TRISTRAM 3   158
    UPON THE BROW-TOP GREW A THORN AND HERE   . . . 155 TRISTRAM 3   205
    THE BLOSSOMD THORN-TREE AND HER SLEEPING LOVER . . 156 TRISTRAM 3   218
    THE GRASS THE ELMS THAT BLOSSOMD THORN . . . 222 EPILOG LAOCOON   52
    THAT NAILD THORN-CROWNED MAN . . . . . 317 OBERMANN MORE   156
    THAT GRACIOUS CHILD THAT THORN-CROWND MAN . . . . 318 OBERMANN MORE   167
    IN THE THORN-CHOKED GULLIES . . . . . . 392 MEROPE   1638

THORNEY
    HUGE IN THE GLOOM ACROSS IN THORNEY ISLE . . . . 444 WESTMIN ABBEY   15
    AND SETS HIS FREIGHT ASHORE ON THORNEY STRAND . . 445 WESTMIN ABBEY   30
    HOW HIS ST PETERS CHURCH IN THORNEY ISLE . . . 445 WESTMIN ABBEY   49

THORNS
    THIS OPEN GLEN WAS STUDDED THICK WITH THORNS . . 155 TRISTRAM 3   191
    UNDER THE THORNS ON THE GREEN SWARD AND STRONG . . 155 TRISTRAM 3   196
    WITH THORNS ONCE STUDDED OLD WHITE-BLOSSOMD TREES   266 THYRSIS   113

THOUGHT
    IS IT HOPE MAKES ME LINGER THE DIM THOUGHT THAT SORROW 19 MODERN SAPPHO   V
    WAS IT A DREAM WE SAILD I THOUGHT WE SAILD . . . 24 DREAM   1
    AND THE HUNGRY THOUGHT THAT MUST BE FED . . . 30 NEW SIRENS   130
    OF THOUGHT SUCH CONTRAST STRANGE . . . . . 36 VOICE   28
    WHICH YEARS AND CURIOUS THOUGHT AND SUFFERING GIVE 43 GIPSY CHILD   38
    THE LONG-MUSED THOUGHT TO NORTH SOUTH EAST AND WEST 45 IN UTRUMQUE PAR   6
    SEES HIS STRONG THOUGHT IN FIERY FLOOD . . . 56 RESIGNATION   156
    HE SPOKE BUT RUSTUM LISTEND PLUNGED IN THOUGHT . 79 SOHRAB RUSTUM   604
    SO DEEMD HE YET HE LISTEND PLUNGED IN THOUGHT . 79 SOHRAB RUSTUM   615
    BUT SOHRAB SAW HIS THOUGHT AND HELD HIS HANDS . 82 SOHRAB RUSTUM   706
    WOULD CHARM THE GAZER TILL HIS THOUGHT . . . 147 TRISTRAM 2   139
    IS IT THIS THOUGHT WHICH MAKES HER MIEN SO STILL . 151 TRISTRAM 3   69
    THIS OR SOME TYRANNOUS SINGLE THOUGHT SOME FIT . 153 TRISTRAM 3   127
    IS IT THIS THOUGHT THAT MAKES HER MIEN SO STILL . 151 TRISTRAM 3   V 69
    OF THOUGHT AND OF AUSTERITY WITHIN . . . . 166 AUSTERITY POET   14
    TWAS NOT THE THOUGHT OF BYRON OF HIS CRY . . . 166 PICT NEWSTEAD   2
    THOUGHT I ABOVE HER STATE THIS SPIRIT TOWERS . . 170 WEST LONDON   9
    TO EVERY THOUGHT THE MASS IGNORE . . . . . 179 FAREWELL   58
    AWHILE LET ME WITH THOUGHT HAVE DONE . . . . 208 ON THE RHINE   11
    FIND ALSO IN THE SOUND A THOUGHT . . . . . 211 DOVER BEACH   19
    THE FAMOUS SPECULATORS THOUGHT . . . . . 219 BACCHANALIA 2   6
    WHATEVER THOUGHT MIGHT THINK IT TOO . . . . 221 BACCHANALIA 2   68
    DIVERGING TO ANOTHER THOUGHT . . . . . 221 EPILOG LAOCOON   7
    HIS THOUGHT MUST FOLLOW WHERE THEY PASS . . . 225 EPILOG LAOCOON   154
    HIS THOUGHT MUST FOLLOW THROUGH THE CROWD . . . 225 EPILOG LAOCOON   156
    HAVE THOUGHT THAT MY SECRET WAS THEIRS . . . 232 YOUTH OF NATURE   130
    HAVE THOUGHT THAT I LIVED BUT FOR THEM . . . 232 YOUTH OF NATURE V 131
    AND TO MY MIND THE THOUGHT . . . . . . 242 SUMMER NIGHT   11
    THE WAVES OF MOURNFUL THOUGHT BY WHICH THEY ARE PREST 243 SUMMER NIGHT   48
    WHO THINKS AS THEY THOUGHT . . . . . . 252 FUTURE   31
    MADE IT A RAY OF THY THOUGHT . . . . . 299 HEINES GRAVE   231
    THE KINGS OF MODERN THOUGHT ARE DUMB . . . 303 GRANDE CHARTR   116
    THY REALM OF THOUGHT IS DREAR AND COLD . . . 309 OBERMANN   107
    THE GLOW OF THOUGHT THE THRILL OF LIFE . . . 309 OBERMANN   V 97
    AN EREMITE WITH THEE IN THOUGHT . . . . 313 OBERMANN MORE   43
    AND PLUNGED IN THOUGHT AGAIN . . . . . 316 OBERMANN MORE   112
    BUT SLOW THAT TIDE OF COMMON THOUGHT . . . 319 OBERMANN MORE   189
    ONE COMMON WAVE OF THOUGHT AND JOY . . . . 323 OBERMANN MORE   323
    ONE MIGHTY WAVE OF THOUGHT AND JOY . . . . 323 OBERMANN MORE V 323
    SPARES NOT A THOUGHT TO HIS HOME . . . . 347 MEROPE   522
    QUICK FROM DISTRESSFUL THOUGHT AND FLOATS IN JOY . . 351 MEROPE   615
    WITHOUT A SINGLE GUILTY THOUGHT . . . . 353 MEROPE   684
    THE NOBLE THOUGHT WHICH IS ALONE THE MAN . . . 385 MEROPE   1409
    THE THOUGHT OF VENGEANCE ON ME NEVER QUITE . . 394 MEROPE   1704
    OF SOLITARY THOUGHT UNSHARED RESOLVE . . . . 403 MEROPE   1969
    AND LEAN UPON THE THOUGHT . . . . . . 420 EMPEDOCLES I 2   239
    WHAT SPRINGS OF THOUGHT THEY USE . . . . 423 EMPEDOCLES I 2   329
    TO HAVE LOVED TO HAVE THOUGHT TO HAVE DONE . . . 425 EMPEDOCLES I 2   400

```
THOUGHT          ( CONTINUED )
        AND HELP HIM TO UNBEND HIS TOO TENSE THOUGHT      • •    435 EMPEDOCLES II       222
        THEN WE COULD STILL ENJOY THEN NEITHER THOUGHT    •      436 EMPEDOCLES II       240
        WHOSE HABIT OF THOUGHT IS FIXD WHO WILL NOT CHANGE       437 EMPEDOCLES II       266
        NOTHING BUT A DEVOURING FLAME OF THOUGHT      • • •  •   438 EMPEDOCLES II       329
        BUT MIND BUT THOUGHT     • • • • • • • •         •      439 EMPEDOCLES II       345
        BAFFLED FOR EVER AND STILL THOUGHT AND MIND       •      439 EMPEDOCLES II       358
        I HAVE IN NO WISE BEEN BUT SLAVE OF THOUGHT       •      440 EMPEDOCLES II       391
        WORN WAS HIS BROW WITH CARES NO THOUGHT COULD SCAN      476 CROMWELL            155
        A LIFE WHOSE WAYS NO HUMAN THOUGHT COULD SCAN     • •    478 CROMWELL            219
        THE THOUGHT THAT SPURRD IT AND A DAUNTLESS WILL   • •    478 CROMWELL            228
        TO READ EACH THOUGHT AND TEACH THAT MASTER MIND   • •    478 CROMWELL            231
        ALL THESE WERE THINE OH THOUGHT OF FEAR AND THOU        479 CROMWELL            233
        LOFTY THOUGHT LIES OFT IN CHILDISH PLAY       • • • •    483 THEKLAS ANSWER       24
        I DROPPD THE BOOK AND OF MY CHILD I THOUGHT       • •    485 S S LUSITANIA         9
        WOMAN I TOO TAKE THOUGHT FOR THIS BUT THEN                  HOMER TRANS          14
                I BETHINK ME

THOUGHTED
        ZEUS AND PURE-THOUGHTED JUSTICE BRAND         • • • •    353 MEROPE              688

THOUGHTEST
        SOHRAB THOU THOUGHTEST IN THY MIND TO KILL    • • • •     77 SOHRAB RUSTUM       528

THOUGHTFUL
        STILL WE WALKD ON IN THOUGHTFUL MOOD • • • • • •         223 EPILOG LAOCOON       61
        YET HAST BEEN LONG AT SCHOOL WITH THOUGHTFUL TIME       394 MEROPE             1708

THOUGHTLESS
        THE THOUGHTLESS WORD THE LACK OF SYMPATHY     • • • •    470 ALARIC AT ROME      220

THOUGHTS
        IF THOUGHTS NOT IDLE WHILE BEFORE ME FLOW     • • • •      7 REP FRIEND          11
        ON HIS OWN SWARMING THOUGHTS AN INTEREST OWN     •        8 RELIGIOUS ISOL       4
        BUT FOR ME MY THOUGHTS ARE STRAYING      • • • • • •     29 NEW SIRENS          93
        OR ARE THOSE OLD THOUGHTS RETURNING      • • • • • •     30 NEW SIRENS         135
        WAFTS NOT FROM THINE OWN THOUGHTS NOR LONGINGS VAIN      42 GIPSY CHILD         10
        WAFTS NOT FROM THINE OWN THOUGHTS OF GRAVER STRAIN      41 GIPSY CHILD      V  10
        WHAT EXILES CHANGING BITTER THOUGHTS WITH GLAD    • •    42 GIPSY CHILD      V  25
        THOSE GIPSIES SO YOUR THOUGHTS I SCAN      • • • •       58 RESIGNATION        203
        AND WONDERS HOW SHE LIVES AND WHAT THE THOUGHTS   •      70 SOHRAB RUSTUM      307
        MUCH CHEERD WITH THOUGHTS OF CHRIST THE LIVING BREAD   169 EAST LONDON          8
        OF WISER THOUGHTS AND FEELINGS BLOT      • • • • •      183 ABSENCE              7
        LIGHT IGNORANCE AND HURRYING UNSURE THOUGHTS           198 FRAG DEJANEIRA        2
        AND SPELL THY LOOKS AND GUESS THY THOUGHTS    • • •     205 CALAIS SANDS        29
        AND WATCH THY AIR AND GUESS THY THOUGHTS      • • •     205 CALAIS SANDS     V  29
        THE THOUGHTS THAT RAIN THEIR STEADY GLOW     • • • •    209 DESPONDENCY          1
        THOUGHTS LIGHT LIKE GLEAMS MY SPIRITS SKY     • • •     209 DESPONDENCY          5
        OF THE THOUGHTS THAT FERMENT IN MY BREAST     • • • •   231 YOUTH OF NATURE    120
        THEIR THOUGHTS FOR FEAR THAT IF REVEALD       • • •     245 BURIED LIFE         17
        WHENCE OUR THOUGHTS COME AND WHERE THEY GO    • • •     246 BURIED LIFE      V  54
        AS WHAT HE SEES IS SO HAVE HIS THOUGHTS BEEN     •      252 FUTURE               7
        HE WOTS OF ONLY THE THOUGHTS     • • • • • • • •        252 FUTURE              25
        AND THEY CAN BIND THEM TO WHAT THOUGHTS THEY WILL      256 SCHOLAR-GIPSY       47
        OF FESTERING THOUGHTS AND PERSONAL FEARS      • • •     271 MEMORIAL VERSES  V
        TRUST ITS OWN THOUGHTS BEFORE YET        • • • • • •    281 HAWORTH CHURCH      42
        THOUGHTS OF THE GENERAL WEAL     • • • • • • •         282 HAWORTH CHURCH    V
        SUCH OF THY THOUGHTS AS THOU WILT        • • • • •      299 HEINES GRAVE       221
        TILL FREE MY THOUGHTS BEFORE ME ROLL     • • • • •      302 GRANDE CHARTR       95
        BUT STOP TO FETCH BACK THOUGHTS THAT STRAY    • •       313 OBERMANN MORE       29
        WHAT THOUGHTS TO ME HIS ROCKS RECALL     • • • • •      313 OBERMANN MORE       35
        NO THOUGHTS THAT TO THE WORLD BELONG     • • • • •      317 OBERMANN MORE      145
        HAVE THOUGHTS AND SMILES AND TEARS       • • • • •      322 OBERMANN MORE      288
        O MEROPE HOW MANY NOBLE THOUGHTS         • • • • • •    335 MEROPE             177
        THEIR THOUGHTS THEIR WAYS THEIR WISHES ARE NOT THINE   429 EMPEDOCLES II       19
        BUT WE RECEIVED THE SHOCK OF MIGHTY THOUGHTS     •      436 EMPEDOCLES II      242
        THE BROW UNBOUND THE THOUGHTS FLOW FREE AGAIN    •      436 EMPEDOCLES II      246
        THOUGHTS SLAVES AND DEAD TO EVERY NATURAL JOY    •      436 EMPEDOCLES II      249
        THOUGHTS OF THE PAST AND OF THE FUTURE TIME      •      467 ALARIC AT ROME     128
        WHILST EVERY CHORD THAT THRILLS AT THOUGHTS OF HOME   467 ALARIC AT ROME     131
        THE THOUGHTS THAT TOUCHT THY BREAST THOU LONELY       468 ALARIC AT ROME     168
                CONQUEROR THEN
        ALAS FAR OTHER THOUGHTS MIGHT WELL BE OURS    • • • •   470 ALARIC AT ROME     199
        TILL ALL BRIGHT THOUGHTS THAT HILLS OR WAVES CAN YIELD 472 CROMWELL            33
        AND THOUGHTS THAT WERE BUT OUTLINES TIME ENGRAVES      473 CROMWELL            47
        AND FLEETING THOUGHTS THAT ON THE LONELY WILD    • •    473 CROMWELL            51
        HIGH THOUGHTS WERE HIS WHEN BY THE GLEAMING FLOOD     473 CROMWELL            65
        HIGH THOUGHTS WERE HIS BUT MEMORYS GLANCE THE WHILE   474 CROMWELL            69
        AND PEACEFUL JOYS AND GENTLER THOUGHTS SWEPT BY   •    474 CROMWELL            71
        THE PEACE OF CHILDHOOD AND THE THOUGHTS THAT ROAM     474 CROMWELL            73
        YOUTH STAIND WITH FOLLIES AND THE THOUGHTS OF ILL     474 CROMWELL            79
        RENT WITH TUMULTUOUS THOUGHTS WHOSE CONFLICT RUNG     478 CROMWELL           223

THOUSAND
        YES WHILE ON EARTH A THOUSAND DISCORDS RING      • •      1 QUIET WORK          9
        REND IN A THOUSAND SHREDS THIS LIFE OF OURS      • •      4 BUTLERS SERMONS     4
        A THOUSAND VIRTUES IN THIS HATED TIME     • • • •       37 YOUTHS AGIT          8
        OF GRIEF AND EASED US WITH A THOUSAND SLEEPS     • •     43 GIPSY CHILD        52
        TEN THOUSAND MOURNERS    • • • • • • • • • •            52 CONSOLATION        64
        THOUGH HE HATH LOOSED A THOUSAND CHAINS       • • •     56 RESIGNATION       150
        THE MURMUR OF A THOUSAND YEARS   • • • • • • •         57 RESIGNATION       188
        SPRANG IN A THOUSAND SHIVERS ON THE HELM      • • •     76 SOHRAB RUSTUM      512
```

THOUSAND   (CONTINUED)
        A THOUSAND YEARS AGO . . . .   149 TRISTRAM 2   193
        THE THOUSAND SWEET STILL JOYS OF SUCH . . . . .   179 FAREWELL   67
        A THOUSAND KNIGHTS HAVE REIND THEIR STEEDS . . . .   204 CALAIS SANDS   1
        COME AS THOU CAMST A THOUSAND TIMES . . . . . .   208 LONGING   5
        BUT MAN HAS A THOUSAND GIFTS . . . .   233 YOUTH OF MAN   32
        AND WE HAVE BEEN ON MANY THOUSAND LINES . . . .   246 BURIED LIFE   57
        OF ALL THE THOUSAND NOTHINGS OF THE HOUR . . . .   247 BURIED LIFE   69
        WITH A THOUSAND CRIES IS ITS STREAM . . . . .   253 FUTURE   54
        AND TIRED UPON A THOUSAND SCHEMES OUR WIT . . . .   259 SCHOLAR-GIPSY   148
        IN A THOUSAND WATER-BREAKS LIGHT . . . . . .   297 HEINES GRAVE   184
        WHAT SOME TWO THOUSAND YEARS SURVEY . . . . .   315 OBERMANN MORE   83
        WELLNIGH TWO THOUSAND YEARS HAVE BROUGHT . . . .   315 OBERMANN MORE   V 81
        THOUGH FENCED BY SANCTION OF A THOUSAND YEARS . . .   353 MEROPE   669
        IN A THOUSAND COUNTRIES A THOUSAND . . . . .   369 MEROPE   1094
        IN A THOUSAND COUNTRIES A THOUSAND . . . . .   369 MEROPE   1094
        IT IS TEN THOUSAND FIERY WILLS IN ONE . . . .   382 MEROPE   1348
        NUMBER IT WITH THE THOUSAND RUMOURS VAIN . . . .   387 MEROPE   1486
        A THOUSAND TIMES HAVE I BEEN HERE ALONE . . . .   406 EMPEDOCLES I 1   7
        I KNOW THESE NOTES AMONG A THOUSAND HARK . . . .   413 EMPEDOCLES I 2   35
        A THOUSAND GLIMPSES WINS . . . .   415 EMPEDOCLES I 2   84
        SEARCH HE A THOUSAND YEARS . . . .   417 EMPEDOCLES I 2   145
        I KNOW THOSE NOTES AMONG A THOUSAND HARK . . . .   413 EMPEDOCLES I 2 V 35
        AND SO CHANGE BACK AND MANY THOUSAND TIMES . . . .   435 EMPEDOCLES II   229
        POUR FROM A THOUSAND HILLS THY WARRIORS OF THE NORTH   465 ALARIC AT ROME   96
        HERE SHOULD A THOUSAND FORMS ON FANCYS WINGS . .   470 ALARIC AT ROME   207
        IN THE PLAIN THERE WERE KINDLED A THOUSAND
            FIRES BY EACH ONE   HOMER TRANS   3

THOUSANDS
        NOT FOR THE THOUSANDS WHOM MY FATHER SLEW . . . .   8 MYCERINUS   2
        THAT THOUSANDS COUNTED EVERY GROAN . . . . . .   303 GRANDE CHARTR   137
        WAS IT THAT YE WITH MAN MIGHT HAVE YOUR THOUSANDS   HOMER TRANS   11
            OF SORROWS

THOUSANDTH
        WEAK WOMEN WITH A THOUSANDTH PART MY WRONGS . .   366 MEROPE   1013

THRACIAN
        THE UNFRIENDLY PALACE IN THE THRACIAN WILD . . . .   201 PHILOMELA   18
        OF THE THRACIAN SEA LET HER LEAVE . . . . . .   361 MEROPE   912

THRALL
        I REST THE THRALL OF HELA AND ENDURE . . . . . .   129 BALDER DEAD 3   545

THREAD
        PAIN TO THREAD BACK AND TO RENEW . . . . . .   53 RESIGNATION   20
        TO CUT THY THREAD OF LIFE AND FREE THY SOUL . .   103 BALDER DEAD 1   303
        ACROSS MY HEART TO SAY THY THREAD . . . . . .   184 TERRACE BERNE   27
        THE THREAD WHICH BINDS IT ALL IN ONE . . . . .   225 EPILOG LAOCOON   141
        A WIND-BLOWN THREAD . . . .   392 MEROPE   1654
        SLOWLY THREAD THEM WHEN BEHOLD . . . .   457 POOR MATTHIAS   183

THREADED
        ARE THREADED QUIET IN THE SUN . . . .   54 RESIGNATION   51
        THREADED AND LIGHTEND BY A TRACK OF FLAME . . . .   473 CROMWELL   60

THREADING
        THREADING THE TARTAR SQUADRONS TO THE FRONT . .   65 SOHRAB RUSTUM   142

THREADS
        OF LITTLE THREADS OUR LIFE IS SPUN . . . . . .   48 HORATIAN ECHO   25

THREAT
        ODIN THOU WHIRLWIND WHAT A THREAT IS THIS . . . .   120 BALDER DEAD 3   248

THREATENED
        EVEN IN THE ACT TO BURST TWICE THREATENED TWICE   465 ALARIC AT ROME   84
            DELAYED

THREATENEST
        THOU THREATENEST WHAT TRANSCENDS THY MIGHT EVEN THINE   120 BALDER DEAD 3   249

THREATENING
        SCARCE CAN ONE THINK IN CALM SO THREATENING   416 EMPEDOCLES I 2   126
            ARE THE GODS

THREATENS
        THREATENS TO BREAK TO DISSOLVE . . . .   291 RUGBY CHAPEL   181

THREATNINGS
        FATES THREATNINGS ARE NOT VAIN THE SPOILER   466 ALARIC AT ROME   120
            COMES NOT SLOW

THREE
        THE ALPINE PEASANTS TWO AND THREE . . . . . .   17 CHURCH BROU 2   18
        THEY THREE IN THAT LONG-DISTANT SUMMER-TIME . .   79 SOHRAB RUSTUM   628
        THREE DAYS SINCE AT THE TIME OF PRAYER . . . .   88 SICK KING BOKH   30
        LO I AM OLD THREE KINGS ERE THEE . . . . . .   92 SICK KING BOKH   143
        THREE MIGHTY CHILDREN TO MY FATHER LOK . . . .   110 BALDER DEAD 2   206
        HER HAND IN TURN FOR GUIDANCE AND THE THREE . .   129 BALDER DEAD 3   551
        THREE HOLLIES SIDE BY SIDE AND MADE A SCREEN . .   150 TRISTRAM 3   20
        THEN ISEULT CALLD THEM TO HER AND THE THREE . .   150 TRISTRAM 3   35
        WARM IN THEIR MANTLES WRAPT THE THREE STOOD THERE   150 TRISTRAM 3   38
        WARM IN THEIR MANTLES WRAPT THE THREE STAYD THERE   TRISTRAM 3   V 38

THREE   (CONTINUED)
         THE VALE THE THREE LONE WEIRS THE YOUTHFUL THAMES   263 THYRSIS   15
         THREE GENERATIONS OF HIS OFFSPRING OUT   •   •   •   •   336 MEROPE   217
         THREE BROTHERS WON THE FIELD   •   •   •   •   •   •   •   344 MEROPE   454
         OF THE THREE HERACLEIDAE   •   •   •   •   •   •   •   •   345 MEROPE   470
         ON SUCH A HUNTING-JOURNEY THREE MORNS SINCE   •   •   355 MEROPE   730
         BY THE THREE FOUNTAINS AND THE ADDERS HILL   •   •   •   356 MEROPE   748
         AND TOOK THREE STRIDES QUARRY AND DOGS WERE GONE   •   •   358 MEROPE   830
         FOR THE THREE CONQUERD KINGDOMS OF THIS ISLE   •   •   389 MEROPE   1549
         WORST OF THE THREE THE STONY SPARTA FELL   •   •   •   •   389 MEROPE   1553
         HE ON A HUNTING PARTY THREE DAYS SINCE   •   •   •   •   364 MEROPE   V 973

THRESHERS
         TO WATCH THE THRESHERS IN THE MOSSY BARNS   •   •   •   •   258 SCHOLAR-GIPSY   104

THRESHING
         BY BARN IN THRESHING-TIME BY NEW-BUILT RICK   •   •   263 THYRSIS   34

THRESHOLD
         BEFORE A STRANGERS THRESHOLD NOT HIS HOME   •   •   •   •   114 BALDER DEAD 3   13
         STANDS ON THE THRESHOLD THE WIND   •   •   •   •   •   •   289 RUGBY CHAPEL   111
         UPON THE THRESHOLD OF OLD AGE ALONE   •   •   •   •   •   334 MEROPE   152

THREW
         AND THREW A WHITE CLOAK ROUND HIM AND HE TOOK   •   •   64 SOHRAB RUSTUM   98
         WHICH IT SENT FLYING WIDE THEN SOHRAB THREW   •   •   73 SOHRAB RUSTUM   405
         AND THREW IT ON HIS HEAD AND SMIRCHD HIS HAIR   •   •   81 SOHRAB RUSTUM   701
         TO HODER AND UNWITTING HODER THREW   •   •   •   •   95 BALDER DEAD 1   7
         AT WHOM THE GODS IN SPORT THEIR WEAPONS THREW   •   •   98 BALDER DEAD 1   103
         ME ON THIS CHEERLESS NETHER WORLD YE THREW   •   •   •   110 BALDER DEAD 2   212
         AND PLACED THEM ON THE PYRE AND ODIN THREW   •   •   •   118 BALDER DEAD 3   172
         AND THREW THEM ON THE PYRE AND ODIN THREW   •   •   •   118 BALDER DEAD 3   V 172
         AND THREW THEM ON THE PYRE AND ODIN THREW   •   •   •   118 BALDER DEAD 3   V 172
         AND THREW HIS TRUNK TO CHOKE THE ABYSMAL VOID   •   •   121 BALDER DEAD 3   V 259
         I SPRANG UP I THREW ROUND ME   •   •   •   •   •   •   186 STRAYED REVEL   29
         TILL WITH HIS DAILY LIFE A LIFE THAT THREW   •   •   •   473 CROMWELL   55

THREWST
         BUT HELA INTO NIFLHEIM THOU THREWST   •   •   •   •   •   121 BALDER DEAD 3   276

THRICE
         AND THRICE IN ARMS AROUND THE DEAD THEY RODE   •   •   115 BALDER DEAD 3   61
         IN SPITALFIELDS LOOKD THRICE DISPIRITED   •   •   •   169 EAST LONDON   4
         AND BY CONTRITION SEALD THRICE SURE   •   •   •   •   •   179 FAREWELL   72
         THRICE ISSUED WITH US FROM THEIR PASTORAL VALES   •   337 MEROPE   226
         THRICE SON FOLLOWD SIRE   •   •   •   •   •   •   •   •   345 MEROPE   467
         O THRICE UNHAPPY HOW I GROAN THY FATE   •   •   •   362 MEROPE   931

THRILL
         A THRILL THROUGH ALL THE TARTAR SQUADRONS RAN   •   •   65 SOHRAB RUSTUM   158
         BACK WITH THE CONSCIOUS THRILL OF SHAME   •   •   •   181 ISOLATION MARG   19
         THE GLOW HE CRIES THE THRILL OF LIFE   •   •   •   •   •   309 OBERMANN   97
         THE GLOW OF THOUGHT THE THRILL OF LIFE   •   •   •   309 OBERMANN   V 97

THRILLD
         HATH NOT BEEN THRILLD BY THEM ALL   •   •   •   •   •   230 YOUTH OF NATURE   82
         HAS NOT BEEN THRILLD BY THEM ALL   •   •   •   •   •   •   230 YOUTH OF NATURE   V 82
         THRILLD WITH A DREAD NO SLUMBER COULD CONTROL   •   •   477 CROMWELL   200

THRILLING
         BLEW SUCH A THRILLING SUMMONS TO MY WILL   •   •   •   •   36 VOICE   37

THRILLS
         THAT THRILLS IN HIS MOURNFULLEST CHORD   •   •   •   •   231 YOUTH OF NATURE   93
         THRILLS AT EACH SMART IS THE PRAISE   •   •   •   •   •   293 HEINES GRAVE   27
         WHILST EVERY CHORD THAT THRILLS AT THOUGHTS OF HOME   467 ALARIC AT ROME   131

THRIVE
         AND SO IT COULD NOT THRIVE   •   •   •   •   •   •   •   •   315 OBERMANN MORE   92
         HAD CEASED TO LIVE AND THRIVE   •   •   •   •   •   •   •   320 OBERMANN MORE   226

THROAT
         WHICH TASKD THY PIPE TOO SORE AND TIRED THY THROAT   269 THYRSIS   225
         PRINKING EARS AND DEWLAP THROAT   •   •   •   •   •   •   454 POOR MATTHIAS   72
         ROUND HIS SMALL THROAT OF BLACK AND BROWN   •   •   •   459 KAISER DEAD   15

THROATED
         THE TAWNY-THROATED   •   •   •   •   •   •   •   •   •   •   200 PHILOMELA   2
         THE INKEN THROATED   •   •   •   •   •   •   •   •   •   •   200 PHILOMELA   V 2

THROATS
         SLAKE THEIR PARCHD THROATS WITH SUGARD MULBERRIES   66 SOHRAB RUSTUM   166
         NOR LET THY BAWLING FELLOWS RACK THEIR THROATS   •   •   255 SCHOLAR-GIPSY   4

THROB
         HAVE RESTLESS HEARTS ONE THROB THE LESS   •   •   •   303 GRANDE CHARTR   144
         THE TEMPLES TIGHTEN AND THROB THERE   •   •   •   •   •   435 EMPEDOCLES II   216

THROBBING
         LET THIS THROBBING PHRYGIAN STRAIN   •   •   •   •   •   •   32 NEW SIRENS   V 168

THROBBING   (CONTINUED)
      FALL ON THE THROBBING BROW FALL ON THE BURNING BREAST   36 VOICE   15
      AND THE SAME VAINLY THROBBING HEART WAS THERE   • •   242 SUMMER NIGHT   24

THROBS
      THE WIDE PLAIN RINGS THE DAZED AIR THROBS WITH BLOWS   137 TRISTRAM 1   235

THROE
      UNFRUITFUL OFT AND AT HER HAPPIEST THROE   • • • •   45 IN UTRUMQUE PAR   27

THROES
      FELT THE DISSOLVING THROES   • • • • • • • • •   229 YOUTH OF NATURE   31

THRONE
      SPRING THE FOUNDATIONS OF THAT SHADOWY THRONE   • •   4 BUTLERS SERMONS   6
      SPRING THE FOUNDATIONS OF THE SHADOWY THRONE   • •   4 BUTLERS SERMONS   V   6
      AND CAME HEAPD WITH MYRTLES TO YOUR THRONE   • • •   27 NEW SIRENS   32
      TO LIDSKIALF AND SATE UPON HIS THRONE   • • • •   96 BALDER DEAD 1   49
      AND BALDER SITTING CROWND AND HELAS THRONE   • • • •   100 BALDER DEAD 1   175
      THE THRONE FROM WHICH HIS EYE SURVEYS THE WORLD   • •   102 BALDER DEAD 1   254
      AND IN THE MIDST ONE HIGHER ODINS THRONE   • • •   106 BALDER DEAD 2   38
      THE SPRING THAT BUBBLES UP BY HELAS THRONE   • • • •   108 BALDER DEAD 2   131
      THESE FLOW BY HELAS THRONE AND NEAR THEIR SPRING   • •   109 BALDER DEAD 2   155
      BUT ALL HE PASSD UNHAILD AND REACHD THE THRONE   • •   109 BALDER DEAD 2   176
      FAR FROM THE OTHER GHOSTS AND HELAS THRONE   • • • •   124 BALDER DEAD 3   391
      ME A SMILING QUEEN UPON MY THRONE   • • • • •   144 TRISTRAM 2   52
      ON A RED GOLD THRONE IN THE HEART OF THE SEA   • •   163 FORSAKEN MERM   51
      AND DROOPD AND SLOWLY DIED UPON THEIR THRONE   • •   239 REVOLUTIONS   16
      HIS SEAT UPON THE INTELLECTUAL THRONE   • • •   260 SCHOLAR-GIPSY   184
      THE MOUNTAIN-TOPS WHERE IS THE THRONE OF TRUTH   • •   267 THYRSIS   144
      AND I AM SEATED ON A PROSPEROUS THRONE   • • •   334 MEROPE   136
      UPON A THRONE NOT THINE TO GIVE IS HEIR   • • • •   336 MEROPE   190
      AND CHAMPION TO THE THRONE I HONOURING MOST   • •   338 MEROPE   268
      WHO SHOOK THE FIERCE NELEIDAE ON THEIR THRONE   • •   338 MEROPE   292
      AND TO MY SON REVERSION TO THY THRONE   • • • •   340 MEROPE   334
      INSTALL HIM IN THY THRONE STILL WITHOUT BLOOD   • •   350 MEROPE   588
      THE BEST THEN TO THE THRONE MAY CARVE HIS WAY   • •   352 MEROPE   658
      THE DARING CLAIMANT OF A PERILOUS THRONE   • • • •   383 MEROPE   1357
      FAST PERMANENCE TO AN ILL-GOTTEN THRONE   • • • •   388 MEROPE   1509
      TO BID HER SHARE THINE UNENDANGERD THRONE   • • • •   395 MEROPE   1740
      TO BEND IN RAPTURE AT SOME IDOL THRONE   • • • •   474 CROMWELL   99
      BETWEEN A RUIND CHURCH AND SHATTERD THRONE   • • • •   477 CROMWELL   188
      YE TOO WHO STAND BESIDE THE HOARY THRONE   • • • •   FRAGMENT 2   1

THRONED
      TERRIBLE DEITIES THRONED • • • • • • • • • •   347 MEROPE   530

THRONES
      OR IN DEAF EASE ON THRONES OF DAZZLING SHEEN   • •   10 MYCERINUS   47
      FILL THE WEALTH-GIVING THRONES • • • • • •   • •   343 MEROPE   415
      GIVE THE THRONES THAT THEY CONQUERD • • • •   •   344 MEROPE   456
      BLOOD-FOUNDED THRONES THOU SAYST ARE INSECURE   • •   389 MEROPE   1532
      THE BROKEN ORDER OF YOUR DORIAN THRONES   • • • •   389 MEROPE   1546

THRONG
      GIRT WITH A THRONG OF REVELLERS BENT HIS WAY   • •   11 MYCERINUS   83
      IN HIS LIGHT YOUTH AMID A FESTAL THRONG   • • • •   166 AUSTERITY POET   3
      A SIGH A TEAR BUT IN THE THRONG   • • • • • • •   225 EPILOG LAOCOON   123
      YES ALL THIS EDDYING MOTLEY THRONG   • • • • • •   226 EPILOG LAOCOON   157
      ABOVE THE LOCKS ABOVE THE BOATING THRONG   • • • •   266 THYRSIS   122
      LOVED NOT WHO TURNEST FROM THE THRONG   • • •   314 OBERMANN MORE   71
      A WORLD THESE SOPHISTS THRONG • • • • • •   •   416 EMPEDOCLES I 2   135
      INCOMMUNICABLY THRONG   • • • • • • • • • •   455 POOR MATTHIAS   104
      AIRY ANTE-MUNDANE THRONG • • • • • • • • • •   456 POOR MATTHIAS   135
      WHILE OER THE DUSTY PLAIN THE MURMUROUS THRONG   • •   473 CROMWELL   43
      THE STRONG BLAST BROUGHT A PIGMY THRONG   • • • •   479 HAYSWATER BOAT   19

THRONGD
      IN THE THRONGD FIELDS WHERE WINNING COMES BY STRIFE   43 GIPSY CHILD   58
      IN EARTHS THRONGD FIELDS WHERE WINNING COMES BY STRIFE   43 GIPSY CHILD   V   58
      WHO THRONGD ME IN THEIR CITIES • • • • • • •   432 EMPEDOCLES II   113

THRONGING
      LET THE WILD THRONGING TRAIN   • • • • • • • • •   185 STRAYED REVEL   3
      LET THE WILD THRONGING TRAIN   • • • • • • • • •   194 STRAYED REVEL   294

THROUGHOUT
      WATCHEST US NATURE THROUGHOUT   • • • • • • • •   232 YOUTH OF MAN   9

THROW
      AND HIGH ROCKS THROW MILDLY • • • • • • • •   • •   165 FORSAKEN MERM   130
      THROW HIM A PEALING WORD OF SUMMONS DOWN   • • •   349 MEROPE   576
      THROW THE DOOR OPEN TIS DONE   • • • • • • • •   372 MEROPE   1152
      SINGLE AND FRIENDLESS THROW TO CERTAIN DEATH   • •   382 MEROPE   V1326
      A MEEK LAST GLANCE OF LOVE DIDST THROW   • • • •   450 GEISTS GRAVE   35

THROWN
      AND YOUR PROUD HEADS BACKWARD THROWN • • • • • •   32 NEW SIRENS   192
      WHICH ALL THE GODS IN SPORT HAD IDLY THROWN   • •   95 BALDER DEAD 1   3
      ONE LITTLE WANDERING ARM IS THROWN   • • • • • •   141 TRISTRAM 1   344

THROWN   (CONTINUED)
        WAS INDEED THE HEAVIEST BURDEN THROWN   . . . .   144 TRISTRAM 2   50
        WITH ECHOING STRAITS BETWEEN US THROWN   . . . .   182 TO MARG CONT   2
        SO FAR APART THEIR LIVES ARE THROWN   . . . . .   206 TOO LATE   3
        LONG SINCE HATH THROWN HER WEEDS AWAY   . . . .   304 GRANDE CHARTR   V 154
        TILL I THROWN OUT AND TIRED CAME TO HALT   . . . .   357 MEROPE   795
        AND ON WHOSE LIGHTNESS BLAME IS THROWN AWAY . .   411 EMPEDOCLES I 1   162
        FROM THAT ON WHICH HIS EXILED AGE IS THROWN . .   436 EMPEDOCLES II   263

THROWS
        WHICH IN A QUEENS SECLUDED GARDEN THROWS   . . . .   70 SOHRAB RUSTUM   315
        AND FROM HER BROWN-LOCKD HEAD THE WIMPLE THROWS . . 156 TRISTRAM 3   216
        IS FRESHEND BY THE LEAPING STREAM WHICH THROWS . .   414 EMPEDOCLES I 2   46

THRUSH
        IN THE PINES THE THRUSH IS WAKING   . . . . . .   35 NEW SIRENS   259
        THE FELL-FARES AND THE SPECKLED MISSEL-THRUSH   . .   150 TRISTRAM 3   30
        SOMETIMES A THRUSH FLIT OVERHEAD   . . . . . .   248 KENSINGTON GARD   11
        THE BROWN THRUSH CROSSES OVERHEAD   . . . . .   KENSINGTON GARD V 11

THRUST
        WOULD THRUST A HAND BEFORE THE LIFTED BOWL . . . .   11 MYCERINUS   105
        THE WORLD SHALL BE THRUST DOWN AND WE UP-BORNE . .   172 IMMORTALITY   4
        THRUST BACK NOW THE BOLT OF THAT DOOR . . . .   372 MEROPE   1147

THUNDER
        GREW BLACKER THUNDER RUMBLED IN THE AIR   . . . .   76 SOHRAB RUSTUM   500
        GREW DEEPER THUNDER CRASHD ALONG THE SKY   . . . .   76 SOHRAB RUSTUM   V 500
        AND HEARD THE THUNDER OF THE STREAMS OF HELL . .   109 BALDER DEAD 2   151
        THUNDER CRASHES FROM ROCK   . . . .   289 RUGBY CHAPEL   91
        PINND BY THE THUNDER TO REAR . . . .   293 HEINES GRAVE   31
        NOT BY THE THUNDER OF SCORN   . . . .   295 HEINES GRAVE   109
        THE EXULTING THUNDER OF YOUR RACE   . . . . .   304 GRANDE CHARTR   164
        SHE LET THE LEGIONS THUNDER PAST   . . . . .   316 OBERMANN MORE   111
        IN THESE EARS THEY THUNDER THEY RING . . . . .   346 MEROPE   500
        NOT RAIN NOT THUNDER   . . . .   398 MEROPE   1803
        THAT THY GROANS LIKE THUNDER PREST   . . . . .   430 EMPEDOCLES II   62
        THAT THY GROANS LIKE THUNDER DEEP   . . . . . .   430 EMPEDOCLES II   V 62

THUNDERED
        INTO THE SOUDANS REALM AND THUNDERED ON   . . . .   154 TRISTRAM 3   149

THUNDERERS
        SPREADING OER THE THUNDERERS FACE   . . . . . .   431 EMPEDOCLES II   68

THUNDERING
        LOUD THUNDERING BORE US BY SWIFT SWIFT IT FOAMD . .   25 DREAM   33
        THUNDERING TO EARTH AND LEAPT FROM RUSTUMS HAND . .   73 SOHRAB RUSTUM   419
        THUNDERING AND BURSTING . . . .   220 BACCHANALIA 2   29
        IN THE RUSHING THUNDERING MAD . . . .   370 MEROPE   1105

THUNDERS
        THERE THE AVALANCHE THUNDERS . . . .   175 PARTING   31
        HAD FELT HIM LIKE THE THUNDERS ROLL   . . . . . .   270 MEMORIAL VERSES   9

THWART
        THAT NATURAL CAUSES THWART THY WELFARE AND NOT FATE   EMPEDOCLES I 2   V

THWARTED
        WHEN HE IS TIED AND THWARTED FROM HIS COURSE . .   LUCRETIUS 2   3

THWARTING
        AND ALL ITS THWARTING CURRENTS OF DESIRE   . . . .   37 YOUTHS AGIT   10
        BY THWARTING SIGNS AND BRAVES . . . .   244 SUMMER NIGHT   60

THYME
        AND FROM THE THYME UPON THE HEIGHT   . . . . .   218 BACCHANALIA 1   10
        HUM OER THE THYME THE GROUSE . . . .   285 HAWORTH CHURCH   121
        AND CRISP THYME TUFTED   . . . .   392 MEROPE   1643
        OUT-PERFUMES THE THYME   . . . .   442 EMPEDOCLES II   442

THYRSIS
        THYRSIS AND I WE STILL HAD THYRSIS THEN   . . . .   263 THYRSIS   10
        THYRSIS AND I WE STILL HAD THYRSIS THEN   . . . .   263 THYRSIS   10
        BUT THYRSIS OF HIS OWN WILL WENT AWAY . . . . .   264 THYRSIS   40
        BUT THYRSIS NEVER MORE WE SWAINS SHALL SEE . . .   265 THYRSIS   77
        YET THYRSIS LET ME GIVE MY GRIEF ITS HOUR . . .   265 THYRSIS   102
        HEAR IT O THYRSIS STILL OUR TREE IS THERE . . .   267 THYRSIS   171
        THOU TOO O THYRSIS ON LIKE QUEST WAST BOUND . .   269 THYRSIS   211
        THYRSIS IN REACH OF SHEEP-BELLS IS MY HOME . . . .   269 THYRSIS   233
        THOU TOO O THYRSIS ON LIKE QUEST WERT BOUND . .   269 THYRSIS   V 211

TIBER
        BY YELLOW TIBER   . . . .   50 CONSOLATION   19

TIBERIUS
        SO TIBERIUS MIGHT HAVE SAT   . . . .   453 POOR MATTHIAS   41
        HAD TIBERIUS BEEN A CAT . . . .   453 POOR MATTHIAS   42

TIDE
          FLOWD THE HUNTERS MERRY TIDE   • • • • • • • •   13 CHURCH BROU 1   8
          WAS AT EASTER-TIDE PUT ON   • • • • • • • •   16 CHURCH BROU 1   110
          WHEN THE SLOW TIDE SETS ONE WAY   • • • • • • • •   33 NEW SIRENS   220
          A GATE SWINGS TO OUR TIDE HATH FLOWD • • • • • • •   53 RESIGNATION   48
          AND ON A FEAST-TIDE IN AFRASIABS HALL • • • • • • •   71 SOHRAB RUSTUM   355
          AND HIS SOUL SET TO GRIEF AS THE VAST TIDE • • • •   79 SOHRAB RUSTUM   616
          RUNNING FAST HOMEWARD WITH THE TURN OF TIDE • • •   69 SOHRAB RUSTUM   V 287
          WATCHING BY THE SALT SEA-TIDE   • • • • • • • •   138 TRISTRAM 1   270
          OF BUFFETING WIND AND SURGING TIDE   • • • • • • •   140 TRISTRAM 1   331
          AND QUIVERING LIPS ON WHICH THE TIDE • • • • • •   146 TRISTRAM 2   118
          BENEATH THE SALT SEA-TIDE   • • • • • • • •   160 NECKAN   32
          BENEATH THE COLD SEA TIDE   • • • • • • • •   160 NECKAN   V 32
          THE EBB-TIDE LEAVES DRY   • • • • • • • •   165 FORSAKEN MERM   135
          THE SALT TIDE ROLLS SEAWARD   • • • • • • • •   164 FORSAKEN MERM   V 110
          THE INFANT CHURCH OF LOVE SHE FELT THE TIDE • • •   172 GOOD SHEPHERD   7
          THE TIDE IS FULL THE MOON LIES FAIR • • • • • •   210 DOVER BEACH   2
          WHERE GAILY FLOWS THE HUMAN TIDE   • • • • • • •   224 EPILOG LAOCOON   108
          SEE LOW ABOVE THE TIDE AT FLOOD   • • • • • • •   274 STANZAS CARNAC   26
          BUT SLOW THAT TIDE OF COMMON THOUGHT • • • • • •   319 OBERMANN MORE   189
          THROUGH POURING TIDE HE PULLS AND DRIZZLING HAZE • •   445 WESTMIN ABBEY   29
          AND MEMORYS GUSHING TIDE SWELLS DEEP AND FULL • • •   464 ALARIC AT ROME   53
          MOURNING AS WIDOWED VENICE OER HER ADRIAN TIDE • •   468 ALARIC AT ROME   162

TIDES
          NOW THE SALT TIDES SEAWARD FLOW   • • • • • •   161 FORSAKEN MERM   5
          WHEN SPRING-TIDES ARE LOW   • • • • • • •   165 FORSAKEN MERM   127
          NOW THE SALT TIDES SEAWARDS FLOW   • • • • • •   161 FORSAKEN MERM   V   5
          THE SPRING-TIDES BRIMMING FLOW   • • • • • •   242 SUMMER NIGHT   16
          FRESHEND BY PLUNGING TIDES BY SHOWERS • • • •   275 STANZAS CARNAC   42
          THE TIDES AND THEN OF MORTAL WARS   • • • • • •   414 EMPEDOCLES I 2   72
          WE MEASURE THE SEA-TIDES WE NUMBER THE SEA-SANDS • •   423 EMPEDOCLES I 2   321
          THE FUTURE ROLLD ITS GATHERING TIDES ALONG • • •   475 CROMWELL   134

TIDINGS
          FOR HE HAD HAD SURE TIDINGS THAT THE BABE • • • •   79 SOHRAB RUSTUM   607
          WILL I SEEK TIDINGS TAKE THE WHILE THIS WORD • •   368 MEROPE   1078

TIE
          ALL TIE WITH ALL BESIDE SEEMD VAIN AND CHEAP • •   173 MONICAS PRAYER   10
          THAT NEITHER GRATITUDE NOR TIE OF RACE • • • •   389 MEROPE   1525
          THOUGH EVERY HOLIEST FEELING EVERY TIE • • • •   467 ALARIC AT ROME   145

TIED
          TIED UNDER THE ARCHEST CHIN   • • • • • • • •   23 MEMORY-PICTURE   27
          HE PASSD AND TIED HIS SANDALS ON HIS FEET • • • •   64 SOHRAB RUSTUM   97
          AND TIED HIM IN A YARD AT AUTUMN SEES • • • • •   129 BALDER DEAD 3   560
          NODDED AND TIED HER PALFREY TO A TREE • • • •   155 TRISTRAM 3   212
          A TRAMP I SAW ILL MOODY AND TONGUE-TIED • • • •   169 WEST LONDON   2
          SEEN BY RARE GLIMPSES PENSIVE AND TONGUE-TIED • •   256 SCHOLAR-GIPSY   54
          WHEN HE IS TIED AND THWARTED FROM HIS COURSE • •   LUCRETIUS 2   3

TIES
          WHICH CONSECRATES THE TIES OF BLOOD FOR THESE INDEED 196 FRAG ANTIGONE   31
          TIES STRAITLY UP FROM MINE THY LOT   • • • • • •   208 ON THE RHINE   8

TIGHT
          THEN HE DISMOUNTED AND DREW TIGHT THE GIRTHS   • •   109 BALDER DEAD 2   146
          YET STARK FROM THE DEATH-STRUGGLE TIGHT-CLENCHD HANDS 373 MEROPE   1174

TIGHTEN
          TIGHTEN THE GIRTHS OF SLEIPNER ODINS HORSE • • • •   100 BALDER DEAD 1   169
          THE TEMPLES TIGHTEN AND THROB THERE • • • • • •   435 EMPEDOCLES II   216

TIGHTNESS
          PUT TIGHTNESS IN THY GOLD-EMBOSSED REIN   • • • •   349 MEROPE   574

TILL
          TILL THAT HOUR SHE NEVER SORROWD   • • • • • • •   14 CHURCH BROU 1   59
          TILL THE CHURCH WAS ROOFD AND DONE   • • • • • •   16 CHURCH BROU 1   102
          TO HUNT THE BOAR IN THE CRISP WOODS TILL EVE   • •   18 CHURCH BROU 3   11
          TILL AT EVENING WE DESCRY   • • • • • • •   27 NEW SIRENS   46
          TILL SHE SEARCH AND LEARN HER OWN   • • • • • •   28 NEW SIRENS   74
          CAUGHT NOT TILL THEN A SENSE   • • • • • • •   47 WORLD QUIETIST   22
          TILL DEATH ARRIVE TO SUPERSEDE   • • • • • • •   56 RESIGNATION   142
          TILL DEATH ARRIVES TO SUPERSEDE   • • • • • •   56 RESIGNATION   V 142
          AND FIGHT BENEATH MY BANNER TILL I DIE   • • • •   71 SOHRAB RUSTUM   332
          OR ELSE THY BONES SHALL STREW THIS SAND TILL WINDS   72 SOHRAB RUSTUM   376
          NEVER TILL NOW DEFILED SANK TO THE DUST   • • • •   76 SOHRAB RUSTUM   498
          AND I WERE THAT WHICH TILL TO-DAY I WAS   • • • •   77 SOHRAB RUSTUM   545
          OH COULD I LIVE TILL I THAT GRIEF HAD SEEN • • •   78 SOHRAB RUSTUM   588
          TILL THEN IF FATE SO WILLS LET ME ENDURE • • •   85 SOHRAB RUSTUM   837
          TILL NOW ALL STRENGTH WAS EBBD AND FROM HIS LIMBS   86 SOHRAB RUSTUM   853
          A FOILD CIRCUITOUS WANDERER TILL AT LAST • • •   87 SOHRAB RUSTUM   888
          NEVER DEFACD TILL NOW SHAMD TO THE DUST   • • •   76 SOHRAB RUSTUM   V 498
          NEVER TILL NOW DEFILED SUNK TO THE DUST   • • •   76 SOHRAB RUSTUM   V 498
          AND I WERE HE WHO TILL TO-DAY I WAS • • • • •   77 SOHRAB RUSTUM   V 545
          I WILL NOT STIR TILL I BE JUDGED   • • • • • •   91 SICK KING BOKH   104
          TILL THAT THE KING STOOD FORTH AND SAID   • • •   91 SICK KING BOKH   107
          TILL THEN IN PERIL OR IN PAIN WE LIVE   • • •   111 BALDER DEAD 2   225
          HOWBEIT WE ABIDE OUR DAY TILL THEN   • • • • • •   111 BALDER DEAD 2   227

TILL   (CONTINUED)
         OF WOOD AND FRAMEDST MEN WHO TILL THE EARTH   • •   121 BALDER DEAD 3   269
         TILL THEY RULE IT TILL HE SEEM • • • • • • •   •   136 TRISTRAM 1   184
         TILL THEY RULE IT TILL HE SEEM • • • • • • •   •   136 TRISTRAM 1   184
         WOULD CHARM THE GAZER TILL HIS THOUGHT   • • • •   147 TRISTRAM 2   139
         AND THEY WOULD STILL HAVE LISTEND TILL DARK NIGHT   151 TRISTRAM 3   56
         TILL FOR ITS SAKE ALONE WE LIVE AND MOVE   • • •   153 TRISTRAM 3   129
         IS MERLIN PRISONER TILL THE JUDGMENT-DAY   • • •   156 TRISTRAM 3   222
         TILL THE SPINDLE DROPS FROM HER HAND • • • • • •   164 FORSAKEN MERM   96
         TILL THE SHUTTLE FALLS FROM HER HAND   • • • • •   164 FORSAKEN MERM   V   96
         MIS-DEFINE THESE TILL GOD KNOWS THEM NO MORE   • •   171 DIVINITY   10
         GO THEN TILL TIME AND FATE IMPRESS   • • • • •   179 FAREWELL   41
         TILL THEY TOO FADE LIKE GRASS THEY CRAWL   • • •   193 STRAYED REVEL   242
         TILL THE FATES COME AGAIN THIS TIME WITH DEATH • • •   195 FRAG ANTIGONE   16
         TILL THE FATES COME AGAIN ALONE WITH DEATH • • • •   195 FRAG ANTIGONE   V   16
         AH MAY SHE SCORN THEM STILL TILL WE   • • • • •   202 URANIA   15
         THEN WILL SHE WEEP WITH SMILES TILL THEN   • • •   202 URANIA   29
         TILL THEN HER LOVELY EYES MAINTAIN   • • • • •   202 URANIA   31
         TILL ALL HAVE BEEN FULFILLD   • • • • • • • •   237 PROGRESS   12
         TILL ALL SHALL BE FULFILLD   • • • • • • • •   237 PROGRESS   V   12
         TILL ALL HATH BEEN FULFILLD   • • • • • • •   237 PROGRESS   V   12
         NOT TILL THE HOURS OF LIGHT RETURN   • • • • •   241 MORALITY   11
         THERE LET ME GAZE TILL I BECOME   • • • • • •   251 WISH   41
         AND HERE TILL SUN-DOWN SHEPHERD WILL I BE   • •   255 SCHOLAR-GIPSY   22
         TILL HAVING USED OUR NERVES WITH BLISS AND TEEN • •   259 SCHOLAR-GIPSY   147
         WOODS WITH ANEMONIES IN FLOWER TILL MAY   • • •   268 THYRSIS   199
         LEFT HUMAN HAUNT AND ON ALONE TILL NIGHT   • • •   269 THYRSIS   230
         WHY FAINTEST THOU I WANDERD TILL I DIED   • • •   269 THYRSIS   237
         FOR FOOD TO KEEP HIM TILL HE END   • • • • •   278 SOUTHERN NIGHT   83
         WE WHO TILL THEN IN THY SHADE   • • • • • •   287 RUGBY CHAPEL   31
         TILL I POSSESS MY SOUL AGAIN   • • • • • •   302 GRANDE CHARTR   94
         TILL FREE MY THOUGHTS BEFORE ME ROLL   • • • •   302 GRANDE CHARTR   95
         BUT TILL THEY RISE ALLOW OUR TEARS   • • • • •   304 GRANDE CHARTR   V 162
         DO THOU TILL FOR THINE ENTRANCE TO THIS HOUSE   332 MEROPE   66
         TILL NOW AND I HAVE STRENGTH TO CHAIN IT STILL   • •   334 MEROPE   150
         TILL THE SINNER THE VENGEANCE BE RIPE   • • • •   347 MEROPE   528
         TILL I THROWN OUT AND TIRED CAME TO HALT   • • •   357 MEROPE   795
         COUNTING TILL I GREW UP THE LAGGARD YEARS   • • •   367 MEROPE   1046
         PERMIT NO PEACE TILL YOUR BEHESTS ARE DONE   • •   367 MEROPE   1057
         THE TOILS OF THY FOUL SERVICE TILL THOU WAKE   •   373 MEROPE   1181
         NOT TILL THE WAYS OF PRUDENCE ALL ARE TRIED   •   384 MEROPE   1386
         TILL PRESENTLY THE KING CAME FORTH IN ROBE • • •   401 MEROPE   1903
         TILL THEN WE ALL SEEMD STONE BUT THEN A CRY   •   402 MEROPE   1930
         HERE WILL I STAY TILL THE SLOW LITTER COMES   •   407 EMPEDOCLES I 1   18
         TILL THE SLOW MULES SHOULD CLIMB IN SIGHT AGAIN • •   408 EMPEDOCLES I 1   48
         CROUCH IN THE WOOD FIRST TILL THE MULES HAVE PASSD   408 EMPEDOCLES I 1   50
         CROUCH IN THE BRUSHWOOD TILL THE MULES HAVE PASSD   411 EMPEDOCLES I 1   166
         THEN PLAY THY KIND PART WELL FAREWELL TILL NIGHT • •   411 EMPEDOCLES I 1   167
         TILL THE ROUGH COW-HERDS DRIVE THEM PAST   • •   413 EMPEDOCLES I 2   40
         CHANGEFUL TILL NOW WE STILL   • • • • • • •   425 EMPEDOCLES I 2   377
         TILL MINE EYES ACHE WITH THE LONG SPECTACLE   •   428 EMPEDOCLES I 2   475
         TILL MY EYES ACHE WITH THE LONG SPECTACLE • • •   428 EMPEDOCLES I 2   V 475
         AND HAUNT HIM TILL THE ABSENCE FROM HIMSELF   •   435 EMPEDOCLES II   225
         TILL THE SAND THY FEATHERS SMIRCH   • • • • •   456 POOR MATTHIAS   129
         TILL WHAT AT MORNINGS HOUR LOOKT WARM AND BRIGHT •   466 ALARIC AT ROME   107
         TILL FANCIFUL REGRET AND DREAMY WOE   • • • •   467 ALARIC AT ROME   125
         TILL ALL BRIGHT THOUGHTS THAT HILLS OR WAVES CAN YIELD   472 CROMWELL   33
         TILL WITH HIS DAILY LIFE A LIFE THAT THREW   • •   473 CROMWELL   55
         TILL LIFE UNSTIRRD BY ACTION LIFE BECAME   • •   473 CROMWELL   59
         TILL THE PALE MONARCH AND THE LONG ARRAY   • • •   477 CROMWELL   197
         STAY THIS HAND FROM FIGHT TILL THE TROJANS   HOMER TRANS   62
              ARE UTTERLY ROUTED

TILLD
         OUT OF A TILLD FIELD INLAND THEN THE WIND   • • •   124 BALDER DEAD 3   363
         CREEPS OVER IT FROM THE TILLD FIELDS BEHIND   •   149 TRISTRAM 3   9
         CREEPS OVER IT FROM THE TILLD LAND BEHIND   • • •   TRISTRAM 3   V   9
         STEALS OVER IT FROM THE TILLD LAND BEHIND   • •   TRISTRAM 3   V   9
         STEALS OVER IT FROM THE TILLD FIELDS BEHIND   • •   TRISTRAM 3   V   9

TILPHUSA
         COLD BUBBLED THE SPRING OF TILPHUSA • • • • •   • •   229 YOUTH OF NATURE   36

TILT
         INTO THE TILT-YARD WHERE THE HEROES FOUGHT • • • •   105 BALDER DEAD 2   30

TIME
         SIX YEARS SIX LITTLE YEARS SIX DROPS OF TIME   • •   10 MYCERINUS   61
         WHERE IN ONE DREAM THE FEVERISH TIME OF YOUTH   • •   11 MYCERINUS   89
         BUT ELSE IT IS A LONELY TIME   • • • • • •   17 CHURCH BROU 2   23
         TIME YOUR MASTER GOVERNS ME   • • • • • • • •   24 MEMORY-PICTURE   54
         TIME IS LAME AND WE GREW WEARY • • • • • • •   28 NEW SIRENS   67
         TIME IS LAME AND WE GROW WEARY • • • • • • •   28 NEW SIRENS   V   67
         A THOUSAND VIRTUES IN THIS HATED TIME   • • •   37 YOUTHS AGIT   8
         WHAT WONDER SHALL TIME BREED TO SWELL THY STRAIN • •   43 GIPSY CHILD   43
         CEASES NOT FROM ALL TIME TO HEAVE AND GROAN   •   45 IN UTRUMQUE PAR   26
         GREY TIME-WORN MARBLES   • • • • • • • • •   50 CONSOLATION   16
         TIME STAND STILL HERE   • • • • • • • • •   51 CONSOLATION   50
         TIME GIVES HIS HOUR-GLASS   • • • • • • •   51 CONSOLATION   53
         TIME SO COMPLAIND OF   • • • • • • • •   52 CONSOLATION   71
         NOT NOW A TIME WILL COME TO EAT AND DRINK   • • •   67 SOHRAB RUSTUM   208

TIME   (CONTINUED)
            BY THEIR DARK SPRINGS THE WIND IN WINTER-TIME   . .   73 SOHRAB RUSTUM   413
            HIS HEAD BUT THIS TIME ALL THE BLADE LIKE GLASS   . .   76 SOHRAB RUSTUM   511
            THEY THREE IN THAT LONG-DISTANT SUMMER-TIME   . .   79 SOHRAB RUSTUM   628
            AND THEY WHO WERE CALLD CHAMPIONS IN THEIR TIME   . .   85 SOHRAB RUSTUM   811
            EVER SINCE PRAYER-TIME HE DOTH WAIT   . . . . . .   88 SICK KING BOKH   14
            THREE DAYS SINCE AT THE TIME OF PRAYER   . .   88 SICK KING BOKH   30
            BUT WHO THROUGH ALL THIS LENGTH OF TIME   . . . .   92 SICK KING BOKH   145
            AND THAT IT BE NOT FROM ALL TIME   . . .   94 SICK KING BOKH   207
            NOW TIME OBSCURES IT AND MENS LATER DEEDS   . . . .   117 BALDER DEAD 3   130
            FOR THE LAST TIME FOR HERE THOU COMST NO MORE . . .   125 BALDER DEAD 3   420
            THEREFORE FOR THE LAST TIME O BALDER HAIL   . . .   126 BALDER DEAD 3   453
            BUT ONE POSSESSD HIS WANING TIME   . . . . . .   132 TRISTRAM 1   70
            CHANGES PLACE AND TIME OF YEAR   . . . . . .   133 TRISTRAM 1   89
            THINND AND PALED BEFORE HIS TIME   . . . . . .   134 TRISTRAM 1   108
            ALL THE SPRING-TIME OF HIS LOVE   . . . . . .   136 TRISTRAM 1   173
            ERASED THE RAVAGES OF TIME   . . . .   147 TRISTRAM 2   140
            TWILL BE EASTER-TIME IN THE WORLD AH ME   . . . .   163 FORSAKEN MERM   58
            AND POINTS US TO A BETTER TIME THAN OURS   . . . .   170 WEST LONDON   14
            GO THEN TILL TIME AND FATE IMPRESS   . . . . . .   179 FAREWELL   41
            PASSD THROUGH THE CRUCIBLE OF TIME   . . . . . .   184 TERRACE BERNE   36
            THIS LONG TIME RUMOURS   . . . .   189 STRAYED REVEL   109
            PARCH THEM IN WINTER-TIME ON THE BARE STEPP   . . .   193 STRAYED REVEL   241
            TILL THE FATES COME AGAIN THIS TIME WITH DEATH . .   195 FRAG ANTIGONE   16
            SPEAK OF THE SURE CONSOLATIONS OF TIME   . . . .   206 SEPARATION   2
            DAYS AND YEARS AND TIME   . . . .   233 YOUTH OF MAN   40
            I KNEW NOT YET THE GAUGE OF TIME   . . . . . .   242 MORALITY   31
            YET STILL FROM TIME TO TIME VAGUE AND FORLORN   . .   247 BURIED LIFE   72
            YET STILL FROM TIME TO TIME VAGUE AND FORLORN   . .   247 BURIED LIFE   72
            ON THE BREAST OF THE RIVER OF TIME   . . . . . .   251 FUTURE   3
            OF THE LANDS WHICH THE RIVER OF TIME   . . . . . .   252 FUTURE   21
            AS SHE WAS BY THE SOURCES OF TIME   . . . . . .   252 FUTURE   28
            THIS TRACT WHICH THE RIVER OF TIME   . . . . . .   253 FUTURE   50
            FOR EVER THE COURSE OF THE RIVER OF TIME   . . . .   253 FUTURE   59
            HAPLY THE RIVER OF TIME   . . . .   253 FUTURE   71
            AND EVERY DOUBT LONG BLOWN BY TIME AWAY   . . . .   261 SCHOLAR-GIPSY   200
            BY BARN IN THRESHING-TIME BY NEW-BUILT RICK   . . .   263 THYRSIS   34
            FOR TIME NOT CORYDON HATH CONQUERD THEE   . . . .   265 THYRSIS   80
            THE CORONALS OF THAT FORGOTTEN TIME   . . . . . .   266 THYRSIS   117
            HERE CAMST THOU IN THY JOCUND YOUTHFUL TIME   . . .   269 THYRSIS   218
            HAD FALLEN ON THIS IRON TIME   . . . .   271 MEMORIAL VERSES   43
            TIME MAY RESTORE US IN HIS COURSE   . . . . . .   272 MEMORIAL VERSES   60
            WAS FALLEN ON THE IRON TIME   . . . .   271 MEMORIAL VERSES V 43
            TIME MAY RESTORE US IN ITS COURSE   . . . . . .   272 MEMORIAL VERSES V 60
            WON CONSECRATION FROM TIME   . . . .   281 HAWORTH CHURCH   46
            THIS SEA OF TIME WHEREON WE SAIL   . . . . . .   303 GRANDE CHARTR   122
            YOU TRIUMPH OVER TIME AND SPACE   . . . . . .   304 GRANDE CHARTR   166
            OF A TREMENDOUS TIME   . . . .   308 OBERMANN   66
            WE HAVE HAD TIME TO BREATHE   . . . .   308 OBERMANN   76
            OF EUROPES STORMIEST TIME   . . . .   308 OBERMANN   V 66
            AND UNSPENT ALL THAT TIME   . . . .   318 OBERMANN MORE   162
            HANG WEEDS OF OUR SAD TIME   . . . .   323 OBERMANN MORE   308
            THE CARES WHICH MIGHT IN ME WITH TIME I FEEL . . .   335 MEROPE   161
            WHILE ALL THIS TIME I BEAR TO LINGER ON   . . . .   366 MEROPE   1017
            MOTHER MY HEART RUNS OVER BUT THE TIME   . . . .   378 MEROPE   1232
            AND THE SLOW-RIPENING TIME AT LAST PREPARES   . . .   379 MEROPE   1264
            ZEAL MAKES HIM MOST UNJUST BUT IN GOOD TIME   . . .   386 MEROPE   1438
            A TIME WILL COME FOR GREETINGS BUT TO-DAY   . . . .   386 MEROPE   1444
            DID EVER BURN IS LONG BY TIME ALLAYD   . . . . . .   387 MEROPE   1471
            TIME PRESSES SO THAT THEME FORBEAR I NOW   . . . .   389 MEROPE   1530
            YET HAST BEEN LONG AT SCHOOL WITH THOUGHTFUL TIME   394 MEROPE   1708
            FOR THE LAST TIME I ASK ASK EARNESTLY   . . . . .   394 MEROPE   1717
            NOT TIME NOT LIGHTNING   . . . .   398 MEROPE   1802
            HE LOVES THAT IN THEE TOO THERE WAS A TIME   . . .   409 EMPEDOCLES I 1   79
            SWELLS WITH THE SWELLING EVIL OF THIS TIME . . . .   410 EMPEDOCLES I 1   113
            WHICH MAKES THE TIME LOOK BLACK AND SAD TO HIM . .   411 EMPEDOCLES I 1   153
            FILL THEE TO SEE OUR TIME   . . . .   416 EMPEDOCLES I 2   113
            SO EACH NEW MAN STRIKES ROOT INTO A FAR FORE-TIME   418 EMPEDOCLES I 2   191
            I HAVE SEEN MANY CITIES IN MY TIME   . . . . . .   428 EMPEDOCLES I 2   474
            TO KNOW THOSE SPELLS OF TIME THAT STAY THEIR HAND   413 EMPEDOCLES I 2 V 25
            WHAT LIFE AND TIME GO HARD WITH THEE TOO AS WITH US   416 EMPEDOCLES I 2 V 116
            SEED-TIME AND HARVEST   . . . .   436 EMPEDOCLES II   254
            YET IN THIS LATTER TIME   . . . .   446 WESTMIN ABBEY   71
            THOUGHTS OF THE PAST AND OF THE FUTURE TIME   . . .   467 ALARIC AT ROME   128
            NOT THIS THE TIME TO WEEP UPON THE BIER   . . . .   467 ALARIC AT ROME   135
            AND THOUGHTS THAT WERE BUT OUTLINES TIME ENGRAVES   473 CROMWELL   47
            TRULY YET THIS TIME WILL WE SAVE THEE MIGHTY ACHILLES   HOMER TRANS   47
            WHERE TIME ELSE DUMB HATH SIGNIFIED HIS SWAY   . .   FRAGMENT 2   2
            SOONER THAN THOSE TWIN REACHES OF GREAT TIME   . .   FRAGMENT 5   7

TIMES
            TIMES GAY MINIONS PLEASED YOU SEE   . . . . . .   24 MEMORY-PICTURE   53
            AH TOO TRUE TIMES CURRENT STRONG   . . . . . .   24 MEMORY-PICTURE   57
            TIMES CHAFING PRISONER ASK IT NOW   . . . . . .   53 RESIGNATION   39
            FOR THEM FOR ALL TIMES BUSY TOUCH   . . . . . .   56 RESIGNATION   126
            FAUSTA TIMES PAST WITH TIMES THAT ARE   . . . .   56 RESIGNATION   137
            FAUSTA TIMES PAST WITH TIMES THAT ARE   . . . .   56 RESIGNATION   137
            THE MEN OF FORMER TIMES HAD CROWND THE TOP   . . .   61 SOHRAB RUSTUM   20
            WAITING THE DARKNESS OF THE FINAL TIMES   . . . .   98 BALDER DEAD 1   124
            IN TIMES LESS ALIEN TO A SPIRIT MILD   . . . . . .   128 BALDER DEAD 3   512

TIMES   (CONTINUED)

NINE TIMES SHE WAVED THE FLUTTERING WIMPLE ROUND	156	TRISTRAM 3	219
UPON TIMES BARREN STORMY FLOW	183	ABSENCE	19
COME AS THOU CAMST A THOUSAND TIMES	208	LONGING	5
AND THE TIMES THAT BRIGHT APOLLO	214	NEW ROME	7
OF THE TIMES WHICH HAD SHELTERD HIS YOUTH	229	YOUTH OF NATURE	30
THE CHILDRENS SHOUTS AND AT TIMES	234	YOUTH OF MAN	72
AND MAN HAS TURND THEM MANY TIMES MADE GREECE	239	REVOLUTIONS	5
AND ABOVE GODSTOW BRIDGE WHEN HAY-TIMES HERE	257	SCHOLAR-GIPSY	91
LOVELY ALL TIMES SHE LIES LOVELY TO-NIGHT	263	THYRSIS	21
BUT A DEAD TIMES EXPLODED DREAM	302	GRANDE CHARTR	98
AND MANY TIMES THAT MORN WE COURSED IN RING	357	MEROPE	793
FIXD YESTERDAY AND TEN TIMES CHANGED SINCE THEN	389	MEROPE	1547
A THOUSAND TIMES HAVE I BEEN HERE ALONE	406	EMPEDOCLES I 1	7
STRAIGHTWAY THOU FALLEST TO ARRAIGN THE TIMES	411	EMPEDOCLES I 1	144
TIS NOT THE TIMES TIS NOT THE SOPHISTS VEX HIM	411	EMPEDOCLES I 1	150
WHICH MAKES THE TIMES LOOK BLACK AND SAD TO HIM	411	EMPEDOCLES I 1 V	153
AND SO CHANGE BACK AND MANY THOUSAND TIMES	435	EMPEDOCLES II	229
AND WE SHALL FLY FOR REFUGE TO PAST TIMES	440	EMPEDOCLES II	383
TO NAME FOR FUTURE TIMES TO KNOW	452	GEISTS GRAVE	79
OR TIMES STERN HAND WHY BLOTS IT NOT AWAY	462	ALARIC AT ROME	5
YES THERE ARE STAINS TIMES FINGERS CANNOT BLOT	462	ALARIC AT ROME	14
TELL OF OLD TIMES AND HOLIEST MEMORIES	467	ALARIC AT ROME	124
HOW EVERY BIRTH OF TIMES MIRACULOUS WOMB	469	ALARIC AT ROME	191
OH THAT PAST TIMES COULD GIVE OUR DAY	482	COURAGE	27
THE COMING SPRING-TIMES EARLIEST STIR	483	ROME-SICKNESS	6

TIMID

OF HIS TIMID YOUTHFUL BRIDE	137	TRISTRAM 1	214

TIMOROUS

THY HOPES GROW TIMOROUS AND UNFIXD THY POWERS	261	SCHOLAR-GIPSY	227
KNOWEST THOU NOT HOW TIMOROUS HOW UNSURE	381	MEROPE	1311

TINGE

A TINGE IT MAY BE OF THEIR SILENT PAIN	244	SUMMER NIGHT	84

TINGED

YET TINGED WITH INFINITE DESIRE	314	OBERMANN MORE	51

TINKLE

THE TINKLE OF THE THIRSTY RILL	217	BACCHANALIA 1	2

TINKLING

WAYS FOR THE TINKLING KINE	312	OBERMANN MORE V	16
THEIR TINKLING BELLS MIXD WITH THE SONG OF BIRDS	407	EMPEDOCLES I 1	28

TINT

HOW EACH BRIGHT TINT OF TREE AND FLOWER AND HEATH	466	ALARIC AT ROME	101

TINTS

A CHEQUER-WORK OF GLOWING SAPPHIRE-TINTS	18	CHURCH BROU 3	23
AND LOOKING DOWN ON THE WARM ROSY TINTS	18	CHURCH BROU 3	28

TINY

WHERE ARE THE MOWERS WHO AS THE TINY SWELL	266	THYRSIS	127
DEAD AND MUTE OUR TINY FRIEND	452	POOR MATTHIAS	14
YET POOR BIRD THY TINY CORSE	454	POOR MATTHIAS	83
TINY THOUGH THOU ART TO STRAY	458	POOR MATTHIAS	208

TIPPD

HER ROSARY-BEADS OF EBONY TIPPD WITH GOLD	152	TRISTRAM 3	93

TIRE

MIGHT WANDER ALL DAY LONG AND NEVER TIRE	11	MYCERINUS	91
THY DAZZLING LIGHT AN EAGLES GAZE SHOULD TIRE	463	ALARIC AT ROME	32

TIRED

SLOW AND TIRED CAME THE HUNTERS	14	CHURCH BROU 1	41
BUT HER HEART WAS TIRED TIRED	21	REQUIESCAT	7
BUT HER HEART WAS TIRED TIRED	21	REQUIESCAT	7
BRUSHES ACROSS A TIRED TRAVELLERS FACE	101	BALDER DEAD 1	231
AND FREA SEALD HER TIRED LIDS WITH SLEEP	103	BALDER DEAD 1	279
AH TIRED MADCAPS YOU LIE STILL	141	TRISTRAM 1	351
ART TIRED WITH HUNTING	188	STRAYED REVEL	72
AND FAIN WOULD ZEUS HAVE SAVED HIS TIRED SON	198	FRAG ANTIGONE	90
THOU ART TIRED BEST BE STILL	215	LAST WORD	8
FROM THEIR TIRED HANDS AND REST	243	SUMMER NIGHT	44
WHERE THE TIRED ANGLER LIES STRETCHD OUT	248	KENSINGTON GARD	18
AND THE TIRED MEN AND DOGS ALL GONE TO REST	255	SCHOLAR-GIPSY	7
WHO TIRED OF KNOCKING AT PREFERMENTS DOOR	256	SCHOLAR-GIPSY	35
AND TIRED UPON A THOUSAND SCHEMES OUR WIT	259	SCHOLAR-GIPSY	148
WHICH TASKD THY PIPE TOO SORE AND TIRED THY THROAT	269	THYRSIS	225
TILL I THROWN OUT AND TIRED CAME TO HALT	357	MEROPE	795
AND THE TIRED CENTAURS COME TO REST	414	EMPEDOCLES I 2	63
SAY MY FATHER DOES THE TIRED		META CLOISTER	29

TIRELESS

YOUR PRIDE OF LIFE YOUR TIRELESS POWERS	304	GRANDE CHARTR	167
BUT KAI A TIRELESS SHEPHERD-LAD	460	KAISER DEAD	44

TIRESIAS
    THEY SEE TIRESIAS . . . . 190 STRAYED REVEL 135
    TIRESIAS BUT THE GODS . . . . 192 STRAYED REVEL 213
    TIRESIAS DRANK AND DIED . . . . 229 YOUTH OF NATURE 45

TISAMENUS
    SLEW THEIR ENEMIES KING TISAMENUS . . . . . . 344 MEROPE 451

TISSUE
    LIKE THE SOILD TISSUE OF WHITE VIOLETS . . . . 86 SOHRAB RUSTUM 844

TITAN
    STORMILY SWEET HIS TITAN-AGONY . . . . 166 PICT NEWSTEAD 3
    THE WEARY TITAN WITH DEAF . . . . 295 HEINES GRAVE 88
    OF THE MOUNTAIN-CRUSHD TORTURED INTRACTABLE TITAN KING 432 EMPEDOCLES II 98

TITANIC
    WHICH SERVED FOR THAT TITANIC STRIFE . . . . . 270 MEMORIAL VERSES 14
    SUFFICD FOR THAT TITANIC STRIFE . . . . . . 270 MEMORIAL VERSES V 14
    WHICH FLOWD FOR THAT TITANIC STRIFE . . . . . 270 MEMORIAL VERSES V 14

TITANS
    THE TOO-DARING TITANS BONES . . . . PILLARS UNIVERS 12

TITLE
    AND TO AN UNSUBSTANTIAL TITLE HEIR . . . . . . 335 MEROPE 170
    NO TITLE FROM THE GODS TO WELFARE AND REPOSE . . 417 EMPEDOCLES I 2 161

TITTLE
    NO JOT NO TITTLE FROM THE LAW SHALL PASS . . . . 237 PROGRESS 11

TMOLUS
    AND TMOLUS HILL AND SMYRNA BAY THOUGH BLIND . . 2 TO A FRIEND 4
    AND TMOLUS HILL AND SMYRNAS BAY THOUGH BLIND . . 2 TO A FRIEND V 4

TOGETHER
    LAST NIGHT WE STOOD EARNESTLY TALKING TOGETHER . . 19 MODERN SAPPHO 9
    TOGETHER AS TWO EAGLES ON ONE PREY . . . . . . 75 SOHRAB RUSTUM 472
    COME RUSHING DOWN TOGETHER FROM THE CLOUDS . . . 75 SOHRAB RUSTUM 473
    DASHD WITH A CLANG TOGETHER AND A DIN . . . . 75 SOHRAB RUSTUM 475
    DREW CLOSE TOGETHER AND CONFERRD . . . . . . 91 SICK KING BOKH 106
    WANDERING TOGETHER THROUGH THAT GLOOMY WORLD . . 104 BALDER DEAD 1 328
    THE GODS HELD TALK TOGETHER GROUPD IN KNOTS . . 113 BALDER DEAD 3 1
    AND THEY RODE HOME TOGETHER THROUGH THE WOOD . . 123 BALDER DEAD 3 329
    SAY I CHARGD HER THAT YE LIVE TOGETHER . . . . 145 TRISTRAM 2 V 95
    THEY SATE THEM DOWN TOGETHER AND A SLEEP . . . 155 TRISTRAM 3 213
    TOGETHER WE HAD GROWN TOGETHER LIVED . . . . . 334 MEROPE 123
    TOGETHER WE HAD GROWN TOGETHER LIVED . . . . . 334 MEROPE 123
    TOGETHER TO THIS ISLE OF PELOPS CAME . . . . . 334 MEROPE 124
    TOGETHER WON THIS FAIR MESSENIAN LAND . . . . . 334 MEROPE 126
    THAT OUR JOINT HANDS MIGHT THEN TOGETHER PAY . . 367 MEROPE 1047
    TOGETHER WE HAD SPRUNG TOGETHER LIVED . . . . . 334 MEROPE V 123
    TOGETHER WE HAD SPRUNG TOGETHER LIVED . . . . . 334 MEROPE V 123
    OR PREST TOGETHER . . . . 460 KAISER DEAD 52
    THOU WONDROUS CHAOS WHERE TOGETHER DWELL . . . . 463 ALARIC AT ROME 43
    THERE THOU TOO SHALT LIVE WITH US TOGETHER . . . 482 THEKLAS ANSWER 13

TOIL
    OF TOIL UNSEVERD FROM TRANQUILLITY . . . . . . 1 QUIET WORK 5
    MANS FITFUL UPROAR MINGLING WITH HIS TOIL . . . 1 QUIET WORK 10
    MANS WEAK COMPLAININGS MINGLING WITH HIS TOIL . . 1 QUIET WORK V 10
    MANS SENSELESS UPROAR MINGLING WITH HIS TOIL . . 1 QUIET WORK V 10
    OUR SENSELESS UPROAR MINGLING WITH OUR TOIL . . 1 QUIET WORK V 10
    TOIL ENDED THROUGH THE SHINING STREETS . . . . 57 RESIGNATION 167
    WHO WHILE THE MOTHER SPAKE HAD CEASED THEIR TOIL . 100 BALDER DEAD 1 195
    MOCKING AND HERMOD KNEW THEIR TOIL WAS VAIN . . 123 BALDER DEAD 3 356
    OF PORT THEY HAD MAKES BITTERER FAR THEIR TOIL . 124 BALDER DEAD 3 367
    NOT WITH LOST TOIL THOU LABOUREST THROUGH THE NIGHT 169 EAST LONDON 13
    THEIR LIVES AND FORMER VIOLENT TOIL IN THEBES . . 193 STRAYED REVEL 256
    OF TOIL AND DOLOUR UNTOLD . . . . 199 FRAG DEJANEIRA 19
    OF TOIL HE MUST LIFES MOVEMENT TELL . . . . . 225 EPILOG LAOCOON 140
    WITH HEADS BENT OER THEIR TOIL THEY LANGUIDLY . . 243 SUMMER NIGHT 39
    WHO THOUGH SO NOBLE SHARE IN THE WORLDS TOIL . . 244 SUMMER NIGHT 81
    WITH PUBLIC TOIL AND PRIVATE TEEN . . . . . . 276 SOUTHERN NIGHT 27
    TOIL OR DEJECTION HAVE TRIED . . . . 290 RUGBY CHAPEL 136
    UNSPARING IN HIS SERVICE OF HIS TOIL . . . . . 404 MEROPE 1975
    THROUGH THIS SHARP TOIL-SET LIFE . . . . . . 421 EMPEDOCLES I 2 268
    HATH TOIL PERPETUALLY . . . . 422 EMPEDOCLES I 2 294
    HAS TOIL PERPETUALLY . . . . 422 EMPEDOCLES I 2 V 294
    NOR DOES HEAVEN TOIL THEREAT . . . . EMPEDOCLES I 2 V
    THE YEARS OF TOIL ALL ALL WERE WRITTEN THERE . . 478 CROMWELL 206

TOILD
    IN WHICH THEY HAVE TOILD ALL NIGHT FROM CATANA . 406 EMPEDOCLES I 1 4

TOILING
    RARER SECRETS THAN THE TOILING HEAD . . . . . 28 NEW SIRENS 80
    AND ONE THE STRONG MUCH-TOILING SAGE . . . . . 308 OBERMANN 51

TOILS

THE TOILS OF THY FOUL SERVICE TILL THOU WAKE • • 373 MEROPE 1181
STILL TOILS TO PERFECT WHAT THE CHILD BEGAN • • 473 CROMWELL 46

TOILSOME

OF TOILSOME MANHOOD IN THE DREAMS OF YOUTH • • • • 474 CROMWELL 98

TOLD

AND NOW THEIR YEARS ARE TOLD • • • • • • • • 48 HORATIAN ECHO 30
HAVE TOLD THEE FALSE THOU ART NOT RUSTUMS SON • • 80 SOHRAB RUSTUM 644
MY MOTHER TOLD ME OF THEE THOU BRAVE STEED • • • 83 SOHRAB RUSTUM 743
BUT WHEN ONE TOLD HIM HE IS DEAD • • • • • • 91 SICK KING BOKH 126
TOLD THEM AN OLD-WORLD BRETON HISTORY • • • • • 150 TRISTRAM 3 37
AND AT HER PRIE-DIEU KNEEL UNTIL SHE HAVE TOLD • 152 TRISTRAM 3 92
SHE HERSELF LOVES THEM STILL AND WHEN THEY ARE TOLD 152 TRISTRAM 3 110
SHE TOLD THEM OF THE FAIRY-HAUNTED LAND • • • • 154 TRISTRAM 3 153
HE TOLD ME THESE THINGS • • • • • • • • • 194 STRAYED REVEL 269
WHEN GOETHES DEATH WAS TOLD WE SAID • • • • • 270 MEMORIAL VERSES 15
YOUNG UNPRACTISED HAD TOLD • • • • • • • 280 HAWORTH CHURCH 10
MAIDENS ASSURE ME IF THEY TOLD ME TRUE • • • • 354 MEROPE 703
WHO TOLD ME THAT THE ROYAL HOUSE WAS HERE • • • 354 MEROPE 704
RIGHTLY THEY TOLD THEE AND THOU ART ARRIVED • • 354 MEROPE 705
NOW TOLD BUT IN ONE FLASHING INSTANT PASSD • • • 358 MEROPE 828
FAITHFUL NOT WELCOME WHEN MY TALE IS TOLD • • • 362 MEROPE 938
HE TOLD HIM OF THE GODS THE STARS • • • • • 414 EMPEDOCLES I 2 71
OF WHAT IS IT TOLD • • • • • • • • • 443 EMPEDOCLES II 458
THAT CITY TOLD OF LANGUOR AND DECAY • • • • • 466 ALARIC AT ROME 106
AND THE WINDS TOLD HIS GLORY AND THE WAVE • • • 476 CROMWELL 157
ERE I HEAR THY CRIES AND THY CAPTIVITY TOLD OF • • HOMER TRANS 38

TOLL

NOR FETCH TO TAKE THE ACCUSTOMD TOLL • • • • • 250 WISH 21

TOLLD

HARK WHAT BELL FOR CHURCH IS TOLLD • • • • • 12 CHURCH BROU 1 4

TOLLS

CRUSHD THEM WITH TOLLS OR FEVER-AIRS • • • • • 193 STRAYED REVEL 251

TOMB

IN THE NAVE A TOMB OF STONE • • • • • • • • 16 CHURCH BROU 1 104
ON THE TOMB TWO FORMS THEY SCULPTURED • • • • 16 CHURCH BROU 1 105
ROUND THE TOMB THE CARVED STONE FRETWORK • • • • 16 CHURCH BROU 1 109
ROUND THE TOMB TO STRAY • • • • • • • • 17 CHURCH BROU 2 35
AND ON THE PAVEMENT ROUND THE TOMB THERE GLINTS • • 18 CHURCH BROU 3 22
ONE DAY TO HARBOUR IN THE TOMB • • • • • • • 22 YOUTH AND CALM 15
MAY SEE MY TOMB A GREAT WAY OFF AND CRY • • • 84 SOHRAB RUSTUM 791
MAY SEE MY TOMB A GREAT WAY OFF AND SAY • • • 84 SOHRAB RUSTUM V 791
I HAVE A FRETTED BRICK-WORK TOMB • • • • • • 94 SICK KING BOKH 221
WHO SEEMS OF MARBLE ON A TOMB • • • • • • 148 TRISTRAM 2 167
WHERE MANY A SPLENDOUR FINDS ITS TOMB • • • • 220 BACCHANALIA 2 22
WE STAND TO-DAY BY WORDSWORTHS TOMB • • • • • 270 MEMORIAL VERSES 5
WE STAND TO-DAY AT WORDSWORTHS TOMB • • • • • 270 MEMORIAL VERSES V 5
WHAT SHALL BE SAID OER WORDSWORTHS TOMB • • • • 270 MEMORIAL VERSES V 5
TENDER VIRGIL NO TOMB • • • • • • • • 294 HEINES GRAVE 59
WHAT DOST THOU IN THIS LIVING TOMB • • • • • 301 GRANDE CHARTR 72
MY HUMBLE TOMB EXPLORE • • • • • • • • 321 OBERMANN MORE 270
DOUBTLESS THEY BEAR THEM TO MY FATHERS TOMB • • 331 MEROPE 55
BEHIND THE SHELTER OF THY FATHERS TOMB • • • • 332 MEROPE 68
IT NEEDS NO YEARLY OFFERINGS AT HIS TOMB • • • 334 MEROPE 119
PRAY AS THOU POURST LIBATIONS ON THIS TOMB • • • 342 MEROPE 382
DRAW DRAW NEAR TO THE TOMB • • • • • • • 342 MEROPE 385
OF HIS UNREVEALD TOMB • • • • • • • • 344 MEROPE 438
THENCE BY THE SEA-GODS SANCTUARY AND THE TOMB • • 356 MEROPE 740
STILL AT HIS MOUNTAIN-TOMB MEN MARVEL BUILT • • 357 MEROPE 782
FROM THE ALTAR THE UNAVENGED TOMB • • • • • 371 MEROPE 1137
AT THE DREAD ALTAR OF HER HUSBANDS TOMB • • • • 385 MEROPE 1414
YET WOULD I NOT DISTURB THEE FROM THY TOMB • • • 449 WESTMIN ABBEY 163
AND WITHER HALF THE LAURELS ON THY TOMB • • • • 463 ALARIC AT ROME 38
SWEPT OFF THE WITHERED LEAVES THAT HIDE THE NAKED TOMB 469 ALARIC AT ROME 192

TOMBS

HER HEAD MID IGNOMINY DEATH AND TOMBS • • • • 172 GOOD SHEPHERD 12
HER HEAD IN IGNOMINY DEATH AND TOMBS • • • • • 172 GOOD SHEPHERD V 12
OVER TOMBS AMID GRAVES • • • • • • • • 220 BACCHANALIA 2 32
PAGEANTS HAVE PASSD AND TOMBS OF MIGHTY KINGS • • 445 WESTMIN ABBEY 53

TOMBSTONE

THAT BLACK TOMBSTONE THE NAME • • • • • • • • 292 HEINES GRAVE 2
THE BLACK TOMBSTONE THE NAME • • • • • • • • 292 HEINES GRAVE V 2

TOME

THE LIBRARY WHERE TRACT AND TOME • • • • • • 300 GRANDE CHARTR 49

TONE

THE SUNK EYES THE WAILING TONE • • • • • • 34 NEW SIRENS 248
SOMETHING ALTERD IN THY COURTLY TONE • • • • • 143 TRISTRAM 2 34
HATH YET AN INFANTINE AND SILVER TONE • • • • 151 TRISTRAM 3 73
HAS YET AN INFANTINE AND SILVER TONE • • • • • 151 TRISTRAM 3 V 73
AND HARDLY YET A GLANCE A TONE • • • • • • • 185 TERRACE BERNE 38

TONE   (CONTINUED)
    KEPT NOT FOR LONG ITS HAPPY COUNTRY TONE   . . . .   269 THYRSIS   222
    THERE SOBS I KNOW NOT WHAT GROUND-TONE   . . . .   307 OBERMANN   35
    TO HEAR A DIM AND LONG FORGOTTEN TONE   . . . .   467 ALARIC AT ROME   123
    FAMILIAR MEANINGS IN YOUR MYSTIC TONE   . . . .   472 CROMWELL   4

TONED
    AND ITS DEEP-TONED MELODIOUS VOICE   . . . . . .   227 EPILOG LAOCOON   195

TONES
    THOSE MELANCHOLY TONES SO SWEET AND STILL   . . . .   36 VOICE   34
    THOSE LUTE-LIKE TONES WHICH IN THE BYGONE YEAR   . .   36 VOICE   35
    THOSE LUTE-LIKE TONES WHICH IN LONG DISTANT YEARS   36 VOICE   V 35
    AGAIN IN TONES OF IRE   . . . .   174 MEETING   10
    IS BY THE TONES OF A LOVED VOICE CARESSD   . . . .   247 BURIED LIFE   83
    SEEMS STRANGELY ECHOED BACK BY TONES OF YESTERDAY   464 ALARIC AT ROME   48
    WHISPERS IN MOURNFUL TONES THY SILENT ELEGY   . .   464 ALARIC AT ROME   66
    AND WITH ITS CLEAR CALM TONES THAT DYING PRAYER   . . 478 CROMWELL   217

TONGUE
    LET THY FOREBODED HOMAGE CHECK THY TONGUE   . . . .   38 WORLDS TRIUMPHS   10
    LET THY FOREBODED TREASON CHECK THY TONGUE   . . . .   38 WORLDS TRIUMPHS V 10
    WITH READIER TONGUE THAN WE   . . . .   48 HORATIAN ECHO   18
    WITH FLANKS A-TREMBLE AND HIS SLENDER TONGUE   . .   114 BALDER DEAD 3   14
    A TRAMP I SAW ILL MOODY AND TONGUE-TIED   . . . .   169 WEST LONDON   2
    TRANSPLANTS THEM TO ANOTHER TONGUE   . . . . . .   224 EPILOG LAOCOON   98
    SEEN BY RARE GLIMPSES PENSIVE AND TONGUE-TIED   .   256 SCHOLAR-GIPSY   54
    SOME YOUTHFUL TROUBADOUR WHOSE TONGUE   . . . .   278 SOUTHERN NIGHT   97
    I THINK OF HER WHOSE GENTLE TONGUE   . . . . . .   279 SOUTHERN NIGHT   121
    LOVE WITHOUT WHICH THE TONGUE   . . . .   295 HEINES GRAVE   101
    HEARD ACCENTS OF THE ETERNAL TONGUE   . . . . . .   310 OBERMANN   125
    ALAS HOW FAIR A COLOUR CAN HIS TONGUE   . . . .   338 MEROPE   278
    THY CROWN CONDEMNS THEE WHILE THY TONGUE ABSOLVES   340 MEROPE   332
    BETTER FROM THINE THAN FROM AN ENEMYS TONGUE   . .   363 MEROPE   950
    A DEED SO AWFUL THAT THE GENERAL TONGUE   . . . .   385 MEROPE   1418
    THE FAITHLESS MURDERERS OWN NO OTHER TONGUE   . .   364 MEROPE   V
    AND THOU A BOY WHOSE TONGUE OUTRUNS HIS KNOWLEDGE   411 EMPEDOCLES I 1   161
    NOR TONGUE OF MAN NOR FEAR NOR SHAME CAN PREACH   . . 467 ALARIC AT ROME   141
    AND THE SAME WORLD HAS TONGUE AND EAR AND EYE   .   470 ALARIC AT ROME   218
    DEEP THRO HIS SOUL AND CHOKD HIS FALTERING TONGUE   478 CROMWELL   224
    AND STEALS THE HONIED MUSIC OF HIS TONGUE   . . . .   FRAGMENT 1   8

TONGUES
    COLD HEARTS AND THANKLESS TONGUES WHERE THANKS ARE DUE   8 MYCERINUS   4
    COLD HEARTS AND THANKLESS TONGUES WHERE THANKS   8 MYCERINUS   V   4
        WERE DUE
    SHARP QUIVERING TONGUES OF FLAME SHOT OUT AND LEAPT   119 BALDER DEAD 3   188
    WHILE TONGUES OF FIRE ON COIGN AND CARVING PLAY   . . 445 WESTMIN ABBEY   36

TOOK
    TOOK MEASURE OF HIS SOUL AND KNEW ITS STRENGTH   . .   12 MYCERINUS   109
    ONCE LIKE US YOU TOOK YOUR STATION   . . . . . .   31 NEW SIRENS   139
    ONCE LIKE ME YOU TOOK YOUR STATION   . . . . . .   31 NEW SIRENS   V 139
    NOT FROM HERSELF HER FAME OF STRENGTH SHE TOOK   . .   37 WORLDS TRIUMPHS   3
    TOOK THEN ITS ALL-SEEN WAY   . . . .   45 IN UTRUMQUE PAR   7
    AND TOOK HIS HORSEMANS CLOAK AND LEFT HIS TENT   . .   61 SOHRAB RUSTUM   9
    HE SPOKE AND PERAN-WISA TOOK THE HAND   . . . .   63 SOHRAB RUSTUM   63
    AND THREW A WHITE CLOAK ROUND HIM AND HE TOOK   .   64 SOHRAB RUSTUM   98
    HE TOOK HIS SPEAR AND TO THE FRONT HE CAME   . . . .   65 SOHRAB RUSTUM   146
    AND YOU WOULD SAY THAT SUN AND STARS TOOK PART   . .   75 SOHRAB RUSTUM   480
    AND SO HE DEEMD THAT EITHER SOHRAB TOOK   . . . .   79 SOHRAB RUSTUM   612
    THEN RUSTUM TOOK IT FOR HIS GLORIOUS SIGN   . . . .   81 SOHRAB RUSTUM   683
    HE SPOKE AND SOHRAB SMILED ON HIM AND TOOK   . . . .   85 SOHRAB RUSTUM   838
    BOTH ARMIES MOVED TO CAMP AND TOOK THEIR MEAL   . .   86 SOHRAB RUSTUM   871
    THE PERSIANS TOOK IT ON THE OPEN SANDS   . . . .   86 SOHRAB RUSTUM   872
    AND THROUGH THE SQUARE HIS WAY HE TOOK   . . . . .   89 SICK KING BOKH   49
    SO SAYING THE KING TOOK A STONE   . . . .   91 SICK KING BOKH   117
    AND THROUGH THE SQUARE HIS PATH HE TOOK   . . . .   89 SICK KING BOKH V 49
    AND LIGHTED TORCHES AND TOOK UP THE CORPSE   . . . .   101 BALDER DEAD 1   204
    WHICH TOOK ON BALDERS TRACK THE WAY BELOW   . . . .   104 BALDER DEAD 1   341
    SO SAID HE AND THE GODS AROSE AND TOOK   . . . . .   106 BALDER DEAD 2   47
    ACROSS THE BRIDGE THEN SHE TOOK POST AGAIN   . . . .   108 BALDER DEAD 2   137
    BUT HERMOD TOOK THE RING AND YET ONCE MORE   . . . .   112 BALDER DEAD 2   282
    NINE DAYS HE TOOK TO GO TWO TO RETURN   . . . .   113 BALDER DEAD 2   293
    HER LONG AGO THE WANDERING ODER TOOK   . . . . .   116 BALDER DEAD 3   93
    SHE IN HER HANDS TOOK BALDERS HEAD AND SPAKE   . .   116 BALDER DEAD 3   98
    AND TOOK THEIR HORSES AND SET FORTH TO RIDE   . .   119 BALDER DEAD 3   215
    WHEN THE GODS HEARD THEY STRAIGHT AROSE AND TOOK   . . 122 BALDER DEAD 3   302
    BUT HERMOD RODE WITH NIORD WHOM HE TOOK   . . . .   122 BALDER DEAD 3   320
    SHE TOOK HIS HANDS IN HERS HER TEARS   . . . . . .   140 TRISTRAM 1   317
    WHEN THE FIERCE PAINS TOOK HER IN THE FOREST   . .   145 TRISTRAM 2   83
    THEN ISEULT TOOK BY THE HAND THOSE CHILDREN FAIR   . . 151 TRISTRAM 3   61
    FORGOT HIS CRAFT AND HIS BEST WITS TOOK FLIGHT   . .   155 TRISTRAM 3   182
    THAT THE SWEET VOICE ITS UPLAND CLEARNESS TOOK   . .   175 PARTING   22
    HE WENT HIS PIPING TOOK A TROUBLED SOUND   . . . .   264 THYRSIS   48
    HE TOOK THE SUFFERING HUMAN RACE   . . . .   270 MEMORIAL VERSES   19
    SHAKING HER HEAD TOOK THE HARP   . . . .   285 HAWORTH CHURCH   126
    AND TOOK THE LAKE TWO HOUNDS ALONE PURSUED   . .   357 MEROPE   809
    AND TOOK THREE STRIDES QUARRY AND DOGS WERE GONE   . . 358 MEROPE   830
    WHERE FIRST THE STAG TOOK WATER FLOATED STILL   . .   358 MEROPE   844
    THE ELDEST MIGHTIEST BROTHER TEMENUS TOOK   . . . .   389 MEROPE   1550

TOOK   (CONTINUED)
        I TOOK MY STAND AND SAW THE UNARMD CROWDS   • • • • •   401 MEROPE   1896
        AND THITHERWARD THE STRANGER TOOK HIS WAY   • • • • •   445 WESTMIN ABBEY   33
        NOT THAT HE TOOK THE COURSE TO DIE   • • • • • •   481 COURAGE   14

TOOLS
        MERE RUTHLESS AND UNCOUNSELLD TOOLS OF WAR   • • • •   381 MEROPE   V1301

TOORKMUN
        AND THE BLACK TOORKMUN TENTS AND ONLY DRUNK   • •   83 SOHRAB RUSTUM   762

TOORKMUNS
        NEXT THE MORE TEMPERATE TOORKMUNS OF THE SOUTH   • •   64 SOHRAB RUSTUM   121

TOOTHLESS
        TOOTHLESS AND OLD SHE GIBES THE PASSERS BY   • • • •   123 BALDER DEAD 3   334

TOP
        ONE MOMENT ON THE RAPIDS TOP OUR BOAT   • • • •   25 DREAM   30
        THE MEN OF FORMER TIMES HAD CROWND THE TOP   • • • •   61 SOHRAB RUSTUM   20
        POISED ON THE TOP OF A HUGE WAVE OF FATE   • • • •   72 SOHRAB RUSTUM   391
        AND ON THE TOP LAY BALDERS CORPSE AND PUT   • • • •   96 BALDER DEAD 1   43
        OF BALDER ON THE HIGHEST TOP THEY LAID   • • • •   118 BALDER DEAD 3   163
        UPON THE BROW-TOP GREW A THORN AND HERE   • • • •   155 TRISTRAM 3   205
        TO THE STONE-ROOFD HUT AT THE TOP   • • • • •   297 HEINES GRAVE   166
        SOMETIMES TO ETNAS TOP AND TO THE CONE   • • • •   409 EMPEDOCLES I 1   95
        ON THE SWARD AT THE CLIFF-TOP   • • • • •   442 EMPEDOCLES II   429

TOPPD
        TOPPD WITH ROUGH-HEWN   • • • • • •   191 STRAYED REVEL   178
        THOSE BLACK-TOPPD RED-BOLED PINE-TREES STAND   • •   248 KENSINGTON GARD V 4
        THOSE DARK-TOPPD RED-BOLD PINETREES STAND   • • • •   KENSINGTON GARD V 4
        IN THE OLD HAUNT AND FIND OUR TREE-TOPPD HILL   • •   265 THYRSIS   103

TOPPED
        ITS FIR-TOPPED HURST ITS FARMS ITS QUIET FIELDS   • •   269 THYRSIS   217

TOPPING
        OUT-TOPPING KNOWLEDGE FOR THE LOFTIEST HILL   • •   2 SHAKESPEARE   3
        OUT-TOPPING KNOWLEDGE SO SOME SOVRAN HILL   • • • •   2 SHAKESPEARE   V   3

TOPS
        THEIR SMOOTH TOPS SHINING SUNWARD AND BENEATH   • •   11 MYCERINUS   87
        THEIR SMOOTH TOPS SHINING SUNWARDS AND BENEATH   • •   11 MYCERINUS   V   87
        ON THE WET UMBRAGE OF THEIR GLOSSY TOPS   • • • •   24 DREAM   4
        AND BURST THEIR ROOTS WHILE TO THEIR TOPS THE GODS   106 BALDER DEAD 2   57
        AND HIGH THE MOUNTAIN-TOPS IN CLOUDY AIR   • • • •   267 THYRSIS   143
        THE MOUNTAIN-TOPS WHERE IS THE THRONE OF TRUTH   • •   267 THYRSIS   144
        TOPS IN LIFES MORNING-SUN SO BRIGHT AND BARE   • •   267 THYRSIS   145

TORCH
        EACH IN HER TURN WITH TORCH UPREARD   • • • • • •   53 RESIGNATION   32
        WAVING HER HUNDRED HANDS A TORCH IN EACH   • • • •   395 MEROPE   1735
        AND STOOD SHOUTING FOR A FIERY TORCH   • • • • • •   399 MEROPE   1835
        PUT THE TORCH TO THE PILE   • • • • • • •   399 MEROPE   1839

TORCHES
        AND LIGHTED TORCHES AND TOOK UP THE CORPSE   • • • •   101 BALDER DEAD 1   204
        AGAINST THE BODIES AND STUCK TORCHES NEAR   • • • •   118 BALDER DEAD 3   167
        SOMETIMES A FAUN WITH TORCHES   • • • • • • •   194 STRAYED REVEL   276
        WHEN THE FLASHING TORCHES APPEAR   • • • • • •   360 MEROPE   896

TORCHLIGHT
        HOME TO OUR HALLS WITH TORCHLIGHT BY OUR KIN   • •   101 BALDER DEAD 1   217

TORE
        THEY OUT-TALKD THEE HISSD THEE TORE THEE   • • • • •   215 LAST WORD   9
        HE TORE US FROM THE PRISON-CELL   • • • • • •   271 MEMORIAL VERSES V
        SHE TORE HER BOOKS SHE SHUT HER COURTS   • • • •   316 OBERMANN MORE   131

TORMENT
        I FELT AS I IN TORMENT LAY   • • • • • •   157 SAINT BRANDAN   33
        THAT OTHER TORMENT GROW UNBEARABLE   • • • • •   435 EMPEDOCLES II   226
        BOTH HE MUST KEEP TORMENT HIM HOW THEY MAY   • • • •   LUCRETIUS 3   V   7
        BOTH HE MUST KEEP TORMENT HIM AS THEY MAY   • • • •   LUCRETIUS 3   V   7

TORMENTING
        MERE PHANTOMS OF MANS SELF-TORMENTING HEART   • •   9 MYCERINUS   25

TORMENTORS
        AND BID THE CHIEF TORMENTORS THERE PROVIDE   • • • •   373 MEROPE   1188

TORMENTS
        AH HOPE CANNOT LONG LIGHTEN TORMENTS LIKE THESE   • •   20 MODERN SAPPHO   32

TORN
        ARTIST WHOSE HAND WITH HORROR WINGD HATH TORN   • •   6 GEO CRUIKSHANK   1
        OF TORN-UP WATER ON THE MAIN   • • • • • • • •   40 HUMAN LIFE   20
        AND STREWN THE CHANNELS WITH TORN BOUGHS SO HUGE   • •   73 SOHRAB RUSTUM   415
        AND STREWN THE CHANNELS WITH TORN BOUGHS SO POUGH   73 SOHRAB RUSTUM   V 415

TORN   (CONTINUED)
        TO THY TORN HEART AND BRAIN   . . . .   200 PHILOMELA   V 14
        AND HURRIED TORN WITH INWARD STRIFE . . . . . .   317 OBERMANN MORE   135
        WITH THY SOILD HUNTING-COAT AND SANDALS TORN   . .   372 MEROPE   1159
        NEVER BEEN TORN FROM THIS BREAST   . . . . . .   377 MEROPE   1231
        AND HAD TORN UP BY THE ROOTS   . . . .   434 EMPEDOCLES II   173
        HIDE HIS TORN HEAD BENEATH HIS SUNLESS CAVE   . .   472 CROMWELL   24

TORPOR
        DULL DID LIFE IN TORPOR FADE   . . . .   28 NEW SIRENS   66
        FROM THAT TORPOR DEEP   . . . .   38 STAGIRIUS   10

TORRENT
        THE CRIMSON TORRENT RAN DIM NOW AND SOILD   . . . .   86 SOHRAB RUSTUM   843
        THE CRIMSON TORRENT POURD DIM NOW AND SOILD   . .   96 SOHRAB RUSTUM   V 843
        THE HOARSE TORRENT DUMB   . . . .   175 PARTING   32
        YET THROUGH THE HUM OF TORRENT LONE   . . . . .   307 OBERMANN   33
        VOICE MOVED ONLY THE TORRENT BROKE   . . . . . .   323 OBERMANN MORE   327
        THE SLENDER TORRENT   . . . .   392 MEROPE   1652
        AND HAVE THIS HOUR SATE BY THE TORRENT HERE   . .   408 EMPEDOCLES I 1   47
        UP BY THE TORRENT-SIDE UNDER THE PINES   . . . .   411 EMPEDOCLES I 1   164
        FAR DOWN THE TORRENT CLEAVES ITS WAY   . . . . .   479 HAYSWATER BOAT   10

TORRENTS
        OF ALL ITS CHAFING TORRENTS AFTER THAW   . . . .   5 DUKE WELLINGTON   5
        THERE THE TORRENTS DRIVE UPWARD   . . . .   175 PARTING   29
        YE TORRENTS I COME . . . .   175 PARTING   34
        IN TORRENTS IN WAVES   . . . .   220 BACCHANALIA 2   30
        ROARING TORRENTS HAVE BREACHD   . . . .   289 RUGBY CHAPEL   94
        I HEAR THE TORRENTS ROAR   . . . .   306 OBERMANN   10
        HE HEARS NOTHING BUT THE CRY OF THE TORRENTS   . .   435 EMPEDOCLES II   213

TORTOISES
        THE BASKING TORTOISES   . . . .   392 MEROPE   1627

TORTURED
        TORTURED THEE BRILLIANT AND BOLD   . . . .   296 HEINES GRAVE   122
        THE PANGS WHICH TORTURED THEM REMAIN . . . . . .   303 GRANDE CHARTR   132
        IS THY TORTURED HEART STILL PROUD   . . . .   430 EMPEDOCLES II   49
        OF THE MOUNTAIN-CRUSHD TORTURED INTRACTABLE TITAN KING   432 EMPEDOCLES II   98

TORTURING
        OF SINNERS PINIOND ON THE TORTURING WHEEL   . . . .   373 MEROPE   1186

TOSS
        CHAMP AND CHAFE AND TOSS IN THE SPRAY   . . . .   161 FORSAKEN MERM   7
        AH TWO DESIRES TOSS ABOUT   . . . .   309 OBERMANN   93
        OR MAN MUST TOSS IN PAIN . . . .   321 OBERMANN MORE   244
        WHILE TROUBLED INNOCENTS TOSS AND LIE AWAKE   . .   372 MEROPE   1155
        AND TOSS AND ROVER . . . .   460 KAISER DEAD   66

TOSSD
        ON THE WAVES OF THE TOSSD FIGHT   . . . .   138 TRISTRAM 1   266
        IN THE WAVES OF THE TOSSD FIGHT   . . . .   138 TRISTRAM 1   V 266
        WAVE-TOSSD WANDERER   . . . .   194 STRAYED REVEL   288
        YEARS THAT WERE SWEET OR SAD BECALMD OR TOSSD   . .   474 CROMWELL   77

TOSSING
        TOSSING CONTINUALLY   . . . .   39 STAGIRIUS   51
        HE HAD LAIN WAKEFUL TOSSING ON HIS BED   . . . .   61 SOHRAB RUSTUM   6
        TOSSING AND WAKEFUL AND I COME TO THEE   . . . .   62 SOHRAB RUSTUM   37
        AND THEY GO LONG DAYS TOSSING UP AND DOWN   . . . .   124 BALDER DEAD 3   365
        TOSSING IN AIR . . . .   218 BACCHANALIA 1   25
        COME WITH THE VOLLEYING RAIN AND TOSSING BREEZE   . .   264 THYRSIS   59
        AND ALL THE TEDIOUS TOSSING TO AND FRO   . . . .   448 WESTMIN ABBEY   150
        THE SUN THAT ON THY TOSSING PAIN   . . . .   482 COURAGE   21

TOST
        MADE MY TOST HEART ITS VERY LIFE-BLOOD SPILL   . .   36 VOICE   39
        OF MEN CONTENTION-TOST OF MEN WHO GROAN   . . . .   269 THYRSIS   224

TOTTERD
        AND HIS KNEES TOTTERD AND HE SMOTE HIS HAND   . .   80 SOHRAB RUSTUM   662

TOTTERING
        TOTTERING A DEATH-STRICKEN HAND   . . . .   281 HAWORTH CHURCH   25

TOTTERS
        AND THEN THE OLD MAN TOTTERS NIGH   . . . .   213 PROGRESS POESY   9

TOUCH
        FOR THEM FOR ALL TIMES BUSY TOUCH   . . . .   56 RESIGNATION   126
        WHO ART THOU THEN THAT CANST SO TOUCH MY SOUL   . .   74 SOHRAB RUSTUM   432
        AND TOUCH THE APATHETIC GHOSTS WITH JOY   . . . .   110 BALDER DEAD 2   196
        TAKE MY HAND AND TOUCH THESE WASTED FINGERS   . .   143 TRISTRAM 2   23
        AN ANGEL TOUCH MINE ARM AND SAY   . . . .   157 SAINT BRANDAN   35
        WHICH TOUCH THEE ARE UNMATING THINGS . . . . . .   181 ISOLATION MARG   32
        I MUST NOT SPRING TO TOUCH THY HAND   . . . . . .   205 CALAIS SANDS   V 25
        THOU HAST INDEED A RARE TOUCH ON THY HARP   . . . .   409 EMPEDOCLES I 1   78
        TOUCH HIS TREMBLING BEAK WITH WINE   . . . . . .   452 POOR MATTHIAS   12

TOUCH (CONTINUED)
```
        DULL OF HEART AND HARD OF TOUCH            .   .   .   .  457 POOR MATTHIAS       168
        TO TOUCH WITH SORROW EVEN A VICTORS MIND   .  .  .  .  468 ALARIC AT ROME      166
        YEA THOUGH HAND TOUCH THEE NOT NOR EYE SHOULD SEE      470 ALARIC AT ROME      209
        TOUCH HIS ROBE AND SAY MY FATHER       .  .  .  .  .      META CLOISTER        27
        TOUCH THE SAME SURFACE WHICH OUR FATHERS TROD     .  .    EVERLASTING SUB       3
        TOUCH THE SAME SURFACE WHICH OUR FATHERS FELT     .  .    EVERLASTING SUB    V  3
        TOUCH THE SAME SURFACE WHICH OUR FATHERS TOUCHD   .  .    EVERLASTING SUB    V  3
```

TOUCHD
```
        BUT NEVER WAS MY HEART THUS TOUCHD BEFORE    .  .  .  .   74 SOHRAB RUSTUM      436
        AND THEN HE TOUCHD IT WITH HIS HAND AND SAID     .  .     81 SOHRAB RUSTUM      686
        FOR IT GREW DARK BUT HODER TOUCHD HIS ARM    .  .  .  .  101 BALDER DEAD 1      229
        PASSD OPPOSITE SHE TOUCHD HER GIRL WHO HIED       .  .   170 WEST LONDON          6
        HE OF THE MYSTIC EAST IS TOUCHD WITH NIGHT     .  .  .   170 EAST AND WEST       14
        HANGS TOUCHD WITH LIGHT ONE SNOWY SAIL    .  .  .  .  .  274 STANZAS CARNAC      32
        HANGS TOUCHD WITH LIGHT ONE DISTANT SAIL     .  .  .  .  274 STANZAS CARNAC   V  32
        TOUCHD SHORE TO DIE       .  .  .  .  .  .  .  .  .  .   278 SOUTHERN NIGHT   V  96
        TOUCHD WITH YELLOW BY HOT          .  .  .  .  .  .  .   292 HEINES GRAVE         5
        I SHOULD HAVE SAID THAT SOME ONE TOUCHD A HARP    .  .   412 EMPEDOCLES I 2      11
        TOUCHD THE HILLS THE STRIFE WAS DONE    .  .  .  .  .    433 EMPEDOCLES II      144
        AND THY TRANSFIGURED WALLS BE TOUCHD WITH FLAME   .  .   449 WESTMIN ABBEY      178
        HAVE THE SAME SURFACE WHICH OUR FATHERS TOUCHD    .  .     EVERLASTING SUB   V   3
        TOUCH THE SAME SURFACE WHICH OUR FATHERS TOUCHD   .  .     EVERLASTING SUB   V   3
```

TOUCHES
```
        AND NEVER TOUCHES THE SHIP-SIDE AGAIN     .  .  .  .  .   41 HUMAN LIFE          24
        THAT TOUCHES BUT HIMSELF      .  .  .  .  .  .  .  .  .  196 FRAG ANTIGONE       33
        TOUCHES AND ON GIBRALTARS ROCK    .  .  .  .  .  .  .  . 276 SOUTHERN NIGHT      47
```

TOUCHEST
```
        THOU TOUCHEST THE WORST OF MY ILLS    .  .  .  .  .  .  345 MEROPE             477
```

TOUCHING
```
        PROFOUND YET TOUCHING SWEET YET STRONG    .  .  .  .    222 EPILOG LAOCOON      28
        TOUCHING THY HARP AS THE WHIM CAME ON THEE    .  .  .  . 407 EMPEDOCLES I 1      33
```

TOUCHT
```
        THE THOUGHTS THAT TOUCHT THY BREAST THOU LONELY        468 ALARIC AT ROME      168
              CONQUEROR THEN
```

TOUGH
```
        RENT THE TOUGH PLATES BUT FAILD TO REACH THE SKIN      76 SOHRAB RUSTUM       493
        RENT THE TOUGH PLATES BUT MISSD TO REACH THE SKIN      76 SOHRAB RUSTUM     V 493
```

TOW
```
        TWO HORSES STRONGLY SWIMMING TOW      .  .  .  .  .  .  191 STRAYED REVEL      185
```

TOWER
```
        SOLE LIKE SOME SINGLE TOWER WHICH A CHIEF     .  .  .    71 SOHRAB RUSTUM      337
        AND LIES A FRAGRANT TOWER OF PURPLE BLOOM     .  .  .    80 SOHRAB RUSTUM      637
        FROM HER LONELY SHORE-BUILT TOWER     .  .  .  .  .  .  131 TRISTRAM 1          43
        ON THE ROOF OF THE BROCKEN-TOWER      .  .  .  .  .  .  297 HEINES GRAVE       168
        THE MORNING MISTS FROM TOWER AND TEMPLE ROLL     .  .   468 ALARIC AT ROME     154
        BY LEAGUERD TOWER AND TENTED FIELD IT CAME    .  .  .   476 CROMWELL           148
```

TOWERD
```
        THAT LONG HAS TOWERD IN THE AIRY CLOUDS     .  .  .  .   73 SOHRAB RUSTUM      401
        HIGH TOWERD THE SPIKES OF PURPLE ORCHISES     .  .  .   266 THYRSIS            115
        THAT THE FLAME TOWERD ON HIGH TO THE HEAVEN     .  .    399 MEROPE            1840
        A FORM THAT TOWERD ABOVE HIS BROTHER MEN    .  .  .  .  476 CROMWELL           145
```

TOWERED
```
        AS TOWERED ON HIGH ABOVE THEIR MOONLIT ROAD     .  .   466 ALARIC AT ROME     113
```

TOWERING
```
        UNDER THE TOWERING TRACHIS CRAGS      .  .  .  .  .  .  198 FRAG ANTIGONE       99
```

TOWERS
```
        AND HERMOD SAW THE TOWERS OF ASGARD RISE    .  .  .    113 BALDER DEAD 2      304
        THE DAY WILL COME WHEN FALL SHALL ASGARDS TOWERS  .  . 127 BALDER DEAD 3      487
        THE DAY WILL COME WHEN ASGARDS TOWERS SHALL FALL  .  . 127 BALDER DEAD 3    V 487
        THE PALACE TOWERS OF TYNTAGIL     .  .  .  .  .  .  .  136 TRISTRAM 1       V 177
        THOUGHT I ABOVE HER STATE THIS SPIRIT TOWERS      .  . 170 WEST LONDON          9
        BEYOND THE ABBEY-TOWERS APPEARD       .  .  .  .  .  . 223 EPILOG LAOCOON      70
        AND THE EYE TRAVELS DOWN TO OXFORDS TOWERS    .  .  . 256 SCHOLAR-GIPSY       30
        YE WITNESS YE NEW-BUILT TOWERS    .  .  .  .  .  .  . 400 MEROPE            1856
        AND OER THY TOWERS THE WINDS HALF UTTERED SIGH    .  . 464 ALARIC AT ROME      65
```

TOWN
```
        FAR FROM TOWN OR HAUNT OF MAN     .  .  .  .  .  .  .   14 CHURCH BROU 1       62
        FROM THE WALLD TOWN BEYOND THE PASS   .  .  .  .  .  .   17 CHURCH BROU 2       26
        BRIGHT COMRADE TO THE NOISY TOWN      .  .  .  .  .  .   54 RESIGNATION         77
        THE TOWN THE HIGHWAY AND THE PLAIN    .  .  .  .  .  .   54 RESIGNATION         79
        CAPPD WITH FAINT SMOKE THE NOISY TOWN     .  .  .  .    55 RESIGNATION         93
        AT SUNSET ON A POPULOUS TOWN      .  .  .  .  .  .  .    57 RESIGNATION        165
        SOME MORN AT MARKET IN A CROWDED TOWN     .  .  .  .   114 BALDER DEAD 3        9
        ONE MORN AT MARKET IN A CROWDED TOWN      .  .  .  .   114 BALDER DEAD 3     V  9
        BY CASTLE FIELD AND TOWN      .  .  .  .  .  .  .  .  . 159 NECKAN              18
        ONE LAST LOOK AT THE WHITE-WALLD TOWN     .  .  .  .   162 FORSAKEN MERM       25
        WHERE THE SEA-STOCKS BLOOM TO THE WHITE-WALLD TOWN    163 FORSAKEN MERM       69
```

TOWN   (CONTINUED)
            SHE SITS AT HER WHEEL IN THE HUMMING TOWN . . . . 164 FORSAKEN MERM   87
            LIGHTS SHINE IN THE TOWN . . . .   164 FORSAKEN MERM   111
            AT THE WHITE SLEEPING TOWN   . . . .   165 FORSAKEN MERM   137
            THE TOWN THE LAKE ARE HERE   . . . .   174 MEETING   2
            FLOWS BY THE TOWN THE CHURCHYARD FAIR   . . . .   184 TERRACE BERNE   10
            IN THE TOWN ROUND THE TEMPLE   . . . .   186 STRAYED REVEL   37
            THE MOORLAND TOWN BUT THE CHURCH   . . . . . .   283 HAWORTH CHURCH   62
            IN THE LORN SYRIAN TOWN . . . .   318 OBERMANN MORE   174
            SET FORTH FROM TEGEA THE ROYAL TOWN . . . . .   355 MEROPE   732
            THERE WITH THE CHIEF OF THAT HILL-TOWN WE LODGED   356 MEROPE   746
            NEAR LYCOSURA BUILDS LYCAONS TOWN . . . . . .   359 MEROPE   848
            O TOWN HIGH STENYCLAROS . . . .   399 MEROPE   1850
            AND NOW AND NOW BACK TO THE TOWN WITH SPEED . .   408 EMPEDOCLES I 1   49
            ANCIENT STREETS OF HASTINGS TOWN   . . . . . .   457 POOR MATTHIAS   182
            A BABY DOG FROM LONDON TOWN . . . .   459 KAISER DEAD   14

TOWND
            FROM THE FOUR-TOWND MOUNTAIN-SHADOWD DORIS . . . . 400 MEROPE   1852

TOWNS
            FROM THE RANK LIFE OF TOWNS THIS LEAF AND FLUNG . .   6 GEO CRUIKSHANK   2
            AND WHEN TIS TRUCE THEN IN AFRASIABS TOWNS . . . . 63 SOHRAB RUSTUM   73
            THE FAMOUS TOWNS OF ITALY . . . .   138 TRISTRAM 1   251
            THE FRET AND MISERY OF OUR NORTHERN TOWNS . . . . 168 RACHEL 2   9
            AS IT GROWS AS THE TOWNS ON ITS MARGE . . . . .   253 FUTURE   72
            THEN THROUGH THE GREAT TOWNS HARSH HEART-WEARYING ROAR 269 THYRSIS   234
            RIVERS AND HIGH-ROOFD TOWNS . . . .   296 HEINES GRAVE   138
            OR WITH THE REVELLERS FROM THE MOUNTAIN-TOWNS . . 406 EMPEDOCLES I 1   8

TOWNSMEN
            OER WHOSE CLIFFS THE TOWNSMEN . . . .   392 MEROPE   1649

TOY
            FOR THE HUMMING STREET AND THE CHILD WITH ITS TOY 164 FORSAKEN MERM   90
            TO TAKE HIS NURSE HIS BROKEN TOY   . . . . . .   248 KENSINGTON GARD   10
            DRAGS TO HIS NURSE HIS BROKEN TOY . . . .   KENSINGTON GARD V 10
            AND BADE THE WINDS THROUGH SPACE IMPEL THE GUSTY TOY 415 EMPEDOCLES I 2   81

TOYS
            WHAT WERE NOW THESE TOYS TO HER   . . . . . .   453 POOR MATTHIAS   35

TRACE
            AND PUT THE SHEPHERDS WANDERER ON THY TRACE . .   257 SCHOLAR-GIPSY   63
            AND LEAVE NO TRACE BEHIND   . . . .   273 EDW QUILLINAN   V 6
            OF OUR OWN ACTIONS DIMLY TRACE THE CAUSES . . .   352 MEROPE   640
            WHAT TRACE OF CARELESS CHILDHOOD LINGERD THERE . . 477 CROMWELL   184

TRACHINIANS
            COMING SWIFTLY THROUGH THE SAD TRACHINIANS . . . . 399 MEROPE   1838

TRACHIS
            UNDER THE TOWERING TRACHIS CRAGS   . . . . . .   198 FRAG ANTIGONE   99
            UP THE PRECIPICES OF TRACHIS   . . . .   399 MEROPE   1828

TRACK
            FOR THIS THY TRACK ACROSS THE FRETFUL FOAM . . . .   5 DUKE WELLINGTON   11
            WHICH TOOK ON BALDERS TRACK THE WAY BELOW . . .   104 BALDER DEAD 1   341
            AND I COME SENT THIS ROAD ON BALDERS TRACK . . .   108 BALDER DEAD 2   116
            AND FLITTED DOWN THE FLOWERY TRACK   . . . . .   184 TERRACE BERNE   19
            THE WOOD-CUTTERS CART-TRACK . . . .   187 STRAYED REVEL   41
            THE TRACK A STRAIGHT BLACK LINE . . . . . .   191 STRAYED REVEL   175
            THE QUIET MOSSY TRACK TO AGE   . . . .   199 EARLY DEATH   7
            THE MOSSY QUIET TRACK TO AGE   . . . .   199 EARLY DEATH   V 7
            IN LESSINGS TRACK AND TRIED TO SEE   . . . . .   221 EPILOG LAOCOON   5
            RUNS IT NOT HERE THE TRACK BY CHILDSWORTH FARM . . 263 THYRSIS   11
            THE TRACK THE STREAM-BED DESCENDS . . . . . .   289 RUGBY CHAPEL   95
            THE MULE-TRACK FROM SAINT LAURENT GOES   . . . .   299 GRANDE CHARTR   4
            IN FRONT THE AWFUL ALPINE TRACK . . . . . .   306 OBERMANN   1
            PEERING TO SPY A GOAT-TRACK DOWN THE CLIFF . . . . 357 MEROPE   804
            THE TRACK WINDS DOWN TO THE CLEAR STREAM   . . .   413 EMPEDOCLES I 2   36
            FAIL TO TRACK THEIR DEEP DISTRESS . . . . . .   455 POOR MATTHIAS   106
            THREADED AND LIGHTEND BY A TRACK OF FLAME . . . . 473 CROMWELL   60

TRACKD
            HAVE YOU TRACKD ITS CLOUDED WAYS   . . . . . .   33 NEW SIRENS   208
            WE TRACKD THE SHY THAMES SHORE   . . . . . .   266 THYRSIS   126
            AND MIST-TRACKD STREAM OF THE WIDE   . . . . .   297 HEINES GRAVE   172
            TRACKD BY MURDERS BLOODY SWORD NO MORE   . . . .   482 THEKLAS ANSWER   16

TRACKING
            IN TRACKING OUT OUR TRUE ORIGINAL COURSE   . . . . 246 BURIED LIFE   50

TRACKS
            AND UP THE DEWY MOUNTAIN-TRACKS THEY FARED . . . . 106 BALDER DEAD 2   51

TRACT
            AND OER A DARKSOME TRACT WHICH KNOWS NO SUN . .   108 BALDER DEAD 2   139
            DOTH A WHOLE TRACT OF HEAVEN DISCLOSE . . . .   242 SUMMER NIGHT   10
            ONLY THE TRACT WHERE HE SAILS . . . .   252 FUTURE   24

TRACT   (CONTINUED)
          THIS TRACT WHICH THE RIVER OF TIME   • • • • • •   253 FUTURE   50
          THE LIBRARY WHERE TRACT AND TOME   • • • • • •   300 GRANDE CHARTR   49
          WE SHALL HAVE LEFT THE WOODY TRACT AND COME   • •   412 EMPEDOCLES I 2   2

TRACTS
          AND IN WILD HUNT THROUGH MAZY TRACTS OF STARS   • •   10 MYCERINUS   45
          HOLDS COUNTLESS TRACTS UNTROD • • • • • • • • •   352 MEROPE   628

TRADE
          TRADE-WINDS WHICH CROSS IT FROM ETERNITY   • • • •   243 SUMMER NIGHT   58
          TRADE-WINDS THAT CROSS IT FROM ETERNITY   • • • •   243 SUMMER NIGHT   V 58
          DENSER THE TRADE ON ITS STREAM • • • • • • • •   253 FUTURE   63

TRADER
          AS SOME GRAVE TYRIAN TRADER FROM THE SEA   • • • •   262 SCHOLAR-GIPSY   232

TRAFFIC
          COME FORTH DENOUNCE THE TRAFFIC AND THE TRAITOR   • •   364 MEROPE   982
          SPOKE AND REVEALD THAT TRAFFIC AND THE TRAITOR   • •   365 MEROPE   V

TRAFFICKERS
          SHY TRAFFICKERS THE DARK IBERIANS COME   • • • •   262 SCHOLAR-GIPSY   249

TRAGIC
          AND YOUR TRAGIC-VAUNTED REVELS • • • • • • • •   26 NEW SIRENS   19
          WAS WOE THAN BYRONS WOE MORE TRAGIC FAR   • • • •   167 PICT NEWSTEAD   14

TRAILD
          HATH TRAILD THE HUNTERS JAVELIN IN HIS SIDE   • •   76 SOHRAB RUSTUM   505
          HAS TRAILD THE HUNTERS JAVELIN IN HIS SIDE • • • •   76 SOHRAB RUSTUM   V 505

TRAILING
          OF THE SOILD GLORY AND THE TRAILING WING   • • • •   43 GIPSY CHILD   56
          TRAILING IN THE COOL STREAM THY FINGERS WET   • •   257 SCHOLAR-GIPSY   75

TRAIN
          SATE AND WATCHD HER WORKING TRAIN   • • • • • •   15 CHURCH BROU 1   94
          I WHO IN YOUR TRAIN AT MORNING • • • • • • • •   26 NEW SIRENS   5
          RUSTUM SHOULD SEEK THE BOY TO TRAIN IN ARMS   • •   79 SOHRAB RUSTUM   611
          RUSTUM SHOULD TAKE THE BOY TO TRAIN IN ARMS   • •   79 SOHRAB RUSTUM   V 611
          A DIRGE AND NANNA AND HER TRAIN REPLIED   • • • •   103 BALDER DEAD 1   274
          ALL THE STRONG BROOD OF HEAVEN TO SWELL MY TRAIN • •   120 BALDER DEAD 3   241
          THE LOVE ALL BEAR TOWARD THEE NOR TRAIN UP • • •   126 BALDER DEAD 3   450
          THE LOVE ALL BEAR TOWARDS THEE NOR TRAIN UP • •   126 BALDER DEAD 3   V 450
          A NOBLER CALMER TRAIN • • • • • • • • • •   183 ABSENCE   6
          LET THE WILD THRONGING TRAIN   • • • • • • •   185 STRAYED REVEL   3
          LET THE WILD THRONGING TRAIN   • • • • • • •   194 STRAYED REVEL   294
          GIRT BY HIS FAR-SHINING TRAIN • • • • • • •   216 LORDS MESSENGER V
          LAID PAUSEFULLY UPON LIFES HEADLONG TRAIN   • • •   266 THYRSIS   137
          WANDERING WITH THE GREAT MOTHERS TRAIN DIVINE   • •   268 THYRSIS   177
          HAVOC IS MADE IN OUR TRAIN   • • • • • • •   289 RUGBY CHAPEL   101
          FRIENDS COMPANIONS AND TRAIN   • • • • • • •   289 RUGBY CHAPEL   122
          THIS DAY AMID THESE RITES THIS BLACK-ROBED TRAIN • •   333 MEROPE   105
          ONE OF THE TRAIN OF CYPSELUS AM I   • • • • •   355 MEROPE   719
          PEACE WITH DELIGHT IN THY TRAIN   • • • • • •   360 MEROPE   891
          IN THE MARRIAGE-TRAIN COMING ON   • • • • • •   360 MEROPE   897
          ONE DEATH-DEALING VENGEFUL TRAIN   • • • • • •   379 MEROPE   1255
          WHEN WITH ELATED HEARTS WE JOIND YOUR TRAIN   • •   436 EMPEDOCLES II   238
          THE GLORIFIED TRAIN   • • • • • • • • • •   442 EMPEDOCLES II   452

TRAIND
          AND TRAIND HIM A BRIGHT BAY WITH LOFTY CREST   • •   69 SOHRAB RUSTUM   V 276
          RULED IN THEIR NAME AND TRAIND THEM TO YOUR WILL • •   339 MEROPE   321
          THEIR CHIEF HATH TRAIND THEM MADE THEM LIKE HIMSELF   381 MEROPE   1303
          A PEOPLE IS NO ARMY TRAIND TO FIGHT • • • • •   382 MEROPE   1339
          WHOSE MIND WAS FED ON OTHER FOOD WAS TRAIND   • •   436 EMPEDOCLES II   264

TRAITOR
          THE TRAITOR JUDAS OUT OF HELL • • • • • • • •   157 SAINT BRANDAN   20
          COME FORTH DENOUNCE THE TRAFFIC AND THE TRAITOR • •   364 MEROPE   982
          SPOKE AND REVEALD THAT TRAFFIC AND THE TRAITOR • •   365 MEROPE   V
          WOULD PLAY THE TRAITOR TO THE STEDFAST WILL • •   475 CROMWELL   108

TRAITOROUS
          BUT FROM THE TRAITOROUS SEED OF LOK THEY COME   • •   120 BALDER DEAD 3   234

TRAMP
          TRAMP OF MEN AND QUICK COMMANDS   • • • • • •   14 CHURCH BROU 1   38
          A TRAMP I SAW ILL MOODY AND TONGUE-TIED   • • •   169 WEST LONDON   2
          HARK HOW THE SHOUTING CROWDS TRAMP HITHERWARD   • •   401 MEROPE   1886

TRAMPLE
          TRAMPLE THE GRASS • • • • • • • • • • • •   218 BACCHANALIA 1   35

TRAMPLING
          UNHALLOWED FEET ARE TRAMPLING ON THIS HAUNTED GROUND   467 ALARIC AT ROME   144

TRAMPS
          SCANND OF TRAMPS AND FISHERMEN • • • • • • • •   457 POOR MATTHIAS   187

TRANCE
        AND LIVED SOME MOONS IN HAPPY TRANCE   . . . . . .   279 SOUTHERN NIGHT   109
        THIRTY LONG DAYS IN A COLD TRANCE OF DEATH . . . . .   410 EMPEDOCLES I 1   110
        IN TRANCE PANTHEIA LAY   . . . .   416 EMPEDOCLES I 2   108
        SHOOK THE DEEP SLUMBER OF HIS DEATHLIKE TRANCE   . .   477 CROMWELL   194

TRANCED
        STAND TRANCED IN JOY   . . . .   51 CONSOLATION   45

TRANCES
        WAS SUBJECT TO THESE TRANCES FROM A GIRL   . . . .   410 EMPEDOCLES I 1   136

TRANQUIL
        A HUNDRED LAMPS BEAMD IN THE TRANQUIL GLOOM   . .   11 MYCERINUS   94
        FROM HER TRANQUIL SPHERE . . . .   35 VOICE   4
        CHANGE DOTH UNKNIT THE TRANQUIL STRENGTH OF MEN   . .   44 QUESTION   3
        AND TRANQUIL FROM WHOSE FLOOR THE NEW-BATHED STARS   87 SOHRAB RUSTUM   891
        HIS TRANQUIL LIFE IN THIS LONE PLACE . . . .   137 TRISTRAM 1   212
        A TRANQUIL SETTLED LOVELINESS   . . . .   147 TRISTRAM 2   145
        WAS TO BE GENTLE TRANQUIL TRUE   . . . .   179 FAREWELL   48
        OF A TRANQUIL LIFE IN THE SHADE   . . . .   199 EARLY DEATH   14
        AND THE SWEET TRANQUIL THAMES   . . . .   200 PHILOMELA   12
        GLIMMERING AND VAST OUT IN THE TRANQUIL BAY   . .   210 DOVER BEACH   5
        OF FEELING AS TRANQUIL AS SURE . . . .   252 FUTURE   40
        AND TRANQUIL AS THE GLACIER-SNOWS   . . . . . .   278 SOUTHERN NIGHT   90
        BACK TO THE TRANQUIL THE COOL   . . . .   296 HEINES GRAVE   150
        YET IN A TRANQUIL WORLD WAS PASSD   . . . . . .   308 OBERMANN   67
        AND THY SAD TRANQUIL LORE   . . . .   313 OBERMANN MORE   48
        OR WONDROUS SOUNDS FROM TRANQUIL SKIES WERE BORNE   472 CROMWELL   35
        SOME SHADOWY VISION OF A TRANQUIL LIFE   . . . .   474 CROMWELL   101
        HIS WERE NO TRANQUIL YEARS NO LANGUID SLEEP   . .   475 CROMWELL   123
        THEY ENVY NOT THIS TRANQUIL BROOD   . . . . . .   484 ROME-SICKNESS   17

TRANQUILLITY
        OF TOIL UNSEVERD FROM TRANQUILLITY   . . . . . .   1 QUIET WORK   5
        SIGHD OUT BY WINTERS SAD TRANQUILLITY   . . . .   12 MYCERINUS   115

TRANQUILLY
        AND TRANQUILLY ABOVE THAT TROUBLED BREAST   . . . .   469 ALARIC AT ROME   195

TRANSCENDS
        THOU THREATENEST WHAT TRANSCENDS THY MIGHT EVEN THINE   120 BALDER DEAD 3   249

TRANSEPT
        ON AISLE AND TRANSEPT AND YOUR MARBLE GRAVE   . .   17 CHURCH BROU 3   6
        NAVE CHOIR AND TRANSEPT GLORIFIED WITH LIGHT   . .   445 WESTMIN ABBEY   35

TRANSFIGURED
        PROPHETS TRANSFIGURED SAINTS AND MARTYRS BRAVE   . .   18 CHURCH BROU 3   20
        AND WITH THAT SMALL TRANSFIGURED BAND   . . . .   311 OBERMANN   145
        AND THY TRANSFIGURED WALLS BE TOUCHD WITH FLAME   . .   449 WESTMIN ABBEY   178

TRANSFIXD
        FALL AND THY SPEAR TRANSFIXD AN UNARMD FOE . . . .   77 SOHRAB RUSTUM   550

TRANSFORMD
        ILSE THE FAIRY TRANSFORMD   . . . .   297 HEINES GRAVE   183
        TRANSFORMD CALLISTO   . . . .   393 MEROPE   1659
        OF HOLIDAY-CLAD CITIZENS TRANSFORMD   . . . . . .   402 MEROPE   1939

TRANSIENT
        FROM SOME TRANSIENT EARTHLY SUN   . . . .   31 NEW SIRENS   152
        FROM SOME TRANSIENT HUMAN SUN   . . . .   31 NEW SIRENS   V 152
        LOVE TRANSIENT POWER AN UNREAL SHOW   . . . . . .   59 RESIGNATION   236
        THAT TRANSIENT GLIMPSE IN SONG THEY SAY   . . . .   226 EPILOG LAOCOON   181
        THAT TRANSIENT SOUND IN SONG THEY TELL   . . . .   226 EPILOG LAOCOON   183

TRANSMITS
        WHERE SIRE TO SON TRANSMITS THE UNQUESTIOND CROWN   388 MEROPE   1517

TRANSPARENCY
        HOW VAST YET OF WHAT CLEAR TRANSPARENCY   . . . .   244 SUMMER NIGHT   89

TRANSPLANTS
        TRANSPLANTS THEM TO ANOTHER TONGUE   . . . . . .   224 EPILOG LAOCOON   98

TRANSPORT
        SHALL TRANSPORT THEE AWAY AND THE DAY OF THY   HOMER TRANS   28
            FREEDOM BE ENDED

TRAPPD
        AND AS A STORK WHICH IDLE BOYS HAVE TRAPPD . . . .   129 BALDER DEAD 3   559

TRAVAIL
        BUT WITH ALL THIS TRAVAIL SAGE . . . .   456 POOR MATTHIAS   147

TRAVAILS
        THAT TRAVAILS SORE AND BRINGS FORTH WIND   . . .   217 NAMELESS EPIT   V
        AND TRAVAILS PANTS AND MOANS   . . . .   422 EMPEDOCLES I 2   295
        AND TRAVAILS STRIVES AND MOANS   . . . .   422 EMPEDOCLES I 2   V 295

TRAVEL
SICK WITH GRIEF I AM AND FAINT WITH TRAVEL   • • • • 142 TRISTRAM 2   15
HIS SHORT COAT TRAVEL-TARNISHD • • • • • • • • 189 STRAYED REVEL   106
HIS EYE MUST TRAVEL DOWN AT FULL   • • • • • 225 EPILOG LAOCOON   145
CLEARD WITH BLITHE TRAVEL AND THE MORNING AIR • • 355 MEROPE   734
WITH MOUNTAIN-TRAVEL AND NIGHT-WATCHING SPENT   • • 359 MEROPE   868
JADED WITH TRAVEL CLAD IN HUNTERS GARB   • • • 363 MEROPE   957
UNARMD AND TRAVEL-SOILD JUST AS HE WAS • • • • 401 MEROPE   1906
IF SO BE THAT TRAVEL THEY   • • • • • • • 454 POOR MATTHIAS   79

TRAVELLD
FOR THEY HAD TRAVELLD FAR AND NOT STOPPD YET • • 154 TRISTRAM 3   172
THE YEAR HAD TRAVELLD ROUND AND ONE BRIGHT DAY • •   TRISTRAM 3   V 1

TRAVELLER
THE TOO IMPERIOUS TRAVELLER ON • • • • • • • • 53 RESIGNATION   37
AND AS A TRAVELLER IN THE EARLY DAWN • • • • • 113 BALDER DEAD 2   295
INVITE TO REST THE TRAVELLER THERE • • • • • 313 OBERMANN MORE   19
ALL ENTERTAINMENT WHICH A TRAVELLER NEEDS • • • 359 MEROPE   870

TRAVELLERS
BRUSHES ACROSS A TIRED TRAVELLERS FACE   • • • 101 BALDER DEAD 1   231
WHERE HOME THROUGH FLOODED FIELDS FOOT-TRAVELLERS GO 258 SCHOLAR-GIPSY   122
WHERE TRAVELLERS NEVER PASS WHERE ONLY COME • • 373 MEROPE   1169
TO TRAVELLERS ON THE PORTSMOUTH ROAD • • • • • 452 GEISTS GRAVE   70
BUT TRAVELLERS IN A HURRY TO ARRIVE • • • • •   LUCRETIUS 6   2

TRAVELLING
LONG FLOCKS OF TRAVELLING BIRDS DEAD ON THE SNOW • • 66 SOHRAB RUSTUM   164
AND AS IN THE DARK NIGHT A TRAVELLING MAN • • • 119 BALDER DEAD 3   V

TRAVELS
PAUSANIAS ON HIS TRAVELS FOUND • • • • • • • 221 EPILOG LAOCOON   16
AND THE EYE TRAVELS DOWN TO OXFORDS TOWERS • • • 256 SCHOLAR-GIPSY   30
OUR SCHOLAR TRAVELS YET THE LOVED HILL-SIDE   • • 269 THYRSIS   240
STUPIDLY TRAVELS HER ROUND • • • • • • • 294 HEINES GRAVE   81
BUT VENGEANCE TRAVELS IN A DANGEROUS WAY • • • 349 MEROPE   580

TRAVERSE
TRAVERSE IN TROOPS WITH CARE-FILLD BREAST • • • • 277 SOUTHERN NIGHT   66

TRAVERSED
THE WAY HE KNEW AND TRAVERSED GIALLS STREAM • • 124 BALDER DEAD 3   375
AND TRAVERSED ALL THE SHADE • • • • • • • 323 OBERMANN MORE   310

TREACHEROUSLY
TREACHEROUSLY PLOTTED TWIXT MY SON AND ME • • • 387 MEROPE   1481

TREACHERY
AND THAT CURST TREACHERY ON THE MOUNT OF GORE • • 430 EMPEDOCLES II   54

TREAD
DIDST TREAD ON EARTH UNGUESSD AT BETTER SO • • • 3 SHAKESPEARE   11
THOSE UPPER REGIONS WE MUST TREAD • • • • 54 RESIGNATION   65
ONCE MORE WE TREAD THIS SELF-SAME ROAD • • • • 55 RESIGNATION   86
ALONE WE TREAD IT YOU AND I • • • • • • • 55 RESIGNATION   88
SLOWLY BEHIND HIS HEAVY TREAD • • • • • • 57 RESIGNATION   184
YET FAUSTA THE MUTE TURF WE TREAD • • • • • 60 RESIGNATION   265
SLOWLY BEHIND THE HEAVY TREAD • • • • • • 57 RESIGNATION   V 184
BUT HE MUST TREAD A DARK UNTRAVELLD ROAD • • • 99 BALDER DEAD 1   143
AND WE SHALL TREAD ONCE MORE THE WELL-KNOWN PLAIN 128 BALDER DEAD 3   537
SINCE THOU AROSEST TO TREAD • • • • • • • 287 RUGBY CHAPEL   27
TREAD THE BORDER-LAND DIM • • • • • • • 288 RUGBY CHAPEL   54
THOU SOLEMN GRAVE WHERE EVERY STEP WE TREAD • • 464 ALARIC AT ROME   49
YEA ON YOUR FATHERS BONES THE AVENGERS TREAD • • 467 ALARIC AT ROME   134
FORMS THAT WITH HIM SHALL TREAD LIFES CHANGING STAGE 476 CROMWELL   161

TREADS
WHERE SORROW TREADS ON JOY • • • • • • • 39 STAGIRIUS   43
WHO TREADS AT EASE LIFES UNCHEERD WAYS • • • • 59 RESIGNATION   237
WHICH IN A DEED LIKE MINE A JUST MAN TREADS • • 341 MEROPE   369
EVEN EARTH WHEREON HE TREADS • • • • • • 352 MEROPE   626
TREADS ON THE SLUMBERING DUST OF OTHER YEARS • • 464 ALARIC AT ROME   50

TREASON
LET THY FOREBODED TREASON CHECK THY TONGUE • • • 38 WORLDS TRIUMPHS   V 10
AH ME WITH WHAT A FOOT DOTH TREASON POST • • • • 363 MEROPE   962

TREASURE
LIKE THOSE KINGS WITH TREASURE STEERING • • • • 26 NEW SIRENS   21
THEIR NAMES CHIEF TREASURE OF ALL • • • • • • 281 HAWORTH CHURCH   V 22
MY NEW-WON TREASURE THY BELOVED LIFE • • • • • 381 MEROPE   1291

TREASURES
AND ROOMS OF TREASURES NOT A FEW • • • • • • 94 SICK KING BOKH   214

TREASURIES
ROAMD ERE BIRTH THE TREASURIES OF GOD • • • • 209 SELF-DECEPTION   6

TREASUURES
          AND SPEND THE GOODLY TREASUURES I HAVE GOT • • • •   68 SOHRAB RUSTUM   238

TREATS
          AND HE TREATS DOUBT THE BEST WHO TRIES TO SEE   415 EMPEDOCLES I 2   101
              LEAST ILL

TREATY
          TREATY AND TO THIS KINGDOM FOR MY SON   • • • • 387 MEROPE   1483

TREE
          FROM TREE TO TREE ALL THROUGH THE TWINKLING GROVE   11 MYCERINUS   95
          FROM TREE TO TREE ALL THROUGH THE TWINKLING GROVE   11 MYCERINUS   95
          NOR WITHERD WHEN THE PALM-TREE PLUMES THAT ROOFD • • 12 MYCERINUS   118
          OR AT A FORD OR SLEEPING BY A TREE • • • • 117 BALDER DEAD 3   118
          OF THAT WORLD-SHADOWING TREE WITH HONEY-DEW • 120 BALDER DEAD 3   222
          WHERE MERLIN BY THE ENCHANTED THORN-TREE SLEEPS • 154 TRISTRAM 3   158
          NODDED AND TIED HER PALFREY TO A TREE • • 155 TRISTRAM 3   212
          THE BLOSSOMD THORN-TREE AND HER SLEEPING LOVER • 156 TRISTRAM 3   218
          WITH TERROR FROM THY TREE • • • • • PHILOMELA   V
          WITH HORROR FROM THY TREE • • • • • PHILOMELA   V
          PAST THE HIGH WOOD TO WHERE THE ELM-TREE CROWNS • 263 THYRSIS   12
          THAT SINGLE ELM-TREE BRIGHT • • • • • 263 THYRSIS   26
          WHILE THE TREE LIVED HE IN THESE FIELDS LIVED ON • 263 THYRSIS   30
          IN THE OLD HAUNT AND FIND OUR TREE-TOPPD HILL • 265 THYRSIS   103
          I KNOW THE FYFIELD TREE • • • • • • 266 THYRSIS   106
          BARE ON ITS LONELY RIDGE THE TREE THE TREE • 267 THYRSIS   160
          BARE ON ITS LONELY RIDGE THE TREE THE TREE • 267 THYRSIS   160
          I CANNOT REACH THE SIGNAL-TREE TO-NIGHT • • 267 THYRSIS   165
          HEAR IT O THYRSIS STILL OUR TREE IS THERE • 267 THYRSIS   171
          THAT LONE SKY-POINTING TREE ARE NOT FOR HIM • 267 THYRSIS   174
          THAT LONELY TREE AGAINST THE WESTERN SKY • • 268 THYRSIS   195
          DOST THOU ASK PROOF OUR TREE YET CROWNS THE HILL • 269 THYRSIS   239
          UP PAST THE WOOD TO WHERE THE ELM-TREE CROWNS • 263 THYRSIS   V 12
          UPON THE BITTER TREE • • • • • • 317 OBERMANN MORE   V 156
          A HEADLAND WITH ONE AGED PLANE-TREE CROWND • 358 MEROPE   817
          SO DIES THE LAST SHOOT OF OUR ROYAL TREE • • 359 MEROPE   857
          HOW EACH BRIGHT TINT OF TREE AND FLOWER AND HEATH   466 ALARIC AT ROME   101
          FRIENDLESS AND HOPELESS LIKE A LONELY TREE • • 477 CROMWELL   189

TREELESS
          STILL ROUGH LIKE THOSE WHICH MEN IN TREELESS PLAINS   73 SOHRAB RUSTUM   410
          LIKE THOSE WHICH MEN WHO DWELL IN TREELESS PLAINS   73 SOHRAB RUSTUM   V 410

TREES
          FROM PALM-GROVE ON TO PALM-GROVE HAPPY TREES • 11 MYCERINUS   86
          TIS HE TIS THEIR FLAG SHOOTING ROUND BY THE TREES   20 MODERN SAPPHO   30
          TIS HE TIS THE BOAT SHOOTING ROUND BY THE TREES   20 MODERN SAPPHO   V 30
          OF BRIGHT-LEAFD CHESTNUTS AND MOSSD WALNUT-TREES • 25 DREAM   8
          ALL PAST AND THROUGH THE TREES WE GLIDE • • 54 RESIGNATION   58
          THE PASTURES AND THE QUIET TREES • • • 57 RESIGNATION   173
          OF HEWING AXES CRASHING TREES SUCH BLOWS • 75 SOHRAB RUSTUM   478
          UNDER SOME MULBERRY-TREES I FOUND • • • 90 SICK KING BOKH   67
          WITH CURIOUS FRUIT-TREES BROUGHT FROM FAR • 94 SICK KING BOKH   201
          WITH CURIOUS FRUIT TREES BOUGHT FROM FAR • 94 SICK KING BOKH   V 201
          UNDER THE TREES IS DIBBLED THICK WITH HOLES • 122 BALDER DEAD 3   312
          BORDERING THE GIANTS WHERE THE TREES ARE IRON • 123 BALDER DEAD 3   331
          ON THE GRASS UNDER THE TREES • • • • 137 TRISTRAM 1   221
          AND FAR BEYOND THE SPARKLING TREES • • • 141 TRISTRAM 1   362
          DOTTED WITH HOLLY-TREES AND JUNIPER • • • 150 TRISTRAM 3   18
          MOVED UP AND DOWN UNDER THE GLOSSY TREES • 150 TRISTRAM 3   43
          THE UNDERWOOD AND TREES BEGAN AGAIN • • • 155 TRISTRAM 3   190
          SPRINKLED WITH HOLLY TREES AND JUNIPER • • TRISTRAM 3   V 18
          MOVD UP AND DOWN UNDER THEIR GLOSSY TREES • TRISTRAM 3   V 43
          BENEATH THE BIRCH-TREES COOL • • • • 160 NECKAN   42
          SERE WITH SEPTEMBER DROOPD THE CHESTNUT-TREES • 167 RACHEL 1   3
          BROWN WITH SEPTEMBER DROOPD THE CHESTNUT-TREES • 167 RACHEL 1   V 3
          LENT IT THE MUSIC OF ITS TREES AT DAWN • • 175 PARTING   20
          WITH ITS COOL TREES AND NIGHT • • • • 200 PHILOMELA   11
          CAME RUSTLING FROM THE GARDEN-TREES • • • 223 EPILOG LAOCOON   66
          THOSE BLACK-CROWND RED-BOLED PINE-TREES STAND • 248 KENSINGTON GARD   4
          SCREEND BY DARK TREES ON EITHER HAND • • 248 KENSINGTON GARD   V 2
          THOSE BLACK-TOPPD RED-BOLED PINE-TREES STAND • 248 KENSINGTON GARD   V 4
          THE BIRDS SING SWEETLY IN THESE TREES • • 248 KENSINGTON GARD   V 5
          THE BIRDS SING SWEETLY IN THEIR TREES • KENSINGTON GARD   V 5
          UNDER A DARK RED-FRUITED YEW-TREES SHADE • • 259 SCHOLAR-GIPSY   140
          FROM THE WET FIELD THROUGH THE VEXT GARDEN-TREES • 264 THYRSIS   58
          AND GROUPS UNDER THE DREAMING GARDEN-TREES • • 264 THYRSIS   69
          WITH THORNS ONCE STUDDED OLD WHITE-BLOSSOMD TREES   266 THYRSIS   113
          WHO MADE THE ROOTS OF TREES HIS BED • • • 277 SOUTHERN NIGHT   79
          COMES SOFTLY THROUGH THE OLIVE-TREES • • • 279 SOUTHERN NIGHT   119
          AT LAST THE ENCIRCLING TREES RETIRE • • • 300 GRANDE CHARTR   21
          MUSICAL THROUGH ITALIAN TREES • • • • 303 GRANDE CHARTR   141
          OFT THROUGH THE TREES THEY CATCH A GLANCE • 305 GRANDE CHARTR   176
          THE BANNERS FLASHING THROUGH THE TREES • • 305 GRANDE CHARTR   187
          AND NEATH THOSE CHESTNUT-TREES WHERE STIFF • • 312 OBERMANN MORE   9
          IN SOME DARK FIR-TREES SHADOW AMID ROCKS • • 373 MEROPE   1167
          OF TREES AND VEINS OF TURF AND LONG DARK SHOOTS • 414 EMPEDOCLES I 2   48
          AND STREAM AND SWARD AND CHESTNUT-TREES • • 414 EMPEDOCLES I 2   52
          UNDERNEATH THE STARLIT TREES • • • • • 434 EMPEDOCLES II   183

TREMBLE
          WHY TREMBLE TRUE THE NOBLENESS OF MAN • • • 6 GEO CRUIKSHANK   11

TREMBLE   (CONTINUED)
 BUT HEAR THOU THIS FIERCE MAN TREMBLE TO HEAR   • •   77 SOHRAB RUSTUM   552
 WITH FLANKS A-TREMBLE AND HIS SLENDER TONGUE   • •   114 BALDER DEAD 3   14
 TREMBLE AND THEIR CHEEKS BE FLAME   • • • • •   135 TRISTRAM 1   148
 AND ARCAS BUT I TREMBLE BOLDLY ASK   • • • • •   375 MEROPE   1211

TREMBLED
 AND THE GODS TREMBLED ON THEIR GOLDEN BEDS   • • • •   102 BALDER DEAD 1   262
 POOR CHANGELING TREMBLED   • • • • • • • •   392 MEROPE   1636
 I TREMBLED FOR OUR PRINCE AND HIS ATTEMPT   • • • •   401 MEROPE   1901

TREMBLER
 BECKONEDST THE TREMBLER AND STILL   • • • • • •   290 RUGBY CHAPEL   132

TREMBLES
 COME YOU SAY OPINION TREMBLES   • • • • • • • •   29 NEW SIRENS   81

TREMBLEST
 FOOLISH BOY WHY TREMBLEST THOU   • • • • • • •   187 STRAYED REVEL   53
 TREMBLEST AND WILT NOT DARE TO TRUST THE JOYS   426 EMPEDOCLES I 2   421
  THERE ARE

TREMBLING
 AND STOOD ERECT TREMBLING WITH RAGE HIS CLUB   • •   74 SOHRAB RUSTUM   449
 TREMBLING I ENTERD BEHELD   • • • • • • • •   187 STRAYED REVEL   46
 AND BLUE-BELLS TREMBLING BY THE FOREST-WAYS   • •   265 THYRSIS   75
 TOUCH HIS TREMBLING BEAK WITH WINE   • • • • • •   452 POOR MATTHIAS   12

TREMENDOUS
 I HEAR A GODS TREMENDOUS VOICE   • • • • • • •   174 MEETING   11
 OF A TREMENDOUS TIME   • • • • • • • • •   308 OBERMANN   66
 OF DARKNESS SO TREMENDOUS THAT ITS AUTHOR   • • • •   385 MEROPE   1420

TREMOR
 WEAK IS THE TREMOR OF PAIN   • • • • • • • •   230 YOUTH OF NATURE   92

TREMULOUS
 AH COOL NIGHT-WIND TREMULOUS STARS   • • • • •   194 STRAYED REVEL   282
 THEN AS NOW THIS TREMULOUS EAGER BEING   • • • •   210 SELF-DECEPTION   9
 WITH TREMULOUS CADENCE SLOW AND BRING   • • • •   211 DOVER BEACH   13
 HOW THICK THE TREMULOUS SHEEP-CRIES COME   • • •   248 KENSINGTON GARD   8
 HOW STRANGE THE TREMULOUS SHEEP-CRIES COME   • • •   KENSINGTON GARD   V 8

TRENCH
 FROM THE DEEP TRENCH SHE PLOUGHD SO STRONG A GOD   • •   118 BALDER DEAD 3   178

TRENCHANT
 I TOO HAVE LONGD FOR TRENCHANT FORCE   • • • • •   178 FAREWELL   33

TRESSES
 WITH BLOWN TRESSES AND WITH BECKONING HANDS   • •   26 NEW SIRENS   16
 AND HER LOAD OF STEAMING TRESSES   • • • • • •   28 NEW SIRENS   71
 MIRTH TO-DAY AND VINE-BOUND TRESSES   • • • • • •   33 NEW SIRENS   197

TRIAL
 IN DANGEROUS TRIAL   • • • • • • • • • •   391 MEROPE   1598

TRIALS
 HIS PUNY CALLOW EAGLETS AND WHAT TRIALS   • • • •   336 MEROPE   214

TRIBE
 FROM TRIBE TO TRIBE UNTIL IT REACH HER EAR   • • •   79 SOHRAB RUSTUM   597
 FROM TRIBE TO TRIBE UNTIL IT REACH HER EAR   • • •   79 SOHRAB RUSTUM   597
 TO LEARN STRANGE ARTS AND JOIN A GIPSY-TRIBE   • •   259 SCHOLAR-GIPSY   135

TRIBES
 KALMUCKS AND UNKEMPT KUZZAKS TRIBES WHO STRAY   • •   65 SOHRAB RUSTUM   132
 KALMUCKS AND UNKEMPD KUZZAKS TRIBES WHO STRAY   • •   65 SOHRAB RUSTUM   V 132
 AND HE WILL SEE THE FEEBLE SHADOWY TRIBES   • • •   100 BALDER DEAD 1   174
 AND FROM THE DARK FLOCKD UP THE SHADOWY TRIBES   •   109 BALDER DEAD 2   156
 BACK THROUGH THE ASTONISHD TRIBES OF DEAD TO HEAVEN   112 BALDER DEAD 2   285
 BELOW AND LOOKD UPON THE SHADOWY TRIBES   • • •   114 BALDER DEAD 3   39
 AND TALKEST WITH THE FEEBLE TRIBES OF GHOSTS   • •   115 BALDER DEAD 3   76
 WHEN I DRAW NIGH AND THE WAN TRIBES OF DEAD   • • •   126 BALDER DEAD 3   464
 THE TRIBES WHO THEN ROAMD ON HER BREAST   • • • •   252 FUTURE   32
 THE TRIBES WHO THEN LIVD ON HER BREAST   • • • •   252 FUTURE   V 32
 WHAT WE FOUND HERE WERE TRIBES OF FAME OBSCURE   • •   337 MEROPE   233
 THESE STURDY AND UNWORN MESSENIAN TRIBES   • • •   338 MEROPE   291
 BEQUEATHS THE ALLEGIANCE OF OUR SHEPHERD-TRIBES   • •   389 MEROPE   1540

TRIBULATIONS
 FROM TRIBULATIONS   • • • • • • • • • • •   38 STAGIRIUS   7

TRIBUNAL
 YET I THINK AT GODS TRIBUNAL   • • • • • • • -   29 NEW SIRENS   91

TRIBUTARIES
 AND WHAT SEDGED BROOKS ARE THAMESS TRIBUTARIES   •   266 THYRSIS   110

TRIBUTE
 TRIBUTE DUE TO THEE A VERSE   • • • • • • • •   453 POOR MATTHIAS   18

TRIBUTE   (CONTINUED)
        TRIBUTE ASKD BY THEE A VERSE . . . . 453 POOR MATTHIAS   V 18

TRICKD
        TRICKD OUT WITH A PARISIAN SPEECH AND FACE . . . . . 168 RACHEL 3   4
        TRICKD IN DISGUISES ALIEN TO THE REST . . . . 245 BURIED LIFE   21

TRICKLE
        WHICH STYXS AWFUL WATERS TRICKLE DOWN . . . . 368 MEROPE   1065

TRICKLED
        TRICKLED IN SILENCE THINE OWN . . . . 296 HEINES GRAVE   126

TRICKS
        WITH THY LIGHT SKIPPING TRICKS AND THY GIRLS WILES   75 SOHRAB RUSTUM   469

TRIED
        AND TRIED AND I HAVE STOOD ON MANY A FIELD . . . . .   71 SOHRAB RUSTUM   326
        BUT MUCH MUST STILL BE TRIED WHICH SHALL BUT FAIL   99 BALDER DEAD 1   130
        THAT SON OF ITALY WHO TRIED TO BLOW . . . . . . 166 AUSTERITY POET   1
        THESE THEY THEMSELVES HAVE TRIED AND KNOWN . . . . 178 FAREWELL   26
        LIKE MINE EACH DAY MORE TRIED MORE TRUE . . . . . . 180 ISOLATION MARG   6
        FROM THE HALF-TRIED BANQUET OF LIFE . . . . . . 199 EARLY DEATH   10
        WOUNDED BY MEN BY FORTUNE TRIED . . . . . . 203 EUPHROSYNE   6
        IN LESSINGS TRACK AND TRIED TO SEE . . . . . . 221 EPILOG LAOCOON   5
        WHICH MUCH TO HAVE TRIED IN MUCH BEEN BAFFLED BRINGS 260 SCHOLAR-GIPSY   165
        TOIL OR DEJECTION HAVE TRIED . . . . 290 RUGBY CHAPEL   136
        TOO FAST WE LIVE TOO MUCH ARE TRIED . . . . . 308 OBERMANN   77
        NOT TILL THE WAYS OF PRUDENCE ALL ARE TRIED . . 384 MEROPE   1386
        AND TRIED IN VAIN THE TURN OF RASHNESS COMES . . 384 MEROPE   1387
        ALL I COULD DO TO SOOTHE THEE HAS BEEN TRIED . . 396 MEROPE   1764
        AND HE WOULD TELL ME AS HIS OLD TRIED FRIEND . . 410 EMPEDOCLES I 1   130
        THY WELL-TRIED FRIENDS THY WILLING MINISTERS . . 429 EMPEDOCLES II   26

TRIES
        AND HE TREATS DOUBT THE BEST WHO TRIES TO SEE   415 EMPEDOCLES I 2   101
                LEAST ILL
        AND FEIGN KIND GODS WHO PERFECT WHAT MAN VAINLY TRIES 422 EMPEDOCLES I 2   316

TRIFLER
        THE ETERNAL TRIFLER BREAKS YOUR SPELL . . . . 304 GRANDE CHARTR   155
        THE ETERNAL TRIFLER BREAKS THEIR SPELL . . . . 304 GRANDE CHARTR   V 155

TRILL
        SONGS TO TRILL IN SURREY AIR . . . . 458 POOR MATTHIAS   197

TRIM
        OF SHAVEN HILL-SWARD TRIM AND GREEN . . . . . .   16 CHURCH BROU 2   V 13
        TRIM MONTMARTRE THE FAINT . . . . 292 HEINES GRAVE   9

TRIMMD
        AND PURGED ITS FAITH AND TRIMMD ITS FIRE . . . . 301 GRANDE CHARTR   68

TRIP
        O VICTOR VICTOR TRIP NOT AT THE GOAL . . . . . . 397 MEROPE   1771

TRIPLE
        THE GUIDE OF OUR DARK STEPS A TRIPLE VEIL . . . .   43 GIPSY CHILD   49
        TRIPLE HIS PULSES WITH FAME . . . . 200 EARLY DEATH   19
        AND LIVES A LONELY MAN IN TRIPLE GLOOM . . . . 410 EMPEDOCLES I 1   124

TRISTRAM
        TRISTRAM OF LYONESS . . . . 131 TRISTRAM 1   23
        WITH TRISTRAM THAT SPICED MAGIC DRAUGHT . . . . 132 TRISTRAM 1   64
        TRISTRAM I PRAY THEE OF THY COURTESY . . . . . 133 TRISTRAM 1   99
        AND TO TRISTRAM LAUGHING SAY . . . . 135 TRISTRAM 1   144
        SIR TRISTRAM OF THY COURTESY . . . . 135 TRISTRAM 1   145
        TRISTRAM NAY NAY THOU MUST NOT TAKE MY HAND . . 135 TRISTRAM 1   166
        TRISTRAM SWEET LOVE WE ARE BETRAYD OUT-PLANND . . 135 TRISTRAM 1   167
        THE TRISTRAM WHO IN BETTER DAYS . . . . . . 136 TRISTRAM 1   202
        UP TRISTRAM UP MEN CRY THOU MOONSTRUCK KNIGHT . . 137 TRISTRAM 1   238
        HOME TRISTRAM TO THY HALLS AGAIN . . . . . . 138 TRISTRAM 1   273
        TRISTRAM AH FOR LOVE OF HEAVEN SPEAK KINDLY . . 142 TRISTRAM 2   13
        TAKE MY HAND DEAR TRISTRAM LOOK ON ME . . . . 142 TRISTRAM 2   16
        ALTERD TRISTRAM NOT IN COURTS BELIEVE ME . . . . 143 TRISTRAM 2   37
        CIRCLED TRISTRAM BY A BAND OF GOLD . . . . . 143 TRISTRAM 2   44
        TRISTRAM TRISTRAM LET THY HEART NOT FAIL . . . . 145 TRISTRAM 2   78
        TRISTRAM TRISTRAM LET THY HEART NOT FAIL . . . . 145 TRISTRAM 2   78
        TRISTRAM ART THOU CALLD FOR MY DEATHS SAKE . . . 145 TRISTRAM 2   86
        TRISTRAM TRISTRAM STAY RECEIVE ME WITH THEE . . 146 TRISTRAM 2   99
        TRISTRAM TRISTRAM STAY RECEIVE ME WITH THEE . . 146 TRISTRAM 2   99
        ISEULT LEAVES THEE TRISTRAM NEVER MORE . . . . 146 TRISTRAM 2   100
        TRISTRAM FOR THE LOVE OF HEAVEN SPEAK KINDLY . . 142 TRISTRAM 2   V 13
        TRISTRAM TRISTRAM STAY I COME AH SORROW . . . . 146 TRISTRAM 2   V 99
        TRISTRAM TRISTRAM STAY I COME AH SORROW . . . . 146 TRISTRAM 2   V 99
        IN CORNWALL TRISTRAM AND QUEEN ISEULT LAY . . . 149 TRISTRAM 3   2
        LAY TRISTRAM AND QUEEN ISEULT DEAD AND COLD . . 149 TRISTRAM 3   V   2

TRISTRAMS
        SHE WHOM TRISTRAMS SHIP OF YORE . . . . . . 132 TRISTRAM 1   59
        EACH HER HOUR OF TRISTRAMS DAY . . . . 132 TRISTRAM 1   69

TRISTRAMS   (CONTINUED)
     WATCHES PALE BY TRISTRAMS BED . . . .   132 TRISTRAM 1   75
     ACROSS THE SHAGGY BROWS OF TRISTRAMS HOUND . . . . 152 TRISTRAM 3   88
     HER WOMEN AND SIR TRISTRAMS AGED HOUND . . . . .   152 TRISTRAM 3   98

TRIUMPH
     AND BRING IN TRIUMPH BALDER BACK TO HEAVEN . . . . . 120 BALDER DEAD 3   244
     WHAT TRIUMPH HARK WHAT PAIN . . . .   200 PHILOMELA   4
     WITH LOVE AND HATE TRIUMPH AND AGONY . . . . . .   201 PHILOMELA   26
     THEREFORE TRIUMPH ITSELF . . . .   296 HEINES GRAVE   123
     YOU TRIUMPH OVER TIME AND SPACE . . . . .   304 GRANDE CHARTR   166
     WHO MADE THAT TRIUMPH THOUGH DEFERRD SECURE . .   336 MEROPE   220
     TO SOUND THY TRIUMPH IN HIS WIDOWS EARS . . . .   395 MEROPE   1739
     CUT SHORT THY TRIUMPH SEEMING AT ITS HEIGHT . .   395 MEROPE   1742
     BUT YET NOT KNOWING THIS I TRIUMPH NOT . . . .   404 MEROPE   1988
     OVER THY CORPSE TRIUMPH NOT NEITHER MOURN . . .   404 MEROPE   1989
     THAT TRIUMPH OF THE SWEET PERSUASIVE LYRE . . . .   432 EMPEDOCLES II   126

TRIUMPHANT
     LORN AUTUMNS AND TRIUMPHANT SPRINGS . . . . . .   181 ISOLATION MARG   34
     TRIUMPHANT AND CONDEMNEST ALL OUR RACE . . . .   367 MEROPE   1051
     SWEPT FROM THY WALLS O ROME ON ITS TRIUMPHANT WAY   465 ALARIC AT ROME   78

TRIUMPHS
     IS IN THEIR FAR-OFF TRIUMPHS PROUD . . . . . .   57 RESIGNATION   163
     LOK TRIUMPHS STILL AND HELA KEEPS HER PREY . . . .   126 BALDER DEAD 3   447
     WITH TRIUMPHS A YET AMPLER BROOD . . . . .   222 EPILOG LAOCOON   24
     THAT DAY THAT HAILD HIS TRIUMPHS SAW HIM DIE . .   478 CROMWELL   212

TRIUMPHT
     SCENES WHERE A CAESAR TRIUMPHT OR A SCIPIO TROD . .   466 ALARIC AT ROME   114

TROD
     FAUSTA WHICH TEN YEARS SINCE WE TROD . . . . .   55 RESIGNATION   87
     I KNOW IT BUT FATE TROD THOSE PROMPTINGS DOWN . .   82 SOHRAB RUSTUM   713
     AND THOU HAST TROD THE SANDS OF SEISTAN . . . .   83 SOHRAB RUSTUM   750
     WHEREWITH THEY STAMPD THEM DOWN AND TROD THEM DEEP   109 BALDER DEAD 2   174
     TWAS WHEN THE HEAVENLY HOUSE I TROD . . . . .   242 MORALITY   35
     FOR SHE HERSELF HAD TROD SICILIAN FIELDS . . . .   265 THYRSIS   93
     SCENES WHERE A CAESAR TRIUMPHT OR A SCIPIO TROD . .   466 ALARIC AT ROME   114
     TOUCH THE SAME SURFACE WHICH OUR FATHERS TROD . .   EVERLASTING SUB   3
     HAVE THE SAME SURFACE WHICH OUR FATHERS TROD . .   EVERLASTING SUB V   3

TRODDEN
     OF THIS OR THAT DOWN-TRODDEN NAME . . . . . .   219 BACCHANALIA 2   16
     BUT IT IS SOMETIMES TRODDEN OH BELIEVE IT . . . .   341 MEROPE   370
     GREAT QUALITIES ARE TRODDEN DOWN . . . . . .   431 EMPEDOCLES II   92

TRODE
     RANG AS HE TRODE THEM WITH THE VOICE OF WAR . .   476 CROMWELL   152

TROJAN
     WHAT THE TROJAN MEN AND TROJAN WOMEN MIGHT MURMUR   HOMER TRANS   15
     WHAT THE TROJAN MEN AND TROJAN WOMEN MIGHT MURMUR   HOMER TRANS   15

TROJANS
     BETWEEN THAT AND THE SHIPS THE TROJANS NUMEROUS FIRES   HOMER TRANS   2
     ALWAYS AND ALWAYS FIGHTING AMONG THE FIRST   HOMER TRANS   18
        OF THE TROJANS
     AND YET NOT THAT GRIEF WHICH THEN WILL BE OF   HOMER TRANS   23
        THE TROJANS
     DID THE TROJANS OBTAIN TO STRIP THE ARMS FROM   HOMER TRANS   51
        PATROCLUS
     STAY THIS HAND FROM FIGHT TILL THE TROJANS   HOMER TRANS   62
        ARE UTTERLY ROUTED

TROOP
     TROOP ACROSS THE FLUSHING SANDS . . . . . .   26 NEW SIRENS   14
     BUT AS A TROOP OF PEDLARS FROM CABOOL . . . .   65 SOHRAB RUSTUM   160
     NO GOD BUT OF THE HERO-TROOP THE CHIEF . . . .   117 BALDER DEAD 3   125
     A TROOP OF OXFORD HUNTERS GOING HOME . . . . .   267 THYRSIS   153

TROOPING
     SWALLOWS TROOPING IN THE SEDGE . . . .   456 POOR MATTHIAS   143

TROOPS
     TROOPS WITH GOLD AND GIFTS APPEARING . . . . .   26 NEW SIRENS   23
     TROOPS LIKE EASTERN KINGS APPEARING . . . . .   26 NEW SIRENS   V   23
     THE ROYAL TROOPS OF PERSIA HORSE AND FOOT . . .   65 SOHRAB RUSTUM   139
     WHO TELLS THE PASSING TROOPS OF DEAD THEIR WAY . .   99 BALDER DEAD 1   150
     AND DOLEFUL ARE THE GHOSTS THE TROOPS OF DEAD . .   104 BALDER DEAD 1   316
     BUT YESTERMORN FIVE TROOPS OF DEAD PASSD BY . .   107 BALDER DEAD 2   104
     TRAVERSE IN TROOPS WITH CARE-FILLD BREAST . . .   277 SOUTHERN NIGHT   66
     OF PASSING TROOPS IN THE SUNS BEAM . . . . .   305 GRANDE CHARTR   177

TROPHIES
     AND BEAR THY TROPHIES TO AFRASIABS TENT . . . .   77 SOHRAB RUSTUM   530

TROPHY
     TROPHY IN MOUTH AGOG TO START . . . .   460 KAISER DEAD   50

TROTTOIRS
     WIDE STREETS WITH FINE DOUBLE TROTTOIRS . . . .   214 NEW ROME   15
     NEW STREETS WITH FINE DOUBLE TROTTOIRS . . . .   214 NEW ROME   V   15

TROUBADOUR
    SOME YOUTHFUL TROUBADOUR WHOSE TONGUE   • • • •   278 SOUTHERN NIGHT   97

TROUBLE
    WHERE COMFORT TURNS TO TROUBLE • • • • • • • •   39 STAGIRIUS   41
    A TROUBLE IN THINE ALTERD AIR • • • • • • • •   178 FAREWELL   14
    SEE YE THE TROUBLE BELOW • • • • • • • •   216 LORDS MESSENGER   2
    IF MEN PROCURED THEE TROUBLE GAVE THEE REST   • •   269 THYRSIS   215
    BUT NOW THAT TROUBLE IS FORGOT • • • • • • •   276 SOUTHERN NIGHT   17
    TEARS WASHD THE TROUBLE FROM HER FACE   • • • •   317 OBERMANN MORE   137
    O MEROPE THE TROUBLE ON THY FACE   • • • • •   393 MEROPE   1684
    THERE IS A SETTLED TROUBLE IN HIS AIR   • • • •   408 EMPEDOCLES I 1   68

TROUBLED
    HE STARES AND STARES WITH TROUBLED FACE   • • • •   148 TRISTRAM 2   157
    INTO HIS MIND THE TROUBLED EBB AND FLOW   • • • •   211 DOVER BEACH   V 17
    HE WENT HIS PIPING TOOK A TROUBLED SOUND   • • •   264 THYRSIS   48
    IN THIS OUR TROUBLED DAY • • • • • • • •   307 OBERMANN   46
    WHILE TROUBLED INNOCENTS TOSS AND LIE AWAKE   • •   372 MEROPE   1155
    AND TRANQUILLY ABOVE THAT TROUBLED BREAST   • • • •   469 ALARIC AT ROME   195
    THEN ALL HIS DREAM WAS TROUBLED AND HIS SOUL   • •   477 CROMWELL   199
    THEN WITH A TROUBLED HEART THE SWIFT ACHILLES   HOMER TRANS   58
        ADDRESSD HIM

TROUBLES
    THEY CLOAK THE TROUBLES OF THE HEART   • • • • • •   48 HORATIAN ECHO   20
    WHILE IT MENDS LITTLE TROUBLES MUCH • • • • • •   56 RESIGNATION   127
    WHICH TROUBLES ALL MY HEART AND MADE MY SHIELD   • •   77 SOHRAB RUSTUM   549
    AH WHAT TROUBLES ON HIS BROW • • • • • • • •   137 TRISTRAM 1   227
    TROUBLES CONFOUND THE LITTLE WIT HE HAS   • • • •   413 EMPEDOCLES I 2   31
    TROUBLES CONFUSE THE LITTLE WIT HE HAS   • • • •   413 EMPEDOCLES I 2   V 31

TROUBLING
    TROUBLING WITH OUR CHATTER VAIN   • • • • • •   456 POOR MATTHIAS   123

TROUBLOUS
    TROUBLOUS AND SAD FOR HER SONS • • • • • •   294 HEINES GRAVE   V 73
    THAT TROUBLOUS NIGHT IS OVER ON THE BROW   • • • •   468 ALARIC AT ROME   151

TROUT
    COUNTS HIS DAYS SPOIL THE SPOTTED TROUT   • • • •   248 KENSINGTON GARD   20
    WHOSE TROUT ARE VOCAL • • • • • • • • • •   391 MEROPE   1611

TROW
    I TROW THE MIGHTY MOTHER DOTH NOT SEE   • • • •   268 THYRSIS   179
    ANOTHER TALE I TROW THY MESSENGER   • • • • •   364 MEROPE   964

TROY
    SEVEN-GATED THEBES OR TROY   • • • • • •   193 STRAYED REVEL   257
    ROUND TROY BUT WHILE THIS STOOD TROY COULD NOT FALL   236 PALLADIUM   8
    ROUND TROY BUT WHILE THIS STOOD TROY COULD NOT FALL   236 PALLADIUM   8
    SO SHONE FORTH IN FRONT OF TROY BY THE BED OF XANTHUS   HOMER TRANS   1
    IT WILL COME WHEN SACRED TROY SHALL GO TO DESTRUCTION   HOMER TRANS   21
    TROY AND WARLIKE PRIAM TOO AND THE PEOPLE OF PRIAM   HOMER TRANS   22
    OF THE HORSEMEN OF TROY IN THE DAY THEY FOUGHT   HOMER TRANS   34
        FOR THEIR CITY

TRUANT
    MY TRUANT ODER I SHALL SEE NO MORE   • • • • •   117 BALDER DEAD 3   120
    ROAMING THE COUNTRY-SIDE A TRUANT BOY   • • • •   261 SCHOLAR-GIPSY   198
    AND LONELY AS A TRUANT CHILD   • • • • • • •   479 HAYSWATER BOAT   3

TRUCE
    AND WHEN TIS TRUCE THEN IN AFRASIABS TOWNS   • • •   63 SOHRAB RUSTUM   73
    LET THERE BE TRUCE BETWEEN THE HOSTS TO-DAY   • •   65 SOHRAB RUSTUM   151
    AND MAKE A TRUCE AND SIT UPON THIS SAND   • • •   74 SOHRAB RUSTUM   440
    SPEAK NOT TO ME OF TRUCE AND PLEDGE AND WINE   • •   75 SOHRAB RUSTUM   465

TRUE
    WHEN TRUE THE LAST IMPOSSIBILITY   • • • • • •   5 HARMONY NATURE   3
    WHY TREMBLE TRUE THE NOBLENESS OF MAN   • • • •   6 GEO CRUIKSHANK   11
    TEACHES THE LIMIT OF THE JUST AND TRUE   • • • •   7 REP FRIEND   7
    AH TOO TRUE TIMES CURRENT STRONG   • • • • •   24 MEMORY-PICTURE   57
    LEAVES US TRUE TO NOTHING LONG • • • • • • •   24 MEMORY-PICTURE   V 58
    ALL TRUE SPEECH AND LARGE AVOWAL   • • • • •   34 NEW SIRENS   227
    SCORES OF TRUE LOVE KNOTS ARE BREAKING   • • • •   35 NEW SIRENS   261
    THY TRUE STRENGTH REVEALING • • • • • • • •   39 STAGIRIUS   V 37
    AND THIS IS TRUE AND SUCH A LOSS IS HEAVENS   • •   111 BALDER DEAD 2   232
    CHILD •TIS NO TRUE DRAUGHT THIS TIS POISOND WINE   • •   133 TRISTRAM 1   103
    SING THEE TALES OF TRUE LONG-PARTED LOVERS   • • •   143 TRISTRAM 2   31
    WHAT BLESSING MUST TRUE GOODNESS SHOWER   • • • •   158 SAINT BRANDAN   V 54
    WITH EYE SUFFUSED BUT HEART INSPIRED TRUE   • • • •   172 GOOD SHEPHERD   10
    TO ALL ALWAYS TRUE • • • • • • • • • •   177 PARTING   82
    WAS TO BE GENTLE TRANQUIL TRUE   • • • • • •   179 FAREWELL   48
    OUR TRUE AFFINITIES OF SOUL   • • • • • •   179 FAREWELL   56
    LIKE MINE EACH DAY MORE TRIED MORE TRUE   • • • •   180 ISOLATION MARG   6
    I MUST NOT SAY THAT THOU WAST TRUE   • • • • •   203 EUPHROSYNE   1
    I MUST NOT SAY THAT THOU WERT TRUE   • • • • •   203 EUPHROSYNE   V 1
    I WILL NOT SAY THAT THOU WAST TRUE   • • • • •   203 EUPHROSYNE   V 1
    I MUST NOT SAY THAT SHE WAS TRUE   • • • • •   203 EUPHROSYNE   V 1
    THY HEART IS MINE TRUE TRUE AH TRUE   • • • • •   207 TOO LATE   7

TRUE   (CONTINUED)
        THY HEART IS MINE TRUE TRUE AH TRUE . . . . . . 207 TOO LATE   7
        THY HEART IS MINE TRUE TRUE AH TRUE . . . . . . 207 TOO LATE   7
        TIS TRUE INDEED AN IRON KNOT . . . . 208 ON THE RHINE   7
        AH LOVE LET US BE TRUE . . . . 211 DOVER BEACH   29
        IN TRACKING OUT OUR TRUE ORIGINAL COURSE . . . . 246 BURIED LIFE   50
        IS ELOQUENT IS WELL BUT TIS NOT TRUE . . . . . 247 BURIED LIFE   66
        IMAGED SO OFT IMAGED SO TRUE . . . . 314 OBERMANN MORE   63
        ITS HEAD WAS CLEAR AND TRUE . . . . 315 OBERMANN MORE   86
        OF LIFE TIS TRUE RECEIVED . . . . 318 OBERMANN MORE   166
        BUT JOY WHOSE GROUNDS ARE TRUE . . . . 320 OBERMANN MORE   238
        TIS TRUE AND LIVING YET . . . . . . 318 OBERMANN MORE   V
        AND JOY WHOSE GROUNDS ARE TRUE . . . . 320 OBERMANN MORE   V 238
        O BROTHER OF MY MOTHER GUARDIAN TRUE . . . . . 330 MEROPE   29
        THE TRUE AVENGERS THESE I LEAVE HIS DEED . . . . 349 MEROPE   555
        THUS MUCH FROM ARCAS MY OLD SERVANT TRUE . . . . 351 MEROPE   616
        ASSIGND US BY THE ACTOR BE THE TRUE ONE . . . . 352 MEROPE   648
        MAIDENS ASSURE ME IF THEY TOLD ME TRUE . . . . . 354 MEROPE   703
        AND HOW THEN RUNS THIS TRUE AND PRIVATE TALE . . 364 MEROPE   967
        TAKE THIS FOR TRUE THE OTHER TALE FOR FEIGND . . 364 MEROPE   984
        WHO LIVES WITNESSES TRUE . . . . 369 MEROPE   1098
        FOR THIS IS THE TRUE STRENGTH OF GUILTY KINGS . . 386 MEROPE   1436
        TRUE BUT WHAT CAUSE TO OUR ARCADIA GIVES . . . 389 MEROPE   1534
        NEPHEW THY FRIENDS ARE SOUNDED AND PROVE TRUE . . 390 MEROPE   1587
        THE TRUE ONE OF A MAN WHAT WAY OF LIFE . . . . 404 MEROPE   1992
        TO RENDER TO MY TRUE MESSENIANS THANKS . . . . 405 MEROPE   2018
        HIS WELFARE HIS TRUE AIM . . . . 418 EMPEDOCLES I 2   174
        TRUE SCIENCE IF THERE IS . . . . 423 EMPEDOCLES I 2   339
        SHALL WE JUDGE WHAT FOR MAN IS NOT TRUE BLISS OR IS 425 EMPEDOCLES I 2   396
        TO HAVE ADVANCED TRUE FRIENDS AND BEAT DOWN . . 425 EMPEDOCLES I 2   401
            BAFFLING FOES
        TO SEE IF WE WILL NOW AT LAST BE TRUE . . . . 440 EMPEDOCLES II   370
        TO OUR OWN ONLY TRUE DEEP-BURIED SELVES . . . . 440 EMPEDOCLES II   371
        SEEMD TO COME TRUE AT LAST O ABBEY OLD . . . . 446 WESTMIN ABBEY   73
        A DACHSHOUND TRUE . . . . 459 KAISER DEAD   18
        STILL WOULD BE TRUE YET STILL GROWS COLD . . . . 481 DESTINY   3
        TRUE WE MUST TAME OUR REBEL WILL . . . . . . 481 COURAGE   1
        TRUE WE MUST BOW TO NATURES LAW . . . . . . 481 COURAGE   2
        YOU SAY TRUE MY DAUGHTER PEACE IS HERE . . . . META CLOISTER   40
        THE TRUE HEART-BREAKING BAFFLED HOPE AND SHAME . . LUCRETIUS 2   13

TRULY
        THESE WE HAD AND WE GAVE TRULY . . . . 34 NEW SIRENS   231
        CLING TO WHAT CAN TRULY CHEER HIM . . . . . . 49 SECOND BEST   19
        STRONGLY SETS AND TRULY BURNS . . . . 49 SECOND BEST   24
        STRONGLY STIRS AND TRULY BURNS . . . . 49 SECOND BEST   V 24
        DEEPLY STIRS AND TRULY BURNS . . . . SECOND BEST   V 24
        AND TRULY WHILE I SPEAK O KING . . . . 92 SICK KING BOKH   129
        BUT COME DECLARE ME THIS AND TRULY TELL . . . . 111 BALDER DEAD 2   243
        TRULY THOU SAYST THE PLANNING GUILTY MIND . . . 125 BALDER DEAD 3   424
        BALDER TOO TRULY THOU FORESAWST A SNARE . . . . 126 BALDER DEAD 3   446
        TRULY I HEAR OF A MAID . . . . 343 MEROPE   425
        AND TRULY IN THIS ILL-RULED WORLD . . . . . . 353 MEROPE   664
        WISHD TRULY WISHD SOLUTION TO OUR BROIL . . . . 360 MEROPE   886
        NONE CAN TRULY CLAIM THAT . . . . 370 MEROPE   1109
        AND TRULY ONE WHO SEES WHAT SEEMD SO STRONG . . 402 MEROPE   1943
        DESIREDST THOU WHAT TRULY SPURRD THEE ON . . . . 404 MEROPE   1980
        AND TRULY HE WHO HERE . . . . 448 WESTMIN ABBEY   141
        TRULY YET THIS TIME WILL WE SAVE THEE MIGHTY ACHILLES HOMER TRANS   47

TRUMP
        ERE DANTE CAME THE TRUMP OF SACRED SONG . . . . 166 AUSTERITY POET   2

TRUMPET
        STILL LIKE A TRUMPET DOST ROUSE . . . . . . 287 RUGBY CHAPEL   52
        TRUMPET IT AS THEY WILL IS BUT THE SAME AS THINE . 417 EMPEDOCLES I 2   141
        THE TRUMPET SWELLS YET LOUDER THEY ARE HERE . . 467 ALARIC AT ROME   133

TRUMPETS
        DANCES AS THE TRUMPETS BLOW . . . . 138 TRISTRAM 1   264

TRUNK
        COULD WIELD AN UNLOPPD TRUNK IT WAS AND HUGE . . 73 SOHRAB RUSTUM   409
        COULD WIELD AN UNLOPPD TRUNK IT WAS STILL ROUGH . 73 SOHRAB RUSTUM   V 409
        AND CAST HIS TRUNK TO CHOKE THE ABYSMAL VOID . . 121 BALDER DEAD 3   259
        AND THREW HIS TRUNK TO CHOKE THE ABYSMAL VOID . . 121 BALDER DEAD 3   V 259

TRUST
        TRUST ME AND GLADLY BRING FOR MY AWARD . . . . 126 BALDER DEAD 3   V 465
        TRUST ITS OWN THOUGHTS BEFORE YET . . . . . 281 HAWORTH CHURCH   42
        AT LEAST IF THOU WILT TRUST THEM TRY THEM FIRST . 381 MEROPE   1319
        HAVE FAITH AND TRUST THE FUTURE AND THE GODS . . 388 MEROPE   1507
        FIRST FOR OUR UNION TRUST ME TWIXT US TWO . . . 395 MEROPE   1733
        REJOICE WITH US AND TRUST ME HE WHO WISHD . . . 403 MEROPE   1958
        TO LEAD THOSE FALSE WHO TRUST IT HIST ONCE MORE . 413 EMPEDOCLES I 2   33
        TREMBLEST AND WILT NOT DARE TO TRUST THE JOYS . . 426 EMPEDOCLES I 2   421
            THERE ARE
        WHO MAY TRUST US TO DIVINE . . . . 457 POOR MATTHIAS   170

TRUSTED
        WHAT FOLLOWD HIS MOST TRUSTED KINSMAN SLEW . . . 389 MEROPE   1555

TRUSTING
    THY TRUSTING LORD DIDST THOU HIS SERVANT SLAY   • • 338 MEROPE   280

TRUTH
    DUMB JUDGES ANSWER TRUTH OR MOCKERY   • • • • • •   4 EMERSONS ESSAYS   14
    BUT IS A CALM LIKE THIS IN TRUTH   • • • • • •   21 YOUTH AND CALM   5
    YET IS A CALM LIKE THIS IN TRUTH   • • • • • •   21 YOUTH AND CALM V   5
    YET AH IS CALM ALONE IN TRUTH • • • • • •   21 YOUTH AND CALM V   5
    ARE SCARCE MORE CHANGED IN TRUTH THAN THEY • • • •   55 RESIGNATION   107
    TRUTH SITS UPON THE LIPS OF DYING MEN • • • • •   80 SOHRAB RUSTUM   656
    BUT EVEN THAT COMES LANGUIDLY IN TRUTH • • • • 151 TRISTRAM 3   74
    BEING IN TRUTH BUT A DISEASED UNREST • • • • • 153 TRISTRAM 3   135
    EVEN IN A PALACE ON HIS TRUTH SINCERE • • • • • 169 WORLDLY PLACE   9
    THIS TRUTH ON THEE BE MINE NO MORE • • • • • 179 FAREWELL   42
    THIS TRUTH TO PROVE AND MAKE THINE OWN • • • • 181 ISOLATION MARG   29
    WHY SHOULD THEY ASK IF TRUTH BE THERE • • • • • 203 EUPHROSYNE   4
    TRUTH WHAT IS TRUTH TWO BLEEDING HEARTS • • • • 203 EUPHROSYNE   5
    TRUTH WHAT IS TRUTH TWO BLEEDING HEARTS • • • • 203 EUPHROSYNE   5
    THEY WILL NOT ASK IF TRUTH BE THERE • • • • • 203 EUPHROSYNE V   4
    THEY SHOULD NOT ASK IF TRUTH BE THERE • • • • • 203 EUPHROSYNE V   4
    COME NOW AND LET ME DREAM IT TRUTH • • • • • 209 LONGING   10
    COME NOW AND LET ME DEEM IT TRUTH • • • • • 209 LONGING V   10
    FOR THESE IN TRUTH WERE EVERYWHERE • • • • • 222 EPILOG LAOCOON   19
    THE MOUNTAIN-TOPS WHERE IS THE THRONE OF TRUTH • • 267 THYRSIS   144
    ART STILL HAS TRUTH TAKE REFUGE THERE • • • • • 271 MEMORIAL VERSES   28
    SHOWD ME THE HIGH WHITE STAR OF TRUTH • • • • 301 GRANDE CHARTR   69
    TO CURSE AND TO DENY YOUR TRUTH • • • • • 301 GRANDE CHARTR   78
    SHOWD ME THE PALE COLD STAR OF TRUTH • • • • • 301 GRANDE CHARTR V 69
    AND WHO BUT THOU MUST BE IN TRUTH • • • • • 313 OBERMANN MORE   37
    AND LOVE HIS CHEERLESS TRUTH • • • • • • 322 OBERMANN MORE   280
    WHOSE TEARS WARRANT HIS TRUTH • • • • • • 369 MEROPE   1091
    SO MUCH IS DUE TO TRUTH EVEN TOWRDS OUR FOE • • 388 MEROPE   1493
    ONE COLOUR IN THY LIFE THE HUE OF TRUTH • • • 404 MEROPE   1996
    WE HAVE THE TRUTH THEY CRY • • • • • • 417 EMPEDOCLES I 2   139
    YET STILL IN SPITE OF TRUTH • • • • • • 424 EMPEDOCLES I 2   367
    AND YET THE VILLAGE-CHURL FEELS THE TRUTH MORE   426 EMPEDOCLES I 2   411
        THAN YOU
    HE FABLES YET SPEAKS TRUTH • • • • • • 431 EMPEDOCLES II   89
    YE SUN-BORN VIRGINS ON THE ROAD OF TRUTH • • • 436 EMPEDOCLES II   239
    SOPHISTICATED NO TRUTH • • • • • • • 441 EMPEDOCLES II   401
    AND GOODNESS WARM AND TRUTH WITHOUT ALLOY • • 446 WESTMIN ABBEY   78
    DOWN THE LONG AGE OF TRUTH THAT RIPENS SLOW • • 448 WESTMIN ABBEY   148
    PERCHANCE HAD QUICKEND WITH A LIVING TRUTH • • • 473 CROMWELL   53
    FOND HEARTS THAT FAIN WOULD CLOTHE THE UNWELCOME TRUTH 474 CROMWELL   97

TRY
    REMEMBER ALL THY VALOUR TRY THY FEINTS • • • •   75 SOHRAB RUSTUM   466
    IS IT A MATTER WHICH A GOD MIGHT TRY • • • • •   99 BALDER DEAD 1   133
    TRY IT BUT I FOR ONE WILL NOT APPLAUD • • • • 121 BALDER DEAD 3   281
    WAS CHRIST A MAN LIKE US AH LET US TRY • • • • 171 BETTER PART   13
    I WILL NOT KNOW FOR WHEREFORE TRY • • • • • 185 TERRACE BERNE   41
    BUT AH HOW FEW OF ALL THAT TRY • • • • • • 226 EPILOG LAOCOON 169
    AND WHILE THEY TRY TO STEM • • • • • • 243 SUMMER NIGHT   47
    AND LONG WE TRY IN VAIN TO SPEAK AND ACT • • • 247 BURIED LIFE   64
    AND WAIVE ALL CLAIM TO BLISS AND TRY TO BEAR • • 260 SCHOLAR-GIPSY   193
    THEY TRY US OFTENEST MAKE US HARD • • • • • 273 EDW QUILLINAN   7
    AS THOSE WHEREWITH WE TRY TO TEST • • • • • 352 MEROPE   634
    POWER FAILS US TO TRY CLEARLY IF THAT CAUSE • • 352 MEROPE   647
    AT LEAST IF THOU WILT TRUST THEM TRY THEM FIRST • • 381 MEROPE   1319
    THEN TRY THE ISSUE AND NOT RUSHING ON • • • • 382 MEROPE   1325
    AS THOSE WITH WHICH WE TRY TO TEST • • • • • 352 MEROPE V 634
    DARED ONE BUT TRY THOU WAST A KIND CHILD EVER • • 408 EMPEDOCLES I 1   76
    YET THOU MAYST TRY THY PLAYING IF THOU WILT • • 409 EMPEDOCLES I 1   85
    AND TRY THY NOBLEST STRAINS MY CALLICLES • • • 409 EMPEDOCLES I 1   97
    DARED ONE BUT TRY THOU WERT A KIND CHILD EVER • • 409 EMPEDOCLES I 1 V 76
    THESE HUNDRED DOCTORS TRY • • • • • • 417 EMPEDOCLES I 2   137
    NEVER TO CEASE TO WRITHE AND TRY TO REST • • • 430 EMPEDOCLES II   60
    NEVER TO CEASE TO WRITHE AND TRY TO SLEEP • • • 430 EMPEDOCLES II V 60

TRYING
    TRYING TO CALL HIM BACK TO LIFE AND LIFE • • • •   81 SOHRAB RUSTUM   697

TRYSTING
    HAD BEEN THE LIKELIEST TRYSTING-PLACE TO-DAY • • 135 TRISTRAM 1   165

TUFTED
    OF HAIR THAT RED AND TUFTED FELL • • • • • • 157 SAINT BRANDAN   18
    OF HAIR THAT BLACK AND TUFTED FELL • • • • • • 157 SAINT BRANDAN V 18
    AND CRISP THYME TUFTED • • • • • • • • 392 MEROPE   1643

TUFTS
    THAT CLIMB FROM THE STREAMS EDGE THE LONG GREY TUFTS 406 EMPEDOCLES I 1   16

TUILERIES
    SERE IN THE GARDEN OF THE TUILERIES • • • • • • 167 RACHEL 1   2
    BROWN IN THE GARDEN OF THE TUILERIES • • • • • 167 RACHEL 1 V   2

TUKAS
    THE TUKAS AND THE LANCES OF SALORE • • • • • •   64 SOHRAB RUSTUM   122

TUMBLING
ROLL TUMBLING IN THE CURRENT OER MY HEAD ▪ ▪ ▪ ▪ 83 SOHRAB RUSTUM 770

TUMULT
REVEALING ALL THE TUMULT OF THE FEAST ▪ ▪ ▪ ▪ 11 MYCERINUS 96
SOME IN THE TUMULT ARE LOST ▪ ▪ ▪ ▪ ▪ ▪ ▪ ▪ 216 LORDS MESSENGER 13
BUT I ON MENS IMPIOUS TUMULT HURLD ▪ ▪ ▪ ▪ ▪ ▪ KENSINGTON GARD V 25
I ON MENS IMPIOUS TUMULT HURLD ▪ ▪ ▪ ▪ ▪ ▪ ▪ KENSINGTON GARD V 25
BY NIGHT IN THAT BLIND TUMULT THEY WERE SLAIN ▪ ▪ ▪ 340 MEROPE 345
TO HEAR ANOTHER TUMULT IN THESE STREETS ▪ ▪ ▪ 349 MEROPE 561

TUMULTUOUS
RENT WITH TUMULTUOUS THOUGHTS WHOSE CONFLICT RUNG 478 CROMWELL 223

TUNES
TO TUNES WE DID NOT CALL OUR BEING MUST KEEP CHIME 418 EMPEDOCLES I 2 196

TUNNIES
GREEN BURSTING FIGS AND TUNNIES STEEPD IN BRINE ▪ ▪ 262 SCHOLAR-GIPSY 239

TURBID
SNATCHD A TURBID INSPIRATION ▪ ▪ ▪ ▪ ▪ ▪ ▪ 31 NEW SIRENS 151
INTO HIS MIND THE TURBID EBB AND FLOW ▪ ▪ ▪ ▪ 211 DOVER BEACH 17
IF NOT THY FIERCE AND TURBID SONG ▪ ▪ ▪ ▪ ▪ ▪ 482 COURAGE 18

TURBULENCE
MUCH TURBULENCE AND LITTLE CONSTANCY ▪ ▪ ▪ ▪ ▪ ▪ 337 MEROPE 234

TURBULENT
TAMED IS THEIR TURBULENT YOUTHFUL GLOW ▪ ▪ ▪ ▪ 208 ON THE RHINE 24

TURF
ON THE TURF DEAD LIES THE BOAR ▪ ▪ ▪ ▪ ▪ ▪ ▪ 13 CHURCH BROU 1 26
IN ITS CLEAR SHALLOW TURF-FRINGED BED ▪ ▪ ▪ ▪ 55 RESIGNATION 91
YET FAUSTA THE MUTE TURF WE TREAD ▪ ▪ ▪ ▪ ▪ ▪ 60 RESIGNATION 265
ITS SLIGHT DARK SHADOW ON THE MOONLIT TURF ▪ ▪ ▪ 70 SOHRAB RUSTUM 316
STARRD THE COOL TURF AND CLUMPS OF PRIMROSES ▪ ▪ 155 TRISTRAM 3 208
PASSING OUT FROM THE WET TURF ▪ ▪ ▪ ▪ ▪ ▪ ▪ 186 STRAYED REVEL 31
WHERE MOST THE GIPSIES BY THE TURF-EDGED WAY ▪ ▪ 258 SCHOLAR-GIPSY 112
OER THE FRESH SHORT TURF OF THE HARTZ ▪ ▪ ▪ ▪ 297 HEINES GRAVE 153
THE TURF THE PINES THE SKY ▪ ▪ ▪ ▪ ▪ ▪ ▪ ▪ 312 OBERMANN MORE 6
SOFT DARKNESS ON THE TURF DID LIE ▪ ▪ ▪ ▪ ▪ ▪ 323 OBERMANN MORE 329
WHILE FROM THE TURF WHEREON I LAY I SPRANG ▪ ▪ 358 MEROPE 829
THEY FEEL THE COOL WET TURF UNDER THEIR FEET ▪ ▪ 406 EMPEDOCLES I 1 2
OF TREES AND VEINS OF TURF AND LONG DARK SHOOTS ▪ ▪ 414 EMPEDOCLES I 2 48
BY MOUNDED TURF AND GRAVEN STONE ▪ ▪ ▪ ▪ ▪ ▪ 451 GEISTS GRAVE 64
GREEN TURF ABOVE AND CRUMBLING DUST BELOW ▪ ▪ ▪ ▪ 464 ALARIC AT ROME 57

TURMOIL
STILL WORKING BLAMING STILL OUR VAIN TURMOIL ▪ ▪ 2 QUIET WORK 13
STILL WORKING CHIDING STILL OUR VAIN TURMOIL ▪ ▪ 2 QUIET WORK V 13
TURMOIL OF DEATH AND OF BIRTH ▪ ▪ ▪ ▪ ▪ ▪ ▪ 216 LORDS MESSENGER V 3
THE TURMOIL FOR A LITTLE BREATH ▪ ▪ ▪ ▪ ▪ ▪ 251 WISH 46
A TURMOIL FOR A LITTLE BREATH ▪ ▪ ▪ ▪ ▪ ▪ ▪ 251 WISH V 46
AND STRANGE AND VAIN THE EARTHLY TURMOIL GROWS ▪ ▪ 267 THYRSIS 148
THE TURMOIL OF EXPIRING LIFE ▪ ▪ ▪ ▪ ▪ ▪ ▪ 271 MEMORIAL VERSES 26

TURN
LET MY TURN IF IT WILL COME BE SWIFT IN ARRIVING ▪ ▪ 20 MODERN SAPPHO 31
BUT WE TURN OUR EYES ARE FLITTING ▪ ▪ ▪ ▪ ▪ ▪ 34 NEW SIRENS 241
BUT IN DISDAINFUL SILENCE TURN AWAY ▪ ▪ ▪ ▪ ▪ 42 GIPSY CHILD 31
EACH IN HER TURN WITH TORCH UPREARD ▪ ▪ ▪ ▪ ▪ 53 RESIGNATION 32
OR ELSE TOO WEAK AND ALL EYES TURN TO THEE ▪ ▪ ▪ 67 SOHRAB RUSTUM 218
IN TURN AND FULL STRUCK RUSTUMS SHIELD SHARP RANG 73 SOHRAB RUSTUM 406
RUNNING FAST HOMEWARD WITH THE TURN OF TIDE ▪ ▪ 69 SOHRAB RUSTUM V 287
ARE IN THEIR TURN OBEDIENT MADE ▪ ▪ ▪ ▪ ▪ ▪ 93 SICK KING BOKH 188
OUT OF OUR SIGHT THAT WE MAY TURN FROM GRIEF ▪ ▪ 115 BALDER DEAD 3 55
HER HAND IN TURN FOR GUIDANCE AND THE THREE ▪ ▪ 129 BALDER DEAD 3 551
IS MY PAGE HERE COME TURN ME TO THE FIRE ▪ ▪ ▪ 139 TRISTRAM 1 298
THEY TURN ON ALL SIDES ▪ ▪ ▪ ▪ ▪ ▪ ▪ ▪ ▪ 190 STRAYED REVEL 131
OH WERT THOU HERE THAT I MIGHT TURN ▪ ▪ ▪ ▪ ▪ 204 CALAIS SANDS V 9
NONE SPEAKS NONE HEEDS AH TURN THY HEAD ▪ ▪ ▪ ▪ 206 RIVER 4
PAGE AFTER PAGE OF MUSIC TURN ▪ ▪ ▪ ▪ ▪ ▪ ▪ 224 EPILOG LAOCOON 103
THE WORLD IN ITS TURN WILL NOT TAKE ▪ ▪ ▪ ▪ ▪ 228 CAUTION POETS 3
AND TURN THOSE LIMPID EYES ON MINE ▪ ▪ ▪ ▪ ▪ 245 BURIED LIFE 10
FROM HER FALSE FRIENDS APPROACH IN HADES TURN ▪ ▪ 261 SCHOLAR-GIPSY 209
TURN WE NEXT TO THE DEAD ▪ ▪ ▪ ▪ ▪ ▪ ▪ ▪ 282 HAWORTH CHURCH 47
TURN O DEATH ON THE VILE ▪ ▪ ▪ ▪ ▪ ▪ ▪ ▪ 281 HAWORTH CHURCH V
TURN ON THE FOOLISH THE STROKE ▪ ▪ ▪ ▪ ▪ ▪ ▪ 281 HAWORTH CHURCH V
I TURN THY LEAVES I FEEL THEIR BREATH ▪ ▪ ▪ ▪ 306 OBERMANN 13
AND THEN WE TURN THOU SADDER SAGE ▪ ▪ ▪ ▪ ▪ ▪ 309 OBERMANN 81
CHOOSEST THOU NOW TO TURN ▪ ▪ ▪ ▪ ▪ ▪ ▪ 314 OBERMANN MORE 74
TURN WITH AVERTED EYES FROM DEEDS OF BLOOD ▪ ▪ ▪ 354 MEROPE 695
A MOMENT MORE I SAW THE PRINCE TURN ROUND ▪ ▪ ▪ 358 MEROPE 831
WHETHER IT TURN AT LAST TO JOY OR WOE ▪ ▪ ▪ ▪ 359 MEROPE 862
AND TRIED IN VAIN THE TURN OF RASHNESS COMES ▪ ▪ 384 MEROPE 1387
MAY IT TURN HAPPIER THAN MY DOUBTS PORTEND ▪ ▪ ▪ 390 MEROPE 1583
THE SACRIFICERS AXE WILL SERVE THY TURN ▪ ▪ ▪ 391 MEROPE 1592
AND IN MY TURN I WISH THE SAME FOR THEE ▪ ▪ ▪ ▪ 396 MEROPE 1763
AND TURN THEE TO THE ELEMENTS THY FRIENDS ▪ ▪ ▪ 429 EMPEDOCLES II 25
DEAR LITTLE FRIEND,AT EVERY TURN ▪ ▪ ▪ ▪ ▪ 450 GEISTS GRAVE 8

TURN (CONTINUED)
WHO WOULD NOT BURST HIS BONDS AND IN HIS TURN BE FREE   465 ALARIC AT ROME   90
WHO WOULD NOT TURN HIM FROM THE BARREN SEA . . . .   470 ALARIC AT ROME   221
THAT CALM EYE FOLLOWD TURN HIM WHERE HE WILL   . .   477 CROMWELL   196

TURND
SHE ENTERD THAT MOMENT HIS EYES TURND FROM ME   . .   19 MODERN SAPPHO   10
HE SPAKE AND PERAN-WISA TURND AND STRODE   . . . .   66 SOHRAB RUSTUM   187
HE SPOKE AND FROWND AND GUDURZ TURND AND RAN   . .   69 SOHRAB RUSTUM   260
AND TURND AWAY AND SPAKE TO HIS OWN SOUL   . . . .   71 SOHRAB RUSTUM   346
AND THEN HE TURND AND STERNLY SPAKE ALOUD   . . . .   72 SOHRAB RUSTUM   364
THE IRON PLATES RANG SHARP BUT TURND THE SPEAR   . .   73 SOHRAB RUSTUM   407
HE SPOKE AND PERAN-WISA TURND AND STRODE   . . . .   66 SOHRAB RUSTUM   V 187
AND TURND AWAY AND SPOKE TO HIS OWN SOUL   . . . .   71 SOHRAB RUSTUM   V 346
IS TO A PUTRID PUDDLE TURND   . . . .   89 SICK KING BOKH   61
AND FAR FROM HEAVEN HE TURND HIS SHINING ORBS   . .   96 BALDER DEAD 1   51
AND HODER TURND AND LEFT HIS MOTHERS HOUSE   . . . .   100 BALDER DEAD 1   197
AND STRAIGHT TO BALDER HERMOD TURND AND SPAKE   . .   111 BALDER DEAD 2   249
HE SPAKE AND TURND TO GO TO THE INNER GLOOM . . . .   125 BALDER DEAD 3   421
TURND TO EACH OTHER THE EYES CLOSED   . . . . . .   141 TRISTRAM 1   338
WAS TURND UPON THE SONS OF MEN . . . .   202 URANIA   10
TO ENGLANDS CLIFFS MY GAZE IS TURND   . . . . . .   205 CALAIS SANDS   19
TO ENGLANDS CLIFFS MY LOOK IS TURND   . . . . . .   205 CALAIS SANDS   V 19
AND MAN HAS TURND THEM MANY TIMES MADE GREECE   . .   239 REVOLUTIONS   5
TURND ONCE TO WATCH WHILE THICK THE SNOWFLAKES FALL   259 SCHOLAR-GIPSY   128
WHEN ALL TURND TOWRDS ME ME HE WOULD HAVE SHOWN   . .   366 MEROPE   1005
BUT HE TURND HIS BEAUTEOUS FACE   . . . .   433 EMPEDOCLES II   159
STILL TURND TO WATCH THE BATTLE STILL FORGOT   . .   476 CROMWELL   171

TURNED
I TURNED BY SOME VAGUE IMPULSE STIRRD   . . . . .   324 OBERMANN MORE   335
YOUR SWEET EYES ARE TURNED ON ME   . . . .   META CLOISTER   20

TURNEDST
STILL THOU TURNEDST AND STILL   . . . .   290 RUGBY CHAPEL   131

TURNEST
LOVED NOT WHO TURNEST FROM THE THRONG   . . . . .   314 OBERMANN MORE   71

TURNING
AND TURNING LEFT THEM THERE AND WITH BRIEF PAUSE   . .   11 MYCERINUS   82
HER LIFE WAS TURNING TURNING   . . . .   21 REQUIESCAT   9
HER LIFE WAS TURNING TURNING   . . . .   21 REQUIESCAT   9
TURNING SICK AND BAFFLED LEARNS   . . . .   SECOND BEST   V 20
TURNING HIM QUICKLY TO GO IN   . . . .   91 SICK KING BOKH   127
THEN TURNING WESTWARD TO THE ADDERS HILL   . . . .   357 MEROPE   779
TURNING WITH PITEOUS   . . . .   393 MEROPE   1662

TURNS
WHERE COMFORT TURNS TO TROUBLE . . . .   39 STAGIRIUS   41
IT TURNS LIFES MIGHTY WHEEL   . . . .   47 WORLD QUIETIST   13
THAT THY POOR HEAD ALMOST TURNS   . . . .   49 SECOND BEST   8
SHE TURNS FROM THAT COLD SUCCOUR WHICH ATTENDS   . .   170 WEST LONDON   12
BANNER BY TURNS AND BUGLE WOO   . . . .   305 GRANDE CHARTR   191
A WOUNDED HUMAN SPIRIT TURNS   . . . .   307 OBERMANN   23
YET WITH A LIGHT UNCAREWORN SPIRIT TURNS   . . . .   351 MEROPE   614
ONE STILL LAGS LAST AND TURNS AND EYES THE PILE   . .   444 WESTMIN ABBEY   14

TURPENTINE
SPLINTERS OF PINE-WOOD SOAKD WITH TURPENTINE   . . .   118 BALDER DEAD 3   168

TURQUOISE
OF TURQUOISE-EARTH AND AMETHYST   . . . .·   191 STRAYED REVEL   195

TURRETS
AND THE GREY TURRETS OF THE CASTLE OLD   . . . . .   151 TRISTRAM 3   59

TWAIN
IN GLOOM THEY TWAIN WERE WRAPPD AND THEY ALONE   . .   75 SOHRAB RUSTUM   486
AGLOW WITH ANGRY FIRE TO KEEP US TWAIN   . . . .   395 MEROPE   1736
SINCE BROILS TEAR US IN TWAIN SINCE THIS NEW SWARM   410 EMPEDOCLES I 1   121

TWELFTH
ON THE TWELFTH DAY THE GODS SHALL BURN HIS CORPSE   106 BALDER DEAD 2   44
AND ON THE TWELFTH MORN SAW THE LIGHT OF HEAVEN   . .   113 BALDER DEAD 2   294

TWELVE
WHERE ARE IN CIRCLE RANGED TWELVE GOLDEN CHAIRS   . .   106 BALDER DEAD 2   37
TWELVE HUNDRED YEARS AND MORE   . . . .   445 WESTMIN ABBEY   51

TWENTIETH
THE TWENTIETH ANNIVERSARY OF STRIFE   . . . . . .   333 MEROPE   115

TWENTY
GLION AH TWENTY YEARS IT CUTS   . . . .   312 OBERMANN MORE   1
YES TWENTY YEARS AGO THIS DAY BEHELD   . . . . . .   333 MEROPE   117
DO TWENTY YEARS WEAR OUT AND SEE EXPIRE   . . . .   335 MEROPE   180
THE SCHEMES PURSUED IN VAIN FOR TWENTY YEARS   . . .   360 MEROPE   876
THROUGH TWENTY YEARS HIS MOURNFUL ANXIOUS ZEAL   . .   387 MEROPE   1477
THE SILENCE THOU HAST KEPT FOR TWENTY YEARS   . . .   395 MEROPE   1726

TWENTY   (CONTINUED)
     FOR TWENTY YEARS FORBORNE TO INTERRUPT   • , • • • 395 MEROPE   1730

TWENTYFOLD
     HOW TWENTYFOLD WORSE ARE YE WHEN YOUR BLOWS   • • 385 MEROPE   1407

TWICE
     HIS BREAST HEAVED HIS LIPS FOAMD AND TWICE HIS VOICE   74 SOHRAB RUSTUM   455
     TWICE ERE THAT DAY OF SHAME THE EMBATTLED FOE   • • 465 ALARIC AT ROME   73
     TWICE HAD THE ETERNAL CITY BOWED HER LOW   • • • • 465 ALARIC AT ROME   75
     TWICE HAD THE PAGEANT OF THAT VAST ARRAY   • • • • 465 ALARIC AT ROME   77
     TWICE FROM WITHOUT THY BULWARKS HATH THE DIN   • • 465 ALARIC AT ROME   79
     TWICE HATH THE CLOUD HUNG OER THEE TWICE BEEN STAYED   465 ALARIC AT ROME   83
     TWICE HATH THE CLOUD HUNG OER THEE TWICE BEEN STAYED   465 ALARIC AT ROME   83
     EVEN IN THE ACT TO BURST TWICE THREATENED TWICE   465 ALARIC AT ROME   84
          DELAYED
     EVEN IN THE ACT TO BURST TWICE THREATENED TWICE   465 ALARIC AT ROME   84
          DELAYED

TWILIGHT
     AT TWILIGHT ON A STORMY EVE IN MARCH   • • • • •   69 SOHRAB RUSTUM   V 286
     WHILE TWILIGHT FELL AND SACRED NIGHT CAME ON   • • 97 BALDER DEAD 1   71
     IN THAT GREAT DAY THE TWILIGHT OF THE GODS   • • • • 115 BALDER DEAD 3   68
     IN TWILIGHT ON THE LONELY VERGE OF HELL   • • • • 124 BALDER DEAD 3   390
     BUT NECKAN IN THE TWILIGHT GREY   • • • • • 161 NECKAN   59
     AND NECKAN IN THE TWILIGHT GREY   • • • • • 161 NECKAN   V 59
     IN THE TWILIGHT AND BATHED IN DEW   • • • • • 234 YOUTH OF MAN   78
     LOOK THROUGH THE SHOWERY TWILIGHT GREY   • • • • 300 GRANDE CHARTR   22

TWIN
     AND FROM THE BLUE TWIN-LAKES IT COMES   • • • • 184 TERRACE BERNE   9
     FROM THE TWIN SOUL WHICH HALVES THEIR OWN   • • • • 206 TOO LATE   4
     FROM THE TWIN SOUL THAT HALVES THEIR OWN   • • • • 206 TOO LATE   V 4
     FROM THOSE TWIN BROOKS THAT BEACHED STRAND   •. • • • 480 HAYSWATER BOAT   21
     SOONER THAN THOSE TWIN REACHES OF GREAT TIME   • •   FRAGMENT 5   7

TWINE
     TWINE ABOUT THEIR HEARTS AGAIN   • • • • • • 135 TRISTRAM 1   152
     WHERE THE SEA-SNAKES COIL AND TWINE   • • • • • 162 FORSAKEN MERM   41
     AND LEAVE IT ROUND THY NECK TO TWINE   • • • • • 461 KAISER DEAD   81
     IF WREATHS MAY TWINE FOR YOU OR LAURELS WAVE   • • 467 ALARIC AT ROME   137
     AND TWINE WITH BOLDER HAND THY LAST MEMORIAL WREATH   471 ALARIC AT ROME   228

TWINES
     WHERE TWINES THE CHAPLET DEALT A MIGHTY BLOW   • • 402 MEROPE   1921

TWINKLE
     BEGAN TO TWINKLE THROUGH THE FOG FOR NOW   • • • •   86 SOHRAB RUSTUM   870
     TWINKLE THE MONASTERY-LIGHTS   • • • • • • • • 156 SAINT BRANDAN   8

TWINKLES
     TWINKLES ON GRASMERE NO MORE   • • • • • • • • 228 YOUTH OF NATURE   19

TWINKLING
     FROM TREE TO TREE ALL THROUGH THE TWINKLING GROVE   11 MYCERINUS   95

TWIRLD
     I SEE THE TAIL LIKE BRACELET TWIRLD   • • • • • • 460 KAISER DEAD   55

TWIRLING
     RAPT TWIRLING IN THY HAND A WITHERD SPRAY   • • • • 258 SCHOLAR-GIPSY   119

TWISTED
     AND FROM THE ROOFS THE TWISTED CHIMNEY-STACKS   • • 263 THYRSIS   5

TWITTERING
     AND THEIR QUICK TWITTERING FILLS THE BANKS AND SHORES   109 BALDER DEAD 2   162
     SO AROUND HERMOD SWARMD THE TWITTERING GHOSTS   • • 109 BALDER DEAD 2   163

TWIXT
     BUT OH LET THERE BE PEACE TWIXT THEE AND ME   • •   74 SOHRAB RUSTUM   447
     PEERD TWIXT THE STEMS AND THE GROUND BROKE AWAY   • • 155 TRISTRAM 3   186
     AND FLUCTUATE TWIXT BLIND HOPES AND BLIND DESPAIRS   236 PALLADIUM   18
     TWIXT MYRTLE-HEDGES ALL IN FLOWER   • • • • • • 278 SOUTHERN NIGHT 103
     TWIXT VICE AND VIRTUE REVIVST   • • • • • • • 288 RUGBY CHAPEL   55
     BUT EVERLASTING HORROR TWIXT US TWO   • • • • • 336 MEROPE   193
     EXTINGUISHES DISTRUST TWIXT HIM AND THEE   • • • • 359 MEROPE   852
     TO PLY TWIXT THE MESSENIAN KING AND HIM   • • • • 364 MEROPE   981
     TREACHEROUSLY PLOTTED TWIXT MY SON AND ME   • • • • 387 MEROPE   1481
     TWIXT THEE AND ME SUSPICION THAT I NURSED   • • • • 394 MEROPE   1699
     FIRST FOR OUR UNION TRUST ME TWIXT US TWO   • • • • 395 MEROPE   1733
     STAND NOT TWIXT HIS SOUL AND OURS   • • • • • 457 POOR MATTHIAS   172

TWO
     ONE LESSON OF TWO DUTIES KEPT AT ONE   • • • • •   1 QUIET WORK   3
     TWO LESSONS NATURE LET ME LEARN OF THEE   • • • •   1 QUIET WORK   V 1
     TWO LESSONS THAT IN EVERY WIND ARE BLOWN   • • • •   1 QUIET WORK   V 2
     TWO BLENDING DUTIES HARMONISD IN ONE   • • • • •   1 QUIET WORK   V 3
     ONE LESSON OF TWO DUTIES SERVD IN ONE   • • • •   1 QUIET WORK   V 3
     ONE LESSON OF TWO DUTIES KEPT IN ONE   • • • • •   1 QUIET WORK   V 3
     HEMMD BY TWO BANKS OF CLOUD PEERS PALE AND WEAK   • •   10 MYCERINUS   57
     ON THE TOMB TWO FORMS THEY SCULPTURED   • • • •   16 CHURCH BROU 1   105

TWO   (CONTINUED)
        THE ALPINE PEASANTS TWO AND THREE   • • • • •   17 CHURCH BROU 2   18
        ON THE BROWN RUDE-CARVED BALCONY TWO FORMS • • • •   25 DREAM   21
        TWO YOUNG FAIR LOVERS   • • • • • • • • •   51 CONSOLATION   41
        SOME TWO HOURS MARCH WITH SERIOUS AIR   • • • •   54 RESIGNATION   68
        LET THE TWO ARMIES REST TO-DAY BUT I • • • • •   62 SOHRAB RUSTUM   55
        I CHALLENGED ONCE WHEN THE TWO ARMIES CAMPD • • •   72 SOHRAB RUSTUM   357
        TOGETHER AS TWO EAGLES ON ONE PREY   • • • • •   75 SOHRAB RUSTUM   472
        THE TWO HOSTS HEARD THAT CRY AND QUAKED FOR FEAR • •   76 SOHRAB RUSTUM   507
        THE CLOUD AND THE TWO ARMIES SAW THE PAIR • • •   77 SOHRAB RUSTUM   524
        AND THE TWO GAZING HOSTS AND THAT SOLE PAIR   • •   86 SOHRAB RUSTUM   866
        THE WATCHERS OF TWO ARMIES STAND   • • • • •   93 SICK KING BOKH   162
        NINE DAYS HE TOOK TO GO TWO TO RETURN   • • •   113 BALDER DEAD 2   293
        SO THEY TWO SOFT TO ONE ANOTHER SPAKE   • • •   114 BALDER DEAD 3   30
        THEY TWO SCOURD EVERY COAST AND ALL THINGS WEPT • •   123 BALDER DEAD 3   328
        ROUND WHERE THEY STOOD AND THEY BEHELD TWO FORMS • • 126 BALDER DEAD 3   442
        AND THE TWO HOSTS ARE MARSHALLD AND IN HEAVEN   • •   127 BALDER DEAD 3   495
        THERE WERE TWO ISEULTS WHO DID SWAY • • • • •   132 TRISTRAM 1   68
        AND ON TWO ANGEL-HEADS DOTH LEAN   • • • • •   141 TRISTRAM 1   337
        TWO SPRINGS WHICH CLOSE BY ONE ANOTHER PLAY   • •   170 EAST AND WEST   2
        TWO SAINTS MET OFTEN WHERE THOSE WATERS FLOW   • •   170 EAST AND WEST   4
        HAVE DREAMD TWO HUMAN HEARTS MIGHT BLEND   • • •   181 ISOLATION MARG   38
        TWO HORSES STRONGLY SWIMMING TOW   • • • • •   191 STRAYED REVEL   185
        BEHOLDING HIM WHERE THE TWO PILLARS STAND   • • •   198 FRAG ANTIGONE   91
        TRUTH WHAT IS TRUTH TWO BLEEDING HEARTS   • • •   203 EUPHROSYNE   5
        THE ONE OR TWO IMMORTAL LIGHTS • • • • • •   220 BACCHANALIA 2   24
        BEETHOVEN TAKES THEM THEN THOSE TWO • • • •   224 EPILOG LAOCOON   95
        TWO SCHOLARS WHOM AT COLLEGE ERST HE KNEW   • •   256 SCHOLAR-GIPSY   42
        BUT WHAT I DREAM TWO HUNDRED YEARS ARE FLOWN • •   259 SCHOLAR-GIPSY   131
        IN THE TWO HINKSEYS NOTHING KEEPS THE SAME   • •   262 THYRSIS   2
        WHICH FOR TWO JADED ENGLISH SAVES   • • • •   277 SOUTHERN NIGHT   58
        I SAW THE MEETING OF TWO • • • • • • •   280 HAWORTH CHURCH   7
        THE TWO HELD CONVERSE THEY WROTE   • • • •   280 HAWORTH CHURCH   7
        TWO FRIENDS MET THERE TWO FAMD • • • • •   280 HAWORTH CHURCH   V   7
        TWO FRIENDS MET THERE TWO FAMD • • • • •   280 HAWORTH CHURCH   V   7
        WANDERING BETWEEN TWO WORLDS ONE DEAD • • •   302 GRANDE CHARTR   85
        I KNOW BUT TWO WHO HAVE ATTAIND   • • • •   307 OBERMANN   47
        AH TWO DESIRES TOSS ABOUT   • • • • • •   309 OBERMANN   93
        WHAT SOME TWO THOUSAND YEARS SURVEY • • • •   315 OBERMANN MORE   83
        WELLNIGH TWO THOUSAND YEARS HAVE BROUGHT   • •   315 OBERMANN MORE   V   81
        BUT EVERLASTING HORROR TWIXT US TWO • • • •   336 MEROPE   193
        TWO UNOFFENDING BABES HIS INNOCENT SONS   • •   339 MEROPE   319
        ADVANCED TWO JAVELINS NOT NOW   • • • • •   342 MEROPE   398
        AND TO TWO DID DESTINY   • • • • • • •   344 MEROPE   455
        WITH CYPSELUS AND TWO DAYS SINCE HE DIED   • •   355 MEROPE   718
        AND TOOK THE LAKE TWO HOUNDS ALONE PURSUED   • •   357 MEROPE   809
        HE ON A HUNTING PARTY TWO DAYS SINCE • • •   364 MEROPE   973
        OF MY TWO ELDER SONS SLAIN LONG AGO • • • •   367 MEROPE   1038
        WE TWO WITH THEE MY MOTHER MAY CONSULT   • •   379 MEROPE   1265
        TWO BROTHERS AND THEIR ORPHAN NEPHEWS STROVE •   389 MEROPE   1548
        FOR TO LIVE DISOBEDIENT TO THESE TWO • • •   390 MEROPE   1575
        FIRST FOR OUR UNION TRUST ME TWIXT US TWO   •   395 MEROPE   1733
        TWO GENERATIONS OF HIS OFFSPRING UP • • •   336 MEROPE   V 217
        AND THERE THEY SAY TWO BRIGHT AND AGED SNAKES •   427 EMPEDOCLES I 2   435
        THERE THOSE TWO LIVE FAR IN THE ILLYRIAN BRAKES •   427 EMPEDOCLES I 2   443
        LIKE DREAMS BETWEEN TWO SORROWS WENT AND CAME • •   474 CROMWELL   96

TWOFOLD
        NONE SINCE A TWOFOLD COLOUR REIGNS IN ALL   • • • •   404 MEROPE   1994

TYNTAGEL
        TO TYNTAGEL TO THE SIDE   • • • • • • • • •   132 TRISTRAM 1   61
        TYNTAGEL ON ITS SURGE-BEAT HILL   • • • • • •   136 TRISTRAM 1   177
        IN KING MARCS CHAPEL IN TYNTAGEL OLD • • • • •   149 TRISTRAM 3   3

TYNTAGELS
        DWELLS ON LOUD TYNTAGELS HILL   • • • • • • • •   134 TRISTRAM 1   134
        DWELLS ON PROUD TYNTAGELS HILL   • • • • • • •   134 TRISTRAM 1   V 134
        SITS ON PROUD TYNTAGELS HILL   • • • • • • • •   134 TRISTRAM 1   V 134
        IN TYNTAGELS PALACE PROUD   • • • • • • • •   146 TRISTRAM 2   115

TYNTAGIL
        TO TYNTAGIL FROM IRELAND BORE   • • • • • • • •   132 TRISTRAM 1   V   60
        KEEPS HIS COURT IN TYNTAGIL   • • • • • • • •   134 TRISTRAM 1   V 134
        THE PALACE TOWERS OF TYNTAGIL   • • • • • • • •   136 TRISTRAM 1   V 177
        IN TYNTAGIL SHE IS ASLEEP IN CORNWALL NOW   • • •   139 TRISTRAM 1   V 301
        IN THE BANQUET-HALL OF TYNTAGIL   • • • • • •   146 TRISTRAM 2   V 115
        AT TYNTAGIL IN KING MARCS CHAPEL OLD • • • • •   149 TRISTRAM 3   V   3

TYPHO
        ONLY TO TYPHO IT SOUNDS HATEFULLY   • • • • • •   430 EMPEDOCLES II   41
        TO TYPHO ONLY THE REBEL OERTHROWN   • • • • • •   430 EMPEDOCLES II   42
        TYPHO SUCH RED JETS OF FLAME   • • • • • • •   430 EMPEDOCLES II   48
        ONLY TO TYPHO THE REBEL OERTHROWN   • • • • • •   430 EMPEDOCLES II   V   42

TYPHOS
        THESE RUMBLINGS ARE NOT TYPHOS GROANS I KNOW   • •   431 EMPEDOCLES II   95

TYR
        VIDAR THE SILENT THE IMPETUOUS TYR   • • • • • • •   127 BALDER DEAD 3   492

TYRANNOUS
    SLAVES OF A TYRANNOUS NECESSITY   • • • • • •   10 MYCERINUS   42
    THIS OR SOME TYRANNOUS SINGLE THOUGHT SOME FIT • • 153 TRISTRAM 3   127
    TYRANNOUS TEMPESTS OF BALE   • • • • • •   293 HEINES GRAVE   35
    OF TYRANNOUS HARSHNESS OR REMISSNESS WEAK • • • • 404 MEROPE   2007
    FROM THE TYRANNOUS EUXINE SEA • • • • • • •   PILLARS UNIVERS V 8

TYRANNY
    TYRANNY PRIDE AND LUST FILL SICILYS ABODES • • • • 416 EMPEDOCLES I 2   121

TYRANT
    INTO A JEALOUS TYRANT SCOURGED WITH FEARS • • • • 335 MEROPE   159
    NOT MUCH A TYRANT THY FREE SPEECH DISPLAYS ME • • 340 MEROPE   350
    OF THIS FAR-SCHEMING TYRANT AND HIS BOON • • • • 366 MEROPE   998
    WITH THIS MESSENIAN TYRANT THAT I KNOW • • • • 380 MEROPE   1275
    THE POWER OF THIS TYRANT AND HIS LORDS • • • • 402 MEROPE   1944

TYRANTS
    FOR TYRANTS MAKE MAN GOOD BEYOND HIMSELF • • • • 331 MEROPE   42
    DEEMING AS TYRANTS DEEM OUR SILENCE HATE • • • • 338 MEROPE   260
    O ARTS ABOVE THE VULGAR TYRANTS REACH • • • • 339 MEROPE   310
    TYRANTS THINK HIM THEY MURDER NOT THEY SPARE • • 340 MEROPE   349
    SHAME RARELY CHECKS THE GENUINE TYRANTS WILL • • 340 MEROPE   352
    AND ONLY SLAVES AND TYRANTS LEFT ALIVE • • • • 383 MEROPE   1378

TYRIAN
    IN A TYRIAN GALLEY STEERING   • • • • • • •   26 NEW SIRENS   V 21
    AS SOME GRAVE TYRIAN TRADER FROM THE SEA • • • • 262 SCHOLAR-GIPSY   232

ULEMA
    BUT WHEN THE ULEMA WERE MET   • • • • • • •   91 SICK KING BOKH   V 109

ULEMAS
    BUT WHEN THE ULEMAS WERE MET   • • • • • • •   91 SICK KING BOKH   109

ULYSSES
    THAN THE CHARMS ULYSSES BORE   • • • • • • •   27 NEW SIRENS   44
    COME FORTH ULYSSES • • • • • • • • • • 188 STRAYED REVEL   71
    I LURED HIM NOT HITHER ULYSSES • • • • • • • 188 STRAYED REVEL   97
    THE WISE ULYSSES • • • • • • • • • 189 STRAYED REVEL   112
    I AM ULYSSES • • • • • • • • • • • 189 STRAYED REVEL   114
    THESE THINGS ULYSSES   • • • • • • • 192 STRAYED REVEL   207
    BUT I ULYSSES • • • • • • • • • 194 STRAYED REVEL   270
    WHICH HID ULYSSES WAVED ITSELF AND SAID • • • 484 S S LUSITANIA   2

UMBRAGE
    ON THE WET UMBRAGE OF THEIR GLOSSY TOPS • • • • 24 DREAM   4

UNABLE
    US UNABLE TO DIVINE • • • • • • • • • 456 POOR MATTHIAS   125

UNADULATING
    UNADULATING GRIEF CONSPIRACY • • • • • • • 338 MEROPE   261

UNAFFRIGHTED
    UNAFFRIGHTED BY THE SILENCE ROUND THEM • • • • 240 SELF-DEPENDENCE   17

UNALLAYD
    THEREFORE WITH CENSURE UNALLAYD • • • • • • 353 MEROPE   686
    AN AIMLESS UNALLAYD DESIRE • • • • • • • 481 DESTINY   8

UNALLIED
    OVER THE UNALLIED UNOPENING EARTH • • • • • • 439 EMPEDOCLES II   360

UNALLOYD
    UNALLOYD MOMENTS • • • • • • • • • • 52 CONSOLATION   62

UNALTERD
    UNALTERD WITH THE YEAR • • • • • • • • 174 MEETING   4
    UNALTERD TO RETAIN • • • • • • • • • 419 EMPEDOCLES I 2   199

UNAPPEASABLE
    GODS UNAPPEASABLE • • • • • • • • • 400 MEROPE   1875

UNAPPEASED
    TO LIE IN GLOOM FOR EVER UNAPPEASED • • • • • 367 MEROPE   1052

UNAPPLAUDED
    UNAPPLAUDED UNSUNG • • • • • • • • 370 MEROPE   1107

UNAPT
    ALBEIT WITH LIPS UNAPT TO SELF-EXCUSE • • • • 336 MEROPE   199

UNARMD
    FALL AND THY SPEAR TRANSFIXD AN UNARMD FOE • • • 77 SOHRAB RUSTUM   550
    UNARMD INGLORIOUS I ATTEND THE COURSE • • • • 128 BALDER DEAD 3   510
    IF PRUDENCE COUNSELS THEE TO GO UNARMD • • • • 391 MEROPE   1591
    I TOOK MY STAND AND SAW THE UNARMD CROWDS • • • • 401 MEROPE   1896
    UNARMD AND TRAVEL-SOILD JUST AS HE WAS • • • • 401 MEROPE   1906

UNASSISTED
    BUT IF SOME SIGNAL UNASSISTED STROKE • • • • • • • 383 MEROPE   1353

UNATONABLE
    DEEDS UNATONABLE • • • • • • • • • • • • 400 MEROPE   1873

UNATTAIND
    FROM HIS UNATTAIND CROWN • • • • • • • • • • • 344 MEROPE   458

UNATTEMPTED
    ALL VENGEANCE UNATTEMPTED AND DESCEND   • • • • 367 MEROPE   1029

UNAVENGED
    A PALACE DEFILED BY A DEATH UNAVENGED   • • • • 346 MEROPE   508
    FROM THE ALTAR THE UNAVENGED TOMB • • • • • • 371 MEROPE   1137
    TO THE DEAD UNAVENGED • • • • • • • • • 400 MEROPE   1868
    THE WIDOW OF A HUSBAND UNAVENGED • • • • • • 403 MEROPE   1955

UNAWAKENING
    THE MORNINGLESS AND UNAWAKENING SLEEP   • • • • 267 THYRSIS   169

UNBAKED
    TO MANTINEIA WITH ITS UNBAKED WALLS • • • • • 355 MEROPE   739
    TO MANTINEA WITH ITS UNBAKED WALLS • • • • • 355 MEROPE   V 739

UNBARRING
    HARK BELOW THE GATES UNBARRING • • • • • • •   14 CHURCH BROU 1   37

UNBEARABLE
    THAT OTHER TORMENT GROW UNBEARABLE   • • • • 435 EMPEDOCLES II   226

UNBEND
    AND UNBEND PLUTOS BROW • • • • • • • • • 265 THYRSIS   V 86
    AND HELP HIM TO UNBEND HIS TOO TENSE THOUGHT • • 435 EMPEDOCLES II   222

UNBENT
    UPHUNG THE SPEAR UNBENT THE BOW • • • • 219 BACCHANALIA 2   11
    OUTSIDE THE WESTERN STRAITS AND UNBENT SAILS • • 262 SCHOLAR-GIPSY   247

UNBLACKEND
    AND STILL THE UNBLACKEND ELMS WERE GAY • • • • 222 EPILOG LAOCOON   39

UNBLAMED
    WHOM AN UNBLAMED SERENITY   • • • • • • •   53 RESIGNATION   23

UNBLEST
    MOST UNBLEST ALSO AT THAT SIGHT • • • • •   90 SICK KING BOKH   86
    UNFREED HAVING SEEN NOTHING STILL UNBLEST • • • 243 SUMMER NIGHT   50
    LIKE US DISTRACTED AND LIKE US UNBLEST • • • 261 SCHOLAR-GIPSY   225
    SOME LIFE OF MEN UNBLEST • • • • • • • • • 264 THYRSIS   46

UNBLOODIED
    UNHACKD UNSMIRCHD UNBLOODIED AND HAVE LEARNT • • 388 MEROPE   1518
    UNHACKD UNSMIRCHD UNBLOODIED AND HAST LEARNT • • 388 MEROPE   V1518

UNBOUND
    AND UNBOUND HAIR • • • • • • • • • • • 278 SOUTHERN NIGHT   V 108
    THE BROW UNBOUND THE THOUGHTS FLOW FREE AGAIN • • 436 EMPEDOCLES II   246
    SKIES THAT UNBOUND BY CLASP OF MOUNTAIN CHAIN • • 473 CROMWELL   37

UNBRAIDED
    DROOPD UNBRAIDED ON YOUR LISTLESS ARMS • • •   30 NEW SIRENS   122

UNBREACHABLE
    UNBREACHABLE THE FORT   • • • • • • • • • 267 THYRSIS   146

UNBRIBED
    WITH THIS TO THOSE UNBRIBED INQUISITORS • • • • 349 MEROPE   553

UNBROKEN
    THE LONE UNBROKEN VIEW SPREADS BRIGHT AND CLEAR • • 150 TRISTRAM 3   12
    FROM ISEULTS LIPS THE UNBROKEN STORY FLOWD • • 150 TRISTRAM 3   45
    THE LONE UNBROKEN VIEW STRETCHD BRIGHT AND CLEAR   TRISTRAM 3   V 12
    THE LONE UNBROKEN VIEW GOES SPREADING CLEAR • • •   TRISTRAM 3   V 12
    WHERE SWEET THE UNBROKEN MOONBEAMS LAY • • • • 177 FAREWELL   2
    OF OCEANS SLEEPING FACE OR HEAVENS UNBROKEN BLUE • • 463 ALARIC AT ROME   36

UNCAREWORN
    YET WITH A LIGHT UNCAREWORN SPIRIT TURNS • • • • 351 MEROPE   614

UNCARING
    UNCARING AND UNDELIGHTED • • • • • • • • • 438 EMPEDOCLES II   297

UNCERTAIN
    WHICH HANGS UNCERTAIN TO WHICH SIDE TO FALL • •   72 SOHRAB RUSTUM   392
    CERTAIN IN THIS THAT TIS UNCERTAIN STILL • • • • 350 MEROPE   601
    MURDERS UNCERTAIN SECRET PERILOUS GAME • • • • 388 MEROPE   1501

UNCERTAINTY
    EDDYING AT LARGE IN BLIND UNCERTAINTY . . . . 246 BURIED LIFE 43
    EDDYING ABOUT IN BLIND UNCERTAINTY . . . . . . 246 BURIED LIFE V 43

UNCHAIND
    OUR HEART AND HAVE OUR LIPS UNCHAIND . . . . . . 245 BURIED LIFE 28

UNCHANGED
    AND YET I KNOW NOT ALL UNCHANGED . . . . 312 OBERMANN MORE 5

UNCHEERD
    WHO TREADS AT EASE LIFES UNCHEERD WAYS . . . . 59 RESIGNATION 237

UNCLASPING
    AND HER BEAUTIFUL ARMS UNCLASPING . . . . . . 197 FRAG ANTIGONE 78

UNCLE
    SECOND AND WAS THE UNCLE OF THE KING . . . . . . 66 SOHRAB RUSTUM 173
    UNCLE AND NEPHEW DISAPPEAR THEIR DEATH . . . . . 364 MEROPE 979
    ARCAS SEEK OUT MY UNCLE LAIAS NOW . . . . . . 379 MEROPE 1260
    THE PRINCE HIS UNCLE LAIAS WHOM HIS WARD . . . . 364 MEROPE V 976

UNCLES
    HIS GRANDSIRE AND HIS UNCLES FEAR THE RISK . . . . 350 MEROPE 603

UNCLIMBD
    UNCLIMBD OF MAN . . . . 392 MEROPE 1648
    UNCLIMBD BY MAN . . . . 392 MEROPE V1648

UNCLOSE
    AND AMETHYST AND RUBY THEN UNCLOSE . . . . . . 18 CHURCH BROU 3 24

UNCLOSED
    UNCLOSED HIS ITCHING FINGERS FROM HIS SWORD . . 394 MEROPE 1705

UNCLOUDED
    NURSING THY PROJECT IN UNCLOUDED JOY . . . . . . 261 SCHOLAR-GIPSY 199
    UNCLOUDED REASON I WOULD NOT DECLINE . . . . . . 335 MEROPE 158
    OF JOYS UNCLOUDED YEARS UNSTIRRD BY STRIFE . . . 474 CROMWELL 102

UNCOMFORTED
    AND I AM LEFT UNCOMFORTED IN HEAVEN . . . . . . 117 BALDER DEAD 3 122

UNCOMPANIOND
    DOWN THE UNCOMPANIOND WAY . . . . 458 POOR MATTHIAS 209

UNCOMPANIONED
    WHERE BROODS THE UNCOMPANIONED LIFE OF GOD . . . . FRAGMENT 6 3

UNCONCEDED
    RIGHTS UNCONCEDED AND DENIED . . . . 352 MEROPE 655

UNCONFINED
    BY MIST AND CHIMNEYS UNCONFINED . . . . . . 223 EPILOG LAOCOON 71

UNCONGENIAL
    THIS UNCONGENIAL PLACE THIS HUMAN LIFE . . . . 440 EMPEDOCLES II 366

UNCONQUERABLE
    WITH ITS UNCONQUERABLE FLOW . . . . 226 EPILOG LAOCOON 168
    STILL NURSING THE UNCONQUERABLE HOPE . . . . . . 261 SCHOLAR-GIPSY 211

UNCONQUERD
    THE UNCONQUERD JOY IN WHICH HER SPIRIT DWELLS . . 176 PARTING 40
    SOME UNCONQUERD ARE CROSSD . . . . 216 LORDS MESSENGER 16

UNCONSCIOUS
    IN HEAVEN AND THOU ART HEAVENS UNCONSCIOUS HAND . . 82 SOHRAB RUSTUM 710
    AND WATCH THEE PASS UNCONSCIOUS BY . . . . . . 205 CALAIS SANDS 28
    AND SEE THEE PASS UNCONSCIOUS BY . . . . . . 205 CALAIS SANDS V 28
    READY TO SLIP ON HIS UNCONSCIOUS PREY . . . . 364 MEROPE 972
    BUT ONE VAST FANE WHERE ALL UNCONSCIOUS SLEEP . . 464 ALARIC AT ROME 59

UNCONSUMED
    BURNS EVER UNCONSUMED . . . . 424 EMPEDOCLES I 2 370

UNCOUNSELLD
    MERE RUTHLESS AND UNCOUNSELLD WOLVES OF WAR . . 381 MEROPE 1301
    MERE RUTHLESS AND UNCOUNSELLD TOOLS OF WAR . . . . 381 MEROPE V1301

UNCOUTHNESS
    OH YOUR PARDON THE UNCOUTHNESS . . . . 27 NEW SIRENS 49

UNCRAVINGLY
    BEARS TO ADMIRE UNCRAVINGLY . . . . 57 RESIGNATION 161

UNCROWNS
    WHO TO THE STARS UNCROWNS HIS MAJESTY . . . . 2 SHAKESPEARE 4
    THAT TO THE STARS UNCROWNS HIS MAJESTY . . . . 2 SHAKESPEARE V 4

UNCRUMPLING
    WITH WHITENING HEDGES AND UNCRUMPLING FERN • • • • 265 THYRSIS 74

UNCURLD
    LIKE LEAVES BY SUNS NOT YET UNCURLD • • • • • • • 59 RESIGNATION 253
    IN MOMENTS OF DISGRACE UNCURLD • • • • • • • • 460 KAISER DEAD 56

UNDAUNTED
    AND UNDAUNTED RETORT • • • • • • • • 293 HEINES GRAVE 33
    ASCENDED WITH UNDAUNTED HEART • • • • • • • • 399 MEROPE 1833

UNDEBARRD
    AWHILE HE HOLDS SOME FALSE WAY UNDEBARRD • • • • 244 SUMMER NIGHT 59

UNDEBASED
    UNWORN UNDEBASED UNDECAYD • • • • • • • • 199 FRAG DEJANEIRA 28

UNDECAYD
    UNWORN UNDEBASED UNDECAYD • • • • • • • • 199 FRAG DEJANEIRA 28

UNDEGENERATE
    THE UNDEGENERATE BLOOD OF HERACLES • • • • • • 383 MEROPE 1356

UNDELIGHTED
    UNCARING AND UNDELIGHTED • • • • • • • • • • 438 EMPEDOCLES II 297

UNDER
    LINKING THEIR CORAL ARMS UNDER THE SEA • • • • 4 BUTLERS SERMONS 10
    TIED UNDER THE ARCHEST CHIN • • • • • • • 23 MEMORY-PICTURE 27
    UNDER THE EAVES PEERD ROWS OF INDIAN CORN • • • 25 DREAM 19
    BLACK UNDER CLIFFS IT RACED ROUND HEADLANDS SHONE 25 DREAM 34
    UNDER OERHANGING PINES THE MORNING SUN • • • • 24 DREAM V 3
    THE PORT LIES BRIGHT UNDER THE AUGUST SUN • • 41 GIPSY CHILD V 5
    UNDER THEIR BURNISHD SYCAMORES • • • • • • 54 RESIGNATION 57
    UNDER THEIR FEET AND MOANING SWEPT THE PLAIN • • 75 SOHRAB RUSTUM 484
    UNDER ITS IRON HEEL FATE FATE ENGAGED • • • 82 SOHRAB RUSTUM 714
    UNDER THE SOLITARY MOON HE FLOWD • • • • • 87 SOHRAB RUSTUM 879
    UNDER SOME MULBERRY-TREES I FOUND • • • • • 90 SICK KING BOKH 67
    FAIR MEN WHO LIVE IN HOLES UNDER THE GROUND • • 97 BALDER DEAD 1 56
    UNDER WHOSE HOOFS THE BRIDGE OER GIALLS STREAM • • 107 BALDER DEAD 2 102
    UNDER THE GATE-HOUSE TO THE SANDS AND FOUND • • 113 BALDER DEAD 2 309
    UNDER THE TREES IS DIBBLED THICK WITH HOLES • • 122 BALDER DEAD 3 312
    ON THE GRASS UNDER THE TREES • • • • • • 137 TRISTRAM 1 221
    AT THIS SOFT HOUR UNDER THIS SWEET MOON • • • 139 TRISTRAM 1 286
    UNDER THE GLITTERING HOLLIES ISEULT STANDS • • • 150 TRISTRAM 3 23
    UNDER THE FEATHERD HATS OF THE SWEET PAIR • • • 150 TRISTRAM 3 33
    CLUSTERD UNDER THE HOLLY-SCREEN AND SHE • • • 150 TRISTRAM 3 36
    UNDER THE HOLLIES IN THE CLEAR STILL AIR • • • 150 TRISTRAM 3 39
    MOVED UP AND DOWN UNDER THE GLOSSY TREES • • • 150 TRISTRAM 3 43
    UNDER THE HOLLIES THAT BRIGHT WINTERS DAY • • • 154 TRISTRAM 3 152
    UNDER THE THORNS ON THE GREEN SWARD AND STRONG • • 155 TRISTRAM 3 196
    UNDER THE BURNISHD HOLLIES ISEULT STANDS   TRISTRAM 3 V 23
    MOVD UP AND DOWN UNDER THEIR GLOSSY TREES • • • TRISTRAM 3 V 43
    MY NAME IS UNDER ALL MENS BAN • • • • • 157 SAINT BRANDAN 27
    AND DRUDGE UNDER SOME FOOLISH MASTERS KEN • • • 169 WORLDLY PLACE 6
    WHO FAILD UNDER THE HEAT OF THIS LIFES DAY • • • 172 IMMORTALITY 7
    UNDER THE TOWERING TRACHIS CRAGS • • • • 198 FRAG ANTIGONE 99
    UNDER THE RUSTLING POPLARS SHADE • • • • 206 RIVER 2
    HOW GREEN UNDER THE BOUGHS IT IS • • • • 248 KENSINGTON GARD 7
    UNDER A DARK RED-FRUITED YEW-TREES SHADE • • • 259 SCHOLAR-GIPSY 140
    AND GROUPS UNDER THE DREAMING GARDEN-TREES • • 264 THYRSIS 69
    UNDER THE FLOWERY OLEANDERS PALE • • • • • 267 THYRSIS 170
    WHERE UNDER LOUGHRIGG THE STREAM • • • • 280 HAWORTH CHURCH 1
    RESTED AS UNDER THE BOUGHS • • • • • • 287 RUGBY CHAPEL 32
    SUMMER BUT UNDER THEM STILL • • • • • • 292 HEINES GRAVE 6
    UNDER THE WINGS OF RENOWN • • • • • • 293 HEINES GRAVE 22
    FAREWELL UNDER THE SKY WE PART • • • • • 312 OBERMANN 181
    ITS PINES UNDER THEIR BRANCHES OPE • • • • 312 OBERMANN MORE 15
    WHO UNDER EARTH WATCH GUILTY DEEDS OF MEN • • • 332 MEROPE 74
    STOUTLY UNDER THE HEADLANDS LEE THEY SWAM • • • 358 MEROPE 822
    FIT DENIZEN THE LAMPLESS UNDER-WORLD • • • 367 MEROPE 1031
    UNDER THE DRIPPING BLACK TARTAREAN CLIFF • • • 368 MEROPE 1064
    THEY FEEL THE COOL WET TURF UNDER THEIR FEET • • 406 EMPEDOCLES I 1 2
    UP BY THE TORRENT-SIDE UNDER THE PINES • • • 411 EMPEDOCLES I 1 164
    STREAMD TO THE GROUND BY THE YOKE ESCAPING HOMER TRANS 45
        FROM UNDER THE COLLAR

UNDERGROUND
    YET HERE THOU LIEST BALDER UNDERGROUND • • • • 127 BALDER DEAD 3 471
    AND WAIT THE ISSUE SLEEPING UNDERGROUND • • • • 448 WESTMIN ABBEY 146

UNDERMINE
    AND DEADLY AIRS HIS STRENGTH DID UNDERMINE • • • • 448 WESTMIN ABBEY 126
    AND DEADLY AIRS HIS FORCE DID UNDERMINE • • • • 448 WESTMIN ABBEY V 126

UNDERNEATH
    CROSS UNDERNEATH THE INDIAN CAUCASUS • • • • • 65 SOHRAB RUSTUM 161
    WIND UNDERNEATH THE INDIAN CAUCASUS • • • • • 66 SOHRAB RUSTUM V 161
    CLIMB UNDERNEATH THE INDIAN CAUCASUS • • • • • 66 SOHRAB RUSTUM V 161
    UNDERNEATH THE STARLIT TREES • • • • • • • 434 EMPEDOCLES II 183

UNDERSTANDS
    TO THAT MANS MIND WHO UNDERSTANDS • • • • • •   93 SICK KING BOKH   172

UNDERSTOOD
    O GENTLE WISDOM LITTLE UNDERSTOOD • • • • • • 339 MEROPE   309

UNDERWOOD
    THE UNDERWOOD AND TREES BEGAN AGAIN • • • • • • 155 TRISTRAM 3   190
    RAN OUT FROM THE DARK UNDERWOOD BEHIND • • • • 155 TRISTRAM 3   209

UNDESCRIED
    AH LIKE YOURS IS UNDESCRIED • • • • • • • • 457 POOR MATTHIAS   164

UNDESIRED
    ARE BY A STROKE THOUGH UNDESIRED COMPLETE • • • • 360 MEROPE   877

UNDID
    AND ON THE BEACH UNDID HIS CORDED BALES • • • • 262 SCHOLAR-GIPSY   250

UNDIMMD
    SOME UNDIMMD HOURS • • • • • • • • •   52 CONSOLATION   75
    OF LIFE WITH VIGOUR UNDIMMD • • • • • • • • 199 FRAG DEJANEIRA   26

UNDISCOVERD
    THAT UNDISCOVERD MYSTERY • • • • • • • • • • 250 WISH   26

UNDISTRACTED
    UNDISTRACTED BY THE SIGHTS THEY SEE • • • • • • 240 SELF-DEPENDENCE   18

UNDISTURBD
    OF HELA AND HOLD CONVERSE UNDISTURBD • • • • • • 126 BALDER DEAD 3   436
    AT LAST SHALL DESCEND UNDISTURBD • • • • • • • 199 FRAG DEJANEIRA   21

UNDIVERTED
    FRESH UNDIVERTED TO THE WORLD WITHOUT • • • • 260 SCHOLAR-GIPSY   162
    UNTHWARTED UNDIVERTED WHEN HE STANDS • • • • • •   LUCRETIUS 2   10

UNDO
    ONE THING TO UNDO WHAT THOU THYSELF HAST RULED • • 120 BALDER DEAD 3   253
    IF YOUR OWN HANDS THE GOOD BEGUN UNDO • • • • 447 WESTMIN ABBEY   103

UNDOING
    FEAR NO UNDOING • • • • • • • • • • • •   40 STAGIRIUS   60

UNDONE
    AND ONLY BAD MEN JOY TO SEE UNDONE • • • • • • 386 MEROPE   1429

UNDOUBTING
    APPROACHES WITH UNDOUBTING HEART • • • • • • 400 MEROPE   1858

UNDOWERD
    LONG LONG SINCE UNDOWERD YET OUR SPIRIT • • • • 209 SELF-DECEPTION   5

UNDRIED
    AT THE UNDRIED FOUNT OF THIS BREAST • • • • • • 378 MEROPE   1236

UNDULLD
    LOOK HOW SO MANY VALOURS LONG UNDULLD • • • •   37 WORLDS TRIUMPHS   7

UNDUPED
    UNDUPED OF FANCY HENCEFORTH MAN • • • • • • 319 OBERMANN MORE   185

UNDYING
    IN FIRES UNDYING OER THE GUILTY HEAD • • • • • • 463 ALARIC AT ROME   28

UNEASY
    HIS PINION AND WITH SHORT UNEASY SWEEPS • • • •   78 SOHRAB RUSTUM   564

UNENDANGERD
    TO BID HER SHARE THINE UNENDANGERD THRONE • • • • 395 MEROPE   1740

UNEPITAPHD
    EVEN AS THOSE DEAD UNEPITAPHD WHO LIE • • • • 356 MEROPE   772

UNEXCEPTING
    THEREFORE WITH UNEXCEPTING BAN • • • • • • • • 353 MEROPE   687

UNEXPRESSD
    BUT THEY COURSE ON FOR EVER UNEXPRESSD • • • • 246 BURIED LIFE   63
    STIRS A HISTORY UNEXPRESSD • • • • • • • • 455 POOR MATTHIAS   102

UNFAITHFUL
    UNFAITHFUL SERVANT DOST THOU TOO DESERT ME • • • • 368 MEROPE   1076
    THIS FAITHFUL IMPULSE OF UNFAITHFUL WILLS • • • •   FRAGMENT 8   4

UNFAMILIAR
    SEE TIS NO FOOT OF UNFAMILIAR MEN • • • • • • 263 THYRSIS   7

UNFATHERD
    BUT IF THE WILD UNFATHERD MASS NO BIRTH • • • •   45 IN UTRUMQUE PAR   22

UNFAVOURD
        NOT UNFAVOURD BY HEAVEN . . . .   360 MEROPE   904

UNFED
        THE ARMIES OF THE HOMELESS AND UNFED . . . . . .   7 REP FRIEND   12
        ALTARS UNFED AND TEMPLES OVERTURND . . . . . .   8 MYCERINUS   3
        NO LONGER LEAVE THY WISTFUL FLOCK UNFED . . . .   255 SCHOLAR-GIPSY   3

UNFINISHD
        STANDS A LONELY CHURCH UNFINISHD . . . .   14 CHURCH BROU 1   63
        AND THE CHURCH UNFINISHD STANDS . . . .   14 CHURCH BROU 1   68

UNFIXD
        THY HOPES GROW TIMOROUS AND UNFIXD THY POWERS . . 261 SCHOLAR-GIPSY   227

UNFLAGGING
        OF THAT UNFLAGGING QUARRY AND THE HOUNDS . . . .   357 MEROPE   800

UNFLINCHING
        WHICH UNFLINCHING AND KEEN . . . .   281 HAWORTH CHURCH   38

UNFLUSHES
        THE WEST UNFLUSHES THE HIGH STARS GROW BRIGHT . . 267 THYRSIS   163

UNFOLD
        I WILL UNFOLD MY SENTENCE AND MY CRIME . . . .   9 MYCERINUS   7

UNFOLLOWD
        SO HERMOD COMES TO-DAY UNFOLLOWD HOME . . . . .   114 BALDER DEAD 3   19
        HE WENDS UNFOLLOWD HE MUST HOUSE ALONE . . . .   269 THYRSIS   209
        SOME SECRET AND UNFOLLOWD VEIN OF WOE . . . . .   411 EMPEDOCLES I 1   152

UNFOOTED
        OF THAT UNFOOTED PRECIPICE WHOSE ROCK . . . . .   358 MEROPE   812

UNFORESEEING
        THOU BAREST ME AND UNFORESEEING SOUL . . . . . .   98 BALDER DEAD 1   99

UNFORESEEN
        OF DEATH AT A CALL UNFORESEEN . . . .   287 RUGBY CHAPEL   29

UNFORGOT
        EYES THAT HE KNEW OLD FACES UNFORGOT . . . . . .   474 CROMWELL   85

UNFORGOTTEN
        O UNFORGOTTEN VOICE THY ACCENTS COME . . . . . .   36 VOICE   29
        O UNFORGOTTEN VOICE THY WHISPERS COME . . . .   36 VOICE   V   29

UNFREED
        UNFREED HAVING SEEN NOTHING STILL UNBLEST . . . . 243 SUMMER NIGHT   50

UNFREQUENTED
        IN THE HIGH UNFREQUENTED MOUNTAIN-SPOTS . . . .   409 EMPEDOCLES I 1   93

UNFRIENDLY
        THE UNFRIENDLY PALACE IN THE THRACIAN WILD . . . . 201 PHILOMELA   18

UNFRUITFUL
        UNFRUITFUL OFT AND AT HER HAPPIEST THROE . . . .   45 IN UTRUMQUE PAR   27
        THE COLD DULL SOIL OF HIS UNFRUITFUL YOUTH . . . . 473 CROMWELL   54

UNFULFILLD
        ACCEPT THEM AND THEY BIND US UNFULFILLD . . . .   120 BALDER DEAD 3   227

UNFURLD
        TO-DAY A HEROS BANNER IS UNFURLD . . . .   3 EMERSONS ESSAYS   4
        US WHO WITH BANNERS UNFURLD . . . .   216 LORDS MESSENGER V

UNFURLED
        THE DOOM PRONOUNCED THE BATTLE-FLAG UNFURLED . .   465 ALARIC AT ROME   93

UNGENIAL
        THOU FLEDST ME WHEN THE UNGENIAL EARTH . . . .   315 OBERMANN MORE   77
        THOU FLEDDST ME WHEN THE UNGENIAL EARTH . . . .   315 OBERMANN MORE   V 77

UNGLOVED
        TO REST UNGLOVED ON HER GREEN RIDING-DRESS . . . . 154 TRISTRAM 3   175

UNGRATEFUL
        WITH NO UNGRATEFUL SOUND . . . .   47 WORLD QUIETIST   18

UNGRATEFULLY
        FORSWORN THEIR BLOOD UNGRATEFULLY HAD THEY . . . . 339 MEROPE   323

UNGRAVEN
        TOO SOON FOR FAME WITH WHITE UNGRAVEN SHIELDS . . 109 BALDER DEAD 2   165

UNGREETING
        FACES UNGREETING AND COLD . . . .   284 HAWORTH CHURCH   76

```
UNGUESSD
        DIDST TREAD ON EARTH UNGUESSD AT BETTER SO   . . . .      3 SHAKESPEARE        11
        DIDST WALK ON EARTH UNGUESSD AT BETTER SO    . . . .      3 SHAKESPEARE      V 11
        DIDST PASS ON EARTH UNGUESSD AT BETTER SO    . . . .      3 SHAKESPEARE      V 11
        DIDST STAND ON EARTH UNGUESSD AT BETTER SO   . . . .      3 SHAKESPEARE      V 11
        DIDST LIVE ON EARTH UNGUESSD AT BETTER SO    . . . .      3 SHAKESPEARE      V 11

UNGUIDED
        UNGUIDED HE REMAINS      . . . . . . . . . .    195 FRAG ANTIGONE         15

UNHACKD
        UNHACKD UNSMIRCHD UNBLOODIED AND HAVE LEARNT   . .    388 MEROPE             1518
        UNHACKD UNSMIRCHD UNBLOODIED AND HAST LEARNT   . .    388 MEROPE            V1518

UNHAILD
        BUT ALL HE PASSD UNHAILD AND REACHD THE THRONE   . .    109 BALDER DEAD 2     176

UNHALLOWD
        WAKE UP IN HELL FROM THINE UNHALLOWD SLEEP  . . . .    373 MEROPE             1183

UNHALLOWED
        UNHALLOWED FEET ARE TRAMPLING ON THIS HAUNTED GROUND    467 ALARIC AT ROME    144

UNHAPPY
        UNHAPPY BUT THAT ART HE DID NOT KNOW   . . .  . . .    101 BALDER DEAD 1      212
        THE VOICE WAS LIKE THE UNHAPPY HODERS VOICE    . .    102 BALDER DEAD 1      243
        UNHAPPY HOW HAST THOU ENDURED TO LEAVE     . . . .    110 BALDER DEAD 2      180
        HODER THE UNHAPPY WHOM HIS OWN HAND SLEW   . . . .    124 BALDER DEAD 3      384
        THE UNHAPPY WITH REPROACH EVEN IN THE GRAVE   . .    124 BALDER DEAD 3      396
        AND WISH THE LONG UNHAPPY DREAM WOULD END   . . . .    260 SCHOLAR-GIPSY     192
        UNHAPPY ELOQUENT THE CHILD     . . . . . . . .    285 HAWORTH CHURCH    105
        UNHAPPY BEAUTIFUL THE CAUSE    . . . . . . . .    285 HAWORTH CHURCH  V 105
        ENDLESS EXTINCTION OF UNHAPPY HATES   . . . . . .    333 MEROPE             102
        SLEEPS AGAMEMNONS UNHAPPY      . . . . . . . .    344 MEROPE             439
        O THRICE UNHAPPY HOW I GROAN THY FATE   . . . .    362 MEROPE             931
        TO OUR UNHAPPY HOUSE THE DEBT WE OWE   . . . . .    367 MEROPE             1048
        UNHAPPY ONE WHAT DEED     . . . . . . . . . .    371 MEROPE             1134
        UNHAPPY ONE THOU STRIKST A MOST JUST BLOW   . . .    374 MEROPE             1200
        UNHAPPY PEOPLE WHERE THE CHIEFS THEMSELVES   . . .    404 MEROPE             2003
        TO ONE UNHAPPY HOUSE THE DEBT WE OWE   . . . . .    367 MEROPE            V1048
        NOR THE UNHAPPY PALACE OF THEIR RACE   . . . . .    427 EMPEDOCLES I 2     441
        MARSYAS THAT UNHAPPY FAUN    . . . . . . . .    433 EMPEDOCLES II      149
        AH UNHAPPY PAIR TO PELEUS WHY DID WE GIVE YOU    . .       HOMER TRANS         9

UNHARNESSING
        ON THE WIDE STEPP UNHARNESSING . . . . . . . .    191 STRAYED REVEL      163

UNHEARD
        UNHEARD ALL DAY ASCENDS AGAIN   . . . . . . . .    217 BACCHANALIA 1        3

UNHURT
        MY CHILD UNHURT ONLY BY OVER JOY     . . . . . .    377 MEROPE             1220

UNIMPEDED
        AN UNIMPEDED WAY    . . . . . . . . . . . .    420 EMPEDOCLES I 2     250

UNIMPROVED
        ENERGIES WASTED UNIMPROVED HOURS    . . . . . .    470 ALARIC AT ROME     201

UNINFRINGED
        I HAVE KEPT UNINFRINGED MY NATURES LAW    . . . .     40 HUMAN LIFE          4

UNION
        AND UNION BEFORE GOD THE ONLY CARE    . . . . .    173 MONICAS PRAYER      11
        KEEP BY THIS LIFE IN GOD AND UNION THERE    . . .    173 MONICAS PRAYER      14
        THE PAST ITS MASK OF UNION ON  . . . . . . .    320 OBERMANN MORE      225
        THE PAST ITS MASK OF UNION GONE   . . . . . .    320 OBERMANN MORE      227
        UNION CEMENTED FOR THIS NATIONS WEAL  . . . . .    333 MEROPE             103
        OUR HANDS IN SOLEMN UNION MAKING FRIENDS    . . .    335 MEROPE             165
        WHO CAN PATCH UNION HERE WHAT CAN THERE BE   . . .    336 MEROPE             192
        THIS HAVING KNOWN LET US A UNION FOUND    . . . .    394 MEROPE            1716
        FIRST FOR OUR UNION TRUST ME TWIXT US TWO   . . .    395 MEROPE            1733
        THIS HAVING LEARND LET US A UNION FOUND   . . . .    394 MEROPE           V1716

UNITE
        SEEK THIS REVIVE UNITE IT GIVE IT HOPE    . . . .    331 MEROPE             45
        LET US IN MARRIAGE KING AND QUEEN UNITE   . . . .    335 MEROPE             167
        OR CONQUERORS WITH CONQUERD TO UNITE  . . . . .    338 MEROPE             289

UNITED
        BREAK YOUR UNITED REPOSE  . . . . . . . . . .    285 HAWORTH CHURCH     124
        AND LITTLENESS UNITED     . . . . . . . . . .    431 EMPEDOCLES II       93

UNITY
        CENTRED IN A MAJESTIC UNITY    . . . . . . . .      4 BUTLERS SERMONS      8

UNIVERSAL
        THE UNIVERSAL ORDER SERVED    . . . . . . . .    314 OBERMANN MORE       55
        THIS UNIVERSAL GOD . . . . . . . . . . . .    422 EMPEDOCLES I 2     298
```

UNIVERSE
    THE MAGIC OF THE UNIVERSE   . . . .   202 URANIA   24
    TO FEEL THE UNIVERSE MY HOME   . . . .   251 WISH   43
    YOU GIVE THE UNIVERSE YOUR LAW   . . . .   304 GRANDE CHARTR   165

UNJUST
    CROWN OF HIS STRUGGLING LIFE AN UNJUST CLOSE   . .   9 MYCERINUS   30
    UNJUST SUSPICION AND ERRONEOUS FEAR   . . . . . .   342 MEROPE   384
    ZEAL MAKES HIM MOST UNJUST BUT IN GOOD TIME   . .   386 MEROPE   1438

UNJUSTLY
    COME HERMES WHO DOST FRIEND THE UNJUSTLY KILLD   . .   367 MEROPE   1058
    COME HERMES WHO DOST WATCH THE UNJUSTLY KILLD   . .   367 MEROPE   V1058

UNKEMPD
    KALMUCKS AND UNKEMPD KUZZAKS TRIBES WHO STRAY   . .   65 SOHRAB RUSTUM   V 132

UNKEMPT
    KALMUCKS AND UNKEMPT KUZZAKS TRIBES WHO STRAY   . .   65 SOHRAB RUSTUM   132

UNKIND
    MURMURING ART THOU STILL UNKIND   . . . . . .   23 MEMORY-PICTURE   36
    IN THE UNKIND SPRING HAVE GNAWN   . . . . . .   193 STRAYED REVEL   238
    IN THE UNKIND SPRING HAVE GNAWD   . . . . . .   193 STRAYED REVEL   V 238
    SUCCUMBD TO THE ENVY OF UNKIND GODS   . . . . . .   197 FRAG ANTIGONE   77

UNKINDNESS
    LOVE NO UNKINDNESS   . . . .   40 STAGIRIUS   58

UNKNIT
    CHANGE DOTH UNKNIT THE TRANQUIL STRENGTH OF MEN   . .   44 QUESTION   3

UNKNOWING
    THE UNKNOWN LITTLE FROM THE UNKNOWING GREAT   . .   170 WEST LONDON   13
    KNOWING HE DID IT UNKNOWING PAYS FOR IT   . . . .   400 MEROPE   1870
    UNKNOWING UNKNOWING   . . . .   400 MEROPE   1871
    UNKNOWING UNKNOWING   . . . .   400 MEROPE   1871

UNKNOWN
    LEAVES HER RIDDLE HALF UNKNOWN   . . . . . .   28 NEW SIRENS   76
    AS CHARTERD BY SOME UNKNOWN POWERS   . . . . . .   41 HUMAN LIFE   26
    THY BROTHER-WORLD STIRS AT THY FEET UNKNOWN   . .   46 IN UTRUMQUE PAR   38
    THY NATIVE WORLD STIRS AT THY FEET UNKNOWN   . . . .   46 IN UTRUMQUE PAR   V 36
    WITH MUCH UNKNOWN AND MUCH UNTRIED   . . . . .   59 RESIGNATION   225
    BUT I WILL FIGHT UNKNOWN AND IN PLAIN ARMS   . . . .   68 SOHRAB RUSTUM   257
    THE UNKNOWN ADVENTUROUS YOUTH WHO FROM AFAR   . .   70 SOHRAB RUSTUM   309
    FOOL THOU ART SLAIN AND BY AN UNKNOWN MAN   . . . .   77 SOHRAB RUSTUM   537
    UNKNOWN THOU ART YET THY FIERCE VAUNT IS VAIN   . .   77 SOHRAB RUSTUM   541
    THE UNKNOWN ADVENTUROUS YOUTH WHO THROUGH THE WORLD   70 SOHRAB RUSTUM   V 309
    BUT HE WILL REACH ITS UNKNOWN NORTHERN SHORE   . .   99 BALDER DEAD 1   162
    UNKNOWN AND LONG AND HAPLY ON THAT WAY   . . . .   116 BALDER DEAD 3   100
    THE UNKNOWN LITTLE FROM THE UNKNOWING GREAT   . .   170 WEST LONDON   13
    STARTLED THE UNKNOWN SEA   . . . .   193 STRAYED REVEL   260
    DEEP IN HER UNKNOWN DAYS EMPLOY   . . . . . .   248 KENSINGTON GARD   12
    SOME COUNTRY-NOOK WHERE OER THY UNKNOWN GRAVE   .   259 SCHOLAR-GIPSY   138
    BAFFLED UNKNOWN SELF-CONSUMED   . . . .   285 HAWORTH CHURCH   98
    WE IN SOME UNKNOWN POWERS EMPLOY   . . . . . .   310 OBERMANN   133
    AN UNKNOWN GUEST WILL ENTER BRINGING WORD   . . . .   331 MEROPE   48
    INGLORIOUS AND SHOULD DROP AT LAST UNKNOWN   . . . .   356 MEROPE   771
    WHICH NO STRANGER UNKNOWN   . . . .   369 MEROPE   1089
    THE UNKNOWN PASSENGER RETURNING STANDS   . . . .   445 WESTMIN ABBEY   43
    BIRDS COMPANIONS MORE UNKNOWN   . . . .   455 POOR MATTHIAS   95
    JOYS THAT HAD COME AND VANISHD HALF UNKNOWN   . .   474 CROMWELL   75

UNLEARNT
    SO MUCH UNLEARNT SO MUCH RESIGND   . . . . . .   301 GRANDE CHARTR   75

UNLED
    UNLED OF FANCY HENCEFORTH MAN   . . . .   319 OBERMANN MORE   V 185

UNLIGHTED
    AND GAVE ME NINE UNLIGHTED REALMS TO RULE   . . . .   110 BALDER DEAD 2   213
    AND GAVST HER NINE UNLIGHTED WORLDS TO RULE   . .   121 BALDER DEAD 3   277
    SOLEMN UNLIGHTED AUSTERE   . . . .   286 RUGBY CHAPEL   10

UNLIKE
    AND WE WHOSE WAYS WERE UNLIKE HERE   . . . . . .   180 FAREWELL   73
    O LIFE UNLIKE TO OURS   . . . .   260 SCHOLAR-GIPSY   166
    AND TO ONE ACT MANY MOST UNLIKE MOTIVES   . . . .   352 MEROPE   645
    UNLIKE THAT OCEAN-CITY GAZING STILL   . . . . .   468 ALARIC AT ROME   159
    BETWIXT SUCH UNLIKE POWERS   . . . .   LUCRETIUS 5   10

UNLIKELY
    A STRANGE UNLIKELY ERRAND SURE IS THINE   . . . .   110 BALDER DEAD 2   203
    THIS STRANGE UNLIKELY TALE THE PRINCE WAS DROWND   . .   364 MEROPE   V

UNLIT
    OF THE UNLIT GULPH OF HIMSELF   . . . .   231 YOUTH OF NATURE   102
    OF THE UNLIT GULF OF HIMSELF   . . . .   231 YOUTH OF NATURE   V 102

UNLIVING
    ALL LIVING AND UNLIVING THINGS TO WEEP . . . . 122 BALDER DEAD 3   292
    ALL LIVING AND UNLIVING THINGS TO WEEP . . . . 122 BALDER DEAD 3   300

UNLOCK
    TO UNLOCK THE HEART AND LET IT SPEAK . . . . . . 245 BURIED LIFE   13

UNLOPPD
    COULD WIELD AN UNLOPPD TRUNK IT WAS AND HUGE . .   73 SOHRAB RUSTUM   409
    COULD WIELD AN UNLOPPD TRUNK IT WAS STILL ROUGH . .   73 SOHRAB RUSTUM V 409

UNLOVEABLE
    OR SOMEWHAT BUT THAT MOST UNLOVEABLE . . . . . .   FRAGMENT 5   9

UNLOVED
    STRANGE UNLOVED UPROAR . . . .   50 CONSOLATION   21
    OF MY UNLOVED PREEMINENCE . . . . 432 EMPEDOCLES II   110

UNLOVELY
    COLD IN THAT UNLOVELY DAWNING . . . .   35 NEW SIRENS   265
    THOU WILT BE MOST UNLOVELY SHALL I CHUSE . . . .   FRAGMENT 5   3

UNMATING
    WHICH TOUCH THEE ARE UNMATING THINGS . . . . . . 181 ISOLATION MARG   32

UNMEANING
    THEIR LIVES TO SOME UNMEANING TASKWORK GIVE . . 243 SUMMER NIGHT   40
    EFFORT UNMEANING AND VAIN . . . . 288 RUGBY CHAPEL   78
    A PALE UNMEANING GHOST POWERLESS TO FRIGHT . . . . 366 MEROPE   1021
    THE CARELESS GLANCE THE COLD UNMEANING SMILE . . 470 ALARIC AT ROME   219

UNMINDFUL
    FOR NOT UNMINDFUL OF THEE ARE THE GODS . . . . 112 BALDER DEAD 2   254

UNMINGLING
    WITH COMMON CARES UNMINGLING AND APART . . . . 473 CROMWELL   57

UNMIXD
    OF BLOOD-UNMIXD FROM POTSDAM CAME . . . . . . 459 KAISER DEAD   20

UNMOORD
    UNMOORD OUR SKIFF WHEN THROUGH THE WYTHAM FLATS . . 266 THYRSIS   123

UNMOVD
    FOOL THOU MISSEST WE ARE BOTH UNMOVD . . . . . . 146 TRISTRAM 2   V 100

UNMOVED
    BEND YE ON THESE INDEED AN UNMOVED EYE . . . .   9 MYCERINUS   35
    FOR THESE THOU SEEST ARE UNMOVED . . . . . 149 TRISTRAM 2   191
    AND IS SHE HAPPY DOES SHE SEE UNMOVED . . . . 151 TRISTRAM 3   64

UNMURMURING
    UNMURMURING IN OUR TENTS WHILE IT IS WAR . . . .   63 SOHRAB RUSTUM   72

UNNAMED
    UNNAMED WHO GOETHE SAID . . . . 295 HEINES GRAVE   99
    AND SPEND OUR WIT TO NAME WHAT MOST EMPLOY UNNAMED   423 EMPEDOCLES I 2 331

UNNATURAL
    IN THAT UNNATURAL CONFLICT FOR A CLOUD . . . .   75 SOHRAB RUSTUM   481
    AND AN UNNATURAL OVERHEAT AT BEST . . . . . 153 TRISTRAM 3   136
    HIS JUST REVENGE TO AN UNNATURAL DEED . . . . 385 MEROPE   1417

UNNEARD
    IN ECHOING UNNEARD SILENCE . . . . 437 EMPEDOCLES II   295

UNNERVED
    BUT THAT BELOVED NAME UNNERVED MY ARM . . . .   77 SOHRAB RUSTUM   547

UNNOTED
    TO SOME SMALL HUMBLE AND UNNOTED STRAND . . . . 395 MEROPE   1745

UNNUMBERD
    OR IS HE MINGLED WITH THE UNNUMBERD DEAD . . . . 125 BALDER DEAD 3   430

UNOBSERVANT
    BOUNDED BY THEMSELVES AND UNOBSERVANT . . . . 240 SELF-DEPENDENCE V 25

UNOERLEAPD
    UNOERLEAPD MOUNTAINS OF NECESSITY . . . . . .   7 REP FRIEND CONT   7

UNOFFENDING
    TWO UNOFFENDING BABES HIS INNOCENT SONS . . . . 339 MEROPE   319

UNOPENING
    SILENT AND WHITE UNOPENING DOWN . . . . . . 242 SUMMER NIGHT   4
    OVER THE UNALLIED UNOPENING EARTH . . . . . 439 EMPEDOCLES II   360

UNPASSIONATE
    ARE YET UNTROUBLED AND UNPASSIONATE . . . . . 244 SUMMER NIGHT   80

UNPASSIONATE   (CONTINUED)
        AND YET UNTROUBLED AND UNPASSIONATE . . . . . . 244 SUMMER NIGHT   V 80

UNPAUSING
        THE LONG UNPAUSING SPECTACLE . . . . 225 EPILOG LAOCOON   146

UNPERMITTED
        AND CROSS THE UNPERMITTED FERRYS FLOW   . . . . 265 THYRSIS   85

UNPIERCED
        IF PERHAPS UNPIERCED BY THE SWORD . . . . . . 370 MEROPE   1116

UNPITYING
        OF THAT UNPITYING PHRYGIAN SECT WHICH CRIED . . 172 GOOD SHEPHERD   3

UNPLUMBD
        THE UNPLUMBD SALT ESTRANGING SEA . . . . . . 182 TO MARG CONT   24
        BUT MORE THAN ALL UNPLUMBD . . . . 352 MEROPE   629

UNPRACTISED
        WHO TAUGHT THIS PLEADING TO UNPRACTISED EYES . . 41 GIPSY CHILD   1
        TO THE UNPRACTISED EYE OF SANGUINE YOUTH . . . 267 THYRSIS   V 142
        YOUNG UNPRACTISED HAD TOLD . . . . 280 HAWORTH CHURCH   10

UNPRAYD
        FORTUNE PRESENTS UNPRAYD . . . . 195 FRAG ANTIGONE   5

UNPROFITABLE
        O MONSTROUS DEAD UNPROFITABLE WORLD . . . . .   3 EMERSONS ESSAYS   1
        IN ITS WEARY UNPROFITABLE LENGTH . . . . . . 235 YOUTH OF MAN   110

UNQUENCHABLE
        ARDENT UNQUENCHABLE FIRES . . . . 288 RUGBY CHAPEL   74

UNQUENCHD
        THAT WILD UNQUENCHD DEEP-SUNKEN OLD-WORLD PAIN . 200 PHILOMELA   8

UNQUESTIOND
        WHERE SIRE TO SON TRANSMITS THE UNQUESTIOND CROWN   388 MEROPE   1517

UNQUIET
        O SOHRAB AN UNQUIET HEART IS THINE . . . . . 63 SOHRAB RUSTUM   65
        NOT LONG A WIFE WHEN HIS UNQUIET HEART . . . . 116 BALDER DEAD 3   107
        THE UNQUIET BRIGHT ATLANTIC PLAIN . . . . . . 148 TRISTRAM 2   174
        ALL OUR UNQUIET PULSES CEASE . . . . 180 FAREWELL   82
        OVER THE LIT SEAS UNQUIET WAY . . . . 240 SELF-DEPENDENCE   14
        HAST THOU THEN STILL THE OLD UNQUIET BREAST . . 243 SUMMER NIGHT   27
        OF FINISTERES UNQUIET BROW . . . . 274 STANZAS CARNAC   36
        WANDER UNQUIET AND MY OWN . . . . 275 SOUTHERN NIGHT   15
        UNQUIET SOULS . . . . 286 HAWORTH CHURCH   134
        UNQUIET DROVE HIM EVER TO PURSUE . . . . . . 355 MEROPE   726

UNRAVEL
        UNRAVEL ALL HIS MANY-COLOURD LORE . . . . . . 43 GIPSY CHILD   34

UNRAVELLING
        SO MEN UNRAVELLING GODS HARMONIOUS WHOLE . . . .   4 BUTLERS SERMONS   3

UNREACHD
        HOW SWEET UNREACHD BY EARTHLY JARS . . . . . 180 FAREWELL   77

UNREAL
        LOVE TRANSIENT POWER AN UNREAL SHOW . . . . . 59 RESIGNATION   236

UNRECOGNISING
        OVER THE UNRECOGNISING SEA WHILE AIR . . . . . 439 EMPEDOCLES II   361

UNRECOVERD
        AN UNRECOVERD PRISONER SHADE WITH SHADES . . . 120 BALDER DEAD 3   229

UNREGARDED
        THE UNREGARDED RIVER OF OUR LIFE . . . . . . 246 BURIED LIFE   39

UNREGARDFUL
        BOUNDED BY THEMSELVES AND UNREGARDFUL . . . . 240 SELF-DEPENDENCE   25

UNRELAXING
        WITH FAITHFUL UNRELAXING FORCE . . . . 225 EPILOG LAOCOON   147

UNRESENTFUL
        BUT CALM BUT UNRESENTFUL I ENDURED . . . . . 366 MEROPE   1014

UNREST
        BEING IN TRUTH BUT A DISEASED UNREST . . . . . 153 TRISTRAM 3   135
        THEREFORE A SECRET UNREST . . . . 296 HEINES GRAVE   121
        KNEW CARE AND KNEW UNREST . . . . 447 WESTMIN ABBEY   122
        THE EYES UNREST . . . . 459 KAISER DEAD   28

UNRESTFUL
        GAZD SADLY DOWN ON HIS UNRESTFUL LOT . . . . . 474 CROMWELL   86

UNRETURND
    AND FAITH MAY OFT BE UNRETURND • • • • • • • • •   180 ISOLATION MARG   10
    AND FAITH IS OFTEN UNRETURND • • • • • • • • •   180 ISOLATION MARG V 10
    AND FAITH MAY WELL BE UNRETURND • • • • • •   180 ISOLATION MARG V 10

UNRETURNING
    OF THAT UNRETURNING DAY • • • • • • • • •   453 POOR MATTHIAS   50

UNREVEALD
    LESS THAN THEY LEFT UNREVEALD • • • • • • • •   231 YOUTH OF NATURE   106
    OF HIS UNREVEALD TOMB • • • • • • • • • •   344 MEROPE   438

UNREVERSED
    GOES AN UNREVERSED DECREE • • • • • • • •   456 POOR MATTHIAS   149

UNROLL
    PROSPECTS UNROLL THEMSELVES • • • • • • • •   50 CONSOLATION   8
    HERE SIT WE AND AGAIN UNROLL • • • • • • • •   55 RESIGNATION   94
    BEFORE HIM HE SEES LIFE UNROLL • • • • • • •   57 RESIGNATION   189

UNROLLD
    AND IN THY COURTS HIS SHINING FREIGHT UNROLLD • •   446 WESTMIN ABBEY   76

UNRULY
    FALSE WE WERE NOT NOR UNRULY • • • • • • • •   34 NEW SIRENS   233

UNSAID
    MY HEART IS SWOLN WITH LOVE UNSAID • • • • • •   206 RIVER   10

UNSATISFIED
    AND WE SHALL BE UNSATISFIED AS NOW • • • • • •   439 EMPEDOCLES II   355

UNSCALED
    AND KEEPS ITS LIQUID SOLITUDES UNSCALED • • • •   351 MEROPE   625
    UNSCALED UNTRODDEN IS THE HEART OF MAN • • • •   352 MEROPE   630

UNSCOURGED
    SIT AND EYE GRIMLY THE VICTIM UNSCOURGED • • • •   347 MEROPE   531

UNSCRUPULOUS
    HAVE PRAISED THE KEEN UNSCRUPULOUS COURSE • • • •   178 FAREWELL   35

UNSEEN
    UNSEEN AND HAVING DRINK TO SPARE • • • • •   90 SICK KING BOKH   71
    SHALL GO AND I WILL BE HIS GUIDE UNSEEN • • •   100 BALDER DEAD 1   191
    AH MIGHT I ALWAYS REST UNSEEN • • • • • •   205 CALAIS SANDS   31
    OH MIGHT I ALWAYS REST UNSEEN • • • • •   205 CALAIS SANDS V 31
    MUST WHEN UNSEEN FROM THE SOUL FADE AWAY • • •   206 SEPARATION   8
    CHILDREN OF MEN THE UNSEEN POWER WHOSE EYE • • •   238 PROGRESS   37
    THE UNSEEN SNOW-BEDS DISLODGE • • • • • •   289 RUGBY CHAPEL   99
    THEY DO NOT ASK WHO PINED UNSEEN • • • • •   311 OBERMANN   153
    THE HAPPY MOMENT COMES LURK HERE UNSEEN • • •   332 MEROPE   67
    BUT THOU MUST KEEP UNSEEN FOLLOW US ON • • •   409 EMPEDOCLES I 1   86
    WITH STERN SLOW STEPS UNSEEN YET STILL THE SAME • •   476 CROMWELL   147

UNSEVERD
    OF TOIL UNSEVERD FROM TRANQUILLITY • • • • • • •   1 QUIET WORK   5

UNSHADED
    BARE UNSHADED ALONE • • • • • • • • • •   287 RUGBY CHAPEL   35

UNSHADOWD
    OF SLEEP UNSHADOWD BY A DREAM OF WOE • • • • •   474 CROMWELL   103

UNSHAKEN
    THAT SPOTLESS HANDS UNSHAKEN SCEPTRES HOLD • • • •   388 MEROPE   1519

UNSHARED
    OF SOLITARY THOUGHT UNSHARED RESOLVE • • • • •   403 MEROPE   1969

UNSHEATHED
    AND NOW MIGHT SOHRAB HAVE UNSHEATHED HIS SWORD • •   73 SOHRAB RUSTUM   422

UNSHUT
    SAIL AND SAIL WITH UNSHUT EYE • • • • • • • •   162 FORSAKEN MERM   44

UNSKILFUL
    OF AN UNSKILFUL GARDENER HAS BEEN CUT • • • •   80 SOHRAB RUSTUM   635

UNSKILFULNESS
    TIS THE SAME UNSKILFULNESS • • • • • • • •   457 POOR MATTHIAS   160

UNSLACKENING
    OUR BUSINESS WITH UNSLACKENING STRIDE • • • •   277 SOUTHERN NIGHT   65

UNSMIRCHD
    UNHACKD UNSMIRCHD UNBLOODIED AND HAVE LEARNT • •   388 MEROPE   1518
    UNHACKD UNSMIRCHD UNBLOODIED AND HAST LEARNT • •   388 MEROPE V1518

UNSMOOTHD
　　STORMS UNSMOOTHD YOUR FOLDED VALLEYS • • • • • •　30 NEW SIRENS　123

UNSOILD
　　UNSOILD AND SO FAREWELL　• • • • • • • • • •　311 OBERMANN　160

UNSOLVED
　　FINDS HIM WITH MANY AN UNSOLVED PLAN • • • • • •　58 RESIGNATION　224

UNSPARING
　　UNSPARING IN HIS SERVICE OF HIS TOIL • • • • • •　404 MEROPE　1975

UNSPEAKABLE
　　THERE RISES AN UNSPEAKABLE DESIRE　• • • • • •　246 BURIED LIFE　47

UNSPENT
　　WITH UNSPENT MIND AND A SOUL　• • • • • • • •　199 FRAG DEJANEIRA　27
　　AND UNSPENT ALL THAT TIME　• • • • • • • •　318 OBERMANN MORE　162

UNSPHERED
　　OF UNSPHERED DISCROWNED CREATURES　• • • • • •　34 NEW SIRENS　249

UNSPOILD
　　THE MEMORY OF A MAN UNSPOILD　• • • • • • • •　273 EDW QUILLINAN　15
　　THE IMAGE OF A MAN UNSPOILD　• • • • • • • •　273 EDW QUILLINAN　V 15

UNSPOTTED
　　UNSPOTTED BY SNOW　• • • • • • • • • • • •　176 PARTING　46
　　UNSPOTTED BY THE WORLD　• • • • • • • • • •　311 OBERMANN　156

UNSTIRRD
　　TILL LIFE UNSTIRRD BY ACTION LIFE BECAME　• • • •　473 CROMWELL　59
　　OF JOYS UNCLOUDED YEARS UNSTIRRD BY STRIFE • • • •　474 CROMWELL　102

UNSTRUNG
　　O UNSTRUNG WILL O BROKEN HEART • • • • • • • •　312 OBERMANN　183

UNSUBSTANTIAL
　　AND TO AN UNSUBSTANTIAL TITLE HEIR　• • • • • •　335 MEROPE　170

UNSUITING
　　WINDS FROM OUR SIDE THE UNSUITING CONSORT RIVE　• •　40 HUMAN LIFE　16

UNSUNG
　　UNAPPLAUDED UNSUNG • • • • • • • • • • • •　370 MEROPE　1107
　　YET THEY DIED AND DIED UNSUNG • • • • • • • •　454 POOR MATTHIAS　56

UNSUNND
　　BURYING THEIR UNSUNND STEMS IN GRASS AND FLOWERS • •　11 MYCERINUS　88
　　AND HE WITH UNSUNND FACE DID ALWAYS GO　• • • •　170 EAST AND WEST　8

UNSURE
　　LIGHT IGNORANCE AND HURRYING UNSURE THOUGHTS　• •　198 FRAG DEJANEIRA　2
　　AND OF HIS UNSURE AGENT WHAT DEMANDS HE　• • •　380 MEROPE　1280
　　KNOWEST THOU NOT HOW TIMOROUS HOW UNSURE　• • •　381 MEROPE　1311
　　AND IF SO USED PROVES AS THOU SAYST UNSURE • • •　382 MEROPE　1341

UNSWERVED
　　MAKES HIS OWN WELFARE HIS UNSWERVED-FROM LAW　• •　195 FRAG ANTIGONE　8

UNTAMED
　　TOO STRANGE TOO RESTLESS TOO UNTAMED • • • • • •　178 FAREWELL　20

UNTASTED
　　AND ON THE TABLES STOOD THE UNTASTED MEATS • • • •　95 BALDER DEAD 1　13

UNTHWARTED
　　UNTHWARTED UNDIVERTED WHEN HE STANDS • • • • • •　LUCRETIUS 2　10

UNTIE
　　GO SHEPHERD AND UNTIE THE WATTLED COTES　• • • •　255 SCHOLAR-GIPSY　2

UNTIED
　　HIS FAWN-SKIN HALF UNTIED　• • • • • • • •　188 STRAYED REVEL　89

UNTIL
　　FROM TRIBE TO TRIBE UNTIL IT REACH HER EAR • • • •　79 SOHRAB RUSTUM　597
　　UNTIL HE CAME TO WHERE A GULLY BREAKS　• • • •　97 BALDER DEAD 1　81
　　NORTHWARD UNTIL HE MEETS A STRETCHING WALL • • • •　100 BALDER DEAD 1　166
　　STILL NORTH UNTIL HE MET A STRETCHING WALL • • • •　109 BALDER DEAD 2　144
　　CURLING AND DARTING HIGHER UNTIL THEY LICKD　• • •　119 BALDER DEAD 3　189
　　AND AT HER PRIE-DIEU KNEEL UNTIL SHE HAVE TOLD　• •　152 TRISTRAM 3　92
　　UNTIL THEY CRUMBLE OR ELSE GROW LIKE STEEL • • • •　153 TRISTRAM 3　121
　　WAIT THEN UNTIL SUFFICIENT HELP APPEARS　• • • •　384 MEROPE　1397
　　UNTIL ANOTHER ROSE AND SMOTE HIM DOWN　• • • •　476 CROMWELL　144

UNTIMELY
　　THE MAN WHO TO UNTIMELY DEATH IS DOOMD　• • • •　359 MEROPE　854

UNTIRED
        UNTIRED ITS MOVEMENT BRIGHT ATTEND • • • • • 227 EPILOG LAOCOON   191
        DROP BY AND LEAVE ITS SEEKER STILL UNTIRED • • • • 268 THYRSIS   207
        AND WHAT BUT GENTLENESS UNTIRED • • • • • • • 279 SOUTHERN NIGHT   129
        EVER FAITHFUL UNTIRED • • • • • • • • • 344 MEROPE   460

UNTO
        AS THOUGH ONE SPAKE OF LIFE UNTO THE DEAD • • • •   3 EMERSONS ESSAYS   8
        AS THOUGH ONE SPAKE OF NOISE UNTO THE DEAD • • • •   3 EMERSONS ESSAYS V   8
        UNTO THEIR ANCIENT HOME • • • • • • • • • 36 VOICE   31
        SEEKING A PREY UNTO HIS HAND • • • • • • • 93 SICK KING BOKH   164
        UNTO A RULE MORE STRONG THAN THEIRS • • • • • • 93 SICK KING BOKH   187
        UNTO A LONELY VILLA IN A DELL • • • • • • • 167 RACHEL 2   1
        REMEMBER EACH UNTO THE END • • • • • • • • 217 NAMELESS EPIT   4
        I SAY UNTO YOU SEE YE KEEP THAT LAW • • • • • 237 PROGRESS   7
        I SAY UNTO YOU SEE THAT YOUR SOULS LIVE • • • • 237 PROGRESS   23
        UNTO ITS HAVEN COMING NIGH • • • • • • • • 276 SOUTHERN NIGHT   46
        UNTO THIS PIOUS HOUSEHOLD TO REPAY • • • • • • 447 WESTMIN ABBEY   108

UNTOLD
        OF TOIL AND DOLOUR UNTOLD • • • • • • • 199 FRAG DEJANEIRA   19
        WITH PIERCING UNTOLD ANGUISH • • • • • • • 235 YOUTH OF MAN   102
        PONDERING GODS MYSTERIES UNTOLD • • • • • • 278 SOUTHERN NIGHT   89

UNTOUCHD
        IS LIFELESS WHILE ITS HEART REMAINS UNTOUCHD • • 382 MEROPE   1343

UNTRAVELLD
        BUT HE MUST TREAD A DARK UNTRAVELLD ROAD • • • • 99 BALDER DEAD 1   143
        IN SILENCE UP THE DARK UNTRAVELLD ROAD • • • • 107 BALDER DEAD 2   79

UNTRIED
        WITH MUCH UNKNOWN AND MUCH UNTRIED • • • • • • 59 RESIGNATION   225

UNTRIMMD
        GERMS YOUR UNTRIMMD PASSION OVERGREW • • • • • • 30 NEW SIRENS   138

UNTROD
        HOLDS COUNTLESS TRACTS UNTROD • • • • • • • • 352 MEROPE   628

UNTRODDEN
        UNTRODDEN LONELY FAR FROM LIGHT AND HEAVEN • • 99 BALDER DEAD 1   136
        PLUNGING THROUGH DEEP UNTRODDEN BANKS OF SNOW • • 107 BALDER DEAD 2   97
        UNSCALED UNTRODDEN IS THE HEART OF MAN • • • 352 MEROPE   630
        UNTRODDEN ON CYLLENES DESOLATE SIDE • • 373 MEROPE   1168
        TO THOSE UNTRODDEN MOUNTAIN-LAWNS AND THERE • • 427 EMPEDOCLES I 2   456

UNTROUBLED
        ARE YET UNTROUBLED AND UNPASSIONATE • • • • • 244 SUMMER NIGHT   80
        AND YET UNTROUBLED AND UNPASSIONATE • • • • • 244 SUMMER NIGHT   V 80
        AND DRINKST UNTROUBLED SLUMBER TO SLEEP OFF • • 373 MEROPE   1180

UNTRUE
        NOR WAS THE LOVE UNTRUE • • • • • • • • • • 196 FRAG ANTIGONE   54

UNUNITED
        BUT SINCE LIVING WE WERE UNUNITED • • • • • • 145 TRISTRAM 2   91

UNUPBRAIDED
        COME UNUPBRAIDED FOR ONCE • • • • • • • • • 283 HAWORTH CHURCH   V

UNUTTERABLE
        ITS ELSE UNUTTERABLE SPELL • • • • • • • • 223 EPILOG LAOCOON   86
        WITH UNUTTERABLE FOREBODING • • • • • • • • 393 MEROPE   1672

UNVISITED
        UNVISITED REMAIN • • • • • • • • • • • • 198 FRAG DEJANEIRA   10

UNVOICED
        THERE IN UNVOICED OBLIVION SINK THY NAME • • • • 395 MEROPE   1751
        THERE IN UNVOICED OBLIVION HIDE THY NAME • • • • 395 MEROPE   V1751

UNWANDERING
        WITH SAFE UNWANDERING FEET EXPLORE • • • • • • 226 EPILOG LAOCOON   190

UNWARND
        FAR OFF WHERE SOME UNWARND MIGHT FAIL TO WEEP • • 122 BALDER DEAD 3   322

UNWAVERING
        THEIR PURE UNWAVERING DEEP DISDAIN • • • • • • 202 URANIA   32
        THEIR GAY UNWAVERING DEEP DISDAIN • • • • • • 202 URANIA   V 32

UNWEARIED
        PROMPT UNWEARIED AS HERE • • • • • • • • • 287 RUGBY CHAPEL   48
        UNWEARIED AS FROM LAND TO LAND • • • • • • • 484 ROME-SICKNESS   29

UNWELCOME
        UNWELCOME SHROUD OF THE FORGOTTEN DEAD • • • • 462 ALARIC AT ROME   1
        FOND HEARTS THAT FAIN WOULD CLOTHE THE UNWELCOME TRUTH 474 CROMWELL   97

UNWILLING
    UNWILLING LINGERERS . . . . 437 EMPEDOCLES II   290

UNWILLINGLY
    UNWILLINGLY THE SPIRIT FLED AWAY . . . . 86 SOHRAB RUSTUM   854
    HER FAIR YOUTH UNWILLINGLY GAVE . . . . . . 197 FRAG ANTIGONE   79
    HIS WHO UNWILLINGLY SEES . . . . 291 RUGBY CHAPEL   166
    AND THEN WE SHALL UNWILLINGLY RETURN . . . . . . 440 EMPEDOCLES II   364

UNWINGD
    AIR TO HIS UNWINGD FORM DENIES A WAY . . . . . . 351 MEROPE   624

UNWINTRY
    OER SOME FAIR UNWINTRY SEA . . . . 133 TRISTRAM 1   91

UNWISHD
    LIFTED AND THAT UNWISHD-FOR HEIRSHIP VOID . . . . 366 MEROPE   1001

UNWITTING
    TO HODER AND UNWITTING HODER THREW . . . . . 95 BALDER DEAD 1   7
    WAS LOKS THE UNWITTING HAND ALONE WAS THINE . . 125 BALDER DEAD 3   425
    UNWITTING FOLLOWD . . . . 393 MEROPE   1660

UNWITTINGLY
    AH SWEET SAINTS UNWITTINGLY . . . . 135 TRISTRAM 1   142

UNWON
    HALF HER LAURELS UNWON . . . . 283 HAWORTH CHURCH   70
    THOUGH MUCH BE STILL UNWON . . . . 322 OBERMANN MORE   290

UNWONTED
    AND AN UNWONTED CALM PERVADES HIS BREAST . . . . 247 BURIED LIFE   95

UNWORLDLY
    WITNESS THEIR UNWORLDLY SONG . . . . 456 POOR MATTHIAS   136

UNWORN
    UNWORN UNDEBASED UNDECAYD . . . . 199 FRAG DEJANEIRA   28
    IN THE SUNSHINE UNWORN BY THE PLOUGH . . . . . 252 FUTURE   30
    THESE STURDY AND UNWORN MESSENIAN TRIBES . . . . 338 MEROPE   291
    THEIR SOUL OF UNWORN YOUTH THEIR BREATH OF GREATNESS 440 EMPEDOCLES II   384

UNWORTHY
    WISHES UNWORTHY OF A MAN FULL-GROWN . . . . . . 8 RELIGIOUS ISOL   8
    HIS NOT UNWORTHY NOT INGLORIOUS SON . . . . . . 62 SOHRAB RUSTUM   52

UNWOUNDED
    O SOHRAB CARRY AN UNWOUNDED SON . . . . . . 63 SOHRAB RUSTUM   77

UNWRINKLED
    AND AS THIS BRIMMD UNWRINKLED RHINE . . . . . 208 ON THE RHINE   12

UNYIELDING
    THY DEEP SECLUSION THINE UNYIELDING GLOOM . . . . 332 MEROPE   84

UP
    FROM FIRST YOUTH TESTED UP TO EXTREME OLD AGE . . 2 TO A FRIEND   10
    CLIMB UP HERE TO PRAY . . . . 17 CHURCH BROU 2   19
    THE GAZING UP MID THE DIM PILLARS HIGH . . . . 18 CHURCH BROU 3   38
    THEN GAZING UP THROUGH THE DIM PILLARS HIGH . . . 18 CHURCH BROU 3 V 38
    FAR UP SHINES THE HOUSE AND BENEATH FLOWS THE RIVER 19 MODERN SAPPHO   3
    FAR UP GLEAMS THE HOUSE AND BENEATH FLOWS THE RIVER 19 MODERN SAPPHO V 3
    AND FROM SOME SWARDED SHELF HIGH UP THERE CAME . . 25 DREAM   11
    LIFE DRIES UP THE HEART DISSEMBLES . . . . . . 29 NEW SIRENS   83
    LIFTING UP YOUR LANGUID EYES . . . . 31 NEW SIRENS   158
    COME BIND UP THOSE RINGLET SHOWERS . . . . . . 32 NEW SIRENS   173
    UP COLD AISLES OF BURIED GLADE . . . . 32 NEW SIRENS   180
    A WILD ROSE CLIMBING UP A MOULDERING WALL . . . . 36 VOICE   20
    OF TORN-UP WATER ON THE MAIN . . . . 40 HUMAN LIFE   20
    SLOPES GRACIOUS UP THE WESTERN RIDGE . . . . . 54 RESIGNATION   53
    MOVE BROWSING UP THE GRAY-WALLD LANE . . . . . 55 RESIGNATION   121
    THE WET FLOWERD GRASS HEAVES UP ITS HEAD . . . . 57 RESIGNATION   185
    AND TO FEROOD HIS BROTHER CHIEFS CAME UP . . . . 66 SOHRAB RUSTUM   170
    FEROOD SHAME BIDS US TAKE THEIR CHALLENGE UP . . . 66 SOHRAB RUSTUM   175
    STAND FORTH THE WHILE AND TAKE THEIR CHALLENGE UP . 66 SOHRAB RUSTUM   183
    AND WITH A CRY SPRANG UP AND DROPPD THE BIRD . . 67 SOHRAB RUSTUM   203
    THERE WOULD I GO AND HANG MY ARMOUR UP . . . . 68 SOHRAB RUSTUM   236
    HAVING MADE UP HIS TALE OF PRECIOUS PEARLS . . . 69 SOHRAB RUSTUM   288
    AND WHETHER IT WILL HEAVE US UP TO LAND . . . . 73 SOHRAB RUSTUM   393
    HYPHASIS OR HYDASPES WHEN HIGH UP . . . . . . 73 SOHRAB RUSTUM   412
    BUT A DARK RUMOUR WILL BE BRUITED UP . . . . . 79 SOHRAB RUSTUM   596
    LIGHTS UP HIS STUDIOUS FOREHEAD AND THIN HANDS . . 81 SOHRAB RUSTUM   676
    THERE WOULD I STAY AND HANG MY ARMOUR UP . . . . 68 SOHRAB RUSTUM V 236
    AND WENT UP ON THE ROOF TO SLEEP . . . . . . 90 SICK KING BOKH   73
    MY LORD HAD COVERD UP HIS FACE . . . . 91 SICK KING BOKH   125
    AND UP FROM THENCE TO ORGUNJE . . . . 93 SICK KING BOKH   168
    GAZING UP HITHER THE POOR MAN . . . . 93 SICK KING BOKH   190
    AND PLUCKING UP THE MARBLE FLAGS . . . . . . 95 SICK KING BOKH   227
    AND UP FROM THENCE TO URGHENDJE . . . . . . 93 SICK KING BOKH V 168
    AND TEARING UP THE MARBLE FLAGS . . . . . . 95 SICK KING BOKH V 227
    UP TO ITS GOLDEN ROOF WITH SOBS AND CRIES . . . . 95 BALDER DEAD 1   12

UP

(CONTINUED)

SO THEY WITH PENT-UP HEARTS AND TEARLESS EYES	• •	97 BALDER DEAD 1	69
THERE HE WENT UP AND PASSD THE OPEN DOORS	• • • •	97 BALDER DEAD 1	87
AND LIGHTED TORCHES AND TOOK UP THE CORPSE	• • •	101 BALDER DEAD 1	204
HIM THE BLIND HODER MET AS HE CAME UP	• •	101 BALDER DEAD 1	226
FORTH FROM THE EAST UP THE ASCENT OF HEAVEN	• •	105 BALDER DEAD 2	1
AND UP THE DEWY MOUNTAIN-TRACKS THEY FARED	• •	106 BALDER DEAD 2	51
AND UP AND DOWN AND SIDE AND SLANT THEY ROAMD	•	106 BALDER DEAD 2	53
IN SILENCE UP THE DARK UNTRAVELLD ROAD	• •	107 BALDER DEAD 2	79
THE SPRING THAT BUBBLES UP BY HELAS THRONE	• • •	108 BALDER DEAD 2	131
AND FROM THE DARK FLOCKD UP THE SHADOWY TRIBES	•	109 BALDER DEAD 2	156
BEHIND FLOCKD WRANGLING UP A PITEOUS CREW	• • •	109 BALDER DEAD 2	170
AND UP FROM THENCE A WET AND MISTY ROAD	• • • •	113 BALDER DEAD 2	289
THE MAST THEY FIXT AND HOISTED UP THE SAILS	• •	118 BALDER DEAD 3	174
BUT THE GODS WENT BY STARLIGHT UP THE SHORE	• •	119 BALDER DEAD 3	207
THAT EMPIRE WILT THOU NOW INVADE LIGHT UP	• • •	121 BALDER DEAD 3	279
AND AS IN WINTER WHEN THE FROST BREAKS UP	• • •	122 BALDER DEAD 3	307
AND THEY GO LONG DAYS TOSSING UP AND DOWN	• •	124 BALDER DEAD 3	365
MY HATED CONVERSE ON THEE CAME I UP	• • •	125 BALDER DEAD 3	414
THE LOVE ALL BEAR TOWARD THEE NOR TRAIN UP	• •	126 BALDER DEAD 3	450
THEY FIXT THE MAST AND HOISTED UP THE SAILS	• •	118 BALDER DEAD 3	V 174
SEES SUDDENLY A SPIRE OF FLAME SHOOT UP	• • •	119 BALDER DEAD 3	V
THE LOVE ALL BEAR TOWARDS THEE NOR TRAIN UP	• •	126 BALDER DEAD 3	V 450
SEE IT SHINE AND TAKE IT UP	• • •	135 TRISTRAM 1	143
THROUGH THE DARK UP THE DROWND SAND	• •	137 TRISTRAM 1	218
UP TRISTRAM UP MEN CRY THOU MOONSTRUCK KNIGHT	•	137 TRISTRAM 1	238
UP TRISTRAM UP MEN CRY THOU MOONSTRUCK KNIGHT	•	137 TRISTRAM 1	238
FILLD UP THE HOLLOW CHEEK AND BROUGHT	• •	147 TRISTRAM 2	141
MOVED UP AND DOWN UNDER THE GLOSSY TREES	• •	150 TRISTRAM 3	43
BORE UP FROM WHERE THE BRIGHT ATLANTIC GLEAMS	•	151 TRISTRAM 3	53
NOT SUFFERING WHICH SHUTS UP EYE AND EAR	• • •	152 TRISTRAM 3	113
BY DRYING UP OUR JOY IN EVERYTHING	• • •	153 TRISTRAM 3	125
THEY STRAIGHTWAY ARE BURNT UP WITH FUME AND CARE	•	153 TRISTRAM 3	139
AND UP AS HIGH AS WHERE THEY STOOD TO LOOK	• • •	155 TRISTRAM 3	188
MOVD UP AND DOWN UNDER THEIR GLOSSY TREES	• • •	TRISTRAM 3	V 43
NOT SUFFERING THAT SHUTS UP EYE AND EAR	• • •	152 TRISTRAM 3	V 113
WHEN HE LOOKD UP TENANTLESS LIES	• • •	158 SAINT BRANDAN	V 75
SHE SIGHD SHE LOOKD UP THROUGH THE CLEAR GREEN SEA		163 FORSAKEN MERM	55
I SAID GO UP DEAR HEART THROUGH THE WAVES	• •	163 FORSAKEN MERM	60
SHE SMILED SHE WENT UP THROUGH THE SURF IN THE BAY		163 FORSAKEN MERM	62
WE WENT UP THE BEACH BY THE SANDY DOWN	• • •	163 FORSAKEN MERM	68
AND WE GAZED UP THE AISLE THROUGH THE SMALL		163 FORSAKEN MERM	75
LEADED PANES			
UP THE STILL GLISTENING BEACHES	• • • •	165 FORSAKEN MERM	132
UP THE CREEKS WE WILL HIE	• • • •	165 FORSAKEN MERM	133
UP THE STEEP PINE-PLUMED PATHS OF THE ESTRELLE	•	167 RACHEL 2	4
OF COMMON LIFE WHERE CROWDED UP PELL-MELL	•	168 WORLDLY PLACE	4
SET UP A MARK OF EVERLASTING LIGHT	• • • •	169 EAST LONDON	10
THE WORLD SHALL BE THRUST DOWN AND WE UP-BORNE		172 IMMORTALITY	4
AND DRY UP MY TEARS	• • • •	177 PARTING	84
UP THE STEEP STREET I HURRIED FAST	• • •	177 FAREWELL	7
LEAND UP AGAINST THE COLUMN THERE	• • •	186 STRAYED REVEL	9
UP AT THE VALLEY-HEAD	• • • •	186 STRAYED REVEL	27
I SPRANG UP I THREW ROUND ME	• • • •	186 STRAYED REVEL	29
I SNATCHD UP MY VINE-CROWN MY FIR-STAFF	• •	186 STRAYED REVEL	33
HEAP UP HIS MOMENTS WITH LIFE	• • • •	200 EARLY DEATH	18
MY PENT-UP TEARS OPPRESS MY BRAIN	• • •	206 RIVER	9
TIES STRAITLY UP FROM MINE THY LOT	• • •	208 ON THE RHINE	8
AT THEIR RETURN UP THE HIGH STRAND	• • •	211 DOVER BEACH	11
AT THEIR RETURN UP THE STEEP STRAND	• • •	211 DOVER BEACH	V 11
AT THEIR RETURN UP THE BARRD STRAND	• • •	211 DOVER BEACH	V 11
WHEN WE ARE FROZEN UP WITHIN AND QUITE	• •	213 GROWING OLD	32
RISE SLOWLY UP INTO THE SKY	• • •	220 BACCHANALIA 2	25
DRINKS UP DELIGHTED ECSTASY	• • •	227 EPILOG LAOCOON	194
YE WHO FROM MY CHILDHOOD UP HAVE CALMD ME	• •	240 SELF-DEPENDENCE	7
BRINGS UP THE STREAM	• • •	254 FUTURE	86
TO-NIGHT FROM OXFORD UP YOUR PATHWAY STRAYS	•	263 THYRSIS	8
AND MAKE LEAP UP WITH JOY THE BEAUTEOUS HEAD	•	265 THYRSIS	87
UP PAST THE WOOD TO WHERE THE ELM-TREE CROWNS	•	263 THYRSIS	V 12
SPIRITS DRIED UP AND CLOSELY FURLD	• • •	272 MEMORIAL VERSES	56
RISE UP ALL ROUND THE CHRISTIAN SPIRES	• •	274 STANZAS CARNAC	22
UP TO THE HEART OF THE MOORS	• • • •	282 HAWORTH CHURCH	56
YE FILL UP THE GAPS IN OUR FILES	• • •	292 RUGBY CHAPEL	204
UP THROUGH THE TALL DARK FIRS	• • •	297 HEINES GRAVE	156
UP BY THE STREAM WITH ITS HUGE	• • •	297 HEINES GRAVE	159
UP OER THE ROCK-STREWN SLOPE	• • •	297 HEINES GRAVE	162
THROUGH FOREST UP THE MOUNTAIN-SIDE	• • •	299 GRANDE CHARTR	6
THE WIND IS UP AND DRIVES THE RAIN	• • •	299 GRANDE CHARTR	8
MOUNTS UP THE STONY FOREST-WAY	• • •	300 GRANDE CHARTR	20
CRAWLS UP ITS ROCKY STAIR	• • •	306 OBERMANN	2
THY MOTHERS KIN RECEIVED THEE AND REARD UP	• •	330 MEROPE	23
THAT THOU IN SECRET NURTUREST UP THY SON	•	334 MEROPE	144
AND HALF-BESTOWD HALF YIELDED UP THEIR SOIL	•	339 MEROPE	294
LIGHT TO SPRING UP TO THY HOUSE	• • •	343 MEROPE	407
THERE ROSE UP A CRY IN THE STREETS	• • •	345 MEROPE	487
UP FROM THE CITY TOWRD THIS GATED HILL	• •	362 MEROPE	935
LOOK UP O QUEEN LOOK UP O MISTRESS DEAR	• •	363 MEROPE	946
LOOK UP O QUEEN LOOK UP O MISTRESS DEAR	• •	363 MEROPE	946
LOOK UP AND SEE THY FRIENDS WHO COMFORT THEE	•	363 MEROPE	947
COUNTING TILL I GREW UP THE LAGGARD YEARS	• •	367 MEROPE	1046
WAKE UP IN HELL FROM THINE UNHALLOWD SLEEP	• •	373 MEROPE	1183

UP   (CONTINUED)
         INEVITABLY HAD SURGED UP PERHAPS   .   .   .   .   .   .   394 MEROPE   1698
         UP THE PRECIPICES OF TRACHIS   .   .   .   .   399 MEROPE   1828
         TWO GENERATIONS OF HIS OFFSPRING UP   .   .   .   .   .   .   336 MEROPE   V 217
         LIGHT TO SPRING UP TO THY RACE   .   .   .   .   343 MEROPE   V 407
         UP FROM THE CITY TOWRDS THIS GATED HILL   .   .   .   .   362 MEROPE   V 935
         WHOSE MULES I FOLLOWD MAY BE COMING UP   .   .   .   .   407 EMPEDOCLES I 1   22
         UP BY THE TORRENT-SIDE UNDER THE PINES   .   .   .   .   411 EMPEDOCLES I 1   164
         SLOPE BEHIND SLOPE UP TO THE PEAK LIES BARE   .   .   414 EMPEDOCLES I 2   55
         A NEW-MADE WORLD UP-SPRINGS   .   .   .   .   418 EMPEDOCLES I 2   179
         FAILD TO FILL UP THE VOID WHICH IN OUR BREASTS WE BEAR   424 EMPEDOCLES I 2   376
         AND HAD TORN UP BY THE ROOTS   .   .   .   .   .   .   434 EMPEDOCLES II   173
         THAT HEAVES ITS WHITE AND BILLOWY VAPOURS UP   .   .   438 EMPEDOCLES II   309
         AH BOIL UP YE VAPOURS   .   .   .   .   441 EMPEDOCLES II   410
         UP THE STILL VALE OF THISBE   .   .   .   .   442 EMPEDOCLES II   427
         THEY STREAM UP AGAIN   .   .   .   .   442 EMPEDOCLES II   450
         HORDE AFTER HORDE STREAMED UP THY FROWNING CAPITOL   464 ALARIC AT ROME   72
         COME FLOATING UP FROM THE ABYSS OF YEARS   .   .   .   469 ALARIC AT ROME   176
         FLOAT UP TO TELL OF AGES THAT ARE GONE   .   .   .   470 ALARIC AT ROME   208
         LAST NIGHT THE WIND WAS UP AND STRONG   .   .   .   479 HAYSWATER BOAT   17
         OR FAR EASTWARD WHERE UP-PILD   .   .   .   .   .   .   PILLARS UNIVERS   6
         THERE OR EASTWARD WHERE UP-PILD   .   .   .   .   .   PILLARS UNIVERS   V   6

UPBORNE
         FROM THE SOULS SUBTERRANEAN DEPTH UPBORNE   .   .   .   .   247 BURIED LIFE   73

UPBRAID
         CONDEMN ME NOR UPBRAID   .   .   .   .   310 OBERMANN   140

UPBRAIDINGS
         UPBRAIDINGS OFTEN ASSAILD   .   .   .   .   294 HEINES GRAVE   71
         BEWARE FROM THEE UPBRAIDINGS I RECEIVE   .   .   .   .   341 MEROPE   360

UPBRAIDS
         BALDER UPBRAIDS ME NOT NOR HATES AT ALL   .   .   .   .   125 BALDER DEAD 3   407
         O MOTHER MOTHER WHO UPBRAIDS ME AH   .   .   .   .   .   376 MEROPE   1213
         UPBRAIDS THEE NO ONE THOU DOST WELL BUT TAKE   .   .   376 MEROPE   1214

UPCLOSE
         THE FLOWERS UPCLOSE THE BIRDS ARE FED   .   .   .   .   249 KENSINGTON GARD   34

UPCROWDING
         BEHIND THE UPCROWDING HILLS   .   .   .   .   324 OBERMANN MORE   342

UPCURLD
         IN WHOSE HOT AIR OUR SPIRITS ARE UPCURLD   .   .   .   .   153 TRISTRAM 3   120

UPFURLD
         ARE SPREAD AND UPFURLD   .   .   .   .   177 PARTING   88

UPHOLD
         AND TO UPHOLD THY DESPERATE CHALLENGING   .   .   .   .   RUDE ORATOR   17

UPHUNG
         UPHUNG THE SPEAR UNBENT THE BOW   .   .   .   .   .   .   219 BACCHANALIA 2   11

UPLAND
         AND WE TOO FROM UPLAND VALLEYS   .   .   .   .   27 NEW SIRENS   25
         OF ITS DARK UPLAND FARMS IS PAST   .   .   .   .   .   .   54 RESIGNATION   55
         PLAY THROUGH THIS GRASSY UPLAND GLEN   .   .   .   .   .   55 RESIGNATION   99
         THAT THE SWEET VOICE ITS UPLAND CLEARNESS TOOK   .   .   175 PARTING   22
         BEFALLS ME WANDERING THROUGH THIS UPLAND DIM   .   .   263 THYRSIS   23
         BUT HUSH THE UPLAND HATH A SUDDEN LOSS   .   .   .   267 THYRSIS   151
         AH VAIN THESE ENGLISH FIELDS THIS UPLAND DIM   .   .   267 THYRSIS   172

UPLANDS
         WHILE TO MY EAR FROM UPLANDS FAR AWAY   .   .   .   .   255 SCHOLAR-GIPSY   17

UPLIFT
         LURD HIM STARWARDS TO UPLIFT HIS EYE   .   .   .   .   .   .   483 THEKLAS ANSWER   18

UPLIFTED
         AND WHITE UPLIFTED FACES STAND   .   .   .   .   300 GRANDE CHARTR   41

UPLIFTS
         OF THE LONG-BATTERD WORLD UPLIFTS ITS WALL   .   .   .   267 THYRSIS   147

UPON
         UPON THE GLISTENING LEADEN ROOF   .   .   .   .   .   .   16 CHURCH BROU 2   1
         AND RISE UPON YOUR COLD WHITE MARBLE BEDS   .   .   .   18 CHURCH BROU 3   27
         THE STRONG SPELL WHICH PASSION UPON HIM HATH HURLD   20 MODERN SAPPHO   V 22
         IF TOO HOTLY MUSED UPON   .   .   .   .   23 MEMORY-PICTURE   10
         UPON THE MOSSY ROCKS AT THE STREAMS EDGE   .   .   .   25 DREAM   14
         THEY BEAT UPON MINE EAR AGAIN   .   .   .   .   36 VOICE   33
         UPON THESE BREATHLESS SOLITUDES   .   .   .   .   .   .   54 RESIGNATION   73
         HE LEANS UPON A GATE AND SEES   .   .   .   .   57 RESIGNATION   172
         UPON THE THICK PILED CARPETS IN THE TENT   .   .   .   .   61 SOHRAB RUSTUM   25
         SHOULD ONE DAY GREET UPON SOME WELL-FOUGHT FIELD   .   .   62 SOHRAB RUSTUM   51
         AND THE OLD TARTAR CAME UPON THE SAND   .   .   .   .   65 SOHRAB RUSTUM   148
         REJOINS HER IN THEIR HUT UPON THE SANDS   .   .   .   .   70 SOHRAB RUSTUM   289

UPON   (CONTINUED)

AND RUSTUM CAME UPON THE SAND AND CAST   . . . .   70 SOHRAB RUSTUM   299
UPON THE SUMMER-FLOODS AND NOT MY BONES   . . . .   74 SOHRAB RUSTUM   428
AND MAKE A TRUCE AND SIT UPON THIS SAND   . . . .   74 SOHRAB RUSTUM   440
AND COMES AT NIGHT TO DIE UPON THE SAND   . . . .   76 SOHRAB RUSTUM   506
SAW RUSTUM STANDING SAFE UPON HIS FEET   . . . .   77 SOHRAB RUSTUM   525
UPON THE CRAGGY ISLE OF A HILL-LAKE   . . . .   78 SOHRAB RUSTUM   558
TO ARMS AND CRY FOR VENGEANCE UPON THEE   . . . .   78 SOHRAB RUSTUM   585
LOVELY IN DEATH UPON THE COMMON SAND . . . .   80 SOHRAB RUSTUM   639
TRUTH SITS UPON THE LIPS OF DYING MEN   . . . .   80 SOHRAB RUSTUM   656
I TELL THEE PRICKD UPON THIS ARM I BEAR   . . . .   80 SOHRAB RUSTUM   658
BUT SOHRAB LOOKD UPON THE HORSE AND SAID   . . . .   83 SOHRAB RUSTUM   741
COME LET ME LAY MY HAND UPON THY MANE   . . . .   83 SOHRAB RUSTUM   746
EMERGE AND SHINE UPON THE ARAL SEA   . . . .   87 SOHRAB RUSTUM   892
AND PERAN WISA CAME UPON THE SAND   . . . .   65 SOHRAB RUSTUM   V 148
ALL RENT AND DUST UPON HIS HAIR   . . . .   88 SICK KING BOKH   32
BEHIND THE DOOR UPON THE GROUND   . . . .   90 SICK KING BOKH   79
WITH A GREAT JOY UPON HIS FACE   . . . .   91 SICK KING BOKH   119
UPON THE RUSSIAN FRONTIER WHERE   . . . .   93 SICK KING BOKH   161
UPON A HILL ON THE RIGHT HAND   . . . .   94 SICK KING BOKH   222
UPON THE ROAD OF SAMARCAND   . . . .   94 SICK KING BOKH   224
UPON THE NORTHERN FRONTIER WHERE   . . . .   93 SICK KING BOKH   V 161
TO LIDSKIALF AND SATE UPON HIS THRONE   . . . .   96 BALDER DEAD 1   49
AND LEFT HIS BODY STRETCHD UPON THE FLOOR   . . . .   97 BALDER DEAD 1   63
UPON HER GOLDEN CHAIR THE MOTHER SATE   . . . .   98 BALDER DEAD 1   92
TEARS STAND UPON THE LASHES OF THINE EYES   . . . .   103 BALDER DEAD 1   289
UPON MY SHIP AND BURN MY CORPSE WITH FIRE   . . . .   103 BALDER DEAD 1   297
AND THEY CAME OUT UPON THE PLAIN AND PASSD   . . . .   106 BALDER DEAD 2   65
UPON MY BRIDGE AND WHEN THEY CROSS I KNOW   . . . .   108 BALDER DEAD 2   121
LET ALL THAT LIVES AND MOVES UPON THE EARTH   . . . .   111 BALDER DEAD 2   236
BELOW AND LOOKD UPON THE SHADOWY TRIBES   . . . .   114 BALDER DEAD 3   39
AND THE GODS STOOD UPON THE BEACH AND GAZED   . . . .   119 BALDER DEAD 3   193
AND THERE FELL JOY UPON THE GODS TO HEAR   . . . .   122 BALDER DEAD 3   319
UPON THE CLIFFS OR SMOKE OF BURNING WEEDS   . . . .   124 BALDER DEAD 3   362
AGAINST THE GODS UPON THE PLAINS OF HEAVEN   . . . .   127 BALDER DEAD 3   481
PROP ME UPON THE PILLOWS ONCE AGAIN   . . . .   130 TRISTRAM 1   2
UPON US ARE THE CHIVALRY OF ROME   . . . .   137 TRISTRAM 1   236
UPON THE WINDOW-PANES THE MOON SHINES BRIGHT   . . . .   139 TRISTRAM 1   299
SHE RAISED HER EYES UPON HIS FACE   . . . .   140 TRISTRAM 1   319
IT SHINES UPON THE BLANK WHITE WALLS . . . .   141 TRISTRAM 1   335
AND UPON EVERY GIANT-BOUGH   . . . .   141 TRISTRAM 1   358
ME A SMILING QUEEN UPON MY THRONE   . . . .   144 TRISTRAM 2   52
HEAVEN HIS HEAD SINKS BACK UPON THE PILLOW   . . . .   145 TRISTRAM 2   77
ONE LAST KISS UPON THE LIVING SHORE   . . . .   145 TRISTRAM 2   98
SHE SINKS UPON THE GROUND HER HOOD   . . . .   146 TRISTRAM 2   103
AND THERE UPON THE WALL YOU SEE   . . . .   147 TRISTRAM 2   V 152
UPON THE BROW-TOP GREW A THORN AND HERE   . . . .   155 TRISTRAM 3   205
FELL UPON MERLIN MORE LIKE DEATH SO DEEP   . . . .   155 TRISTRAM 3   214
HE GAZED UPON ME AS I PASSD   . . . .   158 SAINT BRANDAN   49
HE SITS UPON THE HEADLANDS   . . . .   159 NECKAN   13
MY MARGUERITE SMILES UPON THE STRAND . . . .   174 MEETING   3
THE CALM UPON THE MOONLIT SEA   . . . .   180 FAREWELL   80
UPON THE PINE-GROWN LATMIAN STEEP   . . . .   181 ISOLATION MARG   24
UPON TIMES BARREN STORMY FLOW   . . . .   183 ABSENCE   19
UPON THE BOUNDLESS OCEAN-PLAIN . . . .   185 TERRACE BERNE   46
UPON THEIR CARAVAN OR GREEDY KINGS   . . . .   193 STRAYED REVEL   249
WAS TURND UPON THE SONS OF MEN . . . .   202 URANIA   10
THEY SHINE UPON THE WORLD THEIR EARS . . . .   203 EUPHROSYNE   21
THEY SMILE UPON THE WORLD THEIR EARS . . . .   203 EUPHROSYNE   V 21
WERE GORGEOUS UPON EARTH AGAIN . . . .   204 CALAIS SANDS   8
I SAW UPON THE OPEN SAND   . . . .   204 CALAIS SANDS   10
HANGS DARK UPON THE ROLLING SEA . . . .   205 CALAIS SANDS   22
AND SEE UPON THE LOVELY SAND   . . . .   204 CALAIS SANDS   V 10
LET BEAM UPON MY INWARD VIEW   . . . .   208 ON THE RHINE   17
UPON THE STRAITS ON THE FRENCH COAST THE LIGHT . . .   210 DOVER BEACH   3
UPON THE STRAIT ON THE FRENCH COAST THE LIGHT   . . .   DOVER BEACH   V 3
CARRY MY PEACE UPON EARTH . . . .   216 LORDS MESSENGER   6
AND FROM THE THYME UPON THE HEIGHT   . . . .   218 BACCHANALIA 1   10
AND NOW UPON THE BRIDGE WE STOOD   . . . .   223 EPILOG LAOCOON   62
SOME HANG UPON THE RAILS AND SOME   . . . .   224 EPILOG LAOCOON   113
THIS THROUGH THE RIDE UPON HIS STEED . . . .   224 EPILOG LAOCOON   115
HELEN WILL COME UPON THE WALL TO SEE . . . .   236 PALLADIUM   16
UPON OUR LIFE A RULING EFFLUENCE SEND . . . .   236 PALLADIUM   22
THE MASTER STOOD UPON THE MOUNT AND TAUGHT   . . . .   237 PROGRESS   1
WHILE YET UPON THE VERGE OF HEAVEN HE STOOD   . . .   239 REVOLUTIONS   2
AND DROOPD AND SLOWLY DIED UPON THEIR THRONE   . . .   239 REVOLUTIONS   16
STILL STILL LET ME AS I GAZE UPON YOU . . . .   240 SELF-DEPENDENCE   11
AND LAY UPON THE BREAST OF GOD . . . .   242 MORALITY   36
AN AIR OF COOLNESS PLAYS UPON HIS FACE   . . . .   247 BURIED LIFE   94
THE NIGHT COMES DOWN UPON THE GRASS   . . . .   249 KENSINGTON GARD   35
SITTING UPON THE RIVER BANK OERGROWN . . . .   258 SCHOLAR-GIPSY   97
AND TIRED UPON A THOUSAND SCHEMES OUR WIT   . . . .   259 SCHOLAR-GIPSY   148
HIS SEAT UPON THE INTELLECTUAL THRONE . . . .   260 SCHOLAR-GIPSY   184
LAID PAUSEFULLY UPON LIFES HEADLONG TRAIN   . . . .   266 THYRSIS   137
HE TOO UPON A WINTRY CLIME   . . . .   271 MEMORIAL VERSES   42
KEEP FRESH THE GRASS UPON HIS GRAVE   . . . .   272 MEMORIAL VERSES   71
THIS WAS THY LIFE UPON EARTH   . . . .   288 RUGBY CHAPEL   57
UPON THE WALL THE KNEE-WORN FLOOR   . . . .   300 GRANDE CHARTR   46
ONCE MORE UPON ME ROLL   . . . .   306 OBERMANN   14
UPON HIS CROSS WITH HEAD SUNK LOW   . . . .   317 OBERMANN MORE   155

UPON   (CONTINUED)
         UPON THEM PLIES THE RACE OF MAN   •   •   •   •   •   •   320 OBERMANN MORE   213
         UPON THE BITTER TREE   •   •   •   •   •   •   •   •   317 OBERMANN MORE   V 156
         UPON THEM PLY THE RACE OF MAN   •   •   •   •   •   •   320 OBERMANN MORE   V 213
         UPON THE THRESHOLD OF OLD AGE ALONE   •   •   •   •   •   •   334 MEROPE   152
         UPON A THRONE NOT THINE TO GIVE IS HEIR   •   •   •   •   336 MEROPE   190
         YOUR SONS LEAP UPON THE FOE OF YOUR KIN   •   •   •   344 MEROPE   462
         WE SPRANG UPON OUR FEET WE SNATCHD OUR SPEARS   •   •   357 MEROPE   789
         WASHD AS THE MARKS UPON THE HILLS STILL SHOW   •   •   358 MEROPE   815
         CAME UPON HER STEALING   •   •   •   •   •   •   •   392 MEROPE   1644
         TO HEAVEN AND LAID HIS HAND UPON THE STEER   •   •   •   402 MEROPE   1914
         UPON THE OPEN SHOULDER OF THE HILL   •   •   •   •   •   412 EMPEDOCLES I 2   3
         AND LEAN UPON THE THOUGHT   •   •   •   •   •   •   •   420 EMPEDOCLES I 2   239
         WE NOW WOULD LEAN UPON   •   •   •   •   •   •   •   •   422 EMPEDOCLES I 2   315
         CURSE UPON CURSE PANG UPON PANG   •   •   •   •   •   427 EMPEDOCLES I 2   447
         CURSE UPON CURSE PANG UPON PANG   •   •   •   •   •   427 EMPEDOCLES I 2   447
         SINK UPON HIS MIGHTY KNEES   •   •   •   •   •   •   •   431 EMPEDOCLES II   73
         HANGD UPON A BRANCHING FIR   •   •   •   •   •   •   •   433 EMPEDOCLES II   148
         UPON WHOSE CHARRD AND QUAKING CRUST I STAND   •   •   438 EMPEDOCLES II   307
         UPON THE HEARTH AND PLAYD WITH THEM AND SMILED   •   •   446 WESTMIN ABBEY   90
         SHALL SEE THY GRAVE UPON THE GRASS   •   •   •   •   •   452 GEISTS GRAVE   75
         GREET UPON THE LAWN AT PLAY   •   •   •   •   •   •   •   454 POOR MATTHIAS   68
         SATST UPON THY PERCH TO HEAR   •   •   •   •   •   •   455 POOR MATTHIAS   120
         UPON ITS HEADLONG COURSE WITH SAD PROPHETIC EYE   •   •   463 ALARIC AT ROME   24
         WHEN THE GOTH STOOPED UPON HIS STRICKEN PREY   •   •   464 ALARIC AT ROME   68
         GIRD THEE AND ON UPON THY FATEFUL PATH   •   •   •   465 ALARIC AT ROME   88
         NOT THIS THE TIME TO WEEP UPON THE BIER   •   •   •   467 ALARIC AT ROME   135
         YES THERE HE STOOD UPON THAT SILENT HILL   •   •   •   468 ALARIC AT ROME   157
         SMILINGLY FORTH UPON HER SUNNY BAY   •   •   •   •   468 ALARIC AT ROME   160
         FLASHD FROM THY SOUL UPON THINE INWARD EAR   •   •   •   472 CROMWELL   28
         UPON THE REEFS AND SANDBANKS OF THE WORLD   •   •   •   LUCRETIUS 2   5
         THE CLOUDS OF SICKNESS CAST NO STAIN UPON   •   •   •   FRAGMENT 8   1

UPPER
         A LIGHT THAT FROM SOME UPPER FOUNT DID BEAM   •   •   9 MYCERINUS   21
         THOSE UPPER REGIONS WE MUST TREAD   •   •   •   •   •   54 RESIGNATION   65
         INTO AN UPPER CHAMBER AND LAY DOWN   •   •   •   •   •   103 BALDER DEAD 1   278
         IN THE UPPER GLENS   •   •   •   •   •   •   •   •   •   190 STRAYED REVEL   144
         SET WHERE THE UPPER STREAMS OF SIMOIS FLOW   •   •   •   236 PALLADIUM   1
         THAT PEACE HAS LEFT THE UPPER WORLD   •   •   •   •   249 KENSINGTON GARD   27

UPRAISEST
         STILL THOU UPRAISEST WITH ZEAL   •   •   •   •   •   •   •   287 RUGBY CHAPEL   49

UPREARD
         EACH IN HER TURN WITH TORCH UPREARD   •   •   •   •   •   53 RESIGNATION   32

UPRIGHT
         HIS SWORD UPRIGHT AND FELL ON IT AND DIED   •   •   •   •   102 BALDER DEAD 1   252

UPROAR
         MANS FITFUL UPROAR MINGLING WITH HIS TOIL   •   •   •   •   1 QUIET WORK   10
         MANS SENSELESS UPROAR MINGLING WITH HIS TOIL   •   •   1 QUIET WORK   V 10
         OUR SENSELESS UPROAR MINGLING WITH OUR TOIL   •   •   1 QUIET WORK   V 10
         STRANGE UNLOVED UPROAR   •   •   •   •   •   •   •   •   50 CONSOLATION   21
         I ON MENS IMPIOUS UPROAR HURLD   •   •   •   •   •   •   •   249 KENSINGTON GARD   25
         UPROAR SURELY NOT LOATH   •   •   •   •   •   •   •   •   •   293 HEINES GRAVE   15

UPSTREAMING
         THERE WINDS UPSTREAMING SLOWLY STILL   •   •   •   •   •   54 RESIGNATION   62

UPTORN
         TO FORMS FROM ANTIQUE GREECE AND ROME UPTORN   •   •   168 RACHEL 3   3

UPTURND
         THAT MOMENT WHILE WITH UPTURND EYES HE PRAYD   •   •   402 MEROPE   1918

UPWARD
         AND HAVE DRAWN UPWARD TO THIS VERGE OF HELL   •   •   126 BALDER DEAD 3   439
         THERE THE TORRENTS DRIVE UPWARD   •   •   •   •   •   •   175 PARTING   29

UPWARDS
         AND HAVE DRAWN UPWARDS TO THIS VERGE OF HELL   •   •   126 BALDER DEAD 3   V 439
         THAT KNEW NOT EARTH SOARD UPWARDS TO THE SKY   •   •   477 CROMWELL   178

URGE
         WITH GOAD AND SHOUTING URGE THEIR CATTLE PAST   •   •   107 BALDER DEAD 2   96
         THE PRAYER I CAME TO URGE I WILL DEFER   •   •   •   •   333 MEROPE   109
         TO OFFER THAT I COME NOT BUT TO URGE   •   •   •   •   394 MEROPE   1688
         HENCEFORTH IF WHAT I URGE DISPLEASE I MAY   •   •   •   395 MEROPE   1727
         TO OFFER THAT I CAME NOT BUT TO URGE   •   •   •   •   394 MEROPE   V1688
         I DARE NOT URGE HIM FURTHER HE MUST GO   •   •   •   •   428 EMPEDOCLES I 2   479

URGED
         URGED AND TO FEED WHOSE MOVEMENT SPINNING SAND   •   •   5 DUKE WELLINGTON   6
         BREASTS HER OWN GRIEFS AND URGED TOO FIERCELY SAYS   6 GEO CRUIKSHANK   10
         THIS AT A MOMENT TOO WHEN I HAD URGED   •   •   •   360 MEROPE   879
         ALL THIS NO DOUBT THOU TO THYSELF HAST URGED   •   •   389 MEROPE   1529
         OTHERS HAVE URGED IT TOO   •   •   •   •   •   •   •   •   •   419 EMPEDOCLES I 2   210

URGHENDJE
         AND UP FROM THENCE TO URGHENDJE   • • • • • •   93 SICK KING BOKH   V 168

US
         THE SEEDS OF GODLIKE POWER ARE IN US STILL • • • •   4 EMERSONS ESSAYS   12
         SAY WHAT SHALL CALM US WHEN SUCH GUESTS INTRUDE • •   6 GEO CRUIKSHANK   6
         SPARING US NARROWER MARGIN THAN WE DEEM • • • •   7 REP FRIEND CONT   8
         WHAT MAY CHAIN US WHO CAN SAY • • • • • •   23 MEMORY-PICTURE   22
         LEAVES US FIXT TO NOTHING LONG • • • • • • •   24 MEMORY-PICTURE   58
         LEAVES US TRUE TO NOTHING LONG • • • • • •   24 MEMORY-PICTURE   V 58
         LEAVES US FIRM TO NOTHING LONG • • • • • •   24 MEMORY-PICTURE   V 58
         LEAVES US JOIND TO NOTHING LONG • • • • •   24 MEMORY-PICTURE   V 58
         THEY SAW US THEY CONFERRD THEIR BOSOMS HEAVED • •   25 DREAM   26
         LOUD THUNDERING BORE US BY SWIFT SWIFT IT FOAMD •   25 DREAM   33
         FADED THE MOSS THE ROCKS US BURNING PLAINS • • •   25 DREAM   36
         BRISTLED WITH CITIES US THE SEA RECEIVED • • • •   25 DREAM   37
         ONCE LIKE US YOU TOOK YOUR STATION • • • • •   31 NEW SIRENS   139
         O LET FALL ONE TEAR AND SET US FREE • • • • •   34 NEW SIRENS   226
         OH SET US FREE • • • • • • • • • •   39 STAGIRIUS   48
         AH LET US MAKE NO CLAIM • • • • • •   40 HUMAN LIFE   7
         LET US NOT FRET AND FEAR TO MISS OUR AIM • • •   40 HUMAN LIFE   10
         IF SOME FAIR COAST HAVE LURED US TO MAKE STAY • •   40 HUMAN LIFE   11
         OR SOME FRIEND HAILD US TO KEEP COMPANY • • • •   40 HUMAN LIFE   12
         IF SOME FAIR COAST HAS LURED US TO MAKE STAY • •   40 HUMAN LIFE   V 11
         OF GRIEF AND EASED US WITH A THOUSAND SLEEPS • •   43 GIPSY CHILD   52
         US NOT THE DAILY QUICKENING RACE • • • • •   48 HORATIAN ECHO   7
         AND LET US BEAR THAT THEY DEBATE • • • • •   48 HORATIAN ECHO   13
         WITH PLEASANT SMILE LET US TAKE CARE • • • •   48 HORATIAN ECHO   21
         AND SCORN US AS OUR MISTRESS MAY • • • • •   48 HORATIAN ECHO   33
         TO DIE BE GIVEN US OR ATTAIN • • • • • •   52 RESIGNATION   1
         THERE SPRINGS THE BROOK WILL GUIDE US DOWN • •   54 RESIGNATION   76
         HEMS US ALL IN HE IS NOT BOUND • • • • • •   58 RESIGNATION   210
         THE SOLEMN HILLS AROUND US SPREAD • • • • •   60 RESIGNATION   266
         AND SHARE THE BATTLES COMMON CHANCE WITH US • •   63 SOHRAB RUSTUM   67
         THAT WERE FAR BEST MY SON TO STAY WITH US • •   63 SOHRAB RUSTUM   71
         TO US FAIN THEREFORE SEND THEE HENCE IN PEACE •   63 SOHRAB RUSTUM   89
         FEROOD SHAME BIDS US TAKE THEIR CHALLENGE UP • •   66 SOHRAB RUSTUM   175
         COME DOWN AND HELP US RUSTUM OR WE LOSE • • •   67 SOHRAB RUSTUM   219
         AND WHETHER IT WILL HEAVE US UP TO LAND • • •   73 SOHRAB RUSTUM   393
         OR WHETHER IT WILL ROLL US OUT TO SEA • • • •   73 SOHRAB RUSTUM   394
         WE KNOW NOT AND NO SEARCH WILL MAKE US KNOW • •   73 SOHRAB RUSTUM   396
         ONLY THE EVENT WILL TEACH US IN ITS HOUR • • •   73 SOHRAB RUSTUM   397
         O THOU OLD WARRIOR LET US YIELD TO HEAVEN • • •   74 SOHRAB RUSTUM   438
         PLIES SOME LIGHT FEMALE TASK NOR DREAMS OF US •   80 SOHRAB RUSTUM   647
         OF US SHE DREAMS NOT NOR OF WOUNDS NOR WAR • •   80 SOHRAB RUSTUM   648
         BUT LET US SPEAK NO MORE OF THIS I FIND • • •   82 SOHRAB RUSTUM   716
         NOW THE KING CHARGED US SECRETLY • • • •   91 SICK KING BOKH   113
         AND WITH HIMSELF SET US HIS OFFSPRING FREE • •   111 BALDER DEAD 2   223
         HELPLESS TO BETTER US OR RUIN THEM • • • •   111 BALDER DEAD 2   230
         THY VOICE OF JOYANCE MINDED US AND YOUTH • • •   117 BALDER DEAD 3   143
         ACCEPT THEM AND THEY BIND US UNFULFILLD • • •   120 BALDER DEAD 3   227
         THEN ME THOU MADST OF US THE GODS WERE BORN •   121 BALDER DEAD 3   267
         IT IS THE ACCUSER LOK WHO FLOUTS US ALL • • •   124 BALDER DEAD 3   370
         AND BRING US NEARER TO THE FINAL DAY • • • •   127 BALDER DEAD 3   474
         I MOURN THEE THAT THOU CANST NOT HELP US THEN •   127 BALDER DEAD 3   482
         O HERMOD PRAY THAT THOU MAYST JOIN US THEN • •   129 BALDER DEAD 3   543
         BEFORE US ARE THE SWEET GREEN FIELDS OF WALES •   133 TRISTRAM 1   95
         UPON US ARE THE CHIVALRY OF ROME • • • • •   137 TRISTRAM 1   236
         CHRIST KEEP US FROM SUCH FANTASY • • • • •   147 TRISTRAM 2   130
         HEAVEN KEEP US FROM SUCH FANTASY • • • • •   147 TRISTRAM 2   V 130
         AND LETS US BE WHAT WE WERE ONCE NO MORE • • •   153 TRISTRAM 3   115
         BY WHAT OF OLD PLEASED US AND WILL AGAIN • • •   153 TRISTRAM 3   118
         WHICH KILLS IN US THE BLOOM THE YOUTH THE SPRING •   153 TRISTRAM 3   122
         THIS TOO CAN CHANGE US WHOLLY AND MAKE SEEM • •   153 TRISTRAM 3   131
         HERE LET US HALT SAID MERLIN THEN AND SHE • • •   155 TRISTRAM 3   211
         COME DEAR CHILDREN LET US AWAY • • • • • •   161 FORSAKEN MERM   1
         CHILDREN DEAR LET US AWAY • • • • • •   161 FORSAKEN MERM   8
         WE SHALL SEE WHILE ABOVE US • • • • • •   165 FORSAKEN MERM   116
         IN HER LIKE US THERE CLASHD CONTENDING POWERS •   168 RACHEL 3   11
         WHO RATES US IF WE PEER OUTSIDE OUR PEN • • •   169 WORLDLY PLACE   7
         AND POINTS US TO A BETTER TIME THAN OURS • • •   170 WEST LONDON   14
         NO JUDGE EYES US FROM HEAVEN OUR SIN TO SCAN •   170 BETTER PART   4
         WAS CHRIST A MAN LIKE US AH LET US TRY • • •   171 BETTER PART   13
         WAS CHRIST A MAN LIKE US AH LET US TRY • • •   171 BETTER PART   13
         HARK THE WIND RUSHES PAST US • • • • • •   176 PARTING   43
         BUT A SEA ROLLS BETWEEN US • • • • • •   176 PARTING   65
         BUT HE WHO SEES US THROUGH AND THROUGH • • •   179 FAREWELL   46
         WOULD NEVER LET US SATIATE HERE • • • • •   180 FAREWELL   88
         WITH ECHOING STRAITS BETWEEN US THROWN • • •   182 TO MARG CONT   2
         NOW ROUND US SPREADS THE WATERY PLAIN • • •   182 TO MARG CONT   17
         THEY WILL NOT GIVE US LOVE AND TEARS • • • •   203 EUPHROSYNE   23
         THEY BRING US LIGHT AND WARMTH AND JOY • • •   203 EUPHROSYNE   24
         SILENT THE SWANS BESIDE US FLOAT • • • • •   206 RIVER   3
         SAY WHAT BLINDS US THAT WE CLAIM THE GLORY • •   209 SELF-DECEPTION   1
         STAVED US BACK AND GAVE OUR CHOICE THE LAW • • •   210 SELF-DECEPTION   12
         FOR ALAS HE LEFT US EACH RETAINING • • • •   210 SELF-DECEPTION   17
         STILL THESE WASTE US WITH THEIR HOPELESS STRAINING   210 SELF-DECEPTION   19
         POWERS STIR IN US STIR AND DISAPPEAR • • • • •   210 SELF-DECEPTION   22
         AH LOVE LET US BE TRUE • • • • • • • •   211 DOVER BEACH   29
         TO LIE BEFORE US LIKE A LAND OF DREAMS • • •   211 DOVER BEACH   31

US

(CONTINUED)

AND WHAT CRIES CUPID WILL SAVE US	214	NEW ROME	9
AND WHAT ASKS CUPID WILL SAVE US	214	NEW ROME	V 9
US WHO WITH BANNERS UNFURLD	216	LORDS MESSENGER	V
THEY YIELD US NOT TO SOOTHE OUR PAINS	222	EPILOG LAOCOON	32
BUT HE WAS A PRIEST TO US ALL	229	YOUTH OF NATURE	53
AND MOUNTAINS THAT FILL US WITH JOY	230	YOUTH OF NATURE	61
GIVES US A SENSE OF THE AWE	231	YOUTH OF NATURE	100
THOU SURVIVEST US THIS	232	YOUTH OF MAN	2
THOU WHO SEEST US DIE	232	YOUTH OF MAN	5
SEEST US CHANGE WHILE WE LIVE	232	YOUTH OF MAN	6
WATCHEST US NATURE THROUGHOUT	232	YOUTH OF MAN	9
WELL FOR US THAT WE CHANGE	232	YOUTH OF MAN	11
WELL FOR US THAT THE POWER	232	YOUTH OF MAN	12
BUT LEAVE US NOT WHILE WE LIVE	234	YOUTH OF MAN	60
AH WELL FOR US IF EVEN WE	245	BURIED LIFE	26
SO WILD SO DEEP IN US TO KNOW	246	BURIED LIFE	53
AH YES AND THEY BENUMB US AT OUR CALL	247	BURIED LIFE	71
AND LIVED ITSELF AND MADE US LIVE	251	WISH	40
NOW FLOWS THROUGH WITH US IS THE PLAIN	253	FUTURE	51
BUT WHAT WAS BEFORE US WE KNOW NOT	253	FUTURE	69
AND THEN WE SUFFER AND AMONGST US ONE	260	SCHOLAR-GIPSY	182
TELLS US HIS MISERYS BIRTH AND GROWTH AND SIGNS	260	SCHOLAR-GIPSY	187
WAVE US AWAY AND KEEP THY SOLITUDE	261	SCHOLAR-GIPSY	210
LIKE US DISTRACTED AND LIKE US UNBLEST	261	SCHOLAR-GIPSY	225
LIKE US DISTRACTED AND LIKE US UNBLEST	261	SCHOLAR-GIPSY	225
STOOD WITH SUSPENDED SCYTHE TO SEE US PASS	266	THYRSIS	129
HE TAUGHT US LITTLE BUT OUR SOUL	270	MEMORIAL VERSES	8
WORDSWORTH HAS GONE FROM US AND YE	271	MEMORIAL VERSES	40
HE FOUND US WHEN THE AGE HAD BOUND	271	MEMORIAL VERSES	45
HE LAID US AS WE LAY AT BIRTH	271	MEMORIAL VERSES	48
SMILES BROKE FROM US AND WE HAD EASE	271	MEMORIAL VERSES	50
THE HILLS WERE ROUND US AND THE BREEZE	271	MEMORIAL VERSES	51
TIME MAY RESTORE US IN HIS COURSE	272	MEMORIAL VERSES	60
OTHERS WILL TEACH US HOW TO DARE	272	MEMORIAL VERSES	64
OTHERS WILL STRENGTHEN US TO BEAR	272	MEMORIAL VERSES	66
BUT WHO AH WHO WILL MAKE US FEEL	272	MEMORIAL VERSES	67
WORDSWORTH IS GONE FROM US AND YE	271	MEMORIAL VERSES	V 40
HE TORE US FROM THE PRISON-CELL	271	MEMORIAL VERSES	V
TIME MAY RESTORE US IN ITS COURSE	272	MEMORIAL VERSES	V 60
THEY TRY US OFTENEST MAKE US HARD	273	EDW QUILLINAN	7
THEY TRY US OFTENEST MAKE US HARD	273	EDW QUILLINAN	7
AGE WHOM THE MOST OF US CHIDE	283	HAWORTH CHURCH	V
AH YES SOME OF US STRIVE	288	RUGBY CHAPEL	79
NOTHING TO US THOU WAST STILL	290	RUGBY CHAPEL	138
NOTHING TO US THOU WERT STILL	290	RUGBY CHAPEL	V 138
ALAS TO HELP US FORGET	296	HEINES GRAVE	118
SPIRIT WHO FILLEST US ALL	298	HEINES GRAVE	218
AH LEAVE US NOT THE FRET ALONE	302	GRANDE CHARTR	108
BUT IF YOU CANNOT GIVE US EASE	302	GRANDE CHARTR	109
HERE LEAVE US TO DIE OUT WITH THESE	302	GRANDE CHARTR	111
STILL THE SAME OCEAN ROUND US RAVES	303	GRANDE CHARTR	125
WHICH TELLS US HOW THOU HIDDST THY HEAD	304	GRANDE CHARTR	147
AND CALL US BUT TOO LATE YE COME	305	GRANDE CHARTR	196
TOO LATE FOR US YOUR CALL YE BLOW	305	GRANDE CHARTR	197
AH LEAVE US NOT THE PANG ALONE	302	GRANDE CHARTR	V 108
THEY AWE US BUT THEY ARE NOT OURS	304	GRANDE CHARTR	V 168
LET US CONSULT BEFORE THIS PALACE SENDS	330	MEROPE	26
BUT LET US KEEP THAT PURPOSE WHICH AT HOME	331	MEROPE	35
ASSIST ME TO RULE MILDLY LET US JOIN	335	MEROPE	164
LET US IN MARRIAGE KING AND QUEEN UNITE	335	MEROPE	167
BUT EVERLASTING HORROR TWIXT US TWO	336	MEROPE	193
THRICE ISSUED WITH US FROM THEIR PASTORAL VALES	337	MEROPE	226
WERE THEY WE DISPOSSESSED OF US I SPEAK	337	MEROPE	229
TO HIS NEW SUBJECTS THAN TO US HIS FRIENDS	337	MEROPE	242
IF JEALOUSY OF US IT SHAMED THE MAN	337	MEROPE	253
AT LAST IT REACHD US THAT HE STILL MISTRUSTFUL	338	MEROPE	259
SEND US THE YOUTH WHOM YE HIDE	342	MEROPE	393
HEAR US AND HELP US SHADE OF OUR KING	348	MEROPE	541
HEAR US AND HELP US SHADE OF OUR KING	348	MEROPE	541
POWER FAILS US TO TRY CLEARLY IF THAT CAUSE	352	MEROPE	647
ASSIGND US BY THE ACTOR BE THE TRUE ONE	352	MEROPE	648
TELLING US ARNE MINDED HIM HE TOO	356	MEROPE	768
AND THIS AT LANDING SPIED BY US AND SAVED	358	MEROPE	842
AND YET THE ONLY PEACE TO US ALLOWD	378	MEROPE	1250
ADVISING US A COURSE WHICH WOULD INDEED	382	MEROPE	1337
THOU WILT DESTROY I SEE THYSELF AND US	385	MEROPE	1405
LEGITIMATELY SIRE TO SON WITH US	389	MEROPE	1539
WHO SPARED NOT OTHERS BID NOT US TO SPARE	390	MEROPE	1578
SHALL BE IMPOSED TO US SHALL BE THE DEED	390	MEROPE	1585
THIS HAVING KNOWN LET US A UNION FOUND	394	MEROPE	1716
BASED ON PURE PUBLIC WELFARE LET US BE	394	MEROPE	1718
LET US FORGET OURSELVES FOR THOSE WE RULE	394	MEROPE	1721
FIRST FOR OUR UNION TRUST ME TWIXT US TWO	395	MEROPE	1733
AGLOW WITH ANGRY FIRE TO KEEP US TWAIN	395	MEROPE	1736
HERACLES GAVE US	398	MEROPE	1813
SILENCE AND EXPECTATION HELD US ALL	401	MEROPE	1902
REJOICE WITH US AND TRUST ME HE WHO WISHD	403	MEROPE	1958
FIRST WORK AFTER SUCH VICTORY LET US GO	405	MEROPE	2017
THIS HAVING LEARND LET US A UNION FOUND	394	MEROPE	V1716

US (CONTINUED)
WHY HAST THOU FOLLOWD US THE NIGHT WAS HOT • • • • 407 EMPEDOCLES I 1 36
SOME OF US TO THE PORTICO TO BREATHE • • • • • • 407 EMPEDOCLES I 1 38
BUT THOU MUST KEEP UNSEEN FOLLOW US ON • • • • • 409 EMPEDOCLES I 1 86
SINCE BROILS TEAR US IN TWAIN SINCE THIS NEW SWARM 410 EMPEDOCLES I 1 121
LET US REST HERE AND NOW EMPEDOCLES • • • • • • 412 EMPEDOCLES I 2 7
BUT HEED HIM NOT HE WILL NOT MOUNT TO US • • • • 412 EMPEDOCLES I 2 18
VISIT US AS THEY DO WITH SIGN AND PLAGUE • • • • 413 EMPEDOCLES I 2 24
MIND IS A LIGHT WHICH THE GODS MOCK US WITH • • • 413 EMPEDOCLES I 2 32
WHAT LIFE AND CHANCE GO HARD WITH THEE TOO AS WITH US 416 EMPEDOCLES I 2 116
A BIAS WITH US HERE • • • • • • • • • • 418 EMPEDOCLES I 2 193
AFFECTS US AS WE COME NEAR • • • • • • • • 418 EMPEDOCLES I 2 195
THAT CHANCE WILL BRING US THROUGH • • • • • 420 EMPEDOCLES I 2 240
LIKE US THE LIGHTNING-FIRES • • • • • • • • 420 EMPEDOCLES I 2 247
THE STREAM LIKE US DESIRES • • • • • • • • 420 EMPEDOCLES I 2 249
LIKE US THE LIBYAN WIND DELIGHTS TO ROAM AT LARGE 420 EMPEDOCLES I 2 251
OF NATURE HARM US NOT • • • • • • • • • 421 EMPEDOCLES I 2 265
LET US WITH CHANGELESS WILL • • • • • • • • 425 EMPEDOCLES I 2 379
I THINK MIGHT MAKE US FEAR • • • • • • • • 425 EMPEDOCLES I 2 384
MAKE US NOT FLY TO DREAMS BUT MODERATE DESIRE • • 425 EMPEDOCLES I 2 386
WHAT LIFE AND TIME GO HARD WITH THEE TOO AS WITH US 416 EMPEDOCLES I 2 V 116
NOR OUTWARD THINGS WERE CLOSED AND DEAD TO US • • 436 EMPEDOCLES II 241
THE SMALLEST THING COULD GIVE US PLEASURE THEN • • 436 EMPEDOCLES II 250
WEARY LIKE US THOUGH NOT • • • • • • • • 438 EMPEDOCLES II 299
WITH WHAT ROLLD OF US IN THE STORMY MAIN • • • 439 EMPEDOCLES II 342
IF THESE HAVE BEEN THE MASTER PART OF US • • • 439 EMPEDOCLES II 346
BUT WE SHALL STILL BE IN THEM AND THEY IN US • • 439 EMPEDOCLES II 349
AND KEEP US PRISONERS OF OUR CONSCIOUSNESS • • • 439 EMPEDOCLES II 352
AND NEVER LET US CLASP AND FEEL THE ALL • • • 439 EMPEDOCLES II 353
WILL HURRY US WITH THEM ON THEIR HOMELESS MARCH • 439 EMPEDOCLES II 359
WILL BLOW US FIERCELY BACK TO SEA AND EARTH • • 439 EMPEDOCLES II 362
AND FIRE REPEL US FROM ITS LIVING WAVES • • • 439 EMPEDOCLES II 363
WILL HAVE MORE PERIL FOR US THAN THE LAST • • • 440 EMPEDOCLES II 378
AND THE REALITY WILL PLUCK US BACK • • • • 440 EMPEDOCLES II 385
KNEAD US IN ITS HOT HAND AND CHANGE OUR NATURE • 440 EMPEDOCLES II 386
WITH WHAT ROLLD OF US IN THE STORMY DEEP • • • 439 EMPEDOCLES II V 342
CHEERD US AND NOW IS PASSD INTO THE NIGHT • • • 444 WESTMIN ABBEY 3
CALLD US TO PET THEE OR TO PRAISE • • • • 450 GEISTS GRAVE 7
ON US WHO STOOD DESPONDENT BY • • • • • • 450 GEISTS GRAVE 34
NOR TO US ONLY ART THOU DEAR • • • • • • 451 GEISTS GRAVE 53
IN US WAS ALL THE WORLD TO THEE • • • • • 451 GEISTS GRAVE 60
FRIENDS MORE NEAR US THAN A BIRD • • • • • 453 POOR MATTHIAS 23
LESS THAN THEY TO US ARE YOU • • • • • • 453 POOR MATTHIAS 44
OPEN LIVED TO US AND NEAR • • • • • • • 455 POOR MATTHIAS 88
LIVE BESIDE US BUT ALONE • • • • • • • • 455 POOR MATTHIAS 96
US THY HUMAN KEEPERS HARD • • • • • • • 456 POOR MATTHIAS 122
US UNABLE TO DIVINE • • • • • • • • 456 POOR MATTHIAS 125
TEACH US WHILE THEY COME AND GO • • • • • 456 POOR MATTHIAS 139
PROVE US SO REMOTE IN KIND • • • • • • • 457 POOR MATTHIAS 156
WHO MAY TRUST US TO DIVINE • • • • • • • 457 POOR MATTHIAS 170
WHO ASSURE US SUNDERING POWERS • • • • • • 457 POOR MATTHIAS 171
TO US DECLINING TOWRDS OUR END • • • • • • 459 KAISER DEAD 35
SHOULD FLEET BEFORE US BUT TO MELT AWAY • • • 470 ALARIC AT ROME 212
LIKE SOME FORGOTTEN STRAIN THAT HAUNTS US STILL • 477 CROMWELL 195
THEY LESS THAN US MIGHT RECOGNIZE • • • • • 481 COURAGE 11
KEPT MORE THAN US THEIR STRENGTH OF SOUL • • • 481 COURAGE 12
AND BYRON LET US DARE ADMIRE • • • • • • 482 COURAGE 17
THERE THOU TOO SHALT LIVE WITH US TOGETHER • • • 482 THEKLAS ANSWER 13
AND STRUCK AND OER US THE SEA-WATERS SPREAD • • 484 S S LUSITANIA 8
BUT FOR US WE VIE IN SPEED WITH THE BREATH HOMER TRANS 54
    OF THE WEST-WIND

USD
CONSTRUED AWRY MISPLANND INVASIONS USD • • • • 336 MEROPE V 216

USE
THE JOYS WHICH WERE NOT FOR OUR USE DESIGND • • 41 HUMAN LIFE 28
AH NOT THE NECTAROUS POPPY LOVERS USE • • • • 43 GIPSY CHILD 53
HIS MISTRESS USE HER EMPIRE AS SHE MAY • • • • 155 TRISTRAM 3 184
STILL THE ATTEMPT TO USE THEM PROVES THEM NULL • 210 SELF-DECEPTION 20
AND ITS LOCKD FOUNT OF BEAUTY USE • • • • • 223 EPILOG LAOCOON 84
THEN HERE AT NOON COMES BACK HIS STORES TO USE • 255 SCHOLAR-GIPSY 15
THEN MIGHT I USE THEM THEN FOR ONE WHO THUS • • 383 MEROPE 1362
HAVING LEARNT THIS THEN USE THY KNOWLEDGE NOW • • 388 MEROPE 1520
OR DIDST THOU BUT AS CAUTIOUS SCHEMERS USE • • • 404 MEROPE 1984
BUT HE HAS LAID THE USE OF MUSIC BY • • • • 409 EMPEDOCLES I 1 83
STILL USE OUR BODIES ILL • • • • • • • • 420 EMPEDOCLES I 2 230
WE WANT ALL PLEASANT ENDS BUT WILL USE NO HARSH MEANS 420 EMPEDOCLES I 2 236
WHAT SPRINGS OF THOUGHT THEY USE • • • • • • 423 EMPEDOCLES I 2 329

USED
TILL HAVING USED OUR NERVES WITH BLISS AND TEEN • 259 SCHOLAR-GIPSY 147
THE MIEN OF YOUTH WE USED TO SEE • • • • • 276 SOUTHERN NIGHT 38
MIGHT FROM THE PEOPLE DRAW IF RIGHTLY USED • • • 382 MEROPE 1336
AND IF SO USED PROVES AS THOU SAYST UNSURE • • 382 MEROPE 1341
GREW USED TO THE APPROACH OF GLORYS WINGS • • • 445 WESTMIN ABBEY 56

USELESS
HOW USELESS AN ALLY A PEOPLE IS • • • • • 381 MEROPE 1312
NOT PRONE ALL SAY TO USELESS BLOODSHED NOW • • • 388 MEROPE V1492

USHER
TO USHER FOR A DESTINED SPACE . . . . 53 RESIGNATION   35
GO THOU THE FIRST AND USHER IN THY LORD . . . . . 373 MEROPE   1190

USHERS
THE USHERS RASH AND FEVERISH MELANCHOLY   . . . . .   FRAGMENT 1   5

USURPATION
THE REIGN OF FOLLY USURPATION EVER . . . . 353 MEROPE   668
DO I THEN GIVE TO USURPATION GRACE . . . . 388 MEROPE   1494

UTMOST
AND SET BY OCEANS UTMOST MARGE TO DWELL . . . . . 121 BALDER DEAD 3   275
HAS REACHD THE LIMIT OF HIS UTMOST GROWTH . . . . .   LUCRETIUS 2   9

UTTER
HARDLY HAD SKILL TO UTTER ONE OF ALL . . . . . . 246 BURIED LIFE   61

UTTERD
WHO STOOD AT HAND UTTERD A DREADFUL CRY   . . . . 76 SOHRAB RUSTUM   502
SPEECHLESS AND THEN HE UTTERD ONE SHARP CRY   . . 81 SOHRAB RUSTUM   690
HE SPAKE AND BALDER UTTERD HIM REPLY . . . . . . 112 BALDER DEAD 2   262
THE WORDS ARE UTTERD AND THEY FLEE . . . . 224 EPILOG LAOCOON   90
UTTERD THE VOICE OF MY HILLS . . . . 231 YOUTH OF NATURE   125
HAPPIER HAVE UTTERD IN MINE . . . . 299 HEINES GRAVE   228
LOW MOANS HALF UTTERD . . . . 393 MEROPE   1667

UTTERED
AND OER THY TOWERS THE WINDS HALF UTTERED SIGH . . 464 ALARIC AT ROME   65

UTTEREST
SPIRIT WHO UTTEREST IN EACH . . . . 298 HEINES GRAVE   219

UTTERLY
AH IS FADED UTTERLY . . . . 23 MEMORY-PICTURE   14
NOR LET THEE UTTERLY DEPART . . . . 451 GEISTS GRAVE   39
STAY THIS HAND FROM FIGHT TILL THE TROJANS   HOMER TRANS   62
    ARE UTTERLY ROUTED

UTTERS
WHO IS IT UTTERS THROUGH THE DARK HIS HEST . . . . 102 BALDER DEAD 1   241

VACANT
THE LITTLE FAIR-HAIRD SON WITH VACANT GAZE . . . . 167 PICT NEWSTEAD   10
SOME VACANT AND SOME MUSING WENT . . . . 224 EPILOG LAOCOON   119
WE BID THEE TO THY VACANT CHAIR . . . . 451 GEISTS GRAVE   46

VAGUE
WHO FROM HISTORYS VAGUE NARRATIONS . . . .   SECOND BEST   V 17
A VAGUE DEJECTION . . . . 50 CONSOLATION   4
YET STILL FROM TIME TO TIME VAGUE AND FORLORN   . . 247 BURIED LIFE   72
THY DARK VAGUE EYES AND SOFT ABSTRACTED AIR . . . 258 SCHOLAR-GIPSY   99
WHOSE VAGUE RESOLVES NEVER HAVE BEEN FULFILLD . . 260 SCHOLAR-GIPSY   175
VAGUE HALF-BELIEVERS OF OUR CASUAL CREEDS   . . . 260 SCHOLAR-GIPSY   V 172
I TURNED BY SOME VAGUE IMPULSE STIRRD . . . . . 324 OBERMANN MORE   335
META WITH A VAGUE MISGIVING . . . .   META CLOISTER   19

VAIN
STILL WORKING BLAMING STILL OUR VAIN TURMOIL   . .   2 QUIET WORK   13
STILL WORKING CHIDING STILL OUR VAIN TURMOIL   . .   2 QUIET WORK   V 13
VAIN LABOUR DEEP AND BROAD WHERE NONE MAY SEE   . .   4 BUTLERS SERMONS   5
VAIN DREAMS WHICH QUENCH OUR PLEASURES THEN DEPART   9 MYCERINUS   27
STRINGING VAIN WORDS OF POWERS WE CANNOT SEE   . . 10 MYCERINUS   51
VAIN DREAMS THAT QUENCH OUR PLEASURES THEN DEPART   9 MYCERINUS   V 27
OF MANS LABOUR IS BUT VAIN . . . . 28 NEW SIRENS   58
AND PROCLAIMD YOUR VAIN OVATION . . . . 31 NEW SIRENS   153
MAR THE MUSIC OF YOUR FEASTS IN VAIN . . . . . . 32 NEW SIRENS   170
VAIN IT WASTES AND WE GREW WEARY . . . . 28 NEW SIRENS   V 67
VAIN IT WORE AND WE GREW WEARY . . . . 28 NEW SIRENS   V 67
BLAME THE MUSIC OF YOUR FEASTS IN VAIN . . . . . 32 NEW SIRENS   V 170
SHALL IN VAIN BE SPED . . . . 36 VOICE   12
IN VAIN ALL ALL IN VAIN . . . . 36 VOICE   32
IN VAIN ALL ALL IN VAIN . . . . 36 VOICE   32
WHEN YOUTH HAS DONE ITS TEDIOUS VAIN EXPENSE   . . 37 YOUTHS AGIT   3
WEAKNESS AND WORSE WEAKNESS BESTOWD IN VAIN   . . 40 HUMAN LIFE   15
WAFTS NOT FROM THINE OWN THOUGHTS NOR LONGINGS VAIN 42 GIPSY CHILD   10
THE LIFE HE CRAVES IF NOT IN VAIN . . . . 58 RESIGNATION   196
JUDGE VAIN BEFOREHAND HUMAN CARES . . . . 59 RESIGNATION   232
IN VAIN BUT WHO CAN KEEP THE LIONS CUB   . . . . 63 SOHRAB RUSTUM   91
UNKNOWN THOU ART YET THY FIERCE VAUNT IS VAIN   . 77 SOHRAB RUSTUM   541
IN VAIN THEREFORE WITH WISTFUL EYES . . . . . . 93 SICK KING BOKH   189
IN VAIN HATH A KING POWER TO BUILD . . . . 94 SICK KING BOKH   198
THROUGH MANY STREETS THE POOR BEAST RUNS IN VAIN . 114 BALDER DEAD 3   10
MOCKING AND HERMOD KNEW THEIR TOIL WAS VAIN   . . 123 BALDER DEAD 3   356
LONGING WILL STIR WITHIN MY BREAST THOUGH VAIN   . 127 BALDER DEAD 3   499
ONE LAST KISS FIRST TIS VAIN TO HORSE AWAY   . . 135 TRISTRAM 1   169
OF ME SHE RECKS NOT NOR MY VAIN DESIRE . . . . 140 TRISTRAM 1   303
VAIN AND STRANGE DEBATE WHERE BOTH HAVE SUFFERD . 144 TRISTRAM 2   53
HUSH TIS VAIN I FEEL MY END APPROACHING   . . . 145 TRISTRAM 2   81
ALL TIE WITH ALL BESIDE SEEMD VAIN AND CHEAP   . 173 MONICAS PRAYER   10
BUT SEE TIS IN VAIN . . . . 176 PARTING   62

VAIN   (CONTINUED)
     HOW VAIN A THING IS MORTAL LOVE   . . . . . .   181 ISOLATION MARG   26
     WHO RENDERS VAIN THEIR DEEP DESIRE   . . . . . .   182 TO MARG CONT   21
     FOR EVER LEAVES ITS VAIN EMPLOY   . . . . . .   206 RIVER   18
     VAIN IS THE EFFORT TO FORGET   . . . . . .   207 ON THE RHINE   1
     VAIN IS THE AGONY OF GRIEF   . . . . . .   208 ON THE RHINE   6
     LOOKS IN VAIN FOR ALLS OBSCURE   . . . . . .   215 PIS-ALLER   4
     VAIN THY ONSET ALL STANDS FAST   . . . . . .   215 LAST WORD   3
     ROME ENGLAND FRANCE YES NOR IN VAIN ESSAYD . .   239 REVOLUTIONS   6
     WHO HAVE LONGD DEEPLY ONCE AND LONGD IN VAIN .   244 SUMMER NIGHT   85
     AND LONG WE TRY IN VAIN TO SPEAK AND ACT   . . . .   247 BURIED LIFE   64
     AND WE SHOULD TEASE HER WITH OUR PLAINT IN VAIN . .   265 THYRSIS   100
     WELL WIND-DISPERSED AND VAIN THE WORDS WILL BE . .   265 THYRSIS   101
     AND STRANGE AND VAIN THE EARTHLY TURMOIL GROWS . .   267 THYRSIS   148
     AH VAIN THESE ENGLISH FIELDS THIS UPLAND DIM   . .   267 THYRSIS   172
     HE LONGD FOR IT PRESSD ON IN VAIN   . . . . . .   275 STANZAS CARNAC   45
     HE LONGD IT HE PRESSD ON IN VAIN   . . . . . .   275 STANZAS CARNAC   V   45
     BUT IF THE PRAYER BE IN VAIN   . . . . . .   282 HAWORTH CHURCH   V
     SURELY HAS NOT BEEN LEFT VAIN   . . . . . .   287 RUGBY CHAPEL   39
     EFFORT UNMEANING AND VAIN   . . . . . .   288 RUGBY CHAPEL   78
     STAGGER FOR EVER IN VAIN   . . . . . .   291 RUGBY CHAPEL   186
     LABOUR FOR EVER IN VAIN   . . . . . .   291 RUGBY CHAPEL   V 186
     BATTER FOR EVER IN VAIN   . . . . . .   291 RUGBY CHAPEL   V 186
     IN VAIN MEN STILL WITH HOPING NEW   . . . . . .   318 OBERMANN MOPE   177
     ITS COMMON HOPE WERE VAIN   . . . . . .   321 OBERMANN MOPE   242
     AND KNEW MY LIFE WAS VAIN   . . . . . .   321 OBERMANN MORE   266
     WILLINGLY FED OR NO THEIR MOST VAIN HOPES . . .   334 MEROPE   148
     BE ERROR DEEMD BUT THAT PRETENCE IS VAIN   . . . .   339 MEROPE   315
     STRUGGLING IN VAIN TO CROSS IT SWEPT THEM ON   .   358 MEROPE   825
     THE SCHEMES PURSUED IN VAIN FOR TWENTY YEARS   .   360 MEROPE   876
     AND EYEBALLS STARING FOR REVENGE IN VAIN   . . .   373 MEROPE   1175
     AND TRIED IN VAIN THE TURN OF RASHNESS COMES   .   384 MEROPE   1387
     NUMBER IT WITH THE THOUSAND RUMOURS VAIN   . . .   387 MEROPE   1486
     IN VAIN OUR PENT WILLS FRET   . . . . . .   418 EMPEDOCLES I 2   182
     BORN INTO LIFE IN VAIN   . . . . . .   419 EMPEDOCLES I 2   197
     TO FIND WITH YOU THE JOY WE IN VAIN HERE REQUIRE .   425 EMPEDOCLES I 2   381
     AND PULLULATING RITES EXTERNE AND VAIN   . . .   449 WESTMIN ABBEY   160
     NOW IN VAIN YOU CALL HIS NAME   . . . . . .   452 POOR MATTHIAS   7
     VAIN TO AUGUR THEY OR I   . . . . . .   454 POOR MATTHIAS   76
     TROUBLING WITH OUR CHATTER VAIN   . . . . . .   456 POOR MATTHIAS   123
     FATES THREATNINGS ARE NOT VAIN THE SPOILER   466 ALARIC AT ROME   120
          COMES NOT SLOW
     TO ME IT SEEMS AS VAIN LUCRETIUS   . . . . . .   LUCRETIUS 3   1

VAINLY
     RISE WHEREFORE DOST THOU VAINLY QUESTION THUS . .   72 SOHRAB RUSTUM   365
     SINCE THEN I VAINLY SEEK HIM THROUGH THE WORLD . .   116 BALDER DEAD 3   109
     AND THE SAME VAINLY THROBBING HEART WAS THERE .   242 SUMMER NIGHT   24
     VAINLY DOES EACH AS HE GLIDES   . . . . . .   252 FUTURE   19
     VAINLY FOR HE IN THE GLENS   . . . . . .   347 MEROPE   518
     VAINLY YOU HEDGE HIM FROM THE ASSAULT OF HARM . .   359 MEROPE   855
     AND FEIGN KIND GODS WHO PERFECT WHAT MAN VAINLY TRIES 422 EMPEDOCLES I 2   316
     VAINLY RAISE HIS RIGID FRAME   . . . . . .   452 POOR MATTHIAS   8
     VAINLY WARM HIM IN YOUR BREAST   . . . . . .   452 POOR MATTHIAS   9
     VAINLY KISS HIS GOLDEN CREST   . . . . . .   452 POOR MATTHIAS   10
     THY PASSING BY DOTH VAINLY WAIT   . . . . . .   461 KAISER DEAD   74

VALAIS
     THE VALAIS OPENS FAIR   . . . - . . .   324 OBERMANN MORE   340
     HIGH IN THE VALAIS-DEPTH PROFOUND   . . . . . .   324 OBERMANN MORE   347

VALE
     SEEING THIS VALE THIS EARTH WHEREON WE DREAM   . .   7 REP FRIEND CONT   5
     CLOUDS OF WHITE ROLLING VAPOURS FILL THE VALE . .   113 BALDER DEAD 2   298
     THERE TO WATCH OER THE SUNK VALE   . . . . . .   176 PARTING   47
     AND THE SPERCHEIOS VALE SHAKEN WITH GROANS . . .   198 FRAG ANTIGONE   100
     LONE DAULIS AND THE HIGH CEPHISSIAN VALE   . . .   201 PHILOMELA   27
     THE VALE THE THREE LONE WEIRS THE YOUTHFUL THAMES .   263 THYRSIS   15
     HEAR IT FROM THY BROAD LUCENT ARNO-VALE   . . .   267 THYRSIS   167
     UP THE STILL VALE OF THISBE   . . . . . .   442 EMPEDOCLES II   427
     BEHIND A BURIED VALE DOTH SLEEP   . . . . . .   479 HAYSWATER BOAT   9

VALES
     THRICE ISSUED WITH US FROM THEIR PASTORAL VALES . . 337 MEROPE   226
     LIKE FROZEN WINDS ON SOUTHERN VALES THAT BLOW . .   474 CROMWELL   89

VALHALLA
     WEEPING AND WAILING AND VALHALLA RANG . . . . .   95 BALDER DEAD 1   11
     NOT TO LAMENT IN WAS VALHALLA MADE   . . . . . .   95 BALDER DEAD 1   19
     NOR TOWRD VALHALLA AND THE SORROWING GODS . . .   97 BALDER DEAD 1   58
     BUT IN VALHALLA ALL THE GODS WENT BACK . . . . .   97 BALDER DEAD 1   61
     AND IN VALHALLA ODIN LAID HIM DOWN   . . . . . .   102 BALDER DEAD 1   267
     FEAST IN VALHALLA IN MY FATHERS HALL   . . . . .   104 BALDER DEAD 1   322
     NOR TOWARDS VALHALLA AND THE SORROWING GODS . .   97 BALDER DEAD 1   V   58
     AND IN VALHALLA FROM HIS GABLE-PERCH   . . . . .   105 BALDER DEAD 2   3
     HERMOD LED SLEIPNER FROM VALHALLA FORTH   . . .   106 BALDER DEAD 2   71

VALHALLAS
     AND TO VALHALLAS GATE HE RODE AND LEFT . . . . .   102 BALDER DEAD 1   265
     AND MOUNTED THEM AND IN VALHALLAS COURT   . . .   105 BALDER DEAD 2   13

VALIANT
    VALIANT OR CRAVEN YOUNG OR OLD TO ME . . . .   68 SOHRAB RUSTUM   253
    ALL THE MOST VALIANT CHIEFS LONG HE PERUSED . . .   70 SOHRAB RUSTUM   311
    WITH AGE AND RULES OVER THE VALIANT KOORDS . . .   78 SOHRAB RUSTUM   592
    AND VALIANT HEART OF YOUTH OR MANHOODS FIRM . .   335 MEROPE   157
    OF A VALIANT CHIEF TO HIS OWN . . . .   345 MEROPE   486
    NOR WOULD MY OWN HEART LET ME MY HEART WHICH   HOMER TRANS   17
         HAS BID ME BE VALIANT

VALIANTLY
    SUCH AS ON EARTH WE VALIANTLY HAVE WAGED . . . . 117 BALDER DEAD 3   139

VALKYRIES
    AND THE VALKYRIES CROWND THEIR HORNS WITH MEAD . .   97 BALDER DEAD 1   68
    AND THE VALKYRIES ON THEIR STEEDS WENT FORTH . . 105 BALDER DEAD 2   19

VALLEY
    REACH THE VALLEY WHERE THE FABRIC . . . . .   15 CHURCH BROU 1   87
    IN SOME WINDLESS VALLEY FARTHER DOWN . . . . .   31 NEW SIRENS   146
    IN A WINDLESS VALLEY FURTHER DOWN . . . . .   31 NEW SIRENS   V 146
    THE VALLEY-PASTURES ONE BY ONE . . . . . .   53 RESIGNATION   50
    FOLDS THE STILL VALLEY ALMOST ROUND . . . . .   57 RESIGNATION   175
    TO THE STEEP EDGE OF SOME GREAT VALLEY COMES . . 113 BALDER DEAD 2   296
    UP AT THE VALLEY-HEAD . . . . 186 STRAYED REVEL   27
    DOWN THE DARK VALLEY I SAW . . . . 187 STRAYED REVEL   42
    LOOKING OVER THE VALLEY . . . . 194 STRAYED REVEL   272
    CROWNS THE STILL VALLEY BEHIND . . . . . . 234 YOUTH OF MAN   63
    THE WIDE WIDE VALLEY OUTSPREADS . . . . . 234 YOUTH OF MAN   76
    OER THE VALLEY THE DIZZILY PERCHD . . . . . 297 HEINES GRAVE   187
    HIGH IN THE VALLEY WET AND DREAR . . . . . 299 GRANDE CHARTR   17
    THE LEAVES ARE ON THE VALLEY-PATHS . . . . . 306 OBERMANN   7
    ACROSS THE VALLEY ON THAT SLOPE . . . . . 312 OBERMANN MORE   13
    HERE IN THE VALLEY IS IN SHADE THE SWARD . . . 406 EMPEDOCLES I 1   12
    THE JARS OF MEN REACH HIM NOT IN THY VALLEY . . 435 EMPEDOCLES II   209
    DARK THE VALLEY SLEEPS IN SHADE . . . . . .   META CLOISTER   14

VALLEYS
    VALLEYS AND MEN TO MIDDLE FORTUNE BORN . . . .   6 GEO CRUIKSHANK   4
    DOWN THE SAVOY VALLEYS SOUNDING . . . . . .   12 CHURCH BROU 1   1
    MID THE SAVOY MOUNTAIN VALLEYS . . . . . .   14 CHURCH BROU 1   61
    AND WE TOO FROM UPLAND VALLEYS . . . . . .   27 NEW SIRENS   25
    STORMS UNSMOOTHD YOUR FOLDED VALLEYS . . . . .   30 NEW SIRENS   123
    THE VALLEYS WESTERN BOUNDARY . . . .   53 RESIGNATION   47
    THROUGH VALLEYS DEEP-ENGULPHD WITH ROARING STREAMS .   99 BALDER DEAD 1   146
    THROUGH VALLEYS DEEP-ENGULPHD BY ROARING STREAMS . 107 BALDER DEAD 2   84
    BUT THE VALLEYS ARE FLOODED WITH HAZE . . . . 228 YOUTH OF NATURE   7
    AT THE MEETING VALLEYS . . . . 391 MEROPE   1607

VALLIES
    HER VALLIES AND BLUE HILLS . . . .   FRAGMENT 8   2

VALOUR
    REMEMBER ALL THY VALOUR TRY THY FEINTS . . . .   75 SOHRAB RUSTUM   466

VALOURS
    LOOK HOW SO MANY VALOURS LONG UNDULLD . . . .   37 WORLDS TRIUMPHS   7

VAN
    YE ALIGHT IN OUR VAN AT YOUR VOICE . . . . . . 292 RUGBY CHAPEL   196

VANADIS
    NAMES HATH SHE MANY VANADIS ON EARTH . . . . . . 116 BALDER DEAD 3   96

VANHEIM
    NOT BORN IN HEAVEN HE WAS IN VANHEIM REARD . . . . 122 BALDER DEAD 3   324

VANISHD
    HE VANISHD WITH HIS BRIDE . . . . 160 NECKAN   30
    WITH SPIRIT VANISHD BEAUTY WANED . . . . . . 185 TERRACE BERNE   37
    RAN OFF AND VANISHD OUT OF HAND . . . . . 213 PROGRESS POESY   8
    JOYS THAT HAD COME AND VANISHD HALF UNKNOWN . . 474 CROMWELL   75

VANISHED
    AND VANISHED WITH HIS MULE . . . . 161 NECKAN   58

VANISHT
    THE VANISHT MIGHT OF THAT DISCROWNED HEAD . . . 464 ALARIC AT ROME   46
    BUT OER HER VANISHT MIGHT AND HUMBLED PRIDE . . 468 ALARIC AT ROME   161
    THE VANISHT GLORIES OF THINE EARLY DAY . . . . 471 ALARIC AT ROME   224

VANITY
    THOU HAST FOREKNOWN THE VANITY OF HOPE . . . .   43 GIPSY CHILD   39

VANQUISHD
    BUILT IN STRENGTH AGAINST THE VANQUISHD . . . . 400 MEROPE   1854

VANQUISHED
    MARSYAS THOU ART VANQUISHED . . . . 433 EMPEDOCLES II   146

VAPOUR
    BY THE DIM VAPOUR-BLOTTED LIGHT OF STARS . . . 108 BALDER DEAD 2   126

VAPOUR   (CONTINUED)
        ROUND WHICH THE SULLEN VAPOUR ROLLS ALONE   •   •   •   •   429 EMPEDOCLES II   4

VAPOURS
        CLOUDS OF WHITE ROLLING VAPOURS FILL THE VALE   •   •   113 BALDER DEAD 2   298
        IN A BANK OF VAPOURS AGAIN   •   •   •   •   •   •   •   297 HEINES GRAVE   174
        SWIFT RUSH THE SPECTRAL VAPOURS WHITE   •   •   •   •   299 GRANDE CHARTR   13
        FAST RUSH THE SPECTRAL VAPOURS WHITE   •   •   •   •   299 GRANDE CHARTR   V   13
        THAT HEAVES ITS WHITE AND BILLOWY VAPOURS UP   •   •   438 EMPEDOCLES II   309
        AH BOIL UP YE VAPOURS   •   •   •   •   •   •   •   •   441 EMPEDOCLES II   410

VARIANCE
        TOO WIDE AT VARIANCE WITH THE PEACE I SEEK   •   •   •   •   333 MEROPE   107

VARIED
        AND ALL HIS HOURLY VARIED ANODYNES   •   •   •   •   •   •   260 SCHOLAR-GIPSY   190

VARIOUS
        SO VARIOUS SO BEAUTIFUL SO NEW   •   •   •   •   •   •   •   211 DOVER BEACH   32
        THAT WIDE AND VARIOUS WORLD THE HEART OF OTHERS   •   •   352 MEROPE   637

VASE
        PRICKS WITH VERMILION SOME CLEAR PORCELAIN VASE   •   •   81 SOHRAB RUSTUM   673

VASSALS
        GUIDE ME VASSALS TO THE MOUNTAIN   •   •   •   •   •   15 CHURCH BROU 1   V   75
        WHERE HORN AND HOUND AND VASSALS NEVER COME   •   •   17 CHURCH BROU 3   3

VAST
        IN THE VAST WESTERN WINDOW OF THE NAVE   •   •   •   18 CHURCH BROU 3   21
        THAT VAST SKY-NEIGHBOURING MOUNTAIN OF MILK SNOW   •   •   66 SOHRAB RUSTUM   162
        BEHOLD ME I AM VAST AND CLAD IN IRON   •   •   •   •   •   71 SOHRAB RUSTUM   325
        BEGIN THOU ART MORE VAST MORE DREAD THAN I   •   •   •   72 SOHRAB RUSTUM   385
        AND HIS SOUL SET TO GRIEF AS THE VAST TIDE   •   •   •   79 SOHRAB RUSTUM   616
        A KING WHOSE FAME THEN FILLD THE VAST OF HEAVEN   •   •   117 BALDER DEAD 3   129
        THE VAST RANGE OF SNOW   •   •   •   •   •   •   •   175 PARTING   12
        THE VAST SEAS OF SNOW   •   •   •   •   •   •   •   •   175 PARTING   28
        THE VAST FIELDS OF SNOW   •   •   •   •   •   •   •   •   PARTING   V   28
        ENNOBLED BY A VAST REGRET   •   •   •   •   •   •   •   179 FAREWELL   71
        GLIMMERING AND VAST OUT IN THE TRANQUIL BAY   •   •   210 DOVER BEACH   5
        OF THE NIGHT-WIND DOWN THE VAST EDGES DREAR   •   •   211 DOVER BEACH   27
        FEEL MY SOUL BECOMING VAST LIKE YOU   •   •   •   •   240 SELF-DEPENDENCE   12
        HOW VAST YET OF WHAT CLEAR TRANSPARENCY   •   •   •   244 SUMMER NIGHT   89
        IN THE SOUNDING LABOUR-HOUSE VAST   •   •   •   •   •   287 RUGBY CHAPEL   41
        OF THE TOO VAST ORB OF HER FATE   •   •   •   •   •   295 HEINES GRAVE   96
        TO OBSERVE A WORLD SO VAST   •   •   •   •   •   •   419 EMPEDOCLES I 2   213
        OF FIGURES WITH HER FULNESS VAST   •   •   •   •   •   450 GEISTS GRAVE   25
        BUT ONE VAST FANE WHERE ALL UNCONSCIOUS SLEEP   •   •   464 ALARIC AT ROME   59
        TWICE HAD THE PAGEANT OF THAT VAST ARRAY   •   •   •   465 ALARIC AT ROME   77

VASTNESS
        THE VASTNESS THE GRANDEUR THE GLOOM   •   •   •   •   •   •   231 YOUTH OF NATURE   101

VASTY
        THE VASTY HALL OF DEATH   •   •   •   •   •   •   •   •   •   21 REQUIESCAT   16

VATICAN
        THE ARMLESS VATICAN CUPID   •   •   •   •   •   •   •   •   214 NEW ROME   1
        THE ARMLESS VATICAN CUPID   •   •   •   •   •   •   •   •   214 NEW ROME   17

VAULT
        FROM THE INTENSE CLEAR STAR-SOWN VAULT OF HEAVEN   •   •   240 SELF-DEPENDENCE   13
        AND THUS BENEATH THE CLEAR CALM VAULT OF HEAVEN   •   •   466 ALARIC AT ROME   103

VAUNT
        BY CHALLENGE FORTH MAKE GOOD THY VAUNT OR YIELD   •   •   72 SOHRAB RUSTUM   367
        EITHER THOU SHALT RENOUNCE THY VAUNT AND YIELD   •   •   72 SOHRAB RUSTUM   375
        UNKNOWN THOU ART YET THY FIERCE VAUNT IS VAIN   •   •   77 SOHRAB RUSTUM   541

VAUNTED
        AND YOUR TRAGIC-VAUNTED REVELS   •   •   •   •   •   •   •   26 NEW SIRENS   19
        OUR VAUNTED LIFE IS ONE LONG FUNERAL   •   •   •   •   •   44 QUESTION   10

VAUNTS
        THE YOUNG MAY RISE AT SOHRABS VAUNTS NOT I   •   •   •   •   68 SOHRAB RUSTUM   227
        THEIR VAUNTS THEIR FEATS LET A SARDONIC SMILE   •   •   298 HEINES GRAVE   208

VEHEMENCE
        PASSION VEHEMENCE GRIEF   •   •   •   •   •   •   •   •   •   284 HAWORTH CHURCH   95

VEHEMENT
        OF VEHEMENT ACTIONS WITHOUT SCOPE OR TERM   •   •   •   •   5 DUKE WELLINGTON   12

VEIL
        ONE THE DUCHESS IN HER VEIL   •   •   •   •   •   •   •   16 CHURCH BROU 1   108
        THE GUIDE OF OUR DARK STEPS A TRIPLE VEIL   •   •   •   •   43 GIPSY CHILD   49
        SHE SPOKE AND ON HER FACE LET FALL HER VEIL   •   •   100 BALDER DEAD 1   192
        SHE SPAKE AND ON HER FACE LET FALL HER VEIL   •   •   122 BALDER DEAD 3   295
        I SEE HER VEIL DRAW SOFT ACROSS THE DAY   •   •   •   266 THYRSIS   133
        I TAKE THE OMEN EVE LETS DOWN HER VEIL   •   •   •   267 THYRSIS   161

VEILD
    WITH VEILD FACE AND BOWD HEAD • • • • • • • • •   283 HAWORTH CHURCH   V
    SHE VEILD HER EAGLES SNAPPD HER SWORD • • • • •   316 OBERMANN MORE   125
    NOR KNOWN IT THEN BUT IT WAS VEILD NO MORE • • • •   477 CROMWELL   202

VEILED
    TO-NIGHT THOSE SOFT-VEILED EYES SHALL CLOSE   • •   205 CALAIS SANDS   V 35

VEILS
    BUT THROUGH THEIR FORMS AND MODES AND STIFLING VEILS   439 EMPEDOCLES II   354

VEIN
    AND STRIKES THE ROCK AND FINDS THE VEIN • • • •   213 PROGRESS POESY   2
    SOME SECRET AND UNFOLLOWD VEIN OF WOE • • • •   411 EMPEDOCLES I 1   152

VEIND
    OF VEIND WHITE-GLEAMING QUARTZ AND HERE AND THERE   150 TRISTRAM 3   17

VEINS
    SWELL THEIR LARGE VEINS TO BURSTING IN WILD PAIN • •   192 STRAYED REVEL   226
    OF TREES AND VEINS OF TURF AND LONG DARK SHOOTS • •   414 EMPEDOCLES I 2   48
    THE AIR IS THIN THE VEINS SWELL • • • • • •   435 EMPEDOCLES II   215

VELAN
    AND THE DOMED VELAN WITH HIS SNOWS • • • • •   324 OBERMANN MORE   341

VENGEANCE
    TO ARMS AND CRY FOR VENGEANCE UPON THEE • • • •   78 SOHRAB RUSTUM   585
    WHAT WILL THAT GRIEF WHAT WILL THAT VENGEANCE BE • •   78 SOHRAB RUSTUM   587
    VENGEANCE O KING BUT THE KING SPAKE • • • • •   89 SICK KING BOKH   39
    VENGEANCE O KING BUT THE KING SPOKE • • • • •   89 SICK KING BOKH   V 39
    BY ME SHALL VENGEANCE ON THE MURDERER LOK • • •   96 BALDER DEAD 1   37
    TO GUIDE OUR VENGEANCE TO A PROSPEROUS CLOSE • • •   332 MEROPE   75
    BEACONS OF VENGEANCE NOT TO BE LET DIE • • •   333 MEROPE   93
    DEMANDEST VENGEANCE NOT GRIEF • • • • • •   343 MEROPE   405
    VENGEANCE O QUEEN IS HIS DUE • • • • • •   343 MEROPE   408
    SOMEWHERE FOR VENGEANCE A CHAMPION A LIGHT • • •   346 MEROPE   513
    TILL THE SINNER THE VENGEANCE BE RIPE • • •   347 MEROPE   528
    VENGEANCE ON SINNER AND SIN • • • • •   348 MEROPE   539
    IN CALLING VENGEANCE ON A MURDERERS HEAD • • •   348 MEROPE   549
    CAN VENGEANCE GIVE ME BACK THE MURDERED NO • • •   349 MEROPE   567
    BUT VENGEANCE TRAVELS IN A DANGEROUS WAY • • •   349 MEROPE   580
    ALL VENGEANCE UNATTEMPTED AND DESCEND • • •   367 MEROPE   1029
    STAND AND LET VENGEANCE PASS HOLD O QUEEN HOLD •   374 MEROPE   1198
    FROM THE FIRST-WROUGHT VENGEANCE IS BORN • • •   379 MEROPE   1251
    WHAT HELP WHAT VENGEANCE AT THEIR HANDS HAVE I •   381 MEROPE   1318
    HIS SON FROM VENGEANCE ON HIS MURDERER • • •   385 MEROPE   1415
    THE THOUGHT OF VENGEANCE ON ME NEVER QUITE • • •   394 MEROPE   1704
    NATURAL VENGEANCE MAY MAINTAIN THINE ACT • • •   404 MEROPE   1998
    OF PERSONAL VENGEANCE TO THE PUBLIC WEAL • • •   394 MEROPE   V1712

VENGEFUL
    EITHER A VENGEFUL FURY I SHOULD STALK • • •   366 MEROPE   1019
    ONE DEATH-DEALING VENGEFUL TRAIN • • • •   379 MEROPE   1255
    TO ARMED WARRIORS I HEARD VENGEFUL CRIES • • •   402 MEROPE   1940

VENICE
    WHICH VENICE SHIPS DO FROM SWART EGYPT BRING • •   150 TRISTRAM 3   41
    MOURNING AS WIDOWED VENICE OER HER ADRIAN TIDE • •   468 ALARIC AT ROME   162

VENT
    WHEREON TO VENT THEIR RAGE • • • • • • • •   421 EMPEDOCLES I 2   275

VERDANT
    MORE FRESH MORE VERDANT THAN THE LAST WITH FRUITS   128 BALDER DEAD 3   529
    DOWN ITS STEEP VERDANT SIDES THE AIR • • • • •   414 EMPEDOCLES I 2   45

VERDE
    REACHD CAPE VERDE ISLANDS LUSITANIA • • • • •   485 S S LUSITANIA   14

VERDURE
    SHADOW AND VERDURE AND COOL • • • • • • •   292 HEINES GRAVE   8

VERGE
    THIS IS THE GLIMMERING VERGE OF HEAVEN AND THESE •   19 CHURCH BROU 3   41
    IN TWILIGHT ON THE LONELY VERGE OF HELL • •   124 BALDER DEAD 3   390
    AND HAVE DRAWN UPWARD TO THIS VERGE OF HELL • •   126 BALDER DEAD 3   439
    AND HAVE DRAWN UPWARDS TO THIS VERGE OF HELL • •   126 BALDER DEAD 3   V 439
    WHILE YET UPON THE VERGE OF HEAVEN HE STOOD • •   239 REVOLUTIONS   2
    BUT ON THE HORIZONS VERGE DESCRIED • • • • •   274 STANZAS CARNAC   31

VERGELMER
    WHICH FROM THE FOUNTAIN OF VERGELMER RUN • • •   108 BALDER DEAD 2   130

VERMILION
    AND SHOWD A SIGN IN FAINT VERMILION POINTS • • •   81 SOHRAB RUSTUM   671
    PRICKS WITH VERMILION SOME CLEAR PORCELAIN VASE • •   81 SOHRAB RUSTUM   673

VERSE
```
      AND SO THERE RISE THESE LINES OF VERSE      • • • •   451 GEISTS GRAVE        41
      TRIBUTE DUE TO THEE A VERSE      • • • • • • •   453 POOR MATTHIAS       18
      GEIST HAD VERSE TO MOURN HIS END      • • • • •   454 POOR MATTHIAS       58
      TRIBUTE ASKD BY THEE A VERSE      • • • • • •   453 POOR MATTHIAS     V  18
```

VERY
```
      MADE MY TOST HEART ITS VERY LIFE-BLOOD SPILL    • •    36 VOICE              39
      FOR VERY YOUNG HE SEEMD TENDERLY REARD    • • •    70 SOHRAB RUSTUM     313
      THE VERY SAME WHICH YESTERNIGHT    • • • • •   146 TRISTRAM 2        112
      ATONED THIS VERY DAY PERHAPS IT IS    • • • •   397 MEROPE           1769
      HE GRASPS THE VERY REINS OF LIFE AND DEATH    • • •   410 EMPEDOCLES I 1    125
      YET SOME THERE ARE THEIR VERY LIVES WOULD GIVE    • •   462 ALARIC AT ROME     17
      AND MAKES THY VERY RUIN FRESH AND BEAUTIFUL    • •   464 ALARIC AT ROME     54
      HAVING BEEN FURTHERD TO HIS VERY WISH    • • • •        LUCRETIUS 2        11
```

VESPASIANS
```
      TAUGHT ARRIAN WHEN VESPASIANS BRUTAL SON    • • • •     2 TO A FRIEND         7
```

VESSEL
```
      I SEE THE SMOKE-CROWND VESSEL COME    • • • • • •   276 SOUTHERN NIGHT     30
```

VESSELS
```
      CUT BY AN ONWARD-LABOURING VESSELS PRORE    • • •    41 HUMAN LIFE         23
      THE CALM SEA SHINES LOOSE HANG THE VESSELS SAILS  • •   133 TRISTRAM 1         94
      THOU COMEST YES THE VESSELS CLOUD    • • • • •   205 CALAIS SANDS       21
      AT THIS VESSELS PROW I STAND WHICH BEARS ME    • •   239 SELF-DEPENDENCE     3
      AT THE VESSELS PROW I STAND WHICH BEARS ME    • • •   239 SELF-DEPENDENCE  V  3
      FOLLOWING THE SUN WE SET OUR VESSELS HEAD    • • •   484 S S LUSITANIA       3
```

VESTED
```
      VESTED FOR EVER WITH GREEN    • • • • • • • •   280 HAWORTH CHURCH      3
```

VESTIGE
```
      FLED FLED AT ONCE BE ALL VESTIGE OF THEE    • • • •   206 SEPARATION         10
```

VEVEY
```
      VEVEY AND MEILLERIE    • • • • • • • • •   311 OBERMANN          164
      OR DOT THE SLOPES TO VEVEY DOWN    • • • • • •   483 ROME-SICKNESS      12
```

VEX
```
      NOT BY THEIR HANDS WHO VEX THE PATIENT GROUND    • •     4 DUKE WELLINGTON     3
      MY FATHER WHOM THE ROBBER AFGHANS VEX    • • • •    68 SOHRAB RUSTUM     233
      THINGS WHICH MIGHT VEX HIM SHALL BE FOUND    • • •    92 SICK KING BOKH    160
      VEX ONE ANOTHER NIGHT AND DAY    • • • • • •    93 SICK KING BOKH    174
      I THINK THOU WOULDST NOT VEX HIM NO AND YET    • •   408 EMPEDOCLES I 1     55
      TIS NOT THE TIMES TIS NOT THE SOPHISTS VEX HIM    • •   411 EMPEDOCLES I 1    150
```

VEXD
```
      TO THE VEXD WATERS OF A MOUNTAIN LAKE    • • • •   477 CROMWELL          192
```

VEXT
```
      THESE VEXT BRANCHES AND THIS HOWLING SKY    • • •    27 NEW SIRENS         48
      SOME REACHES OF THY STORM-VEXT STREAM OF LIFE    • •    43 GIPSY CHILD        60
      O MAN WHOM EARTH THY LONG-VEXT MOTHER BARE    • •    46 IN UTRUMQUE PAR    32
      FROM THE WET FIELD THROUGH THE VEXT GARDEN-TREES   • •   264 THYRSIS            58
      VEXT HEART DEPLORE    • • • • • • • • • •   275 SOUTHERN NIGHT     16
```

VIALS
```
      POUR FORTH THE FOAMING VIALS OF THY WRATH    • • • •   465 ALARIC AT ROME     86
```

VICE
```
      TWIΛT VICE AND VIRTUE REVIVST    • • • • • • •   288 RUGBY CHAPEL       55
```

VICIOUS
```
      ARE LIKE THE MOB VICIOUS AND IGNORANT    • • • •   404 MEROPE           2004
```

VICISSITUDE
```
      FOR THEM VICISSITUDE AND NEED    • • • • • • •    56 RESIGNATION       143
```

VICTIM
```
      SIT AND EYE GRIMLY THE VICTIM UNSCOURGED    • • •   347 MEROPE            531
      TO SEE ANOTHER MIGHTY VICTIM BLEED    • • • • •   349 MEROPE            563
      THE FIERCELY-REQUIRED VICTIM    • • • • • •   400 MEROPE           1869
      THE FLOWER-DRESSD VICTIM STOOD A MILK-WHITE BULL   • •   401 MEROPE           1910
```

VICTIMS
```
      NO VICTIMS BLEED NO DRUIDS BOW    • • • • • • •   274 STANZAS CARNAC     15
      IN A KINGS HOUSE THY VICTIMS HERITAGE    • • • •   373 MEROPE           1179
```

VICTOR
```
      SENT FORTH ECHEMUS THE VICTOR THE KING    • • • •   344 MEROPE            442
      O VICTOR VICTOR TRIP NOT AT THE GOAL   • • • • •   397 MEROPE           1771
      O VICTOR VICTOR TRIP NOT AT THE GOAL   • • • • •   397 MEROPE           1771
```

VICTORIES
```
      AS THEY LOOKED STERNLY ON BEHELD NEW VICTORIES    • •   468 ALARIC AT ROME    174
```

VICTORIOUS
```
      FIND THEIR SOLE SPEECH IN THAT VICTORIOUS BROW    • •     3 SHAKESPEARE        14
      FIND THEIR SOLE VOICE IN THAT VICTORIOUS BROW    • •     3 SHAKESPEARE     V  14
```

VICTORIOUS   (CONTINUED)
    SHE HEARD IT THE VICTORIOUS WEST . . . . 316 OBERMANN MORE 121
    THE SOUND BELOVED OF HIS VICTORIOUS BREATH . . . . 448 WESTMIN ABBEY 128

VICTORS
    LET THE VICTORS WHEN THEY COME . . . . 215 LAST WORD 14
    THEREFORE THE VICTORS HEART . . . . 296 HEINES GRAVE 127
    SOWING HIS VICTORS THINLY THROUGH THEM ALL . . 337 MEROPE 250
    WITH NEW WALLS WHICH THE VICTORS . . . . . . 400 MEROPE 1851
    TO TOUCH WITH SORROW EVEN A VICTORS MIND . . . . 468 ALARIC AT ROME 166

VICTORY
    THY VICTORY YET THOU CANST NOT SURELY KNOW . . . . 72 SOHRAB RUSTUM 389
    NOR ELLAS VICTORY ON THE ENGLISH COAST . . . 117 BALDER DEAD 3 147
    THE LATE-RELENTING GODS WITH VICTORY BROUGHT . . 330 MEROPE 6
    VICTORY SURE TO HER RACE . . . . 343 MEROPE 428
    FLIES VICTORY WINGD AND JUSTICE RAISES THEN . . 388 MEROPE 1503
    MY FINAL VICTORY PROVES THE GODS APPEASED . . . 397 MEROPE 1770
    THAT EVEN IN THY VICTORY THOU SHOW . . . . 405 MEROPE 2012
    FIRST WORK AFTER SUCH VICTORY LET US GO . . . 405 MEROPE 2017
    THAT FAMOUS FINAL VICTORY . . . . . 432 EMPEDOCLES II 127
    SAW BUT ANOTHER STEP TO CLIMB TO VICTORY . . . 469 ALARIC AT ROME 186

VIDAR
    VIDAR THE SILENT THE IMPETUOUS TYR . . . . . . 127 BALDER DEAD 3 492

VIE
    BUT FOR US WE VIE IN SPEED WITH THE BREATH   HOMER TRANS 54
        OF THE WEST-WIND

VIENNA
    FROM VIENNA BY THE DANUBE . . . . 13 CHURCH BROU 1 13
    IN VIENNA BY THE DANUBE . . . . 14 CHURCH BROU 1 53
    IN VIENNA BY THE DANUBE . . . . 14 CHURCH BROU 1 57

VIES
    GOLD FURZE WITH BROOM IN BLOSSOM VIES . . . . 274 STANZAS CARNAC 19
    GOLD BROOM WITH FURZE IN BLOSSOM VIES . . . . 274 STANZAS CARNAC V 19

VIEW
    THE LONE UNBROKEN VIEW SPREADS BRIGHT AND CLEAR . . 150 TRISTRAM 3 12
    THE LONE UNBROKEN VIEW STRETCHD BRIGHT AND CLEAR . . TRISTRAM 3 V 12
    THE LONE UNBROKEN VIEW GOES SPREADING CLEAR . . . TRISTRAM 3 V 12
    AND THEY THAT LOVELY FACE WHO VIEW . . . . 203 EUPHROSYNE 3
    LET BEAM UPON MY INWARD VIEW . . . . 208 ON THE RHINE 17
    AND LUMINOUS VIEW TO GAIN . . . . 308 OBERMANN 80
    HE CANNOT ALL THINGS VIEW . . . . 424 EMPEDOCLES I 2 348

VIEWD
    ASK HOW SHE VIEWD THY SELF-CONTROL . . . . . . 241 MORALITY 15

VIEWLESS
    THE FUTURE AND ITS VIEWLESS THINGS . . . . . . 250 WISH 25
    THOU MUST BE VIEWLESS TO EMPEDOCLES . . . . . . 408 EMPEDOCLES I 1 52

VIGOROUS
    HER VIGOROUS PRIMITIVE SONS . . . . 252 FUTURE 33
    OF THY DEAD HUSBANDS FACTION VIGOROUS ONCE . . . 334 MEROPE 139
    A CLOUD OF VULTURES ON THIS VIGOROUS RACE . . . 339 MEROPE 296

VIGOUR
    OF LIFE WITH VIGOUR UNDIMMD . . . . 199 FRAG DEJANEIRA 26
    OF THY RADIANT VIGOUR AGAIN . . . . 286 RUGBY CHAPEL 18
    NO VIGOUR AND SEVERITY MUST CHAIN . . . . 390 MEROPE 1563
    NURSED AN IMMORTAL VIGOUR I ALONE . . . . 438 EMPEDOCLES II 320
    THAT FRAME OF VIGOUR SHALL BE CRUMBLING CLAY . . 469 ALARIC AT ROME 194

VILE
    THEN SAY HE WAS NOT WHOLLY VILE . . . . . . 95 SICK KING BOKH 231
    TURN O DEATH ON THE VILE . . . . 281 HAWORTH CHURCH V
    HIDEOUS AND ARID AND VILE . . . . 290 RUGBY CHAPEL 158

VILLA
    UNTO A LONELY VILLA IN A DELL . . . . 167 RACHEL 2 1

VILLAGE
    THE VILLAGE STREET ITS HAUNTED MANSION LACKS . . 262 THYRSIS 3
    AND YET THE VILLAGE-CHURL FEELS THE TRUTH MORE . . 426 EMPEDOCLES I 2 411
        THAN YOU
    THE VILLAGE-GIRL AT HER WHEEL . . . . . 436 EMPEDOCLES II 257
    WERE KNOWN TO ALL THE VILLAGE-STREET . . . . . 459 KAISER DEAD 8

VILLAGES
    TO VILLAGES AND HOMES OF MAN . . . . . . 278 SOUTHERN NIGHT 82
    TO VILLAGES AND HAUNTS OF MAN . . . . 278 SOUTHERN NIGHT V 82
    O VILLAGES OF OETA . . . . 399 MEROPE 1820
    IN THE MOUNTAIN-VILLAGES . . . . 434 EMPEDOCLES II 184

VINDICATE
    AUGUST LAWS DOTH MIGHTILY VINDICATE . . . . . . 196 FRAG ANTIGONE 49

VINE
        MIRTH TO-DAY AND VINE-BOUND TRESSES   • • • • • •   33 NEW SIRENS   197
        I SNATCHD UP MY VINE-CROWN MY FIR-STAFF   • • • •   186 STRAYED REVEL   33
        OF THY CUP THE BRIGHT GLANCING VINE-LEAVES • • • •   188 STRAYED REVEL   85
        DOTTING THE FIELDS OF CORN AND VINE   • • • • • •   275 SOUTHERN NIGHT   5

VINEDRESSER
        THE VINEDRESSER IN HIS VINEYARD   • • • • • •   436 EMPEDOCLES II   256

VINES
        WHERE AT SUNRISE THROUGH YOUR VINES   • • • • • •   29 NEW SIRENS   94
        WHERE AT SUNRISE THROUGH THE VINES   • • • • • •   29 NEW SIRENS   V 94

VINEYARD
        BETWEEN THE DUSTY VINEYARD-WALLS   • • • • • •   311 OBERMANN   169
        THE VINEDRESSER IN HIS VINEYARD   • • • • • •   436 EMPEDOCLES II   256

VINEYARDS
        VINEYARDS AND CROFTS AND PASTURES BRIGHT WITH SUN   113 BALDER DEAD 2   300

VIOLATE
        I WILL NOT VIOLATE THY NOBLE GRIEF   • • • • • •   333 MEROPE   108

VIOLENCE
        IMPERIOUS SELF-ASSERTING VIOLENCE   • • • • • •   353 MEROPE   689

VIOLENT
        AND BLOOD AND RINGING BLOWS AND VIOLENT DEATH   • •   117 BALDER DEAD 3   140
        FROM VIOLENT ANGUISH SURELY FREE   • • • • • •   137 TRISTRAM 1   233
        THEIR LIVES AND FORMER VIOLENT TOIL IN THEBES   • •   193 STRAYED REVEL   256
        FOR KNOW THOU THIS A VIOLENT HEART HATH BEEN   • •   382 MEROPE   1329
        AND VIOLENT DEATHS TO VIOLENT MEN   • • • • • •   398 MEROPE   1809
        AND VIOLENT DEATHS TO VIOLENT MEN   • • • • • •   398 MEROPE   1809

VIOLET
        VIOLET SEA   • • • • • • • • • • • • • •   192 STRAYED REVEL   204
        THE ORANGE AND PALE VIOLET EVENING-SKY   • • • •   267 THYRSIS   159

VIOLETS
        LIKE THE SOILD TISSUE OF WHITE VIOLETS   • • • •   86 SOHRAB RUSTUM   844
        OF FRESH-PULLD VIOLETS WREATHED AND NODDING OER   • •   431 EMPEDOCLES II   87

VIRGIL
        TENDER VIRGIL NO TOMB   • • • • • • • • • •   294 HEINES GRAVE   59

VIRGILIAN
        SEEMD SURGING THE VIRGILIAN CRY   • • • • • •   450 GEISTS GRAVE   15

VIRGIN
        POURD IN PRAYER BEFORE THE VIRGIN-MOTHER   • • • •   144 TRISTRAM 2   63
        POURD IN GRIEF BEFORE THE VIRGIN-MOTHER   • • • •   144 TRISTRAM 2   V 63
        MOUNTAINS SURROUND IT AND SWEET VIRGIN AIR   • • •   236 PALLADIUM   10
        YES THOUGH THE VIRGIN MOUNTAIN-AIR   • • • • • •   307 OBERMANN   25
        ON EVERY BANK THE VIRGIN SAXIFRAGE   • • • • •   EVERLASTING SUB   5

VIRGINAL
        MORE VIRGINAL AND SWEET THAN OURS   • • • • • •   426 EMPEDOCLES I 2   434
        AS VIRGINAL AND SWEET AS OURS • • • • • • • •   426 EMPEDOCLES I 2   V 434

VIRGINS
        YE SUN-BORN VIRGINS ON THE ROAD OF TRUTH   • • • •   436 EMPEDOCLES II   239

VIRTUE
        AND STILL THE HAUNT BELOVED A VIRTUE YIELDS   • •   269 THYRSIS   220
        TWIXT VICE AND VIRTUE REVIVST   • • • • • • • •   288 RUGBY CHAPEL   55
        BENT ONLY TO SERVE VIRTUE   • • • • • • • •   353 MEROPE   662
        TO GIVE TO VIRTUE HER DOMINION DUE   • • • • • •   353 MEROPE   666

VIRTUES
        THOSE VIRTUES PRIZED AND PRACTISED BY TOO FEW   • •   6 REP FRIEND   2
        A THOUSAND VIRTUES IN THIS HATED TIME   • • • •   37 YOUTHS AGIT   8
        HIS ACTS THE WIFE HE CHOSE WAS FULL OF VIRTUES   • •   337 MEROPE   240
        TO GIVE HIS VIRTUES ROOM • • • • • • • • • •   420 EMPEDOCLES I 2   255
        TO LEAVE HIS VIRTUES ROOM • • • • • • • • •   420 EMPEDOCLES I 2   V 255
        BUT ALL THOSE VIRTUES WHICH COMMEND   • • • • • •   459 KAISER DEAD   31

VISAGE
        AND OER HIS VISAGE SERPENTS DROPPING GALL   • • • •   111 BALDER DEAD 2   221
        BUT LIGHT THE SERIOUS VISAGE GREW   • • • • • •   202 URANIA   11
        EACH TAKES AND THEN HIS VISAGE WAN   • • • • • •   300 GRANDE CHARTR   43

VISION
        AND IN THIS VISION OF THE GENERAL LAW   • • • •   5 DUKE WELLINGTON   8
        AND THAT SOUL-SEARCHING VISION FELL ON ME   • • •   42 GIPSY CHILD   16
        AND THY DARK MOURNFUL VISION RESTS ON ME   • • •   41 GIPSY CHILD   V 16
        WHO GIVE THEM VISION   • • • • • • • • • •   192 STRAYED REVEL   214
        WHO GAVE THEM VISION   • • • • • • • • • •   192 STRAYED REVEL   V 214
        AT THE HEIGHT OF HIS VISION CAN DEEM • • • • • •   253 FUTURE   42
        THE VISION ENDED I AWOKE • • • • • • • • • •   323 OBERMANN MORE   325
        SOME SHADOWY VISION OF A TRANQUIL LIFE   • • • •   474 CROMWELL   101
        AND THE LONG VISION OF THE YEARS TO BE   • • • •   475 CROMWELL   140

VISION   (CONTINUED)
    BY WORCESTERS FIELD THE WARRIOR-VISION PASSD   • •   476 CROMWELL   150
    IN BROAD CLEAR LIGHT THE GHASTLY VISION SHONE   • • • 477 CROMWELL   203
    THEN ALL HIS VISION FADED AND HIS SOUL   • • • • 479 CROMWELL   235

VISIONS
    YET HADST THOU ALWAY VISIONS OF OUR LIGHT   • • • • 269 THYRSIS   227
    THE SADDENING VISIONS OF DEPARTED DAYS   • • • • 470 ALARIC AT ROME   202
    THAT WILDEST VISIONS STILL SHOULD LOVELIEST SEEM • • • 470 ALARIC AT ROME   213
    THEN FANCYS ROVING VISIONS BOLD AND FREE   • • • • 474 CROMWELL   93
    NO SOFTENING RAY NO VISIONS FALSE AND WILD   • • • • 475 CROMWELL   125

VISIT
    MUST VISIT FIRST THEM TOO AND MAKE THEM PALE   • •   193 STRAYED REVEL   246
    WE VISIT IT BY MOMENTS AH TOO RARE   • • • • • 236 PALLADIUM   12
    DISCOVERY OF A VISIT MADE BY STEALTH • • • • • • 351 MEROPE   605
    VISIT OUR STREETS AND THE SOUND   • • • • • • 360 MEROPE   894
    VISIT US AS THEY DO WITH SIGN AND PLAGUE   • • • • 413 EMPEDOCLES I 2   24

VISITANT
    WHICH FLOATS BEFORE A VISITANT FROM HEAVEN • • • • 126 BALDER DEAD 3   438
    AND BID THE SUN THINE ONLY VISITANT • • • • • • 395 MEROPE   1752
    OUR SHINING VISITANT   • • • • • • • • • 444 WESTMIN ABBEY   2

VISITINGS
    SAD COMPUNCTIOUS VISITINGS   • • • • • • • 455 POOR MATTHIAS   86

VISITS
    TOO RARE TOO RARE GROW NOW MY VISITS HERE   • • • 263 THYRSIS   31
    TOO RARE TOO RARE GROW NOW MY VISITS HERE   • • • 269 THYRSIS   231

VITAL
    LIKE MEN WHO LIVE AND DRAW THE VITAL AIR   • • • • 108 BALDER DEAD 2   108

VITALS
    THAT SAPPST THE VITALS OF THIS TERRIBLE MOUNT   • • 438 EMPEDOCLES II   306

VIVIAN
    FOR HERE HE CAME WITH THE FAY VIVIAN • • • • • 154 TRISTRAM 3   159
    MERLIN AND VIVIAN STOPPD ON THE SLOPES BROW   • • 155 TRISTRAM 3   201
    HER FINGER ON HER LIPS THEN VIVIAN ROSE   • • • 156 TRISTRAM 3   215

VIVIANS
    HAD LOOSEND THE BROWN LOCKS OF VIVIANS HAIR   • • 154 TRISTRAM 3   168
    HAD LOOSEND THE BROWN CURLS OF VIVIANS HAIR   • • 154 TRISTRAM 3   V 168

VIZIER
    O MOST JUST VIZIER SEND AWAY   • • • • • • •   87 SICK KING BOKH   1
    O VIZIER WITHOUT LYING DOWN   • • • • • • •   88 SICK KING BOKH   15
    O VIZIER HERE IS THE KINGS DOOR   • • • • •   88 SICK KING BOKH   20
    O VIZIER I MAY BURY HIM • • • • • • • • •   88 SICK KING BOKH   21
    O VIZIER BE IT AS THOU SAYST   • • • • • •   88 SICK KING BOKH   29
    O VIZIER THOU ART OLD I YOUNG • • • • • • •   93 SICK KING BOKH   181
    THITHER O VIZIER WILL I BEAR • • • • • • •   95 SICK KING BOKH   225

VOCAL
    WHOSE TROUT ARE VOCAL   • • • • • • • • • 391 MEROPE   1611

VOGUE
    BY OTHER RULES THAN ARE IN VOGUE TO-DAY   • • • • 436 EMPEDOCLES II   265

VOICE
    FIND THEIR SOLE VOICE IN THAT VICTORIOUS BROW   • •   3 SHAKESPEARE   V 14
    A VOICE ORACULAR HATH PEALD TO-DAY • • • • •   3 EMERSONS ESSAYS   3
    FELL THIS DREAD VOICE FROM LIPS THAT CANNOT LIE   •   8 MYCERINUS   5
    WHERE EARTHLY VOICE CLIMBS NEVER WING THEIR FLIGHT   10 MYCERINUS   44
    FELL THIS LATE VOICE FROM LIPS THAT CANNOT LIE   • •   8 MYCERINUS   V 5
    PERCEIVE BUT A VOICE AS I COME TO HIS SIDE • • • •   20 MODERN SAPPHO   26
    BUT DEEPER THEIR VOICE GROWS AND NOBLER THEIR BEARING   20 MODERN SAPPHO   27
    IT HEARS A VOICE WITHIN IT TELL   • • • • •   22 YOUTH AND CALM   22
    O UNFORGOTTEN VOICE THY ACCENTS COME • • • • •   36 VOICE   29
    O UNFORGOTTEN VOICE THY WHISPERS COME   • • •   36 VOICE   V 29
    O WHERE THY VOICE DOTH COME   • • • • • •   39 STAGIRIUS   52
    IF I MIGHT LEND THEIR LIFE A VOICE • • • • •   **60 RESIGNATION**   2̶8̶9̶
    SO HE SPAKE MILDLY SOHRAB HEARD HIS VOICE   • • • •   **71 SOHRAB RUSTUM**   3̶3̶1̶
    THE MIGHTY VOICE OF RUSTUM AND HE SAW   • • • •   71 SOHRAB RUSTUM   335
    HIS BREAST HEAVED HIS LIPS FOAMD AND TWICE HIS VOICE   74 SOHRAB RUSTUM   455
    FIGHT LET ME HEAR THY HATEFUL VOICE NO MORE   • •   75 SOHRAB RUSTUM   459
    BUT WITH A COLD INCREDULOUS VOICE HE SAID   • • • •   78 SOHRAB RUSTUM   576
    AND WITH A FAILING VOICE SOHRAB REPLIED   • • • •   78 SOHRAB RUSTUM   579
    AND IN A HOLLOW VOICE HE SPAKE AND SAID   • • • •   80 SOHRAB RUSTUM   666
    O BOY THY FATHER AND HIS VOICE CHOKED THERE   • •   81 SOHRAB RUSTUM   691
    AND WITH A SOOTHING VOICE HE SPAKE AND SAID   • •   82 SOHRAB RUSTUM   707
    SO SAID HE AND HIS VOICE RELEASED THE HEART   • •   82 SOHRAB RUSTUM   726
    BUT RUSTUM CHID HIM WITH STERN VOICE AND SAID   • •   82 SOHRAB RUSTUM   737
    BUT WITH A GRAVE MILD VOICE SOHRAB REPLIED   • • • •   84 SOHRAB RUSTUM   771
    AND WITH A MOURNFUL VOICE RUSTUM REPLIED   • •   84 SOHRAB RUSTUM   795
    AND WITH A COLD INCREDULOUS VOICE HE SAID   • • • •   78 SOHRAB RUSTUM   V 576
    AND WITH A SOOTHING VOICE HE SPOKE AND SAID   • •   82 SOHRAB RUSTUM   V 707
    AND WITH A GRAVE MILD VOICE SOHRAB REPLIED • • • •   84 SOHRAB RUSTUM   V 771

VOICE (CONTINUED)

BUT HE PRAISED ALLAH WITH LOUD VOICE		91 SICK KING BOKH	123
THE VOICE WAS LIKE THE UNHAPPY HODERS VOICE		102 BALDER DEAD 1	243
THE VOICE WAS LIKE THE UNHAPPY HODERS VOICE		102 BALDER DEAD 1	243
BUT FEEBLY AS A VOICE FAR OFF HE SAID		112 BALDER DEAD 2	263
AND HE DREW NEAR AND HEARD NO LIVING VOICE		113 BALDER DEAD 2	305
THY VOICE OF JOYANCE MINDED US AND YOUTH		117 BALDER DEAD 3	143
DOUBTLESS THOU FEAREST TO MEET BALDERS VOICE		124 BALDER DEAD 3	392
STRETCHD FORTH HIS HAND AND WITH BENIGNANT VOICE		125 BALDER DEAD 3	410
ABOVE THE DIN HER VOICE IS IN MY EARS		137 TRISTRAM 1	240
HER CHILDRENS SHE MOVES SLOW HER VOICE ALONE		151 TRISTRAM 3	72
HE HEARS A VOICE SIGH HUMBLY WAIT		157 SAINT BRANDAN	23
IN A VOICE THAT SHE WILL KNOW		161 FORSAKEN MERM	12
I HEAR A GODS TREMENDOUS VOICE		174 MEETING	11
BUT ON THE STAIRS WHAT VOICE IS THIS I HEAR		175 PARTING	17
THAT THE SWEET VOICE ITS UPLAND CLEARNESS TOOK		175 PARTING	22
OF THAT FRESH VOICE THE GAY DELIGHT		184 TERRACE BERNE	31
THY VOICE IS SWEET		189 STRAYED REVEL	116
THY VOICE IN GUSHES COMES		200 PHILOMELA	V
THY VOICE BY GUSHES COMES		200 PHILOMELA	V
HIS VOICE LIKE SOUNDS OF SUMMER NIGHTS		202 URANIA	22
HOW EXQUISITE THY VOICE WOULD COME		205 CALAIS SANDS	13
FORTH WITH THY PRAISING VOICE		220 BACCHANALIA 2	47
AND ITS DEEP-TONED MELODIOUS VOICE		227 EPILOG LAOCOON	195
OR THE VOICE WHICH REVEALS WHAT YOU ARE		230 YOUTH OF NATURE	65
IN MYSIAN IDA THE VOICE		230 YOUTH OF NATURE	76
HARDLY HIS VOICE AT ITS BEST		231 YOUTH OF NATURE	99
UTTERD THE VOICE OF MY HILLS		231 YOUTH OF NATURE	125
HERE LET THAT VOICE MAKE END THEN LET A STRAIN		238 PROGRESS	33
O AIR-BORN VOICE LONG SINCE SEVERELY CLEAR		240 SELF-DEPENDENCE	29
IS BY THE TONES OF A LOVED VOICE CARESSD		247 BURIED LIFE	83
YOUNG DAPHNIS WITH HIS SILVER VOICE DOTH SING		268 THYRSIS	185
LET IN THY VOICE A WHISPER OFTEN COME		269 THYRSIS	235
THE LAST POETIC VOICE IS DUMB		270 MEMORIAL VERSES	4
FOR NEVER HAS SUCH SOOTHING VOICE		271 MEMORIAL VERSES	35
AH MAY YE FEEL HIS VOICE AS WE		271 MEMORIAL VERSES	41
HEARS THY VOICE RIGHT NOW HE IS GONE		272 MEMORIAL VERSES	74
WITH GENTLE VOICE AND BROW		273 EDW QUILLINAN	18
VOICE TO ITS CREED ERE THE CREED		281 HAWORTH CHURCH	45
YE ALIGHT IN OUR VAN AT YOUR VOICE		292 RUGBY CHAPEL	196
SCARCE COMPREHENDING THE VOICE		294 HEINES GRAVE	78
VOICE MOVED ONLY THE TORRENT BROKE		323 OBERMANN MORE	327
STILL IN MY SOUL THE VOICE I HEARD		324 OBERMANN MORE	333
ONE VOICE PREACHD PATIENCE AND THAT VOICE WAS MINE		337 MEROPE	258
ONE VOICE PREACHD PATIENCE AND THAT VOICE WAS MINE		337 MEROPE	258
CHEERING WITH HAND AND VOICE AND HORN HIS DOGS		357 MEROPE	805
NOT CONDEMND BY MY VOICE		360 MEROPE	902
OR WITH WHAT VOICE SHALL I THE QUESTIONS MEET		367 MEROPE	1037
ARE THESE WORDS MEROPES IS THIS VOICE MINE		368 MEROPE	1068
HEAR THAT FRESH VOICE AND CLASP THAT GOLD-LOCKD HEAD		387 MEROPE	1460
NOT DECRIED BY MY VOICE		360 MEROPE	V 902
IN THIS CLEAR MOUNTAIN-AIR A VOICE WILL RISE		409 EMPEDOCLES I 1	88
REASON ITS VOICE CONFIRMS		419 EMPEDOCLES I 2	V 224
THE LYRES VOICE IS LOVELY EVERYWHERE		430 EMPEDOCLES II	37
SEND FAR THEIR LIGHT VOICE		442 EMPEDOCLES II	426
THAT VOICE HAD NOTE SO CLEAR OF SWEET COMMAND		445 WESTMIN ABBEY	28
WHICH JOYD MY VOICE TO HEAR		449 WESTMIN ABBEY	162
AND YOUR OWN VOICE GUIDE HIM TO HIS PREY		466 ALARIC AT ROME	118
LEARNS FREEDOMS LESSON FROM YOUR VOICE OF FEAR		471 CROMWELL	2
AND MEMORYS CALM CLEAR VOICE AND MOURNFUL EYE		474 CROMWELL	87
RANG AS HE TRODE THEM WITH THE VOICE OF WAR		476 CROMWELL	152
THE GATHERING TEMPEST WITH ITS VOICE OF FEAR		478 CROMWELL	209
AND HE WAS GIVEN A VOICE BY THE WHITE-ARMD GODDESS HERA		HOMER TRANS	46
THUS FAR HE AND HERE HIS VOICE WAS STOPPED BY THE FURIES		HOMER TRANS	57
AT YOUR VOICE HE RISES SLOWLY		META CLOISTER	33

VOICELESS

WAS COLD AND SAD BENEATH THAT BREATHLESS VOICELESS NIGHT		466 ALARIC AT ROME	108
PEOPLED NIGHTS VOICELESS SHADES WITH FORMS OF LONG AGO		467 ALARIC AT ROME	126
BUT AS ONE VOICELESS BLANK A PLACE OF GRAVES		469 ALARIC AT ROME	182

VOICES

DO ADVERSE VOICES FALL ON THE WORLDS EAR		47 WORLD QUIETIST	19
WITH SWEET JOIND VOICES		51 CONSOLATION	46
HOW WOULD YOUR VOICES RUN AGAIN		141 TRISTRAM 1	361
WHAT VOICES ARE THESE ON THE CLEAR NIGHT-AIR		142 TRISTRAM 1	372
CHILDRENS VOICES SHOULD BE DEAR		161 FORSAKEN MERM	14
CHILDRENS VOICES WILD WITH PAIN		162 FORSAKEN MERM	16
OUR HEARTS OUR VOICES MUST WE TOO BE DUMB		245 BURIED LIFE	25
THEIR VOICES WERE IN ALL MENS EARS		303 GRANDE CHARTR	123
WHAT VOICES ENRAPTURE		442 EMPEDOCLES II	443
FLOAT THERE NOT VOICES ON THE MURMURING WIND		468 ALARIC AT ROME	164
SOUNDS OF DEEP IMPORT VOICES THAT BEGUILE		472 CROMWELL	5

VOICINGS

AT A PAUSE OF SIREN VOICINGS		27 NEW SIRENS	47

VOID

AND CAST HIS TRUNK TO CHOKE THE ABYSMAL VOID		121 BALDER DEAD 3	259
AND THREW HIS TRUNK TO CHOKE THE ABYSMAL VOID		121 BALDER DEAD 3	V 259

872

VOID   (CONTINUED)
    IN THE VOID AIR TOWARDS THEE   . . . .   176 PARTING   63
    AND THROUGH THE VOID AIR SANG   . . . .   197 FRAG ANTIGONE   88
    SHE FELT THE VOID WHICH MINED HER BREAST   . . . .   316 OBERMANN MORE   123
    LIFTED AND THAT UNWISHD-FOR HEIRSHIP VOID   . . . .   366 MEROPE   1001
    HOW MUCH MEN THINK ME ABJECT VOID OF HEART   . . . .   366 MEROPE   1016
    MY DEATH MAKES MY DEBT VOID AND DOUBLES THINE   . .   367 MEROPE   1049
    WE PEOPLING THE VOID AIR   . . . .   421 EMPEDOCLES I 2   278
    FAILD TO FILL UP THE VOID WHICH IN OUR BREASTS WE BEAR   424 EMPEDOCLES I 2   376
    THE HOWLING VOID TO SPAN   . . . .   415 EMPEDOCLES I 2   V   77
    MADE VOID AND HELD THE SORROW AND THE JOY   . . . .   RUDE ORATOR   4

VOLLEYING
    COME WITH THE VOLLEYING RAIN AND TOSSING BREEZE   . .   264 THYRSIS   59

VOLUME
    LIKE THE BROAD VOLUME OF THE INSURGENT NILE   . .   10 MYCERINUS   40

VOLUMES
    OF VOLUMES YET TO READ   . . . .   423 EMPEDOCLES I 2   334

VOTARY
    BUT THE SOLITUDE OPPRESSES THY VOTARY   . . . .   435 EMPEDOCLES II   208
    WHERE SHALL THY VOTARY FLY THEN BACK TO MEN   . .   435 EMPEDOCLES II   220

VOUCHD
    AND VOUCHD BY GLORIOUS RENOWN   . . . .   459 KAISER DEAD   17

VOW
    VOW TO BEAT HENCEFORTH SIDE BY SIDE   . . . . . .   203 EUPHROSYNE   8

VOYAGE
    LIFES VOYAGE DONE HIS HEAVENLY FRIEND   . . . .   40 HUMAN LIFE   2
    I FORGOT THOU COMEST FROM THY VOYAGE   . . . . .   142 TRISTRAM 2   17

VOYAGED
    SHE WHO AS THEY VOYAGED QUAFFD   . . . .   132 TRISTRAM 1   63

VOYAGES
    VOYAGES EXILES HATES DISSENSIONS WARS   . . . . .   195 FRAG ANTIGONE   23

VULGAR
    O ARTS ABOVE THE VULGAR TYRANTS REACH   . . . .   339 MEROPE   310

VULGARITY
    NOT IN AMERICAN VULGARITY   . . . .   480 HUNGARIAN NAT   6

VULTURES
    A CLOUD OF VULTURES ON THIS VIGOROUS RACE   . . . .   339 MEROPE   296
    WILD BEASTS AND VULTURES SAILING OVERHEAD   . . . .   373 MEROPE   1170

VYING
    IN THEIR FLITTING LUSTRE VYING . . . .   131 TRISTRAM 1   27

WADED
    HAVE WADED FOREMOST IN THEIR BLOODY WAVES   . . . .   74 SOHRAB RUSTUM   434

WADING
    WHEN A DREARY DAWN IS WADING   . . . .   33 NEW SIRENS   211
    WHEN A DREARY LIGHT IS WADING   . . . .   33 NEW SIRENS   V 211

WAFT
    ONE MOMENTS SPACE MIGHT WAFT HIM FAR AWAY   . . . .   475 CROMWELL   111

WAFTS
    WAFTS NOT FROM THINE OWN THOUGHTS NOR LONGINGS VAIN   42 GIPSY CHILD   10
    WAFTS NOT FROM THINE OWN THOUGHTS OF GRAVER STRAIN   41 GIPSY CHILD   V 10
    WAFTS HIM HERE AND LETS HIM FIND   . . . .   136 TRISTRAM 1   191

WAGE
    DID ITS NOW SILENT WARFARE WAGE   . . . .   219 BACCHANALIA 2   20
    PERFORMD GOOD SERVICE FOR HIS BLOODY WAGE   . . . .   364 MEROPE   975

WAGED
    SUCH AS ON EARTH WE VALIANTLY HAVE WAGED   . . . .   117 BALDER DEAD 3   139
    ITS WARFARE WAGED WITH PAIN   . . . .   313 OBERMANN MORE   42

WAGGON
    AND ON THE RIDGE A WAGGON CHOKES THE WAY   . . . .   107 BALDER DEAD 2   94

WAIL
    ENOUGH OF TEARS YE GODS ENOUGH OF WAIL   . . . .   95 BALDER DEAD 1   18
    BUT WHEN THEIR SOULS WERE SATISFIED WITH WAIL   . .   103 BALDER DEAD 1   276
    ON BALDERS BREAST AND THUS BEGAN THE WAIL   . . . .   115 BALDER DEAD 3   66
    AND SOON HAD ALL THAT DAY BEEN SPENT IN WAIL   . .   118 BALDER DEAD 3   155
    YE GODS THERE WELL MAY BE TOO MUCH OF WAIL   . . . .   118 BALDER DEAD 3   157
    CARRIED THY LOVELY WAIL AWAY   . . . .   303 GRANDE CHARTR   140
    FROM THE ALTAR OF ZEUS FROM THE CROWD CAME A WAIL   346 MEROPE   489
    HOMES EEN NOW IS THERE WAIL   . . . .   369 MEROPE   1095
    THE PIOUS WAIL FORSAKE   . . . .   416 EMPEDOCLES I 2   134

WAILD
AND FAR INTO THE NIGHT THEY WAILD THEIR DIRGE • • 103 BALDER DEAD 1 275
HE SPAKE AND ALL THE GODS ASSENTING WAILD • • • • 116 BALDER DEAD 3 89
WAILD FROM THE PALACE WITHIN • • • • • • • • 346 MEROPE 496

WAILFUL
THEN MUST HE NOT REGARD THE WAILFUL GHOSTS • • • • 100 BALDER DEAD 1 176
THEN HE MUST NOT REGARD THE WAILFUL GHOSTS • • • • 100 BALDER DEAD 1 V 176

WAILING
THE SUNK EYES THE WAILING TONE • • • • • • • 34 NEW SIRENS 248
WEEPING AND WAILING AND VALHALLA RANG • • • • 95 BALDER DEAD 1 11
WAILING BUT OTHERWISE WAS ODINS WILL • • • • • • 95 BALDER DEAD 1 16
WAILING NO MORE IN SILENCE ATE AND DRANK • • • • 97 BALDER DEAD 1 70

WAILS
AND THE WIND WAILS AMONG THE MOUNTAIN PINES • • 18 CHURCH BROU 3 V 37

WAIN
SILENT THE SWATHS THE RINGING WAIN • • • • • • 217 BACCHANALIA 1 5
SILENT THE SHEAVES THE RINGING WAIN • • • • • • 217 BACCHANALIA 1 V 5

WAIT
SO TO WAIT BUT WHAT NOTES DOWN THE WIND HARK 20 MODERN SAPPHO 29
  ARE DRIVING
THEN TO WAIT BUT WHAT NOTES DOWN THE WIND HARK 20 MODERN SAPPHO V 29
  ARE DRIVING
ARE WILLS SO WEAK THEN LET NOT MINE WAIT LONG • • 38 WORLDS TRIUMPHS 12
OR DO I WAIT TO HEAR SOME GRAY-HAIRD KING • • • • 43 GIPSY CHILD 33
EVER SINCE PRAYER-TIME HE DOTH WAIT • • • • 88 SICK KING BOKH 14
SO QUICKLY AND WILL WAIT FOR NO REPLY • • • • 102 BALDER DEAD 1 242
HERE MUST THOU LIE AND WAIT AN ENDLESS AGE • • • 126 BALDER DEAD 3 452
MY PRINCESS ART THOU THERE SWEET DO NOT WAIT • • 140 TRISTRAM 1 308
HE HEARS A VOICE SIGH HUMBLY WAIT • • • • • • 157 SAINT BRANDAN 23
ONE MOMENT WAIT THOU HOLY MAN • • • • • • • 157 SAINT BRANDAN 25
TO WORK OR WAIT ELSEWHERE OR HERE • • • • • 251 WISH 52
HERE WILL I SIT AND WAIT • • • • • • • • 255 SCHOLAR-GIPSY 16
WHO WAIT LIKE THEE BUT NOT LIKE THEE IN HOPE • • • 260 SCHOLAR-GIPSY 170
HE COULD NOT WAIT THEIR PASSING HE IS DEAD • • • 264 THYRSIS 50
ALIGHT AND SPARELY SUP AND WAIT • • • • • • 300 GRANDE CHARTR 26
LIKE THESE ON EARTH I WAIT FORLORN • • • • • 302 GRANDE CHARTR 88
AND WAIT TO SEE THE FUTURE COME • • • • • • 303 GRANDE CHARTR 118
BUT WHILE WE WAIT ALLOW OUR TEARS • • • • • 304 GRANDE CHARTR 162
AND WAIT FOR WORDS TO COME • • • • • • • 318 OBERMANN MORE 180
WAIT THEN UNTIL SUFFICIENT HELP APPEARS • • • 384 MEROPE 1397
LONGING LISTENING I WAIT I IMPLORE • • • • • 347 MEROPE V
CALLICLES MUST WAIT HERE AND PLAY TO HIM • • • 428 EMPEDOCLES I 2 484
AND WAIT WHILE HE DID THERE A SPACE ABIDE • • • • 445 WESTMIN ABBEY 26
AND WAIT THE ISSUE SLEEPING UNDERGROUND • • • 448 WESTMIN ABBEY 146
WAIT FOR THE LEAVEN TO WORK THE LET TO END • • • 449 WESTMIN ABBEY 170
THY PASSING BY DOTH VAINLY WAIT • • • • • • 461 KAISER DEAD 74
MUST LEARN TO WAIT RENOUNCE WITHDRAW • • • • 481 COURAGE 4

WAITED
SILENT AND WAITED FOR THE SACRED MORN • • • 119 BALDER DEAD 3 212
LONG IVE WAITED LONG IVE FOUGHT MY FEVER • • • • 142 TRISTRAM 2 3
WHILE THEIR MASTERS SATE BY THE FIRE AND WAITED HOMER TRANS 6
  FOR MORNING

WAITEST
THOU WAITEST FOR THE SPARK FROM HEAVEN AND WE • • 260 SCHOLAR-GIPSY 171

WAITING
LADIES WAITING ROUND HER SEAT • • • • • • • 13 CHURCH BROU 1 34
WAITING THE DARKNESS OF THE FINAL TIMES • • • • 98 BALDER DEAD 1 124
WAITING HER PASSAGE • • • • • • • • • • 196 FRAG ANTIGONE 43
AND WAITING FOR THE SPARK FROM HEAVEN TO FALL • • 258 SCHOLAR-GIPSY 120

WAITS
OF HIS PALE WIFE WHO WAITS AND WEEPS ON SHORE • • 69 SOHRAB RUSTUM 285
OF HIS PALE WIFE WHO WAITS AND WEEPS ASHORE • • 69 SOHRAB RUSTUM V 285

WAITST
FOR FATE THOU WAITST NOT LONG SINCE IN THIS HOUR • • 397 MEROPE 1777

WAIVE
AND WAIVE ALL CLAIM TO BLISS AND TRY TO BEAR • • 260 SCHOLAR-GIPSY 193

WAKE
OR IF YE WAKE LET IT BE THEN WHEN FAIR • • • • 18 CHURCH BROU 3 17
AND IF YE WAKE LET IT BE THEN WHEN FAIR • • • • 18 CHURCH BROU 3 V 17
TO WAKE THE GODS AND HEROES TO THEIR TASKS • • • • 105 BALDER DEAD 2 9
BUT THEY HARP EVER ON ONE STRING AND WAKE • • • • 117 BALDER DEAD 3 137
THEIR HOT SEALS AND LET HIM WAKE • • • • • 139 TRISTRAM 1 295
ONCE EVERY YEAR WHEN CAROLS WAKE • • • • • • 158 SAINT BRANDAN 65
SENT ECHOES THROUGH THE NIGHT TO WAKE • • • • 177 FAREWELL 3
THE TOILS OF THY FOUL SERVICE TILL THOU WAKE • • 373 MEROPE 1181
WAKE UP IN HELL FROM THINE UNHALLOWD SLEEP • • • 373 MEROPE 1183
WAKE AMID GLOOM AND HOWLING AND THE NOISE • • • 373 MEROPE 1185
NOR WAKE THE WEARY SOUL THAT SLUMBERS ON BELOW • • 469 ALARIC AT ROME 198
GAZING ON THEE WE WAKE TO FIND IT IS NOT SO • • 470 ALARIC AT ROME 216

WAKED
    HE SEES THE DROWSY NEW-WAKED CLOWN • • • • • • 57 RESIGNATION   181

WAKEFUL
    HE HAD LAIN WAKEFUL TOSSING ON HIS BED • • • • 61 SOHRAB RUSTUM   6
    TOSSING AND WAKEFUL AND I COME TO THEE • • • • 62 SOHRAB RUSTUM   37

WAKENS
    WAKENS O QUEEN REMEMBRANCE IN THY HEART • • • • 333 MEROPE   106

WAKES
    HIST HE WAKES • • • • • • • • • • • • 188 STRAYED REVEL   96
    WHETHER HE WAKES • • • • • • • • • • • 252 FUTURE   8
    WAKES ME THUS KINDLY FROM THE PERILOUS SLEEP • • 375 MEROPE   1203

WAKING
    IN THE PINES THE THRUSH IS WAKING • • • • • 35 NEW SIRENS   259
    O WAKING ON A WORLD WHICH THUS-WISE SPRINGS • • 45 IN UTRUMQUE PAR   8
    BETWIXT THY WAKING AND THE BIRTH OF THINGS • • • 45 IN UTRUMQUE PAR   10
    AGES OR HOURS O WAKING ON LIFES STREAM • • • 45 IN UTRUMQUE PAR   11
    TEN YEARS AND TO MY WAKING EYE • • • • • • 183 TERRACE BERNE   1

WALES
    BEFORE US ARE THE SWEET GREEN FIELDS OF WALES • • 133 TRISTRAM 1   95
    DIE ON THE GREEN FIELDS OF WALES • • • • • 135 TRISTRAM 1   158

WALK
    DIDST WALK ON EARTH UNGUESSD AT BETTER SO • • • 3 SHAKESPEARE   V 11
    AND NEATH THE GARDEN-WALK IT HUMS • • • • 184 TERRACE BERNE   11
    AND WE MUST LEAVE THE OLD FAITHS AND WALK THEREIN   237 PROGRESS   26
    HIS FIXD CONDITION AND PERPETUAL WALK) • • • 404 MEROPE   1993
    BEGUILED HIS WALK • • • • • • • • • 460 KAISER DEAD   72
    AH THEY WALK IN STARRY MUSINGS • • • • • • META CLOISTER   3

WALKD
    ONE MORN AS THROUGH HYDE PARK WE WALKD • • • • 221 EPILOG LAOCOON   1
    STILL WE WALKD ON IN THOUGHTFUL MOOD • • • • • 223 EPILOG LAOCOON   61

WALKING
    LAST WALKING BY THE SEA THOU FOUNDEST SPARS • • 121 BALDER DEAD 3   268
    THEN WALKING BY THE SEA THOU FOUNDEST SPARS • • 121 BALDER DEAD 3   V 268

WALKS
    CHILL BLOWS THE WIND THE PLEASAUNCE-WALKS ARE DREAR   135 TRISTRAM 1   161
    THE PLEASAUNCE-WALKS THE WEEPING QUEEN • • • 136 TRISTRAM 1   178
    WHEN GARDEN-WALKS AND ALL THE GRASSY FLOOR • • • 264 THYRSIS   54
    BORDERD BY STATUES AND WALKS • • • • • • 296 HEINES GRAVE   133

WALL
    ROUND THE WALL TO STRAY • • • • • • • • 16 CHURCH BROU 2   11
    THE CHURCHYARD WALL THAT CLIPS THE SQUARE • • • 16 CHURCH BROU 2   12
    RANGED DIAMOND-BRIGHT THE ETERNAL WALL OF SNOW • • 25 DREAM   13
    A WILD ROSE CLIMBING UP A MOULDERING WALL • • • 36 VOICE   20
    THEIR SHIPS AND THROUGH THE GATE BEYOND THE WALL • • 97 BALDER DEAD 1   75
    THROUGH THE CLIFF-WALL AND A FRESH STREAM RUNS DOWN   97 BALDER DEAD 1   82
    BOTH NIGHT AND DAY AND BY THE INNER WALL • • • • 98 BALDER DEAD 1   91
    NORTHWARD UNTIL HE MEETS A STRETCHING WALL • • • 100 BALDER DEAD 1   166
    BARRING HIS WAY AND IN THE WALL A GRATE • • • 100 BALDER DEAD 1   167
    AGAINST THE HARBOUR BY THE CITY-WALL • • • • 101 BALDER DEAD 1   225
    STILL NORTH UNTIL HE MET A STRETCHING WALL • • • 109 BALDER DEAD 2   144
    BARRING HIS WAY AND IN THE WALL A GRATE • • • 109 BALDER DEAD 2   145
    FOR NEAR THE WALL THE RIVER OF ROARING FLOWS • • 109 BALDER DEAD 2   152
    OR HOW OERLEAP THE GRATE THAT BARS THE WALL • • 110 BALDER DEAD 2   185
    AND TO THE WALL HE CAME AND FOUND THE GRATE • • 113 BALDER DEAD 2   286
    AND CAME BENEATH THE WALL AND FOUND THE GRATE • • 124 BALDER DEAD 3   377
    AND THERE UPON THE WALL YOU SEE • • • • • 147 TRISTRAM 2   V 152
    THE FRORE MOUNTAIN-WALL • • • • • • • 176 PARTING   48
    FIND THY BODY BY THE WALL • • • • • • • 215 LAST WORD   16
    THE FAMOUS PAINTERS FILLD THEIR WALL • • • • 219 BACCHANALIA 2   8
    HELEN WILL COME UPON THE WALL TO SEE • • • • 236 PALLADIUM   16
    DREAMING OF NOUGHT BEYOND THEIR PRISON-WALL • • 243 SUMMER NIGHT   41
    OF THE LONG-BATTERD WORLD UPLIFTS ITS WALL • • 267 THYRSIS   147
    UPON THE WALL THE KNEE-WORN FLOOR • • • • 300 GRANDE CHARTR   46
    BENEATH SOME OLD-WORLD ABBEY WALL • • • • 304 GRANDE CHARTR   170
    AND CRUMBLING WALL AND SULTRY SAND • • • • 318 OBERMANN MORE   183
    TAYGETUS LACONIAS BORDER-WALL • • • • • • 330 MEROPE   17
    A FRETTED WALL OF BLUE AND GREY • • • • • 479 HAYSWATER BOAT   12

WALLD
    FROM THE WALLD TOWN BEYOND THE PASS • • • • 17 CHURCH BROU 2   26
    MOVE BROWSING UP THE GRAY-WALLD LANE • • • • 55 RESIGNATION   121
    ONE LAST LOOK AT THE WHITE-WALLD TOWN • • • 162 FORSAKEN MERM   25
    WHERE THE SEA-STOCKS BLOOM TO THE WHITE-WALLD TOWN   163 FORSAKEN MERM   69
    IN THE WALLD CITIES THE WAY PASSES THROUGH • • 193 STRAYED REVEL   250
    FROM THE GREY-WALLD GARDENS A BREATH • • • • 234 YOUTH OF MAN   67

WALLING
    WHERE THE ROAD ISSUES BETWEEN WALLING ROCKS • • 107 BALDER DEAD 2   89

WALLS
```
        ON THE SMOOTH LEADEN ROOF AND ON THE WALLS  .  .  .  .       18 CHURCH BROU 3      34
        MUFFLED .ITS WALLS AND ON THE STONE-STREWN ROOF    .  .      25 DREAM            17
        IT SHINES UPON THE BLANK WHITE WALLS  .  .  .  .  .  .      141 TRISTRAM 1      335
        SATE IN THE BROUGHAM AND THOSE BLANK WALLS SURVEYD         167 RACHEL 1          8
        ON THOSE WALLS SUBTERRANEAN WHERE SHE HID     .  .  .      172 GOOD SHEPHERD    11
        SLOWLY WITHIN THE WALLS   .  .  .  .  .  .  .  .  .        233 YOUTH OF MAN     46
        AND THERE IN THE DUSK BY THE WALLS    .  .  .  .  .        234 YOUTH OF MAN     83
        THAT THOU WERT WANDERD FROM THE STUDIOUS WALLS            259 SCHOLAR-GIPSY   134
        THE CHAPEL-WALLS IN WHOSE BOUND       .  .  .  .  .        286 RUGBY CHAPEL     12
        BETWEEN THE DUSTY VINEYARD-WALLS      .  .  .  .  .        311 OBERMANN        169
        AND WALLS WHERE BYRON CAME  .  .  .  .  .  .  .  .        313 OBERMANN MORE    24
        TO MANTINEIA WITH ITS UNBAKED WALLS   .  .  .  .  .        355 MEROPE          739
        WALLS ON ONE SIDE THE DEEP STYMPHALIAN LAKE   .  .        358 MEROPE          813
        WITH NEW WALLS WHICH THE VICTORS      .  .  .  .  .        400 MEROPE         1851
        TO MANTINEA WITH ITS UNBAKED WALLS    .  .  .  .  .        355 MEROPE        V 739
        AND THY TRANSFIGURED WALLS BE TOUCHD WITH FLAME          449 WESTMIN ABBEY   178
        SWEPT FROM THY WALLS O ROME ON ITS TRIUMPHANT WAY        465 ALARIC AT ROME   78
```

WALNUT
```
        OF BRIGHT-LEAFD CHESTNUTS AND MOSSD WALNUT-TREES  .  .     25 DREAM            8
```

WALTON
```
        I PASSD TO-DAY OER WALTON HEATH       .  .  .  .  .  .    483 ROME-SICKNESS     5
```

WAN
```
        CAN MEN WORSHIP THE WAN FEATURES      .  .  .  .  .        34 NEW SIRENS      247
        NOR LOOKST THOU PALE AND WAN LIKE MEN DECEASED   .  .     108 BALDER DEAD 2   109
        WHEN I DRAW NIGH AND THE WAN TRIBES OF DEAD      .  .     126 BALDER DEAD 3   464
        EACH TAKES AND THEN HIS VISAGE WAN    .  .  .  .  .       300 GRANDE CHARTR    43
        THAT WAN NAILD FORM WITH HEAD DROOPD LOW   .  .  .        317 OBERMANN MORE V 155
        ROUND THE WAN TEMPLES OF THE HALLOWED DEAD   .  .  .      463 ALARIC AT ROME   26
```

WANDER
```
        MIGHT WANDER ALL DAY LONG AND NEVER TIRE     .  .  .       11 MYCERINUS        91
        WHITHER DOES HE WANDER NOW   .  .  .  .  .  .  .  .       136 TRISTRAM 1      189
        HITHER LET HIM WANDER NOW    .  .  .  .  .  .  .  .       137 TRISTRAM 1      228
        AND WANDER ROUND THE WORLD AGAIN      .  .  .  .  .       206 RIVER            16
        AND ON EARTH WE WANDER GROPING REELING    .  .  .        210 SELF-DECEPTION   21
        WANDER UNQUIET AND MY OWN    .  .  .  .  .  .  .  .       275 SOUTHERN NIGHT   15
        FOR ONE SHORT MOMENT WANDER OER HIS LIPS  .  .  .  .      298 HEINES GRAVE    209
        LETTING THE SEA-STREAM WANDER THROUGH THY HAIR   .  .     430 EMPEDOCLES II    61
```

WANDERD
```
        THERE BY THE RIVER-BANKS HE WANDERD ON    .  .  .  .       11 MYCERINUS        85
        THE SCARED GLENS WE WANDERD ON  .  .  .  .  .  .  .        27 NEW SIRENS       30
        WHICH YOUR LOVERS WANDERD DOWN  .  .  .  .  .  .  .        30 NEW SIRENS      126
        LONG WE WANDERD WITH YOU FEEDING      .  .  .  .  .        34 NEW SIRENS      235
        HAD WANDERD FORTH HER CHILDREN WERE AT PLAY  .  .  .      149 TRISTRAM 3        6
        SINGS HOW A KNIGHT HE WANDERD   .  .  .  .  .  .  .       159 NECKAN           17
        OR HAST THOU LONG SINCE WANDERD BACK  .  .  .  .  .       184 TERRACE BERNE    17
        THAT THOU WERT WANDERD FROM THE STUDIOUS WALLS           259 SCHOLAR-GIPSY   134
        WHY FAINTEST THOU I WANDERD TILL I DIED   .  .  .  .      269 THYRSIS         237
        FROM CHIEF TO CHIEF I WANDERD AT HIS SIDE    .  .  .      355 MEROPE          728
```

WANDEREDST
```
        THOU WANDEREDST WITH ME FOR A LITTLE HOUR    .  .  .      269 THYRSIS         212
```

WANDERER
```
        A FOILD CIRCUITOUS WANDERER TILL AT LAST     .  .  .       87 SOHRAB RUSTUM   888
        WAVE-TOSSD WANDERER    .  .  .  .  .  .  .  .  .  .       194 STRAYED REVEL   288
        O WANDERER FROM A GRECIAN SHORE       .  .  .  .  .       200 PHILOMELA         5
        A WANDERER IS MAN FROM HIS BIRTH      .  .  .  .  .       251 FUTURE            1
        AND PUT THE SHEPHERDS WANDERER ON THY TRACE  .  .        257 SCHOLAR-GIPSY    63
        AH DO NOT WE WANDERER AWAIT IT TOO    .  .  .  .  .       260 SCHOLAR-GIPSY   180
        KNOW HIM A WANDERER STILL THEN WHY NOT ME    .  .  .      268 THYRSIS         200
        A FRENZIED WANDERER A GOD-DRIVEN MAN  .  .  .  .  .       385 MEROPE         1424
        AND THE KIND CHANCE-ARRIVED WANDERER  .  .  .  .  .       399 MEROPE         1836
        THOU KNOWST ME FOR A WANDERER FROM OF OLD    .  .  .      428 EMPEDOCLES I 2  477
        THE INCESSANT WANDERER TAKES HIS WAY  .  .  .  .  .       484 ROME-SICKNESS    30
```

WANDERERS
```
        AUSTRIAN WANDERERS BRING O WARDERS    .  .  .  .  .        15 CHURCH BROU 1    79
        LIKE WANDERERS FROM THE WORLDS EXTREMITY     .  .  .       36 VOICE            30
```

WANDERING
```
        YOU LISTEN BUT THAT WANDERING SMILE  .  .  .  .  .         58 RESIGNATION     199
        AND THEN A SWARM OF WANDERING HORSE WHO CAME  .  .         64 SOHRAB RUSTUM   126
        NEAREST THE POLE AND WANDERING KIRGHIZZES    .  .  .       65 SOHRAB RUSTUM   133
        HIS WANDERING GUEST AND GAVE HIM HIS FAIR CHILD  .  .      79 SOHRAB RUSTUM   626
        SIGHTLESS AND HELPLESS WANDERING WEAK IN HEAVEN  .        98 BALDER DEAD 1    97
        WANDERING TOGETHER THROUGH THAT GLOOMY WORLD     .       104 BALDER DEAD 1   328
        HER LONG AGO THE WANDERING ODER TOOK  .  .  .  .  .       116 BALDER DEAD 3    93
        MY LONG-LOST WANDERING ODER THOU HAST MET    .  .  .      116 BALDER DEAD 3   101
        ONE DAY THE WANDERING ODER WILL RETURN    .  .  .  .      116 BALDER DEAD 3   115
        WANDERING THROUGH THEIR DROOPING SAILS    .  .  .  .      135 TRISTRAM 1      157
        ONE LITTLE WANDERING ARM IS THROWN    .  .  .  .  .       141 TRISTRAM 1      344
        WANDERING IN HEAVEN FAR REMOVED       .  .  .  .  .       181 ISOLATION MARG   27
        SOUND AS OF WANDERING BREEZE BUT SOUND    .  .  .  .      223 EPILOG LAOCOON   75
        AND WANDERING FROM THE STREAM THEY GO .  .  .  .         226 EPILOG LAOCOON  174
        BEFALLS ME WANDERING THROUGH THIS UPLAND DIM     .       263 THYRSIS          23
```

WARDER

SCANT SPACE THAT WARDER LEFT FOR PASSERS BY	• •	107 BALDER DEAD 2	90
HE SPAKE THE WARDER OF THE BRIDGE REPLIED	• • • •	108 BALDER DEAD 2	118

WARDERD

FROM THE DRAGON-WARDERD FOUNTAINS	• • • • • • •	27 NEW SIRENS	33

WARDERS

AUSTRIAN WANDERERS BRING O WARDERS	• • • • • •	15 CHURCH BROU 1	79
FROM THE GATE THE WARDERS ANSWERD	• • • • • •	15 CHURCH BROU 1	81

WARDS

THE GOTH BOUND ROME-WARDS SO THE HUN	• • • • • •	52 RESIGNATION	9

WARFARE

WARFARE OF MAN FROM HIS BIRTH	• • • • • • •	216 LORDS MESSENGER	3
DID ITS NOW SILENT WARFARE WAGE	• • • • • •	219 BACCHANALIA 2	20
ITS WARFARE WAGED WITH PAIN	• • • • • • • •	313 OBERMANN MORE	42

WARLIKE

TROY AND WARLIKE PRIAM TOO AND THE PEOPLE OF PRIAM		HOMER TRANS	22

WARM

AND LOOKING DOWN ON THE WARM ROSY TINTS	• • • •	18 CHURCH BROU 3	28
DREW A WARM SCENT ABROAD BEHIND THE PINES	• • • •	25 DREAM	6
LAY THE WARM GOLDEN GOURDS GOLDEN WITHIN	• • • •	25 DREAM	18
AND THOSE WARM LOCKS MEN WERE PRAISING	• • • •	30 NEW SIRENS	121
MUSED ON WARM THE HEART ANEW	• • • • • •	30 NEW SIRENS	134
WHERE THE WARM JUNE-WIND	• • • • • • •	51 CONSOLATION	42
HIS BED AND THE WARM RUGS WHEREON HE LAY	• •	63 SOHRAB RUSTUM	95
FOR THE WARM PERSIAN SEA-BOARD SO THEY STREAMD	• •	64 SOHRAB RUSTUM	116
AND WARM AND PLEASANT BUT THE GRAVE IS COLD	• •	71 SOHRAB RUSTUM	323
THE BIG WARM TEARS ROLLD DOWN AND CAKED THE SAND	•	82 SOHRAB RUSTUM	736
REGRETTING THE WARM MANSION WHICH IT LEFT	• • •	86 SOHRAB RUSTUM	855
TO RIGHT AND LEFT AND WARM STEAM FILLS THE AIR	•	107 BALDER DEAD 2	98
AND A WARM WEST-WIND BLOWS AND THAW SETS IN	• •	122 BALDER DEAD 3	309
LIKE HELPLESS BIRDS IN THE WARM NEST	• • • • •	140 TRISTRAM 1	328
WARM WITH THE WINTER-SUN OF BURNISHD GREEN	• • •	150 TRISTRAM 3	21
WARM IN THEIR MANTLES WRAPT THE THREE STOOD THERE		150 TRISTRAM 3	38
BUT STILL AS THEY PURSUED THEIR WARM DRY ROAD	• •	150 TRISTRAM 3	44
ONE APRIL WHEN THE WARM DAYS FIRST BEGAN	• • • •	154 TRISTRAM 3	160
WARM IN THEIR MANTLES WRAPT THE THREE STAYD THERE		TRISTRAM 3	V 38
NOR TO THE BROWN HEATHS ROUND THEM WARM AND WIDE	• •	TRISTRAM 3	V 49
ABOVE THE FRAGRANT WARM PROVENCAL SHORE	• • •	167 RACHEL 2	2
ON THE WARM GRASSY	• • • • • • • • •	190 STRAYED REVEL	137
SITTING ON THE WARM STEPS	• • • • • • •	194 STRAYED REVEL	271
ON THE WARM INGLE-BENCH THE SMOCK-FROCKD BOORS	•	256 SCHOLAR-GIPSY	59
AND WATCH THE WARM GREEN-MUFFLED CUMNER HILLS	•	257 SCHOLAR-GIPSY	69
THIS WINTER-EVE IS WARM	• • • • • • • •	263 THYRSIS	16
AND WHAT BUT NOBLE FEELING WARM	• • • • •	279 SOUTHERN NIGHT	130
RUFFLES THE WARM AFTERNOON	• • • • • • •	293 HEINES GRAVE	40
YET WARM IT MOUNTS THE HOUR OF LIFE	• • • • •	322 OBERMANN MORE	291
FOR COURTEOUS ENTERTAINMENT WELCOME WARM	• • •	356 MEROPE	760
THE ADRIATIC BREAKS IN A WARM BAY	• • • •	426 EMPEDOCLES I 2	428
BASK IN THE GLENS OR ON THE WARM SEA-SHORE	• • •	427 EMPEDOCLES I 2	437
AND GOODNESS WARM AND TRUTH WITHOUT ALLOY	• • •	446 WESTMIN ABBEY	78
WARM IN HER BREAST BY DAY	• • • • • • •	446 WESTMIN ABBEY	87
HERE WHERE THE GRASS IS SMOOTH AND WARM	• • • •	451 GEISTS GRAVE	66
FOUND HIM STIFF YOU SAY THOUGH WARM	• • • •	452 POOR MATTHIAS	3
VAINLY WARM HIM IN YOUR BREAST	• • • • • •	452 POOR MATTHIAS	9
TILL WHAT AT MORNINGS HOUR LOOKT WARM AND BRIGHT	• •	466 ALARIC AT ROME	107

WARMD

SOON THE PLANKD COTTAGE BY THE SUN-WARMD PINES	• •	25 DREAM	35
SOON THE PLANKD COTTAGE MID THE SUN-WARMD PINES	• •	25 DREAM	V 35
ABOVE HIS SUN-WARMD FIRS	• • • • • • •	313 OBERMANN MORE	34
FROM THE GRASSY SUN-WARMD PLACE	• • • • •	433 EMPEDOCLES II	161

WARMER

TO WARMER LANDS AND COASTS THAT KEEP THE SUN	• •	129 BALDER DEAD 3	562

WARMING

WARMING THEIR HEADS IN THE SUN	• • • • • • • •	297 HEINES GRAVE	157

WARMLY

THE CHILD SLEEPS WARMLY IN HIS BED	• • • • • •	249 KENSINGTON GARD	36

WARMTH

IN WARMTH LIGHT JOY	• • • • • • • •	52 CONSOLATION	70
THEY BRING US LIGHT AND WARMTH AND JOY	• • •	203 EUPHROSYNE	24
HATH NEITHER BEAUTY NOR WARMTH	• • • • • •	233 YOUTH OF MAN	30
HAS NEITHER BEAUTY NOR WARMTH	• • • • • •	233 YOUTH OF MAN	V 30
WHEN BLOOD AND WARMTH WERE FLED	• • • • •	319 OBERMANN MORE	194
WITH PASSIONATE WARMTH WE CLASP	• • • • •	424 EMPEDOCLES I 2	359
FAR FROM MY OWN SOUL FAR FROM WARMTH AND LIGHT	• •	440 EMPEDOCLES II	396

WARN

AH WARN SOME MORE AMBITIOUS HEART	• • • • • •	174 MEETING	15

WARND

AND WEAKNESS WARND HIM AND HE FEARD DECLINE	• •	447 WESTMIN ABBEY	123

WASTE   (CONTINUED)
```
      BY NASEBYS HILL OER MARSTONS HEATHY WASTE  .  .  .  .  476 CROMWELL              149
      IN A WASTE WOOD A SINGLE BOAT  .  .  .  .  .  .  .  .  479 HAYSWATER BOAT           4
```

WASTED
```
      WILL THE FIRE JOY HATH WASTED  .  .  .  .  .  .  .  .   30 NEW SIRENS             133
      NOT THIS FEVER-WASTED WIGHT  .  .  .  .  .  .  .  .  .  133 TRISTRAM 1             107
      DOWN ON HIS WASTED FINGERS RAIND  .  .  .  .  .  .  .  140 TRISTRAM 1             318
      TAKE MY HAND AND TOUCH THESE WASTED FINGERS  .  .  .  143 TRISTRAM 2              23
      THAT WASTED CHEEK  .  .  .  .  .  .  .  .  .  .  .  .  276 SOUTHERN NIGHT          44
      ENERGIES WASTED UNIMPROVED HOURS  .  .  .  .  .  .  .  470 ALARIC AT ROME         201
```

WASTES
```
      VAIN IT WASTES AND WE GREW WEARY  .  .  .  .  .  .  .   28 NEW SIRENS           V 67
      THE SOLEMN WASTES OF HEATHY HILL  .  .  .  .  .  .  .   55 RESIGNATION             96
      WASTES AND RUNS THINNER EVERY DAY  .  .  .  .  .  .  .   89 SICK KING BOKH          64
```

WASTING
```
      IF SADNESS AT THE LONG HEART-WASTING SHOW  .  .  .  .    7 REP FRIEND               9
      BETRAYD THEM AND OF WASTING AGE THEY DIED  .  .  .  .  109 BALDER DEAD 2          167
```

WATCH
```
      OER THE BRIDGE BIFROST WHERE IS HEIMDALLS WATCH  .  .   99 BALDER DEAD 1          141
      BUT HE MUST EVER WATCH THE NORTHERN BEAR  .  .  .  .    99 BALDER DEAD 1          155
      SLEEP ON I WATCH THEE AND AM HERE TO AID  .  .  .  .  103 BALDER DEAD 1          292
      AND OVER BIFROST WHERE IS HEIMDALLS WATCH  .  .  .  .  105 BALDER DEAD 2           22
      OER THE BRIDGE BIFROST WHERE IS HEIMDALLS WATCH  .  .  119 BALDER DEAD 3          216
      I WILL WATCH THEE TEND THEE SOOTHE THY PAIN  .  .  .  143 TRISTRAM 2              30
      THERE TO WATCH OER THE SUNK VALE  .  .  .  .  .  .  .  176 PARTING                 47
      TO WATCH THIS LINE OF SAND-HILLS RUN  .  .  .  .  .  .  204 CALAIS SANDS             2
      AND WATCH THEE PASS UNCONSCIOUS BY  .  .  .  .  .  .  205 CALAIS SANDS            28
      AND WATCH THY AIR AND GUESS THY THOUGHTS  .  .  .  .  205 CALAIS SANDS          V 29
      WHEN I WHO WATCH THEM AM AWAY  .  .  .  .  .  .  .  .  249 KENSINGTON GARD         30
      AND WATCH THE WARM GREEN-MUFFLED CUMNER HILLS  .  .  257 SCHOLAR-GIPSY           69
      TO WATCH THE THRESHERS IN THE MOSSY BARNS  .  .  .  .  258 SCHOLAR-GIPSY          104
      TURND ONCE TO WATCH WHILE THICK THE SNOWFLAKES FALL  259 SCHOLAR-GIPSY          128
      OR YET LATER IN WATCH  .  .  .  .  .  .  .  .  .  .  .  297 HEINES GRAVE           167
      BUT WE STAND MUTE AND WATCH THE WAVES  .  .  .  .  .  303 GRANDE CHARTR          126
      WE WATCH THOSE YELLOW TAPERS SHINE  .  .  .  .  .  .  305 GRANDE CHARTR          200
      BUT THEY STAND MUTE AND WATCH THE WAVES  .  .  .  .  303 GRANDE CHARTR        V 126
      WHO UNDER EARTH WATCH GUILTY DEEDS OF MEN  .  .  .  .  332 MEROPE                  74
      PEACE PEACE ALLS CLEAR THE WICKED WATCH AND WORK  .  365 MEROPE                 995
      COME HERMES WHO DOST WATCH THE UNJUSTLY KILLD  .  .  367 MEROPE               V1058
      AND I COULD WATCH HIM WITH HIS PROUD SAD FACE  .  .  408 EMPEDOCLES I 1          59
      THEN WATCH HIM FOR HE RANGES SWIFT AND FAR  .  .  .  409 EMPEDOCLES I 1          94
      TO WATCH MAN DOUBT AND FEAR  .  .  .  .  .  .  .  .  .  415 EMPEDOCLES I 2          88
      STILL TURND TO WATCH THE BATTLE STILL FORGOT  .  .  476 CROMWELL               171
```

WATCHD
```
      SATE AND WATCHD HER WORKING TRAIN  .  .  .  .  .  .  .   15 CHURCH BROU 1          94
      THERE SHE SATE AND WATCHD THE BUILDERS  .  .  .  .  .   16 CHURCH BROU 1         101
      SCARFD WITH THE CROSS WHO WATCHD THE MILES  .  .  .  .   52 RESIGNATION             5
      WATCHD MY LORDS COMING FORTH AND PUSHD  .  .  .  .  .   88 SICK KING BOKH          33
      BUT THROUGH THE DARK THEY WATCHD THE BURNING SHIP  .  119 BALDER DEAD 3          197
      WE WATCHD THE FOUNT OF FIERY LIFE  .  .  .  .  .  .  .  270 MEMORIAL VERSES         13
      HE WHO HATH WATCHD NOT SHARED THE STRIFE  .  .  .  .  309 OBERMANN               101
      AND WATCHD THE ROSY LIGHT  .  .  .  .  .  .  .  .  .  .  310 OBERMANN               122
      I WATCHD THE CROCUS FADE AND FLOWER  .  .  .  .  .  .  321 OBERMANN MORE          255
      AND SINCE HAS FONDLY WATCHD HIM NIGHT AND DAY  .  .  351 MEROPE                 618
      AND RESTING THERE TO BREATHE I WATCHD THE CHASE  .  .  357 MEROPE                 797
      THE GUARD-WATCHD BEAR  .  .  .  .  .  .  .  .  .  .  .  393 MEROPE                1678
      WHERE OFT WE WATCHD THY COUCHANT FORM  .  .  .  .  .  451 GEISTS GRAVE            68
      SAD FACES WATCHD AROUND HIM AND HIS BREATH  .  .  .  .  478 CROMWELL               207
```

WATCHER
```
      I A FADED WATCHER BY THY PILLOW  .  .  .  .  .  .  .  144 TRISTRAM 2              61
      BUT ARE LOST WHEN THEIR WATCHER IS GONE  .  .  .  .  .  230 YOUTH OF NATURE         74
```

WATCHERS
```
      FROM THE WATCHERS ON THE MOUNTAINS  .  .  .  .  .  .  .   27 NEW SIRENS             35
      WATCHERS FOR A PURER FIRE  .  .  .  .  .  .  .  .  .  .   31 NEW SIRENS            140
      THE WATCHERS OF TWO ARMIES STAND  .  .  .  .  .  .  .   93 SICK KING BOKH         162
```

WATCHES
```
      WATCHES PALE BY TRISTRAMS BED  .  .  .  .  .  .  .  .  132 TRISTRAM 1              75
      STILL RULES STILL WATCHES AND NUMBRETH THE HOURS  .  .  347 MEROPE                 527
      STILL RULES STILL WATCHES AND NUMBERS THE HOURS  .  .  347 MEROPE               V 527
```

WATCHEST
```
      WATCHEST US NATURE THROUGHOUT  .  .  .  .  .  .  .  .  .  232 YOUTH OF MAN             9
```

WATCHFUL
```
      SAGACIOUS MEN OF IRON WATCHFUL FIRM  .  .  .  .  .  .  .  381 MEROPE                1304
```

WATCHING
```
      AND ON THE BRIDGE A DAMSEL WATCHING ARMD  .  .  .  .  107 BALDER DEAD 2           87
      WATCHING BY THE SALT SEA-TIDE  .  .  .  .  .  .  .  .  138 TRISTRAM 1             270
      THIS COMES OF NURSING LONG AND WATCHING LATE  .  .  .  140 TRISTRAM 1             313
      WATCHING HER CHILDREN PLAY THEIR LITTLE HANDS  .  .  150 TRISTRAM 3              24
      HAVE KNOWN THEE WATCHING ALL AN APRIL-DAY  .  .  .  .  258 SCHOLAR-GIPSY        V 107
```

WATCHING   (CONTINUED)
    WITH MOUNTAIN-TRAVEL AND NIGHT-WATCHING SPENT   • •   359 MEROPE   868
    YE LIE WATCHING FOR THE FOE OF YOUR KIN   • • • •   344 MEROPE   V 462
    WATCHING HOW THE WHETTING SPED • • • • • • • •   434 EMPEDOCLES II   164

WATER
    OF TORN-UP WATER ON THE MAIN   • • • • • • • •   40 HUMAN LIFE   20
    THAT THE GREEN WATER IN THE TANKS   • • • • • •   89 SICK KING BOKH   60
    WITH ALL THE WATER THAT WAS THERE   • • • • • •   90 SICK KING BOKH   69
    THE WATER-PITCHER WHERE IT STOOD   • • • • • •   90 SICK KING BOKH   78
    BRING WATER NARD AND LINEN ROLLS   • • • • • •   95 SICK KING BOKH   229
    FURROWD IT AND THE WATER GURGLED IN   • • • • •   118 BALDER DEAD 3   179
    CHILD TIS NO WATER THIS TIS POISOND WINE   • • •   133 TRISTRAM 1   V 103
    WHO COME AT NOON DOWN TO THE WATER HERE   • • •   155 TRISTRAM 3   194
    WHICH COME AT NOON DOWN TO THE WATER HERE   • • •   155 TRISTRAM 3   V 194
    DOWN AT THE WATER-SIDE   • • • • • • • •   194 STRAYED REVEL   266
    AH GLIMMERING WATER   • • • • • • • • •   194 STRAYED REVEL   283
    AND BRINGS THE WATER FROM THE FOUNT   • • • •   213 PROGRESS POESY   3
    AND DARTING SWALLOWS AND LIGHT WATER-GNATS   • •   266 THYRSIS   125
    MUSICAL WATER HALF-HID   • • • • • • • •   297 HEINES GRAVE   161
    IN A THOUSAND WATER-BREAKS LIGHT   • • • • •   297 HEINES GRAVE   184
    AND SHED THEIR BLOOD LIKE WATER IN OUR CAUSE   • •   337 MEROPE   227
    WHERE FIRST THE STAG TOOK WATER FLOATED STILL   • •   358 MEROPE   844
    THE TALL CRESTED WATER-REEDS   • • • • • • • •   434 EMPEDOCLES II   174
    OUR BLOOD TO WATER   • • • • • • • • • •   439 EMPEDOCLES II   334
    BLACK CHAFING WATER AND AFLOAT   • • • • • •   479 HAYSWATER BOAT   2
    ALL ELSE BLACK WATER AND AFLOAT   • • • • • •   479 HAYSWATER BOAT   15

WATERD
    OUR FATHERS WATERD WITH THEIR TEARS   • • • • •   303 GRANDE CHARTR   121
    THEIR FATHERS WATERD WITH THEIR TEARS   • • • •   303 GRANDE CHARTR   V 121
    OF ALL THE WOODY HIGH WELL-WATERD DELLS   • • • •   414 EMPEDOCLES I 2   42

WATERING
    AND SAW THE NORNIES WATERING THE ROOTS   • • • •   120 BALDER DEAD 3   221
    PAMISUS WATERING THE MESSENIAN PLAIN • • • • •   330 MEROPE   19

WATERS
    AT THE SLEEPLESS WATERS   • • • • • • • • • •   35 VOICE   5
    THE SWINGING WATERS AND THE CLUSTERD PIER   • • •   42 GIPSY CHILD   6
    GAY SHINE THE WATERS AND THE CLUSTERD PIER   • • •   41 GIPSY CHILD   V 6
    HIS LUMINOUS HOME OF WATERS OPENS BRIGHT   • • •   87 SOHRAB RUSTUM   890
    STILL CARRIED OER THE DISTANT WATERS ON   • • •   119 BALDER DEAD 3   198
    GOD TIS HER FACE PLAYS IN THE WATERS BRIGHT   • •   139 TRISTRAM 1   284
    TWO SAINTS MET OFTEN WHERE THOSE WATERS FLOW   • •   170 EAST AND WEST   4
    AND ON THE SPARKLING WATERS PLAYD   • • • • •   223 EPILOG LAOCOON   67
    BY THE FAVOURITE WATERS OF RUTH   • • • • •   229 YOUTH OF NATURE   24
    COLD PLASHING PAST IT CRYSTAL WATERS ROLL   • • •   236 PALLADIUM   11
    AH ONCE MORE I CRIED YE STARS YE WATERS   • • •   240 SELF-DEPENDENCE   9
    AND THE WIDTH OF THE WATERS THE HUSH • • • • •   254 FUTURE   78
    OER THE BLUE MIDLAND WATERS WITH THE GALE   • • •   262 SCHOLAR-GIPSY   244
    SHE KNEW THE DORIAN WATERS GUSH DIVINE   • • •   265 THYRSIS   94
    MEDITERRANEAN WATERS LAVE • • • • • • • •   275 STANZAS CARNAC   39
    SUCH BY THESE WATERS OF ROMANCE   • • • • • •   279 SOUTHERN NIGHT   111
    WHAT ELSE IS ALL THESE WATERS ARE   • • • • •   279 SOUTHERN NIGHT   133
    GENTLY BY HIS YE WATERS GLIDE   • • • • • • •   279 SOUTHERN NIGHT   138
    LAKE LEMANS WATERS FAR BELOW   • • • • • • •   310 OBERMANN   121
    AT LAST THE CRY DREW TO THE WATERS EDGE   • • •   357 MEROPE   806
    THERE THE LAKE-WATERS WHICH IN AGES GONE   • • •   358 MEROPE   814
    WHICH STYXS AWFUL WATERS TRICKLE DOWN   • • • •   368 MEROPE   1065
    MOST BEAUTIFUL OF WATERS • • • • • • • • •   391 MEROPE   1609
    IN THE RIPPLED WATERS GREY   • • • • • • •   433 EMPEDOCLES II   134
    THAT MILD AND LUMINOUS FLOOR OF WATERS LIVES   • •   438 EMPEDOCLES II   315
    THE SUNNY WATERS HOLD THEIR JOYOUS WAY   • • •   469 ALARIC AT ROME   196
    SMOTE LIKE THE RUSH OF WATERS ON HIS EAR   • • •   475 CROMWELL   136
    TO THE VEXD WATERS OF A MOUNTAIN LAKE   • • • •   477 CROMWELL   192
    SPRANG FROM ITS SLEEP AND LO THE WATERS ROLL   • •   479 CROMWELL   236
    THE GREY-STREAKD WATERS LABOUR STILL • • • • •   479 HAYSWATER BOAT   18
    AND STRUCK AND OER US THE SEA-WATERS SPREAD   • •   484 S S LUSITANIA   8

WATERSHED
    IS BUT A QUIET WATERSHED • • • • • • • • • •   59 RESIGNATION   259

WATERY
    TO HEM HIS WATERY MARCH AND DAM HIS STREAMS   • •   87 SOHRAB RUSTUM   882
    OCEAN WHOSE WATERY RING ENFOLDS THE WORLD   • • •   99 BALDER DEAD 1   160
    AND MANY A STRETCH OF WATERY SAND   • • • • •   141 TRISTRAM 1   369
    DOTTING THE SHORELESS WATERY WILD   • • • • •   182 TO MARG CONT   3
    NOW ROUND US SPREADS THE WATERY PLAIN   • • • •   182 TO MARG CONT   17
    AND THERE ACROSS THE WATERY WAY   • • • • • •   274 STANZAS CARNAC   25

WATTLED
    AND ROUND THEM STILL THE WATTLED HURDLES HUNG   • •   109 BALDER DEAD 2   173
    GO SHEPHERD AND UNTIE THE WATTLED COTES   • • • •   255 SCHOLAR-GIPSY   2

WAVD
    WHICH WAVD AND ON THEIR SHOULDERS FLUTTERING PLAYD   25 DREAM   V 25

WAVE
    LIKE THE WAVE   • • • • • • • • • • • • •   44 QUESTION   2

WAVE   (CONTINUED)
POISED ON THE TOP OF A HUGE WAVE OF FATE . . . . .   72 SOHRAB RUSTUM   391
FAR FROM THE KIND SEA-WAVE   . . . . . .   159 NECKAN   16
FAR FROM THE GREEN SEA WAVE   . . . .   159 NECKAN   V 16
WHO SINS ONCE WASHD BY THE BAPTISMAL WAVE   .   172 GOOD SHEPHERD   5
WAVE-TOSSD WANDERER   . . . .   194 STRAYED REVEL   288
THEIR FEET FROM ITS ALLURING WAVE   . . . .   226 EPILOG LAOCOON   166
TALL GRASSES AND WHITE FLOWERING NETTLES WAVE   259 SCHOLAR-GIPSY   139
WAVE US AWAY AND KEEP THY SOLITUDE   . . . . .   261 SCHOLAR-GIPSY   210
INTO THE WORLD AND WAVE OF MEN DEPART   . . .   264 THYRSIS   39
O ROTHA WITH THY LIVING WAVE   . . . . . .   272 MEMORIAL VERSES   72
IT LAY BESIDE THE ATLANTIC WAVE   . . . . .   273 STANZAS CARNAC   6
HOME ROUND INTO THE ENGLISH WAVE   . . . .   275 STANZAS CARNAC   37
OERFROWNS THE WAVE   . . . .   276 SOUTHERN NIGHT   24
AND FROM THE WAVE-KISSD MARBLE STAIR   . . .   278 SOUTHERN NIGHT   106
BURIED A WAVE BENEATH   . . . .   308 OBERMANN   74
THE SECOND WAVE SUCCEEDS BEFORE   . . . . .   308 OBERMANN   75
WHERE WITH CLEAR-RUSTLING WAVE   . . . . .   311 OBERMANN   166
THE BLUE SEINE ROLLS HER WAVE   . . . . .   312 OBERMANN   178
THE SEINE CONDUCTS HER WAVE   . . . . . .   312 OBERMANN   V 178
HAD STOOD AGAINST THE WAVE   . . . . . .   317 OBERMANN MORE   146
ONE COMMON WAVE OF THOUGHT AND JOY   . . .   323 OBERMANN MORE   323
ONE MIGHTY WAVE OF THOUGHT AND JOY   . . .   323 OBERMANN MORE   V 323
ON THE BLACK WAVE BORNE TO AND FRO   . . . .   370 MEROPE   1119
LIKE A SEA-WAVE BETWIXT THE WORLD AND THEE   .   436 EMPEDOCLES II   231
WHY SPEEDST THOU NOT THY DEATHLIKE WAVE TO SHED   462 ALARIC AT ROME   3
OF THE HOARSE ONSET OF THE SURGING WAVE   . . .   466 ALARIC AT ROME   110
IF WREATHS MAY TWINE FOR YOU OR LAURELS WAVE .   467 ALARIC AT ROME   137
TO MARK WITH SHIVERD CREST THE REELING WAVE   .   472 CROMWELL   23
BY HILL OR WAVE THE MOUNTAIN OR THE SHORE   . .   472 CROMWELL   30
AND THE WINDS TOLD HIS GLORY AND THE WAVE   . .   476 CROMWELL   157

WAVED
THEIR LIPS MOVED THEIR WHITE ARMS WAVED EAGERLY . .   25 DREAM   28
OF HORSEHAIR WAVED A SCARLET HORSEHAIR PLUME   . .   69 SOHRAB RUSTUM   269
HE SPOKE AND WAVED FAREWELL AND GAVE HIS HAND   . .   129 BALDER DEAD 3   549
NINE TIMES SHE WAVED THE FLUTTERING WIMPLE ROUND .   156 TRISTRAM 3   219
IT GREEND IT BRANCHD IT WAVED   . . . . . .   160 NECKAN   54
WHICH HID ULYSSES WAVED ITSELF AND SAID   . . .   484 S S LUSITANIA   2

WAVER
YE FADE YE SWIM YE WAVER BEFORE ME   . . . . .   194 STRAYED REVEL   290
DID I THEN WAVER   . . . .   398 MEROPE   1794

WAVERING
OUR WAVERING MANY-COLOURD LINE   . . . . . .   54 RESIGNATION   61
GIVE TO THE WIND THEIR WAVERING SPIRES   . . .   55 RESIGNATION   117
FLING THEIR WAVERING LIGHTS   . . . .   253 FUTURE   73
A FEEBLE WAVERING LINE   . . . .   291 RUGBY CHAPEL   173
STRENGTHEN THE WAVERING LINE   . . . . . .   292 RUGBY CHAPEL   205
EXPECT NO WAVERING NO RETREAT NO CHANGE   . . .   342 MEROPE   378

WAVES
ON THE WILD WHIRLING WAVES MOURNFULLY MOURNFULLY . .   35 VOICE   7
LIKE BRIGHT WAVES THAT FALL   . . . .   36 VOICE   17
PLUNGING ALL DAY IN THE BLUE WAVES AT NIGHT   . .   69 SOHRAB RUSTUM   287
BACK OUT TO SEA TO THE DEEP WAVES OF DEATH   . .   73 SOHRAB RUSTUM   395
HAVE WADED FOREMOST IN THEIR BLOODY WAVES   . .   74 SOHRAB RUSTUM   434
OH THAT ITS WAVES WERE FLOWING OVER ME   . . .   83 SOHRAB RUSTUM   768
THE LONGD-FOR DASH OF WAVES IS HEARD AND WIDE .   87 SOHRAB RUSTUM   889
BETWEEN THE WAVES AND BLACK OERHANGING CLIFFS   97 BALDER DEAD 1   79
AND CAME AGAIN DOWN TO THE ROARING WAVES   . . .   101 BALDER DEAD 1   199
AND THE SHIP FLOATED ON THE WAVES AND ROCKD   .   118 BALDER DEAD 3   180
OF THE NEAR WAVES CAME SADLY GRAND   . . . .   137 TRISTRAM 1   217
ON THE WAVES OF THE TOSSD FIGHT   . . . . .   138 TRISTRAM 1   266
IN THE WAVES OF THE TOSSD FIGHT   . . . . .   138 TRISTRAM 1   V 266
DRAGGING THEIR NETS THROUGH THE ROUGH WAVES AFAR .   151 TRISTRAM 3   80
AND TAKES IT IN HER HAND AND WAVES IT OVER   . .   156 TRISTRAM 3   217
FROM THE SEA-WAVES I COME   . . . .   159 NECKAN   26
I SAID GO UP DEAR HEART THROUGH THE WAVES   . . .   163 FORSAKEN MERM   60
WILL HEAR THE WAVES ROAR   . . . .   164 FORSAKEN MERM   115
THE WAVES ROAR AND WHIRL   . . . .   165 FORSAKEN MERM   117
WAVES THY WHITE ROBE   . . . .   186 STRAYED REVEL   22
THE FAVOURD GUEST OF CIRCE BROUGHT BY THE WAVES .   189 STRAYED REVEL   110
FLOW THE COOL LAKE-WAVES   . . . .   190 STRAYED REVEL   160
OF PARNES WHERE THY WAVES   . . . .   197 FRAG ANTIGONE   62
OF PEBBLES WHICH THE WAVES DRAW BACK AND FLING .   211 DOVER BEACH   10
OF PEBBLES WHICH THE WAVES SUCK BACK AND FLING .   211 DOVER BEACH   V 10
IN TORRENTS IN WAVES   . . . .   220 BACCHANALIA 2   30
LIGHT-PLASHING WAVES AN ANSWER MADE   . . . .   223 EPILOG LAOCOON   68
THE MURMUR OF ITS WAVES DOTH HEAR   . . . . .   226 EPILOG LAOCOON   180
THEN FROM ITS BRIMMING WAVES THEIR EYE   . . .   227 EPILOG LAOCOON   193
BACKWARD AND FORWARD ROLLD THE WAVES OF FIGHT   .   236 PALLADIUM   7
THE WAVES OF MOURNFUL THOUGHT BY WHICH THEY ARE PREST 243 SUMMER NIGHT   48
THE FRESHENING WIND AND BLACKENING WAVES   . . . .   244 SUMMER NIGHT   61
THE YOUNG LIGHT-HEARTED MASTERS OF THE WAVES   .   262 SCHOLAR-GIPSY   241
MORE THAN HE ASKS WHAT WAVES   . . . . . .   288 RUGBY CHAPEL   69
BUT WE STAND MUTE AND WATCH THE WAVES   . . . .   303 GRANDE CHARTR   126
DEEP DEEP THE GREENWOOD ROUND THEM WAVES   . . .   305 GRANDE CHARTR   173
BUT THEY STAND MUTE AND WATCH THE WAVES   . . .   303 GRANDE CHARTR   V 126

WAVES   (CONTINUED)
          THE RIPPLES OF WHOSE BLUE WAVES CHEER   • • • •   311 OBERMANN   163
          IN THE STORMY DESOLATE WAVES • • • • • • • •   361 MEROPE   911
          AND FIRE REPEL US FROM ITS LIVING WAVES   • • •   439 EMPEDOCLES II   363
          AND THE ROUGH WAVES OF LIFE FOR EVER LAID • • • •   449 WESTMIN ABBEY   165
          HIGH FATE IS THEIRS YE SLEEPLESS WAVES WHOSE EAR • •   471 CROMWELL   1
          AROUND WHOSE FEET THE EXULTING WAVES HAVE SUNG •   472 CROMWELL   13
          DID THE WAVES CHAUNT THEIR SONG OF LIBERTY • • • •   472 CROMWELL   16
          TILL ALL BRIGHT THOUGHTS THAT HILLS OR WAVES CAN YIELD   472 CROMWELL   33
          DEEP ON HIS LIFE AND CHILDHOODS BABY WAVES . • • •   473 CROMWELL   48
          ON LIFES WILD WAVES THE LIVING AND THE LOST   •   474 CROMWELL   78
          AMID THE WILD WAVES WELTERING • • • • • • • •   479 HAYSWATER BOAT   8

WAVING
          THE BOUNDLESS WAVING GRASS-PLAINS STRETCH THICK-STARRD   191 STRAYED REVEL   168
          WAVING HER HUNDRED HANDS A TORCH IN EACH • • • •   395 MEROPE   1735
          WAVING HER MYRIADS OF WHITE FAIRY BLOOMS   • • •   EVERLASTING SUB   6

WAVST
          WHAT WAVST THOU OFF THAT MURDEROUS AXE AWAY   • •   376 MEROPE   1215

WAXD
          AND WHEN THE MIRTH WAXD LOUDEST WITH DULL SOUND • •   12 MYCERINUS   123
          WHO SINCE IN YOUR DESPITE HATH WAXD AMAIN • • • •   110 BALDER DEAD 2   210

WAXES
          AND THE NIGHT WAXES AND THE SHADOWS FALL   • • • •   10 MYCERINUS   72

WAXING
          WHEN THE MIND WAXING CLEARER SEES GOD NO NEARER • •   38 STAGIRIUS   V 16

WAY
          THAT THOU CANST HEAR AND HEARING HOLD THY WAY • •   3 EMERSONS ESSAYS   2
          GIRT WITH A THRONG OF REVELLERS BENT HIS WAY   • •   11 MYCERINUS   83
          HO THIS WAY YE LAGGARD HUNTERS • • • • • • •   14 CHURCH BROU 1   43
          CLIMB THE WINDING MOUNTAIN-WAY • • • • • • • •   15 CHURCH BROU 1   86
          DOWN THE MOUNTAIN-WAY   • • • • • • • •   17 CHURCH BROU 2   27
          WHO WHEN SHIPS ARE THAT WAY TENDING • • • • •   26 NEW SIRENS   13
          COULD LIFE RUN NO HAPPIER WAY • • • • • • •   33 NEW SIRENS   200
          WHEN THE SLOW TIDE SETS ONE WAY   • • • • •   33 NEW SIRENS   220
          COULD LIFE RUN NO EASIER WAY   • • • • • • •   33 NEW SIRENS   V 200
          TO TOO EXACT A STEERING OF OUR WAY • • • • •   40 HUMAN LIFE   9
          TOOK THEN ITS ALL-SEEN WAY   • • • • • • •   45 IN UTRUMQUE PAR   7
          AND MANY A MILE OF DUSTY WAY   • • • • • • •   54 RESIGNATION   80
          THE LOOSE DARK STONES ON THE GREEN WAY • • • •   55 RESIGNATION   100
          IN THEIR HEREDITARY WAY • • • • • • • •   56 RESIGNATION   139
          A BELT OR SWORD PERHAPS AND GO HIS WAY • • • •   71 SOHRAB RUSTUM   354
          WAS CHOKED WITH RAGE AT LAST THESE WORDS BROKE WAY   74 SOHRAB RUSTUM   456
          FROM HUNTING AND A GREAT WAY OFF DESCRIES • • •   78 SOHRAB RUSTUM   562
          MAY SEE MY TOMB A GREAT WAY OFF AND CRY   • • •   84 SOHRAB RUSTUM   791
          MAY SEE MY TOMB A GREAT WAY OFF AND SAY   • • •   84 SOHRAB RUSTUM   V 791
          AS THE LAW IS AND GO YOUR WAY • • • • • • •   87 SICK KING BOKH   9
          ARE THIS WAY BRINGING THE DEAD MAN   • • • • •   88 SICK KING BOKH   19
          AND THROUGH THE SQUARE HIS WAY HE TOOK • • • •   89 SICK KING BOKH   49
          OF SAMARCAND IS BROUGHT THIS WAY   • • • • •   89 SICK KING BOKH   63
          YET IF HE SEEK TO FLY GIVE WAY • • • • • • •   91 SICK KING BOKH   115
          BUT FATE WITHSTANDS AND LAWS FORBID THIS WAY • •   98 BALDER DEAD 1   127
          YET IN MY SECRET MIND ONE WAY I KNOW   • • • •   99 BALDER DEAD 1   128
          WHAT WAY IS THIS O MOTHER THAT THOU SHOWST • • •   99 BALDER DEAD 1   132
          WHO GOES THAT WAY MUST TAKE NO OTHER HORSE • • •   99 BALDER DEAD 1   137
          WHO TELLS THE PASSING TROOPS OF DEAD THEIR WAY • •   99 BALDER DEAD 1   150
          BARRING HIS WAY AND IN THE WALL A GRATE • • • •   100 BALDER DEAD 1   167
          MOTHER A DREADFUL WAY IS THIS THOU SHOWST • • •   100 BALDER DEAD 1   185
          TO ASGARD AND DECLARST THIS HIDDEN WAY • • • •   100 BALDER DEAD 1   190
          THY WAY AND THIS AT LEAST MY PRAYERS AVAIL • • •   104 BALDER DEAD 1   309
          WHICH TOOK ON BALDERS TRACK THE WAY BELOW • • •   104 BALDER DEAD 1   341
          THERE IS A WAY WHICH LEADS TO HELAS REALM • • •   99 BALDER DEAD 1   V 135
          AND ON THE RIDGE A WAGGON CHOKES THE WAY   • • •   107 BALDER DEAD 2   94
          SO ON THE BRIDGE THAT DAMSEL BLOCKD THE WAY • •   107 BALDER DEAD 2   99
          BOUND ON THEIR WAY BELOW TO HELAS REALM • • •   107 BALDER DEAD 2   105
          BALDER HATH GONE THIS WAY AND TAEN THE ROAD   •   108 BALDER DEAD 2   122
          BUT NORTHWARD HERMOD RODE THE WAY BELOW • • •   108 BALDER DEAD 2   138
          BARRING HIS WAY AND IN THE WALL A GRATE • • • •   109 BALDER DEAD 2   145
          THEY GO THE ERRAND AND THE WAY IS KNOWN • • •   110 BALDER DEAD 2   191
          WORSE WAS THAT WAY TO GO THAN TO RETURN • • •   113 BALDER DEAD 2   291
          AND LED THE WAY ON SLEIPNER AND THE REST • • •   115 BALDER DEAD 3   59
          UNKNOWN AND LONG AND HAPLY ON THAT WAY • • • •   116 BALDER DEAD 3   100
          BETHINK YE GODS IS THERE NO OTHER WAY • • • •   120 BALDER DEAD 3   236
          SPEAK WERE NOT THIS A WAY THE WAY FOR GODS • • •   120 BALDER DEAD 3   237
          SPEAK WERE NOT THIS A WAY THE WAY FOR GODS • • •   120 BALDER DEAD 3   237
          BUT NORTHWARD HERMOD RODE THE WAY BELOW • •   124 BALDER DEAD 3   374
          THE WAY HE KNEW AND TRAVERSED GIALLS STREAM   •   124 BALDER DEAD 3   375
          WERE FEET LIKE THOSE MADE FOR SO WILD A WAY • •   135 TRISTRAM 1   163
          THEN WENT MY WAY TO KILL AND LIE   • • • • •   158 SAINT BRANDAN   59
          THIS WAY THIS WAY • • • • • • • • •   161 FORSAKEN MERM   9
          THIS WAY THIS WAY • • • • • • • • • •   161 FORSAKEN MERM   9
          THIS WAY THIS WAY • • • • • • • • • •   162 FORSAKEN MERM   19
          THIS WAY THIS WAY • • • • • • • • • •   162 FORSAKEN MERM   19
          WHEN DID MUSIC COME THIS WAY   • • • • • •   162 FORSAKEN MERM   46
          A PROP GAVE WAY CRASH FELL A PLATFORM LO   • • •   166 AUSTERITY POET   8

WAY   (CONTINUED)
      WE LEAVE THE BRUTAL WORLD TO TAKE ITS WAY   . . .   172 IMMORTALITY   2
      SWEET NOTES THIS WAY   . . . .   175 PARTING   24
      SWEET LIPS THIS WAY   . . . .   176 PARTING   42
      IN THE WALLD CITIES THE WAY PASSES THROUGH   . . .   193 STRAYED REVEL   250
      THIS WAY AT NOON   . . . .   193 STRAYED REVEL   264
      ON THE HEIGHT OF THEIR BOLD-FOLLOWD WAY   . . . .   216 LORDS MESSENGER V 17
      FOR ILL-ENDOWD FOR SUCH A WAY   . . . . .   226 EPILOG LAOCOON   171
      NO PAINTER YET HATH SUCH A WAY   . . . . . .   227 EPILOG LAOCOON   201
      FOR ILL PREPARED FOR SUCH A WAY   . . . . .   226 EPILOG LAOCOON   V 171
      TO CLEAR THE NEW WORLDS WAY   . . . . 237 PROGRESS   16
      WAY AFTER WAY CHANGES THAT NEVER CEASE   . . . .   239 REVOLUTIONS   7
      WAY AFTER WAY CHANGES THAT NEVER CEASE   . . . .   239 REVOLUTIONS   7
      OVER THE LIT SEAS UNQUIET WAY   . . . . . .   240 SELF-DEPENDENCE   14
      AWHILE HE HOLDS SOME FALSE WAY UNDEBARRD   . . . . 244 SUMMER NIGHT   59
      PURSUE WITH INDISCERNIBLE FLOW ITS WAY   . . . . 246 BURIED LIFE   40
      MET HIM AND OF HIS WAY OF LIFE ENQUIRED   . . . . 256 SCHOLAR-GIPSY   43
      OR CROSS A STILE INTO THE PUBLIC WAY   . . . . .   257 SCHOLAR-GIPSY   85
      WHERE MOST THE GIPSIES BY THE TURF-EDGED WAY . . . 258 SCHOLAR-GIPSY   112
      AND LONG THE WAY APPEARS WHICH SEEMD SO SHORT . . . 267 THYRSIS   141
      AND SOON THY FOOT RESUMED ITS WANDERING WAY   . . . 269 THYRSIS   229
      AND THERE ACROSS THE WATERY WAY   . . . . .   274 STANZAS CARNAC   25
      WITH STAFF AND GOURD HIS WAY DID BEND   . . . . 278 SOUTHERN NIGHT   81
      COME TO THE END OF OUR WAY   . . . .   289 RUGBY CHAPEL   108
      AH BUT THE WAY IS SO LONG   . . . .   291 RUGBY CHAPEL   176
      POET THE WORLD TO THY WAY   . . . .   295 HEINES GRAVE   107
      MOUNTS UP THE STONY FOREST-WAY   . . . . 300 GRANDE CHARTR   20
      AND THROUGH THE WOOD ANOTHER WAY   . . . . .   305 GRANDE CHARTR   181
      AND THROUGH THE WOODS ANOTHER WAY   . . . . .   305 GRANDE CHARTR   V 181
      SAVE THE TO SEE THEIR WAY   . . . .   307 OBERMANN   48
      WHOM MANY A DIFFERENT WAY   . . . .   311 OBERMANN   146
      AND STONY MOUNTS THE WAY . . . .   312 OBERMANN MORE   10
      ALONG THE APPIAN WAY   . . . .   315 OBERMANN MORE   100
      SIMPLY THE WAY DIVINE   . . . .   319 OBERMANN MORE   188
      WE JUDGED THE BEST CHANCE FINDS NO BETTER WAY . . . 331 MEROPE   36
      WHEN IT SHOULD PLUCK THEE FROM THY HOSTILE WAY . .   333 MEROPE   99
      DIZZY THE PATH AND PERILOUS THE WAY   . . . . .   341 MEROPE   368
      IN THE THIRD GENERATION THE WAY   . . . . 343 MEROPE   412
      SHE LED THE WAY OF DEATH . . . .   344 MEROPE   434
      THE ALL-WEPT WAY   . . . .   344 MEROPE   448
      THE ALL-WEPT WAY   . . . .   345 MEROPE   468
      BUT VENGEANCE TRAVELS IN A DANGEROUS WAY   . . . . 349 MEROPE   580
      THAT WAY IS DUBIOUS FOR A MOTHERS PRAYER   . . . . 349 MEROPE   583
      AIR TO HIS UNWINGD FORM DENIES A WAY   . . . . .   351 MEROPE   624
      MORE THAN ALL SECRETS HID THE WAY IT KEEPS . . . . 352 MEROPE   631
      THE BEST THEN TO THE THRONE MAY CARVE HIS WAY . .   352 MEROPE   658
      THAT HE TO POWER MAKES WAY BY ARMS   . . . . .   353 MEROPE   681
      CROWND WITH SUCCESS NOT IN MY WAY BUT HEAVENS . .   360 MEROPE   878
      APPOINTS THE WAY TO PEACE THROUGH SHEDDING BLOOD .   378 MEROPE   1248
      HATE DUTY INTEREST PASSION CALL ONE WAY   . . . . 383 MEROPE   1382
      I LOATHE FOR HIM THE SLIPPERY WAY OF BLOOD . . . . 387 MEROPE   1464
      WHICH WAY TO LEAN I KNOW NOT BLOODY STROKES   . . . 388 MEROPE   1521
      OF SACRIFICE HIS GUARDS CLEARING THE WAY   . . . . 401 MEROPE   1904
      COULD FIND NO WAY TO FOUND THEM SURE AS THIS . . . 403 MEROPE   1960
      THE TRUE ONE OF A MAN WHAT WAY OF LIFE   . . . . 404 MEROPE   1992
      BUT HIDE THEE IN THE ROCKS A GREAT WAY DOWN   . . . 409 EMPEDOCLES I 1   96
      THE CATTLE LOVE TO GATHER ON THEIR WAY   . . . . 413 EMPEDOCLES I 2   38
      AN UNIMPEDED WAY   . . . .   420 EMPEDOCLES I 2   250
      BUT WE AN EASIER WAY TO CHEAT OUR PAINS HAVE FOUND   421 EMPEDOCLES I 2   271
      THEIR WAY THROUGH LIFE AND BOW   . . . . 425 EMPEDOCLES I 2   389
      O SAGE O SAGE TAKE THEN THE ONE WAY LEFT   . . . . 429 EMPEDOCLES II   24
      HAUGHTILY ANOTHER WAY   . . . .   433 EMPEDOCLES II   160
      BRING HIM TO POISE THERE IS NO OTHER WAY   . . . . 436 EMPEDOCLES II   234
      AND THITHERWARD THE STRANGER TOOK HIS WAY . . . . 445 WESTMIN ABBEY   33
      FOR THIS AND THAT WAY SWINGS   . . . . 448 WESTMIN ABBEY   151
      QUICK RAISED TO ASK WHICH WAY WE GO   . . . . .   451 GEISTS GRAVE   50
      FIRST THE INEVITABLE WAY . . . .   454 POOR MATTHIAS   80
      DOWN THE UNCOMPANIOND WAY   . . . .   458 POOR MATTHIAS   209
      SWEPT FROM THY WALLS O ROME ON ITS TRIUMPHANT WAY   465 ALARIC AT ROME   78
      THINK YE THE AVENGER LOITERS ON HIS WAY   . . . . 466 ALARIC AT ROME   116
      THE SUNNY WATERS HOLD THEIR JOYOUS WAY   . . . . 469 ALARIC AT ROME   196
      FAR DOWN THE TORRENT CLEAVES ITS WAY   . . . . .   479 HAYSWATER BOAT   10
      THE INCESSANT WANDERER TAKES HIS WAY   . . . . .   484 ROME-SICKNESS   30
      THIS WAY MOVES AND PAUSES GAZES   . . . . .   META CLOISTER   11
      THIS WAY MOVES AND PAUSES GAZING   . . . . .   META CLOISTER   V 11

WAYFARER
      IN THE PLACE WHERE THE WAYFARER ONCE . . . . .   289 RUGBY CHAPEL   96
      A STRANGE WAYFARER COMING TO HIS SIDE   . . . . 444 WESTMIN ABBEY   23

WAYFARING
      SOUNDS SUCH AS ERST THE LONE WAYFARING MAN . . . . 473 CROMWELL   39

WAYS
      HAVE YOU TRACKD ITS CLOUDED WAYS   . . . . . .   33 NEW SIRENS   208
      WHO TREADS AT EASE LIFES UNCHEERD WAYS   . . . .   59 RESIGNATION   237
      THEIR ERRANDS TO EACH OTHER OR THE WAYS   . . . . 110 BALDER DEAD 2   190
      THEY ASK NOT KINDNESS GENTLE WAYS   . . . . .   178 FAREWELL   25
      AND WE WHOSE WAYS WERE UNLIKE HERE   . . . . . . 180 FAREWELL   73
      COULD FROM EARTHS WAYS THAT FIGURE SLIGHT . . . . 184 TERRACE BERNE   29

WAYS   (CONTINUED)
          AND BLUE-BELLS TREMBLING BY THE FOREST-WAYS   • •   265 THYRSIS   75
          POACH THE DEEP WAYS COMING DOWN   • • • • •   282 HAWORTH CHURCH   59
          FOR THE WORLD LOVES NEW WAYS   • • • • • •   307 OBERMANN   42
          WAYS FOR THE PASTURING KINE   • • • • • •   312 OBERMANN MORE   16
          WAYS FOR THE TINKLING KINE   • • • • • • •   312 OBERMANN MORE   V 16
          NOT TILL THE WAYS OF PRUDENCE ALL ARE TRIED   • •   384 MEROPE   1386
          WE MARK NOT THE WORLDS WAYS BUT WOULD HAVE   419 EMPEDOCLES I 2   V 221
             IT LEARN OURS
          THEIR THOUGHTS THEIR WAYS THEIR WISHES ARE NOT THINE   429 EMPEDOCLES II   19
          ONLY FOUR YEARS THOSE WINNING WAYS   • • • • •   450 GEISTS GRAVE   5
          SUCH WAYS SUCH ARTS SUCH LOOKS HADST THOU   • • •   451 GEISTS GRAVE   44
          A LIFE WHOSE WAYS NO HUMAN THOUGHT COULD SCAN   • •   478 CROMWELL   219

WAYSIDE
          THAT WAYSIDE INN WE LEFT TO-DAY   • • • • • •   53 RESIGNATION   41

WE
          WE ASK AND ASK THOU SMILEST AND ART STILL   • • • •   2 SHAKESPEARE   2
          GODS ARE WE BARDS SAINTS HEROES IF WE WILL   • • •   4 EMERSONS ESSAYS   13
          GODS ARE WE BARDS SAINTS HEROES IF WE WILL   • • •   4 EMERSONS ESSAYS   13
          SEEING THIS VALE THIS EARTH WHEREON WE DREAM   • • •   7 REP FRIEND CONT   5
          SPARING US NARROWER MARGIN THAN WE DEEM   • • •   7 REP FRIEND CONT   8
          AND THE GREAT POWERS WE SERVE THEMSELVES MAY BE   • •   10 MYCERINUS   41
          STRINGING VAIN WORDS OF POWERS WE CANNOT SEE   • •   10 MYCERINUS   51
          WE WILL BUILD THE CHURCH AGAIN   • • • • •   15 CHURCH BROU 1   76
          SAY WHAT IS THIS WE ARE IN BLISS FORGIVEN   • • •   18 CHURCH BROU 3   30
          LAST NIGHT WE STOOD EARNESTLY TALKING TOGETHER   •   19 MODERN SAPPHO   9
          AH RETAIN WE ALL WE CAN   • • • • • • •   24 MEMORY-PICTURE   60
          AH RETAIN WE ALL WE CAN   • • • • • • •   24 MEMORY-PICTURE   60
          WAS IT A DREAM WE SAILD I THOUGHT WE SAILD   • • •   24 DREAM   1
          WAS IT A DREAM WE SAILD I THOUGHT WE SAILD   • • •   24 DREAM   1
          WE SHOT BENEATH THE COTTAGE WITH THE STREAM   • •   25 DREAM   20
          FLASHD ONCE LIKE FALLING STREAMS WE ROSE WE GAZED   25 DREAM   29
          FLASHD ONCE LIKE FALLING STREAMS WE ROSE WE GAZED   25 DREAM   29
          AND WE TOO FROM UPLAND VALLEYS   • • • • • •   27 NEW SIRENS   25
          THE SCARED GLENS WE WANDERD ON   • • • • • •   27 NEW SIRENS   30
          WE ARE EXILES WE ARE FALLING   • • • • • •   27 NEW SIRENS   37
          WE ARE EXILES WE ARE FALLING   • • • • • •   27 NEW SIRENS   37
          WE HAVE LOST THEM AT YOUR CALL   • • • • •   27 NEW SIRENS   38
          THAT WE SOUGHT YOU WITH REJOICINGS   • • • • •   27 NEW SIRENS   45
          TILL AT EVENING WE DESCRY   • • • • • •   27 NEW SIRENS   46
          AND WE PLEAD AS STAUNCH ADHERENCE   • • • • •   28 NEW SIRENS   59
          AH WE OWN DIVINER FEATURES   • • • • • •   28 NEW SIRENS   63
          TIME IS LAME AND WE GREW WEARY   • • • • • •   28 NEW SIRENS   67
          ONLY WHAT WE FEEL WE KNOW   • • • • • • •   29 NEW SIRENS   84
          ONLY WHAT WE FEEL WE KNOW   • • • • • • •   29 NEW SIRENS   84
          THESE WE HAD AND WE GAVE TRULY   • • • • • •   34 NEW SIRENS   231
          THESE WE HAD AND WE GAVE TRULY   • • • • • •   34 NEW SIRENS   231
          DOUBT NOT WHAT WE HAD WE GAVE   • • • • • •   34 NEW SIRENS   232
          DOUBT NOT WHAT WE HAD WE GAVE   • • • • • •   34 NEW SIRENS   232
          FALSE WE WERE NOT NOR UNRULY   • • • • •   34 NEW SIRENS   233
          LONG WE WANDERD WITH YOU FEEDING   • • • • •   34 NEW SIRENS   235
          BUT WE TURN OUR EYES ARE FLITTING   • • • • •   34 NEW SIRENS   241
          AND WE PLEAD AS FIRM ADHERENCE   • • • • • •   28 NEW SIRENS   V 59
          TIME IS LAME AND WE GROW WEARY   • • • • •   28 NEW SIRENS   V 67
          VAIN IT WASTES AND WE GREW WEARY   • • • • •   28 NEW SIRENS   V 67
          VAIN IT WORE AND WE GREW WEARY   • • • • • •   28 NEW SIRENS   V 67
          WHEREIN WE LANGUISH   • • • • • • • •   38 STAGIRIUS   9
          WHEREIN WE LIE ASLEEP   • • • • • • • •   38 STAGIRIUS   11
          AY WE WOULD EACH FAIN DRIVE   • • • • • • •   40 HUMAN LIFE   13
          WE RUSH BY COASTS WHERE WE HAD LIEF REMAIN   • • • •   40 HUMAN LIFE   17
          WE RUSH BY COASTS WHERE WE HAD LIEF REMAIN   • • • •   40 HUMAN LIFE   17
          EVEN SO WE LEAVE BEHIND   • • • • • • • •   41 HUMAN LIFE   25
          WE STEM ACROSS THE SEA OF LIFE BY NIGHT   • • • •   41 HUMAN LIFE   27
          THE FRIENDS TO WHOM WE HAD NO NATURAL RIGHT   • •   41 HUMAN LIFE   29
          WE STEM ACROSS THE SEA BY NIGHT   • • • • •   41 HUMAN LIFE   V 27
          WE COUNT THE HOURS THESE DREAMS OF OURS   • • • •   44 QUESTION   15
          DO WE GO HENCE AND FIND THEY ARE NOT DEAD   • • • •   44 QUESTION   17
          JOYS WE DIMLY APPREHEND   • • • • • • • •   44 QUESTION   18
          SHALL WE FOLLOW   • • • • • • • • • •   44 QUESTION   21
          SHALL WE GO HENCE AND FIND THEY ARE NOT DEAD   • •   44 QUESTION   V 17
          ARE WHAT WE MEAN TO BE   • • • • • • • •   46 WORLD QUIETIST   8
          OR WHAT WE FIX WITH FOREIGN POWERS   • • • • •   47 HORATIAN ECHO   3
          IF FRANCE AND WE ARE REALLY FRIENDS   • • • • •   47 HORATIAN ECHO   4
          MOURN WILL WE NOT YOUR CLOSING HOUR   • • • • •   48 HORATIAN ECHO   10
          WITH READIER TONGUE THAN WE   • • • • • •   48 HORATIAN ECHO   18
          THE DAY APPROACHES WHEN WE MUST   • • • • • •   48 HORATIAN ECHO   31
          WE LEFT JUST TEN YEARS SINCE YOU SAY   • • • • •   53 RESIGNATION   40
          THAT WAYSIDE INN WE LEFT TO-DAY   • • • • • •   53 RESIGNATION   41
          OUR JOVIAL HOST AS FORTH WE FARE   • • • • • •   53 RESIGNATION   42
          ALL PAST AND THROUGH THE TREES WE GLIDE   • • • •   54 RESIGNATION   58
          THOSE UPPER REGIONS WE MUST TREAD   • • • • •   54 RESIGNATION   65
          THROUGH THE DEEP NOONTIDE HEATS WE FARE   • • • •   54 RESIGNATION   69
          LINGERING WE FOLLOW DOWN WE GAIN   • • • • •   54 RESIGNATION   78
          LINGERING WE FOLLOW DOWN WE GAIN   • • • • •   54 RESIGNATION   78
          PARCHD AND ROAD-WORN WE MADE THAT DAY   • • • •   54 RESIGNATION   81
          WE BATHED OUR HANDS WITH SPEECHLESS GLEE   • • • •   54 RESIGNATION   84
          ONCE MORE WE TREAD THIS SELF-SAME ROAD   • • • •   55 RESIGNATION   86
          FAUSTA WHICH TEN YEARS SINCE WE TROD   • • • • •   55 RESIGNATION   87
          ALONE WE TREAD IT YOU AND I   • • • • • • •   55 RESIGNATION   88

WE   (CONTINUED)

HERE SIT WE AND AGAIN UNROLL	55 RESIGNATION	94
THESE ARE NOT CHANGED AND WE YOU SAY	55 RESIGNATION	106
THE GIPSIES WHOM WE MET BELOW	55 RESIGNATION	108
HE ESCAPES THENCE BUT WE ABIDE	58 RESIGNATION	213
THE WORLD IN WHICH WE LIVE AND MOVE	58 RESIGNATION	215
THIS WORLD IN WHICH WE DRAW OUR BREATH	59 RESIGNATION	229
CROWD AS WE WILL ITS NEUTRAL SPACE	59 RESIGNATION	258
ENOUGH WE LIVE AND IF A LIFE	60 RESIGNATION	261
YET FAUSTA THE MUTE TURF WE TREAD	60 RESIGNATION	265
CROWD AS WE WILL ITS NEUTRAL ROOM	59 RESIGNATION	V 258
YET CHAMPION HAVE WE NONE TO MATCH THIS YOUTH	66 SOHRAB RUSTUM	176
LET SOHRAB ARM AND WE WILL FIND A MAN	66 SOHRAB RUSTUM	186
COME DOWN AND HELP US RUSTUM OR WE LOSE	67 SOHRAB RUSTUM	219
BUT RUSTUM IS FAR HENCE AND WE STAND HERE	72 SOHRAB RUSTUM	384
FOR WE ARE ALL LIKE SWIMMERS IN THE SEA	72 SOHRAB RUSTUM	390
WE KNOW NOT AND NO SEARCH WILL MAKE US KNOW	73 SOHRAB RUSTUM	396
COME PLANT WE HERE IN EARTH OUR ANGRY SPEARS	74 SOHRAB RUSTUM	439
FATHERS WE MUST HAVE WIFE AND CHILD	92 SICK KING BOKH	149
THAT THOUGH WE TAKE WHAT WE DESIRE	94 SICK KING BOKH	211
THAT THOUGH WE TAKE WHAT WE DESIRE	94 SICK KING BOKH	211
WE MUST NOT SNATCH IT EAGERLY	94 SICK KING BOKH	212
THAT THOUGH WE SNATCH WHAT WE DESIRE	94 SICK KING BOKH	V 211
THAT THOUGH WE SNATCH WHAT WE DESIRE	94 SICK KING BOKH	V 211
BUT OURS WE SHALL NOT MEET WHEN THAT DAY COMES	96 BALDER DEAD 1	31
WHY SHOULD WE MEET ANOTHERS PORTION SO	96 BALDER DEAD 1	33
THE FOE THE ACCUSER WHOM THOUGH GODS WE HATE	96 BALDER DEAD 1	38
THE FOE THE ACCUSER WHOM THOUGH GODS WE HATE	98 BALDER DEAD 1	101
WOULD THAT OURSELVES O BALDER WE WERE BORNE	101 BALDER DEAD 1	216
BUT EVEN THERE O NANNA WE MIGHT FIND	104 BALDER DEAD 1	326
AND TALKING OF THE LIFE WE LED IN HEAVEN	104 BALDER DEAD 1	329
WHILE WE YET LIVED AMONG THE OTHER GODS	104 BALDER DEAD 1	330
THOU KNOWST THOU KNOWST WHAT GRIEF WE HAVE IN HEAVEN	110 BALDER DEAD 2	192
TILL THEN IN PERIL OR IN PAIN WE LIVE	111 BALDER DEAD 2	225
HOWBEIT WE ABIDE OUR DAY TILL THEN	111 BALDER DEAD 2	227
WE DO NOT AS SOME FEEBLER HATERS DO	111 BALDER DEAD 2	228
ENEMY MOCKER WHOM THOUGH GODS WE HATE	114 BALDER DEAD 3	22
OUT OF OUR SIGHT THAT WE MAY TURN FROM GRIEF	115 BALDER DEAD 3	55
THEN WE SHALL MISS THY COUNSEL AND THY ARM	115 BALDER DEAD 3	70
FOR WE LOSE HIM WHO SMOOTHED ALL STRIFE IN HEAVEN	116 BALDER DEAD 3	88
WHOM WE MAY BID TO SING THOUGH THOU ART GONE	117 BALDER DEAD 3	134
AND ALL THESE GLADLY WHILE WE DRINK WE HEAR	117 BALDER DEAD 3	135
AND ALL THESE GLADLY WHILE WE DRINK WE HEAR	117 BALDER DEAD 3	135
SUCH AS ON EARTH WE VALIANTLY HAVE WAGED	117 BALDER DEAD 3	139
THOK NOT FOR GIBES WE COME WE COME FOR TEARS	123 BALDER DEAD 3	346
THOK NOT FOR GIBES WE COME WE COME FOR TEARS	123 BALDER DEAD 3	346
THERE RE-ASSEMBLING WE SHALL SEE EMERGE	128 BALDER DEAD 3	527
BUT WE IN HEAVEN SHALL FIND AGAIN WITH JOY	128 BALDER DEAD 3	532
FAMILIAR HALLS WHERE WE HAVE SUPPD OF OLD	128 BALDER DEAD 3	534
AND WE SHALL TREAD ONCE MORE THE WELL-KNOWN PLAIN	128 BALDER DEAD 3	537
THE GOLDEN DICE WHEREWITH WE PLAYD OF YORE	128 BALDER DEAD 3	539
THE GOLDEN DICE WITH WHICH WE PLAYD OF YORE	128 BALDER DEAD 3	V 539
TRISTRAM SWEET LOVE WE ARE BETRAYD OUT-PLANND	135 TRISTRAM 1	167
WE CANNOT KEEP HIM NOW AS THEN	138 TRISTRAM 1	244
WHAT NEW CHANGE SHALL WE NOW SEE	139 TRISTRAM 1	296
I AM HERE WE MEET I HOLD THY HAND	142 TRISTRAM 2	8
JOIND WE ARE HENCEFORTH NOR WILL THY PEOPLE	144 TRISTRAM 2	57
BUT SINCE LIVING WE WERE UNUNITED	145 TRISTRAM 2	91
FOOL THOU MISSEST WE ARE BOTH UNMOVD	146 TRISTRAM 2	V 100
AND LETS US BE WHAT WE WERE ONCE NO MORE	153 TRISTRAM 3	115
NO WE MAY SUFFER DEEPLY YET RETAIN	153 TRISTRAM 3	116
TILL FOR ITS SAKE ALONE WE LIVE AND MOVE	153 TRISTRAM 3	129
ALL WHICH WE DID BEFORE SHADOW AND DREAM	153 TRISTRAM 3	132
ALL THAT WE DID BEFORE SHADOW AND DREAM	153 TRISTRAM 3	V 132
MOTHER DEAR WE CANNOT STAY	162 FORSAKEN MERM	20
WE HEARD THE SWEET BELLS OVER THE BAY	162 FORSAKEN MERM	31
IN THE CAVERNS WHERE WE LAY	162 FORSAKEN MERM	32
CHILDREN DEAR WERE WE LONG ALONE	163 FORSAKEN MERM	64
COME I SAID AND WE ROSE THROUGH THE SURF IN THE BAY	163 FORSAKEN MERM	67
WE WENT UP THE BEACH BY THE SANDY DOWN	163 FORSAKEN MERM	68
BUT WE STOOD WITHOUT IN THE COLD BLOWING AIRS	163 FORSAKEN MERM	73
WE CLIMBD ON THE GRAVES ON THE STONES WORN WITH RAINS	163 FORSAKEN MERM	74
AND WE GAZED UP THE AISLE THROUGH THE SMALL LEADED PANES	163 FORSAKEN MERM	75
SHE SATE BY THE PILLAR WE SAW HER CLEAR	163 FORSAKEN MERM	76
MARGARET HIST COME QUICK WE ARE HERE	163 FORSAKEN MERM	77
DEAR HEART I SAID WE ARE LONG ALONE	163 FORSAKEN MERM	78
WE SHALL SEE WHILE ABOVE US	165 FORSAKEN MERM	116
UP THE CREEKS WE WILL HIE	165 FORSAKEN MERM	133
WE WILL GAZE FROM THE SAND-HILLS	165 FORSAKEN MERM	136
OUR FREEDOM FOR A LITTLE BREAD WE SELL	169 WORLDLY PLACE	5
WHO RATES US IF WE PEER OUTSIDE OUR PEN	169 WORLDLY PLACE	7
CHRIST SOME ONE SAYS WAS HUMAN AS WE ARE	170 BETTER PART	3
WE LIVE NO MORE WHEN WE HAVE DONE OUR SPAN	171 BETTER PART	5
WE LIVE NO MORE WHEN WE HAVE DONE OUR SPAN	171 BETTER PART	5
LIVE WE LIKE BRUTES OUR LIFE WITHOUT A PLAN	171 BETTER PART	8
IF WE THEN TOO CAN BE SUCH MEN AS HE	171 BETTER PART	14
WE LEAVE THE BRUTAL WORLD TO TAKE ITS WAY	172 IMMORTALITY	2
AND PATIENCE IN ANOTHER LIFE WE SAY	172 IMMORTALITY	3
THE WORLD SHALL BE THRUST DOWN AND WE UP-BORNE	172 IMMORTALITY	4
YET WE HER MEMORY AS SHE PRAYD WILL KEEP	173 MONICAS PRAYER	13

WE   (CONTINUED)

LOCKD IN EACH OTHERS ARMS WE STOOD	178	FAREWELL	11
WE SCHOOL OUR MANNERS ACT OUR PARTS	179	FAREWELL	45
AND THOUGH WE WEAR OUT LIFE ALAS	179	FAREWELL	49
IN BEATING WHERE WE MUST NOT PASS	179	FAREWELL	51
IN SEEKING WHAT WE SHALL NOT FIND	179	FAREWELL	52
YET WE SHALL ONE DAY GAIN LIFE PAST	179	FAREWELL	53
WE SHALL NOT THEN DENY A COURSE	179	FAREWELL	57
WE SHALL NOT THEN CALL HARDNESS FORCE	179	FAREWELL	59
THEN WE SHALL KNOW OUR FRIENDS THOUGH MUCH	179	FAREWELL	65
AND WE WHOSE WAYS WERE UNLIKE HERE	180	FAREWELL	73
WE WERE APART YET DAY BY DAY	180	ISOLATION MARG	1
WE MORTAL MILLIONS LIVE ALONE	182	TO MARG CONT	4
FOR SURELY ONCE THEY FEEL WE WERE	182	TO MARG CONT	15
AND WE FORGET BECAUSE WE MUST	183	ABSENCE	11
AND WE FORGET BECAUSE WE MUST	183	ABSENCE	11
AND NOT BECAUSE WE WILL	183	ABSENCE	12
WHILE WE RANGE THE WOODLAND	188	STRAYED REVEL	73
TO BECOME WHAT WE SING	193	STRAYED REVEL	234
BY CITY AND HOUSEHOLD GROUPD WE LIVE AND MANY SHOCKS	195	FRAG ANTIGONE	20
WHILE WE FOR HOPELESS PASSION DIE	202	URANIA	6
AH MAY SHE SCORN THEM STILL TILL WE	202	URANIA	15
ONE OF SOME BETTER RACE THAN WE	202	URANIA	V 18
ONE OF SOME WORTHIER RACE THAN WE	202	URANIA	V 18
SHE SMILES ELSEWHERE WE MAKE A DIN	204	EUPHROSYNE	V
EACH ON HIS OWN STRICT LINE WE MOVE	206	TOO LATE	1
THEN WHEN WE MEET AND THY LOOK STRAYS TOWARD ME	206	SEPARATION	13
THEN WHEN WE MEET AND THY LOOK STRAYS TOWARDS ME	206	SEPARATION	V 13
SAY WHAT BLINDS US THAT WE CLAIM THE GLORY	209	SELF-DECEPTION	1
BUT BEFORE WE WOKE ON EARTH WE WERE	209	SELF-DECEPTION	4
BUT BEFORE WE WOKE ON EARTH WE WERE	209	SELF-DECEPTION	4
MANS NEW SPIRIT SINCE IT WAS NOT WE	210	SELF-DECEPTION	14
AND ON EARTH WE WANDER GROPING REELING	210	SELF-DECEPTION	21
WE BUT DREAM WE HAVE OUR WISHD-FOR POWERS	210	SELF-DECEPTION	25
WE BUT DREAM WE HAVE OUR WISHD-FOR POWERS	210	SELF-DECEPTION	25
ENDS WE SEEK WE NEVER SHALL ATTAIN	210	SELF-DECEPTION	26
ENDS WE SEEK WE NEVER SHALL ATTAIN	210	SELF-DECEPTION	26
SOME END IS THERE WE INDEED MAY GAIN	210	SELF-DECEPTION	28
MANS BLANK SPIRIT SINCE IT WAS NOT WE	210	SELF-DECEPTION	V 14
OF HUMAN MISERY WE	211	DOVER BEACH	18
AND WE ARE HERE AS ON A DARKLING PLAIN	212	DOVER BEACH	35
BUT NOW WE ONLY HEAR	211	DOVER BEACH	V 24
AH TIS NOT WHAT IN YOUTH WE DREAMD TWOULD BE	212	GROWING OLD	12
AND NOT ONCE FEEL THAT WE WERE EVER YOUNG	212	GROWING OLD	22
AND FEEL BUT HALF AND FEEBLY WHAT WE FEEL	213	GROWING OLD	27
WHEN WE ARE FROZEN UP WITHIN AND QUITE	213	GROWING OLD	32
TOO LONG LET WE THEM GROAN	216	LORDS MESSENGER	4
ONE MORN AS THROUGH HYDE PARK WE WALKD	221	EPILOG LAOCOON	1
MY FRIEND AND I BY CHANCE WE TALKD	221	EPILOG LAOCOON	2
AND AFTER WE AWHILE HAD GONE	221	EPILOG LAOCOON	4
WHILE THUS MY FRIEND DISCOURSED WE PASS	222	EPILOG LAOCOON	36
STILL WE WALKD ON IN THOUGHTFUL MOOD	223	EPILOG LAOCOON	61
AND NOW UPON THE BRIDGE WE STOOD	223	EPILOG LAOCOON	62
ONWARD WE MOVED AND REACHD THE RIDE	224	EPILOG LAOCOON	107
WE HEARD AFAR FAINT MUSIC PLAY	224	EPILOG LAOCOON	110
WELL MAY WE MOURN WHEN THE HEAD	229	YOUTH OF NATURE	48
WHICH WE SAW WITH HIS EYES AND WERE GLAD	229	YOUTH OF NATURE	55
O CHARM O ROMANCE THAT WE FEEL	230	YOUTH OF NATURE	64
WE O NATURE DEPART	232	YOUTH OF MAN	1
SEEST US CHANGE WHILE WE LIVE	232	YOUTH OF MAN	6
WELL FOR US THAT WE CHANGE	232	YOUTH OF MAN	11
WE ARE YOUNG AND THE WORLD IS OURS	233	YOUTH OF MAN	26
BUT LEAVE US NOT WHILE WE LIVE	234	YOUTH OF MAN	60
WE VISIT IT BY MOMENTS AH TOO RARE	236	PALLADIUM	12
WE SHALL RENEW THE BATTLE IN THE PLAIN	236	PALLADIUM	13
THEN WE SHALL RUST IN SHADE OR SHINE IN STRIFE	236	PALLADIUM	17
AND FANCY THAT WE PUT FORTH ALL OUR LIFE	236	PALLADIUM	19
AND WHEN IT FAILS FIGHT AS WE WILL WE DIE	236	PALLADIUM	23
AND WHEN IT FAILS FIGHT AS WE WILL WE DIE	236	PALLADIUM	23
AND WHILE IT LASTS WE CANNOT WHOLLY END	236	PALLADIUM	24
AND WE MUST LEAVE THE OLD FAITHS AND WALK THEREIN	237	PROGRESS	26
AH WE SHALL KNOW THAT WELL WHEN IT COMES NEAR	239	REVOLUTIONS	19
WE CANNOT KINDLE WHEN WE WILL	241	MORALITY	1
WE CANNOT KINDLE WHEN WE WILL	241	MORALITY	1
WE DIG AND HEAP LAY STONE ON STONE	241	MORALITY	8
WE BEAR THE BURDEN AND THE HEAT	241	MORALITY	9
ALL WE HAVE BUILT DO WE DISCERN	241	MORALITY	12
ALL WE HAVE BUILT DO WE DISCERN	241	MORALITY	12
YES YES WE KNOW THAT WE CAN JEST	245	BURIED LIFE	4
YES YES WE KNOW THAT WE CAN JEST	245	BURIED LIFE	4
WE KNOW WE KNOW THAT WE CAN SMILE	245	BURIED LIFE	5
WE KNOW WE KNOW THAT WE CAN SMILE	245	BURIED LIFE	5
WE KNOW WE KNOW THAT WE CAN SMILE	245	BURIED LIFE	5
BUT WE MY LOVE DOTH A LIKE SPELL BENUMB	245	BURIED LIFE	24
OUR HEARTS OUR VOICES MUST WE TOO BE DUMB	245	BURIED LIFE	25
AH WELL FOR US IF EVEN WE	245	BURIED LIFE	26
AND THAT WE SHOULD NOT SEE	246	BURIED LIFE	41
AND WE HAVE BEEN ON MANY THOUSAND LINES	246	BURIED LIFE	57
AND WE HAVE SHOWN ON EACH SPIRIT AND POWER	246	BURIED LIFE	58
BUT HARDLY HAVE WE FOR ONE LITTLE HOUR	246	BURIED LIFE	59

WE   (CONTINUED)

```
BEEN ON OUR OWN LINE HAVE WE BEEN OURSELVES      •  •   246 BURIED LIFE        60
AND LONG WE TRY IN VAIN TO SPEAK AND ACT      •  •  •  •  247 BURIED LIFE        64
OUR HIDDEN SELF AND WHAT WE SAY AND DO        •  •  •  •  247 BURIED LIFE        65
AND THEN WE WILL NO MORE BE RACKD       •  •  •  •  •  •  247 BURIED LIFE        67
AND WHAT WE MEAN WE SAY AND WHAT WE WOULD WE KNOW     •   247 BURIED LIFE        87
AND WHAT WE MEAN WE SAY AND WHAT WE WOULD WE KNOW     •   247 BURIED LIFE        87
AND WHAT WE MEAN WE SAY AND WHAT WE WOULD WE KNOW     •   247 BURIED LIFE        87
AND WHAT WE MEAN WE SAY AND WHAT WE WOULD WE KNOW     •   247 BURIED LIFE        87
BUT WE MY LOVE DOES A LIKE SPELL BENUMB       •  •  •  •  245 BURIED LIFE      V  24
AND WE HAVE SHOWN ON EACH TALENT AND POWER    •  •  •  •  246 BURIED LIFE      V  58
AND WE ON ITS BREAST OUR MINDS    •  •  •  •  •  •  •  •  253 FUTURE            55
ARE CONFUSED AS THE CRIES WHICH WE HEAR    •  •  •  •  •  253 FUTURE            56
CHANGING AND SHOT AS THE SIGHTS WHICH WE SEE  •  •  •  •  253 FUTURE            57
AND WE SAY THAT REPOSE HAS FLED      •  •  •  •  •  •  •  253 FUTURE            58
BUT WHAT WAS BEFORE US WE KNOW NOT      •  •  •  •  •  •  253 FUTURE            69
AND WE KNOW NOT WHAT SHALL SUCCEED     •  •  •  •  •  •  253 FUTURE            70
TO THE JUST-PAUSING GENIUS WE REMIT    •  •  •  •  •  •  259 SCHOLAR-GIPSY     149
OUR WORN-OUT LIFE AND ARE WHAT WE HAVE BEEN     •  •  •  259 SCHOLAR-GIPSY     150
AND WE OURSELVES SHALL GO     •  •  •  •  •  •  •  •  •  259 SCHOLAR-GIPSY     156
AND WE IMAGINE THEE EXEMPT FROM AGE    •  •  •  •  •  •  259 SCHOLAR-GIPSY     158
BECAUSE THOU HADST WHAT WE ALAS HAVE NOT   •  •  •  •  •  259 SCHOLAR-GIPSY     160
THOU WAITEST FOR THE SPARK FROM HEAVEN AND WE   •  •  •  260 SCHOLAR-GIPSY     171
FOR WHOM EACH YEAR WE SEE    •  •  •  •  •  •  •  •  •  •  260 SCHOLAR-GIPSY     176
AH DO NOT WE WANDERER AWAIT IT TOO     •  •  •  •  •  •  260 SCHOLAR-GIPSY     180
YES WE AWAIT IT BUT IT STILL DELAYS    •  •  •  •  •  •  260 SCHOLAR-GIPSY     181
AND THEN WE SUFFER AND AMONGST US ONE     •  •  •  •  •  260 SCHOLAR-GIPSY     182
THIS FOR OUR WISEST AND WE OTHERS PINE    •  •  •  •  •  260 SCHOLAR-GIPSY     191
AND WE SHOULD WIN THEE FROM THY OWN FAIR LIFE    •  •  •  261 SCHOLAR-GIPSY     224
OUR WELL-WORN LIFE AND ARE WHAT WE HAVE BEEN    •  •  •  259 SCHOLAR-GIPSY   V 150
THYRSIS AND I WE STILL HAD THYRSIS THEN   •  •  •  •  •  263 THYRSIS            10
WE PRIZED IT DEARLY WHILE IT STOOD WE SAID    •  •  •  •  263 THYRSIS            28
WE PRIZED IT DEARLY WHILE IT STOOD WE SAID    •  •  •  •  263 THYRSIS            28
HERE TOO OUR SHEPHERD-PIPES WE FIRST ASSAYD   •  •  •  •  263 THYRSIS            35
SOON SHALL WE HAVE GOLD-DUSTED SNAPDRAGON   •  •  •  •  •  264 THYRSIS            64
AND WE SHALL HAVE HIM IN THE SWEET SPRING-DAYS  •  •  •  265 THYRSIS            73
BUT THYRSIS NEVER MORE WE SWAINS SHALL SEE    •  •  •  •  265 THYRSIS            77
AND WE SHOULD TEASE HER WITH OUR PLAINT IN VAIN   •  •  265 THYRSIS           100
WE TRACKD THE SHY THAMES SHORE     •  •  •  •  •  •  •  •  266 THYRSIS           126
ROAM ON THE LIGHT WE SOUGHT IS SHINING STILL    •  •  •  269 THYRSIS           238
WE STAND TO-DAY BY WORDSWORTHS TOMB    •  •  •  •  •  •  270 MEMORIAL VERSES     5
WE BOWD OUR HEAD AND HELD OUR BREATH   •  •  •  •  •  •  270 MEMORIAL VERSES     7
WITH SHIVERING HEART THE STRIFE WE SAW    •  •  •  •  •  270 MEMORIAL VERSES    10
WE WATCHD THE FOUNT OF FIERY LIFE      •  •  •  •  •  •  270 MEMORIAL VERSES    13
WHEN GOETHES DEATH WAS TOLD WE SAID    •  •  •  •  •  •  270 MEMORIAL VERSES    15
AH MAY YE FEEL HIS VOICE AS WE    •  •  •  •  •  •  •  •  271 MEMORIAL VERSES    41
HE LAID US AS WE LAY AT BIRTH    •  •  •  •  •  •  •  •  271 MEMORIAL VERSES    48
SMILES BROKE FROM US AND WE HAD EASE   •  •  •  •  •  •  271 MEMORIAL VERSES    50
WE STAND TO-DAY AT WORDSWORTHS TOMB    •  •  •  •  •  •  270 MEMORIAL VERSES  V   5
WE BOWD OUR HEADS AND HELD OUR BREATH      •  •  •  •  •  270 MEMORIAL VERSES  V   7
WHEN GOETHE PASSD AWAY WE SAID    •  •  •  •  •  •  •  •  270 MEMORIAL VERSES  V  15
WHERE WE HAD LONG BEEN DOOMD TO DWELL     •  •  •  •  •  271 MEMORIAL VERSES  V
ONCE MORE WE LAY AS ERST AT BIRTH      •  •  •  •  •  •  271 MEMORIAL VERSES  V  48
NO MORE AND WE RETAIN     •  •  •  •  •  •  •  •  •  •  •  273 EDW QUILLINAN      14
ALIVE WE WOULD HAVE CHANGED HIS LOT    •  •  •  •  •  •  273 EDW QUILLINAN      19
WE WOULD NOT CHANGE IT NOW    •  •  •  •  •  •  •  •  •  273 EDW QUILLINAN      20
THE MIEN OF YOUTH WE USED TO SEE    •  •  •  •  •  •  •  276 SOUTHERN NIGHT     38
IN CITIES SHOULD WE ENGLISH LIE      •  •  •  •  •  •  •  277 SOUTHERN NIGHT     61
WE WHO PURSUE     •  •  •  •  •  •  •  •  •  •  •  •  •  277 SOUTHERN NIGHT     64
BEFORE WE DIE   •  •  •  •  •  •  •  •  •  •  •  •  •  •  277 SOUTHERN NIGHT     72
FIRST TO THE LIVING WE PAY    •  •  •  •  •  •  •  •  •  281 HAWORTH CHURCH     34
TURN WE NEXT TO THE DEAD   •  •  •  •  •  •  •  •  •  •  282 HAWORTH CHURCH     47
HOW SHALL WE HONOUR THE YOUNG      •  •  •  •  •  •  •  282 HAWORTH CHURCH     48
CONSOLE WE CANNOT HER EAR     •  •  •  •  •  •  •  •  •  282 HAWORTH CHURCH     50
HER WHOM WE CANNOT SAVE   •  •  •  •  •  •  •  •  •  •  282 HAWORTH CHURCH    V
WHAT MIGHT WE SAY TO CONSOLE      •  •  •  •  •  •  •  •  282 HAWORTH CHURCH    V
IN THE GLOOM OF NOVEMBER WE PASSD      •  •  •  •  •  •  286 RUGBY CHAPEL       19
WE WHO TILL THEN IN THY SHADE    •  •  •  •  •  •  •  •  287 RUGBY CHAPEL       31
SUNSHINE AND RAIN AS WE MIGHT      •  •  •  •  •  •  •  287 RUGBY CHAPEL       34
WE WE HAVE CHOSEN OUR PATH    •  •  •  •  •  •  •  •  •  288 RUGBY CHAPEL       84
WE WE HAVE CHOSEN OUR PATH    •  •  •  •  •  •  •  •  •  288 RUGBY CHAPEL       84
CHEERFUL WITH FRIENDS WE SET FORTH     •  •  •  •  •  •  289 RUGBY CHAPEL       89
WE WE ONLY ARE LEFT   •  •  •  •  •  •  •  •  •  •  •  •  289 RUGBY CHAPEL      104
WE WE ONLY ARE LEFT   •  •  •  •  •  •  •  •  •  •  •  •  289 RUGBY CHAPEL      104
STERNLY COMPRESSD WE STRAIN ON     •  •  •  •  •  •  •  •  289 RUGBY CHAPEL      106
WHOM IN OUR PARTY WE BRING    •  •  •  •  •  •  •  •  •  289 RUGBY CHAPEL      115
WHOM WE HAVE LEFT IN THE SNOW      •  •  •  •  •  •  •  289 RUGBY CHAPEL      116
SADLY WE ANSWER WE BRING    •  •  •  •  •  •  •  •  •  •  289 RUGBY CHAPEL      117
SADLY WE ANSWER WE BRING    •  •  •  •  •  •  •  •  •  •  289 RUGBY CHAPEL      117
ONLY OURSELVES WE LOST    •  •  •  •  •  •  •  •  •  •  •  289 RUGBY CHAPEL      118
HARDLY OURSELVES WE FOUGHT THROUGH     •  •  •  •  •  •  289 RUGBY CHAPEL      120
STRIPPD WITHOUT FRIENDS AS WE ARE      •  •  •  •  •  •  289 RUGBY CHAPEL      121
WE WERE WEARY AND WE      •  •  •  •  •  •  •  •  •  •  290 RUGBY CHAPEL      128
WE WERE WEARY AND WE      •  •  •  •  •  •  •  •  •  •  290 RUGBY CHAPEL      128
FEARFUL AND WE IN OUR MARCH      •  •  •  •  •  •  •  •  290 RUGBY CHAPEL      129
THY SPIRIT OF THAT WE SAW    •  •  •  •  •  •  •  •  •  290 RUGBY CHAPEL      137
ENGLAND MY COUNTRY FOR WE    •  •  •  •  •  •  •  •  •  294 HEINES GRAVE       72
WE TOO SIGH THAT SHE FLAGS    •  •  •  •  •  •  •  •  •  294 HEINES GRAVE       76
WE TOO SAY THAT SHE NOW   •  •  •  •  •  •  •  •  •  •  294 HEINES GRAVE       77
SO WE ARRAIGN HER HER SONS     •  •  •  •  •  •  •  •  •  295 HEINES GRAVE       86
```

WE   (CONTINUED)

SHALL WE SELECT THAN POLYPHONTES WHAT   • • • •   390 MEROPE   1570
HAVE LEARND THAT WE MUST SACRIFICE THE BENT   • •   394 MEROPE   1711
LET US FORGET OURSELVES FOR THOSE WE RULE   • • • •   394 MEROPE   1721
TILL THEN WE ALL SEEMD STONE BUT THEN A CRY   • •   402 MEROPE   1930
MIGHT ASK WHY WE ENDURED THEIR YOKE SO LONG   •   402 MEROPE   1947
BUT THAT WE KNOW HOW EVERY PERILOUS FEAT   • • • •   402 MEROPE   1948
WHAT MOOD OF SPIRIT THEREFORE SHALL WE CALL   •   404 MEROPE   1991
TOGETHER WE HAD SPRUNG TOGETHER LIVED   • • • •   334 MEROPE   V 123
AS THOSE WITH WHICH WE TRY TO TEST   • • • • •   352 MEROPE   V 634
ON THE SAME SPUR WHERE WE HAD SATE AT MORN   • • •   357 MEROPE   V 796
TO ONE UNHAPPY HOUSE THE DEBT WE OWE   • • • •   367 MEROPE   V1048
HAVE LEARND THAT WE MUST SACRIFICE THE THIRST   • •   394 MEROPE   V1711
AND THE FEAST PAST ITS PRIME SO WE SLIPPD OUT   • •   407 EMPEDOCLES I 1   37
PLAY WHEN WE HALT AND WHEN THE EVENING COMES   •   409 EMPEDOCLES I 1   90
WHEN WE WERE GATHERD WITH PEISIANAX   • • •   410 EMPEDOCLES I 1   127
THE NOON IS HOT WHEN WE HAVE CROSSD THE STREAM   • •   412 EMPEDOCLES I 2   1
WE SHALL HAVE LEFT THE WOODY TRACT AND COME   • •   412 EMPEDOCLES I 2   2
AND WE WERE NOT SO FAR FROM HUMAN HAUNT   • • • •   412 EMPEDOCLES I 2   10
AND WE FEEL DAY AND NIGHT   • • • • • • •   416 EMPEDOCLES I 2   127
WE HAVE THE TRUTH THEY CRY   • • • • • • •   417 EMPEDOCLES I 2   139
BUT WE ARE ALL THE SAME THE FOOLS OF OUR OWN WOES   417 EMPEDOCLES I 2   166
WE MORTALS ARE NO KINGS   418 EMPEDOCLES I 2   177
NO WE ARE STRANGERS HERE THE WORLD IS FROM OF OLD   418 EMPEDOCLES I 2   181
LIMITS WE DID NOT SET   • • • • • • • •   418 EMPEDOCLES I 2   184
CONDITION ALL WE DO   • • • • • • • • •   418 EMPEDOCLES I 2   185
BORN INTO LIFE WE ARE AND LIFE MUST BE OUR MOULD   •   418 EMPEDOCLES I 2   186
BORN INTO LIFE WE BRING   • • • • • • • •   418 EMPEDOCLES I 2   192
AFFECTS US WE COME NEAR   • • • • • • •   418 EMPEDOCLES I 2   195
TO TUNES WE DID NOT CALL OUR BEING MUST KEEP CHIME   418 EMPEDOCLES I 2   196
BORN INTO LIFE TIS WE   • • • • • • • • •   419 EMPEDOCLES I 2   207
BUT WE AS SOME RUDE GUEST   • • • • • • •   419 EMPEDOCLES I 2   217
WE MARK NOT THE WORLDS COURSE BUT WOULD HAVE   419 EMPEDOCLES I 2   221
   IT TAKE OURS
WE SPURN IT AND INVENT   • • • • • • • • • •   419 EMPEDOCLES I 2   225
RICHES WE WISH TO GET   • • • • • • • • •   420 EMPEDOCLES I 2   227
WE WOULD HAVE HEALTH AND YET   • • • • • •   420 EMPEDOCLES I 2   229
WE WOULD HAVE INWARD PEACE   • • • • • •   420 EMPEDOCLES I 2   232
WE WOULD HAVE MISERY CEASE   • • • • • •   420 EMPEDOCLES I 2   234
WE WANT ALL PLEASANT ENDS BUT WILL USE NO HARSH MEANS   420 EMPEDOCLES I 2   236
WE DO NOT WHAT WE OUGHT   • • • • • • • •   420 EMPEDOCLES I 2   237
WE DO NOT WHAT WE OUGHT   • • • • • • • •   420 EMPEDOCLES I 2   237
WHAT WE OUGHT NOT WE DO   • • • • • • • •   420 EMPEDOCLES I 2   238
WHAT WE OUGHT NOT WE DO   • • • • • • • •   420 EMPEDOCLES I 2   238
BUT WE AN EASIER WAY TO CHEAT OUR PAINS HAVE FOUND   421 EMPEDOCLES I 2   271
WE PEOPLING THE VOID AIR   • • • • • • • •   421 EMPEDOCLES I 2   278
THE ILLS WE OUGHT TO BEAR   • • • • • • •   421 EMPEDOCLES I 2   280
GRANT THAT THE WORLD WERE FULL OF GODS WE CANNOT SEE   421 EMPEDOCLES I 2   286
THAT WE WHO RAIL ARE STILL   • • • • • •   422 EMPEDOCLES I 2   289
WITH WHAT WE RAIL AT ONE   • • • • • • •   422 EMPEDOCLES I 2   290
DO WE AT WILL INVENT   • • • • • • • • •   422 EMPEDOCLES I 2   309
BUT NEXT WE WOULD REVERSE   • • • • • • •   422 EMPEDOCLES I 2   312
AND WHAT WE MADE TO CURSE   • • • • • • •   422 EMPEDOCLES I 2   314
WE NOW WOULD LEAN UPON   • • • • • • • •   422 EMPEDOCLES I 2   315
AND WE WOULD KNOW IT ALL   • • • • • • •   423 EMPEDOCLES I 2   318
WE MAP THE STARRY SKY   • • • • • • • • •   423 EMPEDOCLES I 2   319
WE MINE THIS EARTHEN BALL   • • • • • • •   423 EMPEDOCLES I 2   320
WE MEASURE THE SEA-TIDES WE NUMBER THE SEA-SANDS   •   423 EMPEDOCLES I 2   321
WE MEASURE THE SEA-TIDES WE NUMBER THE SEA-SANDS   •   423 EMPEDOCLES I 2   321
WE SCRUTINISE THE DATES   • • • • • • • •   423 EMPEDOCLES I 2   322
WE SEARCH OUT DEAD MENS WORDS AND WORKS OF   423 EMPEDOCLES I 2   326
   DEAD MENS HANDS
WE SHUT OUR EYES AND MUSE   • • • • • • •   423 EMPEDOCLES I 2   327
BUT STILL AS WE PROCEED   • • • • • • • •   423 EMPEDOCLES I 2   332
WE REST OUR FACULTIES   • • • • • • • • •   423 EMPEDOCLES I 2   337
WHICH HENCEFORTH WE RESIGN   • • • • • •   423 EMPEDOCLES I 2   345
WITH PASSIONATE WARMTH WE CLASP   • • • • •   424 EMPEDOCLES I 2   359
NOW DO WE SOON PERCEIVE HOW FAST OUR YOUTH IS SPENT   424 EMPEDOCLES I 2   361
WE SEE IN BLANK DISMAY   • • • • • • • •   424 EMPEDOCLES I 2   363
WE PAUSE WE HUSH OUR HEART   • • • • • •   424 EMPEDOCLES I 2   372
WE PAUSE WE HUSH OUR HEART   • • • • • •   424 EMPEDOCLES I 2   372
FAILD TO FILL UP THE VOID WHICH IN OUR BREASTS WE BEAR   424 EMPEDOCLES I 2   376
CHANGEFUL TILL NOW WE STILL   • • • • • •   425 EMPEDOCLES I 2   377
TO FIND WITH YOU THE JOY WE IN VAIN HERE REQUIRE   • •   425 EMPEDOCLES I 2   381
SHALL WE WITH TEMPER SPOILD   • • • • • •   425 EMPEDOCLES I 2   392
SHALL WE JUDGE WHAT FOR MAN IS NOT TRUE BLISS OR IS   425 EMPEDOCLES I 2   396
THAT WE MUST FEIGN A BLISS   • • • • • •   425 EMPEDOCLES I 2   402
AND WHILE WE DREAM ON THIS   • • • • • •   425 EMPEDOCLES I 2   404
WE MARK NOT THE WORLDS WAYS BUT WOULD HAVE   419 EMPEDOCLES I 2   V 221
   IT LEARN OURS
WE SPURN THEM AND INVENT   419 EMPEDOCLES I 2   V 225
NOR DO WE SOON PERCEIVE HOW FAST OUR YOUTH IS SPENT   424 EMPEDOCLES I 2   V 361
SHALL WE WITH TEMPERS SPOILD   • • • • • •   425 EMPEDOCLES I 2   V 392
SHALL WE JUDGE WHAT FOR MAN IS NOT HIGH BLISS OR IS   425 EMPEDOCLES I 2   V 396
THAT WE DEMAND A BLISS   • • • • • • • •   425 EMPEDOCLES I 2   V 402
THAT WE MUST CLAIM SOME BLISS   • • • • •   425 EMPEDOCLES I 2   V 402
AND WHILE WE DREAM OF THIS   • • • • • •   425 EMPEDOCLES I 2   V 404
WHEN WE WERE YOUNG WHEN WE COULD NUMBER FRIENDS   436 EMPEDOCLES II   236
WHEN WE WERE YOUNG WHEN WE COULD NUMBER FRIENDS   436 EMPEDOCLES II   236
WHEN WITH ELATED HEARTS WE JOIND YOUR TRAIN   • •   436 EMPEDOCLES II   238
THEN WE COULD STILL ENJOY THEN NEITHER THOUGHT   •   436 EMPEDOCLES II   240
BUT WE RECEIVED THE SHOCK OF MIGHTY THOUGHTS   • •   436 EMPEDOCLES II   242
WE HAD THE POWER TO FEEL THE PRESSURE EASED   • •   436 EMPEDOCLES II   245

WE

(CONTINUED)

WE HAD NOT LOST OUR BALANCE THEN NOR GROWN • • • • 436 EMPEDOCLES II 248
AND WE MIGHT GLADLY SHARE THE FRUITFUL STIR • • 439 EMPEDOCLES II 339
WE MIGHT HAVE JOY BLENT WITH THE ALL-BATHING AIR • • 439 EMPEDOCLES II 343
BUT WE SHALL STILL BE IN THEM AND THEY IN US • • 439 EMPEDOCLES II 349
AND WE SHALL BE THE STRANGERS OF THE WORLD • • • • 439 EMPEDOCLES II 350
AND WE SHALL BE UNSATISFIED AS NOW • • • • • 439 EMPEDOCLES II 355
AND WE SHALL FEEL THE AGONY OF THIRST • • • • 439 EMPEDOCLES II 356
AND THEN WE SHALL UNWILLINGLY RETURN • • • • 440 EMPEDOCLES II 364
TO SEE IF WE WILL POISE OUR LIFE AT LAST • • • 440 EMPEDOCLES II 369
TO SEE IF WE WILL NOW AT LAST BE TRUE • • • • 440 EMPEDOCLES II 370
BEING ONE WITH WHICH WE ARE ONE WITH THE WHOLE WORLD • 440 EMPEDOCLES II 372
OR WHETHER WE WILL ONCE MORE FALL AWAY • • • • 440 EMPEDOCLES II 373
AND EACH SUCCEEDING AGE IN WHICH WE ARE BORN • • 440 EMPEDOCLES II 377
AND WE SHALL STRUGGLE AWHILE GASP AND REBEL • • 440 EMPEDOCLES II 382
AND WE SHALL FLY FOR REFUGE TO PAST TIMES • • • 440 EMPEDOCLES II 383
AND WE SHALL FEEL OUR POWERS OF EFFORT FLAG • • 440 EMPEDOCLES II 387
AND WE SHALL SINK IN THE IMPOSSIBLE STRIFE • • 440 EMPEDOCLES II 389
WE SHOULD HAVE JOY BLENT WITH THE ALL-BATHING AIR • 439 EMPEDOCLES II V 343
YET WOULD WE KEEP THEE IN OUR HEART • • • • • 451 GEISTS GRAVE 37
WHILE TO EACH OTHER WE REHEARSE • • • • 451 GEISTS GRAVE 43
WE STROKE THY BROAD BROWN PAWS AGAIN • • • 451 GEISTS GRAVE 45
WE BID THEE TO THY VACANT CHAIR • • • • 451 GEISTS GRAVE 46
WE GREET THEE BY THE WINDOW-PANE • • • • 451 GEISTS GRAVE 47
WE HEAR THY SCUFFLE ON THE STAIR • • • • 451 GEISTS GRAVE 48
WE SEE THE FLAPS OF THY LARGE EARS • • • • 451 GEISTS GRAVE 49
QUICK RAISED TO ASK WHICH WAY WE GO • • • • 451 GEISTS GRAVE 50
AND THOU SHALT LIVE AS LONG AS WE • • • • 451 GEISTS GRAVE 58
WE STRIVE TO CARRY DOWN THY NAME • • • • 451 GEISTS GRAVE 63
WE LAY THEE CLOSE WITHIN OUR REACH • • • • 451 GEISTS GRAVE 65
WHERE OFT WE WATCHD THY COUCHANT FORM • • • 451 GEISTS GRAVE 68
THERE BUILD WE THEE O GUARDIAN DEAR • • • • 452 GEISTS GRAVE 71
WHEN WE TOO LIKE THYSELF ARE CLAY • • • • 452 GEISTS GRAVE 74
THERE CHOOSE WE THEE O GUARDIAN DEAR • • • • 452 GEISTS GRAVE V 71
WE DISMISSD WITHOUT A WORD • • • • • 453 POOR MATTHIAS 24
CHANGED AND AGING THEY AND WE • • • • • 454 POOR MATTHIAS 51
MAX AND KAISER WE TO-DAY • • • • • 454 POOR MATTHIAS 67
WELL WE KNEW WHEN THEY WERE GLAD • • • • 455 POOR MATTHIAS 89
PLAIN WE SAW IF THEY WERE SAD • • • • • 455 POOR MATTHIAS 90
KINDNESS WE BESTOW AND PRAISE • • • • • 455 POOR MATTHIAS 99
WHAT THEY WANT WE CANNOT GUESS • • • • • 455 POOR MATTHIAS 105
EVERY MORNING DID WE PAY • • • • • 455 POOR MATTHIAS 111
CAKE WE OFFERD SUGAR SEED • • • • • 455 POOR MATTHIAS 115
WHEREBY STRANGE ARE THEY AND WE • • • • 456 POOR MATTHIAS 150
DOES IT IF WE MISS YOUR MIND • • • • • 457 POOR MATTHIAS 155
BIRDS WE BUT REPEAT ON YOU • • • • • 457 POOR MATTHIAS 157
WHAT AMONGST OURSELVES WE DO • • • • • 457 POOR MATTHIAS 158
KNOW WE MORE OUR FELLOW MEN • • • • • 457 POOR MATTHIAS 162
DRIVN INSHORE WE FOLLOW DOWN • • • • • 457 POOR MATTHIAS 181
HOME WE BROUGHT HIM YOUNG AND FAIR • • • 458 POOR MATTHIAS 196
WE WITHOUT THEE LITTLE FRIEND • • • • • 458 POOR MATTHIAS 210
BETTER THAN WE SPENT WITH THEE • • • • • 458 POOR MATTHIAS 213
AND KAISERS RACE WE DEEMD THE SAME • • • • 459 KAISER DEAD 21
YES MAX AND WE GREW SLOW AND SAD • • • • 460 KAISER DEAD 43
FAIN WOULD WE DEEM THAT THOU HAST RISEN SO HIGH • • 463 ALARIC AT ROME 31
WHERE ALL WE SEE OR DO OR HEAR OR SAY • • • 464 ALARIC AT ROME 47
THOU SOLEMN GRAVE WHERE EVERY STEP WE TREAD • • 464 ALARIC AT ROME 49
AND DASH OUR HOLIEST RAPTURES WHILE WE GAZE • • 470 ALARIC AT ROME 200
AND WHILE THEY RISE HERE MIGHT WE STAND ALONE • • 470 ALARIC AT ROME 203
THAT WHILE WE FEEL THE WORLD IS DULL AND LOW • • 470 ALARIC AT ROME 215
GAZING ON THEE WE WAKE TO FIND IT IS NOT SO • • 470 ALARIC AT ROME 216
SO PASS WE ON BUT OH TO HARP ARIGHT • • • • 471 ALARIC AT ROME 223
LIT BY A WANDERING GLEAM WE KNOW NOT HOW • • • 475 CROMWELL 128
TRUE WE MUST TAME OUR REBEL WILL • • • • • 481 COURAGE 1
TRUE WE MUST BOW TO NATURES LAW • • • • • 481 COURAGE 2
OUR BANE DISGUISE IT AS WE MAY • • • • • 482 COURAGE 25
DOUBT IT NOT WE MET AND WE ARE ONE • • • • 482 THEKLAS ANSWER 10
DOUBT IT NOT WE MET AND WE ARE ONE • • • • 482 THEKLAS ANSWER 10
WHEN THOU TOO HAST BORNE THE LOVE WE BORE • • • 482 THEKLAS ANSWER 14
OF WHAT WE SAY WE FEEL BELOW THE STREAM • • • 483 BELOW SURFACE 2
OF WHAT WE SAY WE FEEL BELOW THE STREAM • • • 483 BELOW SURFACE 2
AS LIGHT OF WHAT WE THINK WE FEEL THERE FLOWS • • 483 BELOW SURFACE 3
AS LIGHT OF WHAT WE THINK WE FEEL THERE FLOWS • • 483 BELOW SURFACE 3
THE CENTRAL STREAM OF WHAT WE FEEL INDEED • • • 483 BELOW SURFACE 5
TO DAILY TASKS WE SET OUR HAND • • • • • 483 ROME-SICKNESS 1
FOLLOWING THE SUN WE SET OUR VESSELS HEAD • • • 484 S S LUSITANIA 3
WE CHEERD BUT FROM IT RUSHD A BLAST OF MIGHT • • 484 S S LUSITANIA 7
AH UNHAPPY PAIR TO PELEUS WHY DID WE GIVE YOU • HOMER TRANS 9
TRULY YET THIS TIME WILL WE SAVE THEE MIGHTY ACHILLES HOMER TRANS 47
BUT THY DAY OF DEATH IS AT HAND NOR SHALL WE HOMER TRANS 48
  BE THE REASON
BUT FOR US WE VIE IN SPEED WITH THE BREATH HOMER TRANS 54
  OF THE WEST-WIND
ARE WE DISSATISFIED WITH WHAT WE ARE • • • • • LUCRETIUS 3 9
ARE WE DISSATISFIED WITH WHAT WE ARE • • • • • LUCRETIUS 3 9
THAT WE WERE DESTIND TO A HAPPIER STATE • • • • LUCRETIUS 3 11
ARE WE DISSATISFIED WITH WHAT WE HAVE • • • • LUCRETIUS 3 V 9
ARE WE DISSATISFIED WITH WHAT WE HAVE • • • • LUCRETIUS 3 V 9
WE BUT SURVEY HE IS THE ARCHITECT • • • • • LUCRETIUS 5 3
BEFORE A STONE WAS LIFTED AND WE MEMMIUS • • • • LUCRETIUS 5 5
IN FRONT OF SOME GREAT FANE WHEREOF WE KNOW • • LUCRETIUS 5 7
NOTHING BUT THAT WE SEE IT WHAT RESPECT • • • • LUCRETIUS 5 8

WE   (CONTINUED)

WE BUT BEHOLD HE IS THE ARCHITECT	LUCRETIUS 5	V	3
WHAT ARE WE ALL	LUCRETIUS 6		1
WE PRIZE NOT WHEN TIS PRESENT BUT WHEN LOST	LUCRETIUS 7		2
HATH FRAYD AND SLIDDEN DOWN AND WE NO MORE	EVERLASTING SUB		2
THIS LITTLE WHICH WE ARE	FRAGMENT 3		1
SWIMS ON AN OBSCURE MUCH WE MIGHT HAVE BEEN	FRAGMENT 3		2

WEAK

MANS WEAK COMPLAININGS MINGLING WITH HIS TOIL	1 QUIET WORK	V	10
HEMMD BY TWO BANKS OF CLOUD PEERS PALE AND WEAK	10 MYCERINUS		57
NO WEAK NURSLING OF AN EARTHLY SUN	30 NEW SIRENS		112
ARE WILLS SO WEAK THEN LET NOT MINE WAIT LONG	38 WORLDS TRIUMPHS		12
FROM WILD AND WEAK COMPLAINING	39 STAGIRIUS		36
WITH WEAK INDULGENCE	51 CONSOLATION		56
WEAK YET NOT WEAK I MIGHT REPLY	59 RESIGNATION		255
WEAK YET NOT WEAK I MIGHT REPLY	59 RESIGNATION		255
OR ELSE TOO WEAK AND ALL EYES TURN TO THEE	67 SOHRAB RUSTUM		218
AM OLDER IF THE YOUNG ARE WEAK THE KING	67 SOHRAB RUSTUM		222
AND HE HAS NONE TO GUARD HIS WEAK OLD AGE	68 SOHRAB RUSTUM		235
AND WITH MY GREAT NAME FENCE THAT WEAK OLD MAN	68 SOHRAB RUSTUM		237
TO GLAD THY FATHER IN HIS WEAK OLD AGE	77 SOHRAB RUSTUM		536
THEN WITH WEAK HASTY FINGERS SOHRAB LOOSED	81 SOHRAB RUSTUM		669
WITH WOMENS TEARS AND WEAK COMPLAINING CRIES	96 BALDER DEAD 1		32
SIGHTLESS AND HELPLESS WANDERING WEAK IN HEAVEN	98 BALDER DEAD 1		97
THE OLD THE COWARDS AND THE WEAK ARE THERE	104 BALDER DEAD 1		324
WITH WOMANS TEARS AND WEAK COMPLAINING CRIES	96 BALDER DEAD 1	V	32
WHAT KNIGHT IS THIS SO WEAK AND PALE	130 TRISTRAM 1		9
HE IS WEAK WITH FEVER AND PAIN	133 TRISTRAM 1		85
SHOOK HER WEAK BOSOM DAY AND NIGHT	147 TRISTRAM 2		133
SHE WOULD FIND ILL TO BEAR WEAK AS SHE IS	152 TRISTRAM 3		101
THY HUSBAND WEAK AVENGER THROUGH THYSELF	201 PHILOMELA	V	
TOO KEEN TO REST TOO WEAK TO FIND	217 NAMELESS EPIT	V	
THE PUISSANT CROWND THE WEAK LAID LOW	219 BACCHANALIA 2		12
WEAK IS THE TREMOR OF PAIN	230 YOUTH OF NATURE		92
WHICH HAS NOT TAUGHT WEAK WILLS HOW MUCH THEY CAN	238 PROGRESS		41
ALAS IS EVEN LOVE TOO WEAK	245 BURIED LIFE		12
WHOSE WEAK RESOLVES NEVER HAVE BEEN FULFILLD	260 SCHOLAR-GIPSY	V	175
NO SMALL BOAST FOR A WEAK	293 HEINES GRAVE		29
ALL SHIPWRECK IN THY OWN WEAK HEART	307 OBERMANN		19
THOUGH LATE THOUGH DIMMD THOUGH WEAK YET TELL	323 OBERMANN MORE		311
ALL KNOW HOW WEAK THE EAGLE HERACLES	336 MEROPE		212
WEAK WOMEN WITH A THOUSANDTH PART MY WRONGS	366 MEROPE		1013
WHAT ONE WEAK WOMAN CAN ACHIEVE ALONE	368 MEROPE		1074
OF TYRANNOUS HARSHNESS OR REMISSNESS WEAK	404 MEROPE		2007
AS CHILDREN OF WEAK AGE	421 EMPEDOCLES I 2		273
COWARDS TO CONQUER AND THE WEAK TO DIE	467 ALARIC AT ROME		140

WEAKEN

WEAKEN THE SENSE OF HIS LOSS	283 HAWORTH CHURCH	V	

WEAKLY

EACH NERVE MORE WEAKLY STRUNG	212 GROWING OLD	V	10

WEAKNESS

ALL WEAKNESS WHICH IMPAIRS ALL GRIEFS WHICH BOW	3 SHAKESPEARE		13
ALL WEAKNESS THAT IMPAIRS ALL GRIEFS THAT BOW	3 SHAKESPEARE	V	13
BUT FROM THEIR WEAKNESS WHO WOULD WORK HER RUE	37 WORLDS TRIUMPHS		4
WEAKNESS AND WORSE WEAKNESS BESTOWD IN VAIN	40 HUMAN LIFE		15
WEAKNESS AND WORSE WEAKNESS BESTOWD IN VAIN	40 HUMAN LIFE		15
HE READ EACH WOUND EACH WEAKNESS CLEAR	270 MEMORIAL VERSES		20
HE SCANND EACH WOUND EACH WEAKNESS NEAR	270 MEMORIAL VERSES	V	20
IN MORTAL WEAKNESS A LAST	281 HAWORTH CHURCH		32
WEAKNESS IS NOT IN YOUR WORD	292 RUGBY CHAPEL		194
NO WEAKNESS SPOIL OUR LOT	421 EMPEDOCLES I 2		263
FALSE WEAKNESS IN THE WORLD AND IN OURSELVES FALSE POWERS	419 EMPEDOCLES I 2	V	226
AND WEAKNESS WARND HIM AND HE FEARD DECLINE	447 WESTMIN ABBEY		123
IS WEAKNESS IS A FALTERING COURSE	482 COURAGE		26
FOR ANY MAN TO FRET AGAINST HIS WEAKNESS	LUCRETIUS 3		2

WEAL

THOUGHTS OF THE GENERAL WEAL	282 HAWORTH CHURCH	V	
UNION CEMENTED FOR THIS NATIONS WEAL	333 MEROPE		103
WHAT GODS THE GODS OF CONCORD CIVIL WEAL	341 MEROPE		358
MAY BE NAY SHOULD IF FOR THE GENERAL WEAL	352 MEROPE		657
OF PERSONAL FEELING TO THE PUBLIC WEAL	394 MEROPE		1712
OF PERSONAL VENGEANCE TO THE PUBLIC WEAL	394 MEROPE	V	1712
BOTH IN WEAL OF THEIRS AND WOE	455 POOR MATTHIAS		94

WEALTH

CROWNING MOMENTS WITH THE WEALTH OF YEARS	29 NEW SIRENS		88
THEY THINK TO BURN AND ALL MY CHOICEST WEALTH	103 BALDER DEAD 1		299
SIT PALE BESIDE THEIR WEALTH	191 STRAYED REVEL		192
WHAT POWER OF PASSION WEALTH OF CHANGE	223 EPILOG LAOCOON		82
THE WEALTH DIVINE THEY HAVE IN CHARGE	224 EPILOG LAOCOON		102
FILL THE WEALTH-GIVING THRONES	343 MEROPE		415

WEALTHY

WEALTHY IN CORN AND FLOCKS WHICH WHEN AT LAST	330 MEROPE		5

WEAPON
AT BALDER WHOM NO WEAPON PIERCED OR CLOVE • • • • 95 BALDER DEAD 1 4

WEAPONS
AT WHOM THE GODS IN SPORT THEIR WEAPONS THREW • • 98 BALDER DEAD 1 103
I HEARD THE CLASH OF WEAPONS THEN I SAW • • • • 402 MEROPE 1941

WEAR
AND WEAR THIS MAJESTY OF GRIEF AGAIN • • • • • 44 GIPSY CHILD 68
THE CHEEKS THAT STILL THEIR GENTLE PALENESS WEAR • • 175 PARTING 38
AND THOUGH WE WEAR OUT LIFE ALAS • • • • • 179 FAREWELL 49
DO TWENTY YEARS WEAR OUT AND SEE EXPIRE • • • • 335 MEROPE 180
SHALL THEY NOT WEAR ONE HATRED OUT AS WELL • • • • 335 MEROPE 181

WEARIED
AND YOU WEARIED IN DESIRE • • • • • • • • 31 NEW SIRENS 142

WEARINESS
NOR WEARINESS THE FULL-FED SOULS ANNOY • • • • 42 GIPSY CHILD 11
WEARINESS NOT ON YOUR BROW • • • • • • • 292 RUGBY CHAPEL 195
DEEP WEARINESS AND SATED LUST • • • • • • 315 OBERMANN MORE 95
WHOSE WEARINESS NO ENERGY CAN REACH • • • • • 429 EMPEDOCLES II 13
WEARY WITH OUR WEARINESS • • • • • • • • 438 EMPEDOCLES II 300

WEARS
WHAT MOOD WEARS LIKE COMPLEXION TO THY WOE • • • 42 GIPSY CHILD 21
FOR WHAT WEARS OUT THE LIFE OF MORTAL MEN • • • • 259 SCHOLAR-GIPSY 142
BUT THE DAY WEARS GO NOW PAUSANIAS • • • • • 427 EMPEDOCLES I 2 464

WEARY
TIME IS LAME AND WE GREW WEARY • • • • • • 28 NEW SIRENS 67
TIME IS LAME AND WE GROW WEARY • • • • • • 28 NEW SIRENS V 67
VAIN IT WASTES AND WE GREW WEARY • • • • • • 28 NEW SIRENS V 67
VAIN IT WORE AND WE GREW WEARY • • • • • • 28 NEW SIRENS V 67
FOR I AM LONG SINCE WEARY OF YOUR STORM • • • • 127 BALDER DEAD 3 503
FOR SHE WAS PASSING WEARY OF HIS LOVE • • • • 156 TRISTRAM 3 224
TO MONTH WITH WEARY PAIN • • • • • • • 212 GROWING OLD 25
AND DOWN HE LAYS HIS WEARY BONES • • • • • 213 PROGRESS POESY 12
IN ITS WEARY UNPROFITABLE LENGTH • • • • • 235 YOUTH OF MAN 110
WHICH HAS NOT CRIED TO SUNK SELF-WEARY MAN • • • 238 PROGRESS 43
WEARY OF MYSELF AND SICK OF ASKING • • • • • 239 SELF-DEPENDENCE 1
WE WERE WEARY AND WE • • • • • • • • 290 RUGBY CHAPEL 128
GAVEST THE WEARY THY HAND • • • • • • 290 RUGBY CHAPEL 133
THE WEARY TITAN WITH DEAF • • • • • • • 295 HEINES GRAVE 88
NOR DOES BEING WEARY PROVE THAT HE HAS WHERE TO REST 424 EMPEDOCLES I 2 351
THE WEARY MAN THE BANISHD CITIZEN • • • • • 429 EMPEDOCLES II 11
I AM WEARY OF IT • • • • • • • • • 432 EMPEDOCLES II 108
I AM WEARY OF THEE • • • • • • • • 435 EMPEDOCLES II 198
I AM WEARY OF THE SOLITUDE • • • • • • 435 EMPEDOCLES II 199
WEARY LIKE US THOUGH NOT • • • • • • • 438 EMPEDOCLES II 299
WEARY WITH OUR WEARINESS • • • • • • • • 438 EMPEDOCLES II 300
NOR WAKE THE WEARY SOUL THAT SLUMBERS ON BELOW • 469 ALARIC AT ROME 198
AND REST HIS WEARY EYES ON THE GREEN LAND AND THEE 470 ALARIC AT ROME 222
THAT ALL NIGHT LONG ITS WEARY MOAN DOTH MAKE • • 477 CROMWELL 191

WEARYING
THEN THROUGH THE GREAT TOWNS HARSH HEART-WEARYING ROAR 269 THYRSIS 234

WEATHER
OF THIS FAIR SUMMER-WEATHER ON THESE HILLS • • • • 409 EMPEDOCLES I 1 101
IN WINTER WEATHER • • • • • • • • • • • 460 KAISER DEAD 54

WEAVE
AND GARLANDS FOR THEIR FOREHEAD WEAVE • • • • 203 EUPHROSYNE 18

WEAVER
AND THE PALE WEAVER THROUGH HIS WINDOWS SEEN • • 169 EAST LONDON 3

WEAVES
IN EVER-NEARING CIRCLE WEAVES HER SHADE • • • • 266 THYRSIS 132

WEB
EACH FORTIETH WEB OF CLOTH TO ME • • • • • 87 SICK KING BOKH 8
THE TOO CLEAR WEB AND THY DUMB SISTERS SHAME • • 201 PHILOMELA 21

WED
WHERE THE PRINCE WHOM SHE MUST WED • • • • • 134 TRISTRAM 1 133
IN SOUL WITH WHAT I GAZE ON WED • • • • • • 251 WISH 42

WEDDST
SIR KNIGHT WHO WEDDST TO-DAY • • • • • • • 159 NECKAN 24

WEDGED
WEDGED IN THE SNOW THEN PAINFULLY THE HINDS • • 107 BALDER DEAD 2 95

WEED
WHERE THE SALT WEED SWAYS IN THE STREAM • • • • 162 FORSAKEN MERM 38
WITH MANY A WILD WEED OVERGROWN • • • • • • 479 HAYSWATER BOAT 14

WEEDS

UPON THE CLIFFS OR SMOKE OF BURNING WEEDS	• • •	124	BALDER DEAD 3	362
LONG SINCE HATH FLUNG HER WEEDS AWAY • •	• • •	304	GRANDE CHARTR	154
LONG SINCE HATH THROWN HER WEEDS AWAY	• • •	304	GRANDE CHARTR	V 154
MID WEEDS AND WRECKS SHE STOOD A PLACE	• • •	317	OBERMANN MORE	139
HANG WEEDS OF OUR SAD TIME • • • • • •	• •	323	OBERMANN MORE	308

WEEK

WHAT A TALE OF THY LAST WEEK • • • • •	• • •	455	POOR MATTHIAS	110

WEEKS

BUT THE SMOOTH-SLIPPING WEEKS • • • • •	• • •	268	THYRSIS	206

WEEP

I SHALL WEEP BUT THEIR LOVE WILL BE COOLING AND HE		20	MODERN SAPPHO	18
WILL IT WEEP OUR BURNING TEARS • • • • • •	• •	29	NEW SIRENS	86
AND ZAL MIGHT WEEP ABOVE MY GRAVE NOT THINE	•	85	SOHRAB RUSTUM	821
AND SAY O SON I WEEP THEE NOT TOO SORE	• • •	85	SOHRAB RUSTUM	822
IF ANY HERE MIGHT WEEP FOR BALDERS DEATH	• •	96	BALDER DEAD 1	20
I MOST MIGHT WEEP HIS FATHER SUCH A SON	• • •	96	BALDER DEAD 1	21
WEEP HIM AN HOUR BUT WHAT CAN GRIEF AVAIL	• •	96	BALDER DEAD 1	27
WEEP HIM AND ALL THAT IS WITHOUT LIFE WEEP • •	•	111	BALDER DEAD 2	237
WEEP HIM AND ALL THAT IS WITHOUT LIFE WEEP • •	•	111	BALDER DEAD 2	237
AND IN PROCESSION ALL COME NEAR AND WEEP	• • •	115	BALDER DEAD 3	51
AND WEEP FROM SHORE TO SHORE MY GOLDEN TEARS	•	116	BALDER DEAD 3	110
WEEP NOT O FREYA WEEP NO GOLDEN TEARS	• • •	116	BALDER DEAD 3	114
WEEP NOT O FREYA WEEP NO GOLDEN TEARS	• • •	116	BALDER DEAD 3	114
ALL LIVING AND UNLIVING THINGS TO WEEP	• • •	122	BALDER DEAD 3	292
ALL LIVING AND UNLIVING THINGS TO WEEP	• • •	122	BALDER DEAD 3	300
ENTREATING ALL THINGS TO WEEP BALDERS DEATH	• •	122	BALDER DEAD 3	305
FAR OFF WHERE SOME UNWARND MIGHT FAIL TO WEEP	•	122	BALDER DEAD 3	322
THOK WITH DRY EYES WILL WEEP OER BALDERS PYRE	•	123	BALDER DEAD 3	352
WEEP HIM ALL OTHER THINGS IF WEEP THEY WILL	•	123	BALDER DEAD 3	353
WEEP HIM ALL OTHER THINGS IF WEEP THEY WILL	•	123	BALDER DEAD 3	353
I WEEP HIM NOT LET HELA KEEP HER PREY	• • •	123	BALDER DEAD 3	354
NAY ALLS WELL AGAIN THOU MUST NOT WEEP	• • •	144	TRISTRAM 2	72
I WEEP THEBANS • • • • • • • • • • •	• •	196	FRAG ANTIGONE	46
AND KNOW HER FRIEND AND WEEP FOR GLEE	• • •	202	URANIA	27
THEN WILL SHE WEEP WITH SMILES TILL THEN	• • •	202	URANIA	29
THEIR LOT WAS BUT TO WEEP AND MOAN	• • • •	203	EUPHROSYNE	10
AH LET ME WEEP AND TELL MY PAIN	• • • •	206	RIVER	11
AND WEEP AND FEEL THE FULNESS OF THE PAST	• •	212	GROWING OLD	19
I DO NOT STRIVE I DO NOT WEEP • • • • •	• •	241	MORALITY	26
LET THOSE WHO WILL IF ANY WEEP • • • • •	•	250	WISH	7
PRESSES ME CHIDES ME WILL NOT LET ME WEEP	• • •	378	MEROPE	1233
TO MAKE HIM LAUGH OR WEEP • • • • • • •			EMPEDOCLES I 2	V
DO THY BLOODSHOT EYES STILL WEEP • • • •	• •	430	EMPEDOCLES II	55
AND WERE THERE NONE TO STAND AND WEEP ALONE	•	467	ALARIC AT ROME	121
NOT THIS THE TIME TO WEEP UPON THE BIER	• • •	467	ALARIC AT ROME	135

WEEPING

STANDS AT DAYBREAK WEEPING BY MY SIDE	• • •	35	NEW SIRENS	274
AND YOU TOO O WEEPING GRACES • • • • • •	•	34	NEW SIRENS	V 243
WEEPING AND WAILING AND VALHALLA RANG	• • •	95	BALDER DEAD 1	11
WEEPING THE SANDS WERE WETTED AND THEIR ARMS	•	115	BALDER DEAD 3	62
OF ALL THINGS WEEPING TO BRING BALDER BACK • •	•	122	BALDER DEAD 3	318
THE PLEASAUNCE-WALKS THE WEEPING QUEEN	• • •	136	TRISTRAM 1	178
THEE A WEEPING EXILE IN THY FOREST • • •	• •	144	TRISTRAM 2	V 51
HE SINGS HOW SHE SITS WEEPING • • • • •	• •	160	NECKAN	33
BRING HIM A WEEPING CHILD • • • • • • •	•	195	FRAG ANTIGONE	12
WEEPING AT HIS MASTERS END • • • • • •	• •	434	EMPEDOCLES II	167

WEEPS

OF HIS PALE WIFE WHO WAITS AND WEEPS ON SHORE	• •	69	SOHRAB RUSTUM	285
OF HIS PALE WIFE WHO WAITS AND WEEPS ASHORE	• •	69	SOHRAB RUSTUM	V 285
SINCE THEN SHE SEEKS HIM AND WEEPS TEARS OF GOLD	• •	116	BALDER DEAD 3	95
FALSE NECKAN SHARES MY BED SHE WEEPS • • • •	• •	160	NECKAN	35

WEIGH

IS THE CALM THINE OF STOIC SOULS WHO WEIGH • •	• •	42	GIPSY CHILD	29
O AEPYTUS WEIGH WELL HER COUNSEL GIVEN	• • • •	382	MEROPE	1332

WEIGHD

WEIGHD LIKE OSSA ON THE AERY SOUL • • • • •	•	28	NEW SIRENS	V 72

WEIGHING

WHO WEIGHING THAT LIFE WELL • • • • • • •	• •	195	FRAG ANTIGONE	4

WEIGHS

WEIGHS LIKE OSSA ON THE AERY SOUL • • • • •	• •	28	NEW SIRENS	V 72
WEIGHS DOWN MY SOUL • • • • • • • • • •	• •	50	CONSOLATION	5

WEIGHT

CROWNING MOMENTS WITH THE WEIGHT OF YEARS	• • •	29	NEW SIRENS	V 88
A WEIGHT OF MEDITATION MIXD WITH PAIN	• • • •	41	GIPSY CHILD	V 12

WEIGHTY

O KING ALL HAIL I COME WITH WEIGHTY NEWS	• • • •	354	MEROPE	710
ARRIVED FROM TEGEA WITH WEIGHTY NEWS • • • • •	•	361	MEROPE	915

WEIMAR
    GOETHE IN WEIMAR SLEEPS AND GREECE . . . . . 270 MEMORIAL VERSES 1
    IN GERMAN WEIMAR SLEEPS . . . . 308 OBERMANN 52

WEIRD
    AND THE WEIRD CHIPPING OF THE WOODPECKER . . . . 155 TRISTRAM 3 198
    BRIGHT IN THE SUNSET WEIRD AND STILL . . . . . 273 STANZAS CARNAC 5
    FROM THOSE WEIRD DOMES OF MOUNDED GREEN . . . . 480 HAYSWATER BOAT 23

WEIRS
    THE VALE THE THREE LONE WEIRS THE YOUTHFUL THAMES 263 THYRSIS 15

WELCOME
    HAST THOU NO LIP FOR WELCOME SO I SAID . . . . 3 EMERSONS ESSAYS 5
    WELCOME THESE EYES COULD SEE NO BETTER SIGHT . . 67 SOHRAB RUSTUM 205
    WELCOME HE SAID IF THERE BE WELCOME HERE . . . 125 BALDER DEAD 3 411
    WELCOME HE SAID IF THERE BE WELCOME HERE . . . 125 BALDER DEAD 3 411
    I HONOUR AND WELCOME THEE . . . . 189 STRAYED REVEL 129
    AND NIGHT AS WELCOME AS A FRIEND WOULD FALL . . 267 THYRSIS 150
    WELCOME THE SISTER THE FRIEND . . . . 284 HAWORTH CHURCH 86
    FOR COURTEOUS ENTERTAINMENT WELCOME WARM . . . 356 MEROPE 760
    MY FAITHFUL FOLLOWER COMES WELCOME OLD FRIEND . . 362 MEROPE 937
    FAITHFUL NOT WELCOME WHEN MY TALE IS TOLD . . . 362 MEROPE 938
    MY CHILD MY CHARGE BELOVED WELCOME TO LIFE . . . 375 MEROPE 1207
    NOT WELCOME EXCULPATION TO HER KIN . . . . . 386 MEROPE 1453
    BUT THEY WILL GLADLY WELCOME HIM ONCE MORE . . . 435 EMPEDOCLES II 221

WELCOMED
    WELCOMED HERE AND HERE INSTALLD . . . . . . 136 TRISTRAM 1 204

WELFARE
    MAKES HIS OWN WELFARE HIS UNSWERVED-FROM LAW . . 195 FRAG ANTIGONE 8
    BASED ON PURE PUBLIC WELFARE LET US BE . . . . 394 MEROPE 1718
    WELFARE TO THE MESSENIAN STATE AND CALM . . . 403 MEROPE 1959
    NO TITLE FROM THE GODS TO WELFARE AND REPOSE . . 417 EMPEDOCLES I 2 161
    HIS WELFARE HIS TRUE AIM . . . . 418 EMPEDOCLES I 2 174
    THE WORLD DOES BUT EXIST THAT WELFARE TO BESTOW . 418 EMPEDOCLES I 2 176
    HIS WELFARE INSECURE . . . . 420 EMPEDOCLES I 2 245
    THAT NATURAL CAUSES THWART THY WELFARE AND NOT FATE EMPEDOCLES I 2 V

WELL
    IT WAS WELL WITH ME ONCE IF I SAW HIM TO-MORROW . 19 MODERN SAPPHO V
    CALMS NOT LIFES CROWN THOUGH CALM IS WELL . . . 22 YOUTH AND CALM 23
    BY WELL-HEADS IN SUMMER DAYS . . . . 34 NEW SIRENS 240
    THE WORLD SPEAKS WELL YET MIGHT HER FOE REPLY . . 38 WORLDS TRIUMPHS 11
    LIFE WELL AND FIND IT WANTING NOR DEPLORE . . . 42 GIPSY CHILD 30
    WELL PLEASED SEE END . . . . 52 CONSOLATION 65
    BUT FAUSTA I REMEMBER WELL . . . . 54 RESIGNATION 82
    I HAVE STILL SERVED AFRASIAB WELL AND SHOWN . . 62 SOHRAB RUSTUM 44
    SHOULD ONE DAY GREET UPON SOME WELL-FOUGHT FIELD . 62 SOHRAB RUSTUM 51
    FAIN WOULD I KNOW THEE SAFE AND WELL THOUGH LOST . 63 SOHRAB RUSTUM 88
    FOR WELL I KNOW THAT DID GREAT RUSTUM STAND . . 72 SOHRAB RUSTUM 370
    YET THIS THOU HAST SAID WELL DID RUSTUM STAND . . 72 SOHRAB RUSTUM 382
    AND THAT OLD KING HER FATHER WHO LOVED WELL . . 79 SOHRAB RUSTUM 625
    WHOM RUSTUM WERT THOU HIS MIGHT WELL HAVE LOVED . 80 SOHRAB RUSTUM 642
    AND SAID O RUKSH BEAR RUSTUM WELL BUT I . . . 83 SOHRAB RUSTUM 755
    ONE MAN IS NOT WELL MADE TO BEAR . . . . . 92 SICK KING BOKH 154
    FOR WELL HE KNEW THE GODS WOULD HEED HIS WORD . . 97 BALDER DEAD 1 59
    AND WELL I KNOW THAT BY NO STROKE OF DEATH . . 103 BALDER DEAD 1 305
    WHOM THOU SO WELL HAST LOVED BUT I CAN SMOOTH . . 103 BALDER DEAD 1 308
    SO BALDER SAID BUT ODER WELL I KNOW . . . . 117 BALDER DEAD 3 119
    YE GODS THERE WELL MAY BE TOO MUCH OF WAIL . . 118 BALDER DEAD 3 157
    STILL LIFTED WELL WAS HIS RETURN FOREKNOWN . . 124 BALDER DEAD 3 378
    THOU DOEST WELL TO CHIDE ME HODER BLIND . . . 125 BALDER DEAD 3 423
    ESTEEM AND FUNCTION AND SO FAR IS WELL . . . 127 BALDER DEAD 3 470
    AND WE SHALL TREAD ONCE MORE THE WELL-KNOWN PLAIN 128 BALDER DEAD 3 537
    AH TIS WELL HE SHOULD RETRACE . . . . . . 137 TRISTRAM 1 211
    NAY ALLS WELL AGAIN THOU MUST NOT WEEP . . . 144 TRISTRAM 2 72
    WELL-FED WELL-CLOTHED WELL-FRIENDED I . . . 158 SAINT BRANDAN 57
    WELL-FED WELL-CLOTHED WELL-FRIENDED I . . . 158 SAINT BRANDAN 57
    WELL-FED WELL-CLOTHED WELL-FRIENDED I . . . 158 SAINT BRANDAN 57
    SHE COMBD ITS BRIGHT HAIR AND SHE TENDED IT WELL 163 FORSAKEN MERM 53
    FOR THE PRIEST AND THE BELL AND THE HOLY WELL . 164 FORSAKEN MERM 91
    WHO STRUCK IN HEAT HIS CHILD HE LOVED SO WELL . 166 PICT NEWSTEAD 5
    WHO STRUCK IN HEAT THE CHILD HE LOVED SO WELL . 166 PICT NEWSTEAD V 5
    POLYMNIA FULL ON HER DEATH-BED TWAS WELL . . 168 RACHEL 2 8
    EVEN IN A PALACE LIFE MAY BE LED WELL . . . 168 WORLDLY PLACE 1
    WELL THEN FOR CHRIST THOU ANSWEREST WHO CAN CARE . 171 BETTER PART 6
    WELL SPAKE THE IMPETUOUS SAINT AND BORE OF MEN . 171 DIVINITY 6
    HIS SOUL WELL-KNIT AND ALL HIS BATTLES WON . . . 172 IMMORTALITY 13
    AND FAITH MAY WELL BE UNRETURND . . . . . 180 ISOLATION MARG V 10
    WELL HATH HE DONE WHO HATH SEIZED HAPPINESS . 195 FRAG ANTIGONE 1
    WHO WEIGHING THAT LIFE WELL . . . . . . 195 FRAG ANTIGONE 4
    HE DOES WELL TOO WHO KEEPS THAT CLUE THE MILD . 195 FRAG ANTIGONE 9
    HIM I COUNT HIM WELL-STARRD . . . . . . 199 FRAG DEJANEIRA 31
    BY DAY I SHALL BE WELL AGAIN . . . . . . 208 LONGING 2
    BY DAY I SHALL BE WELL AGAIN . . . . . . 209 LONGING 14
    HIS MASTERS ERRAND WELL DONE . . . . . . 217 LORDS MESSENGER 22
    THE POET FEELS THE PAST AS WELL . . . . . 221 BACCHANALIA 2 66
    THEN LET HIM CHOOSE HIS MOMENT WELL . . . . 223 EPILOG LAOCOON 59
    BUT NOT AS THE MUSICIAN WELL . . . . . . 226 EPILOG LAOCOON 184

WELL   (CONTINUED)
        WELL MAY WE MOURN WHEN THE HEAD   . . . . .   229 YOUTH OF NATURE   48
        OR THE POET WHO SINGS YOU SO WELL   . . . . .   230 YOUTH OF NATURE   62
        WELL FOR US THAT WE CHANGE   . . . .   232 YOUTH OF MAN   11
        WELL FOR US THAT THE POWER   . . . .   232 YOUTH OF MAN   12
        WELL I KNOW WHAT THEY FEEL   . . . .   235 YOUTH OF MAN   88
        WELL I KNOW WHAT THEY FEEL   . . . .   235 YOUTH OF MAN   96
        BUT THAT YE THINK CLEAR FEEL DEEP BEAR FRUIT WELL   238 PROGRESS   47
        BUT THAT YOU TOO FEEL DEEPLY BEAR FRUIT WELL   .   238 PROGRESS   V   47
        BUT THAT YOU THINK CLEAR FEEL DEEP BEAR FRUIT WELL   238 PROGRESS   V   47
        AH WE SHALL KNOW THAT WELL WHEN IT COMES NEAR   .   239 REVOLUTIONS   19
        AH WELL FOR US IF EVEN WE   . . . .   245 BURIED LIFE   26
        AND WELL-NIGH CHANGE HIS OWN IDENTITY   . . . .   246 BURIED LIFE   34
        IS ELOQUENT IS WELL BUT TIS NOT TRUE   . . . .   247 BURIED LIFE   66
        AT EVE BY THE PALM-SHADED WELL   . . . .   252 FUTURE   37
        OUR WELL-WORN LIFE AND ARE WHAT WE HAVE BEEN   259 SCHOLAR-GIPSY   V 150
        WELL WIND-DISPERSED AND VAIN THE WORDS WILL BE   265 THYRSIS   101
        THEY ALL ARE GONE AND THOU ART GONE AS WELL   266 THYRSIS   130
        MIGHT WELL REPOSE   . . . .   278 SOUTHERN NIGHT   92
        O BOY IF HERE THOU SLEEPST SLEEP WELL   . . . .   285 HAWORTH CHURCH   107
        BUT WE WE LEARNT YOUR LORE TOO WELL   . . . .   304 GRANDE CHARTR   156
        BUT WE WE LEARNT THEIR LORE TOO WELL   . . . .   304 GRANDE CHARTR   V 156
        TO TELL TOO DEEP ONES IS NOT WELL   . . . .   307 OBERMANN   43
        THOU TOO HAST SCANND IT WELL   . . . . .   309 OBERMANN   84
        THOSE PENSIVE FEATURES WELL I KNEW   . . . .   314 OBERMANN MORE   61
        SO WELL SHE MUSED A MORNING BROKE   . . . .   316 OBERMANN MORE   113
        OUR JOURNEY IS WELL MADE THE WORK REMAINS   .   330 MEROPE   24
        OF MY OWN DEATH BUT LAIAS WELL I HOPE   . . . .   331 MEROPE   49
        REPEATED ARE IN THEE I WELL BELIEVE   . . . .   333 MEROPE   87
        SHALL THEY NOT WEAR ONE HATRED OUT AS WELL   .   335 MEROPE   181
        FOES DAZZLED WITH YOUR PROWESS WELL INCLINED   339 MEROPE   302
        FOR WELL HE KNEW WHAT YOU HIS CHIEFS DID NOT   339 MEROPE   306
        WELL SOMETIMES MAY THE GOOD DESIRE   . . . .   353 MEROPE   665
        WELL MAY HE LONG TO INTERRUPT   . . . . . .   353 MEROPE   667
        WELL THIRST TO DRAG THE WRONGFUL RULER DOWN   .   353 MEROPE   670
        WELL PURPOSE TO PEN BACK   . . . .   353 MEROPE   671
        AND KNOWING WELL MANS INMOST HEART INFIRM   .   353 MEROPE   692
        WHETHER I LEARNT THEIR LESSONS WELL   . . . .   354 MEROPE   698
        OR HAVING LEARNT THEM WELL APPLY   . . . .   354 MEROPE   699
        O WERE BUT ARCAS COME ALL WOULD BE WELL   . . .   362 MEROPE   933
        IF SO ALLS WELL FOR LOOK THE OLD MAN SPEEDS   .   362 MEROPE   934
        MOTHER I WELL BELIEVED THOU LIVEDST ON   . . .   367 MEROPE   1043
        WELL-MOURND BUT ILL-AVENGED   . . . . . .   372 MEROPE   1142
        UPBRAIDS THEE NO ONE THOU DOST WELL BUT TAKE   376 MEROPE   1214
        BEAR WITNESS SEE MARK WELL ON WHAT A HEAD   377 MEROPE   1223
        O AEPYTUS WEIGH WELL HER COUNSEL GIVEN   . . .   382 MEROPE   1332
        CONDEMND BY PRUDENCE HAVE SOMETIMES GONE WELL   383 MEROPE   1385
        HER WELL-KNOWN ENEMY   . . . .   393 MEROPE   1666
        THANKS TO HIM FOR OUR AMITY AS WELL   . . .   395 MEROPE   1724
        NOW FOR THYSELF THOU COMST WITH WELL-CLOAKD JOY   395 MEROPE   1737
        ALL THINGS BUT LIFE THOU LOSE NOT LIFE AS WELL   396 MEROPE   1757
        ONCE MORE MY FRIENDSHIP THOU REJECTEST WELL   398 MEROPE   1783
        THOU SPEAKEST WELL BUT HERE TO GIVE OUR EYES   403 MEROPE   1951
        WELL MAY THEY LONG TO INTERRUPT . . . . . .   353 MEROPE   V 667
        I HAVE MY HARP TOO THAT IS WELL APOLLO   . . .   407 EMPEDOCLES I 1   19
        HE KNEW ME WELL AND WOULD OFT NOTICE ME   . . .   408 EMPEDOCLES I 1   57
        PANTHEIA FOR I KNOW HER KINSMEN WELL   . . .   410 EMPEDOCLES I 1   135
        THEN PLAY THY KIND PART WELL FAREWELL TILL NIGHT   411 EMPEDOCLES I 1   167
        OF ALL THE WOODY HIGH WELL-WATERD DELLS   . . .   414 EMPEDOCLES I 2   42
        WELL THEN THE WISER WIGHT   . . . .   416 EMPEDOCLES I 2   129
        FAIN WOULD DO ALL THINGS WELL BUT SOMETIMES   422 EMPEDOCLES I 2   296
              FAILS IN STRENGTH
        HE EVER LOVED THE THEBAN STORY WELL   . . . .   427 EMPEDOCLES I 2   463
        PAUSANIAS IS FAR HENCE AND THAT IS WELL   . . .   429 EMPEDOCLES II   5
        THY WELL-TRIED FRIENDS THY WILLING MINISTERS   429 EMPEDOCLES II   26
        GODS AND THE RACE OF MORTALS LOVE SO WELL   431 EMPEDOCLES II   65
        AS THE WELL-COUNSELLD ZEUS OPPRESSD   . . .   432 EMPEDOCLES II   102
        THEY WERE WELL BORN THEY WILL BE WELL ENTOMBD   439 EMPEDOCLES II   337
        THEY WERE WELL BORN THEY WILL BE WELL ENTOMBD   439 EMPEDOCLES II   337
        WELL WOULD IT BE   . . . .   439 EMPEDOCLES II   341
        WELL MIGHT IT BE   . . . .   439 EMPEDOCLES II   V 341
        EVEN AS THAT LOVED THAT WELL-RECORDED FRIEND   449 WESTMIN ABBEY   168
        WELL HE KNEW HIS MISTRESS DEAR   . . . . . .   452 POOR MATTHIAS   6
        WELL WE KNEW WHEN THEY WERE GLAD . . . . . .   455 POOR MATTHIAS   89
        SUITED WELL TO HEALTH BUT HOW   . . . . . .   455 POOR MATTHIAS   113
        FARE THEE WELL COMPANION DEAR   . . . . . .   458 POOR MATTHIAS   206
        FARE FOR EVER WELL NOR FEAR   . . . . . .   458 POOR MATTHIAS   207
        FULL WELL MAX KNOWS THE FRIEND IS DEAD   . . .   460 KAISER DEAD   69
        WELL FETCH HIS GRAVEN COLLAR FINE   . . . .   461 KAISER DEAD   79
        MIGHT WELL BE MINGLING AT THAT MURMURED SIGH   469 ALARIC AT ROME   179
        ALAS FAR OTHER THOUGHTS MIGHT WELL BE OURS   . .   470 ALARIC AT ROME   199
        OR BEAR PAILS TO THE WELL OF MESSEIS OR HYPEREIA   HOMER TRANS   30
        I OF MYSELF KNOW WELL THAT HERE I AM DESTIND TO PERISH   HOMER TRANS   60

WELLING
        CAME WELLING FROM THE OPEN GASH AND LIFE . . . .   85 SOHRAB RUSTUM   841

WELLNIGH
        WELLNIGH NOT TO BE BORNE . . . .   295 HEINES GRAVE   95
        WELLNIGH TWO THOUSAND YEARS HAVE BROUGHT . . .   315 OBERMANN MORE   V   81

WEPT   (CONTINUED)
          LISTEND AND WEPT AWAY   . . . .   310 OBERMANN   128
          THE ALL-WEPT WAY   . . . . 344 MEROPE   448
          THE ALL-WEPT WAY   . . . . 345 MEROPE   468
          NO ALL WAS CHANGD THE MONARCH WEPT ALONE   . . . . 477 CROMWELL   187

WEST
          THE LONG-MUSED THOUGHT TO NORTH SOUTH EAST AND WEST   45 IN UTRUMQUE PAR   6
          ONE FROM THE EAST ONE FROM THE WEST THEIR SHIELDS   75 SOHRAB RUSTUM   474
          NORTH SOUTH EAST WEST THEY STRUCK AND ROAMD THE WORLD 122 BALDER DEAD 3   304
          AND A WARM WEST-WIND BLOWS AND THAW SETS IN   . . 122 BALDER DEAD 3   309
          THE SEER FROM THE WEST WAS THEN IN SHADE   . . . . 170 EAST AND WEST   11
          THE MAN OF THE BOLD WEST NOW COMES ARRAYD   . . . . 170 EAST AND WEST   13
          AGAINST THE WEST I MISS IT IS IT GONE   . . . . 263 THYRSIS   27
          THE WEST UNFLUSHES THE HIGH STARS GROW BRIGHT   . . 267 THYRSIS   163
          BROUGHT BY THE WEST-WIND RETURNS   . . . . 285 HAWORTH CHURCH   114
          SHE HEARD IT THE VICTORIOUS WEST   . . . . 316 OBERMANN MORE   121
          SOUTHWARD AND WEST BEHOLD THOSE SNOWY PEAKS   . . 330 MEROPE   16
          TO THE WEST-WINDS MURMUR . . . . 391 MEROPE   1619
          TO WHERE THE WEST-WIND PLAYS   . . . . 427 EMPEDOCLES I 2   454
          BUT FOR US WE VIE IN SPEED WITH THE BREATH   HOMER TRANS   54
                    OF THE WEST-WIND

WESTERING
          CATCHES THE WESTERING SUNS LAST FIRES   . . . . 274 STANZAS CARNAC   24
          AND WHEN NOW THE WESTERING SUN . . . . 433 EMPEDOCLES II   143
          THE WORLD-FAMED ABBEY BY THE WESTERING THAMES   . . 444 WESTMIN ABBEY   20

WESTERN
          ON THE CARVED WESTERN FRONT A FLOOD OF LIGHT   . . 18 CHURCH BROU 3   18
          IN THE VAST WESTERN WINDOW OF THE NAVE   . . . . 18 CHURCH BROU 3   21
          THE VALLEYS WESTERN BOUNDARY   . . . . 53 RESIGNATION   47
          SLOPES GRACIOUS UP THE WESTERN RIDGE   . . . . . 54 RESIGNATION   53
          OER THE SUN-REDDEND WESTERN STRAITS   . . . . . . 198 FRAG ANTIGONE   92
          ON THIS FAIR WESTERN LAWN   . . . . 201 PHILOMELA   V 18
          OUTSIDE THE WESTERN STRAITS AND UNBENT SAILS   . . 262 SCHOLAR-GIPSY   247
          THAT LONELY TREE AGAINST THE WESTERN SKY   . . . 268 THYRSIS   195
          OF GIANT MOUNTAINS BY THE WESTERN MAIN   . . . . 475 CROMWELL   105
          TO WESTERN SHORES THE DEATH-PLACE OF THE DAY   . . 475 CROMWELL   112
          IN THE FARTHEST WESTERN WILD   . . . .   PILLARS UNIVERS   5

WESTWARD
          WESTWARD ON THE SIDE OF FRANCE . . . . 13 CHURCH BROU 1   20
          WIDENS SLOWLY WESTWARD ALL THAT WHILE   . . . . 33 NEW SIRENS   V 218
          ONE CAME FROM PENMON WESTWARD AND A GLOW   . . . 170 EAST AND WEST   5
          THEN TURNING WESTWARD TO THE ADDERS HILL   . . . 357 MEROPE   779
          OF MESSOGIS WESTWARD BREAK   . . . . 433 EMPEDOCLES II   138
          MOUNTING WESTWARD HIGH AND HIGHER   . . . . 433 EMPEDOCLES II   139

WET
          ON THE WET UMBRAGE OF THEIR GLOSSY TOPS   . . . . 24 DREAM   4
          THE WET FLOWERD GRASS HEAVES UP ITS HEAD   . . . 57 RESIGNATION   185
          AND WENT ABROAD INTO THE COLD WET FOG   . . . . 61 SOHRAB RUSTUM   10
          AND DEAR AS THE WET DIVER TO THE EYES   . . . . 69 SOHRAB RUSTUM   284
          AND DEAR AS THE WET FISHER TO THE EYES   . . . . 69 SOHRAB RUSTUM   V 284
          THEIR LIPS STILL WET WHEN I CAME DOWN   . . . . 90 SICK KING BOKH   84
          TEARS WET THE PILLOW BY THY CHEEK BUT THOU   . . 103 BALDER DEAD 1   290
          AND UP FROM THENCE A WET AND MISTY ROAD   . . . . 113 BALDER DEAD 2   289
          OF THOSE OLD OAKS WHOSE WET RED LEAVES   . . . . 141 TRISTRAM 1   359
          THE CASTLE-COURT ALL WET WITH RAIN   . . . . . . 148 TRISTRAM 2   170
          SAY HAS SOME WET BIRD-HAUNTED ENGLISH LAWN . . . 175 PARTING   19
          PASSING OUT FROM THE WET TURF   . . . . 186 STRAYED REVEL   31
          BEHOLD WITH TEARS MINE EYES ARE WET   . . . . . . 245 BURIED LIFE   2
          BEHOLD WITH TEARS MY EYES ARE WET   . . . . 245 BURIED LIFE   V   2
          TRAILING IN THE COOL STREAM THY FINGERS WET   . . 257 SCHOLAR-GIPSY   75
          FROM THE WET FIELD THROUGH THE VEXT GARDEN-TREES . . 264 THYRSIS   58
          WHERE THAT WET SMOKE AMONG THE WOODS   . . . . . 299 GRANDE CHARTR   11
          HIGH IN THE VALLEY WET AND DREAR   . . . . 299 GRANDE CHARTR   17
          AND DARKNESS STEAL OER THE WET GRASS   . . . . . 310 OBERMANN   117
          THEY FEEL THE COOL WET TURF UNDER THEIR FEET   . . 406 EMPEDOCLES I 1   2
          ONE SEES ONES FOOTPRINTS CRUSHD IN THE WET GRASS . . 406 EMPEDOCLES I 1   14
          THAT MUFFLE ITS WET BANKS BUT GLADE   . . . . . . 414 EMPEDOCLES I 2   51

WETTED
          WEEPING THE SANDS WERE WETTED AND THEIR ARMS   . . 115 BALDER DEAD 3   62

WEVE
          SIT SIT BY ME I WILL THINK WEVE LIVED SO   . . . . 143 TRISTRAM 2   35

WHALES
          WHERE GREAT WHALES COME SAILING BY   . . . . 162 FORSAKEN MERM   43

WHEATFIELDS
          AND BOYS WHO IN LONE WHEATFIELDS SCARE THE ROOKS . . 257 SCHOLAR-GIPSY   64

WHEEL
          IT TURNS LIFES MIGHTY WHEEL   . . . . 47 WORLD QUIETIST   13
          YET AS THE WHEEL FLIES ROUND   . . . . 47 WORLD QUIETIST   17
          SHE SITS AT HER WHEEL IN THE HUMMING TOWN   . . . 164 FORSAKEN MERM   87
          FOR THE WHEEL WHERE I SPUN   . . . . 164 FORSAKEN MERM   92
          AND THE WHIZZING WHEEL STANDS STILL   . . . . . . 164 FORSAKEN MERM   97

WHET
    AND BEGAN TO WHET HIS KNIFE . . . . 433 EMPEDOCLES II 150

WHETTING
    WATCHING HOW THE WHETTING SPED . . . . 434 EMPEDOCLES II 164

WHILE
    YES WHILE ON EARTH A THOUSAND DISCORDS RING . . 1 QUIET WORK 9
    IF THOUGHTS NOT IDLE WHILE BEFORE ME FLOW . . . . 7 REP FRIEND 11
    THE REST I GIVE TO JOY EVEN WHILE I SPEAK . . . . 10 MYCERINUS 55
    WHILE THE DEEP-BURNISHD FOLIAGE OVERHEAD . . . . 11 MYCERINUS 98
    BUT SHE DIED WHILE IT WAS BUILDING . . . . . . 14 CHURCH BROU 1 67
    THEY MUST LOVE WHILE THEY MUST BUT THE HEARTS 19 MODERN SAPPHO 15
        THAT LOVE LONGER
    WHILE THE SOVRAN HEART IS DEAD . . . . . . 28 NEW SIRENS 78
    CAN YOUR EYES WHILE FOOLS ARE DOZING . . . . . . 33 NEW SIRENS 209
    SPREADS ITS COLD LIGHT WIDER ALL THAT WHILE . . 33 NEW SIRENS 218
    WHILE THE PRINCELY HEART IS DEAD . . . . . . 28 NEW SIRENS V 78
    WHILE THE DAWNING OF THE MORROW . . . . . . 33 NEW SIRENS V 217
    WIDENS SLOWLY WESTWARD ALL THAT WHILE . . . . 33 NEW SIRENS V 218
    SO IT MUST BE YET WHILE LEADING . . . . . . 49 SECOND BEST 13
    A STRAIND LIFE WHILE OVERFEEDING . . . . . . 49 SECOND BEST 14
    YET WHILE I LANGUISH . . . . 50 CONSOLATION 6
    CROUCHD ON HIS SADDLE WHILE THE SUN . . . . 52 RESIGNATION 10
    WHILE IT MENDS LITTLE TROUBLES MUCH . . . . 56 RESIGNATION 127
    FAUSTA BETRAYS YOU COLD THE WHILE . . . . 58 RESIGNATION 200
    MAN ITERATES WHILE THESE FORBEAR . . . . 60 RESIGNATION 272
    THIS TOO THOU KNOWST THAT WHILE I STILL BEAR ON . . 62 SOHRAB RUSTUM 46
    UNMURMURING IN OUR TENTS WHILE IT IS WAR . . . 63 SOHRAB RUSTUM 72
    STAND FORTH THE WHILE AND TAKE THEIR CHALLENGE UP 66 SOHRAB RUSTUM 183
    SO WILL HE SPEAK PERHAPS WHILE MEN APPLAUD . . . 72 SOHRAB RUSTUM 362
    AND PIERCED THE MIGHTY RUSTUM WHILE HE LAY . . . 73 SOHRAB RUSTUM 423
    HE CEASED BUT WHILE HE SPAKE RUSTUM HAD RISEN . . 74 SOHRAB RUSTUM 448
    AND FALSEHOOD WHILE I LIVED WAS FAR FROM MINE . . 80 SOHRAB RUSTUM 657
    AND TRULY WHILE I SPEAK O KING . . . . . . 92 SICK KING BOKH 129
    WHILE TWILIGHT FELL AND SACRED NIGHT CAME ON . . 97 BALDER DEAD 1 71
    WHO WHILE THE MOTHER SPAKE HAD CEASED THEIR TOIL . . 100 BALDER DEAD 1 195
    WHILE WE YET LIVED AMONG THE OTHER GODS . . . 104 BALDER DEAD 1 330
    AND BURST THEIR ROOTS WHILE TO THEIR TOPS THE GODS 106 BALDER DEAD 2 57
    WHILE ON HIS ISLAND IN THE LAKE AFAR . . . 111 BALDER DEAD 2 214
    AND ALL THESE GLADLY WHILE WE DRINK WE HEAR . . 117 BALDER DEAD 3 135
    AND WHILE THEY GAZED THE SUN WENT LURID DOWN . . 119 BALDER DEAD 3 194
    FOR DEAR-BELOVED WAS BALDER WHILE HE LIVED . . . 120 BALDER DEAD 3 232
    WHILE FROM THE EAST THE GIANT RYMER STEERS . . . 127 BALDER DEAD 3 478
    WHILE THE KNIGHTS ARE AT THE WARS . . . . . 131 TRISTRAM 1 44
    WHILE HE MUTTERS BROKENLY . . . . 133 TRISTRAM 1 93
    WE SHALL SEE WHILE ABOVE US . . . . 165 FORSAKEN MERM 116
    WHILE BY HER BEDSIDE HEBREW RITES HAVE PLACE . . 168 RACHEL 3 8
    WHILE YET THE NIGHT IS CHILL . . . . 183 ABSENCE 18
    AH SHALL I SEE THEE WHILE A FLUSH . . . . 184 TERRACE BERNE 13
    WHILE WE RANGE THE WOODLAND . . . . . . 188 STRAYED REVEL 73
    SITTING BY ME WHILE HIS FAUNS . . . . . . 194 STRAYED REVEL 265
    WHILE WE FOR HOPELESS PASSION DIE . . . . . 202 URANIA 6
    WHILE THUS MY FRIEND DISCOURSED WE PASS . . . 222 EPILOG LAOCOON 36
    WHILE THROUGH THEIR EARTH-MOORD NAVE BELOW . . . 223 EPILOG LAOCOON 73
    WHILE THROUGH THE EARTH-MOORD NAVE BELOW . . . 223 EPILOG LAOCOON V 73
    SEEST US CHANGE WHILE WE LIVE . . . . . . 232 YOUTH OF MAN 6
    BUT LEAVE US NOT WHILE WE LIVE . . . . 234 YOUTH OF MAN 60
    WHILE THE LOCKS ARE YET BROWN ON THY HEAD . . . 235 YOUTH OF MAN 112
    WHILE THE SOUL STILL LOOKS THROUGH THINE EYES . . 235 YOUTH OF MAN 113
    WHILE THE HEART STILL POURS . . . . . . 235 YOUTH OF MAN 114
    ROUND TROY BUT WHILE THIS STOOD TROY COULD NOT FALL 236 PALLADIUM 8
    AND WHILE IT LASTS WE CANNOT WHOLLY END . . . 236 PALLADIUM 24
    WHILE YET UPON THE VERGE OF HEAVEN HE STOOD . . 239 REVOLUTIONS 2
    AND WHILE THEY TRY TO STEM . . . . 243 SUMMER NIGHT 47
    WHILE ALL AROUND IN SILENCE LIES . . . . . 250 WISH 30
    WHILE TO MY EAR FROM UPLANDS FAR AWAY . . . . 255 SCHOLAR-GIPSY 17
    TURND ONCE TO WATCH WHILE THICK THE SNOWFLAKES FALL 259 SCHOLAR-GIPSY 128
    WE PRIZED IT DEARLY WHILE IT STOOD WE SAID . . . 263 THYRSIS 28
    WHILE THE TREE LIVED HE IN THESE FIELDS LIVED ON . . 263 THYRSIS 30
    DESPAIR I WILL NOT WHILE I YET DESCRY . . . . 268 THYRSIS 193
    WHILE BY THE STRAND . . . . 275 SOUTHERN NIGHT 8
    WHILE HARK FAR DOWN WITH STRANGLED SOUND . . . 299 GRANDE CHARTR 9
    SILENT WHILE YEARS ENGRAVE THE BROW . . . . 302 GRANDE CHARTR 113
    BUT WHILE WE WAIT ALLOW OUR TEARS . . . . 304 GRANDE CHARTR 162
    WHILE THUS I MUSED NIGHT GENTLY RAN . . . . 314 OBERMANN MORE 57
    HE LIVED WHILE WE BELIEVED . . . . . . 318 OBERMANN MORE 168
    WHILE WE BELIEVED ON EARTH HE WENT . . . . 318 OBERMANN MORE 169
    WHILE THE WORLD LIES FORLORN . . . . . . 321 OBERMANN MORE 248
    BUT HERE WHILE HARBOURING ON ITS MARGIN LAY . . 332 MEROPE 70
    IT LIVES AND WHILE I SEE THE LIGHT WILL LIVE . . 334 MEROPE 121
    BUT WHILE I SMOTE HIM QUEEN I HONOURD HIM . . 334 MEROPE 132
    RAVIN A LITTLE WHILE IN SPOIL AND BLOOD . . . 339 MEROPE 297
    THY CROWN CONDEMNS THEE WHILE THY TONGUE ABSOLVES 340 MEROPE 332
    TEARS FALL THICKLY THE WHILE . . . . . . 342 MEROPE 389
    A KING A KING WAS HE WHILE HE LIVED . . . 345 MEROPE 472
    WHILE STOOD OER HIM A FORM . . . . . . 346 MEROPE 492
    I SEND AND THESE LIBATIONS POUR THE WHILE . . . 350 MEROPE 595
    THEREFORE WHILE ACTS ARE FROM THEIR MOTIVES JUDGED 352 MEROPE 644
    WHILE FROM THE TURF WHEREON I LAY I SPRANG . . . 358 MEROPE 829

WHILE   (CONTINUED)
          WHILE ALL ELSE GRIEVES HIM THAT HIS GRANDCHILDS DEATH   359 MEROPE   851
          WHILE THE MATRONS COME TO THE DOORS   360 MEROPE   899
          WHILE LOYALTY WITH ALL HER SPEED IS SLOW   363 MEROPE   963
          WHILE THE GOOD SLEEP THE WORKERS HAVE THE DAY   366 MEROPE   996
          WHILE ALL THIS TIME I BEAR TO LINGER ON   366 MEROPE   1017
          WILL I SEEK TIDINGS TAKE THE WHILE THIS WORD   368 MEROPE   1078
          WHILE TROUBLED INNOCENTS TOSS AND LIE AWAKE   372 MEROPE   1155
          IS LIFELESS WHILE ITS HEART REMAINS UNTOUCHD   382 MEROPE   1343
          PROMISE NOT FAIR LET HIM A LITTLE WHILE   388 MEROPE   1506
          THAT MOMENT WHILE WITH UPTURND EYES HE PRAYD   402 MEROPE   1918
          AND WHILE WE DREAM ON THIS   425 EMPEDOCLES I 2   404
          AND WHILE WE DREAM OF THIS   425 EMPEDOCLES I 2 V 404
          WHILE OER HIS SOVRAN EYE   431 EMPEDOCLES II   78
          OVER THE UNRECOGNISING SEA WHILE AIR   439 EMPEDOCLES II   361
          WHILE OER HIS SOVEREIGN EYE   431 EMPEDOCLES II V 78
          AND WAIT WHILE HE DID THERE A SPACE ABIDE   445 WESTMIN ABBEY   26
          WHILE TONGUES OF FIRE ON COIGN AND CARVING PLAY   445 WESTMIN ABBEY   36
          THEN FADES BUT SPEAKS THE WHILE   445 WESTMIN ABBEY   47
          WHILE TO EACH OTHER WE REHEARSE   451 GEISTS GRAVE   43
          GRAVELY THOU THE WHILE POOR DEAR   455 POOR MATTHIAS   119
          TEACH US WHILE THEY COME AND GO   456 POOR MATTHIAS   139
          THE WHILE THERE SLEEPS WITHIN THY PRECINCTS DREAD   464 ALARIC AT ROME   51
          WHILE FULL AND CEASELESS AS THE OCEAN ROLL   464 ALARIC AT ROME   71
          AND DASH OUR HOLIEST RAPTURES WHILE WE GAZE   470 ALARIC AT ROME 200
          AND WHILE THEY RISE HERE MIGHT WE STAND ALONE   470 ALARIC AT ROME 203
          THAT WHILE WE FEEL THE WORLD IS DULL AND LOW   470 ALARIC AT ROME 215
          A LITTLE WHILE ALAS A LITTLE WHILE   470 ALARIC AT ROME 217
          A LITTLE WHILE ALAS A LITTLE WHILE   470 ALARIC AT ROME 217
          WHILE OER THE DUSTY PLAIN THE MURMUROUS THRONG   473 CROMWELL   43
          HIGH THOUGHTS WERE HIS BUT MEMORYS GLANCE THE WHILE   474 CROMWELL   69
          ONLY WHILE THEIR LOVE LIVD LASTED THEY   482 THEKLAS ANSWER   8
          WHILE THEIR MASTERS SATE BY THE FIRE AND WAITED   HOMER TRANS   6
             FOR MORNING
          WHO WHILE I PONDERED ON THE LOT OF SOULS   RUDE ORATOR   2

WHILST
          WHILST OTHER MEN MAKE CHEER AND SING   93 SICK KING BOKH 178
          WHILST EVERY CHORD THAT THRILLS AT THOUGHTS OF HOME   467 ALARIC AT ROME 131

WHIM
          TOUCHING THY HARP AS THE WHIM CAME ON THEE   407 EMPEDOCLES I 1   33

WHIPS
          CHRIST WHAT A NIGHT HOW THE SLEET WHIPS THE PANE   130 TRISTRAM 1   4

WHIRL
          THE WAVES ROAR AND WHIRL   165 FORSAKEN MERM   117

WHIRLD
          IN ACTIONS DIZZYING EDDY WHIRLD   60 RESIGNATION   277
          CAUGHT THEM AS WIND TAKES FEATHERS WHIRLD THEM ROUND   358 MEROPE   824

WHIRLING
          LEAVES WERE WHIRLING IN THE ALLEYS   30 NEW SIRENS   125
          LEAVES ARE WHIRLING IN THE ALLEYS   30 NEW SIRENS   V 125
          ON THE WILD WHIRLING WAVES MOURNFULLY MOURNFULLY   35 VOICE   7
          ALL RED WITH BLOOD THE WHIRLING RIVER FLOWS   137 TRISTRAM 1   234
          WITH SILENCE BALM MY WHIRLING BRAIN   158 SAINT BRANDAN   70
          WHETHER THROUGH WHIRLING SAND   193 STRAYED REVEL   247

WHIRLS
          WHIRLS EARTH AND HEAVEN AND MEN AND GODS ALONG   9 MYCERINUS   V 39
          THAT WHIRLS THE SPIRIT FROM ITSELF AWAY   243 SUMMER NIGHT   30
          FLASHING IN THE DANCES WHIRLS   434 EMPEDOCLES II   182

WHIRLWIND
          AND IN A SANDY WHIRLWIND WRAPPD THE PAIR   75 SOHRAB RUSTUM   485
          FOR DREAD FOR LIKE A WHIRLWIND ODIN CAME   102 BALDER DEAD 1   264
          ODIN THOU WHIRLWIND WHAT A THREAT IS THIS   120 BALDER DEAD 3   248

WHIRLWINDS
          OR LOUDER RUSH OF WHIRLWINDS SWEEPING BY   466 ALARIC AT ROME 111

WHISPER
          LET IN THY VOICE A WHISPER OFTEN COME   269 THYRSIS   235
          A WHISPER THROUGH THE PALACE FLIES OF ONE   361 MEROPE   914
          WHERE YOU WHISPER IS ASSURANCE   META CLOISTER   21

WHISPERD
          HAVE WHISPERD IT TO THE COMPLAINING SEA   8 RELIGIOUS ISOL   11
          AND I WHISPERD FIX ON HIM   458 POOR MATTHIAS   195

WHISPERED
          AND THE DAMES WHISPERED SCOFFINGLY   146 TRISTRAM 2   124

WHISPERING
          WHISPERING A LITTLE SPACE AND THOU ART MINE   11 MYCERINUS   106
          SILKEN COURTIERS WHISPERING HONIED NOTHINGS   144 TRISTRAM 2   47
          SPARE ME THE WHISPERING CROWDED ROOM   250 WISH   13
          WHISPERING HOPE OF A LIFE   369 MEROPE   1088

WHISPERING   (CONTINUED)
     WHISPERING FROM ALL AROUND ALL EARTHLY THINGS MUST DIE 469 ALARIC AT ROME   180

WHISPERS
     O UNFORGOTTEN VOICE THY WHISPERS COME   • • • •   36 VOICE   V 29
     EVEN NOW THEIR WHISPERS PIERCE THE GLOOM   • • • •   301 GRANDE CHARTR   71
     WHISPERS IN MOURNFUL TONES THY SILENT ELEGY   • • 464 ALARIC AT ROME   66
     AND WHISPERS TO THE LISTENING WINDS THAT SWELL   • • 472 CROMWELL   19

WHISTLED
     THE BLACKBIRD WHISTLED FROM THE DINGLES NEAR   • • 155 TRISTRAM 3   197

WHISTLING
     MAKE WHISTLING TOWRD HIS MIST-WREATHED FLOCK   • •   57 RESIGNATION   183
     MAKE WHISTLING TOWARDS HIS MIST-WREATHED FLOCK   • •   57 RESIGNATION   V 183

WHITE
     ON HER PALFREY WHITE THE DUCHESS   • • • • • •   15 CHURCH BROU 1   93
     CLAD IN BLACK ON HER WHITE PALFREY   • • • • • •   15 CHURCH BROU 1   97
     YOU HEAR THE WHITE-ROBED PRIEST SAY MASS • • • •   17 CHURCH BROU 2   29
     AND RISE UPON YOUR COLD WHITE MARBLE BEDS • • • •   18 CHURCH BROU 3   27
     AND RAISE YOU ON YOUR COLD WHITE MARBLE BEDS   • •   18 CHURCH BROU 3   V 27
     FASTEND ON HER DARK HAIR AND HER WREATH OF   19 MODERN SAPPHO   11
          WHITE HEATHER
     CLAD WERE THEY BOTH IN WHITE FLOWERS IN THEIR BREAST 25 DREAM   23
     THEIR LIPS MOVED THEIR WHITE ARMS WAVED EAGERLY • • 25 DREAM   28
     CLAD WERE THEY BOTH IN WHITE FLOWERS IN THEIR BREASTS 25 DREAM   V 23
     SEE THE WHITE EAST AND THE MORNING RAYS   • • • • •   34 NEW SIRENS   242
     A WHITE-ROBED SLAVE STOLE TO THE GREAT KINGS SIDE   47 WORLD QUIETIST   27
     A WHITE-ROBED SLAVE STOLE TO THE MONARCHS SIDE   • • 47 WORLD QUIETIST   V 27
     IN HIS WHITE QUAINT-EMBROIDERD FROCK   • • • • • •   57 RESIGNATION   182
     AND THREW A WHITE CLOAK ROUND HIM AND HE TOOK   • •   64 SOHRAB RUSTUM   98
     FLOWD WITH THE STREAM ALL DOWN HIS COLD WHITE SIDE   86 SOHRAB RUSTUM   842
     LIKE THE SOILD TISSUE OF WHITE VIOLETS   • • • • •   86 SOHRAB RUSTUM   844
     HIS LIMBS GREW SLACK MOTIONLESS WHITE HE LAY   • •   86 SOHRAB RUSTUM   848
     WHITE WITH EYES CLOSED ONLY WHEN HEAVY GASPS   • •   86 SOHRAB RUSTUM   849
     AND I TO TARRY WITH THE WHITE-HAIRD ZAL   • • • •   68 SOHRAB RUSTUM   V 232
     MAKES THE HEAD WHITE AND BOWS THE KNEES   • • • •   92 SICK KING BOKH   152
     FROM HERE THE COLD WHITE MIST CAN BE DISCERND   • •   108 BALDER DEAD 2   124
     TOO SOON FOR FAME WITH WHITE UNGRAVEN SHIELDS   • • 109 BALDER DEAD 2   165
     CLOUDS OF WHITE ROLLING VAPOURS FILL THE VALE   • •   113 BALDER DEAD 2   298
     HER FLOCK ALONG THE WHITE NORWEGIAN BEACH   • • • •   117 BALDER DEAD 3   150
     AS THE DRIVEN SNOW ARE WHITE   • • • • • •   131 TRISTRAM 1   31
     HER SNOW-WHITE HANDS HER GOLDEN HAIR • • • • • •   132 TRISTRAM 1   51
     ISEULT OF THE SNOW-WHITE HAND   • • • • • •   132 TRISTRAM 1   74
     FOR THE GLEAM OF THY WHITE SAIL   • • • • • •   138 TRISTRAM 1   272
     IT SHINES UPON THE BLANK WHITE WALLS   • • • • •   141 TRISTRAM 1   335
     ALL SHINING IN THE WHITE MOON-BEAMS   • • • • • •   141 TRISTRAM 1   370
     SEE MY CHEEK AND LIPS HOW WHITE THEY ARE   • • •   143 TRISTRAM 2   24
     STRUNG LIKE WHITE STARS THE PEARLS STILL ARE   • •   146 TRISTRAM 2   109
     FLASH ON HER WHITE ARMS STILL   • • • • • • •   146 TRISTRAM 2   111
     OF VEIND WHITE-GLEAMING QUARTZ AND HERE AND THERE   150 TRISTRAM 3   17
     ON HER WHITE PALFREY HERE HE MET HIS END   • • • •   154 TRISTRAM 3   162
     HAD SCORED HER WHITE RIGHT HAND WHICH SHE ALLOWS • • 154 TRISTRAM 3   174
     THEN WHITE WITH BLOSSOM AND YOU SAW THE HORNS   • •   155 TRISTRAM 3   192
     ACROSS THE HOLLOW WHITE ANEMONIES   • • • • • •   155 TRISTRAM 3   207
     FROM THE OPEN WASTE WHITE BY THE HEDGEROWS LAY   • •   TRISTRAM 3   V 51
     HE SEES FLOAT PAST AN ICEBERG WHITE   • • • • •   156 SAINT BRANDAN   15
     HE SEES FLOAT NEAR AN ICEBERG WHITE   • • • • •   156 SAINT BRANDAN   V 15
     ON HIS WHITE MULE ACROSS THE BRIDGE   • • • • • •   160 NECKAN   47
     NOW THE WILD WHITE HORSES PLAY • • • • • • •   161 FORSAKEN MERM   6
     THE WILD WHITE HORSES FOAM AND FRET   • • • • •   162 FORSAKEN MERM   21
     ONE LAST LOOK AT THE WHITE-WALLD TOWN   • • • • •   162 FORSAKEN MERM   25
     WHERE THE SEA-STOCKS BLOOM TO THE WHITE-WALLD TOWN   163 FORSAKEN MERM   69
     AT THE WHITE SLEEPING TOWN   • • • • • • •   165 FORSAKEN MERM   137
     A ROBE OF SACKCLOTH NEXT THE SMOOTH WHITE SKIN   • • 166 AUSTERITY POET   11
     HALT AT THE WHITE AND SILENT COLONNADE   • • • •   167 RACHEL 1   5
     ITS WHITE PEAKS IN AIR   • • • • • • • • •   175 PARTING   14
     WHERE THE WHITE MISTS FOR EVER • • • • • •   177 PARTING   87
     ON THY WHITE SHOULDER   • • • • • • • •   186 STRAYED REVEL   18
     WAVES THY WHITE ROBE   • • • • • • • •   186 STRAYED REVEL   22
     WHEN THE WHITE DAWN FIRST   • • • • • • •   186 STRAYED REVEL   24
     IACCHUS WHITE FANE   • • • • • • •   186 STRAYED REVEL   38
     HIS WHITE DELICATE NECK   • • • • • • •   188 STRAYED REVEL   83
     HIS SCORND WHITE HAIRS   • • • • • • • •   192 STRAYED REVEL   219
     IN THE WHITE ACACIA FLOWERS   • • • • • •   201 PHILOMELA   V
     AND FROM THE ELDER-BLOSSOM WHITE   • • • • •   218 BACCHANALIA 1   11
     LOOSE OER THEIR SHOULDERS WHITE   • • • • •   218 BACCHANALIA 1   26
     SILENT AND WHITE UNOPENING DOWN   • • • • •   242 SUMMER NIGHT   4
     HOUSES WITH LONG WHITE SWEEP   • • • • • •   242 SUMMER NIGHT   18
     AND ONLY THE WHITE SHEEP ARE SOMETIMES SEEN   • •   255 SCHOLAR-GIPSY   8
     OF FLOWERS THE FRAIL-LEAFD WHITE ANEMONY   • • • •   257 SCHOLAR-GIPSY   87
     AND GAIND THE WHITE BROW OF THE CUMNER RANGE   • •   259 SCHOLAR-GIPSY   127
     TALL GRASSES AND WHITE FLOWERING NETTLES WAVE   • •   259 SCHOLAR-GIPSY   139
     WITH BLOSSOMS RED AND·WHITE OF FALLEN MAY   • • •   264 THYRSIS   55
     AND THE FULL MOON AND THE WHITE EVENING-STAR   • •   264 THYRSIS   70
     SHE KNEW EACH LILY WHITE WHICH ENNA YIELDS • • • •   265 THYRSIS   95
     I KNOW WHAT WHITE WHAT PURPLE FRITILLARIES • • • •   266 THYRSIS   107
     WITH THORNS ONCE STUDDED OLD WHITE-BLOSSOMD TREES   266 THYRSIS   113
     THE WHITE FOG CREEPS FROM BUSH TO BUSH ABOUT   • •   267 THYRSIS   162
     CETTE WITH ITS GLISTENING HOUSES WHITE   • • • •   275 SOUTHERN NIGHT   9

WHITE   (CONTINUED)
          AND WHITER THAN THY WHITE BURNOUS   • • • • • •   276 SOUTHERN NIGHT   43
          HOAR-HEADED WRINKLED CLAD IN WHITE   • • • • • •   278 SOUTHERN NIGHT   86
          GREY-HEADED WRINKLED CLAD IN WHITE   • • • • • •   278 SOUTHERN NIGHT   V 86
          SHAKING HIS THIN WHITE HAIRS   • • • • •   289 RUGBY CHAPEL   112
          FLOWER OF MARBLE OF WHITE   • • • • • • •   296 HEINES GRAVE   131
          SWIFT RUSH THE SPECTRAL VAPOURS WHITE   • • •   299 GRANDE CHARTR   13
          COWLD FORMS BRUSH BY IN GLEAMING WHITE   • •   300 GRANDE CHARTR   36
          AND WHITE UPLIFTED FACES STAND   • • • • •   300 GRANDE CHARTR   41
          SHOWD ME THE HIGH WHITE STAR OF TRUTH   • •   301 GRANDE CHARTR   69
          FAST RUSH THE SPECTRAL VAPOURS WHITE   • • • •   299 GRANDE CHARTR   V 13
          THE WHITE MISTS ROLLING LIKE A SEA   • • • • •   306 OBERMANN   9
          THE SOUL OF THEIR WHITE SNOWS   • • • • • •   307 OBERMANN   28
          WHITE HOUSES PRANK WHERE ONCE WERE HUTS   • •   312 OBERMANN MORE   3
          CLUSTERING OER THY WHITE FOREHEAD LIKE A GIRLS   •   373 MEROPE   1162
          THE WHITE MOUNTAIN-BIRDS   • • • • • • • •   392 MEROPE   1625
          WHEN THE WHITE-ROBED GARLAND-CROWNED MONARCH   •   400 MEROPE   1857
          THE FLOWER-DRESSD VICTIM STOOD A MILK-WHITE BULL •   401 MEROPE   1910
          I SADDLED MY WHITE MULE AND ALL NIGHT LONG   • •   407 EMPEDOCLES I 1   44
          THE PEAK ROUND WHICH THE WHITE CLOUDS PLAY • • •   414 EMPEDOCLES I 2   56
          AND THE WHITE OLYMPUS-PEAKS   • • • • • •   431 EMPEDOCLES II   80
          HIS WHITE GARMENT TO HIS EYES   • • • • • •   434 EMPEDOCLES II   188
          THAT HEAVES ITS WHITE AND BILLOWY VAPOURS UP   •   438 EMPEDOCLES II   309
          LIE STREWN THE WHITE FLOCKS   • • • • • •   442 EMPEDOCLES II   430
          SO WHITE THROUGH THE GLOOM   • • • • • •   442 EMPEDOCLES II   438
          BY THEIR CHARIOTS STOOD THE STEEDS AND CHAMPD   HOMER TRANS   5
                  THE WHITE BARLEY
          AND HE WAS GIVEN A VOICE BY THE WHITE-ARMD   HOMER TRANS   46
                  GODDESS HERA
          WAVING HER MYRIADS OF WHITE FAIRY BLOOMS   • • • •   EVERLASTING SUB   6

WHITEND
          WHEN THE FROST FLOWERS THE WHITEND WINDOW-PANES • •   70 SOHRAB RUSTUM   306
          WHITEND HIS FACE FROM THE SUNS FRONTING RAY   • •   170 EAST AND WEST   6

WHITENING
          AND YON WHITENING BONE-MOUNDS DO NOT GROW   • • • •   27 NEW SIRENS   56
          AND THOSE WHITENING BONE-MOUNDS DO NOT GROW   • •   27 NEW SIRENS   V 56
          WITH WHITENING HEDGES AND UNCRUMPLING FERN • • • •   265 THYRSIS   74
          THEN FROM THOSE WHITENING LIPS AS DEATH DREW NEAR   478 CROMWELL   213

WHITENS
          GREAT ELBRUIS WHITENS CLEAR   • • • • • • •   PILLARS UNIVERS   10

WHITER
          AND WHITER THAN THY WHITE BURNOUS   • • • • • •   276 SOUTHERN NIGHT   43

WHITHER
          NOW THEREFORE WHAT TO ATTEMPT OR WHITHER FLY   • •   98 BALDER DEAD 1   105
          WHITHER DOES HE WANDER NOW   • • • • • • •   136 TRISTRAM 1   189
          BUT SHE HERSELF WHITHER SHE WILL CAN ROVE   • • •   156 TRISTRAM 3   223
          BUT WHITHER GOST THOU HENCE O QUEEN AWAY   • • •   350 MEROPE   597
          WHITHER FROM WINTRY MAENALUS WERE BROUGHT   • • •   356 MEROPE   741

WHIZZING
          AND THE WHIZZING WHEEL STANDS STILL   • • • • • •   164 FORSAKEN MERM   97

WHOEER
          FLY HENCE POOR WRETCH WHOEER THOU ART   • • • •   307 OBERMANN   17

WHOLE
          WHO SAW LIFE STEADILY AND SAW IT WHOLE   • • • •   2 TO A FRIEND   12
          SO MEN UNRAVELLING GODS HARMONIOUS WHOLE   • • • •   4 BUTLERS SERMONS   3
          THOUGH SLOWLY THE FAMILIAR WHOLE   • • • • •   55 RESIGNATION   95
          A PLACID AND CONTINUOUS WHOLE   • • • • • •   57 RESIGNATION   190
          CREEDS PASS RITES CHANGE NO ALTAR STANDETH WHOLE • •   173 MONICAS PRAYER   12
          CLEAR PROSPECT OER OUR BEINGS WHOLE   • • • • •   179 FAREWELL   54
          WHAT THE PARTS AND WHAT THE WHOLE SHOULD BE   • •   210 SELF-DECEPTION   V 16
          THE STREAM OF LIFES MAJESTIC WHOLE   • • • • • •   226 EPILOG LAOCOON   187
          DOTH A WHOLE TRACT OF HEAVEN DISCLOSE   • • •   242 SUMMER NIGHT   10
          AND NEVER SEES A WHOLE   • • • • • • • • • •   415 EMPEDOCLES I 2   85
          BEING ONE WITH WHICH WE ARE ONE WITH THE WHOLE WORLD   440 EMPEDOCLES II   372
          WHAT WAS FOUR YEARS THEIR WHOLE SHORT DAY   • • •   450 GEISTS GRAVE   20
          WHAT WAS FOUR YEARS THEIR WHOLE SHORT STAY   • • •   450 GEISTS GRAVE   V 20
          WHO THOUGH THE TENDENCE OF THE WHOLE   • • • • •   481 COURAGE   10

WHOLLY
          THEN SAY HE WAS NOT WHOLLY VILE   • • • • • •   95 SICK KING BOKH   231
          AS WHOLLY TO BE PITIED QUITE FORLORN   • • • • •   126 BALDER DEAD 3   458
          THIS TOO CAN CHANGE US WHOLLY AND MAKE SEEM   • •   153 TRISTRAM 3   131
          NOT WHOLLY CLEAR NOR WHOLLY BLIND   • • • • •   217 NAMELESS EPIT   V
          NOT WHOLLY CLEAR NOR WHOLLY BLIND   • • • • •   217 NAMELESS EPIT   V
          AND WHILE IT LASTS WE CANNOT WHOLLY END   • • •   236 PALLADIUM   24
          THE OLD LAW THEY CRIED IS WHOLLY COME TO NOUGHT • •   237 PROGRESS   3
          THE OLD LAW THEY SAID IS WHOLLY COME TO NOUGHT   • •   237 PROGRESS   V 3
          FOR WOES THEY WHOLLY FEEL   • • • • • • • •   320 OBERMANN MORE   236
          WHOLLY FORGET THEIR FIRST SAD LIFE AND HOME   • •   427 EMPEDOCLES I 2   458
          NOT TO DIE WHOLLY NOT TO BE ALL ENSLAVED   • • •   441 EMPEDOCLES II   406

WICKED
          FROWNING GRIM DOWN THOU WICKED KING   • • • • • •   91 SICK KING BOKH   97
          PEACE PEACE ALLS CLEAR THE WICKED WATCH AND WORK • •   365 MEROPE   995

WICKET
    KNOCK PASS THE WICKET THOU ART COME • • • • • • 300 GRANDE CHARTR   29

WIDE
    SAW THE WIDE PROSPECT AND THE ASIAN FEN • • • •   2 TO A FRIEND   3
    THE WIDE EARTH IS STILL • • • • • • • • • •   50 CONSOLATION   V
    THAT NIGHT IN THE WIDE-GLIMMERING SEA • • • •   54 RESIGNATION   85
    NOT DEEP THE POET SEES BUT WIDE • • • • • •   58 RESIGNATION   214
    WHICH IT SENT FLYING WIDE THEN SOHRAB THREW • •   73 SOHRAB RUSTUM   405
    AND THEY STOOD WIDE WITH HORROR AND HE SEIZED • •   81 SOHRAB RUSTUM   699
    THE LONGD-FOR DASH OF WAVES IS HEARD AND WIDE • •   87 SOHRAB RUSTUM   889
    THE WIDE PLAIN RINGS THE DAZED AIR THROBS WITH BLOWS 137 TRISTRAM 1   235
    FIXD ON THEIR MOTHERS FACE IN WIDE SURPRISE • •   151 TRISTRAM 3   47
    NOR TO THE BROWN HEATHS ROUND THEM BRIGHT AND WIDE   151 TRISTRAM 3   49
    IS WITH THEM AND THE WIDE HEATHS WHERE THEY PLAY • • 152 TRISTRAM 3   103
    FIXD ON THEIR MOTHERS FACE IN WIDE SURPRIZE • •   TRISTRAM 3   V 47
    NOR TO THE BROWN HEATHS ROUND THEM WARM AND WIDE • •   TRISTRAM 3   V 49
    ON THE WIDE STEPP UNHARNESSING • • • • • • •   191 STRAYED REVEL   163
    ACROSS THIS WIDE AERIAL PLAIN • • • • • • • •   204 CALAIS SANDS   6
    SPREAD WIDE AWAY THE LUMINOUS PLAIN • • • • •   204 CALAIS SANDS   V 6
    WIDE STREETS WITH FINE DOUBLE TROTTOIRS • • • •   214 NEW ROME   15
    OER THAT WIDE PLAIN NOW WRAPT IN GLOOM • • • •   220 BACCHANALIA 2   21
    THE WIDE WIDE VALLEY OUTSPREADS • • • • • •   234 YOUTH OF MAN   76
    THE WIDE WIDE VALLEY OUTSPREADS • • • • • •   234 YOUTH OF MAN   76
    ON THE WIDE OCEAN OF LIFE ANEW • • • • • • •   243 SUMMER NIGHT   53
    THE WIDE AERIAL LANDSCAPE SPREAD • • • • • •   250 WISH   34
    MID WIDE GRASS MEADOWS WHICH THE SUNSHINE FILLS • • 257 SCHOLAR-GIPSY   68
    MEN WHO THROUGH THOSE WIDE FIELDS OF BREEZY GRASS   257 SCHOLAR-GIPSY   93
    I CLIMBD BENEATH ME BRIGHT AND WIDE • • • • •   273 STANZAS CARNAC   3
    AND BEYOND THAT THE ATLANTIC WIDE • • • • • •   274 STANZAS CARNAC   29
    AND MIST-TRACKD STREAM OF THE WIDE • • • • • •   297 HEINES GRAVE   172
    WIDE GERMAN LAND GOING DOWN • • • • • • • •   297 HEINES GRAVE   173
    WORDSWORTHS SWEET CALM OR GOETHES WIDE • • • •   308 OBERMANN   79
    TOO WIDE AT VARIANCE WITH THE PEACE I SEEK • • •   333 MEROPE   107
    THAT WIDE AND VARIOUS WORLD THE HEART OF OTHERS • • 352 MEROPE   637
    THAT YOUR OWN HANDS MUST OPEN WIDE THE GATE • •   466 ALARIC AT ROME   117
    NEW DREAMS OF WIDE DOMINION MIGHTIER HIGHER • •   469 ALARIC AT ROME   175

WIDEN
    AND WIDEN AND THE PEASANTS HEART IS GLAD • • • •   122 BALDER DEAD 3   316

WIDEND
    WIDEND HER SWEEP AND SURVEYD • • • • • • • •   280 HAWORTH CHURCH   16

WIDENS
    WIDENS SLOWLY WESTWARD ALL THAT WHILE • • • •   33 NEW SIRENS   V 218
    AS THE PALE WASTE WIDENS AROUND HIM • • • • • •   254 FUTURE   83

WIDER
    SPREADS ITS COLD LIGHT WIDER ALL THAT WHILE • •   33 NEW SIRENS   218
    WIDER THAN ONE MANS PASSION THERES NO MOOD • • • •   50 CONSOLATION   V
    OF THESE AFFECTIONS WIDER MADE • • • • • • •   58 RESIGNATION   219
    ON A WIDER STATELIER STREAM • • • • • • • •   253 FUTURE   74

WIDEST
    BEYOND HIS PASSIONS WIDEST RANGE • • • • • •   58 RESIGNATION   221

WIDOW
    FOR YEARS HIS WIDOW IN THEIR SIGHT I STAND • • •   381 MEROPE   1316
    CANST THOU EXPECT WHEN THUS THY WIDOW FAILS • •   386 MEROPE   1433
    THE WIDOW OF A HUSBAND UNAVENGED • • • • • •   403 MEROPE   1955

WIDOWED
    EVEN IN THE LONENESS OF THY WIDOWED YEARS • • •   463 ALARIC AT ROME   22
    MOURNING AS WIDOWED VENICE OER HER ADRIAN TIDE • •   468 ALARIC AT ROME   162

WIDOWHOOD
    OF WIDOWHOOD IN THESE POLLUTED HALLS • • • • •   383 MEROPE   1370

WIDOWS
    TO SOUND THY TRIUMPH IN HIS WIDOWS EARS • • • •   395 MEROPE   1739

WIDTH
    AND THE WIDTH OF THE WATERS THE HUSH • • • • • •   254 FUTURE   78

WIELD
    COULD WIELD AN UNLOPPD TRUNK IT WAS AND HUGE • •   73 SOHRAB RUSTUM   409
    COULD WIELD AN UNLOPPD TRUNK IT WAS STILL ROUGH • •   73 SOHRAB RUSTUM V 409
    TO SNATCH AND WIELD IT WILL NOT SEE • • • • •   282 HAWORTH CHURCH   V
    ALL SKILL I WIELD ARE FREE • • • • • • • •   415 EMPEDOCLES I 2   105

WIFE
    LAY BEFORE HIS YOUTHFUL WIFE • • • • • •   14 CHURCH BROU 1   50
    OF HIS PALE WIFE WHO WAITS AND WEEPS ON SHORE • •   69 SOHRAB RUSTUM   285
    OF HIS PALE WIFE WHO WAITS AND WEEPS ASHORE • •   69 SOHRAB RUSTUM V 285
    FATHERS WE MUST HAVE WIFE AND CHILD • • • •   92 SICK KING BOKH   149
    BUT IN BREIDABLIK NANNA BALDERS WIFE • • • •   102 BALDER DEAD 1   268
    MOST HONOURD AFTER FREA ODINS WIFE • • • • •   116 BALDER DEAD 3   92
    TO HIS NEGLECTED WIFE AND WHAT HE IS • • • • •   116 BALDER DEAD 3   104

WIFE   (CONTINUED)
          NOT LONG A WIFE WHEN HIS UNQUIET HEART   • • • •   116 BALDER DEAD 3   107
          AND WIFE AND CHILDREN AND OUR ANCIENT HOME • • • • 117 BALDER DEAD 3   144
          DAUGHTER AND WIFE OF ODIN THUS SHE SAID   • • • •   120 BALDER DEAD 3   247
          I TOO HAD ONCE A WIFE AND ONCE A CHILD   • • • •   125 BALDER DEAD 3   403
          BUT EMPTY FOR HIS WIFE FOR NANNA CAME   • • • •   125 BALDER DEAD 3   433
          THY LOVELY YOUTHFUL WIFE GROWS PALE   • • • • •   138 TRISTRAM 1   269
          THE LOVELY YOUTHFUL WIFE GROWS PALE   • • • •   138 TRISTRAM 1   V 269
          HIS WIFE AND CHILDREN BE   • • • •   159 NECKAN   8
          GRAVE GAY CHILD PARENT HUSBAND WIFE   • • • •   226 EPILOG LAOCOON   161
          AM MEROPE THY MURDERD MASTERS WIFE   • • • • •   335 MEROPE   184
          HIS ACTS THE WIFE HE CHOSE WAS FULL OF VIRTUES • •   337 MEROPE   240
          THESE WORDS TO THINE INDULGENT EAR THY WIFE   350 MEROPE   594
          APPROVST THOU THY WIFE NOW   • • • • •   372 MEROPE   1143
          A NEW-MADE WIFE I FROM ARCADIA CAME   • • • • •   403 MEROPE   1972
          HIS HARD-TASKD SUNBURNT WIFE   • • • • • •   426 EMPEDOCLES I 2   414
          AND IN THE GRAVE HE LAID A CHERISHD WIFE • • • •   447 WESTMIN ABBEY   124
          AND TO THE GRAVE HE BORE A CHERISHD WIFE • • • •   447 WESTMIN ABBEY   V 124
          SEE THE WIFE OF HECTOR THAT GREAT PRE-EMINENT CAPTAIN HOMER TRANS   33

WIFES
          THY DEAR WIFES ASHES BURIED ARE   • • • • • •   277 SOUTHERN NIGHT   51

WIGHT
          NOT THIS FEVER-WASTED WIGHT   • • • • • • • •   133 TRISTRAM 1   107
          LIKE THAT BALD CAESAR THE FAMED ROMAN WIGHT   • •   153 TRISTRAM 3   143
          SHE LOOKD SO WITCHING FAIR THAT LEARNED WIGHT • •   154 TRISTRAM 3   181
          LIKE THAT BOLD CAESAR THE FAMED ROMAN WIGHT   • •   153 TRISTRAM 3   V 143
          TO A MUCH FEEBLER WIGHT THE HEROIC MAN   • • • •   198 FRAG ANTIGONE   96
          WELL THEN THE WISER WIGHT   • • • • • • • •   416 EMPEDOCLES I 2   129

WILD
          BUSINESS COULD NOT MAKE DULL NOR PASSION WILD   • •   2 TO A FRIEND   11
          AND IN WILD HUNT THROUGH MAZY TRACTS OF STARS   • •   10 MYCERINUS   45
          NOTES OF WILD PASTORAL MUSIC OVER ALL   • • • •   25 DREAM   12
          ON THE WILD WHIRLING WAVES MOURNFULLY MOURNFULLY • • 35 VOICE   7
          A WILD ROSE CLIMBING UP A MOULDERING WALL   • • •   36 VOICE   20
          SO SAD AND WITH SO WILD A START   • • • • •   36 VOICE   23
          FROM WILD AND WEAK COMPLAINING • • • • • • •   39 STAGIRIUS   36
          BUT IF THE WILD UNFATHERD MASS NO BIRTH   • • • •   45 IN UTRUMQUE PAR   22
          STILL THIS WILD BROOK THE RUSHES COOL   • • • •   55 RESIGNATION   104
          IN DARK KNOTS CROUCH ROUND THE WILD FLAME   • • •   55 RESIGNATION   118
          HE HAS THE WILD STAGS FOOT THE LIONS HEART • • •   66 SOHRAB RUSTUM   177
          HE HAS THE WILD STAGS FOOT THE LIONS HEART • • •   67 SOHRAB RUSTUM   216
          HE HATH THE WILD STAGS FOOT THE LIONS HEART • • •   67 SOHRAB RUSTUM   V 216
          ON THIS WILD DECEMBER NIGHT   • • • • • •   130 TRISTRAM 1   14
          WITH A WILD DELICIOUS PAIN   • • • • • • •   135 TRISTRAM 1   151
          WERE FEET LIKE THOSE MADE FOR SO WILD A WAY   • •   135 TRISTRAM 1   163
          AND THAT LONG WILD KISS THEIR LAST   • • • • •   136 TRISTRAM 1   180
          THE WILD BOAR RUSTLES IN HIS LAIR   • • • • •   149 TRISTRAM 2   183
          THE WILD BOAR HARBOURS CLOSE AND FEEDS   • • • •   148 TRISTRAM 2   V
          IN EVERY HUT ALONG THIS SEA-COAST WILD   • • • •   152 TRISTRAM 3   109
          NOW THE WILD WHITE HORSES PLAY • • • • • • •   161 FORSAKEN MERM   6
          CHILDRENS VOICES WILD WITH PAIN   • • • • •   162 FORSAKEN MERM   16
          THE WILD WHITE HORSES FOAM AND FRET   • • • • •   162 FORSAKEN MERM   21
          I COME TO THE WILD • • • • • • • •   177 PARTING   76
          ON THIS WILD EARTH OF HATE AND FEAR   • • • • •   180 FAREWELL   86
          DOTTING THE SHORELESS WATERY WILD   • • • • •   182 TO MARG CONT   3
          LET THE WILD THRONGING TRAIN   • • • • • • •   185 STRAYED REVEL   3
          SWELL THEIR LARGE VEINS TO BURSTING IN WILD PAIN •   192 STRAYED REVEL   226
          SOMETIMES A WILD-HAIRD MAENAD   • • • • • • •   194 STRAYED REVEL   275
          LET THE WILD THRONGING TRAIN   • • • • • • •   194 STRAYED REVEL   294
          SAW AND SNATCHD WILD WITH LOVE • • • • • • •   196 FRAG ANTIGONE   60
          THAT WILD UNQUENCHD DEEP-SUNKEN OLD-WORLD PAIN • •   200 PHILOMELA   8
          THE UNFRIENDLY PALACE IN THE THRACIAN WILD • • •   201 PHILOMELA   18
          SEE THE WILD MAENADS   • • • • • • • •   218 BACCHANALIA 1   28
          SO WILD SO DEEP IN US TO KNOW   • • • • • • •   246 BURIED LIFE   53
          AND ROAMD THE WORLD WITH THAT WILD BROTHERHOOD •   256 SCHOLAR-GIPSY   38
          LEAVING THE REST IN THE WILD   • • • • • • •   290 RUGBY CHAPEL   127
          YEARS THEY HAVE BEEN IN THE WILD   • • • • •   291 RUGBY CHAPEL   177
          STRONG CHILDREN OF THE ALPINE WILD   • • • • •   301 GRANDE CHARTR   57
          AND HEAR THE WILD BEES ALPINE HUM   • • • • •   313 OBERMANN MORE   47
          WILD HOG AND BEAR AND MOUNTAIN-DEER AND ROE   • •   356 MEROPE   758
          WILD BEASTS AND VULTURES SAILING OVERHEAD   • • •   373 MEROPE   1170
          WILD GOOSEBERRIES SCARED HER   • • • • • • •   392 MEROPE   1639
          WITH HEDGES OF THE WILD ROSE   • • • • • • •   399 MEROPE   1821
          FLASHT ON THE RUDE BARBARIANS WILD ARRAY   • • •   464 ALARIC AT ROME   70
          HAST THOU NOT MARKED ON A WILD AUTUMN DAY   • • •   466 ALARIC AT ROME   97
          WAS THE WILD SHOUT THOSE GOTHIC MYRIADS GAVE   • •   466 ALARIC AT ROME   112
          AND FLEETING THOUGHTS THAT ON THE LONELY WILD • •   473 CROMWELL   51
          ON LIFES WILD WAVES THE LIVING AND THE LOST   • •   474 CROMWELL   78
          NO SOFTENING RAY NO VISIONS FALSE AND WILD • • •   475 CROMWELL   125
          A REGION DESOLATE AND WILD   • • • • • • •   479 HAYSWATER BOAT   1
          AMID THE WILD WAVES WELTERING   • • • • • • •   479 HAYSWATER BOAT   8
          WITH MANY A WILD WEED OVERGROWN   • • • • •   479 HAYSWATER BOAT   14
          IN THE FARTHEST WESTERN WILD   • • • • • • •   PILLARS UNIVERS   5

WILDER
          AND CLOSE-SET SKULL-CAPS AND THOSE WILDER HORDES • •   64 SOHRAB RUSTUM   130

WAILD
    AND FAR INTO THE NIGHT THEY WAILD THEIR DIRGE   • • 103 BALDER DEAD 1   275
    HE SPAKE AND ALL THE GODS ASSENTING WAILD   • • • • 116 BALDER DEAD 3   89
    WAILD FROM THE PALACE WITHIN   • • • • • • • • 346 MEROPE   496

WAILFUL
    THEN MUST HE NOT REGARD THE WAILFUL GHOSTS   • • • • 100 BALDER DEAD 1   176
    THEN HE MUST NOT REGARD THE WAILFUL GHOSTS   • • • • 100 BALDER DEAD 1   V 176

WAILING
    THE SUNK EYES THE WAILING TONE   • • • •   34 NEW SIRENS   248
    WEEPING AND WAILING AND VALHALLA RANG   • • •   95 BALDER DEAD 1   11
    WAILING BUT OTHERWISE WAS ODINS WILL • • • •   95 BALDER DEAD 1   16
    WAILING NO MORE IN SILENCE ATE AND DRANK • • •   97 BALDER DEAD 1   70

WAILS
    AND THE WIND WAILS AMONG THE MOUNTAIN PINES   • •   18 CHURCH BROU 3   V 37

WAIN
    SILENT THE SWATHS THE RINGING WAIN   • • • • • 217 BACCHANALIA 1   5
    SILENT THE SHEAVES THE RINGING WAIN   • • • • 217 BACCHANALIA 1   V   5

WAIT
    SO TO WAIT BUT WHAT NOTES DOWN THE WIND HARK   20 MODERN SAPPHO   29
      ARE DRIVING
    THEN TO WAIT BUT WHAT NOTES DOWN THE WIND HARK   20 MODERN SAPPHO V 29
      ARE DRIVING
    ARE WILLS SO WEAK THEN LET NOT MINE WAIT LONG   • •   38 WORLDS TRIUMPHS   12
    OR DO I WAIT TO HEAR SOME GRAY-HAIRD KING • • •   43 GIPSY CHILD   33
    EVER SINCE PRAYER-TIME HE DOTH WAIT • • •   88 SICK KING BOKH   14
    SO QUICKLY AND WILL WAIT FOR NO REPLY • • • 102 BALDER DEAD 1   242
    HERE MUST THOU LIE AND WAIT AN ENDLESS AGE • • 126 BALDER DEAD 3   452
    MY PRINCESS ART THOU THERE SWEET DO NOT WAIT • • 140 TRISTRAM 1   308
    HE HEARS A VOICE SIGH HUMBLY WAIT • • • • 157 SAINT BRANDAN   23
    ONE MOMENT WAIT THOU HOLY MAN • • • 157 SAINT BRANDAN   25
    TO WORK OR WAIT ELSEWHERE OR HERE • • • 251 WISH   52
    HERE WILL I SIT AND WAIT • • • • 255 SCHOLAR-GIPSY   16
    WHO WAIT LIKE THEE BUT NOT LIKE THEE IN HOPE • 260 SCHOLAR-GIPSY   170
    HE COULD NOT WAIT THEIR PASSING HE IS DEAD • • 264 THYRSIS   50
    ALIGHT AND SPARELY SUP AND WAIT • • • 300 GRANDE CHARTR   26
    LIKE THESE ON EARTH I WAIT FORLORN • • • 302 GRANDE CHARTR   88
    AND WAIT TO SEE THE FUTURE COME • • • 303 GRANDE CHARTR   118
    BUT WHILE WE WAIT ALLOW OUR TEARS • • • 304 GRANDE CHARTR   162
    AND WAIT FOR WORDS TO COME • • • 318 OBERMANN MORE   180
    WAIT THEN UNTIL SUFFICIENT HELP APPEARS • • 384 MEROPE   1397
    LONGING LISTENING I WAIT I IMPLORE • • • 347 MEROPE   V
    CALLICLES MUST WAIT HERE AND PLAY TO HIM • • 428 EMPEDOCLES I 2   484
    AND WAIT WHILE HE DID THERE A SPACE ABIDE • • 445 WESTMIN ABBEY   26
    AND WAIT THE ISSUE SLEEPING UNDERGROUND • • 448 WESTMIN ABBEY   146
    WAIT FOR THE LEAVEN TO WORK THE LET TO END • • 449 WESTMIN ABBEY   170
    THY PASSING BY DOTH VAINLY WAIT • • • 461 KAISER DEAD   74
    MUST LEARN TO WAIT RENOUNCE WITHDRAW • • • 481 COURAGE   4

WAITED
    SILENT AND WAITED FOR THE SACRED MORN • • • 119 BALDER DEAD 3   212
    LONG IVE WAITED LONG IVE FOUGHT MY FEVER • • 142 TRISTRAM 2   3
    WHILE THEIR MASTERS SATE BY THE FIRE AND WAITED   HOMER TRANS   6
      FOR MORNING

WAITEST
    THOU WAITEST FOR THE SPARK FROM HEAVEN AND WE   • • 260 SCHOLAR-GIPSY   171

WAITING
    LADIES WAITING ROUND HER SEAT • • • • • • •   13 CHURCH BROU 1   34
    WAITING THE DARKNESS OF THE FINAL TIMES • • •   98 BALDER DEAD 1   124
    WAITING HER PASSAGE • • • • • • • • 196 FRAG ANTIGONE   43
    AND WAITING FOR THE SPARK FROM HEAVEN TO FALL • • 258 SCHOLAR-GIPSY   120

WAITS
    OF HIS PALE WIFE WHO WAITS AND WEEPS ON SHORE • •   69 SOHRAB RUSTUM   285
    OF HIS PALE WIFE WHO WAITS AND WEEPS ASHORE • •   69 SOHRAB RUSTUM V 285

WAITST
    FOR FATE THOU WAITST NOT LONG SINCE IN THIS HOUR • • 397 MEROPE   1777

WAIVE
    AND WAIVE ALL CLAIM TO BLISS AND TRY TO BEAR • • 260 SCHOLAR-GIPSY   193

WAKE
    OR IF YE WAKE LET IT BE THEN WHEN FAIR • • • •   18 CHURCH BROU 3   17
    AND IF YE WAKE LET IT BE THEN WHEN FAIR • • • •   18 CHURCH BROU 3 V 17
    TO WAKE THE GODS AND HEROES TO THEIR TASKS • • • 105 BALDER DEAD 2   9
    BUT THEY HARP EVER ON ONE STRING AND WAKE • • • 117 BALDER DEAD 3   137
    THEIR HOT SEALS AND LET HIM WAKE • • • • 139 TRISTRAM 1   295
    ONCE EVERY YEAR WHEN CAROLS WAKE • • • • 158 SAINT BRANDAN   65
    SENT ECHOES THROUGH THE NIGHT TO WAKE • • • 177 FAREWELL   3
    THE TOILS OF THY FOUL SERVICE TILL THOU WAKE • • 373 MEROPE   1181
    WAKE UP IN HELL FROM THINE UNHALLOWD SLEEP • • • 373 MEROPE   1183
    WAKE AMID GLOOM AND HOWLING AND THE NOISE • • • 373 MEROPE   1185
    NOR WAKE THE WEARY SOUL THAT SLUMBERS ON BELOW • • 469 ALARIC AT ROME   198
    GAZING ON THEE WE WAKE TO FIND IT IS NOT SO • • 470 ALARIC AT ROME   216

WANDERING   (CONTINUED)
      WANDERING WITH THE GREAT MOTHERS TRAIN DIVINE   • •   268 THYRSIS   177
      AND SOON THY FOOT RESUMED ITS WANDERING WAY   • •   269 THYRSIS   229
      SINCE ERST AT MORN SOME WANDERING SHADE   • • • •   271 MEMORIAL VERSES   37
      WANDERING BETWEEN TWO WORLDS ONE DEAD   • • • •   302 GRANDE CHARTR   85
      THOU MASTER OF MY WANDERING YOUTH   • • • •   313 OBERMANN MORE   39
      MY HUSBAND WANDERING WITH HIS STERN COMPEERS   •   367 MEROPE   1033
      THEIR KINDNESS SHOWN ME IN MY WANDERING HOUR   • •   447 WESTMIN ABBEY   109
      PERCHANCE HIS WANDERING HEART WAS FAR AWAY   • • • •   468 ALARIC AT ROME   169
      LIT BY A WANDERING GLEAM WE KNOW NOT HOW   • • •   475 CROMWELL   128
      DARE O FRIEND BE WANDERING DARE BE DREAMING   •   483 THEKLAS ANSWER   23

WANDERINGS
      WHERE THOUGH LONG WANDERINGS INTERVENE   • • • •   55 RESIGNATION   114

WANDERS
      THE EYE WANDERS FAITH IS FAILING   • • • • • •   34 NEW SIRENS   223
      AS HE WANDERS FAR FROM HERE   • • • • • • • •   133 TRISTRAM 1   88
      AH HE WANDERS FORTH AGAIN   • • • • • • • •   138 TRISTRAM 1   243
      SOMETIMES AND WANDERS FAR AMONG THE GLENS   • • • •   412 EMPEDOCLES I 2   17

WANE
      YET SUNS SHALL RISE AND MANY MOONS SHALL WANE   • •   10 MYCERINUS   62

WANED
      ALL DAY AND DAYLIGHT WANED AND NIGHT CAME ON   • •   107 BALDER DEAD 2   81
      WITH SPIRIT VANISHD BEAUTY WANED   • • • • • •   185 TERRACE BERNE   37

WANING
      BUT ONE POSSESSD HIS WANING TIME   • • • • • •   132 TRISTRAM 1   70
      TO THE CLEAR WANING HILL-SIDE   • • • • • • • •   176 PARTING   45

WANT
      THE WANT WHICH RACKD OUR BRAIN   • • • • • • •   323 OBERMANN MORE   314
      THE WANT WHICH CRAZED OUR BRAIN   • • • • • •   323 OBERMANN MORE   V 314
      THE WANT WHICH WORE OUR BRAIN   • • • • • • •   323 OBERMANN MORE   V 314
      OR OUR OWN WANT OF EFFORT BE THE BAR   • • • • • •   352 MEROPE   643
      WE WANT ALL PLEASANT ENDS BUT WILL USE NO HARSH MEANS   420 EMPEDOCLES I 2   236
      FOR WANT OF LIGHT WHICH SHOULD THE BOON CONVEY   • •   446 WESTMIN ABBEY   70
      PENITENT FOR WANT OF RACE   • • • • • • • •   454 POOR MATTHIAS   74
      WHAT THEY WANT WE CANNOT GUESS   • • • • • • •   455 POOR MATTHIAS   105
      MAKING WANT OF THEIRS AND PLAN   • • • • • • •   456 POOR MATTHIAS   151
      AT THY WANT OF A MAN LIKE ME TO SAVE THEE FROM BONDAGE   HOMER TRANS   36
      FOR BY NO SLOW PACE OR WANT OF SWIFTNESS OF OURS   • •   HOMER TRANS   50

WANTED
      HAD EVERY OTHER GIFT BUT WANTED LOVE   • • • • • •   295 HEINES GRAVE   100

WANTING
      LIFE WELL AND FIND IT WANTING NOR DEPLORE   • • • •   42 GIPSY CHILD   30
      SIGNS ARE NOT WANTING WHICH MIGHT RAISE   • • • •   56 RESIGNATION   122
      SIGNS ARE NOT WANTING IF THEY WOULD   • • • • • •   56 RESIGNATION   124

WANTS
      WHAT OUR GIFTS AND WHAT OUR WANTS SHOULD BE   • •   210 SELF-DECEPTION   16
      OUR WANTS HAVE ALL BEEN FELT OUR ERRORS MADE BEFORE   419 EMPEDOCLES I 2   211

WAR
      UNMURMURING IN OUR TENTS WHILE IT IS WAR   • • • •   63 SOHRAB RUSTUM   72
      A SON SO FAMED SO BRAVE TO SEND TO WAR   • • • •   68 SOHRAB RUSTUM   231
      OF WAR I FIGHT IT OUT AND HAND TO HAND   • • • •   75 SOHRAB RUSTUM   464
      WITH SPOILS AND HONOUR WHEN THE WAR IS DONE   • •   79 SOHRAB RUSTUM   595
      OF US SHE DREAMS NOT NOR OF WOUNDS NOR WAR   • • • •   80 SOHRAB RUSTUM   648
      A SON SO PRAISD SO BRAVE TO SEND TO WAR   • • • •   68 SOHRAB RUSTUM   V 231
      AS AMONG THOSE WHOSE JOY AND WORK IS WAR   • • • •   115 BALDER DEAD 3   81
      SOMETHING TOO MUCH OF WAR AND BROILS WHICH MAKE   • •   128 BALDER DEAD 3   505
      WHO THEN SHALL LIVE IN PEACE AS NOW IN WAR   • • • •   128 BALDER DEAD 3   531
      WHO CARRIED THE GREAT WAR FROM MACEDON   • • • •   154 TRISTRAM 3   148
      OF WAR AND ARTS   • • • • • • • • • • •   189 STRAYED REVEL   125
      THE FAMOUS MEN OF WAR HAVE FOUGHT   • • • • • •   219 BACCHANALIA 2   5
      LIGHT FLOWS OUR WAR OF MOCKING WORDS AND YET   • •   245 BURIED LIFE   1
      TO LIFE TO CITIES AND TO WAR   • • • • • • • •   305 GRANDE CHARTR   180
      WAR-CRIES TO FACTION YEAR BY YEAR RENEWD   • • • •   333 MEROPE   92
      MERE RUTHLESS AND UNCOUNSELLD WOLVES OF WAR   • •   381 MEROPE   1301
      HIS KINSMAN HIS RIGHT HAND IN PEACE AND WAR   •   403 MEROPE   1974
      MERE RUTHLESS AND UNCOUNSELLD TOOLS OF WAR   • • • •   381 MEROPE   V1301
      FIERCE DISPUTATIOUS EVER AT WAR WITH MAN   • • • •   440 EMPEDOCLES II   395
      COUNCILS AND ARMIES AND THE POMP OF WAR   • • • •   476 CROMWELL   142
      RANG AS HE TRODE THEM WITH THE VOICE OF WAR   • •   476 CROMWELL   152

WARD
      YES AND I FAIN WOULD ALTOGETHER WARD   • • • • • •   104 BALDER DEAD 1   310
      I DOUBT THEIR CAUTION LITTLE SUITS THEIR WARD   • •   351 MEROPE   608
      OUR PRINCE AND THE GOOD LAIAS WHOM HIS WARD   •   364 MEROPE   976
      THE PRINCE HIS UNCLE LAIAS WHOM HIS WARD   • • • •   364 MEROPE   V 976

WARDED
      THE OTHER WARDED OFF THE DROOPING BOUGHS   • • • •   154 TRISTRAM 3   176

WARDER
    SCANT SPACE THAT WARDER LEFT FOR PASSERS BY   • • 107 BALDER DEAD 2   90
    HE SPAKE THE WARDER OF THE BRIDGE REPLIED • • • 108 BALDER DEAD 2   118

WARDERD
    FROM THE DRAGON-WARDERD FOUNTAINS • • • • • 27 NEW SIRENS   33

WARDERS
    AUSTRIAN WANDERERS BRING O WARDERS • • • • 15 CHURCH BROU 1   79
    FROM THE GATE THE WARDERS ANSWERD • • • • • 15 CHURCH BROU 1   81

WARDS
    THE GOTH BOUND ROME-WARDS SO THE HUN • • • • 52 RESIGNATION   9

WARFARE
    WARFARE OF MAN FROM HIS BIRTH • • • • • • 216 LORDS MESSENGER   3
    DID ITS NOW SILENT WARFARE WAGE • • • • • 219 BACCHANALIA 2   20
    ITS WARFARE WAGED WITH PAIN • • • • • • 313 OBERMANN MORE   42

WARLIKE
    TROY AND WARLIKE PRIAM TOO AND THE PEOPLE OF PRIAM   HOMER TRANS   22

WARM
    AND LOOKING DOWN ON THE WARM ROSY TINTS • • • • 18 CHURCH BROU 3   28
    DREW A WARM SCENT ABROAD BEHIND THE PINES • • • 25 DREAM   6
    LAY THE WARM GOLDEN GOURDS GOLDEN WITHIN • • • • 25 DREAM   18
    AND THOSE WARM LOCKS MEN WERE PRAISING • • • 30 NEW SIRENS   121
    MUSED ON WARM THE HEART ANEW • • • • • • 30 NEW SIRENS   134
    WHERE THE WARM JUNE-WIND • • • • • • 51 CONSOLATION   42
    HIS BED AND THE WARM RUGS WHEREON HE LAY • • • 63 SOHRAB RUSTUM   95
    FOR THE WARM PERSIAN SEA-BOARD SO THEY STREAMD • • 64 SOHRAB RUSTUM 116
    AND WARM AND PLEASANT BUT THE GRAVE IS COLD • • 71 SOHRAB RUSTUM 323
    THE BIG WARM TEARS ROLLD DOWN AND CAKED THE SAND • 82 SOHRAB RUSTUM 736
    REGRETTING THE WARM MANSION WHICH IT LEFT • • • 86 SOHRAB RUSTUM 855
    TO RIGHT AND LEFT AND WARM STEAM FILLS THE AIR • • 107 BALDER DEAD 2   98
    AND A WARM WEST-WIND BLOWS AND THAW SETS IN • • 122 BALDER DEAD 3 309
    LIKE HELPLESS BIRDS IN THE WARM NEST • • • • 140 TRISTRAM 1   328
    WARM WITH THE WINTER-SUN OF BURNISHD GREEN • • • 150 TRISTRAM 3   21
    WARM IN THEIR MANTLES WRAPT THE THREE STOOD THERE 150 TRISTRAM 3   38
    BUT STILL AS THEY PURSUED THEIR WARM DRY ROAD • • 150 TRISTRAM 3   44
    ONE APRIL WHEN THE WARM DAYS FIRST BEGAN • • • 154 TRISTRAM 3   160
    WARM IN THEIR MANTLES WRAPT THE THREE STAYD THERE   TRISTRAM 3 V 38
    NOR TO THE BROWN HEATHS ROUND THEM WARM AND WIDE • • TRISTRAM 3 V 49
    ABOVE THE FRAGRANT WARM PROVENCAL SHORE • • • 167 RACHEL 2   2
    ON THE WARM GRASSY • • • • • • • 190 STRAYED REVEL 137
    SITTING ON THE WARM STEPS • • • • • • 194 STRAYED REVEL 271
    ON THE WARM INGLE-BENCH THE SMOCK-FROCKD BOORS • 256 SCHOLAR-GIPSY   59
    AND WATCH THE WARM GREEN-MUFFLED CUMNER HILLS • 257 SCHOLAR-GIPSY   69
    THIS WINTER-EVE IS WARM • • • • • • 263 THYRSIS   16
    AND WHAT BUT NOBLE FEELING WARM • • • • 279 SOUTHERN NIGHT 130
    RUFFLES THE WARM AFTERNOON • • • • • 293 HEINES GRAVE   40
    YET WARM IT MOUNTS THE HOUR OF LIFE • • • • 322 OBERMANN MORE 291
    FOR COURTEOUS ENTERTAINMENT WELCOME WARM • • 356 MEROPE 760
    THE ADRIATIC BREAKS IN A WARM BAY • • • • 426 EMPEDOCLES I 2 428
    BASK IN THE GLENS OR ON THE WARM SEA-SHORE • • • 427 EMPEDOCLES I 2 437
    AND GOODNESS WARM AND TRUTH WITHOUT ALLOY • • 446 WESTMIN ABBEY   78
    WARM IN HER BREAST BY DAY • • • • • 446 WESTMIN ABBEY   87
    HERE WHERE THE GRASS IS SMOOTH AND WARM • • 451 GEISTS GRAVE   66
    FOUND HIM STIFF YOU SAY THOUGH WARM • • • 452 POOR MATTHIAS   3
    VAINLY WARM HIM IN YOUR BREAST • • • • 452 POOR MATTHIAS   9
    TILL WHAT AT MORNINGS HOUR LOOKT WARM AND BRIGHT • 466 ALARIC AT ROME 107

WARMD
    SOON THE PLANKD COTTAGE BY THE SUN-WARMD PINES • • 25 DREAM   35
    SOON THE PLANKD COTTAGE MID THE SUN-WARMD PINES • • 25 DREAM V 35
    ABOVE HIS SUN-WARMD FIRS • • • • • • • 313 OBERMANN MORE   34
    FROM THE GRASSY SUN-WARMD PLACE • • • • • 433 EMPEDOCLES II 161

WARMER
    TO WARMER LANDS AND COASTS THAT KEEP THE SUN • • 129 BALDER DEAD 3 562

WARMING
    WARMING THEIR HEADS IN THE SUN • • • • • • 297 HEINES GRAVE 157

WARMLY
    THE CHILD SLEEPS WARMLY IN HIS BED • • • • • 249 KENSINGTON GARD   36

WARMTH
    IN WARMTH LIGHT JOY • • • • • • • • 52 CONSOLATION   70
    THEY BRING US LIGHT AND WARMTH AND JOY • • • 203 EUPHROSYNE   24
    HATH NEITHER BEAUTY NOR WARMTH • • • • • 233 YOUTH OF MAN   30
    HAS NEITHER BEAUTY NOR WARMTH • • • • • 233 YOUTH OF MAN V 30
    WHEN BLOOD AND WARMTH WERE FLED • • • • 319 OBERMANN MORE 194
    WITH PASSIONATE WARMTH WE CLASP • • • • 424 EMPEDOCLES I 2 359
    FAR FROM MY OWN SOUL FAR FROM WARMTH AND LIGHT • 440 EMPEDOCLES II 396

WARN
    AH WARN SOME MORE AMBITIOUS HEART • • • • • 174 MEETING   15

WARND
    AND WEAKNESS WARND HIM AND HE FEARD DECLINE • • 447 WESTMIN ABBEY 123

WARNING
```
    HEARD IN SLUMBER SOUNDS OF WARNING        • • • • • •    26 NEW SIRENS           7
    HEARD AT EVENING SOUNDS OF WARNING        • • • • • •    26 NEW SIRENS        V  7
    WARNING THE GODS THAT FOES DRAW NIGH TO HEAVEN  • •     105 BALDER DEAD 2         7
    DEAD AND NO WARNING SHIVER RAN  • • • • •              184 TERRACE BERNE       26
    FOR THAT IN THIS MY WARNING THOU ART PAID  • • • •     396 MEROPE            1765
    OF WONDER TO THE FOOL OF WARNING TO THE WISE  • •      462 ALARIC AT ROME      12
```

WARRANT
```
    WHOSE TEARS WARRANT HIS TRUTH  • • • • • • • •         369 MEROPE            1091
```

WARRIOR
```
    O THOU OLD WARRIOR LET US YIELD TO HEAVEN  • • • •      74 SOHRAB RUSTUM      438
    THOU CAMEST NEAR THE NEXT O WARRIOR THOR  • • • •      115 BALDER DEAD 3       71
    MOUNTED ON SLEIPNER WITH THE WARRIOR THOR  • • •       120 BALDER DEAD 3      239
    MY FATHER AND HIS PRIDE THE WARRIOR THOR  • • •        127 BALDER DEAD 3      491
    WARRIOR STATESMAN HAD SIGND  • • • • • • •             281 HAWORTH CHURCH      21
    WARRIOR STATESMAN HAD LEFT  • • • • • •                281 HAWORTH CHURCH   V  21
    WERE NOT AMONG THE FEUDS OF WARRIOR-CHIEFS  • • • •    388 MEROPE            1512
    WERT NOT AMONG THE FEUDS OF WARRIOR-CHIEFS  • • • •    388 MEROPE           V1512
    BY WORCESTERS FIELD THE WARRIOR-VISION PASSD  • •      476 CROMWELL           150
```

WARRIORS
```
    AT BURNING NOON SO WARRIORS SAID  • • • • • •           52 RESIGNATION          4
    AND PICK THE BRAVEST WARRIORS OUT FOR DEATH  • •       105 BALDER DEAD 2       26
    TO ARMED WARRIORS I HEARD VENGEFUL CRIES  • • • •      402 MEROPE            1940
    POUR FROM A THOUSAND HILLS THY WARRIORS OF THE NORTH   465 ALARIC AT ROME      96
```

WARS
```
    REMEMBRANCE IN OUR SOUL OF WARS ALONE  • • • •        117 BALDER DEAD 3      138
    WHILE THE KNIGHTS ARE AT THE WARS  • • • • • •        131 TRISTRAM 1          44
    VOYAGES EXILES HATES DISSENSIONS WARS  • • • •        195 FRAG ANTIGONE       23
    THE TIDES AND THEN OF MORTAL WARS  • • • • • •        414 EMPEDOCLES I 2      72
```

WASH
```
    OXUS IN SUMMER WASH THEM ALL AWAY  • • • • • •          72 SOHRAB RUSTUM      378
    AND WASH THEM WITH THY TEARS AND SAY MY SON  • •        82 SOHRAB RUSTUM      720
    WASH OFF ALL BLOOD SET SMOOTH EACH LIMB  • • • •        95 SICK KING BOKH     230
    WHAT BLOOD SO MEET AS THINE TO WASH IT OUT  • • • •    402 MEROPE            1924
```

WASHD
```
    WHO ON SHORES AND SEA-WASHD PLACES  • • • • • •         26 NEW SIRENS          11
    WASHD EDDYING FROM THIS BANK THEIR HOME  • • • •        58 RESIGNATION        202
    WHO SINS ONCE WASHD BY THE BAPTISMAL WAVE  • • • •     172 GOOD SHEPHERD        5
    TEARS WASHD THE TROUBLE FROM HER FACE  • • • •         317 OBERMANN MORE      137
    THE SUN SHONE IN THE NEW-WASHD SKY  • • • •            319 OBERMANN MORE      209
    WASHD AS THE MARKS UPON THE HILLS STILL SHOW  • •      358 MEROPE             815
    YET STAINS OUR LAND BE BY THIS BLOOD WASHD OUT  • •    402 MEROPE            1916
```

WASHED
```
    TEARS HAVE WASHED THEIR AUSTERE FACES  • • • • •           META CLOISTER        7
```

WASHES
```
    AND THE WIND WASHES THROUGH THE MOUNTAIN-PINES  • •     18 CHURCH BROU 3       37
    AND THE WIND WASHES IN THE MOUNTAIN PINES  • • • •      18 CHURCH BROU 3    V  37
    AND THE WIND WASHES MID THE MOUNTAIN PINES  • • • •     18 CHURCH BROU 3    V  37
```

WASTE
```
    THROUGH THIS WASTE OF SUNLESS GREENS  • • • • • •       33 NEW SIRENS         212
    DEEP IN THE SANDY WASTE  • • • • • • • • •              51 CONSOLATION         33
    WHO ROAM OER KIPCHAK AND THE NORTHERN WASTE  • •        65 SOHRAB RUSTUM      131
    HATH BUILDED ON THE WASTE IN FORMER YEARS  • • • •      71 SOHRAB RUSTUM      338
    BOKHARA AND LONE KHIVA IN THE WASTE  • • • •            83 SOHRAB RUSTUM      761
    THAT SO THE PASSING HORSEMAN ON THE WASTE  • • •        84 SOHRAB RUSTUM      790
    AND NIGHT CAME DOWN OVER THE SOLEMN WASTE  • • •        86 SOHRAB RUSTUM      865
    REJOICING THROUGH THE HUSHD CHORASMIAN WASTE  • •       87 SOHRAB RUSTUM      878
    WHO COME FROM KIPCHAK AND THE NORTHERN WASTE  • •       65 SOHRAB RUSTUM    V 131
    WHO DWELL IN KIPCHAK AND THE NORTHERN WASTE  • •        65 SOHRAB RUSTUM    V 131
    WHO ROVE OER KIPCHAK AND THE NORTHERN WASTE  • •        65 SOHRAB RUSTUM    V 131
    HAS BUILDED ON THE WASTE IN FORMER YEARS  • • • •       71 SOHRAB RUSTUM    V 338
    HATH BUILDED ON THE WASTE IN FORMER DAYS  • • • •       71 SOHRAB RUSTUM    V 338
    HAS BUILDED ON THE WASTE IN FORMER DAYS  • • • •        71 SOHRAB RUSTUM    V 338
    AT THE CHINKD FIELDS OF ICE THE WASTE OF SNOW  • •     100 BALDER DEAD 1      164
    OUT OF THE BLACK WASTE FOREST FAR BELOW  • • •         119 BALDER DEAD 3     V
    OVER THE WASTE THIS CIRQUE OF OPEN GROUND  • • • •     150 TRISTRAM 3          13
    OVER THE WASTE THIS RING OF OPEN GROUND  • • • •       150 TRISTRAM 3       V  13
    OVER THE WASTE BUT WHERE THIS OPEN GROUND  • • •           TRISTRAM 3       V  13
    OVER THE WASTE ALL THE HOLLOW GROUND  • • • •              TRISTRAM 3       V  13
    FROM THE OPEN WASTE WHITE BY THE HEDGEROWS LAY  • •        TRISTRAM 3       V  51
    THE SUNNY WASTE  • • • • • • • • • • •                 191 STRAYED REVEL      180
    BESIDES WHAT WASTE HE MAKES  • • • • • • • •           195 FRAG ANTIGONE       24
    STILL THESE WASTE US WITH THEIR HOPELESS STRAINING     210 SELF-DECEPTION      19
    ON THE STARLIT ARABIAN WASTE  • • • • • • •            253 FUTURE              47
    AS THE PALE WASTE WIDENS AROUND HIM  • • • • •         254 FUTURE              83
    DIE ONE BY ONE IN THE WASTE  • • • • • • • •           291 RUGBY CHAPEL       187
    ON TO THE BOUND OF THE WASTE  • • • • • • •            292 RUGBY CHAPEL       207
    ON THIS CHARRD BLACKEND MELANCHOLY WASTE  • • • •      428 EMPEDOCLES II        2
    DECKD THE DULL WASTE AND THE FAMILIAR FIELD  • •       472 CROMWELL            34
    FAR OER THE PATHLESS WASTE OF LABOURING FOAM  • •      475 CROMWELL           114
```

WE   (CONTINUED)

WE
(CONTINUED)

YES WE ARRAIGN HER BUT SHE	295	HEINES GRAVE	87
WE KNOW ALL THIS WE KNOW	295	HEINES GRAVE	115
WE KNOW ALL THIS WE KNOW	295	HEINES GRAVE	115
THAT WAS HEINE AND WE	298	HEINES GRAVE	212
WHAT ARE WE ALL BUT A MOOD	298	HEINES GRAVE	214
OF THE SPIRIT IN WHOM WE EXIST	298	HEINES GRAVE	216
OF THE BEING IN WHOM WE EXIST	298	HEINES GRAVE	V 216
THE BRIDGE IS CROSSD AND SLOW WE RIDE	299	GRANDE CHARTR	5
APPROACH FOR WHAT WE SEEK IS HERE	300	GRANDE CHARTR	25
THIS SEA OF TIME WHEREON WE SAIL	303	GRANDE CHARTR	122
BUT WE STAND MUTE AND WATCH THE WAVES	303	GRANDE CHARTR	126
OR ARE WE EASIER TO HAVE READ	304	GRANDE CHARTR	145
BUT WE LEARNT YOUR LORE TOO WELL	304	GRANDE CHARTR	156
BUT WE WE LEARNT YOUR LORE TOO WELL	304	GRANDE CHARTR	156
MORE FORTUNATE ALAS THAN WE	304	GRANDE CHARTR	158
BUT WHILE WE WAIT ALLOW OUR TEARS	304	GRANDE CHARTR	162
ALLOW THEM WE ADMIRE WITH AWE	304	GRANDE CHARTR	163
WE LAUD THEM BUT THEY ARE NOT OURS	304	GRANDE CHARTR	168
WE ARE LIKE CHILDREN REARD IN SHADE	304	GRANDE CHARTR	169
LONG SINCE WE PACE THIS SHADOWD NAVE	305	GRANDE CHARTR	199
WE WATCH THOSE YELLOW TAPERS SHINE	305	GRANDE CHARTR	200
HOW SHOULD WE GROW IN OTHER GROUND	306	GRANDE CHARTR	207
HOW CAN WE FLOWER IN FOREIGN AIR	306	GRANDE CHARTR	208
BUT WE WE LEARNT THEIR LORE TOO WELL	304	GRANDE CHARTR	V 156
BUT WE WE LEARNT THEIR LORE TOO WELL	304	GRANDE CHARTR	V 156
WE MARK THEM BUT THEY ARE NOT OURS	304	GRANDE CHARTR	V 168
WE PRAISE THEM BUT THEY ARE NOT OURS	304	GRANDE CHARTR	V 168
HOW SHOULD WE FLOWER IN FOREIGN AIR	306	GRANDE CHARTR	V 208
CLEARER HOW MUCH THAN OURS YET WE	308	OBERMANN	63
BUT WE BROUGHT FORTH AND REARD IN HOURS	308	OBERMANN	69
WE HAVE HAD TIME TO BREATHE	308	OBERMANN	76
TOO FAST WE LIVE TOO MUCH ARE TRIED	308	OBERMANN	77
AND THEN WE TURN THOU SADDER SAGE	309	OBERMANN	81
TO THEE WE FEEL THY SPELL	309	OBERMANN	82
TO THEE WE COME THEN CLOUDS ARE ROLLD	309	OBERMANN	105
WE IN SOME UNKNOWN POWERS EMPLOY	310	OBERMANN	133
CAN NEITHER WHEN WE WILL ENJOY	310	OBERMANN	135
NOR WHEN WE WILL RESIGN	310	OBERMANN	136
DISTINCTIONS WE ESTEEM SO GRAVE	311	OBERMANN	151
FAREWELL UNDER THE SKY WE PART	312	OBERMANN	181
HELD BY THE WORLD WHICH WE	314	OBERMANN MORE	70
AH ME WE ANCHORITES READ THINGS BEST	314	OBERMANN MORE	75
HE LIVED WHILE WE BELIEVED	318	OBERMANN MORE	168
WHILE WE BELIEVED ON EARTH HE WENT	318	OBERMANN MORE	169
AND OH WE CRIED THAT ON THIS CORSE	319	OBERMANN MORE	197
THE WORN-OUT WORLD WE KNEW	319	OBERMANN MORE	206
AH ME WE ANCHORITES KNEW IT BEST	314	OBERMANN MORE	V 75
SOUL THAT THAN THEY WE TAKE MORE CARE	315	OBERMANN MORE	V
SOUL THAT WE TAKE MORE COUNT AND CARE	315	OBERMANN MORE	V
THE OUT-WORN WORLD WE KNEW	319	OBERMANN MORE	V 206
WHEREON WE PITCH OUR TENT	320	OBERMANN MORE	V 218
SON OF CRESPHONTES WE HAVE REACHD THE GOAL	330	MEROPE	1
WHICH TO PERFORM WE MADE IT MEANS FOR THAT	330	MEROPE	25
WE JUDGED THE BEST CHANCE FINDS NO BETTER WAY	331	MEROPE	36
FOR WE WERE KINSMEN MORE THAN KINSMEN FRIENDS	334	MEROPE	122
TOGETHER WE HAD GROWN TOGETHER LIVED	334	MEROPE	123
WE CALL IT MURDER CRUSH HIM BRAND HIS NAME	336	MEROPE	203
WERE THEY WE DISPOSSESSED OF US I SPEAK	337	MEROPE	229
WHAT WE FOUND HERE WERE TRIBES OF FAME OBSCURE	337	MEROPE	233
LONG WE REFRAIND OURSELVES SUBMITTED LONG	337	MEROPE	254
HOUSE OF THE GRAVE WHAT WE DO	342	MEROPE	391
AS THOSE WHEREWITH WE TRY TO TEST	352	MEROPE	634
YEA AND NOT ONLY HAVE WE NOT EXPLORED	352	MEROPE	636
BOUNDED IN OUR OWN BREAST WE HARDLY KNOW	352	MEROPE	639
WE RODE FROM TEGEA THROUGH THE WOODS OF OAKS	355	MEROPE	735
THERE WITH THE CHIEF OF THAT HILL-TOWN WE LODGED	356	MEROPE	746
FAR IN THE LIQUID LAKE WE SATE AND DREW	356	MEROPE	752
AND AS WE ATE AND RESTED THERE WE TALKD	356	MEROPE	755
AND AS WE ATE AND RESTED THERE WE TALKD	356	MEROPE	755
OF PLACES WE HAD PASSD SPORT WE HAD HAD	356	MEROPE	756
OF PLACES WE HAD PASSD SPORT WE HAD HAD	356	MEROPE	756
AND STRANGELY AS WE TALKD HE WOULD APPLY	356	MEROPE	766
AND THEN HE BADE REMEMBER HOW WE PASSD	356	MEROPE	774
WE CHEERED HIM BUT THAT MOMENT FROM THE COPSE	357	MEROPE	786
WE SPRANG UPON OUR FEET WE SNATCHD OUR SPEARS	357	MEROPE	789
WE SPRANG UPON OUR FEET WE SNATCHD OUR SPEARS	357	MEROPE	789
WE BOUNDED DOWN THE SWARDED SLOPE WE PLUNGED	357	MEROPE	790
WE BOUNDED DOWN THE SWARDED SLOPE WE PLUNGED	357	MEROPE	790
AND MANY TIMES THAT MORN WE COURSED IN RING	357	MEROPE	793
ON THAT SAME SPUR WHERE WE HAD SATE AT MORN	357	MEROPE	796
BOATS AND APPROACH NEAR AS WE DARED THE CHASM	358	MEROPE	838
THE YOUTH THOU SAYST WE SAW AND HEARD BUT NOW	365	MEROPE	985
INTERPRET THEN FOR WE IT SEEMS ARE DULL	365	MEROPE	989
TO OUR UNHAPPY HOUSE THE DEBT WE OWE	367	MEROPE	1048
AS DEAD WE HELD THEE MOURND FOR THEE AS DEAD	375	MEROPE	1208
WE SEE DEAR MISTRESS AND WE SAY THE GODS	377	MEROPE	1225
WE SEE DEAR MISTRESS AND WE SAY THE GODS	377	MEROPE	1225
WE TWO WITH THEE MY MOTHER MAY CONSULT	379	MEROPE	1265
WITH CYPSELUS OUR FATHER WHERE WE SAW	388	MEROPE	1515

WEEDS

```
UPON THE CLIFFS OR SMOKE OF BURNING WEEDS      124 BALDER DEAD 3       362
LONG SINCE HATH FLUNG HER WEEDS AWAY           304 GRANDE CHARTR       154
LONG SINCE HATH THROWN HER WEEDS AWAY          304 GRANDE CHARTR    V  154
MID WEEDS AND WRECKS SHE STOOD A PLACE         317 OBERMANN MORE       139
HANG WEEDS OF OUR SAD TIME                     323 OBERMANN MORE       308
```

WEEK

```
WHAT A TALE OF THY LAST WEEK                   455 POOR MATTHIAS       110
```

WEEKS

```
BUT THE SMOOTH-SLIPPING WEEKS                  268 THYRSIS             206
```

WEEP

```
I SHALL WEEP BUT THEIR LOVE WILL BE COOLING AND HE    20 MODERN SAPPHO    18
WILL IT WEEP OUR BURNING TEARS                  29 NEW SIRENS           86
AND ZAL MIGHT WEEP ABOVE MY GRAVE NOT THINE     85 SOHRAB RUSTUM       821
AND SAY O SON I WEEP THEE NOT TOO SORE          85 SOHRAB RUSTUM       822
IF ANY HERE MIGHT WEEP FOR BALDERS DEATH        96 BALDER DEAD 1        20
I MOST MIGHT WEEP HIS FATHER SUCH A SON         96 BALDER DEAD 1        21
WEEP HIM AN HOUR BUT WHAT CAN GRIEF AVAIL       96 BALDER DEAD 1        27
WEEP HIM AND ALL THAT IS WITHOUT LIFE WEEP     111 BALDER DEAD 2       237
WEEP HIM AND ALL THAT IS WITHOUT LIFE WEEP     111 BALDER DEAD 2       237
AND IN PROCESSION ALL COME NEAR AND WEEP       115 BALDER DEAD 3        51
AND WEEP FROM SHORE TO SHORE MY GOLDEN TEARS   116 BALDER DEAD 3       110
WEEP NOT O FREYA WEEP NO GOLDEN TEARS          116 BALDER DEAD 3       114
WEEP NOT O FREYA WEEP NO GOLDEN TEARS          116 BALDER DEAD 3       114
ALL LIVING AND UNLIVING THINGS TO WEEP         122 BALDER DEAD 3       292
ALL LIVING AND UNLIVING THINGS TO WEEP         122 BALDER DEAD 3       300
ENTREATING ALL THINGS TO WEEP BALDERS DEATH    122 BALDER DEAD 3       305
FAR OFF WHERE SOME UNWARND MIGHT FAIL TO WEEP  122 BALDER DEAD 3       322
THOK WITH DRY EYES WILL WEEP OER BALDERS PYRE  123 BALDER DEAD 3       352
WEEP HIM ALL OTHER THINGS IF WEEP THEY WILL    123 BALDER DEAD 3       353
WEEP HIM ALL OTHER THINGS IF WEEP THEY WILL    123 BALDER DEAD 3       353
I WEEP HIM NOT LET HELA KEEP HER PREY          123 BALDER DEAD 3       354
NAY ALLS WELL AGAIN THOU MUST NOT WEEP         144 TRISTRAM 2           72
I WEEP THEBANS                                 196 FRAG ANTIGONE        46
AND KNOW HER FRIEND AND WEEP FOR GLEE          202 URANIA               27
THEN WILL SHE WEEP WITH SMILES TILL THEN       202 URANIA               29
THEIR LOT WAS BUT TO WEEP AND MOAN             203 EUPHROSYNE           10
AH LET ME WEEP AND TELL MY PAIN                206 RIVER                11
AND WEEP AND FEEL THE FULNESS OF THE PAST      212 GROWING OLD          19
I DO NOT STRIVE I DO NOT WEEP                  241 MORALITY             26
LET THOSE WHO WILL IF ANY WEEP                 250 WISH                  7
PRESSES ME CHIDES ME WILL NOT LET ME WEEP      378 MEROPE             1233
TO MAKE HIM LAUGH OR WEEP                          EMPEDOCLES I 2     V
DO THY BLOODSHOT EYES STILL WEEP               430 EMPEDOCLES II        55
AND WERE THERE NONE TO STAND AND WEEP ALONE    467 ALARIC AT ROME      121
NOT THIS THE TIME TO WEEP UPON THE BIER        467 ALARIC AT ROME      135
```

WEEPING

```
STANDS AT DAYBREAK WEEPING BY MY SIDE           35 NEW SIRENS          274
AND YOU TOO O WEEPING GRACES                    34 NEW SIRENS       V  243
WEEPING AND WAILING AND VALHALLA RANG           95 BALDER DEAD 1        11
WEEPING THE SANDS WERE WETTED AND THEIR ARMS   115 BALDER DEAD 3        62
OF ALL THINGS WEEPING TO BRING BALDER BACK     122 BALDER DEAD 3       318
THE PLEASAUNCE-WALKS THE WEEPING QUEEN         136 TRISTRAM 1          178
THEE A WEEPING EXILE IN THY FOREST             144 TRISTRAM 2       V   51
HE SINGS HOW SHE SITS WEEPING                  160 NECKAN               33
BRING HIM A WEEPING CHILD                      195 FRAG ANTIGONE        12
WEEPING AT HIS MASTERS END                     434 EMPEDOCLES II       167
```

WEEPS

```
OF HIS PALE WIFE WHO WAITS AND WEEPS ON SHORE   69 SOHRAB RUSTUM       285
OF HIS PALE WIFE WHO WAITS AND WEEPS ASHORE     69 SOHRAB RUSTUM    V  285
SINCE THEN SHE SEEKS HIM AND WEEPS TEARS OF GOLD 116 BALDER DEAD 3      95
FALSE NECKAN SHARES MY BED SHE WEEPS           160 NECKAN               35
```

WEIGH

```
IS THE CALM THINE OF STOIC SOULS WHO WEIGH      42 GIPSY CHILD          29
O AEPYTUS WEIGH WELL HER COUNSEL GIVEN         382 MEROPE             1332
```

WEIGHD

```
WEIGHD LIKE OSSA ON THE AERY SOUL               28 NEW SIRENS       V   72
```

WEIGHING

```
WHO WEIGHING THAT LIFE WELL                    195 FRAG ANTIGONE         4
```

WEIGHS

```
WEIGHS LIKE OSSA ON THE AERY SOUL               28 NEW SIRENS       V   72
WEIGHS DOWN MY SOUL                             50 CONSOLATION           5
```

WEIGHT

```
CROWNING MOMENTS WITH THE WEIGHT OF YEARS       29 NEW SIRENS       V   88
A WEIGHT OF MEDITATION MIXD WITH PAIN           41 GIPSY CHILD      V   12
```

WEIGHTY

```
O KING ALL HAIL I COME WITH WEIGHTY NEWS       354 MEROPE              710
ARRIVED FROM TEGEA WITH WEIGHTY NEWS           361 MEROPE              915
```

WELL   (CONTINUED)

WELLING

WELLNIGH

WELLS
    THE ACRID MILK OF CAMELS AND THEIR WELLS   • • • •   64 SOHRAB RUSTUM   125

WELTERING
    SENSELESS WELTERING IN HIS GORE   • • • •   13 CHURCH BROU 1   28
    HIS EYE PLUNGED DOWN THE WELTERING STRIFE • • • •   270 MEMORIAL VERSES   25
    AMID THE WILD WAVES WELTERING • • • • • • •   479 HAYSWATER BOAT   8

WELTERS
    AND WELTERS LIKE A HUMAN THING • • • • • • • •   479 HAYSWATER BOAT   7

WEND
    AND WEND THEMSELVES TO HELAS GLOOMY REALM • • •   98 BALDER DEAD 1   121

WENDED
    FORTH WENDED THEY AND DRAVE THEIR STEEDS BEFORE • •   106 BALDER DEAD 2   50
    FORTH WENDED THEY AND DROVE THEIR STEEDS BEFORE • •   106 BALDER DEAD 2   V 50
    WHERE I AM THOU ASKST AND WHERE I WENDED • • •   482 THEKLAS ANSWER   1

WENDING
    TO ALL REEFS AND NARROWS WENDING • • • • • •   26 NEW SIRENS   15

WENDS
    HE WENDS UNFOLLOWD HE MUST HOUSE ALONE • • • •   269 THYRSIS   209

WENT
    ROSE-CROWND AND EVER WHEN THE SUN WENT DOWN • •   11 MYCERINUS   93
    MARGUERITE SAYS AS LAST YEAR WENT • • • • •   23 MEMORY-PICTURE   17
    WENT LURID DOWN OER FLOODED PLAINS • • • • •   52 RESIGNATION   11
    AND WENT ABROAD INTO THE COLD WET FOG • • •   61 SOHRAB RUSTUM   10
    AND SOHRAB CAME THERE AND WENT IN AND STOOD •   61 SOHRAB RUSTUM   24
    HIS HERALD TO HIS SIDE AND WENT ABROAD • • •   64 SOHRAB RUSTUM   103
    CHANGED GIFTS AND WENT ON EQUAL TERMS AWAY • •   72 SOHRAB RUSTUM   361
    HISSD AND WENT QUIVERING DOWN INTO THE SAND •   73 SOHRAB RUSTUM   404
    AND WENT ABROAD INTO THE COLD DIM AIR • • •   61 SOHRAB RUSTUM   V 10
    WENT SEEKING RUSTUM AND DEFYING FORTH • • •   70 SOHRAB RUSTUM   V 310
    WENT FORTH AGAIN THE HOLY BOOK • • • • •   89 SICK KING BOKH   47
    AND WENT UP ON THE ROOF TO SLEEP • • • •   90 SICK KING BOKH   73
    BUT IN VALHALLA ALL THE GODS WENT BACK • •   97 BALDER DEAD 1   61
    FROM AROUND BALDER ALL THE HEROES WENT • •   97 BALDER DEAD 1   62
    IN ODINS HALL AND WENT THROUGH ASGARD STREETS •   97 BALDER DEAD 1   73
    HE CAME AND SADLY WENT ALONG THE SAND • • •   97 BALDER DEAD 1   78
    THERE HE WENT UP AND PASSD THE OPEN DOORS • •   97 BALDER DEAD 1   87
    AND BACK ALONG THE BEACH TO ASGARD WENT • •   101 BALDER DEAD 1   200
    THEY SPAKE AND EACH WENT HOME TO HIS OWN HOUSE •   101 BALDER DEAD 1   219
    MOST FLEET HE WAS BUT NOW HE WENT THE LAST •   101 BALDER DEAD 1   222
    AND STARTS HIM THAT HE THINKS A GHOST WENT BY •   101 BALDER DEAD 1   234
    AND HE WENT IN AND SHUT THE DOOR AND FIXT • •   102 BALDER DEAD 1   251
    SLEIPNER AND SLEIPNER WENT TO HIS OWN STALL •   102 BALDER DEAD 1   266
    THEY WENT AND LAID THEM DOWN AND NANNA WENT •   103 BALDER DEAD 1   277
    THEY WENT AND LAID THEM DOWN AND NANNA WENT •   103 BALDER DEAD 1   277
    AND THE VALKYRIES ON THEIR STEEDS WENT FORTH •   105 BALDER DEAD 2   19
    BUT THE GODS WENT NOT NOW AS OTHERWHILE •   105 BALDER DEAD 2   29
    BUT THEY WENT ODIN FIRST THE REST BEHIND • •   105 BALDER DEAD 2   35
    WENT STRAINING THROUGH THE CRACKLING BRUSHWOOD DOWN   106 BALDER DEAD 2   62
    AND EVERY GOD WENT HOME TO HIS OWN HOUSE • •   106 BALDER DEAD 2   69
    KNOWING THE GOD THEY WENT TO SEEK HOW DEAR • •   107 BALDER DEAD 2   77
    WHICH BRANCHES FROM THE NORTH OF HEAVEN AND WENT •   107 BALDER DEAD 2   80
    AND WHILE THEY GAZED THE SUN WENT LURID DOWN •   119 BALDER DEAD 3   194
    BUT THE GODS WENT BY STARLIGHT UP THE SHORE •   119 BALDER DEAD 3   207
    THEN I REMEMBERD HOW I WENT • • • • • •   157 SAINT BRANDAN   41
    THEN WENT MY WAY TO KILL AND LIE • • • •   158 SAINT BRANDAN   59
    CALL YET ONCE THAT SHE WENT AWAY • • • •   162 FORSAKEN MERM   49
    SHE SMILED SHE WENT UP THROUGH THE SURF IN THE BAY   163 FORSAKEN MERM   62
    WE WENT UP THE BEACH BY THE SANDY DOWN • •   163 FORSAKEN MERM   68
    SOME VACANT AND SOME MUSING WENT • • • •   224 EPILOG LAOCOON   119
    HIS FRIENDS AND WENT TO LEARN THE GIPSY-LORE •   256 SCHOLAR-GIPSY   37
    BUT THYRSIS OF HIS OWN WILL WENT AWAY • • •   264 THYRSIS   40
    HE WENT HIS PIPING TOOK A TROUBLED SOUND • •   264 THYRSIS   48
    WENT OER THE SUN-LIT FIELDS AGAIN • • • •   271 MEMORIAL VERSES   52
    STILL STILL WENT FORTH THAT CHILDS DEAR FORCE •   318 OBERMANN MORE   163
    WHILE WE BELIEVED ON EARTH HE WENT • • • •   318 OBERMANN MORE   169
    WHEN THY OWN LOT WENT HARD • • • • • •   417 EMPEDOCLES I 2   165
    AND WENT WHERE ALL HIS FATHERS WENT BEFORE • •   447 WESTMIN ABBEY   116
    AND WENT WHERE ALL HIS FATHERS WENT BEFORE • •   447 WESTMIN ABBEY   116
    LIKE SUNSHINE WENT AND CAME AND BADE • • •   460 KAISER DEAD   47
    LIKE DREAMS BETWEEN TWO SORROWS WENT AND CAME •   474 CROMWELL   96
    IN PRIESTLY GARB A FRAIL OLD MAN WENT BY • •   476 CROMWELL   166

WEPT
    THEN YOU WEPT AND SLOWLY RAISING • • • •   31 NEW SIRENS   147
    HE SPOKE AND AS HE CEASED HE WEPT ALOUD • •   79 SOHRAB RUSTUM   602
    HIS ARMS ROUND HIS SONS NECK AND WEPT ALOUD •   82 SOHRAB RUSTUM   728
    RATHER IT FITS YOU HAVING WEPT YOUR HOUR • •   96 BALDER DEAD 1   34
    WHEN YE ENOUGH HAVE WEPT THEN BUILD A PILE • •   115 BALDER DEAD 3   53
    AND ALL THAT LIVED AND ALL WITHOUT LIFE WEPT •   122 BALDER DEAD 3   306
    THEY TWO SCOURD EVERY COAST AND ALL THINGS WEPT •   123 BALDER DEAD 3   328
    WHO WEPT AT READING OF A GRECIAN KNIGHT • •   153 TRISTRAM 3   144
    WEPT BY THE RIVER-POOL • • • • • •   161 NECKAN   60
    HE WEPT THE EARTH HATH KINDNESS • • • • •   161 NECKAN   61

WHEEL   (CONTINUED)
    OF SINNERS PINIOND ON THE TORTURING WHEEL • • • • 373 MEROPE   1186
    THE VILLAGE-GIRL AT HER WHEEL • • • • • • • • 436 EMPEDOCLES II   257

WHEELD
    HIS WHEELD HOUSE AT NOON • • • • • • • • • 191 STRAYED REVEL   164

WHEELS
    WHEREOER THE CHARIOT WHEELS OF LIFE ARE ROLLD • •   4 BUTLERS SERMONS   13
    BECAUSE THOU HAST BELIEVED THE WHEELS OF LIFE • •   4 DUKE WELLINGTON   1

WHELMD
    THE BROAD EARTH OPEND AND WHELMD THEM AND HIM • • 197 FRAG ANTIGONE   87

WHENCE
    HERE WHENCE THE EYE FIRST SEES FAR DOWN • • • •   55 RESIGNATION   92
    WHENCE EQUALLY THE SEAS OF LIFE AND DEATH ARE FED   60 RESIGNATION   260
    THE MOUNT FROM WHENCE HIS EYE SURVEYS THE WORLD • •   96 BALDER DEAD 1   50
    AH WHENCE THIS MERCY LORD I SAID • • • • • • 157 SAINT BRANDAN   37
    WHENCE ISSUED THE WORLD • • • • • • • • • 177 PARTING   90
    WHENCE ART THOU SLEEPER • • • • • • • • • 186 STRAYED REVEL   23
    HIES AH FROM WHENCE WHAT NATIVE GROUND • • • • 225 EPILOG LAOCOON   125
    WHENCE WAS IT FOR IT IS NOT MINE • • • • • • 241 MORALITY   24
    WHENCE OUR LIVES COME AND WHERE THEY GO • • • • 246 BURIED LIFE   54
    WHENCE OUR THOUGHTS COME AND WHERE THEY GO • • • 246 BURIED LIFE   V 54
    WHENCE DROPS THE PATH TO ALLIERE DOWN • • • • 313 OBERMANN MORE   23
    THE BONES OF ARCAS WHENCE OUR RACE IS NAMED • • 356 MEROPE   742
    WHENCE THE RIDGED PINE-WOODED ROOTS • • • • • 433 EMPEDOCLES II   137
    WHENCE THE RIDGD PINE-MUFFLED ROOTS • • • • • 433 EMPEDOCLES II V 137
    NOT IN THAT MADHOUSE FRANCE FROM WHENCE THE CRY • • 480 HUNGARIAN NAT   4

WHEREAT
    WHEREAT HE ANSWERD THAT THE GIPSY-CREW • • • • 256 SCHOLAR-GIPSY   44

WHEREBY
    WHEREBY STRANGE ARE THEY AND WE • • • • • • 456 POOR MATTHIAS   150

WHEREFORE
    OH WHEREFORE CHEAT OUR YOUTH IF THUS IT BE • • •   10 MYCERINUS   49
    O GUDURZ WHEREFORE DOST THOU SAY SUCH WORDS • •   68 SOHRAB RUSTUM   250
    O SOHRAB WHEREFORE WILT THOU RUSH ON DEATH • • •   71 SOHRAB RUSTUM   329
    RISE WHEREFORE DOST THOU VAINLY QUESTION THUS • •   72 SOHRAB RUSTUM   365
    WHEREFORE THAT I MAY COUNSEL THEE • • • • •   88 SICK KING BOKH   26
    WHEREFORE HEAR THOU KNOWST HOW FIERCE • • • •   89 SICK KING BOKH   58
    O HELA WHEREFORE SHOULD THE GODS DECLARE • • • 110 BALDER DEAD 2   189
    I WILL NOT KNOW FOR WHEREFORE TRY • • • • • 185 TERRACE BERNE   41
    TOO QUICK DESPAIRER WHEREFORE WILT THOU GO • • • 264 THYRSIS   61
    WHEREFORE ACCEPT THAT HAPPIER OMEN • • • • • 344 MEROPE   452
    WHEREFORE DOST THOU GROAN SO LOUD • • • • • 430 EMPEDOCLES II   45
    WHEREFORE DO THY NOSTRILS FLASH • • • • • • 430 EMPEDOCLES II   46
    AND WHEREFORE THEN HAVING NO CLAIM TO MORE • • •   LUCRETIUS 3   8
    AND WHEREFORE THEN IF HE CAN NEVER CHANGE • • •   LUCRETIUS 3   V 8

WHEREIN
    WHEREIN EARTHS GREAT ONES ARE DISQUIETED • • • •   7 REP FRIEND   10
    WHEREIN WE LANGUISH • • • • • • • • • •   38 STAGIRIUS   9
    WHEREIN WE LIE ASLEEP • • • • • • • • • •   38 STAGIRIUS   11
    WHEREIN HE DOTH FOR EVER CHASE • • • • • • • 247 BURIED LIFE   92
    WHEREIN AT FIRST WAS DIGHT • • • • • • • • 446 WESTMIN ABBEY   62

WHEREOER
    WHEREOER THE CHARIOT WHEELS OF LIFE ARE ROLLD • •   4 BUTLERS SERMONS   13

WHEREOF
    WHEREOF THY YOUTH FELT ALL THE SPELL • • • • • 323 OBERMANN MORE   309
    IN FRONT OF SOME GREAT FANE WHEREOF WE KNOW • •   LUCRETIUS 5   7

WHEREON
    SEEING THIS VALE THIS EARTH WHEREON WE DREAM • •   7 REP FRIEND CONT   5
    HIS BED AND THE WARM RUGS WHEREON HE LAY • • •   63 SOHRAB RUSTUM   95
    THIS SEA OF TIME WHEREON WE SAIL • • • • • • 303 GRANDE CHARTR   122
    WHEREON MEN PITCH THEIR TENT • • • • • • • 320 OBERMANN MORE   218
    WHEREON WE PITCH OUR TENT • • • • • • • • 320 OBERMANN MORE V 218
    EVEN EARTH WHEREON HE TREADS • • • • • • • 352 MEROPE   626
    WHILE FROM THE TURF WHEREON I LAY I SPRANG • • • 358 MEROPE   829
    TO FIND IN THEE A FAULT WHEREON TO FOUND • • • 404 MEROPE   2006
    WHEREON TO VENT THEIR RAGE • • • • • • • • 421 EMPEDOCLES I 2   275
    WHEREON THOU BUILDEST SUCH A GOODLY PRIDE • • • •   RUDE ORATOR   8

WHERESOEER
    WHERESOEER MEN ARE THERE IS GRIEF • • • • • • 369 MEROPE   1093

WHEREWITH
    WHEREWITH THEY STAMPD THEM DOWN AND TROD THEM DEEP   109 BALDER DEAD 2   174
    THE GOLDEN DICE WHEREWITH WE PLAYD OF YORE • • • 128 BALDER DEAD 3   539
    AS THOSE WHEREWITH WE TRY TO TEST • • • • • • 352 MEROPE   634
    WHEREWITH FROM END TO END ARCADIA RINGS • • • • 362 MEROPE   943
    WHEREWITH FATIGUE AND YOUTH HAD BOUND MINE EYES • • 375 MEROPE   1204
    FIGMENTS OF PLOTS WHEREWITH INTRIGUERS FILL • • 387 MEROPE   1487
    WHEREWITH AT FIRST WAS DIGHT • • • • • • • 446 WESTMIN ABBEY   V 62

WHITE   (CONTINUED)
```
AND WHITER THAN THY WHITE BURNOUS         •   •   •   •   •   •   276 SOUTHERN NIGHT       43
HOAR-HEADED WRINKLED CLAD IN WHITE        •   •   •   •   •   •   278 SOUTHERN NIGHT       86
GREY-HEADED WRINKLED CLAD IN WHITE        •   •   •   •   •   •   278 SOUTHERN NIGHT   V   86
SHAKING HIS THIN WHITE HAIRS              •   •   •   •   •   •   289 RUGBY CHAPEL        112
FLOWER OF MARBLE OF WHITE                 •   •   •   •   •   •   296 HEINES GRAVE        131
SWIFT RUSH THE SPECTRAL VAPOURS WHITE     •   •   •   •   •   •   299 GRANDE CHARTR        13
COWLD FORMS BRUSH BY IN GLEAMING WHITE    •   •   •   •   •   •   300 GRANDE CHARTR        36
AND WHITE UPLIFTED FACES STAND            •   •   •   •   •   •   300 GRANDE CHARTR        41
SHOWD ME THE HIGH WHITE STAR OF TRUTH     •   •   •   •   •   •   301 GRANDE CHARTR        69
FAST RUSH THE SPECTRAL VAPOURS WHITE      •   •   •   •   •   •   299 GRANDE CHARTR    V   13
THE WHITE MISTS ROLLING LIKE A SEA        •   •   •   •   •   •   306 OBERMANN             9
THE SOUL OF THEIR WHITE SNOWS             •   •   •   •   •   •   307 OBERMANN            28
WHITE HOUSES PRANK WHERE ONCE WERE HUTS   •   •   •   •   •   •   312 OBERMANN MORE        3
CLUSTERING OER THY WHITE FOREHEAD LIKE A GIRLS    •   •   •   •   373 MEROPE            1162
THE WHITE MOUNTAIN-BIRDS                  •   •   •   •   •   •   392 MEROPE            1625
WHEN THE WHITE-ROBED GARLAND-CROWNED MONARCH   •   •   •   •   •   400 MEROPE            1857
THE FLOWER-DRESSD VICTIM STOOD A MILK-WHITE BULL   •   •   •   •   401 MEROPE            1910
I SADDLED MY WHITE MULE AND ALL NIGHT LONG    •   •   •   •   •   407 EMPEDOCLES I 1      44
THE PEAK ROUND WHICH THE WHITE CLOUDS PLAY    •   •   •   •   •   414 EMPEDOCLES I 2      56
AND THE WHITE OLYMPUS-PEAKS               •   •   •   •   •   •   431 EMPEDOCLES II       80
HIS WHITE GARMENT TO HIS EYES             •   •   •   •   •   •   434 EMPEDOCLES II      188
THAT HEAVES ITS WHITE AND BILLOWY VAPOURS UP   •   •   •   •   •   438 EMPEDOCLES II      309
LIE STREWN THE WHITE FLOCKS               •   •   •   •   •   •   442 EMPEDOCLES II      430
SO WHITE THROUGH THE GLOOM                •   •   •   •   •   •   442 EMPEDOCLES II      438
BY THEIR CHARIOTS STOOD THE STEEDS AND CHAMPD               HOMER TRANS             5
    THE WHITE BARLEY
AND HE WAS GIVEN A VOICE BY THE WHITE-ARMD                  HOMER TRANS            46
    GODDESS HERA
WAVING HER MYRIADS OF WHITE FAIRY BLOOMS  •   •   •   •         EVERLASTING SUB        6
```
WHITEND
```
WHEN THE FROST FLOWERS THE WHITEND WINDOW-PANES   •   •    70 SOHRAB RUSTUM      306
WHITEND HIS FACE FROM THE SUNS FRONTING RAY       •   •   170 EAST AND WEST        6
```
WHITENING
```
AND YON WHITENING BONE-MOUNDS DO NOT GROW     •   •   •   •    27 NEW SIRENS        56
AND THOSE WHITENING BONE-MOUNDS DO NOT GROW   •   •   •   •    27 NEW SIRENS    V   56
WITH WHITENING HEDGES AND UNCRUMPLING FERN    •   •   •   •   265 THYRSIS           74
THEN FROM THOSE WHITENING LIPS AS DEATH DREW NEAR    •   •   478 CROMWELL         213
```
WHITENS
```
GREAT ELBRUIS WHITENS CLEAR    •   •   •   •   •   •   •   •        PILLARS UNIVERS      10
```
WHITER
```
AND WHITER THAN THY WHITE BURNOUS    •   •   •   •   •   •   276 SOUTHERN NIGHT      43
```
WHITHER
```
NOW THEREFORE WHAT TO ATTEMPT OR WHITHER FLY   •   •    98 BALDER DEAD 1      105
WHITHER DOES HE WANDER NOW        •   •   •   •   •   •   136 TRISTRAM 1         189
BUT SHE HERSELF WHITHER SHE WILL CAN ROVE   •   •   •   •   156 TRISTRAM 3         223
BUT WHITHER GOST THOU HENCE O QUEEN AWAY    •   •   •   •   350 MEROPE             597
WHITHER FROM WINTRY MAENALUS WERE BROUGHT   •   •   •   •   356 MEROPE             741
```
WHIZZING
```
AND THE WHIZZING WHEEL STANDS STILL    •   •   •   •   •   •   164 FORSAKEN MERM       97
```
WHOEER
```
FLY HENCE POOR WRETCH WHOEER THOU ART    •   •   •   •   307 OBERMANN           17
```
WHOLE
```
WHO SAW LIFE STEADILY AND SAW IT WHOLE    •   •   •   •     2 TO A FRIEND        12
SO MEN UNRAVELLING GODS HARMONIOUS WHOLE   •   •   •   •     4 BUTLERS SERMONS     3
THOUGH SLOWLY THE FAMILIAR WHOLE       •   •   •   •   •    55 RESIGNATION        95
A PLACID AND CONTINUOUS WHOLE    •   •   •   •   •   •   •    57 RESIGNATION       190
CREEDS PASS RITES CHANGE NO ALTAR STANDETH WHOLE   •   •   173 MONICAS PRAYER     12
CLEAR PROSPECT OER OUR BEINGS WHOLE    •   •   •   •   •   179 FAREWELL           54
WHAT THE PARTS AND WHAT THE WHOLE SHOULD BE    •   •   •   210 SELF-DECEPTION  V   16
THE STREAM OF LIFES MAJESTIC WHOLE     •   •   •   •   •   226 EPILOG LAOCOON    187
DOTH A WHOLE TRACT OF HEAVEN DISCLOSE     •   •   •   •   242 SUMMER NIGHT       10
AND NEVER SEES A WHOLE    •   •   •   •   •   •   •   •   •   415 EMPEDOCLES I 2     85
BEING ONE WITH WHICH WE ARE ONE WITH THE WHOLE WORLD   440 EMPEDOCLES II     372
WHAT WAS FOUR YEARS THEIR WHOLE SHORT DAY   •   •   •   •   450 GEISTS GRAVE       20
WHAT WAS FOUR YEARS THEIR WHOLE SHORT STAY   •   •   •   •   450 GEISTS GRAVE   V   20
WHO THOUGH THE TENDENCE OF THE WHOLE   •   •   •   •   •   481 COURAGE            10
```
WHOLLY
```
THEN SAY HE WAS NOT WHOLLY VILE    •   •   •   •   •   •    95 SICK KING BOKH    231
AS WHOLLY TO BE PITIED QUITE FORLORN   •   •   •   •   •   126 BALDER DEAD 3     458
THIS TOO CAN CHANGE US WHOLLY AND MAKE SEEM    •   •   •   153 TRISTRAM 3        131
NOT WHOLLY CLEAR NOR WHOLLY BLIND      •   •   •   •   •   217 NAMELESS EPIT    V
NOT WHOLLY CLEAR NOR WHOLLY BLIND      •   •   •   •   •   217 NAMELESS EPIT    V
AND WHILE IT LASTS WE CANNOT WHOLLY END   •   •   •   •   236 PALLADIUM          24
THE OLD LAW THEY CRIED IS WHOLLY COME TO NOUGHT   •   •   237 PROGRESS            3
THE OLD LAW THEY SAID IS WHOLLY COME TO NOUGHT    •   •   237 PROGRESS       V    3
FOR WOES THEY WHOLLY FEEL    •   •   •   •   •   •   •   •   320 OBERMANN MORE    236
WHOLLY FORGET THEIR FIRST SAD LIFE AND HOME    •   •   •   427 EMPEDOCLES I 2    458
NOT TO DIE WHOLLY NOT TO BE ALL ENSLAVED   •   •   •   •   441 EMPEDOCLES II     406
```
WICKED
```
FROWNING GRIM DOWN THOU WICKED KING    •   •   •   •   •   •    91 SICK KING BOKH    97
PEACE PEACE ALLS CLEAR THE WICKED WATCH AND WORK   •   •   365 MEROPE            995
```

INDEX WORDS IN ORDER

OF FREQUENCY

1045 I	**235** O	**149** NIGHT	**123** SAY	**99** BRIGHT
613 WE	**234** US	**145** LIGHT UP	**120** SAID	**98** NEVER OUT
560 ALL	**230** MAN	**144** OWN	**115** EARTH OER WHILE	**97** ONLY
546 MY	**227** COME	**143** KNOW	**114** SON SUCH	**95** HIGH
490 AS	**214** GODS SEE	**142** SOUL	**112** SIDE	**94** FIRST
410 OUR	**212** WORLD	**141** HEAVEN OLD	**109** BACK	**93** BEFORE EVER YEARS
401 ME	**209** DOWN	**139** DEATH	**106** HEAD LAST	**92** MIGHT SAW TIME VOICE
310 WILL	**205** SOME	**134** DEAD	**105** KING	**91** HOME YOUTH
285 ONE	**194** HEART MEN	**132** ONCE UPON WAY	**104** CLEAR MAKE	**90** GRAVE
270 YET	**188** LET LONG	**131** WELL	**102** AIR	**87** DARK SUN
269 LIFE	**177** EYES	**130** THAN	**101** ALONE GO LOVE	**86** BLOOD LIVE STREAM
256 STILL	**170** SEA	**127** HAND ROUND	**100** ART AWAY JOY WHITE	
250 MORE	**163** FAR	**125** DEEP		
247 DAY	**150** CAME			
241 LIKE				

83
LAY
RUSTUM
TILL

82
GONE

81
MANY
OVER
STOOD

80
HEAR

79
SWEET

78
FAIR
NEW

77
EYE
FEEL
LEFT
MOUNTAIN
WIND

76
MADE

75
REST

74
COLD
FORTH
SINCE
VAIN

73
FACE
GREAT

71
GREEN
LITTLE
MINE

69
BALDER

68
TEARS

67
NEAR
PAST

66
FEAR
FIND
FRIENDS
HOUR
PAIN
POWER
STAND
WITHOUT

65
DIE
FATHER

64
CHILD
MOTHER
THINGS

63
COMES
HEARD
THOUGHT
TWO

62
BREAST

61
DAYS
FIRE
MIND
SPAKE

60
EVEN
GOD
TRUE
YOUNG

59
AGE

58
MOST
SAD

57
GLOOM
PASSD
POOR
TAKE

56
BRING
PALE
PEACE
PLAIN

55
DEAR
GIVE
KNEW
MUCH
RACE

54
FRIEND
GOOD
WILD

53
CHILDREN
GOLDEN
HILL
HOUSE
HUMAN
KEEP
SLEEP
SOHRAB

52
END
LOVED
SPIRIT
WENT

51
FIELDS
HALF

50
ARMS
ASK
FEET
FREE
LOOK
MANS
PASS
PLACE
SET
SOFT

49
BORN
CRY
FATE
HANDS
HERMOD
STRONG
THOUGHTS
YES

48
AFTER
CALM
FOUND
GREY
UNDER
WAVES

47
BELOW
BLACK
GRIEF
WORDS

46
BROW
HOPE
ILL

45
BEAR
EVERY
FULL
LAND
SAND
SELF
SOULS
SPRING
STRIFE
TREES

44
AMONG
ERE
FALL
HAPPY
SLOW
TOOK

43
BLUE
HILLS
LIE
TELL

42
GRASS
HAIR
NATURE
OFF
SEEK

41
BEHIND
CALL
DONE
DREAM
FOREST
GROUND
LEAVE
MORN
QUEEN
SAVE
STARS
WORD

40
BREATH
FATHERS
LEAVES
LIVED
LOST
NAME
NOTHING
OURS
SPEAK

39
ALAS
BEHOLD
CITY
MEET
RIGHT
SEES
SHORE
SILENCE
SILENT
SONS
SOON
TRUTH

38
BROUGHT
CHANGE
DIED
LESS
MAKES
PLAY
SEEN
WARM
WEAK

37
ABOVE
FELL
FIELD
INDEED
LONELY
MORNING
SPOKE

WILT
WORK

36
BED
BOUND
EAR
FRESH
GAVE
ROSE
SATE
TURN

35
COURSE
FIGHT
LIES
THINK
WEEP
WINDS
WOOD

34
BENEATH
DREAMS
GOLD
LAKE
LOVELY
THOUSAND
TIMES
WORLDS

33
AGAINST
BROTHER
FAME
GROW
HALL
LAW
LIPS
LIVING
MORTAL
OPEN
POWERS
QUIET
RIVER
SAME
SHADE
SNOW
SOUND
STERN
WASTE
WIDE

32
ACROSS
BEST
CARE
CLOSE
ELSE
FALSE
ISEULT
LOW
MIGHTY
PEOPLE
PURE
RULE
SKY
STAY
STRENGTH
WITHIN

31
CHURCH
COOL
CROSS
GREW
HEARTS
KINGS
LIVES
MOMENT
PINES
REACH
STONE
WATERS
WAVE
YEAR

30
BLOW
DAWN
DIVINE
FILL
FORM
HELP
LATE
LONE
RETURN
SHINING
SMILE
SUMMER
TOMB

29
ARM
BALDERS
BLIND
DESIRE
EVENING
FLOW
FLOWERS
KIND
KNOWN
LABOUR
LAID
MID
MILD
PROUD
QUICK
RISE
SHORT
STANDS
THRONE

28
ALONG
CRIES
DIM
DYING
FELT
HOURS
JUST
NONE
REALM
RED
TREE
WALL

27
BAY
BESIDE
DUST
FAST
LOOKD
MOON

MOUNTAINS
MUSIC
ODIN
PRINCE
SIGHT
SUNK
WAIT

26
BETWEEN
FLY
FOE
GAZE
HENCE
HORSE
HOT
LOT
MASTER
PALACE
ROAD
SORROW
STREAMS
SURE
TOWN

25
AROUND
BETTER
BIRTH
BOY
CROWND
DEEDS
DUMB
FIERCE
GAY
HELAS
LIFES
OFTEN
PRAISE
RARE
SONG
STRAIN
SWORD
TRISTRAM
WANDERING
WATCH
WIFE

24
BEYOND
BORE
BRIDGE
CLOUD
COMMON
COUNTRY
EARS
ETERNAL
GAZING
GRACE
ICE
LORD
MOURNFUL
NEWS
PASSION
SHADOW
SHIP
SINGLE
SOLEMN
SURELY
UNKNOWN
WEARY

23
BREAK
DISTANT
DOOR
DULL
FOLLOWD
HARD
KEPT
MESSENIAN
MUTE
NOON
PINE
PRIME
ROCKS
SEEMS
SPIRITS
STRAND
TOIL
TRAIN
VENGEANCE

22
BLISS
BLOWS
BOAT
BROWN
BUILT
CAUSE
COMING
CROWN
ENOUGH
FILLD
FOES
FORMS
HARK
HATE
MURDER
NORTHERN
PRAYER
SHOW
SLOWLY
SOMETHING
SOMETIMES
SWIFT
TIDE
TRY
TURND
WET
WOE

21
ANY
BEING
BENT
BLOOM
CLOUDS
DREW
FADE
FAITHFUL
FLED
FLOOR
FUTURE
GLORY
GLOW
HAVING
HOPES
KNOWS
LINE
MORROW
MURMUR
ORDER
PASSING
PERHAPS

PRAY
READ
REPOSE
SECRET
SHEEP
SMOOTH
STRANGE
STREETS
TOLD
TONGUE
WAR
WATER
WOODS

20
ALIVE
BROAD
CEASE
CHEEKS
CHIEF
CHIEFS
DOUBT
EARLY
FAINT
FOOT
GLEAM
HARDLY
HARP
HELD
HOST
LEARN
LIGHTS
MET
OXUS
PLEASURE
ROCK
ROLL
SENSE
SPEAR
SPEECH
STATE
SWEPT
THREE
TOGETHER
VAST
WISE

19
ARCADIAN
ASGARD
BEGAN
CHEEK
DRAW
FEAST
FEELING
FORMER
GODDESS
HODER
IMMORTAL
LED
LOOKS
LOUD
MAIDENS
MIST
MOURN
MOVE
NEEDS
PATH
RAIN
REPLIED
RICH
RODE

RUSTUMS
SIGN
SLEIPNER
SPACE
SPENT
STAR
STONES
TALE
TRANQUIL
UNHAPPY

18
BAND
BARE
BELIEVE
CALLD
CORPSE
DARKNESS
DEED
FAIN
FAMOUS
FIERY
FRONT
GRACIOUS
GROWS
HELA
HEROES
HUNTERS
IRON
KNOWST
MARBLE
MARCH
NEXT
POET
RAN
RIDE
SEEMD
SEND
SICK
STREWN
STRUCK
TARTAR
THICK
THING
THIRST
TIRED
VALLEY
YOUTHFUL

17
ANSWERD
BATTLE
BELOVED
BIRDS
BORNE
BOUGHS ·
BOWD
BRAIN
BROKE
CAST
DOOM
EARTHLY
FLAME
FORCE
GIRL
GOAL
HEAVY
HOLD
KNIGHT
LARGE
LORDS
MASTERS

17 (cont.)

MEMORY
MOMENTS
MYSELF
OCEAN
OFT
OURSELVES
PILE
REPLY
SAGE
SHINE
SINGS
SITS
SMALL
SMILED
SOLE
SPELL
SPREAD
STEEDS
STROKE
TENT
TRACK
TRULY
WALLS
WAYS
ZEUS

16

ABOUT
AGO
ALWAYS
ANCIENT
AWE
BEAUTY
BEGIN
BLAME
BREAKS
CHARM
CRIED
DEW
EASE
FEVER
FLOWER
GATE
GAZED
GHOSTS
GLAD
GLORIOUS
HEIGHT
HUSBAND
JUSTICE
LAIAS
MOVED
PITY
PRIDE
PUBLIC
PUT
QUITE
RING
SACRED
SAIL
SANDS
SOLITUDE
SOUNDS
SPRINGS
STORM
SUFFERING
SWEEP
SWELL
TOUCH
TRIED
WINE
WINTER

15

BANKS
BEHELD
BROKEN
CHANCE
CHANGED
DESPAIR
DORIAN
DRINK
EAST
FAITH
FED
GLANCE
GUEST
HEADS
HEAVENLY
HEAVENS
HELL
HENCEFORTH
HUSH
JUDGE
LOSS
MENS
MOOD
MOUNT
NANNA
NIGHTS
NOBLE
ODINS
PART
PLAN
PRESENT
RAISED
ROAR
ROME
ROOM
ROUGH
RUN
SCORN
SHAME
SHINES
SITTING
SLEEPING
SMILES
STRAIGHT
STRAY
TURF
WHENCE
WINDOW
WISDOM
WISH
WON

14

AGES
AMID
AUTUMN
BIRD
BITTER
BOLD
BURN
BURNING
CLAD
CLAIM
CORN
DAILY
DARE
DWELL
FAMED
FARE
FAREWELL
FEEBLE
FINGERS

FIRM

FLOWS
FOLLOW
GRAVES
HAIL
HAUNT
HEATH
HIDE
HUNG
ISLE
KEEPS
LIT
LO
LONGING
LOSE
LOVES
MANKIND
MOTHERS
MUSE
PRIZE
PROOF
RADIANT
REARD
SAILS
SECOND
SEEM
SHARP
SIT
SPEAKS
SPEARS
STIR
STIRS
STORMY
STORY
SUNSHINE
TENTS
TERMS
TOUCHD
TREAD
WATCHD
WEAKNESS
WEPT
WEST
WHEREFORE
WHOLE
WORN

13

ACT
AFAR
APPEAR
BADE
BID
BOON
BRINGS
CHAIN
CLIFFS
COUNSEL
DARED
DECAY
DESERT
DOGS
DROVE
DRY
ERST
FAILD
FEARS
FEW
FIGURE
FORESTS
FRANCE
GLENS
GOES

GROWN

HAIRD
HALLS
HAPPIER
HEAT
HOLDS
HURLD
LEAST
LESSON
LOK
LOVERS
LYING
MARK
MEETS
MEROPE
NINE
OBSCURE
ONES
PERAN
PRESENCE
PRISON
RUSH
SAFE
SHEPHERD
SHOOK
SLAVE
SLEEPS
SLOPE
SLOPES
SOUTH
SPRANG
SPRAY
STIRRD
STRETCHD
TAUGHT
TRIBES
USE
WELCOME
WOMAN
WORE
WROUGHT
YELLOW
YESTERDAY
YIELD

12

AID
ALPINE
ALTAR
ANSWER
AUSTERE
BABE
BANK
BEAUTIFUL
BLOODY
BONES
BREATHE
BREEZE
BROTHERS
BUILD
BURIED
CASTLE
CHEER
CHRIST
CLIFF
CRIME
CUT
DEEPLY
DELIGHT
DEPART
DISCERN
DREAD
DUCHESS

EMPEDOCLES

FEELS
FIRES
FIXD
FORLORN
FRAME
FRUIT
GARDEN
GLADE
GRASSY
GREET
GUIDE
HANGS
HERACLES
HID
HOLLOW
HORSES
HUGE
HUNTER
JOYS
KNOWLEDGE
LEAD
LONGD
LORE
MARGUERITE
MOONLIGHT
MOONLIT
NEED
PAIR
PERSIAN
PLAYD
PRIEST
REACHD
REASON
RESTLESS
ROYAL
RUIN
RUNS
SADLY
SAINT
SAVED
SEED
SENT
SIGH
SING
SMOKE
SMOTE
STEEP
STEPS
THREW
THUNDER
TWIXT
VISION
VOID
WAKE
WIN
WIT
YOUNGER

11

ANGUISH
APOLLO
ARCAS
ARISE
ARTS
ASKS
ATLANTIC
BEACH
BEARS
BETWIXT
BOW
BRAVE
BRIDE

8 (cont.)

FARMS
FATES
FITS
FIXT
FLEET
FLOOD
FLUTE
FLUTTERING
FOG
FOLD
FOLLY
FOOD
FOOLS
FRAIL
FRO
FUNERAL
GLEN
GLISTENING
HANGING
HARSH
HAUNTS
HEATHS
HEED
HOARSE
HOMAGE
HOUSES
HUSBANDS
IMPULSE
KINE
LANDS
LAUGH
LAWN
LEAF
LIGHTNINGS
LISTEN
LOAD
MAD
MAGIC
MAJESTIC
MEADOWS
MEANT
MELT
MESSENGER
MIEN
MILK
MINGLING
MOUTH
MUSED
NOUGHT
PASTORAL
PATHS
PEN
PLAYS
PLEASANT
POLYPHONTES
PRINCESS
PROMISE
PROVE
PURPLE
PYRE
QUENCH
QUICKLY
REMAIN
RENEW
RINGING
RITES
ROARING
ROLLING
RUDE
SAINTS
SCANND
SCENE
SEAS

SEATS
SHADOWY
SHUT
SIGNS
SINNER
SIRE
SIX
SNOWY
SOILD
SOOTHE
SPED
STOLE
STOPS
STORMS
STRAINS
SUSPICION
TABLETS
TEMPER
THENCE
THIN
TIDES
TONES
TOSSING
TOWNS
TRAVEL
TROOPS
TROUBLE
TROUBLED
TURNS
TWILIGHT
ULYSSES
VAGUE
VERY
WANDER
WATCHING
WELFARE
WILLING
WISHD
WITS
WONDER
WORDSWORTHS
WRAPT
YIELDS
ZAL

7

ABROAD
AGONY
ANGRY
APPEARD
ARMD
AUGUST
BAD
BLEST
BOAST
BOOK
BOUGH
BRILLIANT
BRITTANY
BUGLE
BUSINESS
CARVED
CAUGHT
CAVE
CHAMPION
CHARGED
CHIDE
CHILDRENS
CHILL
CLOUDY
COLOUR
CROSSING
CROWNING

CUP
CYPSELUS
DANGEROUS
DATE
DAZZLING
DEATHS
DECLINE
DEEPER
DEPTHS
DIMMD
DOG
DREAMING
EASY
ELMS
ENDS
ENVY
FANCY
FARED
FEVERISH
FINDS
FINE
FLASHING
FLEW
FLIES
FLING
FLOWN
FOLDED
FOLLOWS
FORGOTTEN
FORTUNE
FRAY
FREA
FRIENDLY
FURLD
GALE
GERMAN
GHOST
GIANTS
GIFTED
GLEAMING
GLIMMERING
GOODNESS
GORGES
GRATE
HATES
HATRED
HEALTH
HEATHER
HEAVED
HIDDEN
HISTORY
HOUND
IMPERIAL
INMOST
JEALOUS
JUDGMENT
KEN
KINDNESS
LABOURING
LACK
LAUREL
LIGHTED
LIMBS
LOCKD
LOVELINESS
LURED
MAINTAIN
MARGE
MARKD
MAX
MEMORIAL
MERE
MESSENIANS
MIDST

MINDS
MISERY
MISS
MOB
MOUNTS
MOVEMENT
MULES
MURDERD
NARROW
NATIVE
NATURES
NECK
NIMBLE
NOBLER
NURSLING
OUTWORN
OVERHEAD
OXFORD
PAINS
PAN
PATIENT
PENSIVE
PERCHANCE
PERILOUS
PRAYD
PRINCELY
PROFOUND
QUIVERING
RAPT
REGARD
REMEMBER
REMEMBRANCE
RESTING
RISK
RIVERS
ROBED
ROOF
RUSHES
SANG
SCARLET
SCHOLAR
SEARCH
SEAT
SERVANT
SHIPS
SHOUT
SLAY
SMILING
SNATCH
SOLITARY
SORE
SOUTHERN
SPARKLING
SPEND
SPHERE
SPORT
SPREADS
SQUARE
STEMS
STORE
STRAIT
STRAITS
SUCCOUR
SUFFER
SURFACE
SWEETLY
SYMPATHY
TALL
TEACH
TELLS
TERM
THINKING
THOR
THORN

TIED
TOPS
TORRENTS
TROY
TURMOIL
TURNING
TWENTY
UPLAND
UTTERD
VIEW
VIZIER
WARMTH
WASHD
WEAL
WHEEL
WHEREWITH
WILDERNESS
WREATHED
WRONG
YEA

6

ACCEPT
ACTIONS
ADVANCE
AEPYTUS
AFRASIABS
AGED
ALLEYS
ALLOW
ALLOWD
ALLS
ALMOST
ALOOF
ALOUD
ANON
APART
APPEARS
APRIL
ARGOS
ASIDE
ASKD
ASPECT
AVENGER
AWAIT
BALM
BASE
BEAM
BEASTS
BELL
BIND
BLESSED
BOSOM
BOUNDED
BOUNDLESS
BRANCHES
BRANDAN
BRINGING
BROOD
BROOKS
BROU
BURNISHD
BURNS
BURSTING
CALLICLES
CATTLE
CEASED
CENTURIES
CERTAIN
CHALLENGE
CHESTNUT
CHESTNUTS
CIRCLE

6 (cont.)

CLASH	GAINST	PAUSE	STEER	BANQUET
CLEARER	GARB	PENT	STILLNESS	BARDS
CLUB	GARLANDS	PEOPLES	STRANGELY	BATHING
CLUSTERD	GATHERD	PERISHD	STRUGGLING	BATTLES
COMMAND	GEIST	PILLARS	SURPRISE	BEATS
COMMERCE	GIALLS	PILLOWS	TABLE	BEGUILED
COMPOSED	GIPSY	PLEASE	TALK	BELIEVED
COMST	GLADES	PLOT	TALKD	BESIDES
CONSCIENCE	GLOSSY	POINT	TERROR	BINDS
COUNCIL	GRAND	POISED	THITHER	BLITHE
COUNTLESS	GREATNESS	POOL	THREAD	BLOSSOMD
CRADLE	GREECE	PRAISED	THRICE	BLOWING
CRESPHONTES	GROANS	PRIMAL	TOWER	BOATS
CRUEL	HAILD	PRIVATE	TRACT	BOKHARA
CURRENT	HALT	PROCESSION	TROUBLES	BREAD
DARES	HAPPINESS	PROSPEROUS	TUMULT	BREAKING
DAYLIGHT	HEALING	PULSE	TYNTAGIL	BREATHLESS
DEER	HEDGE	PURPOSE	TYRANTS	BRIEF
DESIRES	HOLLIES	PURSUE	UNBROKEN	BRIMMING
DESTINED	HOPELESS	PURSUED	UPPER	BROODS
DIES	HORNS	QUIT	UPROAR	BROOK
DIFFERENT	HURRY	RAISE	URGE	BUILDED
DISAPPEAR	HUSHD	RANGED	VALIANT	BUOYANT
DOUBTS	HUT	RAPTURE	VAPOURS	BURSTS
DRAWS	ICEBERG	RECEIVED	VEIL	BUSH
DREAMD	IDLY	REJOICE	VERGE	BYRON
DREARY	ILLS	REMAIND	VESSELS	CARRIED
DRESS	IMAGE	REMAINS	VEX	CAVES
DRIED	IMPETUOUS	REMORSE	VIOLENT	CENTRAL
DROP	INNOCENT	RESIGND	VIRTUES	CHANGES
EAGLES	ISSUED	RETAIN	WALK	CHANGING
EASED	JOYLESS	RETURNING	WALLD	CHASM
ECHOING	JUDGED	REVEALD	WAN	CHECK
EDGE	JUNE	RHINE	WARNING	CHEERD
ELSEWHERE	KAI	RIDGE	WASTED	CHEERLESS
ENDED	LAUGHTER	RISES	WATERY	CHERISHD
ENDURED	LAWS	RISING	WAVED	CHILDHOODS
ENEMIES	LEAGUE	ROAMD	WAVERING	CHILDISH
ENERGY	LEAN	ROOFD	WEALTH	CHRISTIAN
ENGLAND	LEISURE	RUSHD	WESTWARD	CHURCHYARD
ENTERD	LIFTING	SAKE	WHIRLING	CLEARD
ETNA	LISTEND	SCENT	WIGHT	CLIMBING
EXACT	LONGER	SCHEMES	WILLD	CLOTHED
EXILE	LOOSED	SCOPE	WINTERS	COLDLY
EXPERIENCE	LUST	SECURE	WINTRY	COLOURD
EXPLORE	LYRE	SEEKING	WISHES	COMFORT
FAUN	MANE	SEEMING	WOKE	COMPANIONS
FEATURES	MATTHIAS	SEER	WONDROUS	COMPANY
FEELINGS	MEANWHILE	SEISTAN	WOUNDED	CONQUER
FEROOD	MEASURE	SEIZED	WRETCH	CONQUERING
FIERCELY	MERLIN	SENSELESS	YON	CONSUMED
FILES	MIDDLE	SENTENCE	ZEAL	COPSE
FILLS	MIDNIGHT	SERPENT		COTTAGE
FINAL	MOAN	SETS		COUNSELLD
FIR	MOCKING	SETTLED	5	COUNTENANCE
FIX	MONTH	SHEEN	ACCOMPLISHD	COURTS
FLAG	MOORD	SHOT	ACTIVE	CRAFT
FLANKS	MOORS	SHOULDER	ACTS	CREATURE
FLASH	MORTALS	SHOUTING	ADDRESSD	CREEDS
FLESH	MOUNTED	SICILIAN	ADER	CREEP
FLIGHT	NAKED	SIGHTS	ALIEN	CREW
FLOATING	NILE	SIMPLE	ALLOWS	CROWDS
FLOCK	NOISY	SINKS	ALOFT	CUMNER
FLOWD	NORTHWARD	SLAVES	ANGER	CUPID
FLOWERY	OBERMANN	SOMEWHAT	ANXIOUS	CYLLENES
FLOWING	OPEND	SOMEWHERE	APPROACH	DANCE
FOREHEAD	OPENING	SPELLS	ARRAY	DARKENING
FORWARD	OUGHT	SPIRES	ARRIVED	DARKSOME
FOUNDED	PAID	SPOT	ASH	DEAF
FOUNTAINS	PALSIED	SPRUNG	ASHES	DEBT
FRINGED	PARTED	STAGE	ATTEMPT	DECK
FURIOUS	PASSAGE	STARRY	ATTEND	DECLARE
FURZE	PASSERS	START	AY	DEEMD
	PASTURES	STAYD	BAIJAN	DEMAND

5 (cont.)
DENIED
DESOLATE
DESPERATE
DESTINY
DISDAIN
DRANK
DRIPPING
DRIVING
DROOPING
DROPPD
DROPPING
DUSTY
ECHO
ELM
EMPTY
ERRAND
ETERNITY
EUROPES
EVERLASTING
EXPECT
EYELIDS
FAINTER
FAIREST
FALLN
FARES
FASTER
FATIGUE
FEEBLY
FETCH
FIGHTS
FIRS
FISHER
FLAMES
FLOCKS
FLOODED
FLOODS
FLOWERD
FOILD
FOND
FORTUNATE
FOUNTAIN
FRANK
FRAUGHT
FREEDOM
FRIENDLESS
FRINGE
FROWNING
FRUITLESS
FUMES
GATES
GATHER
GATHERING
GENEROUS
GLASS
GLOWING
GOETHE
GOETHES
GRATEFUL
GRAY
GREATEST
GREETED
GREETINGS
GRIEVE
GRIEVOUS
GROUNDS
GUARDS
GUILT
GULF
GULPH
HARBOUR
HARVEST
HAY
HEAREST

HEARTH
HEATS
HELM
HERACLEIDAE
HERITAGE
HERO
HEST
HIGHEST
HOLLOWS
HOLLY
HOMES
HOMEWARD
HOURLY
HOWBEIT
HUE
HUTS
IMPERIOUS
INCLINED
INFINITE
INLY
INN
INNER
INSPIRE
INSPIRED
INTEREST
IRELAND
ISLANDS
ISSUE
JEWELLD
KAISER
KINDLED
KINGLY
KINSMAN
KNOWEST
KNOWING
LATTER
LAURELS
LEADS
LENGTH
LEST
LIFELESS
LIGHTNING
LIONS
LIP
LIQUID
LITTER
LODGE
LOFTY
LONDON
LOOKING
LOUDER
LOVING
MAINTAIND
MAJESTY
MANHOOD
MARGARET
MATCHD
MEAL
MEANS
MEED
MEETING
MEMORIES
MIDGARD
MIGHTIEST
MIRTH
MOANS
MOODS
MORNINGS
MOSS
MOSSY
MOURND
MOURNFULLY
MOVING
MULE

MYRIADS
NAMES
NEATH
NECESSITY
NOISE
NUMBER
OBEYD
OBLIVION
ODER
OLYMPUS
OUTSIDE
OUTSPREAD
OUTWARD
PALACES
PALM
PASSES
PEERS
PEISIANAX
PERCH
PERISH
PERSONAL
PIERCED
PIERCING
PILLAR
PLACED
PLACES
PLEASED
PLEASURES
PLEDGE
POLE
POLICY
POMP
POSSESSD
POST
POURD
PRESS
PREVAIL
PROFIT
PROUDLY
PROVED
PROVES
PRUDENCE
PUISSANT
QUEST
RAGE
RANKS
RASH
RAYS
REAPERS
RECALL
REED
REGION
RENOWN
RENT
REPORT
RESOLVE
RESTED
RIGHTEOUS
RIGHTS
RIVAL
ROCKY
ROMAN
ROUSE
SAMARCAND
SANDY
SECRETS
SEEKS
SERENE
SERVE
SERVED
SERVICE
SEVERD
SEVERE
SHAKEN

SHAKES
SHAMED
SHIELD
SHOOT
SHOWD
SHOWER
SIDES
SIGHD
SIGHTLESS
SIGNAL
SILKEN
SINGING
SKIES
SMART
SOIL
SOLITUDES
SOOTHED
SORROWS
SOUNDING
SOUTHWARD
SPARES
SPECTACLE
SPOTS
SPUN
SPUR
SQUADRONS
STAG
STAINS
STAIR
STANDEST
STARTLED
STEALS
STONY
STOPPD
STREAMING
STRETCHING
STREW
STRICKEN
STRIKES
SUBJECTS
SUBTLE
SUCCESS
SUDDENLY
SUFFERD
SUNG
SUNLESS
SWINGS
TALES
TEDIOUS
TEMPEST
TEMPLE
TEND
THEREON
THICKLY
THRONES
THROW
TILLD
TOSS
TRAIND
TRANSIENT
TRAVELLERS
TRAVELS
TREADS
TREMBLE
TREMULOUS
TRISTRAMS
TROJANS
TWIN
TWINE
TYRANNOUS
TYRANT
UNARMD
UNCONSCIOUS
UNGUESSD

UNLIKE
UNTRODDEN
URGED
USED
VEXT
VICTORS
VIGOUR
VIRGIN
VISIONS
VISIT
WAKING
WEAR
WEARINESS
WEEDS
WHEREIN
WHISPERING
WHITHER
WINNING
WITHERD
WOES
WORKING
WOUND
XANTHUS
YEW
YOUNGEST
YOUTHS

4
ABHORRD
ABODE
ABSENCE
ACCENTS
ACCUSER
ACHILLES
ADMIRE
AFIELD
AFRAID
AILS
AIRY
AISLES
ALARM
ALTERD
AMISS
ARCH
ARMOUR
ARMY
ATE
AUGHT
AUSTRIAN
AVAIL
AVENGE
AVERSE
AWAKE
BABY
BALE
BANDS
BANISHD
BANNERS
BARED
BARK
BEGUN
BELT
BESTOWD
BETHINK
BETRAYD
BEWILDERD
BIER
BIFROST
BLAND
BLOODSHOT
BLOSSOM
BLOT
BODIES

4 (cont.)
BONDS
BONE
BORDERD
BORDERS
BOUNDS
BOWER
BOWERS
BOWL
BRAVEST
BRAZEN
BREACH
BREATHED
BREATHING
BRETHREN
BRINE
BRINK
BROOM
BRUSHWOOD
BURDEN
BUSY
BYRONS
CADENCE
CAESAR
CALAIS
CALAMITY
CALLING
CALLS
CAMST
CARELESS
CATANA
CAUSES
CAVERNS
CENTRE
CHAINS
CHAIR
CHAMBERS
CHARGD
CHECKS
CHILDS
CHIME
CHOICE
CHOSEN
CITIZENS
CLASPD
CLAY
CLEARNESS
CLOSING
CLOTH
CLOUDED
COMPANION
COMPLAIN
CONDEMND
CONJECTURED
CONTENT
CONVEY
CORNWALL
COURTEOUS
COURTESY
COURTLY
COVERTS
CRASHING
CREDULOUS
CREEPING
CRIMES
CROWNED
CROWNS
CRUMBLING
CUMBERD
CURE
CURIOUS
CURLS
CURRENTS
CYPRESS

DAMSEL
DANUBE
DAUGHTER
DAWNS
DEATHLIKE
DEJECTION
DENY
DEPARTED
DESCEND
DESCRIED
DESCRY
DESIGN
DESPISE
DEVOURING
DEWS
DIGHT
DIRGE
DISCONTENT
DISMAY
DISTANCE
DIZZY
DOMINION
DRAUGHT
DRAWBRIDGE
DROWN
DROWND
DUKE
DUTIES
EAGLE
EARNESTLY
EASIER
EAT
EFFACE
ENDURING
ENEMYS
EQUAL
EUROPE
EUXINE
EVENT
EXILED
EXIST
EXPRESS
FAILING
FAIRY
FAMILIAR
FATAL
FATED
FAULT
FAY
FEARFUL
FEASTS
FEIGN
FESTAL
FIGHTING
FINGER
FISHERS
FIT
FIVE
FLAGS
FLASHD
FLOATED
FLOATS
FLOWERING
FLUNG
FLUSH
FLUSHING
FLUTES
FOAMD
FOAMING
FOLLOWERS
FOOTED
FORBEAR
FOREIGN
FORWARDS

FREELY
FRENCH
FROSTY
FULNESS
FURIES
GAILY
GENERATIONS
GENTLY
GESTURE
GET
GETS
GIPSIES
GIRLS
GIRT
GLARE
GLEE
GLIDE
GLISTERING
GLORIES
GOATS
GORGE
GOT
GRECIAN
GROVE
GUARDIAN
GUESS
GUESTS
GUIDED
GUIDES
GUST
HAIRS
HARMONY
HATED
HATEFUL
HAUNTED
HAVEN
HAZE
HEADLONG
HEAPS
HEARING
HEATHY
HECTOR
HEEL
HEIR
HEIRSHIP
HELPERS
HERMES
HEROIC
HIST
HOLIDAY
HORN
HORROR
HOSTILE
HUES
HUMMING
HUNT
HURRIED
HURT
IACCHUS
IGNOBLE
INGLORIOUS
INLAND
INTENT
ISLES
ITALIAN
ITALY
IVY
JADED
JAMAN
JEALOUSY
JOINTS
JOYFUL
JOYOUS
KILL

KILLD
KINDLE
KINDLY
KINSMEN
KIPCHAK
KISSD
KNEE
KNEELING
LABOURD
LADIES
LADY
LAIR
LAKES
LAME
LAMPS
LANGUIDLY
LAWNS
LEAND
LEANING
LEANS
LEAVING
LEND
LENT
LICHEN
LINEAGE
LINGER
LIVD
LOATH
LOATHED
LOVER
LUMINOUS
MANTLES
MARGIN
MARRIAGE
MARSHALLD
MARVEL
MAST
MATCH
MATES
MATTED
MEADOW
MERCHANTS
MERLINS
MESSENIA
MILLIONS
MINDED
MIRROR
MISSD
MIXD
MOCKD
MODERATE
MONARCH
MOONS
MOULD
MOWN
MUFFLED
MULTITUDE
MURMURD
MURMURING
MUSES
MUSICIAN
MUSING
MUTTERS
MYRTLE
MYSTERY
NAMED
NAMELESS
NATIONS
NEST
NIFLHEIM
NIORD
NOBLY
NURSED
OFFER

OFFERS
OMEN
ONWARD
OUTGROWS
OUTLASTS
PAGEANT
PAINFUL
PALFREY
PANG
PANTHEIA
PARENT
PARIS
PARTY
PASSIVE
PASTIME
PAVEMENT
PEACEFUL
PEAK
PEERLESS
PELOPS
PEOPLED
PERCEIVE
PERFECT
PERPETUAL
PHANTOMS
PIERCE
PILLOW
PIOUS
PIPE
PITCH
PITCHD
PITEOUS
PLANT
PLOTS
PLUCKD
PLUME
PLUNGING
PLY
PORT
PORTICO
POSSESS
PRACTISED
PRESSD
PREST
PRISONER
PRISONERS
PROCLAIMS
PROMPT
PROW
PULSES
QUAILD
QUESTION
QUITS
RALLY
RAPTURES
RARELY
RAVE
REBEL
RECALLD
RECENT
REFUSED
REPAIR
REPELLD
REQUIRED
RETURND
REVEALING
REVERENCE
RINGS
RIVALS
ROBBER
ROBES
ROOFS
ROUT
RUIND

4 (cont.)

RUSTLING
SADDLE
SCANT
SCEPTRE
SCHOOL
SCORNFUL
SCOURGE
SCREAM
SCREAMS
SCREEND
SEAL
SEAWARD
SEEING
SERIOUS
SERVANTS
SEVEN
SHADOWED
SHELL
SHELTER
SHIVER
SHORES
SHOUTED
SHOWS
SICKNESS
SILVERD
SIR
SKILL
SLENDER
SOLDIER
SOOTHING
SOPHISTS
SORT
SOULD
SPAIN
SPARK
SPARS
SPEAKING
SPITE
SPLENDOUR
SPOIL
SPOILD
SPRINGING
SPURN
STAIND
STARLIT
STATESMAN
STATUES
STAVE
STAYS
STEAL
STEM
STENYCLAROS
STERNER
STRAIND
STRAINING
STRAYS
STREAMD
STRETCH
STRUNG
STYMPHALIAN
SULLEN
SUMMERS
SUNNY
SUNRISE
SURGING
SURVEYS
SWALLOWS
SWARMING
SWAYS
SWEEPING
SWITZERLAND
SYLVAN
TALKING

TANGLED
TARRY
TASKD
TEGEA
TENDER
TERRIBLE
THANK
THANKLESS
THEBAN
THINKS
THRILL
THRUSH
THUNDERING
THYME
TINY
TOMBS
TONGUES
TOPPD
TORCH
TORCHES
TORMENT
TORTURED
TOSSD
TOWERD
TOY
TRACE
TRACKD
TRAITOR
TRANCE
TRAVELLER
TREMBLING
TRIUMPHS
TROOP
TRUCE
TRUNK
TYNTAGELS
TYPHO
UNAVENGED
UNBLEST
UNCLE
UNDERNEATH
UNKIND
UNKNOWING
UNMEANING
UNREST
UNSURE
UNTIRED
UNWILLINGLY
UNWORN
VANISHD
VERSE
VICTIM
VICTORIOUS
VILLAGE
VILLAGES
VINE
VIRTUE
WAILING
WAITING
WALKS
WANDERS
WARD
WARMD
WARRIORS
WARS
WASH
WEEPS
WHISPERS
WHITENING
WIDER
WIELD
WINDING
WINDY
WINGD

WISER
WISTFUL
WOODY
WORDSWORTH
WORKS
WORST
WORTH
WRITTEN
WRONGD
YARD
ZEALOUS

3

ABANDOND
ABIDES
ABODES
ABOUND
ABYSS
ACHIEVE
ACHING
ADDRESS
ADIEU
ADOWN
ADVANCED
AERIAL
AFFECTIONS
AFLOAT
AFRASIAB
AFTERNOON
ALARMS
ALERT
ALIGHT
ALLAH
ALREADY
ALWAY
AMBITION
AMPLER
AMUSE
ANCESTOR
ANCHORITES
ANEMONIES
ANEW
ANTIQUE
APOLLOS
APPEARING
APPEASED
APPLAUD
APPLY
APPOINTED
APPROACHES
APPROVE
ARCHES
ARCHITECT
ARDENT
ARDOUR
ARID
ARIGHT
ARRAIGN
ARRIVE
ARROW
ARROWY
ARTHUR
ARTIST
ARTISTS
ASTRAY
ATONED
ATOSSA
AUTHOR
AVENGED
AVENGERS
AWOKE
AXES
BACKWARD

BAFFLING
BALANCE
BALANCED
BALTIC
BALUSTRADE
BANNER
BAR
BARGE
BARRD
BARS
BASILIS
BASK
BATHE
BEACHES
BEACONS
BEARDED
BEARERS
BEATING
BEE
BEETHOVEN
BEGUILE
BEINGS
BENCH
BENIGNANT
BENUMB
BESTOW
BEWARE
BIDS
BLACKEND
BLEAK
BLEEDING
BLENT
BLESSING
BLEW
BLINDED
BOARD
BODING
BOISTEROUS
BOLT
BOORS
BOTTOM
BOUGHT
BOUNDING
BOWED
BRAKE
BRAKES
BREASTS
BREATHES
BREIDABLIK
BRIMMD
BRINGEST
BROIDERD
BROIL
BROODING
BROTHERHOOD
BROWS
BRUSHD
BRUTES
BUILDERS
BULRUSH
CAKES
CALLISTO
CALMD
CALMS
CANARY
CAP
CAPTIVE
CAPTURED
CASE
CASPIAN
CASUAL
CATCH
CAUCASUS
CEASELESS

CEDARN
CENSURE
CENTAURS
CHAFED
CHAFING
CHAIRS
CHALETS
CHANCED
CHANNEL
CHANNELS
CHARRD
CHATTER
CHEQUER
CHILLY
CHOSE
CHRISTMAS
CILICIAN
CIRCE
CIRCULAR
CITYS
CLAIMS
CLARION
CLEAREST
CLEARLY
CLIMBD
CLIME
CLOSELY
CLOUDLESS
CLOVE
CLUE
CLUSTERS
COCK
COLLIE
COLUMNS
COMER
COMEST
COMPLEXION
CONDEMN
CONFESS
CONQUEST
CONSIDER
CONSTRUED
CONSULT
COUCHD
COWARD
COWARDS
COWSLIPS
CRACKLING
CRAG
CRASH
CREATURES
CREED
CRESTED
CRISP
CROCUS
CROUCH
CROUCHD
CROW
CRUSH
CUCKOO
CUNNING
CURLD
CURTAINS
CUTS
DAM
DAMES
DANCES
DANCING
DANTE
DARLING
DARTING
DAWNING
DAZZLED
DEADENS

3 (cont.)
DEADLY
DEAFEND
DEALT
DEBTS
DECEMBER
DEFILED
DELAYS
DELICATE
DELIGHTED
DELIGHTFUL
DELIGHTS
DELL
DELLS
DEMANDS
DENIES
DEPLORE
DESCENDS
DESCRIES
DESERTED
DESIGND
DESPOTIC
DESTIND
DIMLY
DISAPPEARD
DISEASE
DISMAL
DISMAYD
DISPLAY
DIVINER
DOCTOR
DOING
DOOMD
DOORS
DORIANS
DOUBTFUL
DRAIND
DRAUGHTS
DRENCHD
DRIFTING
DRIFTS
DRINKS
DRUDGE
DUBIOUS
DUSKY
DWELT
EAGERLY
EARNEST
EASTERN
EASTWARD
EBBD
ECHOED
ECHOES
EDDY
EEN
EFFACED
ELDER
ELDEST
ELEMENTS
ELOQUENT
EMBRACE
EMBROILD
EMERGE
EMOTIONS
ENCHANTED
ENCIRCLING
ENGLANDS
ENJOY
ENNOBLED
ENSIGNS
ENTER
ENTERING
ENTREAT
ENVIOUS

ERRANDS
ERROR
ERRS
ESCAPES
ETNAS
EUGENIA
EXPECTATION
EXPIRE
EXULTING
FACTIONS
FADES
FADING
FAINTLY
FAITHS
FALTER
FALTERING
FANE
FANTASTIC
FARM
FEARD
FEARLESSLY
FEATHERD
FEATHERS
FEEDEST
FEIGND
FENCE
FENRIS
FERMENT
FERN
FERRY
FEUDS
FIEND
FIGURES
FILE
FIREPLACE
FITFUL
FLEETS
FLIT
FLITTING
FLOODING
FLUX
FOLDS
FOLK
FONDLY
FORBID
FOREBODES
FOREMOST
FORT
FORTUNES
FOUL
FRAGRANCE
FRAMED
FREED
FREEDOMS
FREEZE
FREIGHT
FRESHEND
FRESHENING
FREYA
FRIENDSHIP
FRORE
FRUITFUL
FUGITIVE
FULFIL
FURROWD
FURY
GAIND
GALL
GARLAND
GARMENT
GATED
GAZD
GAZER
GAZES

GENTLENESS
GERMANY
GHOSTLIKE
GIBRALTARS
GILD
GLADSOME
GLANCING
GLIDES
GLIMPSE
GLION
GLOOMS
GLORIFIED
GLOWS
GOAD
GORE
GOTH
GRACES
GRANDSIRE
GRANTED
GRASP
GRATING
GREEK
GRIEFS
GRIM
GROUP
GROUPD
GROVES
GRUDGE
GULFS
GUSTS
HABIT
HADES
HAG
HAMMER
HARDER
HARM
HARTZ
HASTY
HAT
HATS
HAUGHTY
HEADED
HEAPD
HEAVES
HEAVILY
HEDGES
HEIMDALLS
HEIRS
HELICON
HELPING
HEMMD
HERALD
HERBS
HERDS
HIDEOUS
HIDES
HIMALAYAN
HO
HOLDST
HOLIEST
HOMELESS
HONOURS
HORIZON
HORIZONS
HORSEHAIR
HORSEMEN
HOTLY
HOVER
HUMBLE
HUMBLED
HUMID
HURRYING
ICY
IDAS

IGNORANCE
ILLUMINED
IMAGED
IMMERSED
IMPART
IMPORT
IMPOSSIBLE
INFIRM
INFORM
INSCRUTABLE
INSIGHT
INSTANT
INSTRUCT
INTERRUPT
INVENT
IRAN
ISSUING
IVE
JARS
JEST
JOYFULLY
KINSFOLK
KNEEL
KNIT
KNOTS
LABOURERS
LABOURS
LANES
LAP
LASHES
LASTS
LATEST
LAUD
LAUGHING
LAYS
LEADEN
LEADER
LEAPING
LEAPT
LEARNED
LEARNS
LESSONS
LIBATIONS
LIEST
LIGHTEND
LIGHTER
LIGHTLY
LIGHTNESS
LILAC
LINGERING
LISTENING
LOCK
LOGS
LONGINGS
LONGS
LOOM
LOOSEND
LORN
LOVELIEST
LOVST
LOYAL
LURID
LYCAEUS
MADLY
MAILD
MAKING
MAR
MARC
MARKET
MARSYAS
MASK
MEAD
MEDITATION
MEDITERRANEAN

MEMORYS
MENTAL
MERIT
MIDLAND
MIGHTIER
MILDER
MILDLY
MIMIC
MINED
MINISTER
MINISTERS
MINSTER
MIRACLE
MISCHANCE
MISERABLE
MISTRUST
MOANING
MOCKERY
MONARCHS
MOONSHINE
MOORLAND
MOSSD
MOTION
MOTIVES
MOUNDED
MOUNDS
MOUNTING
MOURNING
MURDERS
MYSTIC
NEER
NEIGHBOUR
NEPHEWS
NIGHTFALL
NIGHTINGALES
NOD
NOISIER
NOOK
NORNIES
NOTING
NURSING
OAK
OAKS
OARS
OBTAIN
OCTOBER
OERHANGING
OFFERINGS
OFFSPRING
ONSET
OPENS
OPPRESSD
ORACULAR
ORDAIND
ORDERD
ORESTES
ORGANS
ORPHAN
ORPHEUS
OSSA
OWND
PACE
PAINTER
PAINTERS
PAMERE
PANES
PANGS
PARK
PARNASSUS
PASTURE
PATHOS
PAUSES
PEAL
PEEP

2

ABANDONS
ABBEYS
ABLAZE
ABYSMAL
ACACIA
ACCEPTANCE
ACCURST
ACHAIAN
ACHE
ACQUIRES
ADAMANTINE
ADDERS
ADHERENCE
ADORE
ADRIATIC
ADVANCING
ADVENTUROUS
ADVISE
AEGAEAN
AERY
AFLAME
AGAMEMNONS
AGENTS
AGITATED
AGREES
AGRIGENTUM
AIMS
AISLE
ALIKE
ALLEGIANCE
ALLY
ALTARS
ALTERNATING
AMAIN
AMAZED
AMBER
AMBUSHD
AMETHYST
AMONGST
AMPLE
ANGEL
ANGERS
ANGLER
ANGRILY
ANNUAL
ANSWERED
ANSWEREST
ANTIGONE
ANTLERD
APACE
APPEARANCE
APPROACHING
APPROVES
ARCADE
ARDRES
ARGIVE
ARMLESS
ARNE
ARRAYD
ARRIVES
ARTHURS
ASGARDS
ASHORE
ASKST
ASOPUS
ASSAILD
ASSAULT
ASSURANCE
ASSURE
ATHENS
ATHIRST
ATTENTIVE
ATTIRE

ATTITUDE
AUGUR
AUTUMNS
AVALANCHE
AVENGING
AVERT
AWARD
AWED
AWRY
AYE
BACKD
BALEFUL
BALES
BALMS
BALMY
BAN
BANE
BANISHMENT
BAREST
BARLEY
BARRIER
BARRING
BASKET
BASKS
BATHES
BATTERD
BEADS
BEAMD
BEAMS
BEAST
BEAUTEOUS
BECK
BECKOND
BECOMES
BEDSIDE
BEES
BEFITS
BEGINNING
BEHOLDING
BELIEVERS
BELONG
BENDING
BENEFICENT
BENUMBING
BERKSHIRE
BERRIED
BERRIES
BESPAKE
BEWAILD
BEWAILING
BEWEEP
BITTERER
BITTEREST
BITTERLY
BLACKBIRD
BLACKER
BLAZED
BLAZING
BLEED
BLEND
BLINDLY
BLINDNESS
BLINDS
BLITHELY
BLOND
BLOODLESS
BLOODSHED
BLOOMS
BLOSSOMS
BLOTTED
BLOTTING
BOASTFUL
BOILING
BOLDER

BOLDEST
BOLDLY
BOLDNESS
BOLED
BOND
BONDAGE
BOOKS
BOOTHS
BOOTS
BORDERING
BOSOMS
BRACELET
BRANCHD
BRAND
BREADTH
BREATHINGS
BREEDEST
BREEDS
BRETHRENS
BRETON
BRIGHTEN
BRIGHTENING
BRIGHTEST
BRIGHTNESS
BRINGER
BROILS
BROKENLY
BROODED
BROUGHAM
BRUSH
BRUTAL
BUBBLING
BUGLES
BUILDING
BUILDS
BURND
BURY
BURYING
BYGONE
CAGES
CALMER
CAMEST
CAMPD
CANAL
CANOPY
CAPITOL
CAPS
CAPTAIN
CAREER
CARNAC
CAROLS
CART
CARTHAGE
CASSOCKD
CASTLED
CATCHES
CATES
CAVERN
CEASES
CEDAR
CEDARS
CELESTIAL
CENTAUR
CENTRED
CHAFE
CHALET
CHAMPIONS
CHANGD
CHANGEFUL
CHANGELESS
CHAPLET
CHARIOT
CHARMED
CHEAP

CHEAT
CHEERFULNESS
CHEERING
CHEERS
CHIDING
CHIPPING
CHIRP
CHIVALRY
CHOIR
CHOKE
CHOPS
CHORASMIAN
CHORD
CIRCLES
CIRCLET
CIRCLING
CITADEL
CLANG
CLASHD
CLEARING
CLIMBS
CLIMES
CLIP
CLOISTER
CLOSER
CLOSES
CLOTHES
CLUMPS
CLUSTERING
CLUTCHD
COASTS
COATED
COFFINS
COLDER
COLLAR
COLT
COMBINED
COMMIT
COMMUNION
COMPACT
COMPOSE
COMRADES
CONCEALD
CONCEALS
CONCEIVE
CONCORD
CONDITION
CONE
CONFEDERATE
CONFERRD
CONFERRING
CONFIRMS
CONFLICT
CONFUSED
CONSCIOUS
CONSCIOUSNESS
CONSECRATION
CONSOLE
CONSOLED
CONSPIRACY
CONTACT
CONTENTION
CONTRITION
CONVENT
CONVOLVULUS
CONVULSED
COOLD
COPE
CORDIAL
CORE
CORNWALLS
CORSE
CORSLET

CORYDON
COURAGEOUS
COURSED
COURSES
COUSINS
COVERING
COW
COWLD
CRAGGY
CRAGS
CRAVEN
CRAZED
CREON
CRIMSON
CRITIAS
CRITICS
CROPPD
CRUSTED
CRYING
CUMBER
CUMNOR
CURDLED
CURSINGS
CURST
CURTAIN
DACHSHOUND
DAISIED
DAISIES
DAME
DARKER
DARKLING
DARTS
DASH
DATES
DAVIDS
DEATHLESS
DEBARRD
DEBATE
DECEASED
DECEIVE
DECKD
DECLAIMS
DECLINES
DECREES
DEEPENING
DEEPS
DEFYING
DEITIES
DELAY
DELICATELY
DELICIOUS
DELIVERD
DELPHI
DELUGE
DELUSION
DELVES
DEN
DENOUNCE
DEPARTING
DESIGNED
DESPITE
DESPONDENCY
DESTRUCTION
DETESTED
DEVOTION
DICE
DIFFERENCE
DIG
DINGLES
DISAPPEARS
DISCERND
DISCROWNED
DISLODGE

2 (cont.)

DISMARBLE
DISPERSED
DISPIRITED
DISSATISFIED
DISSUADES
DISTINCTLY
DISTRACTED
DISTRACTIONS
DISTRESSFUL
DIVIDING
DOME
DOMINE
DONND
DOTTED
DOTTING
DOWNCAST
DRAG
DRAGGD
DRAGGING
DRAGS
DRAVE
DREADED
DREAMER
DREAMERS
DRIFTED
DRIVEN
DROWSY
DRUNK
DULLS
DUN
DUPED
DWELLING
DWINDLING
EARN
EARTHEN
EASILY
EASTER
EAVES
ECSTASY
EDGED
EGYPT
ELATE
ELATION
ELECTRA
EMBATTLED
EMBLEMS
EMBRACED
EMBRACES
EMERGING
EMINENT
ENDEAVOURD
ENDOWD
ENFOLDS
ENFORCED
ENGINE
ENGULPHD
ENJOYD
ENNERDALE
ENNOBLING
ENTANGLED
ENTERTAINMENT
ENTOMBD
ENVIES
ENWOUND
EPOCH
ERECT
ERRORS
ESTEEM
ESTEEMD
ESTRANGED
ESTRANGING
ETERNALLY

EVENTIDE
EVERMORE
EVERYTHING
EVIL
EXCULPATION
EXEMPT
EXISTENCE
EXISTENCES
EXPIRED
EXTREMEST
EYEBALLS
EYESIGHT
FABLES
FACTION
FAINTING
FAIRER
FAITHLESS
FALLOW
FALSEHOOD
FAMD
FANCYS
FANTASY
FARTHEST
FASTNESS
FAVOUR
FAVOURD
FAVOURITE
FAVOURITES
FAWN
FEARLESS
FEARST
FEATHERY
FEATS
FEATURE
FEEBLER
FEEDING
FELLOWS
FELTS
FEN
FENCED
FENSALER
FERVENT
FERVOURS
FEVERD
FEWER
FIERCER
FIFTEEN
FIGURED
FILED
FINALLY
FINDING
FINISHD
FISH
FISHERMEN
FLAMING
FLANDERS
FLAPS
FLATS
FLECKD
FLEETING
FLICKERD
FLINTS
FLOCKD
FLUCTUATE
FLUTTERD
FOILING
FOLIAGED
FOLLOWING
FONDNESS
FOOTSTEP
FORCES
FORD
FORDONE

FORE
FOREBODED
FOREBODING
FOREGO
FOREHEADS
FOREKNOWN
FORETOLD
FORFEIT
FORGED
FORGETFULNESS
FORGETTING
FORGIVENESS
FORGIVES
FORGONE
FORSAKE
FORSAKES
FORSOOK
FORTRESS
FOUNDATION
FOUNDATIONS
FOUNDERD
FOUNDEST
FOWL
FRAGMENT
FRAGMENTS
FRANTIC
FRAYD
FREEZING
FREQUENT
FRESHER
FRESHNESS
FRETFUL
FRETTED
FRIGHT
FRINGES
FRINGING
FRITH
FRIVOLOUS
FRONTIER
FROST
FRUITED
FRUITS
FULFILMENT
FUNCTION
FURTIVE
FYFIELD
GALLANT
GALLANTS
GALLERY
GALLOPD
GAME
GAPE
GARDENS
GARMENTS
GASP
GASPS
GAUDS
GAVEST
GAVST
GEESE
GENTIAN
GENUINE
GIBES
GIRTHS
GLADNESS
GLAMOUR
GLANVILS
GLEAMD
GLIMPSES
GLOOMY
GLORIFY
GLORYS
GODDESSES

GODLIKE
GOING
GOODLY
GOTHIC
GOURD
GOVERND
GOVERNS
GRACEFUL
GRAIN
GRANGE
GRANITE
GRASPD
GRASPING
GRASSES
GRAVELY
GRAVEN
GREATER
GREEDY
GROAND
GROANING
GROPING
GROUSE
GROWTH
GUARDED
GUESSES
GUISE
GUSH
GUSHES
HAGGARD
HALVE
HALVES
HAMAN
HAPLESS
HAPPIEST
HARASSD
HARDNESS
HAUNTING
HEADLAND
HEADY
HEAL
HEARKENS
HEARST
HEAVE
HEAVIEST
HEAVING
HEBE
HEDGEROWS
HEEDLESS
HEEDS
HELEN
HELMUND
HELPS
HEM
HEMS
HERACLEIDAN
HEREAFTER
HERMODS
HEWN
HIDING
HIES
HILT
HINKSEY
HISSD
HITHERWARD
HOARDS
HOARY
HOISTED
HOLES
HOMER
HONEY
HONIED
HONOURING
HOOFS

HOPED
HORDE
HORSEMANS
HOTNESS
HOUSEHOLD
HUDDLING
HUMBLER
HUMBLY
HUNGRY
HUNTED
HURST
HUSK
HUSSEIN
HYACINTHS
HYMN
ICEBERGS
IDA
IDOL
IGDRASIL
IGNOMINY
ILEX
ILIUM
ILLYRIAN
IMMATURE
IMMEMORIAL
IMMENSE
IMMUNITY
IMPAIRD
IMPAIRS
IMPATIENT
IMPELLD
IMPLORING
IMPOTENCE
IMPUNITY
IMPUTE
INCESSANT
INCESSANTLY
INCREDULITY
INCREDULOUS
INDISCERNIBLE
INDIVIDUAL
INDULGED
INDULGENT
INEFFABLE
INFANT
INFANTINE
INFANTS
INFUSE
INHERIT
INHERITOR
INJURIOUS
INJUSTICE
INLETS
INNOCENTS
INNS
INQUIRING
INSANE
INSECURE
INSPIRATION
INSTEAD
INSTINCTS
INSURGENT
INTEND
INVADE
INVADES
INVADING
INVASIONS
INVENTIVE
INVEST
INVESTS
INVINCIBLE
INVITE
INVOLVED

2 (cont.)
IRANS
IRE
ISEULTS
ISTER
ISTHMUS
JAGGD
JAVELIN
JOCUND
JOPPA
JOURNEYD
JOVIAL
JOYD
JUDAS
JUDGES
JUNIPER
KAIS
KALMUCKS
KEENER
KERCHIEF
KHIVA
KHOSROO
KILLS
KINDLING
KNEELD
KNIFE
KNOLL
KUZZAKS
LABOURER
LADEN
LAGGARD
LAMB
LAMENT
LAMP
LANCES
LANDSCAPE
LANGUAGE
LANGUISH
LASTING
LATER
LAVE
LEADING
LEAFD
LEAVED
LENGTHEND
LEPER
LEPERS
LESSINGS
LETTERS
LIBERAL
LIBYAN
LIDSKIALF
LIFELIKE
LIFT
LIKENESS
LIMB
LIMIT
LIMITS
LIMPID
LINKING
LISTLESS
LOADS
LOATHING
LODGED
LOFTIER
LOFTIEST
LOITERS
LONELINESS
LOOKED
LOOMING
LOOSELY
LOPPD
LOVD
LOVELIER

LOWER
LOWERD
LUCENT
LULL
LULLD
LURE
LURING
LUSTRE
LUTE
MADDENING
MADMAN
MAENADS
MAKST
MALIGN
MANHOODS
MANNERS
MANSION
MAP
MARCHD
MARCS
MARES
MARRD
MARS
MARSHAL
MARSHY
MASSD
MASSES
MASTERD
MATTER
MATURE
MAZED
MAZES
MEANING
MEASURED
MEASURES
MEEK
MEETINGS
MELODIOUS
MELON
MELTS
MERCHANT
MERCY
MERRY
MESSAGE
META
METEOR
METHINKS
MIGHTILY
MILES
MINDFUL
MINGLE
MINGLED
MIRACULOUS
MISERERE
MISPLANND
MISRULE
MOAT
MOCK
MODERN
MOMENTARY
MOODY
MOONBEAMS
MOOR
MORROWS
MOSES
MOTLEY
MOULDERING
MOULDS
MOUND
MOUNTAINOUS
MOWERS
MUFFLE
MULLIOND

MUNDANE
MURDERERS
MURDEROUS
MURMURS
MUSICAL
MUSINGS
MUSPELS
MUTELY
MYCENAE
MYSTERIOUS
NAILD
NARROWING
NEARD
NEAREST
NEARING
NEARLY
NEEDED
NEEDLE
NEGLECTED
NEIGHBOURING
NEIGHING
NELEUS
NEPHEW
NERVE
NERVES
NEUTRAL
NEWLY
NICOPOLIS
NIGHER
NIGHTLY
NOBLENESS
NODDED
NOISELESS
NOTHINGNESS
NOTHINGS
NOVEMBER
NULL
NUMB
NUMBERD
NURSES
OBEDIENCE
OBEDIENT
OBEYS
OBTAIND
OCCASION
ODOROUS
OERLABOURD
OERTHROWN
OETA
OFFENDING
OFFERD
OFFERING
OFFICE
OFTENER
OFTENEST
OLDER
OLEANDERS
OMIT
OPENINGS
OPPOSERS
OPPOSITE
OPPRESS
ORACLE
ORANGE
ORATORS
ORCHARD
ORCHISES
ORGUNJE
ORIGINAL
OSCILLATIONS
OUTCAST
OUTGOES
OUTLANDISH

OUTLIVED
OUTLIVES
OUTMOST
OUTRAGED
OUTWEARIED
OVERGROWN
OWE
PAGAN
PAGES
PAILS
PAIND
PAINFULLY
PAINLESS
PAINTED
PAINTING
PALED
PALER
PALMERS
PANE
PANIC
PANTHEIAS
PANTS
PARCELLD
PARCH
PARCHD
PARENTS
PARTIES
PASTURED
PASTURING
PATE
PATHETIC
PATIENTLY
PATROCLUS
PATTERN
PAUPERS
PAVILION
PEALD
PEARLS
PEASANTS
PEBBLES
PEERD
PELEUS
PENITENT
PENITENTIAL
PERCEIVED
PERCHD
PERENNIAL
PERFECTING
PERFUME
PERMANENCE
PERPETUALLY
PERSISTENCE
PERUSE
PETULANT
PHIAL
PICK
PILD
PILED
PILGRIMAGE
PINING
PIPING
PITCHERS
PITILESS
PITYING
PLAGUE
PLAINT
PLANET
PLANKD
PLANKS
PLANND
PLASHING
PLAYER
PLEAD

PLEADING
PLEASAUNCE
PLUCKING
PLUMAGE
PLUMES
PLUNGE
PLUTOS
POEMS
POETRY
POINTS
POISE
POISOND
POLAR
PONDERING
PORTAL
PORTION
POSTING
POURING
POURS
PRAISD
PRAISES
PRAISING
PRECINCT
PRECIOUS
PREDESTINED
PREEMINENCE
PREGNANT
PRESENTLY
PRESENTS
PRESSES
PRESSING
PRETENCE
PRETEXT
PRICKERS
PRIESTS
PRIMROSES
PRIOR
PRISONING
PROCEEDS
PROFANE
PROFFER
PROJECT
PROLONG
PROMPTINGS
PRONOUNCE
PROSERPINE
PULLD
PUNISH
PURER
PURGED
QUARREL
QUARRY
QUARTZ
QUICKEND
QUICKER
QUIVER
RACHEL
RACK
RAINS
RANDOM
RAPHAEL
RAVEN
RAVENNA
RAVES
READS
REAL
REALITY
REALLY
REAP
REAREST
REASONS
REBELLIOUS
RECAST

2 (cont.)

RECESSES
RECKONEST
RECKS
RECOILD
RECOMMENCE
REDOUBLED
REELD
REELING
REFRESHD
REGARDS
REGISTAN
REGNER
REGRET
REHEARSE
REIGNS
REJECT
REJOICING
REJOIND
RELAX
RELEASE
RELIGION
REMORSEFUL
REMOVE
REMOVED
REND
RENOUNCE
REPEAT
REPOSED
REPROACH
RESIDES
RESOLVES
RESOUND
RESTS
RETAIND
RETIRE
RETIRED
RETREAT
REVELLERS
REVELS
REVIVE
REVOLVING
RHYME
RIFTS
RIGOROUS
RILLS
RIPPLES
RITE
ROASTED
ROMANCE
ROOD
ROOTED
ROSY
ROUTED
ROVED
RUB
RUDDY
RUDELY
RUFFLED
RUGS
RULERS
RUMOUR
RUNNING
RURAL
RUSSIAN
RUSTIC
RUSTLE
RUSTLES
RUTHLESS
SACKCLOTH
SACRIFICERS
SADDLED
SAFETY

SAFFRON
SALVATION
SANCTUARY
SANDALS
SANE
SANGUINE
SAT
SATED
SATST
SAVES
SCALDS
SCALE
SCANTY
SCARE
SCATHED
SCATTERD
SCATTERING
SCENES
SCENTS
SCHOLARS
SCIENCE
SCIOLISTS
SCORNS
SCOTT
SCRAWLD
SCREAMD
SCREAMING
SCREEN
SCULPTORS
SCULPTURED
SCYTHIAN
SEAFOWL
SEARCHING
SEARD
SEBERTS
SECLUDED
SECLUSION
SEDGE
SEETHING
SELFISH
SELVES
SEPTEMBER
SERIMNERS
SERPENTS
SHAKING
SHAMD
SHARED
SHAVEN
SHAWL
SHEDDING
SHEET
SHELLS
SHELVING
SHIELDS
SHIRT
SHIVERS
SHOCK
SHOCKS
SHOREWARD
SHORTLY
SHOWERING
SHOWERY
SHOWING
SHOWST
SHROUD
SHROUDED
SHUDDER
SHUTS
SICKLE
SILENTLY
SIMPLER
SINCERE
SINKING

SITTST
SKIFF
SKIM
SLACKEND
SLAKE
SLAUGHTEROUS
SLAYING
SLEEPER
SLEWST
SLIDDEN
SLIPPING
SLIPS
SLUMBERD
SLUMBERS
SLUMBROUS
SMEARD
SMILEST
SMOOTHED
SMOOTHNESS
SNAKE
SNAKES
SNARES
SNATCHES
SNORTING
SNOWDROP
SOARING
SOBBING
SOBERD
SOCIAL
SOLDIERS
SOLID
SONCHAUDS
SONGS
SOONEST
SOOTH
SOPHISTRIES
SORROWD
SORROWFUL
SOULLESS
SOURCE
SPARED
SPARKLE
SPARTA
SPEAKEST
SPECIOUS
SPECTRAL
SPIED
SPILL
SPINNING
SPINS
SPIRE
SPITS
SPURND
SPURS
SQUALLS
STACKS
STAGGER
STAIN
STALKS
STALL
STANCH
STARE
STARES
STARLIGHT
STARLIKE
STARTED
STATELIER
STATES
STATESMEN
STATUE
STEADY
STEAMING
STEDFAST

STEED
STEEPD
STEERS
STEPP
STIFFER
STIFLING
STOCKS
STORED
STORIES
STRENGTHEN
STRENUOUS
STRESS
STRICTLY
STRIPS
STROKES
STUDDED
STUDIOUS
STUPID
SUBDUED
SUBDUES
SUBJECT
SUBSISTS
SUBSTANCE
SUCCEEDS
SUCCESSES
SUCCESSION
SUCKD
SUFFERERS
SUFFEREST
SUFFICIENT
SUFFUSED
SULTRY
SUNDAYS
SUNKEN
SUNLIGHT
SUPERSEDE
SUPPOSED
SURGE
SURVEY
SURVEYD
SURVIVES
SWALLOW
SWARM
SWATH
SWATHE
SWEAT
SWEETEST
SWEETS
SWELLING
SWERVED
SWIFTLY
SWIMMING
SWIMS
SWUNG
SYRIAN
TABLES
TAIL
TAMED
TAPESTRY
TASK
TASTED
TAX
TEARLESS
TELLEST
TEMPERD
TEMPESTUOUS
TENDED
TENDING
TENDRILS
TENSE
TENTH
TERRIBLY
TEST

THAW
THEME
THEREIN
THINKST
THIRSTY
THIRTY
THOUGHTFUL
THRACIAN
THREADED
THRIVE
THROATED
THROATS
THROB
THRONGING
THUNDERS
THWARTING
TIBERIUS
TIDINGS
TIES
TIGHT
TIGHTEN
TIMOROUS
TINKLING
TINTS
TIRE
TIRELESS
TITLE
TMOLUS
TOILING
TOILS
TOMBSTONE
TOPPING
TORPOR
TOST
TOUCHING
TOUGH
TRACHIS
TRACTS
TRAFFIC
TRAGIC
TRAILD
TRAILING
TRANQUILLITY
TRANSEPT
TRAVELLD
TRAVELLING
TRAVERSED
TREASON
TREASURES
TREELESS
TREMBLEST
TRIBUTE
TRICKD
TRIES
TRIFLER
TRIM
TROJAN
TROTTOIRS
TROUBLOUS
TROUT
TROW
TUILERIES
TURNED
TWELFTH
TWELVE
TWINKLE
TWITTERING
TYRIAN
UNALLAYD
UNALTERD
UNBAKED
UNBEND
UNBENT

1 (cont.)

CEUTA
CHAFES
CHAFINGS
CHAIND
CHALCEDONY
CHALLENGED
CHALLENGING
CHAMBERY
CHAMP
CHAMPD
CHANCD
CHANCEL
CHANCES
CHANGELING
CHANT
CHANTING
CHANTS
CHAOS
CHARIOTS
CHARITY
CHARMS
CHART
CHARTERD
CHASED
CHASTE
CHATELAINE
CHATTED
CHATTING
CHAUNT
CHECKD
CHEERED
CHEQUERING
CHERRIES
CHEW
CHIAN
CHID
CHIDES
CHIEFLY
CHIEL
CHILDLESS
CHILDSWORTH
CHILLD
CHILLIEST
CHILLING
CHILLON
CHIMNEY
CHIMNEYS
CHIN
CHINKD
CHINKS
CHIRON
CHISELLD
CHOICEST
CHOKD
CHOKES
CHOOSEST
CHORDS
CHRISTS
CHUCKLE
CHURL
CHUSE
CINCTURED
CIRCLED
CIRCUITOUS
CIRCUMAMBIENT
CIRCUMSTANCE
CIRQUE
CISTERNS
CITHAERON
CITIZEN
CITYWARD
CIVIL
CLAIMANT

CLAIMANTS
CLAIMST
CLAMOURS
CLANKD
CLAP
CLAPS
CLASHING
CLASSES
CLASSIC
CLATTER
CLEANSE
CLEARS
CLEAVES
CLEMENT
CLENCHD
CLERE
CLIMATES
CLIMBEST
CLING
CLINGEST
CLINGST
CLIPS
CLOAKD
CLOCK
CLOG
CLOGS
CLOISTRAL
CLOTHE
CLOTHING
CLOVER
CLOWN
CLOY
CLUSTER
CLUTCHING
COASTER
COBHAM
COFFIN
COHESION
COIGN
COIL
COINER
COLDNESS
COLLEGE
COLLIERS
COLONNADE
COLONUS
COLOURED
COLOURS
COLUMN
COLUMND
COMBAT
COMBATANTS
COMBATINGS
COMBD
COMELY
COMETS
COMFORTABLE
COMFORTED
COMFORTERS
COMMANDMENT
COMMANDS
COMMEND
COMMENT
COMMISSION
COMMITS
COMMITTER
COMMUNED
COMPANIES
COMPARE
COMPARES
COMPARISON
COMPASSION
COMPASSIONATE
COMPEERS

COMPELLD
COMPLAIND
COMPLAINED
COMPLAININGS
COMPLAINT
COMPLETE
COMPOSD
COMPREHEND
COMPREHENDING
COMPRESSD
COMPUNCTIOUS
COMRADE
CONCEAL
CONCEDES
CONCERN
CONCERTING
CONCLUDED
CONCOURSE
CONDEMNEST
CONDEMNS
CONDUCTED
CONDUCTS
CONFER
CONFERS
CONFESSEST
CONFEST
CONFIDENCE
CONFLUENT
CONFOUND
CONFOUNDST
CONFRONT
CONFRONTS
CONFUSE
CONJURING
CONQUEROR
CONSECRATE
CONSECRATES
CONSIDERATE
CONSIGND
CONSOLATION
CONSOLATIONS
CONSORT
CONSPIRE
CONSTANCY
CONSTANT
CONSTRAIND
CONSTRAINT
CONSTRUCTED
CONSTRUCTION
CONSUMD
CONSUMING
CONTAIN
CONTAINING
CONTEMPLATING
CONTEMPLATION
CONTEND
CONTENDING
CONTINENT
CONTINUAL
CONTINUALLY
CONTINUE
CONTINUES
CONTINUOUS
CONTRAST
CONTRIVING
CONTROLLD
CONTROLS
CONTROUL
CONVENTS
CONVEYD
CONVICTION
CONVICTIONS
CONVINCE
CONVULSIVE

COOKS
COOLER
COOLING
COOLNESS
COOMBS
COPAIS
CORAL
CORD
CORDED
CORDS
CORNER
CORNFIELD
CORNISH
CORONALS
CORRIDOR
CORRIDORS
CORRUPT
COST
COTES
COUCHANT
COUNCILS
COUNSELS
COUNTED
COUNTERPANE
COUNTEST
COUNTING
COUNTRIES
COUNTRYS
COUNTS
COURRERIE
COURSER
COURTEOUSLY
COURTIERS
COVE
COVERD
COVERLET
COWERING
COWHERDS
COWL
COY
CRACKLED
CRADLED
CRANES
CRASHD
CRASHES
CRAVE
CRAVES
CRAWL
CRAWLD
CRAWLS
CREAMING
CREATING
CREATION
CREDIT
CREEK
CREEKS
CREEPERS
CREONS
CREPT
CRESSES
CRESTS
CRETE
CREVICD
CRINGE
CRISPS
CROFT
CROFTS
CROON
CROSSES
CROWDING
CRUCIBLE
CRUELLER
CRUMBLE
CRUMBLED

CRUSADING
CRUSE
CRUSHED
CRUSHT
CRUST
CRYSTAL
CUB
CUBIT
CUCKOOS
CUCUMBER
CULPRIT
CULTURE
CURB
CURBD
CURES
CURLING
CURSED
CURVED
CURVES
CURVING
CUTTERS
CYCLAMENS
CYCLOPS
CYLLENE
CZAR
DACHS
DAFFODIL
DAINTILY
DAIS
DALES
DAMNING
DAMSELS
DANCD
DANCED
DANCER
DANCERS
DANGER
DANK
DANTES
DAPHNIS
DAPPLED
DARKD
DARKEN
DARKENS
DARNS
DART
DASHD
DASTARD
DATED
DAULIS
DAUNTLESS
DAUNTLESSLY
DAWND
DAYBREAK
DAZED
DAZZLE
DAZZLINGLY
DEADEN
DEADNESS
DEALING
DEARER
DEARLY
DEBAR
DEBATING
DECAYING
DECEIVER
DECEIVING
DECIDED
DECKS
DECLARED
DECLARST
DECLINING
DECREE
DECREED

1 (cont.)

DECRIED
DEDICATION
DEEMEDST
DEEMING
DEEMS
DEEPEST
DEFACD
DEFEAT
DEFENCE
DEFENCELESS
DEFER
DEFERRD
DEFILEMENT
DEFINE
DEFORMITY
DEGRADE
DEGRADING
DEIGN
DEJECTEDLY
DELAYED
DELIBERATE
DELIGHTING
DELIVER
DELIVERANCE
DELOS
DELPHIAN
DELPHIC
DELUGED
DEMANDEST
DEMONS
DENIZEN
DENMARK
DENSE
DENSER
DEPLORED
DEPRESSD
DERIDE
DERISION
DERISIVE
DESERVED
DESERVES
DESIREDST
DESPAIRD
DESPAIRER
DESPAIRING
DESPAIRS
DESPISED
DESPONDED
DESPONDENT
DESTINATION
DESTROY
DESTROYD
DESTROYEST
DETRACTION
DEVICE
DEVISEDST
DEWLAP
DIAMOND
DIANS
DIBBLED
DIDO
DIEU
DIFFERING
DILIGENCE
DIMENSIONS
DIMINISH
DIMMER
DIMNESS
DINGLE
DINGY
DIPT
DIRE
DIRECT

DISABUSINGS
DISAPPOINTMENTS
DISARMD
DISARRAY
DISARRAYD
DISBAND
DISCERNS
DISCIPLES
DISCLOSE
DISCONTENTED
DISCORD
DISCORDS
DISCOURSE
DISCOURSED
DISCOVERY
DISCREDITING
DISDAINFUL
DISEASED
DISEASES
DISENCHANTED
DISFEATURED
DISFIGURED
DISGRACE
DISGUISE
DISGUISES
DISGUST
DISHONOUR
DISMISSED
DISMOUNT
DISMOUNTED
DISOBEDIENT
DISORDERD
DISPEOPLED
DISPLAYD
DISPLAYS
DISPLEASE
DISPOSE
DISPOSSESSD
DISPOSSESSED
DISPOSSESSORS
DISPUTATIOUS
DISPUTES
DISQUIETED
DISQUIETUDE
DISSEMBLES
DISSENSIONS
DISSEVERS
DISSOLVE
DISSOLVING
DISSUADE
DISSUASIONS
DISTIL
DISTILS
DISTINCTIONS
DISTRAUGHT
DISTRUST
DISTURB
DISUSED
DITTY
DIVER
DIVERGING
DIVERS
DIVIDE
DIVIDED
DIVINATIONS
DIVINELIER
DIVINELY
DIVINITY
DIVORCE
DIVORCED
DIVULGE
DIZZILY
DIZZYING
DOCILE

DOCTORS
DOEST
DOGGD
DOGGISH
DOLEFUL
DOLOUR
DOMED
DOMES
DOOMS
DORIS
DOT
DOUBLES
DOUBTED
DOUBTFULLY
DOUBTING
DOWER
DOWNS
DOWNWARD
DOZED
DOZING
DRAGON
DRAWING
DREADING
DREAMY
DREARILY
DRESSD
DREST
DRIES
DRIFT
DRIFTWOOD
DRINKING
DRINKST
DRIVN
DRIZZLED
DRIZZLING
DROOP
DROOPS
DROPT
DROUGHT
DROWNING
DRUGGING
DRUGS
DRUIDS
DRUNKEN
DRYING
DUES
DULLD
DULLEST
DULY
DUMBLY
DUNBAR
DUNGEON
DURABILITY
DUSTED
DUTY
DWARF
DWELLEST
DYNASTIES
EAGLETS
EARLIER
EARLIEST
EARNING
EARNS
EARTHWARD
EBBS
EBONY
ECHEMUS
EDDIES
EDEN
EDGES
EFFACING
EFFECT
EFFIGY
EFFLUENCE

EFFORTS
EGREMONT
EIGHT
EIGHTEEN
ELASTIC
ELATED
ELBRUIS
ELBURZ
ELECT
ELECTRIFY
ELEGY
ELEMENT
ELEMENTAL
ELEUSINIAN
ELF
ELLA
ELLAS
ELOQUENCE
ELUSIVE
ELYSIAN
EMBERS
EMBITTER
EMBOLDEND
EMBOSSED
EMBREATHED
EMBROIDERD
EMPEROR
EMPERORS
EMPOWERD
EMPRISE
EMPRIZE
EMULATE
ENAMELLD
ENAMOURD
ENCHANTER
ENCHANTMENTS
ENCIRCLED
ENCLASPING
ENCOUNTER
ENCOURAGED
ENCROACHING
ENDEARD
ENDING
ENDURANCE
ENDURES
ENDURETH
ENDYMIONS
ENERGIES
ENFORCEMENT
ENGAGED
ENGARLANDED
ENGRAVE
ENGRAVES
ENHANCE
ENISLED
ENJOIN
ENJOIND
ENJOINS
ENKERCHIEFD
ENMITY
ENNA
ENORMOUS
ENQUIRE
ENQUIRED
ENQUIRERS
ENRAPTURE
ENSHAM
ENSIGN
ENSLAVE
ENSLAVED
ENTEREST
ENTERPRISING
ENTERS
ENTERTAINST

ENTHRALL
ENTHROND
ENTHRONED
ENTOMB
ENTRANCE
ENTREATED
ENTREATING
ENVELOPED
EQUALLY
ERASE
ERASED
EREMITE
EREWHILE
ERINNYS
ERRD
ERREST
ERRONEOUS
ERYMANTHUS
ESCAPD
ESCAPE
ESCAPING
ESPY
ESSAYD
ESTRANGEMENT
ESTRELLE
ESTUARIES
ETERNALISE
ETERNE
ETHER
EUBOEA
EUGENIAS
EURIPUS
EVENINGS
EVERLASTINGLY
EVES
EVIDENCE
EXACTER
EXACTING
EXALTED
EXAMIND
EXAMPLE
EXCEL
EXCHANGE
EXCLAIMD
EXCULPATES
EXCUSE
EXECUTION
EXERCISE
EXHAUST
EXISTS
EXPANSE
EXPECTANT
EXPECTEST
EXPECTING
EXPECTS
EXPENSE
EXPIATE
EXPIATION
EXPIRING
EXPLAIN
EXPLODED
EXPLOIT
EXPLORED
EXPRESSION
EXPRESSIVE
EXQUISITE
EXTEND
EXTERNE
EXTINCT
EXTINCTION
EXTINGUISHES
EXTRACT
EXTRAVAGANT
EXTREME

1 (cont.)
HAMANS
HAMLET
HAMLETS
HAMMERS
HAMPDEN
HANDFUL
HANDMAID
HANGD
HAPPENS
HARBOURING
HARBOURS
HARDIHOOD
HAREBELLS
HARMONIA
HARMONIOUS
HARMONISD
HARNESSD
HARPER
HARSHNESS
HASTENING
HASTINGS
HATEFULLY
HATERS
HATING
HAUGHTILY
HAUNTST
HAVIOUR
HAVOC
HAWK
HAYMAKER
HAZELS
HEADSTRONG
HEALD
HEARERS
HEARTED
HEATED
HEATHEN
HEAVENWARD
HEBREW
HEBRIDES
HECUBAS
HEIGHTEND
HEIGHTENING
HEIGHTS
HEINES
HELMSMAN
HELPD
HELPFUL
HELPLESSLY
HENCEFORWARD
HENRI
HERA
HERAS
HERBAGE
HERD
HEREDITARY
HERETOFORE
HEROICALLY
HEROISM
HEROS
HESITATE
HEW
HEWING
HIDDEST
HIDDST
HIDEST
HIE
HIED
HIGHLAND
HIGHLANDS
HIGHWAY
HILLOCK
HINDER

HINDS
HINKSEYS
HISTORIED
HISTORYS
HITHE
HITHERTO
HIVES
HOAR
HODERS
HOG
HOLDING
HOLIER
HOLLYHOCK
HOLYHOCK
HOMELY
HOMESTEAD
HOMEWARDS
HOMILY
HONEYSUCKLE
HONOURABLY
HONOUREST
HOOD
HOPING
HOPST
HORDES
HORNED
HORRIBLE
HORRORS
HORSEBACK
HORSEMAN
HOSTAGE
HOTELS
HOTLIER
HOUSED
HOUSETOPS
HOUSEWIFE
HOVERING
HOWL
HOWLS
HULL
HUMANE
HUMS
HUN
HUNGARIANS
HUNGER
HUNGRIER
HUNTSMAN
HUNTSMEN
HURDLES
HURL
HURTLING
HURTS
HUSTLE
HUSTLING
HYACINTH
HYDASPES
HYDE
HYLLUS
HYPEREIA
HYPHASIS
IBERIANS
IDENTITY
IDLERS
IDOLS
IGNOMINIOUS
IGNORE
ILLIMITABLE
ILLUMINATES
ILLUMINE
ILLUSION
ILLUSTRIOUS
ILSE
ILSLEY
ILYATS

IMAGINE
IMAGINED
IMAGINES
IMBECILES
IMBECILITY
IMBED
IMBRUE
IMMEASURABLE
IMMEDICABLE
IMMORTALITY
IMMORTALS
IMMOVEABLE
IMMURED
IMPAIR
IMPARTING
IMPEL
IMPENDING
IMPENETRABLE
IMPLACABLE
IMPLIES
IMPLORE
IMPOSED
IMPOSSIBILITY
IMPRACTICABLE
IMPRESS
IMPRESSION
IMPRESSIONS
IMPRISONING
IMPRISONS
INACCESSIBLE
INACCURATE
INACTIVE
INALIENABLE
INCENSE
INCESSANTER
INCITE
INCOGNISABLE
INCOMMUNICABLY
INCONGRUOUS
INCURIOUS
INCURRING
INDEX
INDIFFERENCE
INDIGNANTLY
INDISTINCT
INDOMITABLE
INDOORS
INDULGENCE
INDULGENTLY
INEFFECTUAL
INESTIMABLE
INEVITABLE
INEVITABLY
INEXTINGUISHABLE
INFECTION
INFECTIOUS
INFECTS
INFER
INFERIOR
INFINITELY
INFINITY
INFRINGED
INGLE
INGRAIND
INHABIT
INHERITANCE
INHERITORS
INJURED
INKEN
INLAID
INMATE
INMATES
INNERMOST
INNOCENCE

INQUIRE
INQUISITORS
INSCRIBE
INSCRUTABLY
INSHORE
INSINCERE
INSTALL
INSTALLD
INSTANCES
INSTANTLY
INSTANTS
INSTILLS
INSTINCT
INSULTST
INSURGED
INTELLECTUAL
INTELLIGENT
INTEMPERATE
INTENDS
INTENSE
INTENSER
INTER
INTERCEPTED
INTERIOR
INTERMINABLE
INTERMIXD
INTERPOSED
INTERPRET
INTERRD
INTERRUPTED
INTERTWINE
INTERVALS
INTERVENE
INTESTINE
INTOLERABLE
INTOLERABLY
INTONED
INTRACTABLE
INTRIGUERS
INTRUDE
INTRUDERS
INTRUDES
INVADERS
INVARIABLENESS
INVIOLABLE
INVISIBLE
INVITEST
INWOUND
IRIS
IRKD
IRKS
IRONY
IRRESISTIBLY
IRRETRIEVABLE
IRRUPTION
ISLAND
ISMENIAN
ISMENUS
ISOLATION
ISRAELS
ISSUES
ITCHING
ITERATES
IVIED
IVORY
JACKALS
JANGLE
JANGLED
JAR
JARNVID
JARRD
JASMINE
JASPER
JAVELINS

JAWS
JAXARTES
JEMSHID
JETS
JOCK
JOHN
JOINT
JOKES
JOPPAN
JOT
JOURNEYED
JOURNEYS
JOVES
JOYANCE
JUDGMENTS
JUGGLE
JULIETS
JULY
JUNGFRAU
JUSTIFIED
JUTS
JUTTING
KAFFIRS
KAISERS
KALMUKS
KARA
KEENLY
KEEPERS
KEEPEST·
KEIGHLEY
KEMPIS
KEPTEST
KHELMOS
KHORASSAN
KID
KINDS
KINGDOMS
KIRGHIZZES
KNEAD
KNIGHTLY
KNOCK
KNOCKING
KNOLLS
KNOT
KOHIK
KOORDS
KUL
KYBI
LABEL
LABORIOUS
LABOUREST
LACE
LACEDAEMON
LACING
LACKS
LACONIAS
LAD
LADON
LAERTES
LAGS
LAIN
LAMBETH
LAMBS
LAMENTATION
LAMENTING
LAMPLESS
LANCE
LANDED
LANDING
LANDWARD
LANE
LANTERN
LANTERNS
LAOCOON

1 (cont.)

LAPITHAE	LIKEN	LUSTY	MEANER	MISERABLY
LAPPS	LIKEWISE	LYCAON	MEANINGS	MISERYS
LAPS	LILIES	LYCAONS	MEANST	MISGIVING
LAPSE	LILY	LYCOSURA	MEANTEST	MISINTERPRET
LASHD	LIMBER	LYDIAN	MEANTIME	MISLED
LASHER	LIMES	LYONESS	MEAT	MISRULED
LASSA	LIMESTONE	LYRES	MEATS	MISSEL
LASTED	LINDENS	MACARIA	MECCA	MISSES
LASTLY	LINEAL	MACE	MECHANIC	MISSEST
LATELY	LINEAMENTS	MACEDON	MEDICINE	MISSILE
LATHS	LINEN	MACHINE	MEDITATIVE	MISTAKES
LATMIAN	LINGERD	MADCAP	MEEKLY	MISTLETOE
LATTICES	LINGERERS	MADCAPS	MEETER	MISTRUSTFUL
LAUGHD	LINGERS	MADDEN	MEETEST	MISTY
LAUGHS	LINKD	MADEST	MEILLERIE	MIXT
LAUNCELOTS	LION	MADHOUSE	MELL	MIXTURE
LAUNCH	LIPAREAN	MADMEN	MELLOW	MOCKER
LAURELLD	LIPPD	MADST	MELLOWD	MOCKS
LAURENT	LIQUOR	MAEANDERS	MELONS	MODE
LAVENDER	LIST	MAENAD	MELTED	MODERATION
LAWLESS	LISTETH	MAENALUS	MEMBERS	MODERNISE
LAWLESSNESS	LISTLESSLY	MAIA	MEMMIUS	MODERNISED
LAWNY	LISTS	MAID	MENACING	MODES
LAX	LITHE	MAIL	MENDELSSOHN	MODEST
LAYING	LITTLENESS	MAILED	MENDING	MOISTEND
LEA	LITYERSES	MAIMS	MENDS	MOLE
LEADED	LIVEDST	MALATRAIT	MENTION	MOLES
LEADERS	LIVERY	MALIAC	MENTIOND	MONASTERY
LEAFLESS	LIVST	MALIGNANT	MERELY	MONGREL
LEAGUER	LIZARDS	MALIGNER	MERITS	MONICA
LEAGUERD	LOADED	MANACLES	MERMAIDEN	MONSTROUS
LEANEST	LOATHE	MANGER	MERMAN	MONTMARTRE
LEAPEST	LOAVES	MANIFOLD	MEROPES	MONUMENT
LEARNST	LODGERS	MANKINDS	MERRIMENT	MOOLLAH
LEASH	LODGES	MANNER	MERVE	MOONSTRUCK
LEAVEN	LODGING	MANTINEA	MESSAGES	MOORGHAB
LEAVEST	LOG	MANTINEAN	MESSEIS	MORAL
LEAVINGS	LOIRES	MANTINEIA	MESSENE	MORALITY
LEAVST	LOITERER	MANTLED	MESSENGERS	MORASS
LEE	LOITERING	MANTLING	MESSENIAS	MORNINGLESS
LEFTWARD	LOKS	MANYS	MESSES	MORNS
LEGENDARY	LOLLING	MARATHON	MESSOGIS	MORROWLL
LEGIONS	LOMBARD	MARBLES	METE	MORTALITY
LEGITIMATELY	LONELIER	MARCHES	METHOUGHT	MOSQUE
LEMANS	LONELILY	MARCHING	METST	MOSQUES
LEMNIAN	LONENESS	MARCUS	MICHAEL	MOSSES
LENDING	LONGEST	MARGES	MICHAELS	MOTIONLESS
LENDS	LOOKST	MARGUERITES	MIDMOST	MOULDER
LENGTHEN	LOOKT	MARKED	MIDSUMMER	MOULDERD
LENIENCE	LOOSESTRIFE	MARKING	MIGHTEST	MOULDING
LENTISK	LORDSHIPS	MARKS	MIGHTS	MOURNER
LESSENING	LOSES	MARSTONS	MIGRATORY	MOURNERS
LESSER	LOTS	MARTIN	MILAN	MOURNFULLEST
LETHAEAN	LOUDEST	MARTYRS	MILDNESS	MOUTHD
LETO	LOUGHRIGG	MARVELS	MILE	MOVD
LETTING	LOUIS	MASONS	MILL	MOVETH
LEVELS	LOURD	MASSIER	MILTON	MOWING
LIANDE	LOVDST	MASSY	MIMIR	MOZART
LIBATION	LOVELESS	MASTED	MINES	MULBERRIES
LIBERATED	LOVELORN	MASTERFUL	MINION	MULBERRY
LIBERTY	LOVEST	MASTERY	MINIONS	MULTIPLIED
LIBRARY	LOWERING	MATCHEST	MINISTRY	MURDERED
LICKD	LOWINGS	MATELESS	MINSTERS	MURKY
LIDS	LOYALTY	MATERIAL	MINSTREL	MURMURED
LIEF	LUCID	MATERNAL	MINT	MURMUROUS
LIEFER	LUCIDITY	MATIN	MINUTES	MUSICIANS
LIFELONG	LUCRETIUS	MATRICIDAL	MIRACLES	MUSK
LIFTS	LULLING	MATRONS	MIRED	MUSPEL
LIGHTEN	LUNA	MATTERS	MIRRORD	MUTTER
LIGHTENS	LUNAR	MATTRESS	MIRRORING	MYCENAES
LIGHTHOUSE	LURD	MATURER	MIS	MYRTLES
LIKELIEST	LURK	MAUD	MISAPPLIED	MYSIAN
LIKELY	LURKING	MAZE	MISCHIEF	MYSTERIES
	LUSITANIA	MAZY	MISER	MYSTICS

1 (cont.)

NADIR
NAPLES
NARD
NARRATIONS
NARROWER
NARROWS
NASEBYS
NAYE
NEARS
NECESSITATE
NECESSITYS
NECKANS
NECKD
NECTAROUS
NEEDST
NEGLECT
NELEIDAE
NELLYS
NESTLING
NETHER
NETS
NETTED
NETTLES
NETWORK
NEWNESS
NEWSTEAD
NICHED
NIGHTINGALE
NIPS
NOBLEST
NODDING
NODS
NOISED
NOISES
NON
NONACRIS
NOONTIDE
NORWEGIAN
NOSTRILS
NOTICE
NOURISHD
NOURISHING
NOWHERE
NUMBERS
NUMBING
NUMBRETH
NUMEROUS
NURSD
NURTUREST
NYMPHS
OAR
OATH
OBERLAND
OBJECT
OBJECTS
OBLIVIONS
OBSCURED
OBSCURENESS
OBSCURES
OBSCURITY
OBSERVANCES
OBSERVE
OBSERVED
OBSTINATE
OBTAINED
OBTUSE
OCCUPATION
ODE
ODOURS
OEDIPUS
OERFLOW
OERFROWNS

OERGROWN
OERLEAP
OERLEAPS
OERPASS
OERPAST
OERSHADOW
OERSHADOWD
OERSHADOWING
OERSHADOWS
OERTAXD
OERTOOK
OERWORKD
OETAEAN
OFFEND
OFFENDER
OFFICIAL
OIL
OLEANDER
OLIVE
OLIVES
OLIVIAS
OLYMPIA
OLYMPIAN
OMNIPOTENCE
ONESELF
ONWARDS
ONYX
OOZE
OOZING
OPE
OPED
OPERATIONS
OPINION
OPINIONS
OPIUM
OPPIUS
OPPOSER
OPPOSITION
OPPRESSES
OPPRESSORS
OPPREST
OPTIMISTIC
OPULENT
ORACLES
ORATOR
ORB
ORBS
ORCHIS
ORCHOMENIAN
ORCHOMENUS
ORDAINS
ORDERING
ORGAN
ORIENT
ORPHAND
ORPHANS
OTHERWHILE
OTHERWISE
OUTBUILDING
OUTCRY
OUTERMOST
OUTFIT
OUTGUSHING
OUTLINED
OUTLINES
OUTLIVE
OUTLIVING
OUTLOOK
OUTRUNS
OUTSPREADS
OUTWEIGHD
OVATION
OVERAWE

OVERBLOWN
OVERFEEDING
OVERGREW
OVERHEAT
OVERLAID
OVERMUCH
OVERPEER
OVERTURND
OVERWEIGHD
OWNER
OXFORDS
PACIFY
PACING
PACINGS
PACK
PADDLES
PAGEANTS
PAINTS
PALENESS
PALES
PALFREYS
PALL
PALLADIUM
PALLD
PALMS
PAMISUS
PANS
PANTING
PARALYSING
PARALYTIC
PARAMOUNT
PARDON
PARDONING
PARISIAN
PARLOUR
PARMENIDES
PARNASSIAN
PARNES
PARSONAGE
PARTIALITY
PARTRIDGE
PASSAGES
PASSED
PASSENGER
PASSEST
PASSETH
PASSIVELY
PATCH
PATCHES
PATHLESS
PATHWAY
PATRIARCHAL
PATTER
PATTERS
PAUSANIUS
PAUSEFULLY
PAUSING
PAVED
PAVES
PAWS
PAYS
PEACEFULLY
PEALING
PEALS
PEARL
PEARLED
PEASANT
PEBBLY
PEDLARS
PEER
PEERING
PEEVISH
PEKIN

PELASGUS
PELL
PELLUCID
PENCIL
PENMON
PENNON
PEOPLING
PERCEIVST
PERFECTLY
PERFIDIOUS
PERFORMEST
PERFORMS
PERFUMED
PERILS
PERISHES
PERMISSION
PERMIT
PERMITTING
PERSEPOLIS
PERSEVERING
PERSIA
PERSUADED
PERSUASIVE
PERUSED
PERVADES
PERVERSE
PESTER
PET
PETER
PETERS
PETRARCHS
PHARISEES
PHENEOS
PHIDIAS
PHILIPS
PHILISTINE
PHILOCTETES
PHILOSOPHY
PHOEBUS
PHRASE
PHTHIA
PHYSICIAN
PICKING
PICTURE
PIECE
PIECEMEAL
PIERCD
PIGEONS
PIGMY
PILGRIM
PILGRIMS
PINETREES
PININGS
PINION
PINIOND
PINNACE
PINND
PIONEER
PIPES
PIRATE
PIRATES
PIT
PITEOUSLY
PITIED
PITS
PITT
PLACD
PLAGUED
PLANE
PLANK
PLANNING
PLANS
PLANTING

PLATFORM
PLATFORMS
PLATTER
PLAYERS
PLAYST
PLEA
PLEADED
PLEADER
PLEADERS
PLEASURING
PLIANT
PLIGHT
PLODS
PLOTTED
PLOTTING
PLOUGH
PLOUGHBOYS
PLOUGHD
PLOVER
PLUMB
PLUMED
PLUMMET
PLUNGD
POACH
PODARGA
POETIC
POISONOUS
POISONS
POLES
POLISHD
POLITIC
POLITICS
POLLUTED
POLYMNIA
POLYNICES
POMPOUS
POMPS
PONDER
PONDERED
PONDERS
PONIES
POOLS
POPLAR
POPLARS
POPPIES
POPPY
POPULACE
POPULAR
POPULOUS
PORCELAIN
PORTEND
PORTIOND
PORTSMOUTH
POSEIDON
POSSESSES
POSSESSEST
POSSESSING
POSSESSION
POSSIBLE
POSTED
POSTPONING
POSTURE
POSTURES
POTENT
POTENTLY
POTION
POTIONS
POTSDAM
POUCH
POURST
POURTRAY
POWDERY
PRACTISE
PRANK

1 (cont.)

PRATING	PROSE	RADIANCE	REINDEER	REVELATION
PRAYS	PROSPECTS	RAGES	REINS	REVELLD
PRE	PROSPERITY	RAGGED	REJECTEST	REVELLING
PREACHD	PROTECTED	RAGS	REJOICED	REVENGEFUL
PREACHER	PROTECTORS	RAILD	REJOICINGS	REVERE
PREACHES	PROUDER	RAILS	REJOIN	REVERED
PRECARIOUSLY	PROUDEST	RAISES	REJOINS	REVERENT
PRECEDED	PROVENCAL	RAISING	REKINDLING	REVERIE
PRECEDENTS	PROVIDE	RAKES	RELATIONS	REVERIES
PRECINCTS	PROWESS	RAMBLE	RELAXD	REVERING
PRECIPICE	PRUND	RANGES	RELEASEMENT	REVERSAL
PRECISE	PSYCHE	RANGING	RELEGATE	REVERSE
PREFACE	PUDDLE	RANK	RELENTING	REVERSION
PREFER	PUFF	RAPHAELS	RELICS	REVIEW
PREFERMENTS	PUFFS	RAPIDS	RELIEF	REVIEWS
PREOCCUPIED	PULLING	RARER	RELIGIOUS	REVISIT
PREPARE	PULLS	RASHNESS	RELUCTANT	REVIVED
PREPARED	PULLULATING	RATE	RELUCTANTLY	REVIVING
PREPARES	PULSING	RATES	RELYING	REVIVST
PRESCIENCE	PUNCTUAL	RAVAGES	REMAINING	REVOLUTIONS
PRESCRIBED	PUNCTUALLY	RAVENING	REMEMBERED	REWARD
PRESERVED	PUNISHMENT	RAVIN	REMEMBERS	REWARDS
PRESERVER	PUNT	RAVING	REMINDS	RHEA
PRESIDES	PUNTS	RAVISHD	REMISSLY	RHONE
PRESSURE	PURCHASE	RAYLESS	REMISSNESS	RHONES
PRETENDED	PURELY	REACHING	REMIT	RHYMES
PRETENTIOUS	PURENESS	READEST	REMNANT	RIBBON
PREVAILD	PURGE	READIER	REMOUNT	RIBBOND
PREYING	PURIFIES	REALMS	RENDER	RIBBONS
PRIAMS	PURPOSED	REAPER	RENDERD	RICE
PRICKS	PURPOSELESS	REAPPEAR	RENDERS	RICHES
PRIE	PURPOSES	REAPS	RENOUNCED	RICK
PRIMEVAL	PURPOSEST	REBEKAH	RENOWND	RID
PRIMITIVE	PURSUERS	REBUILD	REPAY	RIDDLE
PRINCIPLES	PURSUES	REBUKE	REPEATS	RIDER
PRINKING	PURSY	REBUKES	REPEL	RIDERS
PRIVILEGED	PUSH	RECEDING	REPELLENT	RIDES
PROBATION	PUSHED	RECEIVD	REPELLEST	RIDGED
PROCEED	PUTRID	RECEIVES	REPENTANT	RIDGES
PROCEEDST	PUTS	RECKD	REPLACE	RIDGING
PROCLAIM	PUTTING	RECKLESSLY	REPOSES	RIDINGS
PROCLAIMD	PYLADES	RECLUSES	REPRESSD	RIFLED
PROCLES	PYLOS	RECOGNISE	REPRESSEST	RIGHTEND
PROCURED	PYMS	RECOGNIZE	REPRESSIVE	RIGHTFUL
PRODIGALITY	PYTHO	RECOLLECT	REPROACHFULLY	RIGID
PRODIGY	QUAFFD	RECOLLECTIONS	REPROACHING	RIGIDLY
PRODUCTS	QUAINT	RECOMPENCE	REPROOF	RILL
PROFESSD	QUAKE	RECONCILED	REPROVED	RIM
PROFITEST	QUAKED	RECONCILEMENT	REPULSED	RINGLET
PROFOUNDEST	QUAKING	RECORD	REQUIEM	RINGLETS
PROFOUNDLY	QUALITIES	RECORDED	REQUIRES	RIOTING
PROMETHEUS	QUALITY	RECORDS	REQUIREST	RIOTOUS
PROMISED	QUANTOCK	RECOVERD	REQUITE	RIPENING
PROMONTORIES	QUARTERS	RECROSS	RESERVES	RIPENS
PROMONTORY	QUEENLY	REDDEND	RESOUNDS	RIPPLE
PROMOTION	QUELL	REDDENING	RESOURCE	RIPPLED
PROMPTED	QUELLD	REDOUBLE	RESPECT	RIVALRY
PROMPTER	QUELLING	REEDS	RESPITE	RIVETS
PROMPTS	QUESTING	REEL	RESPLENDENT	ROADS
PRONOUNCED	QUESTIOND	REELS	RESTORER	ROAMING
PROOFS	QUESTIONINGS	REFLECTED	RESTORERS	ROARS
PROPER	QUESTIONS	REFLEX	RESTORES	ROBBERS
PROPHESY	QUIBERON	REFRAIND	RESULTS	ROBBING
PROPHET	QUICKEN	REFRESH	RESUME	ROBINS
PROPHETESSES	QUICKENED	REFRESHMENT	RESUMED	ROBS
PROPHETS	QUICKENING	REFUSE	RETAINING	ROCKD
PROPOSAL	QUICKEST	REGAL	RETORT	ROD
PROPOSE	QUIETLY	REGARDING	RETRACE	ROE
PROPPING	QUITTING	REGISTERED	RETREATING	ROMANTIC
PROPS	RACED	REGRETTING	RETREATS	ROMPING
PROPT	RACES	REGULAR	RETURNST	ROOKS
PRORE	RACHELS	REIGNING	REVEAL	ROOST
	RACING	REIND	REVEALS	ROPE

1 (cont.)

ROSARY	SCANS	SEVERER	SIRES	SNUFFING
ROSEATE	SCAR	SEVERING	SIROCCO	SNUFFS
ROSILY	SCARFD	SEVERITY	SIRS	SOAKING
ROUGE	SCARS	SEVILLE	SISTERLY	SOAKS
ROUNDED	SCATHING	SEVRES	SISTERS	SOAR
ROUNDS	SCATTER	SHACKLED	SIXTH	SOARD
ROUSED	SCATTERS	SHADED	SKIMMING	SOBER
ROUSES	SCENTED	SHADOWING	SKIMS	SOFTEND
ROVING	SCEPTIC	SHAFT	SKINND	SOFTENING
ROW	SCEPTRES	SHAFTS	SKINNY	SOFTENINGS
RUBBD	SCHEME	SHALLOWS	SKIPPING	SOJOURND
RUBY	SCHEMERS	SHAMEFUL	SKULDA	SOLD
RUFFLE	SCHEMING	SHAPES	SKULKD	SOLUTION
RUFFLES	SCHOOLING	SHAREDST	SKULL	SOMEHOW
RUGGED	SCIPIO	SHARER	SKULLS	SONGSTER
RUMBLED	SCOFF	SHARERS	SKYE	SONOROUS
RUMBLING	SCOFFINGLY	SHARPER	SLAKED	SOPHISTICATED
RUMBLINGS	SCOOP	SHATTERD	SLANT	SOPHOCLES
RUNES	SCORE	SHATTERED	SLAUGHTER	SORELY
RUNG	SCORED	SHEDS	SLAUGHTERD	SORES
RUNIC	SCORES	SHEENY	SLAYS	SOREST
RUNNST	SCORNFULLY	SHEEPFOLD	SLAYST	SORRY
RUSHY	SCOURD	SHELF	SLEEPERS	SOUDANS
RUST	SCOURGED	SHELLEY	SLEEPEST	SOUGHTEST
RUSTING	SCOWLING	SHELTRING	SLEEPST	SOUNDED
RUSTLED	SCRAPES	SHELVES	SLEET	SOUNDST
RUSTLINGLY	SCRATCHD	SHEPHERDESS	SLEEVE	SOURCES
RUTHLESSLY	SCREENS	SHEPHERDING	SLEIPNERS	SOURD
RYDAL	SCRIBE	SHEW	SLIGHTS	SOW
RYMER	SCRIBES	SHIAH	SLIM	SOWING
SACRIFICED	SCRUTINISE	SHIFT	SLIPPD	SPACES
SACRIFICING	SCUFFLE	SHIFTING	SLIPPERY	SPACIOUS
SADDENS	SCULLS	SHIFTS	SLOPED	SPAINS
SADDER	SEAFARING	SHINGLE	SLOPING	SPANGLED
SAFELY	SEALIKE	SHINGLES	SLOUGH	SPANND
SAGACIOUS	SEALING	SHIPBOARD	SLOUGHS	SPAR
SAGEST	SEAWEED	SHIPWRECK	SLUGGISHLY	SPARELY
SAHARAN	SEBERT	SHOALS	SLUMBERETH	SPARING
SAIDST	SECONDS	SHOOTS	SLUMBERING	SPARTANS
SAILORS	SECRETLY	SHORELESS	SLUNG	SPASM
SALAMINIAN	SECT	SHOREWARDS	SMALLEST	SPECIAL
SALLIES	SECURES	SHOWED	SMARTING	SPECKLED
SALORE	SECURITY	SHOWERD	SMELL	SPECKS
SALUTATIONS	SEDGED	SHOWERLESS	SMELLING	SPECULATORS
SALUTES	SEDGY	SHRIEK	SMELT	SPEEDING
SANCTIFY	SEDUCED	SHRILLS	SMILINGLY	SPEEDS
SANCTION	SEEKER	SHRINE	SMIRCH	SPEEDST
SANCTIONS	SEEMED	SHRINES	SMIRCHD	SPENDTHRIFTS
SANDALLD	SEEMST	SHRINK	SMIT	SPERCHEIOS
SANDBANKS	SEIRIOL	SHRIVELLING	SMITHS	SPHERED
SANDFORD	SELECT	SHRUNK	SMITTEN	SPHERES
SANGEST	SELECTED	SHUDDERING	SMOCK	SPHINX
SANKST	SELL	SHUFFLE	SMOKED	SPICED
SAPIENT	SELLERS	SHUFFLES	SMOKELESS	SPIKES
SAPPD	SENDER	SHUNS	SMOKY	SPINDLE
SAPPHIRE	SENESCHAL	SHUTTERS	SMOOTHER	SPINE
SAPPST	SENSITIVE	SHUTTLE	SMYRNA	SPIRITED
SARDONIC	SENTENCED	SIBYLLAS	SMYRNAS	SPITALFIELDS
SATIATE	SENTST	SICILYS	SNAP	SPITEFUL
SATURN	SEPARATE	SIGHINGS	SNAPDRAGON	SPLASHING
SATURNS	SEPTEMBERS	SIGHS	SNAPPD	SPLINTERD
SAUNTER	SEQUESTERD	SIGND	SNAPT	SPLINTERS
SAVIOURS	SERAPHS	SIGNIFIED	SNARE	SPLIT
SAVOYS	SERENELY	SILENUS	SNEERS	SPOILER
SAWING	SERENITY	SILLY	SNIFF	SPOILST
SAWST	SERF	SILT	SNOODED	SPOTLESS
SAXIFRAGE	SERFS	SIMOIS	SNORT	SPRAYS
SAXON	SETTER	SIMPLICITY	SNORTED	SPRENT
SAXONS	SETTING	SIMPLY	SNOWFLAKES	SPRIGHTLIER
SCALD	SETTLES	SINEWY	SNOWILY	SPRITES
SCALES	SEVENTH	SINND	SNOWLOADS	SPURNST
SCANNING	SEVER	SINS	SNUFF	SPY
	SEVERELY	SIREN	SNUFFD	SQUALID

1 (cont.)	STRIPPD	SURVIVOR	TELLST	THWARTED
SQUANDER	STROLLD	SUSAS	TEMPERATE	TIBER
SQUANDERD	STRONGEST	SUSPECT	TEMPERS	TIGHTNESS
SQUAT	STROVE	SUSPEND	TEMPESTS	TILPHUSA
SQUEAMISH	STROWN	SUSPENDED	TEMPTATIONS	TILT
SQUIRES	STRUGGLES	SUSPENSE	TENANT	TIMID
SQUIRRELS	STRUTTING	SUSPICIOUS	TENANTLESS	TINGE
STAB	STUBBLE	SUSTAIND	TENDENCE	TINGED
STABILITY	STUCK	SUSTAINS	TENDERER	TINKLE
STABLISH	STUDIOUSLY	SWAINS	TENDEREST	TINT
STAGES	STUDY	SWALLOWING	TENDERLY	TIPPD
STAGHOUNDS	STUFFD	SWARMD	TENDERNESS	TISAMENUS
STAGSHORN	STUNG	SWARMY	TENERIFFE	TISSUE
STAIRS	STUNND	SWART	TENTED	TITANS
STALE	STUPEFYING	SWATHS	TERRACE	TITTLE
STALK	STUPIDLY	SWEARING	TERRACED	TOILD
STAMPD	STUPIFYING	SWEETER	TERRIFIED	TOILSOME
STANDARD	STUPOR	SWEETNESS	TERRORS	TOLL
STANDETH	STURDY	SWIFTNESS	TERTULLIAN	TOLLD
STARING	STYLE	SWIMMERS	TERTULLIANS	TOLLS
STARK	STYX	SWING	TESTED	TOME
STARLINGS	STYXS	SWIRLING	TETHERS	TONED
STARTING	SUBDUE	SWISS	TETHYS	TOOLS
STARTLING	SUBLIME	SWOLN	THAMESS	TOORKMUN
STARTS	SUBMITTED	SWOONING	THANKFUL	TOORKMUNS
STARWARDS	SUBTLETIES	SWOOPING	THEATRE	TOOTHLESS
STATIOND	SUCCEED	SWORDS	THEBANS	TOPPED
STATUED	SUCCEEDING	SYCAMORES	THEMES	TORCHLIGHT
STATURED	SUCCOUREST	SYLLABLE	THENCEFORTH	TORMENTING
STAUNCH	SUCCOURS	SYMPATHISE	THEREAFTER	TORMENTORS
STAVED	SUCCUMBD	SYRIA	THEREAT	TORMENTS
STAYED	SUCK	SYRTES	THEREOF	TORTOISES
STEADILY	SUFFERER	SYRUP	THEREWITH	TORTURING
STEALING	SUFFERINGS	SYSTEMS	THESEUS	TOTTERD
STEALTHILY	SUFFICD	TABLED	THESSALY	TOTTERING
STEAM	SUFFICES	TACITURN	THETIS	TOTTERS
STEEPING	SUFFICING	TAEN	THEW	TOUCHEST
STEMMD	SUFFRAGE	TAGGD	THICKENS	TOUCHT
STEPPD	SUGAR	TAILS	THINKERS	TOW
STICK	SUGARD	TAINT	THINKEST	TOWERED
STILE	SUGGESTIONS	TAINTED	THINLY	TOWERING
STINGS	SUITED	TAKEN	THINND	TOWND
STIRREST	SUITS	TALENT	THINNER	TOWNSMEN
STOIC	SULLYING	TALKEST	THIRTEEN	TOYS
STOLN	SUM	TAMBOURINE	THISBE	TRACHINIANS
STONED	SUMMITS	TANAGRAEAN	THITHERWARD	TRACKING
STONING	SUMPTUOUS	TANGLE	THOKS	TRACKS
STOOPED	SUNBURNT	TANKS	THORA	TRADER
STOPPED	SUNDERING	TANND	THOUGHTED	TRAFFICKERS
STOPPING	SUNWARD	TARDY	THOUGHTEST	TRAITOROUS
STORIED	SUNWARDS	TARNISHD	THOUGHTLESS	TRAMPLE
STORK	SUP	TARRIED	THOUSANDTH	TRAMPLING
STORMIEST	SUPERFLUITY	TARTAREAN	THRALL	TRAMPS
STORMILY	SUPERPOSED	TASKWORK	THREADING	TRANCED
STOUTLY	SUPERSTITIOUS	TASSELLD	THREADS	TRANCES
STOWS	SUPPD	TASSOS	THREAT	TRANQUILLY
STRAFFORDS	SUPPING	TAUNTS	THREATENED	TRANSCENDS
STRAGGLED	SUPPORT	TAWNY	THREATENEST	TRANSFIXD
STRAGGLERS	SUPPOSE	TAYGETUS	THREATENING	TRANSMITS
STRAITLY	SUPPRESSD	TEACHER	THREATENS	TRANSPARENCY
STRATFORD	SUPREMACY	TEACHERS	THREATNINGS	TRANSPLANTS
STRAYING	SURENESS	TEACHES	THRESHERS	TRANSPORT
STREAK	SURGED	TEAM	THRESHING	TRAPPD
STREAMED	SURPLICED	TEARFUL	THREWST	TRAVAIL
STRETCHES	SURPRISED	TEARING	THRILLING	TRAVERSE
STREWD	SURPRIZE	TEASD	THROBS	TREACHEROUSLY
STRIDE	SURRENDER	TEASE	THROE	TREACHERY
STRIDES	SURREY	TEASED	THROES	TREASURIES
STRIDING	SURROUND	TEEM	THRONED	TREATS
STRING	SURROUNDING	TEEMING	THROUGHOUT	TREATY
STRINGING	SURVIVED	TEEMS	THUNDERED	TREMBLER
STRINGS	SURVIVEST	TEJEND	THUNDERERS	TREMBLES
STRIPED	SURVIVING	TELLER	THWART	TREMOR

1 (cont.)

TRENCH	UNBREACHABLE	UNIMPEDED	UNTASTED	VERDURE
TRENCHANT	UNBRIBED	UNIMPROVED	UNTHWARTED	VERGELMER
TRIAL	UNCAREWORN	UNINFRINGED	UNTIE	VESPASIANS
TRIALS	UNCARING	UNITY	UNTIED	VESSEL
TRIBULATIONS	UNCHAIND	UNKEMPD	UNTIMELY	VESTED
TRIBUNAL	UNCHANGED	UNKEMPT	UNTOUCHD	VESTIGE
TRIBUTARIES	UNCHEERD	UNKINDNESS	UNTRIED	VEXD
TRICKLE	UNCLASPING	UNKNIT	UNTRIMMD	VIALS
TRICKLED	UNCLES	UNLEARNT	UNTROD	VICE
TRICKS	UNCLOSE	UNLED	UNTRUE	VICIOUS
TRILL	UNCLOSED	UNLOCK	UNUNITED	VICISSITUDE
TRIMMD	UNCOMFORTED	UNLOVEABLE	UNUPBRAIDED	VICTORIES
TRIP	UNCOMPANIOND	UNMATING	UNVISITED	VIDAR
TRIUMPHT	UNCOMPANIONED	UNMINDFUL	UNWANDERING	VIE
TRODE	UNCONCEDED	UNMINGLING	UNWARND	VIEWD
TROOPING	UNCONFINED	UNMIXD	UNWILLING	VILLA
TROPHIES	UNCONGENIAL	UNMOORD	UNWINGD	VINDICATE
TROPHY	UNCONSUMED	UNMOVD	UNWINTRY	VINEDRESSER
TROUBADOUR	UNCOUTHNESS	UNMURMURING	UNWISHD	VINEYARDS
TROUBLING	UNCRAVINGLY	UNNEARD	UNWITTINGLY	VIOLATE
TRUMP	UNCRUMPLING	UNNERVED	UNWONTED	VIOLENCE
TRUMPETS	UNDEBARRD	UNNOTED	UNWORLDLY	VIRGIL
TRUSTED	UNDEBASED	UNNUMBERD	UNWOUNDED	VIRGILIAN
TRUSTING	UNDECAYD	UNOBSERVANT	UNWRINKLED	VIRGINS
TRYING	UNDEGENERATE	UNOERLEAPD	UNYIELDING	VISITINGS
TRYSTING	UNDELIGHTED	UNOFFENDING	UPBORNE	VITAL
TUFTS	UNDERSTANDS	UNPAUSING	UPBRAID	VITALS
TUKAS	UNDERSTOOD	UNPERMITTED	UPCLOSE	VOCAL
TUMBLING	UNDESCRIED	UNPIERCED	UPCROWDING	VOGUE
TUMULTUOUS	UNDESIRED	UNPITYING	UPCURLD	VOICINGS
TUNES	UNDID	UNPRAYD	UPFURLD	VOLLEYING
TUNNIES	UNDISCOVERD	UNQUENCHABLE	UPHOLD	VOLUME
TURBULENCE	UNDISTRACTED	UNQUENCHD	UPHUNG	VOLUMES
TURBULENT	UNDOING	UNQUESTIOND	UPLANDS	VOUCHD
TURNEDST	UNDONE	UNRAVEL	UPLIFT	VOW
TURNEST	UNDOUBTING	UNRAVELLING	UPLIFTED	VOYAGED
TURPENTINE	UNDOWERD	UNREACHD	UPLIFTS	VOYAGES
TURQUOISE	UNDRIED	UNREAL	UPRAISEST	VULGAR
TURRETS	UNDULLD	UNRECOGNISING	UPREARD	VULGARITY
TWENTIETH	UNDUPED	UNRECOVERD	UPRIGHT	VYING
TWENTYFOLD	UNDYING	UNREGARDED	UPSTREAMING	WADED
TWINES	UNEASY	UNREGARDFUL	UPTORN	WAFT
TWINKLES	UNENDANGERD	UNRELAXING	UPTURND	WAGGON
TWINKLING	UNEPITAPHD	UNRESENTFUL	URGHENDJE	WAILS
TWIRLD	UNEXCEPTING	UNRESTFUL	USD	WAITEST
TWIRLING	UNFAMILIAR	UNRETURNING	USHERS	WAITST
TWISTED	UNFATHERD	UNREVERSED	UTTER	WAIVE
TWOFOLD	UNFAVOURD	UNROLLD	UTTERED	WAKED
TYPHOS	UNFIXD	UNRULY	UTTEREST	WAKENS
TYR	UNFLAGGING	UNSAID	UTTERS	WALLING
TYRANNY	UNFLINCHING	UNSATISFIED	VALIANTLY	WALNUT
ULEMA	UNFLUSHES	UNSCOURGED	VALLIES	WALTON
ULEMAS	UNFOLD	UNSCRUPULOUS	VALOUR	WANDEREDST
UMBRAGE	UNFOOTED	UNSEVERD	VALOURS	WANDERINGS
UNABLE	UNFORESEEING	UNSHADED	VAN	WANE
UNADULATING	UNFORESEEN	UNSHADOWD	VANADIS	WANTED
UNAFFRIGHTED	UNFORGOT	UNSHAKEN	VANHEIM	WARDED
UNALLIED	UNFREED	UNSHARED	VANISHED	WARDERD
UNALLOYD	UNFREQUENTED	UNSHEATHED	VANITY	WARDS
UNAPPEASABLE	UNFRIENDLY	UNSHUT	VANQUISHD	WARLIKE
UNAPPEASED	UNFULFILLD	UNSKILFUL	VANQUISHED	WARMER
UNAPPLAUDED	UNFURLED	UNSKILFULNESS	VARIANCE	WARMING
UNAPT	UNGLOVED	UNSLACKENING	VARIED	WARMLY
UNASSISTED	UNGRATEFUL	UNSMOOTHD	VASE	WARN
UNATONABLE	UNGRATEFULLY	UNSOILD	VASTNESS	WARND
UNATTAIND	UNGRAVEN	UNSOLVED	VASTY	WARRANT
UNATTEMPTED	UNGREETING	UNSPARING	VEHEMENCE	WASHED
UNAWAKENING	UNGUIDED	UNSPEAKABLE	VEHEMENT	WATCHEST
UNBARRING	UNHAILD	UNSPHERED	VEILED	WATCHFUL
UNBEARABLE	UNHALLOWD	UNSTRUNG	VEILS	WATERSHED
UNBLACKEND	UNHALLOWED	UNSUBSTANTIAL	VEIND	WAVD
UNBLAMED	UNHARNESSING	UNSUITING	VELAN	WAVST
UNBRAIDED	UNHEARD	UNSWERVED	VENT	WAXES
	UNHURT	UNTAMED	VERDE	WAXING

1 (cont.)

WAYFARING
WAYSIDE
WEAKEN
WEAKLY
WEALTHY
WEAPON
WEARIED
WEARYING
WEAVE
WEAVER
WEAVES
WEDDST
WEDGED
WEEK
WEEKS
WEIGHD
WEIGHING
WEIRS
WELCOMED
WELLING
WELLS
WELTERS
WEND
WENDING
WENDS
WETTED

WEVE
WHALES
WHEATFIELDS
WHEELD
WHELMD
WHEREAT
WHEREBY
WHEREOER
WHERESOEER
WHET
WHETTING
WHIM
WHIPS
WHIRL
WHIRLWINDS
WHISPERED
WHISTLED
WHITENS
WHITER
WHIZZING
WHOEER
WICKET
WIDEN
WIDEND
WIDEST
WIDOWHOOD
WIDOWS

WIDTH
WIFES
WILDER
WILDLY
WILE
WILLIAM
WILY
WINDINGS
WINGED
WINGING
WINKS
WINNOWING
WIPE
WIPES
WISDOMS
WISELY
WISEST
WITCHING
WITHDRAW
WITHDRAWING
WITHDRAWN
WITHER
WITHSTANDS
WITLESS
WITNESSES
WOLF
WOLFISH

WOMANLY
WOMENS
WONDERFUL
WONDERMENT
WONT
WOODMAN
WOOLLEN
WORCESTERS
WORDY
WORKERS
WORKINGS
WORKMAN
WORKSHOP
WORLDLINGS
WORMS
WOTS
WOULDEST
WOUNDING
WOUNDLESS
WRANGLING
WRAPPED
WRATHFUL
WRATHS
WREATHES
WRECKS
WREST
WRESTLE

WRESTLES
WRETCHEDER
WRING
WRIST
WRIT
WRITE
WRONGFUL
WRONGLY
WROUGHTEST
WYCHWOOD
WYTHAM
YARDS
YAWNING
YEAND
YEARLL
YEARND
YEARNS
YESTERMORN
YOKD
YONDER
ZEUSS
ZIRRAH
ZOARRAH